LESKO'S INFO-POWER

Third Edition

by

MATTHEW LESKO

Lesko's Info-Power III

Information USA, Inc.
Andrew Naprawa, *Editor*
Mary Ann Martello, *Associate Editor*
Toni Murray, *Contributing Editor*

Denise Burek, Claire Capretta, Patricia Dickey
Eugene Gourevitch, Laura Hovenier
Kim Walker-Klarman, Judy Marcus, Shirley Massman
Roger Munter, Daniel O'Connor, Laurie Orr
Julie Paul, Caroline Pharmer, Debbie Samson, Carol Sargent
Pam Schultz, Elaine Sikorski, *Researchers*

Beth Meserve, *Production Director*

Cover design by Lester Zaiontz; *photo by* Kevin Gilbert

Copyright © 1996 by Matthew Lesko

Published by Visible Ink Press
835 Penobscot Bldg.
Detroit, MI 48226-4094

Visible Ink Press is a registered trademark of Gale Research Inc.

ISBN 1-878346-37-7

Printed in the United States of America
10 9 8 7 6

Other books written by Matthew Lesko:

Getting Yours: The Complete Guide to Government Money

How to Get Free Tax Help

Information USA

The Computer Data and Database Source Book

The Maternity Sourcebook

Lesko's New Tech Sourcebook

The Investor's Information Sourcebook

The Federal Data Base Finder

The State Database Finder

Government Giveaways for Entrepreneurs

The Great American Gripe Book

What To Do When You Can't Afford Health Care

1001 Free Goodies and Cheapies

Free Stuff for Seniors

Everything You Need to Run a Business At Home

T O

all the federal and state bureaucrats who

eagerly share information that empowers us

to pursue our goals and dreams

Introduction

Thank you for buying, borrowing, or stealing my book. I have spent over 25 years using and compiling government information. Even though I've written over 50 books on the subject, it is my hope that with every book, I get better at it. I believe that this is my best ever and I hope you can get good use out of *Info-Power*.

WARNING: THIS BOOK IS OUT OF DATE

You have to realize that the moment any book is printed, it is out of date. Especially this one with its 45,000 sources. A book of this size is sure to have some telephone numbers that have changed. But don't be discouraged. You can live with these small inconveniences. If you are calling a government office listed in the book and the telephone number gets you a local diner, or some other wrong number, here's what you can do.

* Call the operator for the area and ask for the number of the office you're after. The directory assistance operator can be located by dialing the area code followed by 555-1212. To inquire about a toll-free number, call directory assistance at 800-555-1212.

* Call your local Federal Information Centers. These are local telephone numbers listed in the U.S. Government section of your telephone directory, or you can call their main number at 301-722-9000.

* Or, call us at 301-924-0556. We will try and help you in any way we can.

You can keep up to date with the information in this book by ordering our new editions when they become available. Each edition verifies all the sources identified in the book and includes updated information, new and expanded chapters and much more. We hope to be publishing updates every other year.

You can also keep current by accessing this information online, via computer, through CompuServe. We will be constantly updating this information on this computer service. For subscription information to CompuServe call 800-524-3388 and ask for Representative 168. Thanks again for your interest in this book. I hope you will feel free to call with your comments and questions.

Happy Hunting,

Matthew Lesko

TABLE OF CONTENTS

Information Is Power

Information is the key to opportunities. It's essential for all the important aspects of life:

* making the right investment,
* choosing the right career,
* seeking the latest medical cure, or
* buying at the best price.

But why, if we are living in an information society, do most of us base our decisions on hearsay, headlines, outdated or incomplete information? I think there are two reasons which explain this paradox:

* information overload, and
* poor information training.

Information overload is the more obvious of the two. We see it everywhere: the proliferation of magazines, newspapers, databases, and even television channels. I'll talk more about this later. What is an even more distressing problem is our inadequate information training.

Your Library Is Out of Date

Today, most adults and even our children have been trained to believe that if you need information, you go to the library. That's fine for certain subjects, like literature and history, but inadequate for most of the important concerns that affect our lives everyday. Libraries are full of the traditional information resources but you will encounter major problems if you rely on these sources because:

* most books are out of date, and
* libraries represent only a fraction of the information available to us.

Books can tell you only about yesterdays, but the information needed to make critical decisions must reflect what is happening today and tomorrow, not the past. More than ever our world is changing at an ever increasing speed. What once took months, even years to change, now occurs in hours, even minutes.

Those who rely on yesterday's information are the ones who get hurt in our society. Take, for example, the steel workers who thought that they would make $25 per hour forever. What about those who believed all the hype a few years ago about how Individual Retirement Accounts (IRAs) would make their financial lives secure forever. Now the rules have changed and the tax advantage isn't what it used to be. Books published in the traditional way are out of date before they hit the bookstores. How can you depend on a book offering investment advice when the manuscript was completed 18 to 24 months ago? It takes most New York publishers 9 to 12 months just to do the editing, proofing, and printing. With external events changing our landscape every day, like the stock market crash of 1987, or the

fall of the Berlin Wall in 1989, we can no longer rely on such books.

Government Is World's Largest Source of Information

Traditional books represent only a fraction of the really powerful information that is available. Did you know that all of the major commercial publishers in our country generate approximately 50,000 books each year, but one little government publisher, the National Technical Information Service (NTIS), alone sells about 90,000 titles annually. And it's estimated that NTIS titles represent only a tiny portion of the research that is actually published by federal agencies. And computers are not much of a help either. Most databases you access are bibliographies which fail to capture the latest information.

The government is the largest source of information in the world, and very little of it is available in any library. And, more importantly, the information you get from the government is going to be superior to most anything you can ever get commercially. If you purchase a book in the bookstore, you're likely to get the result of one to two years of some author's efforts. On the other hand, if you get a government study, often you are getting the results of hundreds of man years worth of work, along with the telephone number of the actual office that conducted the research. That's just how the government works and chances are the government study will be free.

Information Opportunities

By relying on traditional information sources, you are missing out on information opportunities. Such an opportunity occurs when you have intelligence that is current, comprehensive, reliable, and even cheaper than someone else's information. There is no unique opportunity for you when your stockbroker calls about a chance to invest in some biotechnology company, because the broker probably is sharing that tip with 5,000 other "special" clients. The real opportunity occurs when you have the information before the stockbroker. And you can get it, but not from conventional sources. How can you take advantage of a new cure for your medical ailment if your doctor is not aware of the latest therapies because the *New England Journal of Medicine* hasn't published a recent article on this disease. Or perhaps some scientific journal plans to run an article revealing a potential cure, but it is still in the editing process and won't be published for another three months. You need that information today, and you can get it, but not from traditional sources.

Medicine is typical of the information overload when your doctor — the information provider — cannot possibly keep up on all the latest developments. That physician has got a practice to run, and the information changes too fast and constantly. But the best health information in the world *IS* available and *YOU* can get it.

Information Is Power

Archives vs. Information

Libraries are great storehouses for literature and archival material. They handle traditional published materials very well, but do a relatively poor job in solving more current information problems. This is a pity since we are living in an information society, and information is the most important ingredient in our lives. Doesn't it make sense that libraries should be the most important building in the community? Yet they're not, mainly because information retrieval requires a different set of skills than the archival business. Archiving is more suited for passive, non-people oriented skills, the cloistered scholars. The communication skills needed in today's information society are action oriented and people oriented.

The Information Winners

The winners in this information age are those who learn how to tap into non-traditional sources, and use experts. Finding non-traditional sources of information, however, is no easy task. The government is the world's largest supplier of these non-traditional sources, but it does not advertise. The government spends billions collecting information and expertise but spends barely a nickel advertising its availability. Another problem is that much of the information is not collected for the reason for which you want to use it. Even people in the government who have the information often fail to realize that it can be used to solve your particular problem. Take, for example, the Census data. Every decade we spend billions of dollars collecting information on all the noses and toilets in this country--the census of population and housing. The law which requires us to collect this information is, of course, the Constitution, which mandates that we count all Americans in order to figure out the number of Members of Congress. But the unintentional fallout of this law is a billion dollar market study which no one except the government can do. Not even a Fortune 500 company can afford to collect this amount of data. But when the results come out:

* companies can use the data to identify new markets;
* banks can decide where to locate branch offices;
* families can learn which are the best neighborhoods;
* inventors can determine the demand and need for their products.

Using Experts
to Solve Information Overload

Knowing how to find and use experts is not only the solution to identifying the best in non-traditional information, but it is also the key in dealing with information overload. And what's ideal about this approach is that most all the best experts cost you nothing. The government, because it is the richest source for non-traditional information in the world, is also the richest source of experts. It is full of specialists who spend entire careers studying almost any topic from futures commodities to extraterrestrials. And they are available to anyone just for the price of a telephone call.

Find Out
What Will Be in Books Tomorrow

If you access a computerized database and put in a term or key word, you can get overwhelmed. Immediately it will be apparent that today anybody with a copier machine is a publisher, and once it is published, somebody with a database is indexing it. So a printout from your computer search might total 500 citations. If you want answers now, you are in worse shape than when you started. Why? Because the computer cannot distinguish the relevant articles from the bad ones. Probably you need to retrieve all the articles cited. Also, as I mentioned earlier, much of what databases contain is from outdated published material.

My theory is that in an average of seven telephone calls you can find an expert who has read all of those articles. This specialist can tell you which ones to read, or will know the answer on the spot so there will be no need to track down the articles. These experts also can tell you what will be in the database tomorrow because they are in the process of writing it or reviewing another expert's article. They are tracking developments minute by minute in their field of expertise.

And what's great about our society is that these experts are dying to talk to you. They devote their lives to studying a particular subject in a massive bureaucracy and most feel no one cares about what they do and know. I estimate that there are over 700,000 such experts in the federal government alone, and this does not count state governments, non-profit groups, and international organizations.

The real trick is in how you treat these experts. You must remember that these experts get the same paycheck whether they help you for free for two weeks, or whether they hang up on you right after you say hello. You can't think of getting information in the terms we are taught in school. The best information is no longer in some impersonal book locked up in a dusty library. It's locked up in the heads of experts and other resource people, but now you have to learn a whole new set of skills to get at it. Once you do, you will have the power of information at your fingertips. Here are a few examples of what I am talking about.

* You want to know the best industries to invest in? The government has over 100 industry analysts at the U.S. Department of Commerce studying all the major industries in this country and forecasting what they will be doing in the next 5 years.

* Your teenager has run up a few hundred dollars on pornographic 900 numbers? The dial-a-porn expert at the Federal Communications Commission can tell you about your legal position for not paying the bill.

* You want to know the market for polypropelene resin in 15 developing countries? There is a woman at the U.S. Department of Commerce who collects all the official export and import statistics from every country in the world, and can provide you with latest available data.

The Care and Feeding of Bureaucrats

There is no magic in how you treat experts. Simply remember to treat them the way you want to be treated. But, this is easy to forget when the bureaucratic runaround triggers instant frustration. While making your seven phone calls to find your expert--beware. These are common reactions.

* You get put on hold for what seems like hours.
* Everyone you talk with cannot understand your question and thinks you're off your rocker.
* After getting transferred and trying other numbers, you wind up talking with the same person twice.

What's important is not to lose your composure. Keep in mind that it will take an average of seven phone calls to find the person who can help. Otherwise, by the time you reach the expert you'll be angry and frustrated and that attitude will usually cause this information provider to end the conversation immediately. Remember that the expert wants to help you--if you give them a chance.

How High-Priced Consultants
Stop the World From Getting Ahead

I believe that most of us fail to pursue our dreams because we think that the information and resources needed are not available or that we are going to have to pay a lot to get it from some high-priced consultant. If more people learn the new information skills required, more of us will do what we feel is important to do. You don't have to hire a high-priced consultant to get the pertinent information you need to get started. Even if you do, these consultants usually have archaic information gathering skills and usually sell recycled information.

Let's say you have a crazy idea--selling bridal gowns through the mail and you wonder if there is a market for it. A consultant will charge you a minimum of $10,000 to do a market study. However, about $20 can translate into any State Government Data Center providing you with all the ZIP codes which have high concentrations of unmarried, eligible women, correlated with low concentrations of bridal gown salons, or department stores with bridal salons.

Do you want to start your own non-profit organization to change the world? If you call a local attorney, they will charge you a few thousand dollars to fill out the IRS paperwork. Or, you can call the Non-Profit Office at the IRS in Washington, DC, that provides free help to anyone who runs into difficulty completing the tax-exempt forms.

Recently I even got trapped in this negative thinking when I had the idea of sponsoring "My Favorite Bureaucrat Award." I was worried about the rules and regulations for offering a cash prize. What does "Void Where Prohibited" really mean? I thought about hiring a lawyer to figure all this out until I realized that there must be someone in the government to call. And there was. I found a contest expert, an attorney at the Federal Trade Commission, who told me such a contest had the seal of approval as long as I didn't give away over $5,000. He informed me that two states require you to post a bond and complete tons of paperwork if the prize exceeds $5,000. Until I resolved all these questions I was reluctant to pursue my idea. (Incidentally, there is a lot more about the results of this contest in the My Favorite Bureaucrat Chapter.)

In my 25 years of experience, most experts will outshine private consultants both in terms of the quality of information and the cost of providing it!

Be patient. If any phone number is incorrect, call (area code) 555-1212 and request the new listing.

3

How to Find Mr. Potato

The techniques for locating an expert can best be illustrated by a classic story from the days when I was struggling to start my first information brokerage company in 1975.

At the time the business amounted to just a desk and telephone crowded into the bedroom of my apartment. As so often happens in a fledgling enterprise, my first client was a friend. His problem was this: "I've got to have the latest information on the basic supply and demand of Maine potatoes within 24 hours."

My client represented a syndicate of commodity investors which invests millions of dollars in Maine potatoes. When he called, these potatoes were selling at double their normal price and he wanted to know why. I knew absolutely nothing about potatoes, but thought I knew where to find out. The agreement with my client was that I would be paid only if I succeeded in getting the information (no doubt you've guessed I no longer work that way).

Luck With the First Telephone Call

The first call I made was to the general information office of the U.S. Department of Agriculture. I asked to speak to an expert on potatoes. The operator referred me to Mr. Charlie Porter. I wondered if this Mr. Porter was a department functionary with responsibility for handling crank calls, but the operator assured me that he was an agriculture economist specializing in potatoes. I called Mr. Porter and explained how I was a struggling entrepreneur who knew nothing about potatoes and needed his help to answer a client's urgent request. Charlie graciously gave me much of the information I needed, adding that he would be happy to talk at greater length either over the phone or in person at his office. I decided to go see him and meet a real expert face to face.

Only Problem Was Getting Out of Charlie Porter's Office

For 2 1/2 hours the next morning, the Federal government's potato expert explained in minute detail the supply and demand of Maine potatoes. Charlie Porter showed me computer printouts that reflected how the price had doubled in recent weeks. For any subject that arose during our conversation, Charlie had immediate access to a reference source. Rows of books in his office covered every conceivable aspect of the potato market. A strip of ticker tape that tracked the daily price of potatoes from all over the country lay across his desk.

Here in Charlie's office was everything anyone might ever want to know about potatoes. The problem, it turned out, was not in getting enough information, but how to gracefully leave his office. Once Charlie started talking, it was hard for him to stop. It seemed that Charlie Porter had spent his lifetime studying the supply and demand of potatoes and finally someone with a genuine need sought his expertise on the subject closest to his heart.

One Potato....Two Potato....

When I finally had to tell Charlie that I really had to leave, he pointed across the hall in the direction of a potato statistician whose primary responsibility was to produce a monthly report showing potato production and consumption in the United States. From this statistician I was to learn about all the categories of potatoes that are tallied. It turns out the U.S. Department of Agriculture counts all the potato chips sold every month, even how many Pringle potato chips are consumed in comparison to say, Lay's Potato Chips. The statistician offered to place me on the mailing list to receive all this free monthly data.

The Art of Getting an Expert to Talk

The information explosion requires greater reliance on experts in order to sift through this proliferation of enormous data. Cultivating an expert, however, demands an entirely different set of skills from using a library or a publication. You must know how to treat people so that they are ready, willing, and able to give you the information that you need. It is human nature for almost anyone to want to share their knowledge, but your approach will determine whether you ultimately get the expert to open up to your questions. So it is your job to create an environment that makes an individual want to share his expertise. Remember when dealing with both public and private sector experts, they will get the same paycheck whether they give you two weeks worth of free help or if they cut the conversation short after a minute or two. They will decide whether you'll get all of the information that you're asking for.

Expectations: The 7-Phone Call Rule

There is no magic to finding an expert. It is simply a numbers game which seems to take an average of seven telephone calls to find the answer you're looking for. Telephone enough people and keep asking each for a lead. The magic lies in how much information the expert will share once you find the right individual. This is why it is essential to remember "the 7-phone call rule," and never stop at the second or third lead that seems to be going nowhere.

If you make several calls and begin to get upset because you are being transferred from one person to another, you will be setting yourself up to fail once you locate the right expert. What is likely to happen is that when your "Charlie Porter" picks up his telephone he is going to hear you complaining about how sick and tired you are of getting the runaround from his organization and colleagues. If you don't sound like you are going to be the highlight of Charlie's day, he will instantly figure out how to get rid of you fast.

This explains why some people are able to get information and others fail. Seasoned researchers know it is going to take a number of telephone calls and they will not allow themselves to get impatient. After all, the runaround is an unavoidable part of the information gathering process. Consequently, the first words that come out of your mouth are extremely important because they set the stage for letting the expert want to help you.

Ten Basic Telephone Tips

Here are a few pointers to keep in mind when you are casting about for an expert. These guidelines amount to basic common sense but are very easy to forget by the time you get to that sixth or seventh phone call.

1) Introduce Yourself Cheerfully
The way you open the conversation will set the tone for the entire interview. Your greeting and initial comment should be cordial and cheerful. They should give the feeling that this is not going to be just another telephone call, but a pleasant interlude in his or her day.

2) Be Open and Candid
You should be as candid as possible with your source since you are asking the same of him. If you are evasive or deceitful in explaining your needs or motives, your source will be reluctant to provide you with information. If there are certain facts you cannot reveal such as client confidentiality, explain just that. Most people will understand.

3) Be Optimistic
Throughout the entire conversation you should exude a sense of confidence. If you call and say "You probably aren't the right person" or "You don't have any information, do you?" it makes it easy for the person to say "You're right, I can't help you." A positive attitude will encourage your source to stretch his mind to see what information he might have that could possibly help you.

4) Be Humble and Courteous
You can be optimistic and still be humble. Remember the old adage that you can catch more flies with honey than you can with vinegar. People in general, and experts in particular, love to tell others what they know, as long as their position of authority is not questioned or threatened. In fact, if they are made to feel like an expert by the way you treat them, chances are that they will give you more information than they originally intended.

5) Be Concise
State your problem simply. A long-winded explanation may bore your contact and reduce your chances for getting a thorough response.

6) Don't Be a "Gimme"
A "gimme" is someone who says "give me this" or "give me that," and has little consideration for the other person's time or feelings. Remember to "ask" for information or a particular document that you're interested in.

7) Be Complimentary
This goes hand in hand with being humble. A well placed compliment about your source's expertise or insight about a particular topic will serve you well. In searching for information in large organizations, you are apt to talk to many colleagues of your source, so it wouldn't hurt to convey the respect that your "Charlie Porter" commands, for example, "Everyone I spoke to said you are the person I must talk with." It is reassuring for anyone to know that they have the respect of their peers.

8) Be Conversational
Avoid spending the entire time talking about the information you need. Briefly mention a few irrelevant topics such as the weather, the Washington Redskins, or the latest political campaign. The more social you are without being too chatty, the more likely that your source will open up to you.

9) Return the Favor
You might share with your source information or even gossip you have picked up elsewhere. However, be certain not to betray the trust of either your client or another source. If you do not have any relevant information to share at the moment, it would still be a good idea to call back when you are further along in your research when you might have information of value to offer.

10) Send Thank You Notes
A short note, typed or handwritten, will help ensure that your source will be just as cooperative in the future.

Be patient. If any phone number is incorrect, call (area code) 555-1212 and request the new listing.

5

Coping With Misinformation

One of the major problems encountered by researchers is determining the accuracy of the information that they have collected. If you are doing traditional market research and using primary sources, accuracy is not that complicated. Traditional market researchers are well aware of survey methods, sampling techniques, and computing errors using statistical standard deviation analysis. However, if you are a desk researcher, like Information USA, Inc. which relies on secondary sources and expert opinion, how do you compute the standard deviation for error? The answer is that you cannot use hard statistical techniques, but you can employ other soft forms of error checking.

Major Causes for Error and Prevention Tactics

Problem #1: Lost in the Jargon

It is not uncommon for researchers to be dealing frequently in areas of expertise where they do not have complete command of the industry jargon. In such situations it is easy to believe that you have found the exact information needed only to find out later that you missed the mark considerably. This is a common trap to fall into when fishing in unfamiliar waters. And if you have to do the job quickly, it is easy to believe that you know more than you really do or to avoid getting the complete explanation of specific jargon because you do not want to waste the time of the expert who is giving you the information. Here is an experience of a U.S. Department of Agriculture expert which illustrates this point.

This government expert received a call one day from an assistant at the White House. This hot shot, who acted pretty impressed with himself, said he was in a meeting with both the President and the head of the Meat Packers Association and needed to know right then the official number of cows in the United States. The livestock expert asked the presidential aide if that was exactly what he meant and then when he impatiently responded "Yes," the bureaucrat told him the figure. Within minutes the White House staffer called back and said the president of the Meat Packers Association laughed at him and claimed that there were twice as many cows. The assistant then realized he needed the number of all cows — including "male cows" — as well as all female ones.

The White House aide had a problem with semantics, probably a city slicker who never knew the difference between cows and cattle. This can happen to anyone, not only a cocky Presidential aide. For example, if you want to know the market for computers, a more specific question to ask is are you talking about free standing units or central processing units?

Solution #1: Act a Little Dumb

In order to prevent this type of embarrassment, you have to find an expert with whom you are comfortable. When I say comfortable, I mean someone you can go to and ask dumb questions. You will get the most help if you act very humble in your approach. If you request information with the arrogance of the White House staffer, you may be given only the facts you ask for and nothing more. However, if you call up an expert and say something like "Oh God, can you please help me? I don't really know much about this, but my boss needs to know how many cows there are in the country." With more than a hint of indecision in your voice and honestly admitting you don't know much about the field, the expert is more likely to ask you some key questions that will ensure that you get the right figures. He may even enjoy giving you the information that you need, and not just resent your phone call.

Problem #2: Believing the Written Word or a Computer

This is a more serious problem than the difficulties and confusion surrounding industry jargon. Mastering the terminology just requires a little homework. However, overcoming a deep seated belief that information either from a computer, in published sources, or from the government is always accurate can be like changing your religion. It took me years, as well as dozens of professional embarrassments, to overcome this problem.

Just because a figure appears in print does not make it gospel. Remember the saying, "Figures don't lie, but liars can figure." Keep this in mind before betting the farm on anything you read in print, even if it comes out of a computer. A good illustration which follows pertains to Census Bureau information.

A few years ago we were doing a market study on stereo speakers and discovered that the figures the U.S. Bureau of the Census had for this market were off by over 50 percent. No one in the industry complained to the government because the industry was small and couldn't be bothered. But most of the companies involved knew that the figure was misleading and so had no use for the Census report. Another case is a Fortune 500 company which told us that for over five years it filled out the U.S. Census form under the wrong Standard Industrial Code (SIC). An important caveat—this firm ranks as the number two manufacturer in the industry.

You have to remember that number crunchers at the Census Bureau and other such organizations are not always interested in the meaning behind the numbers. Much of their work is simply taking a number from block A, adding it to the number in block B, and placing the result in block C. Verifying where the numbers come from is not their job.

Published sources are an even bigger problem than government data. Many believe that what you read in a magazine or a newspaper or hear on television or radio must be true. Nonsense! Anyone and their brother can be interviewed by a magazine or newspaper, and usually what they say will get printed in a magazine or quoted on the air as long as it is not too outrageous.

Sometimes you are more likely to get it into print if what you're saying **is** outrageous. After all, most news stories are just accounts of what someone said as interpreted by a journalist.

The more general the media, the less accurate its reporting may be about an industry. In other words, an article in the ice cream industry trade magazine is more likely to be accurate than a similar story in the *New York Times*. The trade journal will have reporters who cover that particular industry and they will more than likely be able to flush out bad data. The newspaper, on the other hand, will do only one ice cream story a year, and will print almost anything it hears. So just because someone is quoted in an article does not mean that the information is correct.

I have seen much of this firsthand when on nationwide book promotion tours. In newspaper interviews or on radio and television talk shows, I can say almost anything and they will print or broadcast it, as is. I will give countless facts and figures based on my own biased research (remember that I am trying to sell books), and hardly ever will I be questioned or seriously challenged about the authenticity of my research. I don't know if it is laziness, apathy, or just plain lack of time that allows so much unchallenged information to be presented in the media. I have even blatantly lied to a reporter who thought of himself as a clone of CBS' Mike Wallace of *60 Minutes*. Before I started doing media interviews, I assumed that any good reporter worth his or her salt could find holes in what I presented and would expose me as some kind of fraud. I didn't know how they would do it, but I guess my own insecurity prompted me to prepare for the worst. The reality is that most reporters spend little or no time studying the topic before they interview you, and if you become annoyed or angry, especially with this Mike Wallace type described above, you can blow them away with an exaggerated fact or half-truth that he will never be able to verify.

Solution #2: Find Another Industry Expert

Whether a figure comes from the Census Bureau, a trade magazine or off a television program, your best bet for determining whether the number is accurate is to track down an industry expert and ask him to comment on the figure. What you are seeking is their biased opinion about the accuracy of the stated figure. If the expert believes the figure is correct but doesn't know why, find another expert.

Problem #3: Trusting an Expert

This may seem to contradict what I just said in the solution to problem #2, but stick with me and you'll see the difference.

There are many times when you cannot start with published or printed data and all you can do is pick the brains of experts within the industry. This means that you will be getting facts and figures based on the best available guess from experts. Many times this is the only way to get the information you need.

Getting this type of soft data can be full of danger. After having worked for hours trying to find a friendly soul to share with you his inner-most thoughts about the facts and figures of an industry or company, you do not want to turn him off with an antagonistic remark about the accuracy of his data.

Solution #3: Ask Why?

The best way to judge whether a source is knowledgeable about the fact or figure they have given you is to ask them how they arrived at that number. Such a question will likely initiate one of the following responses:

"I don't know. It's the best I can think of."
- A response like this will be a clue that the expert may not know what he is talking about and you should continue your search for a more knowledgeable and willing expert.

"This is the figure I read from an industry association study."
- This should lead you to verify that such a study was conducted and to attempt to interview people involved with the report and its findings.

"The industry figure is XX because our sales are half that and we are number 2 in the industry."
- This is probably one of the best types of answers you can get. Any time an industry expert gives you a figure based on something he is positive about, you can almost take it to the bank. The best you can do after this is to find other industry analysts and ask them to comment on the figure you were given.

Misinformation can lead to a decision making disaster. Following the simple techniques described above can take you a long way down the road to making good decisions based on near perfect information.

Case Study: Jelly Beans

In our information society, which produces thousands of databases and other resources every day, it seems that most decision makers rely primarily on traditional information sources. More often than not executives will spend lots of time and money trying to determine the size of a market or information about a competitor, and if the answer cannot be found through conventional sources, the corporate decision is made without the information. This does not have to be the case.

We believe that you can find solid information for almost any problem, no matter how sensitive the issue may be, if you use some unorthodox research techniques. To illustrate this point, here is a step-by-step account of how one of our researchers succeeded in gathering figures on the U.S. market for jelly beans when a Fortune 500 firm came up emptyhanded after exhausting all traditional sources. The prevailing view both inside and outside the industry was that this piece of the information puzzle could not be obtained.

It should be said at the outset that the estimates Information USA, Inc. finally obtained must not be regarded as 100% accurate, but they do represent the best available figures and, most likely, come within 10% to 15% of the actual number.

Opening Round

Faced with the problem of finding the U.S. market for jelly beans, we already knew that our client had contacted the major market research firms, did some literature searches, and came up with practically no useful information. As is evident from this case study, this information hunt occurred when Ronald Reagan was President and jelly beans happened to be the candy of choice of several very high government officials.

1)   The first call was to the U.S. Department of Commerce to locate the government's jelly bean expert. We were referred to Cornelius Kenny, the confectionery industry expert. Mr. Kenny was out that day and would call us back when he returned to the office.

2)   A search of Gale's *Encyclopedia of Associations* identified four relevant trade associations. However, upon contacting them we were told that they provide information only to their members.

3)   The White House seemed like a good bet because of Ronald Reagan's fondness for jelly beans and the resulting publicity. The Public Affairs office at 1600 Pennsylvania Avenue said that it never obtained statistical information on the industry but could tell us tales about a lifesize water buffalo and portraits of the President constructed of jelly beans. However, they suggested that we contact several lobbying organizations. Calls to these groups proved fruitless.

4)   A call to the U.S. Bureau of the Census uncovered John Streeter, an analyst who monitors the panned candy industry. He told us:

*   jelly beans have never been counted and there would be no way to get the answer;

*   the non-chocolate panned candy category within the Bureau's Annual Confectionery Survey contains jelly beans;

*   the seasonal category of the non-chocolate panned candies, according to his estimates, contains 90% jelly beans because most jelly beans are sold during Easter and that jelly beans are about the only non-chocolate panned manufactured candy sold on a seasonal basis;

*   \$37,804,000 worth of non-chocolate panned candy was shipped by U.S. manufacturers in 1984, which represents about 48,354,000 pounds; the figures for total non-chocolate panned candy for 1984 totaled \$251,525,000 and 237,308,000 pounds; and

*   government regulations prohibited him from revealing the names of jelly bean manufacturers, but he did refer us to two trade associations he thought might help.

So this analyst at the Census Bureau, who tried to discourage us with warnings that no such figure for the jelly bean market exists, actually gave us quite a lot of concrete information as well as some valuable leads to pursue.

Armed and Dangerous
With a Little Information

At this point, we had a market estimate from one government expert based on a figure generated by the U.S. Bureau of the Census. It may have sounded like the answer we were after, but taking that figure to our client at this juncture would have been premature and possibly irresponsible. The main drawback was that the estimate reflected only one person's opinion, and although he was an expert, he was not a true industry observer as one would be if they were actually in the business of selling jelly beans. Our strategy now was to find people in the industry who could give us their interpretation of these figures.

The Census expert referred us to one of the trade associations we had already contacted. However, when we called back saying that Mr. Streeter at the Census Bureau suggested we call them, the association promptly responded with a list of the 25 major jelly bean manufacturers. This is an example of how using the name of a government expert can get you in the door and get you the information you're looking for. When we phoned several manufacturers, they laughed when we told them of our effort to ascertain the market for jelly beans. Jelly beans had never been counted, they told us, and their advice was to give up.

At this point Mr. Kenny, the confectionery expert at the U.S. Department of Commerce called us back and he, too, said that the market had never been measured. However, he did hazard a guess that the jelly bean market could be roughly 50% of the total Census figure for Non-Chocolate Panned Candy.

A separate call to a private research group which does trend analysis by surveying grocery stores shared its estimate that 90% of all jelly beans are sold at Easter.

Easier to Be a Critic Than a Source

Our lack of success in dealing with a few manufacturers caused us to change tactics. Instead of asking them to estimate the size of the jelly bean market, we began asking them what they thought of the figures we received from the industry analysts at the Commerce Department, as well as the Census Bureau. We decided to try to find someone who actually filled out the Census survey and get a reaction to the Census figures. We spoke with the owner of Herbert Candies, a small candy company. He gave us his 1984 jelly bean production and cost statistics, told us he filled out the Census report, and readily explained what he thought the Census statistics meant in terms of jelly bean production and cost. Furthermore, using his calculator, he helped us arrive at national figures for 1984. He also told us which companies manufacture 80% of the jelly beans produced in the country.

Now, armed with actual figures for 1984 jelly bean production, average cost per pound, average number of jelly beans in a pound, and the percentage of jelly beans produced during Easter, we resumed calling manufacturers — this time to get their opinion of our figures. This was the real turning point in dealing with the manufacturers. Because everyone in the industry knew that there were no exact numbers on the size of the jelly bean market, as professionals they were afraid to give a figure because anyone could say it was wrong. However, because they were experts in the business, they were not afraid to criticize someone else's information. Reactions from insiders were just what we needed to help hone a good working number. The manufacturers were able to tell us why our figures were good or not and they gave us sound reasons why the numbers should be adjusted, such as "Based on our sales figures your numbers sound a little low," or "Not all manufacturers report to the Bureau of the Census, so that figure may be low."

To show how this tactic prompted many manufacturers to be candid about both the industry and their sales in particular, here are highlights of our conversations with nine companies. What is presented below may seem to be too detailed, but after reviewing them we hope that it proves our point about how open business executives can be about their company.

1) Owner, Herbert Candies (small manufacturer and retailer)

* 90% of jelly beans are sold at Easter
* 60% of Census seasonal category are jelly beans
* average cost of jelly beans is $1 per pound
* when President Reagan first got into office the jelly bean market shot up 150% but now it is back to normal
* four companies have 80% of the market, with E.J. Brach the largest at 40%, Brock the second largest, followed by Herman Goelitz and Maillard
* Herbert Candies sold 30,000 pounds of jelly beans this past year and 90% at Easter; 10,000 were gourmet beans at $3.20

per pound and 20,000 were regular jelly beans at $2.80 per pound

2) Marketing Department, Nabisco Confectionery

* suggested we call SAMI, a private market research firm
* estimated 90% of jelly beans are sold at Easter
* confirmed that E.J. Brach has 40% of the market

3) Vice President of Marketing and Sales, Herman Goelitz (producer of "Bellies," Ronald Reagan's favorite)

* between 35% and 50% of his jelly beans are sold at Easter
* $1.00 per pound could be the average retail price
* a retailer can purchase jelly beans at $.60 per pound
* the retail price ranges between $1.25 and $5 per pound

4) General Manager, Burnell's Fine Candy (manufacturer of hanging bag jelly beans)

* 75% of jelly beans are sold at Easter
* $.60 to $.75 per pound is average manufacturer's price
* $1.59 is the average retail price
* 75% of Census seasonal category is probably jelly beans

5) Senior VP of Marketing and Sales, E.J. Brach (largest manufacturer)

* produces 24 million jelly beans annually at an average price of $.86 per pound
* there are approximately 100 beans per pound
* Brach's selling price is about industry average
* they have about 50% of the market
* 90% of the jelly beans sold at Easter sounds too high

6) Product Manager of Marketing Department, Brock Candy (second largest manufacturer)

* 85% to 95% of all jelly beans are sold at Easter
* average price paid by retailers is $.59 to $.99 per pound
* there are 130 to 140 jelly beans in a pound
* E.J. Brach has 40% to 50% of the jelly bean business — 32 to 45 million jelly beans sold in a year sounds correct given Brock's production figures; but probably it is closer to the high side
* Brock Candy is number 2 in the industry
* there are not many jelly bean manufacturers and basing total production on E.J. Brach's sales figures is a good way to arrive at an industry estimate

7) Traffic Manager, Powell Confectionery (medium size producer)

* 75% of jelly beans are sold at Easter judging from Powell's sales
* average retail price $.75 to $.80 per pound and the average manufacturer's price is $.65 to $.70 per pound

* 35 to 45 million jelly beans per year sounds reasonable
* it seems fair to double E.J. Brach production figures to get the total market because it has about 50% share of the market

8) President, Ferrara Panned Candy (largest panned candy producer)

* familiar with Census data and believes that jelly beans represent about 75% to 80% of the seasonal sales; 80% to 90% of all jelly beans are sold at Easter
* 32 to 45 million pounds per year seems a bit low
* E.J. Brach has 50% of the packaged jelly bean market but has less than half of the bulk jelly bean market

9) New Product Development Manager, Farley Candy

* familiar with Census data and believes that the numbers are understated because not all companies report their figures
* an industry estimate of 32 to 50 million pounds per year seems low

So much for all those who discouraged us from even tackling this issue of the market for jelly beans. All the data poured forth during these telephone conversations provided more information than our Fortune 500 client ever expected.

Deciding on an Estimate

As you can see from the interviews outlined above, traffic managers all the way up to company presidents were willing to give us their best estimate of the size of the market and even divulge their own company's sales figures.

After government experts, the figure seemed to cluster around the 45 to 50 million pound range. It may not be that obvious from just reading the highlights of our interviews, but that consensus became apparent after talking with about a dozen people associated with the industry.

Information Exchange Is a People Business

It is just surprising what company executives and government experts are willing to tell you if they are approached in the right way. You can find the answer to any question (or at least a good estimate) as long as you expect to make many phone calls and you treat each person on the other end of the telephone in a friendly, appreciative way.

The biggest difference between those who succeed in their information quest and those who fail boils down to whether or not they believe the information exists. If you persist in thinking the information can be found, nine times out of ten you will get what you need.

My Favorite Bureaucrat

In 1989, Information USA awarded $5,000 to the best story submitted describing how a bureaucrat was of help to you. Two runner-up awards were also given at $500 each. We received close to 1,000 entries and each one proved once again how important and powerful government resources can be. Listed below are a selection of the stories we received. The entry number at the end of the story reflects the number assigned to the entry at the time of submission. If you would like to know about the winner, contact our office.

* Children's Book Writer Finds Success with Free Marketing, Legal and Tax Help

A man in Seattle, Washington wrote a book called "Bill the Dog and Mr. TV Head," but didn't know what to do with his great idea until he contacted his local Small Business Development Center. He read about the center in Information USA's "Government Giveaways for Entrepreneurs." He made an appointment to meet with a counselor, Bill Jacobs, the very next day. As the writer tells it, Bill Jacobs was great. He went over all the facts and asked twenty more questions that the author, himself, hadn't ever thought about. Since the product was an educational book for children, Mr. Jacobs gathered a bundle of marketing information from the U.S. Department of Education. He helped the author settle on objectives and determined how to best meet them. He also secured a government mailing list of those interested in the book, and arranged to get him lower mailing rates at the post office as well as help in filing his taxes. All these services were free of charge. (Entry #3)

* Public Works Worker Passes Buck Quickly to Save Credit Manager's Job

A credit manager for the Sherwin-Williams company had trouble collecting on an old debt of $2,220 worth of paint sold to the Public Works Department of the City of Oakland, California. His boss said that if he didn't collect the check by the end of the month, he would have to suffer the consequences, both financially and emotionally. He kept calling Public Works and didn't receive any attention until a Ms. Perle Goins heard about his predicament. Perle processed the check immediately and called him to see if he would like to come down in person to pick it up. Although the San Francisco earthquake had recently occurred making travel difficult, he went down immediately to pick up the check. The credit manager says that Perle saved his job and possibly his career because "she cares and is willing to do what it takes to get the job done." (Entry #8)

* HUD Auditor Helps Co-Op Owners in Arizona

An auditor for HUD was sent to the Concord Village Co-Op in Tempe, Arizona to investigate a report of irregularities sent into HUD's Inspector General's Office. Since his initial visit he continues to return to investigate when aggravated co-op owners call on him. The owners feel that this auditor is their only recourse in dealing with management. (Entry #16)

* State Official Returns Kidnapped Son to Mom

In August, 1979, a separated woman living in Wisconsin came home one day to find her son had been kidnapped by his father. She contacted Christopher Foley, Wisconsin's Attorney General, and found that she had very little recourse because the father and boy had left the state. A year later Mr. Foley called the mother to tell her that the laws had changed so they now had the right to go after the father and return the boy. By searching telephone records Mr. Foley was able to locate the father in Houston, Texas and had him arrested. Mom flew down to pick up her son. The mother feels she would never have had her child back if it were not for Mr. Foley's efforts to act above and beyond the call of duty by making that extra phone call one year later. (Entry #18)

* Inmate Says Welding Instructor Is Saving the World

An inmate at the Oregon State Penitentiary has a welding instructor named Joe Karvandi who is dedicated to helping inmates learn a trade or skill. Joe believes that inmates who respond to training are likely to be become productive members of society, because they've been given an example of a normal, responsible life style. The inmate feels that without this man's determination and concern for society, the percentage of repeat criminals would be much higher. He believes that Joe is reaching at least one in ten inmates and that his contribution is making our society a better and safer place to live. (Entry #30)

* County Official's House Call Is Highlight of Plumber's Life

A woman named Sheri moved to rural Mississippi with her husband, three year old daughter, and seventy-eight year old father. Within months of moving, her father was diagnosed with throat cancer. Her father's income came from a New York plumber's union pension which needed notarized documents in order to continue sending him checks to pay his medical bills. Sheri's father was bedridden so she couldn't leave the house to see a notary. Mr. Bobby Parker, a county beat supervisor, heard about the problem. He not only took the time to drive way out to their house to see her father and handle the paperwork, but he also visited with her father and made him feel like the most important appointment on his schedule--something much needed by a lonely, terminally ill, elderly man. Her father died a few months later taking with him the memory of his last and gratefully finest outside contact. (Entry #32)

* County Commissioner Is Last Hope for Dying Cancer Victim

A woman living on the East Coast traveled 1,100 miles to Oklahoma to care for her mother who was dying of stomach cancer. When she got there she found her mother in a messy situation. Her mother was living on $400 per month and the doctors and health care providers wanted to charge as much as $92 per visit. Everywhere she turned she was told that her mother was not eligible for any special medical programs. In desperation she called a friend who in turn called County Commissioner Elton Lamb. Within an hour Elton was at her house, took one look at her mother, and within minutes returned with the county nurse. The nurse proceeded to give her morphine, along with instructions on how to administer more when needed. Mr. Lamb took the woman's daughter aside and said "No widow-lady should have to suffer like this, just because she can't afford help. I am very sorry that happened and it is all taken care of now." That night her mother died in her arms. She will never - as long as she lives - forget the compassion of County Commissioner Elton Lamb. (Entry #41)

* State Librarian Saves Government Contractor Hundreds in Documents Costs

A contracts administrator in Utah works for a business that relies on government contracts. He relies on Ferne Kelso, Procurement Consultant at Utah's Military Specification Library, to deliver military specifications quickly and inexpensively when he needs them. In recent months he has sent three different people over to her office to get documents. None had any prior knowledge about how to find the documents they needed, but by the end of their first library visit, they could easily find all of them. When they came across documents the library didn't have, Ferne directed them to the necessary sources and always recommended alternative sources with specific names and telephone numbers. Through her friendliness and wonderful, helpful attitude, she has saved his company hundreds of dollars in labor and documents costs. (Entry #44)

* Delinquent Taxpayer Finds a Helpful Hand at the IRS

A woman in Virginia Beach owed the IRS a lot of back taxes as well as penalties. Revenue Agent L.R. Phelps was assigned to find Mary and collect. When Ms. Phelps located Mary, she was very helpful in solving her problem and worked out a payment schedule. Ms. Phelps performed her job in a manner that was friendly but

My Favorite Bureaucrat

professional, understanding but firm, and patient but aggressive. Mary says she is embarrassed to admit she found a helpful bureaucrat and she's glad Ms. Phelps is in the position. (Entry #53)

* Iowa Governor Keeps Trucks Rolling for Small Businessman

A dispatcher who works for Morgan Drive Away in Iowa, was trying to make sure one of the trucks loaded with gym equipment would make it in time to meet a ship in California. The ship would deliver the equipment to U.S. servicemen overseas. Along the way ,the truck driver was stopped in a southern state and told by authorities that he couldn't travel that day because it was Columbus Day. If the driver didn't travel that day, he would miss the boat. The driver called the dispatcher. The dispatcher told management and somehow Governor Terry Brandstad called Sandy to tell him that he personally talked to the Governor of the southern state involved and everything was now on its way. (Entry #54)

* Local Agency Worker Gets Money in Hours to Save Family from Losing Home

A mortgage company in South Carolina had a client who was about to lose his house if he didn't make his payment the next day. The mortgage company took the client in to see Johnny Ruth Jenkins at the local Human Resource Center. She immediately sized up the situation and realized it was an emergency. She stopped what she was doing, skipped lunch, and within a few hours was able to get the funds from another government agency to pay the bill. Since the incident, the family has been back on their feet, but would have been homeless if it weren't for Ms. Jenkins. (Entry #70)

* Motor Vehicles Clerk Shows Driver How to Beat the System

A woman in Massachusetts and her husband moved and had to change their motor vehicle registrations. The woman took the necessary paperwork for her and her husband's car to the Registry of Motor Vehicles to make the necessary changes. Changing the registration for her car was a snap. But when it came to her husband's car the clerk said, "We can't process this without your husband's signature." Her heart sank. She told the clerk it was going to take another day or two to get the signature because her husband worked a long way off. The clerk said, "Go outside, get your husband's signature and bring it back to me." The clerk kept repeating this phrase to her and she kept telling the clerk it was going to take two days. They kept going back and forth. She thought the clerk had no brains, and that there was a total breakdown in communication, so she left. On the way out the door she realized what the clerk was telling her to do. She went behind a tree and forged her husband's signature. When she came back into the office the clerk said, "You didn't have to go all the way outside." (Entry #72)

* State Tax Auditor Shows Small Business How to Reduce Tax

A woman was running a small business in New Jersey when the state tax auditor walked into her office one day and asked to see all of her records. After reviewing the documentation for several days, it was clear that she was due a heavy fine for not having the necessary paperwork to identify which customers were tax exempt, and a problem in her payroll records. However the agent was terrific. He was friendly and personable and told her exactly what to say in a letter to his supervisor to try and get the fine reduced. In a few weeks she received word that she would only have to pay a token fine. (Entry #77)

* Bureau of Mines Asbestos Researcher Saves the Day for Litigator

A legal researcher working on a class action asbestos case identified an important study at the National Archives that was 50 years old. The study concluded that asbestos is one of the most hazardous substances known to man. The study was signed, but the credentials of the author could not be found until the legal researcher contacted Bob Virta, staff asbestos researcher at the Bureau of Mines. Bob spent that afternoon in the Bureau's library and immediately faxed the researcher chapter and verse about the author in question. Bob sent articles with his comments on the side, information on his academic awards, the accession number of his correspondence file when he worked at the Bureau and even the location of the cemetery where he's buried. He also included a list of people who attended the funeral back in 1972. (Entry #78)

* Ex-Corporate Executive Saves Over $5,000 in Tax Accounting Charges by Using IRS Hotline

An ex-corporate executive in Delaware was used to having his taxes prepared by high priced tax consultants. When he retired he decided to try it himself, but ran into problem because he didn't know how to handle something called "passive activity losses". He called the IRS "800" number and found Mrs. Pat Phillips who researched his question and called him back within a day. She also followed up by sending him some sample work sheets explaining the solution in detail. The next tax season he called the IRS hotline again and continued to get excellent responses. He estimates that this free service has saved him at least $5,000 in tax consulting services. (Entry #83)

* Postal Service Consumer Affairs Gets Results for Lousy Delivery

A computer company in New Jersey moved their offices to a new location on the second floor of a building. The new postal carrier disliked having to climb up the flight of stairs and started harassing the company and obstructing mail delivery. The company called the carrier's supervisor, with no results. They contacted the regional office and also got no results. Then they called the U.S. Postal Service's Office of Consumer Affairs in Washington, DC. They wrote a letter as advised, and promptly got a visit from an official at the regional office, followed by an apology from the postal carrier. (Entry #84)

* New Jersey Chemical Company Succeeds in Business Thanks to Many Helpful Bureaucrats

A manager at Moeller Chemicals recalls Thomas Jefferson who said, "My God, how little do my countrymen know what precious blessing they are in possession of and which no other people on earth enjoy." He believes helpful bureaucrats are one of these precious blessings Jefferson referred to in his writings. He has used Nina McGlone, a clerk at the U.S. Department of Treasury, to help him through a tax problem which dates back to 1985. Special DEA Agent Leslie D. Hoppy at the U.S. Department of Justice was a great help to him in showing their company how to fight against the illicit use of chemicals for the manufacture of narcotics. And, John Markus, Chief of Manufacturing and Quality Control for FDA's Center for Veterinary Medicine, has spent many valuable hours helping him through tedious animal drug applications both over the telephone and through the mail. (Entry #84)

* Young Woman Buys Condo with Help of Little-Known Money Program

A woman living in the District of Columbia thought that at the age of 27 she would never be able to afford her own home--but she was wrong. A little-known local program allowed her to put down 5% on a one bedroom condo, gave her a loan at 3% for $16,000, and gave her a loan at 0% interest to cover the $4,000 closing costs. The rest was financed conventionally. (Entry #93)

* Customer Service Manager for Machinery Corporation Learns Real Customer Service from Government Trade Specialist

The customer service manager for a U.S. subsidiary of a Japanese company was making calls all over the government trying to obtain the necessary forms for exporting and then re-importing repaired circuit boards from Japan. Someone eventually directed him to Mary at the U.S. Department of Commerce. She listened to the problem and said she would find the answer. She got the answer, called him back immediately and volunteered to send him the necessary forms. She also volunteered to make the calls necessary to find out where he should send the forms. She was uncommonly courteous, polite and eager to help. She also called him back in a few days after he received the forms to see if everything had gone smoothly. This customer service manager said he "learned some principles about customer service" from her. (Entry #94)

* Congressional Assistant Helps Citizens Committee Turn NIKE Site into Community Golf Course

Ed Murnane, while working as an assistant to Congressman Philip M. Crane, worked with the Citizens Committee of Arlington Heights, IL to convince the government to give up their plans to build a grandiose Army reserve center in the middle of their town and to instead deed the property over to the city to be used as a park. He went to bat for the community by helping to motivate, inspire and formulate a plan of action that was eventually effective. The city now has a 90 acre golf course that gets over 60,000 rounds of play a year. (Entry #97)

* Smiling Immigration and Naturalization Service Official Takes Pride in Helping Adopted Babies

A few years ago a couple living in New Jersey started the long, arduous and frustrating process of filing for a foreign adoption. It involved standing in lines for hours to pick up a single form and took them to city, state and federal offices. After one year of paperwork, they got a call from their adoption agency saying there was a baby girl waiting for them in Chile. They immediately went to work on the final paperwork because they were told it would take six weeks to process. After many telephone calls to the Newark INS Office, the woman finally reached a HUMAN who asked how she could help. When she heard about the baby, she said, "How wonderful - you must be so excited. Come over to my office right away." When the woman arrived she was greeted by a smiling woman, Mrs. Pollard, who had an entire wall covered with pictures of "her babies" that she had helped get adopted in the U.S. What was supposed to take 6 weeks, this smiling bureaucrat did in only 30 minutes. On the way out the door, Mrs. Pollard wished her luck in her new role as a mother and said she expected a picture for her wall. (Entry #103)

* State Legislative Researcher Finds Money for Struggling Artists

Any time a researcher from the South Carolina Chamber of Commerce needs some information for one of her members, she calls Len Marini, researcher at the Joint Committee on Cultural Affairs. Although he has an amazing scope of professional and volunteer commitments, he always responds immediately to any of her needs. More astounding is his dedication to the cultural community at a grass roots level. He devotes much of his time to help struggling artists, actors, photographers, et. al. He is creative in seeking ways to fund their projects, as well as providing moral support and guidance. He also participates in the arts. He serves on the boards of the local theater and library, works the theater concessions, and has had leading roles in productions such as A Streetcar Named Desire. (Entry #105)

* Call to County Consumer Office Gets Two Free T-Bones

A man in Nassau County, New York was walking into a local food market when he saw a sign on the window that read "Sirloin Steak $1.19 per pound" (this was a few years ago). When he walked over to the meat counter he saw only one badly cut steak in the case. He rang the bell and asked for another cut but was told there was nothing more to cut from. He asked to speak to the meat manager and got no results. He asked to see the store manager and got no results. He went home and called James Picken, Jr., Commissioner of Consumer Affairs. Later that night after he finished dinner, the doorbell rang and standing there was the store manager with two free 2-inch sirloins as a peace offering, thanks to the commissioner's phone call to the store. (Entry #111)

* Michigan Banker Gets the Law Changed in an Afternoon on the Hill

A Michigan banker visiting Capitol Hill with other bankers overheard talk about a piece of legislation which would affect his bank and a handful of other banks in the county. After talking to his Congressman's aide, who called other congressional aides, they were able to get the legislation changed within hours. (Entry #114)

* Government Helps Firearms Entrepreneur on Consulting Fees

An Air Force employee was very active in target shooting and decided to get into the business. He realized that he needed the proper licenses from the U.S. Office of Alcohol, Tobacco and Firearms, when he saw advertisements in gun magazines for consultants who would charge big money to get this information. When he called the office directly he found that the government would send him the information for free, let him attend free seminars on the topic, and provide him with an 800 number to answer any special questions. (Entry #117)

* Bureaucrat Barred Thalidomide

During the early 1960's, thousands of pregnant women in Europe took a new sedative called thalidomide that resulted in the birth of babies without arms or legs or with other deformities. A low level GS-14 bureaucrat, Dr. Frances Lesey at the Food and Drug Administration, held off the pressures from the drug companies and even from within the FDA to approve the drug before she had finished testing it. (Entry 119)

* Coordinator of Vital Records Saves Families and Funeral Directors Valuable Time

Until recently it took 120 to 150 days to have either a major or minor correction made to a death certificate in New York City. When Mrs. Francine Benjamin went to work for the city Department of Health, she cut this time down to 10 days even though it had been done the other way for 20 years. (Entry #121)

* U.S. Attorney's Public Service Includes Towing Stranded Automobiles

Two women driving through Montana on the way to a wedding found themselves stranded in the middle of a Crow Indian Reservation. Along came a very kind man who stopped, drove them to the nearest town, got a tow chain, drove them back to their car, and towed them to a town 40 miles away where they could get help. He was the U.S. Attorney for Billings. He wouldn't take money and said he hoped they would do the same if they found someone stranded.

* Social Security Administration Tracks Down Missing Father of 20 Years

The parents of Mr. James divorced in 1943, while he was serving in the U.S. Army Air Corps. Although he kept up with his mother, he could not find his father no matter how much searching he did through government organizations and public records. Twenty years later his congressman's office told him to write his father a letter explaining that he wanted to contact him, and they would have the Social Security Administration forward it to his last known address. In this way, confidentiality would be maintained. Within a week his father contacted him and arranged for an immediate two week visit. (Entry #124)

* Genealogy Researcher Gets a Surprise Bonanza from County Clerk

When a man in Illinois wrote to the County Clerk's office in Salem, Indiana, he was in for a pleasant surprise. His letter was a request for marriage records from the 1850's for some of his wife's ancestors. The clerk at the office not only sent him copies of the old marriage records, but gave him her home address and said that he could write her personally if he needed more information. He did write her and received so much family history information that it extended his wife's family line back to the pre-Revolutionary War era. Over the years he wrote to her a few more times and each time she responded quickly and efficiently. (Entry #135)

* State Geological Office Saves Residents from Collapsing Mines.

An area in Ohio was plagued by abandoned mines that were collapsing and seriously damaging houses. Property owners were descending on the local library to obtain precise information on the location of the mines. The library didn't have such information, but the head of reference services contacted the state Geological Survey Division and was put in touch with Mr. Rea. Mr. Rea saved the day. He patiently explained the terminology to the librarian in detail so that she could order the proper documents. There were different scale maps available and he advised her to first look at a small-scale map covering the whole county (which he sent free of charge), and then decided for which areas more detailed maps were needed. After the first phone call he even called back to explain that the maps were on light sensitive paper and should be kept away from light. Within days, and with his help, all the necessary maps were available for library patrons. (Entry #137)

* Local HUD Official Saves Mother of Two from Living in the Streets

A young woman in Ohio living in HUD subsidized housing was about to be evicted because she was behind in rent. The woman had two children and also received aid for dependent children. Her sister called the local HUD office and asked to make arrangements for the woman and her children to remain in their home if the rent was caught up and advance payments were made. The answer was a resounding no. The only immediate solution would have been to have her and her two children move into her mother's two bedroom apartment. Her mother had recently undergone a serious back operation and had no income, therefore the solution was not practical. Her sister called HUD again and had an opportunity to speak with Ms. Prince. Ms Prince superseded the system, allowed the woman to pay back rent, and gave her an extension on her lease pending an inspection. The woman was very grateful because she knew that once evicted from federal housing, she wouldn't be eligible to apply for subsidized rent again. If this had occurred, she would have been forced to live in a crowded situation or on the street. (Entry #138)

My Favorite Bureaucrat

* Attorney General Retrieves $1,000 for Couple from Phantom Furniture Store

When a woman in Seattle got married she and her husband fell victim to a furniture scam. They paid $1,000 up front on $1,500 worth of furniture and waited for delivery. The furniture was never delivered. When they returned to the store a few days later the store was completely empty. They called the office of the state Attorney General and were told that there were many people ahead of them who had similar complaints against the company. They also told them that the owners had opened another store 20 miles away. They were given a choice of either waiting in line for legal action, or going to the new store and asking for a refund. They went to the new store, and were given a refund thanks to the information supplied by the Attorney General. (Entry #148)

* IRS Agent Shows Taxpayer How to Beat the System

A young man from Kansas who had recently married reworked his tax return dozens of times because he could not believe that he was going to owe the IRS $750. This was $750 he didn't have. He decided to go to the local IRS office and have them check it. The agent confirmed his worst fears, that he had computed his taxes correctly. But the agent also told him what to do if he couldn't pay the bill. "Do not send in your return until April 15th. Save every cent you can. Then on the 15th, go down to the post office just before midnight and mail your return. Enclose a check for as much as you have saved and a note stating that you cannot pay your tax liability in full at the present time, but you intend to as soon as possible. If you wait until the last minute to send in your return they won't get to it until July, and then it will go into a group of problem returns. They probably won't get to it until October. By then you should have saved enough to pay it off in full, plus interest on the late portion. It's all legal and you ought to come out fine." The man followed the agent's instructions, and just as the agent had predicted, it all worked out. (Entry #153)

* It Only Takes Hours for Newlyweds to Make Their First Move

A man from Detroit, Michigan married a Canadian in Winnipeg, Manitoba. He had heard many horror stories about how long they would have to be separated until they could get the proper documentation allowing his wife to reside with him in the United States. When they went to the U.S. Consulate in Winnipeg, they were met with long lines and were expecting the worst. Instead they met a consulate official named Jeffrey Baron. In less than an hour, he processed all the required paperwork to allow them to both enter the United States. He also explained everything they needed to cross the border into the United States. Instead of waiting weeks, they were able to go into the U.S. that same day. (Entry #168)

* State Senator Saves Beerman's Business

The state of Arizona passed a law which prevented a small beer business from ever doing business again. The owner thought he had lost everything until he contacted State Senator Pat Wright. She took the time to explain his rights to him and all the procedures required to change his situation. With her help and support he ended up in front of the State Senate Hearing Committee and had the law changed. (Entry #174)

* Local Official Pulls All the Stops to Help Woman Get Stop Light

A woman in Michigan wanted to get a traffic light at a dangerous corner near her home. She began collecting signatures, attending city council meetings, and writing city and state officials, but didn't get anywhere. She even collected accident data and understood the ins and out of the "Michigan Manual for Uniform Traffic Control Devices." Then state representative Alvin J. Hoekman got involved and gave her all the assistance he could. The light was installed shortly thereafter. (Entry #178)

* Consumer Utility Official Saves Customers Money, Returns Part of Its Budget to the Treasury and Even Offers Free Meals

A report from the Attorney General of Colorado shows that in its first three years of operation, Colorado's Office of Consumer Counsel was solely responsible for $4.7 million in savings to utility customers, and was primarily responsible for $50 million in annual savings and $73 million more in one-time savings. During this same period of time their expenditures were $1.7 million and each year they returned part of their budget to the state treasury. After long meetings far away from home, the head of

the office, Ron Binz, often invited committee members to stay at his home for dinner and a night's sleep. (Entry #180)

* IRS Agents Shows How Ignorance Does Not Have to Be Taxing

A taxpayer in New Jersey had a windfall in 1988, and in April of 1989 filed and paid a tax based primarily on his windfall. Then in August he received a notice of a penalty of $1,200 for not filing an Estimated Tax Payment. He knew nothing about such a filing and called the IRS 800 number for help. Mr. LeFleur answered the telephone and spent a good deal of time explaining the rules concerning Estimated Taxes. He also read and explained the categories under which he could claim an exception and not pay the penalty. It was obvious that his situation did not fit any of the exceptions. Mr. LeFleur suggested that he write a detailed letter asking to have the penalty removed. He felt that someone reading the letter might accept "Ignorance of the Law" as an excuse. The man wrote the letter and shortly thereafter was notified that his penalty had been lifted based on his explanation. (Entry #181)

* AID Official Helps U.S. Company Get Turkish Contract

A U.S. Company was bidding on a contract in Turkey to build a national radio transmission monitoring system. However, a Canadian company was about to get the contract because the Canadian government was going to throw in a $100,000 feasibility study to sweeten the deal. The U.S. Agency for International Development (AID) decided to match the Canadian deal and, as a result the U.S. company got the contract. (Entry #182)

* Generous Census Worker Helps Woman with Marketing Plan

A woman in Omaha needed to know the concentration of people between the ages of 40 and 60 in order to develop a marketing plan. She didn't know where to start so she called the clerk of her community for help. This call led to four additional calls. All of the kind and generous people she spoke to were willing to explain what data was available and the best place for her to obtain it. Within four hours, including lunch, she was back in her office with all the latest data she needed to solve her problem. (Entry #183)

* Third Grader Gets Help for Science Project from Senator's Office

A third grader in Louisiana had to do a project for science class on a famous astronaut. He and his mom went to the library and couldn't find anything very interesting to report on. When they got home they decided to call Senator John Glenn's Office in Washington, DC for help. Within one week the boy had a wonderful autographed picture of the ex-astronaut along with a bunch of background articles to make him the envy of his class. (Entry #185)

* Transportation Secretary Gets Parachutist Out of Jail

In October, 1986, Michael Sergio showed his enthusiasm for the Mets baseball team by parachuting into the middle of Shea Stadium during the 6th game of the World Series, without permission. The criminal court of Queens treated it as a harmless venture and sentenced Sergio to 100 hours of community service and a $500 fine. However, the FAA held Sergio in contempt of court for not revealing the name of the pilot who flew his plane and sentenced him to six months in jail and a $100 a day fine for each day he continued his silence. As soon as Michael went to jail his parents wrote a letter of appeal to the Secretary of Transportation, Elizabeth Dole. Not only were his parents upset about the cruel and unusual punishment he was receiving, they were also very concerned because Michael's youngest brother was dying of cancer and his brother did not want Michael to be in jail when the end of his life came. Ms. Dole responded quickly and Michael was home with his brother within three weeks. (Entry #188)

* State Counselor Helps Vet When Congressman Fails

When a man from upstate New York received his military discharge, he had a service connected disability but was turned away by the Veterans Administration to receive financial compensation. He contacted his Congressman and even he couldn't help. Years later when a co-worker asked about his limping, he told him his military disability story. The co-worker suggested that he see his brother-in-law who was a veteran's counselor for the state of New York. After a thorough medical exam, a review of the paperwork, and a hearing in front of the appeal board, the Veterans Administration approved him for compensation. (Entry #202)

Be patient. If any phone number is incorrect, call (area code) 555-1212 and request the new listing.

* Postal Supervisor Bucks the System to Get a Company Its Money Sooner

When a small company moved their offices from Hillsdale to Lakewood, New Jersey, they encountered a big problem. The business depended on the mail for its survival. All their orders and money came in by mail. But because of their move, for some reason their mail was taking up to six weeks to catch up to them. When they called their old post office to investigate the trouble, the supervisor who answered the telephone took it upon himself to change the system and have their mail handled as first class mail each day and not as forwarded mail. This meant that they received the mail within one or two days instead of six weeks. (Entry #206)

* Senator Helps Flight Trainer Business Take Off

An entrepreneur in Milwaukee had been trying for nine months to get federal, state and city agencies to look at his proposal for flight training, but no one would help him. As a last resort he sent a letter to Senator Proxmire detailing his proposal. Within a short period of time he received calls and letters of response from those agencies the Senator had contacted and his business was off and flying. (Entry #208)

* Commerce Official Bends the Rules to Refund $1,000 to Exporter

A management consultant in Chicago put down a $1,000 deposit to participate in an upcoming trade show in India sponsored by the U.S. Department of Commerce. He hoped to represent a number of U.S. companies at the show, but despite his best efforts he could not get a single company interested. When he called the Department of Commerce to cancel, he was told the registration dates had been extended and he still had time to solicit companies. The allotted time passed and he still didn't have a customer. He ask for a refund on his deposit but was informed that the 90 day stipulation had passed and that he was not entitled to the refund. He argued, however, that since they had extended the registration time he should be entitled to the refund. A letter to the supervisor of the person he had been dealing with got him his refund. (Entry #209)

* City Planner Shows Citizens How to Beat the System

A number of citizens in St. Petersburg were worried that a city ordinance might be overturned that required neighbor notification of the installation of satellite dishes. When they contacted Bernice Darling, a planner at the City Planning Department, she gave them great advice. She provided them with copies of the ordinance and the application for change. She also informed them of an upcoming city council meeting concerning the matter. With her help they were able to attend the meeting and stop the ordinance from being changed. (Entry #211)

* Federal Reserve Worker Finds Missing $10,000 for Lady from the Bronx

When a woman in the Bronx had a $20,000 Treasury Note ready to mature, she wrote to the Federal Reserve Board asking that the note be rolled over into two $10,000 notes maturing in two and four years, respectively. She also instructed them to transfer all the interest into her account at Chase Manhattan Bank. When she got her statement from Chase she noticed that she only received interest on one note for $10,000. She called the New York Federal Reserve Bank thinking that all would be lost, but instead found Carol Hayes. Carol really understood the problem completely. She asked a few questions and took her number to call her back. Carol was able to follow the money through the Federal Reserve and into the computers of Chase. During the long process Carol continued to call and give progress reports. She assured the distraught woman that she hadn't forgotten her, and that the $10,000 would be found. When she did find the funds, the lady from the Bronx thanked her to no end. Carol simply said, "Just doing my job." (Entry #212)

* IRS Lets Delinquent Taxpayer Work Out a Deal

A fellow in Oklahoma City was making payments of $1,000 per month to the IRS to satisfy back taxes. However, before he had completed his payments he had back surgery and was laid up for two months unable to earn any money. When payments stopped, the IRS issued a "Notice to Levy" and had his checking and other accounts seized. Although he was truly in the wrong, he called the IRS and spoke to a Mrs. Petrie in the Dallas office. After she listened to his problem she rescinded the "Notice to Levy" and reinstated the repayment plan at half his original monthly payments. He says "this truly was an act of compassion by a caring woman, to whom I am grateful." (Entry #216)

* Woman with Special Title Problem Gets Special Help

A woman purchased a car in Vermont and took it to New York for registration. Due to special circumstances they said it would require eight to ten weeks to process the registration. The woman needed the car for local transportation to work as well as for medical reasons for her son, so she contacted her local assemblyman for assistance. His office said they could not help because they were Republican and the Commissioner of Motor Vehicles was a Democrat. She wrote to the local Department of State and they replied saying they could do nothing. At this time she called the main office of the Division of Motor Vehicles, and after five or six transfers finally contacted Louise in the Titles Department. After explaining her situation, Louise contacted the Director of Titles and worked out a plan to personally walk her title through the bureaucracy. (Entry #217)

* Elderly Mugging Victim Gets Losses Back from State Program

While an elderly man was going through the turnstiles of the New York subway system a young punk snatched his wallet and ran away. The man pursued the culprit but he was too fast to catch. He found two transit police and the three of them spent about a half an hour looking around, but with no luck. The transit police reported the crime to the local police station. A few days later the man read in the newspaper about a state program that compensates elderly residents who are victims of violent crimes. He applied thinking that nothing would happen. Lo and behold, in a few weeks, he received a check in the mail for all the money he lost. (Entry #218)

* Labor Statistics Economist Contributes to Writer's Third Shift

A writer in Baltimore was struggling with a chapter on "How to Survive the Third Shift" for her new book about jobs. She wrote to a regional office of the Bureau of Labor Statistics and received a wonderful response from their office in Dallas. The person in charge of the office sent the writer two articles which served as the basis for the entire chapter in her book. The articles were titled "Late-Shift Employment in Manufacturing Industries" and "Workers on Late Shifts in a Changing Economy." (Entry #219)

* Balloonist Flying High with Help from FAA

When a fellow purchased a foreign registered hot air balloon he dreaded the inspection process required by the FAA. However, he was pleasantly surprised when he ran into Phil and Ernie who are specialists at the FAA. Although getting the balloon ready for inspection was a tedious process with many phone calls over a period of several months, he was very impressed by the two officials. They both had a "we want to help you get this done" attitude, and they always showed an interest in any questions or problems he had. Any forms he requested were sent out the same day and all of his phone calls were promptly returned. On the day of inspection, the balloonist was very late for his appointment, but Ernie stayed even though it put him behind schedule. Ernie also followed up the inspection to see if he was encountering any problems clearing up a few discrepancies. When he sent in his application for air worthiness, Ernie mailed back the necessary forms the following afternoon. (Entry #220)

* Management Consultant Gets the Business from Small Business Office

When a management consultant decided to try to get business from the federal government, he called over 50 small business offices in federal agencies. All but one simply sent him literature on how to do business with their agency. The one standout was Ila Burnell, Small Business Specialist at the Customs Service. She immediately made a personal appointment to meet with him, and gave him other names to contact at Customs. In addition, she referred him to procurement people at NASA where she had formerly worked for many years. Using her name, he contacted these people and was able to set up appointments immediately. Although it's too early to tell if business will come of this yet, he certainly has a running start thanks to Ila. (Entry #221)

* A Bureaucratic Belly Laugh Drops Homeowner's Taxes by $16,000

When a man in Mississippi found out that his property taxes had increased because his house was reassessed at a higher value, he called around asking how he could get his taxes reduced. The general consensus of opinion (and accompanying horselaughs) was that he talk to the county tax assessor. Not to be intimidated he called the county tax assessor, who answered his own telephone, and talked to him. When he explained that he might have been treated unfairly, the assessor asked if he was home during the day. He replied, "Hell no, I'm working two jobs to pay for my home." The tax

Be patient. If any phone number is incorrect, call (area code) 555-1212 and request the new listing.

15

man had an out and out belly laugh over the comment and said he would send someone out the next morning to reassess his house. The house was reassessed and the man's taxes were reduced by $16,000. (Entry #223)

* State Acts as Super Travel Agent

When a couple in Michigan wanted to travel to Niagara Falls and New York City last summer they called the 800 number for the New York State Department of Tourism. They could request packets of information by pressing numbers on their touch tone phone, and if they needed to talk to someone they were able to talk to an operator. The person answering the phone was friendly, courteous and to the point. They discussed special subjects the couple wanted information on, and the tourism official suggested other subjects they might find interesting. In a few weeks the couple had brochures showing the places of interest, maps of everything, dining and lodging information bracketed by prices, as well as helpful tips on using mass transit. Based on all this information, they made their plans and had an excellent vacation. (Entry #233)

* State Employee Gives Immediate Answers to Employer's Questions

A business owner in the state of Washington called the state capital several times for help interpreting a new state law affecting him, but didn't get anywhere. Everyone was in a meeting and he was told that someone from a local office would call him back shortly. He thought to himself, "Oh Sure." The very next day, Candy Hansen, the Employment Standards Supervisor for the local agency called him. She listened to the question, but her initial perusal of the law did not identify the section pertaining to his question. She apologized for not being able to cite chapter and verse immediately, and said that she didn't want to tie up his valuable time - could she call him back? Within a half an hour she called him back with the answer and the next day he received a copy of the bill in the mail. (Entry #236)

* Labor Official Explains New Pension Law to Taxpayer

A man from Ohio called the U.S. Department of Labor in Washington to get some information on a new pension law. The person he was directed to not only explained the law to him, but also sent him literature about the law and then called him back and quizzed him on the particulars to ensure that he really understood it. (Entry #240)

* FAA Official Keeps Aircraft Company Flying High

A few years ago a small aircraft company in Kentucky purchased the assets of another aircraft company that was going out of business. The one thing they were unable to purchase was the Type Certificate which is issued by the FAA and authorizes the company to manufacture new aircraft. They petitioned the FAA to revoke the original certificate on the grounds that it had been dormant for 25 years and to re-award it to their company. The official from the FAA assigned to the case could have easily recommended a denial of the petition on the grounds that the procedure was unprecedented, and could have saved himself a tremendous amount of work. Instead, he researched the case fully, visited the facility to see if they could support the responsibilities of a certificate, investigated the legal aspects of the case, contacted the State Corporate Commission to determine the bankruptcy status of the old company, and forwarded a detailed file to FAA headquarters with a recommendation that the petition be honored. An official from the Kentucky company told the FAA official that in 30 years of doing business he had never encountered a bureaucrat who went so far out of his way to help. The bureaucrat's response was, "The taxpayers pay me to do a service - I am just doing that." (Entry #242)

* Banking Commission Official Lowers Mortgage Rate of Divorced Mother and Saves Her $20,000

A woman in Massachusetts had a "locked-in" deal with a bank to finance her new home at 8.75% interest. However, on the day before closing, a bank official called to tell her that because of current banking conditions they could not be held to the 8.75% rate and recalculated the rate to 11 percent. She had already paid the bank a non-refundable fee of $2,000. As a divorced mother of two, with no family in the area, and ready for settlement the following day, she felt helpless. A call to the State Banking Commission changed this. After she called, an official at the Commission made numerous calls to the bank as well as to the attorney handling the closing. The next day the woman went to the closing as advised by the Commission official, signed the mortgage, and immediately told the lawyers she wanted to cancel the mortgage she had just signed. The Commission official spent the next few days reprimanding the president of the bank. The bank president promptly sent the woman

an apology along with a new mortgage at the 8.75% rate. The difference would have cost her $20,000 in extra interest.

* U.S. Border Patrol Favors Canadian Student Who Doesn't Lie

A young Canadian couple was attending a college in Michigan on student visas. They were aware of the many difficulties others had encountered with proper papers and officials at the border. Once when returning from Canada, the wife discovered she had lost her official documents she needed to cross the border that day. They knew they could lie to the border officials so that she could enter on her husband's student visa. But they decided to be honest and explain the situation to the officials. They could have been sent back to Canada, but they weren't. The officials told them that many people lie to them and that they appreciated their honesty. The officials immediately found a way they both could enter the country and get back to school. (Entry # 248)

* IRS Official Helps Woman in Illinois Turn $1,550 Loss into $669 Gain

A woman in Illinois knew she would owe the IRS some money for the Self Employment Tax, but didn't expect to owe the $1,550 stated on a form she received from the IRS. After being unsuccessful trying to get someone at the IRS to explain why she owed that much money, she finally ran into Jean Doughty at the Kansas City IRS Office. Jean listened carefully and then offered to search out and actually look at the original document. She called back and they were going through the return together when Jean suddenly noticed that the woman had listed her income twice. She then offered to rework the whole return - all eight pages, and check it out. About two weeks later the woman in Illinois got a corrected return and a refund check for $669. (Entry # 258)

* State Insulation Expert Offers Expert Advice to New Homeowner

A lady in Scottsdale is very grateful to Dennis Craston who works for the Arizona Risk Assessment Office. Thanks to his advice, she is living in a new home, secure in the knowledge that her children will be growing up surrounded by safe housing insulation. He made himself readily available by telephone to answer all of her environmental quality questions about Urea-Formaldehyde Form insulation and different ways to test for any dangerous toxins it released into the atmosphere. He was willing to listen and not pass the buck. "He offered realistic and helpful advice on testing, how to, where to, etc. He was like finding a lighthouse in a sea of indifference." (Entry #261)

* Sam at the County Government Makes a Heroine Out of Real Estate Consultant

A woman in Northern Virginia thanks Sam Demme at the County Department of Environmental Management for making her a success at her job. While working for a real estate management consulting firm, Sam turned her into an expert on the general procedure, forms, and processes involved in bonding and releasing commercial real estate projects. Over the four and 1/2 years she dealt with Sam, each visit was met with a smile and each question, an answer.

* Government Librarian Overwhelms Student Seeking Fellowship

When a student from Milwaukee decided she wanted to apply for a Fulbright grant to do research in Uruguay, she was overwhelmed by the paperwork and turned to Mr. Dorn, the Hispanic Culture Specialist at the Library of Congress, for help. This specialist was able to supply what she needed to complete the application including: 1) someone in Uruguay who would collaborate with her on the project, 2) the name, address, and telephone number for the National Library in Uruguay which she contacted directly for further information; and 3) a lengthy computer search, to verify that no publication existed which might have the same results as her intended research. (Entry #272)

* State Representative Shows That One Letter Can Make a Difference in Changing the Law

A man in North Carolina who usually felt insulated against politically related problems, was upset when he read in the paper that the North Carolina Legislature was about to change the requirements for children entering elementary school. They were planning to move the cut-off date for 5-year-olds from October 15th to July 1st so that the average age of children would be 3 and 1/2 months older and they would be likely to score better than states who kept the later cut-off date. He became angry and decided to call his State representative at home. The representative came in from cutting the grass to answer the phone and told the concerned man that he just happened to be chairman of the education committee and would be discussing that proposal the coming week. He suggested that he write a letter stating his opposition. The man was relieved to hear that shortly after writing his letter, the proposal to change was dropped.

* Single Mom Realizes Dream Home Through Little-Known Government Program

A young, single parent living in Pennsylvania thought she would never be able to afford her own home. She checked out the traditional, conventional, and FHA mortgages, and quickly realized that she would not be able to do it without some kind of miracle. Then she learned about a little known program aimed at low income people which made her dream come true. This program, at the Farmers Home Administration, subsidizes her mortgage payments, and the subsidy decreases as her mortgage increases until she is able to assume the full mortgage payment. Any interest the government paid on her behalf over the years is recaptured (based on a formula) when she sells the house. (Entry #282)

* Clerk Helps Couple Outfox Foxy Lawyer in Small Claims Court

A young couple, recently out of college, was moving to another town to start a new job. All was going along smoothly until the landlord decided not to refund their deposit of $100. The couple filed in small claims court and won, but were sent back when the landlord's attorney filed an evasive legal maneuver which stopped them from receiving their money. The couple had no attorney but with the help of Eileen, a clerk at the courthouse, they blocked the attorney's smart maneuver. She spent a lot of her time at the courthouse and on the telephone ensuring that the couple had correctly filled out the proper forms, enabling them to circumvent the landlord's action and collect the judgement. (Entry #282)

* Ohio Man Sends in $100 for Info - Gets a Bunch Back Along with His Check

A man in Ohio recently sent in a request for information concerning measuring instruments to the National Institutes of Standards and Technology along with a $100 check as payment for the information. He was quite surprised to discover his refunded check enclosed inside a massive packet of information relevant to his project, along with the assurance that more information was forthcoming.

* City Clerk Shows Young Ice Cream Entrepreneur How to Fight City Hall

A young man in Colorado was trying to set up a business selling ice cream from bicycles fitted with freezers. When he inquired about getting the proper licenses from the city he was told that he would need to pay $50 for a license for each vendor he employed. Since the turnover among adolescent drivers is rapid, the cost would have been prohibitive. A woman in the city office explained the step-by-step process to try to change the law. He followed her advice and after he presented his case to the city council, the ordinance was revised to allow his business to be licensed on a per vehicle basis. (Entry #297)

* Banker Finds a Friendly Banking Official When Starting a New Bank

When a banker in South Carolina submitted a charter for a new bank he was surprised when Mr. Fasbender, the government official assigned to handle the case, demonstrated a personal interest in the banker's efforts and took the time to explain the detailed procedures involved. He was not your "typical" government official. He maintained the high degree of professionalism required, and yet demonstrated that he truly was interested in the bank's success and that he cared. The banker says all this preceded his charter's approval. (Entry #300)

* City Clerk Helps Contest Winner Get $10,000 Prize

A man in Brooklyn was notified that he won $10,000 in a sweepstakes Money Magazine sponsored. But much to his surprise, a follow up letter a few months later informed him he was disqualified after an independent investigation into his application. The man didn't understand the disqualification and believed he was still a winner. He found help from a clerk at the New York City Office of Business

Licensing who helped him compose a letter in response along with proper documentation to tell Money Magazine where they were mistaken. It worked, and he received the $10,000 prize. (Entry #305)

* Motor Vehicle Examiner's Advice is Better than the Doctor's

When a 70-year-old woman in California went to have her driver's license renewed she knew she would have trouble passing the exam because she had just undergone cataract surgery in one eye. She passed the written exam but was unable to read the eye chart, even with her glasses on, and was told to go see a doctor and then return. After the doctor performed some minor corrective surgery she was sent back to motor vehicles with a note from the doctor recommending that she be given a license for two years. When she went back she again failed the eye test and was tested by a cold, impersonal driving examiner who scared the heck out of her. She tried to play on the examiner's sympathies but got nowhere. He was unbelievably nasty. After her driving test he said that he would test her vision again. When she started the eye test, the examiner told her to read from the upper or distance part of the bifocals (previous examiners never told her that). Then the nasty instructor said, "I don't care what your doctor says, I'm approving your license for another four years. You can see perfectly." (Entry #307)

* Customs Official Shows Trust to Free Man's $15,000 Dust Collector

A man in Utah unwittingly purchased a BMW that was improperly cleared through U.S. Customs. As a result it sat in his garage because motor vehicles would not register it without the proper Customs form. Over the weeks he was shuffled unendingly through the Customs Offices at Terminal Island until someone finally told him what to send to obtain the form. He sent the required materials, then waited. Weeks passed and nothing happened. In a second series of calls he learned that he had been given poor advice and he was to send further materials. He sent them, and waited. Weeks passed and again, nothing happened. Finally he contacted Barbara Smith. The visits were formal at first, but soon they became chummy little talks. Then she did an amazing thing -- she decided to waive the most troubling of the paperwork, trusted in him, and sent the customs release form. Now his $15,000 dust collector is his daily transportation. (Entry #310)

* Helpful IRS Agent Shows Couple How to Appeal a Penalty

A couple in Michigan got a notice from the IRS to pay $2,583 in back taxes. After going through their paperwork, they determined that they did indeed owe the taxes, but did not think they had to pay the interest and penalty. They walked into their local IRS office and talked to Tim Whaley about the problem. He understood and explained how to write an appeal letter to get the interest and penalty removed. He worked with them over the weeks to ensure that all steps were taken properly by both the taxpayers and the IRS. The couple is now waiting for their answer. (Entry #311)

* Forest Service Ranger Helps Mountain Guide Find His Way Through the Paper Trail

When a mountain guide applied for a license in the Olympic National Forest in Washington, he knew he was in for trouble. The forest is made up of many autonomous ranger districts, creating inconsistencies in the application procedure and a monumental paper chase. Many of the districts seem most concerned with logging, and consider alternative uses of the forest an annoyance. Many districts don't even consider mountain guide applications in the same year they are submitted, and in some cases the permit fee costs more than a mountain guide can afford. This mountain guide was fortunate to have the help of Carol Both at the Quilcene Ranger Station. She discovered an obscure regulation that allowed her to create a master permit that would work in all districts of the forest. It not only saved the guide time and money, but streamlined the permit process as well. (Entry #317)

* Firehouse Gets Loan for Expansion After Being Denied

The Lawrence Township Fire Company waited years to be able to purchase a tract of land next to its firehouse. When opportunity finally knocked, they applied to the PA Emergency Management Volunteer Loan Assistance Program for a low-interest loan. The person who processed the application, for some unknown reason, by-passed normal procedure and stamped it "denied." After many calls, the fire company reached Ms. Sandra Lowan in the office of the loan program, who did some investigating. She discovered that the person who had denied the application had

My Favorite Bureaucrat

never even looked at it. Ms. Lowan took it upon herself to review the application again, found that it was in order, and set the necessary money aside in a special account awaiting the completion of further paperwork. (Entry #320)

* State Treasurer Sends Milwaukee Man $176 Surprise

In 1989 a man living in Wauwatosa received a letter from the State Treasurer of Wisconsin stating that if he could prove that he once lived on 78th Street in Milwaukee they would send him $176. He did so, and they sent him the money. It seems that in 1959 he owned some stock in a company called Curtis Wright. They couldn't find him to send a dividend, so the state had been sitting on his money all that time. (Entry #322)

* Social Worker Goes Out of Her Way to Keep Brothers in Foster Home Together

Two boys had to be placed in foster homes because their mother was entering drug rehabilitation. The two boys, eight and five years old, were not able to be placed in the same house and their homes were 35 miles apart. The social worker who placed the boys tried to get them together, but when she couldn't she did the next best thing. She would personally take them together to visit their mom. She would also pick them up and take them to their grandparents for visits which would mean five or six hours on the road. The grandmother, who cares deeply for the boys, says they have responded wonderfully. (Entry # 327)

* Temporary Postmaster Didn't Give Up to Save Small Business Thousands on Postage

A small company in Wyoming was sending out their magazine to their customers at $1.05 a piece, and the postage was killing their business. They talked to their local postmaster about getting a lower rate, such as second class postage, but the local postmaster said there was no way they could ever qualify. Then one day a temporary postmaster took over and the businessman thought it couldn't hurt to ask a new person. When he asked, the temporary postmaster was excited about finding a way to get the small business to qualify for the second class postage rate. Although it took him nine months, he finally found a way, and it saved the business thousands of dollars. (Entry #333)

* Damage to Beehive from Bear Is Reimbursed from Wild Bear Attack Grant Program

A man in Denver, Colorado had his beehives broken into by a wild bear. He estimated the damage to be $8,000 and was surprised when he learned that he qualified for a grant from the Colorado Division of Wildlife which would reimburse him for the damage. In addition to immediately agreeing to repay him for his losses, they also placed traps, snares, and electric fences to prevent such an attack from happening again. (Entry # 341)

* State Attorney General Gets Retired School Teacher a Windfall After She's Stuck with Two Timeshares

A retired school teacher in Texas was talked into a time share deal, even though she already owned one time share. The salesman told her if she purchased their property, they would take over responsibility for her old property. She purchased the new property, but, of course, the smooth talking salesman was wrong, and she was still responsible for the old property. She called the state Attorney General's office and they were terrific. They worked out a deal in which the company took back their property, and paid the woman's damages--including all the payments she'd ever made on the first property plus an additional year's maintenance fee and interest. When she continued to receive literature in the mail describing how she could win a new car or $5,000 if she purchased a time-share from this same company she'd just won a judgement from, she sent the literature to the Attorney General. A few months later she received a check for $50 from the U.S. Department of Justice. The literature she and others had received from the company, was sent on to the Department of Justice to be used to win a case against them for false advertising. The judgement was distributed among all those who had complained, just as she had. (Entry #348)

* Newspaper Man Claims State Safety Official Saved 107 Traffic Deaths Last Year

A newspaper man who covers the Montana state capital watched the Highway Traffic Safety Administrator cut the highway traffic death rate in the state from 300 to 193 last year. His research and steady advocacy were instrumental in winning stiffer anti-drunken driving laws and mandatory seat belt legislation in a climate where heavy

drinking, heavier driving, and damn the torpedoes is practically a state motto. He reasoned that nothing educates better than a stern patrolman at the driver-side window, and aimed funding at boosting DWI arrests. He literally turned the DWI picture around in many communities. Many in the state's powerful tavern industry protested, but they couldn't argue with the result of his efforts--a major decrease in DWI crashes. (Entry #350)

* Government Researchers Help Student Get an A+ and Reach the Finals of a Fulbright Scholarship

A 39-year-old woman in Florida working on a paper in Irish Studies, contacted an Irish Studies expert at the Congressional Research Service on Capitol Hill. When she contacted him about a paper she was doing he spent close to an hour providing her with information which would have taken her months to locate, if she'd been able to locate it at all. He also gave her a number of other sources which proved to be invaluable. She got an A on her paper. Shortly thereafter, she contacted him again for some information she needed in order to apply for a Fulbright Scholarship. He didn't have the esoteric information she needed, but he gave her the names of two contacts at the Irish Embassy who were able to provide her with the needed information. She didn't believe that she stood much of a chance of getting a Fulbright, but with this bureaucrat's help she is a finalist. (Entry #354)

* Alaska Natural Resources Officer Saves Mining Entrepreneur from a $25,000 Mistake

A man in Alaska was about to purchase the rights to certain mines in Alaska for $25,000. He went to the State Office of Natural Resources where a Ms. Rosenau helped him do research to see if the person selling the mines actually owned them. In her thorough investigation of the documents, she found that the apparent owner did not own clear title and could not sell the mining claims. This could have easily been a $25,000 mistake. (Entry #358)

* Single Parent Finishes College with Financial Assistance from State Pregnant Women's Program

A single woman in Michigan in her senior year of college, found out she was pregnant. Her baby was due shortly after the end of the semester in which she would receive her degree. As her due date approached, she felt great emotional, physical, academic, and financial pressures. At that point she heard about the Pregnant Woman's Program at the State Department of Social Services. This program provided financial assistance to pregnant women in need. She definitely felt she needed help. Her case worker was wonderful. She guided her step-by-step through the application process and made sure she got the financial help she needed to finish college and have her baby with as little stress as possible. (Entry #384)

* Office of Civil Rights Official is the Only Person to Take Grandmother's Charge of Sexual Harassment Seriously

Officials at the school where a grandmother was taking courses would not take her charges against a teacher for sexual harassment seriously. Everyone she turned to in the administration thought her charge was laughable. The college ignored their harassment policies. When she took her complaint to the Community College Board of Directors they stonewalled her. She finally contacted Bera Lee at the San Francisco Office of Civil Rights who took her complaint seriously. They investigated the case but could not officially find evidence for the grandmother since the case came down to her word against his. However, she found them to be very understanding and fair. (Entry #391)

* State Labor Official is One of the Best at Finding Jobs for Disabled Vets

He works 50 to 60 hours a week and spends his own money and time to get the job done. As a result he is one of the best in the country at getting jobs for disabled veterans. Each time Dan Bloodsworth negotiates with an employer to hire a disabled veteran, another man or woman is placed on the road to a new life and not one of them is accepting something for nothing from the government. (Entry #395)

* Apartment Manager Stuck Out His Can and Got Help from the Garbage Man

A man in California had trouble managing an apartment building. The donut shop next door continually littered the back of his property and used his dumpster. He called the police and the city sanitation departments, but didn't get any response. He

Be patient. If any phone number is incorrect, call (area code) 555-1212 and request the new listing.

finally got in touch with Gunter Moors, an Environmental Inspector with the city, who changed the situation around. In 15 minutes he was at the donut shop, established new rules for the shop to follow, and arranged for the dumpsters to be emptied twice a week. (Entry #397)

* When Local Government Gets Him $368 for Stolen Radio, Man Believes Paying Some Taxes May Be Worth It

Last year a man in Brooklyn had his radio and equalizer stolen while his car was parked in a commercial parking garage. He called the police to report the accident. He spent the next month trying to get his money back from the garage company. They wouldn't pay and he didn't have time to go to small claims court. He had filed a complaint with the Department of Consumer Affairs, but had never followed up on it. A few months later he got a call from a Consumer Affairs office asking if his problem had been settled. It seemed that the garage owner was standing in the office right at that moment seeking a renewal of his owner's license. The official was calling to see if his claim had been settled. Within a few days of the call the man received a check for $368. This makes it a little easier for him to pay taxes. (Entry #399)

* Soil Conservation Official a Friend to Farmers, Sportsmen and Environmentalists

Mr. Lloyd Wright, a land-use planner for the U.S. Soil Conservation Service, designed an agricultural Land Evaluation and Site Assessment (LESA) system which requires federal agencies to assess the negative reaction of any federal projects on farmers. He is also responsible for the wetlands program which helps wildlife, as well as fishermen, hunters, and environmentalists, through efforts to ensure that federal farm programs do not negatively impact wetlands. (Entry #400)

* City Tax Commissioner Gives Back More Taxes

The City Tax Commission of the City of Norfolk has expanded their program to ensure that more people are aware of the possible ways to reduce their real estate taxes. A certain commissioner helps his staff get the limelight for the work he has done. He is very active in the community. For instance, he throws birthday parties at senior citizen homes for those patients who turn 100 years old. (Entry #413)

* State Health Official Makes Life Easier for Parents of Deaf Child

A couple in Pennsylvania finally decided they were ready for children after five years of marriage. When their first child was born, they were crushed to learn that the child was deaf. The woman quit her job to take care of the child's special needs. Shortly after this, the husband lost his job because of a plant closing. The woman turned to the state government for assistance and was happy to find Mr. Tornbloom who gave them a considerable amount of time, a wealth of information about programs and possibilities, and approved payment by the state for the child's hearing aid. The couple remarked, "He genuinely seemed to value his job." (Entry #416)

* Vital Records Supervisor Opens Express Lane for Woman in Need

A woman living near Chicago was concerned about her sister in Indianapolis whose 14-year-old son had just died of cardiac arrest. Her sister's other son was in a hospital in Germany suffering from a collapsed lung. On the day after the funeral, the bereaved mother decided to go immediately to Germany to see her other son, but needed a passport. She called her sister and asked if she would be able to go to Chicago and pick up a copy of her birth certificate which she needed in order to get an emergency passport. The woman had to have the birth certificate in six hours so she could make her flight to Germany. The driving time alone took a good five hours, and when the woman's sister arrived at Vital Records in Chicago, she was told the process of getting a copy of the certificate would take one hour, no matter what the circumstances. She then asked for the supervisor and explained her situation. The supervisor immediately took her hand, expressed his condolences, disappeared for a few minutes and returned with the certificate saying "you better get going." (Entry #418)

* Student in Wheel Chair Thanks to Fast Moving Rehabilitation Counselor

A student at the University of Missouri was used to bureaucratic paperwork. With a post-polio handicap, she often dealt with a state rehabilitation counsellor who drove her crazy by constantly insisting that rules be followed in minute detail. It seemed that he required every scrap of paper pertaining to her existence dating back to the

time of her birth. The student got around campus in an electric wheel-chair she received from the state. One day when the batteries failed, she had to ask campus transportation to drive her around to her classes. To her surprise, when she called her counsellor about the problem, he processed the paperwork immediately and in twenty hours she had her new batteries and was able to get herself to class. (Entry #420)

* IRS Auditor Finds Extra Bonus for Accountant

An accountant in a Texas company was worried when she heard that she would be the one responsible for working with an IRS auditor to audit the company's profit sharing plan. However, the experience changed her mind about IRS auditors. She found the auditor to be warm, friendly and extremely professional. More importantly, during the audit, a mistake in the vesting schedule was uncovered. When the company changed its year end a few years ago, the head of the company did not count the short year as a full year for vesting as required by law. This counting of the short year made the accountant completely vested in the plan, instead of 60% vested as she was told by her employer. An unexpected windfall thanks to the IRS. (Entry #421)

* IRS Problem Resolution Center Saves Home Over $65

The IRS wrote letters to a lady in Baltimore telling her they were going to seize her house if she didn't pay them $65. A few years before, she and her husband had a cleaning woman once a week and erroneously filed the incorrect form when sending in her employment taxes. The poor lady tried for six months to straighten out the IRS computer with no success. Then came Mrs. Stapleton from the IRS Problem Resolution Center to the rescue. She straightened it all out for the grateful couple and they were able to save their house. (Entry #422)

* Lead Poisoning Expert Provides Worried Mother with Expert Advice

A woman in Maryland was frightened and confused when she learned that her daughter tested positive for lead poisoning. She called a number of different agencies attempting to discover the causes, treatments, and effects of lead poisoning. Although she found a number of offices which she thought might be able to help her, no one could give her any clear answers until she spoke with Dr. Susan Binder at the Centers For Disease Control in Atlanta. The doctor listened to her story in detail and outlined the possible causes of the poisoning. Together they arrived at the conclusion that recent house renovations were the likely culprit. She then discussed the potential long-term effects, some of the basic steps she could take to help her daughter, current research and controversies on the subject, and sent current literature. But most importantly, Dr. Binder referred her to local experts and resources in her area where she could turn for further assistance. (Entry #423)

* State Worker Helps Couple Identify Little-Known Program to Pay for Baby's Skull Surgery

A couple in Illinois felt the financial pinch when they learned that their insurance coverage did not cover the C-section birth of their new daughter. They were also devastated to learn that their insurance would not cover the expenses associated with skull surgery which was needed immediately for their new baby. A case worker for the state Office of Crippled Children solved their problem by helping them through the maze of forms and questions needed to qualify for a program which would pay for their baby's operation. (Entry #525)

* Head of State Surplus Property Helps with Computer Bargain

When a college professor went to Utah's Federal Surplus Division to investigate buying a used computer, the clerk was unable to provide him with enough technical information to make an educated purchase. He later called Bill Arseneau, head of the state's surplus division, who personally saw to it that the professor got all the information he needed to make his purchasing decision. (Entry #426)

* Supercrat Writes Comic Strip for State Department as Well as Saving Cambodian Refugees from the Khmer Rouge

Chip Beck, a diplomat at the State Department, is an accomplished cartoonist who writes a Doonesbury type strip for a State Department magazine which makes fun of diplomats. During the Indochina War he also found himself responsible for 40,000 people fleeing communism in central Cambodia. They were encircled by two Khmer Rouge regiments and cut off from normal supply routes. He drove Ambassador John

My Favorite Bureaucrat

Gunther Dean around in an open air jeep during a torrential downpour to witness the plight of the unsheltered families in the midst of a war zone. He jokingly said to the Ambassador, "Sir, I wanted you to see what these people have to endure for the next six months if we don't provide shelter in a hurry."
(Entry #431)

* Social Services Official Provides Hotline for Inner-City Pastor

A Michigan pastor works closely with John Rosendall at the Michigan Department of Social Services. Over 60% of the pastor's people are on some form of public assistance. John gave the pastor a special number so that he can call him almost any time of day to handle the problems of his parishioners. He will also check on many of the people who come to the church for help to see if they really need it. Once a family came to the church's food bank for free food and the pastor, questioning their story, contacted John about their background. John found out that the family was earning more money than many of the working families in the parish and most of their money was tax free. (Entry #434)

* Export Expert Provides Fast Info to Business

Bernadine at the Chicago office of the Department of Commerce goes well beyond the requirements of her job according to a researcher who regularly uses her services. Many times she has answered a critical request from an unknown caller to get export or import numbers on some esoteric data. Her expertise is a positive reflection on all U.S. government workers and a godsend to researchers. (Entry #441)

* State Small Business Specialist Helps 20-Year-Old Entrepreneur

A 20-year-old entrepreneur in New Jersey didn't have money to hire consultants to get answers to all the questions he had about starting his own business. When he called the State Business Assistance Office all his questions were taken care of for free. The woman counselor informed him of the procedures for incorporation, how to protect the name of his business, as well as what forms and fees would be required. She also counselled him on the advantages of forming a partnership, and when he was unsure of taxes she helped him fill out the necessary forms. (Entry #442)

* Poultry Industry Expert Captures Consultant to Tell Him More Than He Ever Wanted to Know About Eggs

A consultant from Silver Spring, Maryland was trying to get some information about the outlook and trends for chicken and eggs for a client who was in the business. After six telephone calls he made contact with Mr. Weimer, whom he was told from previous calls was the government's authority on the poultry industry. He made an appointment to meet with him and when he arrived, Mr. Weimer began a most in depth discussion with hand-outs, sheets and graphs that spelled everything out in a clear and concise manner. (Entry #444)

* Morton Downey Participant Gets Postal Official to Understand the Rules

While a postal worker from Brooklyn was sitting in the audience of the Morton Downey Jr. Show, he met an aging hippie from Colorado. The man in the audience said that he had difficulty cashing a $3,000 postal money order at the Lenox Hill, New York Post Office. The manager of the post office told him he needed two forms of identification when he only showed him one. The Brooklyn postal worker went home and researched the regulations and found that only one form of identification was required. He called the manager of the Lenox Hill office, and was assured that the station will now comply with regulations. (Entry #447)

* Dental Clinic Clerk Helps Homeless with Bad Teeth

A young man in Chicago who grew up in an upper middle class family found himself homeless for six years. When he finally began to get his life back together and had a full time job as a doorman he began to have problems with his teeth. His hard life had taken its toll. His teeth hurt so badly he couldn't sleep at night and he couldn't afford a dentist. He visited the dental clinic at Northwestern University whose prices were very reasonable but he still couldn't afford it. A young woman in the records office, who understood his situation, took it upon herself to call his brother and arrange payment. (Entry #451)

* FHA Official Helps Those with Late Payment Mortgages

A woman in Indiana is grateful to the woman who runs the local office of the Farmers Home Administration. Without the FHA she would not have been able to buy a home of her own. Soon after she moved in she was involved in an accident and was unable to work or pay her mortgage payments. The woman at the FHA Office was very understanding and arranged a repayment program for her once she started working again. (Entry 453)

* Postal Employee Fishes Out No Postage Birthday Cards from Mailbox - on a Sunday

A man in New Jersey waited until the very last minute to buy birthday cards for his wife. One was to be from himself, the other from his one-year-old son. His wife's birthday was on Monday and it was now Sunday. The man knew his wife only liked cards that arrived in the mail, so he drove to the next town which had a Sunday pick-up hoping they would be delivered the next day. When he reached the mailbox and started writing out the cards, an impatient motorist pulled up behind him and started blowing his horn. Hurriedly he posted the cards. When he got home he realized that he didn't place stamps on his cards. It was Sunday, but he decided to call the post office. The man who answered the phone agreed to help. When he returned to the post office the man unlocked the door and came outside to the mailbox to retrieve the cards. He also advised him that if he wanted to have his wife receive her cards by the next day, he would have a better chance if he used another Sunday pickup box near by. He did, and his wife received both of the cards the next day on her birthday, thanks to the Sunday postal official. (Entry #455)

* State Attorney General Gets Alimony Check for Retired Woman

A woman from New York was shocked when her ex-husband told her that he was no longer going to pay her alimony after he retired. He was due to retire soon and she knew she could not make it on her Social Security check alone. She contacted two lawyers to get copies of the laws regarding her situation but they never sent the right ones. When she ran out of money for lawyers, she contacted the Assistant Attorney General of New York and he sent her copies of the laws which showed that her husband had to continue his alimony. She quickly sent him what she received from the state, and he agreed to live up to his responsibility. (Entry #457)

* Industry Expert Saves the Day for Consultant

A consultant in California received the book "Information USA" as a gift for his birthday last year only to leave it collecting dust on a shelf. The man never bothered opening up the first chapter since he believed the phrase, "I am from the government and I'm here to help you" to be one of the world's biggest lies. He changed his mind when a client walked in who knew and wanted to buy something called Vanadium Slags. He couldn't find anyone who knew anything about them. But by chance he picked up "Information USA" and after three calls found Gordon Schmidt at the Department of Commerce. Gordon not only told him over the phone what it is, he also faxed him important information on the product within 15 minutes. The unexpected eagerness made him wonder if he was on Mars. He now believes that conscientious bureaucrats can make a big difference. (Entry #460)

* Opera Company Gets State Grant to Perform in Nursing Homes

A new opera company that wished to perform in nursing homes went to the state arts council for help. They weren't expecting much assistance, but to their surprise, they received moral support, encouragement, and $1,100 to get their opera going. (Entry #465)

* Official Makes State Day Center Happen with Her Own Time and Money

The Governor of Pennsylvania wanted to establish a model State Day Care Center program quickly. Jane Snyder, who was given the project, first worried about how parents, already overburdened with jobs and child care, were going to form the Parents Association required by complex regulations. Diving right in, she helped start the association herself. She paid the application fees from her own pocket and never requested reimbursement. She didn't get overtime pay, but she felt the Day Care project was worth the many extra hours she worked. She got the center running on time and under budget. When the center opened, they needed to write a newsletter but no one could find the time to do it. That is, no one except Jane, who squeezed in the extra hours on Sunday afternoons. Gifts for the center's Christmas in July arrived compliments of Ms. Snyder as well as other incidentals which the budget didn't cover. At the grand opening, the Governor got all the attention and Jane was off camera consoling a crying youngster and helping a little boy fix his shoe laces. (Entry #476)

* State Program Provides Van for Wheelchair Dependent Man to Pursue His Dreams

A young man in Arizona had spinal surgery at the age of twelve and was confined to a wheelchair for the rest of his life. He dreamt of getting up and putting one foot in front of another and going wherever he wanted. His life improved dramatically in his teens when he got an electric wheelchair. With his new freedom and confidence, he started to do things like play drums in the school's marching band. He began to realize that perhaps his options weren't so limited as he once believed. Later on in college he dreamt of being a sportscaster, but realized at graduation that he needed a way of transporting himself around. What he needed was his own van, so that he could start knocking on doors, meeting with people, and volunteering for internships--all requirements for getting a job in broadcasting. Believing himself unable to arrange for such a vehicle, he put his dreams of sportscasting on hold. In the meantime he took a job in telemarketing because it provided wheelchair transportation. All this changed when he met Bill Butler at the state rehabilitation department. Bill arranged for him to buy a $17,000 wheelchair equipped van so that he could pursue his choice of career. To his delight, he soon received his big break at a large local radio station. (Entry #470)

* Bureaucrat Gives Human Response to Environmental Impact Statement

A federal official was working with a large Arizona utility company to prepare an environmental impact statement for their new coal-fired power plant. The statement had to pass muster from the state regulatory agencies. A letter of response from the state agency commented on the artist's rendering of the proposed power plant. The picture showed the main buildings, tall stacks, some landscaping, and a nondescript background with a few clouds drawn in. The letter asked if the sky would actually look like the drawing in the picture. They guessed the state was trying to imply that the sky would fill up with black smoke even though the impact statement showed millions of dollars of state of the art air pollution control equipment. The federal official wrote back to the state saying the sky would look like the picture "Only on partly cloudy days."

* Older Arizonian Writes Governor About Setting Up a Program to Help People Like Her, and Gets a Call to Set Up the Program

An unemployed, elderly American in Arizona had trouble finding work. In desperation, she wrote directly to the Governor about her problem. In her letter she also described, in some detail, a California program called Network Employment Unlimited that was successful in solving her kind of problem and suggested there should be something like this in Arizona. She also mentioned that she would be willing to help establish such a program. To her surprise, she got an immediate call from another state office wishing to meet with her and discuss setting up the program she had described in her letter. She met with the official and is currently involved in establishing the state program she suggested. (Entry #483)

* Writer Gets New and Old Help from IRS

When a freelance writer was working on an article about the first 1040 used 75 years ago, she got more help than she expected from Josie Downing at the IRS in Washington, DC. Josie tracked down several internal publications unavailable outside the agency, and provided her with access to the IRS's vaults and files. She provided her with desk space when she came to town and complimentary photocopies. Josie also directed her to the right official at the National Archives for a copy of the first 1040. (Entry #486)

* A Call to the Interstate Commerce Commission Gets Goods Delivered

National Van Lines was holding the personal goods of a woman from Chicago while they disputed an apparent overcharge on the bill. The woman called the Interstate Commerce Commission in Washington, DC, which in turn contacted the moving company and showed them where they were mistaken. They quickly delivered her goods. (Entry 487)

* Church Board Gets Census Demographics to Select New Pastor

A woman on a committee to select a new pastor for her church, took on the responsibility to find demographic information about the neighborhoods surrounding the church. She wrote to a regional office of the Bureau of the Census requesting the information. To her surprise, she received all the information she needed and more within five days. (Entry #489)

* Controller of Currency Clears Up Credit Rating for Credit Card Holder

A man living in Arizona didn't realize that he had a bad credit rating until he applied for credit at a local shopping center. He once had a credit card with the Bank of Boston and had tried to cancel the card but never got a response from the bank. The bank continued sending him a bill for the annual fee. When he didn't pay they also charged him interest on the fee and placed it in his credit report showing that he didn't pay his bills. The man wrote to Senator Kennedy of Massachusetts who contacted the Controller of Currency in Washington, DC. The Controller wrote to the bank, which cleared up the matter immediately. The bank sent a letter of apology to the man in Arizona. (Entry #490)

* City Code Official Helps Homeowner with Broken Bathroom

A man in Illinois accepted a $400 bid from a freelance repairman to have his bathroom re-tiled. It was considerably less than the $1,000 estimate he had received from a local store. When the freelancer started the job he kept asking for more money and he ended up charging $2,500. The homeowner later found out the man was not a licensed plumber and was wanted in another county for writing bad checks. It cost the homeowner another $2,000 to have a reputable firm repair the job. A code enforcement officer for the city encouraged the homeowner to take the freelancer to court, and helped him through the legal paperwork. He also offered consumer tips on what he did wrong and how to avoid such an incident in the future. Now, the man contacts the code enforcement officer to have him check the credentials and reputation of a tradesman before hiring. (Entry # 492)

* Election Commission Official Helps Biographer Over Five Year Period

Kent Cooper is a public servant in the disclosure unit of the Federal Election Commission. He believes that people who live in a democracy should be told clearly how their system of government can be used. When a young writer was living in Washington, DC, Kent was always available to help him piece together campaign finance puzzles. Even after the writer moved thousands of miles away, Kent continued to help. For five years while the writer was working on a biography of Armand Hammer, Kent, almost always on his own initiative, informed the writer about Hammer's campaign contributions on the public record. He also sent printouts of PAC reports that Hammer had directed. (Entry #496)

* Forest Ranger Fulfills Dream in Life

A 47-year-old woman with no job experience had always dreamed of working outdoors. When she applied to work as a Forest Technician at the Sierra National Forest, it was a local forest ranger who renewed her faith in truth, justice and the American way by promoting equal opportunity and hiring her. She now spends her days planting aspens in beautiful green meadows, and building fences, bridges and gully plugs in an effort to save the environment. (Entry #507)

* State Licensing Official Cut Application Process from Twelve Months to Five Weeks

A woman from Michigan moved to Illinois to work as a nurse. It wasn't until after she got her job that she realized she needed an Illinois nursing certificate to work. The process to obtain a certificate took six to twelve months and she had to start work in six weeks. A call to Ms. Paoni at the Illinois Department of Professional Regulations made it all happen in just five weeks. Ms. Paoni personally walked every piece of paperwork through the system. (Entry #508)

* Conservation Officer Gets Rid of Raccoon Family for Sleepless Homeowner

A female raccoon decided to deliver her babies in a crawl space under a woman's bedroom in Indiana. The woman tried everything to get rid of the mother raccoon and her noisy children including traps, mothball fumes, recordings of barking dogs, and professional exterminators, but nothing worked. After six weeks of insomnia she called Phil, a friendly state conservation officer, who suggested she try rags dipped in ammonia. She did as he had recommended, and the noisy, pesky coons finally left. (Entry #509)

* Librarian Helps Visually Handicapped Want to Live

A woman in Alabama discovered that due to her failing vision she would soon be unable to read, watch television, or drive a car. She went to the local library and the woman in charge of services for the blind literally changed her life. She encouraged her to get a seeing eye dog, and told her about the many free services available through the library, such as talking books. Although her life is different than before, it is still full. (Entry #514)

* State Insurance Commissioner Shows How a Cancerous Mole is More Serious than Breast Enlargements

A woman in North Carolina got a notice from her insurance company that they were not going to pay for her claim to have a cancerous mole removed from her back. She knew of a fellow worker who had just been paid by the same insurance company to have her breasts enlarged and thought she was being treated unfairly. She contacted the state insurance commissioner and within the month received payment for her medical care. (Entry #527)

* FHA Official Shows Realtor How to Get Money for His Clients

A realtor in Montana gave up trying to take advantage of government programs to help his clients purchase homes. But he changed his mind fourteen months ago when John Walkup took over the FHA office. John holds monthly meetings to explain the programs that are available. He explains the need for each document, goes through the processes, and makes people feel better. He also holds educational meetings for realtors and streamlines their jobs. In just over a year he has managed to turn a clumsy, bumbling department into a thriving hub of loan activity.

* State Health Care Official Gets Money and Private Bill to Help Terminally Ill Boy

A Wisconsin couple's insurance company would not cover the medical expenses for their terminally ill son. They turned to a state counselor for help. An attorney who works for the service was able to get an insurance company to pay the $17,000 disputed bill. The attorney also got the Governor to pass a law so that their son was included in a new program. This program provided special funds that allowed him to come home from the hospital for visits three times a week when he was stable. (Entry #540)

* State Assemblyman Corrals Wild Steer with 4-Wheel Drive Bronco

A young girl watched as her prize steer, Boggie, bolted out of a California county fair gate. Several men attempted unsuccessfully to grab his rope. Boggie darted past the midway and out a gate onto Highway 86. He was on his way to becoming hamburger meat. As he ran down the highway, California highway patrolmen halted traffic and the chase continued. The steer sought refuge in an adjoining airport. Assemblyman Steve Peace was eating at a restaurant near the airport and saw the steer pursuit. He dashed from the restaurant and jumped into his Bronco to join the chase. Boggie loped down the runway with Steve in hot pursuit. The persuasive, gentle nudging of the Bronco against Boggie's hind quarters, soon coaxed him into submission against a fence. A livestock trailer was secured and Boggie returned safely to the fairgrounds. Despite the stressful event, Boggie did receive a gold ribbon. The assemblyman deserved one, too. (Entry #542)

* State Director of Children Saves Money and Children's Welfare

The former Permanency Planning Director in the state of Michigan works in behalf of children who are developmentally disabled. She has a philosophy that all children have a right to a permanent home. As a result of her work, the federal government provided a small grant to establish a state-wide program in 1983 to support families as they care for their children with special needs at home. The program is now six years old, and has benefited hundreds of children and their families. The program has also enabled the state of Michigan to recover millions of dollars by averting the cost of placing children in institutions. (Entry #545)

* USDA Instructor Teaches Woman How to Give Out Federal Money and Not Succumb to Special Interest Groups

A woman in Washington, DC was placed in charge of giving out state grants for historic preservation. She took a grant managers course at the local U.S. Department of Agriculture Extension Service. Her instructor instilled in her an attitude of fair play and honesty under pressure. On the job she quickly realized that when large amounts of public monies are at stake, there is great pressure to accommodate special interest groups. Those who do the accommodating rise rapidly on the pay scale until they are not needed anymore. She learned the valuable lesson that maintaining integrity is difficult to do, but possible. (Entry #568)

* Mayor Helps Couple Eliminate Flood Insurance

A young couple who could barely afford their Veterans Administration mortgage payments on their new house, learned that the VA required them to carry flood insurance in an area that had next to no chance of flooding. They wrote to the mayor of the town and in two weeks he sent engineers to designate the area as one that did not require flood insurance. (Entry #573)

* Free Trees Available from City Official

The head of the Tree Shade Commission of Paramus, New Jersey promotes the planting, nurturing, and appreciation of trees in the borough. He has a tree nursery where baby trees, when they are big enough, are given to homeowners free of charge. He makes house-calls free of charge to check on the trees and to see if they are sick and whether or not they can be cured. If a tree dies, he'll replace it with a new one. On Community Health Day he runs a booth demonstrating how to maintain the good health of trees and plants. His staff organizes marathons through the park, allowing the runners to pass by and enjoy the trees. He provides wonderful Paramus Mulch free of charge for gardens or lawns. His accomplishments are well known in surrounding towns, and he is often asked to speak to groups in the surrounding areas. (Entry #583)

* Chief Probation Official Saves Secretary's Life

In 1988 a woman in Michigan became painfully ill after finishing dinner in her apartment. The next morning she called her boss, the county's Chief Probation Official. He came over immediately and took her to the emergency room. After surgery it was learned that she had Chrohn's Disease and would have died if the state official hadn't gone out of his way to get her to the hospital. (Entry #584)

* Hang Up Causes Attorney to Get Satisfaction

A woman in Illinois who made a purchase by phone was dissatisfied with the product. She called the company and requested a refund, but the company hung up on her. The Illinois state Attorney General's Office got her the refund in 90 days. (Entry #585)

* Canadian Bureaucrat Helps New York

A businessman in New York praises a Canadian government official. Although the official was due to retire, he did not lose the desire to see the project he was responsible for through to the end. He was working with the state of New York to develop a new energy saving dry wall product. The dry wall absorbs heat when the room is too hot and discharges heat when the room is too cold. The project could have easily been lost in the cracks if he hadn't made it his duty to see it through to completion. (Entry #588)

* County Conservation Official Helps Homeowner Manage Runoff

When the county highway administration widened a road that ran through a woman's property in upper state New York, she was troubled because they stripped thousands of feet of vegetation away and diverted run-off water into her pond. She called the county soil and water department and spoke with Fred Sinclair who arrived within days offering his knowledge and assistance. He gave her literature on water management and lent her his personal reference materials. He even gave her his home telephone number. When she occasionally called him he was extremely helpful, even after a long day at work. He gave her free government materials to help her re-seed the land and offered his know-how to help with the planting. He has revisited the site many times and intends to do so until the problem is solved. (Entry #592)

* State Helps Single Mother Recover $55,000 in Child Support

A man left his wife and two-year-old daughter in 1977. Over time he accumulated a debt of $55,000 in child support payments. The state office of the Attorney General located him in another state through Department of Labor information files. They were also able to obtain his current salary, social security number, address, and the name of his employer. With this information they were able to serve him with a court summons and collect the money he owed for the child. (Entry #608)

* HUD Official Helps Couple Get House

The performance of Jim LaZott, a HUD official in Des Moines, Iowa was like a beacon of hope in a sea of chaos. When a young couple began working with the local HUD office to purchase a home, they found it nearly impossible to get even the basic information on HUD programs. That all changed when they met Jim. Everything was smooth sailing from there. (Entry #612)

* U.S. Agriculture Official Gives Moscow Bears a Taste of Freedom

When the Moscow Circus was visiting the United States, an official from the Michigan Humane Society contacted the U.S. Department of Agriculture concerning the circus' violation of the federal Animal Welfare Act. Together they tried to get the circus to voluntarily comply with the laws governing the cage sizes for wild animals in captivity. The circus' performing bears were transported and housed in cages that were so small they couldn't even turn around freely, let alone stand up and stretch. The animals were exhibiting stereotypical behavior characteristic of intensive confinement. But because federal laws do not specify exact cage dimensions, circus officials attempted to play a "catch 22" game to get around the law. Although the agriculture official realized that at any moment he or his superiors could receive a call from the U.S. State Department instructing them to leave the circus alone for political reasons, he pursued his mission. After many months of negotiations he was able to work out a compromise in which the circus built a large exercise cage to the Department of Agriculture's specifications and all the bears had four hours of daily access to this cage. (Entry #619)

* States Labor Official Cuts Insurance Rates for Small Business by 30 Percent

The owners of a small foundry in Michigan cite an official from the Michigan Department of Labor as the reason their workman's compensation insurance rates are 30% lower than their competitors'. This official showed up as soon as they opened their doors for business. He pointed out many areas that had to be addressed to eliminate potential hazards and also set up a program where he made monthly visits to teach employees about safety. As a result, the company has never had an OSSA, EPA or Michigan Department of Public Health violation, and received an award for going three years in a row without a lost time accident. This exemplary safety record caused their insurance rates to be 30% lower than their nearest competitor. (Entry #621)

* A Call to Washington, DC Results in Hand Delivered Tax Forms in Arizona

A tax lawyer in Arizona had trouble getting a form from a local IRS office. He decided to contact the IRS Ombudsman's office in Washington, DC to complain about the problem. When he heard about the complaint, the Ombudsman called a local office and had an IRS agent hand deliver the form to the attorney. (Entry #626)

* Forest Service Helps Survival School Survive

A survival school located in Arizona has nothing but praise for the local forest service. They are a small business and whenever they can't meet the payments to obtain their necessary permits, the forest service allows them whatever time they need to make the payments, without penalizing them. Whenever they need to extend the range of their permit, the forest service will always accommodate them. Even when they failed to meet a deadline to sign some papers, a forest service official brought the papers to them, so they didn't have to pay a penalty. (Entry #627)

* State Nurse Helps Mothers Cope with Premature Babies

A woman in Delaware was devastated to learn that her baby would be born fourteen weeks early. She began working with a nurse from the state Early Intervention Program. After the birth of her son, the nurse visited him frequently throughout his four month hospital stay, and after the baby had returned to his home, she visited him many times to thoroughly evaluate his developmental progress. She was the first to spot his hearing loss and helped the couple obtain a state-funded hearing aid for him. She diagnosed his need for speech, physical, and occupational therapy, and helped enroll him in an excellent school. At this time the nurse was experiencing difficulties of her own at home. Her husband was dying of cancer. Despite this, she continued to be an extremely dedicated and compassionate person. (Entry #636)

* FDA Official Helps Inventor Get Clearance

The inventor of a medical device had to get clearance from the Food and Drug Administration before he could start selling his product to manufacturers. His initial call to the FDA resulted in pounds of booklets and forms. When he called back a second time, he not only got exact answers to his questions, but he also received the know-how to achieve his dream. An FDA staffer sent him samples of successful applications to copy from, and told him exactly what was required of him to be accepted by the FDA. With this help, the inventor got his approval in record time. Most companies he spoke with were surprised at how quickly he had managed to cut through the bureaucratic red tape. (Entry #646)

* Student Gets Government Doctor to Help with Term Paper

In 1983, a student studying organizational psychology used the book "Information USA" to identify a physician at the National Institutes of Health to help him obtain information for a term paper. This doctor spoke to the student for over an hour helping him gain a basic understanding of the subject matter. The doctor's assistant sent the student an index of federally funded grants on the subject, a list of publications available from their office, and a thick annotated bibliography enabling him to do further research on the subject. All of this was free of charge. He also obtained the names of other researchers to contact and references to explore. (Entry #652)

* Counselor Takes 61-Year-Old from Potential Suicide to Great Potential

A draftsman in Ohio was laid off at the age of 61. He couldn't find another job and became so depressed, he even considered suicide. By chance, he met a state vocational counselor and she changed his life. She helped him enroll in a computer aided drafting school to update his skills and found him a new job. (Entry #659)

* State Consultant Doubles Income for Small Business Owner for Free

A free consultant from Tennessee's Small Business Development Center helped a small metal products company on the verge of not making it. He helped double the company's income and gave the owner confidence in the future. The consultant suggested the business would benefit if it were to sell to the government. He showed them how to get on the state government's bidders list. Once they had been accepted, he helped them figure out the cost of materials so that they could make a proper bid. The consultant also called the state to get answers to their many unanswered questions, and helped them locate materials and get credit extensions from suppliers. He taught the owner's wife how to do the payroll and other accounting functions. When the company was filling its biggest order, the owner hurt his leg and the doctors told him to stay off of it. Hearing this, the state consultant came by after he got off work, put on a pair of cover-alls and painted grills. One day the company was having trouble with their hydropic press. The owner was so frustrated he was about to scream, when the state official stopped by on his way home from work and fixed it himself, to the owner's amazement. The consultant has been checking up on the business for six months and has gotten them on three more bidders lists. (Entry #666)

* Unemployed Couple Learns About Program Where Employer Can Get Money if They Are Hired

In 1983 a couple moved to Tonawanda, New York to try to get jobs in their respective fields. However, when they couldn't find good jobs they were forced to live on their earnings from part-time jobs and buy food stamps. Then they encountered an official with the local Jobs Training Partnership Act. He showed them how to make themselves more marketable by informing potential employers that they would be entitled to cash benefits if they hired them. This made the difference. The husband was hired and within the year he more than doubled his salary. The man realizes the Jobs Training Partnership Act was the main reason he was able to find employment. (Entry #679)

Be patient. If any phone number is incorrect, call (area code) 555-1212 and request the new listing.

23

My Favorite Bureaucrat

* Commerce Expert Helps Market Researcher

When a market researcher called the Material Handling Specialist at the Department of Commerce for some marketing data, he was told that the data he needed had not been collected by the government for the last three years. But the specialist, undaunted, said she would try to find some additional information and call him back. A couple of days later she called back and gave him a number of additional sources likely to provide the information he needed. She also went out of her way to apologize for not being able to help him directly and wished him luck. She encouraged him to call back if she could be of any further assistance.

* City Manager Pays for White Shirts Ruined in Washing Machine

A man in Elmhurst, Illinois got his first white collar job and purchased eight new white shirts. When his wife laundered his new shirts, to her surprise they all turned to a rust color. The called the city water department to see if there was anything wrong with the water and got a negative response. They then called the city manager trying to get a refund for his ruined shirts. After a couple of phone calls back and forth and a letter from the city attorney, his request was denied. He then showed up at the city manager's office and asked to see the water department's work sheets for the day in question. The city manager said it would take too much time to accommodate his request. After a few minutes of silence the man asked him if he would take a check for half the cost of the shirts now and the other half in about a week. (Entry #700)

* Judge Straightens Out Life of Gambler

In 1987 a man from South Carolina found himself broke, out of a job, and in jail for writing bad checks to support his gambling habit. He was easily looking at spending the next five years in jail for his crimes. While in jail he wrote to a local judge for help. The judge called him to his office along with all the people to whom he had written bad checks. Together they worked out a payment plan and got him a job with the water department. Within a year he was made supervisor, paid off all his debts, got married again and is raising a family.

* Fifty-Six Year Old Woman Thought She Was Unemployable

A 56 year old woman in Seattle suddenly found herself out of work and she thought she was unemployable. The Women's Bureau at the U.S. Department of Labor made an appointment for her with the Mayor's Office for Senior Employment. There a counselor showed her the worth of her skills and got her a job as an editor. (Entry #712)

* Wife Who Works with County Crippled Children Teaches Husband Meaning of Life

A man from Grand Rapids nominates his wife, who works for the Crippled Children Division of the Kent County Health Department, for the favorite bureaucrat award. She spends a considerable amount of time working out problems, expressing love, and offering understanding to parents who learn that their children will never be like other children. Many of the children die at a very young age. Her understanding of human needs has taught him compassion and tenderness which he would never have learned without her example.

* Congressman Teaches Constituent How to Expect Good Things from People

A congressman from Michigan manages a summer vegetable stand in front of his house. He manages the stand by the honor system with a note asking patrons to place the money for the produce they purchase in an empty coffee can. A constituent recently learned while talking to the congressman, that he empties the can each night and in several years of operation he has never been cheated. The congressman said he believes that people respond to the expectations of others. If we assume others will betray us, people have nothing to lose by doing so; however, if we sincerely respect their potential for good, most people do not want to show themselves to be unworthy. (Entry #716)

* U.S. Postal Service Employees Have Special Programs to Help the Needy at Christmas

During the Christmas season a committee at a local post office goes through hundreds of letters to Santa. The requests from children who ask for food, clothing, or blankets instead of toys, are granted from a special fund set up by postal workers. Fun letters from children asking for toys are also answered personally by postal workers. Mail carriers also submit names of families on their routes that are struggling. These families are adopted by groups of postal workers who donate money to purchase groceries, clothing, and toys for them.

* Job Service Helps Homeless Ex-Marine and His Family

Last year a Vietnam Veteran and his family were homeless and broke. They were living in the back of their station wagon in West Virginia. They decided to go to Mesa, Arizona where they met a veterans affairs representative at the job service office who worked closely with the family to get them food, shelter, and work. By the end of the year, they had a Christmas tree in their own living room with presents under it. (Entry #722)

* EPA Makes Sure Woman Business Owner Gets Contract

A woman in Mississippi was running her husband's subcontracting business for some time while he was ill. When he died, a number of prime government contractors took away her business believing that she could not do the job alone. She contacted the EPA's Minority and Women's Business Representative who took up her case and made sure that the subcontracts were returned to her. She says that this official reaffirmed her belief that the compassion of an individual along with the power of a bureaucracy can protect small business in America.

* Transportation Expert Puts Inventor into Big Business

An inventor in New Jersey had a great idea for an automobile anti-theft device. The product would enable the customer to permanently etch a federal number on car windows. This would cut down on thefts because a thief would have to replace the windows in the vehicle if he wanted to resell it. This would make car theft too expensive and time consuming. The inventor had trouble identifying insurance companies that offered premium discounts for such devices. Without this information the product would not have credibility or perceived value. He checked through Information USA newsletters for sources of assistance and came across the U.S. Department of Transportation's Office of Motor Vehicle Theft Rulemaking Group. When he contacted the group, the woman he spoke with on the phone listed the insurance companies she thought might offer the discounts he was looking for. While on the line, she located a 52-page report that had been presented to Congress concerning motor vehicle theft, which added more states to the list that required insurance companies to provide a discount for this type of anti-theft device. She also gave him contacts to obtain further information and sent him a copy of the 52-page report, which arrived two days later. One of the contacts provided a free report from the state police agencies which demonstrated how such an anti-theft device substantially increased the recovery rate of stolen vehicles from 20% to over 70%. This information was critical to the future growth and well being of this small business. (Entry #730)

* Government Expert on Paper Preservation Helps Comic Book Collector

A comic book collector in California was worried about the best way to preserve his rare, valuable comic book collection. Certain plastics used for comic storage are intensely destructive to paper, and he had no way of knowing which plastics were this type. Advertisements in trade magazines were deceptive and confusing. Using the copy of "Information USA" he'd received for Christmas, he contacted Carole Zimmermann, head of the Preservation Office at the Library of Congress. This cheerful public servant not only identified the plastic in question to be highly destructive, but also clarified confusing advertisements, explained the latest laboratory research, and suffered his ignorant questions with grace and an easy laugh. She shared her expansive knowledge in a relaxed, personable, and enjoyable conversation and saved him hundreds of dollars in potential damages. (Entry #736)

* Rehabilitation Counselor Helps Woman in Illinois to See Again

As a result of a spinal tap, a woman in Illinois contracted Multiple Sclerosis. The effects of her disease caused her to lose her eyesight, her job, and have a car accident. In addition to the financial strains she already faced, the roof on her house also had to be replaced. She went to the state's Office of Rehabilitation to see if they could help her find employment since she was blind. The counselor questioned the diagnosis of her eye condition and paid for another eye test. As a result of the test, she had eye surgery and regained her eyesight. (Entry #756)

Info-Power Greatest Hits

We've put together this quick reference guide of the hundred or so topics that people most often ask us about, whether it's money to start a business, government auctions, a vacation in the Virgin Islands, free medical care, summer jobs, or birthday cards from the President.

The list is arranged alphabetically, with key words first. You'll find a brief description of the program, a telephone number to get you started, and then a reference to the chapter in *Info-Power* where you can find more information on the topic and lots of other related sources you might also be interested in.

If you don't find what you're looking for in this section, be sure to check the index at the back of *Info-Power*. If you still can't find what you're looking for, call us at 301-924-0556, and we'll get you headed in the right direction.

* Adopt-A-Horse
Public Affairs
Bureau of Land Management
Suite 5600, 1849 C Street, NW
Washington, DC 20240   202-208-5717
If you've got the proper place to put it, the Bureau of Land Management will let you adopt a burro or horse for about $125. *(See the chapter on Environment and Nature.)*

* Aerial Photos of Your Neighborhood
EROS Data Center
Sioux Falls, SD 57198   605-594-6151
The government has taken aerial photos of almost every square foot of the U.S., including your neighborhood. *(See the chapter on Weather and Maps.)*

* Aerospace Workshops for Teachers
Education Division
NASA
300 E Street, SW, Code FE
Washington, DC 20546   202-358-1519
NASA holds free workshops all over the U.S. for teachers on astronomy, life in space, rocketry, remote sensing, and more. *(See the chapter on Science and Technology.)*

* Age Discrimination
Publications Center
Equal Employment Opportunity Commission
P.O. Box 12549
Cincinnati, Oh 45212   800-669-3362 (publications)
Population's getting older, but companies still want younger employees. Unfortunately, that's illegal. *(See the chapters on Careers and Workplace, and Law and Social Justice.)*

* AIDS Hotline
National AIDS Information Clearinghouse
P.O. Box 6003   800-458-5231
Rockville, MD 20850   Fax: 301-738-6616
                              TDD: 800-243-7012
Know the difference between fact and fiction when it comes to AIDS. Free publications, videos, posters, and research results. *(See the chapter on Health and Medicine.)*

* Airline Passenger Complaint Center
Consumer Affairs
U.S. Department of Transportation, C-75
Washington, DC 20590   202-366-2220
Was your flight attendant rude? Were you bumped off a flight even though you had a prepaid ticket? Get some action fast. *(See the chapter on Consumer Power.)*

* Air Traffic Controller Job Bank
Federal Aviation Administration
800 Independence Ave., SW
Washington, DC 20591   202-267-3456
Lost your airline job during the recession? Maybe you can get another through the Airline Rehire Program. *(See the chapter on Careers and Workplace.)*

* Ansel Adams Prints
National Archives, NNSP
8601 Adelphi Rd.
College Park, MD 20740   301-713-6625
Want copies of selected still photos in the National Archives holdings? *(See the chapter on Books and Libraries.)*

* Artists and Creative Writers: Free Money
National Endowment for the Arts
1100 Pennsylvania Avenue, NW
Washington, DC 20506   202-682-5464
Starving writer or artist? The National Endowment of the Arts gives out millions in grants each year. *(See the chapter on Arts and Humanities.)*

* Art Slide Shows on Free Loan
National Gallery of Art
Slide Library
Constitution and 6th Streets, NW
Washington, DC 20565   202-842-6273
The National Gallery of Art loans all kinds of slides and videos on their collection. *(See the chapter on Arts and Humanities.)*

* Astronomy Hotline
See Star Gazer Hotline

* Auctions at the Postal Service
Claims and Inquiries
U.S. Postal Service
2970 Market Street, Room 531A
Philadelphia, PA 19104   215-895-8140
What happens to all those packages that go unclaimed through the mail? They're auctioned off. *(See the chapter on Government Auctions and Surplus Property.)*

* Auto Safety Hotline
National Highway Traffic Safety Administration
Auto Safety Hotline
NEF-11.2HL
400 7th Street, SW
Washington, DC 20590   800-424-9393

Info-Power Greatest Hits

Safety problems with your new car and the dealer is no help? The government is a good persuader. *(See the chapter on Consumer Power.)*

* Banking Complaint Action
Federal Deposit Insurance Corporation (FDIC)
Division of Compliance and Consumer Affairs
550 17th St., NW   800-934-3342
Washington, DC 20429   202-942-3100
If you've got a problem with any FDIC-insured bank, call this hotline and have it investigated. *(See the chapter on Consumer Power.)*

* Bird Watchers Paradise
See Wildlife Refuges

* Birthday Greetings from the President
White House Greetings Office
Room 39   202-456-2724
Washington, DC 20500   Fax: 202-395-1232
The President will send anyone who's 80 or over a birthday card. To request one, write the above office. You may also send your request by fax. *(See the chapter on More Info-Power Hits.)*

* Boating Lessons
Commandant, (G-NAB-5)
U.S. Coast Guard Headquarters   800-368-5647
Washington, DC 20593-0001   202-267-0780 in DC
The Coast Guard offers all kinds of free boating and safety courses. *(See the chapter on Vacations and Business Travel.)*

* Boating Safety Hotline
Commandant, (G-NAB-5)
U.S. Coast Guard Headquarters   800-368-5647
Washington, DC 20593-0001   202-267-0780
Information on safety courses, product recalls, publications, coloring books for kids, and general complaints. *(See the chapter on Vacations and Business Travel.)*

* Burros
See Adopt-A-Horse

* Business Start-Up Money
Answer Desk
U.S. Small Business Administration (SBA)
409 Third Street, SW
Washington, DC 20416   800-827-5722
The SBA guarantees small business loans for those who can't qualify through their regular bank. Also contact your state's Department of Economic Development, or your local Small Business Development Center, for information on money sources closer to home. *(See the chapter on Small Business and Entrepreneuring.)*

* Business Loans for Teens
Farmer Programs Loan Making Division
Farmers Home Administration
U.S. Department of Agriculture
South Agriculture Building, Room 5420
Washington, DC 20250   202-720-4323
Kids can get thousands to finance their own farm-related businesses from the local Farmers Home Administration, Production Loan Division. *(See the chapter on Small Business and Entrepreneuring.)*

* Cancer Answers
National Cancer Institute
Building 31, Room 10A24
9000 Rockville Pike
Bethesda, MD 20892-2580   800-4-CANCER
Everything you needed to know about cancer, plus physician referrals, latest research and publications. *(See the chapter on Health and Medicine.)*

* Capitol Hill Guided Tours
U.S. Capitol
Washington, DC 20510
Before you go to Washington, DC, ask your member of congress for a VIP tour pass to get free red carpet treatment. *(See the chapter on Vacations and Business Travel.)*

* Cars
See Auctions

* Cholesterol Info-Line
National Heart, Lung, and Blood Institute Information Center
P.O. Box 30105
Bethesda, MD 20824   301-251-1222
Get the newest facts and research results on cholesterol and your diet. *(See the chapter on Health and Medicine.)*

* Christmas Trees and Firewood
For a nominal permit fee, you can cut your own Christmas tree or collect firewood on public lands. Contact your nearest National Forest or local Bureau of Land Management, U.S. Department of Interior, for details. *(See the chapter on Environment and Nature.)*

* Condom Testing Results
Center for Population Research
6100 Executive Boulevard, Room 8B07
Bethesda, MD 20892   301-496-4924
How reliable is that brand of condom you're using? The government has expert testers. *(See the chapter on Health and Medicine.)*

* Congressional Salaries and Expenses
House Documents Room
2nd and D Street, SW, Room B18
Washington, DC 20515   202-225-3456
How much did your congressional representative spend on meals and entertainment last year? *(See the chapter on Information from Lawmakers.)*

* Consultants Can Make Millions
Each year government agencies spend millions on freelancers to advise them on everything from engineering and accounting problems to environmental studies and pesticides. Contact the Office of Small and Disadvantaged Business Utilization for whichever agency you're interested in for more details. *(See the chapter on Selling to the Government.)*

* Consumer Products and Toy Recall Hotline
Office of Information and Public Affairs
U.S. Consumer Product Safety Commission
Washington, DC 20207   800-638-2772
Want to find out if a toy you bought for your kid is being recalled because it's dangerous? *(See the chapter on Consumer Power.)*

* Country Home Loans
Fannie Mae
Public Information Office
3900 Wisconsin Avenue, NW
Washington, DC 20016-2899   800-732-6643
FmHA provides low-interest loans to qualified buyers to purchase homes in rural areas. *(See the chapter on Housing and Real Estate.)*

* Country Inn Start-Up Money: $100,000
Office of Rural Affairs and Economic Development
U.S. Small Business Administration
409 Third Street, SW
Washington, DC 20416   202-205-6485
A catalog called, *Working Together: A Guide to Federal and State Resources for Rural Economic Development*, describes money and ways to help start businesses in small towns. *(See the chapter on Small Business and Entrepreneuring.)*

* Credit Counseling for Home Buyers

If you own a HUD-insured home, and you're having trouble meeting your bills, you can receive free financial counseling. Contact your bank that handles the loan for more information. *(See the chapter on Housing and Real Estate.)*

* Credit Repair Help for Free

Don't pay to have your credit improved. Your local County Cooperative Extension Service will show you how to do it for free. *(See the chapter on Consumer Power.)*

* Crime Insurance at Bargain Prices

Federal Crime Insurance Program
P.O. Box 6301
Rockville, MD 20849-6301   800-638-8780
Residents in 12 states qualify for federally-subsidized crime insurance for their homes. *(See the chapter on Law and Social Justice.)*

* Crime Victims Assistance

A mugger stole your rent money, and you missed two weeks of work while in the hospital. Get money by contacting your state's Crime Victims Assistance office. *(See the chapter on Law and Social Justice.)*

* Dead Beat Dads: Tracking Him Down

He says it wasn't him. He won't pay child support he owes you. Contact your state Child Support Enforcement Office. *(See the chapter on Your Community.)*

* Dental Care: Free and Low-Cost

Contact your state's Dental Society or the Dental School at the university near you for information on how to get dental care at a fraction of the cost that a private dentist would charge. *(See the chapter on Health and Medicine.)*

* Dental Implants for Free

National Institute of Dental Research
Clinical Center
Bethesda, MD 20892   301-496-4261
Lost a tooth along the way? If government dental researchers are studying new dental implants and looking for volunteer patients, you could get one for free. *(See the chapter on Health and Medicine.)*

* Drug Dealers' Boats and Cars

U.S. Custom Service
Public Auction Line
EG&G Dynatrend, Attn: PAL
2300 Clarendon Blvd., Suite 705
Arlington, VA 22201   703-351-7887
U.S. Customs and Marshals Services confiscate and auction cars, boats, jewelry, and real estate of drug dealers. Call the above number, and look in the Wednesday edition of *USA Today*. *(See the chapter on Government Auctions and Surplus Property.)*

* Drugs, Free

See Prescription Drugs

* Earthquake Safety Checklist

Publications
Federal Emergency Management Agency (FEMA)
500 C Street, SW   800-480-2520
Washington, DC 20472   202-646-3484
Obviously you think living in California is worth it. But the FEMA still thinks you should be prepared. *(See the chapter on Your Community.)*

* Environmental Question Line

Environmental Protection Agency
Public Information Center, 3404
401 M Street, SW   202-260-7751
Washington, DC 20460   Fax: 202-260-6257
How should you dispose of motor oil? Indoor air quality problems? Removing asbestos? *(See the chapter on Environment and Nature.)*

* Export Advice Hotline

Trade Information Center
International Trade Administration
U.S. Department of Commerce
14th and Constitution Avenue, NW, Room HCHB 7424
Washington, DC 20230   800-USA-TRADE
Want to sell your gizmo or doodad in the Soviet Union but don't know how? Experts are waiting to help. A fax service is also available. *(See the chapter on International Trade.)*

* Family Budget Help

See Home Economics

* Films and Lectures on Art

National Gallery of Art
Constitution and 4th Street, NW
Washington, DC 20565   202-737-4215
National Gallery holds all kinds of free lectures and films on the arts. Call the above number for a schedule. *(See the chapter on Arts and Humanities.)*

* Firewood

See Christmas Trees

* Flags over the U.S. Capitol

U.S. Capitol
Washington, DC 20515   202-224-3121
Want to buy a flag that's flown over the U.S. Capitol in Washington, DC? Contact your local Senator or Congressman for details, or call the above number. *(See the chapter on More Info-Power Hits.)*

* FmHA Money Waiting for You

Support Service Center
U.S. Department of Housing and Urban Development
P.O. Box 23699
Washington, DC 20026-3699   703-235-8117
Ever taken out a FmHA-insured home loan? You may have a chunk of money waiting for you. One call will tell. *(See the chapter on Housing and Real Estate.)*

* Foster Grandparents Volunteers

AmeriCorps   800-424-8867
1100 Vermont Avenue, NW   202-606-4849
Washington, DC 20525   TDD: 800-833-3722
Over 60 and looking for something new? Help out under-privileged children. Call ACTION for details. *(See the chapter on Your Community.)*

* Franchise Buying Assistance: Laws and Guidelines

Franchise Rule Information
Federal Trade Commission
Sixth Street and Pennsylvania Avenue, NW
Washington, DC 20580   202-326-3220
Call the Federal Trade Commission Franchise Rule Information Hotline. *(See the chapter on Small Business and Entrepreneuring.)*

* Freelancer Artists, Writers, Consultants

The government spends millions each year on these freelance services. Contact the Office of Small and Disadvantaged Business Utilization for whichever agency you're interested in for more details. *(See the chapter on Selling to the Government.)*

* Genealogical Workshops

National Archives
Washington, DC 20408   202-501-5410

Info-Power Greatest Hits

Want to find out who your great-grandfather was? The National Archives runs three-hour workshops to show you the ropes of genealogical research for $10. The Archive's calendar of events includes registration details. *(See the chapter on Arts and Humanities, and Books and Libraries.)*

* Geographic Names Information Database

Geographic Names Branch
U.S. Geological Survey
12201 Sunrise Valley Drive
Reston, VA 22092   703-648-4547

Thinking of starting a new town in Alaska? Make sure there already isn't another town with the same name. *(See the chapter on Government Databases and Bulletin Boards.)*

* Health Care: Best in the World for Free

National Institutes of Health
Communications Office
Building 10, Room 1C255
Bethesda, MD 20892   301-496-2563

Each year hundreds of thousands of people across the country receive free medical care for everything from breast cancer and toothache to diabetes and writer's cramp, from the best researchers in the country. *(See the chapter on Health and Medicine.)*

* Health Information Hotline

National Health Information Center
P.O. Box 1133   800-336-4797
Washington, DC 20013-1133   301-565-4167

Want to know about health care issues such as Lyme Disease, cancer, AIDS, Medicare and Medicaid? The National Health Information Center has both answers and free publications. *(See the chapter on Health and Medicine.)*

* Health Profession Scholarships From U.S. Department of Veterans Affairs

Health Professional Educational Assistance Programs
U.S. Department of Veterans Affairs
Office of Academic Affairs
810 Vermont Avenue, NW
Washington, DC 20420   202-565-7091

If you're willing to work for the VA for at least a year after you graduate, you might be in line for a scholarship. *(See the chapter on Health and Medicine.)*

* Historic Home Renovation Loans

History Division
National Park Service
800 N. Capitol Street, NE
Washington, DC 20002   202-343-8169

Think your home has local historic significance? If it makes it on the National Register, you may qualify for low-interest loans to pay for upkeep and renovation. Contact your state Historic Registration or call the number above. *(See the chapter on Your Community, and Housing and Real Estate.)*

* Historic Preservation Ideas

Superintendent of Documents
Government Printing Office   202-512-1800
Washington, DC 20402   Fax: 202-512-2250

Is there a special way to rehang wooden windows or put a new roof on an historic home? Get a free Government Printing Office bibliography of publications on historic preservation. *(See the chapter on Your Community and Housing and Real Estate.)*

* Home-based Business Tips

Answer Desk
U.S. Small Business Administration
409 Third Street, SW
Washington, DC 20416   800-827-5722

Want to run a business out of your home? Get a free start-up guide from the Small Business Administration (SBA). Contact your local SBA or call the above number. *(See the chapter on Small Business and Entrepreneuring.)*

* Home Economics Workshops

Your local County Cooperative Extension Service will help you select, prepare, and budget a healthy menu for your family. *(See the chapter on Health and Medicine.)*

* Horses to Adopt

See Adopt-A-Horse

* Housing Discrimination Hotline

Housing Discrimination Hotline
U.S. Department of Housing and Urban Development
451 Seventh Street, SW
Washington, DC 20410   800-669-9777

Can't get a housing loan because the house is in the "wrong" kind of neighborhood? Landlord won't rent to you after seeing you in person? *(See the chapter on Consumer Power.)*

* Houses for $1?

You probably won't get a house for a dollar, but you just may be able to get one for pennies on the dollar at HUD auctions. Consult the Real Estate section in your paper for upcoming auctions and available properties. For information on low-interest, government-insured housing loans, call your local HUD office. *(See the chapter on Housing and Real Estate.)*

* Ice Breaker Expeditions

Ice Operations
U.S. Coast Guard
2100 2nd Street, SW
Washington, DC 20593   202-267-1450

Need to go to the South Pole to write your next book? *(See the chapter on Vacations and Business Travel.)*

* Information on Demand

Reference
Library of Congress
101 Independence Avenue, SE
Washington, DC 20540   202-707-5534

Got a quick question that a staff member at Library of Congress could answer? *(See the chapter on Books and Libraries.)*

* Inmate Locator Line

Federal Bureau of Prisons
Inmate Locator
320 First Street, NW
Washington, DC 20534   202-307-3126

You've just got to get letters to Jim Bakker and Charles Manson. *(See the chapters on Law and Social Justice, and Information on People, Companies and Mailing Lists.)*

* Insurance Complaints and Questions

Insurance company won't honor your claim? Canceled without a reason? Your state's insurance commissioner will get what's coming to you. *(See the chapter on Information on People, Companies and Mailing Lists.)*

* Interstate Land Sales Fraud-Line

Interstate Land Sales Registration Division
U.S. Department of Housing and Urban Development
451 7th Street, SW
Washington, DC 20410   202-708-0502

Bought some swamp land in Florida that was supposed to be luxury condos? *(See the chapter on Consumer Power.)*

* Inventors Become Millionaires

Office of Technology Innovation
National Institute of Standards and Technology
Division 241
Gaithersburg, MD 20899   301-975-5500

The Energy Related Invention Assistance Program will evaluate your invention and help you get a grant to turn your idea into a business. *(See the chapter on Science and Technology.)*

* Job Retraining for Free

Get free technical and vocational training under a federal job training program through your local employment office. *(See the chapter on Careers and Workplace.)*

* Job Safety Inspections On-Site

Consumer Affairs
Occupational Safety and Health Administration (OSHA)
200 Constitution Avenue, NW, Room N3637
Washington, DC 20210   800-321-OSHA

Asbestos falling from your ceiling at work? Repetitive movements causing pain in your joints? OSHA will inspect for free. Contact your local OSHA office for information. For emergencies, contact the 800 number listed above. *(See the chapter on Careers and Workplace.)*

* Jobs With the Federal Government

Most federal agencies have job line recordings for immediate openings that need filling. Consult the U.S. Government listings in your phone book for the appropriate agency and number, or see the chapter on Federal Government Databases for the listings in Washington, DC headquarters.

* Job Trends: What's Hot, What's Not

Office of Employment Projectors
U.S. Department of Labor
2 Massachusetts Avenue, NE, Room 2135
Washington, DC 20212   202-606-5709

Find out what jobs will be hot and what will not before you spend money on college. *(See the chapter on Careers and Workplace.)*

* Lie Detector Reliability

National Criminal Justice Reference Service
Box 6000   800-851-3420
Rockville, MD 20850   301-251-5500

How reliable are lie detector tests? The Justice Department will send you the findings of their study. *(See the chapters on Careers and Workplace, Law and Social Justice.)*

* Lost Loved Ones

See Missing People

* Medical Care: Free and Low-Cost

Office of Health Facilities
Health Resources and Services Administration
U.S. Department of Health and Human Services
5600 Fishers Lane, Room 11-03   800-638-0742
Rockville, MD 20857   800-492-0359 in MD

Under the Hill-Burton law, many low-income individuals qualify for free health care at over 2,500 health facilities. *(See the chapter on Health and Medicine.)*

* Medications, Free

See Prescription Drugs

* Missing People: Be Your Own Private Eye

Find your lost friend or loved one on your own and save big money. Use state motor vehicles records, voter registration records, armed services locator program, professional licensing offices, and much more. *(See the chapter on Information on People, Companies and Mailing Lists.)*

* Money Programs: Billions for Everyone

The federal government loans and gives away billions every year for everything from houses and businesses, to writers and painters. Look through the *Catalog of Federal Domestic Assistance* at your library. *(See the chapters on Small Business and Entrepreneuring, and Housing and Real Estate.)*

* Money to Start a Business

See Business Start-Up Money

* Moon Rocks for Teachers

Johnson Space Center
Education Coordinator
National Aeronautics and Space Administration (NASA)
Houston, TX 77058   713-483-0123

NASA will loan science teachers lunar rock samples for classroom use after an orientation seminar. *(See the chapter on Education.)*

* Motor Vehicle Records: Locate Anyone Who Drives

Don't hire a private eye--do what they do: use your state's motor vehicle and license records to track anyone down. *(See the chapter on Information on People, Companies and Mailing Lists.)*

* NASA Space Videos

Lorain County Joint Vocational School
NASA Core
15181 Route 58 South
Oberlin, OH 44074   216-774-1051, ext. 293

Want some great NASA videos on moon walks, the Space Shuttle, the Apollo Missions? Get them at a fraction of retail cost directly from NASA. *(See the chapter on Education.)*

* Native American Ancestry Census

U.S. Department of the Interior
Bureau of Indian Affairs
Tribal Enrollment
Mail Stop 2611-MIB
Washington, DC 20245   202-208-3702

Think you might be part Cherokee or Apache? The Bureau of Indian Affairs can help you in your search. Call the Branch of Tribal Enrollment. *(See the chapter on Arts and Humanities.)*

* Neighborhood Watch Programs

National Sheriff's Association
1450 Duke Street
Alexandria, VA 22314   703-836-7827

Want to make your neighborhood a safer place for your kids? Get help setting up a Watch program. *(See the chapter on Law and Social Justice.)*

* Nuclear Fallout Shelter Plans

Publications
Federal Emergency Management Agency
500 C Street, SW   800-480-2520
Washington, DC 20472   202-646-3484

Want to build a snack bar that also serves as a nuclear fallout shelter? Call the number above for plans. *(See the chapter on Your Community.)*

* Nuclear War Survival Guide

NETC Home Study Program
Federal Emergency Management Agency (FEMA)
16825 S. Seton Ave.
Emmsburg, MD 21727   301-447-1076

Still worried about the Russian A-bombs? FEMA will send a home-study course on surviving a nuclear war. *(See the chapter on Your Community.)*

* Overseas Travel Advisory Hotline

Citizens Emergency Center
Overseas Citizens Services
U.S. Department of State
2201 C Street, NW, Room 4800
Washington, DC 20520   202-647-5225

Before you book three weeks in Beirut or Yugoslavia, you might want to get some advice from the State Department. *(See the chapter on Vacations and Business Travel.)*

* Painters and Sculptors: Money for Your Work

202-501-1256

New federal buildings have to set aside a portion of construction and renovation budgets for art work. *(See the chapter on Small Business and Entrepreneuring.)*

* Paternity Testing

See Dead Beat Dads

* Peace Corps Volunteering

Peace Corps
1400 Wilson Blvd.
Suite 400
Arlington, VA 22209   703-235-9191

Want to see Prague and Budapest but can't afford it? The Peace Corps has sent hundreds to Eastern Europe. *(See the chapter on Your Community.)*

* Pension Protection Guides for Employees

Public Affairs
Pension Benefits Guaranty Corporation
2020 K Street, NW
Washington, DC 20005-4026   202-326-4000

Know your rights about pensions, including the federal program that insures certain plans. *(See the chapter on Careers and Workplace.)*

* Pesticides Hotline

National Pesticide Telecommunications Network
Texas Tech University
Thompson Hall, Room 5129   800-858-7378
Lubbock, TX 79430   Fax: 806-743-3094

Need to know how to safely handle and use certain pesticides in your garden? Call the Environmental Protection Agency at the above number. *(See the chapter on Environment and Nature.)*

* Plant Care Answer Line

Horto-Line   202-225-8333

Why is your bonsai dying? Do dandelions have any medicinal use? How do you grow your own herbs? Call on Tuesdays and Thursdays between 9 and 11 am. *(See the chapter on Housing and Real Estate.)*

* Plant and Lawn Workshops

You've decided you don't want a yellow lawn again this year. Call your local County Cooperative Extension Service for free expertise. *(See the chapter on Housing and Real Estate.)*

* Polar Expeditions for Civilians

Ice Operations
U.S. Coast Guard
2100 2nd Street, SW
Washington, DC 20593   202-267-1450

Need to go to the South Pole to write your next book? *(See the chapter on Vacations and Business Travel.)*

* Police Radar Guns

See Radar Buster Reports

* Polygraph Testing Rights

202-523-7640

Before you agree to taking a lie detector test at your job, you should know the law that prohibits its use. *(See the chapter on Careers and Workplace.)*

* Prescription Drugs for Free

Pharmaceutical Manufacturer's Association
1100 15th Street, NW
Washington, DC 20005   800-726-7504

If you have to choose between eating and taking a much-needed medication, then you might be able to get your drug prescription filled free of charge directly from the drug company. Call the Pharmaceutical Manufacturer's Association for a directory of drug companies that participate. *(See the chapter on Health and Medicine.)*

* Presidential Birthday Cards

See Birthday Cards

* Prospecting for Gold

The Bureau of Mines publishes a free guide on prospecting for gold. Contact your local library and ask for Information Circular (IC) 8517. This publication can also be found in Federal Depositories, on many university campuses. *(See the chapter on Business and Industry.)*

* Puerto Rico on Uncle Sam

VISTA
1100 Vermont Avenue, NW, Suite 8100   800-424-8867
Washington, DC 20525   TDD: 800-833-3722

Always wanted to spend time in Puerto Rico but couldn't afford it? Volunteer to fight poverty there and Uncle Sam will pay you to go for a year and even forgive a portion of your student loans. *(See the chapter on Your Community.)*

* Radar Buster Reports: Beating a Speeding Ticket

Office of Law Enforcement Standards
National Institute of Standards and Technology
Building 225, Room A-323
Gaithersburg, MD 20899   301-975-2757

Busted for speeding? A report on the reliability of police radar might be what you're looking for. *(See the chapter on Science and Technology.)*

* Radon Gas Leaks

National Safety Council
Environmental Health Center
Environmental Protection Agency
1019 19th St., NW, Suite 401
Washington, DC 20036   800-SOS-RADON

For information on how to get your home tested for radon and locating a contractor to make any necessary repairs, call the above number. *(See the chapter on Environment and Nature.)*

* Rental Rates Across the U.S.

Valuation Branch
Multi-Family Housing
U.S. Department of Housing and Urban Development
451 7th Street, SW
Washington, DC 20410   202-708-0624

Negotiating a rental agreement and think the landlord is asking too much? Show him or her what the government thinks the place should go for. *(See the chapter on Housing and Real Estate.)*

* Scholarships and Internships

U.S. Capitol
Washington, DC 20510   202-224-3121

Millions of dollars are available to students each year in the form of fellowships and scholarships. Write your member of congress and ask for a copy of Info-Pack *Internships and Fellowships* (#IP0631) or call the above number. *(See the chapter on Education.)*

* Second Surgical Opinion Line

Health Care Financing Administration
330 Independence Avenue, SW
Washington, DC 20201   800-638-6833

Just maybe you don't need a hysterectomy or your gall bladder removed. If you're on Medicare or Medicaid, you can get help with a second opinion. *(See the chapter on Health and Medicine.)*

* Small Business Loans
Answer Desk
U.S. Small Business Administration (SBA)
409 Third Street, SW
Washington, DC 20416   800-827-5722
Everything you needed to know and more about starting and running your own small business. *(See the chapter on Small Business and Entrepreneuring.)*

* Small Business Mentors
Answer Desk
U.S. Small Business Administration (SBA)
409 Third Street, SW
Washington, DC 20416   800-827-5722
Need some free marketing advice or accounting help? A retired business executive will help. *(See the chapter on Small Business and Entrepreneuring.)*

* Smoking: Free Help to Quit
National Cancer Institute
Building 31, Room 10A24
9000 Rockville Pike
Bethesda, MD 20892   800-4-CANCER
Everything you need to know about smoking and how to quit, new research, local programs, and more. *(See the chapter on Health and Medicine.)*

* Space Camp for Kids and Adults
U.S. Space Camp and Rocket Center
P.O. Box 070015
Huntsville, AL 35807-7015   800-637-7223
Astronaut training, rocketry classes, simulated space missions, and everything. *(See the chapter on Education.)*

* Space Photos
EROS Data Center
Sioux Falls, SD 57198   605-594-6511
What does Montana look like from space? How about Sheboygan? You can buy it and hang it on your wall. *(See the chapter on Weather and Maps.)*

* Star Gazer Hotline
                    202-357-2000
When is Jupiter next visible? The next eclipse? Find out the latest astronomical news. *(See the chapter on Science and Technology.)*

* Stock Broker Complaint Line
Consumer Affairs
Securities and Exchange Commission (SEC)
Mail Stop 11-2
450 5th Street, NW
Washington, DC 20546   202-942-7040
Your broker drained your account and blew it in Las Vegas? The SEC can help. *(See the chapter on Investments and Finance Services.)*

* Student Loans Forgiven
VISTA
1100 Vermont Avenue, NW   800-942-2677
Washington, DC 20525   202-606-5000
If you join Volunteers in Service to America (VISTA) and work to help the poor for a year, you can have a portion of your student loans forgiven; up to 50%, if you stay in for three years. *(See the chapter on Your Community.)*

* Student Loan Hotline
Federal Student Aid Information Center
P.O. Box 84
Washington, DC 20044   800-433-3243
Interested in finding out what federal financial aid is available for college? *(See the chapter on Education.)*

* Summer Jobs in Conservation
Forest Service
U.S. Department of Agriculture
Personnel
1621 N. Kent
Rosslyn, VA 22209   703-235-8102
or
Office of Human Resources
U.S. Fish and Wildlife Resources
4040 Fairfax Dr.
Arlington, VA 22203   703-358-1724
The Forest Service and Fish and Wildlife Service hire teens during the summer for conservation work on public lands. *(See the chapter on Careers and Workplace.)*

* Summer Jobs: Thousands for Teens and Older
Job Information Center
Office of Personnel Management
1900 E St., NW, Room 1416
Washington, DC 20415   202-606-2700
Each summer the federal government hires thousands of kids across the U.S. Apply before April 15. *(See the chapter on Careers and Workplace.)*

* Tax Preparation Courses Free to All
Internal Revenue Service
1111 Constitution Avenue, NW
Public Affairs
Washington, DC 20224   800-829-1040
The Internal Revenue Service will train you to prepare returns in return for helping others who need tax help. *(See the chapter on Taxes.)*

* Teenage Business Loans
See Business Loans for Teens

* Term Papers: 10,000 Free for the Asking
U.S. Capitol
Washington, DC 20515
By writing your member of Congress, you can get a research paper written on practically any subject on current events. *(See the chapter on Current Events and Homework.)*

* Travel Emergency Center
Citizen Emergency Center
Overseas Citizens Services
U.S. Department of State
2201 C Street, NW
Washington, DC 20520   202-647-5225
Did your father go to Spain and not return? Need to get money to your son who's homeless in Paris? *(See the chapter on Vacations and Business Travel.)*

* Treasury Securities Info-Line
Public Affairs
U.S. Savings Bond Division
U.S. Department of Treasury
999 E St., NW
Room 353
Washington, DC 20239   202-874-4000
What's a T-Bill? Is it different from a Savings Bond? Can I buy one and avoid paying a broker a commission? *(See the chapter on Investments and Financial Services.)*

* Turkey Cooking Hotline
Meat and Poultry Hotline   800-535-4555
                    202-720-3333
Just how long should you cook a thirteen pound turkey to make sure it's safe to eat? The U.S. Department of Agriculture knows. *(See the chapter on Health and Medicine.)*

Info-Power Greatest Hits

* Unconventional Cancer Treatments

Office of Technology Assessment (OTA)
Health Program
U.S. Congress
Washington, DC 20515-8025   202-228-6590

OTA is studying the safety, effectiveness, and availability of new, unconventional cancer treatments. *(See the chapter on Health and Medicine.)*

* Urban Homesteading Program

Willing to live in a run-down city neighborhood if you can get a house for $250 and agree to fix it up? Call your regional U.S. Department of Housing and Urban Development office or County Housing Community Development Office for details. *(See the chapter on Housing and Real Estate.)*

* Videos and Films: 8,000 From Uncle Sam

National Audiovisual Center
Multi-Media Publications   800-788-6282
8700 Edgeworth Drive   703-487-4650
Capitol Heights, MD 20743   301-763-1896

Looking for a video on prospecting, worker safety, or even concentration camps? Try the National Audiovisual Center. *(See the chapter on Arts and Humanities.)*

* Virgin Islands Vacation

VISTA
1100 Vermont Avenue, NW   800-942-2677
Washington, DC 20525   202-606-5000

Camp out at the National Park on the Virgin Islands for a fraction of what a hotel there costs. If you want to spend a whole year there on Uncle Sam, join VISTA and request to be sent there to work on eliminating poverty. *(See the chapter on Vacations and Business Travel.)*

* Watergate Tapes and Trial Transcripts

Nixon Materials Project Staff
National Archives
8601 Adelphi Rd.
College Park, MD 20740   301-713-6800

Want to hear Nixon, Haldeman, and Ehrlichman cooking up a conspiracy? Transcripts of tapes available, too. *(See the chapter on Arts and Humanities.)*

* Wildlife Refuges: National Guide

Superintendent of Documents
Government Printing Office (GPO)   202-512-1800
Washington, DC 20402   Fax: 202-512-2250

The ultimate animal watcher's vacation idea: tour some National Wildlife Refuges. Ask for *National Wildlife Refuges: A Visitor's Guide.* (See the chapter on Vacations and Business Travel.)

* Writers: Free Grants to Create

National Endowment for the Arts
1100 Pennsylvania Avenue, NW
Washington, DC 20506   202-682-5400

Starving writer? The National Endowment for the Arts gives out millions in grants each year. *(See the chapter on Arts and Humanities.)*

* Woodsy Owl Cleanup For Kids

Forest Service
Woodsy Owl, SNPF
U.S. Department of Agriculture
P.O. Box 96090
Washington, DC 20090-6090   202-205-1483

Give a hoot, show kids how to not pollute with stickers, coloring sheets, patches, and song sheets. *(See the chapter on Environment and Nature.)*

Information Starting Places
Free Help in Finding a Free Expert

See also Experts Chapter

Not only is the world full of experts who are willing to help resolve your information problems for free, there are organizations whose sole mission is to put you in touch with these specialists. Here is a list of some of these clearinghouses arranged by subject area. Don't forget to use the Experts Chapter, which includes the names and phone numbers of experts who specialize in everything from aquaculture to zinc. Remember that these experts spend their lives studying specific areas and are waiting to help you for free. Just keep in mind that a polite, courteous phone attitude can do wonders.

* Agriculture and Commodities

Office of Public Affairs
U.S. Department of Agriculture
Room 413A
Washington, DC 20250   202-720-4623
A staff of research specialists are available to provide specific answers or direct you to an expert in any agricultural-related topic.

National Agricultural Library
10301 Baltimore Boulevard
Beltsville, MD 20705-2351   301-504-5755
The National Agricultural Library serves as an information clearinghouse for agricultural-related topics.

National Agricultural Statistics Service
U.S. Department of Agriculture, NAS
14th and Independence Avenue SW
Room 4117 S. Bldg.
Washington, DC 20250   202-720-3896
The Agricultural Statistics Service (ASS) provides contacts for agricultural production, stocks, prices and other data.

* Arts and Entertainment

Performing Arts Library
John F. Kennedy Center
Washington, DC 20566   202-416-8000
This center which works jointly with the Library of Congress offers reference services on any aspect of the performing arts.

* Best and Worst Industries and Companies

Bureau of the Census
U.S. Department of Commerce
Washington, DC 20230   301-763-4040
Over 100 analysts monitor all the major industries in the United States and the companies within these industries, which range from athletic products to truck trailers.

Office of Industries
U.S. International Trade Commission
500 E Street SW, Room 504
Washington, DC 20436   202-205-3296
Experts analyze impact of world trade on United States industries ranging from audio components to x-ray apparatus.

* Business Advice

Roadmap Program
U.S. Department of Commerce
14th and Constitution Avenue, NW
Washington, DC 20230   202-482-3176
Roadmap Program provides reference services on all aspects of commerce and business.

Library
U.S. Department of Commerce
14th and Constitution Avenue, NW
Washington, DC 20230   202-482-5511
This library also provides reference services on all aspects of business.

* Country Experts

Country Officers
U.S. Department of State
2201 C Street NW
Washington, DC 20520   202-647-4000
Hundreds of experts are available to provide current political, economic, and other background information on the country they study. Call to ask for the number of a specific country officer.

U.S. Department of Commerce
International Trade Administration
Washington, DC 20230   202-482-3809
Teams of experts from these regions can provide information on marketing and business practices for every country in the world.

Commercial Agriculture
Economics Research Service
U.S. Department of Agriculture
14th and Independence Ave.
Washington, DC 20005-4788   202-219-0700
This office provides information on agricultural-related aspects of foreign countries.

Foreign Agricultural Service (FAS)
Information Division
U.S. Department of Agriculture
14th and Independence Avenue, SW
Washington, DC 20250   202-720-3935
The Foreign Agricultural Service (FAS) provides data on world crops, agricultural policies, and markets.

Division of International Minerals
Bureau of Mines
U.S. Department of Interior
810 7th Street, NW
MS 5205
Washington, DC 20241   202-501-9666
Foreign country experts monitor all aspects of foreign mineral industries.

* Crime

National Criminal Justice Reference Service
National Institute of Justice
Box 6000   800-851-3420
Rockville, MD 20850   301-251-5500
Database and reference services provide bibliographies and expertise free or sometimes for a nominal fee.

Uniform Crime Reporting Section
Federal Bureau of Investigation (FBI)
U.S. Department of Justice
409 7th St., NW
Washington, DC 20535   202-324-3000
Statistics are available from this office on eight major crimes against person and property.

* Demographics, Economic and Industry Statistics

Data Users Service Division
Bureau of the Census
Customer Service
Washington, DC 20233   301-457-4100
Staff will guide you to the billions of dollars worth of taxpayer supported data.

Be patient. If any phone number is incorrect, call (area code) 555-1212 and request the new listing.

33

Information Starting Places

* Economics: National, Regional and International

Bureau of Economic Analysis
U.S. Department of Commerce
Washington, DC 20230   202-606-9900
This office is the first place to call for economic data.

* Education

Office of Educational Research and
    Improvement (OERI)
U.S. Department of Education
555 New Jersey Ave., NW
Washington, DC 20208-1235   202-219-2050
A network of 16 information clearinghouses that identify literature, experts,
audiovisuals, funding, etc.

National Library of Education
U.S. Department of Education
555 New Jersey Avenue, NW
Washington, DC 20208   800-424-1616
This hotline provides referrals to other information sources on any aspect of
education.

* Energy

National Energy Information Center
U.S. Department of Energy
1F048 Forrestal Building
1000 Independence Ave., SW
Washington, DC 20585   202-586-8800
This office provides general reference services on U.S. Department of Energy data.

Conservation and Renewable Energy Inquiry
    and Referral Service
P.O. Box 3040
Merrifield, VA 22116   800-523-2929
Free help on how to save energy as well as information on solar, wind, or any other
aspect of renewable energy.

U.S. Department of Energy
Office of Scientific and Technical Information
P.O. Box 62
Oak Ridge, TN 37831   615-576-1301
This office provides research and other information services on all energy related
topics.

* Health

National Health Information Center
P.O. Box 1133   800-336-4797
Washington, DC 20013-1133   301-565-4167 in MD
Contact this center for leads to both public and private sector health organizations,
research centers and universities.

National Center for Health Statistics
U.S. Department of Health and Human Services
6525 Belcrest Rd., Room 1064
Presidential Building
Hyattsville, MD 20782   301-436-8500
This clearinghouse can provide data on any aspect of health.

* Housing

Library and Information Services Center
U.S. Department of Housing and Urban Development
451 7th Street SW
Washington, DC 20410   202-708-2370
This library provides information on all aspects of housing, and staff will direct you
to a program which meets your needs.

* Import and Export Statistics

Foreign Trade Reference Room
U.S. Department of Commerce
14th and Constitution Ave., NW
Washington, DC 20230   202-482-2185
This library can provide data on many aspects of United States trade.

* Metals and Minerals

Division of Mineral Commodities (Domestic)
Bureau of Mines
U.S. Department of the Interior
810 7th Street, NW
Washington, DC 20241   202-501-9450
Dozens of commodity specialists collect, analyze, and disseminate information on the
adequacy and availability of the mineral base for the national economy.

* Prices, Employment, Productivity And Living Conditions Statistics

U.S. Department of Labor
Bureau of Labor Statistics
Washington, DC 20212   202-606-7828
There are subject specialists in such areas as plant closings, labor force projections,
producer price indexes, work stoppages.

* World Import and Export Statistics

World Trade Statistics
U.S. Department of Commerce
Room 2233, Herbert Hoover Building
14th and Constitution Ave.
Washington, DC 20230   202-482-3809
This is place for numbers concerning trade for most countries.

General Sources

These three offices are the places to get help in locating experts
in government as well as the private sector and trade associations.

* Associations

Information Central
American Society of Association Executives
1575 Eye Street NW
Washington, DC 20005   202-626-2723
If you cannot find a relevant association after referring to *Gale's Encyclopedia of
Associations* (which is available in most libraries), this organization will help find
the right one.

* Government Experts

Federal Information Center
P.O. Box 600
Cumberland, MD 21501-0600   301-722-9000
Federal Information Centers are located throughout the country and the staff will find
you an expert in the government on most any topic.

* Technical Research

Science and Technology Division
Reference Section
Library of Congress
1st and Independence, SE
Washington, DC 20540   202-707-5639
This reference section offers both free and fee-based reference and bibliographic
services.

State Starting Places for Finding Experts

If you have trouble locating the exact office you need from the listings elsewhere in the book, this is the section for you. The first place you should start is with State Information Offices listed below. The operators at these offices are normally trained to handle information requests from people who don't know where to go within the state bureaucracy. If you are not successful, try either or both of the other offices listed.

Governor's Office

Because the responsibilities of various state offices often overlap, it may be helpful to begin your data search by contacting the state governor's office. While every state has a central switchboard to field inquiries regarding state business, the number is usually helpful only if you already know which agency is responsible for gathering and interpreting the information you are after. If you are hazy in this regard, the state governor's office will certainly know the appropriate agency department and, if you are lucky, even the name of the special contact person to call.

State Library

A vast amount of research information is available from the state library. After all, it is the official repository of state agency documents and the first place to start if you want to do all of the footwork yourself. In addition, most state libraries also shelve copies of federal government documents and publications.

State libraries are paid for with tax dollars and are open to the public. Collections usually include state legal codes, state historical documents, archival records, genealogy type information, business and economic records, statistical abstracts and annual reports.

In each library these is generally a government information person who can provide telephone and personal assistance to researchers. In addition, there is often a staff specialist to help with statistical questions.

The following is a list of state operators, librarians, and governor's offices.

State Information and Governor's Offices

Alabama
State Information: 334-242-8000

Governor's Office: Office of the Governor, Statehouse, 11 South Union St., Montgomery, AL 36130; 334-242-7100.

State Library: Alabama Public Library Service, 6030 Monticello Drive, Montgomery, AL 36130; 334-213-3900.

Alaska
State Information: 907-465-2111

Governor's Office: Office of the Governor, P.O. Box 110001, Juneau, AK 99811; 907-465-3500.

State Library: Libraries and Museums, P.O. Box 110571, Juneau, AK 99811-0571; 907-465-2921.

Arizona
State Information: 602-542-4900

Governor's Office: Office of the Governor, 1700 West Washington St., Phoenix, AZ 85007; 602-542-4331.

State Library: Department of Library Archives and Public Records, State Capitol, 1700 W. Washington St., Phoenix, AZ 85007; 602-542-4159.

Arkansas
State Information: 501-682-3000

Governor's Office: Office of the Governor, State Capitol Building, Room 250, Little Rock, AR 72201; 501-682-2345.

State Library: Arkansas State Library, 1 Capitol Mall, Little Rock, AR 72201; 501-682-1527.

California
State Information: 916-322-9900

Governor's Office: Office of the Governor, State Capitol, Sacramento, CA 95814; 916-445-2841.

State Library: California State Library, Library and Courts Building, Sacramento, CA 95814; 916-654-0174.

Colorado
State Information: 303-866-5000

Governor's Office: Office of the Governor, 136 State Capitol Building, Denver, CO 80203-1792; 303-866-2471.

State Library: Colorado State Library, 201 East Colfax Ave., Denver, CO 80203; 303-866-6900.

Connecticut
State Information: 203-566-2211

Governor's Office: Office of the Governor, Executive Chambers, Room 202, Hartford, CT 06106; 203-566-4840.

State Library: Connecticut State Library, 231 Capitol Ave., Hartford, CT 06115; 203-566-4777.

Delaware
State Information: 302-739-4000

Governor's Office: Office of the Governor, Tatnall Bldg., William Penn Street, Dover, DE 19901; 302-739-4101.

State Library: Delaware State Library, 43 South DuPont Highway, Dover, DE 19901; 302-739-4748.

Be patient. If any phone number is incorrect, call (area code) 555-1212 and request the new listing.

35

Information Starting Places

District of Columbia
Information: 202-727-1000

Mayor's Office: Executive Office of the Mayor, 441 4th NW, Room 1100, 1 Judiciary Square, Washington, DC 20001; 202-727-2980.

Central Library: Martin Luther King, Jr. Memorial Library, 901 G St. NW, Washington, DC 20001; 202-727-1101.

Florida
State Information: 904-488-1234

Governor's Office: Office of the Governor, The Capitol, Tallahassee, FL 32399-0001; 904-488-4441.

State Library: Florida State Library, R.A. Gray Building, 500 Bruno St., Tallahassee, FL 32399; 904-487-2651.

Georgia
State Information: 404-656-2000

Governor's Office: Office of the Governor, 203 State Capitol, Atlanta, GA 30334; 404-656-1776.

State Library: Georgia State Library, 156 Trinity Ave, Atlanta, GA 30303; 404-657-6220.

Hawaii
State Information: 808-546-2211

Governor's Office: Office of the Governor, State Capitol, Honolulu, HI 96813; 808-548-5420.

State Library: Hawaii State Library, 478 South King St., Honolulu, HI 96813; 808-548-4775.

Idaho
State Information: 208-334-2411

Governor's Office: Office of the Governor, State House, Boise, ID 83720-0034; 208-334-2100.

State Library: Idaho State Library, 325 West State St., Boise, ID 83702; 208-334-5124.

Illinois
State Information: 217-782-2000

Governor's Office: Office of the Governor, State Capitol, Springfield, IL 62706; 217-782-6830.

State Library: Illinois State Library, 300 S. 2nd Street, Springfield, IL 62701; 217-782-7596.

Indiana
State Information: 317-232-1000

Governor's Office: Office of the Governor, State House, 100 N. Capitol Ave. Indianapolis, IN 46204; 317-232-4567.

State Library: Indiana State Library, 140 North Senate, Indianapolis, IN 46204; 317-232-3675.

Iowa
State Information: 515-281-5011

Governor's Office: Office of the Governor, State Capitol, Des Moines, IA 50319; 515-281-5211.

State Library: Iowa State Library, East 12th and Grand Streets, Des Moines, IA 50319; 515-281-4118.

Kansas
State Information: 913-296-0111

Governor's Office: Office of the Governor, State House, Topeka, KS 66612; 913-296-3232.

State Library: Kansas State Library, State House, Topeka, KS 66612; 913-296-3296.

Kentucky
State Information: 502-564-3130

Governor's Office: Office of the Governor, State Capitol Building, Frankfort, KY 40601; 502-564-2611.

State Library: Kentucky State Library, 700 Capitol Ave., #200, Frankfort, KY 40601-3489; 502-564-8300.

Louisiana
State Information: 504-342-6600

Governor's Office: Office of the Governor, P.O. Box 94004, Baton Rouge, LA 70804; 504-342-7015.

State Library: Louisiana State Library, P.O. Box 131, Baton Rouge, LA 70821; 504-342-4923.

Maine
State Information: 207-582-9500

Governor's Office: Office of the Governor, State House Station 1, Augusta, ME 04333; 207-287-3531.

State Library: Maine State Library, State House, Station 83, Augusta, ME 04333; 207-287-5600.

Maryland
State Information: check your local telephone directory or information operator.

Governor's Office: Office of the Governor, State House, Annapolis, MD 21401; 410-974-3901.

State Library: Maryland State Archives, Hall of Records, 350 Rowe Boulevard, Annapolis, MD 21401; 410-974-3914.

Massachusetts
State Information: 617-722-2000

Governor's Office: Office of the Governor, State House, Boston, MA 02133; 617-727-3600.

State Library: 341 State House, Boston, MA 02133; 617-727-2590.

Michigan
State Information: 517-373-1837

Governor's Office: Office of the Governor, State Capitol Building, Lansing, MI 48913; 517-373-3400.

State Library: Michigan State Library, 717 W. Allegan, Lansing, MI 48909; 517-373-5400.

Minnesota
State Information: 612-296-6013

Be patient. If any phone number is incorrect, call (area code) 555-1212 and request the new listing.

Governor's Office: Office of the Governor, 130 State Capitol, St. Paul, MN 55155; 612-296-3391.

State Library: Legislative Reference Library, State Office Building, St. Paul, MN 55155; 612-296-3398.

Mississippi
State Information: 601-359-1000

Governor's Office: Office of the Governor, P.O. Box 139, Jackson, MS 39205; 601-359-3150.

State Library: Department of Archives and History Library, P.O. Box 571, Jackson, MS 39205; 601-359-6850.

Missouri
State Information: 314-751-2000

Governor's Office: Office of the Governor, State Capitol, P.O. Box 720, Jefferson City, MO 65102-0720; 314-751-3222.

State Library: Missouri State Library, P.O. Box 387, Jefferson City, MO 65102-0387; 314-751-3615.

Montana
State Information: 406-444-2511

Governor's Office: Office of the Governor, State Capitol, Helena, MT 59620; 406-444-3111.

State Library: Montana State Library, 1515 East 6th Ave., Helena, MT 59620; 406-444-3115.

Nebraska
State Information: 402-471-2311

Governor's Office: Office of the Governor, State Capitol, P.O. Box 94848, Lincoln, NE 68509-4848; 402-471-2244.

State Library: Nebraska State Library, P.O. Box 98910, Lincoln, NE 68509-8910; 402-471-3189.

Nevada
State Information: 702-687-5000

Governor's Office: Office of the Governor, State Capitol Bldg., Carson City, NV 89710; 702-687-5670.

State Library: Nevada State Library, 100 Stewart St., Carson City, NV 89710; 702-687-5160.

New Hampshire
State Information: 603-271-1110

Governor's Office: Office of the Governor, State House, Concord, NH 03301; 603-271-2121.

State Library: New Hampshire State Library, 20 Park St., Concord, NH 03301; 603-271-2144.

New Jersey
State Information: 609-292-2121

Governor's Office: Office of the Governor, 125 West State St., State House, Trenton, NJ 08625; 609-292-6000.

State Library: New Jersey State Library, State House Annex, CN 520, Trenton, NJ; 609-292-6220.

New Mexico
State Information: 505-827-4011

Governor's Office: Office of the Governor, State Capitol Building, Santa Fe, NM 87503; 505-827-3000.

Governor's Office: State Library: New Mexico State Library, 325 Don Gaspar, Santa Fe, NM 87503; 505-827-3800.

New York
State Information: 518-474-2121

Governor's Office: Office of the Governor, State Capitol, Albany, NY 12224; 518-474-8390.

State Library: New York State Library, Empire State Plaza, Madison Avenue, Albany, NY 12230; 518-474-5355.

North Carolina
State Information: 919-733-1110

Governor's Office: Office of the Governor, State Capitol, Raleigh, NC 27603; 919-733-5811.

State Library: North Carolina State Library, 109 East Jones St., Raleigh, NC 27611; 919-733-2570.

North Dakota
State Information: 701-328-2000

Governor's Office: Office of the Governor, State Capitol, Bismarck, ND 58505; 701-328-2200.

State Library: North Dakota State Library, State Capitol, Bismarck, ND 58505; 701-328-2490.

Ohio
State Information: 614-466-2000

Governor's Office: Office of the Governor, State House, Columbus, OH 43215; 614-466-3555.

State Library: Ohio State Library, 65 South Front St., Columbus, OH 43266; 614-644-7061.

Oklahoma
State Information: 405-521-2011

Governor's Office: Office of the Governor, 212 State Capitol, Oklahoma City, OK 73105; 405-521-2342.

State Library: Oklahoma State Library, 200 N.E. 18th St., Oklahoma City, OK 73105; 405-521-2502.

Oregon
State Information: check your local telephone directory or information operator.

Governor's Office: Office of the Governor, 254 State Capitol, Salem, OR 97310; 503-378-3111.

State Library: Oregon State Library, State Library Building, Salem, OR 97310; 503-378-4274/4277.

Pennsylvania
State Information: 717-787-2121

Governor's Office: Office of the Governor, 225 Main Capitol Bldg., Harrisburg, PA 17120; 717-787-5962.

Information Starting Places

State Library: Pennsylvania State Library, P.O. Box 1601, Harrisburg, PA 17105; 717-787-5718.

Rhode Island
State Information: 401-277-2000

Governor's Office: Office of the Governor, 222 State House, Providence, RI 02903; 401-277-2080.

State Library: Rhode Island State Library, Room 208, State House, Providence, RI 02903; 401-277-2473.

South Carolina
State Information: 803-734-1000

Governor's Office: Office of the Governor, P.O. Box 11369, Columbia, SC 29211; 803-734-9818.

State Library: South Carolina State Library, P.O. Box 11469, Columbia, SC 29225; 803-734-8666.

South Dakota
State Information: 605-773-3011

Governor's Office: Office of the Governor, State Capitol, Pierre, SD 57501; 605-773-3212.

State Library: South Dakota State Library, 500 E. Capitol, Pierre, SD 57501; 605-773-3131.

Tennessee
State Information: 615-741-3011

Governor's Office: Office of the Governor, State Capitol, Nashville, TN 37219; 615-741-2001.

State Library: Tennessee State Library, 403 7th Ave. North, Nashville, TN 37243; 615-741-2764.

Texas
State Information: 512-463-4630

Governor's Office: Office of the Governor, P.O. Box 12428, Austin, TX 78711; 512-463-2000.

State Library: Texas State Library, P.O. Box 12927, Austin, TX 78711; 512-463-5455.

Utah
State Information: 801-538-3000

Governor's Office: Office of the Governor, Room 210, State Capitol, Salt Lake City, UT 84114; 801-538-1000.

State Library: Utah State Library, 2150 South 300 West, Suite 16, Salt Lake City, UT 84115; 801-466-5888.

Vermont
State Information: 802-828-1110

Governor's Office: Office of the Governor, 109 State Street, Montpelier, VT 05609-0101; 802-828-3333.

State Library: Vermont State Library, 109 State Street, Montpelier, VT 05609-0601; 802-828-3261.

Virginia
State Information: 804-786-0000

Governor's Office: Office of the Governor, P.O. Box 1475, Richmond, VA 23212; 804-786-2211.

State Library: Virginia State Library, 11th St and Capitol Square, Richmond, VA 23219; 804-786-8929.

Washington
State Information: 360-753-5000

Governor's Office: Office of the Governor, Legislative Building, Olympia, WA 98504; 360-753-6780.

State Library: Washington State Library, Capitol Campus, Mail Stop AJ-11, Olympia, WA 98504; 360-753-5590.

West Virginia
State Information: 304-558-3456

Governor's Office: Office of the Governor, Main Capitol Complex, Charleston, WV 25305; 304-558-2000.

State Library: West Virginia State Library, Cultural Center, Charleston, WV 25305; 304-558-2041.

Wisconsin
State Information: 608-266-2211

Governor's Office: Office of the Governor, 115 E. Capitol, Madison, WI 53702; 608-266-1212.

State Library: State Historical Society, 816 State St., Madison, WI 53706; 608-264-6534.

Wyoming
State Information: 307-777-7011

Governor's Office: Office of the Governor, State Capitol, Cheyenne, WY 82002; 307-777-7434.

State Library: Wyoming State Library, Supreme Court Building, 23rd and Capitol, Cheyenne, WY 82002; 307-777-7283.

Be patient. If any phone number is incorrect, call (area code) 555-1212 and request the new listing.

Federal Public Information Offices

Almost every federal department, agency, and commission has a special staff to respond to inquiries from the public and the press. These public information offices are particularly helpful in providing details about new programs, proposed legislation, data, statistics, reports and other materials. Keep in mind that the public information office may not be aware or may not be in a position to share with you information that has not been officially released by the government agency. The policy of each office differs; some public information offices, like many at the National Institutes of Health, tend to offer to send photocopies of medical article abstracts and also provide the names and phone numbers of experts and NIH researchers. If others are reluctant to suggest whom you should talk with, refer to the relevant chapter in *Info-Power* and place calls to other offices within the agency or department.

BRANCHES

Legislative Branch

The U.S. Senate
Washington, DC 20510
202-224-3121

The U.S. House of Representatives
Washington, DC 20510
202-224-3121

Architect of the Capitol
U.S. Capitol Building
Room SB15
Washington, DC 20515-8000
202-228-1793

U.S. Botanic Garden
245 First Street, SW
Washington, DC 20024
202-225-8333

General Accounting Office
441 G Street, NW
Washington, DC 20548
202-512-3000

Government Printing Office
710 N. Capitol Street, NW
Washington, DC 20401
202-512-0000

Library of Congress
101 Independence Ave., SE
Washington, DC 20540
202-707-5000

Office of Technology Assessment
U.S. Congress
600 Pennsylvania Ave., SE
Washington, DC 20510-8025
202-224-9241

Congressional Budget Office
2nd and D Sts., SW
Washington, DC 20515
202-226-2621

Judicial Branch

Supreme Court of the U.S.
1 1st St., NE
Washington, DC 20543
202-479-3000

U.S. Court of International Trade
1 Federal Plaza
New York, NY 10278-0001
212-264-2814

Judicial Panel on Multidistrict Litigation
1 Columbus Circle, NE
Room 255, North Lobby
Washington, DC 20002
202-273-2800

U.S. Federal Claims Court
717 Madison Place, NW
Washington, DC 20005
202-219-9657

U.S. Court of Military Appeals
450 E. St., NW
Washington, DC 20442-0001
202-761-1448

Office of Policy Development
10th and Constitution Ave., NW
Room 4234
Washington, DC 20530
202-514-4601

U.S. Tax Court
400 2nd St., NW
Washington, DC 20217
202-606-8751

Administrative Office of the United States
Court of Appeals
717 Madison Place, NW
Washington, DC 20439
202-633-6588

Federal Judicial Center
1 Columbus Circle, NE
Washington, DC 20002
202-273-4004

Executive Branch

The White House Office
1600 Pennsylvania Ave.
Washington, DC 20500
202-456-1414

Office of Management and Budget
Office of Public Affairs
725 17th St., NW, Room 9026
Washington, DC 20503
202-395-7250

Information Starting Places

Information Security Oversight
18th and F St., NW, Room 530
Washington, DC 20405
202-634-6150

Council of Economic Advisers
Room 314, Old Executive Office Bldg.
17th and Pennsylvania Ave., NW
Washington, DC 20500
202-395-5084

National Security Council
Old Executive Office Bldg.
17th and Pennsylvania Ave., NW
Washington, DC 20506
202-456-9272

Office of the U.S. Trade Representative
600 17th St., NW
Washington, DC 20508
202-395-3230

Council on Environmental Quality
722 Jackson Place, NW
Washington, DC 20503
202-395-5754

Office of Science and Technology Policy
Old Executive Office Bldg.
Room 431
Washington, DC 20500
202-395-7347

Office of National Drug Control Policy
Executive Office of the President
750 17th St., NW, 8th Floor
Washington, DC 20500
202-395-6700

Office of Administration
725 17th St., NW
Washington, DC 20503
202-395-6963

Office of the Vice President of the United States
Old Executive Office Bldg.
Washington, DC 20501
202-456-2326

DEPARTMENTS

Department of Agriculture
14th and Independence Ave., SW
Washington, DC 20250
202-720-8732

Small Community and Rural Development
Farmers Home Administration
14th and Independence Ave., SW
Room 5037-S
Washington, DC 20250
202-720-4323

Rural Business and Cooperative Development Service
U.S. Department of Agriculture
Room 5045
14th and Independence Ave., SW
Washington, DC 20250
202-690-4730

Rural Electrification Administration
Room 4043S
14th and Independence, Ave., SW
Washington, DC 20250
202-720-1255

Federal Crop Insurance Corporation
14th and Independence Ave., SW
Washington, DC 20250
202-254-8460

Marketing and Inspection Services
Agricultural Cooperative Service
P.O. Box 96576
Washington, DC 20090-6576
202-720-2556

Agricultural Marketing Service
U.S. Department of Agriculture
P.O. Box 96456
Room 3510, South
Washington, DC 20090-6456
202-720-8999

Animal and Plant Health Inspection Service
Jamie L. Whitten Bldg., Room 312E
Washington, DC 20250-3401
202-720-3861

Food Safety and Inspection Service
14th and Independence Ave., SW
Washington, DC 20250
202-720-7943

Packers and Stockyards Administration
14th and Independence Ave., SW, Room 3039
Washington, DC 20250-2800
202-720-7051

Food and Consumer Services
Food and Nutrition Service
3101 Park Center Drive
Alexandria, VA 22302
703-305-2276

Human Nutrition Information Service
6505 Bellcrest Road
Hyattsville, MD 20782
301-436-7725

Office of Consumer Affairs
3101 Park Center Drive, 813B
Alexandria, VA 22302
703-305-2281

Consolidated Farm Service Agency
3624 South Bldg.
P.O. Box 2415
Washington, DC 20013
202-720-5237

Commodity Credit Corporation
14th and Independence Ave., SW, Room 4521-S
Washington, DC 20250-1000
202-720-3448

Foreign Agricultural Service
14th and Independence Ave., SW, Room 5074-S
Washington, DC 20250
202-720-3448

Office of International Corporation and Development
14th and Independence Ave., SW
Room 3005
Washington, DC 20250-4300
202-690-1823

Science and Education
Agricultural Research Service
14th and Independence Ave., SW
302A Jamie L. Whitten Federal Bldg.
Washington, DC 20250-0300
202-720-3656

Be patient. If any phone number is incorrect, call (area code) 555-1212 and request the new listing.

Cooperative State Research Service
14th and Independence Ave., SW
305A Jamie L. Whitten Federal Bldg.
Washington, DC 20250-2201
202-720-4423

USDA Extension Service
Room 3328 South
14th and Independence Ave., SW
Washington, DC 20250-0900
202-720-3029

National Agricultural Library
10301 Baltimore Blvd.
Beltsville, MD 20705-2351
301-504-5248

Natural Resources and Environment
Forest Service
201 14th St., SW
Washington, DC 20250
202-205-1760

Soil Conservation Service
P.O. Box 2890
Washington, DC 20013
202-205-0027

Economic Research Service
1301 New York Ave., NW
Washington, DC 20005
202-219-0515

National Agricultural Statistics Service
14th and Independence Ave., SW, Room 5829
Washington, DC 20250
202-720-4020

Office of Energy and New Uses
USDA/OE
1301 New York Ave., NW, Room 1212
Washington, DC 20005-4788
202-219-1941

World Agricultural Outlook Board
Room 5143 South
14th and Independence Ave., SW
Washington, DC 20250-3800
202-720-6030

Economics Research
1301 New York Ave., NW, Room 237
Washington, DC 20005-4788
202-219-0504

Graduate School, U.S. Department of Agriculture
14th and Independence Ave., SW, Room 1103
Washington, DC 20250
202-690-4280

Sources of Information for the Department of Agriculture
Contracts and Small Business Activities
14th and Independence Ave., SW
Room 1550, South Building
Washington, DC 20250

Films
Office of Public Affairs
Room 1614 South
14th and Independence Ave., SW
Washington, DC 20250-1300
202-720-6072

Waste and Fraud Hotline
14th and Independence Ave., SW
Washington, DC 20250
800-424-9121

Speakers
Office of Public Liaison
14th and Independence Ave., SW
Jamie L. Whitten Federal Bldg., Room 412A
Washington, DC 20250-1320
202-720-2798

USDA Locator
14th and Independence Ave., SW
Washington, DC 20250
202-720-8732

Public Affairs
14th and Independence Ave., SW
Room 412A, Administration Bldg.
Washington, DC 20250-1320
202-720-2798

Freedom of Information Office
14th and Independence Ave., SW
Room 536-A
Washington, DC 20250-1300
202-720-8164

Rural Information Center
National Agricultural Library
Room 304
10301 Baltimore Blvd.
Beltsville, MD 20705
800-633-7701

Department of Commerce
Herbert C. Hoover Bldg.
14th and Constitution Ave., NW
Washington, DC 20230
202-482-2000

Office of the Secretary
14th and Constitution Ave., NW, Room 5516
Washington, DC 20230
202-482-2112

Competitive Assessment and Business Policy
Office of Business Analysis
HCHB Room 4885
Washington, DC 20230
202-482-1986

Minority Business Development Agency
14th and Constitution Ave., NW
Room 6707
Washington, DC 20230
202-482-1936

Bureau of the Census
Public Information Office
Room 2705-3
Washington, DC 20233
301-457-2794

Office of Census Publications
Washington, DC 20233
301-457-4100

Bureau of Economic Analysis
1441 L St., NW
Washington, DC 20230
202-606-9900

Bureau of Export Administration
Room HCHB 3895
BXA/OCPA, Room 3897
14th and Constitution Ave., NW
Washington, DC 20230
202-482-2721

Be patient. If any phone number is incorrect, call (area code) 555-1212 and request the new listing.

41

Information Starting Places

Economic Development Administration
14th and Constitution Ave., NW, Room 7810
Washington, DC 20230
202-482-5113

International Trade Administration
14th and Constitution Ave., NW, Room 3414
Washington, DC 20230
202-482-3808

National Oceanic and Atmospheric Administration (NOAA)
14th and Constitution Ave., NW, Room 5230
Washington, DC 20230
202-482-2985

NOAA Publications
NOAA Central Library
6009 Executive Blvd.
Rockville, MD 20852
301-413-0900

Patent and Trademark Office
Commission of Patents and Trademarks
Washington, DC 20231
703-305-8341

Technology Administration
Room 4824
14th and Constitution Ave., NW
Washington, DC 20230
202-482-3037

National Institute of Standards and Technology (NIST)
Gaithersburg, MD 20899-0001
301-975-2758

NIST Publications
TB416, Room 118
Gaithersburg, MD 20899
301-975-3058

National Technical Information Service
5285 Port Royal Road
Springfield, VA 22161
703-487-4650

United States Travel and Tourism Administration
14th and Constitution Ave., NW
Room 1520
Washington, DC 20230
202-482-3811

Sources of Information for the Department of Commerce
Age and Citizenship Information
Bureau of the Census
P.O. Box 1545
Jeffersonville, IN 47131
812-285-5314

Public Affairs
Room 5610
14th and Constitution Ave., NW
Washington, DC 20230
202-219-3605

Locator
14th and Constitution Ave., NW
Washington, DC 20230
202-482-2000

Publications
Office of Secretary
Publications Division
Room 2830B
14th and Constitution Ave.
Washington, DC 20230
202-482-2108

Freedom of Information Office
14th and Constitution Ave., NW, Room 6020
Washington, DC 20230
202-482-4115

Fraud and Waste Hotline
Office of Inspector General
P.O. Box 612
Ben Franklin Station
Washington, DC 20044
800-424-5197

Department of Defense
Army Public Affairs Office
Defense Intelligence Agency
Attention: Public Liasion Office
Pentagon
Washington, DC 20340
703-695-0071

Naval Public Affairs Office
Defense Intelligence Agency
Pentagon, 2E340
Washington, DC 20350
703-697-7491

Publications Office
Office of the Assistant Secretary of Defense
(Public Affairs)
Directorate for Public Communications
Room 2 Echo 777
Pentagon
Washington, DC 20301-1400
703-697-5737

Freedom of Information Office
Office of the Assistant Secretary for Defense
Chief, Freedom of Information and Privacy Acts Division
DFOISR, Room 2C757
1400 Defense Pentagon
Washington, DC 20301-1400
703-697-1180

Locator
Pentagon
Washington, DC 20350
703-545-6700

Defense Hotline
Pentagon
Washington, DC 20301-1900
800-424-9098

American Forces Information Service
601 N. Fairfax St.
Suite 311
Alexandria, VA 22314
703-274-4839

DOD Dependent Schools
4040 Fairfax Dr.
Arlington, VA 22203
703-696-4413

Office of Civilian Health and Medical
Program of the Uniformed Services
Aurora, CO 80045-6900
303-361-1000

Office of Civilian Health and Medical
Program of the Uniformed Services
Defense Medical Systems Support Center
5109 Leesburg Pike
Skyline 6
Falls Church, VA 22041
703-681-9530

Be patient. If any phone number is incorrect, call (area code) 555-1212 and request the new listing.

Office of Economic Adjustment
400 Army Navy Drive, Room 200
Arlington, VA 22202-2884
703-604-6020

Washington Headquarters Service
Office of Secretary of Defense
Room 3D972, Pentagon
Washington, DC 20301-1155
703-695-4436

Department of the Air Force
Office of the Assistant to the Secretary of Defense
Directorate of FOI and Security Review
Room 2C757
1400 Defense Pentagon
Washington, DC 20301-1400
703-697-8120

Department of the Army
Office of Chief of Public Affairs
Attn: SAPA-PCD
Pentagon
Washington, DC 20310
703-697-1736

Office of the Secretary of the Army
Room 3E718
Pentagon
Washington, DC 20310-0101
703-695-3211

United States Army Forces Command
Office of Public Affairs
Attn: AFCS-PA
Ft. McPherson, GA 30330-6000
404-669-5607

United States Army Material Command
5001 Eisenhower Ave.
Alexandria, VA 22333-0001
703-274-9625

United States Army Information Systems Command
Headquarters
Ft. Huachuca, AZ 85613-5000
602-538-6161

United States Army Intelligence and Security Command
Headquarters
8825 Beulah St.
Attn: IACS
Ft. Belvoir, VA 22060
703-706-1232

United States Army Health Service Command
Headquarters
Ft. Sam Houston, TX 78234
210-221-6313

United States Army Criminal Investigation Command
Dept. of Army
6010 6th St.
Fort Belvoir, VA 22060-5506
703-806-0403

Military Traffic Management Command
5611 Columbia Pike
Falls Church, VA 22041-5050
703-681-6724

United States Army Military District of Washington
Building 42
Ft. McNair
Washington, DC 20319
202-475-0897

United States Army Corps of Engineers
Chief of Engineers
U.S. Army Corps of Engineers
Attn CECS
Washington, DC 20314-1000
202-761-0001

Department of the Navy
Public Affairs Office
Secretary of the Navy
Washington, DC 20350-1000
703-697-7491

Space and Naval Warfare Systems Command
Office of Public Affairs
2451 Crystal Park 5
Washington, DC 20363-5200
703-602-8954

Supply Systems
Naval Supply Systems Command
1931 Jefferson Davis Hwy.
Arlington, VA 22248-5360
703-607-2883

Strategic Systems
Air Force Programs
1250 Pentagon
Washington, DC 20330-1250
703-614-6407

Naval Computer and Tele-communications Command
Administrative Offices
4401 Massachusetts Ave., NW
Washington, DC 20394-5460
202-764-0356

Office of the Assistant Secretary for Defense
Freedom of Information Office
Room 2C757, Pentagon
Washington, DC 20301-1400
703-697-1180

Naval Inspector General
Washington Navy Yard
Building 200
901 M St., SE
Washington, DC 20374-5006
202-433-2000

Judge Advocate General
200 Stovall St.
Alexandria, VA 22332-2400
703-614-7420

Comptroller
Room 4E768, Pentagon
Washington, DC 20350-1000
703-697-2325

Auditor General
5611 Columbia Pike
Room 506B Nassas Bldg.
Falls Church, VA 22041-5080
703-681-9117

Office of Information
Chief of Information
Pentagon, Room 2E335
Washington DC 20350-1200
703-695-0965

Chief of Naval Research
800 North Quincy St.
Suite 907
Arlington, VA 22217-5660
703-696-4258

Information Starting Places

Personnel Boards
801 N. Randolph St.
Suite 907
Arlington, VA 22203
703-696-4356

Naval Records
Bureau of Naval Personnel
Office of the Files
PERS 313C1 REC
2 Navy Annex, Room 3048
Washington DC 20370-3130
703-614-1402

Naval Air Systems Command
Commander of Naval Air Systems
1421 Jefferson Davis Hwy.
Arlington, VA 22243
703-604-2201

Naval Sea Systems Command
Office of the Commander
2531 Jefferson Davis Highway
Arlington, VA22242-5160
703-602-3328

Naval Personnel
Navy Annex
Federal Bldg., #2
S/HHRO
Washington, DC 20370-5000
703-614-1271

Naval Medicine
2300 E St., NW
Washington, DC 20372-5120
202-653-1327

Oceanographer of the Navy
Chief of Naval Operations (N096)
U.S. Naval Observatory
3450 Massachusetts Ave., NW
Washington, DC 20392-5421
202-653-1295

Legal Services
Judge Advocates Office
200 Stovall St.
Alexandria, VA 22332-2400
703-325-9820

Naval Security Group Command
Office of the Commander
3801 Nebraska Ave., NW
Washington, DC 20393-5442
202-764-0444

Intelligence Command
Office of Inspector General
901 M St., SE, Building 200
Washington Navy Yard
Washington, DC 20374-5006
202-433-2000

Naval Investigative Service
901 M St., SE
Building 111
Washington, DC 20388
202-433-9323

Chief of Naval Education and Training
250 Dallas St.
Pensacola, FL 32508-5220
904-452-4858

United States Marine Corps
Office of Public Affairs (PA)

HQ USMC
Washington, DC 20380-0001
703-614-4080

United States Naval Academy
Admissions Division
117 DeCater Road
Annapolis, MD 20412-5018
800-638-9156

Defense Agencies
Advanced Research Projects Agency
3701 N. Fairfax Dr.
Arlington, VA 22203-1714
703-696-2444

Defense Commissary Agency
Bldg. 11200
Ft. Lee, VA 23801-6300
804-734-8721

Defense Contract Audit Agency
8725 John J. Kingman Rd., Suite 2135
Fort Belvoir, VA 22060-6219
703-767-3200

Defense Finance and Accounting Service
1931 Jefferson Davis Highway
Arlington, VA 22240-5291
703-607-2616

Defense Information Systems Agency
701 S. Courthouse Road
Arlington, VA 22204-2199
703-607-6900

Defense Intelligence Agency
Public Liaison Office
Washington, DC 20340-2033
703-695-0071

Defense Investigative Service
1340 Braddock Place
Alexandria, VA 22314-1651
703-325-5324

Defense Legal Services Agency
1600 Defense, Pentagon
Washington, DC 20301-1600
703-695-3341

Defense Logistics Agency
8725 John J. Kingman Rd.
Fort Belvoir, VA 22060-6221
703-767-6200

Defense Mapping Agency
8613 Lee Highway
Fairfax, VA 22031
703-285-9368

Defense Security Assistance Agency
Office of the Director
1111 Jefferson Davis Hwy., Suite 303
Arlington, VA 22202
703-604-6513

National Security Agency
9800 Savage Road
Ft. George G. Mead, MD 20755-6000
301-688-6524

On-Site Inspection Agency
Dulles International Airport
201 W. Service Rd.
Washington, DC 20041-0498
703-803-4326

Be patient. If any phone number is incorrect, call (area code) 555-1212 and request the new listing.

Ballistic Missile Defense Organization
71 Defense Pentagon
Washington, DC 20301-7100
703-697-4040

Joint Service Schools
Joint Military Intelligence College
Attn: MCA-2
Washington, DC 20340-5100
202-373-4545

Defense Systems Management College
Ft. Belvoir, VA 22060-5426
703-805-3360
800-845-7646

National Defense University
National War College
Fort Lesley J. McNair
Washington, DC 20319-6000
202-475-1954

National Defense University
Industrial College of the Armed Forces
Ft. L.J. McNair
Washington, DC 20319
202-475-1832

Armed Forces Staff College
7800 Hampton Blvd.
Norfolk, VA 23511-1702
804-444-5302

National Defense University
Information Resource Management College
Ft. Lesley J. McNair
Washington, DC 20319-6000
202-287-9321

Department of Education
600 Independence Ave., SW
Washington, DC 20202
202-401-5986

Federally Sided Corporations
American Printing House for the Blind
P.O. Box 6085
Louisville, KY 40206
502-895-2405

Gallaudet University
800 Florida Ave., NE
Washington, DC 20002
202-651-5000

Howard University
2400 6th St., NW
Washington, DC 20059
202-806-6100

National Technical Institute for the Deaf
52 Lomb Memorial Drive
Rochester, NY 14623-5604
716-475-6400

Department of Energy
1000 Independence Ave., SW
Washington, DC 20585
202-586-5000

Public Affairs
1000 Independence Ave., SW
Room 7A145
Washington, DC 20585

202-586-4940
202-586-6827

Office of Nuclear Safety
Room 78121
1000 Independence Ave., SW
Washington, DC 20585
202-586-2407

Office of Energy Research and Resource Management
ER-60, GTN
19901 Germantown Rd.
Germantown, MD 20874-1290
301-903-4944

Office of Environmental Restoration and Waste Management
EM 121, Room 18203
1000 Independence Ave., SW
Washington, DC 20585
202-586-2661

Assistant Secretary for Fossil Energy
4F033
1000 Independence Ave., SW
Washington 20585
301-586-6600

Defense Programs
1000 Independence Ave., SW
Washington, DC 20585
202-586-2295

Nuclear Energy
Office of Public Affairs
1000 Independence Ave., SW
Washington DC 20585
202-586-1941

Civilian Radioactive Waste Management
1000 Independence Ave., SW
Washington, DC 20585
202-586-6842

National Energy Information Center
1000 Independence Ave., SW
Washington, DC 20585
202-586-8800

Economic Regulatory Administration
1000 Independence Ave., SW
Room 5B148
Washington, DC 20585
202-523-3053

Federal Energy Regulatory Commission
825 N. Capitol
Washington, DC 20426
202-208-0300

Power Administrations
Bonneville Power Administration
P.O. Box 3621
Portland, OR 97208
503-230-5101

Southeastern Power Administration
Samuel Elbert Bldg.
2 Public Square
Elberton, GA 30635
706-213-3805

Alaska Power Administration
2770 Sherwood Lane
Suite 2B
Juneau, AK 99801-8545
907-586-7405

Be patient. If any phone number is incorrect, call (area code) 555-1212 and request the new listing.

45

Information Starting Places

Southwestern Power Administration
P.O. Box 1619
Tulsa, OK 74101
918-581-7474

Western Area Power Administration
1627 Cole Blvd., Bldg. 18
Golden, CO 80401
303-275-1111

Department of Health and Human Services
Information Center
200 Independence Ave., SW
Washington, DC 20201
202-619-0257

Administration on Aging
330 Independence Ave., SW, Suite 4661
Washington, DC 20201
202-619-0556

Administration for Children and Families
370 L'Enfant Promenade, SW, Suite 600
Washington, DC 20447
202-401-9200

Developmental Disabilities
200 Independence Ave., SW
Washington, DC 20201
202-690-6590

Native Americans
370 L'Enfant Promenade, SW
Washington, DC 20447
202-690-7776

Child Support Enforcement
370 L'Enfant Promenade, SW
Washington, DC 20447
202-401-9373

Community Services
5th Floor, West
370 L'Enfant Promenade, SW
Washington, DC 20447
202-401-9333

Program Support
370 L'Enfant Promenade, SW
Washington, DC 20447
202-401-9238

Office of Information Systems Management
200 Independence Ave., SW
Washington, DC 20201
202-401-9257

Financial Management
370 L'Enfant Plaza, SW
Washington, DC 20447
202-401-9238

Public Affairs
901 D St., SW
Washington, DC 20447
202-401-9215

Refugee Resettlement
370 L'Enfant Promenade, SW
Washington, DC 20447
202-401-9246

Office of Family Assistance
370 L'Enfant Promenade
Washington, DC 20447
202-401-9275

Public Health Service
613 G St., NW, Room 304
Washington, DC 20001
202-727-0014

Employment
5600 Fishers Lane
Rockville, MD 20857
301-443-6900

Films, Publications, and Other Information
Office of Communications
200 Independence Ave., SW
Room 738G
Washington, DC 20201
202-690-6867

Agency for Health Care Policy and Research
2101 E. Jefferson St.
Rockville, MD 20852-4908
301-594-1360

Grants Management
Executive Office
Suite 601
2101 E. Jefferson St.
Rockville, MD 20852
301-594-1447

Contracts
Executive Office Center
Suite 400
2101 E. Jefferson St.
Rockville, MD 20852
301-594-1398

Employment
2101 E. Jefferson St.
Suite 501
Rockville, MD 20852
301-594-1360

Publications Clearinghouse
P.O. Box 8547
Silver Spring, MD 20907
800-358-9295

Substance Abuse and Mental Health Service Administration
Parklawn Bldg.
5600 Fishers Lane
Room 12-105
Rockville, MD 20857
301-443-3875

National Institute on Alcohol Abuse and Alcoholism
5600 Fishers Lane
Rockville, MD 20857
301-443-4373

National Institute on Drug Abuse
Room 1005
5600 Fishers Lane
Rockville, MD 20857
301-443-6487

National Institute of Mental Health
Extramural Programs
Parklawn Bldg.
Room 17-99
Rockville, MD 20857
301-443-3877

Office for Substance Abuse Prevention
5600 Fishers Lane
Rockwall II Bldg.
Rockville, MD 20857
301-443-5266

Be patient. If any phone number is incorrect, call (area code) 555-1212 and request the new listing.

Center For Substance Abuse Treatment
618 Rockwall II Bldg.
5515 Security Lane
Rockville, MD 20852
301-443-6501

Grants and Contracts
5600 Fishers Lane
Rockville, MD 20857
301-443-4147

Employment
5600 Fishers Lane, Room 14C-14
Rockville, MD 20857
301-443-5407

Centers for Disease Control and Prevention
Public Affairs Office
1600 Clifton Rd., NE
Atlanta, GA 30333
404-639-3286

Employment
1600 Clifton Rd., NE
Atlanta, GA 30333
404-639-3615

Films
1600 Clifton Rd., NE
Atlanta, GA 30333
404-639-2412

Publications
1600 Clifton Rd., NE
Atlanta, GA 30333
404-639-3534

Agency for Toxic Substances and Disease Registry
1600 Clifton Rd., NE
Mailstop E60
Atlanta, GA 30333
404-639-0727

Food and Drug Administration
5600 Fishers Lane
Rockville, MD 20857
301-443-1544

Office of Consumer Affairs
5600 Fishers Lane
Rockville, MD 20857
301-443-3170

Center for Drug Evaluation and Research
5600 Fishers Lane, HFD-1
Rockville, MD 20857
301-594-6740

Center for Biologics Evaluations Evaluation and Research
1401 Rockville Pike
Rockville, MD 20852
301-827-0377

Division of Consumer Affairs and Center for Devices and Radiological Health
1901 Chapman Ave.
Rockville, MD 20857
301-443-4190

Center for Veterinary Medicine
Metro Park North 2
HFV1
7500 Standish Place
Rockville, MD 20855
301-443-3450

Regional Operations
Office of Regulatory Affairs

5600 Fishers Lane, Room 1490
Rockville, MD 20857
301-443-1594

Consumer Activities
Room 16-75
5600 Fishers Lane
Rockville, MD 20857
301-443-5006

Employment
5600 Fishers Lane, Room 759
Rockville, MD 20857
301-443-2234

Publications
5600 Fishers Lane
Rockville, MD 20857
301-443-3220

Freedom of Information Office
5600 Fishers Lane
Room 12A16
Rockville, MD 20857
301-443-1813

Health Resources and Services Administration
Office of Communications
5600 Fishers Lane, Room 1445
Rockville, MD 20857
301-443-2086

Bureau of Primary Health Care
4350 East West Hwy., 11th Floor
Bethesda, MD 20814
301-594-4110

Bureau of Health Professions
5600 Fishers Lane, Room 805
Parklawn Building
Rockville, MD 20857
301-443-5194

Bureau of Health Resources Development
5600 Fishers Lane
Room 705
Parklawn Building
Rockville, MD 20857
301-443-1993

Maternal and Child Health Bureau
Room 18-05
Parklawn Building
5600 Fishers Lane
Rockville, MD 20857
301-443-2170

Employment
Room 14A-46
Parklawn Building
5600 Fishers Lane
Rockville, MD 20857
301-443-5460

Films
Room 14-45
Parklawn Building
5600 Fishers Lane
Rockville, MD 20857
301-443-2086

Office of Communications
Room 14-45
Parklawn Building
5600 Fishers Lane
Rockville, MD 20857
301-443-2086

Be patient. If any phone number is incorrect, call (area code) 555-1212 and request the new listing.

47

Information Starting Places

Publications
Room 14-45
Parklawn Building
5600 Fishers Lane
Rockville, MD 20857
301-443-2086

Indian Health Service
Room 6-05
Parklawn Building
5600 Fishers Lane
Rockville, MD 20857
301-443-1087

Employment
Room 4B-44
Parklawn Building
5600 Fishers Lane
Rockville, MD 20857
301-443-6520

Publications
5600 Fishers Lane, Room 6-35
Rockville, MD 20857
301-443-1397

Office of Communications
5600 Fishers Lane
Room 6-35
Rockville, MD 20857
301-443-1397

National Institutes of Health
9000 Rockville Pike
Bethesda, MD 20892
301-496-4000

National Cancer Institute
Building 31, Room 10A24
9000 Rockville Pike
Bethesda, MD 20892-2580
301-496-6631

National Heart, Lung, and Blood Institute
Office of Communications and Public Information
Building 31, Room 4A21
31 Center Dr., MSC 2840
Bethesda, MD 20892-2840
301-496-4236

National Library of Medicine
Office of Inquiries
Building 38, Room 2S10
8600 Rockville Pike
Bethesda, MD 20894
301-496-6193

National Institute of Diabetes and Digestive and Kidney Diseases
Office of the Director
Building 31, Room 9A52
31 Center Dr., MSC 2560
Bethesda, MD 20892-2560
301-496-5741

National Institute of Allergy and Infectious Diseases
Office of Communications
Building 31, Room 7A50
31 Center Dr., MSC 2520
Bethesda, MD 20892-2520
301-496-5717

National Institute of Child Health and Human Development
Office of the Director
Building 31, Room 2A20
31 Center Dr., MSC 2420
Bethesda, MD 20892-2420
301-496-5133

National Institute on Deafness and Other Communicative Disorders
Office of the Director
Building 31, Room 3C02
31 Center Dr., MSC 2320
Bethesda, MD 20892-2320
301-402-0495

National Institute of Dental Research
Office of the Director
Building 31, Room 2C27
31 Center Dr., MSC 2290
Bethesda, MD 20892-2290
301-496-6621

National Institute of Environmental Health Sciences
Office of Communications
Building 101, Room A202
Research Triangle Park, NC 27709
919-541-3665

National Institute of General Medical Sciences
Office of Administrative Management
Building 45, Room 3AS25
9000 Rockville Pike
Bethesda, MD 20892
301-496-7714

National Institute of Neurological Disorders and Stroke
Public Inquiries Section
Building 31, Room 8A06
31 Center Dr., MSC 2540
Bethesda, MD 20892-2540
301-496-5751

National Eye Institute
Office of the Director
Building 31, Room 6A03
31 Center Dr., MSC 2510
Bethesda, MD 20892-2510
301-496-7425

National Institute on Aging
Office of Administrative Management
Building 31, Room 5C32
31 Center Dr., MSC 2292
Bethesda, MD 20892-2292
301-496-5345

National Institute of Arthritis and Musculoskeletal and Skin Diseases
Office of the Director
Building 31, Room 4C32
31 Center Dr., MSC 2350
Bethesda, MD 20892-2350
301-496-4353

Clinical Center
Office of the Director
Building 10, Room 2C146
10 Center Dr., MSC 1504
Bethesda, MD 20892-1504
301-496-3227

Fogarty International Center
Building 31, Room B2C29
31 Center Dr., MSC 2220
Bethesda, MD 20892-2220
301-496-4625

National Center for Human Genome Research
Building 31, Room 4B09
31 Center Dr., MSC 2152
Bethesda, MD 20892-2152
301-496-0844

National Center for Nursing Research
Building 31, Room 5B03
31 Center Dr., MSC 2178

Bethesda, MD 20892-2178
301-496-8230

Division of Computer Research and Technology
Executive Office
Building 12A, Room 3025
12 South Dr., MSC 5650
Bethesda, MD 20892-5650
301-496-5206

National Center for Research Resources
Executive Office
Building 12A, Room 4003
12 South Dr., MSC 5660
Bethesda, MD 20892-5660
301-496-5605

Division of Grants and Procurement and Management
Executive Office
5660 Fishers Lane
Rockville, MD 20875
301-443-1433

Contracts
6100 Executive Blvd., Room 6D01A
Rockville, MD 20852
301-496-6431

Employment
Office of Personnel Management
Building 1, Room B1-60
9000 Rockville Pike
Bethesda, MD 20892
301-496-4197

Division of Commissioned Personnel
5600 Fishers Lane, Room 436
Rockville, MD 20875
301-594-3000

Films
National Library of Medicine
8600 Rockville Pike
Bethesda, MD 20894
301-496-6308

Publications
Editorial Operations Branch
Building 31, Room 2B03
9000 Rockville Pike
Bethesda, MD 20892
301-496-4143

Office of Communications
Building 31, Room 2B03
9000 Rockville Pike
Bethesda, MD 20892
301-496-4143

Health Care Financing Administration
6325 Security Blvd.
364 East Highrise Building
Baltimore, MD 21207
410-966-3000

Contracts and Small Business Activities
Office of Grants
364 East Highrise Bldg.
6325 Security Blvd.
Baltimore, MD 21207
410-966-5157

Employment
634 Highrise Building
6325 Security Blvd.
Baltimore, MD 21207
410-966-5489

Publications
555 E. Highrise Building
6325 Security Blvd.
Baltimore, MD 21207
410-966-3215

Social Security Administration
Office of Public Inquiries
1-A-2 Gwyn Oak Ave.
6401 Security Blvd.
Baltimore, MD 21235
410-965-7700

Contracts and Small Business Activities
Office of Acquisition and Grants
1710 Gwyn Oak Ave.
Baltimore, MD 21207
410-965-9498

Reading Rooms
Library
Altmeyer Building, Room G-44
Baltimore, MD 21235
410-965-6111

Employment
Personnel Office
6401 Security Blvd.
Baltimore, MD 21235
410-965-4506

Publications, Speakers and Films
1-A-2 Gwyn Oak Ave.
6401 Security Blvd.
Baltimore, MD 21235
410-965-7700

Sources of Information for Health and Human Services
Civil Rights Office
330 Independence Ave., SW
Washington, DC 20201
202-619-0403
202-863-0100 (Hotline)

Locator
330 Independence Ave., SW
Washington, DC 20201
202-619-0257

Publications
330 Independence Ave., SW
Washington, DC 20201
202-619-1587

Department of Housing and Urban Development
451 Seventh St., SW
Washington, DC 20410
202-708-1422

HUD Hotline
Office of the Inspector General
451 Seventh St., SW
Washington, DC 20410
800-347-3735 or
202-708-4200

Program Areas
Assistant Secretary for Housing-Federal Housing Commissioner
451 Seventh St., SW, Room 9100
Washington, DC 20410-8000
202-708-3600

Assistant Secretary for Community Planning and Development
451 Seventh St., SW, Room 7100
Washington, DC 20410
202-708-2690

Information Starting Places

*Assistant Secretary for Policy
Development and Research*
451 Seventh St., SW, Room 8100
Washington, DC 20410
202-708-1600

*Lead-Based Paint Abatement
and Poisoning Prevention*
451 Seventh St., SW, Room 3202
Washington, DC 20410
202-755-1785

*Assistant Secretary for Fair Housing
and Equal Opportunity*
451 Seventh St., SW, Room 5100
Washington, DC 20410
202-708-4252

*Assistant Secretary for Public
and Indian Housing*
Room 4100
451 Seventh St., SW
Washington, DC 20410
202-708-0950

Government National Mortgage Association
Room 6100
451 Seventh St., SW
Washington, DC 20410
202-708-0926

Locator
451 Seventh St., SW
Washington, DC 20410
202-708-1112

Contracts
Room 5272
451 Seventh St., SW
Washington, DC 20410
202-708-1290

Property Disposition Division
Room 9172
451 Seventh St., SW
Washington, DC 20410
202-708-0740

Employment
Room 2258
451 Seventh St., SW
Washington, DC 20410
202-708-0408

Program Information Center
451 Seventh St., SW
Washington, DC 20410
202-708-1420

Freedom of Information Act Requests
Room 10139
451 Seventh St., SW
Washington, DC 20410
202-708-3054

Office of Public Affairs
451 Seventh St., SW
Washington, DC 20410
202-708-0980

Department of the Interior
Office of Communications
1849 C St., NW
Mail Stop 7013
Washington, DC 20240
202-208-3171

Office of Inspector General
Mailstop 5341
1849 C St., NW
Washington, DC 20240
202-208-4356

Office of Hearings and Appeals
4015 Wilson Blvd.
Arlington, VA 22203
703-235-3810

Bureaus:
United States Fish and Wildlife Service
1849 C St., NW
Washington, DC 20240
202-208-5634

Contracts
4401 N. Fairfax Dr., Room 212
Arlington, VA 22203
703-358-1728

Office of Current Information
1849 C St., NW
Washington, DC 20240
202-208-5634

Publications
4401 N. Fairfax Dr.
Mailstop 130, Webb Building
Arlington, VA 22203
703-358-1711

National Park Service
1849 C St., NW
Washington 20013-7127
202-208-6843

Contracts
4401 N. Fairfax Dr., Suite 212
Arlington, VA 22203
703-358-1901

Employment
1849 C St., NW, Room 2013
Washington, DC 20240
202-208-5093

Publications
Harpers Ferry Historical Association
P.O. Box 197
Harpers Ferry, WV 25425
304-535-6881

Grants-in-Aid
800 N. Capitol St., NW
Suite 400
Washington, DC 20002
202-343-3700

United States Bureau of Mines
810 Seventh St., NW
Washington, DC 20241
202-501-9649

Contracts
Procurement Office
Mailstop 2140
810 Seventh St., NW
Washington, DC 20241
202-501-9259

Public Affairs
Mailstop 1040
810 Seventh St., NW
Washington, DC 20241
202-501-9649

Be patient. If any phone number is incorrect, call (area code) 555-1212 and request the new listing.

Employment
Mailstop 2130
810 Seventh St., NW
Washington, DC 20241
202-501-9630

Publications
Publication Distributions
P.O. Box 18070
Cochrans Mill Road
Pittsburgh, PA 15236
412-892-4338

United States Geological Survey
National Center
12201 Sunrise Valley Drive
Reston, VA 22092
703-648-4460

Contracts, Grants, and Cooperative Agreements
Office of Procurement and Contracts
205 National Center
12201 Sunrise Valley Drive
Reston, VA 22092
703-648-7373

Employment
215 National Center
12201 Sunrise Valley Drive
Reston, VA 22092
703-648-6131

Exhibits
Branch of Visual Service
790 National Center
12201 Sunrise Valley Drive
Reston, VA 22092
703-648-4357

Films
Branch of Visual Service
790 National Center
12201 Sunrise Valley Drive
Reston, VA 22092
703-648-4357

Maps
Distribution Branch
Box 25286, Denver Federal Center
Denver, CO 80225
303-202-4700

Public Affairs
119 National Center
12201 Sunrise Valley Drive
Reston, VA 22092
703-648-4460

Publications
Distribution Branch
Box 25286
Denver Federal Center
Denver, CO 80225
303-202-4700

Water Data
National Water Data Exchange
421 National Center
12201 Sunrise Valley Drive
Reston, VA 22092
703-648-5663

Office of Surface Mining Reclamation and Enforcement
1951 Constitution Ave., NW
Washington, DC 20240
202-208-2553

Contracts
Procurement Branch
Office of Surface Mining
1951 Constitution Ave., NW
Washington, DC 20240
202-343-9120

Employment
Chief, Division of Personnel
Office of Surface Mining
1951 Constitution Ave., NW
Washington, DC 20240
202-208-2965

Bureau of Indian Affairs
Department of the Interior
1849 C St., NW
Mail Stop 4140
Washington, DC 20240
202-208-7315

Contracts
Chief, Contracting and Grants Administration
Department of the Interior
1951 Constitution Ave., NW
Washington, DC 20240
202-208-2825

Employment
Personnel Office
1951 Constitution Ave., NW
Washington, DC 20240
202-208-2547

Reading Room
National Resources Library
Main Interior Building
Department of the Interior
1951 Constitution Ave., NW
Washington, DC 20240
202-208-5815

Speakers and Films
Office of Public Affairs
1849 C St., NW
Mail Stop 1340
Washington, DC 20240
202-208-7315

Public Affairs
Office of Public Affairs
1849 C St., NW
Mail Stop 1340
Washington, DC 20240
202-208-7315

Minerals Management Service
1849 C St., NW
Washington, DC 20240
202-208-3983

Public Affairs
1849 C St., NW, Room 4213
Washington, Dc 20240
202-208-3983

Bureau of Land Management
Department of the Interior
1849 C St., NW
Washington, DC 20240
202-208-5717

Contracts
Office of Procurement
1620 L St., Suite 1075
Washington, DC 20036
202-452-5170

Information Starting Places

Public Affairs
1849 C St., NW
Room 5600
Washington, DC 20240
202-208-5717

Small Business Activities
(for Western States except Oregon)
Office of Procurement
Building 50
Denver Federal Center
P.O. Box 25047
Denver, CO 80225-0047
303-969-6502

Bureau of Reclamation
Office of Public Affairs
Room 7640
1849 C St., NW
Washington, DC 20240
202-208-4662

Contracts
Office of Procurement
Building 67
Denver Federal Center
Denver, CO 80225
303-236-8040, ext. 227

Employment
Personnel Office
P.O. Box 25007
Denver Federal Center
Denver, CO 80225
303-236-3820

Publications
Office of Publications
P.O. Box 25286
Denver Federal Center
Denver, CO 80225
303-202-4700

Speakers and Films
Office of Public Affairs
Room 7640
1849 C St., NW
Washington, DC 20240
202-208-4662

Office of Public Affairs
Room 7640
1849 C St., NW
Washington, DC 20240
202-208-4662

Sources of Information for the Department of the Interior
Contracts
Office of Acquisition and Property Management
1849 C St., NW
Mailstop 5512-MIB
Washington, DC 20240
202-208-6431

Departmental Museum
1849 C St., NW
Mailstop 5412-MIB
Washington, DC 20240
202-208-4743

Employment
Office of Personnel
1849 C St., NW
Mail Stop 5203
Washington, DC 20240
202-208-6761

Publications
Office of Printing and Publications
Mailstop 1307-MIB
1849 C St., NW
Washington, DC 20240
202-208-4841

Office of Public Affairs
Mailstop 7013
1849 C St., NW
Washington, DC 20240
202-208-3171

Freedom of Information Office
1849 C St., NW
Mail Stop 6013
Washington, DC 20240
202-208-5342

Reading Room
Library Reading Room
Mailstop 1151
1849 C St., NW
Washington, DC 20240
202-208-5815

Locator
1849 C St., NW
Washington, DC 20240
202-208-7220

Department of Justice

Constitution Ave. and Tenth St., NW
Washington, DC 20530
202-514-2000

Community Relations Service
Suite 330, 5550 Friendship Blvd.
Chevy Chase, MD 20815
301-492-5929

Office for U.S. Trustees
Suite 700
901 E St., NW
Washington, DC 20530
202-307-1391

Divisions
Antitrust Division
FOIA Unit
200 Liberty Place Bldg.
Washington, DC 20530
202-514-2692

Civil Division
Office of the Asst. Attorney General
10th St. and Pennsylvania Ave., NW
Washington, DC 20530
202-514-3301

Civil Rights Division
Executive Officer
1425 New York Ave.
Washington, DC 20005
202-514-4224

Criminal Division
Office of the Asst. Attorney General
10th St. and Constitution Ave., NW
Room 2107
Washington, DC 20530
202-514-2601

Environment and Natural Resources Division
Office of the Attorney General
10th St. and Pennsylvania Ave., NW

Be patient. If any phone number is incorrect, call (area code) 555-1212 and request the new listing.

Washington, DC 20530
202-514-2701

Tax Division
Office of the Asst. Attorney General
10th St. and Constitution Ave., NW
Room 4143
Washington, DC 20530
202-514- 2901

Office of Special Counsel for Immigration Related Unfair
Employment Practices
P.O. Box 27728
Washington, DC 20035-5490
800-255-7688

Bureaus
Drug Enforcement Administration
Department of Justice
Washington, DC 20537
202-307-7977

Federal Bureau of Investigation
9th St. and Pennsylvania Ave., NW
Washington, DC 20535
202-324-3000

Bureau of Prisons
320 First St., NW
Washington, DC 20534
202-307-3198

United States Marshal Service
600 Army Navy Drive
Arlington, VA 22202-4210
202-307-9000

United States National Central Bureau-
International Criminal Police Organization
Washington, DC 20530
202-616-9000

Immigration and Naturalization
425 I St., NW
Washington, DC 20536
202-514-4316

Office of Justice Programs
633 Indiana Ave., NW
Washington, DC 20531
202-307-0781

Boards
Executive Office for Immigration Review
5107 Leesburg Pike
Suite 2400
Falls Church, VA 22041
703-305-0169

United States Parole Commission
5550 Friendship Blvd., Suite 420
Chevy Chase, MD 20815
301-492-5821

Foreign Claims Settlement Commission of
the United States
Office of the Chairman
600 E St., NW
Washington, DC 20579
202-616-6975

Sources of Information for the Department of Justice
Controlled Substances Act Registration
P.O. Box 28083
Central Station
Washington, DC 20038
202-307-7255

Employment
Personnel Management
10th St. and Constitution Ave., NW
Washington, DC 20530
202-514-6877
202-514-6818

Reading Rooms
Bureau of Prisons
320 First St., NW
Washington, DC 20534
202-307-3029

Immigration and Naturalization
425 I St., NW
Washington, DC 20536
202-514-2837

Foreign Claims Settlement Commission
600 E St., NW
Washington, DC 20579
202-616-6975

Board of Immigration Appeals
Suite 1609
5107 Leesburg Pike
Falls Church, VA 22041
703-305-0168

National Institute of Justice
9th Floor
633 Indiana Ave., NW
Washington, DC 20531
202-307-5883

Publications and Films
Room 1228
10th and Constitution Ave., NW
Washington, DC 20530
202-514-2007

Office of Public Affairs
Room 1228
10th and Constitution Ave., NW
Washington, DC 20530
202-514-2007

Freedom of Information Officer
Office of Information and Privacy
Flag Bldg., Suite 570
Washington, DC 20530
202-514-3642

Reference Service
Criminal Justice Reference Service
Box 6000
Rockville, MD 20850
800-851-3420

Small Business Activities
Office of Small and Disadvantaged Business Utilization
1331 Pennsylvania Ave., NW, Room 1010
Washington, DC 20530
202-616-0521

Locator
10th St. and Pennsylvania Ave., NW
Washington, DC 20530
202-514-2000

Fraud Hotline
Inspector General's Hotline
P.O. Box 28188
Central Station
Washington, DC 20038
800-869-4499
24 hr. Fax: 202-616-9898

Information Starting Places

Aliens Inquiries Information
Office of Information
Immigration and Naturalization
425 I St., NW
Washington, DC 20536
202-514-4316

Department of Labor
200 Constitution Ave., NW
Washington, DC 20210
202-219-5000

Inspector General
200 Constitution Ave., NW
Washington, DC 20210
800-347-3756

Public Affairs
200 Constitution Ave., NW
Room S1032
Washington, DC 20210
202-219-7316

Women's Bureau
200 Constitution Ave., NW
Room S3002
Washington, DC 20210
202-219-6611

Deputy Secretary of Labor
200 Constitution Ave., NW
Room S2018
Washington, DC 20210
202-219-6151

Administrative Appeals
Room S4309
200 Constitution Ave., NW
Washington, DC 20210
202-219-4728

Office of Small and Disadvantaged Business Utilization
Room C2318
200 Constitution Ave., NW
Washington, DC 20210
202-219-9148

Office of Administrative Law Judges
Suite 400
800 K St., NW
Washington, DC 20001-8001
202-565-5330

Benefits Review Board
Suite 500 North
800 K St., NW
Washington, DC 20001-8001
202-565-7501

Wage Appeals Board
200 Constitution Ave.
Room N1651
Washington, DC 20210
202-219-9039

Department of Labor Academy
Room N2305
200 Constitution Ave., NW
Washington, DC 20210
202-219-7401

Solicitor of Labor
Room S2002
200 Constitution Ave., NW
Washington, DC 20210
202-219-7705

Employment Training Administration
200 Constitution Ave., NW, Room 4700N
Washington, DC 20210
202-219-6871

Federal Unemployment Insurance Service
200 Constitution Ave., NW, Room S4231
Washington, DC 20210
202-219-8600

United States Employment Service
Room N4470
200 Constitution Ave., NW
Washington, DC 20210
202-219-5257

Office of Apprenticeship and Training
Room N4649
200 Constitution Ave., NW
Washington, DC 20210
202-219-5921

Office of Trade Adjustment Assistance
200 Constitution Ave., NW, Room C4318
Washington, DC 20210
202-219-5555

Job Training Partnership Act
Room N4459
200 Constitution Ave., NW
Washington, DC 20210
202-219-6236

Senior Community Service Employment Program
Room N4641
200 Constitution Ave., NW
Washington, DC 20210
202-219-5904

Office of Policy and Research
200 Constitution Ave., NW, Room N5637
Washington, Dc 20210
202-219-7664

Financial and Administrative Management Service
Room S5526
200 Constitution Ave., NW
Washington, DC 20210
202-219-7801

Labor-Management Standards
Room N5605
200 Constitution Ave., NW
Washington, DC 20210
202-219-7337

Pension and Welfare Benefits Administration
200 Constitution Ave., NW
Washington, DC 20210
202-219-8784

Office of the American Workplace
Room N5402
200 Constitution Ave., NW
Washington, DC 20210
202-219-6045

Employment Standards Administration
Room C4325
200 Constitution Ave., NW
Washington, DC 20210
202-219-8743

Federal Contract Compliance Programs
200 Constitution Ave., NW, Room C3310
Washington, DC 20210
202-219-9371

Be patient. If any phone number is incorrect, call (area code) 555-1212 and request the new listing.

Office of Workers' Compensation Program
800 N. Capitol St., NW
Washington, DC 20211
202-565-9770

Occupational Safety and Health Administration
200 Constitution Ave., NW, Room N3647
Washington, DC 20210
202-219-8148

Bureau of Labor Statistics - Recording
2 Massachusetts Ave., NE
Washington, DC 20212
202-606-7828

Veterans' Employment and Training Service
200 Constitution Ave., NW, Room 1316
Washington, DC 20210
202-219-9110

Sources of Information for the Department of Labor
Public Affairs
Bureau of Labor Statistics
2 Massachusetts Ave., NE, Room 4110
Washington, DC 20212
202-606-5900

Procurement and Policy
Room S1522
200 Constitution Ave., NW
Washington, DC 20210
202-219-8904

Employment
200 Constitution Ave., NW
Washington, DC 20210
202-219-6666

Publications
200 Constitution Ave., NW, Room N4700
Washington, DC 20210
202-219-6871

Reading Rooms
200 Constitution Ave., NW, Room N2445
Washington, DC 20210
202-219-6992

Locator
200 Constitution Ave., NW
Washington, DC 20210
202-219-6666

Freedom of Information Officer
Room N2428
200 Constitution Ave., NW
Washington, DC 20210
202-219-8188

Fraud and Waste Hotline
Office of Inspector General
Attn: CAO, Room S5514
200 Constitution Ave., NW
Washington, DC 20210
800-347-3756

Labor Statistics - Price Index
2 Massachusetts Ave., NE, Room 3615
Washington, DC 20212-0001
202-606-7000

Department of State
2201 C St., NW
Washington, DC 20520
202-647-4000

Functional Areas
Diplomatic Security
2201 C St., NW
Washington, Dc 20520
202-663-0063

Economic and Business Affairs
2201 C St., NW, Room 6828
Washington, DC 20520
202-647-7971

Intelligence and Research
Room 6639
2201 C St., NW
Washington, DC 20520
202-647-1080

International Communications and Information Policy
Room 4826
2201 C St., NW
Washington, DC 20520
202-647-5832

International Narcotics Matters
Room 7333
2201 C St., NW
Washington, DC 20520
202-647-8464

International Organization Affairs
Room 6323
2201 C St., NW
Washington, DC 20520
202-647-9600

Legislative Affairs
Room 5913
2201 C St., NW
Washington, DC 20520
202-647-2163

Medical Services
Room 2906
2201 C St., NW
Washington, DC 20520
202-647-3617

Public Affairs
Room 5827
2201 C St., NW
Washington, DC 20520
202-647-6575

Consular Affairs
Room 6831
2201 C St., NW
Washington, DC 20520
202-647-1488

Politico-Military Affairs
Room 7319
2201 C St., NW
Washington, DC 20520
202-647-6968

Oceans and International Environmental and Scientific Affairs
Room 7821
2201 C St., NW
Washington, DC 20520
202-647-3622

Protocol
Room 1238
2201 C St., NW
Washington, DC 20520
202-647-2663

Human Rights and Humanitarian Affairs
Room 7802
2201 C St., NW
Washington, DC 20520
202-647-2126

Refugee Programs
Room 1244
2201 C St., NW
Washington, DC 20520
202-663-1520

Sources of Information for the Department of State
Audiovisual Materials
Video Transfer, Inc.
5709-B Arundel Avenue
Rockville, MD 20852
301-881-0270

Conferences, Seminars, Speaking Engagements, Briefings
Office of Public Liaison
Bureau of Public Affairs
Department of State, Room 1212A
Washington, DC 20520
202-647-1076

Contracts
Office of Acquisitions (A/OPR/ACQ)
Department of State
1800 N. Kent St.
Arlington, VA 22209
703-875-6884

Diplomatic and Official Passports
Passport Services
Diplomatic and Congressional Travel Branch
1111 19th St., NW
Washington, DC 20522-1705
202-955-0217

Employment
  Foreign Service Employment
  PER/REE/REC
  P.O. Box 9317
  Rosslyn Station
  Arlington, VA 22210
  703-875-7490
  703-875-7252

  Civil Service Positions
  Office of Civil Service Personnel
  Department of State
  P.O. Box 18657
  Washington, DC 200236-8657
  202-647-7252

  Civil Service Job Information Line
  202-647-7284

Freedom of Information Officer
Office of Freedom of Information, Privacy, and Classification Review
2201 C St., NW
Washington, DC 20520-1512
202-647-8484

Missing Persons, Emergencies, Deaths of Americans Abroad
Citizens Emergency Center
2201 C St., NW
Washington, DC 20520
202-647-5225

Citizenship, International Parental Child Abduction,
Judicial Assistance, Overseas Voting
Bureau of Consular Affairs
Citizens Overseas Service, Room 4817
Washington, DC 20520
202-647-3666

Passports
Passport Service
Bureau of Consular Affairs
1111 19th St., NW
Washington, DC 20522
202-647-0518

Publications
Public Information
Bureau of Public Affairs
2201 C St., NW, Room 5831
Washington, DC 20520
202-647-6575

Reading Room
2201 C St., NW, Room 3239
Washington, DC 20520
202-647-1099

Visas
2201 C St., NW
Washington, DC 20520
202-663-1225

Locator
2201 C St., NW
Washington, DC 20520
202-647-4000

Fraud and Waste Hotline
Office of the Inspector General
P.O. Box 9778
Arlington, VA 22219
202-647-3320

Department of Transportation
400 Seventh St., SW
Washington, DC 20590
202-366-4000

United States Coast Guard
2100 Second St., SW
Washington, DC 20593-0001
202-267-2229

Search and Rescue
Commandant (G-NRS)
2100 Second St., SW
Washington, DC 20593
202-267-1948

Maritime Law Enforcement
Commandant (G-OLE)
2100 Second St., SW
Washington, DC 20593
202-267-1890

Marine Inspection
Merchant Vessel Inspection and Documentation Division
2100 Second St., SW
Washington, DC 20593
202-267-1464

Marine Licensing
U.S. Coast Nation Maritime Center
4200 Wilson Blvd., Suite 510
Arlington, VA 22203
703-235-1864

Marine Environmental Response
2100 Second St., SW
Washington, DC 20593
202-267-0518

Port Safety and Security
Room 1104

2100 Second St., SW
Washington, DC 20593
202-267-0489

Waterways Management
2100 Second St., SW, Room 4120
Washington, DC 20593
202-267-0980

Aids to Navigation
2100 Second St., SW, Room 1116
Washington, DC 20593
202-267-1965

Bridge Division
Room 1408, 2100 Second St., SW
Washington, DC 20593
202-267-0368

Ice Operations
NIO
Room 1202-A
2100 Second St., SW
Washington, DC 20593
202-267-1450

Compliance Branch
2100 Second St., SW
Washington, DC 20593
202-267-0495

Boating Safety
2100 Second St., SW
Washington, DC 20593
202-267-1077

Coast Guard Auxiliary
Room 1504
2100 Second St., SW
Washington, DC 20593
202-267-1001

Military Readiness
Room 3300
2100 Second St., SW
Washington, DC 20593
202-267-2039

Reserve Training
Room 5412
2100 Second St., SW
Washington, DC 20593
202-267-1240

Marine Safety Regulations
Room 3406
2100 Second St., SW
Washington, DC 20593
202-267-1477

Information Office
Headquarters Information
2100 Second St., SW
Washington, DC 20593
202-267-2229

Federal Aviation Administration
Office of Public Affairs
800 Independence Ave., SW
Washington, DC 20591
202-267-3484

Federal Highway Administration
Public Affairs Office
400 Seventh St., SW
Washington, DC 20590
202-366-0660

Office of Management Systems
400 Seventh St., SW
Washington, DC 20590
202-366-9062

Federal Railroad Administration
400 Seventh St., SW
Washington, DC 20590
202-366-0881

Transportation Test Center
P.O. Box 11130
Pueblo, CO 81001
719-584-0501

Public Affairs Office
400 Seventh St., SW, Room 8125
Washington, DC 20590
202-366-0881

National Highway Traffic Safety Administration
Office of Public and Consumer Affairs
400 Seventh St., SW, Room 5232
Washington, DC 20590
202-366-9550

Federal Transit Administration
Office of Public and Consumer Affairs
400 Seventh St., SW, Room 90400
Washington, DC 20590
202-366-4043

Maritime Administration
Office of External Affairs
Room 7219, 400 Seventh St., SW
Washington, DC 20590
202-366-5807

Saint Lawrence Seaway Development Corporation
Director of Communications
400 Seventh St., SW, Room 5424
Washington, DC 20590
202-366-0091

Research and Special Programs
Administration
400 Seventh St., SW
Washington, DC 20590
202-366-4433

Office of Hazardous Materials Safety
400 Seventh St., SW, Room 8420
Washington, DC 20590
202-366-0656

Office of Pipeline Safety
400 Seventh St., SW, Room 2335
Washington, DC 20590
202-366-4595

Office of Research, Technology, and Analysis
Room 9402
400 Seventh St., SW
Washington, DC 20590
202-366-4434

Office of Emergency Transportation
Room 8404
400 Seventh St., SW
Washington, DC 20590
202-366-5270

Office of Airline Statistics
Room 4125
400 Seventh St., SW
Washington, DC 20590
202-366-9059

Information Starting Places

Office of University Research and Education
400 Seventh St., SW, Room 10309
Washington, DC 20590
202-366-5442

Office of Automated Tariffs
400 Seventh St., SW, Room 6424
Washington, DC 20590
202-366-4381

Office of Research Policy and Technology Transfer
Room 9402
400 Seventh St., SW
Washington, DC 20590
202-366-4208

Volpe National Transportation Systems Center
55 Broadway, Kendall Square
Cambridge, MA 02142
617-494-2224

Office of Management and Administration
400 Seventh St., SW, Room 8321
Washington, DC 20590
202-366-4347

Office of Aviation and International Affairs
Room 10232
400 Seventh St., SW
Washington, DC 20590
202-366-8834

Policy and Transportation
Room 10228
400 Seventh St., SW
Washington, DC 20590
202-366-4544

Budget and Programs
Room 10101
400 Seventh St., SW
Washington, DC 20590
202-366-9191

Office of Civil Rights
Room 10215
400 Seventh St., SW
Washington, DC 20590
202-366-4648

Public Affairs
Room 10413
400 Seventh St., SW
Washington, DC 20590
202-366-5580

Small and Disadvantaged Business Utilization
400 Seventh St., SW, Room 9414
Washington, DC 20590
800-532-1169

Contract Appeals
Room 5101
400 Seventh St., SW
Washington, DC 20590
202-366-4305

Commercial Space Transportation
Room 5415
400 Seventh St., SW
Washington, DC 20590
202-366-5770

Inspector General- Fraud and Waste
P.O. Box 23178
Washington, DC 20026-0178
800-424-9071

**Sources of Information for the
Department of Transportation**
Coast Guard Career
U.S. Coast Guard Academy
2100 Second St. SW
Washington, DC 20590
202-267-2229 or
203-444-8444

Consumer Protection
Department of Transportation
C-75
Washington, DC 20590
202-366-2220

Contracts
Office of Acquisition and Grant Management
Room 9401
400 Seventh St., SW
Washington, DC 20590
202-366-4285

Employment
DOT Connection
PL 402
400 Seventh St., SW
Washington, DC 20590
202-366-9392

Environmental Affairs
Regulatory Affairs
Environmental Division
400 Seventh St., SW
Washington, DC 20590
202-366-4366

Reading Rooms/Dockets
PL 401
400 Seventh St., SW
Washington, DC 20590
202-366-9322

Locator
400 Seventh St., SW
Washington, DC 20590
202-366-4000

Publications Request Line
Publications Section
400 Seventh St., SW
Washington, DC 20590
202-366-0039
Fax: 202-366-2795

Freedom of Information Officer
Room 5432
400 Seventh St.
Washington, DC 20590
202-366-4542

Department of Treasury
1500 Pennsylvania Ave., NW
Washington, DC 20220
202-622-2000

Bureau of Alcohol, Tobacco and Firearms
Public Affairs
Room 8290
650 Massachusetts Ave., NW
Washington, DC 20226
202-927-8500

Communications Office
650 Massachusetts Ave., NW
Washington, DC 20226
202-927-7777

Be patient. If any phone number is incorrect, call (area code) 555-1212 and request the new listing.

Office of the Comptroller of the Currency
250 E St., SW
Washington, DC 20219
202-874-5000

Public Affairs
250 E St., SW
Washington, DC 20219
202-874-5770

Contracts
250 E St., SW
Washington, DC 20219
202-874-5040

Employment
250 E St., SW
Washington, DC 20219
202-874-4490

United States Customs Service
1301 Constitution Ave., NW
Washington, DC 20229
202-927-2095

Public Affairs
1301 Constitution Ave., NW
Washington, DC 20229
202-927-1770

Publications
Office of Public Affairs
1301 Constitution Ave., NW
Washington, DC 20229
202-927-1770

Reading Rooms
Customs Library
1301 Constitution Ave., NW
Washington, DC 20229
202-927-1617

Speakers
Office of Public Relations
1301 Constitution Ave., NW
Washington, DC 20229
202-927-1770

Contracts
Office of Contracts and Procurements
1301 Constitution Ave., NW
Washington, DC 20229
202-927-0990

Freedom of Information Officer
1301 Constitution Ave., NW
Washington, DC 20229
202-482-6970

Bureau of Engraving and Printing
14th and C Streets, SW
Washington, DC 20228
202-874-3019

Contracts and Small Business Activities
Office of Procurement
Room 705A, 14th and C Streets, SW
Washington, DC 20228
202-874-2534

Employment
Office of Personnel
14th and C Streets, SW
Room 202A
Washington, DC 20228
202-874-3747

Freedom of Information Act Requests
14th and C Streets, SW, Room 321-A
Washington, DC 20228
202-874-2058

Public Affairs
14th and C Streets, SW, Room 533M
Washington, DC 20228
202-874-3019

Product Sales
14th and C Streets, SW, Room 515M
Washington, DC 20228
202-874-3316

Federal Law Enforcement Training Center
Glynco, GA 31524
912-267-2447 or
202-927-8940 (Washington, DC, number)

Public Affairs
Bldg. 94
Glynco, GA 31524
912-267-2447

Financial Management Service
401 14th St., SW, Room 548
Washington, DC 20227
202-874-6740

Office of Public Affairs
401 14th St., SW
Washington, DC 20227
202-874-6740

Contracts
Acquisitions
Room 427
401 14th St., SW
Washington, DC 20227
202-874-6910

Employment
Room 120
401 14th St., SW
Washington, DC 20227
202-874-7090

Internal Revenue Service
1111 Constitution Ave., NW
Washington, DC 20224
800-829-1040
202-622-5000

Contracts
Office of Procurement
Room 3425
1111 Constitution Ave., NW
Washington, DC 20224
202-622-8480

Educational Programs
1111 Constitution Ave., NW
Washington, DC 20224
800-829-1040

Employment
Public Affairs - Job Hotline
1111 Constitution Ave., NW
Washington, DC 20224
202-622-5560

Publications and Forms
P.O. Box 25866
Richmond, VA 23260
800-829-3676

Be patient. If any phone number is incorrect, call (area code) 555-1212 and request the new listing.

59

Information Starting Places

Reading Rooms
1111 Constitution Ave., NW
Washington, DC 20224
202-622-5164

Taxpayer Service
1111 Constitution Ave., NW
Washington, DC 20224
800-829-1040

United States Mint
633 Third St., NW
Washington, DC 20220
202-874-6000

Office of Public Affairs
Room 74
633 Third St., NW
Washington, DC 20220
202-874-6450

Numismatic Services
Customer Service Department
10001 Arrowspace Rd.
Lanham, MD 20706
202-283-COIN

Bureau of the Public Debt
999 E St., NW
Washington, DC 20239-0001
202-219-3300

Office of Public Affairs
Room 553
E St. Bldg.
Washington, DC 20239-0001
202-219-3302

Employment
Office of Personnel
P.O. Box 1328
Parkersburg, WV 26106
304-480-7708

Savings Bonds
Office of Bond Consultants
P.O. Box 1328
Parkersburg, WV 26106-1328
304-480-6112

Treasury Securities
Customer Service
1300 C St., SW, Room 240
Washington, DC 20239
202-874-4000 (press #1 and ext. 300 for personal assistance)

United States Savings Bonds Division
999 E St., NW
Washington, DC 20239
202-219-4235

Office of Public Affairs
999 E St., NW
Washington, DC 20226
202-219-3302

Current Rate Information
800 K St., NW
Washington, DC 20226
800-4US-BOND
202-377-7715

United States Secret Service
1800 G St., NW
Washington, DC 20223
202-435-5708

Public Affairs
1800 G St., NW
Suite 805
Washington, DC 20223
202-435-5708

Employment
Office of Personnel
1800 G St., NW, Suite 912
Washington, DC 20223
202-435-5800

Publications
Office of Public Affairs
1800 G St., NW
Suite 805
Washington, DC 20223
202-435-5708

Office of Thrift Supervision
1700 G St., NW
Washington, DC 20552
202-906-6000

Public Affairs
1700 G St., NW
Washington, DC 20552
202-906-6913

Sources of Information for the Department of Treasury
Contracts
Office of Procurement
1500 Pennsylvania Ave., NW
Room 6083
Washington, DC 20220
202-622-0530

Public Affairs
1500 Pennsylvania Ave., NW
Room 2315
Washington, DC 20220
202-622-2960

Reading Room
Library
1500 Pennsylvania Ave., NW, Room 5310
Washington, DC 20220
202-622-0990

Small and Disadvantaged Business Activities
1500 Pennsylvania Ave., NW
Room 6083
Washington, DC 20220
202-622-0530

Tax Legislative Council
Room 3064
1500 Pennsylvania Ave., NW
Washington, DC 20220
202-622-0140

Inspector General- Fraud and Waste Hotline
1500 Pennsylvania Ave., NW
Washington, DC 20220
800-359-3898

Freedom of Information Office
Room 1054
1500 Pennsylvania Ave., NW
Washington, DC 20220
202-622-0930

Locator
1500 Pennsylvania Ave., NW
Washington, DC 20220
202-622-2000

Be patient. If any phone number is incorrect, call (area code) 555-1212 and request the new listing.

Department of Veterans Affairs

810 Vermont Ave., NW
Washington, Dc 20420
202-273-5400

National Cemetery System
Office of Public Affairs
MS 402-E
810 Vermont Ave., NW
Washington, DC 20420
202-273-5221

Veterans Benefits Administration
810 Vermont Ave., NW, MS 20A1
Washington, DC 20420
202-273-6767

Veterans Health Administration
810 Vermont Ave., NW, MS 10D
Washington, DC 20420
202-273-5664

**Sources of Information for the
Department of Veterans Affairs**
Office of Public Affairs
810 Vermont Ave., NW, MS 80F
Washington, DC 20420
202-273-5700

Audiovisual Services
810 Vermont Ave., NW
Mail Stop 032B3
Washington, DC 20420
202-273-5373

Contracts and Small Business Activities
Office of Acquisition and Review
810 Vermont Ave., NW, Room 703
Washington, DC 20420
202-273-5686

Employment
Office of Human Resources
810 Vermont Ave., NW
Mail Stop 055
Washington, DC 20420
202-273-4950

Freedom of Information Act Requests
810 Vermont Ave., NW
Mail Stop 045A4
Washington, DC 20420
202-565-8272

Reading Room
Library
810 Vermont Ave., NW
Mail Stop 026H
Washington, DC 20420
202-273-6558

Publications
Mail Stop 97
811 Vermont Ave., NW
Washington, DC 20420
202-565-9347

Inspector General- Fraud and Waste Hotline
P.O. Box 50410
Washington, DC 20091-0410
800-488-8244

Locator
810 Vermont Ave., NW
Washington, DC 20420
202-273-5400

INDEPENDENT AGENCIES

Corporation for National Service
AmeriCorps
1201 New York Ave., NW
Washington, DC 20525
800-94-ACORPS
202-606-5000

Foster Grandparents
1201 New York Ave., NW
Washington, DC 20525
800-424-8867
TDD: 800-833-3722

Retired Senior Volunteers
1201 New York Ave., NW
Washington, DC 20525
800-424-8867
TDD: 800-833-3722
202-606-5000, ext. 189

Senior Companions
1201 New York Ave., NW
Washington, DC 20525
800-424-8867
TDD: 800-833-3722

Volunteers in Service to America
VISTA
1201 New York Ave., NW
Washington, DC 20525
800-424-8867
TDD: 800-833-3722

Student Community Service Projects
1201 New York Ave., NW
Washington, DC 20525
800-94-ACORPS
202-606-5000

Program Demonstration and Development Division
1201 New York Ave., NW
Washington, DC 20525
800-94-ACORPS
202-606-5000

Publications
1201 New York Ave., NW
Washington, DC 20525
800-94-ACORPS
202-606-5000

Public Affairs
1201 New York Ave., NW
Washington, DC 20525
800-94-ACORPS
202-606-5000

Administrative Conference of the United States

Suite 500
2120 L St., NW
Washington, DC 20037-1568
202-254-7020

African Development Foundation

7400 I St., NW
Washington, DC 20005
202-673-3916

Central Intelligence Agency

Washington, DC 20505
703-482-1100

Information Starting Places

Commission on Civil Rights
624 9th St., NW
Washington, DC 20425
202-376-8177

Public Affairs
624 9th St., NW
Washington, DC 20425
202-376-8312

Commodity Futures Trading Commission
2033 K St., NW
Washington, DC 20581
202-254-6970

Office of Communication and Education Services
2033 K St., NW
Washington, DC 20581
202-254-8630

Consumer Product Safety Commission
Information and Public Affairs
East West Towers
4330 East West Hwy.
Bethesda, MD 20814
301-504-0580

Defense Nuclear Facilities Safety Board
625 Indiana Ave., NW, Suite 700
Washington, DC 20004
202-208-6400

Environmental Protection Agency
401 M St., SW
Washington, DC 20460
202-260-2090

Activities
Air and Radiation
Room 937 West Tower
401 M St., SW
Washington, DC 20460
202-260-7400

Office of Water
Room 1035 East Tower
401 M St., SW
Washington, DC 20460
202-260-5700

Solid Waste and Emergency Response
401 M St., SW, Room 363
Washington, DC 20460
202-260-4610

Prevention, Pesticides and Toxic Response
635 East Tower Bldg.
401 M St., SW
Washington, DC 20460
202-260-2902

Research and Development
913 West Tower Bldg.
401 M St., SW
Washington, DC 20460
202-260-7676

Sources of Information
Contracts
Procurement and Contracts Management
401 M St., SW
Washington, DC 20460
202-260-5020

Employment
Office of Human Resources
401 M St., SW
Washington, DC 20460
202-260-3144

Freedom of Information Act Requests
Freedom of Information Officer
401 M St., SW
Washington, DC 20460
202-260-4048

Reading Room
Information Management and Services Division
401 M St., SW, MS 3404
Washington, DC 20460
202-260-5921

Public Affairs
Office of Communications, Education and Public Affairs
401 M St., SW
Washington, DC 20460
202-260-7963

Public Information Center
401 M St., SW
Washington, DC 20460
202-260-7751

Equal Employment Opportunity Commission
1801 L St., NW
Washington, DC 20507
202-663-4900
800-USA-EEOC

Sources of Information
Employment
Personnel Office
1801 L St., NW
Washington, DC 20507
202-663-4306

General Inquiries
1801 L St., NW
Washington, DC 20507
800-669-4900

Publications
1801 L St., NW
Washington, DC 20507
800-669-EEOC

Reading Room
EEOC Library
1801 L St., NW
Washington, DC 20507
202-663-4630

Speakers
1801 L St., NW
Washington, DC 20507
202-663-4900

Export-Import Bank of the United States
811 Vermont Ave., NW
Washington, DC 20571
202-565-3200

Farm Credit Administration
1501 Farm Credit Drive
McLean, VA 22102-5090
703-883-4000

Be patient. If any phone number is incorrect, call (area code) 555-1212 and request the new listing.

Public Affairs
1501 Farm Credit Drive
McLean, VA 22102-5090
703-883-4056

Federal Communications Commission
1919 M St., NW
Washington, DC 20544
202-418-0200

Personnel Locator
1919 M St., NW
Washington, DC 20544
202-418-0126

Activities
Mass Media
1919 M St., NW
Washington, DC 20554
202-418-2610

Common Carrier Communications
1919 M St., NW
Washington, DC 20554
202-418-1370

Private Radio Communications
2025 M St., NW
Washington, DC 20554
202-418-0600

Engineering and Technology
2000 M St., NW
Room 480
Washington, DC 20554
202-739-0700

Office of Compliance
1919 M St., NW
Room 728
Washington, DC 20554
202-418-1130

Sources of Information
General Council
1919 M St., NW
Washington, DC 20554
202-418-1720

Consumer Assistance and Small Business Division
1919 M St., NW, Room 254
Washington, DC 20554
202-418-0190

Contracts
Office of Acquisitions
1919 M St., NW
Washington, DC 20554
202-418-0930

Employment
Office of Personnel
1919 M St., NW, Room 212
Washington, DC 20554
202-418-0100

Equal Employment Practices by Industry
Office of Workplace Diversity
2033 M St., NW
Washington, DC 20554
202-776-1887

Ex-Parte Presentations
Room 222, 1919 M St., NW
Washington, DC 20554
202-418-0300

Copying Fee Information
Document Retrieval Service
2100 M St., NW, Room 140
Washington, DC 20037
202-857-3800

Information Available for Public Inspection
Office of the Managing Director
1919 M St., NW, Room 852
Washington, DC 20554
202-418-1919

Public Affairs
1919 M St., NW
Washington, DC 20554
202-418-0500

Federal Deposit Insurance Corporation
550 17th St., NW
Washington, DC 20429
202-393-8400

Sources of Information
Bank Depositors and Customers
Director, Office of Consumer Affairs
550 17th St., NW
Washington, DC 20429
202-942-3100

Employment
Personnel Office
550 17th St., NW
Washington, DC 20429
202-942-3501

FDIC Rules and Related Acts
1776 F St., Room 415
Washington, DC 20429
202-898-3823

Corporate Communications Office
550 17th St., NW
Washington, DC 20429
202-898-6996

Federal Election Commission
999 E St., NW
Washington, DC 20463
202-219-3420
800-424-9530

Sources of Information
Clearinghouse on Election Administration
999 E St., NW
Washington, DC 20463
800-424-9530

Public Affairs
Press Office
999 E St., NW
Washington, DC 20463
202-219-4155 or
800-424-9530

Employment
Director
Personnel and Labor Management Relations
999 E St., NW
Washington, DC 20463
202-219-4290

Reading Room
FEC Library
999 E St., NW
Washington, DC 20463
202-219-3312

Be patient. If any phone number is incorrect, call (area code) 555-1212 and request the new listing.

63

Information Starting Places

Federal Emergency Management Agency
500 C St., SW
Washington, DC 20472
202-646-4600

Contracts
500 C St., SW
Washington, DC 20472
202-646-3744

Employment
500 C St., SW
Washington, DC 20472
202-646-3964

Freedom of Information Officer
Office of General Counsel
500 C St., SW
Room 840
Washington, DC 20472
202-646-4105

Public Affairs
500 C St., SW
Washington, DC 20472
202-646-4600

Federal Housing Finance Board
1777 F St., NW
Washington, DC 20006
202-408-2500

Public Affairs
1777 F St., NW
Washington, DC 20006
202-408-2986

Federal Labor Relations Authority
607 14th St., NW
Washington, DC 20424
202-482-6550

Director of Information Resources and Research Services
607 14th St., NW
Washington, DC 20424
202-482-6550

Federal Maritime Commission
800 N. Capitol St., NW
Washington, DC 20573-0001
202-523-5707

Employee Locator
800 N. Capitol St., NW
Washington, DC 20573-0001
202-523-5773

Informal Complaints
800 N. Capitol St., NW
Washington, DC 20573-0001
202-523-5807

Office of the Secretary
800 N. Capitol St., NW
Washington, DC 20573-0001
202-523-5725

Federal Mediation and Conciliation Service
2100 K St., NW
Washington, DC 20427
202-606-8080

Office of Public and International Affairs
2100 K St., NW
Washington, DC 20427
202-606-8080

Arbitration
2100 K St., NW
Washington, DC 20427
202-606-5111

Mediation Services
2100 K St., SW
Washington, DC 20427
202-606-8140

Federal Mine Safety and Health Review Commission
1730 K St., NW
Washington, DC 20006
202-653-5633

Federal Reserve System
Board of Governors of the Federal Reserve System
20th St. and Constitution Ave., NW
Washington, DC 20551
202-452-3000

Publications Services (MS-138)
20th St. and Constitution Ave., NW
Washington, DC 20551
202-452-3244

Reading Room
Library
20th St. and Constitution Ave., NW
Washington, DC 20551
202-452-3684

Office of Public Affairs
20th St. and Constitution Ave., NW
Washington, DC 20551
202-452-3204

Federal Retirement Thrift Investment Board
1250 H St., NW, Suite 400
Washington, DC 20005
202-942-1600

Director of External Affairs
1250 H St., NW
Washington, DC 20005
202-942-1640

Federal Trade Commission
Pennsylvania Ave. at 6th St., NW
Washington, DC 20580
202-326-2222

Contracts
Office of Procurement
Pennsylvania Ave. at 6th St., NW
Washington, DC 20580
202-326-2275

Employment
Office of Personnel
Room H-148
Pennsylvania Ave. at 6th St., NW
Washington, DC 20580
202-326-2022

Publications
Public Reference Branch

Be patient. If any phone number is incorrect, call (area code) 555-1212 and request the new listing.

Pennsylvania Ave. at 6th St., NW
Washington, DC 20580
202-326-2222

Office of Public Affairs
Room 421
Pennsylvania Ave. at 6th St., NW
Washington, DC 20580
202-326-2180

General Services Administration

General Services Building
18th and F St., NW
Washington, DC 20405
202-708-5082

Information Resources Management Service
18th and F St., NW
Washington, DC 20405
202-501-1000

Federal Supply Service
General Services Administration
1941 Jefferson Davis Hwy., CM #4
Washington, DC 20406
703-305-6667

Public Buildings Service
18th and F St., NW, Room 6344
Washington, DC 20405
202-501-1100

Federal Property Resources Service
18th and F St., NW
Washington, DC 20405
202-501-0210

Acquisition Policy
Room 4040
18th and F St., NW
Washington, DC 20405
202-501-1043

Small and Disadvantaged Business Utilization
Room 6029
18th and F St., NW
Washington, DC 20405
202-501-1021

Workplace Initiative
Room 6119
18th and F St., NW
Washington, DC 20405
202-501-3965

Governmentwide Policy Division
Room 6215
18th and F St., NW
Washington, DC 20405
202-501-0507

Contract Appeals
Room 7022
18th and F St., NW
Washington, DC 20405
202-501-0720

Office of the Inspector General
18th and F St., NW
Washington, DC 20405
202-501-0466

Fraud and Waste Hotline
18th and F St., NW
Washington, DC 20405
800-424-5210

Office of Management Services and Human Resources
Room 6125
18th and F St., NW
Washington, DC 20405
202-501-0945

Chief Financial Officer
Room 2140
18th and F St., NW
Washington, DC 20405
202-501-1721

Equal Employment Opportunities
Room 5129
18th and F St., NW
Washington, DC 20405
202-501-0767

Ethics
Room 5135
18th and F Sts., NW
Washington, DC 20405
202-501-0765

Federal Telecommunications System 2000
7980 Boeing Court
Vienna, VA 22182
703-760-7790

Office of Information Technology Integration
5203 Leesburg Pike
Suite 400
Falls Church, VA 22041
703-756-4100

Office of Information Resources
Procurement
Room 3024
18th and F St., NW
Washington, DC 20405
202-501-3535

Emerging Technologies
Suite G242
18th and F St., NW
Washington, DC 20405
202-501-0308

GSA Information Systems
18th and F St., NW
Washington, DC 20405
202-501-1800

Federal Information Center
P.O. Box 600
Cumberland, MD 21502-0600
301-722-9098

Domestic Assistance Catalogue
300 7th St., SW
Reporters Building
Room 101
Washington, DC 20407
202-708-5126

Federal Supply Service
Office of the Public Liaison
1941 Jefferson Davis Highway
Arlington, VA 22202
703-305-6646

Commercial Broker
Room 2341
18th and F St., NW
Washington, DC 20405
202-501-1025

Information Starting Places

Fee Developer
Room 3338
18th and F St., NW
Washington, DC 20405
202-501-0887

Office of Real Property Management and Safety
Room 4340
18th and F St., NW
Washington, DC 20405
202-501-0971

Office of Physical Security and Law Enforcement
18th and F St., NW
Washington, DC 20405
202-501-0907

Portfolio Management
Room 6331
18th and F St., NW
Washington, DC 20405
202-501-0638

Office of Procurement
18th and F St., NW
Washington, DC 20405
202-501-0907

Sources of Information for
General Services Administration
Consumer Information Center
Pueblo, CO 81009
719-948-3334

Employment
Personnel Operations Division (CPS)
Office of Personnel
18th and F St., NW, Room 1100
Washington, DC 20405
202-501-0370

Freedom of Information Act Request
Attn: Privacy Act Officer
18th and F St., NW, Room 7102
Washington, DC 20405
202-501-2691

Publications
Director of Publications
Office of Communications (XS)
18th and F St., NW, Room 6022
Washington, DC 20405
202-501-1235

Speakers
Office of Public Affairs (X)
General Services Administration
Washington, DC 20405
202-501-0705

Public Affairs
Office of Public Affairs (X)
General Services Administration
Washington, DC 20405
202-501-0705

Inter-American Foundation

901 North Stuart St., 10th Floor
Arlington, VA 22203
703-841-3800

Office of the President
10th Floor
901 North Stuart St.
Arlington, VA 22203
703-841-3810

Interstate Commerce Commission

12th and Constitution Ave., NW
Washington, DC 20423
202-927-7119

Sources of Information
Consumer Affairs
Office of Compliance and Consumer Assistance
12th and Constitution Ave., NW
Washington, DC 20423
202-927-5500

Contracts
Procurement and Contracting Branch
12th and Constitution Ave., NW
Washington, DC 20423
202-927-5370

Employment
Director of Personnel
12th and Constitution Ave., NW
Washington, DC 20423
202-927-7288

Public Affairs
Office of External Affairs
12th and Constitution Ave., NW, Room 3130
Washington, DC 20423
202-927-5350

Publications
Public Affairs
Office of External Affairs
12th and Constitution Ave., NW, Room 3392
Washington, DC 20423
202-927-7328

Reading Rooms
Office of the Secretary
Room 2215, ICC Building
12th and Constitution Ave., NW
Washington, DC 20423
202-927-7428

Small Business Activities
Office of Public Assistance
Room 3148, 12th and Constitution Ave., NW
Washington, DC 20423
202-927-7597

Speakers
Public Affairs
Office of External Affairs
Room 3130
12th and Constitution Ave., NW
Washington, DC 20423
202-927-5350

Merit Systems Protection Board

8th Floor, 1120 Vermont Ave., NW
Washington, DC 20419
202-653-7124

National Aeronautics and Space Administration

300 E St., SW
Washington, DC 20546-0001
202-358-1000

Office of Aeronautics
NASA Headquarters
Code R
300 E St., SW
Washington, DC 20546
202-358-2693

Be patient. If any phone number is incorrect, call (area code) 555-1212 and request the new listing.

Space Access and Technology
NASA Headquarters
Code D
300 E St., SW
Washington, DC 20546
202-358-4600

Space Science and Applications
NASA Headquarters
Code S
300 E St., SW
Washington, DC 20546
202-358-0370

Space Flight
NASA Headquarters
Code M
300 E St., SW
Washington, DC 20546
202-358-2015

Space Communications
NASA Headquarters
Code O
300 E St., SW
Washington, DC 20546
202-358-2020

Sources of Information
Contracts
Office of Procurement
NASA Headquarters
Code H
300 E St., SW
Washington, DC 20546
202-358-2090

Employment
NASA Headquarters
Code FPH
300 E St., SW
Washington, DC 20546
202-358-1562

Reading Room
NASA Headquarters
300 E St., SW
Washington, DC 20546-0001
202-358-0168

Headquarters Information Center
NASA Headquarters
300 E St., SW
Washington, DC 20546-0001
202-358-1000

National Archives and Records Administration

National Archives Bldg.
7th St. and Pennsylvania Ave., NW
Washington, DC 20408
202-501-5400

References Services Branch (NNRS)
7th St. and Pennsylvania Ave., NW
National Archives Bldg.
Washington, DC 20408
202-501-5400

Presidential Libraries
National Archives Bldg., Room 104
7th St. and Pennsylvania Ave., NW
Washington, DC 20408
202-501-5700

Federal Records Centers
8601 Adelphi Rd.

College Park, MD 20740-6001
301-713-7200

Records Administration
8601 Adelphi Rd.
College Park, MD 20740-6001
301-713-7100

Office of the Federal Register
800 N. Capitol St., NW, Suite 700
Washington, DC 20408
202-523-5240

Public Programs
Room G12
7th St. and Pennsylvania Ave., NW
Washington, DC 20408
202-501-5200

National Archives Trust Fund Board
8601 Adelphi Rd.
College Park, MD 20740-6001
301-713-6405

National Historical Publications and Records Commission
7th St. and Pennsylvania Ave., NW, Room 607
Washington, DC 20408
202-501-5600

Sources of Information
Calendar of Events
National Archives Building
Office of Public Affairs
7th St. and Pennsylvania Ave., NW
Washington, DC 20408
202-501-5525

Recorded Messages
7th St. and Pennsylvania Ave., NW
Washington, DC 20408
202-501-5000

Speakers
Office of Public Affairs
7th St. and Pennsylvania Ave., NW
Washington, DC 20408
202-501-5525

Workshops
Office of Education
7th St. and Pennsylvania Ave., NW
Washington, DC 20408
202-501-6172

Publications
Publication Services
7th and Pennsylvania Ave., NW
Washington, DC 20408
202-501-5235

Teaching Aids
Office of Education
7th and Pennsylvania Ave., NW
Washington, DC 20408
202-501-6172

Guided Tours
Room G8
7th and Pennsylvania Ave., NW
Washington, DC 20408
202-501-5205

Audiovisual Sales and Rentals
National Audiovisual Center
8700 Edgeworth Drive
Capitol Heights, MD 20743-3701
800-788-6282

Information Starting Places

Educational Opportunities
Office of Public Programs
7th and Pennsylvania Ave., NW
Washington, DC 20408
202-501-5200

Volunteers
National Archives Bldg.
7th and Pennsylvania Ave., NW
Washington, DC 20408
202-501-5205

Congressional and External Affairs
Office of Public Affairs
7th St. and Pennsylvania Ave., NW
Washington, DC 20408
202-501-5525

Reading Rooms
National Archives Library
8601 Adelphi Rd.
College Park, MD 20740-6001
301-713-6778

Freedom of Information Act
Policy and Planning Analysis Division
8601 Adelphi Rd.
College Park, MD 20740-6001
301-713-6730

Contracts
Acquisitions Management Branch
8601 Adelphi Rd.
College Park, MD 20740-6001
301-713-6755

Employment
Personnel Operations Branch
Room 2002
9700 Page Blvd.
St. Louis, MO 63132
800-827-4898

Records Administration Information Center
8601 Adelphi Rd.
College Park, MD 20740-6001
301-713-6677

National Capital Planning Commission

Suite 301
801 Pennsylvania Ave., NW
Washington, DC 20576
202-724-0174

National Credit Union Administration

1775 Duke St.
Alexandria, VA 22314-3428
703-518-6300

Office of Examination and Insurance
1775 Duke St.
Alexandria, VA 22314-3428
703-518-6360

Sources of Information
Employment
Human Resources
1775 Duke St.
Alexandria, VA 22314-3428
703-518-6510

Federally Insured Credit Unions
Freedom of Information Officer
National Credit Union Administration

1775 Duke St.
Room 4026
Alexandria, VA 22314-3428
703-838-0401

Office of Public and Congressional Affairs
National Credit Union Administration
1775 Duke St.
Alexandria, VA 22314-3428
703-518-6330

National Foundation on the Arts and the Humanities

National Endowment for the Arts
1100 Pennsylvania Ave., NW
Washington, DC 20506
202-682-5400

National Endowment for the Humanities
1100 Pennsylvania Ave., NW
Washington, DC 20506
202-606-8438

Education Grants
Arts and Education Programs
1100 Pennsylvania Ave., NW
Washington, DC 20506
202-682-5426

Research
Division of Research Programs
1100 Pennsylvania Ave., NW
Washington, DC 20506
202-682-5432

State Grants
Division of State Programs
1100 Pennsylvania Ave., NW
Washington, DC 20506
202-682-5753

Challenge Grants
Office of Challenge Grants
1100 Pennsylvania Ave., NW
Washington, DC 20506
202-682-5436

Public Affairs
1100 Pennsylvania Ave., NW
Washington, DC 20506
202-682-5400, ext. 4

Institute of Museum Services
Program Director
Room 510
1100 Pennsylvania Ave., NW
Washington, DC 20506
202-606-8536

National Labor Relations Board

1099 14th St., NW
Washington, DC 20570
202-273-1000

Information Division
1099 14th St., NW
Washington, DC 20570
202-273-1991

National Mediation Board

1301 K St., NW
Suite 250E
Washington, DC 20572
202-523-5920

Be patient. If any phone number is incorrect, call (area code) 555-1212 and request the new listing.

National Railroad Passenger Corporation (AMTRAK)
60 Massachusetts Ave., NE
Washington, DC 20002
202-906-3000

Public Affairs
Public Affairs Department
60 Massachusetts Ave., NE
Washington, DC 20002
202-906-3860

National Science Foundation
4201 Wilson Blvd.
Arlington, VA 22230
703-306-1234

Sources of Information
Board and Committee Minutes
National Science Board Office
4201 Wilson Blvd., Room 1220N
Arlington, VA 22230
703-306-2000

Contracts
4201 Wilson Blvd., Room 475
Arlington, VA 22230
703-306-1242

Employment
Division of Human Resource Management
4201 Wilson Blvd., Room 3048
Arlington, VA 22230
703-306-1182

Fellowships
Directorate for Education and Human Resources
4201 Wilson Blvd., Room 805N
Arlington, VA 22230
703-306-1600

Freedom of Information Act
FOIA REQUEST
General Council
4201 Wilson Blvd., Room 1265
Arlington, VA 22230
703-306-1060

Inspector General
Office of Inspector General
4201 Wilson Blvd., Room 1135S
Arlington, VA 22230
703-306-2100

Privacy Act Requests
General Council
4201 Wilson Blvd., Room 1265
Arlington, VA 22230
703-306-1060

Publications
National Science Foundation
Forms and Publications
4201 Wilson Blvd., Room P-15
Arlington, VA 22230
703-306-1130

Reading Room
National Science Foundation Library
4201 Wilson Blvd., Room 225
Arlington, VA 22230
703-306-0658

Small Business Activities
Office of Small Business and Disadvantaged Business Utilization
4201 Wilson Blvd., Room 590
Arlington, VA 22230
703-306-1390

Legislative and Public Affairs
4201 Wilson Blvd., Room 1245S
Arlington, VA 22230
703-306-1070

National Transportation Safety Board
490 L'Enfant Plaza, SW
Washington, DC 20594
202-382-6600

Sources of Information
Contracts
Contracting Officer
Financial Management Division
490 L'Enfant Plaza
Washington, DC 20594
202-382-6539

Employment
Human Resources Division
490 L'Enfant Plaza, SW
Washington, DC 20594
202-382-6717

Publications
Public Inquiries Section
490 L'Enfant Plaza, SW
Washington, DC 20594
202-382-6735

Reading Room
Public Inquiries Section
490 L'Enfant Plaza, SW
Washington, DC 20594
202-382-6735

Public Affairs
490 L'Enfant Plaza, SW
Washington, DC 20594
202-382-0660

Nuclear Regulatory Commission
11555 Rockville Pike
Rockville, MD 20852
301-415-7000

Sources of Information
Contracts
Small and Disadvantaged Business Utilization and Civil Rights
11555 Rockville Pike
Rockville, MD 20852
301-415-7380

Employment
Office of Personnel
Nuclear Regulatory Commission
11555 Rockville Pike
Rockville, MD 20852
301-415-7530

Freedom of Information Act Requests
Director
Division of Freedom of Information and Publication Services
Nuclear Regulatory Commission
11555 Rockville Pike
Rockville, MD 20852
301-415-7175

Reading Rooms
Public Document Room
2120 L St., NW

Washington, DC 20555
202-634-3273

Records
Director
Division of Freedom of Information
 and Publication Services
Nuclear Regulatory Commission
11555 Rockville Pike
Rockville, MD 20852
301-415-7175

Office of Governmental and Public Affairs
Nuclear Regulatory Commission
11555 Rockville Pike
Rockville, MD 20852
301-415-8200

Occupational Safety and Health Review Commission

1120 20th St., NW, 9th Floor
Washington, DC 20036-3419
202-606-5100

Office of Government Ethics

Suite 500
1201 New York Ave., NW
Washington, DC 20005-3917
202-619-5757

Office of Personnel Management

1900 E St., NW
Washington, DC 20415-0001
202-606-1800

Inspector General
1900 E St., NW
Room 6400
Washington, DC 20415
202-606-1200

Sources of Information
Contracts
Chief
Procurement Division
Administration Group
1900 E St., NW, Room SB427
Washington, DC 20415
202-606-2240

Employment
Office of Personnel
Room 1447
1900 E St., NW
Washington, DC 20415
202-606-2400

Publications
1900 E St., NW
Washington, DC 20415
202-606-1822

Office of Communications
1900 E St., NW, Room 5F12
Washington, DC 20415-0001
202-606-1800

Office of Special Counsel

Suite 216
730 M St., NW
Washington, DC 20036
202-653-7188
800-872-9855

Panama Canal Commission

1825 I St., NW, Suite 1050
Washington, DC 20006-5402
202-634-6441

Peace Corps

1990 K St., NW
Washington, DC 20526
202-606-3886; 800-424-8580

Sources of Information
Recruiting
Public Response Unit
1990 K St., NW
Washington, DC 20526
800-424-8580
202-606-2445

Employment
Office of Personnel Management
1990 K St., NW
Washington, DC 20526
202-606-3336

Office of External Affairs
Press Office
1990 K St., NW
Washington, DC 20526
202-606-3010

Pennsylvania Avenue Development Corporation

Suite 1220 North
1331 Pennsylvania Ave., NW
Washington, DC 20004-1703
202-724-9091

Director of Corporate Affairs
Suite 1220 North
1331 Pennsylvania Ave., NW
Washington, DC 20004-1703
202-724-9062

Pension Benefit Guaranty Corporation

1200 K St., NW
Washington, DC 20005-4026
202-326-4000

Postal Rate Commission

1333 H St., NW, Suite 300
Washington, DC 20268-0001
202-789-6800

Secretary
1333 H St., NW, Suite 300
Washington, DC 20268-0001
202-789-6840

Railroad Retirement Board

844 North Rush St.
Chicago, IL 60611-2092
312-751-4500

Office of Public Affairs
844 North Rush St.
Chicago, IL 60611-2092
312-751-4777

Washington Legislative/Liaison Office
1310 G St., NW, Suite 500
Washington, DC 20005-3004
202-272-7742

Resolution Trust Corporation

(The Resolution Trust Corporation was discontinued in December, 1995.
Its business was taken over by the Federal Deposit Insurance Corporation.)

Securities and Exchange Commission

450 5th St., NW
Washington, DC 20549
202-942-8088

Office of Public Affairs
450 5th St., SW
Washington, DC 20549
202-942-0020

Publications - a monthly summary of security transactions is available through:
Superintendent of Documents
Government Printing Office
Washington, DC 20402
202-512-1800

Contracts
Office of Administrative Services
450 5th St., SW
Washington, DC 20549
202-942-4990

Employment
Office of Human Resources Management
450 5th St., SW
Washington, DC 20549
202-942-4144

Reading Rooms
Library
450 5th St., SW
Washington, DC 20549
202-942-7090

Small Business Activities
450 5th St., SW
Washington, DC 20549
202-942-2950

Selective Service System

National Headquarters
1515 Wilson Blvd.
Arlington, VA 22209-2425
703-235-2555

Office of Public Affairs
National Headquarters
1515 Wilson Blvd.
Arlington, VA 22209-2425
703-235-2053

Employment
Director, Selective Service System
Attn: RMH
1515 Wilson Blvd.
Arlington, VA 22209-2425
703-235-2258

Procurement
Director, Selective Service System
Attn: RML
1515 Wilson Blvd.
Arlington, VA 22209-2425
703-235-2209

Small Business Administration

409 Third St., SW
Washington, DC 20416
202-205-6533

Locator
409 Third St., SW
Washington, DC 20416
202-205-6600

Answer Desk
409 Third St., SW
Washington, DC 20416
800-U-ASK-SBA

Office of Financial Assistance
409 Third St., SW, 8th Floor
Washington, DC 20416
202-205-6490

Disaster Assistance
409 Third St., SW
Washington, DC 20416
202-205-6734

Investment
Divesture Insurance
409 Third St., SW, Suite 8100
Washington, DC 20416
202-205-6510

Surety Guarantee
Suite 8600
409 Third St., SW
Washington, DC 20416
202-205-6540

Procurement Assistance
409 Third St., SW
Washington, DC 20416
202-205-6460

Business Initiatives, Education and Training
409 Third St., SW
Washington, DC 20416
202-205-6665

Minority Small Business Development
409 Third St., SW
Washington, DC 20416
202-205-6410

Advocacy
Suite 7800
409 Third St., SW
Washington, DC 20416
202-205-6533

Women's Business Ownership
409 Third St., SW
Washington, DC 20416
202-205-6673

Veterans Affairs
409 Third St., SW
Washington, DC 20416
202-205-6773

Office of Technology
409 Third St., SW
Washington, DC 20416
202-205-6450

International Trade
409 Third St., SW
Washington, DC 20416
202-205-6720

Small Business Development Centers
409 Third St., SW
Washington, DC 20416
202-205-6766

Be patient. If any phone number is incorrect, call (area code) 555-1212 and request the new listing.

71

Information Starting Places

Public Affairs
409 Third St., SW
Washington, DC 20416
202-205-6533

Tennessee Valley Authority

1 Massachusetts Ave., NW
Washington, DC 20444-0001
202-289-2999
or
400 West Summit Hill Dr.
Knoxville, TN 37902
615-632-2101

Citizen Participation
Corporate Communications and Education
ET PB 25H
400 West Summit Hill Dr.
Knoxville, TN 37902-1499
615-632-8033

Contracts
Division of Purchasing
1101 Market St.
Chattanooga, TN 37401-2127
615-751-2624

Electric Power Supply and Rates
Electrical Systems Operations
1101 Market St.
Chattanooga, TN 37402-2801
615-751-8678

Employment
Human Resources Services
ET 5D 93U
400 West Summit Hill Drive
Knoxville, TN 37902-1499
615-632-7744
Fax: 615-632-7152

Environmental and Energy Education
TVA Energy Education/Information Programs
4125 Greenway Rd.
Knoxville, TN 37918
615-673-2270

Environmental Management
Resource Development
400 W. Summit Hill Dr.
Knoxville, TN 37902-1499
615-632-6578

Economic Development
Resource Group in Economic Development
400 Summit Hill Drive
Knoxville, TN 37901-1499
615-632-4405

Maps
Geographic Information and Engineering
HBIA
311 Broad St.
Chattanooga, TN 37402-2801
615-751-6277

Medical Program
Health Services
1101 Market St.
Chattanooga, TN 37402-2801
615-751-2091

Publications
Public Relations
ET 7 D-K
400 W. Summit Hill Drive

Knoxville, TN 37902-1499
615-632-8039

Recreation
Land Resources
Forestry Bldg.
Ridgeway Road
Norris, TN 37828
615-632-1600

Technical Library
Technical Library Services
ETPC-K
400 W. Summit Hill Drive
Knoxville, TN 37902-1499
615-632-3033

Public Affairs
Regional Communications
Tennessee Valley Authority
400 West Summit Hill Dr.
Knoxville, TN 37902-1499
615-632-8000
or
Washington Office
1 Massachusetts Ave., NW
Suite 300
Washington, DC 20001
202-898-2999

Thrift Depositor Protection Oversight Board

808 17th St., NW
Washington, DC 20232
202-416-2650

Public Affairs
808 17th St., NW
Washington, DC 20232
202-416-2622

United States Arms Control and Disarmament Agency

320 21st St, NW
Washington, DC 20451
202-647-8677

Contracts
Contracting Office
320 21st St., NW
Washington, DC 20451
703-235-3288

Public Affairs
Room 5843
320 21st St., NW
Washington, DC 20451
202-647-8677

Speakers
320 21st St., NW
Washington, DC 20451
202-647-8677

United States Information Agency

301 4th St., SW
Washington, DC 20547
202-619-4700 (recording)
202-619-5618

Public Affairs
Office of the Public Liaison
301 4th St., SW
Washington, DC 20547
202-619-4355

Be patient. If any phone number is incorrect, call (area code) 555-1212 and request the new listing.

Administrative Regulations
Directives, Forms, and Records
Management Staff
301 4th St., SW
Washington, DC 20547
202-619-5680

Contracts
Office of Contracts
301 4th St., SW
Washington, DC 20547
202-205-5498

Employment
Special Recruitment Staff
Office of Personnel
301 4th St., SW, Room 518
Washington, DC 20547
202-619-4659

United States International Development Cooperation Agency

320 21st St., NW
Washington, DC 20523-0001
202-647-9620

Agency for International Development
320 21st St., NW
Washington, DC 20523-0001
202-647-9620

Public Affairs
Office of the Public Liaison
320 21st St., NW
Washington, DC 20523-0001
202-647-4274

Congressional Affairs
Bureau for Legislative Affairs
Agency for International Development
320 21st St., NW
Washington, DC 20523-0001
202-647-4274

Employment
Recruiting Division
Office of Human Resources Development
2401 E St., NW, Room 1026
Washington, DC 20523-0001
202-663-2368

Contracts
Office of Small and Disadvantaged Business Utilization
1100 Wilson Blvd.
Roslyn, VA 22201
703-875-1551

Trade and Development Program
Director
Room 309, State Annex 16
Washington, DC 20523
703-875-4357

Overseas Private Investment Corporation
Information Office
1100 New York Ave., NW
Washington, DC 20527
202-336-8400

United States International Trade Commission

500 E St., SW
Washington, DC 20436
202-205-2000

United States Postal Service

475 L'Enfant Plaza, SW
Washington, DC 20260
202-268-2000

Consumer Advocate
475 L'Enfant Plaza, SW
Washington, DC 20260
202-268-2284

Marketing Department
475 L'Enfant Plaza, SW
Washington, DC 20260
202-268-3916

Postal Inspection
475 L'Enfant Plaza, SW
Washington, DC 20260
202-268-4293

Contracts
Purchasing, Supply, and Diversity
475 L'Enfant Plaza, SW
Washington, DC 20260
202-268-4140

Employment
Labor Relations
475 L'Enfant Plaza, SW
Washington, DC 20260
202-268-3783

Films
Corporate Relations
475 L'Enfant Plaza, SW
Washington, DC 20260
202-268-2191

Philatelic Information
Stamp Marketing
475 L'Enfant Plaza, SW
Washington, DC 20260-2420
202-268-2312

Philatelic Sales
Philatelic Sales Branch
U.S. Postal Service
8300 NE Underground Dr., Pillar 210
Kansas City, MO 64144-9998
816-545-1100

Reading Rooms
11th Floor North
Library Division
475 L'Enfant Plaza, SW
Washington, DC 20260
202-268-2900

Speakers
Corporate Relations
475 L'Enfant Plaza, SW
Washington, DC 20260
202-268-2155

Hotlines

- *A database on foreign owned agricultural land in the U.S.;*
- *Audiovisual materials on foreign language instruction;*
- *Recalls on automobiles purchased in the past 10 years;*
- *Just about any kind of map ranging from road maps to highly specialized maps;*
- *Finance records of political candidates;*
- *Inventory of houses acquired from failed savings and loan companies;*
- *Assistance to small businesses in complying with environmental regulations;*
- *Status of bills pending in State legislatures;*
- *Free eye care for the elderly;*
- *A hearing test by telephone; and*
- *Recorded messages of job vacancies in federal government agencies.*

Do you know that this kind of information can be obtained by one toll-free telephone call? These "hotline" numbers may be set up by state or federal agencies or nonprofit organizations, who are more than willing to answer your inquiries or provide you with publications, most of which will be sent to you free of charge.

Hotline numbers often are thought of as emergency numbers or numbers to be called in a crisis situation. Although many hotline numbers are emergency response numbers such as the Chemical Manufacturers Association chemical spills or explosions emergency assistance hotline or U.S. Department of Health and Human Services food and drug emergency advice line, the majority of hotlines are informational. They are staffed by experts who can answer your questions or are clearinghouses with personnel eager to send you their publications.

Many hotlines are simply recorded messages of information, providing the answers to the organization's most asked questions. The U.S. Department of Commerce/Bureau of Economic Analysis has four such recorded messages, including information on leading economic indicators, quarterly estimates of the gross national product, statistical information on personal income, and U.S. international transactions. The U.S. Department of Health and Human Services/Centers for Disease Control has three recorded messages on AIDS giving you statistical information such as the number of cases and deaths among age groups, the ten states with the highest number of cases, and projections of deaths by 1992.

Hotline numbers are usually, but not necessarily, toll-free 800 numbers. Due to budget cuts, many numbers of the Federal government, which were previously toll free, are now commercial numbers, although their function remains the same.

Some of the 800 numbers of hotlines listed below cannot be reached from all calling areas. An 800 number sometimes cannot be used when dialing within the same metropolitan area, state, or area code where the organization is located. In these instances, the commercial number is given in addition to the toll free number. Generally, the toll-free numbers for state government agencies are valid only within the state. There are a few exceptions to this, such as 800 numbers for State Offices of Tourism and some State tax information hotlines.

Hotlines provide many types of assistance, ranging from informational to direct financial or other types of direct intervention assistance. Here are some examples of the types of assistance individuals have received from hotline organizations:

National Health Organizations Help Disabled Child Win Medicaid and SSI Benefits
A child with congenital brain damage, mental retardation, eye problems, and paralysis on the right side was denied Supplemental Security Income (SSI) and Medicaid by the Social Security Administration based on insufficient disability. The decision was appealed and brought before the U.S. Supreme Court. The American Academy of Pediatrics, the National Organization for Rare Disorders and the Spina Bifida Association among others filed an Amicus brief on behalf of the child. Making reference to the Amicus brief, the Supreme Court ruled that Social Security benefits are improperly being denied because child claimants are held to a higher standard than adults. As a result of this decision, the child, as well as many others previously denied benefits, will now receive them.

New York State Receives Assistance with Drug Prevention Program
The State of New York's Section V (an 11-county area) decided to implement a long-range chemical health program for student athletes. The steering committee of Operation Offense, the name adopted for their program, asked State High School Associations' TARGET professionals to come to New York to train athletic directors or coaches to become workshop leaders. In the next eight months, over 5,000 coaches, parents and athletes were reached by the Operation Offense program.

Counseling and Morale Support from MADD
Parents who lost a child as a result of drunk driving phone Mothers Against Drunk Driving and talk to a counselor who lost a daughter to a drunk driver. The counselor talks to them, subsequently helps them through the criminal justice system, and even goes to court with them to provide them with morale support.

Women's Sports Foundation Gives Financial Assistance to Athletes
Bonnie Blair, a speed skater, who received the WSF Up and Coming Athlete Award in 1986, went on to win a gold medal at

the 1988 Olympics. Sheila Conover, a luger, received a grant from WSF and became a double gold medalist in the 1987 Pan American Games.

A list of hotlines follows, in alphabetical order by agency or organization under main subject headings:

Agriculture and Botany

U.S. Department of Agriculture (USDA)
Recorded message of agricultural news
202-488-8358

U.S. Department of Agriculture (USDA)
Meat and Poultry Hotline
800-535-4555

U.S. Department of Agriculture (USDA)
USDA Information Center
202-720-2791

U.S. Department of Agriculture (USDA)
Office of Inspector General
202-720-8001

U.S. Department of Agriculture (USDA)
To order publications, databases and subscriptions on agricultural trade and economics
800-999-6779

USDA/Ag NewsFax Service
Up to 10 documents may be requested per call
202-690-3944

USDA/Agricultural Research Service
Information on activities of ARS
202-344-2340

USDA/Economic Research Service
To order database on Foreign Owned Agricultural Land (No. 87015)
800-999-6779

USDA/Foreign Agricultural Service
To access foreign agricultural news releases by Fax machine
202-720-7115; Fax: 202-690-3944

USDA/National Agricultural Library (ALF)
An electronic bulletin board for the exchange of agricultural information
301-504-6510, 5111, 5496, 5497
Technical Assistance: 301-504-5113

U.S. Botanic Gardens
Recorded message of upcoming events
202-225-7099

U.S. Botanic Gardens
Talk to a botanist about plant care
202-226-4082

Banks and Investments

Commodity Futures Trading Commission
To file complaints about commodity brokers or firms
202-254-3067

Federal Deposit Insurance Corporation (FDIC)
For information and to file complaints about FDIC insured banks
800-934-3342

Federal Deposit Insurance Corporation (FDIC) Fax and Bulletin Board Systems
Documents are available via fax machine or may be downloaded to your computer
Fax: 804-642-0003; BBS: 804-642-2737

Federal Reserve Banks throughout the USA with recorded messages announcing future auctions of Treasury securities (Bills, Bonds, and Notes) and interest rates and other auction results:

Atlanta, Georgia:	404-521-8500
Birmingham, Alabama:	205-731-8500 x702
Boston, Massachusetts:	617-973-3000
Buffalo, New York:	716-849-5000
Chicago, Illinois:	312-322-5322
Denver, Colorado:	303-572-2300
Detroit, Michigan:	313-961-6880
Kansas City, Missouri:	816-881-2000
Louisville, Kentucky:	502-568-9200
Miami, Florida:	305-591-2065 general information
	305-471-6257 interest rates
New Orleans, Louisiana:	504-593-3200
N.Y., New York:	212-720-5000
Oklahoma City, Oklahoma:	405-270-8400
Omaha, Nebraska:	402-221-5500
Philadelphia, Pennsylvania:	215-574-6000
Pittsburgh, Pennsylvania:	412-261-7800
Portland, Oregon:	503-221-5900 (future auction schedules)
	503-221-5921 (results of recent auctions)
Salt Lake City, Utah:	801-322-7900
San Antonio, Texas:	210-978-1200 x330
San Francisco, California:	415-974-2000
Seattle, Washington:	206-343-3600
St. Louis, Missouri:	314-444-8444

Federal Reserve Board
Recorded message on statistical releases, board meetings, testimony, etc.
202-452-3206

Federal Reserve Board
Recorded message regarding bank holding companies' applications and orders
202-452-3207

Federal Reserve System
Consumer Affairs Line
202-452-3946

Securities and Exchange Commission
Recorded message of information on publications, investor inquiries/complaints, broker/dealer registration, etc.
800-SEC-0330

U.S. Department of the Treasury/Bureau of Public Debt
Recorded message on Treasury Bill, Note, and Bond offerings, auction results, U.S. Savings Bond information, etc.
202-874-4000

Recorded message of information on U.S. Savings Bonds, etc.
800-US-BONDS

Books, Audiovisual Materials, Libraries, and Records

Government Printing Office (GPO)
To place an order or obtain information on new government books
202-512-1800

Government Printing Office (GPO)
To order special publications such as regulations
202-512-2457

Government Printing Office (GPO)
To check on a subscription
202-512-2303

Library of Congress
Information about the Library of Congress and its holdings
202-707-5522

Library of Congress
Recorded message regarding major exhibitions on display
202-707-8000

Library of Congress
Recorded message on using the Library of Congress
202-707-6400

Information Starting Places

National Archives and Records Administration
  Recorded message on events at the National Archives
  202-501-5000

National Audiovisual Center
  Audiovisual materials on foreign languages, fire safety, wildlife, etc.
  800-222-0109

Smithsonian Institution
  To order Smithsonian records and books, including *A Smithsonian Book of Comic-Book Comics*
  800-927-7377

U.S. Department of Defense (DOD)/Public Communications
  To inquire about or order DOD publications
  703-697-5737

Business and the Economy

Nebraska Department of Economic Development
  Nebraska marketing, demographic and economic information
  800-426-6505

Senior Corps of Retired Executives (SCORE)
  Information about SCORE and referrals
  202-205-6762

Small Business Administration (SBA)
  Small Business facts, financing and development programs, including SCORE information and the SBA Bulletin Board
  800-827-5722
  202-205-6533

U.S. Department of Commerce
  Information/assistance to small businesses
  202-482-1472

U.S. Department of Labor
  Recorded message of departmental news
  202-606-7828

Civil Rights

Commission on Civil Rights
  To file civil rights complaints
  202-376-8513
  800-552-6843

Equal Employment Opportunity Commission
  How to file EEO complaints
  800-669-3362

U.S. Department of Justice
  Redress information for Japanese Americans interred during World War II
  202-219-6900

U.S. Department of Justice/Community Relations Service
  Assist people with discrimination cases and hate groups in neighborhoods
  202-514-1026

Commerce, Interstate
(For Foreign Commerce see Trade)

Interstate Commerce Commission (ICC)
  Recorded message giving diesel fuel price for the day, ICC news releases, telephone directory, and other information
  202-927-7600

Communications

Federal Communications Commission (FCC)
  Actions taken by FCC and public notices are available via Internet at http://www.fcc.gov or ftp.fcc.gov or by fax service
  202-632-7000; Fax Service: 202-418-2830

Consumer Power

Consumer Product Safety Commission
  Consumer product safety information, recalls, complaints, and publications
  800-638-2772; 800-638-8270 TDD
  800-492-8104 TDD in Maryland; Fax Service: 301-504-0124

Consumer Product Safety Commission
  Recorded message announcing meetings
  301-504-0709

Interstate Commerce Commission
  Complaints about household movers
  202-927-5500

Postal Rate Commission
  Recorded message regarding hearings on postal rates and mail classifications
  202-789-6874

State consumer protection offices for information on filing complaints and access to records, by state (all numbers are in-state only):

Alabama . . . . 800-392-5658; 800-392-8050 Utility Company Complaints
Arizona . . . . 800-352-8431; 800-222-7000 Utility Company Complaints
Arkansas 800-482-8982
  800-482-1164 Utility Company Complaints
California . . . . 800-649-7570 Utility Company Complaints
  800-952-5210 Auto Repair Complaints
  800-927-4357 Insurance Information and Complaints
Connecticut 800-842-2649
  800-538-2277 Lemon Law complaints for new automobile purchases
  800-382-4586 Utility Company Complaints
Delaware . . . . 800-443-2179 Sussex County
  800-282-8574 Utility Company Complaints
Florida . . . . 800-321-5366 Toll Free Lemon Law
  800-851-7352
  800-342-2762 Insurance Company Complaints
  800-342-3552 Utility Company Complaints
Georgia 800-869-1123
  800-282-5813 Utility Company Complaints
Illinois . . . . 800-252-8666 complaints and information only
Idaho 800-432-3545
Indiana 800-382-5516
  800-851-4268 Utility Company Complaints
Kansas 800-432-2310
  800-662-0027 Utility Company Complaints
Louisiana . . . . 800-256-2413 Utility Company Complaints
Maine 800-332-8529
Maryland . . . . 800-685-0123 Utility Company Complaints
Michigan . . . . 800-292-9555 Utility Company Complaints
  also 800-443-8926 TDD
Minnesota . . . . 800-657-3782 Consumer Affairs
  800-652-9747 Utility Company Complaints
Mississippi . . . . 800-356-6428 Utility Company Complaints North District
  800-356-6430 Utility Company Complaints Central Districts
  800-356-6429 Utility Company Complaints South District
Missouri 800-392-8222
  800-392-4211 Utility Company Complaints
Nebraska . . . . 800-526-0017 Utility Company Complaints
Nevada 800-992-0900
New Hampshire . . . . 800-852-3793 Utility Company Complaints
New Jersey . . . . 800-242-5846 Tapes on various subjects,
  including Lemon Law, Truth-in-Lending
  800-624-0241 Utility Company Complaints
New Mexico 800-678-1508
  800-663-9782 Utility Company Complaints
New York . . . . 800-342-3377 Utility Company Complaints
  800-342-3355 Utility Company Complaints--
  unwarranted shut-off of a utility (emergencies)
North Dakota 800-472-2600
  800-932-2400 Utility Company Complaints
Ohio 800-899-5253
  800-282-0515 Business and Product Complaints
  800-686-7826 Utility Company Complaints
Oklahoma . . . . 800-522-8154 Utility Company Complaints
Oregon . . . . 800-522-2404 Utility Company Complaints
Pennsylvania . . . . 800-782-1110 Utility Company Complaints
  800-441-2555 Consumer Affairs

Be patient. If any phone number is incorrect, call (area code) 555-1212 and request the new listing.

Rhode Island	800-852-7776
	800-341-1000
South Carolina	800-922-1594
	800-922-1531 Utility Company Complaints
South Dakota	800-300-1986 Consumer Affairs
	800-332-1782 Utility Company Complaints
Tennessee	800-342-8385
	800-342-8359 Utility Company Complaints
Vermont	800-622-4496 Utility Company Complaints
	800-649-2424 Consumer Affairs
Virginia	800-552-9963
	800-552-7945 Utility Company Complaints
Washington	800-551-4636
	800-300-1846 Utility Company Complaints
West Virginia	800-368-8808
	800-344-5113 Utility Company Complaints
	800-247-8789 Motor Carrier Complaints
Wisconsin	800-362-8189
	800-225-7729 Utility Company Complaints

U.S. Department of Agriculture
Food safety information and to report illness from meat, poultry or eggs
800-535-4555

U.S. Department of Labor/Bureau of Labor Statistics
Recorded message regarding indicators, including consumer and producer price indexes, employment cost index, etc.
202-606-7828

Copyright Information
Library of Congress
Copyright information
202-707-3000

Courses
Boating correspondence course entitled "The Skipper's Course"
719-544-3142

National Credit Union
Examiner training programs
202-682-9640

National Federation of State High School Associations
Under TARGET Program, training seminars for teachers and other professionals on chemical use and prevention
816-464-5400

National Resource Center on Child Sexual Abuse
Training for professionals
800-KIDS-006

U.S. Department of State
One-day seminar on foreign policy and business opportunities abroad for Vice Presidents of companies doing business
202-647-4000

U.S. Department of the Treasury/Internal Revenue Service
Under VITA program, free courses in return for tax preparation and small business tax education course
800-829-1040, x9049

Crimes, Criminals and Criminal Law
Anonymous Witness Reporting System
To report major crimes
800-782-7463; 800-78-CRIME in California

U.S. Department of Justice/Bureau of Justice Statistics
Publications providing statistical information on prisoners
800-732-3277

Justice/Bureau of Justice Statistics
Information on juvenile justice publications and database searches
800-638-8736

Justice/National Institute of Justice
Publications and database searches for criminal justice-related information, statistics and publications
800-851-3420

U.S. Secret Service
Information about criminal activities and protective responsibilities
202-435-5800

Defense and the Military
Defense/Air Force
Health Profession Scholarships in return for military service
800-531-5980

Defense/Army
Recorded message of information for problems with army retirees' paychecks
800-428-2290

Defense/Civilian Health and Medical Program of the Uniformed Services
Information regarding benefits
303-361-1000

Defense/Defense Mapping Agency
Guidance on obtaining maps and charts of the Defense Mapping Agency
800-826-0342

Defense/Defense Nuclear Agency
Radiation exposure by veterans in Hiroshima/Nagasaki or participating in nuclear tests
800-462-3683

Defense/Navy
Naval recruitment and opportunities
800-327-NAVY

U.S. Naval Academy
Recorded message (M-F 5pm-8pm, weekends and holidays) regarding admissions information, nominations and appointments, application materials, etc.
800-638-9156

U.S. Naval Reserves
Recorded message to leave name/number for someone to call back
800-USA-USNR

Selective Service
Selective Service registration and status
708-688-6888

Veterans Administration
Prisoners of War assistance with receiving checks, hospital problems, etc.
800-827-1000

Veterans Administration
Information on CHAMPVA, medical benefits for dependents of disabled veterans or veterans whose death was service related
800-733-8387

Disaster Relief
Federal Emergency Management Agency (FEMA)
Information on National Flood Insurance Program regulations, claims, conferences and maps
800-638-6620; 301-731-5300 in DC

FEMA - National Emergency and Training Learning Resource Center
Publications and bibliographies on emergency management information
800-638-1821; 301-447-1030

FEMA
To order maps showing flood-prone areas
800-358-9616

FEMA
Document available via fax
202-646-FEMA

Information Starting Places

Drugs and Chemical Dependency

Al-Anon
    Referral service to support group meetings
    800-344-2666

Alcohol and Chemical Dependency Rehabilitation for the Elderly
    Treatment center at Hopedale Hall, Hopedale, Illinois
    800-354-7089
    800-344-0824 in Illinois

Alcohol and Drug Help Referral Hotline
    Information, referrals and 24 hour a day counseling
    800-252-6465

Drug Free Workplace Helpline/U.S. Department of Health and Human Services
    Assistance on implementing drug-free workplace programs
    800-843-4971

Just Say No! International
    Publications, consultations, grant information
    800-258-2766

Mothers Against Drunk Driving (MADD)
    Information, victims assistance, and referrals
    800-438-6233

Health Connection
    Publications, videos, display posters on drug, alcohol, and smoking prevention
    and education
    800-548-8700

National Clearinghouse for Alcohol and Drug Information
    Publications and grant information
    800-729-6686
    301-468-2600

National Cocaine Hotline
    Information and referrals
    800-COC-AINE

National Council on Alcoholism and Drug Dependence Hope Line
    Information and publications on alcoholism and drug addiction
    800-NCA-CALL

National Family Partnership
    Parent information line and training about drugs
    314-968-1322; 314-845-1933
    Fax: 314-845-2117

National Institute on Drug Abuse Hotline/HHS
    Information and referrals
    800-662-HELP

Pride Institute - Chemical Dependency Treatment Center
    Inpatient facility in Eden Prairie, Minnesota, treating alcohol- and/or drug-
    dependent lesbians and gay men
    800-54-PRIDE

State High School Associations Target Programs
    Information, publications and drug and alcohol education for K-12
    800-366-6667

U.S. Department of Education
    To order What Works--Schools Without Drugs and
    A Parent's Guide to Prevention
    800-624-0100

U.S. Department of Health and Human Services/Alcohol, Drug Abuse and
Mental Health Administration
    Information about drugs in the workplace program
    800-843-4971

U.S. Department of the Interior/No Drugs in the Workplace
    Recorded message of information regarding AIDS, alcohol, illegal drugs, drug
    testing procedures, personal counseling, etc.
    800-628-DRUG

Education

Bilingual and minority language training and technical assistance:
    Evaluation Assistance Center--Georgetown University
    800-925-EACE
    RMC Research Corp.
    800-258-0802

ERIC Clearinghouse on Adult Career and Vocational Education
    Adult vocational and continuing education programs
    800-848-4815, x3

ERIC Document Reproduction Service
    To order copies of ERIC documents announced in Resources in Education
    800-443-ERIC

National Clearinghouse for Bilingual Information
    Bilingual education information for educators
    800-321-6223

State Clearinghouses for Adult Education for Virginia
    Information to improve basic skills
    800-237-0178; 804-828-6521
    804-828-6161

U.S. Department of Education
    Educational research and improvement statistics
    800-424-1616

Education/Federal Student Aid Information Center
    General and technical information regarding application process and Federal
    policy
    800-433-3243

Education/Office of Educational Research and Improvement
    OERI Electronic Bulletin Board for accessing education information
    800-424-1616; Data: 800-222-4922

Education/Office of Intergovernmental Affairs
    Information regarding the application process for the President's Academic
    Fitness Line
    202-401-3644

Education/Office of Postsecondary Education
    Information on Pell Grant Program
    800-433-3243

ERIC Clearinghouse for Rural Education and Small Schools
    800-624-9120

ORYX Press
    Publishes Current Index to Journals in Education, the Thesaurus of ERIC
    Descriptors and other ERIC publications
    800-279-ORYX

Access ERIC
    Provides referral services for the Educational Resources Information Center
    800-LET-ERIC

Employment and Job Training

AmeriCorps
    Volunteers in Service to America information on applying or services
    800-94-ACORPS; 202-606-5000

Administrative Office of the U.S. Courts
    Job vacancy number
    202-273-2777

National Archives and Records Administration
    Job information and vacancies
    800-827-4898

National Science Foundation
    Job information and vacancies
    800-628-1487

Be patient. If any phone number is incorrect, call (area code) 555-1212 and request the new listing.

Office of Personnel Management Career America Connection
Recorded message of information about jobs with the U.S. Government
202-606-2700

Peace Corps
Recorded message of information about activities, application procedures and job vacancies
800-424-8580 x2

U.S. Department of Labor
Recorded message about job information and vacancies
800-366-2753

Labor/Employment and Training Administration
Recorded message of information on Job Corps for Youths
800-733-JOBS

Labor/Women's Bureau
Technical information and papers regarding workforce quality
800-827-5335

U.S. Navy
Naval recruitment and opportunities
800-327-NAVY

Energy

Nuclear Regulatory Commission (NRC)
Recorded message announcing Nuclear Reactor Regulations meetings
301-415-1292

Nuclear Regulatory Commission (NRC)
NRC Local Public Document Rooms
800-638-8081

Energy/Energy Efficiency and Renewable Energy Clearinghouse (EREC)
Conservation and renewable energy information, publications and referrals
800-363-3732; 800-523-2929; BBS: 800-273-2955

Energy/Energy Efficiency and Renewable Energy Network (EREN)
Energy; appropriate technology assistance service and conservation information
303-275-4035; Data: 305-275-INFO

Energy/Federal Energy Regulatory Commission (FERC)
FERC Hotline Enforcement Task Force: Complaints or questions concerning gas and electric power companies or to report violations of FERC regulations
202-208-1390

Energy/Federal Energy Regulatory Commission (FERC)
FERC Daily Issuance Hotline: Recorded message of FERC documents and orders issued daily
202-208-1371; BBS: 202-208-1397

Energy/National Energy Information Center
Information, research and orders for publications
202-586-8800

Environment

Chemical Manufacturers Association
Chemical spills, explosions, etc., emergency response assistance
800-424-9300

Chemical Manufacturers Trade Association
Referrals for health and safety information on industrial chemicals
800-CMA-8200

Environmental Protection Agency (EPA)/Small Business Ombudsman Hotline
Asbestos handling and abatement in schools, home and workplace information and assistance to small businesses in complying with regulations
800-368-5888; 703-305-5938 in Washington, DC

Environmental Protection Agency (EPA)
Chemical spills; community planning and procedural information
800-535-0202; 703-412-9877
TDD: 800-553-7672

Infoterra
International environmental information
202-260-5917

Environmental Protection Agency (EPA) Headquarters, Washington, DC
EPA/Hazardous Waste Ombudsman assistance on hazardous waste issues
202-260-9361; 800-262-7937

Environmental Protection Agency (EPA)
Resource Conservation and Recovery Act and the Comprehensive Environmental Response, Compensation and Liability Act information and requests for documents (Superfund)
800-424-9346; 703-412-9810
TDD: 800-553-7272

Environmental Protection Agency (EPA)
Safe drinking water information
800-426-4791; 202-260-7908 in Washington, DC

Environmental Protection Agency (EPA) TSCA Hotline
Toxic Substances Control Act regulations and asbestos program information
202-554-1404

Environmental Protection Agency program information by region:

Region I (CT, MA, ME, VT, NH, RI)
Hazardous Waste Ombudsman 617-573-5758
Small Business Ombudsman 617-565-3617
Unleaded Fuel Hotline 800-532-3394
Public Information 617-565-8300

Region II (NY, NJ, Puerto Rico and Virgin Islands)
Public Affairs 212-637-3663
RCRA Hotline 800-424-9346
Superfund Hotline 800-535-0202
Public Information Office (Niagara Falls) 716-285-8842

Region III (Washington, DC; DE, MD, PA, VA, WV)
Hazardous Waste Ombudsman 215-597-2842
Small Business Ombudsman 215-597-9807
Public Environmental Education Center 800-438-2474

Region IV (AL, FL, GA, KY, MS, NC, SC, TN)
General Number 404-347-4727
Hazardous Waste Ombudsman 404-347-3004
Small Business Ombudsman 404-347-7109
Public Information Center 404-347-2316

Region V (IN, MI, IL, MN, OH, WI)
General Number 800-621-8431
Public Affairs 312-353-2072

Region VI (AR, LA, NM, OK, TX)
General Number 214-655-6444
Environmental Emergency Hotline--24 hours 214-655-2222
Hazardous Waste Ombudsman 214-655-8527
Small Business Ombudsman 214-655-2200

Region VII (NE, IA, KS, MO)
General Number 913-551-7000
Action Line 800-223-0425

Region VIII (CO, MT, ND, SD, UT, WY)
General Number 800-277-8917
Hazardous Waste Ombudsman 303-294-1111
Small Business Ombudsman 303-294-1111

Region IX (AZ, CA, HI, NV, Guam, Samoa, Northern Mariana Islands, Palau, Micronesia, and Marshall Islands)
Hazardous Waste Ombudsman 415-744-2124
RCRA Hotline 415-744-2074
Small Business Ombudsman 415-744-1635
Superfund Hotline 800-231-3075

Region X (WA, OR, ID, AS)
General Number 206-553-4973
Public Information Center 800-424-4EPA

Information Starting Places

EPA/Center for Environmental Research Information
> To order EPA research reports
> 513-569-7562

EPA Institute
> Clearinghouse for all EPA training activities
> 202-260-6678

EPA/National Radon Hotline
> Information on radon issues
> 800-SOS-RADON

EPA\Solid Waste Assistance Program
> Waste reduction and minimization information
> 800-677-9424

National Pesticide Telecommunications Network (EPA and Texas Tech University)
> Pesticide information on safe use and effects
> 800-858-7378; OR 806-743-3091 in Texas
> 800-858-7377 (medical and government personnel)

National Small Flows Clearinghouse
> Information on wastewater treatment technologies for small communities
> 800-624-8301; 304-293-4191
> BBS: 800-544-1936

Nuclear Regulatory Commission
> Recorded message announcing DOE/NRC meetings on waste management
> 301-415-1292

U.S. Department of Agriculture
> Rural Information Center Hotline
> 800-633-7701

U.S. Department of Agriculture/Soil and Water Conservation Society
> Information on conserving soil and water resources and on volunteering
> 800-THE SOIL

U.S. Department of the Interior/Mineral Management Service-
Pacific Regional Office
> For information about Outer Continental Shelf oil and gas exploration off California
> 805-389-7502

Interior/Office of Surface Mining Reclamation and Enforcement
Eastern Support Center
> Emergency response number regarding abandoned land mines
> 412-937-2146

U.S. Department of Transportation/Coast Guard
> To report adverse environmental acts (oil spills, etc.) by boats
> 800-424-8802; 202-426-2675 in Washington DC

Wetlands Information Hotline
> Provides you with information on wetlands and their protection
> 800-832-7828

Firearms and Explosives

U.S. Department of the Treasury/Alcohol, Tobacco and Firearms Administration
> Firearms, explosives, and licensing information
> 404-679-5040

Treasury/Alcohol, Tobacco and Firearms Administration
> To report stolen or missing explosives
> 800-800-3855; 202-927-7777 in DC

Fraud Hotlines
(see Whistleblower Hotlines)

Government

White House Comments Office
> Leave messages or express opinions
> 202-456-2461

Executive Office of the President
> Recorded message of information on White House tours
> 202-456-7041

Executive Office of the President
> Recorded message of information on tours of the Old Executive Office Building
> 202-395-5895

Federal Election Commission
> Political candidates and committees finance records
> 800-424-9530

Federal Information Centers
> For information about Federal services, programs, and regulations:
> Eastern time zone: 800-347-1997
> Central time zone: 800-366-2998
> Mountain time zone: 800-359-3997
> Pacific time zone: 800-726-4995
> Alaska: 800-729-8003
> Hawaii: 800-733-5996

National Archives and Records Administration/Office of the Federal Register
> Information on documents (regulations, etc.) published in the *Federal Register*
> 202-523-6641; 202-523-5229 (TTY)
> BBS: 202-275-0920

Office of Press Secretary
> Recorded message of President's daily schedule
> 202-456-2343

Office of the Special Counsel
> To report prohibited personnel practices, political activities and other violations by federal and certain state/local employees
> 800-872-9855

State legislatures, status, copies, etc., of bills:
(For a complete state by state listing, see the section "Tracking State Legislation," in the chapter *Information from Lawmakers*.)
> Delaware 800-282-8545; 302-739-4114
> Florida 800-342-1827; 904-488-4371
> Georgia 404-656-5015
> Illinois 800-252-6300; 217-782-3944
> Maryland 800-492-7122; 410-841-3870
> Montana 406-444-3064
> Nebraska 800-742-7456; 402-471-2271
> New Jersey 800-792-8630; 609-292-4840
> New York 800-342-9860; 518-455-4218
> Ohio 800-282-0253; 614-466-8842
> South Carolina 800-922-1539; 803-734-2060
> Washington 800-562-6000; 206-786-7573
> West Virginia 800-642-8650; 304-347-4831
> Wisconsin 800-362-9472; 608-266-1304

U.S. Congress
> Recorded messages of floor votes on legislation:
> U.S. House of Representatives
> > Democratic Cloakroom
> > 202-225-7400
> > Republican Cloakroom
> > 202-225-7430
>
> U.S. Senate
> > Democratic Cloakroom
> > 202-224-8541
> > Republican Cloakroom
> > 202-224-8601

U.S. Department of the Treasury/Financial Management Services
> To report lost or stolen Federal Government checks
> 202-874-7620

The White House Office
> To comment on any subject
> 202-456-1111

The White House Office
> Information on obtaining greeting cards from the President
> 202-456-2724

Be patient. If any phone number is incorrect, call (area code) 555-1212 and request the new listing.

White House Switchboard
  To transfer to another White House telephone line
  202-456-1414

National Archives and Records Administration Public Events Line
  Recorded message on visitors information
  202-501-5000

Handicapped Services and Information

American Council of the Blind
  Legislation affecting and resource materials for the blind
  800-424-8666
  703-467-5081 in Virginia

American Foundation for the Blind
  Referral service
  800-232-5463

American Speech Language Hearing Association
  Consumer hearing and speech hotline
  301-897-5700; 301-897-0039

Blind Children's Center
  Nursery School, infant to age 5, in Los Angeles, California
  800-222-3566; 800-222-3567 in California

National Information Center for Children and Youth with Disabilities
  Publications and referrals
  202-416-0300

Family Resource Center on Disabilities
  Information and referrals
  312-939-3513

Deafness Research Foundation
  Information and referrals
  800-535-3323

Devereux Foundation
  Residential treatment in 11 states for emotionally disturbed, retarded or autistic individuals
  800-345-1292

Federation of the Handicapped
  Referrals and training program for the handicapped
  212-727-4200

Foundation for the Blind
  Referral services
  800-232-5463; 212-502-7600 in New York

Gallaudet Library
  Information about library holdings
  202-651-5216 TDD only; 202-651-5217 voice and TDD

Guide Dog Foundation for the Blind
  Free guide dogs for the blind
  800-548-4337

Heath Resource Center
  Post-secondary education for people with disabilities
  800-544-3284; 202-939-9320 in Washington, DC

Information Center for Individuals with Disabilities
  Information and referrals for the disabled
  617-727-5540

Heart Spring
  Residential school in Wichita, Kansas, for multiple-handicapped children
  800-835-1043

Job Accommodation
  Information/consulting referral service for accommodating people with disabilities in the workplace
  800-526-7234; 304-293-7186 in West Virginia; 800-526-2262 in Canada

Library of Congress/National Library for the Blind
  Provides books and tapes to individuals with sight disabilities
  800-424-8567; 202-707-5100

Massachusetts Commission for the Blind
  Job counseling and job referral services
  800-392-6450 (voice); 800-392-6556 (TDD), Boston office
  800-332-2772 (voice and TDD), Springfield office; 617-727-5550

National Center for Youth with Disabilities
  Information including database searches for adolescents
  800-333-NCYD

National Down Syndrome Congress
  Information and publications
  800-232-6372

National Down Syndrome Society Hotline
  Publications, information about educational, respite and research grants programs
  800-221-4602
  212-460-9330 in New York

National Hearing Aid Society Hearing Aid Helpline
  Assistance in locating qualified hearing instrument specialists, consumer information kit, referrals for financial assistance
  800-521-5247
  810-478-2610 in Michigan

National Information Center for Children and Youth with Disabilities
  Locating services for the handicapped and information on learning disabilities
  800-999-5599; 800-695-0285

National Information Clearinghouse for Infants with Disabilities and Life-Threatening Conditions
  Referral service for ill or seriously disabled infants
  800-922-9234

National Information System for Health Related Services
  Information regarding children born with disabilities
  800-922-9234

National Rehabilitation Information Center (NARIC)
  Information and referral on disability and rehabilitation
  800-346-2742 voice and TDD; 301-588-9284 voice and TDD
  Fax: 301-587-1967; BBS: 301-589-3563

Tripod/Grapevine
  Information and referral service regarding deafness in children
  800-352-8888 voice and TDD; 800-2-TRIPOD voice and TDD;

U.S. Department of Education/American Printing House for the Blind
  Information on publications regarding the blind
  800-223-1839

Health

Aerobics and Fitness Association
  Information on diet and exercise
  800-BE FIT 86

AIDS Clinical Trials Information Service/HIV AIDS Treatment Service
  Information on federally and privately sponsored clinical trials
  800-TRIALS-A

Al-Anon Family Group Headquarters
  Information and counseling for family and children of alcoholics
  800-356-9996

Alcohol and Drug Information, National Clearinghouse
  Publications, posters and referrals
  800-729-6686

Allergy and Asthma Information Line
  Publications and referrals
  800-822-ASMA

Information Starting Places

Alzheimer's Disease Education Center, National Institute on Aging
Information packets and referrals
800-438-4380

AMC Cancer Information and Counseling Line of the National Cancer Institute
Information, publications, nursing and counseling services
800-525-3777

American Academy of Pediatrics
Although primarily an association for pediatricians, also is an advocacy center for children
800-433-9016

American Association of Poison Control Centers
For information on accidental ingestion of chemicals, poisons or drugs (unless otherwise noted, toll-free numbers are valid only within each state):

Alabama:
Children's Hospital of Alabama - Regional Poison Control Center, Birmingham
800-292-6678; 205-939-9201; 205-933-4050
Alabama Poison Control Center, Tuscaloosa
800-462-0800; 205-345-0600

Alaska:
Anchorage Poison Center, Anchorage
800-478-3193

Arizona:
Arizona Poison and Drug Information Center, Tucson
800-362-0101; 602-626-6016
Samaritan Regional Poison Center, Phoenix
602-253-3334

Arkansas:
Arkansas Poison and Drug Info Center, Little Rock
800-376-4766

California:
Fresno Regional Poison Control Center
800-346-5922; 209-445-1222
Los Angeles County Medical Association Regional Poison Control Center
800-77-POISN
San Diego Regional Poison Center
800-876-4766; 619-543-6000
San Francisco Bay Area Regional Poison Control Center
800-523-2222
Santa Clara Regional Poison Center
800-662-9886; 408-885-6000
UCDMC Regional Poison Control Center, Sacramento
800-342-9293; 916-734-3692
University of CA, Davis Medical Center Poison Control Center, Sacramento
800-342-9293

Colorado:
Rocky Mountain Poison and Drug Center, Denver
800-332-3073; 303-629-1123
800-446-6179 (NV); 800-525-5042 (MT)

Connecticut:
Connecticut Poison Center, Farmington
800-343-2722

District of Columbia:
National Poison Control Center Hotline (Georgetown University Hospital, Washington, DC)
202-625-3333; TDD: 202-362-8563

Florida:
Florida Poison and Toxicology Resource Center, Tampa
800-282-3171; 813-253-4444
Florida Poison Information Center, Tampa
800-282-3171; 904-549-4480

Georgia:
Georgia Poison Control Center, Atlanta
800-282-5846; 404-525-3323 (TTY)
404-616-9000

Idaho:
Idaho Poison Center, Boise
800-632-8000

Illinois:
Chicago and NE Illinois Poison Center, Chicago
800-942-5969
St. Johns Hospital Poison Center for Central and Southern Illinois, Springfield
800-252-2022

Indiana:
Indiana Poison Center, Indianapolis
800-382-9097; 317-929-2323

Iowa:
Mid-Iowa Poison Center, Des Moines
800-362-2327
Poison Control Center, Iowa City
800-272-6477
St. Lukes Poison Center, Sioux City
800-352-2222

Kansas:
Mid-America Poison Center
800-332-6633

Kentucky:
Kentucky Regional Poison Center of Kosair, Louisville
800-722-5725; 502-629-7275

Louisiana:
Louisiana Drug and Poison Info Center, Monroe
800-256-9822

Maine:
Maine Poison Center, Portland
800-442-6305

Maryland:
Maryland Poison Center, Baltimore
800-492-2414; 410-528-7701
National Capital Poison Center (DC Suburbs only)
202-625-3333; TDD: 202-362-8563

Massachusetts:
Massachusetts Poison Control System, Boston
800-682-9211; 617-232-2120

Michigan:
Poison Control Center, Children's Hospital of Michigan, Detroit
800-764-7661; TDD: 800-356-3232

Minnesota:
Hennepin Regional Poison Center
612-347-3141
TDD: 612-337-7474
Petline: 612-337-7387
Minnesota Regional Poison Center
800-222-1222; 612-221-2113

Missouri:
Cardinal Glennon Children's Hospital Regional Poison Center, St. Louis
800-392-9111; 800-366-8888
TDD: 314-577-5615; 314-772-5200

Montana:
Rocky Mountain Poison and Drug Center, Denver, Colorado
800-525-5042; 303-629-1123

Nebraska:
Mid-Plains Poison Control Center, Omaha
800-955-9119 (NE, WY); 402-390-5555

New Hampshire:
New Hampshire Poison Info Center, Lebanon
800-562-8236

Be patient. If any phone number is incorrect, call (area code) 555-1212 and request the new listing.

New Jersey:
New Jersey Poison Information and Education System, Newark
800-962-1253; 800-764-7661

New Mexico:
New Mexico Poison and Drug Information Center, Albuquerque
800-432-6866; 505-843-2551

New York:
Central New York Poison Center, Syracuse
800-252-5655
Finger Lakes Poison Center, Rochester
800-333-0542
Hudson Valley Regional Poison Center, N. Tarrytown
800-336-6997; 914-366-3030
Long Island Regional Poison Control Center, East Meadow
516-542-2323, 516-542-2324
516-524-2325, 516-542-3813
New York City Poison Control Center, New York, NY
212-340-4494; 212-POISONS
TDD: 212-689-9014
Western NY Region Poison Center, Buffalo
800-888-7655

Nevada:
Rocky Mountain Poison and Drug Center, Denver, Colorado
800-446-6179 for Las Vegas

North Carolina:
North Carolina Poison Center, Charlotte
800-848-6946; 704-355-4000
Triad Poison Center, Greensboro
800-953-4001

North Dakota:
North Dakota Poison Center, Fargo
800-732-2200

Ohio:
Akron Regional Poison Center, Akron
800-362-9922
Central Ohio Poison Center, Columbus
800-682-7625; 614-228-2272 (TTY)
614-228-1323; 614-461-2012
Northeast Ohio Poison Center, Canton
800-456-8662
Regional Poison Control System, Cincinnati Drug and Poison
Information Center
800-872-5111; 513-558-5111

Oklahoma:
Oklahom Poison Center, Oklahoma City
800-522-4611

Oregon:
Oregon Poison Center, Portland
800-452-7165; 503-494-8968

Pennsylvania:
Central Pennsylvania Poison Center, Hershey
800-521-6110
Delaware Valley Regional Poison Control Center, Philadelphia
215-386-2100
Pittsburgh Poison Center
412-681-6669

Rhode Island:
Rhode Island Poison Center - Rhode Island Hospital, Providence
401-277-5727

South Carolina:
Palmetto Poison Center, Columbia
800-922-1117

South Dakota:
McKennan Poison Control Center, Sioux Falls
800-952-0123

Tennessee:
Mid-Tennessee Poison Center, Nashville
800-289-9999
Southern Poison Center, Inc., Memphis
800-288-9999

Texas:
North Texas Poison Center, Dallas
800-441-0040; 214-590-5000
Texas Poison Center Network, Amarillo
800-764-7661
Texas State Poison Center, Galveston
409-765-1420; [800-392-8548--medical professionals only]
713-654-1701 (Houston)

Utah:
Intermountain Regional Poison Control Center, Salt Lake City
800-456-7707; 801-581-2151

Virginia:
Blue Ridge Poison Center, Charlottesville
800-451-1428; 804-924-5543
National Capital Poison Center, Washington, DC
202-625-3333; 202-362-8563 (northern VA only)
Virginia Poison Center, Richmond
800-552-6337

Washington:
Washington Poison Center, Seattle
800-732-6985

West Virginia:
West Virginia Poison Center, Charleston
800-642-3625; 304-348-4211

Wisconsin:
University of Wisconsin Poison Control Center, Madison
800-815-8855

Wyoming:
Rocky Mountain Poison and Drug Center, Denver, Colorado
800-442-2702; 402-390-5555 (Omaha)
800-955-9119 (NE, WY)

American Cancer Society
Information, publications and referrals
800-ACS-2345 (within each state with a divisional office)

American Cleft Palate Association
Publications and referrals
800-24-CLEFT

American Diabetes Association
Information and publications
800-ADA-DISC; 703-549-1500 in Virginia and Washington, DC

American Kidney Fund
Publications, information and financial assistance
800-638-8299

American Liver Foundation
Information and referrals
800-223-0179

National Mental Health Association Information Center
Call to receive brochure
800-433-5959; 800-969-6642

American Paralysis Foundation
Spinal Cord Injury Hotline
Information, counseling and referral service
800-526-3456

American Parkinson Disease Association
Information and referrals to doctors and hospitals
800-223-2732

Be patient. If any phone number is incorrect, call (area code) 555-1212 and request the new listing.

Information Starting Places

American Sudden Infant Death (SIDS) Institute
Clinical research, educational seminars and treatment facilities
800-232-SIDS; 800-847-7437 in Georgia

American Society of Plastic and Reconstructive Surgeons
Referral service
800-635-0635

American Trauma Society
Publications and information
800-556-7890; 301-420-4189 in Maryland

Amyotrophic Lateral Sclerosis Association
Information, publications and referrals
800-782-4747

Arthritis Foundation
Information and referrals
800-283-7800

ASPO/Lamaze (American Society for Psychoprophylaxis in Obstetrics)
Information regarding certification of educators and class referrals
800-368-4404

Better Hearing Institute
Information and educational publications
800-EAR-WELL
703-642-0580 in Virginia

Birth Control Care Center
Information, referrals and treatment
800-255-7889

Children's Hospice International
Referral network
800-242-4453

Clearinghouse on Child Abuse and Neglect Information
Publications and information on child abuse
800-FYI-3366

Cornelia de Lange Syndrome Foundation
Supportive education and referrals for families with children with Cornelia de Lange syndrome
800-223-8355; 203-693-0159 in Connecticut
800-753-2357 in Canada

Cystic Fibrosis Foundation
Publications and referrals
800-344-4823; 301-951-4422 in Maryland

Deafness and Other Communication Disorders, National Institute on Deafness
Publications and referrals
800-241-1044

Drug Free Workplace Helpline
Publications and referrals to corporations, businesses and organizations
800-843-4971

Drug Abuse, Information on
NIDA, National Drug and Alcohol Treatment Routing Service
800-662-HELP

Eldercare Hotline
Referrals to local resources nationwide
800-677-1116

Endometriosis Foundation
Leave name/address on recorded message to get information
800-992-ENDO; 414-355-2200 in Wisconsin

Epilepsy Foundation of America
Information
800-EFA-1000; 301-459-3700 in Maryland

Facial Plastic Surgery Information Service
To receive information packet

800-332-FACE (USA); 800-332-FACE (Canada)
202-842-4500

Foundation Center
Information on foundations and types of grants they provide
800-424-9836

Hill-Burton Hospital Free Care
Information on hospitals and other health facilities with provide free care
800-638-0742; 800-492-0359 (in Maryland)

Homeless and Mental Illness, National Resource Center on
Information about services for homeless and mentally ill population
800-444-7415

Hospice Education Institute Hospicelink
Referral network
800-331-1620; 203-767-1620 in Connecticut
800-544-2213

Human Growth Foundation
Information regarding physical growth disorders in children
800-451-6434

Huntington's Disease Society of America
Information Line
800-345-4372; 212-242-1968 in New York

Joseph and Rose Kennedy Institute of Ethics National Reference Center for Bioethics Literature
Free online searches of database on bioethic research
800-MED-ETHX

Juvenile Diabetes Foundation
Information, publications and volunteer programs
800-JDF-CURE; 212-889-7575 in New Jersey

The Living Bank
Organ donor registry and referral service
800-528-2971

Lung Line National Asthma Center
Information and publications on immune system and respiratory disorders
800-222-5864; 303-355-LUNG in Denver

Lupus Foundation of America
For free information packet
800-558-0121

March of Dimes Birth Defects Foundation
Health services grants to individuals or institutions
914-428-7100

Mercer Center for Eating Disorders
Information and counseling
800-33-ABTEC; 410-332-9800 in Maryland

Minority Health Resource Center, Office of
Publications, referrals and assistance
800-444-6472

Myasthenia Gravis Foundation
Patient and professional literature and grants for research
800-541-5454

Names Project
Orders for "Common Threads," a documentary on the AIDS quilt
800-USA-NAME

National AIDS Hotline (funded by Centers for Disease Control)
AIDS information
800-342-AIDS; 800-344-SIDA (Spanish);
TDD: 800-243-7889

National AIDS Information Clearinghouse
AIDS publications, posters, databases, videos, fax service is available
800-458-5231

National Association for Sickle Cell Disease
    Publications and referrals
    800-421-8453; 213-936-7205 in California

National Child Safety Council
    Safety materials for children
    800-222-1464; 517-764-6070

National Eye Care Project Helpline
    Assistance/care for the elderly
    800-222-EYES

National Foundation for Depressive Illness
    Information on recorded message
    800-248-4344

National Foundation for Ileitis and Colitis
    Free brochures, counseling, doctor referrals and support groups
    800-343-3637

National Headache Foundation
    Information and publications
    800-843-2256; 800-243-2256 in Illinois

National Health Information Clearinghouse
    To obtain publications on health, such as those contained in *Healthfinder series*
    and referrals to laser surgery experts
    800-336-4797

National Hepatitis Hotline of the American Liver Foundation
    Information regarding tests, availability of vaccines, etc.; physicians referral
    service
    800-223-0179

National Hospice Organization
    Referral and information helpline on hospices
    800-658-8898

National Institute of Mental Health
    Fax service for information on mental health
    301-443-5158; Fax: 301-443-4515

National Institute for Occupational Safety and Health Information
    Publications/database searches on occupational safety and health, including
    hazards associated with fetal development and pregnancy and list of cancer-
    causing products
    800-35-NIOSH
    Fax Service: 404-332-4565

National Kidney Foundation
    Information regarding organ and tissue donation
    800-ACT-GIVE

National Library of Medicine
    Information and reference database searches on publications from 1913 and
    audiovisuals from 1970
    800-272-4787

National Lymphedema Network
    Information and referrals
    800-541-3259

National Multiple Sclerosis Society
    800-344-4867

National Native American AIDS Prevention Center/Indian AIDS Hotline
    Information on AIDS and AIDS prevention
    800-283-AIDS

National Neurofibromatosis Foundation
    To receive information packet
    800-323-7938; 212-344-6633 in New York

National Parkinson Foundation
    Information and neurologists referrals
    800-327-4545; 800-433-7022 in Florida; 305-547-6666 in Maine

National Rehabilitation Information Center (NARIC)
    Information and referral on disability and rehabilitation
    800-34-NARIC; 301-588-9284 voice and TDD
    Fax: 301-587-1967; BBS: 301-589-3563

National Reyes' Syndrome Foundation
    Information and referrals
    800-233-7393; 419-636-2679

National Safety Council
    Recorded message of information and to leave name/address to receive
    publications
    800-621-7619

National Sexually Transmitted Diseases Resource Center
    Information, publications and referrals
    800-227-8922

National Spinal Cord Injury Association
    Information and referrals
    800-962-9629

National Sudden Infant Death Syndrome (SIDS) Foundation
    Publications, information and referrals
    800-221-SIDS

National Tuberous Sclerosis Association
    Research, information and referrals
    800-225-6872; 301-459-9888 in Maryland

Neurological Disorders and Stroke, National Institute of
    Information and referrals
    800-352-9424; 301-496-5751

Occupational Hearing Service
    Hearing/screening test by telephone
    800-222-EARS; 610-544-7700

Organ Donor Hotline
    Information
    800-24-DONOR

Orton Dyslexia Society
    Information and referrals
    800-ABCD-123; 410-296-0232 in Maryland

Parkinson's Education Program
    714-250-2975 for information and referrals; 800-344-7872 for free information
    packet; 800-457-6676

PMS Access
    Information packet, referrals, and pharmacy
    800-222-4767

AIDS, and HIV Infection
    Information packet and newsletter on experimental drugs for AIDS, and HIV
    infection
    800-822-7422; 415-558-8669; 415-558-9051

Sarcoidosis Family Aid and Research Foundation
    Information, publications, research
    800-223-6429

Shriner's Hospital Referral Line
    800-237-5055; 813-281-0300

Simon Foundation
    Information regarding loss of bladder control
    800-23-SIMON; 708-864-3913

Spina Bifida Information and Referral
    Publications, information and referrals
    800-621-3141

Sturge-Weber Foundation
    Literature, Support Services and education on Sturge-Weber syndrome
    800-627-5482

Be patient. If any phone number is incorrect, call (area code) 555-1212 and request the new listing.

Tourette Syndrome Association
    To receive information packet
    800-237-0717

United Scleroderma Foundation
    Information and publications
    800-722-HOPE
    408-728-2202 in California

U.S. Department of Agriculture
    Food safety information and to report illness from meat, poultry or eggs
    800-535-4555
    202-447-3333 in Washington, DC

U.S. Department of Health and Human Services (HHS)
    Health information referral service
    800-336-4797

HHS/Centers for Disease Control
    AIDS: Recorded message on number of cases, deaths, and distribution among age groups; fax service is available
    404-332-4555

HHS/Centers for Disease Control
    AIDS: Recorded message on distribution of total cases among transmissions categories and among male and female adults, adolescents and children; fax service is available
    404-332-4555

HHS/Centers for Disease Control
    AIDS: Recorded message on ten states with highest number of cases, current public health service estimates of HIV infections and projections of cases and deaths by 1992; fax service is available
    404-332-4555

HHS/Food and Drug Administration
    Reporting of problems with drugs by health professionals
    800-638-6725

HHS/Food and Drug Administration
    Food and drugs; complaints and advice on emergencies
    202-443-1240
    202-857-8400 weekends and holidays

HHS/Health Care Financing Administration
    Medicare Hotline
    800-638-6833; 800-492-6603 in Maryland

HHS/National Institutes of Health/National Cancer Institute
    Cancer information and publications
    800-4-CANCER; 808-524-1234 in Hawaii

HHS/Office of Minority Health Resource Center
    Information, publications and database searches
    800-444-6472

HHS/Social Security Administration
    Information on retirement, survivor, disability, medicare and SSI benefits
    800-772-1213

U.S. Department of Labor/Mine Safety and Health Administration
    For reporting health and safety hazards; your call will be directed to the proper authority
    703-235-1452

Women's Spots Foundation
    Information packet, educational travel and training grants for individual athletes
    800-227-3988

Housing, Real Estate and Home Improvement

Cooperative Extension Service Headquarters throughout the USA, which provide home and garden assistance, information, and education:

Amherst, Massachusetts	413-545-4800
Athens, Georgia	706-542-3824
Auburn, Alabama	205-844-4444
Baton Rouge, Louisiana	504-388-6083
Blacksburg, Virginia	703-231-6705
Bozeman, Montana	406-994-4371
Brookings, South Dakota	605-688-4792
Burlington, Vermont	802-656-2980
Clemson, South Carolina	803-656-3382
College Park, Maryland	301-405-2906
College Station, Texas	409-845-7967
Columbia, Missouri	314-882-7754
Columbus, Ohio	614-292-4067
Corvalis, Oregon	503-737-2713
District of Columbia	202-274-6900
Durham, New Hampshire	603-862-1520
Fargo, North Dakota	701-231-8944
Fairbanks, Alaska	907-474-7246
Fort Collins, Colorado	303-491-6281
Gainesville, Florida	904-392-1761
Honolulu, Hawaii	808-956-8397
Ithaca, New York	607-255-2237
Kingston, Rhode Island	401-792-2474
Knoxville, Tennessee	615-974-7114
Kolonia, Pohnpei, Micronesia	691-320-2728
Lansing, Michigan	517-355-2308
Laramie, Wyoming	307-766-5124
Las Cruces, New Mexico	505-646-3016
Lincoln, Nebraska	402-472-2966
Little Rock, Arkansas	501-761-2000
Lexington, Kentucky	606-257-4772
Logan, Utah	801-750-2200
Madison, Wisconsin	608-262-3786
Mangilao, Guam	617-734-2562
Manhattan, Kansas	913-532-7137
Mayaguez, Puerto Rico	809-265-3850
Mississippi State, Mississippi	601-325-3036
Morgantown, West Virginia	304-293-5691
Moscow, Idaho	208-885-6639
Newark, Delaware	302-831-2504
New Brunswick, New Jersey	908-932-9306
Oakland, California	510-987-0505
Orono, Maine	207-581-3186
Pullman, Washington	509-335-2933
Raleigh, North Carolina	919-515-2811
Reno, Nevada	702-784-1614
St. Croix, Virgin Islands	809-692-4022
Saint Paul, Minnesota	612-624-2703
Saipan, Marianas	670-234-9022
Stillwater, Oklahoma	405-744-5398
Storrs, Connecticut	203-486-6271
Tucson, Arizona	602-470-8086
University Park, Pennsylvania	814-865-2541
Urbana, Illinois	217-333-2660

Federal National Mortgage Association (Fannie Mae)
    Information on accessing Fannie Mae's mortgage network
    800-471-5554; 202-752-7000

State housing assistance program information for the following states:

Maine	800-452-4668
Minnesota	800-652-9747
Vermont	800-287-VHFA

U.S. Department of Agriculture/Economic Research Service
    To order database on Foreign Owned Agricultural Land (No. 87015)
    800-999-6779

U.S. Department of Housing and Urban Development (HUD)
    Fair housing information or complaints regarding housing discrimination
    800-669-9777

U.S. Department of Housing and Urban Development (HUD)
    Home Equity Conversion Reverse Mortgage Programs, drug information, searchable database, publications, etc.
    800-245-2691; 301-251-5154 in Maryland

U.S. Department of the Treasury/Office of Thrift Supervision
    Recorded message of indexes used to compute mortgage rates
    202-906-6988

Immigration

U.S. Department of Justice/Immigration and Naturalization Service
Recorded message of information on visas, passports, family fairness policy, permanent residency status, etc.
202-514-4316

Immigration-Related Unfair Employment Practices Hotline
To report employment problems
800-255-7688

Amnesty Program/Legislation General Information
To find out information regarding the process to request amnesty or become a legal immigrant
800-755-0777; 202-514-4316

Insurance

Federal Crime Insurance
Insurance coverage for robbery and burglary
800-638-8780
301-251-1660 in Washington, DC

Hill-Burton
Information on free or low-cost health care, complaints about facilities or denial of treatment due to medicare/medicaid coverage
800-638-0742
800-492-0359 in Maryland

Office of Personnel Management/Office of Retirement and Insurance Policy
Recorded message of information on federal employees special benefits
202-606-0777

U.S. Department of Defense/Civilian Health and Medical Program of the Uniformed Services (CHAMPUS)
Information regarding benefits
303-361-1000

Veterans Administration
Information on CHAMPVA, medical benefits for dependents of disabled veterans or veterans whose death was service related
800-733-8387

Veterans Administration
GI life insurance information
800-669-8477

Veterans Administration
To contact your VA regional offices
800-827-1000

International Organizations

Peace Corps
Recorded message of information about activities, application procedures and job vacancies
800-424-8580 x214

Judicial System

Administrative Office of the U.S. Courts
Recorded message regarding pending legislation affecting the courts
202-273-1138

U.S. Supreme Court
Information on dockets and activities
202-479-3011

U.S. Department of Justice
To report hate crimes
202-514-1026

Maps

Federal Emergency Management Agency
To order maps showing flood-prone areas
800-358-9616

U.S. Department of Defense/Defense Mapping Agency
Guidance on obtaining maps and charts of the Defense Mapping Agency
800-826-0342

U.S. Geological Survey
To order maps: Antarctic, moon and planets, land use, photoimage, etc.
800-USA-MAPS

U.S. Department of the Interior/National Park Service
Civil War troop movement maps
303-969-2130

Maritime

St. Lawrence Seaway Ship Arrival
Recorded message of shipping schedule
315-769-2422

U.S. Department of Transportation (DOT)/Coast Guard
Boating safety information, complaints or violations and referrals to local CG offices for subscriptions to *Local Notice to Mariners*
800-368-5647

U.S. Department of Transportation (DOT)/Coast Guard
Coast Guard Auxiliary public education courses
800-336-BOAT; or 800-245-BOAT in Virginia

U.S. Department of Transportation (DOT)/Coast Guard
To report adverse environmental acts (oil spills, etc.) by boats
800-424-8802; 202-426-2675 in Washington, DC

U.S. Department of Transportation (DOT)/Coast Guard
To report hazardous conditions, drug smuggling or improper boarding
800-323-7233

Money and Coins

American Eagle
To receive a free regional edition buyer's guide to U.S. mint and eagle coins
800-USA-GOLD

Professional Ordering Service for Various Products
For information on obtaining Presidential Bicentennial Gold Coins
800-822-6500

U.S. Department of the Treasury/Bureau of Engraving and Printing
Recorded message of information on tours
202-874-3188

Patent and Trademark

U.S. Department of Commerce/Patent and Trademark Helpline
703-305-8747; 800-888-8062 (Trademark Registration)

Patent and Trademark Office Bulletin Board
BBS: 703-305-8950; voice 703-308-0322

Pension Plans

Pension Benefits Guarantee Corporation
Recorded message of current interest rates on pension plans
202-326-4141

Tennessee Valley Authority (TVA)
Information regarding TVA retirement system
615-632-2672

Recreation

U.S. Department of Agriculture (USDA)/Forest Service
Reservations at National Forests and free camping information
800-280-CAMP

U.S. Department of Agriculture (USDA)/Forest Service
Information and publications on wildlife, rangers, etc.
202-205-0957

Be patient. If any phone number is incorrect, call (area code) 555-1212 and request the new listing.

87

Information Starting Places

U.S. Department of the Interior/National Park Service
Documents, prints of drawings, brochures, aerial photos, etc., on National Parks
303-969-2130

Senior Citizens Services

American Association of Retired Persons and state and Washington, DC governments
Free legal counsel for the elderly
800-622-2520; 202-234-0970

National Eye Care Project Helpline
Assistance/care for the elderly
800-222-EYES

National Institute on Aging
A free copy of *Don't Take It Easy - Exercise* is available as well as a catalog of other publications
800-222-2225

National Technical Information Service
To order 30-page study entitled *Aging and Health Promotion: Market Research for Public Health*
800-553-NTIS

Elder Care
This service helps locate state or local offices that can assist with the needs of the elderly
800-677-1116

State agencies on aging for information on services, assistance and benefits:
Illinois 800-252-8966
Maryland 800-243-3425
Missouri . . . . 800-392-0210 elderly abuse
800-235-5503 aging information and referrals
New Hampshire 800-351-1888
Oregon . . . . 800-232-3020 program monitoring
800-282-8096 administration of senior services (voice/TDD)
Texas 800-252-9240

Social Services

Center for Substance Abuse Treatment
Referral service to appropriate agencies and sources in your area
800-662-HELP

Covenant House
Crisis counseling and referral service for all types of problems
800-999-9999

Edna Gladney Center
Maternity home and adoption center
800-433-2922
800-772-2740 in Texas

Kevin Collins Foundation for Missing Children
Advice and immediate response to families of stranger-abducted children
800-272-0012

MADD - Mothers Against Drunk Driving
National headquarters that can refer you to your local office
800-438-6233

National Child Abuse Hotline - Child Help USA
Information, counseling and referral service
800-422-4453

National Council on Child Abuse and Family Violence
Referral assistance, information and publications
800-222-2000

National Hotline for Missing and Exploited Children
Reports from parents and law enforcement officers and sightings of missing children
800-843-5678

National Organization for Victim Assistance
Referral service for victims and survivors of violent crime
800-TRY-NOVA; 202-232-6682

National Resource Center on Child Sexual Abuse
Child sexual abuse information, publications and training
800-KIDS-006

National Sexually Transmitted Disease Hotline
Provides free information on specific diseases and provides counseling and referrals
800-227-8922

Runaway hotline
With information, resources and message delivery for runaways and their parents
800-621-4000; TDD: 800-621-0394

Tough Love
Referral service for parents with problem children
800-333-1069

U.S. Department of Labor/Women's Bureau
Publications on childcare and work and family life
800-827-5335

Space

Smithsonian Institution
Recorded *Sky Watcher's Report* on stars and constellations
202-357-2000

Space and Rocket Center
Space Camp programs for children, adults, and educators
800-63-SPACE

Taxes

Internal Revenue Service/U.S. Department of the Treasury
To speak to a tax specialist for account-related information, to set up payment plans, etc.
800-829-1040

Internal Revenue Service
To order IRS forms
800-829-3676

Internal Revenue Service
IRS telephone assistance services for deaf taxpayers with TDD equipment
800-829-4059

Internal Revenue Service
Status of tax return and recorded topics
800-829-4477

State tax assistance numbers, which are toll free only for the following states:
Arizona 800-352-4090
Connecticut 800-322-9463
Delaware 800-292-7826
Hawaii . . . . 800-222-3229 (information)
800-222-7572 (forms)
Illinois . . . . 800-732-8866 (information, forms)
800-624-2459 (forms during filing season)
Maine 800-773-7895
Michigan 800-487-7000
Minnesota 800-657-3676
800-657-3777 (corporate)
800-422-4618 (personal)
Nebraska . . . . 800-742-7474 (corporate)
New Jersey 800-323-4400
New York . . . . 800-225-5829 (information)
800-443-3200 (refunds)
800-462-8100 (forms)
Ohio 800-282-1780

Technology

National Small Flows Clearinghouse
   Wastewater treatment technologies for small communities
   800-624-8301, #2

National Technical Information Service/U.S. Department of Commerce
   To order publications on U.S. and foreign government technology, including medical technology
   800-553-NTIS

Time

U.S. Naval Observatory
   Recorded message giving the time (within milliseconds)
   202-653-1800

Trade

Export-Import Bank
   Export financing, marketing and insurance programs; fax service is available
   800-565-3946

International Trade Commission
   To order ITC publications
   202-205-1807

International Trade Commission
   Petitions and complaints recording line
   202-205-2196

International Trade Commission
Trade Remedy Assistance Office
   Information regarding trade laws and help for small business with technical assistance
   800-343-9822

Overseas Private Investment Corporation
   Information on programs, press releases, and employment opportunities; fax service is available
   202-336-8799

U.S. Department of Agriculture/Foreign Agricultural Service
   Information/assistance/training for projects in developing countries and scientific exchanges with developed countries
   202-720-7115

U.S. Department of Commerce
   Leave message to have a trade specialist contact you
   800-USA-TRADE

U.S. Department of Commerce
   Recorded message of Commerce Department news
   202-393-1847

U.S. Department of Commerce/Foreign Trade Statistics
   Recorded message of information on current goods and services, and trade figures
   301-457-3041, #5

U.S. Department of Commerce/Bureau of Economic Analysis
   Recorded message of leading economic indicators with analysis and data for composite indexes
   202-606-5361

U.S. Department of Commerce/Bureau of Economic Analysis
   Recorded message of revised quarterly estimates of gross national products
   202-606-5306

U.S. Department of Commerce/Bureau of Economic Analysis
   Recorded message of personal income and outlays statistical information
   202-606-5303

U.S. Department of Commerce/Bureau of Economic Analysis
   Recorded message on merchandise trade, balance of payments basis or U.S. international transactions
   202-606-5362

U.S. Department of Commerce/Export Administration Bureau
   Information on export regulations, forms, commodity classifications and seminar program
   202-482-4811

U.S. Department of Commerce/International Trade Administration
   Small-to-medium sized businesses counseling number for assistance in export development; fax service is available
   800-USA-TRADE

U.S. Department of the Treasury/Office of Foreign Assets Control
   Information on economic sanctions against Iraq, Libya, Nicaragua, Panama, South Africa, etc.
   202-622-2410

U.S. Trade Representative
   Recorded message on recent activities and regulation under section 301 of the Trade Act, 1974
   202-395-3871

Transportation

AMTRAK
   AMTRAK tickets or travel information
   800-USA-RAIL

U.S. Department of Transportation (DOT)/Federal Aviation Administration
   Non-safety transportation complaints such as lost baggage
   202-366-2220

U.S. Department of Transportation (DOT)/Federal Aviation Administration
   To report possible safety or Federal Aviation Administration (FAA) Regulations violations
   800-255-1111

U.S. Department of Transportation (DOT)/Federal Aviation Administration
   Consumer complaints regarding carry-on baggage, aircraft security, child infant seat, aircraft and airmen verification and noise abatement
   800-FAA-SURE

U.S. Department of Transportation (DOT)/National Highway Traffic Safety Administration
   Highway safety information and to report auto safety defects and recall information on autos manufactured in the past 10 years
   800-424-9393; 202-366-0123 in Washington, DC

Travel/Tourism

Nation's Capital Events Hotline
   Recorded message of activities at parks, embassies, etc.
   202-789-7000

State Offices of Tourism; information about the following states:

Alabama	800-ALABAMA
Alaska	907-465-2012
Arizona	800-842-8257
Arkansas	800-628-8725
California	800-862-2543
Colorado	800-265-6723
Connecticut	800-282-6863
Delaware	800-441-8846
Florida	904-488-5607
Georgia	800-847-4842
Hawaii	808-586-2550
Idaho	800-635-7820
Illinois	800-CONNECT
Indiana	800-289-6646
Iowa	800-345-4692
Kansas	800-252-6727
Kentucky	800-225-8747
Louisiana	800-334-8626
Maine	800-533-9595
Maryland	800-543-1036
Massachusetts	800-447-6277
Michigan	800-543-2937
Minnesota	800-657-3700

Be patient. If any phone number is incorrect, call (area code) 555-1212 and request the new listing.

89

Information Starting Places

Mississippi 800-WARMEST
Missouri 800-877-1234
Montana 800-VISIT-MT
Nebraska 800-228-4307
Nevada 800-638-2328
New Hampshire 800-386-4664
New Jersey 800-537-7397
New Mexico 800-545-2040
New York State 800-CALL-NYS
North Carolina 800-847-4862
North Dakota 800-HELLO-ND
Ohio 800-BUCKEYE
Oklahoma 800-652-6552
Oregon 800-547-7842
Pennsylvania 800-VISIT-PA
Rhode Island 800-556-2484
South Carolina 800-346-3634
South Dakota 800-SDAKOTA
Tennessee 800-836-6200
Texas 800-888-8839
Utah 800-200-1160
Vermont 800-VERMONT
Virginia 800-847-4882
Washington State 800-544-1800
West Virginia 800-225-5982
Wisconsin 800-432-8747
Wyoming 800-225-5995
American Samoa 684-633-1091
Guam 800-873-4826
Marianas Island 670-234-8327
Puerto Rico 800-866-7827
U.S. Virgin Islands 809-774-8784

U.S. Congress
Information on tours of the U.S. Capitol
202-225-6827

U.S. Department of Health and Human Services/Centers for Disease Control
Vaccination requirements, disease outbreaks, AIDS and the foreign traveler, etc., information; fax service is available
404-332-4559

U.S. Department of State/Bureau of Consular Affairs (BCA/State)
Citizens Emergency Center, which gives assistance to Americans traveling or arrested abroad
202-647-5225

U.S. Department of State/Bureau of Consular Affairs (BCA/State)
Information about visas
202-663-1225

U.S. Department of State/Bureau of Consular Affairs (BCA/State)
Information about passports
202-647-0518

Volunteerism
U.S. Geological Survey
Recorded message of information on "Volunteer for Science" program
703-648-7440; 703-648-7452

Weather
U.S. Department of Commerce/National Oceanic and Atmospheric Administration
National Climatic Data Center Archives on weather and data for the nation
704-271-4800; Fax: 704-271-4876
Internet: orders@ncdc.noaa.gov

Whistleblower Hotlines
Unless otherwise noted, Whistleblower Hotlines are established as a means of reporting fraud, waste, abuse or mismanagement within a particular federal agency. The agencies with these hotlines are listed below:

U.S. Department of Agriculture
800-424-9121; 202-727-2540

Department of the Army
800-752-9747; 800-572-9000 (VA); 703-545-6700

U.S. Department of Commerce
800-424-5197; 202-482-4661

U.S. Department of Defense
To report fraud or corruption by employees of DOD contractors
800-424-9098; 703-545-6700

U.S. Department of Education
800-647-8733; 202-755-5770

U.S. Department of Energy
800-541-1625; 202-586-5000

Federal Bureau of Investigation
202-324-2901; 800-869-4499

U.S. Department of Health and Human Services
800-368-5779; 410-965-7420

U.S. Department of Housing and Urban Development
800-347-3735; 202-708-4200

U.S. Department of the Interior
800-424-5081; 202-208-3424

U.S. Department of Justice
800-869-4466; 202-514-3435

U.S. Department of Labor
800-347-3756; 202-219-7296

U.S. Department of State
202-647-3320

U.S. Department of Transportation
800-424-9071; 202-366-1461

U.S. Department of Treasury
800-359-3898; 202-622-1090

U.S. Department of Veterans Affairs
202-233-5394; 800-488-8244

Agency for International Development
703-875-4999; 800-230-6539

Environmental Protection Agency
202-260-4977; 800-424-4000

Equal Employment Opportunity Commission
202-663-7020; 800-849-4230

General Accounting Office
To report fraud, waste, abuse or illegal acts within federal government
202-512-7470; 800-424-5454

General Services Administration
800-424-5210; 202-501-1780

Interstate Commerce Commission
use DOT hotline

Merit Systems Protection Board
800-872-9855; 202-653-9125

National Aeronautics and Space Administration
800-424-9183; 202-358-1233

Navy Department
To report waste, fraud or abuse within Navy or by Navy contractors
800-522-3451

Nuclear Regulatory Commission
800-233-3497; 301-415-5930

Be patient. If any phone number is incorrect, call (area code) 555-1212 and request the new listing.

Office of Personnel Management
202-606-2423

Railroad Retirement Board
800-772-4258; 312-751-4336

Social Security Administration
800-368-5779

Small Business Administration
202-205-7151; 800-767-0385

Tennessee Valley Authority
800-323-3835
800-423-3071 (Tennessee only); 615-632-3550

U.S. Information Agency
202-401-7202

Recorded Messages

You'll find many other recorded messages in every chapter, particularly in Health and Medicine as well as Federal Jobs Banks in the Careers and Workplace Chapter. Dozens of taped information spots prepared by the Immigration and Naturalization Service are included in the Law and Social Justice Chapter.

Agriculture Department News	202-488-8358
Botanic Garden Upcoming Events	202-225-7099/8333
Career America Hotline	912-757-3000
Centers for Disease Control, U.S. Travel	404-332-4555
Centers for Disease Control, Foreign Travel	404-332-4559
Commerce Department News	202-393-1847
Consumer Price Index	202-606-7828
Consumer Product Safety Commission Investigations	800-638-CPSC
Current Labor Statistics	202-606-7828
Education Department Financial Aid	800-433-3243
Employment Lost Index	202-606-7828
Employment Situation Information	202-606-7828
Engraving and Printing	202-622-2000
Federal Job Information Center (Career America Connection)	202-606-2700
Federal Trade Commission Meetings	202-326-2711
Geological Survey Volunteers	703-648-7440
Immigration and Naturalization	202-307-1501
Labor Department News	202-606-7828
Nation's Capitol Events Hotline	202-PA 4-0009

Naval Academy	800-638-9156
Overseas Citizens Service Travel Tips	202-647-5225
Passport Services Information	202-647-0518
Peace Corps	800-424-8580
Producer Price Index	202-606-7828
Public Debt	202-874-4000
Public Health Corps Scholarships (recorded message only after 5 p.m.)	800-638-0824
Radon Hotline	800-SOS-RADON
Savings Bonds	202-447-1775
SBA Answer Desk	800-827-5722
Smithsonian Dial-A-Museum	202-357-2020
Smithsonian Skywatchers Report	202-357-2000
Time (within milliseconds)	202-653-1800
Thrift Supervision	202-906-6988
Treasury Bills	202-874-4000

US House of Representatives Floor Votes
Democratic Cloakroom — 202-225-7400
Republican Cloakroom — 202-225-7430

US International Transactions Weekend Preview — 202-393-4102

US Senate Floor Votes
Democratic Cloakroom — 202-224-8541
Republican Cloakroom — 202-224-8601

Consumer Power
General Sources

* *See also Investments and Financial Services Chapter*
* *See also Health and Medicine Chapter*
* *See also Agriculture and Farming Chapter*

When you find yourself the victim of an unfair business practice, you don't have to sit there and feel helpless. This chapter includes a wide variety of programs that offer information and advice on consumer complaints such as mail fraud, deceptive advertising, and warrantee enforcement. You'll find answers to consumer questions on everything from tanning salons to funeral practices. You should also see the Expert Chapter for subject specific experts on all kinds of consumer issues.

* Advertising Practices
Federal Trade Commission (FTC)
Advertising Practices
601 Pennsylvania Ave., NW
Washington, DC 20580   202-326-3131
This division of the FTC promotes the distribution of truthful information to the public through law enforcement and oversight activities in the following areas: 1) General advertising for deceptive claims at the national and regional level. 2) Advertising claims for food and over-the-counter drugs, particularly claims relating to safety or effectiveness. 3) Tobacco advertising, which includes monitoring for unfair practices or deceptive claims, implementing cigarette and smokeless tobacco labeling laws, and reporting to Congress on cigarette and smokeless tobacco labeling, advertising, and promotion. 4) Performance and energy-savings claims for solar products, furnaces, window coverings, room heaters, wood burning products, gas-saving products and motor oils, and other products featuring energy conservation. For more information about any of these programs, contact this office.

* Advocacy Program
Federal Trade Commission
Bureau of Economics
601 Pennsylvania Ave., NW
Washington, DC 20580   202-326-3131
Under the Advocacy Program, the Federal Trade Commission's (FTC) three bureaus--Economics, Competition, and Consumer Protection--present comments to other Federal agencies concerning the effect of regulation on competition and consumers. Some recent studies have analyzed the effect of state entry regulation on retail automobile markets, certificate of need regulation in the health care field, and consumer information regulations in the insurance industry. For more information on these and other advocacy program studies, contact this bureau.

* Air Travelers' Rights and Complaints
Consumer Affairs Division
Intergovernmental and Consumer Affairs
Governmental Affairs
Office of the Secretary of Transportation
U.S. Department of Transportation
400 7th Street, SW   800-424-9393
Washington, DC 20690   202-366-2220
If your problem cannot be resolved directly with the airline, contact this office for information on air travelers' rights and for assistance in resolving problems with airlines and charter flights. Complaints about delayed or canceled flights, reservations, lost baggage, smoking, refunds, and overbooking can also be handled here.

* Alcohol, Tobacco, and Firearms Information
Communications Center
Bureau of Alcohol, Tobacco, and Firearms
U.S. Department of the Treasury
650 Massachusetts Ave., Room 5200
Washington, DC 20226   202-927-8120
This Center functions as a 24 hours a day, seven days a week clearinghouse for those seeking assistance from the Bureau of Alcohol, Tobacco, and Firearms.

* Alcohol, Tobacco, and Firearms: Laws and Regulations
Superintendent of Documents
Government Printing Office
Washington, DC 20402   202-512-1800
The *Alcohol, Tobacco, and Firearms Quarterly Bulletin* announces all new laws, regulations, codes, and rulings or changes related to alcohol, tobacco, and firearms. The subscription price is $13 per year (S/N 748-001-00000-0).

* Automobile Fuel Economy
Motor Vehicle Requirements Division
Office of Market Incentives
Rulemaking
National Highway Traffic Safety Administration (NHTSA)
U.S. Department of Transportation
400 7th Street, SW
Room 5320   800-424-9393
Washington, DC 20690   202-366-0486
The National Highway Traffic Safety Administration (NHTSA) issues fuel economy standards and collects information on the technological and economic capabilities of automobile manufacturers to maximize fuel efficiency. Contact this office for information and referrals.

* Auto Safety Hotline
Office of Defects Investigation (NEF-10)
National Highway Traffic Safety Administration
U.S. Department of Transportation
400 7th Street, SW
Room 5326   800-424-9393
Washington, DC 20690   202-366-0123
This toll-free hotline is accessible in all 50 states, Puerto Rico, and the Virgin Islands. Consumers may call to report automobile safety problems or to request information on recalls, defects, investigations, child safety seats, tires, drunk driving, crash test results, seat belts, air bags, odometer tampering, and other related topics. Staff will also make referrals to state and other agencies. Also ask about the New Car Assessment Program (NCAP), which provides comparable data on the frontal crashworthiness of selected new vehicles.

* Buying By Phone
Federal Trade Commission (FTC)
Joel Brewer
Enforcement Division
601 Pennsylvania Ave., NW
Washington, DC 20580
Recording for orders or complaints   202-326-3027
The Federal Trade Commission (FTC) receives complaints indicating that businesses and other organizations have problems with some telephone solicitors who use illegal tactics to make sales or send unordered merchandise. For more information about these illegal solicitors, often called "WATS-line hustlers" because they use long-distance phone lines, contact your local FTC office, or the office above.

Consumer Power

* Care Labeling
Federal Trade Commission (FTC)
Enforcement Division
601 Pennsylvania Ave., NW
Washington, DC 20580   202-326-3034

Under the Federal Trade Commission's (FTC) Care Labeling Rule concerning textile clothing, a care label must be attached to most clothing--except articles that are used to primarily to cover or protect the head and hands--giving care instructions. For more information on the Care Labeling Rule and your rights, or to report clothing you have purchased that has no care label attached, contact the FTC.

* Consumer Affairs
Office of Consumer Affairs (OCA)
U.S. Department of Health and Human Services
Washington, DC 20201   202-634-4140

The Office of Consumer Affairs (OCA) is responsible for providing the President and federal agencies with advice and information regarding the interests of American consumers. The OCA encourages and assists in developing new consumer programs; makes recommendations to improve federal consumer programs; cooperates with state agencies and voluntary organizations in advancing consumer interests; promotes improved consumer education; recommends legislation and regulations to help consumers; and encourages the exchange of ideas among industry, government, and consumers. *The Consumer's Resource Handbook* and *Consumer Information Catalog* are available free from Consumer Information Center, P.O. Box 100, Department 635H, Pueblo, CO 81009, or by calling 719-948-4000.

* Consumer Affairs - International
Commercial, Legislative and Business Affairs
Bureau of Economic and Business Affairs
U.S. Department of State
2201 C St., NW, Room 6822
Washington, DC 20520   202-647-1942

This office monitors developments in international consumer affairs and coordinates U.S. participation in international organizations dealing with consumer affairs policy.

* Consumer Complaint Letters to the FTC
Federal Trade Commission (FTC)
Correspondence Branch
601 Pennsylvania Ave., NW
Washington, DC 20580   202-326-2222

Letters from consumers are very important to the work of the Federal Trade Commission (FTC). They are often the first indication of a problem in the marketplace and may provide the initial evidence to begin an investigation. Although the FTC is not authorized to resolve individual consumer complaints, it can act when it sees a pattern of possible law violations. If you have witnessed an incidence of unfair trade practice, write a letter to the FTC to help them determine if any federal action is warranted.

* Consumer Information Catalog
Catalog, P.O. Box 100
Pueblo, CO 81002

Published quarterly, The *Consumer Information Catalog* includes a descriptive listing of approximately 200 booklets from a variety of federal agencies. The publications cover health, federal benefits, money management, housing, child care, employment, small business, education, food and nutrition, consumer protection, and more. Some booklets are free and some are available at cost. The Center also has a list of over 100 booklets available free in Spanish. They include a variety of subjects such as health, money management, children, federal benefits, and more. To obtain a copy, write to LISTA, Pueblo, CO 81002. Here is a brief list of some of the subjects you will find:

Auto
Nine Ways to Lower Your Auto Insurance
Collecting Used Oil for Recycling/Reuse

Children
Helping Your Child Learn to Read
Books for Children, #10

Parenting
Growing Up Drug Free
Kids Aren't Just Small Adults

Employment
Tips for Finding the Right Job
Working For Us in the 1990s

Federal Programs
Guide to Health Insurance for People with Medicare
Medicare Q and A
Understanding Social Security

Food and Nutrition
The Food Guide Pyramid

Health
Lead Threat Lessens, but Mugs Pose Problems
Secondhand Smoke
Lyme Disease

Housing
Fair Housing: It's Your Right
Home Buyers Vocabulary

Money
Consumer Handbook to Credit Protection Laws
Managing Money Throughout Life
Investment Swindles...How They Work and How to Avoid Them
Your Guaranteed Pension
Investment Swindlers: How They Work and How to Avoid Them

Sources of Assistance
Getting Information from FDA
U.S. Government TDD Directory
Your Right to Federal Records

* Consumer Information Center
Pueblo, CO 81002   202-501-1794

The Consumer Information Center (CIC) was established in 1970 to help federal agencies and departments release consumer information they wish to bring to the public's attention and to help build public awareness and use of this information. CIC is a separately funded operation located in the General Services Administration, and it is under the policy guidance of the Special Adviser to the President for Consumer Affairs. CIC has a small staff of consumer information specialists available on a selected basis to speak at or participate in national conferences. CIC's exhibit, which includes free catalogs, is also available for major conferences.

* Consumer Information Media Hotline
Pueblo, CO 81002   202-501-1794

Members of the Consumer Information Center (CIC) media staff are ready to help reporters research consumer stories and can put reporters in touch with contacts who will answer questions directly.

* Consumer Publications
Federal Trade Commission (FTC)
Public Reference Branch
601 Pennsylvania Ave., NW, Room 130
Washington, DC 20580   202-326-2222 - Recording

The following publications are available free of charge by visiting the Federal Trade Commission (FTC) in person, but if that is not possible, the FTC will send you any of them free of charge except those marked with an asterisk (*), which are available for a nominal fee from the Consumer Information Center, Pueblo, CO 81002.

Art Fraud
"Bargain" Jewelry
Buying a Safer Car* $.50
Buying By Phone
Buying Native American Jewelry
Care Labels: Caring For Your Clothes
Consumer Alert: Investing In Rare Coins
Consumer Guide to the FTC Funeral Rule* $.50
Consumer Quiz
Contest Cons
Dollars for Dancing
Door to Door Sales
Eye Wear* $.50

Eyeglasses
Franchise and Business Opportunities
Generic Drugs
Health Claims: Separating Fact From Fiction
Health Questions: How To Talk To and Select Physicians, Pharmacists, Dentists, and Vision Care Specialists
Health Spas: Exercise Your Rights
How To Buy A Manufactured Home* $.50
How To Write A Wrong: Complain Effectively And Get Results
Job-Hunting: Should You Pay?
Layaway Purchase Plans
Real Estate Brokers
Service Contracts
Shopping by Mail
Shopping by Phone and Mail
Smart Buying for Young Consumers
Swindlers Are Calling* $.50
Telephone Investment Fraud
Unordered Merchandise
Vacation Time Sharing Tips
Varicose Veins Treatments* $.50
Warranties
What's New About Care Labels
Work-At-Home Schemes

Automobile
Automatic Transmission Repair*
Buying a Used Car* $.50
Car Rental Guide
Car Ads: Low Interest Loans and Other Offers
General Motors Consumer Mediation/Arbitration Program
New Car Buying Guide* $.50
Volkswagen Consumer Mediation/Arbitration Program
Water Treatment Units* $.50

Consumer Financing
Choosing and Using Credit Cards* $.50
Consumer Handbook on Adjustable Rate Mortgages $.50
Cosigning A Loan
Credit and Charge Card Fraud
Credit and Divorce* $.50
Credit and Older Americans
Credit Practices Rule
Electronic Banking
Equal Credit Opportunity
Escrow Accounts For Home Mortgages
Facts About Financial Planners* $.50
Fair Credit Reporting
Fair Credit Reporting Act
Fair Credit Billing
Fair Debt Collection* $.50
Fix Your Own Credit Problems and Save Money
Getting a Loan: Your Home As Security
How to Dispute Credit Report Errors* $.50
Income Tax Preparation Services
Invention Program Firms* $.50
Lost or Stolen: Credit and ATM Cards* $.50
Mortgage Servicing* $.50
Money Matters: How To Talk To and Select Lawyers, Financial Planners, Tax Preparers, and Real Estate Brokers
Mortgage Money Guide* $1.25
Refinancing Your Home
Second Mortgage Financing
Scoring for Credit
Solving Credit Problems* $.50
Swindlers are Calling* $.50
Using Plastic: A Young Adult's Guide To Credit Cards
Women and Credit Histories

* Crashworthiness: Air Bags, Child Seats, Helmets, Seat Belts

Office of Crashworthiness Research (NRD-10)
Research and Development
National Highway Traffic Safety Administration
U.S. Department of Transportation

400 7th Street, SW   800-424-9393
Washington, DC 20690   202-366-4862

Research is conducted on vehicle crashworthiness and crash avoidance. To determine how drivers and passengers fare in head-on collisions, information is collected on seat belts, air bags, child safety restraints, motorcycle helmets, fuel systems, rearview mirrors, tires, door locks, seats, bumpers, and school busses. The annual publication, *Federal Motor Vehicle Safety Standards and Regulations*, is available for $134 (S/N 950-031-00000-0) from the Government Printing Office. Superintendent of Documents, Washington, DC 20402; 202-512-1800. New Car Assessment Program information on selected models is available from the Auto Safety Hotline: 800-424-9393.

* Essential Air Service

Office of Aviation Analysis
Policy and International Affairs
Office of the Secretary of Transportation
U.S. Department of Transportation
400 7th Street, SW, Room 6401   800-424-9393
Washington, DC 20690   202-366-5903

The Department's Essential Air Service Program ensures that certain cities will be served by air transportation. The program establishes subsidy levels, selects carriers, processes applications to change service levels, and reviews fitness of carriers. Contact the office listed for information about this program.

* Explosives/Stolen Weapons Hotline

Explosives Enforcement Branch
Bureau of Alcohol, Tobacco, and Firearms (ATF)
U.S. Department of the Treasury
650 Massachusetts Ave., Room 5200   202-927-7930
Washington, DC 20226   202-927-8120

Those with information on a major arson incident or bombing, or those aware of stolen/lost weapons or explosives, may call the above hotline. One of four national response teams will be rushed to the scene within 24 hours. A report will be taken by those answering the phone, and the information will be transferred to the nearest agent in the area. Each of the four response teams is composed of 10 special agents, a forensic chemist, and an explosive specialist from ATF's Explosives Technology Branch. A state or local law enforcement or fire service official can request the services of a National Response Team by contacting an ATF Special Agent in charge at one of 22 strategic office locations throughout the United States:

Atlanta, GA: 404-331-6526
Birmingham, AL: 205-731-1205
Boston, MA: 617-565-7042
Brentwood, TN: 615-781-5364
Charlotte, NC 704-344-6125
Dallas, TX: 214-767-2250
Detroit, MI: 313-393-6000
Houston, TX: 713-449-2073
Kansas City, MO: 816-421-3440
Los Angeles, CA: 213-894-4812
Louisville, KY: 502-582-5211
Miami, FL: 305-536-4368
Middleburg Heights, OH: 216-522-7210
Nashville, TN: 615-781-5368
New Orleans, LA: 504-589-2048
New York, NY: 212-264-4657
Oak Brook, IL: 708-971-8422
Philadelphia, PA: 215-597-7266
San Francisco, CA: 415-744-7001
Seattle, WA: 206-220-6440
St. Louis, MO: 314-425-5560
St. Paul, MN: 612-290-3092
Washington, DC: 202-927-8500

* Eye Care

Federal Trade Commission (FTC)
Reilly Dolal
Service Industry Practices
601 Pennsylvania Ave., NW
Washington, DC 20580   202-326-3277

Under the Federal Trade Commission (FTC) Rule, an eye care specialist is required to provide you with your eyeglass prescription, immediately after the examination,

Be patient. If any phone number is incorrect, call (area code) 555-1212 and request the new listing.

95

so that you can then comparison shop for eyeglasses. The specialist, however, is not required to provide you with your contact lens fitting specifications. For more information on eye care products and services and your consumer rights, contact the Federal Trade Commission.

* Firearms and Explosives
Licensing Center
Bureau of Alcohol, Tobacco and Firearms
U.S. Department of the Treasury
650 Massachusetts Ave.   202-566-7135
Washington, DC 20226   800-366-5423
This office provides license information.

* Firefighting, Prevention, and Forest Fires Bibliography
Superintendent of Documents
Government Printing Office
Washington, DC 20402   202-512-1800
Fire safety publications are listed, including improving the fire safety of cigarettes and the effect of cigarettes on the ignition of furnishings. Free.

* Funeral Rule
Federal Trade Commission (FTC)
Service Industry Practices
601 Pennsylvania Ave., NW
Washington, DC 20580   202-326-3064
Each year Americans arrange more than two million funerals for family and friends, and the Federal Trade Commission (FTC) has developed a trade regulation rule concerning funeral industry practices to enable consumers to obtain information about funeral arrangements. For a free brochure on the funeral rule, including price disclosures, embalming information, and cremation, contact this FTC office.

* Gangs, Guns, Drugs...Had Enough
Bureau of Alcohol, Tobacco and Firearms
U.S. Department of the Treasury
650 Massachusetts Ave.   202-566-7135
Washington, DC 20226   800-ATF-GUNS
Information is accepted at this office regarding illegal use, buying or selling of firearms. Any suspicious gang activity may also be reported here. If you wish, information may be given anonymously.

* General Motors Consumer Mediation Program
Federal Trade Commission (FTC)
Enforcement Division
601 Pennsylvania Ave., NW
Washington, DC 20580   202-326-3027
Under the terms of a 1983 Federal Trade Commission (FTC) order, all owners of General Motors (GM) cars and light trucks with engine or transmission problems have an opportunity to get money back spent on repairs, or to get repairs by GM at no charge. For a free handbook about this mediation/arbitration program, call 800-824-5109, or contact the FTC for a free fact sheet outlining your rights.

* Geologic Hazards
Geologic Inquiries
U.S. Geological Survey
911 National Center
Reston, VA 22092   703-648-4380
This division evaluates environmental hazards which are associated with earthquakes, volcanoes, floods, droughts, toxic materials, landslides, subsidience, and other ground failures. Methods of hazards prediction are developed through the study of the Earth's internal structure. Engineering problems are identified and solved, including problems in the selection of sites for power stations, highways, bridges, dams, and hazardous waste disposal.

* Grape Wine Label Information
Distribution Center
Bureau of Alcohol, Tobacco, and Firearms
U.S. Department of the Treasury
7943 Angus Ct.
Springfield, VA 22153   703-455-7801

The free brochure, *What You Should Know About Grape Wine Labels*, describes the elements written on a label for grape wine and what can be learned from the label. These include brand, vintage date, varietal designations, alcohol content, appellation of origin, viticultural area, name or trade name, and estate bottled.

* Health and the Environment
American Council on Science and Health
1995 Broadway, 2nd Floor
New York, NY 10023-5860   212-362-7044
The American Council on Science and Health (ACSH) is a consumer education association providing the public with scientifically balanced evaluations of food, chemicals, the environment and health. Publications: *ACSH News and Views, Inside ACSH, ACSH Media Update*.

* Health Fraud
Federal Trade Commission (FTC)
Service Industry Practices
601 Pennsylvania Ave., NW
Washington, DC 20580   202-326-3128
Each year billions of consumer dollars are wasted on useless remedies and devices. This Federal Trade Commission (FTC) office can provide you with information on how to spot worthless, fraudulent claims involving products which "cure" arthritis, cancer, weight loss, cellulite, baldness, and much more.

* Health Spa Complaints
Federal Trade Commission
Service Industry Practices
601 Pennsylvania Ave., NW
Washington, DC 20580   202-326-3128
The most frequent complaints about health spas concern high pressure sales tactics, misrepresentations about facilities and services, and spas that go out of business. This office can provide you with information about your rights or how to file a complaint.

* Interstate Bussing, Trucking, Railroad Complaints
The Interstate Commerce Commission has three regional offices which serve a variety of functions, one of which is to answer inquiries and assist the public with concerns regarding interstate bus, trucking, and railroad companies. The most frequent calls involve moving companies.

Eastern
Interstate Commerce Commission, 3535 Market St., Room 16400, Philadelphia, PA 19104; 215-596-4040. States served: AL, CT, DE, DC, FL, GA, KY, MA, MD, ME, MS, OH, PA, NC, NH, NJ, NY, RI, SC, TN, VA, VT, WV.

Central
Interstate Commerce Commission, 55 W. Monroe, Suite 550, Chicago, IL 60603; 312-353-6204. States served: AR, IA, IL, IN, KS, LA, MI, MO, MN, NE, ND, OK, SD, TX, WI.

Western
Interstate Commerce Commission, 211 Maine St., Suite 500, San Francisco, CA 94105; 415-744-6520. States served: AK, AZ, CA, CO, ID, MT, NV, NM, OR, UT, WA, WY.

* Legal Action Against Companies
Federal Trade Commission (FTC)
Office of the General Counsel
601 Pennsylvania Ave., NW
Washington, DC 20580   202-326-2481
During an investigation, the Federal Trade Commission (FTC) staff may find reason to believe that an individual company has violated the law. If the case is not settled by a formal agreement with the company (a consent order), the FTC may decide to sue the company. Depending on the circumstances, the case will be tried before an administrative law judge or in federal court. The FTC may seek a cease and desist order, a preliminary or permanent injunction, consumer redress, or other appropriate relief.

* Loss and Damage of Cargo Claims
Office of Compliance and Consumer Assistance
Interstate Commerce Commission
12th St. and Constitution Ave., NW

Room 4412
Washington, DC 20423   202-927-5520

While the Commission does not have specific binding authority to adjudicate a dispute claim, it will render all possible assistance. There are several publications available to inform the consumer of his or her rights. *Loss and Damage Claims! Can You Collect?* provides the basic information on cargo claim problems. *Administrative Ruling 120* deals with concealed loss or damage claims. For a copy of these publications and further assistance, contact the Office of Compliance and Consumer Assistance.

* Marketing Practices

Federal Trade Commission (FTC)
Marketing Practices
601 Pennsylvania Ave., NW
Washington, DC 20580   202-326-3128

This division of the Federal Trade Commission (FTC) brings law enforcement actions with regard to unfair or deceptive marketing and warranty practices. Although the FTC is not authorized to resolve individual consumer complaints, it can act when it sees a pattern of possible law violations. Deceptive sales programs areas include the following: business opportunities, multi-level marketing plans, and pyramid sales schemes; business and office supply sales schemes; counterfeit goods; fraudulent health spa practices; health or safety risks or defects in major consumer products, such as cars; rebate coupon problems; travel clubs or coupons and vacation certificates; and vacation timesharing or campground plans. This division also enforces actions regarding warranties, franchising rules, and funeral rules. For more information on these or other advertising issues, contact this office.

* Maximum Speed Limit

Police Traffic Services Division
Office of Enforcement and Emergency Services
Traffic Safety Programs
National Highway Traffic Safety Administration
U.S. Department of Transportation
400 7th Street, SW, Room 6124   800-424-9393
Washington, DC 20690   202-366-5440

The National Maximum Speed Limit is 65 miles per hour on certain interstate highways. This office processes annual certifications of maximum speed limit enforcement programs throughout the U.S. and assists states in developing and improving enforcement efforts.

* Meat and Poultry Hotline

Food Safety and Inspection Service
U.S. Department of Agriculture   202-720-3333
Washington, DC 20250   800-535-4555

This service takes calls from consumers on cases of meat or poultry food poisoning or complaints about meat or poultry spoilage due to improper packaging or processing. They can also provide you with health-oriented information on safe handling and storage of meats and poultry.

* Moving

Office of the Secretary
Interstate Commerce Commission
12th St. and Constitution Ave., NW
Washington, DC 20423   202-927-5520

When You Move: Your Rights and Responsibilities is a pamphlet your mover gives you to provide information about your rights and responsibilities as a shipper of household goods. It includes information on estimates, contracts, weight of shipment, pick-up and delivery, notification of charges, and payments. Also included is a section on filing of loss or damage claims.

* Moving and Trucking Complaint and Performance Data

Office of Compliance and Consumer Assistance
Interstate Commerce Commission (ICC)
12th St. and Constitution Ave., NW
Washington, DC 20423   202-927-5520

Among the many consumer-oriented services of the ICC is a series of advisory bulletins alerting the public and prospective transportation users of the existence of certain transportation problems, and of a regulation requiring household goods carriers to furnish an information bulletin to each prospective customer. You may obtain these advisories by calling or writing this office.

* News Releases From FTC

Federal Trade Commission (FTC)
Office of Public Affairs (OPA)
601 Pennsylvania Ave., NW
Washington, DC 20580   202-326-2710

This office provides information to the public through the media. It issues news releases on all significant Commission actions, responds to reporters' inquiries and arranges television, radio, and print interviews for Federal Trade Commission (FTC) officials. The Office of Public Affairs (OPA) also issues a weekly calendar of Commission events and a weekly summary of press releases, called *News Notes*, which are available to the public. To be placed on the mailing list for *News Notes*, contact this office. Weekly Calendar: Call 202-326-2711 on Monday mornings for current weeks' activities.

* Odometer Tampering

Odometer Fraud Staff
Office of Chief Counsel
National Highway Traffic Safety Administration (NHTSA)
U.S. Department of Transportation
400 7th Street, SW, Room 5219   800-424-9393
Washington, DC 20690   202-366-9511

Federal law requires that the seller of a car sign a disclosure statement that the mileage on the odometer is accurate and has not been rolled back. NHTSA enforces the odometer law via inspections and criminal charges. Information on odometer tampering is also available from the Auto Safety Hotline: 800-424-9393.

* Postal Inspection Service

Inspection Service Department
U.S. Postal Service
475 L'Enfant Plaza, SW
Washington, DC 20260-2100   202-268-4267

As the law enforcement arm of the Postal Service, The Postal Inspection Service protects the mails, postal funds, and property; investigates internal conditions and needs that may affect postal security and effectiveness; apprehends those who violate the postal laws; and audits financial and nonfinancial operations. Information on past and present schemes used to defraud the public is available as well. Help is available if you experience difficulty with a company or suspect that you have been the victim of mail fraud. There is a Regional Chief Inspector in each of the five postal regions. Information and complaints of postal violations should be presented to the nearest Postal Inspector in charge.

Inspection Service Operational Support Group
Central Division
Chicago
Main Post Office Bldg., Chicago, IL 60607-5401; 312-669-5650
433 W. Van Buren St., Chicago, IL 60669-2201; 312-669-5633

Denver
P.O. Box 329, Denver, CO 80201-0329; 303-295-5320

Des Moines
P.O. Box 566, Des Moines, IA 50302-0566; 515-253-9060

Detroit
P.O. Box 330119, Detroit, MI 48232-6119; 313-226-8184

Indianapolis
7188 Lakeview Pkwy. W. Dr., Indianapolis, IN 46268-4101; 317-328-2500

Kansas City
3101 Broadway, Suite 850, Kansas City, MO 64111-2416; 816-932-0400

Milwaukee
P.O. Box 788, Milwaukee, WI 53201-0788; 414-287-2200

St. Louis
1106 Walnut St., St. Louis, MO 63199-2201; 314-539-9300

St. Paul
P.O. Box 64558, St. Paul, MN 55164-0558; 612-293-3202/3200

Eastern Division
Cynwyd
P.O. Box 3000, Bala Cynwyd, PA 19004; 610-668-4500

Be patient. If any phone number is incorrect, call (area code) 555-1212 and request the new listing.

Baltimore
P.O. Box 1856, Baltimore, MD 21203; 410-347-4380

Charlotte
2901 I-85 S., Charlotte, NC 28228-3000; 704-329-9120

Cincinnati
P.O. Box 14487, Cincinnati, OH 45250-0487; 513-684-5700

Cleveland
P.O. Box 5726, Cleveland, OH 44101-0726; 216-443-4000

Harrisburg
P.O. Box 60035, Harrisburg, PA 17106-0035; 717-257-2330

Philadelphia
P.O. Box 7500, Philadelphia, PA 19101-9000; 215-895-8450

Pittsburgh
1001 California Ave., Pittsburgh, PA 15290-9000; 412-359-7900

Richmond
P.O. Box 25009, Richmond, VA 23260-5009; 804-418-6100

Washington, DC
P.O. Box 96096, Washington, DC 20066-6096; 202-636-2339/2300

Northeast Division
Newark
Gateway #2, McCarter Hwy. and Market St., Newark, NJ 07175-0001; 201-621-5500
P.O. Box 509, Newark, NJ 07101-5901; 201-596-5450

Boston
P.O. Box 2217, Boston, MA 02202-2217; 617-464-8000

Buffalo
685 Ellicott Sq., Buffalo, NY 14203-2545; 716-856-3674

Hartford
P.O. Box 2169, Hartford, CT 06145-2169; 203-524-6060

New York
421 8th Ave., New York, NY 10116-9998; 212-330-3844

San Juan
P.O. Box 3667, San Juan, PR 00936-9614; 809-749-7600

Southern Division
Memphis
10th Fl., 1407 Union Ave., Memphis, TN 38161-0001; 901-722-7700
P.O. Box 3180, Memphis, TN 38173-0180; 901-576-2137

Atlanta
P.O. Box 16489, Atlanta, GA 30321-0489; 404-765-7369

Birmingham
P.O. Box 2767, Birmingham, AL 35202-2767; 205-521-0270

Fort Worth
P.O. Box 162929, Fort Worth, TX 76161-2929; 817-625-3411

Houston
P.O. Box 1276, Houston, TX 77251-1276; 713-238-4400

Miami
P.O. Box 520772, Miami, FL 33152-0772; 305-470-0379

New Orleans
P.O. Box 51690, New Orleans, LA 70151-1690; 504-589-1200

Tampa
P.O. Box 22526, Tampa, FL 33622-2526; 813-281-5200

Western Division
San Bruno
850 Cherry Ave., San Bruno, CA 94098-0100; 415-952-2900

Oakland
7717 Edgewater Dr., Oakland, CA 94621-3013; 510-251-3300

Pasadena
P.O. Box 2000, Pasadena, CA 91102-2000; 818-405-1200

Phoenix
P.O. Box 20666, Phoenix, AZ 85036-0666; 602-223-3660

Portland
Suite 790, 921 SW Washington, Portland, OR 97205-2898; 503-279-2060

San Diego
P.O. Box 2110, San Diego, CA 92112-2110; 619-233-0610

San Francisco
P.O. Box 882000, San Francisco, CA 94188-2000; 415-550-5602/5700

Seattle
P.O. Box 400, Seattle, WA 98111-4000; 206-442-6300

* Radon
Public Information Center
Environmental Protection Agency
401 M St., SW, PM-211 B   202-382-2491
Washington DC 20460   202-382-2491

A Citizen's Guide to Radon helps readers understand the radon problem and decide if they need to take action to reduce radon levels in their homes. It explains what radon is, how it is detected, and what the results mean. Contact this office for your free copy.

* Reference Guides on Consumer Concerns
Science and Technology Division
Reference Section, Library of Congress
Washington, DC 20540   202-707-5580

Informal series of reference guides are issued free from the Science and Technology Division under the general title, *LC Science Tracer Bullet*. These guides are designed to help readers locate published material on subjects about which they have only general knowledge. New titles in the series are announced in the weekly Library of Congress *Information Bulletin* that is distributed to many libraries including:

80-14 Automotive Maintenance and Repair
80-18 Health Foods
81-6 Pets and Pet Care
81-9 Cable Television (Cable TV)

* Service Industry Practices
Federal Trade Commission (FTC)
Service Industry Practices
601 Pennsylvania Ave., NW
Washington, DC 20580   202-326-3321

This Federal Trade Commission (FTC) division focuses on deception and misrepresentation in the advertising of professional services. Law enforcement activities are directed toward restrictions on advertising and other business practices of professionals that may impede competition and consumer choice. Other activities include investigating investment schemes; monitoring industry standards and certification programs and the Retail Food Advertising and Marketing Practices Rule. Program areas include advertising, eyeglasses, employment counseling services, health care services, and legal services. This division's current investment fraud investigations focus on gemstones, cellular phone lotteries, rare coins, and art. Contact this division for more information on any of these programs or investigations.

* Shopping By Mail
Federal Trade Commission (FTC)
Enforcement Division
601 Pennsylvania Ave., NW
Washington, DC 20580   202-326-3768

Ordering merchandise by mail can be a convenient way to save time, energy, and sometimes money, but if your merchandise arrives late or not at all, you need to know your rights. The Federal Trade Commission (FTC) can furnish you with information concerning the Mail Order Merchandise Rule, but to resolve a complaint against a company, contact your local Postmaster, your local consumer protection agency, or the Direct Marketing Association at 6 E. 43rd St., New York, NY 10017.

* State Motor Vehicle Inspections

Records and Motor Vehicle Services Division (NTS-43)
National Highway Traffic Safety Administration (NHTSA)
U.S. Department of Transportation
400 7th Street, SW   800-424-9393
Washington, DC 20690   202-366-2676

The National Highway Traffic Safety Administration's (NHTSA) Motor Vehicle Inspection Program is aimed at providing car owners with preventive information on what repairs are needed to achieve greater safety, lower pollution, and better mileage. The annual *Study of the State Motor Vehicle Inspection Program* is available from this office.

* Telemarketing Travel Fraud

Federal Trade Commission
Marketing Practices
601 Pennsylvania Ave., NW
Washington, DC 20580   202-326-3128

Have you ever been tempted to buy one of those bargain-priced travel packages sold over the telephone? Be careful. Your dream vacation may turn into a misadventure if you fall victim to one of the many travel scams being sold over the phone which are defrauding consumers out of millions of dollars each month. If you feel you are a victim of just such a scam, or you want information on how to avoid them, contact this office for their free brochure.

* Trade Regulation Enforcement

Federal Trade Commission (FTC)
Enforcement Division
601 Pennsylvania Ave., NW
Washington, DC 20580   202-326-3027

This division of the Federal Trade Commission (FTC) monitors compliance with Commission orders and, along with the Regional Offices, enforces a number of trade regulations and specific laws. What follows is a brief listing of some of the FTC laws and regulations, along with the respective FTC expert in that area:

Appliance Labeling Rule, which requires the disclosure of energy costs of home appliances. Stephen Ecklund, 202-326-3034.

Cooling-Off Rule, which requires sellers to give consumers notice of their three-day cancellation rights for sales made away from the seller's place of business. George Brent Mickum, 202-326-3132.

Games of Chance in the Food Retailing and Gasoline Industries Rule, which requires disclosure of the odds of winning prizes, the random distribution of the winning prize pieces, and the publication of the winners' names. John Mendenhall, Cleveland Regional Office, 216-522-4210.

Negative Option Rule, which requires sellers who use negative option purchase plans, such as book and record clubs, to give members at least 10 days to reject the monthly selection. Erwin Rodriguez, 202-326-3647

Octane Posting and Certification Rule, which requires the posting of octane ratings on gasoline dispensers. Neil Blickman, 202-326-3038.

R-value Rule, which requires sellers to disclose the thermal efficiency of home insulation. Kent Howerton, 202-326-3013.

Used Car Rule, which requires dealers to post on each used car a "Buyers Guide" that gives information about the warranty coverage, tells the meaning of an "as is" sale, and suggests that consumers ask about getting an independent inspection before buying the car. George Brent Mickum, 202-326-3132.

Fair Packaging and Labeling Act, which requires consumer commodities to be accurately labeled to describe the product's identity and net quantity. Stephen Ecklund, 202-326-3034.

Hobby Protection Act, which requires imitation coins, medals, and other monetary items to be marked "copy," and imitation political items to be marked with the year of manufacture. Robert Easton, 202-326-3029.

Textile, Wool, and Fur Acts, which protect consumers against mislabeling, false advertising, and false invoicing of textile, wool, and fur products. Bret Smart, Los Angeles Regional Office, 310-235-7975.

Amended Wool Products Labeling and Textile Fiber Products Identification Acts, which require all wool and textile items, domestic or imported, to be labeled with the country of origin. Steve Ecklund, 202-326-3034.

Unordered Merchandise Statute, which permits consumers to keep, as a free gift, merchandise they received through the U.S. mail but did not order. Vada Martin, 202-326-3768.

Made in USA, requires labeling and advertising to state country of origin. Steve Ecklund, 202-326-3034.

* Transportation Issues

Office of Public Interest Groups
Intergovernmental and Consumer Affairs
Governmental Affairs
Office of the Secretary of Transportation
U.S. Department of Transportation (DOT)
400 7th Street, SW   800-424-9393
Washington, DC 20690   202-366-1524

This office acts as a liaison between Congress, state and local governments, business and industry, and public interest groups to ensure that their needs are considered when Department policy decisions are made. Public and private organizations can contact this office to communicate needs and comment on DOT programs and regulations.

* Transportation Safety Institute

Transportation Safety Institute (DMA-60)
Research and Special Programs Administration
U.S. Department of Transportation
6500 South MacArthur Blvd.
Oklahoma City, OK 73169   405-680-3153

The Institute supports the Department's efforts to reduce transportation accidents. It develops and conducts training programs for Federal, state, and local governments; industry; and foreign personnel. Courses are offered in aviation, highway, marine, pipeline, and railroad safety; materials analysis; transportation security; and other subjects. Mail: P.O. Box 25082, Oklahoma City, OK 73125-5050.

* Vehicle Importation

Public Information Division
U.S. Customs Service
U.S. Department of the Treasury
P.O. Box 7407
Washington, DC 20044   202-927-6724

The pamphlet, *Importing a Car*, outlines the provisions for dutiable entry or free entry of automobiles, trucks, and motorcycles. Prior arrangements, documentation, safety and emissions standards, and federal tax guidelines are also discussed.

* Vehicle Manufacturer Safety Compliance

Vehicle Manufacturer Safety Compliance (NEF-30)
Enforcement
National Highway Traffic Safety Administration
U.S. Department of Transportation
400 7th Street, SW   800-424-9393
Washington, DC 20690   202-366-2832

To ensure that foreign and domestic vehicle and equipment manufacturers comply with federal motor vehicle safety standards, this office performs compliance testing, inspections, and investigations involving about 150 performance requirements and nearly 3000 equipment items.

* Vehicle Research and Testing

Vehicle Research and Test Center
Research and Development
National Highway Traffic Safety Administration (NHTSA)
U.S. Department of Transportation
P.O. BOX 37
East Liberty, OH 43319   513-666-4511

The National Highway Traffic Safety Administration (NHTSA) evaluates the effectiveness of Federal Motor Vehicle Safety Standards. This engineering facility performs tests to obtain basic data used to establish standards for safety and fuel efficiency of motor vehicles.

Be patient. If any phone number is incorrect, call (area code) 555-1212 and request the new listing.

99

Consumer Power

* Warranties

Federal Trade Commission (FTC)
Division of Marketing Practices
601 Pennsylvania Ave., NW
Washington, DC 20580   202-326-3128

Although the Federal Trade Commission (FTC) cannot intervene in individual disputes and does not handle private cases, the FTC does want to know if companies are meeting their warranty obligations. To report violations of the Warranty Act or warranty-related problems, or to request information concerning warranties in general, contact this office.

* Work-At-Home Schemes

Division of Marketing Practices
Federal Trade Commission (FTC)
6th and Pennsylvania Ave., NW
Washington, DC 20580   202-326-3128

Be careful about work-at-home ads--stuffing envelopes, assembling work, and others--especially ones that promise you large profits in a short period of time. While some of these plans are legitimate, many are not, and if you feel you've been taking advantage of, or if you'd like to know precautions to take against fraudulent schemes, contact the Better Business Bureau, your local Postmaster, your state's Attorney General's office, or the FTC.

State Consumer Protection Offices

You are interested in investing in a company that sells educational courses to the public, but you want to know if they are getting any complaints about their sales practices. How can you find out? Or perhaps you are the manufacturer of a potato peeler which is sold with a warning against using the product on anything other than potatoes. Are you protected from a law suit brought against you by a consumer who cut his finger while using your potato peeler on an orange? On the consumer side, you may have a problem with a product or service, and the retailer has ignored your complaints or given you the run around. What are your rights? In any of these cases, you will probably need consumer protection advice, and quickly. Instead of hiring a high-priced consumer lawyer to solve your problems, contact your state Consumer Affairs Office, which can give you as much, if not more, of the information and advice you may need as the lawyer can give you, but for free.

The kinds of information available from these offices varies from state-to-state; however, most of them can help you with your inquiry or complaint. Aside from just handling complaints, many states publish valuable consumer information on their in-state companies. For example, Alabama will provide you with a listing of all companies that have gone out of business; Arkansas publishes a Buyer Beware List of companies that have been brought to court; New York and Iowa publish yearly reports naming companies that have had complaints filed against them; and Oklahoma and New Mexico release periodic press releases to warn the public of companies that have had court actions taken against them.

If you have yet to purchase a product and want to make sure that you don't get a lemon, state Consumer Offices can help you, too. Most states will provide some information by phone about companies that have had complaints filed against them in the state. Some states, however, require that you speak directly with the investigator assigned to the case, while in others your request must be in writing. Currently, the following states will provide listings of all companies that have had complaints filed against them: Alabama, Arkansas, Delaware, Maine, Maryland, Michigan, Vermont. And 18 states have toll free numbers for in-state consumers to file complaints or to search out information about whether a company has had complaints filed against it. Only five states--Colorado, Illinois, Nevada, Missouri, and West Virginia--do not provide any consumer protection information at all.

Most offices will advise you to take the following steps when lodging a complaint of your own. First, contact the retailer in person or by phone and let them know the nature of the problem. If that doesn't yield the proper response, take step two: write an angry letter that clearly states the problem, the date of purchase, a copy of the receipt, canceled check, or itemized charge bill, and what you would consider a fair and equitable settlement. If you still get no satisfactory response, contact the Consumer Affairs Office.

If you purchased an offending product in another state, start with that state's Consumer Affairs Office. Most offices offer a wide selection of information and educational materials, and most will be glad to answer your questions or direct you toward someone who can. But before you even start, it is very important that you have copies of any relevant sales receipts, other sales documents, and all correspondence between yourself and the retailer and/or manufacturer.

State Consumer Protection Offices

Alabama
Office of Attorney General, Consumer Protection Division, 11 South Union St., Montgomery, AL 36130; 334-242-7334, 800-392-5658. Information on a specific company can be obtained by writing to this office. A listing of complaints filed against a company as well as a listing of companies that have gone out of business can be obtained.

Alaska
The Consumer Protection Section in the Office of the Attorney General has been closed. Consumers with complaints are being referred to the Better Business Bureau. 3380 C Street, Suite 103, Anchorage, AK, 99503, 907-562-0704.

Arizona
Financial Fraud Division, Office of Attorney General, 1275 W. Washington St., Phoenix, AZ 85007; 602-542-3702, 542-5763. Information on complaints on a specific company can be given over the phone. A listing of companies in their files with complete name, address and zip code is also available.

Arkansas
Consumer Protection Division, Office of Attorney General 200 Tower Bldg., 323 Center St., Little Rock, AR 72201; 501-682-2341/TDD, 800-482-8982. Information can be given over the phone on current lawsuits pending, or the names of companies who have failed to respond to a complaint after it has been issued. A Buyer Beware List is distributed which informs consumers which companies have been brought to court.

California
State Department of Consumer Protection, 400 R St., Suite 1040, Sacramento, CA 95814; consumer information, 916-445-1254. Data is computerized and available on computer readable formats. A disclosure policy prohibits the release of company information. This office will refer consumers to appropriate licensing boards if necessary. 916-522-1700/TDD, 800-344-9940.

Colorado
Consumer Protection Unit, Office of Attorney General, 1625 Broadway, Denver, CO 80202; 303-620-4500. A disclosure policy prohibits the release of any company information. No publications available.

Connecticut
Department of Consumer Protection, State Office Building, 165 Capitol Ave., Hartford, CT 06106; 203-566-4999, 800-842-2649, 800-538-2277. Requests for specific information on a company must be made in writing. Information is given on the company's license, and complaint record over the last 2 years.

Delaware
Division of Consumer Affairs, Department of Community Affairs, 820 North French St., Wilmington, DE 19801; 302-571-4080, 800-443-2179, 800-736-4000. A list of companies with registered complaints can be obtained from this office.

Consumer Power

District of Columbia
Department of Consumer and Regulatory Affairs, 614 H. St., NW, Washington, DC 20001; 202-727-7000. Specific information on some companies may be given over the phone, including the name of the company president or officer. For detailed information a request must be made in writing.

Florida
Department of Agriculture and Consumer Services, Division of Consumer Services, 218 Mayo Building, Tallahassee, FL 32399; 904-488-1234, 800-342-2176/TDD, 800-342-2175, 800-327-3382. Information on complaints of a specific company can be given over the phone. Some information is available on computer readable formats.

Georgia
Office of Consumer Affairs, 2 Martin Luther King, Jr. Dr., Suite 356, Atlanta, GA 30334; 404-656-3790, 404-651-8600, 800-869-1123.

Hawaii
Office of Consumer Protection, Department of Commerce and Consumer Affairs, P.O. Box 3767, Honolulu, HI 96812; 808-586-2630. Information on the number of complaints filed, date of complaints and a public review of a specific company can be given over the phone.

Idaho
Office of Consumer Protection, 650 W. State, Lower Level, Boise, ID 83720; 208-334-2424, 800-432-3545. Consumer brochures are available. Data is computerized but business status reports are not given to the general public.

Illinois
Consumer Protection Division, Office of Attorney General, 222 S. College St., Springfield, IL 62706; 217-782-0244, 800-252-8666. Information on a specific company is not given over the phone. Data is computerized but not released. Mediation consumer brochures are available.

Indiana
Consumer Protection Division, Office of Attorney General, 219 State House, Indianapolis, IN 46204; 317-232-6330, 800-382-5516. All company information is available for public record but must have the permission of the specific company before it can be released to the public. Data files are computerized and available on computer readable formats with company consent.

Iowa
Consumer Protection Division, Office of Attorney General, 1300 E. Walnut, Des Moines, IA 50319; 515-281-5926. Information on the number of complaints filed on a specific company can be given over the phone by an assigned investigator. A yearly report is published and available to the public. No computer listings are available.

Kansas
Consumer Protection Division, Office of Attorney General, 301 West 10th, Topeka, KS 66612; 913-296-3751, 800-432-2310. Complaint or information on a lawsuit for a specific company can be given over the phone by talking with the case attorney. Data files are computerized but a complete listing of companies in the file is considered confidential.

Kentucky
Consumer Protection Division, Office of Attorney General, 209 Saint Clair St., Frankfort, KY 40601; 502-564-2200, 800-432-9257. Information on complaints of a specific company can be given over the phone. Various consumer brochures are published.

Louisiana
Department of Urban and Community Affairs, P.O. Box 94005, Baton Rouge, LA 70804; 504-342-7373. Litigation information on a specific company can be given over the phone.

Maine
Bureau of Consumer Credit Protection, State House Station # 35, Augusta, ME 04333-0035; 207-624-8527, 800-332-8529. Investigation results of a specific company can be given over the phone. Staff will also advise you on registration or license information for a specific company. Consumer purchasing brochures are available. Data is in the process of becoming computerized. A listing of all companies in their file including name, address and zip code is available in hand written form.

Maryland
Consumer Protection Division, Office of Attorney General, 200 St. Paul Place, Baltimore, MD 21202; 410-528-8662 (9 a.m.-3 p.m.), 800-969-5766. Information on the number of complaints within a 3 year period a company has received can be obtained over the phone. Data files are computerized, and are available on computer readable formats. A listing of all companies in their file is available to the public.

Massachusetts
Consumer Protection Division, Department of Attorney General, 200 Portland St., Boston, MA 02114; 617-727-8400. Information on complaints and specific fees charged by a specific company can be obtained over the phone. Data files are computerized. For specific company requests, the name, address and zip code is provided.

Michigan
Consumer Protection Division, Office of Attorney General, P.O. Box 30213, Lansing, MI 48909; 517-373-1140. Information on the number of complaints or written inquiries of a specific company can be given over the phone (limited to 2 requests at a time). Computer listings of companies and their addresses are available for a fee.

Minnesota
Office of Consumer Services, Office of Attorney General, 117 University Avenue, St. Paul, MN 55155; 612-296-2331. The status of legal action and information on complaints of a specific company can be given over the phone. No computer listings are available.

Mississippi
Consumer Protection Division, Office of Attorney General, P.O. Box 22947, Jackson, MS 39225-2947; 601-354-6018. Information on complaints filed for a specific company can be given over the phone. Data files are not computerized.

Missouri
Department of Economic Development, P.O. Box 899, Jefferson City, MO 65102; 314-751-3321. There is no Consumer Protection Agency in Missouri; for specific information contact this office.

Montana
Consumer Affairs Unit, Department of Commerce, P.O. Box 20051, Helena, MT 59620; 406-444-4312, 800-332-2272. Information on complaints on a specific company can be given over the phone. All investigative information is confidential. Data files are not computerized.

Nebraska
Consumer Protection Division, Department of Justice, 2115 State Capital Bldg., Lincoln, NE 68509; 402-471-2682. A computer check detailing the nature of a complaint for a specific company, and if the complaint was resolved is available from this office. Data files are computerized.

Nevada
Consumer Affairs Office, Department of Commerce, State Mail Room Complex, Las Vegas, NV 89158; 702-486-7355. A disclosure policy prohibits the release of any company information.

New Hampshire
Consumer Protection Bureau, Office of Attorney General, 33 Capital St., Concord, NH 03301; 603-271-3641. Information on court actions for a specific company can be given over the phone. Some data is computerized, entire files are not available to the public.

New Jersey
Division of Consumer Affairs, P.O. Box 45027, Newark, NJ 07101; 201-648-4010, 800-242-5846. Information on the nature of complaints filed for a specific company can be given over the phone. Data files are computerized but an entire listing of all companies is not available.

New Mexico
Consumer and Economic Crime Division, Office of Attorney General, P.O. Drawer 1508, Santa Fe, NM 87504; 505-827-6000. Information on complaints on a specific company can be given over the phone. A press release is published every two weeks warning consumers of current scams. Data files are not computerized.

New York
New York State Consumer Protection Board, 99 Washington Ave., Albany, NY 12210; 518-474-8583. An annual report is available to the public. Data files are

computerized in the complaint unit located in Buffalo and Rochester. Call this office for referral.

North Carolina

Consumer Protection Section, Office of Attorney General, P.O. Box 629, Raleigh, NC 27602; 919-733-7741. Information on the number of complaints filed for a specific company can be obtained from the specialist who handled the case. Published information is available on complaint laws. Data files are computerized, but a listing of all companies on file is not released.

North Dakota

Consumer Fraud Division, Office of Attorney General, State Capitol Building, Bismarck, ND 58505; 701-328-2210, 800-472-2600. Information on the complaint record of a specific company can be given over the phone. Various consumer brochures are published. Data files are not computerized.

Ohio

Consumer Frauds and Crimes Section, Office of Attorney General, 30 East Broad St., State Office Tower, Columbus, OH 43266; 614-466-4986, 800-282-0515, 614-466-1393/TDD. Only information concerning a law suit against a specific company can be given over the phone. Various consumer brochures are published. Names of businesses with complaints filed against them are released with a written request.

Oklahoma

Consumer Affairs, Office of Attorney General, 4545 N. Lincoln Blvd., Suite 260, Oklahoma City, OK 73105; 405-521-4274. Information on the number of complaints, and legal action taken against a specific company can be given over the phone. Consumer brochures and press releases are available. Data files are not computerized.

Oregon

Financial Fraud Section, Department of Justice, Justice Building, Salem, OR 97310; 503-378-4320. Information on the number of complaints and a brief summary of the complaints against a specific company can be given over the phone. Various consumer brochures are available including the Unlawful Trade Practices Act. Data files are computerized, but no listings are available.

Pennsylvania

Bureau of Consumer Protection, Office of Attorney General, Strawberry Square, 14th Floor, Harrisburg, PA 17120; 717-787-9707, 800-441-2555. Only information concerning a court case of a specific company can be given over the phone. Data files are computerized, no listings are available.

Rhode Island

Consumer Protection Division, Department of Attorney General, 72 Pine St., Providence, RI 02903; 401-277-2104, 401-274-4400, ext. 354/TDD, 800-852-7776. Information concerning cases of consumer fraud are available. Data is computerized and available on computer readable formats. A complete listing of all companies in their files with the name, address, zip code of each company is available.

South Carolina

Consumer Protection Office, Office of Attorney General, P.O. Box 5757, Columbia, SC 29250; 803-734-9452, 803-734-9455/TDD, 800-922-1594. Information on complaints and the closing of a specific company can be obtained over the phone. Information is also available on the company's credit rating and certification (if it applies).

South Dakota

Division of Consumer Affairs, Office of Attorney General, 500 East Capital, Pierre, SD 57501; 605-773-4400. Information on complaints on a specific company can be given over the phone, including the firm's name and address. Data files are compu-

terized but a complete listing of all businesses in the file is not available. A consumer handbook is published.

Tennessee

Antitrust and Consumer Protection Division, Office of Attorney General, 450 James Robertson Parkway, Nashville, TN 37243-0485; 615-741-2672. Information on whether or not a complaint has been filed against a specific company is available over the phone. For more detailed information the investigator on the case must be contacted. A Consumer Survival Kit is distributed as well as various consumer brochures.

Texas

Consumer Protection Division, Office of Attorney General, 714 Jackson, Suite 700, Dallas, TX 75202; 214-742-8944. Information on complaints on a specific company can be given over the phone. Some data is computerized. No lists are available.

Utah

Division of Consumer Protection, Department of Business Regulation, P.O. Box 45804, Salt Lake City, UT 84145-0804; 801-530-6601. Information on complaints taken to court are available over the phone. Various consumer information publications are available including the Unfair Practice Act, Lemon Law, and other brochures on fraud and pyramid schemes. Data files are not computerized.

Vermont

Public Protection Division, Office of Attorney General, 109 State St., Montpelier, VT 05609; 802-828-3171. A listing of complaints made, how many, a brief summary and how and if the complaint was resolved is available for a specific company. Data files are computerized; a computer listing can be generated. Various consumer brochures are available on housing, credit, mail order, auto, health, and money matters.

Virginia

Office of Consumer Affairs, P.O. Box 1163, Richmond, VA 23219; 804-786-2042. Information on if a complaint exists, if it was resolved and how, is available for a specific company over the phone. Various brochures concerning Virginia consumer laws are published. Data files are computerized from 1986 to the present. No listings are available.

Washington

Attorney General's Office, Consumer and Business Fair Practices Division, 900 Fourth Ave., Suite 2000, Seattle, WA 98164; 206-464-6431, 800-551-4636. To have access to complaint files, a public disclosure agreement form must be filled out. The only information given out over the phone is if a company has been sued.

West Virginia

Consumer Protection Division, Office of Attorney General, 812 Quarrier St., Charleston, WV 25301; 304-348-8986, 800-368-8808. A disclosure policy prohibits the release of any information on a specific company.

Wisconsin

Office of Consumer Protection, Department of Justice, P.O. Box 7856, Madison, WI 53707; 608-266-1852, 800-362-8189. Information on complaints filed on a specific company can be given over the phone. Various consumer brochures are published. Some data are computerized.

Wyoming

Consumer Protection Office, Office of Attorney General, 123 Capitol Building, Cheyenne, WY 82002; 307-777-7874. Information on complaints on a specific company can be given over the phone. Some data are computerized. No listings are available.

Money, Banking, and Credit

* Banking and Credit Problem Hotline

Office of Consumer Affairs
Federal Deposit Insurance Corporation (FDIC)
550 17th St., NW, Room F-130   800-934-3342
Washington, DC 20456   202-898-3536

This office answers questions and addresses complaints regarding FDIC-insured banks. A computerized system helps to track complaints from their initial filing to their resolution. A follow-up complaint satisfaction survey is also conducted periodically. Banking questions may be directed to the nearest regional FDIC office, or call the FDIC's toll-free customer service hotline between 9 a.m. and 4 p.m. EST, Monday through Friday.

* Consumer Banking and Finance Publications

Public Information Materials Directory. Catalogues most publications and audiovisual materials prepared by the 12 Federal Reserve Banks and the Board of Governors of the Federal Reserve System. This information is designed to increase public understanding of the functions and operations of the Federal Reserve System, monetary policy, financial markets and institutions, consumer finance and the economy. Copies of this directory can be obtained from the Federal Reserve Bank in your district.

What follows is a list of the Federal Reserve Banks across the U.S., along with their free consumer publications available:

Board of Governors of the Federal Reserve System
Publications Services, MS-138
20th St. and Constitution Ave., NW
Washington, DC 20551   202-452-3000

Consumer Handbook on Adjustable Rate Mortgages. Explains adjustable rate mortgages and some of the risks and advantages.
Consumer Handbook to Credit Protection Laws. Tells how consumer credit laws can help in shopping for and applying for credit and in keeping a good credit record.
Consumer's Guide to Mortgage Closings. Explains the mortgage closing process.
Consumer's Guide to Mortgage Lock-Ins. Describes various aspects of mortgage lock-ins.
Consumer's Guide to Mortgage Refinancing. Discusses the process and some of the risks and advantages to mortgage refinancing.
Guide to Business Credit and the Equal Credit Opportunity Act. Advises consumers of their rights under the Act when applying for a business loans and helps consumers prepare effective loan presentations.
Guide to Federal Reserve Regulations. Explains the goals and scope of Federal Reserve regulations.
How to File a Consumer Credit Complaint. Tells how to file a complaint against a bank.
Welcome to the Federal Reserve. Structure and function of the System.
What You Should Know About Home Equity Lines of Credit. Describes what the equity plan does, how it works and obtaining the credit. Also includes checklist and glossary.

Federal Reserve Bank of Atlanta
Public Affairs Department
104 Marietta St. NW
Atlanta, GA 30303-2713   404-521-8500

Bank Examiner Flimflam. Information on what to do if you are a victim of the "bank examiner" or "policeman" scam. Warns bank customer against possible theft by deception.
Economic Review. A bimonthly publication presenting new research and articles on the economy of the Southeast.

Federal Reserve Bank of Boston
Bank and Public Services Department
P.O. Box 2076
Boston, MA 02106-2076   617-973-3000

Checkpoints. Explains how to write, deposit, and cash checks; also available in Spanish and Portuguese.
Home Improvement Credit: Avoiding Second Mortgage Fraud. Homeowners' rights when in need of credit for home improvement projects.

Massachusetts in the 1990's: The Role of the State Government. Focuses on expenditures and summarizes the recent revenue experience and outlook.
New England Economic Indicators. Monthly report of statistical data for the nation and New England states.
New England Economic Review. Publishes articles of broad economic interest bi-monthly.
Right Checks. Outlines the use of specialized checks. Certified, personal, travelers, government, cashier and postal money orders.
Wishes and Rainbows. Touches on the economic problem of scarce resources and society's reaction through a children's story.

Federal Reserve Bank of Chicago
Public Information Center
230 S. LaSalle St.
P.O. Box 834
Chicago, IL 60690-0834   312-322-5322

ABC's of Figuring Interest. Ways of calculating interest and how the dollar amount paid was affected.
Credit Guide. Basic guidelines for obtaining and using consumer credit.
Economic Perspectives. Bimonthly publication on banking, business, and agriculture.
Great Lakes Economy. Looking North and South. Economic trends, performances and linkage within the region through agriculture, energy, research and development.
Home Improvement Credit: Avoiding Second Mortgage Fraud. Homeowners' rights when in need of credit for home improvement projects.
Seventh District Economic Data. Provides statistical data on population, business, agriculture, foreign trade, and finance for the five states of the 7th Federal Reserve District.

Federal Reserve Bank of Cleveland
Public Information Department
P.O. Box 6387
Cleveland, OH 44101-1387   216-579-2000

Economic Review. Quarterly publication featuring monetary, economic, and banking topics of district and national interest.
Economic Trends (Chartbook). Charts latest economic statistics and briefly discusses the current economy. Monthly.

Federal Reserve Bank of Dallas
Public Affairs Department
2200 N. Pearl
Dallas, TX 75201   214-922-6000

Quarterly Survey of Agricultural Credit Conditions. Discusses regional agricultural developments.
Southwest Economy. Bimonthly publication of articles on economic and financial topics.
United States Savings Bonds. Basic information.
United States Treasury Securities. Basic information on investing in Treasury bills, notes and bonds.

Federal Reserve Bank of Kansas City
Public Affairs Department
925 Grand Ave.
Kansas City, MO 64198-0001   816-881-2000

Banking Regulation: Its Purposes, Implementation and Effect. A look at today's regulatory system and recent changes in banking.
Economic Review. Discusses a variety of economic and financial topics; quarterly.
Financial Market Volatility and Economy. How to cope with market volatility.

Federal Reserve Bank of Minneapolis
Public Affairs
250 Marquette Ave.
Minneapolis, MN 55401-0291   612-340-2345

Agricultural Credit Conditions. Quarterly survey of district farm economy.
Consumer Credit Protection: Do You Know Your Rights? Easy-to-understand summary of consumers' credit protection rights.

Fedgazette. Quarterly business and economics newspaper for the ninth district. Features include opinion survey results, current business news, economic indicators and commentary.

Quarterly Review. Includes feature articles on the district economy.

Federal Reserve Bank of New York
Public Information Department
33 Liberty Street
New York, NY 10045   212-720-5000

Consumer Credit Regulators (Fedpoints 17). Reviews the responsibilities of the 12 federal organizations charged with administering consumer regulations.

Debit and Deficits. Their size and impact and measures for bringing them under control.

Primer on Inflation. Process, causes, transmittion and alternatives for dealing with the problem.

Quarterly Review. Reports on business activities and the money and bond markets.

Story of Foreign Trade and Exchange. Explains basic principle. Comic-style booklet.

Federal Reserve Bank of Philadelphia
Public Information Department
P.O. Box 66
Philadelphia, PA 19105   215-574-6000

Applying for Credit and Charge Cards: What Consumers Should Know About the Cost and Terms of Credit. Explains the Fair Credit Act.

Business Outlook Survey. Reports on manufacturing in the district and provides forecasts for the next six months; monthly.

Business Review. Bimonthly articles for readers with a general interest in economics.

Buying Treasury Securities. Provides basic information on investing in Treasury bills, notes, and bonds.

Electronic Banking for Today's Consumer. Explains electronic services such as ATMs, direct deposit, bill-paying services, and point-of-sale terminals, as well as consumer protections of Regulation E.

Fair Debt Collection Practices Act. Summarizes the main provisions of the Act.

Frauds and Scams: Protect Yourself and Your Money. Protecting yourself against old and new scams.

Give Yourself Credit. Guides consumers through various credit protection laws.

How the New Equal Credit Opportunity Act Affects You. Outlines the Act's main provisions for consumers.

Plastic Fraud: Getting a Handle on Debit and Credit Cards. Discusses consumer awareness concerning credit and debit card fraud and the regulations protecting consumers.

Quarterly Regional Economic Report. Analyzes the economy of the district.

Your Credit Rating. Describes the importance of credit histories and consumers' rights when using credit, including ways to correct records.

Federal Reserve Bank of Richmond
Public Services Department
P.O. Box 27622
Richmond, VA 23261   804-697-8000

Black Banks. Profiles operating revenue and distribution by profit/loss size of black banks.

Community Affairs Officers at Federal Reserve Banks. Outlines the Community Affairs Officer's role, duties, and responsibilities, particularly those related to the Community Reinvestment Act.

Cross Sections. Quarterly reviews of business and economic developments.

Homeownership. Guidelines for buying and owning a home.

How Much Are You Worth. Monitoring the finances and economics of the household.

Where Banks Get Their Money. Information of banks' sources of funds.

Federal Reserve Bank of St. Louis
Public Information Office
P.O. Box 442
St. Louis, MO 63166   314-444-8444

Agriculture: an Eighth District Perspective. Quarterly summary of national and district agricultural developments.

Annual U.S. Economic Data. Provides selected economic statistics.

Pieces of Eight: An Economic Perspective on the Eighth District. Summarizes national and district business developments.

Review. Examines national and international economic developments; analyzes various sectors of the district; ten issues per year.

Federal Reserve Bank of San Francisco
Public Information Department
P.O. Box 7702
San Francisco, CA 94120   415-974-2000

Give Yourself Credit. Guides the consumer through various credit protection laws.

Economic Review. Discusses selected economic, banking, and financial topics; quarterly.

Weekly Letter. Highlights a major economic issue each week.

Teaching Materials. Audiovisual Materials. Films, filmstrips, slides and video cassettes, in most cases, may be borrowed from within the district of the issuing Bank and do require return postage. Exceptions include the educational filmstrips issued by the Federal Reserve Bank of New York which are sold at nominal cost. For a listing of titles and the issuing Bank, request the Public Information Materials directory from your districts' Bank.

* Consumer Expenditure and Family Budgets
Consumer Expenditure Surveys Division
Office of Prices and Living Conditions
Bureau of Labor Statistics
U.S. Department of Labor
2 Massachusetts Ave. NE, Room 3985
Washington, DC 20212   202-606-6872

The *Consumer Expenditure Studies*, a continuing annual survey of consumer expenditures and income, is the basic source of data for the revision of items and weights in the market basket of consumer purchases to be priced for the Consumer Price Index. Selected data is classified by income class, family size, and other demographic and economic characteristics of consumer units. Coverage includes the urban population of the U.S. through 1983, and the total population in 1984 and after.

* Consumer's Financial Guide
Publications Section
Printing Branch, Stop C-11
U.S. Securities and Exchange Commission
Washington, DC 20549   202-272-7040

The free publication, *Consumer's Financial Guide*, contains basic information on choosing investments and keeping them safe, trading securities, and the different protections guaranteed by law. To obtain this publication, contact this office.

* Consumer Price Index Within 24 hours
National Technical Information Service
U.S. Department of Commerce
5285 Port Royal Road
Springfield, VA 22161   703-487-4630

A Consumer Price Index data summary is available by mailgram within 24 hours of the CPI release. It provides unadjusted and seasonally adjusted U.S. City Average data for All Urban Consumers and for Urban Wage Earners and Clerical Workers. The cost of this service is $190 per year.

* Consumer Prices
Office of Prices and Living Conditions
Bureau of Labor Statistics
U.S. Department of Labor
2 Massachusetts Ave. NE, Room 3615
Washington, DC 20212   202-606-7000

The Labor Department measures consumer price changes for a predetermined market basket of consumer goods and services for two population groups: all urban consumers, and urban wage earners and clerical workers. The fixed market basket includes 382 entry level items representing all goods and services purchased for everyday living by all urban residents. Monthly and bimonthly indexes are available for various geographic regions.

* Consumer Purchasing Power Index
Superintendent of Documents
Government Printing Office
Washington, DC 20402   202-512-1800

Each monthly issue of the *Consumer Price Index Detailed Report* provides a comprehensive summary of price movements for the month, plus statistical tables, charts, and technical notes. The report covers two indexes, the Consumer Price Index for All Urban Consumers, and the Consumer Price Index for Wage Earners and Clerical Workers. The indexes reflect data for the U.S. city average and selected areas. An annual subscription is available for $23. (S/N 729-001-00000-3).

Consumer Power

* Credit and ATM Cards

Federal Trade Commission
Credit Practices
6th and Pennsylvania Ave., NW
Washington, DC 20580 202-326-3233

Loss or theft of credit and ATM cards is a serious consumer problem; however, there are laws which establish procedures for you and your creditors to follow to resolve problems with these cards. This office investigates credit card fraud and can give you information on what to do if any of your cards are missing or stolen.

* Credit Card and Computer Fraud

Fraud Division
Office of Investigations
U.S. Secret Service
U.S. Department of the Treasury
1800 G St., NW
Washington, DC 20223 202-535-5850

The fraudulent use of credit and debit cards is a federal violation. Investigations are conducted by the Secret Service, including stolen or lost credit cards, the misuse of credit card account numbers, automated teller machine fraud, telephone fraud involving long distance calls, and other types of access device fraud. Computer fraud is a recent concern of the Secret Service. New law enforcement techniques are being pioneered in an effort to identify computer criminals.

* Credit Pamphlets

Office of Consumer Affairs
Federal Deposit Insurance Corporation (FDIC)
550 17th St., NW, Room F-130 800-934-FDIC(3342)
Washington, DC 20429 202 898-3536

The following Federal Deposit Insurance Corporation (FDIC) pamphlets are free and are available in English and Spanish.

Consumer Information. Provides an overview of the FDIC, its regional offices, and the major consumer and civil rights laws and regulations that protect bank customers.
Equal Credit Opportunity and Age. Describes Credit Law and age discrimination.
Equal Credit Opportunity and Women. Describes Credit Law and issues of sex and marital status.
Fair Credit Billing. Offers consumers advice on handling disputes regarding billing errors and defective merchandise in ways designed to protect their credit rating.
Fair Credit Reporting Act. Details consumers' rights to know what credit and personal information has been obtained about them by "Consumer Reporting Agencies" and what their rights are to challenge inaccurate information.
Truth in Lending. Explains how the Truth in Lending Law protects consumers from hidden finance charges when obtaining credit.

* Credit Practices

Federal Trade Commission (FTC)
Credit Practices Division
6th and Pennsylvania Ave., NW
Washington, DC 20580 202-326-3233

This division of the Federal Trade Commission (FTC) works to ensure that creditors, credit counselors, certain mortgage lenders, and others who grant credit do not engage in unfair or deceptive acts or practices in providing credit or credit-related services. It also enforces the specific consumer protection statutes and rules listed below. Contact this division for more information about these topics. *Consumer Leasing Act*, which requires lessors to give consumers specific information on lease costs and terms. *Electronic Fund Transfer Act*, which requires institutions to disclose in writing important terms, such as charges for electronic fund transfers. *Equal Credit Opportunity Act*, which prohibits any creditor from denying credit to a consumer on the basis of sex, marital status, color, race, religion, national origin, age, or receipt of public assistance. *Truth in Lending Act*, which requires creditors to disclose in writing certain cost information, such as the annual percentage rate (APR), before consumers enter into credit transactions. *Credit Practices Rule*, which prohibits certain security interests and collection remedies in consumer credit contracts--namely, confessions of judgment, wage assignments, waivers of exemption, and security interests in certain household goods. *Holder-in-Due Course Rule*, which preserves consumers' claims and defenses involving performance of merchandise bought on credit against a non-seller owner of the credit contract.

* Credit Problems

Federal Trade Commission
Bureau of Consumer Protection
Credit Practices Division
6th and Pennsylvania Ave., NW
Washington, DC 20580 202-326-3233

Before you pay a credit repair clinic to "fix" your credit record, learn what the law says and consider saving your money by making some phone calls yourself. This office can give you information on how to "fix" your own credit rating, along their free brochure.

* Credit Protection Laws

Publication Services
MS-138, Board of Governors
Federal Reserve System
Washington, DC 20456 202-452-3244

The *Consumer Handbook to Credit Protection Laws*, which can help you better understand how the credit protection laws can help you, is available free from this office.

* Damaged Currency Redemption

Office of Currency Standards
Bureau of Engraving and Printing
U.S. Department of the Treasury
Room 344A, BEPA
P.O. Box 37048
Washington, DC 20013 202-662-2361

All mutilated currency may be sent to the above address where trained personnel will determine if it can be exchanged at face value. All final decisions for redemption of this currency are made by the Treasurer of the United States. Currency should be sent by registered mail to the P.O. box address above.

* Direct Deposit of Social Security Payments

Office of the Assistant Commissioner Field Operations
Financial Management Service
U.S. Department of the Treasury
401 14th St., SW
Washington, DC 20227 202-874-7328

Presumed Direct Deposit is an approach of establishing Direct Deposit as the "normal" way to receive Social Security benefit payments. Sign-up techniques are simplified. Customer Service is being increased in over-the-counter and over-the-phone contacts. Beneficiaries may still choose to receive a check if they prefer or if they do not have a banking relationship.

* Donations to the Public Debt

Office of the Commissioner
Bureau of the Public Debt
U.S. Department of the Treasury
999 E St., NW
Washington, DC 20239 202-219-3300

Since the U.S. government maintains a public debt of more than $1.9 trillion dollars, and is currently paying $176 billion in interest to pay off this debt, they are asking for donations from the general public to pay off the debt. The Treasury has an account into which money received as gifts is deposited. The money is used to pay at maturity, or to redeem or buy before maturity, an obligation of the Government included in the public debt. You can send donations to: Bureau of the Public Debt, Department G, Washington, DC 20239-0601.

* Fair Credit Billing

Federal Trade Commission
Division of Credit Practices
6th and Pennsylvania Ave., NW
Washington, DC 20580 202-326-3233

Credit card billing errors do occur, but they are simple to resolve if you know how to use the Fair Credit Billing Act, which protects your rights as a card user. For a free brochure on this Act or on credit billing laws in general, contact the Federal Trade Commission (FTC).

* Fair Credit Reporting

Federal Trade Commission
Credit Practices
6th and Pennsylvania Ave., NW
Washington, DC 20580   202-326-3233

If you've ever applied for a charge account, a personal loan, insurance, or a job, someone is probably keeping a file on you. This file might contain information on how you pay your bills, or whether you've been sued, arrested, or have filed for bankruptcy. Credit bureaus gather and sell this information as "consumer reports" to creditors, employers, and other businesses, but the Fair Credit Reporting Act protects you by requiring credit bureaus to furnish correct and complete information. This office can give you more information on your rights.

* Fair Debt Collection

Federal Trade Commission
Credit Practices
6th and Pennsylvania Ave., NW
Washington, DC 20580   202-326-3233

If you use credit cards, owe money on a loan, or are paying off a home mortgage, you are a "debtor." And although you may never come in contact with a debt collector, if you do, you should know the law to make sure you are treated fairly. This office can provide you with information about your rights as a debtor.

* Women and Credit Histories

Federal Trade Commission (FTC)
Bureau of Consumer Protection
6th and Pennsylvania Ave., NW
Washington, DC 20580   202-326-3233

Each year many women are denied credit because they cannot show how they have used it, but two federal laws, the Equal Credit Opportunity Act and the Fair Credit Reporting Act, give you specific rights that help protect your credit history and make it easier for you to obtain credit. For more information, including a brochure on how to establish your credit, contact the Federal Trade Commission.

Product Safety

* Accident Investigations Database

National Injury Information Clearinghouse

U.S. Consumer Product Safety Commission (CPSC)	800-638-2772
Washington, DC 20207	301-504-0424

Consumer Product Safety Commission (CPSC) accident investigation reports provide information about an accident's sequence, human behavior, and role of the consumer product in the accident. Following is a description of the information in the CPSC's Accident Investigations database, which includes accidents occurring after mid-1972: the state in which the accident occurred; the victim's background, including age, race sex, education, and number of days incapacitated; the injury diagnosis; the consumer product involved; the product manufacturer; and more. Most information requests are answered without charge within 10 working days, but there is a charge for costs in excess of $25.

* Consumer Commission Meetings and Reports

Office of the Secretary

U.S. Consumer Product Safety Commission (CPSC)	800-638-2772
Washington, DC 20207	301-504-0800

Commission meetings and meetings of the commissioners or Commission staff with persons outside of government are generally open to the public. In addition, records of what was discussed at those meetings are available for public inspection. Notices of meetings are generally published in the Commission's Public Calendar at least seven days before the meetings take place. Contact this office for a free copy of the Public Calendar.

* Consumer Deputy Program

U.S. Consumer Product Safety Commission (CPSC)

5401 Westbard Avenue	800-638-2772
Washington, DC 20207	301-504-0788

As an unpaid volunteer, you can work with district and regional Commission offices to visit retail stores to make sure that the stores are complying with CPSC guidelines. Volunteers identify themselves to the store, check the inventory, and then report their findings back to the CPSC. The most recent Deputy program involves monitoring stores for the illegal sale of lawn darts.

* Consumer Injury Surveillance System

National Injury Information Clearinghouse

U.S. Consumer Product Safety Commission (CPSC)	800-638-2772
Washington, DC 20207	301-504-0424

The National Electronic Injury Surveillance System (NEISS) collects injury data from a sample of hospitals with emergency rooms across the U.S. and its territories. This data provides national estimates of the number and severity of injuries associated with but not necessarily caused by consumer products and treated in hospital emergency rooms. Information gathered from these and other sources, such as death certificates and reported incidents, guides the Commission in setting priorities for selecting types of products for further investigation and action. NEISS data are available in various computer formats. Any of the standard reports may be requested from this office, while custom reports are available at variable rates.

* Consumer Outreach Programs

U.S. Consumer Product Safety Commission (CPSC)	800-638-2772
Washington, DC 20207	301-504-0580

By contacting the Commission's main office in Washington, DC, or your local CPSC regional office, you can arrange to have a consumer education specialist visit your business, school, community group, or organization for a presentation on consumer product hazards and safety strategies.

* Consumer Product/Product-Related Injury Hotline

Office of Information and Public Affairs
U.S. Consumer Product Safety Commission (CPSC)

Washington, DC 20207	800-638-2772

To report a hazardous product or product-related injury, call this toll-free number.

This hotline handles more than 200,000 calls each year. Operators are on duty from 10:30 a.m. to 4:00 p.m. Eastern Standard Time, Monday through Friday.

* Consumer Product Safety Commission Library

U.S. Consumer Product Safety Commission (CPSC)	800-638-2772
Washington, DC 20207	301-504-0044

The Consumer Product Safety Commission (CPSC) library's collection includes reference materials on engineering, economics, and health sciences, which CPSC staff and other researchers may use for background on product safety issues. The library does not include CPSC documents and publications.

* Consumer Safety Databases

U.S. Consumer Product Safety Commission (CPSC)	800-638-2772
Washington, DC 20207	301-504-0424

Although the Commission does not maintain databases which are accessible to outside users, specific requests for data are handled by the Commission's National Injury Information Clearinghouse or the Division of Automated Data Processing. Data may be provided to the requestor in the form of printouts, 9 track tapes, or 5.25" floppy diskettes. All information disclosed must first meet the disclosure requirements of the Consumer Product Safety Act. What follows is sampling of the Commission's databases.

American Association of Poison Centers: Information on childhood poisoning incidents received annually and prepared on various substance categories.

All Terrain Vehicle (ATV) Deaths: Information on ATV-related deaths, including investigation and injury reports, and death certificates.

Chemicals in Products: Contains complete chemical and biological information on consumer products.

Childhood Drowning Study: Contains information of swimming pool-related deaths of children.

Death Certificates: Information on death certificates involving product-related deaths in the U.S.

Establishment Inventory System: Maintains information on businesses which CPSC monitors or otherwise contacts, including data on firms, products, inspections, samples, and violations.

Fire Incident Reporting System: Contains information on electrical and range/oven fires collected from fire departments throughout the U.S.

Lawn Mower Special Survey: Maintains reports of lawn mower-related injuries over the last four years.

PCAT Data Collection: Contains children poisoning information, including records of ingestion by product categories for children under 5 years of age.

Product Defect Identification: contains manufacturer and retail reports to CPSC of product defects with injury risks, along with complaints and injuries of which the companies are aware.

* Consumer's Resource Handbook

Office of Information and Public Affairs
U.S. Consumer Product Safety Commission (CPSC)

Washington, DC 20207	800-638-2772

This free *Consumer's Resource Handbook* shows you how to communicate more effectively with manufacturers, retailers, and service providers. The first section features tips on avoiding purchasing problems and getting the most for your money by giving steps for handling your own complaint and writing an effective complaint letter. The second section, the *Consumer Assistance Directory*, lists consumer offices in both public and private sectors that provide assistance for consumer complaints. Available from the Consumer Information Center, Pueblo CO 81009.

* Explosives Hotline

Explosives Enforcement Branch
Bureau of Alcohol, Tobacco, and Firearms

U.S. Department of the Treasury	800-424-9393
650 Massachusetts Ave.	202-927-7930
Washington, DC 20226	202-927-8120

Those with information on a major arson incident or bombing, or those aware of stolen explosives, may call the above hotline. One of four national response teams will be rushed to the scene within 24 hours. A report will be taken by those answering the phone, and the information will be transferred to the nearest agent in the area. Each of the four response teams is composed of 10 special agents, a forensic chemist, and an explosive specialist from ATF's Explosives Technology Branch. A state or local law enforcement or fire service official can request the services of a National Response Team by contacting an ATF Special Agent in charge at one of 22 strategic office locations throughout the United States:

Atlanta, GA:	404-331-6526
Birmingham, AL:	205-731-1205
Boston, MA:	617-565-7042
Brentwood, TN:	615-736-5412
Charlotte, NC	704-371-6125
Dallas, TX:	214-767-2250
Detroit, MI:	313-226-4830
Houston, TX:	713-229-3511
Kansas City, MO:	816-374-7188
Los Angeles, CA:	213-894-4812
Louisville, KY:	502-582-5211
Miami, FL:	305-536-4368
Middleburg Heights, OH:	216-522-7210
New Orleans, LA:	504-589-2048
New York, NY:	212-264-4657
Oak Brook, IL:	312-620-7824
Philadelphia, PA:	215-597-7266
San Francisco, CA:	415-974-9589
Seattle, WA:	206-442-4485
St. Louis, MO:	314-425-5560
St. Paul, MN:	612-290-3092
Washington, DC:	703-285-2543

* Explosives Incidents Statistics

Explosives Division
Office of Law Enforcement
Bureau of Alcohol, Tobacco, and Firearms
U.S. Department of the Treasury
650 Massachusetts Ave.   800-424-9393
Washington, DC 20226   202-927-7930

The annual *Explosives Incidents Report* highlights statistics of explosive incidents and stolen explosives and recoveries. Tables include incidents by state, by target, and by types of explosives used. Significant explosives incidents during the year are also described. To obtain a copy of the report, contact Distribution Center, Bureau of Alcohol, Tobacco, and Firearms, U.S. Department of the Treasury, 7943 Angus Ct., Springfield, VA 22153.

* Firearms: Federal Regulations

Distribution Center
Bureau of Alcohol, Tobacco, and Firearms
U.S. Department of the Treasury
7943 Angus Ct.
Springfield, VA 22153   703-455-7801

Federal firearms laws are outlined in the free book, *Your Guide to Federal Firearms Regulation: 1988-1989*. Regulations concerning state firearms control assistance; machine guns, destructive devices, and certain other firearms; certain firearms administered by other federal agencies; commerce in firearms and ammunition, and the importation of arms, ammunition and implements of war are included. For questions on Federal Firearms Laws, regulations, procedures or policies, contact the ATF compliance operations office nearest you, seen in the list below (alphabetical by state).

Birmingham, AL 35209	205-731-0400
Little Rock, AR 72201	501-378-6457
Los Angeles, CA 90053	213-894-4817
Sacramento, CA 95814	916-551-1323
San Francisco, CA 94107	415-974-7778
San Jose, CA 95113	408-291-7464
Santa Ana, CA 92712	714-836-2946
Santa Rosa, CA 95404	707-576-0184
Denver, CO 80294	303-844-5027
Hartford, CT 06103	203-722-2037
Miami, FL 33166	305-592-9967
Tampa, FL 33602	813-228-2346

Atlanta, GA 30340	404-986-6075
Chicago, IL 60604	312-353-3797
Frankfort, KY 40601	502-223-3350
Louisville, KY 40202	502-582-5217
Baltimore, MD 21201	301-962-3200
Boston, MA 02222-1079	617-565-7073
Farmington Hills, MI 48331	313-226-4735
St. Paul, MN 55101	612-290-3496
Kansas City, MO 64106	816-426-2464
St. Louis, MO 63101	314-539-2251
Parsippany, NJ 07054	201-334-7058
Buffalo, NY 14202	716-846-4048
New York, NY 10008	212-264-4650
Charlotte, NC 28209	704-371-6127
Cincinnati, OH 45203	513-684-3351
Middleburg Hts.,OH 44130	216-522-3374
Portland, OR 97218	503-231-2331
Lansdale, PA 19446	215-248-5252
Pittsburgh, PA 15222	412-644-2919
Hato Rey, PR 00918	809-753-4082
Dallas, TX 75242	214-767-9461
Houston, TX 77024	713-220-2157
San Antonio, TX 78206	512-229-6168
Richmond, VA 23240	804-771-2877
Seattle, WA 98174	206-442-5900
Milwaukee, WI 53202	414-291-3991

* Firearms Identification

Distribution Center
Bureau of Alcohol, Tobacco, and Firearms
U.S. Department of the Treasury
7943 Angus Ct.
Springfield, VA 22153   703-455-7801

The free publication, *Identification of Firearms*, helps individuals in identifying weapons classified as firearms, including destructive devices. Pictures and descriptions are included of machine guns and machine pistols, shotguns, rifles, silencers, and other weapons and destructive devices.

* Fishery Products Grading and Inspection

Utilization Research and Services
National Marine Fisheries Service
National Oceanic and Atmospheric Administration
U.S. Department of Commerce
1335 East-West Hwy., Room 6142
Silver Spring, MD 20910   301-713-2245

The National Marine Fisheries Service conducts a voluntary seafood inspection program on a fee-for-service bases. A wide range of inspection services are available to any interested party, including harvesters, processors, food-service distributors, and importers and exporters. These services include vessel and plant sanitation inspection, product evaluation (in-plant and warehouse lot), product specification review, label review, laboratory analyses (microbiological tests, chemical contaminant/indices of decomposition, species identification), training, and education and information. This office has a great deal of information concerning inspections, grading of products, and regulations. They also publish a document listing fishery products that have been produced in fish establishments approved by the National Marine Fisheries Service.

* National Injury Information Clearinghouse

U.S. Consumer Protection Safety Commission (CPSC)
5401 Westbard Avenue, Room 625
Washington, DC 20207   301-504-0424

This clearinghouse collects, investigates, analyzes, and distributes injury data and information relating to the causes and prevention of death, injury, and illness associated with consumer products. It maintains thousands of detailed investigative reports of injuries associated with consumer products and has access to automated databases with several million incidents of injuries that have been reported by a nationwide network of hospital emergency departments. Technical analysts prepare publications, such as hazard analyses, special studies, and data summaries, a catalog of which is available by contacting the clearinghouse.

* Publications

Office of Information and Public Affairs
U.S. Consumer Product Safety Commission (CPSC)
EXPA

Be patient. If any phone number is incorrect, call (area code) 555-1212 and request the new listing.

109

Consumer Power

Washington, DC 20207   Recording: 800-638-2772
The following consumer publications describe some of the common hazards associated with the use of consumer products and recommend ways to avoid these hazards. They come in the form of fact sheets (F.S.), brochures, and materials developed especially for use by classroom teachers. Some of the publications listed here can also be requested from the Commission's Regional Offices. Direct your request to the above address on a post card.

General Information
Who We Are and What We Do
Compilation of Laws
Consumer Resource Handbook (1988)
CPSC Hotline Brochure
Some Federal Consumer Oriented Agencies (F.S. 52)

Annual Reports
Annual Report 1987
Annual Report 1986
Annual Report 1984 Part II
Annual Report 1983 Part II
Annual Report 1982
Annual Report 1981 Parts I,II

Bicycle Safety
Sprocketman (a comic book for high school age students)
Bicycle Safety

Children's Furniture
Cribs (F.S. 43)
High Chairs (F.S. 70)
Bunk Beds (F.S. 71)
Tips for Your Baby's Safety - Nursery Equipment Checklist
(English and Spanish)
The Safe Nursery - A Buyer's Guide to Nursery Equipment
(English and Spanish)
Be Sure It's Safe For Your Baby

Children's Safety
Skateboards (F.S. 93)
Protect Your Child
Bumps Teachers Guide
Super Sitter

Compliance Publications
Retailers Guide (1/86)
Guide for Manufacturers, Distributors, and Retailers
Guide for Retailers (9/84)

Curriculum Guides and Lessons for Use By Educators
It's No Accident - Consumer Product Safety
 Guide for Teachers of Grades 3-6
Flammable Products: A Guide for Teachers of Secondary Grades
Flammable Products: A Guide for Teachers of Elementary Grades
(Spanish)
Flammable Fabrics: Teacher's Guide (4T)
Flammable Fabrics: Student Readings (4-S)
Halloween Safety Teacher's Guide (9T)
Holiday Safety Teacher's Guide (7T)
Poison Prevention Teacher's Guide (6T)

Electric Safety
Ranges and Ovens (F.S. 9)
TV Fire and Shock (F.S. 11)
Electric Blenders (F.S. 50)
Clothes Dryers (F.S. 73)
Ground Fault Circuit Interrupters (F.S. 99)
CPSC Guide to Electrical Safety
Consumer Product Safety Alert on Antennas
Electrical Safety Room by Room Audit Checklist (English and Spanish)
(This is also available on "slow play disc" for the blind.)

Final Reports
Final Report of the National Conference on Product Safety (1982)
Final Report of the National Conference on Product Safety (1984)
Final Report of the National Consumer Product Safety Conference for
 Retailers
Final Report of the National Conference on Fire Toxicity

Fire Safety
Fireworks (F.S. 12)
Upholstered Furniture (F.S. 53)
Halloween Safety (F.S. 100)
What You Should Know About Smoke Detectors
Give a Gift--Give a Smoke Detector (poster)
Home Fire Safety Checklist

Hazardous Substances
School Science Laboratories: A Guide to Some Hazardous Products
Asbestos in the Home
List of Asbestos in Hair Dryers
Methylene Chloride Safety Alert

Holiday Safety
Merry Christmas With Safety

Home Heating Equipment
Space Heaters (F.S. 34)
Fireplaces (F.S. 44)
Furnaces (F.S. 79)
Wood Burning Stoves (F.S. 92)
Kerosene Heaters (F.S. 97)
Electric Space Heaters (F.S. 98)
464 Chimneys Safety Alert (1984)
Caution: Choosing and Using Gas Space Heaters
What You Should Know About Kerosene Heaters
What You Should Know About Space Heaters

Home Insulation
Installing Insulation Safety
Insulation Installers Guide
Q&A Urea Formaldehyde Foam Insulation

Indoor Air Quality
The Inside Story: A Guide to Indoor Air Quality

Outdoor Power Equipment
Power Mowers (F.S. 1)
Chain Saws (F.S. 51)
Chain Saw Safety Guide
Consumer Product Safety Alert on Chain Saws
Mower Hazards and Safe Practices (poster)
Power Mower and Maintenance Storage Tips
Safety, Sales, and Services
Power Lawn Mower Safety Kit--Teachers Manual
Power Mower Hazards and Safety Features (poster)

Older Consumers Safety
Home Safety Checklist for Older Consumers (English and Spanish)

Playground Equipment
Play Happy, Play Safely: Little Big Kids (3-5 years)
Handbook for Playground Safety, Volume I, General Guidelines

Poison Prevention
First Aid Brochure
Locked-up Poisons (English and Spanish)
Poison Lookout Checklist
Poison Prevention Packaging: A Text for Pharmacies and Physicians

Pool Safety
Children and Pool Safety Checklist
 Backyard Pool--CPSC Safety Alert (5/87)

Spanish Fact Sheets
Power Mowers (F.S. 1)
Kitchen Ranges (F.S. 61)
Carbon Monoxide (F.S. 13)
Infant Falls (F.S. 20)
Mobile Homes (F.S. 39)
Older Consumers and Stairway Accidents (F.S. 48)
Kitchen Knives (F.S. 83)
Trampolines (F.S. 85)

Toys Safety
For Kids Sake, Think Toy Safety Pamphlet (English and Spanish)
Toy Safety Coloring Book (English and Spanish)

* Safety Standard Changes

U.S. Consumer Product Safety Commission (CPSC) 800-638-2772
Washington, DC 20207 301-504-0580

If you think that the current safety specifications on a certain product, such as a toy or a kitchen appliance, aren't tough enough, you can petition the Consumer Product Safety Commission (CPSC) to make the changes and possibly have your recommendations used in the new specifications. Contact this office for more details.

Be patient. If any phone number is incorrect, call (area code) 555-1212 and request the new listing.

111

Post Office and Mailing

* Administrative Support Manual

Consumer Affairs
U.S. Postal Service
475 L'Enfant Plaza, SW
Washington, DC 20260-3121   202-268-2284

This subscription service consists of a basic manual and supplementary material for an indeterminate period. This manual describes matters of internal administration in the Postal Service. It includes functional statements as well as policies and requirements regarding security, communications (printing directives, forms, records, newsletters), government relations, procurement and supply, data processing systems, maintenance, and engineering. A subscription is available for $16 domestic, $20 foreign, S/N 039-000-00281-7, from: Superintendent of Documents, Government Printing Office, Washington, DC 20402-0001; 202-512-1800.

* A Consumer's Guide to Postal Crime Prevention

Public Affairs Branch
The Postal Inspection Service
U.S. Postal Service
475 L'Enfant Plaza, SW
Washington, DC 20260-2100   202-268-5169

The free booklet, *A Consumer's Guide to Postal Crime Prevention*, is full of tips and ideas on how to discourage mail thieves and how to help put mail fraud con artists out of business. Consumers who believe they are victims of mail fraud should write the nearest office of the Postal Inspection Service or refer the information through their local postmaster.

* A Guide to Business Mail Preparation

Marketing Department
Regular Mail Services Division
U.S. Postal Service
475 L'Enfant Plaza, SW, Room 5541
Washington, DC 20260-6336   202-268-2222

This free guide provides voluntary guidelines for postal customers and their suppliers regarding the preparation of letter mail for successful processing on the latest in high-speed automated mail sorting equipment. Computerized mail processing is faster, more efficient, economical, and accurate than older manual or mechanized sorting and mailing methods. Information on addressing for automation, postnet bar codes, and FIM patterns is covered.

* Business Guide to Postal Crime Prevention

Public Affairs Branch
The Postal Inspection Service
U.S. Postal Service
475 L'Enfant Plaza, SW
Washington, DC 20260-2100   202-268-5169

The booklet, *Postal Crime Prevention: A Business Guide*, shows business owners how to protect themselves from con artists and thieves whose business is mail fraud and mail theft. It includes information on different types of mail fraud to watch for, check cashing precautions, guidelines for mailroom security, bombs in the mail, and additional information.

* Business Mailer Information

Communications Department
U.S. Postal Service
475 L'Enfant Plaza, SW
Washington, DC 20260   202-268-2158

The free monthly publication, *Memo to Mailers*, advises business mailers of all rate and classification changes as well as other postal news. It is available from *Memo to Mailers*, Post Office Box 999, Springfield, VA 22150-0999.

* Business Reply Mail

Rates and Classification Department
U.S. Postal Service
475 L'Enfant Plaza, SW
Washington, DC 20260   202-268-5311

Businesses and others who want to encourage responses to their mailings by paying the postage for those responses might consider using business reply mail. Under this service, all responses are returned to the sender from any U.S. post office to any valid address in the United States. Business reply mail must be prepaid according to a specified format, and a small annual fee is charged for each permit issued. The mailer guarantees to pay the postage for all replies returned to him or her at the regular first class rate plus a business reply fee. For additional information, contact this office.

* Business Reply Mailgram

Rates and Classification Department
U.S. Postal Service
475 L'Enfant Plaza, SW
Washington, DC 20260   202-268-5311

A Business Reply Mailgram is now available for customers who require a quick turnaround response. This mailgram provides all of the features of a regular Mailgram with the addition of a built-in response device using a Business Reply envelope. Contact this office for more information, or call a Western Union company in your area.

* Carrier Alert Program

Communications Department
U.S. Postal Service
475 L'Enfant Plaza, SW
Washington, DC 20260   202-268-2158

Pioneered by the Postal Service and the National Association of Letter Carriers, the Carrier Alert Program encourages letter carriers to watch participants' mailboxes for mail accumulations that might signal illness or injury. Accumulations of mail are reported by carriers to their supervisors who then notify a sponsoring agency, through locally developed procedures, for follow-up action. Since its founding in 1982, this lifeline has been cited for saving dozens of lives.

* Consumer Advocate

The Consumer Advocate
U.S. Postal Service
475 L'Enfant Plaza, SW, Room 5821
Washington, DC 20260-2202   202-268-2281

The Consumer Advocate, a postal ombudsman, represents the interest of the individual mail customer in matters involving the Postal Service by bringing complaints and suggestions to the attention of top postal management and solving the problems of individual customers. Contact your postmaster if your problem cannot be solved by your local post office.

* Consumer's Directory of Postal Services and Products

Consumer Advocate
U.S. Postal Service
475 L'Enfant Plaza West, SW
Washington, DC 20260-2202   202-268-2281

This directory, which discusses the various services and products the Postal Service offers, will help you choose the right service to meet your individual needs and save time and money. Included is information on mail services, addressing and packaging, special services, stamp collecting and mail fraud. To obtain a copy, contact this office or your local post office.

* Current Mail Rates, Fees and Services

Rates and Classification Department
U.S. Postal Service
475 L'Enfant Plaza, SW
Washington, DC 20260   202-268-5169

This department can give you information on current mail rates, fees, and services.

* Customer Service Representatives

Marketing and Sales Group
U.S. Postal Service
475 L'Enfant Plaza, SW
Washington, DC 20260   202-268-2267

The U.S. Postal Service has a local sales staff of Customer Service Representatives found in main post offices. Their services include helping you get the most for your postage dollar; showing you how to set up a mail room; resolving your business mail problems and selling services. Contact this office for more information on getting these services.

* Customs

U.S. Customs Service
Treasury Department
1301 Constitution Ave., NW
Washington, DC 20229-0001   202-566-2957

All mail originating in foreign countries and most United States territories is subject to U.S. Customs Service examination upon entering the United States. Many imported goods are subject to U.S. customs duty. When goods enter by mail, the duty assessed by Customs is collected by the Postal Service, as is a customs clearance and delivery fee on each mail piece on which customs duty is paid.

* Design Licenses

Law Department
U.S. Postal Service
475 L'Enfant Plaza, SW
Washington, DC 20260   202-268-2329

Designs of postage stamps issued after January 1, 1978, are copyrighted and may not be reproduced except under license granted by the U.S. Postal Service. Earlier designs are in the public domain and may be reproduced without permission for philatelic, educational, historical, and newsworthy purposes.

* Directives and Forms Catalog

Document Control Division
Office of Information Services
Information Resource Management Department
U.S. Postal Service
Washington, DC 20260-1571

This document is a catalog of all national directives and forms currently used in the Postal Service. A complete edition of this publication is published three times a year. Interim changes appear regularly in the "Directives Update" and "Forms Update" in the *Postal Bulletin*. Also included is a list of directives which the public may obtain free of charge at main post offices.

* Domestic Mail Manual

Superintendent of Documents
Government Printing Office
Washington, DC 20402   202-512-1800

The manual is designed to assist customers in obtaining maximum benefits from domestic postal services. It includes applicable regulations and information about rates and postage, classes of mail, special services, wrapping and mailing requirements, and collection and delivery services. The subscription service consists of four cumulative issues a year and is available for $36 domestic, $45.75 foreign, S/N 739-003-00000-8.

* Freedom of Information Requests

General Counsel
Postal Rate Commission
1333 H St., NW, Suite 300
Washington, DC 20268-0001   202-789-6820

Contact this office for information requests under the Freedom of Information Act.

* Hazardous and Illegal Items

Postal Inspection Service
U.S. Postal Service
475 L'Enfant Plaza, SW
Washington, DC 20260-2186   202-268-5169

It is illegal to send through the U.S. Mail any article, composition, or material which may kill or injure another person, or obstruct mail service or damage property.

Harmful matter includes, but is not limited to poisons, poisonous animals, insects, and reptiles, including all types of snakes and spiders; all disease germs or scabs, and all explosives, flammable material, dangerous machines, and mechanical, chemical or other devices or compositions which may catch fire or explode. Contact this office for more information on the guidelines.

* History of Rural Post Offices

Administrative Office
Postal Rate Commission
1333 H St., NW, Suite 300
Washington, DC 20268-0001   202-789-6840

At the Crossroads: An Inquiry into Rural Post Offices and the Communities They Serve investigates the sociological implications and community effects resulting from the closing of a post office in a small rural community. The study shows the history and development of postal delivery and the Postal Service as it affects rural areas. Write or call for a free copy.

* International Mail Manual

International Postal Affairs Department
U.S. Postal Service
475 L'Enfant Plaza, SW
Washington, DC 20260   202-268-2445

This manual sets forth the policies, regulations, and procedures governing international mail services offered to the public by the Postal Service. It includes the postage rates, fees, and mail preparation information for Postal Union mail, parcel post, and International Express Mail, as they apply to each individual country. A subscription is available for $17 domestic, and $21 foreign, S/N 739-004-00000-4, from: Superintendent of Documents, Government Printing Office, Washington, DC 20402-0001; 202-512-1800.

* International Surface Airlift

International Postal Affairs
U.S. Postal Service
475 L'Enfant Plaza, SW
Washington, DC 20260   202-268-2445

International Surface Air Lift service provides fast delivery, at a cost lower than airmail, for publications and printed matter sent overseas at surface rate. The postage rate is a per pound rate.

* Legal Restrictions

Postal Inspection Service
U.S. Postal Service
475 L'Enfant Plaza, SW
Washington, DC 20260-2186   202-268-5169

There are legal restrictions on the mailing of radioactive material, firearms, knives, and sharp instruments, drugs and narcotics, and other controlled substances as defined by Federal law and related Federal regulations. Certain potentially harmful or dangerous articles and substances may be mailed if special packaging and labeling requirements are met. Your local postmaster or account representative can provide more details.

* Library

Library
U.S. Postal Service
475 L'Enfant Plaza SW, Room 11800
Washington, DC 20260-1641   202-268-2904

Along with a working collection of materials in law, the social sciences, and technology, the Postal Library contains a unique collection of postal materials, legislative files from the 71st Congress to date, reports, pamphlets, clippings, photographs, general postal histories, periodicals of the national postal employee organizations, Universal Postal Union studies, and Postal laws and regulations handbooks and manuals. The library is open to the public weekdays from 9 a.m. to 4 p.m. Reading Rooms are located on the 11th Floor North.

* Mail Fraud

Chief
Postal Inspection Service
U.S. Postal Service
475 L'Enfant Plaza, SW, Room 3021
Washington, DC 20260-2186   202-268-5169

Consumer Power

Postal Crime Hotline
800-654-8896

Mail fraud is a scheme to get money, or anything of value from the public by offering a product, service, or investment opportunity that does not live up to its claims. Prosecutors must prove the claims were intentionally misrepresented and that the mails were used to carry out the scheme. The Postal Inspection Service investigates violations of the mail fraud law. Consumer complaints are the primary basis for investigation by Postal Inspectors. Some of the more common mail fraud schemes include medical fraud, work-at-home-schemes, land fraud, charity fraud, insurance fraud, investment fraud, and home improvement fraud.

* Mailing Free Matter For Blind and Visually Handicapped Persons

Office of Consumer Affairs
US Postal Service
475 L'Enfant Plaza, SW
Washington, DC 20260
202-268-2284

The free pamphlet, *Mailing Free Matter For Blind and Visually Handicapped Persons,* is designed to answer the most often asked questions about mailing free matter for the visually handicapped. It discusses qualifying, eligibility, conditions and restrictions on mailings, and the steps to make special arrangements for delivery.

* Mailing Services for the Blind and Handicapped

Office of the Consumer Advocate
U.S. Postal Service
L'Enfant Plaza, SW
Washington, DC 20260-6320
202-268-2281

Persons who are blind or who cannot use or read conventionally-printed material due to a physical handicap may qualify to mail items free of postage. To be eligible, a competent authority must submit a statement to the post office where postage-free mailings will be made or received, certifying that the individual is unable to read conventional reading material. Certain conditions and restrictions apply. The same general rules apply to both domestic and international mail service. Special arrangements for delivery or pickup of free mail for eligible persons may be arranged through local post offices depending on the circumstances. Contact this office for more information.

* Mailing to the Soviet Union

International Postal Affairs Department
U.S. Postal Service
475 L'Enfant Plaza, SW
Washington, DC 20260-6500
202-245-4575

Of all countries of the world with which the U.S. Postal Service exchanges mail, none has created more problems for U.S. mailers than the Soviet Union. U.S. mailers can reduce many of their frustrations by getting clear information on how to send mail to the Soviet Union, and how to seek redress if problems are encountered. Contact this office for more information on prohibited items, restricted articles, and size and weight limits.

* National Zip Code and Post Office Directory

Delivery Distribution Department
U.S. Postal Service
475 L'Enfant Plaza, SW
Washington, DC 20260
202-268-6990

Proper Zip Code information is essential for speedy and economic delivery of your mail. The *Zip Code Directory* is an up-to-date and comprehensive listing of Zip Code information by state and post office. It includes instructions for quickly finding a Zip Code number when an address is known. The Zip Code Directory also includes official lists of post offices, named stations, named branches, and community post offices in the United States. The volume includes a wealth of handy information about Zip Codes, postal abbreviations, and basic postal procedures, and is an indispensable aid that is worth its price many times over. Available for $15, foreign $18.75 from: Superintendent of Documents, Government Printing Office, Washington, DC 20402-0001; 202-512-1800.

* Pornography

Postal Inspection Service
U.S. Postal Service
475 L'Enfant Plaza, SW
Washington, DC 20260-2186
202-268-5169

To stop the mailing of unsolicited sexually-oriented advertisements to yourself or your minor children, fill out *Application for Listing Pursuant of 39 USC 3010,* at

your local post office. Thirty days after your name has been added to the Postal Service reference list, any mailer who sends you sexually oriented advertisements is subject to legal action by the U.S. Government. To stop the mailing of any further advertisements to yourself which you consider "erotically arousing or sexually provocative," fill out *Notice for Prohibitory Order Against Sender of Pandering Advertisement in the Mails,* at your local post office.

* Postal Answer Line (PAL)

Consumer Advocate
U.S. Postal Service
475 L'Enfant Plaza, SW, Room 5821
Washington, DC 20260-2200
202-268-2281

The Postal Answer Line (PAL) is the Postal Serivce's automated telephone information service. With a touchtone phone, answers to your questions are only a call away. This service is available 24 hours a day. By selecting and listening to prerecorded messages, you can obtain information on many postal products and services. PAL can also assist you in calculating postal costs for commonly used mail services if you know the weight of the item you want to mail. PAL is presently available in 80 cities. Publication 349, *Postal Answer Line Directory,* lists the PAL phone number for each of the cities offering this service.

* Postal Bulletin

Superintendent of Documents
Government Printing Office
Washington, DC 20402
202-512-1800

This weekly publication contains current orders, instructions and information relating to the Postal Service, including philatelic, airmail, money order, parcel post, etc. The subscription is available for $63 domestic, and $78.75 foreign per year, (S/N 739-001-0000-5) from: Superintendent of Documents, Government Printing Office, Washington, DC 20402-0001; 202-512-1800.

* Postal Commission Procedures

Administrative Office
Postal Rate Commission
1333 H St., NW, Suite 300
Washington, DC 20268-0001
202-789-6840

The publication, *The Postal Rate Commission in Brief,* outlines the steps of various cases and decisions for which the Commission is responsible. The steps in a postal rate case and the decision procedure are outlined, as well as those of a mail classification case. Change in nationwide service, the appeal process for closing or consolidating a small post office, and the way in which rate or service complaints are handled are also described. Contact this office to receive a copy.

* Postal Financial Management Manual

Superintendent of Documents
Government Printing Office
Washington, DC 20402-0001
202-512-1800

The *Financial Management Manual* presents an overview of the financial activities of the Postal Service. It summarizes the following topics: general accounting, post office accounting, accounts receivable and accounts payable, budget and planning, payroll accounting and control of assets.

* Postal Inspection Service

Inspection Service Department
U.S. Postal Service
475 L'Enfant Plaza, SW
Washington, DC 20260-2100
202-268-4267

As the law enforcement arm of the Postal Service, The Postal Inspection Service protects the mails, postal funds, and property; investigates internal conditions and needs that may affect postal security and effectiveness; apprehends those who violate the postal laws; and audits financial and nonfinancial operations. Information on past and present schemes used to defraud the public is available as well. Help is available if you experience difficulty with a company or suspect that you have been the victim of mail fraud. There is a Regional Chief Inspector in each of the five postal regions. Information and complaints of postal violations should be presented to the nearest Postal Inspector in charge.

Central Division
Chicago
Main Post Office Bldg., Chicago, IL 60607-5401; 312-669-5650
433 W. Van Buren St., Chicago, IL 60669-2201; 312-669-5633

Denver
P.O. Box 329, Denver, CO 80201-0329; 303-295-5320

Des Moines
P.O. Box 566, Des Moines, IA 50302-0566; 515-253-9060

Detroit
P.O. Box 330119, Detroit, MI 48232-6119; 313-226-8184

Indianapolis
7188 Lakeview Pkwy.W. Dr., Indianapolis, IN 46268-4101; 317-328-2500

Kansas City
3101 Broadway, Suite 850, Kansas City, MO 64111-2416; 816-932-0400

Milwaukee
P.O. Box 788, Milwaukee, WI 53201-0788; 414-287-2200

St. Louis
1106 Walnut St., St. Louis, MO 63199-2201; 314-539-9300

St. Paul
P.O. Box 64558, St. Paul, MN 55164-0558; 612-293-3202/3200

Eastern Division
Cynwud
P.O. Box 3000, Bala Cynwyd, PA 19004; 610-668-4500

Baltimore
P.O. Box 1856, Baltimore, MD 21203-1856; 410-347-4380

Charlotte
2901 I-85 S., Charlotte, NC 28228-3000; 704-329-9120

Cincinnati
P.O. Box 14487, Cincinnati, OH 45250-0487; 513-684-5700

Cleveland
P.O. Box 5726, Cleveland, OH 44101-0726; 216-443-4000

Harrisburg
P.O. Box 60035, Harrisburg, PA 17106-0035; 717-257-2330

Philadelphia
P.O. Box 7500, Philadelphia, PA 19101-9000; 215-895-8450

Pittsburgh
1001 California Ave., Pittsburgh, PA 15290-9000; 412-359-7900

Richmond
P.O. Box 25009, Richmond, VA 23260-5009; 804-418-6100

Washington, DC
P.O. Box 96096, Washington, DC 20066-6096; 202-636-2339/2300

Northeast Division
Newark
Gateway No. 2, McCarter Hwy. and Market St., Newark, NJ 07175-0001; 201-621-5500
P.O. Box 509, Newark, NJ 07101-5901; 201-596-5450

Boston
P.O. Box 2217, Boston, MA 02202-2217; 617-464-8000

Buffalo
685 Ellicott Sq., Buffalo, NY 14203-2545; 716-856-3674

Hartford
P.O. Box 2169, Hartford, CT 06145-2169; 203-524-6060

New York
421 8th Ave., New York, NY 10116-9998; 212-330-3844

San Juan
P.O. Box 3667, San Juan, PR 00936-9614; 809-749-7600

Southern Division
Memphis
10th Fl., 1407 Union Ave., Memphis, TN 38161-0001; 901-722-7700
P.O. Box 3180, Memphis, TN 38173-0180; 901-576-2137

Atlanta
P.O. Box 16489, Atlanta, GA 30321-0489; 404-765-7369

Birmingham
P.O. Box 2767, Birmingham, AL 35202-2767; 205-521-0270

Fort Worth
P.O. Box 162929, Fort Worth, TX 76161-2929; 817-625-3411

Houston
P.O. Box 1276, Houston, TX 77251-1276; 713-238-4400

Miami
P.O. Box 520772, Miami, FL 33152-0772; 305-470-0379

New Orleans
P.O. Box 51690, New Orleans, LA 70151-1690; 504-589-1200

Tampa
P.O. Box 22526, Tampa, FL 33622-2526; 813-281-5200

Western Division
San Bruno
850 Cherry Ave., San Bruno, CA 94098-0100; 415-952-2900

Oakland
7717 Edgewater Dr., Oakland, CA 94621-3013; 510-251-3300

Pasadena
P.O. Box 2000, Pasadena, CA 91102-2000; 818-405-1200

Phoenix
P.O. Box 20666, Phoenix, AZ 85036-0666; 602-223-3660

Portland
Suite 790, 921 SW Washington, Portland, OR 97205-2898; 503-279-2060

San Diego
P.O. Box 2110, San Diego, CA 92112-2110; 619-233-0610

San Francisco
P.O. Box 882000, San Francisco, CA 94188-2000; 415-550-5602/5700

Seattle
P.O. Box 400, Seattle, WA 98111-4000; 206-442-6300

* Postal Life: The Magazine for Postal Employees

Consumer Affairs
U.S. Postal Service
475 L'Enfant Plaza, SW
Washington, DC 20260   202-268-2284

This bimonthly periodical contains articles, with illustrations, about new methods, techniques and programs of the U.S. Postal Service. Its purpose is to keep postal employees informed and abreast of developments in the U.S. Postal Service. The subscription is available for $11 domestic, and $13.75 foreign per year, S/N 739-002-00000-1, from: Superintendent of Documents, Government Printing Office, Washington, DC 20402-0001; 202-512-1800.

* Postal Publications

The following postal publications are available free from your local post office, business center, or on a subscription basis. Please refer to the publication numer in parentheses when requesting publications.

Designing Business Letter Mail (Publication 25). A technical guide for designing letter mail for automation. Provides guidelines for machinability, readability, and barcoding.

Postal Addressing Standards (Publication 28). Provides guidelines on address format standards and options for the best service.

Address Information Systems (Publication 40). A guide to addressing products for improving the quality of your address files.

Business Reply Mail Accounting System (Notice 46). Describes a system to reduce costs for business reply mail users.

National Change of Address (NCOA) (Notice 47). Describes the National Change of Address system, which makes available current change-of-address information.

Third-Class Mail Preparation (Publication 49). Describes third-class bulk business mail including rate categories, payment options, sorting, and filling out mailing forms.

Designing Flat Mail (Publication 63). A technical guide for designing flat mail for automation.

Metering (Notice 125). A pamphlet on how to use postage meters including tips on proper metering.

Addressing for Success (Notice 221). Addressing for compatibility with automated processing equipment. Describes automation process and how to benefit from it.

Designing Reply Mail (Publication 353). A technical guide for designing reply mail.

* Postal Publications and Handbooks

Data Information Center
Document Control Division
U.S. Postal Service
475 L'Enfant Plaza, SW
Washington, DC 20260   202-268-2852

Postal Service Publication No. 223 lists all technical publications available, including titles of publications and their supply source.

* Postal Rate Commission

Postal Rate Commission
1333 H St., NW
Suite 300
Washington, DC 20268-0001   202-789-6800

The Postal Rate Commission considers proposed changes in postal rates, fees, and mail classifications and issues recommendations to the Governors of the Postal Service. It also considers changes in the nature of available postal service. Postal Service decisions to close or consolidate post offices are also reviewed. The Commission also investigates complaints concerning postal rates and service on the national level. Five Commissioners serve a six-year term of office and are appointed by the President.

* Postal Rate Commission Open Meetings

General Counsel
Postal Rate Commission
1333 H St., NW
Suite 300
Washington, DC 20268-0001   202-789-6820

The Commission meetings are the forums where postal rates, fees, mail classifications, service changes, and post office closings and consolidations are discussed. They are open to the public, except in special circumstances, but public participation is not permitted. Documents from these meetings are also available to the public at the headquarters offices.

* Postal Rate Complaints

General Counsel
Postal Rate Commission
1333 H St., NW, Suite 300
Washington, DC 20268-0001   202-789-6820

Written complaints may be addressed to the above office if you feel changes are needed in the rate and classification structure of mail or if you believe the nationwide system of the Postal Service can be improved. Local problems must be addressed to the U.S. Postal Service directly.

* Postal Rate Consumer Information

Consumer Advocate
Postal Rate Commission
1333 H St., NW, Suite 300
Washington, DC 20268-0001   202-268-2281

Information on the activities of the Postal Rate Commission is distributed by the Consumer Advocate. If a postal rate case is pending, the newspapers and other media are alerted. Consumer groups are also notified.

* Postal Service Changes

Postal Rate Commission
1333 H St., NW
Suite 300
Washington, DC 20268-0001   202-789-6800

The Postal Service asks the Postal Commission for their advisory opinion on proposed changes in nationwide postal services, rates, and classifications. These formal requests are then published in the *Federal Register*.

* Postal Service Films

Communications Department
The U.S. Postal Service
475 L'Enfant Plaza, SW
Washington, DC 20260   202-268-2156

A few general films are available for loan to the public. One film, for example, traces the route of a letter as it goes through the postal service system, and another film demonstrates the importance of letters in people's lives.

* Postal Speakers Network

Assistant Postmaster General
Communications Department
U.S. Postal Service
475 L'Enfant Plaza, SW
Room 5300
Washington, DC 20260   202-268-2143

Speakers may be scheduled free of charge provided two to three months notice is given and provided those interested give preliminary information. It is also possible to coordinate Postal Service participation in meetings of national organizations and associations. Speakers for meetings that are regional or local in nature are scheduled by the appropriate Regional Postmaster General's office or the Regional Chief Inspector's office.

* Practice and Procedures

Administrative Office
Postal Rate Commission
1333 H St., NW, Suite 300
Washington, DC 20268-0001   202-789-6840

Rules of Practice and Procedure describes in detail the methods for handling the Postal Rate Commission's responsibilities. First is a listing of rules that apply to general business matters, including term definitions, the docket and hearing calendar, inquiries, and public attendance at Commission meetings. Rules are also written for rates or fees changes, for changing the mail classification schedule, for postal service changes, and for rate and service complaints. The method for filing testimony by those who wish to intervene in rate and classification proceedings is also included, as well as the procedure for an appeal to a decision to close or consolidate small post offices.

* Products and Services

The Marketing Department
The U.S. Postal Service
475 L'Enfant Plaza, SW
Room 5014
Washington, DC 20260   202-268-2222

For information on specific Postal Service products and services, contact this office.

* Public Hearings on the Postal System

Docket Section
Postal Rate Commission
1333 H St., NW
Suite 300
Washington, DC 20268-0001   202-789-6845

When a proposed change in the national Postal Service is recommended before the Postal Rate Commission, public hearings are held. Testimony is given on the program, and those in attendance are given an opportunity to address questions. The records of these public hearings are used in making the final decisions on postal system changes. To be placed on the mailing list to receive notices of these hearings, contact the office above. A hearing calendar and a docket of all proceedings from the hearings is also available for public inspection. Office hours are 8 a.m. to 5 p.m., Monday through Friday. You must have the docket number of the proceeding you wish to examine.

* Regional and Field Division Offices

U.S. Postal Service
475 L'Enfant Plaza, SW
Washington, DC 20260-0010

In addition to the national headquarters, regional and field division offices supervise more than 40,000 post offices, branches, stations, and community post offices throughout the United States. Each of the five Regional Postmasters General manage postal activities in a geographical area as indicated below.

Central Division
433 W. Van Buren St., Chicago, IL 60699-0100; 312-669-5633. Areas served: CO, IL, IN except ZIP Codes 420, 423, 424, 470, 476, 477), IA, KS, MI, MN, MO, NE, ND, SD, WI, WY.

Eastern Division
P.O. Box 7500, Philadelphia, PA 19197-9000; 215-895-8450. Areas served: DC, DE, IN (ZIP Codes 420, 423, 424, 470, 476, 477), KY, MD, NJ (ZIP Codes 080-084), NC, OH, PA, SC, VA, WV.

Northeast Division
6 Griffin Park Rd. N, Windsor, CT 06006-0100; 203-524-6060. Areas served: CT, MA, ME, NH, NJ (ZIP Codes 070-079, 085-089), NY, Puerto Rico, RI, VT, Virgin Islands.

Southern Division
1407 Union Ave., Memphis, TN 38166-0100; 901-722-7700. Areas served: AL, AR, FL, GA, LA, MS, OK, TN, TX (except ZIP Codes 797-799).

Western Division
850 Cherry Ave., San Bruno, CA 94099-0100; 415-952-2900. Areas served: AK, AZ, CA, HI, ID, MT, NV, NM, OR, TX (ZIP Codes 797-799), UT, WA, Pacific Possessions and Trust Territories.

* Rural or Highway Contract Route

Rural Delivery Division
Delivery and Distribution and Transportation Department
U.S. Postal Service
Washington, DC 20260   202-268-6990

General distribution of third class mail to each boxholder on a rural or highway contract route, or for each family on a rural route, or for all boxholders at a post office that does not have city or village carrier service, may have the mail addressed omitting the names of individuals and box or route numbers if the mailer uses this form of address: "Postal Customer," or, to be more specific: "Rural (or Highway Contract Route) Boxholder, City (or town), State." On request, a Postmaster will furnish mailers with the number of families and boxes served on each route.

* Small Post Office Closings

Delivery Distribution and Transportation Department
U.S. Postal Service
475 L'Enfant Plaza, SW
Washington, DC 20260   202-268-6990

Contact this office for information on small post office closings or consolidations.

* Stamp Collecting

Philatelic Fulfillment Service Center
U.S. Postal Service
P.O. Box 449997
Kansas City, MO 64144-9997

Stamp collecting is an enjoyable hobby that does not require any specific skills or expensive equipment. A good place to start your collection is your local post office. You can also buy philatelic products, such as stamp collecting kits, the *Postal Service Guide to U.S. Stamps*, and mint sets of commemorative and special stamps for recent years. For a free mail order catalog of philatelic products, write to the address above.

* Third-Class Mail Preparation

Marketing and Sales
U.S. Postal Service
475 L'Enfant Plaza, SW
Washington, DC 20260-3121   202-268-2143

If you're planning to mail at the third-class bulk rates, this publication explains what bulk business mail is, and how to get the most out of it. If you already have the necessary permits to mail at the bulk third-class rates, this publication will serve as a valuable reference. (Publication 49)

* Unsolicited Merchandise

Consumer Advocate
U.S. Postal Service
475 L'Enfant Plaza, SW, Room 5821
Washington, DC 20260-2200   202-268-2281

or

Bureau of Consumer Protection
Federal Trade Commission
Washington, DC 20580-0001

Federal law prohibits the shipment of unordered merchandise. Such a practice may constitute an unfair trade practice. Merchandise mailed in violation of the federal code may be treated as a gift by the recipient without any obligation to the sender.

Housing and Real Estate
General Sources

* See also Your Community Chapter

This chapter provides good starting places for finding information in the housing and real estate industry. You'll find sources on such topics as surplus property, urban homesteading, construction standards, and even historic preservation. There's information here for anyone interested in housing and real estate, including first time home buyers, urban planners, and real estate speculators. Whether you're looking for mortgage counseling, foreclosed properties, or information on housing discrimination, you should be able to find what you're looking for.

* American Housing Survey for the United States
HUD User
P.O. Box 6091   800-245-2691
Rockville, MD 20849   301-251-5154
TDD: 800-483-2209
Internet: huduser@aspensys.com

This survey is the result of personal and telephone interviews of approximately 190,000 households in 44 selected metropolitan areas conducted by the Census Bureau for HUD. Information is provided on the size and composition of the U.S. housing inventory, occupant characteristics, changes in the stock due to new construction, indicators of housing and neighborhood quality, and the characteristics of recent movers. The study contains hundreds of different kinds of information on such housing-related topics as age, race sex, and income of households; source of income--wages, pensions, dividends, welfare, Social Security; reasons for moving from last home; type and condition of housing; amount of rent or mortgage payment, value of property, purchase price, downpayment; number of rooms, bedrooms, baths; repairs, alterations, additions; plumbing, heating, cooling equipment, and other appliances; cost of fuel and utilities, type of fuel used; neighborhood quality--police protection, hospitals; neighborhood problems--crime, pollution, street noise.

The information from this survey can be used in many ways. Mortgage lenders, developers, marketing analysts, and demographers can use the survey information to examine economic and social trends for planning and decisionmaking. Manufacturers, housing analysts, financial institutions, and planners may study particular markets, which builders and real estate brokers can rely on to help them better understand their housing markets. Data is also available on magnetic tape or compact disc. If you need microdata, the survey is now available in CD-ROM (compact disc-read only memory) in two formats: ASCII and SAS internal format. The cost is $3 for the information in hard copy, and $125 for the data on CD-ROM.

* Assisted Housing - Section 8
HUD USER
P.O. Box 6091   800-245-2691
Rockville, MD 20849   301-251-5154
Fax: 301-251-5747
TDD: 800-483-2209
Internet: huduser@aspensys.com

This section includes publications on the administration, effectiveness, and demographics of HUD rental assistance, such as Section 8 housing certificates and vouchers. Publications available include:

Administrative Costs of the Housing Voucher and Certificate Programs, 1988, ACCN-5223, $4.

Assessment of the HUD-Insured Multifamily Housing Stock, Final Report, Vol. I: Current Status of HUD-Insured (or Held) Multifamily Rental Housing, 1993, ACCN-6261, $4.

Capital Needs Assessment: Multifamily Rental Housing with HUD-Insured (or Held) Mortgages, 1992, ACCN-6092, $4.

Characteristics of HUD-Assisted Renters and Their Units in 1989, ACCN-5961, $4.

Final Comprehensive Report of the Freestanding Housing Voucher Demonstration Volume I, 1990, ACCN-5555, $4.

    Volume II, Appendixes, 1990, ACCN-5556, $4.

Financial Management System Package for the Housing Voucher Program (Computer Package), 1989, ACCN-5409, $20.

Housing Quality Standards (2 videotapes), 1989, ACCN-5353, $60.

Operation Bootstrap, 1994

    Volume I, Program Administration, ACCN-6491, $4.

    Volume II, Outcomes of Participation, ACCN-6492, $4.

    Volume III, Case Studies, ACCN-6493, $4.

Recipient Housing in the Housing Voucher and Certificate Programs, 1990, ACCN-5597, $4.

Section 8 Administrative Fees: A Report to Congress, 1994, ACCN-6445, $4.

Section 8 Rental Voucher and Rental Certificate Utilization Study: Final Report, 1994, ACCN-6505, $4.

Tenant Integrity Program: Training Guide for Public Housing and Section 8 Certificate, Voucher, and Moderate Rehabilitation Program, 1992, ACCN-6053, $20 (reproduction document).

Tenant Integrity Program (videotape), 1989, ACCN-5423, $20.

For information of related interest, see: Public and Indian Housing, and Homeownership.

* Beginning Farmer Loans
Information Staff
Farmers Home Administration (FmHA)
U.S. Department of Agriculture (USDA)
14th and Independence Ave., SW
Washington, DC 20250   202-720-4323

Special assistance is available to beginning farmers and ranchers in the form of down payment farm ownership loans and special operation loans. To receive a down payment loan, the applicant must either be a first-time farm or ranch operator or not have operated one for more than 10 years, and meet certain other requirements. The applicant must provide 10 percent of the purchase price or appraised value, and the Farmers Home Administration (FmHA) will make a down payment loan for 30 percent of the purchase price or appraised value, which may not exceed $250,000. More information is available by contacting the office listed above.

* Building Environment
Building Environment Division
B304 Building and Fire Research Lab
National Institute of Standards and Technology (NIST)
Gaithersburg, MD 20899   301-975-5851

The Building Environment Division develops fundamental data, measurement techniques, test methods, and models for the design, construction, and operation of the building envelope and building mechanical and electrical systems. The division also develops software performance criteria, interface standards, and test methods needed to make effective use of modern computer-aided design hardware and software and database management systems within the disaggregated construction industry. Sample outputs for the division include testing and rating procedures and computer models for the performance of heating and air conditioning systems, predictive models for estimating peak heating/cooling requirements and annual building energy use, and indoor air quality, criteria for improving thermal performance of insulting materials, and criteria for measuring and improving the lighting in buildings. The division also has computer aids to assist in formulating building standards and expert systems. Contact this office for more information.

* Building Materials Research

Building Materials Division
B348 Building and Fire Research Lab
National Institute of Standards and Technology (NIST)
Gaithersburg, MD 20899   301-975-6707

The Building Materials Division conducts laboratory, field and analytical research and develops methods for evaluating the performance and durability of building materials and components. The division also develops chemical, physical, microstructural, and mechanical characterization procedures and mathematical methods for describing microstructures for building materials. Also, the division conducts voluntary laboratory inspection and proficiency sample programs to aid maintenance of quality in execution of standard tests on materials used in building and highway construction. Researchers at NIST are working to gain a better understanding of the lifespan of inorganic materials such as cement and concrete used in building. Artificial intelligence systems are being developed for optimizing the selection of materials and for diagnosing the causes of material degradation. Researchers are also looking into the lifespans of organic building materials such as protective coatings for steel, roofing materials, and asphalt. Contact this office for guidelines for selecting building materials, or for more information on the ongoing research in building materials.

* Building Technology

Building and Fire Research Lab
National Institute of Standards and Technology (NIST)
Gaithersburg, MD 20899   301-975-5900

The Center for Building Technology is the national building research laboratory. It works cooperatively with other organizations, private and public, to improve building practices. It conducts laboratory, field, and analytical research. It develops technologies to predict, measure, and test the performance of building materials, components, systems, and practices. This knowledge is required for responsible and cost effective decisions in the building process and cannot be obtained through proprietary research and development. The Center provides technologies needed by the building community to achieve the benefits of advanced computation and automation. It does not distribute building standards or regulations, but its technologies are widely used in the building industry and adopted by governmental and private organizations which have standards and codes responsibilities. Contact this Center for more information.

* Building Technology

HUD USER
P.O. Box 6091   800-245-2691
Rockville, MD 20849   301-251-5154
TDD: 800-483-2209
Internet: huduser@aspensys.com

The following is a sampling of publications of interest to real estate developers, builders, and others in the housing construction industry. $3 is charged per document for handling.

Adaptable Housing: A Technical Manual for Implementing Adaptable Dwelling Unit Specification, 1987, ACCN-4981, $4.
Alternative Framing Materials for Residential Construction: Three Case Studies, 1994, ACCN-6512, $4.
Alternatives to Lumber and Plywood in Home Construction, 1993, ACCN-6135, $4.
Assessment of Damage Caused by Hurricanes Andrew and Iniki, 1993, ACCN, $4.
Blueprint Catalog, 1986, ACCN-BLU0000, Free.
Cost of Accessible Housing, 1993, ACCN-6180, $4.
Design Guide for Frost-Protected Shallow Foundations, 1994, ACCN-6507, $4.
Frost-Protected Shallow Foundations in Residential Construction
    Phase I, 1993, ACCN-6143, $4.
    Phase II, 1994, ACCN-6498, $4.
Home Building Cost Cuts: Construction Methods and Materials for Affordable Housing (Looseleaf Bulletin), 1983, ACCN-2930, $4.
Market Rental Housing Energy Efficient: Guide to Performing Energy Retrofit During Multi-family Property Rehabilitation, 1990, ACCN-5650, $4.
Measurement and Determination of Radon Source Potential: A Literature Review, ACCN-6368, $15.
Rehabilitation Guidelines 1986:
1. *Setting and Adopting Standards for Building Rehabilitation*, 1986, ACCN-50783, $4.
2. *Approval of Building Rehabilitation*, 1986, ACCN-50785, $4.
3. *Guideline for Building Rehabilitation*, 1986, ACCN-50785, $4.
4. *Guideline for Managing Official Liability Associated With Building Rehabilitation*, 1986, ACCN-50786, $4.
5. *Egress Guideline for Residential Rehabilitation*, 1986, ACCN-50787, $4.
6. *Electrical Guideline for Residential Rehabilitation*, 1986, ACCN-50788, $4.
7. *Plumbing DWV Guideline for Residential Rehabilitation*, 1986, ACCN-50789, $4.
8. *Guideline on Fire Ratings of Archaic Materials and Assemblies*, 1986, ACCN-50790, $4.
9. *Guidelines for Structural Assessment*, 1986, ACCN-50791, $4.
10. *Guideline on the Rehabilitation of Walls, Windows, and Roofs*, 1986, ACCN-50792, $4.
11. *Guideline for Residential Building Systems Inspection*, 1986, ACCN-50793, $4.
Rehabilitation Technology: A State of the Art Overview, 1987, ACCN-4718, $10 (reproduction copy).

For information of related interest, see: Housing for Special Needs, Housing Production/Rehabilitation, Lead-Based Paint, and Public and Indian Housing.

* Building Technology Presentations and Symposia

B222 Building and Fire Research Lab
National Institute of Standards and Technology (NIST)
Gaithersburg, MD 20899   301-975-5900

Staff at the Center for Building Technology make a number of presentations at professional societies and at technical meetings of building community organizations. Also, the center presents a monthly series of Building Technology Symposia, in cooperation with other organizations concerned with building research and practice. Contact this Center for further information.

* Community and Urban Planning Information

HUD USER
P.O. Box 6091   800-245-2691
Rockville, MD 20849   301-251-5154
TDD: 800-483-2209
Internet: huduser@aspensys.com

The following is a sampling of publications of interest to community and urban planners available for a $3 handling charge. The information in this section document innovative strategies for enhancing housing and economic opportunity in urban neighborhoods through community development programs, public-private partnerships, and enterprise zones.

Annual Report to Congress on the Community Development Block Grant Program, 1993, ACCN-6277, $10 (reproduction copy).
Case Study Examples in Neighborhood Development and Grass Roots Fundraising
    Round 1, 1987, ACCN-5129, $4.
    Round 2, 1989, ACCN-5540, $4.
Cityscape, Volume 1, No. 1, August 1994, ACCN-6488, $4.
Entrepreneurial Approach to Funding Social Services: The Story of Pioneer Human Services, 1992, ACCN-6009, $4.
Hurricanes Andrew and Iniki Data Graph Files (Computer Package), 1993, ACCN-AV10029, $15.
Interim Evaluation of the Single Family Property Disposition Demonstration, 1993, ACCN-6146, $4.
Keeping Ahead: A Directory of Technical Assistance Documents, 1989, ACCN-5405, $4.
Local Comprehensive Housing Affordability Strategy (CHAS): A Preliminary Assessment of First-Year Submissions, 1992, ACCN-5997, $4.
National Analysis of Housing Affordability, Adequacy, and Availability: A Framework for Local Housing Strategies, 1994, ACCN-6365, $4.
Nonprofit Housing: Costs and Funding, Final Report
    Volume I, Findings, 1993, ACCN-6291, $4.
    Volume II, Case Studies, 1993, ACCN-6290, $4.
Planning and Implementing Small Business Incubators, 1986, ACCN-4961, $4.
Proposed Model Land Development Standards and Accompanying Model State Enabling Legislation, 1993, ACCN-6212, $4.
State-Designated Enterprise Zones: Ten Case Studies, 1986, ACCN-4570, $4.
State Enterprise Zone Update, 1991, ACCN-HUD5808, $10 (reproduction copy).

For information of related interest, see: Energy/Infrastructure.

* Consumer Housing Publications

Consumer Information Center
Pueblo, CO 81002

Write to the above address to order any of the following publications:

Consumer Handbook on Adjustable Rate Mortgages. Basic features, advantages and risks, and terminology associated with adjustable rate mortgages. (1984, Federal Reserve Board, 423 Y., $.50).

A Consumer's Guide to Mortgage Lock-ins. What they are and how you can lock-in interest rates and points when applying for a mortgage. (1988, Federal Reserve Board, 424 Y., $.50).

A Consumer's Guide to Mortgage Refinancing. What the costs are and how to tell if the time is right to refinance your home. (1988, Federal Reserve Board, 425 Y., $.50).

Guide to Single Family Home Mortgage Insurance. Protects lenders against losses on mortgages so they can offer you terms you might not have otherwise. Learn about these options and your responsibilities. (1990 Housing and Urban Development, 120 Y. $1)

Home Buyer's Vocabulary. Defines common words and terms used in the real estate world. Especially useful for the first time buyer. (1987 Housing and Urban Development, 121 Y. $1)

Home Mortgages: Understanding the Process and Your Right to Fair Lending. Describes your responsibilities and legal protections regarding application and credit evaluation (1990, Federal Reserve Board, 426 Y. $.50)

How to Buy a Manufactured (Mobile) Home. Helpful tips on selection, placement transportation warranties installation, and inspection. (1992, Federal Trade Commission, 427 Y., $.50).

Reverse Mortgages. Learn how to convert home equity into cash. Explains the three different types of reverse mortgages available, and how to get more information on home equity conversion plans. (1991 Federal Trade Commission, 475 Y., $.50)

When Your Home is On the Line. Your home serves as collateral for a home equity loan. Here are questions, terms, tips, and more - all to help you find the best deal. (1989, Federal Reserve Board, 428 Y. $.50)

Wise Home Buying. Here's help in finding the right house: when to use a broker, inspection, and shopping for a mortgage (1987, Housing and Urban Development, 123 Y. $1)

Simple Home Repairs Inside. Step-by-step directions with pictures on how to repair or replace doors, faucets, plugs, windows, screens, tiles, and more. (1986 U.S. Department of Agriculture, 125 Y. $1.50)

* Counseling for Homebuyers, Homeowners, and Tenants

Single Family Servicing Branch
Counseling Services
U.S. Department of Housing and Urban Development
Washington, DC 20410-8000   202-708-3664

To help reduce delinquencies, defaults, and foreclosures, the U.S. Department of Housing and Urban Development (HUD) provides free counseling to homeowners and tenants under its programs through HUD- approved counseling agencies. The counselors advise and assist homeowners with budgeting, money management, and buying and maintaining their homes. Contact this office or your local HUD office of information on the counseling agency nearest you.

* Country Homes

Farmers Home Administration
U.S. Department of Agriculture (USDA)
Single Family Housing Division
14th and Independence Ave., SW
Washington, DC 20250   202-720-4323

The Farmers Home Administration makes low-interest loans to qualified applicants to purchase homes or farms in rural areas. They are also charged with disposing of properties that are foreclosed. First, the Farmers Home Administration makes any necessary repairs to the property, then offers them for sale to people who have the same qualifications as those applying for loans. Eligible applicants also qualify to purchase at special low interest rates (as low as 1%). If no eligible applicants purchase a property, it is then put up for sale to the general public at competitive prices. If the property is not sold within 10 days, it is reduced by 10%.

* Directory of Information Resources in Housing and Urban Development

HUD USER
P.O. Box 6091   800-245-2691
Rockville, MD 20849   301-251-5154
                                   TDD: 800-483-2209
                          Internet: huduser@aspensys.com

The most recent edition of this directory lists 150 trade and professional organizations, public agencies, advocacy groups, and research and educational institutes in housing and urban development. Each entry describes the organization's purpose and services and includes an address and telephone number. These contacts can provide current relevant information on today's key housing issues. The *Directory* also describes 40 online databases available in the field. This publication is available for $26 (ACCN-6200).

* Directory of Private Fair Housing Organizations

Clearinghouse Division
U.S. Commission on Civil Rights
624 Ninth St., NW
Washington, DC 20425   202-376-8128

This directory lists by locality more than 200 organizations that have fair housing activities and describes types of activities each performs and number of staff involved. It also lists the Community Housing Resource Boards funded by the U.S. Department of Housing and Urban Development. This publication is available free of charge, order number 005-902-00042-8 (172pp). Other publications available include:

The Federal Fair Housing Enforcement Effort, 235pp., #005-901-00020-1, free.
An Annotated Bibliography on Selected Fair Housing Issues, 52pp, #005-902-00048-7, free.

* Earth Sheltered Buildings

Science and Technology Division
Reference Section
Library of Congress
Washington, DC 20540-5580   202-707-5580

An informal series of reference guides are issued free from the Science and Technology Division under the general title, *LC Science Tracer Bullet.* These guides are designed to help readers locate published material on subjects about which they have only general knowledge. New titles in the series are announced in the weekly Library of Congress *Information Bulletin* that is distributed to many libraries. The relevant study is No. 82-3 *Earth Sheltered Buildings.*

* Energy/Infrastructure

HUD USER
P.O. Box 6091   800-245-2691
Rockville, MD 20849   301-251-5154
                                   Fax: 301-251-5747
                                   TDD: 800-483-2209
                          Internet: huduser@aspensys.com

The documents and software listed below promote efficient energy management for homes, developments, and entire communities.

Carriage Gas Utility System (5-1/4 diskette), 1990, ACCN-AVI5648, $15.
How to Save Money on Monthly Gas Utility Bills for Public Housing Agencies: A Simple Step-by-Step Procedure, 1989, ACCN-5435, $10 (reproduction copy).
Life-Cycle Cost Analysis for Utility Combinations (computer package), 1989, ACCN-5432, $10.
Making Rental Housing Energy Efficient: Guide to Performing Energy Retrofit During Multifamily Property Rehabilitation, 1990, ACCN-5650, $4.
Model Energy Code Thermal Compliance Protection (MECCP) Version 1.1 (computer package), 1993, ACCN-6266, $20.
Model Energy Code Thermal Compliance Guide, 1994, ACCN-6366, $4.
Program for Energy Analysis of Residences (PEAR 2.2 microcomputer package), 1993, ACCN-5434, $10.
Reducing Energy Costs in Multifamily Housing: Guidelines for Using Energy Management Companies, 1986, ACCN-4609, $4.
Residual Solar Viability Program, Version 3.0 (computer package), 1992, ACCN-6000, $20.
Utility Accounting Package (computer package), 1988, ACCN-5390, $20.

* Fair Housing

HUD USER
P.O. Box 6091   800-245-2691
Rockville, MD 20849   301-251-5154
                                   Fax: 301-251-5747
                                   TDD: 800-483-2209
                          Internet: huduser@aspensys.com

U.S. Department of Housing and Urban Development (HUD) research, information, and evaluation documents in this section examine the incidence of housing discrimination, as well as the statutes and programs designed to promote fair housing practices.

Fair Housing Amendments of 1988: A Selected Resource Guide, 1990, ACCN-5771,
$10 (reproduction copy).
Housing Discrimination Study: Analyzing Racial and Ethnic Steering, 1991,
ACCN-5096, $4.
Housing Discrimination Study: Incidence and Severity of Unfavorable Treatment,
1991, ACCN-5908, $4.
*Housing Discrimination Study: Incidence of Discrimination and Variations in
Discriminatory Behavior*, 1991, ACCN-5910, $4.
*Housing Discrimination Study: Mapping Patterns of Steering for Five Metropolitan
Areas*, 1991, ACCN-5905, $4.
Housing Discrimination Study: Methodology and Data Documentation, 1991,
ACCN-5909, $4.
*Housing Discrimination Study: Replication of 1977 Study Measures with Current
Data*, 1991, ACCN-5907, $4.
Housing Discrimination Study: Synthesis, 1991, ACCN-5827, $4.
Housing Discrimination Study Data Tape (computer package), 1991,
ACCN-AVI0028, $75.

For information of related interest see: Housing for Special Needs.

* Fair Housing and Equal Opportunity

Assistant Secretary for Fair Housing and Equal Opportunity
U.S. Department of Housing and Urban Development (HUD)
451 7th St., SW
Washington, DC 20410   202-708-4252
This office administers: fair housing laws and regulations prohibiting discrimination
in public and private housing on the basis of race, color, religion, sex, age, or
national origin, handicap, or familial status; and equal opportunity laws and
regulations prohibiting discrimination in HUD-assisted housing and community
development programs on the basis of race, handicap, sex, age, or national origin.

* Fair Housing Complaints

Fair Housing Enforcement Division
Office of Fair Housing and Equal Opportunity
U.S. Department of Housing and Urban Development (HUD)
Washington, DC 20410-2000
For filing complaints: 202-619-8041
The U.S. Department of Housing and Urban Development (HUD) administers the
law that prohibits discrimination in housing on the basis of race, color, religion, sex,
and national origin; investigates complaints of housing discrimination; and attempts
to resolve them through conciliation. Two common forms of discrimination are
redlining and steering. Redlining is the illegal practice of refusing to originate
mortgage loans in certain neighborhoods on the basis of race or ethnic origin.
Steering is the illegal act of limiting the housing shown by a real estate agent to a
certain ethnic group. If you have experienced housing discrimination, you should file
a complaint with any HUD office in person, by mail, or by telephone at the numbers
listed here. HUD refers complaints to state and local fair housing agencies.

* Fair Housing: Voluntary Compliance

Office of Voluntary Compliance
Office of Fair Housing and Equal Opportunity
U.S. Department of Housing and Urban Development (HUD)
Washington, DC 20410-2000   202-708-1992
HUD promotes voluntary compliance in the private sector and with other Federal
agencies in the area of fair housing activities nationwide. HUD executes Voluntary
Affirmative Marketing Agreements with housing industry groups, both locally and
nationwide. Comprehensive fair housing plans are also developed with local units of
government. HUD also organizes volunteer citizen groups to work with these plans
and agreements. Trade and professional organizations in housing and related fields,
including homebuilders, real estate brokers, mortgage lenders, and rental property
managers are asked to comply.

* Federal National Mortgage Association (Fannie Mae)

Federal National Mortgage Association
3900 Wisconsin Ave., NW
Washington, DC 20016   202-752-7000
This governmental financial institution has been created to serve as a secondary
source of mortgage funds. By purchasing loans from lenders, it serves as a conduit
for funds from investors into the loan industry. Even though it is a privately-owned,
profit-motivated corporation, the Secretary of HUD has regulatory authority over
Fannie Mae's operations.

* Federal Real Estate Bulletin Board

Federal Supply Service
General Services Administration (GSA)   800-472-1313
Washington, DC 20406   Data: 800-776-7872
                                               Data: 202-501-6510
The General Services Administration (GSA) sells most surplus government real
estate. A number of other federal agencies, including the Department of Housing and
Urban Development and the Department of Veterans Affairs, also sell real estate.
Consult local real estate agents or contact the agencies directly. You may also request
a free copy of U.S. Real Property Sales List from the Consumer Information Center,
Department 514A, Pueblo, CO 81009. If you have a computer equipped with a
modem, you can access the Federal Real Estate Bulletin Board for information on
real estate sales. Set communications software to 8 data bits, no parity, and 1 stop
bit.

* Foreign Investments in the U.S.

Land Branch, ERS
U.S. Department of Agriculture
1301 New York Ave., NW
Washington, DC 20005-4788   202-219-0420
Foreign investment in U.S. agricultural land has been reported for 14.8 million acres
in 1,918 of the 3,041 counties in the U.S. *Foreign Ownership of U.S. Agricultural
Land through December 31, 1993* lists data for each county to show the number of
acres, its value, country of origin, and use of the land. This publication is available
at no cost from this office. An electronic database is available for $35, order #7015,
by calling 800-999-6779. This database is also available on the internet. For access:
1) Gopher client - gopher.usda.mannlib.cornell.edu.70; 2) Telnet - telnet usda.
mannlib.cornell.edu (login as "usda"); 3) FTP - ftp usda.mannlib.cornell.edu (login
as anonymous with your ID name or e-mail address as the password, then cd usda).
For technical assistance, call 607-255-7960 or e-mail oyr1@cornell.edu.

* Ginnie Mae Mortgage-Backed Securities

Government National Mortgage Association
U.S. Department of Housing and Urban Development (HUD)
Washington, DC 20410-9000   202-708-0926
The Government National Mortgage Association guarantees the timely payment of
principal and interest on securities issued by lenders and backed by pools of
Government-underwritten residential mortgages. The program's purpose is to attract
non-traditional investors into the residential mortgage market by offering them a
high-yield, risk-free, Government-guaranteed security which has none of the
servicing obligation associated with a mortgage loan portfolio. GNMA II, which
supplements the original program, has a central paying agent, Chemical Bank, which
makes consolidated payments to investors. Larger, geographically-dispersed,
multiple-issuer mortgage pools, as well as custom pools, are offered. A mix of
interest rates is also provided among the mortgages within the pool. Securities under
this program are privately issued and backed by pools of FHA or Veteran's
Administration mortgages. Included in the mortgage pools are single-family level
payment, graduated payment, growing equity, and manufactured housing loans.
Lending institutions under this program must be in good standing and have adequate
net worth, staffing, and experience.

* Handicapped Access to Buildings

U.S. Architectural and Transportation Barriers
Compliance Board (Access Board)
1331 F St., NW, Suite 1000   202-272-5434, ext. 7-36
Washington, DC 20004-1111   Fax: 202-272-5447
                                       Voice and TDD: 800-872-2253
                                                 TDD: 800-993-2822
                                                 TDD: 202-272-5449
                              Access Bulletin Board: 202-272-5448
The Access Board produces or distributes publications of interest to people with
disabilities. Single copies in regular print, Braille, cassette, disk, or large type are
available at no cost. You may also download these publications through the Access
Bulletin Board at no cost. The bulletin board operates 24 hours a day. If you need
technical assistance using the bulletin board, call 202-272-5434. Some of the
publications available include:

American with Disabilities Act Accessibility Guidelines; accessibility requirements
for new construction and alteration of buildings and facilities covered by the
Americans with Disabilities Act. ($14).
Hands-on Architecture; contains pertinent information from a Board-sponsored
research project with suggested standards for specifying controls and operating
mechanisms. (A26).

Housing and Real Estate

Technical Paper on Accessibility Codes and Standards; compares the Minimum Guidelines and Requirements for Accessible Design and the Uniform Federal Accessibility Standards with local, state, and foreign access codes and standards. (S06).

Uniform Federal Accessibility Standards (UFAS); design, construction and alteration standards for access to federally funded building. (S04). (UFAS Checklist - S05).

UFAS Retrofit Manual; This 300 page document, based on UFAS, contains easy to understand, practical solutions to often encountered alteration situations (S07).

There is also an ongoing series of technical assistance bulletins for design professionals developed from frequently asked questions about specific ADAAG provisions. The publications list may be ordered through the Board's telephone or fax numbers.

* Handicapped Housing Information for Developers
Office of Elderly and Assisted Housing
U.S. Department of Housing and Urban Development (HUD)
Washington, DC 20410-8000   202-708-2866
This office can provide you with complete information on the procedure to obtain Section 202 funding for handicapped housing projects. An information packet, which outlines the program requirements and the specifications for the construction of the project to be funded, is available.

* Historic Preservation
Superintendent of Documents
Government Printing Office (GPO)   202-512-1800
Washington, DC 20402   Fax: 202-512-2250
The following publications on historic preservation are available from the Government Printing Office (GPO):

Applied Decoration for Historic Interiors: Preserving Composition Ornament (1994). Describes the historical uses of composition ornament. Demonstrates how to repair or replace composition ornament as a part of the preservation and restoration of historic buildings. #024-005-01137-4. $1.50.

Federal Historic Preservation Laws, 1994, 96pp, #024-005-01138-2, $3.

Guiding Principles of Sustainable Design, 1993. Provides a basis for achieving sustainability in facility planning and design. #014-005-01132-3, $11.

Heating, Ventilating, and Cooling Historic Buildings: Problems and Recommended Approaches, 1991. Discusses the importance of careful planning in order to balance the preservation objectives with interior climate needs of the building. #024-005-01090-4, $1.

Keeping It Clean: Removing Exterior Dirt, Paint, Stains, and Graffiti From Historic Masonry Buildings, 1988. Provides basic information and technical advice on all aspects of planning and carrying out a cleaning project. #024-005-01035-1, $2.50.

Maintenance and Repair of Architectural Cast Iron, 1991. Provides general guidance on approaches to the preservation and restoration of historic cast iron. #024-995-01088-2, $1.

Making Historic Properties Accessible, 1993. Discusses methods of making historic properties accessible to people with disabilities while preserving their historic character. #024-005-01121-8, $1.50.

Metals in America's Historic Buildings, Uses and Preservation Treatments, Part 1, A Historical Survey of Metals; Part 2, Deterioration and Methods of Preserving Metals, 1992. Intended for use by owners, architects, and building managers responsible for the preservation and maintenance of America's architectural heritage. #024-005-01108-1, $10.

Mothballing Historic Buildings, 1993. Describes the process of closing a historical building temporarily to protect it from damage by weather, insects, and vandals, until it can be restored to its original condition. #024-005-01120-0, $1.50.

Painting Historic Interiors, 1992. Discusses manufacturing and use of paint for the interiors of American buildings, from the colonial era to the present. #014-005-01089-1, $1.

Preservation and Repair of Historic Clay Tile Roofs, 1993. Reviews the history of clay roofing tiles. #024-005-01110-2, $1.25.

Preservation and Repair of Historic Log Buildings, 1991. Presents a concise history and description of the diversity of American log buildings and provides basic guidance regarding their preservation and maintenance. #024-005-01087-4, $1.

Preservation and Repair of Historic Stained and Leaded Glass, 1993. Provides a short history of stained and leaded glass in America. #024-005-01122-6, $1.50.

Preservation Briefs: Recognizing and Resolving Common Preservation Problems: Brochures 1-14, 1975-1987. Provides guidance to owners, architects, and developers of historic buildings with information on cleaning and waterproof

coating for historic masonry; repointing mortar joints; conserving energy; roofing for historic buildings; historic adobe buildings; dangers of abrasive cleaning, historic glazed architectural terra-cotta; aluminum and vinyl siding on wood frame buildings; repairing historic wooden windows; exterior painting problems on historic woodwork; and rehabilitating historic storefronts, 14 folders. #$024-005-02102602, $13.

Preservation Briefs: Brochures 15-23, 1988-1990. Assists owners of historic buildings, architects and contractors in recognizing and resolving common preservation problems prior to work, 9 folders. #025-005-01085-8, $5.

Preservation of Historic Signs, 1991. Describes the historic sign types and practices in the pre-nineteenth century, nineteenth century, and twentieth century. #024-005-01086, $1.

Preservation Tech Notes:

Exterior Woodwork: Protecting Woodwork Against Decay Using Borate Preservatives, 1993. Describes the use of borate preservatives to protect the totem pole collection at Sitka National Park. #024-005-01131-5, $1.25.

Temporary Protection: Specifying Temporary Protection of Historic Interiors During Construction and Repair, 1993. Describes how to protect historic interiors and collections from potential damage during construction work in historic buildings. #024-005-01130-7, $1.25.

Preserving Historic Building Materials: Wood, Paint, Masonry, Concrete, 20th Century Materials, 1993. Contains books on preserving wood features in historic buildings; painting historic buildings, materials and techniques; historic masonry deterioration and repair techniques; historic concrete; and twentieth century building materials, 1990-1950. #024-005-01128-5, $24.

Repair, Replacement, and Maintenance of Historic Slate Roofs, 1992. Assists property owners, architects, preservationists, and building managers in understanding the causes of slate roof failures and undertaking the repair and replacement of slate roofs. #024-005-01109-9, $1.25.

Secretary of the Interior's Standards for Rehabilitation and Illustrated Guidelines for Rehabilitation Historic Buildings, 1992. Enhances overall understanding of basic preservation principles. #024-005-01091-2, $8.

Sources of Federal Assistance Preservation and Revitalization, 1993, 164pp., #024-005-01129-3, $6.

* Home Improvements for Veterans
Public Affairs and Outreach Staff
Veterans Benefits Administration
U.S. Department of Veterans Affairs
1800 G St., NW   202-275-5249
Washington, DC 20420   800-827-1000
The Home Improvements and Structural Alterations (HISA) program helps pay for home improvements necessary to provide access to the home and its essential lavatory and sanitary facilities. For alterations, VA will pay up to $4100 for veterans being treated for a service-connected disability or a veteran with a disability rating of 50 percent or more. Up to $1200 will be paid to other veterans eligible for outpatient care. To apply, contact the nearest VA medical center.

* Homelessness
HUD USER
P.O. Box 6091   800-245-2691
Rockville, MD 20849   301-251-5154
                                     Fax: 301-251-5747
                                     TDD: 800-483-2209
                            Internet: huduser@aspensys.com
HUD USER makes available information on federal, state, and local policy responses to America's continuing homelessness crisis.

Allocation Homeless Assistance by Formula: Report to Congress, 1992, ACCN-6102, $4.

Entrepreneurial Approach to Funding Social Services: The Story of Pioneer Human Services, 1992, ACCN-6009, $4.

Evaluation of the Emergency Shelter Grants Program, 1994
    Volume I, Findings, ACCN-6501, $4.
    Volume II, Site Profiles, ACCN-6502, $4.
    Volume III, Technical Appendices, ACCN-6503, $4.

Evaluation of the Supplemental Assistance for Facilities to Assist the Homeless Program, 1994, ACCN-6367, $4.

Federal Programs to Help Homeless People, 1993, ACCN-6130, $4.

Homelessness (standard search), ACCN-SCH0016, $5.

Housing Special Populations: A Resource Guide, 1987, ACCN-5040, $4.

Initiatives for the Homeless: A Collection of Program Descriptions, 1991, ACCN-5778, $4.

The McKinney Act - A Program Guide, 1991, ACCN-BRO0005, free.

Nation Concerned: Report to the President and Congress on the Response to Homelessness in America, 1989, ACCN-5362, $4.

Practical Methods for Counting Homeless People: A Manual for State and Local Jurisdictions, 1992, ACCN-5970, $4.

Publications Relating to Homelessness: A Working Bibliography, 1989, ACCN-5451, $4.

Working to End Homelessness: A Manual for States, 1991, ACCN-5870, $4.

* Homeownership

HUD USER
P.O. Box 6091
Rockville, MD 20849

800-245-2691
301-251-5154
Fax: 301-251-5747
TDD: 800-483-2209
Internet: huduser@aspensys.com

The publications in this section describe the various federal mortgage insurance and homeownership assistance programs that are making homeownership a reality for many low-income Americans.

Escrow Management for Single-Family Residential Property: Phase 1 Report, 1991, ACCN-5829, $10 (reproduction copy)

Escrow Management for Single-Family Residential Property, Phase 2, Report on Servicer Survey, 1992, ACCN-6101, $4.

FHA Home Equity Conversion Mortgage Insurance Demonstration: A Model to Calculate Borrower Payments and Insurance Risks, 1991, ACCN-5802, $4.

Homeownership and Affordable Housing: The Opportunities, 1991, ACCN-5536, $4.

Interim Evaluation of the Single Family Property Disposition Demonstration, 1993, ACCN-6146, $4.

Options for Elderly Homeowners: A Guide to Reserve Mortgages and Their Alternatives, 1989, ACCN-5395, $4.

Preliminary Evaluation of the Home Equity Conversion Mortgage Insurance Demonstration: Report to Congress, 1992, ACCN-6094, $4.

Public Housing Homeownership Demonstration Assessment, 1990, ACCN-5537, $4.

Public Housing Homeownership Demonstration Assessment Case Studies, 1990, ACCN-5538, $4.

For information of related interest see: Regulatory Barriers to Affordable Housing.

* Homeownership and Opportunity for People Everywhere (HOPE)

Assistant Secretary for Public and Indian Housing
Office of Resident Initiatives
U.S. Department of Housing and Urban Development (HUD)
Washington, DC 20410-5000   800-955-2232

Homeownership and Opportunity for People Everywhere (HOPE) implementation grants provide for the actual conveyance of property. This includes rehabilitation, replacement reserves and housing, legal fees, resident relocation, economic development activities, and administrative costs. The overall amount of an implementation grant is not capped, although there are specific cost caps on eligible activities. Implementation grants require a local match from non-federal sources. Eligible HOPE sponsors include no profit organizations, housing cooperatives, public bodies, public and Indian housing authorities, resident councils, and resident management corporations.

* Homeownership Publications

Veterans Assistance Office
U.S. Department of Veterans Affairs (VA)
810 Vermont Ave., NW
Washington, DC 20420   202-418-4343

The following publications are available to veterans from this office or your VA regional office:

Pointers for the Veteran Homeowner. A guide for veterans whose home mortgage is guaranteed or insured under the GI Bill.

To the Home-Buying Veteran. A guide for veterans planning to buy or build homes with a VA loan.

VA-Guaranteed Home Loans for Veterans. To help you understand what the VA can and cannot do for the home purchaser.

* HOPE for Homeownership of Single Family Homes

Assistant Secretary for Community Planning and Development
U.S. Department of Housing and Urban Development (HUD)

Washington, DC 20410-7000   202-708-2690

HOPE is a national program offering homeownership opportunities to lower-income families and individuals by providing federal assistance to finance an eligible homebuyer's direct purchase and rehabilitation of eligible single family properties. The program funds may also be used for the acquisition and rehabilitation of single family properties for sale and occupancy by families at affordable prices. More information is available from this office or HUD Field Offices.

* Housing Consumer Publications

Superintendent of Documents
Government Printing Office   202-512-1800
Washington, DC 20402   Fax: 202-512-2250

The following publications are geared toward home buyers, and prospective home buyers, who may not be familiar with such issues as consumer rights, mortgages, financing, and much more. Each publication is followed by the GPO order number and price.

Wise Home Buying (S/N 023-000-00752-5, $1). Instructs the first-time home buyer in selecting and financing a house. Discusses the relation of housing costs to income, new versus old houses, mortgage loans, real estate brokers, and more.

Home Buyer's Vocabulary (S/N 023-000-00751-7, $1). Provides general, nontechnical definitions of terms the potential home buyer will encounter in buying and financing a home.

Guide to Single Family Home Mortgage Insurance (#023-000-00809-2, $1.25). Explains: how FHA mortgage insurance works; how to shop for a HUD-approved lender; how to apply for a FHA-insured loan; how your payment schedule will operate; what restrictions apply to FHA-insured mortgages; and which specific FHA program can best help you.

Homebuyer's and Seller's Guide to Radon (#055-000-00428-4, $1.50). Prepared for anyone buying or selling a home who wants to learn about radon, an invisible, cancer-causing, radioactive gas. This pamphlet tells how to test for radon.

Mortgage Money Guide (#018-000-00341-4, $74). Explains some of the basic concepts needed to shop for a home loan. Summarizes more than a dozen financing plans. Includes monthly payment tables for loans from $25,000 to $100,000, covering spans of 5 to 30 years, with interest rates from 8 to 15 percent. Sold in packages of 100 only.

* Housing Discrimination

Fair Housing Enforcement Division
Office of Fair Housing and Equal Opportunity
U.S. Department of Housing and Urban Development (HUD)
Washington, DC 20410-2000   202-708-2213

Technical assistance is available to state and local agencies, private and public groups, and profit or nonprofit organizations to help them prevent or eliminate discriminatory housing practices.

* Housing Finance Statistics

Financial Policy Division
Office of Housing
U.S. Department of Housing and Urban Development (HUD)
Washington, DC 20410   202-755-7450

Studies are conducted by the Financial Policy Division of HUD in areas relating to the mortgage market, securities, taxation, market trends, and interest rates, among others. If you are interested in receiving information about these subjects or want to be placed on the mailing list, contact this office.

* Housing for Special Needs

HUD USER
P.O. Box 6091
Rockville, MD 20849

800-245-2691
301-251-5154
Fax: 301-251-5747
TDD: 800-483-2209
Internet: huduser@aspensys.com

These publications discuss housing and supportive service options for the elderly and physically or mentally disabled Americans.

Adaptable Housing: A Technical Manual for Implementing Adaptable Dwelling Unit Specifications, 1987, ACCN-4981, $4.

Cost of Accessible Housing, 1993, ACCN-6180, $4.

Creating Community: Integrating Elderly and Severely Mentally Ill Persons in Public Housing, 1993, ACCN-6213, $4.

Housing and Real Estate

FHA Home Equity Conversion Mortgage Insurance Demonstration: A Model to Calculate Borrower Payments and Insurance Risks, 1991, ACCN-5802, $4.

Housing for the Elderly, (standard search), ACCN-SCH0005, $5.

Housing Special Populations: A Resource Guide, 1987, ACCN-5040, $4.

Options for Elderly Homeowners: A Guide to Reverse Mortgages and Their Alternatives, 1989, ACCN-5395, $4.

Preliminary Evaluation of the Home Equity Conversion Mortgage Insurance Demonstration: Report to Congress, 1992, ACCN-6094, $4.

Report to Congress: Housing Mentally Disabled Persons in Public Housing Projects for the Elderly, 1990, ACCN-5798, $10 (reproduction copy).

For information of related interest see: Building Technology, Fair Housing, Homeownership, and Regulatory Barriers to Affordable Housing.

* Housing Policy

HUD USER
P.O. Box 6091   800-245-2691
Rockville, MD 20849   301-251-5154
                                                Fax: 301-251-5747
                                               TDD: 800-483-2209
                                     Internet: huduser@aspensys.com

This section contains documents that discuss current and proposed federal housing policies and provide data on housing needs and information resources.

Allocating Homeless Assistance by Formula: Report to Congress, 1992, ACCN-6102, $4.

Cityscape, Volume I, No. I (August 1994), ACCN, 6488, $4.

Directory of Information Resources in Housing and Urban Development, Third Edition (Resource Guide), 1993, ACCN-6200, $4.

Federal Housing Programs (standard search), ACCN-SCH0010, $5.

Federal Programs to Help Homeless People, 1993, ACCN-6130, $4.

Guidelines for Unsolicited Proposals Submitted to the Office of Policy Development and Research, 1989, ACCN-5959, $4.

Local Comprehensive Housing Affordability Strategy (CHAS): A Preliminary Assessment of First-Year Submissions, 1992, ACCN-5997, $4.

Location of Worst Case Needs in the Late 1980's: A Report to Congress, 1992, ACCN-6102, $4.

Median Family Incomes for Fiscal Year 1993
National, ACCN-DOC1600, $20.
State (choose one), ACCN-DOC1601, $5 (reproduction copy).
Area Definitions, ACCN-DOC1602, $10 (reproduction copy)/

President's National Urban Policy Report, 1991, ACCN-5915, $4.

Priority Housing Problems and "Worst Case" Needs in 1989, A Report to Congress, ACCN-5825, $4.

Rediscovering Urban America: Perspectives on the 1980's, 1993, ACCN-6106, $4.

Report to Congress on the Federal Home Loan Bank System, 1994
Volume 1: Summary Analysis and Policy Recommendations, ACCN-6370
Volume 2: Analytical Studies, ACCN-6371, $4.

State and Local Pension Fund Financing of Housing: A Report to Congress, 1992, ACCN-5981, $4.

Third Report to Congress on HUD's Program Monitoring and Evaluation Activities, ACCN-6361, $4.

U.S. Housing Market Conditions:
4th Quarter, 1994, ACCN-6359, $4.
1st Quarter, 1994, ACCN-6410, $4.
2nd Quarter, 1994, ACCN-6490, $4.
3rd Quarter, 1994, ACCN-6514, $4.

Urban Policy Brief: Residential Mobility Programs, 1994, ACCN-6510, free.

Worst Case Needs for Housing Assistance in the United States in 1990 and 1991, 1994, ACCN-6457, $4.

1993 Income Limits for "Low Income" and "Very Low Income" Families Under the Housing Act of 1937
National, ACCN-DOC1700, $25 (reproduction copy).
State (choose one), ACCN-DOC1701, $5 (reproduction copy).
Area Definitions, ACCN-DOC1602, $10 (reproduction copy).

1994 Income Limits for "Low Income" and "Very Low Income" Families Under the Housing Act of 1937
National, ACCN-DOC1900, (reproduction copy).
State (choose one), ACCN-DOC1901, $5 (reproduction copy).
Area Definitions, ACCN-DOC1802, $10 (reproduction copy).

For information of related interest see: American Housing Survey, Assisted Housing/Section 8, Community Planning/Urban Development, Fair Housing, Homelessness, Homeownership, Housing Production/Rehabilitation Programs, and Public and Indian Housing.

* Housing Production/Rehabilitation Programs

HUD USER
P.O. Box 6091   800-245-2691
Rockville, MD 20849   301-251-5154
                                                Fax: 301-251-5747
                                               TDD: 800-483-2209
                                     Internet: huduser@aspensys.com

These publications discuss federal and local programs designed to increase the supply of safe, decent, and affordable housing through new construction and rehabilitation.

Evaluation of the Low-Income Housing Tax Credit, Final Report, 1991, ACCN-5927, $4.

Federal Housing Programs (standard search), ACCN-SCH0010, $5.

Housing Rehabilitation (standard search), ACCN-SCH0019, $5.

Local Comprehensive Housing Affordability Strategy (CHAS): A Preliminary Assessment of First-Year Submissions, 1992, ACCN-5997, $4.

Nonprofit Housing: Costs and Funding, Final Report
Volume I: Findings, 1993, ACCN-6291, $4.
Volume II: Case Studies, 1993, ACCN-6290, $4.

Rural Rental Rehabilitation Demonstration: Report to Congress, 1993, ACCN-6103, $4.

* Housing Programs for Rural America

Housing Assistance Council (HAC)
1025 Vermont Ave., NW   202-842-8600
Washington, DC 20005   Fax: 202-347-3441

The Housing Assistance Council's (HAC) basic funding has been provided by the U.S. Department of Housing and Urban Development (HUD), supplemented by grants from foundations, and by contracts with the state housing and development agencies and nonprofit housing organizations. HAC's staff includes professional housing technicians and specialists in government housing programs, finance, research, information, and training. Basic technical services are generally available without charge to public and nonprofit agencies serving the rural poor. Predevelopment loans are available at less than market rates. For further information, contact this office.

* Housing Research and Policy

Assistant Secretary for Policy Development and Research
U.S. Department of Housing and Urban Development (HUD)
Washington, DC 20410-6000   202-708-1600

This office is responsible for economic and policy analyses, research, demonstrations, and evaluations of national housing and community development. All policy development data generated by the U.S. Department of Housing and Urban Development (HUD) are made available to interested parties, such as state and local governments, financial institutions, builders, developers, neighborhood groups, and universities and colleges. The research addresses many issues, including the management, operation, and maintenance of the insured and assisted multi-family housing inventory; the stability of the nation's housing finance system; the design of sound mortgage instruments and improvements in FHA programs; the increase of housing affordability through technological and regulatory improvements; the improvement of public housing; the assurance of a supply of affordable rental housing units; the promotion of fair and nondiscriminatory housing; and the study of housing-related health problems.

* Housing the Homeless

Information Staff
Farmers Home Administration (FmHA)
U.S. Department of Agriculture (USDA)
14th and Independence Ave., SW
Washington, DC 20250   202-720-4323

The Farmers Home Administration (FmHA) offers single family housing inventory property to nonprofit organizations or public bodies for transitional housing for the homeless. Qualifying organizations may lease nonprogram property if they can show a documented need in the community for the type of housing use proposed and the financial ability to meet proposed housing costs.

* HUD Counseling Agency Program

Single Family Servicing Branch
Counseling Services
U.S. Department of Housing and Urban Development (HUD)
Washington, DC 20410-8000   202-708-3664

Housing counseling grants are awarded on a competitive basis to HUD-approved counseling agencies to reimburse them partially for costs. These agencies and private and public organizations must be competent and have knowledge and experience in housing counseling. The maximum grant available is $40,000 per agency.

* HUD Library and Information Service

Program Information Center
U.S. Department of Housing and Urban Development (HUD)
Washington, DC 20410   202-708-1420

If you need additional assistance and direction to particular programs within the U.S. Department of Housing and Urban Development (HUD), or have questions about how HUD can work for you, contact the Program Information Center, and they will gladly assist you.

* HUD Major Publication Sources

HUD USER
P.O. Box 6091   800-245-2691
Rockville, MD 20849   301-251-5154
                                                      TDD: 800-483-2209
                                            Internet: huduser@aspensys.com

HUD USER, the research information service sponsored by the U.S. Department of Housing and Urban Development's (HUD) Office of Policy Development and Research, distributes the latest research in the fields of housing and urban development in a variety of formats tailored to your needs. These include:

Document delivery - Printed copies of recently published reports and photocopies of unpublished and out-of-print materials.

Resource guides - illustrated collections of abstracts on topics of special interest, such as housing rehabilitation, enterprise zones, public housing, alternative housing arrangements, affordable housing, fair housing, elderly housing, homelessness, and accessible environments for the disabled.

Directory of Information Resources in Housing and Urban Development- a valuable reference tool providing descriptions of 114 organizations and 37 online databases in the housing, construction, and planning fields.

Searches on HUD USER ONLINE - performed by HUD USER reference specialists to help you locate documents containing information in your area of interest.

Microfiche - copies of any non-copyrighted documents in HUD USER ONLINE in an economical and space-saving format.

Audiovisual programs - to stimulate discussion at group meetings on improving housing and neighborhoods.

* HUD Programs Investigation Division

Office of Investigation
U.S. Department of Housing and Urban Development (HUD)
Washington, DC 20410-2000   202-708-0390

The U.S. Department of Housing and Urban Development (HUD) determines the extent to which its programs comply with Federal laws forbidding discrimination in all federally funded activities. This office investigates complaints and reviews HUD programs to eliminate discrimination. Activities are made more responsive to minorities and promote their participation in HUD programs. Technical assistance is available to state and local agencies with civil rights problems.

* HUD USER

HUD USER
P.O. Box 6091   800-245-2691
Rockville, MD 20849   301-251-5154
                                                      Fax: 301-251-5747
                                                      TDD: 800-483-2209
                                            Internet: huduser@aspensys.com

HUD USER is a research information service and clearinghouse for people who are working toward improving housing and strengthening community development. HUD USER collects, develops, and distributes housing-related information that can help you perform your work more efficiently and effectively. Reference Specialists are available to access the information you need. Resources and services available include: documents, audiovisual programs, Recent Research Results, HUD USER database, resource guides, Directory of Information in Housing and Urban Development, referrals, microfiche copies, computer packages, and blueprints.

* Land Sale Fraud

Federal Trade Commission
Marketing Practices
6th and Pennsylvania Ave., NW
Washington, DC 20580   202-326-3128

This office investigates fraud as it relates to the sale of land to the public, and can provide you with information about your rights and how to avoid fraudulent practices.

* Land Sales

Interstate Land Sales Registration
U.S. Department of Housing and Urban Development (HUD)
Washington, DC 20410-8000   202-708-0502

The registration of interstate land sales protects subdivision lot purchasers by prohibiting fraudulent practices requiring of land developers and promoters full financial disclosure. Before a lot can be sold or leased, two conditions must be met by developers: 1) A Statement of Record must be filed with HUD, containing full and current disclosure about the ownership of the land, the state of title, planned physical characteristics, planned availability of roads, services, utilities, and other matters; and 2) A printed Property Report must be delivered to each purchaser or lessee in advance of signing the contract or agreement. Anti-fraud provisions apply to subdivisions containing 25 or more lots. HUD may seek an injunction against any developer whom it can show is violating or about to violate the law, and may suspend the registration of a developer whose Statement of Record or Property Report contains misrepresentation or omits material facts.

* Lead Based Paint

Office of Lead-Based Paint Abatement and Poisoning Prevention
U.S. Department of Housing and Urban Development (HUD)
Washington, DC 20410   202-755-1785

The responsibilities of this office include increasing awareness by the public and the building industry of the dangers of lead-based paint poisoning and the options for detection, risk reduction, and abatement. It also encourages state and local governments to develop lead-based paint programs covering primary prevention, including public education, contractor certification, hazard reduction, financing, and enforcement.

* Lead Based Paint

HUD USER
P.O. Box 6091   800-245-2691
Rockville, MD 20849   301-251-5154
                                                      Fax: 301-251-5747
                                                      TDD: 800-483-2209
                                            Internet: huduser@aspensys.com

HUD USER offers an excellent selection of training kits, manuals, and guidelines for public housing officials and others on the assessment, control, and abatement of lead-based paint hazards in residential buildings.

Comprehensive and Workable Plan for the Abatement of Lead-Based Paint in Privately Owner Housing: A Report to Congress, 1990, ACCN-5716, $20.
Environmental Hazards (standard search), ACCN-ACH0018, $5.
HUD Lead-Based Paint Abatement Demonstration (FHA), 1991, ACCN-5845, $4.
HUD Lead-Based Paint Abatement Demonstration (FHA), Appendixes:
    Volume I: Appendixes A-H, 1991, ACCN-5846, $25.
    Volume II: Appendixes I-P, 1991, ACCN-5847, $30.
HUD Lead-Based Paint Abatement Demonstration (FHA), Unit Sample on Diskette, 1992, ACCN-AVI0019, $15.
Lead Abatement Training for Supervisors and Contractors, (training kit), 1992, ACCN-AVI6059, $310.
Lead-Based Paint (videotape), 1991, ACCN-ANI0009, $20.
Lead-Based Paint Bibliographies:
    Problem Identification, 1991, ACCN-BIB0018, $4.
    Strategies, 1992, ACCN-BIB0019, $4.
Lead-Based Paint Interim Guidelines for Hazard Identification and Abatement in Public and Indian Housing (training kit), 1990, ACCN-AVI5579, $310.
Lead-Based Paint: A Threat to Your Children, 1993, ACCN-BRO0026, single copies free.
Lead-Based Paint Risk Assessment Protocol, 1992, ACCN-6026, $15.
Lead Inspector Training: U.S. Environmental Protection Agency Model Training Course Curriculum
    Inspector's Manual and Slides, 1993, ACCN-6140, $115.
    Student Manual, 1993, ACCN-6141, $5.

Be patient. If any phone number is incorrect, call (area code) 555-1212 and request the new listing.

125

Housing and Real Estate

Residential Lead-Based Paint Abatement Model Training Course (training kit), 1994
  Training Kit, ACCN-AVI6500, $310.
  Student Manual, ACCN-AVI6501, $25.
  Tool Box Guide, ACCN-AVI6502, $3.

For information of related interest see: Public and Indian Housing.

* Lenders Offering FHA-Insured Mortgages
  Office of Insured Single Family Housing
  U.S. Department of Housing and Urban Development (HUD)
  Washington, DC 20410-8000   202-708-2700
This U.S. Department of Housing and Urban Development (HUD) office maintains a listing of lenders who participate in FHA-insured mortgage programs. You can get this information by contacting your local Field Office.

* Manufactured Housing
  HUD USER   800-245-2691
  P.O. Box 6091   301-251-5154
  Rockville, MD 20849   Fax: 301-251-5747
                                           TDD: 800-483-2209
                              Internet: huduser@aspensys.com
This section presents a sample of the many research documents available from HUD USER on the safety, efficiency, and durability of manufactured and mobile homes, and on planning for their use at the local level.

Evaluation of Manufactured Home Safety for 1982-1983, 1987, ACCN-4815, $10.
Final Report of National Commission on Manufactured Housing, 1994, ACCN-6482, $4.
Indoor Ventilation Requirements for Manufactured Housing, 1991, ACCN-5799, $10 (reproduction copy).
Manufactured Home Fire Experience Through 1990 Fires: Final Report, 1993, ACCN-6133, $15 (reproduction copy).
Manufactured Housing: A HUD USER Resource Guide, 1993, ACCN-6245, $4.
Overall U-Values and Heating/Cooling Loads - Manufactured Homes (computer package), 1992, ACCN-5945, $15.
Permanent Foundations Guide to Manufactured Housing, 1989, ACCN-5433, $20 (reproduction copy).
Revision of the Energy Conservation Requirements in the Manufactured Housing Construction and Safety Standards, 1992, ACCN-5946, $20 (reproduction copy).
Ventilation, Moisture Control, and Indoor Air Quality in Manufactured Houses, 1993, ACCN-6250, $10 (reproduction copy).
Wind Load Provisions of the Manufactured Home Construction and Safety Standards - A Review and Recommendations for Improvement, 1993, ACCN-6142, $15 (reproduction copy).

For information on related interests see: Regulatory Barriers to Affordable Housing.

* Mobile Home Construction and Safety Standards
  Office of Single Family Housing
  Office of Manufactured Housing and Regulatory Functions
  Manufactured Housing and Construction Standards Division
  U.S. Department of Housing and Urban Development (HUD)
  Washington, DC 20410-8000   202-755-7430
The U.S. Department of Housing and Urban Development (HUD) issues Federal manufactured home construction and safety standards to reduce the number of personal injuries and deaths, and the amount of insurance costs and property damage resulting from manufactured home accidents. The program also strives to improve the quality and durability of manufactured homes. Standards are enforced by HUD directly or by various States which have established State administrative agencies that participate in the program. HUD inspects factories and obtains records needed to enforce the standards, and if standards are not met, the manufacturer is forced to notify the consumer and to correct any defects found.

* Multifamily Property Disposition
  Multifamily Property Disposition Branch
  Office of Multifamily Housing
  U.S. Department of Housing and Urban Development (HUD)
  Washington, DC 20410   202-275-7471
Multifamily properties are sold through sealed-bid auctions across the country. This office maintains a listing of the current available properties. To be placed on the mailing list for current and new apartments that become available, contact this office.

* Native American Indians and Housing
  Office of Public Affairs
  Bureau of Indian Affairs
  U.S. Department of the Interior
  18th and C Sts., NW
  Washington, DC 20240   202-208-3710
The free booklet, *American Indians Today: Answers to Your Questions*, contains useful information on the Native American Indians and their relationship to the Bureau of Indian Affairs. Programs within the Bureau, including education, health services, and housing are briefly outlined and contain recent statistics. Many questions are answered within the booklet, including the rights of the Indians to own land and have their own governments. A map locates the Indian lands and communities, showing Federal and State Indian Reservations and other Indian groups. An excellent bibliography, prepared by the Smithsonian Institution, is included.

* Public and Indian Housing
  Office of Public and Indian Housing
  U.S. Department of Housing and Urban Development (HUD)
  Washington, DC 20410   202-708-0950
This office administers public and Indian housing programs, including rental and homeownership programs, and provides technical and financial assistance in planning, developing, and managing low-income projects. For more information, contact the office listed above.

* Public and Indian Housing
  HUD USER
  P.O. Box 6091   800-245-2691
  Rockville, MD 20849   301-251-5154
                                           Fax: 301-251-5747
                                           TDD: 800-483-2209
                              Internet: huduser@aspensys.com
Residents and Managers of public and Indian housing will find useful information in these publications on the administration, operation, maintenance, and modernization of public housing developments, as well as opportunities for resident empowerment and self-sufficiency.

Characteristics of HUD-Assisted Renters and Their Units in 1989, ACCN-5961, $4.
Comprehensive Grant Program (videotape)
  Part 1: Developing a Successful Plan, 1992, ACCN-AVI0014, $20.
  Part 2: HUD Review and Monitoring, 1992, ACCN-AVI0015, $20.
Creating Community: Integrating Elderly and Severely Mentally Ill Persons in Public Housing, 1993, ACCN-6213, $4.
Evaluation of Resident Management in Public Housing, 1992, ACCN-6093, $4.
Family Data on Public and Indian Housing (computer package), 1994, ACCN-AVI0027, $15.
Future Accrual of Capital Repair and Replacement Needs of Public and Indian Housing, 1989, ACCN-5401, $4.
Guide to Financial Management for Resident Management Corporations, Parts 1 and 2, ACCN-5912/5913, $4.
Housing Quality Standards (2 videotapes), 1989, ACCN-5353, $60.
How to Save Money on Monthly Gas Utility Bills for Public Housing Agencies: A Simple Step-by-Step Procedure, 1989, ACCN-5435, $10 (reproduction copy).
Life-Cycle Cost Analysis for Utility Combinations (computer package), 1989, ACCN-5432, $10.
Managing Maintenance in Public Housing: A Guide for Administrators and Supervisors, 1993, ACCN-6260, $10 (reproduction copy).
The Occupancy Challenge (videotape), 1990, ACCN-AVI10003, $20.
Operation Bootstrap, 1994
  Volume 1: Program Administration, ACCN-6491, $4.
  Volume 2: Outcomes of Participation, ACCN-6492, $4.
  Volume 3: Case Studies, ACCN-6493, $4.
An "Ounce of Prevention": Preventive Maintenance in HUD Communities (videotape), 1990, ACCN-AVI0006, $20.
Program for Energy Analysis of Residences (microcomputer program), 1989, ACCN-5434, $10.
Project-Based Accounting Guidebook, 1990, ACCN-5673, $4.
Public Housing Drug Elimination Program Resource Document, 1994
  Final Report, ACCN-6462, $4.
  Case Studies, ACCN-6463, $4.
  Executive Summary, ACCN-6464, $4.
Public Housing Homeownership Demonstration Assessment, 1990, ACCN-5537, $4.
Public Housing Homeownership Demonstration Assessment Case Studies, 1990, ACCN-5538, $4.
Public Housing (standard search), ACCN-SCH0017, $5.

Report on Emerging Resident Management Corporations in Public Housing, 1993, $6108, $4.

Report to Congress on Alternative Methods for Funding Public Housing Modernization, 1990, ACCN-5535, $4.

Revised Methods of Providing Federal Funding to Public Housing Agencies, 1994, ACCN-6476, $4.

A Standard Project-Based Accounting System for Public Housing Agencies: Final Report, 1990, ACCN-5672, $4.

Study of Modernization Needs of the Public and Indian Housing Stock: National, Regional, and Field Office Estimates: Backlog of Modernization Needs and HUD Perspective on Public Housing Modernization, 1988, ACCN-5105/5106, $4.

Tenant Integrity Program: Training Guide for Public Housing and Section 8 Certificate, Voucher, and Moderate Rehabilitation Program, 1992, ACCN-6053, $20 (reproduction copy).

Tenant Integrity Program (videotape), 1989, ACCN-5423, $20.

For information of related interest see: Assisted Housing/Section 8, and Lead Based Paint.

* Real Estate Settlements

Real Estate Settlement Procedures Act (RESPA)
Office of Insured Single Family Housing
U.S. Department of Housing and Urban Development (HUD)
Washington, DC 20410-8000   202-708-4560

RESPA requires that lenders give all borrowers of federally-insured mortgage loans a HUD-prepared booklet with information about real estate transactions, settlement services, cost comparisons, and relevant consumer protection laws. When applying for a loan, borrowers must receive the booklet along with the lender's good faith estimate of the settlement costs they are likely to incur. One day before settlement, the borrower may request that the person conducting the settlement provide information on the actual settlement costs. At settlement, both the buyer and seller are entitled to a settlement statement that itemizes the costs they paid in connection with the transaction.

* Recent Research Results (RRR)

HUD USER
P.O. Box 6091   800-245-2691
Rockville, MD 20850   301-251-5154

This newsletter contains short summaries of reports recently published under the auspices of the HUD Office of Policy Development and Research. To be put on the mailing list, contact this office.

* Regulatory Barriers to Affordable Housing

HUD USER
P.O. Box 6091   800-245-2691
Rockville, MD 20849   301-251-5154
                                         Fax: 301-251-5747
                                         TDD: 800-483-2209
                                Internet: huduser@aspensys.com

The HUD documents in this section provide policy research, guidelines, and case studies on regulatory reforms that states and localities can undertake to enhance the affordability of their housing stock.

Affordable Housing Challenge and Response:
Volume 1: *Affordable Residential Land Development*, 1987, ACCN-5039, $4.
Volume 2: *Affordable Residential Construction*, 1987, ACCN-5051, $4.

Affordable Housing: Development Guidelines for State and Local Government, 1992, ACCN-5940, $15 (reproduction copy).

Creating a Local Advisory Council on Regulatory Barriers to Affordable Housing, 1992, ACCN-AHC0004, $4.

Home Building Cost Cuts: Construction Methods and Materials for Affordable Housing (looseleaf bulletin), 1983, ACCN-2930, $4.

Homeownership and Affordable Housing: The Opportunities, 1991, ACCN-5536, $4.

Impact Fees and the Role of State: Guidance for Drafting Legislation, 1994, ACCN-6315, $4.

Local Comprehensive Housing Affordability Strategy (CHAS): A Preliminary Assessment of First-Year Submissions, 1992, ACCN-5997, $4.

National Analysis of Housing Affordability, Adequacy and Availability: A Framework for Local Housing Strategies, 1994, ACCN-6365, $4.

"Not In My Back Yard": Removing Barriers to Affordable Housing, 1991, ACCN-5806, $4.

Proposed Model Land Development Standard and Accompanying Model State

Enabling Legislation, 1993, ACCN-6212, $4.

Regulatory Barriers to Affordable Housing: A Resource Guide, 1991, ACCN-5800, $4.

Removing Regulatory Barriers to Affordable Housing: How States and Localities are Moving Ahead, 1993, ACCN-AHC0009, $4.

Report to Congress on Rent Control, 1991, ACCN-5868, $4.

For information of related interest see: Fair Housing, Housing for Special Needs, and Manufactured Housing.

* Rehabilitation Mortgage Insurance

Assistant Secretary for Housing
Federal Housing Commissioner
U.S. Department of Housing and Urban Development (HUD)
Washington, DC 20410-8000   202-708-3600

HUD insured rehabilitation loans to 1) finance rehabilitation of an existing property; 2) finance rehabilitation and refinancing of the outstanding indebtedness of a property; and 3) finance purchase and rehabilitation of a property. An eligible rehabilitation loan must involve a principal obligation not exceeding the amount allowed under Section 203(b) home mortgage insurance. More information is available from this office or HUD Field Offices.

* Rental Rates

Technical Support Division
Office of Multifamily Housing
U.S. Department of Housing and Urban Development (HUD)
Washington, DC 20410   202-708-0035

The *Federal Register* contains a yearly listing of the fair market rental rates in 450 market areas around the country. The data show the rental rates for various types of dwellings.

* Research in Assisted Housing

Assistant Secretary for Policy
Development and Research
U.S. Department of Housing and Urban Development (HUD)
Washington, DC 20410-6000   202-708-1600

This office conducts research and evaluations to develop more efficient, effective, and equitable ways to assist low-income households. HUD's assisted housing programs are monitored and evaluated, and alternatives are investigated. Data is collected and analyzed by the Department's staff and made available to interested parties, to federal agencies, and to Congress. Assisted housing research conducted includes the following areas: administrative costs of operating assisted housing programs, development costs of assisted housing programs, alternative assisted housing demonstrations, efficient, effective management of public housing projects, benefits to participants in assisted housing programs, and environmental hazards in assisted housing.

* Safe Drinking Water

Office of Water Resource Center
401 M St., SW, 4100 (P)   202-250-7786
Washington, DC 20460   Fax: 202-260-4383

The Resource Center distributes ground water and drinking water documents, water quality criteria documents, and related videotapes, and some wastewater treatment documents free of charge while supplies last. A catalog of publications is available at no cost from this office. Publications available include:

Drinking Water from Household Wells, #570/9-90-013
Fact Sheet: Home Water Testing, #570/9-91-500
Ground Water Protection: A Citizen's Action Checklist, #810/F-93-005
Home Water Treatment Units: Filtering Fact Sheet, #570/9-90-HHH
Protecting Our Ground Water, #440/6-85-006
What You Can Do to Keep Your Drinking Water Safe, #570/9-90-500

* Single Family Property Auctions

Sales Promotion Branch
Office of Single Family Housing
U.S. Department of Housing and Urban Development (HUD)
Washington, DC 20410   202-708-0740

Single-family homes are sold by sealed-bid auction in every city in the country. These properties are advertised in local newspapers.

Housing and Real Estate

* So...Now You Own a Septic System

National Small Flows Clearinghouse
Environmental Protection Agency (EPA)
West Virginia University   800-624-8301
P.O. Box 6064   304-293-4191
Morgantown, WV 26506-6064   Fax: 304-293-3161
                                  Bulletin Board: 800-544-1936

The purpose of the Clearinghouse is to collect, classify, and disseminate information on small alternative wastewater technology. They distribute publications and videotapes, perform literature searches, operate a toll-free hotline, produce free newsletters, and operate a computer bulletin board. *So...Now You Own a Septic System* is one of the free brochures available describing how to care for a septic tank (#WWBRPE20). You can request a free copy of the *Guide to Products and Services* from the office listed above. Other publications available include:

The Care and Feeding of Your Septic Tank (#WWBRPE18). This brochure describes septic tanks and absorption fields, as well as rules to protect them and to prolong their usefulness. Free.

Groundwater Protection (#WWBRPE21). This brochure discusses groundwater contamination from septic systems and how to prevent it. Free.

Septic Tank Siting to Minimize the Contamination of Ground Water by Micro-organisms (#WWPCGN39). This book contains a rating system using readily available data that could be used as a tool in septic tank siting. 97pp, $9.30.

Septic Tank Effluent Pump Pressure Sewer Systems Information Package (STEP), (#WWPCGN41). This package of information contains general system characteristics, design information, performance data, and tips on septage characteristics and disposal alternatives. 192pp, $16.40.

Your Septic System: A Guide for Homeowners (#WWVTPE16). This 11 minute videotape discusses septic system operation and maintenance, covering 10 basic rules for homeowners to follow. $27.

Septic Systems - A Guide for Homeowners (#WWBRPE17). This brochure describes a conventional septic system and how it should be cared for to achieve optimal results. Tips for trouble-free operation are provided. Free.

* Solar Heated Homes

Superintendent of Documents
Government Printing Office   202-512-1800
Washington, DC 20420   Fax: 202-512-2250

The following publications concerning solar energy will be of interest to those considering alternative heating methods for their homes.

Design Contest, 1989, 155pp, #061-000-00780-6, $9. Defines in a checklist format the issues that are unique to energy conserving, passive solar design that must be considered early in the design process. Issues discussed include site and climate analysis, building organization and design, building system options, space conditioning options, user influence, and building codes and zoning ordinances.

Passive Solar Homes: Case Studies, 1990, 149pp, #061-000-00769-5, $8.50. Discusses 13 passive solar houses in Europe and the United States, showing the architectural impact of energy conservation and passive/hybrid solar features. Each house is presented as a case study on the design, construction, and performance results.

Solar Collector Manufacturing Activity, 1992, 76pp, #061-003-00830-5, $5. Presents data provided by United States based manufacturers and importers of solar collectors. It summarized data on solar thermal collector shipments for the years 1974 through 1992, and on photovoltaic cell and module shipments for the years 1982 through 1992. It also details information for solar thermal collectors.

* Surplus Property

Public Benefit Program
Division of Health Facilities Planning

Public Health Service (PHS), Room 17A10
5600 Fishers Lane
Rockville, MD 20857   301-443-2265

The Public Health Service has real estate property available for use under two programs. The first program allows the property to be used for a public health purpose by local and state governments and private nonprofit organizations certified under the Internal Revenue Service (IRS) code. The property can be used for such projects as nursing homes, clinics, or mental health centers. You are deeded the property with a thirty year period of restriction. The second program allows the property to be used by local government or private nonprofit organizations for homeless shelters.

* Surplus Veterans Homes

U.S. Department of Veterans Affairs
810 Vermont Ave, NW
Washington, DC 20420   202-418-4270, ext. 3336

The U.S. Department of Veterans Affairs sells foreclosed properties through private real estate brokers. Properties are frequently advertised in local newspapers. Almost any real estate agent can show you the property. Local Veterans offices are the best sources of information on the procedures involved in purchasing these properties. Prices drop on those homes that are not sold in a certain period of time. Veterans financing is possible, but you get a 10% discount if you pay cash. See the Section on Computerized Electronic Bulletin Boards for getting this information online with your modem.

* Urban Policy Report to Congress

Assistant Secretary for Policy
Development and Research
U.S. Department of Housing and Urban Development (HUD)
Washington, DC 20410-6000   202-708-1600

Under the Urban Growth and New Community Development Act of 1970, Congress is required to develop a national urban growth policy report every two years. This report summarizes trends, identifies significant problems, evaluates the effectiveness of federal efforts to deal with the problems, and makes recommendations for legislative and administrative actions.

* Urban Trees Money

Public Affairs Office
Forest Service
U.S. Department of Agriculture (USDA)
P.O. Box 96090
Washington, DC 20090-6090   703-720-3760
OR: Your regional Forest Service Office

The U.S. Department of Agriculture (USDA) will provide financial, technical, and related assistance in order to plant and protect trees, maintain and use wood from trees in open spaces, green belts, roadside screens, parks woodlands, curb areas, and residential developments in urban areas.

* Veterans Foreclosed Homes

U.S. Department of Veterans Affairs
810 Vermont Ave, NW
Washington, DC 20420   202-418-4270, ext. 3336

The U.S. Department of Veterans Affairs sells foreclosed properties through private real estate brokers. Properties are frequently advertised in local newspapers, giving information such as address, number of bedrooms and bathrooms, particular defects in the property and price. Almost any real estate can show you the property. Local Veterans offices are the best source of information on the procedures involved in purchasing these properties. Many local offices maintain the information on local online bulletin boards. See the Chapter on Government Databases and Bulletin Boards.

Be patient. If any phone number is incorrect, call (area code) 555-1212 and request the new listing.

Federal Money for Housing and Real Estate

The following is a description of the federal funds available to renters, homeowners, developers, and real estate investors for housing in urban and rural areas. This information is derived from the *Catalog of Federal Domestic Assistance* which is published by the U.S. Government Printing Office in Washington, D.C. The number next to the title description is the official reference for this federal program. Contact the office listed below the caption for further details. The following is a description of the terms used for the types of assistance available:

Loans: money lent by a federal agency for a specific period of time and with a reasonable expectation of repayment. Loans may or may not require payment of interest.

Loan Guarantees: programs in which federal agencies agree to pay back part or all of a loan to a private lender if the borrower defaults.

Grants: money given by federal agencies for a fixed period of time and which does not have to be repaid.

Direct Payments: funds provided by federal agencies to individuals, private firms, and institutions. The use of direct payments may be "specified" to perform a particular service or for "unrestricted" use.

Insurance: coverage under specific programs to assure reimbursement for losses sustained. Insurance may be provided by federal agencies or through insurance companies and may or may not require the payment of premiums.

* Money for Conserving the Water and Soil During an Emergency

(10.054 Emergency Conservation Program (ECP))
Agricultural Stabilization and Conservation Service
U.S. Department of Agriculture
P.O. Box 2415
Washington, DC 20013   202-720-6221
Objectives: To enable farmers to perform emergency conservation measures to control wind erosion on farmlands, or to rehabilitate farmlands damaged by wind erosion, floods, hurricanes, or other natural disasters and to carry out emergency water conservation or water enhancing measures during periods of severe drought. Types of assistance: direct payments for specified use. Estimate of annual funds available: (Direct payments) $19,489,000.

* Money to Insure Your Soil and Land Remains Intact

(10.063 Agricultural Conservation Program (ACP))
Agricultural Stabilization and Conservation Service
U.S. Department of Agriculture
P.O. Box 2415
Washington, DC 20013   202-720-6221
Objectives: Control of erosion and sedimentation, encourage voluntary compliance with Federal and State requirements to solve point and nonpoint source pollution, improve water quality, encourage energy conservation measures, and assure a continued supply of necessary food and fiber for a strong and healthy people and economy. The program will be directed toward the solution of critical soil, water, energy, woodland, and pollution abatement problems on farms and ranches. Types of assistance: direct payments for specified use. Estimate of annual funds available: (Direct payment) $146,618,000.

* Money to Insure That Your Water is Clean

(10.068 Rural Clean Water Program (RCWP))
Agricultural Stabilization and Conservation Service
U.S. Department of Agriculture
P.O. Box 2415
Washington, DC 20013   202-720-6221
Objectives: To achieve improved water quality in the most cost-effective manner possible in keeping with the provisions of adequate supplies of food, fiber, and a quality environment, and to develop and test programs, policies, and procedures for control of agricultural nonpoint source pollution. Types of assistance: direct payments for specified use. Estimate of annual funds available: (Direct payments) $43,000.

* Money to Improve Your Water and Soil

(10.069 Conservation Reserve Program (CRP))
Agricultural Stabilization and Conservation Service
U.S. Department of Agriculture
P.O. Box 2415
Washington, DC 20013   202-720-6221
Objectives: To protect the Nation's long-term capability to produce food and fiber; to reduce soil erosion; to reduce sedimentation; to improve water quality; to create a better habitat for fish and wildlife; to curb production of some surplus commodities; and to provide some needed income support for farmers. Types of assistance: direct payments for specified use. Estimate of annual funds available: $1,808,578,000.

* Money to Change Your County Property Into a Wetlands

(10.070 Colorado River Basin Salinity Control Program (CRBSCP))
Agricultural Stabilization and Conservation Service
U.S. Department of Agriculture
P.O. Box 2415
Washington, DC 20013   202-720-6221
Objectives: To provide financial and technical assistance to: (1) Identify salt source areas; (2) develop project plans to carry out conservation practices to reduce salt loads; (3) install conservation practices to reduce salinity levels; (4) carry out research, education, and demonstration activities; (5) carry out monitoring and evaluation activities; and (6) to decrease salt concentration and salt loading which causes increased salinity levels within the Colorado River and to enhance the supply and quality of water available for use in the United States and the Republic of Mexico. Types of assistance: direct payments for specified use. Estimate of annual funds available: (Direct payments) $8,394,000.

* Loans to Help Your Country Property Recover From an Emergency

(10.404 Emergency Loans)
Administrator
Consolidated Farm Service Agency
U.S. Department of Agriculture
Washington, DC   202-720-1632
Objectives: To assist established (owner or tenant) family farmers, ranchers and aquaculture operators with loans to cover losses resulting from major and/or natural

disasters, which can be used for annual farm operating expenses, and for other essential needs necessary to return disaster victims' farming operations to financially sound bases in order that they will be able to return to private sources of credit as soon as possible. Types of assistance: direct loans. Estimate of annual funds available: $100,000,000.

* Money to Build Houses for Your Employees

(10.405 Farm Labor Housing Loans and Grants (Labor Housing))
Multi-Family Housing Processing Division
Consolidated Farm Service Agency
U.S. Department of Agriculture
Washington, DC 20250   202-720-1604

Objectives: To provide decent, safe, and sanitary low-rent housing and related facilities for domestic farm laborers. Types of assistance: project grants; guaranteed/insured loans. Estimate of annual funds available: (Loans) $16,012,000. (Grants) $11,297,000.

* Money to Buy, Fix Up or Build Houses in Small Towns

(10.410 Very Low to Moderate Income Housing Loans
(Section 502 Rural Housing Loans))
Administrator
Consolidated Farm Service Agency
U.S. Department of Agriculture
Washington, DC 20250   202-720-7967

Objectives: To assist lower-income rural families through direct loans to buy, build, rehabilitate, or improve decent, safe, and sanitary dwellings and related facilities for use by the applicant as a permanent residence. Subsidized funds are available only on direct loans for low and very low-income applicants. Nonsubsidized Funds (loan making) are available for very low- and low-income applicants who are otherwise eligible for assistance, but based on the amount of the loan requested, the interest credit assistance formula results in no interest credit. Nonsubsidized funds (loan servicing) are available to very low-, low- and moderate-income applicants/borrowers who do not qualify for interest credit assistance for: (1) Subsequent loans for repair and rehabilitation; and (2) subsequent loan part only (repair or rehabilitation or the payment of equity) in connection with transfers by assumption or credit sales. Loan guarantees are also available to assist moderate income rural families in home acquisition. Types of assistance: direct loans; guaranteed/insured loans. Estimate of annual funds available: (Direct Loans) $1,400,000,000 (for subsidized low or moderate-income loans for servicing and repairs). (Guaranteed loans) $1,000,000,000.

* Money for Non-Profits to Build Rental Houses in Small Towns

(10.415 Rural Rental Housing Loans)
Director
Multi-Family Housing Processing Division
Consolidated Farm Service Agency
U.S. Department of Agriculture
Washington, DC 20250   202-382-1604

Objectives: To provide economically designed and constructed rental and cooperative housing and related facilities suited for independent living for rural residents. Types of assistance: direct loans. Estimate of annual funds available: (Direct Loans) $220,000,000.

* Money to Improve Your Water for a House in the Country

(10.416 Soil and Water Loans (SW Loans))
Administrator
Consolidated Farm Service Agency
U.S. Department of Agriculture
Washington, DC 20250   202-720-1632

Objectives: To facilitate improvement, protection, and proper use of farmland by providing adequate financing and supervisory assistance for soil conservation, water resource development, conservation and use, forestation, drainage of farmland, the establishment and improvement of permanent pasture, the development of pollution abatement and control facilities on farms, development of energy conserving measures and other related conservation measures. Types of assistance: direct loans; guaranteed/insured loans. Estimate of annual funds available: (Direct Loans) $2,894,700. (Guarantee Loans) $832,290.

* Loans and Grants to Fix Up Your House in the Country ($5,000 Grants)

(10.417 Very Low-Income Housing Repair Loans and Grants
(Section 504 Rural Housing Loans and Grants)
Director
Single-Family Housing Processing Division
Consolidated Farm Service Agency
U.S. Department of Agriculture
Washington, DC 20250   202-720-1474

Objectives: To give very low-income rural homeowners an opportunity to make essential repairs to their homes to make them safe and to remove health hazards to the family or the community. Types of assistance: direct loans; project grants. Estimate of annual funds available: (Loans) $25,000,000. (Grants) $25,000,000.

* Money to Conserve Soil and Water in Small Towns

(10.900 Great Plains Conservation)
Deputy Chief for Programs
Soil Conservation Service
U.S. Department of Agriculture
P.O. Box 2890
Washington, DC 20013   202-720-1868

Objectives: To conserve and develop the Great Plains soil and water resources by providing technical and financial assistance to farmers, ranchers, and others in planning and implementing conservation practices. Types of assistance: direct payments for specified use; advisory services and counseling. Estimate of annual funds available: (Grants) $2,045,000. (Salaries and expenses) $8,892,000.

* Money to Fix Up an Abandoned Coal Mine

(10.910 Rural Abandoned Mine Program (RAMP))
Deputy Chief for Programs
Soil Conservation Service
U.S. Department of Agriculture
P.O. Box 2890
Washington, DC 20013   202-720-2847

Objectives: To protect people and the environment from the adverse effects of past coal mining practices, and to promote the development of soil and water resources of unreclaimed mined lands. Types of assistance: direct payments for specified use; advisory services and counseling. Estimate of annual funds available: (Grants) $8,524,403. (Salaries and expenses) $4,854,550.

* Loans to Fix Up Houses That Are More Than One Year Old

(14.108 Rehabilitation Mortgage Insurance (203(k)))
Director
Single Family Development Division
Office of Insured Single Family Housing
U.S. Department of Housing and Urban Development
Washington, DC 20410   202-708-2720

Objectives: To help families repair or improve, purchase and improve, or refinance and improve existing residential structures more than one year old. Types of assistance: guaranteed/insured loans. Estimate of annual funds available: (Loans insured) $201,259,000.

* Loans to Buy Trailers

(14.110 Manufactured Home Loan Insurance-Financing Purchase of Manufactured Homes as Principal Residences of Borrowers (Title I))
Director, Title I Insurance Division
U.S. Department of Housing and Urban Development   800-733-4663
Washington, DC 20410   202-708-2880

Objectives: To make possible reasonable financing of manufactured home purchases. Types of assistance: guaranteed/insured loans. Estimate of annual funds available: Loans reported under program No. 14.142.

* Loans to Co-op Investors

(14.112 Mortgage Insurance for Construction or Substantial Rehabilitation of Condominium Projects (234(d) Condominiums))
Policies and Procedures Division
Office of Insured Multifamily Housing Development
U.S. Department of Housing and Urban Development
Washington, DC 20410   202-708-2556

Objectives: To enable sponsors to develop condominium projects in which individual units will be sold to home buyers. Types of assistance: guaranteed/insured loans. Estimate of annual funds available: (Mortgages insured) $0.

* Loans to Homeowners Anywhere With 1 to 4 Family Units

(14.117 Mortgage Insurance-Homes (203(b)))
Director
Single Family Development Division
Office of Insured Single Family Housing
U.S. Department of Housing and Urban Development
Washington, DC 20410   202-708-2700

Objectives: To help people undertake home ownership. Types of assistance: guaranteed/insured loans. Estimate of annual funds available: (Mortgages insured-including funding for 14.119, 14.121, 14.163 and 14.175) $52,610,678,000.

* Loans to Buy Single Family Homes for Disaster Victims

(14.119 Mortgage Insurance-Homes for Disaster Victims (203(h)))
Director
Single Family Development Division
Office of Insured Single Family Housing
U.S. Department of Housing and Urban Development
Washington, DC 20410   202-708-2700

Objectives: To help victims of a major disaster undertake homeownership on a sound basis. Types of assistance: guaranteed/insured loans. Estimate of annual funds available: (Mortgages insured) reported under Program No. 14.117.

* Money for Low to Moderate Income Families Hurt by a Disaster or Urban Renewal

(14.120 Mortgage Insurance-Homes for Low and Moderate Income Families (221(d)(2)))
Director, Single Family Development Division
Office of Insured Single Family Housing
U.S. Department of Housing and Urban Development
Washington, DC 20410   202-708-2700

Objectives: To make homeownership more readily available to families displaced by a natural disaster, urban renewal, or other government actions and to increase homeownership opportunities for low-income and moderate-income families. Types of assistance: guaranteed/insured loans. Estimate of annual funds available: (Mortgages insured) $127,193,000.

* Money for Homes in Outlying Areas

(14.121 Mortgage Insurance-Homes in Outlying Areas (203(i)))
Director, Single Family Development Division
Office of Insured Single Family Housing
U.S. Department of Housing and Urban Development
Washington, DC 20410   202-708-2700

Objectives: To help people purchase homes in outlying areas. Types of assistance: guaranteed/insured loans. Estimate of annual funds available: (Mortgages insured) reported under program No. 14.117.

* Money for Homes in Urban Renewal Areas

(14.122 Mortgage Insurance-Homes in Urban Renewal Areas (220 Homes))
Director, Single Family Development Division
Office of Insured Single Family Housing
U.S. Department of Housing and Urban Development
Washington, DC 20410   202-708-2700

Objectives: To help families purchase or rehabilitate homes in urban renewal areas. Types of assistance: guaranteed/insured loans. Estimate of annual funds available: (Mortgages insured) $47,000.

* Money for Homes in Older Areas of Town

(14.123 Mortgage Insurance-Housing in Older, Declining Areas (223(e)))
For Single Family:
Single Family Development Division
Office of Insured Single Family Housing
U.S. Department of Housing and Urban Development
                                         202-708-2700

For Multifamily:
Policies and Procedures Division
Office of Insured Multifamily Housing Development
U.S. Department of Housing and Urban Development
Washington, DC 20410   202-708-2556

Objectives: To assist in the purchase or rehabilitation of housing in older, declining urban areas. Types of assistance: guaranteed/insured loans. Estimate of annual funds available: (Mortgages insured - single family and multifamily) $16,794,000.

* Money to Buy a Co-op Apartment

(14.126 Mortgage Insurance-Cooperative Projects (213 Cooperatives))
Policies and Procedures Division
Office of Insured Multifamily Housing Development
U.S. Department of Housing and Urban Development
Washington, DC 20410   202-708-2556

Objectives: To make it possible for nonprofit cooperative ownership housing corporations or trusts to develop or sponsor the development of housing projects to be operated as cooperatives and to allow investors to provide good quality multifamily housing to be sold to such nonprofit corporations or trusts upon completion of construction or rehabilitation. Types of assistance: guaranteed/insured loans. Estimate of annual funds available: (Mortgages insured-including funding for 14.132) $0.

* Money to Buy a Trailer-Home Park

(14.127 Mortgage Insurance-Manufactured Home Parks (207(m) Manufactured Home Parks))
Policies and Procedures Division
Office of Insured Multifamily Housing Development
U.S. Department of Housing and Urban Development
Washington, DC 20410   202-708-2556

Objectives: To make possible the financing of construction or rehabilitation of manufactured home parks. Types of assistance: guaranteed/insured loans. Estimate of annual funds available: (Mortgages insured) Reported under program No. 14.134.

* Money to Buy a Hospital

(14.128 Mortgage Insurance-Hospitals (242 Hospitals))
Hospital Mortgage Insurance Staff
U.S. Department of Housing and Urban Development
Washington, DC 20410   202-708-0599
or
Division of Facilities Loans
U.S. Department of Health and Human Services
Rockville, MD 20857   301-443-5317

Objectives: To facilitate the affordable financing of hospitals for the care and treatment of persons who are acutely ill or who otherwise require medical care and related services of the kind customarily furnished only or most effectively by hospitals. Types of assistance: guaranteed/insured loans. Estimate of annual funds available: (Mortgages insured) $350,000,000.

* Money to Buy a Nursing Home

(14.129 Mortgage Insurance-Nursing Homes, Intermediate Care Facilities and Board and Care Homes (232 Nursing Homes))
Policies and Procedures Division
Office of Insured Multifamily Housing Development
U.S. Department of Housing and Urban Development
Washington, DC 20412   202-708-2556

Objectives: To make possible financing for construction or rehabilitation of nursing homes, intermediate care facilities and board and care homes, to allow purchase or refinancing with or without repairs of projects currently insured by HUD, but not requiring substantial rehabilitation, and to provide loan insurance to install fire safety equipment. Types of assistance: guaranteed/insured loans. Estimate of annual funds available: (Mortgages insured) $1,019,908,000.

* Money to Buy Your House if It is in a Long Term Ground Lease

(14.130 Mortgage Insurance-Purchase by Homeowners of Fee Simple Title From Lessors (240))
Director, Single Family Development Division
Office of Insured Single Family Housing
U.S. Department of Housing and Urban Development
Washington, DC 20410   202-708-2700

Be patient. If any phone number is incorrect, call (area code) 555-1212 and request the new listing.

131

Objectives: To help homeowners obtain fee-simple title to the property which they hold under long-term leases and on which their homes are located. Types of assistance: guaranteed/insured loans. Estimate of annual funds available: (Mortgages insured) $0.

* Money to Buy Your Co-op

(14.132 Mortgage Insurance-Purchase of Sales-Type Cooperative Housing Units (213 Sales))
Director
Single Family Development Division
Office of Insured Single Family Housing
U.S. Department of Housing and Urban Development
Washington, DC 20410   202-708-2700
Objectives: To make available, good quality, new housing for purchase by individual members of a housing cooperative. Types of assistance: guaranteed/insured loans. Estimate of annual funds available: (Mortgages insured) Reported under program 14.126.

* Money to Buy a Condominium

(14.133 Mortgage Insurance-Purchase of Units in Condominiums (234(c)))
Director, Single Family Development Division
Office of Insured Single Family Housing
U.S. Department of Housing and Urban Development
Washington, DC 20410   202-708-2700
Objectives: To enable families to purchase units in condominium projects. Types of assistance: guaranteed/insured loans. Estimate of annual funds available: (Mortgages insured) $4,844,885,000.

* Money to Invest in Apartment Buildings for Middle Class Families

(14.135 Mortgage Insurance-Rental and Cooperative Housing for Moderate Income Families and Elderly, Market Interest Rate (221(d)(3) and (4) Multifamily - Market Rate Housing))
Policies and Procedures Division
Office of Insured Multifamily Housing Development
U.S. Department of Housing and Urban Development
Washington, DC 20410   202-708-2556
Objectives: To provide good quality rental or cooperative housing for moderate income families and the elderly and handicapped. Single Room Occupancy (SRO) may also be insured under this section (see 14.184). Types of assistance: guaranteed/insured loans. Estimate of annual funds available: (Mortgages insured excluding coinsurance) $444,913,000.

* Money to Invest in Rental Housing for the Elderly

(14.138 Mortgage Insurance-Rental Housing for the Elderly (231))
Policies and Procedures Division
Office of Insured Multifamily Housing Development
U.S. Department of Housing and Urban Development
Washington, DC 20410   202-708-2556
Objectives: To provide good quality rental housing for the elderly. Types of assistance: guaranteed/insured loans. Estimate of annual funds available: (Mortgages insured) $0.

* Money to Invest in Rental Housing in Urban Renewal Areas

(14.139 Mortgage Insurance-Rental Housing in Urban Renewal Areas (220 Multifamily))
For production information:
Policies and Procedures Division
Office of Insured Multifamily Housing Development
U.S. Department of Housing and Urban Development
Washington, DC 20410   202-708-2556
For management information:
Director, Office of Multifamily Housing Management
U.S. Department of Housing and Urban Development
Washington, DC 20410   202-708-3730
Objectives: To provide good quality rental housing in urban renewal areas, code enforcement areas, and other areas designated for overall revitalization. Types of assistance: guaranteed/insured loans. Estimate of annual funds available: (Mortgages insured) $0.

* Money to Fix Up Your Home

(14.142 Property Improvement Loan Insurance for Improving All Existing Structures and Building of New Nonresidential Structures (Title I))
Director, Title I Insurance Division
U.S. Department of Housing and Urban Development   800-733-4663
Washington, DC 20410   202-708-7400
Objectives: To facilitate the financing of improvements to homes and other existing structures and the building of new nonresidential structures. Types of assistance: guaranteed/insured loans. Estimate of annual funds available: (Loans insured including funding for programs 4.110 and 14.162) $1,289,200,000.

* Money to Fix Up Multi-Family Projects

(14.151 Supplemental Loan Insurance-Multifamily Rental Housing (241(a)))
Policies and Procedures Division
Office of Insured Multifamily Housing Development
U.S. Department of Housing and Urban Development
Washington, DC 20411   202-708-2556
Objectives: To finance repairs, additions and improvements to multifamily projects, group practice facilities, hospitals, or nursing homes already insured by HUD or held by HUD. Major movable equipment for insured nursing homes, group practice facilities or hospitals may be covered by a mortgage under this program. Types of assistance: guaranteed/insured loans. Estimate of annual funds available: (Loans) $43,630,000.

* Money to Investors to Purchase or Refinance Multifamily Housing

(14.155 Mortgage Insurance for the Purchase or Refinancing of Existing Multifamily Housing Projects (Section 223(f) Insured Under Section 207))
Office of Insured Multifamily Housing Development
Policies and Procedures Division
U.S. Department of Housing and Urban Development
Washington, DC 20410   202-708-2556
Objectives: To provide mortgage insurance to lenders for the purchase or refinancing of existing multifamily housing projects, whether conventionally financed or subject to federally insured mortgages at the time of application for mortgage insurance. Types of assistance: guaranteed/insured loans. Estimate of annual funds available: (Mortgages Insured) (Excludes coinsurance) $894,910,000.

* Money to Build Housing for the Elderly That Also Provides Support Services

(14.157 Supportive Housing for the Elderly (202))
Housing for the Elderly and Handicapped People Division
Office of Elderly and Assisted Housing
U.S. Department of Housing and Urban Development
Washington, DC 20410   202-708-2730
Objectives: To expand the supply of housing with supportive services for the elderly. Types of assistance: project grants. Estimate of annual funds available: (Reservations for Capital Grants, Rental Assistance and Service Coordinators) $166,300,000.

* Money to Buy a House With Graduated Mortgage Payments

(14.159 Section 245 Graduated Payment Mortgage Program)
Director, Single Family Development Division
Office of Insured Single Family Housing
U.S. Department of Housing and Urban Development
Washington, DC 20410   202-708-2700
Objectives: To facilitate early home ownership for households that expect their incomes to rise. Program allows homeowners to make smaller monthly payments initially and to increase their size gradually over time. Types of assistance: guaranteed/insured loans. Estimate of annual funds available: (Mortgages Insured - includes 14.172) $414,624,000.

* Money to Buy a Trailer and Trailer Lot

(14.162 Mortgage Insurance-Combination and Manufactured Home Lot Loans (Title I))
Director, Title I Insurance Division
U.S. Department of Housing and Urban Development
Room B-133
Washington, DC 20410   202-755-7400
Objectives: To make possible reasonable financing for the purchase of a

manufactured home and a lot on which to place the home. Types of assistance: guaranteed/insured loans. Estimate of annual funds available: (Guaranteed/Insured Loans) Reported under program No. 14.110.

* Money to Finance Coop Buildings

(14.163 Mortgage Insurance-Single Family Cooperative Housing (203(n)))
Director, Single Family Development Division
Office of Insured Single Family Housing
U.S. Department of Housing and Urban Development
Washington, DC 20410   202-708-2700

Objectives: To provide insured financing for the purchase of the Corporate Certificate and Occupancy Certificate for a unit in a cooperative housing project. Ownership of the corporate certificate carries the right to occupy the unit located within the cooperative project. Types of assistance: guaranteed/insured loans. Estimate of annual funds available: Reported under program No. 14.117.

* Money to Developers in Financial Trouble

(14.164 Operating Assistance for Troubled Multifamily Housing Projects (Flexible Subsidy Fund) (Troubled Projects))
Director
Office of Multifamily Housing Management
U.S. Department of Housing and Urban Development
Washington, DC 20420   202-708-3730

Objectives: To provide loans to restore or maintain the physical and financial soundness, to assist in the management and to maintain the low-to moderate-income character of certain projects assisted or approved for assistance under the National Housing Act or under the Housing and Urban Development Act of 1965. Types of assistance: direct payments for specified use. Estimate of annual funds available: (Reservations) $125,000,000.

* Money to Buy Houses in Areas Hurt by Defense Cuts

(14.165 Mortgage Insurance-Homes-Military Impacted Areas (238(c)))
Director
Single Family Development Division
Office of Insured Single Family Housing
U.S. Department of Housing and Urban Development
Washington, DC 20410   202-708-2700

Objectives: To help families undertake home ownership in military impacted areas. Types of assistance: guaranteed/insured loans. Estimate of annual funds available: (Mortgages Insured) $16,259,000.

* Money for Active Duty Military to Buy Houses

(14.166 Mortgage Insurance-Homes for Members of the Armed Services (Section 222))
Director, Single Family Development Division
Office of Insured Single Family Housing
U.S. Department of Housing and Urban Development
Washington, DC 20410   202-708-2700

Objectives: To help members of the armed services on active duty to purchase a home. Types of assistance: guaranteed/insured loans. Estimate of annual funds available: (Mortgages Insured) $1,776,000.

* Loans to Developers in Trouble During Their First Two Years of Operation

(14.167 Mortgage Insurance-Two Year Operating Loss Loans, Section 223(d) (Two Year Operating Loss Loans))
For program information:
Policies and Procedures Division
Office of Insured Multifamily Housing Development
U.S. Department of Housing and Urban Development
Washington, DC 20410   202-755-2556
For management information:
Director
Office of Multifamily Housing Management
U.S. Department of Housing and Urban Development
Washington, DC 20410   202-708-3730

Objectives: To insure a separate loan covering operating losses incurred during the first two years following the date of completion of a multifamily project with a HUD-insured first mortgage. Types of assistance: guaranteed/insured loans. Estimate of annual funds available: (Loans) $19,100,000.

* Money to Buy a Home Using Increased Equity Payments

(14.172 Mortgage Insurance-Growing Equity Mortgages (GEMs))
Director, Single Family Development Division
Office of Insured Single Family Housing
U.S. Department of Housing and Urban Development
Washington, DC 20410   202-708-2700

Objectives: To provide a rapid principal reduction and shorter mortgage term by increasing payments over a 10-year period, thereby expanding housing opportunities to the homebuying public. Types of assistance: guaranteed/insured loans. Estimate of annual funds available: (Mortgages insured) Reported under program 14.159.

* Money to Buy a Home Using an Adjustable Rate Mortgage

(14.175 Adjustable Rate Mortgages (ARMS))
Director, Single Family Development Division
Office of Insured Single Family Housing
U.S. Department of Housing and Urban Development
Washington, DC 20410   202-708-2700

Objectives: To provide mortgage insurance for an adjustable rate mortgage which offers lenders more assurance of long term profitability than a fixed rate mortgage, while offering consumer protection features. Types of assistance: guaranteed/insured loans. Estimate of annual funds available: Reported under 14.117.

* Money for Non-Profits to Build Houses for Lower-Income Families

(14.179 Nehemiah Housing Opportunity Grant Program (Nehemiah Housing))
Morris E. Carter, Director
Single Family Development Division
U.S. Department of Housing and Urban Development
451 7th Street, SW
Washington, DC 20410   202-708-2700

Objectives: To provide an opportunity for those families who otherwise would not be financially able to realize their dream of owning a home, to increase the employment opportunities of the residents in neighborhoods where the housing is proposed and to create sound and attractive neighborhoods. Types of assistance: project grants. Estimate of annual funds available: (Grants) $16,552,000.

* Money to Invest in Houses for Those With Disabilities

(14.181 Supportive Housing for Persons with Disabilities (811))
Housing for Elderly and Handicapped People Division
Office of Elderly and Assisted Housing
U.S. Department of Housing and Urban Development
Washington, DC 20410   202-708-2730

Objectives: To provide for supportive housing and related facilities for persons with disabilities. Types of assistance: project grants. Estimate of annual funds available: (Reservations for Capital Grants and Rental Assistance) $387,000,000.

* Rental Supplements for Investors Who Provide Houses to Low Income Families

(14.182 Lower Income Housing Assistance Program-Section 8 New Construction/Substantial Rehabilitation (Section 8 Housing Assistance Payments Program for Very Low Income Families-New Construction/ Substantial Rehabilitation))
For management information:
Director
Office of Multifamily Housing Management
U.S. Department of Housing and Urban Development
Washington, DC 20410   202-708-3730

Objectives: To aid very low income families in obtaining decent, safe and sanitary rental housing. Types of assistance: direct payments for specified use. Estimate of annual funds available: (Outlays for N/SR units under payment) $4,077,884,000.

* Money to Help Elderly Homeowners Convert Their Equity into a Monthly Income

(14.183 Home Equity Conversion Mortgages (255))
Director
Insured Family Development Division

Office of Single Family Housing
U.S. Department of Housing and Urban Development
Washington, DC 20410   202-708-2700
Objectives: To enable elderly homeowners to convert equity in their homes to monthly streams of income or lines of credit. Types of assistance: guaranteed/insured loans. Estimate of annual funds available: (Mortgages insured): $34,763,000.

* Money for Low-Income Housing Tenants to Buy Their Building

(14.186 Mortgage Insurance-Equity Loans (241(f) Equity Loans))
For program information:
Policies and Procedures Division
Office of Insured Multifamily Housing Development
U.S. Department of Housing and Urban Development
Washington, DC 20410   202-708-2556
For management information:
Director
Office of Preservation and Property Disposition
U.S. Department of Housing and Urban Development
Washington, DC 20410   202-708-3555
Objectives: To insure a separate equity loan to owners of eligible low income multifamily properties who wish to extend the low income affordability restrictions or to insure an acquisition loan for select purchasers who will maintain such restrictions. Types of assistance: guaranteed/insured loans. Estimate of annual funds available: (Loans) $53,630,000.

* Grants to Non-Profits Who Lend Money to Low Income Families to Buy Houses

(14.240 HOPE for Homeownership of Single Family Homes (Hope 3))
Cliff Taffet
Office of Affordable Housing Programs
U.S. Department of Housing and Urban Development
Room 7168, 451 7th Street, SW
Washington, DC 20410   202-708-3226
Objectives: To provide homeownership opportunities to lower-income families and individuals by providing grantees with Federal assistance to finance an eligible homebuyer's direct purchase and rehabilitation of eligible single family properties or to fund the grantee's acquisition and rehabilitation of single family properties for sale and occupancy by families at affordable prices. Types of assistance: project grants. Estimate of annual funds available: (Grants) $50,000,000.

* Money for Homes That Use New Building Ideas

(14.507 Mortgage Insurance-Experimental Homes (ExTech 233-Homes))
Assistant Secretary for Policy Development and Research
Division of Innovative Technology
U.S. Department of Housing and Urban Development
451 7th Street, SW
Washington, DC 20410   202-708-4370
Objectives: To help finance the development of homes that incorporate new or untried construction concepts designed to reduce housing costs, raise living standards, and improve neighborhood design by providing mortgage insurance. Types of assistance: guaranteed/insured loans. Estimate of annual funds available: Mortgages are insured and experimental features are guaranteed to the home owner. No direct funding or subsidies are provided for the project.

* Money for Doctor's Offices and Hospitals That Use New Building Ideas

(14.508 Mortgage Insurance-Experimental Projects Other Than Housing (ExTech 233-Projects Other Than Housing)
Assistant Secretary for Policy Development and Research
Division of Innovative Technology
U.S. Department of Housing and Urban Development
451 7th Street, SW
Washington, DC 20410   202-708-4370
Objectives: To provide mortgage insurance to help finance the development of group medical facilities that incorporate new or untried construction concepts intended to reduce construction costs, raise living standards and improve neighborhood design. Types of assistance: guaranteed/insured loans. Estimate of annual funds available: (Mortgages insured - reported under program No. 14.509).

* Money for Apartment Buildings That Use New Ideas

(14.509 Mortgage Insurance-Experimental Rental Housing (ExTech 233 - Experimental Rental Housing))
Assistant Secretary for Policy Development and Research
Division of Innovative Technology
U.S. Department of Housing and Urban Development
451 7th Street, SW
Washington, DC 20410   202-708-4370
Objectives: To provide mortgage insurance to help finance the development of multifamily housing that incorporates new or untried construction concepts designed to reduce housing costs; raise living standards; and improve neighborhood design. Types of assistance: guaranteed/insured loans. Estimate of annual funds available: Mortgages are insured and experimental features are guaranteed. No funds or subsidies are available.

* Rent Supplements to Building Owners With Tenants That Have Low Incomes

(14.856 Lower Income Housing Assistance Program-Section 8 Moderate Rehabilitation (Section 8 Housing Assistance Payments Program for Very Low Income Families-Moderate Rehabilitation))
For program information:
Office of Assisted Housing
Rental Assistance Division
U.S. Department of Housing and Urban Development
Washington, DC 20410   202-708-7424
Objectives: To aid very low income families and homeless individuals in obtaining decent, safe and sanitary rental housing. Types of assistance: direct payments for specified use. Estimate of annual funds available: (Contract replacements to certificates) $54,000,000.

* More Rent Supplements for Building Owners With Tenants That Have Low Incomes

(14.857 Section 8 Rental Certificate Program (Section 8 Rental Certificates))
Office of Assisted Housing
Rental Assistance Division
U.S. Department of Housing and Urban Development
Washington, DC 20410   202-708-0477
Objectives: To aid low income families in obtaining decent, safe, and sanitary rental housing. Types of assistance: direct payments for specified use. Estimate of annual funds available: Reported under Program 14.156.

* Grants to Organizations Who Help Low-Income Families Buy Houses

(14.858 HOPE for Public and Indian Housing Homeownership (HOPE for Public and Indian Housing (HOPE 1)))
Gary Van Buskirk
Homeownership Division for Public and Indian Housing
U.S. Department of Housing and Urban Development   202-708-4233
Washington, DC 20410   TDD 202-708-9300
Objectives: To provide homeownership programs for eligible public and Indian housing residents and other low income families through the sale of eligible public and Indian housing. Types of assistance: project grants. Estimate of annual funds available: (Grants) $266,800,000.

* Money to Have Your State Buy Your Old Farm and Turn It into a Park

(15.916 Outdoor Recreation-Acquisition, Development and Planning (Land and Water Conservation Fund Grants))
Chief, Recreation Grants Division
National Park Service
U.S. Department of the Interior
P.O. Box 37127
Washington, DC 20013-7127   202-343-3700
Contact: Sam L. Hall
Objectives: To provide financial assistance to the States and their political subdivisions for the preparation of Statewide Comprehensive Outdoor Recreation Plans (SCORPs) and acquisition and development of outdoor recreation areas and facilities for the general public, to meet current and future needs. Types of assistance: project grants. Estimate of annual funds available: (Grants) $24,750,000.

* Grants to Build Houses on Indian Reservations

(15.141 Indian Housing Assistance)
Chief, Division of Housing Assistance
Division of Housing Assistance
Office of Tribal Services
Room 4640, Main Interior Building
Bureau of Indian Affairs
1849 C St., NW
Washington, DC 20240   202-208-5427

Objectives: To use the Indian Housing Improvement Program (HIP) and Bureau of Indian Affairs resources to substantially eliminate substandard Indian housing. This effort is combined with the Indian Health Service (Department of Health and Human Services). Types of assistance: project grants (contracts); dissemination of technical information. Estimate of annual funds available: (Total HIP program costs including grant funding, self governance compact funding, salaries, and expenses) $19,083,000.

* Money for Veterans Who Want to Buy a House

(64.114 Veterans Housing-Guaranteed and Insured Loans
(VA Home Loans))
U.S. Department of Veterans Affairs
Washington, DC 20420

Objectives: To assist veterans, certain service personnel, and certain unremarried surviving spouses of veterans, in obtaining credit for the purchase, construction or improvement of homes on more liberal terms than are generally available to non-veterans. Types of assistance: guaranteed/insured loans. Estimate of annual funds available: (Closed Loans Guaranteed) $30,256,320,000.

* Loans for Disabled Veterans to Buy a House

(64.118 Veterans Housing-Direct Loans for Disabled Veterans)
U.S. Department of Veterans Affairs
Washington, DC 20420

Objectives: To provide certain severely disabled veterans with direct housing credit in connection with grants for specially adaptive housing with special features or movable facilities made necessary by the nature of their disabilities. Types of assistance: direct loans. Estimate of annual funds available: (Loans) $33,000.

* Money for Veterans to Buy Mobile Homes

(64.119 Veterans Housing-Manufactured Home Loans)
U.S. Department of Veterans Affairs
Washington, DC 20420

Objectives: To assist veterans, servicepersons, and certain unremarried surviving spouses of veterans in obtaining credit for the purchase of a manufactured home on more liberal terms than are available to non-veterans. Types of assistance: guaranteed/insured loans. Estimate of annual funds available: (Guaranteed Loans) $2,557,000.

* Loans for Native American Veterans to Buy or Build a Home

(64.126 Native American Veteran Direct Loan Program
(VA Native American Home Loan Program))
U.S. Department of Veterans Affairs
Washington, DC 20420

Objectives: To provide direct loans to certain Native American veterans for the purchase or construction of homes on trust lands. Types of assistance: direct loans. Estimate of annual funds available: (Loans): $11,202,000.

* Grants for Storm Windows or to Weatherize Your Home

(81.042 Weatherization Assistance for Low-Income Persons)
Jeanne Van Viandren, Director
Weatherization Assistance Programs Division
Mail Stop CE-532
Conservation and Renewable Energy
U.S. Department of Energy
Forrestal Building
Washington, DC 20585   202-586-2204

Objectives: To insulate the dwellings of low-income persons, particularly the elderly and handicapped low-income, in order to conserve needed energy and to aid those persons least able to afford higher utility costs. Types of assistance: formula grants. Estimate of annual funds available: $230,000,000.

* Government Subsidized Flood Insurance to Homeowners

(83.100 Flood Insurance)
James M. Rose
Federal Insurance Administration
Federal Emergency Management Agency
Washington, DC 20472   202-646-2780

Objectives: To enable persons to purchase insurance against losses from physical damage to or loss of buildings and or contents therein caused by floods, mudflow, or flood-related erosion in the United States and to promote wise flood plain management practices in the Nation's flood-prone and mudflow-prone areas. Types of assistance: insurance. Estimate of annual funds available: $808,220,000.

* Money For Non-Profits to Provide Rural Housing Site Loans

(10.411 Rural Housing Site Loans
(Section 523 and 524 Site Loans))
Director, Single-Family Housing Processing Division
Farmers Home Administration
U.S. Department of Agriculture
Washington, DC 20250   202-720-1474

Objectives: To assist public or private nonprofit organizations interested in providing sites for housing, to acquire and develop land in rural areas to be subdivided as adequate building sites and sold on a cost development basis to families eligible for low and very low income loans, cooperatives, and broadly based nonprofit rural rental housing applicants. Types of assistance: direct loans. Estimate of annual funds available: (Loans) $616,000.

* Money to Fix Up Your Home in the Country

(10.433 Rural Housing Preservation Grants)
Multiple Family Housing Processing Division
Farmers Home Administration
U.S. Department of Agriculture
Washington, DC 20250   202-720-1606

Objectives: To assist very low- and low-income rural residents individual homeowners, rental property owners (single/multi-unit) or by providing the consumer cooperative housing projects (co-ops) the necessary assistance to repair or rehabilitate their dwellings. These objectives will be accomplished through the establishment of repair/rehabilitation, projects run by eligible applicants. This program is intended to make use of and leverage any other available housing programs which provide resources to very low and low-income rural residents to bring their dwellings up to development standards. Types of assistance: project grants. Estimate of annual funds available: (Grants) $23,000,000.

* Money for Homes for Low-Income Indian Families

(14.850 Public and Indian Housing)
Assistant Secretary for Public and Indian Housing
U.S. Department of Housing and Urban Development
Washington, DC 20410   202-708-0950

Objectives: To provide and operate cost-effective, decent, safe and affordable dwellings for lower income families through an authorized local Public Housing Agency (PHA) or Indian Housing Authority (IHA). Types of assistance: direct payments for specified use. Estimate of annual funds available: (Includes obligations for 14.851, 14.852, 14.853 and 14.854) $0. Indian Development: $263,000,000.

* Loans for Families With Bad Credit Histories

(14.140 Mortgage Insurance-Special Credit Risks)
For production information:
Director, Single Family Development Division
Office of Insured Single Family Housing
U.S. Department of Housing and Urban Development
Washington, DC 20410   202-708-2700
For management information:
Director, Single Family Servicing Division
Secretary-Held and Counseling Services Branch
Office of Insured Single Family Housing
U.S. Department of Housing and Urban Development
Washington, DC 20410   202-708-1672

Objectives: To make homeownership possible for low and moderate-income families who cannot meet normal HUD requirements. Types of assistance: guaranteed/insured loans. Estimate of annual funds available: (Mortgages insured) $13,000.

Housing and Real Estate

* Money to Provide Affordable Rental Housing for Low-Income Families

(14.239 HOME Investment Partnerships Program)
Gordon McKay, Director
Office of Affordable Housing Programs
Community Planning and Development
U.S. Department of Housing and Urban Development
451 7th Street, SW
Washington, DC 20410   202-708-2685

Objectives: (1) To expand the supply of decent and affordable housing, particularly rental housing, for low and very low income Americans; (2) To strengthen the abilities of State and local governments to design and implement strategies for achieving adequate supplies of decent, affordable housing; (3) To provide both financial and technical assistance to participating jurisdictions, including the development of model programs for developing affordable low income housing and; (4) To extend and strengthen partnerships among all levels of government and the private sector, including for-profit and nonprofit organizations, in the production and operation of affordable housing. Types of assistance: formula grants. Estimate of annual funds available: (Grants) $1,400,000,000.

* Rental Voucher Program for Low-Income Indian Families

(14.855 Section 8 Rental Voucher Program)
Office of Assisted Housing
Rental Assistance Division
U.S. Department of Housing and Urban Development
Washington, DC 20410   202-708-0477

Objectives: To aid very low income families in obtaining decent, safe, and sanitary rental housing. Types of assistance: direct payments for specified use. Estimate of annual funds available: Reported under Program 14.177.

* Money to Invest in Rental Housing for Lower-Income Families

(14.856 Lower Income Housing Assistance Program-Section 8 Moderate Rehabilitation)
For program information:
Office of Assisted Housing

Rental Assistance Division
U.S. Department of Housing and Urban Development
Washington, DC 20410   202-708-7424

Objectives: To aid very low income families in obtaining decent, safe and sanitary rental housing. Types of assistance: direct payments for specified use. Estimate of annual funds available: (Contract replacements to certificates) $54,000,000.

* Loans to Investors, Builders, Developers of Affordable Housing

(14.189 Qualified Participating Entities QPE Risk Sharing Pilot Program)
Policies and Procedures Division
Office of Insured Multifamily Housing Development
U.S. Department of Housing and Urban Development
Washington, DC 20410   202-708-2556

Objectives: Under this program HUD will provide reinsurance on multifamily housing projectmily housing projects whose loans are originated, under-written, serviced, and disposed of by qualified participating entities (QPEs) and/or its approved lenders, up to 15,00 units through fiscal year 1994. The program is a pilot designed to assess the feasibility of risk-sharing partnerships between HUD and QPEs, including Government Sponsored Enterprises, State and local housing finance agencies, financial institutions and the Federal Housing Finance Board, in providing affordable housing for the nation. Types of assistance: guaranteed/insured loans. Estimate of annual funds available: $640,000,000.

* Money for Developers, Investors, and Builders of Low Income Housing

(14.188 HFA Rick Sharing Pilot Program)
Policies and Procedures Division
Office of Insured Multifamily Housing Development
U.S. Department of Housing and Urban Development
Washington, DC 20412   202-708-2556

Objectives: Under this program, HUD will provide full mortgage insurance on multifamily housing projects whose loans are under-written, processed, serviced, and disposed of by HFAs, up to 30,000 units through fiscal year 1995. The program is a pilot designed to assess the feasibility of risk-sharing partnerships between HUD and qualified State and local Housing Finance Agencies (HFA) in providing affordable housing for the nation. Types of assistance: guaranteed/insured loans. Estimate of annual funds available: $539,000,000.

State Money For Housing and Real Estate

State Initiatives

While affordable housing has long held an important place on the federal government's policy agenda, budget cutbacks in recent years have forced the government to turn over many housing responsibilities to the states. Housing finance agencies (HFAs) have been created by states to issue tax-exempt bonds to finance mortgages for lower-income first-time home buyers and to build multi-family housing.

States are involved in a host of initiatives throughout the broad spectrum of housing finance and development. Interim construction financing programs which can reduce the basic costs of lower-income housing projects have been initiated in a number of states, together with innovative home ownership programs and programs directed toward rehabilitation and improved energy conservation.

States are also venturing into areas which have not received as much public sector attention until recently. By encouraging non-traditional types of housing, such as accessory units, shelters, and single room occupancy housing, states are addressing important elements of the housing market.

In Colorado, the state Housing and Finance Authority (CHFA) has issued more than $2.6 billions of bonds and notes since its establishment in 1973, providing housing for more than 47,000 families and individuals of low and moderate income; 27,200 first-time home buyers and over 20,500 rental housing units. In recent years the state has broadened CHFA's authority to allow it to develop finance programs to assist the growth of small business, help exports with insurance on goods sold overseas, and similar projects.

Colorado has done more than simply help its citizens find housing: the programs have resulted in construction employment of more than 20,000 jobs, with wages estimated at almost $20 million in new local real estate taxes and an indirect gain of $1.6 billion for the state.

Wisconsin, Maine and New York each have between 18 and 20 programs including special ones for women and minorities, for disabled persons, and for environmental hazard removal.

Maryland operates 26 programs, including those to help people with closing costs and settlement expenses. It also has special funds available for the elderly and is developing an emergency mortgage fund to help people who have fallen behind in their payments. Non-profit developers can also tap the state for money to build low-cost rental units.

Among Michigan's 29 programs and Minnesota's 25 are several for neighborhood revitalization. Minnesota also offers programs targeting the needs of urban Indians and migrant farm workers. Alaska, Oregon and Vermont offer financing for tenant acquisition of mobile home parks.

Funds are also available for persons who take steps to make their homes more energy efficient, for home owners and landlords who remove lead paint from dwelling units, for houses without plumbing or those with plumbing that is dysfunctional, for handicapped persons, and to help landlords defray the costs of bringing low-income housing into compliance with state and local housing codes. There are also funds for non-profit organizations to acquire or renovate existing houses and apartments for use as group homes for special needs such as mentally retarded.

In many states, elderly home owners can look to the HFA to obtain financing and/or support services they need to remain in their homes and avoid institutionalization. Some of the states have more than one agency dedicated to housing and we have attempted to list them all here. Also, many cities and counties have quasi-federal/quasi-local "housing authorities" with additional programs. Check your local government listings for these.

The following is a complete listing of state housing programs.

Housing Offices

Alabama
Alabama Housing Finance Authority, P.O. Box 230909, Montgomery, AL 36123-0909; 205-244-9200 or 800-325-2432.
1) Mortgage Revenue Bond Program: low-rate loans for income-eligible first-time home buyers.
2) Downpayment Assistance Program: matching funds for lower-income home buyers.
3) Mortgage Credit Certificate Program: provides a 20% federal tax credit on mortgage loan interest for lower-income home buyers.
4) Low-Income Housing Tax Credit Program: federal tax credits for owners of low-income rental housing.
5) Multi-Family Bond Program: tax-exempt bonds for financing multi-family projects with units affordable to low-income tenants.
6) Home Program: provides additional opportunities for the production of affordable housing for low income families.

Alaska
Alaska Housing Finance Corp., P.O. Box 101020, 520 East 34th Avenue, Anchorage, AK 99510; 907-561-1900.
1) Home Ownership Assistance Program: interest subsidy to as low as 6%.
2) Mobile Home Loan Program: low downpayment.
3) Taxable Mortgage Program: for others than first time home buyers and veterans.
4) FmHA Guaranteed Rural Housing Loan Program: lower downpayments to those that qualify in rural Alaska's "small communities".
5) Tax Exempt Mortgage Program: loans up to $157,190 for single family and $176,996 for duplexes.
6) Second Mortgage Program: up to $99,900 for single family homes and $127,800 for duplexes can be used for home purchase or home improvement.
7) Veterans Mortgage Program: low interest loans to veterans and members of the reserve and National Guard.
8) Refinance Program: reduce monthly payments on existing loans.
9) Non-Conforming Property Program: homes which cannot be financed through traditional financing.
10) Rural Owner-Occupied or Nonowner- Occupied Loan Program: financing to qualified borrowers for the purchase, construction or rehabilitation of owner occupied or nonowner occupied housing in a "small Community in rural Alaska.
11) Section 8 New Construction and Additional Assistance: provides housing for the elderly, disabled and or handicapped in Fairbanks, Cordova, Wrangell, Seward and Anchorage.
12) Low to Moderate Income Home Ownership Programs: provides assistance on loans made to persons of low to moderate incomes for the purchase of owner

occupied residences.

13) Refinance Program of a Non-AHFC Loan: refinancing for a loan not held by AHFC.

14) Second Mortgage Program for Health and Safety Repairs: for AHFC loan borrowers to bring property up to safety and health requirements.

15) Multi-Family, Congregate and Special Needs Housing Loans: assists qualified non-profit housing providers and for-profit companies in financing multi-family complexes for low and moderate income housing.

16) Emergency Housing Grants: grants to assist with meeting the housing needs of homeless persons.

17) Senior Housing Plan: potential borrowers may apply for financing to purchase, construct, rehabilitate or improve various kinds of housing that would meet the needs of persons 60 or older.

18) Low-Income Weatherization: eligible families can receive improvements to their home resulting in a reduction of their heating bills by an average of 25 percent.

Arizona

Arizona Department of Commerce, Office of Housing and Infrastructure Development, 3800 North Central Suite 1200, Phoenix, AZ 85012, 602-280-1365, TDD 602-280-1301; FAX: 602-280-1470.

1) Low-Income Housing Tax Credits: federal income tax credits for owners of low-income housing units.

2) Low Interest Mortgage Programs: typically below 9% interest loans for eligible Arizonans to purchase homes.

3) Arizona Housing Trust Fund: construction, housing rehabilitation, down payment, and closing cost assistance for low/moderate income home buyers.

4) Rental Rehabilitation Program: assists owners in rehabilitating rental housing for low/moderate income households.

5) HOME Program: provides help for low-income families with various housing needs from rehabilitation to rental assistance.

6) Community Development Block Grant Program: develop viable communities by providing housing and a suitable living environment.

Arkansas

Arkansas Development Finance Authority, P.O. Box 8023, 100 Main St., Suite 200, Little Rock, AR 72203; 501-682-5900.

1) HOME Program: funds are used for a variety of activities to develop and support affordable housing for low income. Eligible activities include: Tenant Based Rental Assistance, Rental Rehabilitation, and New Construction and Assistance for Homebuyers and Home Buyers.

2) Single-Family: below market rate loans to first time home buyers for the purchase of a single-family home.

3) Low-Income Housing Tax Credit Program: federal tax credits for owners of low-income rental housing.

California

California Housing Finance Agency, 1121 L Street, 7th Floor, Sacramento, CA 95815; 916-322-3991.

1) Multi-Family Program: permanent financing for builders and developers of multi-family unit, elderly and congregate rental housing.

2) Development Loan Program: 7% loans to small and minority developers.

3) Self-Help Housing Program: funds to non-profit developers in order to produce self-help housing.

4) Home Purchase Assistance Program: low interest loans for low/moderate income first-time home buyers.

5) 3% Down Payment Loan Program: enables first time home buyers to purchase a home with only a 3 percent downpayment.

6) CHFA Resale Program: below market-rate loans to first-time home buyers who meet income limits and are purchasing previously-owned property within CHFA sales price limits.

7) Compensating Balance Program: construction financing to minority/women-owned business enterprises and self-help program developers.

8) Self-Help Builder Assistance Program: construction financing for self-help builders.

9) Self-Help Housing Program: finances self-help homes under supervision of non-profit organizations.

Non-Profit Housing Program: permanent financing for contractor built single family homes developed and sold by nonprofit organizations which serve low income households.

10) Rental Housing Program: provides affordable rental housing to lw income families.

11) Equity Link Program: the home buyer makes no down payment.

California Department of Housing and Community Development, P.O. Box 952054, Sacramento, CA 94252-2050; 916-322-1560.

1) California Indian Assistance Program (CIAP): assist tribal organizations to obtain and administer housing, infrastructure comminity and economic development project funds provided by federal and state agencies.

2) California Housing Rehabilitation Program-Owner Component: low-rate loans to bring homes up to code, make general improvements, or to make adaptations for handicapped.

3) Natural Disaster Assistance Program: rehabilitation loans for property damaged by natural disaster.

4) HOME Program: assist communities and community housing development organizations (CHDO's) in activities that create or retain affordable housing.

5) Mobile Home Park Assistance Program: loans and technical assistance to mobile home park resident organizations that are purchasing their park.

6) Rental Housing Construction Program: very low-rate loans for development and construction costs associated with new rental housing units for low-income households.

7) Family Housing Demonstration Program: very low-rate loans to develop new, or rehabilitate existing, rental or co-op housing that provides on-site support programs for low-income households.

8) Permanent Housing for the Handicapped Homeless Program: partial funding to acquire, rehabilitate, and operate housing for the disabled homeless.

9) State Rental Rehabilitation Program: partial funding to rehabilitate low/ moderate-income rental housing in small rural communities.

10) California Energy Conservation Rehabilitation Program: grants of up to $5,000 per unit to assist energy conservation rehabilitation of low-income owner and renter farmworker housing, residential hotels, and rental housing for the elderly and handicapped.

11) Pre-Development Loan Program: low-rate, 3-year loans for pre-development costs of low-income housing projects.

12) PLP Natural Disaster Component: low-rate, 3-year loans for pre-development costs of reconstruction or rehabilitation of subsidized housing damaged by natural disaster.

13) Emergency Housing Assistance Program: grants to provide emergency shelter for homeless households.

14) Farmworker Housing Grant Program: grants to provide owner-occupied and rental units for year-round, low-income agricultural workers and to rehabilitate those damaged by natural disaster.

15) Community Development Block Grant (CDBG) Program: funds are used for housing or housing related activities and economic development.

16) Section 8 Housing Assistance Program: rental assistance payments for very low-income households.

17) State (CDBG) General, Native American, and Colonias Allocations: funding for housing, community, and economic development projects serving lower income people in rural communities.

18) Senior Citizen Shared Housing Program: grants to assist seniors in obtaining shared housing or for development of group residences.

Colorado

Colorado Housing & Finance Authority, 1981 Blake Street, Denver, CO 80202; 303-297-7427 or 800-877-2432.

1) Single-Family Program: lower-than-market interest rates available to first- time home owners.

2) Commercial Division Programs: financial assistance provided to assist small businesses with expansion of their facilities.

3) Rental Acquisition Program: offers affordable multi-family housing for low-income households.

4) Section 8 Moderate Rehabilitation Program: incentives to property owners who rehabilitate substandard rental housing for low-income tenants qualifying for rent subsidies.

5) Low-Income Housing Tax Credit Program: federal tax credits for owners of low-income rental housing.

6) Mortgage Credit Certificates: reduction of federal income tax for home buyers.

7) Tax-Exempt Bond Program: financing for acquisition and/or rehabilitation of low-income rental housing.

8) Special Needs Housing Fund: financing for housing for frail elderly, mentally ill, battered persons, runaways, etc.

9) Shelter Housing Assistance Program: financing for emergency or transitional housing.

10) Construction Loan Fund: Short-term loans to non-profits for acquisition, rehab, construction and development costs of low-income housing to be sold.

11) Housing Development Loan Fund: short-term loans to non-profits for pre-development costs or acquisition of property for low-income multi-family housing projects.

12) Special Projects Program: short-term loans to non-profits for acquisition, rehab, or construction of projects such as group homes, shelters, co-ops, mobile home parks.

13) Rural Development Loan Program: loans for businesses in rural areas of Colorado.

14) Mortgage Revenue Bond Program: CHFA sells tax-exempt bonds and makes

proceeds available to qualified home buyers under two options: Below-Market Interest Rate Program or Cash Assistance Program.

15) Recycled Funds Program: provides a limited number of mortgage loans originated by affordable housing and community reinvestment lenders.

Connecticut

Connecticut Housing Finance Authority, 40 Cold Spring Road, Rocky Hill, CT 06067; 203-721-9501.

1) Home Mortgage Program: low-interest mortgages for low-and moderate- income persons and families.

2) Rehabilitation Mortgages: loans to protect or improve livability or energy efficiency of a home.

3) Reverse Annuity Mortgages (RAM): allows senior citizens to convert their home's equity into monthly tax-free cash payments.

4) Market Rate Multi-Family Program: below conventional-rate financing to develop or rehabilitate multi-family housing with units affordable to low-income households.

5) Low-Income Housing Tax Credit Program: federal tax credits for owners of low-income rental housing.

6) Private Rental Investment Mortgage and Equity Program: financing for mixed-income rental developments.

7) Apartment Conversion for the Elderly: loans to home owners 62 years of age or older for additions or conversions to their homes to create income-producing rental units.

8) Corporation for Supportive Husing Program: provides housing with special support services to people who have severe prolonged mental illness, AIDS and related disorders, chronic substance abusers, are homeless or at risk of being homeless.

9) Mortgage Revenue Bond Program: provides assistance for first time home buyers who are of low and moderate income.

Delaware

Delaware State Housing Authority, Division of Housing and Community Development, 18 The Green, P.O. Box 1401, Dover, DE 19901; 302-739-4263.

1) Single-Family Mortgage Program: low-interest loans to first-time home buyers.

2) Housing Development Funds: loans to developers of housing for low- and moderate-income persons and families.

3) Housing Rehabilitation Loan Program: $15,000 for ten years at 3% to fix up single-family homes.

4) Rent Subsidy Programs: money to provide subsidies for low- and moderate-income rental housing.

5) Public Housing Home Ownership Program: provides public housing tenants and families on the waiting list the opportunity to purchase affordable homes in residential neighborhoods.

6) Rental Rehabilitation Program: loans to cover up to 50% of rehab costs for low/moderate income housing.

7) Emergency Shelter Grants Program: to assist emergency housing shelters for the homeless.

8) Community Development Block Grants: funding to maintain or improve housing of low/moderate-income households.

9) Multi-Family Mortgage Revenue Bonds: financing for profit and non-profit developers of low-income housing.

10) Low-Income Housing Tax Credit Program: federal tax credits for owners of low-income rental housing.

11) Family Assisted Interest Rate Loans: first time homebuyers mortgage assitance at exceptionally low interst rates.

12) Second Mortgage Assistance Program: downpayment and closing cost assistance for first time homebuyers.

13) Emergency Shelter Grant Program: federal funds for local communities to rehabilitate, expand and operate shelter and transitional housing.

14) HOME Program: designed to expand affordable housing through tenant and homebuyer assistance, rehabilitation, and new construction.

15) Family Self-Sufficiency Program: designed to coordinate services that assisted housing residents need to achieve economic independence.

16) Delaware Housing Partnership Program: Second mortgages for settlement assistance to low to moderate income families purchasing homes in targeted new construction subdivisions.

District of Columbia

DC Housing Finance Agency, 1275 K Street, NW, Suite 600, Washington, DC 20005; 202-408-0415; FAX: 202-408-2766.

1) Single-Family Purchase Program: loans to first-time home buyers with 5% down and 7.5% interest.

2) Multi-Family Program: construction and permanent financing for developers of multi-family housing with at least 20% of the units designated for low-income households.

District of Columbia Department of Housing and Community Development, 51 N Street, NE, Washington, DC 20002; 202-535-1353.

1) Home Purchase Assistance Program: low or no interest loans for low- and moderate-income home buyers.

2) First Right Purchase Assistance Program: low-cost loans for low- and moderate-income individuals and tenant groups to exercise their right to purchase their rental housing that is being offered for sale.

3) Homestead Housing Preservation Program: repossessed properties are sold to eligible District residents at low cost and with deferred payment loans.

4) Multi-Family Housing Rehabilitation Loan Program: low-rate financing for construction and rehabilitation of multi-family housing.

5) Rental Rehabilitation Program: low or no interest deferred loans for rehabilitation and rent subsidies for property owners and tenants of low-income housing.

6) Distressed Properties Program: tax incentives to encourage the development of new rental housing or for the rehabilitation of vacant rental housing; similar benefits for occupied properties in economic difficulty.

7) Housing Finance for the Elderly, Dependent and Disabled: loans for the development of housing for special needs households.

8) Low-Income Housing Tax Credit Program: tax credits for owners of low-income rental housing.

9) Single-Family Housing Rehabilitation Program: low-cost financing for the rehabilitation of one to four unit low-income housing in designated areas.

10) Home Improvements for the Handicapped: grants to remove barriers and improve accessibility; for home owners or landlords on behalf of handicapped tenants.

Florida

Florida Housing Finance Agency, 227 North Bronough Street, Suite 5000, Tallahassee, FL 32301-1329; 904-488-4197.

1) First-Time Homebuyer Mortgage Revenue Bond Program: below-market rate financing for first-time home buyers with low/moderate income.

2) Home Ownership Assistance Program: $2,500 zero interest, due-on-sale loan to defer closing costs.

3) Affordable Housing Guarantee Program: below market financing for developers/home buyers of rental and for-sale housing.

4) State Apartment Incentive Loan Program: low-rate financing for developers who build or rehabilitate rental housing with 20% of units for low-income households and to eligible non-profit sponsors of housing projects.

5) Low-Income Housing Tax Credit Program: federal tax credits for owners of low-income rental housing.

6) Rental Housing Bond Program: below-market financing to developers of rental housing with 20% for low-income households.

7) Section 8 Program: federal rent subsidies for low-income tenants.

8) HOME Investment Partnerships Program: provides states their opportunity to administer federally funded homeownership and rental housing programs.

9) Single Family Mortgage Revenue Bond (MRB) Program: bonds used to finance below-market interest rate mortgage loans for first time home buyers with low to middle incomes.

10) State Housing Initiatives Partnership Program (SHIP): funds for the development and maintenance of affordable housing.

11) Community Homebuyer's Program (CHBP): provides less costly Conventional financing for low and moderate income buyers.

Georgia

Georgia Residential Finance Authority, 60 Executive Parkway South, Suite 250, Atlanta, GA 30329; 404-679-4840.

1) Single-Family Home Ownership Loan Program: 1.5% below prevailing interest rates for first-time home owners.

2) Homeowner Rehabilitation: HOME funded loans for homeowner rehabilitation programs.

3) Nonprofit Housing Development Program: provides technical and financial assistance to nonprofit housing developers.

4) Multi-family Bond Program: below-market interest rate loans to develop or rehabilitate multi-family rental housing.

5) Low-Income Housing Tax Credit Program: federal income tax credits to construct or rehabilitate low-income rental housing.

6) Section 8 Existing Housing Assistance: rental assistance subsidy payments to landlords of low-income individuals or families.

7) Housing Trust Fund for the Homeless: grants to homeless emergency shelters and service organizations in communities.

8) Appalachian Regional Commission: grants and loans for site development, technical assistance and others for low-and moderate-income housing projects.

9) HOME Investment Partnership Program: grants used to assist with state and local housing concerns.

10) Emergency Shelter Grant Programs: grants to shelter facilities for building improvements and renovation.

Be patient. If any phone number is incorrect, call (area code) 555-1212 and request the new listing.

139

Housing and Real Estate

Hawaii

Hawaii Housing Authority, 1002 North School Street, P.O. Box 17907, Honolulu, HI 96817; 808-832-6020.

1) Homeless Program: shelter and social services for homeless families and individuals.

2) State Rent Supplement Program: rent subsidies to tenants in approved projects.

3) Modernization and Maintenance: funds for the preservation and maintenance of existing housing.

4) Section 8 Certificate/Voucher Programs: rental housing subsidies.

5) Public Housing Projects: low rent housing for eligible families, elderly or disabled.

Housing Finance and Development Corporation, 677 Queen Street, Suite 300, Honolulu, HI 96813; 808-587-0597.

1)Hula Mae Single Family Program: low interest loans to first-time home buyers.

2) Tax Reform: Multi-Family Program: tax credits to investors in qualified low-income rental housing projects.

3) Housing Finance Revolving Fund: long-term mortgage financing in geographic areas for projects where private mortgage insurers will not insure.

Idaho

Idaho Housing Agency, 565 W. Myrtle, P.O. Box 7899, Boise, ID 83707-1899; 208-331-4882, TDD 800-219-2285.

1) Mortgage Credit Certificates: home buyers who have not owned a home in the last three years can claim 20% of their mortgage interest as a tax credit.

2) Single Family Mortgage Loan Program: below-market rate loans for first-time and limited-income home buyers.

3) Section 8 New Construction/Substantial Rehab Program: financing of multi-family housing affordable to very low-income households via rent subsidies.

4) Section 8 Moderate Rehab Program: incentives for property owners to upgrade substandard rental units to be occupied by low-income tenants qualifying for rent subsidies.

5) Section 8 Existing Certificate and Voucher Program: assistance for low-income households to meet costs of rental housing.

6) Rental Rehabilitation Program: funding for private property owners to make improvements to rental units in eligible locations.

7) Low-Income Housing Tax Credit Program: tax credit for owners/developers of housing for low-income households.

8) Stewart B. McKinney Permanent Housing Program for Handicapped Homeless: grant funds for private non-profit project sponsors.

9) Multi-Family Housing Financing: loans for new construction or substantial rehab of multi-family housing with a percentage rented to low-income tenants.

10) HOME Program: funds used for the construction and rehabilitation of affordable rental housing for low-income families across the state.

11) 5/15 Low-Interest Home Repair Loan Program: loans ranging from $5,000 to $15,000 are available for specific repairs under this program, with repayment terms from five to fifteen years.

12) Interest Qualifier Loan: allows borrowers to pay a lower interest rate for the first three years of their mortgage and then a one time interest increase in the fourth year for the remaining mortgage.

Illinois

Illinois Housing Development Authority, 401 N. Michigan Ave., Suite 900, Chicago, IL 60611; 312-836-5200 or 800-942-8439, TDD 312-836-5222.

1) Tax Exempt Bonds: low-interest loans to rehabilitate low- income housing.

2) Congregate Housing Finance Program: loans for congregate housing for the elderly.

3) First Time Homebuyer Program: low-interest mortgages for first-time income-eligible home buyers.

4) Affordable Housing Trust Fund: grants and loans to profit and non-profit developers of low-income housing projects.

5) HOME Program: this program is designed to expand the availability of affordable housing for low and very low income persons.

6) Tax Credits: help finance developments ranging from a single family house to a multi-family project.

Indiana

Indiana Housing Finance Authority, 115 West Washington Street, Suite 1350, South Tower, Indianapolis, IN 46204; 317-232-7777 or 800-872-0371.

1) First Home Program: loans to home buyers at 1 to 2 percentage points below the market rate.

2) Multi-Family Program: loans for developers of low- and moderate- income housing.

3) Mortgage Credit Certificate Program: tax credits to families purchasing mobile homes.

4) Low-Income Housing Tax Credit: federal tax credit to owners of low-income

rental housing.

5) Low-Income Housing Trust Fund: matching funds for development of low-income housing, permanent or transitional.

6) Mortgage Revenue Bonds: low-interest mortgages for working families that are financed through the sale of tax-exempt bonds.

7) Equity Fund: provides financial and technical assistance to non-profit and smaller for profit developers who want to use Low Income Tax Credits.

8) Housing Development Fund: funds to build local capacity in non-metropolitanareas.

9) HOME Program: funds used for a number of different purposes to create affordable housing.

10) First Home Program: allows qualified buyers to purchase homes using minimal amount of their own cash.

Iowa

Iowa Finance Authority, 100 East Grand Avenue, Suite 250, Des Moines, IA 50309; 515-281-4058.

1) Single-Family Mortgage Loans: low-interest loans to home buyers

2) Mortgage Credit Certificate Program: tax credits of up to 20% of the interest paid annually on home loans.

3) Small Business Loan Program: loans for small business.

4) Title Guaranty Program: to guaranty (insure) titles to Iowa real estate.

5) Economic Development Loan Program: for businesses exceeding the limitations of the Small Business Loan Program.

6) Targeted Area Assistance Program: assistance with origination fees and discount points.

7) Closing Cost Assistance: up to 3% or $1200 to help with closing costs of eligible buyers.

8) Low-Income Housing Tax Credit Program: federal tax credits for owners of low-income rental housing.

9) Housing Assistance Fund Program: funding for multi-family rehab and construction, rent subsidies, group homes, shelters, and other housing projects.

10) Homeless Shelter Assistance: funding for homeless shelters.

Kansas

Kansas Department of Commerce and Housing, 700 S.W. Harrison Suite 1300,Topeka, KS 66603; 913-296-3481 or 800-752-4422.

1) Tax Credits for Low-Income Housing: tax credits for developers who rent to low-income families.

2) Rental Rehabilitation Loan Program: loans up to $5,000 per rental unit to bring unit up to city code standard.

3) Emergency Shelter Grant Program: grants to local government agencies to provide emergency shelters for homeless households.

4) Permanent Housing for Handicapped Homeless: grants for acquisition, rehabilitation, and operation of multi-unit and group home projects for disabled homeless.

5) HOME/HOPE Program: emphasis is on assistance for first time home buyers with low to very low income.

6) Weatherization: a multi-funded program used to decrease fuel consumption in low income homes.

7) Community Service Block Grant Program: grants to community action agencies and migrant and seasonal farm worker organizationsto assist low income Kansans.

8) Section 8 Rental Assistance: monthly assistance payments to project owners.

9) Emergency Community Services Homeless Funding: services are the same as the Community Service Block Grant Program with the stipulation that the target population must be homeless.

10) Rural Operation Homeless: families from specific counties who are homeless receive financial assistance toward the payment of rent.

11) Sunflower Supportive Services Program: provides supportive services for older residents of Kansas.

12) Housing Outreach Program: this program is designed to assess local community needs and to develop local resources.

Kentucky

Kentucky Housing Corporation, 1231 Louisville Road, Frankfort, KY 40601; 502-564-7630 or 800-633-8896.

1) Single-Family Home Ownership: low-interest loans to home buyers who currently do not own property.

2) Elderly Rural Rehabilitation Program: grants to elderly in rural areas for the installment of indoor plumbing facilities.

3) Grants to the Elderly for Energy Repairs (GEER): grants to elderly for home energy repairs.

4) Housing Trust: single-family loans for eligible low-income families.

5) EPIC (Equity Partners Investing in the Commonwealth) Program: financing for eligible Kentuckians for downpayment and closing costs.

6) KHC Urban Program: initiatives to produce affordable housing in designated

Be patient. If any phone number is incorrect, call (area code) 555-1212 and request the new listing.

urban areas.

7) KHC Rural Program: loans and administrative assistance to non-profit organizations for construction or rehab of low-income housing.

8) Kentucky Appalachian Housing Program: site development grants and loans for housing developments in 49 eastern KY counties.

9) Country Home Program: low-rate construction financing for families in 63 counties.

10) Field Services/Special Population Needs Emergency Fund: loans for emergency repairs for low-income Kentuckians.

11) Permanent Housing for Homeless Handicapped Persons: funds for acquisition/rehabilitation of housing for homeless handicapped persons.

12) Section 8 Programs: rent subsidies and other assistance to low-income households.

13) Rental Housing Finance Program: below-market financing for low-income rental housing.

14) Rental Deposits Surety Program: assistance with utility and security deposits for low-income households.

15) Residential Investment Program: fixed-rate mortgages for non-profit sponsors of new rental units in rural counties.

16) Low-Income Housing Tax Credits: federal tax credits for owners of low-income rental housing.

Louisiana

Louisiana Housing Finance Agency, 200 Lafayette Street, Suite 300, Baton Rouge, LA 70801; 504-342-1320.

1) Single-Family: lower-interest rate 8.8% for 30 yr. FHA/VA financing for first-time home buyers.

2) Multi-Family: financing available for developers of low-moderate income housing development.

3) Tax Credit Programs: federal and state income tax credit provisions provided to developers of low-to-moderate multi-family development.

4) Housing Development Action Grants: financing for multi-family housing developments.

5) ACCESS Program: qualified individuals receive a reduced rate 30 year mortgage or qualify for additional financing for up to 3.0 percent of their total mortgage loan applied towards their downpayment and closing costs.

6) HOME Assistance Program: assistance when purchasing a home for qualified individuals.

7) Builder's Program: provides take out financing of new construction or substantial rehabilitation of single-family homes made available to low and moderate income families.

Maine

Maine State Housing Authority, P.O. Box 2669, 353 Water Street, Augusta, ME 04338-2669; 207-626-4600, 800-452-4668.

1) Statewide Housing Aquisition/Rehabilitation Program (SHARP): loans to purchase and rehabilitate small (3 to 20 units) rental housing developments.

2) Fix-Me Program: low interest loans for home improvements for very low-income home owners.

3) Production Incentive Demonstration Program: financial incentive for the formation of Community Housing Development Organizations (CHDOs) and their involvment in affordable housing.

4) Home Purchase Program: low downpayment and low-rate financing for first-time income-eligible home buyers.

5) Purchase Plus Improvement: home improvement loans for borrowers in the Home Purchase or Home Start programs.

6) Underground Oil Storage Tank Removal Program: grants or interest-free loans to property owners for removal and disposal of environmentally hazardous underground oil storage tanks and pipes and installation of replacements.

7) Home Equity Conversion Mortgage: supplies elderly home owners with cash for some of the equity in their homes.

8) Home Improvement Program: low-rate home improvement loans.

9) Rental Loan Program: below market rate loans for new or rehabilitated rental housing affordable to low/moderate income households.

10) Rental Rehabilitation Program: low-interest deferred payment loans to repair substandard apartments.

11) Consumer Residential Opportunity Program: low-rate loans for housing the mentally ill.

12) Land Acquisition Program: low-rate deferred payment loans to non-profit housing corporations to buy land for affordable housing.

13) Homeless Shelter Assistance: funding to operate or improve shelters.

14) Supportive Housing Initiative Program (SHIP): low-rate, no/low down payment loans for non-profit organizations developing housing for special needs households.

15) Low-Income Housing Tax Credit: tax credits to developers of housing for low-income households.

16) Section 8 New Construction: rent subsidies for low-income households.

17) Section 8 Moderate Rehabilitation: rent subsidies for low-income households in rehabilitated rental units.

18) Section 8 Certificates and Vouchers: rental assistance for low-income tenants.

19) Low Income Heating Assistance Program: offers assistance to fuel vendors to provide heating for low income home owners and renters.

20) Weatherization Assistance: provides energy assistance for low income home owners.

Maryland

Department of Housing and Community Development, 100 Community Place, Crownsville, MD 21032-2023; 410-514-7500 or 800-492-7127.

1) Rental Housing Production Program: loans to developers or non-profit organizations to cover the costs of construction, rehabilitation, acquisition or related development costs through interest rate writedowns or rent subsidies.

2) Mortgage Program: below-market interest rate mortgage financing for low- and moderate-income home buyers.

3) Home and Energy Loan Program: below-market interest rate loans for home and energy conservation improvements for single-family homes.

4) Multi-Family Home & Energy Loan Program: rehabilitation and energy conservation loans for multi-family rental projects and single scattered-site rental properties.

5) Housing Rehabilitation Program: loans to limited income home owners, owners of multi-unit residential buildings and owners of small nonresidential properties.

6) Group Home Financing Program: low-interest, no interest deferred payment loans to non-profit organizations to purchase and modify housing for use as group homes and shelters.

7) Residential Lead Paint Abatement Program: loans to finance the abatement of lead paint in rental properties.

8) Elderly Rental Housing Program: new construction financing for rental housing for elderly citizens.

9) Rental Allowance Program: subsidies to very low-income individuals with emergency needs.

10) Emergency Mortgage Assistance: assists home owners in imminent danger of losing homes to foreclosure after loss of income due to critical circumstances.

11) Reverse Equity Program: enables low-income elderly to access home equity to pay housing and other expenses that facilitate continued occupancy.

12) Settlement Expense Loan Program: low-rate loans up to $5000 toward settlement expenses for low-moderate income home buyers.

13) Multi-Family Bond Program: below-market financing for low-income multi-family rental housing development.

14) Non-Profit Rehabilitation Program: low-rate loans to non-profit organizations to rehabilitate low-income rental housing.

15) Partnership Rental Housing Program: loans for local governments and housing authorities for development or acquisition of low-income rental housing.

16) Construction Loan Program: low-rate financing for development of affordable single-family or multi-family housing.

17) Preferred Interest Rate Loan Program: offers preferred rates for those who qualify.

18) Housing Rehabilitation Program-Single Family: low-rate financing for rehabilitation of small residential properties for low-income households.

19) Accessory, Shared and Sheltered Housing Program: low-rate loans to finance additions and improvements to create accessory, shared or sheltered housing for low-income households.

20) Indoor Plumbing Program: low-rate loans to provide indoor plumbing.

21) Energy Bank Program: matching funds to low-income home owners for energy conservation improvements.

22) Section 8 Existing Voucher Program: rent subsidies for low-income households.

23) Moderate Rehabilitation Program: incentives to property owners for improvements to deteriorating housing units to be rented to households eligible for rent subsidies.

24) Rental Rehabilitation Program: rehab funds for property owners renting to low-income households.

25) Low-Income Housing Tax Credit Program: federal tax credits to owners of low-income rental housing.

26) Transitional Housing and Emergency Shelter Program: provides grants to improve or create transitional housing and emergency shelters.

Massachusetts

Massachusetts Housing Finance Agency, One Beacon Street, Boston, MA 02190; 617-854-1000, TDD 617-854-1025.

1) Real Estate-Owned Program: offers assistance to both lenders and borrowers.

2) General Lending: special loans for Vietnam Era Veterans, low-income and minority borrowers and physically handicapped.

3) Neighborhood Rehabilitation Programs: funds for people who buy and/or rehabilitate homes in locally designated neighborhoods.

4) New Construction Set-Aside: funds for purchasers of new homes and

condominiums built by specific developers.

5) Home Improvement Program: loans for owner-occupied, one- to four-family homes.

6) State Housing Assistance for Rental Productions (SHARP): interest rate subsidies to developers for production of rental housing where at least 25% are available to low-income households.

7) Project TAP (Tenant Assistance Program): training for project residents for drug- and alcohol-related problems.

8) Low-Income Housing Tax Credit Program: federal tax credits for owners of low-income rental housing.

9) Elder Choice Program: fills the gap between independent living and a nursing home by providing a home-like setting coupled with on-site services that support the needs of frail elderly persons.

10) Mortgage Credit Certificate Program: federal tax credits for eligible first-time home buyers.

11) Mortgage Insurance Program: lower premium private mortgage insurance available to HOP- and MHFA-assisted borrowers.

12) Rental Acquisition Development Initiative: low-rate financing for developers of rental properties with units affordable to low-income households.

13) Supportive Services in Elderly Housing: assists elderly residents in avoiding premature placement in nursing homes by delivering affordable homemaking, health care, and other services.

14) Acquisition Set-Aside Program: allows builders to offer lower interest mortgages to eligible home buyers as a sales incentive in return for reducing cost of units.

15) Reverse Equity Mortgage Program (REM): a pilot program that allows senior citizens to use a portion of their home equity to cover expenses and meet basic needs without having to sell their homes.

16) Home Advantage Program: provides low interest rate mortgages to buyers of discounted Fannie Mae properties.

17) Get the Lead Out Program: provides loans of up to $15,000 -- some at zero percent interest for borrowers under court order to delead.

Executive Office of Communities and Development, Commonwealth of Massachusetts, 100 Cambridge Street, Room 1804, Boston, MA 02202; 617-727-7765.

1) Section 8 Certificate/Voucher Programs: rent subsidies for low-income households.
2) Rental Voucher Program: rent subsidies similar to Section 8 Certificate Program.
3) Mc Kinney Emergency Community Services Homeless Grant: helps homeless individuals and those at risk of becoming homeless through eviction or forclosure.
4) Low-Income Home Energy Assistance: provides help with home heating costs for low-income, elderly and handicapped clients.
5) Low-Income Weatherization Assistance: funds for weatherization improvements in units occupied by low income persons.
6) Indian Affairs and Assistance: provides a broad spectrum of services to Native Americans.
7) Community Service Block Grant: provides funds for designated community action agencies to enhance the quality of life among the poor.
8) HOME: produces affordable housing units for rent or purchase by low or moderate income households.
9) Elderly Low Income Housing: provides housing for the low income elderly as well as individuals with disabilities.

Michigan

Michigan State Housing Development Authority, Plaza One, Fourth Floor, 401 South Washington Square, P.O. Box 30044, Lansing, MI 48909; 517-373-8370 or 800-327-9158, TDD 800-382-4568.

1) Single-Family Home Mortgage: low-interest loans for single-family homes and condominiums.
2) Michigan Mortgage Credit Certificates: federal income tax credits that give home buyers more income to qualify for a mortgage.
3) Home and Neighborhood Improvement Loans: home improvement loans for homes over 20 years old at interest rates from 1 to 9 percent.
4) Section 8 Existing Rental Allowance Program: rent subsidies for low-income persons who find their own housing in private homes and apartment buildings.
5) Moderate Rehabilitation Loans to Landlords: loans to landlords for rehabilitation of units.
6) 1% Tax Exempt Bond, Family Housing Program: offers developers 1 percent interest rate loans for constructing or rehabilitating rental housing units for families in distressed areas.
7) Housing for the Homeless: grants to organizations to operate shelters for the homeless.
8) Rehabilitation Assistance Program: provides a ten year forgiveable loan to very low income families to make improvements on their homes.
9) Low-Income Housing Tax Credit Program: federal tax credits for owners/ developers of low-income rental housing.
10) 70/30 Rental Housing Program: low interest loans to construct or rehabilitate low-income rental housing.

11) Contractor's Assistance Program: provides working capital loans to small contractors who have been selected to work on rental housing projects.
12) Community Development Block Grant (Small Cities) Program: for neighborhood revitalization and improvements to infrastructure and rental housing.
13) Comprehensive Neighborhood Rehabilitation Competition: for neighborhood revitalization projects.
14) Emergency Housing Apartment Program (EHAP): pilot project; loans and grants for purchase and renovation of a homeless shelter.
15) Home Improvement Loan Program (HIP/CHIP): low cost home improvement loans.
16) Homeless Children's Fund: funds raised for shelters and transitional housing.
17) HOME Single Family Purchase Program : grants to be used to rehabilitate or construct single family homes.
18) Housing Assistance Program: targeted technical and financial assistance to local governments.
19) 21st Initiative: for neighborhood revitalization of single-family and rental housing.
20) Neighborhood Builders Alliance: targeted technical and financial assistance to local governments and non-profits.
21) Neighborhood Housing Grant Program: assistance to non-profits for neighborhood revitalization of single-family and rental housing.
22) Neighborhood Preservation Program (NPP): targeted technical and financial assistance for local governments sponsoring neighborhood infrastructure improvements and building preservation.
23) Pass Through Program: loans for low-income rental housing development.
24) Set-Asides for Non-Profits: homebuyer assistance for low-income households participating in programs of non-profit organizations.
25) Special Housing Program: for handicapped group homes and other housing needs of the handicapped.
26) Supported Independent Living Program and Respite Program: for housing needs of the handicapped.
27) Taxable Bond Program: rental housing construction and renovation.
28) Urban Development Initiative: targeted technical assistance to local governments.
29) MSHDA Housing Initiative: low downpayment loans with liberal eligibility requirements; not restricted to first-time buyers.

Minnesota

Minnesota Housing Finance Agency, 400 Sibley Street, St. Paul, MN 55101; 612-296-9951, 612-296-7608, or 800-657-3769, TDD 612-297-2361.

1) Indian Housing Programs: mortgage and home improvement financing for tribal housing as well as home ownership loans at below-market interest rates.
2) Innovative Housing Loan Program: no-interest and low-interest loans to develop housing that is innovative in design, construction, marketing and/or financing.
3) Deferred Loan Program: interest-free loans to households with a disabled member.
4) Rental Rehabilitation Program: grants to rental property owners.
5) Rental Rehabilitation Loan Program: low-interest loans to rental property owners.
6) Section 8 Housing Assistance: rents subsidies for low-income renters.
7) Home Sharing Program: grants to non-profits who assist elderly in sharing homes.
8) Purchase Plus Program: financing for both purchase and rehabilitation of existing housing for median income or below.
9) Minnesota Mortgage Program: below-market rate loans for low/moderate income first-time home buyers.
10) Home Ownership Assistance Fund: downpayment and monthly payment assistance to lower income MHFA mortgage recipients.
11) Urban Indian Housing Program: below-market financing for Indians in Duluth, Minneapolis and St. Paul.
12) Urban and Rural Homesteading Program: grants to organizations to acquire and rehabilitate vacant and condemned properties for sale to first-time "at risk" home buyers.
13) Deferred Loan Program: deferred payment loans to assist low-income home owners making home improvements.
14) Great Minnesota Fix-Up Fund: below-market home-improvement loans for low/moderate income credit-worthy home owners.
15) Home Energy Loan Program: low-rate loans for increasing energy-efficiency of homes; no maximum income limits.
16) Low and Moderate Income Program: property improvement loans for low/moderate income households or owners of low/moderate income rental housing in designated areas.
17) Revolving Loan Program: rehabilitation financing for low/moderate income home owners who don't qualify for other programs.
18) Housing Trust Fund: zero-interest deferred loans for development of low-income rental and co-op housing.
19) $1.00 Home Set-Aside Program: HUD lease program for non-profit use of repossessed HUD homes to house the homeless.
20) Intermediate Care Facilities for the Developmentally Disabled: below-market financing for non-profit sponsors to develop residential facilities for the developmentally disabled.

21) Low-Income Housing Tax Credit Program: federal tax credit for owners of low-income rental housing.

22) Affordable Rental Investment Fund: zero-interest deferred loans to rehabilitate small family low-income rental housing.

23) Low-Income Large Family Rental Housing Program: financing for construction of large rental units for low-income families.

24) HOME Disaster Grant Program: provides grants to low-income households for housing improvements due to weather related damages.

25) New Construction Tax Credit Mortgage/Bridge Loan Program: for construction/rehabilitation of rental units for low-income households.

Mississippi

Mississippi Home Corporation, 840 River Place, Suite 605, Jackson, MS 39201; 601-354-6062.

1) Mortgage Certificate Program: low-rate financing for income-eligible first-time home buyers.

2) Low-Income Housing Tax Credit Program: tax credits for owners of low-income rental housing.

3) Downpayment Assistance Program: for buyers who can afford mortgage payments but not a downpayment.

4) Rental Rehabilitation Program: (under development).

5) Energy Conservation Revolving Loan Fund: (under development).

Missouri

Missouri Housing Development Commission, 3770 Broadway, Kansas City, MO 64111; 816-756-3790, TDD 816-756-2744.

1) Multi-Family Program: low-interest rate mortgages to developers of multi-family developments.

2) Single-Family Down Payment Assistance Program: below-market interest rate mortgages for first-time home buyers.

3) Neighborhood Loan Program: loans to neighborhood organizations and/or developers for acquiring and rehabilitating residential properties.

4) Home Improvements/Weatherization Loan Program: low-interest loans to assist qualified home owners in home improvements that will increase energy efficiency.

5) Affordable Housing Production Program: low-interest rates to developers to stimulate production of housing for low-and moderate-income families and individuals.

6) RTC Home Purchase Program: low-rate financing to purchase reduced cost housing.

7) HUD Repo Properties: HUD-insured low-rate loans for low-income households to purchase HUD-foreclosed properties.

8) Low-Income Housing Tax Credit Program: tax credits for owners of low-income rental housing.

9) Section 8 Programs: subsidies and financial assistance for low-income tenants.

10) Operation Homeless: provides homeless households with Section 8 certificates or vouchers to secure affordable subsidized rental housing.

11) Housing Trust Fund Program: non-Section 8 rental assistance payments for low-income households.

12) Housing Inventory Recycling Program: funds to facilitate purchase of foreclosed homes by lower income households.

13) FmHA Supplemental Subsidy Program: rent subsidies for low-income elderly in FmHA housing projects.

14) Missouri Low-Income Housing Tax Credit Program: supplements the federal Low-Income Housing Tax Credit Program.

15) Risk Sharing Program: designed to produce and preserve affordable multifamily rental housing.

16) HANDS Program: provides low interest loans to officers who relocate to targeted city neighborhoods.

17) Mortgage Credit Certificate Program: certificates for home mortgage loans for low and moderate income homebuyers.

16) Equity Fund: capital for construction or renovation of housing unitsfor lower income families.

17) Unusual Need Loan Program: designed to produce affordable rental units.

18) HOME Rental Housing Program: provides financing for the acquisition and rehabilitation of housing for low and moderate income families.

19) Flood Recovery Programs: assistance for those who wish to relocate from the flood plain.

20) Bridge Loan Program: encourages and facilitates low income housing.

21) Single Family Mortgage Revenue Bond Program: mortgage financing at interest rates below conventional market rates.

Montana

Montana Board of Housing, 2001 Eleventh Avenue, Helena, MT 59620; 406-444-3040.

1) Single-Family Programs: low-interest loans to low-income families.

2) Multi-Family Program: construction loans to developers of multi-family units for persons and families of lower income.

3) Homebuyers Cash Assistance Program: assist those credit worthy persons lacking the financial assistance to purchase a home under any other program.

4) Low-Income Housing Tax Credit Program: federal tax credits for owners of low-income housing.

5) Reverse Annuity Mortgage Loans: home-equity loans for senior 68+ home owners.

6) Recycled Mortgage Purchase Program: assists lower income households who cannot purchase homes through the Single-Family Mortgage Program; grant funds help lower construction costs for developers, reduce home prices, create low-interest loans, and assist with downpayments and closing costs.

7) Disabled Accessible Affordable Homeownership Program: assists people with disabilities to acquire affordable architecturally accessible homes enabling them to live independently.

Nebraska

Nebraska Investment Finance Authority, 1033 O Street, Suite 218, Lincoln, NE 68508; 402-434-3900.

1) Single-Family Mortgage Program: low-cost loans for single family homes, townhomes, condominiums, mobile homes, and up to 4-unit dwellings.

2) Tax Credit Program: attractive interest rates for developers of rental housing for low- and moderate-income households.

3) Agricultural Finance Programs:
First-Time Farmer Loan: loans to purchase agricultural real estate.
FmHA: loans to refinance existing agricultural loans.

4) Low-Income Housing Tax Credit Program: federal tax credits for owners of low-income housing.

Nevada

Department of Commerce, Housing Division, 1802 N. Carson St., Suite 154, Carson City, NV 89710; 702-687-4258.

1) Single Family Mortgage Purchase Program: loans to moderate-income families with no previous home ownership interest within the last 3 years.

2) Industrial Development Bonds: low financing costs for new construction or expansion manufacturing projects.

3) Rural Area Housing Program: low-interest mortgage loans to developers to develop affordable rental units outside metropolitan areas.

Nevada Rural Housing Authority, 2100 California Street, Carson City, NV 89701; 702-687-5747.

New Hampshire

Housing Finance Authority, P.O. Box 5087, Manchester, NH 03108; 603- 472-8623 or 800-640-7239.

1) Housing Expense Loan Program (HELP): provides limited financial assistance to eligible borrowers to enable them to meet a portion of the downpayment and closing costs of a single family home.

2) Single-Family Mortgage Program: low-interest mortgage funds to qualifying individuals and households.

3) Multi-Family Housing Program: construction loans for small rental projects for private for profit developers and non-profit organizations.

4) Borrower Assistance Program: provides assistance to selected borrowers on the Authority's Single Family Mortgage Program who are delinquent in mortgage payments due to unexpected financial problems.

5) Affordable Housing Fund: financing primarily for non-profit or co-op multi-family projects.

6) HOPE 3 Program: for borrowers who can afford mortgage payments but lack downpayment and closing costs.

7) Home Equity Conversion Program: loans to help seniors meet living and medical expenses while retaining ownership and residence in their own homes.

8) Section 8 Housing Programs: rental assistance for low-income households.

9) Low-Income Housing Tax Credit Program: tax credits for owners of low-income rental housing.

10) Supportive Services Program: funding for seniors to receive services they need to remain independent.

11) Home of Your Own Program: provides homeownership opportunities for developmentally disabled people.

12) Housing Preservation Grant Program: provides funds for rehabilitationof low income, owner occupied housing in rural ares ofthe state.

13) HOME Rental Housing Production Program: provides funds to support the development of rental housing opportunities for low and very low income households.

14) Affordable Home Ownership Program: financing for developers of single family homes to be sold at below market cost.

15) Direct Acquisition Program: develop low income multi-family housing opportunities using existing stock.

16) Affordable Housing Fund: funds are used for the acquisition, development and

preservation of low income housing.

17) Emergency Assistance Fund: funds used to correct problems which threaten the livability of property.

New Jersey

New Jersey Housing Agency, 3625 Quakerbridge Road, Trenton, NJ 08650-2085; 609-890-8900 or 800-NJ-HOUSE.

1) Home Buyers Program: low-interest loans to urban area first-time buyers with a 5% downpayment.

2) Seed Money Loan Program: funding of pre-development costs for non-profits seeking to develop affordable housing.

3) Continuing Care Retirement Communities: construction loans and lower-than-market mortgage interest rates for residential communities for senior citizens.

4) Home Buyers Program: low-rate financing and low downpayments for income-eligible first-time home buyers or home buyers in 41 targeted urban areas.

5) Home Buyers 100% Financing Program: for low/moderate-income first-time or urban buyers.

6) Home Ownership for Performing Employees (HOPE) Program: financial assistance from sponsoring employers to reduce downpayment, closing costs and monthly payments for their employees.

7) Development Set-Aside Program: mortgage funding for purchasers of housing units in Agency-approved housing developments.

8) Multi-Family Rental Housing Program: low-rate financing for developers of rental housing for low/moderate income households.

9) Low-Income Housing Tax Credit Program: federal tax credits for owners of low-income rental housing.

10) Revolving Loan Program: financing for the production of small and medium-sized rental housing projects with units affordable to low-income households.

11) Services for Independent Living Program: support services that enable senior citizens in Agency-financed housing to avoid institutionalization.

12) Boarding House Life Safety Improvement Loan Program: low-rate loans to finance safety improvements in boarding homes.

13) Transitional Housing Program: financing for the construction of transitional housing for the homeless.

New Mexico

Mortgage Finance Division, P.O. Box 2047, Albuquerque, NM 87103; 505-843-6880 or 1-800-444-6880.

1) Mortgage Saver Program: below-market loans to first-time home buyers.

2) Multi-Family Programs: financing of multi-family housing for low- and moderate-income tenants.

New Mexico State Housing Division, 1100 St. Francis Drive, Santa Fe, NM 87503; 505-827-7124.

1) Low-Income Housing Tax Credit Program: federal tax credits for owners of low-income rental housing.

2) State Housing Rehabilitation Program: rehabilitation grants for low-income elderly, handicapped and disabled home owners.

3) Section 8 Housing Assistance Payments Program (Voucher): rent subsidies for low-income households who locate their own housing.

4) HUD Rental Rehabilitation Program: grants to rehabilitate sub-standard rental units for rental to low-income tenants qualifying for rent subsidies.

5) HOME Program: expands the supply of affordable housing for low income families.

New York

State of New York, Executive Department, Division of Housing and Community Renewal, One Fordham Plaza, Bronx, NY 10458; 718-563-5700.

1) Special Needs Housing Program: grants to non-profit sponsors for single room occupancy dwellings units for low-income individuals.

2) Low-Income Housing Trust Fund: funds to non-profit sponsors to rehabilitate existing properties into affordable low-income housing.

3) Housing Development Fund: temporary financing to non-profit sponsors developing housing with private or government-aided mortgages

4) Rental Rehabilitation Program: up to $8,500 per unit to subsidize up to 50% of the cost of moderate rehabilitation of residential units in lower-income neighborhoods.

5) Rural Preservation Program: funds to local not-for-profit organizations engaging in a variety of activities for the benefit of low- and moderate-income persons.

6) Rural Rental Assistance Program: monthly rent subsidy payments to owners of multi-family projects on behalf of low-income tenants.

7) Turn Key/Enhanced Housing Trust Fund: financing for developers of low-income rental housing.

8) Infrastructure Development Demonstration Program: grant funds for infrastructure improvements (water lines, roads, sidewalks, utility lines) that serve affordable housing projects.

9) Urban Initiative Program: funding for community preservation and improvement in designated urban areas.

10) Rural Area Revitalization Program: funding for not-for-profit organizations to make housing improvements in designated areas.

11) Housing Opportunities Program for the Elderly-RESTORE: funds for not-for-profit organizations to make emergency home repairs for elderly home owners.

12) Shared Housing Development Program: funding for boarding houses, accessory apartments and "granny flats" in designated areas.

13) Clinton Preservation Program: financing to preserve and improve the Clinton neighborhood in NYC.

14) Low-Income Housing Tax Credit Program: federal tax credits for owners of low-income housing rental.

15) Neighborhood Preservation Program: funding to defray administrative costs of not-for-profit organizations performing neighborhood preservation activities.

16) Rural Home Ownership Assistance Program: funds to defray administrative costs of not-for-profit organizations assisting low-income households in the acquisition, financing, and rehabilitation of affordable housing.

17) Neighborhood Redevelopment Demonstration Program: funds for planning, administration and project costs for activities that promote affordable housing or improve neighborhoods.

18) Section 8 Moderate Rehabilitation Program: incentives for property owners to upgrade substandard rental housing for tenants qualifying for rent subsidies.

19) Section 8 Existing Housing Program: rent subsidies for low-income households.

20) Senior Citizen Rent Increase Exemption: exemption from rent increases for tenants 62 years of age or older who live in rent-controlled apartments in NYC and 15 other areas; landlords are compensated with certificates to pay real estate taxes or to convert to cash.

21) HOME Program: provides funds for a variety of housing needs for low income families.

New York State Housing Authority, 250 Broadway, New York, NY 10007; 212-306-3000.

North Carolina

North Carolina Housing Finance Agency, P.O. Box 28066 Raleigh, NC 27611-8066; 919-781-6115.

1) Single-Family Mortgage Loan Program: below-market, fixed-rate loans for first-time home buyers with low/moderate income.

2) Builder Bonus Program: improves the affordability of new single family homes in nonmetropolitan counties.

3) Catalyst Home Ownership Program: encourages nonprofit organizations to develop new single family homes by providing loans and grants.

4) Mortgage Credit Certificate Program: tax-credit for first-time home buyers paying mortgage interest.

5) Home Ownership Challenge Fund: funding to non-profits that create home ownership opportunities for low-income households.

6) Maxwell/Fuller Self-Help Housing Program: zero-interest loans to nonprofits managing self-help or owner-built housing projects for low-income households.

7) Multi-Family Loan Program: below-market financing for developers of low/moderate-income rental housing.

8) Multi-Family Subsidized Program: rent subsidies for low-income tenants.

9) Low-Income Housing Tax Credit Program: federal tax credits for owners of low-income housing.

10) Catalyst Loan Program: funding for non-profits for front-end costs in the development of low-income rental housing.

11) Housing Rehabilitation Program: rehabilitation funds for privately-owned rental housing for low-income households.

12) HOME Program: provides federal funds for developing affordable housing for very low, low and moderate income households.

13) Housing Production Program: financing for new or rehabilitated housing for low-income households.

14) Housing LINC Loan Fund: revolving loan fund to pay predevelopment costs for assisted living projects for the elderly.

15) Resolution Trust Corporation Clearinghouse: property information for purchasers, allowing qualified purchasers right of first refusal for single family and multi-family properties affordable to low/moderate income households.

16) Multifamily Unsubsidized Loan Program: provides morgage financing at a lower interest rate.

17) Security and Utility Deposit Loan Program: provides loans and guarantees for security and utility deposits to help people move from homeless shelters and transitional housing into permanent housing.

North Dakota

Housing Finance Agency, P.O. Box 1535, Bismarck, ND 58502; 701-328-3434.

1) Housing Assistance: rental assistance program for low-income renter households and mobile home space renters.

2) Single Family Program: low interest loans for low- to moderate-income first- time home buyers.

3) Housing Assistance Program: certificates and vouchers to assist low-income tenants with rent payments.

4) Moderate Rehabilitation Program: incentives for rehabilitation of substandard housing for rental to low-income tenants qualifying for rent-subsidies.

5) Low-Income Housing Tax Credit Program: federal tax credits for owners of low-income rental housing.

Ohio

Ohio Housing Finance Agency, 775 High St., 26th Floor, Columbus, OH 43266; 614-466-0400.

1) Seed Money Loan Program: no-interest loans to non-profit, public and limited profit entities to arrange financing for low- and moderate-income rental housing developments.

2) First-Time Homebuyer Program: below-market financing for first-time home buyers.

3) Home Ownership Incentive Programs: low interest rates and downpayments for non-profit developers of housing to meet special needs (single parents, minorities, disabled, rural, inner city).

4) Development Loan Program: financing for construction and development costs of low/moderate income housing by non-profit and limited profit sponsors.

5) Low-Income Housing Tax Credit Program: federal tax credits for owners of low-income rental housing.

6) 403 Rental Housing Gap Financing Program: financial assistance to non-profit organizations for development of low-income rental housing.

7) Rental Housing Energy Conservation Program: funds to non-profits for energy-efficient rehabilitation or new construction of low-income rental housing.

8) Multi-Family Rental Development Program: financing for purchase, construction, and rehabilitation of multi-family rental housing for the elderly.

9) Section 8 Rental Assistance Program: rent subsidies.

10) Downpayment Assistance Program: offers up to $2,500 in downpayment assistance for eligible homebuyers to purchase homes.

Oklahoma

Oklahoma Housing Finance Agency, P.O. Box 26720, Oklahoma City, OK 73126-0720; 405-848-1144 or 1-800-256-1489.

1) Single-Family Mortgage Revenue Bond Program: low-rate loans to first-time home buyers.

2) Multi-Family Mortgage Revenue Bond Program: funds for the purchase, construction or rehabilitation of housing for low/moderate income families.

3) Homeless Program: support for homeless families while they await funds for housing.

4) Section 8 Existing Housing Assistance Program: rent subsidies for low-income tenants.

5) Section 8 Rental Rehabilitation Program: matching funds for property owners who renovate rental units for low/moderate-income households.

6) Section 8 Voucher Assistance Program: rent subsidies for low-income households who locate their own housing.

Oregon

Oregon Housing Agency, Housing Division, 1600 State St., Suite 100, Salem, OR 97310; 503-986-2000.

1) Elderly and Disabled Housing Program: below-market interest rate mortgage loans for multi-family housing for elderly and disabled.

2) Family Rental Housing Program: financing for multi-unit rental housing for low-income families.

3) Seed Money Advance Program: no-interest advances to non-profits to cover pre-construction costs.

4) Low-Income Housing Tax Credit: federal income tax credits to developers who construct, rehabilitate, or acquire qualified low-income rental housing.

5) Single-Family Mortgage Program: below-market interest rate loans to low- and moderate-income Oregon home buyers.

6) Mortgage Credit Certificate Program: federal tax credit for low- and moderate-income Oregonians to purchase, improve or rehabilitate a single-family residence.

7) Oregon Lenders' Tax Credit Program: very low interest loans to non-profits from qualified Oregon financial institutions for low-income multi-family housing.

8) Low-Income Rental Housing Fund: rental assistance for low-income families.

9) Mobile Home Park Purchase Program: financial and technical assistance for tenants' associations to purchase their mobile home parks.

10) Partnership Housing Team: technical assistance to local governments and non-profits developing low-income housing.

11) Community Development Corporation Program: grants and technical assistance for local community development corporations to increase their skills in establishing low-income housing.

Pennsylvania

Pennsylvania Housing Finance Agency, 2101 North Front St. Harrisburg, PA 17105; 717-780-3800.

1) Home Owners Emergency Mortgage Assistance Program: loans to keep delinquent home owners from losing their homes to foreclosure.

2) PennHOMES Program: provides interim and permanent mortgage financing to developers of low-income rental housing.

3) Lower Income Home Ownership Program: provides mortgage loans to low income first time homebuyers who meet income and home purchase price guidelines.

4) Rental Housing Tax Credit Program: federal income tax credits to developers of affordable rental housing.

5) Statewide Home Ownership Program: low-interest financing for first-time home buyers or buyers of property in targeted areas.

6) Pennsylvania HomePlus Program: allows Pennsylvanians who are 62 or older to "convert" the equity in their property into cash.

7) Closing Cost Assistance Program: pays up to $2,000 toward closing costs for houses that are bought by participants in the Lower Income Home Ownership Program, qualified participants must have dependent children or be disabled.

8) Supportive Services Program: to help elderly residents of subsidized senior citizen rental apartments meet routine needs that enable them to remain in their own homes.

Rhode Island

Rhode Island Housing and Mortgage Finance Corporation, 60 Eddy St., Providence, RI 02903; 401-751-5566 or 800-427-5560, TDD 401-421-9799.

1) Home Repair: fixed rate-loans to make needed repairs on 1 to 6 unit dwellings owned or occupied by low- and moderate-income persons.

2) Rental Housing Production Program: tax-exempt and/or taxable bond financing for developers for projects where a minimum of 20% of the units are rented to low-income tenants.

3) First Homes Program: low-rate mortgages for income-eligible first-time home buyers.

4) Down Payment Assistance: down payment and closing cost assistance to lower income first time home buyers.

5) Energy-Efficient Homes Program: additional assistance to FIRST HOMES mortgagees if their home receives a high energy-efficiency rating.

6) HOME Program: grants and low interest loans to encourage the construction or rehabilitation of affordable housing.

7) Home Equity Conversion Mortgage Program: reverse mortgages to enable older home owners to remain in and retain ownership of their homes.

8) Access Independence Program: provides low-interest financing to cover the cost of modifying a home for persons with age or disability related permanent functional limitations.

9) Mortgage Credit Certificates: tax credit for first-time home buyers.

10) Construction Loan Program: below market rate loans to build/rehab affordable 1-4 family homes for low/moderate-income persons.

11) Cooperative Housing Demonstration Program: funding packages for non-profit organizations to develop cooperative housing.

12) Land Bank Program: below market rate loans for purchase or refinancing of undeveloped land to be used for low/moderate-income housing.

13) Housing Equity Pool I and II: funds to purchase Low Income Housing Tax Credits and from developers of affordable rental housing.

14) Low-Income Housing Tax Credit Program: tax credits for owners of rental housing for low-income households.

15) Pre-Development Loan Program: short-term loans to cover pre-development costs for non-profit developers.

16) Preservation Loan Fund: below-market rate loans to preserve affordability of existing subsidized rental housing.

17) Emergency Housing Assistance Program: assistance to qualified low-income households facing a temporary housing crisis.

18) Employer Assisted Housing: employer resources combine with existing programs to provide affordable housing for employees.

19) Opening Doors: pilot program to assist the minority community with buying their first home.

20) Extra assistance: Lower-income buyers may be eligible for deferred payment second mortgages of up to 10 percent of the purchase price of the home they buy.

South Carolina

South Carolina State Housing Finance and Development Authority, 919 Bluff Road, Columbia, SC 29201; 803-734-2000.

1) Multi-Family Development Programs: construction loans to construct houses for rental to low and moderate-to-low income persons.

2) Moderate Rehabilitation Program: mortgage financing for the upgrade of substandard rental housing.

3) Home Ownership Mortgage Purchase Program: below market rate financing for income-eligible home buyers.

4) Community Home Ownership Opportunity Partnership (CHOP): below market rate

financing for purchase of affordable homes by qualified borrowers in conjunction with local communities' contributions.

5) Low-Income Housing Tax Credit Program: tax credits for developers of low-income rental housing.

6) Section 8 Certificates and Vouchers: rental assistance for low-income households.

7) Section 8 Moderate Rehabilitation Program: rent subsidies for low-income households.

9) HOME Program: affords state and local governments the flexibility to fund a wide range of low income housing activities.

South Dakota

South Dakota Housing Development Authority, P.O. Box 1237, Pierre, SD 57501; 605-773-3181.

1) Mortgage Assistance Program: provides down payment and closing cost assistance.

2) Mortgage Assistance Grant Program: provides an interest free second loan of up to $1,000 to assist borrowers with down payment and closing costs.

3) Single Family Homeownership Program: low-rate financing for eligible single families to build, rehabilitate or buy homes.

4) Multi-Family Bond Financing Program: permanent and temporary mortgage loans to finance the construction of multi-family housing.

5) Low-Income Housing Tax Credit Program: federal tax credits for developers/ owners of low-income housing.

6) Emergency Shelter Grants Program: financing of shelters for homeless and special needs households.

7) HOME Rental Rehab Program: financing for owners of rental properties occupied by low-income households.

8) Step Rate Mortgage Program: provides low-interest mortgage loans to qualified, first time homebuyers.

9) HOME Programs: designed to encourage creative ways to produce housing for low income families.

10) 100 Cooperative Home Improvement Program: low interst loans for up to seven years for the improvement, repair, or addition to the borrower's home.

11) Sweat Equity Down Payment Program: provides short term sweat equity loans for outside work which cannot be completed during the fall or winter seasons.

Tennessee

Tennessee Housing Development Agency, 404 James Robertson Parkway, Suite 1114, Nashville, TN 37243-0900; 615-741-4979, TDD 800-228-THDA.

1) Home Ownership Program: reduced interest rate loans to low- and moderate-income families.

2) Veterans: permanent mortgage financing available for disabled Veterans who need specially designed homes.

3) Rental Rehabilitation: lower-than-market loans to owners of rental property to rehabilitate units. This program also offers a grant of up to $5000 per unit to keep the cost of rehabilitation down.

4) Owner-Built Homes: permanent financing for homes built by the owners. Sweat equity serves as the downpayment.

5) Turn Key III: subsidized rent to bring economically viable residents into personal home ownership.

6) Section 8 Rental Assistance Program: subsidy funds to low-income households.

7) Technical Assistance Program: technical assistance to public and private sponsors of low- and moderate-income housing.

8) Low-Income Housing Tax Credit: tax credits for owners of low-income housing.

9) Moderate Rehabilitation Program: incentives for property owners to upgrade substandard rental units to be occupied by low-income tenants qualifying for rent subsidies.

10) HOUSE Program: funding for special needs housing projects.

Texas

Texas Department of Housing and Community Affairs, PO Box 13941 811 Barton Springs Road, Suite 100, Austin, TX 78711; 512- 475-3800.

1) Mortgage Credit Certificate Program: up to $2,000 of federal tax credits for first-time home owners.

2) Low-Income Rental Housing Tax Credit: federal tax credits for those who wish to acquire, construct, or rehabilitate rental housing for low-income families.

3) Single-Family Bond Program: low-rate financing for low/moderate income first-time home buyers.

4) Section 8 Housing Assistance Program: rental assistance via subsidies for low-income households.

5) Multi-Family Bond Program: finances below market loans to non-profit and for profit developers of apartment projects that agree to set aside 20% for rental to low income families.

6) Down Payment Assistance Program: Assits low income families with interest free loans of up to $1,500 to be used for a downpayment on a home purchased through the First Time Homebuyer Program.

7) Home Improvement Loan Program: provides interest free loans of up to $15,000

to low and very low income homeowners for improving or protecting the livability of their residence.

8) Housing Trust Fund: assistance for persons and families of low and very low income in financing, rehabilitating and aquiring safe housing.

9) HOME Program: funds are used to address the state's most critical housing needs which include owner occupied and rental housing rehabilitation and tenant-based assistance.

10) Community Development Block Grant: assists local governments in the development of viable communities.

11) Community Development Fund: provides funds for public facility improvements and housing rehabilitation.

12) Emergency Shelter Grants Program: grants are awarded to counties and nonprofit organizations to assist with the prevention of homelessness, this includes shelters and services.

13) Permanent Housing For Handicapped and Homeless Persons: provides assistance to help establish housing for for homeless individuals with mental disabilities or other handicaps.

14) Weatherization Assistance Program: helps low income households make their homes energy efficient.

Utah

Utah Housing Finance Agency, 554 South 300 East, Salt Lake City, UT 84147-0069; 801-521-6950 or 800-284-6950, TDD 801-298-9484.

1) Single-Family Home Ownership Program: money to first-time home buyers or home buyers in targeted areas with required downpayment.

Vermont

Vermont Housing Finance Agency, One Burlington Sq., PO Box 408, Burlington, VT 05402; 802-864-5743, 1-800-222-VFHA.

1) Mortgage Plus: federal income tax credit for up to 20% of interest on a home loan.

2) Mortgages for Vermonters: low-interest mortgages for first-time buyers.

3) Energy-Rated Homes of Vermont Mortgage Program: money to modify homes to make them energy efficient.

4) New Home Financing: low-rate financing for qualified borrowers purchasing new homes.

5) Mobile Home Financing: mortgage financing for modular or permanently fixed mobile homes; financing for non-profit or tenant acquisition of mobile home parks.

6) Perpetually Affordable Housing Program: low-rate financing for non-profit housing developers providing home ownership opportunities that will remain affordable over the long term.

7) Rural Vermont Mortgage: low-rate financing for low-income households in rural areas.

8) Home Energy/Improvement Loan Program: low-rate loans for low/ moderate-income home owners to make energy improvements.

9) Multi-Family Financing: financing to eligible housing sponsors who wish to build or renovate low/moderate-income rental or cooperative housing.

10) Low-Income Housing Tax Credit Program: tax credits for developers/ owners of rental housing for low-income households.

11) Vermont Housing Ventures: low-rate financing to cover pre-development costs of locally based non-profit housing.

12) Housing Foundation, Inc.: purchases and preserves housing units threatened with conversion to unsubsidized stock; aids in tenant acquisition of mobile home parks.

13) Housing Vermont: develops affordable housing in partnership with non-profit organizations throughout the state.

14) Vermont Home Mortgage Guarantee Board (VHMGB): low-cost mortgage insurance for low/moderately-priced housing.

15) Vermont Housing and Conservation Board: grants and loans to projects which meet both affordable housing and conservation goals.

16) ENABLE Program: low-rate loans to finance modifications designed to make housing more accessible for the elderly and disabled.

Vermont State Housing Authority, P.O. Box 397, Montpelier, VT 05601-0397; 802-828-3295.

Virginia

Virginia Housing Development Authority, 601 S. Belvedere Street, Richmond, VA 23220; 804-782-1986.

1) Home Mortgage Loan Program: below-market loans to eligible home buyers with required downpayment.

2) Virginia Housing Fund: flexible, below-market rate loans for lower-income people.

3) Home Rehabilitation Loan Program: loans at 8% interest for 6 months to 8-year terms.

4) Targeted Area Program: below-market loans with low downpayments for purchasers of homes in designated areas.

5) Multi-Family Loan Program: below-market loans to developers of low/moderate-price rental housing.

6) Low-Income Housing Tax Credit Program: federal tax credits for owners of low-income rental housing.

7) Rental Rehabilitation Program: grants for up to 50% of rehab costs for low-income rental housing.

8) Section 8 Rent Subsidy Programs: subsidies to assist low-income households in meeting rental housing costs.

9) Joint Program for Housing Persons with Mental Disabilities and Recovering Substance Abusers: below-market loans to assist non-profit sponsors in developing supportive housing facilities.

10) Rental Assistance Programs: provide low and moderate income families and individuals with rents they can afford.

11) FHA Plus Program: assists qualified borrowers who need down payment assistance.

Washington

Washington State Housing Finance Commission, 1000 Second Avenue, Suite 2700, Seattle, WA 98104-1046; 206-464-7139 or 800-767-4663.

1) Streamlined Tax-Exempt Placement (STEP): provides tax-exempt financing to nonprofit and for profit organizations for new construction or purchasing of residential housing.

2) Multi-Family Program: financing to developers of multi-family projects where at least 20% or more units will be rented to lower- to mid-income persons, the elderly or the handicapped.

3) Low-Income Housing Tax Credit Program: federal tax credits to developers/owners of low-income rental housing.

4) House Key Program: below market rate loans for income-eligible first time home buyers and buyers of residences in targeted areas.

5) Housing for the Elderly Program: tax-exempt financing for group homes, congregate housing, and retirement housing (non-medical).

6) Multi-Family Tax Exempt Bond Financing Program: tax exempt financing for developers/owners of multi-family housing with a percentage set aside for low-income households; new construction, acquisition and rehabilitation.

West Virginia

West Virginia Housing Development Fund, 814 Virginia St., East, Charleston, WV 25301; 304-345-6475 or 800-933-9843.

1) Mortgage Credit Certificate Program: federal tax credit for home buyers.

2) Single Family Mortgage Program: financing for single family homes with deferred payment loans to pay downpayment and closing costs.

3) Multi-Family Construction Loan Incentive Program: construction financing for sponsors of low-income multi-family housing.

4) Building Revitalization/Reutilization Program: funds for rehabilitation of existing downtown residential and commercial buildings.

5) Emergency Shelters Program: financing for construction, rehabilitation, and acquisition of shelters.

6) Community Provider Financing Program: low-interest loans to non-profits for financing the acquisition or construction of health facilities.

7) Home Rehab Program: low-cost loans to repair flooded homes.

8) Low-Income Housing Tax Credit Program: federal tax credits for developers/owners of low-income multi-family housing.

9) Land Development Program: low-rate financing for developers of raw land to support housing developments.

10) Rental Rehab Program: grants for upgrading rental units for low-income households.

11) HOME Program: funding for housing for low income families.

Wisconsin

Wisconsin Division of Housing, Department of Administration, 101 East Wilson Street, 4th Floor, Madison, WI 53702-0001 or P.O. Box 8944, Madison WI 53708-8944; 608-266-0288.

1) HOME Program: low interest, fixed rate, 30-year loans.

2) Lease Purchase Program: allows nonprofit organizations to aquire affordable single family housing and lease it to a low income home buyer who will purchase it within three years.

3) DEER Program: money to non-profits to acquire and rehabilitate older single-family and two-family homes with special emphasis on energy conservation. Restored homes are then sold.

4) Rental Housing Programs: financing of rental housing for low-and moderate-income individuals and families, elderly and disabled.

5) Community Housing Alternatives Program: loans for construction, purchase or rehabilitation of projects to house those who are chronically disabled due to mental illness, development disability, physical disability, or alcohol- or other drug-related dependence, or those over 60 years of age.

6) Rental Rehabilitation Program: money for rehabilitation of rental units for low-income households.

7) Low-Income Housing Tax Credits: federal tax credits for low-income rental housing in Wisconsin.

8) WHEDA Foundation Grants: grants to non-profit housing project sponsors.

9) Business Development Bond Program: financing for small- and medium-sized businesses.

10) Linked Deposit Loan Program: loans to businesses that are more than 50% owned by women or minorities.

11) Multifamily Mortgage Programs: federally tax exempt and taxable financing for the development of multifamily rental housing.

12) Credit Relief Outreach Program: agricultural related families can receive interest rate reduction and loan guarantees of up to $20,000.

13) Home Improvement Loan Program: below-market financing for low/moderate income home owners to make eligible home improvements such as energy-conserving improvements.

14) Section 8 Rent Subsidy Program: rent subsidies for low/moderate income rental households.

15) Small Business Loan Guarantee Program: funding necessary to guarantee conventional loans needed by businesses to fulfill awarded contracts.

16) Neighborhood Housing Program Fund: supports development and improvement of low-income housing and urban and rural neighborhood revitalization.

17) Elderly Housing Program Fund: supports development and improvement of non-institutional housing facilities for frail or low-income elderly persons.

18) Wisconsin Partnership for Housing Development: development financing and technical assistance to community-based organizations providing housing to low-income households.

Wyoming

Wyoming Community Development Authority, 123 S. Durbin St., P.O. Box 634, Casper, WY 82602; 307-265-0603.

Funding for single-family homes, multi-family projects, and economic development.

1) Single Family Mortgage Program: low-rate financing for first-time home buyers.

2) Section 8 Rental Assistance Program: certificates and vouchers to assist low-income rental households.

3) HOME Program: funds for the development of affordable housing for low and very low income households.

4) Urban Homesteading Program: sale of deteriorating government-owned residences to "urban homesteaders" who agree to restore and live in them.

5) WCDA CDBG Revolving Loan Fund: for housing rehabilitation that benefits low/moderate income households.

6) Low-Income Tax Credit Program: tax credits for owners of rental housing affordable to low-income households.

Gardening

* Alternative Farming Systems

Alternative Farming Systems
U.S. Department of Agriculture
10301 Baltimore Blvd.
Beltsville, MD 20705   301-504-5204
This center covers organized farming or gardening that includes low-input, sustainable, or regenerative agriculture. Conservation tillage and other cultivation practices, such as intercropping, crop rotation, and use of green manures, are also covered. You can receive a listing of information products that are available. These products are free of charge. Most of the publications on the list are available in either hardcopy or electronic format. A few are available only in one or the other. In addition, all electronically available publications are available on the Internet via National Agricultural Library's (NAL) Gopher: <gopher.nalusda.gov>; Alternative Farming Systems Information Center's (AFSIC) World Wide Web Page: <http://www.inform.umd.edu/EdRes/Topic/AgrEnv/AltFarm>; or NAL's Electronic Bulletin Board System: Agricultural Library Forum (ALF), 301-504-6510.

An example of publications available include:
Acid Rain (QB 95-03) 1995, 132pp.
Alternative Crops (QB 93-53), 1993, 34pp.
Double Cropping and Interplanting (QB 94-51), 1994, 111pp.
Fish Farming (QB 94-44), 1994, 32pp.
Irrigating Efficiently (QB 94-35), 1994, 64pp.
Nonpoint Source Pollution Issues (QB 95-01), 1995, 51pp.
Precision Farming (AT 95-01), 1994, 15pp.
Resource Guide to Growing and Using Herbs (SBR 93-01), 15pp.
Sustainable or Alternative Agriculture (QB 93-03), 84pp.

* Aquaculture Information Center

Aquaculture Information Center
National Agricultural Library
U.S. Department of Agriculture (USDA)
10301 Baltimore Blvd.   301-504-5558
Beltsville, MD 20705-2351   Fax: 301-504-5472
                                         E-mail: aic@nalusda.gov
Major subject areas covered by the Aquaculture Information Center (AIC) are: controlled cultivation of fish, shellfish, and aquatic plants; diseases; nutrition; culturing systems; water quality; financial assistance; legislation and regulations; and economics and marketing of aquaculture products. AIC serves as a national depository of aquaculture information materials. The center publishes cooperative bibliographies and factsheets. Publications are free of charge and currently include:
Aquaculture (July 1992)
Aquaculture and Hydroponics (August 1993)
Aquaculture in Intensive Systems: 1989-1994
Potentials of Aquaculture: An Overview and Bibliography (1989)
Recirculation - Aeration Bibliography for Aquaculture (1993)
Water Quality in Aquaculture Ponds (June 1992)

* Botanic Garden: 10,000 Plant Species

U.S. Botanic Garden
Office of Director
2245 First St., SW
Washington, DC 20024   202-225-8333
The Botanic Garden is a living museum open daily, free of charge, containing noteworthy collections, including Economic Plants, Cycads, Orchids, Begonias, Cacti and Succulents, Carnivorous Plants, Bromeliads, Ferns, Roses, Palms, and other miscellaneous tropical and subtropical plants, many of which are rare species. There are special displays during most of the year, and in their proper seasons banana, papaya, orange, lemon, tangerine, kumquat, averrhoa, coffee, and surinam cherry are displayed in luxuriant fruiting. Included in its glasshouse collections are many of the plants brought to the U.S. Botanic Garden from the Wilkes Expedition to the South Seas in 1842. The entire collection of the Garden includes over 10,000 species and varieties of plant growth. The collection attracts many visitors annually, including botanists, horticulturists, students, and garden club members. The horticultural and botanical library is available by appointment only.

* Botanical Garden Tours

Public Programs Office
U.S. Botanic Garden
245 1st St., SW
Washington, DC 20024   202-226-4082
The Botanic Garden is open to the public from 9 a.m. to 9 p.m. daily June through August, and from 9 a.m. to 5 p.m. the rest of the year. Tours are given to interested groups, including garden clubs, professional organizations, and school children.

* Botanical Specimens for Plant Breeders

U.S. Botanic Garden
Office of Director
2245 First St., SW
Washington, DC 20024   202-225-8333
Though not operated as a scientific institution, the Botanic Garden does make educational facilities available for study to students, botanists, and floriculturists on many rare and interesting botanical specimens. Working with scientists, the Garden grows, displays, and keeps records on significant botanical collections for study and for exchange with other institutions. The Garden is a gene pool resource for plant breeders. It is also involved in the preservation of rare or endangered plants and is actively building and displaying economic plants. Every year botanical specimens are received from all over the world with requests for identification, and one of the services offered by the Garden to the public is the identification of such specimens and the furnishing of information relating to the proper care for them, and methods of growing them.

* Christmas Tree Diseases

Superintendent of Documents
Government Printing Office   202-512-1800
Washington, DC 20402   Fax: 202-512-2250
Tree publications are listed, including those of interest to tree growers and the lumber industry. Also featured is a guide to Christmas Tree diseases and books listing the tropical timbers of the world. The list of publications is available free of charge. You can request a copy from the office listed above or by using the Government Printing Office Fax Watch System by calling 202-512-1716 and requesting document number 086.

* Compost and Improved Soil

Soil Microbial Systems
U.S. Department of Agriculture
Building 318, Room 108 BARC-E
Beltsville, MD 20705   301-504-8163
This office provides technical assistance on the production and use of compost, soil, and microbes. The information from this office is of a highly scientific nature. More practical information is available through your local county extension service. To find the office nearest you, call 202-720-4651.

* Desert and Tropical Plants Museum

The Conservatory
Maryland Avenue
1st to 2nd Sts., SW
Washington, DC 20024   202-225-6647
The Conservatory houses permanent collections of tropical, subtropical, and desert plants in an exhibition area of 38,000 square feet. Just across from the Conservatory on Independence Avenue, the Frederic Auguste Bartholdi Park features displays of bulbs, annuals, and perennials.

* Environmental Impact on Plant Species

U.S. Botanic Garden
Office of Director
2245 First St., SW
Washington, DC 20024   202-225-8333

In these times of global changes, with climate changes, the greenhouse effect, and the need for species diversity, strategically placed at the foot of our nation's Capitol, the Botanic Garden's spectacular displays of significant plant collections can have a strong impact on people's awareness of the environment.

* Gardening and Plant Propagation Workshops

Poplar Point
700 Howard Road, SE
Anacostia, DC 20020   202-563-2220

The Poplar Point Production Facility is a nursery and greenhouse range responsible for plant production for the U.S. Botanic Garden and the entire Capitol Hill Complex. The facility is open by appointment and occasionally tours of the facility are conducted for the public. Next year a new nursery will be built and many hands-on classes and workshops on gardening and plant propagation will be held there.

* Gypsy Moth Control

Printing and Distribution Management Branch
Animal and Plant Health Inspection Service (APHIS)
U.S. Department of Agriculture
4700 River Rd.
Riverdale, MD 20737   301-734-7799

The following publication is available free of charge from APHIS: *Don't Move the Gypsy Moth* (July l985). This tells how to make sure outdoor household articles don't spread gypsy moths.

* Horticulture

Reference Desk
National Agricultural Library (NAL)
U.S. Department of Agriculture
10301 Baltimore Blvd.
Beltsville, MD 20705   301-504-5479

Most questions concerning horticultural or botanical questions, economic botany, wild plants of possible use, herbs, bonsai, and floriculture can be answered here. For more information you will be referred to the appropriate information center depending on the nature of your interests.

* Horticultural Classes: Medicinal Plants to Lawn Care

Public Programs Office
U.S. Botanic Garden
245 1st St., SW
Washington, DC 20024   202-226-4082

Horticultural classes are held throughout the year on timely subjects related to botanical, horticultural, and environmental interests. Many leading scientists are featured as lecturers and all classes are free of charge. Classes consist of a lecture incorporating slides or demonstrations, tours or workshops. Some examples of recent classes include Fall Lawn Care, Decorating With Exotics, Native Medicinal Plants, and The Dynamics of Horticultural Therapy. A calendar of all classes is available.

* Indoor and Outdoor Insects Identification

Contact your local USDA
Extension Service Agent

Technical assistance is available to help you identify and eliminate any problems you may have which are caused by insects and bugs. You are encouraged to catch one of the insects causing the problem and send it in for analysis. Contact your local Extension Service for more information. To find the extension service nearest you, call 202-720-4651.

* Landscaping

Landscape Architect
Engineering Division
Soil Conservation Service
U.S. Department of Agriculture (USDA)
6129 South Building
Washington, DC 20250   202-720-6858

Assistance is available to help anyone with landscaping-related problems from your local U.S. Department of Agriculture (USDA) Extension Service agents. Help is also available to those having problems with larger projects involving conservation. Contact the above office.

* Lawn Care Pesticides

U.S. General Accounting Office (GAO)
P.O. Box 6015   202-512-6000
Gaithersburg, MD 20884-6015   Fax: 301-258-4066

The professional lawn care business has developed into a billion dollar industry as more people have turned to such companies for lawn maintenance. To create beautiful lawns free of weeds and pests, lawn care companies rely on chemical pesticides. Many homeowners purchase this service, while others purchase and apply these pesticides themselves. Concerns have been raised about protecting the public from exposure to the risk of lawn care pesticides. The General Accounting Office reviewed the information that lawn care pesticides industry — manufacturers, distributors, and professional applicators — provides to the public about the safety of its products, federal enforcement actions taken against lawn care pesticide safety advertising claims, and the reregistration status of 34 lawn care pesticides. The first copy of this GAO report is free. Additional copies are $2. Orders for 100 or more copies mailed to a single address are discounted 25%.

* National Arboretum

U.S. National Arboretum
3501 New York Ave.
Washington, DC 20002   202-245-2726

Various woody ornamental and outdoor plants are grown and cared for on the 444 acres comprising the U.S. National Arboretum. Admission and parking are free, and guided tours for 10 or more are available with 3 weeks advance notice. Many free classes are offered, along with many special events and functions associated with gardening and growing plants. A free monthly newsletter lists the monthly calendar.

* National Arboretum Library

Administration Building
U.S. National Arboretum Library
3501 New York Ave., NE
Washington, DC 20002   202-475-4828

The library contains a collection of several thousand botanical and horticultural works. Covering the range of plant sciences from taxonomy to home gardening, this collection is particularly strong in floras of the world and books on bonsai, herbs, and ornamental plant production. About 175 journals are on display in the Library's reading room, with another 300 journals in the bookstacks. The Arboretum Library's hours are 8:30 am to 4:30 pm, Tuesdays and Thursdays, by appointment only.

* Patents on Seeds

Plant Variety Protection Office
Commodities Scientific Support Division
AMS
National Agricultural Library (NAL), Room 500
Beltsville, MD 20705-2351   301-504-5518

Unique seeds, with few exceptions, that are sexually reproduced can be protected by patents. The protection, which extends for 18 years, provides owners with exclusive rights to sell, reproduce, export, and produce the seed.

* Pest and Weed Control

Superintendent of Documents
U.S. Government Printing Office   202-512-1800
Washington, DC 20402   Fax: 202-512-2250

The following publications concerning pest and weed control are available from the Government Printing Office. For a complete listing of all titles available, including order numbers and prices, you can call the Government Printing Office Fax Watch at 202-512-1716 and follow the voice prompts to request document number 227.

Christmas Tree Pest Manual, (1983), #001-001-0064106, $14. Provides a "hands on" approach to the identification and control of various Christmas tree pests. The book is illustrated with color photographs.

How to Control House and Stable Flies Without Using Pesticides, (1994), #001-000-04604-7, $1. Advises on the control of the house fly and the stable fly with minimum use of insecticides.

Pesticide Containers: A Report to Congress, (1992), #055-000-00405-6, $15. Investigates the options for encouraging or requiring the return, refill, and reuse of pesticide containers; ways of facilitating the removal of residues from the containers; and the use of bulk storage facilities to reduce the number of pesticide containers requiring disposal.

Housing and Real Estate

Protect Yourself From Pesticides: Guide for Pesticide Handlers, (1994), #055-000-00467-6, $6.50. Presents all the information required for training pesticide handlers under the Environmental Protection Agency Worker Protection Standard.

* Plant and Flower Shows

Office of the Director
U.S. Botanic Garden
245 1st St., SW
Washington, DC 20024   202-225-8333

Spectacular seasonal plant and flower shows are scheduled throughout the year. The Annual Spring Flower Show features spring flowering plants and is held from Palm Sunday through Easter Sunday. The Summer Terrace Display is held on the patio in front of the Conservatory from late May through September. Hundreds of flowering and foliage plants in hanging baskets highlight this event. Mid-November through Thanksgiving Day features The Annual Chrysanthemum Show. The Annual Poinsettia Show takes place from mid-December through the Christmas holidays. The Garden also hosts various plant and flower shows sponsored by area garden clubs and plant societies each year. Each show has a theme and offers excellent ideas for new plants, innovative garden designs, and uses state-of-the-art gardening techniques. Special exhibits are prepared for the U.S. Botanic Garden. Call 202-225-7099 for more information about shows.

* Plant Care and Botanical Garden Calendar

Public Programs Office
U.S. Botanic Garden
245 1st St., SW
Washington, DC 20024   202-226-4082

Handouts are provided on plant culture, sources for plants and care for certain plants. A pamphlet offers a self-guided tour of the Garden. Brochures including schedules for shows and horticultural classes, and historical information about the Garden are also available.

* Plant Care Telephone Line and Information Service

Plant Information Service
U.S. Botanic Garden
245 1st St., SW
Washington, DC 20024   202-226-4082

The Garden serves as a center for plant information offering a telephone information service as well as responding to written inquiries Monday through Friday from 9:00 a.m. to 11:30 a.m.

* Plant Protection and Rescue Center

U.S. Botanic Garden
Office of Director
2245 First St., SW
Washington, DC 20024   202-225-8333

Serving as a Plant Rescue Center for the U.S. Department of Agriculture's (USDA) Animal and Plant Health Inspection Service, the Botanic Garden is legally obligated to care for and preserve the multitude of protected plants it receives that are illegally shipped into the U.S. Through this program, the Garden helps visitors recognize the value of preservation and protection of plants.

* Plants: Research and Reference

National Arboretum Library
3501 New York Ave., NE
Washington, DC 2000   202-245-2726

This library provides information on many aspects of indoor plants and gardening. Due to a limited staff, most calls will be referred to their local cooperative extension service where trained horticulturists and volunteer master gardeners can answer your questions. To find the extension service nearest you, call 202-720-4651.

* Seed Quality and Inspection Labs

Federal Seed Lab
U.S. Department of Agriculture
Beltsville, MD 20705   301-504-8089

The federal government can test seeds to determine their quality and whether they are free from contamination. They will also prosecute any agent that transfers contaminated or mislabeled seeds from state to state. Seeds are examined by or at a state agent's request, and there may be some fee involved.

* Sick House Plants, Pets, Trees, and Lawns

Contact your local U.S. Department of Agriculture
Extension Service Agent

Free technical assistance is available to help diagnose and cure diseases of plants and animals. Services range from telephone consultations and free literature, to analyzing your pets' stools or your plants' leaves for disease. To find the extension service nearest you, call 202-720-4651.

* Solar Greenhouses

Superintendent of Documents
U.S. Government Printing Office   202-512-1800
Washington, DC 20402   Fax: 202-512-2250

Solar Greenhouses and Sunspaces: Lessons Learned, is a 35-page book available from the Government Printing Office which presents information from the experiences of 200 of 2,200 grantees who studied, built, managed, and improved greenhouses or sunspaces. Six major categories are covered: design; construction tips; management; maintenance and safety; agriculture; greenhouse construction workshops; and information sources. The order number is #061-000-00622-2, and the cost is $2.50.

* Sustainable Agriculture Network (SAN)

Gabriel Hegyes, SAN Coordinator
Alternative Farming System Information Center, Room 304
National Agricultural Library/ARS
U.S. Department of Agriculture
10301 Baltimore Blvd.   301-504-2351
Beltsville, MD 20705-2351   Fax: 301-504-6409
                                  Internet: gopher.ces.ncsu.edu

The Sustainable Agriculture Network (SAN) is a cooperative effort of university, government, business, and nonprofit organizations dedicated to the exchange of scientific and practical information on sustainable agricultural systems. It is a network supporting the exchange of information with a variety of users. The networking takes many forms: print, meetings, and electronic access. You will have access to SAN databases including SARE/ACE Research Reports; summaries of the projects funded by the USDA/CSRS Sustainable Agriculture Research and Education program; The Directory, a listing of detailed characteristics by individuals and organizations that are willing to share their expertise in sustainable agriculture; *Showcase*, annotated bibliography of educational and informational materials; *Managing Cover Crops Profitably*, a guide for farmers looking for alternatives to chemical fertility and weed control; Discussion Group, members who share sources of information and help answer each other's questions (subscribe sanet-mg); and information on more Internet resources (send internet exploring-internet to the address: almanac@esusda.gov). For more information or help accessing SAN, contact the office above.

* Tracer Bulletins to Gardening References

Science and Technology Division
Reference Section
Library of Congress
Washington, DC 20540   202-707-5580

An informal series of reference guides are issued free from the Science and Technology Division under the general title, *LC Science Tracer Bullet*. These guides are designed to help readers locate published material on subjects about which they have only general knowledge. New titles in the series are announced in the weekly Library of Congress *Information Bulletin* that is distributed to many libraries. The following is a list of *Tracer Bullets* currently available:

80-1	*The Green Revolution*
81-2	*Medicinal Plants*
81-15	*History of American Agriculture*
82-2	*Gardening*
82-6	*Biological Control of Insects*
83-5	*Plant Exploration and Introduction*
84-2	*Edible Wild Plants*
85-1	*Herbs and Herb Gardening*
85-2	*Landscape Gardening*
85-10	*Rose Culture*
86-3	*Jojoba and Other Oilseed Plants*
86-4	*Composite Materials*
88-5	*Soil Erosion*
89-6	*Endangered Species (plants)*
90-4	*Poisonous Plants*

*U.S. Department of Agriculture (USDA) Plant Hardiness Zone Map
Superintendent of Documents
U.S. Government Printing Office   202-512-1800
Washington, DC 20402   Fax: 202-512-2250

This map consists of a waterproof chart showing ten different zones, each of which represents an area of winter hardiness of the plants of agriculture and natural landscape. It also introduces Zone 11 to represent areas that have average annual minimum temperatures above 40 degrees Fahrenheit (44 degrees Celsius) and that are therefore essentially frost free. The stock number is #001-000-04550-4, and the price is $6.50. Other publications available from the Government Printing Office include:

Selecting and Growing House Plants, #001-000-00863-3, $1
Growing Veggies in the Home Garden, #001-000-04454-1, $2.25

Mini Gardens for Veggies, #001-000-3834-6, $2.25
Mulches for Your Garden, #001-000-01172-3, $1

* Wood Pests
Public Affairs Office
U.S. Forest Service
U.S. Department of Agriculture (USDA)
P.O. Box 96090
Washington, DC 20090-6090   202-720-3760
OR: Your local Forest Service or Extension Office

The USDA provides technical assistance for insects and diseases to wood, whether it is in use or stored, wood products, or urban trees. All insect and disease suppression projects must meet specific criteria for federal participation.

Education
School: Grades K-12

* *See also Careers and Workplace Chapter*
* *See also Drugs and Chemical Dependence Chapter*
* *See also Weather and Maps Chapter*
* *See also Current Events and Homework Chapter*

Studies and new assessments of American education abound. Take advantage of the numerous clearinghouses which are excellent starting points for information. Resources on pre-school and early childhood development are sprinkled here. Vocational education is included in the next section on postsecondary education. Students and teachers alike will find very relevant information in the Current Events and Homework Chapter toward the end of the book. And, of course, additional classroom materials and lesson plans are identified throughout the book.

* Academic Affairs
Academic Affairs
Veterans Health Administration
U.S. Department of Veterans Affairs (VA)
810 Vermont Ave., NW, Room 876
Washington, DC 20420   202-565-7091
The VA conducts the largest coordinated health professions education and training efforts of its kind in the U.S. Its purpose is to assure high quality health care for veterans and to develop a sufficient number of all categories of professional and other health personnel. For more information contact the office above.

* Alternative versus Traditional Schools
ERIC Clearinghouse on Educational Management
5207 University of Oregon
1787 Agate St.
Eugene, OR 97403-5207   503-346-5043
Subject areas include all aspects of the administration, leadership, finance, governance, and structure of public and private education organizations at the elementary, middle, and secondary levels, including facility planning, design, construction, equipment and furnishing, and maintenance; and pre-service and in-service preparation of administrators. Topics covered include the social, technological, political, and legal contexts of education organizations, and of State and Federal programs and policies, and traditional and alternative schools.

* America Goes Back to School
Information Resource Center
U.S. Department of Education
600 Independence Ave. SW   800-USA-LEARN
Washington, DC 20202   202-401-2000
The Family Involvement Partnership for Learning is sponsoring America Goes Back to School with hopes of getting communities involved to improve education. The goals of the program are to: improve the basics and core academics; create safe and drug free school environments; make college more accessible; get technology and computers into the classroom as fast as possible; raise standards of achievement and discipline; and connect schools and families with community resources and school-to-work programs.

* American Educators Teaching Abroad
Superintendent of Documents
Government Printing Office (GPO)   202-512-1800
Washington, DC 20402   Fax: 202-512-2250
The United States Information Agency (USIA) publishes many teaching materials, including books, maps, complete teaching modules, and 14 magazines in 20 languages. By law most USIA publications may be distributed only in foreign countries. However, by congressional action, *English Teaching Forum*, a quarterly for English teachers worldwide, published by USIA's English Language Programs Division, is available in the United States through the GPO for $9.50, order #725-001-00000-2.

* American Studies for Foreigners
Division of Study of the U.S.
United States Information Agency
301 Fourth St., SW
Washington, DC 20547   202-619-4562
The Division for the Study of the U.S. promotes foreign education through conferences, seminars, exchange programs for foreign educators, grants, and development of school resource materials. The Academic Specialist Branch provides grants for American teachers to instruct their peers at foreign educational institutions. Contact this office for more information.

* Army Reserve Community Projects: From Baseball to Language Training
Chief of U.S. Army Reserve
Public Affairs, The Pentagon
Washington, DC 20310   703-697-3961
The Army Reserve provides a variety of community services through their special programs. Requests are handled on a case by case basis based on their current ability to help. Projects might involve building a community playground or a baseball field. Through the Adopt-a-School Program, Corps people with special skills or training teach special courses, such as a foreign language or communications, or may be involved in extra-curricular activities. Contact your local Army Reserve headquarters or the above office for further information.

* Arts and Education Linked Through Technology
Scott D. Stone, Director
ARTSEDGE
The Kennedy Center
Washington, DC 20566-0001   202-416-8800
E-mail: stoner@artsedge.kennedy-center.org]
Internet: http/artsedge.kennedy-center.org/db/kc/kc-ed.html
ARTSEDGE represents an investment in the future of the arts in American education. It has been designed to literally place and maintain the arts alongside science, math, and other subject areas among the vast resources of the Internet. ARTSEDGE was established in response to a national advisory group's recommendations to the Secretary of Education for ensuring that the arts are included in national education reform initiatives. ARTSEDGE basic goals are to: develop a cohesive and strong arts education community that learns from each other; showcase contributions of teachers, artist-educators, and others who have demonstrated successful interdisciplinary programs and practices; and to create a central clearinghouse and laboratory that stimulates and supports innovative learning and teaching about the through the arts.

* Arts Education
National Arts Education Research Center
St. Johns University
8000 Utopia Parkway
Jamaica, NY 11439   718-990-6250

Established in 1987 as a joint project of the U.S. Department of Education and the National Endowment for the Arts, the Center develops teaching strategies and curricula in arts education. The Center's research design is unique in that it comprises teacher-centered, classroom based collaborations among teachers, university researchers, professional artists, aestheticians and critics. The Center has a network of more than 60 practicing arts educators in 23 states. Work in the Center focuses on secondary education in music, visual arts and theater arts with a special concentration on interdisciplinary and multicultural studies.

* Arts Education Research Publications

National Arts Education Research Center
School of Music
University of Illinois at Urbana-Champaign
1114 West Nevada Street
Urbana, IL 61801   217-333-1027

While the Center concluded its work in 1991, there are still ten publications available including: *Status of Arts Education in American Public Schools: Summary and Conclusions*; *Dance Education in American Public Schools* (case studies); *Guide to Curriculum Development in Elementary School Drama/Theatre Education*; and others.

* Art Slides, Films, Video Loan Program

Department of Education Resources
National Gallery of Art
Constitution and 6th St., NW
Washington, DC 20565   202-842-6273

Color slide programs, films, and videocassettes are loaned at no cost to schools, libraries, community organizations, and individuals across the nation. The programs deal with a wide range of subjects drawn from the Gallery's permanent collections and special exhibitions. A free catalog listing all free-loan Extension Programs is available.

* Bilingual Education Clearinghouse

National Clearinghouse for Bilingual Education (NCBE)
George Washington University   800-321-6223
1118 22nd Street NW   202-467-0867
Washington, DC 20037   Fax: 800-531-9347

The National Clearinghouse for Bilingual Education (NCBE) provides information to practitioners in the field on curriculum materials, program models, methodologies, and research findings on the education of limited English proficient (LEP) individuals. They also offer an electronic information system, free to users, where you may access a database of curriculum materials and literature related to the education of LEP persons. An electronic bulletin board (800-752-1860) is also available which contains news from federal, state, and local education agencies, conference announcements, and other current information. NCBE also develops and publishes three types of publications: a bimonthly newsletter, occasional papers, and program information guides. Their newsletter, *FORUM*, is available free of charge. Below is a sampling of other publications available through this organization at $3.50 each. The NCBE's on line library can be accessed at http://www.ncbe.gwa.edu

Assessing Language Development in Bilingual Preschool Children
Bilingual Education: A Look to the Year 2000
Bilingualism and Bilingual Education: A Research Prospective
Distance Learning: The Challenge for a Multicultural Society
Family Literacy for Language Minority Families: Issues for Program Implementation
For All Students: Limited English Proficient Students and Goals 2000
Implementing Bilingual Programs is Everybody's Business
Multicultural Education: Strategies for Linguistically Diverse Classrooms
Restructuring the Bilingual Special Education Interface
Whole School Bilingual Education Programs: Approaches for Sound Assessment

* Books and Reading

Center for the Book
Library of Congress
Washington, DC 20540   202-707-5221

A partnership between the federal government and private industry, the Center for the Book works closely with other organizations to explore important issues dealing with books and educational communities. The Center encourages reading and research about books and reading and serves as a catalyst by bringing together authors, publishers, librarians, booksellers, educators, scholars, and readers to discuss common concerns. Each year the Center promotes a theme such as "The Year of the Lifetime Reader," "Explore New Worlds - READ!", "Books Change Lives," and

"Books and Beyond." The Center also honored Thomas Jefferson for his dedication to education in the promotion of liberty. Four primary concerns are: television and the printed word, reading development, international role of the book, and publishing. The center is funded by tax-deductible contributions.

* Braille U.S. Constitution

National Braille Press, Inc.
88 St. Stephen St.
Boston, MA 02115   617-266-6160

Individuals may request free copies of the U.S. Constitution in Braille at the above address.

* Captioned Movies and Videos for the Hearing Impaired

Education Services
4707 140th Ave. N, Suite 105
Clearwater, FL 34622   813-532-0706

This company's captioned film/video program provides a free loan service of educational and theatrical films and videos for various groups to assist deaf/hearing impaired persons in educational and recreational pursuits. Comprehensive, free catalogs list over 3,500 films and videocassettes. Language controlled open-captions (subtitles) appear on each film and video.

* Chapter 1 Education Grants

Office of Elementary and Secondary Education
U.S. Department of Education
600 Independence Ave. SW
Washington, DC 20202-6132   202-260-0820

Chapter 1 provides financial assistance to local school districts to meet the special needs of educationally disadvantaged children who live in areas that have large concentrations of low-income families. Deprived children at the preschool, elementary, and secondary school level are eligible for assistance. In 1992-93 almost 6 million children will participate in the program. The estimated budget for the program is $6.7 billion.

* Children's Literature

Children's Literature Center
National Programs
Library of Congress
Washington, DC 20540   202-707-5535

The Center prepares lists and scholarly bibliographies and provides other reference services for individuals who serve children, including scholars, writers, teachers, librarians, and illustrators. The center also has many publishers' catalogs that list titles to be published in the upcoming year, a wide range of periodicals about children's literature, and lists from rare and used book sellers. The Center can also provide you with reading lists for your children grouped by age and type of literature. *Books for Children*, a guide to reference sources for children's literature published annually for $1 per issue, is available from the Superintendent of Documents, Government Printing Office, Washington, DC 20402; 202-512-1800. Order #030-001-00160-1, $1.00.

* Consumer Publications for Students and Teachers

Office of Information and Public Affairs
U.S. Consumer Product Safety Commission (CPSC)   301-504-0580
Washington, DC 20207   800-638-2772

The Consumer Product Safety Commission (CPSC) has publications available describing some of the common hazards associated with the use of consumer products and recommend ways to avoid these hazards. These are in the form of fact sheets, brochures, and materials developed for use by consumers. CPSC protects the public from 15,000 types of products under the agency's jurisdiction. Publications of interest to teachers would include toy safety, children's safety, playground equipment, poison prevention, fire safety, holiday safety, and arts and crafts. You can request a Publications Listing (Item #107) by phone or mail from the office listed above or one of the Commission's Regional Offices. To order documents through the CPSC fax-on-demand system, call 301-504-0051 from the handset of your fax machine and follow the instructions for ordering. You can obtain news releases and recall information via Internet gopher service at cpsc.gov

* Cooperative Education

United States Agency for International Development (USAID)
Attention: Student Programs Coordinator

Education

Recruitment
Room 1026, SA-1
2401 F St. NW
Washington, DC 20523   703-302-4128

The Cooperative Education Program (Co-op) combines classroom learning with practical, on-the-job experience. It enables the student to apply the theory and skills learned in the classroom to a job situation. In addition to providing students with paid work experience in their field of study, co-ops may have the opportunity for full-time professional employment through non-competitive appointment to government service upon successful completion of their work study program. The program is open to full-time high school, undergraduate and graduate college students in accredited institutions who are working towards a certificate, diploma, or degree. Students must be at least 16 years old, a U.S. citizen, maintain at least a 2.5 grade point average, and pass a background investigation.

* Counseling and Student Services Information

ERIC Clearinghouse on Counseling and Student Services
University of North Carolina at Greensboro
School of Education   800-414-9769
101 Park Building   910-334-4114
Greensboro, NC 27412-5001   Fax: 910-334-4116
                            Internet: ericcass@iris.uncg.edu

Subject areas cover the preparation, practice, and supervision of counselors at all educational levels and in all settings; theoretical development of counseling and guidance; personnel procedures such as testing and interviewing and the analysis and distribution of the resulting information; group work and case work; nature of pupil, student, and adult characteristics; personnel workers and their relation to career planning, family consultations, and student orientation activities. The Center also publishes the quarterly newsletter *CAPS Capsule*. Also ask for the CAPS publication list. One of the most popular CAPS products is the *CounselorQuest*, a compilation of 165 ERIC digests designed to answer counselor's questions on a wide range of subjects. It is available for $19.95.

* Creation and Presentation

National Endowment for the Arts
Nancy Hanks Center
1100 Pennsylvania Ave. NW   202-682-5452
Washington, DC 20506-0001   TDD: 202-682-5496

The Arts Endowment offers assistance for a full range of arts disciplines and types and sizes of organizations involved in the arts. Through its Creation and Presentation theme, the Arts Endowment seeks to nurture American culture in all its variety. Support is available for artistic work of all cultures and periods. This theme recognizes the role of both individuals and organizations in sustaining and making available to the American public our rich cultural legacy and artistic creativity in all their forms. Projects may range from the creation of new works to the presentation of existing works. Criteria considered during the review of applications are artistic excellence and artistic merit, impact of the project, and the ability to carry out the project. Grants generally range from $5,000 to $200,000 and require a match of at least 1 to 1. For more information request a copy of the free publication *Grants to Organizations: Application Guidelines*. Application forms are also available.

* Creative and Analytical Thinking Skills

Commissioner of Patents and Trademarks
Patent and Trademark Office
U.S. Department of Commerce
2121 Crystal Dr., Crystal Park Two, Suite 0100
Arlington, VA 22202   703-305-8292/8341

Project XL is an outreach program of the U.S. Patent and Trademark Office designed to encourage the development of inventive thinking and problem-solving skills through: designing national and regional workshops which "teach teachers to teach" creative thinking; creating special teaching materials and lecture kits which stress the importance of creativity and problem-solving skills; partnering with the National Inventive Thinking Association and other private and public organizations, to promote the teaching of creative thinking, problem-solving skills and the inventing process, throughout America's public and private schools; and encouraging professionals to support and promote Project XL in their local communities by sponsoring teachers to attend conferences and workshops, participating in the development of school programs and offering assistance in providing creative thinking materials to local area schools. Free copies of the following publications are available: Inventive Thinking Curriculum Project (available in Spanish); Black Innovators in Technology: Inspiring a New Generation; and Inventive Thinking Resources Directory.

* Current Education Information On-Line

OERI Electronic Bulletin Board
Office of Educational Research and Improvement (OERI)   202-219-1526
U.S. Department of Education   BBS: 800-222-4922
555 New Jersey Ave. NW   BBS: 202-219-1511
Washington, DC 20208   Technical Assistance: 202-219-1857

This free service offers a means of obtaining current tables of education data, bulletins, grant information, publication summaries and full texts, legislation, phone directories, links to ERIC and regional labs, and announcements of data tapes and reports. In operation 24 hours a day, this bulletin board can be accessed toll-free, using a modem and almost any type of microcomputer with communications software.

* Curriculum and Student Standards

Consortium for Policy Research in Education
The Eagleton Institute of Politics Rutgers
The State University of New Jersey
86 Clifton Avenue
New Brunswick, NJ 08901   908-932-1331

Major research areas include curriculum and student standards, teacher policies, indicators and monitoring, new roles and responsibilities; and evolution of reform. Publications are available in the following areas: Curriculum and Standards, Educational Indicators, Evolution of the Reform Movement, New Roles and Responsibilities (for education), Teacher Policy. Also available from the Center are numerous publications on school finance.

* Deaf Children's Education

Gallaudet University
800 Florida Avenue, NE
Washington, DC 20002

On agreement with the U.S. Department of Education, Gallaudet operates a model Secondary School for the Deaf for students from the District of Columbia, Maryland, Virginia, West Virginia, Pennsylvania, and Delaware. The University also operates the Kendall Elementary Demonstration School, which experiments in techniques and materials and disseminates information to educational facilities for deaf children. For more information, contact Gallaudet.

* Department of Education Flash Fax

Information Resource Center
U.S. Department of Education
600 Independence Ave. SW   800-USA-LEARN
Washington, DC 20202   202-401-2000

The Information Resource Centers fax information line allows you to access Department of Education information 24 hours a day, 7 days a week. Follow voice prompts to the fax system and to receive an index of available documents.

* Disabilities Information Clearinghouse

Clearinghouse on Disability Information Program
Information and Coordination Staff
U.S. Department of Education
Mary Switzer Building, Room 3132
Washington, DC 20202-2524   202-205-8241

The Clearinghouse responds to inquiries on a wide range of topics. Information is especially strong in the areas of Federal funding for programs serving individuals with disabilities, Federal legislation affecting the disability community, and Federal programs benefitting people with disabilities. Free publications from the Clearinghouse include the following:

The Pocket Guide to Federal Help for Individuals with Disabilities
A Summary of Existing Legislation Affecting Persons with Disabilities - a history of all relevant federal laws enacted through 1987. An update will be published in August 1992.

The Clearinghouse can also steer you to other publications on disabilities and federal programs. The following are some examples:

Adult Basic Education Programs for Disabled Adults.
Educating Students with Learning Problems: A Shared Responsibility.
Free Appropriate Public Education for Students with Handicaps: Requirements under Section 504 of the Rehabilitation Act of 1973.
EEO and Affirmative Action for Employment of Handicapped Persons by Federal Contractors.

Employers are Asking about Accommodating Workers with Disabilities. Identifies common barriers in the workplace and provides suggestions for accommodation.

Fact Sheet No. 7, Handicapped Assistance Loans. Explains the qualifications and conditions for loan approval to small business owners with physical handicaps.

Hiring the Mentally Restored Makes Dollars and Sense. Includes the following publications: Affirmative Action to Employ Mentally Restored People; Eight Questions Employers Ask about Hiring the Mentally Restored; and The Mentally Restored and Work: A Successful Partnership.

A Summary Guide to Social Security and Supplemental Income with Incentives for the Disabled and Blind. This booklet was designed to assist professionals who need to know the work incentive provisions for working with potential or actual SSI or SSDI beneficiaries.

Your Medicare Handbook: A Comprehensive Guide to Your Medicare Hospital and Medical Insurance Benefits.

Facts about Down Syndrome.

Caring about Kids: Helping the Hyperactive Child. Discusses the causes, diagnosis, and treatment of hyperactivity in children.

Periodontal Disease and Diabetes: A Guide for Patients.

Housing and Disabled People--Q and A's for the Disabled.

Statistics Related: SSA Research and Statistics Publications Catalog. Bibliography listing studies conducted or funded by the Social Security Administration. A number of the studies deal with disability related topics.

* Documents on Education

General Accounting Office (GAO) 202-512-6000
P.O. Box 6015 Fax: 301-258-4066
Gaithersburg, MD 20884-6015 TDD: 301-413-0006
Internet: info@www.gao.gov

GAO Reports: Health, Education, Employment, Social Security, Welfare, and Veterans Issues is a 42 page document available from the General Accounting Office (GAO) Document Distribution Center (GAO/HEHS-95-58W). This booklet lists GAO documents on government programs related to health, education, employment, social security, welfare, and veterans issues, which are primarily run by the Departments of Health and Human Services, Labor, Education, and Veterans Affairs. One section identifies reports and testimony issued during the past month and summarizes key products. Another section lists all documents published during the past year, organized chronologically by subject. Order forms are included. A single copy of this document is free of charge, $2.00 each additional copy. Orders for 100 documents or more to be delivered to one address are discounted 25 percent. A check or money order made out to the Superintendent of Documents should accompany orders when necessary.

* Dropout Prevention Demonstrations

National Dropout Prevention Network (NDPN)
Clemson University
205 Martin St., Box 345111 800-656-2599
Clemson, SC 29634-5111 Fax: 803-656-0136

The National Dropout Prevention Network (NDPN) is a membership organization of more than 3,000 teachers, counselors, school administrators, state department of education staff, and business and community leaders who are concerned with dropout issues. The National Dropout Prevention Center (NDPC), a major partner with the Network, provides information and technical assistance to members located in all 50 states and several foreign countries. The NDPC advocates a comprehensive, systematic approach that embraces efforts in the following four areas related to public policy and educational practice: restructuring schooling processes; increasing access to education and employment; forming public-private partnerships; and increasing awareness and developing skills.

* Drug Free Schools and Communities Program

National Programs Division
Drug Free Schools and Communities Staff
Office of Elementary and Secondary Education
U.S. Department of Education
Portals Bldg., 600 Independence Ave. SW
Washington, DC 20202-6123 202-260-3954

This program provides grant funds for several programs designed to promote drug free schools. State Formula Grants fund Governor's funds which go to local governments and non-profit groups drug prevention programs as well as funding teacher training in this area. The State Formula Grants also fund local and state agencies to operate drug education and rehabilitation activities in elementary and secondary schools.

* Drug Prevention Videos

National Programs Division
Drug Planning and Outreach Staff
U.S. Department of Education
Portals Bldg.
600 Independence Ave. SW
Washington, DC 20202 202-260-3954

Eight productions, close-captioned for the hearing impaired, have been designed to inform students, attending kindergarten through 12th grade, about the dangers of drug use in an engaging and entertaining manner. Contact this office for further information on borrowing or purchasing these videos.

* Early Childhood Development and Education

National Institute on Early Childhood Development and Education
Office of Educational Research and Improvement (OERI)
U.S. Department of Education
555 New Jersey Ave. NW
Washington, DC 20208-5520 202-219-1935

The Institute sponsors coordinated and comprehensive research, development, and dissemination activities that will investigate factors, including services and support, in order to improve the learning, cognitive, and social-emotional development, and general well-being of children from birth through age 8, and their families. The Institute supports the following activities aimed at improving early childhood development and education: The Early Childhood Research Working Group, the 21st Century Community Learning Centers Program, The Policy Research Project on Inclusion, The Family School Partnership Program, and The Ready-to-Learn Television Program. Contact this office for information on publications, announcements, and topical papers; presentations; sharing information at meetings and conferences; on-line conferencing; and networking activities with public and private organizations.

* Early Start Program

Office of Migrant Education
Office of Elementary and Secondary Education
U.S. Department of Education
600 Independence Ave. SW
Washington, DC 20202 202-260-1124

This program is designed to provide assistance to states to establish and improve programs for meeting the special educational needs of children of migratory agricultural workers by integrating early childhood education and adult education into a unified program.

* Education and Access

National Endowment for the Arts
Nancy Hanks Center
1100 Pennsylvania Ave. NW 202-682-5438
Washington, DC 20506-0001 TDD: 202-682-5496

The Arts Endowment offers assistance for a full range of arts disciplines and types and sizes of organizations involved in the arts. Through Education and Access, the Endowment supports projects that seek to expose the public to excellence in the arts, while broadening understanding and appreciation of our heritage and culture. Access entails a deliberate effort to reach audiences that have not been reached before or that have been limited in their opportunities. It seeks to expand appreciation for and awareness of art forms to which exposure has been limited or non-existent criteria considered during the review of applications are artistic excellence and artistic merit, impact of the project, and the ability to carry out the project. Grants generally range from $5,000 to $200,000 and require a match of at least 1 to 1. For more information request a copy of the free publication *Grants to Organizations: Application Guidelines.* Application forms are also available.

* Education Grant Programs Guide

Office of Public Affairs
Education Programs Office
U.S. Department of Education
600 Independence Ave. SW
Washington, DC 20202 202-401-0078

Published annually, the *Guide* to U.S. Department of Education programs gives a brief description of the financial assistance programs available through the U.S. Department of Education. Contact this office to receive a copy and have your name added to their mailing list.

Education

* Education Information and Assistance

Office of Public Affairs
U.S. Department of Education
600 Independence Ave. SW
Washington, DC 20202   202-401-1576

If you need information about a particular educational issue, this is a useful starting place.

* Education Information on the Internet

Information Resource Center
U.S. Department of Education   800-872-5327
Washington, DC 20202   202-401-2000

The Internet contains a vast collection of Department of Education Information including general information about the Department of Education, information on key department initiatives, full text publications of interest to teachers, parents and researchers, press releases, and information on grants programs. Access may be obtained via Gopher dot.ed.gov, URL http//www.ed.gov/, FTP ftp.ed.gov (use anonymous log on) and e-mail almanac@inet.ed.gov (message should be "sendcatalog"). More information is available from the Resource Information Center by phone, mail or fax.

* Education Information Processing and Reference

ERIC Processing and Reference Facility
Computer Sciences Corporation
Systems Engineering Division   800-799-ERIC
1301 Piccard Dr., Suite 300   301-258-5500
Rockville, MD 20850-4305   Fax: 301-948-3695
    Internet: ericfac@inet.ed.gov

The ERIC Processing and Reference Facility is a central editorial and computer processing agency that coordinates document processing and database-building activities for ERIC: Performs acquisition, lexicographic, and reference functions; and maintains systemwide quality control standards. The ERIC Facility also prepares Resources in Education (RIE), ERIC Ready Reference, and other products.

* Education of At-Risk Students

National Institute on the Education
of At-Risk Students (ATRISK)
Office of Educational Research and Improvement (OERI)
U.S. Department of Education
555 New Jersey Ave. NW
Washington, DC 20208-5521   202-219-2239

The institute provides national leadership and support for the expansion of research-based knowledge and strategies that will promote excellence and equity in the education of children and youth placed at risk of educational failure. A major component of the At-Risk Institute is the Research and Development Center program with missions created to complement the work of the institute. They are: The Center for Research on the Education of Students Placed at Risk; the National Center for Research on Cultural Diversity and Second Language Learning; The National Resource Center on Education in the Inner Cities; and The National Research Center on the Gifted and Talented. Contact the Institute for more information on grants, competitions, and publications. You can reach the Institute's Internet home page at: http://www.ed.gov/prog-info/At-Risk.

* Education Publications

Superintendent of Documents
U.S. Government Printing Office   202-512-1800
Washington, DC 20402-9371   Fax: 202-512-2250

The following is a sample of publications available from the Government Printing Office. Complete Subject Bibliographies are available at no cost by phone, mail, or through the GPO FaxWatch system at 202-512-1716.

Access to Early Childhood Programs for Children at Risk, $7, #065-000-00649-9
America's High School Sophomores: A Ten Year Comparison, $7.50, #065-000-00572-7
Beginning Reading Instruction Study, $7.50, #065-000-00575-1
Characteristics of the 100 Largest Elementary and Secondary School Districts in the United States, 1991-1992, $4, #065-000-00650-2
Continuing Child Protection Emergency: A Challenge to the Nation, $14, # 017-092-00105-3
Digest of Education Statistics, 1994, $33, #065-000-00693-6
Directory of Public Elementary and Secondary Education Agencies, $25, #065-000-00684-7

Dropout Rates in the United States, 1993, $12, #065-000-00690-1
Drug Abuse Among Minority Youth: Advances in Research and Methodology, $14, #017-024-01506-7
Drug Use Among American High School Seniors, College Students and Young Adults, 1975-1990: Volume 2, College Students and Young Adults, $10, #017-024-01461-3
Educating Young Children Prenatally Exposed to Drugs and at Risk, $6, $065-000-00583-2
Filling the Gaps: An Overview of Data on Education in Grades K Through 12, $4.25, #065-000-00540-9
Goals 2000, Educate America Act, $5.50, #065-000-0017-1
Helping Your Child Learn Science, $36, #065-000-00520-4
Improving America's Schools Act of 1994, $20, #065-000-00172-1
NAEP Writing Report Card, 1992, $14, #065-000-00654-5
Preventing Tobacco Use Among Young People: A Report of the Surgeon General, $19, #017-001-00491-0
Projections of Education Statistics to 2004, $13, #065-000-00608-1
Public School Kindergarten Teachers' Views on Children's Readiness for School, $7.50, #065-000-00596-4
Smoking, Drinking and Illicit Drug Use Among American Secondary School Students, College Students and Young Adults, Volume 1, Secondary School Students, $14, #017-024-01497-4
Soozie and Katy: We're Teaming Up for Your Good Health, $1.25, #027-004-0036-9
Sticking Together 2, Strengthening Linkages and the Transition Between Early Childhood Education and Early Elementary School: Summary of the Second National Policy Forum, $3.25, #065-000-00612-0
Student Data Handbook for Early Childhood, Elementary, and Secondary Education, $20, #065-000-00658-8
Youth Indicators, 1993: Trends in the Well-Being of American Youth, $11, #065-000-00611-1

* Education Savings Bonds

U.S. Savings Bonds Marketing Division
U.S. Department of the Treasury
Washington, DC 20226   202-219-4235

Savings Bonds Operations Office
Office of Bond Consultants
Bureau of the Public Debt
U.S. Department of the Treasury
P.O. Box 1328
Parkersburg, WV 26106-1328   304-480-6112

The new education savings bond program permits qualified taxpayers to exclude from their gross income all or a portion of the interest earned on eligible Series EE savings bonds issued after 1989. To qualify for this exclusion, tuition and fees must be incurred by the taxpayer, the taxpayer's spouse, or the taxpayer's dependent at postsecondary educational institutions. These institutions are those that meet federal financial aid program standards. In addition, there are income and age limitations on participation in the program. Contact this office for more information on the program.

* Educational Videos

Office of Civil Rights
U.S. Patent and Trademark Office   800-243-6877
Washington, DC 20231   703-305-8292

The following educational videos are available through your local Patent and Trademark Depository Library or through the office listed above.
Project XL: A Quest for Excellence, highlights Project XL and its goal of encouraging inventive thinking among Americas' youth.
From Dreams to Reality: A Tribute to Minority Inventors, is an award winning video designed to inspire young audiences through the experiences of minority inventors. It shows students that dreams can become reality through hard work and dedication.

* Educators for Social Responsibility

475 Riverside Drive
Room 450
New York, NY 10115   212-870-3318

Educators for Social Responsibility (ESR) works to promote social responsibility and awareness through education in the hopes of developing people who can work effectively with others to help create a just, peaceful, ecologically sound world. Core components of the program include teacher training in conflict resolution and peer mediation of conflict. ESR also sponsors a Multicultural Education Project. Contact ESR for information on programs and for a list of the regional ESR chapters.

* Eisenhower Mathematics and Science Education

Office of Reform Assistance and Dissemination
Office of Educational Research and Improvement
U.S. Department of Education
555 New Jersey Ave, NW, Suite 522
Washington, DC 20208-5524   202-219-2206

The purpose of the Eisenhower program is to support innovative projects of national significance directed at improving the quality of teaching and instruction in mathematics and science in the schools and to increase the access of all students to that instruction. Programs focus on teacher training and curriculum change at the K-12 levels. Strong emphasis is placed on reaching students who have been relatively underrepresented in the past as well as those who are relatively more gifted and talented. At the elementary level, most projects incorporate an increased emphasis on practical hands on problem solving and higher order thinking skills. At the secondary level, a curriculum improvement project awarded to the National Science Teachers Association will have students study physics, chemistry, biology, and earth/space science every year for six years instead of the traditional year long segments in each area. The Office of Educational Research and Improvement can provide you with a booklet listing current projects under the Eisenhower program.

* Elementary and Early Childhood Education
Information

ERIC Clearinghouse on Elementary and
 Early Childhood Education
University of Illinois   800-583-4135
805 West Pennsylvania Ave.   217-333-1386
Urbana, IL 61801-4897   Fax: 217-333-3767
                               Internet: eric.eece@ux1.cso.uiuc.edu

Subject areas cover all aspects of the cognitive, emotional, social, and physical development and education of children from birth through early adolescence, excluding specific elementary school curriculum areas. Among the topics covered are prenatal and infant development and care; child care programs and community services for children at local, state, and federal levels; parent, child, and family relationships; home and school relationships; technology and children; preparation of early childhood teachers and caregivers; foster care and adoption; theoretical and philosophical issues related to children's development and education.

* Environmental Education Materials

Public Information Center
Environmental Protection Agency (EPA)
401 M St., SW, Mail Stop 3404
Washington DC 20460   202-260-2080

The Environmental Protection Agency (EPA) can provide you with a teacher package with materials for teachers of students in grades 1-12. In particular, *Environmental Education Materials For Teachers and Young People* is a free annotated list of educational materials on environmental issues. Entries include diverse materials ranging from workbooks and lesson plans to newsletters, films, and computer software intended for young people. Educational materials available from sources other than EPA are listed alphabetically following the name of their sponsoring organization or group. A separate listing of selected EPA publications and other material available from EPA's Public Information Center is included in this pamphlet. *Earth Notes* is an EPA publication aimed at grades 1-6 and contains information on Earth Day and trees. Also included in the package are posters you can put up in the classroom. Contact this office to order your free package.

* Evaluation, Standards, and Testing

Center for Research on Evaluation, Standards
 and Student Testing (CRESST)
Regents of the University of California
Center for the Study of Evaluation
University of California at Los Angeles
10920 Wilshire Blvd., Suite 900
Los Angeles, CA 90024-1522   310-206-1532

Major research areas include testing for the improvement of learning; systems for evaluating and improving educational quality; the impact of testing and evaluation on educational standards, policy, and practice; and school reform. The Center for Research on Evaluation, Standards and Student Testing (CRESST) publishes a newsletter, *CRESST Line* as well as a research periodical entitled *Evaluation Comment*, which highlights a single theme in each issue. Contact this office to have your name added to their mailing list to receive these publications which are published 3 to 4 times a year.

* Family Involvement in Learning

Information Resource Center
Family Involvement Partnership for Learning
U.S. Department of Education   800-872-5327
Washington, DC   202-219-2050

This program is designed to encourage and support efforts by families, communities, schools, and businesses to take a more active role in childrens' learning through the formation of family, school, and community partnerships. Research shows that family involvement in child learning is a critical link to achieving high quality education. Seven tips for parents and families are: find time for families to learn together; challenge your children to reach their full potential; limit television watching on school nights to 2 hours; read together; encourage your children to take tough courses and find time to check their homework; make sure children go to school daily and are off the streets late at night; and talk to children about drugs and alcohol and the values you want your children to have. More information is available form the Information Resource Center by phone, mail, or fax.

* Follow Through Educational Program

Compensatory Education Programs
Office of Elementary and Secondary Education
U.S. Department of Education
600 Independence Ave. SW
Washington, DC 20202   202-260-0826

This program provides grants to local education agencies, private agencies and organizations for the purpose of developing and disseminating information and services to improve the school performance of children from low-income families in grades K-3. Research grants are also available to public and non-profit agencies, institutions, or organizations to conduct research directly related to the Follow Through Program.

* Foreign Languages Assistance Program

Office of School Improvement Programs
Office of Elementary and Secondary Education
Office of Bilingual Education
U.S. Department of Education
600 Independence Ave. SW, MES Bldg.
Washington, DC 20202-6510   202-205-8766

This program is designed to provide financial assistance to states for foreign language instruction at both the elementary and secondary education levels in all languages with preference given to the less common languages such as Chinese, Japanese, Korean, Arabic, and Russian. These languages have been identified as important to the economic and security interests of the United States.

* Geography Education

American Geographical Foundation
156 Fifth Avenue, Room 600
New York, NY 10010   212-242-0214

The Society presents lectures, conferences and symposia, awards honors to scholars and explorers, conducts research on a wide range of geographical topics, and has amassed the largest geographical research library in the Western Hemisphere. It is also involved in improving geographical education, sponsors educational travel programs, and promotes better geographical education for grades K-12.

* Gifted and Talented National Clearinghouse

ERIC Clearinghouse on Disabilities and Gifted Education
Council for Exceptional Children   800-328-0272
1920 Association Dr.   703-264-9474
Reston, VA 22091-1589   Fax: 703-620-2521
                                          TDD: 703-264-9449
                               Internet: erecec@inet.ed.gov

Subject areas include all aspects of the education and development of handicapped persons, including prevention of handicaps, identification and assessment of handicaps, and intervention and enrichment programs for the handicapped both in special settings and within the mainstream. All aspects of the education and development of gifted persons are also covered.

* Goals 2000

Information Resource Center
Goals 2000
U.S. Department of Education

Be patient. If any phone number is incorrect, call (area code) 555-1212 and request the new listing.

157

Education

600 Independence Ave. SW   800-872-5327
Washington, DC 20202   202-401-2000

In response to the growing concern that American schools were not producing graduates with sufficient skills to meet the challenges of the 21st century, President Bush kicked off Goals 2000. Aims of Goals 2000 include: increasing graduation rate to 90%, putting American students first in the world in science and math, and ensuring all schools are free of drugs and violence. Goals 2000 will be implemented at the Community level. Periodic Satellite Town Meetings are held on the goals of Goals 2000. Contact the Goals 2000 staff for information on Goals 2000 schools and meetings in your area.

* Goals 2000 Arts Partnership

Goals 2000
Office of Education Research and Improvement
U.S. Department of Education
600 Independence Ave. SW
Washington, DC 20202   202-401-0769

Arts have been incorporated into the larger Goals 2000 project through the joint cooperation of the U.S. Department of Education and the National Endowment for the Arts. Current plans include the seven following components: Developing World Class Standards in the Arts; Involving Goals 2000 Communities; Helping States Implement High National Standards; Creating a National Center for Arts Education; Expanding the National Assessment of Educational Progress (NAEP); Developing a Research Agenda in Arts Education; and Designing a National Arts Education Dissemination Network.

* Hawaiian Family Based Education Centers

Office of School Improvement Programs
Office of Elementary and Secondary Education
U.S. Department of Education
600 Independence Ave. SW
Washington, DC 20202   202-260-2502

This program is designed to develop and operate family based education centers throughout the Hawaiian Islands. These centers include parent, infant and preschool programs, as well as research, development and assessment of the activities.

* Head Start Development Program for Low-Income 3-5 Year Olds

Publications Desk
Head Start Bureau
U.S. Department of Health and Human Services
P.O. Box 1182
Washington, DC 20013   202-205-8560

Project Head Start, a comprehensive child development program, was launched by the Federal Government in 1965 to help young children from low-income families get a better start in life. The education program is administered by the Administration for Children, Youth and Families. Grants are awarded by Health and Human Services Regional Offices to local public agencies and private non-profit organizations for the purpose of operating a Head Start program at the community level. There are special programs for Indian and migrant farmworker children. Head Start also publishes a pamphlet entitled *Easing the Transition from Preschool to Kindergarten*. Contact Head Start for more information about its programs.

* Heritage and Preservation

National Endowment for the Arts
Nancy Hanks Center
1100 Pennsylvania Ave. NW   202-682-5428
Washington, DC 20506-0001   TDD: 202-682-5496

The Arts Endowment offers assistance for a full range of arts disciplines and types and sizes of organizations involved in the arts. The purpose of Heritage and Preservation is to: 1) honor, assist and make visible those artists and forms of artistic expression that are rooted in and reflective of the many cultural groups that make up our nation; 2) preserve our most significant artistic accomplishments for future generations; and 3) conserve important works or art. Heritage and Preservation projects should represent clearly defined strategies to accomplish these goals. Criteria considered during the review of applications are artistic excellence and artistic merit, impact of the project, and the ability to carry out the project. Grants generally range from $5,000 to $2000,000 and require a match of at least 1 to 1. For more information request a copy of the free publication Grants to Organizations: Application Guidelines. Application forms are also available.

* High School and Intercollegiate Debate Topics

Your Congressman's Office

A series of free reports are prepared by the Congressional Research Service of the Library of Congress that contain pertinent excerpts, bibliographic references, and other materials related to debate topics for that year. For high school debate teams, the topics are selected by the National University Extension Service Association, and for college, the topics are selected by the American Speech Association.

* High School Student Pages at U.S. Congress

Switchboard
The Capitol
Washington, DC 20515   202-224-3121

Being a Page is an opportunity to live in the nation's capitol and see Congress at work. Pages are selected by Representatives and Senators whose seniority permits this privilege. Pages must be at least juniors in high school. They serve principally as messengers carrying documents, letters, and messages between the House and Senate, Members' offices, committees, and the Library of Congress. They also prepare the House and Senate Chambers for each day's business. Pages serve one or two terms of an academic year and also during the summer months. Their tenure depends on ability, conduct, academic performance, and their sponsor's term in office.

* High School Training

Education Service (225B)
Veterans Benefits Administration
U.S. Department of Veterans Affairs
810 Vermont Ave., NW
Washington, DC 20420   202-273-7293

A veteran may pursue high school training or training to pass the GED examination and may receive educational assistance allowance without a charge against basic entitlement. Additional secondary school training, such as refresher courses or deficiency courses, are permitted if needed to qualify for admission to an appropriate educational institution. Contact your VA regional office for more information.

* Homeless Children Education

Compensatory Education Programs
Office of Elementary and Secondary Education
U.S. Department of Education
600 Independence Ave. SW
Washington, DC 20202   202-260-0826

Through this program, grants for state activities are provided to State educational agencies to ensure that homeless children have access to free, appropriate public education.

* HOTS (High Order Thinking Skills)

University of Arizona
College of Education
Tucson, AZ 85721   602-621-1305

HOTS is a general thinking skills program designed primarily for Chapter 1 and mildly impaired Learning Disabled students in grades 4-7. The thinking skills are designed to enhance social interaction and basic skills. HOTS represents a new approach to compensatory education in that instead of reteaching the information the students did not previously learn, HOTS provides the types of thinking skills that students need to be able to learn the material the first time it is taught. Contact the University of Arizona for more information about the program.

* Improving America's Schools Act

Information Resource Center
U.S. Department of Education   800-872-5327
Washington, DC 20202   202-401-2000

The Improving America's Schools Act of 1994, which authorizes Elementary and Secondary Education Act (ESEA), provides nearly 11 billion dollars to school districts and schools to improve teaching and learning for all students. The overhauled ESEA encourages states and schools to set high academic standards for student academic achievements, addresses the problems of school violence and drug use, provides resources for professional development to teachers, creates incentives for educational innovation through charter schools, and improved access to technology. In addition the Act eliminates federal red tape and redesigned federal programs to strengthen and reinforce state and local school reform. The main program, Title 1, provides supplemental support in various forms to economically disadvantaged students in all 50 states and territories. More information is available by phone, mail, or fax from the Information Resource Center.

* Indian Education

Office of Indian Education
Bureau of Indian Affairs
U.S. Department of the Interior
1849 C St. NW
Washington, DC 20240   202-208-6123

The Office of Indian Education provides funding for both public and private Indian schools. Also sponsored are adult education classes and college scholarships. To receive information regarding Indian Education statistics and various programs sponsored by the Bureau of Indian Affairs, contact this office.

* International Youth Exchange

The Bureau of Educational and Cultural Affairs
Youth Exchange Programs Division
United States Information Agency (USIA)
301 Fourth St., SW, Room 357
Washington, DC 20547   202-619-6299

This office administers grants to non-profit organizations for international educational and cultural exchanges for youths 15 to 25 years of age. Organizations wishing to become sponsors, or individuals wishing to be put in contact with sponsoring organizations, can receive free information from this office. A list of prior fiscal year awards is also available. The Division also manages the Congress-Bundestag Youth Exchange Program which sends 400 American high school students to work in the German parliament and an equal number of Germans to work in the U.S. Congress. The Samantha Smith Memorial Exchange Program supports grants for exchanges with Eastern Europe and the former U.S.S.R. When contacting USIA, ask for the *Advisory List of International Educational Travel and Exchange Programs* which lists organizations that sponsor travel programs.

* Languages and Linguistics Education Information

ERIC Clearinghouse on Languages and Linguistics
Center for Applied Linguistics   800-276-9834
1118 22nd St., NW   202-429-9551
Washington, DC 20037-0037   Fax: 202-659-5641
    Internet: eric@cal.org

Subject areas cover languages and language sciences; theoretical and applied linguistics; all areas of foreign language, second language and linguistics pedagogy or methodology; psycholinguistics and the psychology of language learning; cultural and intercultural context of languages; application of linguistics in language teaching; bilingualism and bilingual education; sociolinguistics; study abroad and international exchanges; teacher training and qualifications specific to the teaching of a foreign language and second language; commonly and uncommonly taught languages, including English as a second language; and related curriculum developments and problems.

* Literature Education

Center for Learning and Teaching of Literature
State University of New York at Albany
School of Education
1400 Washington Ave.
Albany, NY 12222   518-442-5026

Major research areas include current emphases in curriculum and instruction; teaching and learning processes; and assessment.

* Magnet Schools Assistance Program

Office of School Improvement Programs
Office of Elementary and Secondary Education
U.S. Department of Education
600 Independence Ave. SW
Washington, DC 20202   202-260-3770

This program is designed to provide grants to eligible local educational agencies to develop and operate magnet schools that are a part of an approved desegregation plan. The criteria used to define a magnet school in this program are the following: a distinctive school curriculum based on a special theme or method of instruction; a unique district role and purpose for voluntary desegregation; a voluntary choice of the school by student and parent; and open access to school enrollment beyond a regular attendance zone.

* Migrant Education Programs

Office of Migrant Education
Office of Elementary and Secondary Education
U.S. Department of Education
600 Independence Ave. SW
Washington, DC 20202   202-260-1124

This program is designed to provide financial assistance to State Educational Agencies to establish or improve programs designed to meet the special educational needs of children of migratory agricultural workers or fishers aged 3-21. The program includes a basic grant component, a record transfer system, and a coordination program for the state agencies.

* NASA Education Workshops for Elementary School Teachers (NEWEST)

Education Division
Mail Code FE
NASA Headquarters
Washington, DC 20546   202-358-1520

NEWEST is for elementary school teachers (grades 1-6) in all disciplines. Selected teachers are awarded a two-week, expense-paid workshop at a NASA field center, with each center hosting about 20 teachers. The workshops vary from center to center. Although all focus on current NASA programs, each center conducts activities unique to its work. During their stay, teachers meet with scientists, technicians, and educational specialists. Teachers are instructed how to apply their experiences to their elementary curriculum.

* NASA Minority Summer High School Apprentice Research Program (SHARP)

SHARP Program Manager
Education Division
National Aeronautics and Space Administration (NASA)
Mail Code FE
Washington, DC 20546   202-358-1631

SHARP provides an opportunity for targeted underrepresented minority students in grades 10-12 who live within commuting distance of a participating NASA field center to take part in an eight-week, paid apprenticeship, where they work directly with NASA scientists or engineers. Interested students submit an application and references from a school administrator, teacher, or guidance counselor. Chosen students work with scientists or engineers whose work is related to his or her career aspirations, which may include computers, research, navigation, or guidance systems.

* National Center for Geographic Education

Indiana University of Pennsylvania
Geography Department
16 A Leonard Hall
Indiana, PA 15705-1087   412-357-6290

The Council is overseeing the development of World Class Standards in geography. It encourages the training of teachers in geographic concepts, practices, and teaching methods and improves the teaching and learning of geography in schools as well as among adult groups outside schools. Publications include the *Journal of Geography*, the newsletter *Perspective*, and *Pathways in Geography*, a series of publications for teachers, students, teacher trainers and curriculum planners.

* National Center for History in the Schools

University of California
Moore Hall 234
405 Hilgard Avenue
Los Angeles, CA 90024-1521   310-825-8388

This Center is leading a national effort to develop World Class Standards in American history and world history. It has also developed curricular units on subjects such as the ancient Near East, China under the Han dynasty, and America in colonial times. It is supported by the U.S. Department of Education and the National Endowment for the Arts.

* National Council for History Education

26915 Westwood Road
Suite B-2
Westlake, OH 44145-4656   216-835-1776

This is the successor organization to the Bradley Commission on History in Schools, which published *Building a History Curriculum: Guidelines for Teaching History in*

School ($3.00). It acts as a clearinghouse for information on history in education, provides a network for history educators as well as publishing a monthly newsletter for parents, educators, and policy makers.

* National Council for the Social Studies

3501 Newark Street, NW
Washington, DC 20016   202-966-7840
The Council promotes the teaching of social studies at all levels and provides information and resources to social studies teachers in all 50 states and more than 69 foreign countries. For a catalog of publications available call 800-683-0812.

* National Geographic Society Geography Education Program

Geographic Education Division
National Geographic Society
P.O. Box 37138
Washington, DC 20013-7138   202-775-6701
The Society brings together academic geographers and K-12 teachers through a network of state geographic alliances based on university campuses across the country. Interested K-12 teachers may ask to be placed on the mailing list. All teachers on the mailing list will receive a packet of information during Geographic Awareness Week. It publishes the newsletter *Update*, which includes lesson plans. It also sponsors teacher workshops in Washington, DC, and in all states and territories.

* National Library of Education

National Library of Education (NLE)
Office of Educational Research and Improvement (OERI)
U.S. Department of Education   800-424-1616
555 New Jersey Ave. NW   202-219-1692
Washington, DC 20208-5721   Fax: 202-219-1696
Internet: Library@inet.ed.gov
The National Library of Education (NLE) is the largest federally funded library devoted entirely to education; it is the federal government's principal center for one-stop information and referral on education. The Library offers a CD-ROM catalog of the collection, individual study room, group and individual orientation seminars; houses more that 200,000 books and more that 750 periodicals; has a special collection of pre-1800 rare books, Early American textbooks, 1775-1900; modern American textbooks, 1900-1959; education reports, bibliographies, and studies; archived speeches, correspondence, policy papers, and reports; and children's classics; maintains an electronic repository of information; has a Technology Resources Center; shares information through the resources and services of the 16 Educational Resources Information Center (ERIC) Clearinghouses; and has a Legislative Reference Service for information on the law (202-401-1045). The Library responds to phone, mail, and electronic inquiries with information on publications, education materials from other federal agencies, services and resources available through ERIC, the research institutes, and the national education dissemination systems, and statistics from the National Center for Education Statistics.

* Native American Indians

Office of Public Affairs
Bureau of Indian Affairs (BIA)
U.S. Department of the Interior
1849 C St. NW
Washington, DC 20240   202-208-3710
The free booklet, *American Indians Today: Answers to Your Questions, 1988*, contains useful information on the Native American Indians and their relationship to the Bureau of Indian Affairs. Programs within the Bureau, including education, health services, and housing are briefly outlined and contain recent statistics. Many questions are answered within the booklet, including the rights of the Indians to own land and have their own governments. A map locates the Indian lands and communities, showing Federal and State Indian Reservations and other Indian groups. An excellent bibliography, prepared by the Smithsonian Institution, is included.

* Native American Indian Education Programs

Office of Indian Education Programs
Bureau of Indian Affairs
U.S. Department of the Interior
1849 C St. NW
Washington, DC 20240   202-208-6175
The Office of Indian Education Programs can provide you with information on

efforts to improve Native American education. Part of this program has integrated Indian schools into the America 2000 education program. Numerous programs are also available for disadvantaged and handicapped Indian children. Other BIA sponsored programs are the following: Solo Parent, for single parents to finish high school while living at school with their children; Close Up, for civic education; Junior Achievement, for applied economics; and Family and Child Education, a family literacy program for children 1-5 years old and their parents. The Bureau of Indian Affairs publishes an *Education Directory* which is an invaluable source for information on programs as well as for contacts in BIA.

* Natural History Museum Education Program

National Museum of Natural History
Office of Education
10th and Constitution Ave. NW, MSC 158
Washington, DC 20560   202-357-2747
The museum has an extensive educational school program with film and workshops available at your school or the museum, including museum lesson tours, the Discovery Room, the Naturalist Center, and instructional kits. A catalog of services can be sent to you. The Office also publishes a quarterly calendar of films and events at the Museum.

* Performing Arts Education

Education Department
Kennedy Center for the Performing Arts
New Hampshire Avenue at Rock Creek Pkway
Washington, DC 20566-0001   202-416-8800
The Kennedy Center takes a leadership role in national performing arts education policy and programs, commissioning, creating, and touring performances for families, school groups, and teachers; offering professional development opportunities in the arts for teachers; developing model programs for use by other performing arts centers and schools; developing and encouraging national and community outreach programs; and serving as a clearinghouse for arts education information and as an advocate for arts education on a national level.

* Physical/Recreational Education

ERIC Clearinghouse on Teaching and Teacher Education
American Association of Colleges for Teacher
 Education (AACTE)   800-822-9229
One Dupont Circle, NW   202-293-2450
Suite 610   Fax: 202-293-2450
Washington, DC 20036-2412   Internet: ericsp@inet.ed.gov
This clearinghouse can provide you with information on all aspects of physical, health, and recreation education. The adjunct ERIC Clearinghouse on Clinical Schools is associated with this clearinghouse and can be reached at the same address and phone number.

* Planning and Stabilization in the Arts

National Endowment for the Arts
Nancy Hanks Center
1100 Pennsylvania Ave. NW   202-682-5429
Washington, DC 20506-0001   TDD: 202-682-5496
The Arts Endowment offers assistance for a full range of arts disciplines and types and sizes of organizations involved in the arts. The Endowment recognizes that there is a continuing struggle on the part of America's arts organizations to achieve stability, and that arts organizations are engaged in various efforts to develop structure that will enable them to carry on their work effectively and creatively. Planning and Stabilization offers assistance to applicants to assess carefully their organizational strengths, weaknesses and financial health. Projects can also focus on the strategies for building partnerships and resources among a group of organizations that are linked by geography, programming, mission, etc. Projects can focus on organizational planning, stabilization or both. Criteria considered during the review of applications are artistic excellence and artistic merit, impact of the project, and the ability to carry out the project. Grants generally range from $15,000 to $500,000 and require a match ranging from at least 1 to 1, to at least 5 to 1. For more information request a copy of the free publication *Grants to Organizations: Application Guidelines*. Application forms are also available.

* Presidential Honor Students

White House Commission on Presidential Scholars
U.S. Department of Education
600 Independence Ave. SW

Washington, DC 20202 202-401-0961

This annual program honors 141 students chosen among the nation's most outstanding graduating high school seniors. Those students who become Presidential Scholars are chosen on the basis of their accomplishments in many areas--academic and artistic success, demonstrated leadership, and involvement in school and community. Students may not apply individually to the program nor may their schools nominate them. The Scholars are given a medallion and are invited to Washington, DC where they are honored. There is no monetary award.

* President's Council on Physical Fitness and Sports

Communications Office
701 Pennsylvania Ave., NW, Suite 250 202-272-3421/3431
Washington, DC 20004 Fax: 202-504-2064

The Council serves as a catalyst to promote, encourage, and motivate the development of physical fitness and sports programs for all Americans. To receive President's Challenge materials call 800-258-8146.

* Reading and Communication Skills Information

ERIC Clearinghouse on Reading and Communication Skills
Indiana University
Smith Research Center 800-759-4723
2805 East 10th St., Suite 150 812-855-5847
Bloomington, IN 47408-2698 Fax: 812-855-4220
Internet: ericcs@ucs.indiana.edu

Subject areas include reading, English and communication skills (verbal and nonverbal) preschool through college; education research and development in reading, writing, speaking, and listening; identification, diagnosis, and remediation of reading problems; speech communication, mass communication, interpersonal and small group interaction, interpretation, rhetorical and communication theory, instructional development, speech sciences, and theater. Preparation of instructional staff and related personnel in these areas are also covered.

* Reading Is Fundamental

Reading Is Fundamental (RIF)
600 Maryland Ave., SW, Suite 600 202-287-3220
Washington, DC 20024-2569 Fax: 202-287-3196

The RIF Guide to Encouraging Young Readers ($12.00). Hundreds of kid-tested activities designed to engage children from infancy to age 11 in the fun of reading; an annotated reading list of 200 children's books; resource listing of book clubs and magazines, parent's books and concerned organizations. RIF can also send you information on how to establish a RIF Center in your community or how to become a volunteer at a RIF center near you. Below is a list of publications that can be ordered from RIF.

Books to Grow On ($2). Magazine for parents including reading tips and games and puzzles for young readers.
Children Who Can Read, But Don't ($.50). How to help readers aged 9-12 discover the fun of reading.
Choosing Good Books for Children ($.50). Information and resources to help parents find appropriate books for children to age 12.
Encouraging Soon-to-Be Readers ($.50). How to excite preschoolers about books and help them to develop skills that lead to reading.
Family of Readers Activity Book ($2). Fun-to-do reading and writing activities. Available in English and Spanish.
Family Fact Brochure ($1.25) 24 page booklet provides a place to keep important information about your children. Also features tips on raising readers.
Magazines and Family Reading ($.50). Ways that magazines can get the whole family turning pages.
Reading Aloud to Your Children ($.50). The why's, when's, where's, what's and how's of reading aloud.
Reading is Fun! ($1). Tips for parents to prepare young children for reading.
Reading: What's In It for Teenagers/Teenagers and Reading ($.50). Two brochures in one, perforated for parents to keep their half and give the other half to their teenager.
Summertime Reading ($.50) How to encourage your children to keep books open after school is closed.
Upbeat and Offbeat Activities to Encourage Reading ($.50). Playful projects and activities to help preschoolers and beginning readers build skills.

* Reading Research Center

Center for the Study of Reading
University of Illinois

174 Children's Research Center
51 Gerty Drive
Champaign, IL 61820 217-333-2552

Major research areas include acquisition of knowledge and skills, instruction in reading, text characteristics, and reading proficiency. The Center can send you a list of their technical reports, video tapes and publications which are available for a fee. Publications and video tapes from the Center include the following:

Monographs:
Beginning to Read: Thinking and Learning about Print--A Summary
Becoming a Nation of Readers: The Report of the Commission on Reading

Videotapes:
Teaching Reading: Strategies from Successful Classrooms, set of six tapes with print guides.
    Individual tapes-
    Emergent Literacy
    The Reading/Writing Connection
    Teaching Word Identification
    Literacy in Content Area Instruction
    Fostering a Literate Culture
    Teaching Reading Comprehension
Teaching Reading: Strategies from Successful Classrooms--Preview Tape

Pamphlets and Booklets:
Reading and Your Adolescent
10 Ways to Help Your Children Become Better Readers
Teacher and Independent Reading: Suggestions for the Classroom

Special Reports:
The At-Risk Situation: A Synthesis of Reading Research
Academic Libraries and Research in the Teaching of English
Teachers' Views of Chapter 1 Programs
Research Programs at the Center for the Study of Reading, 1987-1992

Guides:
A Guide to Selecting Basal Reading Programs
A Guide to Selecting Basal Reading Programs--Overhead Masters
A Guide to Selecting Basal Reading Programs and Overhead Masters

Technical Reports:
A listing of Technical Reports is available upon request.

* READ*WRITE*NOW

Information Resource Center
U.S. Department of Education
600 Independence Ave. SW 800-USA-LEARN
Washington, DC 20202 202-401-2000

The READ*WRITE*NOW program will bring together children and reading partners--parents, summer project leaders, senior citizens, teachers, librarians, students in grades seven and up to help children grow in their reading and writing skills over the summer. Each reading team of child and reading partner will receive a READ*WRITE*NOW kit consisting of a book of fun activities that support reading and writing. The child and reading partner will meet one or more times each week to complete activities together. Each child will try to reach the goal of reading about 20 minutes every day throughout the summer. Other partner activities may include a trip to the library, discussing books being read, writing to a pen pal, or setting up a young readers club. In addition to the activities book, the kit will include a funbook for children pre-kindergarten through kindergarten; recommended reading lists; a Strong Families Read Together bookmark; and a certificate of participation.

* Research on Teaching

Institute for Research on Teaching (IRT)
Michigan State University
252 Erickson Hall
College of Education
East Lansing, MI 48824-1034 517-355-5522

The Institute's goal is to study the whole teacher, i.e., teacher's role as related to society, the school district, and the students; the professional planning, thinking, and decision making involved in playing these roles; and the strategies for setting and reaching goals related to student needs. Current research at the IRT focuses on the relationship between teacher behavior and student achievement. IRT ongoing projects include the following: Elementary Subjects Center - focuses on effective elementary school teaching; Writing Strategies Instruction - teaches elementary school teachers

Be patient. If any phone number is incorrect, call (area code) 555-1212 and request the new listing.

161

how to teach effective writing skills; Science Achievement - this project is working to rewrite a commercial science textbook prototype unit; Responsive Reading Strategies - the focus here is on the relationship between responsive elaboration and student achievement; Reciprocal Teaching; Dilemma Management in Mathematics Teaching; and more. The IRT also publishes a newsletter entitled *Communications Quarterly*. A publications list and catalog are also available.

* Rural Education and Small Schools Clearinghouse

ERIC Clearinghouse on Rural Education and Small Schools
Appalachia Educational Laboratory, Inc.
1031 Quarrier St.
P.O. Box 1348   800-624-8841
Charleston, WV 25325-1348   304-347-0400
                                                    Fax: 304-347-0487
                                               Internet: Lanhamb@ael.org

Subject areas cover economic, cultural, social, or other factors related to education programs and practices for rural residents; American Indians/Alaska Natives, Mexican Americans, and migrants; education practices and programs in all small schools; and outdoor education. This includes programs, practices, and materials that provide learning experiences designed to meet the special needs of rural populations and schools where conditions of smallness are a factor.

* School Administrators and Management Clearinghouse

ERIC Clearinghouse on Educational Management
5207 University of Oregon
1787 Agate St.   800-438-8841
Eugene, OR 97403-5207   503-686-5043
                                                    Fax: 503-346-2334
                                       Internet: ppiele@oregon.uoregon.edu

Subject areas include all aspects of the administration, leadership, finance, governance, and structure of public and private education organizations at the elementary, middle, and secondary levels, including facility planning, design, construction, equipment and furnishing, and maintenance; and pre-service and in-service preparation of administrators. Topics covered include the social, technological, political, and legal contexts of education organizations, and of State and Federal programs and policies, and traditional and alternative schools.

* School Discipline, Phonics and Other Publications

U.S. Department of Education
Office of Educational Research and Improvement
555 New Jersey Ave., NW
Washington, DC 20208-5721   800-424-1616

Elementary School Recognition Program (brochure) (PIP 88-821): Describes the program, requirements, characteristics of successful schools, and information on how to apply.
Improving School Discipline (IS 88-161).
Students at Risk (IS 89-540).
Ten Steps to a Successful Magnet Program (OR 88-510).
Ten Ways to Help Your Children Become Better Readers.
What We Know About Phonics (IS 88-163).
Employment Outcomes of Recent Master's and Bachelor's Degree Recipients (CS 88-251).
Students Report Job Success More Important Than Making Money (CS 88-436).
Check This Out Fact Sheet: Literacy for Every Adult Project (LP 89-732).
Check This Out Fact Sheet: Read-Aloud Programs for the Elderly (LP 89-731).
Helping Your Child Use the Library (LP 89-712).
Approaches to Drug and Alcohol Abuse (PIP 89-857).
Drug Prevention Curricula: A Guide to Selection and Implementation (PIP 88-835).
Five Tips to Improving Teaching (IS 87-127).
The Impact on Children's Education: TV's Influence on Cognitive Development (OR 88-507).
School Climate and Reading Performance (CS 88-605).
Education Statistics - 1988 Pocket Digest (OERI # 88611, Series: PD-88). Selected key statistics from the Digest of Education.
Pocket Projections, 1977-78 to 1997-98. (OERI No. 88612, Series: PP-88). Pocket-sized pamphlet of projections of key elementary/secondary and higher education statistics.
American Education at a Glance (OERI No. 89618, Series: NA). A variety of charts and tables providing an overview of American education.
Young Adult Literacy and Schooling (OERI No. 88604).
Teacher Incentive Programs in Public Schools (OERI No. 89063, Series: PUP-85).

* School-to-Work Opportunities

The National School-to-Work Learning and Information Center
400 Virginia Ave. SW, Room 210   800-251-7236
Washington, DC 20024   202-401-6222
                                                    Fax: 202-401-6211
                                               E-mail: stw-lc@ed.gov

This Center, sponsored by the Department of Education and the Department of Labor, provides information, assistance, and training to build School-to-Work opportunities in the United States. The Center utilizes the latest information technology to help increase the capacity of professionals, and to develop and implement School-to-Work systems across the nation. Its services are available to state and local School-to-Work offices, employers, schools, labor, parents, students, and to the general public. The Center is open from 8:00 a.m. to 6:00 p.m. and is also accessible via the Internet at http://www.stw.ed.gov

* Secondary Schools

Center on Organization and Restructuring of Schools
University of Wisconsin - Madison
1025 West Johnson St.
Madison, WI 53706   608-263-7575

Major research areas include a clearinghouse on academic achievement; non-instructional influences on adolescent engagement and achievement; the stratification of learning opportunities in middle and high schools; higher-order thinking in the high school curriculum; programs and policies to serve at risk students; and alternative structures and the quality of teacher worklife. The Center also publishes a quarterly newsletter entitled *Issues*, and also publishes occasional issues-oriented *Briefs*. A publications list is also available.

* Secondary School Teaching

Center for Research on the Context of Secondary School Teaching
Stanford University - School of Education
CERAS Building
Stanford, CA 94305-3084   415-723-4972

Major research areas include conceptualization and development; the relationship of context to school workplace conditions, teaching and student outcomes; state reform and teacher contexts; inner city, high poverty schools; and alternative schools. The center is funded by federal and private grants.

* Social Organization of Schools

Center for Social Organization of Schools
Johns Hopkins University
3505 North Charles St.
Baltimore, MD 21218-2498   410-516-8800

The purpose of the Center is to study how changes in the social organization of schools can make them more effective for all students in promoting academic achievement, development of potential, and later-life career success. A publications list is also available.

* Social Studies and Curriculum Kits

Social Issues Research Service (SIRS) Documents
Education Branch
National Archives and Records Administration
7th St. and Pennsylvania Ave., NW, Room 505
Washington, DC 20408   202-501-6172

A catalog is available which contains supplemental teaching units with primary sources from the National Archives. Each unit is a package of materials that serves as a complete classroom set. Each unit contains about 50 reproductions of documents, with some also including cassette tapes. The materials deal with certain key issues of the period, with governmental and political responses to these issues, and with public attitudes. Each unit includes a detailed teachers' guide containing developmental exercises to help students examine the documents. Each unit costs $40 except *U.S. At War, 1944*, which includes 3 video tapes and sells for $95.00. The following 7 units are currently available.

The Constitution - Evolution of a Government.
The Bill of Rights - Evolution of Personal Liberties.
The United States Expands West, 1785-1842.
Westward Expansion, 1842-1912.
World War II - The Home Front.
Peace and Prosperity, 1953-1961.

To order The Constitution or The Bill of Rights contact the National Archives at 800-234-8861. To order all other units contact SIRS at 800-232-7477.

* Social Studies/Social Science Education Information

ERIC Clearinghouse on Social Studies/Social Science Education
Social Studies Development Center
Indiana University
Smith Research Center · · · 800-266-3815
2805 East Tenth St., Suite 120 · · · 812-855-3838
Bloomington, IN 47408-2698 · · · Fax: 812-855-0455
Internet: ericso@indiana.edu

Subject areas include all levels of social science education (history, geography, anthropology, economics, sociology, social psychology, and political science); applications of theory and research to social science education; values education; contribution of social science disciplines; comparative education (K-12); social studies content and curriculum materials on such subjects as law-related education, bias and discrimination, and aging. Subjects also include the humanities (music and art).

* Social Studies Teachers Workshops

Education Branch
National Archives and Records Administration
7th St. and Pennsylvania Ave., NW, Room 505
Washington, DC 20408 · · · 202-501-6172

This workshop, sponsored each summer, provides a varied program of lectures, demonstrations analysis of documents, independent research, and group work that introduces teachers to the holdings and organization of the National Archives. Participants learn how to use Archives materials to develop teaching units. The cost of the program for 1993 will be $100.

* Stay in School Program

U.S. Agency for International Development
Attention: Student Programs Coordinator
Recruitment
Room 1026, SA-1
2401 F St. NW
Washington, DC 20523 · · · 703-302-4128

This program offers employment to students who, because of financial constraints, may not be able to continue their education without paid employment. This program is open to high school students and undergraduates. Students must be at least 16 years of age, U.S. citizens, enrolled in school full-time, able to pass a background investigation, maintain a 2.5 grade point average, and type at least 40 words per minute. In addition, students must have certified financial need according to the economic guidelines established by the U.S. Office of Personnel Management.

* Student Achievement, Curriculum, and Assessment

National Institute on Student Achievement, Curriculum and Assessment (SAI)
Office of Educational Research and Improvement (OERI)
U.S. Department of Education
555 New Jersey Ave. NW
Washington, DC 20208-5573 · · · 202-219-2079

SAI supports basic and applied research in the areas of learning, teaching, and assessment; monitors the research and development center on improving student learning and achievement; monitors the research and development center on improving student assessment and educational accountability; works to identify, develop, and evaluate innovative and exemplary methods to advance student knowledge; and serves as an expert resource for current civics and economics education, core academic content areas, and technology use. The Institute provides national leadership in education through cooperation with national organizations in the subject-matter disciplines and state departments of education and local school districts to promote student achievement; supports evaluation of research to identify successful education practices and assessments, provides technical assistance and guidance by converting research findings into classroom applications; manages programs to support graduate student fellowships and senior fellows; and disseminates and exchanges information through publications, scholarly papers and presentations, conferences, workshops, consensus panels, and electronic releases.

* Students with Disabilities National Clearinghouse

ERIC Clearinghouse on Disabilities and Gifted Education
Council for Exceptional Children · · · 800-328-0272
1920 Association Dr. · · · 703-264-9474
Reston, VA 22091-1589 · · · TDD: 703-264-9449
Fax: 703-620-2521
Internet: ericed@inet.ed.gov

Subject areas include all aspects of the education and development of handicapped persons, including prevention of handicaps, identification and assessment of handicaps, and intervention and enrichment programs for the handicapped both in special settings and within the mainstream. All aspects of the education and development of gifted persons are also covered.

* Teacher Education Clearinghouse

ERIC Clearinghouse on Teaching and Teacher Education
American Association of Colleges for Teacher
Education (AACTE) · · · 800-822-9229
One Dupont Circle, NW, Suite 610 · · · 202-293-2450
Washington, DC 20036-1186 · · · Fax: 202-293-2450
Internet: ericsp@inet.ed.gov

Subject areas cover school personnel at all levels; teacher selection and training; pre-service and in-service preparation and retirement; the theory, philosophy, and practice of teaching; and curricula and general education not specifically covered by other clearinghouses. Also included are all aspects of physical education, health, dance, and recreation education.

* Teacher Education Research

National Center for Research on Teacher Learning
College of Education
Michigan State University
116 Erickson Hall
East Lansing, MI 48824-1034 · · · 517-355-9302

This Center focuses on the area of teacher learning. Currently, the Center is working on three projects that encompass 11 individual studies. Project A looks at the beliefs teachers acquire about teaching before they enter the profession. Project B is split into two studies. The first of these examines the subject matter teachers learn in college to gain insight into the substantive knowledge base of teachers. The second looks at programs designed to prepare teachers for work in multicultural learning environments. Project C, an amalgam of 8 studies, focuses on how teachers weave different kinds of knowledge together. The Center also puts out a publications list and publishes a quarterly magazine entitled *Colloquy*, which examines issues relevant to teaching different subjects.

* Teacher of the Arts Summer Fellowships

Council for Basic Education
1319 F St. NW, Suite 900
Washington, DC 20005 · · · 202-347-4171

Fellowships under this program are awarded for four to eight weeks of independent study. Eligible teachers must be currently working with K-12 students. Teacher-Fellows use personally developed plans for serious independent study of the arts or related issues. Call for more information.

* Teacher's Guide to Selective Service Registration

Public Affairs
Selective Service System
1515 Wilson Blvd., 4th Floor
Arlington, VA 22209 · · · 703-235-2053

A Teacher's Guide to Selective Service Registration is designed to assist teachers in their preparation of lessons covering the Selective Service System and describes the purpose, history, organization, and function of the System. With a summary of important teaching points, and questions and answers at the end of each chapter, this guide assists teachers in teaching their students about the Selective Service System. Also available is a fact pack that contains information on state laws relating to registration, student loans and registration, and job training benefits and registration. For additional information, contact this office.

* Testing Educational Achievement

National Assessment of Educational Progress
Educational Testing Service
P.O. Box 2923, 6710 Rosedale Rd. · · · 609-921-9000
Princeton, NJ 08541 · · · 800-223-0267

NAEP surveys the educational achievement of 9-year-olds, 13-year-olds, 17-year-olds, and at grades 4, 8, and 12, and periodically, young adults. The surveys are conducted in such areas as art, career and occupational development, citizenship, literature, mathematics, music, reading, science, social studies, and writing. Different learning areas are assessed every two years, and all areas are periodically reassessed to measure changes in educational achievement. A publications brochure is available through this office, and surveys may be purchased. Below is a sampling of other publications available through NAEP:

Education

Becoming Literate About Literacy: A Policy Information Report ($7.50)
Capturing the Power of Classroom Assessment (Free)
Computer Competence: The First National Assessment ($14)
Developing a Test (Free)
Effective Schools in Mathematics ($14)
Exploring the Age of Space (Videotape $50)
The Geography Learning of High School Seniors ($10)
Increasing Minority Faculty: An Elusive Goal (Free)
Performance Assessment Sampler: A Workbook ($11.25)
Science Learning Matters: An Interpretive Overview to the Science Report Card
    (Free)
Trends in Academic Progress ($19)
The Writing Report Card ($12)

* Tests, Measurement, and Evaluation Clearinghouse

ERIC Clearinghouse on Assessment and Evaluation
The Catholic University of America   800-464-3742
210 O'Boyle Hall   202-319-5120
Washington, DC 20064   Fax: 202-319-6692
                                   Internet: eric_ae@cua.edu
Subject areas include the assessment and evaluation of education projects or
programs; tests and other measurement devices; methodology of measurement and
evaluation; research design and methodology; human development; and learning
theory in general.

* Urban Community Enrichment Program (UCEP)

Education Division
Mail Code FE
NASA Headquarters
Washington, DC 20546   202-358-1110
UCEP is specifically targeted toward middle-school students in urban areas with high
percentages of minorities. NASA specialists will meet with school representatives to
formulate a custom-tailored program to fit the school's needs. Typically a program
begins with teacher orientation workshops followed by assemblies, a series of student
workshops, and classroom visits. In the classroom, NASA specialists work with
students on various hands-on activities, such as building rockets or airplanes or
learning about how information is transmitted from space back to Earth.

* Urban Education Clearinghouse

ERIC Clearinghouse on Urban Education
Teachers College, Box 40   800-601-4868
Columbia University   212-678-3433
New York, NY 10027-6696   Fax: 212-678-4048
                                   Internet: eric_cue@columbia.edu
Subject areas include programs and practices in schools in urban areas and the
education of racial/ethnic minority children and youth in various settings--local,
national, and international; the theory and practice of education equity; urban and
minority experiences; and urban and minority social institutions and services.

* Volunteer Intern Program

United States Agency for International Development (USAID)
Attention: Student Programs Coordinator
Recruitment
Room 1026, SA-1
2401 F St. NW
Washington, DC 20523   703-302-4128
Professional work experiences are available for qualified college students who are
considering careers in international relations. This program offers students the
opportunity to gain knowledge of the USAID mission through a supervised work
experience involving assignments related to their academic studies. Internships are
available to currently enrolled undergraduate and graduate students who will continue
their education immediately upon completion of the internship. Students must be at
least 16 years of age, a U.S. citizen, maintain at least a 2.5 grade point average, and
pass a background investigation. Presently, internships are available in Washington,
DC only. USAID has several other programs available to students such as the
Volunteer Intern Program, Stay-In-School program, Summer Employment Program,
Presidential Management Intern Program, and the Intern Investment Program.
Contact this office for more information on eligibility requirements and application
procedures.

* Women's Educational Equity Program

Office of School Improvement Programs
Office of Elementary and Secondary Education
U.S. Department of Education
600 Independence Ave. SW
Washington, DC 20202   202-260-2670
This program is designed to provide educational equity for women who suffer
discrimination based on sex and/or race, age, ethnic origin, or disability. Grant
programs provide financial assistance to public agencies, private non-profit
organizations and institutions and individuals for the development of educational
materials and model programs that promote equity for women and girls.

* Writing Skills: Students and Instructors

Center for the Study of Writing and Literacy
University of California at Berkeley
5513 Tolman Hall
Berkeley, CA 94720-1670   510-643-7022
                                   Internet: writ@violet.berkeley.edu
The Center supports an extensive program of research to improve the teaching and
learning of writing, from the early years of schooling through adulthood. Through
this research it is seeking to understand more explicitly how students from a variety
of backgrounds acquire writing and literacy skills, the types of instructional practices
that address the diverse needs of students, and ways in which schools can be
structured to support and sustain responsive approaches to education. In conjunction
with the National Writing Project, *The Quarterly*, a journal on the teaching and
learning of writing. The Center also offers seminars for teachers. A publications list
is available upon request.

College and Continuing Education

* Adult and Vocational Curriculum National Network

National Network for Curriculum Coordination
in Vocational and Technical Education
Office of Vocational and Adult Education
U.S. Department of Education
Switzer Bldg.
600 Independence Ave. SW, Room 4512   202-205-9673
Washington, DC 20202-7242   Fax: 202-205-8793

The six coordination centers provide leadership in curriculum coordination activities and offer a variety of curriculum-related activities, which include collecting and distributing curriculum information and products and assisting individuals, schools, and groups in addressing and resolving problems.

Western Curriculum Coordination Center, College of Education, University of Hawaii, 1776 University Ave., Wist. 216, Honolulu, HI 96844-0001; 808-956-7834, Fax 808-956-3374. Serving: American Samoa, Arizona, California, Guam, Hawaii, Nevada, and Trust Territory Government of Northern Marianas.

East Central Curriculum Coordination Center, Sangamon State University, K-80, Shepherd Rd., Springfield, IL 62708; 217-786-6375, 800-252-4822, Fax 217-786-6036. Serving: Delaware, District of Columbia, Indiana, Illinois, Maryland, Michigan, Minnesota, Ohio, Pennsylvania, Virginia, West Virginia, and Wisconsin.

Southeast Curriculum Coordination Center, Mississippi State University, Department of Tech/Ed, P.O. Drawer NU, Mississippi State, MS 39762; 601-325-1552, Fax 601-325-1837. Serving: Alabama, Florida, Georgia, Kentucky, Mississippi, North Carolina, South Carolina, and Tennessee.

Northeast Curriculum Coordination Center, New Jersey Vocational Education Resource Center, Rutgers University, Crest Way, Aberdeen, NJ 07747; 908-290-1900. Serving: Connecticut, Maine, Massachusetts, New Hampshire, New Jersey, New York, Puerto Rico, Rhode Island, Vermont, and Virgin Islands.

Mideast Curriculum Coordination Center, State Department of Vocational and Technical Education, 1500 West Seventh Ave., Stillwater, OK 74074-4364; 405-377-2000, Ext. 252, Fax 405-743-5541. Serving: Arkansas, Iowa, Kansas, Louisiana, Missouri, Nebraska, New Mexico, Oklahoma, and Texas.

Northwestern Curriculum Coordination Center, Bldg. 15, Clover Park Technical College, 4500 Steilacoom Blvd. SW, Tacoma, WA 98499-4098; 206-589-5764, Fax 206-589-5503. Serving: Alaska, Colorado, Idaho, Montana, North Dakota, Oregon, South Dakota, Utah, Washington, and Wyoming.

* Adult Continuing Education Clearinghouse

ERIC Clearinghouse on Adult, Career and Vocational Education
Ohio State University Center on Education and   800-848-4815
  Training for Employment   614-292-4353
1900 Kenny Rd.   Fax: 614-292-1260
Columbus, OH 43210-1090   Internet: ericacve@magnus.acs.ohio-state.edu

Subject areas cover all levels of adult and continuing education from basic literacy training through professional skill upgrading; vocational and technical education covering all service areas for secondary, postsecondary, and adult education populations; and career education and career development programs for all ages and populations in educational, institutional, business, and industrial settings. The Clearinghouse also now has subprofessional fields in industrial arts, corrections education, entrepreneurship, and adult retraining.

* Adult Educators

Clearinghouse on Adult Education
U.S. Department of Education
Office of Vocational and Adult Education
330 C St., SW
Washington, DC 20202   202-205-9872/9996

This clearinghouse links the adult education community with existing resources in adult education. The Bibliography of Resource Materials provides a complete list of

materials available from the clearinghouse. Examples include a directory of adult education-related programs, fact sheets on such topics as literacy and disabled adults, and materials concerning English as a second language.

* American and Foreign Teachers Exchange Program

Office of Academic Programs
United States Information Agency
301 Fourth St., SW, Room 353
Washington, DC 20547   202-619-4360

The Advising, Teaching, and Specialized Programs Division serves overseas education advising centers, foreign exchange students in the U.S., and administers the International Student Exchange Program for one-to-one exchange of university students. Its Teacher Exchange Branch arranges one and two way exchanges of U.S. and foreign teachers, and summer seminars for U.S. teachers to study abroad. Free brochures and applications are available.

* American Educators Teaching Abroad

Superintendent of Documents
Government Printing Office   202-512-1800
Washington, DC 20402   Fax: 202-512-2250

The United States Information Agency (USIA) publishes many teaching materials, including books, maps, complete teaching modules, and 14 magazines in 20 languages. By law most USIA publications may be distributed only in foreign countries. However, by congressional action, two magazines are available in the United States. English Teaching Forum, a quarterly for English teachers worldwide, is published by USIA's English Language Programs Division. This magazine is available through the GPO for $9.50, order #725-001-00000-2.

* Black Universities and Agricultural Sciences

Special Advisor to the Deputy Secretary
Agricultural Stabilization and Conservation Service
P.O. Box 2415
Washington, DC 20013   202-720-6346

The U.S. Department of Agriculture (USDA) has a unique relationship with 17 historically black universities that began in 1890 when these schools were designated by Congress as Land-Grant Institutions. In 1988 a symposium was sponsored by USDA at one of these institutions to re-examine the partnership between USDA and the universities.

Work is underway on a number of recommendations that came from this conference:

- Programs of financial assistance are being developed to help minorities through college.
- Liaison officers are working at each school to recruit students into the agricultural sciences and from there into careers at USDA.
- A marketing program is being developed for careers in agriculture and home economics and for educational opportunities at the 1990s.
- A K-12 career awareness initiative program is underway in food and agricultural sciences.
- More than 400 summer jobs were created around the country in the agricultural sciences for students.
- Partnerships are being developed between predominantly white land-grant institutions and the historically black schools.
- A program is being developed to work with the agricultural high schools in areas of higher education and career development.

* Career Education

ERIC Clearinghouse on Adult, Career and Vocational Education
Ohio State University Center on Education and   800-848-4815
  Training for Employment   614-292-4353
1900 Kenny Rd.   Fax: 614-292-1260
Columbus, OH 43210-1090   Internet: ericacve@magnus.acs.ohio-state.edu

Subject areas cover all levels of adult and continuing education from basic literacy training through professional skill upgrading; vocational and technical education

Education

covering all service areas for secondary, postsecondary, and adult education populations; and career education and career development programs for all ages and populations in educational, institutional, business, and industrial settings.

* College Environmental Curricula Grants

Office of Environmental Education
Environmental Protection Agency
401 M St., SW, Room A107
Washington DC 20460   202-260-4958

The Office of Environmental Education awards money to colleges to support the development of environment-related curriculum, allowing these colleges to then train State employees. The office also awards fellowships to State employees to continue their education concerning the environment. The fellowship applications are given out through the individual States. Other grants are awarded for a variety of environmentally related projects. These grants are coordinated by the EPA's regional offices. Contact this office for more information.

* College Courses

Information Office
U.S. Department of Agriculture Graduate School
Capital Gallery Building
600 Maryland Ave. SW, Room 129
Washington, DC 20024   202-720-4419

The U.S. Department of Agriculture (USDA) Graduate School, which is open to the public, offers college courses on nonagricultural subjects at reasonable prices. Although the school does not grant degrees, college credits are awarded and can be transferred to other universities. Some lectures are available on film, videotape, and in manuscript form.

* College Library Technology Grants

Library Development Staff
Library Programs/OERI
U.S. Department of Education
555 New Jersey Ave., NW, Room 404
Washington, DC 20208-5571   202-219-1315

The purpose of these grants is to encourage resource-sharing projects among the libraries of institutions of higher education through the use of technology and networking; to improve resource sharing services provided with public and private non-profit organizations, and to conduct innovative research and demonstration projects which meet special needs in utilizing technology to enhance library services. The Department of Education can send you an application form and a list of past awardees.

* Community Colleges Clearinghouse

ERIC Clearinghouse on Community Colleges
University of California at Los Angeles   800-832-8256
3051 Moore Hall   310-825-3931
Los Angeles, CA 90024-1564   Fax: 310-206-8095

Subject areas include the development, administration, and evaluation of two-year public and private community and junior colleges, technical institutes, and two-year branch university campuses. This covers the organization, administration, finance, governance, role and mission, and futures of such institutions; staff preparation, development, and evaluation; curricula and program; teaching methods; student services; libraries and learning resource centers; and methodologies of research applied to two-year colleges.

* Congress-Bundestag Exchange Program

CDS International Inc.
330 Seventh Ave.
New York, NY 10001   212-760-1400

Through this program, Americans between the ages of 18 and 24 have the opportunity to live and work in Germany. The program lasts for one year and successful applicants will spend their year learning German, further developing skills at a German technical school or University, and working in an internship with a German company. Contact the program for more information and an application.

* Cooperative Education Program (CO-OP)

Michael Parrish
Co-op Coordinator
Goddard Space Flight Center, Mail Code 114

Greenbelt, MD 20771   301-286-7206

Co-op gives high school, college, and graduate students an opportunity to work at a NASA field center while completing their education. Participating students usually alternate working one semester with studying one semester. In addition to job experience, the program also serves as a recruitment tool. Interested students must be attending school, be enrolled in their school's co-op program, maintain at least a 2.0 overall grade point average, and be recommended by the school. Each NASA field center negotiates its own cooperative agreements with school in its geographic area, and it is usually the responsibility of a school to initiate the venture.

* Cultural and Educational International Exchange

Academic Division
United States Information Agency (USIA)
301 Fourth St., SW, Room 234
Washington, DC 20547   202-619-4360

The U.S. Information Agency (USIA) can provide you with information on public and private organizations which sponsor international exchange activities. The book *Fulbright Grants and Other Grants for Graduate Study Abroad* contains a lot of valuable information both on the Fulbright program and on other organizations sponsoring exchanges.

* Exchange Programs with Eastern Europe

Council for International Exchange of Scholars (CIES)
3007 Tilden St. NW, Suite 5M
Washington, DC 20008-3009   202-686-7863

The U.S. Information Agency has contracted the Council for International Exchange of Scholars (CIES) to provide you with information on several new programs to exchange scholars with and accept students from Eastern Europe and the former Soviet Union. Notable programs include the Benjamin Franklin Fellowship, the Samantha Smith Program, the Alexander Hamilton Program for business students, and the John Marshall program for students in law and political science. Contact CIES for the list of programs.

* Fellowships: Latin America

Inter-American Fellowship Programs
901 N. Jewett Street, 10th Floor
Arlington, VA 22203   703-841-3800

This grant program stresses practical solutions to obstacles in grassroots development by fostering increased attention within the academic community on micro-level development in Latin America and the Caribbean. Part of the fellowships go to scholars and professionals from research and development institutions in Latin America and the Caribbean whose work would benefit from graduate-level study at U.S. universities, while other fellowships go to doctoral candidates and master's-level students enrolled in U.S. universities to conduct field research in Latin America or the Caribbean.

* Financial Aid Received by Legal Immigrants

General Accounting Office (GAO)   202-512-6000
P.O. Box 6015   Fax: 301-258-4066
Gaithersburg, MD 20884-6015   TDD: 301-413-0006
     Internet: info@www.gao.gov

Higher Education: Selected Information on Student Financial Aid Received by Legal Immigrants is a 26 page report available from the General Accounting Office (GAO) Document Distribution Center (GAO/HEHE-96-9). According to records at the Education Department, about 390,000 legal immigrant students received Pell grant aid in academic year 1992-1993. This was about 10 percent of all students receiving Pell grants. In total, immigrants received $662 million, or about 11 percent, of Pell grant aid in that year. GAO was unable to determine the total number of legal immigrants who received Stafford loans because citizenship data are not maintained in the Education Department's loan files. Some immigrants who received Pell grants, however, also received Stafford loans totaling $257 million. You can receive one copy of this report free of charge, additional copies are $2.00 each. Orders for 100 or more copies to be mailed to a single address are discounted 25 percent. A check or money order made out to the Superintendent of Documents should accompany orders when necessary.

* Foreign Exchange Students and Agriculture

Office of International Cooperation
International Training Division
U.S. Department of Agriculture
South Building, Room 3121

Washington, DC 20250-4300   202-690-2796

Students from developing countries can obtain assistance in identifying where to train in agriculture in the U.S. and in other countries.

* Foreign Language Materials Acquisition

Library Development Staff
Library Programs/OERI
U.S. Department of Education
555 New Jersey Ave., NW, Room 404
Washington, DC 20208-5571   202-219-1315

The Department of Education has grants available for state and local libraries for the acquisition of foreign language materials such as books, periodicals, newspapers, microforms, and various audio-visual materials. Contact the Library Development Staff for details.

* Foreign Language Training

Defense Language Institute
Foreign Language Center
OPP-PP
Presidio of Monterey, CA 93944   408-242-5000

The Defense Language Institute is one of the world's largest language training centers. The holdings of its library--over 100,000 books in 50 languages--are available through a national inter-library loan program. The non-resident division offers foreign language courses for sale. A catalog of the languages available and items available for sale may be obtained for $5.25. Write or call for brochures on the Institute and information regarding inter-library loans.

* Foreign Student Support Services

Advising, Teaching, and Specialized Programs Division
Office of Academic Programs
Bureau of Educational and Cultural Affairs
United States Information Agency (USIA)
301 Fourth St., SW, Room 349
Washington, DC 20547   202-619-5434

The U.S. Information Agency (USIA) develops a variety of programs to aid foreign students in the United States. Free information is available.

* Foreign Training for Veterans, Inservice Students and Eligible Dependents

Veterans Education Service Benefits Administration (225B)
U.S. Department of Veterans Affairs (VA)
810 Vermont Ave., NW
Washington, DC 20420   202-273-7293

The pamphlet, *Foreign Training for Veterans, Inservice Students and Eligible Dependents*, provides general information about the approval of courses at foreign schools. It also provides specific information for veterans, inservice students and dependents planning to pursue training at a foreign school. This pamphlet lists those foreign schools which offer at least one course approved for training. Note, however, that not all the courses at a listed school are necessarily approved for training. Please read the pamphlet carefully. It is available from your regional VA office.

* Fulbright Foreign Studies Scholarships

Office of Academic Programs
The Bureau of Educational and Cultural Affairs
United States Information Agency (USIA)
301 Fourth St., SW, Room 234
Washington, DC 20547   202-619-4360

This office develops and runs all academic programs of USIA, including the best-known educational exchange, the Fulbright Scholarship program. About 5,000 Fulbright grants are awarded each year to American students, teachers, and scholars to work abroad and to foreign citizens to teach, study, and conduct research in the U.S. The book *Fulbright Scholar Program: Grants for Faculty and Professionals* contains information on the application process for grants, the fields of study necessary, and a directory of country programs/requirements. In addition to the Fulbright program, the Academic Exchange Programs Division of this office administers grants to private agencies conducting complementary programs to the Fulbright academic exchanges, and has responsibilities for foreign research centers, Fulbright commissions, and seminars for foreign Fulbright students. Contact this office for more information and application forms for the Fulbright program.

* Grants Administration Manual

Superintendent of Documents
Government Printing Office   202-512-1800
Washington, DC 20402   Fax: 202-512-2250

This manual is designed to provide guidelines on the fiscal and administrative aspects of grants management to all granting agencies of the Department of Health and Human Services. Subscription service consists of a basic manual and updated transmittal letters for an indeterminate period in looseleaf form, punched for 3-ring binder. Subscription price is $38.00, order #917-002-00000-2. A complete *Subject Bibliography on Grants and Awards* is available by phone or mail and via the Government Printing Office Faxwatch at 202-512-1716.

* Health Care Training Programs

Veterans Health Education Service Benefits (225B)
U.S. Department of Veterans Affairs (VA)
810 Vermont Ave., NW
Washington, DC 20420   202-273-7293

The Department of Veterans Affairs (VA) has over 2,000 training relationships between VA health care facilities and schools of medicines, dentistry, nursing, pharmacy, social work, and other allied health professions and occupations at the graduate and undergraduate levels. For more information, contact the office above.

* Health Professional Scholarship Program

Associated Health Professions
Education Programs Services
Veterans Health Administration (143)
U.S. Department of Veterans Affairs (VA)
810 Vermont Ave., NW, Room 878
Washington, DC 20420   202-565-7134

The VA Health Professional Scholarship Program assists in the recruitment of health professionals in the VA health care system. In return for scholarship support while in college, participants agree to serve a minimum of one year in VA medical centers in the discipline for which degree was awarded. For more information, contact the office above. Ask in particular about the Scholarship Awards and the Reserve Member Stipend Awards.

* Higher Education Clearinghouse

ERIC Clearinghouse on Higher Education
George Washington University   800-773-3742
One Dupont Circle NW, Suite 630   202-296-2597
Washington, DC 20036-1183   Fax: 202-296-8379
    Internet: eriche@inet.ed.gov

Subject areas cover education beyond the secondary level that leads to a four-year, masters, doctoral, or professional degree and includes courses and programs designed to enhance or update skills obtained in these degree programs. Also included are student programs, conditions, and problems at colleges and universities. Other areas include academic advising, university and college faculty; graduate and professional education; professional continuing education; governance and management of higher education institutions; legal issues and legislation; financing; planning and evaluation; facilities--their structural design, management implications, curriculum and instructional problems, programs, and development; and business or industry education programs leading to a degree.

* Higher Education Partnerships

Higher Education Programs
Room 3914A
Administration Building
U.S. Department of Agriculture
14th and Independence SW
Washington, DC 20250   202-720-1973

In order to maintain superior scientific and professional expertise in the food and agricultural sciences, higher education must make major shifts in such areas as instructional emphasis, faculty competencies, and scientific instrumentation. Working with colleges and universities, business, and industry, the U.S. Department of Agriculture's (USDA) Higher Education Program (HEP) has initiated several national projects aimed at federal-state and public-private partnerships; assessing competencies needed by scientists; revitalizing curricula; improving faculty development programs; strengthening industry-academia networks to stimulate outstanding students; developing student recruitment programs; and gathering manpower supply-demand statistics and career information.

Education

* Higher Education Programs

Higher Education Programs
Room 3914A
Administration Building
U.S. Department of Agriculture
14th and Independence SW
Washington, DC 20250   202-720-1973

Although the U.S. Department of Agriculture (USDA) does not make individual loans or scholarships to students, it does makes grants to universities to carry out various programs. For information on individual monetary awards, contact your local cooperative extension agent. The USDA administers the following programs:

Food and Agricultural Sciences National Needs Graduate Fellowship Grants: This program consists of competitive institutional grants to recruit and support new graduate students in areas with shortages of expertise in biotechnology, agricultural engineering, food and agricultural marketing, food science, and human nutrition. The fellowship program is a national investment strategy to attract outstanding students to pursue advanced degrees in food and agricultural sciences. Institutions with Master's or doctoral programs in these fields are eligible to participate. Two year stipends for masters students are $10,000 annually, three year stipends for doctoral students are $17,000 annually. For more information, contact Dr. Wm. Jay Jackman.

Higher Challenge Grants: These competitive grants are open to all colleges and universities to ameliorate national problems affecting the quality of education, to foster university partnerships with industry and with other universities, and to stimulate non-Federal support for education. Awards are $80,000 to $160,000 for up to three years. Matching support is required. For more information, contact Dr. Wm. Jay Jackman.

1994 Land Grant Institutions Endowment Fund: This program will enhance educational opportunities for Native Americans by strengthening instructional programs at one of the 29 Tribal Colleges specified as 1994 Land Grant Institutions the areas of student recruitment and retention, curricula development, faculty preparation, instruction delivery systems, and equipment and instrumentation for teaching. For more information, contact Ms. Deborah Cavett or Dr. Jeffrey Gilmore at 202-720-1973.

Higher Education Multicultural Scholars Program: This department-wide initiative is open to all U.S. colleges and universities with baccalaureate and higher degree programs in agriculture, medicine, and closely allied disciplines. The program provides for each student selected for a scholarship. Scholars receive approximately $6,000 per year for up to 4 years. For more information, contact Dr. Wm. Jay Jackman at the office above.

1890 Institution Capacity Building Grants Program: The program addresses the need to 1) attract more minority students into the food and agricultural sciences, 2) expand the linkages among the 1890 institutions and with other colleges and universities, and 3) strengthen the teaching and research capacity of the 1890 land grant institutions to more firmly establish then as full partners in the food and agricultural science and education projects ranging from 1-3 years duration. Research proposals may request up to a maximum or $350,000. For more information, contact Mr. Richard Hood at 202-720-1973.

Tribal Colleges Educational Equity Grants Program: This formula grants program is designed to promote and strengthen higher education in the food and agricultural sciences at the 29 Tribal Colleges designated as 1994 Land Grant Institutions in the Equity in Educational Land Grant Status Act of 1994. Plans of work should focus on one or more of the following areas: Curricula Design and materials Development; Faculty Development and Preparation for Teaching; Instruction Delivery System; Student Experiential Learning; Equipment and Instrumentation for Teaching; or Student Recruitment and Retention. Institutions will receive $50,000 upon approval of an annual Plan of Work. For more information, contact Ms. Deborah Cavett or Dr. Jeffrey Gilmore at 202-720-1973.

Agency grant information is also available on the Internet at http://www.reeusda.gov/

* Higher Education Publications

Superintendent of Documents
Government Printing Office   202-512-1800
Washington, DC 20402   Fax: 202-512-2250

You can receive a Subject Bibliography describing information available for sale from the Government Printing Office. Subject Bibliographies are free and can be requested by mail or phone. You may also have this document delivered directly to your fax machine by calling 202-512-1716. Ask for Subject Bibliography #217.

* Historically Black Colleges and Universities Program

Office of White House Initiatives on the HBCUs.
U.S. Department of Education
7th and D Sts. SW   202-708-8667
Washington, DC 20202   Fax: 202-708-7872

Through the Historically Black Colleges and Universities Program, the Department of Education is tasked to design a program to achieve an increase by the Historically Black Colleges and Universities (HBCU) in federally sponsored programs. The Department of Education can provide you with the annual Federal Performance Report on Executive Agency Actions to Assist HBCUs and answer any questions you may have about the program. Below is a list of contact numbers in the Federal Departments and agencies for the HBCU program.

Agency for International Development	703-875-4502
U.S. Information Agency	202-619-6409
U.S. Department of Agriculture	202-720-6346
Appalachian Regional Commission	202-884-7666
Central Intelligence Agency	703-874-2421
Corporation for National Service	202-606-5000 ext. 234
U.S. Department of Commerce	202-482-8118
U.S. Commission on Civil Rights	202-376-8356
U.S. Department of Defense	703-697-1481
U.S. Department of Education	202-708-8669
U.S. Department of Energy	202-586-8383
U.S. Environmental Protection Agency	202-260-2566
Equal Employment Opportunity Commission	202-663-4402
U.S. Department of Health and Human Services	202-690-7000
U.S. Department of Housing and Urban Development	202-401-6367
U.S. Department of the Interior	202-208-3866
U.S. Department of Justice	202-616-4811
U.S. Department of Labor	202-219-9151
National Aeronautics and Space Administration	202-358-0970
National Endowment for the Arts	202-682-5454
National Science Foundation	703-306-1633
National Endowment for the Humanities	202-606-8273
National Credit Union Administration	703-518-6326
U.S. Nuclear Regulatory Commission	301-415-5097
Office of Personnel Management	202-606-4306
U.S. Department of State	202-647-9295
U.S. Small Business Administration	202-205-7736
Social Security Administration	410-965-2660
U.S. Department of Transportation	202-366-7037
U.S. Department of the Treasury	202-622-0338
U.S. Department of Veterans Affairs	202-482-6719

* International Auditor Fellowship Program

Director,
Office of International Liaison
General Accounting Office (GAO)
441 G St., NW, Room 7806
Washington, DC 20548   202-512-4707

The General Accounting Office (GAO) attempts to share its knowledge and experience with other nations, particularly from the developing world. The most visible effort is the Comptroller General's International Auditor Fellowship Program, established in 1979, through which a small number of auditors from developing countries are selected annually to spend three to six months in an academic and on-the-job experience program in the U.S. Although GAO cannot pay travel and subsistence for the Fellows, it provides the training itself at no cost, and assists many participants in obtaining financial aid from the U.S. Agency for International Development, and the United Nations Development Program, and Fellows are increasingly receiving aid from their own governments. This is GAO's lead office in dealing with representatives of international audit organizations, and those of individual foreign governments.

* Internships in the Performing Arts

Darrell M. Ayers
Internship Program Coordinator
Education Department
The Kennedy Center
Washington, DC 20566   202-416-8807

Internships are designed to offer meaningful learning experiences for people interested in careers in performing arts management and/or arts education. Upper-level undergraduate students (juniors and seniors), graduate students, and students who have graduated but have not been out of school for more than two years are eligible to apply. Contact this office for more information intern responsibilities, benefits, participating components of the Kennedy Center, and the application procedure.

* Land-Grant Colleges

Cooperative State Research and Education Extension Service
U.S. Department of Agriculture
Room 3328, South Building
Washington, DC 20250   202-720-3029

Congress originally mandated that federal funds be used to support a college or university in each state in 1862, which established the land-grant college network. In 1890 additional legislation was passed to include 17 traditionally black institutions. Today, a large variety of initiatives are taking place at these institutions aimed at building and improving programs to educate students in the agricultural sciences. Cooperative Extension Offices, which provide practical education and information to scientists, researchers, farmers, as well as the general public, are located at each land-grant institution. Liaison work with educational, research, government, business, and public and private organizations is conducted. The state agricultural experiment stations--located at the land grant institutions--conduct agricultural research geared at critical state, regional, and national issues. The Office of Higher Education Programs sponsors the 1890 Institution Capacity Building Grants for 1890 Land-Grant universities and Tuskegee university to advance university teaching and research capabilities. Grants range from $50,000 to $350,000 for up to three years.

* Lecturing Opportunities in Hungary

Office of Academic Programs
The Bureau of Educational and Cultural Affairs
United States Information Agency (USIA)
301 Fourth St., SW
Washington, DC 20547   202-619-4420

The U.S. Information Agency (USIA) can provide you with information on the Hamilton and Marshall Chairs which provide for the sending of distinguished American scholars in Economics and Political Science, respectively, to lecture in Hungary.

* Libraries and Lifelong Learning

National Institute on Postsecondary Education
Libraries, and Lifelong Learning (PLLI)
Office of Educational Research and Improvement (OERI)
U.S. Department of Education
555 New Jersey Ave. NW
Washington, DC 20208-5531   202-219-2207

The Institute conducts research and development activities designed to promote quality and access in the education and training received by adults. These activities will help accomplish the major objectives of an important National Education Goal: That every adult American will be literate and possess the knowledge and skills necessary to compete in a global economy and exercise the rights and responsibilities of citizenship. The work is concentrated in postsecondary education, adult literacy, libraries and community-based education, and special mission institutions such as tribal colleges. A major component of the mission are the Research and Development Centers created to complement the work of the institute.

* Library Career Training Grants

Library Development Staff
Library Programs/OERI
U.S. Department of Education
555 New Jersey Ave., NW, Room 404
Washington, DC 20208-5571   202-219-2293

The Department of Education awards grants for professional education or retraining in librarianship through fellowships, institutes, or traineeships in order to establish, develop, and expand programs of library and information science, including new techniques of information transfer and communication technology.

* Library Resources Program

Library Development Staff
Library Programs/OERI
U.S. Department of Education
555 New Jersey Ave., NW, Room 404
Washington, DC 20208-5571   202-219-2293

The Department of Education promotes high quality research and education

nationwide by providing funds to major research libraries to preserve and strengthen their collections as well as expanding resources available to university researchers.

* Lunar Samples for University Educators

NASA Johnson Space Center
Curator's Office, Code SN2   713-483-3274
Houston, TX 77058-3696   Fax: 713-483-5347

Under the Thin Section Program a set of lunar thin sections is available for instructive and study purposes by college and university science instructors. The materials consist of twelve samples of lunar soils and rocks and a description booklet. Information about this and other programs is available from the regional Teacher Resource Centers. See listing in the science teachers and students section.

* Montgomery GI Bill for Education - Active Duty

Education Services (22)
Veterans Benefits Administration
U.S. Department of Veterans Affairs
810 Vermont Ave, NW
Washington, DC 20420   202-273-7132

You may be eligible for benefits under the Montgomery GI Bill if you are on active duty or have served three years in the active duty military or two years active plus four years in the reserve. You must have served in the military after June 30, 1985 and been honorably discharged if no longer in the service. Contact the Benefits Administration for the free booklet *Summary of Education Benefits Under the Montgomery GI Bill-Active Duty Educational Assistance Program, Chapter 30 of Title 38 U.S. Code*. This booklet contains information on eligibility and benefits.

* Montgomery GI Bill for Education - Selected Reserve Duty

Education Services (22)
Veterans Benefits Administration
U.S. Department of Veterans Affairs
810 Vermont Ave, NW
Washington, DC 20420   202-273-7132

Reservists who have or have had a 6 year obligation to serve in the Selected Reserve after June 30, 1985, have completed the Initial Active Duty Training, and are in good standing with their units may be eligible for educational benefits under the Montgomery GI Bill. Contact the Benefits Administration for the free booklet *Summary of Educational Benefits Under the Montgomery GI Bill-Selected Reserve Educational Assistance Program, Chapter 106 of Title 10 U.S. Code*. This booklet contains information on eligibility and benefits.

* NASA University Programs Branch

Education Division
Mail Code FE
NASA Headquarters
Washington, DC 20546   202-358-1531

This program awards grants to graduate students on a competitive basis whose research interests are compatible with NASA research programs. Fellowships are for one year and are renewable, based on progress reports, of up to three years. The fellowships also allow students to carry out a plan of study or research at their home university, but those awarded by NASA field centers require fellows to spend some time at the center, usually from a few weeks to a summer each year.

* National Center on Adult Literacy

University of Pennsylvania
3910 Chestnut Street
Philadelphia, PA 19104-3111   215-898-2100

The National Center on Adult Literacy (NCAL) heads a national initiative to focus research and development on adult literacy. The center sponsors innovative research, works with practitioners to improve instruction, and gives decision-makers the tools to form sound practices. Current project areas include: motivational factors in adult literacy participation, families and literacy learning, workplace literacy, and adult literacy and English as a second language. The Center publishes the quarterly newsletter *NCAL Connections*. Also ask for a publications list.

* Native American Programs

Office of Indian Education Programs
Bureau of Indian Affairs

U.S. Department of the Interior
1849 C St. NW
Washington, DC 20240   202-208-6175

The Bureau of Indian Affairs sponsors several programs to promote higher education for Native Americans. The Higher Education Grant Program provides grants to Indians to work toward an undergraduate degree. The Special Higher Education Grant Program provides funds for Indians to pursue a graduate degree. The Adult Education Program provides funds for Indian adults to pursue a GED. The Summer Law Program provides funding for 30 Indian Students who have been accepted into an accredited law school to participate in a summer institute which will prepare them for the first year of law school. A good source of information on Indian education in general is the annual *Office of Indian Education Programs Education Directory*.

* Occupational Safety and Health Education

Educational Resource Development Branch
Division of Training and Manpower Development
National Institute of Occupational Safety and Health (NIOSH)
6474 Columbia Parkway
Cincinnati, OH 45336   513-533-8241

Training grants are awarded by the National Institute of Occupational Safety and Health (NIOSH) to support educational programs in the fields of industrial hygiene, occupational health nursing, occupational/industrial medicine, occupational safety, and other specialized areas. The objective of this program is to award funds to eligible institutions or agencies to assist in providing an adequate supply of qualified professional and para-professional occupational safety and health personnel to carry out the purposes of the Occupational Safety and Health Act. NIOSH does not provide direct assistance to students. Student financial assistance may be offered by NIOSH training grantees and students should contact those schools in which they are interested. To receive additional written information call 404-332-4561 and refer to announcement #123. If you still have questions you can contact the office above or the Grants Management Specialist at 404-842-6630.

* Postsecondary Education National Center

National Center for Research to Improve
   Postsecondary Teaching and Learning
School of Education
University of Michigan
Ann Arbor, MI 48198-1259   313-936-2741

Major research areas include classroom teaching and learning strategies; curricular design: influences and impact; faculty as a key resource; organizational context for teaching and learning; learning, teaching and technology; research leadership, and design and integration. Publications are available through ERIC at 800-443-3742.

* Postsecondary School Administration

Center for Higher Education Governance and Leadership
University of Maryland
College of Education, Room 4114
CSS Building
College Park, MD 20742-2435   301-405-5582

Major research areas cover the examination of postsecondary education finance and governance.

* Publications on Higher Education

Superintendent of Documents
Government Printing Office   202-512-1800
Washington, DC 20402   Fax: 202-512-2250

Adult Literacy and New Technologies: Tools for a Lifetime, 1993, ($16.00, #052-003-01330-4)

Basic Student Charges at Postsecondary Institutions: Academic Year 1993-1994, Tuition and Required Fees and Room and Board Charges at 4-Year, 2-Year, and Public Less-Than-2-Year Institutions, 1994 ($11.00, #065-000-00701-1)

Beginning Postsecondary Students Longitudinal Study First Follow-up (BPS:90/92) 1994, Data Analysis System CD-ROM ($14.00, #065-000-00718-5) *Final Public Technical Report*, Book, 1994 ($17.00 #065-000-00659-6)

Campus Security: A First Look at Promising Practices, 1994 ($2.25 #065-000-00681-2)

Characteristics of Nation's Postsecondary Institutions: Academic Year 1994-1994, 1994 ($2.50, #065-000-00696-1)

Compilation of Federal Education Laws, Volume 3, Higher Education Laws (1993, $23.00, #052-070-06850-7)

Compliance Supplement for Audits of Institutions of Higher Learning and Other Non Profit Institutions (1991, $56.50, #041-001-00363-1)

Contractor Reports:

Changes in Undergraduate Student Financial Aid: Fall 1986 to Fall 1989 (1993, $11.00, #065-000-00592-1)

National Postsecondary Student Aid Study, Students at Less-Than-4-Year Institutions (1992, $4.25, #065-000-00541-7)

Occupational and Educational Outcomes of Recent College Graduates One Year After Graduation, 1991 (1993, $6.00, #065-000-00617-1)

Profile of Undergraduates in United States Postsecondary Education Institutions, 1989-1990 (1993, $7.50, #065-000-00590-5)

Undergraduates Who Work While Enrolled in Postsecondary Education 1989-1990 (1994, $6.00, #065-000-00676-2)

Current Funds Revenues and Expenditures of Institutions of Higher Education, Fiscal Years 1984 Through 1992 (1994, $3.25, #065-000-00682-1)

Deaf and Hard of Hearing Students in Postsecondary Education (1994, $4.75, #065-000-00637-5)

Degrees and Other Awards Conferred by Institutions of Higher Education: 1991-1992 (1994, $3.25, #065-000-00694-4)

Digest of Education Statistics, 1994 (1994, $33.00, #065-000-00693-6)

Directory of Postsecondary Institutions, 1991-1992, Volume 2, Less-Than-2-Year (1992, $22.00, #065-000-00534-4)

EDsearch: Education Statistics on Disk (CD-ROM, 1994, $14.00, #065-000-00690-1)

Financial Investigations: A Financial Approach to Detecting and Resolving Crimes: Instructor's Guide (1991, $48.00, #048-004-02328-8) *Student Workbook* (1994, $13.00, #048-004-02327-0)

Higher Education Amendments of 1992 (1992, $12.00, #869-016-00083-7)

Higher Education Opportunities for Minorities and Women: Annotated Selection (1994, $7.50, #065-000-00687-1)

Higher Education Technical Amendments of 1993 ($1.50, #869-012-00208-6)

Military Cutbacks and the Expanding Role of Education (1992, $13.00, #065-000-00545-0)

National Assessment of College Student Learning: Getting Started, A Summary of Beginning Activities (1993, $12.00, #065-000-00566-2)

Identification of the Skills to be Taught, Learned and Assessed (1994, $20.00, #065-000-00674-0)

National Household Education Survey, Adult Education: Employment Related Training (1994, $2.75, #065-000-00652-9)

National Postsecondary Student Aid Study: Financing Undergraduate Education, 1990 (1993, $9.00, #065-000-00571-9)

National Survey Results on Drug Use From the Monitoring the Future Study, 1975-..., Volume 2, College Students and Young Adults (1992: $13.00, #017-024-01512-1; 1993, $13.00, #017-024-1537-7)

Postsecondary Education Facilities Inventory and Classification Manual (1992, $13.00, #065-000-00644-8)

Postsecondary Student Outcomes: A Feasibility Study (1992, $5.50, #065-000-00489-5)

Projections of Education Statistics to 2004 (1993, $13.00, #065-000-00608-1)

Reaching the Goals, Goal 2, High School Completion (1993, $2.75, #065-000-00613-8)

Research and Intervention: Preventing Substance Abuse in Higher Education (1994, $8.00, #065-000-00643-0)

Residence and Migration of First-Time Freshman Enrolled in Higher Education Institutions: Fall 1992 (1995, $2.50, #065-000-0735-5)

Science and Engineering Indicators (1991. $29.00, #038-000-00587-1; 1993, $39.00, #038-000-00589-8)

Smoking, Drinking and Illicit Drug Use Among American Secondary School Students, College Students and Young Adults, 1975-1991 ($14.00, #017-024-01497-4)

State Higher Education Profiles: A Comparison of State Higher Education Data for Fiscal Year 1991 (1994, $39.00, #065-000-00712-6)

Study of Selected Non-sampling Errors in the 1991 Survey of Recent College Graduates (1994, $13.00, #065-000-00721-5)

Trends in Our Own Land: Cultural Literacies and the College Curriculum (1992, $5.00, #065-000-00535-2)

Trends in Degrees Conferred by Institutions of Higher Education: 1984-1985 Through 1990-1991 (1993, $4.25, #065-000-00591-3)

* Resident Research Associate Program

Education Division
Mail Code FE
NASA Headquarters
Washington, DC 20546   202-358-1531

This program gives postdoctoral scientists and engineers an opportunity to perform research at specified National Aeronautics and Space Administration (NASA) field centers, working full time on the research that their award is based on. They must be in residence at the sponsoring field center during the entire associateship. Awardees must hold a PhD, ScD, or other earned research doctoral degree recognized in U.S. academic circles as equivalent to the PhD, and must also demonstrate superior ability for creative research.

* Sea-Grant Colleges

Office of National Sea-Grant College Programs
National Oceanic and Atmospheric Administration
U.S. Department of Commerce
1315 East-West Hwy.
Silver Spring, MD 20910   301-713-2431 ext. 150
The National Sea Grant College Program is a national network of over 300 colleges, universities, research institutions, and consortia working in partnership with industry and the federal government to support Great Lakes and marine research, education, and extension services. This program provides support for institutions engaged in comprehensive marine research, education, and advisory service programs, supports individual projects in marine research and development, and sponsors education of ocean scientists and engineers, marine technicians, and other specialists at selected colleges and universities.

* Service Academy Appointments

For those seeking appointments to the service academies, it is necessary to write your U.S. Senator or Representative for a recommendation. Call the Capitol switchboard to reach your Member of Congress at 202-224-3121.

* State Resource Centers for Adult Education

The following are sources of adult education information at the state level:

Alabama
Alabama Adult Literacy Resource Center (AALRC), Joe Macaluso, State Department of Education, 5343 Gordon Persons Bldg., 50 North Ripley St., P.O. Box 30201, Montgomery, AL 36104-2101; 334-242-8182, Fax 334-242-2236, E-mail: mcaluso@sdenet.alsde.edu

Alaska
Northwest Regional Literacy Resource Center, Alan Waugh, 1701 Broadway, Seattle, WA 98122; 206-507-3882, Fax 206-344-4377, E-mail: awaugh@seaccd.sccd.ctc.edu

Governor's Contact for Alaska, Constance Munro, Supervisor, Adult Basic Education, Department of Education, 801 West 10th St., Suite 200, Juneau, AK 99801-1894; 907-465-8714, Fax 907-465-8714, E-mail: none

Arizona
The Arizona Adult Literacy & Technology Resource Center, Inc., Maureen Ambrose, Executive Director, 703 East Highland, Phoenix, AZ 85014; 602-265-0231, Fax 602-265-7403, E-mail: maaltrek@aol.com

Arkansas
Arkansas Adult Education/Literacy Resource Center, Janie Carter, Director, University of Arkansas, Monticello Campus, Southeast Arkansas Education Service Cooperative, Box 3507, Willard Hall, 1st Floor, Monticello, AR 71655-3507, 501-367-6848, Fax 501-367-9877, E-mail: jcarter@seaesc.kiz.us

California
California Literacy Resource Center, Carol Talan, Executive Director, 9738 Lincoln Village Dr., Sacramento, CA 95827-3399; 916-228-2760, Fax 916-228-2726, E-mail: talan@connectinc.com

Colorado
Colorado State Literacy Resource Center, Debra Fawcette, Coordinator, Department of Education, State Library & Adult Education Office, 201 East Colfax Ave., Room 100, Denver, CO 80203; 303-866-6611, Fax 303-830-0793, E-mail: dfawcette@csn.org

Connecticut
Literacy Resource Center, Betty Huckabee, Coordinator, Adult Training and Development Network (ATDN), 785 Unquowa Rd., Fairfield, CT 06430; 302-365-8800 ext. 306, Fax 203-259-7067, E-mail: none

Delaware
Delaware State Literacy Resource Center, Daphne Mathews, Director, Genevieve R. Motley, Administrative Assistant, ACE Network, Delaware State University, Education and Humanities Center, 1200 North DuPont Hwy., Dover, DE 19901; 302-739-6959, Fax 302-739-6017, E-mail: acenetwork@aol.com

District of Columbia
District of Columbia Literacy Resource Center, Marcia Harrington, Director, Martin Luther King Memorial Library, 901 G Street NW, Room 300, Washington, DC 20001; 202-727-1616/2431, Fax 202-727-1129, E-mail: marcia_harrington@csgi.com

Florida
The Florida Adult Literacy Resource Center discontinued effective July 1, 1995

Georgia
Georgia Literacy Resource Center, Kimberly E. Lee, Curriculum Coordinator, Georgia Department of Technical & Adult Education, 1800 Century Pl. NE, Atlanta, GA 30345-4304; 404-679-1624, Fax 404-679-1630, E-mail: none

Hawaii
Literacy Office, Sue Berg, Literacy Coordinator, 465 South King St., Room B-1, Honolulu, HI 96813; 808-586-7188, Fax 808-586-7191, E-mail: none

Idaho
Northwest Regional Literacy Resource Center, Alan Waugh, 1701 Broadway, Seattle, WA 98122

Governor's contact for Idaho: Shirley Spencer, Director, Adult Education, State Department of Education, P.O. Box 83720, Boise, ID 83720-0027; 208-334-2187, Fax 317-232-9121, E-mail: stspence@sde.id.us

Illinois
Illinois Network of Literacy/Adult Education Resources, Judith Rake, Literacy Program Director, 431 South 4th St., Springfield, IL 62701; 217-785-6921, Fax 217-785-6927, E-mail: jrake@library.sos.il.us

Indiana
Indiana Literacy & Technical Education Resource Center, Gael Deppert, Director, Indiana State Library, 140 North Senate Ave., Room 208, Indianapolis, IN 46204; 317-233-5200, In-state 800-233-4572, Fax 317-233-5333, E-mail: none

Iowa
Northeast Iowa Regional Library System, James E. Sixta, Administrator, 415 Commercial St., Waterloo, IA 50701; 319-233-1200, 800-772-2023, Fax 319-233-1964, E-mail: sixta@cobra.uni.edu

Kansas
Kansas State Literacy Resource Center, Diane Glass, Co-Director, 913-296-7159, Janet Stotts, Co-Director, 913-296-3192, Kansas State Board of Education, 120 South E. 10th Ave., Topeka, KS 66612; Fax 913-296-7933, E-mail: dglass@sml.pgw.ksbe.state.us and jstotts@smtpgw.ksbe.state.ks.us

Kentucky
Kentucky Center for Adult Education and Literacy, Kay Beall, Coordinator, 1049 US 127 South, Suite 3, Frankfort, KY 40601; 502-564-6624, 800-928-6485, Fax 502-564-6407, E-mail: kykay.bea@dial-in.nw.dc.us or gsullivan wfdccpt.wfdc.internet@msmail.state.ky.us

Louisiana
Louisiana State Literacy Resource Center, Jerry Pinsel, Executive Director, Office of Lifelong Learning, Office of the Governor, P.O. Box 94004, Baton Rouge, LA 70804-9004; 504-342-2462, Fax 504-342-1494, E-mail: oll@tyrell.net

Maine
Center for Adult Learning and Literacy, Sandy Brawders, Director, Adult Learning and Literacy, University of Main, 5766 Shibles Hall, Orono, ME 04469-5766; 207-581-2498, Fax 207-581-2423, E-mail: brawders@maine.maine.edu

Maryland
Maryland State Adult Literacy Resource Center, Patricia Thomas-Towns, Resource Specialist, 301 North Broadway, Baltimore, MD 21231; 410-327-2512, 800-358-3010, Fax 410-396-0979, E-mail: none

Michelle Frazier/DCTAL, 200 West Baltimore St., Baltimore, MD 21201; 410-767-0161

Massachusetts
Massachusetts State Literacy Resource Center System for Adult Basic Education Support (SABES), Sally Waldron, Director, World Education, 210 Lincoln St., Boston, MA 02111; 617-482-9485, Fax 617-482-0617, E-mail: sally_waldron@jsi.com

Michigan
State Literacy Resource Center, Virginia Watson, Director, Central Michigan University, Room 219A, Ronana Hall, Mt. Pleasant, MI 48859; 517-774-7690/7691, Fax 517-774-2181, E-mail: 3431Z67@cmuvm.csv.cmich.edu

Minnesota
MN/South Dakota Regional Literacy Resource Center, Virginia Heinrich, Director,

University of St. Thomas, 2115 Summit Ave., St. Paul, MN 55105; 612-962-5570, Fax 612-962-5406, E-mail: vmheinrich@stthomas.edu

Mississippi
Mississippi State Literacy Resource Center
Judy Williams, Director, Governor's Office of Literacy, 3825 Ridgewood Rd., Jackson, MS 39211; 601-982-5691, in-state 800-325-7323, Fax 601-364-2319, E-mail: judy@gol.state.ms.us

Missouri
Literacy Investment for Tomorrow (LIFT), Diana Schmidt, Executive Director, 300 South Broadway, St. Louis, MO 63192; 314-421-1970, in-state 800-539-5170, Fax 314-539-5170, E-mail: stodea@aol.com

Montana
Montana State Literacy Resource Center, Richard Miller, Librarian for Special Population, Montana State Library, 1515 East 6th Ave., Helena, MT 59620-1800; 406-444-5351, Fax 406-444-5612, E-mail: none

Nebraska
Nebraska Institute for the Study of Adult Literacy, John M. Dirkx, Director and Terri Deems, Coordinator, Department of Vocational and Adult Education, Room 511, University of Nebraska, P.O. Box 880515, Lincoln, NE 685888-0515; 608-472-8331, Fax 608-472-5907, E-mail: nisal@unlinfo.unl.edu

Nevada
Nevada State Literacy Resource Center, Emmy Bell, Coordinator, Nevada Literacy Coalition, Nevada Literacy Library & Archives, 1000 Steward St., Capitol Complex, Carson City, NV 89710; 702-687-8340, in-state 800-445-9673, Fax 702-687-8311, E-mail: nlcnevada@connectinc.com

New England
Nashua Adult Learning Center, Silja Kallenbach, Coordinator, World Education, 210 Lincoln St., Boston, MA 02111; 617-482-9485, Fax 617-482-0617, E-mail: ssk@world.std.com

New Hampshire
Nashua Adult Learning Center, Terri Viens, JOBS Coordinator, 4 Lake St., Nashua, NH 03060; 603-882-9080, Fax 603-882-0069, E-mail: none

New Jersey
Adult Literacy Enhancement Center, Janet F. Buongiomo, Manager, Professional Development Office, 1090 King George Post Rd., Bldg. #9, Edison, NJ 08837; 908-225-4545, Fax 908-225-0235, E-mail: none

New Mexico
New Mexico Coalition for Literacy Resource Center, Sylvia Sandoval, Interim Director, Michelle Jaschke, Resource Developer, 1510 St. Francis Dr., P.O. Box 6085, Santa Fe, NM 87502; 505-982-3997, Fax 505-982-4095, E-mail: ssnmcl@aol.com

New York
New York State Literacy Resource Center, Joseph Mangano, Director, State University of New York, 135 Western Ave., Room 208 Husted, Albany, NY 12222; 518-442-5510, Fax 518-442-3933, E-mail: sharonlrc@aol.com

North Carolina
North Carolina Literacy Resource Center, Mary Dunn Siedow, Director, 530 North Wilmington St., Raleigh, NC 27604; 919-715-5794, Fax 919-715-5796, E-mail: nclrc@cybernetics.net

North Dakota
Statewide Adult Education Resource Center (SAERC), G. David Massey, Director, Department of Public Instruction, Division of Adult Education and Literacy, 600 East Boulevard Ave., Bismarck, ND 58505-0440; 701-328-2393, Fax 701-328-4770, E-mail: dmassey@c01as400.state.nd.us

Ohio
The Ohio Literacy Resource Center, Jean Stephens, Director, Kent State University, 414 White Hall, P.O. Box 5190, Kent, Ohio 44242-0001; 216-672-4841, Fax 216-672-4841, E-mail: jstephen@kentvm.kent.edu

Oklahoma
Oklahoma Literacy Resource Center, Ira L. Isch, Director, Oklahoma Department of Libraries, 200 Northeast 18th St., Oklahoma City, OK 73105-3298; 405-521-2502 ext. 249, 800-522-8116 ext. 249, E-mail: iisch@aol.com

Oregon
Northwest Regional Literacy Resource Center, Alan Waugh, 1701 Broadway, Seattle, WA 98122; 206-507-3882, Fax 206-344-4377, E-mail: awaugh@seaccd.sccd.ctc.edu

Governor's contact for Oregon:
Donna Lane, Assistant State Commissioner, Oregon Office of Community College Services, 255 Capitol St. NE, Salem, OR 97310; 503-378-8648 ext. 329, Fax 503-378-8434, E-mail: donna.lane@state.or.us

Pennsylvania
ADVANCE Clearinghouse and Resource Center, Evelyn Werner, Director, Pennsylvania Department of Education, 333 Market St., 11th Floor, Harrisburg, PA 17126-0333; 717-783-5420, in-state 800-992-2283, Fax 717-783-783-5420, E-mail: werner@hslc.org

Western Pennsylvania Adult Literacy Resource Center (WPALRC), Christina Kemp, Resource Specialist, 347 William Flynn Hwy., Route 8, Gibsonia, PA 15044-9463; 412-961-0294, 800-446-5607, Fax 412-443-1310

Puerto Rico
Literacy and Adult Education Resource Center, Gladys Perez, Director, Centro de Recursos para lo Alfabetizacion y Educacion de Adultos, Education Department, 6TO, Piso, P.O. Box 190-759, Hato Rey, PR 00919-0759; 809-759-2000 or 281-0271, Fax 809-754-0843, E-mail: none

Rhode Island
Rhode Island Literacy Resource Center, Howard L. Dooley, Jr., Director, 645 Elmwood Ave., Providence, RI 02907; 401-785-3050, Fax 401-785-3090, E-mail: rilrc@aol.com

South Carolina
South Carolina Literacy Resource, Dianna Deaderick, South Carolina Department of Education, 1722 Mail St., Suite 104, Columbia, SC 29201; 803-929-2574, Fax 803-929-2571, E-mail: diannadsc@aol.com

South Dakota
South Dakota Literacy Resource Center, Dan Boyd, Coordinator, State Library, 800 Governor's Dr., Pierre, SD 57501; 605-773-3131, Fax 605-773-4950, E-mail: dan.b@stlib.state.sd.us

Tennessee
Tennessee Literacy Resource Center, Brenda Bell, Associate Director, Center for Literacy Studies, University of Tennessee, 600 Henley St., Knoxville, TN 37996-4531; 615-974-4109, Fax: 615-974-3857, E-mail: bbell@ukvx.utk.edu OR literacy@ukvx.utk.edu

Texas
Texas Literacy Resource Center, JoAnn Martin, Director, College of Education, Texas A&M University, 618 Harrington, College Station, TX 77843-3256; 409-845-5965, Fax 409-845-0409, E-mail: jmartin@acs.tamu.edu

Utah
Utah Literacy and Adult Education Resource Center, Murray Meszaros, Specialist, Utah State Office of Education, 250 East 500 South St., Salt Lake City, UT 84111; 801-538-78701, Fax 801-538-7868, E-mail: murray.meszaros@usoe.k12.ut.us

Vermont
Vermont Literacy Resource Center, Wendy Ross, Director, Literacy Board, Department of Education, 120 State St., Montpelier, VT 05602; 802-828-3131 or Cara Herring 802-828-3132, Fax 802-828-3146, E-mail: none

Virginia
Adult Education and Literacy Resource Center, Evelyn Nunes, Director, Adult Education Centers for Professional Development, Virginia Commonwealth University, Oliver Hall S., Room 4080, 1015 West Main St., Box 2020, Richmond, VA 23284-2020; 804-828-6521, Fax 804-828-2001, E-mail: enunes@cabell.vcy.edu

Washington
Northwest Regional Literacy Resource Center, Alan Waugh, 1701 Broadway, Seattle, WA 98122; 206-587-3882, Fax 206-344-4377, E-mail: awaugh@seaccd.sccd.ctc.edu

Northwest Regional Literacy Resource Center, Patricia Green, Director, O.A.L.-S.B.C.T.C., Box 24295, Olympia, WA 98504-2495; 206-753-3662, Fax 206-664-8808, E-mail: none

West Virginia
The Center for Adult Literacy & Learning (CALL) has been closed.

Wisconsin

Wisconsin Literacy Resource Center, James A. Mueller, Director, Board of Vocational/Technical & Adult Education, 310 Price Place, Madison, WI 53707; 608-266-3497, Fax 608-266-1690, E-mail: muellerj@board.tec.wi.us

Wyoming

Wyoming Literacy Resource Center, Donna Amstutz, Assistant Professor, Division of Lifelong Learning and Instruction, College of Education, Room 16, Education Bldg., P.O. Box 3374; 307-766-3969, Fax 307-766-6668, E-mail: amstutz@uwyo.edu

* Veterans Continuing Education

Continuing Education Service (145)
Academic Affairs
Veterans Health Administration
U.S. Department of Veterans Affairs (VA)
810 Vermont Ave., NW
Washington, DC 20420   202-565-7523

The Department of Veterans Affairs conducts system-wide continuing education programs to bring the latest in scientific, medical and management knowledge to VHS & RA employees. These programs include workshops, seminars and individual training, and all forms of audiovisual, print, and transmission media. Contact the office above for more information.

* Vocational Education Clearinghouse

ERIC Clearinghouse on Adult, Career and
Vocational Education
Ohio State University Center on Education and   800-848-4815
Training for Employment   614-292-4353
1900 Kenny Rd.   Fax: 614-292-1260
Columbus, OH 43210-1090   Internet: ericacve@magnus.acs.ohio-state.edu

Subject areas cover all levels of adult and continuing education from basic literacy training through professional skill upgrading; vocational and technical education covering all service areas for secondary, postsecondary, and adult education populations; and career education and career development programs for all ages and populations in educational, institutional, business, and industrial settings.

* Vocational Education Research

National Center Clearinghouse
National Center for Research in Vocational Education (NCRVE)
2150 Shattuck Ave., Suite 1250   800-762-4093
University of California   510-642-4004
Berkeley, CA 94704   Fax: 510-642-2124
E-mail: askncrve@vocserve.berkeley.edu
Gopher: gopher://vocserve.berkeley.edu

WWW: http://vocserve.berkeley.edu

The National Center for Research in Vocational Education (NCRVE) is the nation's largest center for research and development in work-related education. NCRVE has played a key role in developing a new concept of vocational education as the Center works towards fulfilling its mission to strengthen education to prepare all individuals for lasting and rewarding employment, and lifelong learning. This new concept of vocational education has been developed through NCRVE research, development, dissemination, and outreach in the areas of: changing skill demands; the integration of academic and vocational curricula; the integration of secondary and postsecondary programs (tech prep); characteristics and effects of work-based learning; performance measures and standards; methods for serving special populations; staff development; and institutional collaboration. Among the materials offered by the Center are resource papers and research syntheses; newsletters and periodicals; and monographs and reports. Among the services offered are conferences; summer institutes and teleconferences; electronic communications and networking; and information referral services. Technical assistance is offered in the areas of recruiting, hiring and advancing minorities; professional leadership development; and program improvement for special population students. The Center can provide you with an extensive publications catalog as well as a Human Resource directory for all members of the affiliated universities involved in the program.

* White House Fellowship Program

President's Commission on White House Fellowships
712 Jackson Place, NW
Washington, DC 20503   202-395-4522

The White House Fellowship program is a highly competitive opportunity to participate in and learn about the Federal government from a unique perspective. For one year, 20 Fellows are selected to work in the Executive Office of the President or in an Executive Branch department or agency. The qualities being sought are high levels of achievement, demonstrated leadership, commitment to serve others, and the skill which would make one a good special assistant in the short run and a national leader in the long run. Although there is no age limit, the program is designed to encourage future leaders rather than reward established leaders. For further information, contact the above office. Information is also available via the internet at http://www.whitehouse.gov/white_house/wh_fellows/html/fellows1.html

* Workplace Safety and Health Courses

Division of Training and Manpower Development
National Institute for Occupational Safety and health
4676 Columbia Parkway
Cincinnati, OH 45226   513-533-8221

This division offers courses for industry and health care professional on such topics as occupational safety, industrial hygiene, and safety in the laboratory. For a course listing and description, contact this office.

Education

Science Teachers and Students

* Aerospace Education

National Headquarters
Civil Air Patrol
Maxwell AFB, AL 36112-5572   334-293-5463

The Civil Air Patrol (CAP), the civilian auxiliary of the U.S. Air Force, offers workshops, materials, and programs for all grade levels, from kindergarten through the postgraduate level. Resources include activity books, posters, guides to aerospace education and careers, textbooks for one-year high school elective courses in aerospace, and a guide to additional educational resources available from the U.S. Dept. of Defense that includes resources available from military installations, the Air National Guard, Air Force Recruiting Services, military museums, and other sites.

* Aerospace Education Services Program (AESP)

Education Division
Mail Code FE
NASA Headquarters
Washington, DC 20546-0001   202-358-1110

The Aerospace Education Services Program (AESP) is one of NASA's premier outreach programs, reaching millions of students each year with its traveling aerospace education units, which bring the aerospace program into our nation's schools. These units travel to all parts of the country, conducting classroom and assembly programs on the principles of rocketry, living and working in space, aeronautics, space science, and NASA's history and accomplishments. They also provide the most up-to-date information about current and future NASA projects. Prior to a visit, AESP specialists, all of whom are former teachers, make an initial contact with the school to identify any specific educational topics of interest. This information is used by the specialist to customize the program to meet a school's curricula needs. The specialist also encourages inclusion of an in-service workshop prior to the visit to familiarize teachers with the program content and further identify specific areas of interest.

* Aerospace Computer Software

Technology and Evaluation Branch
Education Division
Mail Code FET
NASA Headquarters
Washington, DC 20546   202-358-1540

Several needed enhancements in the availability of software have been identified by NASA's review of computer programs for aerospace education. Instructional enhancements through computer-assisted instruction packages, simulations and databases are being developed. Programs related to astronomy, graphics files, and various reference databases are also among the items being developed. The software development capability is being enhanced through *The Classroom of the Future* project, which is expected to result in a greater number of available titles. Many software packages are available for download via NASA Spacelink.

* Aviation and Space Science Instruction

Aviation Education Officer
Federal Aviation Administration (FAA)
U.S. Department of Transportation
800 Independence Ave., SW
Washington, DC 20591   202-267-3190

The FAA's Aviation Education Program offers volunteer assistance to the nation's schools through the following programs: career guidance; tours of airports, control towers, and other facilities; classroom lectures and demonstrations; aviation safety information; aviation education resource materials; computerized clearinghouse of aviation and space information; aviation science instruction programs for home/school computers; "Partnerships-in-Education" activities; and teachers' workshops. Write to the above office for more information.

* Aviation Materials for Educators

Office of Public Affairs
Federal Aviation Administration
Aviation Education Program

800 Independence Ave., SW
Washington, DC 20591   202-267-3190

The Federal Aviation Administration (FAA), as part of its effort to promote better understanding of aviation and air transportation, offers educational materials and publications to both teachers and students. These include instructional materials, films, aviation career information, historical publications, and a guide to additional materials from other sources.

* Challenger Center for Space Science Education

Challenger Center for Space Science Education
1055 N. Fairfax St., Suite 100
Alexandria, VA 22314   703-683-9740

The Challenger Center for Space Science Education is an international network of facilities and programs founded by the families of the seven crew members of Challenger flight 511, to continue the crew's educational mission. Currently 14 high-tech space simulators are located in science centers, museums, school districts, and soon, universities throughout the United States and Canada. The simulators fly middle school students through two-hour missions, where they learn science and develop problem-solving and communication skills. Challenger Center has developed a wide range of student programs which support the learning center experience as well as teacher workshops, led by teachers from Challenger Center's International Faculty. The center also offers international, interactive, live teleconferences.

* Community Involvement Program

Education Division
Mail Code FE
NASA Headquarters
Washington, DC 20546-0001   202-358-1439

Through a series of meetings, NASA staff members and community educators custom-tailor each Community Involvement Program (CIP) to match the community where it is held. A typical CIP might include school assemblies, teacher workshops, a visit by an astronaut, exhibits in shopping centers and schools, presentations by NASA scientists, competitions for students, and public events.

* Cooperative Education Program (CEP)

Education Division
Mail Code FHP
NASA Headquarters
Washington, DC 20546-0001   202-358-1570

The Cooperative Education Program (CEP) gives high school, college, and graduate students an opportunity to work at a National Aeronautics and Space Administration (NASA) field center while completing their education. Participating students usually alternate working one semester with studying one semester. In addition to job experience, the program also serves as a recruitment tool. Interested students must be attending school, be enrolled in their school's coop program, maintain at least a 2.0 overall grade point average, and be recommended by the school. Each NASA field center negotiates its own cooperative agreements with school in its geographic area, and it is usually the responsibility of a school to initiate the venture.

* Educational Horizons

Education Division
NASA Headquarters
Educational Horizons
Mail Code FE
Washington, DC 20546-0001   202-358-1110

Educational Horizons is the National Aeronautics and Space Administration's (NASA) triannual publication for educators. Each issue announces opportunities for educators and students to interact with NASA and NASA's Field Centers through participation in inservice programs, acquisition of educational publications and multimedia products, as well as through cable television programming and teleconferencing. *Educational Horizons* is published in the fall, winter and spring, and is available free by subscription to educators. *Educational Horizons* is also available in electronic format through NASA Spacelink.

* Environmental/Energy Education

Environmental/Energy Education
Land Resources Division
Resource Development
Tennessee Valley Authority (TVA)
Norris, TN 37828   615-632-1640

Much of the Tennessee Valley Authority's (TVA) environmental education effort is accomplished through university-based environmental education centers. The TVA has worked with several universities and colleges across the Valley and seven states to develop environmental education teaching aids and programs for schools, along with workshops for teachers. At the national level, the TVA has been involved in coordinating programs with the Environmental Protection Agency. In addition, TVA offers teacher workshops and interpretive programs for groups at Land Between the Lakes, an experimental area for schools and the public to study total resource management. Contact this office for more information on the TVA's environmental education programs.

* Graduate Student Researchers Program

Education Division
Mail Code FE
NASA Headquarters
Washington, DC 20546-0001   202-358-1517

This program awards grants to graduate students on a competitive basis whose research interests are compatible with National Aeronautics and Space Administration (NASA) research programs. Fellowships are for one year and are renewable, based on progress reports, of up to three years. The fellowships also allow students to carry out a plan of study or research at their home university, but those awarded by NASA field centers require fellows to spend some time at the center, usually from a few weeks to a summer each year.

* Lunar Rocks On Loan

SN2/Lunar Sample Curator
NASA Johnson Space Center   713-483-3274
Houston, TX 77058-3696   Fax: 713-483-5347

Under the Educational Disk Program, NASA will loan teachers six samples of lunar material (three lunar soils and three lunar rocks) encapsulated in a six-inch diameter clear lucite disk, accompanied by written and graphic descriptions of each sample in the disk; a film; a sound and slide presentation; a teacher workbook; and additional printed material. Science teachers may qualify for the use of the disk by attending one of the many workshops sponsored by NASA's Space Science Education Specialists scheduled during the year at different locations throughout the U.S.

* Math Competition: MATHCOUNTS

Education Division
Mail Code FE
NASA Headquarters
Washington, DC 20546-0001   202-358-1516

MATHCOUNTS is an annual math competition for 7th and 8th grade students that brings a number of organizations together, including the National Aeronautics and Space Administration (NASA) and the U.S. Department of Education, to promote and reward excellence in mathematics. Competition begins each September with a qualifying test, and those who qualify are then coached by their teachers for the regional competition in February, the State competition in April, and the national competition in May in Washington, DC.

* Mathematics Education

Center for the Learning and Teaching of Mathematics
Wisconsin Center for Education Research
University of Wisconsin at Madison
1025 West Johnson St.
Madison, WI 53706   608-263-4285

Major research areas include cognitively guided instruction in mathematics education; learning and instruction of algebra, early arithmetic, geometry, and rational numbers; mathematics curriculum study; and the assessment of mathematics.

* NASA CORE

NASA CORE
Lorain County Joint Vocational School
15181 Route 58 South
Oberlin, OH 44074   216-774-1051, x293 or x294

The National Aeronautics and Space Administration's (NASA) Central Operation of

Resources for Educators (CORE) was established for the national and international distribution of NASA-produced educational materials in audiovisual format. Submit a written request on your school letterhead for a catalogue and order forms. Orders are processed for a small fee that includes the cost of the media.

* NASA Education Satellite Videoconference Series

Videoconference Producer
NASA Teaching From Space Program
308A CITD
Oklahoma State University
Stillwater, OK 74078-0422   403-744-7015
                    E-mail: nasaedutv@smtpgate.osu.hq.nasa.gov

The Education Satellite Videoconference Series for Teachers is offered as an inservice education program for educators through the school year. The content of each program varies, but includes aeronautics or space science topics of interest to elementary and secondary teachers. NASA program managers, scientists, astronauts, and education specialists are featured presenters. The videoconference series is free to registered educational institutions. To participate, the institution must have a C-band satellite receiving system, teacher release time, and an optional long distance telephone line for interaction. Arrangements may also be made to receive the satellite signal through the local cable television system. The programs may be videotaped and copied for later use.

* NASA Education Workshops for Elementary School Teachers (NEWEST)

Education Division
Mail Code FE
NASA Headquarters
Washington, DC 20546   202-358-1516

NEWEST is for elementary school teachers (grades 1-6) in all disciplines. Selected teachers are awarded a two-week, expense-paid workshop at a NASA field center, with each center hosting about 20 teachers. The workshops vary from center to center. Although all focus on current NASA programs, each center conducts activities unique to its work. During their stay, teachers meet with scientists, technicians, and educational specialists. Teachers are instructed how to apply their experiences to their elementary curriculum.

* NASA Education Workshop for Math and Science Teachers (NEWMAST)

Education Division
Mail Code FE
NASA Headquarters
Washington, DC 20546-0001   202-358-1516

NEWMAST makes awards to math, science, and technology teachers in grades 7-12 with a two week, expense-paid workshop at a NASA field center each year. Applications must be submitted in the winter, and the winners are announced in the spring. Teachers are chosen on the basis of educational background, teaching experience, recommendations, personal and professional goals, and an essay explaining how selection for NEWMAST will benefit the applicant's students, colleagues, and community.

* Resident Environmental Education

Environmental/Energy Education
Land Between The Lakes
Resource and Development
Tennessee Valley Authority
Golden Pond, KY 42231   502-924-1606

The Youth Station and Brandon Spring at Land Between The Lakes operates the residential education program to promote better environmental understanding, aesthetic appreciation, and man's place in nature. These dorm-style activity areas are open year-round and accommodate kindergarten through college-level groups. Groups are welcome to carry out their own programs, or the staff can help in developing them. Activities include canoeing, pond studies, and nature walks. With Murray (Kentucky) State University Center for Environmental Education, the staff provides additional workshops for area teachers and in-service students.

* Resident Research Associate Program

Education Division
Mail Code FE
NASA Headquarters

Education

Washington, DC 20546   202-358-1531

This program gives postdoctoral scientists and engineers an opportunity to perform research at specified National Aeronautics and Space Administration (NASA) field centers, working full time on the research that their award is based on. They must be in residence at the sponsoring field center during the entire associateship. Awardees must hold a PhD, ScD, or other earned research doctoral degree recognized in U.S. academic circles as equivalent to the PhD, and must also demonstrate superior ability for creative research.

* Science and Engineering Fairs

Education Division
Mail Code FE
NASA Headquarters
Washington, DC 20546   202-358-1631

The National Aeronautics and Space Administration (NASA) takes part in the International Science and Engineering Fair for high school students by awarding certificates of merit at the regional and state levels of competition, and sending a team of judges to the international fair, where they select up to 12 students to receive an expense-paid trip with their teachers to a NASA field center. Local science fairs that are not affiliated with the international fair can take part in NASA's award system by requesting information from the field center serving their geographical area.

* Science Education

National Center for Improving Science Education
The Network, Inc.
300 Brickstone Sq., Suite 900
Andover, MA 01810   508-470-1080
or

Washington DC Office
2000 L St., NW, Suite 603
Washington, DC 20036   202-467-0652

Major research areas include the assessment of science; science curriculum study; and science instruction study.

* Science, Mathematics, and Environmental Education Information

ERIC Clearinghouse on Science, Mathematics,
  and Environmental Education   800-276-0462
Ohio State University   614-292-6717
1929 Kenny Rd.   Fax: 614-292-0263
Columbus, OH 42310-1080   Internet: ericse@osu.edu

Subject areas cover science, mathematics, environmental, and engineering education at all levels, and within these broad subject areas, the following topics: development of curriculum and instructional materials; teachers and teacher education; learning theory/outcomes (including the impact of such factors as interest level, intelligence, values, and concept development upon learning in these fields); education programs; research and evaluative studies; media applications; and computer applications.

* Science, Technology, and Social Science Database

General Reading Rooms
Library of Congress
Washington, DC 20540   202-707-5522

The *Science, Technology, and Social Science Database* is a computerized directory of more than 14,000 organizations or individuals who will provide information to the general public on topics primarily in science, technology, and the social sciences. Citations generally contain the name of the organization or person, mailing address, telephone number, areas of interest, special collections, publications, and special services.

* Space Camp

U.S. Space and Rocket Center
One Tranquility Base   800-63-SPACE
Huntsville, AL 35805-3399   205-837-3400

Space Camp and Space Academy, sponsored by the Space and Rocket Center, give both children and adults an opportunity to take part in mission-oriented programs similar to an actual space mission. Participants spend from three to ten days learning about the principles of rocketry and living in space, and then go through a simulated mission. Prices range from $400 to $800, depending on the program and age of the participant.

* Space Education Resource Center

U.S. Space Foundation
2860 S. Circle Dr., Suite 2301
Colorado Springs, CO 80906-4184   719-576-8000

The U.S. Space Foundation serves as a national resource for research and educational information on all aspects of space. The foundation has developed or assisted other organizations and individuals in developing space-related educational materials and offering teacher workshops. The staff is also available for classroom visits.

* Spacelink

Spacelink Administrator
Education Programs Office
NASA Marshall Space Flight Center
Mail Code CL-01
Huntsville, AL 35812-0001   205-544-6360

NASA Spacelink is an electronic information system designed to provide current educational information to teachers, faculty and students. Spacelink offers a wide range of materials (computer text files, software, and graphics) related to the space program. Documents on the system include science, mathematics, engineering, and technology education lesson plans, historical information related to the space program, current status reports on NASA projects, news releases, information on NASA educational programs, NASA educational publications, and other materials, such as computer software and images, chosen for their educational value and relevance to space education. The system may be accessed by computer through direct-dial modem or the Internet.

* Space Museum Education Programs

Office of Education
National Air and Space Museum
Smithsonian Institution
Room 211, MRC 305
Washington, DC 20560   202-786-2106

The National Air and Space Museum offers a wide variety of educational activities, including making personnel available for teacher workshops, assistance in preparing resource materials, and making many of its resource materials available in the museum's Education Resource Center. The museum also offers teacher workshops year-round and produces classroom activities and materials for use in conjunction with a planned trip to the museum or as enrichment materials.

* Space Orientation Course for Educators

U.S. Space and Rocket Center
One Tranquility Base   800-63-SPACE
Huntsville, AL 35805-3399   205-837-3400

This orientation course for educators is a five-day program that introduces educators to space-related topics and shows them how to incorporate what they learn there into classroom activities.

* Space Science Student Involvement Program

Education Division
Mail Code FE
NASA Headquarters
Washington, DC 20546-0001   202-358-1631

The Space Science Student Involvement Program (SSIP), an annual program that involves students in creating experiments, art, and newspaper articles in areas of interest to NASA, honors outstanding student work through awarding various prizes, but the awards are secondary to participation in classroom activities. Students complete in five categories, some of which are broken down into separate competitions for different grade levels. Depending on the category, winners receive expense-paid trips to NASA field centers or national science symposia, and cash awards.

* Summer Faculty Fellowship Program

Education Division
Mail Code FE
NASA Headquarters
Washington, DC 20546-0001   202-358-1524

This fellowship program gives faculty fellows in various academic disciplines the opportunity to use NASA field centers to perform research. Those selected spend 10 weeks at a field center and received a stipend. The program is open to U.S. citizens with teaching or research appointments in universities or colleges; priority is given to applicants with two years of experience, and most have doctorate degrees and

Be patient. If any phone number is incorrect, call (area code) 555-1212 and request the new listing.

carry an academic title of assistant, associate, or full professor. About 200 fellowships are awarded each year.

* Summer High School Apprentice Research Program (SHARP)

Education Division
National Aeronautics and Space Administration
Mail Code FE
Washington, DC 20546-0001   202-358-1631

SHARP provides an opportunity for targeted underrepresented minority students in grades 10-12 who live within commuting distance of a participating NASA field center to take part in an eight-week, paid apprenticeship, where they work directly with NASA scientists or engineers. Interested students submit an application and references from a school administrator, teacher, or guidance counselor. Chosen students work with scientists or engineers whose work is related to his or her career aspirations, which may include computers, research, navigation, or guidance systems.

* Teacher Resource Centers (TRC)

Education Division
Mail Code FE
National Aeronautics and Space Administration Headquarters
Washington, DC 20546   202-358-1110

These resource centers contain a wealth of information for educators interested in space- and science-related material: publications, reference books, slides, audio cassettes, video cassettes, telelecture programs, computer programs, lesson plans and activities, and lists of publications available from government and nongovernment sources. Much of the material is free. In the case of media such as videocassettes, however, educators are asked to supply their own media; copying facilities are available at all field centers. What follows is a list of the TRCs and the regions they serve:

NASA Teacher Resource Center, Mail Stop T12-A, NASA Ames Research Center, Moffett Field, CA 94035-1000; 415-604-3574. Areas served: Alaska, Arizona, California, Hawaii, Idaho, Montana, Nevada, Oregon, Utah, Washington, Wyoming.

NASA Teacher Resource Laboratory, Mail Code 130.3, NASA Goddard Space Flight Center, Greenbelt, MD 20771-0001; 301-286-8570. Areas served: Connecticut, Delaware, District of Columbia, Maine, Maryland, Massachusetts, New Hampshire, New Jersey, New York, Pennsylvania, Rhode Island, Vermont.

NASA Teacher Resource Room, Mail Code AP 2, NASA Johnson Space Center, 2101 NASA Road 1, Houston, TX 77058-3696; 713-483-8696. Areas served: Colorado, Kansas, Nebraska, New Mexico, North Dakota, Oklahoma, South Dakota, Texas.

NASA Educators Resource Laboratory, Mail Code ERL, NASA Kennedy Space Center, Kennedy Space Center, FL 32899-0001; 407-867-4090. Areas served: Florida, Georgia, Puerto Rico, Virgin Islands.

NASA Teacher Resource Center for Langley Research Center, Virginia Air and Space Center, 600 Settler's Landing Rd., Hampton, VA 32669-4033; 804-727-0900, x757. Areas served: Kentucky, North Carolina, South Carolina, Virginia, West Virginia.

NASA Teacher Resource Center, Mail Stop 8-1, NASA Lewis Research Center, 21000 Brookpark Rd., Cleveland, OH 44135-3191; 216-433-2017. Areas served: Illinois, Indiana, Michigan, Minnesota, Ohio, Wisconsin.

NASA Teacher Resource Center for Marshall Space Flight Center, U.S. Space and Rocket Center, P.O. Box 070015, Huntsville, AL 35807-7015; 205-544-5812. Areas served: Alabama, Arkansas, Iowa, Louisiana, Missouri, Tennessee.

NASA Teacher Resource Center, Building 1200, NASA John C. Stennis Space Center, Stennis Space Center, MS 29529-6000; 601-688-3338. Areas served: Mississippi.

NASA Teacher Resource Center, Mail Stop CS-530, NASA Jet Propulsion Laboratory, 4800 Oak Grove Dr., Pasadena, CA 91109-8099; 818-354-6916. The Jet Propulsion Laboratory (JPL) serves inquiries related to space and planetary exploration and other JPL activities.

NASA Teacher Resource Center, Public Affairs Office (Trl. 42), NASA Dryden Flight Research Facility, Edwards, CA 93523-0273; 805-258-3456. Areas served: California (mainly cities near Dryden Flight Research Facility).

NASA Goddard Space Flight Center, Wallops Flight Facility, Education Complex, Visitor Center, Building J-17, Wallops Island, VA 23337-5099; 804-824-2297/2298. Areas served: Virginia and Maryland's Eastern Shores.

* Teacher Resource Network

Education Division
Mail Code FE
National Aeronautics and Space Administration Headquarters
Washington, DC 20546   202-358-1110

To make information available to the educational community, NASA has created the Teacher Resource Network made up of Teacher Resource Centers, Regional Teacher Resource Centers, and the Central Operation of Resources for Educators.

* Teaching Materials for Geology

Geologic Inquiries Group
U.S. Geological Survey
907 National Center
Reston, VA 22092   703-648-4383

Packets of geological teaching aids for different grade levels and geographic location are available from the Geologic Inquiries Group and from the Earth Science Information Centers listed elsewhere in this book. These packets include lists of reference materials, various maps and map indexes, and a selection of general interest publications. Requests for teachers packets should be sent on school letterhead, indicating the grade level and subject of interest.

* Urban Community Enrichment Program (UCEP)

Education Division
Mail Code FE
NASA Headquarters
Washington, DC 20546-0001   202-453-2991

The Urban Community Enrichment Program (UCEP) is specifically targeted toward middle-school students in urban areas with high percentages of minorities. NASA specialists will meet with school representatives to formulate a custom-tailored program to fit the school's needs. Typically a program begins with teacher orientation workshops followed by assemblies, a series of student workshops, and classroom visits. In the classroom, NASA specialists work with students on various hands-on activities, such as building rockets or airplanes or learning about how information is transmitted from space back to Earth.

Innovation and Trends

* Appalachia Education Research Center

Appalachia Educational Laboratory, Inc.
1031 Quarrier St.
P.O. Box 1348   800-624-9120
Charleston, WV 25325-1348   304-347-0400

Major activity areas include classroom instruction, school governance and administration, policy and planning, professional preparation and research, regional liaison center, school service center, and rural and small schools. States served: Kentucky, Tennessee, Virginia, and West Virginia.

* Arts Education Research and Testing

University of Illinois at Urbana - Champaign
College of Applied and Fine Arts
110 Agricultural Bldg.
608 E. Lorado Taft Dr.
Champaign, IL 61820   217-333-6061

Major research areas include the development and validation of standardized achievement tests in the area of artistic processes and techniques in art history; national study on literacy and art education; role of music in general education; status surveys in art, visual, dance and drama in the elementary and secondary schools; drama/theatre, visual and dance; influence on culture condition on the learning of arts; development of computer assisted testing (music education); design of studies in dance; designs of studies in theatre; status survey of music education in elementary and secondary schools; and arts education field work: and observational studies.

* Center on Education in the Inner Cities (CEIC)

Mid-Atlantic Regional Educational Laboratory
Temple University Center for Research in Human Development and Education
933 Ritter Annex
13th St. and Cecil B. Moore Ave.   215-204-3030
Philadelphia, PA 19122   Fax: 215-204-5130
         http://blue.temple.edu/-crhde

The Center on Education in the Inner Cities (CEIC) is conducting systematic studies of innovative initiatives that take bold steps to improve the capacity for education in inner cities. CEIC consists of three research and development programs: 1) Family and the Education Process, 2) School Resilience and Learning Success, and 3) The Communities Connection with Education.

* Comprehensive Assistance Centers

Arthur Cole
Comprehensive Assistance Centers
U.S. Department of Education
600 Independence Ave. SW
Washington, DC 20202-6140   202-260-3693

There are 15 federally funded Regional Comprehensive Assistance Centers designed to assist federal, state, and local education agencies in creating educational systems that will assure that all students meet high content and performance standards. The following is a list of these centers and the state or area each one serves. Contact centers for additional information.

Region I
Education Development Center, Inc.
55 Chapel Street
Newton, MA 02158-1060
617-969-7100 ext. 2201
Serving: CT, ME, MA, NH, RI, VT

Region II
New York Technical Assistance Center
32 Washington Place
New York, NY 10003
212-998-5100
Serving: New York State

Region III
Comprehensive Technical Assistance Center
1730 North Lynn Street, Suite 401
Arlington, VA 22209
703-528-3588
Serving: DE, MD, NJ, OH, PA, DC

Region IV
Appalachia Educational Laboratory, Inc.
P.O. Box 1348
Charleston, WV 25325-1348
304-347-0400
Serving: KY, NC, SC, TN, VA, WV

Region V
Southwest Educational Development Laboratory
211 East 7th Street
Austin, TX 78701-6861
512-476-6861
Serving: AL, AR, GA, LA, MS

Region VI
Comprehensive Regional Assistance Center
1025 West Johnson St.
Madison, WI 53706
608-263-4326
Serving: IA, MI, MN, ND, SD, WI

Region VII
Comprehensive Assistance Center
555 Constitution St., Suite 128
Norman, OK 73072-7820
405-325-1711
Serving: IL, IN, KS, MO, NE, OK

Region VIII
Intercultural Development Research Association
5835 Callaghan Rd., Suite 350
San Antonio, TX 78228-1190
210-684-8180
Serving: Texas

Region IX
Southwest Comprehensive Regional Assistance Center
121 Tijeras, NE, Suite 2100
Albuquerque, NM 87102
505-242-7447
Serving: AZ, CO, NM, NV, UT

Region X
Northwest Regional Educational Laboratory
101 SW Main St., Suite 500
Portland, OR 97204
503-275-9479
Serving: ID, MT, OR, WA, WY

Region XI
Far West Laboratory for Education Research
730 Harrison St.
San Francisco, CA 94107
800-64-LEARN
Serving: Northern CA

Region XII
Southern California Comprehensive Regional Assistance Center
9300 Imperial Highway
Downey, CA 90242-2890
310-922-6343
Serving: Southern CA

Region XIII
Alaska Comprehensive Regional Assistance Center
210 Ferry Way, Suite 200
Juneau, AK 99801
Serving: Alaska

Region XIV
Educational Testing Service
1979 Lake Side Parkway, Suite 400
Tucker, GA 30084
770-723-7443
Serving: FL, PR, VI

Region XV
Pacific Comprehensive Regional Assistance Center
(The Pacific Center)
828 Fort Street Mall, Suite 500
Honolulu, HI 96813-4321
808-533-6000
Serving: American Samoa, Federated States of Micronesia, Commonwealth of the Northern Mariana Islands, Guam, Hawaii, Republic of the Marshall Islands, and the Republic of Palau

* Document Reproduction of Education Research

ERIC Document Reproduction Service (EDRS)
Dyn Corp   800-443-ERIC
7420 Fullerton Rd., Suite 110   Fax: 703-440-1408
Springfield, VA 22153   Internet: edrs@inet.ed.gov
This service is responsible for microfilming the ERIC documents announced in *Resources in Education*. Once microfilmed, the RIE documents can be purchased as either microfiche or paper reproductions by simply calling the ERIC Document Reproduction Service (EDRS). You can expect to receive your requests within 3 to 5 working days. EDRS supplies more than 1 million microfiche each month to over 750 locations around the world.

* Educational Abstracts Journal

Superintendent of Documents
U.S. Government Printing Office   202-512-1800
Washington, DC 20402-9371   Fax: 202-512-2250
Published for the U.S. Department of Education in twelve monthly issues, *Resources in Education*, a monthly abstract journal of ERIC, covers the document literature of education. It is indexed by subject institution, personal author, and publication type. A year's subscription to the journal is $77, order #RIE.

* Education and Employment

Institute on Education and the Economy
Teachers College
Columbia University, Box 174   212-678-3091
New York, NY 10027   Fax: 212-678-3699
Major research areas include education and the labor market; the role of family background, school characteristics, and school curriculum in the link between education and labor market outcomes; youth participation in job training and labor market outcomes; knowledge acquisition at work; and community-based planning for work-related education.

* Educational Institutions Providing the ERIC System

ERIC Processing and Reference Facility
Computer Sciences Corp.
Systems Engineering Division   800-799-ERIC
1301 Piccard Dr., Suite 300   301-258-5500
Rockville, MD 20850-4305   Fax: 301-948-3695
                                        Internet: ericfac@inet.ed.gov
The free *Directory of ERIC Information Service Providers* lists all of the service providers, primarily colleges and universities, within the ERIC system according to geographical region. It includes organizations that provide computerized searches of the ERIC database, that have sizeable collections of ERIC microfiche, and that subscribe to and collect the various ERIC publications.

* Education Reform and Policy Research

Center for Policy Research in Education
The Eagleton Institute of Politics Rutgers
The State University of New Jersey

86 Clifton Ave.
New Brunswick, NJ 08901   908-932-1331
Major research areas include curriculum and student standards, teacher policies, indicators and monitoring, new roles and responsibilities; and evolution of reform.

* Educational Research and Databases

Center for Electronic Records
National Archives and Records Administration
8601 Adelphi Rd.
College Park, MD 20740-6001   301-713-6630
This center holds a variety of records pertaining to educational research, including data from the U.S. Department of Education, Office of Education, U.S. Department of Health, Education, and Welfare, as well as other government agencies. Some of the data consists of basic skills test scores, teacher questionnaires, and principal questionnaires.

* Educational Resources Information Center (ERIC)

Access ERIC
1600 Research Blvd.   800-538-3742
Rockville, MD 20850-3172   301-251-5264
                                            Fax: 301-309-2084
                                Internet: acceric@inet.ed.gov
The Educational Resources Information Center (ERIC) is a national education information system responsible for developing, maintaining, and providing access to the world's largest education research database. The ERIC system includes a network of clearinghouses, each of which acquires and reviews documents and prepared indexes and abstracts, which are then entered into the ERIC database, which contains over 650,000 abstracts. ERIC is made available to a wide variety of users through multiple means, including microfiche collections (available in over 700 libraries around the world) and through vendor-provided online and compact disk-read only memory (CD-ROM) searching. Periodic reports, digests, and other documents are prepared by the clearinghouses, each of which covers education research and practice in an assigned topic area. Each clearinghouse also provides a variety of user services, including training, and responds to numerous requests for information. *A Pocket Guide to ERIC* and *All About ERIC* are available free of charge from this office to clarify the activities of the ERIC system.

* Educational Technology

Educational Technology Center
Harvard Graduate School of Education
337 Gutman Library
6 Appian Way
Cambridge, MA 02138   617-495-9373
Major research areas include mathematics, science, computer education, and new technologies.

* Far West Educational Research and Development

Far West Laboratory for Educational Research
  and Development
730 Harrison
San Francisco, CA 94107-1242   415-565-3000
Major activity areas include teaching and learning, improving organizational effectiveness, professional preparation and development, students at risk, Center for Educational Policy, Southern Service Center, rural and small schools, planning and evaluation, and publication services. States served: Arizona, California, Nevada, and Utah.

* Grants and Contracts Service

Office of Management Grants and Contract Service
U.S. Department of Education
Mail Stop 4725
Washington, DC 20202   202-708-8810
This office publishes the pamphlet, *GCMS: Grants and Contracts Management System*, which gives you over-all information about the on-line information system which monitors the educational grant and procurement contract awards of the U.S. Department of Education. It also contains a telephone list of contacts within the system to call for information and inquiries on the status of your application. For information concerning GCMS, contact the Director, Management Support Division, Grants and Contracts Service, 202-732-2773.

Education

* Guidelines for Publishing Educational Material with ERIC

Access ERIC
1600 Research Boulevard
Rockville, MD 20850-3238

800-538-3942
301-251-5506
Fax: 301-309-2084
Internet: acceric@inet.ed.gov

Submitting documents to the Educational Resources Information Center (ERIC) is a free pamphlet outlining the types of documents suitable for ERIC publication and the procedure for submitting the documents to ERIC.

* Guide to the Department of Education Office of Educational Research and Improvement

National Library of Education
Office of Educational Research and Improvement (OERI)
U.S. Department of Education
555 New Jersey Ave., NW
Washington, DC 20208

800-424-1616
202-219-1692
Fax: 202-219-1696

OERI--Who We Are and What We Can Do for You is free pamphlet is an overview of the functions of the Office of Educational Research and Improvement (OERI). It also contains important phone numbers to call for specific projects within the department, including Research, Library Programs, and Information Services.

* Information Resources Clearinghouse

ERIC Clearinghouse on Information Resources and Technology
Syracuse University School of Education
4-194 Center for Science and Technology
Syracuse, NY 13244-2340

315-443-3640
Fax: 315-443-5448
Internet: eric@eric/r.syr.edu

Subject areas cover educational technology and library and information science at all levels. This includes instructional design, development and evaluation with emphasis on educational technology, along with the media of educational communication; computers and microcomputers, telecommunications (cable, broadcast, satellite); and audio and video recordings, film and other audiovisual materials, as they pertain to teaching and learning. Within library and information science, the focus is on the operation and management of information services for education-related organizations. All aspects of information technology related to education are considered within this scope.

* Languages and Linguistics Education Information

ERIC Clearinghouse on Languages and Linguistics
Center for Applied Linguistics
1118 22nd St., NW
Washington, DC 20037-0037

800-276-9834
202-429-9292
Fax: 202-659-5641
Internet: eric@cal.org

Subject areas cover languages and language sciences; theoretical and applied linguistics; all areas of foreign language, second language and linguistics pedagogy, or methodology; psycholinguistics and the psychology of language learning; cultural and intercultural context of languages; application of linguistics in language teaching; bilingualism and bilingual education; sociolinguistics; study abroad and international exchanges; teacher training and qualifications specific to the teaching of a foreign language and second language; commonly and uncommonly taught languages, including English as a second language; and related curriculum developments and problems.

* Leadership in Education

The Principals' Center
Graduate School of Education
Harvard University
336 Guttman Library
6 Appian Way
Cambridge, MA 02138-3704

Fax: 617-495-5900
617-495-3575

The Principals' Center is an organization which attempts to improve the quality of life and learning in schools by encouraging different ways of thinking about common problems; by transforming school problems into opportunities for school improvement; by encouraging clarification of assumptions guiding practice; by offering opportunities for shared problem-solving and reflection; and by providing a context of mutual support and trust in which personal relationships may be established and developed.

* Learning Skills

Center for the Study of Learning
Learning, Research and Development Center
University of Pittsburgh
3939 O'Hara St.
Pittsburgh, PA 15260

412-624-7020

Major research areas include mathematics, science, social studies learning, and learning skills.

* Mid-Atlantic Laboratory for Student Success (LSS)

Mid-Atlantic Regional Educational Laboratory
Temple University Center for Research in Human Development and Education
933 Ritter Annex
13th Street and Cicil B. Moore Ave.
Philadelphia, PA 19122

215-204-3030
Fax: 215-204-5130
http://blue.temple.edu/-crhde

The Laboratory will focus on developing products, program models, and exemplary strategies that are useful and usable for widespread dissemination and application to achieve high academic standards for all children and youth in the mid-Atlantic region. Key areas of programmic emphasis include: enhance functioning and coordination of education; work to create a system of research-based educational reform; emphasize the needs of the most severely disadvantaged students, schools and communities; and link all efforts with those of their regions, states, and the nation. LSS will develop and implement an urban education enhancement program and will focus on building this nation's capacity for fostering educational resilience and learning success of children and youth in urban schools with a concentration of students from a variety of circumstances that place them at risk of school failure.

* Midwest Regional Education Research Lab

Mid-Continent Regional Educational Laboratory
2550 S. Parker Rd., Suite 500
Aurora, CO 80014

303-337-0990

or

3100 Broadway, Suite 209
Kansas City, MO 64111-2413

816-756-2401

Their major activities are to foster regional communication and networks; distribute information, and provide technical assistance to improve educational practice; strengthen the region's capacity to design and implement policies that support school improvement; develop databases on economic, social, political, and educational trends in the region; develop new resources aimed at improving education for students most in need; and rural and small schools. States served: Colorado, Kansas, Nebraska, Missouri, Wyoming, North Dakota, and South Dakota.

* National Longitudinal Study Public Information Division

National Library of Education
Office of Educational Research and Improvement
U.S. Department of Education
555 New Jersey Ave. NW
Washington, DC 20208-5641

800-424-1616
202-219-1522

NELS:88 is a longitudinal study that begins with a survey in 1988 of eighth grade students, their schools, teachers, and their parents. This study will track the critical transitions experienced by young adults as they progress through junior high school, high school, and postsecondary education into the world of work. This study will yield policy-relevant information about such topics as high school effectiveness, discipline, homework, coursetaking patterns, cognitive ability, dropouts, private schools, vocational education, special education, instruction for limited-English-speaking students, postsecondary access and choice, student financial assistance, employment during high school and college, transfer behaviors, vocational training, on-the-job training, labor force participation, employment stability, family formation, and graduate/professional training. Conducted every two years, published information concerning the survey is available in June of the year following the actual survey.

* North Central Region Lab

North Central Regional Educational Laboratory
1900 Spring Rd.
Oakbrook, IL 60521-1480

708-571-4700

Major activity areas include improving student performance, strengthening the quality of instruction, developing the education professions, and rural and small schools. States served: Illinois, Indiana, Iowa, Michigan, Minnesota, Ohio, and Wisconsin.

Be patient. If any phone number is incorrect, call (area code) 555-1212 and request the new listing.

* Northeast Education Research Lab

Regional Laboratory for Educational Improvement
of the Northeast and Islands
300 Brickstone Sq., Suite 950
Andover, MA 01810   508-470-0098
Major activity areas include leadership for school improvement, teacher development, public policy for school improvement, at-risk youth, rural and small schools, and program governance and support. Areas served: Connecticut, Maine, Massachusetts, New Hampshire, New York, Rhode Island, Vermont, Puerto Rico, and the Virgin Islands.

* Northwest Regional Lab

Northwest Regional Educational Laboratory
101 SW Main St., Suite 500   800-547-6339
Portland, OR 97204-3212   503-275-9500
Major activity areas include evaluation assessment, cultural understanding, and equity; business and human resource agencies; professional development, rural and small schools, school improvement; and technology. Other Laboratory Programs include education and work; evaluation and assessment; institutional development and communication; literacy and language; planning and service coordination; R&D for Indian education; school improvement program; technology program; and the Western Center for Drug-Free Schools and Communities. Areas served: Alaska, Idaho, Montana, Oregon, Washington, American Samoa, Guam, Hawaii, and the Northern Mariana Islands.

* Pacific Region Educational Laboratory (PREL)

Pacific Region Educational Laboratory
828 Fort Street Mall, Suite 500   808-533-6000
Honolulu, HI 96813-4321   Fax: 808-533-7599
The Pacific Region Educational Laboratory (PREL) helps schools improve educational outcomes for children, youth, and adults ba assisting education, families, government, community agencies, business, and labor in maintaining cultural literacy and improving quality and equality in educational programs and processes. Publications available at no cost include: *Young Children and Education in the Pacific: A Look at the Research; Year-Round Schools: The Star of the Sea Model;* and *Research Summary Series: Pacific Region School Finance and Facilities Study.*

* Regional Educational Laboratories Programs For the Improvement of Practice

Educational Networks Division
Office of Reform Assistance and Dissemination
555 New Jersey Ave., NW
Washington, DC 20208   202-219-2187
This office funds ten regional laboratories which carry out applied research, development, and technical assistance for educators, parents, and decisionmakers in the 50 states, the District of Columbia, Puerto Rico, the Virgin Islands, and the Pacific Basin Region. Each laboratory serves a geographic region and is governed by an independent board of directors. These laboratories plan programs through an ongoing assessment of regional needs, a knowledge of the current trends in research practice, and interaction with the many other agencies and institutions that assist communities and schools with educational improvement. The laboratories also are being asked to help coordinate field-based services for department funded technical assistance providers, such as the new Comprehensive Regional Assistance Centers, the Regional Technology Consortia, and the Regional Mathematics and Science Education Consortia. Under a 5 year contract the laboratories are asked to: link researchers and teachers in activities designed to find out--in actual schools and classrooms--how research findings can be translated into effective practice; provide states and localities with objective, research-based information, training and technical assistance, to help them with their school improvement and reform efforts; develop and try out innovative strategies to help districts and schools that serve high concentrations of economically disadvantaged children and rural populations; and, use advanced technologies as an integral part of their operations and help other educational agencies to do the same. Each of the following laboratories have a specialty area which works toward achieving national prominence within its respective field.

Northeastern Region: Brown University, 164 Angell St., Box 1929, Providence, RI 02910, 401-863-2777
Specialty Area: Language and Cultural Diversity
States Served: CT, MA, ME, NH, NY, PR, VI, VT

Mid-Atlantic Region: Temple University, 933 Ritter Annex, 13th and Cecil B. Moore, Philadelphia, PA 19122, 215-204-3001
Specialty Area: Urban Education
States Served: DC, DE, MD, NJ, PA

Appalachian Region: Appalachia Educational Laboratory, Inc., 1030 Quarrier St., P.O. Box 1348, Charleston, WV 25325, 800-624-9120, http://www.ael.org
Specialty Area: Rural Education
States Served: KY, TN, VA, WV

Southeastern Region: Southeastern Regional Vision for Education, P.O. Box 5367, Greensboro, NC 27435, 800-755-3277, http://www.serv.org
Specialty Area: Early Childhood Education
States Served: AL, FL, GA, MS, NC, SC

Midwestern Region: North Central Regional Educational Laboratory, 1900 Spring Road, Suite 300, Oak Brook, IL 60521-1480, 708-571-4700, http://www.ncrel.org
Specialty Area: Technology
States Served: IA, IL, IN, MI, MN, OH, WI

Southwestern Region: Southwest Educational Development Laboratory, 211 East Seventh St., Second Floor, Austin, TX 78701-3281, 512-476-6861, http://www.sedl.org
Specialty Area: Language and Cultural Diversity
States Served: AR, LA, NM, OK, TX

Central Region: Mid-continent Regional Educational laboratory, 2550 South Parker Rd., Suite 500, Aurora, CO 80014, 303-337-0990, http://www.mcrel.org
Specialty Area: Curriculum, Learning, and Instruction
States Served: CO, KS, MO, NB, ND, SD, WY

Western Region: Far West Laboratory for Educational Research and Development, 730 Harrison Street, San Francisco, CA 94107-1242, 415-565-3000, http://www.fwl.org
Specialty Area: Assessent and Accountability
States Served: AZ, CA, NV, UT

Northwestern Region: Northwest Regional Educational laboratory, 101 SW Main St., Suite 500, Portland, OR 97204-3212, http://www.nwrel.org
Specialty Area: School Change Processes
States Served: AK, ID, MT, OR, WA

Pacific Region: Pacific Region Educational Laboratory, 828 Fort Street Mall, Suite 500, Honolulu, HI 96813, 808-533-6000, http://pres-oahu-1.prel.hawaii.edu
Specialty Area: Language and Cultural Diversity
Region Served: American Samoa, Commonwealth of the Northern Mariana Islands, Republic of Palau

* Research and Development Centers Nationwide

National Research and Development Centers
Office of Educational Research and Development
U.S. Department of Education
555 New Jersey Ave., NW
Washington, DC 20208   202-219-2232
These university-based centers focus research on topics of national significance to educational policy and practice. Each center works in a defined field on a multi-year (and usually multi-disciplinary) program of research and development. Each center's role is to: 1) exercise leadership in its mission area; 2) conduct programmatic research and development; 3) attract the sustained attention of the best researchers to education problems; 4) create a long-term interaction between researchers and educators; 5) participate in a network for collaborative exchange in the education community; and 6) engage in an information distribution program.

* Research for Better Schools

Research for Better Schools
444 North Third St.
Philadelphia, PA 19123   215-574-9300
Major activity areas include institutional development, cooperative school improvement, state leadership assistance, applied research, products for special populations, national networking, and rural and small schools. Areas served: Delaware, District of Columbia, Maryland, Pennsylvania, and New Jersey.

Education

* Southeastern Education Research Lab

Southeastern Educational Vision for Education

P.O. Box 5347	800-755-3277
Greensboro, NC 27435	910-334-3211

Major activity areas include improving writing, math, and leadership skills; making effective use of technology; state policy and educational reform; the teaching profession; dropout prevention; and rural and small schools. States served: Alabama, Florida, Georgia, Mississippi, North Carolina and South Carolina.

* Southwest Regional Education Research Lab

Southwest Educational Development Laboratory

211 East Seventh St., 2nd Floor

Austin, TX 78701-3281   512-476-6861

Major activity areas include improving teacher and administrator performance, improving school and classroom productivity, facilitating student achievement, information services for education decisionmakers, and rural and small schools. States served: Arkansas, Louisiana, New Mexico, Oklahoma, and Texas.

* Statistics and Information

National Center for Education Statistics

Office of Educational Research and Improvement (OERI)

555 New Jersey Ave., NW

Washington, DC 20208-5574   202-219-1828

The Center's function is to collect, collate, analyze, and report complete statistics on the condition of American education; conduct and publish reports, and review and report on education activities internationally. To acquire statistical information or obtain a copy of the Digest of Education Statistics or the condition of education contact the National Library of Education Information Division at 800-424-1616.

* Technology in Education

Center for Technology in Education

916 Morton St., 7th Floor

New York, NY 10014   212-807-4200

Major research areas include integrating technology into learning and instruction; assessing learning; linking reform and restructuring to learning and technology; and adapting and designing advanced technologies.

Money for Teachers and Schools

Grants from the federal government are available not only to educators and faculty, but to universities and other educational institutions. In addition to the money programs identified here for medical school and other fields, more grants are listed in the Careers and Workplace Chapter. The information is taken from the *Catalog of Federal Domestic Assistance* which is published by the U.S. Government Printing Office in Washington, DC. The number next to the title description is the official reference number listed in this catalog. Contact the office listed below the title for details.

* Airway Science (AWS) 20.107

Office of Training and Higher Education, ANT 30
Federal Aviation Administration
400 7th St., SW, Plaza Room PL-10
Washington, DC 20591   202-366-7996
To assist recognized colleges and/or universities in the need for facilities and equipment for Airway Science (AWS) curriculum students. Types of assistance: grants. Estimate of annual funds available: $ not known.

* State Marine Schools 20.806

Taylor Jones, Director
Office of Maritime Labor and Training
Maritime Administration
U.S. Department of Transportation
Washington, DC 20590   202-366-5755
To train merchant marine officers in state marine schools. Types of assistance: direct payments. Estimate of annual funds available: $ 11,271,000.

* Promotion of the Arts - Arts in Education 45.003

Arts in Education Program
Room 602, National Endowment for the Arts
The Nancy Hanks Center
1100 Penn. Ave., NW
Washington, DC 20506   202-682-5426
To encourage state and local arts agencies to develop long-term strategies in assisting appropriate state and local education authorities to establish the arts as basic in education. Types of assistance: grants. Estimate of annual funds available: $ 7,110,000.

* Promotion of the Humanities - Summer Seminars for College Teachers 45.116

Summer Seminars for College Teachers
Division of Fellowships and Seminars
National Endowment for the Humanities, Room 316
Washington, DC 20506   202-606-8463
To provide opportunities for teachers in five, four, and two-year colleges; for scholars employed in libraries, museums, historical associations, and other humanities institution to work during the summer in their areas of interest under the direction of distinguished scholars at institutions with library resources suitable for advanced study and research. Types of assistance: grants. Estimate of annual funds available: $ 4,470,000.

* Promotion of the Humanities - Summer Stipends 45.121

Division of Research Programs
Summer Stipends
National Endowment for the Humanities, Room 316
Washington, DC 20506   202-606-8551
To provide support for individual faculty and staff members at universities and two-year and four-year colleges and for others who have made or have demonstrated promise of making significant contributions to the humanities. Types of assistance: grants. Estimate of annual funds available: $ 876,000.

* Promotion of the Humanities Institutional Programs and Resources 45.122

Division of Research Programs
Institutional Programs and Resources
Room 318
National Endowment for the Humanities
Washington, DC 20506   202-606-8359
To provide support for humanities research programs that are administered by independent research centers and scholarly organizations. Types of assistance: grants. Estimate of annual funds available: $2,985,000.

* Promotion of the Humanities-Elementary and Secondary Education in the Humanities 45.127

Elementary and Secondary Education in the Humanities
National Endowment for the Humanities, Room 302
Washington, DC 20506   202-606-8377
To increase the effectiveness of humanities teaching in our nation's elementary, middle, and secondary schools. Types of assistance: grants. Estimate of annual funds available: $ 6,769,000.

* Promotion of the Humanities-Fellowships for University Teachers 45.142

Fellowships for University Teachers
Division of Fellowships and Seminars
National Endowment for the Humanities, Room 316
Washington, DC 20506   202-606-8466
To provide time for uninterrupted study and research to university teachers, and faculty members of postgraduate professional schools who can make significant contributions to thought and knowledge in the humanities. Types of assistance: grants. Estimate of annual funds available: $ 3,117,000.

* Promotion of the Humanities - Fellowships for College Teachers and Independent Scholars 45.143

Fellowships for College Teachers and Independent Scholars
Division of Research Programs, Room 316
National Endowment for the Humanities
Washington, DC 20506   202-606-8467
To provide opportunities for college teachers and independent scholars to pursue independent study and research that will enhance their capacities as teachers, scholars, or interpreters of the humanities. Types of assistance: grants. Estimate of annual funds available: $ 3,117,000.

* Promotion of the Humanities-Reference Materials/Tools 45.145

Division of Research Programs
Reference Materials/Tools
National Endowment for the Humanities
Washington, DC 20506   202-606-8358
To fund, wholly or partially projects which create research tools important for scholarly research. Types of assistance: grants. Estimate of annual funds available: $ 3,364,000.

Education

* Promotion of the Humanities-Higher Education in the Humanities 45.150

Higher Education in the Humanities
National Endowment for the Humanities
Room 302
Washington, DC 20506   202-606-8380

To assist institutions of higher education in their efforts to improve the teaching of the humanities. Types of assistance: grants. Estimate of annual funds available: $ 6,768,000.

* Promotion of the Humanities-Summer Seminars for School Teachers 45.151

Summer Seminars for School Teachers
Division of Education
National Endowment for the Humanities
Room 316
Washington, DC 20506   202-606-8463

To provide opportunities for school teachers to work during the summer under the direction of a distinguished teacher and active scholar at colleges and universities throughout the country, studying seminal works in the humanities in a systematic and thorough way. Types of assistance: grants. Estimate of annual funds available: $ 4,914,000.

* Air Pollution Control Manpower Training 66.003

Environmental Protection Agency
Grants Administration Division, PM 216
Washington, DC 20460

To develop career-oriented personnel qualified to work in pollution abatement and control. Types of assistance: grants. Estimate of annual funds available: $ 400,000.

* Air Pollution Control - Technical Training 66.006

Deborah Miller
Air Pollution Training Institute
Environmental Protection Agency (EPA)
Research Triangle Park, NC 27711   919-541-3724

To provide technical training to personnel from state and local air pollution control agencies. Types of assistance: training. Estimate of annual funds available: $ 300,000.

* Environmental Education and Training Program 66.950

Kathleen MacKinnon
Environmental Education Specialist
Office of Environmental Education 1707
Environmental Protection Agency
401 M St., SW
Washington, DC 20460   202-260-3335

To train educational professionals in the development and delivery of environmental education and training programs and studies. Types of assistance: grants. Estimate of annual funds available: $2,000,000.

* Environmental Education Grants 66.951

George Walker
Environmental Education Specialist
Office of Environmental Education 1707
Environmental Protection Agency
401 M St., SW
Washington, DC 20460   202-260-8691

To support projects to design, demonstrate, or disseminate practices, methods, or techniques related to environmental education and training. Types of assistance: grants. Estimate of annual funds available: $3,000,000.

* National Gallery of Art Extension Services 68.001

Department of Extension Programs
National Gallery of Art
Washington, DC 20565   202-737-4215

To provide educational material on the Gallery's collections and exhibitions free of charge except for transportation costs, to schools, colleges, and libraries across the Nation. Types of assistance: other. Estimate of annual funds available: $ 857,000.

* University-Laboratory Cooperative Program 81.004

Larry L. Barker
Division of University and Industry Programs
Office of Energy Research
U.S. Department of Energy (DOE)
Washington, DC 20585   202-586-8947

To provide college and university science and engineering faculty and students with energy-related training and research experience in areas of energy research at DOE facilities. Types of assistance: grants, other. Estimate of annual funds available: $ 5,500,000.

* Energy Policy, Planning and Development 81.080

Joseph Benedik, Resource Management Office
Policy Planning and Analysis
Forrestal Bldg., 1000 Independence Ave., SW
Washington, DC 20585   202-586-2431

To provide financial assistance for gathering outside experts for seminars, conferences and work groups to discuss specific energy policy issues and write recommendations and reports. Types of assistance: grants. Estimate of annual funds available: $ 450,000.

* Educational Exchange - University Lecturers (Professors) and Research Scholars (Fulbright-Hays Program) 82.002

Council for International Exchange of Scholars
3007 TIlden St., NW, Suite 5M
Washington, DC 20008

To improve and strengthen the international relations of the U.S. by promoting mutual understanding among the peoples of the world through educational exchanges. Types of assistance: grants. Estimate of annual funds available: $ 24,689,000.

* Bilingual Education 84.003

Rudolph Munis
Office of Bilingual Education and Minority Languages Affairs
U.S. Department of Education
330 C St., SW, Room 5086
Washington, DC 20202   202-205-9700

To develop and carry out programs of bilingual education in elementary and secondary schools. Types of assistance: grant, direct payments. Estimate of annual funds available: $ 151,690,000.

* Civil Rights Technical Assistance and Training 84.004

Equity and Educational Excellence Division
Office of Elementary and Secondary Education
1250 Maryland Ave., SW
Washington, DC 20202-6438.   202-260-2495

To provide technical assistance and training services to school districts to cope with educational problems occasioned by discrimination from race, sex, and national origin. Types of assistance: grants. Estimate of annual funds available: $ 21,606,000.

* Educationally Deprived Children - Local Educational Agencies (Chapter 1, of Title I, ESEA) 84.010

Compensatory Education Programs
Office of Elementary and Secondary Education
U.S. Department of Education
1250 Maryland Ave., SW
Washington, DC 20202   202-260-0826

To provide financial assistance to local educational agencies to meet the special needs of educationally deprived children selected in accordance with Section 1014 of Chapter 1. Types of assistance: grants. Estimate of annual funds available: $6,698,356,000.

* Migrant Education-Basic State Formula Grant Program (State Migrant Education Program) 84.011

Office of Migrant Education
Office of Elementary and Secondary Education
U.S. Department of Education
1250 Maryland Ave., SW
Washington, DC 20202   202-260-1164

To establish and improve programs to meet the special educational needs of migratory children of migratory agricultural workers or migratory fishers. Types of assistance: grants. Estimate of annual funds available: $ 299,475,000.

* Neglected and Delinquent Children (Chapter 1 ESEA; Neglected and Delinquent) 84.013

Compensatory Education Programs
Office of Elementary and Secondary Education
U.S. Department of Education
1250 Maryland Ave., SW, Room 2043
Washington, DC 20202   202-260-0826

To provide financial assistance to State agencies to meet the special needs of institutionalized neglected or delinquent children and children in community day programs for whom they have an educational responsibility. Types of assistance: grants. Estimate of annual funds available: $ 39,311,000.

* National Resource Centers and Fellowships Program for Language and Area or Language and International Studies 84.015

Joseph F. Belmonte, Advanced Training and Research Branch
Center for International Education
600 Independence Ave., SW
Washington, DC 20202   202-401-9782

To promote instruction in those modern foreign languages area and international studies critical to national needs by supporting the establishment, strengthening and operation of such programs at colleges and universities. Types of assistance: grants. Estimate of annual funds available: $ 19,040,000.

* Undergraduate International Studies and Foreign Language Programs 84.016

International Studies Branch
Center for International Education
Office of Postsecondary Education
U.S. Department of Education
600 Independence Ave., SW
Washington, DC 20220   202-401-9783

The Undergraduate International Studies and Foreign Language program issues awards to institutions of higher education and public and nonprofit private agencies and organizations. Types of assistance: grants. Estimate of annual funds available: $ 3,907,000.

* International Research and Studies (HEA Title VI Research and Studies) 84.017

Division of Advanced Training and Research
Center for International Education
U.S. Department of Education
600 Independence Ave., SW
Washington, DC 20202   202-401-9784

To improve foreign language and area studies training through support of research and studies, experimentation and development of specialized instructional materials. Types of assistance: grants. Estimate of annual funds available: $ 2,731,000.

* Fulbright-Hays Seminars Abroad - Special Bilateral Projects (Fulbright Exchange) 84.018

International Studies Branch
Center for International Education
U.S. Department of Education
600 Independence Ave., SW
Washington, DC 20202   202-401-9798

To increase mutual understanding and knowledge between the people of the U.S. and those in other countries by offering qualified U.S. educators opportunities to participate in short-term study seminars. Types of assistance: grants. Estimate of annual funds available: $ 956,530.

* Fulbright-Hays Training Grants - Faculty Research Abroad 84.019

Advanced Training and Research Branch
Center for International Education

U.S. Department of Education
600 Independence Ave., SW
Washington, DC 20202   202-401-9777

To help universities and colleges strengthen their language and area studies programs by enabling faculty members to conduct research abroad in order to improve their skill in languages. Types of assistance: grants. Estimate of annual funds available: $ 809,920.

* Fulbright-Hays Training Grants - Group Projects Abroad 84.021

International Studies Branch
U.S. Department of Education
490 L'Enfant Plaza East, SW, 2100 Corridor
Washington, DC 20202   202-708-7283

To help educational institutions improve their programs in modern foreign language and area studies. Types of assistance: grants. Estimate of annual funds available: $ 2,119,000.

* Handicapped-Innovation and Development (Research in Education for the Handicapped) 84.023

Division of Innovation and Development
Office of Asst. Secretary for Special Education and Rehabilitative Services
U.S. Department of Education
400 Maryland Ave., SW
Washington, DC 20202   202-205-8125

To improve the education of handicapped children through research and development projects and model programs (demonstrations). Types of assistance: grants. Estimate of annual funds available: $ 19,885,000.

* Handicapped Early Childhood Education (Early Education Program) 84.024

Division of Educational Services
Special Education Programs
U.S. Department of Education
600 Independence Ave., SW
Washington, DC 20202   202-205-9045

To support demonstrations, dissemination and implementation of effective approaches to preschool and early childhood education handicapped children. Types of assistance: grants. Estimate of annual funds available: $ 25,167,000.

* Handicapped Education-Deaf-Blind Centers (Services for Deaf-Blind Children and Youth) 84.025

Division of Educational Services
Special Education Service
U.S. Department of Education
600 Independence Ave., SW
Washington, DC 20202   202-205-8165

To provide technical assistance to state education agencies and to improve services to deaf-blind children and youth. Types of assistance: grants. Estimate of annual funds available: $ 12,832,000.

* Handicapped Media Services and Captioned Films (Media Materials; Technology for the Handicapped) 84.026

Division of Educational Services
Special Education Programs
U.S. Department of Education
Washington, DC 20202   202-205-9172

To maintain a free loan service of captioned films for the deaf and instruction media for the educational, cultural, and vocational enrichment of the handicapped. Types of assistance: direct payments. Estimate of annual funds available: $ 19,142,000.

* Handicapped-State Grants (Part B, Education of the Handicapped Act) 84.027

Division of Assistance to States
Office of Special Education
U.S. Department of Education
600 Independence Ave., SW

Education

202-205-8825
To provide grants to states to assist them in providing a free appropriate public
education to all handicapped children. Types of assistance: grants. Estimate of annual
funds available: $ 2,322,915,000.

* Handicapped Regional Resource and Federal Centers 84.028

Division of Educational Services
Office of Special Education
U.S. Department of Education
600 Independence Ave., SW
Washington, DC 20202   202-205-8451
To establish regional resource centers which provide advice and technical services
to educators for improving education of handicapped children. Types of assistance:
grants. Estimate of annual funds available: $ 7,218,000.

* Handicapped Education-Special Education Personnel Development (Training Personnel for the Education of the Handicapped) 84.029

Norm How
Division of Personnel Preparation
Special Education Programs
U.S. Department of Education
Washington, DC 20202   202-732-1070
To address identified shortages of special education teachers and related service
personnel. Types of assistance: grants. Estimate of annual funds available:
$ 67,095,000.

* Clearinghouses for the Handicapped Program 84.030

Division of Educational Services
Office of Asst. Secretary for Special Education
  and Rehabilitative Services
U.S. Department of Education
400 Maryland Ave, SW
Washington, DC 20202   202-205-5809
To disseminate information regarding education programs and services for
handicapped children. Types of assistance: grants. Estimate of annual funds available:
$ 2,162,000.

* Higher Education-Institutional Aid Special Needs Program 84.031

Institutional Aid Programs
Office of Postsecondary Education
U.S. Department of Education
600 Independence Ave., SW
Washington, DC 20202   202-708-8816
To help eligible colleges and universities to strengthen their management and fiscal
operations. Types of assistance: grants. Estimate of annual funds available:
$ 74,135,000.

* Library Services (LSCA-Title I) 84.034

Robert Klaassen
Public Library Support Staff
Library Programs
U.S. Department of Education
Washington, DC 20208   202-219-1303
To assist in extending public library services to areas without service or with
inadequate service. Types of assistance: grants. Estimate of annual funds available:
$ 81,562,000.

* Interlibrary Cooperation and Resource Sharing (LSCA-Title III) 84.035

Robert Klaassen, Public Library Support Staff
Library Programs
Office of Educational Research and Improvement
U.S. Department of Education
Washington, DC 20208   202-219-1303
To plan and take steps leading to the development of cooperative networks. Types
of assistance: grants. Estimate of annual funds available: $ 23,226,000.

* Library Career Training (HEA Title II-B) 84.036

Louise Sutherland
Library Development Staff, Library Programs
U.S. Department of Education
555 New Jersey Avenue, NW
Washington, DC 20208   202-219-1315
To assist institutions of higher education and library organizations and agencies in
training or retraining persons in areas of library specialization where there are
shortages. Types of assistance: grants. Estimate of annual funds available:
$ 4,916,000.

* Library Research and Demonstration (HEA Title II-B) 84.039

Neal Kaske
Library Development Staff
U.S. Department of Education
555 New Jersey Ave., NW
Washington, DC 20208-1430   202-219-1315
To award grants and contracts for research and/or demonstration projects in areas of
specialized services intended to improve library and information science practices.
Types of assistance: grants. Estimate of annual funds available: $ 6,500,000.

* Student Support Services 84.042

Division of Student Services
Office of Postsecondary Education
U.S. Department of Education
3066 ROB-3, 7th and D St., SW
Washington, DC 20202   202-708-4804
To provide supportive services to disadvantaged college students to enhance their
potential for successfully completing the postsecondary education program in which
they are enrolled. Types of assistance: grants. Estimate of annual funds available:
$ 144,100,000.

* Vocational Education-Basic Grants to States 84.048

Division of Vocational Education
Winifred I. Warnat
U.S. Department of Education
600 Independence Ave., SW
Washington, DC 20202   202-205-9441
To assist states in expanding, improving, modernizing, and developing quality
vocational education programs. Types of assistance: grants. Estimate of annual funds
available: $ 955,626,000.

* Vocational Education - Consumer and Homemaking Education 84.049

Winifred I. Warnat
Director, Division of Vocational Education
U.S. Department of Education
600 Independence Ave., SW
Washington, DC 20202   202-205-9441
To assist states in conducting programs in consumer and homemaking education.
Types of assistance: grants. Estimate of annual funds available: $ 35,234,000.

* National Vocational Education Research 84.051

Jackie Friederich
U.S. Department of Education
Division of National Programs
600 Independence Ave., SW
Washington, DC 20202   202-205-9071
To provide support for the National Center for Research in Vocational Education and
six curriculum coordination centers and special research projects. Types of assistance:
grants. Estimate of annual funds available: $ 17,268,000.

* Higher Education-Cooperative Education (Cooperative Education Program) 84.055

Division of Higher Education Incentive Programs
Office of Postsecondary Education
U.S. Department of Education
Washington, DC 20202   202-260-3291

To provide federal support for planning, establishing, expanding, and carrying out projects of cooperative education in institutions of higher education. Types of assistance: grants. Estimate of annual funds available: $ 6,927,000.

* Indian Education-Adult Indian Education (Indian Education Act-Subpart 3) 84.062

Indian Education Programs
Office of Elementary and Secondary Education
U.S. Department of Education
600 Independence Ave., SW
Washington, DC 20202   202-260-1612

To plan develop and implement programs for Indian adults to decrease the rate of illiteracy, increase the mastery of basic skills, and increase the number who earn high school equivalency diplomas. Types of assistance: grants. Estimate of annual funds available: $ 5,420,000.

* Educational Opportunity Centers 84.066

Division of Student Services
Education Outreach Branch
U.S. Department of Education
600 Independence Ave., SW
Washington, DC 20202   202-708-4804

To provide information on financial and academic assistance available for qualified adults desiring to pursue a program of postsecondary education, and to assist them in applying for admission to institution of postsecondary education. Types of assistance: grants. Estimate of annual funds available: $ 24,700,000.

* National Diffusion Network (NDN: National Diffusion Network) 84.073

Steve Balkcom
National Diffusion Network
Recognition Division
655 New Jersey Ave., NW
Washington, DC 20208   202-219-2089

To promote and accelerate the systematic, rapid dissemination and adopting by public and nonpublic educational institutions nationwide. Types of assistance: grants. Estimate of annual funds available: $ 14,480,000.

* Postsecondary Education Programs for Handicapped Persons (Postsecondary Programs) 84.078

Michael Ward
Division of Educational Services
Special Education Programs
U.S. Department of Education
600 Independence Ave., SW
Washington, DC 20202   202-205-8163

To develop and operate specially designed model programs of vocational, technical, postsecondary or adult education for deaf or other handicapped persons. Types of assistance: grants. Estimate of annual funds available: $ 8,839,000.

* Women's Educational Equity (Women's Educational Equity Act Program) 84.083

Equity and Educational Excellence Division
Office of Elementary and Secondary Education
U.S. Department of Education
600 Independence Ave., SW, Room 4500
Washington, DC 20202   202-260-2670

To promote educational equity for women and girls at all levels of education and to provide financial assistance to local educational institutions to help them meet the requirements of Title IX. Types of assistance: grants. Estimate of annual funds available: $ 3,964,000.

* Handicapped Education-Severely Handicapped Program (Programs for Severely Handicapped Children and Youth) 84.086

Dawn Hunter, Division of Educational Services
U.S. Department of Education
600 Independence Ave., SW

Washington, DC 20202   202-205-5809

To improve and expand innovative educational/training services for severely handicapped children and youth. Types of assistance: grants. Estimate of annual funds available: $ 10,030,000.

* Strengthening Research Library Resources (HEA Title II-C) 84.091

Discretionary Library Programs Division
Office of Educational Research and Improvement
Library Programs
U.S. Department of Education
Washington, DC 20208-5571   202-219-1315

To promote research and education of high quality throughout the U.S by providing financial assistance. Types of assistance: grants. Estimate of annual funds available: $ 5,808,160.

* Bilingual Vocational Instructor Training 84.099

Division of National Programs
Office of Vocational and Adult Education
U.S. Department of Education
600 Independence Ave., SW
Washington, DC 20202   202-205-5864

To provide training for instructors and other ancillary personnel in bilingual vocational training programs. Types of assistance: grants, direct payments. Estimate of annual funds available: $ 441,900.

* Bilingual Vocational Materials, Methods, and Techniques 84.100

Cindy Townser
Division of National Programs
Office of Vocational and Adult Education
U.S. Department of Education
600 Independence Ave., SW
Washington, DC 20202   202-205-5864

To develop instructional materials, methods, techniques, to encourage research programs and demonstration projects and to overcome the shortage of instructional materials available for bilingual vocational training programs. Types of assistance: grants. Estimate of annual funds available: $ 218,090.

* Training for Special Programs Staff and Leadership Personnel 84.103

Patricia Lucas
Division of Student Services
Office of Postsecondary Education
U.S. Department of Education
600 Independence Ave., SW
Washington, DC 20202   202-708-4804

To provide training for staff and leadership personnel employed in, or preparing for employment in, projects funded under the Special Programs for Students from Disadvantaged Backgrounds. Types of assistance: grants. Estimate of annual funds available: $ 2,100,000.

* Fund for the Improvement of Postsecondary Education (FIPSE) 84.116

Fund for the Improvement of Postsecondary Education
Office of the Asst. Secretary for Postsecondary Education
7 and D Sts., SW, Room 3100
Washington, DC 20202   202-708-5750

To provide assistance for innovative programs which improve the access to and the quality of postsecondary education. Types of assistance: grants. Estimate of annual funds available: $ 17,543,000.

* Educational Research and Development 84.117

U.S. Department of Education
Office of Educational Research and Improvement
55 New Jersey Ave., NW
Washington, DC 20208   202-219-2079

To provide grants, contracts and cooperative agreements to individuals and institutions seeking to advance knowledge about education policy and practice. Types of assistance: grants. Estimate of annual funds available: $ 86,200,000.

* Minority Science Improvement (MSIP) 84.120

Argelia Velez-Rodriguez
Division of Higher Education Incentive Programs
U.S. Department of Education
Washington, DC 20202 202-260-3261

To assist institutions to improve the quality of preparation of their students for graduate work or careers in science. Types of assistance: grants. Estimate of annual funds available: $ 5,839,000.

* Law-Related Education 84.123

Equity and Educational Excellence Division
Office of Elementary and Secondary Education
600 Independence Ave., SW
Washington, DC 20202 202-260-2738

To support programs at the elementary and secondary school levels by developing and implementing model projects designed to institutionalize law-related. Types of assistance: grants. Estimate of annual funds available: $ not known.

* Rehabilitation Services - Basic Support (Basic Support) 84.126

Office of Program Operations
Rehabilitation Services Administration
U.S. Department of Education
Washington, DC 20202 202-205-9406

To provide vocational rehabilitation services to persons with mental and/or physical handicaps. Types of assistance: grants. Estimate of annual funds available: $ 2,043,874,000.

* Rehabilitation Training 84.129

Rehabilitation Services Administration
Office of Special Education and Rehabilitative Services
U.S. Department of Education
Washington, DC 20202 202-205-9400

To support projects to increase the numbers and improve the skills of personnel trained in providing vocational rehabilitation services to handicapped individuals in areas targeted as having personnel shortages. Types of assistance: grants. Estimate of annual funds available: $ 22,400,813.

* Migrant Education-High School Equivalency Program (HEP) 84.141

Office of Migrant Education
Office of Elementary and Secondary Education
U.S. Department of Education
600 Independence Ave., SW
Washington, DC 20202 202-260-1164

To assist students who are engaged or whose families are engaged in migrant and other seasonal farm work to obtain the equivalent of a secondary school diploma. Types of assistance: grants. Estimate of annual funds available: $ 8,161,000.

* Business and International Education 84.153

International Studies Branch
Center for International Education
U.S. Department of Education
600 Independence Ave., SW
Washington, DC 20202 202-401-9778

To promote innovation and improvement in international business education curricula at institutions of higher education and serve the needs of the business community. Types of assistance: grants. Estimate of annual funds available: $ 3,355,000.

* Secondary Education and Transitional Services for Handicapped Youth 84.158

Division of Educational Services
Office of Special Education Program
600 Independence Ave., SW
Washington, DC 20202 202-205-8163

To strengthen and coordinate education, training, and related services for handicapped youth. Types of assistance: grants. Estimate of annual funds available: $ 23,966,000.

* Training Interpreters for Deaf Individuals 84.160

Office of Special Education and
 Rehabilitative Services
U.S. Department of Education
Washington, DC 20202 202-205-9152

To support projects, increase the numbers and improve the skills of manual and oral interpretors who provide services to deaf individuals. Types of assistance: grants. Estimate of annual funds available: $ 1,510,000.

* National Programs for Strengthening, Teaching, and Administration in Mathematics and Science Programs 84.168

U.S. Department of Education
FIRST
Office of Educational Research and Improvement
Washington, DC 20208 202-219-2206

To provide support for projects designed to improve the quality of instruction in mathematics and science. Types of assistance: grants. Estimate of annual funds available: $ 21,356,000.

* Technology, Educational Media and Materials for the Handicapped (Technical Development) 84.180

Division of Innovation and Development
Office of Assistant Secretary for Special Education
 and Rehabilitative Services
U.S. Department of Education
600 Independence Ave., SW
Washington, DC 20202 202-205-8123

To provide contracts, grants, or cooperative agreements for the purpose of advancing the use of new technology. Types of assistance: grants. Estimate of annual funds available: $ 10,362,000.

* Handicapped Infants and Toddlers (Early Intervention Grants) 84.181

Division of Educational Services
Office of Special Education Program
U.S. Department of Education
600 Independence Ave., SW
Washington, DC 20202 202-205-9084

To assist each state and territory to develop a state-wide comprehensive, coordinated multidisciplinary, interagency system to provide early intervention services for handicapped infants and toddlers and their families. Types of assistance: grants. Estimate of annual funds available: $ 325,632,000.

* National Programs for Drug-Free Schools and Communities 84.184

Division of Drug Free Schools and Communities
U.S. Department of Education
Office of Elementary and Secondary Education
600 Independence Ave., SW
Washington, DC 20202 202-260-2844

To assist in drug and alcohol abuse education and prevention, personnel training and curriculum demonstration activities, as authorized by the Drug Free Schools and Communities Act of 1986. Types of assistance: grants. Estimate of annual funds available: $ 25,000,000.

* Drug-Free Schools and Communities - State Grants (Drug-Free Schools and Communities) 84.186

Safe and Drug Free Schools Program
U.S. Department of Education
Office of Elementary and Secondary Education
600 Independence Ave., SW, Room 604
Washington, DC 20202 202-260-3954

To provide financial assistance to establish programs of alcohol and drug abuse education and prevention coordinated with related community efforts and resources. Types of assistance: grants. Estimate of annual funds available: $ 456,962,000.

* Supported Employment Services for Individuals with Severe Handicaps (Supported Employment Services Program) 84.187

Mark E. Shob
Office of Program Operations
Rehabilitation Services Administration
U.S. Department of Education
Washington, DC 20202-2574   202-205-9406

To provide grants for training and traditionally time limited post employment services leading to supported employment for individuals with severe handicaps. Types of assistance: grants. Estimate of annual funds available: $ 36,536,000.

* Christa McAuliffe Fellowships (CMFP) 84.190

U.S. Department of Education
Office of the Asst. Secretary for Elementary and
 Secondary Education
School Effectiveness Division
600 Independence Ave., SW
Washington, DC 20202   202-260-2715

To reward excellence in teaching by providing financial assistance to outstanding teachers to continue their education. Types of assistance: grants. Estimate of annual funds available: $ 1,946,000.

* National Adult Education Research 84.191

Division of National Programs
Office of Vocational and Adult Education
U.S. Department of Education
600 Independence Ave., SW
Washington, DC 20202   202-205-9650

Types of assistance: grants. Estimate of annual funds available: $ 3,900,000.

* Adult Education for the Homeless 84.192

Division of Adult Education
Office of Vocational and Adult Education
U.S. Department of Education
600 Independence Ave. SW
Washington, DC 20202   202-205-5499

To provide literacy training and basic skills remediation for adult homeless individuals, including a program of outreach activities. Types of assistance: grants. Estimate of annual funds available: $ 19,082,000.

* Bilingual Education Support Services 84.194

Office of Bilingual Education and Minority Languages Affairs
330 C St., SW, Room 5086
Washington, DC 20202   202-205-9907

To provide in-service training and technical assistance to parents and educational personnel participating in, or preparing to participate in bilingual education programs. Types of assistance: grants. Estimate of annual funds available: $ 14,330,000.

* Bilingual Education Training Grants 84.195

Division of National Programs
Office of Bilingual Education and Minority Languages Affairs
330 C St., SW, Room 5086
Washington, DC 20202   202-205-8722

To provide financial support for programs designed to meet the training needs for additional or better trained education personnel in Bilingual Education. Types of assistance: grants. Estimate of annual funds available: $ 25,189,000.

* College Library Technology and Cooperation Grants (HEA Title II-D) 84.197

Neal Kaske
Discretionary Library Programs Division
Library Development Staff, Library Programs
U.S. Department of Education
Washington, DC 20208   202-219-1315

To encourage resource sharing activities among the libraries in institutions of higher education through the use of technology and networking. Types of assistance: grants. Estimate of annual funds available: $ 3,873,000.

* Workplace Literacy 84.198

Jeanne Williams
Division of National Programs
Office of Vocational and Adult Education
U.S. Department of Education
600 Independence Ave., SW
Washington, DC 20202   202-205-5977

The Adult Education Act was amended to establish workplace literacy partnerships. Types of assistance: grants. Estimate of annual funds available: $ 37,516,000.

* Vocational Education-Cooperative Demonstration 84.199

Richard Smith
Division of National Programs
Office of Vocational and Adult Education
U.S. Department of Education
600 Independence Ave., SW
Washington, DC 20202   202-205-9249

To support exemplary cooperative demonstration programs for high technology training pertaining to vocational education. Types of assistance: grants. Estimate of annual funds available: $ 5,496,100.

* STAR Schools Program (Star Schools) 84.203

Gregory Dennis
Office of Educational Research and Improvement
U.S. Department of Education
Washington, DC 20208-5644   202-219-1919

To provide demonstration grants to eligible telecommunications partnerships to develop, construct and acquire audio and visual facilities and equipment. Types of assistance: grants. Estimate of annual funds available: $ 30,000,000.

* School, College, and University Partnership (SCUP) 84.204

Frances Bergeron
U.S. Department of Education
Division of Student Services
Suite 600D, Portals Bldg.
1250 Maryland Ave., SW
Washington, DC 20202   202-708-4804

To encourage partnerships between institutions of higher education and secondary schools serving low-income students to support programs that improve the academic skills of public and private nonprofit secondary school students. Types of assistance: grants. Estimate of annual funds available: $ 3,893,000.

* Native Hawaiian Family Based Education Centers 84.209

Beth Baggett, School Improvement Programs
Equity and Educational Excellence Division
U.S. Department of Education
600 Independence Ave, SW
Washington, DC 20202   202-260-2502

To develop and operate a minimum of eleven family based education centers throughout the Hawaiian Islands. Types of assistance: direct payments. Estimate of annual funds available: $ 5,600,000.

* Even Start - Local Education Agencies 84.213

Donna Conforti-Campbell
U.S. Department of Education
Compensatory Education Programs
Office of Elementary and Secondary Education
600 Independence Ave., SW
Washington, DC 20202   202-260-0996

To provide family centered education projects to help parents become full partners in the education of their children. Types of assistance: grants. Estimate of annual funds available: $ 102,024,000.

Education

* **Even Start - Migrant Education 84.214**
Bayla White, Migrant Education
Office of Elementary and Secondary Education
U.S. Department of Education
600 Independence Ave., SW
Washington, DC 20202   202-260-1164
To establish and improve programs to meet the special educational needs of the children of migratory agricultural workers. Types of assistance: grants. Estimate of annual funds available: $ 2,940,720.

* **The Secretary's Fund for Innovation in Education 84.215**
U.S. Department of Education, FIE
Office of Educational Research and Improvement
Washington, DC 20208   202-219-1301
To conduct projects that offer the promise of identifying and disseminating innovative educational approaches at the preschool, elementary and secondary level. Types of assistance: grants. Estimate of annual funds available: $ 36,750,000.

* **Center for International Business Education 84.220**
Susanna Easton
International Studies Branch
Center for International Education
U.S. Department of Education
600 Independence Ave. SW
Washington, DC 20202   202-401-9780
To serve the international needs of the business community by promoting improved business strategies in international trade. Types of assistance: grants. Estimate of annual funds available: $ 6,810,000.

* **Native Hawaiian Special Education 84.221**
Linda Glidewell   202-205-9097
To operate projects addressing the special education needs of Native Hawaiian Students. Types of assistance: grants. Estimate of annual funds available: $ 1,200,000.

* **Language Resource Centers 84.229**
Advanced Training and Research Branch
Center for International Education
Office of Higher Education Programs
Office of Postsecondary Education
U.S. Department of Education
600 Independence Ave., SW
Washington, DC 20202   2020-401-9785
To improve the Nation's capacity to teach and learn foreign languages effectively by supporting the establishment, strengthening, and operations of language resource centers at institutions of higher education. Types of assistance: grants. Estimate of annual funds available: $2,400,000.

* **Special Education- Program for Children with Serious Emotional Disturbance 84.237**
Dores Andres   202-205-8125
To establish projects for the purpose of improving special education and related services to children and youth with serious emotional disturbance. Types of assistance: grants. Estimate of annual funds available: $4,147,000.

* **National Institute for Literacy 84.257**
National Institute for Literacy
800 Connecticut Ave., NW
Washington, DC 20006
To enhance the national effort to reach the goal that all Americans will be literate. Activities funded include research and development, database of practices, funding fellowships, and supporting a national literacy hot line. Types of assistance: grants. Estimate of annual funds available: $4,900,000.

* **Minority Teacher Recruitment 84.262**
U.S. Department of Education
Higher Education Programs
Office of Postsecondary Education
600 Independence Ave., SW
Washington, DC 20202   202-260-3207
To improve the recruiting and training opportunities in education for minority teachers in elementary and secondary schools. Types of assistance: grants. Estimate of annual funds available: $2,458,000.

* **Faculty Development Fellowship 84.271**
U.S. Department of Education
Higher Education Programs
Division of Higher Education Incentive Programs OPE
CY-80, Portals
600 Independence Ave., SW
Washington, DC 20202   2020-260-3209
To identify talented faculty from under represented groups wishing to obtain a doctoral degree and remain in the higher education professorate. Types of assistance: grants. Estimate of annual funds available: $3,732,000.

* **GOALS 2000 84.276**
Goals 2000
Office of Elementary and Secondary Education
U.S. Department of Education
600 Independence Ave., SW
Portals Bldg., Room 4000
Washington, DC 20202   202-401-0039
To provide grants to support the development and implementation of comprehensive reform plans to improve the teaching and learning of all children. Types of assistance: grants. Estimate of annual funds available: $402,821,000.

* **Safe Schools Discretionary Grants to Local Education Agencies 84.277**
Director
Division of Drug-Free Schools and Communities
U.S. Department of Education
Office of Elementary and Secondary Education
400 Maryland Ave., SW
Portals Bldg.
Washington, DC 20202   202-260-1683
To help local schools achieve goals of the National Education Goals stating that by the year 2000 every school in America will be free of drugs and violence. Types of assistance: grants. Estimate of annual funds available: $20,000,000.

* **GOALS 2000- Opportunity to Learn Development Grants 84.280**
U.S. Department of Education
Office of Educational Research and Improvement (OERI)
555 New Jersey Ave., NW
Washington, DC 20208   202-219-2079
To provide grants to help defray the cost of developing, testing, and evaluating State assessments tied to content standards. Types of assistance: grants. Estimate of annual funds available: $5,000,000.

* **Public Charter Schools 84.282**
Public Charter Schools Program
Equity and Educational Excellence Division
Office of School Improvement Programs
Office of Elementary and Secondary Education
Washington, DC 20202   202-260-2671
To increase national understanding of the Charter Schools Model by providing financial assistance for the design and initial implementation of charter schools and evaluating the effects of such schools. Types of assistance: grants. Estimate of annual funds available: $6,000,000.

* **Family and Community Endeavor Schools Grant Program 84.285**
Safe and Drug-Free Schools Program
OESE
U.S. Department of Education
600 Independence Ave., SW, Suite 604

Be patient. If any phone number is incorrect, call (area code) 555-1212 and request the new listing.

Portals Building
Washington, DC 20202   202-260-3954
To improve the overall social and academic development of at-risk children in communities that experience significant violent crime and poverty. Types of assistance: grants. Estimate of annual funds available: $11,100,000.

* Technical Support and Professional Development Consortia for Technology 84.302
U.S. Department of Education
Office of Educational Research and Improvement
Office of Reform Assistance and Dissemination
Washington, DC 20208   202-219-8070
To help State, local education agencies, teachers, school library and media personnel, administrators, and others successfully integrate advanced technology into kindergarten through twelfth grade classrooms, library media centers, and other settings. Types of assistance: grants. Estimate of annual funds available: $9,900,000.

* Challenge Grants for Technology in Education 84.303
Interagency Technology Office
U.S. Department of Education
Washington, DC 2020   202-708-6001
To support the development, interconnection, improvement, and maintenance of an effective educational technology infrastructure, including activities to promote and provide equipment, training and technical support. Types of assistance: grants. Estimate of annual funds available: $27,000,000.

* International Education Exchange 84.304
National Research Institute on Student Achievement,
    Curriculum, and Assessment
Office of Educational Research and Improvement
U.S. Department of Education
Washington, DC 20208   202-219-2079
To support international education exchange activities between the United States and eligible countries in civics, government, education, and economics. Types of assistance: grants. Estimate of annual funds available: $3,000,000.

* Grants for Faculty Training Projects in Geriatric Medicine and Dentistry (Geriatric Fellowships) 93.156
Susan Klein
Division of Associated Dental and
    Public Health Professions, BHP
Health Resources and Services Administration
Public Health Service (PHS)
Room 8C-103, 5600 Fishers Lane
Rockville, MD 20857   301-443-6887
To assist in the operation of postdoctoral training preparing current and future faculty for leadership roles in geriatric medicine and dentistry. Types of assistance: grants. Estimate of annual funds available: $ 2,841,596.

* Programs of Excellence in Health Professions Education for Minorities 93.157
Grants Management Officer
Health Resources and Services Administration
Room 8C-26, 5600 Fishers Lane
Rockville, MD 20857   301-443-6857
To strengthen the national capacity to train minority students in the health professions; and to support the health professions schools which have trained a significant number of the nation's minority health professionals. Types of assistance: grants. Estimate of annual funds available: $ 23,246,000.

* Nurse Training Improvement - Special Projects (Special Projects, Grants and Contracts for Improvement in Nurse Training) 93.359
Dr. Mary Hill
Division of Nursing
Health Resources and Services Administration
Public Health Service

5600 Fishers Lane, Room 9-36
Rockville, MD 20857   301-443-6193
To help schools of nursing and other institutions improve the quality and availability of nursing education through projects for specified purposes such as providing continuing education for nurses, demonstrating improved geriatric training, increasing nursing personnel in rural areas. Types of assistance: grants. Estimate of annual funds available: $ 9,474,000.

* Minority Biomedical Research Support (MBRS) 93.375
Director
Minority Biomedical Research Support
Program Branch, Division of Research Resources
National Institutes of Health
45 Center Dr., MSC 6200
Bethesda, MD 20892   301-594-3900
To address the lack of representation of minorities in biomedical research by increasing the pool of minorities pursing research careers. Types of assistance: grants. Estimate of annual funds available: $ 37,105,000.

* Cancer Research Manpower 93.398
Dr. Vincent J. Cairoli, Chief
Cancer Training Branch
Division of Cancer Prevention and Control
National Cancer Institute, EPN/232B
Bethesda, MD 20892   301-496-8580
To make available support for nonprofit institutions interested in providing biomedical training opportunities for individuals interested in careers in basic and clinical research to support important areas of the National Cancer Program. Types of assistance: grants. Estimate of annual funds available: $ 60,831,000.

* Administration on Developmental Disabilities - University Affiliated Programs 93.632
Program Development Division
Administration on Developmental Disabilities
U.S. Department of Health and Human Services
Washington, DC 20201   301-690-6961
To defray the cost of administration and operation of programs that provide interdisciplinary training for personnel concerned with developmental disabilities. Types of assistance: grants. Estimate of annual funds available: $ 18,979,174.

* Child Welfare Services Training Grants 93.648
Director
Program Support Division
Children's Bureau
Administration for Children, Youth, and Families
P.O. Box 1182
Washington, DC 20013   202-401-7626
To develop and maintain an adequate supply of qualified and trained personnel for the field of services to children and their families, and to improve educational programs and resources for preparing personnel for this field. Types of assistance: grants. Estimate of annual funds available: $ 4,398,087.

* Health Careers Opportunity Program 93.822
Grants Management Officer
Health Resources and Services Administration
Room 8C-26, 5600 Fishers Lane
Rockville, MD 20857   301-443-6857
To identify, recruit, and select individuals from disadvantaged backgrounds for education and training in a health or allied health professions school. Types of assistance: grants. Estimate of annual funds available: $ 24,000,000.

* Area Health Education Centers (AHEC) 93.824
Dr. Marc Rivo, Director
Division of Medicine
Health Resources and Services Administration (HRSA)
Public Health Service
5600 Fishers Lane, Room 9A-27
Rockville, MD 20857   301-443-6190
To improve the distribution, supply, quality, utilization, and efficiency of health

Be patient. If any phone number is incorrect, call (area code) 555-1212 and request the new listing.

191

personnel in the health service delivery system and for the purpose of increasing the regionalization of educational responsibilities of health professions schools. Types of assistance: grants. Estimate of annual funds available: $ 19,900,000.

* Medical Library Assistance 93.879

Extramural Programs
National Library of Medicine
Bethesda, MD 20894   301-496-4221

To improve health information services by providing funds to train professional personnel, strengthen library and information services, support biomedical publication, and conduct research in information science and in medical information. Types of assistance: grants. Estimate of annual funds available: $ 24,330,000.

* Minority Access to Research Careers (MARC) 93.880

Adolphus Toliver
Program Director (MARC Program)
National Institute of General Medical Sciences
National Institutes of Health
45 Center Dr., MSC 6200
Bethesda, MD 20892   301-594-3900

To assist minority institutions to train greater numbers of scientist and teachers in health related fields. Types of assistance: grants. Estimate of annual funds available: $ 16,653,000.

* Grants for Physician Assistant Training Program (Physical Assistant Training Program) 93.886

Dr. Marc Rivo, Director
Division of Medicine
Bureau of Health Professions
Health Resources and Services Administration (HRSA)
Public Health Service (PHS)
U.S. Department of Health and Human Services (DHHS)
Parklawn Bldg., Room 9A-27, 5600 Fishers Lane
Rockville, MD 20857   301-443-6190

To enable public or nonprofit private health or educational entities to meet the cost of projects to plan, develop and operate programs for the training of physicians assistants. Types of assistance: grants. Estimate of annual funds available: $ 2,400,000.

* Resource and Manpower Development in the Environmental Health Sciences (Core Centers and Research Training Program) 93.894

Director
Division of Extramural Research and Training
National Institute of Environmental Health Sciences
P.O. Box 12233
Research Triangle Park, NC 27709   919-541-7634

To provide long-term, stable support for broadly based multidisciplinary research and training on environmental health problems in Environmental Health Sciences Center. Types of assistance: grants. Estimate of annual funds available: $ 31,718,000.

* Grants for Faculty Development in Family Medicine 93.895

Dr. Marc Rivo, Director
Division of Medicine
Health Resources and Services Administration (HRSA)
Public Health Service (PHS)
Room 9A-27, 5600 Fishers Lane
Rockville, MD 20857   301-443-6190

To increase the supply of physician faculty available to teach in family medicine programs and to enhance the pedagogical skills of faculty presently teaching in family medicine. Types of assistance: grants. Estimate of annual funds available: $ 6,300,000.

* Residency Training and Advanced Education in the General Practice of Dentistry 93.897

Dr. Rosemary Duffy, Dental Education and Special Initiatives
Division of Assoc. and Dental Health Professions
Health Resources and Services Administration (HRSA)
Public Health Service (PHS)
5600 Fishers Lane
Rockville, MD 20857   301-443-6837

To assist schools of dentistry and institutions conducting post-graduate dental training in defraying the costs of projects to plan, develop, and operate an approved residency or advanced educational program in the general practice of dentistry. Types of assistance: grants. Estimate of annual funds available: $ 3,285,000.

* Grants for Faculty Development in General Internal Medicine and/or General Pediatrics (GIM/GP Faculty Development) 93.900

Dr. Marc Rivo, Director, Division of Medicine
Health Resources and Services Administration (HRSA)
Public Health Service (PHS)
Room 9A-27, 5600 Fishers Lane
Rockville, MD 20857   301-443-6190

To promote the development of faculty skills in physicians (full-time, part-time, volunteer, fellows and/or residents) who are currently teaching or who plan teaching careers in general internal medicine and/or general pediatrics training programs. Types of assistance: grants. Estimate of annual funds available: $ 3,600,000.

* Grants for the Training of Health Professions in Geriatrics 93.969

Ms. Bernice Parlak
Health Resources and Services Administration (HRSA)
Public Health Service (PHS)
U.S. Department of Health and Human Services
5600 Fishers Lane, Room 8-103
Rockville, MD 20857   301-443-6887

To develop regional resource centers focused on strengthening multidisciplinary training of health professionals in geriatric health care. Types of assistance: grants. Estimate of annual funds available: $ 5,926,000.

* Health Professions Recruitment Program for Indians (Recruitment Program) 93.970

Division of Grants and Contracts
Grants Management Branch
Indian Health Service
Public Health Service (PHS)
U.S. Department of Health and Human Services (DHHS)
12300 Twinbrook Pkwy., Suite 100
Rockville, MD 20852   301-443-5204

To identify Indians with a potential for education or training in the health professions and to encourage and assist them to enroll in health or allied health professional schools. Types of assistance: grants. Estimate of annual funds available: $ 945,000.

* Grants for Establishment of Departments of Family Medicine (Family Medicine Departments) 93.984

Dr. Marc Rivo, Director
Division of Medicine
Health Resources and Services Administration (HRSA)
BHPR, Public Health Service (PHS)
Room 4C-25, 5600 Fishers Lane
Rockville, MD 20857   301-443-6190

To assist in establishing, maintaining or improving family medicine academic administrative units to provide clinical instruction in family medicine in order that these units are comparable in status, faculty and curriculum to those other clinical units at the applying school. Types of assistance: grants. Estimate of annual funds available: $ 8,483,000.

Federal Money for Students

Both the federal government and state governments have student loan programs and other financial assistance to pursue higher education. And these programs are not limited to young adults, but include the elderly as well. The federal programs identified here are taken from the *Catalog of Federal Domestic Assistance* which is published by the U.S. Government Printing Office in Washington, DC. The number next to the title is the official reference. In the case of the federal agency, contact the office listed below the title for more details. Refer to the next section for a state-by-state listing of financial aid and scholarships for students.

* Money to Study Farming, Flowers, Clothing, and Food

(Special Emphasis Outreach Grants - 10.140)
McKinely Mays, CSREES
Special Emphasis Outreach Programs
U.S. Department of Agriculture
3345 South Building, AG ox 0910
14th and Independence Avenue, SW
Washington, DC 20250-0910   202-720-2471

To provide rapid financial support to assist public, private, state and/or other colleges and universities whose activities relate to the 1890 Morrill Act special emphasis areas. Overall goals of this program are to assist these institutions in their efforts to increase minority participation in agricultural and related fields, and to improve higher educational programs and resources that prepare students to enter into these fields. Estimate of annual funds available: $100,000.

* Fellowships to Study Food and Agriculture Science

(Food and Agricultural Science National Needs Graduate Fellowship Grants - 10.210)
Grant Programs Manager
Office of Higher Education Programs
U.S. Department of Agriculture
CSREES-HEP
South Building, Room 3914
14th and Independence Avenue, SW
Washington, DC 20250-2251   202-720-1973

To award grants to colleges and universities that have superior teaching and research competencies in the food and agricultural sciences. These grants are to be used to encourage outstanding students to pursue and complete a graduate degree at such institutions in an area of the food and agricultural sciences for which there is a national need for development of scientific expertise. Therefore, institutions that currently have excellent programs for graduate study and research in the food and agricultural sciences dealing with targeted national needs are particularly encouraged to apply. Estimate of annual funds available: $3,400,000.

* Help Prepare for College Math and Science

(Youth Competency, Math and Science - 11.449)
Lesa Morris
Colorado Alliance for Science
University of Colorado
Campus Box 456
Boulder, CO 80309-0456   303-492-6392

To increase the number of minority students enrolling in college and majoring in math, science, and engineering from the St. Vrain and Boulder Valley School districts, and to recruit scientists and engineers from the Boulder County area to serve as science/math tutors for primarily girls and minority students in the Boulder Valley and St. Vrain school districts. Estimate of annual funds available: N/A.

* Money for School and Even Flight Training for Joining the National Guard

(Selected Reserve Educational Assistance Program - 12.609)
Assistant Secretary of Defense
Reserve Affairs
Pentagon, Room 2D517
Washington, DC 20301   703-695-7459

To encourage and sustain membership in the National Guard and Reserve. Estimate of annual funds available: $68,400,000.

* Money from the Department of Defense to Study Mathematics

(Mathematical Sciences Grants Program - 12.901)
Dr. Charles F. Osgood, Director
NSA Mathematical Science Programs
National Security Agency, ATTN: R51A
U.S. Department of Defense
Fort George G. Meade, MD 20755-6000   301-688-0400

The National Security Agency (NSA) is concerned over the steadily declining pool of American citizens making careers in those areas of mathematics most strongly identified with cryptology. This alarming trend, along with lagging federal compensation could imperil NSA's carrying out its cryptologic mission. This grant program exists in order to make careers in these fields of mathematics seem more attractive to Americans and to make NSA known as a possible employer of such mathematicians. Estimate of annual funds available: $1,000,000.

* Money to Study Community Planning and Development

(Community Development Work-Study Program - 14.234)
John Hartung
U.S. Department of Housing and Urban Development
Office of Policy Development and Research
Office of University Partnerships
451 7th St., SW, Room 8130
Washington, DC 20410   202-708-3061, ext. 261

The Community Development Work-Study Program makes grants to institutions of higher education to provide assistance to economically disadvantaged and minority students. Students take part in community development work-study programs while they are enrolled full time in graduate or undergraduate programs with that major. Estimate of annual funds available: $3,000,000.

* Money to Study Housing Issues

(Doctoral Dissertation Research Grant Program - number to be announced)
Mr. Charles Taylor
Division of Budget, Contracts, and Program Control
Office of Policy Development and Research
U.S. Department of Housing and Urban Development
451 7th St., SW, Room 8230
Washington, DC 20410   202-708-1796

To encourage doctoral candidates to engage in policy-related housing and urban development research and to assist them in its timely completion. Estimate of annual funds available: N/A.

* Money for Members of Indian Tribes to Go to College

(Indian Education — Higher Education Grant Program - 15.114)
Bureau of Indian Affairs
Office of Indian Education Programs
U.S. Department of the Interior
1849 C St., NW, MS 3512-MIB

Washington, DC 20240   202-208-4871

To provide financial aid to eligible Indian students to enable them to attend accredited institutions of higher education. Estimate of annual funds available: $29,280,000.

* Money for Graduate Students in Criminal Justice

(Criminal Justice Research and Development — Graduate Research Fellowships - 16.562)
National Institute of Justice
633 Indiana Ave., SW
Washington, DC 20531   202-307-0645

To improve the quality and quantity of knowledge about crime and the criminal justice system. Additionally, the program seeks to increase the number of persons who are qualified to teach in collegiate criminal justice programs, to conduct research related to criminal justice issues, and to perform more effectively within the criminal justice system. Estimate of annual funds available: $125,000.

* Money for Graduate Students Who Want to Study the Break Up of the USSR

(Russian, Eurasian, and East European Research and Training - 19.300)
Program Officer
Eurasian and East European Research and Training Program
INR/RES
U.S. Department of State
Suite 404, Box 19, 1250 23rd St., NW
Washington, DC 20037   202-736-9060

To sustain and strengthen American expertise on the Commonwealth of Independent States, Georgia, the Baltic countries, and countries of Eastern Europe by supporting graduate training; advanced research; public dissemination of research data, methods, and findings; contact and collaboration among Government and private specialists; and first hand experience of the (former) Soviet Union and Eastern European countries by American specialists, including on-site conduct of advanced training and research. Estimate of annual funds available: $9,961,000.

* $3,000 a Year to Study at a State School to Become a Merchant Marine

(State Marine Schools - 20.806)
Martha Johnson
Office of Maritime Labor, Training and Safety
Maritime Administration
U.S. Department of Transportation
400 7th St., SW
Washington, DC 20590   202-366-5755

To train merchant marine officers in State Marine Schools. Estimate of annual funds available: $10,847,000.

* All Expenses Plus $543 a Month to Study at the Merchant Marine Academy

(U.S. Merchant Marine Academy - 20.807)
Office of Maritime Labor, Training and Safety
Maritime Administration
U.S. Department of Transportation
400 Seventh St., SW, Room 7302
Washington, DC 20590   202-366-5755

To train merchant marine officers. Estimate of annual funds available: $27,845,000.

* Money for Minorities and Women to Study Transportation

(Student Training and Education Program - 20.902)
Yvonne Strowbridge
Office of Small and Disadvantaged Business Utilization
U.S. Department of Transportation
S-40, Office of the Secretary
400 Seventh St., SW
Washington, DC 20590   800-532-1169

To support Historically Black Colleges and Universities (HBCU) in advancing the development of potential by providing quality education to minority students. This project will provide opportunities for students to enhance their knowledge and skills in the field of transportation through their involvement with the HBCUs and minority students. Estimate of annual funds available: $800,000.

* Part-Time Jobs in the Government for Students 16 and Older Who Have Trouble Paying Tuition

(Federal Employment For Disadvantaged Youth — Part-Time - 27.003)
Office of Affirmative Recruiting and Employment
Career Entry Group
Office of Personnel Management
1900 E St., NW
Washington, DC 20415   202-606-2605

The Stay-In-School Program is designed to give disadvantaged students (16 years and older), an opportunity for part-time temporary employment with federal agencies to allow them to continue their education without interruptions caused by financial pressures. Students enrolled full time in high school or college, and who meet the financial need criteria, are permitted to work up to 20 hours per week during school and 40 hours during school breaks. A *Career America-Student Employment* brochure is available. Estimate of annual funds available: N/A.

* Summer Jobs in the Government for Students 16 and Over Who Have Trouble Paying Tuition

(Federal Employment For Disadvantaged Youth — Summer - 27.004)
Office of Affirmative Recruiting and Employment
Career Entry Group
Office of Personnel Management
1900 E St., NW
Washington, DC 20415   202-606-2605

The Summer Aid program allows kids 16 and older to work for the Federal Government during the summer to earn money to enable them to return to school in the fall. To be eligible, a youth must meet the program's economic needs criteria. Interested youths should apply early (January-April) for summer work. Estimate of annual funds available: N/A.

* Summer Jobs in the Government for College and High School Students

(Federal Summer Employment - 27.006)
Staffing Operations Division
Career Entry Group
Office of Personnel Management
1900 E St., NW
Washington, DC 20415   202-606-0950

Most federal agencies employ individuals during summer vacation periods. The jobs may be clerical, crafts and trades, administrative, or subprofessional related to career interests. Employees are paid at the regular federal pay rate for the position. Summer jobs are filled through agency staffing plans as outlined in the Office of Personnel Management's *Summer Jobs*, (Announcement 414), issued in January of each year. Estimate of annual funds available: N/A.

* Internships for Graduate Students to Work at 54 Government Agencies

(Presidential Management Intern Program - 27.013)
Jamie Langlie, Projects Manager
Presidential Management Intern Program
Office of Personnel Management   703-807-0324
1400 Wilson Blvd., Suite 1200   703-807-0313
Washington, DC 22203   Fax: 703-235-1411

The PMI Program is a two-year, entry-level employment and career development program designed to attract to the federal civil service men and women with graduate degrees from diverse cultural and academic backgrounds who have demonstrated academic excellence, possess management and leadership potential, and have a commitment to and a clear interest in a public service career. Nominees for the PMI Program undergo a rigorous, competitive screening process. Being selected as a PMI Finalist is a first step, but does not guarantee a job. Agencies designate positions for PMIs and each establishes its own procedures for considering and hiring PMIs. Once hired by agencies, PMIs are encouraged to work with their agencies to establish an "individual development plan". PMIs participate in training conferences, seminars, and Congressional briefings. Estimate of annual funds available: N/A.

* $2,500 for High School and College Students to Study and Travel During the Summer

(Promotion of the Humanities — Younger Scholars - 45.115)
Division of Fellowships and Seminars
Younger Scholars Program
National Endowment For the Humanities

1100 Pennsylvania Ave., NW
Room 316
Washington, DC 20506   202-606-8463
To support humanities projects in progress during the summer by college students and advanced high school students. Grants are awarded for the research and writing of a paper, in one or more of the fields included in the humanities: history, philosophy, language, linguistics, literature, archaeology, art history, and criticism. Estimate of annual funds available: $375,000.

* $4,000 to Study the Humanities for the Summer

(Promotion of the Humanities — Summer Stipends - 45.121)
Division of Fellowships and Seminars
Summer Stipends
National Endowment for the Humanities
1100 Pennsylvania Ave., NW
Room 316
Washington, DC 20506   202-606-8551
To provide support for individual faculty and staff members at universities and two-year and four-year colleges and for others who have made or have demonstrated promise of making significant contributions to the humanities, in order to pursue two consecutive months of full-time study or research on a project in the humanities. Estimate of annual funds available: $ 1,000,000.

* Money for Ph.D. Students in Humanities to Complete Their Dissertation

(Promotion of the Humanities — Dissertation Grants - 45.157)
Division of Fellowships and Seminars
Dissertation Grants
National Endowment for the Humanities
1100 Pennsylvania Ave., NW, Room 316
Washington, DC 20506   202-606-8465
To provide support for individual Ph.D candidates in the humanities to complete the writing of their doctoral dissertations. Estimate of annual funds available: $987,000.

* Money for Social, Behavioral, and Economic Sciences Students

(Social, Behavioral, and Economic Sciences - 47.075)
Assistant Director
Social, Behavioral, and Economic Research (SBER)
National Science Foundation
4201 Wilson Blvd., Room 995
Arlington, VA 22230   703-306-1700
To promote the progress of the social, behavioral, and economic sciences; to facilitate cooperative research activities with foreign scientists, engineers, and institutions; and to support understanding of the resources invested in science and engineering in the U.S. Estimate of annual funds available: $98,960,000.

* Money for Science, Math, and Engineering Students

(Education and Human Resources - 47.076)
Assistant Director
Education and Human Resources
National Science Foundation
4201 Wilson Blvd.
Arlington, VA 22230   703-306-1600
To provide leadership and support to the nation's efforts to improve the quality and effectiveness of science, mathematics and engineering education, with the ultimate goal being a scientifically literate society, a technically competent work force, and a body of well-educated scientists and engineers able to meet the nation's needs. Estimate of annual funds available: $487,500,000.

* Money for Disabled Veterans to Go to College

(Vocational Rehabilitation For Disabled Veterans - 64.116)
Department of Veterans Affairs
Central Office
Washington, DC 20420   800-827-1000
To provide all services and assistance necessary to enable service-disabled veterans and service persons hospitalized pending discharge to achieve maximum independence in daily living and, to the maximum extent possible, to become employable and to obtain and maintain suitable employment. Estimate of annual funds available: Direct payments: $245,070,000. Loan advances: $2,387,000.

* Money for Spouses and Children of Deceased or Disabled Veterans to Go to School

(Survivors and Dependents Educational Assistance - 64.117)
Department of Veterans Affairs
Central Office
Washington, DC 20420   800-827-1000
To provide partial support to those seeking to advance their education who are qualifying spouses, surviving spouses, or children of deceased or disabled veterans who, as a result of their military service, have a permanent and total (100 percent) service connected disability, or are service personnel who have been listed for a total of more than 90 days as currently Missing in Action, or as Prisoners of War. Estimate of annual funds available: $109,072,000.

* Money for Veterans Who Served Between 1977-1985 to Go to School or Receive Training

(Post-Vietnam Era Veterans' Educational Assistance - 64.120)
Department of Veterans Affairs
Central Office
Washington, DC 20420   800-827-1000
To provide educational assistance to persons entering the Armed Forces after December 31, 1976, and before July 1, 1985, in obtaining an education they might otherwise not be able to afford; and to promote and assist the all volunteer military program of the United States by attracting qualified persons to serve in the Armed Forces. Estimate of annual funds available: $183,530,000.

* Money for Retired Veterans to Get Two Years of Training to Start a New Career

(Vocational Training For Certain Veterans Receiving VA Pensions - 64.123)
Department of Veterans Affairs
Central Office
Washington, DC 20420   800-827-1000
To assist new pension recipients to resume and maintain gainful employment by providing vocational training and other services. Estimate of annual funds available: $475,000.

* Money for Retired Veterans to Go to School

(All-Volunteer Force Educational Assistance - 64.124)
Department of Veterans Affairs
Central Office
Washington, DC 20420   800-827-1000
To help service persons readjust to civilian life after their separation from military service; to assist in the recruitment and retention of highly qualified personnel in the active and reserve components in the Armed Forces; to extend the benefits of a higher education to those who may not otherwise be able to afford it; to restore lost educational opportunities to those who served on active duty; and to enhance the Nation's competitiveness through a more highly educated work force. Estimate of annual funds available: $783,571,000.

* Pay Off Student Loans by Becoming a Community Volunteer

(Volunteers In Service To America (VISTA) - 72.003)
Corporation for National Service
AmeriCorps
1201 New York Ave., NW
Washington, DC 20525   800-942-2677
To supplement efforts of private, nonprofit organizations, and federal, state, and local government agencies to eliminate poverty and poverty-related problems by encouraging persons from all walks of life and all age groups to perform meaningful and constructive services as volunteers. Estimate of annual funds available: $36,236,000.

* Volunteer and Earn Money to Pay for School

(AmeriCorps - number to be announced)
Corporation for National and Community Service
AmeriCorps
1201 New York Ave., NW
Washington, DC 20525   800-942-2677
AmeriCorps is an initiative designed to achieve direct results in addressing the Nation's critical education, human, public safety, and environmental needs at the

community level. The program provides meaningful opportunities for people to serve their country in organized efforts, fostering citizen responsibility, building their community, and providing educational opportunities for those who make a serious commitment to service. Estimate of annual funds available: $153,000,000.

* Money for Science and Engineering Students to Travel to and Work in Energy Labs

(University-Laboratory Cooperative Program - 81.004)
Larry L. Barker
Postsecondary Programs Division
Science Education Programs
Scientific Education and Technology Information, EP-31
U.S. Department of Energy (DOE)
Washington, DC 20585   202-586-8947

To provide college and university science and engineering faculty and students with energy-related training and research experience in areas of energy research at Department of Energy research facilities. Estimate of annual funds available: $5,500,000.

* Money for Minority Students to Go to Energy-Related Conferences

(Minority Educational Institution Research Travel Fund - 81.083)
Annie Whatley
Office of Minority Economic IMPACT, MI-1
U.S. Department of Energy
Forrestal Building, Room 5B-110
Washington, DC 20585   202-586-0281

To provide travel funds to faculty members and students of minority postsecondary educational institutions to encourage and assist in initiating, improving, renewing, and expanding energy-related research. Estimate of annual funds available: $50,000.

* Money for Minority Students at Junior Colleges Who Are Energy Majors

(Minority Honors Training and Industrial Assistance Program - 81.084)
Annie Whatley
Office of Minority Economic IMPACT, MI-1
U.S. Department of Energy
Forrestal Building, Room 5B-110
Washington, DC 20585   202-586-0281

To provide scholarship funding to financially needy minority honor students pursuing training in energy-related technologies and to develop linkages with energy industries. Estimate of annual funds available: $418,000.

* Spend a Semester in a Department of Energy Lab

(Science and Engineering Research Semester - 81.097)
Donna Prokop
Office of Science Education Programs
U.S. Department of Energy
1000 Independence Ave., SW, Room 5B168, Code ET-30
Washington, DC 20585   202-586-8910

To give juniors and seniors the opportunity to participate in hands-on research at the cutting edge of science at Department of Energy laboratories, and to provide training and experience in the operation of sophisticated state-of-the-art equipment and instruments. Estimate of annual funds available: $3,600,000.

* Money for Minority Science, Engineering, and Math Majors

(Minority Undergraduate Training For Energy Related Careers - 81.098)
U.S. Department of Energy
1000 Independence Ave., SW, Room 5B-110
Washington, DC 20585   202-586-1593

To improve minority representation in energy-related technological areas associated with science, engineering, and mathematics by providing institutional grants to support the development and implementation of a structured set of activities tailored to the individual school. Estimate of annual funds available: $2,119,000.

* $15,000 for Graduate Students to Study Overseas

(Educational Exchange — Graduate Students - 82.001)
Institute of International Education

Attn: U.S. Student Programs
809 United Nations Plaza
New York, NY 10017   212-984-5330

To improve and strengthen international relations of the United States by promoting better mutual understanding among the peoples of the world through educational exchanges. Estimate of annual funds available: $10,500,000.

* $4,000 Grant for Students Having Trouble Paying for Tuition

(Federal Supplemental Educational Opportunity Grants - 84.007)
Division of Policy Development
Student Financial Assistance Programs
Office of Assistant Secretary for Postsecondary Education
U.S. Department of Education
600 Independence Ave., SW
Portals Bldg., Suite 3045
Washington, DC 20202   202-708-4690

To provide eligible undergraduate postsecondary students who have demonstrated financial need with grant assistance to help meet educational expenses. Estimate of annual funds available: $499,892,000.

* Money for a Foreign Language Degree

(National Resource Centers and Fellowships Program For Language and Area or Language and International Studies - 84.015)
Advanced Training and Research Branch
Center for International Education
Office of Postsecondary Education
U.S. Department of Education
600 Independence Ave., SW
Washington, DC 20202-5331   202-401-9774

In this global world, foreign languages and international studies are becoming increasingly important. The Department of Education has funds to support centers which promote instruction in foreign language and international studies at colleges and universities. In addition, there are graduate fellowships to pursue this course of study in order to develop a pool of international experts to meet our Nation's needs. Estimate of annual funds available: Grants: $18,029,000; Fellowships: $12,767,000.

* Money for Students and Teachers to Travel Overseas

(Fulbright-Hays Training Grants — Group Projects Abroad - 84.021)
Center for International Education
Office of Assistance Secretary for Postsecondary Education
U.S. Department of Education
600 Independence Ave., SW
Washington, DC 20202   202-401-9798

To help educational institutions improve their programs in modern foreign language and area studies through overseas study/travel seminar group research, advanced foreign language training, and curriculum development. Estimate of annual funds available: $2,203,000 plus $8,463,780 Indian rupees.

* Money for Ph.D. Students to Do Research Overseas

(Fulbright-Hays Training Grants — Doctoral Dissertation Research Abroad - 84.022)
Advanced Training and Research Branch
Center for International Education
Office of Assistant Secretary for Postsecondary Education
U.S. Department of Education
600 Independence Ave., SW
Washington, DC 20202   202-401-9798

To provide opportunities for graduate students to engage in full-time dissertation research abroad in modern foreign language and area studies, with the exception of Western Europe. This program is designed to develop research knowledge and capability in world areas not widely included in American curricula. Estimate of annual funds available: $1,735,000 plus 2,500,000 Indian rupees.

* Money to Study to Be a Special Education Teacher

(Special Education — Special Education Personnel Development and Parent Training - 84.029)
Division of Personnel Preparation
Special Education Programs
Office of Assistant Secretary for Special Education
and Rehabilitative Services

U.S. Department of Education
330 C St., SW, Room 3072
Washington, DC 20202   202-205-9554

To address identified shortages of special education teachers and related service personnel; to improve the quality and increase the supply of teachers, supervisors, administrators, researchers, teacher educators, speech correctionists, educational interpreters for the hearing impaired, and other special personnel such as specialists in physical education and recreation, paraprofessionals, vocational/career education, volunteers; and to provide parent training and information services. Estimate of annual funds available: $102,522,000.

* Guaranteed Student Loans

(Guaranteed Student Loans - 84.032)
Federal Student Aid Information Center
P.O. Box 84
Washington, DC 20044   800-433-3248

To authorize guaranteed loans for educational expenses available from eligible lenders such as banks, credit unions, savings and loan associations, pension funds, insurance companies, and schools, to vocational, undergraduate, and graduate students enrolled at eligible postsecondary institutions. Estimate of annual funds available: $19,961,182,000.

* Get Loans Directly from Your School

(Federal Direct Student Loan Program - number to be announced)
Federal Student Aid Information Center
P.O. Box 84
Washington, DC 20044   800-433-3248

To provide loans directly to students through schools, rather than through private lenders. Direct lending will save taxpayers an estimated $4.8 billion dollars, and make borrowing simpler, faster, and easier. Estimate of annual funds available: N/A.

* Work-Study Programs to Pay for School

(Federal Work-Study Program - 84.033)
Federal Student Aid Information Center
P.O. Box 84
Washington, DC 20044   800-433-3248

To provide part-time employment to eligible postsecondary students to help meet educational expenses and encourage students receiving program assistance to participate in community service activities. Estimate of annual funds available: $526,941,000.

* Grants to Study Library Science

(Library Education and Human Resource Development - 84.036)
Discretionary Library Programs Division
Library Programs
Office of Educational Research and Improvement
U.S. Department of Education
555 New Jersey Ave., NW, Room 300
Washington, DC 20208   202-219-1315

To assist institutions of higher education and library organizations and agencies in training or retraining persons in areas of library specialization where there are shortages, in new techniques of information acquisition, transfer and communication technology; in library leadership through advanced training in library management, in library education, in advanced training in management of new organizational formats (networks, consortia, etc.), and in serving the information needs of the elderly, the illiterate, disadvantaged or rural residents. Estimate of annual funds available: $4,960,000.

* Low-Interest Student Loans

(Federal Perkins Loan Program — Federal Capital Contributions - 84.038)
Federal Student Aid Information Center
P.O. Box 84
Washington, DC 20044   800-433-3248

To provide low-interest loans to eligible postsecondary students with demonstrated financial need to help meet educational expenses. Estimate of annual funds available: $144,037,000.

* Get Help to Study

(Upward Bound - 84.047)
Division of Student Services

Education Outreach Branch
Office of Postsecondary Education
U.S. Department of Education
600 Independence Ave., SW
Portals Bldg., Suite 600D
Washington, DC 20202   202-708-4804

To generate skills and motivation necessary for success in education beyond high school among low-income and potential first-generation college students and veterans. The goal of the program is to increase the academic performance and motivational levels of eligible enrollees so that they have a better chance of completing secondary school and successfully pursuing postsecondary educational programs. Estimate of annual funds available: Grants: $145,938,000; Math/Science Regional Centers: $14,600,000.

* $2,300 Grants to Go to School

(Federal Pell Grant Program - 84.063)
Division of Policy Development
Student Financial Assistance Programs
Office of Postsecondary Education
U.S. Department of Education
600 Independence Ave., SW
Washington, DC 20202   202-708-4607

To provide eligible undergraduate postsecondary students who have demonstrated financial need with grant assistance in meeting educational expenses. Estimate of annual funds available: $6,096,087,000.

* $5,000 from Your State to Go to College

(Grants to States For State Student Incentives - 84.069)
Division of Policy Development
Student Financial Assistance Programs
Office of Postsecondary Education
U.S. Department of Education
600 Independence Ave., SW
Washington, DC 20202   202-708-4607

To provide grants to the States for use in programs that provide financial assistance to eligible postsecondary students. Estimate of annual funds available: $72,555,000.

* Grants to Graduate Students

(Patricia Roberts Harris Fellowships - 84.094)
Cosette Ryan
Division of Higher Education Incentive Programs
Office of Postsecondary Education
U.S. Department of Education
600 Independence Ave., SW
Washington, DC 20202   202-260-3608

In order to help students achieve the master's level, professional, or doctoral education, grants are given to colleges and universities to fund fellowships, particularly for women and members of minority groups who are obtaining degrees in fields of high national priority. Estimate of annual funds available: $21,796,000.

* Money for Students Interested in Helping People with Disabilities

(Rehabilitation Training - 84.129)
Richard Melia
Rehabilitation Services Administration
Office of Developmental Programs
U.S. Department of Education
Mail Stop 2649
Washington, DC 20202-2649   202-205-9400

To support projects that provide new personnel and improve the skills of existing personnel trained in providing vocational rehabilitation services to individuals with disabilities in areas targeted as having personnel shortages. Estimate of annual funds available: $24,743,974.

* Money for Minorities and Low-Income Students to Go to Law School

(Assistance for Training in the Legal Profession - 84.136)
Janice Wilcox
Office of Postsecondary Education
Higher Education Programs

Education

U.S. Department of Education
600 Independence Ave., SW
Washington, DC 20202   202-708-4653
To assist minority, low income, and educationally disadvantaged college graduates
to train in the legal profession. Estimate of annual funds available: $2,991,000.

* Aid for Students Who Want to Be Interpreters for the Deaf

(Training Interpreters For Individuals Who Are Deaf and Individuals
Who Are Deaf-Blind - 84.160)
Office of Developmental Programs
Rehabilitation Services Administration
U.S. Department of Education
Mail Stop 2649
Washington, DC 20202-2649   202-205-9001
To support projects that train new interpreters and improve the skills of manual, oral,
and cued speech interpreters already providing services to individuals who are deaf
and individuals who are deaf-blind. Estimate of annual funds available: $1,510,000.

* $9,500 Per Year for Ph.D. Students

(Jacob K. Javits Fellowships - 84.170)
Division of Higher Education Incentive Programs
Office of Postsecondary Education
U.S. Department of Education
600 Independence Ave., SW
Washington, DC 20202-5329   202-260-3371
To provide fellowships to individuals of superior ability for doctoral study in
specified subfields within the arts, humanities, and social sciences. Estimate of annual
funds available: $8,664,000.

* $20,000 for Students Who Want to Become Teachers

(Douglas Teacher Scholarships - 84.176)
U.S. Department of Education
Office of Assistance Secretary for
   Postsecondary Education
Division of Higher Education Incentive Programs
Room 3022, ROB No. 3
600 Independence Ave., SW
Washington, DC 20202-5329   202-260-3392
To provide scholarships through the States that enable and encourage outstanding
high school graduates to pursue teaching careers at the pre-school, elementary, or
secondary level. Estimate of annual funds available: $15,379,000.

* $1,500 Per Year Grants to College Students

(Robert C. Byrd Honors Scholarships - 84.185)
Darleen Collins
U.S. Department of Education
Office of Student Financial Assistance
Office of the Assistant Secretary for
   Postsecondary Education
Division of Higher Education Programs
600 Independence Ave., SW
Washington, DC 20202-5329   202-260-3394
To provide scholarships to promote student excellence and achievement and to
recognize exceptionally able students who show promise of continued academic
achievement. Estimate of annual funds available: $18,940,000.

* Money for Students Who Want to Become Bilingual Education Teachers

(Bilingual Education Training Grants - 84.195)
Cynthia Ryan
Division of National Programs
Office of Bilingual Education and
   Minority Languages Affairs
U.S. Department of Education
600 Independence Ave., SW, Room 5628
Washington, DC 20202   202-205-9727
To provide financial support for programs designed to meet the training needs for
additional or better trained education personnel in bilingual education, including
support for program improvement. In certain cases, financial support is available for

students pursuing post-baccalaureate degrees in areas related to programs for limited
English proficient persons. Estimate of annual funds available: $36,672,000

* Money to Graduate Students Who Are Studying in Areas of National Need

(Graduate Assistance In Areas Of National Need - 84.200)
Division of Higher Education Incentive Programs
Office of Postsecondary Education
U.S. Department of Education
600 Independence Ave., SW
Washington, DC 20202-5329   202-260-3265
To provide fellowships through graduate academic departments to graduate students
of superior ability who demonstrate financial need and are able to of enhance the
capacity to teach and conduct research in areas of national need. For the academic
year 1993-94 the designated academic areas are: biology, chemistry, engineering,
foreign languages, mathematics, and physics. Estimate of annual funds available:
$35,623,000.

* Money for Women and Minority Students to Go to Graduate School

(Grants To Institutions To Encourage Women and Minority Participation In
Graduate Education - 84.202)
Vicky Paine
Division of Higher Education Incentive Programs
Office of Postsecondary Education
U.S. Department of Education
Washington, DC 20202-5329   202-260-3291
To provide grants to institutions of higher education to identify talented
undergraduate students that demonstrate financial need and are from minority groups
underrepresented in fields of study in graduate education. Estimate of annual funds
available: $6,004,000.

* Grants for Undergraduate and Graduate Students Who Have Trouble Paying Tuition

(Ronald E. McNair Post Baccalaureate Achievement - 84.217)
U.S. Department of Education
Division of Student Services
Office of Postsecondary Education
600 Independence Ave., SW
Portals Bldg., Suite 600D
Washington, DC 20202   202-708-4804
To provide grants for institutions of higher education to prepare low-income,
first-generation college students and students underrepresented in graduate education
for graduate study. Estimate of annual funds available: $9,859,000.

* Scholarships for Computer Science, Mathematics, and Engineering Students

(National Science Scholars - 84.242)
Charles Brazil
Division of Higher Education Incentive Programs
U.S. Department of Education
600 Independence Ave., SW
Portals Bldg., Suite C-80
Washington, DC 20202-5329   202-260-3245
To provide scholarships to graduating high school seniors to help cover the costs of
undergraduate postsecondary education that promote participation and excellence in
the life, physical, and computer sciences, mathematics and engineering (medical
studies and social sciences are excluded). Estimate of annual funds available:
$6,048,000.

* Money for Students Who Want to Study Early Childhood Education and Violence Counseling

(Training In Early Childhood Education And Violence Counseling -
84.266)
Robert Alexander
U.S. Department of Education
600 Independence Ave., SW
4400 Portals
Washington, DC 20202-6132   202-260-0994
To recruit and train students for careers in early childhood development, care, and

Be patient. If any phone number is incorrect, call (area code) 555-1212 and request the new listing.

counseling of young children and their care givers affected by community violence. Estimate of annual funds available: $4,960,000.

* Money for Students Interested in Careers in Public Service

(Harry S. Truman Scholarship Program - 85.001)
Louis Blair, Executive Secretary
Truman Scholarship Foundation
712 Jackson Place, NW
Washington, DC 20006   202-395-4831

A special scholarship program for college juniors has been established to encourage students to pursue careers in public service. Estimate of annual funds available: $3,060,000.

* Health Education Assistance Loans

(Health Education Assistance Loans - 93.108)
Division of Student Assistance
Bureau of Health Professions
Health Resources and Service Administration
Public Health Service
U.S. Department of Health and Human Services
Room 8-37, 5600 Fishers Lane
Rockville, MD 20857   301-443-1540

To authorize Health Education Assistance Loans, which are available from lenders such as banks, credit unions, savings and loan associations, and more to cover the costs for education in a health profession. Estimate of annual funds available: $350,000,000.

* Health Professions Scholarships for American Indians

(Health Professions Pregraduate Scholarship Program For Indians - 93.123)
Rosh Foley
IHS Scholarship Program
Indian Health Service (IHS)
Public Health Service
U.S. Department of Health and Human Services
Twinbrook Metro Plaza
Suite 100, 12300 Twinbrook Parkway
Rockville, MD 20852   301-443-6197

To provide scholarships to American Indians and Alaska Natives for the purpose of completing pre-graduate education leading to a baccalaureate degree in the areas of pre-medicine or pre-dentistry. Estimate of annual funds available: $1,636,500.

* Money to Train to Become a Nurse Anesthetist

(Nurse Anesthetist Traineeships - 93.124)
Erin Stevens
Division of Nursing
Bureau of Health Professions
Health Resources and Services Administration
Public Health Service
U.S. Department of Health and Human Services
Parklawn Building, Room 9-36
5600 Fishers Lane
Rockville, MD 20857   301-443-5763

To support registered nurses to become nurse anesthetists by providing funds for a maximum 18-month period of full-time study. Nurses must complete 12 months of study in a nurse anesthetist program. Estimate of annual funds available: $900,000.

* Financial Assistance for Disadvantaged Health Professions Students

(Financial Assistance For Disadvantaged Health Professions Students - 93.139)
Division of Student Assistance
Bureau of Health Professions
Health Resources and Services Administration
Public Health Service
U.S. Department of Health and Human Services
Parklawn Building, Room 8-34
5600 Fishers Lane
Rockville, MD 20857   301-443-4776

To assist disadvantaged health professions students who are of exceptional financial need to obtain a degree in medicine, osteopathic medicine, or dentistry by providing

financial support to defray the costs of their education. Estimate of annual funds available: $6,441,000.

* Money for Minorities Pursuing a Health Professions Education

(Programs of Excellence In Health Professions Education For Minorities - 93.157)
Dr. Garcia, Division of Disadvantaged Assistance
Bureau of Health Professions
Health Resources and Services Administration
Public Health Service
U.S. Department of Health and Human Services
Room 8A-09, Parklawn Building
5600 Fishers Lane
Rockville, MD 20857   301-443-2100

To strengthen the national capacity to train minority students in the health professions, and to support health professions schools which train a significant number of minority health professionals. Estimate of annual funds available: $23,500,000.

* Money for Health Professionals to Repay Their Student Loans

(National Health Service Corps Loan Repayment - 93.162)
National Health Service Corps
Loan Repayment Program
8201 Greensboro Drive, Suite 600
McLean, VA 22102   800-221-9393

To help assure an adequate supply of trained health professionals, the National Health Service Corps provides for the repayment of educational loans for health professionals who agree to serve in a health manpower shortage area. Priority is given to primary care physicians, dentists, certified nurse midwives, certified nurse practitioners, and physicians assistants. Estimate of annual funds available: $45,000,000.

* Money for Health Professionals to Repay Their Student Loans if They Serve with the Indian Health Service

(Indian Health Service Educational Loan Repayment - 93.164)
Mr. Charles Yepa
Loan Repayment Program
Indian Health Service
Public Health Service
U.S. Department of Health and Human Services
12300 Twinbrook Parkway, Suite 100
Rockville, MD 20852   301-443-3396

To help insure an adequate supply of trained health professionals, the Indian Health Service provides for the repayment of loans to those professionals who agree to serve in an Indian Health Service facility. Estimate of annual funds available: $15,182,000.

* Money for Disadvantaged Students to Study Nursing

(Nursing Education Opportunities For Individuals From Disadvantaged Backgrounds - 93.178)
Division of Nursing
Bureau of Health Professions
Health Resources and Services Administration
Public Health Service
U.S. Department of Health and Human Services
Room 8C-26, Parklawn Building
5600 Fishers Lane
Rockville, MD 20857   301-443-6915

To provide financial assistance to eligible schools of nursing and other applicants to meet the costs of projects that increase nursing education opportunities for individuals from disadvantaged backgrounds. Estimate of annual funds available: $3,811,000.

* Grants for Podiatric Primary Care Residency Training

(Grants For Podiatric Primary Care Residency Training - 93.181)
Division of Medicine
Bureau of Health Professions
Health Resources and Services Administration

Public Health Service
U.S. Department of Health and Human Services
Room 9A-20, Parklawn Building
5600 Fishers Lane
Rockville, MD 20857   301-443-1467

To provide grants to hospitals and schools of podiatric medicine to support residency programs for primary care podiatric practice. Funds can be used to cover the development and establishment of Podiatric Primary Care Residency programs and to provide resident stipends for those planning to specialize in podiatric primary care. Estimate of annual funds available: $706,345.

* Money for Health Care Students Who Want to Train in Rural Areas

(Interdisciplinary Training For Health Care For Rural Areas - 93.192)
Division of Associated, Dental and Public Health Professions
Bureau of Health Professions
Health Resources and Services Administration
Room 8C02, Parklawn Building, 5600 Fishers Lane
Rockville, MD 20857   301-443-6763

To help fulfill the health care needs in rural areas, money is set aside to recruit and retain health care professionals in rural health care settings. Funds can be used for student stipends, post-doctoral fellowships, faculty training, and the purchase or rental of necessary transportation and telecommunication equipment. Estimate of annual funds available: $4,146,000.

* Money for Health Care Students to Study Job Safety and Health

(Occupational Safety and Health — Training Grants - 93.263)
National Institute for Occupational Safety and Health (NIOSH)
Centers for Disease Control and Prevention
Public Health Service
U.S. Department of Health and Human Services
4676 Columbia Parkway
Cincinnati, OH 45226   513-533-8241
NIOSH Information Line   800-356-4674

To develop specialized professional and paraprofessional personnel in the occupational safety and health field with training in occupational medicine, occupational health nursing, industrial hygiene, and occupational safety. Estimate of annual funds available: $11,354,000.

* Scholarships for National Health Service Corps

(National Health Service Corps Scholarship Program - 93.288)
National Health Service Corps Scholarships
8201 Greensboro Drive, Suite 600
McLean, VA 22102   800-221-9393

To provide service-conditioned scholarships to health professions students to assure an adequate supply of physicians, dentists, certified nurse midwives, certified nurse practitioners, and physician assistants in Health Professional Shortage Areas. Estimate of annual funds available: $39,453,484.

* Health Professionals Student Loans

(Health Professions Student Loans, Including Primary Care Loans/Loans For Disadvantaged Students - 93.342)
Division of Student Assistance
Bureau of Health Professions
Health Resources and Services Administration
Public Health Service
U.S. Department of Health and Human Services Administration
Parklawn Building, Room 8-34
5600 Fishers Lane
Rockville, MD 20857   301-443-4776

In order to increase educational opportunities for students in need of financial assistance to pursue degrees in health professions, long-term low-interest loans are available. Estimate of annual funds available: $8,179,000.

* Money to Train to Be a Professional Nurse

(Professional Nurse Traineeships - 93.358)
Erin Stevens
Division of Nursing
Bureau of Health Professions

Health Resources and Services Administration
Public Health Service
U.S. Department of Health and Human Services
Room 9-36, Parklawn Building
5600 Fishers Lane
Rockville, MD 20857   301-443-5763

To prepare individuals who have completed basic nursing preparation as nurse educators, public health nurses, nurse midwives, and nurse practitioners, or as other clinical nursing specialists. Estimate of annual funds available: $14,420,000.

* Nursing Student Loans

(Nursing Student Loans - 93.364)
Division of Student Assistance
Bureau of Health Professions
Health Resources and Services Administration
Public Health Service
U.S. Department of Health and Human Services
Parklawn Building, Room 8-34
5600 Fishers Lane
Rockville, MD 20857   301-443-4776

Long-term, low-interest loans are available at the rate of five percent to students in need of financial assistance to pursue a course of study in professional nursing education. Students may pursue a course of study leading to a diploma, associate, baccalaureate, or graduate degree in nursing. Estimate of annual funds available: $4,000,000.

* Grants for Graduate Training in Family Medicine

(Grants For Graduate Training In Family Medicine - 93.379)
Division of Medicine
Bureau of Health Professions
Health Resources and Services Administration
Public Health Service
U.S. Department of Health and Human Services
Room 4C25, 5600 Fishers Lane
Rockville, MD 20857   301-443-6190

To increase the number of physicians practicing family medicine, particularly to those willing to work in medically under-served communities, grants are available to cover the cost of developing and operating residency training programs, and to provide financial assistance to participants in the programs. A grant may be made to a residency program in family practice; an internship program in osteopathic medicine which emphasizes family medicine; or a residency program in osteopathic general practice. Estimate of annual funds available: $14,319,000.

* Scholarships for Students in Child Development

(Child Development Associate Scholarships - 93.614)
Council for Early Childhood Professional Recognition
Head Start Bureau
P.O. Box 1182
1341 G St., Suite 400   800-424-4310
Washington, DC 20005   Fax: 202-265-9161

To support the cost of training, application, assessment, and credentialing of candidates for certification as Child Development Associates (CDA), who can then work in pre-school programs such as Head Start and other day care programs. Estimate of annual funds available: $1,371,936.

* Scholarships for Students of Exceptional Financial Need

(Scholarships for Students of Exceptional Financial Need - 93.820)
Division of Student Assistance
Bureau of Health Professions
Health Resources and Services Administration
Public Health Service
U.S. Department of Health and Human Services
Room 8-34, Parklawn Building
5600 Fishers Lane
Rockville, MD 20857   301-443-4776

To make funds available to health professions schools to award scholarships to health professions students of exceptional financial need. These scholarships are awarded with an obligation to serve in an area of the country designated a Health Professional Shortage Area. Estimate of annual funds available: $10,767,000.

* Health Careers Opportunity Program

(Health Careers Opportunity Program - 93.822)
Division of Disadvantaged Assistance
Bureau of Health Professions
Health Resources and Services Administration
Public Health Service
U.S. Department of Health and Human Services
Room 8A-09, 5600 Fishers Lane
Rockville, MD 20857   301-443-2100

The Health Careers Opportunity Program provides assistance to individuals from disadvantaged backgrounds to obtain a health or allied health profession degree. Stipends are available to students of financial need who attend schools of medicine, osteopathic medicine, public health, veterinary medicine, optometry, pharmacy, allied health, chiropractic, podiatric medicine, clinical psychology, or dentistry. Other services include counseling, preliminary education before entry into a health profession education program, facilitating entry, retention, financial aid information dissemination, and more. Estimate of annual funds available: $24,100,00.

* Money for Dental Students for Advanced Residency Training

(Residency Training And Advanced Education In General Practice Of Dentistry - 93.897)
Dental Education and Special Initiatives Branch
Division of Associated Dental and Public Health Professions
Bureau of Health Professions
Health Resources and Services Administration
Public Health Service
U.S. Department of Health and Human Services
5600 Fishers Lane
Rockville, MD 20857   301-443-6837

To assist schools of dentistry or dental training to institute residency training and advanced educational programs in the general practice of dentistry. The grant can be used to support personnel, residents, or trainees who are in need of financial assistance, to purchase equipment, and for other expenses necessary to conduct the program. Estimate of annual funds available: $3,849,000.

* Grants for Nurse Anesthetists

(Grants For Nurse Anesthetist Faculty Fellowships - 93.907)
Erin Stevens, Division of Nursing
Bureau of Health Professions
Health Resources and Services Administration
Public Health Service
Room 9-36, Parklawn Building, 5600 Fishers Lane
Rockville, MD 20857   301-443-5763

To provide financial assistance and support through fellowships to certified registered nurse anesthetists (CRNAs) who are faculty members of accredited nurse anesthetist programs to enable them to obtain advanced education relevant to their teaching functions. Estimate of annual funds available: $160,000.

* Money for Nursing Students to Repay Their Loans by Working at a Public Health Facility After Graduation

(Nursing Education Loan Repayment Agreements For Registered Nurses Entering Employment At Eligible Health Facilities - 93.908)
Loan Repayment Programs Branch
Division of Scholarships and Loan Repayment
Bureau of Primary Health Care
Health Resources and Services Administration
4350 East-West Highway
Rockville, MD 20857   800-435-6464

As an incentive for registered nurses to enter into full-time employment at health facilities with nursing shortages, this program assists in the repayment of their nursing education loans. The program is designed to increase the number of registered nurses serving designated nurse shortage areas. Estimate of annual funds available: $2,050,000.

* Scholarships and Money to Repay Loans of Disadvantaged Health Professionals

(Disadvantaged Health Professions Faculty Loan Repayment and Fellowship Program - 93.923)
Division of Disadvantaged Assistance
Bureau of Health Professions

Health Resources and Services Administration
Public Health Service
Parklawn Building, Room 8A-09
5600 Fishers Lane
Rockville, MD 20857   301-443-3680

To attract and retain disadvantaged health professions faculty members for accredited health professions schools of medicine, nursing, osteopathic medicine, dentistry, pharmacy, podiatric medicine, optometry, veterinary medicine, public health, or a school that offers a graduate program in clinical psychology for at least two years. The program repays the annual educational loan balance of the students for those years. Estimate of annual funds available: $1,156,000.

* Grants to States to Give Scholarships to Those Who Want to Serve the Community

(Demonstration Grants To States For Community Scholarships - 93.931)
Division of National Health Service Corps
Bureau of Primary Health Care
Health Resources and Services Administration
Public Health Service
4350 East-West Highway
Rockville, MD 20814   301-594-4260

To fill the need in health professional shortage areas, grants are given to community organizations, who in turn provide educational scholarships to individuals serving as health professionals in these areas. The community organizations provide scholarships to recipients to become physicians, certified nurse practitioners, physician assistants, or certified nurse midwives. The scholars must agree to serve in the health professional shortage area in which the community organization is located. Estimate of annual funds available: $500,000.

* Money for Health Professionals Who Want to Be in Public Health

(Public Health Traineeships - 93.964)
Anne Kahl
Public Health Branch
Division of Associated, Dental, and Public Health Professions
Bureau of Health Professions
Health Resources and Services Administration
Public Health Service
Parklawn Bldg., Room 8C-09
5600 Fishers Lane
Rockville, MD 20857   301-443-6757

To help support graduate students who are studying in the field of public health, grants are given to colleges and universities offering graduate or specialized training in the public health field. Support is limited to the fields of epidemiology, environmental health, biostatistics, toxicology, and public health and nutrition. Estimate of annual funds available: $2,587,000.

* Money for American Indians Who Want to Be Health Care Professionals

(Health Professions Recruitment Program For Indians - 93.970)
Mr. Larry S. Thomas, Director
Division of Health Professions Recruitment and Training
Indian Health Service
Public Health Service
U.S. Department of Health and Human Services
Twinbrook Metro Plaza
12300 Twinbrook Parkway, Suite 100
Rockville, MD 20852   301-443-4242

To increase the number of American Indians and Alaskan Natives who become health professionals, money has been set aside for non-profit health or educational entities, Indian tribes, or tribal organizations to help identify students interested in the field and to assist them in enrolling in schools. Some of the projects funded include the recruitment of American Indians into health care programs, a variety of retention services once students have enrolled, and scholarship support. Estimate of annual funds available: $1,500,000.

* Money for American Indians Who Need Extra Studies Before Acceptance into a Health Care Program

(Health Professions Preparatory Scholarship Program For Indians - 93.971)
Rosh Foley
Indian Health Service Scholarship Program

Education

Indian Health Service (IHS)
U.S. Department of Health and Human Services
Twinbrook Metro Plaza
Suite 100, 12300 Twinbrook Parkway
Rockville, MD 20852   301-443-6197

To make scholarships available to American Indians and Alaskan Natives who need to take some extra courses in order to qualify for enrollment or re-enrollment in a health profession school. Estimate of annual funds available: $1,636,500.

* Scholarships for Health Care Professionals

(Health Professions Scholarship Program - 93.972)
Rosh Foley
Indian Health Service Scholarship Program
Indian Health Service (IHS)
U.S. Department of Health and Human Services
Twinbrook Metro Plaza
Suite 100, 12300 Twinbrook Parkway
Rockville, MD 20852   301-443-6197

To provide scholarships to American Indians and Alaska Natives attending health professions schools interested in serving other Indians. Upon completion, scholarship recipients are obligated to serve in the Indian Health Service (IHS) one year for each year of scholarship support, with a minimum of two years. The health professions needed by the IHS include allopathic and osteopathic medicine, dentistry, nursing, public health nutrition, medical social work, speech pathology/audiology, optometry, pharmacology, and health care administration. Estimate of annual funds available: $8,717,000.

* Loans for Health Service Corps Doctors to Enter Private Practice

(Special Loans For National Health Service Corps Members To Enter Private Practice - 93.973)
National Health Service Corps
Health Resources and Services Administration
Public Health Service
U.S. Department of Health and Human Services
8201 Greensboro Dr., Suite 600   301-443-2900
McLean, MD 22102   800-221-9393

To assist individuals who received National Health Service Corps scholarships and have completed their period of service with the Corps by giving one loan to help them enter private full-time clinical practice. To receive the loan, the person must agree to operate the practice in a health professional shortage area for not less than two years. Estimate of annual funds available: N/A.

The World's Largest Educational Database

What Is ERIC

The Educational Resources Information Center (ERIC) is a federally funded, nationwide information network designed to provide you with ready access to education literature. At the heart of ERIC is the largest education database in the world containing more than 850,000 records of journal articles, research reports, curriculum and teaching guides, conference papers, and books. Each year approximately 30,000 new records are added. The ERIC database is available in many formats at hundreds of locations. ERIC also offers customized assistance through a network of subject-specific education clearinghouses that provide toll-free reference and referral, and free or low-cost publications on important education topics. The ERIC system manages by the U.S. Department of Education's Office of Educational Research and Improvement (OERI) consists of 16 clearinghouses and a number of adjunct clearinghouses, and additional support components.

How to Use ERIC

The ERIC clearinghouses collect, abstract, and index educational materials for the ERIC database; respond to requests for information in their subject areas; and produce special publications on current research, programs, and practices.

The ERIC Document Reproduction Service (EDRS) produces and sells microfiche and paper copies of documents announced in the ERIC database. Back collections of ERIC documents, annual subscriptions, cumulative indexes, and other ERIC related products are also available from EDRS. For more information on how to order documents call 800-443-ERIC.

The ERIC Processing and Reference Facility is the technical hub of the ERIC system that produces and maintains the database and systemwide support products. The ERIC Facility also prepares Resources in Education (RIE), ERIC Ready Reference, and other products. Their toll-free number is 800-443-ERIC.

ACCESS ERIC is the main center for the ERIC clearinghouses information. ACCESS ERIC coordinates ERIC's outreach and systemwide dissemination activities; develops new ERIC publications; and provides general reference and referral services. ACCESS ERIC's publications and directories, including *A Pocket Guide to ERIC, All About ERIC, The ERIC Review, ERIC Users' Interchange, the Catalog of ERIC Clearinghouse Publications*, and several reference directories, help the public understand and use ERIC as well as provide information about current education-related issues, research, and practice. Contact ACCESS ERIC at 800-LET-ERIC.

Internet Access to ERIC

If you have a computer with a modem, and have Internet, e-mail, gopher, or World Wide Web access, you can tap into a vast array of ERIC information. For questions about education, child development and care, parenting, learning, teaching, information technology, and other related topics, send an e-mail message to askeric@ericir.syr.edu.

More than a dozen ERIC Clearinghouses, Adjunct Clearinghouses, and support components host gopher and World Wide Web sites. For general information about ERIC and links to all ERIC Internet sites, start with the ERIC systemwide sites: gopher: aspensys.aspensys.com:74/11/ericor URL: http://www/aspensys.com/eric2/welcome.html.

You can also use the Internet to connect to sites that offer free public access to the ERIC database. For a list of public Internet access points to the ERIC database and step-by-step log-in instructions, send an e-mail message to ericdb@aspensys.com.

Commercial networks feature ERIC information including Digests, Parent Brochures, articles from the ERIC Review, bibliographies, and more. For help finding ERIC on these networks, contact ACCESS ERIC at 800-LET-ERIC.

If your computer has a CD-ROM drive and you have frequent need for searches of the education literature, a subscription to the ERIC database is now available for as little as $100 per year. To find a CD-ROM vendor call 800-799-ERIC.

Elementary and Early Childhood

This Clearinghouse provides information on the development and education of children from birth through early adolescence. Among the topics covered are: prenatal and infant development and care; child care programs and community services for children at local, state, and federal levels; family relationships; home and school relationships; technology and children; preparation of early childhood teachers and caregivers; foster care and adoption; and theoretical and philosophical issues related to children's development and education.

The clearinghouse provided a couple with guides, publications and checklists to help them select a day care center. They also directed them on where to search for more information on day care centers, and provided a guide to assess their preschooler's development.

A reporter called the clearinghouse to obtain information for a news story on the quality of foster care. After conducting a database search, the clearinghouse sent articles, research reports, and statistics.

ERIC/EECE Digests and Resource Lists are free; publications and ReadySearches are individually priced. Contact: Eric Clearinghouse On Elementary And Early Childhood Education, University of Illinois, 805 West Pennsylvania Ave., Urbana, IL 61801-4897, 217-333-1386, 800-583-4135.

Education

Teaching and Teacher Education

The ERIC Clearinghouse on Teaching and Teacher Education provides comprehensive information on health, physical education, recreation, and dance and movement education.

Many administrators and researchers call the clearinghouse to get answers to questions on the reform movement in teacher certification: What are the requirements? How do they vary from state to state? What are the current objectives and priorities?

A math teacher wanted to expand his horizons in the classroom by introducing some computer games to help his students learn to multiply and divide. The Clearinghouse sent him a bibliography called *Simulations and Games* which has over 2,000 entries in 60 categories reflecting the growing interest in applying computer games to education.

Contact: Eric Clearinghouse On Teaching and Teacher Education, American Association of Colleges for Teacher Education, One Dupont Circle, NW, Suite 610, Washington, DC 20036-1186, 202-293-2450, 800-822-9229.

Disabled and Gifted

This Clearinghouse provides information on the education and development of disabled persons, including prevention of disabilities, identification and assessment of disabilities, and intervention and enrichment programs for the disabled both in special settings and within the mainstream. All aspects of the education and development of gifted persons are covered as well.

A teacher was helped to mainstream a handicapped student in her vocational education classes. She obtained information on how to make the child feel more comfortable, and ways to adapt her teaching style to the child's needs. She received research briefs on being at ease with handicapped children, and managing stress for the learning disabled.

A graduate student needed information on the post-school status of learning disabled students. The clearinghouse provided research and resource summaries, a bibliography of selected publications, suggestions for database searching, and referrals to other sources of information.

For pricing information contact Information Services at Eric Clearinghouse on Disabled and Gifted Education, The Council for Exceptional Children, 1920 Association Dr., Reston, VA 22091-1589, 703-264-9474, 800-328-0272.

Educational Management

This Clearinghouse distributes information on the leadership, management, and structure of public and private educational organizations, and many facets of administration and methods of organizational change. The Clearinghouse also provides information on sites and equipment and aspects of planning and operating an educational facility.

A policymaker formulating educational policy needed to understand the nature of teachers' work. The clearinghouse sent literature to answer questions such as How do teachers preserve the quality of instruction in the face of never-ending task demands? What benefits do teachers derive from their interactions with students? and What would a cooperative alliance between policymakers and teachers look like?

A high school principal was concerned about racism in school. The clearinghouse provided a bulletin explaining why racism is on the rise and reporting on effective programs to foster cultural acceptance.

Publications vary in price from $4 to $25. Database searches range from $7.50 to $30+ according to the type and length of search. Other short product series are available free. For a pricing list, contact Eric Clearinghouse On Educational Management, College of Education, University of Oregon, 1787 Agate Street, Eugene, OR 97403-5207, 503-346-5043, 800-438-8841.

Languages and Linguistics

This Clearinghouse provides information on language and language sciences and all areas of language instruction methodology and learning, including foreign language. Additionally it monitors bilingualism and bilingual education, study abroad and international exchanges, and teacher training.

A public policy maker obtained information on the problems facing illiterate adults who are not native English speakers, and what the most effective education strategies have been.

A business owner wanted information on teaching English as a second language for to improve communication in the workplace. He received an annotated bibliography with abstracts and call numbers of documents relative to the topic.

Single copies of mini-bibliographies and fact sheets are free. Ready-made computer search printouts are available for $10 each, prepaid. Prices vary for a tailor-made search. Contact Eric Clearinghouse On Languages and Linguistics, Center for Applied Linguistics, 1118 22nd St., NW, Washington, DC 20037-0037, 202-429-9292, 800-276-9834.

Assessment and Evaluation

The Clearinghouse provides information on the assessment and evaluation of education projects or programs; tests and other measurement devices; methodology of measurement and evaluation; research design and methodology; human development; and learning theory in general.

Many researchers call the clearinghouse to obtain statistics on the various states that deal with testing for teachers. What percentage of would-be teachers certify? Which states have more stringent standards? and How do the standards for certification vary from state to state?

Many educators and researchers obtain information on the effectiveness of the Scholastic Aptitude Test to determine college entrance. Do statistics show that the tests discriminate against certain minority groups? Are the tests effective tools for measurement? The clearinghouse can provide this information.

For pricing information and a listing of publications contact Eric Clearinghouse On Assessment And Evaluation, The Catholic University of America, 210 O'Boyle Hall, Washington, DC 20064, 202-319-5120, 800-464-3742.

Urban Education

The Clearinghouse provides information on the programs and practices in schools in urban areas and the education of racial/ethnic minority children and youth in various settings; theory and practice of education equity; and urban and minority experiences and social institutions and services.

Members of school boards of education obtain research and current studies from the clearinghouse on the most effective programs for reducing the dropout rates among inner city high school students.

Federal government employees and media personnel often call the clearinghouse to obtain data on how much money is spent on programs to reduce drop-out rates, especially around the time of appropriations.

For pricing information and a list of publications contact Eric Clearinghouse On Urban Education, Box 40, Teachers College, Columbia University, New York, NY 10027-6696, 212-678-3433, 800-601-4868.

Rural Education, Small Schools

The Clearinghouse provides information on economic, cultural, social, and other factors of education for rural residents, including American Indians/Alaska Natives, Mexican Americans, and migrants; and education in all small schools.

A policymaker obtained information about the emerging problem of maintaining and replacing school buildings in rural areas. The clearinghouse sent reports analyzing the available options, outlining implications for educators, and developing recommendations for possible consideration by state-level policymakers.

A teacher with several children whose immigration status placed them at risk in his classes contacted the clearinghouse to obtain publications describing the plight of these children in American schools, the legal issues and pertinent court rulings, and prohibited and recommended practices.

For pricing information and a list of publications contact: Eric Clearinghouse On Rural Education And Small Schools, Appalachia Educational Laboratory, Inc., 1031 Quarrier St., P.O. Box 1348, Charleston, WV 25325-1348, 800-624-9120 (outside WV), 800-344-6646 (in WV).

Adult, Career and Vocational Learning

The Clearinghouse provides materials covering all levels of adult and continuing education from basic literacy training through professional skill upgrading; vocational and technical education covering all service areas for secondary, postsecondary, and adult populations; and career education and career development programs for all ages and populations in educational, institutional, business, and industrial settings.

The clearinghouse conducted a database search for a businessman on the latest information in robotics and their applications.

An employer wanted to implement flex time, work share and several pre-retirement plans for his employees. The clearinghouse provided him with information on various experimental models, resources to help him set up and start the programs, and research on the effectiveness of the programs in other worksites.

For pricing information and a list of publications contact: Eric Clearinghouse On Adult, Career And Vocational Learning, Ohio State University Center on Education and Training for Employment, 1960 Kenny Rd., Columbus, OH 43210-1090, 800-848-4815, 614-292-4353.

Higher Education

The Clearinghouse provides information covering education beyond the secondary level that leads to a four-year, masters, doctoral, or professional degree and that includes courses and programs designed to enhance or update skills obtained in these degree programs. It also covers business or industry education programs leading to a degree.

What research and assessments are available on the trends and issues in higher education? What are students really learning? The clearinghouse maintains up-to-date research and information on these issues.

A graduate student, interested in what percentage of state university faculty are minorities and women, obtained data on the diversity in state university faculties. Another student obtained figures on the number of female Hispanic school administrators in Ohio.

A basic bibliographic printout consists of up to 100 current citations. The cost varies: $80 corporate; $40 academic institutions; $25 students. Contact Eric Clearinghouse On Higher Education, George Washington University, One Dupont Circle NW, Washington, DC 20036-1183, 202-296-2597, 800-773-3742.

Community Colleges

This Clearinghouse provides information on the development, administration, and evaluation of two-year public and private community and junior colleges, technical institutes, and two-year branch university campuses. It also deals with linkages between two-year colleges and business/industrial organizations.

A researcher obtained information on the graduation rates of nursing students working on A.A. degrees from junior colleges. How many of these students are returning women and mothers?

Another researcher requested information on recruiting minorities and women, and efforts to retain them in community colleges.

Education

Contact: Eric Clearinghouse On Community Colleges, University of California at Los Angeles, 3051 Moore Hall, Los Angeles, CA 90024-1521, 310-825-3931, 800-832-8256.

Information and Technology

This Clearinghouse provides information covering educational technology and library and information science at all levels. Within library and information science, the focus is on the operation and management of information services for education-related organizations. All aspects of information technology related to education are considered within this scope.

A school administrator called the clearinghouse to obtain the latest research on the value of using computers and applying video technology to enhance learning. He received some of the clearinghouse's own materials and learned how to access the database to obtain more specific information.

A software company needed information on the advantages of the CD-ROM over floppy disks. The clearinghouse sent the company various studies comparing the different types of computer base media.

ERIC digests and mini-bibliographies are free. More exhaustive database searches vary in cost. Contact Eric Clearinghouse On Information and Technology, Syracuse University, 4-194 Center for Science and Technology, Syracuse, NY 13244-4100, 315-443-3640, 800-464-9107.

Science, Math and the Environment

The ERIC Clearinghouse for Science, Mathematics, and Environmental Education acquires educational literature on the following topics: development of curriculum and instructional materials; teachers and teacher education; learning theory/outcomes; educational programs; research and evaluative studies; media applications; and computer applications.

A sixth-grade teacher obtained information to help her teach a lesson on environmental education. She received a publication suggesting activities related to proper use and disposal of hazardous materials found in the home. She also received a list of suggested activities to involve her students in examining the nature and importance of recycling along with a list of films, readings, and organizations to contact for further information.

The clearinghouse can provide materials to answer questions such as How are microcomputers being used in laboratory activities? What are the recent developments in college mathematics? What are the common safety hazards in science classrooms? What resources are available for teaching mathematics in a bilingual classroom? What are the environmental education objectives, activities, accomplishments, and plans of the agencies of the Federal Government?

There is a minimal charge for certain publications and bibliographies. In-depth database searches cost a minimum of $25 or $35 per hour. Contact: Eric Clearinghouse For Science, Mathematics, And Environmental Education, Ohio State University, 1929 Kenney Rd., Columbus, OH 43210-1080, 614-292-6717, 800-276-0462.

Reading, English and Communication Skills

This Clearinghouse makes available hard-to-find educational materials such as research reports, literature reviews, curriculum guides, conference papers, projects or program reviews, and government reports. Each year ERIC/RCS helps thousands of people find useful information related to education in reading, English, journalism, theater, speech and mass communications.

The clearinghouse can provide materials to answer questions such as: How can newspapers, television and film be used as effective teaching tools? What strategies help Dyslexic students? What are specific problems in media ethics? How does bias affect the perception of journalists? and What models have been used to foster cognitive development in college students?

An English teacher wished to incorporate computers into her classroom at the elementary level. The clearinghouse provided guidelines on the sequential organization of word-processing skills, software selection, class organization, desktop publishing, and a variety of other lessons for the effective integration of computers into the instructional program.

ERIC/RCS Focused Access to Selected Topics Bibliographies, newsletters, and Digests with information and references on topics of current interest are free of charge. Multiple copies of publications for workshop distribution are available at no-cost. Question-answering is also a free service. Customized computer searches of the ERIC database are conducted for $20 for the first 50 citations. Contact Eric Clearinghouse On Reading English And Communication Skills, Indiana University, Smith Research Center, Suite 150, 2805 East Tenth Street, Bloomington, IN 47408-2698, 812-855-5847, 800-759-4723.

Social Studies and Social Science

This Clearinghouse describes journal articles and documents at all levels of social studies and social science education, including anthropology, economics, geography, sociology, social psychology, civics, and political science. It also covers materials on history and on social topics such as law-related education, ethnic studies, bias and discrimination, aging, adoption, women's equity, and sex education.

A curriculum policy maker obtained information from the clearinghouse focusing on what is happening now in computer use and what might be expected in the future for social studies.

A middle school world geography teacher wished to supplement her lessons on Africa and African culture. The clearinghouse provided essays on what, why, and how to teach about people and places of Africa, provided teaching materials, and listed resources including a select bibliography on teaching about Africa and listings of national centers of African studies and other organizations with resources in Africa.

You can obtain a customized computer search of the ERIC database on a requested topic for $10 to $25 to yield an annotated bibliography of up to 50 documents and journal articles in the ERIC system. For more information, contact Eric Clearinghouse For Social Studies/social Science Education, Social Studies Development Center, Indiana University, Smith Research Center,

2805 East Tenth St., Suite 120, Bloomington, IN 47405, 812-855-3838.

Counseling and Student Services

This Clearinghouse provides documents covering all levels of counseling and student services including preparation, practice, and supervision of counselors at all education levels and in all settings; theoretical development of counseling and guidance; personnel procedures such as testing and interviewing and the analysis and dissemination of the resultant information; group work and case work; nature of pupil, student, and adult characteristics; personnel workers and their relation to career planning, family consultations, and student orientation activities.

The clearinghouse can provide materials to answer questions from the public and professionals such as How can I enhance a student's self-esteem through counseling? How can counselors effectively intervene in the problems of child abuse? What are the emerging priorities for counseling in the 1990's? What counseling relevant software programs are available and how can the software be used? and What dropout prevention programs have been effective?

For information on pricing and publications, contact Eric Clearinghouse On Counseling And Student Services, University of North Carolina at Greensboro, School of Education, 101 Park Bldg., Greensboro, NC 27412-5001, 910-334-4114, 800-414-9769.

Adjunct ERIC Clearinghouses

Adjunct ERIC Clearinghouses are associated with the ERIC Clearinghouse whose scope overlaps the narrower scope of the adjunct. Each adjunct identifies and acquires significant literature within its scope area. The clearinghouse with which the adjunct is associated then catalogs, indexes, and abstracts the documents for inclusion in the ERIC database. Like the larger clearinghouses, the adjuncts provide free reference and referral services in their subject areas.

Adjunct ERIC Clearinghouse for ART Education
Indiana University
Social Studies Development Center   800-266-3815
2805 E. 10th St., Suite 120   812-855-3838
Bloomington, IN 47408-2698   Fax: 812-855-0455
                    Internet: eric@indiana.edu
All aspects of visual arts education, including painting, sculpture, and aesthetics; training of art education teachers; the role of visual arts education in the overall school curriculum; and curriculum materials for art education and for integration of art into other subject areas.

Adjunct ERIC Clearinghouse on Chapter 1
    (Compensatory Education)
Chapter 1 Technical Assistance Center
PRC, Inc.
2601 Fortune Circle East   800-456-2380
One Park Fletcher Bldg., Suite 300-A   317-244-8160
Indianapolis, IN 46241-2237   Fax: 317-244-7386
                    Internet: princ@delphi.com
Helps state and local education agencies evaluate and improve their compensatory education programs; acquires and maintains workshop materials and documents produced by the nationwide network of Chapter 1 Technical Assistance Centers.

Adjunct ERIC Clearinghouse for Child Care
National Child Care Information Center
301 Maple Ave. West, Suite 602   800-616-2242
Vienna, VA 22180   Fax: 800-716-2242
                    Internet: agoldstein@acf.dhhs.gov
Covers all areas of child care information; current research; acquisition of documents; listings and abstracts of publications and resources; and the development of electronic child care information resources for Internet access on a World Wide Web server.

Adjunct ERIC Clearinghouse on Clinical Schools
American Association of Colleges for
    Teacher Education   800-822-9229
One Dupont Circle NW, Suite 610   202-293-2450
Washington, DC 20036-1186   Fax: 202-457-8095
                    Internet: iabdalha@inet.ed.gov
Provides a source of information on clinical schools, professional development schools, professional practice schools, and similar institutions; acquires, abstracts, and processes literature on clinical schools for ERIC database; produces bibliographies, periodic papers, digests, and other material on issues related to clinical schools; and conducts research on clinical schools.

Adjunct ERIC Clearinghouse for Consumer Education
National Institute for Consumer Education
207 Rackham Bldg., West Circle Dr.   800-336-6423
Eastern Michigan University   313-487-2292
Ypsilanti, MI 48197-2237   Fax: 313-487-7153
                    Internet: nice@emuvax.emich.edu
Consumer and personal finance education throughout the life cycle; examines decision making, problem solving, identifying values and goals, obtaining resources, spending and borrowing, saving and investing, protecting resources, purchasing goods and services, rights and responsibilities, laws and regulation, and consumer assistance and advocacy within economic, political, and social contexts.

Adjunct ERIC Clearinghouse for Literacy Education
Center for Applied Linguistics
1118 22nd St. NW   202-429-9292 ext. 200
Washington, DC 20037   Fax: 202-659-5641
                    Internet: ncle@cal.org
All aspects of literacy education for adults and out-of-school youth with limited English proficiency. Specific topics covered include development of reading, writing, computational, and communication skills; programs and projects in employment or in occupational or vocational training; workplace literacy programs; family literacy programs; intergenerational literacy programs; program design, development, implementation, and evaluation; outreach, including student assessment and placement; teaching methods, approaches, and techniques; technologies in the teaching of limited English proficient (LEP) adults; training and resource materials for teachers, instructors, and volunteers; training of trainers; student curricular materials; learning styles; cross-cultural considerations in literacy education; English as a second language for LEP adults; native language literacy for LEP adults; research on second language literacy; and citizenship instruction for adults of limited English proficiency.

Adjunct ERIC Clearinghouse for Law-Related Education
Indiana University
Social Studies Development Center   800-266-3815
2805 East 10th St., Suite 120   812-855-3838
Bloomington, IN 47408-2698   Fax: 812-855-0455
          Internet: ericso@indiana.edu
All areas of law-related education, including citizenship education, the United States Constitution, the law and legal issues, and the Bill of Rights.

Adjunct Test Collection Clearinghouse   609-734-5737
Educational Testing Service   Fax: 609-683-7186
Princeton, NJ 08541   Internet: mhalpern@est.org
Prepares descriptions of commercially available and non-commercially available tests, checklists, instruments, questionnaires, and other assessment and evaluation tools.

National Clearinghouse for U.S.-Japan Studies
Indiana University
Social Studies Development Center   800-266-3815
2805 East 10th St., Suite 120   812-855-3838
Bloomington, IN 47408-2698   Fax: 812-855-0455
          Internet: eabrooks@indiana.edu
Covers all aspects of teaching and learning about Japanese society and culture, including economics, language training, politics, and U.S.-Japan relations.

State Money for College Students

Students seeking financial assistance should ask the State higher education agency in their home state for information about State aid — including aid from a program jointly funded by individual states and the U.S. Department of Education. Each State has its own name for this program, as well as its own award levels, eligibility criteria, and application procedures.

Your State can also give you information about the Paul Douglas Teacher Scholarship Program, which is a Federal program administered at the State level. These scholarships are for outstanding high school graduates who want to pursue teaching careers after they finish college. A Douglas scholarship provides up to $5,000 per year to students who graduate from high school in the top 10% of their class, and who meet other selection criteria their State may establish. Generally, students are required to teach two years for each year of scholarship assistance they receive.

The agency in your State responsible for public elementary and secondary schools can also give you information on the Robert C. Byrd Honors Scholarship Program and the National Science Scholars Program (NSSP). Under the Byrd Program, students who demonstrate outstanding academic achievement and show promise of continued excellence may receive $1,500 for their first year of postsecondary education. Under the NSSP, graduating high school seniors (or those who will obtain the equivalent of a certificate of graduation) who have demonstrated excellence and achievement in the physical, life, or computer sciences, mathematics, or engineering may receive funds to continue their studies at the postsecondary level. Scholarships of up to $5,000 per year of undergraduate study, or the cost of education, whichever is less, are awarded to two students from each Congressional district.

Federal loans, grants and work-study programs are also available. Contact your school's financial aid administrator to find out details and to determine which ones are available at your school. First-time undergraduates may receive all three types of financial aid. Graduate students may apply for loans or Work-Study, but not for Pell Grants or SEOG. The State aid totals below reflect State grant and scholarship amounts and do not include Federal funding.

The U.S. Department of Education offers the following major financial aid programs:

Loans:
1) Stafford Loans are low-interest loans made to students attending school at least half-time. Loans are made by a lender such as a bank, credit union, or savings and loan association. Sometimes a school acts as a lender. These loans are insured by the guarantee agency in each State and reinsured by the Federal Government. Students must repay this loan. To find out the name, address, and telephone number of the guarantee agency in your State, as well as information about borrowing, call the Federal Student Aid Information Center at 800-4-FED AID.

2) PLUS loans are for parents who want to borrow to help pay for their children's education. Supplemental Loans for Students (SLS) are for student borrowers. Both loans provide additional funds for educational expenses, and, like Stafford Loans, are made by a lender such as a bank, credit union, or savings and loan association.

3) Perkins Loans: This low-interest (5 percent) loan is for first-time undergraduates and graduate students with exceptional financial need, as determined by the school. For undergraduate students, priority is given to Pell Grant recipients. Loans are made through a school's financial aid office; the school is the lender. These loans must be repaid. Students may borrow up to $4,500 if they have completed less than two years of a program leading to a first bachelor's degree, or if they are enrolled in a vocational program. Students may borrow up to $9,000 if they have already completed two years of study toward a first bachelor's degree and have achieved third-year status. Up to $18,000 may be borrowed for graduate or professional study. See your school's financial aid department for details.

Grants:
1) Pell Grant: This award helps first-time undergraduates pay for their education after high school. Eligibility for those who receive a Pell Grant for the first time is usually limited to five to six years of undergraduate study, not including remedial coursework. Awards for the 1992-93 academic year will depend upon program funding. The maximum award for the 1991-92 academic year was $2,400. Students must attend school at least half-time. Grants do not have to be paid back. For more information, contact the financial aid administrator of the college or university you are attending.

2) Supplemental Educational Opportunity Grant (SEOG): This award helps first-time undergraduates with exceptional financial need, as determined by the school. Priority is given to Pell Grant recipients. An SEOG does not have to be paid back. Students can get up to $4,000 a year, depending upon available funding.

Work-Study:
1) College Work-Study (CWS): This program provides jobs for first-time undergraduates and for graduate students who need financial aid. CWS lets you earn money to help pay your educational expenses. Students are paid at least the current Federal minimum wage, but the pay may also be related to the type of work done and the skills required. Schools set individual work schedules and must pay students directly at least once a month.

State Money for Students

Alabama
Alabama Commission on Higher Education, 3465 Norman Bridge Rd., Montgomery, AL 36105-2310, 205-281-1921. The following programs are open to Alabama residents attending an in-state school. Estimated annual funds available: $8,014,799.

Education

1) Grants To Students Who Can't Afford Tuition

Alabama Student Assistance Program: These need-based, state/federal grants range from $300 to $2,500 per academic year. At most institutions, awards are limited to undergraduate study. Nearly 90 Alabama institutions participate in this program.

2) Grants To Students Attending Private Colleges

Alabama Student Grant Program: This award of grant assistance is open to undergraduates attending an eligible independent Alabama college or university. Up to $1,200 is available per academic year for each eligible student that applies to the program.

3) $65,000 In Low-Interest Loans For All Your College Expenses

Alabama Guaranteed Student Loan Program (AGSLP): This is a need-based, low-interest loan program. Full-time undergraduates can borrow up to $2,625 for the first year, $3,500 if you've completed your first year of study, and $5,500 a year, if you've completed two years of study. If you're a graduate student, you can borrow up to $8,500 a year. The total debt you are allowed as an undergraduate may not exceed $23,000. The total debt for graduate or professional study is $65,500, including any Stafford loans you received as an undergraduate.

4) Join The National Guard And Get $1,000 A Year For College

Alabama National Guard Assistance Program: Awards are used for tuition, educational fees, and book/supplies for Alabama National Guard members to attend a state public postsecondary educational institution. Awards are limited to $500 per term, cannot exceed $1,000 per year, and are not based on financial need.

5) Grants and Loans To Nursing Students

Alabama Nursing Scholarships: Scholarship/loans of varying amounts are awarded to students enrolled in eligible nursing programs at participating institutions.

6) Tuition, Fees, And Books To Spouses and Children Of Veterans

Alabama GI Dependents Educational Benefit Program: Tuition, fees, and book assistance are available to children and spouses of eligible Alabama veterans who attend state public postsecondary schools. This program is available to undergraduates only.

7) Grants To Children and Grandchildren of Veterans

American Legion Scholarship and American Legion Auxiliary Scholarship Programs: Open to students who are the sons, daughters, grandsons, or granddaughters of veterans of World War I, World War II, Korea or Vietnam. Grants must be used for tuition, fees, and board expenses to attend a public postsecondary school. Awards are restricted to students who attend institutions with on-campus housing.

8) Free Tuition If You're Over 60

Senior Adult Scholarships: This free tuition program is available to individuals, 60 years of age or older, who attend public two-year postsecondary education institutions.

9) Money For Jocks Going To Junior College

Junior and Community College Athletic Scholarships: Awards are based on demonstrated athletic ability determined through tryouts. Awards fund total tuition. Students must attend state public junior and community colleges. Awards are not based on financial need.

10) Money For Dancers, Singers, and Actors Attending Junior College

Junior and Community College Performing Arts Scholarships: Awards are based on demonstrated talent determined through competitive auditions. Students must attend state public junior and community colleges. Awards are used to fund total tuition, and are not based on financial need.

11) Grants To Children Of The Blind

Alabama Scholarships for Dependents of Blind Parents: This award covers instructional fees and tuition for children from families in which the head of the household is blind and whose family income is insufficient to provide educational benefits to minors.

12) Grants For Dependents Of Fire Fighters And Police Officers Killed In The Line Of Duty

Police Officers and Fire Fighters Survivor's Educational Assistance Program: The grant covers fees, books, and supplies for dependents and eligible spouses of Alabama police officers and fire fighters killed in the line of duty. There is no limit on the amount awarded to recipients. Applicants must enroll in an undergraduate program at a state public postsecondary educational institution.

13) Loans That Guarantee The Price Of Your Future Tuition

Wallace-Folsom Prepaid College Tuition Program: Parents, grandparents, friends, or any other sponsor may purchase a contract to guarantee tuition payment for a determined number of credit hours for a baccalaureate degree. Age limits apply to students enrolled in this program. Lump-sum or periodic payment plans may be selected.

14) $5,000 Per Year To Become A School Teacher

Paul Douglas Teaching Scholarship: These scholarships are available to full-time undergraduate and high school seniors who graduated in the top 10% of their high school graduating class or scored at least 62 on the GED and are pursuing certification to teach at the pre-school, elementary, or secondary level. Scholarships are for $5,000 per academic year. After graduation, recipients are required to teach two years for each year of scholarship assistance to receive total loan forgiveness.

Alaska

Alaska Commission on Postsecondary Education, Student Loan Office, 330 Vintage Blvd., Juneau, AK 99801-7109, 907-465-2962, Fax: 907-465-5316. The following programs are open to Alaskan residents attending an in-state or out-of-state school. Estimated annual funds available: $61,050,000.

1) Free Money To Go To School If You Work In Law Enforcement

Michael Murphy Memorial Scholarship Loan: Funds up to $1,000 per year for undergraduates are awarded to full-time students pursuing a degree program at an accredited college or university in law enforcement, law, probation and parole, penology, or closely related fields. Loans are non-interest bearing and, upon degree completion, the scholarship loan recipient receives forgiveness of 20% of total loan indebtedness for each period he or she is employed full time in Alaska law enforcement or a related field.

2) Free Money To Go To School If You Become A Teacher Or Work For The Government

Robert C. Thomas Memorial Scholarship Loan Fund: This scholarship provides loans to students wishing to pursue a degree at an accredited college or university that will lead to a career in education, public administration, or other closely related fields. Funds up to $1,000 per year are available for full-time study, and undergraduates and graduates are eligible to apply. Loans are non-interest bearing and, upon degree completion, the loan recipient receives forgiveness of 20% of total loan indebtedness for each period he or she is employed full time in an education or public administration field position.

3) Money For 8 Years Of College If You Study Food Or Wildlife

A.W. "Winn" Brindle Memorial Scholarship Loan: This program provides educational loans to Alaska residents who are pursuing full-time undergraduate or graduate study at accredited schools in the following degree or certificate programs: fisheries, fishery management, food technology, fishery science, seafood processing, and other related fields. Awards cover the cost of tuition and fees, books and supplies, room and board, and transportation costs for up to two round trips between the recipient's home and school each year. A loan may be made for up to five years of undergraduate study, five years of graduate study, or a combined maximum of eight years of study.

4) $1,500 Toward Your First Year Of College

Alaska State Educational Incentive Grant Program: This program provides grants to eligible students enrolled in their first undergraduate program at in-state or out-of-state postsecondary educational institutions. Grants range from $100 to $1,500, depending upon financial need.

5) $7,500 A Year and Travel Money If You Study To Be A Teacher In A Small Town

Teacher Scholarship Loan Program: This program encourages Alaska high school graduates to pursue teaching careers in rural elementary and secondary schools in the state. Students may borrow up to $7,500 per year for in-state or out-of-state study. Loans may be used for tuition, room and board, books, and supplies, and transportation costs of up to two round trips between the student's home community and the school of attendance. Loans are awarded for a maximum of five years of undergraduate study.

6) $5,000 Per Year To Become A School Teacher

Paul Douglas Teaching Scholarship: These scholarships are available to full-time undergraduate and high school seniors who graduated in the top 10% of their high school graduating class or scored at least 62 on the GED and are pursuing certification to teach at the pre-school, elementary, or secondary level. Scholarships are for $5,000 per academic year. After graduation, recipients are required to teach two years for each year of scholarship assistance to receive total loan forgiveness.

Arizona

Arizona Commission for Postsecondary Education, 2020 North Central, Suite 275, Phoenix, AZ 85004, 602-229-2590. Arizona administers a "decentralized" form of student aid in higher education. Monies are allocated based on a formula to postsecondary schools, and each college or university sets their own individual funding limits. Students should contact the Financial Aid office at the college they plan to attend for applicable scholarship, grant, and loan information. State residency is required for the programs listed. In 1992-93, $3,500,000 was awarded.

1) $2,500 Grants For Students Having Trouble Paying Tuition

Arizona State Student Incentive Grant Program: This program provides grants from $100 to $2,500 to needy students who attend participating postsecondary educational institutions in Arizona. It is available to both undergraduate and graduate students who are attending school on at least a half-time basis in an eligible program.

2) Money And Help To Educate Students With Physical and Mental Disabilities

Vocational Rehabilitation Assistance: Persons with a physical or mental disability that substantially interferes with obtaining employment may be eligible for assistance from this program. Each qualified individual works with a counselor to develop an appropriate rehabilitative program. This program is tailored to the individual and may

Be patient. If any phone number is incorrect, call (area code) 555-1212 and request the new listing.

include classroom training, in addition to work experience. Depending upon need, support services such as day care, allowances for transportation, books, and other supplies are provided. Supplemental training stipends are available on a limited basis. Additional information may be obtained by contacting the Vocational Rehabilitation Division of the nearest office of the Arizona Department of Economic Security.

3) Reduced Tuition To Take Courses Not Offered In Arizona

Student Exchange Program: The Western Interstate Commission for Higher Education (WICHE) helps Arizona students obtain access to five fields of professional education not available in Arizona, but made available at participating institutions in other western states at a reduced tuition rate. The reduced tuition usually amounts to the in-state rate at public schools and one-third the regular tuition rate at private schools.

4) $5,000 Per Year To Become A School Teacher

Paul Douglas Teaching Scholarship: These scholarships are available to full-time undergraduate and high school seniors who graduated in the top 10% of their high school graduating class or scored at least 62 on the GED and are pursuing certification to teach at the pre-school, elementary, or secondary level. Scholarships are for $5,000 per academic year. After graduation, recipients are required to teach two years for each year of scholarship assistance to receive total loan forgiveness.

Arkansas

Arkansas Department of Higher Education, 114 East Capitol, Little Rock, AR 72201, 501-324-9300. Applicants must be current residents of Arkansas. In 1992-93, $7,037,860 was awarded.

1) $624 Per Year On First-Come, First-Served Basis

Student Assistance Grants: Full-time undergraduate and high school seniors may apply for grants of up to $624 per year. Grants are awarded for financial need, on a first-come, first- served basis.

2) $2,000 For High School Graduates With At Least 3.6 Averages

Governor's Scholars: Scholarships of $2,000 per academic year are awarded to 100 high school seniors in recognition of outstanding academic achievement and leadership. Students with at least an ACT score of 27 or a grade point average of 3.6 may apply.

3) $1,000 For High School Graduates With At Least 2.5 Averages

Arkansas Academic Challenge Scholarship: Scholarships of $1,000 per academic year are awarded to high school seniors with financial need, an ACT score of 19, and a grade point average of 2.50 in the precollegiate core course curriculum.

4) $5,000 Per Year To Become A School Teacher

Paul Douglas Teaching Scholarship: These scholarships are available to full-time undergraduate and high school seniors who graduated in the top 10% of their high school graduating class or scored at least 62 on the GED and are pursuing certification to teach at the pre-school, elementary, or secondary level. Scholarships are for $5,000 per academic year. After graduation, recipients are required to teach two years for each year of scholarship assistance to receive total loan forgiveness.

5) Free Money For School If You Become a Math, Science, or Special Education Teacher, or a Guidance Counselor

Emergency Secondary Education Loan: Loans of $2,500 are available to full-time undergraduates or graduate students pursuing a secondary education teaching certificate in the following categories: foreign language, math, science, special education, guidance/counseling or gifted/talented. Repayment of the loan is forgiven at 20% for each year taught in approved subject shortage areas in Arkansas secondary schools after graduation.

6) Free Tuition, Room, Board, and Fees To Dependents and Spouses of MIA's and POW's

MIA/KIA Dependent's Scholarship: This scholarship is open to full-time undergraduate/graduate students and high school seniors who are dependents or spouses of persons identified as Killed in Action, Missing in Action or Prisoners of War. The award provides a waiver of in-state tuition, on-campus room, board, and fees at state higher education institutions. Students must attend an approved two or four year state supported college, university, or vocational/technical school. Graduate students must not have received their undergraduate education in Arkansas.

7) Grants To Dependents Of Law Enforcement Officers Killed Or Totally Disabled In The Line Of Duty

Law Enforcement Officer's Dependents Scholarship: This scholarship is available to full-time undergraduates and high school seniors who are dependents of persons who were killed or totally disabled in the line of duty as law enforcement officers. The award is limited to eight semesters and does not include board, books, materials and supplies, dues, or extracurricular activity fees. Spouses lose their eligibility for this program if they remarry.

8) $1,000 To Top Ten GED Scorers

Second Effort Scholarship: The Arkansas Department of Higher Education contacts the individuals with the top ten GED scores and offers this scholarship. Awards are for $1,000 per academic year.

California

California Student Aid Commission, P.O. Box 510845, Sacramento, CA 94245-0845, 916-445-0880. Applicants must be residents of California. Approximately $155,000,000 is awarded in new and renewable A, B, and C Cal Grants to 75,060 students each year.

1) Grants For Tuition, Living Expenses, and Vocational Training

Cal Grants A: Helps low- and middle-income students with tuition/fee costs. Grant recipients are selected based on financial need and grade point average.

Cal Grants B: This grant provides a living allowance (and occasionally tuition/fee assistance) for very low-income students.

Cal Grant C: Helps vocational school students with tuition and training costs.

2) Help To Work Your Way Through College

State Work-Study Program: This program offers eligible college and university students the opportunity to earn money to defray educational expenses. Jobs may be available with public institutions or non-profit or profit-making enterprises. Students will be paid at rates comparable to other paid positions within the employing organization.

3) $8,000 To Become A Teacher

Assumption Program of Loans for Education (APLE): Teacher candidates may apply for up to $8,000 in loan-assumption benefits through this program. The Commission annually accepts up to 500 new APLE program applicants who are selected by participating postsecondary institutions with approved teacher preparation programs. To receive benefits, participants must provide three consecutive years of teaching in a California public school in a designated subject matter shortage area or in a school serving a high proportion of low-income students.

4) Grants To Graduate Students Who Want To Become College Teachers

Graduate Fellowship Program: Candidates must be pursuing recognized advanced or professional degrees on at least a half-time basis at an eligible California graduate or professional school. Applicants must demonstrate their intent to become college or university faculty members. Awards are made based on grades, graduate admissions test scores, and consideration of the applicant's disadvantaged background.

5) Grants To Dependents Of Fire Fighters, Police Officers, and Correctional Officials Killed Or Totally Disabled In The Line Of Duty

Law Enforcement Personnel Dependents Scholarship: This program provides educational grants to needy dependents and spouses of California peace officers, officers and employees of the Department of Corrections or Youth Authority, and permanent and full-time fire fighters who have been killed or totally disabled in the line of duty. Grants at four-year colleges range from $100 to $1,500 per year, with a maximum of $6,000 in a six-year period. Grants at community colleges range from $100 to $500 per year, for up to four years.

6) Money to Dependents of Deceased or Disabled Veterans

State Veterans Benefits: Dependents of California veterans who are current totally service-connected disabled or deceased, wives of totally disabled veterans, and widows of deceased veterans may be eligible to receive benefits from the California Department of Veteran's Affairs. The benefits include a $100 per month subsistence allowance and a waiver of registration and tuition fees at the University of California, California State University, and community colleges.

7) $5,000 Per Year To Become A School Teacher

Paul Douglas Teaching Scholarship: These scholarships are available to full-time undergraduate and high school seniors who graduated in the top 10% of their high school graduating class or scored at least 62 on the GED and are pursuing certification to teach at the pre-school, elementary, or secondary level. Scholarships are for $5,000 per academic year. After graduation, recipients are required to teach two years for each year of scholarship assistance to receive total loan forgiveness.

Colorado

Colorado Commission on Higher Education, 1300 Broadway, 2nd Floor, Denver, CO 80203, 303-866-2723. Applicants must be residents of Colorado. Estimated annual funds available: $42,200,000.

1) Grants To Students From Families Who Don't Normally Go To College

Colorado Diversity Grants: These grants are available as part of a state-wide effort to increase participation of underrepresented groups in the Colorado public higher education system.

2) Grants To Students Who Are Having Trouble Paying For Tuition

Colorado Student Incentive Grants (CSIG): Grants are available to qualified undergraduates with substantial financial need. Student grants under this program are comprised of both federal and state funds.

3) More Grants To Students Who Are Having Trouble Paying For Tuition

Colorado Student Grants (CSG): Grants are available to qualified undergraduates with documented financial need.

4) Money For Students Going To College Part-Time

Colorado Part-time Grants: These need-based grants are for less than full-time

Education

students attending eligible Colorado institutions.

5) State Jobs For Students Having Trouble Paying Tuition
Colorado Work-Study: This part-time employment program is designed to help students with financial need as well as those who need to acquire work experience.

6) Money For Smart Students Going To College In Colorado
Undergraduate Merit Awards: Awards are available to students who demonstrate superior scholarship or talent as defined by the Colorado college or university they attend.

7) Money For Graduates Who Have Trouble Paying Tuition
Colorado Graduate Grants: Graduate students with financial need may apply for this program.

8) Money For Smart Graduate Students
Colorado Graduate Fellowships: This program provides merit-based awards to graduate students.

9) Grants To Dependents Of POW/MIA's or Fire Fighters, Police Officers, and Correctional Officials Killed Or Totally Disabled In The Line Of Duty
Law Enforcement/POW-MIA Dependents Tuition Assistance: This award, of approximately $5,000, pays tuition for dependents of Colorado law enforcement officers, fire, or national guard personnel killed or disabled in the line of duty, and for dependents of prisoners of war or service personnel listed as missing in action. Dependents of disabled personnel must have demonstrated financial need for assistance to be awarded.

10) Money To Be A Nurse And Practice In Colorado
Colorado Nursing Scholarship: These scholarships provide assistance to individuals who wish to pursue a nursing education and also agree to practice in Colorado. Applications are available from the Commission on Higher Education in April of each year.

11) $5,000 Per Year To Become A School Teacher
Paul Douglas Teaching Scholarship: These scholarships are available to full-time undergraduate and high school seniors who graduated in the top 10% of their high school graduating class or scored at least 62 on the GED and are pursuing certification to teach at the pre-school, elementary, or secondary level. Scholarships are for $5,000 per academic year. After graduation, recipients are required to teach two years for each year of scholarship assistance to receive total loan forgiveness.

Connecticut
Connecticut Board of Higher Education, 61 Woodland Street, Hartford, CT 06105-2391, 203-566-8118. Applicants must be Connecticut residents for in-state and out-of-state schools programs. Estimated annual funds available: $19,697,418.

1) $2,000 A Year If You Are In Top 20% Of Your High School Class
Scholastic Achievement Grant: Grants of up to $2,000 a year are awarded to Connecticut high school seniors who rank in the top 20% of their class or who achieve SAT scores of at least 1,100 (27 on the ACT test). Awards are based on financial need and must be used at a Connecticut college or in states that have reciprocity agreements with Connecticut.

2) $6,384 A Year To Attend A Private College
Connecticut Independent College Student Grant: Up to $6,384 a year is available in grants to state residents attending Connecticut independent colleges. Awards are based on financial need.

3) Money For Students Who Need Help Paying Tuition At A Public University
Connecticut Aid for Public College Students: Awards of up to the amount of unmet financial need are available for students attending Connecticut public colleges. In 1993-94, $ 5,562,888 was appropriated in funding.

4) Money To Dependents Of Deceased, Disabled, Or MIA Veterans
Aid to Dependents of Deceased, Disabled, or MIA Veterans: This award is available to students whose parent was a Connecticut resident upon entry into the U.S. Armed Forces and served during the war; death must be service-related; disability must be rated as permanent and 100% by the Veterans Administration. Awards of $400 a year are based on financial need.

5) Money To Be A Nurse
Connecticut Nursing Scholarship: This scholarship is available to students enrolled full-time in a three-year hospital school of nursing in Connecticut, or in a two- or four-year nursing program at a Connecticut college. The amount of the award varies and is based both on academic standing and financial need.

6) Loans Up To $20,000 A Year To Attend College Full or Part Time Anywhere
Family Education Loan Program (FELP): Loans that range from $2,000 to $20,000 a year at a fixed rate are available to students enrolled at least half time in Connecticut non-profit colleges, or Connecticut residents enrolled at least half time in a non-profit college anywhere in the U.S.

7) Free Tuition To Veterans
Tuition Waiver for Veterans: This program is available to veterans who are Connecticut residents when enrolling in college and upon entry in the U.S. Armed Forces. It is also available to the children of Vietnam veterans declared MIA/POW attending Connecticut public colleges. The waiver is equal to tuition only.

8) Free Tuition To Students Over 62

Tuition Waiver for Senior Citizens: This program is available to students, age 62 and over, attending Connecticut public colleges. The waiver is equal to tuition only.

9) $5,000 Per Year To Become A School Teacher
Paul Douglas Teaching Scholarship: These scholarships are available to full-time undergraduate and high school seniors who graduated in the top 10% of their high school graduating class or scored at least 62 on the GED and are pursuing certification to teach at the pre-school, elementary, or secondary level. Scholarships are for $5,000 per academic year. After graduation, recipients are required to teach two years for each year of scholarship assistance to receive total loan forgiveness.

Delaware
Delaware Postsecondary Education Commission, Carvel State Office Bldg., 820 N. French Street, Wilmington, DE 19801, 302-577-3240. Applicants must be Delaware residents for in-state or out-of-state colleges. Estimated annual funds available: $130,200,000.

1) Up To $1,000 A Year For Students Having Trouble Paying Tuition
Delaware Postsecondary Scholarship Fund: This need-based grant program helps Delaware students in meeting college costs. Funds awarded are not repaid by the students or their parents. Grants may be used at Delaware colleges, and under certain conditions, in states other than Delaware. The maximum grant is $1,000 per year. Reapplication is required each year that funds are requested.

2) Money To Be A Teacher In Delaware
Christa McAuliffe Teacher Scholarship Loan: This scholarship loan awards scholarships to academically talented Delaware students who agree to pursue teaching careers at the elementary and secondary levels in Delaware public schools. This merit-based award of $1,000 minimum is renewable for up to four years, and must be repaid with teaching service.

3) $1,000 A Year For Undergraduate Students
Diamond State Scholarship: This program promotes academic achievement among Delaware students. The Diamond State Scholars are awarded scholarships of $1,000 that are renewable for four years of undergraduate study. Approximately 50 awards are made each year to graduating high school seniors.

4) Full Tuition, Room and Board To Smart High School Seniors
B. Bradford Barnes Scholarship: This program was established by the state to honor the memory of a Speaker of the House who died while serving in the General Assembly. One merit-based, renewable scholarship is awarded annually to an outstanding high school senior who has accepted an offer of admission from the University of Delaware. The scholarship pays full tuition, fees, and room and board at the University of Delaware.

5) $3,000 A Year To Be A Registered Or Practical Nurse And Practice In A State-Owned Hospital
Delaware Nursing Incentive Scholarship Loan: This scholarship loan program was established to encourage academically talented Delaware students to pursue education leading to certification as a Registered or Practical Nurse. Awards may be up to $3,000 per year, renewable for up to four years of study, and must be repaid with nursing practice at a Delaware state-owned hospital.

6) Money For Students From Delaware To Study Optometry In Pennsylvania
Delaware Optometric Institutional Aid: This program maintains an agreement with the Pennsylvania College of Optometry (PCO) to help Delawareans obtaining a degree in optometry. Under this agreement, the state provides $4,000 per year for up to four years for a limited number of Delaware residents who qualify for admission. PCO applies the entire $4,000 to the student's tuition. The student must repay 25% of the state support and practice optometry in Delaware for the same number of years he/she received state support.

7) $5,000 Per Year To Become A School Teacher
Paul Douglas Teaching Scholarship: These scholarships are available to full-time undergraduate and high school seniors who graduated in the top 10% of their high school graduating class or scored at least 62 on the GED and are pursuing certification to teach at the pre-school, elementary, or secondary level. Scholarships are for $5,000 per academic year. After graduation, recipients are required to teach two years for each year of scholarship assistance to receive total loan forgiveness.

District of Columbia
Office of Postsecondary Education, 2100 Martin Luther King, Jr. Ave., SE, Suite 401, Washington, DC 20020, 202-727-3685. Applicants must be District Of Columbia residents for in-state or out-of-state school programs. Estimated annual funds available: $703,033.

1) Money For College Anywhere
D.C. State Student Incentive Program: Between $400 and $1,500 is available to students who have been permanent D.C. residents for at least 15 months, and attend school full-time at an accredited postsecondary institution in the U.S.

2) Money To Study To Be A Nurse If You Work For Two Years For DC

Government

D.C. Nurses Training Corps Program: This renewable program is open to nursing students who plan to attend or are attending the University of D.C., Catholic University of America, Howard University, Georgetown University, or the Margaret Murray Washington Career Development Center. Students must agree to work at D.C. General Hospital, D.C. Office on Aging, or the Commission of Public Health. Up to $22,000 per year is available based on the cost of attendance at school. Students must work two years for every year of scholarship received.

3) Special Loans Up To $20,000 A Year

TERI Supplemental Loan: This private loan provides funding from $2,000 to $20,000 a year at a fixed or variable rate. Undergraduate or graduate students attending a participating college or university in the U.S. may apply. Contact the Financial Aid Office at a participating college or university for details, or contact The Education Resources Institute (TERI) at 1-800-255-TERI.

4) $5,000 Per Year To Become A School Teacher

Paul Douglas Teaching Scholarship: These scholarships are available to full-time undergraduate and high school seniors who graduated in the top 10% of their high school graduating class or scored at least 62 on the GED and are pursuing certification to teach at the pre-school, elementary, or secondary level. Scholarships are for $5,000 per academic year. After graduation, recipients are required to teach two years for each year of scholarship assistance to receive total loan forgiveness.

Florida

Florida Office of Student Financial Assistance, State Programs Unit, 1344 Florida Education Center, Tallahassee, FL 32399-0400, 904-488-1034. Applicants must be Florida residents for in-state or out-of-state school programs. Estimated annual funds available: $86,000,000.

1) Money For Students Who Have Trouble Paying Their Tuition

Florida Student Assistance Grants (FSAG): These need-based grants range from $200 to $1,500 per academic year. The program is open to full-time undergraduate students with financial need who are attending an eligible public or private Florida institution.

2) Free Tuition At Private Colleges In Florida

State Tuition Voucher (STV): This undergraduate award is used for tuition and fees at eligible independent Florida colleges or universities. This award is not based on need and the amount awarded is dependent on the number of eligible students and level of funding.

3) Up To $2,500 For Smart High School Graduates

Florida Undergraduate Scholars' Fund: This merit scholarship program provides awards to outstanding Florida high school graduates. Initial awards are for $1,000, $1,500 or $2,500, depending on eligibility. Renewal awards are $2,500.

4) Work Your Way Through College With A Job At A Local Elementary School

Public School Work Experience (PSWEP): This program supports employment for undergraduate students as teacher aides or science laboratory assistants in public schools; as reading tutors in adult basic skills education programs; or as tutors/counselors for educationally disadvantaged first-year students in public postsecondary schools.

5) Jobs For Full Or Part-Time Students Who Need Help Paying Tuition

College Career Work Experience Program (CCWEP): This need-based program is open to undergraduates with financial need who are enrolled at least half time at an eligible Florida institution. It provides jobs related to their declared major areas of study or career interest. The amount of award varies according to financial need.

6) Money For Smart High School Graduates Who Want To Be Teachers In Florida

"Chappie" James Most Promising Teacher Scholarship Loan Program: This scholarship loan program provides up to $1,500 per academic year to outstanding Florida high school seniors who intend to enter the public school teaching profession in Florida. The loan is repaid by teaching service or a cash repayment.

7) Money For College Students Who Want To Be Teachers

Critical Teacher Shortage Scholarship Loan Program: This scholarship loan program was created to attract capable students to the teaching profession in critical teacher shortage areas. Up to $4,000 per academic year is available for a maximum of two years. The loan is repaid by teaching service or a cash repayment.

8) $3,000 A Year To Smart High School Graduates

Mary McLeod Bethune Scholarship Challenge Grant Fund: This need-based scholarship provides $3,000 per academic year to outstanding high school seniors who will attend Florida Agricultural and Mechanical University, Bethune-Cookman College, Edward Waters College, or Florida Memorial College. Applicants must be enrolled as full-time undergraduate students.

9) Grants For American Indians To Go To College

Seminole/Miccosukee Indian Scholarship: This program provides scholarships for Seminole and Miccosukee Indians of Florida who are enrolled as full-time or part-time undergraduate or graduate students. The amount of scholarship is determined by the respective tribe.

10) Money To Descendants Of The Confederacy Army Who Want To Go To College

Confederate Memorial Scholarship: This scholarship for lineal descendants of Confederate soldiers and sailors provides $150 for an academic year.

11) Money For Dependents Of Deceased or Disabled Veterans And POW/MIA's

Scholarships for Children of Deceased or Disabled Veterans: This scholarship provides funding for dependent children of deceased or 100% disabled veterans or servicemen officially classified as Prisoners of War or Missing in Action. The amount equals tuition and fees for an academic year at a public Florida institution. Residency requirements varies.

12) $2,000 For Hispanic Americans Who Want To Go To College

Jose Marti Scholarship Challenge Grant Fund: This need-based scholarship for Hispanic Americans provides $2,000 for an academic year. It is available for undergraduate or graduate study and the amount available is contingent upon matching contributions from private sources. Applicants may apply for the first year of undergraduate study or the first year of graduate study.

13) $2,000 NOT To Go To College But To Vocational School Instead

Vocational Gold Seal Endorsement Scholarship: This scholarship program is available to high school graduates who wish to pursue postsecondary vocational-technical education. Up to $2,000 per academic year is provided.

14) $10,000 For Minority Students To Study Medicine

Florida Minority Medical Education Program: This program encourages minorities to enter the medical profession. The maximum award is $10,000 per year for three students at each of the state's four participating medical schools: University of Florida, University of South Florida, University of Miami, and Southeastern University of Health Sciences. The program requires two years of primary care service in a medically underserved area of Florida or repayment of all scholarship money with interest.

15) $6,000 Plus Tuition and Fees For Teachers To Return To Get A Graduate Degree

Masters' Fellowship Loan Program for Teachers: This fellowship loan program was created to attract liberal arts graduates, science graduates, and mid-career returning students to teaching in Florida public schools. Awards of $6,000 are provided in addition to an amount equal to the average tuition and fees at the state universities for up to two semesters or three quarters and one summer term.

16) Money For Teachers To Take Part-Time Graduate Courses

Critical Teacher Shortage Tuition Reimbursement Program: This tuition reimbursement program encourages public school district employees certified to teach to become certified in, or gain a graduate degree in, a critical teacher shortage area. Up to $78 per credit hour is provided for up to nine credit hours per academic year. The maximum total is 36 credit hours.

17) Free College Money If You Teach In Florida Public Schools

Critical Teacher Shortage Student Loan Forgiveness Program: This loan forgiveness program was created to attract qualified personnel to seek employment in Florida public schools in designated critical teacher shortage areas. It provides repayment of educational loans in return for teaching in a critical teacher shortage area. Up to $2,500 per year is available for four years for teachers with undergraduate loans, or $5,000 per academic year for up to two years for teachers with graduate loans.

18) Money For Minority Students To Go To Law School

Virgil Hawkins Fellowship: Fellowships are available for minority students attending Florida State University and the University of Florida Law School. An award of $5,000 is provided for a maximum of three years.

19) Money For Teachers To Get Retrained

Exceptional Student Education Training Grant for Out-of-Field Teachers: This tuition reimbursement program is available to teachers holding a valid Florida teaching certificate but who are not fully certified in the areas of exceptionality in which they teach. Up to $200 per course for a maximum of three courses or nine semester hours per term is available.

200 $5,000 Per Year To Become A School Teacher

Paul Douglas Teaching Scholarship: These scholarships are available to full-time undergraduate and high school seniors who graduated in the top 10% of their high school graduating class or scored at least 62 on the GED and are pursuing certification to teach at the pre-school, elementary, or secondary level. Scholarships are for $5,000 per academic year. After graduation, recipients are required to teach two years for each year of scholarship assistance to receive total loan forgiveness.

Georgia

Georgia Department of Education, Division of General Instruction, 2054 Twin Towers East, Atlanta, GA 30334-5040, 404-656-5812. Estimated annual funds available: $1,078,000.

1) Georgia provides no state grants but does offer the merit-based Georgia Scholar Program. This program identifies and recognizes high school seniors who have achieved excellence in school and community life. Requirements include: a minimum score of 1300 on the SAT test; a score of 31 on the ACT; or a ranking in the upper 10% of his or her graduating class. As a recipient of the award, the student may

receive a Governor's Scholarship if he or she continues their postsecondary education in an approved public or private college or the University of Georgia, and meets other program requirements. The scholarship is used to defray the cost of tuition for a maximum of four years eligibility. The maximum amount awarded is $1,540.

2) $5,000 Per Year To Become A School Teacher

Paul Douglas Teaching Scholarship: These scholarships are available to full-time undergraduate and high school seniors who graduated in the top 10% of their high school graduating class or scored at least 62 on the GED and are pursuing certification to teach at the pre-school, elementary, or secondary level. Scholarships are for $5,000 per academic year. After graduation, recipients are required to teach two years for each year of scholarship assistance to receive total loan forgiveness.

Hawaii

Hawaii Department of Education, Student Personnel Services, 2530 10th Ave., Honolulu, HI 96816, 808-733-9100. Applicants must be residents of Hawaii. Estimated annual funds available: $780,000.

1) Free Tuition

Hawaii Student Incentive Grants (HSIG): These grants provide tuition waivers for undergraduates. A student must be eligible for a Pell Grant and be a Hawaii resident, as defined by the Board of Regents for tuition purposes.

2) $5,750 Plus Free Tuition And Travel To High School Graduates With 3.5 Grade Point Averages

Regents Scholarship for Academic Excellence: This scholarship of $5,750 per year and a full tuition waiver is provided to 20 entering first- year students with a combined SAT score of 1200 and a high school grade point average of 3.5. This scholarship is renewable for four years if the student continues to meet eligibility requirements. This program also includes a one-time $2,000 grant that pays for an approved study abroad/exchange program during the student's junior year.

3) $4,000 Plus Free Tuition And Travel To High School Graduates With 3.7 Grade Point Averages

Presidential Achievement Scholarship: These scholarships provide $4,000 per year plus a full tuition waiver to those juniors with a cumulative grade point average of 3.7 showing superior academic achievement or creative efforts. They are renewable for one year if eligibility requirements are again met by the student. This program also includes a one-time $2,000 grant that pays for an approved study abroad/exchange program during the student's junior year.

4) Money For Students Planning To Study Pacific/Asian Studies

Pacific Asian Scholarships: These are waivers of tuition to students for academic merit (3.5 cumulative grade point average or better), who are pursuing study relevant to the Pacific and Asian region.

5) $5,000 Per Year To Become A School Teacher

Paul Douglas Teaching Scholarship: These scholarships are available to full-time undergraduate and high school seniors who graduated in the top 10% of their high school graduating class or scored at least 62 on the GED and are pursuing certification to teach at the pre-school, elementary, or secondary level. Scholarships are for $5,000 per academic year. After graduation, recipients are required to teach two years for each year of scholarship assistance to receive total loan forgiveness.

Idaho

Office of the State Board of Education, 650 West State Street, 307 Len B. Jordan Building, Boise, ID 83702, 208-334-2270. Applicants must be Idaho residents. Estimated annual funds available: $251,600.

1) $2,650 To Study In Idaho

Idaho Scholarship Program: This program provides awards of $2,650 per year to graduating Idaho high school seniors who wish to pursue their postsecondary education at an Idaho college or university. The award is based on academic merit and is automatically renewed each year, provided the student maintains satisfactory grades. Twenty-five percent of the initial scholarships each year are given to vocational students. Students must be enrolled full time in an academic or vocational program at an Idaho college or university.

2) $2,830 For Students In Idaho, Washington and Oregon To Study ANYWHERE

Paul L. Fowler Memorial Scholarship Program: This memorial scholarship provides assistance to outstanding students in Idaho, Washington, and Oregon. There are no geographic restrictions included. The one-year awards are for $2,830 and recipients are selected on the basis of rank in class and ACT scores.

3) $3,000 For Student Activists

Idaho Governor's Scholarship Program: Scholarships of $3,000 are awarded based on scholastic achievement, leadership, and community involvement. Students must have a cumulative grade point average of 3.5 or rank in the top 10% of his/her graduating class and score in the top 5% of the ACT. Recipients must enroll as full-time students in an academic program at an Idaho college or university.

4) Disadvantaged High School Students Can Get $2,500 To Go To College

Idaho Minority and "At-Risk" Student Scholarship: Awards of $2,500 are available to help talented students who may not be able to attend college because of cultural, economic, or physical circumstances. Recipients must be full-time undergraduates at one of the following eligible postsecondary institutions: Boise State University, Idaho State University, North Idaho College, Eastern ID Technical College, Lewis-Clark State College, University of Idaho, College of Southern Idaho, and the College of Idaho. For further details, contact the Financial Aid office of the college or university you plan to attend.

5) Free Money For Students Studying To Be Teachers Or Nurses

Education Incentive Loan Forgiveness: This program provides loan forgiveness to Idaho students who wish to pursue a teaching career or professional nursing career within the state. Recipients must rank within the upper 15% of his/her graduating class or have earned a cumulative grade point average of 3.0 or higher. They must also pursue a teaching career or a nursing career within Idaho for a minimum of two years or pay back their loans in cash, including interest.

6) $5,000 Per Year To Become A School Teacher

Paul Douglas Teaching Scholarship: These scholarships are available to full-time undergraduate and high school seniors who graduated in the top 10% of their high school graduating class or scored at least 62 on the GED and are pursuing certification to teach at the pre-school, elementary, or secondary level. Scholarships are for $5,000 per academic year. After graduation, recipients are required to teach two years for each year of scholarship assistance to receive total loan forgiveness.

Illinois

Illinois Student Assistance Commission, 1755 Lake Cook Rd., Deerfield, IL 60015, 708-948-8550. Applicants must be Illinois residents. Estimated annual funds available: $358,612,000 for 218,584 students.

1) Grants Up To $3,500 No Matter What Your Grades Are

Monetary Award Program: The Monetary Award Program provides grants for students that demonstrate financial need. Students are not required to submit high school grades or test scores when applying for a MAP grant. Students must enroll at an approved Illinois MAP institution (more than 200 qualify), and enroll for at least six credit hours per term. MAP grants can only be applied toward tuition and mandatory fees. Therefore, all awards are paid directly to the college or university. Grants are awarded up to $3,500.

2) $1,000 For Students In The Top 5% Of Their Class

Illinois Merit Recognition Scholarship Program: This program provides a one-time $1,000 award to Illinois high school students who rank in the top 5% of their class at the end of the seventh semester. Financial need is not a factor in determining recipients. The scholarship can be used for tuition, fees, or other expenses at approved Illinois institutions.

3) Join The National Guard For Free Tuition For Graduate Or Undergraduate Studies

National Guard/Naval Militia Grant Program: Members of the Illinois Naval Militia are eligible for payment of tuition and some fees for either undergraduate or graduate education. The individual must be registered as enlisted personnel or be an officer up to the rank of captain, be enrolled at an Illinois state-supported college or university, and have one full year of service in the National Guard or Naval Militia.

4) Veterans Living In Illinois Can Get Free Tuition and Fees

Illinois Veteran Grant Program: The Illinois Veteran Grant (IVG) Program pays tuition and certain fees at all Illinois state-supported colleges, universities, and community colleges for Illinois residents. Recipients may use their grant assistance for either undergraduate or graduate study for a period of up to 16 calendar years or a maximum of 120 eligibility points, whichever comes first.

5) Grants To Dependents Of Fire Fighters Or Police Officers Killed In The Line Of Duty

Police Officer/Fire Officer Dependent's Grant Program: The spouse and children of Illinois police and fire personnel killed in the line of duty may be eligible for grant assistance to meet college tuition and mandatory fees at approved Illinois colleges and universities. Children who apply for this program must be 25 years old or younger, attend college in Illinois, and meet several other eligibility requirements.

6) Grants To Dependents Of Correctional Officers Killed Or Disabled In The Line Of Duty

Correctional Officer's Survivor's Grant Program: The spouse and children of a state of Illinois Department of Corrections worker killed or at least 90% disabled in the line of duty may be eligible for grant assistance. This grant may only be used for tuition and mandatory fees at approved Illinois colleges and universities.

7) $5,000 Per Year To Become A School Teacher

Paul Douglas Teaching Scholarship: These scholarships are available to full-time undergraduate and high school seniors who graduated in the top 10% of their high school graduating class or scored at least 62 on the GED and are pursuing certification to teach at the pre-school, elementary, or secondary level. Scholarships are for $5,000 per academic year. After graduation, recipients are required to teach two years for each year of scholarship assistance to receive total loan forgiveness.

Indiana

State Student Assistance Commission of Indiana, 150 W. Market St., Suite 500, Indianapolis, IN 46204, 317-232-2350. Applicants must be Indiana residents. Estimated annual funds available: $77,167,437.

1) Indiana College Students Who Have Trouble Paying Tuition
Indiana Higher Education Grant: This award focuses on tuition and fees and is "need-based," with students with the least ability to finance a college education receiving the largest grants.

2) $5,000 Per Year To Become A School Teacher
Paul Douglas Teaching Scholarship: These scholarships are available to full-time undergraduate and high school seniors who graduated in the top 10% of their high school graduating class or scored at least 62 on the GED and are pursuing certification to teach at the pre-school, elementary, or secondary level. Scholarships are for $5,000 per academic year. After graduation, recipients are required to teach two years for each year of scholarship assistance to receive total loan forgiveness.

Iowa

Iowa College Student Aid Commission, 914 Grand Avenue, Suite 201, Des Moines, IA 50309-2824, 515-281-3501. Applicants must be Iowa residents. Estimated annual funds available: $45,000,000 to 30,000 students.

1) Money For High School Graduates In The Top 15% Of Their Class
State of Iowa Scholarship Program: State Scholar applicants must rank in the top 15% of their class and take the ACT test by October of their senior year. Each scholar is eligible to receive an award ranging from $100 to $400 per year. Award amounts are determined by academic index and the number of units that each student takes in the subject of math, science, social studies, foreign language, and language arts. Awards may be used at eligible Iowa schools.

2) Grants To Pay For Tuition At Private Colleges
Iowa Tuition Grants: This grant provides students with the option of attending Iowa private colleges and universities. The grant is based on financial need, with priority given to the neediest applicants. The maximum grant is $2,650 for each year of full-time undergraduate study. The award may also be prorated for less than full-time study.

3) $600 To Take A Vocational Education Course
Iowa Vocational-Technical Tuition Grants: This program provides need-based grants for Iowa students enrolled in career education courses at area community colleges. The maximum grant is $600 for a full year (four quarters or two semesters and a summer session).

4) Grants To Students Who Need Money For Education
Iowa Grants: This grant assists exceptional need students enrolled in an undergraduate program at an Iowa state university, independent college or university, or area community college. The maximum grant is $1,000 for each year of full-time undergraduate study (12 or more semester hours). The award may also be prorated for less that full-time study.

5) $5,000 Per Year To Become A School Teacher
Paul Douglas Teaching Scholarship: These scholarships are available to full-time undergraduate and high school seniors who graduated in the top 10% of their high school graduating class or scored at least 62 on the GED and are pursuing certification to teach at the pre-school, elementary, or secondary level. Scholarships are for $5,000 per academic year. After graduation, recipients are required to teach two years for each year of scholarship assistance to receive total loan forgiveness.

Kansas

Kansas Board of Regents, 700 SW Harrison, Suite 1410, Topeka, KS 66603, 913-296-3517. Applicants must be Kansas residents. Estimated annual funds available: $12,045,000.

1) $1,500 A Year For Minority Students
Kansas Minority Scholarship: This program provides need-based awards to ethnic minority students attending Kansas two-or four-year institutions. Selection is based on academic performance, ethnic category, and financial need. Up to $1,500 is available per academic year, for up to four years. Funding assists approximately 135 students.

2) $500 To Take A Vocational Training Course
Vocational Education Scholarship: This merit-only award assists students enrolling in eligible vocational programs. Applicants must take the vocational exam and be among the top 100 scorers. Up to $500 is available per academic year. Funding assists approximately 100 students.

3) $5,000 A Year If You Study To Be A Teacher In Kansas
Kansas Teacher Scholarship: This service-based award encourages high academic achievers to enter teaching, teach in Kansas, and teach in "hard-to-fill" disciplines. Undergraduates without prior teacher certification eligibility may be considered. Up to $5,000 per academic year is available and is limited to four years, unless the student is enrolled in a five-year program. Funding assists approximately 100 students.

4) $3,500 A Year To Be A Nurse
Kansas Nursing Scholarship: This service-based award encourages students to study nursing and then practice nursing in Kansas. The program is jointly sponsored with health care agencies. Students must secure sponsorship. After passing the licensing exam, a student must be employed by the sponsor for one year for each year of funding or repay the funds at a 15% interest rate. $2,500 per academic year is available for LPN study, $3,500 per academic year for RPN study. Approximately 270 students are funded each year.

5) $1,000 To High School Graduates Who Have Trouble Paying Tuition
Kansas State Scholarship: This need-based award assists students designated during their high school senior year as state scholars. Funding is provided by both federal and state sources and ranges from $50 to $1,000 per academic year. Funding assists approximately 1,350 students and is limited to four academic years, unless the student is enrolled in a designated five-year program.

6) $5,000 Per Year To Become A School Teacher
Paul Douglas Teaching Scholarship: These scholarships are available to full-time undergraduate and high school seniors who graduated in the top 10% of their high school graduating class or scored at least 62 on the GED and are pursuing certification to teach at the pre-school, elementary, or secondary level. Scholarships are for $5,000 per academic year. After graduation, recipients are required to teach two years for each year of scholarship assistance to receive total loan forgiveness.

Kentucky

Kentucky Higher Education Assistance Authority, 1050 U.S. 127 South, Suite 102, Frankfort, KY 40601, 502-564-7990. Applicants must attend an eligible Kentucky college; be enrolled in an undergraduate degree program; be state residents; establish financial need; and meet program requirements. Funds are limited, so students who file by April 1 have the best chance of receiving awards. Estimated annual funds available: $20,300,000.

1) Grants To Financially Needy Full-Time and Part-Time Students
College Access Program Grants (CAP): A CAP Grant is awarded to financially needy undergraduates enrolled for a minimum of six semester hours at a two- or four-year public or private non-profit college or proprietary school. The grant amount each year is equal to the community college tuition rate. CAP recipients must have an expected family contribution of $3,000 or less.

2) More Grants To Financially Needy Full-Time and Part-Time Students
Kentucky State Student Incentive Grant Program: Program requirements are the same as the CAP program listed above.

3) Grants To Students
Kentucky Tuition Grants (KTG): This program provides need-based grants to qualified applicants to attend one of the Commonwealth's independent, non-profit colleges. The program assists full-time students with the higher tuition charges at these schools. The maximum KTG award for each eligible applicant is $1,200 per academic year.

4) $5,000 Per Year To Become A School Teacher
Paul Douglas Teaching Scholarship: These scholarships are available to full-time undergraduate and high school seniors who graduated in the top 10% of their high school graduating class or scored at least 62 on the GED and are pursuing certification to teach at the pre-school, elementary, or secondary level. Scholarships are for $5,000 per academic year. After graduation, recipients are required to teach two years for each year of scholarship assistance to receive total loan forgiveness.

Louisiana

Office of Student Financial Assistance, P.O. Box 91202, Baton Rouge, LA 70821-9202, 504-922-1011, Fax: 504-522-1089. Applicants must be Louisiana residents. Estimated annual funds available: $7,600,000.

1) Free Tuition To Attend State Schools
Louisiana Tuition Assistance Plan: This need-based award pays undergraduate tuition at a state public college or university. The recipient must have been a Louisiana resident for at least two years prior to application or have a parent or guardian who is a domiciliary of Louisiana. Approximately 3,000 awards are presented annually.

2) Money For Smart Kids
Louisiana T.H. Harris Scholarship: This academic merit scholarship is awarded to Louisiana high school graduates who have achieved a 3.0 high school grade point average. The award amount is $400 per year, up to $2,000. Students must be enrolled as full-time undergraduates at a Louisiana public college or university. 3,750 awards are given out annually.

3) $7,000 Grant To Study Forestry Or Marine Sciences
Louisiana Rockefeller State Wildlife Scholarship: This program was designed to

Be patient. If any phone number is incorrect, call (area code) 555-1212 and request the new listing.

215

Education

attract graduates in wildlife forestry, or marine sciences to Louisiana. Grant amounts are $1,000 per year up to $7,000 for undergraduates, or up to two years of graduate study. Students must attend a Louisiana public college or university on a full-time basis. They must also obtain a wildlife, forestry, or marine science degree or repay the scholarship, plus interest. Sixty scholarships are awarded each year.

4) $5,000 Per Year To Become A School Teacher
Paul Douglas Teaching Scholarship: These scholarships are available to full-time undergraduate and high school seniors who graduated in the top 10% of their high school graduating class or scored at least 62 on the GED and are pursuing certification to teach at the pre-school, elementary, or secondary level. Scholarships are for $5,000 per academic year. After graduation, recipients are required to teach two years for each year of scholarship assistance to receive total loan forgiveness.

Maine

Maine Department of Higher Education, Maine Education Assistance Division, State House Station 33, One Weston Court, Augusta, ME 04333-0023, 207-287-5803. Applicants must be Maine residents. Estimated annual funds available: $4,800,000.

1) Money For Students From Maine To Study In New England States, Alaska, Delaware, DC, Maryland, and Pennsylvania
Maine Student Incentive Scholarship Program (MSISP): Applicants must be at least half-time undergraduate students and attend any eligible post-secondary institution in New England, Alaska, Delaware, the District of Columbia, Maryland, and Pennsylvania. Full-time students may receive up to $500 at a public institution and up to $1,000 at a private institution. Part-time students will receive one half of the full-time award. These awards are based on a student's financial needs.

2) Money For Students In The Upper Half Of Their Class Who Want To Be Teachers
Blaine Scholars Program: Any high school senior who will graduate from high school in the upper half of his class may apply. Scholar loans are competitive and based on academic achievement. The program also offers Teachers Loans for Maine teachers employed at least half-time by a Maine school. Students may borrow up to $1,500 per year, renewable, up to a $6,000 limit. Loans may be forgiven for teaching service.

3) Money For Dependents Of Veterans Killed Or Disabled In Military Service
State Veterans Benefits: Spouses or children, widows or widowers of veterans killed or permanently disabled as a result of military service may apply for a maximum of $300 per year for private schools. Free tuition is offered for state- supported post-secondary schools.

4) Loans Up To $20,000 A Year To Go To College
Maine Educational Loan Authority (MELA) Supplemental Education Program: Qualified applicants may borrow from $2,000 to $20,000 a year to cover education-related expenses with a supplemental loan from the Maine Education Loan Authority. The amount is determined by the school.

5) Free Tuition To Members Of Indian Tribes
Indian Scholarships: Waivers covering tuition and fees are available through the University of Maine System for members of the Passamaquoddy and Penobscot Tribes. They are also available for others who have resided in Maine for at least one year and who have at least one parent or grandparent on the census of a North American Indian Tribe, or with a band number of the Micmac or Maliseet Tribes. In addition, room and board charges are subsidized for those eligible students residing in university dormitories.

6) Free Tuition To Dependents Of Law Enforcement Officers And Fire Fighters Killed In The Line Of Duty
Tuition Waiver Program for Children of Fire Fighters and Law Enforcement Officers Killed in the Line of Duty: This program provides a tuition waiver at schools in the University of Maine System for children of fire fighters and law enforcement officers who have been killed in the line of duty or injured during the performance of their duties which resulted in death.

7) $5,000 Per Year To Become A School Teacher
Paul Douglas Teaching Scholarship: These scholarships are available to full-time undergraduate and high school seniors who graduated in the top 10% of their high school graduating class or scored at least 62 on the GED and are pursuing certification to teach at the pre-school, elementary, or secondary level. Scholarships are for $5,000 per academic year. After graduation, recipients are required to teach two years for each year of scholarship assistance to receive total loan forgiveness.

Maryland

Maryland Higher Education Commission, State Scholarship Administration, The Jeffrey Building, 16 Francis Street, Suite 209, Annapolis, MD 21401-1781, 410-974-5370. Applicants must be Maryland residents, unless specified for in-state or out-of-state schools. $26,000,000 is available in scholarships to over 20,000 students. State funding for the State Incentive Program totaled $11,757,932.

1) $2,500 For Full-Time Undergraduate Students
Maryland State Scholarship Program: This award provides $200 to $2,500 per year, up to four years with a possible fifth year, to qualified undergraduates. Students must attend a Maryland degree-granting or nursing institution. Limited out-of-state awards are given to approximately 10% of applicants. Students must attend school full time, except for part-time nursing students.

2) $2,000 To Full- Or Part-Time Students
Senatorial Scholarship Program: This program provides from $400 to $2,000 to full-time and part-time students enrolled in undergraduate, graduate, and certain vocational programs. The awards are made by the State Senators to students in their districts and are automatically renewed until their degrees are granted (up to four years maximum).

3) $200 To Full-Time Or Part-Time Students
House of Delegates Award: These awards are made by State Delegates to students in their districts. The amount of the award varies, with a minimum of $200 offered. The program is open to full-time and part-time students in undergraduate, graduate, and certain vocational programs. The renewable award is offered for one to four years. Students should apply directly to their Delegates for this program.

4) $1,500 To Take A Vocational Education Course
Tolbert Grant: This one-year award of $200 to $1,500 is open to full-time students attending vocational programs in Maryland private career schools. Applicants may reapply up to a two year maximum.

5) $3,000 A Year For Smart Students
Distinguished Scholar Program: This program is open to National Merit and Achievement Finalists and academically or artistically gifted and talented students. Awards of $3,000 are granted, up to a maximum of four years. Students must attend an accredited Maryland postsecondary school on a full-time basis and maintain a 3.0 grade point average.

6) $4,800 To Get A Degree In Nursing
Maryland State Nursing Scholarship: This program provides up to $2,400, with a need-based additional grant of up to $2,400, to undergraduate and graduate nursing students. Recipients must serve in a Maryland area experiencing a shortage of nurses for one year for each year of the award.

7) $3,000 A Year To Become A Teacher In Maryland
Teacher Education Distinguished Scholar Program: These awards are open to students who have received a Distinguished Scholar Award. Awards of $3,000 are granted, up to a maximum of four years. Students must attend an accredited Maryland postsecondary school on a full-time basis and maintain a 3.0 grade point average. Recipients must teach in a Maryland public school for one year for each year of the award.

8) Grants To Dependents Of POW's, Fire Fighters, Police Officers, and Safety Personnel Killed Or Disabled In The Line Of Duty
Edward Conroy Grant: This program is open to disabled public safety employees, children of POW's, dependents of military and public safety personnel, deceased or disabled in the line of duty. The award provides tuition and mandatory fees up to $2,400 for full-time and part-time undergraduate and graduate students. A maximum of eight years of funding is available. Maryland residency is not required for this program.

9) Grants To Study Physical Therapy
Physical and Occupational Therapists and Assistants Scholarships: This program provides $2,000 per year, up to four years, for full-time undergraduate students pursuing a career in physical and occupational therapy. Recipients must provide one year of service in a state hospital, or to handicapped students for each year of the award.

10) $7,500 A Year To Study Family Practice Medicine
Family Practice Medical Scholarship: This program provides $7,500 per year, up to four years, for full-time graduate students planning a career in family practice medicine. Two new awards are made each year. Students must attend the University of Maryland at Baltimore and be willing to practice medicine for three years in Maryland following graduation. A minimum of five years Maryland residency is required.

11) $5,000 Per Year To Become A School Teacher
Paul Douglas Teaching Scholarship: These scholarships are available to full-time undergraduate and high school seniors who graduated in the top 10% of their high school graduating class or scored at least 62 on the GED and are pursuing certification to teach at the pre-school, elementary, or secondary level. Scholarships are for $5,000 per academic year. After graduation, recipients are required to teach two years for each year of scholarship assistance to receive total loan forgiveness.

12) Grants To Study Law, Dentistry, Medicine, Nursing Or Pharmacy
Professional Scholarship: Eligible applicants must be enrolled in a degree or diploma program in dentistry, law, medicine, nursing, or pharmacy. This program provides $200 to $1,000 per year, up to four years, for full-time undergraduate, graduate, and nursing students.

13) Tuition, Fees, Room and Board To Become A Teacher
Sharon Christa McAuliffe Critical Shortage Teacher Scholarship: This program provides up to $700 in tuition, fees, room, and board for full-time undergraduate and graduate students planning to enter the teaching profession. Awards are offered up

to five semesters. Recipients must teach in a Maryland public school for one year for each year of the award.

14) $2,000 To Study Child Care, Full or Part Time
Child Care Provider Scholarship: Full-time and part-time undergraduates who are planning a career in child care are eligible for this program. Awards are renewable and range from $500 to $2,000 per year. Recipients must provide one year of child care service for each year of scholarship assistance.

15) Free Tuition To Fire Fighters and Rescue Squad Members Who Want To Study Full Or Part Time
Reimbursement of Fire Fighters and Rescue Squad Members: Tuition of up to $2,200 per year is provided for fire fighters and rescue squad members attending a Maryland degree-granting program. Applicants may be full-time or part-time undergraduate or graduate students. The award is renewable. Reimbursement is made one year after completion of course work and recipients must continue to be active in Maryland as a fire fighter or rescue squad member.

16) Student Loans If You Work For A Non-Profit
Loan Assistance Repayment Program (LARP): Applicants must be a graduate of a Maryland institution and be employed by the state or local government or a non-profit organization. Renewable loans of up to $7,500 per year are offered. Priority is given to critical shortage employment fields.

Massachusetts
Board of Regents of Higher Education, Scholarship Office, 330 Stuart Street, Boston, MA 02116, 617-727-9420. Applicants must be Massachusetts residents. Estimated annual funds available: $38,000,000.

1) $1,900 For Full-Time Students
Massachusetts General Scholarship: This scholarship provides funding in amounts ranging from $200 to $1,900 to students attending full-time, state-approved Massachusetts postsecondary schools.

2) Money To Attend Private Colleges In Massachusetts
Gilbert Matching Scholarship: This scholarship is available to full-time students attending an independent regionally accredited Massachusetts school. The amount of the award is determined by the school's Financial Aid Office.

3) Free Tuition At State Schools
Tuition Waiver Program: This program waives up to the cost of tuition for students enrolled in Massachusetts state-supported colleges or universities. The amount of the award varies and is determined by the institution's Financial Aid Office.

4) Loans To Families With College Students
Massachusetts Family Education Loan: This loan provides up to 100% of the cost of attendance at a Massachusetts state-approved postsecondary school. Specific eligibility criteria is available at individual participating Massachusetts colleges and universities.

5) $20,000 A Year In Loans For College
TERI Supplemental Loan (TERI): This private loan provides funding from $2,000 to $20,000 a year, at a fixed or variable rate. Undergraduate or graduate students attending a participating college or university in the U.S. may apply. Contact the Financial Aid office at a participating college or university for details or contact The Education Resources Institute (TERI) at 1-800-255-TERI.

6) $7,500 For Graduate Students
Professional Education Plan (PEP): Graduate students may borrow up to $7,500 on their own signature, depending on their cumulative education debt. Students with a credit worthy co-borrower may borrow up to $20,000.

7) $5,000 Per Year To Become A School Teacher
Paul Douglas Teaching Scholarship: These scholarships are available to full-time undergraduate and high school seniors who graduated in the top 10% of their high school graduating class or scored at least 62 on the GED and are pursuing certification to teach at the pre-school, elementary, or secondary level. Scholarships are for $5,000 per academic year. After graduation, recipients are required to teach two years for each year of scholarship assistance to receive total loan forgiveness.

Michigan
Michigan Department of Education, Student Financial Assistance Services, P.O. Box 30008, Lansing, MI 48909, 517-373-3394. Applicants must be Michigan residents. Estimated annual funds available: $79,067,000.

1) Money For Smart Kids Who Have Trouble Paying Tuition
Competitive Scholarships: This program is limited to high school graduates favorably recommended by an appropriate educational institution who achieve a semifinalist score on the American College Test (ACT). Those who demonstrate financial need are eligible for monetary consideration. Awards are limited to undergraduates enrolled at least half time at an eligible Michigan college. Students enrolled in a program leading to a degree in theology, divinity, or religious education are ineligible for state scholarships or tuition grants. A student may not concurrently

receive state scholarship and tuition grant assistance.

2) Money For Students Attending Private Colleges
Tuition Grants: This program is open to students attending an independent non-profit Michigan college or university. Tuition grants are available to both undergraduates and graduates enrolled at least half time and are based on financial need.

3) $5,000 Per Year To Become A School Teacher
Paul Douglas Teaching Scholarship: These scholarships are available to full-time undergraduate and high school seniors who graduated in the top 10% of their high school graduating class or scored at least 62 on the GED and are pursuing certification to teach at the pre-school, elementary, or secondary level. Scholarships are for $5,000 per academic year. After graduation, recipients are required to teach two years for each year of scholarship assistance to receive total loan forgiveness.

Minnesota
Minnesota Higher Education Coordinating Board, Capitol Square Building, 550 Cedar Street, Suite 400, St. Paul, MN 55101-2292, 612-296-3974. Applicants must be residents of Minnesota, unless otherwise specified. Estimated annual funds available: $81,050,000.

1) Money To Pay Half Your College Expenses
State Grant Program: This award is based on financial need and goes toward the cost of attendance at a postsecondary institution. All applicants must contribute at least 50% of their cost of education. The award is $1,200. Eligible students must be enrolled at least half time in any year of undergraduate study and attend eligible Minnesota colleges.

2) Money For Part-Time Students
State Part-Time Grant Program: This grant is awarded to students who are enrolled less than half time in a college or university, and are pursuing a program or course of study that applies to a degree, diploma, or certificate. The amount of the award is determined by the individual school's Financial Aid Office.

3) Money To Be A Nurse If You Practice For 3 to 5 Years In A Small Town
Rural Nursing Grants: This award is available to students entering or enrolled in a registered or licensed practical nursing program who have no previous nurse training or education. Applicants must agree to practice at least three of their first five years in a designated rural area. Awards are based upon financial need and must provide 20% of an applicant's combined state and federal Pell Grant awards. The minimum amount awarded is $100.

4) Money For American Indians To Attend College
Minnesota Indian Scholarship Program: This scholarship is based on financial need and is awarded to students who are one-fourth or more Indian ancestry, residents of Minnesota, and members of a recognized Indian tribe. The student must be a high school graduate or have a GED and show an ability to benefit from advanced education. Recipients must be accepted by an approved Minnesota institution and be approved by the Minnesota Indian Scholarship Committee. The average award is $1,450.

5) Money To Go To School If You Lost Your Job In A Small Town
Dislocated Rural Workers Program: This program is open to rural Minnesotans enrolled in an adult farm management program or programs providing preparation for available employment; a person who has lost or is about to lose their job; or a displaced homemaker or farmer demonstrating a severe financial need. The program includes spouses. Awards are based on financial need and are determined by the Financial Aid Office of the individual school.

6) Money For Child Care While You Go To School Or Work Part Time
Non-AFDC Child Care Grant Program: Students who do not receive Aid to Families With Dependent Children funding who have children 12 and under and demonstrate financial need may receive assistance to help pay for child care from the Financial Aid Administrator at the school they plan to attend. Assistance may cover the hours necessary for education and up to 20 hours of employment. Eligible institutions include all public postsecondary schools and private, baccalaureate degree granting colleges or universities in Minnesota. Students should apply to the Financial Aid Office at their school.

7) $1,000 For High School Students To Take Summer Courses At A College
Summer Scholarships for Academic Enrichment: This program provides financial assistance of up to $1,000 to Minnesota students in grades 7-12 who attend eligible summer academic programs sponsored by Minnesota postsecondary schools. These include the University of Minnesota campuses, state universities, community colleges, private colleges, and technical colleges. Awards are based on financial need. Students must have earned at least a B average for the most recently recorded school term, or have a B average in the subject area of the enrichment course.

8) Grants For Dependents Of MIA/POW's To Attend Private Colleges
State Veterans' Dependents Assistance Program: This program provides aid to dependents of POWs and MIAs. The award provides up to $250 per year for tuition and fee assistance at Minnesota private postsecondary institutions.

9) Grants To Dependents Of Safety Officers Killed In The Line Of Duty
Safety Officers' Survivor Program: Dependent children less than 23 years of age and the surviving spouse of a public safety officer killed in the line of duty on or after

Be patient. If any phone number is incorrect, call (area code) 555-1212 and request the new listing.

217

January 1, 1973, are eligible to receive these educational benefits. For students attending public institutions, the award is the actual tuition and fees charged by the institution or the highest tuition and fees charged by a public institution in Minnesota. Awards are renewable for a maximum of six semesters or nine quarters or their equivalent.

10) Free College Money For Doctors Willing To Practice One Year In A Small Town

Rural Physicians Loan Forgiveness Program: Medical students who agree to serve at least three of their first five years in practice following residency in a designated rural area are eligible to apply for this program. Up to eight applicants may participate each year. Participants may designate up to $10,000 as a qualified loan for each year of medical school, to a maximum of four years. For each year the physician serves in a designated rural area, an award will be paid that is equal to one year of qualified loans and the interest accrued on them.

110 $5,000 Per Year To Become A School Teacher

Paul Douglas Teaching Scholarship: These scholarships are available to full-time undergraduate and high school seniors who graduated in the top 10% of their high school graduating class or scored at least 62 on the GED and are pursuing certification to teach at the pre-school, elementary, or secondary level. Scholarships are for $5,000 per academic year. After graduation, recipients are required to teach two years for each year of scholarship assistance to receive total loan forgiveness.

Mississippi

Student Financial Aid Office, Mississippi Postsecondary Education, Financial Assistance Board, 3825 Ridgewood Rd., Jackson, MS 39211-6453, 601-982-6570. Applicants must be Mississippi residents. Estimated annual funds available: $1,900,000.

1) Money To Pursue Degrees In Another State That Are Not Offered In Mississippi

Academic Common Market Program: This program is an interstate agreement among southern states for sharing academic programs. Participating states make arrangements for their residents who qualify to enroll in specific programs in other states on an in-state tuition basis. The waiver of out-of-state tuition is not granted to Mississippi residents pursuing degree programs that are available in Mississippi. There are no repayment requirements for assistance under this program.

2) Grants To Full-Time Students Who Have Trouble Paying Tuition

State Student Incentive Grant Program: This program is administered by the Financial Aid Office on the campus of each participating college/university. Each participating college/university recommends the recipients for this grant from the eligible students on its campus through the regular financial aid award process. Applicants must demonstrate financial need and be enrolled as a full-time undergraduate at a non-profit state college/university. Awards range from $200 to $1,500 per academic year. There are no repayment requirements for assistance under this program.

3) Graduate Students Can Make $1,000 A Month As Student Interns

Mississippi Public Management Graduate Internship Program: This program offers assistance to United States residents (or those possessing "green cards") enrolled at Jackson State University, Mississippi State University, University of Mississippi, or University of Southern Mississippi. Participants must have a grade point average of 3.0 or higher and have completed at least one semester of course work, earning a B or higher in a quantitative research methods course. Participants are awarded a $1,000 stipend per month plus 1% fringe benefits, up to eight months. Approximately 10 participants are selected per year.

4) Money To Dental Students

State Dental Education Loan/Scholarship Program: This program is available to students who have been accepted for admission to the University of Mississippi School of Dentistry and who meet program academic qualifications. Awards of $4,000 per year are made to three to five recipients. This annual award is limited to four years. Participants can discharge their financial obligation by serving for one year in their field of training for every year of financial assistance.

5) Money To Full-Time Students Who Want To Become Teachers

William Winter Teacher Scholar Loan Program: The program is open to Mississippi students enrolled full time in any accredited program that leads to a baccalaureate degree and a Class A teaching certificate. Students intending to teach in a critical subject will be given priority in selection. This merit-based program provides $1,000 per academic year for freshmen/sophomore participants, while junior/senior participants receive $3,000 per academic year. Approximately 50 participants per grade level are selected each year. The award is made on an annual basis with priority given to renewal students and a program participation limit of four years.

6) $10,000 A Year To African-American Ph.D. Students

African-American Doctoral Teacher Loan/Scholarship Program: This program is open to full-time students pursuing a career in teaching at an accredited public Mississippi college or university. Participants must also meet the program's academic qualifications. Under the program, $10,000 is awarded per academic year, and approximately five participants are selected per year. The award is made on an annual basis with priority given to renewal students and a program participation limit

of three years. Obligation can be discharged on the basis of one year's teaching service at an accredited public Mississippi college or university for one year's loan/scholarship.

7) Money To Study Optometry Or Osteopathic Medicine

Southern Regional Educational Board (SREB) Loan/ Scholarship Program: This program assists students enrolled in an approved accredited School of Optometry or Osteopathic Medicine who meet the program's academic qualifications. The amount of the award is determined by the SREB Board and is dependent upon the availability of funds. The award is made on an annual basis with priority given to renewal students and a program participation limit of four years. The number of recipients is designated by the Board. Obligation can be discharged on the basis of one year's service in the field of approved training in Mississippi for one year's loan/scholarship.

8) Tuition, Room and Board and Fees To Dependents Of Police Officers and Fire Fighters Who Died Or Became Disabled In The Line Of Duty

Law Enforcement Officers and Firemen Scholarship Program: This program provides scholarships for the spouse and children of full-time Mississippi law enforcement officers and firemen/fire fighters who were fatally injured or totally disabled from injuries which occurred in the line of duty. The applicant must be enrolled or accepted for enrollment at a Mississippi state-supported college or university. Awards cover the cost of tuition and the average cost of a dormitory room, plus required fees, including applicable course fees. Recipients are entitled to eight semesters of scholarship assistance. Children are entitled to the scholarship until the age of 23. There are no repayment requirements.

9) Tuition, Room and Board and Fees To Dependents Of POW/MIA's

Southeast Asia POW/MIA Scholarship Program: This program provides scholarships for children of Mississippi veterans presently or formerly listed as Missing in Action in Southeast Asia. Children of Mississippi veterans who have been prisoners of a foreign government as the result of a military action against the U.S. naval vessel Pueblo are also eligible. The applicant must be enrolled or accepted for enrollment at a Mississippi state-supported college or university. The scholarship covers the cost of tuition and the average cost of a dormitory room, plus required fees, including applicable course fees. Children are entitled to the scholarship until the age of 23.

10) Money To Professional Students Who Have To Go Out Of State To Get Their Degrees

Graduate and Professional Degree Loan/Scholarship Program: This program is open to students seeking a professional degree not available at a Mississippi university and who, as a result, enroll in an accredited out-of-state institution. Participants must also meet the program's academic qualifications. The approved fields of study are limited to health-related professions including chiropractic medicine, orthotics/prosthetics, and podiatric medicine. An average of $3,000 is awarded each year to each participant. Approximately ten participants per grade level are selected in each academic year. Participants can discharge their financial obligation by serving for one year in their field of training for every year of financial assistance.

11) Money To Professional Students Who Study In Mississippi

State Medical Education Loan/Scholarship Program: This program offers assistance to state students who have been accepted for admission to the University of Mississippi School of Medicine and who meet program academic qualifications. Acceptable fields of study, training, and practice include family medicine, internal medicine, pediatrics, or obstetrics/ gynecology. Awards of $6,000 per year are made to approximately five to ten recipients per grade level. This annual award is limited to four years. Obligation can be discharged on the basis of one year's service in a geographical area of critical need in Mississippi designated by the Mississippi State Department of Health, or entry into full-time public health work at a state health institution or community health center for one year's loan/scholarship.

12) Money For Registered Nurses Who Want To Go Back And Get A Bachelor's Degree In Nursing

Career Ladder Nursing Loan/Scholarship Program: This program is available to students who have graduated from an accredited high school and an accredited school of nursing, and who are a Mississippi licensed registered nurse seeking a Bachelor's degree (BSN). Under the program, $1,500 is awarded per academic year, and participation is limited to two years. Participants can discharge their financial obligation by serving for one year in their field of training for every year of financial assistance.

13) Up To $5,000 Per Year For Nursing Students

Nursing Education Loan/Scholarship Program: This program offers assistance to students enrolled full- or part-time in a school of nursing approved by the Board of Trustees and who meet the program's academic qualifications. Those pursuing a BSN Degree are eligible to receive up to $2,000 per academic year, up to two years of full-time study. Those pursuing an MSN Degree are eligible to receive up to $3,000 per year, up to one year of full-time study. Those pursuing a DSN degree are eligible to receive up to $5,000 per academic year for two years of full-time study. Participants can discharge their
financial obligation by serving for one year in their field of training for every year of financial assistance.

14) $4,000 For Nursing Students
Special Nursing Education Loan/Scholarship for Study in Baccalaureate Nursing Education Program: This privately-funded scholarship is sponsored by the Vicksburg Foundation. The program assists state residents studying toward a baccalaureate degree in nursing and is based on financial need and the Pre-Nursing Exam (NLN) score. The applicant must be a junior or senior enrolled full time in an approved, accredited Mississippi school of nursing. The total amount of assistance available is $4,000, and $2,000 is payable per academic year. Participants can discharge their financial obligation by serving for one year in their field of training for every year of financial assistance.

15) Money For Studying Psychology, Speech Pathology, Occupational Therapy, and Physical Therapy
Health Care Professions Loan Scholarship Program: This program is available to full-time junior or senior students who are enrolled in an accredited training program of critical need in the state. Programs include: speech pathology, psychology, occupational therapy, physical therapy, and other allied health programs in critical demand. Awards of $1,500 are made to one recipient per critical training program each year. Program participation is limited to two years. Participants can discharge their financial obligation by serving for one year in their field of training for every year of financial assistance.

16) Money For Medical Students
Special Medical Education Loan/Scholarship Program: This privately-funded scholarship is sponsored by the Vicksburg Foundation. The program offers assistance to junior and senior students enrolled at the University of Mississippi School of Medicine. Assistance of up to $12,000 (payable $6,000 per academic year), is awarded based on class rank. Medical study, training, and practice must be in specialty areas other than primary care. Participants can discharge their financial obligation by serving for one year in their field of training for every year of financial assistance.

17) $5,000 Per Year To Become A School Teacher
Paul Douglas Teaching Scholarship: These scholarships are available to full-time undergraduate and high school seniors who graduated in the top 10% of their high school graduating class or scored at least 62 on the GED and are pursuing certification to teach at the pre-school, elementary, or secondary level. Scholarships are for $5,000 per academic year. After graduation, recipients are required to teach two years for each year of scholarship assistance to receive total loan forgiveness.

Missouri

Missouri Coordinating Board of Higher Education, P.O. Box 6730, 3515 Amazonis St., Jefferson City, MO 65109, 314-751-3940. Applicants must be Missouri residents. Estimated annual funds available: $21,000,000 awarded to 14,000 students. In 1992-93, $10,895,560 was awarded to 8,863 students through the Missouri Student Grant Program. The Higher Education Academic Scholarship Program awarded $10,299,000 to 5,450 students.

1) $2,000 A Year To Students With ACT Scores In The Top 3%
Missouri Higher Education Academic Scholarship Program: The Missouri Higher Education Academic Scholarship Program, also known as "Bright Flight," provides maximum scholarship awards of $2,000 per year to eligible students. Recipients must attend a participating Missouri postsecondary institution full time and have a composite score on the American College Testing Program (ACT) in the top 3% of all Missouri students taking those tests. These scholarships may be renewed annually up to five years of study.

2) Grants To Full-Time Students In Financial Need
Missouri Student Grant Program: Missouri Student Grants are awarded to undergraduate students who demonstrate financial need and are enrolled full time at an approved Missouri school. Missouri grants do not have to be paid back. The award amount will vary from school to school, depending on the total cost of education. The minimum annual grant award is $1,500 and is divided equally into semester or quarter payments.

3) Tuition For Dependents Of Public Safety Officers Or Department Of Highway Officers Who Were Killed In The Line Of Duty
Public Service Officer or Employee's Child Survivor Grant Program: This program provides tuition grants to eligible undergraduate students enrolled in participating Missouri postsecondary institutions. This program is open to dependent children of a public safety officer or employee of the Department of Highways and Transportation (engaged in the construction or maintenance of the state's highways, roads, and bridges) who was killed in the line of duty. The maximum tuition grant amount per academic year is the least of: the actual tuition charged at the institution where the student is enrolled full-time; or the amount of tuition charged a Missouri undergraduate resident enrolled full-time in the same class level and in the same academic major as an applicant at the University of Missouri.

4) $5,000 Per Year To Become A School Teacher
Paul Douglas Teaching Scholarship: These scholarships are available to full-time

undergraduate and high school seniors who graduated in the top 10% of their high school graduating class or scored at least 62 on the GED and are pursuing certification to teach at the pre-school, elementary, or secondary level. Scholarships are for $5,000 per academic year. After graduation, recipients are required to teach two years for each year of scholarship assistance to receive total loan forgiveness.

Montana

Office of the Commissioner of Higher Education, 2500 Broadway, Helena, MT 59620-3103, 406-444-6594. Applicants must be Montana residents. Estimated annual funds available: $725,000.

1) $1350 To Top Ranking High School Seniors
High School and Community College Honor Scholarships: In 1992-93, the commission provided $725,000 to academic achievers. Students received $1,350 each in fee waivers that they could apply to attend Montana State University, the University of Montana, Eastern Montana College, Northern Montana College, Western Montana College, or Montana Tech.

2) Grants To Students Who Can't Afford Tuition
State Student Incentive Grants (SSIG): Awards are based on financial need, and the maximum award is $900 per year. To be eligible, state residents must be full-time undergraduates attending a participating Montana school. Montana administers a "decentralized" form of student aid in higher education. Monies are allocated based on a formula to postsecondary schools and each college or university sets their own funding limits. Students should contact the Financial Aid Office at the college they plan to attend for scholarship, grant, and loan information.

3) Free Tuition For Senior Citizens, Veterans, War Orphans, Etc.
Fee Waivers: The Montana University system grants fee waivers to a limited number of students enrolled at Montana colleges or universities. Fee waivers may be available to: Native Americans, senior citizens, some veterans, war orphans, dependents of Prisoners of War, residents of Mountain View and Pine Hill schools, and similar public and private non-sectarian Montana charitable institutions, and athletes. Fees waived vary and are granted on the basis of financial need and academic or athletic achievement.

4) $5,000 Per Year To Become A School Teacher
Paul Douglas Teaching Scholarship: These scholarships are available to full-time undergraduate and high school seniors who graduated in the top 10% of their high school graduating class or scored at least 62 on the GED and are pursuing certification to teach at the pre-school, elementary, or secondary level. Scholarships are for $5,000 per academic year. After graduation, recipients are required to teach two years for each year of scholarship assistance to receive total loan forgiveness.

Nebraska

Nebraska Coordinating Commission for Postsecondary Education, 140 N. Eighth St., Suite 300, P.O. Box 95005, Lincoln, NE 68508, 402-471-2847. Nebraska administers a "decentralized" form of student aid in higher education. Monies are allocated based on a formula to postsecondary schools. A limited number of state programs are administered directly through postsecondary schools. Students should contact the Financial Aid Office at the college they plan to attend for scholarship, grant, and loan information. State residency is required. Estimated annual funds available: $13,161,449 total appropriations, which include $2,600,000 in state scholarships.

1) $5,000 Per Year To Become A School Teacher
Paul Douglas Teaching Scholarship: These scholarships are available to full-time undergraduate and high school seniors who graduated in the top 10% of their high school graduating class or scored at least 62 on the GED and are pursuing certification to teach at the pre-school, elementary, or secondary level. Scholarships are for $5,000 per academic year. After graduation, recipients are required to teach two years for each year of scholarship assistance to receive total loan forgiveness.

Nevada

Nevada Department of Education, Student Incentive Grant Program, 400 West King Street, Carson City, NV 89710, 702-687-5915. Nevada has no state scholarships. The Nevada Student Incentive Grant Program is the only source of state grants. It administers renewable, need-based awards of up to $2,500 per year. In fiscal year 1993, the program awarded $204,665 in funding. Students should contact the Financial Aid Office at the college they plan to attend for further information. State residency is required. Estimated annual funds available: $204,665.

1) $5,000 Per Year To Become A School Teacher
Paul Douglas Teaching Scholarship: These scholarships are available to full-time undergraduate and high school seniors who graduated in the top 10% of their high school graduating class or scored at least 62 on the GED and are pursuing certification to teach at the pre-school, elementary, or secondary level. Scholarships

Be patient. If any phone number is incorrect, call (area code) 555-1212 and request the new listing.

219

Education

are for $5,000 per academic year. After graduation, recipients are required to teach two years for each year of scholarship assistance to receive total loan forgiveness.

New Hampshire

New Hampshire Postsecondary Education Commission, 2 Industrial Park Drive, Concord, NH 03301, 603-271-2555. Applicants must be New Hampshire residents, for programs involving colleges in and out of state. Estimated annual funds available: $250,872.

1) $2,000 Grants To Attend Colleges In The New England States
New Hampshire Incentive Program: Grants from $100 to $2,000 are provided to New Hampshire undergraduate students attending eligible postsecondary institutions with the six New England states accredited by the New England Association for Schools and Colleges. Students must demonstrate financial need and academic ability.
2) Money For Dependents Of Veterans Who Died In Service
Scholarships for Orphans of Veterans: Scholarships of $1,000 per year are offered to students whose parent(s) died as a result of service in World War I, World War II, the Korean Conflict, or the Southeast Asian Conflict. The deceased parent(s) must have been residents of New Hampshire at the time of their death. Applicants must be between the ages of 16 and 25. Students are eligible for tuition waivers at New Hampshire public postsecondary institutions.
3) Grants For Nurses Who Agree To Practice In New Hampshire
New Hampshire Nursing Grants: Grants are provided to students who agree to practice nursing in New Hampshire one year for every year they receive the grant following graduation from state approved nursing schools. The grant amount is dependent upon need and is awarded for a maximum of two years.
4) $5,000 Per Year To Become A School Teacher
Paul Douglas Teaching Scholarship: These scholarships are available to full-time undergraduate and high school seniors who graduated in the top 10% of their high school graduating class or scored at least 62 on the GED and are pursuing certification to teach at the pre-school, elementary, or secondary level. Scholarships are for $5,000 per academic year. After graduation, recipients are required to teach two years for each year of scholarship assistance to receive total loan forgiveness.

New Jersey

New Jersey Department of Higher Education, Office of Student Assistance, 4 Quakerbridge Plaza, CN 540, Trenton, NJ 08625, 609-588-3288. Applicants must be New Jersey residents. Estimated annual funds available: $122,000,000.

1) $4,580 A Year In Grants To Full-Time Students
Tuition Aid Grants: These grants are available to students who are or intend to be full-time undergraduates at an approved New Jersey college or university. Grants range in value from $400 to $4,580 per year, based upon the student's need and college choice. Grants are renewable annually.
2) Grants, Tutoring, and Counseling To Students On Limited Income
Educational Opportunity Fund Grants (EOF): This program is available to students from educationally disadvantaged backgrounds with demonstrated financial need. Generally, family income for dependent students cannot exceed $15,320 for a two-person household. Single independent student income cannot exceed $9,450, and the income for independent students with a two-person household cannot exceed $11,780. Applicants must be full-time matriculated students in a New Jersey college or university. Undergraduate grants range from $200 to $1,950 per year and graduate grants are awarded up to $4,000 per year. Grants are renewable. Campus EOF programs include summer sessions, tutoring, counseling, and development courses.
3) Grants To Students With High SAT Scores
Edward J. Bloustein Distinguished Scholar Program: Students demonstrating high academic achievement based upon their secondary school records and junior year SAT scores will be selected for consideration by their secondary schools. Additional scholarships are awarded to the state's urban and economically distressed areas based on class rank and grade point average. Recipients must enroll at a New Jersey college or university as full-time undergraduate students. Financial need is not a factor in determining eligibility. Awards are $1,000 per year, but students demonstrating financial need may receive up to an additional $1,000 per year.
4) Grants To Smart High School Juniors
Garden State Scholars Program: Students demonstrating high academic achievement based upon their secondary school records and junior year SAT scores will be selected for consideration by their secondary schools. Recipients must enroll at a New Jersey college or university as full-time undergraduate students. Awards are granted for $500 per year throughout their undergraduate program, regardless of financial need. Students demonstrating financial need may receive an additional $500 per year.
5) Free Tuition To Dependents Of Emergency Service Personnel and Law Enforcement Officers Killed In The Line Of Duty
Public Tuition Benefits Program: Eligible applicants include dependents of emergency service personnel and law enforcement officers killed in the line of duty who are residents of New Jersey and attend a New Jersey college or university as full-time undergraduates. Grants pay the actual costs of tuition up to the highest tuition charged at a New Jersey college or university.
6) $5,000 Per Year To Become A School Teacher
Paul Douglas Teaching Scholarship: These scholarships are available to full-time undergraduate and high school seniors who graduated in the top 10% of their high school graduating class or scored at least 62 on the GED and are pursuing certification to teach at the pre-school, elementary, or secondary level. Scholarships are for $5,000 per academic year. After graduation, recipients are required to teach two years for each year of scholarship assistance to receive total loan forgiveness.

New Mexico

New Mexico Commission On Higher Education, 1068 Cerrillos Road, Santa Fe, NM 87501, 505-827-7383. Applicants must be New Mexico residents, unless otherwise stated. Estimated annual funds available: $15,000,000.

1) Free Tuition To Students With "Good Moral Character"
Three Percent Scholarship Program: This program is a gratis scholarship that provides tuition and fee grants to undergraduate and graduate students who possess "good moral character, satisfactory initiative, scholastic standing, and personality." Students must be enrolled at a public post-secondary institution in New Mexico. At least one-third of the scholarships must be awarded based on financial need.
2) Tuition, Books, and Fees For High School Students In Top 5% Of Class
New Mexico Scholars Program: This program encourages New Mexico high school graduates to attend college in New Mexico by providing scholarships that pay for tuition, required student fees, and books for an academic year at eligible postsecondary institutions. Eligible students must have graduated in the upper 5% of his/her high school class or obtained a composite score of at least 25 on the American College Test (ACT). Students may receive up to four annual awards based on academic progress. A combined family income may not exceed $30,000 per year.
3) Part-Time Jobs To Undergraduate and Graduate Students
New Mexico Work-Study Program: The New Mexico Work-Study Program provides employment opportunities for qualified undergraduate and graduate students. Employment is limited to postsecondary non-profit institutions, state political subdivisions, state agencies, and non-profit organizations approved by the Commission on Higher Education. One third of the awards are based on financial need.
4) Money For Osteopathic Students Willing To Practice In New Mexico
Osteopathic Medical Student Loan Program: This loan-for-service program works to increase the number of osteopathic physicians in medically underserved areas in New Mexico. Loans may be forgiven through service or repaid. Students may borrow a maximum of $10,000 per year up to five years. Highest priority is given to students who can demonstrate financial need.
5) Grants To Half-Time and Full-Time Students In Financial Need
New Mexico Student Incentive Grant: Grants ranging from $200 to $2,500 per year are awarded to students attending public and private state institutions. Grants are based on financial need. Students must be enrolled at least half time as undergraduates.
6) Tuition, Books, And Fees To Vietnam Vets
Vietnam Veterans' Scholarship Program: The Vietnam Veterans' Scholarship provides tuition payments, book allowance, and required student fees to Vietnam Veterans. A student's eligibility must be certified by the New Mexico Veterans' Service Commission. Scholarships are awarded on a first-come, first-served basis. The program is open to undergraduate and graduate students.
7) Athletes From Anywhere Attending College In New Mexico
Athlete Scholarship Program: The Athlete Scholarship Program provides a tuition and required student fee grant to eligible athletes attending the University of New Mexico, New Mexico State University, Eastern New Mexico University, New Mexico Highlands University, Western New Mexico University, and New Mexico Junior College. Eligibility includes New Mexico residents and non-residents. No more than 75% of the awards may go to out-of-state residents.
8) $10,000 For Nursing Students Willing To Practice In New Mexico
New Mexico Nursing Student Loan for Service Program: This is a loan-for-service program that is designed to increase the number of nurses in medically underserved areas in New Mexico. Loans may be forgiven through service or repaid in cash. Undergraduates and graduates may borrow a maximum of $2,500 per year up to an aggregate total of $10,000. Students must be enrolled in an approved nursing education program preparing for a Licensed Practical Nursing degree (LPN), Associate Degree in Nursing (ADN), or a Baccalaureate of Science degree in Nursing (BSN).
9) $7,200 Per Year For Women And Minorities To Go To Graduate School
Graduate Scholarship Program: This program's goal is to increase graduate enrollment, particularly for minorities and women, in academic fields in the state's public universities. Preference is given to students enrolled in business, engineering, computer science, mathematics, and agriculture. The award pays a maximum of

$7,200 per academic year which may be renewed annually. Recipients must serve ten hours per week in an unpaid internship or assistantship.

10) Money For Students Attending Private Colleges
Student Choice: Student Choice grants are made to residents attending private independent institutions of higher education. Students must be enrolled for at least six semester credit hours at the College of Santa Fe, St. John's College in Santa Fe, or the College of the Southwest in Hobbs.

11) Money To Take Courses Out-Of-State Not Offered By New Mexico Colleges
Professional Student Exchange Program: This exchange program provides New Mexico residents access to academic professional programs at out-of-state institutions at reduced tuition rates on a preferred admission basis. State support is provided for programs not offered at in-state colleges. Categories include: dentistry, veterinary medicine, occupational therapy, optometry, osteopathic medicine, podiatry, graduate library studies, and public health.

12) Money For Medical Students Willing To Practice In New Mexico
New Mexico Physician and Physician Assistant Student Loan for Service Program: This loan-for-service program was created to increase the number of physicians and physician assistants in medically underserved rural areas in New Mexico. Students may borrow a maximum of $10,000 per academic year. Loans may be forgiven through service or repaid in cash. Students must declare intent to practice as a physician or physician assistant in New Mexico and be enrolled and accepted by an accredited school. Highest priority is given to students who demonstrate financial need.

13) Money For Women And Minority Ph.D. Students
Minority Doctoral Assistance Loan for Service Program: This loan-for-service program was created to increase the number of ethnic minorities and women available to teach engineering, physical or life sciences, mathematics, and other academic disciplines that are underrepresented in New Mexico colleges and universities. Students must attend a sponsoring New Mexico four-year institution and be approved by their academic committee.

14) $5,000 Per Year To Become A School Teacher
Paul Douglas Teaching Scholarship: These scholarships are available to full-time undergraduate and high school seniors who graduated in the top 10% of their high school graduating class or scored at least 62 on the GED and are pursuing certification to teach at the pre-school, elementary, or secondary level. Scholarships are for $5,000 per academic year. After graduation, recipients are required to teach two years for each year of scholarship assistance to receive total loan forgiveness.

New York
New York Higher Education Services Corporation, Grants and Scholarship Information, 99 Washington Ave., Albany, NY 12255, 518-474-1137. Applicants must be residents of New York. Estimated annual funds available: $632,400,000.

1) $4,125 Grant For Full-Time Students
Tuition Assistance Program (TAP): This program offers awards up to $4,125, or tuition, whichever is less, to help students pay tuition at postsecondary institutions in the state. A TAP award is a grant that students do not have to repay. Undergraduate students may receive up to four years of assistance for full-time study or up to five years in certain programs. Graduate or professional students may also receive up to four years of TAP for full-time study for a combined undergraduate-graduate total of eight years.

2) $2,000 Grant For Part-Time Students
Aid for Part-Time Study (APTS): These grants provide aid for part-time study up to $2,000 per year, but an award cannot exceed tuition. The amount of the award is established by the participating college.

3) $5,000 For Accounting, Veterinary, and Students Pursuing 19 Other Professional Careers
New York Regents Professional Opportunity Scholarships: Full-time students pursuing one of 21 professional careers may be eligible for this scholarship. Professions range from accounting to veterinary medicine. Contact the New York Higher Education Services Corporation for a complete listing. Awards range from $1,000 to $5,000 per year for up to four years of study. If an approved program requires more than four years of study, a student will be eligible for payments for the required duration of study. Students must work one year for each annual payment received. Employment must be in the studied profession and be within New York State. If the student does not begin practice within one year of program completion, the student must repay twice the amount of all scholarship monies received, plus interest.

4) $5,000 Per Year To Become A School Teacher
Paul Douglas Teaching Scholarship: These scholarships are available to full-time undergraduate and high school seniors who graduated in the top 10% of their high school graduating class or scored at least 62 on the GED and are pursuing certification to teach at the pre-school, elementary, or secondary level. Scholarships are for $5,000 per academic year. After graduation, recipients are required to teach two years for each year of scholarship assistance to receive total loan forgiveness.

5) $10,000 A Year For Students Studying Medicine Or Dentistry
New York Regents Health Care Opportunity Scholarships: This annual scholarship awards between $1,000 to $10,000 per year to students studying medicine and dentistry. Students must attend an approved program in New York State on a full-time basis. Awards are dependent upon family income and are available for up to four years. Upon completion of study, the student must work one year for each annual payment received. However, the minimum service requirement is two years, even if only one annual payment was received. Employment must be in the studied profession and must be in a designated physician-shortage area of New York State. The same penalties apply as above to those students who do not meet their service obligation.

6) $15,000 For Students Studying To Be Dental Hygienists, Midwives, Therapists, And Speech-Language Pathologists
New York State Health Service Corps Scholarships: This competitive scholarship provides up to $15,000 per year for two years of full-time study. The award is presented to students studying to become: dental hygienists, midwives, nurse practitioners, occupational therapists, pharmacists, physical therapists, physician assistants, registered nurses, or speech-language pathologists. Students must have been accepted or enrolled full-time in an approved professional program and be within two years of becoming eligible for New York state licensure in their chosen field. Students must agree to work 18 months in a state-operated facility or certain state-licensed voluntary agencies for each year of scholarship support received. Selection is based on academic achievement, previous work experience in the chosen health profession, and demonstrated interest in working with institutionalized populations.

7) $3,000 A Year To Become Teachers, Guidance Counselors, And College Administrators
Empire State Challenger Scholarship for Teachers: This program provides up to $3,000 per year to those planning a career in the teaching profession. Contact your high school guidance counselor, college Financial Aid Administrator or the New York State Education Department for program details.

8) $1,350 To Native Americans To Attend College
State Aid to Native Americans: Up to $1,350 may be awarded yearly to enrolled members of Indian tribes within New York State for half-time or full-time study in the state.

9) Grants To Dependents Of Deceased Or Disabled Veterans
Regents Award for Children of Deceased or Disabled Veterans: Awards of $450 per year are provided to children whose parent(s) served during World War I, World War II, Korean War, or Vietnam War. Parents may also have served as Merchant Seamen during World War II, or during military operations in Lebanon, Grenada, Panama, or the Persian Gulf. Undergraduate work in all programs of study are funded.

10) Grants To Dependents Of Deceased Police Officers, Fire Fighters, Or Correction Officers
Regents Awards for Children of Deceased Police Officers, Fire Fighters, and Correction Officers: Awards of $450 per year are provided in all programs of study to students in this category. Undergraduate work in all study programs are funded.

11) Tuition And Fees For Dependents Of Deceased Police Officers and Fire Fighters
Memorial Scholarships for Children of Police Officers and Fire Fighters: Undergraduate students who qualify under this category are eligible to receive the actual tuition or tuition and fees at the State University of New York, whichever is less, plus allowances for room, board, books, supplies, and transportation.

12) Money, Counseling, and Tutoring To Academically And Financially Troubled Students
Opportunity Programs: New York State provides financial aid for students who are both academically and economically disadvantaged. The financial aid is combined with programs of special counseling, tutoring, and remedial course work. Assistance is limited and is made at the discretion of the college. Awards vary with financial need.

13) $1,000 Per Semester For Vietnam Veterans
Vietnam Veterans Tuition Awards: This program provides tuition assistance to eligible Vietnam Veterans enrolled in an undergraduate program at a degree-granting institution or an approved vocational school. Awards are $1,000 per semester for full-time study and $500 per semester for part-time study, but cannot exceed tuition costs.

North Carolina
North Carolina State Education Assistance Authority, P.O. Box 2688, Chapel Hill, NC 27515-2688, 919-549-8614. Applicants must be residents of North Carolina. Estimated annual funds available: $85,486,851.

1) Grants For Full-Time And Part-Time Students
Appropriated Grants: This category includes funds for both full-time and part-time undergraduates plus graduate and first-year professional students attending the University of North Carolina (UNC). Awards are based on financial need and vary depending upon the cost of education at the institution, other available financial aid, and the financial resources of the student or family.

Be patient. If any phone number is incorrect, call (area code) 555-1212 and request the new listing.

221

2) $5,000 A Year For Preschool, Elementary, Or Secondary Level Teachers

Paul Douglas Teacher Scholarship Program (PDTS): Although this is a federally funded scholarship, the program in this state is administered by the North Carolina State Education Assistance Authority. These scholarships are for outstanding high school graduates who want to pursue teaching careers after they finish college. A Douglas scholarship provides up to $5,000 a year to students who graduate from high school in the top 10% of their class, and have a cumulative GPA of 3.0 on a 4.0 scale. Students must express an interest in becoming a teacher at the preschool, elementary, or secondary level, especially in North Carolina. Students are required to teach two years for each year of scholarship assistance they receive.

3) $3,000 For Smart High School Students Active In Public Service

Incentive Scholarship Program: These renewable awards are open to undergraduate students who enroll at Elizabeth City State University, Fayetteville State University, North Carolina Agricultural and Technical State University, North Carolina Central University, Pembroke State University, and Winston-Salem University. Awards vary, but annual awards may not exceed $3,000 for any recipient. To be eligible, students must meet certain admissions standards, including specified grade-point averages, submit to standardized assessments, and participate in required public service activities.

4) Grants For Minorities Studying Part Time Or Full Time

Minority Presence Grant Program: Grants are available to North Carolina students taking at least three hours of degree-credit course work per semester at a UNC institution where their race is in the minority. The amount of the award depends upon the financial need of the recipient and the availability of funds.

5) Grants For Minorities Studying Law, Veterinary Medicine, Or Working On A Ph.D.

Minority Presence Grant Program: Doctoral/Law/Veterinary Medicine Program: These grants are available to Afro-American North Carolinians who are enrolled full time in a doctoral degree program at East Carolina University, North Carolina State University, UNC-Chapel Hill, and UNC-Greensboro, or the UNC-Chapel Hill Law School. Each recipient is awarded $4,000 (up to $4,000 for law) for the academic year, with an option of $500 in additional support for study during the summer.

6) Grants For Students Going Part Time To Junior Colleges

North Carolina Community College Scholarship Program: North Carolina students enrolled at least part time at one of the 58 state community colleges may apply. This renewable program awards 950 scholarships at $375 each annually. Priority is given to students enrolled in college transferable curriculum programs, those seeking new job skills, women in non-traditional curricula, and students who participated in an ABE, GED, or High School Diploma program.

7) $1,500 To Full-Time Undergraduate Students

North Carolina Student Incentive Grant: This program is open to full-time undergraduates who demonstrate substantial financial need and are enrolled in a state college or university. Awards range from $200 to $1,500 per year, depending on need. The average award is approximately $750.

8) Grants Given By State Legislators To Students Who Don't Even Need The Money

North Carolina Legislative Tuition Grant Program: This program assists full-time undergraduates attending a North Carolina private college or university. This program is not based on financial need. Students must be eligible for in-state tuition rates under the terms and conditions of the current UNC residence manual and meet program conditions.

9) $7,500 A Year For Undergraduate Or Graduate Students In Health, Science, Or Mathematics

North Carolina Student Loan Program for Health, Science, and Mathematics: Applicants must be accepted as full-time students in accredited associate, baccalaureate, master's, or doctoral programs leading to a degree. Maximum loans range from $2,500 to $7,500 a year, depending on the degree level. Rewards are renewable and recipients are chosen according to major academic capabilities and financial need.

10) $5,000 A Year To Students Who Want To Be Teachers

North Carolina Teaching Fellows Scholarship Program: Selection is based upon high school grades, class standing, SAT scores, writing samples, community service, and references. Up to 400 Teaching Fellows are selected annually from area high schools. Scholarships of $5,000 per year are renewable for four years of college. Recipients must attend one of the following institutions: Appalachian State University, East Carolina University, Elon College, Meredith College, North Carolina A&T University, North Carolina Central University, North Carolina State University, UNC campuses at Asheville, Chapel Hill, Charlotte, Greensboro, Wilmington, and Western Carolina University.

11) Grants To Dependents Of Deceased Or Disabled Veterans Or POW/MIA's

North Carolina Veterans Scholarship: This award is available to children of certain deceased or disabled veterans or of veterans who were listed as POW/MIA. The veteran must have been a legal resident of North Carolina at the time of entry into service, or the child must have been born in North Carolina and resided there continuously. Full scholarships are provided for four academic years of free tuition, room and board, and fees at state-supported institutions. Limited scholarships provide free tuition and mandatory fees. The yearly value at private institutions is $3,000

(full) and $1,200 (limited). Awards may be used for undergraduate or graduate study.

12) Grants To Full-Time Or Part-Time Native American Students

American Indian Student Legislative Grant Program: This special program provides grants to needy resident North Carolina Indians. Grants of up to $500 per academic year are provided for full-time undergraduate or graduate students and a reduced amount proportional to academic load is available to part-time students. Fellowships at the doctoral level are awarded in the amount of $4,000 annually to eligible students who study at one of the UNC constituent institutions. Awards may be renewed annually.

13) Money For Students In 2-Year Or 4-Year Nursing Programs

Nurse Education Scholarship Loan Program: These awards range from $400 to $5,000, depending on financial need, for students studying for the Bachelor of Science Degree in Nursing. Awards range from $400 to $3,000 for students enrolled in the Associate Degree in Nursing and LPN programs.

14) $6,000 A Year For Nursing Students Willing To Practice In North Carolina

Nursing Scholars Program: This new program is a competitive, renewable, merit-based scholarship/loan available to students planning a nursing career. Recipients are selected based on academic achievement, leadership potential, and a desire to practice nursing on a full-time basis in North Carolina. Financial need is not a criterion. Candidates for an associate degree in nursing receive $3,000 per year; for a diploma in nursing, $3,000; and for a bachelor of science in nursing, $5,000 or $3,000 per year. Up to 450 scholarship/loans are funded annually. An annual award of $6,000 is available for a second year of full-time study toward a masters degree in nursing.

15) $5,000 Plus Tuition And Fees For Dental Students

Board of Governors Dental Scholarship: A student must be accepted for admission to the UNC School of Dentistry, have financial need, and express an intent to practice dentistry in the state. This scholarship provides an annual stipend of $5,000 plus tuition, mandatory fees, and approved costs for certain instruments and supplies. Awards are renewable annually for a period of four years, dependent upon program specifications.

16) $5,000 Plus Tuition And Fees For Medical Students

Board of Governors Medical Scholarship Program: Students must be accepted for admission to one of the following North Carolina medical schools: Bowman Gray of Wake Forest University, Duke University, East Carolina University, and UNC-Chapel Hill. An applicant must demonstrate financial need and express an intent to practice medicine in the state. This scholarship provides an annual stipend of $5,000 plus tuition and mandatory fees. The student must be nominated for the award by one of the four medical schools. Twenty recipients are chosen annually, subject to budget restrictions.

17) Free Loans For Studying Psychology, Counseling, Or Speech

Prospective Teacher Scholarship Loans: Recipients are selected on the basis of GAP, SAT scores, class rank, congressional district, recommendations, and certification areas of need. Students must attend one of the 45 public or private state colleges or universities with a North Carolina-approved education program or enroll in a technical institute or community college with a transfer program. Awards of up to $2,000 are made per academic year for up to four years of undergraduate study. Recipients in special services areas (i.e., school psychologists, counselors, speech language specialists, and audiologists) receive up to $2,000 per academic year for the minimum number of years required to earn an entry level degree. One year of the loan will be forgiven for each full year the recipient teaches or works as a special services professional in a state public school.

18) Grants To Part-Time Or Full-Time Students Attending Private Colleges

State Contractual Scholarship Program: This program provides scholarship funds to private state colleges or universities for needy North Carolina full or part-time undergraduates. Each eligible school receives up to $450 per state resident undergraduate enrolled. Awards based on financial need are at the discretion of the Financial Aid Office.

19) Tuition, Fees, And Day Care For the Physically Or Mentally Disabled

Vocational Rehabilitation Program: Persons with a physical or mental disability that substantially interferes with obtaining employment may be eligible for assistance from this program. Each qualified individual works with a counselor to develop an appropriate rehabilitative program. This program is tailored to the individual and may include classroom training, as well as work experience. Depending upon need, support services such as day care and allowances for transportation, books, and supplies are provided. Supplemental training stipends are available on a limited basis. Additional information may be obtained by contacting the Vocational Rehabilitation Division nearest the student's home or the North Carolina Department of Rehabilitation Services.

North Dakota

North Dakota Student Financial Assistance Program, State Capitol, 600 East Boulevard, Bismarck, ND 58505, 701-328-4114. Applicants must be residents of North Dakota. Estimated annual funds available: $2,018,600.

1) $600 To Students Attending Any College

North Dakota Student Financial Assistance Program: Grants of up to $600 are available to students to attend any public or private, non-profit postsecondary training institution in North Dakota. To qualify, students must enroll in a course of study of at least nine months in duration, with a minimum of 12 credits for each enrollment period.

2) 50% Tuition Awarded To Top High School Students

North Dakota Scholars Program: This program provides approximately 50 tuition scholarships to high school seniors who rank in the top 5% of all North Dakota students taking the ACT assessment and ranking in the top 20% of their high school graduation class. This scholarship must be used at a North Dakota college or university.

3) Money For Students Studying Nursing

North Dakota Nursing Scholarship/Loan Program: This scholarship provides funds for qualified students who express an interest in pursuing a career in nursing and show an appropriate financial need. Each recipient must sign and execute a note for each payment. The maximum amount of the scholarships are: $5,000 to professional nurse graduates, $3,000 to professional nurse students, and $2,000 to practical nurse students.

4) $2,000 For Students With 1/4 Indian Blood

North Dakota Indian Scholarship: The North Dakota University System provides renewable grants ($2,000 maximum) for Indian students who have been admitted to a postsecondary institution in North Dakota. Awards are made for one academic year. The applicant must be either a resident of North Dakota with 1/4 degree Indian blood or an enrolled member of a tribe, now considered resident in North Dakota. Residency for each student is determined by the postsecondary institution that the student is attending.

5) $5,000 Per Year To Become A School Teacher

Paul Douglas Teaching Scholarship: These scholarships are available to full-time undergraduate and high school seniors who graduated in the top 10% of their high school graduating class or scored at least 62 on the GED and are pursuing certification to teach at the pre-school, elementary, or secondary level. Scholarships are for $5,000 per academic year. After graduation, recipients are required to teach two years for each year of scholarship assistance to receive total loan forgiveness.

Ohio

Ohio Board of Regents, Ohio Student Aid Commission, State Grants and Scholarship Department, 309 S. 4th St., Columbus, OH 43215, 614-466-7420. Applicants must be residents of Ohio. Estimated annual funds available: $90,300,000.

1) Grants For Middle Income Families To Pay Tuition

Ohio Instructional Grants: This grant program assists low and middle income families in meeting tuition costs. The amount of each award is based on reported family income and the total number of dependent children. Grants range from $216 to $1,326 for full-time undergraduates attending public colleges and universities; $540 to $3,306 for students attending private institutions of higher education; and from $372 to $2,268 for students attending proprietary institutions. This grant pays instructional and general fees (tuition) only.

2) Grants To Pay Tuition At Private Colleges

Ohio Student Choice Grant Program: This program provides tuition assistance to students attending Ohio non-profit colleges or universities to reduce the gap between tuition costs at public and private institutions. Eligible applicants include students enrolled full-time in a bachelor's degree program in an Ohio non-profit college or university. Award amounts vary from year to year. This grant pays instructional and general fees (tuition) only.

3) Grants To Dependents Of Deceased Or Disabled Veterans And POW/MIAs

Ohio War Orphans Scholarship Program: This program assists in meeting college costs of the children of deceased or disabled Ohio war veterans and children of Vietnam conflict MIAs or POWs. Students must be between the ages of 16 and 21, and enrolled or intend to enroll full-time at an Ohio public college or university or an eligible private non-profit institution of higher education. The scholarship provides general and instructional fees for students attending public colleges or universities. Children of Vietnam conflict MIAs or POWs also receive benefits for room, board, and books. Students attending private, non-profit institutions receive the average dollar equivalent of the public college costs. The scholarship may be used for instructional and general fees. Dependents of Vietnam conflict MIAs or POWs may use scholarship benefits for instructional and general fees, room and board, and books.

4) $1,000 A Year To Smart High School Students Who Attend Ohio Colleges

Ohio Academic Scholarship Program: This scholarship recognizes an outstanding senior scholar from each high school in Ohio and encourages enrollment in Ohio institutions of higher education. Scholars receive $1,000 per year for a maximum of four academic years. Scholarships of $1,000 are awarded annually to each participating chartered high school in Ohio.

5) $3,500 A Year For Graduate Students

Regents Graduate/Professional Fellowship Program: This program recognizes the outstanding academic achievement of Ohio's baccalaureate graduates and encourages their pursuit of graduate or professional degrees in Ohio. Eligible applicants include college or university seniors or baccalaureate degree candidates who will enroll as full-time graduate students in eligible Ohio graduate or graduate professional schools. Regents Fellows receive $3,500 per year for a maximum of two academic years.

6) Free Tuition To Dependents Of Fire Fighters And Police Officers Killed In The Line Of Duty

Police and Fire Fighter Tuition Benefits: This program provides benefits for children of Ohio fire fighters and peace officers killed in the line of duty. Eligible applicants include Ohio residents under 26 years, or under 30 years (if honorably discharged from the armed services). The award covers instructional and general fees at a state college or university or the average equivalent at a participating private college. The maximum grant covers four years of undergraduate study.

7) $1,500 A Year For Students With 1/4 American Indian Blood

Bureau of Indian Affairs Educational Assistance: This scholarship provides up to $1,500 per year to students of American Indian heritage. An applicant must be at least 1/4 blood American Indian or an enrolled member of a federally recognized tribe. Preference is given to full-time students who live on or near a reservation. Individual tribes may set priorities for available funds.

8) $13,000 For Nursing Students

This program provides financial assistance to nursing students based on financial need. Students must be enrolled at least half time in participating schools of nursing. The loan maximum is $2,500 for years one and two of study, and up to $4,000 for years three and four of study. A portion of the loan may be canceled for specified career service.

9) $5,000 Per Year To Become A School Teacher

Paul Douglas Teaching Scholarship: These scholarships are available to full-time undergraduate and high school seniors who graduated in the top 10% of their high school graduating class or scored at least 62 on the GED and are pursuing certification to teach at the pre-school, elementary, or secondary level. Scholarships are for $5,000 per academic year. After graduation, recipients are required to teach two years for each year of scholarship assistance to receive total loan forgiveness.

Oklahoma

Oklahoma State Regents for Higher Education, 500 Education Building, State Capitol Complex, Oklahoma City, OK 73105-4503, 405-524-9100. Applicants must be Oklahoma residents. Estimated annual funds available: $13,282,967.

1) $1,000 For Students Having Trouble Paying Tuition

Oklahoma Tuition and Grant Program: This need-based grant program is open to Oklahoma students who attend approved colleges, universities, and vocational-technical schools in Oklahoma. Awards are approved for full-time or part-time students and are meant for undergraduate or graduate study. The maximum annual award is 75% of enrollment costs or $1,000, whichever is less.

2) Tuition, Fees, And Room And Board For Financially Troubled Students

William P. Willis Scholarship Program: Eligible applicants include low-income, full-time students attending one of Oklahoma's public colleges or universities. Scholarships are awarded on a yearly basis, renewable for up to three years, and covers general enrollment fees, books, materials, and room and board.

3) Grants To Top 15% High School Students Who Want To Be Teachers

Future Teachers Scholarship Program: This competitive scholarship is available to outstanding high school graduates who demonstrate an interest in teaching in fields where there is a teacher shortage in Oklahoma. Eligible applicants must rank in the top 15% of their high school graduating class. Scholarships are awarded for up to $1,500 per year for full-time students and up to $750 per year for half-time students. The scholarship may be renewed for up to four years.

4) $5,000 Per Year To Become A School Teacher

Paul Douglas Teaching Scholarship: These scholarships are available to full-time undergraduate and high school seniors who graduated in the top 10% of their high school graduating class or scored at least 62 on the GED and are pursuing certification to teach at the pre-school, elementary, or secondary level. Scholarships are for $5,000 per academic year. After graduation, recipients are required to teach two years for each year of scholarship assistance to receive total loan forgiveness.

Oregon

Oregon State Scholarship Commission, 1500 Valley River Drive, Suite 100, Eugene, OR 97401, 503-687-7400. Applicants must be residents of Oregon. Estimated annual funds available: $13,403,500.

1) Grants To Smart High School Students

A) Oregon State Grants: The commission awards state grants to Oregon resident undergraduate students who enroll full-time at a non-profit college or university in Oregon. Both state grants are awarded on the basis of financial need. Either grant may be received for twelve terms or eight semesters, provided a student maintains

Be patient. If any phone number is incorrect, call (area code) 555-1212 and request the new listing.

223

Education

satisfactory academic progress and files a new need analysis form each year to demonstrate continued financial need.

B) Cash Awards: These grants are awarded to graduating high school seniors with high academic potential, as well as financial need. Cash Awardees are selected on the basis of high school GPA, as well as SAT or ACT scores, reported by high schools for the top 10% of graduating seniors. During 1992-93, the amount of a Cash Award was $864.

2) Grants To College Students In Financial Need

Need Grants: Eligibility for this program is based entirely on financial need. The amount of the award depends on the level of need and the cost of education. For Oregon schools, the 1992-93 maximum award for a community college is $756, the maximum award at a public four-year school is $966, and at private schools the maximum ranges from $2,352 to $3,150.

3) State Scholarships For High School Seniors, Graduate, and Undergraduate Students

The Oregon State Scholarship Commission administers a number of private award programs with very specific eligibility requirements. Scholarships are available to high school seniors, high school graduates, undergraduates, and graduate students. Students may receive a listing of individual programs and their requirements directly from the Commission.

4) $5,000 Per Year To Become A School Teacher

Paul Douglas Teaching Scholarship: These scholarships are available to full-time undergraduate and high school seniors who graduated in the top 10% of their high school graduating class or scored at least 62 on the GED and are pursuing certification to teach at the pre-school, elementary, or secondary level. Scholarships are for $5,000 per academic year. After graduation, recipients are required to teach two years for each year of scholarship assistance to receive total loan forgiveness.

Pennsylvania

Pennsylvania Higher Education Assistance Agency, 1200 N. 7th St., Harrisburg, PA 17102-1444, 717-257-2550. Applicants must be Pennsylvania residents for in-state schools, unless otherwise specified. Estimated annual funds available: $175,000,000 awarded to 130,000 students.

1) 80% Of Tuition And Fees For Financially Needy Students

Pennsylvania State Grants: Full-time undergraduate students who demonstrate financial need are eligible for these grants. Awards are limited to 80% of tuition and fees, up to $2,300 at approved institutions in Pennsylvania. At approved institutions outside of the state, the grant limit is $600. Pennsylvania also requires that grant recipients file for aid in the Federal Pell Grant Program. The remainder of the costs are then met through borrowing, working, or other aid programs. Awards are made for a maximum of one academic year at a time. Grants do not have to be repaid in any form.

2) 80% Of Tuition And Fees To Veterans And Dependents Of POW/MIAs

Grants for Veterans and POW/MIA Dependents: Qualified veterans of the U.S. Armed Services are eligible for consideration for state grants while they are full-time undergraduate students. Grants are limited to 80% of tuition and fees, up to a maximum of $2,300 at a Pennsylvania school or $800 at out-of-state schools.

3) Grants To Dependents Of POW/MIAs

Undergraduate state grants are also available to dependents of military service personnel, who were officially declared Prisoners of War or Missing in Action after January 31, 1955. Students must demonstrate financial need, be state residents, and attend a PHEAA- approved Pennsylvania college or university on at least a half-time basis.

4) $5,000 Per Year To Become A School Teacher

Paul Douglas Teaching Scholarship: These scholarships are available to full-time undergraduate and high school seniors who graduated in the top 10% of their high school graduating class or scored at least 62 on the GED and are pursuing certification to teach at the pre-school, elementary, or secondary level. Scholarships are for $5,000 per academic year. After graduation, recipients are required to teach two years for each year of scholarship assistance to receive total loan forgiveness.

Rhode Island

Rhode Island Higher Education Assistance Authority, 560 Jefferson Boulevard, Warwick, RI 02886, 401-736-1100. Applicants must be residents of Rhode Island. Estimated annual funds available: $9,200,000.

1) $2,000 For Part-Time And Full-Time Students

State Scholarship: Scholarships are based on grades or test scores, as well as financial need. Students must be enrolled or accepted in a college, university, or technical school on at least a half-time basis. Awards range from $250 to $2,000, depending on state money provided and student need.

2) $5,000 A Year For High School Students Who Want To Be Teachers

Best and Brightest Scholarship: This competitive academic scholarship is available

to graduating seniors at Rhode Island high schools who want to become teachers when they finish college. Recipients must have been accepted as full-time students at colleges or universities in a program leading to teacher certification. The maximum award amount given is $5,000 per year. Recipients must fulfill a teaching obligation of two years for each year of scholarship. If this is not met, the scholarship becomes a loan.

3) Money For Top 10% High School Students Who Want To Be Teachers

Paul Douglas Scholarship: Although this is a federally funded scholarship, the program in this state is administered by the Rhode Island Higher Education Assistance Authority. These scholarships are for outstanding high school graduates who want to pursue teaching careers after they finish college. A Douglas scholarship provides up to $5,000 a year to students who graduate from high school in the top 10% of their class, and have a cumulative GPA of 3.0 on a 4.0 scale. Students must express an interest in becoming a teacher at the preschool, elementary, or secondary level, especially in Rhode Island. Students are required to teach two years for each year of scholarship assistance they receive.

South Carolina

South Carolina Commission on Higher Education, 1333 Main Street, Suite 200, Columbia, SC 29201, 803-737-2260. Applicants must be residents of South Carolina. Estimated annual funds available: $1,600,000.

1) $3,320 For Students In Financial Need

South Carolina Tuition Grants: This program is open to students accepted for full-time enrollment in eligible private institutions in the state. Grants are based upon financial need and range up to $3,320 per year depending upon tuition cost.

2) $10,000 For Graduate Students

South Carolina Graduate Incentive Fellowship Program: This program is open to full-time graduate and first-year professional students with strong academic records. To be eligible, the student must be a member of a minority race at the institution to be attended. South Carolina residency requirements do not apply to students enrolled in doctoral programs. Recipients may receive a maximum of $5,000 per year for masters and first professional studies, and a maximum of $10,000 per year for doctoral studies.

3) $1,000 For Minority Students

South Carolina "Other Race" Program: Eligible applicants include members of a minority race at the institution to be attended. Eligible institutions include all public senior colleges and Denmark Technical College. Students must meet certain academic requirements. The college selects recipients based on academic performance and related criteria. Awards are given up to $1,000 per year.

4) $5,000 For High School Seniors With High Test Scores

Palmetto Fellows Scholarship: Eligible applicants include students who have attained an established qualifying score on the PSAT and plan to attend in-state institutions. Students may apply in the fall of their senior year. Recipients may receive up to $5,000 per year, and awards are renewable for three years.

5) $2,000 For College For Students With Physical And Mental Disabilities

Vocational Rehabilitation Benefits: This program is available to students who have physical or mental handicaps that limit vocational opportunities. Awards up to $2,000 per year are given based on financial need and are meant to cover educational fees. Additional funds are available for special services.

6) $10,000 A Year For Medical And Dental Students

South Carolina Medical and Dental Scholarship Fund: This program is available to students who are accepted for enrollment in an approved, accredited medical or dental school in the U.S. Applicants must be willing to practice in manpower shortage areas. Loans are forgivable under certain conditions. Loans of $10,000 per academic year are awarded for up to four years.

7) Free Tuition For Students Over 60 Years Old

Tuition Waiver for Senior Citizens: Tuition waivers are available to students, age 60 and over, attending South Carolina public colleges. Students must meet institution admissions policies. The waiver is equal to tuition only in the public college to be attended.

8) Free Tuition For Dependents Of Disabled Or Deceased Veterans

Free Tuition for Children of Deceased or Disabled South Carolina Veterans: A waiver of tuition is available to students attending any public institution in South Carolina, if they are children of deceased or totally disabled veterans. This waiver is not based upon financial need.

9) Free Tuition For Dependents Of Deceased Or Disabled Fire Fighters, Law Officers, and Members Of The Civil Air Patrol

Free Tuition for Children of Deceased or Disabled South Carolina Fire Fighters, Law Officers, and Members of Civil Air Patrol or Organized Rescue Squad: A waiver of tuition is available to students attending any public postsecondary institution in South Carolina, if they are children of deceased or totally disabled personnel, as described above. This waiver is not based upon financial need.

10) $5,000 Per Year To Become A School Teacher

Paul Douglas Teaching Scholarship: These scholarships are available to full-time undergraduate and high school seniors who graduated in the top 10% of their high school graduating class or scored at least 62 on the GED and are pursuing certification to teach at the preschool, elementary, or secondary level. Scholarships are for $5,000 per academic year. After graduation, recipients are required to teach two years for each year of scholarship assistance to receive total loan forgiveness.

South Dakota

South Dakota Department of Education and Cultural Affairs, Office of the Secretary, 700 Governors Drive, Pierre, SD 57501, 605-773-3134. Applicants must be residents of South Dakota. Estimated annual funds available: $400,000.

1) $2,500 Per Year For Students In Financial Need
South Dakota State Student Incentive Grant Program: Grants ranging from $200 to $2,500 per year are awarded to students attending public and private state institutions. Grants are based on financial need, and students must be enrolled at least half time as undergraduates.
2) $250 For Students Attending Private Colleges
South Dakota Tuition Equalization Grant Program: This program is available to financially needy students who are enrolled as full-time undergraduate students at an eligible South Dakota private college. The maximum grant is the total amount of tuition and mandatory fees charged by the institution for the academic year, or $250, whichever is less. Students may apply annually for the award for up to four years, or until they receive a baccalaureate degree.
3) $5,000 Per Year To Become A School Teacher
Paul Douglas Teaching Scholarship: These scholarships are available to full-time undergraduate and high school seniors who graduated in the top 10% of their high school graduating class or scored at least 62 on the GED and are pursuing certification to teach at the preschool, elementary, or secondary level. Scholarships are for $5,000 per academic year. After graduation, recipients are required to teach two years for each year of scholarship assistance to receive total loan forgiveness.

Tennessee

Tennessee Student Assistance Corporation, 404 James Robertson Parkway, Suite 1950, Parkway Towers, Nashville, TN 37243-0820, 615-741-1346. Applicants must be residents of Tennessee. Estimated annual funds available: $14,570,178.

1) $1,482 For Financially Needy Students
Tennessee Student Assistance Award: This need-based, non-repayable grant provides up to $1,482 per year for undergraduate students attending eligible Tennessee postsecondary institutions. Students must also be eligible for a Pell Grant.
2) $4,000 To High School Seniors In Top 5% Of Class
Tennessee Academic Scholars Program: This highly competitive scholarship is available to entering freshmen with a 3.5 high school GPA who achieve an ACT or SAT score in the top 5% nationally. The award provides up to $4,000 annually for a maximum of four years to attend an eligible Tennessee institution.
3) $6,000 For Students Who Want To Teach Grades K Thru 12
Teacher Loan Program for Disadvantaged Areas of Tennessee: This program is available to students pursuing teacher certification at the kindergarten through twelfth grade level. Recipients must pledge to teach in a disadvantaged geographic area in Tennessee. Funds are awarded up to $1,500 per academic year, with a maximum of $6,000 available for a four-year period.
4) $1,500 To Become An Art Or Music Teacher
Teacher Loan/Scholarship Program: This program is available to students pursuing teacher certification in art/music at the kindergarten through eighth grade level, math/science at the seventh through twelfth grade level, elementary education, or special education. Recipients must pledge to teach in a Tennessee public school in one of the areas listed for a minimum of four years. Up to $1,500 per academic year is available for a maximum of four years to students attending an eligible Tennessee institution.
5) Money For Minorities To Study Teacher Education At Community Colleges
Community College Education Recruitment Scholarship for Minorities: This program is available to entering freshmen who are members of minorities and plan to enroll in a teacher education program at a Tennessee community college. Eligible high school students must have achieved a grade point average of 2.5 on a 4.0 scale, at least 20 on the ACT or SAT tests, and to have graduated in the top 25% of their graduating class. Awards of $2,000 per academic year are available ($1,000 for half-time enrollment).
6) $5,000 A Year For Minorities In The Top 25% Of Class To Become Teachers
Minority Teaching Fellows Program: This program is available to entering freshmen with a 2.5 high school GPA on a 4.0 scale. Applicants must achieve at least 18 on the ACT test or 780 on the SAT or be in the top 25% of their high school class. Recipients must agree to teach at the kindergarten through twelfth grade level in a Tennessee public school. Funds are awarded up to $5,000 per academic year, with a maximum of $20,000 available.
7) $5,000 Per Year To Become A School Teacher

Paul Douglas Teaching Scholarship: These scholarships are available to full-time undergraduate and high school seniors who graduated in the top 10% of their high school graduating class or scored at least 62 on the GED and are pursuing certification to teach at the pre-school, elementary, or secondary level. Scholarships are for $5,000 per academic year. After graduation, recipients are required to teach two years for each year of scholarship assistance to receive total loan forgiveness.

Texas

Texas Coordinating Board on Higher Education, Box 12788, Capitol Station, Austin, TX 78711-2788, 512-483-6200. Applicants must be residents of Texas, unless otherwise specified. Estimated annual funds available: $141,787,017. Approximately $68,787,017 is awarded in state funded scholarships and grants, and an additional $73,000,000 is available in tuition and fee waivers and exemptions.

1) Money To Attend Public Colleges In Texas
Texas Public Education Grant: This grant is available to state residents, non-residents, and foreign students attending public colleges in Texas. Grants are for undergraduate and graduate programs. The maximum award is based on individual financial need.
2) Money To Attend Private Colleges In Texas
Tuition Equalization Grant: This program is available to Texas residents or National Merit Scholarship recipients. Eligible students are undergraduates or graduates enrolled at least half-time at independent Texas colleges. The maximum award is the lesser of the student's need or $1,900.
3) $1,250 For Half-Time Or Full-Time Students
Student Incentive Grant: This grant is available to residents or non-residents enrolled at least half time in an undergraduate or graduate program at a Texas public college. The maximum award is the lesser of the student's need or $1,250.
4) Grants To Financially Needy Students
Texas Tuition Assistance Grant: This program is available for undergraduates enrolled on a full-time basis who attend public or non-profit independent Texas colleges. The initial award must be applied for within two years of high school graduation. To be eligible, a student's high school grade point average must be equal to 80 on a scale of 100. For continuation of the award, college grade point average must be 2.5 on a 4.0 scale. The maximum award is the amount of tuition charged at a public senior level institution.
5) $1,000 For Members Of An Ethnic Group
State Scholarship Program for Ethnic Recruitment: To be eligible, a student must be a member of an ethnic group comprising less than 40% of a college's enrollment. The maximum award is $1,000. The program is available to undergraduate and graduate students enrolled on a full-time basis at a public senior Texas college. Entering freshmen must have a minimum 800 SAT or 18 ACT score or new transfer students with a minimum of 2.75 college grade point average.
6) Money To Study To Be A Nurse
State Scholarships are available for a number of nursing programs in Texas. Programs exist for ethnic minorities, rural professionals, vocational and graduate nursing students, and for licensed vocational nurses working toward becoming professional nurses. Information may be obtained through the Director of Vocational or Professional Nursing or the Director of Financial Aid at any non-profit institution in Texas offering an accredited program in nursing. Applications may be obtained through the relevant Director of Financial Aid.
7) Tuition And Fees For Blind Or Deaf Students
Blind or Deaf Students are exempted from tuition and fees at public colleges and universities in Texas. Students must provide certification of deafness or blindness from the appropriate state vocational or rehabilitation agency to the Registrar's Office of the institution to be attended.
8) Money For Dependents Of Disabled Or Deceased Firemen, Peace Officers, Custodial Employees of the Department Of Corrections, Or Game Wardens
Children of Disabled Firemen and Peace Officers are exempt from tuition and fees at public colleges and universities in Texas. To be eligible, the student must be the child of deceased or disabled firemen, peace officers, custodial employees of the Department of Corrections, or game wardens, whose death or disability was sustained in the line of duty while serving in Texas. The award must be applied for prior to the student's 21st birthday.
9) Money For Dependents Of POW/MIAs
Children of Prisoners of War or Persons Missing in Action: A dependent child of a Texas resident who is either a Prisoner of War or Missing in Action is exempt from tuition and fees at public colleges or universities in Texas. Students must provide proof of the parent's status from the Department of Defense.
10) Tuition And Fees For Fire Fighters To Take Science Courses
Fire Fighters Enrolled in Fire Science Courses: This program is open to residents and non-residents who are enrolled in fire science courses offered as part of a fire science curriculum. The program provides exemption from tuition and laboratory fees at public colleges or universities in Texas.
11) Free Tuition And Fees For Veterans
Veterans and Dependents (The Hazelwood Act): This program provides exemption

Be patient. If any phone number is incorrect, call (area code) 555-1212 and request the new listing.

225

Education

from tuition and certain fees at some Texas private colleges and universities to honorably discharged veterans who were residents of Texas when they entered the service. Exemptions may also apply to children whose parent(s) died while in the Armed Forces and to children of members of the Texas National Guard and Texas Air National Guard who died since Jan. 1, 1946, while on active duty.

12) Money For The Smartest High School Students
Highest Ranking High School Graduate: To be eligible, the student must be the highest ranking graduate of an accredited high school in the state. The program provides exemption from tuition for two semesters only, of the first regular session at public colleges and universities following high school graduation.

13) Money For Foreign Students From Central America
Students from Other Nations of the American Hemisphere (Good Neighbor Scholarship): The program provides exemption from tuition only, at Texas public colleges and universities to native-born citizens and residents from another nation of the American (Western) Hemisphere. The student must be scholastically qualified for admission to a public college or university in Texas. A maximum of 235 students may participate in this program per year. Students should apply through the Financial Aid Office or Foreign Student Office of his or her university.

14) Up To $1,500 For Undergraduates
Texas Educational Opportunity Grant: This program provides grants to undergraduates enrolled at least half time at a public or non-profit Texas independent college. Priority is given to minorities, first-generation college students, and students with high financial need. The maximum award is $1,500.

15) $5,000 Per Year To Become A School Teacher
Paul Douglas Teaching Scholarship: These scholarships are available to full-time undergraduate and high school seniors who graduated in the top 10% of their high school graduating class or scored at least 62 on the GED and are pursuing certification to teach at the pre-school, elementary, or secondary level. Scholarships are for $5,000 per academic year. After graduation, recipients are required to teach two years for each year of scholarship assistance to receive total loan forgiveness.

Utah

Utah System for Higher Education, 355 West North Temple, 3 Triad Center, Suite 550, Salt Lake City, UT 84180-1205, 801-321-7100. Utah administers funding to state residents. The state uses a decentralized system. Students should contact the Financial Aid Office at the college they plan to attend. Estimated annual funds available: $591,010.

1) Grants For Students In Financial Need
State Student Incentive Grant Program: This program makes Federal and state funds available to students with substantial financial need. The Utah Board of Regents administers this program. A maximum of $2,500 per student per academic year may be awarded to students who meet eligibility criteria.

2) $5,000 Per Year To Become A School Teacher
Paul Douglas Teaching Scholarship: These scholarships are available to full-time undergraduate and high school seniors who graduated in the top 10% of their high school graduating class or scored at least 62 on the GED and are pursuing certification to teach at the pre-school, elementary, or secondary level. Scholarships are for $5,000 per academic year. After graduation, recipients are required to teach two years for each year of scholarship assistance to receive total loan forgiveness.

Vermont

Vermont Student Assistance Corporation, Champlain Mill, P.O. Box 2000, Winooski, VT 05404, 802-655-9602. Applicants must be Vermont residents, unless otherwise stated. Estimated annual funds available: $10,727,605.

1) Grants For Students In Financial Need
Vermont Incentive Grants: Applicants may include any full-time undergraduate who attends or plans to attend an approved post-high school degree program and has not already received a bachelor's degree. Applicants may also include students enrolled at the University of Vermont College of Medicine or students enrolled in a Doctor of Veterinary Medicine program at an accredited school of veterinary medicine. Grants are based upon financial need.

2) Grants For Part-Time Students
Vermont Part-Time Student Grants: This need-based grant program is open to students accepted or enrolled in a degree, diploma, or certificate program at the undergraduate level. Applicants must take fewer than 12 credits per semester and have not received a bachelor's degree. Awards vary depending upon credit hours taken.

3) $325 Per Course If You're NOT Working Toward A Degree
Vermont Non-Degree Student Grant Program: This program is open to students enrolled in any non-degree course that will improve employability or encourage further study. Awards are based upon financial need and total up to $325 for one course per semester. The award may be used for tuition and fees.

4) Extra Loans For College Students
Vermont EXTRA Loans (Supplemental): This program is available to students enrolled in a Vermont postsecondary school or Vermont residents attending out-of-state schools. Borrowers and co-borrowers must meet established credit standards. EXTRA borrowers must first apply for the maximum PLUS or SLS Loan. Loans do not exceed the student's estimated cost of attendance, less the estimated financial assistance awarded.

5) $5,000 Per Year To Become A School Teacher
Paul Douglas Teaching Scholarship: These scholarships are available to full-time undergraduate and high school seniors who graduated in the top 10% of their high school graduating class or scored at least 62 on the GED and are pursuing certification to teach at the pre-school, elementary, or secondary level. Scholarships are for $5,000 per academic year. After graduation, recipients are required to teach two years for each year of scholarship assistance to receive total loan forgiveness.

Virginia

Virginia State Council of Higher Education, Office of Financial Aid, James Monroe Building, 101 North 14th Street, Richmond, VA 23219, 804-371-7941. Applicants must be Virginia residents. Estimated annual funds available: $73,600,000.

1) $2,000 For Students In Financial Need
Virginia College Assistance Program (CSAP): CSAP is available to undergraduate students who demonstrate financial need as determined by the institution. The amount of the award ranges from $400 to $2,000.

2) $3,000 A Year For The Brightest High School Students
Virginia Scholars Program (VSP): VSP is a merit-based scholarship program to encourage Virginia's brightest high school seniors and two-year college students to attend school in Virginia. The maximum award amount is $3,000 per year.

3) Grants For Students Even Though They Don't NEED The Money
Virginia Tuition Assistance Grant Program (TAGP): This program is available to undergraduate and graduate/ professional students who are residents of Virginia and enrolled full-time in a degree-seeking program at eligible private colleges or universities in Virginia. There is no financial need requirement for this grant. The award amount is determined yearly by the General Assembly.

4) Free Tuition For White Students To Attend Black Colleges
Virginia Transfer Grant Program (VTGP): VTGP is available to "other race" students who are enrolled in a traditionally white or black four-year Virginia public college or university. Applicants must meet minimum criteria and qualify for entry as a first-time transfer student. The grant is administered by the institution and provides up to full tuition and mandatory fees.

5) Part-Time Jobs For Students Having Trouble Paying Tuition
Virginia Work-Study Program: This need-based program allows undergraduate and graduate students to earn money to contribute toward their education expenses. The amount of the award varies with the hourly wage and the number of hours worked.

6) Grants To Black Undergraduate Students
Last Dollar Program: The Last Dollar Program awards grants to black undergraduate students enrolled for the first time in a state supported college or university in Virginia. Financial need must be demonstrated and the size of the award cannot exceed financial need.

7) $5,000 A Year To Become A Teacher
Paul Douglas Teacher Scholarship: Although this is a federally funded scholarship, the program in this state is administered by the Virginia State Council of Higher Education. This scholarship encourages outstanding high school graduates to pursue teaching careers. It awards scholarships on a competitive basis to qualified students who rank in the top 10% of their high school graduating class. Applicants must enroll for full-time study in a program which leads to teacher certification. The maximum award per year is $5,000.

8) Nursing Students Receive $100 A Month For Every Month They Agree To Work In Virginia
Nursing Scholarship Program: This program assists students who agree to engage continuously in nursing work in Virginia for one month for each $100 of scholarship funds.

9) Money For Medical Students Who Agree To Work In Virginia
Medical Scholarship Program: This program provides funds to students at Virginia medical schools who are studying to be primary care physicians. Recipients must agree to practice in an area of need in Virginia or to serve as an employee of state health, welfare, or corrections programs for a period of years equal to the number of years for which the scholarship is awarded. The amount of the award is $10,000. Contact the Department of Health at 804-786-4891 for further details.

10) $2,500 To Dental Students Who Agree To Work In Small Virginia Towns
Rural Dental Scholarships: Ten scholarships are awarded at $2,500 per year to dental students. Recipients must agree to work in an area of need in the state one year for every year of scholarship awarded. Call 804-786-9196 for more information.

11) $2,000 A Year For Teaching Students For Every Year They Agree To Work In Virginia
Virginia Teaching Scholarship: This program provides scholarships to college juniors

and seniors to help increase the supply of properly endorsed teachers in special need teaching fields. The amount of the award is $2,000 per academic year, and the recipient must teach one year in public schools for each year of the award.

12) Free Tuition For Police Officers To Take College Courses
State Law Enforcement Officers Educational Program: This program provides reimbursement for law enforcement officers who wish to attend college.

13) $450 For Teachers To Take Courses In Special Education
Traineeship for Special Education Personnel: This program provides $450 to encourage teachers to become endorsed in Special Education. Applicants must possess a teaching degree and endorsement and be recommended by their school board.

14) Free Tuition, Fees, And Room and Board For State Cadets
State Cadetships: This program provides tuition, required fees, and room and board for qualified state cadets. Call 703-464-7208 for further information.

15) Free Tuition For Dependents Of Deceased Or Disabled Veterans
Virginia War Orphan Education Act: This program provides 100% of tuition and required fees for any child of a veteran who was killed in action or 100% permanently disabled as a result of a wartime service-related injury. Recipients must attend a public college or university in Virginia. Call 703-857-7104 for further information.

16) Free Tuition And Fees For Students Who Want To Study Soil Science
Soil Scientist Program: This award covers tuition and required fees for four soil students at Virginia Tech. Recipients must agree to work one year for each year of scholarship awarded. Call 703-231-9778 or 703-231-9786 for further information.

17) Free Tuition For Students Over 60
Senior Citizens Tuition Waiver: This program provides tuition waivers for credit courses for Virginia residents aged 60 and older who have individual taxable income from the previous year of $10,000 or less. Information is available from the Admissions Office at any public Virginia college or university.

18) Loans To Middle Class Families Having Trouble Paying For Tuition
EDVANTAGE: This long-term, educational loan program is designed for families who wish to supplement, or do not qualify for, other forms of financial assistance. Loans are made through banks, credit unions, and savings and loan associations, and the program is administered by the State Assistance Authority. Edvantage loans are credit based, and the interest rates are variable throughout the life of the loan. Loans are available from $1,000 to $15,000 per year, up to $60,000 over the college career.

Washington

Higher Education Coordinating Board, 917 Lakeridge Way, Olympia, WA 98504-3430, 206-753-7800. Applicants must be Washington residents for in-state or out-of-state programs, when specified. Estimated annual funds available: $72,000,000.

1) College Students Who Have Trouble Paying Tuition
Washington State Need Grant Program: This grant program provides educational assistance to needy or disadvantaged students who enroll at one of Washington's public or private, two-year, four-year or vocational-technical institutions, or selected proprietary schools.

2) Part-Time Employment To Students Who Need Money
Washington State Work-Study Program: This program offers financial aid to needy students through part-time employment at Washington state public or private institutions of postsecondary education. The state reimburses the employer for a major share of the wages. Wherever possible, employment will be related to the student's academic pursuits or area of career interest.

3) Money to High School Students In The Top 1%
Washington Scholars Program: This program recognizes and honors three high school seniors from each legislative district. Eligible students representing the top 1% of the senior class are nominated by the high school principals based on academic accomplishments, leadership, and community service. Scholars attending a Washington public college or university receive a full tuition and fee waiver for undergraduate studies. Scholars attending a Washington independent college or university receive a grant that is matched by the school on a dollar-for-dollar basis.

4) $15,000 If You Teach 10 Years In A Washington Public School
Future Teachers Conditional Scholarship Program: This state scholarship was established to recruit future teachers from students who have distinguished themselves through academic achievement and students who act as role models for children, including targeted ethnic minorities. The $3,000 scholarships are renewable for up to five years and require a ten-year Washington public school teaching commitment or repayment of the scholarship, plus interest. This program is not based on need.

5) $3,000 to Study Nursing If You Practice For Five Years In Washington
Nurses Conditional Scholarship: This state scholarship encourages qualified individuals to serve in nursing shortage areas. Recipients agree to nurse in a state defined shortage area for five years or repay the scholarship, plus interest. The renewable scholarship pays the cost of attendance for the nursing program, up to $3,000 per year. This is a non-need based program.

6) $2,500 A Year For Math And Science Teachers
Teacher Incentive Loan for Mathematics and Science: The Math-Science Loan program provides need-based loans of up to $2,500 per year to students who intend to teach math or science at the middle or secondary level. Applicants must be declared majors in math or science who have been accepted into a program of teacher preparation. The loan is canceled for recipients who teach math or science for ten years in Washington's public middle or secondary schools; otherwise it must be repaid with interest over a ten-year period. This is a need-based program.

7) Money To Study Optometry In Other States
Western Interstate Commission for Higher Education (WICHE) Professional Exchange Program: This is a program for optometry students providing state support to needy Washington residents enrolled in out-of-state optometry programs.

8) Money To Get A Master's Or Ph.D. In Out-Of-State Schools
Western Interstate Commission for Higher Education (WICHE) Regional Graduate Program: Under this category, qualified Washington residents may enroll at reduced tuition rates in out-of-state master's and doctoral programs not offered in Washington. Programs are primarily in the science and liberal arts, rather than in the professional fields.

9) Free Tuition And Fees To Financially Needy Students
Tuition Waiver Program: This program enables public two- and four-year colleges and universities to waive all or part of the tuition and fees of needy or disadvantaged students from revenue generated by tuition and fees. Application is automatic when a student applies for financial aid from a public Washington State institution. In the most recent year for which statistics were available, more than 6,000 students received approximately $3.4 million through the program, with an average waiver equivalent to $523.

10) $5,000 Per Year To Become A School Teacher
Paul Douglas Teaching Scholarship: These scholarships are available to full-time undergraduate and high school seniors who graduated in the top 10% of their high school graduating class or scored at least 62 on the GED and are pursuing certification to teach at the pre-school, elementary, or secondary level. Scholarships are for $5,000 per academic year. After graduation, recipients are required to teach two years for each year of scholarship assistance to receive total loan forgiveness.

West Virginia

West Virginia Higher Education Program, P.O. Box 4007, Charleston, WV 25364, 304-347-1211. Applicants must be residents of West Virginia. Estimated annual funds available: $6,375,233.

1) Money For Financially Needy Students
West Virginia Higher Education Grant: This grant program is the primary state-funded financial aid program for West Virginia students at the postsecondary level. The program is designed to assist needy undergraduate West Virginia residents who require financial assistance in order to meet their educational goals. The amount of non-repayable grants fluctuates from year to year according to available funding and the number of applicants.

2) Money To Study Teaching At The Graduate Or Undergraduate Level
Underwood-Smith Teacher Scholarship Program:
A) Undergraduate Level: This state-funded student aid program encourages outstanding high school graduates to pursue teaching careers and graduate scholarships. Scholarships do not exceed $5,000 and are awarded on the basis of academic qualifications and interest in teaching. To qualify, students must graduate in the top 10% of his or her class, have a cumulative GPA of 3.25 after successfully completing two years of course work at an approved institution, or score in the top 10% statewide of those students taking the ACT. In 1992-93, $572,040 was awarded through this program.
B) Graduate Level: To qualify, students must have or will be graduating in the top 10% of his or her college or university class and be enrolled or accepted at a West Virginia institution of higher education in a program which leads to teacher certification. Recipients must agree to teach at a public preschool, elementary, or secondary school level in West Virginia for two years for each year of scholarship assistance unless entering a teacher shortage area, an exceptional children's program, or an economically disadvantaged area. Otherwise, students must repay all scholarship money, with interest.

3) Money For Medical Students
Central Office of the State College and University Systems Medical Student Loan Program: This program provides loans to students who demonstrate financial need, meet academic standards, and are enrolled or accepted for enrollment at the West Virginia University School of Medicine, the Marshall University School of Medicine, or the West Virginia School of Osteopathic Medicine. Award amounts are determined annually and cannot exceed $5,000 per year.

4) $5,000 Per Year To Become A School Teacher
Paul Douglas Teaching Scholarship: These scholarships are available to full-time undergraduate and high school seniors who graduated in the top 10% of their high school graduating class or scored at least 62 on the GED and are pursuing certification to teach at the pre-school, elementary, or secondary level. Scholarships

Be patient. If any phone number is incorrect, call (area code) 555-1212 and request the new listing.

227

Education

are for $5,000 per academic year. After graduation, recipients are required to teach two years for each year of scholarship assistance to receive total loan forgiveness.

Wisconsin

State of Wisconsin Higher Educational Aids Board, P.O. Box 7885, Madison, WI 53707-7885, 608-267-2206. Applicants must be residents of Wisconsin. Estimated annual funds available: $45,141,565 awarded to 48,000 students.

1) Grants To College Or Vocational Students
Wisconsin Higher Education Grant: This undergraduate grant program is open to students enrolled at least half time at the University of Wisconsin or vocational/technical institutions. The maximum award is $1,800, with ten semesters of eligibility. All awards are based on student financial need.

2) Grants To Students Attending Private Colleges In Wisconsin
Wisconsin Tuition Grant: This undergraduate grant program is open to students enrolled in independent, non-profit Wisconsin institutions. All awards are based on financial need and the difference between the tuition actually paid by the student and the tuition which would have been paid if the student attended the University of Wisconsin at Madison. The maximum award is $2,172, with ten semesters of eligibility.

3) Grants For Deaf And Blind Students
Visual and Hearing Impaired Program: This program provides grants for undergraduate study to students who are legally deaf and blind. To be eligible for the grant, the student must have financial need as determined by the institution the student attends. If the impairment prevents the student from studying in a Wisconsin institution, he or she may attend an out-of-state institution that specializes in teaching the blind or deaf and still receive a maximum grant of $1,800 per year. Eligibility cannot exceed ten semesters.

4) Grants To Blacks, Hispanics, Native Americans, And Former Citizens Of Laos, Vietnam, and Cambodia
Minority Retention Grant: This program provides financial assistance to Black, Hispanic, and Native American students to improve their opportunities for retention and graduation. Eligible applicants also include students admitted to the U.S. after December 31, 1975 who are either a former citizen of Laos, Vietnam, or Cambodia or whose ancestor was a citizen of those countries. Eligibility cannot exceed eight semesters. The University of Wisconsin has a similar program.

5) Grants To Non-Traditional Students
Talent Incentive Program: This program provides grants to severely needy nontraditional students. The maximum award is $1,800. The program is open to freshmen and upperclassmen who continue to be enrolled and have financial need. Eligibility cannot exceed ten semesters.

6) $2,200 A Year To Students With At Least 25% Native American Blood
Wisconsin Native American Student Grant: Awards under this program are made to students who are at least 25% Native American heritage. Applicants must attend a Wisconsin institution, either public, independent, or proprietary. Awards are made to graduate students as well as undergraduates. Maximum award is $2,200 a year with a limit of ten semesters of eligibility.

7) Grants To Smart High School Students
Academic Scholarships: The graduate with the highest grade point average from each Wisconsin high school is eligible for a scholarship to attend any accredited Wisconsin public or private non-profit institution of higher education. High schools with over 1,000 students will have one or more additional scholars. Awards vary, but are at least $1,500. Scholars who continue to attend full time with a 3.0 grade point average will have their awards renewed for up to three additional years.

8) $1,000 A Year For Every Year You Work As A Nurse In Wisconsin
Nursing Student Stipend Loans: State-funded forgivable loans are available to students enrolled as full-time second year vocational or technical students or collegiate juniors and seniors in a program which provides an associate degree Diploma, or bachelor's degree in nursing. Borrowers may receive up to $2,500 per year, based on financial need, for a total of $5,000. Funds are also available to masters candidates who intend to teach nursing. Recipients must provide one year of service in a Wisconsin hospital, nursing home, or public agency for twelve months for each $1,000 in stipend they receive or they must repay the loan.

9) Cheap Tuition For Attending Minnesota Universities
Minnesota-Wisconsin Reciprocity Program: Wisconsin residents may attend a Minnesota public college or university and pay the reciprocity tuition charged by that institution. All academic programs are eligible except for the doctoral programs in medicine, dentistry, and veterinary medicine.

10) $5,000 Per Year To Become A School Teacher
Paul Douglas Teaching Scholarship: These scholarships are available to full-time undergraduate and high school seniors who graduated in the top 10% of their high school class or scored at least 62 on the GED and are pursuing certification to teach at the pre-school, elementary, or secondary level. Scholarships are for $5,000 per academic year. After graduation, recipients are required to teach two years for each year of scholarship assistance to receive total loan forgiveness.

Wyoming

Programs Unit, Wyoming Department of Higher Education, Hathaway Building, 2nd Floor, Cheyenne, WY 82002, 307-777-6213. Applicants must be residents of Wyoming. Estimated annual funds available: $2,248,470.

1) Grants and Loans To Education Majors
Scholarship/Loan Fund for Superior Students in Education: These scholarship/loans are available to high school graduates who have demonstrated high scholastic achievement and qualities of leadership and who plan to teach in Wyoming public schools. Each year, 20 scholarships may be awarded to Wyoming high school graduates to attend the University of Wyoming or any community college in the state. Students must declare a major in education. Awards are available up to eight semesters, with no more than four awarded for study at a community college.

2) Grants To High School Students With 3.01 Averages
Pent's Honor Scholarship: High school seniors who have demonstrated outstanding academic achievement and leadership potential are eligible for this scholarship. Nominations are made by high school officials and the number of awards is dependent upon the size of the high school graduating class. Scholarships may be used at any state community college, as well as the University of Wyoming. Recipients must have a high school GPA of 3.01 out of 4.0 to qualify. The value of the scholarship generally equals full in-state tuition and fees. No more than eight semesters of scholarship is awarded.

3) Grants Given By County Governments
County Commissioners Scholarship: These scholarships are available to students who are residents of Wyoming and who graduate from a Wyoming high school. Funds are provided by appropriation from the Wyoming State Legislature. The awards are generally made for the amount of tuition and fees. Scholarships may be used at any public institution in Wyoming. Students should apply directly to the Board of County Commissioners in their county of residence.

4) Grants To Students With 25% Native American Blood
Bureau of Indian Affairs Scholarship and Loan: This program offers grants to students who are at least one fourth American Indian, Eskimo or Aleut, who are members of tribes served by the Bureau for educational purposes. Students must be enrolled or accepted for enrollment and have a definite financial need.

5) Grants To Members Of The Northern Arapaho Tribe
Northern Arapaho Tribal Scholarship: These scholarships are available to high school graduates who are enrolled members of the Northern Arapaho Tribe. Scholarships may be used for full-time study at any public institution in Wyoming.

6) Grants To Members Of The Wind River Shoshone Tribe
Shoshone Tribal Scholarship: These scholarships are available to high school graduates who are enrolled members of the Wind River Shoshone Tribe. Scholarships may be used at any public institution in Wyoming for full-time study. Applications should be made to the Community Development Office listed above.

7) $5,000 Per Year To Become A School Teacher
Paul Douglas Teaching Scholarship: These scholarships are available to full-time undergraduate and high school seniors who graduated in the top 10% of their high school graduating class or scored at least 62 on the GED and are pursuing certification to teach at the pre-school, elementary, or secondary level. Scholarships are for $5,000 per academic year. After graduation, recipients are required to teach two years for each year of scholarship assistance to receive total loan forgiveness.

State Education Information

A friend recently had the idea of marketing "Class of 2001" T-shirts to the parents of the kindergarten class of '88. Faced with the problem of estimating the size of the market, he did what any sharp young entrepreneur would do -- he turned to his state department of education for all of the little details...and a mailing list to boot.

It would probably take some effort to come up with a service or product that a school district doesn't buy short of military hardware (but that, too, might be changing). Like the federal government, schools purchase just about everything under the sun. Each state has a department of education or public instruction which collects and disseminates information on students, staff, school finances, and other related matters. And this data can help you sell a lot more than just T-shirts.

You can use the data to find the names and addresses of science teachers if you've got a great new product for demonstrating chemical reactions or cell osmosis; of math teachers if you've got 3-D geometry models or a novel new software idea; or PE teachers if you're designing football gear for the next century. Remember, teachers are usually the first to lobby for specific new textbooks and learning tools.

Information on the student population of a given school district can yield a pretty accurate picture of who lives where, what their parents earn and how they spend it -- priceless marketing information available at no or little cost to you. If you sell real estate or insurance, having accurate school district information may be essential in closing a sale or targeting new clients.

In addition, there is plenty of money to be made with accurate information on high school seniors. From yearbooks to class rings, prom gowns to SAT tutorials, the senior class is an industry unto itself. So, rather than wait for the "Class of 2001" to grow up, many businesses are already using state education information to get a edge over the competition.

Each state has a Department of Education or Public Instruction which collects and disseminates information pertaining to students, staff, finances and general matters. A representation of types of data collected and maintained is as follows:

Students:
- by grade
- by sex
- by ethnicity
- by special programs (special education, vocational education, bilingual and English as a second language, compensatory education, gifted and talented, migrant)
- by curriculum enrollment, graduates, dropouts, accidents, immunizations, projected enrollment and attendance, test scores.

Educators and Staff:
- Professional job assignments (teachers, administrators, support staff and aides, secretaries)
- sex
- ethnicity
- salaries
- program areas
- highest college degree attained
- months of contract
- days employed
- certification/permits granted
- tenure
- experience.

School District Finances:
- district budgeting and audited accounting data on revenues
- expenditures
- assets
- liabilities
- fund balances
- bond/loan requirements
- local school tax information
- district detailed state aid calculations
- total receipts and disbursements
- taxable property values.

General:
- number of districts
- demographic data
- address and telephone numbers of school campuses within district
- maps
- census.

By observing trends in statistical data, a school system can monitor school programs, improve data management, and address changing economic perspectives in education. In each state a statistical service department is responsible for the identification, implementation, and operation of data collection procedures. Within each state, various offices are responsible for:

* Analyzing, interpreting, and disseminating data relating to public and private elementary and secondary schools. Some offices also include data on colleges and universities of the state;

* Coordinating data collection procedures within the department;

* Recommending policies and procedures for processing statistics;

* Conducting special statistical studies; and

* Preparing projections and estimates.

Education

The information each education department needs is collected annually, and by using machine-readable forms and electronic data processing, various outputs are produced.

Descriptive Reports

These are the major sources of information that states regarding their school programs. Data include enrollment by grade and race, daily session data, distribution of graduating class, number of dropouts, special programs, availability of resources (videos, computers etc.), and a faculty listing.

Statistical Reports

A wide variety of statistical analyses of characteristics of public school professional staff are produced, including such factors as salary, degree status, certification status, experience, sex, and age. Summaries of various factors are usually available by school, school district, county, geographic region and for the total state. Also, a number of student statistics can be easily generated including: enrollment by grade, racial/ethnic characteristics, course registrations, student staff ratios, class size, and teacher load.

Special Requests

Requests for special data are handled in a variety of ways. Simple requests can be resolved by referencing a publication. Other more complex requests require custom searching of the databases and may require computer programming. In some cases there is a cost recovery fee, and in most cases a written request is preferred and will receive a higher priority.

List of State Department of Education Offices

Alabama

Alabama Department of Education, Montgomery, AL 36130; 334-242-9590. The computer services department provides computer printouts, and information on magnetic tape or computer diskette. There is a basic charge of $50 per hour for searches. Printouts of information over 50 pages cost an additional $.05 per page. There is a charge of $10 per diskette and $25 per tape. The basic fee for mailing labels is $65 plus an additional $.05 per label for those that run over 1,300. The Department of Education also publishes an *Annual Report*.

Alaska

Alaska Department of Education, Data Processing, P.O.F, Juneau, AK; 907-465-2808. This office provides computer searches and printouts. Specialized requests should be in writing. Publications include an *Annual Report*.

Arizona

Arizona Department of Education, 1535 West Jefferson, Phoenix, AZ 85007; 602-542-5295. The data processing department provides services such as computer searches, printouts and magnetic tapes. Requests should be in writing, and the fee varies depending upon the extent of programming necessary. The office publishes an *Annual Report*.

Arkansas

Arkansas Department of Education, Office of Accountability, 4 State Capitol Mall, Little Rock, AR 72201; 501-682-4229. The Office of Accountability provides computer searches and information via printouts and diskettes. Requests may be made directly over the telephone, but those of a complex nature should be put in writing. There is no fee for services. Publications include: *Affecting Basic Skills Achievement Through Technology - A Research Report, Arkansas Policy Statements, Federal Focus, Needs Assessment: Education for Economic Security Act - Title II, EESA, Networking Strategies: Community Education Proven Practice II, Private Schools in Arkansas, Statistical Summary for the Public Schools of Arkansas*.

California

California Department of Education, 721 Capitol Mall, P.O. Box 944272, Sacramento, CA 94244; 916-657-2676. The Demographics Services Department provides computer searches and printouts. There is no charge for publications or small searches, but detailed requests require a fee. Requests should be in writing. The office's publications include: *Enrollment Data, Racial or Ethnic Distribution of Staff and Students in California Public Schools*, and *Language Census Report*.

Colorado

Colorado Department of Education, 201 E. Colfax, Denver, CO 80203; 303-866-6837. This office provides computer searches if data are readily available on staff and student enrollment. Requests should be in writing. Publications include *Status of K-12 Public Education in Colorado, Certificated Personnel and Related Information*, and *Pupil Membership and Related Information*. A fee of $5 is charged for each report.

Connecticut

Connecticut Department of Education, Public Information Office, Box 2219, Hartford, CT 06145; 203-566-5667. This office provides information through computer searches, printouts and magnetic tapes. They very rarely charge for services and publish an *Annual Report*. Brochures are available describing the different areas of research and the types of information available.

Delaware

Delaware Department of Public Instruction, John Townsend Building, P.O. Box 1402, Dover, DE 19903; 302-739-4583. This office provides board approved reports listing statistics on school enrollments, number of teachers, educational statistics, and teacher personnel reports. They publish a *Report of Educational Statistics* which is available free of charge and an educational directory priced at $10.

Florida

Florida Department of Education, 275 Knott Building, Tallahassee, FL 32399; 904-487-1234. This service provides computer searches and printouts. If you send in a computer diskette they will transfer the information requested. Their publications include *MIS Statistical Brief* (monthly), *Profiles of Florida School Districts* and administrative support briefs.

Georgia

Georgia Department of Education, Twin Towers East, Atlanta, GA 30334; 404-656-2400. The Statistical Services Department provides information such as basic attendance data and enrollment data, some financial information, types of enrollment, and the expenditure and cost per child. Computer searches and printouts of existing data are available. There is a charge of $.10 per page if the printout is over 20 pages long. Handouts of specific summaries are available.

Hawaii

Hawaii Department of Education, Office of Information Resource Management, P.O. Box 2360, Honolulu, HI 96804. Enrollment data can be obtained free of charge from this office in printout form. At present, computer diskettes and magnetic tapes are not available. Specialized requests should be in writing. Publications include *Education Today in Hawaii* and the *Annual Financial Report*.

Idaho

Idaho Department of Education, Len B. Jordan Office Building, P.O. Box 83720, Boise, ID 83720-0027; 208-334-3330. The Department of Statistical Services provides limited computer searches and free printouts if data exists. There is a base charge of $25 for labels. Their publications include *Financial Summaries*, and an *Annual Statistical Report of Public School Certified Personnel and Employees in Non-Certified Positions*. They also provide an *Educational Directory* for $5.

Illinois

Illinois State Board of Education, 100 North First St., Springfield, IL 62777; 217-782-3950. The Department of Statistics provides computer searches and printouts free of charge. There is a charge for magnetic tapes or disks. Their publications include *Annual Statistical Report of Illinois Public School Districts* and *Schools and School Directories are free*. A nominal fee is charged for searches depending on the amount of information requested.

Indiana

Indiana Department of Education, Education Information Systems, Room 229, State House, Indianapolis, IN 46204; 317-232-0808. This office provides computer searches, printouts and magnetic tapes. Types of information available include enrollment figures, graduation rate, average teacher, and teacher to pupil ratio. Their publications include the *Fall Enrollment Report, Indiana Public School Professional Personnel Data*, and *Non-Certified Personnel Data*. There is a $5 set up fee for computer printout information and a charge of $.15 per page for xeroxed pages.

Be patient. If any phone number is incorrect, call (area code) 555-1212 and request the new listing.

Iowa

Iowa Department of Education, Grimes State Office Building, Des Moines, IA 50319; 515-281-5294. This office provides computer searches, printouts and magnetic tapes. There is no charge for standard enrollment and staff reports, but individual reports may require a charge, depending upon the degree of difficulty it took to gather the information. Teachers' names and school addresses are released. Their publications include the *Commission of Education Annual Report* and the *Educational Directory*.

Kansas

Kansas State Department of Education, Deputy Commissioners Office, 120 East 10th St., Topeka, KS 66612; 913-296-3871. This office provides free computer searches, and printouts. Requests should be in writing. Publications include: *A Strategic Plan for Kansas Public Education for the Year 2005, Annual Report, Profile of Kansas Schools, Profiles of Kansas Education Personnel: Superintendents, Teachers, Elementary Principals, Principals, AVTS Directors, and Community College Presidents, 125 Years of Kansas History: How Should Educators Approach It?*

Kentucky

Kentucky Department of Education, Frankfort, KY 40601; 502-564-4770. Services: This office provides computer searches, printouts and bulletins. While the bulletins and most statistical searches are free, stylized reports require a charge. Their publications include: *Profiles of Kentucky Public Schools, Public School Financial Analysis, Local District Annual Financial Reports, Receipts and Expenditures, Public School Salaries.*

Louisiana

Louisiana Department of Education, P.O. Box 94064, Baton Rouge, LA 70804; 504-342-3731. The Bureau of School Accountability provides computer searches, printouts and magnetic tapes. Publications include the *Annual Financial and Statistical Report*.

Maine

Maine Department of Educational and Cultural Services, Educational Building, Station No. 23, Augusta, ME 04333; 207-287-5841. This office provides computer searches and printouts plus magnetic tapes upon special request. Requests should be in writing. The cost is $.02 per name, with a $3 minimum. The cost for labels is $.05 each. Information on grades kindergarten through the twelfth grade is available. Teacher names and school addresses are released. Publications include: *Maine School Statistics, Students Educated at Public Expense, Resident Per Pupil Operating Costs, Maine Educational Facts.* All publications are $3 and less.

Maryland

Maryland Department of Education, Office of Management and Information Systems, 200 West Baltimore St., Baltimore, MD 21201; 410-767-0073. This office's services include computer searches and printouts from large databases only (enrollment, finance, staff). The information that was previously printed in the *Annual Report* is now distributed in specific smaller releases. There is no charge for printouts or reports.

Massachusetts

Massachusetts Department of Education, 350 Main St., Malden, MA 02148; 617-388-3300. Computer searches and printouts are available throughout this office, free of charge. They are currently in the process of converting to an electronic access system. Information available includes: attendance data and drop out reports. Publications include: *Distribution of High School Graduates, Per Pupil Expenditure.*

Michigan

Michigan Department of Education, Information Center Data Services, P.O. Box 30008, Lansing, MI 48909; 517-873-3324. This office provides computer searches and printouts on a limited basis., Diskettes are available. At present, there is no base charge for services, but this would depend upon the extent of the request. All information requests should be in writing. Publications include *Financial Data Statistics* and *Fingertip Facts.*

Minnesota

Minnesota Department of Education, Data Management Information, 550 Cedar St., Capitol Square Bldg., St. Paul, MN 55101; 612-296-2751. This office provides computer searches, printouts and diskettes, free of charge. Teachers' names and school addresses are available on labels from the Bookstore at 800-657-3757. Their publications include their *Annual Report.*

Mississippi

Mississippi Department of Education, P.O. Box 771, Jackson, MS 39205; 601-359-3527. Management Information Services provides computer searches, printouts and magnetic tapes. Requests should be in writing. Fees vary depending upon the scope

of the request and whether or not a program has to be specifically written. Their publications are $5 each and include the *Annual Report, Statistical Report,* and *School Dropouts by Reasons.*

Missouri

Missouri Department of Education School Data Section, P.O. Box 480, Jefferson City, MO 65102-0480; 314-751-2569. Computer searches and printout requests are evaluated individually. This office's publications include the *Report of the Public Schools of Missouri,* and *Missouri School Director,* which they sell for $6.

Montana

Montana Office of Public Instruction, State Capitol, Helena, MT 59620; 406-444-3656. This office provides computer searches and printouts. Special requests should be in writing. They also publish a report on *Public Education in Montana.*

Nebraska

Nebraska Department of Education Management Information Systems, Box 94987, 301 Centennial Mall, South Lincoln, NE 68509-4987; 402-471-2367. This office's services include computer searches, printouts, disks, and magnetic tapes. Fees vary depending upon the scope of the project. The office prefers that requests be in writing. Labels and listings of names are also provided for a fee. Teachers' names and school addresses are released in the School Directories. The office's publications include an *Annual Report,* and a series of reports called *Information Tabs* for $10 and the *Education Directory* for $15.

Nevada

Nevada Department of Education, 400 W. King St., Carson City, NV 89710; 702-687-3100. This office provides computer searches and printouts based upon aggregated student demographic data. Requests should be written. Their publications include a *Status Report,* and reports on *Student Dropout* and *Math and Science.*

New Hampshire

New Hampshire Department of Education, State Office Park South, 101 Pleasant St., Concord, NH 03301; 603-271-2778. The office of Information Services. Mailing labels for $.03 each. Teachers' names and school addresses are released. The office's publications a variety of statistical reports. To request the moving packet for $2.00, which contains comparative results, call 603-271-6333.

New Jersey

New Jersey Department of Education, 225 West State St., Trenton, NJ 08625; 609-292-7629. Services include computer searches, printouts and magnetic tapes upon individual request. There is no set fee for services, since it varies according to the scope of the request. The office's major publications include reports on *Vital Education Statistics,* and *Enrollment Projections.*

New Mexico

New Mexico Department of Education, Education Building, Santa Fe, NM 87501; 505-827-6524. This office provides computer searches and printouts, free of charge. Requests for computer information should be in writing. Teachers' names and school addresses released under certain circumstances. The office publishes the *New Mexico School District Profile.*

New York

New York Department of Education, Information Center on Education, Albany, NY 12234; 518-474-3852. This office provides computer searches, printouts and magnetic tapes. Requests should be in writing. Teachers names and addresses are not released. Publications include: *Projections of Public and Non-public School Enrollment and High School Graduates, Public School Professional Personnel Report, Non-public School Enrollment and Staff, Distribution of High School Graduates and College-Going Rate, Racial/Ethnic Distribution of Public School Students and Staff,* and *Education Statistics.*

North Carolina

Planning & Institutional Research, East Carolina University, 710 Spillman, Greenville, NC 37858-4353; 919-328-6288. This office provides computer searches and printouts. Fees vary, depending upon the complexity of the request. The office's publications include the *Annual Data Plan* and *Selected Financial Data Report.*

North Dakota

North Dakota Department of Public Instruction, Bismarck, ND 58505; 701-328-2268. This office provides computer searches, printouts and magnetic tapes. If the request involves a special computer program to be run, a minimum charge of $10 is required. Information requests can be given directly over the telephone. Teachers' names and school addresses are released. The office's publications include *Finance Facts* and a *Statewide Summary on Personnel.*

Education

Ohio

Ohio Department of Education, Computer Services, Division of Information Management, 2151 Karmack Rd., Columbus, OH 43211-3595; 614-466-7000. This office provides computer searches, printouts, disks, and magnetic tapes. There is a $75 minimum charge for services. Requests should be in writing. Publications include a *Salary Study Guide* and *Cost Per Pupil Report*.

Oklahoma

Oklahoma State Department of Education, Data Research Services, 2500 N. Lincoln Blvd., Oklahoma City, OK 73105; 405-521-3308. This office provides computer searches and printouts. The cost is $.05 per page, with a $10 minimum, plus shipping. The department will send you the material with an invoice in six to eight working days. Publications include an Educational Directory and Dropout Report. Nonprofit organizations can receive the information on diskette or magnetic tape for $15 per disk with a $50 minimum.

Oregon

Oregon Department of Education, Data Processing, 700 Pringle Parkway S.E., Salem, OR 97310; 503-378-3569. This office provides computer searches and printouts. If you send in your own formatted 3.5 diskette, they will transfer the information to it for you. Requests should be in writing and services are free. Publications include: *Oregon School District Census by ESD Lines, School District Budget Summary, Status of School District Tax Bases, Oregon School Districts - Organization, Location and Size,* and *Oregon Public and Private High School Graduates - Actual and Projected*.

Pennsylvania

Pennsylvania Department of Education, Office of Data Services, 333 Market St., Harrisburg, PA 17126; 717-787-2644. This office provides computer searches and printouts. In general, services are free, but a large request for a printout or mailing labels may require a fee. Requests should be in writing. They publish the *Status Report On Education In Pennsylvania* and numerous other reports.

Rhode Island

Rhode Island Department of Education, 22 Hayes St., Providence, RI 02908; 401-277-2841. This office provides computer searches and printouts on a limited basis. Although there is no charge for services at the present time, a fee scale is being developed. Requests should be in writing and take two weeks to fulfill. Their major publications include the *Annual Report on Statistical Tables* and the *Report on Education Indicators*.

South Carolina

South Carolina Department of Education, Rutledge, Management Information Section, Office of Research, Room 605, Rutledge Building, Columbia, SC 29201; 803-253-6464. This office provides computer searches and printouts. Special requests should be in writing. Fees vary for the use of computer time, and are dependent upon the complexity of the request. Their list of publications includes: *Pupils in South Carolina Schools, Supplemental Salary Study of Selected School, District, and County Personnel,* and an *Annual Salary Study*.

South Dakota

South Dakota Department of Education and Cultural Affairs, Richard F. Kneip Building, 700 Governors Dr., Pierre, SD 57501; 605-773-3134. This office provides computer searches and printouts. Special requests should be in writing. They also publish the *Educational Statistics Digest*.

Tennessee

Tennessee Department of Education, Office of Education Technology, Gateway Plaza Bldg., 7th Floor, Nashville, TN 32743-0381; 615-741-0728. This office does not normally provide computer searches but will provide you with a free copy of their *Annual Statistics Report* or *School Directory* for a fee. Call 615-741-3034.

Texas

Texas Department of Education, Division of Public Information, 1701 N. Congress, Austin, TX 78701-1494; 512-463-9000. This office provides computer searches, printouts and diskettes. Requests should be in writing. The charge is $10 per diskette, $16 per hour of programming and $.35 per second of computer time. Publications include *Public Education and You*.

Utah

Utah Board of Education, Department of Finance, 250 East 500 South, Salt Lake City, UT 84111; 801-538-7500. Printouts of information are provided free of charge. The department prefers requests to be in writing. Publications available include the *Annual Report*.

Vermont

Vermont Department of Education, Statistics and Information Unit State Office Building, 120 State St., Montpelier, VT 05602; 802-828-3151. This office provides information via printouts and diskettes. There is a $25 charge for diskettes unless the requestor is a non-profit organization. Requests should be in writing. They also publish an *Annual Statistical Report of Schools*.

Virginia

Virginia Department of Education, Division of Information Services, 101 N. 14th St., Richmond, VA 23219; 804-225-2949. The Division of Information Services provides computer searches and distributes information via printouts and booklets. Requests must be in writing. Diskette and magnetic tapes are available through special, written requests. Service fees vary according to the complexity of the request. The office publishes the *Superintendent's Annual Report* which summarizes student, faculty and finance information. The current publication, which is free, contains information based on the 1989-90 school year.

Washington

Washington Superintendent of Public Instruction, Old Capitol Building, FG-11, Olympia, WA 98504; 360-753-1700. Services: This office conducts computer searches and provides information via printouts, diskettes and computer tapes. There is a charge of $5 per diskette and $25 per tape. Special requests should be in writing. Publications include *Dropout and Graduation Statistics, Minority Enrollment Report,* and *Facts on Washington*.

West Virginia

West Virginia Department of Education, Department of Statistical Information, Capitol Complex, Charleston, WV 25305; 304-558-6300. This office provides computer searches and printouts. Although they do not normally provide information on diskette or magnetic tape, they can do so if you specify your required format. Requests for information can be made directly over the phone as well as in writing. The office does charge a fee if they write an individual computer program to handle a request. Most information is provided through free printout reports. The office publishes an *Annual Report*.

Wisconsin

Wisconsin Department of Public Instruction, 125 S. Webster, P.O. Box 7841, Madison, WI 53707; 608-266-3390. Printouts of information are provided free of charge. At present, diskettes and magnetic tapes are not available, but will be accessible at a later date. Specialized requests should be made in writing. Computer searches are run, if data exists. An *Annual Report* is published.

Wyoming

Wyoming Department of Education, Statistical Department, Hathaway Building, 2nd Floor, Cheyenne, WY 82002; 307-777-7673. This office provides computer searches and printouts free of charge. A written request for information is required. Publications include the *Statistical Report Series I-III*. At present, information is not provided on diskette or magnetic tape.

Be patient. If any phone number is incorrect, call (area code) 555-1212 and request the new listing.

Careers and Workplace
General Sources

* *See also Your Community: Money for Communities and Non-Profits Chapter*
* *See also Business and Industry Chapter*
* *See also Economics, Demographics, and Statistics Chapter*

Each month, several federal and state agencies collect, analyze, and publish data which reflect the current employment and unemployment situation around the country. This information often reveals changing profiles of the U.S. work force, future trends, and even the impact of technological innovations on the work force. Besides employment statistics, you'll also find information on such hot topics as child care, foreign labor trends, genetic testing, and literacy in the workplace.

* 800 Labor Publications
Office of Information and Public Affairs
U.S. Department of Labor
200 Constitution Ave., NW, Room S1032
Washington, DC 20210   202-219-7316
This office can provide you with a free catalog of publications of the U.S. Department of Labor. It contains over 800 title listings in 26 labor categories, and provides ordering information.

* Affirmative Action: Successful Strategies
Office of Federal Contract Compliance
U.S. Department of Labor
200 Constitution Ave., NW, Room 3310
Washington, DC 20210   202-219-9368
Opportunity 2000: Creative Affirmative Action Strategies for a Changing Workforce is a study which profiles the strategies that companies use to ease the conflict between work and family responsibilities and to recruit, develop, and retain minority and economically disadvantaged workers, disabled workers, older workers, and veterans. This publication is available for $5 from the Government Printing Office, SN #029-014-00242-9; 202-512-1800.

* American Workforce in the Year 2000
Superintendent of Documents
U.S. Government Printing Office   202-512-1800
Washington, DC 20402   Fax: 202-512-2250
Workforce 2000 is a U.S. Department of Labor funded study that looks into the workplace and workforce changes that will take place by the year 2000. The department is using this study to rethink their policies and programs in order to prepare the country for the changes ahead. The study looks at the forces shaping the American economy, scenarios for the year 2000, work and workers in the year 2000 and six challenges the country will face. This publication is available for $4.25, SN #029-014-00240-2.

* Caregiving for the Elderly
Women's Bureau
U.S. Department of Labor
200 Constitution Ave., NW, Room S3315   800-827-5335
Washington, DC 20210   202-219-6631
Caring for the dependent elderly will become a major issue for the 21st century labor force. The issue arises with the aging of the U.S. population and the restructuring of the American family as women, the traditional care-givers, move into the workforce in increasing numbers. The Women's Bureau can provide you with the factsheet *Eldercare: An Overview*, which discusses important issues related to eldercare in the next century.

* Caribbean Basin Employment and Trade
Office of International Economic Affairs
Bureau of International Labor Affairs
U.S. Department of Labor
200 Constitution Ave., NW, Room S5325

Washington, DC 20210   202-219-7610
The annual report, *Trade and Employment Effects of the Caribbean Basin Economic Recovery Act (CBERA)*, describes the provisions included in the CBERA, along with the benefits they provide to beneficiary countries. It also analyzes changes in U.S. trade with CBERA countries, and looks at trends in U.S. employment in those industries which have undergone the most significant changes in trade flows. Contact this office for more information on the report.

* Changing Workplace and Labor Force
Superintendent of Documents
Government Printing Office   202-512-1800
Washington, DC 20402   Fax: 202-512-2250
Many of the Bureau of Labor Statistics' major surveys and research studies are available in the BLS bulletin series, which include more than 100 area and industry wage studies each year and about 40 volumes dealing with a wide range of economic subjects. Here are examples of publications in this series.

New Worklife Estimates contains detailed working life tables and is widely used in liability litigations ($3.25).
Women at Work: A Chartbook focuses on women's economic activity: labor force trends; occupational and industrial employment patterns; and market work of women in a family context ($4).
Children of Working Mothers, part of the Special Labor Force Report series, discusses the increases in the number of children with working mothers and the two major reasons for this growth ($3).
Occupational Projections and Training Data serves as a statistical and research supplement to the *Occupational Outlook Handbook*. It provides detailed data on careers and projected occupational employment, replacement needs, and education and training program completions ($5.50).

* Child Care Survey and Trends
Information Office
U.S. Department of Labor
200 Constitution Ave., NW, Room S1032
Washington, DC 20210   202-219-6652
The free report, *Child Care: A Workforce Issue*, is a product of a U.S. Department of Labor internal task force on child care, and is the first step toward understanding child care as a workforce issue. It includes a survey of current activities on the government and private level, examines work-related trends and needs, and analyzes potential problems.

* Child Labor Laws
Special Employment Branch
Wage and Hour Division
Employment Standards Administration
200 Constitution Ave., NW, Room S3510
Washington, DC 20210   202-219-7640
The Fair Labor Standards Act protects young workers from employment that might interfere with their educational opportunities or be hazardous to their health or well-being. There are different standards for work allowed, depending upon the age of the child. Contact the Child Labor Programs office for more information.

Careers and Workplace

* Civil Service Employment

Superintendent of Documents
Government Printing Office   202-512-1800
Washington, DC 20402   Fax: 202-512-2250

The 1988 book *Civil Service 2000* outlines the expected demographic changes in the Federal workforce and the changes in skills that the Government will need between now and the year 2000. It includes an appendix which discusses Federal child care programs and policies. Cost - $2.50, SN #006-000-01337-6.

* Commission on Achieving Necessary Skills

Employment and Training Administration (ETA)
U.S. Department of Labor
200 Constitution Ave, NW, Room N4700
Washington, DC 20210   202-219-6871

The Secretary's Commission on Achieving Necessary Skills has released its first report, which outlines the skills and skill levels necessary for entry level work in today's economy. For information on the report, contact the ETA.

* Commissions on Women

Women's Bureau
U.S. Department of Labor
200 Constitution Ave., NW, Room S3315
Washington, DC 20210   202-219-6631

This Bureau provides funds and other assistance to support regional conferences of women's commissions and the annual convention of The National Association of Commissions for Women, an umbrella organization. The women's commission movement continues to grow, and now 247 state, regional, and local commissions for women are reported.

* Compensation and Working Conditions

Superintendent of Documents
Government Printing Office   202-512-1800
Washington, DC 20402   Fax: 202-512-2250

Each monthly issue of *Compensation and Working Conditions* includes selected wage and benefit changes, work stoppages, major agreements that expire during the next month, calendar of features, and statistics on compensation changes. The cost is $23 per year, SN #729-003-00000-0. For more information on this data, contact Office of Compensation and Working Conditions, Bureau of Labor Statistics, U.S. Department of Labor, 441 G St., NW, Room 2021, Washington, DC 20212; 202-606-6275.

* Competitiveness in the Workplace

National Technical Information Service (NTIS)
U.S. Department of Commerce   800-553-6847
5285 Port Royal Rd.   703-487-4650
Springfield, VA 22161   Fax: 703-321-8547

The Office of Technology Assessment has numerous reports on issues related to competitiveness, employment, and training. The following is a list of reports completed in the last several years.

Performance Standards for the Food Stamp Employment and Training Program, PB92-157932
The Use of Integrity Tests for pre-employment screening. PB91-107011
Worker Training: Competing in the new international economy. PB91-106716 1990.
Technology and structural unemployment: reemploying displaced adults. PB86-206174
Plant Closing: advance notice and rapid response.PB87-118212
Displaced homemakers: programs and policy. PB86-120276
Demographic trends and the scientific and engineering workforce. PB86-206182
Automation and the workplace: selected labor, education, and training issues. PB83-191320.

* Consumer Price Index and Labor Data on Computer Diskette

Division of Information Services
Bureau of Labor Statistics
U.S. Department of Labor
Postal Square Bldg.
2 Massachusetts Ave., NE, Room 2860
Washington, DC 20212   202-606-5886

Computer diskettes offer an easy-to-use way to manipulate data for economists, other social scientists, researchers, managers, and policymakers with an interest in measuring employment, prices, productivity, injuries and illnesses, and wages. BLS diskette users need an IBM-compatible microcomputer and Lotus 1-2-3 Version 1A or Version 2. Each diskette contains the named data series and a brief technical description that highlights regular revisions, if any, and typical uses for statistics. A flyer is available which describes the diskettes available and their cost.

* Current Employment Analyses

Office of Employment and Unemployment Statistics
Bureau of Labor Statistics
U.S. Department of Labor
Postal Square Bldg.
2 Massachusetts Ave., NE
Washington, DC 20212   202-606-6378

Labor force statistics from the *Current Population Survey* provide a comprehensive body of information on the employment and unemployment experience of the nation's population, classified by age, sex, race, and a variety of other characteristics. The data is published in a variety of sources, including the monthly news release, *The Employment Situation*, and the monthly periodical, *Employment and Earnings*. Data uses include economic indicators, measure of potential labor supply, and evaluation of wage rates and earnings trends for specific demographic groups.

* Employer Resource Kit on Employees' Family Needs

Work and Family Clearinghouse
Women's Bureau
U.S. Department of Labor
200 Constitution Ave., NW, Room S3306
Washington, DC 20210   800-827-5335

The *Work and Family Resource Kit* is designed to help employers understand the range of family needs emerging in the workplace and the numerous ways a company can respond. It provides a state-of-the-art review of these options as well as advantages and disadvantages. Also listed are references and resources to help employers select the most appropriate response for their employees' family needs. Two recent publications included in the Resource Kit are *Women Workers: Outlook to 2005* and *Women With Work Disabilities*.

* Employment and Earnings: Monthly Publication

Editors
Bureau of Labor Statistics
U.S. Department of Labor
Postal Square Bldg.
2 Massachusetts Ave., NE
Washington, DC 20212   202-606-6373

Employment and Earnings is a monthly publication prepared by the Office of Employment and Unemployment Statistics, with data collected by the Bureau of the Census and state employment security agencies. Detailed information is given according to employment status and characteristics of the employed and unemployed. The data are also categorized into employment setting, hours and earnings, and state and labor force data. Subscriptions can be ordered for $31 per year (SN #729-004-00000-6) by contacting: Superintendent of Documents, Government Printing Office, Washington, DC 20402; 202-512-1800.

* Employment and Training Administration Projects and Publications

Office of Worker Retraining and Adjustment Programs
Employment and Training Administration (ETA)
U.S. Department of Labor
200 Constitution Ave., NW, Room N4469
Washington, DC 20210   202-219-5577

The Employment and Training Administration (ETA) has recently completed several studies related to employment issues and worker training. In addition, it has also initiated several new studies. The publication *America and the New Economy* discusses a wide range of evolving forces that will affect industries, workers, and their occupations and the standing of the U.S. in world markets. ETA has also completed several studies of displaced workers and the implementation of assistance to them through the Economic Dislocation and Worker Adjustment Assistance Act. *America and the New Economy* may be purchased for $30 from the American Society for Training and Development, 1640 King St. Box 1443, Alexandria, VA 22313-2043; 703-683-8129. Contact ETA for other publications available.

* Employment and Unemployment: Monthly Data and Estimates

Office of Employment and Unemployment Statistics
Bureau of Labor Statistics
Postal Square Bldg.
2 Massachusetts Ave., NE, Room 4675
Washington, DC 20212   202-606-6378

This office collects, analyzes, and publishes detailed industry data on employment, wages, hours, and earnings of workers on payrolls of non-agricultural business establishments. It also publishes monthly estimates of state and local area unemployment for use by federal agencies in allocating funds as required by various federal laws. In addition, the office provides current data on occupational employment for most industries for economic analysis and for vocational guidance and education planning.

* Employment Projections: 650 Occupations and 300 Industries

Office of Economic Growth and Employment Projections
U.S. Department of Labor
Postal Square Bldg.
2 Massachusetts Ave., NE, Room 2135
Washington, DC 20212   202-606-5720

This office produces national occupational employment projections for over 650 detailed occupations for all industries combined and within over 300 detailed industries.

* Employment Research and Evaluation Studies

Office of the Assistant Secretary of Policy
U.S. Department of Labor
200 Constitution Ave., NW, Room S2006
Washington, DC 20210   202-219-6181

A free listing is available of all the employment research and evaluation projects completed since 1980 by the U.S. Department of Labor, along with information on how to obtain copies of the reports. The inventory is broken down into the following major topic areas and the reports are listed chronologically: Discrimination/Minorities; Drug Abuse and AIDS Issues in the Workplace; Labor Market Issues and Studies (includes mobility, minimum wage, and farmworker shortage); Labor Market Theory; Miscellaneous and Cross-Program Studies; Occupational Disease; Occupational Safety and Health; Pensions; Public Employment; Quality of Work Life (includes productivity, job satisfaction); Training; Unemployment (includes unemployment insurance); Unions/Labor Relations; Youth; and Price Schedule.

* Employment Statistics for 800 Occupations and 400 Industries

Office of Employment and Unemployment
Bureau of Labor Statistics
U.S. Department of Labor
Postal Square Bldg.
2 Massachusetts Ave., NE
Washington, DC 20212   202-606-6515

Available occupational employment statistics include data on employment by occupation and industry for about 800 occupations and 400 industries. Published in bulletins, such as *Occupational Employment* in (industries), data are used for evaluation of current and historical employment by industry and occupation and vocational planning.

* Foreign Economic Impact on U.S. Employment

Office of International Economic Affairs
Bureau of International Labor Affairs
200 Constitution Ave., NW
Room S5325
Washington, DC 20210   202-219-7610

The Labor Department's foreign economic research program evaluates the effects of foreign economic developments on the earnings and employment of U.S. workers. This includes quantitative analysis of the impact of policies on international trade, investment, and technology transfer. Often undertaken in response to congressionally-mandated studies or to requests from other executive branch agencies, research is conducted by staff economists and supplemented by outside research contractors. A complete list of the research is available by contacting this office.

* Foreign Labor Trends

Office of Foreign Relations
Bureau of International Labor Affairs
U.S. Department of Labor
200 Constitution Ave., NW, Room S5006
Washington, DC 20210   202-219-6257

The U.S. Department of State has 47 labor foreign service attaches placed in embassies all over the world. They monitor and report foreign labor developments, as well as educate other countries on U.S. labor developments. They submit annual reports, including an additional 70 embassy reports, to the U.S. Department of Labor, which then publishes the *Foreign Labor Trends Series*. Available through Superintendent of Documents, Government Printing Office, Washington DC 20402; 202-512-1800; cost $36 per year. Country labor profiles for some 55 nations are also available.

* Foreign Visitor Program

Jim Fowler
International Affairs
Federal Mediation and Conciliation Service (FMCS)
2100 K St., NW
Washington, DC 20427   202-606-9143

Representatives of labor, management, and governments from around the world can see how arbitration, mediation, collective bargaining, and employee involvement programs function in the U.S. by participation in this visitor program. Industrial labor relations are targeted. For more information, contact the International Affairs office listed.

* Future Jobs in Over 200 Industries

Office of Economic Growth
Bureau of Labor Statistics
U.S. Department of Labor
601 D St., NW, Room 4000
Washington, DC 20212   202-606-5700

This program provides a framework for studying the factors affecting long-range economic growth and employment by industry and occupation. Information available includes: projections of gross domestic product (GDP), demand and income composition of GDP, and aggregate components of demand specified by 228 industry groups under alternative assumptions for basic economic variables (labor force, unemployment, productivity, etc.) and government economic policies; industry projections, including final demand (consumers, government, business investment, exports, imports), output, and employment; projected input-output data including interindustry employment data. This information can be found in articles in *Monthly Labor Review* and is also available on tape or diskette.

* Government Contractors Employment Standards

Office of Federal Contract Compliance Program
Employment Standards Administration
U.S. Department of Labor
200 Constitution Ave., NW
Room C3325
Washington, DC 20210   202-219-9475

This office ensures that federal contractors and subcontractors or contractors with federally-assisted construction contracts do not discriminate against any employee or applicant for employment because of race, color, religion, or national origin, and that these contractors take affirmative action to hire and promote qualified handicapped people, Vietnam-era veterans, and disabled veterans of all wars. This office also investigates complaints to determine whether federal contractors are meeting these obligations.

* Government Labor Statistics Programs

Division of Information Services
Bureau of Labor Statistics
U.S. Department of Labor
Postal Square Bldg.
2 Massachusetts Ave., NE, Room 2860
Washington, DC 20212   202-606-5886

The free publication, *Major Programs of the Bureau of Labor Statistics*, presents in concentrated form the scope of the Bureau's major statistical programs, the data available, the form of publication, some of the uses of the data, and selected publications and data tapes.

Careers and Workplace

* Handicapped Persons Affirmative Action

Office of Federal Compliance Programs
Employment Standards Administration
U.S. Department of Labor
200 Constitution Ave., NW, Room C3325
Washington, DC 20210   202-219-9384

The Rehabilitation Act of 1973 prohibits most employers doing business with the federal government from discriminating in employment against handicapped persons. Employers with contracts in excess of $2,500 must take affirmative action to hire and promote qualified handicapped persons.

* History of Labor in the U.S.

Departmental Historian
U.S. Department of Labor
200 Constitution Ave., NW, Room N2445
Washington, DC 20210   202-501-6438

The Labor Department Historian can answer any historical inquiries regarding the Department. Questions usually come from Congressional offices, newspapers, and students. As well as conducting his own research on various aspects of Department history, the historian also assists those researching the Department of Labor.

* Home-Based Manufacturing Operations

Wage and Hour Division
Employment Standards Administration
U.S. Department of Labor
200 Constitution Ave., NW, Room S3516
Washington, DC 20210   202-219-8743

Home-based industry work has always been permitted except in seven industries: knitted outerwear, women's apparel, jewelry manufacturing, gloves and mittens, button and buckle manufacturing, handkerchief manufacturing, and embroidery. In 1984, the U.S. Labor Department lifted the total ban on home work in knitted outerwear, and is now considering a proposal to lift the ban on all industries except women's apparel and those jewelry manufacturing operations in the home that may be hazardous. Contact this office for more information on homework and FLSA enforcement.

* Hours and Earnings Monthly Survey

Office of Employment and Unemployment Statistics
Bureau of Labor Statistics
U.S. Department of Labor
Postal Square Bldg.
2 Massachusetts Ave., NE
Washington, DC 20212   202-606-6555

A monthly survey provides hours and earnings data collected from payroll records of business establishments. The data available includes gross hours and earnings of production or nonsupervisory workers in 454 industries, and overtime hours in 323 manufacturing industries. The data are published in a variety of sources, and are used as economic indicators, wage negotiations, and economic research and planning.

* Industry and Employment Projections

Office of Economic Growth and Employment Projections
Bureau of Labor Statistics
U.S. Department of Labor
Postal Square Bldg.
2 Massachusetts Ave., NE, Room 2135
Washington, DC 20212   202-606-5720

State and area employment data classified by industry division, and gross weekly hours and earnings for production and related workers in manufacturing is available, as is other data, including demographic employment/unemployment, monthly labor force and unemployment, occupational employment, and area wage surveys.

* Industry-Occupation Employment Matrix

Office of Economic Growth and Employment Projections
Bureau of Labor Statistics
U.S. Department of Labor
Postal Square Bldg.
2 Massachusetts Ave., NE
Washington, DC 20212   202-606-5730

The National Industry-Occupation Employment Matrix provides detailed information on the distribution of occupational employment by industry. Coverage is for over 650 detailed occupations--wage and salary, self-employed, and unpaid family workers, and wage and salary workers only for over 300 detailed industries.

* Industry Technological Trends

Industry Productivity Studies Division
Office of Productivity and Technology
U.S. Department of Labor
200 Constitution Ave., NW, Room S4320
Washington, DC 20210   202-606-5624

This office looks at a variety of technological trends. One study analyzes major impending changes in products, materials, and production methods in selected industries; their present and future applications; and their effect on output, productivity, employment, skill levels, training, and occupational requirements. Another study analyzes technological changes that have major effects on more than one industry. Coverage includes selected innovations such as computers and numerical control of machine tools, with an emphasis on innovations that will be important in the next five to 10 years.

* International Labor Affairs

International Labor Organization
Bureau of International Organization Affairs
U.S. Department of State
2201 C St., NW, Room 5336
Washington, DC 20520   202-647-4196

As a United Nations affiliate, the International Labor Organization (ILO) is comprised of three parts: government, worker, and employee delegations from 150 countries. Headquartered in Geneva, the ILO meets three times a year and holds an annual conference. The ILO serves as a multilateral technical assistance agency designed to promote free labor in a free market system, along with investigating international human rights complaints. They also take a major role in workers rights, such as the right to bargain collectively, and protection from discrimination.

* Job Counseling and Placement Fraud

Federal Trade Commission (FTC)
Bureau of Consumer and Business Education
6th and Pennsylvania Ave., NW, Room H-403
Washington, DC 20580   202-326-3650

The FTC often receives complaint letters about job counseling and placement services which charge large fees and misrepresent their services. The FTC publishes an Alert Sheet entitled *Job Ads, Job Scams, and "900" Numbers*. Other information is available in the FTC brochures *Job Hunting: Should You Pay* and *"900" Numbers*. For information on how to select a legitimate employment service or to complain about one which you feel has misrepresented itself, contact your local FTC office.

* Job Corps Statistics

Office of Job Corps
Employment and Training Administration
U.S. Department of Labor
200 Constitution Ave., NW   800-733-JOBS
Washington, DC 20001   202-219-8550

Job Corps statistics are available, including cost statistics, enrollee demographics, and enrollee outcomes. Contact this office for further information.

* Job Search Booklet

Employment and Training Administration
U.S. Department of Labor
200 Constitution Ave, NW, Room N4700
Washington, DC 20210   202-219-6871

The Education and Training Administration publishes a booklet entitled *Tips for Finding the Right Job*. This booklet contains information on all aspects of the job search including resume writing, interviewing, test taking, cover letters, post interview follow up, and time management. It is available free.

* Job Training for the Homeless

Employment and Training Administration
U.S. Department of Labor
200 Constitution Ave., NW, Room N5637
Washington, DC 20210   202-219-7674

This program is authorized by the Stewart B. McKinney Homeless Assistance Act and has the objective of providing training, support and housing programs to increase the employment opportunities, job retention, and the attainment of permanent housing for homeless persons.

* Labor Force: A National Profile

Office of Employment and Unemployment Statistics
Bureau of Labor Statistics
U.S. Department of Labor
Postal Square Bldg.
2 Massachusetts Ave., NE
Washington, DC 20212   202-606-6378

The labor force statistics available include employment status of the U.S. population 16 years and over by age, sex, race, hispanic ethnicity, martial status, family relationships, Vietnam-era Vietnam status, educational attainment, school enrollment, and residence in metropolitan/nonmetropolitan areas and poverty/nonpoverty areas. Also included is information concerning employed and unemployed persons by occupation, industry, and class of worker, as well as characteristics, work history, and job seeking intentions of persons not in the labor force. Special topics, such as the labor force status of particular groups of the population, occupational mobility and work experience, are also available.

* Labor Force Population Trends

Office of Employment and Unemployment Statistics
Bureau of Labor Statistics
U.S. Department of Labor
Postal Square Bldg.
2 Massachusetts Ave., NE
Washington, DC 20212   202-606-6378

This office analyzes and publishes data from the *Current Population Survey (CPS)* on the labor force, employment, unemployment, as well as on persons not in the labor force. Studies based on the CPS data cover a broad range of topics, including annual analyses of labor market developments, occupational analyses, characteristics of special worker groups (such as minorities and women maintaining families), and employment-related economic hardship.

* Labor Statistics Availability

Division of Information Services
Bureau of Labor Statistics
U.S. Department of Labor
Postal Square Bldg.
2 Massachusetts Ave., NE
Washington, DC 20212   202-606-7828

The Bureau of Labor Statistics can provide you with a tentative release schedule for BLS major economic indicators. The schedule lists the information available (i.e., employment situation, consumer price index, productivity and costs, etc.), as well as the date and time of the information release. The *BLS Update* also contains the release dates for the quarter.

* Labor Statistics Catalog

Office of Publications
Bureau of Labor Statistics
U.S. Department of Labor
Postal Square Bldg.
2 Massachusetts Ave., NE
Washington, DC 20212   202-606-7828

The free quarterly publication, *BLS Update*, contains a complete list of new BLS publications, including a brief description and ordering information. Also included are BLS summaries, data services, telephone numbers for recorded summaries of BLS data, as well as general information concerning BLS.

* Labor Statistics Monthly Review

Superintendent of Documents
Government Printing Office   202-512-1800
Washington, DC 20402   Fax: 202-512-2250

Each issue of the *Monthly Labor Review* includes analytical articles, 47 pages of current statistics, reports on industrial relations, book reviews, and other features for a cost of $25 per year, SN #729-007-00000-5.

* Labor Surplus Areas and Government Contracts

Superintendent of Documents
Government Printing Office   202-512-1800
Washington, DC 20402   Fax: 202-512-2250

Area Trends in Employment and Unemployment is a list of labor surplus areas, which are designated as such by the U.S. Department of Labor. This list is used to give priority in awarding government contracts. Once an area has been placed on the list,

it remains there for one year. This monthly publication is available for $41 per year, SN #729-001-00000-7. For more information on the labor surplus issues, contact: Employment Service, Employment and Training Administration, U.S. Department of Labor, 200 Constitution Ave., NW, Room N4456, Washington, DC 20210; 202-535-0189.

* Library on Labor Movement and Occupational Evolution

U.S. Department of Labor
200 Constitution Ave., NW, Room N2445
Washington, DC 20210   202-219-6992

This library has a wealth of historical labor material, as well as collections of state labor department reports, documents, and trade union journals. The library is open to the public and staffed by reference librarians, who will assist you in locating materials. The library is open 8:15-4:45 Monday through Friday. Appointments are not necessary. The library also participates in the Inter-Library Loan system.

* Local Area Employment and Unemployment

Office of Employment and Unemployment Statistics
Bureau of Labor Statistics
U.S. Department of Labor
Postal Square Bldg.
2 Massachusetts Ave., NE
Washington, DC 20212   202-606-6392

This office provides laborforce, employment, and unemployment data estimated by state employment security agencies. These data are used primarily to allocate federal funds to local jurisdiction. The coverage includes annual average data with demographic detail for 50 states, the District of Columbia, 50 large metropolitan areas, and 17 of their central cities, and monthly data to include 50 states, 330 areas, 3,100 counties, and 1200 cities of 25,000 or more. The data are published in a variety of sources, including the annual bulletin, *Geographic Profile of Employment and Unemployment*, and the monthly periodical, *Employment and Earnings*. This data is also available on tape and diskette.

* Longitudinal Employment Surveys

Office of Economic Research
Bureau of Labor Statistics
U.S. Department of Labor
Postal Square Bldg.
2 Massachusetts Ave., NE
Washington, DC 20212   202-606-7386

Every couple of years, this office updates *The National Longitudinal Surveys*, which study employment profiles of certain age groups . The groups include: young women who were 14-24 in 1968; mature women who were 30-44 in 1967; and youth who were 14-21 in 1979. Information available includes labor market activities, characteristics of jobs, earnings, unemployment, social and demographic characteristics, education, and training.

* Minimum Wage and Overtime Pay Standards

Office of Information and Consumer Affairs
Employment Standards Administration
U.S. Department of Labor
200 Constitution Ave., NW, Room S3325
Washington, DC 20210   202-219-8743

The Fair Labor Standards Act establishes minimum wages, overtime pay, recordkeeping, and child labor standards which affect some 73 million employees. It requires employers to pay at least the federally-standardized minimum wage per hour to all covered and nonexempt employees, and to pay one and one-half times their regular pay for all hours worked over 40 in the work week.

* Minimum Wage Exemptions

Special Employment Branch
Wage and Hour Division
Employment Standards Administration
U.S. Department of Labor
200 Constitution Ave., NW, Room S3510
Washington, DC 20210   202-219-7640

This office issues certificates allowing employers to pay subminimum wages to full-time students, trainees, and handicapped workers. Contact this office for more information regarding these certificates.

Careers and Workplace

* Multifactor Productivity Trends

Industry Productivity Studies Division
Office of Productivity and Technology
U.S. Department of Labor
200 Constitution Ave., NW, Room S4320
Washington, DC 20210   202-606-5624

This program develops indexes of multifactor productivity-output per unit of combined labor and capital inputs-for major sectors of the economy and for manufacturing industries at the 2-digit Standard Industrial Classification level. Indexes are published in the publication *Multifactor Productivity Indexes for Private Business, Private Nonfarm Business, and Manufacturing Sectors.*

* Necessary Job Skills in Today's and Tomorrow's Labor Force

Superintendent of Documents
U.S. Government Printing Office (GPO)   202-512-1800
Washington, DC 20402   Fax: 202-512-2250

Building A Quality Workforce suggests that businesses and schools need to work together to help entry level workers be better prepared for employment. It states that the basic skills gap between what business needs and the qualifications of the entry level workers available to business is widening. Also discussed are community partnerships that have worked in Prince Georges County, Maryland, Cincinnati, Ohio, and Portland, Oregon. The cost is $4.50, SN #029-000-00425-1 (1988, 85 pgs).

* Occupational and Economic Outlook Projections

Office of Economic Growth
Bureau of Labor Statistics
U.S. Department of Labor
601 D St., NW, Room 4000
Washington, DC 20212   202-606-5702

The BLS publication *Outlook: 1993 - 2005* contains projections for the following occupational and economic categories: Gross National Product; Labor Force Growth; Industry Employment; Occupational Employment; and other issues. The Bureau has detailed employment projections for more than 500 occupations.

* Occupational Outlook Handbook, 1994-95

Superintendent of Documents
Government Printing Office   202-512-1800
Washington, DC 20402   Fax: 202-512-2250

This set of 20 individual booklets includes all categories of occupations listed in the *Occupational Outlook Handbook.* Each booklet covers a specific occupational field or area. These reprints are especially useful for jobseekers who want to know about a single field or counselors who need to make the contents of a single book accessible to many jobseekers. Cost - $24 per set, SN #029-001-03159-9.

* Occupational Titles and Classifications Dictionary

Superintendent of Documents
Government Printing Office   202-512-1800
Washington, DC 20402   Fax: 202-512-2250

A compendium of approximately 12,000 occupations, the *Dictionary of Occupational Titles,* 4th Edition defines each occupation and provides a classification structure that groups them in terms of related duties and activities. It also includes sections on the purpose of the dictionary and how to use the data bank for job placement. All occupational titles are arranged alphabetically and by industry for easy reference. The cost is $40, SN #029-013-00094-2.

* On-site Child Care

Women's Bureau
U.S. Department of Labor
200 Constitution Ave., NW
Room S3309
Washington, DC 20210   202-219-6652

The free publication, *Employers and Child Care: Benefiting Work and Family,* is designed for employers and employees concerned with developing programs and policies to assist in quality and cost-efficient child care programs while parents are at work. Created to help in a vast array of situations, it provides guidance to those who wish to improve employee productivity and business' ability to recruit and retain the best workers. It is designed for people who are concerned about fulfilling two essential and often conflicting responsibilities--working and caring for their families. The Women's Bureau can also provide you with the fact-sheet entitled

Child Care: An Overview, which can provide you with more general information on issues related to child care and the workplace.

* Pension Benefit Guaranty Corporation

Public Affairs
Pension Benefit Guaranty Corporation (PBGC)
1200 K St., NW, Room 930
Washington, DC 20005-4026   202-326-4000

The PBGC works to ensure the solvency and viability of company sponsored pension plans. It directly pays the benefits of some 142,000 retirees from terminated pension plans. The corporation is financed from premiums charged to companies that sponsor insured pension plans. The PBGC also works to ensure that underfunded programs are brought up to full funding within a reasonable time period. For more information, contact the PBGC.

* Plant Closings Notifications

Notification (WARN)
Office of Employment and Training Programs
Employment and Training Administration
U.S. Department of Labor
200 Constitution Ave., NW, Room N4669
Washington, DC 20210   202-219-5577

WARN requires that employers with 100 or more employees provide 60 days advance notice of a plant closing or mass layoff. A plant closing is a permanent or temporary shutdown of a single site of employment or one or more facilities or operating unit within a single site or employment, resulting in an employment loss at the site during any 30-day period for 50 or more employees. A mass layoff is a reduction in force at a single site during any 30 day period which results in the employment loss of at least 1/3 of the employees and at least 50 employees or at least 500 employees.

* Productivity and Technology Statistics

Office of Productivity and Technology Studies
Bureau of Labor Statistics
U.S. Department of Labor
Postal Square Bldg.
2 Massachusetts Ave., NE
Washington, DC 20210   202-606-5624

This office is responsible for three major research programs. The productivity program compiles and analyzes productivity and related statistics on the U.S. business economy and its major sectors, and on individual industries and government. The technological studies program investigates trends in technology and their impact on employment and productivity. And the international labor statistics program compiles and analyzes data on productivity and related factors in foreign countries for comparison with the U.S. experience. The free directory, *BLS Publications on Productivity and Technology,* lists all the publications of each program.

* Self Employment Demonstration Projects

Employment and Training Administration (ETA)
U.S. Department of Labor
200 Constitution Ave., NW, Room S2431
Washington, DC 20210   202-219-4620

The U.S. Department of Labor has been exploring the viability of self-employment for people receiving unemployment insurance. In two demonstration projects the Department provided eligible UI claimants interested in self-employment with a package of assistance designed to help them start their own businesses. Call ETA for more information on and results from this project.

* Trade-Related Employment Issues

Bureau of International Labor Affairs
U.S. Department of Labor
200 Constitution Ave., NW, Room S2235
Washington, DC 20210   202-219-6043

The Bureau of International Labor Affairs represents the U.S. Department of Labor in the development of international economic and trade policies that affect the welfare of U.S. workers. This role includes conducting research on trade-related employment issues, coordinating advice received from Labor Advisory Committees on Trade authorized by the Trade Agreements Act of 1979, and acting as a liaison between other federal departments, agencies, and organized labor. The Bureau is also a member of various interagency committees charged with trade policy functions, and continues to participate in the formulation of U.S. immigration policy.

* Trade Adjustment Assistance

Employment and Training Administration (ETA)
Office of Trade Adjustment Assistance
U.S. Department of Labor
200 Constitution Ave, NW, Room C-4318
Washington, DC 20210   202-219-4756

Trade Adjustment Assistance is available to workers who lose their jobs or whose hours and wages are reduced as a result of increased imports. Workers may be eligible for training, a job search allowance, a relocation allowance, and other reemployment services. Weekly trade readjustment allowances may be payable to workers following their exhaustion of unemployment benefits. Information on the program is available from the U.S. Department of Labor in Washington or at any of the 10 ETA regional offices around the country, or your state employment security agency.

* Unemployment Insurance for Lost Wages

Office of Occupational and Administrative Standards
Bureau of Labor Statistics (BLS)
U.S. Department of Labor
Postal Square Bldg.
2 Massachusetts Ave., NE
Washington, DC 20212   202-606-6515

Insured Employment and Wages data are collected quarterly by state employment security agencies in cooperation with BLS. The data available include monthly employment, total quarterly wages, taxable wages, employer contributions, and reporting units, by industry, county, and state, for workers covered by state unemployment insurance laws and by the Unemployment Compensation for Federal Employees program.

* Union Membership Database

Bureau of Labor Statistics
U.S. Department of Labor
Postal Square Bldg.
2 Massachusetts Ave., NE
Washington, DC 20212   202-606-6304

The BLS maintains a database of union contracts searchable by company name and dating back one year. This program provides annual data on wage and salary workers who are union members, who are represented by a union whether or not they are members, and who are not represented by a union. Data available includes number of workers and usual median weekly earnings by industry division, occupations, and related demographic characterizations. Publications available include the *Annual News Release Union Members*.

* Veterans and Federal Contracts

Veterans Employment and Training
U.S. Department of Labor
200 Constitution Ave., NW, Room S1316   800-442-2VET
Washington, DC 20210   202-219-9110

Federal government contractors and subcontractors (with government contracts of $10,000 or more) are required by law to take affirmative action to employ and to advance in employment qualified special disabled and Vietnam-era Veterans. All suitable employment openings must be given to the nearest local State Employment Office. A Veterans Employment and Training Representative is located in each office to provide employment advice and assistance to veterans. Contact the Office of Federal Contract Compliance Programs if it appears that a contractor has failed to comply. Complaints can be made to: Office of Federal Contract Compliance Programs, U.S. Department of Labor, 200 Constitution Ave., NW, Room C3325, Washington, DC 20210; 202-219-9475.

* Veterans Employment Program

Assistant Secretary for Veterans
Employment and Training
U.S. Department of Labor
200 Constitution Ave., NW, Room S1316   800-442-2VET
Washington, DC 20210   202-219-9110

Employment-related services designed to aid veterans include counseling, testing, and skills training; unemployment compensation for newly separated ex-service members while they look for civilian employment; tax credits for private employers who hire certain target groups of veterans; placement in private and public sector jobs; and reemployment rights assistance. For more information, contact the Veterans' Employment and Training Office.

* Wage and Hour Investigations

Employment Standards Administration
U.S. Department of Labor
200 Constitution Ave., NW, Room S3028
Washington, DC 20210   202-219-8353

This division administers the Fair Labor Standards Act, which includes minimum wage, overtime pay, and child labor provisions. Its responsibilities also have grown to include other laws and regulations which protect worker's wages and working conditions. Wage and Hour Division compliance officers across the country conduct investigations of employers covered by the various laws which the division administers, to determine whether workers are being paid in compliance with the laws. They are also responsible for investigating complaints filed by employees who allege that their employers discriminated against them for actions they took to further the purposes of various environmental protection laws, and for improving conditions for migrant farm workers.

* Wage and Industrial Relations Information

Office of Compensation and Working Conditions
Bureau of Labor Statistics
U.S. Department of Labor
Postal Square Bldg.
2 Massachusetts Ave., NE
Washington, DC 20210   202-606-6220

The Bureau of Labor Statistics conducts three major types of occupational wage surveys: 1) area surveys, 2) industry surveys, and 3) a national white-collar salary survey. Non-wage compensation is covered in a comprehensive survey of the incidence and characteristics of employee benefit plans. They also develop measures of trends in employee compensation. The office's program of studies in labor-management relations includes analyses of wage and benefit changes in major collective bargaining agreements, statistics on work stop pages, and reports on pending labor-management negotiations in major bargaining units.

* Wage and Price Indexes on Computer Tape and Diskette

Bureau of Labor Statistics (BLS)
U.S. Department of Labor
Postal Square Bldg.
2 Massachusetts Ave., NE
Washington, DC 20212   202-606-5888

The Bureau of Labor Statistics (BLS) major data series are available on magnetic tape. The standard format is 9-track, 6250 BPI. In addition to the data files listed, BLS makes some microdata tapes and also prepares customized data files on a cost-for-service basis. Available data files include consumer expenditures, consumer price index, export-import price indexes, and labor force, as well as many others. Brochures are available which describe the tapes or diskettes, ordering information, and the cost of each tape.

* Wage Surveys: Area, Industry and White Collar Earnings

Office of Compensation and Working Conditions
Bureau of Labor Statistics
U.S. Department of Labor
Postal Square Bldg.
2 Massachusetts Ave., NE
Washington, DC 20210   202-606-6220

This office conducts three different types of wage surveys. The area and industry surveys provide annual data on averages and distributions of earnings for selected occupations in major industry groups in metropolitan areas. The white-collar salary survey is the annual *Professional, Administrative, Technical, and Clerical Survey* which is used in the Federal pay-setting process and provides data on salaries in white-collar occupations from a national sample of establishments.

* White-Collar Salaries

Benefit Levels Division
Office of Compensation Levels and Trends
Bureau of Labor Statistics
U.S. Department of Labor
Washington, DC 20210   202-606-6225

The annual white-collar salary survey provides data on salaries in white-collar occupations from a national sample of establishments. The data available includes averages and distributions of salary rates for about 50 blue collar and 100

Careers and Workplace

professional, administrative, technical, and clerical work levels. The results are published in the annual news release, *White-Collar Salaries*, and the annual bulletin, *National Survey of Occupational Pay*.

* Women and Office Automation

Women's Bureau
U.S. Department of Labor
200 Constitution Ave., NW, Room S3309
Washington, DC 20210   202-219-6652

The impact of automation on the quality of worklife as well as on the economic well-being of clerical workers and their families is a matter of priority for the Women's Bureau. The free publication, *Women and Office Automation: Issues for the Decade Ahead*, discusses the quality of work, training and retraining, home-based clerical work, and health and safety issues.

* Women in the Workforce Clearinghouse

Women's Bureau
U.S. Department of Labor
200 Constitution Ave., NW, Room S3315   800-827-5335
Washington, DC 20210   202-219-6665

The Women's Bureau offers a free listing of publications they have available. They have eighteen fact sheets on women workers, as well as information on women in technology, careers/job options, child care, and standards and legislation affecting women. The Bureau has a variety of program models available dealing with employment of women and several conference models. Currently, the staff is focusing on identifying the characteristics of cities presently experiencing labor shortages and other economic stresses expected to be more widespread by the year 2000, the impact of trade competition on women's jobs, child care for women workers, and many other women's issues. *There's No Such Thing As Women's Work* is a video which reviews the history of women in the workforce and provides information about meeting present day work and family challenges.

* Women Worker Data

Office of Publications
Bureau of Labor Statistics
U.S. Department of Labor
441 G St., NW, Room 2421
Washington, DC 20212   202-606-7828

This office publishes a wide array of information about women in the labor force. This information is presented to the public through a variety of publications, including news releases, periodicals, bulletins, reports, tapes, and diskettes.

* Work and Family Clearinghouse

Women's Bureau
U.S. Department of Labor
200 Constitution Ave., NW, Room S3306
Washington, DC 20210   800-827-5335

The Work and Family Clearinghouse was designed and established to assist employers in identifying the most appropriate policies for responding to the dependent care (child and/or elder care) needs of employees who are seeking to balance their dual responsibilities. Information and guidance are available in five broad areas: direct services, information services, financial assistance, flexible policies, and public-private partnership. Technical assistance includes national and state information sources, bibliographic references, conference information, research and statistics. *Program Profiles* are available which describe employer-related child and elder care systems already in place.

* Work Based Learning Programs

Office of Work Based Learning
Employment and Training Administration
U.S. Department of Labor
200 Constitution Ave., NW, Room N4703
Washington, DC 20210   202-219-5577

In September 1990 six seed money grants were awarded to test innovative approaches to improve the school-to-work transition for youth. During fiscal year 1991 the grantees developed models to redesign school curriculum so students learn job-related subjects. Major findings from this study have been summarized and published in the report entitled *Formula for Success*. Contact ETA for information on how to obtain the report.

* Work Permits for Foreigners

Labor Certification Division
Employment Service
Employment and Training Administration
U.S. Department of Labor
200 Constitution Ave., NW, Room N4456
Washington, DC 20210   202-219-5263

If an employer wishes to hire foreign workers, he must first obtain a foreign labor certificate, which is a statement from the U.S. Department of Labor stating that there is no U.S. citizen available to fill the job. The Department investigates to make sure that the wages and working conditions of the foreign workers will not seriously affect the wages and working conditions of U.S. workers. An employer applies for a foreign labor certificate through the local state employment service office, which then conducts a job hunt before sending the application form to the area regional office for approval or disapproval.

* Worker Training

Superintendent of Documents
Government Printing Office   202-512-1800
Washington, DC 20402   Fax: 202-512-2250

The publication *Worker Training: Competing in the New International Economy* focuses on ways in which public and private firms can develop and tap their employees skills, making them and America more competitive. It compares education and training offered by foreign countries and discusses new training organizations, support structures, and training approaches that can enhance the scope and quality of training at all levels of the workplace. Cost - $12, SN #052-003-01214-6.

* Workplace Literacy, Youth Training and Other Projects

Office of Strategic Planning and Policy Development
Employment and Training Administration
U.S. Department of Labor
200 Constitution Ave., NW, Room N5637
Washington, DC 20210   202-219-7674, x153

Research, Demonstration, and Evaluation includes studies concerning: the development or improvement of federal, state, local, and privately supported employment and training programs; labor market processes and outcomes, including improving workplace literacy; policies and programs to reduce unemployment; productivity of labor; improved means of using projections of labor supply and demand; methods of improving the wages and employment opportunities of low-skilled, disadvantaged, and dislocated workers; methods of addressing the needs of at-risk populations, such as the homeless; methods of developing information on immigration, international trade and competition; and methods of easing the transition from school to work, from one job to another, and from work to retirement.

* Work Stoppages and Strikes

Office of Compensation and Working Conditions
Bureau of Labor Statistics
U.S. Department of Labor
Postal Square Bldg.
2 Massachusetts Ave., NE
Washington, DC 20212   202-606-6275

This office generates monthly and annual data on major strikes and lock outs. The coverage includes all strikes and lock outs involving 1,000 workers or more and lasting more than one shift. This information measures collective bargaining and economic effects of work stoppages.

* Youth Fair Chance Program

Office of Strategic Planning and Policy Development
Employment and Training Administration
U.S. Department of Labor
200 Constitution Ave., NW, Room N5637
Washington, DC 20210   202-219-7674, x153

The purpose of the Youth Fair Chance program is to ensure access to education and job training assistance for youth residing in high poverty areas of urban and rural communities; provide a comprehensive range of education, training, and employment services to disadvantaged youth who ar not currently in job training programs; enable communities with high concentrations of poverty to establish and meet goals for improving the opportunities available to youth in the community; and facilitate the coordination of comprehensive services to serve youth in these communities.

Career and Job Training Opportunities

For anyone looking for help choosing a career, changing jobs, or finding a job, there is plenty of help at little or no cost. Not only can you find where the job opportunities are, you can also see what the job market will be for any profession next year, or even five years from now. If you want to know what part of the country is the best market for, say nurses or engineers, you can find out in one phone call. If you want to choose a major in college that will be marketable when you graduate, that's available too. There are even national computerized job banks and job matching programs listed here that will help match your background and abilities with available jobs. Besides help in finding a job, you'll also find job training and retraining vocational programs, along with plenty of assistance for such special groups as the disabled, displaced homemakers, the elderly, veterans, and those suffering lay-offs from large industries.

* Airline Jobs Bank
Office of Labor-Management Programs
Bureau of Labor-Management Relations
U.S. Department of Labor
200 Constitution Ave., NW, Room N5411
Washington, DC 20210   202-219-6231

The Airline Rehire Program gives displaced airline workers first-right-of-hire preference for jobs with pre-deregulation air carriers if the workers were dislocated between 1978 and 1988. One of the key features of this program is a national listing of airline vacancies compiled and kept at the New York State employment service. All carriers are required to list openings with the Job Bank, and anyone may use the list to obtain information about airline vacancies.

* Aviation Careers
Aviation Education Officer
Federal Aviation Administration
U.S. Department of Transportation
800 Independence Ave., SW
Washington, DC 20591   202-267-3190

The FAA's Aviation Education Program offers volunteer assistance to the nation's schools through the following programs: career guidance; tours of airports, control towers, and other facilities; classroom lectures and demonstrations; aviation safety information; aviation education resource materials; computerized clearinghouse of aviation and space information; aviation science instruction programs for home/school computers; "Partnerships-in-Education" activities; and teachers' workshops. Write to the above office for more information.

* Career Encyclopedia and Prospects
Office of Information
Bureau of Labor Statistics
U.S. Department of Labor, 441 G St., NW
Washington, DC 20212   202-606-7828

The *Occupational Outlook Handbook* is an encyclopedia of careers covering 250 occupations. For each of these, information is included on what the work is like, 1986 employment figures, educational and training requirements, advancement possibilities, job prospects through the year 2000, earnings-related occupations, and where to find additional information. The cost of the handbook is $26 (SN #029-001-03159-2). The *Occupational Outlook Quarterly* can help students, guidance counselors, and employment counselors keep abreast of current occupational and employment developments between editions of the *Occupational Outlook Handbook*. The quarterly supplement provides you with advice on how to get a job, articles on new occupations, addresses and phone numbers for more information on apprenticeships and training, and information on special scholarships for talented students. The cost of the *Quarterly* is $9.50 per year (SN #729-008-00000-4). Both books can be ordered by contacting: Superintendent of Document, Government Printing Office, Washington, DC 20402; 202-512-1800. Both of these books are available at public libraries.

* Career Guide to Industries
Superintendent of Documents
U.S. Government Printing Office
Washington, DC 20402   202-512-1800
                              Fax: 202-512-2250

This book provides information on the nature of the industry, employment, working conditions, occupations in the industry, training and advancement, earnings, and outlook. It is organized by Standard Industrial Classification (SIC) major categories. This publication is intended as a companion to the *Occupational Outlook Handbook*. The *Guide* costs $14, SN #029-001-03200-5.

* Careers in Dozens of Fields
Superintendent of Documents
Government Printing Office   202-512-1800
Washington, DC 20402   Fax: 202-512-2250

The following reprints are available from the *Occupational Outlook Handbook*:

Business, Managerial, and Legal Occupations. $2.50
Clerical and Other Administrative Support Occupations. $1.75
Communications, Design, Performing Arts, and Related Occupations. $1.50
Computer and Mathematics-Related Occupations. $1.50
Construction and Extractive Occupations. $1.75
Dietetics, Nursing, Pharmacy and Therapy Occupations. $1.50
Education, Social Service, and Related Occupations. $2
Engineering, Scientific, and Related Occupations. $1.75
Health Technologists and Technicians. $1.50
Mechanics, Equipment Installers, and Repairers. $2
Medical and Dental Practitioners and Assistants. $1.25
Metalworking and Woodworking Occupations. $1.50
Production and Transportation Occupations. $2
Protective Service Occupations and Compliance Inspectors. $1
Sales Occupations. $1.25
Service Occupations: Food, Cleaning, Health and Personal. $1.50
Technologists and Technicians, Except Health. $1.25
Tomorrow's Jobs: Overview. $1.25

* Coast Guard Training
U.S. Coast Guard
U.S. Department of Transportation
Aeronautical Center
MPB 237, P.O. Substation 18
Oklahoma City, OK 73169-6999   405-954-7293/7240

Coast Guard personnel are trained for advancement through a nonresident course program developed by this Institute. For more information about Guard training or for referral to Institute staff members, contact the number listed.

* Creative Writers Publishing Grants
Literature Program
National Endowment for the Arts
1100 Pennsylvania Ave., NW
Room 723
Washington, DC 20506   202-682-5451

The Literature Program assists individual creative writers and literature translators, encourages wider audiences for contemporary literature, and assists non-profit literary organizations. Fellowships enable writers and translators to set aside time for writing and research. Publishing grants provide assistance to literary magazines, small presses, and various distribution projects. Grants are also available to support residencies for writers to allow them to interact with their public. Literary centers may request funds but must offer a regular format of readings, workshops, and technical assistance for writers. Grants can be made to individuals or to non-profit organizations if such donations qualify as charitable deductions under Section 170(c) of the Internal Revenue Code of 1954. Grants range from $2,000 to $50,000.

* Dictionary of 20,000 Occupational Titles

Superintendent of Documents
Government Printing Office   202-512-1800
Washington, DC 20402   Fax: 202-512-2250

A compendium of approximately 20,000 occupations, the *Dictionary of Occupational Titles* defines each occupation and provides a classification structure that groups them in terms of related duties and activities. It also includes sections on the purpose of the dictionary and how to use the data bank for job placement. All occupational titles are arranged alphabetically and by industry for easy reference. The cost is $40, SN #029-013-00094-2.

* Disabilities Program

Employment and Training Administration (ETA)
U.S. Department of Labor
200 Constitution Ave, NW
Washington, DC 20210   202-219-5904

The ETA funds several projects to increase the number and quality of job opportunities for disabled individuals under the Job Training Partnership Act. These projects provide services which address each of the major conditions which constitute barriers to labor market participation - sight, hearing, epilepsy, mental retardation and other physical and emotional impairments.

* Disabled Veterans: Job Matching Service

Veterans Employment and Training
U.S. Department of Labor
200 Constitution Ave., NW
Room S1316   800-442-2VET
Washington, DC 20210   202-219-9110

Located in most employment service offices, the Disabled Veterans' Outreach Program is staffed by veterans who provide special assistance to other veterans and help them obtain employment and training services. The DVOP staff develop networks of employer contacts and work with community groups and veterans organizations in their effort to find jobs for their clients. Unique to this program is the emphasis to seek out and help disabled and Vietnam-era veterans.

* Dental Health Professions

Division of Associated and Dental Health Professions
Health Resources and Services Administration
5600 Fishers Lane, Room 8-101
Rockville, MD 20857   301-443-6854

This division serves as a principle focus with regard to health professions education, practice, and service research, in the fields of dentistry, optometry, pharmacy, veterinary medicine, public health, and allied health professions. It supports and conducts programs, surveys, and studies to analyze and improve the quality, development, organization, utilization, and credentialing of personnel in these fields. It also supports and conducts special educational initiatives. A publications list for professionals is available.

* Disease Control and Environmental Health Training

Training and Laboratory Program Office
Centers for Disease Control
1600 Clifton Rd.
Atlanta, GA 30333   404-639-2142

The Centers for Disease Control offers course work on such topics as environmental health sciences, communicable disease control, and vector-born disease control. Anyone can take these courses; however, they are designed for hospital personnel and health care providers. These classes are offered at a variety of locations, as well as many being available as self-study training courses.

* Displaced Homemakers Job Network

Women Work! National Network for Women's Employment
1625 K St., NW
Suite 300
Washington, DC 20006   202-467-6346

Supported by the Women's Bureau at the U.S. Department of Labor, the Displaced Homemakers Network is the only national organization which addresses the specific concerns of displaced homemakers. Through its Washington, DC, office, it works to increase displaced homemakers' options for economic self-sufficiency, to provide information about the public policy issues which affect displaced homemakers, to provide technical assistance resources for service providers, and to help program staff around the country locate the information and expertise they need to develop programs that work for displaced homemakers. There are many publications and newsletters available, and the staff can assist you in locating a displaced homemakers program near you.

* Employment for People With Severe Disabilities

Committee for Purchase from People Who are Blind or Severely Disabled
Crystal Square 3, Suite 403
1735 Jefferson Davis Hwy.
Arlington, VA 22202-3461   703-603-7740

The Javis-Wagner-O'Day (JWOD) Program provides nonprofit agency employees with invaluable vocational opportunities not otherwise available, which result in additional income and increased independence. Two advantages are: long term work experience and stable employment for individuals who are blind or have other severe disabilities; and attainment of marketable job skills that offer opportunities for individual advancement. You can contact this office to find a state contact near you to receive more information about this program.

* Employment in the Manufacturing Industry

Superintendent of Documents
U.S. Government Printing Office   202-512-1800
Washington, DC 20402   Fax: 202-512-2250

Occupational Employment in the Manufacturing Industries, 1992 provides data from a 1992 survey of occupational employment in manufacturing industries. The book costs $7.50, SN #029-001-03184-0 (1994, 123pg).

* Employment in Transportation

Office of Personnel
U.S. Department of Transportation
400 7th St., SW, Room 9113
Washington, DC 20590   202-366-9417

Employment inquiries for positions in Washington, DC, should be submitted to this office. Regional and district offices handle employment in their areas. Civil Service positions include air traffic controller; electronics maintenance technicians; civil, aeronautical, automotive, electronic, and highway engineers; and administrative, management, and clerical positions.

* Employment Search Strategies

Superintendent of Documents
Government Printing Office   202-512-1800
Washington, DC 20402   Fax: 202-512-2250

A new ETA publication, *Tips for Finding the Right Job,* can help you take advantage of successful job-hunting strategies and find out what you need to know before your job interview. It can be ordered from GPO for $1.25, SN #029-014-00244-5.

* Environmental Protection Job Opportunities

Superintendent of Documents
Government Printing Office   202-512-1800
Washington, DC 20402   Fax: 202-512-2250

We've Got the Whole World in Our Hands: Environmental Careers (1994, 11pg), describes employment and working conditions and training requirements for selected environmental occupations. The book sells for $1.25, SN #029-001-03208-1.

* Epidemic Intelligence Service

Epidemiology Program Office
Centers for Disease Control
1600 Clifton Rd., NW, Room 5127
Atlanta, GA 30333   404-639-3588

The Epidemic Intelligence Service is a two-year program of service and on-the-job training for health professionals, most of whom are physicians, in the practice of epidemiology. The officers have opportunities to investigate disease outbreaks, conduct epidemiologic studies, teach, travel, and present and publish their work. The class begins with a training course, and then the class responds to inquiries, monitors reports of disease, investigates outbreaks, and analyzes epidemiologic data.

* Experimental Job Training Opportunities

Office of Strategic Planning and Policy Development
Employment and Training Administration
U.S. Department of Labor
200 Constitution Ave., NW, Room N5637
Washington, DC 20210   202-219-7674, x153

This office plans and implements Pilot and Demonstration Programs to provide job training, employment opportunities, and related services for individuals with specific disadvantages. These programs address industry-wide skill shortages and offer technical expertise to particular client groups. They also develop information networks among organizations with similar Job Training Partnership Act-related objectives. Administered at the National level and operated at the state and local level, these programs cover disadvantaged groups in the labor market, including offenders, individuals with limited English language proficiency, handicapped person, women, single parents, displaced homemakers, youth, older workers, those who lack educational credentials and public assistance recipients.

* Federal Aviation Administration Academy

Federal Aviation Administration
U.S. Department of Transportation
P.O. Box 25082, AMA-1
Oklahoma, OK 73125   405-954-6900

The Academy is the principal source of technical information on U.S. civil aviation. It conducts training for FAA personnel through resident or correspondence courses and occasional on-site training. Air traffic training is available for specialists who man the FAA airport traffic control towers, air route traffic control center, and flight service stations. Electronic training is also available for engineers and technicians who install and maintain navigation and traffic control communications facilities. Initial and recurrent training is also conducted for air carrier and general operations inspectors. The Academy provides air navigation facilities and flight procedures analysis to flight inspection personnel.

* Fish Husbandry Training Academy

Education and Training Center
National Fisheries Center
U.S. Fish and Wildlife Service
U.S. Department of the Interior
Route 3, Box 49
Kearneysville, WV 25430   304-725-8461, x2

This facility contains a training academy of fish husbandry and numerous other training programs. Contact this office for a catalog describing the programs available and who to contact.

* Foreign Service Career Counseling

Personnel Office, Special Services Branch
United States Information Agency
301 Fourth St., SW, Room 525
Washington, DC 20547   202-619-3732

Information on career opportunities in the Foreign Service is available from this office. This office can also send you an application for the Foreign Service Exam.

* Future Job Trends by Occupation

Superintendent of Documents
Government Printing Office   202-512-1800
Washington, DC 20402   Fax: 202-512-2250

A supplement to the latest edition of the *Occupational Outlook Handbook*, *Occupational Projections and Training Data* provides detailed, comprehensive statistics and technical data supporting the information presented in the *Handbook*. It also presents a broad overview of expected trends in employment in the mid 1990's and provides employment data for approximately 250 occupations profiled in the *Handbook*. This supplement is a key reference source for training officials, education planners, and vocational and employment counselors. The cost is $5.50, SN #029-001-03189-1.

* Health Professions and Training Programs

Division of Public Health Professions
Health Resources and Services Administration
5600 Fishers Lane, Room 8-101
Rockville, MD 20857   301-443-6854

This division supports programs and provides grants for the following areas: Geriatric Education Centers; Rural Areas Health Care; Dentistry; Schools of Public Health; Preventive Medicine Residency Training; and Graduate Programs in Health Administration. Call for more information on programs.

* Highly Skilled Jobs Apprenticeship

Bureau of Apprenticeship and Training
Employment and Training Administration
U.S. Department of Labor
200 Constitution Ave., NW, Room N4649
Washington, DC 20210   202-219-5540

Apprenticeship is a combination of on-the-job training and related classroom instruction in which workers learn the practical and theoretical aspects of a highly skilled occupation. Apprenticeship programs are operated on a voluntary basis by employers, employer associations, or management and labor groups. The role of the federal government is to encourage and promote the establishment of apprenticeship programs and provide technical assistance to program sponsors. The related classroom instruction is given in the program sponsor's training facility or a local technical school or junior college.

* Homeless Veterans Projects

Veterans Employment and Training Service
U.S. Department of Labor
200 Constitution Ave., NW, Room S-1316   800-442-2VET
Washington, DC 20210   202-219-9110

The Homeless Veterans' Reintegration Projects (HVRP) helps homeless veterans get and retain jobs. It is assisted by other providers, such as veterans' affairs offices and medical facilities, Job Training Partnership Act entities and social service agencies. These providers offer access to benefits, substance abuse treatment, job training, transitional housing and other services needed to stabilize the homeless veteran and remove such barriers to employment as lack of clothing, medical care and job skills. The HVRP program uses veterans who have experienced homelessness themselves to reach out to homeless veterans.

* Indians and Job Training

Job Placement Service
Bureau of Indian Affairs
U.S. Department of the Interior
1849 C St., NW
Washington, DC 20240   202-208-2570

This office serves as a cross between the Health and Human Services, Labor, Justice, and Housing and Urban Development Departments for the Indian population. The needy are paid welfare subsidies and provided job training. This office also operates 19 special federal courts and funds 127 tribal courts, along with administering the police force for Indian reservations, and a rehabilitation program for Indian homes.

* Information and Records Management Training

Records Administration Information Center
National Archives and Records Administration
8601 Adelphi Rd., Room 2200, Mail Stop NI
College Park, MD 20740-6001   301-713-6677

The Directory of Records Administration Training Programs in the Washington, DC Area lists classes available from government, academic, and private sources in such subject areas as records management, Information Resource Management, micrographics, and optical disks. Basic courses currently being offered include: Introduction to Records Management; Files Improvement; and Records Disposition. Contact this office for a copy.

* International Trade Commission Jobs

Office of Personnel
U.S. International Trade Commission
500 E St., SW, Room 314
Washington, DC 20436   202-205-2651

Information on employment can be obtained from the Personnel Director. Personnel employed include international economists, attorneys, accountants, commodity and industry specialists and analysts, and clerical and other support personnel.

* Job Corps Conservation Centers

Office of Historically Black College
and University Programs and Job Corps
U.S. Department of the Interior
18th and C Sts., NW

Washington, DC 20240   202-208-6403
This residential program provides job training for disadvantaged youth throughout the country. You must be between the ages of 16 and 22 to participate. Conservation centers are located throughout the country for training purposes.

* Job Corps for Youths

Office of Job Corps
Employment and Training Administration
U.S. Department of Labor
200 Constitution Ave., NW   800-733-JOBS
Washington, DC 20001   202-219-8550
The Job Corps, a Federally administered national employment and training program, is designed to serve severely disadvantaged youth 16-21 years old. Enrollees are provided food, housing, education, vocational training, medical care, counseling, and other support services. The program prepares youth for stable, productive employment and entrance into vocational/technical schools or other institutions for further education or training. Job Corps centers range in capacity from 175 to 2,600 enrollees. Some of the centers are operated by the U.S. Departments of Interior and Agriculture (civilian conservation centers), while the remaining centers are operated under contracts with the U.S. Department of Labor primarily by major corporations. Vocational training is given in such occupations as auto repair, carpentry, painting, nursing, business and clerical skills, as well as preparation for the General Education Development high school equivalency examination. To apply, contact a Job Service office, or call the Job Corps Alumni Association's toll-free number: 800-424-2866.

* Jobs For Seniors 55 Years and Up

Office of Special Targeted Programs
Employment and Training Administration
U.S. Department of Labor
200 Constitution Ave., NW, Room N4643   202-219-5904
Washington, DC 20210   TDD: 800-326-2577
Sponsored by state and territorial governments and ten national organizations, the Senior Community Service Employment Program (SCSEP) promotes the creation of part-time jobs in community service activities for jobless, low-income persons who are at least 55 years of age and have poor employment prospects. Individuals work in part-time jobs at senior citizens centers, in schools or hospitals, in programs for the handicapped, in fire prevention programs, and on beautification and restoration projects. This program makes possible and array of community services to the elderly. SCSEP participants must be at least 55 years of age, have family income of not more than 25% above the Federal poverty level, and be capable of performing the tasks to which they are assigned. For more information, contact state offices for the aging, area agencies on aging, local job service offices, or this office.

* Job Training and Employment Publications

Superintendent of Documents
Government Printing Office   202-512-1800
Washington, DC 20402   Fax: 202-512-2250
The Government Printing Office (GPO) sells hundreds of publications on employment and occupations. Call GPO and ask for Subject Bibliographies 044 and 202, which contain lists of available publications and their prices. The Subject Bibliographies are free. You can have these documents faxed to you by using GPO Faxwatch at 202-512-1716.

* Job Training and Employment Services

Office of the Assistant Secretary for Employment and Training
U.S. Department of Labor
200 Constitution Ave., NW, Room S2321
Washington, DC 20210   202-219-6050
The Job Training Partnership Act provides job training and employment services for economically disadvantaged adults and youth, dislocated workers, and others who face significant employment barriers. The goal of this Act is to move the jobless into permanent, unsubsidized, self-sustaining employment. State and local governments have primary responsibility for the management and administration of job training programs. In addition, a new public/private partnership has been created to plan and design training programs as well as to deliver training and other services.

* Job Training and Workplace Research and Development

Office of Strategic Planning and Policy Development
Employment and Training Administration
U.S. Department of Labor

200 Constitution Ave., NW, Room N5637
Washington, DC 20210   202-219-7674, x153
Research, Demonstration, and Evaluation Projects summarizes the projects funded by the Employment and Training Administration. The most recent focus has been on workplace literacy, youth, worker adjustment, women-families-welfare, and improving employment and training programs. This free catalog provides several indexes and ordering information.

* Job Training for Ex-Offenders

Office of the Assistant Secretary for Employment and Training
U.S. Department of Labor
200 Constitution Ave., NW, Room S2321
Washington, DC 20210   202-219-6050
The ETA has several programs and services available that can help ex-offenders find employment. Programs include the following: Job Training Partnership Act programs, U.S. Employment Service, Targeted Jobs Tax Credit Program, Apprenticeship programs, Job Corps, Federal Bonding Program, and Tips for Finding the Right Job. Call ETA for more information.

* Junior Foreign Service Officer Trainee Program

Personnel Office
Special Services Branch
United States Information Agency
301 Fourth St., SW, Room 525
Washington, DC 20547   202-619-4659
Each December the Foreign Service Officer Examination is held at many locations in this country and overseas to screen candidates for the Junior Officer Trainee Program. Date, locations, and other information is available from this office.

* Literature Translators Opportunities

Literature Program
National Endowment for the Arts
1100 Pennsylvania Ave., NW, Room 723
Washington, DC 20506   202-682-5451
The Literature Program assists individual creative writers and literature translators, encourages wider audiences for contemporary literature, and assists non-profit literary organizations. Fellowships enable writers and translators to set aside time for writing and research. Publishing grants provide assistance to literary magazines, small presses, and various distribution projects. Grants are also available to support residencies for writers to allow them to interact with their public. Literary centers may request funds but must offer a regular format of readings, workshops, and technical assistance for writers. Grants can be made to individuals or to non-profit organizations if such donations qualify as charitable deductions under Section 170(c) of the Internal Revenue Code of 1954. Grants range from $2,000 to $50,000.

* Local Help for Job Seekers

Employment and Training Administration
U.S. Department of Labor
200 Constitution Ave., NW, Room N4470
Washington, DC 20210   202-219-5257
The U.S. Employment Service, through affiliated state employment agencies, operates almost 2,000 local employment service (job service) offices. They assist job seekers in finding employment and assist employers in filling job vacancies. They administer occupational aptitude tests and circulate information about jobs and training opportunities.

* Matching Yourself with the Workworld

Superintendent of Documents
Government Printing Office   202-512-1800
Washington, DC 20402   Fax: 202-512-2250
Designed to assist you in comparing job characteristics with your skills and interests, the publication, *Matching Yourself with the World of Work*, lists and defines 17 occupational characteristics and requirements, and matches these characteristics with 200 occupations chosen from the 1988-89 *Occupational Outlook Handbook*. It is available for $1, SN #029-001-02910-1.

* Medical/Scientist Training

Dr. Bert Schapiro
Medical Scientist Training Program (MSTP)
National Institute of General Medical Sciences

Westwood Building
Bethesda, MD 20892   301-594-3830

The MSTP provides assistance to students attempting to receive the dual degree of MD-PHD. Candidates must show evidence of high academic performance and significant prior research experience. Up to six years of support is given, and candidates must attend MSTP support institutions.

* Migrant and Seasonal Farmworker Opportunities

Employment and Training Administration
U.S. Department of Labor
200 Constitution Ave., NW, Room N4641
Washington, DC 20210   202-219-5500

This office administers a national program to help combat chronic unemployment, underemployment, and substandard living conditions among migrant and seasonal farm workers and their families. Supportive services are available to farm workers who seek alternative job opportunities that will enable them to secure stable employment at an income above the poverty level, and improve the living standard of those who remain in the agricultural labor market. Through grants to public and private non-profit institutions, economically disadvantaged farmworker families are furnished training and other employment--related services, including classroom training, on-the-job training, work experience, and supportive services. Supportive services include day care, health care, legal aid, transportation assistance and food and housing in emergency situations. You can contact this office for help in finding a local sponsor.

* Military Careers

Superintendent of Documents
U.S. Government Printing Office   202-512-1800
Washington, DC 20402   Fax: 202-512-2250

Military Careers is prepared especially to help educators and youth learn about the many career opportunities the military has to offer. The first section contains descriptions of 197 enlisted and officer occupations. The second section, military career paths, describes the typical duties and assignments a person might expect when advancing along the path of a 20-year military career. Indexed alphabetically and by Dictionary of Occupational Titles classification numbers. The book costs $30, SN #008-000-00614-8 (1992, 485pg).

* Minority Access to Biomedical Research Careers

Minority Access to Research Careers Program
National Institute of General Medical Sciences
Westwood Buildings, Room 2AS37
Bethesda, MD 20892   301-594-3900

This program provides special training opportunities in biomedical science for students and faculty at institutions with substantial minority enrollments. There are four types of support: 1) Honors Undergraduate Research Training Program, which provides support to institutions to teach and provide research training to honors students in their junior or senior year who plan biomedical research careers. 2) The Predoctoral Fellowship provides support for graduates of the MARC honors undergraduate program to pursue a graduate degree in the biomedical sciences (not medical school). 3) The Faculty Fellowship Program provides opportunities for research training for faculty members of colleges with high minority enrollment. 4) The Visiting Scientist Fellowship provides support for outstanding scientists-teachers to serve as visiting scientists at colleges with substantial minority enrollments.

* Modern Archives Management Training

Office of Public Programs
National Archives and Records Administration
8601 Adelphi Rd.   800-827-4898
College Park, MD 20740-6001   301-713-6760

The "Modern Archives Institute: Introduction to Modern Archives Administration," is a two-week archival training course that offers an introduction to archival theory and practice for participants. It is sponsored by the National Archives Trust Fund Board, and includes lectures, discussions, workshops, and visits to the Manuscript Division of the Library of Congress and various units of the National Archives. The Institute is offered twice a year.

* National Computerized Job Bank

United States Employment Service
Employment and Training Administration
U.S. Department of Labor
200 Constitution Ave., NW, Room N4470

Washington, DC 20210   202-219-5257

A computerized network connecting more than 2,000 Job Service (Employment Service) Offices, the Interstate Job Bank (IJB) is your opportunity to explore available jobs listed in all 50 states. During any given week there are over 20,000 job openings available in the IJB. During a year approximately 42,000 job orders containing 97,000 job openings are distributed through the IJB. When an employer cannot fill a job with local talent, the job than gets listed with the Interstate Job Bank. Jobs are listed three ways; as a detailed job description, and on two indexes, one listed by State and one by occupation. You may have access to any one of these listings through the Job Service Office. After you have selected the jobs you are interested in, a review with your local Job Service representative is in order. A proper plan is developed which may include sending your resume directly to an employer or to a Job Service office in another State. The Interstate Job Bank is a free service.

* National Health Service Corps

National Health Service Corps Scholarship Program
2070 Chain Bridge Rd., Suite 450
Vienna, VA 22182   800-221-9393

The National Health Service Corps helps alleviate the shortage of health professionals in geographically isolated or rural areas by offering a loan repayment program. The program pays the participants' lenders up to $20,000 a year toward their qualified health professions education loans during their contracted service periods.

* Native Americans: Job Training

Office of Special Targeted Programs
Employment and Training Administration
U.S. Department of Labor
200 Constitution Ave., NW, Room N4643
Washington, DC 20210   202-219-8502

The U.S. Department of Labor sponsors special employment and training programs designed to help jobless Native Americans. Those eligible include Indians, Eskimos, Aleuts, Hawaiians, and other persons of native American descent who are economically disadvantaged, unemployed, or underemployed. In addition to job referrals, these programs offer job training, counseling, and other employment-related services to help Native Americans prepare for and hold productive jobs. To make participation easier, child care, transportation, and training allowances are included as part of the programs. You can apply by contacting tribal or other grantees representing the reservations or villages who receive Labor Department grants, or you can get further information by contacting the office above.

* New Teachers in the Job Market

Superintendent of Documents
U.S. Government Printing Office   202-512-1800
Washington, DC 20402   Fax: 202-512-2250

New Teachers in the Job Market, 1991 Update summarizes findings from the Recent College Graduates study, with focus on the number, characteristics, and labor force and teaching status of newly qualified teachers. It provides information on teachers who obtained a bachelor's or master's degree in the 1989-1990 academic year who fit the definition of newly qualified teachers given in this publication. The book costs $6, SN #065-000-00602-2 (1993, 88pg).

* Nursing Research Training

National Institute for Nursing Research
National Institutes of Health
Building 31, Room 5B13
9000 Rockville Pike
Bethesda, MD 20892   301-496-0207

The National Institute for Nursing Research (NINR) supports nursing research and research training related to patient care, the promotion of health, and the prevention of disease. NCNR also supports studies of nursing interventions, procedures, and delivery methods, as well as the ethics of patient care. Publications are available regarding NCNR and its research grant process.

* Occupational Skill Standards Projects

Superintendent of Documents
U.S. Government Printing Office   202-512-1800
Washington, DC 20402   Fax: 202-512-2250

This book contains abstracts of 22 projects funded by the Departments of Education and Labor to develop voluntary skill standards covering 19 major industrial areas. Each project is depicted in terms of the occupations within the industry for which skill standards are being developed; the various public and private-sector agencies and groups assisting in the identification of relevant skill standards; a status report in terms of when standards and other deliverables will be available; and the identification of a project contact person. The cost is $3, SN #065-000-00679-1 (1994, 41pg).

* Oceanographic Corps Jobs

Commission Personnel Division, NOAA Corps
National Oceanic and Atmospheric Administration (NOAA)
U.S. Department of Commerce
1315 East West Hwy, 12th Floor
Silver Spring, MD 20910   301-713-1045

The NOAA Corps is the uniformed service of the U.S. Department of Commerce responsible for operating and managing NOAA's fleet of hydrographic, oceanographic, and fisheries-research ships and for supporting NOAA scientific programs. Engineering, computer science, mathematics, and science baccalaureate or higher degree graduates are sought for positions in the Corps.

* Office Automation Impact on Women

Women's Bureau
U.S. Department of Labor
200 Constitution Ave., NW, Room S3309   800-827-5335
Washington, DC 20210   202-219-6652

The impact of automation on the quality of worklife as well as on the economic well-being of clerical workers and their families is a matter of priority for the Women's Bureau. The free publication, *Women and Office Automation: Issues for the Decade Ahead*, discusses the quality of work, training and retraining, home-based clerical work, and health and safety issues.

* One-Stop Career Center System

Division of Acquisition and Assistance
Employment and Training Administration
U.S. Department of Labor
200 Constitution Ave., NW, Room S4203   202-219-8395
Washington, DC 20210   Fax: 202-219-5024
                          Internet: last name first initial @doleta.gov

All population groups have access to a wide array of jobseeking and employment development services, including the initial assessment of skills and abilities, self-help information relating to career exploration and skill requirements of various occupation, consumer report information on the performance of local education and training providers, and quality labor market information.

* Programs and Services for Women

Superintendent of Documents
U.S. Government Printing Office   202-512-1800
Washington, DC 20402   Fax: 202-512-2250

The *Directory of Nontraditional Training and Employment Programs Serving Women* provides information on 125 programs and services for women seeking jobs in trades and technology. The programs are divided according to those that primarily focus on: training, information and technical assistance, and outreach. The *Directory* costs $9, SN #029-002-00080-1 (1991, 165pg).

* Reemployment Help for the Jobless

Office of Employment and Training Programs
Employment and Training Administration
U.S. Department of Labor
200 Constitution Ave., NW, Room N4469
Washington, DC 20210   202-219-5577

The Economic Dislocation and Worker Adjustment Assistance Act (EDWAA) provides assistance to dislocated workers whose employment loss means they are unlikely to return to their previous industries or occupations. This includes workers who lose their jobs because of plant closings or mass lay-offs; long-term unemployed persons with limited local opportunities; and farmers, ranchers, and other self-employed persons who become jobless due to general economic conditions or national disasters. EDWAA has a local service-delivery system through which sub-state areas and grantees provide assistance to workers. Major activities and services under EDWAA include: 1) rapid response: the state's Dislocated Worker Unit (DWU) must be alerted to plant closings and mass lay-offs, and responds with on-site services to assist workers facing job losses; 2) retraining services, including basic education, occupational skills and/or on-the-job training; 3) needs-related payments: dislocated workers may receive payments to complete their training once

their unemployment insurance is exhausted; and 4) reemployment services, such as job search and placement, and relocation assistance. Contact this office for further information.

* Report on the American Workforce

Superintendent of Documents
U.S. Government Printing Office   202-512-1800
Washington, DC 20402   Fax: 202-512-2250

Report on the American Workforce provides a status report on the American workforce. It contains chapters on: labor market developments, key long term trends, the likely future, the structure of earnings, and safety and health in the workplace. Also included are statistical tables. The book costs $7, SN #029-001-03194-7 (1994, 208pg).

* School to Work Opportunities

Learning and Information Center
National School to Work Opportunities Office   800-251-7236
400 Virginia Ave., Room 210   202-401-6222
Washington, DC 20024   Fax: 202-401-6211
                                        e-mail: stw-lc@ed.gov
                                 Internet: http://www.stw.ed.gov

Operating under the School to Work Opportunities Act, this Center serves as a broker of technical assistance expertise in the fields of School to Work system building, school-based learning, work-based learning, and connecting activities. Information is available on: successful school to work systems, professional development strategies, management of state and local partnerships, integrated curricula, and methods for involving employers; labor market analyses, surveys, and other information related to the economic environment; and research and evaluation concerning school to work, skill certificates, skill standards, and related assessment technologies. Guided by experts in the field, the Center offers customers access through six different services: a resource bank of select technical assistance providers; an 800-number Answer Line; an Internet Home Page/Information Network; databases on key School to Work contacts, organizations, and practices; relevant publications; and meetings, conferences, and training sessions.

* Securities and Exchange Commission Jobs

The Director of Personnel
U.S. Securities and Exchange Commission
450 5th St., NW
Washington, DC 20549   202-942-4065

With the exception of the attorney category, positions are in the competitive civil service and are filled generally by selection from lists of eligibles who have taken civil service examinations. The Commission operates a college and law school recruitment program, including on-campus visitations for interview purposes. Inquiries should be directed to this office.

* Skills Needed for Specific Jobs

Superintendent of Documents
Government Printing Office   202-512-1800
Washington, DC 20402   Fax: 202-512-2250

Selected Characteristics of Occupations Defined in the Dictionary of Occupational Titles ($40, SN #029-014-00246-1) is a supplement to the *Dictionary of Occupational Titles* ($40, SN #029-013-00094-2)which can save you time in matching individual skills and qualifications to available positions. It provides information on the training time, the physical demands, and environmental conditions for particular jobs. For more information regarding this publication and other career and occupation publications contact: Office of Public Affairs, Employment and Training Administration, 200 Constitution Ave., NW, Room S2322, Washington, DC 20210; 202-219-6871.

* Special Help to Workers Laid Off

Office of Trade Adjustment Assistance
Employment and Training Administration
U.S. Department of Labor
601 D St., NW, Room 6434
Washington, DC 20210   202-219-5555

The Trade Act of 1974 provides assistance to workers who become totally or partially separated from employment because of increased import competition. Such assistance may consist of training, job search and relocation allowances, special help in finding a new job, and weekly cash benefits equal to the level of regular unemployment compensation payable in the separated worker's state (A worker must exhaust all unemployment insurance benefits available in his state before collecting weekly cash benefits under the Trade Act). Petitioning worker groups may be certified eligible to apply for worker adjustment assistance if the department determines that increased imports of articles like or directly competitive with those produced by the petitioning worker's firm contributed importantly to decreased sales or production and to worker separations.

* State Employment Services for the Unemployed
Employment and Training Administration
U.S. Department of Labor
200 Constitution Ave., NW, Room N4470
Washington, DC 20210   202-219-5257

This administration's threefold responsibilities cover: 1) training programs, including the Job Training Partnership Act (JTPA), which prepares unskilled and dislocated workers for productive employment; 2) the network of state employment service offices, which helps place people in jobs; and 3) income maintenance for those who lose their jobs through no fault of their own. Under JTPA alone, more than two million persons are provided employment and training services each year. Federal funds are apportioned to the states, which provide the training and other services, working with local governments, business and industry, labor, education, and nonprofit groups. About 2,200 state employment service offices across the country make over three million job placements annually. For those out of work, state unemployment insurance offices, operating under federal guidelines, provide weekly cash benefits which become an important revenue source in local communities.

* Summer Youth Employment and Training Programs
Office of Employment and Training Programs
U.S. Department of Labor
200 Constitution Ave., NW, Room N-4469
Washington, DC 20210   202-219-7533

The Summer Youth Employment and Training Program is a federally administered national program under the Job Training Partnership Act (JTPA). The legislative purposes of the summer programs is; to enhance the basic educational skills of youth; to encourage school completion or enrollment in supplementary or alternative school programs; to provide eligible youth with exposure to the world of work; and to enhance citizenship skills of youth. Young men and women, aged 14-21 and economically disadvantaged may apply. Contact your state JTPA office for the closest Private Industry Council, Service Delivery Area. Interested employers may call the National Alliance of Business at 800-787-2848.

* Tomorrow's Jobs in 250 Industries
Office of Economic Growth
Bureau of Labor Statistics
U.S. Department of Labor
Postal Square Bldg.
2 Massachusetts Ave., NE
Washington, DC 20212   202-606-5702

This office has information on 250 industries regarding employment requirements, specifically on the demand for employment in the future. Industries covered follow the *1972 Standard Industrial Classification Manual*. The November, 1989, issue of the *Monthly Labor Review* provides an overview of the data available.

* Training Information Program, Version 1.0
Associate Director for Administration
Office of Personnel Management (OPM)
1900 E St., NW, Room 5542   202-606-2000
Washington, DC 20415-0001   Fax: 202-606-2214
To order:
National Technical Information Service (NTIS)
U.S. Department of Commerce   800-553-6847
5285 Port Royal Rd.   703-487-4650
Springfield, VA 22161   Fax: 703-321-8547

The Training Information Program is a PC-based interactive software system developed by the U.S. Office of Personnel Management to help federal employees obtain relevant information about training and career development opportunities. Users of the program can quickly access information on more than 1000 training courses available nationwide to any federal employee. The courses include classroom, correspondence, and computer-based courses as well as long-term development opportunities. A search for courses can be done by course title, skill category, subject matter, course provider, location, type of training, length and cost. A detailed description of each course includes its objectives, intended audience, locations and dates of the course, and the name and telephone number of the course provider. This

program is available on one diskette for $55, 3.5" high density (PB93-500148CBX); 5.25" high density (PB93-500130CBX).

* U.S. Merchant Marine Academy
Maritime Administration
U.S. Department of Transportation-Kings Point
Long Island, NY 11024   516-773-5000

Future merchant marine officers are trained here in navigation instrumentation, ship maneuvering, ship management, and communications. The Academy also administers a Federal assistance program for maritime academies in California, Maine, Massachusetts, Michigan, New York, and Texas.

* Veterans' Employment and Training Help
Veterans' Employment and Training Service (VETS)
U.S. Department of Labor
200 Constitution Ave., NW, Room S1316   800-442-2VET
Washington, DC 20210   202-219-9110

The Veterans' Employment and Training Service is responsible for administering veterans' employment and training programs and activities through VETS to ensure that legislative and regulatory mandates are accomplished. The field staff of VETS works closely with and provides technical assistance to State Employment Security Agencies and Job Training Partnership Act grant recipients to ensure that veterans are provided the priority services required by law. They also coordinate with employers, labor unions, veterans, service organizations, and community organizations through planned public information and outreach activities.

* Veterans' Reemployment Rights
Veterans' Employment and Training
U.S. Department of Labor
200 Constitution Ave., NW, Room S1316   800-442-2VET
Washington, DC 20210   202-219-9110

The law provides that any employee enlisting in or inducted into the Armed Services, who leaves a position in order to perform military service, will be given back his or her position that he or she otherwise would have achieved had it not been for his or her military service. For more information on qualifications and eligibility, or if you need to register a complaint, contact this office.

* Veterans' Transition Assistance Program
Veterans' Employment and Training
U.S. Department of Labor
200 Constitution Ave., NW, Room S1316   800-442-2VET
Washington, DC 20210   202-219-9110

The veterans Transition Assistance Program was established to meet the needs of active duty servicemembers scheduled for separation by offering them job search assistance. The TAP has been increased due to the downsizing of America's standing forces with the end of the Cold War. TAP workshops provide servicemembers with information on conducting a successful job search, information on career decision-making, a realistic evaluation of employability, current occupational and labor market information, and information on veterans benefits.

* Welfare to Work Program
Administration for Children and Families
U.S. Department of Health and Human Services
370 L'Enfant Promenade, SW
Washington, DC 20447   202-401-9215

The Job Opportunities and Basic Skills Training (JOBS) Program provides recipients of Aid to Families with Dependent Children (AFDC) with the opportunity to take part in job training, work, and education-related activities that lead to economic self-sufficiency. JOBS also provides welfare recipients with necessary support services, such as transportation and child care. Responsibility for the JOBS program rests with the state welfare agency. However, in some areas, JOBS is under the administration of an Indian tribe or Alaska Native organization. More information is available from this office.

* Women in Non-Traditional Careers
Superintendent of Documents
Government Printing Office   202-512-1800
Washington, DC 20402   Fax: 202-512-2250

For use by career counselors and educators, *Women in Non-traditional Careers: Journal and Curriculum Guide*, contains a comprehensive selection of ideas,

Careers and Workplace

activities, and resources. It can help women to learn more about careers in carpentry, mechanics, printing, engineering, architecture, and other non-traditional fields. Included with the *Guide* is a sample journal which can be used in the classroom to allow women to record their thoughts in diary format. The journal contains questions, facts, and quotes intended to enhance self-understanding with regard to non-traditional roles. The cost is $47, SN #029-002-00074-6.

* Women's Jobs in Highway Construction

Women's Bureau
U.S. Department of Labor
200 Constitution Ave., NW, Room S3309
Washington, DC 20210   202-219-6652

Women in Highway Construction, a jointly-funded project of the Women's Bureau, the Employment and Training Administration, and the Federal Highway Administration, will identify the barriers women face in the construction trades and develop a model program to be used by State Highway Departments and highway construction contractors in recruiting and hiring women.

* Work-Based Learning

Employment and Training Administration
U.S. Department of Labor
200 Constitution Ave, NW, Room N4700
Washington, DC 20210   202-219-6871

America's economic future will increasingly depend on highly skilled workers. In 1987 the U.S. Department of Labor launched an initiative to determine what role the apprenticeship concept might play in raising the skill levels of American workers. The results are summarized in the report *Work Based Learning: Training America's Workers*. It is available free from the U.S. Dept. of Labor.

* Youth Conservation Corps: Conservation

United States Youth Conservation Corps
U.S. Fish and Wildlife Service
National Park Service
Washington, DC 20240   202-208-4635

The Park Service's Youth Conservation Corps is a summer employment program for young men and women, ages 15 through 18, who work, learn, and earn wages accomplishing needed conservation work on public lands. The program is also administered by the Forest Service of the U.S. Department of Agriculture. Projects include constructing trails, building campground facilities, planting trees, collecting litter, clearing streams, improving wildlife habitats, and office work. Limited positions are available.

* Youth Conservation Corps Regional Offices

Youth Program Officer
National Park Service

U.S. Department of the Interior
Room 4415
P.O. Box 37127
1100 L St., NW
Washington, DC 20013-7127   202-343-5514

Alaska
National Park Service, 2525 Gambell St., Room 107, Anchorage, AK 99503; 907-257-2698. Serving: Alaska

Mid-Atlantic Region
National Park Service, 143 S. Third St., Philadelphia, PA 19106; 215-597-3679. Serving: Delaware, Maryland, Pennsylvania, Virginia, and West Virginia

Midwest Region
National Park Service, 1709 Jackson St., Omaha, NE 68102; 402-221-3448. Serving: Illinois, Indiana, Iowa, Kansas, Minnesota, Michigan, Missouri, Nebraska, Ohio, and Wisconsin

Washington, DC
National Park Service, 1100 Ohio Dr., SW, Washington, DC 20242; 202-619-7222. Serving: DC, Maryland, and Virginia

North Atlantic Region
National Park Service, 15 State St., Boston, MA 02109; 617-223-5199. Serving: Maine, Massachusetts, New Hampshire, New Jersey, New York, Rhode Island, Vermont, and Connecticut

Pacific Northwest Region
National Park Service, 909 First Ave., Suite 212, Seattle, WA 98104-1060; 206-442-1006. Serving: Washington, Oregon, and Idaho

Rocky Mountain Region
National Park Service, 12795 West Alameda Parkway, P.O. Box 25287, Lakewood, CO 80225; 303-969-2500. Serving: Colorado, Montana, North Dakota, South Dakota, Utah, and Wyoming

Southeast Region
National Park Service, 75 Spring St., SW, Atlanta, GA 30303; 404-331-4998. Serving: Alabama, Florida, Georgia, Tennessee, Mississippi, Kentucky, North Carolina, South Carolina, Puerto Rico, and the Virgin Islands

Southwest Region
National Park Service, P.O. Box 728, Santa Fe, NM 87504; 505-988-6011. Serving: Arkansas, Louisiana, New Mexico, Oklahoma, and Texas

Western Region
National Park Service, 600 Harrizon St., Suite 600, San Francisco, CA 94102; 415-556-1866. Serving: Arizona, California, Nevada, and Guam

Employee Benefits and Rights

Pension plans, lie detector tests, affirmative action, and many other issues of worker protection are covered here. With these sources you'll be able to find out how your employee benefits compare with thousands of others across the country, how to protect your pension, or even how to contest the findings of a lie detector test. Additional sources on union grievance procedures and rights are included in the next section on Labor-Management Cooperation.

* Affirmative Action of Handicapped Persons

Office of Federal Compliance Programs
Employment Standards Administration
U.S. Department of Labor
200 Constitution Ave., NW, Room C3325
Washington, DC 20210   202-219-9384

The Rehabilitation Act of 1973 prohibits most employers doing business with the federal government from discriminating in employment against handicapped persons. Employers with contracts in excess of $2,500 must take affirmative action to hire and promote qualified handicapped persons.

* Age or Pay Discrimination

Equal Employment Opportunity Commission
1801 L Street, NW   800-669-4000
Washington, DC 20507   202-663-4395
                                        TDD: 800-800-3302

Discrimination on the basis of age is illegal under the 1964 Civil Rights Act. In addition, it is illegal to differentiate pay scales on the basis of sex for the same work. For information or to file a complaint, contact the EEOC.

* Child Labor Laws

Special Employment Branch
Wage and Hour Division
Employment Standards Administration
200 Constitution Ave., NW, Room S3510
Washington, DC 20210   202-219-7640

The Fair Labor Standards Act protects young workers from employment that might interfere with their educational opportunities or be hazardous to their health or well-being. There are different standards for work allowed, depending upon the age of the child. Contact this office for information on Child Labor Programs.

* Coal Miners' Benefits

Coal Mine Workers' Compensation Division
Employment Standards Administration
U.S. Department of Labor
200 Constitution Ave., NW
Room C3526
Washington, DC 20210   202-219-6795

Benefits are available for medical treatment and monthly payments to coal miners totally disabled from pneumoconiosis (black lung) arising from employment in the nation's coal mines. There are also benefits for the miner's dependents and to certain survivors of miners who died while totally disabled from pneumoconiosis. A copy of the *Black Lung Benefits Act* is available by contacting this office.

* Disabilities Discrimination

Equal Employment Opportunity Commission
1801 L Street, NW   800-669-4000
Washington, DC 20507   202-663-4395
                                        TDD: 800-800-3302

Title I of the Americans with Disabilities Act of 1990, prohibits private employers, state and local governments, employment agencies and labor unions from discriminating against qualified individuals with disabilities in job application procedures, hiring, firing, advancement, compensation, job training, and other terms, conditions and privileges of employment. For more information or to file a complaint, contact the EEOC.

* Employee Benefits National Survey

Office of Compensation and Working Conditions
Bureau of Labor Statistics
U.S. Department of Labor
Postal Square Bldg.
2 Massachusetts Ave., NE
Washington, DC 20212   202-606-6302

This office conducts an annual survey of employers in the private sector and sample data on the incidence and characteristics of employee benefit plans. Data available includes incidence and detailed characteristics of 15 private sector employee benefits paid for, at least in part, by the employer. The data are presented separately for three occupational groups: professional-administrative; technical-clerical; and production workers.

* Employee Pay and Benefits Cost Index

Office of Compensation and Working Conditions
Bureau of Labor Statistics
U.S. Department of Labor
Postal Square Bldg.
2 Massachusetts Ave., NE
Washington, DC 20212   202-606-6200

The quarterly *Employment Cost Index* measures changes in total compensation (wages, salaries, and employer costs for employee benefits) in wages and salaries only. Coverage includes all private industry and state and local government workers, but excludes Federal government, farm, household, self-employed, proprietors, and unpaid family workers. This information is also available on tape or diskette, and on the bureau's 24 hour information line at 202-606-7828.

* Employee Protection on Garnishing Wages

Wage-Hour Division
Employment Standards Administration
U.S. Department of Labor
200 Constitution Ave., NW
Room 3502
Washington, DC 20210   202-219-8305

The Federal Wage Garnishment Law limits the amount of an employee's disposable earnings which may be withheld in any one week by an employer to satisfy creditors. "Disposable Earnings" means that part of an employee's earnings remaining after deduction of any amount required by law. This law does not apply to bankruptcy court orders and debts for state and federal taxes. This law also prohibits an employer from discharging an employee whose earnings have been subjected to garnishment for any one indebtedness. Contact this office for more information on wage garnishments.

* Employee Whistleblower Abuse and Waste Hotline

Inspector General's Office
U.S. Department of Commerce
P.O. Box 612
Ben Franklin Station
Washington DC 20230   800-424-5197

This hotline was established so that consumers and employees could report fraud, abuse, or waste within any office in the U.S. Department of Commerce. All reports are investigated and reports can be made anonymously. The Pentagon, the U.S. Department of Housing and Urban Development (HUD), and other government departments also have whistleblower hotlines.

Careers and Workplace

* Employer's and Employee's Pension Guides

Public Affairs
Pension Benefit Guaranty Corporation
1200 K Street, NW
Washington, DC 20005-4026 202-326-4000
This office will provide you with the following publications free of charge:

Employer's Pension Guide. This is a cooperative project of the Pension and Welfare Benefits Administration of the U.S. Department of Labor, the Internal Revenue Service, and the Pension Benefit Guaranty Corporation to provide a general overview of the responsibilities under federal law of employers who sponsor single-employer defined benefit pension plans. It describes federal pension law effective as of 1989. However, it is not intended to be, nor is it, all-inclusive; for specific legal or technical information, consult these federal agencies or a private sector employee benefits specialist.

Your Guaranteed Pension. This booklet answers some of the most frequently asked questions about the Pension Benefit Guaranty Corporation and its termination insurance program for single-employer defined benefit pension plans. The answers in it apply to pension plan terminations taking place in 1989. For terminations that occurred in previous years, different rules may apply.

Your Pension: Things You Should Know About Your Pension Plan. This publication is intended to serve as a handy explanation of pension plans; what they are, how they operate, and the rights and options of participants. It should not be relied upon for information about your specific pension plan. That information should be obtained from your Plan Administrator or the Summary Plan Description of your pension plan.

* Equal Employment Opportunity

Office of Federal Contract Compliance Programs
Employment Standards Administration
U.S. Department of Labor
200 Constitution Ave., NW
Room N3424
Washington, DC 20210 202-219-9428
Executive Order 11246 requires that equal opportunity be provided for all persons without regard to race, color, religion, sex or national origin, employed or seeking employment with Government contractors or subcontractors. It also applies to construction contractors who are performing on construction projects being built with Federal financial assistance. Contact the above office for more information.

* Family and Medical Leave Act

Wage and Hour Division
Employment Standards Administration
U.S. Department of Labor
200 Constitution Ave., NW
Washington, DC 20210 202-219-8412
The Family Medical Leave Act (FMLA) of 1993 entitles eligible employees to take up to 12 weeks of unpaid, job-protected leave in a 12-month period for specified family and medical reasons. To be eligible for FMLA benefits, an employee must: work for a covered employers; have worked for the employer for a total of 12 months; have worked at least 1,250 hours over the previous 12 months; and work at a location in the U.S. or territory or possession of the U.S. where at least 50 employees are employed by the employer within 75 miles. Leave entitlement reasons include: the birth and care of a newborn child of the employee; placement with the employee of a son or daughter for adoption or foster care; to care for an immediate family member with a serious health condition; or to take medical leave when the employee is unable to work because of a serious health condition. More detailed information is available from this office or the nearest office of the Wage and Hour Division, listed in most telephone directories.

* Farm Worker Protection and Rights

Farm Labor Programs
Employment Standards Administration
U.S. Department of Labor
200 Constitution Ave., NW, Room S3510
Washington, DC 20210 202-219-7605
The Migrant and Seasonal Agricultural Workers Protection Act requires agricultural employers, agricultural associations, and farm labor contractors to observe certain labor standards when employing migrant and seasonal agricultural workers, unless exemptions apply. Certain persons and organizations, such as family businesses, small businesses, some seed and tobacco operations, labor unions, and their employees, are exempt. MSPA requires farm labor contractors to register with the U.S. Department of Labor. Contact this office for more information about the Act and for a list of workers' rights.

* Foreigners and Work Permits

Labor Certification Division
Employment Service
Employment and Training Administration
U.S. Department of Labor
200 Constitution Ave., NW, Room N4456
Washington, DC 20210 202-5263
If an employer wishes to hire foreign workers, he must first obtain a foreign labor certificate, which is a statement from the U.S. Department of Labor stating that there is no U.S. citizen available to fill the job. The U.S. Department investigates to make sure that the wages and working conditions of the foreign workers will not seriously affect the wages and working conditions of U.S. workers. An employer applies for a foreign labor certificate through the local state employment service office, which then conducts a job hunt before sending the application form to the area regional office for approval or disapproval.

* Formal Labor Complaints

Office of the General Counsel
National Labor Relations Board
1099 14th St., NW, Room 10100
Washington, DC 20570 202-273-3700
The General Counsel issues and prosecutes formal complaints before the National Labor Relations Board.

* Freedom on Information Act Requests

Public Affairs
Pension Benefit Guaranty Corporation
1200 K St., NW
Washington, DC 20005-4026 202-778-8839
Contact the office above for Freedom of Information Act requests.

* Garnishment of Wages

Wage-Hour Division
U.S. Department of Labor
200 Constitution Ave., NW, Room S3502
Washington, DC 20210 202-219-8305
The Federal Wage Garnishment Law limits the amount of an employee's disposable earnings which may be withheld in any one week by an employer to satisfy creditors. The law also prohibits an employer from discharging an employee whose earnings have been subjected to garnishment for any one indebtedness.

* Handicapped Workers

Office of Federal Contract Compliance Programs
Employment Standards Administration
U.S. Department of Labor
200 Constitution Ave., NW, Room N3424
Washington, DC 20210 202-219-9428
Under the Rehabilitation Act of 1973 Government Contractors and subcontractors are required to take affirmative action to employ and advance employment of qualified handicapped individuals.

* Job Counseling and Placement Fraud

Federal Trade Commission
Office of Consumer and Business Education
6th and Pennsylvania Ave., NW, H-403
Washington, DC 20580 202-326-3650
The FTC often receives complaint letters about job counseling and placement services which charge large fees and misrepresent their services. For information on how to select a legitimate employment service or to complain about one which you feel has misrepresented itself, contact your local FTC office.

* Lie Detector Testing

Wage and Hour Division
Employment Standards Administration

Be patient. If any phone number is incorrect, call (area code) 555-1212 and request the new listing.

U.S. Department of Labor
200 Constitution Ave., NW, Room S3502
Washington, DC 20210   202-219-8305

The Employee Polygraph Protection Act prohibits most private employers from using lie detector tests either for pre-employment screening or during the course of employment. Federal, State, and local government employers are exempted for the Act. The law provides several limited exemptions which permit the use of polygraph tests. For more information on the law and the use of polygraphs, contact this office.

* Longshore and Harbor Workers Benefits

Longshore and Harbor Worker's
Compensation Division
U.S. Department of Labor
200 Constitution Ave., NW
Room C4315
Washington, DC 20210   202-219-8572

The Longshore and Harbor Worker's Compensation Act covers all maritime workers for job-related injury, illness, or death on the navigable waters of the U.S., as well as employees working on adjoining piers, docks, and terminals. Compensation is paid by insurance carriers or by employers who are self-insured.

* Minorities/Women in Management

Program Development and Research Division
Employment Standards Administration
U.S. Department of Labor
200 Constitution Ave., NW, Room 3319
Washington, DC 20210   202-219-7342

The *Report on the Glass Ceiling Initiative* was released in August 1991. This study sought to identify artificial barriers that prevent women and minorities from advancing to mid and upper level management positions in the corporate world and to determine how such barriers could be removed. Information on the study and its findings are available from the Employment Standards Administration.

* National Origin or Religious Discrimination

Equal Employment Opportunity Commission
1801 L Street, NW   800-669-4000
Washington, DC 20507   202-663-4395
                                            TDD: 800-800-3302

Discrimination on the basis of national origin or religious orientation is illegal under the 1964 Civil Rights Act. For information or to file a complaint, contact the EEOC.

* Pension and Retirement Audits

Office of the Chief Accountant
Pension and Welfare Benefits Administration
U.S. Department of Labor
200 Constitution Ave., NW, Room N5510
Washington, DC 20210   202-219-8818

This office serves as the U.S. Department of Labor's primary advisor on accounting, auditing, and actuarial issues stemming from its responsibilities under the Employee Retirement Income Security Act and the Federal Employees' Retirement System Act (FERSA). It serves as the primary agency contact with accounting and actuarial organizations, as well as with federal and state agencies on accounting matters. It also administers a comprehensive system of compliance audits under FERSA and reviews annual financial reports.

* Pension Benefit Annual Report

Public Affairs
Pension Benefit Guaranty Corporation (PBGC)
1200 K St., NW
Washington, DC 20005-4026   202-326-4000

This publication contains information on Pension Benefit Guaranty Corporation (PBGC), including financial statements and an actuarial report. To obtain a copy contact the office above.

* Pension Benefit Guaranty Corporation Interest Rates

National Technical Information Service (NTIS)
U.S. Department of Commerce   800-553-6847
5285 Port Royal Rd.   703-487-4630
Springfield, VA 22161   Fax: 703-321-8547

The Pension Benefit Guaranty Corporation (PBGC) is a federal agency that administers a single-employer and a multi-employer pension insurance program which ensures that retirement benefits earned by American workers are paid when they die, using its own funds if necessary. In administering its program, the PBGC uses several distinct interest rates; late payment interest rate, withdrawal liability interest rate; variable rate premium valuation interest rate; and valuation interest rates. This is available by subscription for $125, order #SUB-9244.

* Pension Benefits

Office of Research and Economic Analysis
Pension and Welfare Benefits Administration
U.S. Department of Labor
200 Constitution Ave., NW, Room N5647
Washington, DC 20210   202-219-4505

This office can provide you with a list of reports prepared under contract to the U.S. Department of Labor concerning pensions. Some of the more recent studies include pension plan terminations with asset reversions, study of the investment performance of Employment Retirement Income Security Act (ERISA) plans, and the effect of job mobility on pension plans.

* Pension Failure Early Warning

Public Affairs
Pension Benefit Guaranty Corporation
1200 K St., NW
Washington, DC 20005-4026   202-326-4000

An "early warning system" is provided under the Employee Retirement Income Security Act (ERISA) of 1974, which requires that PBGC be notified within 30 days if an insured pension plan or plan sponsor is experiencing certain problems. Contact this office for more information. This notice is intended to provide PBGC with an opportunity to determine whether action is necessary to protect the interests of either the plan participants or the pension insurance program. PBGC may assess a penalty of up to $1,000 a day for failure to provide such required information. Contact the office above for more information including information on filing reportable events.

* Pension Insurance Premiums

Public Affairs
Pension Benefit Guaranty Corporation
1200 K St., NW
Washington, DC 20005-4026   202-326-4000

The Pension Benefit Guaranty Corporation's (PBGC) insurance is financed by premiums paid by covered plans or employers sponsoring these plans, and employer liability owed to PBGC when underfunded plans terminate. The PBGC administers two pension insurance programs: the single-employer program and the multiemployer program. Under the single-employer program, a company can voluntarily terminate its plan using either a standard termination procedure or a distress termination procedure. In addition, the PBGC may seek termination of a plan when necessary to protect the interests of the plan participants, of the plan, or of the PBGC. The PBGC must seek plan termination when a plan cannot pay current benefits. Multiemployer pension plans are maintained under collectively-bargained agreements between employee representatives and two or more unrelated employers. If a PBGC-insured multiemployer plan becomes insolvent, it receives financial assistance from the PBGC, thus enabling the plan to pay participants their guaranteed benefits. Contact the office above for more information.

* Pension Plan Financial Statements

Public Affairs
Pension Benefit Guaranty Corporation
1200 K St., NW, Room 6000
Washington, DC 20005-4026   202-326-4000

Contact the office above to obtain information on the PBGC combined financial statements which include the assets and liabilities of all defined benefit pension plans for which the Corporation is trustee.

* Pension Plan Insurance Coverage

Public Affairs
Pension Benefit Guaranty Corporation
1200 K St., NW
Washington, DC 20005-4026   202-326-4000

For additional information or assistance on the single-employer defined benefit pension plan insurance program, or on defined benefit plan terminations, contact the office above.

Careers and Workplace

* Pension Plans: Disclosure Requirements

Public Disclosure Room
Pension and Welfare Benefits Administration
U.S. Department of Labor
200 Constitution Ave., NW, Room N5638
Washington, DC 20210   202-219-8771

If you are covered by a pension plan and/or a welfare benefit plan, the administrator of your plan must give you a summary plan description (SPD), written in a manner easily understood, which provides information about eligibility, benefits, and procedures. Plan administrators also are required to provide you with a summary of any important changes in the SPD; a summary of the annual report that is filed with the Internal Revenue Service; a statement of accrued and vested benefits when you leave employment or have a break in service; and a written explanation if your claim for benefits has been denied. Administrators file copies of the SPD and certain other reports with the U.S. Department of Labor and are available to the public.

* Pension Plans Publications

Division of Public Information
Pension and Welfare Benefits Administration
U.S. Department of Labor
200 Constitution Ave., NW, Room N5656
Washington, DC 20210   202-219-8921

The publications listed below are available free of charge from this office:

What You Should Know About the Pension Law
How to File a Claim for Your Benefit
Your Pension
Often-Asked Questions About Employee Retirement Benefits
Trouble-Shooter's Guide to Filing the ERISA Annual Reports
Know Your Pension Plan
How to Obtain Employee Benefit Documents From the Labor U.S. Department
Reporting and Disclosure Guide for Employee Benefit Plans
Summary Plan Description Requirements Under ERISA
The Prudence Rule and Pension Plan Investments Under ERISA
Fiduciary Standards: Employee Retirement Income Security Act
Exemptions From ERISA Prohibited Transactions Provision
ERISA Reports to Congress
U.S. Department of Labor Highlights
PWBA Fact Sheets
PWBA: Administering The Pension and Welfare Law
A Brief Look at Pension Plan Chargers Under the Tax Reform Act of 1986

* Pension Protection and Retirement Equity

Pension and Welfare Administration
U.S. Department of Labor
200 Constitution Ave., NW, Room N5656
Washington, DC 20210   202-219-8921

The Retirement Equity Act of 1984 was designed to provide greater pension equity for women and for all workers and their spouses by taking into account changes in work patterns and marriage as an economic partnership. The new provisions lower the age for earning pension credits, provides for leaves of absences from work, and allow for greater benefits relating to marriage. Contact this office for further information.

* Pension Public Records

Disclosure Officer
Pension Benefit Guaranty Corporation
1200 K St., NW, Room 7100
Washington, DC 20005-4026   202-326-4000

Trusteeship plans, opinion letters, opinion manuals, litigation, termination case data sheets, and case log terminating plans updated quarterly are available for inspection from the office above. Also, *Annual Premium Reports* on microfilm filed by pension plans may be inspected. Contact the office above.

* Pension Terminations

Coverage and Inquiries Branch
Insurance Operations U.S. Department
Pension Benefit Guaranty Corporation
1200 K St., NW
Washington, DC 20005-4026   202-326-4000

Employers may end ("terminate") a defined benefit pension plan, but only if they meet safeguards designed to protect the plan participants. This can be accomplished either through a standard termination or a distress termination. In addition, PBGC may take action to terminate a plan if certain statutory criteria are met. PBGC encourages employers who are considering plan termination to explore alternatives that may enable them to preserve the plan and avoid benefit losses for their employees. Such alternatives may include "freezing" a plan or continuing to maintain and fund a plan although the facility has been shut down and its employees laid off. Employers should consult with private employee benefit specialists, the IRS, or PBGC for more information on these and other alternatives.

* Pension Trusteeships

Coverage and Inquiries Branch
Insurance Operations U.S. Department
Pension Benefit Guaranty Corporation
1200 K St., NW
Washington, DC 20005-4026   202-326-4000

If a plan qualifies for distress termination and can pay all of its benefit liabilities, PBGC will authorize the plan administrator to distribute the assets and complete the termination as in a standard termination. If the plan cannot pay all of its benefit liabilities, the plan administrator may be authorized to distribute the assets or PBGC may become trustee of the plan, either by agreement with the plan administrator or by order of a U.S. District Court. As trustee, PBGC will acquire the plan's records and assets, if any, as well as responsibility for benefit payments. PBGC will use its insurance funds to the extent necessary to pay the plan participants their guaranteed benefits. The plan's sponsor and its controlled group then become liable to PBGC for unpaid contributions and for unfunded benefit liabilities. Contact the office above for further information.

* Pregnancy Discrimination

Equal Employment Opportunity Commission
1801 L Street, NW   800-669-4000
Washington, DC 20507   202-663-4395
                                        TDD: 800-800-3302

Discrimination on the basis of pregnancy, childbirth or related medical conditions constitutes unlawful sex discrimination under Title VII of the 1964 Civil Rights Act. Women affected by pregnancy or related conditions must be treated in the same manner as other applicants or employees with similar limitations or abilities. For more information or to file a complaint, contact the Equal Employment Opportunity Commission (EEOC).

* Private Pension and Welfare Protection

Pension and Welfare Benefits Administration
U.S. Department of Labor
200 Constitution Ave., NW, Room N5656
Washington, DC 20210   202-219-8921

The Retirement Equity Act (1984) is designed to provide greater pension equity for women and for all workers and their spouses. It liberalizes such rules as those affecting participation, vesting, break in service, joint-and-survivor annuity, and alienation and assignment of benefits. This new law also protects the benefits of millions of workers and their beneficiaries in private pension plans and sets minimum standards to protect the interest of participant and their beneficiaries. Contact this office for more information.

* Railroad Retirement

Railroad Retirement Board
844 North Rush Street
Chicago, IL 60611-2092   312-751-4777

The Railroad Retirement Board (RRB) is an independent federal agency whose primary function is to administer comprehensive retirement-survivor and unemployment-sickness benefit programs for the nation's railroad workers and their families, under the Railroad Retirement and Railroad Unemployment and Insurance Acts. RRB publications include: *Annual Reports* (available from the Government Printing Office, 202-512-1800), *Federal Income Tax and Railroad Retirement Benefits*; *Medicare for Railroad Workers and Their Families*; *Railroad Unemployment and Sickness Insurance Benefits*; *Railroad Retirement Handbook*; *Monthly Benefits Statistics* (available from the Government Printing Office, 202-512-1800); *RRB News* (restricted to members); and *Railroad Retirement Information*. For further information or publications, contact the RRB.

* Sexual Harassment

Equal Employment Opportunity Commission
1801 L Street, NW   800-669-4000

Washington, DC 20507

202-663-4395
TDD: 800-800-3302

Unwelcome sexual advances, requests for sexual favors, and other verbal or physical conduct of a sexual nature constitute sexual harassment when submission to or rejection of this conduct explicitly or implicitly affects an individuals employment, unreasonably interferes with an individual's work performance or creates an intimidating, hostile or offensive work environment. This type of behavior violates Title VII of the Civil Rights Act of 1964. For more information or to file a complaint, contact the EEOC.

* Statistical History of Pension Claims

Corporate Policy and Research U.S. Department
Pension Benefit Guaranty Corporation
1200 K St., NW, Room 7300
Washington, DC 20005-4026   202-326-4000

Contact the office above to obtain information on pension liabilities guaranteed by the PBGC which includes assets of terminated plans, statutory employer liability, and the resulting net claims.

* Transit System Employee Protection

Office of Labor-Management Programs
Bureau of Labor-Management Relations
U.S. Department of Labor
200 Constitution Ave., NW, Room N5411
Washington, DC 20210   202-219-4473

Federal law requires that arrangements be made to protect the rights of transit system employees when a state or local body uses federal funds to acquire or improve that system. This requirement is one of several laws administered by the U.S. Department of Labor to protect specific employees who might be adversely affected by a federal program. The protective arrangements must include preservation of rights, privileges, and benefits under existing collective bargaining agreements, continuation of collective bargaining rights, protection of individual employees against a worsening of their positions, assurances of employment and priority of reemployment, and paid training or retraining programs. An employee who believes he or she has been adversely affected as a result of federal transit assistance can make a claim with the U.S. Department of Labor.

* Unemployment Insurance and Reemployment

Unemployment Insurance Service
Employment and Training Administration
U.S. Department of Labor
200 Constitution Ave., NW, Room S4231
Washington, DC 20210   202-219-7831

The Employment and Training Administration has begun to review a number of nontraditional approaches to the Unemployment Insurance system. These alternative approaches involve several demonstration projects and include the following reemployment services: job search assistance, referral to training, relocation assistance, monetary incentives to search for work faster, and grants for self-employment. For more information about these projects, contact this office.

* Unemployment Insurance Help

Unemployment Insurance Service
Employment and Training Administration
U.S. Department of Labor
200 Constitution Ave., NW, Room S4231
Washington, DC 20210   202-219-7831

Unemployment Insurance programs provide limited compensation to workers who lose their jobs through no fault of their own. The Federal government establishes guidelines and pays state administrative costs from funds collected under the Federal Unemployment Tax Act, and the states operate the program under these guidelines. Claimants must be able to work, available to work, and seeking work.

* Unemployment Insurance Laws: State Comparisons

Superintendent of Documents
Government Printing Office   202-512-1800
Washington, DC 20402   Fax: 202-512-2250

The Comparison of State Unemployment Insurance Laws analyzes State unemployment insurance statutes. It provides text and tables on coverage, taxation, benefits, eligibility, administration of program, and temporary disability benefits. A one year subscription is available for $45 (SN #929-002-00000-8). For more information on the laws contact: Unemployment Insurance, Employment and

Training Administration, U.S. Department of Labor, 200 Constitution Ave., NW, Room C4512, Washington, DC 20210; 202-219-0200.

* Unemployment Insurance Surveys

Division of Actuarial Services
Employment and Training Administration
U.S. Department of Labor
200 Constitution Ave., NW, Room S4519
Washington, DC 20210   202-219-4630

The UI Data Summary is produced quarterly from state-reported data contained in the Unemployment Insurance Data Base, as well as UI-related data from outside sources. This report is intended to provide the user with a quick overview of the status of the unemployment insurance system at the national and state levels. Tables are provided for each state, and many data items are repeated on summary tables. This report is available at no cost.

* Veteran Reemployment Rights

Veterans Employment and Training
U.S. Department of Labor
200 Constitution Ave., NW, Room S1316   800-442-2VET
Washington, DC 20210   202-219-9110

The law provides that any employee enlisting in or inducted into the Armed Services, who leaves a position in order to perform military service, will be given back his or her position that he or she otherwise would have achieved had it not been for his or her military service. For more information on qualifications and eligibility, or if you need to register a complaint, contact this office.

* Veteran Job Training Program

Assistant Secretary For Veterans
Employment and Training
U.S. Department of Labor
200 Constitution Ave., NW, Room S1316   800-442-2VET
Washington, DC 20210   202-219-9110

Employment-related services designed to aid veterans include counseling, testing, and skills training; unemployment compensation for newly separated ex-service members while they look for civilian employment; tax credits for private employers who hire certain target groups of veterans; placement in private and public sector jobs; and reemployment rights assistance. For more information, contact the Veterans Employment and Training Office.

* Vietnam and Disabled Vets Job Placement

Veterans Employment and Training
U.S. Department of Labor
200 Constitution Ave., NW, Room S1316   800-442-2VET
Washington, DC 20210   202-219-9110

Federal government contractors and subcontractors (with government contracts of $10,000 or more) are required by law to take affirmative action to employ and to advance in employment qualified special disabled and Vietnam-era Veterans. All suitable employment openings must be given to the nearest local State Employment Office. A Veterans Employment and Training Representative is located in each office to provide employment advice and assistance to veterans. Contact the Office of Federal Contract Compliance Programs if it appears that a contractor has failed to comply. Complaints can be made to: Office of Federal Contract Compliance Programs, U.S. Department of Labor, 200 Constitution Ave., NW, Room C3325, Washington, DC 20210; 202-219-9475.

* Workers' Compensation for Federal Employees

Federal Employees' Compensation Division
Office of Workers' Compensation Programs
Employment Standards Administration
U.S. Department of Labor
200 Constitution Ave., NW, Room S3229
Washington, DC 20210   202-219-7552

This office can provide you with a variety of free publications which explain the Federal Employees' Compensation Act, claim forms for work-related disabilities or deaths, as well as checklists for evidence required in support of claims for occupational diseases, such as work-related coronary illness, pulmonary disease, and hearing loss. Federal Injury Compensation is a free publication which lists questions and answers regarding the Federal Employees' Compensation Act. Contact this office for a list of publications, and further information.

Be patient. If any phone number is incorrect, call (area code) 555-1212 and request the new listing.

253

Labor-Management Relations

Reducing tensions between management and workers and improving the quality of worklife are emerging issues for companies nationwide. Here you will find all kinds of information on such issues as collective bargaining agreements, union contracts, cooperative workshops, and pending legislation. You can find additional sources on productivity, one of the underlying goals of labor-management cooperation, in the Business and Industry chapter.

* Alternative Dispute Resolution

Directors Office
Federal Mediation and Conciliation Service (FMCS)
2100 K St., NW
Washington, DC 20427   202-606-8100

The term "Alternative Dispute Resolution" is used to describe a variety of approaches that are alternatives to courtroom or agency adjudication and rulemaking. Under the Administrative Disputes Resolution Act of 1990 (PL 101-552), FMCS was officially authorized to share its expertise in all aspects of dispute resolution with federal agencies, including third-party dispute resolution assistance; dispute resolution training for agency personnel; and consultation systems design. A one day "awareness" workshop which explores the various ADR techniques of negotiation, mediation, fact finding, settlement, judges, facilitation, mini-trials, arbitration, negotiated rule-making, and consensual decision-making. This workshop includes a combination of lecture, discussions, exercises, and mock mediations. Call the FMCS for more information.

* Arbitrators and Mediators

Directors Office
Federal Mediation and Conciliation Service (FMCS)
2100 K St., NW
Washington, DC 20427   202-606-8100

Through its regional offices and suboffices, FMCS assists federal agencies, private sector employers, and labor organizations in resolving labor-management disputes. When there is no local or state resource available, the parties involved may contact the regional FMCS office to be assigned a qualified mediator or arbitrator, on call 24 hours a day. Upon request, mediators will assist the parties in resolving disputes, and arbitrators will make a final decision. Technical assistance includes training for one or both parties in developing constructive methods of dispute resolution, help in forming committees, and collective bargaining workshops. Contact your local FMCS office for any of these services.

* Best Practices Clearinghouse

Information Office
Office of the American Workplace
U.S. Department of Labor
200 Constitution Ave., NW, Room N5411   202-219-5769
Washington, DC 20210   Fax: 202-219-5338

The Bureau has developed a national information clearinghouse to help with the exchange of information among employers, unions, and others interested to joint labor-management programs, and innovative workplace practices. A computerized database contains basic information on programs operating in a variety of firms and organizations in the private and public sectors, including the names of individuals in these organizations who can provide additional information. Listings from the clearinghouse are available to all interested parties upon request. Database information can be accessed easily according to type of industry and employer size, geographic area, program type/features, program scope and workplace issues addressed, union involvement and year program began. You can access this information through their bulletin board at 202-219-7088, or via the Internet at http://www.dol.gov/dol/oaw.

* Case Processing of Worker Grievances

Management and Information Systems Branch
National Labor Relations Board (NLRB)
1099 14th St., NW
Washington, DC 20570   202-273-4030

This service monitors all NLRB cases from their initial filing to their final

resolution. Information regarding regional cases is tabulated and detailed in reports issued periodically to Board members for their use only. Summaries and statistical tables regarding these cases are published in the Annual Report available from the U.S. Government Printing Office, 202-512-1800.

* Collective Bargaining Agreements and Case Files

Office of Research and Information Management
National Mediation Board
1301 K Street, NW, Suite 2506
Washington, DC 20572   202-523-5920

The public may inspect copies of collective bargaining agreements between labor and management of rail and air carriers at this office. Copies of awards and interpretations issued by the National Railroad Adjustment Board are also available. Write or visit the office listed above to access copies of collective bargaining agreements. Some National Railroad Adjustment Board documents may require a Freedom of Information Act request. Submit FOIA requests to the National Mediation Board at above address, telephone 202-523-5996.

* Collective Bargaining Annual Report

Office of Public Affairs
Federal Mediation and Conciliation Service (FMCS)
2100 K St., NW, 9th Floor
Washington, DC 20427   202-606-8080

Booklets about collective bargaining, arbitration, and mediation in the private, federal, State, and local sectors are available from this office. The *FMCS Annual Report* summarizes major negotiations and important developments of the year. To obtain these publications and for further information, contact Public Affairs.

* Collective Bargaining Units

Division of Information
National Labor Relations Board (NLRB)
1099 14th St., NW, Room 9404
Washington, DC 20570-0001   202-273-1994

A bargaining unit, in general, is a group of two or more employees whose mutual interests form a reasonable basis for collective bargaining. The National Labor Relations Board is responsible for determining units appropriate for collective bargaining purposes. Questions concerning bargaining units should be directed to this office, or to the regional office in the area where the employee unit is located.

* Employers Register with OLMS

Office of Labor-Management Standards (OLMS)
U.S. Department of Labor
200 Constitution Ave., NW, Room S2203
Washington, DC 20210   202-219-6045

This register contains the names of companies and individuals which have filed employer reports with OLMS from 159 to 1986. It includes the city and state in which the employer is located, the file number assigned by OLMS, and last fiscal year for which the employer filed an LM-10 report.

* Federal Labor Relations Documents

Office of Case Control
Federal Labor Relations Authority (FLRA)
607 14th St., NW
Washington, DC 20424   202-482-6690, x416

Case file information is maintained on FLRA hearings and cases prosecuted to ensure compliance with the rights and obligations of federal employees to organize, bargain collectively, and participate in labor organizations. To view FLRA case dockets and decisions, call ahead to this office to arrange for a visit.

* Federal Labor Relations Authority Publications

Office of Information Resources and Research Service
Federal Labor Relations Authority (FLRA)
607 14th St., NW
Washington, DC 20424   202-482-6550

The Federal Labor Relations Authority has several free publications available including the following: *Federal Service Labor-Management Statute; A Guide to the Federal Service Labor-Management Relations Statute;* and the *Annual Report of the Federal Labor Relations Authority* and the *Federal Services Impasses Panel.*

* Federal Labor Relations Freedom of Information

Solicitors Office
Federal Labor Relations Authority (FLRA)
607 14th St., NW
Washington, DC 20424   202-482-6620

The Public Information Office listed above is the Freedom of Information Act contact for the Authority.

* Federal Labor Relations Library

Library
Federal Labor Relations Authority (FLRA)
607 14th St., NW
Washington, DC 20424   202-482-6695, x352

A small specialized collection is housed here. Material covers federal service labor-management relations and the Federal Labor Relations Authority. The library is open to the public, but due to tight security in the building, you are advised to call ahead for an appointment.

* Foreign Visitor Program

Office of International Affairs
Federal Mediation and Conciliation Service (FMCS)
2100 K St., NW, Room 212
Washington, DC 20427   202-606-9143

Representatives of labor, management, and governments from around the world can see how arbitration, mediation, collective bargaining, and employee involvement programs function in the U.S. by participation in this visitor program. Industrial labor relations are targeted. For more information, contact the Special Mediation Services office listed.

* Labor-Management Cooperation Program

Directors Office
Federal Mediation and Conciliation Service (FMCS)
2100 K St., NW
Washington, DC 20427   202-606-8100

This program provides grants to support the establishment and operation of joint labor-management committees in public and private sectors. Labor-management committees operate at the plant level, on a community or area wide basis, within a particular industry, and in public sector organizations at various levels. Contact the FMCS for more information on getting involved in this program.

* Labor Practices in Federal Service

Office of Information Resources and Research Service
Federal Labor Relations Authority (FLRA)
607 14th St., NW
Washington, DC 20424   202-482-6550

Contact this office to obtain a copy of the *FLRA Annual Report*, which describes significant decisions of the FLRA and case processing statistics of the General Counsel of the Authority. Cases of alleged unfair labor practices in federal service are investigated and prosecuted by the General Counsel and are heard by the FLRA's Office of Administrative Law Judges.

* Labor Union Regulations

Office of Labor-Management Standards
U.S. Department of Labor

200 Constitution Ave., NW, Room S1032
Washington, DC 20210   202-219-6098

Labor-Management Standard is a newsletter sent to approximately 200 international unions, informing the union presidents about OLMS compliance assistance and enforcement programs. As part of the publication, OLMS includes *Labor-Management Reporting and Disclosure Act Compliance Tips*, which are detachable sheets that can be distributed to affiliated locals to assist them in complying with various LMRDA provisions.

* Mediation Board Publications

Office of Executive Secretary
National Mediation Board
1301 K St., NW, Room 250E
Washington, DC 20572   202-523-5920

There are three annual subscription mailing lists available from the Board. Costs may be reduced or waived when it is in the public interest to do so.

Subscription List #1, $175: *Annual Reports of the NMB; Certifications and Dismissals; Determination of Craft or Class; Findings Upon Investigation; Emergency Board Reports*

Subscription List #2, $ 50: *Annual Reports of the NMB; Emergency Board Reports; Determination of Craft or Class*

Subscription List #3, $ 35: *The Representation Manual* and amendments

* Mediation Cases

Legal Services Office
Federal Mediation and Conciliation Service (FMCS)
2100 K St., NW, Room 712
Washington, DC 20427   202-606-8140

This office represents FMCS in legal cases. In unusually complex and technical mediation efforts, Legal Services staff participate as part of the mediation team. Contact this office for more information on labor-management conciliation cases.

* Mediation National Board Freedom of Information

General Council
National Mediation Board
1301 K St., NW, Room 250
Washington, DC 20572   202-523-5996

This office handles Freedom of Information Act requests regarding the National Mediation Board.

* Mediation Programs

Federal Mediation and Conciliation Service (FMCS)
2100 K St., NW
Washington, DC 20427   202-606-8150

The FMCS sponsors a variety of workshops in labor-management dispute resolution. Workshops focus on two principal themes: the development of effective labor-management committees and the promotion of effective labor-management communication. FMCS programs include:

Labor-Management Committee (LMC) - The LMC represents an ongoing forum for dealing provocatively with common problems ranging from attitudes to productivity improvements. FMCS can assist the parties to not only design the framework for an effective LMC, but can provide training in the application of proven problem solving processes necessary to promote the success of Labor-Management Committee Operations.

* Mediation Service Freedom of Information

General Council
Federal Mediation and Conciliation Service (FMCS)
2100 K St., NW, Room 712
Washington, DC 20427   202-606-5444

This office handles FMCS Freedom of Information Act requests.

* National Labor Relations Act

Division of Information
National Labor Relations Board (NLRB)
1099 14th St., NW

Washington, DC 20570-0001   202-632-4950

The National Labor Relations Act states and defines the rights of employees to organize and to bargain collectively with their employers through representatives of their own choosing. The Act ensures that labor representatives are chosen by secret ballot and also defines certain practices of employers and unions as unfair labor practices. The NLRB can provide you with a free guide to the National Labor Relations Act that explains its provisions in detail.

* National Labor Relations Board (NLRB) Election Reports

Joyce Paige
Management Information
National Labor Relations Board
Washington, DC 20570   202-273-4039

National Labor Relations Boards yearly union election results for the United States are available on disk from this office free of charge. You can request what year(s) you would like to receive. Years dating back to 1984 are readily available, but you can request results for years prior to that date. A printed copy of the 300-character election file is also available at no cost.

* Negotiation Impasses

Federal Services Impasses Board
Federal Labor Relations Authority (FLRA)
607 14th St., NW
Washington, DC 20424   202-482-6680, x232

When negotiation impasses develop between Federal agencies and employee representatives, this panel provides assistance in resolving the stalemate. The following publications are available: *Guide to Hearing Procedures of the Federal Services; Impasses Panel; Subject Matter Index; Table of Cases; and the Annual Report.*

* NLRB Annual Report

Division of Information
National Labor Relations Board (NLRB)
1099 14th St., NW, Room 9431
Washington, DC 20570-0001   202-273-1994

The National Labor Relations Board's activities and its significant case decisions for the previous fiscal year are highlighted in its Annual Report. Included are summaries of unique and/or precedent setting unfair labor practice decisions and representation elections. Statistical tables break down case information into such categories as geographic location, type of industry involved, actions taken, and final case disposition. Questions regarding the report should be directed to this office, and to purchase the report, contact the Superintendent of Documents, Government Printing Office, Washington, DC 20402; 202-512-1800.

* NLRB Cases

Office of the Executive Secretary
National Labor Relations Board (NLRB)
1099 14th St., NW, Room 11602
Washington, DC 20570-0001   202-273-1935

All pertinent information regarding current cases before the NLRB is tracked by this service. Summaries include such information as the type of allegation, industries involved, location of the incident, and actions already taken. This document is for internal National Labor Relations Board use only. The office also communicates on behalf of the board with employees, employers, members of Congress, labor organizations, other agencies, and the general public.

* NLRB Elections

Division of Information
National Labor Relations Board (NLRB)
1099 14th St., NW, Room 9401
Washington, DC 20570-0001   202-273-1994

Secret ballot elections, conducted by the National Labor Relations Board, are held by employees to determine whether union representation is desired for the purpose of collective bargaining. The Board publishes a monthly update, *National Labor Relations Board Monthly Election Report*, available for $17 per year from Superintendent of Documents, Government Printing Office, Washington, DC 20402; 202-512-1800. Contact this office for more information regarding petitioning for an election as well as Certification of Representative, Decertification, Withdrawal of Union-Shop Authority, Employer Petition, Unit Clarification, and Amendment of Certification.

* NLRB Freedom of Information

Division of Advice
National Labor Relations Board (NLRB)
1099 14th St., NW
Washington, DC 20570-0001   202-273-3847

The Regional Advice Branch advises the general counsel and regional directors on special issues of law and policy and performs legal research. This branch prepares the general counsel's quarterly reports and guideline memoranda on important legal issues for regional directors and for the public. It also coordinates compliance with the Freedom of Information Act.

* NLRB Legal Advisor

Office of the Solicitor
National Labor Relations Board (NLRB)
1099 14th St., NW, Room 11812
Washington, DC 20570-0001   202-273-2910

The solicitor is the chief legal officer for the board. The office advises the board on questions of law and procedure, on intervention in court proceedings to protect the board's jurisdiction, on the board's exercise of its discretion regarding injunctive relief and on the enforcement of the boards orders. The office also serves as the boards liaison with members of Congress, the White House, state officials or other agencies and members of the bar.

* NLRB Meetings

Division of Information
National Labor Relations Board (NLRB)
1099 14th St., NW, Room 9431
Washington, DC 20570-0001   202-273-1994

The public is usually allowed to attend National Labor Relations Board meetings. Information regarding upcoming meetings is published in the *Federal Register* or can be attained through this office.

* NLRB Publications

Division of Information
National Labor Relations Board (NLRB)
1099 14th St., NW, Room 9431
Washington, DC 20570-0001   202-273-1994

Contact this office to obtain a free list of the National Labor Relations Board publications. The list includes information regarding the documents' frequency of publication, stock numbers, and cost. The following pamphlets are available free in limited quantity:

A Career in Labor: Management Relations as an Attorney.
A Career in Labor: Management Relations as a Field Examiner.
The National Labor Relations Board and You. (Representation Cases)
The National Labor Relations Board and You. (Unfair Labor Practices)
The National Labor Relations Board: What It Is, What It Does.
Your Government Conducts an Election for You on the Job.

* NLRB Public Information Room

Records Management
National Labor Relations Board (NLRB)
1099 14th St., NW, Room 9201
Washington, DC 20570-0001   202-273-2840

This facility provides for public inspection of the Board's decisions, appeals, and advice papers.

* NLRB Speakers

Division of Information
National Labor Relations Board (NLRB)
1099 14th St., NW, Room 9401
Washington, DC 20570-0001   202-273-1994

Personnel from Washington headquarters and the regional offices serve as speakers and panelists before bar associations, labor and management organizations, as well as education and civic groups. For more information regarding the speaker program, contact this office or your nearest National Labor Relations Board regional office.

* NLRB Weekly Summary

Superintendent of Documents
Government Printing Office   202-512-1800
Washington, DC 20402   Fax: 202-512-2250

The NLRB's publication, *Weekly Summary of National Labor Relations Board Cases,* is available through the Government Printing Office for $84 per year.

* Office of Labor Management Standards Publications
Division of Liaison and Compliance Assistance and Training
Office of Labor-Management Standards (OLMS)
U.S. Department of Labor
200 Constitution Ave, NW, Room N5605
Washington, DC 20210   202-219-7320

The OLMS publishes a variety of pamphlets explaining the rights and obligations of employers, employees, unions, and union officers under the under the Labor-Management Reporting and Disclosure Act (LMRDA) of 1959. Available publications include:

Brochures:
Bonding Requirements Under the LMRDA and the Civil Service Reform Act (CSRA)
Checklist for Conducting Local Union Officer Elections
Election Union Officials
Electing Local Unions Officers by Mail
Election of Officers of Labor Organizations
Labor-Management Reporting and Disclosure Act of 1959
LMRDA Regulations and Interpretative Bulletins
Reports Required Under the LMRDA and CSRA
Rights and Responsibilities Under the LMRDA and CSRA
Standard of Conduct Regulations (for federal employee organizations)
Conducting Local Union Officer Elections - A Guide for Election Officials (available from the Government Printing Office, #029-014-11250-0, $6, 202-512-1800)

Program Highlights:
Fact Sheet #1: *Labor-Management Reporting and Disclosure Act*
Fact Sheet #2: *Office of Labor-Management Standards (OLMS)*

Compliance Tips:
#1 *Retention of Union Records*
#2 *How to Run a Polling Place*
#3 *Mail Ballot Election*
#5 *Bonding Requirements*
#6 *Internal Financial Controls*

Contact the OLMS for copies of these publications.

* President's Advisory Committee on Mediation and Conciliation
Directors Office
Federal Mediation and Conciliation Service (FMCS)
2100 K St., NW
Washington, DC 20427   202-606-8100

Between 1985 and 1987 this committee heard testimony from business, labor, and the public sector regarding the health of their relationship, the role of mediation and arbitration in sustaining that relationship, and the future of collective bargaining in America. The report is available free from the FMCS.

* Preventive Mediation
Directors Office
Federal Mediation and Conciliation Service (FMCS)
2100 K St., NW
Washington, DC 20427   202-606-8100

FMCS preventive mediation is increasingly used by business and labor to anticipate problems before they obstruct the collective bargaining process from functioning as it should. Mediators use a variety of preventive mediation activities, including, among others, Labor-Management committees, a diversity of training programs, and for serious cases, Relationship by Objective Programs. Entire industries are addressed through conferences and seminars designed to raise the consciousness of the participants of the consequences of the failing relationship. Contact the FMCS for more information.

* Quality-of-Worklife
National Technical Information Service (NTIS)
U.S. Department of Commerce
5285 Port Royal Rd.   800-553-6847
Springfield, VA 22161   703-487-4650

Work Worth Doing is a two-part news documentary which describes how six progressive companies and their unions are using a variety of cooperative labor relations practices and quality-of-work-life programs not only to survive in the market place, but to thrive. *Part I* is an overview of several types of programs instituted in various organizations, and *Part II* provides more detailed information about how these programs were implemented and are maintained. Each part costs $90. (Part I, #AVA-16639-VNBI; Part II, #AVA-16642-VNBI.)

* Railroad Carrier Employee Grievances
National Railroad Adjustment Board
National Mediation Board
219 S. Dearborne, Room 1364
Chicago, IL 60604   312-886-7303

The Railroad Adjustment Board handles carrier employee grievances and disputes related to the interpretation and application of existing contracts which cannot be resolved in the usual manner. Disputes may concern rates of pay or working conditions, for example. Disputes are referred by petition of either or both parties to the appropriate Adjustment Board division.

- First Division: Train and yard service employees including engineers, firemen, hostlers, conductors, and trainmen.

- Second Division: Machinists, boilermakers, blacksmiths, sheet metal workers, carmen, coach cleaners, powerhouse employees, and railroad shop laborers.

- Third Division: Clerical employees, station and tower employees, telegraph employees, dispatchers, maintenance of way men, freight handlers, store employees, signalmen, sleeping car conductors, porters, maids, and dining car employees.

- Fourth Division: Employees of carriers directly or indirectly engaged in transportation of passengers or cargo by water and employees not coming under the jurisdiction of the other three divisions.

For further information, contact the office listed.

* Statistics on Dispute Mediation
Federal Mediation and Conciliation Service (FMCS)
2100 K St., NW, Room 712
Washington, DC 20427   202-606-8740

The FMCS can provide you with statistics on dispute mediation, preventive mediation, work stoppages, and contract mediation analysis for calendar years 1985-1990.

* Unfair Labor Practice Charges
Office of Appeals
National Labor Relations Board (NLRB)
1099 14th St., NW, Room 9404
Washington, DC 20570-0001   202-273-3760

Unfair labor practice charges may be filed by employees, employers, and unions against businesses and\or labor organizations at the nearest National Labor Relations Board regional office. If the regional office refuses to issue a complaint, contact this main office..

* Unfair Labor Practice Hearings
Division of Administrative Law Judges
National Labor Relations Board (NLRB)
1099 14th St., NW, Room 5400E
Washington, DC 20005-0001   202-501-8800

Administrative law judges conduct formal hearings regarding unfair labor practices. In addition to ruling on these cases, the judges assign hearing dates and maintain the calendar of upcoming cases.

* Union Bylaws and Public Information
Disclosure Room
Office of Labor-Management Standards
U.S. Department of Labor
200 Constitution Ave., NW, Room N5610
Washington, DC 20210   202-219-8861

Unions must file information reports, constitutions and bylaws, and annual financial reports with the Secretary of Labor. Officers and employees of labor unions must report any loans and gifts received from, or certain financial interests in, employers whose employees the union represents. Employers who engage in certain financial dealings with their employees, unions, and labor-relations consultants must file reports, as well as labor-relations consultants who enter into agreements with employers to persuade employees as to the manner of exercising their rights. All reports are public information, and may be examined at the OLMS national and regional offices. The publication, *Reports Required*, gives detailed information on who needs to file reports, and general rules relating to these reports. It is available from the Office of Policy Program and Support, 202-219-7373.

* Union Contracts Bargaining Calendar

Superintendent of Documents
Government Printing Office   202-512-1800
Washington, DC 20402   Fax: 202-512-2250

The Bureau of Labor Statistics' publishes *Bargaining Calendar*, a yearly schedule of information on anticipated contract adjustments between labor and management negotiators. Major situations by company and union are identified in which contracts will terminate, deferred wage increases will become due, changes in the Consumer Price Indexes will be reviewed, and contracts will be renewed. The price is $3.50, SN #029-001-03201-3.

* Union Contracts Clearinghouse

Public File of Collective Bargaining Agreements
Labor-Management Relations
Bureau of Labor Statistics
U.S. Department of Labor
Postal Square Bldg.
2 Massachusetts Ave., NE
Washington, DC 20212   202-606-6288

The Bureau of Labor Statistics maintains for public examination and use a file of collective bargaining agreements, including an annual and monthly calendar of contract expirations. The file covers 5,000 agreements in private industry and government, including virtually all those covering bargaining units with 1,000 employees or more, exclusive of railroads and airlines. Negotiators for both labor and management use this data. Copies of specific agreements are available at the cost of copying. Monthly listings of major agreement expirations are published in the *Monthly Labor Review* and the *Bargaining Calendar*.

* Union Contracts Database

Legal Services Office
Federal Mediation and Conciliation Service (FMCS)
2100 K Street, NW, Room 712
Washington, DC 20427   202-606-8140

The office also maintains a database of union contracts searchable by company name and dating back one year. Information can be obtained by written request.

* Union Contracts: Help Getting Copies

Office of Labor-Management Standards
U.S. Department of Labor
200 Constitution Ave., NW, Room S2203
Washington, DC 20210   202-219-6045

Every employee (whether or not a union member) is entitled, on request, to receive from a local union a copy of each collective bargaining agreement made by the local which directly affects that person's rights as an employee. OLMS should be notified if the union fails to furnish copies of the agreements.

* Union Information

Office of Labor-Management Standards
U.S. Department of Labor
200 Constitution Ave., NW, Room S2203
Washington, DC 20210   202-219-6045

The OLMS keeps a registry by location and name, each of the unions that files reports under the LMRDA or the CSRA. It also contains addresses of national unions and a series of statistical appendices such as the number of reporting affiliates per national union. This publication is available from the Government Printing Office.

* Union Investigations

Office of Labor-Management Standards
U.S. Department of Labor
200 Constitution Ave., NW, Room S2203
Washington, DC 20210   202-219-6045

The Labor-Management Reporting and Disclosure Act authorizes the Secretary of Labor to investigate any union to determine whether a violation has occurred. The investigation can be prompted by an analysis of reports a union files or in response to specific complaints. If the investigation is based on a complaint, information such as the complainant's name and the specific details of the complaint will not be disclosed, and the union will not be allowed to review the complaint or obtain a copy of it. Criminal violations will be referred to the Justice Department.

* Union Members' Bill of Rights

Office of Labor-Management Standards
U.S. Department of Labor
200 Constitution Ave., NW, Room S2203
Washington, DC 20210   202-219-6045

The Labor-Management Reporting and Disclosure Act grants certain rights to union members and protects their interests by promoting democratic procedures within labor organizations. The Act establishes a Bill of Rights for union members; reporting requirements for labor organizations, union officers, and employees, employers, labor-relations consultants, and surety companies; standards for the regular election of union officers; and certain safe guards for labor organization funds. Copies of the law and additional information are available from this office.

* Union Officer Elections Case Digest

Office of Labor-Management Standards
U.S. Department of Labor
200 Constitution Ave., NW, Room S2203
Washington, DC 20210   202-219-6045

The Digest and supplements present summaries of LMRDA and CSRA union officer election cases and trusteeship cases. Entries are excerpted from reported and unreported judicial opinions and court documents, and OLMS case records and deal with the legal aspects of the cases. The first 2 volumes of the digest, which cover from 1959-1982 are out of print, but information on them may be available from OLMS. The third volume, covering 1983 through 1986 is available from GPO for $23.

Occupational Health and Safety

* See also Drug and Chemical Dependence Chapter

All sorts of work-related health and safety issues are covered here, including radiation from computer screens, high blood pressure screening, smoking restrictions, and exposure to hazardous materials. These sources can tell you whom to contact for the latest scientific data on work-related injuries and safety, and can assist businesses in helping them follow federal and state safety guidelines. You'll find additional sources mentioned in the Health and Medicine Chapter in the section on Hazards: Chemicals and Toxins.

* Accident Reporting Network

Office of Field Programs
Occupational Safety and Health Administration
U.S. Department of Labor
200 Constitution Ave., NW, Room N3603
Washington, DC 20210   202-219-7725

All employers are required to report all accidents which result in a work-related death or five or more hospitalizations to the nearest OSHA office within 48 hours. You can not be discriminated against, fired, demoted, or otherwise penalized for complaining about a hazard to your employer, requesting an OSHA inspection, or participating in union safety and health activities. OSHA can take action, including going to court if necessary, to force your employer to restore your job, earnings, and benefits. You will not have to pay and legal fees.

* Agency for Toxic Substances and Disease Registry (ATSDR) Hotline

Division of Toxicology (DT)
Agency for Toxic Substances and Disease Registry (ATSDR)
1600 Clifton Rd., Mail Stop E-29
Atlanta, GA 30333   404-639-6000

The Division of Toxicology (DT) has a 24-hour information service to help callers with frequently asked questions about DT activities. A touchtone phone is needed to use this system. Callers with rotary dials should call during regular business hours for operator assistance. DT updates the information regularly. The Hotline provides the following information: how to get a list of hazardous substances, ranked by priority, that pose a significant health threat to people; how to get draft and final toxicological profiles; status of toxicological profiles being developed; ongoing and planned research activities; technical help on chemicals of interest or concern; how to qualify for the DT mailing list for free publications; and how to get more information on DT materials. For more information, call 404-639-6300 or fax 404-639-6315.

* Airline Pilots Medical Certification

Civil Aeromedical Institute
Federal Aviation Administration
U.S. Department of Transportation
Mike Monroney Aeronautical Center
P.O. Box 25082
Oklahoma, OK 73125   405-954-1000

CAMI operates a program for the medical certification of airmen, and educates pilots and physicians in matters related to aviation safety. It is also responsible for developing and producing brochures, slides, and training films for distribution to aviation groups and organizations. Contact CAMI for more information on certification or these education programs.

* Appealing an OSHA Standard

Office of the Assistant Secretary
Occupational Safety and Health Administration
U.S. Department of Labor
200 Constitution Ave, NW, Room S2315
Washington, DC 20210   202-219-8151

No decision on a permanent standard is ever reached without due consideration of the arguments and data received from the public in written submissions and at hearings. However, any person who may be adversely affected by a final or emergency standard may file a petition within 60 days for judicial review of the standard with the U.S. Court of Appeals for the circuit in which the objector lives or has his business.

* Appealing OSHA Citations

Office of Information
Occupational Safety and Health Review Commission
1120 20th St., NW
Washington, DC 20036-3419   202-606-5100

If an employer disagrees with any aspect of an Occupational Safety and Health Administration citation, issued by an inspector in the workplace, the employer must notify OSHA of that disagreement within 15 working days of receiving the citation. The employer is then entitled to have its dispute resolved by this Commission. A case that comes before the Commission is first heard and decided by an Administrative Law Judge. The judge's decision may be reviewed at the discretion of the Commission members, who have the authority to change that decision. Commission decisions and Judges' decisions not reviewed by the Commission can be appealed to the United States Court of Appeals.

* Audiovisuals on Occupational Safety and Health

Audiovisual Training Programs
National Audiovisual Center
Customer Services Section
8700 Edgeworth Dr.
Capitol Heights, MD 20743   800-778-6282

The *Occupational Safety and Health Audiovisual Training Programs* catalog lists over 65 high quality, low-cost hazard training programs from the safety experts at OSHA, NIOSH, and other federal agencies. It features OSHA's popular *Hazard Recognition Series* that teaches people what they need to know to work safety in a variety of situations. Contact this office for your free catalog, #PR996.

* Aviation Medicine

Research and Special Projects Medical Division
Office of Aviation Administration
Federal Aviation Administration
U.S. Department of Transportation
800 Independence Ave., SW, Room 325
Washington, DC 20591   202-366-6910

The FAA conducts aeromedical research in the biomedical and behavioral sciences.

* Census of Fatal Occupational Injuries

William Eisenberg, Data Manager
Office of Safety, Health, and Working Conditions
Bureau of Labor Statistics (BLS)
U.S. Department of Labor (DOL)
2 Massachusetts Ave., NE
Washington, DC 20212   202-606-6304

This program provides information on all fatal work injuries by state during a given year. The source of data includes death certificates, state worker compensation reports, state coroner reports, and other documents. Information is updated yearly and only information for the current year is available. Data is available free of charge in printed form only from the Office of Publications at the address above, or call 202-606-6304.

Careers and Workplace

* Chemical Hazards

Clearinghouse for Occupational Safety and Health Information
National Institute of Occupational Safety and Health (NIOSH)
4676 Columbia Parkway   800-35-NIOSH
Cincinnati, OH 45226   513-533-8471
                                          Fax: 513-533-8573

This clearinghouse can answer a wide range of questions regarding chemical hazards in the workplace and occupational safety by using their databases (National Occupational Hazard Survey and NIOSH Technical Information Center) to research your questions. They have many publications, such as *Prevention of Leading Work-Related Diseases* and *NIOSH Recommendations for Occupational Safety*, including a free catalog.

* College Courses

Educational Information
National Institute for Occupational Safety and Health
4676 Columbia Parkway
Cincinnati, OH 45226   513-533-8221

This division offers courses for industry and health care professionals on such topics as occupational safety, industrial hygiene, and safety in the laboratory. For a course listing and description, contact this office.

* Companies Inspected by OSHA

Office of Management Data Systems
Directorate of Administrative Programs
Occupational Safety and Health Administration (OSHA)
U.S. Department of Labor
200 Constitution Ave, NW, Room N3661
Washington, DC 20210   202-219-7888

This office can provide you with the entire range of inspection data, including who, what, when, where, and why companies were inspected, and the violations that were found.

* Cumulative Trauma Disorders

Superintendent of Documents
Government Printing Office (GPO)   202-512-1800
Washington, DC 20402   Fax: 202-512-2250

Ergonomics: The Study of Work discusses the types of work patterns that may cause Cumulative Trauma Disorders and other musculoskeletal or nervous system disorders resulting from ergonomic hazards, and the methods employers can use to control or prevent their occurrence. The term "ergonomics" can simply be defined as the study of work. Ergonomics helps adapt the job to fit the person, rather than force the person to fit the job. References, bibliography, and states with approved plans are included. This book costs $1, SN #029-016-00124-7 (1991, 28 pg).

* Educational Resource Centers for Health/Safety Training

Division of Training and Manpower Development
National Institute of Occupational Safety and Health (NIOSH)
4676 Columbia Parkway
Cincinnati, OH 45226-1998   513-533-8241

The National Institute of Occupational Safety and Health (NIOSH) supports Educational Resource Centers (ERCs) at 14 American universities to help ensure an adequate supply of trained occupational safety and health professionals.

* Emerging Trends in Work and Health

Institute for Alternative Futures
108 N. Alfred St., Second Floor
Alexandria, VA 22314   703-684-5880

The Future of Work and Health: Implications for Health Strategies (1987, 46 pg), summarizes emerging trends in work and health and explores issues concerning the development of health care strategies for worksites in the future. The cost of this publications is $7.

* Employee Safety Program

Consumer Product Safety Commission
5401 Westbard Avenue
Bethesda, MD 20207   301-504-0580

Through one of its regional offices, the Commission will send you information on safety hazards and accident prevention on-the-job.

* Equipment for Determining Hazards in the Workplace

Occupational Safety and Health Administration (OSHA)
U.S. Department of Labor
U.S. Post Office Bldg.
Fifth and Walnut Sts.
Cincinnati, OH 45202   513-684-3721

The OSHA Cincinnati Laboratory develops, evaluates, calibrates, and repairs hazard measurement instrumentation and equipment. They can provide you with information on all aspects of this equipment.

* Fatal Accident Investigations

Mr. Ted Petit
National Institute for Occupational Safety and Health (NIOSH)
1095 Willowdale Rd.
Morgantown, WV 26505-2888   304-285-6020

The Fatality Assessment and Control Evaluation (FACE) research project conducts investigations to gather information on factors that may have contributed to traumatic occupational fatalities.

* Hazards Detection

National Institute for Occupational Safety and Health (NIOSH)
4676 Columbia Parkway
Cincinnati, OH 45226   800-356-4674

NIOSH is responsible for conducting research to make the nation's workplaces healthier and safer by responding to urgent requests for assistance from employers, employees, and their representatives where imminent hazards are suspected. They conduct inspections, laboratory and epidemiologic research, publish their findings, and make recommendations for improved working conditions to regulatory agencies. NIOSH trains occupational health and safety workers and communicates research results to those concerned.

* Hazards Outreach Program

Office of Field Programs
U.S. Department of Labor
200 Constitution Ave., NW, Room N3603
Washington, DC 20210   202-219-7725

Local offices of the Occupational Safety and Health Administration carry out many different programs: enforcement, standard setting, state programs, voluntary compliance programs, and training and education. OSHA personnel are available to speak at civic clubs, union meetings, and trade association gatherings to explain new OSHA standards, encourage participation in OSHA rule makings, and answer questions about the agency's approach to workplace safety and health. OSHA also demonstrates, to the extent possible, technical equipment and materials. Prepackaged training programs are available to unions or trade groups. Contact you local OSHA office for more information.

* Health Hazard Evaluation

National Institute of Occupational Safety and Health (NIOSH)
4676 Columbia Parkway, R-9
Cincinnati, OH 45226   800-35-NIOSH

A typical Health Hazard Evaluation (HHE) involves studying a workplace, such as a particular department in a factory, industrial plant or other worksite. The study is done by NIOSH in response to concern expressed by employees, employee representatives, or employers, to find out whether there is a health hazard caused by exposure to hazardous materials (chemical or biological contaminants) in the workplace. NIOSH also evaluates other potentially hazardous working conditions, such as exposures to heat, noise, radiation, or musculoskeletal stresses. Requests for HHE's must be submitted in writing, specifying those work areas and potential hazards which need to be evaluated. Forms for requesting an HHE are available from the office listed above or a NIOSH regional office.

* Health Initiatives in the Workplace

National Clearinghouse for Alcohol and Drug Information (NCADI)
P.O. Box 2345   800-729-6686
Rockville, MD 20847-6686   TDD: 800-487-4889

"NCADI at Work" (VHA60) is a free videotape which shows the faces and services of the federal government's national clearinghouse for information about alcohol and other drugs. An ideal tape for use in conferences and workshops to alert anyone who is interested in prevention to this national resource for materials, statistics, reference checking, and other information services.

Be patient. If any phone number is incorrect, call (area code) 555-1212 and request the new listing.

* Health Promotion at Work

National Health Information Clearinghouse
P.O. Box 1133   800-336-4797
Cincinnati, OH 45226   301-565-4167

Health Promotion Goes to Work (1993, 73 pg), was produced on behalf of the National Coordinating Committee on Worksite Health Promotion. This compendium presents examples of worksite health programs with documented results. This publication, order #W0021, is available for a $5 handling fee.

* Health Promotion in the Workplace

Office of Disease Prevention and Health Promotion
Public Health Service
200 Independence Ave., SW, Room 738G
Washington, DC 20201   202-205-8611

This office works on developing policies for the Year 2000 objectives for health promotion. Their Preventive Services Task Force is developing recommendations for clinical practice, in addition to a worksite Health Promotion Task Force and a Nutrition Branch. This office also operates the Health Promotion Clearinghouse which offers many publications.

* Healthy Worksite Directory

National Health Information Clearinghouse
P.O. Box 1133   800-336-4797
Cincinnati, OH 45226   301-565-4167

The Healthy Worksites Directory of Federal Initiatives in Worksite Health Promotion (1992, 24 pg), is a compilation of projects and research sponsored by the federal government to stimulate and improve worksite health promotion in public and private sectors. It includes agency contacts, brief project descriptions, and available resources. This booklet, order #W0019 is available for $3.

* Industrial Hygiene

National Institute for Occupational Safety and Health (NIOSH)
4676 Columbia Parkway
Cincinnati, OH 45226   800-356-4674

The National Institute of Occupational Safety and Health (NIOSH) is responsible for conducting research to make the nation's workplaces healthier and safer by responding to urgent requests for assistance from employers, employees, and their representatives where imminent hazards are suspected. They conduct inspections, laboratory and epidemiologic research, publish their findings, and make recommendations for improved working conditions to regulatory agencies. NIOSH trains occupational health and safety workers and communicates research results to those concerned.

* Industry Health Studies

Division of Surveillance
Hazard Evaluation and Field Studies
National Institute for Occupational Safety and Health (NIOSH)
4676 Columbia Parkway
Cincinnati, OH 46226   800-356-4674

The National Institute of Occupational Safety and Health (NIOSH) conducts a wide range of studies regarding occupational health. They look at exposure to chemicals, PCB, and asbestos in the workplace, as well as other occupational health hazards. This information is made public to companies, unions, and private citizens.

* Industry Injuries and Illnesses Data

Superintendent of Documents
Government Printing Office   202-512-1800
Washington, DC 20402   Fax: 202-512-2250

Occupational Injuries and Illnesses, Counts, Rates and Characteristics (#029-001-3210-2, $17) is an annual report with detailed tables showing the job-related injury and illness experience of employees in a wide range of industries. For more information on available publications on occupational injury and illness statistics, call the Bureau of Labor Statistics at 202-606-6167.

* Information Clearinghouse

Information Office
Occupational Safety and Health Administration (OSHA)
U.S. Department of Labor
200 Constitution Ave., NW, Room S2315

Washington, DC 20210   202-219-4667

This office can provide you with information regarding the various OSHA programs, and can direct your inquiries to the appropriate office. The staff also schedules and coordinates public hearings and supports advisory committees in their development of recommendations to the Assistant Secretary of OSHA. A good starting place for information on OSHA is the booklet *All About OSHA*. It is available free of charge from OSHA.

* Injured Workers Statistics

Office of Safety, Health and Working Conditions
Bureau of Labor Statistics
U.S. Department of Labor
Postal Square Bldg.
2 Massachusetts Ave., NE
Washington, DC 20210   202-606-6167

This office maintains the nationwide employer record keeping system on job-related injuries and illnesses, conducts the annual survey based on these records and analyzes the results, and compiles supplementary statistics from other sources. States provide additional information on occupational accidents and exposures from workers' compensation records which give a sharper definition of occupational safety and health problems, associated characteristics, and possible action indicators. The *Work Injury Report* examines selected types of work injures to develop a detailed profile of characteristics associated with the injuries data from questionnaires completed by injured workers.

* Injuries and Illnesses On-the-Job

Office of Safety, Health and Working Conditions
Bureau of Labor Statistics
U.S. Department of Labor
Postal Square Bldg.
2 Massachusetts Ave., NE
Washington, DC 20210   202-606-6167

An annual survey, conducted by State employment security agencies on a cooperative basis with Bureau of Labor Statistics, provides data on the incidence of occupational injuries and illnesses by industry and State. Data available include incidence votes by private industry for injuries and illnesses, with estimates of numbers of fatal and nonfatal cases, and lost workday cases. *Work Injury Report Surveys* provide data collected from employees on characteristics of selected types of injuries. Data available include type of equipment involved, availability and use of protective devices, worker activity at time of accident, amount of training worker received, and presence of hazardous conditions.

* Job Safety and Health Information Clearinghouse

Technical Data Center
Occupational Safety and Health Administration (OSHA)
U.S. Department of Labor
200 Constitution Ave, NW, Room N2625
Washington, DC 20210   202-219-7500

This center houses technical information on all industries covered by OSHA. They maintain a library of 8,000 volumes and 250 journals, as well as an extensive microform collection of industry standards and OSHA rule making records. They have access to a wide variety of databases, including Dialog and two of their own. The Center is also the docket office and holds the hearing records on standards, the comments, and final rules, and can provide certified copies. The center is open to the public 8:15 a.m. to 4:45 p.m., Monday through Friday.

* Manufacturing Plants and Chemical Registry

National Institute of Occupational Safety and Health (NIOSH)
Division of Surveillance Hazard Evaluation
4676 Columbia Parkway
Cincinnati, OH 45226   513-841-4491

NIOSH maintains two databases, the National Occupational Hazard Survey Databases I & II, which contain surveys of 5,000 manufacturing plants each. NIOSH administers a questionnaire, investigates health and safety programs, and conducts an inventory of chemicals. Through the databases, NIOSH can identify potential exposure agents, describe health and safety programs, and by chemical can develop estimates of number of people exposed.

* Mine Accident Prevention Training

Division of Policy and Program Coordination
Education and Training

Careers and Workplace

Mine Safety and Health Administration
U.S. Department of Labor
4015 Wilson Blvd., Room 531
Arlington, VA 22203   703-235-1400

Training is an important tool for preventing accidents and avoiding unsafe and unhealthful working conditions. Training specialists coordinate their districts various training and miners to tailor programs specifically to individual needs. Training specialists conduct examinations to certify miners for certain specialized work, review training plans submitted by the mine operators, conduct various accident prevention programs, and assist at regional mine rescue contests.

* Miner Health and Safety Training Academy

Continuing Education Department
National Mine Safety and Health Academy
P.O. Box 1166
Beckley, WV 25801   304-256-3100

The National Mine Health and Safety Academy is the world's largest educational institution devoted solely to safety and health in mining. The academy serves as the central training facility for federal mine inspectors and mine safety professionals from other government agencies, the mining industry, and labor. Courses are offered on safety and inspection procedures, accident prevention, investigations, industrial hygiene, mine emergency procedures, mining technology, and management theory and techniques. The academy also provides field training and serves as a technical resource to help meet the mining community's instructional needs.

* Mine Safety and Health Case Files

Docket Office
Federal Mine Safety and Health Review Commission
1730 K St., NW, 6th Floor
Washington, DC 20006   202-653-5629

Transcripts of hearings and written decisions on mine safety and health cases brought before the Commission are housed here. Cases may involve mine closure orders, citations, or violations of mandatory safety and health standards, for example. Records may be freely accessed on a walk-in basis, but if a case is not recent, call ahead as old files are archived and may require a couple of weeks to retrieve.

* Mine Safety Clearinghouse

Office of Information and Public Affairs
Mine Safety and Health Administration
U.S. Department of Labor
4015 Wilson Blvd.
Arlington, VA 22203   703-235-1452

This office can provide you with general information regarding the Mine Safety and Health Administration, as well as brochures, manuals, and other publications regarding mine safety and health.

* Mine Safety Reviews

Acting Chairman
Federal Mine Safety and Health Review Commission
1730 K St., NW, 6th Floor
Washington, DC 20006   202-653-5644

Cases are brought before this commission and its Administrative Law Judges by the Mine Safety and Health Administration, mine operators, and miners or their representatives. Cases reviewed usually revolve around actions of the Mine Safety and Health Administration, which enforces occupational safety standards in U.S. surface and underground mines. Hearings are held as close as practical to locations of the mines involved. The Office of Administrative Law Judges operates from the following locations: 2 Skyline Plaza, 5203 Leesburg Pike, Falls Church, VA 22041, 703-756-6200; and at the Colonnade Center, Room 280, 1244 Speer Blvd., Denver, CO 80204; 303-844-5266. For further information on Commission activities, contact the Chairman's office listed above.

* Miners X-Rays

National Institute of Occupational Safety and Health (NIOSH)
944 Chestnut Ridge Road
Morgantown, WV 26505-2888   304-285-5724

The National Institute of Occupational Safety and Health (NIOSH) assures periodic chest X-rays to coal miners to facilitate early detection of coal workers pneumoconiosis through the Coal Worker Surveillance Program.

* Mining Hazards: Safety and Prevention Assistance

Office of Information
Mine Safety and Health Administration (MSHA)
U.S. Department of Labor
4015 Wilson Blvd
Arlington, VA 22203   703-234-1452

Specialists from MSHA's technical support facilities can provide technical and engineering assistance in helping to reduce hazards in their operations' mining systems. MSHA's engineers, scientists, and industrial hygienists often suggest possible solutions to difficult problems dealing with the safe design or maintenance of mining equipment and machinery, roof support or ventilation systems and mine waste facilities, and with the regular measurement and control of miners' exposure to health hazards such as noise, radiation, or harmful dust.

* Mining Industry Training Products

National Mine Health and Safety Academy
Attention: Business Office
P.O. Box 1166
Beckley, WV 25802   304-256-3257

The free catalog, *Training Products for the Mining Industry*, is divided into three major sections: films and videotapes; training materials such as instructional programs and safety manuals; and a complete listing of available MSHA informational reports. Each item includes a brief description, ordering information, and cost.

* Mining Injury and Illness Registry

MSHA Safety and Health Technology Center
Mine Safety and Health Administration (MSHA)
U.S. Department of Labor
P.O. Box 25367
Denver, CO 80225   303-231-5425

MSHA specialists collect, analyze, and publish data obtained from mine operators on the prevalence of work-related injuries and illnesses in the mining industry. This information helps MSHA's own staff, mining companies, and labor organizations gauge the effectiveness of their safety programs and to make needed improvements. MSHA specialists also publish a number of analytical studies and reports each year for use by the mining industry and the general public.

* NIOSH Databases

National Institute of Occupational Safety and Health (NIOSH)
4676 Columbia Parkway
Cincinnati, OH 45226-1998   513-533-8326

NIOSH maintains an extensive database of occupational safety and health information from around the world.

Registry of Toxic Effects of Chemical Substances (RTECS): this is a database of toxicological information compiled, maintained, and updated by NIOSH. RTECS currently contains over 125,000 chemicals. Six types of toxicity data are included in the file; primary irritation; mutagenic effects; reproductive effects; tumorigenic effects; acute toxicity; and other multiple dose toxicity. Available online and CD-ROM.

NIOSHTIC: is a bibliographic database of literature in the field of occupational safety and health. About 160 current, English language technical journals provide approximately 35 percent of the additions to NIOSHTIC annually. Types of information includes: behavioral sciences; biochemistry, physiology, and metabolism; toxicology; pathology and histology; chemistry; control technology; education and training; epidemiological studies of diseases and disorders; ergonomics; health physics; occupational medicine; safety; biological hazards; and hazardous waste. Available online and CD-ROM.

NIOSH Manual of Analytical Methods (NMAM): is a compilation of methods for sampling and analysis of contaminants in workplace air, and in the blood and urine of worker who are occupationally exposed to that air. These methods have been developed specifically to have adequate sensitivity to detect the lowest concentrations and sufficient flexibility of range to detect concentrations exceeding safe levels of exposure. Available on diskette.

NIOSH Pocket Guide to Chemical Hazards (NPG): is intended as a source of general industrial hygiene information quick and convenient for workers, employers, and occupational health professionals. The NPG presents key information and data in abbreviated tabular form for chemicals or substance groupings that are found in the work environment. Available on CD-ROM and diskette.

* NIOSH Publications

National Institute of Occupational Safety and Health (NIOSH)
4676 Columbia Parkway, C-13   800-35-NIOSH
Cincinnati, OH 45226-1998   513-537-8471
                         Fax: 513-533-8573

The *NIOSH Bookshelf* lists the publications available from NIOSH. It contains listings for publications containing recommendations for chemical, physical and other hazards in the workplace. it also lists NIOSH bibliographies as well as technical publications available. It is free. This listing can also be delivered directly to your fax machine by calling 404-332-4565.

* Occupational Health and Safety TVA Investigations

Human Resources
Tennessee Valley Authority
MPB 1E 215B-M
Muscle Shoals, AL 35660   205-386-2893

This office formulate and oversees the implementation of TVA's occupational health and safety policies and plans. It develops and issues standards for control of hazards in the workplace, supports the investigation of serious accidents, and ensures appropriate follow-through. The staff coordinates TVA review of regulatory requirements and industry trends relating to safety practices, and develops agency comments on proposed regulations. Staff develops and delivers management and employee safety orientation and training in health and safety. The program provides industrial hygiene services for the agency, including surveys to measure employee exposure to toxic chemicals and physical agents, and recommends appropriate administrative and engineering control methods. It is responsible for handling workplace and community noise prevention programs, and by-product material licensing support and radiation safety services.

* Occupational Safety and Health Administration CD-ROM Subscription Service

Occupational Safety and Health Administration (OSHA)
U.S. Department of Labor (DOL)
200 Constitution Ave., NW
Washington, DC 20210   801-487-0680

This CD-ROM contains major Occupational Safety and Health Administration (OSHA) data. Included are OSHA information files of standards, selected interpretations, directives, Federal Register Index (OSHA) fact sheets, speeches, and other data issued quarterly. Annual subscriptions are available from the Superintendent of Documents, Government Printing Office, Washington, DC 20402-9325; 202-512-1800, fax: 202-512-2250. The stock number is 729-013-00000-5, and the cost is $88 per year.

* Occupational Safety and Health Publications

Superintendent of Documents
Government Printing Office   202-512-1800
Washington, DC 20402   Fax: 202-512-2250

The Government Printing Office (GPO) can provide you with a bibliography that lists hundreds of source materials on occupational safety and health issues. Call the GPO and ask for *Subject Bibliography 213*. It's free. This document can be delivered directly to your fax machine by calling GPO FaxWatch at 202-512-1716.

* Occupational Safety and Health Administration Regional Offices

Atlanta
1375 Peachtree St., NE, Room 587, Atlanta, GA 30367; 404-347-3573

Boston
133 Portland St, 1st Floor, Boston, MA 02114; 617-565-7159

Chicago
230 South Dearborn Street, Room 3244, Chicago, IL 60604; 312-353-2220.

Dallas
525 Griffin Street, Room 602, Dallas, TX 75202; 214-767-4731

Denver
1999 Broadway, Suite 1690, Denver, CO 80202; 303-391-5858

Kansas City
1100 Main St., Suite 800, City Center Square Bldg., Kansas City, MO 64105; 816-426-5861.

New York
201 Varick Street, Room 670, New York, NY 10014; 212-337-2378.

Philadelphia
Gateway Building, Suite 2100, 3535 Market Street, Philadelphia, PA 19104; 215-596-1201.

Santa Rosa
1221 Farmers Lane, Suite 300, Santa Rosa, CA 95405; 510-557-8640

Seattle
1111 Third Avenue, Suite 715, Seattle, WA 98101-3212; 206-553-5930.

* OSHA Certificate of Service

Executive Secretary
Occupational Safety and Health Review Commission
1120 20th St., NW, 9th Floor
Washington, DC 20036-3419   202-606-5100

Documents that have been filed with the Commission or an Administrative Law Judge of the Commission must be copied and given to all parties in a case, either by first-class mail or by hand. A statement must also be submitted showing the date and manner of the delivery and the names of the persons receiving copies of the documents.

* OSHA Commission Decisions Index

Executive Secretary
Occupational Safety and Health Review Commission (OSHRC)
1120 20th St., NW, 9th Floor
Washington, DC 20036-3419   202-606-5100

The *Index to Decisions of the OSHRC*, which lists company names and OSHRC docket numbers, is sold based on the number of pages and the years requested. For a price quote, contact the above office. Subscriptions to microfiche copies of OSHRC decisions, called *OSHRC Reports*, are available from the Superintendent of Documents, Government Printing Office, Washington, DC, 202-512-1800.

* OSHA Commission Docket

Office of Information
Occupational Safety and Health Review Commission
1120 20th St., NW, 9th Floor
Washington, DC 20036-3419   202-606-5100

Copies of the proceedings of any of the cases decided by the Commission and Administrative Law Judges are available for public inspection. An appointment in advance is needed with the office above.

* OSHA Commission Publications

Office of Information
Occupational Safety and Health Review Commission
1120 20th St., NW, 9th Floor
Washington, DC 20036-3419   202-606-5100

The following information booklets are free upon request describing the function of the Commission: *Simplified Proceedings, Rules of Procedure, A Guide to Procedures of the OSHRC*, and the *Annual Report to the President*.

* OSHA Complaint and Response

Executive Secretary
Occupational Safety and Health Review Commission
1120 20th St., NW, 9th Floor
Washington, DC 20036-3419   202-606-5100

Within 30 calendar days of the date on which the Commission receives an employer's Notice of Contest, the Secretary of Labor must file a written complaint with the Commission. A copy must be sent to the employer and any other parties in the case. The complaint sets forth in detail the alleged violation for which the employer received the citation. The employer must then file a written answer to the complaint with the Commission within 30 calendar days after receipt of the complaint. This answer must admit or deny each paragraph and subparagraph of the complaint. The answer is filed by mailing it to the address above.

* OSHA Employer Notice of Contest

Office of Information
Occupational Safety and Health Review Commission
1120 20th St., NW, 9th Floor

Washington, DC 20036-3419   202-606-5100

There are two steps that must be taken by an employer who wishes to contest all or part of a citation received from the Occupational Safety and Health Administration. Within 15 working days from receipt of the proposed penalty, the employer must notify the Labor Department of the employer's intent to contest all or part of the citation, the penalty proposed, or the time allowed for the correction of the alleged violation. This notification is called a *Notice of Contest*. After the U.S. Department of Labor notifies the Review Commission that the citation has been contested, the employer will receive a notice from the Review Commission that the case has been filed. Forms will also be supplied to notify affected employees and their union that a notice of contest has been filed.

* OSHA Freedom of Information Act Requests

Freedom of Information Act Officer
Occupational Safety and Health Review Commission
1120 20th St., NW, 9th Floor
Washington, DC 20036-3419   202-606-5100

Freedom of Information requests should be sent to the officer above.

* OSHA Publications

Publications
Occupational Safety and Health Administration (OSHA)
U.S. Department of Labor
P.O. Box 37535
Washington, DC 20013-7535   202-219-4667

Occupational Safety and Health Administration (OSHA) can provide you with a list of publications related to safety and health issues free of charge. Government Printing Office (GPO) publications are also listed in this publication.

* OSHA Simplified Appeals Process

Executive Secretary
Occupational Safety and Health Review Commission
1120 20th St., NW, 9th Floor
Washington, DC 20036-3419   202-606-5100

Simplified proceedings are designed to expedite the resolution of cases, to make it easier for those appearing before the Commission to proceed without an attorney, to reduce paperwork, and to reduce the expense of litigation. This process is used in cases where the issues are less involved and a formal procedure is not needed for a fair hearing. Contact this office for more information.

* Petition for Modification of Abatement

Executive Secretary
Occupational Safety and Health Review Commission
1120 20th St., NW, 9th Floor
Washington, DC 20036-3419   202-606-5100

If an employer has made a good faith effort to correct an OSHA violation within the given abatement period but has not been able to do so because of reasons beyond his/her control, he/she may file a petition for modification of abatement. This petition is filed with the Occupational Safety and Health Administration Area Director no later than the end of the next working day following the day on which abatement was to have been completed.

* Petitioning the Government on Safe Working Conditions

Office of the Assistant Secretary
Occupational Health and Safety Administration (OSHA)
U.S. Department of Labor
200 Constitution Ave., NW, Room S2315
Washington, DC 20210   202-219-8151

OSHA can begin standards-setting procedures on its own initiative, or in response to petitions from other parties, including the Secretary of Health and Human Services, the National Institute for Occupational Safety and Health, State and local governments, any nationally-recognized standards-producing organization, employer or labor representative, or any other interested party. Contact this office for more information on the standard setting procedure.

* Publications and Training Materials

OSHA Publications
Occupational Safety and Health Administration (OSHA)

U.S. Department of Labor
P.O. Box 37535
Washington, DC 20013-7535   202-219-4667

Contact this office for a list of OSHA free publications and *Federal Register* reprints pertaining to OSHA. These publications are available at no charge.

* Regulations

Subscription Service
Superintendent of Documents
Government Printing Office   202-512-1800
Washington, DC 20402   Fax: 202-512-2250

The OSHA subscription service was developed to assist the public in keeping current with OSHA standards. This service provides all standards, interpretations, regulations, and procedures in easy to use loose-leaf form, punched for use in a three-ring binder. All changes and additions are issued for and indefinite period of time. The following volumes are available:

General Standards and Interpretations (includes agriculture)
Maritime Standards and Interpretations
Construction Standards and Interpretations
Other Regulations and Procedures
Field Operations Manual
Industrial Hygiene Field Operations Manual

* Review Commission

Occupational Safety and Health Review Commission
1120 20th St., NW, 9th Floor
Washington, DC 20036-3419   202-606-5100

The Occupational Safety and Health Review Commission serves as a court to resolve disputes that arise under the Occupational Safety and Health Act of 1970, which involves workplace inspections. The Commission is not connected in any way with the U.S. Department of Labor or the Occupational Safety and Health Administration.

* Safety and Health Training Institute

Occupational Safety and Health Administration (OSHA)
U.S. Department of Labor
1555 Times Dr.
Des Plaines, IL 60018   708-297-4810

The OSHA Training Institute in Des Plaines, Illinois, provides basic and advanced training and education in safety and health for federal and state compliance officers; state consultants; other federal agency personnel; private sector employers; and employees and their representatives. Institute courses cover such areas as electrical hazards, machine guarding, ventilation, and ergonomics. Many courses are available for personnel in the private sector dealing with such subjects as safety and health in the construction industry and methods of voluntary compliance with OSHA standards.

* Safety and the Workplace: Onsite Consultation

OSHA Publications
Occupational Safety and Health Administration (OSHA)
U.S. Department of Labor
P.O. Box 37535
Washington, DC 20013-7535   202-219-4667

Using a free consultation service, employers can find out about potential hazards at their worksites, improve their safety management systems, and even qualify for a one-year exemption from routine OSHA inspections. Primarily targeted for smaller businesses, this safety and health consultation program is completely separate from the OSHA inspection effort. In addition, no citations are issued or penalties proposed. These consultations are carried out through State OSHA consultation programs. Contact this OSHA office for a listing of these state programs.

* Scientific and Medical Issues

Directorate of Technical Support FPB
Occupational Safety and Health Administration
U.S. Department of Labor
200 Constitution Ave., NW, Room N3653
Washington, DC 20210   202-219-7031

This office serves as the principal source of agency expertise with respect to scientific, engineering, and medical issues involved in the overall occupational safety and health field. The Directorate manages a centralized program to provide technical interpretations and clarifications of OSHA standards, rule making and related matters.

* Small Business Health and Safety

National Institute for Occupational Safety and Health
4676 Columbia Parkway
Cincinnati, OH 45226

800-35-NIOSH
513-533-8471
Fax: 513-533-8573

Many publications are available through this office regarding safety, occupational hazards, and occupational safety and health programs for a variety of business settings. Contact this office for a free catalog of publications.

* Smoke Free Workplaces

Publications Catalog
Office of Smoking and Health
Mail Stop K-50
Atlanta, GA

Secondhand Smoke in the Workplace is one of the publications available from the Center for Disease Control's Office of Smoking and Health. This contains information on secondhand smoke, the benefits of a smoke free workplace, and how to get your workplace to be smoke free. All of the publications are free, most of the information is available in written form, and some is available by fax. By calling the number listed, you can request a free catalog of publications by mail, or receive a listing by fax of the publications that are available via fax machine.

* Speakers from OSHA

Occupational Safety and Health Review Commission
1120 20th St., NW, 9th Floor
Washington, DC 20036-3419

202-606-5100

The Chairman, General Counsel, and members of the Commission have participated as speakers for various industry and civic organizations. A written request to the individual is necessary for a confirmation of availability and attendance.

* Standards on Occupational Safety and Health

Superintendent of Documents
Government Printing Office
Washington, DC 20402

202-512-1800
Fax: 202-512-2250

The *Federal Register* is one of the best sources of information on standards, since all OSHA standards are published there when adopted, as are all amendments, corrections, insertions, or deletions. Annual subscriptions are available from the Government Printing Office. Each year the office of the *Federal Register* publishes all current regulations and standards in the *Code of Federal Regulations*, available at many libraries and from the Government Printing Office. OSHA's regulations are collected in Title 29 of the CFR, Part 1900-1999.

* Substance Abuse Information Database (SAID) Diskette

Office of the Assistant Secretary for Policy (OASP)
U.S. Department of Labor (DOL)
200 Constitution Ave., NW
Washington, DC 20210

800-808-0965

This is a free software program from the Department of Labor. The program is designed to provide employers with information for establishing employee drug abuse awareness programs and employee counseling. SAID also includes guidelines for employers in dealing with drug-addicted employees. The OASP does plan on establishing a SAID Bulletin Board service in the future.

* Survey of Worksite Health Promotion Activities

National Health Information Clearinghouse
P.O. Box 1133
Cincinnati, OH 45226

800-336-4797
301-565-4167

The Executive Summary of the 1992 National Survey of Worksite Health Promotion Activities (1992, 26 pg), measures the growth of worksite health promotion activities since the first national survey in 1985. A major focus of the survey was to assess progress toward worksite objectives in Healthy People 2000, a national initiative to improve the health of all Americans through prevention. It is driven by 300 specific national health promotion and disease prevention objectives within 22 priority areas, targeted for achievement by the year 2000. This booklet, order #W0020, is available for a $2 handling fee.

* Toxic Hazards in the Workplace

Salt Lake City Laboratory
Occupational Safety and Health Administration (OSHA)
U.S. Department of Labor
P.O. Box 65200
Salt Lake City, UT 84165-0200

801-487-0267

The OSHA Analytical Laboratory conducts extensive analyses, tests, and studies of all samples submitted by safety and health compliance officers and others to evaluate toxicity and the existence of health hazards.

* Wellness Outreach at Work Program

National Institutes of Health
National Heart, Lung, and Blood Institute (NHLBI)
P.O. Box 30105
Bethesda, MD 20824-0105

301-251-1222

The Wellness Outreach at Work program was developed by the Worker Health Program, a research unit of the Institute of Labor and Industrial Relations at the University of Michigan. The program offers comprehensive risk reduction services to all employees at a workplace. It encompasses screening for cardiovascular risks, referral for medical treatment, followup counseling, and health improvement programs. It also suggests ways to organize the worksite to create an environment that supports risk reduction and health improvement. The Wellness Outreach at Work Program has been implemented in more than 100 worksites and has reached more than 75,000 employees in organizations ranging in size from 5 employees to 6,000 employees, both blue collar and white collar.

* Worker Health and Safety Standards

Directorate of Health Standards Programs
Occupational Safety and Health Administration (OSHA)
U.S. Department of Labor
200 Constitution Ave., NW, Room N3718
Washington, DC 20210

202-219-7075

OSHA develops mandatory health standards for such varied fields as manufacturing, construction, longshoring, agriculture, law and medicine, charity and disaster relief, organized labor, and private education. Contact this office about these standards.

* Workplace Safety and Health Awards

Occupational Safety and Health Administration (OSHA)
U.S. Department of Labor
200 Constitution Ave., NW, Room N3700
Washington, DC 20210

202-219-7266

Designed to augment OSHA's enforcement efforts, the Star, Merit, and Demonstration Programs encourage and recognize excellence in occupational safety and health. Only those companies which demonstrate commitments to workplace safety and health beyond the requirements of the OSHA standards are eligible. Participation in the programs exempts a worksite from OSHA's programmed inspections. Companies must have strong safety and health programs, along with employee participation. Contact this office for an application, information, and complete details regarding the various programs.

* Worksite Health Programs

National Health Information Clearinghouse
P.O. Box 1133
Washington, DC 20013-1133

800-336-4797
301-565-4167 (MD and DC)

Worksite Wellness Media Reports illustrate examples of worksite health promotion programs and also present comprehensive reports on health facts. These reports are designed for the media covering the business community. The latest report totaling 318 pages (Order No.W0015) is available for $3.

* Worksite Nutrition Program

National Health Information Clearinghouse
P.O. Box 1133
Cincinnati, OH 45226

800-336-4797
301-565-4167

The Healthy Menu Program Kit provides the *Healthy Menu Manual*, the *Healthy Menu Theme Planner*, the *Healthy Menu Cookbook*, the Healthy Menu newsletters, and the Nutrition Information handouts. This presents strategies for employers and health promotion professionals interested in implementing a worksite nutrition program. The Kit, order #W0018, is available for a $3 handling fee.

Be patient. If any phone number is incorrect, call (area code) 555-1212 and request the new listing.

265

Federal Employment

As the largest single employer in the country, the federal government has plenty of benefits, programs, and services for its employees, many of whom may not know all that's available to them. Here federal employees will find information sources on pensions, compensation, new job opportunities, health benefits, merit pay, and countless other programs.

* Affirmative Employment

Office of Affirmative Employment Programs
Office of Personnel Management
1900 E St., NW, Room 6355
Washington, DC 20415   202-606-1059

The Office of Personnel Management (OPM) seeks to eliminate nonmerit considerations such as race, color, religion, sex, national origin, or age from all aspects of federal employment through its affirmative employment efforts. OPM also operates selective placement programs for physically and mentally handicapped persons, and programs for other groups including veterans, youths, and women. Contact this office for more information.

* Alcoholic and Drug Treatment Programs

Labor Relations
Office of Personnel Management
1900 E St., NW
Washington, DC 20415   202-606-1046

All government employee health and alcoholism/drug abuse programs are overseen by this office. Contact this office for more information.

* Annuities

Retirement and Insurance Group
Annuitant Services Division
Office of Retirement Programs
Office of Personnel Management
1900 E St., NW, Room 3321
Washington, DC 20415   202-606-2039

This office has free pamphlets describing annuity benefits under the civil service retirement system. Contact this office for more information.

* Appeals Process

Office of the Appeals Counsel
Merit Systems Protection Board
1120 Vermont Ave., NW, Room 864
Washington, DC 20419   202-653-8888

The Office of Appeals Counsel assists the Board in judicially settling petitions for review from initial decisions issued by administrative judges in the regional offices. The office receives and analyzes the petitions, researches applicable laws, rules, and precedents, and submits proposed opinions to the board members for their final settlement. When an agency issues a decision notice to an employee on a matter that is appealable to the Board, the agency must provide the employee with a notice of the time limits for the appeal and the address for filing the appeal, a copy of or access to a copy of the Board's regulations, a copy of the appeal form, and a notice of any right the employee has to file a grievance.

* Appeals Regional Offices

Office of Policy and Evaluation
Merit Systems Protection Board
1120 Vermont Ave., NW, Room 800
Washington, DC 20419   202-653-8900

The Merit Systems Protection Board (MSPB) Regional Offices are located in 11 major metropolitan areas throughout the United States: Atlanta, Boston, Chicago, Dallas, Denver, New York, Philadelphia, St. Louis, San Francisco, Seattle, and Washington, DC. These offices receive and process the initial appeals filed with the Board. Administrative judges in the regional offices have the primary function of issuing fair, timely, and well-reasoned decisions on all appeals. Contact this office for a listing of these offices and more information.

* Aviation Careers

Aviation Education Officer
Federal Aviation Administration (FAA)
U.S. Department of Transportation
800 Independence Ave., SW, Room 575
Washington, DC 20591   202-267-3190

The Federal Aviation Administration's (FAA) Aviation Education Program offers volunteer assistance to the nation's schools through the following programs: career guidance; tours of airports, control towers, and other facilities; classroom lectures and demonstrations; aviation safety information; aviation education resource materials; computerized clearinghouse of aviation and space information; aviation science instruction programs for home/school computers; "Partnerships-in-Education" activities; and teachers' workshops. Write to the above office for more information.

* Civil Service Exams

Federal Job Information Center
General Information
Office of Personnel Management
1900 E St., NW, Room 1416
Washington, DC 20415   202-606-2700/2701

Information on Civil Service Exams is contained in the pamphlet, *Current Federal Examination Announcements* (AN-2279). This free pamphlet is available from any Federal Job Information Center.

* Compensation Benefits

Office of Worker's Compensation Programs
Employment Standards Administration
U.S. Department of Labor
200 Constitution Ave., NW, Room S3524
Washington, DC 20210   202-219-7503

The Federal Employees' Compensation Act (FECA) provides compensation benefits to civilian employees of the U.S. for disability due to personal injury sustained while in the performance of duty. The Act also provides compensation for employment-related disease. Benefits also available to injured employees include rehabilitation, medical, surgical, and hospital services and supplies, and necessary transportation expenses. FECA provides compensation to dependents if the injury or disease causes the employees's death.

* Employee and Annuitant Information Center

Retirement Information Branch
Retirement Programs
Retirement and Insurance Group
Office of Personnel Management
1900 E St., NW, Room 1323B
Washington, DC 20415   202-606-0500

This clearinghouse offers guidance on federal retirees' annuities.

* Employee Conduct Regulations

Office of Government Ethics
1201 New York Ave., Suite 500
Washington, DC 20005   202-523-5757

Ethics in Government, federal regulations, and a digest of opinions since 1979 is outlined in the *Agency Relations Packet*, which is available free from the above office.

* Environmental Protection Agency Job Hotline

Recruitment
Environmental Protection Agency (EPA)
401 M Street, SW
Washington, DC 20460   202-260-5055

This EPA National Recruitment Program Number enables potential hirees to contact the Agency for employment information and assists EPA managers in locating and hiring qualified employees to fill vacant positions. The number operates Monday through Friday, 8:30 a.m. to 4:30 p.m. (EST).

* Ethics in Federal Workplace

Office of Government Ethics
1201 New York Ave., Suite 500
Washington, DC 20005   202-523-5757

To prevent conflicts of interest on the part of officers and employees of any executive agency, overall direction of executive branch policies is provided by this office. Rules and regulations are developed here pertaining to employee conduct and post-employment conflicts of interest, and public financial disclosure is monitored. Contact this office for more information.

* Executive Development Center

Federal Executive Institute
Office of Personnel Management
1301 Emmet St.
Charlottesville, VA 22903   804-980-6200

The Federal Executive Institute (FEI) is an interagency executive development center which responds to the training and development needs of federal executives. FEI programs schedule courses that are designed to facilitate executive improvement. Programs in four categories are conducted: The Executive leadership and Management Program, the Senior Executive Education program, FEI alumni Follow-up Conferences, and Special Programs.

* Ex-Railroad Workers Placement Service

Unemployment and Sickness Insurance
Railroad Retirement Board
844 N. Rush St.
Chicago, IL 60611   312-751-4800

The Board operates a free job placement service for experienced railroad workers who have lost their jobs. It is available to those claiming unemployment benefits. Contact this office or the nearest Railroad Retirement Board Office for more information.

* Federal Contracts

Contracting Division
Office of Personnel Management
1900 E Street, NW, Room 1452
Washington, DC 20415   202-606-2240

Information on contracts can be obtained by contacting one of the field service centers listed below.

Atlanta Region
Jacquelyn Moses, Federal Building, 75 Spring Street, SW, Atlanta, GA 30303-3019; 404-331-3455. Serving: Alabama, Florida, North Carolina, South Carolina, Georgia, Mississippi, Tennessee, and Virginia

Chicago Region
Karen Johnson, Federal Building, 230 South Dearborn Street, Chicago, IL 60604; 312-353-2930. Serving: Illinois, Indiana, Iowa, Kansas, Kentucky, Michigan, Minnesota, Missouri, Nebraska, North Dakota, Ohio, South Dakota, West Virginia, and Wisconsin

Philadelphia Region
Joseph Stix, Federal Building, 600 Arch Street, Philadelphia, PA 19106-1596; 215-597-7670. Serving: Connecticut, Delaware, Maine, Maryland, Massachusetts, New Hampshire, New Jersey, New York, Pennsylvania, Puerto Rico, Rhode Island, Vermont, and Virgin Islands

San Francisco Region
Linda Peterson, 120 Howard, Room 735, San Francisco, CA 94105; 415-281-7094. Serving: Alaska, California, Hawaii, Idaho, Nevada, Oregon, Pacific Ocean Area, and Washington

* Federal Employees' Attitudes Surveys

Center for Electronic Records
National Archives and Records Administration
8th St. and Pennsylvania Ave., NW, Room 20E
Washington, DC 20408   202-501-5402

This center has data pertaining to federal employees' attitudes on a variety of topics, and can provide you with a complete list of the survey samples.

* Federal Employees Current Attitudes

Office of Communications
Office of Personnel Management
1900 E St., NW
Washington, DC 20415   202-606-1212

A government-wide attitude survey of federal employees was administered to establish a baseline of employee attitudes about their jobs and work environment. Groupings include federal agencies, pay levels, pay systems, and supervisory and non-supervisory personnel. *Federal Employee Attitudes: Phase 2--Follow Up*, a report, can be purchased from the Superintendent of Documents, Government Printing Office, Washington, DC 20402; 202-512-1800.

* Federal Job Information Centers

Federal Job Information Center
Career America Connection
Office of Personnel Management
1900 E Street, NW, Room 1416   912-757-3000
Washington, DC 20415   202-606-2700

Federal Job Information Centers are located in major metropolitan areas. This network of centers provides information on summer employment, necessary application forms, exams, and all other aspects pertaining to federal employment. *Federal Job Information Centers,* a free directory, is available from the above office. By using the government pages of your local phone directory, you will be able to locate the center nearest you.

* Federal Job Opportunity Bulletin Board (F-JOB)

Staffing Service Center
Office of Personnel Management (OPM)
75 Spring St   404-331-4315
Atlanta, GA 30303   Data: 912-757-3100

This bulletin board provides complete information about jobs that are currently available in the federal government as well as information on a variety of employment topics. You are also able to network with others who are also looking for federal government jobs. You cannot submit applications through the bulletin board. If there is a job you would like to apply for, you must contact the agency that posted that job.

* Federal Labor Relations Authority
Freedom of Information

Office of Information Resources and Research Services
Federal Labor Relations Authority (FLRA)
607 14th St., NW
Washington, DC 20424-0001   202-482-6550

The Public Information Office listed above is the Freedom of Information Act contact for the Authority.

* Federal Occupational and Career Information System (FOCIS)

Associate Director for Administration
Office of Personnel Management (OPM)
1900 E St., NW, Room 5542   202-606-2000
Washington, DC 20415-0001   Fax: 202-606-2214

To order:
National Technical Information Service (NTIS)
U.S. Department of Commerce   800-553-6847
5285 Port Royal Rd.   703-487-4650
Springfield, VA 22161   Fax: 703-321-8547

The Federal Occupational and Career Information System (FOCIS) is a PC-based interactive software program developed by the U.S. Office of Personnel Management (OPM) to help federal employees and job seekers to obtain information about federal careers, occupations, agencies, current job openings, and training. Job seekers use FOCIS for career guidance and for exploring the federal world of work. Typing, clerical, and interest tests can be taken on the computer. FOCIS contains a database of information on almost 600 federal occupations and 500 federal organizations. Users with modems can dial into OPM Mainstreet Bulletin Board, electronically transfer current job vacancy listings to their computer, and search for job openings using FOCIS. Federal employees can use FOCIS to access information on more than one thousand nationwide training courses. This program is available on diskette for $55. 3.5" high density, PB93-502557CBX; 5.25" high density, PB93-502540CBX: 3.5" double density, PB93-502532CBX; 5.25" double density, PB93-502524CBX.

* Forest Ranger Jobs

Forest Service
U.S. Department of Agriculture
Recruitment
P.O. Box 2417
Washington, DC 20013   703-235-2730
Contact this office for information on a career as a forest ranger.

* General Schedule Classification

Office of Public Affairs
Office of Personnel Management
1900 E St., NW, Room 5F12
Washington, DC 20415   202-606-1212
A variety of publications on government service classifications are available. Single copies are free, including *A Report on Study of Position Classification Accuracy in Executive Branch on Occupation Under the General Schedule*. The *Handbook of Occupational Groups and Series of Classes* ($120) is sold by the Superintendent of Documents, Government Printing Office, Washington, DC 20402; 202-512-1800.

* Health Benefits

Insurance Programs
Retirement and Insurance Programs
Office of Personnel Management
1900 E St., NW, Room 3439
Washington, DC 20415   202-606-0191
This office oversees the federal employees health benefits program which includes various types of hospital, surgical and medical benefits for federal employees. Contact this office for more information.

* Health Professions in U.S. Public Health Corps

Office of Research and Planning
Bureau of Health Professions
5600 Fishers Lane, Room 8-43
Rockville, MD 20857   301-443-6936
The Bureau of Health Professions supports the development of human resources needed to staff the U.S. health care system. It is concerned with health professions education, credentialing of health care personnel, and analysis of data to project needs for health care personnel. They also support student assistance and analyze current and future personnel supply, requirements and distribution. This office can supply you with data regarding health profession supply distribution on the level of nursing training in any area of the country. This information is often used by consultants, corporations involved with medical technology, and other government agencies.

* Incentive Awards

Performance Management
Office of Personnel Management
1900 E St., NW, Room 7412
Washington, DC 20415   202-606-2828
Cash and honor awards are available under the incentive award program to employees for effecting improvements in government operations or services through their suggestions, inventions, and superior performance. The publication *Achievements* is available for free. Information from this office is also available in newsletters, info-packs, and on the Office of Personnel Management (OPM) Mainstreet Bulletin Board at 202-606-4800. Contact this office for more information.

* Index To OPM Information

Publishing Management Branch
Office of Personnel Management (OPM)
1900 E St., NW, Room B430
Washington, DC 20415   202-606-1822

The *Handbook of Publications and Periodicals* is available at no cost from this office. This index lists all Office of Personnel Management publications, including information required to be available under the Freedom of Information Act. Requests must be submitted in writing.

* Job Grading System

Standard Development Staff
Office of Classifications
Personnel Systems and Oversight Group
Office of Personnel Management
1900 E St., NW, Room 7H29
Washington, DC 20415   202-606-2970
The publication, *Job Grading System for Trades and Labor Occupations*, is available on a subscription basis ($69, #906-031-00000-2) from the Superintendent of Documents, Government Printing Office, Washington, DC 20402; 202-512-1800. For additional information contact the office above.

* Labor Agreement Information Retrieval System (LAIRS)

Labor Agreement Information Retrieval System
Office of Labor Relations and Workforce Performance
Personnel Systems and Oversight Group
Office of Personnel Management
1900 E St., NW, Room 7431
Washington, DC 20415   202-606-2940
The LAIRS system provides current and historic information about the federal labor relations program. The information is provided in the form of computer searches, microfiche of full text decisions, published analytic reports, current periodicals, and variety of audio-visual training aids. The file contains negotiated agreements, arbitration awards, and significant Federal labor relations decisions. A fee schedule is included. This system publishes labor-management reports, surveys, digests, and other related publications. A publications list and additional information can be obtained from the above office.

* Labor Management Information

Labor Agreement Information Retrieval Systems
Office of Personnel Management
1900 E St., NW, Room 7429
Washington, DC 20415   202-606-2940
This public reference room has labor-management reports, surveys, and analyses available for public viewing. An appointment is suggested.

* Labor-Management Relations

Employee Labor and Agency Relations
Personnel Systems and Oversight Group
Office of Personnel Management
1900 E St., NW, Room 7412
Washington, DC 20415   202-606-2930
This office provides information, guidance, and assistance to agencies, unions, and the public on federal labor-management relations. Eligible labor organizations are consulted in the development and revision of government-wide personnel policies.

* Labor Management Surveys

Labor Agreement Information Retrieval System (LAIRS)
Office of Personnel Management
1900 E St., NW, Room 7431
Washington, DC 20415   202-606-2940
The LAIRS (Labor Agreement Information Retrieval System) generates numerous surveys and analytical studies, including:

A Survey of Unfair Labor Practice Complaints in The Federal Government
Maternity/Sick Leave Provisions in Federal Agreements
Productivity Clauses in Federal Agreements

Single copies of these publications are available free of charge.

* Labor Practices in Federal Service

Office of Information Resources and Research Services
Federal Labor Relations Authority (FLRA)

607 14th St., NW
Washington, DC 20424-0001   202-482-6550

Contact this office to obtain a copy of the *FLRA Annual Report*, which describes significant decisions of the FLRA and case processing statistics of the General Counsel of the Authority. Cases of alleged unfair labor practices in federal service are investigated and prosecuted by the General Counsel and are heard by the FLRA's Office of Administrative Law Judges.

* Labor Relations Documents

Office of Case Control
Federal Labor Relations Authority (FLRA)
607 14th St., NW
Washington, DC 20424-0001   202-482-6690, x416

Case file information is maintained on FLRA hearings and cases prosecuted to ensure compliance with the rights and obligations of federal employees to organize, bargain collectively, and participate in labor organizations. To view FLRA case dockets and decisions, call ahead to this office to arrange for a visit.

* Labor Relations Reading

Library
Federal Labor Relations Authority (FLRA)
607 14th St., NW
Washington, DC 20424-0001   202-482-6695, x352

A small specialized collection is housed here. Material covers federal service labor-management relations and the Federal Labor Relations Authority. The library is open to the public, but due to tight security in the building, you are advised to call ahead for an appointment.

* Loans Available to Federal Retirees

External Affairs
Federal Retirement Thrift Investment Board
1250 H St., NW
Washington, DC 20005   202-942-1640

Federal Employee's Retirement System and Civil Service Retirement System employees may borrow their own contributions and earnings from the Thrift Savings Plan account for the purchase of a primary residence, medical expenses, educational expenses, and financial hardships. The minimum loan is $1,000, and the loan is repaid through regular payroll allotments. For more information about loans, federal employees should ask their employing agency for copies of the *Thrift Savings Plan* loan program materials.

* Merit Systems Protection Board (MSPB)

Office of Policy and Evaluation
1120 Vermont Ave., NW, Room 800
Washington, DC 20419   202-653-8900

The Merit Systems Protection Board (MSPB) is an independent agency in the Executive branch of the Federal Government whose job it is to see that Federal employees are protected against abuses by agency management, that Executive branch agencies make employment decisions in accordance with the merit system principles, and that Federal merit systems are kept free of prohibited personnel practices. The booklet *An Introduction to the MSPB* describes its basic functions. A publications list is also available.

* Merit Systems Protection Personnel Practices

Office of Policy and Evaluation
Merit Systems Protection Board (MSPB)
1120 Vermont Ave., NW, Room 800
Washington, DC 20419   202-653-8900

The Merit Systems Protection Board conducts special studies on the civil service and other executive branch merit systems and reports to the President and the Congress on whether the federal work force is being adequately protected against political abuses and prohibited personnel practices. You can receive a list and free copies of MSPB reports by contacting the office. Some recently released reports include *First-Line Supervisory Selection in the Federal Government*, and *U.S. Office of Personnel Management and the Merit System: A Retrospective Assessment*.

* Military Personnel Records Archives Center

National Personnel Records Center
National Archives and Records Administration
9700 Page Ave.

St. Louis, MO 63132   314-263-3901

The National Personnel Records Center stores the personnel records of former federal employees. The Center can answer requests for information, most of which are inquiries relating to claims for benefits. All requests for information must be submitted in writing.

* Negotiation Impasses

Federal Services Impasses Board
Federal Labor Relations Authority (FLRA)
607 14th St., NW
Washington, DC 20424-0001   202-482-6680, x232

When negotiation impasses develop between Federal agencies and employee representatives, this panel provides assistance in resolving the stalemate. The following publications are available: *Guide to Hearing Procedures of the Federal Services*; *Impasses Panel*; *Subject Matter Index*; *Table of Cases*; and the *Annual Report*.

* Office of Personnel Management Resource Center

Resource Center
Office of Personnel Management (OPM)
1900 E Street, NW, Room 5L44
Washington, DC 20415   202-606-1432

The OPM Library contains a comprehensive collection of materials on personnel management and the federal civil service. The library also issues *Personnel Literature*, a monthly with an annual index ($22, #706-007-00000-8) which is available from the Superintendent of Documents, Government Printing Office, Washington, DC 20402; 202-512-1800.

* Office of Personnel Management Publications

Superintendent of Documents
Government Printing Office (GPO)   202-512-1800
Washington, DC 20402   Fax: 202-512-2250

The GPO has a list of OPM publications available for a fee. The list is free. Ask for *Subject Bibliography 300*. You can also have this document delivered directly to your fax machine by calling GPO FaxWatch at 202-512-1716.

* Pay and Benefits Inquiries

Agency Services
Office of Personnel Management
1900 E St., NW, Room 4330
Washington, DC 20415   202-606-0788

Questions about federal holidays, salary schedules, group life insurance, health benefits, occupational health insurance, sick leave, retirement, and so on, can be answered by this office.

* Pension and Retirement Audits

Office of the Chief Accountant
Pension and Welfare Benefits Administration
U.S. Department of Labor
200 Constitution Ave., NW
Room N5677
Washington, DC 20210   202-219-8951

This office serves as the U.S. Department of Labor's primary advisor on accounting, auditing, and actuarial issues stemming from its responsibilities under the Employee Retirement Income Security Act and the Federal Employees' Retirement System Act (FERSA). It serves as the primary agency contact with accounting and actuarial organizations, as well as with federal and state agencies on accounting matters. It also administers a comprehensive system of compliance audits under FERSA and reviews annual financial reports filed under ERISA.

* Personnel Investigations

Office of Federal Investigations
Investigation Group
Office of Personnel Management
PO Box 886
Washington, DC 20044   202-376-3800

Used in support of the selection and appointment processes, these investigations serve several purposes: to determine the suitability of applicants under consideration for appointment; to check on applicants or employees under consideration for appointment to positions having either national security or special professional or administrative qualifications requirements, or both; and to enforce civil service regulations. The Office of Personnel Management also makes loyalty determinations of United States citizens employed or under consideration for employment by international organizations of which the United States is a member. Contact this office for more information.

* Personnel Investigator

        Office of the Special Counsel
        1120 Vermont Ave   202-653-7188
        Washington, DC 20419   800-872-9855

The Office of the Special Counsel is an independent investigative and prosecuting agency that litigates before the Merit Systems Protection Board. The office is responsible for investigating allegations of prohibited personnel practices, prohibited political activities by federal and certain state and local employees, arbitrary or capricious withholding of information in violation of the Freedom of Information Act, prohibited discrimination when found by appropriate authority, and other activities prohibited by any civil service law, rule, or regulation. The office is also responsible for receiving and referring to the appropriate agency information that indicates a violation of any law, rule, or regulation, mismanagement, a gross waste of funds, an abuse of authority, or a substantial and specific danger to public health or safety. The Special Counsel may request the Merit Systems Protection Board to order disciplinary action against any employee who violates civil service laws, rules, and regulations. Any federal employee may file a complaint with the office.

* Personnel Management

        Personnel and EEO Division
        Office of Personnel Management
        1900 E St., NW, Room 1469
        Washington, DC 20415   202-606-1402

This office manages the following personnel management responsibilities: government-wide classification system, administration of government pay systems; development and operation of information systems to support and improve federal personnel management decisionmaking; and independent evaluation of agency personnel management systems. Contact this office for more information.

* Personnel Publications

        Superintendent of Documents
        Government Printing Office   202-512-1800
        Washington, DC 20402   Fax: 202-512-2250

Personnel Literature is a monthly publication that includes about 200 or so personnel management subjects, such as performance evaluation, productivity, executives, employee training and development, and labor management relations. It includes federal, state, and local governments, foreign governments, and private organizations. It is sold for $22, SN #706-007-00000-8.

* Personnel Records Archives

        National Personnel Records Center
        National Archives and Records Administration
        111 Winnebago Street
        St. Louis, MO 63118   314-425-5761

Federal employees' personnel records are transferred and stored in the National Personnel Records Center. The Center can answer questions regarding the information available, and can provide copies of documents. Only civilian records are stored here. Contact the Center for more information.

* Personnel Records System

        Office of Workforce Information
        Office of Personnel Management
        1900 E St., NW
        Washington, DC 20415   202-606-2868

Operating Manual: Guide to Personnel Record Keeping describes the personnel records system of the Office of Personnel Management. This publication is available by subscription for $93 (SN #906-005-00000-0) from the Superintendent of Documents, Government Printing Office, Washington, DC 20402; 202-512-1800.

* Postal Career Executive Service

        Employee Relations Department
        U.S. Postal Service
        475 L'Enfant Plaza, SW
        Washington, DC 20260   202-268-3643

The postal career executive program develops qualified managers and supervisors through training, educational and work experiences. Contact this office for more information about this program.

* Postal Inspector Jobs

        Chief Postal Inspector
        U.S. Postal Service
        475 L'Enfant Plaza, SW
        Washington, DC 20260   202-268-4267

Information about Inspection Service employment may be obtained from the Chief Postal Inspector.

* Postal Service Employee/Labor Relations Manual

        Employee Relations Department
        U.S. Postal Service
        475 L'Enfant Plaza, SW
        Washington, DC 20260   202-268-3643

This subscription service consists of a basic manual and updated transmittal letters for an indeterminate period. This manual sets forth the personnel policies and regulations governing employment with the Postal Service. Topics covered include organization management, job evaluation, employment and placement, pay administration, employee benefits, employee relations, training, safety and health, and labor relations. The subscription is available for $29 domestic, and $36.25 foreign per year from: Superintendent of Documents, Government Printing Office, Washington, DC 20402-0001; 202-512-1800.

* Postal Service Employment

        Employee Relations Department
        U.S. Postal Service
        475 L'Enfant Plaza, SW
        Washington, DC 20260   202-268-3643

General information about jobs such as clerk, letter carrier, etc., including information about programs for veterans, may be obtained by contacting the nearest post office. Individuals, generally college graduates interested in engineering, management, finance, personnel work, or in employment as physicists, mathematicians, and operations research analysts, may obtain information by contacting the above office.

* Postal Service Handicapped Employment

        Employee Relations Department
        U.S. Postal Service
        475 L'Enfant Plaza, SW
        Washington, DC 20260   202-268-3643

The Postal Service created a noncompetitive hiring process for severely handicapped applicants. This program allows the Veterans Administration and State agencies for the disabled (once certified by the Postal Service as having appropriate screening and development capabilities) to refer severely handicapped individuals for direct career appointments.

* Postal Service Union Negotiations

        Labor Relations
        U.S. Postal Service
        475 L'Enfant Plaza, SW Room 9021
        Washington, DC 20260   202-268-3619

The Postal Service is the only Federal agency whose employment policies are governed by a process of collective bargaining. Labor contract negotiations, affecting all bargaining unit personnel, as well as personnel matters involving employees not covered by collective bargaining agreements, are administered by the Human Resources Group.

* Presidential and Vice-Presidential Financial Reporting

        Office of Government Ethics
        Office of Personnel Management
        1201 New York Ave., NW, Suite 500
        Washington, DC 20005   202-523-5757

This office is responsible for the financial statements of top personnel in the Executive Branch, including the President, Vice President, and anyone with a basic rate of pay equal to or above a General Schedule-16. All appointees file with the agency in which they are employed. The financial statements of the U.S. President and the Vice President are available.

* Presidential Management Intern Programs

Philadelphia Service Center
ATTN: PMI Program Office
Office of Personnel Management
Federal Building
600 Arch St.
Philadelphia, PA 19106   918-757-3000

The Presidential Management Intern (PMI) Program is open to students who have completed or will complete an advanced degree by the end of the school year and have an interest in public service. The PMI Program is a two-year program offering challenging career experience and training. To be eligible, you must be nominated by the Dean, Director or Chairperson of a credited college or university. For more information, you can contact your Graduate Program Office or Career Guidance and Placement Office at your school. To receive more information, you should first contact Career American Connection at the phone number listed above. If you need additional assistance, you can call the PMI Program Office at 215-597-7671.

* Productivity Among Civil Servants

Industry Productivity Studies Division
Office of Productivity and Technology
Bureau of Labor Statistics
U.S. Department of Labor
Postal Square Bldg.
2 Massachusetts Ave., NE
Washington, DC 20212   202-606-6222

Productivity measures are developed annually for various functional levels within the Federal government. The information available includes annual indexes of output per employee year, unit labor costs, compensation per employee year, and out put and employee years. Data come from 455 organizations within 48 Federal departments and agencies.

* Railroad Certificate of Service Months and Compensation

Research and Employment Accounts
Railroad Retirement Board
844 N. Rush St.
Chicago, IL 60611   312-751-4968

Each year railroad employees receive a Certificate of Service Months and Compensation (Form BA-6) from their employers or from the Board, which provides a current record of service and compensation. Contact the above listed office to report incorrect information.

* Railroad Employees Benefit Statistics

Office of Public Affairs
Railroad Retirement Board
844 N. Rush St.
Chicago, IL 60611   312-751-4777

Information on Board operations and on the laws it administers is available. Publications include *Annual Report, Statistical Supplement, Monthly Benefit Statistics*, and several informational pamphlets. The *Annual Report* can be ordered from the Superintendent of Documents, Government Printing Office, Washington, DC 20402; 202-512-1800.

* Railroad Retirement and Survivor Benefits

Bureau of Retirement Claims
Railroad Retirement Board
844 N. Rush St.
Chicago, IL 60611   312-751-4600

Railroad retirement benefits include regular employee retirement annuities after 10 year of service, supplemental annuities, spouse annuities, cost-of-living increases in employee and spouse retirement benefits, and other survivor benefits. *Railroad Retirement and Survivor Benefits* describes these benefits and provides practical information on how to claim them. It also includes relevant tax information.

* Railroad Retirement Appeals Process

Bureau of Hearings and Appeal
Railroad Retirement Board
844 N. Rush St.
Chicago, IL 60611   312-751-4790

Railroad employees can demand an official review of any determination to deny their benefits. If the review still denies the benefits, the employee can appeal.

* Railroad Retirement Benefit Conferences

Labor Member
Railroad Retirement Board
844 N. Rush St.
Chicago, IL 60611   312-751-4905

The Board conducts conferences to describe the benefits available under its retirement-survivor, unemployment-sickness, and Medicare programs. Attendants receive a copy of the *Informational Conference Handbook*--a comprehensive source of information on Board programs--plus pamphlets and other materials highlighting Board programs.

* Railroad Retirement Board Field Offices

Office of Public Affairs
Railroad Retirement Board
844 N. Rush St.
Chicago, IL 60611   312-751-4777

Railroad Retirement Board offices are located across the country in localities accessible to large numbers of railroad workers. Personnel are on hand to explain benefit rights and responsibilities, assist employees in applying for benefits, and to answer questions related to the Board's programs. To locate the nearest Board office check the telephone directory under "United States Government", your Post Office, or a Federal Information Center. If there is no Board office nearby, call the nearest district office to set up an appointment to meet with a traveling Board representative.

* Railroad Retirement Board Freedom of Information

Office of Information Resources Management
Railroad Retirement Board
844 N. Rush St.
Chicago, IL 60611   312-751-4692

For Freedom of Information Act requests, contact the above office.

* Railroad Employee Service and Earnings Records

Research and Employment Accounts
Railroad Retirement Board
844 N. Rush St.
Chicago, IL 60611   312-751-4980

Records of service and earnings are kept on all railroad employees since 1936. The records are kept under the employee's Social Security number. Businesses covered by this program include railroads engaged in interstate commerce and some of their subsidiaries, railroad associations, and national railway labor organizations. Contact this office for more information on the records and how to access them.

* Railroad Workers Sickness and Unemployment Benefits

Bureau of Unemployment and Sickness Insurance
Railroad Retirement Board
844 N. Rush St.
Chicago, IL 60611   312-751-4800

Railroad unemployment insurance provides cash benefits in the form of unemployment benefits and sickness benefits. Under the Railroad Unemployment Insurance Act, an employee's eligibility is generally based on railroad service and earnings in the previous calendar year. Contact this office or your nearest Railroad Retirement Board regional office for more information on benefits.

* Retiree Interfund Transfers

External Affairs
Federal Retirement Thrift Investment Board
1250 H St., NW
Washington, DC 20005   202-942-1640

Open seasons for Federal employees provide the opportunity for Federal Employees' Retirement System employees to transfer a portion of their previously invested contributions and all earnings on their own contributions among three investment Plans: the Government Securities Investment Fund, the Common Stock Index Investment Fund, and the Fixed Income Index Investment Fund. Contact the above office or your employing Federal agency for further information.

* Retirees Health and Life Insurance

Office of Insurance Programs
Office of Personnel Management

1900 E Street, NW
Room 3H37
Washington, DC 20415   202-606-0239

Comparisons of various types of medical benefits and life insurance for retired federal employees are available from this office.

* Retirement Benefits

Office of Retirement Programs
Retirement and Insurance Group
Adjudication Division
Retirement Information Office
Office of Personnel Management
1900 E St., NW, Room 1323
Washington, DC 20415   202-606-0500

All claims for benefits under the retirement system must be adjudicated. Benefits are not paid automatically. Information on how to apply for retirement benefits, death benefits, and refunds is available from this office.

* Retirement Thrift Personnel Training Program

External Affairs
Federal Retirement Thrift Investment Board
1250 H St., NW
Washington, DC 20005   202-942-1640

The Board annually trains personnel in Federal agencies, particularly benefits officers, on the summary of the Thrift Benefits Plan. These persons are then prepared to explain the plan to other Federal employees and to answer questions concerning the options under the plan.

* Retirement Thrift Savings Plan

External Affairs
Federal Retirement Thrift Investment Board
1250 H St., NW
Washington, DC 20005   202-942-1640

Federal employees may benefit from this retirement savings and investment plan, which provides tax deferral on up to 5 percent for Civil Service Retirement System employees and 10 percent for Federal Employees' Retirement System employees from their basic pay. It also provides secure investments in the Government Securities Investment Fund, immediate vesting in one's own contributions and their earnings, a loan program, portability if leaving Government service, and a choice of withdrawal options. For further information, contact the above office for the brochure, *Thrift Savings Plan for Federal Employees.*

* Salary Schedules

Advisory Services Division
Office of Pay and Benefits
Office of Personnel Management
1900 E St., NW, Room 7434
Washington, DC 20415   202-606-2848

Salary and grade rates are available for General Schedule, Executive Schedule, and Senior Executive Schedule employees. Contact this office for more information.

* Senior Executive Candidates

Office of Executive Resources
Office of Personnel Management
1900 E. Street, NW
Washington, DC 20415   202-606-1610

This program prepares senior federal managers and other employees at a certain level to enter the Senior Executive Service by providing opportunities to improve upon and/or acquire the management and executive competencies required for the SES. Details about the program are available from the office listed above.

* Senior Executive Service

Senior Executive Service Division (SES)
Office of Personnel Management
1900 E Street, NW
Washington, DC 20415   202-606-1728

SES provides every eligible senior manager the chance to shift top career managers around to meet the senior executive's needs. Additional information on the service is available from this office.

* Speakers About Public Service

Office of Public Affairs
Office of Personnel Management
1900 E St., NW
Washington, DC 20415   202-606-1212

Professional societies, business and labor groups, and other organizations can contact this office to arrange for representatives of the Office of Personnel Management to speak on federal personnel policies and changes.

* Special Benefits

Advisory Service Division
Office of Retirement Insurance and Policy
Retirement and Insurance Policy
Office of Personnel Management
1900 E St., NW
Washington, DC 20415   202-606-0777

Information on special civil service benefits is available from the Advisory Service. This is a recorded message.

* Standards for Federal Employment

Office of Classifications
Standards Development Staff
Career Entry and Employee Development Group
Office of Personnel Management
199 E St., NW, Room 6515
Washington, DC 20415   202-606-2970

Standards for evaluating employment requirements for most government occupations are developed by this office. Minimum qualification standards are provided to individual agencies, and they can then add more qualifications of their own if necessary. Contact this office for more information.

* Summer Job Announcements

Federal Job Information Center
Career America Connection
Office of Personnel Management
1900 E Street, NW   912-757-3000
Washington, DC 20415   202-606-2700

Announcements and information on summer employment opportunities with federal agencies is available.

* Tax Savings and the Retirement Thrift Savings Plan

External Affairs
Federal Retirement Thrift Investment Board
1250 H St., NW
Washington, DC 20005   202-942-1640

Thrift Savings Plan contributions are deducted from Federal pay before Federal and, in most cases, State income taxes are calculated. Until you withdraw your TSP account, you pay no income tax on the money you contribute, the money your agency contributes (if you are a Federal Employees' Retirement System employee), or the earnings on your account. For further information, contact your Federal employing agency or the above office for a copy of *Summary of the Thrift Savings Plan for Federal Employees.*

* Thrift Plan Investment Options

External Affairs
Federal Retirement Thrift Investment Board
1250 H St., NW
Washington, DC 20005   202-942-1640

Under present law, most Plan assets in the early years of investing, including some contributions (all of them if you are a Civil Service Retirement System employee) and all agency contributions, must be invested in a fund consisting of short-term, nonmarketable U.S. Treasury securities specially issued to the Thrift Savings Plan. This is the Government Securities Investment Fund or the G Fund. Federal Employee' Retirement System employees may make some of their own contributions, and beginning in 1993, may allocate some of their agency's contributions, to either the Common Stock Index Investment Fund or the Fixed Income Index Investment Fund or both. For a description of the advantages and risks of these investment options, contact your federal agency or the office above for a copy of *Summary of the Thrift Savings Plan for Federal Employees.*

* Thrift Savings Annuities

External Affairs
Federal Retirement Thrift Investment Board
1250 H St., NW
Washington, DC 20005   202-942-1640

The Thrift Savings Plan provides a number of life annuity choices for Federal employees. A life annuity is a monthly benefit paid to you for life. You may choose to receive equal monthly payments or choose initially lower payments that increase each year. Some choices also provide your surviving spouse or other designated survivor with a monthly benefit for life after you die. The joint life annuities provide either a 100 percent or 50 percent survivor benefit. Contact the benefit officer at your employing Federal agency for more details.

* Thrift Savings Plan Investment Management

External Affairs
Federal Retirement Thrift Investment Board
1250 H St., NW
Washington, DC 20005   202-942-1640

The five member Board of the Federal Retirement Thrift Investment Board establishes the Plan's investment policies. The actual management of the money in the Plan is handled differently for each of the three investment funds. The Government Securities Investment Fund is managed directly by experienced financial/investment analysts on the Board staff following the policies adopted by the Board. The other two funds, the Common Stock Index Investment Fund and the Fixed Income Index Investment Fund, are handled by private sector investment managers. The firms are selected by the Executive Director of the Board through the competitive procurement process.

* Whistleblower Abuse and Waste Hotlines

Inspector General's Office
U.S. Department of Commerce
P.O. Box 612
Ben Franklin Station
Washington, DC 20044   800-424-5197

This hotline was established so that consumers and employees could report fraud, abuse, or waste within any office in the U.S. Department of Commerce. All reports are investigated and reports can be made anonymously. The Pentagon, the U.S. Department of Housing and Urban Development (HUD), and other government departments also have whistleblower hotlines.

* Withdrawing Money under the Thrift Savings Plan

External Affairs
Federal Retirement Thrift Investment Board
1250 H St., NW
Washington, DC 20005   202-942-1640

You cannot withdraw any portion of your Thrift Savings Plan account while you are still employed by the Federal government. The basic purpose of the plan is to provide a retirement income. For further information, contact the above office.

* Work Force Analysis and Statistics

Superintendent of Documents
Government Printing Office   202-512-1800
Washington, DC 20402   Fax: 202-512-2250

Statistics and analyses are available on the Federal Civilian Work Force. A bi-monthly publication, *Federal Civilian Work Force Statistics*, contains information on current employment by branch, agency, and area; trends of employment and payroll, and accessions and separations. Summary tables and narrative analyses are given. This can be purchased for $11 a year from the Government Printing Office, #706-002-00000-6.

* Working for the U.S.A.

Federal Job Information Center
General Information
Office of Personnel Management
1900 E St., NW, Room 1416
Washington, DC 20415   202-606-2700

This free pamphlet is available from any Federal Job Information Center.

Federal Job Banks

Here you will find the offices within each of the government agencies and departments which have responsibility for personnel. Recorded messages inform callers about immediate job openings. Future employment prospects, the interview process, and other questions about the civil service can be directed to these offices which are staffed with knowledgeable federal employees. In the cases of those agencies which are not listed here, or only have a recorded message, refer to the Federal Public Information Offices section in the Information Starting Places Chapter. If you run into any difficulties with a particular federal office, contact either of your U.S. Senators or Representatives.

African Development Foundation
1400 I Street, NW
Washington, DC 20005
202-673-3916

Agriculture, U.S. Department of
14th St. and Independence Ave., SW
Washington, DC 20250
202-720-5626
202-720-2436
202-720-2108

Agricultural Research Service Job Line
Beltsville, MD
301-344-2288 recorded message
301-344-1124

Air Force, U.S. Department of the
The Pentagon
Civilian Personnel
Washington, DC 20310
703-545-6700
703-693-6550 recorded message

Alcohol Tobacco and Firearms Bureau
Employment Branch
650 Massachusetts Ave., NW, Room 4150
Washington, DC 20226
202-927-8610

American Battle Monument Commission
Pulaski Building
20 Massachusetts Ave., NW, Room 5127
Washington, DC 20314
202-761-0534

Appalachian Regional Commission
1666 Connecticut Ave., Suite 721 NW
Washington, DC 20235
202-884-7799

Arms Control and Disarmament Agency
320 21st Street, NW
Washington, DC 20451
202-647-2034

Army, U.S. Department of
Personnel and Employment Service
The Pentagon
Washington, DC 20310-6800
703-695-2589

Bureau of Public Debt
Personnel Office
U.S. Department of the Treasury
200 Third St.

Parkersburg, WV 26101
304-480-6144 recorded message

Census Bureau
Personnel Division
U.S. Department of Commerce
Room 1412, Bldg. 3
Washington, DC 20233
301-457-1722

Central Intelligence Agency
Recruitment Branch
P.O. Box 12727
Arlington, VA 22209-8727
800-562-7242

Civil Rights Commission
Washington, DC 20425
202-376-8364

Commerce, U.S. Department of
Office of the Secretary
Human Resources Management
14th & Constitution Ave., NW, Room 1069
Washington, DC 20230
202-482-5257
202-482-5138 recorded message

Commission of Fine Arts
441 F Street, NW, Suite 312
Pension Bldg.
Washington, DC 20001
202-504-2200

Commodity Futures Trading Commission
Human Resources
1155 21st St., Suite 7200
Washington, DC 20581
202-418-5003
202-418-5009 recorded message

Comptroller of the Currency
Personnel Division
U.S. Department of the Treasury
250 E St., SW
Washington, DC 20219
202-874-4490

Consumer Product Safety Commission
5401 Westbard Ave.
Bethesda, MD 20207
301-504-0100

Corporation for National Service
Human Resources
1201 New York Ave., NW

Washington, DC 20525
202-565-2800 recorded message

Defense Intelligence Agency
Civilian Personnel
Attn: DAH-2
200 Mac Dill Blvd.
Washington, DC 20340-5100
800-525-4629, x41710
703-907-1280

Defense, U.S. Department of
Directorate for Personnel
Washington Headquarters Services
Room 2E148, The Pentagon
Washington, DC 20301-1155
703-614-4066

Defense Logistics Agency
Personnel
8725 John J. Kingman Rd.
0119 - Room 1739
Ft. Belvoir, VA 22060
703-767-7100

Education, U.S. Department of
600 Independence Ave.
Washington, DC 20202
202-401-0553
202-401-0559 recorded message

Equal Employment Opportunity Commission
1801 L St., NW
Washington, DC 20507
202-663-4337
202-663-4306

Employment Standards Administration
U.S. Department of Labor
200 Constitution Ave., NW
Washington, DC 20210
202-219-7516

Energy, U.S. Department of
1000 Independence Ave., SW
Washington, DC 20585
202-586-4333 recorded message
202-586-8851

Environmental Protection Agency
401 M Street, SW
Washington, DC
202-260-9686
202-260-5055 recorded message

Executive Office of the President
725 17th Street, NW
Washington, DC 20503
202-395-3000

Export-Import Bank of the U.S.
811 Vermont Avenue, NW
Washington, DC 20571
202-565-3300
202-565-3946 recorded message

Farm Credit Administration
Human Resources Division
1501 Farm Credit Drive
Mclean, VA 22102-5090
703-883-4135
703-883-4139 recorded message.

Federal Aviation Administration
800 Independence Avenue, SW
Washington, DC 20591
202-267-8008

Federal Bureau of Investigation
9th and Pennsylvania Ave., NW
Washington, DC 20535
202-324-6223
202-324-3674 recorded message

Federal Communications Commission
Personnel Branch
1919 M Street, NW, Room 212
Washington, DC 20554
202-418-0130

Federal Deposit Insurance Corporation
Personnel Management
550 17th Street, NW
Washington, DC 20429
202-942-3000

Federal Election Commission
Personnel Officer
999 E St., NW, Suite 236
Washington, DC 20463
202-219-4290
800-424-9530

Federal Emergency Management Agency
Office of Personnel
500 C St., SW
Washington, DC 20472
202-646-3962 vacancy hotline number

Federal Home Loan Bank Board
Human Resources
1700 G Street, NW
Washington, DC 20552
202-906-6060

Federal Labor Relations Authority
Director of Personnel
607 14th Street, NW
Washington, DC 20424-0001
202-482-6660

Federal Maritime Commission
Personnel Office
800 N. Capitol, NW
Washington, DC 20573
202-523-5773

Federal Mediation and Conciliation Service
Personnel Office
2100 K St., NW, Room 718
Washington, DC 20427
202-653-5260

Federal Mine Safety and Health Review Commission
Administrative Officer
1730 K St., NW
Washington, DC 20006
202-653-5615

Federal Reserve System
Board of Governors
Human Resources Management
20th and C Street, NW, MS 156
Washington, DC 20551
202-452-3880
202-452-3038 recorded message

Careers and Workplace

Federal Retirement Thrift Investment Board
Personnel Officer
1250 H Street, NW, Suite 400
Washington, DC 20005
202-942-1680

Federal Trade Commission
600 Pennsylvania Ave., NW
Washington, DC 20591
202-326-2020 recorded message
202-326-2021

Forest Service
General Employment
PM - Room 900 RPE
P.O. Box 96090
Washington, DC 20090-6090
703-235-2730

General Accounting Office
Office of Recruitment
441 G Street, NW, Room 1157
Washington, DC 20548
202-512-4900

General Services Administration
Office of Personnel
General Services Building
18th and F St., NW, Room 1100
Washington, DC 20405
202-501-0398

Government Printing Office
Office of Personnel
North Capitol and H Street, NW
Washington, DC 20401
202-512-1198

Health and Human Services, U.S. Department of
Personnel
Program Support Division
5600 Fishers Lane, Room 1748
Rockville, MD 20857
301-443-6900

Health and Human Services, U.S. Department of
Substance Abuse and Mental Health Services
Division of Personnel
5600 Fishers Lane
Rockville, MD
301-443-5407
301-443-2282 recorded message

Health and Human Services, U.S. Department of
Health Resources and Services Administration
5600 Fishers Lane, Room 14A-46
Rockville, MD 20857
301-443-1230 recorded message

Health and Human Services, U.S. Department of
Division of Career Resources
National Institutes of Health
Room B3C15
31 Center Dr., MSC-2207
Bethesda, MD 20892-2207
301-496-2403 recorded message

House of Representative
Offfffice of Human Resources
Canon House Office Bldg.
Room 263
Washington, DC 20515-6610
202-226-6731
202-226-0098 fax

Housing and Urban Development, U.S. Department of
Office of Personnel
451 7th Street, SW
Washington, DC 20410
202-708-0408
202-708-3203 recorded message

Immigration and Naturalization Service
Office of Personnel
U.S. Department of Justice
425 I Street, NW
Washington, DC 20536
202-514-3088

Inter-American Foundation
901 N. Stuart Street
10th Floor
Arlington, VA 22203
703-841-3866

Interior, U.S. Department of
Office of Personnel
1849 C St., NW
Washington, DC 20240
202-208-6702
202-501-9630 Bureau of Mines
703-358-1743 Fish and Wildlife
202-208-7581 Indian Affairs
202-208-4648 Park Service

Internal Revenue Service (IRS)
Personnel Office
U.S. Department of the Treasury
1111 Constitution Ave., NW
Washington, DC 20224
202-622-6310

International Trade Commission
Personnel Office
500 E Street, SW
Washington, DC 20436
202-205-2000

Interstate Commerce Commission
Personnel Office
12th and Constitution Ave., NW
Washington, DC 20423
202-927-7119

Justice, U.S. Department of
Personnel Office
10th St. and Constitution Ave., NW
Washington, DC 20530
202-514-6818 recorded message

Labor, U.S. Department of
Human Resources
200 Constitution Avenue, NW
Washington, DC
202-219-6677
202-606-2700 recorded message

Library of Congress
101 Independence Avenue, NW
Washington, DC 20594
202-707-5000

Marine Corp, U.S. Department of the
Human Resources Office
Headquarters, Marine Corps
Room 1215
Washington, DC 20380
703-614-1046

Merit Systems Protection Board
Human Resources Management
1120 Vermont Ave., NW
Washington, DC 20419
202-653-5916

National Aeronautics and Space Administration
Human Resources Management Division
NASA Headquarters
Code FM
Washington, DC 20546-0001
202-358-2215

National Archives and Records Administration
Personnel Services Division
8601 Adelphi Rd.
College Park, MD 20740-6001
301-713-6760
800-827-4898 recorded message

National Art Gallery
Personnel Office
Washington, DC 20594
202-842-6282
202-842-6298 recorded message

National Capitol Planning Commission
Office of Personnel
801 Pennsylvania Ave., NW
Suite 301
Washington, DC 20576
202-724-0170

National Credit Union Administration
Human Resources
1775 Duke St.
Alexandria, VA 22314-3428
703-518-6510

National Endowment for the Arts
Human Resources
1100 Pennsylvania Ave., NW
Washington, DC 20506
202-682-5405

National Endowment for the Humanities
Human Resources
100 Pennsylvania Ave., NW, Room 417
Washington, DC 20506
202-606-8438

National Labor Relations Board
Personnel
1099 14th St., NW
Washington, DC 20750
202-273-3900

National Mediation Board
Human Resources
1301 K St., NW
Washington, DC 20572
202-523-5950

National Oceanic and Atmospheric Administration
Human Resources
U.S. Department of Commerce
1315 East West Hwy
Attn: 215
Silver Spring, MD 20910
301-713-0530

National Science Foundation
Division of Human Resources Management
4201 Wilson Blvd., Room 3048

Arlington, VA 22230
703-306-1182

National Security Agency
ATT: M 322
Fort Meade, MD 20755-6000
410-859-6444

National Technical Information Service
Personnel Office
5285 Port Royal Rd.
Springfield, VA 22161
703-487-4680

National Transportation Safety Board
Attn: Human Resources Division, AD-31
490 L'Enfant Plaza E, SW
Washington, DC 20594-2000
202-382-6717
202-382-6619 recorded message

Navy, U.S. Department of
Human Resources Office
2531 Jefferson Davis Hwy
CM2, Room 430
Arlington, VA 22242-5161
703-607-1722
703-602-4190 vacancies

Nuclear Regulatory Commission
Office of Personnel
11555 Rockville Pike
Rockville, MD 20852
301-415-7530

Occupational Safety and Health Administration
Personnel
200 Constitution Ave., NW
Washington, DC 20210
202-219-8013

Occupational Safety and Health Review Commission
Personnel
1120 20th Street, NW, 9th Floor
Washington, DC 20036-3419
202-606-5390

Office of Personnel Management
Congressional Liaison OPM
Rayburn House Office Building
Washington, DC 20515
202-225-4955
912-757-3000 recorded message

Overseas Private Investment Corporation
Personnel
1100 New York Ave., NW
Washington, DC 20527
202-336-8529
202-336-8682 recorded message

Panama Canal Commission
1825 I St., NW
Washington, DC 20006-5402
202-634-6441

Peace Corps
1990 K Street, NW, Suite 4100
Washington, DC 20526
202-606-3120
800-424-8580 toll-free job info (press #2, then x2225)

Pennsylvania Avenue Development Corporation
1331 Pennsylvania Ave., NW, Suite 1220 North

Be patient. If any phone number is incorrect, call (area code) 555-1212 and request the new listing.

Washington, DC 20004-1703
202-724-9091

Pension Benefit Guaranty Corporation

1200 K St., NW, Room 3700
Washington, DC 20005
202-778-8808

Postal Rate Commission

Administrative Office
1333 H St., Suite 300, NW
Washington, DC 20268-0001
202-789-6840

Railroad Retirement Board

Director of Personnel
844 Rush Street
Chicago, IL 60611
312-751-4580

Securities and Exchange Commission

450 5th Street, NW
Room 20549, Mail Stop 2-3
Washington, DC 20549
202-272-2550
202-272-3100 Recorded message

Selective Service System

Attn: RMH
1515 Wilson Blvd.
Arlington, VA 22209-2425
703-235-2258

Senate

Hart Senate Office Building
Room S H 142 B
Washington, DC 20510
202-224-9167

Small Business Administration

409 3rd Street, SW, Room 4200
Washington, DC 20416
202-205-6780

Smithsonian Institution

Human Resources
955 L'Enfant Plaza, SW, Suite 2100
Washington, DC 20560
202-287-3100

State, U.S. Department of

2201 C Street, NW
Washington, DC 20520
or
Personnel
P.O. Box 18657
Washington, DC 20036-8657
202-647-7284 recorded message
703-875-7490 Foreign Service

Tennessee Valley Authority

Personnel Office
400 West Summit Hill Drive
ET - 5D - 936
Knoxville, TN 37902
423-632-7744

Transportation, U.S. Department of

DOT Connection
400 7th St., SW, PL-402
Washington, DC 20590
202-366-9391

Treasury, U.S. Department of

Personnel Office
15th St. and Pennsylvania Ave., NW, Room 1334
Washington, DC 20220
202-622-1470

U.S. Information Agency

301 4th St., SW, Room 518
Washington, DC 20547
202-619-4659

U.S. Agency for International Development

Room 1026 - SA - 1
Washington, DC 20523-0116
703-302-4128

U.S. International Trade Commission

Office of Personnel
500 E St., SW, Room 314
Washington, DC 20436
202-205-2651

U.S. Postal Service

475 L'Enfant Plaza, SW
Room 1813
Washington, DC 20260-4261
202-268-3646
800-JOB-USPS recorded message.

U.S. Tax Court

400 2nd St., NW, Room 146
Washington, DC 20217
202-606-8724

U.S. Trade and Development Program

Personnel
State Annex 16, Room 309
Washington, DC 20523-1602
703-875-4357

Veterans Affairs, U.S. Department of

Human Resources
810 Vermont Avenue, NW, MS -055
Washington, DC 20420
202-273-4950

Research Grants in Every Field

You'll discover from this list of federal grants that research opportunities exist in almost every occupational field from forestry to injury prevention to library development. The following is a description of the federal dollars available to researchers, organizations, and universities. Grants to teachers and those involved in education are listed separately in the Education Chapter. This information is taken from the *Catalog of Federal Domestic Assistance* which is published by the U.S. Government Printing Office in Washington, DC. The number next to the title description is the official reference number listed in this catalog. Contact the office listed below the title for more details.

* **Special Emphasis Outreach Programs Grants 10.140**
  Special Emphasis Outreach Programs
  Office of Advocacy and Enterprise
  U.S. Department of Agriculture
  14th and Independence Ave., SW
  Washington, DC 20250   202-720-4097

* **Grants for Agricultural Research, Special Research Grants (Special Research Grants) 10.200**
  Administrator
  Cooperative State Research Service
  U.S. Department of Agriculture
  Ag Box 2201
  Washington, DC 20250   202-720-4423

* **Cooperative Forestry Research (McIntire-Stennis Act) 10.202**
  Administrator
  Cooperative State Research Service
  U.S. Department of Agriculture
  Washington, DC 20250   202-720-4423

* **Payments to 1890 Land-Grant Colleges and Tuskegee University 10.205**
  Administrator, Cooperative State Research Service
  U.S. Department of Agriculture
  Washington, DC 20250   202-720-4423

* **Grants for Agricultural Research-Competitive Research Grants 10.206**
  National Research Initiative
  Competitive Research Grants Office
  U.S. Department of Agriculture
  Aerospace Bldg., Room 323
  14th and Independence Ave, SW
  Washington, DC 20250   202-401-5022

* **Animal Health and Disease Research 10.207**
  Administrator, Cooperative State Research Service
  U.S. Department of Agriculture
  Ag Box 2201
  Washington, DC 20250   202-720-4423

* **Morrill-Nelson Funds for Food and Agricultural Higher Education 10.214**
  Deputy Administrator
  Office of Higher Education Programs
  Administration Bldg., Room 3912 South
  U.S. Department of Agriculture
  Washington, DC 20250   202-720-7854

* **Sustainable Agriculture Research & Education 10.215**
  Administrator, Cooperative State Research Service
  U.S. Department of Agriculture
  Ag Box 2201
  Washington, DC 20250   202-720-4423

* **Technical Agricultural Assistance 10.960**
  Mr. Harry Mattox
  Office of International Cooperation and Development
  Development Resources Division
  U.S. Department of Agriculture
  Washington, DC 20250   202-690-1924

* **International Agricultural Research (International Research) 10.961**
  L. Whetten Reed
  Office of International Cooperation and Development
  Research & Scientific Exchange Division
  U.S. Department of Agriculture
  Washington, DC 20250   202-690-4872

* **International Training-Foreign Participant 10.962**
  Dr. Frank A. Fender
  Office of International Cooperation and Development
  Food Industries Division
  U.S. Department of Agriculture
  Washington, DC 20250   202-690-1339

* **Research and Evaluation Program 11.312**
  Richard Hage, Room H-7315
  EDA, U.S. Department of Commerce
  Washington, DC 20230   202-482-4085

* **Anadromous Fish Conservation Act Program 11.405**
  Director, Office of Fisheries Conservation and Management
  National Marine Fisheries Service
  1315 East-West Highway
  Silver Spring, MD 29010   301-713-2334

* **Interjurisdictional Fisheries Act of 1986 11.407**
  Director
  Office of Fisheries Conservation and Management
  National Marine Fisheries Service
  1315 East-West Hwy
  Silver Spring, MD 20910   301-713-2334

* **Sea Grant Support 11.417**
  Director, National Sea Grant College Program
  National Oceanic and Atmospheric Administration

1315 East West Hwy
Silver Spring, MD 20910   301-713-2448

* Financial Assistance for Ocean Resources Conservation and Assessment Program 11.426

National Oceanic and Atmospheric Administration
National Ocean Service
Office of Ocean Resources Conservation & Marine Assessment
(N/ORCA), 1305 East West Hwy.
Silver Spring, MD 20910   301-713-3125

* Fisheries Development and Utilization Research and Development Grants and Cooperative Agreements Program 11.427

Office of Trade and Industry Services
National Marine Fisheries Service
National Oceanic and Atmospheric Administration (NOAA)
U.S. Department of Commerce
1315 East-West Hwy.
Silver Spring, MD 20910   301-713-2358

* Marine Sanctuary Program 11.429

Chief, Sanctuaries and Reserves Division
Office of Ocean and Coastal Resource Management
National Ocean Service
National Oceanic and Atmospheric Administration (NOAA)
1305 East West Hwy.
Silver Spring, MD 20910   301-713-3125

* Undersea Research 11.430

Director, Office of Undersea Research
National Oceanic and Atmospheric Administration
1315 East-West Hwy
Silver Spring, MD 20910   302-713-2427

* Climate and Atmospheric Research 11.431

Director, Office of Global Programs
National Oceanic and Atmospheric Administration
1100 Wayne Ave.
Silver Spring, MD 20910   303-427-2089

* Measurement and Engineering Research and Standards 11.609

National Institute of Standards & Technology
Gaithersburg, MD 20899

* Regional Centers for the Transfer of Manufacturing Technology 11.611

Mr. Kevin Carr
Manufacturing Extension Partnership
National Institute of Standards and Technology (NIST)
Building 301, Room C121
Gaithersburg, MD 20899   301-975-5020

* Minority Business Development Centers (MBDC) 11.800

Assistant Director, Office of Program Development
Room 5096, Minority Business Development Agency
U.S. Department of Commerce
14th & Constitution Ave., NW
Washington, DC 20230   202-482-5770

* American Indian Program (AIP) 11.801

Assistant Director, Office of Program Development
Room 5096, Minority Business Development Agency

U.S. Department of Commerce
14th & Constitution Ave., NW
Washington, DC 20230   202-482-5770

* Procurement Technical Assistance for Business Firms (Procurement Technical Assistance (PTA)) 12.002

Defense Logistics Agency
Cameron Station
Office of Small and Disadvantaged
 Business Utilization (DLA-U)
5010 Duke St.
Building 6, Door 5, Room 6-170
Alexandria, VA 22304-6100   202-274-6471

* Corrections-Research and Evaluation and Policy Formulation 16.602

Chief, Community Services Division
National Institute of Corrections
320 First St., NW, Room 5007
Washington, DC 20534   800-307-3106

* Employment and Training Research and Development Projects 17.248

Chief, Division of Research and Demonstration
Employment and Training Administration
U.S. Department of Labor
Washington, DC 20210   202-219-5677

* Urban Mass Transportation Grants for University Research and Training 20.502

Office of Technical Assistance and Safety
Office of Training
Research and Rural Transportation (TTS-31)
Urban Mass Transit Administration
400 7th St., SW, Room 6100
Washington, DC 20590   202-366-0242

* Urban Mass Transportation Technical Studies Grants (Technical Planning Studies) 20.505

Director, Office of Planning (TGM 20)
Office of Grants Management
Federal Transit Administration
U.S. Department of Transportation
400 7th St., SW
Washington, DC 20590   202-366-2360

* Promotion of the Humanities-Regrants/Centers for Advanced Study 45.122

Division of Research Programs
Institutional Programs and Resources, Room 318
National Endowment for the Humanities
Washington, DC 20506   202-606-8359

* Promotion of the Humanities-Division of Preservation and Access 45.149

Division of Preservation & Access
National Endowment for the Humanities, Room 802
Washington, DC 20506   202-606-8570

* Engineering Grants 47.041

Glen Larsen
Program Analyst
Directorate for Engineering
National Science Foundation, Room 1126E
4201 Wilson Blvd.
Arlington, VA 22230   703-306-1303

* Mathematical and Physical Sciences 47.049

Assistant Director
Mathematical and Physical Sciences
National Science Foundation
4201 Wilson Blvd.
Arlington, VA 22230   703-306-1800

* Geosciences 47.050

Dr. Richard Greenfield
Atmospheric Sciences
National Science Foundation
4201 Wilson Blvd.
Arlington, VA 22230   703-306-1520

* Computer and Information Science and Engineering (SISE) 47.070

Assistant Director
Computer and Information Science and Engineering
National Science Foundation
4201 Wilson Blvd.
Arlington, VA 22230   703-306-1900

* Science and Technology Centers 47.073

Director
Office of Science and Technology Infrastructure
National Science Foundation
4201 Wilson Blvd.
Arlington, VA 22230   703-306-1040

* Environmental Protection-Consolidated Research 66.500

Environmental Protection Agency
Grants Administration Division, 3909F
Washington, DC 20460   202-260-7473

* Solid Waste Disposal Research 66.504

Director
Research Grants Staff
RD-675, Environmental Protection Agency
Washington, DC 20460   202-260-7473

* Water Pollution Control-Research, Development, and Demonstration 66.505

Director, Research Grants Staff
RD 675, Environmental Protection Agency
Washington, DC 20460   202-260-7473

* Safe Drinking Water Research and Demonstration 66.506

Director, Office of Research Grants
RD-675, Environmental Protection Agency
Washington, DC 20460   202-260-7473

* Toxic Substances Research 66.507

Director, Research Grants Staff
RD-675, Environmental Protection Agency
Washington, DC 20460   202-260-7473

* Superfund Technical Assistance Grants for Citizen Groups at Priority Sites 66.806

Office of Emergency and Remedial Response
Mail Code 5203G
Environmental Protection Agency
401 M St., SW
Washington, DC 20460   703-603-8842

* University-Laboratory Cooperative Program 81.004

Larry L. Barker
Division of University and Industry Programs
Office of Energy Research
U.S. Department of Energy (DOE)
Washington, DC 20585   202-586-8947

* Energy-Related Inventions 81.036

George Lewitt, Director
Office of Technology Evaluation and Assessment
National Institute of Standards and Technology
Gaithersburg, MD 20899   301-975-5500

* Basic Energy Sciences--University and Science Education 81.049

William Burrier
Division of Acquisition and Assistance Management
Office of Energy Research, Mail Stop G-236
U.S. Department of Energy (DOE)
Washington, DC 20545   301-353-5544

* Energy Conservation for Institutional Buildings 81.052

Robert Volk, Director
Institutional Conservation Programs Division
Office of Conservation and Renewable Energy
MS G-236
U.S. Department of Energy (DOE)
Washington, DC 20585   301-903-5541

* University Coal Research 81.057

Office of Advanced Research
Assistant Secretary of Fossil Energy
Washington, DC 20585   301-903-2786

* University Research Instrumentation 81.077

Michael Wolfe
Postsecondary Programs Division
Office of University and Science Education (ER-82)
Office of Energy Research
U.S. Department of Energy (DOE)
Washington, DC 20585   202-586-8949

* Regional Biomass Programs 81.079

Mike Voorhies
Office of National Programs, EE-522
U.S. Department of Energy (DOE)
Washington, DC 20585   202-586-1480

* Domestic and International Energy Policy Development 81.080

Resource Management Office
Office of Domestic and International Energy Policy (EP-3)
7E-090, Forrestal Bldg.
1000 Independence Ave., SW
Washington, DC 20585   202-586-2431

* Conservation Research and Development 81.086

Energy Efficiency and Renewable Energy
Office of Building Technologies
Conservation and Renewable Energy
Washington, DC 20585   202-586-0098

* Renewable Energy Research and Development 81.087

Energy Efficiency and Renewable Energy
Office of Building Technologies

Conservation and Renewable Energy
Washington, DC 20585   202-586-0098

* Fossil Energy Research and Development 81.089

Mary Roland
U.S. Department of Energy
Fossil Energy Program
FE-122
Germantown, MD 20545   202-903-3514

* Socioeconomic and Demographic Research, Data and Other Information 81.091

Georgia R. Johnson
U.S. Department of Energy
Forrestal Building
Room 5B-110
Washington, DC 20585   202-586-1593

* International Research and Studies (HEA Title VI Research and Studies) 84.017

Division of Advanced Training and Research
Center for International Education
U.S. Department of Education, ROB-3
7 & D St., SW
Washington, DC 20202-5331   202-401-9784

* Disabled--Innovation and Development 84.023

Division of Innovation and Development
Office of Asst. Secretary for Special Education
 and Rehabilitative Services
U.S. Department of Education
400 Maryland Ave., SW
Washington, DC 20202   202-205-8125

* Library Research and Demonstration 84.039

Discretionary Library Programs
Library Programs
Office of Educational Research and Improvement
U.S. Department of Education
555 New Jersey Ave., NW
Washington, DC 20208-5571   202-219-1315

* National Vocational Education Research 84.051

Jackie Friedrich
U.S. Department of Education
Division of National Programs
Office of Vocational and Adult Education
400 Maryland Ave., SW
Washington, DC 20202-7242   202-205-9071

* Educational Research and Development 84.117

Jackie Jenkins
U.S. Department of Education
Office of Educational Research and Improvement
555 New Jersey Ave., NW
Washington, DC 20208   202-219-2079

* National Institute on Disability and Rehabilitation Research 84.133

Director
National Institute on Disability
 and Rehabilitation Research
Office of Assistant Secretary for Special
 Education and Rehabilitation Services
U.S. Department of Education
600 Independence Ave., SW
Washington, DC 20202-2572   202-205-5450

* Disabled--Special Studies and Evaluations 84.159

Lou Danielson
Division of Innovation and Development
Office of Special Education Programs
400 Maryland Ave., SW
Washington, DC 20202   202-205-8119

* National Adult Education Discretionary Program 84.191

Howard Hjelm
Division of National Programs
Office of Vocational and Adult Education
U.S. Department of Education
600 Independence Ave., SW
Washington, DC 20202-7242   202-205-9650

* Grants for Preventive Medicine and Dental Public Health 93.117

Division of Associated Dental and Public Health Professions
Bureau of Health Professions, HRSA
Public Health Service (PHS)
U.S. Department of Health and Human Services (DHHS)
5600 Fishers Lane
Rockville, MD 20857   301-443-6757

* Food and Drug Administration-Research 93.103

Robert L. Robins, Chief
Grants and Assistance Agreements Section
Div. of Contracts and Grants
Food and Drug Administration
HFA-520, Room 3-40
Parklawn Bldg., 5600 Fishers Lane
Rockville, MD 20857   301-443-6170

* Maternal and Child Health Federal Consolidated Programs (Special Projects of Regional and National Significance (SPRANS) 93.110

Maternal and Child Health Bureau
HRSA, Public Health Service
Room 18-05, 5600 Fishers Lane
Rockville, MD 20857   301-443-2170

* Adolescent Family Life Research Grants 93.111

Eugenia Eckard
Office of Adolescent Pregnancy Programs
Office of Population Affairs
Office of the Assistant Secretary of Health
West Tower, Suite 200
5600 Fishers Lane
Rockville, MD 20857   301-594-4008

* Biological Response to Environmental Health Hazards 93.113

Director
Division of Extramural Research and Training
National Institute of Environmental Health Sciences
Public Health Service
Department of Health and Human Services
P.O. Box 12233
Research Triangle Park, NC 27709   919-541-7628

* Applied Toxicological Research and Testing (Bioassay of Chemicals and Test Development) 93.114

Director
Division of Extramural Research and Training
National Institute of Environmental Health Sciences

Public Health Service
Department of Health and Human Services
P.O. Box 12233
Research Triangle Park, NC 27709   919-541-7628

* Biometry and Risk Estimation-Health Risks From Environmental Exposures 93.115

Director, Division of Extramural Research and Training
National Institute of Environmental Health Sciences
Public Health Service
U.S. Department of Health and Human Services
P.O. Box 12233
Research Triangle Park, NC 27709   919-541-7628

* Project Grants and Cooperative Agreements for Tuberculosis Control Programs 93.116

Chief, Grants Management Branch
Centers for Disease Control, Public Health Service
U.S. Department of Health and Human Services
225 E. Paces Ferry Rd., NE
Atlanta, GA 30305   404-842-6640

* Acquired Immunodeficiency Syndrome (AIDS) Activity (AIDS) 93.118
Grants Management Branch

Procurement and Grants Office
Centers for Disease Control
U.S. Department of Health and Human Services
255 E. Paces Ferry Rd., NE
Atlanta, GA 30305   404-842-6575

* Oral Diseases and Disorders Research 93.121

Extramural Program
National Institute of Dental Research
National Institutes of Health
Bethesda, MD 20892   301-496-7884

* Centers for Research and Demonstration for Health Promotion and Disease Prevention (Prevention Centers) 93.135

Diane Jones, Project Officer
NCCDPHP, Centers for Disease Control
Public Health Service (PHS)
4770 Buford Hwy., NE, K-30
Atlanta, GA 30333   404-488-5395

* Injury Prevention and Control Research Projects 93.136

Division of Injury Epidemiology and Control
Center for Environmental Health and Injury Control
Centers for Disease Control, Public Health Service
Atlanta, GA 30333   404-488-4265

* Intramural Research Training Award (IRTA Program) 93.140

Associate Director for Intramural Affairs
National Institutes of Health
Shannon Bldg. Room 140
Rockville, MD 20892   301-496-4920

* NIEHS Hazardous Waste Worker Health and Safety Training (Superfund Worker Training Program) 93.142

Director, Division of Extramural Research and Training
National Institute of Environmental Health Sciences
P.O. Box 12233
Research Triangle Park, NC 27709   919-541-7628

* NIEHS Superfund Hazardous Substances-Basic Research and Education 93.143

Director, Division of Extramural Research and Training
National Institutes of Environmental Health Sciences
P.O. Box 12233
Research Triangle Park, NC 27709   919-541-0797

* AIDS Education and Training Centers 93.145

Marc Rivo, MD, Director
Division of Medicine
Bureau of Health Professions
Health Resources and Services Administration
Room 9A-27, 5600 Fishers Lane
Rockville, MD 20857   301-443-6190

* Human Genome Research 93.172

Mark Guyer, MD
National Center for Human Genome Research
National Institutes of Health, Public Health Service
U.S. Department of Health and Human Services (DHHS)
Bethesda, MD 20892   301-496-0844

* Biological Research Related to Deafness and Communicative Disorders 93.173

Dr. Ralph F. Naunton
National Institute of Deafness and Other
  Communication Disorders
Executive Plaza South, Room 400-B
Bethesda, MD 20892   301-496-1804

* Conference Grant (Substance Abuse) 93.174

Center for Substance Abuse Prevention (CSAP)
Substance Abuse and Mental Health Administration
Rockwall II Bldg., 5600 Fishers Lane
Rockville, MD 20857   301-443-0377

* Health Services Research and Development Grants 93.226

Agency for Health Care Policy and Research
Public Health Service (PHS)
U.S. Department of Health and Human Services (DHHS)
Suite 601, Executive Office Center
2101 E. Jefferson St.
Rockville, MD 20852   301-594-1447

* Mental Health Research Grants 93.242

Dr. Stephen Koslow, Director
Division of Neuroscience & Behavioral Sciences
National Institute of Mental Health
5600 Fishers Lane
Rockville, MD 20857   301-443-3563

* Occupational Safety and Health Research Grants 93.262

Henry Cassell, Procurement and Grants Office
Centers for Disease Control (CDC)
U.S. Department of Health and Human Services (DHHS)
255 E. Paces Ferry Rd., NE, MS-E13
Atlanta, GA 30333   404-842-6798

* Alcohol Scientist Development Award and Research Scientist Development Award for Clinicians (Research Center ("K") Awards) 93.271

Dr. William Lands, Director
Division of Basic Research
National Institute on Alcohol Abuse and Alcoholism

Be patient. If any phone number is incorrect, call (area code) 555-1212 and request the new listing.

Public Health Service (PHS)
5600 Fishers Lane
Rockville, MD   301-443-1206

* Alcohol National Research Service Awards for Research Training (NRSA Program) 93.272

Dr. William Lands, Director
Division of Basic Research
National Institute on Alcohol Abuse and Alcoholism
Public Health Service (PHS)
5600 Fishers Lane
Rockville, MD   301-443-1206

* Alcohol Research Programs 93.273

Dr. William Lands, Director
Division of Basic Research
National Institute on Alcohol Abuse and Alcoholism
Public Health Service (PHS)
5600 Fishers Lane
Rockville, MD   301-443-1206

* Drug Abuse National Research Service Awards for Research Training (NRSA Program) 93.278

Dr. James Dingell, Director
Division of Basic Research
National Institute on Drug Abuse
5600 Fishers Lane
Rockville, MD 20857   301-443-1887

* Drug Abuse Research Programs 93.279

Dr. James Dingell, Director
Division of Basic Research
National Institute on Drug Abuse
5600 Fishers Lane
Rockville, MD 20857   301-443-1887

* Mental Research Scientist Development Award and Research Scientist Development Award for Clinicians (Career Development ("K") Awards) 93.281

Dr. Stephen Koslow, Director
Division of Neuroscience and Behavioral Sciences
National Institute of Mental Health
Parklawn Building
5600 Fishers Lane, Room 11-103
Rockville, MD 20857   301-443-3563

* General Clinical Research Centers 93.333

General Clinical Research Centers Program
National Center for Research Resources
National Institutes of Health
Bethesda, MD 20892   301-594-7945

* Biomedical Research Support 93.337

Marjorie Tingle, MD
National Center for Research Resources
National Institutes of Health
Bethesda, MD 20892   301-594-7947

* Nursing Research - Health Promotion and Disease Prevention 93.361

National Institute of Nursing Research
National Institutes of Health
Public Health Service
Natcher Bldg.
Room 3AN-12, MSC 6300
Bethesda, MD 20892   301-594-5969

* Biomedical Research Technology 93.371

Biomedical Research Technology Program
National Center for Research Resources
National Institutes of Health
Bethesda, MD 20892   301-594-7934

* Research Centers in Minority Institutions (RCMI) 93.389

Dr. Sidney A. McNairy, Director
RCMI
National Center for Research Resources
National Institutes of Health (NIH)
Bethesda, MD 20892   301-594-7944

* Academic Research Enhancement Award (AREA) 93.390

Office of Research Training and Special Programs
Office of Extramural Research
National Institutes of Health
Bethesda, MD 20892   301-496-1968

* Cancer Cause and Prevention Research 93.393

Dr. Richard H. Adamson, Director
Division of Cancer Etiology
National Cancer Institute
Bethesda, MD 20892   301-496-5946

* Cancer Detection and Diagnosis Research 93.394

Sheila Taube
Extramural Research Program
National Cancer Institute
Bethesda, MD 20892   301-496-1591

* Cancer Treatment Research 93.395

Robert Wittes
Division of Cancer Treatment
National Cancer Institute
Bethesda, MD 20892   301-496-4291

* Cancer Biology Research 93.396

Dr. Faye Austin, Associate Director
Extramural Research Program
National Cancer Institute
Bethesda, MD 20892   301-496-8636

* Cancer Centers Support 93.397

Dr. Margaret Holmes
Training and Resources Program
Division of Cancer Biology and Diagnosis
National Cancer Institute
EPN/502
Bethesda, MD 20892   301-496-8531

* Cancer Control 93.399

Dr. Edward Sondick, Deputy Director
Division of Cancer Prevention and Control
National Cancer Institute
Bethesda, MD 20892   301-496-9569

* Child Welfare Research and Demonstration 93.608

Cecilia Sudia
Children's Bureau
Administration for Children and Families
P.O. Box 1182
Washington, DC 20013   202-205-8764

* Social Services Research and Demonstration 93.647

Richard Greenberg, Director
Division of Research and Evaluation
Office of Policy & Evaluation
Administration of Children and Families
370 L'Enfant Promenade SW, 7th Floor
Washington, DC 20447　　　　　202-401-6971

* Adoption Opportunities 93.652

Ronald Snead
Children's Bureau
Administration for Children, Youth and Families
P.O. Box 1182
Washington, DC 20013　　　　　202-205-8710

* Child Abuse and Neglect Discretionary Activities 93.670

Director
National Center on Child Abuse and Neglect (NCCAN)
P.O. Box 1182
Washington, DC 20013　　　　　202-205-8586

* Biophysics and Physiological Sciences 93.821

Dr. James Cassatt, Director
Division of Cell Biology and Biophysics
National Institute of General Medical Sciences
MSC 6200
National Institutes of Health
Bethesda, MD 20892　　　　　301-594-0828

* Heart and Vascular Diseases Research 93.837

Director
Division of Heart and Vascular Diseases
National Heart, Lung, and Blood Institute
Bethesda, MD 20892　　　　　301-496-1857

* Lung Diseases Research 93.838

Director
Division of Lung Diseases
National Heart, Lung, and Blood Institute
Bethesda, MD 20892　　　　　301-594-7430

* Blood Diseases and Resources Research 93.839

Director
Division of Blood, Diseases, and Resources
National Heart, Lung, and Blood Institute
Bethesda, MD 20892　　　　　301-496-4868

* Arthritis, Musculoskeletal and Skin Diseases Research 93.846

Dr. M. Lockshin, Director
Extramural Activities Program
National Institute of Arthritis and
　Musculoskeletal and Skin Diseases
Natcher Bldg., Room 5AS-13F
45 Center Dr., MSC 6500
National Institutes of Health (NIH)
Bethesda, MD 20892　　　　　301-594-2463

* Diabetes, Endocrinology and Metabolism Research 93.847

Dr. Richard Eastman, Director
Division of Diabetes, Endocrinology and Metabolic Diseases
MSC 2560, Bldg. 31
National Institute of Diabetes and Kidney Diseases
National Institutes of Health
Bethesda, MD 20892　　　　　301-496-7348

* Digestive Diseases and Nutrition Research 93.848

Dr. Jay Hoofnagle, Director
Division of Digestive Diseases and Nutrition
MSC 2560, Bldg. 31
National Institutes of Health (NIH)
Bethesda, MD 20892　　　　　301-496-1333

* Kidney Diseases, Urology and Hematology Research 93.849

Dr. G. Striker, Director
Division of Kidney, Urologic and Hematologic Diseases
MSC 2560, Bldg. 31
National Institutes of Health
Bethesda, MD 20892　　　　　301-496-6325

* Biological Basis Research in the Neurosciences 93.854

Division of Extramural Activities
NINDS, National Institutes of Health (NIH)
Federal Bldg. Room 1016
Bethesda, MD 20892　　　　　301-496-9231

* Allergy, Immunology and Transplantation Research 93.855

Grants Management Branch
National Institute of Allergy and Infectious Diseases
National Institutes of Health
Bethesda, MD 20892　　　　　301-496-7075

* Microbiology and Infectious Diseases Research 93.856

Grants Management Branch
National Institute of Allergy and Infectious Diseases
National Institutes of Health
Bethesda, MD 20892　　　　　301-496-7075

* Pharmacological Sciences 93.859

Michael Rogers, Program Director
National Institute of General Medical Sciences
National Institutes of Health, MSC 6200
Bethesda, MD 20892　　　　　301-594-3827

* Genetics Research 93.862

Dr. Judith H. Greenberg, Program Director
National Institute of General Medical Sciences
National Institutes of Health (NIH), MSC 6200
Bethesda, MD 20892　　　　　301-594-0943

* Population Research 93.864

Donald E. Clark, Chief
Office of Grants and Contracts
National Institute of Child Health and Human Development
National Institutes of Health
Bethesda, MD 20892　　　　　301-496-5001

* Research for Mothers and Children 93.865

Donald E. Clark, Chief
Office of Grants and Contracts
National Institute of Child Health and Human Development
National Institutes of Health
Bethesda, MD 20892　　　　　301-496-5001

* Aging Research 93.866

Dr. Richard L. Sprott
National Institute of Aging
National Institutes of Health (NIH)
Bethesda, MD 20892　　　　　301-496-4996

* Retinal and Choroidal Diseases Research 93.867

Carolyn Grimes
Extramural Services Branch
National Eye Institute
National Institutes of Health
Bethesda, MD 20892

301-496-5884

* Alcohol Research Center Grants 93.891

Dr. Ernestine Vanderveen
Division of Basic Research
National Institute on Alcohol Abuse and Alcoholism
Public Health Service (PHS)
6000 Executive Blvd., MSC 7003
Rockville, MD 20892

301-443-2530

* Resource and Manpower Development in the Environmental Health Sciences 93.894

Director, Division of Extramural Research and Training
National Institute of Environmental Health Sciences
P.O. Box 12233
Research Triangle Park, NC 27709

919-541-7634

* Family Planning-Services Delivery Improvement Research Grants (SDI) 93.974

Eugenia Eckard
Office of Population Affairs
Office of the Asst Secretary for Health
U.S. Department of Health and Human Services (DHHS)
West Tower, Suite 200, East West Hwy.
5600 Fishers Lane
Rockville, MD 20857

301-594-4008

* Preventive Health Services - Sexually Transmitted Diseases Research, Demonstrations, and Public Information and Education Grants 93.978

Chief
Grants Management Branch
Procurement and Grants Office
Centers for Disease Control
Public Health Service
U.S. Department of Health and Human Services (DHHS)
255 E. Paces Ferry Rd., NE
Atlanta, GA 30305

404-842-6640

Arts and Humanities
Artists, Designers, Performers

* See also Careers and Workplace; Research Grants in Every Field Chapter

Here is a sampling of the opportunities for dancers, fashion designers, sculptors, theater companies, musicians, and other artists. A complete list of federal grants for artists is outlined in "Money for the Arts" in this chapter. The Performing Arts Library listed below serves as a clearinghouse for information and reference assistance on dance, theater, opera, music as well as film and broadcasting.

* Actors, Mimes, and Playwrights Grants
Heritage and Preservation Division
National Endowment for the Arts
1100 Pennsylvania Ave., NW, Room 608
Washington, DC 20506   202-682-5428

The Theater Program provides financial assistance for the creation and presentation of work by professional artists, primarily in companies, and to bring the work to locales where theater is generally not available. The Professional Theater Training category is designed to encourage efforts to raise professional standards by assisting professional training of theater artists. Grants are also available to organizations and publishers for projects and services that address the needs of the theater. Grants can be made to individuals and non-profit organizations if such donations qualify as charitable deductions under Section 170(c) of the Internal Revenue Code of 1954.

* American Culture and Folk Art Grants
Heritage and Preservation Division
National Endowment for the Arts
1100 Pennsylvania Ave., NW, Room 725
Washington, DC 20506   202-682-5428

The Folk Arts Program supports the traditional arts that have grown through time within the many groups that make up the United States. The Program's objectives are to present and enhance this multi-cultural artistic heritage and to make it more available to a wider public audience. The Program offers grants for the presentation and documentation of traditional arts and artists, as well as for supporting the development of state- or regionally-based folk arts programs.

* Art Grant Application Guide
Public Information Offices
National Endowment for the Arts
1100 Pennsylvania Ave., NW, Room 617
Washington, DC 20506   202-682-5400

The National Endowment for the Arts offers a free publication, the *Guide to the National Endowment for the Arts*, which outlines its various programs and grants, and provides a calendar of deadlines, as well as application information for the grants. Regional offices and other related agencies are also listed.

* Arts Education and Successful Teaching
National Arts Education Research Center
School of St. John's University
8000 Utopia Pkwy.
Jamiaca, NY 11439   718-990-1300

Major research areas include the processes of successful teaching and curriculum in arts education; videotape documentation of successful teaching in arts education; and educational relationships among the schools and cultural institutions.

* Artists as Teachers Grants
Arts-In-Education
Education and Access Division
National Endowment for the Arts
1100 Pennsylvania Ave., NW, Room 602
Washington, DC 20506   202-682-5426

The Arts-In-Education Program is a partnership program through cooperative efforts of the Arts Endowment, state arts and education agencies, local communities, and other organizations. The Program's overall goal is to advance the arts as part of basic education. Grants are awarded to place practicing artists in a variety of educational settings and to support other projects designed to enhance arts education in schools. Arts in Schools Basic Education Grants encourage plans and projects that promote the arts in schools as a basic component of the curriculum in kindergarten through high school.

* Classical Music Concerts
Public Affairs Office
Library of Congress
Washington, DC 20540   202-707-2905

A variety of cultural programs takes place each year in the Library, including poetry and other literary readings, lectures, and musical presentations. Among the most popular musical events are the Julliard String Quartet concerts featuring five Stradivari instruments given to the Library in the 1930s. Other gifts have brought the Library a variety of musical pieces including two Bach cantatas and sketches for portions of two Beethoven quartets. Recordings of Julliard concerts and many other programs are played on radio stations across the country, and lectures are often published for distribution. Also prints and photographs, maps and musical scores, rare books, and manuscripts are drawn from the collections and displayed in the Library in continually changing exhibitions. Many exhibits are sent on tour to libraries and museums across the nation. A free monthly calendar of events is available by written request.

* Dance and Choreography Grants
Creation and Presentation Division
National Endowment for the Arts
1100 Pennsylvania Ave., NW, Room 621
Washington, DC 20506   202-682-5452

The Dance Program focuses on American dance, and offers grants to dance companies, choreographers, and dance organizations to allow for the improvement of their staffs, as well as supporting performers and performances and the commissioning of new work. The program also offers grants to organizations who provide services to dancers, choreographers and companies, such as those that provide performance space or communication within the dance world. Grants can be made to non-profit organizations if such donations qualify as charitable deductions under Section 170(c) of the Internal Revenue Code of 1954.

* Duck Stamp Design Competition
Federal Duck Stamp Office
U.S. Fish and Wildlife Service
1849 C St., NW
Washington DC 20240   202-208-4354

Each year, a Duck Stamp Design Competition is held, with the winning design chosen by a panel of waterfowl and art experts. Any artist can enter the contest by submitting a 7 X 10 inch waterfowl design and paying an entry fee. The winner receives a pane of stamps bearing his or her design. Winning artists also sell prints of their prize entries which are eagerly sought by collectors.

* Fashion, Graphic, Industrial Designers Grants
Heritage and Preservation Division
Design Arts Program
National Endowment for the Arts

Arts and Humanities

1100 Pennsylvania Ave., NW, Room 625
Washington, DC 20506   202-682-5428
The Design Arts Program supports projects in the fields of architecture, landscape architecture, urban design, historic preservation, urban planning, interior design, industrial design, graphic design, and fashion design. Grants are given to projects that advance design through practice, theory and research, media, and education concerning design. Some examples may be to produce a new graphic system, to study the theory of landscape architecture, or to produce a film on design issues. Grants can be made to non-profit organizations, including arts groups and local and state governments if such donations qualify as charitable deductions under Section 170(c) of the Internal Revenue Code of 1954. Grants can range from $5,000 to $40,000.

* Folklife Crafts and American Traditions

Center for Folklife Programs and Cultural Studies
Smithsonian Institution
955 L'Enfant Plaza, Suite 2600
Washington, DC 20590   202-287-3424
Through its annual Festival of American Folklife, the Smithsonian created a program of folklife presentations for the general public for two weeks each summer. The Office also carries on research in folklife traditions, publishes documentary and analytical studies, develops and organizes exhibitions with folklife themes, and cooperates with Universities and other institutions in presentation projects involving traditional craftsman and performing artists.

* Free National Gallery Concerts

National Gallery of Art
Constitution and 6th St., NW
Washington, DC 20565   202-737-4215
Free concerts are presented in the East Garden Court every Sunday evening, September to June. The National Gallery Orchestra performs and features guest musicians as well. Concerts are announced in the Calendar of Events.

* Jazz Performers, Choruses and Grants for Other Musicians

Education and Access Division
Music Program
National Endowment for the Arts
1100 Pennsylvania Ave., NW, Room 702
Washington, DC 20506   202-682-5438
The Music Program provides support for the creation and performance of music, with an emphasis on assisting the growth of American music and musicians. Support is available for single-music and multi-music presenters and for music festivals. Grants help jazz organizations hire professional management personnel and assist organizations with innovative projects that benefit the field of jazz. Music ensembles, choruses, and orchestras can receive grants to help pay a variety of expenses, such as salaries, touring, or collaboration with other groups. Music professional training supports music and advanced training on programs leading to professional careers in music. Grants also assist non-profit organizations in recording and distributing American music, and to establish a variety of residencies for composers or ensembles.

* Museum Artistic Initiative Grants

Creation and Presentation Division
Museum Program
National Endowment for the Arts
1100 Pennsylvania Ave., NW, Room 624
Washington, DC 20506   202-682-5452
The Museum Program is designed to meet the needs of the museum field by providing funding for a variety of projects. Utilization of Museum Resources is designed to help organizations make greater use of museum collections and other resources. Grants help with reinstallation, exhibitions, and collection sharing. Grants can be used to develop related programs and events that enrich these presentations, including the preparation and publication of exhibition catalogs. The Education category provides for educational programs for the community, which can include outside specialists, and the Catalog category supports the cataloging of a permanent museum collection and the publication of materials related to the collection. Special Artistic Initiatives is designed to encourage long-term programming by museums and should include a unifying, thematic framework. The Museum Program helps museums conserve collections by providing grants for planning, conservation, and training. Grants also aid in collection maintenance through solving problems in climate control, security, and storage. Museums are encouraged to purchase works by living American artists, as well as to mount or participate in special exhibitions.

* Musicians Overseas Concert Tours

Artistic Ambassador Program
Office of Private Sector Programs
Bureau of Educational and Cultural Affairs
U.S. Information Agency
301 Fourth St., SW, Room 224
Washington, DC 20547   202-619-4779
This program, begun in 1983, sends gifted American musicians who are not under professional management on overseas tours, where they give public concerts and work with music students and faculties. The program began with pianists, and now also includes piano-violin-cello trios. Contact this office for information on the selection process and tour itineraries.

* Opera and Musical Theater Funding

Creation and Presentation Division
Opera-Musical Theater Program
National Endowment for the Arts
1100 Pennsylvania Ave., NW, Room 703
Washington, DC 20506   202-682-5452
The Opera-Musical Theater Program assists all forms of music theater generally involving voice. Grants support professional opera and musical theater production organizations, and the creation, development, rehearsal, and production of new American or seldom-produced works. Funds are available to bring performances to areas where they generally do not take place. Independent producers can also receive support for the development of new works. National service organizations and special projects. Individual and non-profit organizations can apply for grants, if such donations qualify as charitable deduction under Section 170(c) of the Internal Revenue Code of 1954.

* Overseas Speaking Opportunities for Artists

Thematic Programs
Office of Program Coordination and Development
U.S. Information Agency (USIA)
301 Fourth St., SW, Room 550
Washington, DC 20547   202-619-4764
U.S. Speakers are experts in a field--usually economics, international affairs, literature, the arts, U.S. political and social processes, sports, science, or technology--sent abroad by U.S. Information Agency (USIA) to meet with groups or individual professional counterparts. Recruited on the basis of requests of USIA staff in other countries, U.S. speakers often engage in informal lecture/discussions with small groups, grant media interviews, or speak before larger audiences. Those interested in the American Participant program are invited to submit a brief letter indicating times of availability, along with a curriculum vitae and at least two lecture topics with brief talking points.

* Performing Artists International Tours

Partnership Planning Division
International Partnerships Office
National Endowment for the Arts
1100 Pennsylvania Ave., NW, Room 517
Washington, DC 20506   202-682-5562
The Rockefeller Foundation, the United States Information Agency, and the Arts Endowment jointly fund performing artists invited to international festivals abroad and fund U.S. representation at major international exhibitions of visual art. Fellowships are also available to artists in various disciplines to work and study in Japan, Canada, and Mexico.

* Performing Arts and Visual Arts Copyright

Entries Catalogs
Superintendent of Documents
Government Printing Office
Washington, DC 20402   202-512-1800
The following copyright catalogs, which list materials registered only during the period covered by each issue, are available on microfiche only and are sold as individual subscriptions:

Part 1: Nondramatic Literary Works (quarterly) $14 per year.
Part 2: Serials and Periodicals (semi-annually) $5 per year.
Part 3: Performing Arts (quarterly) $13 per year.
Part 4: Motion Pictures and Filmstrips (semi-annually) $5 per year.
Part 5: Visual Arts (excluding maps) (semi-annually) $5 per year.

* Performing Arts Clearinghouse

John F. Kennedy Center for the Performing Arts
2700 F St. N.W.
Washington, DC 20566   202-416-8780

The Performing Arts Library is a joint project of the Library of Congress and the Kennedy Center, and offers information and reference assistance on dance, theater, opera, music, film, and broadcasting.

* Performing Arts Resource Center

Performing Arts Reading Room
Room LM113
Library of Congress
Washington, DC 20540   202-707-5507

The Performing Arts Reading Room houses the Library of Congress's non-book collections in the performing arts area: music, dance, sound recordings, motion pictures, and television. The collection includes more than 4,000,000 pieces of music and manuscripts, some 300,000 books and pamphlets, and about 350,000 sound recordings reflecting the development of music in Western civilization from earliest times to the present. Reference services are available. Adjacent to the reading room is the Recorded Sound Reference Center for users primarily interested in sound recordings and radio materials. Listening facilities are available in the reading room, but their use is limited of those doing research of a specific nature leading to publication or production. Musicians who wish to play music drawn from the Library's collection may use the piano available in an adjacent sound proof room.

* Polar Expeditions for Artists and Photographers

Ice Operations Division
Office of Navigation Safety and Waterways Services
U.S. Coast Guard
U.S. Department of Transportation
2100 2nd St., SW, Room 1202 A
Washington, DC 20593-0001   202-267-1450

The Coast Guard furnishes vessels to other agencies, such as the National Science Foundation, U.S. Geological Survey, and the Navy, to conduct research and ice operations in Arctic and Antarctic waters. The agencies sponsoring the missions select scientists, researchers, students, and in some cases, journalists, photographers, and artists to accompany the mission when space is available. This office is a good starting point for obtaining information on the pertinence of a mission to your field, to be directed to the appropriate agency sponsors, and for information about the data collected during missions.

* Surveys of Educational Schooling

University of Illinois at Urbana - Champaign
Grants and Contracts
109 Coble Hall
801 South Wright St.
Champaign, IL 61820-6242   217-333-2186

Major research areas include the development and validation of standardized achievement tests in the area of artistic processes and techniques in art history; national study on literacy and art education; role of music in general education; status surveys in art, visual, dance and drama in the elementary and secondary schools; drama/theater, visual and dance; influence on culture condition on the learning of arts; development of computer assisted testing (music education); design of studies in dance; designs of studies in theater; status survey of music education in elementary and secondary schools; and arts education field work: observational studies.

* Theater Company Funding

Heritage and Preservation Division
Theater Program
National Endowment for the Arts
1100 Pennsylvania Ave., NW, Room 608
Washington, DC 20506   202-682-5428

The Theater Program provides financial assistance for the creation and presentation of work by companies, and to bring the work to locales where theater is generally not available. The Professional Theater Training category is designed to encourage efforts to raise professional standards by assisting professional training of theater artists. Grants are also available to organizations and publishers for projects and services that address the needs of the theater. Grants can be made to non-profit organizations if such donations qualify as charitable deductions under Section 170(c) of the Internal Revenue Code of 1954.

* Theater Playbills and Rare Books Collection

Rare Book and Special Collections Division
Library of Congress, Deck B
Washington, DC 20540   202-707-5434

The Rare Books Division contains about 300,000 volumes and 200,000 pamphlets, broadsides, theater playbills, title pages, manuscripts, posters, and photographs. The collection includes documents of the first fourteen congresses of the United States, the personal libraries of Thomas Jefferson and Harry Houdini, incunabula; miniature books and dime novels, and the Russian Imperial collection. The division has its own central card catalog plus special card files that describe individual collections or special aspects of books from many collections.

* Transportation Architecture and Beautification

Environment Division
Policy and International Affairs
Office of the Secretary of Transportation
U.S. Department of Transportation (DOT)
400 7th Street, SW, Room 9217
Washington, DC 20590   202-366-4366

This is the DOT contact point for environmental issues. Staff can provide you with information and referrals on such subjects as highway beautification, transportation architecture, bicycle paths, historic preservation activities, and environmental impact statements.

* Travel Abroad for Artists and Performers

Office of Arts America
The Bureau of Educational and Cultural Affairs
United States Information Agency (USIA)
301 Fourth St., SW, Room 567
Washington, DC 20547   202-619-4779

Arts America recruits artists and performers to visit other countries and provides some assistance to artists traveling privately. The USIA sends some 15 large fine arts exhibitions and 25 performing arts groups overseas annually. Panels set up by the National Endowment for the Arts recommends a group of candidates, from which the USIA selects the programs participants. A Speakers Program recruits artists from the fields of literature, film, and the plastic and performing arts, on the basis of requests from overseas posts. AculSpecs are American specialists, in one of the plastic or performing arts, who visit a foreign country for two to six weeks with a local host institution for a program of master classes, workshops, and demonstrations. Arts America sponsors about 30 of these programs a year. This office also provides support materials for major fine and performing arts projects; publishes a quarterly list of privately traveling artists; and tries to assist overseas posts in programming these performers.

* Visual Media Grants to Artists

Creation and Presentation Division
Visual Arts Program
National Endowment for the Arts
1100 Pennsylvania Ave., NW, Room 729
Washington, DC 20506   202-682-5452

The Visual Arts Program awards grants to organizations that assist visual artists and support public art projects, such as art in parks, plazas, and airports. Funding is available for a variety of projects that enable visual artists to communicate with their peers and the public, and for a variety of on-going visual arts programs, including exhibitions and access to working facilities. Grants can be made to non-profit organizations if such donations qualify as a charitable deduction under Section 170(c) of the Internal Revenue Code of 1954.

Film, Photography, and Media Arts

Numerous archives on broadcast and film are readily available not only to researchers but to the public at large. The government produces new audiovisuals every year on virtually every field of interest. These films, slide shows, video and audio tapes can be purchased and often rented. Grants available to the media arts community are listed in "Money for the Arts" in this chapter.

* 8,000 Government Films, Videos and Other Audiovisuals

National Audiovisual Center
National Archives and Records Administration
Customer Services Section P2
8700 Edgeworth Dr.   800-553-NTIS
Capitol Heights, MD 20743   703-487-4650

The National Audiovisual Center was established to serve as the central source for all federally-produced audiovisual materials and to make them available to the public through information and distribution services. Through the Center's distribution programs, the public has access to more than 8,000 titles covering a wide range of subjects. Major subject concentrations in the Center's collection include history, medicine, dentistry and the allied health sciences, safety, aviation and space technology, vocational and management training, and the environmental sciences. The audiovisual materials are available for sale, rental, or preview. A *Media Resources Catalog* is available at no charge and lists the materials by subject and title.

* Aerial Photographs and Surveys

Cartographic and Architectural Branch
Non-Textual Division
National Archives and Records Administration
8601 Adelphi Rd.
College Park, MD 20740   301-713-7030

The Cartographic and Architectural Branch has over 11 million maps, charts, aerial photographs, architectural drawings, patents, and ship plans, which constitute one of the world's largest accumulations of such documents. Some of the holdings are grouped under subject areas such as Mapping, which contains exploration and scientific surveys (as from the Lewis and Clark Expedition), public land surveys, Indian affairs, topography and natural resources, navigation, census mapping, and maps of foreign countries. All the holdings can be examined in the research room from 8:45 a.m. to 5:00 p.m., Monday through Friday, with some evening and Saturday hours as well. Reproductions can be furnished for a fee.

* African Art and Culture Photographic Archives

National Museum of African Art
950 Independence Ave., SW
Washington, DC 20560   202-357-4654

The Eliot Elisofon Photographic Archives is devoted to the collection, preservation, and management of visual resources of sub-Saharan African Art. It conducts picture research and collaborates with art historians, anthropologists, filmmakers, and other interested specialists in the publication and exhibition of its images. In addition, it serves as an international clearinghouse for information about African art and cultural history. The collection is divided into two major categories: art, which includes photographs of art objects in the permanent collection, as well as in public and private collections; and field, which contains images of African life. An overall guide to the collection and a price list are available upon request.

* Air and Space Archival Videodiscs

Smithsonian Institution Press
c/o Order Dept. 900
Blue Ridge Summit, PA 17214   800-782-4612

The National Air and Space Museum is reproducing its entire photo archives on videodiscs. Ten discs are planned, featuring color and black and white photographs of the U.S. and foreign aircraft, as well as of the artifacts and people associated with the development of aviation and space flight.

* American Slides and Photographs Databases

Research and Scholars Center
National Museum of American Art
9th and G Sts. N.W.
Washington, DC 20560   202-357-1348

The Office of Research Support maintains seven research projects totaling over 530,000 art data records and over 250,000 photographic images. Each of the projects uses automation in cataloging information and images, thus providing the user with access to art information and reproductions in a variety of ways. The Peter A. Juley and Son Collection of more than 127,000 photographic negatives documenting American art and artists photographed between 1896 and 1975 by this New York City firm; and the Slide and Photograph Archives, a collection of over 90,000 slides and 200,000 photographs available for study and 20,000 slides available for loan. Please call in advance for an appointment.

* Art Slides, Films, Video Loan Program

Education Resources Programs
National Gallery of Art
Extension Services
Constitution and 6th St., NW
Washington, DC 20565   202-842-6273

Color slide programs, films, and videocassettes are loaned at no cost to schools, libraries, community organizations, and individuals across the nation. The programs deal with a wide range of subjects drawn from the Gallery's permanent collections and special exhibitions. A free catalog listing all free-loan Extension Programs is available.

* Film and Broadcast Resource Center

Education Resource Center
John F. Kennedy Center for the Performing Arts
2700 F St. N.W.
Washington, DC 20566-0001   202-416-8780

The Performing Arts Library is a joint project of the Library of Congress and the Kennedy Center, and offers information and reference assistance on dance, theater, opera, music, film, and broadcasting.

* Film and Sound Recordings Archives

Motion Picture and Video and Sound Branch
National Archives and Records Administration
8601 Adelphi Rd.
College Park, MD 20740   301-713-7060

The Motion Picture, Sound, and Video Branch has 150,000 reels of motion picture film and several thousand videotapes from government sources as well as private individuals and organizations. The films consist of edited and nonedited footage, documentaries, newsreels, news films, combat films, and research and development test films. The collection generally covers 1914 to the present. The Archives also hold a collection of more than 115,000 sound recordings received from federal and private agencies, and commercial and foreign sources. There are several card catalogs to assist you in research, and copies can be made upon request. It is best to call ahead for an appointment to reserve a viewing room.

* Filming on Public Lands

Bureau of Land Management
U.S. Department of the Interior
18th and C Sts., NW
Washington, DC 20240   202-452-5125

The Bureau of Land Management issues leases, rights-of-way, and use permits for a wide variety of public lands including parks; power transmission and distribution lines; petroleum products collection and transmission systems; advertising and motion picture filming; and recreational events.

* Fish and Wildlife Photographs
Audio Visuals
U.S. Fish and Wildlife Service
18th and C Sts., NW
Washington, DC 20240   202-208-5611
The Audio Visual Department of the U.S. Fish and Wildlife Service has an extensive collection of both black and white pictures and color slides of fish and wildlife. There is no charge for their lending service, which extends 30 or 90 days. If the photographs or slides are used in publications, the photographer and the U.S. Fish and Wildlife Service must be given credit.

* Folkways Musical Recordings Archive
Office of Folklife Programs
955 L'Enfant Plaza, SW, Suite 2600
Washington, DC 20560   202-287-3251
The Folkways Records Archive, comprising the Moses and Frances Asch Collection, contains material related to the 2,200 published recordings of Folkways Records. The Folkways collection documents world-wide musical traditions, the spoken words of significant American figures, historical events, and nonmusical sounds of technology and nature. A catalog of the archives holdings is available which includes information on how to purchase recordings of the music.

* Historical Sound Recordings
Motion Picture, Broadcasting, and Recorded Sound Division
3rd Floor, Room 338
Library of Congress
Washington, DC 20540   202-707-5840
The sound recording collection reflects the entire spectrum of history of sound from wax cylinders to quadraphonic discs and includes such diverse media as wire recordings, aluminum discs, zinc discs, acetate-covered glass discs, rubber compound discs, and translucent plastic discs. The division has also recently made all of its materials recorded prior to 1909 available on 8-inch compressed audio discs for individual users in the Recorded Sound Reading Room using a micro computer. Included are the Berliner collection, from the company which invented and introduced disc recording, radio news commentaries from 1944 to 1946, eyewitness descriptions of marine combat and House of Representatives debates. For purchase by researchers, the Division's laboratory is prepared to make taped copies of recordings in good physical condition, when not restricted by copyright, performance rights, or provisions of gift or transfer. The requester is responsible for any necessary search--by mail or in person--of Copyright Office records to determine the copyright status of specific recordings. The Division also offers copies of some of its holdings for sale in disc form. These include a number of LP records of folk music, poetry, and other literature.

* Interactive Video Project
National Demonstration Laboratory for Interactive Educational Technologies
Library of Congress
Madison Building
1st and Independence SE
Smithsonian Institution
Washington, DC 20540   202-884-8906
The National Demonstration Laboratory is a testing center for educational applications of interactive technologies and a clearinghouse of information about the technologies. It was established as a joint effort of the Smithsonian Institution and the Interactive Video Consortium, a group of public television stations actively involved with interactive technologies. The NDL clearinghouse database eventually will be accessible electronically. This online database will be available free of charge to all NDL Affiliates and to the public through paid subscription. The database will include information about basic attributes of interactive technologies, specific educational applications, bibliographic references, and equipment and software options. The coupling of interactive computer programs with multimedia materials offers educators the ability to maximize scarce resources, to address curriculum problems, and to reach new groups of learners. NDL conducts seminars and workshops which bring together educators, public broadcasters, and developers of software and hardware. They also identify elements of educational curricula that would be suitable for interactive video applications and distributes an assessment of interactive video user training and funding needs. Call or write for more information.

* Media Arts and Filmmaker Grants
Creation and Presentation Division
National Endowment for the Arts
1100 Pennsylvania Ave., NW, Room 726
Washington, DC 20506   202-682-5452
This program provides support to non-profit organizations that help artists carry out their projects. The program also offers funding for a limited number of major public television and radio series that bring other art forms to a wide public. Grants are available to support productions in film and video that emphasize the use of these media as art forms. Grants assist organizations that distribute significant films and videotapes, and sponsor conferences, workshops, and publications. Grants can be made to non-profit organizations, including arts centers, if such donations qualify as charitable deductions under Section 170(c) of the Internal Revenue Code of 1954.

* Motion Picture and Broadcasting Collection
Motion Picture, Broadcasting, and Recorded Sound Division
3rd Floor Room 338
Library of Congress
Washington, DC 20540   202-707-5840
The Library's film and television collections contain more than 100,000 titles and more than 1,000 titles are added each month through copyright deposit, purchase, gift, or exchange. Items selected from copyright deposits include feature films and short works of all sorts, fiction and documentary, exemplifying the range of current film and video production. The collections also include some 90,000 stills. The film and television collections are maintained for research purposes. Limited viewing and listening facilities for individual users are provided in the reading rooms.

* Motion Picture and Sound Recordings
Copyright Entries Catalogs
Superintendent of Documents
Government Printing Office
Washington, DC 20402   202-512-1800
The following copyright catalogs, which list materials registered only during the period covered by each issue, are available on microfiche only and are sold as individual subscriptions:
Part 4: Motion Pictures and Filmstrips (semi-annually) $5 per year.
Part 5: Visual Arts (excluding maps) (semi-annually) $5 per year.
Part 6: Maps (semi-annually) $5 per year.
Part 7: Sound Recordings (semi-annually) $7.50 per year.
Part 8: Renewals (semi-annually) $5 per year.

* Motion Picture Archives
Human Studies Film Archives (HSFA)
National Museum of Natural History
10th St. and Constitution Ave., NW
Washington, DC 20560   202-357-3349
The Human Studies Film Archives (HSFA) was established to collect and preserve Motion picture film and video recordings of Western and nonwestern cultures. The growing collection consists of over three million feet of ethnographic film and video records of diverse cultures from every major geographical region in the world. Access to the holdings is available though SIRIS. The HSFA performs a full range of archival functions, including locating and collecting ethnographic footage, conducting film preservation work, refining techniques for storing and maintaining archival film collections, and developing a system for cataloging ethnographic film and video materials. The HSFA sponsors public screenings and lectures, and serves as a national clearinghouse for information about ethnographic film. Researchers must make appointments forty-eight hours in advance.

* Panama Canal Photographs
Office of Public Affairs
Panama Canal Commission
APO Miami, FL 34011-5000   011-507-52-3165
8 x 10 glossy, black and white photographs are available free of charge showing the Locks towing locomotives helping ease container ships into locks of the Panama Canal. Contact this office for more information.

* Park System Photographs
Photo Library, Office of Public Affairs
National Park Service
U.S. Department of the Interior

Arts and Humanities

18th and C Sts., NW
Washington, DC 20240 202-208-4997
This library contains photos and transparencies of the National Park Service that can be borrowed free of charge. Geologic features, living history, and natural history subjects are available.

* Photographic and Microform Archives
National Gallery of Art
Constitution and 6th St., NW
Washington, DC 20565-0046 202-842-6039
The Photographic Archives is a study and research collection of black-and-white photographs, negatives, microforms and reproductive prints, which documents works of art and architecture and consists of over 1,232,000 photographs and negatives and 4,183,000 microform images. A summary listing of the current holdings is available. The Archives is open to all Gallery library users.

* Photographs from the U.S. Geological Survey
Photographic Library
MS 914
U.S. Geological Survey
Box 25046, Federal Center
Denver, CO 80225 303-236-1010
The Photographic Library of the U.S. Geological Survey contains a special collection of approximately 250,000 photographs. The Library may be used by the public as well as by personnel of other government agencies. Persons who wish to obtain prints, copy negatives, and duplicate transparencies from the collection are encouraged to visit the library. If this is not possible, the staff will prepare lists of specific photographs in response to requests. Many photographs are selected by searching U.S. Geological Survey publications and are identified by title and number of the publication as well as the number of the page and plate of the figure found. To obtain information on purchasing prints, negatives, or transparencies, contact the library directly.

* Photographs of Masterpieces
National Gallery of Art
Office of Photographic Services
Constitution and 6th St., NW
Washington, DC 20565 202-842-6231
Black and white, 8 x 10 photographs of works from the National Gallery of Art's permanent collections are available for purchase, either by visiting the Office of Photographic Services or by mail. Color transparencies of works from the Gallery, to be used for publication, are available for rental only and must be requested in writing.

* Photographic Views of the U.S. Capitol
The Curator's Office
Architect of the Capitol
The Capitol Building, Room SB15
Washington, DC 20515 202-225-1222
Views of the U.S. Capitol, a collection of seven popular views of the United States Capitol, are compiled from the Capitol collection maintained by the Architect of the Capitol. Reproductions may be purchased from the following office, but no photographs from this collection may be used for commercial purposes: Photo-duplication Service, Library of Congress, Washington, DC 20540.

* Prints and Photographs Archives
Prints and Photographs Division
Library of Congress
LM 337
Washington, DC 20540 202-707-6394
More than 10 million items in the Library of Congress chronicle American life and society from its earliest days to the present through its prints and photographs. Items include architectural plans, posters, cartoons, drawings, and advertising labels. Reference librarians will assist those doing their own research, and they can furnish names of freelance picture researchers for individuals who cannot get to the Library.

* Public Lands Photos
Office of Public Affairs
Bureau of Land Management
U.S. Department of the Interior

18th and C Sts., NW
Washington, DC 20240 202-452-5125
Thousands of black and white photographs and color slides are available, including forestry, realty, minerals, and range subjects.

* Smithsonian Collection Slides and Photographs
Photographic Services
Smithsonian Institution
14th and Constitution Ave.
Washington, DC 20560 202-357-1933
Slides, transparencies, and prints (black and white and color) are available of photographs in the Smithsonian's collections. You can also order their seven slide series on a variety of topics, and most include a booklet and cassette tape. For a slide series catalog or ordering information, contact Photographic Services.

* Slide Lending Series on Art
Slide Library
National Gallery of Art
Constitution and 6th St., NW
Washington, DC 20565 202-842-6100
The National Gallery maintains a lending slide collection of over 50,000 images, which are loaned to the public free of charge. There is no list of the slide lending collection, but selections for National Gallery objects can be made from Gallery catalogs. Up to 50 slides can be borrowed at one time and may be kept for a period of two weeks. The slide library is open to the public.

* Six Million Still Pictures
Still Pictures Branch
National Archives and Records Administration
8601 Adelphi Rd.
College Park, MD 20740 301-713-6625, x234
There are approximately six million still pictures in the Archives, including posters and photographs of artwork. Among the photographers represented in the Archives holdings are Matthew Brady, Carleton Watkins, William Henry Jackson, and Ansel Adams. There are leaflets which describe available selected photographs and slides in a variety of areas. Copies of still photographs are available as copy negatives and color and black-and-white prints and slides. Contact the office for information about photographs and a current price list.

* Sound Recordings of Poetry and Other Literature
Motion Picture, Broadcasting, and Recorded
Sound Division
Library of Congress
Washington, DC 20540 202-707-5840
The Library of Congress offers copies of some of its poetry and literature holdings for sale in disc form. Contact this office for information on what's available, along with prices.

* Space Photographs
Customer Services
Earth Resources Observation System
Data Center (EROS)
U.S. Geological Survey
Sioux Falls, SD 57198 605-594-6546
The EROS Data Center maintains photographs from many of the space missions, including those of the space shuttle, Apollo, and Gemini. Contact the center directly for information concerning specific topics.

* TV and Radio Production Funding
Humanities Projects in Media
Division of Public Programs
National Endowment for the Humanities
1100 Pennsylvania Ave., NW, Room 420
Washington, DC 20506 202-606-8278
The Humanities Projects in Media supports the planning, writing, or production of television and radio programs in the humanities, which are intended for general audiences. Awards are made for both adult and children's programming. The collaboration of scholars in the humanities with experienced writers, producers, and directors is required. Nonprofit institutions, organizations and groups, including public television and radio stations may apply for grants.

* Washington Architecture Photographs
United States Commission of Fine Arts (CFA)
441 F St., Suite 312
Washington, DC 20001   202-504-2200

The Commission of Fine Arts (CFA) maintains a file of photographs of past and present Washington, DC, architectural projects which involve the CFA. Reproductions are available to the public for a processing fee upon written request. Call this office for information on what photographs are available in their files.

Money for the Arts

The following is a description of money programs available to artists and other interested parties from the federal government. The information is taken from the *Catalog of Federal Domestic Assistance* which is published by the U.S. Government Printing Office in Washington, DC. The number next to the title description is the reference number listed in this *Catalog*. Contact the office listed below the title for more information about any of these programs.

* $25,000 For Graphic Artists, Interior And Product Designers

(Promotion Of The Arts — Design Arts - 45.001)
Design Art Program
National Endowment For The Arts
1100 Pennsylvania Ave., NW, Room 627
Washington, DC 20506   202-682-5437

Through a combination of grants and leadership initiatives, the Design Arts Program supports excellence in the disciplines that comprise the design arts: architecture, landscape architecture, urban design and planning, historic preservation, interior design, industrial and product design, and graphic design. Grants are awarded to professional designers, non-profit organizations, arts groups, colleges and universities, and local and state governments. There are project grants for individuals, individual grants for design innovation, and project grants for rural and small communities, design education and design history and documentation. There are even USA Fellowships which provide up to $20,000 for designers and other individuals working in design-related professions to study and travel independently within the United States. Estimate of annual funds available: $3,450,000.

* $45,000 For Dancers

(Promotion Of The Arts — Dance - 45.002)
Dance Program
National Endowment for the Arts
1100 Pennsylvania Ave., NW, Room 620
Washington, DC 20506   202-682-5435

The Dance Program provides support for professional choreographers, dance companies, and to organizations and individuals that service dance. Estimate of annual funds available: $7,350,000.

* Grants For Art Teachers

(Promotion of the Arts — Arts In Education - 45.003)
Arts In Education Program
National Endowment for the Arts
1100 Pennsylvania Ave., NW, Room 602
Washington, DC 20506   202-682-5426

The Arts in Education Program's goal is to advance the arts as a basic part of education, and to encourage the development and implementation of arts education programs. Estimate of annual funds available: $7,800,000.

* $20,000 For Freelance Writers

(Promotion of the Arts — Literature - 45.004)
Literature Program
National Endowment for the Arts
1100 Pennsylvania Ave., NW, Room 722
Washington, DC 20506   202-682-5451

To aid creative writers of fiction, poetry, creative non-fiction, and translators of literary works into English through fellowships; and to support residencies for writers and reading series, non-commercial literary magazines, small presses, and more. Estimate of annual funds available: $4,325,000.

* $35,000 For Musicians

(Promotion of the Arts — Music - 45.005)
Music Program
National Endowment for the Arts
1100 Pennsylvania Ave., NW, Room 702

Washington, DC 20506   202-682-5445

To support excellence in music performance and creativity, and to develop informed audiences for music throughout the country. Estimate of annual funds available: $11,325,000.

* $35,000 For Radio, TV, And Film Producers

(Promotion of the Arts — Media Arts - 45.006)
Media Arts Program
National Endowment for the Arts
1100 Pennsylvania Ave., NW, Room 720
Washington, DC 20506   202-682-5452

To provide grants in support of projects that advance the media arts and encourage their practice and wider appreciation. The media arts include documentary, experimental, animated and narrative film/video works, as well as radio programming and audio art. Estimate of annual funds available: $10,600,000.

* $37,500 To Exhibit A Local Art Show

(Promotion of the Arts — State and Regional Program - 45.007)
State and Regional Program
National Endowment for the Arts
1100 Pennsylvania Ave., NW, Room 602
Washington, DC 20506   202-682-5429

To assist state and regional public arts agencies in the development of programs that encourage the arts and artists, and to assist organizations providing services at the national level to state or local arts agencies. Estimate of annual funds available: $33,000,000.

* $37,500 For Struggling Actors And Theaters

(Promotion of the Arts — Theater - 45.008)
Theater Program
National Endowment for the Arts
1100 Pennsylvania Ave., NW, Room 608
Washington, DC 20506   202-682-5425

To provide grants to aid professional non-profit theater companies, individual theater artists, national theater service organizations, and professional theater training institutions. Fellowships for solo theater artists can include puppeteers, mimes, storytellers, monologists, clowns, new vaudevillians, and others. There are also fellowships for playwrights, directors, actors, and designers. Estimate of annual funds available: $8,675,000.

* $20,000 For Painters, Sculptors, And Craft Artists

(Promotion of the Arts — Visual Arts - 45.009)
Visual Arts Program
National Endowment for the Arts
1100 Pennsylvania Ave., NW, Room 729
Washington, DC 20506   202-682-5448

To provide grants to visual artists including: painters, sculptors, photographers, crafts artists, printmakers, artists specializing in drawing, artists creating artists books, video artists, performance artists, conceptual artists, and visual artists working in new genres. Grants are intended to support institutions devoted to the development of the visual arts in America. Estimate of annual funds available: $5,125,000.

* Money To Local Theater And Dance Companies

(Promotion of the Arts — Expansion Arts - 45.010)
Expansion Arts Program

National Endowment for the Arts
1100 Pennsylvania Ave., NW, Room 711
Washington, DC 20506   202-682-5443

To provide grants to professionally directed arts organizations of high artistic quality that are deeply rooted in and reflective of culturally diverse, inner-city, rural, or tribal communities. Matching grants are available to help create, exhibit, or present works representative of the culture of a community, and to provide a community with access to all types of quality art. Estimate of annual funds available: $5,600,000.

* Money For Regional Art Programs

(Promotion of the Arts — Presenting and Commissioning - 45.011)
Presenting and Commissioning Program
National Endowment for the Arts
1100 Pennsylvania Ave., NW, Room 726
Washington, DC 20506   202-682-5444

To provide grants for arts projects that potentially have national or regional impact. Estimate of annual funds available: $5,875,000.

* Money For Art Institutions

(Promotion of the Arts — Challenge Grants - 45.013)
Challenge and Advancement Grant Programs
National Endowment for the Arts
1100 Pennsylvania Ave., NW, Room 617
Washington, DC 20506   202-682-5436

To provide a special opportunity for art institutions to strengthen long-term institutional capacity and to enhance their organization's artistic quality and diversity. Challenge grantees must match every federal dollar with at least three dollars from other sources. Grants are available to arts institutions, state and local arts agencies, regional organizations, and others. Estimate of annual funds available: $13,487,000.

* Money For Opera Singers And Opera Companies

(Promotion of the Arts — Opera-Musical Theater - 45.014)
Opera-Musical Theater Program
National Endowment for the Arts
1100 Pennsylvania Ave., NW, Room 703
Washington, DC 20506   202-682-5447

The Opera-Musical Theater Program is committed to diverse forms of music theater, such as the great operas of the past, contemporary works, the Broadway musical, and the richness of the multi-cultural heritage. Estimate of annual funds available: $5,500,000.

* $10,000 For American Folk Artists

(Promotion of the Arts — Folk Arts - 45.015)
Folk Arts Program
National Endowment For The Arts

1100 Pennsylvania Ave., NW, Room 710
Washington, DC 20506   202-682-5449

The Folk Arts Program supports traditional arts that have grown through time within the many groups that make up our nation — groups that share the same ethnic heritage, language, occupation, religion, or geographic area. These folk arts include music, dance, poetry, tales, oratory, crafts, and various types of visual art forms. The Program's main objectives are to preserve and enhance this multi-cultural artistic heritage and to make it more widely available. Estimate of annual funds available: $3,000,000.

* Grants To Non-Profits To Produce Radio And Television Shows

(Promotion of the Humanities — Humanities Projects In Media - 45.104)
Division of Public Programs
Humanities Projects in Media
National Endowment for the Humanities
1100 Pennsylvania Ave., NW, Room 420
Washington, DC 20506   202-606-8278

To encourage and support radio and television production that advances public understanding and appreciation of the humanities. Estimate of annual funds available: $10,500,000.

* $5,500 Plus Travel Expenses For 11-Week Course In Arts Administration

(Promotion of the Arts — Arts Administration Fellow's Program - 45.021)
Arts Administration Fellows Program
National Endowment for the Arts
1100 Pennsylvania Ave., NW
Washington, DC 20506   202-682-5786

A limited number of 11-week fellowships are available for professionals in arts management and related fields. This program is designed to acquaint fellows with the policies, procedures, and operations of the Endowment and to give them an overview of art activities in the United States. It is open to people who have a bachelor of arts degree and a minimum of three years professional arts management experience and/or an advanced degree. Estimate of annual funds available: $225,000.

* Money For Arts Groups To Have Better Management

(Promotion of the Arts — Advancement Grants - 45.022)
Challenge and Advancement Grant Programs
National Endowment for the Arts
1100 Pennsylvania Ave., NW, Room 617
Washington, DC 20506   202-682-5436

To help improve the management of arts organizations, grants have been set aside to help these organizations develop specific strategies to eliminate deficiencies in organizational management practice and to take carefully planned steps toward achievement of long-range goals. Estimate of annual funds available: $3,300,000.

Money for the Humanities

The following is a description of the money programs available to those interested in the humanities. The information is taken from the *Catalog of Federal Domestic Assistance* which is published by the U.S. Government Printing Office in Washington, DC. The number next to the title description is the reference number listed in this *Catalog*. Contact the office listed below the title for more information about any of the programs listed.

* Promotion of the Humanities - Humanities Projects in Media 45.104

Division of General Programs
Humanities Projects in Media
National Endowment for the Humanities, Room 420
Washington, DC 20506   202-606-8278

To encourage and support radio and television production that advances public understanding and appreciation of the humanities by adults and young people of junior high and high school age. Types of assistance: grants. Estimate of annual funds available: $ 10,264,000.

* Promotion of the Humanities - Public Humanities Projects 45.113

Public Humanities Projects
Division of General Programs
National Endowment for the Humanities, Room 426
Washington, DC 20506   202-606-8272

To support humanities projects addressed to out-of-school audiences. All projects must draw upon resources and scholars in the fields of the humanities. Types of assistance: grants. Estimate of annual funds available: $ 2,476,000.

* Promotion of the Humanities - Summer Seminars for College Teachers 45.116

Summer Seminars for College Teachers
Division of Fellowships and Seminars
National Endowment for the Humanities, Room 316
Washington, DC 20506   202-606-8463

To provide opportunities for teachers in five, four, and two-year colleges; for scholars employed in libraries, museums, historical associations, and other humanities institution to work during the summer in their areas of interest under the direction of distinguished scholars at institutions with library resources suitable for advanced study and research. Types of assistance: grants. Estimate of annual funds available: $ 4,470,000.

* Promotion of the Humanities - Summer Stipends 45.121

Division of Fellowships and Seminars, Summer Stipends
National Endowment for the Humanities, Room 316
Washington, DC 20506   202-606-8551

To provide support for individual faculty and staff members at universities and two-year and four-year colleges and for others who have made or have demonstrated promise of making significant contributions to the humanities. Types of assistance: grants. Estimate of annual funds available: $ 876,000.

* Promotion of the Humanities - Regrants/Centers for Advanced Study 45.122

Division of Research Programs
Institutional Programs and Resources, Room 318
National Endowment for the Humanities
Washington, DC 20506   202-606-8359

To support interrelated research in well-defined subject areas at independent centers for advanced study, American research centers overseas, and independent research libraries and museums. Types of assistance: grants. Estimate of annual funds available: $ 2,985,000.

* Promotion of the Humanities - Humanities Projects in Museums and Historical Organizations 45.125

Humanities Projects in Museums and Historical Organizations
Division of Public Programs, Room 420
National Endowment for the Humanities
Washington, DC 20506   202-606-8284

To assist museums, historical organizations, and other similar cultural institutions to plan and implement effective and imaginative programs which use material culture to convey and interpret the humanities to the general public. Types of assistance: grants. Estimate of annual funds available: $ 9,916,000.

* Promotion of the Humanities - Elementary and Secondary Education in the Humanities 45.127

Elementary and Secondary Education in the Humanities
National Endowment for the Humanities, Room 302
Washington, DC 20506   202-606-8377

To increase the effectiveness of humanities teaching in our Nation's elementary, middle, and secondary schools. Types of assistance: grants. Estimate of annual funds available: $ 6,769,000.

* Promotion of the Humanities - State Programs 45.129

Federal-State Partnerships
National Endowment for the Humanities, Room 411
Washington, DC 20506   202-606-8254

To promote local humanities programming through renewable program grants to humanities councils within each of the 50 states, the District of Columbia, Puerto Rico, and the U.S. Virgin Islands for the purpose of regranting funds to local non-profit organizations. Types of assistance: grants. Estimate of annual funds available: $ 28,014,000.

* Promotion of the Humanities - Challenge Grants 45.130

Office of Challenge Grants, Room 429
National Endowment for the Humanities
Washington, DC 20506   202-606-8309

To support educational and cultural institutions and organizations in order to increase their financial stability and to sustain or improve the quality of humanities programs. Types of assistance: grants. Estimate of annual funds available: $ 13,973,000.

* Promotion of the Humanities - Texts/Publication Subvention 45.132

Division of Research Programs, Scholarly Publications
National Endowment for the Humanities, Room 318
Washington, DC 20506   202-606-8207

To ensure through grants to publishing entities the dissemination of works of scholarly distinction in the humanities. Types of assistance: grants. Estimate of annual funds available: $ 5,711,000.

* Promotion of the Humanities - Humanities Projects in Libraries and Archives 45.137

Division of Public Programs
Humanities Projects in Libraries
National Endowment for the Humanities, Room 420

Washington, DC 20506   202-606-8271

To encourage public understanding o the humanities and an interest in academic and public libraries' humanities resources through thematic programs, exhibitions, publications, and other library activities to stimulate use of the resources. Types of assistance: grants. Estimate of annual funds available: $ 2,481,000.

* Promotion of the Humanities - Interpretive Research/ Projects 45.140

Interpretive Research/Projects
Division of Research Programs, Room 318
National Endowment for the Humanities
Washington, DC 20506   202-606-8210

To advance important original researching all fields of the humanities. Types of assistance: grants. Estimate of annual funds available: $ 4,071,000.

* Promotion of the Humanities - Fellowships for University Teachers 45.142

Fellowships for University Teachers
Division of Research Programs
National Endowment for the Humanities, Room 316
Washington, DC 20506   202-606-8466

To provide time for uninterrupted study and research to university teachers, and faculty members of postgraduate professional schools who can make significant contributions to thought and knowledge in the humanities. Types of assistance: grant. Estimate of annual funds available: $ 3,117,000.

* Promotion of the Humanities - Fellowships for College Teachers and Independent Scholars 45.143

Fellowships for College Teachers and Independent
Scholars
Division of Research Programs
Room 316
National Endowment for the Humanities
Washington, DC 20506   202-606-8467

To provide opportunities for college teachers and independent scholars to pursue independent study and research that will enhance their capacities as teachers, scholars, or interpreters of the humanities. Types of assistance: grants. Estimate of annual funds available: $ 3,117,000.

* Promotion of the Humanities - Reference Materials/ Tools 45.145

Division of Research Programs
Reference Materials/Tools, Room 318
National Endowment for the Humanities
Washington, DC 20506   202-606-8358

To fund, wholly or partially projects which create research tools important for scholarly research. Types of assistance: grants. Estimate of annual funds available: $ 3,364,000.

* Promotion of the Humanities - Office of Preservation 45.149

Division of Preservation and Access
National Endowment for the Humanities
Room 802
Washington, DC 20506   202-606-8570

To fund, wholly or partially, projects which will promote the preservation of research resources (library, archival, and other collections) relating to the humanities in the U.S. Types of assistance: grants. Estimate of annual funds available: $ 24,502,000.

* Promotion of the Humanities - Higher Education in the Humanities 45.150

Higher Education in the Humanities
National Endowment for the Humanities, Room 302
Washington, DC 20506   202-606-8380

To assist institutions of higher education in their efforts to improve the teaching of the humanities. Types of assistance: grants. Estimate of annual funds available: $ 6,768,000.

* Promotion of the Humanities - Summer Seminars for School Teachers 45.151

Summer Seminars for School Teachers
Division of Education
National Endowment for the Humanities, Room 316
Washington, DC 20506   202-606-8463

To provide opportunities for school teachers to work during the summer under the direction of a distinguished teacher and active scholar at colleges and universities throughout the country, studying seminal works in the humanities in a systematic and thorough way. Types of assistance: grant. Estimate of annual funds available: $ 4,914,000.

* Promotion of the Humanities - Dissertations 45.157

Dissertation Grants
Division of Research Programs
National Endowment for the Humanities, Room 316
Washington, DC 20506   202-606-8465

To offer support for doctoral candidates in the writing of their dissertations in the humanities. All requirements for a Ph.D must be completed except for their dissertation. Types of assistance: grants. Estimate of annual funds available: $354,000.

* Promotion of the Humanities - Integrating Undergraduate Education 45.158

Science and Humanities Integrating Undergraduate Education
National Endowment for the Humanities, Room 302
Washington, DC 20506   202-606-8384

To develop undergraduate courses and curricula that integrate the study of sciences and the humanities. Type of assistance: grants. Estimate of annual funds available: $ 1,500,000.

* Institute of Museum Services 45.301

Institute of Museum Services
1100 Pennsylvania Ave, NW, Room 510
Washington, DC 20506   202-606-8536

To support the efforts of museums to conserve the nation's historic, scientific and cultural heritage. Types of assistance: grants, direct payments. Estimate of annual funds available: $ 21,976,000.

* National Historical Publications and Records Grants 89.003

National Archives and Records Administration
National Historical Publications and Records
Commission
National Archives Bldg.
Washington, DC 20408   202-501-5610

To carry out the National Historical Documents Program which will help preserve important historical documents. Types of assistance: grants. Estimate of annual funds available: $ 9,000,000.

Historians, Scholars, and Writers

In addition to source documents and other materials available to researchers, courses in historical editing and works of archivists are included in the listings below. The section, "Money for the Humanities," in this chapter identifies additional funding and scholarship opportunities.

* Advertising Labels, Cartoons, Posters, Prints Archives
Prints and Photographs Division
Library of Congress, LM 337
Washington, DC 20540   202-707-6394
More than 10 million items in the Library of Congress chronicle American life and society from its earliest days to the present through its prints and photographs. Items include architectural plans, posters, cartoons, drawings, and advertising labels. Reference librarians will assist those doing their own research, and they can furnish names of freelance picture researchers for individuals who cannot get to the Library.

* Air and Space History Archives
Archives, National Air and Space Museum
7th St. and Independence Ave., SW
Washington, DC 20590   202-357-3133
The National Air and Space Archives assembles and preserves documentary materials that chronicle the history and development of aerospace technology and exploration. Collection-level descriptions are available to researchers through SIRIS in the *Guide to the Collections of the National Air and Space Archives*. The Archives also includes the U.S. Air Force Pre-1954 Still Photograph Collection and videodisc viewing facilities. Direct mail to: Smithsonian Institution, MRC 322, Washington, DC 20506.

* Alexander Graham Bell and History of American Science
Joseph Henry Papers
Arts and Industries Building, 2188
900 Jefferson Dr. S.W.
Washington, DC 20560   202-357-2787
The Joseph Henry Papers conducts research on the life of Joseph Henry (1797-1878), first secretary of the Smithsonian Institution, the early history of the Smithsonian, and the development of American science during the mid-nineteenth century. It has over ninety thousand manuscripts, as well as research aids and reference guides. In addition, the Joseph Henry Papers curates the Bell-Henry Library, which contains the scientific library of Alexander Graham Bell and the personal library of Henry. Appointments should be made in advance.

* American Civilization Studies
American Studies Program
Barney Studio House
Smithsonian Institution.
Washington, DC 20560   202-357-4800, x255
This office conducts a program in the material aspects of American civilization for graduate students enrolled in cooperating Universities. Interested students should apply to the American Studies department of the George Washington University or the University of Maryland, or the Office of American Studies.

* American Ethnology Archive of Historical Manuscripts
National Museum of Natural History
10th St. and Constitution Ave. N.W.
Washington, DC 20560   202-357-1986
The NAA holds the collection of historical manuscripts that relates to the linguistics, ethnology, archeology, physical anthropology, and history of North American Natives. It also has the administrative records of the Department of Anthropology. The photograph collection incorporates 150,000 original negatives and prints made by photographers who worked with American Indian subjects. Other pictorial materials are available through SIRIS. In the near future, all publications and annual reports will be available via the World Wide Web.

* American History and Advertising History Archives
National Museum of American History
12th St. and Constitution Ave. N.W.
Washington, DC 20560   202-357-3270
The Archives Center provides research materials for museum staff, scholars, students, writers and other researchers. The collections are organized in four areas: Manuscripts (personal papers and records of businesses and other organizations); Advertising history; Historical photographs; and Films, audiotapes, and videotapes covering a number of subject areas. Holdings are described through SIRIS. Researchers are urged to call in advance.

* American History Branch Library
National Museum of American History
Room 5016, MRC 630
12th and Constitution Ave., NW
Washington, DC 20560   202-357-2414
The Library houses a collection of 165,000 volumes of book and bound journals on engineering, transportation, military history, science, applied science, decorative arts, and domestic and community life in addition to American history and the history of science and technology. They have special collections of trade literature and materials about world fairs. The Library is open to the public by appointment.

* American Portraits Research Center
National Portrait Gallery
8th and F Sts., NW
Washington, DC 20560   202-357-2578
The Catalog of American Portraits, administered by the National Portrait Gallery, is a national reference center whose files contain photographs and documentation for more than 100 thousand likenesses of historically important Americans. Arranged alphabetically by subject, the files are extensively cross-referenced by artist. A continuing Automated National Portrait Survey has made its holdings more readily accessible to researchers. Computerized indices by subject, artist, occupation, location, and medium make the catalog a valuable resource.

* Anthropology, Archeology, Bibliography and Other Interpretative Research Funding
Research and Education Division
National Endowment for the Humanities
1100 Pennsylvania Ave., NW, Room 318
Washington, DC 20506   202-606-8200
The purpose of this Program is to support scholarly research and interpretation that will advance knowledge and deepen or broaden understanding of major topics in the humanities. Projects supported in this program include biographies, research in various humanities disciplines, cultural anthropology, and archeology.

* Archeological Assistance
Archeological Assistance Division (AAD)
National Park Service (NPS)
U.S. Department of the Interior
800 N. Capital St. NW, Suite 210
Washington, DC 20002   202-343-4101
This division of National Park Service (NPS) provides technical assistance to federal and state agencies on the identification, evaluation, and preservation of archeological properties. The Archeological Assistance Division (AAD) is developing a series of technical publications, including *Archeological Assistance Program Technical Briefs*. The National Archeological Database is maintained, along with other archeological clearinghouses.

* Architectural Drawings and Cartographic Archives

Cartographic and Architectural Branch
National Archives and Records Administration
8601 Adelphi Rd.
College Park, MD 20740-6001   301-713-7040

The Cartographic and Architectural Branch has over 11 million maps, charts, aerial photographs, architectural drawings, patents, and ship plans, which constitute one of the world's largest accumulations of such documents. The Branch holds architectural and engineering drawings created by civilian and military agencies. All the holdings can be examined in the research room. Reproductions can be furnished for a fee.

* Architecture in the National Parks

Park Historic Structures and Cultural Landscape
National Park Service
U.S. Department of the Interior
800 N. Capital St. NW, Suite 360
Washington, DC 20002   202-343-8146

Activities related to the preservation of historic and prehistoric structures and cultural landscapes within the National Park System are administered by this office. *A List of Classified Structures* is maintained, which is an inventory of all historic and prehistoric structures in the System. A bibliography of Cultural Resources Management is also administered, listing all reports that address cultural resources in the Park System.

* Archives Center

National Museum of American History
12th St. and Constitution Ave. N.W.
Washington, DC 20560   202-357-3270

The Archives Center provides research materials for museum staff, scholars, students, writers and other researchers. The collections are organized in four areas: Manuscripts (personal papers and records of businesses and other organizations); Advertising history; Historical photographs; and Films, audiotapes, and videotapes covering a number of subject areas. Holdings are described through SIRIS. Researchers are urged to call in advance.

* Continental Congress and Other Diplomatic Papers

Civil Reference Branch
National Archives and Records Administration
8th St. and Pennsylvania Ave., NW, Room 11
Washington, DC 20408   202-501-5395

The Civil Reference Branch holds the records of all government civilian agencies, including records of the Continental Congress.

* Creative Writers Publishing Grants

Creation and Presentation Division
National Endowment for the Arts
1100 Pennsylvania Ave., NW
Washington, DC 20506-0001   202-682-5428

The Creation and Presentation program assists individual creative writers and literature translators, encourages wider audiences for contemporary literature, and assists non-profit literary organizations. Fellowships enable writers and translators to set aside time for writing and research. Publishing grants provide assistance to literary magazines, small presses, and various distribution projects. Grants are also available to support residencies for writers to allow them to interact with their public. Literary centers may request funds but must offer a regular format of readings, workshops, and technical assistance for writers. Grants can be made to individuals or to non-profit organizations if such donations qualify as charitable deductions under Section 170(c) of the Internal Revenue Code of 1954. Grants range from $5,000 to $200,000.

* Declassified Government Documents

Records Declassification Division
Office of the National Archives
National Archives and Records Administration
8601 Adelphi Rd.
College Park, MD 20740-6001   301-713-6600

This office performs systematic review and research-initiated review of security-classified records using guidelines prepared by federal agencies having jurisdiction over the information. These guidelines provide the National Archives with the authority to systematically review and declassify most records more than 25 years old. With research-initiated review, requests are submitted under the provisions of the Freedom of Information Act. The Archives then refers the classified document to the responsible agency for possible release.

* Decorative and Interior Arts Research Center

Doris and Henry Dreyfuss Study Center and Library
Cooper-Hewitt Museum
Smithsonian Institution's National Museum of Design
2 East 91st St. 3rd Floor
New York, NY 10128   212-860-6887

The Study Center and Library serve as a resource for scholars, researchers, designers, and students for the study of design. The library contains fifty thousand volumes, with specialized holdings in decorative arts, textiles, and needlework, wallcoverings, architecture, pattern and ornament, landscape design, industrial design, interior design, theater design, and graphic design. Researchers are asked to call or write in advance. Photographs may be ordered through the museum's Photographic Services Department.

* Education and Access Grants

National Endowment for the Arts
Education and Access
1100 Pennsylvania Avenue, NW
Washington, DC 20506-0001   202-682-5428

The Arts Endowment believes that all Americans should have opportunities to experience the arts. This grant program supports projects that seek to expose the public to excellence in the arts. Their intent is to broaden understanding and appreciation of our heritage and culture. Access entails a deliberate effort to reach audiences that have not been reached before or have limited opportunities.

* Every Book Published Since 1454

Catalog Management and Publications Division
LA 2004, Library of Congress
Washington, DC 20540   202-707-5965

The *National Union Catalog* lists the world's books published since 1454 and held in approximately 1,100 North American libraries and other union catalogs that record the location of books in Slavic, Hebraic, Japanese, and Chinese languages (if Romanizad). The catalog is produced on microfiche, and many libraries have it.

* Federal Government's Watchdog History

Information Handling and Support Facilities
General Accounting Office
P.O. Box 6015
Gaithersburg, MD 20877   202-512-6000

The free book, *GAO: An Administrative History 1966-1981*, describes the role and operations of the General Accounting Office (GAO), and its evolution over the past fifteen years. The activities of the GAO offices and divisions are detailed, and their functions and accomplishments are described.

* Fellowship Program for Researchers and Scholars

Woodrow Wilson International Center for Scholars
Smithsonian Institution
1000 Jefferson Dr., SW
Washington, DC 20560   202-357-2841

The Center conducts a fellowship program for advanced research, and awards approximately 35 residential fellowships fellowships annually in an international competition to individuals with outstanding project proposals representing the entire range of scholarship, with strong emphasis on the humanities and social sciences. Where appropriate, Fellows may be associated with one of the Center's seven programs: the Asia Program; the East and West European Program; the Historical, Cultural, and Literary Studies Program; the International Studies Program; the Kennan Institute for Advanced Russian Studies; the Latin American Program; or the United States Studies Program. The Center sponsors an extensive series of meetings, information discussions, and formal colloquia on special topics. They also publish the *Wilson Quarterly* and *Dialogue*.

* Folk Culture Archive

American Folklife Center
Library of Congress
Washington, DC 20540   202-707-6590

This Center collects and maintains archives, conducts scholarly research, and

Arts and Humanities

coordinates the development of field projects, performances, exhibitions, festivals, workshops, publications, and audiovisual programs on American folklife. *Folk Life Center News* is a free quarterly newsletter on folklife activities and programs. The Center maintains and administers an extensive collection of folk music, folk culture, ethnomusicology, and grass-roots oral history--both American and international--in published and unpublished forms. The Archive houses more than 30,000 hours of folk-related recordings, manuscripts, and raw materials. The Archive Reading Room, 202-707-5510, contains more than 4,000 books and periodicals, plus unpublished thesis, and dissertations, field notes, and many textual and some musical transcriptions and recordings. A free listing of the Archive's publications is available.

* Folklife Studies Worldwide

Office of Folklife Programs Archive
Folkways Records Archive
Office of Folklife Programs
955 L'Enfant Plaza, Suite 2600
Washington, DC 20560   202-287-3251

The Office of Folklife Programs Archive contains folkloristic materials generated through research for and documentation of the Festival of American Folklife Studies Monograph/Film Series. These materials document hundreds of folk culture traditions from the United States and forty-five other countries. Researchers should call for an appointment.

* Fulbright Foreign Exchange Scholarships

Office of Academic Programs
Bureau of Educational and Cultural Affairs
U.S. Information Agency
301 Fourth St., SW, Room 234
Washington, DC 20547   202-619-6409

This office develops and runs all academic programs of USIA, including the best-known educational exchange, the Fulbright Scholarship program. About 5,000 Fulbright grants are awarded each year to American students, teachers, and scholars to work abroad and to foreign citizens to teach, study, and conduct research in the U.S. In addition to the Fulbright program, the Academic Exchange Programs Division, 202-619-4360, of this office administers grants to private agencies conducting complementary programs to the Fulbright academic exchanges, and has responsibilities for foreign research centers, Fulbright commissions, and seminars for foreign Fulbright students. Contact this office for more information and application forms for the Fulbright program.

* Gettysburg Address and Other Manuscripts

Manuscript Division
LH 101, Library of Congress
Washington, DC 20540   202-707-5387

More than 40 million pieces of manuscript material are housed in the Manuscript Division, including the letters, diaries, speech drafts (including the copy of the Gettysburg Address), scrapbooks, telegrams, and so forth of influential people. For instance, the Library owns the papers of 23 of the presidents from George Washington to Calvin Coolidge, as well as materials of Clara Barton, Sigmund Freud, and Benjamin Franklin. The Manuscript is open to persons engaged in serious research who present proper identification. Hours of operation are 8:30 a.m. to 5:00 p.m., Monday through Saturday (except national holidays).

* Government Agencies' Significant Records

Office of the National Archives
National Archives and Records Administration
8601 Adelphi Rd.
College Park, MD 20740-6001   301-713-6645

The Center for Electronic Records administers computer files having enduring value that have been transferred to the National Archives from other federal agencies. A free copy of the *Center for Electronic Records Title List (A Partial and Preliminary List of the Datasets in Custody of the National Archives)* is available, as is information regarding their reference services and charges.

* Government Humanities Grants News

Public Information Office
National Endowment for the Humanities
1100 Pennsylvania Ave., NW, Room 410
Washington, DC 20506   202-606-8443

Humanities is a bimonthly magazine published by the National Endowment for the Humanities (NEH) features articles by nationally known scholars and writers on current humanities topics, listings of recent grants by discipline, calendars of grant application deadlines, guide sections for those who are thinking of applying for an NEH grant, and essays about noteworthy NEH-supported projects. A subscription for $15 per year is available from the Superintendent of Documents, Government Printing Office, Washington, DC 20402; 202-512-1800.

* Government Record Management News

Records Administration Information Center
Agency Services Division
National Archives and Records Administration
8601 Adelphi Rd.
College Park, MD 20740-6001   301-713-6800

The Records Administration Information Center is a valuable resource for all records managers. This Center can answer your specific records management questions and direct you to useful publications and other sources of assistance, along with arranging for individual assistance with planning for training, electronic records systems, developing records schedules, and other projects.
Recordfacts Update is published by the Records Administration Information Center to share news about records administration throughout the federal records community. The newsletter provides information on National Archives programs and initiatives, agency records management programs, and available resources. This free publication is directed mostly to federal records managers, but is an excellent resource for any records managers.

* Grants for Archival History and Preservation

National Archives and Records Administration
8th St. and Pennsylvania Ave., NW
Room 300
Washington, DC 20408   202-501-5200

The Commission awards grants to promote a variety of historically-oriented projects, such as archival programs, documentary publications projects, and archival and editorial education. The Publications Program provides grant money for printed and microfilm publications of the papers of famous American diplomats, politicians, reformers, scientists, labor figures, as well as corporate and organizational records. A subsidy program provides grants to non-profit presses to help support publication costs of sponsored editions. The Records Program makes grants to state and local governments, historical societies, archives, libraries, and associations for the preservation, arrangement, and description of historical records. Education programs include an institute to train scholars in documentary editing and fellowships in the fields of documentary editing and archival administration.

* Handbook of North American Indians

Smithsonian Institution Press
P.O. Box 960
Herndon, VA 22070   800-782-4612

This twenty-volume encyclopedia summarizes knowledge about all Native peoples north of Mesoamerica, including cultures, languages, history, prehistory, and human biology. This bound series is a standard reference work for anthropologists, historians, students, and the general public. It contains chapters by authorities on each topic, including one on each tribe.

* Heritage and Preservation Grants

National Endowment for the Arts
Heritage and Preservation
1100 Pennsylvania Avenue, NW
Washington, DC 20506-0001   202-682-5428

The National Endowment for the Arts supports those artists and forms of artistic expression that are reflective of the many cultural groups that make up our nation. Other primary objectives include the preservation of our most significant artistic accomplishments for future generations and to conserve important works of art.

* Historical Documents Editing Classes

National Historical Publications and
  Records Commission
National Archives and Records Administration
8th St. and Pennsylvania Ave., NW, Room 607
Washington, DC 20408   202-501-5610

The NHPRC Institute for the Editing of Historical Documents is held for two weeks each summer at the University of Wisconsin, Madison. Admission is competitive and applicants should hold a Masters degree in American History or American Studies or have equivalent training.

* Historical Grants for Humanities Disciplines Study

Division of Research and Education
National Endowment for the Humanities
1100 Pennsylvania Ave., NW, Room 318
Washington, DC 20506   202-606-8200

In this category, the Endowment supports research that employs the theories and methods of humanities disciplines to study science, technology, and medicine. Historical studies and studies of the fundamental concerns that lie behind current issues are eligible for funding. An example would be a historian studying the history of the Islamic hospital to better understand the development of Western medicine.

* Historical Handbook Series Bibliography

Superintendent of Documents
Government Printing Office
Washington, DC 20402   202-512-1800

Historical landmarks are described in the historical handbooks featured in this listing. Sites include Antietam Battlefield, Devil's Tower in Wyoming, Ford's Theater, Glacier Bay, Lincoln Memorial, and Nez Perce National Historical Park in Idaho, among others. Free.

* Historic American Buildings Survey

Historic American Buildings Survey
National Park Service
U.S. Department of the Interior
P.O. Box 37127
Washington, DC 20013-7127   202-343-9625

The *Historic American Buildings Survey* has led the approach of preservation through the documentation of historic buildings, and landscape architectural and streetscape recording. Priority is given to those buildings administered by the National Park Service, to nationally significant structures (including National Historic Landmarks), and to historic buildings that are threatened by demolition. Collections of the *Survey* are accessible to the public in the Library of Congress' Prints and Photographs Division in Room 339 of the James Madison Building, First and Independence, SE, Washington, DC. All records can be reproduced.

* Historic American Engineering Record

Historic American Engineering Record
National Park Service
U.S. Department of the Interior
P.O. Box 37127
Washington, DC 20013-7127   202-343-9625

Historic American Engineering Record was established to document historic engineering, industrial, and technological works throughout the country. It is conducted by the Park Service in cooperation with the American Society of Civil Engineers and the Library of Congress. The records take the form of measured drawings, professional photographs, historical reports, technical analyses, and motion pictures. This collection, like the *Historic American Building Survey*, is also accessible to the public at the Library of Congress' Prints and Photographs Division, Room 339, James Madison Building, First and Independence Ave., SE, Washington, DC.

* Historic Landmarks

The National Historic Landmarks Program
National Park Service
U.S. Department of the Interior
800 N. Capital St. NW
Washington, DC 20002   202-343-8167

Under the National Historic Landmarks Program, historic sites are identified for their national significance. Sites and structures found nationally significant by the Secretary are eligible for designation as National Historic Landmarks and are included in the *National Register* and listed monthly in the *Federal Register*. Upon the owner's agreement to adhere to accepted preservation precepts, landmark designation is recognized by the award of a bronze plaque and a certificate.

* Historic Preservation Assistance

Preservation Assistance Division
National Park Service
U.S. Department of the Interior
800 N. Capital St. NW
Washington, DC 20002   202-343-9573

The Preservation Assistance Division guides Federal and state agencies and the general public in historic preservation project work. Standards and guidelines are established, information on technical preservation is distributed, and training is given on technical preservation approaches and treatments. This office also administers the Preservation Tax Incentives program, the status of National Historic Landmarks, and the Historic Preservation Fund grant-in-aid program.

* Historic Preservation Council

Advisory Council on Historic Preservation
1100 Pennsylvania Ave., NW
Suite 809
Washington, DC 20004   202-606-8503

Affiliated with the U.S. Department of the Interior, this council advises Congress and the President on matters of historic preservation. The Council is composed of the Secretaries of the Interior, Housing and Urban Development, Commerce, Treasury, Transportation, and Agriculture; the Attorney General; the Administrator of the General Services Administration; the Chairman of the National Trust for Historic Preservation; the Secretary of the Smithsonian Institution; and 10 non-federal members appointed by the President.

* Historic Preservation Publications

Cultural Resources Programs
National Park Service
U.S. Department of the Interior
800 N. Capitol St. NW
Washington, DC 20002   202-343-9596

The *Catalog of Historic Preservation Publications* is a valuable listing of books on the subject of historic preservation. Books on the actual preservation of old buildings are included, as well as the procedures to follow to register buildings in the National Register. Archeological research, architecture, historic landmarks, and anthropology are also featured subjects.

* History of the U.S. Capitol

Superintendent of Documents
Government Printing Office
Washington, DC 20402   202-512-1800

The Capitol provides a pictorial and narrative history of the U.S. Capitol building and the Congresses that have served there. Included are sections devoted to the Architects of the Capitol, the Speaker of the House, House and Senate Leadership, pages of the U.S. Congress, Congress in international affairs, elected officers of the Senate, a profile of the 100th Congress, women in American politics, and related information. The cost is $10 from the Government Printing office, S/H 052-071-00687-7, but if you contact your congressman's office, you can get a complimentary copy.

* Humanities Publication Funding

Division of Research and Education
National Endowment for the Humanities
1100 Pennsylvania Ave., NW, Room 318
Washington, DC 20506   202-606-8200

This Program provides support for the preparation for publication of texts that promise to make major contributions to the study of the humanities. Support is available for editions of works and documents, for translation of works into English, and for the publication and distribution of scholarly books in all fields of the humanities.

* Indian Ancestry

Office of Public Affairs
Bureau of Indian Affairs
U.S. Department of the Interior
18th and C Sts., NW
Washington, DC 20240   202-208-3711

Tracing your Indian ancestry requires that you first do basic genealogical research to obtain the following information: the names of your Indian ancestors; dates of birth, marriages, and death; where they lived; their brothers and sisters; and very importantly, their tribal affiliations. To verify that your ancestors are on official tribal rolls or censuses, contact the National Archives and Records Administration, Civil Resources Division, 8th and Pennsylvania Ave., NW, Washington, DC 20408, (please do not call). You may also receive assistance from the office above. The requirements of the particular tribe of your Indian ancestors will determine whether you are eligible for membership.

Arts and Humanities

* Information On Demand

Humanities and Social Services
Library of Congress
LJ 109
Washington, DC 20540   202-707-5530

If you need information that is contained in the material in the Library of Congress collections, the reference staff will find it for you and relay it over the phone. If the information you require is too extensive, however, the reference staff will refer you to private researchers who work on a fee basis.

* International Peace Fellowships

Jennings Randolph Program for International Peace
United States Institute of Peace
1550 M St., NW
Washington, DC 20005-1708   202-429-3886

This Program provides fellowships to scholars and leaders in peace to undertake research and other appropriate forms of communication on issues of international peace and the management of international conflict. The Fellowship Program has three levels: Jennings Randolph Distinguished Fellows are individuals whose careers show extraordinary accomplishment concerning questions of international peace; United States Institute of Peace Fellows are individuals also of accomplishment, but of somewhat less eminence; and United States Institute of Peace Scholars are individuals working on doctoral dissertations in the field.

* International Research and Advanced Study Grants

Division of Research and Education
National Endowment for the Humanities
1100 Pennsylvania Ave., NW, Room 318
Washington, DC 20506   202-606-8200

Grants in the Centers for Advanced Study category support interrelated research efforts at independent research libraries and museums, American research centers overseas, and centers for advanced study. Grants awarded by the centers enable individual scholars to pursue their own research and to participate in the interchange of ideas among the Centers' scholars. Grants in the International Research category provide funds to national organizations and learned societies to enable scholars to pursue research abroad, to attend or participate in international conferences, and to engage in collaborative work with foreign colleagues.

* International Scholars Exchange Programs

International Activities
3123 S. Dillon Ripley Center
1100 Jefferson Dr., SW
Smithsonian Institution
Washington, DC 20560   202-357-4282

Handbook for Foreign Opportunities serves as a basic reference document for Smithsonian staff who travel abroad on official business or who engage in international scholarly or museum exchanges. Although directed toward Smithsonian staff, this publication can give others helpful tips for conducting research and exchanges abroad, including visas, research permits and money concerns, and also covers issues surrounding immigration and international visitors.

* John F. Kennedy Assassination Records Collection

JFK Liaison
National Archives and Records Administration
8601 Adelphi Rd.
College Park, MD 20740-6001   301-713-6620

This collection includes documentation from both the Warren Commission and the Rockfeller Commission. Holdings also include donated historical materials from the Dallas Police Department. Additionally, transcripts of the telephone conversations between Lyndon Johnson and J. Edgar Hoover, Richard Russell and others concerning issues relating to the assassination, such as the establishment of the Warren Commission.

* Korean War Data Files

Center for Electronic Records
National Archives and Records Administration
8601 Adelphi Rd.
College Park, MD 20740-6001   301-713-6645

The Center for Electronic Records maintains military data files for all branches of the military and a variety of records on Korean War.

* Library of Congress Reading Rooms

Main Reading Room
Library of Congress
Washington, DC 20540   202-707-5522

Located on the first floor of the Thomas Jefferson Building, the main reading room contains material on American history, economics, fiction, language and literature, political science, government documents, and sociology. A reference collection for these materials is also housed there. These reading rooms are not equipped to answer reference questions over the telephone, but will provide information on their collections, hours of operation, and the like.

Social Science	202-707-5522
Microfilm	202-707-5522
Local History and Genealogy	202-707-5522
Newspapers and Current Periodicals	202-707-5690
Science	202-707-5639
Law Library	202-707-5079
Performing Arts	202-707-5507
Performing Arts Library at the Kennedy Center	202-707-6245
Motion Picture, Broadcasting, and Recorded Sound	202-707-8572
Archive of Folk Culture	202-707-5510
Prints and Photographs	202-707-6394
Manuscripts	202-707-5387
Rare Book and Special Collections	202-707-5434
Geography and Map	202-707-6277
Hispanic	202-707-5397
European	202-707-4514
Asian	202-707-5423
African and Middle Eastern Division	202-707-5528
Music	202-707-5507

* Manuscript Preservation Archive

National Endowment for the Humanities
1100 Pennsylvania Ave., NW
Room 802
Washington, DC 20506   202-606-8570

Vast numbers of source documents are in danger of destruction due to the disintegration of the paper on which they are written. This program provides support to projects that deal with this problem, such as those that save informational content, improve collection maintenance, and develop preventive care practices. Non-profit institutions and organizations may apply.

* Minority Research Grants

Fellowships and Grants
Smithsonian Institution
Washington, DC 20560   202-287-3271

The Smithsonian offers fellowships and internships for research and study in fields which are actively pursued by the museums and research organizations of the Institution. Both predoctoral and postdoctoral fellowships are available, as well as Minority Faculty Fellowships. The length of the term and size of the stipend vary. The Minority and Native American Internship Programs are performed under direct supervision of Smithsonian staff, as tutorial situations.

* Modern Archives Management Training Course

Office of Public Programs
National Archives and Records Administration
8601 Adelphi Rd.
College Park, MD 20740-6001   301-713-7390, x260

The "Modern Archives Institute: Introduction to Modern Archives Administration," is a two-week archival training course that offers an introduction to archival theory and practice for participants. It is sponsored by the National Archives Trust Fund Board, and includes lectures, discussions, workshops, and visits to the Manuscript Division of the Library of Congress and various units of the National Archives. The Institute is offered twice a year.

* National Air and Space Museum Branch Library

National Air and Space Museum
7th and Independence Ave. S.W.
Room 3100
Washington, DC 20560   202-357-3133

This library houses more than 30,000 books, 4700 periodical titles, 6,000,000 technical reports, and is enriched by a documentary archival collection which includes 900,000 photographs, drawings, and other documents. The scope of the collection covers history of aviation and space, flight technology, aerospace industry, biography, lighter-than-air technology and history, rocketry, earth and planetary sciences, and astronomy. The Library is open to the public by appointment.

* National Anthropological Archives

National Museum of Natural History
10th St. and Constitution Ave. N.W.
Washington, DC 20560   202-357-1986

The NAA holds the Bureau of American Ethnology's collection of historical manuscripts that relates to the linguistics, ethnology, archeology, physical anthropology, and history of North American Natives. It also has the administrative records of the Department of Anthropology. The photograph collection incorporates 150,000 original negatives and prints made by photographers who worked with American Indian subjects. Other pictorial materials are available through SIRIS.

* National Archives Conferences and Workshops

Office of Public Affairs
National Archives and Records Administration
8th St. and Pennsylvania Ave., NW
Washington, DC 20408   202-501-5525

A free, monthly Calendar of Events is available which includes information on free films and lectures, as well as information on workshops, exhibitions, and tours.

* National Archives Posters and Publications

Publications Sales
National Archives and Records Administration
7th St. and Pennsylvania Ave., NW
Washington, DC 20408   800-234-8861

There are several brochures which list publications available from the National Archives and Records Administration. *Select List of Publications of the National Archives and Records Administration* includes publications of several finding aids to records held by NARA that are currently in print. Also included are professional archival papers and books, and other materials of interest to researchers. *Publications from the National Archives* includes guide and indices to collections in specific areas and publications that will be useful to archivists, historians and researchers, as well as general-interest books concerning U.S. history of the National Archives. *Full-Color High Quality Posters from Your National Archives* illustrates 29 popular historical and contemporary posters and postcards.

* National Register of Historic Places

Interagency Resources Division
National Park Service
U.S. Department of the Interior
800 N. Capital St. NW
Suite 250
Washington, DC 20002   202-343-9500

The National Register of Historic Places is administered by the Interagency Resources Division of the National Park Service (NPS). Along with the Preservation Assistance Division, this office administers the Historic Preservation Fund grants-in-aid to states and the National Trust for Historic Preservation. Technical workshops and other assistance is provided on preservation planning, and a database of historic information is maintained.

* National Registry of Natural Landmarks

National Registry Branch
National Park Service
U.S. Department of the Interior
800 N. Capital St. NW, Suite 250
Washington, DC 20002   202-343-9536

The Park Service conducts natural region studies to identify areas that are of potential national significance. These areas are then studied in the field by scientists. Natural areas considered of national significance are cited by the Secretary of the Interior as eligible for recognition as Registered Natural Landmarks. The owner may apply for a certificate and bronze plaque designating the site.

* Native American Indian Publications

Office of Public Affairs
Bureau of Indian Affairs
U.S. Department of the Interior
18th and C Sts., NW

Washington, DC 20240   202-208-3711

The following is a listing of free publications from the Bureau of Indian Affairs Public Affairs office. Due to the limited supply and small staff only one copy of each publication may be requested.

Booklists:
Book List for Young Readers
General Reading List for Adults
Languages
Legends and Myths
Music
Religions and Ceremonials
Wars and Local Disturbances
Origin

* Natural History Library

Natural History Library
10th and Constitution Ave. N.W.
Washington, DC 20560   202-357-1496

This library houses 330,000 books and bound journals and receives 1,963 journal subscriptions. The library consists of a main location and several subject-based locations. Topics covered include biology, geology, paleontology, ecology, anthropology, botany, entomology, and mineral sciences. Call to make an appointment or for information on the location of the subject-based libraries.

* Newspapers and Periodicals From Around the World

Library of Congress
Washington, DC 20540   202-707-5650

Hundreds of different newspapers and periodicals from all fifty states and countries around the world are available on microfilm for $35 for domestic and $40 for foreign publications. Subscriptions are available or single issues can be ordered. Orders must be prepaid or charged to a standing account at the Library of Congress.

* North American Indian Handbook

Superintendent of Documents
Government Printing Office
Washington, DC 20402   202-512-1800

Handbook of North American Indians is the first to be published of a set of volumes that will give a summary of the prehistory, history, and cultures of the native peoples of America who lived north of central Mexico.

Arctic. Vol.5, 1984 (S/N 047-000-00398-9, $29)
Subarctic. Vol. 6, 1981 (S/N 047-000-00374-1, $25)
California. Vol. 8, 1981. (S/N 047-000-00347-4, $25)
Southwest. Vol. 9, 1979. Covers Puebloan peoples and general Southwest
    prehistory and history. (S/N 047-000-00361-0, $48)
Southwest. Vol. 10, 1983. Contains 56 articles about the non-Puebloan peoples
    of the Southwest and some surveys on the entire Southwest. (S/N
    047-000-00390-3, $25)
Great Basin. Vol. 11, 1986. Surveys the Shoshone, Bannock, Ute, Paiute,
    Washoe, and Kawaiisu peoples who once inhabited the entire Great Basin
    region of western North America.(S/N 047-000-00401-2, $27)
Northeast. Vol. 15, 1978. (S/N 047-000-00351-2, $27)
History of Indian-White Relations. Vol. 4 ($47)
Northwest Coast. Vol. 7 ($38)

* Online Access to Smithsonian Resources for Research

Smithsonian Institution
900 Jefferson Dr., SW, Suite 2310
Washington, DC 20560   202-357-1385

Smithsonian Institution Research Information System (SIRIS) is a computerized collection of research catalogs maintained by the Smithsonian Institution's libraries, archives and research units. SIRIS contains information about books, serials, archives and manuscripts, films, sound recordings, paintings, sculptures and other material.

* Overseas Research Grants

Fellowships and Grants
Smithsonian Institution
Washington, DC 20560   202-287-3271

The office also administers a Special Foreign Currency Program, a nationally competitive grants program for research carried out by U.S. institutions in countries where the United States owns local currencies deemed by the Treasury Department to be in excess of normal U.S. needs. Write or call for more information or applications.

* Overseas Tour for Scholars

Thematic Program
Office of Program Coordination and Development
United States Information Agency
301 Fourth St., SW, Room 550
Washington, DC 20547   202-619-4700

The Thematic Program participants are experts in a field -- usually economics, international affairs, literature, the arts, U.S. political and social processes, sports, science, or technology -- sent abroad by USIA to meet with groups or individual professional counterparts. Recruited on the basis of requests of USIA staff in other countries, the Thematic Program participants often engage in informal lecture/discussions with small groups, grant media interviews, or speak before larger audiences. Those interested in the Thematic Program are invited to submit a brief letter indicating times of availability, along with a curriculum vitae and at least two lecture topics with brief talking points. A free brochure on the program is available from this office.

* Peace and International Relations Research Studies

United States Institute of Peace
1550 M Street, NW, Suite 700
Washington, DC 20005-1708   202-457-1700

The Institute of Peace designs and directs research and studies projects carried out through a process which includes the production of working papers on selected topics and their discussion by experts in public session. Working-group projects proceed through four or more public sessions involving a core group of experts. Studies are conceived on the same scale, but with a changing cast of experts. Public workshops are three-hour, monthly events designed for group discussion around a discrete topic of current concern.

* Peale Family Papers (1735-1885)

Peale Family Papers
National Portrait Gallery
AAPG322
Smithsonian Institute
8th and F Sts., NW
Washington, DC 20560   202-357-2565

The Peale Family Papers is a project that carries on research in eighteenth and early nineteenth century art and cultural history, with particular attention to Maryland and Philadelphia from 1735 to 1885. The project's files contain documents, correspondence, diaries, manuscripts, writings, secondary literature and some photographs of Charles Wilson Peale, his children and his relatives. The files may be consulted by appointment.

* Planning and Stabilization Grants

National Endowment for the Arts
Planning and Stabilization
1100 Pennsylvania Avenue, NW
Washington, DC 20506-0001   202-682-5428

The National Endowment for the Arts recognizes that there is a continuing struggle on the part of America's art organizations, and that art organizations are engaged in various efforts to develop structures that will enable them to carry on their work effectively and creatively. This program helps eligible organizations to clarify and strengthen their identities and missions. They support the arts in an era of constant and profound change. The Endowment also builds partnerships which strengthen the arts infrastructure.

* Political Science Fellowships

United States Institute of Peace
1550 M St., NW, Suite 700
Washington, DC 20005   202-457-1700

The Grants Program provides financial support to nonprofit organizations, official public institutions, and individuals to fund projects on various themes and topics of interest. Past projects have included the role of third-party negotiators in the resolution of regional conflicts, religious and ethical questions in war and peace, and the use of non-violent sanctions in confronting political violence. Call or write for more information regarding grant application procedures.

* Preservation of Library Materials

National Preservation Directorate Office
Library of Congress, LMG 21
Washington, DC 20540   202-707-1840

The Preservation Office is involved in a constant race against time to preserve its millions of items from disintegration. Newspapers are immediately microfilmed, motion pictures are rushed to refrigerated vaults, manuscripts are put in fumigating vaults, and maps are encased in polyester envelopes. But the main problem for preservationists is acid and its affect on paper. Recently the Library's chemists developed a technique whereby wood pulp books are placed in huge vacuum tanks which are flooded with diethyl zinc gas, thus deacidifying them for another hundred years. Research continues on longstanding preservation problems. A series of leaflets on various preservation and conservation topics is available from the office.

* Presidential Documents and Public Papers

Office of the Federal Register
National Archives and Records Administration
8th St. and Pennsylvania Ave., NW, Room 8401
Washington, DC 20408   202-523-5230

The *Weekly Compilation of Presidential Documents* is published each week and contains all of the President's statements, nominations, acts he approves, weekly schedules, transcripts of speeches; basically all of his actions. A subscription for $75 a year is available by contacting the Superintendent of Documents, Government Printing Office, Washington, DC, 20402; 202-512-1800.

* Presidential Libraries

National Archives and Records Administration
8th St. and Pennsylvania Ave., NW, Room 104
Washington, DC 20408   202-501-5709

Through the Presidential Libraries, which are located on sites selected by the presidents and built with private funds, the National Archives preserves and makes available for use the Presidential records and personal papers that document the actions of a particular president's administration. In addition to providing reference services on Presidential documents, each library prepares documentary and descriptive publications and operates a museum to exhibit documents, historic objects, and other memorabilia of interest to the public. Each library provides research grants to scholars and graduate students for the encouragement of research in Presidential libraries' holdings and of publication or works based on such research. Public programs of the libraries include conferences, lectures, films, tours, commemorative events, and seminars. For further information, contact the Presidential library of your choice.

Herbert Hoover Library, West Branch, IA, 52358, 319-643-5301
Franklin D. Roosevelt Library, Hyde Park, NY, 12538, 914-229-8114
Harry S. Truman Library, Independence, MO, 64050; 816-833-1400
Dwight D. Eisenhower Library, Abilene, KS, 67410; 913-263-4751
John F. Kennedy Library, Boston, MA, 02125; 617-929-4500
Lyndon B. Johnson Library, Austin, TX, 78705; 512-482-5137
Gerald R. Ford Library, Ann Arbor, MI, 48109; 313-741-2218
Gerald R. Ford Museum, Grand Rapids, MI, 49504; 616-451-9263
Jimmy Carter Library, Atlanta, GA, 30307; 404-331-3942
Ronald Reagan Library, Simi Valley, CA; 805-522-8444
Bush Presidential Materials Project, College Station, TX 77840; 409-260-9554

* Private Library Space for Researchers

Research Facilities Section
General Reading Rooms
Library of Congress
Washington, DC 20540   202-707-5211

For increased convenience, full-time scholars and researchers may apply for study desks in semi-private areas within the Library of Congress.

* Regional Archive Centers Nationwide

Regional Archives System
National Archives and Records Administration
8th St. and Pennsylvania Ave., NW
Washington, DC 20408   202-501-5510

This periodic newsletter includes information regarding activities at the various regional archives centers, including workshops, exhibits, publications, and networking information.

* Regional Archives

Research services include textual and microfilm research rooms, extensive National Archives microfilm publication, research assistance on-site and by mail or phone, reference library of aids to research in the National Archives and photoduplication of regional archives archival holdings.

National Archives - New England Region
380 Trapelo Rd., Waltham, MA 02154; 617-647-8100.
CT, ME, MA, NH, RI, VT

National Archives - Northeast Region
201 Varick St., New York, NY 10014; 212-337-1300.
NJ, NY, PR, VI

National Archives - MidAtlantic Region
9th and Market Sts., Room 1350, Philadelphia, PA 19107; 215-597-3000.
DE, MD, PA, VA, WV

National Archives - Southeast Region
1557 St. Joseph Ave., East Point, GA 30344; 404-763-7477.
AL, FL, GA, KY, MS, NC, SC, TN

National Archives - Great Lakes Region
7358 S. Pulaski Rd., Chicago, IL 60629; 312-581-7816.
IL, IN, MI, MN, OH, WI

National Archives - Central Plains Region
2312 E. Bannister Rd., Kansas City, MO 64131; 816-926-6272.
IA KS, MO, NE

National Archives - Southwest Region
501 W. Felix St., P.O. Box 6216, Ft. Worth, TX 76115; 817-334-5525.
AR, LA, NM, OK, TX (Most records from federal agencies in New Mexico are at the Rocky Mountain Region)

National Archives - Rocky Mountain Region
Building 48, Denver Federal Center, Denver, CO,80225-0307; 303-236-0817.
CO, MT, NK, SD, UT, WY, NM

National Archives - Pacific Southwest Region
24000 Avila Rd., Laguna Niguel, CA 92656; 714-643-4241.
AZ, Southern CA, Clark County, NV

National Archives - Pacific Sierra Region
1000 Commodore Dr., San Bruno, CA 94066; 415-876-9009. Northern CA, HI, NV (except Clark County), the Pacific Trust Territories, American Samoa

National ARchives - Pacific Northwest Region
6125 Sand Point Way, NE, Seattle, WA 98115; 206-526-6507.
ID, OR, WA

National Archives - Alaska Region
654 W. Third Ave., Anchorage, AK 99501; 907-271-2441.
AK

* Reproductions and Help for Researchers

National Archives and Records Administration
8th St. and Pennsylvania Ave., NW, Room 205
Washington, DC 20408   202-501-5403

Staff members provide reference service on records by responding in person, over the telephone, and in writing to requests for information from or about records, making original records available to researchers in research rooms, providing researchers with copies of records for a fee, and preparing microform publications of heavily used series of records. The Reference Services Branch refers requests to the branch in the National Archives that has custody of the relevant records. *Ordering Reproductions From the National Archives* is a helpful brochure which outlines the information needed to fill your request. Contact the References Services Branch for more information.

* Smithsonian Archives Guide

Smithsonian Archives
Smithsonian Institution
900 Jefferson Dr. S.W.
Washington, DC 20560   202-357-1420

This free *Guide to Smithsonian Archives* is a reference resource to the holdings of the Archives, giving a detailed listing of the records, papers, and projects the Archives has, as well as information regarding their use.

* Smithsonian Institution Library Services

Smithsonian Institution Libraries
10th St. and Constitution Ave., NW
Washington, DC 20560   202-357-2139

The libraries of the Smithsonian Institution include approximately 950,000 volumes, with strengths in natural history, museology, history of science, and the humanities. Inquiries on special subjects or special collections should be addressed to the appropriate branch library or to the Central Reference and Loan.

* State Historical Records

National Historical Publications and Records Commission
National Archives and Records Administration
8th St. and Pennsylvania Ave., NW, Room 607
Washington, DC 20408   202-501-5600

The governor of each state appoints a State Historical Records Coordinator, who is in charge of either the state archival agency or the state-funded historical agency. The governor also appoints a State Historical Records Advisory Board, which is the central advisory body for state projects and records planning. The Board makes funding recommendations to the National Historical Publications and Records Commission concerning records grant applications from institutions and organizations in the state. The Board may also undertake projects and studies of its own, solicit or develop proposals for Commission-funded projects, and review the progress of State Category Grants funded by the Commission. The grants fund projects for the preservation, arrangement, and description of historical records.

* State and Regional Arts Agencies

Following is a list of state arts agencies and regional arts organizations working with the Arts Endowment utilizing funds mandated by the Congress as well as funds from state governments and other sources.

State Arts Agencies

Alabama
Alabama State Council on the Arts, One Dexter Ave., Montgomery, Al 36130; 334-242-4076

Alaska
Alaska State Council on the Arts, 411 W. 4th Ave., Suite 1E, Anchorage, AK 99501-2343; 907-269-6610

American Samoa
American Samoa Council on Arts, Culture and Humanities, P.O. Box 1540, Pago Pago, American Samoa 96799; 011-684-633-4347

Arizona
Arizona Commission on the Arts, 417 W. Roosevelt, Phoenix, AZ 85003; 602-255-5882

Arkansas
Arkansas Arts Council, 1500 Tower Bldg, 323 Center St., Little Rock, AR 72201; 501-324-9766

California
California Arts Council, 1300 I St., #930, Sacramento, CA 95814; 916-322-6555

Colorado
Colorado Council on the Arts, 750 Pennsylvania St., Denver, CO 80203-3699; 303-894-2617

Connecticut
Connecticut Commission on the Arts, 755 Main St., Hartford, CT 06103; 203-566-4770

Delaware
Delaware Division of the Arts, State Office Bldg., 820 N. French St., Wilmington, DE 19801; 302-577-3540

District of Columbia
District of Columbia Commission on the Arts and Humanities, 410 8th St., NW, Washington, DC 20004; 202-724-5613

Florida
Division of Cultural Affairs, Florida Department of State, The Capitol, Tallahassee, Fl 32399-0250; 904-487-2980

Georgia
Georgia Council for the Arts, 530 Means St., NW, Suite 115, Atlanta, GA 30318-5730; 404-651-7920

Guam
Guam Council on the Arts and Humanities, Office of the Governor, P.O. Box 2950, Agana, GU 96910; 011-671-647-2242

Hawaii
State Foundation on Culture and the Arts, 44 Merchant St., Honolulu, HI 96813; 808-586-0300

Idaho
Idaho Commission on the Arts, P.O. Box 83720, Boise, ID 83720-0008; 208-334-2119

Illinois
Illinois Arts Council, State of Illinois Center, 100 W. Randolph, Suite 10-500, Chicago, IL 60601; 312-814-6750

Indiana
Indiana Arts Commission, 402 W. Washington St., Room 072, Indianapolis, In 46204-2741; 317-232-1268

Iowa
Iowa Arts Council, 600 E. Locust, State Capitol Complex, Des Moines, IA 50319; 515-281-4451

Kansas
Kansas Arts Commission, Jayhawk Tower, 700 Jackson, Suite 1004, Topeka, KS 66603; 913-296-3335

Kentucky
Kentucky Arts Council, 31 Fountain Place, Frankfort, KY 40601; 502-564-3757

Louisiana
Division of the Arts, Louisiana Department of Culture, Recreation and Routism, 1051 N. Third St., P.O. Box 44247, Baton Rouge, LA 70804; 504-342-8180

Maine
Maine Arts Commission, 55 Capitol St., State House Station 25, Augusta, ME 04333; 207-287-2724

Maryland
Maryland State Arts Council, 601 N. Howard St., 1st Floor, Baltimore, MD 21201; 410-333-8232

Massachusetts
Massachusetts Cultural Council, 120 Boylston St, 2nd Floor, Boston, MA 02116-4600; 617-727-3668

Michigan
Michigan Council for Arts and Cultural Affairs, 1200 6th St., Executive Plaza, Detroit, MI 48226; 313-256-3731

Minnesota
Minnesota State Arts Board, 400 Sibley St., Suite 200, St. Paul, MN 55101-1949; 612-215-1600, 800-8MN-ARTS

Mississippi
Mississippi Arts Commission, 239 N. Lamar St., Second Floor, Jackson, MS 39201; 601-359-6030

Missouri
Missouri State Council on the Arts, Wainwright Office Complex, 111 N. Seventh St., Suite 105, St. Louis, MO 63101; 314-340-6845

Montana
Montana Arts Council, 316 N. Park Ave., Room 252, Helena, MT 59620; 406-444-6430

Nebraska
Nebraska Arts Council, The Joslyn Castle Carriage House, 3838 Davenport St., Omana, NE 68131-2329; 402-595-2122

Nevada
Nevada State Council on the Arts, Capitol Complex, 602 N. Curry St., Carson City, NY 89710; 702-687-6680

New Hampshire
New Hampshire State Council on the Arts, Phenix Hall, 40 N. Main St., Concord, NH 03301; 603-271-2789

New Jersey
New Jersey State Council on the Arts, 20 W. State St., 3rd Floor, Trenton, NJ 08625-0306; 609-292-6130

New Mexico
New Mexico Arts Division, 228 E. Palace Ave., Santa Fe, NM 87501; 505-827-6490

New York
New York State Council on the Arts, 915 Broadway, New York, NY 10010; 212-387-7000

North Carolina
North Carolina Arts Council, Department of Cultural Resources, Raleigh, NC 27601-2807; 919-733-2821

North Dakota
North Dakota Council on the Arts, 418 E. Broadway Ave., Suite 70, Bismarck, ND 58501-4086; 701-328-3954

Northern Mariana Islands
Commonwealth Council for Arts and Culture, P.O. Box 553, CHRB, CNMI Convention Center, Commonwealth of the Northern Mariana Islands, Saipan, MP 96950; 011-670-322-9982

Ohio
Ohio Arts Council, 727 E. Main St., Columbus, OH 43205; 614-466-2613

Oklahoma
State Arts Council of Oklahoma, P.O. Box 52001-2001, Oklahoma City, OK 73152-2001; 405-521-2931

Oregon
Oregon Arts Commission, 775 Summer St., NE, Salem, OR 97310; 503-986-0082

Pennsylvania
Commonwealth of Pennsylvania Council on the Arts, Finance Bldg., Room 216A, Harrisburg, PA 17120; 717-787-6883

Puerto Rico
Institute of Puerto Rican Culture, Apartado Postal 4184, San Juan, PR 00902-4184; 809-724-3210

Rhode Island
Rhode Island State Council on the Arts, 95 Cedar St., Suite 103, Providence, RI 02903; 401-277-3880

South Carolina
South Carolina Arts Commission, 1800 Gervais St., Columbia, SC 29201; 803-734-8696

South Dakota
South Dakota Arts Council, Office of Arts, 800 Governors Drive, Pierre, SD 57501-2294; 605-773-3131

Tennessee
Tennessee Arts Commission, Parkway Towers, Suite 160, 404 James Robertson Pkwy., Nashville, Tn 37243-0780; 615-741-1701

Texas
Texas Commission on the Arts, P.O. Box 13406, Capitol Station, Austin, TX 78711; 512-463-5535

Utah
Utah Arts Council, 617 East South Temple Street, Salt Lake City, UT 84102; 801-533-5895

Vermont
Vermont Council on the Arts, 136 State St., Montpelier, VT 05633-6001; 802-828-3291

Virginia
Virginia Commission for the Arts, 223 Governor St., Richmond, VA 23219; 804-225-3132

Virgin Islands
Virgin Islands Council on the Arts, 41-42 Norre Gade, 2nd Floor, P.O. Box 103, St. Thomas, VI 00802; 809-774-5984

Washington
Washington State Arts Commission, 234 East 8th Ave., P.O. Box 42675, Olympia, WA 98504-2675; 360-753-3860

West Virginia
Arts and Humanities Section, West Virginia Division of Culture and History, 1900 Kanawha Blvd. East, Capitol Complex, Charleston, WV 25305-0300; 304-558-0220

Wisconsin
Wisconsin Arts Board, 101 E. Wilson St., 1st Floor, Madison, WI 53702; 608-266-0190

Wyoming
Wyoming Arts Council, 2320 Capitol Ave., Cheyenne, WY 82002; 307-777-7742

Regional Arts Organizations

Arts Midwest, Hennepin Center for the Arts, 528 Hennepin Ave., Suite 310, Minneapolis, MN 55403; 612-341-0755

Consortium for Pacific Arts and Cultures, 2141C Atherton Rd., Honolulu, HI 96822; 808-946-7381

Mid-America Arts Alliance, 912 Baltimore Ave., Suite 700, Kansas City, MO 64105; 816-421-1388

Mid Atlantic Arts Foundation, 11 E. Chase St., Suite 2-A, Baltimore, MD 21202; 410-539-6659

New England Foundation for the Arts, 330 Congress St., 6th Floor, Boston, MA 02210-1216; 617-951-0010

Southern Arts Federation, 181 14th St., NE, Suite 400, Atlanta, GA 30309; 404-874-7244

Western States Arts Federation, 237 Montezuma Ave., Santa Fe, NM 87501; 505-988-1166

* Status of Presidential Documents
Executive Clerks Office
The White House
Washington, DC 20500   202-456-2226
The Executive Clerks Office reviews, processes, and records all documents signed by the President. To find out the status of any official Presidential proclamation, Executive order, nomination, appointment or legislation, contact the office above.

* Telephone Reference Service at Library of Congress
Library of Congress
Washington, DC 20540   202-707-5522
This service provides information to callers about the collections within the Library of Congress and how they can be used. In planning your research, remember that the Library of Congress is the library of last resort -- all other inter-library loan avenues must be exhausted before you may borrow a book from the Library of Congress. Always begin your research with your local library.

* Thomas Jefferson's Library and Other Rare Books Collection
Rare Book and Special Collections Division
Library of Congress, LJ 256
Washington, DC 20540   202-707-5434
The Rare Books Division contains about 300,000 volumes and 200,000 pamphlets, broadsides, theater playbills, title pages, manuscripts, posters, and photographs. The collection includes documents of the first fourteen congresses of the United States, the personal libraries of Thomas Jefferson and Harry Houdini, incunabula; miniature

books and dime novels, and the Russian Imperial collection. The division has its own central card catalog plus special card files that describe individual collections or special aspects of books from many collections.

* Vice-Presidential Papers
Office of Presidential Libraries
National Archives and Records Administration
8th St. and Pennsylvania Ave., NW, Room 104
Washington, DC 20408   202-501-5700
Vice-Presidential records are subject to the same provisions as Presidential records and become property of the United States Government.

* Vietnam War Records
Center for Electronic Records
National Archives and Records Administration
8601 Adelphi Rd.
College Park, MD 20740-6001   301-713-6645
The Center has records created between 1954 and 1975 by U.S. Army-Vietnam, U.S. Military Assistance Command-Thailand, and U.S. Military Assistance Command-Vietnam. Together they constitute the central documentary record on the war in Southeast Asia. They have divisional and brigade records, as well as records of combat units, which include those performing infantry, armor, aviation, artillery, and calvary functions, and those support units performing engineering signal, maintenance, and medical functions.

* Visual Arts Fellowships
National Gallery of Art
Center for Advanced Study in the Visual Arts
Constitution and 6th St., NW
Washington, DC 20565   202-842-6480
The Center has a four-part program of fellowships, meetings, publications, and research in the field of visual arts. The Center offers a series of discussions, symposia, and lectures. Nine pre-doctoral fellowships are available for productive scholarly work in the history of art, architecture, and urban form, as well as senior fellowships and visiting senior fellowships for post-doctoral studies. Center 8 is a publication which contains research reports by members of the Center, as well as a record of the activities of the Center. The Center also publishes an annual listing of research in the history of art sponsored by a number of granting institutions.

* Washington, DC Historic Street Plans
Public Information Office
Pennsylvania Avenue Development Corporation
1311 Pennsylvania Ave., NW
Suite 1220 North
Washington, DC 20004   202-724-9091
The following publications are available:

Pennsylvania Avenue Development Corporation, Annual Report, 1988
The Pennsylvania Avenue Plan, 1974
Amendments to the Pennsylvania Avenue Plan
The Avenue Report (a quarterly newsletter)

* Weekly Presidential Documents
Superintendent of Documents
U.S. Government Printing Office
Washington, DC 20402   202-512-1800
The *Weekly Compilation of Presidential Documents*, compiles transcripts of the President's news conferences, messages to Congress, public speeches and statements, and other presidential materials released by the White House. The *Compilation* carries a *Monthly Dateline* and covers materials released during the preceding week. Each issue carries an index of contents and a cumulative index to prior issues. Separate indexes are published quarterly, semiannually, and annually. Other finding aids include lists of laws approved by the President and of nominations submitted to the Senate, and a checklist of White House releases. Subscriptions are $75 per year S/N-769-007-00000-8, and single copies are $3.

* White House Publications Listing
National Tech Information Service
5285 Port Royal Rd.
Springfield, VA 22161   703-487-4650

Arts and Humanities

Publications of the Executive Office of the President is a listing of the documents issued from the Executive Office of the President (EOP), including where to obtain them. Contact the office above to get your free copy.

* White House Watergate Tapes and Transcripts

Nixon Presidential Materials Project
Office of Presidential Libraries
National Archives and Records Administration
8601 Adelphi Rd.
College Park, MD 20740-6001   301-713-6800

The Nixon tapes include 4,000 hours of secretly recorded conversations in the Oval Office of the White House. As of May 17, 1993, 63 hours of White House related tapes were made open to the public. Of the 44 million textual records, 5 million pages of Nixon materials are now open for research and include some of the most sensitive of the White House files. Nixon Project audiovisual records include over 400,000 official White House photographs. Researchers are encouraged to call or wirte in advance of any research visit to ensure the materials you need are available.

* World War II Military Data Files

Center for Electronic Records
National Archives and Records Administration
8601 Adelphi Rd.
College Park, MD 20740-6001   301-713-6645

The Center for Electronic Records maintains military data files for all branches of the military and a variety of records from World War II.

* World War II Nazi Records

National Archives and Records Administration
8601 Adelphi Rd.
College Park, MD 20740-6001   301-713-7250

This office holds all the records of the German Army that were captured during World War II, and can direct you to guides to the collection.

* World Wide Web Sites

National Endowment for the Arts	http://arts.endow.gov
National Endowment for the Humanities	http://neh.fed.us
National Archives	http://www.nara.gov
The Library of Congress	http://www.loc.gov
National Park Service U.S. Department of the Interior	http://www.nps.gov
Smithsonian Institution	http://www.si.edu

The World Wide Web offers researches and historians a wealth of information 24 hours a day, 7 days a week. You can research the Gettysburg Address via the Library of Congress Home Page or seek grant information via the National Endowment for the Humanities Home Page. You can surf through the main home page of a department to get to a particular program within it. For example, you can get to the National Air and Space Museum Home Page through the Smithsonian Institutes Home Page.

Be patient. If any phone number is incorrect, call (area code) 555-1212 and request the new listing.

Museums and Cultural Resources

The national museums and libraries span geographical and cultural boundaries to allow anyone to tap into arts, ethnography, anthropology, craft, architecture, archeology, history, oral tradition and folklore as well as natural history. The Museological Clearinghouse may serve as a good point of departure to locate the collections and experts in a particular time in history as well as to learn about trends in the museum world. Also refer to the section on Money for the Arts in this chapter which includes federal funding for exhibits and promotion of the arts.

* African Art National Museum

National Museum of African Art
Smithsonian Institution
950 Independence Ave., SW
Washington, DC 20560   202-357-4600 ext.286

The National Museum of African Art is dedicated to the collection, exhibition, and study of traditional arts of sub-Saharan Africa. Included in the collection are sculptures, textiles, jewelry, architectural elements, decorative arts, and utilitarian objects. They have an extensive education program, in addition to gallery lectures, programs for families and films for children. A free calendar of exhibitions and programs is available.

* African Art and Culture Photographic Archives

National Museum of African Art
950 Independence Ave., SW
Washington, DC 20560   202-357-4600 ext.280

The Eliot Elisofon Photographic Archives is devoted to the collection, preservation, and management of visual resources of sub-Saharan African Art. It conducts picture research and collaborates with art historians, anthropologists, filmmakers, and other interested specialists in the publication and exhibition of its images. In addition, it serves as an international clearinghouse for information about African art and cultural history. The collection is divided into two major categories: art, which includes photographs of art objects in the permanent collection, as well as in public and private collections; and field, which contains images of African life. An overall guide to the collection and a price list are available upon request.

* African Art Library

Smithsonian Institution
950 Independence Ave., SW
Washington, DC 20560   202-357-4600 ext.285

The Library maintains a collection of 15,000 books and 280 periodical titles on traditional and contemporary arts of Africa, including sculptural and decorative arts, ethnography, anthropology, craft, architecture, archeology, history, oral tradition and folklore, and African retentions in the New World. The Library is open to the public by appointment.

* Afro-American History and Cultures Exhibit

Anacostia Neighborhood Museum
Smithsonian Institution
1901 Fort Place, SE
Washington, DC 20020   202-287-3306

This museum presents exhibitions on the history and cultures of Afro-Americans. The Research Department, open for use by scholars, conducts independent studies in the areas of Afro-American history, minority and ethnic studies, and history of Washington, DC. The Education Department develops independent programs and activities to serve the needs and interests of the local school community. These activities include a traveling puppet troupe, teacher workshops and seminars, and a circulating library of children's books for use by teachers.

* Air Force Art Collection

Secretary of the Air Force
Art and Museum Branch
The Pentagon, Room 4A120
Washington, DC 20330   703-697-6629

The Air Force Museum has available 8 x 10 reproduction photographs of the Air Force art collection. They will accept written requests.

* American Art Collections Nationwide

Archives of American Art
Smithsonian Institution
8th and G Sts., NW
Washington, DC 20560   202-357-2781

The Archives of American Art publishes a quarterly *Journal* that contains articles based on its collections and features reports from the regional centers. Separate publications include: *The Card Catalog of the Manuscript Collections of the Archives of American Art*; *Archives of American Art Collection of Exhibition Catalogs*; *Archives of American Art, A Directory of Resources*; and *Archives of American Art, A Checklist of the Collection.*

* American Art Museum

Barney Studio House
National Museum of American History
Smithsonian Institution
Washington, DC 20560

The house, a curatorial department of the National Museum of American Art, was built by artist Alice Pike Barney in 1902 to be her home, studio and salon. Now being renovated, this unique showplace is filled with paintings by Mrs. Barney and her friends, ornate furniture, oriental rugs and decorative bibelots. It is open by reservation for guided visits, and an annual series of programs is presented in the spirit of the salons given by Mrs. Barney. Closed until further notice.

* American Arts and Industries Museum

Smithsonian Institution
Arts and Industries Building
900 Jefferson Dr., SW
Washington, DC 20560   202-357-3224

The Arts and Industries Building is made up of four exhibition halls. Currently, three of the halls contain portions of the "1876: A Centennial Exhibition", which recreates the United States Centennial Exhibition held in Philadelphia in 1876. One hall is a changing exhibition of African American History and Culture. The building also houses the Smithsonian's Discovery Theater, which, from October to June, offers a changing series of live performances designed for young people and their families, including presentations by puppeteers, dancers, actors, mimes, and singers. Hours of operation - 10 a.m. to 4 p.m. For information regarding the Discovery Theater, call 202-357-1500.

* American Crafts and Designers

Renwick Gallery
17th and Pennsylvania Ave., NW
Washington, DC 20560   202-357-2531

The Renwick Gallery of the National Museum of American Art exhibits the creative achievements of designers and craftspeople in the United States. The programs include lunchtime films, concerts, and other musical events, lectures and craft demonstrations, and children's programs related to current exhibitions. A free monthly calendar is available.

* American Culture and Folk Art Grants

Heritage and Preservation
National Endowment for the Arts

Be patient. If any phone number is incorrect, call (area code) 555-1212 and request the new listing.

309

Arts and Humanities

1100 Pennsylvania Ave., NW, Room 725
Washington, DC 20506   202-682-5428

The Heritage and Preservation Program supports the traditional arts that have grown through time within the many groups that make up the United States. The Program's objectives are to present and enhance this multi-cultural artistic heritage and to make it more available to a wider public audience. The Program offers grants for the presentation and documentation of traditional arts and artists, as well as for supporting the development of state- or regionally-based folk arts programs. Fellowships are given to master folk artists to provide national recognition.

* American History Branch Library

National Museum of American History
14th and Constitution Ave., NW
Room 5016
Washington, DC 20560   202-357-2414

The Library houses a collection of 165,000 volumes of book and bound journals on engineering, transportation, military history, science, applied science, decorative arts, and domestic and community life in addition to American history and the history of science and technology. They have special collections of trade literature and materials about world fairs. The Library is open to the public by appointment.

* American History National Museum

National Museum of American History
Directors Office
Smithsonian Institution
14th Sts. and Constitution Ave., NW
Washington, DC 20560   202-357-2510

The museum's mission is to illuminate through collections, exhibitions, research, publications, and educational programs, the entire history of the United States, including the external influences that have helped to shape the national character. From the patent model Eli Whitney's cotton gin to a Ford Model T, objects on display at the Museum embody the nation's scientific, technological, and cultural heritage. Recent major reinstallations treat everyday life in America just after the Revolutionary War, the American Industrial Revolution, and the diverse origins of the American people. You will find exhibits on agriculture, medicine, armed forces history, graphic arts, ceramics, glass, political history, and many other areas. Educational activities are directed toward both children and adults. Musical programs are offered regularly. Demonstration Centers offer participatory educational experiences where visitors may touch and handle objects.

* American Painting and Sculpture Databases

Research and Scholar Center
National Museum of American Art
8th and G Sts., NW
Washington, DC 20560   202-357-1626

The Research and Scholar Center maintains seven research projects totaling over 530,000 art data records and over 250,000 photographic images. Each of the projects uses automation in cataloging information and images, thus providing the user with access to art information and reproductions in a variety of ways. The research databases are: the Inventory of American Paintings Executed before 1914, a computerized index to over 250,000 paintings; the Inventory of American Sculpture, an on-line interactive database accessible through SIRIS, containing information on sculpture and outdoor monuments; the Pre-1877 Art Exhibition Catalog Index, recording works of art listed in catalogs of art exhibitions held in the U.S. and Canada; the Smithsonian Art Index, which lists drawings, prints, paintings, and sculptures located in Smithsonian scientific, technical, and historical collections; the Permanent Collection Database, comprising over 32,000 objects in the museum's collection; the Peter A. Juley and Son Collection of more than 127,000 photographic negatives documenting American art and artists photographed between 1896 and 1975 by this New York City firm; and the Slide and Photograph Archives, a collection of over 90,000 slides and 200,000 photographs available for study and 20,000 slides available for loan. Please call in advance for an appointment.

* American Portraits Research Center

National Portrait Gallery
8th and F Sts., NW
Washington, DC 20560   202-357-1886

The Catalog of American Portraits, administered by the National Portrait Gallery, is a national reference center whose files contain photographs and documentation for more than eighty thousand likenesses of historically important Americans. Arranged alphabetically by subject, the files are extensively cross-referenced by artist. A continuing Automated National Portrait Survey has made its holdings more readily accessible to researchers. Computerized indices by subject, artist, occupation, location, and medium make the catalog a valuable resource.

* Antiques and Historical Design

National Cooper-Hewitt Museum of Design
Smithsonian Institution
2 E. 91st St.
New York, NY 10128   212-860-6868

The Cooper-Hewitt Museum is the only museum in the United States devoted exclusively the study and exhibition of historical and contemporary design. The collection contains textiles, wallpaper, furniture, ceramics, glass, architectural ornaments, metalwork, woodwork, drawings and prints. Educational programs offered include lectures, craft workshops, repair clinics, seminars, young people's classes, and performing arts demonstrations.

* Archeological Policies for National Parks

Anthropology Division
National Park Service
U.S. Department of the Interior
800 N. Capital St. NW
Washington, DC 20002   202-343-4101

The Anthropology Division of the National Park Service (NPS) is responsible for developing service-wide archeological and ethnographic program policies, guidelines, and standards. This function is concerned with preservation, protection, and visitor use activities related to the archeological aspects of the cultural resources of the Park System.

* Architectural and Engineering Drawings

Cartographic and Architectural Branch
National Archives and Records Administration
8601 Adelphi Rd.
College Park, MD 20740-6001   301-713-7040

The Cartographic and Architectural Branch has over 11 million maps, charts, aerial photographs, architectural drawings, patents, and ship plans, which constitute one of the world's largest accumulations of such documents. The Branch holds architectural and engineering drawings created by civilian and military agencies. Reproductions can be furnished for a fee.

* Architecture of the U.S. Capitol

The Curator's Office
Architect of the Capitol
The Capitol Building, Room SB15
Washington, DC 20515   202-288-2700

A packet of fact sheets on the various features and artifacts of the Capitol is available free of charge. It includes information on the Statue of Freedom; the tile floor of the Capitol; the history of the old subway transportation system connecting the Capitol and the Russell Office Building; the Rotunda Frieze; the "cornstalk" or "corncob" columns and capitals; the dome; the historic catafalque; Washington's tomb; those who have lain in state in the rotunda; the flags over the east and west central fronts; and the architects and architecture of the Capitol.

* Art Donations and Bequests

Development Department
National Gallery of Art
Constitution and 6th St., NW
Washington, DC 20565   202-842-6372

The Gallery seeks gifts-in-kind of American and Western European works of art. All donations should be discussed with the Development Department.

* Art Exhibits for American Embassies

Bureau of Administration
U.S. Department of State
21st and Virginia Ave., NW, Room B-258
Washington, DC 20520   202-647-5723

The State Department is responsible for placing original American art in U.S. Embassies. Based on cooperation between the government and the private sector, museums, corporate and private collectors, commercial galleries, and artists donate or lend American art representing all styles, periods, and media. Currently, more than 3,000 works of art valued at more than $35.2 million are being circulated in 123 countries. Write for an information brochure.

* Art Exhibits Insurance Coverage

Arts and Artifacts Indemnity Museum
National Endowment for the Arts
1100 Pennsylvania Ave., NW, Room 624
Washington, DC 20506   202-682-5442

This program provides grants for insurance against loss or damage for art works borrowed for international exhibitions. Individuals, non-profit institutions, and government agencies may apply. A single object can be insured for up to $50 million. A single exhibition can be insured for up to $300 million, while an entire show can be insured for $3 billion.

* Art Exhibits in the Halls of Congress

Secretary of the Senate
U.S. Capitol
Washington, DC 20510   202-224-3121

Most people tour the Capitol and admire its art work, but miss the works of art throughout all the buildings in the Capitol complex. The Rayburn House Office Building displays a statue of Sam Rayburn. The basement rotunda in the Cannon House Office Building displays a large model of the Capitol. The Hart Senate Office Building has an impressive Alexander Calder sculpture which fills the entire atrium courtyard space. Large, stately, richly detailed caucus rooms are historic places where major public hearings over the past three quarters of a century have taken place. The subway tunnel between the Cannon House Office Building and the Capitol is the site for a display of paintings done by high school artists who enter their works in congressional district competitions sponsored by the Congressional Arts Caucus.

* Art Exhibits Overseas

Office of Arts America
The Bureau of Educational and Cultural Affairs
United States Information Agency
301 Fourth St., SW, Room 567
Washington, DC 20547   202-619-4779

Arts America recruits artists and performers to visit other countries and provides some assistance to artists traveling privately. The USIA sends some 15 large fine arts exhibitions and 25 performing arts groups overseas annually. Panels set up by the National Endowment for the Arts recommends a group of candidates, from which the USIA selects the programs participants. A Speakers Program recruits artists from the fields of literature, film, and the performing arts, on the basis of requests from overseas posts. AculSpecs are American specialists, in one of the plastic or performing arts, who visit a foreign country for two to six weeks with a local host institution for a program of master classes, workshops, and demonstrations. Arts America sponsors about 30 of these programs a year. This office also provides support materials for major fine and performing arts projects; publishes a quarterly list of privately traveling artists; and tries to assist overseas posts in programming these performers.

* Art History Archive from 18th Century On

Archives of American Art
American Art and Portrait Gallery
8th and F Sts., NW
Washington, DC 20560   202-357-2781

The Archives of American Art is dedicated to the collection, preservation, and study of papers and other primary records of the history of the visual arts in America. Its collections, comprising more than eight million items, are the world's largest single source for such information. The collections include correspondence, journals, business papers, and other documentation of artists, dealers, critics, art historians, and art institutions from the eighteenth century to the present. Microfilm copies of many of the collections are available through interlibrary loan. Holdings of the Archives are described in a published card catalog (1980 -) and on SIRIS. In addition to its headquarters in Washington DC, the Archives of American Art maintains offices in four cities: Boston: 617-565-8444; Detroit: 313-226-7544; New York City: 212-399-5015; and Los Angeles: 818-583-7847, all of which serve as regional collecting and research centers, and provide microfilm of the collections to researchers. The Archives publishes the Archives of American Art Journal quarterly and sponsors symposia and lectures on art history subjects. Subscription 1 yr. - $35, 2 yr. - $65, 3 yr. - $90, single copy - $10.

* Art in the Capitol

The Curator's Office
Architect of the Capitol
The Capitol Building, Room SB15
Washington, DC 20515   202-228-2700

The U.S. Capitol is a recognized work of art. The classical architecture and the interior embellishments set the backdrop for the variety and scope of American history and culture. Much of the Capitol's art collection is catalogued in *Art in the Capitol*, published by the Architect of the Capitol under the direction of the Joint Committee on the Library.

* Arts in Education Initiatives

Education and Access
National Endowment for the Arts
1100 Pennsylvania Ave., NW, Room 602
Washington, DC 20506   220-682-5426

The Education and Access Program is a partnership program through cooperative efforts of the Arts Endowment, state arts and education agencies, local communities, and other organizations. The Program's overall goal is to advance the arts as part of basic education. Grants are awarded to place practicing artists in a variety of educational settings and to support other projects designed to enhance arts education in schools. Arts in Schools Basic Education Grants encourage plans and projects that promote the arts in schools as a basic component of the curriculum in kindergarten through high school.

* Art Slides, Films, Video Loan Program

Education Resources Programs
National Gallery of Art
Extension Services
Constitution and 6th St., NW
Washington, DC 20565   202-842-6099

Color slide programs, films, and videocassettes are loaned at no cost to schools, libraries, community organizations, and individuals across the nation. The programs deal with a wide range of subjects drawn from the Gallery's permanent collections and special exhibitions. A free catalog listing all free-loan Extension Programs is available. Call to book a program.

* Asia and Near East Art National Collection

Sackler Gallery
Smithsonian Institution
1050 Independence Ave. SW
Washington, DC 20560   202-357-4880

Opened in 1987, the Sackler Gallery has over 1000 art objects from China, South and Southeast Asia, and the ancient Near East given to the museum by the late Arthur M. Sackler. Future programs at the gallery include major international shows offering both surveys of distinctive traditions and comparative exhibitions showing the art of different centuries, geographic areas, and types of patronage. Most exhibitions will be accompanied by public programs and scholarly symposia. The Sackler has a library and a slide study room which are open to the public. *Asian Art and Culture* is published three time a year.

* Asian and Near Eastern Art Museum

Freer Gallery of Art
Smithsonian Institution
1050 Independence Ave. SW
Washington, DC 20560   202-357-4880

The Freer Gallery of Art is a museum of Asian and Near Eastern Art from the third millennium B.C. to the early 20th century. It also houses a group of works by late 19th and early 20th century American artists. The building, the original collection, and an endowment fund were the gift of Charles Lang Freer. The 26,800 Art works now in the Freer's Asian and Near Eastern collections include paintings, ceramics, manuscripts, metalwork, and sculpture. The Freer and the Sackler Gallery have joined together to share staff and research facilities, as well as a library housed at the Sackler. The Technical Laboratory conducts research and conservation of objects from the Freer and Sackler collections. It undertakes technical analyses of Asian art, investigates and rectifies conservation problems, and ensures that art works are in stable condition for exhibition. A free public lecture series is held where scholars present illustrated lectures on Asian and Near Eastern Art.

* Attracting Wider Audience to Smithsonian Museums

Wider Audience Development Programs
Arts and Industries Building
Suite 2472
Smithsonian Institution
Washington, DC 20560   202-786-2403

The role of this Office is to extend the reach of Smithsonian programs to segments

---

Be patient. If any phone number is incorrect, call (area code) 555-1212 and request the new listing.

of the public that traditionally have been under-represented in the institution's audience. The office helps museums, offices, and bureaus throughout the institution in their outreach efforts. The OCWA systematically ensures participation in minority groups at receptions and special events.

* Audiovisual Materials for Art Exhibits

National Gallery of Art
Audiovisual Department
Constitution and 6th St., NW
Washington, DC 20565   202-842-6099

This office produces multi-image programs which accompany major exhibitions, as well as archival videotaping of exhibitions, special events, and lectures.

* Central Museological Clearinghouse

Center for Museum Centers
Art and Industries Building
900 Jefferson Dr. S.W.
Washington, DC 20560   202-357-3101

This information center and library has a working collection of resources on all aspects of museum operations. The Center has the only central source of museological information in the United States, also contains evaluation studies, visitor surveys, volunteer manuals, long-range development plans, sample by-laws, and characters and museum collection management records. The Center is open to the public by appointment.

* Color Reproductions of National Collection

National Gallery of Art
Constitution and 6th St., NW
Washington, DC 20565   202-842-6466

The Publications Sales Department offers a large selection of color reproductions and scholarly publications related to the collections, exhibits, and other activities of the Gallery. Additional offerings include books and videocassettes on fine art and architecture, slide sets from the permanent collection, framed and matted reproductions and games. A free color reproductions mail order catalog is available. Call 202-357-2995.

* Conservators and Archacometry Training

Conservation-Analytical Laboratory
Smithsonian Institution
Museum Support Center
4210 Silver Hill Rd.
Suitland, MD 20560   301-238-3700, x134

The Conservation-Analytical Laboratory engages in research in the conservation, technical study, and analysis of museum objects and related materials. Conservation-related information is made available to museum professionals nationwide and to the general public. In the archacometry program, physical scientists engage in analytical and technical studies of artifacts. The laboratory performs conservation treatments on objects from the Smithsonian collections that present special problems. The conservation training program provides internship training for conservation students and organizes advanced specialist training courses for practicing conservators.

* Conservation and Preservation Survey

National Institute for the Conservation
of Cultural Property, Inc (NIC)
3299 K St. NW, Suite 403
Smithsonian Institution
Washington, DC 20007   202-625-1495

This clearinghouse for museums and conservationists is currently undertaking several projects, including the Conservation Assessment Survey Program, which is designed to help museums organize and weed out their collections; and the Save Outdoor Sculpture (SOS) project, which catalogs, inventories, and ensures that outdoor sculptures are treated properly.

* Contemporary and Historical Design

National Cooper-Hewitt Museum of Design
Smithsonian Institution
2 E. 91st St.
New York, NY 10128   212-860-6868

The Cooper-Hewitt Museum is the only museum in the United States devoted exclusively to the study and exhibition of historical and contemporary design. The collection contains textiles, wallpaper, furniture, ceramics, glass, architectural ornaments, metalwork, woodwork, drawings and prints. Educational programs offered include lectures, craft workshops, repair clinics, seminars, young people's classes, and performing arts demonstrations.

* Dial-A-Museum

Visitor Information Center
Smithsonian Institution
1000 Jefferson Dr., SW
Washington, DC 20560   202-357-2020

By calling this number, you will hear a taped telephone message with daily announcements on new exhibits and special events.

* Disabled Smithsonian Visitors

Visitor Information and
Associates' Reception Center
Smithsonian Institution
1000 Jefferson Dr. SW
Washington, DC 20560   202-357-1300

A free guide book to the Smithsonian is available for disabled visitors, which includes information on parking, transportation, wheelchair access, bathrooms, and telephones. Sign language and oral interpreter services may be arranged three days in advance. Several museums have large-print brochures available.
Hours 9AM-4PM.

* Elderly and Disabled Access to the Arts

Office for Special Constituencies
National Endowment for the Arts
1100 Pennsylvania Ave., NW
Room 605   202-682-5532
Washington, DC 20506   202-682-5496 TDD

The Office for Special Constituencies assists individuals and organizations in making arts activities accessible to older adults, disabled people, and those in institutions. Contact this Office for assistance and materials, including examples of how other arts groups have made their programs available to special groups, along with model project guidelines.

* Endowment for the Arts Grant Application Guide

Public Information Offices
National Endowment for the Arts
1100 Pennsylvania Ave., NW
Room 617
Washington, DC 20506   202-682-5400

The National Endowment for the Arts offers a free publication, the *Grants to Organizations*, which outlines its various programs and grants, and provides a calendar of deadlines, as well as application information for the grants. Regional offices and other related agencies are also listed.

* Family Art Programs in Washington

National Gallery of Art
Education Division
Constitution and 6th St., NW
Washington, DC 20565   202-842-6246

Family programs are offered on Saturday mornings for families with children ages 6 to 12. These events usually include a film or special activity and a tour and lasts about 1 1/2 hours. Advance registration is required.

* Famous American Portraits

National Portrait Gallery
Publications Office
Smithsonian Institution
8th and F Sts., NW
Washington, DC 20560   202-357-2995

The National Portrait Gallery's collection consists of paintings, sculpture, prints, drawings, and photographs of figures significant to the history of the United States. At any given time, any number of research projects may be in progress on topics in American history, biography, and portraiture. This unique reference facility contains documentation on nearly 70,000 portraits of noted Americans. The Gallery provides a full range of educational services both within the museum and out in the community, including a Speakers' Bureau, a Lunchtime Lectures Series, and

"Portraits in Motion" performance series, which presents actors and musicians in readings, concerts, and plays. Education office 202-357-2920.

* Films and Lectures on Art
National Gallery of Art
Adult Programs
Constitution and 6th St., NW
Washington, DC 20565   202-842-6247
Free films on art, along with feature films, are presented at the Gallery. The *Calendar of Events* lists the titles and times of the showings. Free lectures are given by distinguished scholars on Sundays. No reservations are needed, but seating is limited. Andrew W. Mellon Lectures in the Fine Arts, a six-lecture series given at the Gallery, encompasses the history, criticisms, and theory of the visual and performing arts. All lectures also are announced in the Gallery's *Calendar*.

* Folklife Crafts and American Traditions
Center for Folklife Programs and Cultural Studies
Smithsonian Institution
955 L'Enfant Plaza, Suite 2600
Washington, DC 20590   202-287-3424
Through its annual Festival of American Folklife, the Smithsonian created a program of folklife presentations for the general public for two weeks each summer. The Office also carries on research in folklife traditions, publishes documentary and analytical studies, develops and organizes exhibitions with folklife themes, and cooperates with Universities and other institutions in presentation projects involving traditional craftsman and performing artists.

* Folklife Studies Worldwide
Office of Folklife Programs Archive/
Folkways Records Archive
Office of Folklife Programs
955 L'Enfant Plaza, SW, Suite 2600
Washington, DC 20560   202-287-3251
The Office of Folklife Programs Archive contains folkloristic materials generated through research for and documentation of the Festival of American Folklife Studies Monograph/Film Series. These materials document hundreds of folk culture traditions from the United States and forty-five other countries. Researchers should call for an appointment.

* Folkways Musical Recordings Archive
Office of Folklife Programs Archives
955 L'Enfant Plaza, SW, Suite 2600
Washington, DC 20560   202-287-3251
The Folkways Records Archive, comprising the Moses and Frances Asch Collection, contains material related to the 2,200 published recordings of Folkways Records. The Folkways collection documents world-wide musical traditions, the spoken words of significant American figures, historical events, and nonmusical sounds of technology and nature. A catalog of the archives holdings is available which includes information on how to purchase recordings of the music.

* Hirshhorn Museum and Sculpture Garden
Smithsonian Institution
7th St. and Independence Ave. S.W.
Washington, DC 20560   202-357-3091
The Hirshhorn Museum and Sculpture Garden is devoted to the exhibition, interpretation, and study of modern and contemporary art. The Collection consists of 19th and 20th century sculpture, paintings, prints and drawings. Children's events and a supplementary program of lectures, documentary films, art films, and performing arts are offered. Outreach programs provide on-site classroom preparation, lecture services for adult community groups, and a teachers' workshop course.

* Historic Architecture in the National Parks
Park Historic Architecture Division
National Park Service
U.S. Department of the Interior
800 N. Capitol St. NW, Suite 360
Washington, DC 20002   202-343-8146
Activities related to the preservation of historic and prehistoric structures and cultural landscapes within the National Park System are administered by this office. *A List of Classified Structures* is maintained, which is an inventory of all historic and prehistoric structures in the System. A bibliography of Cultural Resources Management is also administered, listing all reports that address cultural resources in the Park System.

* Humanities Exhibits at Museums and Historical Organizations Grants
Division of Public Programs and Enterprise
National Endowment for the Humanities
1100 Pennsylvania Ave., NW
Room 420
Washington, DC 20506   202-606-8267
This Program provides support for the planning and implementation of temporary and permanent exhibitions, historic site interpretations, publications, lectures and other educational programs, which engage the public in a greater appreciation and understanding of the humanities. Grants allow institutions to plan projects that interpret collections and to carry out permanent or temporary projects. Grants can support the cataloguing of a collection to make possible their use in programs on the humanities, as well as allowing for planning of computerized documentation. Self-study grants allow an organization to evaluate its humanities resources and develop long-range plans. Grants can be made to non-profit organizations, including local and state governments, if such donations qualify as charitable deductions under Section 170(c) of the Internal Revenue Code of 1954.

* Import Controls on Cultural Property
Cultural Property Advisory Committee
Bureau of Educational and Cultural Affairs
U.S. Information Agency
301 Fourth St., SW, Room 247
Washington, DC 20547   202-619-6612
This Presidential committee, comprised private citizens who are archaeologists, art dealers, representatives of the museum community, or the general public, advises the deputy USIA director, who determines whether the U.S. should impose import controls on endangered archaeological and ethnological materials at the request of foreign countries. The Cultural Property staff investigates and reports to the committee, and serves as liaison to federal agencies and to the archaeological, art dealer, museum, and preservation communities affected by U.S. actions under the 1983 Cultural Property Act.

* Indian Arts and Crafts Development
Indian Arts and Crafts Board
Bureau of Indian Affairs
U.S. Department of the Interior
18th and C Sts., NW
Washington, DC 20240   202-208-3773
The Indian Arts and Crafts Board promotes the development of Native Indian arts and crafts so that the artists will achieve economic stability. Three museums are operated by the Board: the Sioux Indian Museum in Rapid City, South Dakota; the Museum of the Plains Indian in Browning, Montana; and the Southern Plains Indian Museum in Anadarko, Oklahoma. These museums contain historic artifacts of these Indian tribes, but primarily function as contemporary showcases of Indian art. The Board also provides advisory services for Indian artists and craftsmen. In the near future, a directory of many locations where Indian art can be seen and purchased will be available. For more information, contact the office above.

* Indian Arts and Crafts Directory
Indian Arts and Crafts Board
Bureau of Indian Affairs, Room 4004
U.S. Department of the Interior
Washington, DC 20240   202-208-3773
The Indian Arts and Crafts Board has compiled a source directory of arts and crafts businesses owned and operated by Indians, Eskimos and Aleuts. The free directory lists the name, address, and phone number of each business and the types of products sold. The Indian Arts and Crafts Board's goal is to make the Indian populations more economically independent through their native arts and crafts.

* Indian Craft Shops
Indian Craft Shop
Bureau of Indian Affairs
U.S. Department of the Interior
18th and C Sts., NW
Washington, DC 20240   202-208-4056

Be patient. If any phone number is incorrect, call (area code) 555-1212 and request the new listing.

313

Arts and Humanities

These shops contain Indian crafts that can be purchased by the public. The hours at the Main Building location are 8:30 a.m. to 4:30 p.m., Monday through Friday.

* Indian Museums

Southern Plains Indian Museum
P.O. Box 749
Anadarko, OK 73005   405-247-6221

Museum of the Plains Indian
P.O. Box 400
Browning, MT 59417   406-338-2230

Sioux Indian Museum
P.O. Box 1504
Rapid City, SD 57709   605-348-0557

These three Indian museums are administered by the Indian Arts and Crafts Board of the Bureau of Indian Affairs, U.S. Department of the Interior. The museums issue free informational pamphlets and brochures about their respective programs and exhibition activities. Contact the museums directly to be placed on their mailing lists.

* Indian Publications and Audiovisuals

Indian Arts and Crafts Board
Bureau of Indian Affairs
Room 4004
U.S. Department of the Interior
Washington, DC 20240   202-208-3773

The Indian Arts and Crafts Board has compiled a listing of their publications and audiovisuals available to the public. Titles include *Contemporary Southern Plains Indian Metalwork*, *Painted Tipis by Contemporary Plains Indian Artists*, *Coyote Tales of the Montana Salish*, *Contemporary Indian Artists - Montana/Wyoming*, and *Contemporary Southern Plains Indian Painting*. Two slide lecture kits are available for purchase at $50 each: *Contemporary Indian and Eskimo Crafts of the United States* and *Contemporary Sioux Painting*.

* International Museum Scholars Exchange

International Activities
3123 S. Dillon Ripley Center
1100 Jefferson Dr. S.W.
Smithsonian Institution
Washington, DC 20560   202-357-4282

Handbook of Foreign Opportunities serves as a basic reference document for Smithsonian staff who travel abroad on official business or who engage in international scholarly or museum exchanges. Although directed toward Smithsonian staff, this publication can give others helpful tips for conducting research and exchanges abroad, including visas, research permits and money concerns, and also covers issues surrounding immigration and international visitors.

* Military Photographic Archives

Still Picture Branch (NNSP)
National Archives Records Administration
8601 Adelphi Rd.
College Park, MD 20740-6001   301-713-6660

The archives holds the official photographic collection for the Army, Navy, and Marine Corps dating 1955 back to the founding of the country. Patrons can order photographic reproductions and posters for a small fee. Write or call for a price sheet, a "Select List" of period topics--including The Civil War, World War II, the Old West, the American Revolution, and American Cities--and a catalog entitled *War and Conflict*.

* Museum Career Training Grants

National Museum Act
Smithsonian Institution
Arts and Industries Building
900 Jefferson Dr.S.W.
Washington, DC 20560   202-357-2987

The National Museum Act authorizes the Smithsonian to make grants that would enhance professionalism in museums. Awards are made for training career employees in museum practices, for research on museum-related problems and for projects involving the distribution of technical information. Grants are made to museums, museum-related organizations, academic institutions, and sponsored individuals pursuing careers in conservation practices.

* Museum Collections in National Parks

Museum Management
National Park Service (NPS)
U.S. Department of the Interior
800 N. Capital St. NW
Washington, DC 20002   202-343-8138

National Park Service museum collections are managed by this branch of NPS. The office's *NPS Museum Handbook* provides guidelines on the acquisition, documentation, cataloging, conservation, storage, use, and disposition of museum objects. The Automated National Catalog System maintains the centralized records of museum pieces belonging to the Park System.

* Museum Conservation Science Center

Museum Support Center Library
Smithsonian Institution
4210 Silver Hill Rd., MRC 534
Suitland, MD 20746   301-238-3666

This library provides information about conservation of materials and museum objects, conservation science, which includes archaeometry, the study of museum environments, and the analysis of materials by such means as X-ray, diffraction, and gas chromatography. This library is open to the public by appointment.

* Museum Contracts and Small Business

Office of Procurement Property Management
Smithsonian Institution
Washington, DC 20560   202-287-3238

This office provides information regarding contract application for services such as supplies, construction, equipment, and research. They can answer questions regarding the application process, and can direct you to offices possibly in need of your services.

* Museum of the U.S. Department of the Interior

Departmental Museum
U.S. Department of the Interior
18th and C Sts., NW, Room 1240
Washington, DC 20240   202-208-4743

The highlights of this museum's exhibit include Native American artifacts and dioramas depicting the history of each of DOI's Bureaus. Of particular interest to children is a collection of fossils and a display of fragments from the moon's surface. The display is oriented to children in the fourth grade and older, but younger children are welcome. The hours of operation are 8 a.m. to 4 p.m., Monday through Friday. Admission is free.

* Museum Programs Clearinghouse

Smithsonian Institution
Center for Museum Studies
900 Jefferson Dr. S.W. Room 2235
Washington, DC 20560   202-357-3101

The Center for Museum Studies provides professional development training, advisory assistance, and research services to the national and international museum community and the Smithsonian staff through sponsorship of workshops, internships, and professional visitor programs, an audiovisual production and loan program, a museum reference center, a native American training program, and publications. The Audio-visual Program distributions slide-cassette and video-tape programs on conservation, exhibitions, museum education, security, museum careers, and folklife. The Native American Museums Program provides information services and educational opportunities for employees of tribal and urban native American museums and cultural Centers. The Program offers workshops, short-term residencies, technical assistance, publications, and audio-visual materials on museums.

* National Air and Space Museum

Public Affairs Office
Smithsonian Institution
7th St. and Independence Ave. S.W.
Washington, DC 20560   202-357-1552

The National Air and Space Museum was established to memorialize the development of air and space flight, and to collect, display, and preserve aeronautical and space flight artifacts. The 23 galleries contain items ranging from the Wright 1903 Flyer to Apollo 11. The Langley Theater, with a giant screen presentation, shows a variety of films every half hour, as does the Albert Einstein Planetarium. Both charge a small fee. There are live, free presentations concerning the current

Be patient. If any phone number is incorrect, call (area code) 555-1212 and request the new listing.

night sky, and there are monthly sky lectures by staff and guest speakers. A summer concert series is presented on the terrace. The Museum's Education Resource Center provides air-and-space-related materials for teachers. The Office of Education produces three new publications: *Discovery*, a curriculum package for kindergarten through third grade; 5, 4, 3, 2, 1, a guide for the very young visitor; and *Skylines*, a quarterly newsletter for educators.

* National American Art Collection
National Museum of American Art
Smithsonian Institution
8th and G Sts., NW
Washington, DC 20560   202-357-3095

The National Museum of American Art's collections of American paintings, sculptures, graphics, folk art, and photographs exhibit a broad range of artistic achievement in America from the 18th century to the present. The museum holds extensive public programs which include lectures, symposia, concerts, poetry readings, and other special events. A free calendar of events is available. NMAA conducts extensive research on American Art and has implemented seven discrete research databases totalling over 530,000 records. They also publish a scholarly journal, *Smithsonian Studies in American Art*, with articles ranging from interviews with artists to discussions of artistry in films.

* National Gallery of Art Extension Services
Education Resources
National Gallery of Art
Washington, DC 20565   202-842-6246

Education Resources provides educational material on the Gallery's collections and exhibitions free of charge except for transportation costs, to schools, colleges, and libraries across the nation. A free catalog is available.

* National Gallery Collection Catalogs
Division of Records and Loans
National Gallery of Art
Constitution and 6th St., NW
Washington, DC 20565   202-842-6234

The Gallery is publishing a systematic catalog of its entire collection of paintings, sculpture, decorative arts, and Steiglitz photographs. Twenty-five volumes are planned, and the first volume, *Early Netherlandish Paintings*, is available now at the Museum for $14.95.

* National Gallery's Permanent Collection Catalog Museum Shop
National Portrait Gallery
Smithsonian Institution
8th and F Sts. N.W.
Washington, DC 20560   202-357-1447

This book contains photographs of the entire collection of the National Portrait Gallery, including the sculptures. Cost: $24.95 ($3.95 shipping and handling).

* Native American Internship Opportunities
Fellowships and Grants
Smithsonian Institution
Washington, DC 20560   202-287-3271

The Smithsonian offers fellowships and internships for research and study in fields which are actively pursued by the museums and research organizations of the Institution. Both predoctoral and postdoctoral fellowships are available, as well as Minority Faculty Fellowships. The length of the term and size of the stipend vary. The Minority and Native American Internship Programs are performed under direct supervision of Smithsonian staff, as tutorial situations.

* Natural History Collection: Anthropology to Zoology
Museum of Natural History, Directors Office
Smithsonian Institution
10th and Constitution Ave., NW
Washington, DC 20560   202-357-2664

The Museum of Natural History is responsible for the largest natural history collections in the world. The collections are organized into eight major research and curatorial units: the departments of Anthropology, Botany, Entomology, Invertebrate Zoology, Mineral Sciences, Paleobiology, and Vertebrate Zoology and the

Smithsonian Oceanographic Sorting Center. Some of the objects and specimens include minerals and gems, meteoritic geology, sea life, insects, ice age mammals, origins and traditions of Western Civilization, and the splendors of nature. The size of the collection increases by up to a million new specimens annually. The museum conducts research on a wide variety of topics, and more than 2,000 scholars visit the museum each year. A free calendar of events is available outlining programs, symposia, lectures, and films available.

* Natural History Library
Natural History Library
10th and Constitution Ave. N.W.
Washington, DC 20560   202-357-2240

This library houses 330,000 books and bound journals and receives 1,963 journal subscriptions. The library consists of a main location and several subject-based locations. Topics covered include biology, geology, paleontology, ecology, anthropology, botany, entomology, and mineral sciences. Call to make an appointment or for information on the location of the subject-based libraries.

* Natural History Museum Education Program
National Museum of Natural History
Office of Education
Room 212, Mail Stop 158
Washington, DC 20560   202-357-2747

The museum has an extensive educational school program with film and workshops available at your school or the museum, including museum lesson tours, the Discovery Room, the Naturalist Center, and instructional kits. A catalog of services can be sent to you. The Office also publishes a quarterly calendar of films and events at the Museum.

* Numismatic Collection: Coins, Medals, Paper Money
National Museum of American History
Smithsonian Institution
12th and Constitution Ave. N.W.
Washington, DC 20560   202-357-1798

The Numismatic Collection contains 900,000 coins, medals, and paper money from ancient times to the present day.

* Outdoor Sculpture (SOS) Project
National Institute for the Conservation
of Cultural Property, Inc (NIC)
3299 K St. NW, Suite 403
Smithsonian Institution
Washington, DC 20007   202-625-1495

This clearinghouse for museums and conservationists is currently undertaking several projects, including the Conservation Assessment Survey Program, which is designed to help museums organize and weed out their collections; and the Save Outdoor Sculpture (SOS) project, which catalogs, inventories, and ensures that outdoor sculptures are treated properly.

* Post-Byzantine Art to Present Library
National Gallery of Art
Reference Desk
Constitution and 6th St., NW
Washington, DC 20565   202-842-6511

The Gallery's library has over 150,000 volumes with a specialty in Renaissance and Baroque art. The collection covers the period from Post-Byzantine to the present, focusing on the history and criticism of art. The stacks themselves are closed; however, the library is open to the public, but you should call for the hours and to make an appointment.

* Philatelic Collection: Stamps and Postal Memorabilia
National Museum of American History
12th and Constitution Ave. N.W.
Washington, DC 20560   202-357-1796

This is the largest and most extensive collection of postage stamps and postal memorabilia in the world, and is the third most valuable collection in the Smithsonian. It comprises 16 million objects, including a pair of confederate stamps, Amelia Earhart's flight jacket, and the mail wrapper the Hope Diamond was sent in when it was donated to the Smithsonian. The museum has slide programs available free of charge to civic groups, postal unions, and philatelic organizations.

Be patient. If any phone number is incorrect, call (area code) 555-1212 and request the new listing.

315

Arts and Humanities

* Photographs of Masterpieces

National Gallery of Art
Office of Visual Services
Constitution and 6th St., NW
Washington, DC 20565   202-842-6231

Black and white, 8 x 10 photographs of works from the National Gallery of Art's permanent collections are available for purchase, either by visiting the Office of Photographic Services or by mail. Color transparencies of works from the Gallery, to be used for publication, are available for rental only and must be requested in writing.

* Slide Lending Series on Art
Slide Library

National Gallery of Art
Constitution and 6th St., NW
Washington, DC 20565   202-842-6100

The National Gallery maintains a lending slide collection of over 50,000 images, which are loaned to the public free of charge. There is no list of the slide lending collection, but selections for National Gallery objects can be made from Gallery catalogs. Up to 50 slides can be borrowed at one time and may be kept for a period of two weeks. The slide library is open to the public.

* Smithsonian Archives Guide

Smithsonian Archives
Smithsonian Institution
900 Jefferson Dr. S.W.
Washington, DC 20560   202-357-1420

This free Guide to Smithsonian Archives is a reference resource to the holdings of the Archives, giving a detailed listing of the records, papers, and projects the Archives has, as well as information regarding their use.

* Smithsonian Central Exhibits Office

Smithsonian Institution
1111 N. Capitol St.
Washington, DC 20560   202-357-3118

The Office provides design, editorial production, installation and other specialized exhibition services for a variety of Smithsonian programs. For instance, their exhibitions include a life-size model of the jaw of a prehistoric shark, and also provided texts, graphic panels, maps, and time lines for a traveling exhibit on Ancient Syria.

* Smithsonian Institution Library Services

Smithsonian Institution Libraries
10th St. and Constitution Ave., NW
Washington, DC 20560   202-357-2240

The libraries of the Smithsonian Institution include approximately 950,000 volumes, with strengths in natural history, museology, history of science, and the humanities. Inquiries on special subjects or special collections should be addressed to the appropriate branch library or to the Central Reference and Loan.

* Smithsonian Institution Press

Smithsonian Institution
1111 North Capitol St.
Washington, DC 20560   202-287-3738

The Smithsonian has been publishing books since its foundation and functions like a university press. It publishes 70 scholarly books each year, in addition to several hundred popular books on topics such as science, art, American history and architecture. Call for a free catalog. To place an order call 800-927-7377.

* Smithsonian Museum Internships

Office of Museum Programs
Arts and Industries Building, Room 2235
Smithsonian Institution
Washington, DC 20560   202-357-3101

Three publications are available for interns: Internships and Fellowships describes the majority of internship and fellowship programs at the Smithsonian. The Handbook for Smithsonian Interns provides information about Smithsonian procedures, facilities, services and activities available to interns. Housing Information for Interns and Fellows is a guide to short-term housing in the Washington metropolitan area. A new publication, Internship Opportunities at the Smithsonian, is a comprehensive listing of all the internships available at each of the museums.

* Smithsonian Museum Merchandise

Capital Gallery Building
600 Maryland Ave. S.W
Suite 295B   202-287-3563
Washington, DC 20560   mail order catalog 202-287-3566

Many of the Smithsonian museums run shops which sell books, crafts, games, toys, posters, and cards. They also have a mail-order service which publishes three merchandise catalogs each year.

* Smithsonian Slides and Photographs

Photographic Services
Smithsonian Institution
14th and Constitution Ave.
Washington, DC 20560   202-357-1933

Slides, transparencies, and prints (black and white and color) are available of photographs in the Smithsonian's collections. You can also order their seven slide series on a variety of topics, and most include a booklet and cassette tape. For a slide series listing or ordering information, contact Photographic Services.

* Smithsonian Records and Books

Smithsonian Institution
P.O. Box 700
Holmes, PA 19043   800-927-7377 (PRESS)

The Smithsonian Institution produces and markets recordings of both modern and classical works, illustrating research in music history developed by Smithsonian staff and, in many cases, performed on instruments from the Institute's extensive collection. The Recordings include a wide range of music from country and western, to jazz to Bach. The Smithsonian also publishes quality illustrated books and a free catalog. For information on the Smithsonian Magazine membership programs call 1-800-533-7901.

* Traveling National Gallery Exhibits

Exhibit Lending Service
National Gallery of Art
Constitution and 6th St., NW
Washington, DC 20565   202-842-6083

The National Lending Service was established to make the collections of the Gallery accessible to museums throughout the U.S. This is accomplished through two programs: the Extended Loan Program which allows a museum to borrow up to five works of art for a year; and the Special Exhibition Program which provides exhibitions of up to 50 works in groups of 10, for periods of 4 to 6 weeks. Call or write for information on qualifications and costs.

* Visual Arts Fellowships

National Gallery of Art
Center for Advanced Study in the Visual Arts
Constitution and 6th St., NW
Washington, DC 20565   202-842-6480

The Center has a four-part program of fellowships, meetings, publications, and research in the field of visual arts. The Center offers a series of discussions, symposia, and lectures. Nine pre-doctoral fellowships are available for productive scholarly work in the history of art, architecture, and urban form, as well as senior fellowships and visiting senior fellowships for post-doctoral studies. The Center publishes an annual report which contains research reports by members of the Center, as well as a record of the activities of the Center. The Center also publishes an annual listing of research in the history of art sponsored by a number of granting institutions.

State Money for the Arts and Artists

Listed below are the money programs available from each state for the arts and artists. Although every state has different requirements for their programs, certain guidelines hold true for every state arts program. Individuals applying for fellowships must meet state residency requirements. Fellowships are granted to professional artists, not students. Organizations must be non-profit and tax exempt and provide arts programming and/or services.

Matching grants are often required for organizations requesting funding. Matching grants require that the recipient of the grant raise funds in some proportion to the amount awarded. In some instances, in-kind goods and services may be used in place of matching grants. An in-kind contribution of goods is a contribution of any tangible, useable item that the organization would have otherwise had to purchase to obtain. An in-kind contribution of a service includes intangible contributions such as donations of volunteer time, or the use of facilities or equipment.

Individuals or organizations interested in applying for a grant should determine their basic eligibility through the information in the *Guide to the National Endowment for the Arts* which is available from the Public Information Office, National Endowment for the Arts, Nancy Hanks Center, 1100 Pennsylvania Ave., NW, Washington, DC 20506.

Potential applicants should then request application guidelines from the appropriate state program office. These guidelines contain application forms and instructions as well as more detailed information on grants. Most organizations have seen severe budget cutbacks since the 1990-91 fiscal year. As a result, the figures listed below for overall funding are often higher than what is now available.

State Arts Programs

Alabama

Alabama Arts Council, 1 Dexter Ave., Montgomery, AL 36130-5810, 205-242-4076. For individual artist programs state residency is required, unless otherwise specified. Grants to organizations must be matched by at least an equal amount from other sources located by the applicant. In 1993-94, the Council awarded $333,000 in state funding to non-profit organizations, while $45,000 went to individual artists through fellowships.

1) $5,000 To Art Administrators
Fellowship in Arts Administration: Awards of $5,000 are given to any administrator or artist who has been employed by an Alabama Arts organization in a full-time paid position for at least two years prior to submitting the application.
2) $10,000 For Artists, Craftsmen, Photographers
Artists Fellowships: Grants of $5,000 or $10,000 are available for individual artists in the following disciplines: design, literature, media/photography, music, theater, visual arts, and crafts.
3) $1,000 To Develop Administrative Skills
Technical Assistance: Limited funds of up to $1,000 are available to help arts organizations develop specific administrative and technical skills. To be eligible for this program, as well as the artists fellowship program described above, an artist must be a legal resident of Alabama and have lived in the state for two years prior to application.
4) Money To Be An Artist In Residence

Artist Residences: In-state and out-of-state practicing artists are reviewed for school and community residencies. Residency length varies from two weeks to ten months. Alabama residency requirements are not applicable under this program.
5) $5,000 For Master Folk Artists
Folk Art Apprenticeships: Cash awards up to $5,000 are given to master folk artists willing to take students and teach them their specific craft. Students who have entered into an agreement with a master folk artist may also apply.
6) Grants To Large Arts Organizations
Advanced Institutional Assistance: This category applies to the state's larger cultural organizations. Grants are based on the organization's actual cash income for the three years prior to application.
7) Money For Schools To Hire Artists
Arts in Education Projects: Provides support for projects and residencies in private and public elementary and secondary schools. Minimum support is $500. Grants provide up to 50% of the total project budget or 60% of the total cost of an artist residency.
8) $500 For Designers
Design Arts Projects: This category provides state support for projects that increase public awareness of the role of design. Minimum support is $500 and funding is available for up to 50% of the total project budget.
9) $500 For Folk Artists
Folklife Program: This program helps preserve and present Alabama folklife culture. It includes the annual Alabama Folk Heritage Award to a Master folk artist and an apprenticeship program. Applications must be for a minimum of $500 and not more than 50% of the total project budget.
10) $7,500 For Local Arts Councils
Local Arts Councils: This program provides specialized support and structure for local arts councils. Grants range from $2,500 for technical assistance and planning funds, to $7,500 for special projects.
11) Money To Put On A Show Or Exhibition
Presenter Program: Grants are available to offset the costs of presenting performances and exhibitions. For basic presenter activities, applicants may request up to 25% of the engagement fee of a performance event or 25% of the combined cost of the shipping fee and insurance cost for an exhibition.
12) $1,000 For Community Arts Projects
Project Assistance Programs: This program offers financial assistance for a wide range of community-oriented arts projects. Minimum funding is $1,000. Up to 50% of the total cost for a project or service is eligible for this type of funding.

Alaska

Alaska State Council on the Arts, 411 W. 4th Ave., Suite E, Anchorage, AK 99501-2343, 907-279-1558. State residency is required for individual grants to artists. The Council awards funds only to Alaskan non-profit organizations, schools or government agencies. In 1992-93, Alaska provided $1,119,322 in grant funding to non-profit organizations and artists.

1) $5,000 For Artists To Develop New Works
Individual Artist Fellowships: Non-matching $5,000 awards are given to experienced, professional artists to assist them in creating new works and/or in the development of their careers.
2) $600 For Artists To Travel To Art Conferences
Travel Grant Program: This category allows professional artists to attend in-state, national, or international art events. It pays two-thirds of travel expenses up to a maximum of $600.
3) $2,000 To Study With A Master Craftsperson, Musician, Dancer, Or Storyteller
Master Arts and Apprentice Grants in Traditional Native Arts: Grants of up to $2,000 are awarded for study with a master craftsperson, musician, dancer, or storyteller. These grants pay the fee of the master artist and other essential costs of the apprenticeship.
4) Money For Local Art Agencies
Grants to Local Arts Agencies: This category encourages arts development at the local level for community oriented projects.
5) Grants To Help Pay For Art Administration Costs
Season Support: These grants help with a portion of an organization's on going artistic and administrative functions.
6) Money To Support a Local Art Project
Project Grants: This program provides matching funds twice a year to non-profit

Be patient. If any phone number is incorrect, call (area code) 555-1212 and request the new listing.

317

Arts and Humanities

organizations, schools, and government agencies for specific local arts projects and programs.

7) Money To Pay Artists To Speak At Workshops
Workshop Grants: These grants provide an opportunity to hold short-term workshops using artists and other professionals as instructors. Grants provide all but $50 of the instructor's fee and in-state travel costs.

8) Money For Schools To Have An Artist In Residence Program
Artist Residency Grants: This category provides matching funds to Alaskan schools to support artists' residencies. It offers artists an opportunity to work with students in on-site residency situations for extended periods of up to four months.

Arizona

Arizona Arts Commission, 417 W. Roosevelt St., Phoenix, AZ 85003, 602-255-5882. Individual Artist Fellowships require state residency. Priority for organizational funding is given to projects in rural areas of the state and projects coordinated by ethnic-run organizations or those that primarily serve ethnic communities. In 1991-92, the Commission awarded $3,224,116 to state arts organizations and artists. State funding amounted to $1,345,900.

1) $7,500 For Artists and Writers
Fellowships: Awards between $5,000 and $7,500 are given in creative writing, performing arts, and visual arts.

2) $5,000 For Artists To Use For Research And Travel
Artist Projects: This category supports individual artists in all disciplines, and collaborations between artists. Awards up to $5,000 are granted to provide assistance, such as travel funds or research and development time.

3) Money To Support Special Art Projects
Project Support: This is a flexible category designed to respond to the changing needs of the arts community within the state. Artists in residence, consultant services, and festivals are included in this group. A funding scale can be obtained directly from the Arts Commission.

4) Grants To Help Run Art Organizations
Administrative/General Operating Support: This category provides grants that help with administrative expenses of arts organizations. The program is divided into three levels based upon the size of the organization's operating budget and amount of assistance needed.

5) Money For Schools To Have Artists In Residence Programs
Artists in Residence: This program provides an opportunity for artists, educators, and students to work together on in-depth creative projects. Residences usually range from two weeks to a month. Artists participating in this program are included in the Commission's Artist Roster. Schools and other community organizations use the Artist Roster to select artists for residencies. Different types of residencies include: individual artist, performing company, folklorist, teacher resource, and interdisciplinary (two or more artists in different disciplines).

6) Money For Schools With New Ideas In Art
Education Initiatives: Schools or organizations may apply for assistance to sponsor projects that include new initiatives, new elements of an existing program, or ones that expand current work being conducted in the area of arts education. Some initiatives may take multiple years to carry out and complete.

7) Help For Sponsors Who Wish To Contract With Artists
Project Support: Project support is available to sponsors who wish to contract with artists who are not on the Artist Roster.

Arkansas

Arkansas Arts Council, 1500 Tower Bldg., 323 Center St., Little Rock, AR 72201, 501-324-9150. State residency is required for individual artist programs. Funds awarded to non-profit organizations and educational institutions must be at least equally matched by the applicant organization with cash from sources other than the Council or National Endowment for the Arts (NEA). In 1993-94, $1,006,233 was awarded in grants to non-profit arts organizations. Eight fellowships were awarded for the year totalling $40,000.

1) $5,000 To Craftspersons and Artists
Fellowships: The Individual Artist Fellowship Program makes unconditional awards to professional artists in recognition of their artistic accomplishments. It is a non-matching cash award. In recognition of 1993 as the Year of American Craft, a maximum of ten $5,000 fellowships in the categories of crafts and three-dimensional visual arts were funded.

2) Grants To Arts Organizations
General Operating Support Grants: These grants provide support for non-profit agencies that produce or promote the performing, visual, or literary arts. Applicants may apply for up to 20% of their preceding year's actual income.

3) Grants To Put On Art Shows For The Public
Program Support Grants: This program assists non-profit organizations in producing, presenting, and promoting public arts events or activities that meet a specific need.

4) Money For Arts Organizations To Hire Consultants
Professional and Organizational Development Grant: This grant helps emerging Arkansas arts organizations in obtaining professional assistance. Awards are for a one-year period, although recipients may reapply the following year for further assistance.

5) Money For Schools Or Communities To Have An Artist In Residence
Arts-in-Education: Funding is used to place professional artists in school and community residences. Funds may also support educational projects to help make the arts basic in grades kindergarten through 12. Applicants must provide an equal cash match the first year with increased cash matches in subsequent years.

6) $1,000 For Emergency Arts Funding
Mini-Grants: This category provides funding throughout the year for unanticipated expenses or emergencies. Generally, grants will be less than $1,000, with most falling in the range of $500 or less.

7) More Money For Schools Or Communities To Have An Artist In Residence
Artists In Residence: This program includes several categories of grants as well as assistance for developmental activities on the local level. This program places professional artists in elementary, middle, and high schools for residencies varying in length from one week to one semester.

8) Money To Support Community Arts Activities
Community Arts Development Grants: Local arts councils may apply for project support for art service activities. Regional organizations may also be eligible.

California

California Arts Council, Public Information Council, 2411 Alhambra Blvd., Sacramento, CA 95817, 916-227-2550. State residency is required for individual artists programs. In 1992-93, the Council administered $13,800,000 in funding to non-profit arts organizations and artists. Individual artist fellowships totalled $50,000.

1) $2,500 Award To Artists, Choreographers, and Writers
Artists Fellowship Program: Each year, fellowships of $2,500 each are awarded to exemplary California resident artists. These are not project grants, but are given to recognize and honor the creative work and careers of artists. Thus, choreographers may, but dancers may not apply, playwrights but not actors, etc. At present, artists may apply only once in a four-year cycle. Categories include: 1993-94, visual arts; 1994-95, performing arts; 1995-96, media arts and new genre, and, 1996-97, literature. In 1992-93, 20 fellowships were awarded.

2) Be An Artist In Residence And Get $1,300 For 80 Hours
Artists in Residence Program: This program offers long-term interaction between professional artists and the public, in workshops sponsored by schools, government units, non-profit arts organizations, and tribal councils. The Arts Council does not maintain rosters of eligible artists or sponsors. Projects are locally developed by the artist and sponsor organization and last at least three months; most are for nine to eleven months. The Council funds two types of residencies. In an individual residency, one or two artists work with a sponsor on a project. In a multi-residency, eligible non-profit arts organizations coordinate the work of several artists at one or more sites. The individual artist earns $1,300 a month for 80 hours of project time, while multi-residency artists have varied fees and hours.

3) Money For Organizations Interested In Art-Related Activities
Organizational Support Program: This program awards grants for general operations or for projects that aid artistic or administrative development. Applicants must show two consecutive years of arts programming in California. A non-arts organization may apply if arts programming is integral to its activities. This program supports small to mid-size organizations, as well as large organizations with budgets over $1,000,000.

4) $6,000 For Multi-Cultural Arts Activities
Multi-Cultural Entry Grant Program: This program aids the development of ethnic arts groups and organizations. Awards are granted only in three-year cycles (current cycle: fiscal years 1993-95). Organizations receive $2,000 per year, for each of the three consecutive years. For the first year, grantees are free from matching requirements; thereafter, the amount of the match increases each year — 25% during the second year of the cycle and 50% for the third year. Categories include multi-cultural entry and multi-cultural advancement programs.

5) $40,000 For Multi-Cultural Grant Activities
Multi-Cultural Advancement Program: This program, also offered in three-year cycles, awards grants of up to $40,000 per year to mid-sized multi-cultural organizations to assist them in advancing to the next level of institutional development. To be eligible, an organization must have garnered a successful record of awards in the Organizational Support Program over each of the three years preceding the application.

6) Money For Organizations To Hire Performing Artists
Performing Arts Touring and Presenting Program: This program helps bring performances of high artistic quality to California audiences. Qualified non-profit organizations and government agencies may request fee support when hiring artists included in the Touring Artists Directory. Fee support consists of partial reimbursement for fees paid to the artists.

Be patient. If any phone number is incorrect, call (area code) 555-1212 and request the new listing.

7) Matching Grants For Arts Organizations
California Challenge Program: This program encourages opportunities for innovation in the arts, and requires the raising of new private sector contributions. Organizations must have annual incomes over $100,000 to be eligible for these funds. Awards must be matched two or three times the award amount in new, private contributions, depending on specific program guidelines.

Colorado

Colorado Council on the Arts CCAH, 750 Pennsylvania, Denver, CO 80203, 303-894-2617. For individual artist programs, state residency is required, unless otherwise specified. Colorado's Arts Organizations Program awarded $220,000 in 1993-94 to approximately 100 programs.

1) Grants To Individual Artists
Colorado Visions Project Grants: These grants provide direct financial support for projects undertaken by individual artists.
2) Grants To Learn From A Master Artist
Folk Arts Master/Apprentice Program: Provides direct financial support for a master artist to train a practicing artist in a traditional folk art form.
3) $5,000 To Arts Groups Serving Minorities Or Rural Areas
Entry Grants: This category supports organizations that represent minorities, underserved constituencies, rural communities, and emerging organizations. In 1993-94, 21 grants were awarded that ranged from $2,000 to $5,000.
4) Grants To Groups Who Have Been In Operation For Three Years Or More
Institutional Partnership Program: These funds support annual operating budgets for Colorado-based major institutions. Participants must have a budget of $250,000 or more for at least a three-year period prior to application to qualify for these funds.
5) Money For Special Projects
Project Grants: These grants provide support for projects designed to enhance artistic achievement, improve management, or provide the public with accessible art experiences.
6) Grants For Arts Programs In Small Towns
Rural Arts Initiatives: This program serves rural areas of the state and projects coordinated by ethnic-run organizations or serving ethnic communities.
7) Funding For Arts Programs In The Summer
Summer Activities Programs: Eligible organizations are those that produce their programming between May 15 and September 15 of each year.
8) Free Help With Managing An Arts Organization
Organizational Assistance Program: This program supplies a variety of technical and management assistance services to Colorado non-profit cultural organizations. Service areas range from grassroots fund raising to programmatic cost accounting. This is a referral program handled by CCAH staff.
9) Grants To Local Arts Councils
Community Arts Development Grants: Local arts councils may apply for project support for arts service activity or for community-based activities. Local arts councils may apply for collaborative projects with individual artists or organizations.
10) Money For Schools To Have An Artist In Residence
Artists in Residence Program: This program places professional Colorado artists in elementary, middle, and high schools for residencies varying in length from one week to one semester. Residencies are available in all disciplines.

Connecticut

Connecticut Commission on the Arts, 227 Lawrence St., Hartford, CT 06106, 203-566-4770. Individual Artist Programs: State residency is required, unless otherwise specified. In 1992-93, the Commission awarded grants totalling $904,788. Individual artist grants are federally funded.

1) $5,000 For Visual Artists
Artist Grants: Provides direct support to resident artists who have lived and worked in Connecticut for a minimum of four years at the time of application. Twenty awards of $5,000 each are distributed based on a professional peer review selection process. In 1993, grant awards were devoted to the visual arts.
2) Money For Organizations To Hire An Artist In Residence
Artists Residencies: The resource directory at the back of Artsbook lists "Brokers of Arts-in-Education Services", listing organizations which provide artists for residencies. Through the Arts in Education program, residencies are supported with Commission funding. Schools, senior centers, correctional institutions, non-profit sites and community arts centers may apply for matching funds to hire artists.
3) Money To Help Art Organizations With Long Range Planning
Multi-Year Funding: This category is designed to assist the long term development of organizations through better strategic planning, improved programs, and more stable funding. The program operates on a three-year funding cycle.
4) Grants To Arts Groups To Afford Administrative Help
Professional Development Funding: This funding assists smaller arts organizations

in obtaining professional assistance. Awards are for a one-year period, although the program will attempt to provide assistance for a maximum of three years on an annually decreasing basis, beginning with up to 50% of the position's salary for the first year, 33% for the second year, and 25% for the third year.
5) $10,000 To Produce A Show, A Festival, Or A Book
Arts Project Grants: Grants are available to organizations to produce exhibitions, festivals, literary publications, dance, music, theater, or film productions. Grants are also available to pay consultant fees for professional assistance in areas such as promotion or budgeting. The maximum award is $10,000, and the minimum award is $500.

Delaware

Delaware Division of the Arts, Carvell State Office Building, 820 North French St., Wilmington, DE 19801, 302-577-3540. Individual artist programs require state residency, unless otherwise specified. In 1993-94, the Division awarded $1,858,191 in funding. This included $65,000 in individual artist fellowships.

1) Money For New Or Established Artists
Individual Artist Fellowships: These grants provide assistance for professional development based on demonstrated creativity and skills in an art form. Grants are divided into two categories: A) Emerging Professionals with grants of $2,000 and B) Established Professionals with grants of $5,000. Recipients in the Emerging Artist category may apply in the Established Professional category after a three-year period.
2) Matching Grants For Arts Groups
Project Support Grants: These grants provide funding on a matching basis for specific arts projects. Grants may fund up to 50% of the total cash expense of each project, although awards are often less. Matching funds must be in cash and may not come from the National Endowment for the Arts.
3) Money For Operating Expenses
General Operating Support Grants: These grants support overall activities of established arts institutions. Each organization is eligible to receive a single General Operating Grant in lieu of several project grants. The two categories of General Operating Support are Primary Institutions and Program Support.
4) $500 Emergency Money For Arts Groups
Emergency Grants: Grants of up to $500 can be obtained in response to an emergency situation which requires financial assistance. Annual events or other recurring events do not qualify in this category.
5) Money For New Arts Groups To Help With Management
Grants to Emerging Organizations: Organizations may apply for matching grants of up to 50% of their budget for arts projects and/or administrative costs such as marketing, membership development, or management.
6) Money For Schools To Have An Artist In Residence
Arts in Education Residencies: This program provides matching funds to place professional literary, visual, and performing artists in educational settings for residencies of ten days to one year. A five-day residency may be approved for first-time sites and for special populations.

District of Columbia

District of Columbia Council of Arts, 410 Eight St., NW, 5th Floor, Stables Art Center, Washington, DC 20004, 202-724-5613. Individual artist programs require residency in the District of Columbia for at least one year prior to application deadline and the applicant must maintain residency during the grant period. Individuals and arts organizations may apply in one of the following disciplines: crafts, dance, interdisciplinary/performance art (individuals only), literature, media, multi-disciplinary, music, theater, and the visual arts. In 1992-93, the Commission awarded $710,000. Individuals are awarded grants which range from $1,000 to $5,000. There is no matching fund requirement.

1) $5,000 For Theater, Visual, And Literary Artists
Individuals are awarded grants which range from $1,000 to $5,000. There is no matching fund requirement.
2) $40,000 For Art Groups
Organizational Funding: Organizations are eligible to apply for grant amounts up to $40,000. Grants in this category are usually awarded in the $5,000 to $20,000 range. These funds must be matched dollar for dollar, i.e., an organization requesting $15,000 must document $30,000 in expenses. In-kind services may not be used to satisfy the matching requirement.

Florida

Florida Arts Council, Division of Cultural Affairs, Department of State, Tallahassee, FL 32399-0250, 904-487-2980. Individual Artist Programs: State residency is required, unless otherwise specified. Florida funded $2,173,800 in grants to statewide arts organizations. Fellowships for individual artists totalled $200,000 in 1992-1993.

Be patient. If any phone number is incorrect, call (area code) 555-1212 and request the new listing.

319

Arts and Humanities

1) $5,000 To Professional Artists

Individual Artist Fellowship Program: Fellowships of $5,000 each are awarded to Florida professional creative artists who have demonstrated exceptional talent and ability. In 1993-94, the Division received approximately 400 applications and awarded 40 fellowships. Fellowships may be awarded in: dance, folk art, interdisciplinary arts, literature, media arts, music, theater, and visual arts and crafts.

2) $40,000 For Arts Groups

General Program Support: This category funds day-to-day operations and programs. This type of funding is broad in scope. Grants are funded in the following disciplines: dance, folk arts, interdisciplinary arts, literature, media arts, multi-disciplinary arts, music, sponsor/presenter, theater, and visual arts. Arts organizations must meet specific discipline requirements. Grants range from $1,000 to $40,000.

3) $20,000 For Arts Related Activities

Specific Project Support: This program funds a particular project, program, or series within the applicant organization's total operations. No more than one application may be submitted in any grant cycle. Non-arts organizations may also request funding of up to $20,000. Non-profit organizations are those whose primary mission or more than half of the operating budget is not dedicated to activity in the arts. Specific projects are also funded under this category.

4) Up To $100,000 For Arts Organizations

Challenge Grant Program: This program provides funding incentives to cultural institutions or groups of institutions. Challenge grants range from $10,000 to more than $100,000 and must be matched by the applicant institution(s) on at least a three-to-one basis. In 1993-1994, $300,000 in funding was allocated.

5) $1,000 To Hire An Arts Consultant

Technical Assistance Grants: Promotes professional development for arts organizations within five funding categories including: mini-grants, staff exchange grants, consultant grants, in-service training grants, and special grants. Grants are funded up to $1,000 and generally require a dollar-for-dollar match. However, as a general rule, funding is only given for up to one-third of the project cost.

6) $20,000 For Schools To Improve Their Arts Program

Arts Education Project Support: This program has been designed to develop or strengthen arts curricula for pre-kindergarten through twelfth grade students. Grants are awarded up to $20,000.

7) $20,000 For School Teachers To Work With Artists

Special Projects: Grants fund projects addressing areas of educational significance and those with possible statewide impact. Projects may involve artist-teacher collaborations, or special populations (such as mentally or physically challenged students or the elderly) in school or non-school settings. Funding is available up to $20,000.

Georgia

Georgia Council for Arts, 530 Means St., NW, Suite 115, Atlanta, GA 30318, 404-651-7920. Individual artist programs require state residency, unless otherwise specified. In general, grant categories include: architecture/environmental arts, dance, arts-related education, film-making, folk arts/heritage arts and crafts, arts-related historic preservation, literary arts, multi-media, museums, music, photography, public radio and television, theater and visual arts. The total amount of organizational funding in 1993-94 was $2,727,660. Grants for individuals totalled $117,500.

1) $5,000 For Artists, Choreographers, And Playwrights

Individual Artist Grants: Georgia offers individual artist grants only for the creative and not for the performing arts. Thus, choreographers may, but dancers may not apply; playwrights but not actors, etc. This grant category provides support for individual Georgia artists on the basis of artistic merit. Funded artists must complete the specific projects funded. Grants range from $500 to $5,000.

2) $150,000 To Arts Organizations

Major Arts Organization Grants: This grant category provides general or project support to arts organizations which have been certified as major arts organizations, based on factors such as budget size and leadership. The maximum grant request is $150,000 and organizations must apply for funding on at least a four-to-one cash matching basis.

3) $55,000 For Arts Organizations

Arts Organization Grants: These grants provide general or project support to arts organizations and community arts councils/agencies. Grants are available in amounts of $5,000, $22,500 and $55,000, depending on the size of the non-profit organization and the length of time that it has been in operation. Organizations which apply for amounts up to the $22,500 maximum must match the request on a one-to-one basis. Organizations which apply for amounts above $22,500 up to the $55,000 maximum must match the request on a three-to-one basis. At least 75% of the match must be cash. The match also may include in-kind income-donated materials, space, or services.

4) Grants To Schools, Local Governments, And Non-Profits

Civic/Education Government/Other Grants: This grant category provides support for arts programming offered by civic, education, government, and other organizations, including educational institutions and units of local/state government. Grants fund project support for arts-related programming. Grant categories and matching requirements are the same as those listed above for arts organizations grants.

5) Money To Set Up A Local Arts Council

Arts Council/Agency Development Grants: This three-year program develops community arts councils and agencies state-wide that strengthen and encourage arts activities at the local level. Two options are available, depending upon the level of Council funding and local support. Option One provides for employment of a full-time local director/coordinator, assisted by a part-time secretary. Option Two provides for employment of a part-time director/coordinator. The Council provides in-service training and continuing consultation for the local director/coordinator, who administers a budget developed by the Council. Funding ranges from $5,000 to $15,000. This is a matching fund program.

6) Grants For Art Groups To Tour

Georgia Touring Grants: This grant category provides fee support to presenters to promote touring by groups/individuals on the Georgia Touring Roster. Presenters may request up to 25% of the fee.

7) $500 To Hire An Arts Consultant

Technical Assistance Grants: These grants provide support to improve artistic quality or managerial effectiveness through employment or consultants. Consultants may then give intensive, short-term professional advice in specific problem or growth areas. The maximum grant request is $500.

8) Georgia Folklife Program

Georgia Folklife Program: This program brings the public into contact with Georgia's indigenous, ethnic, and immigrant traditional arts through documentation and programming. During 1992-93, the Folklife Advisory Panel will assist the Council in developing a three-year plan to establish funding and programming priorities. Technical assistance is currently available to artists, arts organizations, and the general public.

9) Money For Schools To Have An Artist In Residence

Artist in Education Program: This program hires artists for residencies lasting from three to eighteen weeks, and as consultants for shorter periods. The program hires creative artists and places them in schools in all grade levels throughout the state. Disciplines include: architecture/environmental design, dance, literature, media arts, music theater, folk arts, and visual arts. The artist spends half of the time working with students and teachers and the remaining time working on his or her own creative projects in an on-site studio, open to observers by invitation. Artists in residence become temporary employees of the State of Georgia. Depending upon length and relocation needs, salaries range from $500 to $600 per week.

Hawaii

Hawaii State Foundation on Culture and Arts (SFCA), 335 Merchant St., Room 202, Honolulu, HI 96813, 808-586-0300. No fellowships were awarded this year, although a new individual artist program is being developed. For 1993-94, grants appropriated by the legislature to non-profit organizations totalled $5,950,586.

1) Grants For Concerts, Performances, Workshops, and Lectures

Organizational Funding: Grants are provided to organizations that provide services and carry out activities such as concerts, performances, workshops, lectures, exhibits, etc. Proposals are considered in eight program areas: Arts in Education, Community Arts, Ethnic Heritage and Folk Arts, Humanities, Literary Arts, Media Arts, Performing Arts (Dance/Theater and Music/Opera), and Visual and Environmental Arts.

2) $2,700 For Artists To Study As An Apprentice

The Folk Arts Program: This program provides Apprenticeship Awards, ranging from $1,600 to $2,700, that fund one-on-one instruction between a master traditional artist and an experienced apprentice.

Idaho

Idaho Commission on Arts, 304 West State St., Boise, ID 83720, 208-334-2119. Individual artist programs require state residency, unless otherwise specified. In 1993-94, the Commission funded 130 projects in 43 towns for a total of $462,347. All funds are matched by local communities. The Commission also awarded $152,200 in funding for local arts council salary assistance, rural touring fee support, FastFunds, sudden opportunity grants for artists, and traditional arts apprenticeship grants.

1) $5,000 For Artists, Dancers, Designers, and Craftspersons

Fellowship Awards: Fellowships of $5,000 are awarded in literature, music, theater, dance, media, visual arts, crafts, and design.

2) $5,000 For Artists To Work With A Master

Worksites Awards: Worksites are awarded to artists to work with a master, either in a small group, a studio, in workshops, seminars, or in a one-on-one arrangement. They are also awarded for artist residencies. Awards are funded up to $5,000.

3) $1,000 To Support An Artist's Work

Sudden Opportunity Awards: Grants of up to $1,000 are awarded to support an artist's work and/or career, and special, time-limited opportunities.

4) $1,000 Plus Travel To Study With A Master Craftsperson

Traditional Native Arts Apprenticeship Program: Supports master/apprenticeship opportunities. The usual amount awarded is $1,500. This includes approximately $10 per hour for 100 hours of instruction, plus travel and materials expenses.

5) $10,000 To Be A Writer In Residence

Writer in Residence: This $10,000 award provides recognition and financial support to a distinguished Idaho writer. The award is distributed over a two-year term.

6) $25,000 For An Arts Group

General Operating Support: Applicants may apply for single year funding of up to $15,000 or multi-year funding of up to $25,000.

7) $10,000 For Special Art Projects

Project Support: This category encourages a variety of high-quality arts activities in Idaho communities. Applicants may request up to one-half of the project costs with a minimum of $1,500 and a maximum of $10,000.

8) $5,000 For Touring Arts Groups

Performing Arts Touring: This program supports performances of exceptional quality in Idaho communities. The maximum grant available is $5,000. There is no minimum for an applied grant.

9) Grants To Bring Art To Small Towns

Arts in Rural Towns: This three-year grant encourages the creation and growth of local arts councils and presenters in rural communities. Funding is non-competitive once the organization has been accepted into the program.

10) Money For Running A Local Arts Council

Local Arts Council Salary Assistance: This category strengthens local arts councils by supporting paid management positions. This is a three-year grant. Personnel costs will be funded based on declining percentages.

11) $3,700 For An Arts Council In A Small Town

Arts in Rural Towns (ARTs): Encourages the creation and growth of local arts councils and presenters in Idaho's rural communities. This three-year funding commitment totals $3,700.

12) FastFunds: This category provides timely assistance to meet unanticipated opportunities for presenting or producing the arts. Grants are available for up to one-half of the project costs, up to $1,500.

13) Money To Build A Cultural Facility

Cultural Facilities Grants: These grants encourage local support, both public and private, for feasibility studies, renovation, or construction of performance, exhibition, or artist spaces. Organizations may apply for up to $10,000. Grant funds must be matched with an equal amount of cash.

14) $500 To Artists and Schools To Improve Arts Education

Technical Assistance: This flexible program provides grants from $100 to $500 to artists, (including folk artists), arts educators, arts organizations, and school administrators to improve their effectiveness in the arts or through arts education.

15) Money For Schools Or Nursing Homes To Have An Artist In Residence

Artists in Residence: This category provides opportunities for artists to work in school and community residencies. Artists and companies are selected for inclusion in Idaho's Roster of Arts in education, and touring artists. Artists are then contacted directly by the sponsoring organization regarding available residencies. Minimum residency length is ten days. In most cases, grants range from $850 to $2,400 and pay up to 50% of the projects's total costs.

16) $600 For Creative Art Teachers

Master Teacher Awards: Grants of up to $600 are awarded to assist Idaho teachers in the development of innovative arts education curriculum.

17) $3,500 For New Ideas In Arts Education

Special Projects Awards: Grants from $700 to $3,500 are awarded to encourage innovative efforts in arts education. Grants cover up to 50% of total project costs.

Illinois

Illinois Arts Council, State Of Illinois Center, 100 West Randolph, Suite 10-500, Chicago, IL 60601, 312-814-6750. Individual artist programs require state residency, unless otherwise specified. In fiscal year 1993, the Commission awarded over $6,056,031 in federal and state funding to non-profit arts organizations. Individuals received $217,000 in funding. In addition to the programs detailed, grants are funded for choral music and opera, dance, ethnic and folk arts, symphonies and ensemble, theater, and visual arts programs.

1) $10,000 for Artists, Photographers, Writers, and Poets

Fellowships: Non-matching fellowships in fixed amounts of $5,000 and $10,000 and Finalist Awards of $500 are awarded to exceptional Illinois artists. Fellowships are awarded in: choreography, crafts, ethnic and folk arts, interdisciplinary/ performance arts, media arts, music composition, photography, playwriting/screenwriting, poetry, prose, and the visual arts.

2) Grants To Artists To Study As Apprentices

Apprenticeship Program: This program provides grants which recognize and foster the master/artist apprenticeship relationship.

3) $1,000 For Writers And Non-Profit Magazines

Literary Awards: Awards of $1,000 are given each year for the publication of new quality writing by Illinois writers appearing in non-profit magazines.

4) Money To Provide Art To Communities Normally Deprived Of Art

Access Program: This category supports projects designed to explore new strategies that enrich the artistic diversity of the state and involve the culture of under-represented populations.

5) Grants To Groups That Support Creative Writers

Literature Programs: This category supports organizations which promote the creation, publication, and distribution of creative writing.

6) Money For Film and Video Production

Media Program: This program funds organizations engaged in the production of film, video, and audio art, as well as exhibition and service organizations that promote the creation, distribution, and public awareness of the media arts.

7) Funding For Interdiscipline Art Programs

Multi-Disciplinary Programs: These programs support and assist projects and institutions whose activities combine or involve two or more art disciplines.

8) Grants For Performing Arts

Presenters Development Programs: Programming/operation support is provided to presenters of quality performing arts activities.

9) Money For Touring Art Groups

ArtsTour: This program provides fee support to presenting organizations for Illinois performing groups/artists.

10) Special Money For Arts Programs and Projects

Special Assistance Grants: These grants are available throughout the year to address specific artistic, programming, administrative, or technical needs.

11) Money For Schools Or Other Organizations To Have An Artist In Residence

Artists in Residence: This category supports artist residencies in school and community-based organizations.

12) Grants For Schools To Develop Special Art Classes

Arts Resource: This program assists schools with their efforts to develop curriculum for comprehensive arts programs.

Indiana

Indiana Arts Commission, 402 W. Washington St., Room 072, Indianapolis, IN 46204-2741, 317-232-1268. Individual Artist Programs: State residency is required, unless otherwise specified. Grants are awarded in 16 categories: dance, design arts, education, expansion arts, folk arts, literature, local arts agencies, media arts, multi-arts, museums, music, presenters, statewide arts service organizations, theater, and visual arts. In fiscal year 1993, the Commission awarded $2,492,319 in grants awards and services and $105,000 in Individual Artist Fellowships to 30 Indiana artists.

1) Grants To Individual Artists

Individual Artist Fellowships: Non-matching cash grants are awarded to help develop the careers of visual, performing, media, literary, and folk artists. Artists may use the grants for specific projects, to purchase supplies, or to develop new techniques.

2) Grants To Arts Organizations

General Operating Support: This category assists arts organizations that create, produce, present, or otherwise service the arts. The program helps established institutions support their overall activities, and grants are awarded to organizations for a complete organization plan rather than for a specific project. The grant is awarded to organizations that have received at least two previous IAC Arts Projects and Series grants in at least two of the last three fiscal years.

3) Grants To Local Arts Organizations

State and Local Partnership: This category provides grants that assist local arts or community agencies throughout Indiana. The grant is awarded to organizations that have received at least two previous IAC Arts Projects and Series grants in at least two of the last three fiscal years.

4) Grants To Run Special Art Projects

Arts Projects and Series: Funds arts organizations and other non-profit organizations that conduct high-quality arts activities. Funding is provided for a single activity or a series of activities. Individual artists seeking funding must have the sponsorship of a non-profit applicant organization that is responsible for the project and will administer the funds. Up to 50% of a project's cost may be funded.

5) Money For Artists In Residence Programs

Arts in Education Grants: These grants place professional artists in educational settings throughout Indiana. During the program, artists spend one-half of their time as practicing artists in educational settings and the other half in independent, creative work. Residencies range from one to eight months and artists are paid on a per diem basis.

6) $2,000 To Bring Artists Into Schools

Visiting Arts Program: This program brings artists into Indiana sites with on going educational programming for short-term residencies, student or teacher workshops, or educational performances. The IAC offers grants of up to $2,000 for educational programs.

Be patient. If any phone number is incorrect, call (area code) 555-1212 and request the new listing.

321

7) Money For Multi-Cultural Or Rural Art Activities

Arts: Rural and Multi-cultural (ARM) Program: ARM grants support activities in Indiana's rural and multi-cultural communities. Grants are available for touring, technical assistance, and arts projects. The IAC covers 75% of an activity's fees, while applicants must provide the remaining portion.

8) Money For Art Administrators To Attend Workshops

Technical Assistance: Grants in this category fund consultant services for organizations on technical matters, administrative functions, and problem-solving techniques. Arts professionals can get financial assistance through these grants to attend conferences and workshops.

9) $4,000 To Put On An Art Show

Presenter Touring Program: This category encourages the presentation of high-quality art throughout the state. Grants of up to $4,000 are given to presenters to assist with the fees for sponsoring and presenting the groups and exhibitions listed in the IAC's adjudicated Artist Directory.

Iowa

Iowa Council On Arts, Capitol Complex, Des Moines, IA 50319, 515-281-4451. Individual artist programs require state residency, unless otherwise specified. In 1992-93, non-profit institutions such as schools and libraries received $138,441 in funding. Non-profit arts organizations received $288,524. Grants to individual artists totalled $10,240.

1) Money For Individual Artists

Individual Artist Programs: Artist Mini-Grants provide direct financial assistance to Iowa artists to support opportunities in the grants listed below. Project Mini-Grants, Professional Development Mini-Grants, and Arts Education Mini-Grants are limited to $500. Training grants are limited to $200. State residency is required.

2) Money For Artists To Work On Special Projects

Artist Project Grants: Grants support projects that are designed and managed by artists. The type of projects funded in this category are intentionally broad so artists may develop projects which meet their individual needs. Projects may include research and development or the completion or presentation of a work in progress.

3) Money To Help Artists With Financial, Legal, Or Marketing Problems

Artist Professional Development Grants: Grants support individual artists seeking professional development opportunities. Examples may include career planning, financial management, legal aspects, marketing, professional presentations, and technical assistance.

4) Money For Artists To Attend Out-Of-State Seminars

Artist Training Grants: These grants support individual artists who attend training opportunities such as seminars, workshops, and conferences. Out-of-state travel is an allowable expense.

5) Grants For Artists To Learn More About Their Craft

Artist Arts Education Grants: These awards support opportunities for artists to develop, enhance, or expand their knowledge and materials of their art form for use in educational settings. Projects may include research, development and/or implementation of arts education projects.

6) $1,000 For Local Artists To Show Their Work

Community Folk Arts Residency Program: This program allows apprentice and master artists the opportunity to showcase their skills in their local community or region of Iowa. Residencies should take place at a public location such as a local arts council, school, local museum, library, or city/county historical society. Residency costs should be kept between $500 and $1,000.

7) $1,000 For Artists To Work Towards A College Degree In Art

Iowa Scholarship for the Arts: This annual award encourages the development of high school seniors and college students who excel in the arts and who have enrolled in educational programs leading to careers in the arts. Up to five scholarships of $1,000 each may be awarded. Awards are for undergraduate study only, and must be used for tuition at the institution where recipients are enrolled.

8) $1,000 For Poets And Writers

Iowa Literary Awards Prospectus: This competition recognizes outstanding Iowa poets and fiction writers. There are two awards in each category. First prize is a $1,000 cash award and second prize is a $500 cash award.

9) Money To Provide Art To Those Who Normally Don't Participate

Special Constituencies Program: This program supports arts residencies for the traditionally unserved and underserved audiences, e.g., the elderly, institutionalized, disadvantaged and at-risk populations, including youth, and projects for people with physical and/or mental disabilities. Residencies vary in length from one day to one year and in frequency (daily, monthly, etc.). A two-hour minimum project is required. Artist fees are $650 per week, $150 per day, and $30 per hour.

10) $3,000 To Produce Visual Or Performance Art

Arts to Go Presenter Program: Provides Iowa non-profit organizations financial assistance in presenting high quality music, theater, and dance performance or literary readings in their communities. The presenter should contact one or more artists/companies on the Arts to Go Roster and confirm contractual arrangements. Presenters may request up to 50%, or $3,000, whichever is less, for each artist/company booked.

11) $500 To Help Art Groups

Technical Assistance: Matching grants of up to $500 are available to assist organizations in strengthening the effectiveness of their structure, programs, or services.

12) Grants To Arts Organizations

Operational Support Grants: A limited number of grants are awarded for general operating support to large-budgeted and mid-sized organizations that provide cultural and managerial excellence on a continuing basis. Large-budgeted organizations are funded on a two-year cycle. Mid-sized organizations may receive up to $10,000 annually and must demonstrate the ability to match the award in cash.

13) $1,600 To Non-Profits To Develop Art Projects

Project Support: These grants provide financial incentives for non-profit organizations to develop and maintain art projects that make the arts accessible to Iowa residents at the grassroots level. The funding average in this matching grant category is $1,600.

14) $500 In Emergency Art Money For Organizations

Emergency Project Support: This category provides up to $500 in emergency support for projects unforeseen at the time of deadline for Project Support Grants.

15) $200 To Help Train Art Administrators

Training Grants: Up to $200 in non-matching funds is available to organizations wanting to strengthen the administrative skills of staff or volunteers.

16) $1,000 For Arts Education Programs

Area Education Agencies Grants: The Council provides matching grants of up to $1,000 per project to agencies to fund arts education opportunities within their area. Projects must provide professional staff development or in-service training in one or more of the major arts disciplines.

17) Money For Schools To Have An Artist In Residence

Artists in Schools/Communities Residencies: Residencies encourage collaborations between schools and local organizations. Projects must be at least five days in length and no more than four-and-a-half hours per day. Artists are available in the following disciplines: literature, theater, music, folk arts, dance, visual arts, opera/music theater, design arts, crafts, photography/ holography/media art, or interdisciplinary. The applicant organization must contact an artist for the project from the residency roster available prior to submitting an application. The standard artist's fee, $750 for a one-week project, must be matched in cash by the applicant organization.

18) Money For Art Management Training

Arts Education Mini-Grants: Matching grants are available to organizations to develop and implement arts education programs or projects. Funding may be used for conferences, in-service training, or innovative projects. Grants must be matched dollar-for-dollar in cash.

Kansas

Kansas Arts Commission, Jayhawk Tower, 700 Jackson, Suite 1004, Topeka, KS 66603-3714, 913-296-3335. Individual Art programs require state residency. The Commission provides direct or indirect funding to artists, schools, government units, and cultural, social and educational organizations as well as non-profit organizations. Major grants are awarded each May for the following fiscal year. In 1992-93, $946,748 was awarded in funding to 241 non-profit organizations. Three individual artists were awarded fellowships of $5,000 each. The Folk Artist Apprenticeship Program was awarded $22,000.

1) $5,000 For Artists And Writers

Fellowships in the Performing Arts: The Commission awards up to four fellowships to outstanding Kansas artists. Fellowships are $5,000 each. A rotating cycle has been established to offer fellowships in a different field each year. Fellowships in literature will be awarded in 1994.

2) $500 For Artists Creating Original Work

Professional Development Grant Program: Grants of up to $500 each are awarded to individual creative artists from a $5,000 funding pool. Awards encourage the development of Kansas-resident artists who are creating original work in any discipline. Grants are designed to help cover up to 50% of project expenses. These expenses must clearly demonstrate the next step of the artist's development.

3) Money For Folk Artists To Work As Apprentices

Folk Arts Apprenticeship Program: This program preserves traditional, folk and ethnic crafts, trades, music, and dance by bringing together qualified apprentices with recognized master artists living in Kansas. Each approved apprenticeship is eligible for grant support to help cover expenses.

4) Money To Start A Community Art's Organization

Local Arts Agency Support: This category provides up to 50% of basic operating expenses to a publicly accountable community organization or city or county government agency that provides cultural planning and development.

5) Money To Support Local Art Agencies

Basic Program Support: This program provides 50% of the operating costs for arts agencies, and for arts programs at non-arts agencies with a structure similar to a separate non-profit agency (with a governing board or advisory group and a separate budget).

6) Grants To Produce Art Publications, Workshops, Exhibits, and Performances
Project Support: Grants provide up to 50% of the expenses for one-time or stand-alone arts events. These may include workshops, exhibitions, publications, performances, and lectures or demonstrations.

7) Money To Groups That Help Artists
Statewide Arts Service Organizations: This category funds up to 50% of basic operating and programming expenses for organizations that provide professional development, networking, and educational services to a specific arts constituency that is intrastate or statewide.

8) $2,000 To Schools To Improve Their Art Education
Planning Education in the Arts in Kansas (PEAK): PEAK offers grants of up to $2,000 to schools or school districts that express a commitment to improve education opportunities for children.

9) Money For Schools and Organizations To Have An Artist In Residence
Artist in Residency and Visiting Artist Grants: These grants provide schools, organizations, and institutions with matching funds and a roster of professional artists in most disciplines for symbiotic residencies of varying lengths. Residencies vary in length from one day to a full academic year. The Visiting Artist component offers residencies of one to five days.

Kentucky

Kentucky Arts Council, 31 Fountain Place, Frankfort, KY 40601, 502-564-3757. Matching grants from the Council are available to Kentucky non-profit organizations committed to providing arts programs and services to the public. Grant amounts vary from year to year and depend upon the availability of funds. Non-matching fellowships are available to Kentucky artists. Interim Grants are available in all program areas to provide one-time funding for emergencies or for unexpected and outstanding opportunities in the arts. In 1992-93, non-profit organizations received $956,466 in state and federal funding. Individual artists received $111,000 in fellowships.

1) Money To Produce Art Projects
Project and Touring Grants: These grants provide opportunities to enhance or complement an arts organization's artistic development.

2) Money To Hire An Arts Management Consultant
Consultant Grants: Funding in this category provides technical assistance for artistic and management improvements.

3) Grants To Arts Organizations
Challenge Grants: Grants in this category act as incentives for broad-based, on going private support of arts organizations.

4) Money To Help Pay Artists And Art Administrators
Arts Development Grants: Grants are designed for long-term organizational and artistic improvements and salary assistance supplements for top-level professional artistic and management positions.

5) Grants For Local Art Projects
Project and Touring Grants: Funding is provided for community and folk art projects that strengthen and stimulate local and neighborhood arts activity or share local arts with other Kentucky communities.

6) Grants To Support Rural Art Projects
Special Initiatives: Funding is provided for specific issues such as rural arts development.

7) Money For Communities Which Have Little Access To Art
Consultant Grants: Funding encourages on going arts programming to communities where little presently exists.

8) Money For Communities To Have An Artist In Residence
Community Artist Residencies: Residencies support outstanding artists.

9) Money For Schools To Have An Artist In Residence
Artists in Residence Grants: These grants place outstanding professional artists in educational and community settings.

10) Grants For Teachers To Put Art In Their Classrooms
Teacher Incentive Project Grants: Grants fund projects, designed by teachers in collaboration with professional artists, which use artists residencies to integrate the arts into the regular classroom or to strengthen and enrich teaching in the arts.

11) Funding For Art Projects In Education
Project and Touring Grants: These grants fund projects which demonstrate the value of arts in education.

Louisiana

Louisiana State Division of the Arts, P.O. Box 44247, Baton Rouge, LA 70804, 504-342-8180. Individual artist programs require state residency. In 1992-93, only federal funds were available. The Division of the Arts administered $467,503 in grants to non-profit organizations. Individual fellowships totalled $25,800.

1) $5,000 For Artists, Craftspersons, Designers, and Musicians
Artist Fellowships: Non-matching artist fellowships of $5,000 are awarded to artists of exceptional talent from the following disciplines: crafts, dance, design arts, folklife, literature, media, music, theater, and visual arts.

2) $5,000 For Artists To Work With A Master
Folklife Apprenticeships: Non-matching apprenticeship grants of up to $5,000 are available to master folk artists and apprentices who will work together during an apprenticeship period.

3) $15,000 For Art Organizations
Project Assistance Program: This program provides project support for specific activities or services, growth and administrative development, increased arts services for the community, opportunities for involvement of individual professional artists, and contributions to the cultural enrichment of the general public. Grants are available in the following disciplines: dance, design arts, folklife, literature, media, multi-discipline, music, theater, and visual arts and crafts. Grants do not exceed $15,000 and must be matched at least dollar for dollar in either cash or in a combination of cash and in-kind contributions. At least 50% of the amount requested must be matched with cash.

4) $1,000 For Arts Management Training
Technical Assistance: This pilot project promotes professional development in emerging arts organizations. Grants are available to assist organizations to obtain artistic or management consultation or training. Grants are offered up to $1,000 and must be matched on a one-to-one basis in cash.

5) Up To $350,000 For Local Arts Agencies
Local Arts Agency Program: This program is divided into two categories:
A) Local Arts Agency Level One: This category funds established arts agencies that provide diverse programs and services in their communities or region. Organizations must have had annual operating revenues of $100,000 or more for the preceding fiscal year and have at least one full-time, paid professional staff member. Grants do not exceed $350,000 or 50% of the projected year's cash budget, excluding Division of the Arts Grants.
B) Local Arts Agency Level Two: Local arts agencies in the early stages of development fall under this category. Grants may be used for planning, operations, special projects, or organizational and professional staff development. Grants do not exceed $10,000 or 50% of the projected year's budget. Grants must be matched dollar for dollar in either cash or a combination of cash and in-kind services. At least 50% of the amount requested must be matched with cash.

6) Up To $350,000 For Art Groups
General Operating Support: This program provides support for organizations whose programming has a major impact on their communities and on the state's cultural environment. There are two funding levels:
A) Level One provides support for organizations whose annual budget is $500,000 or more. Grants cannot exceed $350,000, or 50% of the projected year's cash budget, excluding Division of the Arts grants.
B) Level Two provides support for organizations whose budget is at least $100,000, but less than $500,000. Funding does not exceed $75,000, or 50% of the projected year's cash budget, excluding Division of the Arts Grants.

7) Money For Schools To Develop Art Programs
Educational Funding: Louisiana's Arts in Education Programming provides support for the Arts Basic Program, Residencies, and Projects. Grants may be requested for up to 50% of the total cost of a project or artist residency. Grants must be matched at least dollar for dollar in cash or a combination of cash and in-kind contributions. At least 50% of the amount requested must be matched with cash.
A) Arts Basic: This category provides planning or programming grants which assist in making the arts basic to the kindergarten through twelfth grade curriculum in Louisiana schools.
B) Arts in Education Residencies: Residencies place professional artists or folklorists in public and private, elementary and secondary schools to work and demonstrate their art forms. Visiting Artists (1-10 days per site or school), Short-Term Residencies (11-40 days per semester), and Long-Term Residencies (41 or more days per semester) are funded.
C) Arts in Education Projects support specific arts-related activities which relate to the artistic educational development of elementary and secondary school students.

Maine

Maine Arts Commission, State House Station 25, Augusta, ME 04333, 207-287-2724. Individual artist programs require state residency. Maine offers an Institutional Support Program which provides two-year funding for established professional, non-profit cultural organizations, schools, and other organizations for specific local arts projects and programs. In 1992-93, $811,471 was awarded in state funding to Maine non-profit organizations. Individual artists were awarded $33,351 in fellowships.

1) $3,000 To Artists
Fellowships: A limited number of fellowships are provided to Maine artists in recognition of artistic excellence. Up to six awards of $3,000 may be awarded

annually.

2) $1,200 For Master Artists To Teach Others

Traditional Arts Apprenticeships: Up to seven awards of $1,200 each are given to master artists to teach apprentices their respective arts.

3) Grants To Arts Organizations

Operating Support: This multi-year grant supports the on going work of the state's leading cultural institutions. The grant amount requested is determined by a formula that takes a base dollar amount, plus a percentage of the applicant's operating budget. For 1992-93 this amount was $3,000, plus 1% of the applicant's total revenues.

4) Up To $20,000 For Special Art Programs

Project Support: This highly competitive grant funds innovative projects in the arts and creative projects within the on going work of the organization. Grants do not exceed $20,000 for the two-year grant period, or more than 30% of an organization's annual operating budget.

5) $850 For Community Arts Programs

Regional Arts Program: This program was designed to generate interest and participation in the arts at the community level. The Commission selects seven non-profit arts organizations from seven regions of the state as regranting sites. Grants do not exceed $650. All grants must be matched on a one-to-one cash basis.

6) $2,500 For Multi-Cultural Arts Programs In Schools

Special Projects in Arts Education: This pilot program encourages non-cultural institutions and schools to collaborate with one another. Applicants may request up to $2,500. A 50/50 cash match is required. Both collaborators must show a cash commitment to the project.

7) $2,000 For School Teachers To Go To Art Seminars

Professional Development for Teachers: Funding is available for teacher conferences, seminars, workshops, and long term summer institutes. Applicants may request up to $2,000. A 50/50 cash match is required. Requests in the $500 - $1,000 range are encouraged.

Maryland

Maryland State Arts Council, 601 N. Howard St., Baltimore, MD 21201, 410-333-8232. The Council provides direct grants to individual artists, offers professional advice, and initiates projects that provide services and opportunities for Maryland artists. State residency is required for participation. The Council's Community Arts Development program supports county arts council organizations in each of the 23 counties of Maryland and Baltimore City. Funds are used in each county to regrant to local arts organizations, support various arts programs, assist local arts groups with fund raising, publicity, promotion and planning, and to support the operating expenses of the county arts council. In 1993, the Council awarded $5,352,792 in state funding to organizations through 251 grants. Eighty-two grants to individual artists totalled $173,000.

1) $6,000 For Creative Artists

Individual Artist Awards: Awards range from $1,000 to $6,000 and are based solely on the basis of creative excellence.

2) Money For Large Arts Organizations

Grants to Major Institutions: These grants offer general operating support to established non-profit, tax exempt Maryland cultural institutions which offer high quality arts programming and services. Organizations must have had an independent board of directors and professional staff and an operating budget of at least $1,000,000 for the two most recently completed fiscal years.

3) Grants To Groups Who Provide Art To Children And Communities

General Operating Grants: These grants are designed for arts organizations whose programming have substantial impact on their communities. Grants are awarded in: children's events, dance, folk arts/heritage, literature, media, multi-discipline, music, theater and visual arts. Eligible organizations are those that produce or present the arts through public programs or services. All grants must be matched at minimum on a three-to-one basis. Up to 10% of an arts organization's operating cash expenses may be funded.

4) Money To Support Innovative Art Projects

Special Project Grants: Under this category, grants are awarded to organizations involved in clearly innovative activities. The minimum grant request is $1,000 and funding cannot exceed more than 50% of the project's total cost. All Special Project Grants must be matched at least dollar for dollar with funds from non-Maryland state sources.

5) Grants To Non-Arts Groups

Grants to Non-Arts Organizations: The Council offers program and project grant assistance to non-arts organizations that provide arts programming to the general public. These settings may include colleges, libraries, churches, and community services.

6) Help For Those Interested In Maryland Folklife

Maryland Folklife Program: Provides research and technical support to individuals and organizations engaged in the study and interpretation of Maryland's folk culture. Activities include public talks, film screening to community groups, and advice in the design of exhibitions, festivals, concerts, and other main events.

8) Money For Poets, Artists, and Performers To Be At Schools

Artists in Education Program: This program provides funds, augmented by a grant from the National Endowment for the Arts, for residencies and visits to schools and other educational settings by poets, artists, and performers. Schools and other sponsoring organizations provide partial funding for projects that vary from one-day visits to three-month residencies. Disciplines include poetry, visual arts, and performing arts.

9) Help With Managing Arts Organizations

Arts Advancement Program: This program provides technical assistance and management support services to producing and presenting arts organizations throughout the state. The program includes workshops, organizational analysis, management audits, and long-term planning and development constituencies.

Massachusetts

Massachusetts Cultural Council, 80 Boylston St., 10th Floor, Boston, MA 02116, 617-727-3668. Individual artist programs require state residency, unless otherwise specified. The Massachusetts Cultural Council (MCC) offers grants and services to 2,500 schools, 335 local arts lottery councils in 348 communities, 1,500 non-profit cultural organizations and individual practitioners. The Commission's 1993-94 budget is $5,408,839. In 1993-94, $100,000 was appropriated for individual fellowships.

1) $5,000 To Creative Artists, Craftspersons, and Scientists

Individual Project Support: This category provides an opportunity for individual artists, humanists, and interpretive scientists to apply directly to the council for support of creative and innovative projects. Categories for fiscal year 1993 include crafts and new approaches to science literacy. Awards range from $2,000 to $5,000. Projects must culminate in a formal public presentation in cooperation with a cultural organization, community center, government agency, or corporation.

2) $15,000 For Arts Organizations

General Project Support: This program supports cultural programs and services of excellence for the general public. A project can be a single event or a series of activities. The Council encourages collaborations. Organizations must have completed one year of cultural programming prior to application deadline and have a minimum operating budget of $2,500. Applicants can request up to 50% of the total project cost. Grants range from $2,000 to $15,000 and must be matched on a one-to-one basis with cash and in-kind goods and services.

3) $15,000 To Provide Art To Children

Education Project Support: This category provides direct services to children, particularly inner-city youth, those in rural areas, and those in low-income communities, as well as those with differing abilities and bilingual students. Organizations must have completed one year of cultural programming prior to application deadline and have a minimum operating budget of $2,500. The Council will fund up to 50% of the total project cost. Grants range from $2,000 to $15,000 and must be matched on a one-to-one basis with cash and in-kind goods and services.

4) Money To Provide Artist In Residence To Schools

Residency Program: Residencies provide the opportunity for students and teachers to work with an artist from five to forty or more days. The artist must spend a minimum of two days per week in the school throughout the length of the residency. The Council will pay from 40% to 70% of an artist's fee of $150 per day, depending on the length of the residency.

Michigan

Michigan Council for the Arts, 1200 Sixth St., Detroit, MI 48226, 313-256-3731. The Council for the Arts was recently restructured. Grant programs are arranged in three general funding programs: Arts Organizations, Arts Projects, and Individual Artists. Any non-profit organization or institution, artist, local government, school or community group in Michigan is eligible to apply for MCA grant funds. All funded activities must take place within the state and comply with Equal Opportunity Standards. Contact the Council for specific program guidelines. In 1992-93, $4,094,908 was awarded in state funding of arts programming.

Minnesota

Minnesota State Arts Board, 432 Summit Ave., St. Paul, MN 55102, 612-297-2603. Individual artist programs require state residency, unless otherwise specified. In 1992-93, the Board administered $3,936,126 in funding to 173 non-profit organizations. Thirty-four individual fellowships were awarded totalling $204,000. Grants to individual artists totalled $254,500.

1) $6,000 For Visual, Literary, Or Performing Artists

Fellowships: These year-long fellowships recognize outstanding professional artists working in the visual, literary, and performing arts. All fellowships are $6,000.

2) $1,000 For Artists To Improve Their Careers

Career Opportunity Grants: These awards help artists take advantage of impending, concrete opportunities that will significantly advance their work or careers. Projects must be unique short-term opportunities. Grants are available in variable amounts from $100 to $1,000. A total of $5,500 is available during each review cycle.

3) Money For Art Studio In Sausalito, California
Headlands Residency Project: This residency program for Minnesota creative artists is at Headlands Center for the Arts in Sausalito, CA, near San Francisco. Artists receive a travel allowance, living stipend, housing, and studio space for three to five months to live and work with other artists.

4) $4,000 To Be An Apprentice Craftsperson
Folk Arts Apprenticeship Grants: These non-matching grants are given for the serious study of traditional arts between a master artist and apprentice. Grant awards range from $100 to $4,000.

5) $4,000 For Folk Art Research And Festivals
Folk Arts Sponsorship Grants: This category provides annual matching grants for research and presentation of Minnesota folk arts events. Grants range from $100 to $4,000.

6) $3,000 For Artists To Travel More Than 60 Miles From Home
Minnesota Touring Arts: This three-year program promotes increased touring by performing artists within the state and 60 miles or more from their home base. Selected groups will receive up to 30% of their artistic fees for touring performances. The maximum grant for each performance is $3,000. Selected groups may also receive up to $1,000 for technical assistance.

7) $10,000 To Organizations Who Help Artists
Operating Support Program: This program provides unrestricted operating support to arts organizations that produce or exhibit works of art or offer a broad range of services to artists. Grant amounts are up to 10% of their cash income budget. Minimum grants range between $5,000 and $10,000.

8) $5,000 To Organizations That Help More Than 5 Artists
Series Presenters Programs: This category funds non-profit, tax exempt groups which present five or more professional artists or artistic companies in a community during an annual season. Grants are awarded up to 20% of cash expenses. The minimum grant is $5,000.

9) Money For Schools To Improve Their Arts Program
Organizational Support Grants: This category encourages and expands the delivery of cost efficient quality arts programs to Minnesota schools. Grants are awarded to Minnesota arts organizations that offer school residencies of at least five days in length. Matching grants are available in variable amounts and do not exceed one-half of residency expenses.

10) Money For Schools To Have An Artist In Residence
School Support Grants: Matching grants are awarded to elementary and secondary schools to sponsor individual arts residencies which range from five days to one year in length. Schools may request up to one-half of residency expenses.

Mississippi
Mississippi Arts Commission, 239 North Lamar St., Suite 207, Jackson, MS 39201, 601-359-6030. Individual artist programs require state residency. In 1992-93, the Commission awarded $619,045 in organizational funding. Four individual artist fellowships were awarded totalling $19,000. Four folk art apprenticeships were also funded totalling $7,794.

1) $5,000 For Writers, Composers, Video Producers
Artist Fellowships: Non-matching fellowships of up to $5,000 are awarded to individual artists in disciplines designated each year. Awards are based on the quality of past work. For 1994, categories include the visual arts, choreography, and film, video, and media.

2) $30,000 For Arts And Cultural Organizations
General Operating Support: This category provides funds for on going activities within arts and cultural organizations (not local arts agencies) or major arts divisions of non-profit organizations. Grant awards average between $10,000 and $30,000. Organizations are encouraged to apply for 10% of the actual cash revenues they received the previous fiscal year.

3) $25,000 For Local Arts Agencies
Local Arts Agencies: Applicants are encouraged to apply for 25% their income. Grants average between $5,000 and $25,000.

4) $9,000 For New Arts Organizations
Organizational Development: This category provides support for on going activities of new arts and cultural organizations, incorporated for seven years or less. Organizations with a full-time professional director working at least 35 hours per week may apply for up to $9,000. Organizations with part-time or volunteer staff may apply for up to $5,000.

5) $5,000 For Special Art Projects
Project Support: This category funds a wide variety of arts projects and/or arts components of larger projects. Organizations may apply for funding for more than one project. However, the total for all projects cannot exceed $5,000 in any fiscal year.

6) $2,000 To Help Touring Artists

Mississippi Touring Arts: Fifty percent of an artist's fees, up to $2,000, are covered from the Touring Arts Rosters program.

7) $7,000 For Local Schools To Improve Their Art Programs
Arts in Education: This program advances basic arts education for all students, including the gifted and talented, in kindergarten through the twelfth grade. Up to $7,000 in matching funds are awarded.

Missouri
Missouri State Council on the Arts, Wainwright Office Complex, 111 N. 7th St., Suite 105, St. Louis, MO 63101-2188, 314-340-6845. The Council offers financial assistance through seven art areas: dance, literature, media, multi-discipline, music, theater, and visual arts. A program administrator supervises applications in each area. In 1992-93, Missouri granted $4,414,799 to 227 non-profit, tax exempt state-based arts organizations. The Council is unable to fund fellowships to individuals.

1) Money For Smaller Arts Organizations
Community Arts Program (CAP): This program helps non-metropolitan community arts councils and other local arts coordinating agencies sponsor projects in more than one art form. It also helps arts agencies upgrade their management abilities. Financial assistance is available for up to 50% of project support, arts agency administration salary support, and office support. See Council guidelines for geographic restrictions.

2) $2,000 For New Art Projects
Community Arts Special Projects: Organizations may apply for up to $2,000 for new projects not covered in its Community Arts Program application. Priority is given to new CAP applicants.

3) Money For Arts Groups Serving The Entire State
Statewide Arts Service Organizations: This category provides financial assistance to organizations in the delivery of service to their statewide (or multi-state) arts constituency. Eligible organizations must be governed by a board of directors that has representation throughout the state and/or from a multi-state area.

4) $2,000 To Help Art Organizations With Management Development
Technical Assistance: This category helps arts organizations develop specific administrative and technical skills. Eligible activities might include contracting with a consultant to assist the organization in a particular area, or defraying the cost of attending a workshop or conference that will help the organization develop needed skills and expertise. Funding of up to $2,000 may be requested. Applicants must provide at least 25% of the project's cost.

5) Money For Schools To Have An Artist In Residence
Artist Residency Program: This program offers Missouri students and adults the opportunity to participate in artist residencies which promote and enrich existing arts curricula. It offers artists an opportunity to work with students in on-site residency situations for extended periods of time. Artists are paid on a per diem basis.

6) Money To Learn From Folk Art Masters
Traditional Arts Apprenticeship Program: This program provides opportunities for qualified apprentices to learn style, technique, and repertoire from recognized folk art masters. This program is administered by the University of Missouri Cultural Heritage Center in Columbia. Funding is provided by the Council and the National Endowment of the Arts (NEA).

Montana
Montana Arts Council, 48 N. Last Chance Gulch, Helena, MT 59620, 406-444-6430. Individual artist programs require state residency. In the 1992-93 biennium, $1,300,000 was awarded for 101 projects in 32 communities. Grants ranged from $1,000 to $73,400. The average grant was approximately $13,000. It is estimated that $670,000 may be available for each year of the 1994-95 grant period.

1) $2,000 To Individual Artists
Individual Artist Fellowships: Awards of $2,000 are presented annually to artists of merit. Decisions are based on the quality of an artist's work and are awarded in a variety of disciplines.

2) $6,000 For Arts Organizations
Organizational Funding: Each dollar in grant funds must be matched by the applicant with one dollar in cash or in-kind goods and services. At least one-third of the amount requested must be matched in cash. Grants seldom exceed $6,000 and the average grant is $1,500.

3) Grants For Arts Preservation, Media Arts, Archaeology, and Folklore
Cultural and Aesthetic Project Grants: These grants are awarded by the legislature for a two-year period. Grants are awarded in: visual, performing, literary and media arts, history, archaeology, folklore, archives, collections, research, historic preservation, and the construction or renovation of cultural facilities. Categories include:

A) Special Project Grants: Grants are awarded for specific activities, services or events of limited duration, the expansion of on going programs to meet defined needs, and to support projects which generate new sources of revenue.

Be patient. If any phone number is incorrect, call (area code) 555-1212 and request the new listing.

325

Arts and Humanities

B) Operational Support Grants: Grants are available for cultural organizations which have been in existence for at least two years. Generally, each grant dollar must be matched with one dollar in cash or in-kind goods and services.

C) Capital Expenditure Grants: Grants are available for additions to a collection or acquisition of works of art, artifacts or historical documents, historic preservation, and the renovation or construction of cultural facilities. Each grant dollar generally must be matched with three dollars in cash or in-kind goods and services.

D) Challenge Grants: Grants are awarded for the expansion of permanent endowments to support non-profit cultural organizations and activities. Each grant dollar must be matched with three dollars in cash, irrevocable planned or deferred gifts or life insurance, devises, and bequests.

E) Immediate Action Grants: These grants are awarded throughout the year to enable the Council to respond to unanticipated opportunities or emergencies which occurred after the regular grant request deadline. Grants generally do not exceed $500.

F) Underwriting Assistance Grants: Grants are given as "courage money" to sponsors of professional performing arts touring companies and artists. Grants are awarded on a first-come, first-served basis and preference is given to small communities. Grants are limited to a maximum of $300.

G) Folklife and Traditional Arts Grant Program: Matching grants are available to non-profit groups such as community and cultural organizations, tribes, professional societies, local arts agencies, and libraries for projects designed to support folklife and traditional arts.

4) Money For Schools To Have An Artist In Residence
Artists in Schools/Communities: These grants allow professional artists to work in residencies in schools or community settings. Nationally selected poets and writers, musicians, dancers, visual artists, theater artists, folk artists, and video artists may participate. Artists are paid on a per diem basis.

Nebraska

Nebraska Arts Council, Jocelyn Castle Carriage House, 3838 Davenport St., Omaha, NE 68131-2329, 402-595-2122. Individual artist programs require state residency. In fiscal year 1993, the Council awarded 374 grants totalling $1,206,453 to non-profit organizations. Sixteen individual artists received a total of $32,000.

1) Money For Writers, Artists, and Performers
Individual Artist Fellowships: Fellowships operate on a two-year alternating cycle. The award pool is equally divided each year between visual arts and one other discipline area. Literature and performing arts are eligible in alternating years. Dollar amounts depend on federal funds available at that time.

2) Grants To Arts Organizations
Basic Support Grant: This grant category provides general operating support throughout the year to arts organizations. Applicants are divided into four categories, based on their previous year's fiscal budget. The minimum basic level of funding is $500.

3) $2,000 For New Arts Organizations
Community Challenge Grant: The Challenge Grant provides a year of activities to new and emerging arts organizations. Applicants may request up to $1,000 during the first year, $1,500 during the second year, and $2,000 in the third year. All grants require matching funds.

4) $1,000 For High Risk Art Projects
Director's Fund: Grants are available to arts and non-arts organizations for emergency or contingency funds, high risk ventures, professional development, pilot projects, and collaborative new work/projects between Nebraska arts organizations and individual artists. Grants may cover up to one-half of the total project and range from $100 to $1,000.

5) $10,000 For Art Festivals, Exhibitions, and Poetry Readings
Special Projects: Funding is available for specific arts projects such as exhibitions, festivals, or poetry readings. One-half of the total cost of the project may be funded. Grants range from $500 to $10,000.

6) Money For Touring Exhibits and Programs
Nebraska Touring Program/Exhibits Nebraska: This program provides grants to sponsors of performances or exhibits selected from a roster of eligible artists or organizations.

7) Money For Educational Organizations To Use Art
Arts as Basic in the Curriculum/Community: This category supports fees for projects sponsored by arts or non-arts organizations which integrate the arts into the basic curriculum of a school district or emphasize collaborations with an arts education focus.

8) $500 For Artists and Groups To Tour
Nebraska Touring Program/Exhibits Nebraska (NTP) Technical Assistance Program: NTP provides up to $500 per year for non-performance production/exhibit expenses to artists, groups, or non-profit arts organizations.

9) Money For Art Projects At Schools
Artists in Schools/Communities: This category supports fees for artists' residencies sponsored by non-arts organizations in school or community settings. Residencies can be short term, long term or for an extended term.

Nevada

Nevada State Council on the Arts, Capitol Complex, 100 S. Stewart St., Carson City, NV 89701, 702-687-6880. Individual artist programs require state residency. In 1993-94, the Council awarded $513,594 in funding to non-profit arts organizations. Individual artist fellowships and apprenticeships totalled $32,000.

1) $10,000 For Artists To Create New Works
Artists Fellowships: Fellowships assist in the creation of new works and support artists' efforts to advance their careers. Fellowships range from $2,000 to $10,000 and are available to artists with at least one year of Nevada residency at the time of application.

2) $2,500 For Master Folk Artists To Teach Apprentices
Folk Arts Apprenticeships: This category funds master-apprentice learning relationships that perpetuate Nevada's traditional arts and cultures. Awards of $2,500 are available to master folk artists and one or two apprentices, with at least one participant being a Nevada resident.

3) $22,500 For Arts Organizations
Grants to Organizations: These grants provide funding to strengthen and improve arts organizations. Grants range from $1,000 to $22,500, depending on the size of the non-profit organization. Public institutions are eligible for project support only.

4) $7,500 For Art Groups To Make Presentations
Grants to Presenters: These grants are awarded to presenting organizations to support the presentation of performing or visual arts seasons. Grants are awarded on a competitive basis. Grants range from $1,001 to $7,500 for non-profit organizations and from $1,001 to $5,000 for public institutions.

5) $15,000 To Bring Art To Small Towns
Rural Arts Development: This category provides support to develop stronger arts in Nevada's rural communities. Non-matching grants of up to $5,000 are awarded to non-profit, tax exempt community organizations or local government entities. Grants of up to $15,000 are awarded to developing arts organizations. Funds require a one-to-two local match to state/federal dollars and should be used to undertake new or expanded community initiatives, or assist in programming.

6) $30,000 To Help Art Organizations
Challenge Grant Program: Established tax exempt, non-profit organizations may apply for grants up to $30,000 that may be used to strengthen long-term operations and financial stability. Funds may be used for creating a new, or adding to an existing, endowment or cash reserve; capital expenditures for building acquisition or renovation; land acquisition directly related to the organization's mission; major equipment (over $1,000); or collections acquisition.

7) $1,000 For Artists Or Art Groups
Mini-Grants: Grants of up to $1,000 are provided for specific, short-term assistance which fills an immediate need. New or established tax exempt, non-profit organizations, public institutions, individual artists, administrators, art educators, and board members may apply for funding.

8) Money For Schools To Have An Artist In Residence
Artist in Residence Program: This program provides an opportunity for artists around the country to spend one month in a work/instruction arrangement within elementary and high schools, community centers, and other organizations. Applicant sites must match Council funds on at least a one-to-one basis. In 1993-94, the Arts and Education program was awarded $31,000 in funding.

New Hampshire

New Hampshire Division of Arts, Council of the Arts, 40 North Main St., Concord, NH 03301-4974, 603-271-2789. Individual artist programs require state residency, unless otherwise specified. In 1992-93, the Council awarded approximately $580,000 in grants to organizations and schools. Funding to individual artists totalled $35,000.

1) $3,000 For Individual Artists
Individual Artist Fellowships: Fellowships are awarded to professional artists in recognition of excellence and range from $1,500 to $3,000.

2) $500 For Individual Artists
Artist Opportunity Grants: These awards are open only to artists who have been designated as finalists for the current fellowship year. Grants up to $500 are awarded.

3) $500 For Artists Who Don't Normally Get Money
Discovery Award: This award was designed to find artists who may "fall through the gaps" of the Council's grants. The first award was presented in October, 1993. The maximum amount awarded is $500.

4) $8,000 To Help The Management Of Arts Groups
Operating Grants: These grants provide funds for on going administrative and arts programming needs of non-profit community arts organizations. Funding is for 20% of the organization's annual operating income, or $8,000, whichever is less.

5) $4,000 To Community Arts Organizations
Program Grant: Cash match grants of up to $4,000 are available to community arts organizations without paid staff, and to non-arts organizations.

6) $5,000 To Pay For Staff At Arts Groups

Salary Assistance Grants: These grants are open to incorporated community arts councils seeking administrative staff for the first time or securing additional staff or staff hours. Maximum funding is $5,000 with a minimum match of $2,500. An arts council may apply for second-year funding up to $3,000 with a minimum match of $1,500. By year three, the organization must be able to assume full payment of the salary.

7) $4,000 For Special Art Projects
Special Project Grants: Matching grants of up to $4,000 are awarded to support specific arts programming activities.

8) $3,000 For Artist In Residence In Small Towns
Rural Residency Grants: Grants of up to 50% of total residency costs or $2,000, whichever is less, are available for three to ten day community-based artist residencies. Full-time residency applicants are eligible for up to 75%, or $3,000, whichever is less.

9) $500 For Groups To Hire Consultants
Technical Assistance Grants: Three types of grants are offered: Consultancies ($500), Scholarship Aid/Travel Fund ($250), and Grants to New Arts Organizations ($750).

10) $16,000 To Help Art Groups With Fund Raising
Arts Institution (A1) Grants: This category consists of A-1 Development and Operating Grants. While both grants can be used to help with operating expenses, Development Grants incorporate a challenge grant to help organizations raise funds from new or established donors. Funding ranges from $9,000 to $16,000.

11) $4,500 Grants For Special Projects
Project Grants: Grants support specific arts programming for the general public. Programming may be a single event or a thematically linked set of events. Up to $4,500 is available in funding.

12) $4,000 For Schools To Bring In Artists
Artist in Residence Grants: This category supports the costs of bringing artists to sites where they will work with students and teachers, kindergarten through twelfth grade, over time from three to sixty days. Depending upon the length of residency, grants range from $400 to $4,000.

13) $5,000 For Arts Education In Schools
AIE Initiatives: This category provides arts education programs for students pre-kindergarten through twelfth grade and to education professionals who serve this group. Grants range from $2,000 to $5,000.

14) $1,490 For School Teachers To Develop Art Classes
Teacher/Artist Curriculum Collaborations: This category is designed for a two-year cycle and provides incentives for teachers to integrate new arts curricula with educational programs. Funding is available up to $1,000 in the first year, and up to $1,490 in the second year.

New Jersey

New Jersey State Council on the Arts, 20 West State St., CN 306, Trenton, NJ 08625, 609-292-6130. Individual artist programs require state residency, unless otherwise specified. In 1992-93, the Council awarded $9,107,209 in grants to non-profit organizations. Sixty-eight individual fellowships were awarded totalling $434,000.

1) Grants For Artists, Mimes, Sculptors, Poets, and Opera Singers
Fellowships: Fellowships are awarded to professional New Jersey artists. No students are eligible. Categories include: choreography, music composition, opera/music theater composition, theater (mime), experimental art, graphics, painting, sculpture, design arts, crafts, photography, media arts (film/video), prose, play writing, poetry, and interdisciplinary arts. An artist may apply in only one discipline and in one category.

2) Grants To Arts Organizations
Organizational Funding: This category is open to non-profit, tax exempt organizations that have been in existence and active for at least two years at the time of application. All organizations applying for support must apply for either a general operating support grant or a special project grant. All grants offered through this program are matching grants, and all matches must be cash matches.

3) Money For Regional and State-Wide Organizations
General Operating Support: This category provides discretionary, non-project oriented funding to support overall administrative as well as artistic operations. Organizations must be multi-regional or statewide in public impact. Awards generally do not exceed 20% of total projected expenditures.

4) Grants To Support Special Art Projects
Special Project Support: Grants are awarded specifically for an arts project/event of an eligible non-profit organization, agency or local government institution. Projects must be multi-regional or statewide in public impact.

5) Money For Art Programs In Local Schools
Arts Basic to Education Awards: These awards support arts education organizations and agencies that provide art-in-education services to children in kindergarten through twelfth grade.

6) Funding For Arts Organizations
Major Impact Arts Organizations: Funding is granted to a limited number of arts organizations which meet the Council's highest standards of excellence and administrative and fiscal responsibility. Designations are made for a three-year period.

7) Matching Grants To Arts Organizations
Challenge Grants: Grants may be offered to help the arts organization leverage increased contributed support from corporations, foundations, and other public and private sources. Funds must be matched and may be applied to general operations.

8) Grants To Improve The Management Of Art Organizations
Technical Assistance: Grants are offered that assist organizations in obtaining needed expertise and management skills. These grants usually do not require a match.

9) Money For Public Or Parochial School Art Programs
Educational Funding: Arts in Education Programs (AIE) are available to public, private and parochial schools, school districts, non-profit community organizations, non-profit local arts centers, and organizations that sponsor not-for-profit community projects. The NJSCA awards sponsors matching funds to pay for artists' fees only.

10) Money For Jazz, Folk, And Theater Artists In Residence
Artists in Education Programs: Residencies range from five-day short-term residencies to long-term residencies lasting 100 days. Disciplines include: architecture, dance, folk arts, jazz, media arts, theater/drama, visual arts/crafts, and writing.

11) Summer Programs For Artists and Teachers
Artist/Teacher/Institute: This ten-day summer program offers educators the same opportunities for artistic growth that students experience in AIE residencies. Workshops and in-depth arts experiences are available in all disciplines.

New Mexico

New Mexico Cultural Affairs, Arts Division, 228 East Palace Ave., Santa Fe, NM 87501, 505-827-6490. The New Mexico Art Division is unable to fund fellowships to individuals. It strongly encourages applicant organizations to involve resident New Mexico artists. However, the Division does support local sponsorship of out-of-state artists or organizations to enrich a resident group or when the services fill a need that is not being met locally. In 1993-94, the Division awarded $918,400 in grant funding to non-profit organizations.

Organizational Funding: New Mexico administers awards to non-profit organizations. Generally, award applicants must provide at least a one-to-one cash match.

1) $120,000 For Arts Organizations
Established Arts Organizations: This category purchases art services on behalf of New Mexico residents from established professional organizations. Applicants fall into three categories: those whose cash operating incomes for the preceding year were greater than $500,000, less than $500,000 and less than $100,000. Grants range from $10,000 to $120,000 depending on the specific category's guidelines.

2) $15,000 For Local Art Groups
Civic and Community Arts Organizations: This category supports those organizations that promote, produce, and/or present quality arts experiences but do not meet the requirements to apply as Professional Arts Organizations. The maximum grant available is 50% of the cash operating income, excluding grants from the Arts Division, or $15,000, whichever is less.

3) $15,000 For Ethnic Arts Projects
Culturally Diverse Organizations: This category was designed to develop stronger ethnic arts organizations on a long-term basis. The maximum grant available is 50% of cash operating income, excluding grants from the Arts Division, or $15,000, whichever is less.

4) $5,000 For Folk Art Programs
Arts Projects: This program purchases short-term arts services on behalf of New Mexico residents. The maximum request is $5,000 for Folk Arts, Culturally Diverse Arts, and other Arts Projects.

5) Money For Artists To Tour The State
Incentives to Present New Mexico Touring Artists: This program assists presenters in obtaining the services of New Mexico touring performing artists on behalf of their communities. Presenters may be awarded up to 50% of any given fee on the application.

6) Money For An Artist In Residence For Schools And Community Homes
Artists Residencies: This program places qualified artists in various community, rural, and institutional settings through grants for collaborative residencies or rural and institutional residencies. There is a ten-day minimum residency length. Artists are paid a minimum of $110 per working day.

New York

New York State Council on the Arts, 915 Broadway, New York, NY 10010, 212-387-7000. Individual artist programs require state residency. Non-profit organizations can obtain support in 17 areas including: architecture, planning and design, arts in education, capital funding initiative, dance, electronic media and film, folk arts, individual artists, literature, museum, music, musical instrument revolving loan fund,

Be patient. If any phone number is incorrect, call (area code) 555-1212 and request the new listing.

327

Arts and Humanities

presenting operations, special arts services, state local partnership, theater, and the visual arts. In 1992-93, New York awarded $26,172,900 in grants to non-profit arts organizations.

1) $25,000 For Artists

Individual Artist Programs: The Council and local regrant agencies are unable to make grants directly to individuals. All applications must be sponsored by non-profit organizations. Grants of up to $25,000 are awarded through Cultural Service Contracts with the non-profit organizations which direct the funds to the individual's project. Funding categories include: composers' commissions, film production, media production, visual arts, and theater. State residency is required.

2) Grants For Arts Organizations

General Operating Support: Through this program, unrestricted support is provided for on going institutional activities. Each program has its particular criteria and restrictions. In general, a group must have at least three years prior support from the program in order to be eligible for funding.

3) Money For More Than One Year For Art Groups

Multi-Year Support: Many programs offer multi-year support in areas other than General Operating Support. In these instances, organizations do have the option of applying for more than one year of support.

4) $5,000 For Local Art Groups

In addition to providing support to non-profit arts organizations through its own funding process, the Council also supports a statewide local regranting system called Decentralization. Grants up to $5,000 are funded to support professional and avocational arts activities in all artistic disciplines within local communities.

5) Money For School Art Programs In Music, Theater, and Media

Arts in Education is a collaboration between the Council and the State Education Department. Non-profit cultural and environmental organizations based in New York may submit applications. Funding categories include general operating support, planning grants, implementation grants, special projects, evaluation/research and long-term projects. Arts and education, dance groups, museums, theater, and folk arts are among the eligible categories. Individual artists are funded through sponsoring organizations. These individual grants are available in five areas: film production, media production, visual artist sponsored projects, theater commissions, and music commissions. The amount of funding available is dependent on the proposed project.

North Carolina

North Carolina Arts Council, Department of Cultural Resources, Raleigh, NC 27601-2807, 919-733-2821. Individual artist programs require state residency. Money for arts organizations is in eight categories: community development, dance, folklife, literature, music, theater, touring/presenting, and the visual arts. Support includes funding for program support, interdisciplinary/special projects, and organizational development grants. The Council provides over 1,700 grants each year to artists and non-profit organizations for arts programming throughout the state. In 1993-94, the Council awarded $3,388,696 in grants to non-profit organizations. Individual artists received $131,000 in fellowships.

1) $8,000 For Artists, Dancers, Musicians, and Writers

Fellowships: Awards recognize the contribution of exemplary artists and provide funds for continued creative development. Fellowships of $8,000 are available in dance, literature, music, theater, and the visual arts.

2) $8,000 For Specific Dance, Folk Art, or Literature Projects

Artist Project Grants: These grants support professional artists for specific artistic projects. Grants are available in dance, folklife, literature, and visual arts and range from $5,000 to $8,000.

3) Money For Artists To Work With Schools And Community Colleges

Residencies: Residencies provide opportunities for artists to work in schools and community colleges. Residency opportunities at out-of-state arts centers are also available in some categories.

4) $3,000 For Local Folk Artists

Folk Heritage Awards: These awards recognize the lifetime achievement of folk artists who have made outstanding contributions to the state's cultural heritage. A non-matching cash amount of $3,000 is awarded.

5) $10,000 To Make A Documentary Of State Folk Artists

Folklife Documentary Project Grants: Grants provide support for the preservation of the state's traditional culture through the use of modern documentary technology. Grants rarely exceed $10,000.

6) Help For Local Artists To Tour The State

Touring Artists Roster: This roster contains a list of selected performing artists receiving fee support for touring performances in the state. Current artists on the roster and recent alumni may also apply for scholarship and project assistance.

7) $500 For Writers To Attend Conferences

Writers Scholarships: Grants provide support to writers to attend workshops, conferences, book fairs, or other educational events. Awards do not exceed $500.

8) Money To Train As An Art Administrator

Internships: Programs are available to individuals for training in arts administration.

9) Money For Dance, Music, And Visual Arts Groups

Major Organization Support: This category provides funding for the artistic programs and administration of the state's major dance, music, and visual arts organizations.

10) Money For Theater And Literary Organizations

General Support: Provides funding for artistic programs and administration of established theater and literary organizations through this category.

11) Money For Local Governments To Support Art Groups

Local Government Challenge: These grants match new allocations provided by county and municipal governments for local arts council programming.

12) Money For Statewide Arts Groups

Management Service Organization: Grants support statewide organizations serving community arts programming.

13) Grants To Schools For Art Projects

Arts in Education: This category supports the arts in education and assists the Basic Education Program through artist residencies, program development grants, and Arts in Education project grants. The Council plans to hold a statewide conference on arts education. It also plans to publish a directory on model projects, as well as develop an audiovisual program to encourage arts in education.

North Dakota

North Dakota Council On Arts, Black Building, #606, 118 Broad Way, Fargo, ND 58102, 701-239-7150. Individual artist programs require state residency, unless otherwise specified. In 1992-93, the Council awarded approximately $600,000 to non-profit organizations. Individuals received $42,000 in fellowship grants.

1) Money For Artists, Dancers, Opera Singers, Photographers, and Writers

Artists Fellowships Program: Fellowships assist North Dakota artists in furthering their professional artistic careers. Fellowship funds come from individual and business donations and interest from the state's Cultural Endowment. Fellowships are awarded in the following disciplines: dance, music, opera/ musical theater, theater, visual arts, architecture/design, crafts, photography, media arts, literature, interdisciplinary arts, and folk arts.

2) Money To Hire Consultants Or Arts Advisors

Professional Development Program: This program provides financial assistance for informational/educational opportunities relating to the arts and arts development, or to benefit arts organizations by providing support for consultants and technical or artistic advisors. Only one grant of up to $300 will be provided per artist or organization per year. Grants do not require matching funds.

3) Grants To Small Arts Organizations

ACCESS Grant Program: The ACCESS Program provides state funds to non-profit organizations for general operating expenses, as well as for special projects. Generally, the program serves small, rural, or emerging groups, or those making special efforts to provide arts experiences to previously underserved audiences.

4) $500 For Special Art Projects

Institutional Support: This category supports non-profit organizations for general operating expenses as well as for performances, exhibitions, workshops, and other special projects in all arts disciplines. Mini-grant requests of $500 are accepted throughout the year.

5) Grants For Arts Projects In Small Towns

Rural Arts Initiative: This category combines federal, state, and local funding to assist the significant organizational, programmatic, and artistic growth of selected local arts organizations in small, rural towns.

6) Money For Artistic Touring Events

Touring Arts Program: This program provides a roster of high quality, low cost touring events, and grants state funds to non-profit organizations sponsoring these events in North Dakota communities.

7) Money For Schools To Have An Artist In Residence

Artists in Residence: This program provides a roster of qualified artists who can work with students in elementary and secondary schools for sustained periods of time, and provides federal funds to non-profit organizations and local school districts for sponsoring these artists.

8) Money For Schools To Develop Art Programs

Local Education in the Arts Planning: (LEAP) Program regrants federal funds to assist local school districts in developing five-year education plans.

Ohio

Ohio Council on Arts, 727 East Main St., Columbus, OH 43205, 614-466-2613. State residency is required, unless otherwise specified. In 1992-93 Ohio awarded $6,119,360 in grants to non-profit organizations and artists.

1) $10,000 For Artists And Art Critics

Individual Artist Fellowships: Fellowships of $5,000 or $10,000 are awarded to artists of exceptional talent based on the quality of their work. Categories include: choreography, crafts (contemporary and traditional), creative writing, design arts, interdisciplinary and performance art, media arts, music composition, photography, and visual arts. The category of criticism supports critical writing that investigates, evaluates, or analyzes modern and contemporary art activity, including the visual arts, photography, crafts, dance music, theater, literature, design arts, media arts, and traditional arts.

2) Study Your Art In Long Island, NY Or Sausalito, CA
The Individual Artist Program also offers residency opportunities. Residencies at P.S.I. in Long Island, NY and Headlands Center for the Arts in Sausalito, CA are open to artists who have received Individual Artists Fellowships.

3) $1,000 For Artists To Attend Workshops
Professional Development Assistance: This program provides assistance of up to $1,000 to help an artist pay for a variety of activities such as workshops, conferences, colonies, seminars, symposia, and studio facilities. It is designed for short-term assistance only.

4) $2,000 For An Artist To Work With A Master
Traditional and Ethnic Arts Apprenticeship Program: Grants are offered up to $2,000 and are based on the quality of the master's and apprentice's work and the apprenticeship plan they develop together. A traditional master artist and apprentice artist apply together for a one-year apprenticeship.

5) Grants To Arts Organizations
Major Institution Support: This category helps fund operational expenses for Ohio institutions with operating incomes over $500,000. Support for organizations include funding for: art in public places, dance, design arts, literature, media arts, multi-arts, music, theater, traditional and ethnic arts, and visual arts and crafts.

6) Money To Support Special Projects
Project Support: Partial funding is provided through this program toward year-long projects or short-term projects sponsored by arts and non-arts organizations.

7) Money For Administrative Expenses
Operating Support: This category funds the on going artistic and administrative functions of arts organizations with operating incomes under $500,000 for a full year of services, from July 1 to June 30.

8) $2,000 For Special Art Opportunities
Sudden Opportunity Grants: Money is provided through this category for an unforeseen arts opportunity that may occur between council Board meetings. Grants are limited to $2,000 and may fund a wide variety of activities.

Oklahoma
State Arts Council of Oklahoma, 2101 N. Lincoln Blvd., Oklahoma City, OK 73105, 405-521-2931. The Council is unable to fund individuals. Applications are accepted from non-religious, non-profit, tax exempt organizations. Colleges, schools, and universities which receive funding through the State Regents for Higher Education or substantial private sources, are a lower funding priority, except in areas where the university or college is the sole source of arts events in a community. All funding for the Advanced Request, Over $2,000 and Under $2,000 Project Assistance categories must be matched dollar for dollar by the applicant. Fifty percent of the matching funds must be cash. The Council will fund personnel or administrative costs associated with a project. The Council does not fund general administrative expenses or general organizational support. In 1992-93, Oklahoma provided $2,844,042 in state funding to non-profit organizations.

1) Grants For Arts Organizations
Advanced Request Funding: This category encourages project planning 16 months in advance of the fiscal year in which activities will occur. It allows for the inclusion of Advanced Request Category recommendations in the State Arts Council's budget request to the Governor and Legislature in September of each year.

2) Money For Projects Over $2,000
Project Assistance Over $2,000: This category supports programs or projects for which the total financial assistance requested from the Council exceeds $2,000. Applicants are reviewed by advisory panels which make funding recommendations to the Council. Projects must be submitted no later than December 10.

3) Money For Projects Under $2,000
Project Assistance Under $2,000: This category provides assistance for smaller or low-cost projects. Applications are reviewed monthly on a first-come, first-served basis by the Executive Committee of the State Arts Council. Applications must be submitted no later than 60 days prior to the project beginning date.

4) $5,000 For Minority Arts Organization
Minority Arts: This category is for requests of under $5,000 to be used primarily for technical assistance to minority arts organizations or for special projects designed for audience development, community participation, or projects directed toward youth. The match for the projects may be in the form of in-kind services. Limited funds are available. The deadline for submission is 60 days prior to the project start date.

5) Grants For Community Arts Celebrations
Fairs and Festival Funding: Fairs and festivals are defined as one-day indoor or outdoor community celebrations of the arts. Financial assistance for a one-day fair or festival is generally under $500. Applications for one-day fair and festival events should be submitted under the Under $2,000 category. Applications for fairs and festivals lasting two or more days should be submitted in the Under $2,000, Over $2,000 or Advanced Request categories depend upon the amount of funding requested. Applications will be judged on an individual basis.

6) Money For An Artist In Residence In Schools Or Community Groups
Artists in Residences Program: Applications are accepted from local education agencies and non-profit, tax exempt community organizations. A residency's structure is determined by the on- site arts planning team and consists mostly of class sessions. Teacher or adult workshops, lecture, and mini-performances are some of the other possible activities. A school or community residency may last up to 36 weeks and is based on a 40-hour work week. Half of that time is spent with residency participants, the remaining time is designated as studio time for the artist. The artist's compensation for an approved residency is $520 per week. There is a set relocation fee for travel to residencies outside the artist's home town. Artists are responsible for their own transportation, board, and lodging.

7) Money For Artists To Tour
Oklahoma Touring Program: This program enables the Council to share the cost of quality Oklahoma performing events with local community organizations. Producers of dance, music, opera and theater, along with storytellers and folk artists are chosen on the basis of artistic quality. Any non-religious, non-profit, tax exempt organization, governmental unit, tribal government, or educational institution is eligible for assistance. Touring costs are shared by the Council and the presenter. Funding is available for 50% of the contracted performance or exhibition fee.

Oregon
Oregon Arts Commission, 550 Airport Road, SE, Salem, OR 97310, 503-378-3625. Individual artist programs require state residency, unless otherwise specified. In 1992-93, the Commission awarded $1,690,163 in grants to non-profit arts organizations. Individuals received $40,000 in fellowships.

1) $3,000 To Artists, Photographers, And Performers
Artist Fellowships: This program recognizes Oregon's professional artists working in all media with cash awards of $3,000. Fellowships are awarded on the basis of the quality of work presented by the individual artist, and that artist's record of sustained professional achievement. Funds may be used as the artist's needs require. This category is open to artists working in the visual arts, crafts, photography, design and interdisciplinary arts, literature, music/opera, media arts, theater, and dance. Full-time students and non-professionals who produce art as a hobby are not eligible.

2) $7,000 For Artists Living In 13 Western States
Western States Regional Media Arts Fellowships: These fellowships are available to artists living in the thirteen western states, including Oregon, and the Pacific territories. Project grants up to $7,000 are available for production expenses for proposed new work or works in progress.

3) Money For Authors and Publishers In 13 Western States
Western States Book Awards: These awards recognize authors and small publishers of outstanding literary works in the West. Each year the Western States Arts Federation (WESTAF) provides cash prizes to the winning authors and their publishers, and provides outstanding opportunities for critical attention. For information, contact WESTAF, 236 Montezuma Avenue, Santa Fe, NM 87501. Phone: 505-988-1166.

4) Grants For Arts Organizations
Economic Development Grants: Non-profit arts organizations which have been in existence at least two years may apply. Grants contribute to an organization's entire year's programming. Economic Development Grants are intended for arts organizations with operating budgets greater than $50,000. Grants must be matched at least dollar for dollar with either earned or contributed cash. Arts organizations that had previously applied for Challenge grants, Program grants, or Presenting grants are encouraged to apply. Applications will be scored based on four broad areas: artistic quality, economic impact, outreach, and relationship to the community. The Commission encourages grant applications in all disciplines. All grants must be spent within a one-year period.

5) Grants For Artists and Small Art Groups
Regional Regranting: In general, this category is intended for individual artists and arts organizations with annual budgets under $50,000. Grants must be made for arts projects in Oregon. Projects must have artistic merit and relate in some way to the community. Contact your regional arts council for complete guidelines.

6) Money To Be An Artist In Residence
Artist Residencies: Residencies are offered in all arts disciplines: visual arts, crafts, design, architecture, creative writing, dance, music, film and video, folk arts, theater, and interdisciplinary projects. Short-term and long-term residencies are available. Artists are paid on a per diem basis.

7) $3,000 For Arts Programs In Schools
Arts Education Project Grants: Supports projects that make the arts basic to education within the schools and extends arts education opportunities for Oregon students beyond the schools. Grants of up to $3,000 are awarded for one-time projects or as seed money to develop a program.

Arts and Humanities

Pennsylvania

Pennsylvania Council on the Arts, Room 216, Finance Bldg., Harrisburg, PA 17120, 717-787-6883. For individual artist programs, applicants must have lived in Pennsylvania for two years prior to applying for funding and should have had a minimum of three years professional experience in their field. Organizational funding programs require that organizations must be non-profit, tax exempt corporations that provide arts programming and/or services to Pennsylvania. Categories include: broadcast of the arts, crafts, inter-disciplinary arts, dance, literature, local arts services, local government, media arts, museums, music, presenting organizations, theater, and visual arts. Non-profit organizations may apply on behalf of an unincorporated arts group. In this capacity, the organization becomes a "conduit" for grant funds and is financially, administratively, and programmatically responsible for a grant. In 1992-93, non-profit organizations received $9,212,960 in funding. Fellowships were awarded to 105 individual artists totalling $439,700.

1) Grants To Dancers, Jazz Composers, Writers, And Artists
Fellowships: Limited fellowships are available to established or emerging artists. Categories include: crafts, dance, folklife, literature, media arts (audio/radio), music (composers, jazz composers and performers, and solo recitalists), inter-disciplinary arts, theater and screenwriter and visual arts. Awards are made directly to the individual primarily on the basis of the creative excellence of the work submitted for review.
2) Grants To Arts Organizations
General Support: This category assists arts organizations which have been regularly receiving Council support for the costs of their annual activities. First-time applicants should not apply for General Support. Organizations must have been in operation for at least three years prior to application and be under professional, artistic, and managerial leadership on a year-round basis. These are matching grants.
3) $1,000 To Hire A Consultant For Your Art Group
Technical Assistance: Non-matching grants are available to engage consultants to review programs and operations and to advise in organization planning and development. Maximum funding is $1,000. Conference grants of up to $250 are also available.
4) $250 To Bus Artists To A Performance
Busing Program: Busing grants are provided to non-profit organizations if they are transporting groups to art activities. Non-matching grants are awarded up to $250 per trip.
Residencies: The Arts in Education Program (AIE) places practicing artists in schools and community settings, particularly where quality arts experiences are not readily available. AIE covers all disciplines. Priority is given to Pennsylvania artists. In cases where extreme financial needs can be demonstrated, the normal 50% matching requirements may be waived. Residencies last from a minimum of 10 days in length to a maximum of 80 days. The cost of a residency is $150 per day for the resident artist's fees. Applicants may also apply for funds for travel and daily expenses.

Rhode Island

Rhode Island State Council on The Arts, 95 Cedar St., Suite 103, Providence, RI 02903, 401-277-3880. Applicants for the individual artist programs must be eighteen years of age or older and have lived in the state for at least one year prior to application. Minimum grants awarded to organizations is $100 and funds must be expended during the fiscal year of the award. Program grants, with the exception of general operating support, are divided into two categories. Level I grants range from $100 to $2,000. Level II grants range from $2,001 to $5,000. A dollar for dollar cash match is required. In fiscal year 1993, the Council awarded $518,092 to non-profit arts organizations. Individual artists received $118,305 in fellowships.

1) $5,000 For Artists To Create New Works
Artist Projects: This category enables an artist to create new work and/or complete works-in-progress by providing direct financial assistance. Grants range from $2,000 to $5,000.
2) $3,000 For Artists, Choreographers, Designers, and Printmakers
Fellowships: Fellowships are offered in: choreography, crafts, design, drawing and printmaking, film and video, folk arts, literature, music composition, new genres, painting, photography and three-dimensional art. Grant recipients each receive $3,000. A runner-up in each category, if awarded, will receive a $500 honorarium.
3) $2,000 For Folk Art Apprenticeships
Folk Arts Apprenticeships: This program fosters the sharing of traditional (folk) artistic skills between a master and an apprentice who is already familiar with the genre. Grants range from $100 to $2,000. For exceptional projects, higher amounts may be awarded. Most of the support is for the master's fee.
4) Grants To Groups Providing Art To Underserved Groups
Access Initiatives: This category provides funds for projects that assure equal opportunity and access for hunderserved groups and individuals.
5) Grants For Special Art Projects
Arts Programming: Matching funds are provided under this category for a wide variety of arts-related projects planned and executed by eligible non-profit organizations.
6) Grants To Help Manage Art Organizations
Organizational Development: This category supplies funds to advance an organization's artistic, management, and technical capabilities.
7) Money For Operating Expenses
General Operating Support: Under this category, partial operating costs are provided for the state's established arts producing/exhibiting organizations. Organizations are eligible for single-year funding if they have had a three-year grant history with the Council. Organizations that have made a statewide impact may apply for multi-year funding if their budget is over $100,000 and if they have had a five-year grant history with the Council.
8) $12,000 To Have An Artist In Residence At A School
Artist Residency Grants: Grants sponsor both professional and folk artists for residencies in educational settings. Residencies are carried out by artists from the Arts in Education Artist Roster and are long term (15 to 100 days for professional artists, a minimum of five days for folk artists). Grants are funded up to $12,000.
9) $2,500 To Develop Art For Schools
Arts as Basic in Curriculum (ABC) Grants: Grants of up to $2,500 are available to help make the arts a basic part of kindergarten through twelfth grade education.
10) $2,000 For A Public School To Plan An Art Program
Rhode Island Comprehensive Arts Planning Grants: This category is open to Rhode Island public school districts with a need to coordinate and improve educational programs in dance, theater, music, visual arts, and creative writing for its students. $2,000 will be awarded to each year's chosen districts.

South Carolina

South Carolina Arts Commission, 1800 Gervais St., Columbia, SC 29201, 803-734-8696. Individual artist programs require state residency. For fiscal year 1993, state funding to non-profit arts organizations totalled $1,249,578.

1) $7,500 For Artists, Performers, Writers, And Craftsmen
Fellowships: Six fellowships are available annually in the following disciplines: visual arts, crafts, literature, and music performance. These non-matching awards are for $7,500.
2) $7,500 For Artists To Do Special Projects
Project Support: Project grants are given to help pay actual project costs such as assistance for one specific arts activity for professional development or career advancement. Grants are funded up to $7,500. Artists may submit one project grant only. Up to one half of the cash match (i.e., 25% of the total project budget) may be accounted for by the cash value of the artist's creative time.
3) $1,000 To Be Used For Professional Development
Quarterly Grants: Grants of up to $1,000 are funded to assist in pilot projects for professional development or career development. Ordinary living expenses during the project are not eligible costs.
4) Up To $500,000 To Arts Groups
General Support Grants: These matching grants provide assistance for programs and general operating expenses. It is offered to applicants in two categories: 1) arts producing, presenting, and discipline service organizations and 2) arts councils/agencies. Grants to applicants in Category One range from $10,000 to $500,000, depending on the applicant's total operating budget of the last completed fiscal year. Grants to applicants in Category Two, range from $1,000 to $150,000. Major Grantees (arts organizations receiving grants of over $1,000) are eligible for professional development assistance through Quarterly Grants.
5) $20,000 For Special Art Projects
Project Support: These matching grants are intended to assist one specific arts activity, event or series. Applicants may include arts producing, presenting, and service organizations and other (non-arts) organizations. Maximum funding is up to $20,000.
6) $1,000 To Help Develop Art Management Skills
Quarterly Grants: Matching grants of up to $1,000 are awarded to assist specific arts activity or professional development for artistic and managerial staff which may arise.
7) Money To Bring Art Programs To Schools
Arts in the Basic Curriculum: Provides grants and assistance designed to help the arts become part of the basic curriculum in South Carolina schools.
8) Money For Schools To Have An Artist In Residence
Arts in Education: Provides grants to schools and organizations for residencies, performances, and special projects in educational settings.
9) $350 For Teachers To Work On Art Projects In School
Teacher Incentive Grants: Provides non-matching grants of up to $350 to teachers for innovative arts projects.
10) Grants To Bring Performances Or Screenings To Schools
Visiting Artists: Provides fee support for performances, readings, and film screening in educational institutions not participating in the Arts in Education grant program.

South Dakota

South Dakota Arts Council, 230 S. Phillips Ave., Suite 204, Sioux Falls, SD 57102, 605-339-6646. Individual artist programs require state residency. All grants (except Emerging Artist Grants and Fellowships) are intended as seed money. Applicant organizations and individuals are funded up to 50% of projected costs. Funding is available in the following arts disciplines: dance, music, opera/music theater, theater, visual arts, design arts, crafts, photography, media arts, literature, and folk arts. In 1993-94, the Council distributed $741,422 in grants to non-profit arts organizations. Individual fellowships totalled $40,000.

1) $5,000 For Artists In Any Arts Discipline
Artist Fellowship Grants: Grants under this category recognize South Dakota artists of exceptional talent in any arts discipline. Non-matching grants of $5,000 are awarded.
2) $1,000 For Artists Who Want To Grow
Emerging Artists Grants: This category recognizes artists for their potential for growth and contribution to the arts. This non-matching grant of $1,000 can only be awarded to an individual artist once every three years.
3) Grants For Artists To Work On Specific Projects
Project Grants: Grants assist individual artists in the presentation of projects for the general public or an activity which meets specific needs of the applicant artist. Up to 50% of the total project costs are funded. Grants must be matched at least dollar for dollar in cash or in combination with an in-kind service.
4) Grants To Arts Groups and Art Councils
General Operating Support: This category provides operating assistance to South Dakota non-profit presenting or producing arts institutions and community arts councils. Grants are funded up to 10% of the applicant's annual eligible cash operating expenses.
5) Grants To Groups For Special Projects
Project Grants: Grants under this category assist non-profit organizations in the presentation of an activity or series of activities for the general public which meet specific needs of the applicant organization. Funds are awarded up to 50% of the total project costs. Grants must be matched at least dollar for dollar in cash or in combination with an in-kind service.
6) $500 For New Art Organizations
Interim Project Grants: This category is open to organizations that have not received a General Operating Support or Project Grant. Up to $500 in matching funds may be awarded in special cases involving new sites, new events, or new organizations.
7) $500 For Art Groups Who Need Emergency Support
Emergency Grants: Up to $500 in funds may be awarded to organizations which need emergency support, but for a legitimate reason could not apply on the February 1 deadline.
8) $1,000 For A Community Art Project
Arts Bank: The Arts Bank provides underwriting to remove fear of financial loss in producing and sponsoring performances, workshops, and other arts events for local audiences without removing the community effort required to support the event. An organization cannot receive more than $1,000 from the Arts bank within a fiscal year.
9) $500 For Arts Groups To Hire Consultants
Technical Assistance: Matching funds are provided for professional advice on technical matters, specific programs, projects, and/or administrative functions of non-profit arts organizations. Grants up to $500 are provided to match 50% of the consultant's negotiated fee and travel/lodging/meals at state government rates.
10) $500 For Art Group Managers To Improve Their Skills
Professional Development: This category assists individuals associated with arts organizations in improving their ability to work for arts in South Dakota. Grants up to $500 are provided to match 50% of the consultant's negotiated fee and travel/lodging/ meals at state government rates. Funds are awarded to the applicant's organization.
11) Money For Touring Art Groups
Touring Arts: This program category helps make the arts available in all regions of the state by providing matching funds to individuals for touring in any arts discipline. In 1993-94, this program received $109,110 in funds.
12) Money For Schools To Have An Artist In Residence
Artists in Schools: Under this program, practicing artists conduct residences of one week or longer in South Dakota schools. Preference is given to public and private elementary and secondary schools. Artist fees are supported on a matching funds basis between the sponsoring organization and the Council. In 1993-94, $85,970 was awarded in grants.
13) Grants For Teachers To Develop Art In Schools
Art Educator Grants: Grants assist teachers from all arts disciplines in the development of arts education curricula for students in kindergarten through twelfth grade.

Tennessee

Tennessee Art Commission, 320 6th Ave., North, Suite 100, Nashville, TN 37243-0780, 615-741-1701. Individual artist programs require state residency. In 1993-94, the Commission will award $3,857,940 in matching grants to non-profit arts organizations. Eight individual fellowships of $2,500 each will be awarded totalling $20,000.

1) $2,500 For Artists, Musicians, Writers, And Dancers
Individual Artists Fellowships: This category provides as many as eight awards to outstanding Tennessee artists in each of the following disciplines: crafts, dance, literature, media, music, opera, theater, and visual arts. Each fellowship will be at least $2,500 or more. Honorable mention grants, if given, usually are for less than $2,500.
2) Grants For Arts Organizations
Arts Build Communities: This pilot project works in direct partnership with one or more designated agencies in each of Tennessee's nine developmental districts to increase arts awareness and involvement throughout the state. Each designated agency receives a "block grant" of a per capita share of $41,000,000 appropriated to the Arts commission for community grants. All funds received by a designated agency must be matched on a one-to-one basis. See the Commission's Guideline to Grants for complete details.
3) $6,000 For Special Art Projects
Arts Projects: This category provides funds for a wide variety of quality arts projects and programs. Grants range from $500 to $6,000. Funds are available to those counties not being served by a designated agency under Arts Build Communities. Non-profit organizations in the following counties only may apply for an Arts Project matching grant: Cheatham, Dickson, Giles, Hickman, Houston, Humphreys, Lawrence, Lewis, Maury, Montgomery, Perry, Robertson, Rutherford, Stewart, Wayne, Williamson, and Wilson.
4) $15,000 For Community Orchestras
Community Orchestra Challenge Grants: These grants provide matching funds for Tennessee's community orchestras in amounts ranging from $1,000 to $15,000. To be eligible, an orchestra must have an annual operating income of under $500,000 (excluding all in-kind contributions).
5) Grants To Operate An Arts Organizations
General Operating Support: This category provides general, non-project support to established non-profit, tax exempt organizations exclusively involved in on going, continuous arts activities or services. Funding is divided into organizations with operating expenses under $499,999, and over $500,000. Funding is available for up to 10% of an organization's total operating expenses for their last year's income.
6) $25,000 For Underserved Art Forms
Partnerships for Access and Appreciation: This program provides matching funding for underserved and underrepresented art disciplines and forms. Each funded project must involve at least two non-profit Tennessee organizations or at least one artist and one non-profit Tennessee organization. Grants generally range from $10,000 to $25,000.
7) $500 For Unexpected Art Activities
Special Opportunity Grants: Grants provide funds for unexpected but important arts activities. Matching grants of up to $500 are offered for activities of modest size.
8) $2,500 To Hire Out-Of-Town Consultants
Technical Assistance Program: This program provides funds for special technical assistance, often by out-of-state consultants. Grants range from $500 to $2,500 and may require a cash and/or in-kind match.
9) $5,000 For Artists To Go On Tour
Touring Arts Program: This program brings professional performers to communities by providing financial assistance to qualified presenters/sponsors. Performers are available for one or two-day residencies. Grants range from $1,000 to $5,000, and matching funds are required.
10) $10,000 For A Non-Profit Agency To Have An Artist In Residence
Artists Residencies: Residencies place professional artists in educational settings. They serve primarily as a resource to existing teaching staff. Grants range between $500 and $10,000, depending upon the arts discipline and length of residency. Organizations must supply matching funds. Residences are available in architecture/environment, dance/ movement, film/video, folk arts, multi-arts, music, poetry/ creative writing, theater, and visual arts/crafts. Individual elementary, middle, and secondary schools may apply. Community arts councils, museums, statewide arts organizations, and other Tennessee chartered non-profit organizations may apply as a coordinating agency.

Texas

Texas Commission on the Arts, 920 Colorado, P.O. Box 13406, Capitol Station, Austin, TX 78711-3406, 512-463-5535. Texas does not offer direct funding to individuals. Individual artists are funded indirectly through the Arts in Education and the Touring Programs. In addition, individual artists may apply to the Commission under the umbrella of a non-profit organization or government entity. In 1991-92, the Commission awarded $2,988,023 in funding to non-profits arts organizations.

1) Grants To Arts Organizations
Organizational Assistance: This category provides financial assistance for operational

support for a 12-month period. This program is available to: major institutions, cultural and artistic organizations, local arts agencies, cultural/arts service organizations, regional organizations, and private non-profit education organizations. Matching requirements are one to one with the exception of major institutions, which must provide a two-to-one match. All match funds must be in cash.

2) Money To Support Art Projects

Project Assistance: This category provides support for a specific event, project, or activity, either programmatic or administrative. This program is available to all groups. Applicant matching funds must be a minimum of 50% of the cost. Half of these funds may be in-kind contributions, which are the value of goods and services directly donated to a project, where no dollars are exchanged.

3) Grants For Artists To Go On Tour

Touring Assistance: Up to 50% of artist fee support is provided to presenters who present companies/artists for both visual and performing events. Performers are chosen from the Texas Touring Program Company/Artist Roster. Presenters are approved for a two-year period.

4) Money For Schools To Have An Artist In Residence

Arts in Education: This program is available to professionally staffed organizations for up to 50% of project costs for an artist in residence. Priority is given to programs involving students in kindergarten through twelfth grade, teacher training, and that show evidence of community involvement. Artists are required to provide 20 hours of service of artist development time during a normal 40-hour week and are paid on a per diem basis.

Utah

Utah Arts Council, 617 E. South Temple, Salt Lake City, UT 84102, 801-533-5895. Individual artist programs require state residency, unless otherwise specified. In 1992-93, 181 grants were awarded to organizations totalling $1,000,349.

1) $5,000 For Artists, Printmakers, Photographers, and Video Artists

Visual Artist Fellowships: The Council awards two $5,000 visual artists fellowships annually through the Visual Arts Program. Fellowships are available for individual artists practicing crafts, painting, drawing, printmaking, photography, sculpture, artist's bookmaking, and working in new genres, performance arts, conceptual arts, and video. These grants do not require matching funds.

2) $2,500 For An Artist To Learn From A Master

Folk Arts Apprenticeship Program: This program assists traditional artists and their communities by providing up to $2,500 to support one-on-one teaching between master artists and qualified apprentices.

3) $5,000 For Creative Writers

Creative Writing Award: The Council awards a $5,000 publication prize to an outstanding Utah writer.

4) $130,000 To Art Groups

Grants Program: The Council supports non-profit organizations through grants awarded on the basis of program quality. Annual grants are awarded to a wide variety of recipients, ranging from the Utah Symphony to the smallest community arts council. Grants range from $300 to $130,000 and include general support grants, Challenge grants (to $2,500), and Community Arts Development grants. Currently, total grant program funds are matched approximately 24-to-1 by funds from other sources.

5) Money For Community Art Councils

Community/State Partnership Program: This program assists community arts councils in incorporating, fund raising, presenting arts events, and initiating board development.

6) Money For Performing Artists To Tour The State

Utah Performing Arts Tour: This program encourages and supports professional residency activities that otherwise might not take place. Each winter a Roster of Performing Artists and companies is selected through applications and auditions. While Utah artists are highly encouraged to apply, out-of-state-artists are included on the tour each season. Technical assistance is provided in such areas as audience development, ticket-pricing, publicity, and program development.

7) $25 An Hour For Artists To Work At Local Schools

Arts in Education: This program encourages the recognition of the arts as part of basic education, primarily through school and community residencies and project grants in arts education. Residencies range from 10 days to a year in length. Artists receive $25 per hour and work four hours per day.

Vermont

Vermont Council on Arts, 133 State St., Montpelier, VT 05633-6001, 802-828-3291. Individual artist programs require state residency. The Vermont Council on Arts is an independent non-profit organization and not part of the State Government. In 1992-93, the Council awarded $524,870 in grants to non-profit organizations including schools and libraries. Individuals received $45,030 in funding, including $38,000 in Individual Artist Fellowships. The Artist Development Program awarded 29 grants totalling $7,030.

1) $1,000 For Artists To Attend Classes and Workshops

Artist Development Grants: These grants assist artists' professional development by supporting master classes, workshops, project development, documentation and more. Awards range from $100 to $500 for individual submissions and up to $1,000 for collaborative applications.

2) $3,500 For Artists

Fellowships: The Council awards $3,500 for Fellowships, and $500 for Finalist awards in recognition of artistic accomplishment. The program is highly competitive with only 5% to 8% of all applicants receiving awards.

3) Money To Support Special Art Projects

Project Grants: Grants fund specific arts projects within the general scope of arts organizations or non-arts organizations. Individual artists may apply for Project Grants in cooperation with an organization serving as Fiscal Agent.

4) $15,000 For Arts Groups

Operating Grants: Grants under this category provide general support for Vermont non-profit, tax exempt organizations for one year. Based on their most recently completed fiscal year, eligible organizations with an annual cash income of at least $15,000 and less than $125,000 may apply for a maximum of 10% of its annual operating budget. Grants rarely exceed $6,000. Eligible organizations with an annual cash income of more than $125,000 may apply for a maximum of 5% of its annual operating budget. Grants rarely exceed $15,000. Applications for grants must be for at least $1,500 a year.

5) $3,000 For Special Art Projects

Project Grants: Funding is available for specific arts projects within the general scope of arts organizations, non-arts organizations, or for artist's projects. Artists may work individually, in collaboration, or in partnership with an organization. Matching grants fund up to 50% of the project's cash cost or $3,000, whichever is less.

6) $5,000 For Arts Organizations To Develop

Service Organization Grants: Grants support non-profit organizations by providing resources and developmental opportunities. Grants range from $500 to $5,000, but are limited to half of the applicant's total operating budget, based on the applicant's most recently completed fiscal year.

7) $750 For Schools And Groups To Hire Artists

Options Programs: This program provides partial support to arts presenters and schools which hire culturally diverse artists who are not on the current Vermont Council on the Arts (VCA) Touring or Art in Education Rosters. Sponsors may request up to $100 a day for performances, and for workshops and residencies up to $750 per year.

8) Money To Have An Artist Perform For Your Organization

Touring Artists Program: This program provides partial support to local non-profit sponsors, including schools and municipalities, for performances of artists who are on the VCA Artists Register.

9) $160 A Day Plus Expenses To Be An Artist In Residence

Residency Program: This program brings working professional artists, including architects, craftsmen, dancers, musicians, poets, writers, media, theater, and visual artists into schools and other educational settings for residencies of one week to several months. Artists are paid a minimum of $160 per day, plus materials, mileage and hospitality, as negotiated with a sponsor.

10) Grants To Develop Art-Related Courses

Development Grants: Supports projects that advance the goal of the arts becoming a basic part of education in Vermont public schools. Non-profit arts organizations, Vermont public schools, and professional organizations may apply for these funds.

11) Money To Have An Artist In Residence

Residency Grants for Sponsors: These grants provide support for schools and non-profit educational organizations which host residencies by practicing artists from the Vermont Council on the Arts Register.

Virginia

Virginia Commission for the Arts, Lewis House, 223 Governor St., Richmond, VA 23219-2010, 804-225-3132. Individual artist programs require state residency. In 1993-94, grant awards will total over $1,400,000. In addition, the Commission approved 40 performing artists and ensembles for its 1994-95 Tour Directory. The Commission awarded grants totalling $1,106,700 to non-profit arts organizations under its General Operating Support Program.

1) $5,000 For Professional Artists To Advance Their Careers

Project Grants: A limited number of non-matching grants of $5,000 each are available to professional artists to support projects that will advance their art form or careers. One arts discipline will be eligible for support each year on a rotating basis. In 1993-94, 18 writers across the state received grants totalling $65,000.

2) $250 For Readings and Workshops Conducted By Writers

Writers in Virginia: This grant program provides subsidy for readings and workshops by Virginia writers in a wide variety of settings. Funding is available up to 50% of the writer's fee, with a maximum of $250 available. Sponsors may receive a total of $500 in any year. Grants are awarded on a first-come, first-served basis.

Organizational Funding: Maximum grants do not exceed more than 30% of an organization's income for the previous year. Most applicants receive much less than 30% of their income in Commission grants.

3) $15,000 To Run An Arts Organization
General Operating Support: This program provides funding to non-profit arts organizations to maintain stability and encourage advancement. Eligible activities include general operating expenses, special projects, construction or renovation costs, and reserve funds. Applicants may apply for 10% of their previous year's cash income for each year of the grant period, less Commission support and money raised for capital purposes in the previous year. Grants range from $500 to $150,000 per year.

4) $1,500 To Hire Management Consultants
Technical Assistance Grants: Non-matching grants provide outside help for organizations on particular problems. Organizations with annual incomes of $50,000 or more can apply for up to $1,000 in grants. Organizations with incomes of less than $50,000 can apply for up to $1,500 in grants.

5) Money To Produce Music, Opera, Theater, and Dance
Performing Arts Endowment Matching Program: This pilot program matches the interest earned by performing arts organizations on their endowment funds. It is open to organizations which produce music, opera, theater, and dance and pay its performers professional level salaries. Funds may either be used for performers' salaries or placed in the principal of the endowment fund.

6) $5,000 To Help Local Governments Support The Arts
Local Government Challenge Grants: The competitive program will match up to $5,000 in tax monies given by independent town, city, and county governments to arts organizations in their jurisdictions. Seventy-three towns, counties, and cities received support totalling $150,180 through this program. These are matching grants, and the maximum grant was $2,230.

7) Money For Artists To Tour The State
Touring Assistance Programs: This grant program supports touring by Virginia performing artists and arts organizations within the state. The Commission will fund up to 50% of the fee for any touring program listed in the Virginia Commission for Arts Tour Directory.

8) Money For Schools To Have An Artist In Residence
Artist in Education Residencies: This program places professional artists of various disciplines in residencies directed toward elementary and secondary students and their teachers. Generally, the Commission will award no more than 50% of the total cash cost of the residency program. First-time applicants, however, may request up to two-thirds of the total cash cost of the residency.

9) Grants For Community Colleges To Have An Artist In Residence
Community College Artist Residencies: This program places professional artists of a variety of disciplines in long-term residencies in community colleges of six to nine months. Eligible sponsors include all Virginia Community Colleges. Any professional artist in the discipline selected each year may apply to be included on the roster of eligible artists. Funding is tied to current faculty salary levels.

10) Funding For Workshops and Consultants In Arts Education
Arts in Education Development Grants: This program is available to all Virginia public schools and private schools. The program promotes the planning and development of sequential arts instruction in schools that do not currently offer arts education in the curriculum. Up to 50% of a project's cash cost can be funded. Funding can be used for projects such as workshops, consultants, or in-service training.

11) $300 For Teachers To Develop Innovative Art Programs
Teacher Incentive Grant Program: Financial assistance, up to $300, is provided to classroom teachers (pre-kindergarten through twelfth grade) to develop innovative ways of integrating the arts into the basic curriculum. The program is available to certified elementary and secondary classroom teachers, in any discipline, currently employed by Virginia educational institutions.

12) Money To Hire Consultants Or Attend Conferences In Arts Education
Arts In Education Technical Assistance: This program provides arts education associations, educators, arts administrators, etc., with opportunities for training, assistance, and services in the area of arts education. Grants of up to $1,000 are available for activities such as short-term consultancies by arts education specialists or attendance at arts education conferences or seminars.

Washington
Washington State Arts Commission, 110-9th and Columbia Bldg., MS-GH11, Olympia, WA 98504-2675, 206-753-3860. Individual artist programs require state residency. For fiscal year 1993, $1,152,000 was awarded to non-profit, community-based arts organizations. Individual fellowships totalled $60,000.

1) $5,000 To Professional Literary, Performing, and Two-Dimensional Artists
Artist Fellowship Awards: Awards of $5,000 are given to nine Washington practicing professional artists. Awards are made in the two-dimensional arts and literary arts in even-numbered years, and in the three-dimensional and performing arts (choreography, composition, and playwriting) in odd-numbered years. The tenth fellowship is awarded in the media arts.

2) Money For Outstanding Artists
Governor's Arts Awards: These awards honor the state's outstanding artists, arts supporters, and arts organizations.

3) Grants To Ethnic Heritage Artists
Governor's Ethnic Heritage Awards: These awards recognize individuals who have enhanced the state's individual cultures.

4) $2,000 For Short-Term Art Projects
Project Support: This program provides smaller arts organizations an opportunity to apply for as much as $2,000 for short-term endeavors.

5) $10,000 For Arts Organizations
Organizational Support: Under this category, mid-sized arts organizations grants may apply for grants of up to $10,000. Funding is made in three general categories:
A) Arts Organizations: This category includes arts producing, arts service, and arts education organizations such as theaters, orchestras, museums, dance companies, professional arts schools, cultural heritage associations, media arts centers, etc.
B) Arts Series Presenters: Rather than producing a single artistic event for their community, a "presenter" organizes, selects, and presents works by producing arts organizations and artists in a season, or series of events. A series presenter must sponsor three or more arts events during the year which are promoted as a series rather than as separate events.
C) Local Arts Agencies: Provides support to a non-profit local arts agency, arts council, arts commission, or entity.

6) Money To Support Arts Organizations
Institutional Support Program: This program helps fund 19 of Washington's major music, dance, theater, and visual arts organizations which annually bring some 2,500 artists before audiences of more than 2,000,000.

7) Money To Bring Performances To Schools
Cultural Enhancement Program (CEP): CEP offers elementary and secondary schools performances in music, dance, and drama. A school may hire an artist to do follow-up workshops for a class or school or apply for an AIR grant, described below.

8) Money For Schools To Have An Artist In Residence
Artists in Residence Program (AIR): In a typical year, 90 AIR artists and art critics will complete approximately 275 two-week residencies in schools, prisons, hospitals, community centers, and for special populations. Longer residencies of four weeks are also available. This is a cost-sharing (matching) program between the Commission and a sponsor. It is a competitive program, and successful applicants will receive a grant for 50% of the artist/scholar fees. A sponsor will spend approximately $608 per week per residency with an out-of-town artist/scholar and approximately $400 per residency week for an artist/scholar local to the site. The sponsor will also spend approximately $50 on artist's mileage and fees for the residency pre-planning meeting.

West Virginia
Arts and Humanities Division, Division of Culture and History, Cultural Center, 1900 Kanawha Blvd. East, Charleston, WV 25305-0300, 304-558-0220. In 1993-94, the Division awarded $912,872 in grants to non-profit arts organizations and $20,000 in eight individual fellowships. The majority of programs offer award grants to local sponsors for a project involving an individual artist. Artists arrange the proposed project with a sponsor who then applies for the grant.

1) Money For Individual Artists
Individual Artist Programs: This is a pilot program for individual fellowships based on artistic merit. Categories include: literature, music composition, crafts, the visual arts, and an award for artistic merit. At present, the following programs do not provide direct financial assistance to individual artists, but they do provide opportunities for sponsors to present artists in alternative ways. Artists are encouraged to contact potential sponsors about applying to present these programs. State residency is required.

2) Money For The Professional Development Of Artists
Support for Artists Program: This program assists artists with professional development through exhibitions, performances, commissions, and other projects.

3) Artists Lists and Register
West Virginia Artists List and Register: This register contains a comprehensive listing of performing, visual, and literary artists.

4) Money For Craftsman and Artists
West Virginia Juried Exhibition: This biennial statewide exhibition for visual artists and craftsmen provides direct awards to artists through competitive juring. Nationally recognized jurors select artists whose works receive purchase awards and merit awards totalling $33,000.

5) $15,000 For An Art Exhibition
Presenting West Virginia Artists Program: Museums and galleries may select a West Virginia artist who has been accepted in a minimum of three juried exhibitions or who has documentation of significant professional accomplishment and present the artist in a one-person exhibition. A maximum of $15,000 per exhibition is available for two projects each year.

Arts and Humanities

6) Money For Special Art Exhibits

Showcase of Visual Arts Program: Museums and galleries may request assistance to present a showcase exhibition of West Virginia artists who have been award winners in juried exhibitions or have documentation of significant professional accomplishment. Three to five artists, each of who agree to exhibit up to six recently created works, can be eligible. A maximum of $15,000 per exhibition is available for these projects.

7) $125,000 For Art Organizations

Major Institutions Support Grant: This program supports and stabilizes existing non-profit organizations by providing financial assistance toward their overall programming budget. Organizations must have a minimum operating base of at least $500,000, been in existence for five years, and serve a large audience that represents a broad cross-section of citizens. Up to $125,000 is available in funding.

8) $25,000 For Theaters, Galleries, and Museums

Support for Arts Institutions/Arts Organizations: Performing arts institutions, galleries, museums, and other arts organizations with boards of directors are eligible for this program. Funds may be used to support programming and exhibition costs. Maximum funding is $25,000.

9) $10,000 To Pay For Performing Artists

Residencies for Performing Arts Organizations and Institutions: This category is open to organizations such as orchestras, chamber groups, dance groups, and theater companies that include guest artists who are presented on their season of programs. Up to $10,000, or 50% of the contract fees for each artist will be awarded.

10) Grants To Bring Art To Local Schools And Communities

Arts in the Community: This program assists public schools and communities with up to 50% ($1,000 maximum) of the contractual fees and expenses of West Virginia performing, literary, media, and visual arts. This program is designed for individual schools or communities that present a single arts event for the year. A maximum of $12,000 in bookings is available for each individual artist and $30,000 for each touring company in a fiscal year.

11) Money To Fund Art Programs

Touring Program: This program enables sponsors to present performing, literary, and visual artists or exhibitions in their communities and schools. Sponsors of national touring companies can request up to 50% of the contract fee involved.

12) $10,000 For Film, Video, And Audio Projects

Media Arts Projects: This category supports media arts projects (film, video, and audio) in the areas of artist's fees, production and post-production costs, and presentation costs. Arts organizations may apply for 50% of the costs mentioned above, up to $10,000 per project. Non-matching grants up to $5,000 are also available to individual artists.

13) Money To Support New Works Of Composers, Playwrights, Writers, and Choreographers

Performing Arts: This category provides support for competitive commissions of new works and new productions. It encourages the creation of new works by composers, playwrights, writers, and choreographers. Applicants are strongly encouraged to work with West Virginia artists. Organizations may request up to 50% of funding.

14) Money To Artists and Art Administrators To Attend Conferences

Travel Fund: This category provides financial assistance to artists and arts administrators to attend professional events outside the state. Eligible applicants include volunteer or professionally staffed arts organizations. Expenses up to $200 are funded.

15) Grants For Groups And Communities To Develop Long Range Arts Programs

Project 20/21: This project encourages individual arts organizations and communities to develop long-range plans to strengthen and advance their administrative and technical development. Non-profit arts organizations, city or council governments, or similar organizations are eligible to apply. Typically, grants are awarded for up to 50% of fees and expenses.

16) Money to Develop Special Art Programs For Schools

Arts in Education provides assistance with the planning and development of various projects involving schools and the community. Performances, demonstrations, artist residencies, teacher training, and other innovative arts education projects are eligible for support. Artist in Residencies projects range from a minimum of one week to one year.

Wisconsin

Wisconsin Arts Board, 101 E. Wilson St., Suite 301, Madison, WI 53702, 608-266-0190. Individual artist programs require state residency. For most programs, recipients must match state awards with cash or donated services. In 1992-93, $2,982,570 was awarded to non-profit organizations and individuals.

1) $5,000 For Artists, Writers, and Folk Artists

Fellowships: Awards of $5,000 each are granted in the following disciplines: dance, music, opera/musical theater, theater, visual arts, design arts, crafts, photography, media arts, literature, interdisciplinary arts, and folk arts.

2) $3,500 For New Artistic Works

New Work Awards: These awards fund the creation of new artistic works through grants of $3,500 each. In 1992-93, $52,500 was awarded under this category.

3) $1,000 To Support An Artist's Professional Development

Development Grants: These grants provide awards of $1,000 each to support the artist's professional development.

4) Money For Artists To Work With A Master

Folk Art Apprenticeships: Under this category, funding is provided for master artists to pass skills on to apprentices.

5) Grants To Larger Arts Organizations

Artistic Program Support I: This category promotes artistic quality, organizational and financial stability, and long-range planning for producing arts organizations which have state-wide impact and budgets of $400,000 or more.

6) Grants To Smaller Arts Organizations

Artistic Program Support II: Supports same goals as above for organizations with budgets of $50,000 to $400,000. State and private universities may also apply to this category for specific project support.

7) $3,000 For Small Groups And Individual Artists

Small Organization Support: This category provides project funding of up to $3,000 to organizations with budgets of less than $50,000. Individual artists engaged in entrepreneurial activities may also be eligible.

8) Grants To Community Art Programs

Community Arts Program: Under this program, matching grants are provided to local arts agencies and arts service organizations for community projects. The Arts Board will support up to 50% of the total expense of the project. Applicants must show at least one-half of the match as a cash contribution.

9) Support For The Performing Arts Network

Performing Arts Network (PAN)-Wisconsin: PAN provides support to arts organizations that sponsor a series of four or more performances engaging professional touring artists.

10) Money For Organizations To Bring In Professional Touring Artists

Wisconsin Touring Program: This program provides support for organizations to sponsor a performance by a Wisconsin professional touring artist.

11) $5,000 For Folk Artists

Folk Arts Opportunity Grants: Grants support projects that help preserve and present Wisconsin folklife culture. Generally, grants range from $1,000 to $5,000. Applicants must provide support that matches the Arts Board's funding.

12) Grants For Culturally Diverse Art Projects

Cultural Diversity Initiative: This program provides funds to strengthen and stabilize cultural diverse arts organizations with annual budgets under $300,000, based in underserved communities.

13) Money To Pay For Art Administrators

Salary Assistance Grants: Grants under this category provide partial support for new, permanent artistic or administrative personnel for non-profit arts organizations.

14) Money For Schools To Have An Artist In Residence

Artists in Education Residency: Residencies provide funds to schools and community agencies to cover expenses of five-day to year-long artist residencies. Artists are selected form the AIE Artists Directory.

15) Money For Schools To Bring Artists Into The Classroom

Educational Opportunity Grants: Grants are awarded to schools so that they may use individuals listed in the AIE Artists Directory to provide hands-on service for kindergarten through twelfth grade teacher training.

Wyoming

Wyoming Arts Council, 2320 Capitol Ave., Cheyenne, WY 82002, 307-777-7742. Individual artist programs require state residency. For educational funding, grants require a one-to-one cash match. In 1992-93, $339,267 was awarded in grants to non-profit organizations. Individual fellowships totalled $32,000. Individual artist grants totalled $6,750.

1) $2,500 For Artists, Mimes, And Costume Designers

Performing Arts: This program incorporates music, theater, dance, stage, light and costume design, mime, opera and many other disciplines. It includes the Performing Arts Fellowships, with up to four $2,500 awards given, Individual Artist Grants, and supports the block-booking efforts of Wyoming's presenters.

2) $2,500 To Exhibit Wyoming Artists

Visual Arts: This program sponsors six exhibits annually in the Council gallery, as well as the biennial fellowship exhibition with tours throughout the Rocky Mountain West. The program coordinates the Visual Arts Fellowships, which award up to four $2,500 awards. It also provides specialized training opportunities, such as the 1991-92 Professional Development Series for visual artists and maintains a registry of over 400 Wyoming artists for review by galleries, corporations, and other seeking commissioned works.

3) $2,500 To Writers

Literature: This program provides fellowships and individual artist grants and brings nationally known writers to the state. It also sponsors readings for Wyoming writers. Under the Literary Fellowship Program, up to four $2,500 awards given. The Blanchan/Doubleday Memorial Awards provides awards of $1,000.

4) Grants For Arts Organizations

Organizational Funding: Wyoming's Community Service Program provides direct grants, training, technical assistance, and information to non-profit arts organizations. All grant requests must be matched a minimum of one-to-one with foundation, corporate, or local cash funding. Generally, no more than 20% of an organizations' total cash expenses is awarded.

5) Grants For Operating An Arts Organization

General Operating Support Grant: This grant covers the cost of administration and operation of the organization, as well as its artistic programming, excluding touring. Eligible organizations must have an annual budget greater than $100,000 and have at least one paid, full-time staff member.

6) Grants For One-Time Arts Events

Project Grants: These grants fund a specific, one-time arts project, event or a limited series of events. Projects may involve performing, visual, literary, media, folk, or multi-disciplinary arts.

7) Grants For Art Productions

Presenting and Producing Grants: These grants support organizations and presenting groups that take productions out of the local area and/or present events of regional, state, and national interest.

8) Grants To Strengthen An Arts Organization

Technical Assistance: Grants assist with program and board development, or any area that may prove to be helpful in strengthening the organization. Maximum funding is 50% of the project's total cash expense.

9) Grants To Schools And Organizations To Plan Arts Programs

Art is Essential Grant: This program encourages schools and organizations to plan for an entire year of arts in education. Applicants may apply at one deadline only for year-long projects, multiple projects, or projects that occur yearly and require constant planning. Generally, no more than 30% of an organization's total cash budget is funded.

10) Grants For Schools To Have An Artist In Residence

Artist In Residence Grants: These grants fund professional artists in schools, institutions, and communities for projects ranging from one week to one year. The Council sets a minimum artist fee of $100 per day for residences up to three weeks in length, and $1,600 per month for long-term residencies. Sponsors pay the artists' travel fees and per diem costs for the length of the residency.

11) Money To Develop Art Courses In Schools

Project Grants: These grants provide funding assistance to schools and organizations to strengthen their on going curriculum, or develop new curriculum with the assistance of roster artists and/or consultants.

12) Money To Bring Scholars and Experts To School Art Programs

Technical Assistance/In-service Grants: Schools and organizations may apply for funding to provide training for teachers and administrators. The program brings scholars and experts in to provide specific training and sends school or organization personnel to workshops and classes where they learn skills to train others.

13) Money For Trailblazer Art Programs

Trailblazer Projects: Arts programs which demonstrate an exciting, replicable activity, as determined by the grants review panels, may receive a special Trailblazer award to provide additional funding to document the project. This additional funding does not require matching funds and is an option for the applicant to accept.

Be patient. If any phone number is incorrect, call (area code) 555-1212 and request the new listing.

335

Your Community
Urban and Rural Resources

* *See also Housing and Real Estate Chapter*
* *See also Education Chapter*
* *See also Careers and Workplace Chapter*
* *See also Government Financial Help to Individuals Chapter*
* *See also Drugs and Chemical Dependence Chapter*
* *See also Government Auctions and Surplus Property Chapter*

On nearly every page of this book there are numerous resources mentioned that can benefit your community. Non-profit and service organizations are eligible to apply for federal loans and grants which are intended for education, job training, housing and economic development. The most relevant money programs for cities and towns are identified in this chapter but others appear throughout this book. Regional offices which dot the country bring the resources and experts of the federal government closer as well. Also browse through the index and discover thousands of films and other audiovisuals which are available for community groups.

* Arson Prevention Traveling Exhibit

U.S. Fire Administration
Office of Fire Prevention and Arson Control
Federal Emergency Management Agency
16825 South Seton Ave.
Emmitsburg, MD 21727   301-447-1200
Arson Trailers tour the country to provide technical and educational assistance to State, local, and national fire service and community groups. Their public educations demonstrations include fire safety issues, local fire problems, and smoke detector usage and maintenance.

* Appalachian Communities Aid

Appalachian Regional Commission
News and Public Affairs
1666 Connecticut Avenue, NW, Room 624
Washington, DC 20235   202-673-7968
The Commission provides various grants and loans for economic, physical, and social development of the 13-state Appalachian region, which includes parts of Alabama, Georgia, Kentucky, Maryland, Mississippi, New York, North Carolina, Ohio, Pennsylvania, South Carolina, Tennessee, Virginia, and all of West Virginia. The Commission publishes the *Appalachian Regional Commission Annual Report* which provides financial statistics, activities and programs over the past year.

* Community and Rural Economic Development

Valley Resource Center
Resource Group
Tennessee Valley Authority
600 W. Summit Hill Dr.
Knoxville, TN 37902-2801   615-632-3215
The Valley Resource Center can be contacted for information on community and rural economic development programs.

* Community Health Services Grants

Bureau of Health Care Delivery and Assistance
Health Resources and Services Administration
5600 Fishers Lane, Room 7-05, Parklawn Bldg.
Rockville, MD 20857   301-443-2320
                    Publications 301-443-1050
The Bureau of Health Care Delivery and Assistance Services focuses nationally on efforts to ensure the availability and delivery of health care services in health manpower shortage areas, to medically undeserved populations, and to special services populations, such as migrants or the homeless. The Bureau provides project grants to community-based organizations to meet the health needs of the undeserved or special needs populations.

* County Cooperative Extension Service

Executive Officer
U.S. Department of Agriculture (USDA)
Room 340A Administration Building
Washington, DC 20250   202-720-0987
The USDA operates an extension program in 3,050 counties located in all of the 50 states and the U.S. territories. Federal, state, and local governments share in financing and conducting cooperative extension educational programs to help farmers, processors, handlers, farm families, communities, and consumers apply the results of food and agricultural research. The Extension Service has targeted 7 national initiatives to provide a new focus for educational efforts.

1) Improving Nutrition, Diet, and Health: Extension offers up-to-date information about the relationship of dietary practices to lifestyle factors; the safety, quality, and composition of foods; and consumers' needs and perceptions about the food industry.

2) International Marketing:

3) Revitalizing Rural America: In cooperation with local governments, Extension programs emphasize how to increase competitiveness and efficiency of rural programs, explore methods to diversify local economies and attract new business, adjust to impact of change, develop ways to finance and deliver services, and train leaders to make sound policy decisions for rural communities.

4) Sustainable Agricultrue:

5) Waste Management:

6) Water Quality: Work with consumers, producers and local government to learn more about the importance of high-quality ground water and the conservation of water resources. Emphasis is also on the effects of agricultural chemicals and contaminants on water quality.

7) Youth at Risk: Extension is helping expand youth outreach resources to meet the needs of youth, develop programs for the most susceptible youth populations, provide leadership and job skills, and increase training of professionals and volunteers to work in communities to prevent and treat problems.

* County Governments Environmental Activities

National Association of Counties (NACo)
440 1st St., NW, 8th Floor
Washington, DC 20001   202-393-6226
NACo serves as a forum for improving the nation's county governments and to communicate the county viewpoint to national officials. NACo acts as a liaison with other levels of government, serves as a national advocate for counties, and achieves a public understanding of the role of counties in the intergovernmental system. *County News* is published bi-weekly, $75 a year.

* Dredging Permits

Regulatory Branch
U.S. Army Corps of Engineers
20 Massachusetts Ave., NW
Room 6235
Washington, DC 20314   202-272-0199

You must obtain a Corps permit if you plan to locate a structure, excavate, or discharge dredged or fill material in waters of the United States, including wetlands, or if you plan to transport dredged material for the purpose of dumping it into ocean waters. Contact the appropriate District Engineer office for current information and to apply for a permit. You may contact the above office for addresses and telephone numbers of the District offices.

* Economic Research Studies

Public Affairs
Economic Development Administration
U.S. Department of Commerce
14th St. and Constitution Ave., NW
Washington, DC 20230   202-377-5113

Economic Research Studies of the Economic Development Administration is an annotated bibliography listing economic research reports published by the Economic Development Administration (EDA). Each of the 210 entries includes an abstract and ordering information. The reports cover a broad range of topics and concentrate on the causes of economic distress and of economic growth, the basic remedy for distress. Contact EDA for your free copy.

* Election Assistance

Federal Election Commission (FEC)
Information Services
999 E Street, NW
Washington, DC 20463   202-219-3420

In an effort to promote voluntary compliance with the law, this office provides technical assistance to candidates and committees and others involved in elections. Staff will research and answer questions on the Federal Election Campaign Act and FEC regulations, procedures, and advisory opinions; direct workshops on the law; and publish a wide range of materials.

* Fair Lending Practices

Fair Lending Analyst
Office of Consumer Affairs
Federal Deposit Insurance Corporation (FDIC)
550 17th St., NW, Room F-130
Washington, DC 20429   202-898-3535

The Community Reinvestment Act of 1977 empowers the Federal Deposit Insurance Corporation (FDIC) to monitor FDIC-insured, state-chartered banks to make sure that the banks are meeting the credit needs of the communities they serve, including low- and middle-income areas. Questions regarding community reinvestment should be directed to the nearest FDIC regional office or to the Fair Lending Analyst at the above office.

* Free Experts on Loan to Community Organizations

Pearson Program
Bureau of Personnel
U.S. Department of State
2101 C St. NW, Room 2807
Washington, DC 20520   202-647-3308

The two objectives of this program are to allow State and local governments and related organizations to utilize the experience and expertise of Foreign Service Officers and to permit Foreign Service Officers to be assigned to positions with substantial program management responsibilities. Frequently officers are assigned to serve as special assistants to governors, mayors, city managers, and county commissioners. They have been assigned to a State department of social services, a regional local government innovation group, and to the Pan American Games organizing group. Interested organizations should discuss requests with the Office of Training and Liaison, and then submit a proposal. The U.S. Department of State will then attempt to identify an interested officer for the position.

* Free Food For Non-Profit Institutions

Food Distribution Division
Food and Nutrition Service
3101 Park Center Dr., Room 503

Alexandria, VA 22302   703-305-2680

Charitable and rehabilitation institutions are usually eligible to receive surplus commodities stored by U.S. Department of Agriculture. The commodities available are dairy products, grain oil, and peanuts.

* Geographic Names Information

Branch of Geographic Names
U.S. Geological Survey (USGS)
National Center, MS 523
Reston, VA 22092   703-648-4547

The USGS Branch of Geographic Names maintains a national research, coordinating, and information center to which all problems and inquiries concerning domestic geographic names can be directed. This office compiles name information, manages a names data repository, maintains information files, and publishes materials on domestic geographic names. The USGS, in cooperation with the Board on Geographic Names, maintains the *National Geographic Names Data Base* and compiles *The National Gazetteer of the United States of America* on a state-by-state basis.

* Health Services for Indigents

Bureau of Health Care Delivery and Assistance
Health Resources and Services Administration
5600 Fishers Lane
Room 7-05
Rockville, MD 20857   301-443-2320

The Bureau of Health Care Delivery and Assistance Services focuses nationally on efforts to ensure the availability and delivery of health care services in health manpower shortage areas, to medically underserved populations, and to special services populations, such as migrants or the homeless. It also administers the National Health Service Corps Program which recruits health care practitioners and places them in areas having shortages of people trained in health-related fields.

* Historic Places National Register

Interagency Resources Division
National Park Service
U.S. Department of the Interior
1100 L St., NW
Washington, DC 20005   202-343-9500

The National Register of Historic Places is administered by the Interagency Resources Division of the National Park Service (NPS). Along with the Preservation Assistance Division, this office administers the Historic Preservation Fund grants-in-aid to states and the National Trust for Historic Preservation. Technical workshops and other assistance is provided on preservation planning, and a database of historic information is maintained.

* Local Environmental Health Managers

National Conference of Local
  Environmental Health Administrators (NCLEHA)
Summit County Health Department
1100 Graham Circle
Cuyahoga Falls, OH 44224   216-923-4891

The National Conference of Local Environmental Health Administrators promotes efficient and effective local environmental health programs. NCLEHA is affiliated with the National Environmental Health Association.

* Local Government Environmental Activities

International City Managers Association (ICMA)
77 N. Capital, NE, Suite 500
Washington, DC 20002   202-289-4262

The purposes of the International City Managers Association (ICMA) are to enhance the quality of local government and to nurture and assist professional local government administrators in the United States and other countries.

* Mayors of Large Cities

U.S. Conference of Mayors
1620 I St., NW, 4th Floor
Washington, DC 20006   202-293-7330

The United States Conference of Mayors is the official nonpartisan organization of cities with populations of 30,000 or more. It has taken the lead in calling national attention to the problems and the potential of urban America.

Your Community

* Medical Services and Personnel Shortages Survey

National Clearinghouse for Primary Care Information
8201 Greensboro Dr., Suite 600
McLean, VA 22102   703-821-8955

This clearinghouse provides information services to support the planning, development, and delivery of ambulatory health care to urban and rural areas where shortages of medical personnel and services exist. Its primary audience is health care providers who work in community health centers. They have a list of publications and can make referrals to other health-related organizations. This clearinghouse also publishes a newsletter, *Primary Care Perspectives*.

* Military Base Closures: Community Adjustment

Office of Economic Adjustment
U.S. Department of Defense
The Pentagon, Room 4C767
Washington, DC 20301-4000   703-545-6700

The Office of Economic Adjustment assists local communities, areas or states affected by U.S. Department of Defense actions, such as base closures, establishment of new installations, and cutbacks or expansion of activities. It publishes a number of free publications on these issues, including *Communities in Transition, Economic Recovery*, and *Twenty-five Years of Civilian Re-use*. Write or call for more information.

* National Governor's Association

National Governor's Association (NGA)
444 North Capitol St., NW
Suite 250
Washington, DC 20001   202-624-5300

NGA serves as a vehicle through which governors influence the development and implementation of national policy and apply creative leadership to state problems.

* National League of Cities

National League of Cities (NLC)
1301 Pennsylvania Ave., NW
Suite 600
Washington, DC 20004   202-626-3000

NLC is dedicated to making cities efficient and improving the delivery of municipal services by providing answers to questions about the day-to-day realities of running a city or town including refuse collection, employment practices, police management, cable television, hazardous waste management and international trade.

* Non-Profits and Foreign Exchange Programs

Bureau of Education and Cultural Affairs
United States Information Agency (USIA)
301 Fourth St., SW, Room 216
Washington, DC 20547   202-619-4700

Grants and assistance are given to private non-profit organizations for exchange programs which further USIA goals of promoting mutual understanding between Americans and others. Any non-profit organization can submit proposals for partial funding.

* Place and Feature Names: State-by-State Dictionary

U.S. Geological Survey (USGS)
Books and Open File Reports
Box 25425, Federal Center
Denver, CO 80225   303-236-7476

The National Gazetteer of the United States of America is a geographic dictionary of place and feature names, published on a state-by-state basis. It includes a glossary of terms and abbreviations, a map of counties in a state, and an alphabetical listing of USGS topographic quadrangle maps of the state, in addition to the information contained in the *National Geographic Names Data Base*. Also listed are names of features from other historical sources. Variant names are listed and cross-referenced to their official names. A variant name is any other known name or spelling applied to a feature other than the official name. Also available at USGS, Branch of Distribution, P.O. Box 25286, Denver, CO 80225.

* Planned Approach to Community Health (PATCH)

Centers for Chronic Disease Prevention and Health Promotion
Centers for Disease Control

1600 Clifton Rd., NE
Bldg 3, Room 117
Atlanta, GA 30333   404-488-5401

Centers for Chronic Disease Prevention and Health Promotion (CCDPHP) staff work with State and local health departments and community members to organize local intervention programs. The center provides materials and technical assistance, and the communities invest their time and resources and make the program work. Programs have focused on cholesterol screening and nutrition, smoking cessation, alcohol misuse, and prevention of injuries from falls. The PATCH program also conducts international training conferences.

* Public Works Engineering

American Public Works Association (APWA)
1313 East 60th St.
Chicago, IL 60637   312-667-2200

The American Public Works Association consists of government officials, engineers, administrators and others engaged in the various aspects of public works and published *APWA Reporter and APWA Directory*.

* Resource Development

Resource Development
Tennessee Valley Authority (TVA)
P.O. Box 1010, Reservation Rd.
Muscle Shoals, AL 35660   205-386-2601

The TVA plans to fund several future development programs. These include the stewardship of TVA facilities and landholdings; the improvement of water resources; the development of the Land Between the Lakes to reach its potential as a national demonstration model; and the production of fertilizer technology that supports a profitable and competitive agriculture. Group economic and rural development programs will also be funded in the Valley Resource Center to expand the Valley's service sector, upgrade literacy and job skills, promote a competitive manufacturing section, and expand employment in natural resource-based industries.

* Rural Agricultural Processing Industries

Science and Education
Agricultural Research Service (ARS)
U.S. Department of Agriculture
Washington, DC 20250   202-720-5923

The ARS administers fundamental and applied research to solve problems in animal and plant protection and production; the conservation and improvement of soil, water and air; the processing, storage, and distribution of farm products; and human nutrition. The research applies to a wide range of goals, commodities, natural resources, fields of science and geographic, climatic, and environmental conditions.

Research activities are carried out at 138 domestic locations, including Puerto Rico, the Virgin Islands, and in 8 foreign countries. Much of this research is conducted in cooperation with State partners in the universities and experiment stations, other Federal agencies, and private organizations. A national program staff, headquartered at Beltsville, MD, is the focal point in the overall planning and coordination of the Service's national research programs. Day-to-day management of the various national research programs for specific field locations is assigned to 8 area offices.

* Rural Communities Clearinghouse

Rural Information Center
U.S. Department of Agriculture
10301 Baltimore Blvd., Room 304
Beltsville, MD 20705   301-504-5719

This center handles matters of economic competitiveness, economic development, local government, rural communities, community leadership, and natural resources. This center is a joint project of USDA's Extension Service and NAL.

* Rural Communities Financial Assistance

Farmers Home Administration (RDA)
U.S. Department of Agriculture
Washington, DC 20250   202-720-4323

RDA provides financial assistance to rural people and communities that cannot obtain commercial credit at affordable terms. Applicants must be unable to obtain credit from usual commercial sources. Examples of the types of loans available are Emergency Loans, Youth Project Loans, Housing Repair Loans and Grants, Business and Industry Loan Guarantees, Community Facilities Loans and Loan Guarantees, and Farm Operating Loans.

Be patient. If any phone number is incorrect, call (area code) 555-1212 and request the new listing.

* State Legislatures Coordination

National Conference of State Legislatures (NCSL)
444 North Capitol St., NW
Suite 500
Washington, DC 20001   202-624-5400

NCSL is a national organization of state legislators and legislative staff whose aims are to improve the quality and effectiveness of state legislators, to ensure states a strong, cohesive voice in the federal decision-making process and to foster interstate communication and cooperation.

* Telecommunications and Computing Technology

Office of Technology Assessment
600 Pennsylvania Ave., SE
Washington, DC 20003   202-228-6760

Recent advances in information storage and transmission technologies, occurring in a new deregulated and intensely competitive economic climate, are rapidly changing the Nation's communication networks. OTA is studying the role of the Federal government in this area, along with how to coordinate them, resolve potential conflicts between them, and examine new communication systems abroad and their potential relationships to the U.S. systems. Contact Linda Garcia, the project director, for more information.

* Telecommunications Expertise for Libraries, Schools, Fire Departments

Public Telecommunications Facilities Program
National Telecommunications and Information Administration
U.S. Department of Commerce
14th St. and Constitution Ave., NW
Room 4625
Washington, DC 20230   202-377-5802

By identifying public service telecommunications needs, NTIA assists schools, hospitals, libraries, policy, fire departments, and government agencies in using advanced telecommunications systems and technology to achieve their goals.

* Towns and Townships Advocacy

National Association of Towns and Townships (NATT)
1522 K St., NW
Suite 600
Washington, DC 20005   202-737-5200

NATT is a federation of state organizations and individual communities which provide technical assistance, educational services and public policy support to local government officials of small communities across the country.

Neighborhood Improvements

* Aerial Photographs of Your Neighborhood

Customer User Services
Earth Resources Observation System Data Center (EROS)
U.S. Geological Survey
Mundt Federal Bldg.
Sioux Falls, SD 57198 605-594-6511
Aerial photographs are available from the Earth Resources Observation System Data Center for most geographical regions of the country. Prices range from $6 to $65, depending on whether they are black and white or color photographs. Contact this office for ordering information.

* Afro-American and Minority Health Projects

Office of Minority Health
U.S. Department of Health and Human Services
200 Independence Ave., SW
Room 118F
Washington, DC 20201 202-245-0020
This office serves as the focal point for the implementation of the recommendations and findings from the Report of the Secretary's Task Force on Black and Minority Health. Community-based projects are being designed to reduce the more than 60,000 excess deaths each year among minority Americans. Major activities include conferences, grants for innovative community health strategies developed by minority coalitions, and research on risk factors affecting minority health. The Report may be obtained from Minority Health Resource Center, 301-589-1938.

* Aircraft Noise

Noise Abatement Division
Office of Environment and Energy
Federal Aviation Administration
U.S. Department of Transportation
800 Independence Ave., SW, Room 432
Washington, DC 20591 202-267-3553
This Federal Aviation Administration (FAA) division conducts research on reducing noise levels of new aircraft, and retrofitting older aircraft to reduce noise levels.

* Air Force Bands

U.S. Air Force
Bands and Music Branch
The Pentagon, SAF/PAG
Washington, DC 20330-1000 202-767-5658
If there is an Air Force band stationed near you, you can request a public performance in your town. For information on where the bands are located and who to contact to schedule a performance, call the above coordinating office.

* Air Shows

Headquarters
U.S. Marine Corps
Community Relations
Washington, DC 20380-0001 703-614-1054
The Marine Corps can provide aviation demonstrations for community events. Contact your local Marine Corps headquarters or the above office for a referral.

* Anti-Drug Abuse Community Grants

Drug Abuse Prevention Oversight Staff
Office of the Secretary
U.S. Department of Education
400 Maryland Ave., SW, Room 1073
Washington, DC 20202-0100 202-401-1599
State and Local Grants Program: This is a formula grant program which allocates funds to States based on school-age enrollment. Funds are to be used for anti-drug abuse efforts in schools and community-based organizations. Contact Allen King, 202-401-1599.

* Army Band and Chorus

Community Relations Division
U.S. Army Public Affairs
The Pentagon, Room 2E631
Washington, DC 20310 703-614-0739
To arrange for a performance in your community by the Army Field Band and Soldiers Chorus, the Golden Knights paratrooper unit, color guards, and other marching units, contact your nearest Army installation, or the above office for a referral.

* Army Paratroopers and Color Guards

Community Relations Division
U.S. Army Public Affairs
The Pentagon, Room 2E631
Washington, DC 20310 703-614-0739
To arrange for a performance in your community by the Golden Knights paratrooper unit, color guards, and other marching units, contact your nearest Army installation, or the above office for a referral.

* Army Reserve Band and Color Guard

Chief of U.S. Army Reserve
Public Affairs
Washington, DC 20310 703-696-3963
To request an Army Reserve band performance in your town, or to arrange for a color guard at a former military person's funeral,
contact your local Army Reserve headquarters or the above office for a referral.

* Army Reserve Community Projects: Baseball to Language Training

Chief of U.S. Army Reserve
Public Affairs, The Pentagon
Washington, DC 20310 703-696-3962/3
The Army Reserve provides a variety of community services through their special programs. Requests are handled on a case by case basis based on their current ability to help. Projects might involve building a community playground or a baseball field. Through the Adopt-a-School Program, Corps people with special skills or training teach special courses, such as a foreign language or communications, or may be involved in extra-curricular activities. Contact your local Army Reserve.

* Art Exhibits: Parks, Plazas, Airports

Visual Arts Program
National Endowment for the Arts
1100 Pennsylvania Ave., NW, Room 729
Washington, DC 20506 202-682-5448
The Visual Arts Program awards fellowships to artists in a wide variety of visual media, enabling them to set aside time to pursue their work. It also awards grants to organizations that assist visual artists and support public art projects, such as art in parks, plazas, and airports. Funding is available for a variety of projects that enable visual artists to communicate with their peers and the public, and for a variety of on-going visual arts programs, including exhibitions and access to working facilities.

* Bank Loans and Community Reinvestment

Community Affairs Officer
Federal Reserve System
20th St. and Constitution Ave., NW
Washington, DC 20551 202-452-3000
The Community Reinvestment Act encourages banks and other institutions to help meet the credit needs for housing and other purposes in their communities. In accordance with this Act, the Community Affairs Officer and staff at each of the 12 Federal Reserve Banks are responsible for advising depository institutions of private and public resources for community development. The officers also facilitate communications between borrowers, lending institutions, local government agencies,

and others involved with community development financing. A pamphlet outlining the Community Reinvestment Act responsibilities of the Community Affairs Officers may be requested from the Federal Reserve Bank of Richmond, or the Community Affairs Officer at any Federal Reserve Bank.

* Cities in Schools: Truancy, Dropouts, Violence

Office of Juvenile Justice and Delinquency Prevention
U.S. Department of Justice
633 Indiana Ave., NW
Washington, DC 20531   202-307-0751

Cities in Schools, a public-private partnership that addresses the problems of dropouts and school violence, is designed to reduce school absenteeism and dropout rates by coordinating services for at-risk youngsters. Five regional offices help serve the 26 operating programs throughout the country and assist other local communities to initiate new Cities in Schools programs.

* Community Action Against Alcohol and Drug Addiction

National Clearinghouse on Alcohol and Drug Information
P.O. Box 2345
Rockville, MD 20847   301-468-2600

Communities: What You Can Do About Drug and Alcohol Abuse is a booklet that discusses various strategies for parent groups, schools, and workplaces and details various educational materials available. Single copies of this booklet (No. 84-1310) are available free.

* Community Anti-Drug Alliance

ACTION
Drug Alliance Office
1100 Vermont Ave., NW, Suite 8200
Washington, DC 20525   202-606-4857

ACTION supports community-based prevention and education efforts with grants, contracts, conferences, and technical assistance. Nonprofit organizations and state and local governments are eligible to receive grants from ACTION. An announcement is made in the *Federal Register* regarding the type of activities that the ACTION grant is available for and organizations are encouraged to apply. ACTION also maintains a mailing list which sends copies of the notices appearing in the *Federal Register* directly to those on the list. To get the name of your organization on this list, call the number above.

* Community Business Development

Public Affairs
Economic Development Administration
U.S. Department of Commerce
14th St. and Constitution Ave., NW
Room 7810
Washington, DC 20230   202-377-5113

The Economic Development Administration provides loan guarantees to industrial and commercial firms, and technical assistance and grants to enable communities and firms to find solutions to problems that stifle economic growth. Contact this office for more information.

* Community Drug Abuse Situation

Information Systems Unit
Office of Diversion Control
Drug Enforcement Administration
U.S. Department of Justice
1405 Eye St. NW, Room 719
Washington, DC 20537   202-307-1000

For those who want to understand and evaluate the scope and magnitude of drug abuse in the United States, this network is an invaluable information source. Whether you are a local public administrator considering programs, a reporter on the heels of a story, or just a concerned parent, the Drug Abuse Warning Network (DAWN) can provide you with needed information. More than 900 hospital emergency rooms and medical examiner facilities supply data to the program. DAWN identifies drugs currently in vogue, determines existing patterns and profiles of abuse/abuser in Standard Metropolitan Statistical Areas, monitors systemwide abuse trends, detects new abuse entities and polydrug combinations, and provides data needed for rational control and scheduling of drugs being abused. It is the full-information source on the drug problem in America.

* Community Involvement with Workplace Drug Abuse

National Audiovisual Center
Customer Service Section
8700 Edgeworth Drive
Capitol Heights, MD 20743-3701   301-763-1896

National Clearinghouse for Alcohol and Drug Information
P.O. Box 2345
Rockville, MD 20847   301-468-2600

Finding Solutions portrays drug abuse in the workplace as a community-wide problem; thus the solutions offered through education and prevention are presented as personal, workplace, and community responsibilities. Specific emphasis is placed on the need to effectively deliver accurate and credible information to the workforce, to promote workplace peer involvement and build community partnerships. It is available for sale and rental.

* Crime Insurance for Homeowners and Business

Federal Crime Insurance
P.O. Box 6301   800-638-8780
Rockville, MD 20849-6301   301-251-1660 in DC

The Federal Crime Insurance Program is a federally subsidized program sponsored by the Federal Emergency Management Adminstration for homeowners and commercial businesses to insure against burglary and robbery. To find out if your state is eligible and for further information, contact the office above. Those living in Maryland outside DC should call collect: 301-251-1660.

* Ethnic or Racial Tensions Resolution

Community Relations Service (CRS)
U.S. Department of Justice
5550 Friendship Blvd., Suite 330
Chevy Chase, MD 20815   301-492-5929

If your community is being torn apart by ethnic disputes or police-citizen conflicts, you may need help from this special service, set up by the Civil Rights Act of 1964. The Community Relations Service exists to resolve such disputes. The agency provides direct conciliation and mediation assistance to communities to facilitate the peaceful, voluntary resolution of racial and ethnic disputes or conflicts, and the peaceful co-existence of police and citizens' groups in the rapidly changing neighborhoods of today's cities. The CRS regularly provides conferences, training workshops, and publications to any and all communities in an attempt to forestall such disputes. However, when tensions do break out, the CRS will initiate whatever steps are necessary to begin making progress toward bringing about a resolution. They normally begin with extensive informal discussions with public or police officials and local community leaders, but if the agency and the parties determine that formal negotiations offer the best hope for a settlement, the agency arranges and mediates the negotiations.

* Fire Prevention and Education

Office of Fire Prevention and Arson Control
U.S. Fire Administration
16825 South Seton Ave.
Emmitsburg, MD 21727   301-447-1122

For information on technical and educational assistance to State, local, and national fire services and community groups, contact the office above. Information on fire safety, residential sprinkler trailers and smoke detector usage and maintenance can be obtained from this office. Various forms of educational assistance (pamphlets, books, tapes) can be obtained. Call the office above to receive the following publications, and to find out how to receive the monthly newsletter, *Operation Life Safety.*

After the Fire: Returning (#5-0027)
America's Burning (#5-0025)
Check Your Hotspots Kit (#5-0101)
Home Fire Protection Fire Sprinkler (#5-0007)
It's Alarming (#5-0035) poster
Fire in the U.S. (#5-0135)
Organizing Your Community (#5-0068)
Public Fire Education Today (#5-0139)
Safety and Your Christmas Tree (#5-0029)
Smoke Detector and Fire Safety Guide (#5-0039)
Smoke Detector Kit (#5-0051)
Smoke Detectors: Don't Stay at Home (#5-0104)
U.S. Fire Administration Brochure (#5-0067)
Winter Fires (#5-0031)

Your Community

* Fire Safety for Children

U.S. Fire Administration
16825 South Seton Ave.
Emmitsburg, MD 21727   301-447-1122

Contact the office above to obtain materials on fire safety for children. The following materials are available, in addition to Sesame Street education materials on fire safety education:

Adolescent Firesetter Handbook, ages 14 - 18 (#5-0091) FA-80
Child Firesetter Handbook, ages 7 - 13 (#5-0107) FA-82
Child Firesetter Handbook, ages 0 - 7 (#5-0106) FA-83
Curious Kids Kit (#5-0121) K-71
Juvenile Firesetter Handbook - Dealing with Children Ages 7-14 (FA-63)
Fire Safety Book (#5-0069) cass. (#5-0090)

* Free Christmas Trees

Division of Forestry
Bureau of Land Management (BLM)
U.S. Department of the Interior
1849 C St., NW
Washington, DC 20240   202-208-5717

The Bureau of Land Management (BLM) officials issue permits to cut Christmas trees for a nominal fee on Bureau of Land Management-administered lands in the 11 Western states and Alaska. Free-use permits are available from the Bureau to non-profit organizations for timber and trees to be used exclusively by that organization. This excludes the resale of any free timber or trees by those organizations.

* Historic Preservation Assistance

Preservation Assistance Division
National Park Service
U.S. Department of the Interior
1100 L St., NW
Washington, DC 20005   202-208-7394

The Preservation Assistance Division guides Federal and state agencies and the general public in historic preservation project work. Standards and guidelines are established, information on technical preservation is distributed, and training is given on technical preservation approaches and treatments. This office also administers the Preservation Tax Incentives program, the status of National Historic Landmarks, and the Historic Preservation Fund grant-in-aid program.

* Homeless, Migrants, Refugees: Health Services

Bureau of Health Care Delivery and Assistance
Health Resources and Services Administration
5600 Fishers Lane
Room 7-05
Rockville, MD 20857   301-443-2320

The Bureau of Health Care Delivery and Assistance Services focuses nationally on efforts to ensure the availability and delivery of health care services in health manpower shortage areas, to medically underserved populations, and to special services populations, such as migrants or the homeless. It also administers the National Health Service Corps Program which recruits health care practitioners and places them in areas having shortages of people trained in health-related fields.

* Job Creation Assistance

Technical Assistance Division
Economic Development Administration (EDA)
U.S. Department of Commerce
14th St. and Constitution Ave., NW
Washington, DC 20230   202-377-2127

The Technical Assistance Division of Economic Development Administration (EDA) sponsors programs of technical assistance to local communities which are designed to discover new ways to generate jobs. Local governments, non-profit organizations, and private firms can apply. Contact this office for more information.

* Marine Corps Air Show

Commandant of the Marine Corps (OLAC)
Headquarters Marine Corps
Community Relations
Washington, DC 20380   703-614-1034

Watch the AV8 Harrier jump jet (it shoots straight up and turns around in mid-air), the Drum and Bugle Corps, and Marine bands perform. You may write to the above address or your nearest Corp installation for their brochure explaining Marine Corps programs and how to complete the forms to arrange for these units' performance in your community. They can also provide you with a patriotic speaker for Veterans Day and Memorial Day events.

* Marine Corps Bands and Color Guards

Headquarters
U.S. Marine Corps
Code P.A.C.
Washington, DC 20380   703-614-1034

The Marine Corps can provide bands and color guards for community events. The Corps supports the Devil Pup program. Contact your local Marine Corps headquarters or the above office for a referral.

* Marine Corps Summer Camp

Headquarters
U.S. Marine Corps
Code P.A.C.
Washington, DC 20380-0001   703-614-1034

The Marine Corps sponsor a summer camp for high school youth. Contact your local Marine Corps headquarters or the above office for a referral.

* National Guard Community Participation

National Guard Bureau
Attn: NGB-PAC
Skyline #6
5109 Leesburg Pike, Suite 4013
Falls Church, VA 22041-3201   703-756-1923

Local National Guard units provide bands, color guards, and flight demonstrations for community events upon request of civic groups. The Guard also sponsors annual open houses and conducts tours of the local bases. A Speakers Bureau will provide experts to speak on defense and local issues, and the Guard sponsors orientation trips for civic leaders. Call or write for more information on the Guard's varied community assistance programs, including the loan of equipment to civic groups.

* Navy Bands and Concerts

U.S. Navy Band
Public Affairs Office
Washington Navy Yard
Washington, DC 20374-5054   202-433-2394

The U.S. Navy Concert Band and its specialty units--including the Topside Quartet (jazz, rock), Brass Navy Band, Saxaphone Quartet, Fairwinds Quartet (vocal), Windjammers, Tuba-Euphonium Quartet, Sea Chanters, Country Current, and the Commodores--are available to perform at community events nationwide. Units of the band perform a wide range of musical styles, from jazz, folk, and blue grass to classical chamber and cocktail music. Write or call for information on how to request the Band.

* Neighborhood Crime Comparison Information

Uniform Crime Reporting Section
Federal Bureau of Investigation
U.S. Department of Justice
9th and Pennsylvania Ave., NW, GRB
Washington, DC 20535   202-324-5015

If you'd like to know how safe your prospective new neighborhood is, contact the Uniform Crime Reporting Section. This annual report, *Crime In the United States* contains an exact reading of the crime rates of any city in America (down to the types of crimes committed most frequently in which neighborhoods). Also, local police departments of most major cities have neighborhood crime reports available and will actually rate the safety factor of your new address for you.

* Neighborhood Safety Videos and Publications

National Institute of Justice (NIJ)
NCJRS, Box 6000
Dept. AID   800-851-3420
Rockville, MD 20850   301-251-5500 in DC

The National Institute of Justice (NIJ) has these and other publications and videos on crime prevention and the law. Many of the documents are free of charge, while others are available for a modest fee. When ordering or inquiring about an NIJ publication, refer to its NCJ number.

Crime Stoppers: A National Evaluation (RIB). 1986, 5 pp. (NCJ 102292).
The Growing Role of Private Security (RIB). 1984, 5 pp. (NCJ 94703).
*Guardian Angels: An Assessment of Citizen Response to Crime: Executive
   Summary.* 1986, 31 pp. (NCJ 1009111).
Improving the Use and Effectiveness of Neighborhood Watch Programs (RIA).
   1988, 4 pp. (NCJ 108618).
Neighborhood Safety (Crime file videotape). 1985 (NCJ 97227). VHS, Beta, or
   3/4-inch.
*Taking a Bite Out of Crime: The Impact of a Mass Media Crime Prevention
   Campaign.* 1984, 78 pp. (NCJ 93350). N.C.P. Council 202-466-6272

* Neighborhood Watch Programs

Office of Crime Prevention
National Institute of Justice
U.S. Department of Justice
633 Indiana Ave. NW
Washington, DC 20531   202-307-2942

If you're interested in starting a Neighborhood Watch Program in your town, or want
to know how you can make yours better, contact the Neighborhood Watch Specialists
at the National Institute of Justice. They will be glad to help you make your
neighborhood a safer place.

* Recycling Efforts

Public Information Center
Environmental Protection Agency
401 M St., SW
PM-211 B
Washington DC 20460   202-260-2080

Recycling Works! is a free booklet that provides information about successful
recycling programs initiated by state and local agencies. It also describes private
recycling efforts and joint recycling ventures of government and businesses.
Publications are available through Resource Conservation and Recovery Act, 202-
260-9327.

* Residential Fire Sprinklers

Federal Emergency Management Agency (FEMA)
16825 South Seton Ave.
Emmitsburg, MD 21727   301-447-1021

Through its regional offices, Federal Emergency Management Agency (FEMA)
conducts demonstrations of how residential fire sprinklers operate. Contact your
regional FEMA office or the office above for more information.

* Telecommunications Expertise for Libraries, Schools, Fire Departments

Public Telecommunications Facilities Program
National Telecommunications and
   Information Administration (NTIA)
U.S. Department of Commerce
14th St. and Constitution Ave., NW, Room 4625
Washington, DC 20230   202-377-5802

By identifying public service telecommunications needs, NTIA assists schools,
hospitals, libraries, policy, fire departments, and government agencies in using
advanced telecommunications systems and technology to achieve their goals.

* Toys for Tots

Commanding General (PAO)
4th Marine Division (Rein.), FMF
U.S. Marine Corps Reserve
4400 Dauphine St.
New Orleans, LA 70146-5400   504-948-1457

The Marine Corps Reserve sponsors an annual Christmas "Toys for Tots" project,
which collects toys for needy children. To learn how to donate or provide a
collection point at your place of business, contact your local Marine Corps Reserve
office or the above office for more information.

* Waste Management Policy

Association of Metropolitan Sewerage Agencies (AMSA)
1000 Connecticut Ave., NW, Suite 1006
Washington, DC 20036   202-833-2672

The Association of Metropolitan Sewerage Agencies consists of sewerage agencies
in areas with more than 250,000 people. It serves to exchange technical data and
deals with the federal government on environmental and regulatory matters.

* Woodsy Owl: Litter Cleanup

U.S. Department of Agriculture
Forest Service
P.O. Box 96090
Washington, DC 20090-6090   202-205-1760

To increase children's awareness of our delicate environment, the Forest Service's
Woodsy Owl campaign has a variety of free materials available, including coloring
sheets, detective sheets, song sheets, patches, *Woodsy Owl on Camping* (brochure),
and stickers. A Woodsy Owl costume is available to some community groups to
compliment "Give A Hoot! Don't Pollute" campaign.

Traffic and Transportation

* Commuter and Air Taxi Services

Commuter and Air Taxi Branch
Transportation Division
Office of Federal Aviation Administration
800 Independence Ave., SW, Room 303
Washington, DC 20591   202-267-8086

Contact this office for information regarding policy, regulations, and directives for commuter and air taxi aircraft. A list is available of air taxi operators and commercial operators of small aircraft. This list available in Oklahoma City through F.V.N., 405-680-4391.

* Essential Air Passenger Service

Aviation Analysis
U.S. Department of Transportation
400 7th St., SW, Room 6401
Washington, DC 20591   202-366-5903

This office guarantees that certain cities will be served by airlines. It also represents community views. Contact this office for more information on airport service.

* Funded Traffic Safety Projects

Evaluation Staff (NTS-31)
Traffic Safety Programs
National Highway Traffic Safety Administration
U.S. Department of Transportation
400 7th Street, SW
Washington, DC 20590   202-366-2759

Once known as the National Project Reporting System, funded project information collected by this office from each state is stored in a database. Projects are funded in areas such as occupant safety and alcohol. Findings are assembled annually in a published report providing an overview of the projects, their status, and how funding is apportioned, such as amounts to each project and within each project, amount to education, to enforcement, and to other areas. Contact the Evaluation Staff for details.

* Handicapped Assistance and Mass Transit

Office of Research, Training, and Rural Transportation
Urban Mass Transit Administration
400 7th St., SW, Room 6102
Washington, DC 20590   202-366-4995

The Urban Mass Transit Administration (UMTA) is involved in a Congressionally-mandated project with the National Easter Seals Committee to study accessibility problems faced by the handicapped who use mass transit. The office runs a series of demonstrations on improved arrangements to help the handicapped.

* Highway Safety Accident Prevention

Office of Highway Safety (HHS-21)
Associate Administrator for Safety and Operations
Federal Highway Administration
U.S. Department of Transportation
400 7th St., SW
Washington, DC 20590   202-366-1153

Highway construction safety programs are funded to remove, relocate, or shield roadside obstacles; to identify and correct hazards at railroad crossings; and to improve signing, pavement markings, and signalization. For information and referral, contact the Office of Highway Safety. The following publications are also available:

Highway Safety Improvement Programs, Annual Report.
Status Report of Federal Funds Used for Highway Safety Programs.

Several other reports prepared by this office are available from National Technical Information Service, 5285 Port Royal Road, Springfield, VA 22161; 703-487-4650. A sampling of titles follows:

Inexpensive Accident Countermeasures at Narrow Bridges
Legibility and Driver Response to Selected Lane and Road Closure Barricades
Rollover Potential of Vehicles on Embankments, Sideslopes, and Other Roadside Features; Final Report
Constant Warning Time Devices for Railroad-Highway Crossings: Technical Summary
Studies of the Road Marking Code

* Highway Traffic Safety Records

U.S. Department of Transportation
National Highway Traffic Safety Administration (NHTSA)
Technical Reference Division (NAD-52)
Office of Administrative Operations
400 7th Street, SW
Washington, DC 20590   202-366-2768

The National Highway Traffic Safety Administration (NHTSA) reports and records are available for public inspection at this location, and database searches can be requested for a fee. Holdings include vehicle research and test reports; investigation reports on accidents and defects; recall information; compliance reports; consumer complaints; consumer advisories; filmed records of research and tests; NHTSA *Technical Reports*; engineering specifications; and certification information. Both light and heavy highway vehicles are covered. Call ahead to ensure that the records you need will be on hand.

* Mass Transit Program Evaluation

Program Evaluation Division
Federal Transit Administration (FTA)
U.S. Department of Transportation
400 7th St., SW, Room 9306
Washington, DC 20590   202-366-1727

This office can provide you with information on its recent and on-going evaluations of projects and programs implemented by the Federal Transit Administration (FTA). For information on earlier evaluations regarding bus, subway, and other modes of urban transit.

* Maximum Speed Limit

U.S. Department of Transportation
National Highway Traffic Safety Administration,
Police Traffic Services Division
Office of Enforcement and Emergency Services
Traffic Safety Programs
400 7th Street, SW
Room 5119
Washington, DC 20590   202-366-5440

The National Maximum Speed Limit is 65 miles per hour on certain interstate highways. This office processes annual certifications of maximum speed limit enforcement programs throughout the U.S. and assists states in developing and improving enforcement efforts.

* National Driver Register

National Driver Register (NTS-24)
Traffic Safety Programs
National Highway Traffic Safety Administration
U.S. Department of Transportation
400 7th Street, SW, Room 6124
Washington, DC 20590   202-366-4800

The *National Driver Register* is a central, computerized index of state records on drivers whose operator licenses have been revoked, denied, or suspended for more than 6 months. Data includes name, birthdate, height, weight, eye color, date and reason for action, and date of reinstatement. Applications for driver licenses are routinely checked against the register, and states exchange information via an electronic system.

* Occupants Displaced by Highway Construction

Office of Right-of-Way (HRW-22)
Office of Right-of-Way and Environment
Federal Highway Administration (FHWA)
U.S. Department of Transportation
400 7th St., SW, Room 3219
Washington, DC 20590   202-366-0342

This office administers the Federal Highway Administration's (FHWA) lead role in implementing the Uniform Relocation Assistance and Real Property Acquisition Policies Act. When Federally funded highway construction projects involve displacing residents from acquired property, this Act sets policies for purchase of the land and relocating the people on it. The publication, *Your Rights and Benefits as Displaced Under the Federal Relocation Assistance Program*, is available from this office.

* Pedestrian and Driver Research

Office of Program Development and Evaluation (NTS-30)
National Highway Traffic Safety Administration
U.S. Department of Transportation
400 7th Street, SW, Room 6240
Washington, DC 20590   202-366-9591

This office studies factors affecting the safety of drivers and pedestrians. Research areas include determining the causes of unsafe driving and developing counter-measures; the effectiveness of vehicle occupant safety restraints; the effect of alcohol and drugs; the safety concerns of bicycles, motorcycles, and mopeds; driver license standards; and young drivers. This office can refer you to staff researching the topic of your interest.

* Pedestrian Safety

Geometric and Roadside Design Branch
Engineering Division
Office of Engineering Program Development
Federal Highway Administration
U.S. Department of Transportation
400 7th St., SW, Room 3128
Washington, DC 20590   202-366-1315

Highway design and roadside facilities are studied by this office to determine their impact on pedestrians and bicyclists. The publication, *Pedestrian and Bicycle Facilities* provides you with information about the roadside designs and structures used in safety-related applications.

* Private Sector Initiatives in Mass Transit

Office of Private Sector Initiatives
Office of Budget and Policy
Federal Transit Administration
U.S. Department of Transportation
400 7th St., SW, Room 9300
Washington, DC 20590   202-366-1666

This office encourages private sector involvement in mass transit throughout the United States. Specifically, they work through the following four areas:

1) Competitive Contracting: Local transit authorities are encouraged to open the provisioning of services up to private sector competition.

2) Entrepreneurial Services: Groups in the private sector are encouraged to start self-sustaining transit services (such as taxi and bus) in cooperation with local transit authorities.

3) Joint Development: Federal assistance is available to help plan public/private sector joint ventures at transit facilities.

4) Demand Management Program: Federal funds are available to encourage local employers and merchants to develop techniques to help manage transportation and mobility problems in their areas.

* Public Private Transportation Network (PPTN)

8737 Colesville Rd
Suite 1100
Silver Spring, MD 20910   800-522-7786

The *Transis Information Exchange* is a free technical assistance program sponsored by the Federal Transit Administration. PPTN assists public transit agencies, private transit operators, federal, state, and local officials, and others seeking guidance on transportation issues, especially concerning identification and fostering of public/private partnerships. Assistance includes site visits by a network of industry professionals; speakers and facilitators for seminars, conferences, and workshops; and a library of technical assistance materials.

* Road Signs

Traffic Control Development Applications
Division (HTO-21)
Traffic Operations Division
Office of Safety and Operations
Federal Highway Administration
U.S. Department of Transportation
400 7th St., SW, Room 3419
Washington, DC 20590   202-366-2184

Efforts by this division improve the effectiveness and uniformity of such traffic control devices as road signs, signal lamps, and highway markings throughout the country. Standards are developed for designing signs and using other traffic control devices. The meanings of road signs and markings are described in *Road Symbol Signs*, which can be obtained by contacting the office listed above. Two other publications on the subject, listed below, are available from the Superintendent of Documents, Government Printing Office, Washington, DC 20402; 202-512-1800. *Manual on Uniform Traffic Control Devices*, ($22) *Standard Highway Signs Book*, ($30).

* Roadway Beautification

Special Programs and Evaluation Branch (HRW-12)
Program Requirements Division
Office of Right-of-Way and Environment
Federal Highway Administration
U.S. Department of Transportation
400 7th St., SW, Room 3221
Washington, DC 20590   202-366-2017

Junkyards and outdoor advertising along federally aided and interstate highways are regulated under a program conducted through this office. The publication, *Junkyards, the Highway, and Visual Quality*, offers information on this program. To obtain a copy, or to request further details on highway beautification programs, contact the branch listed.

* Traffic Accident Data

Information Management and Anaylsis Branch
Office of Highway Safety
Federal Highway Administration
U.S. Department of Transportation
400 7th St., SW, Room 3407
Washington, DC 20590   202-366-2159

Statistics are kept here on fatal and injury accident rates for the Nation's highways. An extensive list of publications related to accidents and highway safety is also maintained. Call or write this office to request the data you need.

* Urban Mass Transportation Research

Manager, UMTRIS
Transportation Research Board
National Research Council
PO Box 289
Washington, DC 20055   202-334-3214

The Urban Mass Transportation Research Information Service is a computerized database on worldwide transportation research. Administered by the Transportation Research Board (TRB), it covers all phases of conventional, new, and automated public transportation. UMTRIS features database storage/ retrieval of abstracts of technical papers, journal articles, research reports, computer program descriptions, and statistical sources, as well as state-of-the-art bibliographies. Descriptions of ongoing research, especially that sponsored by UMTA, are also included. UMTRIS offers the public nearly 20,000 information references to ongoing and completed research activities, and adds 2,000 new references annually to the database. In addition to serving as the central source of technical information to the public and private sectors, UMTRIS also serves as an institutional memory for UMTA projects and project reports. The database can be searched online by any computer with a modem through DIALOG Information Services File 63. UMTRIS is supported by a National Network of Transportation Libraries (18), and they serve both as repositories that house and make UMTA documents available to the general public, as well as document delivery centers that provide UMTRIS users with full text copies of citations retrieved from the database.

Fires, Floods, and Disaster Relief

* Arson Control and Clearinghouse

U.S. Fire Administration
Federal Emergency Management Agency (FEMA)
16825 South Seton Ave.
Emmitsburg, MD 21727   301-447-1122

The Arson Resource Center is available to help answer your questions and locate resources related to arson. It was established several years ago by the U.S. Fire Administration, and has developed an impressive collection of arson-related materials. Federal Emergency Management Agency (FEMA) personnel and NETC students can borrow materials from the Center, and books and research reports are available to the general public through area libraries (interlibrary loan). Audio-visual and general references are stored in the Center for in-house use. The following publications and source materials on arson are available from the U.S. Fire Administration free of charge:

Arson Victims: Suggestions (#5-0034)
Arson Resource Directory (#5-0087)
Arson Prosecution Issues (#5-0086)
Rural Arson Control (#5-0110)
Establishing an Arson Strike Force (#5-0111)

* Bomb Shelters Designs

Federal Emergency Management Agency (FEMA)
P.O. Box 70274
Washington, DC 20024   202-646-3484

The following free publications will show you the ins and outs of bomb shelters and their construction:

Shelters in New Homes (TR-60). Shows how any home builder or owner can provide an area that protects against fallout radiation and windstorm without sacrificing its day-to-day usefulness. It includes examples of multi-purpose areas, shelter designs and details, and radiation shielding principles.
Cost Benefits in Shelters (TR-69). Explores various areas of cost savings resulting from the incorporation of basic fallout shelter design techniques in new buildings.
Home Fallout Shelter--Snack Bar--Basement Location Plan D (H-12D). A snack bar built of brick and concrete block can be converted into shelter.
Home Fallout Shelter: Outside Concrete Shelter (H-12-1).
Home Fallout Shelter: Aboveground Home Shelter (H-12-2).
Home Blast Shelter: Underground Concrete Shelter (H-12-3).
Technical Standards for Fallout Shelter Designs (TM 72-1). Shows the technical architectural and environmental standards for fallout shelter design.

* Dam Safety and Hazards

Federal Emergency Management Agency (FEMA)
P.O. Box 70274
Washington, DC 20024   202-646-3484

The following publications are available from the Federal Emergency Management Agency (FEMA) office above and contain information on dam safety:

Civil Preparedness Guide: National Dam Safety Program for S & L (CPG 1-39) #8-0709
Dam Safety: An Owner's Guidance Manual (FEMA 145) #8-0648
Dam Safety: Know the Potential Hazard (L-152) #8-0607
Federal Guidelines for Dam Safety (FEMA-93) #8-0047
Financial Assistance Guidelines (CPG 1-32) #8-0404
Glossary of Terms for Dam Safety (FEMA-148) #8-0676

* Disaster Relief Grants and Loans

Federal Emergency Management Agency (FEMA)
P.O. Box 70274
Washington, DC 20024   202-646-3484

The following free publications will help you through the application process for Federal disaster relief grants and loans:

Handbook for Applicants (DR&R-1) #8-0056. Prescribes policy and procedures for requesting, obtaining, and administering FEMA grants for public assistance under the Disaster Relief Act of 1974.
Community Disaster Loan Handbook (DAP-5). For local governments and state and federal officials outlying FEMA Community Disaster Loan Program.
Financial Assistance Guidelines (CPG 1-32) #8-0404.

* Disaster Relief and Recovery Help

Federal Emergency Management Agency (FEMA)
P.O. Box 70274
Washington, DC 20024   202-646-3484

The Digest of Federal Assistance Programs (DAP-21) #8-0729, is designed to serve as an initial source of information for private citizens and public officials who need disaster assistance. It is a compendium of Federal programs specifically designed to supplement State and local relief and recovery efforts, as well as programs that may serve to lessen the effects of civil disasters or emergencies. It includes programs that either require a Presidential declaration of a major disaster or emergency and those which do not.

* Earthquakes and Small Businesses

Federal Emergency Management Agency (FEMA)
P.O. Box 70247
Washington, DC 20024   202-646-3484

Guidelines for Local Small Businesses in Meeting the Earthquake Threat is a booklet designed to help small businesses prepare for and respond to a catastrophic earthquake. It contains information on assessing earthquake risks and provides a planning framework for preparation, response, and long-term recovery for a small business. (FEMA-87) #8-0500

* Earthquake Hazard Reduction Program

Federal Emergency Management Agency (FEMA)
P.O. Box 70274
Washington, DC 20024   202-646-3484

The publication, National Earthquake Hazard Reduction Program Five Year Plan, presents an overview of FY 1985-89 program plans for the National Earthquake Hazard Reduction Program (NEHRP). It emphasizes the goals, objectives, and funding requirements for each of the participating major program elements. It also provides a comprehensive and coherent presentation of the activities projected by each participating agency for 5 fiscal years. It is available from the office above.

* Earthquake Safety Checklist

Federal Emergency Management Agency (FEMA)
P.O. Box 70274
Washington, DC 20024   202-646-3484

The following publications provide information on earthquake preparedness and safety:

Family Earthquake Safety Home Hazard Hunt and Drill (FEMA-113) #8-0871. Discusses how to identify and correct hazards in the home and practice what to do if an earthquake occurs.
Coping With Children's Reactions to Earthquakes and Other Disasters (FEMA-48) #8-0750. Deals with children's fears and anxieties following a disaster. In Spanish (FEMA-184) #8-0849
Earthquake Safety Checklist (FEMA-46) #8-0820. Safety tips for preparation, response to, and immediate aftermath of an earthquake.
Earthquakes (L-111) #8-0821. Offers safety tips for potential victims of earthquakes.

* Emergency and Fire Professionals Protection

Federal Emergency Management Agency (FEMA)
P.O. Box 700274
Washington, DC 20024   202-646-3484

The *U.S. Fire Administration Brochure* (L-160) #5-0067, describes the programs offered by the U.S. Fire Administration, including those that help fire service professionals manage fire data that gets the public involved, educates fire and emergency professionals, helps protect firefighters, and promotes life-saving technology.

* Emergency Broadcast System

Federal Emergency Management Agency (FEMA)
P.O. Box 70274
Washington, DC 20024   202-646-3484

The leaflet, *Emergency Broadcast System* (L-93), cites the Emergency Broadcast System (EBS) as a method of communicating with the American public in the event of war, threat of war, or grave national crisis.

* Emergency Education Network

Emergency Education Network (EENET)
National Emergency Training Center
16825 South Seton Ave.
Emmitsburg, MD 21727   301-447-1068

The Emergency Education Network (EENET) is owned and operated by the Federal Emergency Management Agency (FEMA) to provide State and local emergency management personnel with quality education and training. Several shows per year are produced to be shown to live audiences via satellite or by cable. Contact the office above for further information.

* Emergency Management Institute

Emergency Management Institute
National Emergency Training Center
16825 South Seton Ave,
Emmitsburg, MD 21727   301-447-6771

The Emergency Management Institute provides courses on several different topics in emergency management and civil defense. For more information on these courses, contact the office above.

* Emergency Management Materials

Federal Emergency Management Agency (FEMA)
P.O. Box 70274
Washington, DC 20024   202-646-3484

Publications on emergency management which are available from the above office are listed below:

Emergency Management in Public Administration Education (FEMA-106) #6-0009
Emergency Management, USA (HS-2) #6-0141
In Time of Emergency - A Citizen's Handbook on Emergency Management (H-14) #8-0819
This is The Federal Emergency Management Agency #0-0058

* Emergency Medical Services

Federal Emergency Management Agency (FEMA)
P.O. Box 70274
Washington, DC 20024   202-646-3484

Introduction to Emergency Medical Services (SM 220) is a student manual which includes lectures, discussions, slide/tape presentations, case studies, and an optional workshop. Lessons cover topics on the historical perspective, system design, resources, medical control, EMS councils, legal and medical issues, communications, and mutual aid.

* Emergency Planning Educational Teleconferences

U.S. Fire Administration
Federal Emergency Management Agency (FEMA)
16825 South Seton Ave.
Emmitsburg, MD 21727   301-447-1122

The Federal Emergency Management Agency (FEMA) holds an annual series of educational teleconferences for fire service and emergency management audiences on such topics as stress management, public affairs, residential sprinklers, flammable gases and liquids, AIDS, and radiation transportation accidents, and hazardous materials training. Copies of previous 52 shows are available for a charge, or could be borrowed from the State Emergency Management Offices, or one of the 10 FEMA Regional Offices.

* Emergency Plans for Acutely Toxic Chemicals

Emergency Planning and Community
Right to Know
U.S. Environmental Protection Agency (EPA)
401 M St., SW   800-535-0202
Washington, DC 20460   703-920-9877

This Environmental Protection Agency (EPA) hotline provides communities with help in preparing for accidental releases of toxic chemicals. Communities can call to obtain interim guidelines regarding *Acutely Toxic Chemicals*. These guidelines cover Organizing a Community, Developing a Chemical Contingency Plan, and gathering site-specific information. The hotline also provides a list of more than 400 acutely toxic chemicals.

* Emergency Preparedness Offices Nationwide

The Federal Emergency Management Administration (FEMA) has regional offices throughout the country.

Region I
Federal Emergency Management Agency (FEMA), J.W. McCormack Post Office and Courthouse Building, Room 442, Boston, MA 02109; 617-223-9540. Serving: Connecticut, Maine, Massachusetts, New Hampshire, Rhode Island, and Vermont.

Region II
Federal Emergency Management Agency (FEMA), 26 Federal Plaza, Room 1338, New York, NY 10278. Serving: New Jersey, New York, Puerto Rico, and Virgin Islands.

Region III
Federal Emergency Management Agency (FEMA), Liberty Square Building (Second Floor), 105 South Seventh St., Philadelphia, PA 19106; 215-931-5500. Serving: Delaware, District of Columbia, Maryland, Pennsylvania, Virginia, and West Virginia.

Region IV
Federal Emergency Management Agency (FEMA), 1371 Peachtree Street, NE, Suite 700, Atlanta, GA 30309; 404-853-4200. Serving: Alabama, Florida, Georgia, Kentucky, Mississippi, North Carolina, South Carolina, and Tennessee.

Region V
Federal Emergency Management Agency (FEMA), 175 Jackson Blvd, 4th Floor, Chicago, IL 60604; 312-408-5500. Serving: Illinois, Michigan, Minnesota, Ohio, and Wisconsin.

Region VI
Federal Emergency Management Agency (FEMA), Federal Regional Center, Room 206, 800 North Loop 288, Denton, TX 76201; 817-898-9399. Serving: Arkansas, Louisiana, New Mexico, Oklahoma, and Texas.

Region VII
Federal Emergency Management Agency (FEMA), Federal Official Building, 911 Walnut Street, Room 200, Kansas City, MO 64106; 816-283-7061. Iowa, Kansas, Missouri, and Nebraska.

Region VIII
Federal Emergency Management Agency (FEMA), Denver Federal Center Building 710, PO Box 25267, Denver, CO 80225; 303-235-4800. Serving: Colorado, Montana, North Dakota, South Dakota, Utah, and Wyoming.

Region IX
Federal Emergency Management Agency (FEMA), Presidio of San Francisco, Building 105, San Francisco, CA 94129; 415-923-7100. Serving: Arizona, California, Hawaii, and Nevada. (Pacific Commonwealth and Territories)

Region X
Federal Emergency Management Agency (FEMA), Federal Regional Center, 130 228th Street, SW, Bothell, WA 98021-9796; 206-481-8800. Serving: Alaska, Idaho, Oregon, and Washington.

* Emergency Preparedness Publications

Federal Emergency Management Agency (FEMA)
P.O. Box 70274
Washington, DC 20024   202-646-3484

The *FEMA Publications Catalog* (FEMA-20) lists FEMA publications which are available to help meet the needs of citizens in emergency management matters. These

Your Community

publications are on subjects such as civil defense, earthquakes, floods, hurricanes, tornadoes, fire, nuclear accidents, acts of terrorism, dam safety, and hazardous materials incidents.

* Emergency Preparedness Responsibilities

Federal Emergency Management Agency (FEMA)
P.O. Box 70274
Washington, DC 20024   202-646-3484

The *Data Base Guide* (FPG 47.101) #07281, is a complete inventory of the automated data files used in support of the Federal Emergency Management Agency (FEMA) program offices. Included are data files which are the result of a cooperative effort between FEMA and other federal departments and agencies having delegated emergency preparedness responsibilities. These files have detailed information on virtually all of the resources important to the defense of, or--in the event of enemy attack--the survival and recovery of, the United States.

* Emergency Relief and Excess Food

Commodity Operations Division
U.S. Department of Agriculture
ASCS, Room 6745, South Building
Washington, DC 20250   202-720-4785

The Commodity Credit Corporation buys, stores, and distributes such commodities as dry milk, wheat, rice, and corn, which are acquired through price support programs. The commodities are sent overseas as donations, distributed to domestic food programs, or given to relief agencies in times of emergencies.

* Emergency Training National Center

National Emergency Training Center (NETC)
Federal Emergency Management Agency (FEMA)
The Learning Resource Center
16825 South Seton Ave.   800-638-1821
Emmitsburg, MD 21727   301-447-1032

The Learning Resource Center is the National Emergency Training Center (NETC) campus library for students in all areas of training at the National Emergency Training Center, and for the U.S. Fire Administration. Services include all types of reference work and interlibrary loans. Contact the office above for further information.

* Firefighters Safety and Health

Office of Firefighter Health and Safety
U.S. Fire Administration
16825 South Seton Ave.
Emmitsburg, MD 21727   301-447-6771

This office develops national standards for firefighter's health and safety and also researches and analyzes data concerning the well-being of firefighters while exposed to such hazards as fire, heat, toxic chemicals. Research on firefighters protective clothing and equipment and a hazardous chemical materials response suit is also being studied. Contact the office above for more information.

* Fire Incident Reporting System

National Fire Data Center
U.S. Fire Administration
16825 South Seton Ave.
Emmitsburg, MD 21727   301-447-1313

This office quantifies and analyzes fire loss experienced at the local, State, and federal levels. Data are available on standard fire incidents. This office offers participants both mainframe and microcomputer applications for data collection and analysis. For more information and information on the Management Application Project (MAP) and the National Fire Incident Reporting System (NFIRS), contact the office above.

* Flood Damage Prevention

Flood Protection Branch, Air and Water Resources
Tennessee Valley Authority (TVA)
River Basin Operations
Resource Development
Liberty Bldg.
524 Union Ave., Room 1A-37902
Knoxville, TN 37902   615-632-4455

The Tennessee Valley Authority's (TVA) local flood damage prevention program helps communities avoid flood damages through a variety of measures, including floodplain zoning, flood proofing, and flood insurance. To assess flood risks, a field staff of engineers gathers data which is used when considering community development proposals. The TVA promotes the wise use of flood hazard areas with information, guidance, and assistance for individuals and businesses to avoid and adjust to flood areas. Staff works with local officials to assess community flood situations, and evaluate and install prevention and warning programs. A great emphasis is placed on environmental aspects as the program tries to maintain the natural benefits of flood plains and meet community needs through use and management of river corridors.

* Flood Insurance for Property Owners

Federal Emergency Management Agency (FEMA)
Federal Insurance Administration
500 C Street, SW
Washington, DC 20472   800-638-6620

The National Flood Insurance Program (NFIP) helps property owners to purchase flood insurance. This insurance is designed to provide an insurance alternative to disaster assistance to meet the escalating costs of repairing damage. Contact the office above for information about the laws, regulations, or administrative policies related to the NFIP. Maryland residents outside of DC should call: 800-492-6605, and those in Alaska, Guam, Hawaii, Puerto Rico, and Virgin Islands residents should call: 800-638-6831.

Questions and Answers on the National Flood Insurance Program (FIA-2) #30002 contains questions and answers about the National Flood Insurance Program. There are six regional offices.

* Flood Plain Management Assistance

U.S. Army Corps of Engineers
Attn: CECW-PF
20 Massachusetts Ave., NW
Washington, DC 20314   202-272-0169

The Army Corps of Engineers provides information, guidance, and technical assistance to civic groups and organizations in developing regulations for flood plain use. These services help communities understand the extent and magnitude of flood hazards in their areas. For information, contact the above office.

* Flood Preparedness Publications

Federal Emergency Management Agency (FEMA)
P.O. Box 70274
Washington, DC 20024   202-646-3484

The Flood Insurance Administration series of publications provide information on specific topics within the National Flood Insurance Program. The following publication can be obtained from the office above:

Flood Emergency and Residential Repair Handbook (FIA-13) #3-0123. Provides homeowners, residential contractors, and local government officials with procedures for dealing with flood hazards and damages to homes and their contents.

* Flood-Prone Areas

Federal Emergency Management Agency (FEMA)
P.O. Box 70274   202-646-3484
Washington, DC 20024   800-333-1363

The Federal Emergency Management Agency publishes the *Flood Hazard Boundary Map* which shows the flood-prone areas within the community. Each map consists of one Map Index Page and one or more map sheets for all of the areas within the community's corporate limits subject to flooding. Call the number above for more information and map requests. *Guide To Flood Insurance Rate Map* (FIA-14) #3-0138 is a guide to help identify and understand key features of the Flood Insurance Rate Map.

* General Hazard Insurance

Federal Emergency Management Agency (FEMA)
P.O. Box 70274
Washington, DC 20024   202-646-3484

The *Insurance Handbook for Public Assistance* (DR&R-3) #8-0075, is a policy and procedural handbook for local, State, and Federal officials concerned with administering general hazard insurance and flood insurance requirements under the Disaster Relief Act of 1974.

* Hazardous Materials and Emergency Response

Toxicology Information Program (TIP)
National Library of Medicine
8600 Rockville Pike
Bethesda, MD 20894   301-496-6308

(TIP) was established to provide national access to information on toxicology. The program is charged with setting up computerized databases of information from the literature of toxicology and from the files of both governmental and non-governmental organizations. Among the databases are TOXLINE (Toxicology Information Online) and CHEMLINE, a chemical dictionary file. TIP implemented the TOXNET (Toxicology Data Network) system of toxicologically-oriented data banks, including the HSDB (Hazardous Substances Data Bank), which is useful in chemical emergency response. TIP also supports the Toxicology Information Response Center, which provides reference services to the scientific community.

* Hazardous Material Transportation Accidents

Office of Hazardous Materials and Planning and Analysis (DHM-63)
Research and Special Programs Administration
U.S. Department of Transportation
400 7th Street, SW, Room 8112
Washington, DC 20590   202-366-4555

This division collects and analyzes accident data from transporters of hazardous materials by highway, rail, air, and water and from container manufacturers. Information stored in the database includes the hazardous material involved, transporter name and mode, packaging used, cause of accident, and results. Contact the above office for searches. There may be a charge.

* Hurricane Safety for Kids

Children's Television Workshop
One Lincoln Plaza, Dept. CES/NH
New York, NY 10023   212-595-3456

The Federal Emergency Management Agency (FEMA) funded the creation of the *Big Bird Gets Ready for Hurricanes* kit, which is intended to help teachers and parents teach kids about hurricanes in a non-frightening way. The kit contains a 16-page booklet, a record of "The Hurricane Blues," and a board game (K-68) #8-0647. There is a charge.

* Legal Services for Disaster Victims

Federal Emergency Management Agency (FEMA)
P.O. Box 70274
Washington, DC 20024   202-646-3484

The *Manual for Disaster Legal Services* has been prepared by FEMA and the Young Lawyers Division (YLD) of the American Bar Association. Its purpose is to orient new and potential volunteers to the FEMA-YLD Program for offering legal services to victims following major disasters. In order to facilitate this orientation, the *Manual* emphasizes schematic diagram, paraphases statutes and regulations, and simplifies many issues relating to the program.

* Mental Health Services Response to Emergencies, Disasters and Crises

Emergency Services Branch, Violence and Tramatic Stress
National Institutes of Health
National Institute of Mental Health
5600 Fishers Lane, Room 18105
Rockville, MD 20857   301-443-3728

The Emergency Services Branch oversees three programs: 1) The Emergency Research Program studies the psychosocial response to mass emergencies; 2) The Crisis Counseling Program administers crisis counseling grants to states in which there has been a Presidentially-declared disaster; 3) The Emergency Preparedness Program plans for alcohol, drug abuse, and mental health disaster-related services nationwide. The program provides technical assistance and public education materials to states and local agencies in times of emergencies, and has three publications designed for non-mental health emergency workers (police, fire, emergency medical personnel) which focus on mental health issues.

* Natural Disaster and Nuclear Attack Planning for Families

Federal Emergency Management Agency (FEMA)
P.O. Box 70274
Washington, DC 20024   202-646-3484

In Time of Emergency: A Citizen's Handbook on Emergency Management (H-14) #8-0819, is addressed directly to the individual and the family to provide information and guidance on what can and should be done to prepare for a major natural disaster or nuclear attack.

* Natural Disaster Relief

Office of Government and Public Affairs
U.S. Department of Agriculture (USDA)
Washington, DC 20250   202-720-8732

This free publication provides an overview of the U.S. Department of Agriculture's disaster assistance programs. It describes types of assistance available and where to apply for assistance. Local extension agents in each county can approve disaster applications for the following: conservation structures (when located on eligible lands); rehabilitation of farm lands destroyed by disaster; crop payment subsidies for disruption caused by disaster to regular crop schedules; sale of animal feed at below market price in emergency situations; animal grazing on reserve or conservation lands in emergency situations; donation of animal feed to Indian reservations when needed; and donation of grain to migratory wildfowl domains. The federal government will also remove debris from a major disaster from publicly- or privately-owned lands or waters.

* Nuclear Crisis Planning

Federal Emergency Management Agency (FEMA)
P.O. Box 70274
Washington, DC 20024   202-646-3484

Preparedness Planning for a Nuclear Crisis (HS-4) #6-0178, is a FEMA home-study course that will help you better prepare for a nuclear attack by providing information on the following: the effects of nuclear weapons; evacuation and sheltering; preparation of stocking of fallout shelters; and development of emergency plans to improve the chance of survival for individuals and families.

* Nuclear Fallout Shelters

Federal Emergency Management Agency (FEMA)
P.O. Box 70274
Washington, DC 20024   202-646-3484

The free booklet, *HUD Aids for Fallout Shelter Development* (TR-58), describes the principal programs of the U.S. Department of Housing and Urban Development (HUD) which can be used to promote and develop fallout shelters when the requirements of the specific programs are met. Call HUD, 202-275-0635.

* Posters: Natural and Civil Disasters

Federal Emergency Management Agency (FEMA)
P.O. Box 70274
Washington, DC 20024   202-646-3484

The following natural disaster informational posters are from FEMA:

Flood Insurance
Winter Watch for Kids
Earthquake
Emergency Poster
Accidental Launch Warning Message Threat Areas
NEW *Civil Defense* #8-0839
NEW *Flood Safety Rules* #0-0054.

* Temporary Housing

Federal Emergency Management Agency (FEMA)
P.O. Box 70274
Washington, DC 20024   202-646-3484

The Mobile Home Sales Handbook (DAP-20) #8-0376, establishes the Federal Emergency Management Agency policy regarding the sale of mobile homes, under Section 404 of the Disaster Relief Act of 1974, to eligible temporary housing occupants. It prescribes the methods, techniques, and procedures utilized in the sales transaction.

* Tornadoes, Hurricanes, and Flash Floods

Federal Emergency Management Agency (FEMA)
P.O. Box 70274
Washington, DC 20024   202-646-3484

The following FEMA publications will better help you prepare for severe weather disasters:

Be patient. If any phone number is incorrect, call (area code) 555-1212 and request the new listing.

349

Hurricane Safety: Tips for Hurricanes (L-105) #0-0017
Tornado Safety Tips (L-148) #0-0164
Survival in a Hurricane Wallet Card
Tips for Tornado Safety Wallet Card #0-0117
Big Bird Gets Ready for Hurricane Kit (K-68) #8-0647

* Winter Storm Safety

Federal Emergency Management Agency (FEMA)
P.O. Box 70274

Washington, DC 20024   202-646-3484

These Federal Emergency Management Agency (FEMA) publications will help you prepare for the winter storm season:

Safety Tips for Winter Storms (L-96) #0-0172
Winter Survival Coloring Book (FEMA-26). Includes safety tips on winter for children.
Winter Survival Test #0-0179. A test about safety precautions to be taken around the home before winter storms strike, including heating systems, room heaters and fireplaces, kitchen pipes, and emergency supplies.

Money For Communities and Non-Profits

The federal money programs outlined here are designed to help communities solve many of today's difficult problems. Economic development opportunities such as job training funds are identified. Community improvement programs for emergency shelters, rural housing, senior centers, and mass transit services are described as well as airport modernization loans and grants. You will discover various services such as school lunch and nutrition programs, runaway halfway houses and health clinics. This information is derived from the *Catalog of Federal Domestic Assistance* which is published by the U.S. Government Printing Office in Washington, DC. The number next to the title description is the reference number listed in this *Catalog*. Contact the office listed below the title for more details.

* Rural Self-Help Housing Technical Assistance (Section 523 Technical Assistance) 10.420

Administrator
Rural Housing and Community Development Service
U.S. Department of Agriculture
Washington, DC 20250   202-720-1474

To provide financial support for the promotion of a program of technical and supervisory assistance that will aid needy very low and low-income individuals and their families in carrying out mutual self-help housing efforts in rural areas. Types of assistance: grants. Estimate of annual funds available: $ 12,650,000.

* Housing Application Packaging Grants 10.442

Director
Single Family Housing Processing Division
Rural Housing and Community Development
U.S. Department of Agriculture
Washington, DC 20250   202-720-1474

To package single family housing applications for very low- and low-income rural residents in colonials and designated counties who wish to buy, build, or repair houses for their own use and to package applications for organizations wishing to develop rental units for lower income families. Types of assistance: grants. Estimate of annual funds available: $2,000,000.

* Cooperative Extension Service 10.500

Cooperative State Research Education and Extension Service
U.S. Department of Agriculture
Washington, DC 20250   202-720-2810

To help people and communities identify and solve their farm, home, and community problems through the practical application of research findings of USDA and the Land-Grant Colleges and Universities. Types of assistance: grants. Estimate of annual funds available: $ 426,140,000.

* Food Distribution 10.550

Food Distribution Division
Food and Consumer Service
U.S. Department of Agriculture
Alexandria, VA 22302   703-305-2680

To improve the diets of school and preschool children; the elderly; needy persons in charitable institutions; other individuals in need of food assistance; and to increase the market for domestically produced foods acquired under surplus removal or price support operations. Types of assistance: sale, exchange, or donation. Estimate of annual funds available: $118,808,152.

* Child Nutrition: State Administrative Expenses 10.560

Director, Child Nutrition Division
Food and Consumer Service
U.S. Department of Agriculture
Alexandria, VA 22302   703-305-2590

To provide each state agency with funds for its administrative expenses in supervising and giving technical assistance to local schools, school districts and institutions in their conduct of child nutrition programs. Types of assistance: grants. Estimate of annual funds available: $ 92,196,000.

* Nutrition Education and Training Program (NET Program) 10.564

Nutrition and Technical Services Division
Food and Consumer Service
U.S. Department of Agriculture
Alexandria, VA 22302   703-305-2554

To help subsidize State and local programs that encourage the dissemination of nutrition information to children participating, or eligible to participate in the school lunch and related child nutrition programs. Types of assistance: grants. Estimate of annual funds available: $ 10,271,000.

* Temporary Emergency Food Assistance (Administrative Costs) 10.568

Food Distribution Division, FNS
U.S. Department of Agriculture (USDA)
Room 502, Park Office Center
3101 Park Center Drive
Alexandria, VA 22302   703-305-2680

To make funds available to States for storage and distribution costs incurred by nonprofit eligible recipient agencies in providing food assistance to needy persons. Types of assistance: grants. Estimate of annual funds available: $ 40,010,000.

* Temporary Emergency Food Assistance (Food Commodities) 10.569

Food Distribution Division, FNS, USDA
Room 502, Park Office Center
3101 Park Center Drive
Alexandria, VA 22302   703-305-2680

To make food commodities available to States for distribution to the needy. Types of assistance: grants. Estimate of annual funds available: $ 25,000,000.

* Food Commodities for Soup Kitchens 10.571

Food Distribution Division
Food and Nutrition Service
U.S. Department of Agriculture
Alexandria, VA 22302   703-305-2680

To improve the diets of the homeless. Types of assistance: grants. Estimate of annual funds available: $ 40,000,000.

* Community Economic Adjustment Planning Assistance For Reductions 10.611

Director
Office of Economic Adjustment
OASD (ES)
400 Army Navy Dr., Suite 200
Arlington, VA 22202   703-604-6020

To assist States on behalf of local governments and local governments to undertake economic adjustment planning activities to respond to major reductions in defense industry employment resulting from the cancellation, termination or failure to proceed with a major DoD acquisition. Types of assistance: grants. Estimate of annual funds available: $1,720,000.

* Cooperative Forestry Assistance 10.664

Deputy Chief
State and Private Forestry
Forest Service
U.S. Department of Agriculture
P.O. Box 96090
Washington, DC 20090-6090   202-205-1657
With respect to nonfederal forest and other rural lands to assist in the advancement of forest resources management; the encouragement of the production of timber; the control of insects and diseases affecting trees and forests. Types of assistance: grants. Estimate of annual funds available: $ 91,521,000.

* Schools and Roads - Grants to States (25 Percent Payments to States) 10.665

Al Smith
Director of Procurement and Property
Forest Service, Room 706 RPE
U.S. Department of Agriculture (USDA)
P.O. Box 96090
Washington, DC 20090-6090   703-235-8007
To share receipts from the National Forests with the States in which the National Forests are situated. To be used for the benefit of the public schools and public roads of the county or counties in which the National Forest is situated. Types of assistance: grants. Estimate of annual funds available: $ 324,538,000.

* Schools and Roads - Grants to Counties (Payments to Counties) 10.666

Al Smith
Director of Procurement and Property
Forest Service, Room 701 RPE
U.S. Department of Agriculture (USDA)
P.O. Box 96090
Washington, DC 20090-6090   703-235-8007
To share receipts from National Grasslands and Land Utilization Projects with the counties in which the National Grasslands and Land Utilization Projects are situated. To be used for school or road purposes or both. Types of assistance: grants. Estimate of annual funds available: $ 4,790,000.

* Empowerment Zones Program 10.772

U.S. Department of Agriculture
Rural Business and Cooperative Development Servicing
EZ/EC Team
300 7th St., SW, Room 701
Washington, DC 20024   202-619-7981
Provides for the establishment of empowerment zones and enterprise communities in rural areas to stimulate the creation of new jobs, particularly for the disadvantaged and long-term unemployed, and to promote revitalization of economically distressed areas. Types of assistance: grants. Estimate of annual funds available: $140,000,000.

* Livestock, Meat and Poultry Market Supervision 10.800

Administrator for Packers and Stockyards Administration
Room 3039, South Building
U.S. Department of Agriculture
Washington, DC 20250   202-720-7051
To protect producers and consumers against unfair business practices in the marketing of livestock, meat and poultry; and members of the livestock marketing and meat and poultry industries against unfair, deceptive, discriminatory, and monopolistic practices of competitors. Types of assistance: grants. Estimate of annual funds available: $11,989,000.

* Rural Electrification Loans and Loan Guarantees 10.850

Administrator
Rural Utilities Service
U.S. Department of Agriculture
Washington, DC 20250   202-720-9540
To assure that people in eligible rural areas have access to electric services comparable in reliability and quality to the rest of the Nation. Types of assistance: direct loans. Estimate of annual funds available: $610,488,922.

* Rural Telephone Loans and Loans Guarantees 10.851

Assistant Administrator
Rural Utilities Service
U.S. Department of Agriculture
Washington, DC 20250   202-720-9554
To assure that people in eligible rural areas have access to telecommunications services comparable in reliability and quality to the rest of the Nation. Types of assistance: direct loans. Estimate of annual funds available: $85,283,784.

* Rural Telephone Bank Loans 10.852

Assistant Governor, Rural Telephone Bank
U.S. Department of Agriculture
Washington, DC 20250   202-720-9554
To provide supplemental financing to extend and improve telecommunications services in rural areas. Types of assistance: direct loans. Estimate of annual funds available: $175,000,000.

* Rural Economic Development Loans and Grants 10.854

Administrator
Rural Business and Cooperative Development Service
U.S. Department of Agriculture
Washington, DC 20250   202-720-1400
To promote rural economic development and job creation projects, including funding for project feasibility studies, start-up costs, incubator projects, and other reasonable expenses for the purpose of fostering rural development. Types of assistance: direct loans. Estimate of annual funds available: $12,347,512.

* Distance Learning and Medical Link Grants 10.855

Assistant Administrator
Telecommunications, Rural Utilities Service
Room 4056, South Building
U.S. Department of Agriculture
14th and Independence Ave., SW
Washington, DC 20250   202-720-9554
To encourage and improve the use of telecommunications, computer networks, and related advanced technologies to provide educational and medical benefits to people living in rural areas. Types of assistance: grants. Estimate of annual funds available; $7,500,000.

* Great Plains Conservation 10.900

Deputy Chief for Programs
Natural Resources Conservation Service
U.S. Department of Agriculture
P.O. Box 2890
Washington, DC 20013   202-720-4527
To conserve and develop the Great Plains soil and water resources by providing technical and financial assistance to farmers, ranchers, and others in planning and implementing conservation practices. Types of assistance: direct payment. Estimate of annual funds available: $ 6,231,084.

* Resource Conservation and Development 10.901

Deputy Chief for Programs
Natural Resources Conservation Service
U.S. Department of Agriculture
P.O. Box 2890
Washington, DC 20013   202-720-4527
To encourage and improve the capability of state and local units of government and local nonprofit organizations in rural areas to plan, develop and carry out programs for resource conservation and development. Types of assistance: grants. Estimate of annual funds available: $ 2,464,000.

* Watershed Protection and Flood Prevention (Small Watershed Program; PL-566 Program) 10.904

Deputy Chief for Programs
Natural Resources Conservation Service
U.S. Department of Agriculture
P.O. Box 2890
Washington, DC 20013   202-720-4527

To provide technical and financial assistance in planning and carrying out works of improvement to protect, develop, and utilize the land and water resources in small watersheds. Types of assistance: grants. Estimate of annual funds available: $107,746,516.

* Watershed Protection and Flood Prevention 10.904

Deputy Chief for Natural Resource Programs
Natural Resources Conservation Service
U.S. Department of Agriculture
P.O. Box 2890
Washington, DC 20013   202-720-4527

To provide technical and financial assistance in planning and carrying out works of improvement to protect, develop and utilize the land and water resources in small watersheds. Types of assistance: grants. Estimate of annual funds available: $44,000,000

* Rural Abandoned Mine Program (RAMP) 10.910

Deputy Chief for Programs
Natural Resources Conservation Service
U.S. Department of Agriculture
P.O. Box 2890
Washington, DC 20013   202-720-4527

To protect people and the environment from the adverse effects of past coal mining practices, and to promote the development of soil and water resources of unreclaimed mined lands. Types of assistance: direct payments. Estimate of annual funds available: $ 3,900,030.

* Rural Abandoned Mine Program 10.910

Deputy Chief for Programs
Natural Resources Conservation Service
U.S. Department of Agriculture
P.O. Box 2890
Washington, DC 20013   202-720-2847

To protect people and the environment from the adverse effects of past coal mining practices, and to promote the development of soil and water resources of unreclaimed mined lands. Types of assistance: direct payments. Estimate of annual funds available: $3,900,030.

* Economic Development - Grants for Public Works and Development Facilities 11.300

David L. McIlwain, Director, Public Works Division
Economic Development Administration
Room H7326, Herbert Hoover Bldg.
U.S. Department of Commerce
Washington, DC 20230   202-482-5265

To promote long-term economic development and assist in the construction of public works and development facilities needed to initiate and encourage the creation or retention of permanent jobs in the private sector in areas experiencing severe economic distress. Types of assistance: grants. Estimate of annual funds available: $ 195,000,000.

* Economic Development-Support for Planning Organizations (Development District Program; Redevelopment Area Program; and Indian Program) 11.302

Luis F. Bueso, Director Planning Division
Economic Development Administration
Room H7023, Herbert Hoover Bldg.
Washington, DC 20230   202-377-2873

To assist in providing administrative aid to multi-county district and redevelopment area (primarily Indian reservations and lands) economic development planning and implementation capability and thereby promote effective utilization of resources in the creation of full-time permanent jobs for the unemployed and the underemployed in high distress areas. Types of assistance: grants. Estimate of annual funds available: $ 21,484,000.

* Economic Development-Technical Assistance 11.303

Richard E. Hage, Technical Assistance Programs
Economic Development Administration

Room H7319, Herbert Hoover Bldg.
U.S. Department of Commerce
Washington, DC 20230   202-482-2127

To promote economic development and alleviate under-employment and unemployment in distressed areas, EDA operates a technical assistance program. Types of assistance: grants. Estimate of annual funds available: unknown.

* Economic Development-Public Works Impact Projects 11.304

David L. McIlwain
Director, Public Works Division
Economic Development Administration
Room H7326, Herbert Hoover Bldg.
Washington, DC 20230   202-482-5265

To promote long-term economic development and assist in providing immediate useful work (i.e., construction jobs) to unemployed and underemployed persons in designated project areas. Types of assistance: grants. Estimate of annual funds available: unknown.

* Economic Development-State and Local Economic Development Planning (302(a) Grants-State and Urban Planning Programs) 11.305

Luis F. Bueso
Director, Planning Division
Economic Development Administration
Room 7319, Herbert Hoover Bldg.
U.S. Department of Commerce
Washington, DC 20230   202-482-3027

To help state and/or local governments formulate and implement economic development plans designed to reduce unemployment and increase incomes. Types of assistance: grants. Estimate of annual funds available: $ 4,873,000.

* Special Economic Development and Adjustment Assistance Program-Sudden and Severe Economic Dislocation and Long-term Economic Deterioration (SSED and LTED) 11.307

David Witschi, Director
Economic Adjustment Division
Economic Development Administration
Room H7327, Herbert Hoover Bldg.
U.S. Department of Commerce
Washington, DC 20230   202-482-2659

To assist state and local areas develop and/or implement strategies designed to address adjustment problems resulting from sudden and severe economic dislocation such as plant closings (SSED), or from long-term economic deterioration in the area's economy (LTED). Types of assistance: grants. Estimate of annual funds available: $ 291,213,000.

* Research and Evaluation Program 11.312

Richard Hage
Room H-7315, EDA
U.S. Department of Commerce
Washington, DC 20230   202-482-4085

To assist in the determination of causes of unemployment, under-employment, underdevelopment, and chronic depression in various areas and regions of the nation. Types of assistance: grants. Estimate of annual funds available: $ 500,000.

* Anadromous and Great Lakes Fisheries Conservation 11.405

Director
Office of Fisheries Conservation and Management
National Marine Fisheries Service
1315 East-West Hwy
Silver Spring, MD 29010   202-713-2334

To cooperate with the states and other nonfederal interests in the conservation, development, and enhancement of the nation's anadromous fish and the fish in the Great Lakes and Lake Champlain that ascent streams to spawn, and for the control of sea lamprey. Types of assistance: grants. Estimate of annual funds available: $ 2,003,000.

Be patient. If any phone number is incorrect, call (area code) 555-1212 and request the new listing.

353

* Interjurisdictional Fisheries Act of 1986 11.407

Director
Office of Fisheries Conservation and Management
National Marine Fisheries Service
1315 East-West Hwy
Silver Spring, MD 20910   301-713-2334
To assist states in managing interjurisdictional fisheries resources. Types of assistance: grants. Estimate of annual funds available: $ 3,156,000.

* Coastal Zone Management Program Administration Grants 11.419

Chief, Coastal Programs Division
Office of Ocean Coastal Resource Management
National Ocean Service
National Oceanic and Atmospheric Administration (NOAA)
U.S. Department of Commerce
1305 East West Highway
Silver Spring, MD 20910   301-713-3102
To assist states in implementing and administering Coastal Zone Management programs that have been approved by the Secretary of Commerce. Types of assistance: grants. Estimate of annual funds available: $ 53,500,000.

* Coastal Zone Management Estuarine Research Reserves 11.420

Chief, Marine and Estuarine Management Div.
Office of Ocean and Coastal Resource Management
National Ocean Service
National Oceanic and Atmospheric Administration (NOAA)
U.S. Department of Commerce
1305 East West Highway
Silver Spring, MD 20910   301-713-3125
To assist states in the acquisition, research, development and operation of national estuarine research reserves for the purpose of creating natural field laboratories to gather data and make studies of the natural and human processes occurring within the estuaries of the coastal zone. Types of assistance: grants. Estimate of annual funds available: $ 3,300,000.

* Fisheries Development and Utilization Research and Development Grants and Cooperative Agreements Program 11.427

Office of Trade and Industry Services
National Marine Fisheries Service
National Oceanic and Atmospheric Administration (NOAA)
U.S. Department of Commerce
1315 East West Hwy.
Silver Spring, MD 20910   301-713-2358
To foster the development and strengthening of the fishing industry of the United States and increase the supply of wholesome, nutritious fish and fish products available to consumers. Types of assistance: grants. Estimate of annual funds available: $ 7,000,000.

* Intergovernmental Climate-Programs 11.428

Climate Analysis Center
National Oceanic and Atmospheric Administration (NOAA)
U.S. Department of Commerce
5200 Auth Rd.
Camp Springs, MD 20746   301-763-8071
To aid states in the initiation of regional climate centers which will supply guidance, information and climate data to users in the private and public sectors. Types of assistance: grants. Estimate of annual funds available: $ 3,200,000.

* Marine Sanctuary Program 11.429

Chief, Marine and Estuarine Management Division
Office of Ocean and Coastal Resource Management
National Ocean Service
National Oceanic and Atmospheric Administration (NOAA)
U.S. Department of Commerce
1305 East West Hwy., 12th Floor
Silver Spring, MD 20910   301-713-3125
To identify areas of the marine environment of special national significance due to their resource or human-use values; to provide authority for comprehensive and coordinated conservation and management of these marine areas that will complement existing regulatory authorities. Types of assistance: grants. Estimate of annual funds available: $ 1,600,000.

* Regional Centers for the Transfer of Manufacturing Technology 11.611

Mr. Kevin Carr
Director, NIST MTC Program
Room C121, Metrology Bldg
National Institute of Standards and Technology (NIST)
Gaithersburg, MD 20899   301-975-5020
To establish regional centers, the functions of which are to accelerate the transfer of advanced manufacturing technology from the National Institute of Standards and Technology (NIST) automated manufacturing research facility and similar research and development laboratories to small and medium sized U.S. based manufacturing firms. Types of assistance: grants. Estimate of annual funds available: $ 105,379,000.

* Minority Business and Industry Association - Minority Chambers 11.802

Assistant Director
Office of Program Development
Minority Business Development Agency
U.S. Department of Commerce (MB and IA/C of C)
14th and Constitution Ave, NW, Room 5096
Washington, DC 20230   202-482-5770
To provide financial assistance for Minority Business and Industry Association/Minority Chambers of Commerce (MB and IA/C of C) which act as advocates for their members and the minority community. Types of assistance: grants. Estimate of annual funds available: $ 3,295,000.

* Payments to States in Lieu of Real Estate Taxes 12.112

HQ, U.S. Army Corps of Engineers
Attn: CERM-F
20 Massachusetts Ave., NW
Washington, DC 20314-1000   202-272-1931
To compensate local taxing units for the loss of taxes from federally acquired lands, 75 percent of all monies received or deposited in the Treasury during any fiscal year for the account of leasing of lands acquired by the United States for flood control, navigation and allied purposes. Types of assistance: grants. Estimate of annual funds available: $ 5,124,521.

* Military Construction, Army National Guard 12.400

Director of Engineering
NGB-AEN, ARNG Readiness Center
111 S. George Mason Dr.
Arlington, VA 22204   703-607-7900
To provide a combat-ready reserve force and facilities for training and administering the Army National Guard units in the 50 states, District of Columbia, Commonwealth of Puerto Rico, Virgin Islands, and Guam. Types of assistance: grants. Estimate of annual funds available: $ 65,800,000.

* Community Economic Adjustment Planning Assistance 12.607

Director, Office of Economic Adjustment
OASD (ES)
400 Army Navy Dr., Suite 200
Arlington, VA 22202   703-604-6020
To assist local governments or States, on behalf of local government to undertake community economic adjustment planning activities to respond to military base closures and realignments. Types of assistance: grants. Estimate of annual funds available: $39,127,000.

* Joint Military/Community Comprehensive Land Use Plans 12.610

Director, Office of Economic Adjustment, OASD
400 Army Navy Dr., Suite 200
Arlington, VA 22202   703-604-6020

To enable the Army, Navy, Air Force, and Marine Corps to participate in development and implementation of *Joint Military/Community Comprehensive Land Use Plans.* Types of assistance: grants. Estimate of annual funds available: $200,000.

* Community Base Reuse Plans 12.612

Director
Office of Economic Adjustment
OASD (ES)
400 Army Navy Dr., Suite 200
Arlington, VA 22202   703-604-6020

To assist local governments or States, on behalf of local governments, to conduct community base reuse plans at closing or realigning military installations. Types of assistance: grants. Estimate of annual funds available: $400,000.

* Mortgage Insurance-Hospitals (242 Hospitals) 14.128

Insurance Division
Office of Insured Multifamily Housing Development
U.S. Department of Housing and Urban Development
Washington, DC 20410   202-708-0599

To make possible the financing of hospitals. Types of assistance: loan guarantee. Estimate of annual funds available: $ 515,000,000.

* Mortgage Insurance-Nursing Homes, Intermediate Care Facilities and Board and Care Homes (232 Nursing Homes) 14.129

Insurance Division
Office of Insured Multifamily Housing Development
U.S. Department of Housing and Urban Development
Washington, DC 20412   202-708-2556

Types of assistance: loan guarantee. Estimate of annual funds available: $ 999,252,000.

* Congregate Housing Services Program (CHSP) 14.170

Assisted Elderly and Handicapped Housing Division
Office of Elderly and Assisted Housing
U.S. Department of Housing and Urban Development
Washington, DC 20410   202-708-3291

To prevent premature or unnecessary institutionalization of elderly-handicapped, non-elderly handicapped, and temporarily disabled, to provide a variety of innovative approaches for the delivery of meals and non-medical supportive services while utilizing existing service programs and to fill gaps existing service systems. Types of assistance: grants. Estimate of annual funds available: $ 7,747,000.

* Nehemiah Housing Opportunity Grant Program (Nehemiah Housing) 14.179

Morris E. Carter, Director
Single Family Housing Development Division
U.S. Department of Housing and Urban Development (HUD)
451 7th St., SW
Washington, DC 20410

To provide an opportunity for those families who otherwise would not be financially able to realize their dream of owning a home. Types of assistance: grant. Estimate of annual funds available: $ 18,877,000.

* Community Development Block Grants/Entitlement Grants 14.218

Entitlement Cities Division
Office of Block Grant Assistance
Community Planning and Development
451 7th St., SW
Washington, DC 20410   202-708-1577

To develop viable urban communities, by providing decent housing and a suitable living environment. Types of assistance: grants. Estimate of annual funds available: $ 3,157,000,000.

* Community Development Block Grants/Small Cities Program (Small Cities) 14.219

State and Small Cities Division
Office of Block Grant Assistance Community Planning and Development
U.S. Department of Housing and Urban Development (HUD)
451 7th St., SW
Washington, DC 20410   202-708-1322

The primary objective of this program is the development of viable urban communities by providing decent housing, a suitable living environment, and expanding economic opportunities. Types of assistance: grants. Estimate of annual funds available: $ 54,360,000.

* Community Development Block Grants/Secretary's Discretionary Fund/Insular Area 14.225

Office of Program Policy Development
Community Planning and Development
U.S. Department of Housing and Urban Development (HUD)
451 7th St., SW
Washington, DC 20410   202-708-1322

To provide community development assistance to American Samoa, Guam, the Northern Mariana Islands, Palau and the Virgin Islands. Types of assistance: grants. Estimate of annual funds available: $ 7,000,000.

* Community Development Block Grants/State's Program 14.228

State and Small Cities Division
Office of Block Grant Assistance
Community Planning and Development
U.S. Department of Housing and Urban Development (HUD)
451 7th St., SW
Washington, DC 20410   202-708-1322

The primary objective of this program is the development of viable urban communities by providing decent housing, a suitable living environment and expanding economic opportunities principally for persons of low and moderate income. Types of assistance: grants. Estimate of annual funds available: $ unknown.

* Emergency Shelter Grants Program (ESGP) 14.231

Barbara Richards
Division of Special Needs Assistance
U.S. Department of Housing and Urban Development (HUD)
451 7th St., SW, Room 7262
Washington, DC 20410   202-708-4300

The program is designed to help improve the quality of existing emergency shelters for the homeless, to help make available additional emergency shelters, and to help pay the costs of operating emergency shelters. Types of assistance: grants. Estimate of annual funds available: $ 47,302,000.

* Empowerment Zones Program 14.244

Office of Community Planning and Development
U.S. Department of Housing and Urban Development   800-998-9999

To provide for the establishment of Empowerment Zones and Enterprise Communities in urban areas, to stimulate the creation of new jobs, particularly for the disadvantaged and long-term unemployed, and to promote revitalization of economically distressed areas. Types of assistance: grants. Estimate of annual funds available: $140,000,000.

* Fair Housing Assistance Program-State and Local (FHAP) 14.401

Assistant Secretary for Fair Housing
and Equal Opportunity
U.S. Department of Housing and Urban Development (HUD)
451 7th St., SW
Washington, DC 20410   202-708-0455

To provide to those agencies to whom the U.S. Department of Housing and Urban Development (HUD) must refer Title VIII complaints both the incentives and resources required to develop an effective work force to handle complaints and provide technical assistance and training. Types of assistance: grants. Estimate of annual funds available: $ 7,375,000.

* Employment Opportunities for Lower Income Persons and Businesses 14.412

Maxine Cunningham
Office of Fair Housing and Equal Opportunity
U.S. Department of Housing and Urban Development
451 7th St., SW
Washington, DC 20410   202-708-0800

To promote affirmative action by Public Housing Agencies (PHAs) and to expand the Department's Title VI Compliance Program beyond the HUD-initiated compliance review process. Types of assistance: advisory services and counseling. Estimate of annual funds available: not known.

* Community Outreach Partnership Program 14.511

HUD USER
P.O. Box 6091
Rockville, MD 20849   800-245-2691

This program is a five-year demonstration program to determine the feasibility of facilitating partnerships among institutions of higher education and communities to solve urban problems through research, outreach and exchange of information. Types of assistance: grants. Estimate of annual funds available: $7,500,000,000.

* Community Development Work-Study Program 14.512

HUD USER
P.O. Box 6091
Rockville, MD 20849   800-245-2691

To make grants to institutions of higher education for the purpose of providing assistance to economically disadvantaged and minority students who participate in community development work-study programs are enrolled in full-time graduate or undergraduate programs in community and economic development and community planning. Types of assistance: grants. Estimate of annual funds available: $3,000,000.

* Mariel-Cubans 16.572

Louise Lucas
Bureau of Justice Assistance
Office of Justice Programs
633 Indiana Avenue, NW
Washington, DC 20531   202-307-1065

To provide financial reimbursements to states for their expenses by reason of Mariel-Cubans having to be incarcerated in state facilities for terms requiring incarceration for the period of October 1, 1988 through September 30, 1989, following their conviction of a felony committed after having been paroled into the U.S. by the Attorney General during the 1980 influx of Mariel-Cubans. Types of assistance: grant. Estimate of annual funds available: $ unknown.

* Emergency Federal Law Enforcement Assistance 16.577

Luke Galant
Bureau of Justice Assistance
Office of Justice Programs
U.S. Department of Justice
633 Indiana Ave., NW
Washington, DC 20531   202-616-3211

To provide necessary assistance to and through a state government to provide an adequate response to an uncommon situation which requires law enforcement, which is or threatens to become of serious or epidemic proportions and with respect to which state and local resources are inadequate to protect the lives and property of citizens or to enforce the criminal law. Types of assistance: grants. Estimate of annual funds available: $ 1,123,000.

* Narcotics Control Discretionary Grant Program (Discretionary Program) 16.580

Office of Justice Programs
Bureau of Justice Assistance
U.S. Department of Justice
633 Indiana Ave., NW
Washington, DC 20531   202-514-5947

To enhance the capacity of each state to define the drug problem and to focus on program development on areas of greatest need. Types of assistance: grant. Estimate of annual funds available: $ 67,352,000.

* Drug Law Enforcement Program-Prison Capacity (Prison Capacity Program) 16.581

Tom Albrecht
Office of Justice Programs
Bureau of Justice Assistance
U.S. Department of Justice
Washington, DC 20531   202-514-5943

To provide technical assistance, training and financial support to state, local and private nonprofit organizations dealing with state prison capacities and their alternatives. Types of assistance: grants. Estimate of annual funds available: $ 8,441.

* Crime Victim Assistance/Discretionary Grants 16.582

Marti Speights
Division Director
Office for Victims of Crime
Office of Justice Programs
U.S. Department of Justice
633 Indiana Ave., NW
Washington, DC 20531   202-616-3582

One percent of the Crime Victims Fund is statutorily reserved by the Office for Victims of Crime for grants to provide training and technical assistance services to eligible crime victims assistance programs and for financial support of services to victims of federal crime by eligible crime victims assistance programs. Types of assistance: grants, direct payments. Estimate of annual funds available: $ 5,802,000.

* Children's Justice Act Discretionary Grants for Native American Indian Tribes (Children's Justice Act for Native American Indian Tribes) 16.583

Marti Speights
Division Director
Office for Victims of Crime
Office of Justice Programs
U.S. Department of Justice
633 Indiana Ave., NW
Washington, DC 20531   202-616-3578

Fifteen percent of the funds from the Crime Victims Services that are transferred to the U.S. Department of Health and Human Services as part of the Children's Justice Act are to be statutorily reserved by the Office for Victims of Crime to make grants for the purpose of assisting native American Indian tribes in developing, establishing and operating programs. Types of assistance: grants, direct payments. Estimate of annual funds available: $ 1,621,000.

* Corrections-Training and Staff Development 16.601

National Institute of Corrections
320 First St., NW, Room 5007
Washington, DC 20534   202-307-3156

To devise and conduct in various geographical locations, seminars, workshops and training programs for law enforcement officers, judges and judicial personnel, probation and parole personnel, correctional personnel, welfare workers and other personnel, including lay ex-offenders and paraprofessionals, connected with the treatment and rehabilitation of criminal and juvenile offenders. Types of assistance: grants. Estimate of annual funds available: $ 1,876,325.

* Corrections-Technical Assistance/Clearinghouse 16.603

Technical Assistance Coordinator
National Institute of Corrections
320 First St., NW, Room 5007
Washington, DC 20534   202-307-3106

To encourage and assist federal, state, and local government programs and services, and programs and services of other public and private agencies, institutions, in their efforts to develop and implement improved corrections programs. Types of assistance: grants. Estimate of annual funds available: $ 2,646,715.

* Employment Service 17.207

John Robinson
Director
United States Employment Service
Employment and Training Administration
U.S. Department of Labor

Washington, DC 20210 202-219-5257

To place persons in employment by providing a variety of placement-related services without charge to job seekers and to employers seeking qualified individuals to fill job openings. Types of assistance: grants. Estimate of annual funds available: $ 845,912,000.

* Dislocated Workers: Employment and Training Assistance 17.246

Employment and Training Administration
U.S. Department of Labor
200 Constitution Ave., NW, Room N5426
Washington, DC 20210 202-219-5577

To assist dislocated workers obtain unsubsidized employment through training and related employment services using a decentralized system of state programs. Types of assistance: grants. Estimate of annual funds available: $ 1,036,800,000.

* Migrant and Seasonal Farmworkers (Migrant and Other Seasonally Employed Farmworker Programs) 17.247

Office of Special Targeted Programs
Division of Seasonal Farmworker Programs
Employment and Training Administration
U.S. Department of Labor
Room N4641
200 Constitution Ave., NW
Washington, DC 202-219-5500

To provide job training, job search assistance, and other supportive services for those individuals who suffer chronic seasonal unemployment and underemployment in the agricultural industry. Types of assistance: grants. Estimate of annual funds available: $ 85,710,000.

* Employment Services and Job Training-Pilot and Demonstration Programs 17.249

Administrator
Office of Policy and Research
Employment and Training Administration
U.S. Department of Labor
200 Constitution Ave., NW
Washington, DC 202-219-5677

To provide, foster, and promote job training and other services which are most appropriately administered at the national level and which are operated in more than one state to groups with particular disadvantage in the labor market. Types of assistance: grants. Estimate of annual funds available: $ 35,522,000.

* Job Training Partnership Act (JTPA) 17.250

Donald Kulick
Employment and Training Administration
U.S. Department of Labor
200 Constitution Ave., NW
Washington, DC 20210 202-219-6236

To provide job training and related assistance to economically disadvantaged individuals and others who face significant employment barriers. Types of assistance: grants. Estimate of annual funds available: $ 1,054,813,000.

* Native American Employment and Training Programs 17.251

Division of Indian and Native American Programs
Employment and Training Administration
U.S. Department of Labor
200 Constitution Ave., NW, Room N4641
Washington, DC 202-219-8502

To afford job training to Native Americans facing serious barriers to employment, who are in special need of such training to obtain productive employment. Types of assistance: grants. Estimate of annual funds available: $ 64,080,040.

* Mine Health and Safety Grants 17.600

Assistant Secretary of Labor for Mine Safety and Health
Mine Safety and Health Administration
U.S. Dept. of Labor
4015 Wilson Blvd.

Arlington, VA 22203 703-235-8264

To assist states in developing and enforcing effective mine health and safety laws and regulations. Types of assistance: grants. Estimate of annual funds available: $ 5,851,000.

* Disabled Veterans Outreach Program 17.801

Veterans Employment and Training Service
Office of the Assistant Secretary for Veterans
Employment and Training
U.S. Department of Labor
200 Constitution Ave., NW, Room S-1316
Washington, DC 20210 202-219-9105

To provide funds to states to provide job and job training opportunities for disabled and other veterans through contacts with employers. Types of assistance: grants. Estimate of annual funds available: $ 83,601,000.

* Local Veterans Employment Representative Program (LVER Program) 17.804

Veterans Employment and Training Service
Office of the Asst. Secretary for Veterans
Employment and Training
U.S. Dept. of Labor, Room S1316
200 Constitution Ave., NW
Washington, DC 20210 202-219-9105

To provide funds to State Employment Service/Job Service Agencies to ensure that there is local supervision of compliance with federal regulations, performance standards, and grant agreement provisions in carrying out requirements of 38 USC 2004 in providing veterans with maximum employment and training opportunities. Types of assistance: grants. Estimate of annual funds available: $ 77,593,000.

* Boating Safety Financial Assistance 20.005

Commandant
U.S. Coast Guard
Washington, DC 20593-0001 202-267-0857

To encourage greater state participation and uniformity in boating safety, particularly to permit the states to assume the greater share of boating safety education , assistance, and enforcement activities. Types of assistance: grants. Estimate of annual funds available: $ 3,850,000.

* Airport Improvement Program (AIP) 20.106

Federal Aviation Administration (FAA)
Office of Airport Planning and Programming
Grants-in-Aid Division, APP-500
800 Independence Ave., SW
Washington, DC 20591 202-267-3831

To assist sponsors, owners, or operators of public-use airports in the development of a nationwide system of airports adequate to meet the needs of civil aeronautics. Types of assistance: grants. Estimate of annual funds available: $ 1,450,000,000.

* Highway Planning and Construction (Federal-Aid Highway Program) 20.205

William Weseman, Director
Office of Engineering
Federal Highway Agency (FHA)
400 7th St., SW
Washington, DC 20590 202-366-4853

To assist state highway agencies (SHA) in the development of an integrated, interconnected network of highways by constructing and rehabilitating the interstate highway system and building or improving primary, secondary and urban systems roads, and streets. Types of assistance: grants. Estimate of annual funds available: $ 19,649,127,000.

* Motor Carrier Safety Assistance Program (MCSAP) 20.218

Associate Administrator for Motor Carriers
Federal Highway Agency (FHA)
Washington, DC 20590 202-366-2519

To reduce the number and severity of accidents and hazardous materials incidents involving commercial motor vehicles by substantially increasing the level of

Be patient. If any phone number is incorrect, call (area code) 555-1212 and request the new listing.

357

enforcement activity and the likelihood that safety defects, driver deficiencies, and unsafe carrier practices will be detected and corrected. Types of assistance: grants. Estimate of annual funds available: $ 73,078,400.

* Grants-In-Aid for Railroad Safety-State Participation (State Participation in Railroad Safety) 20.303

Associate Administrator for Safety
Federal Railroad Administration
Room 8320A, 400 7th St., SW
Washington, DC 20590   202-366-0895

To promote safety in all areas of railroad operations; reduce railroad related accidents and casualties; and to reduce damage to property caused by accidents involving any carrier of hazardous materials by providing State participation in the enforcement and promotion of safety practices. Types of assistance: grants. Estimate of annual funds available: $ not known.

* Local Rail Service Assistance (National Rail Service Continuation Grants) 20.308

Office of Railroad Development
Federal Railroad Administration
Room 5410, 400 7th St., SW
Washington, DC 20590   202-366-1677

To maintain efficient local rail freight services. Types of assistance: Grant. Estimate of annual funds available: $ 17,000,000.

* Urban Mass Transportation Capital Improvement Grants (Capital Grants) 20.500

Federal Transit Administration
U.S. Department of Transportation
400 7th St., SW
Washington, DC 20590   202-366-1660

To assist in financing the acquisition, construction, reconstruction and improvement of facilities and equipment for use, by operation, lease, or otherwise in mass transportation service in urban areas. Types of assistance: grants. Estimate of annual funds available: $ 1,924,904,000.

* Urban Mass Transportation Managerial Training Grants (Mass Transit Technology and Technical Assistance Program) 20.503

Office of Technical Assistance and Safety
Federal Transit Administration
U.S. Department of Transportation
400 Seventh St., SW
Washington, DC 20590   202-366-0234

To provide fellowships for training of managerial, technical and professional personnel employed in the urban mass transportation field. Types of assistance: grants. Estimate of annual funds available: $ not known.

* Urban Mass Transportation Technical Studies Grants (Technical Planning Studies) 20.505

Director, Office of Planning Assistance
Office of Grants Management
Federal Transit Administration
U.S. Department of Transportation (DOT)
400 7th St., SW
Washington, DC 20590   202-366-6385

To assist in planning, engineering and designing of urban mass transportation projects, and other technical studies in a program for a united or officially coordinated urban transportation system. Types of assistance: grants. Estimate of annual funds available: $ 43,528,000.

* Urban Mass Transportation Capital and Operating Assistance Formula Grants 20.507

Director
Office of Planning Assistance
Office of Grants Management
Federal Transit Administration
U.S. Department of Transportation (DOT)

400 7th St., SW
Washington, DC 20590   202-366-1662

To assist in financing the acquisition, construction, cost effective leasing, planning and improvement of facilities and equipment for use by operation or lease or otherwise in mass transportation service. Types of assistance: grants. Estimate of annual funds available: $ 2,933,761,000.

* Public Transportation for Nonurbanized Areas (Section 18) 20.509

Federal Transit Administration
Office of Grants Management
Office of Capital and Formula Assistance
400 7th St., SW
Washington, DC 20590   202-366-6385

To improve, initiate, or continue public transportation services in nonurbanized areas by providing financial assistance for the acquisition, construction and improvement of facilities and equipment and the payment of operating expenses by operating contract, lease or otherwise. Types of assistance: grants. Estimate of annual funds available: $ 87,318,000.

* Urban Mass Transportation Technical Assistance 20.512

Associate Administrator for Technical
  Assistance and Safety (TTS-1)
Federal Transit Administration
U.S. Department of Transportation (DOT)
400 7th St., SW, Room 6431
Washington, DC 20590   202-366-4052

To improve mass transportation service, to contribute toward meeting total urban transportation needs at a minimum cost, and to assist in the reduction of urban transportation needs by improving the ability of transit industry operating officials to plan, manage, and operate their systems more effectively and safely. Types of assistance: grants. Estimate of annual funds available: $ not known.

* Capital Assistance Program for Elderly and Handicapped Persons (Section (b)(2)) 20.513

Federal Transit Administration
Office of Grants Management
Office of Capital and Formula Assistance
400 7th St., SW
Washington, DC 20590   202-366-2053

To provide financial assistance in meeting the transportation needs of elderly and handicapped persons where public transportation services are unavailable. Types of assistance: grants. Estimate of annual funds available: $ 59,192,000.

* State and Community Highway Safety 20.600

Adele Derby
Coordinator of Regional Operations
National Highway Traffic Safety Administration
Washington, DC 20590   202-366-6902

To provide a coordinated national highway safety program to reduce traffic accidents, deaths, injuries, and property damage. Types of assistance: grants. Estimate of annual funds available: $ 123,000,000.

* Pipeline Safety 20.700

Tom Fortner
Research and Special Programs Administration
U.S. Department of Transportation
400 7th St., SW
Washington, DC 20590   202-366-4564

To develop and maintain state natural gas, liquified natural gas, and hazardous liquid pipeline safety programs. Types of assistance: grants. Estimate of annual funds available: $ 12,000,000.

* Tax Counseling for the Elderly 21.006

Tax Counseling for the Elderly
Taxpayer Service Division
Internal Revenue Services
1111 Constitution Ave., NW

Washington, DC 20224 202-622-7664

To authorize the Internal Revenue Service to enter into agreement with private or public nonprofit agencies or organizations to establish a network of trained volunteers to provide free income tax information and return preparation assistance to elderly taxpayers. Types of assistance: direct payment. Estimate of annual funds available: $ 3,700,000.

* Appalachian Supplements to Federal Grant-In-Aid Community Development 23.002

Executive Director
Appalachian Regional Commission
1666 Connecticut Avenue, NW
Washington DC 20235 202-884-7700

To meet the basic needs of local areas and assist in improving creation of jobs and private sector involvement and investment by funding development facilities such as water and sewage systems, sewage treatment plants, industrial sites and providing basic water and sewer facilities. Types of assistance: grants. Estimate of annual funds available: $ 100,370,000.

* Appalachian Development Highway System (Appalachian Corridor) 23.003

Executive Director
Appalachian Regional Commission
1666 Connecticut Ave., NW
Washington, DC 20235 202-884-7700

To provide a highway system which, in conjunction with other federally-aided highways, will open areas with development potential within the Appalachian region where commerce and communication have been inhibited by lack of adequate access. Types of assistance: grants. Estimate of annual funds available: $233,479,000.

* Appalachian Health Programs (Appalachian 202 Health Programs) 23.004

Executive Director
Appalachian Regional Commission
1666 Connecticut Avenue, NW
Washington DC 20235 202-884-7700

To make primary health care accessible, reduce infant mortality and recruit needed health manpower in designed "health-shortage" areas. Types of assistance: grants. Estimate of annual funds available: $ 1,800,000.

* Appalachian Housing Project Planning Loan, Technical Assistance Grant and Site Development and Off-Site Improvement Grant 23.005

Executive Director
Appalachian Regional Commission
1666 Connecticut Ave., NW
Washington, DC 20235 202-884-7700

To stimulate the creation of jobs and private sector investment through low and moderate income housing construction and rehabilitation, and to assist in developing site and off-site improvements for low and moderate income housing in the Appalachian Region. Types of assistance: grant. Estimate of annual funds available: $ 650,000.

* Appalachian Local Access Roads 23.008

Executive Director
Appalachian Regional Commission
1666 Connecticut Ave., NW
Washington, DC 20235 202-884-7700

To provide access to industrial, commercial, educational, recreational, residential and related transportation facilities which directly or indirectly relate to the improvement of the areas determined by the states to have significant development potential. Types of assistance: grant. Estimate of annual funds available: $ 1,800,000.

* Appalachian Local Development District Assistance (LDD) 23.009

Executive Director
Appalachian Regional Commission

1666 Connecticut Ave., NW
Washington, DC 20235 202-884-7700

To provide planning and development resources in multicounty areas; to help develop the technical competence essential to sound development assistance. Types of assistance: grant. Estimate of annual funds available: $ 5,631,000.

* Appalachian Mine Area Restoration 23.010

Executive Director
Appalachian Regional Commission
1666 Connecticut Ave., NW
Washington, DC 20235 202-884-7700

To further the creation of jobs by rehabilitating areas presently damaged by deleterious mining practices and by controlling or abating mine drainage pollution. Types of assistance: Grant. Estimate of annual funds available: $ not known.

* Appalachian State Research, Technical Assistance, and Demonstration Projects (State Research) 23.011

Executive Director
Appalachian Regional Commission
1666 Connecticut Ave., NW
Washington, DC 20235 202-884-7700

To expand the knowledge of the region to the fullest extent possible by means of state-sponsored research studies, technical assistance and demonstration projects in order to assist the Commission in accomplishing the objectives of the Act. Types of assistance: grant. Estimate of annual funds available: $ 900,000.

* Appalachian Vocational and Other Education Facilities and Operations 23.012

Executive Director
Appalachian Regional Commission
1666 Connecticut Ave., NW
Washington DC 20235 202-884-7700

To provide the people of the region with the equipment, renovation and operating funds for training and education necessary to obtain employment at their best capability for available job opportunities. Types of assistance: grants. Estimate of annual funds available: $ 29,735,000.

* Appalachian Child Development 23.013

Executive Director
Appalachian Regional Commission
1666 Connecticut Ave., NW
Washington, DC 20235 202-884-7700

To provide child development services throughout the region which meet the needs of industry and its employees. Types of assistance: grants. Estimate of annual funds available: $ 500,000.

* Training Assistance to State and Local Government 27.009

Office of Training Operations
Workforce Training Service
Office of Personnel Management
1400 Wilson Blvd.
Arlington, VA 22209 703-312-7282

To assist state and local governments and Indian tribal governments in training professional, administrative, and technical personnel to increase their capability for mission accomplishment. Types of assistance: training. Estimate of annual funds available: $ not known.

* Presidential Management Intern Program 27.013

Office of Marketing and Information
Workforce Training Service
Office of Personnel Management
1400 Wilson Blvd.
Arlington, VA 22209 703-312-7282

To attract to the federal service graduate students of exceptional potential who are receiving advanced degrees in a variety of academic disciplines and who have a clear interest in and commitment to a career in the analysis and management of public programs and policies. Types of assistance: federal employment. Estimate of annual funds available: $ not known.

Be patient. If any phone number is incorrect, call (area code) 555-1212 and request the new listing.

359

Your Community

* Employment Discrimination-State and Local Anti-Discrimination Agency Contracts 30.002

Lawrence Koziarz, State and Local Programs Division
Office of Program Operations
Equal Employment Opportunity Commission (EEOC)
1801 L St., NW, Room 8030
Washington, DC 20507   202-663-4856

To assist EEOC in the enforcement of Title VII of the Civil Rights Act of 1964, as amended and of the age discrimination in employment act of 1967 by investigating and resolving charges of employment discrimination based on race, color, religion, sex, national origin, etc. Types of assistance: direct payment. Estimate of annual funds available: $ 26,500,000.

* Employment Discrimination Project Contracts - Indian Tribes 30.009

Lawrence Koziarz, State and Local Programs Division
Office of Program Operations
Equal Employment Opportunity Commission (EEOC)
1801 L St., NW, Room 8030
Washington, DC 20507   202-663-4856

To insure the protection of employment rights of Indians working on reservation. Types of assistance: grants. Estimate of annual funds available: $ not known.

* Labor-Management Cooperation 34.002

Division of Labor Management Grant Programs
Federal Mediation and Conciliation Service
2100 K St., NW
Washington, DC 20247   202-606-8181

Types of assistance: grants. Estimate of annual funds available: $ 1,500,000.

* Community Development Revolving Loan Program for Credit Unions (CDCU) 44.002

Mr. Floyd Lancaster
Community Development Revolving Loan Program for Credit Unions
National Credit Union Administration
1775 Duke St.
Alexandria, VA 22314   703-518-6610

To support community based credit unions in their efforts to stimulate economic development activities which result in increased income, ownership and employment opportunities for low-income residents and to provide basic financial and related services to residents of their communities. Types of assistance: direct loans. Estimate of annual funds available: $ 1,620,000.

* Promotion of the Arts-State Programs 45.007

Directors, State Program
National Endowment for the Arts
1100 Pennsylvania Ave., NW
Washington, DC 20506   202-682-5429

To assist state and regional public arts agencies in the development of programs for the encouragement of the arts and artists, and to assist organizations providing services at a national level to state or local arts agencies. Types of assistance: grants. Estimate of annual funds available: $ 31,075,000.

* Promotion of the Arts-Expansion Arts 45.010

Expansion Arts Program
National Endowment for the Arts
1100 Pennsylvania Ave., NW
Washington, DC 20560   202-682-5443

To provide grants to professionally directed arts organizations of high artistic quality which are deeply rooted in and reflective of the culture of a minority. Types of assistance: grants. Estimate of annual funds available: $ 6,700,000.

* Promotion of the Arts: Inter-Arts 45.011

Director, Presenting Program
National Endowment for the Arts
1100 Pennsylvania Ave., NW
Washington, DC 20506   202-682-5444

To provide grants for projects that potentially have national or regional impact. Types of assistance: grants. Estimate of annual funds available: $ 5,035,000.

* Promotion of the Arts - Challenge Grants 45.013

Challenge and Advancement Grant Programs
Room 617, National Endowment for the Arts
1100 Pennsylvania Ave., NW
Washington, DC 20506   202-682-5436

To assist on a one-time basis, projects designed to have a lasting impact that can help move the National forward in achieving excellence in the arts, access to, and/or appreciation of such excellence. Types of assistance: grants. Estimate of annual funds available: $ 12,670,000.

* Promotion of the Arts-Folk Arts 45.015

Director, Folk and Traditional Arts Program
National Endowment for the Arts
1100 Pennsylvania Ave., NW
Washington, DC 20506   202-682-5449

To provide grants to assist, foster, and make publicly available the diverse traditional American folk arts throughout the country. Types of assistance: grants. Estimate of annual funds available: $ 3,375,000.

* Promotion of the Arts (Local Programs) 45.023

Local Arts Agencies Programs
National Endowment for the Arts
Nancy Hawks Center
1100 Pennsylvania Ave., NW
Washington, DC 20506   202-682-5431

To enhance to the quality and availability of the arts by fostering expansion of public support for the arts at the local level and to strengthen the local arts agency as a mechanism for arts planning, financial support and development and to encourage joint planning for the arts by Federal, state, and local art agencies, community leaders, public officials, art organizations, and artists. Types of assistance: grants. Estimate of annual funds available: $ 2,065,000.

* Management and Technical Assistance for Socially and Economically Disadvantaged Businesses: 7(j) Development Assistance Program 59.007

Associate Administrator for Minority Small Business
409 3rd St., SW
Washington, DC 20416   202-205-6410

To provide management and technical assistance through qualified individuals, public or private organizations to existing or potential businesses which are economically and socially disadvantaged or which are located in areas of high concentration of unemployment. Types of assistance: grants. Estimate of annual funds available: $ 8,073,000.

* Physical Disaster Loans (7(b) Loans (DL)) 59.008

Office of Disaster Assistance
Small Business Administration (SBA)
409 3rd St., SW
Washington, DC 20416   202-205-6734

To provide loans to the victims of designated physical-type disasters for uninsured loans. Types of assistance: loans, loan guarantee. Estimate of annual funds available: $ 1,152,502,000.

* Service Corps of Retired Executives Association (SCORE) 59.026

National SCORE Office
Small Business Administration (SBA)
409 3rd St., SW
Washington, DC 20036   202-205-6762

To utilize the management experience of retired and active business executives to counsel and train potential in existing small businesses. Types of assistance: grants, other. Estimate of annual funds available: $ 3,250,000.

* Small Business Development Center (SBDC) 59.037

Small Business Administration
Office of Small Business Development Center
409 3rd St., SW, 4th Floor
Washington, DC 20416   202-205-6776

To provide management counseling, training and technical assistance to the small

Be patient. If any phone number is incorrect, call (area code) 555-1212 and request the new listing.

business community through Small Business Development Centers (SBDCs). Types of assistance: grants. Estimate of annual funds available: $ 76,986,000.

* Veterans State Domiciliary Care 64.014

Assistant Chief
Medical Director for Geriatrics and Extended Care
U.S. Department of Veterans Affairs
Washington, DC 20420   202-535,7538

To provide financial assistance to states furnishing domiciliary care to eligible veterans in State Veterans Homes which meet the standards prescribed by the Secretary of Veterans Affairs. Types of assistance: grants. Estimate of annual funds available: $ 19,716,661.

* Veterans State Nursing Home Care 64.015

Assistant Chief
Medical Director for Geriatrics and Extended Care
U.S. Department of Veterans Affairs
Washington, DC 20420   202-535,7538

To provide financial assistance to states furnishing nursing home care to eligible veterans in State Veterans Homes which meet the standards prescribed by the Secretary of Veterans Affairs. Types of assistance: grants. Estimate of annual funds available: $ 161,078,694.

* Veterans State Hospital Care 64.016

Assistant Chief Medical Director for Geriatrics and Extended Care
U.S. Department of Veterans Affairs
Washington, DC 20420   202-535,7538

To provide financial assistance to states furnishing hospital care to eligible veterans in State Veterans Homes which meet the standards prescribed by the Secretary of Veterans Affairs. Types of assistance: grants. Estimate of annual funds available: $ 4,621,798.

* State Cemetery Grants 64.203

Director, State Cemetery Grant Program
National Cemetery System
U.S. Department of Veterans Affairs
810 Vermont Ave., NW
Washington, DC 20420   202-273-5350

To assist states in the establishment, expansion and improvement of veterans cemeteries. Types of assistance: grants. Estimate of annual funds available: $ 10,305,000.

* Air Pollution Control Program Support 66.001

Steve Hitte, Air Quality Management Division
Office of Air and Radiation
Environmental Protection Agency (EPA)
Research Triangle Park, NC 27711   919-541-0876

To assist state, municipal, intermunicipal, and interstate agencies in planning developing, establishing, improving and maintaining adequate programs for prevention and control of air quality standards. Types of assistance: grants. Estimate of annual funds available: $ 180,709,300.

* Air Pollution Control-Technical Training 66.006

Deborah Miller, Air Pollution Training Institute
Environmental Protection Agency (EPA)
Research Triangle Park, NC 27711   919-541-3724

To provide technical training to personnel from state and local air pollution control agencies. Types of assistance: training. Estimate of annual funds available: $ 300,000.

* Water Pollution Control-State and Interstate Program Support (106 Grants) 66.419

Carol Crow, Director
Analysis and Evaluation Division
Office of Water Regulations and Standards
Office of Water
Environmental Protection Agency (EPA)
Washington, DC 20460   202-260-6742

To assist states, territorial Indian Tribes and interstate agencies in establishing and maintaining adequate measures for prevention and control of surface and ground water pollution. Types of assistance: grants. Estimate of annual funds available: $ 79,534,000.

* Water Quality Control Training Seminars, Data and Monitoring Publications (STORET-Storage and Retrieval System) 66.423

Monitoring Branch
Assessment and Watershed Protection Division
Office of Wetlands
Washington, DC 20460   202-260-6549

To provide state, interstate and other water pollution control and water resource management agencies orientation and where requested training in the use of the storage and retrieval system used by EPA. Types of assistance: Training. Estimate of annual funds available: $ 2,550,000.

* State Public Water System Supervision 66.432

Craig Damron, Office of Drinking Water
Office of Water
Environmental Protection Agency (EPA)
Washington, DC 20460   202-260,5556

To foster development and maintenance of state programs which implement the Safe Drinking Water Act. Types of assistance: Grant. Estimate of annual funds available: $ 70,000,000.

* State Underground Water Source Protection 66.433

Francoise Brasier, Chief
Underground Injection Control Branch
Office of Drinking Water
Office of Water
Environmental Protection Agency (EPA)
401 M St., SW
Washington, DC 20460   202-260-7077

To foster development and implementation of underground injection control (UIC) programs under the Safe Drinking Water Act. Types of assistance: grants. Estimate of annual funds available: $ 9,923,000.

* Water Pollution Control-Lake Restoration Cooperative Agreements (Clean Lakes Program) 66.435

Environmental Protection Agency
Grants Administration Division (3903F)
Washington, DC 20460   202-260-7105

To provide financial assistance to states for assessing the water quality of publicly-owned freshwater lakes, diagnosing the causes of degradation in publicly owned lakes, developing lake restoration and protection plans. Types of assistance: grants. Estimate of annual funds available: $ 3,200,000.

* Construction Management Assistance (Construction Grants Delegation to States) 66.438

Arnold Speiser, Delegation Management Branch
Municipal Support Division, 4204
Environmental Protection Agency
Washington, DC 20460   202-260-7377

To assist and serve as an incentive in the process of delegating the states a maximum amount of authority for conducting day-to-day matters related the management of the construction grant program. Types of assistance: Grant. Estimate of annual funds available: $ not known.

* Water Quality Management Planning (205(j)) 66.454

Don Kunkoski, Director
Assessment and Watershed Protection Division
Office of Water
Environmental Protection Agency (EPA)
401 M St., SW, 4503F
Washington, DC 20460   202-260-7103

To assist states (including territories and the District), public comprehensive planning organizations, and interstate organizations in carrying out water quality management planning. Types of assistance: grants. Estimate of annual funds available: $ 13,300,000.

Be patient. If any phone number is incorrect, call (area code) 555-1212 and request the new listing.

361

* National Estuary Program 66.456

Marilyn Mlay, Chief
Oceans and Coastal Protection Division
Office of Wetlands, Oceans, and Watersheds Protection
Environmental Protection Agency (EPA)
Washington, DC 20460   202-260-1952

To authorize the Agency to convene Management Conferences with participants from states, legislatures, etc., to develop programs to protect and restore coastal resources in estuaries of national significance. Types of assistance: grants. Estimate of annual funds available: $ 14,168,600.

* Capitalization Grants for State Revolving Funds (State Revolving Fund) 66.458

Don Niehus
Delegation Management Branch
Municipal Construction Division
Office of Municipal Control
Environmental Protection Agency (EPA)
Washington, DC 20460   202-260-7366

To create State Revolving Funds through a program of capitalization grants to states which will provide a feasible transition to state and local financing of municipal wastewater treatment facilities. Types of assistance: grants. Estimate of annual funds available: $ 1,235,200,000.

* Air Pollution Control Research 66.501

Environmental Protection Agency
Grants Administration, 3903F
Washington, DC 20460

Types of assistance: grants. Estimate of annual funds available: $ 39,224,200.

* Environmental Protection Consolidated Grants - Program Support (Consolidated Program Support Grants) 66.600

Richard Mitchell
Grants Administration Division
PM 3903, Environmental Protection Agency
Washington, DC 20460   202-260-6077

The consolidated program support grant is an alternative assistance delivery mechanism which allows a state or local agency responsible for continuing pollution control programs to develop an integrated approach to pollution control. Types of assistance: grants. Estimate of annual funds available: $ 38,384,050.

* Pesticides Enforcement Program 66.700

John Neylan, Director
Office of Compliance Monitoring
Office of Pesticides and Toxic Substances, 2222A
Environmental Protection Agency (EPA)
Washington, DC 20460   202-564-2385

To assist states in developing and maintaining comprehensive pesticide enforcement programs. Types of assistance: grants. Estimate of annual funds available: $ 16,135,800.

* Toxic Substances Compliance Monitoring Cooperative Agreements 66.701

John Neylan, Director
Office of Compliance Monitoring
Office of Pesticides and Toxic Substances, 2222A
Environmental Protection Agency (EPA)
Washington, DC 20460   202-564-2385

To assist states in developing and maintaining comprehensive Toxic Substance enforcement programs. Types of assistance: grants. Estimate of annual funds available: $ 4,150,000.

* Hazardous Waste Management State Program Support 66.801

Grants Administration Division
PM-216F
Environmental Protection Agency (EPA)

Washington, DC 20460   703-308-8757

To assist state governments in the development and implementation of an authorized hazardous waste management program for the purpose of controlling the generation, transportation, treatment, storage and disposal of hazardous waste. Types of assistance: grants. Estimate of annual funds available: $ 97,049,700.

* Hazardous Substance Response Trust Fund (Superfund) 66.802

Carolyn Offutt, Chief
State Involvement Section
Office of Emergency and Remedial Response
Environmental Protection Agency (EPA)
Washington, DC 20460   703-603-8797

To determine level of hazard at sites listed in the CERCLA Information System. Types of assistance: grants. Estimate of annual funds available: $ 100,000,000.

* State Underground Storage Tanks Program (UST Program) 66.804

Dana Tulis, Director
Implementation Division
Underground Storage Tank Program (OSWER)
Environmental Protection Agency (EPA)
401 M St., SW
Washington, DC 20460   703-308-8891

To assist states in Development and implementation of their own underground storage tank programs to operate in lieu of the federal Program. Types of assistance: grants. Estimate of annual funds available: $ 9,000,000.

* Underground Storage Tank Trust Fund Program 66.805

Dana Tulis, Director
Implementation Division
Office of the Underground Storage Tanks
Environmental Protection Agency (EPA)
Waterside Mall
401 M St., SW
Washington, DC 20460   703-308-8891

To support the development of state corrective action and enforcement programs that address releases from underground storage tanks containing petroleum. Types of assistance: grants. Estimate of annual funds available: $ 64,550,000.

* Superfund Technical Assistance Grants for Citizen Groups at Priority Sites 66.806

Nicole Lacoste
Office of Emergency and Remedial Response
Environmental Protection Agency (EPA)
401 M St., SW
Washington, DC 20460   703-603-8842

To provide resources for community groups to hire technical advisors who can assist them in interpreting technical information concerning the assessment of potential hazards and the selection and design of appropriate remedies. Types of assistance: grants. Estimate of annual funds available: $ 5,540,000.

* Energy Conservation for Institutional Buildings 81.052

Robert Volk
Institutional Conservation Programs Division
Office of Conservation and Renewable Energy
CE-231
U.S. Department of Energy
Washington, DC 20585   202-586-8034

Types of assistance: grants. Estimate of annual funds available: $ 28,915,000.

* Nuclear Waste Disposal Siting (Consultation and Cooperation Financial Assistance) 81.065

Jerome Saltzman
Office of Civilian Radioactive Waste Management
Washington, DC   202-586-2277

To provide for the development of a repository for the disposal of high level radioactive waste and spent nuclear fuel. Types of assistance: direct payment. Estimate of annual funds available: $ 32,200,000.

* Energy Task Force for the Urban Consortium 81.081

Linda J. DelaCroix, Project Manager
Building Services Division
Office of Conservation and Renewable Energy
U.S. Department of Energy (DOE)
1000 Independence Ave., SW
Washington, DC 20585   202-586-1851

To develop the capability to address energy related problems and to evaluate and test community energy supply and conservation techniques. Types of assistance: grants. Estimate of annual funds available: $ 1,843,000.

* Reimbursement for Firefighting on Federal Property 83.007

Clyde A. Bragdon, Jr., Administrator,
U.S. Fire Administration
16825 S. Seton Ave.
Emmitsburg,, MD 21727   301-447-1080

To provide that each fire service organization which engages in firefighting operations on Federal property may be reimbursed for their direct expenses and direct losses incurred in firefighting Types of assistance: direct payment. Estimate of annual funds available: $ not known.

* Community-Based Anti-Arson Program 83.008

Management
U.S. Fire Administration
Office of Fire Prevention and Arson Control
16825 S. Seton Ave., Room 732
Emmitsburg, MD 21727   301-447-1181

To assist local community based anti-arson organizations increase and intensify arson mitigation efforts. Types of assistance: grants. Estimate of annual funds available: $ 300,000.

* Civil Defense - State and Local Emergency Management Assistance (Emergency Management Assistance) 83.503

Dwight Poe
Preparedness, Policy and Guidance Branch
State and Local Preparedness Directorate
Federal Emergency Management Agency (FEMA)
Washington, DC 20472   202-646-3492

To develop civil defense organizations in the states and their political subdivisions in order to plan for and coordinate emergency activities in the event of attack or natural disaster. Types of assistance: grants. Estimate of annual funds available: $74,628,000.

* State Disaster Preparedness Grants (Disaster Preparedness Improvement Grant) 83.505

Dwight Poe
Preparedness, Policy and Guidance Branch
State and Local Preparedness Division
Federal Emergency Management Agency (FEMA)
Washington, DC 20472   202-646-3492

To assist states in developing and improving state and local plans, programs, and capabilities for disaster preparedness and prevention. Types of assistance: grants. Estimate of annual funds available: $ 2,500,000.

* Disaster Assistance 83.516

Patricia Stahlschmidt
Response and Recovery Directorate
Federal Emergency Management Agency (FEMA)
Washington, DC 20472   202-646-4066

To provide supplemental assistance to states, local government, certain private nonprofit organizations and individuals in alleviating suffering and hardship resulting from major disasters or emergencies declared by the President. Types of assistance: grants, direct payment. Estimate of annual funds available: $ 4,300,000,000.

* Hurricane Preparedness Grants (Hurricane Preparedness) 83.520

Cynthia Keegan
Mitigation Directorate
Federal Emergency Management Agency (FEMA)
Washington, DC 20472   202-646-2711

Major objectives of the Hurricane Preparedness Program are to provide technical and financial assistance to state and local governments to conduct a Hurricane Preparedness Study that addresses the unique consequences of hurricanes in high-risk, high-population areas, reduce hurricane-caused injuries and save lives by assisting in the preparation of a hurricane evacuation plan, and reduce property damage caused by hurricanes. Types of assistance: grants. Estimate of annual funds available: $ 1,110,000.

* Earthquake Hazards Reduction Grants (Earthquake Hazards Reduction) 83.521

Sheila Donahoe
Mitigation Directorate
Federal Emergency Management Agency (FEMA)
Washington, DC 20472   202-646-3121

To reduce, abate and mitigate the potential loss of life and property as the result of the occurrence of an earthquake by fostering the increase in public awareness. Types of assistance: Grant. Estimate of annual funds available: $ 3,692,700.

* Federal Emergency Management Food and Shelter Program (Emergency Food and Shelter) 83.523

Fran McCarthy
Preparedness, Training, and Exercises Directorate
Federal Emergency Management Agency (FEMA)
Washington, DC 20472   202-646-3652

To supplement and expand on-going efforts to provide shelter, food and supportive services for needy families and individuals. Types of assistance: grants. Estimate of annual funds available: $ 130,000,000.

* National Defense/National Direct/Perkins Loan Cancellations (formerly National Direct Student Loan (NDSL) 84.037

Susan Morgan
Policy Development Division
Student Financial Assistance Programs
Office of Assistant Secretary for Postsecondary Education
1600 Independence Ave., SW
Washington, DC 20202   202-708-8242

To reimburse institutions for their share of loans cancelled for National Defense Student Loan recipients who become teachers or who perform active military service in the U.S. Armed Forces. Types of assistance: direct payment. Estimate of annual funds available: $ 14,500,000.

* Impact Aid-Construction (Impact Aid; Construction) 84.040

Charles E. Hansen
Program Operations
Impact Aid Program
U.S. Department of Education
1250 Maryland Ave., SW
Washington, DC 20202-6244   202-260-3907

To provide assistance for the construction of urgently needed minimum school facilities in school districts which have had substantial increases in school membership as a result of new or increased Federal Activities. Types of assistance: grants. Estimate of annual funds available: $ 28,593,000.

* Impact Aid-Maintenance and Operation (Impact Aid/Disaster Aid) 84.041

Charles Hansen
Impact Aid Program
Office of Elementary and Secondary Education
U.S. Department of Education
1250 Maryland Ave., SW
Washington, DC 20202   202-260-3907

Your Community

To provide financial assistance to local educational agencies when enrollments or availability of revenue are adversely affected by federal activities. Types of assistance: direct payment. Estimate of annual funds available: $ 728,000,000.

* Vocational Education-State Councils 84.053

Division of Vocational Education
Office of Asst Secretary for Vocational
and Adult Education
U.S. Dept. of Education
600 Independence Ave., SW
Washington, DC 20202   202-205-9441

To advise the State Board for Vocational Education on the development and administration of the State Plan. Types of assistance: grants. Estimate of annual funds available: $ 9,006,000.

* Indian Education-Formula Grants to Local Educational Agencies (Indian Education Act - Subpart 1) 84.060

Office of Indian Educations
U.S. Department of Education
600 Independence Ave., SW
Washington, DC 20202   202-260-1441

To develop and carry out elementary and secondary school programs designed to meet the special educational and culturally related academic needs of Indian children. Types of assistance: grants. Estimate of annual funds available: $ 59,686,000.

* Rehabilitation Services-Basic Support (Basic Support) 84.126

Office of Program Operations
Rehabilitation Services Administration
U.S. Department of Education
Washington, DC 20202   202-205-9406

To provide vocational rehabilitation services to persons with mental and/or physical handicaps. Types of assistance: grants. Estimate of annual funds available: $ 2,043,874,000.

* Rehabilitation Services-Service Projects (Rehabilitation Service Projects) 84.128

Rehabilitation Services Administration
Office of Asst. Secretary for Special Education
and Rehabilitative Services
U.S. Department of Education
Washington, DC 20202   202-205-9297

To provide funds to state vocational rehabilitation agencies and public nonprofit organizations for projects and demonstration which hold promise of expanding and otherwise improving services for groups of mentally and physically handicapped individuals over and above those provided by the Basic Support Program. Types of assistance: grants. Estimate of annual funds available: $ 45,030,000.

* Migrant Education - Interstate and Intrastate Coordination Program 84.144

Office of Migrant Education
Office of Elementary and Secondary Education
U.S. Department of Education
600 Independence Ave., SW, Room 4104
Washington, DC 20202   202-260-1164

To carry out activities to improve the interstate and intrastate coordination of migrant education between state and local education agencies. Types of assistance: grants. Estimate of annual funds available: $ 5,985,000.

* Public Library Construction (LSCA Title II) 84.154

State Programs Division
Library Programs
U.S. Department of Education
Washington, DC 20208   202-219-1303

To assist with public library construction. Types of assistance: grants. Estimate of annual funds available: $ 30,400,000.

* Client Assistance For Handicapped Individuals (CAP) 84.161

U.S. Department of Education
Associate Commissioner for Program Operations
Office of Special Education and Rehabilitative Services
Washington, DC 20202   202-205-9406

To provide assistance in informing and advising clients and client applicants of available benefits under the Rehabilitation Act. Types of assistance: grants. Estimate of annual funds available: $ 9,824,000.

* Library Services for Indian Tribes and Hawaiian Natives 84.163

Library Development Staff, Library Programs
Office of Educational Research and Improvement
U.S. Department of Education
Washington, DC 20208   202-219-1670

To promote the extension of public library services to Indian people living on or near reservations; for Indian tribes and Indian in Oklahoma. Types of assistance: grants. Estimate of annual funds available: $ 2,494,380.

* Magnet Schools Assistance 84.165

Equity and Educational Excellence Division
600 Independence Ave., SW
Washington, DC 20202   202-260-2476

To provide grants to eligible local educational agencies for use in magnet schools that are part of approved desegregation plans. Types of assistance: grants. Estimate of annual funds available: $ 107,985,000.

* Library Literacy (LSCA Title VI) 84.167

Library Development Staff, Library Programs
Office of Educational Research and Improvement
U.S. Department of Education
Washington, DC 20208   202-219-1315

To provide support to state public libraries for coordinating and planning library literacy programs and making arrangements for training librarians and volunteers to carry out such programs. Types of assistance: grants. Estimate of annual funds available: $ 8,026,000.

* Handicapped-Preschool Grants 84.173

Division of Educational Services
Office of the Asst. Secretary for Special Education
and Rehabilitative Services
U.S. Department of Education
600 Independence Ave., SW
Washington, DC 20202   202-205-9097

To provide grants to states to assist them in providing a free appropriate public education to preschool age handicapped children. Types of assistance: grants. Estimate of annual funds available: $ 360-265,000.

* Vocational Education-Community Based Organizations 84.174

U.S. Department of Education
Office of Asst. Secretary for Vocational and
Adult Education
600 Independence Ave., SW
Washington, DC 20202   202-205-9441

To provide educational assistance to severely disadvantaged youth, through the collaboration of public agencies, community based organizations and business concerns to enable them to succeed in vocational education. Types of assistance: grant. Estimate of annual funds available: $ 11,499,000.

* Adult Education- Literacy Training and Homeless Adults 84.192

Division of National Programs
Office of Vocational and Adult Education
U.S. Department of Education
600 Independence Ave., SW
Washington, DC 20202   202-205-5499

To provide literacy training and basic skills remediation for adult homeless individuals including a program of outreach activities. Types of assistance: grants. Estimate of annual funds available: $19,082,000.

* State Activities - Education of Homeless Children and Youth 84.196

Compensatory Education Programs
Office of Elementary and Secondary Education
U.S. Department of Education
600 Independence Ave., SW
Washington, DC 20202   202-260-2777

To establish or designate an office in each state educational agency and Outlying Area for the coordination of education for homeless children and youth. Types of assistance: grants. Estimate of annual funds available: $ 28,811,000.

* Workplace Literacy Partnerships 84.198

Division of National Programs
Office of Vocational and Adult Education
U.S. Department of Education
600 Independence Ave., SW
Washington, DC 20202   202-205-5977

To provide demonstration grants to exemplary education partnerships for workplace literacy programs. Types of assistance: grants. Estimate of annual funds available: $37,516,000.

* Native Hawaiian Family Based Education Centers 84.209

Beth Baggett
School Improvement Programs
U.S. Department of Education
600 Independence Ave., SW
Washington, DC 20202   202-260-2502

To develop and operate a minimum of eleven family based education centers throughout the Hawaiian Islands. Types of assistance: direct payment. Estimate of annual funds available: $ 5,600,000.

* Capital Expenses (Chapter 1 - Capital Expenses) 84.216

Mary Jean LeTendre
Compensatory Education Programs
U.S. Department of Education
600 Independence Ave., SW
Washington, DC 20202   202-260-0826

To provide payments to local educational agencies for increases in capital expenses paid from Chapter 1 funds for the purpose of regaining levels of instructional services to eligible private school children. Types of assistance: grants. Estimate of annual funds available: $ 41,434,000.

* State Improvement (Chapter 1 State Improvement Program Grants) 84.218

Compensatory Education Programs
Office of Elementary and Secondary Education
U.S. Department of Education
600 Independence Ave., SW
Washington, DC 20202   202-260-2777

To provide payments to state and local educational agencies to operate Chapter 1 program improvement plans. Types of assistance: grants. Estimate of annual funds available: $ 27,560,000.

* Native Hawaiian Special Education 84.221

Lynda Glidewell   202-205-9099

To operate projects addressing the special education needs of Native Hawaiian Students. Types of assistance: grants. Estimate of annual funds available: $ 1,200,000.

* Mental Health Planning and Demonstration Projects 93.125

Community Support Programs Section
Division of Demonstration Programs

National Institute of Mental Health (NIMH)
Parklawn Bldg., Room 11C-22
5600 Fishers Lane
Rockville, MD 20857   301-443-3653

To promote the development of community support systems for the long-term mentally ill, including inappropriately institutionalized individuals, mentally disturbed children and youth, and homeless individuals in communities. Types of assistance: grants. Estimate of annual funds available: $ 41,000,000.

* Emergency Medical Services Children (EMS for Children) 93.127

Maternal and Child Health Bureau
Health Resources and Services Admin.
Room 18A-39, 5600 Fishers Lane
Rockville, MD 20857   301-443-4026

To support demonstration projects for the expansion and improvement of emergency medical services for children who need treatment for trauma or critical care. Types of assistance: grants. Estimate of annual funds available: $ 10,000,000.

* Technical and Non-Financial Assistance to Community and Migrant Health Centers 93.129

Director, Division of Community and Migrant Health
Bureau of Primary Health Care
Health Resources and Services Admin.
4350 East West Hwy., 7th Floor
Bethesda, MD 20814   301-594-4310

To provide assistance to community health centers (CHCs) in the following areas: the initiation of new shared services activities involving specific CHCs within a state or region; and the enhancement of the clinical capability of centers within a state or region including assistance in retention and recruitment of providers. Types of assistance: grants. Estimate of annual funds available: $ 8,700,000.

* Primary Care Services-Resource Coordination and Development Cooperative Agreements (Primary Care Services Cooperative Agreements) 93.130

Director, Div. of Community and Migrant Health
Bureau of Primary Health Care
Health Resources and Services Admin., Room 7A-55
4350 East West Hwy., 7th Floor
Bethesda, MD 20894   301-594-4310

To coordinate local, state, and federal resources contributing to primary care service delivery in the state to meet the needs of medically under-served populations through community and migrant health centers, and the retention, recruitment and oversight of the National Health Service Corps and other health professions. Types of assistance: grants. Estimate of annual funds available: $ 9,000,000.

* Assistance for Organ Procurement Organizations 93.134

Director, Division of Organ Transplantation
BMCH & RD, Health Resources and Services Admin.
Room 7-18, 5600 Fishers Lane
Rockville, MD 20857   301-443-7577

To provide for the planning, establishment, initial operation, and expansion of qualified organ procurement organizations. Types of assistance: grants. Estimate of annual funds available: $ 100,000.

* Minority Community Health Coalition Demonstration 93.137

Ms. Sonia Hunt Gray
Office of Minority Health
Rockwall II Bldg., Suite 1000
5515 Security Lane
Rockville, MD 20852   301-594-0769

To demonstrate that coalitions of local community agencies can be formed to effectively impact on the disease risk factors and related health problems of minority groups, through unique and innovative methods of modifying behavioral and environmental factors involved. Types of assistance: grants. Estimate of annual funds available: $ 3,200,000.

* Protection and Advocacy for Mentally Ill Individuals (Mentally Ill P and A Services) 93.138

Ms. Natalie Reatig
Division of State and Community Systems Development
National Institute of Mental Health (NIMH)
Parklawn Bldg., Room 15C-17
5600 Fishers Lane
Rockville, MD 20857   301-443-3667

To enable the establishment and administration of a new system in each state to: protect and advocate the rights of mentally ill individuals and investigate incidents of abuse and neglect of mentally ill individuals. Types of assistance: grants. Estimate of annual funds available: $ 21,517,861.

* Drug and Alcohol Abuse Prevention - High-Risk Youth Demonstration Grants 93.144

Dr. Stephen Gardner, Chief
Demonstration Operations Branch
Div. of Demonstrations for High Risk Populations
Substance Abuse and Mental Health Services Admin.
Room 13A45
Rockville, MD   301-443-0353

To support prevention demonstration programs that will develop client and/or service systems targeted toward: decreasing the incidence and prevalence of drug and alcohol use among high-risk youth. Types of assistance: grant. Estimate of annual funds available: $ 59,249,000.

* AIDS Education and Training Centers 93.145

Director
Division of Medicine
Bureau of Health Professions
Health Resources and Services Admin.
Room 9A27, 5600 Fishers Lane
Rockville, MD 20857   301-443-6190

To provide education and training to primary care providers and others on the treatment and prevention of acquired immune deficiency syndrome (AIDS) in collaboration with health professions schools, local hospitals and health departments. Types of assistance: grants. Estimate of annual funds available: $ 16,435,000.

* Mental Health Services for the Homeless Block Grant (MHSH) 93.150

Mr. Stephen Hudak
Grants Management Officer
Block Grant Programs
ADAMHA, Room 15C-05
Parklawn Bldg., 5600 Fishers Lane
Rockville, MD 20857   301-443-4456

To provide financial assistance to states to support services to chronically mentally ill individuals who are homeless or who are subject to a significant probability of becoming homeless. Types of assistance: grants. Estimate of annual funds available: $ 29,462,000.

* Project Grants for Health Services to the Homeless (Homeless Assistance Program) 93.151

Harold Dame, Director
Health Care Services for the Homeless Program
Health Resources and Services Admin.
4350 East West Hwy., 11th Floor
Bethesda, MD 20814   301-594-4260

To provide health care services to homeless persons. Types of assistance: grants. Estimate of annual funds available: $ 65,445,000.

* Rural Health Research Centers 93.155

Office of Rural Health Policy
Health Resources and Services Admin.
Parklawn Bldg., Room 14-22
5600 Fishers Lane
Rockville, MD 20857   301-443-0835

To support the development of rural health research centers to provide an information base and policy analysis capacity on the full range of rural health issues. Types of assistance: grants. Estimate of annual funds available: $ 2,750,000.

* Health Program for Toxic Substances and Disease Registry 93.161

Dr. Barry Johnson, Assoc. Administrator
Centers for Disease Control, Public Health Service (PHS)
1600 Clifton Rd., NE, Mail Stop E28
Atlanta, GA 30333   404-639-0700

To work closely with state, local, and other federal agencies to reduce or eliminate illness, disability and death resulting from exposure to the public and workers to toxic substances at spill and waste disposal sites. Types of assistance: grants. Estimate of annual funds available: $ 6,000,000.

* Health Services in the Pacific Basin 93.163

Howard Lerner
Bureau of Primary Health Care
Public Health Service (PHS)
4350 East West Hwy, 9th Floor
Bethesda, MD 20814   301-594-4260

To develop projects to build capacity and improve health services and systems, particularly preventive health services in the Commonwealth of the Northern Mariana Islands, American Samoa, Guam, Federated States of Micronesia, and Republic of Palau, and to provide technical assistance in support of such projects. Types of assistance: grants. Estimate of annual funds available: $ 1,364,000.

* Model Projects for Pregnant and Postpartum Women and Their Infants (Substance Abuse) 93.169

Ulonda Shomwell, Director
Division of Demonstrations for High Risk Populations
Substance Abuse and Mental Health Services Admin.
5600 Fishers Lane
Rockville, MD 20857   301-443-4564

To promote the involvement and coordinated participation of multiple organizations in the delivery of comprehensive services for substance-abusing pregnant and postpartum women. Types of assistance: grants. Estimate of annual funds available: $ 19,903,000.

* Childhood Lead Poisoning Prevention Projects 93.197

Mr. David Forney
Lead Poisoning Prevention Branch
Division of Environmental Hazards and Health Effects
National Center for Environmental health
Centers for Disease Control and Prevention
MSF-42, Public Health Service
4770 Buford Highway
Atlanta, GA 30341   404-488-7330

To assure that children in communities with demonstrated high risk for lead poisoning are screened; to identify infants and young children with elevated lead levels; to identify possible sources of lead exposure; and to provide information on childhood lead poisoning. Types of assistance: grants. Estimate of annual funds available: $24,500,000.

* Family Planning-Services (Umbrella Councils) 93.217

Deputy Asst. Secretary for Population Affairs
U.S. Department of Health and Human Services
West Tower, Suite 200
East West Hwy.
5600 Fishers Lane
Rockville, MD 20857   301-594-4000

To provide educational, counseling, comprehensive medical and social services necessary to enable individuals to freely determine the number and spacing of their children, and by doing so helping to reduce maternal and infant mortality and promote the health of mothers and children. Types of assistance: grants. Estimate of annual funds available: $ 179,561,000.

* Community Health Centers 93.224

Director, Division of Community and Migrant Health
Health Resources and Services Admin.
4350 East West Hwy., 7th Floor
Bethesda, MD 20814   301-594-4300

To support the development and operation of community health centers which provide primary health services, supplemental health services and environmental health services to medically under-served populations. Types of assistance: grants. Estimate of annual funds available: $ 616,555,000.

* Indian Health Service-Health Management Development Program Indian Health) 93.228

Division of Community Services
Indian Health Service
Public Health Service (PHS), Room 6A-05
5600 Fishers Lane
Rockville, MD 20857   301-443-6840

To improve the quality of the health of American Indians and Native Alaskans by providing a full range of curative, preventative and rehabilitative health services. Types of assistance: grants. Estimate of annual funds available: $ 5,283,000.

* Mental Health Clinical or Service Related Training Grants 93.244

Paul Wohlford
Human Resource Planning and Development Branch
SAMHSA
Parklawn Bldg., Room 15C-18
5600 Fishers Lane
Rockville, MD 20857   301-443-3606

To encourage mental health specialists to work in areas and settings where severe shortages exist; to increase the number of qualified minority personnel in the mental health professions. Types of assistance: grants. Estimate of annual funds available: $ 2,000,000.

* Migrant Health Centers Grants 93.246

Director, Migrant Health Branch
Health Resources and Services Administration
4350 East West Hwy., 7th Floor
Bethesda, MD 20814   301-594-4303

To support the development and operation of migrant health centers and projects which provide primary health care services, supplemental health services and environmental health services which are accessible to migrant and seasonal agricultural farm workers and their families. Types of assistance: grants. Estimate of annual funds available: $ 65,000,000.

* National Health Service Corps 93.258

Dr. Audrey Manley, Director
National Health Service Corps
Health Resources and Services Admin.
Room 7A-39, Parklawn Bldg.
5600 Fishers Lane
Rockville, MD 20857   301-443-2900

To improve the delivery of health care services to residents in areas critically short of health personnel by the assignment of additional medical personnel. Types of assistance: loans. Estimate of annual funds available: $ 39,866,000.

* Family Planning-Personnel Training 93.260

Office of the Assistant Secretary for Health
U.S. Department of Health and Human Services
West Tower, Suite 200, East West Hwy
Rockville, MD 20857   301-594-4008

To provide job specific training for personnel to improve the delivery of family planning services. Types of assistance: grants. Estimate of annual funds available: $ 5,131,000.

* Childhood Immunization Grants (Section 317, Public Health Service Act; Immunization Program) 93.268

Kathy Cahill
Centers for Disease Control
Public Health Service (PHS)
U.S. Department of Health and Human Services
1600 Clifton Rd., NE
Atlanta, GA 30333   404-639-8208

To assist states and communities in establishing and maintaining preventive health service programs to immunize individuals against vaccine-preventable diseases. Types of assistance: grants. Estimate of annual funds available: $ 355,783,230.

* Centers for Disease Control - Investigations and Technical Assistance 93.283

Dr. David Satcher, Acting Director
Centers for Disease Control
Public Health Service (PHS)
U.S. Department of Health and Human Services
1600 Clifton Rd., NE
Atlanta, GA 30333   404-639-3291

To assist state and local health authorities and other health related organizations in controlling communicable disease, chronic diseases, and other preventable health conditions. Types of assistance: grants. Estimate of annual funds available: $ 93,282,696.

* Transitional Living for Homeless Youth 93.550

Associate Commissioner
Family and Youth Services Bureau
Administration for Children and Families
P.O. Box 1182
Washington, DC 20013   202-205-8076

To provide resources to assist older homeless youth (age 16-21) in making a successful transition toward a productive adulthood and self-sufficiency. Types of assistance: grants. Estimate of annual funds available: $13,648,533.

* Abandoned Infants 93.556

Children's Bureau
Division of Child Welfare
Assistance Branch
P.O. Box 1182
Washington, DC 20013   202-205-8657

To prevent the abandonment of infants and young children including the provision of services; to identify and address their needs, especially those who have been infected with HIV or who have been prenatally exposed to the virus or a dangerous drug; to assist children to reside with their natural families or in foster care; and to conduct residential programs for abandoned infants. Types of assistance: grants. Estimate of annual funds available: $14,406,174.

* Family Preservation and Support Services 93.556

Commissioner
Administration on Children, Youth and Families
P.O. Box 1182
Washington, DC 20013   202-205-8618

To fund community-based family support services that promote the well-being of children and families by enhancing family functioning and child development. Types of assistance: grants. Estimate of annual funds available: $145,000,000.

* Refugee Assistance-Voluntary Agency Programs 93.567

Barbara Chesnik
Office of Refugee Resettlement
Administration for Children and Families
U.S. Department of Health and Human Services
6th Floor
370 L'Enfant Promenade SW
Washington, DC 20447   202-401-4558

To assist refugees in becoming self-supporting and independent members of American society, by providing grant funds to private nonprofit organizations to support case management, transitional assistance, and social services for new arrivals. Types of assistance: grants. Estimate of annual funds available: $41,897,000.

* Emergency Community Services for the Homeless 93.572

Office of Community Services
Administration for Children and Families
U.S. Department of Health and Human Services
370 L'Enfant Promenade, SW
Washington, DC 20447   202-401-9233

To use public and resources and programs to meet the needs of the homeless and to provide funds for programs to assist the homeless with special emphasis on elderly, handicapped, families with children, native Americans, and veterans. Types of assistance: grants. Estimate of the annual funds available: $19,752,000.

Be patient. If any phone number is incorrect, call (area code) 555-1212 and request the new listing.

367

* Refugee and Entrant Assistance 93.576

Allan Gall
Office of Refugee Resettlement
Administration for Children and Families
U.S. Department of Health and Human Services
370 L'Enfant Promenade, SW, 6th Floor
Washington, DC 20447   202-401-9251

To decrease the numbers of refugees on public assistance, to promote refugee community and family stability, to enhance services to refugees and to encourage placement of families in good locations. Types of assistance: grants. Estimate of the annual funds available: $11,720,300.

* Family Support Center and Gateway Demonstration Program 93.578

Community Demonstration Programs
Administration for Children and Families
Office of Community Services
370 L'Enfant Promenade, SW
Washington, DC 20447   202-401-9233

To reduce the rate of repeated incidence of homelessness among center clientele and to decrease the incidence of first time homelessness among community participants. Types of assistance: grants. Estimate of annual funds available: $7,371,000.

* Empowerment Zones Program 93.585

Ms. Margaret Washnitzer
Director
Division of State Assistance
Office of Community Services
Administration for Children and Families
370 L'Enfant Promenade, SW
Washington, DC 20447   202-401-2333

To provide grants to States for social services in Empowerment Zones and Enterprise Communities in order to prevent the neglect and abuse of children and to assist disadvantaged adults and youths in achieving and maintaining self-sufficiency. Types of assistance: grants. Estimate of annual funds available: $640,000,000.

* Native American Programs - Financial Assistance Grants 93.612

Administration for Native Americans
U.S. Department of Health and Human Services
Room 348-F, 200 Independence Ave., SW
Washington, DC 20201   202-690-5780

To provide financial assistance to public and private nonprofit organizations including Indian Tribes, urban Indian centers, Native Alaskan villages, Native Hawaiian organizations, rural off-reservation groups, and Native American Pacific Island groups for the development and implementation of social and economic development strategies that promote self-sufficiency. Types of assistance: grants. Estimate of annual funds available: $ 1,000,000.

* Administration for Children, Youth and Families - Runaway and Homeless Youth 93.623

Associate Commissioner
Family and Youth Services Bureau
U.S. Department of Health and Human Services
P.O. Box 1182
Washington, DC 20013   202-205-9843

To develop local facilities to address the immediate needs of runaway and homeless youth and their families. Types of assistance: grants. Estimate of annual funds available: $ 40,457,946.

* Administration on Developmental Disabilities - Basic Support and Advocacy Grants 93.630

Director
Program Operations Division
U.S. Department of Health and Human Services
Washington, DC 20201   202-690-5962

To assist states in the development of a comprehensive system and a coordinated array of services in order to support the developmentally disabled to achieve their maximum potential and ensure the protection of their legal and human rights. Types of assistance: grants. Estimate of annual funds available: $ 97,156,000.

* Administration on Developmental Disabilities - Projects of National Significance 93.631

Program Development Division
Administration on Developmental Disabilities
U.S. Department of Health and Human Services
Washington, DC 20201   202-690-6961

To provide grants and contracts for projects of national significance to increase and support the independence, productivity, and integration into the community of persons with developmental disabilities. Types of assistance: grants. Estimate of annual funds available: $ 5,714,906.

* Children's Justice Grants to States 93.643

James Auchter
National Center on Child Abuse and Neglect
Administration for Children, Youth and Families
P.O. Box 1182
Washington, DC 20013   202-205-8807

To encourage states to enact child protective reforms which are designed to improve the handling of child abuse cases and the investigation and prosecution of cases of child abuse. Types of assistance: grants. Estimate of annual funds available: $ 9,325,000.

* Child Welfare Services - State Grants 93.645

Daniel Lewis, Associate Commissioner
Children's Bureau
Administration for Children, Youth and Families
P.O. Box 1182
Washington, DC 20013   202-205-8618

To establish, extend, and strengthen child welfare services provided by state and local public welfare agencies to enable children to remain in their own homes. Types of assistance: grants. Estimate of annual funds available: $ 291,989,000.

* Social Services Research and Demonstration 93.647

Richard Greenberg, Director
Division of Research and Evaluation
U.S. Department of Health and Human Services
370 L'Enfant Promenade SW, 7th Floor
Washington, DC 20447   202-401-6971

To promote effective social services for dependent and vulnerable populations such as the poor, the aged, children and youth, Native Americans, and the handicapped. Types of assistance: grants. Estimate of annual funds available: $ 14,961,000.

* Adoption Opportunities: Administration for Children, and Families 93.652

Delmar Weathers
Children's Bureau
Administration for Children, Youth and Families
P.O. Box 1182
Washington, DC 20013   202-205-8710

To provide financial support for demonstration projects to improve adoption practices; to gather information on adoptions; and to provide training and technical assistance to improve adoption services. Types of assistance: grants. Estimate of annual funds available: $ 13,000,330.

* Drug Abuse Prevention and Education for Runaway and Homeless Youth (Runaway Youth Drug Abuse Prevention and Education) 93.657

Family and Youth Services Bureau
Administration for Children, Youth and Families
P.O. Box 1182
Washington, DC 20013   202-205-8030

To expand and improve existing drug abuse and prevention services to runaway and homeless youth and their families. Types of assistance: grants. Estimate of annual funds available: $ 14,465,683.

* Foster Care - Title IV-E 93.658

Associate Commissioner
Children's Bureau
P.O. Box 1182

Washington, DC 20013 202-205-8618

To provide Federal Financial Participation (FFP) in assistance on behalf of eligible children needing care away from their families (in foster care) who are in the placement and care of the state agency administering the program. Types of assistance: grant. Estimate of annual funds available: $ 3,128,023,000.

* Adoption Assistance 93.659

Associate Commissioner
Children's Bureau
P.O. Box 1182
Washington, DC 20013 202-205-8618

To provide Federal Financial Participation (FFP) to states which meet certain eligibility tests, in the adoption subsidy costs for the adoption of children with special needs. Types of assistance: grants. Estimate of annual funds available: $ 425,639,000.

* Drug Abuse Prevention and Education Relating to Youth and Gangs 93.660

Family and Youth Services Bureau
Administration for Children, Youth and Families
P.O. Box 1182
Washington, DC 20013 202-205-8078

To prevent and reduce the participation of youth in gangs that engage in illicit drug-related activities. Types of assistance: grants. Estimate of annual funds available: $ 10,519,523.

* Comprehensive Child Development Centers 93.666

Mary Bogle
Administration for Children, Youth and Families
P.O. Box 1182
Washington, DC 20013 202-205-8891

To plan for and carry out projects for intensive, comprehensive, integrated and continuous supportive services for infants, toddlers, and pre-schoolers from low-income families to enhance their intellectual, social, emotional and physical development. Types of assistance: grants. Estimate of annual funds available: $46,560,000.

* Social Services Block Grant (Social Services) 93.667

Director
Office of Policy, Planning and Legislation
Office of Community Services
370 L'Enfant Promenade, SW
Washington, DC 20447 202-401-2333

To enable each State to furnish social services best suited to the needs of the individuals residing in the State. Types of assistance: grant. Estimate of annual funds available: $ 2,800,000,000.

* Administration for Children, Youth and Families - Child Abuse and Neglect State Grants 93.669

Donna Litton
National Center on Child Abuse and Neglect
Children's Bureau
P.O. Box 1182
Washington, DC 20013 202-205-8640

To assist states in improving and increasing activities for the prevention and treatment of child abuse, and to develop, strengthen, and carry out the program objectives through State grants. Types of assistance: grants. Estimate of annual funds available: $ 22,854,000.

* Family Violence Prevention and Services 93.671

Office of Policy, Planning and Legislation
Office of Community Services
370 L'Enfant Promenade SW, 5th Floor
Washington, DC 20447 202-401-5529

To demonstrate the effectiveness of assisting states and Indian Tribes in the prevention of family violence and to provide immediate shelter and related assistance for victims of family violence and their dependents. Types of assistance: grants. Estimate of annual funds available: $ 27,133,200.

* Grants to States for Planning and Development of Dependent Care Programs (Dependent Care Planning and Development) 93.673

Children's Bureau
Administration for Children, Youth and Families
200 Independence Ave., SW
Washington, DC 20013 202-690-6782

To assist states in the planning, development, establishment, expansion or improvement of services related to dependent care resource and referral and services related to school age child care before and after school. Types of assistance: grants. Estimate of annual funds available: $ 12,823,000.

* Independent Living 93.674

Michael Ambrose, Director
Children's Bureau
Administration for Children, Youth and Families
P.O. Box 1182
Washington, DC 20013 202-205-8740

To assist states and localities in establishing and carrying out programs designed to assist children, with respect to whom foster care maintenance payments are being made by the state and who have attained age 16, in making the transition from foster care to independent living. Types of assistance: grants. Estimate of annual funds available: $ 70,000,000.

* State Medicaid Fraud Control Units 93.775

James Wright, Director
State Fraud Branch, Office of the Secretary
U.S. Department of Health and Human Services (DHHS)
Room 5449, North Bldg.
330 Independence Ave., SW
Washington, DC 20201 202-619-3557

To control provider fraud in the states Medicaid program. Types of assistance: grants. Estimate of annual funds available: $ 76,000,000.

* State Survey and Certification of Health Care Providers and Suppliers 93.777

Wayne Smith, Ph.D., Director
Office of Survey and Certification
Health Standards and Quality Bureau
Health Care Financing Administration
6325 Security Blvd.
Baltimore, MD 21207 410-966-6810

To provide financial assistance to any state which is able and willing to determine through its state health agency or other appropriate state agency that providers and suppliers of health care services are in compliance with federal regulatory health and safety standards. Types of assistance: grants. Estimate of annual funds available: $ 145,800,000.

* Project Grants for Non-Acute Care, Intermediate and Long-Term Care Facilities (1610(b) Program) 93.887

Ms. Charlotte Pascoe, Office of Health Facilities
Bureau of Health Resources Development
Room 7A-31, 5600 Fishers Lane
Rockville, MD 20857 301-443-5656

To renovate, expand, repair, equip, or modernize non-acute care intermediate and long-term care facilities for patients with AIDS. Types of assistance: grants. Estimate of annual funds available: $ 15,000,000.

* Coal Miners Respiratory Impairment Treatment Clinics and Services (Black Lung Clinics) 93.965

Director, Div. of Primary Health Care
Health Resources and Services Administration
4350 East West Hwy
Bethesda, MD 20814 301-594-4420

To develop high quality, patient oriented, integrated systems of care which assure access to and continuity of appropriate primary, secondary and tertiary care with maximum use of existing resources. Types of assistance: grants. Estimate of annual funds available: $ 4,142,000.

* Preventive Health Services - Sexually Transmitted Diseases Control Grants 93.977

Dr. Judith Wasserheit, Acting Director
Centers for Disease Control
Public Health Service
U.S. Department of Health and Human Services (DHHS)
1600 Clifton Road, NE
Atlanta, GA 30333   404-639-8258

To reduce morbidity and mortality by preventing cases and complications of sexually transmitted diseases (STD). Types of assistance: grants. Estimate of annual funds available: $ 72,702,578.

* Mental Health Disaster Assistance and Emergency Mental Health 93.982

Dr. Brian Flynn, Chief
Emergency Services and Disaster Relief Branch
National Institute of Mental Health
5600 Fishers Lane
Rockville, MD 20857   301-443-4735

Provision of supplemental emergency mental health counseling to individuals affected by major disasters, including the training of volunteers to provide such counseling. Types of assistance: grants. Estimate of annual funds available: $ 30,000,000.

* Cooperative Agreements for State-Based Diabetes Control Programs 93.988

Chief
Grants Management Office
Procurement and Grants Office
Centers for Disease Control
Public Health Service
U.S. Department of Health and Human Services (DHHS)
255 E. Paces Ferry Rd.
Atlanta, GA 30305   404-842-6640

To implement comprehensive programs which will ensure that persons with diabetes who are at high risk for certain complications of diabetes are identified, entered into the health are system and receive on going state-of-the-art preventive care and treatment. Types of assistance: grants. Estimate of annual funds available: $ 11,166,818.

* National Health Promotion 93.990

Deputy Director
Office of Disease Prevention and Health Promotion
U.S. Department of Health and Human Services (DHHS)
330 C St, SW, Room 2132
Washington, DC 20201   202-205-8611

To engage national membership organizations from various sectors as a means of expanding and coordinating health promotion efforts. Types of assistance: grants. Estimate of annual funds available: $ 600,000.

* Preventive Health and Health Services Block Grant (PHS Block Grants) 93.991

Chief
Grants Management Branch
Centers for Disease Control
255 E. Paces Ferry Rd.
Atlanta, GA 30305   404-842-6508

To provide states with resources for comprehensive preventive health services including: emergency medical services, health incentive activities, hypertension programs, rodent control, etc. Types of assistance: grant. Estimate of annual funds available: $ 151,952,987.

* Maternal and Child Health Services Block Grant 93.994

Maternal and Child Health Bureau
Health Resources and Services Administration
Public Health Service (PHS)
Room 18A-55, 5600 Fishers Lane
Rockville, MD 20857   301-443-3163

To enable states to maintain and strengthen their leadership in planning, promoting, coordinating and evaluating health care for mothers and children and in providing health services for mothers and children who do not have access to adequate health care. Types of assistance: grants. Estimate of annual funds available: $ 572,259,000.

* Adolescent Family Life-Demonstration Projects 93.995

Office of Adolescent Pregnancy Programs
Office of the Assistant Secretary for Health
U.S. Department of Health and Human Services (DHHS)
East West Tower S, Suite 200, West Tower
Rockville, MD 20857   301-594-4004

To promote adoption as an alternative for adolescent parents. Types of assistance: grants. Estimate of annual funds available: $ 4,013,000.

* Foster Grandparent Program (FGP) 94.011

Program Officer, Foster Grandparent Program
Corporation for National Service
1201 New York Ave., NW
Washington, DC 20525   202-606-5000

To provide part-time volunteer service opportunities for low income persons age 60 and over and to give supportive person-to-person service in health, education welfare and related settings to help alleviate the physical mental and emotional problems of infants, children or youth having special or exceptional needs. Types of assistance: grants. Estimate of annual funds available: $ 67,762,000.

* Retired Senior Volunteer Program (RSVP) 94.002

Program Officer
Retired Senior Volunteer Program
Corporation for National Service
1201 New York Ave., NW
Washington, DC 20525   202-606-5000

To provide a variety of opportunities for retired persons, aged 60 or over to serve their community through significant volunteer service. Types of assistance: grants. Estimate of annual funds available: $ 35,808,000.

* Service-Learning Programs 94.005

Student Community Service Programs
Corporation for National Service
1201 New York Ave., NW
Washington, DC 20525   202-606-5000

To encourage and enable students in secondary, vocational and post-secondary schools to participate in community service projects addressing poverty related problems. Types of assistance: grants. Estimate of annual funds available: $ 12,500,000.

* Senior Companion Program 94.016

Program Officer
Senior Companion Program
Corporation for National Service
1201 New York Ave., NW
Washington, DC 20525   202-606-5000

To provide volunteer opportunities for low income people aged 60 and older which enhance their ability to remain active and provide critically needed community services. Types of assistance: grants. Estimate of annual funds available: $31,394,000.

Volunteerism

* ACTION/VISTA Activities
ACTION
1100 Vermont Ave., NW
Room 1100
Washington, DC 20525   202-606-4857
ACTION Update contains articles on the latest ACTION programs and projects, along with notices of upcoming volunteer-related events and publications of interest.

* Anti-Drug Programs in Your Community
ACTION
Drug Alliance Office
1100 Vermont Ave., NW
Washington, DC 20525   202-606-5108
Created in response to the Anti-Drug Act of 1986, ACTION's anti-drug effort encourages and promotes volunteer, community-based programs for the nation's at-risk youth and the elderly. The free booklet, *Take Action Against Drug Abuse: How to Start a Volunteer Anti-Drug Program in Your Community*, outlines the "how to" strategies of getting started, fundraising, grantsmanship, long-term fundraising, volunteer recruitment and management, and publicity. Contact this office to receive a free booklet and for more information on setting up an anti-drug program in your community.

* Community Volunteer Service Programs
ACTION
Drug Alliance Office
1100 Vermont Ave., NW
Washington, DC 20525   202-606-5108
ACTION is the principal agency in the Federal Government for administering volunteer service programs. Many of the various components of ACTION, such as Foster Grandparents and VISTA, are involved in community drug abuse education, prevention or treatment programs. The Drug Alliance Office coordinates the agency's drug abuse activities, awards grants that strengthen and expand local volunteer activities combatting illegal drug use among youth and the misuse of prescription and over-the-counter drugs by the elderly, provides training and technical assistance, and conducts public awareness and education efforts.

* Fish and Wildlife Service
U.S. Fish and Wildlife Service
4401 N. Fairfax Dr.
Arlington, VA 22203   703-358-1700
Would you like to spend some time banding birds at a national wildlife refuge, feeding fish at a national fish hatchery, or doing research in a laboratory? Then consider volunteering with the U.S. Fish and Wildlife Service. There are no age requirements; however, anyone under 18 must have written parental approval. Young people under 16 years of age are encouraged to volunteer as part of a supervised group, such as a Boy Scout troop, Girl Scout troop, or 4H Club. Contact one of the U.S. Fish and Wildlife regional offices for possible volunteer programs in your area.

* Forest Service Volunteers
Public Affairs Office
U.S. Department of Agriculture
P.O. Box 96090
Washington, DC 20090-6090   202-205-1760
The Forest Service has a volunteer program for almost everyone--retirees, professionals, housewives, students, teenagers, and youngsters. Typical jobs include working with specialists in resource protection and management, cooperative forestry, or research. You may also work at a Visitor Information Center by conducting interpretive natural history walks.

* Foster Grandparents Volunteers
Foster Grandparent Program
ACTION
1100 Vermont Ave., NW
Washington, DC 20525   202-606-4857
As Foster Grandparents, low-income persons 60 and over provide companionship and guidance to mentally, physically, or emotionally handicapped children who are abused, neglected, in the juvenile justice system, or who have other special needs. Foster Grandparents are assigned to individual children on a one- to-one basis. Most Grandparents serve in "volunteer stations" such as public schools, day care centers, residential facilities and hospitals for mentally retarded, emotionally disturbed and physically handicapped children; in correctional facilities and in homes of abused/neglected children. Typically, Foster Grandparents devote two hours daily to each of two children during a 20-hour service week. Volunteers receive a modest tax-free stipend to cover the cost of volunteering; transportation, a meal while in service, accident and liability insurance, and an annual physical examination. For more information on becoming a foster grandparent, or on having a foster grandparent program in your community, contact this office.

* Health Research Volunteers
Normal Volunteer Program
Clinical Center
Building 10, Room 1C-121B
Bethesda, MD 20892   301-496-4763
Many of the research programs at National Institutes of Health require normal volunteers who can provide clinicians with indices of normal body functions. There is a small compensation for their participation.

* National Archives and Geneaology
National Archives and Records Administration
8th St. and Pennsylvania Ave., NW, Room G-8
Washington, DC 20408   202-501-5402
Volunteers are needed to lead tours, welcome visitors at the information desk, assist staff with information and administrative services, and to become genealogical staff aides to assist new genealogical researchers.

* National Park Service
Office of Public Affairs
National Park Service
U.S. Department of the Interior
18th and C Sts., NW
Washington, DC 20240   202-208-6843
The National Park Service provides many opportunities for volunteers to help at their many parks and historic sites. Contact the National Park nearest you for more information.

* National Volunteer Week
Office of National Service
Old Executive Office Building, Room 100
The White House
Washington, DC 20500   202-456-6266
Each spring, the President sets aside a week for the special recognition of volunteers and their achievements. ACTION promotes National Volunteer Week among federal agencies, state and local governments, and private organizations that use volunteers nationwide.

* Retired Business Executives
Service Corps of Retired Executives (SCORE)
National SCORE Office
U.S. Small Business Administration
1129 20th Street, NW, Room 410   800-827-5722
Washington, DC 20416   202-634-1500, ext. 287
Retired business executives volunteer their time and services to help small business solve their operating and management problems. Assigned SCORE counselors visit the owners in their places of business to analyze the problems and offer guidance.

Your Community

In addition to learning more about the SCORE program by calling the toll-free SBA Answer Desk, also refer to your local telephone directory to contact the community-based SCORE center.

* Retired Peace Corps Volunteers

> Office of Private Sector Relations
> Peace Corps
> 1990 K. St., NW, Room 8400
> Washington, DC 20526   202-606-3406

This office serves as the link between the corporate community and the Peace Corps' Office of Returned Volunteer Services.

* Retired Senior Volunteers (RSVP)

> ACTION
> 1100 Vermont Ave., NW
> Washington, DC 20525   202-606-4857

RSVP offers opportunities for older citizens to use their talents and experience in community service, ranging from first aid to tutoring. RSVP operates through grants to public and private non-profit organizations in local communities. Anyone retired and aged 60 or over is eligible to be an RSVP volunteer. Volunteers services include adult basic education, guardians ad litum, tax aides, consultancy services, Meals on Wheels, museum tour guides, low-cost weatherization and home repair, classroom aides, health care and substance abuse counseling, home visitation and long term care, telephone reassurance and many others. Contact this office for more information on becoming a retired senior volunteer, or if you would like to set up a program in your community.

* Senior Companions

> ACTION
> 1100 Vermont Ave., NW
> Washington, DC 20525   202-606-4857

Senior Companions, all low-income persons 60 or over, provide care and companionship to other adults, especially the elderly, in an effort to help them maintain their highest level of independent living. The supportive services given by Senior Companions helps prevent the inappropriate institutionalization of homebound persons. Special emphasis areas include acute care discharge planning, mental health, substance abuse, and care of the terminally ill. Applicants must be at least 60 years old, physically able, and willing to serve 20 hours per week and meet income eligibility guidelines, which vary from state to state. Contact this office for more information on becoming a senior companion, or if you would like to set up a program in your community.

* Smithsonian Curatorial-Aides

> Visitor Information and Associates' Reception Center
> Smithsonian Institution
> 1000 Jefferson Drive S.W.
> Washington, DC 20560   202-357-2627

Volunteers can participate in an independent program in which their educational and professional backgrounds are matched with curatorial or research requests from within the Smithsonian Institution.

* Smithsonian Museums Tour Guides

> Visitor Information and Associates' Reception Center
> Smithsonian Institution
> 1000 Jefferson Drive S.W.
> Washington, DC 20560   202-357-2627

Volunteers are needed and welcomed at the Smithsonian Institution to serves as information volunteers or tour guides at many of the museums and Smithsonian programs and activities.

* Smithsonian Research Expeditions

> Smithsonian National Associates
> Smithsonian Institution
> 490 L'Enfant Plaza SW
> Room 4210
> Washington, DC 20560   202-357-4800

The Smithsonian Research Expeditions Program gives volunteers an opportunity to provide assistance to Smithsonian researchers and scholars. Expedition participants contribute their labor and financial support to projects led by Smithsonian scientists, curators, and research associates that result in exhibitions, publications, and collections for the Smithsonian Institution. Collaborating with staff, expedition volunteers work in field settings, laboratories, and archives to collect, organize, and interpret data. Expeditions cover a range of topics from archaeological digs to photographing radios. Financial Support contributed by participants is used for direct project expenses and follow-up work related to these projects.

* Speakers for Community Groups

> See all other Chapters.

Every federal department and many government agencies have a speakers bureau to inform interested organizations and citizen groups about many of the major community concerns. Many resources are available on medical issues such as health fairs and cholesterol screening. Public education, space programs, housing programs, weapons systems are some of the other areas where federal experts might be available to come to speak.

* Student Community Service

> Student Service Learning Program
> ACTION
> 1100 Vermont Ave., NW
> Washington, DC 20525   202-606-4857

Student Community Service projects are designed to encourage students to undertake volunteer service in their communities to enhance the educational value of the service experience and to serve the needs of the low-income community. Volunteers are non-stipended and must be enrolled in secondary, secondary vocational, or post-secondary schools on an in-school or out-of-school basis. Contact this office for more information on becoming a student volunteer, or if you would like student volunteers assigned to your community.

* Veterans Voluntary Service

> Chief of Voluntary Services
> Veterans Administration Medical Center

Refer to your local telephone directory for the nearest VA hospital or medical center. Many opportunities exist for volunteers to help veterans.

* Volunteers In Service To America (VISTA)

> ACTION
> 1100 Vermont Ave., NW   800-424-8580
> Washington, DC 20525   202-606-4857

VISTA volunteers work to alleviate poverty in the United States. They are assigned to serve on a full-time, full-year basis at the request of public or private non-profit organizations. Volunteers live and work among the poor, serving in urban areas, rural areas, or on Indian reservations, and share their skills and experience in such fields as literacy, employment training, food distribution, shelter for the homeless, and neighborhood revitalization. Volunteers must be citizens or permanent residents of the U.S. and at least 18 years of age. They receive a basic subsistence allowance covering housing, food and incidentals. An additional $75 a month is paid as a stipend upon completion of service. Also, while in service, VISTA volunteers may be eligible for deferment of repayment of certain types of student loans, or under certain circumstances cancellation of a portion of National Direct Student loans. Contact this office for more information on becoming a VISTA volunteer or getting VISTA volunteers to help out in your community.

Government Financial Help To Individuals
Poor, Elderly, Disabled, and Unemployed

* See also Housing and Real Estate Chapter
* See also Your Community Chapter

Besides the well-known federal programs like food stamps and job training for dislocated workers, there are many other financial assistance plans such as compensation to crime victims, health benefits for refugees, temporary child care and crisis nurseries. The following is a description of these money programs available along with community organizations which in turn distribute government assistance to needy Americans. The information is taken from the *Catalog of Federal Domestic Assistance* which is published by the U.S. Government Printing Office in Washington, DC. The number next to the title description is a reference number listed in this *Catalog*. Contact the office listed below the title for more details.

* Food Stamps 10.551

Yvette Jackson
Deputy Administrator
Food Stamp Programs
Food and Consumer Service
U.S. Department of Agriculture
Alexandria, VA 22302   703-305-2026

To improve diets of low-income households by increasing their food purchasing ability. Types of assistance: direct payment. Estimate of annual funds available: $ 25,207,492,000.

* School Breakfast Program 10.553

Director
Child Nutrition Division
Food and Consumer Service
U.S. Department of Agriculture
Alexandria, VA 22302   703-305-2590

To assist states in providing a nutritious nonprofit breakfast service for school students, through cash grants and food donations. Types of assistance: grants. Estimate of annual funds available: $ 1,053,786,000.

* National School Lunch Program 10.555

Director, Child Nutrition Division
Food and Consumer Service
U.S. Department of Agriculture
Alexandria, VA 22302   703-305-2590

To assist states, through cash grants and food donations, in making the school lunch program available to school students of all incomes and to encourage the domestic consumption of nutrition agricultural commodities. Types of assistance: grants. Estimate of annual funds available: $4,484,668,000.

* Special Milk Program for Children 10.556

Alberta Frost, Director
Child Nutrition Division
Food and Consumer Service
U.S. Department of Agriculture
Alexandria, VA 22302   703-305-2590

To provide subsidies to schools and institutions to encourage the consumption of fluid milk by children of high school grade and under. Types of assistance: grants. Estimate of annual funds available: $ 18,063,000.

* Special Supplemental Food Program for Women, Infants, and Children (WIC Program) 10.557

Stanley Garnett, Director
Supplemental Food Programs Division
Food and Consumer Service
U.S. Department of Agriculture
Alexandria, VA 22302   703-305-2746

To supply, at no cost, supplemental nutrition foods and nutrition eduction as an adjunct to good health care to low-income pregnant and postpartum women, infants and children identified to be at nutritional risk. Types of assistance: grants. Estimate of annual funds available: $ 2,674,861,627.

* Child Care Food Program 10.558

Alberta Frost, Director
Director, Child Nutrition Division
Food and Consumer Service
U.S. Department of Agriculture
Alexandria, VA 22302   703-305-2590

To assist states, through grants-in-aid and other means, to maintain nonprofit food service programs for children in public and private nonprofit non-residential institutions providing child care; family day care homes and private for-profit centers that receive compensation under title XX for at least 25 persons. Types of assistance: grants. Estimate of annual funds available: $ 1,481,349,000.

* Summer Food Service Program for Children 10.559

Alberta Frost, Director
Director, Child Nutrition Division
Food and Consumer Service
U.S. Department of Agriculture
Alexandria, VA 22302   703-305-2590

To assist states, through grants-in-aid and other means, to conduct nonprofit food service programs for needy children during the summer months. Types of assistance: grants. Estimate of annual funds available: $ 256,456,000.

* State Administrative Matching Grants for Food 10.561

Stamp Program
Yvette Jackson
Deputy Administrator
Food Stamp Programs
Food and Consumer Service
U.S. Department of Agriculture
Alexandria, VA 22302   703-305-2026

To provide federal financial aid to state agencies for costs incurred to operate the Food Stamp Program. Types of assistance: grants. Estimate of annual funds available: $1,719,564,000.

* Commodity Supplemental Food Program 10.565

Supplemental Food Programs Division
Food and Consumer Service
U.S. Department of Agriculture
Alexandria, VA 22302   703-305-2746

To improve the health and nutritional status of low income pregnant, postpartum and breastfeeding women, infants, and children up to age of 6, and elderly persons through the donation of supplemental foods. Types of assistance: sale, exchange, or donation. Estimate of annual funds available $73,949,017.

Government Financial Help to Individuals

* Nutrition Assistance for Puerto Rico (NAP) 10.566

Yvette Jackson
Deputy Administrator
Food Stamp Programs
Food and Consumer Service
U.S. Department of Agriculture
Alexandria, VA 22303   703-305-2026

A cash grant alternative to the food stamp program to improve diets of needy persons residing in the Commonwealth of Puerto Rico. Types of assistance: direct payment. Estimate of annual funds available: $ 1,130,528,000.

* Food Distribution Program on Indian Reservations 10.567

Les Johnson
Food Distribution Division
Food and Consumer Service
U.S. Department of Agriculture
Alexandria, VA 22302   703-305-2680

To improve the diets of needy persons in households on or near Indian reservations and to increase the market for domestically produced foods acquired under surplus removal or price support operations. Types of assistance: grants. Estimate of annual funds available: $ 20,347,000.

* Nutrition Program for the Elderly (Commodities) (NPE) 10.570

Food Distribution Division
Food and Consumer Service
U.S. Department of Agriculture
Alexandria, VA 22302   703-305-2680

To improve the diets of the elderly and to increase the market for domestically produced foods acquired under surplus removal or price support operations. Types of assistance: grants. Estimate of annual funds available: $ 150,333,317.

* Food Commodities for Soup Kitchens 10.571

Food Distribution Division
Food and Consumer Service
U.S. Department of Agriculture
Alexandria, VA 22302   703-305-2680

To improve the diets of the homes by donating food to non-profits. Types of assistance: grants. Estimate of annual funds available: $40,000,000.

* WIC Farmers Market Nutrition Program 10.572

Supplemental Food Programs Division
Food and Consumer Service
U.S. Department of Agriculture
3101 Park Center Dr., Room 540
Alexandria, VA 22302   703-305-2746

To provide fresh, nutritious unprepared foods to low-income, at-risk women, infants, and children from farmers' markets. Types of assistance: grants. Estimate of annual funds available: $6,750,000.

* Congregate Housing Services Program (CHSP) 14.170

Assisted Elderly and Handicapped Housing Division
Office of Elderly and Assisted Housing
U.S. Department of Housing and Urban Development
Washington, DC 20410   202-708-3291

To prevent premature or unnecessary institutionalization of elderly-handicapped, non-elderly handicapped, and temporarily disabled, to provide a variety of innovative approaches for the delivery of meals and non-medical supportive services while utilizing existing service programs and to fill gaps in existing service systems. Types of assistance: grants. Estimate of annual funds available: $ 7,747,000.

* Public Safety Officers Benefits Program 16.571

Public Safety Officers Benefits Program
Bureau of Justice Assistance
Washington, DC 20531   202-307-0635

To provide a $100,000 death benefit to the eligible survivors of federal, state or local public safety officers whose death is the direct and proximate result of a personal injury sustained in the line of duty. Types of assistance: direct payment. Estimate of annual funds available: $ 31,129,000.

* Crime Victim Assistance 16.575

State Compensation and Assistance Division
Office for Victims of Crime
Office of Justice Programs
U.S. Department of Justice
633 Indiana Ave., NW
Washington, DC 20531   202-307-5947

Each year provide up to 45 percent of the Crime Victims Fund generated through federal criminal fines, penalty assessments, forfeited appearance bonds to be distributed to the states to support crime victim assistance programs. Types of assistance: grants. Estimate of annual funds available: $ 79,749,450.

* Crime Victim Compensation 16.576

State Compensation and Assistance Division
Office for Victims of Crime
Office of Justice Programs
U.S. Department of Justice
Washington, DC 20531   202-307-5947

To provide up to 49.5 percent per year of the Crime Victims fund generated through federal criminal fines, penalty assessment, forfeited appearance bonds, bail bonds, etc., to be distributed among the states to the direct benefit derived by victims from the program. Types of assistance: grants. Estimate of annual funds available: $ 64,674,000.

* Unemployment Insurance 17.225

Esther Johnson, Unemployment Insurance Service
Employment and Training Administration
U.S. Department of Labor
Washington, DC 20210   202-219-7831

To administer program of unemployment insurance for eligible workers through federal and state cooperation; to administer payment of Trade Adjustment Assistance Types of assistance: grant, direct payment. Estimate of annual funds available: $ 2,373,995,000.

* Senior Community Service Employment Program (SCSEP) (Older Worker Program) 17.235

Office of Special Targeted Programs
Employment and Training Administration
U.S. Department of Labor, Room N4641
200 Constitution Ave., NW
Washington, DC 20210   202-219-5500

To provide foster and promote useful part-time work opportunities in community service activities for low income persons who are 55 years old and older. Types of assistance: grant. Estimate of annual funds available: $ 410,500,000,000.

* Trade Adjustment Assistance - Workers 17.245

Vic Trunzo, Director
Office of Trade Adjustment Assistance
Employment and Training Administration
U.S. Department of Labor
200 Constitution Ave., NW, Room C-4318
Washington, DC   202-219-5555

To provide adjustment assistance to workers adversely affected by increased imports of articles like or directly competitive with articles produced by such workers firm. Types of assistance: direct payment. Estimate of annual funds available: $ 179,000,000.

* Dislocated Workers: Employment and Training Assistance 17.246

Employment and Training Administration
U.S. Department of Labor
200 Constitution Ave., NW, Room N5426
Washington, DC 20210   202-219-5577

To assist dislocated workers obtain unsubsidized employment through training and related employment services using a decentralized system of State programs. Types of assistance: grants. Estimate of annual funds available: $ 1,026,800,000.

* Migrant and Seasonal Farmworkers (and Other Seasonally Employed Farmworkers) 17.247

Office of Special Targeted Programs
Division of Seasonal Farmworker Programs
Employment and Training Administration
U.S. Dept. of Labor, Room N4641
200 Constitution Ave., NW
Washington, DC 20210   202-219-5500

To provide job training, job search assistance, and other supportive services for those individuals who suffer chronic seasonal unemployment and underemployment in the agricultural industry. Types of assistance: grants. Estimate of annual funds available: $ 85,710,000.

* Employment Services and Job Training - Pilot and Demonstration Programs 17.249

Administrator
Office of Strategic Planning and Policy Development
Employment and Training Administration
U.S. Department of Labor
200 Constitution Ave., NW
Washington, DC   202-219-5677

To provide foster, and promote job training and other services which are most appropriately administered at the national level and which are operated in more than one State to groups with particular disadvantage in the labor market. Types of assistance: grants. Estimate of annual funds available: $ 35,522,000.

* Job Training Partnership Act (JTPA) 17.250

Donald Kulick
Employment and Training Administration
U.S. Department of Labor
200 Constitution Ave., NW
Washington, DC 20210   202-219-6236

To provide job training and related assistance to economically disadvantaged individuals and others who face significant employment barriers. Types of assistance: grants. Estimate of annual funds available: $ 1,054,813,000.

* Native American Employment and Training Programs 17.251

Division of Indian and Native American Programs
Employment and Training Administration
U.S. Department of Labor
Room N4641
200 Constitution Ave., NW
Washington, DC   202-219-8502

To afford job training to Native Americans facing serious barriers to employment, who are in special need of such training to obtain productive employment. Types of assistance: grants. Estimate of annual funds available: $ 64,080,040.

* Longshore and Harbor Workers' Compensation 17.302

Office of Workers's Compensation Programs
Division of Longshore and Harbor Workers' Compensation
Washington, DC 20210   202-219-8721

To provide compensation for disability or death resulting from injury, including occupational disease, to eligible private employees. Types of assistance: direct payment. Estimate of annual funds available: $ 4,000,000.

* Coal Mine Workers Compensation (Black Lung) 17.307

Division of Coal Mine Workers Compensation
Office of Workers Compensation Programs
Employment Standards Administration
U.S. Dept. of Labor
Washington, DC 20210   202-219-6692

To provide benefits to coal miners who have become totally disabled due to coal workers pneumoconiosis (CWP) and to widows and other surviving dependents of miners who have died of this disease, or who were totally disabled from the disease at the time of death. Types of assistance: direct payment. Estimate of annual funds available: $ 540,725,000.

* Tax Counseling for the Elderly 21.006

Marion L. Butler
Tax Counseling for the Elderly
Taxpayer Service Division
Internal Revenue Service
1111 Constitution Ave., NW
Washington, DC 20224   202-622-7664

To authorize the Internal Revenue Service to enter into agreement with private or public nonprofit agencies or organizations to establish a network of trained volunteers to provide free income tax information and return preparation assistance to elderly taxpayers. Types of assistance: direct payment. Estimate of annual funds available: $ 3,700,000.

* Appalachian Vocational and Other Education Facilities and Operations 23.012

Executive Director
Appalachian Regional Commission
1666 Connecticut Ave., NW
Washington, DC 20235   202-884-7700

To provide the people of the region with the equipment, renovation and operating funds for training and education necessary to obtain employment at their best capability for available job opportunities. Types of assistance: grants. Estimate of annual funds available: $ 29,735,000.

* Federal Employment Assistance for Veterans 27.002

Armando Rodriguez
Office of Diversity
Office of Personnel Management
1900 E St., NW, Room 6332
Washington, DC 20415   202-606-1059

To provide assistance to veterans in obtaining federal employment. Types of assistance: employment. Estimate of annual funds available: $ not known.

* Federal Employment for Disadvantaged Youth 27.003

Staffing Reinvention Office
Employment Service
Office of Personnel Management
1900 E St., NW
Washington, DC 20415   202-606-0830

To give students 16 years of age and older, an opportunity for part-time temporary employment with Federal agencies in order to allow them to continue their education without interruptions caused by financial pressures. Types of assistance: federal employment. Estimate of annual funds available: not applicable.

* Federal Employment for Individuals with Disabilities (Selective Placement Program) 27.005

Office of Diversity
Office of Personnel Management
1900 E St., NW
Washington, DC 20414   202-606-1015

To encourage federal agencies to provide assistance to persons with disabilities in obtaining and retaining federal employment. Types of assistance: federal employment. Estimate of annual funds available: $ not known.

* Social Insurance for Railroad Workers 57.001

Public Affairs Railroad Retirement Board
844 N. Rush St.
Chicago, IL 60611   312-751-4777

To pay rail social security, rail industry pensions, special windfalls, supplemental annuities, permanent and occupational disability and sickness and unemployment benefits to workers and their families. Types of assistance: direct payment. Estimate of annual funds available: $8,186,000,000.

* Pension to Veterans' Surviving Spouse and Children (Death Pension) 64.105

U.S. Department of Veterans Affairs
Washington, DC 20420

Be patient. If any phone number is incorrect, call (area code) 555-1212 and request the new listing.

375

Government Financial Help to Individuals

To assist needy surviving spouses, and children of deceased war-time veterans whose deaths were not due to service. Types of assistance: direct payment. Estimate of annual funds available: $ 838,100,000.

* Senior Environmental Employment Program (SEE) 66.508

Environmental Protection Agency
Office of Research and Development of Exploratory Research
Washington, DC 20460

To use the talents of older Americans to provide technical assistance to federal, state and local environment agencies for projects of pollution prevention abatement and control. Types of assistance: grants. Estimate of annual funds available: $ 45,000,000.

* Weatherization Assistance for Low-Income Persons 81.042

Weatherization Assistance Programs, Branch 232
Conservation and Renewable Energy
U.S. Department of Energy
Forrestal Bldg., Mail Stop EE-532
Washington, DC 20585   202-426-1698

To insulate the dwellings of low income persons, particularly the elderly and handicapped low income, in order to conserve needed energy and to aid those persons least able to afford higher utility costs. Types of assistance: grants. Estimate of annual funds available: $ 226,300,000.

* Centers for Independent Living 84.132

Office of Developmental Programs
Rehabilitation Services Administration, OSERS
U.S. Department of Education
330 C St., SW
Washington, DC 20202   202-205-9315

To provide independent living services to individuals with severe handicaps to assist them to function more independent in family and community settings or secure and maintain appropriate employment. Types of assistance: grants. Estimate of annual funds available: $ 40,533,000.

* Comprehensive Services for Independent Living (Comprehensive Services Part A) 84.169

Suzanne Choiser
Office of Asst. Secretary for Special Education
and Rehabilitative Services
U.S. Department of Education
Washington, DC 20202   202-205-8937

To provide independent living services for individuals with severe handicaps in assisting them to function independently in family and community settings or to secure and maintain appropriate employment. Types of assistance: grants. Estimate of annual funds available: $ 21,859,000.

* Rehabilitation Services - Independent Living Services for Older Blind Individuals 84.177

Raymond Melhoff
Rehabilitation Services Administration
OSERS
U.S. Department of Education
MES Building, Room 3416
330 C St., NW
Washington, DC 20202   202-205-9320

To provide independent living services to older blind individuals. Types of assistance: grants. Estimate of annual funds available: $ 8,952,000.

* Supported Employment Services for Individuals with Severe Handicaps (Supported Employment Services Program) 84.187

Mark E. Shoob
Office of Program Operations
Rehabilitation Services Administration
U.S. Department of Education

Washington, DC 20202-2574   202-205-9406

To provide grants for training and traditionally time limited post employment services leading to supported employment for individuals with severe handicaps. Types of assistance: grants. Estimate of annual funds available: $ 36,536,000.

* State Grants for Technology and Related Assistance to Individuals with Disabilities (Technology Assistance Program) 84.224

NIDRR
600 Independence Ave., SW
Washington, DC 20202   202-205-5666

To provide grants to states to assist them in developing and implementing comprehensive consumer responsive state-wide programs of technology related assistance for individuals with disabilities. Types of assistance: grants. Estimate of annual funds available: $39,249,000.

* Pension Plan Termination Insurance (ERISA) 86.001

Pension Benefit Guaranty Corporation
1200 K St., NW
Washington, DC 20005   202-326-4000

To encourage the continuation and maintenance of voluntary private pension plans for the benefit of their participants. Types of assistance: Insurance of annual funds available: $ 834,950,000.

* Family Support Payments to States Assistance Payments 93.560

Office of the Director
Office of Family Assistance
U.S. Department of Health and Human Services
5th Flr, Aerospace Bldg
370 L'Enfant Promenade, SW
Washington, DC 20447   202-401-9275

To set general standards for state administration; provide the federal financial share to states for Aid to Families with Dependent Children (AFDC). Types of assistance: grants. Estimate of annual funds available: $ 16,205,697,000.

* Job Opportunities and Basic Skills Training (JOBS) 93.561

Office of the Director
Family Support Administration
5th Floor, Aerospace Bldg.
370 L'Enfant Promenade, SW
Washington, DC 20447   202-401-9275

To assure that needy families with children obtain the education, training, and employment that will help them avoid long-term welfare dependence. Types of assistance: grants. Estimate of annual funds available: $ 980,000,000.

* State Legalization Impact Assistance Grants (SLIAG) 93.565

David Smith, Director
Division of State Legalization Assistance
Office of Refugee Resettlement
370 L'Enfant Promenade, SW
Washington, DC 20447   202-401-9255

To offset part of the costs state and local governments incur in providing public subsistence assistance, public health assistance, and educational services to eligible legalized aliens. Types of assistance: grants. Estimate of annual funds available: $ 811,901,000.

* Low-Income Home Energy Assistance 93.568

Janet Fox, Director
Division of Energy Assistance
Administration for Children and Families
370 L'Enfant Promenade, SW
Washington, DC 20447   202-401-9351

To make grants available to states and other jurisdictions to assist eligible households to meet the costs of home energy. Types of assistance: grants. Estimate of annual funds available: $1,319,202,000.

* Community Services Block Grant 93.569

Division of State Assistance
Office of Community Services
Administration for Children and Families
U.S. Department of Health and Human Services
370 L'Enfant Promenade, SW
Washington, DC 20447   202-401-9343

To provide activities designed to assist low-income participants including the elderly poor; to secure and retain meaningful employment; attain an adequate education; and other employment-related assistance. Types of assistance: grants. Estimate of annual funds available; $391,500,000.

* Community Service Block Grants-Discretionary Awards 93.570

Joseph Carroll
Division of Community Discretionary Programs
Office of Community Services
Administration for Children and Families
370 L'Enfant Promenade, SW
Washington, DC 20447   202-401-9345

To support full-time permanent jobs for poverty level project area residents; to improve housing; and to improve income and/or ownership opportunities for low-income community members. Types of assistance: direct payments. Estimate of annual funds available: $45,015,000.

* Community Service Block Grant Discretionary Awards-Community Food and Nutrition 93.571

Community Demonstration Programs
Administration for Children and Families
Office of Community Services
370 L'Enfant Promenade, SW
Washington, DC 20447   202-401-9233

To provide community-based, local statewide and national programs which coordinate existing private and public food assistance resources to better serve low income populations. Types of assistance: grants. Estimate of annual funds available: $8,676,000.

* Child Care for Families At Risk of Welfare Dependency 93.574

Office of the Director
Office of Family Assistance
Administration for Children and Families
U.S. Department of Health and Human Services
5th Floor, Aerospace Building
370 L'Enfant Promenade, SW
Washington, DC 20447   202-401-9275

To provide child care to low income families who are receiving Aid To Families With Dependent Children (AFDC), who need child care in order to work, and who would otherwise be at-risk of becoming eligible for AFDC. Types of assistance: grants. Estimate of annual funds available: $375,000,000.

* Child Care and Development Block Grant 93.575

Child Care Bureau
Administration on Children, Youth, and Families
Administration for Children and Families
U.S. Department of Health and Human Services
200 Independence Ave., SW
3rd Floor,, Room 352-G
Washington, DC 20201

To assist low income families with child care services by increasing the availability, affordability, and quality of child care and to increase the availability of early childhood development and before and after school programs. Types of assistance: grants. Estimate of annual funds available: $934,641,777.

* Temporary Child Care and Crisis Nurseries 93.656

Ory Cuellar
Children's Bureau, Assistance Branch
P.O. Box 1182
Washington, DC 20013   202-205-8899

To provide temporary, non-medical care for handicapped children and children with chronic or terminal illnesses to alleviate social, emotional and financial stress among the families of such children. Types of assistance: grants. Estimate of annual funds available: $ 11,835,000.

* Adoption Assistance 93.659

Daniel Lewis, Associate Commissioner
Children's Bureau
P.O. Box 1182
Washington, DC 20013   202-205-8618

To provide Federal Financial Participation (FFP) to states which meet certain eligibility tests, in the adoption subsidy costs for the adoption of children with special needs. Types of assistance: grants. Estimate of annual funds available: $ 425,639,000.

* Medicare-Hospital Insurance (Medicare) 93.773

Carol Walton
Bureau of Program Operations
Room 300, Meadows East Building
Health Care Financing Administration
Baltimore, MD 21207   410-965-8050

To provide hospital insurance protection for covered services to persons age 65 or above, to certain disabled persons and to individuals with chronic renal disease. Types of assistance: direct payment. Estimate of annual funds available: $ 110,166,000,000.

* Medicare-Supplemental Medical Insurance (Medicare) 93.774

Carol Walton
Bureau of Program Operation
Room 300, Meadows East Bldg.
Health Care Financing Administration
Baltimore, MD 21207   410-965-8050

To provide medical insurance protection for covered services to persons age 65 or over, to certain disabled persons and to individuals with chronic renal disease who elect this coverage. Types of assistance: direct payment. Estimate of annual funds available: $ 64,016,000,000.

* Medical Assistance Program (Medicaid; Title XIX) 93.778

Sally Richardson
Health Care Financing Administration
U.S. Department of Health and Human Services
Room 200, E. High Rise Bldg.
6325 Security Blvd.
Baltimore, MD 21207   410-965-3870

To provide financial assistance to states for payments of medical assistance on behalf of cash assistance recipients, children, pregnant women, and the aged who meet income and resource requirements, and other categorically eligible groups. Types of assistance: grants. Estimate of annual funds available: $ 88,438,360,000.

* Health Programs for Refugees (Immigration and Nationality Act) 93.987

Mr. Richard Moyer, Acting Director
Centers for Disease Control (CDC)
Public Health Service (PHS)
U.S. Department of Health and Human Services (DHHS)
Atlanta, GA 30333   404-639-8111

To assist states and localities in providing health assessment and follow-up activities to new refugees and in addressing refugee health problems of public health concern. Types of assistance: grants. Estimate of annual funds available: $ 2,400,000.

* Cooperative Agreements for State-Based Diabetes Control Programs 93.988

Chief
Grants Management Office
Procurement and Grants Office
Centers for Disease Control (CDC)
Public Health Service (PHS)
U.S. Department of Health and Human Services (DHHS)

Government Financial Help to Individuals

255 E Paces Ferry Rd., NE
Atlanta, GA 30305   404-842-6640

To implement comprehensive programs which will ensure that persons with diabetes who are at high risk for certain complications of diabetes are identified, entered into the health are system and receive on going state-of the-art preventive care and treatment. Types of assistance: grants. Estimate of annual funds available: $ 11,166,818.

* Social Security-Disability Insurance 96.001

Office of Public Inquiries
Room 4100, Annex
Social Security Administration
Baltimore, MD 21235   410-965-2736

To replace part of the earning lost because of a physical or mental impairment severe enough to prevent a person from working. Types of assistance: direct payment. Estimate of annual funds available: $ 40,394,000,000.

* Social Security - Retirement Insurance 96.002

Office of Public Inquiries
Room 4100, Annex
Social Security Administration
Baltimore, MD 21235   410-965-2736

To replace part of the earnings lost due to retirement. Types of assistance: direct payment. Estimate of annual funds available: $ 213,235,000,000.

* Social Security - Special Benefits for Persons Aged 72 and Over 96.003

Office of Public Inquiries
Room 4100, Annex
Social Security Administration
Baltimore, MD 21235   410-965-2736

To assure some regular income to certain persons age 72 and over who had little or no opportunity to earn Social Security protection during their working years. Types of assistance: direct payment. Estimate of annual funds available: $ 3,000,000.

* Social Security - Survivors Insurance 96.004

Office of Public Inquiries
Room 4100, Annex
Social Security Administration
Baltimore, MD 21235   410-965-2736

To replace part of the earnings lost to dependents because of the worker's death. Types of assistance: direct payment. Estimate of annual funds available: $66,458,000,000.

* Special Benefits for Disabled Coal Miners (Black Lung) 96.005

Office of Public Inquiries
Room 4100, Annex
Social Security Administration
6401 Security Blvd.   800-772-1213
Baltimore, MD 21235   410-965-2736

To pay benefits to coal miners who have become disabled due to pneumoconiosis (black lung disease) or other chronic lung disease arising from coal mine employment and their dependents or survivors. Types of assistance: direct payment. Estimate of annual funds available: $ 712,000,000.

* Supplemental Security Income 96.006

Office of Public Inquiries
Room 4100, Annex
Social Security Administration
Baltimore, MD 21235   410-965-2736

To assure a minimum level of income to persons who have attained age 65 or are blind or disabled, whose income and resources are below specified levels. Types of assistance: direct payment. Estimate of annual funds available: $ 24,990,000,000.

Veterans and Dependents

* See also International Relations and Defense

This section identifies the offices, mostly at the U.S. Department of Veterans Affairs, which compensate Americans who have served in the U.S. Armed Forces and their dependents. A number appears by some of the caption headings which is the official reference from the U.S. Government Printing Office's *Catalog of Federal Domestic Assistance*. Contact the office listed below the title for more details.

* Agent Orange or Nuclear Radiation Exposure

Veterans Assistance Office
U.S. Department of Veterans Affairs (VA)
810 Vermont Ave., NW
Washington, DC 20420   202-872-1151

The U.S. Department of Veteran Affairs is authorized by law to provide certain health care services to any veteran of the Vietnam Ear (August 5, 1964 through May 7, 1975) who, while serving in Vietnam, may have been exposed to dioxin or to a toxic substance in a herbicide or defoliant used for military purposes. VA has an ongoing program for examining veterans concerned about the possible health effects of Agent Orange exposure. Vietnam veterans are encouraged to request an examination at their nearest VA healthcare facility. A veteran who participates will receive a comprehensive physical examination and be asked to complete a questionnaire about service experience in Vietnam. The veteran is advised, through personal consultation, of the results of that examination. The examination determines the current health status of the veteran and assists in detecting any illness or injury the veteran may have, regardless of origin, which may serve as the basis for follow-up. The finding of these examinations are entered into a registry. The same process is available for any veteran who exposed while serving on active duty to ionizing radiation from the detonation of a nuclear device in connection with the veteran's participation in the test of a nuclear device or with the American occupation of Hiroshima and Nagasaki, Japan during the period beginning on September 11, 1945, and ending on July 1, 1946. The veteran should contact the nearest VA medical center for an examination.

* Alcohol and Drug Dependence Treatment

Veterans Assistance Office
U.S. Department of Veterans Affairs (VA)
810 Vermont Ave., NW
Washington, DC 20420   202-872-1151

After hospitalization for alcohol or drug treatment, veterans may be eligible for outpatient care, or may be authorized to continue treatment or rehabilitation in facilities such as halfway houses or therapeutic communities at VA expense. For more information contact your VA medical center.

* All Volunteer Force Educational Assistance 64.124

U.S. Department of Veterans Affairs (VA)
Central Office
Washington, DC 20420

To help service persons readjust to civilian life after their separation from military service and to extend the benefits of a higher education to those who may otherwise not afford it. Estimate of annual funds available: $911,853,000.

* Appealing Veterans Benefit Claims

Veterans Assistance Office
U.S. Department of Veterans Affairs (VA)
810 Vermont Ave., NW
Washington, DC 20420   202-872-1151

Veterans who believe they have VA benefits coming to them but have been denied those benefits have the right to appeal. Not all VA findings are appealable, but those dealing with compensation or pension benefits, education benefits, waiver of recovery of overpayments, and reimbursement of unauthorized medical services are typical issues which may be appealed to the Board of Veterans Appeals. Additional information on appeals may be found in VA pamphlet 1-1, *Board of Veterans Appeals, Appeals Regulations and Rules of Practice*, available from the office above.

* Automobiles and Adaptive Equipment for Certain Disabled Veterans and Members of the Armed Forces 64.100

U.S. Department of Veterans Affairs (VA)
Washington, DC 20420

To provide financial assistance to certain disabled servicepersons and veterans toward the purchase price of an automobile or other conveyance and an additional amount for adaptive equipment. Types of assistance: direct payment. Estimate of annual funds available: $ 26,401,000.

* Benefits Assistance Service

Veterans Assistance Office
U.S. Department of Veterans Affairs (VA)
810 Vermont Ave., NW
Washington, DC 20420   202-872-1151

This office provides veterans on their first visit with information about and assistance is applying for various federal benefits. The information provided can also be found in the VA regional offices.

* Benefits Information

Veterans Assistance Office
U.S. Department of Veterans Affairs (VA)
810 Vermont Ave., NW
Washington, DC 20420   202-872-1151

The U.S. Department of Veterans Affairs provides a full range of benefits for eligible veterans and dependents. Toll-free benefits information is available to all veterans at VA regional offices. Check your local telephone directory under United States Government, Department of Veterans Affairs, for the benefits information in your area--or ask your directory assistance operator. Other sources that provide information about benefits are service organizations and state and local offices of veterans affairs.

* Board of Veterans Appeals Decisions

Board of Veterans Appeals (BVA)
U.S. Department of Veterans Affairs (VA)
Washington, DC 20420   202-233-3336

The appellate decisions of the Board of Veterans Appeals (BVA) have been indexed to facilitate access to the contents of decisions (BVA Index 1-01-1). The index is published quarterly in microfiche form with an annual cumulation. It is organized to provide citations to BVA decisions under subject terms chosen to describe the issues adjudicated in the appeals. For information on obtaining the index or purchasing a microfiche copy, contact your regional VA office or the office above.

* Burial Expenses

Veterans Assistance Office
U.S. Department of Veterans Affairs (VA)
810 Vermont Ave., NW
Washington, DC 20420   202-872-1151

Benefits are available to help with the burial expenses of veterans and certain dependents or survivors. Assistance for burial of dependents and survivors is limited to interment in a national cemetery. For more information contact your regional VA office.

Government Financial Help to Individuals

* Burial Expenses Allowance for Veterans 64.101

U.S. Department of Veterans Affairs (VA)
Washington, DC 20420

To provide a monetary allowance not to exceed $150 toward the plot or interment expense for certain veterans not buried in a national cemetery. Types of assistance: direct payment. Estimate of annual funds available: $ 108,739,000.

* Burial Flags

Veterans Assistance Office
U.S. Department of Veterans Affairs (VA)
810 Vermont Ave., NW
Washington, DC 20420   202-872-1151

An American flag is available to drape the casket of an eligible veteran, after which it may be given to the next of kin, a close friend, or an associate of the deceased. The VA may also issue a flag for a veteran who is missing in action and is later presumed dead. Apply at any VA regional office or most local post offices.

* Burial in Arlington National Cemetery

Superintendent
Arlington National Cemetery
Arlington, VA 22211   703-697-2131

The Arlington National Cemetery is under the jurisdiction of the Department of the Army, and burial is limited to specific categories of military personnel and veterans except in the case of cremated remains to be placed in the columbarium. For more information contact the office above.

* Burial in National Cemeteries

Veterans Assistance Office
U.S. Department of Veterans Affairs (VA)
810 Vermont Ave., NW
Washington, DC 20420   202-872-1151

Burial in a VA national cemetery is available to any eligible veteran, spouse, unremarried widow/widower, minor children, and under certain conditions, unmarried adult children. Detailed information regarding eligibility and interments is contained in the VA pamphlet, *Interments in National Cemeteries*. Contact your regional VA office for this pamphlet and for more information and assistance in filing burial benefit claims.

* Chaplain Service

Chaplain Service (125)
U.S. Department of Veterans Affairs (VA)
810 Vermont Ave., NW
Washington, DC 20420   202-535-7594

The Chaplain Service provides for the spiritual welfare of the patients at VA facilities. The program includes opportunities for religious worship in the appropriate setting, pastoral ministry to individual patients and administration in crises situations, opportunities for sacramental ministry and pastoral counseling and other supportive services to aid in the total care and treatment of veteran patients. For more information, contact the office above.

* Compensation

Veterans Assistance Office
U.S. Department of Veterans Affairs (VA)
810 Vermont Ave., NW   800-827-1000
Washington, DC 20420   202-872-1151

Veterans who are disabled by injury or disease incurred or aggravated during active service in the line of duty during wartime or peacetime service and discharged or separated under other than dishonorable conditions are eligible for VA compensation. Eligible veterans are entitled to monthly disability payments. For more information on eligibility and benefits, contact your regional VA office.

* Compensation for Service-Connected Deaths for Veterans Dependents (Death Compensation) 64.102

U.S. Department of Veterans Affairs (VA)
Washington, DC 20420

To compensate surviving spouses, children, and dependent parents for the death of any veteran who died before January 1, 1957, because of a service-connected disability. Types of assistance: direct payment. Estimate of annual funds available: $ 6,213,000.

* Dental Treatment

Veterans Assistance Office
U.S. Department of Veterans Affairs (VA)
810 Vermont Ave., NW
Washington, DC 20420   202-827-1151

The VA provides dental services to eligible veterans on an outpatient basis. Outpatient dental treatment begins with an intraoral examinations and may include the full spectrum of modern diagnostic, surgical, restorative, and preventive techniques. In some instances, the dental care may be comprehensive in nature, while in other cases, the type and extent of treatment may be limited. The measure of treatment is determined by specific eligibilities, service-connection, and/or correlation of the dental conditions with the veteran's medical problems. For more information, including eligibility, contact the nearest VA medical center.

* Dietetic Service

Dietetic Service
Veterans Health Services and Research Administration
U.S. Department of Veterans Affairs (VA)
810 Vermont Ave., NW, Room 927
Washington, DC 20420   202-535-7485

VA dietitians direct nutritional care veterans in all settings by providing active programs which encompass the entire range of nutrition services. There are 13 VA sponsored Dietetic Internships which graduate registration eligible dietitians each year. For more information, contact the office above.

* Disabled Veterans Outreach Program 17.801

Veterans Employment and Training Service
Office of the Assistant Secretary for
Veterans Employment and Training
U.S. Dept. of Labor, Room 5-1316
200 Constitution Ave., NW
Washington, DC 20210   202-219-9105

To provide funds to states to provide job and job training opportunities for disabled and other veterans through contacts with employers. Types of assistance: grants. Estimate of annual funds available: $ 83,601,000.

* Domiciliary Care

Veterans Assistance Office
U.S. Department of Veterans Affairs (VA)
810 Vermont Ave., NW
Washington, DC 20420   202-872-1151

The VA provides care on an ambulatory self-care basis for veterans disabled by age or disease who are not in need of acute hospitalization and who do not need the skilled nursing services provided in nursing homes. For information on eligibility and general information, contact any VA office.

* Domiciliary Care (VA Domiciliary Care) 64.008

Asst. Chief, Medical Director for Geriatrics
and Extended Care (181)
U.S. Department of Veterans Affairs (VA)
Washington, DC 20420   202-535-7530

To provide the least intensive level of VA inpatient care for ambulatory veterans disabled by age or illness who are not in need of more acute hospitalization and who do not need the skilled nursing provided in nursing homes. Types of assistance: specialized services. Estimate of annual funds available: $ 239,314,000.

* Driver Training for the Handicapped

Rehabilitation Medicine Service
U.S. Department of Veterans Affairs (VA)
810 Vermont Ave., NW
Washington, DC 20420   202-535-7273

The VA provides driver education and training for all eligible handicapped veterans and certain military personnel. The DVA has established 40 driver training centers for the handicapped throughout the U.S. For more information, contact the office above.

* Education and Training

Veterans Assistance Office
U.S. Department of Veterans Affairs (VA)

Be patient. If any phone number is incorrect, call (area code) 555-1212 and request the new listing.

810 Vermont Ave., NW
Washington, DC 20420 202-872-1151

The U.S. Department of Veterans Affairs (VA) administers basic programs for veterans and servicepersons seeking assistance for education and training. For eligible persons with service between February 1, 1955, and December 31, 1976, such assistance is available under the noncontributory GI Bill. Veterans and servicepersons who entered the military from January 1, 1977, through June 30, 1985, may receive educational assistance under a contributory plan. Individuals entering on active duty after June 30, 1985, may receive benefits under the Montgomery GI Bill. Contact your regional VA office for specific information on eligibility and benefits.

* Employment and Training Program 17.802

Veterans Employment and Training Service
Office of the Assistant Secretary for
Veterans Employment and Training
200 Constitution Ave., NW, Room S1316
Washington, DC 20210 202-523-9110

To develop programs to meet the employment and training needs of service-connected disabled veterans, veterans of the Vietnam era and veterans who were recently separated from the military service. Types of assistance: grants. Estimate of annual funds available: $ 8,880,000.

* Fee-Basis Medical Program

Veterans Assistance Office
U.S. Department of Veterans Affairs (VA)
810 Vermont Ave., NW
Washington, DC 20420 202-872-1151

The U.S. Department of Veterans Affairs (VA) authorizes veterans to receive medical services from other individuals or organizations by compensating participating members for services performed and paying the veteran for travel expenses incurred for the visit. For more information, contact the nearest VA Medical Center or regional VA office.

* Federal Benefits for Veterans and Dependents

Superintendent of Documents
U.S. Government Printing Office
Washington, DC 20402 202-512-1800

The booklet, *Federal Benefits for Veterans and Dependents*, stock #051-000-00198-2, provides information on the many benefits made available to veterans and dependents. It is available from the Government Printing Office (GPO) for $2.75.

* Fiduciary and Field Examinations

Veterans Assistance Office
U.S. Department of Veterans Affairs (VA)
810 Vermont Ave., NW
Washington, DC 20420 202-872-1151

For information on payment of VA benefits on behalf of adult beneficiaries who are incompetent or under some other legal disability, contact the VA regional office. Information on payments of benefits to minor beneficiaries who are not in care of a natural or adoptive parent can also be obtained from the VA regional office.

* Headstone or Grave Marker

Director, Monument Service (42)
National Cemetery System
U.S. Department of Veterans Affairs (VA)
Washington, DC 20420 202-275-1480

Headstones and markers are provided for the gravesites of eligible veterans buried in private or national cemeteries. Eligibility is the same as for burial in a national cemetery. The headstone or grave marker is provided without charge and shipped at government expense to the consignee designated. The cost of placing the marker in a private cemetery must be borne by the applicant. Forward applications (VA Form 40-1330) to the address above. VA regional offices will provide information and other assistance. For more information contact the office above.

* Health Care Product Support

Director
Marketing Center
U.S. Department of Veterans Affairs (VA)
P.O. Box 76
Hines, IL 60141 708-216-2479

The Marketing Center (MKC) is the largest combined contracting activity within the U.S. Department of Veterans Affairs. It is responsible for supporting the health care delivery systems of the DVA and other government agencies by providing and validating a centralized acquisition program for health care products in a cost effective manner. The primary responsibility of the MKC is assuring contracts are in place to support the DVA's Central Distribution System. Contact the office above for more information.

* Health Care System

Veterans Assistance Office
U.S. Department of Veterans Affairs (VA)
810 Vermont Ave., NW
Washington, DC 20420 202-872-1151

Perhaps the most visible of all VA benefits and services are its hospitals and medical care services, which make up the largest health care system in the free world. More than 90 percent of VA employees are associated with medical care. Of VA's 172 medical centers, some 140 are affiliated with 104 medical schools. More than half of America's practicing physicians receive training in VA medical centers. In addition to medical centers, the health care system includes nursing homes, domiciliaries, and readjustment counseling Vet centers. Contact the nearest VA medical center for specific information.

* High School Training

Veterans Assistance Office
U.S. Department of Veterans Affairs (VA)
810 Vermont Ave., NW
Washington, DC 20420 202-872-1151

A veteran may pursue high school training or training to pass the GED examination and may receive educational assistance allowance without a charge against basic entitlement. Additional secondary school training, such as refresher courses or deficiency courses, are permitted if needed to qualify for admission to an appropriate educational institution. Contact your VA regional office for more information.

* Homeless Veterans Reintegration Project 17.805

Office of the Assistant Secretary for Veterans
and Employment and Training
Room S1316
200 Constitution Ave., NW
Washington, DC 20210 202-219-9105

To provide funds for demonstration programs to expedite the reintegration of homeless veterans into the labor force. Estimate of annual funds available: $5,011,000.

* Home Ownership Publications

Veterans Assistance Office
U.S. Department of Veterans Affairs (VA)
810 Vermont Ave., NW
Washington, DC 20420 202-872-1151

The following publications are available to veterans from their VA regional office:

Pointers for the Veteran Homeowner. A guide for veterans whose home mortgage is guaranteed or insured under the GI Bill.
To the Home-Buying Veteran. A guide for veterans planning to buy or build homes with a VA loan.
VA-Guaranteed Home Loans for Veterans. To help you understand what the VA can and cannot do for the home purchaser.

* Insurance

Veterans Assistance Office
U.S. Department of Veterans Affairs (VA).
810 Vermont Ave., NW
Washington, DC 20420 202-872-1151

Low cost insurance is available for veterans with service-connected disabilities. Veterans who are totally disabled may apply for a waiver of premiums on these policies. For more information on GI life insurance and Servicemen's Group Life Insurance (SGLI), Veterans Group Life Insurance (VGLI), and Veterans Mortgage Life Insurance (VMLI), contact the nearest VA office. The Insurance Information Toll-Free Number, 800-669-8477, is a nationwide source for insurance inquiries and requests for service. It is also useful for policyholders and beneficiaries who are covered by a VA administered life insurance policy. Calls can be made to the number above from 8:00 a.m. to 5:30 p.m. EST.

Be patient. If any phone number is incorrect, call (area code) 555-1212 and request the new listing.

381

Government Financial Help to Individuals

* Job-Finding Assistance

Veterans Assistance Office
U.S. Department of Veterans Affairs (VA)
810 Vermont Ave., NW
Washington, DC 20420   202-872-1151

Assistance in finding jobs is provided to veterans through state employment/job service local offices throughout the country. The Local Veterans Employment Representatives provide functional supervision of job counseling, testing, and employment referral and placement services provided to veterans. Priority in referral to job openings and training opportunities is given to eligible veterans, with preferential treatment for disabled veterans. In addition, the job service assists veterans who are seeking employment by providing information about job markets on-the-job and apprenticeship training opportunities in cooperation with VA Regional Offices and Vet Centers. Veterans should apply for this kind of help at their nearest local state employment service/job service office, not VA.

* Life Insurance (GI Insurance 64.103)

U.S. Department of Veterans Affairs (VA)
Regional Office and Insurance Center
P.O. Box 8079
Philadelphia, PA 19101   800-669-8477

To provide life insurance protection for veterans of World War I, World War II, Korean conflict and service-disabled veterans separated from active duty on or after April 25, 1951, and to provide mortgage protection life insurance for those disabled veterans who are given a VA grant to secure specially adapted housing under Chapter 21, Title 38, USC. Types of assistance: direct loan, insurance. Estimate of annual funds available: $ 94,151,000.

* Loans

Veterans Assistance Office
U.S. Department of Veterans Affairs (VA)
810 Vermont Ave., NW
Washington, DC 20420   202-233-2044

Certain veterans and dependents are eligible for GI loans for homes, condominiums, and manufactured homes. Also, certain disabled veterans of military service may be entitled under certain conditions to a grant from VA for a home specially adapted to their needs. For more information on these loans and grants, contact the nearest VA regional office.

* Medical Care for Dependents or Survivors

CHAMPVA Registration Center
U.S. Department of Veterans Affairs Medical Center
1055 Clermont St.
Denver, CO 80220   303-782-3800

The Civilian Health and Medical Program is a medical benefits program through which VA helps pay for medical services and supplies that eligible dependents and survivors of certain veterans obtain from civilian, non-VA sources. Normally, care under this program will be provided in non-VA facilities. VA facilities may be utilized for treatment when (1 they are equipped to provide the care, and (2 use of these facilities does not interfere with care and treatment of veterans. For more information, including eligibility, contact the office above.

* Medical Service

Medical Service
Veterans Health Services and Research Administration
U.S. Department of Veterans Affairs (VA)
810 Vermont Ave., NW
Washington, DC 20420   202-535-7577

This office is the representative, advocate, and monitoring office of Internal Medicine which constitutes the major bed and clinic service in the VA. It includes Cardiology, Pulmonary Disease, Gastroenterology, Hematology, Oncology, Endocrinology, Infectious Disease, Nephrology, Rheumatology, Dermatology, General Internal Medicine, Nutrition, Geriatrics, and Clinical Pharmacology. As such, this Service is responsible for a variety of important functions designed to maintain high standards of patient care, education, research, and administration. Contact the office above for further information.

* Memorial Markers and Memorial Plots

Veterans Assistance Office
U.S. Department of Veterans Affairs (VA)
810 Vermont Ave., NW

Washington, DC 20420   202-872-1151

A memorial headstone or marker may be furnished on application by a close relative recognized as the next of kin to commemorate any eligible veteran, including a person who died in active military service, whose remains have not been recovered or identified; who was buried at sea; who was donated to science; or who was cremated and the ashes scattered without interment of any portion of the ashes. The memorial may be erected in a private cemetery in a plot provided by the applicant or in a memorial section of a national cemetery. Contact the nearest VA regional office for more information.

* National Cemeteries 64.201

Director, Field Operations (401)
National Cemetery System
U.S. Department of Veterans Affairs (VA)
Washington, DC 20420   202-275-5225

To provide for interment in national cemeteries of veterans and members of the Armed Forces of the United States whose service terminated other than dishonorably and certain eligible dependents. Types of assistance: other. Estimate of annual funds available: $ 69,313,000.

* Native American Veteran Direct Loan Program 64.126

U.S. Department of Veterans Affairs (VA)
Washington, DC 20420

To provide direct loans to Native American veterans for the purchase or construction of homes on trust lands. Estimate of annual funds available: $13,293,000.

* Nursing Home Care

Veterans Assistance Office
U.S. Department of Veterans Affairs (VA)
810 Vermont Ave., NW
Washington, DC 20420   202-872-1151

For admission or transfer to VA Nursing Home Care Units, it is essentially the same as for hospitalization. Direct admission to private nursing homes at VA expense is limited to (1 veterans who require nursing care for a service-connected disability after medical determination by VA; (2 any person in an Armed Forces hospital who required a protracted period of nursing care and who will become a veteran upon discharge from the Armed Forces; and (3 a veteran who had been discharged from a VA medical center and is receiving VA medical center based home health services. VA may transfer veterans who need nursing home care to private nursing homes at VA expense from VA medical centers, nursing homes or domiciliaries. For more information, contact and VA medical facility.

* Office of Systems Planning, Policy, and Acquisition Control (004M)

U.S. Department of Veterans Affairs (VA)
810 Vermont Ave., NW
Washington, DC 20420   202-872-1151

Contact the office above to obtain a copy of *Veterans Affairs Information Systems Plan: Fiscal year 1987-1993.*

* Overseas Medical Benefits

Veterans Assistance Office
U.S. Department of Veterans Affairs (VA)
810 Vermont Ave., NW
Washington, DC 20420   202-872-1151

Reimbursed fee-basis medical care is available outside of the U.S. to veterans for treatment of service-connected disabilities and conditions adjunct to the rated disabilities. Prior to treatment, an authorization must be obtained from the nearest American embassy or consulate. In Canada, veterans should contact the local office of the Canadian Department of Veterans Affairs. In emergency situations, treatment should be reported within 72 hours. Nursing care is not available in foreign jurisdiction.

* Patient Treatment File

Reports and Statistics (10A4Z)
Veterans Health Services and Research Administration
U.S. Department of Veterans Affairs (VA)
810 Vermont Ave., NW
Washington, DC 20420   202-233-2424

The *Patient Treatment File* is a discharge oriented database which contains medical and administrative data for the following types of care provided or paid for by the U.S. Department of Veterans Affairs: VA and non-VA hospitals, VA and non-VA nursing homes, and VA domiciliaries. The file is maintained in fiscal year segments so that complete data for a particular year is not available until some months after the end of the fiscal year. For more information, including the types of data collected, contact the office above.

* Paraplegic Housing - Specially Adapted Housing for Disabled Veterans 64.106
U.S. Department of Veterans Affairs (VA)
Washington, DC 20420

To assist certain severely disabled veterans in acquiring suitable housing units, with special fixtures and facilities made necessary by the nature of the veterans disabilities. Types of assistance: direct payment. Estimate of annual funds available: $ 14,839,000.

* Pensions
Veterans Assistance Office
U.S. Department of Veterans Affairs (VA)
810 Vermont Ave., NW
Washington, DC 20420   202-872-1151

Those eligible for VA pensions include wartime veterans with limited income discharged under other than dishonorable conditions after 90 or more days service who are permanently and totally disabled for reasons not traceable to service, nor due to willful misconduct or vicious habits. Veterans 65 years of age or older and not working are considered permanently and totally disabled. A pension is not payable to those who have estates that can provide adequate maintenance. For more information on eligibility and benefits, contact your regional VA office.

* Pension for Non-Service-Connected Disability for Veterans (Pension) 64.104
U.S. Department of Veterans Affairs (VA)
Washington, DC 20420

To assist wartime veterans in need whose non-service connected disabilities are permanent and total, preventing them from following a substantially gainful occupation. Types of assistance: direct payment. Estimate of annual funds available: $ 2,228,200,000.

* Pension to Veterans, Surviving Spouses, and Children (Death Pension) 64.105
U.S. Department of Veterans Affairs (VA)
Washington, DC 20420

To assist needy surviving spouses, and children of deceased war-time veterans whose deaths were not due to service. Types of assistance: direct payment. Estimate of annual funds available: $ 838,100,000.

* Presidential Memorial Certificates
Veterans Assistance Office
U.S. Department of Veterans Affairs (VA)
810 Vermont Ave., NW
Washington, DC 20420   202-872-1151

Presidential Memorial Certificates expressing the country's grateful recognition of the person's service in the armed forces and bearing the signature of the President are made available to the next of kin of deceased eligible veterans or of persons who were members of the Armed Forces at time of death. Eligible recipients include the next of kin, a relative or friend upon request, or an authorized representative acting on behalf of such relative or friend. Notice of a veteran's death is normally received in one of VA's regional offices, and that facility identifies the next of kin from the veteran's records and requests the certificates from Washington, DC. Next of kin of veterans need not apply. Others should apply to a VA regional office.

* Procurement of Headstones and Markers 64.202
Director
Office of Memorial Programs
National Cemetery System
U.S. Department of Veterans Affairs (VA)
810 Vermont Ave., NW
Washington, DC 20420   202-523-3964

To provide headstones or markers for all unmarked graves in national, post and state Veterans cemeteries and upon receipt of application for the unmarked graves of eligible veterans interred in private cemeteries. Types of assistance: direct payments. Estimate of annual funds available: $ 27,684,000.

* Prosthetic Devices
Veterans Assistance Office
U.S. Department of Veterans Affairs (VA)
810 Vermont Ave., NW
Washington, DC 20420   202-872-1151

Veterans may be provided prosthetic appliances necessary for treatment of any condition when receiving hospital, domiciliary, or nursing home care in a facility under the direct jurisdiction of the U.S. Department of Veterans Affairs (VA). For more information, contact the Prosthetic Activity at VA medical center.

* Readjustment Counseling Service
Readjustment Counseling Service (10B/RC)
U.S. Department of Veterans Affairs (VA)
810 Vermont Ave., NW, Room 851
Washington, DC 20420   202-535-7554

The Readjustment Counseling Service Vietnam Era Veterans Outreach Centers (Vet Centers) are community-based, Department of Veterans Affairs (VA) services which were established following a recognition of the special readjustment needs of veterans who served during the Vietnam War, and from a desire to provide needed readjustment assistance to both top combat veterans and to support personnel of the Vietnam Era. The mission of the Readjustment Counseling Service (RCS) is to provide a wide range of outreach and direct psychosocial counseling services through storefront operations to veterans of the Vietnam era in order to help them make a satisfactory post-war readjustment to civilian life. For more information, including obtaining the address of your nearest Vet Center, contact the office above.

* Recreation Service
Recreation Service (11K)
Veterans Health Services and Research Administration
U.S. Department of Veterans Affairs (VA)
Washington, DC 20420   202-233-2424

The U.S. Department of Veterans Affairs' (VA) recreational programs attempt to improve the quality of patient's lives and facilitate their reentry into the community. For more information, contact the office above.

* Rehabilitation Research
Rehabilitation Research and Development (110)
U.S. Department of Veterans Affairs (VA)
810 Vermont Ave., NW
Washington, DC 20420   202-535-7152

This program focuses directly on the needs of the veteran who is functionally impaired as a result of amputation, paralysis, or the loss or impairment of his or her vision, hearing, or speech. The latest computer and other technological advances are used to develop devices, techniques, and concepts in rehabilitation that will minimize the disability and promote functional independence among disabled veterans. Information and technology transfer is distributed through interagency agreements and collaborative efforts with the private sector. Contact the office above for more information.

* Social Work
Social Work Service (122)
U.S. Department of Veterans Affairs (VA)
810 Vermont Ave., NW
Washington, DC 20420   202-535-7588

Social Work Service is an integral part of the overall U.S. Department of Veterans Affairs (VA) health-care program and operates in close concert with all medical services. Its purpose is to provide help to veterans and their families in resolving the psychosocial, emotional, and economic problems in dealing with the stresses of illness and disability. Social workers furnish psychosocial, diagnostic, and treatment services to the comprehensive treatment of veteran patients moving through admission, hospitalization, and post-hospital care back into the community. Social workers are also actively involved in outreach, readmission, and aftercare phases of the Department of Veterans Affairs' health care programs. For further information, contact the office above.

Government Financial Help to Individuals

* Survivors and Dependents Educational Assistance 64.117

U.S. Department of Veterans Affairs (VA)
Central Office
Washington, DC 20420

To provide partial support to those seeking to advance their education who are qualifying spouses, surviving spouses, or children of deceased or disabled veterans, or of service personnel who have been listed for a total of more than 90 days as missing in action, or as prisoners of war. Types of assistance: direct payment. Estimate of annual funds available: $ 100,874,000.

* Veterans' Court of Appeals

Court of Veterans Appeals
1625 K St., NW, Suite 400
Washington DC 20006   202-501-5970

A Court of Veterans Appeals reviews benefit claims that are appealed on or after November 18, 1988. The Court has exclusive jurisdiction to review decisions of the Board of Veterans Appeals.

* Veterans Compensation for Service-Connected Disability (Compensation) 64.109

U.S. Department of Veterans Affairs (VA)
Washington, DC 20420

To compensate veterans for disabilities incurred or aggravated during military service according to the average impairment in earning capacity such disability would case in civilian occupations. Types of assistance: direct payment. Estimate of annual funds available: $ 11,457,695,000.

* Veterans Dependency and Indemnity Compensation for Service-Connected Death (DIC) 64.110

U.S. Department of Veterans Affairs (VA)
Washington, DC 20420

To compensate unmarried surviving spouses, unmarried children, and parents for the death of any veteran who died on or after January 1, 1957, because of a service-connected disability, or while in the active military, naval or air service. Types of assistance: direct payment. Estimate of annual funds available: $ 2,962,240,000.

* Veterans Hospital Based Home Care 64.022

Asst. Chief Medical Director for Geriatrics and Extended Care
U.S. Department of Veterans Affairs (VA)
Washington, DC 20420   202-535-7530

To provide individual medical, nursing, social and rehabilitative services to eligible veterans in their home environment by VA hospital staff. Types of assistance: specialized services. Estimate of annual funds available: $ 37,000,000.

* Veterans Nursing Home Care (VA Nursing Home Care) 64.010

Asst. Chief Medical Director for Geriatrics and Extended Care (114A)
U.S. Department of Veterans
Washington, DC 20402   202-535-7530

To accommodate eligible veterans who are not acutely ill and not in need of hospital care, but who require skilled nursing care, related medical services, supportive personal care and individual adjustment services. Types of assistance: other. Estimate of annual funds available: $ 1,140,335,000.

* Veterans Outpatient Care 64.011

Director for Administration (161B2)
U.S. Department of Veterans Affairs (VA)
Washington, DC 20420   202-535-7384

To provide medical and dental services, medicines and medical supplies to eligible veterans on an outpatient basis. Types of assistance: specialized services. Estimate of annual funds available: $ 4,729,420,000.

* Veterans Prescription Service (Medicine for Veterans) 64.012

Asst. Chief, Medical Director for Clinical Affairs (111H)
U.S. Department of Veterans Affairs (VA)

Washington, DC 20420   202-535-7302

To provide eligible veterans and certain dependents and survivors of veterans with prescription drugs and expendable prosthetic medical supplies from VA pharmacies upon presentation of prescriptions from a licensed physician. Types of assistance: Other. Estimate of annual funds available: $ 1,054,961,000.

* Veterans Prosthetic Appliances (Prosthetics Services) 64.013

Director
Prosthetic and Sensory Aids (117C)
U.S. Department of Veterans Affairs (VA)
Washington, DC 20420   202-535-7293

To provide through purchase and/or fabrication, prosthetic and related appliances, equipment and services to disabled veterans so that they may live and work as productive citizens. Types of assistance: other. Estimate of annual funds available: $ 274,520,762.

* Veterans Rehabilitation - Alcohol and Drug Dependence (Alcohol and Drug Dependence Treatment Program, Mental Health and Behavioral Sciences Service) 64.019

Director, Mental Health and Behavioral Sciences
Services (111C)
U.S. Department of Veterans Affairs (VA)
Washington, DC 20420   202-535-7316

To provide medical, social and vocational rehabilitation to eligible alcohol and drug dependent veterans. Types of assistance: other. Estimate of annual funds available: $ 563,323,000.

* Vocational and Educational Counseling for Servicemembers and Veterans 64.125

U.S. Department of Veterans Affairs (VA)
Central Office
Washington, DC 20420

To offer vocational and educational counseling to servicemembers within 180 days of their projected discharge and to veterans within 1 year from date of discharge. Estimate of annual funds available: $5,000,000.

* Vocational Rehabilitation for Disabled Veterans (Vocational Rehabilitation) 64.116

U.S. Department of Veterans Affairs (VA)
Central Office
Washington, DC 20420

To provide all services and assistance necessary to enable service-disabled veterans and service persons hospitalized pending discharge to achieve maximum independence in daily living and, to the maximum extent feasible to become employable and to obtain and maintain suitable employment. Types of assistance: direct payment. Estimate of annual funds available: $ 100,874,000.

* Vocational Training for Certain Veterans Receiving VA Pension 64.123

U.S. Department of Veterans Affairs (VA)
Central Office
Washington, DC 20420

To assist new pension recipients to resume and maintain gainful employment by providing vocational training and other services. Types of assistance: direct payment. Estimate of annual funds available: $ 748,000.

* Voluntary Service

Veterans Assistance Office
U.S. Department of Veterans Affairs (VA)
810 Vermont Ave., NW
Washington, DC 20420   202-872-1151

The U.S. Department of Veterans Affairs encourages and trains volunteers to work at VA facilities in a variety of assignments beneficial to veterans and rewarding to volunteers. For complete information on voluntary service, contact the Chief of Voluntary Service at the nearest VA Medical Center.

* Work-Study Program

Veterans Assistance Office
U.S. Department of Veterans Affairs (VA)
810 Vermont Ave., NW
Washington, DC 20420   202-872-1151

Veteran-students enrolled as full-time students may agree to perform VA-related services and receive an additional allowance. The veterans who are 30 percent or more disabled from service-connected disabilities will be given preference. Contact your regional VA office for more information.

Vacations and Business Travel
Tourist Adventures

See also Arts and Humanities; Museums and Cultural Resources Chapter
See also Weather and Maps Chapter for long-range weather forecasts and maps
See also Selling Overseas: International Trade Chapter for overseas promotion opportunities

Here you'll find new ideas for your vacations that you'll probably never get from a travel agent. What about a polar expedition on an icebreaker? If you plan to travel to Europe, what about seeing if the U.S. Information Agency has any interest in paying you to give a lecture? Even if you don't have the energy to visit campgrounds or glaciers, you can still travel to those places simply by writing away for brochures, posters, and other publications available from the National Park Service. Boaters will find all sorts of information about rules, regulations, and safety, including coloring books for the youngsters. You'll also find handy tips for airborne travelers, on both domestic and international flights. We've also compiled a complete listing of each state's travel and tourism hotlines, which can help you map out any trip you want to take in the U.S.

* Agricultural Research Center Tours

Tour Coordinator, Agricultural Research Center
U.S. Department of Agriculture
Building 302
BARC East
10300 Baltimore Ave.
Beltsville, MD 20705-2350   301-504-9403
Tour Reservations   301-504-8483

Visitors to the Beltsville Agricultural Research Center can arrange for guided tours by appointment from 8:00 am to 4:30 pm, Monday through Friday. The center is closed to the public on Saturdays, Sundays, and holidays.

* Air Force Base Tours

Secretary of the Air Force
Office of Public Affairs
Community Relations Branch
The Pentagon, Room SC945
Washington, DC 20330-1690   703-697-1128

Attend an annual open house on your local Air Force base, where you will tour the base, view aircraft on display, and watch an air show. Contact the Air Force installation nearest you, or the above office for a referral.

* Air Force Test Flight Center Tours

Air Force Flight Test Center
Public Affairs Office AFFTC/PA
15 E. Mojave
Edwards Air Force Base, CA 93524-1115   805-277-3510

The Test Center sponsors an annual open house, usually in October, when the public is invited on a six-hour tour of the base. You can view the aircraft up close, watch a demonstration of the military "working" dogs, and view historical films of the base. Write or call the Public Affairs Office for more information.

* Airport and Control Tower Tours

Aviation Education Officer
Federal Aviation Administration (FAA)
U.S. Department of Transportation
NASSIF Building
PL 100, 400 7th St.   202-267-3476
Washington, DC 20590   202-267-3469

The FAA's Aviation Education Program offers volunteer assistance to the nation's schools through these programs: career guidance; tours of airports, control towers, and other facilities; classroom lectures and demonstrations; aviation safety information; aviation education resource materials; computerized clearinghouse of aviation and space information; aviation science instruction programs for home/school computers; "Partnerships-in-Education" activities; and teachers' workshops. Write to the above office for more information.

* American War Memorials

The American Battle Monuments Commission
Casimir Pulaski Building
20 Massachusetts Avenue, NW
Washington, DC 20314-0001   202-272-0533

Presently 124,921 U.S. War Dead are interred in U.S. administered cemeteries around the world, including 24 military burial grounds on foreign soil, and 15 separate monuments, 4 memorials, and 2 tablets in the United States. Each year the Commission publishes attractive, free pamphlets which highlight individual memorials, and include locations, site descriptions and photographs, brief histories of the battles in which the deceased fought, and directions from the nearest major airports. Back issues covering specific memorials are also available at no charge.

* Army Facilities Tours

Community Relations Branch
U.S. Army Public Affairs
The Pentagon, Room 2E637
Washington, DC 20310-1500   703-695-4462
Public Inquiries   703-697-7500
Community Relations   703-697-5081

The Army arranges tours of its facilities and special exhibits for the public. You may watch paratroopers jump, rangers train, tanks and artillery fire, and personally talk to soldiers about their jobs. Contact your nearest army installation for more information, or the above office which will refer you to the appropriate contact.

* Botanical Garden Tours

Public Programs Office
U.S. Botanic Garden
245 1st St., SW
Washington, DC 20024   202-226-4082

The Botanic Garden is open to the public from 9 a.m. to 5 p.m. 7 days a week. Tours are given to interested groups, including garden clubs, professional organizations, and school children at 10:00 a.m. and 2:00 p.m. by appointment on weekdays only. The gardens are located at 1st and Maryland Avenue, SW, Washington, DC; 202-225-7099.

* Buffalo and Cattle Refuges

Division of Refuges
U.S. Fish and Wildlife Service
4401 N. Fairfax Dr., Room 670
Arlington, VA 22203   703-358-1744

Buffalo and Texas longhorn cattle, as well as deer and elk, can be enjoyed at wildlife refuges maintained by the U.S. Department of the Interior. Wichita Mountains in Oklahoma and Fort Niobrara in Nebraska preserve these animals in their natural habitat. The government periodically auctions these animals to the public at these locations. For more information, contact the refuge managers directly: Fort Niobrara National Wildlife Refuge, Hidden Timber Route, HC 14, Box 67, Valentine, NE

69201; 402-376-3789. Witchita Mountains Wildlife Refuge, Rt. 1, Box 448, Indiahoma, OK 73552; 405-429-3221. You can see Buffalo also at the National Bison Range in Moiese, Montana. For more information on this refuge, contact National Bison Range, Moiese, MT 59824; 406-644-2211.

* Capitol Hill Guided Tours

Capitol Guide Service
The Capitol
Washington, DC 20510   202-225-6827

Before leaving home for vacation, write your Representative and/or Senator--as far in advance as possible--for tickets to the morning VIP congressional tour specifying the date you wish to visit. Tickets are limited, but it's worth a try. Also request a Visitor's Pass for each member of your party to view a session of the House and/or Senate. House and Senate passes are not interchangeable, and they do not admit the bearer to special events and to a joint session of the Congress. House Gallery passes are good for both sessions of Congress. Senate Gallery passes are good for only one session. Sometimes visitors get a chance to speak with their elected representatives or their staff. Foreigners wishing to enter need only to come to the door.

The Capitol is located between Constitution and Independence Avenues at First Street. The East Front entrance at East Capitol Street is open daily, 9:00-4:30, except Thanksgiving, Christmas, and New Year's. Free 40-minute guided tours for the public leave from the Rotunda every 10 minutes (more frequently in the summer) between 9 a.m. and 3:45 p.m. You'll view the National Statuary Hall, the House and Senate Chambers, and the Rotunda. The Capitol Rotunda and Statuary Hall are open in the summer until 10 p.m. The House and Senate Wings are also open when either of those legislative bodies is in night session.

* Currency Engraving and Printing Tours

Bureau of Engraving and Printing
U.S. Department of the Treasury
14th and C Streets, SW
Washington, DC 20228   Recorded Messages: 202-874-3188

A continuous self-guided tour at the Bureau features actual currency production. Visitors are able to view the various production steps, and tour guides are available to answer questions and assist visitors. Visitors may purchase uncut sheets of currency, engraved prints, small bags of shredded currency, and souvenir cards at the Visitor's Center. Tours may be taken Monday through Friday and admission is free. Call for information and time of tours, which vary during the year.

* Diplomatic Reception Rooms

Tour Office
U.S. Department of State   202-736-4474
23rd Street Entrance   202-647-3241
Washington, DC 20520   FAX: 202-736-4232

Diplomatic reception rooms, which showcase American cultural heritage of the 18th century, are furnished with priceless antiques that have been donated or loaned to the State Department. These rooms are used for official functions by the President, the Vice President, the Secretary of State, and other governmental officials. The tour office can arrange public tours upon request by reservation only, for up to 50 people.

* Engineering Inventions and Tours

Tours
National Institute of Standards and Technology
Gaithersburg, MD 20899   Recorded Message: 301-975-3585

Free tours of the various facilities at the National Institute of Standards and Technology (NIST) are given on Thursdays at 9:30 a.m. They generally last for one and one-half hours, and the public is welcome, but should schedule reservations in advance through Jan Hauber at the office above.

* Federal Reserve Visitors

Office of Protocol
Board of Governors Office
Federal Reserve System
Room B2214
20th St. and Constitution Ave., NW
Washington, DC 20551   202-452-3149

Those interested in visiting the Federal Reserve Board in Washington, DC, should contact this office. At least one tour is conducted every Thursday at 2:30 p.m., and special arrangements may be made to accommodate groups of 10 or more.

* Glacier Bay and Other Historical Landmarks

Superintendent of Documents
Government Printing Office
Washington, DC 20402   202-512-1800

Historical landmarks are described in the historical handbooks featured in this listing. Sites include Antietam Battlefield, Devil's Tower in Wyoming, Ford's Theatre, Glacier Bay, Lincoln Memorial, and Nez Perce National Historical Park in Idaho, among others. Free.

* House of Representatives Passes

Your Member of Congress
U.S. House of Representatives
Washington, DC 20515   202-224-3121

The U.S. House of Representatives meets in the House Chamber in the south wing of the Capitol. The public is seated in the side and rear galleries; seats are available to those who secure passes from their Representative on a first come, first served basis.

* Indian Museums

Southern Plains Indian Museum
P.O. Box 749
Anadarko, OK 73005   405-247-6221

Museum of the Plains Indian
P.O. Box 400
Browning, MT 59417   406-338-2230

Sioux Indian Museum
P.O. Box 1504
Rapid City, SD 57709   605-348-0557

These three Indian museums are administered by the Indian Arts and Crafts Board, U.S. Department of the Interior. The museums issue free informational pamphlets and brochures about their respective programs and exhibition activities. Contact the museums directly to be placed on their mailing lists.

* Indian Reservations

If you are interested in visiting an Indian reservation on your vacation, or even if you are just interested in finding out more firsthand information about a particular tribe or reservation, you should contact any of the following offices listed below. Since not every Indian reservation allows public tours, you'll have to contact each individually to find out any tourism programs.

Field Offices

Anadarko Agency
P.O. Box 309, Anadarko, OK 73005; 405-247-6673

Anchorage Agency
1675 C Street, Anchorage, AK 99501; 907-271-4088

Ardmore Agency
P.O. Box 997, Ardmore, OK 73402; 405-223-6767

Bethel Agency
P.O. Box 347, Bethel, AK 99559; 907-543-2727

Blackfeet Agency
Box 850, Browning, MT 59417; 406-338-7544

Central California Agency
1824 Tribute Road, Suite 5, Sacramento, CA 95815; 916-978-4337

Cherokee Agency
Cherokee, NC 28719; 704-497-9131

Cheyenne River Agency
P.O. Box 325, Eagle Butte, SD 57625; 605-964-6611

Chinle Agency
P.O. Box 6003, Chinle, AZ 86503; 602-674-5201

Chickasaw Agency
P.O. Box 2240, Ada, OK 74821; 405-436-0784

Be patient. If any phone number is incorrect, call (area code) 555-1212 and request the new listing.

387

Choctaw Agency
421 Powell, Philadelphia, MS 39350; 601-656-1523

Colorado River Agency
Rt. 1, Box 9-C, Parker, AZ 85344; 602-669-7111

Colville Agency
P.O. Box 111, Nespelem, WA 99155; 509-634-4901

Concho Agency
1635 E. Highway 66, El Reno, OK 73036-5769; 405-262-7481

Crow Agency
Crow Agency, MT 59022; 406-638-2672

Crow Creek Agency
P.O. Box 139, Ft. Thompson, SD 57339; 605-245-2311

Eastern Navajo Agency
P.O. Box 328, Crownpoint, NM 87313; 505-786-6149

Eastern Nevada Agency
P.O. Box 5400, Elko, NV 89801; 702-738-0569

Fairbanks Agency
Federal Building and Courthouse, 101 12th Avenue, Box 16, Fairbanks, AK 99701; 907-456-0222

Flathead Agency
Box A, Pablo, MT 59855; 406-675-2700

Fort Apache Agency
P.O. Box 560, Whiteriver, AZ 85941; 602-338-5353

Fort Belknap Agency
P.O. Box 98, Harlem, MT 59526; 406-353-2901 ext. 23

Fort Berthold Agency
P.O. Box 370, New Town, ND 58763; 701-627-4707

Fort Defiance Agency
P.O. Box 110, Fort Defiance, AZ 86504; 602-729-5041

Fort Hall Agency
P.O. Box 220, Fort Hall, ID 83203; 208-238-2301

Fort Peck Agency
P.O. Box 637, Poplar, MT 59255; 406-768-5312

Fort Totten Agency
P.O. Box 270, Fort Totten, ND 58335; 701-766-4545

Fort Yuma Agency
P.O. Box 1591, Yuma, AZ 85364; 619-572-0248

Great Lakes Agency
615 Main West, Ashland, WI 54806; 715-682-4527

Hopi Agency
P.O. Box 158, Keams Canyon, AZ 86034; 602-738-2228

Horton Agency
P.O. Box 31, Horton, KS 66439; 913-486-2161

Jicarilla Agency
P.O. Box 167, Dulce, NM 87528; 505-759-3651

Laguna Agency
P.O. Box 1448, Laguna, NM 87026; 505-522-6001/6002

Lower Brule Agency
P.O. Box 190, Lower Brule, SD 57548; 605-473-5512

Makah Agency
P.O. Box 116, Neah Bay, WA 98357; 206-645-2229

Menominee Area Rep
Minneapolis Area Office, 331 2nd Avenue, Minneapolis, MN 55401-2241; 612-373-1000

Mescalero Agency
P.O. Box 189, Mescalero, NM 88340; 505-671-4423

Metlakatla Field Station
P.O. Box 458, Metlakatla Field Station, Metlakatla, AK 99926; 907-886-3791

Miami Agency
P.O. Box 391, Miami, OK 74355; 918-542-3396

Michigan Agency
2901.5 I-75 Business Spur, P.O. Box 884, Sault Ste. Marie, MI 49783; 906-632-6809

Minnesota Agency
Route 3, P.O. Box 112, Cass Lake, MN 56633; 218-335-6913

Minnesota Sioux Field Rep
Minneapolis Area Office, 331 2nd Avenue E, 6th Floor, Minneapolis, MN 55402; 612-349-3382

Muskogee Area Office
Old Federal Bldg., Muskogee, OK 74401; 918-687-2296

New York Liaison Office
P.O. Box 7366, Syracuse, NY 13261-7366; 315-423-5476

Nome Agency
P.O. Box 1108, Nome, AK 99762; 907-443-2284

Northern California Agency
P.O. Box 494879, Redding, CA 96049-4879; 916-246-5141

Northern Cheyenne Agency
P.O. Box 40, Lame Deer, MT 59043; 406-477-8242

Northern Idaho Agency
P.O. Box 277, Lapwai, ID 83540; 208-843-2300

Northern Pueblos Agency
P.O. Box 4269, Fairview Station, Espanola, NM 57533; 505-753-1400

Okmulgee Agency
P.O. Box 370, Okmulgee, OK 74447; 918-756-3950

Olympic Peninsula Agency
P.O. Box 120, Hoquiam, WA 98550; 206-533-9100

Osage Agency
P.O. Box 1539, Pawhuska, OK 74056; 918-287-1032

Papago Agency
P.O. Box 578, Sells, AZ 85634; 602-383-3286

Palm Springs Agency
P.O. Box 2245, Palm Springs, CA 92263; 619-322-3086

Pawnee Agency
P.O. Box 440, Pawnee, OK 74058; 918-762-2585

Pima Agency
P.O. Box 8, Sacaton, AZ 85247; 602-562-3326

Pine Ridge Agency
P.O. Box 1203, Pine Ridge, SD 57770; 605-867-5125

Puget Sound Agency
3006 Colby St., Federal Bldg., Everett, WA 98201; 206-258-2651

Ramah-Navajo Agency
Rt. 2, Box 14, Ramah, NM 87321; 505-775-3235

Red Lake Agency
Red Lake, MN 56671; 218-679-3361

Rocky Boy's Agency
RR #1, Box Elder, MT 59521; 406-395-4476

Rosebud Agency
P.O. Box 550, Rosebud, SD 57570; 605-747-2224

Sac & Fox Area
Tama, IA 52339; 515-484-4041

Salt River Agency
Rt. 1, P.O. Box 117, Scottsdale, AZ 85256; 602-640-2842

San Carlos Agency
P.O. Box 209, San Carlos, AZ 85550; 602-475-2321

Seattle Support Center
P.O. Box 80947, Seattle, WA 98108; 206-764-3328

Seminole Agency
6075 Stirling Rd., Hollywood, FL 33024; 305-581-7050, Extension 356-7288

Shawnee Agency
624 W. Independence, Suite 114, OK 74801; 405-273-0317

Shiprock Agency
P.O. Box 3239, Shiprock, NM 87420; 505-368-4427

Siletz Agency
P.O. Box 569, Siletz, OR 97380; 503-444-2679

Sisseton Agency
P.O. Box 688, Agency Village, SD 57262; 605-698-7676

Southeast Agency
P.O. Box 3-8000, Juneau, AK 99802; 907-586-7304

Southern California Agency
3600 Lime Street, Suite 722, Riverside, CA 92501; 714-276-6624

Southern Paiute Field Station
Box 720, St. George, UT 84771; 801-674-9720

Southern Pueblos Agency
P.O. Box 1667, Albuquerque, NM 87103; 505-766-3020

Southern Ute Agency
P.O. Box 315, Ignacio, CO 81137; 303-563-4511

Spokane Agency
P.O. Box 389, Wellpinit, WA 99040; 509-258-4561

Standing Rock Agency
P.O. Box E, Ft. Yates, ND 58538; 701-854-3433

Tahlequah Agency
P.O. Box 948, Tahlequah, OK 74465; 918-456-0671

Talihina Agency
P.O. Drawer H, Talihina, OK 74571; 918-567-2207

Truxton Canon Agency
P.O. Box 37, Valentine, AZ 86437; 602-769-2286

Turtle Mountain Agency
P.O. Box 60, Belcourt, ND 58316; 701-477-3191

Uintah & Ouray Agency
P.O. Box 130, Fort Duchesne, UT 84026; 801-722-2406

Umatilla Agency
P.O. Box 520, Pendleton, OR 97801; 503-276-3811

Ute Mountain Agency
General Delivery, Towaoc, CO 81334; 303-565-8471

Wahpeton Indian School
Wahpeton Indian School, Wahpeton, ND 58075; 701-642-3796

Wapato Irrigation Project
P.O. Box 220, Wapato, WA 98951; 509-877-3155

Warm Springs Agency
P.O. Box 1239, Warm Springs, OR 97761; 503-553-2411

Western Navajo Agency
P.O. Box 746, Tuba City, AZ 86045; 602-283-4531

Western Nevada Agency
1677 Hot Springs Rd., Carson City, NV 89706; 702-887-3500

Wewoka Agency
P.O. Box 1060, Wewoka, OK 74884; 405-257-6257

Wind River Agency
P.O. Box 158, Ft. Washakie, WY 82514; 307-332-7810

Winnebago Agency
Rt. 1, Box 18, Winnebago, NE, 68071; 402-878-2502

Yakima Agency
P.O. Box 632, Toppenish, WA 98948; 509-865-2255

Yankton Agency
P.O. Box 557, Wagner, SD 57380; 605-384-3651

Zuni Agency
P.O. Box 369, Zuni, NM 87327; 505-782-5591

Area Offices

Aberdeen Area Director
Bureau of Indian Affairs, 115 4th Avenue, SE, Aberdeen, SD 57401-4382; 605-226-7343. Serving Nebraska, North Dakota, South Dakota.

Albuquerque Area Director
Bureau of Indian Affairs, 615 1st Street, NW, Box 26567, Albuquerque, NM 87125-6567; 505-766-3754. Serving Colorado, New Mexico, Texas.

Anadarko Area Director
Bureau of Indian Affairs, WCD Office Complex, Box 368, Anadarko, OK 73005-0368; 405-247-6673. Serving Kansas, Western Oklahoma, Texas.

Billings Area Director
Bureau of Indian Affairs, 316 North 26th Street, Billings, MT 59101; 406-247-7943. Serving Montana, Wyoming.

Eastern Area Director
Bureau of Indian Affairs, 3701 N. Fairfax Dr., MS260-VASQ, Arlington, VA 22203; 703-235-3006. Serving New York, Maine, Florida, North Carolina, Louisiana, Mississippi, Rhode Island, Connecticut, Alabama, Massachusetts.

Juneau Area Director
Bureau of Indian Affairs, Federal Building, 9109 Menden Hall, Suite 5, P.O. Box 25520, Juneau, AK 99802-5520; 907-586-7177. Serving Alaska.

Minneapolis Area Director
Bureau of Indian Affairs, 331 S. Second Ave., Minneapolis, MN 55401-2241; 612-373-1000. Serving Minnesota, Iowa, Michigan, Wisconsin.

Muskogee Area Director
Bureau of Indian Affairs, 101 N. 5th St., Muskogee, OK 74401; 918-687-2296. Serving Eastern Oklahoma, Missouri.

Navajo Area Director
Bureau of Indian Affairs, P.O. Box 1060, Gallup, NM 87305; 602-863-8314. Serving Navajo Reservation only--Arizona, Utah, New Mexico.

Phoenix Area Director
Bureau of Indian Affairs, 1 North First Street, P.O. Box 10, Phoenix, AZ 85001-0010; 602-379-6600. Serving Arizona, Nevada, Utah, California.

Portland Area Director
Bureau of Indian Affairs, 911 Eleventh Avenue, NE, Portland, OR 97232-4169; 503-231-6702. Serving Oregon, Idaho, Washington, Montana, Alaska (Metlakatla).

Be patient. If any phone number is incorrect, call (area code) 555-1212 and request the new listing.

389

Vacations and Business Travel

Sacramento Area Director
Bureau of Indian Affairs, 2800 Cottage Way, Sacramento, CA 95825-1864; 916-978-4691. Serving California.

* Korean War Veterans Memorial

The American Battle Monuments Commission (ABMC)
Casimir Pulaski Building
20 Massachusetts Avenue, NW
Room 5127
Washington, DC 20314-0001   202-272-0533

In 1986 a new law authorized the American Battle Monuments Commission (ABMC) to erect a memorial in the Washington, DC, area to honor all servicemen and women of the Armed Forces of the United States who served during the Korean War, particularly those who were killed in action, are still listed as Missing in Action, or were held as prisoners of war. The memorial is under construction and should be completed by June, 1995. For information on its concept, construction, and fund raising efforts, contact the ABMC.

* Lawrence Livermore Computer Facility Tours

Visitors Center
Lawrence Livermore National Laboratory
Greenville Road
P.O. Box 808
Livermore, CA 94550   510-422-9797

The National Laboratory conducts public tours of its facility center, highlighting the NOVA Laser, by reservation only. You must, however, be 18 years of age or older. For information, contact the Visitors Center. The facility is closed weekends.

* Missile Testing Center Tours

U.S. Department of the Army
Public Affairs Office
Building 122
White Sands Missile Range, NM 88002-5047   505-678-1134

This research and missile testing center invites the public to an open house twice a year, which includes a visit to the "Trinity Site" where the first atomic detonation took place. The center publishes a brochure and fact sheets on its history, mission, and wide range of programs. The test range also functions as a wildlife preserve. Write or call for their free publications and information on open house days.

* Museum of the U.S. Department of the Interior

Departmental Museum
U.S. Department of the Interior (DOI)
1849 C St., NW, Mail Stop 5412
Washington, DC 20240   202-208-4743

The highlights of this museum's exhibit include Native American artifacts and dioramas depicting the history of each of DOI's Bureaus. Of particular interest o children is a collection of fossils mineral samples. The hours of operation are 8 a.m. to 5 p.m., Monday through Friday. You must have a photo ID to enter the building.

* Music at the Capitol

Architect's Office
Room SB-15
U.S. Capitol Building
Washington, DC 20515   202-228-1793

The Capitol and the House and Senate office buildings resound, especially during the spring and summer months, with all types of music. The American Festival/Concerts at the Capitol are sponsored by the Congress and the Secretary of the Interior. They are performed by the National Symphony and have been conducted by various maestros. The Service bands and choral groups of the Air Force, Army, Marine Corps, and Navy provide summer night entertainment for the public in concerts that have become a Capitol tradition. Concerts are free and seating on the lawn and picnics are in order. In addition, the Capitol and its various office buildings are filled throughout the year, but especially during the winter holiday season, with the joyous voices of choral groups. These appearances are arranged well in advance by the Senators or Representatives through the Architect of the Capitol.

* NASA Tours

Dryden Flight Research Facility
POB 273, TR-42
Edwards, CA 93523   805-258-3460

NASA offers its own base tours with a 20 minute film showing Dryden's current project testings and concluding with a 45 minute walking tour of two active hangers. Tours are Monday-Friday, 10:15 and 1:15. The tours are free, but reservations are required.

* National Aquarium

U.S. Department of Commerce Building
14th St. and Constitution Ave., NW   202-482-2826
Washington, DC 20230   Recorded Information: 202-482-2825

This public aquarium houses both fresh water and marine animals. Exhibits are representations of our natural environment and demonstrate basic biological concepts and principles. The admission fee is $2 for adults and $.75 for children ages 2-12. Children 1 and under are admitted free. The hours are 9-5.

* National Arboretum Tours

U.S. National Arboretum
3501 New York Ave., NE
Educational Department
Washington, DC 20002   Recorded Information: 202-475-4815

Various woody ornamental and outdoor plants are grown and cared for on the 444 acres comprising the U.S. National Arboretum. Admission and parking are free, and guided tours for 10 or more are available with 3 weeks advance notice. Many free classes are offered, along with many special events and functions associated with gardening and growing plants. A free quarterly newsletter lists the monthly calendar.

* National Park Service Folders Bibliography

Superintendent of Documents
Government Printing Office
Washington, DC 20402   Recorded Information: 202-512-1800

National Park Service brochures are featured, including the lesser-known areas of the national parks and a Washington, DC, guide. Also included are books on the preservation of historic structures. The cost is $1.50.

* Nation's Capitol Walker's Guide

Public Information Office
Pennsylvania Avenue Development Corporation
1331 Pennsylvania Ave., NW
Suite 1220 North
Washington, DC 20004-1703   202-724-9091

A Walker's Guide to Pennsylvania Avenue provides the locations and architects of the PADC projects on Pennsylvania Avenue. This guide is free.

* Natural Landmarks Registry

National Registry of Natural Landmarks
Wildlife and Vegetation Division
National Park Service
U.S. Department of the Interior
P.O. Box 37127
Washington, DC 20013-7127   202-343-8129

The Park Service conducts natural region studies to identify areas that are of potential national significance. These areas are then studied in the field by scientists. Natural areas considered of national significance are cited by the Secretary of the Interior as National Natural Landmarks. The owner may apply for a certificate and bronze plaque designating and recognizing the site.

* Panama Canal Tours

Orientation Services
The Office of Public Affairs
c/o Panama Canal Commission
Unit 2300 APOAA 34011   011 50 752-3165

The Canal Guide Service, operated by the Panama Canal Commission, offers free tours of the Panama Canal to the public. Tours are given seven days a week from 9:00 a.m. to 5:00 p.m. The tour takes less than an hour and include a slight briefing, a topographical model of the Canal to view, and a film. Visitors are welcome at the Miraflores Locks on the Pacific side of the Isthmus where a pavilion provides a vantage point for viewing transiting ships. Interested members of the public should call two days in advance to make a reservation. Another attraction is the high doomed ceiling, the dramatic murals, and the marble columns and floor make the rotunda the main attraction of the Administration Building at Balboa Heights. The murals depict the digging of Gaillard Cut at Gold Hill, the erection of a lock gate,

     Be patient. If any phone number is incorrect, call (area code) 555-1212 and request the new listing.

and the construction of the Gatun Dam spillway and Miraflores Locks. Please note the Panama Canal Commission does not provide for transits through the canal. For more information, contact this office.

* Pentagon Art Tours

Director, Pentagon Tours
OASD-PA(DCR)
The Pentagon
Room 1E776
Washington, DC 20301   703-695-1776

Free tours of the Pentagon art collection are conducted Monday through Friday, except holidays, every half hour from 9:30 a.m. to 3:30 p.m. All you need is a valid I.D. to sign up; children under 16 must be accompanied by an adult. Go to the ticket window at the main concourse by the Metro entrance. The tour lasts 1 hour 15 minutes and is one mile in length. The tour is conducted in English only with no translations permitted. Only if you have a group of 9 or more do you need to write for a reservation; otherwise, just come, first come, first served.

* Polar Expeditions with Civilians

Ice Operations Division
Office of Navigation Safety and Waterways Services
U.S. Coast Guard
U.S. Department of Transportation
2100 2nd Street, SW
Room 1202 A
Washington, DC 20593-0001   202-267-1450

The Coast Guard furnishes vessels to other agencies, such as the National Science Foundation, U.S. Geological Survey, and the Navy, to conduct research and ice operations in Arctic and Antarctic waters. The agencies sponsoring the missions select scientists, researchers, students, and in some cases, journalists, photographers, and artists to accompany the mission when space is available. This office is a good starting point for obtaining information on the pertinence of a mission to your field, to be directed to the appropriate agency sponsors, and for information about the data collected during missions.

* Public Buildings and Historic Sites of the United States

Superintendent of Documents
Government Printing Office (GPO)
Washington, DC 20402   202-512-1800

The GPO bibliography of public buildings, landmarks, and historic Sites of the United States is divided into the categories of historic sites, posters, preservation methods for historic buildings, and descriptions of public buildings. Highlights include a poster of the Statue of Liberty and an historic guide to the White House. Free.

* Statue of Liberty

Superintendent of Documents
Government Printing Office
Washington, DC 20402   Recorded Message: 202-512-1800

The Statue of Liberty Exhibit is a full-color pamphlet describing the museum of the Statue of Liberty. It recounts the history of the Statue, describes the intricacies of its architecture and design, and provides information on its French designers and its massive refurbishing. 1988 (S/N 024-005-01025-4, $2.50).

* U.S. Congress Memorial and Historic Trees

Architect of the Capitol
U.S. Capitol Building
Washington, DC 20515   202-224-6645

Since the early 1900s, 191 memorial and historic trees have been planted. 138 are still living on the Capitol grounds. Trees have been planted to memorialize different senators and congressman as well as such people as mothers of America and Vietnam veterans. To obtain a chart which will help you locate various dedicatory trees, contact the Architect's office.

* Voice of America Radio Public Tours

Office of External Affairs
Voice of America (VOA)
United States Information Agency

330 Independence Ave., SW
Washington, DC 20547   Recorded Message: 202-619-4700

Tours of the main headquarters of the Voice of America (VOA), which produces radio programming in 46 languages heard all over the world, are given each weekday except legal holidays. A guide shows visitors the technical operations center, the newsroom, several studios, where either live broadcasts or recordings are being sent out, and a film on the VOA. The 45 minute free tours are scheduled for 8:40, 9:40 and 10:40 a.m., and 1:40 and 2:40 p.m. Reservations are preferred.

* Washington, DC Art Museums

For tour information, contact the appropriate office listed below, or call 202-357-2700 (202-357-1729 TTY) for tour information.

Anacostia Museum
Education Department, Anacostia Museum, 1901 Fort Place S.E., Washington, DC 20020; 202-287-3369.

Cooper-Hewitt Museum
Membership Department, Cooper-Hewitt Museum, 2 East 91st St., New York, NY 10128; 212-860-6868.

Freer Gallery of Art
Tour Information, Freer Gallery of Art, 12th St. and Jefferson Drive SW, Washington, DC 20560; 202-357-2104.

Hirshorn Museum and Sculpture Garden
Office of Education, Hirshorn Museum and Sculpture Garden, 8th St. and Independence Ave. S.W., Washington, DC 20560; 202-357-3235.

Kennedy Center
Tour Information, Friends of the Kennedy Center, Washington, DC 20566; 202-416-8340.

National Air and Space Museum
Office of Volunteer Service, National Air and Space Museum, 7th St. and Independence Ave., S.W., Washington, DC 20560; 202-357-1400.

National Gallery of Art
Education Office, National Gallery of Art, Washington, DC 20565; 202-842-6246. Adult tours, 202-842-6247; School tours, 202-842-6249.

National Museum of African Art
Department of Education, National Museum of African Art, 950 Independence Ave., S.W., Washington, DC 20560; 202-357-4600, ext 221 or 222.

National Museum of American Art
Division of Museum Programs, Office of Educational Programs, National Museum of American Art, Smithsonian Institution, 8th and G Streets, NW, Room 181, Washington, DC 20560; 202-357-4511 or Tour Coordinator, 202-357-3111.

National Museum of American History
Office of Public Programs, National Museum of American History, 14th Street and Constitution Avenue NW, Washington, DC 20560; 202-357-1481; 202-357-1563 TDD.

National Museum of Natural History
Office of Education, National Museum of Natural History, 10th St. and Constitution Ave. N.W., Washington, DC 20560; 202-357-2747.

National Portrait Gallery
Curator of Education, National Portrait Gallery, Eighth and F Sts. N.W., Washington, DC 20560; 202-357-2920.

National Zoological Park
Friends of the National Zoo, National Zoological Park, 3000 Connecticut Ave., N.W., Washington, DC 20008; 202-673-4960. Visitor Information 202-357-2700.

Smithsonian Environmental Research Center
Department of Education, Smithsonian Environmental Research Center, P.O. Box 28, Edgewater, MD 21037; 301-261-4190.

Smithsonian Institutions
1000 Jefferson Drive SW, Washington, DC 20560; 202-357-2700. Visitor Center and Assoc. Reception Center. Info for the Deaf, TDD 202-357-1729.

Vacations and Business Travel

* Washington, DC Landmarks and Points of Interest

Superintendent of Documents
Government Printing Office
Washington, DC 20402   202-512-1800

Washington, DC: Official National Park Guidebook is a colorful descriptive handbook of the Nation's Capitol and nearly Maryland, Virginia and West Virginia. It includes full-color photographs of Washington's landmarks, guide maps, and descriptive histories of all points of interest. 1989 (S/N 024-005-01034-3, $5).

* Washington, DC Pennsylvania Avenue Events

Public Information Office
Pennsylvania Avenue Development Corporation
1331 Pennsylvania Ave., NW
Suite 1220 North
Washington, DC 20004-1703   202-724-9091

Throughout the year, various events are held on Pennsylvania Avenue. Dial 202-724-0009 to hear a recorded message providing daily information about events on Pennsylvania Avenue.

* White House Tours

The White House Office
1600 Pennsylvania Ave., NW   202-456-1414
Washington, DC 20500   Recording: 202-456-7041

Tours of the White House are held every Tuesday through Saturday from 10:00 a.m. to 12:00 noon, unless the White House is closed due to an official function. Tickets are required March through September; otherwise admission is allowed on a first come-first served basis at 8:00 am. Visitors must return at the specified time for the tour. For more information, call the number above.

* Witness Congressional Committee Hearings and Meetings

Contact your Congressman or Senator, or
Senate or House Press Galleries   202-224-3121

Most House and Senate committee hearings and meetings are open to the public. Your Representative or Senator's office should be able to brief you on the subject matter of the hearing and give you a copy of the bill which will be discussed, or a summary of the previous testimony they have heard. By attending committee meetings, you can gain an understanding of the issues gaining the attention of lawmakers and see the legislative process at work. Another type of committee hearing is an "oversight" or investigative session. Members examine the operations of a government agency or search some area of public life that may require future legislation. Hearings are conducted for a variety of reasons; principal among them are to gather information, generate publicity, and assess the level of support. Informed and interested witnesses may appear before the committee, including Federal officials, interest group representatives, academic experts, and private citizens. A civics lesson in action, the committee "mark-up session" occurs after all the testimony has been received and when the drafting of the legislation and voting on provisions actually takes place. This is the heart of the legislative process, where all the political pressures collide with policy questions. It is at this stage when the language of the bill is determined by the committee. Contact your Senator and Representative or call the Senate or House Press Galleries at 202-224-3121 for news about the schedule for committee activities. When in the DC area, check the Washington Post front section (Today in Congress) for House/Senate committee activities.

Be patient. If any phone number is incorrect, call (area code) 555-1212 and request the new listing.

Parks and Camping

* Architecture in the Parks

Historic Architectural Division
National Park Service
U.S. Department of the Interior
800 N. Capitol Street NW
Washington, DC 20002   202-343-8146

Activities related to the preservation of historic and prehistoric structures and cultural landscapes within the National Park System are administered by this office. *A List of Classified Structures* is maintained, which is an inventory of all historic and prehistoric structures in the System. A bibliography of Cultural Resources Management is also administered, listing all reports that address cultural resources in the Park System.

* Apostle Islands

Superintendent of Documents
Government Printing Office
Washington, DC 20402   202-512-1800

Apostle Islands: A Guide to Apostle Islands Lakeshore, Wisconsin recounts the history of these islands, describes the geographical features, and looks at the inland sea. It provides tips on where to visit, wild animal life, and plant life. Full-color photographs are included. (S/N 024-005-01023-8, $2.25).

* Bicycle Paths and Other Transit Environments

Environment Division
Office of Regulatory Affairs
U.S. Department of Transportation (DOT)
400 7th Street, SW, Room 9217
Washington, DC 20590   202-366-4366

This is the DOT contact point for environmental issues. Staff can provide you with information and referrals on such subjects as highway beautification, transportation architecture, bicycle paths, historic preservation activities, and environmental impact statements.

* Campgrounds on Public Lands

Office of Public Affairs
Bureau of Land Management
U.S. Department of the Interior
18th and C Sts., NW
Washington, DC 20240   202-452-5125

The *Recreation Guide to BLM Public Lands* features a map outlining all of the public lands used as recreational areas. Designations on the map include campgrounds, visitors centers, national wild and scenic rivers, national wilderness areas, and national historic and scenic trails. Also included are the states that contain public lands, and state and district offices to contact for additional information. Alaska, Arizona, California, Colorado, Idaho, Montana, Nevada, New Mexico, Oregon, Utah, Washington, and Wyoming are the key states described. To obtain this free guide, write Office of Public Affairs, 1849 C St., NW, Washington, DC 20240.

* Camping and Hiking East of the Mississippi

Land Between the Lakes
Resource and Development
Tennessee Valley Authority
100 Van Morgan Drive
Golden Pond, KY 42211-9001   502-924-5602

Land Between the Lakes offers recreation for tourists on over 300 miles of undeveloped shoreline. The Woodlands Nature Center offers animal exhibits both animals and special programs for the public, including over 200 miles of hiking trails. Wrangler's Camp offers horseback riding on its 26 miles of trails, along with barns, tethers, and posts for riders. Turkey Bay offers an area reserved for off-road vehicle recreation. Three primary campgrounds offer over 1,000 sites and numerous informal shoreline campgrounds. Land Between the Lakes also boasts their own resident buffalo herd--the largest publicly-owned herd east of the Mississippi River. For more information on recreation opportunities at Land Between the Lakes, contact this office.

* Federal Recreation Passport Program

National Park Service Information Office
Office of Public Affairs
National Park Service
P.O. Box 37127
Washington, DC 20013-7127   202-208-6843

The following fee options are available for entrance into federal recreation areas (national parks, and national wildlife refuges). Reservations may be made by contacting: Mistix, P.O. Box 85705, San Diego, CA 92138-5705, 800-365-2267 (camp). For more information on fees and programs, contact your regional national park office.

Single Visit Entrance Fee
Fees range from $1-$4 per person to $10 per vehicle as set by the individual areas. At national park units, fees are charged of visitors 17 through 61 years of age; at national wildlife refuges, visitors 16 through 61 years of age. This fee allows entry to the specific national park or national wildlife unit (where fees are paid). It is good daily or other term, as posted.

Golden Eagle Passport
$25 annually. At national park units, fees are charged of visitors 17 through 61 years of age; at national wildlife refuges, visitors 16 through 61 years of age. This fee allows entry to all federal entrance fee areas, from January 1 through December 31.

Golden Age Passport
Free, for visitors 62 years or older. This allows entry to all federal entrance fee areas plus 50 percent discount on recreation use fees, and is good for the bearer's lifetime.

Golden Access Passport
Free, for visitors who are blind or permanently disabled. This allows entry to all federal entrance fee areas plus 50 percent discount on recreation use fees, and is good for the bearer's lifetime.

Park Pass
$10-$15 annually, for visitors 17 through 61 years of age. This allows entry to the national park unit at which the pass is purchased, from January 1 through December 31.

Duck Stamp
$12.50 annually, for visitors 16 through 61 years of age. This allows entry to all national wildlife refuges which charge entrance fees, from July 1 through June 30.

* Lesser-Known Parks

Superintendent of Documents
Government Printing Office
Washington, DC 20402   202-512-1800

This publication of the National Park Service is *The National Parks: Lesser-Known Areas* (024-005-00911-6, $1.50).

* National and Historical Parks, Monuments and Preserves

Alabama
Horseshoe Bend National Military Park, Route 1, Box 103, Daviston, AL 36256
Russell Cave National Monument, Route 1, Box 175, Bridgeport, AL 35740

Alaska
Aniakchak National Monument and Preserve, P.O. Box 7, King Salmon, AK 99613
Bering Land Bridge National Preserve, P.O. Box 220, Nome, AK 99762
Cape Krusenstern National Monument, P.O. Box 1029, Kotzebue, AK 99752
Denali National Park and Preserve, P.O. Box 9, McKinley Park, AK 99755
Gates of the Arctic National Park and Preserve, P.O. Box 74680, Fairbanks, AK 99707
Glacier Bay National Park and Preserve, Gustavus, AK 99826

Vacations and Business Travel

Katmai National Park and Preserve, P.O. Box 7, King Salmon, AK 99613
Kenai Fjords National Park, P.O. Box 1727, Seward, AK 99664
Klondike Gold Rush National Historical Park, P.O. Box 517, Skagway, AK 99840
Kobuk Valley National Park, P.O. Box 1029, Kotzebue, AK 99752
Lake Clark National Park and Preserve, 701 C St., P.O. Box 61, Anchorage, AK 99513
Noatak National Preserve, P.O. Box 1029, Kotzebue, AK 99752
Sitka National Historical Park, P.O. Box 738, Sitka, AK 99835
Wrangell-St. Elias National, Park and Preserve, P.O. Box 29, Glenallen, AK 99588
Yukon-Charley Rivers, National Preserve, P.O. Box 64, Eagle, AK 99738

Arizona
Coronado National Memorial, Rural Route 2, P.O. Box 126, Hereford, AZ 85615
Grand Canyon National Park, P.O. Box 129, Grand Canyon, AZ 86023
Hot Springs National Park, P.O. Box 1860, Hot Springs, AZ 71902
Petrified Forest National Park, Petrified Forest National Park, AZ 86028
Saguaro National Monument, 36933 Old Spanish Trail, Tucson, AZ 85730
Tumacacori National Historic Park, P.O. Box 67, Tumacacori, AZ 85640

Arkansas
Arkansas Post National Memorial, Route 1, P.O. Box 16, Gillett, AR 72055
Buffalo National River, P.O. Box 1173, Harrison, AR 72601
Hot Springs National Park, P.O. Box 1860, Hot Springs, AR 71902
Pea Ridge National Military Park, Pea Ridge, AR 72751

California
Channel Islands National Park, 1901 Spinnaker Drive, Ventura, CA 93001
Death Valley National Monument, Death Valley, CA 92328
Golden Gate National Recreation Area, Fort Mason, Bldg. 201, San Francisco, CA 94123
Joshua Tree National Monument, 74485 National Monument Drive, Twenty Nine Palms, CA 92277
Kings Canyon National Park, Three Rivers, CA 93271
Lassen Volcanic National Park, P.O. Box 100, Mineral, CA 96063
Pinnacles National Monument, Paicines, CA 95043
Point Reyes National, Seashore, Point Reyes, CA 94956
Redwood National Park, 1111 Second St., Crescent City, CA 95531
San Francisco Maritime National Historical Park, Fort Mason, Bldg. 201, San Francisco, CA 94123
Santa Monica Mountains, National Recreation Area, 22900 Ventura Blvd, Suite 140, Woodland Hills, CA 91364
Sequoia National Park, Three Rivers, CA 93271
Whiskeytown-Shasta-Trinity, National Recreation Area, P.O. Box 188, Whiskeytown, CA 96095
Yosemite National Park, P.O. Box 577, Yosemite National Park, CA 95389

Colorado
Colorado National Monument, Fruita, CO 81521
Curecanti National Recreation Area, 102 Elk Creek, Gunnison, CO 81230
Dinosaur National Monument, P.O. Box 210, Dinosaur, CO 81610
Florissant Fossil Beds National Monument, P.O. Box 185, Florissant, CO 80816
Great Sand Dunes National Monument, Mosca, CO 81146
Mesa Verde National Park, Mesa Verde National Park, CO 81330
Rocky Mountain National Park, Estes Park, CO 80517

District of Columbia
Constitution Gardens, 900 Ohio Dr., SW, Washington, DC 20242
John F.Kennedy Center for the Performing Arts, National Park Service, 2700 F St., NW, Washington, DC 20566
Lyndon B.Johnson Memorial, Grove on the Potomac, c/o NCP - George Washington Memorial Parkway, Turkey Run Park, McLean, VA 22101
National Capital Parks, National Capitol Region, 1100 Ohio Drive SW, Washington, DC 20242
Rock Creek Park, 5000 Glover Rd., NW, Washington, DC 20015
Theodore Roosevelt Island, c/o George Washington Memorial Pkwy, Turkey Run Park, McLean, VA 22101
Thomas Jefferson Memorial and Tidal Basin, c/o NCP - Central, 900 Ohio Dr., SW, Washington, DC 20242
Vietnam Veterans Memorial, c/o National Capitol Parks, Central, 900 Ohio Drive SW, Washington, DC 20242

Florida
Big Cypress National Preserve, Star Route, P.O. Box 110, Ochopee, FL 33943
Biscayne National Park, P.O. Box 1369, Homestead, FL 33090
Canaveral National Seashore, P.O. Box 6447, Titusville, FL 32782
DeSoto National Memorial, 75th St., NW, Bradenton, FL 33529

Everglades National Park, P.O. Box 279, Homestead, FL 33030
Fort Caroline National Memorial, 12713 Fort Caroline Rd., Jacksonville, FL 32225
Fort Jefferson National Monument, c/o Everglades National Park, P.O. Box 279, Homestead, FL 33030
Fort Matanzas National Monument, c/o Castillo de San Marcos, 1 Castillo Drive, St. Augustine, FL 32084
Gulf Islands National Seashore, 1801 Gulf Breeze Parkway, Gulf Breeze, FL 32561
Timucuan Ecological and Historic Preserve, 12713 Fort Caroline Road, Jacksonville, FL 32225

Georgia
Chattahoochee River National Recreation Area, 1978 Island Ford Pkwy, Dunwoody, GA 30350
Chickamauga and Chattanooga National Military Park, P.O. Box 2128, Fort Oglethorpe, GA 30742
Cumberland Island National Seashore, P.O. Box 806, St. Marys, GA 31558
Kennesaw Mountain National, Battlefield Park, P.O. Box 1167, Marietta, GA 30061
Ocmulgee National Monument, 1207 Emery Highway, Macon, GA 31201

Guam
War in the Pacific National Historic Park, P.O. Box FA, Agana, GU 96910

Hawaii
Haleakala National Park, P.O. Box 369, Makawao, HI 96768
Hawaii Volcanoes National Park, Hawaii National Park, HI 96718
Kalaupapa National Historical Park, Kalaupapa, HI 96742
National Park of American Samoa, c/o Pacific Area Office, P.O. Box 50165, Honolulu, HI 96850
Pu'uhonua o Honaunau National Historical Park, P.O. Box 128, Honaunau Kona, HI 96726
USS Arizona Memorial, 1 Arizona Memorial Place, Honolulu, HI 96818

Idaho
City of Rocks National Reserve, 963 Blue Lake Blvd., Suite 1, Twin Falls, ID 83301
Craters of the Moon National Monument, P.O. Box 29, Arco, ID 83213

Indiana
George Rogers Clark National Historical Park, 401 S. Second St., Vincennes, IN 47591
Indiana Dunes National Lakeshore, 1100 N. Mineral Springs Rd., Porter, IN 46304

Iowa
Effigy Mounds National Monument, RR 1, Box 25A, Harpers Ferry, IA 52146

Kansas
Fort Larned National Historic Site, Route 3, Larned, KS 67550

Kentucky
Cumberland Gap National Historical Park, P.O. Box 1848, Middlesboro, KY 40965
Mammoth Cave National Park, Mammoth Cave, KY 42259

Louisiana
Jean Lafitte National Historical Park and Preserve, 423 Canal St., Room 210, New Orleans, LA 70130-2341

Maine
Acadia National Park, P.O. Box 177, Bar Harbor, MED 04609

Maryland
Antietam National Battlefield, P.O. Box 158, Sharpsburg, MD 21782
Assateague Island National Seashore, Rt. 2, P.O. Box 294, Berlin, MD 21811
Catoctin Mountain Park, 6602 Foxville Rd., Thurmont, MD 21788
Chesapeake and Ohio Canal Historical Park, P.O. Box 4, Sharpsburg, Md. 21782
Fort Washington Park, NCP - East, 1900 Anacostia Dr., SE, Washington, DC 20020
Greenbelt Park, 6565 Greenbelt Rd., Greenbelt, MD 20770
Piscataway Park, c/o NCP - East, 1900 Anacostia Drive SE, Washington, DC 20019

Massachusetts
Boston National Historical Park, Charlestown Navy Yard, Boston, MA 02129
Cape Cod National Seashore, South Wellfleet, MA 02663
Lowell National Historical Park, 169 Merrimack St., Lowell, MA 01852

Be patient. If any phone number is incorrect, call (area code) 555-1212 and request the new listing.

Minute Man National Historical Park, P.O. Box 160, 174 Liberty St., Concord, MA 01742

Michigan
Isle Royale National Park, 87 N. Ripley St., Houghton, MI 49931
Pictured Rocks National Lakeshore, P.O. Box 40, Munising, MI 49862
Sleeping Bear Dunes National Lakeshore, P.O. Box 277, 9922 Front St., Empire, MI 49630

Minnesota
Pipestone National Monument, P.O. Box 727, Pipestone, MN 56164
Voyageurs National Park, P.O. Box 50, International Falls, MN 56649

Mississippi
Brices Cross Roads National Battlefield Site, c/o Natchez Trace Pkwy, Rural Route 1, NT-143, Tupelo, MS 38801
Gulf Islands National Seashore, 3500 Park Road, Ocean Springs, MS 39564
Natchez Trace Parkway, Rural Route 1, NT-143, Tupelo, MS 38801
Tupelo National Battlefield, c/o Natchez Trace Pkwy, Rural Route 1, NT-143, Tupelo, MS 38801
Vicksburg National Military Park, 3201 Clay St., Vicksburg, MS 39180

Missouri
Jefferson National Expansion Memorial, 11 North 4th Street, St. Louis, MO 63102
Ozark National Scenic Riverways, P.O. Box 490, Van Buren, MO 63965
Wilson's Creek National Battlefield, Postal Drawer C, Republic, MO 65738

Montana
Big Hole National Battlefield, P.O. Box 237, Wisdom, MT 59761
Bighorn Canyon National Recreation Area, P.O. Box 458, Fort Smith, MT 59035
Custer Battlefield National Monument, P.O. Box 39, Crow Agency, MT 59022
Glacier National Park, West Glacier, MT 59936
Grant-Kohrs Ranch National Historic Site, P.O. Box 790, Deer Lodge, MT 59722

Nebraska
Agate Fossil Beds National Monument, P.O. Box 27, Gering, NE 69341

Nevada
Great Basin National Park, Baker, NV 89311
Lake Mead National Recreation Area, 601 Nevada Hwy, Boulder City, NV 89005-2426

New Jersey
Edison National Historic Site, Main St. and Lakeside Ave., West Orange, NJ 07052
Morristown National Historical Park, Washington Place, Morristown, NJ 07960

New Mexico
Carlsbad Caverns National Park, 3225 National Parks Highway, Carlsbad, NM 88220
Chaco Culture National Historical Park, Star Route 4, P.O. Box 6500, Bloomfield, NM 87413
El Malpais National Monument, P.O. Box 939, Grants, NM 87020
Pecos National Historical Park, P.O. Box Drawer 418, Pecos, NM 87522

New York
Federal Hall National Memorial, Manhattan Sites, 26 Wall St., New York, NY 10005
Fire Island National Seashore, 120 Laurel St., Patchogue, NY 11772
Gateway National Recreation Area, Floyd Bennett Field, Bldg. 69, Brooklyn, NY 11234
General Grant National Memorial, 122nd St. and Riverside Dr., New York, NY 10027
Hamilton Grange National Memorial, 287 Convent Avenue, New York, NY 10031
Saratoga National Historical Park, R.D. 2, P.O. Box 33, Stillwater, NY 12170
Women's Rights National Historical Park, P.O. Box 70, Seneca Falls, NY 13148

North Carolina
Blue Ridge Parkway, 700 Northwestern Plaza, Asheville, NC 28801
Cape Hatteras National Seashore, Rt. 1, P.O. Box 675, Manteo, NC 27954
Cape Lookout National Seashore, P.O. Box 690, Beaufort, NC 28516
Guilford Courthouse National Military Park, P.O. Box 9806, Greensboro, NC 27429
Moores Creek National Battlefield, P.O. Box 69, Currie, NC 28435
Wright Brothers National Memorial, Cape Hatteras Group, Rt. 1, P.O. Box 675, Manteo, NC 27954

North Dakota
Knife River Indian Village National Historic Park, RR 1, Box 168, Stanton, ND 58571
Theodore Roosevelt National Park, P.O. Box 7, Medora, ND 58645

Ohio
Cuyahoga Valley National Recreation Area, 15610 Vaughn Rd., Brecksville, OH 44141
Mound City Group National Monument, 16062 State Route 104, Chillicothe, OH 45601
Perry's Victory and International Peace Memorial, P.O. Box 549, 93 Delaware Ave., Put-in-Bay, OH 43456

Oklahoma
Chicksaw National Recreation Area, P.O. Box 201, Sulphur, OK 73086

Oregon
Crater Lake National Park, P.O. Box 7, Crater Lake, OR 97604
Fort Clatsop National Memorial, Rt. 3, P.O. Box 604-FC, Astoria, OR 97103
Oregon Caves National Monument, 19000 Caves Highway, Cave Junction, OR 97523

Pennsylvania
Delaware Water Gap National Recreation Area, Bushkill, PA 18324
Fort Necessity National Battlefield, The National Pike, R.D. 2, P.O. Box 528, Farmington, PA 51437
Gettysburg National Military Park, Gettysburg, PA 17325
Independence National Historical Park, 313 Walnut Street, Philadelphia, PA 19106
Johnstown Flood National Memorial, c/o Allegheny Portage Railroad NHS, P.O. Box 247, Cresson, PA 16630
Thaddeus Kosciuszko National Memorial, c/o Independence NHP, 313 Walnut St., Philadelphia, PA 19106
Upper Delaware Scenic and Recreational River, P.O. Box C, Narrowsburg, NY 12764
Valley Forge National Historical Park, Valley Forge, PA 19481

Rhode Island
Roger Williams National Memorial, P.O. Box 367, Annex Station, Providence, RI 02901

South Carolina
Cowpens National Battlefield, P.O. Box 308, Chesnee, SC 29323
Kings Mountain National Military Park, P.O. Box 40, Kings Mountain, NC 28086

South Dakota
Badlands National Park, P.O. Box 6, Interior, SD 57750
Jewel Cave National Monument, RR 1, Box 60AA, Custer, SD 57730
Mount Rushmore National Memorial, P.O. Box 268, Keystone, SD 57751
Wind Cave National Park, Hot Springs, SD 57747

Tennessee
Big South Fork National River and Recreation Area, P.O. Drawer 630, Oneida, TN 37841
Fort Donelson National Battlefield, P.O. Box 434, Dover, TN 37058-0434
Great Smoky Mountains National Park, Gatlinburg, TN 37738
Obed Wild and Scenic River, P.O. Box 429, Wartburg, TN 37887
Shiloh National Military Park, P.O. Box 61, Shiloh, TN 38376
Stones River National Battlefield, Rt. 10, P.O. Box 495, Old Nashville Hwy, Murfreesboro, TN 37130

Texas
Amistad Recreation Area, P.O. Box 420367, Del Rio, TX 78842-0367
Big Bend National Park, Big Bend National Park, TX 79834
Big Thicket National Preserve, 3785 Milam, Beaumont, TX 77701
Chamizal National Memorial, c/o Federal Bldg., 700 E. San Antonio, Suite D-301, El Paso, TX 79901
Guadalupe Mountains National Park, H.C. 60, P.O. Box 400, Salt Flat, TX 79847-9400
Lake Meredith Recreation Area, P.O. Box 1438, Fritch, TX 79036
Lyndon B. Johnson National Historical Park, P.O. Box 329, Johnson City, TX 78636
Padre Island National Seashore, 9405 S. Padre Island Dr., Corpus Christi, TX 78482-5597
San Antonio Missions National Historical Park, 2202 Roosevelt Ave., San Antonio, TX 78210-4919

Be patient. If any phone number is incorrect, call (area code) 555-1212 and request the new listing.

395

Utah

Arches National Park, P.O. Box 907, Moab, UT 84532

Bryce Canyon National Park, Bryce Canyon, UT 84717

Canyonlands National Park, 125 W. 200 South, Moab, UT 84532

Capital Reef National Park, Torrey, UT 84775

Glen Canyon National Recreation Area, P.O. Box 1507, Page, UT 86040

Natural Bridges National Monument, Box 1, Lake Powell, UT 84533

Zion National Park, Springdale, UT 84767-1099

Virginia

Appomattox Court House National Historical Park, P.O. Box 218, Appomattox, VA 24522

Arlington House, The Robert E. Lee Memorial, c/o George Washington Memorial Pkwy, Turkey Run Park, McLean, VA 22101

Colonial National Historical Park, P.O. Box 210, Yorktown, VA 23690

Fredericksburg and Spotsylvania National Military Park, P.O. Box 679, Fredericksburg, VA 22404

George Washington Memorial Parkway, Turkey Run Prk, McLean, VA 22101

Great Falls Park, 9200 Old Dominion Dr., Great Falls, VA 22066

Jamestown National Historic Site, c/o Colonial Park, P.O. Box 210, Yorktown, VA 23690

Manassas National Battlefield Park, P.O. Box 1830, Manassas, VA 22110

Petersburg National Battlefield, P.O. Box 549, Rt. 36 East, Petersburg, VA 23804

Prince William Forest Park, P.O. Box 209, Triangle, VA 22172

Richmond National Battlefield Park, 3215 E. Broad St., Richmond, VA 23223

Shenandoah National Park, Rt. 4, P.O. Box 348, Luray, VA 22835

Wolf Trap Farm Park for the Performing Arts, 1551 Trap Rd., Vienna, VA 22180

Virgin Islands

Buck Island Reef National Monument, P.O. Box 160, Christiansted, St. Croix, VI 00820

Virgin Islands National Park, P.O. Box 7789, Charlotte Amalie, St. Thomas, VI 00801

Washington

Coulee Dam National Recreation Area, P.O. Box 37, Coulee Dam, WA 99116

Ebey's Landing National Historical Reserve, P.O. Box 774, 23 Front St., Coupeville, WA 98239

Klondike Gold Rush National Historical Park, 117 S. Main St., Seattle, WA 98104

Lake Chelan National Recreation Area, 2105 Hwy 20, Sedro Woolley, WA 98284

Mount Ranier National Park, Tahoma Woods Star Route, Ashord, WA 98304

North Cascades National Park, 2105 Hwy 20, Sedro Woolley, WA 98284

Olympic National Park, 600 E. Park Ave., Port Angeles, WA 98362

Ross Lake National Recreation Area, 2105 Hwy 20, Sedro Woolley, WA 98284

San Juan Island National Historical Park, P.O. Box 429, Friday Harbor, WA 98250

West Virginia

Appalachian National Scenic Trail, P.O. Box 807, Harpers Ferry, WV 25425

Harpers Ferry National Historical Park, P.O. Box 65, Harpers Ferry, WV 25425

New River Gorge National River, P.O. Box 2289, Oak Hill WV 25901

Wisconsin

Apostle Islands National Lakeshore, Rt. 1, P.O. Box 4, Bayfield, WI 54814

St. Croix and Lower St. Croix, National Scenic Riverways, P.O. Box 708, St. Croix Falls, WI 54024

Wyoming

Devils Tower National Monument, Devils Tower, WY 82212

Fossil Butte National Monument, P.O. Box 527, Kemmerer, WY 83101

Grand Teton National Park, P.O. Drawer 170, Moose,WY 83012

John D. Rockefeller Memorial Parkway, c/o Grand Teton National Park, P.O. Drawer 170, Moose, WY 83012

Yellowstone National Park, P.O. Box 168, Yellowstone National Park, WY 82190

* National Parks Exhibits and Programs

Division of Interpretation
National Park Service
U.S. Department of the Interior
800 N. Capitol, NW, Room 560
Washington, DC 20002   202-523-5270

The National Park Service assists its facilities in planning and carrying out their exhibits and visitor programs. Their future plans include more involvement in environmental education programs to be offered at the Park Service sites.

* National Park Service Clearinghouse

Technical Information Center
National Park Service
Denver Service Center
12795 W. Alameda Parkway
P.O. Box 25287
Denver, CO 80225-0287   303-969-2130

The Technical Information Center has been designated by the National Park Service (NPS) as the central repository for all National Park Service-generated planning, design, and construction maps, drawings, and reports as well as related cultural, environmental, and other technical documents. Bibliographic data on aerial photography is also maintained. The Center reproduces and delivers copies of the available materials for the Service, other agencies, and the public, both here and abroad. Today, the system has a holding of 100,000 data records, which represent about 500,000 microfilm aperture cards of maps, plans, and drawings; 1,000 records of resource and site aerial photography; and 25,000 planning, design, environmental, cultural resource, and natural resource documents. There is a fee depending on the material requested.

* National Park Service Films

National Audiovisual Center
8700 Edgeworth Dr.
Capitol Heights, MD 20743-3701   301-763-1896

The National Audiovisual Center contains more than 2,700 titles of videocassettes, films and slide/sound programs. Among them are some wonderful presentations produced by the National Park Service and the U.S. Fish and Wildlife Service. Materials may be previewed or purchased. Contact the AV Center for specific information. Some titles include:

Everglades: Seeking a Balance
Gulf Island Beaches, Bays, Sands, and Bayous
California Gray Whale
Environmental Awareness
Giant Sequoia
One Man's Alaska
Sanctuary: The Great Smoky Mountains
Crater Lake
Yellowstone
Washington, DC: Fancy Free
Glacier Bay
Bighorn Canyon Experience
Cape Cod
What is a Mountain?
Living Waters of the Big Cypress
National Parks: Our Treasured Lands
Mt. McKinley
America's Wetlands
Parrots of Luquillo
Where the Fish Will Be
Patuxent Wildlife Research Center
Minnesota Valley National Wildlife Refuge

* National Park Service Management and Programming

Park Practice Program
National Park Service
Technical Publications Program
U.S. Department of the Interior
P.O. Box 37127
Washington, DC 20013-7127   202-343-7067

The Park Practice Program is a cooperative effort between the National Park Service and the National Recreation and Park Association. Three publications are produced quarterly in an effort to instruct recreational and park directors on the latest information in the field:

TRENDS. Discusses topics of general interest in park and recreation management and programming. $35.

GRIST. Contains practical solutions to everyday problems in park and recreation operations including energy conservation, cost reduction, safety, and maintenance and designs for small structures.

DESIGN. Offers plans for park and recreation structures which demonstrate quality design accessibility and intelligent use of materials. $35.

These publications are available as a set in an annual subscription of $55. *GRIST* is also available separately for a yearly price of $30. Subscription inquiries should be addressed to: National Recreation and Park Association, 2775 S. Quincy Street, Suite 300, Arlington, VA 22206; 703-820-4940.

* National Parks Service Posters and Charts

Superintendent of Documents
Government Printing Office (GPO)
Washington, DC 20402   202-512-1800

The following National Park Service posters and charts are available from GPO. Several titles can be purchased at special discounts when buying 100-count lots.

The Alpine Northwest
The Atlantic Barrier
The Canyon Country
The Desert
Edgar Allan Poe
Everglades
George Washington Carver
Glacier Bay
Greater Yellowstone Panorama
Hawaii Volcanoes
North Cascades Panorama
The Rocky Mountains
The Sierra Range
Statue of Liberty
Yosemite Panorama
National Park Service
American/British Charts

Six charts were produced jointly with the Sunday Times of London to commemorate the American bicentennial. Each poster is illustrated in full color and presents many facts about life during the Revolutionary War era and the war itself. They may be purchased individually, in a set of one each, or in cartons of 100 per subject.

The American Navies 1775-1783
The Continental Soldier
Philadelphia 1776
The British Navy 1775-1783
The British Redcoat
London 1776

* National Park Service Regional Offices

Alaska
2525 Gambell St., Room 107, Anchorage, AK 99503; 907-257-2696

Mid-Atlantic
143 S. 3rd Street, Philadelphia, PA 19106; 215-597-1085. Serving: PA, VA, WV, DE, MD

Midwest
1709 Jackson St., Omaha, NE 68102; 402-221-3448. Serving: NE, MO, KS, IA, IL, IN, WI, MI, MN, OH

Washington, DC
1100 Ohio Dr., SW, Washington, DC 20242; 202-619-7222

North-Atlantic
15 State St., Boston, MA 02109-3572; 617-223-5199. Serving: NY, NJ, CT, RI, MA, NH, VT, ME

Pacific Northwest
900 First St., Suite 212, Seattle, WA 98104; 206-220-4013. Serving: WA, OR, ID

Rocky Mountain
P.O. Box 25287, Denver, CO 80225; 303-969-2503. Serving: MT, ND, SD, WY, UT, CO

Southeast
75 Spring St., Atlanta, GA 30303; 404-331-4998. Serving: MS, TN, AL, GA, FL, SC, NC, KY, Virgin Is., PR

Southwest
1100 Old Santa Fe Trail, Santa FE, NM 87501; 505-988-6091. Serving: NM, TX, LA, OK, AR

Western
600 Harrison Street, Suite 600, San Francisco, CA 94107; 415-744-3929. Serving: CA, AZ, NV, HI, Guam, Northern Marianas Is., Am Samoa, Micronesia, Marshall Is., Palau

* National Park Service Reservations

MISTIX
P.O. Box 9029
Clearwater, FL 34618   800-365-2267

or

Nationwide Reservations
P.O. Box 37127
Washington, DC 20013-7129   202-208-4747

Reservations to the following national park sites are available from the agent listed above. Advanced notice of eights weeks is needed for individual campsites. Phone reservations must be made directly with those parks accepting them; this information is listed in the Camping Reservation form. The parks include: Acadia National Park, Maine; Assateague Island National Seashore, Maryland/Virginia; Cape Hatteras National Seashore, North Carolina; Death Valley Monument, California; Grand Canyon National Park, Arizona; Great Smoky Mountains National Park, North Carolina/Tennessee; Joshua Tree National Monument, California; Rocky Mountain National Park, Colorado; Sequoia-Kings Canyon National Park, California; Shenandoah National Park, Virginia; Whiskeytown National Recreation Area, California; Yosemite National Park, California.

* National Park Service Statistical Abstract

Socio-Economic Studies
WASO-TNT
National Park Service
U.S. Department of the Interior
P.O. Box 25287
Denver, CO 80225   303-969-6977

National Park Service statistics from 1982-1988 are included in the *Park Service Statistical Abstract*. Recreation visits in the Service are summarized in information tables, such as visitor use, total visits, visits by region and state, visits by urban-rural location, overnight stays, and number of tour buses.

* National Park Service Videos and Literature

Harpers Ferry Historical Association, Inc.
P.O. Box 197
High St.
Harpers Ferry, WV 25425   800-821-5206

This historical society serves as a distributing agency for the sale and rental of materials produced for the National Park Service. A catalog is available listing videos and handbooks, and another 80 historic films are available from the Association for purchase or three-day rental. Some video titles include: *Challenge of Yellowstone*, *Great Sand Dunes*, *Shenandoah: The Gift*, *Cape Cod Treasury*, *Gulf Islands*, *Antietam Visit*, *Civil War Artillery*, *A Lasting Victory (Robert E. Lee)*, and *Blessings of Liberty* (produced for the 200th birthday of the U.S. Constitution). The handbooks describe historical events and different locations within the Park Service. Inquire about a current listing of materials.

* National Parks Index

Superintendent of Documents
Government Printing Office
Washington, DC 20402   202-512-1800

Published yearly, *The National Parks: Index* describes the National Park System and provides information on the available facilities. 1995 edition, S/N 024-005-01160-9, $4.25.

* National Parks Visitor Facilities and Services

National Park Hospitality Association
P.O. Box 27
Manmmoth Cave, KY 42259   502-773-2191

The publication, *National Park Visitor Facilities and Services*, lists all concessioner lodging and service information for the National Parks. To obtain a copy, send $4.50 to 1331 Pennsylvania Ave., NW, Suite 724, Washington, DC 20004.

Vacations and Business Travel

* National Wildlife Refuges Guide

Superintendent of Documents
Government Printing Office
Washington, DC 20402   202-512-1800

National Wildlife Refuges: A Visitor's Guide is a foldout map of the United States including locations of all national wildlife refuges, a list of their names and addresses, and a description of available activities. 1991 (S/N 024-010-00690-1, $1).

* Recreation and Outdoor Activities Bibliography

Superintendent of Documents
Government Printing Office
Washington, DC 20402   202-512-1800

This bibliography is divided into the categories of boating and water activities, camping and hiking, fishing and hunting, national recreation areas, winter activities, and general information. Free.

* Recreation Guide to BLM Public Lands

Office of Public Affairs
Bureau of Land Management (BLM)
U.S. Department of the Interior
18th and C Sts., NW
Washington, DC 20240   202-208-5717

The *Recreation Guide to BLM Public Lands* features a map outlining all of the public lands used as recreational areas. Designations on the map include campgrounds, visitors centers, national wild and scenic rivers, national wilderness areas, and national historic and scenic trails. Also included are the states that contain public lands, and state and district offices to contact for additional information. Alaska, Arizona, California, Colorado, Idaho, Montana, Nevada, New Mexico, Oregon, Utah, Washington, and Wyoming are the key states described.

* Recreation Market Study

Recreation Resources Assistance Division
National Park Service
National Trails and Recreational Branch
U.S. Department of the Interior
P.O. Box 37127, Code 0728
800 N. Capitol Street NW
Washington, DC 20013-7127   202-343-3780

The *National Recreation Survey* provides current information on what Americans do for recreation in the outdoors and their expectations of recreational opportunities. The survey contains valuable market data on such topics as favorite activities, importance of recreation areas and their distance from home, characteristics of trips and outings, characteristics of respondents who spend money on outdoor recreation, and reasons for discontinuing a recreation activity. Various tables that relate to the National Park System and its participants are included.

* State Parks, Forest Camping Areas and Other Recreation Areas

Public Relations
Tennessee Valley Authority (TVA)
400 W. Summit Hill Dr.
Knoxville, TN 37902   615-632-4402

Contact this office for all generic information on the TVA Agency, including the history behind the agency. A brochure is available with questions and answers most frequently asked about the TVA agency, lakes and dams.

Recreation on TVA Lakes
TVA
Natural Resources Building
Ridgeway Road
Norris, TN 37828   615-632-1600

This office can provide you with a free pamphlet which describes recreation areas on the Tennessee Valley Authority lakeshores, including boat docks, resorts, state parks, U.S. Forest Service camp areas, and those county, national, city, state, and municipal parks which have docks or camping areas. Maps are also available.

* Tourism Programs on Public Lands

Office of Public Affairs
Bureau of Land Management
U.S. Department of the Interior
1849 C St., NW
Washington, DC 20240   202-208-5717

In recognition of the importance of outdoor recreation to Americans, *Recreation 2000 Executive Summary* sets forth the commitment of the Bureau of Land Management to the management of outdoor recreation resources in the public lands. The plan highlights the areas in which the Bureau intends to concentrate future efforts, such as visitor information, resource protection, land ownerships, partnerships, volunteers, tourism programs, facilities, and permits, fees, and concessions. This publication also features a map outlining all of the public lands used as recreational areas. Designations on the map include campgrounds, visitors centers, national wild and scenic rivers, national wilderness areas, and national historic and scenic trails. Also included are the states that contain public lands, and state and district offices to contact for additional information. Alaska, Arizona, California, Colorado, Idaho, Montana, Nevada, New Mexico, Oregon, Utah, Washington, and Wyoming are the key states described.

* United States Service Police

National Capital Region
National Park Service
U.S. Department of the Interior
1100 Ohio Dr., SW
Washington, DC 20242   202-619-7310

The U.S. Park Police have the same authority and powers as the Washington, DC metropolitan police. They also act as hosts to park visitors.

* Whale Watching

Office of Protected Resources
National Marine Fisheries Service
National Oceanic and Atmospheric Administration
U.S. Department of Commerce
1335 East-West Hwy.
Silver Spring, MD 20910   301-713-2332

The Marine Mammal Protection Act commits the United States to long-term management and research programs to conserve and protect these animals. The National Marine Fisheries Service grants or denies requests for exemptions, issues permits, carries out research and management programs, enforces the Act, participates in international programs, and issues rules and regulations to carry out its mission to conserve and protect marine mammals. An annual report is available for the Office of Protected Resources, which gives detailed information regarding the activities of the Office. This office can also provide you with copies of the Act, and other publications relating to marine mammals or endangered species.

* Wild and Scenic Rivers

Land and Renewable Resources
Bureau of Land Management
U.S. Department of the Interior
1849 C St., NW, W0200
Washington, DC 20240   202-208-4896

The Bureau of Land Management manages about 2,200 miles of the Wild and Scenic River System, primarily in the western United States. These areas are located in the directory, *Recreation Guide to BLM Public Lands*, available from the Office of Public Affairs, Bureau of Land Management, U.S. Department of the Interior, Washington, DC 20240.

* Woodsy Owl and Children's Materials

U.S. Department of Agriculture
Forest Service
P.O. Box 96090
Washington, DC 20090-6090   202-205-1785

To increase children's awareness of our delicate environment, the Forest Service's Woodsy Owl campaign is in the process of developing a variety of materials which should be available in 1995.

Boating and Fishing

* Advanced Marine Vehicles
Planning Branch
Research and Development Staff
Office of Engineering and Development
U.S. Coast Guard
U.S. Department of Transportation
2100 2nd St., SW, Room 6208
Washington, DC 20593-0001   202-267-1018

Information can be obtained here about research conducted by the Coast Guard in support of its operations and responsibilities. Areas of study include ice operations, law enforcement, marine environmental protection, port safety and security, navigation aids, search and rescue procedures, and recreational boating. For referral to specific personnel working in these areas, contact the Planning Branch.

* Aids to Navigation
Office of Navigation Safety and Waterways Services
U.S. Coast Guard
U.S. Department of Transportation
2100 2nd St., SW, Room 1116
Washington, DC 20593-0001   202-267-1965

The Coast Guard maintains aids to navigation such as lighthouses and lights, buoys, beacons, fog signals, and long-range radionavigation aids like LORAN-C and OMEGA. The aids are established to assist navigators in plotting safe courses on waters under U.S. jurisdiction and in certain international areas. The seven volumes of *Light Lists*, which detail the navigation aids in seven geographic areas, are available at varying cost and are available from the Superintendent of Documents, Government Printing Office, Washington, DC 20402; 202-512-1800. The *LORAN-C User Handbook*, which explains the radionavigation system and how to use it, is also available from GPO for $15.

* Army Corps of Engineers Recreational Facilities Films
U.S. Army Corps of Engineers
Directorate of Information Management
Visual Information Branch
CEHEC-IM-V
20 Massachusetts Ave., NW
Washington, DC 20314   202-272-0717

This office maintains a still photographic library and offers a free film loan and video distribution program. The Corps has educational and public relations films on their recreational facilities, navigation, flood control, hydro-electric power, and environmental systems. Write for information on the how to participate in the program.

* Boating Correspondence Course
U.S. Government Bookstore
Norwest Banks Building
201 W. 8th Street
Pueblo, CO 81003-3091   719-544-3142

Designed for boaters who can't attend a boating class, *The Skipper's Course* covers basic navigation, legal requirements, anchoring, weather, emergency procedures, boat handling, and safety. A certificate of completion is awarded. Stock No: 050012002258. Price: $6.50. This publications is out of print. however, a new edition is in process.

* Coast Guard Courses and Textbooks
Coast Guard Auxiliary National Board, Inc.
9949 Watson Industrial Park
St. Louis, MO 63126

The following are textbooks used in Coast Guard Auxiliary public education courses. They can be ordered by writing to the above address, or you can get each textbook by taking the course of the same title through the Coast Guard. To find out where courses are offered near you, call the Courseline at 800-336-BOAT; or 800-245-BOAT in VA.

Boating Skills and Seamanship. Boating laws and regulations, boat handling, and navigation ($8).
Sailing and Seamanship. Same basic text as above, geared to sailboats ($8).
Advanced Coastal Piloting. How to read charts, plot courses, predict tides, and use navigation aids ($8).

* Coast Guard Rescue Service
SAR Database Manager
Search and Rescue Division
Commandant (G-NRS-1)
Office of Navigation Safety and Waterways Services
U.S. Coast Guard
U.S. Department of Transportation
2100 2nd Street, SW
Room 1422
Washington, DC 20593-0001   202-267-1579

The Search and Rescue (SAR) program maintains a comprehensive system of resources to save lives and prevent personal injury and property damage on the navigable waters of the U.S. This system includes rescue vessels, aircraft, and communication facilities. A cooperative international distress response system is also maintained for incidents on the high seas. For more information about the Guard's SAR program, contact the branch listed above.

* Free Boat Inspection
Courtesy Marine Examination (CME)
BOAT/U.S. Foundation
880 S. Pickett St.   800-336-BOAT
Alexandria, VA 22304   800-245-BOAT (in VA)

The U.S. Coast Guard Auxiliary offers a free safety inspection called a Courtesy Marine Examination. A specially trained Coast Guard Auxiliarist will examine your craft to determine if it has all the necessary and recommended equipment. If properly equipped, you'll be awarded a CME decal. To arrange for your CME, call the toll-free number or contact your local Coast Guard Auxiliary.

* Land Between the Lakes
Land Between The Lakes
Natural Resources
Resource and Development
Tennessee Valley Authority (TVA)
Golden Pond, KY 42211-9001   502-924-5602

Land Between The Lakes is a 40-mile-long peninsula located between Kentucky and Barkley Lakes in west Kentucky and Tennessee. In its 25th year of operation, Land Between The Lakes is managed by TVA to provide an outstanding outdoor recreation experience. A living history farm exhibit called "Homeplace-1850," recreates life as it existed on a typical farmstead in the area before the Civil War. Exhibitors tend crops and animals, prepare meals, and perform hundreds of other farm chores in the same manner as their forebears did. Recreation programs at Land Between the Lakes are for everyone, but many programs are tailored to groups with special needs.

* Marine Advisory Service
National Sea-Grant College Program
National Oceanic and Atmospheric Administration
U.S. Department of Commerce
1315 East-West Hwy.   301-713-2483 (Maryland)
Silver Spring, MD 20910   202-482-6090 (DC)

Operated through the Sea-Grant Colleges, the marine advisory service consists of agents and specialists who are experts in areas such as seafood technology, marine economics, coastal engineering, commercial fishing, recreation, and communications. These specialists provide a link between the people who live and work in coastal areas and researchers in the universities. They sponsor workshops, conferences, and seminars on marine issues for the public and representatives of industry and government agencies. They talk to high school science classes, as well as publish bulletins, fact sheets, newsletters, technical papers, and audio-visual materials

Vacations and Business Travel

concerning marine affairs. The following is a list of Sea-Grant Colleges, and people you can contact for more information.

Sea Grant Colleges

Alabama
See Mississippi

Alaska
Alaska Sea Grant College Program
University of Alaska Fairbanks
138 Irving II
Fairbanks, AK 99775-5040   907-474-7086

Arizona
Environmental Research Laboratory
University of Arizona
2601 E. Airport Drive
Tucson, AZ 85706-6985   602-741-1990

California
California Sea Grant
University of California/San Diego
9500 Gilman Drive
La Jolla, CA 92093-0232   619-534-4444

Sea Grant Program
University of Southern California
University Park
Los Angeles, CA 90089-1231   213-740-1961

Connecticut
Connecticut Sea Grant
Marine Sciences Institute
University of Connecticut
Building 24, Avery Point
Groton, CT 06340   203-445-8664

Delaware
University of Delaware Sea Grant
Marine Communications Office
263 E. Main Street
Newark, DE 19716   302-831-8083

Florida
Florida Sea Grant
Building 803
University of Florida
Gainesville, FL 32611-0341   904-392-2802

Georgia
Georgia Sea Grant
Ecology Building
University of Georgia
Athens, GA 30602   404-542-7671

Hawaii
University of Hawaii
Sea Grant College Program
1000 Pope Road, MSB 200
Honolulu, HI 96822   808-956-7410

Illinois
Illinois-Indiana Sea Grant
University of Illinois
65 Mumford Hall
1301 W. Gregory Drive
Urbana, IL 61801   217-333-9448

Indiana
See Illinois

Louisiana
Louisiana Sea Grant
Center for Wetland Resources
Louisiana State University
Baton Rouge, LA 70803   504-388-6449

Maine
Maine Sea Grant Communications
30 Coburn Hall
University of Maine
Orono, ME 04469   207-581-1440

Marine Law Institute
University of Maine School of Law
246 Deering Avenue
Portland, ME 04102   207-780-4474

Maryland
Maryland Sea Grant
1123 Taliaferro Hall
University of Maryland
College Park, MD 20742   301-405-6371

National Sea Grant College Program
NOAA, SSMB-1/5206
1335 East-West Hwy.
Silver Spring, MD 20910   301-713-2431

Massachusetts
MIT Sea Grant
Building E-38, Room 300
Massachusetts Inst. of Technology
292 Main Street
Cambridge, MA 02139   617-253-7041

Sea Grant Program
Woods Hole Oceanographic Institution
Woods Hole, MA 02543   508-548-1400

Michigan
Michigan Sea Grant Publications
University of Michigan
2200 Bonisteel Blvd.
Ann Arbor, MI 48109-2099   313-764-1138

Minnesota
Minnesota Sea Grant
University of Minnesota
1518 Cleveland Ave. N, Room 302
St. Paul, MN 55108   612-625-9288

Mississippi
Mississippi-Alabama Sea Grant Consortium
P.O. Box 7000
Ocean Springs, MS 39564-7000   601-875-9341

New Hampshire
New Hampshire Sea Grant
Kingman Farm
University of New Hampshire
Durham, NH 03824   603-749-1565

New Jersey
Sea Grant Program
New Jersey Marine Sciences Consortium
Building No. 22
Fort Hancock, NJ 07732   908-872-1300

New York
New York Sea Grant Institute
Dutchess Hall Room 137
SUNY at Stony Brook
Stony Brook, NY 11794-5001   516-632-6905

North Carolina
North Carolina Sea Grant
North Carolina State University
Box 8605
Raleigh, NC 27695   919-515-2454

Ohio
Ohio Sea Grant
Ohio State University

1314 Kinnear Road
Columbus, OH 43212   614-292-8949

Oklahoma
Department of Chemistry
Attn. F. Schmitz
University of Oklahoma
620 Parrington Oval, Room 208
Norman, OK 73019   405-325-5581

Oregon
National Coastal Resources Research and
 Development Inst.
528 SW Mill, Suite 222
P.O. Box 751
Portland, OR 97207   503-725-5725

Oregon Sea Grant
Oregon State University
AdS 402
Corvallis, OR 97331-2134   503-737-2716

Publications Orders
Agricultural Communications
Oregon State University
AdS 422
Corvallis, OR 97331-2119   503-737-2513

Puerto Rico
Puerto Rico Sea Grant Program
Communications Office
RUM-UPR P.O. Box 5000
Mayaguez, PR 00709-5000   809-834-4726

Rhode Island
National Sea Grant Depository
Pell Library Building
Bay Campus
University of Rhode Island
Narragansett, RI 02882   401-792-6114

Rhode Island Sea Grant
Publications Unit
University of Rhode Island
Bay Campus
Narragansett, RI 02882-1197   401-792-6842

South Carolina
South Carolina Sea Grant Consortium
287 Meeting Street
Charleston, SC 29401   803-727-2078

Texas
Texas Sea Grant
Texas A&M-Galveston
P.O. Box 1675
Galveston, TX 77553-1675   409-762-9800

Virginia
Virginia Sea Grant
Madison House
University of Virginia
170 Rugby Road
Charlottesville, VA 22903   804-924-5965

Washington
Washington Sea Grant, HG-30
University of Washington
3716 Brooklyn Avenue, NE
Seattle, WA 98105   206-543-6600

Wisconsin
Sea Grant Institute
University of Wisconsin
1800 University Avenue
Madison, WI 53705   608-263-3259

* Marine Environmental Information
Pollution Response Branch
Marine Environmental Protection Division
Office of Marine Safety, Security,
 and Environmental Protection
U.S. Coast Guard
U.S. Department of Transportation
2100 2nd Street, SW
Room 2100   202-267-0518
Washington, DC 20593-0001   202-267-2611

This office responds to requests for marine environmental protection information from Congress and other federal agencies, state agencies, schools, industries, and the general public. Data is available on laws relating to the protection of the marine environment, incidents involving releases of oil or other hazardous substances, and federally funded spill response operations.

* Marine Fire and Rescue Technology
Library
Coast Guard Research and Development Center
U.S. Coast Guard
U.S. Department of Transportation
1082 Shennecossett Road
Groton, CT 06340-6096   203-441-2648

Marine research is conducted here in areas such as ice technology, navigation instrumentation technology, ocean dumping surveillance, pollution, search and rescue techniques, and marine fire and safety technology. This library is a good starting point for obtaining specific information about what research is done by the Center and for referrals to appropriate experts.

* Mariners Weather Log
National Oceanographic Data Center
National Oceanic and Atmospheric Administration
Universal North Building
Room 406
Washington, DC 20235   202-606-4561

The Mariners Weather Log is a unique source of information on marine weather and climate and their effects on operations at sea. Published quarterly by the National Oceanographic Data Center, the *Mariners Weather Log* provides comprehensive coverage of major storms of the North Atlantic and North Pacific, reports and annual summaries on tropical cyclones, information on the National Weather Service's Marine Observation Program, selected shipboard gale and wave observations, and general articles about weather and climate, hazards and safety precautions, and related marine lore. An annual subscription is available for $12 from the Superintendent of Documents, Government Printing Office, Washington, DC 20402; 202-512-1800.

* Navigation Regulations
Navigation Rules and Information Branch
Short-Range Aids to Navigation Division
Office of Navigation and Waterways Services
U.S. Coast Guard
U.S. Department of Transportation
2100 2nd Street, SW
Room 1416E
Washington, DC 20593-0001   202-267-0357

The Coast Guard establishes regulations for waterways safety that must be followed by U.S. vessels on the high seas and inland waters. These include rules on maneuvering and requirements for lights, sound signals, and radio telephones. For information on the rules, contact the above office or obtain a copy of *Navigation Rules, International and Inland,* available for $8.50 from the Superintendent of Documents, Government Printing Office, Washington, DC 20402; 202-512-1800. This rulebook is required by law to be carried on all vessels 39.4 feet or more in length.

* Pleasure Boating on the St. Lawrence Seaway
Public Affairs Office
Saint Lawrence Seaway Development Corporation
U.S. Department of Transportation
P.O. Box 520
Massena, NY 13662-0520   315-764-3261

The publication, *Pleasure Craft Guide: The Seaway,* provides you with information on boating in the St. Lawrence River. Contact this office to obtain your free copy.

Vacations and Business Travel

* Recreational Fishing

Public Affairs
National Marine Fisheries Service
National Oceanic and Atmospheric Administration
U.S. Department of Commerce
1335 East-West Highway, Room 9300
Silver Spring, MD 20910   301-713-2245

The National Marine Fisheries Service manages the country's stocks of saltwater fish and shellfish for both commercial and recreational interests. NMFS administers and enforces the Magnuson Fishery Conservation and Management Act to assure that fishing stays within sound biological limits, and that U.S. commercial and recreational fishermen have the opportunity to harvest all the available fish within these limits. Several hundred Fisheries Service scientists conduct research relating to these management responsibilities in science and research centers in 15 states and the District of Columbia. Many of these laboratories have evolved a major field of interest, and have special knowledge of the fish in their geographical area that leads to predictions of abundance, economic forecasts, and direct assistance to sport fishermen and commercial fishing businesses.

* Recreational Maps and Navigational Charts

TVA Maps and Surveys
Tennessee Valley Authority (TVA)
HB1A, 1101 Market Street
Chattanooga, TN 37402-2801   615-751-MAPS

Many recreational maps and navigational charts of TVA lakes are available to the public for a small fee. Detailed routes to shoreline recreation areas. The maps show water depths, the location of and detailed routes to the public recreation areas, boat docks, resorts, and roads. The navigational charts for the main lakes show navigation channels, buoys, lights, and other navigational aids, while maps for tributary lakes show the numbered signs TVA has installed at strategic locations on shore to aid fishermen and recreation boaters in locating their position. A map showing TVA dams and steam plants, including important facts about each of them, is available, along with cadastral and topographic maps, aerial photographs, and survey control data. Each request should specify the lake(s) of interest.

* National Recreation Survey

Recreation Resources Assistance Division
National Park Service
U.S. Department of the Interior
P.O. Box 37127
Washington, DC 20013-7127   202-343-3780

The *National Recreation Survey* provides current information on what Americans do for recreation in the outdoors and their expectations of recreational opportunities. The survey contains valuable market data on such topics as favorite activities, importance of recreation areas and their distance from home, characteristics of trips and outings, characteristics of respondents who spend money on outdoor recreation, and reasons for discontinuing a recreation activity. Various tables that relate to the National Park System and its participants are included. This publication is out of print. Selected sections may be available on an individual basis.

* Recreation on Public Lands

Office of Public Affairs
Bureau of Land Management
U.S. Department of the Interior
1849 C St., NW
Washington, DC 20240   202-208-5717

In recognition of the importance of outdoor recreation to Americans, *Recreation 2000 Executive Summary* sets forth the commitment of the Bureau of Land Management to the management of outdoor recreation resources in the public lands. The plan highlights the areas in which the Bureau intends to concentrate future efforts, such as visitor information, resource protection, land ownerships, partnerships, volunteers, tourism programs, facilities, and permits, fees, and concessions.

* Safety Information for Marine Dealers

Marine Dealer Visitation Program
Office of Navigation Safety and Waterway Services
U.S. Coast Guard
U.S. Department of Transportation
2100 2nd St., SW   800-368-5647
Washington, DC 20593-0001   202-267-0780 (in DC)

Through the Marine Dealer Visitation Program, boating equipment dealers can receive updates on regulations, information on Courtesy Marine Examinations, and

details about boating safety education courses. Participating dealers will be visited quarterly by a local Coast Guard Auxiliarist, be given a literature rack with boating brochures and pamphlets for customers, and will receive a "Cooperating Marine Dealer" decal for shop door or window. Marine dealers can participate by calling the Boating Safety Hotline listed above.

* Safety on Small Passenger Vessels

Marine Inspection Office
Your Local Coast Guard Office

Most small passenger vessels (less than 100 tons and carrying more than 6 people) are required to adhere to certain Coast Guard safety regulations. These include having a safety orientation procedure for passengers (announcement or placard), posting of emergency instructions, a life preserver for every person on board, and a Coast Guard safety certification. Marine Inspection Offices around the country issue the certificates. To find an Inspection Office near you, or to report a violation or complaint, call the Boating Safety Hotline 800-368-5647; or 202-267-0780 in DC.

* Scenic River Study

Recreation Program
Lands, River Basin Operations
Tennessee Valley Authority (TVA)
Norris, TN 37828   615-632-1606

The recreation staff completed a TVA river system evaluation, which identifies streams with recreation and aesthetic values, such as the French Broad River in western North Carolina, the eastern Tennessee River, and the Bear Creek streams in northern Alabama. This study also addresses one of the major problems which inhibits full enjoyment of these resources by Valley residents: a lack of easy access to the rivers. Contact this office for more information on this study and its findings.

* Swimming Areas and Aquatic Plants

Aquatic Biology Department
Resource Development
River Basin Operations
Water Resources
Tennessee Valley Authority (TVA)
311 Broad St.
Chattanooga, TN 37402-2801   615-751-0011

The Tennessee Valley Authority's (TVA) two major weapons for controlling the spread of pesky aquatic plants, such as Eurasian watermilfoil, spiney-leaf naiad, and hydrilla in its reservoirs, is the winter and summer draw downs and the selective spraying of herbicides. Reservoir levels may be lowered several feet in the late summer to dry out and kill the roots of these plants embedded in shallow areas of the reservoirs; while at other times, lake levels may be held higher than normal to prevent sunshine from penetrating to the bottom and thus prevent germination and growth of new colonies. Selective use of approved herbicides in high priority use areas, such as swimming beaches, developed shoreline, and marinas, is another effective control method. Several experimental control strategies also are being tested on TVA lakes. One of the most promising is a cooperative effort between TVA and the U.S. Army Corps of Engineers. TVA proposes to conduct large scale demonstrations on Guntersville reservoir on the use of Grass Carp, hydrilla fly, a fungus to control watermilfoil, and other methods being currently tested on a smaller scale by the Corps Waterways Experiment Station.

* Toll-Free Help for Boaters

Boating Safety Hotline
Consumer and Regulatory Affairs Branch (G-NAB-5)
Auxiliary, Boating, and Consumer Affairs Division
Office of Navigation Safety and Waterways Services
U.S. Coast Guard
U.S. Department of Transportation
2100 2nd Street, SW, Room 1109   800-368-5647
Washington, DC 20593-0001   202-267-0780 (in DC)

This service is toll-free throughout the U.S., including Alaska, Hawaii, Puerto Rico, and the Virgin Islands. Staff can provide you with information on such topics of interest to boaters as safety recalls, publications, Coast Guard department contacts and addresses, public education courses, and free Coast Guard services. If hotline operators cannot answer your question directly, you'll get a call back from someone who can. Ask for a consumer information packet, and you'll receive a group of publications and consumer *Fact Sheets* on topics like safe boating, getting help on the water, floatation devices, federal regulations, sanitation devices, and sources of boating education. The *Boater's Source Directory*, included in the packet, is a guide to a wide variety of federal, state, private, and non-profit agencies that provide literature, technical information, free services, and other assistance to recreational boaters. Among the freebies you can request is the *Water 'N Kids* coloring book for 4-8 year olds, which explains basic concepts of water safety. The hotline also takes consumer complaints about safety defects and violations. Operators answer between 8 a.m. and 4 p.m. Eastern Time, and an answering machine takes messages after hours.

* Updates for Mariners

Local Notice to Mariners
District Commander
Your local Coast Guard Office   800-368-5647

The free *Local Notice to Mariners* is issued weekly by each Coast Guard District. Intended for small craft owners, it advises you of changes in the status of aids to navigation (buoys, radiobeacons, etc.); chart updates; drawbridge operations; and safety warnings for particular areas. This *Local Notice* often includes temporary changes not included in the Defense Mapping Agency's *Notice to Mariners*. To order a subscription for the *Local Notice*, send a written request to the District Commander of your local Coast Guard office. For referral to the correct address, call the Boating Safety Hotine 800-368-5647; or 202-267-0780 in DC.

* Water Recreation Areas

U.S. Army Corps of Engineers
Directorate of Civil Works
Natural Resources Management Branch, CECW-ON

20 Massachusetts Ave., NW
Washington, DC 20314-1000   202-761-0660

The Corps has a brochure and map showing the extensive recreational facilities available at U.S. Army Corps of Engineers lakes throughout the country. They offer camp sites, picnic areas, swimming beaches, hiking trails, boating, canoeing, fishing, ice fishing, hunting, and snowmobiling. The Corps also offers safety training classes in water-related sports. To arrange for a speaker to come to your school, call or write the office above. To order the brochure entitled *Lakeside Recreation*, write or call OCE Publication Depot, 2803 52nd Ave., Hyattsville, MD 20781-1102; 301-394-0081.

* Wild Rivers and Other Public Lands

Office of Public Affairs
Bureau of Land Management (BLM)
U.S. Department of the Interior
1849 C St., NW
Washington, DC 20240   202-208-5717

The *Recreation Guide to BLM Public Lands* features a map outlining all of the public lands used as recreational areas. Designations on the map include campgrounds, visitors centers, national wild and scenic rivers, national wilderness areas, and national historic and scenic trails. Also included are the states that contain public lands, and state and district offices to contact for additional information. Alaska, Arizona, California, Colorado, Idaho, Montana, Nevada, New Mexico, Oregon, Utah, Washington, and Wyoming are the key states described.

International Travel

* American Experts Overseas Lecture Tour

Office of Program Coordination and Development
United States Information Agency (USIA)
301 Fourth St., SW, Room 550
Washington, DC 20547　　　　　　　　202-619-4764

U.S. Speakers are experts in a field--usually economics, international affairs, literature, the arts, U.S. political and social processes, sports, science, or technology--sent abroad by the United States Information Agency (USIA) to meet with groups or individual professional counterparts. Recruited on the basis of requests of USIA staff in other countries, U.S. Speakers often engage in informal lecture/discussions with small groups, grant media interviews, or speak before larger audiences. Those interested in the U.S. Speakers program are invited to submit a brief letter indicating times of availability, along with a curriculum vitae and at least two lecture topics with brief talking points. A free brochure on the program is available from this office.

* Animals and Plants Quarantine

APHIS
U.S. Department of Agriculture
Room G-110 Federal Building
6505 Belcrest Rd.
Hyattsville, MD 20782　　　　　　　　301-436-7799

This office will advise travelers about what agriculture and related products may be brought into the U.S. from foreign countries.

* Arctic and Antarctic Polar Expeditions with Civilians

Ice Operations Division
Office of Navigation Safety and Waterways Services
U.S. Coast Guard
U.S. Department of Transportation
2100 2nd St., SW, Room 1202 A
Washington, DC 20593-0001　　　　　　202-267-1450

The Coast Guard furnishes vessels to other agencies, such as the National Science Foundation, U.S. Geological Survey, and the Navy, to conduct research and ice operations in Arctic and Antarctic waters. The agencies sponsoring the missions select scientists, researchers, students, and in some cases, journalists, photographers, and artists to accompany the mission when space is available. This office is a good starting point for obtaining information on the pertinence of a mission to your field, to be directed to the appropriate agency sponsors, and for information about the data collected during missions.

* Binational Libraries and Cultural Centers Worldwide

Library Programs Division
Bureau of Educational and Cultural Affairs
United States Information Agency (USIA)
301 Fourth St., SW, Room 314
Washington, DC 20547　　　　　　　　202-619-4915

The United States Information Agency (USIA) maintains or supports 156 libraries and reading rooms in 95 countries, as well as library programs at 111 binational centers in 24 countries. Collections focus on fostering foreign understanding of U.S. people, history, and culture. A bi-weekly bibliography, listing 80-100 titles on international relations and developments in the U.S., is one of many library services provided for the overseas posts, including reference and research assistance.

* Booklets for Travelers

Government Printing Office
Superintendent of Documents
Washington, DC 20402　　　　　　　　202-512-1800

The U.S. Department of State offers several brochures and pamphlets regarding traveling abroad. ($1 each):

A Safe Trip Abroad. Provides suggestions for avoiding and coping with potential problems and crises abroad.

Tips for Americans Residing Abroad. Includes basic travel information and suggestions, as well as health, insurance, and assistance information of interest to senior citizens traveling abroad.

Your Trip Abroad. Provides basic information on such matters as passport applications, visas, and other documents; obtaining services and help overseas from U.S. consuls; and foreign legal requirements.

Tips for Travelers to the Caribbean.
Tips for Travelers to the People's Republic of China.
Tips for Travelers to Eastern Europe and Yugoslavia.
Tips for Travelers to Russia.
Tips for Travelers to Sub-Saharan Africa.
Tips for Travelers to the Middle East and North Africa.
Tips for Travelers to Mexico.
Tips for Travelers to Central and South America.

* Certification for Travel Abroad

Authentications
Foreign Affairs Center
Bureau of Administration
U.S. Department of State
2400 M Street, NW, Room 101
Washington, DC 20520　　　　　　　　202-647-5002
Executive Office　　　　　　　　　　　202-647-9415

Several steps are necessary in order to get a document authenticated for a use by a foreign government. For legal papers to do business in a foreign government (such as a power of attorney), the papers must be notarized, signed by the Clerk of Court, and then sent to the Secretary of State for the State seal. This Office authenticates the State seal, verifying that it is a legal document. Foreign governments often require that any legal document, whether personal, educational or business related, be authenticated. This includes birth certificates, marriage licenses, divorce papers, or school transcripts.

* CIA World and Country Maps

National Technical Information Service (NTIS)
U.S. Department of Commerce
5285 Port Royal Road
Springfield, VA 22161　　　　　　　　703-487-4650

Hundreds of maps generated by the Central Intelligence Agency are sold through the National Technical Information Service (NTIS). There are country maps as well as maps of continents are available. smaller geographical areas and city maps such as Moscow and Vicinity; Middle East Area Oilfields and Facilities; Israeli Settlement in the Gaza Strip; South Africa: Industrial Activity and Production; Africa Ethnolinguistic Groups; and street maps for Moscow, Shanghai and many other cities.

* Citizens Arrested Overseas

Citizens Emergency Center
Overseas Citizens Service
Bureau of Consular Affairs
2201 C St., NW, Room 4800
Washington, DC 20520　　　　　　　　202-647-5225

The Citizens Emergency Center monitors the cases of Americans arrested abroad and acts as a liaison between the prisoner's family and consular officers overseas. A consular officer visits the American as soon as possible, provides information regarding the foreign legal system and a list of attorneys, and offers other assistance such as contacting family or friends. The consular officer's role in arrest cases is one of observation and support, regularly visiting the prisoner and checking his or her welfare, monitoring human rights, and the status of the case. The Center assists in transferring of funds, and when a prisoner's health or life is endangered by inadequate diet or medical care provided by the local prison, dietary food supplements and/or medical care may be arranged through a U.S. Government loan authorized under the Emergency Medical and Dietary Assistance Program.

* Citizens Emergency Center

Overseas Citizens Service
Bureau of Consular Affairs
2201 C St., NW, Room 4800
Washington, DC 20520   202-647-5225

This center provides assistance to and protects the welfare of U.S. citizens abroad in the following Ways:

Arrests - See "Citizens Arrested Overseas"

Financial Assistance - Assists Americans overseas who find themselves in financial trouble. They first attempt to locate private sources of funds from family or friends, and then assist with the transfer of funds to the individual. If none can be found, the Center will approve a repatriation loan which will pay for the individual's direct return to the nearest port of entry in the U.S.

Medical Assistance - Assists with handling the problems of Americans who become physically or mentally ill while traveling or living abroad. Locates and notifies family or friends, and transmits private funds. When necessary they will assist in the return of the ill or injured person to the U.S. with appropriate medical escort. Full expenses must be borne by citizen.

Deaths - The consular officer reports the death of a U.S. citizen to the next of kin, and will assist in making arrangements for local burial or for return of the body to the U.S. Cost must be borne by family members.

Welfare/Whereabouts - The Center relays the request for assistance and all pertinent data available on the individual to the U.S. Embassy or consulate responsible for the area where the individual is believed to be traveling or residing, and the consular officer then attempts to locate these individuals. In cases of disasters such as earthquakes, or plane crashes, the Center ascertains the names of U.S. citizens involved and informs their families.

Travel Advisories - The Center gives advice to the public and U.S. Foreign Service posts on the advisability of travel to certain countries or areas.

Search and Rescue - The Center monitors the search and rescue efforts outside the U.S., such as attempting to locate missing planes or boats that might be carrying Americans.

* Commercial Library Program Publications List

Library
U.S. Department of State
2201 C St., NW, Room 3239
Washington, DC 20520   202-647-1062

This list provides a wide-ranging selection of publications useful to commercial reference facilities. It contains annotated bibliographies of directories, buyers' guides, yearbooks, atlases, etc., in general and in special product areas. State manufacturing and industrial directories are included, as are telex directories.

* Country and Territory Info Pamphlets

Superintendent of Documents
Government Printing Office
Washington, DC 20402   202-512-1800

Background Notes, a series of short, factual pamphlets about various countries and territories of the world, plus selected international organizations, contain up-to-date information on each country's people, culture, geography, history, government, political conditions, economy, defense, and foreign relations with other countries, including the United States. A reading list provides additional sources of information about the country, and travel notes, maps, and occasional photographs are often included. A complete set can be purchased from the Government Printing Office for $63.

* Cruise the Panama Canal

The Panama Canal Commission
1825 I St., NW
Washington, DC 20006   202-634-6441

Office of Public Affairs
Panama Canal Commission
Unit 2300, APOAA 34011   800-622-2625, ext. 52-5463

Information on cruises of the Panama Canal is available through the above offices. At the Panama Canal you don't have to leave the ship to see the sights. Passengers can watch as their northbound cruise ship enters Pedro Miguel Locks on a northbound transit. In the distance they can see Gaillard Cut where the Canal passes through the Continental Divide. For more information, contact either of the above offices.

* Customs Information for Travelers

Public Information Office
U.S. Customs Service
U.S. Department of the Treasury
P.O. Box 7407
Washington, DC 20044   202-927-6724

Know Before You Go contains Customs hints for residents returning to the U.S. from abroad. Topics include declaration of articles acquired abroad, Customs exemptions, gifts, dutiable articles and those free of duty, rates of duty, prohibited and restricted articles, and other pointers. Publication Number 512.

* Customs Rules for Government Personnel: Civilian and Military

Public Information Office
U.S. Customs Service
U.S. Department of the Treasury
P.O. Box 7407
Washington, DC 20044   202-927-6724

The free leaflet, *U.S. Customs Highlights for Government Personnel*, provides customs information for civilian employees and military personnel of the U.S. Government when returning to the States with personal and household effects after an extended tour of duty abroad and when returning on leave or TDY. Subjects include customs declarations and limitations, gifts, automobiles, and prohibited and restricted importations. Publication Number 518.

* Guide for Private Flyers

Smuggling Investigations Division
Office of Enforcement Regulations
U.S. Customs Service
U.S. Department of the Treasury
1301 Constitution Ave., NW
Washington, DC 20229   202-927-0650

Private, corporate, and charter pilots on business or pleasure flights to and from foreign countries should become acquainted with the booklet, *Guide for Private Flyers*, available from the Public Information Office, U.S. Customs Service, P.O. Box 7407, Washington, DC 20044. It sets forth basic Customs requirements, provides a list of airports at which Customs processing may be obtained, and explains overtime charges. Publication Number 513.

* Pocket Hints for Visitors

Information Services Division
Office of Logistics Management
U.S. Customs Service
U.S. Department of the Treasury
1301 Constitution Ave., NW
Washington, DC 20229   202-927-5980

The free flyer, *Pocket Hints for Visitors*, briefly describes the customs regulations for foreign visitors to the United States. Personal exemptions and a list of items that must meet certain requirements are featured. For further information on customs requirements for foreign visitors, the free pamphlet, *Customs Hints for Visitors*, is also helpful in outlining declarations, exemptions, gifts, duty, and prohibited and restricted articles. To obtain a copies of these publications, write to Public Information Office, U.S. Customs Service, P.O. Box 7407, Washington, DC 20044. Publication Number 521.

* Executive-Diplomat Seminars

Office of Public Programs
U.S. Department of State
Bureau of Public Affairs
2201 C St., NW, Room 5831
Washington, DC 20520-6810   202-647-1433

The State Department holds seminars designed for corporate vice-presidents who do business abroad. These two day seminars, offered twice yearly, begin with a discussion of global foreign policy objectives, and then focus on economic topics and business opportunities. Contact this office for information on scheduling.

Be patient. If any phone number is incorrect, call (area code) 555-1212 and request the new listing.

405

Vacations and Business Travel

* Importing of Articles from Developing Countries

Public Information Office
U.S. Customs Service
U.S. Department of the Treasury
P.O. Box 7407
Washington, DC 20044   202-927-6724

Generalized System of Preferences (GSP) is a system used by many developed countries to help developing nations improve their financial or economic condition through export trade. It provides for the duty-free importation of a wide range of products from certain countries which would otherwise be subject to customs duty. The free pamphlet, *GSP and the Traveler*, lists popular tourist items eligible for duty-free treatment under GSP and the beneficiary countries. Publication Number 515.

* Importing Pleasure Boats

Carrier Rulings Branch
Office of Regulations and Rulings
U.S. Customs Service
U.S. Department of the Treasury
Franklin Court
1099 14th Street NW
Washington, DC 20005   202-482-6940

When a pleasure boat or yacht arrives in the United States, the first landing must be at a Customs port or designated place where Customs service is available. The pamphlet, *Pleasure Boats*, explains the Customs formalities involving pleasure boats to help you plan your importation and reporting requirements, overtime charges, and provides other information relating strictly to pleasure boats. You can get a copy of *Pleasure Boats* from the Public Information Office, U.S. Customs Service, P.O. Box 7407, Washington, DC 20044. Publication Number 544.

* Overseas Citizens Services

U.S. Department of State
2201 C Street, NW
Room 4800   Non-Emergency 202-647-3444
Washington, DC 20520   Emergency 202-647-5225

Overseas Citizens Services is responsible for administering laws, formulating regulations, and implementing policies relating to the broad range of consular services provided to U.S. citizens abroad. These services include providing assistance to and protecting the welfare of U.S. citizens abroad, overseeing the payment of Federal benefits overseas, documenting U.S. citizens born abroad, and making determinations concerning acquisition and nationality abroad. Overseas Citizens Services serves as a liaison between concerned family members, friends, and members of Congress in the United States and consular posts and citizens abroad.

* Overseas Security Advisory Council (OSAC)

Bureau of Diplomatic Security
DA/OSAC
U.S. Department of State
Washington, DC 20522-1003   202-663-0533

Overseas Security Advisory Council (OSAC) was established to promote security for American business interests abroad. In 1987, OSAC was extended overseas through the establishment of "mini-councils" in some of the world's most important business centers. Business representatives in these areas meet locally with Diplomatic Security Officers to promote security for Americans and American interests. Besides regular meetings to plan and exchange information, OSAC also produced a number of well-received publications, such as Security Guidelines for American Families Living Abroad and distributed the Diplomatic Security-produced children's security video, Are You A-OK. OSAC also sends threat advisories and general security information to more than 1,400 companies, and is now providing this information through a computer information database.

* Panama Canal Tours

Orientation Services
The Office of Public Affairs
c/o Panama Canal Commission
Unit 2300
APOAA 34011   800-622-2625, ext. 52-5463

The Canal Guide Service, operated by the Panama Canal Commission, offers free tours of the Panama Canal to the public. Tours are given seven days a week from 9:00 a.m. to 5:00 p.m. The tour takes less than an hour and include a slight briefing, a topographical model of the Canal to view, and a film. Visitors are welcome at the Miraflores Locks on the Pacific side of the Isthmus where a pavilion provides a vantage point for viewing transiting ships. Interested members of the public should call two days in advance to make a reservation. Another attraction is the high doomed ceiling, the dramatic murals, and the marble columns and floor make the rotunda the main attraction of the Administration Building at Balboa Heights. The murals depict the digging of Gaillard Cut at Gold Hill, the erection of a lock gate, and the construction of the Gatun Dam spillway and Miraflores Locks. For more information, contact this office. The history of the Panama Railroad has been closely linked with that of the Panama Canal since long before the waterway was opened to traffic. The first railroad built through the tropical jungles of the New World served for almost 60 years as the only means of transportation across the narrow Isthmus of Panama. Before the Canal was opened in 1914, the Panama Railroad was reported to have the heaviest traffic per mile of all the railroads in the world. The railroad makes five trips per day across the Isthmus, Monday through Friday, and three trips per day on Saturday and Sunday. The train takes an hour and a half to cross the Isthmus. For more information, contact this office.

* Passport Agent's Manual

Passport Services
Bureau of Consular Affairs
U.S. Department of State
2201 C Street, NW, Room 5813
Washington, DC 20520   202-647-6633

The material in this manual is furnished for the passport agent's guidance and is intended to cover the most frequently encountered situations. It has information on evidence of citizenship, names allowed on passports, evidence of identity, and application procedures. A list of travel-related forms and brochures is also included. This publication is not available to the general public. It is available only to passport agents.

* Passport Information

Passport Services
Bureau of Consular Affairs
U.S. Department of State
2201 C Street, NW, Room 5813
Washington, DC 20520   202-647-0518

Passport Services provides a recorded message at 202-647-0518 which explains the documents you need and application process for obtaining a passport, as well as reporting the loss or theft of your passport. It also explains how you can obtain a copy of the report of a birth or death of a U.S. citizen abroad. The message will direct you to the proper agencies for information regarding naturalization, travel advisories, customs regulations, and shots required by various countries.

* Passport Offices Throughout America

You may apply for a passport at any passport agency and at many Clerks of Court Offices or Post Offices designated to accept passport applications. The regional offices are as follows:

Boston
Thomas P. O'Neill Federal Building, 10 Causeway Street, Suite 247, Boston, MA 02202-1094; 617-565-6990.

Chicago
Kluczynski Office Building, 230 S. Dearborn St., Room 380, Chicago, IL 60604-1564; 312-353-7155.

Honolulu
New Federal Building, 300 Ala Moana Blvd., Room C-106, Honolulu, HI 96850-0001; 808-541-1918.

Houston
Mickey Leland Federal Building, 1919 Smith Street, Suite 1100, Houston, TX 77002-8049; 713-653-3153.

Los Angeles
Federal Bldg., 11000 Wilshire Blvd., Suite 13100, Los Angeles, CA 90024-3615; 310-575-7070.

Miami
Claude Pepper Federal Office Building, 51 Southwest 1st Ave., 3rd Floor, Miami, FL 33130-1680; 305-536-4681.

New Orleans
701 Loyal Ave., Postal Services Bldg., T-12005, New Orleans, LA 70113-1931; 504-589-6728/6729/6161/6162/6163.

New York
Rockefeller Center, International Bldg., 630 5th Ave., Room 270, New York, NY 10111-0031; 212-399-5290.

Philadelphia
Federal Building, 600 Arch St., Room 4426, Philadelphia, PA 19106-1685; 215-597-7480.

San Francisco
Tishman Speyer Building, 525 Market St., Room 200, San Francisco, CA 94105-2773; 415-744-4019/4020 or 415-744-4444 (recording).

Seattle
Federal Building, 915 2nd Ave., Room 992, Seattle, WA 98174-1091; 206-220-7777/7788.

Stamford
One Landmark Square, Broad and Atlantic Sts., Stamford, CT 06901-2767; 203-325-3538/3539/3530/4401 (recording).

Washington, DC
Room G62, 1425 K St., NW, Room 214, Washington, DC 20522-1705; 202-326-6060 or 202-647-0518 (recording). This office will relocate September, 1994.

* Pet and Wildlife Importation

Public Information Office
U.S. Customs Service
U.S. Department of the Treasury
P.O. Box 7407
Washington, DC 20044   202-927-6724

The Public Health Service, U.S. Department of Agriculture, U.S. Fish and Wildlife Service, and the U.S. Department of the Treasury have combined efforts to describe the regulations on the importing of pets and wildlife into the United States. Pets, particularly dogs, cats, and turtles, brought into this country must be examined for possible evidence of disease that can be transmitted to humans. Certain animals are prohibited from entry that have been exposed to foot and mouth disease. Endangered species, both plant and animal, may not be imported without special permits. *Pets, Wildlife* explains these regulations in further detail. Publication Number 509.

* Returning U.S. Residents and Customs

Public Information Office
U.S. Customs Service
U.S. Department of the Treasury
P.O. Box 7407
Washington, DC 20044   202-927-6724

Pocket Hints is a brief outline of customs responsibilities of returning residents. Duty free exemptions, restricted or prohibited articles, and customs declarations are summarized. Publication Number 506.

* Security Guidelines for American Enterprises

Bureau of Diplomatic Security
Overseas Security Advisory Council (OSAC)
U.S. Department of State
Washington, DC 20522-1003   202-663-0533

This publication provides security guidelines for American private sector and personnel abroad. This publication is printed and distributed by the State Department. The implementation of security guidelines contained in this publication could reduce the vulnerability of American private sector enterprises abroad to criminal or terrorist acts, and emphasize site selection and operational security. Previous publications include *Crisis Management Guidelines* and *Security Guidelines for American Families Living Abroad.*

* Terrorism and Diplomatic Security

Public Information
Bureau of Diplomatic Security
DS/SA
U.S. Department of State
2121 Virginia Ave., NW, SA-10
Washington, DC 20520   703-204-6212

The Bureau of Diplomatic Security was created in 1985 in an effort to deal with terrorist attacks against overseas missions. All but the smallest of American overseas missions have a Regional Security Officer (RSO) on staff to manage security and keep employees safe on the job and at home. The bureau is responsible for the physical security of the mission, as well as construction and information security. Diplomatic Security Analysts study and analyze intelligence information from a variety of sources, including specific terrorist groups to better understand their tactics and anticipate their actions. They have also developed security awareness materials for the American tourist, business traveler, and Foreign Service family. DS has produced educational videotapes and instructional materials that teach the basics of security to Americans living and working abroad. Other videos focus on professional conduct in foreign cultures. The pamphlet, *Countering Terrorism*, lists several suggestions for security measures for your home, family, and business, as well as what to do in the event of a kidnapping.

* Travel Advisories on Civil Unrest Around-the-World

Citizens Emergency Center (CEC)
Overseas Citizens Services
U.S. Department of State
2201 C Street, NW, Room 4800
Washington, DC 20520   202-647-5225

CEC is responsible for issuing travel warnings when events abroad are likely to adversely affect traveling Americans. Travel warnings often concern international conflict, civil unrest within individual countries, natural disasters, or disease outbreaks. Many of the warnings refer to temporary conditions and are cancelled when the problem no longer poses a threat to travelers.

* Travel Tips for Senior Citizens

Overseas Citizens Services
U.S. Department of State
2201 C Street, NW, Room 4800
Washington, DC 20520   202-647-5226

This publication includes information on insurance, medication, travel advisories, and passports. They include a list of relevant publications, some practical travel tips, as well as the assistance you can expect from U.S. Embassies and consulates. Contact the Government Printing Office for this publication at 202-512-1800.

* Vessel Owners and Masters: Customs Rules

Public Information Office
U.S. Customs Service
U.S. Department of the Treasury
P.O. Box 7407
Washington, DC 20044   202-927-6724

Masters or vessel owners may incur penalties for violations of United States Customs laws, including violations committed by members of their crews. The brochure, *Notice to Masters of Vessels*, notifies the masters of proper precautions in the areas of arrival and entry, and merchandise in order to avoid penalties for violations. Publication Number 581.

* Visa Information for U.S. Citizens Wishing to Travel to Foreign Countries

Overseas Citizens Services
U.S. Department of State
2201 C St., NW, Room 4800
Washington, DC 20520   202-647-5225

This office can provide you with visa requirements for U.S. citizens wishing to travel to foreign countries. They stress that this information is subject to change and that the definitive information regarding visas can come only from the foreign embassies. This taped message lists all the countries, their current visa requirements, travel advisories for the countries, as well as the embassies' phone numbers.

* Visiting and Living Abroad

Office of Citizens Consular Services
Bureau of Consular Affairs
U.S. Department of State
2201 C St., NW, Room 4817
Washington, DC 20520   202-647-3444

This office provides services to U.S. citizens abroad in a variety of ways:

Acquisition and Loss of Citizenship: Determination of an individual's citizenship status is a function of the office if the person is not in the United States.

Passport and Registration Services Abroad: Issues passports, as well as Cards of Identity and Registration as proof of U.S. citizenship. This office officially records a person's U.S. citizenship and/or makes his/her residence a matter of record.

Vacations and Business Travel

Consular Report of Birth: This official record is considered a basic citizenship document setting forth detailed information regarding the facts of birth and parentage, as basis for child's claim to citizenship.

Child Custody Disputes: Helps parents locate children abroad, monitors their welfare upon request, and provides general information about child custody laws and procedures.

Federal Benefits: Assists in processing claims and distributing checks.

International Adoption: Provides general information on adoptions, makes inquiries regarding status of cases, and assists in clarifying documentary requirements.

Judicial Services: Provides advice on the assistance which consular officers can render to U.S. citizens overseas engaged in private legal suits and maintains lists of attorneys. They also administer notarial and authentication functions.

Estates and Property Claims: Consular Officer has statutory responsibility for the personal estates of U.S. citizens who die abroad if the deceased has no legal representative in the country where the death occurred. The Office gives general information regarding property claims and provides a list of attorneys.

Selective Service Registration: Registers people for selective service.

Shipping and Seamen: This office has statutory responsibility to protect the interests of American seamen, vessels, and shipping firms abroad.

Voting: Provides non-partisan voting information and assists in requesting absentee ballots.

Be patient. If any phone number is incorrect, call (area code) 555-1212 and request the new listing.

Domestic Tourism and Trends

* Airline Passenger Safety

Community and Consumer Liaison Division
Office of Public Affairs
Federal Aviation Administration
U.S. Department of Transportation
800 Independence Ave., SW
Washington, DC 20591   202-267-3481

Airline passengers who have inquiries or complaints regarding airplane safety should contact this office. The FAA Consumer Hotline (800-FAA-SURE) can also provide assistance.

* Air Travelers' Rights and Complaints

Consumer Affairs Division, I-25
Intergovernmental and Consumer Affairs
Governmental Affairs
Office of the Secretary of Transportation
U.S. Department of Transportation
400 7th Street, SW
Washington, DC 20590-0001   202-366-2220

If your problem cannot be resolved directly with the airline, contact this office for information on air travelers' rights and for assistance in resolving problems with airlines and charter flights. Complaints about delayed or canceled flights, reservations, lost baggage, smoking, refunds, and overbooking can also be handled here.

* AMTRAK Passenger Services

AMTRAK
60 Massachusetts Ave., N.E.
Washington, DC 20002   202-906-2733

The Passenger Services Department handles all of the onboard service aspects of AMTRAK, including all of its employees across the country.

* AMTRAK Customer Relations

AMTRAK
Customer Relations
60 Massachusetts Ave. N.E.
Washington, DC 20002   202-906-2121

You may call or write the Customer Relations Office concerning any comments or problems with AMTRAK service. Please include your ticket receipt and dates of travel to help with the resolution of your problem.

* Auto Safety Hotline

Office of Defects Investigation (NEF-10)
National Highway Traffic Safety Administration
U.S. Department of Transportation
400 7th Street, SW, Room 5319   Recording: 202-366-0123
Washington, DC 20590-0001   Recording: 800-424-9393

This toll-free hotline is accessible in all 50 states, Puerto Rico, and the Virgin Islands. Consumers may call to report automobile safety problems or to request information on recalls, defects, investigations, child safety seats, tires, drunk driving, crash test results, seat belts, air bags, odometer tampering, and other related topics. Staff will also make referrals to state and other agencies. Also ask about the New Car Assessment Program (NCAP), which provides comparable data on the frontal crashworthiness of selected new vehicles.

* World Tourism in the Millennium

U.S. Travel and Tourism Administration (USTTA)
U.S. Department of Commerce
Office of Policy and Planning
Room 1510
Washington, DC 20230   202-482-4752

World Tourism in the Millennium: A handbook for executives and scholars dealing with international tourism as it relates to commercial and economic activity, political and foreign policy implications, socio-cultural and environmental aspects and implications through the year 2000. Available free from USTTA, Office of Research. (1993, 97 pages).

* Handicapped Visitors

Office of Research
United States Travel and Tourism Administration
U.S. Department of Commerce
14th St. and Constitution Ave., NW
Room 1868
Washington DC 20230   202-482-4028

The United States Welcomes Handicapped Visitors is a publication designed to give advice and guidance to handicapped visitors wishing to travel to and within the United States. It explains Federal regulations and policies of the various modes of transportation, as well as offering information regarding destinations, resources, publications, organizations, and some practical advice. Contact this office for your free copy.

* Multilingual Receptionists

United States Travel and Tourism Administration (USTTA)
Office for Tourism Marketing
U.S. Department of Commerce
14th St. and Constitution Ave., NW
Room 1860
Washington, DC 20230   202-482-1904

To ensure that international visitors enter the U.S. with minimal difficulty, USTTA sponsors a uniformed corps of multilingual receptionists at 12 gateway airports who provide interpreter and allied services required for U.S. entry formalities. International gateways offering this service include New York (Kennedy); Seattle; San Juan; Philadelphia; Miami; Boston; Los Angeles; Honolulu; Bangor; Atlanta; New Orleans and Baltimore-Washington International.

* Rail Tickets or Travel Information

AMTRAK
60 Massachusetts Ave., N.E.
Washington, DC 20002   1-800-USA-RAIL

For information regarding tickets or travel on AMTRAK, call 1-800-USA-RAIL. AMTRAK also publishes a travel planner which provides travel tips and services, as well as a listing AMTRAK's vacation packages.

* Tourism Planning and Development in the U.S.A.

United States Travel and Tourism Administration
Office for Tourism Marketing
U.S. Department of Commerce
14th St. and Constitution Ave. NW
Room 1860
Washington, DC 20230   202-482-1904

Tourism USA is a book produced as an aid to communities interested in initiating or developing tourism as a part of their economic development plan, and has been revised and expanded to also include international marketing and visitor services for special populations. Statistical data has been revised to reflect the most current facts available. This publication covers guidelines for tourism development, including appraising tourism potential, planning for tourism, assessing product and market, marketing tourism, visitor services, and sources of assistance. The first book is free; additional copies are $5 each.

* Tourism Offices

United States Travel and Tourism Administration
Office of Tourism Marketing
U.S. Department of Commerce
14th St. and Constitution Ave., NW

Vacations and Business Travel

Room 1860
Washington, DC 20230   202-482-1904
This publication contains a complete listing of addresses and phone numbers for all state and territorial tourism offices. Contact the office listed above for your free copy.

* Tourism Revenue

Office for Tourism Marketing
United States Travel and Tourism Administration (USTTA)
U.S. Department of Commerce
14th St. And Constitution Ave. NW
Room 1860
Washington, DC 20230   202-482-1904
This office's goal is to increase the U.S. share of international visitors. This is accomplished through several means, one of which is cooperative marketing and advertising overseas. This office often puts together special advertising sections designed for foreign countries. A free publication, *Marketing U.S. Tourism Abroad: A Manual of Cooperative Marketing Programs In USTTA Markets,* lists cooperative advertising opportunities, travel shows, seminars, and travel missions. The *Manual* includes costs, formats, and deadlines. This Office also assists State and local travel organizations, and private industry around issues such as marketing tourism and visitor services.

* Travel Industry Market Research

Office of Research
United States Travel and Tourism Administration (USTTA)
U.S. Department of Commerce
14th St. and Constitution Ave., NW
Room 1868
Washington, DC 20230   202-482-4028
USTTA gathers, analyzes and published international travel statistics, which define the direction and impact of foreign trends, determine foreign market potential, and guide marketing efforts. USTTA's *Inflight Survey* gathers essential marketing information on international travelers to and within the United States, as well as Americans traveling abroad. Conducted with public and private sector tourism organizations and 35 major international air carriers, the *Survey* provides data on travel patterns and preference of foreign visitors. The *Bibliography of Selected USTTA Research Publications and Marketing Manuals* is available at no charge, and includes a description and ordering information for the following USTTA publications:

Recap of International Travel To and From the United States. Summarizes annual developments in inbound/outbound tourism (free).
Summary and Analysis of International Travel to the United States. Provides monthly foreign visitor arrival statistics by region and for 90 different countries. Tables include a variety of travel data (price varies depending on year).
Outlook for International Travel To and From the United States. Provides one-year forecast of international travel to/from the U.S. (free).
Canadian Travel to the United States: 1992. Details Canadian tourism to the U.S. (free).
Impact of Foreign Visitors' Spending on State Economies 1985-1986. (free)
In-Flight Survey of International Air Travelers. Overseas and Mexican Visitors to the United States and (2) *U.S. Travelers to Mexico and Overseas Countries.* Provides survey data on travel characteristics and spending patterns of international air travelers to and from the U.S. Free inbound and outbound profile sheets are available, along with an informational brochure and order form (prices range from $100 to $1000).
Analysis of International Air Travel To and From the United States on U.S./Foreign Flag Carriers (free).
Pleasure Travel Markets to North America. The studies of travel behavior provide information on past travel characteristics, trip planning information, attitudes toward overseas travel, the image of the U.S., and travel market segments. An information packet and free *Highlights* publication for each years study is available (prices range from $25 to $1000).
Marketing Tourism Abroad: USTTA's International Cooperative Marketing Manual. Provides information concerning the cooperative marketing programs offered by USTTA (free).
The United States Welcomes Handicapped Visitors- Designed to give advice and guidance to handicapped visitors wishing to travel to and within the United States (free).

* Traveling to the United States

Tourism Marketing
United States Travel and Tourism Administration (USTTA)
U.S. Department of Commerce
14th St. and Constitution Ave., NW
Washington, DC 20230   202-482-1904
Headquartered in Washington, DC, USTTA has six regional tourism offices in Toronto, Mexico City, Tokyo, London, Paris, and Frankfurt. These offices deal with foreign travel agents and tour operators and facilitate familiarization programs for foreign travel writers and tour operators seeking information on American travel destinations.

Be patient. If any phone number is incorrect, call (area code) 555-1212 and request the new listing.

State Travel Hotlines

If you are interested in travel related industries, planning a dramatic coast-to-coast sightseeing trip, or scouting out possible areas for relocation, your efforts can be made somewhat easier with the help of state offices of tourism. These offices will provide you with maps, brochures, and other valuable information. If you are planning to visit a particular city--say Sioux Falls--someone in the South Dakota state tourist office might send you a booklet of fascinating historical attractions in the areas. If you want to know where to find the hotels, motels or restaurants, cafes, diners, movie theaters, supermarkets, drug stores or churches, this is the place to start.

If you are interested in a specific activity, not just travel advice and information on tourist attractions, these offices can help you as well. Say, you want to pan for gold or visit an authentic western ghost town. By checking with the state tourism office you can get information on these sites, and perhaps also the name of a good book to prepare you for your visit. They might even be able to provide you with the name of a special guide or tour once you are in the area.

Other information from state tourism offices might include highway conditions, weather advice, local hotel/motel rates, and the best places to eat. In general, each state will provide information packages containing a travel guide, a calendar of events, state maps, and brochures from private, state, and regional tourist attractions.

State Travel and Tourism Hotlines

Alabama
205-242-4169
800-ALABAMA

Alaska
907-465-2012

American Samoa
684-633-1091-2-3

Arizona
602-542-4764

Arkansas
501-682-1088
800-NATURAL

California
916-322-2881
800-TO CALIF

Colorado
303-592-5510
800-COLORADO

Connecticut
203-258-4286
800-CT BOUND

Delaware
302-739-4271
800-441-8846

District of Columbia
202-789-7000
800-422-8644

Florida
904-488-5607/9187

Georgia
404-656-3553
800-VISIT GA

Guam
671-646-5278-79
800-US3 GUAM

Hawaii
808-586-2550

Idaho
208-334-2470
800-635-7820

Illinois
312-814-4732
800-223-0120

Indiana
317-232-8860
800-289-6646

Iowa
515-242-4705
800-345-IOWA

Kansas
913-296-2009
800-2 KANSAS

Kentucky
502-564-4930
800-225-TRIP

Louisiana
504-342-8125
800-33 GUMBO

Maine
207-287-5711
800-533-9595

Marianas
670-234-8327

Maryland
410-333-6611
800-543-1036

Massachusetts
617-727-3201
800-447-MASS

Be patient. If any phone number is incorrect, call (area code) 555-1212 and request the new listing.

411

Vacations and Business Travel

Michigan
517-373-0670
800-543-2937

Minnesota
612-296-2755
800-657-3700

Mississippi
601-359-3297
800-WARMEST

Missouri
314-751-3051
800-877-1234

Montana
406-444-2654
800-VISIT MT

Nebraska
402-471-3794
800-228-4307

Nevada
702-687-4322
800-NEVADA 8

New Hampshire
603-271-2665

New Jersey
609-292-6963
800-JERSEY 7

New Mexico
505-827-7400
800-545-2040

New York
518-474-4116
800-CALL NYS

North Carolina
919-733-4171
800-VISIT NC

North Dakota
701-224-2525
800-435-5663

Ohio
614-466-8844
800-BUCKEYE

Oklahoma
405-521-3981
800-652-6552

Oregon
503-986-0000
800-547-7842

Pennsylvania
717-787-5453
800-VISIT PA

Puerto Rico
212-223-6530
800-866-STAR

Rhode Island
401-277-2601
800-556-2484

South Carolina
803-734-0136

South Dakota
605-773-3301
800-S DAKOTA

Tennessee
615-741-2159

Texas
512-462-9191
800-8888 TEX

Utah
801-538-1030

Vermont
802-828-3237
800-338-0189

Virginia
804-786-2051
800-VISIT VA

Virgin Islands
809-774-8784
800-372-8784

Washington
206-753-5600
800-544-1800

West Virginia
304-348-2200
800-225-5982

Wisconsin
608-266-2345
800-432-TRIP

Wyoming
307-777-7777
800-225-5996

Be patient. If any phone number is incorrect, call (area code) 555-1212 and request the new listing.

Investments and Financial Services
General Sources

* *See also Information on People, Companies, and Mailing Lists Chapter*
* *See also Experts Chapter*

This section contains more information about those companies which offer investments rather than investments themselves. More information about specific investments can be found in the Information on People, Companies and Mailing Lists Chapter as well as the Experts Chapter. A great starting place for any information is the Consumer Information Hotline in this chapter's Banking section. Elsewhere in this chapter are answers to numerous other questions about financial institutions such as the viability of your savings and loan or guides to establishing a credit union. You'll also find the names and addresses of appropriate offices which can help you with such nightmares as lost government bonds or stolen government checks. And, what about that $20 bill that barely survived getting washed along with your pants? You probably can redeem the damaged money by sending it to the federal office identified in the Money section.

* Access to Appraisals

Federal Reserve System
Division of Consumer and Community Affairs
20th Street and Constitution Ave. NW
Washington, DC 20551   202-452-3693

Under new rules from the Federal Reserve Board, consumers will find it easier to obtain the property appraisal used by a lender in approving or denying a mortgage or business loan. The rules carry out a 1991 change in the Equal Credit Opportunity Act that gives loan applicants the right to receive the appraisal report as one way to prevent illegal discrimination against minorities or their consumers. For more information write to the Federal Reserve.

* Credit Card and Computer Fraud

Financial Crime Division
U.S. Secret Service
U.S. Department of the Treasury
1800 G St., NW
Washington, DC 20223   202-435-5850

The fraudulent use of credit and debit cards is a federal violation. Investigations are conducted by the Secret Service, including stolen or lost credit cards, the misuse of credit card account numbers, automated teller machine fraud, telephone fraud involving long distance calls, and other types of access device fraud. Computer fraud is a recent concern of the Secret Service. New law enforcement techniques are being pioneered in an effort to identify computer criminals.

* Credit Card Collections

Office of the Assistant Commissioner Federal Finance
Financial Management Service
U.S. Department of the Treasury
401 14th St., SW
Washington, DC 20227   202-874-6540

Under the Credit Card Collection Network, Federal agencies are able to accept MasterCard and VISA from the public for payment of sales, services, fees, fines, and certain types of debts.

* Direct Deposit of Federal Payments

Office of the Assistant Commissioner
Regional Operations
Financial Management Service
U.S. Department of the Treasury
401 14th St., SW
Washington, DC 20227   202-874-6780

This system electronically deposits Federal payments into the beneficiary's checking or savings account. It does away with the costs associated with checks, reducing the cost to 6 cents versus 36 cents for check processing.

* Electronic Benefit Services

Office of the Assistant Commissioner
Federal Finance
Financial Management Service
U.S. Department of the Treasury
401 14th St., SW
Washington, DC 20227   202-874-6720

The Financial Management Service is implementing a government-wide plan to electronically deliver benefits to recipients, such as Social Security, welfare payments, and disability payments, through automated teller machines and point-of-sale terminals. The recipient will not need to have an account with the bank that operates the ATM or point-of-sale terminal.

* Electronic Data Interchange

Office of the Assistant Commissioner Regional Operations
Financial Management Service (FMS)
U.S. Department of the Treasury
401 14th St., SW
Washington, DC 20227   202-874-6780

The Financial Management Service is establishing an electronic funds transfer system, which would fully automate purchase, delivery, and payment cycles with agencies and businesses. As the Federal agencies expand, the number of automated trading partnerships would increase, and reductions in paperwork and delays in processing should significantly decrease.

* Electronic Federal Tax Deposit System

Office of the Assistant Commissioner Federal Finance
Financial Management Service (FMS)
U.S. Department of the Treasury
401 14th St., SW
Washington, DC 20227   202-874-6560

Plans have been initiated by the Financial Management Service (FMS) for the design, development, and implementation of a new electronic-oriented system to replace the outmoded, paper-based, error-prone Federal Tax Deposit System. Employers would use this system to remit withholding and other payroll payments to the government.

* Eximbank Bulletin Board Service (EEB)

Export-Import Bank of the U.S.
811 Vermont Ave. NW   Voice: 202-566-4690
Washington, DC 20571   Data: 202-565-3835

The bulletin board offers descriptions of some of the bank's lending programs and the Foreign Credit Insurance Associations' policies. It includes application forms, press releases, seminar schedules, a referral list of banks in the Export-Import Bank (EIB) programs and an EIB staff directory. Callers are allotted 30 minutes at a time on the electronic bulletin board and it is available 24 hours a day.

Investments and Financial Services

* Federal Deposit Insurance Corporation (FDIC) Affordable Housing

Federal Deposit Insurance Corporation (FDIC)
Office of Consumer Affairs
550 17th St. NW   800-934-3342
Washington, DC 20429   202-898-3773

The Affordable Housing Program (AHP) was established by a 1991 law to provide financial assistance to low and moderate income households who wish to purchase homes the agency acquires from failed institutions. From the start of the program in March 1992, through November 1993, the FDIC sold 1,432 properties at an average price of about $40,000 (85% of the appraised value). To find out more about what's available for sale from the FDIC contact a regional service center of the Division of Depositor and Asset Service listed below.

Northeast Service Center
Newport Towers, 525 Washington Blvd., Jersey City, NJ 07310; 201-653-0100. (CT,ME,NH,NJ,NY,PA,PR,RI,VT,VI)

Southeast Service Center
285 Peachtree Center Ave. NE, Marquis Tower II, Suite 30, Atlanta, GA 30303; 404-880-3000. (AK,DE,DC,FL,GA,KY,MD,MS,NC,SC,TN,VA,WV)

Midwest Service Center
30 S. Wacker Dr., 32nd Floor, Chicago, IL 60606; 312-207-0200. (IL,IN,IA,KS,MI,MN,MO,NE,ND,OH,SD,WI)

Southwest Service Center
1910 Pacific Ave., Suite 1700, Dallas, TX 75201; 214-754-0098. (AR,CO,LA,NM,OK,TX)

Western Service Center
25 Ecker St., Suite 1900, San Francisco, CA 94105; 415-546-1810. (AJ,AZ,CA,GU,HI,ID,MT,NV,OR,UT,WA,WY)

* Federal Deposit Insurance Corporation (FDIC) Consumer News

Federal Deposit Insurance Corporation
550 17th St. NW, Room 7118
Washington, DC 20429

FDIC Consumer News is produced by the Office of Corporate Communications, in cooperation with other FDIC Divisions and Offices. It is intended to present information in a nontechnical way and is not intended to be a legal interpretation of FDIC regulations and policies. *FDIC Consumer News* is published quarterly and subscriptions are available free of charge by writing to the address above.

* Federal Deposit Insurance Corporation (FDIC) Deposit Insurance

Federal Deposit Insurance Corporation
Office of Consumer Affairs
550 17th St. NW   800-934-3342
Washington, DC 20429   202-898-3773

Most rules on Federal Deposit Insurance Corporation (FDIC) deposits have not changed, however, for certain types of retirement and other employee benefit plans the rules have changed. The FDIC has available the 1993 version of the booklet *Your Insured Deposit*. It is a broad description of the insurance rules and is available to consumers free of charge from banks and savings and loans, and from the FDIC's Office of Consumer Affairs. A Spanish version is also available.

* Federal Deposit Insurance Corporation (FDIC) News Releases Via Fax and Internet

Federal Deposit Insurance Corporation (FDIC)
550 17th St. NW   Voice: 800-326-5708
Washington, DC 20429   Fax: 804-642-0003
       Internet: listserv@nic.sura.net

The Federal Deposit Insurance Corporation (FDIC) is now using a new service to provide news releases on a 24-hour basis via facsimile transmission. This service provides press releases back to April 1, 1994, and is updated within an hour of the issuing of a new release. To obtain an index of available releases on the data base, use the phone attached to your fax machine, dial in the number listed above, and follow voice prompts. After you receive the index, repeat the process to receive the news releases you want. You may receive all the news releases issued during a particular week, or only releases of interest to you. The only charge is for calling the

804 number, there is no additional charge for accessing releases. FDIC Press Releases are also available on the Internet. You can have complete instructions on how to access this information on the Internet using the fax service.

* Federal Reserve Economic Data (FRED) Bulletin Board

Research and Public Informaiton
The Federal Reserve Bank of St. Louis
P.O. Box 442
St. Louis, MO 63166   Voice: 314-444-8562 ext. 8807
       Data: 314-621-1824

The Federal Reserve Economic Data (FRED) bulletin board provides current U.S. and international economic and financial data, including daily U.S. interest rates, historical data on money and business indicators, and regional economic data for Arkansas, Illinois, Indiana, Kentucky, Mississippi, Missouri and Tennessee. Weekly U.S. monetary data are updated on FRED Thursday by 5:30 PM Central time. The Master File (file directory 15) contains a listing of all FRED files that are available for viewing or downloading and new user information. Once connected the system will instruct you on how to register and enter your password. FRED is a free service that is available 24 hours a day, 7 days a week, limited to 1 hour of log on time a day.

* Federal Reserve Statistical Releases

Board of Governors
Federal Reserve System
Washington, DC 20551-0001   202-482-1986

The Board of Governors of the Federal Reserve System makes some of its statistical releases available to the public through the U.S. Department of Commerce's economic bulletin board. Information on the the system includes Aggregate Reserves, Factor Affecting Reserve Balances, Money Stock, Assets and Liabilities of Insured Domestically Chartered and Foreign Related Banking Institutions, Foreign Exchange Rates, Selected Interest Rates, Industrial Production and Capacity Utilization, Consumer Installment Credit, and Flow of Funds. Computer access to the releases can be obtained by subscription. Contact this office for further informaiton regarding a subscription to the economic bulletin board.

* Federal Reserve System Resource Materials

Publication Services
MS-127, Board of Governors
Federal Reserve System
Washington, DC 20551   202-452-3244

The free guide, *Public Information Materials of the Federal Reserve System*, describes publications and audiovisual materials available from the Federal Reserve System. It lists materials appropriate for students, consumer groups, economists, bankers, and the general public. Copies of the booklet may be obtained from any Federal Reserve Bank or from the office above.

* Fed Flash Electronic Database

Research Department
Federal Reserve Bank of Dallas   Voice: 214-922-5189
2200 N. Pearl St.   Data: 214-922-5199
Dallas, TX 75201-2272   800-333-1953

Fed Flash is updated daily providing regional and national financial information such as Treasure securities auction results, Eleventh District economic and financial statistics and macroeconomic data. Fed Flash carries selected Federal Reserve Bank of Dallas publication, including *Economic Review* and *Southwest Economy*, and provides historical information about Federal Reserve Bank of Dallas. This is a free service that allows users to call and download information 24 hours a day, 7 days a week.

* Fedlink

Public Information Center
Federal Reserve Bank of Chicago
P.O. Box 834
Chicago, IL 60690-0834   Voice: 312-322-2378
       Data: 312-322-2137

Fedlink is the Federal Reserve Bank of Chicago's electronic bulletin board, featuring current and historical statistics plus a variety of newsletters and other publications. Information available includes selected interest rates, foreign exchange rates, consumer prices, employment and unemployment statistics, industrial production figures, regional economic data, Federal Reserve reports on current economic activity, Federal Reserve Bank of Chicago pamphlets and periodicals, calendar of upcoming events and information on educational programs. All information on Fedlink is updated on a regular basis so you can get current information quickly and easily. Menus, command lines, and help screens will guide you through the bulletin board. Fedlink is a free service that is available 24 hours a day, 7 days a week.

* Fedwire Deposit System

Office of the Assistant Commissioner Federal Finance
Financial Management Service
U.S. Department of the Treasury
401 14th St., SW
Washington, DC 20227   202-874-7167

This system electronically processes 200,000 transactions and $90 billion in receipts annually, providing same-day information to the Treasury and the agencies about these deposits. Continuous access to the system is available through terminals linked to the computer.

* Financial Markets

Patrick Decker
Financial Markets
International Section
Federal Reserve Bank
Washington, DC 20551-0001   202-452-3314

To order:

National Technical Information Service (NTIS)
U.S. Department of Commerce   800-553-6847
5285 Port Royal Rd.   703-487-4650
Springfield, VA 22161   Fax: 703-321-8547

Publications Department
Board of Governors
Federal Reserve Bank
Washington, DC 20551-0001   202-452-3244

This office continuously compiles data on foreign exchange rates and foreign time deposit rates. This information is available through yearly subscriptions (on tape only) through the National Technical Information Service (NTIS). To order ask for International Financial Statistics, order number PB93-592430-XDD, cost is $2,880. Information on daily exchange rates is available weekly in paper form through yearly subscriptions costing $15.00 by contacting the Publications Department of the Federal Reserve.

* KIMBERELY Electronic Database

Carol Dvoracek
Public Affairs
Federal Reserve Bank of Minneapolis
250 Marquette Ave.   Voice: 612-340-2443
Minneapolis, MN 5548?   Data: 612-340-2489

KIMBERELY is a public service electronic database available from the Federal Reserve Bank of Minneapolis that provides economic and financial information and a variety of data and texts. Menus, command lines and help screens will guide you through the process of accessing more than 25 categories of information that are updated regularly. There are more than 500 downloadable files in the areas of, Biographies and Speeches by Federal Officials, National and District Economic and Financial Data, Federal Reserve System and Monetary Policy, Minneapolis Fed News and Information, Ninth District and Naitonal Summary Publications, Regulatory Information and Consumer Finance, and U.S. Coin and Currency, Gold and the Gold Standard. The system can be accessed 24 hours a day, 7 days a week.

* Liberty Link Bulletin Board

Bart Sotnick
Staff Director of Press and Community Relations
Federal Reserve Bank
33 Liberty St.   Voice: 212-720-6143
New York, NY 10045   Data: 212-720-2652

Liberty Link is an electronic bulletin board provided to the public as a free service by the New York Federal Reserve Bank. Data currently available are: Daily, 10AM and 12 noon, Foreign exchange rates; 3:30 PM, Treasury Securities quotes; Weekly,

Aggregate Reserves, Factors Affecting Reserve balances, Money Stock, Market Interest Rates, and Weekly Bulletin of Banking Applications-NY District; Monthly, Commercial Paper news release, Bankers' Acceptances news releases, and Foreign Exchange Volatility Rate report; Quarterly, Foreign Exchange Intervention report and release; and Unscheduled, News releases issued by New York Federal Reserve Bank and Speech texts by key New York Federal Reserve officers.

* The Treasury Fax System

Hamilton Dix
Office of Public Affairs
U.S. Department of the Treasury
1500 Pennsylvania Ave. NW   202-622-2960
Washington, DC 20220   Fax: 202-622-2040

The Treasury Fax service provides 24 hour a day access to Treasury press releases, statements, results of Treasury auctions of 9, 13, 26, and 52 week bills, Treasury weekly bill offerings, Treasury auction of 2 and 5 year bills, savings bond information, media advisories, and other public documents. The system is updated daily and an index of documents that are available on the system can be faxed to you when you call. The Treasury Fax can be reached by calling from a touchtone phone, directing the system to send you documents to a fax machine of you choice, or the system can be directed to send the documents directly to the fax machine you are calling from. Voice prompts will direct you through the system. There is no charge form the Treasury Department for this service.

* Thrift Institutions Supervision

Office of Thrift Supervision (OTS)
U.S. Department of the Treasury
1700 G St., NW
Washington, DC 20552   202-906-6677

The Office of Thrift Supervision (OTS) is the regulatory successor to the Federal Home Loan Bank Board. It oversees the supervision of savings institutions by regulatory staff in its regional offices. Regulations, directives, and policies are developed for the safe and sound operation of savings institutions and to ensure their compliance with federal law and regulations.

* Treasury's Public World Wide Web Server

Senena H. Eriksen
Office of Telecommunications Management
Office of the Deputy Assistant Secretary, Information Systems
U.S. Department of the Treasury
1425 New York Ave., Suite 2150   202-622-1558
Washington, DC 20220   Fax: 202-622-1595
                                    E-mail: serena.eriksen@treas.sprint.com
                                           Internet: http://www.ustreas.gov

The Treasury's public World Wide Web (WWW) server began providing services to the public in October, 1994. The server contains information on Treasury bureaus, services, who's who, and what's new. As might be expected during tax season, the most popular feature is the IRS tax forms and instructions found under the heading "Treasury Bureaus" on the Treasury home page. An impressive feature is the full color photo tour of the historic rooms in the Treasury building, which are not usually open to the public. Based on very faorable comments received from the public to date, the information of the Bureau of Public Debt, and the Mint is most sought after. Helpful hints for navigating the Treasury WWW server can be obtained by clicking on : "For a brief description on how to navigate...click here", in the center of the home page.

* Unclaimed Money at Failed Banks

Federal Deposit Insurance Corporation (FDIC)
550 17th St. NW   800-934-3342
Washington, DC 20429   202-898-3773

A new law could go a long way toward protecting consumers who do not claim their insured deposits after their bank fails. Most depositors claim and receive their funds within days of the closing. But for those who, for one reason or another, do not, this new law gives the depositor more time to claim their money, in some cases up to 11 1/2 years after the bank fails. For more information contact your state office of consumer affairs or the Federal Deposit Insurance Corporation (FDIC).

Banking

* Automated Clearinghouse Returns Compliance

Office of the Assistant Commissioner Regional Operations
Financial Management Service
U.S. Department of the Treasury
401 14th St., SW
Washington, DC 20227   202-874-6810

The Automated Clearinghouse program was developed to assure the return of Direct Deposit funds if they cannot be properly posted to the accounts of recipients by financial institutions. This could involve the funds of either the Federal Government and its agencies, or the public, depending on the Direct Deposit program being used.

* Bank Customer and Financial Industry Affairs

Community Development
Comptroller of the Currency (OCC)
U.S. Department of the Treasury
250 E. Street, SW
Washington, DC 20219   202-874-4930

Consumer banking groups and other industries involved in the financial market are assisted by this office. It acts as a liaison as well as a provider of technical expertise in an effort to inform these groups of OCC policies and to foster a working relationship.

* Bank Education Programs

Consumer Activities
Bank Supervision
Comptroller of the Currency (OCC)
U.S. Department of the Treasury
250 E. Street, SW
Washington, DC 20219   202-874-4700

This office coordinates educational activities with banks, trade associations within the banking industry, and local consumer groups. Training professionals address issues relevant to the banking industry and OCC guidelines and assist in the development of compliance programs.

* Bank Examiners District Offices

Human Resources
Comptroller of the Currency
U.S. Department of the Treasury
250 E. Street, SW
Washington, DC 20219   202-874-4590

Northeastern District: 1114 Avenue of the Americas, Suite 3900, New York, NY 10036; 212-819-9860

Southeastern: 245 Peachtree Center Ave., NE, Marquis One Tower, Suite 600, Atlanta, GA 30303; 404-659-8855

Central: 440 S. LaSalle St., One Financial Place, Suite 2700, Chicago, IL 60605; 312-360-8800

Midwestern: 2345 Grand Ave., Suite 700, Kansas City, MO 64108; 816-556-1800

Southwestern: 1600 Lincoln Plaza, 500 N. Akard, Dallas, TX 75201-3394; 214-720-0656

Western: 50 Fremont St., Suite 3900, San Francisco, CA 94105; 415-545-5900

* Bank Holding Companies

Division of Bank Supervision and Regulation
Federal Reserve System
MS-206
20th St. and Constitution Ave., NW
Washington, DC 20551   202-452-2638

Bank holding companies must register with and report to the Federal Reserve System. A registered bank holding company must obtain the approval of the Board of Governors before acquiring more than 5% of the shares of either additional banks or permissible nonbanking companies. For more information on bank holding companies, contact this office.

* Banking Industry Research

Division of Research and Statistics
Federal Deposit Insurance Corporation (FDIC)
550 17th Street, NW, Room 2028
Washington, DC 20429   202-898-3741

The Federal Deposit Insurance Corporation (FDIC) continually researches and monitors trends in the economy and banking industry. Existing and proposed legislation is studied, as are banking reforms and the effect of interest and inflation rates.

* Banking Law Library

Federal Reserve System (FRS)
Room B1066
20th St. and Constitution Ave. NW
Washington, DC 20551   202-452-3284

For information on specific banking laws, contact the FRS Banking Law Library. The library hours are 9am to 5pm, Monday through Friday. The library is open to the public, but you must call for an appointment.

* Bank Liquidation

Division of Liquidation
Federal Deposit Insurance Corporation (FDIC)
1776 F Street, NW, 8th Floor
Washington, DC 20429   202-898-7350

This office oversees the liquidation of failed banks which are insured by the FDIC, and cases are documented and maintained on file. For more information on accessing these files, contact this office or one of the regional liquidation offices.

* Bank Mergers

Division of Bank Supervision and Regulation
Federal Reserve System
MS-206
20th St. and Constitution Ave., NW
Washington, DC 20551   202-452-2638

The Federal Reserve Board must give prior approval to all proposed bank mergers between insured state-chartered member banks. Contact this office for more information on bank mergers.

* Banks in Developing Countries

Office of the Assistant Secretary of the Treasury
for International Affairs
U.S. Department of the Treasury
1500 Pennsylvania Ave., NW, Room 3430
Washington, DC 20220   202-622-1080

This office assists in the development and operation of multinational banks in developing countries. These include the World Bank, Inter-American Development Bank, Asian Development Bank, and the African Development Bank.

* Bank Supervision and Regulation

Federal Reserve System
20th St. and Constitution Ave., NW
Washington, DC 20551   202-452-2773

The Federal Reserve Board (FRS) supervises and regulates all state member banks and holding companies. Under the Depository Institutions Deregulation and Monetary Control Act of 1980, the FRS sets reserve requirements for, and provides services to, all U.S. depository institutions, not just to national banks and state-chartered member banks. The Board authorizes the acquisition of banks and closely related nonbanking activities by bank holding companies and other changes of control and mergers of banks and bank holding companies. Its responsibilities extend to many foreign activities of U.S. banking institutions and to foreign banking organizations operating in this country.

* Board of Governors

Federal Reserve System
20th St. and Constitution Ave., NW
Washington, DC 20551   202-452-2773

The responsibilities of the Board of Governors include supervising state member banks and all bank holding companies, overseeing Reserve Bank activities, writing consumer credit regulations, approving changes in the discount rate, setting reserve requirements, and establishing margin requirements. The seven members of the Board are appointed for 14-year terms by the U.S. President with the advice and consent of the Senate.

* Call Reports

Financial Disclosure Group
Federal Deposit Insurance Corporation (FDIC)
550 17th Street, NW, Room F-518
Washington, DC 20429   800-688-3342

Prepared quarterly by all FDIC-insured banks and mutual savings banks, Report of Condition and Income Statements of Banks, or Call Reports, include balance sheets, income statements, and supporting statements. Banks can call the toll-free number listed above for assistance in filling out Call Reports. When requesting a previously filed call report (currently available from March 1984), include the name of the bank and the quarter desired. Send requests to this office.

* Community Reinvestment

Fair Lending Analyst
Office of Consumer Affairs
Federal Deposit Insurance Corporation (FDIC)
550 17th Street, NW, Room F-130
Washington, DC 20429   202-898-3535

The Community Reinvestment Act of 1977 empowers the FDIC to monitor FDIC-insured, state-chartered banks to make sure that the banks are meeting the credit needs of the communities they serve, including low- and middle-income areas. Questions regarding community reinvestment should be directed to the nearest FDIC regional office or to the Fair Lending Analyst at the above office.

* Compliance Information

Office of Consumer Affairs
Federal Deposit Insurance Corporation (FDIC)
550 17th Street, NW
Room F-130   800-934-3342
Washington, DC 20429   202-898-6777

For information regarding FDIC-insured, state-chartered banks complying with consumer laws and the Truth-in-Lending Act, contact any FDIC-insured bank, FDIC regional office, or the office above.

* Consumer Information

Office of Consumer Affairs
Federal Deposit Insurance Corporation (FDIC)
550 17th Street, NW, Room F-130   202-898-6777
Washington, DC 20429   800-934-3342

This office answers questions and addresses complaints regarding FDIC-insured banks. A computerized system helps track complaints from their initial filing to their resolution. A follow-up complaint satisfaction survey is also conducted periodically. Banking questions may be directed to the nearest regional FDIC office, or call the FDIC's toll-free customer service hotline between 9 a.m. and 4 p.m. EST, Monday through Friday.

* Comptroller of the Currency Publications

Information Office
Comptroller of the Currency (OCC)
U.S. Department of the Treasury
250 E. Street, SW
Washington, DC 20219   202-874-5000

The Comptroller of the Currency's Information Office requires that all requests for a publications listing or other information be in writing to the Washington address above. All publications must be ordered from the Washington address, 202-874-4960. Selected publications include the following:

Comptroller's Manual for Corporate Activities. This book makes available, in one place, OCC policies and procedures for processing applications for forming a new national bank. The manual can also be used by other institutions entering the national banking system, and by existing national banks expanding and restructuring. ($90)

Comptroller's Manual for National Banks. This looseleaf legal reference contains laws applicable to national banks with sections dealing with regulations and interpretive rulings issued by the OCC. ($50)

Comptroller's Manual to Consumer Compliance. This looseleaf publication is intended to assist the examiner in understanding portions of consumer laws and regulations pertinent to national bank examinations. It contains questions and answers about consumer legislation and interagency statements. ($30)

Comptroller's Handbook for National Bank Examiners. Policies and procedures for the commercial examination of national banks are included in this looseleaf publication. ($90)

Comptroller's Handbook for Fiduciary Activities. Policies and procedures are outlined for the examination of fiduciary activities of national banks. The handbook also assists the examiner in the preparation of examination reports of national bank trust departments, subsidiaries, and affiliates of national banks and their holding companies engaging in fiduciary activities. ($25)

Comptroller's Handbook for Compliance. Written for compliance examinations, this handbook is intended for use by examiners as a supervisory tool in performing compliance examinations, and by bankers as a self-assessment tool for analyzing bank compliance systems. ($25)

Banking Bulletins and Circulars. Circulars provide information of continuing concern to national banks regarding OCC or OCC-supported policies and guidelines. Bulletins inform readers of pending regulation changes and other general information. ($25 each; $100 annual)

OCC Applications for Consumer Activities. A guide to calculating Annual Percentage Rates. The package includes instructions and a 5.25" diskette (MS-DOS) for use in IBM-compatible microcomputers. ($20)

Interpretations and Actions. This subscription provides legal staff interpretations, trust interpretive letters, and investment securities letters. This monthly package represents the informal views of the Comptroller's staff concerning the applications of banking law to contemplated activities or transactions. ($125)

Weekly Bulletin. Contains all corporate decisions made by the Comptroller's office nationwide each week. Applications, approvals or denials, and consummations are noted for new banks, mergers, consolidations, and purchases and assumptions that result in national banks. This publication also carries branch and title changes, changes in controlling ownership, and other corporate changes for national banks. ($250)

Quarterly Journal. Serves as a journal of record for the most significant actions and policies of the OCC. It is published in March, June, September, and December. The journal includes policy statements, decisions on banking structure, selected speeches, testimony, material released in the interpretive letter series, summaries of enforcement actions, statistical data, and other information of interest to the administration of national banks. ($60 annually or $15 per single copy)

* Deposit Data

Financial Disclosure Group
Federal Deposit Insurance Corporation (FDIC)
550 17th St., NW, Room F-518
Washington, DC 20429   800-688-3342

Summary of Deposits is an survey conducted among all FDIC-insured banks every June 30, the results of which are published annually. The *Annual Report of Trust Assets*, a similar survey, is conducted every December 31, among all financial institutions with trust departments. Computer printouts of both surveys are available for all banking offices within a given county, Metropolitan Statistical Area (MSA), or state. Magnetic tapes of *Summary of Deposit* data and the *Annual Report of Trust Assets* data for all U.S. banks for a given year are available for $75 each. Requests for computer printouts and magnetic tapes are handled by this office, which offers a toll-free number for customer assistance.

Be patient. If any phone number is incorrect, call (area code) 555-1212 and request the new listing.

Investments and Financial Services

* Enforcement and Supervision

Office of Supervision and Applications
Division of Supervision
Federal Deposit Insurance Corporation (FDIC)
550 17th St., NW
Room 5025
Washington, DC 20429   202-898-6915

This office monitors insured banks for compliance with Federal Deposit Insurance Corporation (FDIC) regulations and has authority to approve bank applications for deposit insurance and branch formation. This office also initiates cease-and-desist orders against insured banks in the event they fail to correct violations of laws, regulations, or agreements with the FDIC.

* Farm Credit Publications

Office of Congressional and Public Affairs
Farm Credit Administration
1501 Farm Credit Drive
McLean, VA 22102   703-883-4056

Information on obtaining publications and documents can be obtained from the office above. Some of the documents available include the following:

New releases issued since January 1, 1990
Biographies of Farm Credit Administration officials
Speeches by FCA officials
FCA Handbook - Statutes and Regulations (Set fee charged)
FCA Examination Manual (Set fee Charged)
FCA Bulletin
FCA Orders
FCA Organization Chart
FCA Board Policies
FCA Annual Report

* Farm Credit System

Office of Congressional and Public Affairs
Farm Credit Administration
1501 Farm Credit Drive
McLean, VA 22102   703-883-4056

The Farm Credit System is a network of farmer-owned lending institutions and specialized service organizations. More than 70 years ago Congress created the System to provide American agriculture with a dependable source of credit at competitive rates. Today the System provides about one-third of the total credit used by America's farmers, ranchers, and their cooperatives. The *Farm Credit System Information Guide*, which provides information on the Farm Credit System, including a list of the System's banks, is available free from the office above.

* Federal Cash Concentration System

Office of the Assistant Commissioner Federal Finance
Financial Management Service (FMS)
U.S. Department of the Treasury
401 14th St., SW
Washington, DC 20227   202-874-7167

CASH-LINK has transformed the Government's worldwide banking and cash operations. Through the resources of the banking community, the new system electronically captures and reports activity for government-wide collections. The system encompasses seven collection systems: Treasury General Account Cash Concentration System; Financial Management Service Lockbox Network; Credit Card Collection Network; Fedwire Deposit System; Federal Reserve System; Farmers Home Administration Cash Concentration System; and Commodity Credit Corporation Cash Concentration System.

* Federal Information Change Notification

Office of Legislative and Public Affairs
Financial Management Service
U.S. Department of the Treasury
401 14th St., SW
Washington, DC 20227   202-874-6740

This is an automated procedure that financial institutions can use to notify Federal agencies that an error or change has occurred in the depositor's account number, the routing/transit number of the financial institution (small numbers on the bottom of checks), or the type of account (checking or savings) of an Automated Clearinghouse Payment.

* Federal Lockbox Network

Director of Cash Management
Office of the Assistant Commissioner Federal Finance
Financial Management Service
U.S. Department of the Treasury
401 14th St., SW
Washington, DC 20227   202-874-7092

The above office oversees the Lockbox Network which consists of seven banks in nine cities: Atlanta, Chicago, Dallas, Los Angeles, Newark, Philadelphia, Pittsburgh, San Francisco, and St. Louis. Lockboxes, actually post office boxes, are used to collect and deposit mailed payments. More than 363 agency accounts are involved, and about $100 billion is collected and processed annually. All 10 Internal Revenue Service centers utilize the lockbox network.

* Federal Reserve Banks and Treasury Servicing Offices

This is a list of every Treasury Direct servicing office in the U.S. Contact the servicing office closest to you to make transactions on your account, or to receive information about your Treasury security investments.

Federal Reserve Bank Atlanta, 104 Marietta St., NW, Atlanta, GA 30303; 404-521-8500 (Recording)/404-521-8657

Federal Reserve Bank Baltimore, 502 S. Sharp St., P.O. Box 1378, Baltimore, MD 21203; 410-576-3500 (Recording)/410-576-3300

Federal Reserve Bank Birmingham, 1801 Fifth Ave., N., P.O. Box 830447, Birmingham, AL 35283-0447; 205-731-8500, Ext. 215 (Recording)/205-731-8702 (Ext 264)

Federal Reserve Bank Boston, 600 Atlantic Ave., P.O. Box 2076, Boston, MA 02106; 617-973-3805 (Recording)/617-973-3810

Federal Reserve Bank Buffalo, 160 Delaware Ave., P.O. Box 961, Buffalo, NY 14240-0961; 716-849-5046 (Recording)/716-849-5000

Federal Reserve Bank Charlotte, 530 E. Trade St., P.O. Box 30248, Charlotte, NC 28202; 704-358-2100

Federal Reserve Bank Chicago, 230 South LaSalle St., P.O. Box 834, Chicago, IL 60690; 312-322-5322 (Recording)/312-322-2202

Federal Reserve Bank Cincinnati, 150 East Fourth St., Cincinnati, OH 45202 or P.O. Box 999, Cincinnati, OH 45201-0999; 513-721-4787, Ext. 334

Federal Reserve Bank Cleveland, 1455 East Sixth St., P.O. Box 6387, Cleveland, OH 44101; 216-579-2490 (Recording)/216-579-2000

Federal Reserve Bank Dallas, 400 South Akard St., Dallas, TX 75222; 214-651-6362

Federal Reserve Bank Denver, 1020 16th St., P.O. Box 5228, Terminal Annex, Denver, CO 80217; 303-572-2300 (Recording)/303-572-2475

Federal Reserve Bank Detroit, 160 W. Fort St., P.O. Box 1059, Detroit, MI 48231; 313-961-6880 (Recording)/313-963-4936

Federal Reserve Bank Houston, 1701 San Jacinto St., P.O. Box 2578, Houston, TX 77002; 713-652-1688 (Recording)/713-659-4433

Federal Reserve Bank Jacksonville, 800 Water St., P.O. Box 929, Jacksonville, FL 32231-0444; 904-632-1177 (Recording)/904-632-1000

Federal Reserve Bank Kansas City, 925 Grand Ave., P.O. Box 440, Kansas City, MO 64198; 816-881-2000 (Recording)/816-881-2409

Federal Reserve Bank Little Rock, 325 West Capitol Ave., P.O. Box 1261, Little Rock, AR 72203-1261; 501-324-8275 (Recording)/501-324-8300

Federal Reserve Bank Los Angeles, 950 S. Grand Ave., P.O. Box 2077, Terminal Annex, Los Angeles, CA 90051; 213-688-0068 (Recording)/213-683-2100

Federal Reserve Bank Louisville, 410 South Fifth St., P.O. Box 32710, Louisville, KY 40232-2710; 502-568-9200

Federal Reserve Bank Memphis, 200 N. Main St., P.O. Box 407, Memphis, TN 38101-0407; 901-523-7171 Ext. 225 or 641

Be patient. If any phone number is incorrect, call (area code) 555-1212 and request the new listing.

Federal Reserve Bank Miami, 9100 NW Thirty-Sixth St., P.O. Box 520847, Miami, FL 33152-0847; 305-591-2065

Federal Reserve Bank Minneapolis, 250 Marquette Ave., Minneapolis, MN 55401-2171; 612-340-2075 (Recording)/612-340-2345

Federal Reserve Bank Nashville, 301 Eighth Ave., N., Nashville, TN 37203; 615-251-7236 (Recording)/615-251-7100

Federal Reserve Bank New Orleans, 525 St. Charles Ave., P.O. Box 61630, New Orleans, LA 70161-1630; 504-593-3200 (Recording)/504-593-5893

Federal Reserve Bank New York, 33 Liberty St., Federal Reserve P.O. Station, New York, NY 10045; 212-720-5000 (Recording)/212-720-6619

Federal Reserve Bank Oklahoma City, 226 Dean A. McGee Ave., P.O. Box 25129, Oklahoma City, OK 73125; 405-270-8400 (Recording)/405-270-8660

Federal Reserve Bank Omaha, 2201 Farnam St., Omaha, NE 68102; 402-221-5500 (Recording)/402-221-5633

Federal Reserve Bank Philadelphia, 10 Independence Mall, Philadelphia, PA 19106; 215-574-6000 (Recording)/215-574-6188

Federal Reserve Bank Pittsburgh, 717 Grant St., P.O. Box 867, Pittsburgh, PA 15230-0867; 412-261-7800 (Recording)/412-261-7910/7988

Federal Reserve Bank Portland, 915 SW Stark St., P.O. Box 3436, Portland, OR 97208; 503-221-5900 (Recording)/503-221-5932

Federal Reserve Bank Richmond, 701 East Byrd St., P.O. Box 27622, Richmond, VA 23261; 804-697-8355 (Recording)/804-697-8000

Federal Reserve Bank Salt Lake City, 120 South State St.,P.O. Box 30780, Salt Lake City, UT 84125; 801-322-7900 (Recording); 801-355-7844

Federal Reserve Bank San Antonio, 126 E. Nueva St., P.O. Box 1471, San Antonio, TX 78295; 210-224-2141, Ext. 330

Federal Reserve Bank San Francisco, 101 Market St., P.O. Box 7702, San Francisco, CA 94120; 415-974-2000 (Recording)/ 415-974-2330

Federal Reserve Bank Seattle, 1015 Second Ave., P.O. Box 3567, Terminal Annex, Seattle, WA 98124; 206-343-3600 (Recording)/206-343-3605

Federal Reserve Bank St. Louis, 411 Locust St., P.O. Box 442, St. Louis, MO 63166; 314-444-8444 (Recording)/314-444-8703

* FDIC Publications

Office of Corporate Communications
Federal Deposit Insurance Corporation (FDIC)
550 17th St., NW, Room 7118
Washington, DC 20429   202-898-6996

This office distributes the following free publications:

Annual Report. Summarizes the FDIC's operations, regulatory activities, and financial statements. Also included are statistical tables summarizing FDIC assistance to problem and failed banks.

Data Book. This six-volume set contains deposit information for all commercial and mutual savings banks, including U.S.-based branches of foreign banks. Each volume focuses on a different geographic area and includes a national summary with tables on bank structure, class, and size.

Merger Decisions. An annual summary of the FDIC's approvals and denials of bank mergers.

Statistics on Banking. This annual report details bank statistical data, including the total number of banks and branches, and information on incomes, assets, and liabilities of insured banks.

Symbol of Confidence. Provides an overview of the FDIC's history, responsibilities, and operations.

Trust Assets of Financial Institutions. Summarizes trust department data collected from all insured commercial banks. Data is presented by type of account, asset distribution, and size of account.

Your Insured Deposit. Provides examples of the FDIC's insurance coverage for common types of bank accounts.

* Financial Disclosure Group

Federal Deposit Insurance Corporation (FDIC)
550 17th St. NW
Washington, DC 20429   800-945-2186

The Federal Deposit Insurance Corporation (FDIC) disclosure group provides various products and guides. A recorded message will instruct you on how to receive this information. Listed below is a guide to find the information you need and a brief description of the products available.

1. Uniform Bank Production Reports (UBPR's)
2. Call Reports
3. Annual Report of Trust Assets
4. Summary of All Deposits
5. Other products regarding Financial Lists and Labels, Mailing Lists and Labels and Tables for Changes Among Operating Financial Institutions

* International Banking

Analysis Section
Division of Bank Supervision
Federal Deposit Insurance Corporation (FDIC)
550 17th St., NW, Room 5053
Washington, DC 20429   202-898-6821

FDIC-insured banks must first obtain FDIC approval before they establish, operate, or relocate a branch in a foreign country. FDIC approval is also needed before these banks acquire any ownership interest in a foreign bank. Insured branches of foreign banks located in the U.S. are also monitored by the FDIC. For more information, contact the nearest regional FDIC office listed below.

Atlanta Regional Office: Lyle V. Helgerson, Regional Director - Bank Supervision, FDIC, Marquis One, Suite 1200, 1201 W. Peachtree Ave., NE, Suite 1800, Atlanta, GA 30309; 404-817-2500. Serves AL, FL, GA, NC, SC, VA, WV.

Boston Regional Office: Paul H. Wiechman, Regional Director - Bank Supervision, FDIC, Westwood Executive Center, 200 Lowder Brook Drive, Westwood, MA 02090; 617-320-1600. Serves CT, ME, MA, NH, RI, VT.

Chicago Regional Office: Simone L. Frank, Regional Director - Bank Supervision, FDIC, 500 W. Monroe, Suite 3200, Chicago, IL 60661; 312-207-0210. Serves IL, IN, MI, OH, WI.

Dallas Regional Office: Kenneth L. Walker, Regional Director - Bank Supervision, FDIC, 1910 Pacific Ave., Suite 1900, Dallas, TX 75201; 214-220-3342. Serves CO, NM, OK, TX.

Kansas City Regional Office: James O. Leese, Regional Director - Bank Supervision, FDIC, 2345 Grand Ave., Suite 1500, Kansas City, MO 64108; 816-234-8000. Serves IA, KS, MN, MO, NE, ND, SD.

Memphis Regional Office: Bill C. Housten, Regional Director - Bank Supervision, FDIC, 5100 Poplar Ave., Suite 1900, Memphis, TN 38137; 901-685-1603. Serves AR, KY, LA, MS, TN.

New York Regional Office: Nicholas J. Ketcha Jr., Regional Director - Bank Supervision, FDIC, 452 Fifth Ave., 19th Floor, New York, NY 10018; 212-704-1200. Serves DE, DC, MD, NJ, NY, PA, PR, VI.

San Francisco Regional Office: George J. Masa, Regional Director - Bank Supervision, FDIC, 25 Ecker St., Suite 2300, San Francisco, CA 94105; 415-546-0160. Serves AK, AZ, CA, GU, HI, ID, MT, NV, OR, UT, WA, WY.

* International Finance

Office of Development Finance
Bureau of Economic and Business Affairs
U.S. Department of State
2201 C St., NW, Room 2529
Washington, DC 20520   202-647-9426

As the liaison with multilateral development banks, such as the World Bank, African Development Bank, Asian Development Bank, and InterAmerican Bank, this office works on such development issues as coordinating official U.S. Government assistance to promote economic security in developing countries. This office also coordinates with the Export-Import Bank on trade issues.

Be patient. If any phone number is incorrect, call (area code) 555-1212 and request the new listing.

419

Investments and Financial Services

* Law, Regulations, and Related Acts

Office of Corporate Communications
Federal Deposit Insurance Corporation (FDIC)
550 17th St., NW
Room 7118
Washington, DC 20429   202-898-3823

FDIC Law, Regulations, and Related Acts is a three-volume, loose-leaf bound publication containing the FDI Act, Federal Deposit Insurance Corporation (FDIC) rules and regulations, advisory opinions, pertinent statutes, and consumer protection material, among other information. Revisions and updates are published bimonthly. For $280, subscribers receive the three-volume set and updates through December of that year, and they are billed $280 each December to renew the update service.

* Legislation on Financial Institutions

Office of Financial Institutions Policy
Office of the Assistant Secretary of
  Financial Institutions
U.S. Department of the Treasury
1500 Pennsylvania Ave., NW
Washington, DC 20220   202-622-2610

Policy and legislation on the development and administration of banks and other financial institutions is handled by this office. A recent effort involved the study of the ailing thrift institutions, resulting in the formation of the Office of Thrift Supervision.

* Liquidation Litigation

Office of Corporate Communications
Federal Deposit Insurance Corporation (FDIC)
550 17th St., NW
Room 7118
Washington, DC 20429   202-898-6996

This office oversees liquidation litigation among FDIC-insured banks, as well as liquidation and insurance activities for the Federal Savings and Loan Insurance Corporation (FSLIC). Outside counsel is hired to help litigate an estimated 40,000 cases annually. Contact your regional office for more information on liquidation litigation issues.

Regional Offices - Liquidation

Chicago Regional Office: Bart L. Federici, Regional Director - Liquidation, Federal Deposit Insurance Corporation (FDIC), 500 W. Monroe, Lobby Level, Chicago, IL 60661; 312-207-0210. Serves AL, AR, DE, DC, FL, GA, IL, IN, IA, KS, KY, LA, MD, MI, MN, MS, MO, NE, NC, ND, OH, SC, SD, TN, VA, WV, WI.

Dallas Regional Office: G. Michael Newton, Regional Director - Liquidation, Federal Deposit Insurance Corporation (FDIC), 1910 Pacific Ave., Suite 1700, Dallas, TX 75201; 214-754-0098. Serves OK, TX.

New York Regional Office: Thomas A. Beshara, Regional Director - Liquidation, Federal Deposit Insurance Corporation (FDIC), 452 Fifth Ave., 21st Floor, NEw York, NY 10018; 212-704-1200. Serves CT, ME, MA, NH, NJ, NY, PA, RI, VT, PR, VI.

San Francisco Regional Office: Keith W. Seibold, Regional Director - Liquidation, Federal Deposit Insurance Corporation (FDIC), 25 Ecker St., Suite 1900, San Francisco, CA 94105. Serves AK, AZ, CA, CO, GU, HI, ID, MT, NV, NM, OR, UT, WA, WY.

* Office of Thrift Supervision District Offices

One Financial Center, Boston, MA 02111 or P.O. Box 9106 GMF, Boston, MA 02205-9106; 617-542-0150

One World Trade Center, FL 103, New York, NY 10048; 212-912-4600

One Riverfront Center, 20 Stanwix St., Pittsburgh, PA 15222-4893; 412-288-3400

P.O. Box 105217, Atlanta, GA 30348-5217; 404-888-0771

P.O. Box 598, Cincinnati, OH 45201-0598; 513-852-7500

111 E. Wacker Dr., Suite 800, Chicago, IL 60601-4360; 312-540-5900

907 Walnut St., Des Moines, IA 50309; 515-281-1100

P.O. Box 619027, Dallas/Fort Worth, TX 75261-9026; 214-281-2000

P.O. Box 7165, San Francisco, CA 94120; 415-616-1500

101 Stewart St., Suite 1210, Seattle, WA 98101; 206-553-5196

* Office of Thrift Supervision Publications

Office of Thrift Supervision
U.S. Department of the Treasury
1700 G. Street, NW
Washington, DC 20552   202-906-6682

Thrift Activities Regulatory Handbook. Addresses all of the major areas of concern to examiners and supervisors regarding the safety and soundness of regulated institutions. (Price: $50 - members; $75 - non-members)

Compliance Activities Regulatory Handbook. Addresses compliance examination matters related to consumer protection laws and regulations, such as the Truth in Lending Act, and those related to the public interest, such as the Community Reinvestment and Bank Secrecy Acts. (Price: $25 - members; $25 - non-members)

Service Corporations Regulatory Handbook. Addresses issues that primarily arise in dealing with service corporations and discusses relationships between those entities and the parent thrift. (Price: $50 - members; $75 - non-members)

Holding Companies Regulatory Handbook. Addresses areas of particular interest when reviewing holding company operations. (Price: $50 - members; $75 - non-members)

Trust Activities Regulatory Handbook. Designed to assist in the examination of those thrift institutions and their subsidiaries that engage in trust activities. (Price: $50 - members; $75 - non-members)

Application Processing Regulatory Handbook. Contains guidance on how to process and analyze thrift and holding company applications. (Price: $50 - members; $75 - non-members)

Federal Financial Institutions Examination Council (FFIEC) EDP Handbook. This handbook is published by the FFIEC and is currently used by all financial regulatory agencies as a guide for conducting EDP examinations. (Price: $75)

Membership Directory of Institutions. Published during the first quarter of each year, this free directory lists all savings institutions insured by the Savings Association Insurance Fund (SAIF) and the Federal Deposit Insurance Corporation (FDIC), as well as those institutions that are members of the Federal Home Finance Board but are not federally insured. For a copy, call 202-898-8909.

Compliance: A Self-Assessment Guide. This guide will help thrift institutions develop or improve internal policies and programs to ensure compliance with consumer and public interest laws. ($20)

CEBA Guide: Questions and Answers. The questions answered in this guide are those most commonly asked by examination and supervisory staff during the Comprehensive Equality Banking Act of 1987 (CEBA) training programs. ($3)

Bulletin Subscription Series. Thrift Bulletins provide national guidance to alert regulated institutions to practices or events of concern to the thrift industry. The annual subscription price is $175.

* Problem Banks

Office of Corporate Communications
Federal Deposit Insurance Corporation (FDIC)
550 17th Street, NW
Room 7118
Washington, DC 20429   202-898-6996

The Federal Deposit Insurance Corporation (FDIC) uses the Uniform Interagency Bank Rating System to evaluate a bank's performance with respect to capital adequacy, asset quality, management/administration, earnings, and liquidity (known by the acronym CAMEL). Banks are rated on a scale from 1 to 5, with 1 indicating a very sound banking institution. Banks with ratings of 4 or 5 are considered to be problem banks, possibly requiring FDIC intervention and payoff. Individual bank ratings are not available to the public. Contact this office for more information about the rating system.

Be patient. If any phone number is incorrect, call (area code) 555-1212 and request the new listing.

* Registration and Reporting

Public Files Registration and Disclosure
Federal Deposit Insurance Corporation (FDIC)
550 17th St., NW, Room F643
Washington, DC 20429   202-898-8909

The Federal Deposit Insurance Corporation (FDIC) enforces the registration and reporting provisions of the 1934 Securities Exchange Act among FDIC-insured, nonmember banks. Banks with assets totalling more than $1 million and 500 or more security holders are required to file an initial registration statement which summarizes the bank's history, business operations, and overall financial condition. These banks are also required to file periodic reports which include Reports of Condition and Income Statements. The registration statements and periodic reports are filed and maintained in this office.

* Uniform Bank Performance Reports

Financial Disclosure Group
Federal Deposit Insurance Corporation (FDIC)

550 17th St. NW
Washington, DC 20429   800-945-2186

A Uniform Bank Production Report (UBPR) is a computer-generated report for each insured bank. The data is presented in ratio, percentage and dollar formats and compares data in previous years. A recorded message will instruct you on what products and services are available and ordering instructions. Listed below are the 7 UBPR's currently available.

1. *Individual Finance Report*. Contains approximately 13 pages of ratio, percentage and dollar amounts. $45.00
2. *Peer Group Average Report*. Contains 25 peer groups with ratios, percentages, and dollar amounts for each. $65.00
3. *Peer Group Distribution Report*. Contains peer group information for 1 reporting period distributed over a range of percentages. $65.00
4. *State Average Report*. Consolidates all UBPR's in each state. $45.00
5. *State Average Distribution Report*. Contains state average information for 1 reporting period distributed over a range of percentages. $45.00
6. *Users Guide*. Instruction book for UBPR's. $25.00
7. *UBPR magnetic tape*.

Investments and Financial Services

Money

* Congressional Coins
Customer Service Center
U.S. Mint
U.S. Department of the Treasury
10001 Aerospace Dr.
Lanham, MD 20706   301-436-7400
The mint produces and sells numismatic coins, American Eagle gold and silver bullion coins, and national medals. Contact the center for more information.

* Counterfeit and Forgery Statistics
Public Affairs
U.S. Secret Service
U.S. Department of the Treasury
1800 G St., NW, Room 805
Washington, DC 20223   202-435-5708
A statistical summary of activity within the Secret Service investigative area is available, including information on counterfeiting, check forgery, bond forgery, fraud, protective intelligence, and other criminal and noncriminal acts. Data includes investigative activity by fiscal year; counterfeiting trends of notes and coins; trends of counterfeit plant operations, including the production of counterfeit notes, office machine copies, food coupons, false IDs, and domestic and foreign currency; counterfeit notes received by major city and dollar amount; arrests; and forged checks and bonds received.

* Counterfeiting Investigations
U.S. Secret Service
Counterfeit Division
U.S. Department of the Treasury
1800 G St., NW
Washington, DC 20223   202-435-5756
Information may be obtained concerning facts about paper currency and recognizing counterfeit bills and coins. Guidelines are also available on what to do when you receive a counterfeit bill. For additional information, contact Public Affairs at 202-435-5708.

* Counterfeit Money and Forged Checks
Superintendent of Documents
Government Printing Office   202-512-1800
Washington, DC 20402   Fax: 202-512-2250
Know Your Money describes and illustrates ways to recognize counterfeit bills and forged U.S. government checks. Price $1.75; order number S/N 048-006-00010-8.

* Currency and Stamp Production
Associate Director, Chief Operations Director, Operations
Bureau of Engraving and Printing
U.S. Department of the Treasury
14th and C Sts., SW
Washington, DC 20228   202-874-2002
The Bureau of Engraving and Printing designs, engraves, and prints United States paper currency; United States postage and revenue stamps; and miscellaneous engraved items for approximately 75 departments and independent agencies of the Federal Government. White house invitations, commissions, diplomas, certificates, identification cards, and liquor strip stamps are some of the approximately 700 miscellaneous products printed by the Bureau.

* Daily Treasury Statement
Superintendent of Documents
Government Printing Office
Washington, DC 20402   202-512-1800
Published daily except Saturdays, Sundays, and holidays, the subscription service, *Daily Treasury Statement*, outlines the cash and debt operations of the United States Treasury. The annual price is $401. (S/N 748-003-00000-2)

* Damaged Money Redemption
Office of Currency Standards
Bureau of Engraving and Printing
U.S. Department of the Treasury
Room 344A, BEPA
P.O. Box 37048
Washington, DC 20013   202-874-2194
All mutilated currency may be sent to the above address where trained personnel will determine if it can be exchanged at face value. All final decisions for redemption of this currency are made by the Treasurer of the United States. Currency should be sent by registered mail to the P.O. box address above.

* Federal Check Cashing Period
Financial Information
U.S. Department of the Treasury
3700 East West Highway
Room 800 D
Hyattsville, MD 20782   202-874-8400
Effective October 1, 1989, all Treasury checks must be cashed or deposited within 12 months of issuance for payment to be valid. If this time lapses, the holder of the check must contact the agency from where the check was drawn and ask to have another check issued. Entitlement of the funds never ceases. This program within the Financial Management Service (FMS) is called Limited Payability.

* Federal Collections
Office of the Assistant Commissioner Federal Finance
Financial Management Service
U.S. Department of the Treasury
401 14th St., SW, Room 504
Washington, DC 20227   202-874-6530
The Financial Management Service (FMS) is responsible for the largest collection system in the world--approximately $1 trillion annually. These collections include tax deposits, custom duties, loan repayments, fines, services, and proceeds from leases. FMS provides transaction processing to Federal agencies, manages the systems by which Government collections are made, and sets policy for the use of the collection systems.

* Federal Open Market Committee
Division of Monetary Affairs
Federal Reserve System
Room B3022
20th St. and Constitution Ave., NW
Washington, DC 20551   202-452-3761
The Federal Open Market Committee exercises broad control over the growth of the nation's money supply and is in charge of the System's operations in both domestic securities markets and in foreign exchange markets. The Committee is composed of the seven members of the Board of Governors and five Reserve Bank presidents, including the president of the New York Reserve Bank, which conducts foreign and domestic operations for the Committee. For information on the nation's money supply and securities markets, contact this office.

* Federal Payments
Office of Legislative and Public Affairs
Financial Management Service
U.S. Department of the Treasury
401 14th St., SW
Washington, DC 20227   202-874-6740
The issuance of payments is a central financial operation of the Financial Management Service. The Service disburses approximately 800 million payments annually, and issues payments for virtually all Federal civilian agencies, or approximately 85 percent of total Government payments. Payments are issued from seven Regional Financial Center locations on the basis of payment vouchers certified by Federal agencies.

* Forgery Investigations

Forgery Division
U.S. Secret Service
U.S. Department of the Treasury
1800 G St., NW
Washington, DC 20223   202-435-5100

Since there are more than 800 million U.S. Government checks issued each year, they are attractive to criminals who specialize in stealing and forging them. Retail merchants often unknowingly aid the forger by failing to request proper identification. For additional information on precautions to take, contact Public Affairs at 202-435-5708.

* Gold and Silver Bullion Coins

Public Information Office
U.S. Mint
U.S. Department of the Treasury
633-3rd St., NW
Washington, DC 20220   202-874-6450

The American Eagle Gold and Silver Bullion Coins are being minted to purchase as investments. The gold coins are available in one ounce, half-ounce, quarter-ounce and tenth-ounce weights. The silver coins are minted only in the one ounce size. To determine their worth, simply check listings in your daily newspaper. The coins may be purchased from various brokerage companies, participating banks, coin dealers, and precious metal dealers. To obtain a listing of sales locations in your area, contact the office above.

* Lost Government Checks

Financial Information
U.S. Department of the Treasury
3700 East West Highway
Room 800 D
Hyattsville, MD 20782   202-874-8400

To make a claim against the Treasury for a lost check or one you believe has been cashed with a forged endorsement, you first must contact the agency that issued the check and obtain a copy of it along with a claim form. The agency will then contact Treasury to handle your claim. The office above ultimately handles the claim, but requests that it be contacted only when all else fails.

* Monetary Policy

Division of Monetary Affairs
Federal Reserve System (FRS)
Room B3022
20th St. and Constitution Ave., NW
Washington, DC 20551   202-452-3761

This Federal Reserve System (FRS) division analyzes issues in monetary policy, including open market operations, member bank discount borrowing at Federal Reserve Banks, and changes in reserve requirements.

Credit Unions

* CAMEL Rating System

Office of Examination and Insurance
National Credit Union Administration
1775 Duke St.
Alexandria, VA 22314-3428   703-518-6360

Assigned following an examination of a credit union's safety and soundness, a CAMEL rating is a reliable indicator of future success or failure. The CAMEL rating looks at the key areas of a credit union's operations--capital adequacy, asset quality, management, earnings, and liquidity. Ratings range from Code 1, which is good, to Code 5, which is poor. For more information, contact the Office of Examination and Insurance.

* Central Liquidity Facility

Office of Examination and Insurance
National Credit Union Administration (NCUA)
1775 Duke St.
Alexandria, VA 22314-3428   703-518-6360

The Central Liquidity Facility (CLF) is a mixed-ownership government corporation governed by the NCUA Board. CLF is a central source of short-term funds for the credit union system. It has a loan portfolio of $120.4 million and provides lines of credit totalling $13.5 million. To become a CLF member, a credit union or its designated agent must purchase stocks equal to one-half of one percent of the credit union's unimpaired capital and surplus.

* Chartering

Public and Congressional Affairs
National Credit Union Administration (NCUA)
1775 Duke St.
Alexandria, VA 22314-3428   703-518-6330

The NCUA Board grants Federal Credit Union charters to groups sharing a common bond of occupation or association, or to groups within a well-defined neighborhood, community, or rural district. A preliminary investigation is made to determine if certain minimum standards are met before granting a federal charter. Call or write to the regional offices listed at the end of this section for more information on the chartering process.

* Consumer Complaints

Public and Congressional Affairs
National Credit Union Administration
1775 Duke St.
Alexandria, VA 22314-3428   703-518-6330

The Administration investigates the complaints of members who are unable to resolve problems with their federal credit union where these problems relate to a possible violation of the Federal Credit Union Act or to consumer protection regulations. Complaints should be sent directly to the appropriate office. Regional offices are listed at the end of this section.

* Credit Union Information

Public and Congressional Affairs
National Credit Union Administration (NCUA)
1775 Duke St.
Alexandria, VA 22314-3428   703-518-6330

Several publications are available to assist you in starting a federal credit union. *Chartering and Organizing of Federal Credit Unions* provides basic information about credit unions and their membership policies. The *Federal Credit Union Handbook* is intended to assist the board of directors in conducting the credit union's affairs. Contact the regional NCUA office near you for further information.

* Credit Union Supervision

Office of Examination and Insurance
National Credit Union Administration
1775 Duke St.
Alexandria, VA 22314-3428   703-518-6360

Supervisory activities are carried out through annual examiner contacts and through periodic policy and regulatory releases from the Administration. The Administration also maintains a warning system designed to identify emerging problems as well as to monitor operations between examinations.

* Examiner Training Programs

National Credit Union Administration
1775 Duke St.
Alexandria, VA 22314-3428   703-518-6630

This office offers classroom, as well as on-the-job training for new examiners, and offers technical seminars for senior examiners. These seminars cover such topics as consumer lending, investments, and dealing with problem case credit unions. The training programs are open to state supervisory personnel without charge.

* Liquidation

Asset Liquidation Management Center
National Credit Union Administration
4807 Spicewood Springs Rd., Suite 5100
Austin, TX 78759-8490   512-795-0999

Liquidation of federal credit unions is conducted according to the manual *Voluntary Liquidation Procedure for Insured Federal Credit Unions*. The major responsibility of the board is to conduct the liquidations in such a manner that the interest of the members, the insurance fund, and the creditors of the credit union are safeguarded. For information regarding liquidations, contact the Department of Insurance.

* Financial Performance Report

Office of Examination and Insurance
National Credit Union Administration
1775 Duke St.
Alexandria, VA 22314-3428   703-518-6360

The *Financial Performance Report* (FRP), an analytical tool created for management and supervisory purposes, is designed to provide a long-term picture of the financial trends and operating results of the credit union. The *FPR* is updated twice a year, with the December *FPR* providing percentile rankings that show where the credit union stands in relation to **all** other credit unions in key areas of financial performance. This publication breaks down the *FPR* and explains what each category means. A member has the right to inspect a federal credit union's books and records, including the board of directors' minutes.

* Insured Funds

Office of Examination and Insurance
National Credit Union Administration (NCUA)
1775 Duke St.
Alexandria, VA 22314-3428   703-518-6360

Share insurance is mandatory for federal credit unions and for state-chartered credit unions in many states, while optional for other state-chartered credit unions that meet NCUA standards. Credit union members' accounts are insured up to $100,000. The National Credit Union Share Insurance Fund (NCUSIF) requires each insured credit union to place and maintain a one-percent deposit of its insured savings with the NCUSIF. The publication, *Your Insured Funds*, offers further explanation concerning insurance.

* Listing of Federal Credit Unions

Freedom of Information Officer
National Credit Union Administration (NCUA)
1775 Duke St.
Alexandria, VA 22314-3428   703-518-6540

A master list of the names and addresses of all federally insured credit unions is available for public inspection in the Washington and regional offices. Copies of the list may be obtained at a nominal cost by writing to the Freedom of Information Officer. You may also receive a free list of National Credit Union Administration (NCUA) regional offices.

* National Credit Union Administration Bulletin Board System

Cary Savage
Office of Public and Congressional Affairs
National Credit Union Administration
1775 Duke St.   703-518-6330
Alexandria, VA 22314-3428   Data: 703-518-6480

The information contained in this system includes National Credit Union Administration (NCUA) press releases; NCUA rules and regulations; legal opinions; letter to credit unions; interpretive rulings and policy statements; accounting bulleting; and messages. The Bulletin Board system is continuously updated as information becomes available. All of the information is available to the public free of charge. The only costs for using this system are telephone toll charges. The system operates 24 hours a day, 7 days a week, but telephone assistance is only available Monday through Friday from 8 am to 4:30 pm. This bulletin board can also be accessed through the National Technical Information Service (NTIS) bulletin board Fedworld Gateway #128.

* National Credit Union Administration Regional Offices

Region 1

National Credit Union Administration, 9 Washington Square, Washington Ave., Extension, Albany, NY 12205; 518-464-4180. Serves CT, ME, MA, NH, NY, RI, VT

Region 2

National Credit Union Administration, 1775 Duke St., Suite 4206, Alexandria, VA 22314-3437; 703-838-0401. Serves DE, DC, MD, NJ, PA, VA, WV.

Region 3

National Credit Union Administration, 7000 Central Parkway, Suite 1600, Atlanta, GA 30328; 404-396-4042. Serves Al, AR, FL, GA, KY, LA, MS, NC, PR, SC, TN, VI.

Region 4

National Credit Union Administration, 4225 Nappaville Rd., Suite 125, Lisle, IL 60532; 708-245-1000. Serves IL, IN, MI, MO, OH, WI.

Region 5

National Credit Union Administration, 4807 Spicewood Springs Rd., Suite 5200, Austin, TX 78759-8490; 512-482-4500. Serves AZ, CO, IA, KS, MN, NE, NM, ND, OK, SD, TX, UT, WY.

Region 6

National Credit Union Administration, 2300 Clayton Rd., Suite 1350, Concord, CA 94520; 510-825-6125. Serves AK, AS, CA, GU, HI, ID, MT, NV, OR, WA.

* Publications

Publications
National Credit Union Administration (NCUA)
1775 Duke St.
Alexandria, VA 22314-3428   703-518-6340

A listing of National Credit Union Administration (NCUA) publications is available from the Administrative office. These publications include the annual report, the credit union directory, as well as technical reports, such as *Chartering and Organizing of a Federal Credit Union*. There is a nominal charge for each publication.

Be patient. If any phone number is incorrect, call (area code) 555-1212 and request the new listing.

425

Investments and Financial Services

Stocks and Bonds

* Accounting

Office of the Chief Accountant
U.S. Securities and Exchange Commission
450 5th St., NW
Washington, DC 20549   202-942-4400

The Securities and Exchange Commission's (SEC) Chief Accountant consults with representatives of the accounting profession and other standard-setting bodies that promote new or revised accounting and auditing standards. One of the Securities and Exchange Commission's major objectives is to improve accounting and auditing standards and to maintain high standards of professional conduct by the independent accountants. This office also drafts rules and regulations that dictate the requirements for financial statements, and rules which require that accountants examining financial statements filed with the SEC be independent of their clients. For more information accounting procedures, contact this office.

* American Depository Receipts

Office of International Corporate Finance
U.S. Securities and Exchange Commission
450 5th St., NW
Washington, DC 20549   202-942-2770

U.S. investors who are interested in foreign securities may purchase American Depository Receipts. These are negotiable receipts, registered in the name of a U.S. citizen, which represent a specific number of shares of a foreign corporation. For more information about American Depository Receipts, contact this office.

* Annual Reports to Shareholders

Public Reference Branch
U.S. Securities and Exchange Commission
450 5th St., NW, Room 1024   202-942-8090
Washington, DC 20549-1002   TDD: 202-942-8092

Although not a required Securities and Exchange Commission (SEC) filing, the *Annual Report to Shareholders* is the main document most public companies use to give information about corporations to shareholders. It is usually a state-of-the-company report which includes an opening letter from the Chief Executive Officer, financial data, results of continuing operations, market segment information, new product plans, subsidiary activities and research and development activities on future programs. Some filings are available in printed form, but all are available on microfiche.

* Annual (10-K) Reports: Investment Information

Public Reference Room
U.S. Securities and Exchange Commission
450 5th St., NW   202-942-8090
Washington, DC 20549   TDD: 202-942-8092

Many companies whose stock is traded over the counter or on a stock exchange must file "full disclosure" reports on a regular basis with the Securities and Exchange Commission (SEC). The annual report, or *Form 10-K*, is the most comprehensive of these. It describes and contains statistical information on the company's business operations, properties, parents, and subsidiaries; its management, including their salaries and their security ownership in the company; any matters which have been submitted to a vote of shareholders; and significant legal proceedings which involve the company. *Form 10-K* also contains the audited financial statements of the company, including a balance sheet, an income statement, and a statement of where funds come from and how they are used. The public may obtain copies for a small fee by visiting or writing the office above.

* Arbitration Procedures

Publications Section
Printing Branch, Stop C-11
U.S. Securities and Exchange Commission
Washington, DC 20549   202-942-4040

Arbitration Procedures is a free publication available from this office which discusses procedures for disputes with brokerage firms involving financial claims.

* Broker/Dealer Registration

Registration
U.S. Securities and Exchange Commission (SEC)
450 5th Street, NW
Washington, DC 20549   202-942-8980

The registration of brokers and dealers who solicit and execute securities transactions is an important part of the work of the Securities and Exchange Commission (SEC). Broker-dealers must abide by the securities laws, the rules of the self-regulatory organization of which they are members, and SEC rules. Registrations must be kept up to date and must reflect any changes in financial conditions over time. The registration form shows: form of organization; if it is a corporation, the date and state of incorporation, and class of equity security; if it is a sole proprietorship, the person's residence and Social Security number; if it is a successor to a previous broker or dealer, the SEC file number of the predecessor; persons with controlling interests; how the business is financed; the firm's or person's standing with the SEC and other regulatory agencies, including disclosure of having made false statements to the SEC in the past, been convicted in the last 10 years of a related felony, been prohibited in the last 10 years from financial activities, aided anyone in violating related laws or rules, been barred or suspended as a broker-dealer, been the subject of a cease and desist order, been associated with a similar firm that went bankrupt, information about the person or business that maintains the applicant's records and holds funds of the applicant or its customers; details about companies which control or are controlled by the applicant; whether the applicant is an investment adviser; types of business done (such as floor activity, underwriting or mutual fund retailing); descriptions of any nonsecurity business; and information about principals, including positions, securities held, Social Security numbers, education and background. Customers have the right to expect that trades will be executed promptly and that the broker will try to secure the best price, for example. They should expect to receive written confirmation of trading, with information including the date of the transaction, the identity of the security bought or sold, and the number of shares, units, or principal amount of the security. Customers can expect information on the cost of the transaction, including commissions charged, from the broker.

* Broker-Dealer Revocations

Office of Chief Counsel
Division of Market Regulation
U.S. Securities and Exchange Commission
450 5th Street, NW
Washington, DC 20549   202-942-4168

In the case members of an exchange or association, registered brokers or dealers, or individuals associated with any such firm, the Commission can issue an order specifying alleged illegal acts or practices and can direct that a hearing take place. If the Commission finds that the law has been violated, it may impose sanctions or bar a firm from conducting a securities business in interstate commerce or on exchanges, or an individual from association with a registered firm.

* Capital Formation for Small Businesses

The Office of Small Business Policy
Division of Corporation Finance
U.S. Securities and Exchange Commission
450 5th Street, NW
Washington, DC 20549   202-942-2950

The Securities and Exchange Commission's (SEC) main responsibility under the securities laws is to protect investors and to make sure the capital markets operate fairly and orderly. However, the Commission is careful not to let its regulations impair capital formation by small businesses. Therefore, the SEC has taken a number of steps to help small businesses raise capital and to ease the burden of undue regulations under the federal securities laws. The Commission is continually examining other ways to meet these goals. For more information, contact this office.

* Commission Meetings

Office of the Secretary
U.S. Securities and Exchange Commission
450 5th St., NW

Washington, DC 20549 202-942-7070

The Commission meets several times each month to debate and decide on regulatory issues. Like other regulatory agencies, the Commission has two types of meetings. Under the Government in the Sunshine Act, meetings may be open to the public and to members of the press; however, if it is necessary to protect the Commission's ability to conduct investigations and/or protect the rights of individuals and entities which may be the subject of Commission inquiries, meetings may be closed. Commission meetings are generally held to discuss and resolve issues the staff brings before the Commissioners. Issues may be interpretations of federal securities laws, amendments to existing rules under the laws, new rules (often to reflect changed conditions in the marketplace), actions to enforce the laws or to discipline those subject to direct regulation, legislation to be proposed by the Commission, and matters concerning administration of the Commission itself. Issues may be resolved in the form of new rules or amendments to existing ones, enforcement actions, or disciplinary actions. Notices of open and closed Commission meetings and the agendas of open meetings are published the preceding week in the *SEC News Digest*. For more information on weekly meetings, contact this office.

* Confirmation of Transaction

Office of Consumer Affairs
U.S. Securities and Exchange Commission
450 5th St., NW 202-942-7040
Washington, DC 20549 TDD: 202-942-7065

There is a fundamental distinction between a broker and a dealer. The broker is the customers' agent who buys or sells securities for them. The broker owes the customer the highest fiduciary responsibility and can charge only the agency commission that the customer agreed to. On the other hand, a dealer acts as a principal and buys securities from or sells securities to customers. The dealer's profit is the difference between the prices for which the securities are bought and sold. The dealer normally will not disclose the fee or commission charged for services rendered. The law requires that the customer receive a written "confirmation" of each securities transaction. This confirmation discloses whether the securities firm is acting as a dealer (a principal for its own account) or as a broker (an agent for the customer). If the firm is acting as a broker, the confirmation must also disclose the broker's compensation from all sources, as well as other information about the transaction. For more information contact your regional office or contact the above Securities and Exchange Commission (SEC) office.

* Consumer Complaints

Office of Consumer Affairs and Information Services
Investor Services Branch
U.S. Securities and Exchange Commission
450 5th St., NW 202-942-7040
Washington, DC 20549 TDD: 202-942-7065

The Investor Services Branch reviews complaints from the investing public nationwide concerning their dealings with the securities industry and typically obtains written responses from firms mentioned in the complaint. Complaints regarding banks, broker-dealers, investors, junk bonds, investment advisers, and so on are all available for review by the general public. This office strives to improve and upgrade the Securities and Exchange Commission's (SEC) complaint processing effort, analyze trends that surface as a result of complaints received, and increase the Commissions' activities in consumer education. Information suggesting a possible violation of federal securities laws is referred to appropriate Commission staff. When complaints entail private disputes between parties, Commission staff attempt informally to assist the parties in resolving the problem. The SEC also welcomes inquiries and reports about questionable securities practices. Investors should remember, however, that the SEC cannot function as a collection agency or directly represent them in a dispute. Direct investor complaints and grievances to the office above.

* Consumer Information Line

Consumer Information Line
U.S. Securities and Exchange Commission (SEC)
450 5th St. NW
Washington, DC 20549 800-SEC-0330

This information line provides information on proposed Securities and Exchange Commission (SEC) rules to improve prices investors receive when buying and selling, SEC brochures that are available, securities which the commission has syspended trading, the commission's insider trading bounty program, disciplinary history of particular brokers, information about the SEC public reference rooms, corporate filings, and other topics. This service is available 24 hours a day, 7 days a week.

* Consumer's Financial Guide

Publications Section
Printing Branch, Stop C-11
U.S. Securities and Exchange Commission
Washington, DC 20549 202-942-4040

The free publication, *Consumer's Financial Guide*, contains basic information on choosing investments and keeping them safe, trading securities, and the different protections guaranteed by law. To obtain this publication contact this office.

* Corporate Finance Policy

Office of Government Financial Policy
Office of the Assistant Secretary of the Treasury
for Domestic Finance
U.S. Department of the Treasury
1500 Pennsylvania Ave., NW
Washington, DC 20220 202-535-6334

This office is the Department of the Treasury's effort to influence the financial policy directives of corporations. The staff can help answer questions on federal intergovernmental lending.

* Corporate Reorganization

Division of Corporation Finance
U.S. Securities and Exchange Commission (SEC)
450 5th St., NW
Washington, DC 20549 202-942-2800

Reorganization proceedings in the U.S. Courts are begun by a debtor, voluntarily, or by its creditors. Federal bankruptcy law allows a debtor in reorganization to continue operating under the court's protection while it attempts to rehabilitate its business and work out a plan to pay its debts. If a debtor corporation has publicly issued securities outstanding, the reorganization process may raise many issues that will directly affect the rights of public investors. The Securities and Exchange Commission (SEC) is authorized to appear in any reorganization case and to present its views on any issue. However, the Commission gets involved only in proceedings which involve significant public investor interest--protecting public investors holding the debtor's securities, and participating in legal and policy issues concerning public investors. The SEC also continues to address matters of traditional Commission expertise and interest relating to securities. Where appropriate, it reviews reorganization plan disclosure statements and participates in some aspects of law enforcement. The court can confirm a reorganization plan if it is accepted by creditors for at least two-thirds of the amounts of allowed claims, more than one-half the number of allowed claims, and at least two-thirds in amount of the allowed shareholder interest. The biggest protection for public investors is the required disclosure statement issued by the debtor to seek votes on the reorganization plan. In addition, plans involving publicly held debtors usually provide for issuing new securities to creditors and shareholders which may be exempt from registration. For more information on reorganization, contact this office.

* Corporate Reporting

Public Reference Room
U.S. Securities and Exchange Commission (SEC)
450 5th St., NW 202-942-8090
Washington, DC 20549 TDD: 202-942-8092

Companies that want their securities registered and listed for public trading on an exchange have to file a registration application with both the exchange and the SEC. Companies that meet a specific size test, whose equity securities are traded over-the-counter, must file a similar registration form. Commission rules dictate the content and nature of these registration statements and require certified financial statements. Once their securities are registered, companies must file annual and other periodic reports to keep the file updated. Also, issuers must send certain reports to shareholders if they request them. Reports may be read at the public reference rooms, and copied there for a small fee, or obtained at reasonable rates from a copying service under contract to the Commission. For more information on registration, contact this office.

* Directory of Companies

Public Reference Room
U.S. Securities and Exchange Commission
450 5th St., NW, Room 1024 202-942-8090
Washington, DC 20549-1002 TDD: 202-942-8092

The annual *Directory of Companies* is a compendium of all companies which are required to file annual reports with the Securities and Exchange Commission under the Securities Exchange Act of 1934. It lists companies alphabetically and classifies

Be patient. If any phone number is incorrect, call (area code) 555-1212 and request the new listing.

427

Investments and Financial Services

them by industry group according to the *Standard Industrial Classification Manual of the Budget* (1992). It is available for $28 (SN #046-000-00151-6) from: Superintendent of Documents, Government Printing Office, Washington, DC 20402; 202-512-1800.

* EDGAR User Manual

The Office of EDGAR Management
U.S. Securities and Exchange Commission
450 5th St., NW
Washington, DC 20549   202-942-8900

Investors, securities analysts, and other members of the public have access to EDGAR information through a variety of subscriptions and services. A copy of the *EDGAR Filing Manual*, which provides detailed information and directions for making filings on EDGAR, is available by contacting this office.

* Electronic Security Processing

The Office of EDGAR Management
U.S. Securities and Exchange Commission (SEC)
450 5th St., NW
Washington, DC 20549   202-942-8900

The EDGAR management system permits corporations to make their required filings electronically via direct transmission, diskettes, or tapes to the Commission. EDGAR will help to speed up the processing and handling of the 11 million pages of disclosure information that are currently filed with the SEC each year. Private companies are encouraged to offer filer training and support on a competitive basis. The public portions of these filings are available in hardcopy printouts and on microfiche. For more information on the EDGAR Management system, contact this office.

* Enforcement Activities

Division of Enforcement
U.S. Securities and Exchange Commission (SEC)
450 5th St., NW
Washington, DC 20549   202-942-4500

The Securities and Exchange Commission's (SEC) enforcement activities are designed to make sure that the Federal securities laws administered by the Commission are obeyed. These activities include measures to:

- Compel obedience to the disclosure requirements of the registration and other conditions of the act;
- Stop fraud and dishonesty in buying and selling securities;
- Obtain court orders prohibiting acts and practices that operate as a fraud upon investors or otherwise violate the laws;
- Suspend or revoke the registrations of brokers, dealers, and investment companies and investment advisers who willingly engage in fraudulent acts and practices;
- Suspend or bar from association persons associated with brokers, dealers, investment companies, and investment advisers who have violated any conditions of the Federal securities laws; and
- Prosecute persons who have engaged in fraudulent activities or other willful violations of those laws.

In addition, attorneys, accountants, and other professionals who violate the securities laws can loose their right to practice before the Commission. To this end, private investigations are conducted into complaints or other suspected securities violations. Evidence of law violations is used to revoke registration or used in Federal courts to control dishonest activities. If the evidence points to criminal fraud or some other type of intentional violation of the securities laws, the facts are referred to the Attorney General for criminal prosecution of the offenders. The Commission may assist in such prosecutions. For more information on enforcement contact this office.

* Exchange Registration

Registration
U.S. Securities and Exchange Commission (SEC)
450 5th St., NW
Washington, DC 20549   202-942-8980

Registration with the Commission is required of National securities exchanges with a substantial securities trading volume, brokers and dealers who conduct securities business in interstate commerce, transfer agents, clearing agencies, government and municipal brokers and dealers, and securities information processors. To register, exchanges must show that they are organized to comply with the provisions of the statute as well as the rules and regulations of the Commission. The registering

exchanges must also show that their rules ensure fair dealing and protect investors. Each exchange is a self-regulatory organization. Its rules must provide for the expulsion, suspension, or other disciplining of member broker-dealers for unjust and unfair trading conduct. Exchanges shall have full opportunity to establish self-regulatory measures ensuring fair dealing and investor protection. However, the SEC approves--by order, rule, or regulation--any rule changes of exchanges concerning various activities and trading practices if necessary. Exchange rules and revisions, proposed by exchanges or by the Commission, generally reach their final form after discussions between representatives of both bodies. For more information, contact this office.

* Fair and Orderly Markets

Division of Market Regulation
U.S. Securities and Exchange Commission (SEC)
450 5th St., NW
Washington, DC 20549   202-942-4168

The Securities and Exchange Commission (SEC) supervises the securities markets and the conduct of securities professionals. It also serves as a watchdog to protect against fraud in the sale of securities, illegal sales practices, market manipulation, and other violations of investors' trust by broker/dealers. Generally, individuals who buy and sell securities professionally must register with a self-regulatory organization (SRO), meet certain qualifications requirements, and obey the rules of conduct adopted by the SRO. The broker/dealer firms for which they work must in turn register with the SEC and obey its rules relating to financial conditions and sales practices. They also must obey the rules of the exchange they belong to, and the rules of the National Association of Securities Dealers.

* Foreign Securities

Office of International Corporate Finance
U.S. Securities and Exchange Commission (SEC)
450 5th St., NW
Washington, DC 20549   202-942-2770

Foreign corporations that want to sell securities in the U.S. must register those securities with the Securities and Exchange Commission (SEC). They are generally subject to the same rules and regulations that apply to securities of U.S. companies, although the nature of information which foreign companies make available to investors may be somewhat different.

* Form 10-Q: Financial Background on Companies

Public Reference Room
U.S. Securities and Exchange Commission (SEC)
450 5th St., NW   202-942-8090
Washington, DC 20549   TDD: 202-942-8092

The *Form 10-Q* is a report filed quarterly by most public companies, containing information that is important for investors to know. It includes unaudited financial statements and provides a continuing view of the company's financial position during the year. The information includes the income statement; balance sheet; description of important changes since the previous quarter; legal processing; changes in securities; default upon senior securities; and other important events. The report must be filed for each of the first three fiscal quarters and is due within 45 days of the close of the quarter. For more information on these reports, contact this office.

* Fraudulent Securities Schemes

Publications Section
Printing Branch, Stop C-11
U.S. Securities and Exchange Commission (SEC)
Washington, DC 20549   202-942-4040

Several free publications are available through the Securities and Exchange Commission that warn investors against various fraudulent schemes. These include *How to Avoid Ponzi and Pyramid Schemes*, and *Warning to Investors About Get-Rich-Quick Schemes*. To obtain copies of these publications contact the above office.

* Help in Choosing an Investment

Office of Public Affairs
U.S. Securities and Exchange Commission (SEC)
450 5th St., NW
Washington, DC 20549   202-942-0020

If you are thinking about investing your money, you might need assistance in making the most suitable choices for your needs. The Securities and Exchange Commission (SEC) is a good source of information on securities with many publications, a public reference room, disclosure reports, and ready information on how to protect yourself.

* Holding Companies Acquisitions

Division of Investment Management
Office of Public Utility Regulation
U.S. Securities and Exchange Commission (SEC)
450 5th Street, NW
MS 10-6
Washington, DC 20549   202-942-0545

To be authorized by the Securities and Exchange Commission (SEC), holding companies and their subsidiaries that acquire securities and utility assets must meet the following standards: 1) The acquisition must not tend toward interlocking relations or concentrating control to the point that it is harmful to investors or the public interest; 2) Any fees, commissions, or other payments for the acquisition must be reasonable; 3) The acquisition must not complicate the capital structure of the holding company system or harm system functions; and 4) The acquisition must help develop an integrated public utility system that is economical and efficient. Contact this office for more information on these standards.

* Holding Companies Issuance and Sales of Securities

Division of Investment Management
Office of Public Utility Regulation
U.S. Securities and Exchange Commission (SEC)
450 5th Street, NW
MS 10-6
Washington, DC 20549   202-942-0545

Proposed security issues by any holding company must be analyzed, evaluated, and approved by the SEC staff to make sure that the security issues meet the following tests: 1) They conform to the security structure of the issuer and of other companies in the same holding company system; 2) They be proportionate to the earning power of the company; 3) They must be fitting and needed to help the company's business operate economically and efficiently; 4) The fees, commissions, and other payments in connection with the issue must be reasonable; and 5) The terms and conditions of the issue or sale of the security must not damage public or investor interest.

Other regulatory provisions regulate dividend payments (in circumstances where payments might result in corporate abuses); inter-company loans; solicitation of proxies, consents, and other authorizations; and insider trading. "Upstream" loans from subsidiaries to their parents and "upstream" or "cross-stream" loans from public utility companies to any holding company in the same holding company system require Commission approval. All services performed for any company in a holding company system by a service company in that system must be rendered at a fair cost. Contact this office for more information.

* Inquiry Processing

Office of Consumer Affairs and Information Services
Investor Services Branch
U.S. Securities and Exchange Commission (SEC)
450 5th St., NW   202-942-7040
Washington, DC 20549   TDD: 202-942-7065

The Commission's consumer affairs staff received approximately 49,000 investor complaints and inquiries last year. These written or telephone complaints and inquiries are routinely tracked and analyzed through a computer program. In addition to tracking basic information about the specific entity named, investor information, and dates of correspondence, special codes are used to identify the type of entity and the nature of the complaint. Consumer affairs specialists research reference materials and/or databases in order to respond to inquiries. An investor must submit a complaint in writing if he or she wants Commission assistance in obtaining an explanation or resolution. In processing the majority of written complaints, the consumer affairs specialist requests a review of the complaint by the compliance or legal department of the appropriate broker-dealer, mutual fund, or issuer, along with a report of that department's findings. This report is then reviewed to determine whether it responds to the issues raised in the complainant's letter. In many cases, the firm will take action to resolve the problem. In others, the investor's claims or allegations are disputed. Since the Commission is not authorized to serve as a judge or arbitrator, the specialist advises the investor of his or her general rights of private recourse.

* Insider Securities Trading

Superintendent of Documents
Government Printing Office   202-512-1800
Washington, DC 20402   Fax: 202-512-2250

The *Official Summary of Securities Transactions and Holdings* is a monthly report of securities transactions and holdings reported by "insiders" (officers, directors, and certain others) under clauses and agreements in the Federal securities laws. The *Summary* (SN #746-001-00000-2) sells for $23 a copy, or $115 per year for a subscription in the U.S.; and $28.75 a copy, or $143.75 per year subscription foreign.

* Insider Trading

Office of Disclosure Policy
Chief Counsel's Office of Corporation Finance
450 5th St., NW
Washington, DC 20549   202-942-2573

Insider trading controls curb misuse of important confidential information which is not available to the general public. Examples of such misuse are buying or selling securities to make a profit or to avoid losses based on nonpublic information--or by telling others of the information so that they may buy or sell securities--before such information is generally available to all shareholders. Fines are imposed up to three times the profit gained, or loss avoided, through the use of nonpublic information. To further control the misuse of nonpublic information, the Securities and Exchange Commission (SEC) requires all company officers and directors to file an initial report with them, and with the exchange on which the stock may be listed, which shows their holdings. Thereafter, they must file reports for any month during which there was any change in those holdings. Also, profits gained from purchases and sales (or sales and purchases) of such equity securities within any six-month period may be recovered by the company or by any security holder on its behalf in U.S. District Court. Such "insiders" are also not allowed to make short sales of their company's equity securities.

* Internationalization of Capital Markets

Office of International Corporate Finance
U.S. Securities and Exchange Commission (SEC)
450 5th St., NW
Washington, DC 20549   202-942-2770

The Securities and Exchange Commission (SEC) has made special efforts to get a wide range of viewpoints on issues that affect investors and the securities industry. One of the issues Commissioners and industry and investor representatives discuss is internationalization. The Commission has worked out agreements with several nations and is in the process of discussing the need for greater coordination among the international capital markets. For more information, contact this office.

* Interstate Holding Companies

Division of Investment Management
Office of Public Utility Regulation
U.S. Securities and Exchange Commission (SEC)
450 5th Street, NW
MS 10-6
Washington, DC 20549   202-942-0545

Interstate holding companies engaged, through subsidiaries, in the electric utility business or those that sell natural or manufactured gas are subject to SEC regulations on matters such as structure of the system, acquisitions, combinations, and issue and sales of securities. These systems must register with the Commission and file initial and periodic reports containing detailed information about their organization, financial structure, and operations. For more information on these reports, contact this office.

* Investment Advisers Registration

Division of Investment Management
Office of Disclosure and Investment Adviser Regulation
U.S. Securities and Exchange Commission (SEC)
450 5th Street, NW
Washington, DC 20549   202-942-0589

Persons or firms who make money advising others about securities investment must register with the SEC and conform to standards designed to protect investors. The Commission may deny, suspend, or revoke investment adviser registrations if, after notice and hearing, it finds that a statutory disqualification exists and that the action is in the public interest. Persons or firms can be disqualified if they are convicted for financial crimes or securities violations, mail fraud, knowingly filing false reports with the Commission, and willfully violating the Advisers Act, the Securities Act, the Securities Exchange Act, the Investment Company Act, or the rules of the Municipal Securities Rulemaking Board. In these cases, registrations are denied, suspended, or revoked. The Commission may obtain injunctions to prevent these violations of the law from happening again in the future. The SEC may also recommend prosecution by the U.S. Department of Justice for fraudulent misconduct or willful violation of the law or Commission rules. The Commission has adopted rules that define fraudulent, deceptive, or manipulative acts and practices. Investment advisers are required to:

Investments and Financial Services

- Make known the reason they are selling securities to their clients;
- Maintain books and records according to Commission rules, and
- Make books and records available to the Commission for inspections.

* Investment Company Registration

Public Reference Room
U.S. Securities and Exchange Commission (SEC)
450 5th St., NW   202-942-8090
Washington, DC 20549   TDD: 202-942-8092

Activities of companies who invest, reinvest, and trade in securities, and who offer their securities to the public, are subject to the following SEC regulations: 1) They must disclose their financial condition and investment policies to provide investors complete information about their activities; 2) They cannot substantially change the nature of their business or investment policies without stockholder approval; 3) They may not have officers or directors who are guilty of securities fraud; 4) Underwriters, investment bankers, or brokers must constitute only a minority of the directors; 5) They must submit management contracts (and any material changes) to security holders for their approval; 6) They may not perform transactions with their directors, officers, or affiliated companies or persons without SEC approval; 7) They are forbidden to issue senior securities except under specified conditions and terms; and 8) They are prohibited from pyramiding and cross-ownership of their securities. Other provisions involve the following: advisory fees that don't conform to an adviser's fiduciary duty; sales and repurchases of securities issued by investment companies; exchange offers; and other activities of investment companies, including special provisions for periodic payment plans and face-amount certificate companies. Investment companies must not only be registered, but must also file periodic reports and are subject to the SEC's proxy and "insider" trading rules. For more information, contact this office.

* Legal Interpretation and Guidance

Office of the Chief Counsel
Division of Corporation Finance
U.S. Securities and Exchange Commission (SEC)
450 5th St., NW
Washington, DC 20549   202-942-2900

The Securities and Exchange Commission is willing to help the public, prospective registrants, and others, interpret the securities laws and regulations. In this way they can help answer legal questions about how laws apply and are regulated in certain situations, and to aid them in following the laws. For example, this advice might include an informal opinion about whether the offering of a particular security is subject to registration requirements and, if it is, advice on the type of information that must go on the registration form. By interpreting the rules and laws, the SEC makes sure registrants conform to them. For help with interpreting laws, or guidance, contact this office.

* Lost and Stolen Securities

Securities Information Center, Inc.
P.O. Box 9151
Boston, MA 02205-9151   617-345-4910

Every insured bank, broker, and registered transfer agent must be registered with the Securities Information Center. The Center maintains a computerized reporting and inquiry system for lost, stolen, counterfeit, and forged securities. All FDIC-insured banks are required to contact the Securities Information Center when they take custody of stocks or bonds valued in excess of $10,000 in order to verify their validity.

* Lost and Stolen Securities Database

Division of Market Regulation
U.S. Securities and Exchange Commission (SEC)
450 5th St., NW
Washington, DC 20549   202-942-4168

The SEC has a computer-assisted reporting and inquiry system for lost, stolen, counterfeit, and forged securities. All insured banks and brokers, members of the federal reserve, dealers, and other securities firms are required to register with the Securities Information Center, Inc., P.O. Box 9151, Boston, MA 02205-9151; 617-345-4910, where a central database records reported thefts and losses. Contact this office for more information.

* Margin Trading

Office of Legal Policy and Trading Practices
Division of Market Regulation

U.S. Securities and Exchange Commission (SEC)
450 5th Street, NW
Washington, DC 20549   202-942-0772

The Board of Governors of the Federal Reserve System sets limits on the amount of credit available to purchase or carry securities, and then periodically reviews them. This is to make sure that too much of the nation's credit isn't used in the securities markets. While the credit restrictions are set by the Board, the SEC handles investigations and enforcement.

* Market Investigations

Office of Inspections and Financial Responsibility
U.S. Security and Exchange Commission (SEC)
450 5th Street, NW
Washington, DC 20549   202-942-0756

The Securities and Exchange Commission (SEC) regional offices and its Division of Market Regulation conduct surprise investigations to check the books and records of regulated people and organizations to make sure their business practices are legal. Inquiries are also conducted into changes in the market, especially stocks which don't appear to result from general market trends or from known developments affecting the issuing company. For more information, contact your regional office or contact or the office above.

* Market Surveillance

Market Surveillance
Division of Enforcement
U.S. Securities and Exchange Commission (SEC)
450 5th St., NW
Washington, DC 20549   202-942-4731

Securities and Exchange Commission regulates securities trading practices in the exchange and the over-the-counter markets, and it has adopted regulations which, among other things, 1) define acts or practices which constitute a "manipulative or deceptive device or contrivance" prohibited by the statute; 2) regulate short selling, stabilizing transactions, and similar matters; 3) regulate the hypothecation of customers' securities; and 4) provide safeguards with respect to the financial responsibility of brokers and dealers. For more information on market surveillance, contact this office.

* Meeting Notes

Office of the Secretary
U.S. Securities and Exchange Commission (SEC)
450 5th St., NW
Washington, DC 20549   202-942-7070

For cassette tapes of the open meeting minutes, send your request in writing to this office.

* New Rules: Securities

Publications Unit
U.S. Securities and Exchange Commission (SEC)
450 5th Street, NW
C3-38
Washington, DC 20549   202-942-4040

For copies of recently adopted rules contact this office.

* Opening an Account

Public Reference Room
U.S. Securities and Exchange Commission (SEC)
450 5th St., NW   202-942-8090
Washington, DC 20549   TDD: 202-942-8092

Before opening an account with a broker, talk with registered representatives at several firms to find the person who best suits your needs. It is added protection to know that most broker/dealers registered with the SEC are members of the Securities Investor Protection Corporation, a nonprofit membership corporation which administers laws to help protect investors securities and funds held in brokerage accounts. Also, before choosing a broker, to get more factual information about the firm itself, you may order a copy of the firm's registration statement (Form BD) from the office above.

* Opinions and Orders

The Office of Administrative Law Judges
U.S. Securities and Exchange Commission (SEC)

450 5th St., NW
Washington, DC 20549   202-942-0399

Associate of Adjudication, General Council
U.S. Securities and Exchange Commission (SEC)
450 5th St., NW
Washington, DC 20549   202-942-0964

The administrative law judges are responsible for scheduling and conducting hearings on administrative proceedings instituted by others. Opinions and orders resulting from these hearings are prepared by the Office of Opinions and Review. For more information on these hearings contact either of the offices above.

* Ponzi or Pyramid Schemes

Office of Consumer Affairs and Information Services
Investor Services Branch
U.S. Securities and Exchange Commission (SEC)
450 5th St., NW   202-942-7040
Washington, DC 20549   TDD: 202-942-7065

The Securities and Exchange Commission will provide warnings against investing in a Ponzi or pyramid scheme. These schemes are varied, but usually promise very high yield, quick return, a "once in a lifetime" opportunity, and the chance to "get in on the ground floor." To notify the Securities and Exchange Commission of a fraudulent scheme and for further information, contact this office.

* Proxy Filings

Public Reference Room
U.S. Securities and Exchange Commission (SEC)
450 5th Street, NW, Room 1024   202-942-8090
Washington, DC 20549-1002   TDD: 202-942-8092

A proxy statement is a document which lets people know who holds stock in a company so they can cast educated votes on matters which are brought up at company meetings. Typically, a security holder is also given a "proxy" who can vote his or her securities if the holder does not attend the meeting. Definitive (final) copies of proxy statements and proxies are filed with the Commission at the time they are sent to security holders. Preliminary proxy filings are nonpublic upon filing, but may be obtained under FOIA once the definitive proxy has been filed and released. Some definitive filings are available in printed copy and on microfiche.

* Proxy Solicitations

Office of Chief Counsel
Division of Corporation Finance
U.S. Securities and Exchange Commission (SEC)
Washington, DC 20549   202-942-2900

The Securities and Exchange Commission (SEC) administers laws which check the votes from holders of registered securities, both listed and over-the-counter, to elect directors and/or to approve corporate action. Solicitations, whether by management or minority groups, must give all important information needed for holders to vote. Holders also must be given an opportunity to vote "yes" or "no" on each matter. In a contest for control of corporate management, the rules require the names and interests of all "participants" in the proxy contest be made known so that holders can vote intelligently on corporate actions that require their approval. The Commission's rules require that proposed proxy material be filed early so the Commission can examine it to be sure all the information needed is given. In addition, the rules allow shareholders vote at the annual meetings. For more information on proxy solicitations, contact this office.

* Publications Listing

Publications
U.S. Securities and Exchange Commission (SEC)
450 5th Street, NW
Mail Stop C-11
Washington, DC 20549   202-942-4040

You can obtain a listing of current Securities and Exchange Commission (SEC) publications by visiting Publications in Room 3C38 or writing to the office above.

* Reference Microfiche

Public Reference Room
U.S. Securities and Exchange Commission
450 5th Street, NW, Room 1024   202-942-8090
Washington, DC 20549-1002   TDD: 202-942-8092

The public may use the following reference microfiche in the Public Reference Room:

Workload List by File Name. Includes cumulative history and a quarterly supplement.
Workload List by File Number. Includes a cumulative history and a quarterly supplement.
SEC Public Reference. An alphabetical list of all registrants since 1934, including numbers of all files for each named registrant.
Ownership Report System: Cumulative. Contains the cumulative data in the *Official Summary of Security Transactions and Holdings* of corporate affiliates and "insiders."

* Registered Company Disclosure Statements (Prospectus)

Public Reference Room
U.S. Securities and Exchange Commission
450 5th St., NW   202-942-8090
Washington, DC 20549   TDD: 202-942-8092

Before any company offers its securities for sale to the general public, (with certain exceptions) it must file with the Securities and Exchange Commission (SEC) a registration statement known as a "prospectus." The prospectus contains the basic business and financial information on an issuer dealing with a particular security that's being offered to help investors evaluate an investment and thereby helps them make an educated investment decision. In its registration statement, the company must provide information on the nature of its business, the company's management, the type of security it offers and its relation to other securities the company may have on the market, and the company's financial statements as certified by independent public accountants. Many companies must continue to update this information periodically, even if no new securities are being offered, and copies of the prospectus must be provided to investors. The SEC reviews registration statements for accuracy and completeness. Investors who purchase securities and suffer losses have important recovery rights under the law if they can prove that there was incomplete or inaccurate disclosure of important facts in the registration statement or prospectus. Investors may sue to recover losses through the courts if false or misleading statements were made in the prospectus. Some filings are available in paper form, and all filings are available on microfiche from the above office.

* Registration Exemptions for Securities

Registration
U.S. Securities and Exchange Commission
450 5th St., NW
Washington, DC 20549   202-942-8980

In general, registration requirements apply to securities of both domestic and foreign issuers, and to securities of foreign governments (or their instrumentalities) sold in domestic securities markets. However, some securities and transactions are exempt from registration provisions. Among these are:

- Private offerings to a limited number of persons or institutions who already have access to the information that registration would disclose and who do not propose to redistribute the securities;
- Offerings restricted to residents of the state in which the issuing company is organized and doing business;
- Securities of municipal, state, federal, and other governmental instrumentalities as well as charitable institutions, banks, and carriers subject to the Interstate Commerce Act;
- Offerings not exceeding certain specified amounts according to regulations of the Commission; and
- Offerings of "small business investment companies" made in accordance with rules and regulations of the Commission.

Whether or not the securities are exempt from registration, antifraud provisions apply to all sales of securities involving interstate commerce or the mails. For more information, contact this office.

* Reviewing a Prospectus

Public Reference Room
U.S. Securities and Exchange Commission (SEC)
450 5th St., NW   202-942-8090
Washington, DC 20549   TDD: 202-942-8092

If you are considering an investment in an open-end investment company, unit investment trust, or variable annuity, you should obtain and read a current prospectus before looking at other sales literature. Do not hesitate to seek advice if there is anything in the prospectus you do not understand. And if you do buy shares in the company, save the prospectus to refer to in the future. Some of the things the

Investments and Financial Services

prospectus will tell you are the company's investment objectives--in other words, how it is designed to provide income, protect capital, minimize taxes, and so forth, the amount of any sales charges and the procedures for redeeming shares, and what risks may be involved in placing your money in that particular company. Registration is there to give you the facts about the company you're dealing with, and to thereby help you to make an informed decision. Keep in mind, however, that the Commission does not supervise the investment activities of these companies and that regulation by the Commission does not imply safety of investment. To obtain a current prospectus, contact this office.

* Revocations of Securities Registration

Office of Chief Counsel
Division of Market Regulation
U.S. Securities and Exchange Commission (SEC)
450 5th St., NW
Washington, DC 20549   202-942-4168

The SEC can deny registration to securities firms and, in some cases, may impose sanctions against a firm and/or individual in a firm for violation of Federal securities laws (such as manipulation of the market price of a stock, misappropriation of customer funds or securities, or other abuse of customer trust). The Commission polices the securities industry through its own inspections and by working with other securities groups. Brokers and dealers who violate regulations risk suspension or loss of registration with the Commission (and thus the right to continue conducting an interstate securities business) or suspension or expulsion from a self-regulatory organization. For more information, contact this SEC office.

* Rulemaking

Office of Public Affairs
U.S. Securities and Exchange Commission (SEC)
450 Fifth Street NW
Washington, DC 20549   202-942-0020

Rulemaking is one of the most common activities the divisions perform. The rules and registration forms that the SEC uses must constantly be evaluated and reviewed to make sure they are as practical and efficient as possible. If a particular rule appears to be burdensome or isn't achieving its objective, a staff members can recommend changes to the Commissioners. Many suggestions for rule changes follow consultation with industry representatives and others who are affected. The Commission normally gives advance public notice when they are planning to adopt new rules or registration forms, or to amend forms so that interested members of the public can comment on them. For information on rulemaking contact the individual divisions at the SEC.

* Section 13F Securities

Public Reference Room
U.S. Securities and Exchange Commission (SEC)
450 5th Street, NW
Room 1024   202-942-8090
Washington, DC 20549-1002   TDD: 202-942-8092

The quarterly publication, *13F Securities*, is a list of all current Section 13(f) securities, that is, securities of a class described in Section 13(d)(1) of the Exchange Act.

* Securities and Exchange Annual Reports

Superintendent of Documents
Government Printing Office (GPO)   202-512-1800
Washington, DC 20402   Fax: 202-512-2250

The First through 55th SEC annual reports to Congress are out of print and available only for reference purposes in the SEC and Regional Offices. *The Fifty-Sixth Annual Report (1990)* sells for $5.50, the *Fifty-Seventh (1991)* sells for $6, the *Fifty-Eighth (1992)* sells for $6, and the *Fifty-Ninth (1993)* sells for $6.

* Securities and Exchange Commission (SEC) Records and Filings

FOIA Privacy Act Operations Branch
Office of the Executive Director
Securities and Exchange Commission (SEC)
Washington, DC 20549-2011   202-942-4320

The Freedom of Information Act (FOIA) allows you to obtain information from various agencies of the federal government, including the Securities and Exchange Commission (SEC). In general you can inspect or obtain copies of public filings maintained by the SEC through the public reference facilities in the Commission's

office. You can request access to agency records not available through the public reference facilities by filing a FOIA request. To find out more about what information available call or write the office listed above.

* Securities and Exchange Commission (SEC) News Digest Online

Public Reference Room
Securities and Exchange Commission (SEC)
450 Fifth St. NW
Washington, DC 20549   202-942-8090

The SEC News Digest is a daily summary of important Securities and Exchange Commission (SEC) developments including listings of registration, acquisition and 8-K filings received by the Commission. It lists certain no-action letters issued by the Commission. It also lists time, date, place and subject of Commission Open Meetings. This information is available from LEXIS or DIALOG, who has available data from June 1985 to the present.

* Securities and Exchange Docket

The Commerce Clearing House, Inc.
4025 West Peterson Avenue
Chicago, IL 60646   312-583-8500

The *SEC Docket* is a weekly collection of the full text of SEC releases, including the full texts of *Accounting Series* releases, corporate reorganization releases, and litigation releases. It is sold for $290 per year or $265 per year for two years. Subscriptions may be ordered from the company listed above.

* Securities and Exchange: How It Works

Publications Section
Printing Branch
Stop C-11
U.S. Securities and Exchange Commission (SEC)
Washington, DC 20549   202-942-4040

The Work of the SEC discusses the laws administered by the Commission, its organization, and public information about it. To obtain a copy contact this office.

* Securities and Exchange Information Line

SEC Information Line
U.S. Securities and Exchange Commission (SEC)
450 5th St., NW   202-942-8088
Washington, DC 20549   TDD: 202-942-7114

The Security and Exchange Commission's Information Line provides general information about the SEC; registration information for participants in the securities industry; information for users of the commissions electronic filing system, EDGAR; voice responses to information requests; and if you are calling from a fax machine, you can access the SEC Information Line fax service. All automated features of this system are available 24 hours a day, 7 days a week. If you want to reach an operator or the publications department, you will have to call between 9 am and 5:30 pm (EST).

* Securities and Exchange Monthly Statistical Review

The Office of Economic Analysis
U.S. Securities and Exchange Commission (SEC)
450 5th St., NW
Washington, DC 20549   202-942-8020

The *SEC Monthly Statistical Review* contains data on odd lot and round lot transactions, block distributions, working capital of U.S. corporations, assets of noninsured pension funds, Rule 144 filings, and 8K reports. This publication has been discontinued, but information from the old copies is available from this office.

* Securities and Exchange News Digest

Washington Service Bureau
655 15th Street, NW
Washington, DC 20005   202-508-0600

Mead Data Central - LEXIS
1150 18th St., NW
Washington, DC 20036   202-785-3550

The *News Digest* is a daily summary of important SEC developments, including listings of registration, acquisition, and 8-K filings received by the Commission. It also lists certain no-action letters issued by the Commission, and time, date, place, and subject of Commission Open Meetings. The private firms listed above offer subscriptions to the *SEC News Digest*.

* Securities and Exchange Public Reference Room

Public Reference Room
U.S. Securities and Exchange Commission (SEC)
450 5th St., NW, Room 1024   202-942-8090
Washington, DC 20549-1002   TDD: 202-942-8092

The Securities and Exchange Commission (SEC) ordinarily makes public most of the information filed with it, including registration statements, proxy material, quarterly and annual reports, applications, and similar documents filed by corporations, mutual funds, or broker-dealers. Public Reference Rooms are located in Chicago, New York, and Washington, DC, regional offices where individuals can review and copy all public documents. In addition, copies may be ordered by writing or phoning the Commission. This information filed with the Commission is available for inspection weekdays from 9:00 a.m. to 5:00 p.m., and copies of the text of this material can be obtained from a private contractor. For a cost estimate or to order materials, contact this office.

* Securities and Public Offerings

Center for Electronic Records (NNX)
National Archives and Records Administration
8601 Adelphi Rd.
College Park, MD 20740-6001   301-713-6630

The National Archives maintains wide variety of archival information regarding the Securities and Exchange Commission, such as a broker-dealer directory, a corporation index system, an investment company datafile (updated through February 1988), an investment advisory directory, an ownership reporting system, and a proposed for sale security system. These datafiles, which are often continuously updated, are for sale on 9 track computer tape or 3480 class tape cartridge on a cost recovery basis. For a complete list of the data available, along with a current price list, contact the Center for Electronic Records.

* Securities Databases

Public Reference Room
U.S. Securities and Exchange Commission (SEC)
450 5th St., NW, Room 1024   202-942-8090
Washington, DC 20549-1002   Fax: 202-942-8092

Computer terminals which access certain SEC databases are located in the Reference Room for use by the public. You are welcome to use the terminals at any time during the business hours of the Public Reference Room. The databases are as follows:

Workload Teleprocessing Display System (WRKD). Provides an up-to-date listing of filings made by registrants. Filings are maintained on this index for approximately 40 months. Information on earlier filings may be found by using the history microfiche.

Securities Reporting System (SIRS). Provides information on securities transactions by company officers, directors, and beneficial owners. For each transaction, SIRS will list the trading date, name of the owner, number of shares involved, price per share, SEC received date, and the type of transaction (stock dividend, acquisition by gift, private purchase, open market purchase, stock split, etc.).

Proposed Sale of Securities Inquiry System (PSSI). An online retrieval system which lets the public access information filed on Forms 144. The system contains six months of historical data. Monthly updates are done around the 10th of each month. Searching by either the Issuer's Name or the Seller's Name or both, you will receive information such as the name of the issuer, the seller, the class of security being sold, date acquired and acquisition codes, number of securities to be sold, market value, shares outstanding, and more.

Proceedings and Litigation Action Display System (PLAD). An online, public system capable of reviewing public litigation data. The data displayed includes the type of action, name, address, jurisdiction, action date, violation, and disposition. The types of actions are federal, state and Canadian, National Association of Securities Dealers, and Stock Exchange.

* Securities Laws: Legal Assistance

The Office of Small Business Policy
Division of Corporation Finance
U.S. Securities and Exchange Commission (SEC)
450 5th St., NW

Washington, DC 20549   202-942-2800

The staff of the Office of Small Business Policy, as well as the personnel of the SEC Regional Offices, will assist you with any questions you may have regarding federal securities laws. For information about state securities laws, contact the appropriate state securities commissioner, whose office is usually located in the capital city.

* Securities Violations: Litigation, Actions, and Proceedings

Public Reference Room
U.S. Securities and Exchange Commission (SEC)
450 5th Street, NW
Room 1024   202-942-8090
Washington, DC 20549-1002   Fax: 202-942-8092

The quarterly *Litigation, Actions and Proceedings Bulletin* contains information of official actions with respect to securities violations reported to the Commission. In addition, the *Bulletin* contains a supplement which lists the names of individuals reported as being wanted on charges of violations of law in connection with securities transactions. Contact this office for more information on obtaining copies.

* Small Business and the SEC

Publications Section
Printing Branch
Stop C-11
U.S. Securities and Exchange Commission (SEC)
Washington, DC 20549   202-942-4040

The free booklet, *Q&A: Small Business and the SEC*, discusses capital formation and the federal securities laws and is designed to help you understand some of the basis, necessary requirements that apply when you wish to raise capital by selling securities. It answers such questions as:

What are the federal securities laws?
Is any special help available for a small business that wants to sell its securities?
Should my company "go public"?
How does my small business "go public"?
If my company becomes "public," what are its disclosure obligations?
Are there legal ways to sell securities without registering with the SEC?
Are there state law requirements in addition to those under the federal securities laws?
Where can I go for more information?

* Small Business Policy

The Office of Small Business Policy
Division of Corporation Finance
U.S. Securities and Exchange Commission (SEC)
450 5th St., NW
Washington, DC 20549   202-942-2800

This office directs the Securities and Exchange Commission's (SEC) small business rulemaking goals, reviews and comments on the impact the SEC rule proposals have on small issuers, and serves as a liaison with Congressional committees, government agencies, and other groups concerned with small business. Information on security laws that pertain to small business offerings may be obtained from this office.

* Standards for Securities Registration

Registration
U.S. Securities and Exchange Commission (SEC)
450 5th St., NW
Washington, DC 20549   202-942-7272

Registering securities with the SEC does not stop the sale of stock in risky, poorly managed, or unprofitable companies. Nor does the Commission approve or disapprove securities on their merits. The only standard which must be met when registering securities is adequate and accurate disclosure of required information on the company and its securities it wants to sell. The fairness of the terms, the issuing company's chances of successful operation, and other factors affecting the merits of investing in the securities have no bearing on the question of whether or not securities may be registered. Contact this office for more information on SEC securities standards.

* Statutory Sanctions

Division of Enforcement
U.S. Securities and Exchange Commission (SEC)
450 5th St., NW

Washington, DC 20549   202-942-4500

Commission investigations are conducted privately to determine whether there is valid evidence of a law violation; whether action should begin to determine if a violation actually occurred; and, if so, whether some sanction should be imposed. The following provisions of the law, along with disclosure requirements, tend to inhibit fraudulent stock promotions and operations to help build the public's confidence in securities investments. When facts show possible fraud or other law violations, the laws provide several courses of action the Commission may take:

- Civil injunction: where the SEC may apply to a U.S. District Court for an order forbidding the acts or practices claimed to violate the law or Commission rules

- Administrative remedy, where the Commission may take specific action after hearings. It may issue orders to suspend or expel members from exchanges or over-the-counter dealers association; deny, suspend, or revoke broker-dealer registrations; or censure for misconduct or bar individuals from employment with a registered firm temporarily or permanently.

* Stop Orders

Office of Chief Counsel
Division of Corporation Finance
U.S. Securities and Exchange Commission (SEC)
450 5th St., NW
Washington, DC 20549   202-942-2900

The Securities and Exchange Commission (SEC) may conclude that the lack of important information in some registration statements appears to be deliberate attempts to conceal or mislead. They may also conclude there is an attempt to conceal or mislead if the deficiencies are not corrected through the informal letter process. In these cases, the Commission may decide that it is in the public interest to conduct a hearing to develop the facts by evidence which determines if a "stop order" should be issued to refuse or suspend the statement. Although losses which may have been suffered in the purchase of securities are not restored to investors by the stop order, the Commissions's order stops future public sales. Also, the decision and the evidence on which it is based may help notify investors of their rights and aid them in their own recovery suits. For more information on stop orders, contact this SEC office.

* Tender Offer Solicitations

Office of Tender Offers
Division of Corporation Finance
U.S. Securities and Exchange Commission (SEC)
450 5th St., NW
Washington, DC 20549   202-942-2920

The Commission requires that important information be made known by anyone seeking to acquire over five percent of a company's securities by direct purchase or by tender offer. This information must also be given by anyone seeking shareholders to accept or reject a tender offer. Thus, as with the proxy rules, public investors holding stock in these corporations may make more informed decisions on takeover bids. These disclosure provisions are supported by certain other controls which help ensure investor protection in tender offers.

* The October 1987 Market Break

The Office of Consumer Affairs
U.S. Securities and Exchange Commission (SEC)
450 5th St., NW
Washington, DC 20549   202-942-7040

The Office of Consumer Affairs participated with other Securities and Exchange Commission (SEC) organizations in developing the staff report on the October 1987 market break. The office analyzed the "market break complaints" that the SEC and Self-regulatory organizations received from October 14th through the 30th in 1987. Over 1,500 written complaints resulted from the market break. An additional 9,300 telephone complaints and questions were received during a six-week period, beginning October 19. Findings resulting from the consumer complaint analysis are contained in Chapter 12 of the staff report entitled, *The October 1987 Market Break*. The report is available for $38 from the Superintendent of Documents, Government Printing Office, Washington, DC 20402; 202-512-1800.

* Transaction Complaint Investigations

Division of Enforcement
U.S. Securities and Exchange Commission (SEC)
450 5th St., NW
Washington, DC 20549   202-942-4500

Under the laws it administers, the Securities and Exchange Commission (SEC) investigates complaints and other suspected law violations in securities transactions. Most of the Commission's investigations are private and are often about selling securities without registration or distorting facts about securities for sale are distorted or left out. Other types of inquiries relate to manipulating market prices of securities, misappropriating or illegally hypothecating customers' funds, conducting a securities business while bankrupt, broker-dealers buying or selling securities from or to customers at unfair prices, and broker-dealers who don't treat customers fairly. Inquiries and complaints by investors and the general public are the main sources of leads for detecting law violations in securities transactions. For more information on securities violations, contact this office.

* Treasury Securities

Federal Reserve Bank of Richmond
Public Affairs Department
P.O. Box 27622
Richmond, VA 23261   804-697-8000

On behalf of the U.S. Treasury, the Federal Reserve Banks handle public sales, transfers, and redemptions of U.S. government securities. *Investing In Government Securities* outlines procedures for purchasing marketable U.S. government securities and is available free from the Federal Reserve Bank of Richmond, or by contacting any Federal Reserve Bank for additional information.

* Treasury Securities Booklet

Federal Reserve Bank of Richmond
Public Affairs Department
P.O. Box 27622
Richmond, VA 23261   804-697-8000

The booklet, *Buying Treasury Securities at Federal Reserve Banks*, which provides detailed information on buying treasury bills, notes, and bonds, can be purchased for $4.50 from this office. (Book only at this PO Box)

* Trust Indentures

Division of Corporation Finance
U.S. Securities and Exchange Commission (SEC)
450 5th St., NW
Washington, DC 20549   202-942-2573

The SEC ensures that bonds, debentures, notes, and similar debt securities offered for public sale and issued under trust indentures with more than $7.5 million of securities outstanding at any one time, conform to certain statutory standards. In an effort to protect the rights and interests of purchasers, the SEC works to:

- Prohibit the indenture trustee from conflicting interests which might affect its duties on behalf of the securities purchasers,
- Require the trustee to be a corporation with as little combined capital and surplus as possible,
- Impose high standards of conduct and responsibility on the trustee,
- Stop special collection of certain claims the issuer owes the trustee if there is default,
- Assure that the issuer supply the trustee with evidence of following indenture terms and conditions (such as those relating to the release or substitution of mortgaged property, issue of new securities, or satisfaction of the indenture), and
- Require the trustee to provide reports and notices to security holders.

They also work to make sure that the security holder's have a right to sue individually for principal and interest, except under certain circumstances. To help security holders communicate with each other on their rights as security holders, a list must be maintained. The SEC examines applications to qualify for trust indenture for compliance with the law and the Commission's rules. For more information on trust indentures, contact this office.

Government Bonds, Bills, and Notes

* Education Savings Bonds

U.S. Savings Bonds Marketing Office
U.S. Department of the Treasury
800 K. St., NW, Suite 800
Washington, DC 20226   202-377-7925

The new education savings bond program permits qualified taxpayers to exclude from their gross income all or a portion of the interest earned on eligible Series EE savings bonds issued after 1989. To qualify for this exclusion, tuition and other post-secondary educational expenses must be incurred by the taxpayer, the taxpayer's spouse, or the taxpayer's dependent at postsecondary educational institutions. These institutions are those that meet federal financial aid program standards. In addition, there are income limitations on participation in the program. Contact this office for more information on the program.

* Federal Debt Management

Federal Finance
Office of the Assistant Secretary of the Treasury
 for Domestic Finance
U.S. Department of the Treasury
1500 Pennsylvania Ave., NW, Room 2334
Washington, DC 20220   202-622-2037

Federal debt instruments are administered by this office, including public debt securities, nonmarketable public issues, federal agency securities, and government-sponsored agency securities.

* Government Securities Claims

Claims Section
Office of Securities and Accounting Services
Bureau of the Public Debt
U.S. Department of the Treasury
300 13th St., SW
Washington, DC 20239   202-874-4000

This office handles claims for lost, stolen, mutilated, or destroyed government securities.

* Retirement Bonds

Bureau of the Public Debt
U.S. Department of the Treasury
200 Third St.
Parkersburg, WV 26106-1328   304-480-6112

Retirement plan bonds and individual retirement bonds are no longer being issued. Redemption tables with the current value of the bonds, beginning with those issued in 1963, are available.

* Savings Bond Buyer's Guide

Office of Public Affairs
U.S. Savings Bonds Marketing Office
U.S. Department of the Treasury
800 K. St., NW, Suite 800
Washington, DC 20226   202-377-7925

Building Security, Fulfilling Dreams: U.S. Savings Bonds Buyer's Guide describes the information you need to purchase savings bonds, such as available series and denominations, interest rates, where to buy, registration, annual limitation on purchases, redemption, tax status, exchange of series HH bonds, and safety features.

* Savings Bonds Information Guide

Consumer Information Center
P.O. Box 100
Pueblo, CO 81002   719-948-3334

The *Savings Bonds Question and Answer Book* explains everything about the savings bond program, including information on purchase, interest, maturity, replacement, redemption, exchange, and taxes. (347A - $.50)

* Savings Bonds: Lost, Stolen or Destroyed

Bond Consultant Branch
Bureau of the Public Debt
U.S. Department of the Treasury
200 Third St.
Parkersburg, WV 26106-1328   304-480-6112

If your Savings Bonds are lost, stolen, or destroyed, you can apply for free replacement to the address above.

* Savings Bonds Rate Information

U.S. Savings Bonds Division
U.S. Department of the Treasury
800 K. St., NW, Suite 800
Washington, DC 20226   800-US-BONDS

For the current market rate of U.S. Savings Bonds, call the above number 24 hours a day, seven days a week.

* Savings Bonds Statistics

Market Analysis Office
Planning and Product Development Branch
U.S. Savings Bonds Marketing Office
U.S. Department of the Treasury
800 K. St., NW, Suite 800
Washington, DC 20226   202-377-7925

To obtain statistics on sales, redemption, and retention of U.S. Savings Bonds, contact the office above.

* Savings Bonds Volunteer Activities

Office of Banking and Volunteer Activities
U.S. Savings Bonds Marketing Office
U.S. Department of the Treasury
800 K. St., NW, Suite 800
Washington, DC 20226   202-377-7925

Volunteers within the Savings Bond marketing effort are the chief executive officers within industry who promote the purchase of bonds through payroll deductions. Contact the above office for additional information.

* Savings Bonds: Where to Buy

Savings Bonds Operations
Bureau of the Public Debt
U.S. Department of the Treasury
200 Third St.
Parkersburg, WV 26106-1328   304-480-6112

Series EE Bonds may be purchased over the counter from or through most commercial banks, as well as many savings and loans and other financial institutions qualified as issuing agents. They may also be purchased in person or by mail from Federal Reserve Banks and the Treasury Department, Bureau of the Public Debt. EE Bonds may also be purchased through payroll savings plans offered by employers and through Bond-a-Month plans offered by some financial institutions. Series HH Bonds are available only on exchange for eligible Series EE/E Bonds, and U.S. Savings Notes, with total redemption values of $500 or more, and through the authorized reinvestment of the redemption proceeds of matured Series H Bonds. They are issued only by Federal Reserve Banks and the Bureau of the Public Debt.

* Savings Notes

Bureau of the Public Debt
U.S. Department of the Treasury
200 Third St.
Parkersburg, WV 26106-1328   304-480-6112

If you are a holder of savings notes, you may obtain information concerning their value and redemption from the office above.

Investments and Financial Services

* Treasury Direct

Securities Transactions Branch
Bureau of Public Debt
U.S. Department of the Treasury
300 13th St.
Washington, DC 20239-0001   202-874-4000, ext. 3
Hearing Impaired TTD Line: 202-874-4026

Treasury Direct is the book-entry system within the Bureau of the Public Debt whereby new issues of bills, notes, and bonds are maintained as accounting records in a nationwide computer system with the Treasury and Federal Reserve, rather than in definitive form as engraved certificates. This involves only securities issued since July, 1986. The entire investment portfolio is maintained in a single master account. Direct access to your account is available nationwide from Federal Reserve Banks. Direct deposit of the refund, interest, and principal interest payments is also available. Multiple automatic reinvestment options can be used, enabling you to request reinvestment for up to two years after the first maturity date without having to complete and mail a reinvestment request. To mail tenders, address to: Bureau of the Public Debt, Department N, Washington, DC 20239-1500.

* Treasury Information Line

Customer Services
Bureau of Public Debt
U.S. Department of the Treasury
300 13th St.
Washington, DC 20239-0001   202-874-4000

This phone number is the path to discovering all the information you need to know concerning Treasury bills, notes, bonds, securities, savings Bonds, and other related topics. The following is a guide to finding the information you need on this electronic recorded message system:

3 - Securities Analyst Assistance
4 - Savings Bond Information
211 - Treasury Bill Offerings
212 - Treasury Note and Bond Offerings
221 - Treasury Bill Auction Results
222 - Treasury Note and Bond Auction Results
231 - Treasury Bill General Information
232 - Treasury Notes and Bonds General Information
241 - Forms, Statement of Account, or IRS Form 1099 (Interest Earned)
251 - Treasury Securities Information
252 - Non-Receipt of Payment: Discount, Semi-Annual Interest, or Principal
253 - How to Report Change of Address
254 - Redeem Matured Registered and Bearer Treasury Securities
255 - Treasury Direct Payments
260 - Mail Gift to Reduce Public Debt

State Banking Information

With bank failures increasing and a major savings and loan crisis in progress, it makes good sense to know as much as possible about your bank and its officers. If the security of your hard-earned nest egg concerns you, it might not be a bad idea to investigate your bank through the state banking department. Each state maintains records on banks under its jurisdiction, and often this information is available to the public, as long as you know how to go about getting it.

State banking offices are the best source of information on the financial status of all state chartered banks. They will provide information on the number and location of banks in your state, their assets, and recent corporate changes (new board members, new branches). In addition, requesting a fiduciary statement can provide you with a full list of bank officers and stockholders. States also maintain information on other lending institutions, such as savings and loans and credit unions.

For whatever reasons, not all states are as forthcoming as others when it comes to providing information on specific banks and lenders. Georgia is the only state that does not provide any information on banks within its borders, while the District of Columbia began doing so in mid-1989. Colorado, North Dakota, and Washington state will only answer written requests for banking data.

The following are examples of the types of information state banking departments provide.

Reports

Most state banking departments provide some type of financial information on the institutions that they regulate. Alaska and Maine will provide performance and status reports on specific institutions, while twenty-nine states provide annual reports to the public. Louisiana and Missouri provide quarterly reports containing the names and addresses of all regulated banks and savings and loan institutions. Only Alaska provides daily earnings statements on its banks.

Connecticut's annual report contains the following information:
- consolidated Call Reports for all financial institutions.
- comparative, consolidated report of conditions of financial institutions.
- listing of all banks with the names of officers and directors
- addresses of all financial institutions, including motor vehicle finance companies, licensed dealers, sale of check companies, transportation of money and valuables companies, and pre-need funeral contract companies
- number and location of branch offices.

Phone Information

Information on regulated financial institutions is available by phone in fifteen states (see specific state).

Audits

In most states, bank audits are performed every 12 to 18 months. Louisiana, Oklahoma, Oregon and Vermont perform audits every two years and Tennessee every three years. Texas is the only state that performs audits every six months. Audit information is confidential in most states, but Vermont will provide such information to the public. California, Delaware, Nevada, New York, North Dakota, and Washington provide limited information.

Directories

Washington, DC has a directory of financial institutions free of charge. The following states have directories available for a fee: Alaska, California, Kansas, Montana, and Texas.

Call Reports

Thirty nine states allow public review of banking call reports -- simply a balance sheet and an income statement. Institutions must submit this information on a quarterly basis. Some states will give you this information over the telephone. Information from call reports is available on any insured bank from the Federal Deposit Insurance Corporation (FDIC), 800-688-3342.

Mailing Lists

Thirty one states provide mailing lists. Some provide this list in the bank's annual report. The following states provide this list at no charge: Arkansas, Delaware, Florida, Idaho, Kentucky, New Hampshire, North Carolina, and West Virginia.

List of State Banking Departments

Alabama
Kenneth R. McCartha, Acting Superintendent of Banks, State Banking Department, 101 South Union Street, Montgomery, AL 36130-0901; 205-242-3452. Regulates: 163 banks, 1 state chartered trust company, and 1 savings and loan. An audit of each institution is done once a year. All information is sent to the Federal Reserve in Atlanta and to the FDIC. All information is confidential. General information on a specific institution can be given over the phone. A mailing list of chartered banks is available for a fee. December and June publisher's statements are free.

Alaska
Willis F. Kirkpatrick, Director, Banking Securities and Corporations, P.O. Box 110807, Juneau, AK 99811-0807; 907-465-2521. Regulates: 15 banks, 1 savings and loan, 3 small loan companies, 14 premium financing companies, 2 state chartered credit unions, 17 federally regulated credit union, and 15 Federal Reserve banks (114 offices total). An audit of each institution is done once a year and all information is confidential. All information is sent to the Federal Deposit Insurance Corporation (FDIC). Quarterly earnings statements are available. A directory of all financial institutions is available for $10. Call Report and mailing lists are available.

Arizona
Richard C. Houseworth, Superintendent of Banks, State Banking Department, 2910 N. 44th St., Suite 310, Phoenix, AZ 85018; 602-255-4421. Regulates: 23 banks, 1 savings and loan, 417 mortgage brokers, 29 credit unions, and 593 used car dealers. An audit of each institution is done once a year. All information on the audit is confidential and sent to the Federal Deposit Insurance Corporation (FDIC), Federal

Investments and Financial Services

Reserve Bank Board and the National Credit Union Administration. Call Reports can be reviewed in the office or by mail for a fee, per copy or yearly rates. A mailing list of financial institutions is available for a fee.

Arkansas
Bill J. Ford, Assistant Bank Commissioner, State Banking Department, Tower Bldg., 323 Center St., Suite 500, Little Rock, AR 72201-2613; 501-324-9019. Regulates 184 state chartered banks. Each institution is audited every 2 years, and information is confidential. Performance reports of each bank are available for a fee. Annual reports are available as well as a mailing list of financial institutions. Some data is available on magnetic tape. Information from call reports is available.

California
James E. Gilleran, Superintendent of Banks, State Banking Department, 111 Pine St., Suite 1100, San Francisco, CA 94111-5613; 415-557-3535. Regulates: 250 state chartered banks, 23 trust companies, and 96 foreign bank departments. Each institution is examined every two years. Information is confidential and sent to the Federal Deposit Insurance Corporation (FDIC). Annaul reports are made public. Information concerning a bank's assets can be given over the phone. A statistical table is available for free. A directory of financial institutions is available for a fee. Call report information from trust companies is also available.

Colorado
Barbara M.A. Walker, State Banking Commission, 1560 Broadway, Suite 1175, Denver, CO 80204; 303-894-7575. Regulates: 151 state chartered banks, 6 industrial banks, 8 money order companies, 9 trust companies, 27 trust departments, 4 debt adjusters, and 13 electronic data processing services. Information on call reports requires a written request or can be inspected at the office. For specific information on a bank, a written request is required.

Connecticut
Ralph M. Shulanski, Jr., Banking Commissioner, Department of Banking, 44 Capitol Ave., Hartford, CT 06106; 203-566-4560. Regulates: state banks, credit unions and savings and loans. Each institution is examined once a year, and all information is confidential. Information from Call Reports is available over the phone, or can be inspected at the office. A mailing list of all financial institutions is available.

Delaware
Christen M. Evan, Acting Commissioner, Office of the State Bank Commissioner, State Banking Commission, 55 E. Loockerman St., Suite 210, Dover, DE 19901; 302-739-4235. Regulates: state chartered commercial banks, and savings and loan institutions. Audits are done annually or as needed. Some information is available to the public. Annual reports are available as well as a free mailing list of all financial institutions. Call reports are available for a fee or can be inspected at the office.

District of Columbia
Linda Fleming McGhee, Acting Director, Office of Banking and Financial Institutions, 717 14th St., NW, Washington, DC 20006; 202-727-1563. Regulates: 1 trust company and 2 banks. Audits are done every two years. All information is confidential and sent to the Federal Deposit Insurance Corporation (FDIC). Some portions of the annual report are available to the public. A directory of financial institutions is available free of charge.

Florida
Gerald Lewis, State Comptroller, Department of Banking and Finance, Division of Banking, Capitol Building, Plaza Level, Tallahassee, FL 32301; 904-488-0370. Regulates: banks, savings and loans, credit unions and international agencies. Institutions are audited once every 18 months and data is kept confidential. Information is sent to the Federal Deposit Insurance Corporation (FDIC). Call Report information can be given over the phone. A mailing list of all financial institutions is available at no charge.

Georgia
Edward D. Dunn, Commissioner, Department of Banking and Finance, 2990 Brandywine Rd., Suite 200, Atlanta, GA 30341; 404-986-1633. Regulates: state chartered banks, sellers holding companies, mortgage companies, credit unions and international banking offices. Institutions are audited between 12 and 18 months depending on size and age. Data files are kept confidential. For specific information on a bank, you must contact the bank individually. Data files are computerized but not available to the public.

Hawaii
Raymond K. Nuraoka, Commissioner, Department of Commerce and Consumer Affairs, Division of Financial Institutions, P.O. Box 2054, Honolulu, HI 96805; 808-586-2820. Regulates: 7 banks, 2 saving and loans, 4 trust companies, 34 finance

companies, 4 credit union, and 10 financial service loan companies. Each institution is audited every 18 months and data files are confidential. Information is sent to the Federal Deposit Insurance Corporation (FDIC). General comparative information on banks requires a written request. A mailing list of financial institutions is available for $.25 per page, and the annual report is available free of charge.

Idaho
Belton J. Patty, Director, Department of Finance, 700 West State St., Boise, ID 83720; 208-334-3319. Regulates: 155 branch banks, 116 finance companies, and 48 credit unions. Audits are done between 18 months and 2 years depending on type of institution. All data files are kept confidential. Information is sent to the Federal Deposit Insurance Corporation (FDIC), Federal Reserve, Federal Home Loan Bank, and the National Credit Union Administration. Annual Reports are available to the public as well as a mailing list of all financial institutions. There is no charge for the list.

Illinois
Richard N. Luft, Commissioner of Bank and Trust Companies, 500 E. Monroe St., Springfield, IL 62701; 217-785-2837. Regulates: 730 state chartered banks. Banks are audited once a year and data files are kept confidential. Data files are sent to the Federal Deposit Insurance Corporation (FDIC). A mailing list of financial institutions is available in alphabetical order, or by county order for a fee of $25. A written request is required for information from call reports.

Indiana
Charles Phillips, Director of Financial Institutions, 402 W. Washington Street, Room WO66, Indianapolis, IN 46204; 317-232-3955. Regulates: 179 banks, 63 credit unions, 13 savings and loans, 232 consumer credit loan companies, 25 check cashers, 25 money transmitters, and 105 pawn brokers and car dealerships. Each institution is audited once a year and information is confidential. Data files are sent to the Federal Deposit Insurance Corporation (FDIC). Annual reports are made public. A mailing list of all financial institutions is available for $100. Computerized data files include banks opened, closed, or those with a new credit license. Data files are available to the public.

Iowa
Richard H. Buenneke, Superintendent of Banking, Department of Banking, 200 E. Grand St., Suite 300, East Grand Office Park, Des Moines, IA 50309; 515-281-4014. Regulates: 445 state chartered banks, 117 loan companies, 341 holding companies, and 1 trust company. Institutions are audited every 18 months. Data files are confidential and information is sent to the Federal Deposit Insurance Corporation in Kansas City. Information from call reports can be obtained for a fee of $5 each. Corporate files and stockholder lists are available for public inspection at the office.

Kansas
Frank D. Dunnick, State Bank Commissioner, State Banking Department, 700 Jackson St., Suite 300, Topeka, KS 66603; 913-296-2266. Regulates: 354 state banks, 98 trust departments, 7 trust companies, and 1 savings and loan. Each institution is audited every 18 months and data is confidential. Information is sent to the Federal Deposit Insurance Corporation (FDIC). A Kansas International Bank Directory is available for a fee. Call 816-421-7941. Call reports are available by mail for a fee or information from call reports is available over the phone.

Kentucky
Edward B. Hatchett Jr., Commissioner, Department of Financial Institutions, 477 Bersailles Rd., Frankfort, KY 40601; 502-573-3390. Regulates: state chartered banks, credit unions, finance companies selling and registering securities, mortgage companies. Financial institutions are audited once a year. All information is kept confidential and sent to the Federal Deposit Insurance Corporation (FDIC). An annual report which gives bank locations and licenses received is available for free. Some financial information and mailing list information is available in computer readable formats. Call report information is available by phone, mail, or at the office at no cost.

Louisiana
Larry L. Murray, Commissioner of Financial Institutions, Office of Financial Institutions, P.O. Box 94095, Baton Rouge, LA 70804; 504-925-4660. Regulates: 208 state chartered banks, 50 savings and loans, 85 credit unions, and 1200 consumer loan companies. Institutions are audited every two years, and all data files are kept confidential. A quarterly report is available for $10. Requests for information from call reports must be made in writing.

Maine
H. Donald DeMatteis, Superintendent, Bureau of Banking, Department of Professional and Financial Regulations, State House Station #36, Augusta, ME

Be patient. If any phone number is incorrect, call (area code) 555-1212 and request the new listing.

04333; 207-582-8713. Regulates: 17 chartered banks, 4 savings and loans, 12 credit unions and 14 trust companies. Institutions are audited every 2 years and all data is confidential. Data files are sent to the Federal Deposit Insurance Corporation (FDIC). Call reports and balance sheet information is available over the phone. A status report is done on an annual basis for the state legislature and is available to the public. A mailing list of all financial institutions is available as well as information in computer readable formats. For residents of Maine, there are four Consumer Outreach Booklets and videos for middle and high school level on money management issues free of charge.

Maryland

Margie Muller, State Bank Commissioner, Department of Licensing and Regulation, 501 St. Paul Place, 13th Floor, Baltimore, MD 21202; 410-333-6808. Regulates: 78 state chartered banks, and 18 credit unions. Institutions are audited once a year. All data files are kept confidential. Call report information and balance sheet data can be obtained at this office.

Massachusetts

Thomas J. Curry, Acting Commissioner, Division of Banks, 100 Cambridge St., 20th Floor, Boston, MA 02202; 617-727-3120. Regulates: state chartered banks, trust companies, credit unions, finance companies, loan agencies, mortgage companies, credit agencies, auto financing, and retail institutions. Audits are done once a year and all data is confidential. Call reports are available for a fee of $8 per report. A mailing list of executives is available for $30 per year. Bulletins, summary complaints, financial statements, bank roster and information on other financial institutions is available for a fee.

Michigan

Russell S. Kropschot, Commissioner, Financial Institutions Bureau, P.O. Box 30224, Lansing, MI 48909; 517-373-3460. Regulates: 171 banks, 372 credit unions and 3 savings and loans. Institutions are audited annually and data files are kept confidential. An annual report is available to the public as well as a mailing list and computer readable formats of the financial institutions they regulate.

Minnesota

James G. Miller, Deputy Commissioner of Commerce, Financial Examinations Division, Department of Commerce, 133 E. 7th St., St. Paul, MN 55101; 612-296-2135. Regulates: state chartered banks, mortgage companies, small loan companies and loan and thrifts (total of 5000). Each institution is audited every 18 months and data files are kept confidential. Data files are sent to the Federal Deposit Insurance Corporation (FDIC). An annual report is available as well as Call Reports for 50 cents per copy.

Mississippi

Department of Banking and Consumer Finance, P.O. Drawer 23729, Jackson, MS 39205-3729; 601-359-1031. Regulates: 100 banks, 750 small loan companies, 80 credit unions. Institutions are audited once a year and data files are kept confidential. Information from a branch application can be inspected at this office.

Missouri

Earl L Manning, Commissioner's Office, Division of Finance, Department of Economic Development, Regulation and Licensing, P.O. Box 716, Jefferson City, MO 65102; 314-751-2545. Regulates: 425 banks and 370 loan companies. Audits are done every year on banks and every two years on loan companies. Information is confidential and is sent to the Federal Deposit Insurance Corporation (FDIC). Quarterly reports are available to the public. Call reports are available over the phone or by mail for a fee.

Montana

Donald W. Hutchinson, Commissioner of Financial Institutions, P.O. Box 200512, Helena, MT 59620-2091; 406-444-2091. Regulates: 106 state banks, sales finance companies, credit unions, consumer loans and escrows. Each bank is audited once a year, and data files are reported to the Federal Deposit Insurance Corporation (FDIC). Call report information, assets, and liability statements can be given over the phone. A mailing list and directory are available from the Montana Bankers Association for a fee, 406-443-4121.

Nebraska

James Hansen, Director of Banking and Finance, P.O. Box 95006, Lincoln, NE 68509-5006; 402-471-2171. Regulates: 252 commercial banks, one industrial bank, credit unions, sales finance companies, installment companies and trust companies. Banks are audited every one to two years. All data files are confidential, and information is sent to the Federal Deposit Insurance Corporation (FDIC). The annual report is available to the public. Call reports are available over the phone and printed in local papers on a quarterly basis.

Nevada

L. Scott Walshaw, Department of Commerce, Financial Institutions Division, 406 E. 2nd St., Carson City, NV 89710; 702-687-4259. Regulates: banks, savings and loans, credit unions, thrift and loan companies, consumer finance companies and debt collection organizations. Institutions are audited once a year, and data files are sent to the Federal Deposit Insurance Corporation (FDIC). Some financial information is available over the phone. A mailing list of all financial institutions is available for a fee. Some data files are available in computer readable formats.

New Hampshire

A. Rolland Roberge, Bank Commissioner, Department of Banking, 169 Manchester St., Concord, NH 03301; 603-271-3561. Regulates: state chartered banks, trust companies and savings and loans. Institutions are audited every 18 months. All data files are kept confidential. An annual report and monthly bulletin is available to the public, as well as a list of pending applications. A mailing list of financial institutions is available at no cost.

New Jersey

Jeff Connor, Commissioner, Department of Banking, 20 W. State St., P.O. Box CN-040, Trenton, NJ 08625; 609-292-3420. Regulates: commercial and savings banks, credit unions, mortgage companies and small loan companies (6,000 total). Institutions are audited once a year and data files are kept confidential. An annual report and press releases are available. A mailing list of all financial institutions can be obtained at no charge. Some data may be available on computer magnetic tape.

New Mexico

Robert I. LaGrange, Director, Financial Institution Division, P.O. Box 25101, Santa Fe, NM 87504; 505-827-7100. Regulates: 49 state banks, 27 credit unions, one savings and loan, 141 finance companies, 25 escrow companies, 147 mutual sales finance companies, 116 collection agencies, 22 endowment centers, 129 mortgage companies, and 10 trust companies. Institutions are audited once a year. Data files are confidential and are sent to the Federal Deposit Insurance Corporation (FDIC). Information regarding the total asset of an institution can be given over the phone. An annual report, containing a list of financial institutions, is available to the public. Call reports are available.

New York

Superintendent of Banks, State Banking Department, 2 Rector St., New York, NY 10006; 212-618-6642. Regulates: state chartered banks, commercial banks, savings and loans, credit unions, and branches of foreign banks. Audits are done on an annual basis. Most data files are confidential. Brochures are available from the consumer division.

North Carolina

William T. Graham, Commissioner of Banks, Banking Commission, Department of Economic and Community Development, P.O. Box 29512, Raleigh, NC 27626; 919-733-3016. Regulates: 65 state chartered banks, and finance companies. Institutions are audited once a year. Data files are kept confidential and are sent to the Federal Deposit Insurance Corporation (FDIC). Profit/loss statements are public information. A mailing list of all financial institutions is available at no charge.

North Dakota

Gary D. Preszler, Commissioner of Banking, State Capitol, 600 E. Blvd. Ave., 13th Floor, Bismarck, ND 58505; 701-224-2253. Regulates: 117 state chartered banks, 54 credit unions and money brokers. Institutions are audited every 3 years. Some data files are available to the public with a written request to the Commissioner. Data files are sent to the Federal Deposit Insurance Corporation (FDIC). Information from a bank's call report is available over the phone. A mailing list of all financial institutions is available for a fee.

Ohio

John Burns, Deputy Superintendent of Banks, Division of Banks, Department of Commerce, 77 S. High St. 21st Floor, Columbus, OH 43266; 614-466-2932. Regulates: state chartered banks. Banks are audited every 18 months. All data files are kept confidential. A copy of data is sent to the Federal Deposit Insurance Corporation (FDIC). No mailing lists available.

Oklahoma

Mick Thompson, Bank Commissioner, Oklahoma Banking Association, 4545 Lincoln Blvd., Oklahoma City, OK 73105; 405-521-2783. Regulates: state chartered banks, credit unions, savings and loans, and trust companies. Institutions are audited every 2 years. All data is confidential and is sent to the Federal Deposit Insurance Corporation (FDIC). Financial information and letters of correspondence can be reviewed by the public. Call reports are available. The handbook *Report of the Bank*

Be patient. If any phone number is incorrect, call (area code) 555-1212 and request the new listing.

439

Investments and Financial Services

Commissioner, containing information from 1988 to the present on all financial institutions, is available.

Oregon

Cecil R. Monroe, Administrator, Department of Insurance and Finance, Division of Finance and Capital Securities, 21 Labor and Industry Building, Room 410, Salem, OR 97310; 503-378-4140. Regulates: banks, trust companies, pawn brokers. Audits are performed every 2 years or when needed. All data files are confidential and are sent to the Federal Deposit Insurance Corporation (FDIC). Annual reports are available to the public. A mailing list of all financial institutions is available. Information from call reports is available.

Pennsylvania

Sara W. Hargrove, Secretary of Banking, 333 Market St., 16th Floor, Harrisburg, PA 17101; 717-787-6991. Regulates: state chartered savings and loans, commercial banks, foreign banks, credit unions, consumer discount companies, and mortgage banks and brokers. Audits are done on a yearly basis. All data files are confidential and are sent to the Federal Deposit Insurance Corporation (FDIC). An annual report, which contains a listing of all financial institutions, is available to the public.

Rhode Island

Edward D. Pare Jr., Associate Director, Superintendent of Banking, Banking Insurance and Securities Administration, Department of Business Regulation, 233 Richmond St., Suite 231, Providence, RI 02903; 401-277-2405. Regulates: 5 saving banks and 11 trust companies, 1 savings and loan, 46 credit unions, and 450 finance companies. Audits are done once a year. All data files are kept confidential and are sent to the Federal Deposit Insurance Corporation (FDIC). An annual report listing all depositors is available for $25. Information from a call report is available from the office. Balance sheet data is computerized and available in various reports.

South Carolina

Louie A Jacobs, Commissioner of Banking, Bank Examining Division, 1015 Sumter St., Room 309, Columbia, SC 29201; 803-734-2001. Regulates: 51 state chartered banks, 2 trust companies, 27 credit unions, and 6 savings and loans. Institutions are audited once a year. All data files are confidential and are sent to the Federal Deposit Insurance Corporation (FDIC). Information from a call report is available over the phone or by mail. An annual report is available which contains a list of all financial institutions and their addresses.

South Dakota

Richard A. Duncan, Director, Division of Banking, State Capitol Building, 500 E. Capital Ave., Pierre, SD 57501-5070; 605-773-3421. Regulates: 103 banks, 3 savings and loans, 22 mortgage companies, and 19 finance companies. Audits are done annually. All data files are confidential. An annual report is available to the public.

Tennessee

Talmadge Gilly, Commissioner, Department of Financial Institutions, John Sevier Bldg., 4th Floor, Nashville, TN 37243-0705; 615-741-2236. Regulates: state banks, credit unions, savings and loans and mortgage companies. Audits are done every 3 years. All data files are confidential. An annual report and information on a bank's total assets are available by visiting the office or by mail for a fee. Call reports are available.

Texas

Catherine Ghiglieri, Banking Commissioner, Department of Banking, 2601 N. Lamar Ave., Austin, TX 78705; 512-475-1300. Regulates: 510 state banks, and 22 foreign bank agencies. Audits are done every 6 months. All data files are confidential. Information is sent to the Federal Reserve and the Federal Deposit Insurance Corporation (FDIC). Information on a call report is available by visiting the office or by written request. A directory of all financial institutions is available for a fee of $15.

Utah

G. Edward Leary, Commissioner, Department of Financial Institutions, P.O. Box 89, Salt Lake City, UT 84110; 801-538-8830. Regulates: 37 banks. Audits are done yearly. All data files are kept confidential and are sent to the Federal Deposit Insurance Corporation (FDIC) and the Federal Reserve. Information on a report of condition can be given over the phone. Annual reports are available to the public.

Vermont

Elizabeth R. Costle, Commissioner, Department of Banking and Insurance, 89 Main St., Drawer 20, Montpelier, VT 05620-3010; 802-828-3301. Regulates: 16 banks, 3 savings and loans, 46 credit unions, 1 trust company, and 164 license lenders. Audits are done every 2 years and data files are available to the public. Information is sent to the Federal Deposit Insurance Corporation (FDIC). An annual report is available to the public. Call report information is available.

Virginia

Sidney A. Bailey, Commissioner, Bureau of Financial Institutions, State Corporation Commission, P.O. Box 640, Richmond, VA 23205; 804-371-9657. Regulates: state chartered banks, credit unions, industrial loans, savings and loans, and mortgage brokers (total of 500). Audits are done once a year. Data files are kept confidential. An annual report is available containing a list of financial institutions and the proper addresses. Quarterly balance sheets are available.

Washington

Patty Brombacker, Supervisor of Banking, Division of Banking, Department of General Administration, 1400 S. Evergreen Park Dr., SW, Suite 120, P.O. Box 41203, Olympia, WA 98504; 206-753-6520. Regulates: 99 state banks. Audits are done once a year. Data can be obtained with a written request. Data files are sent to the Federal Deposit Insurance Corporation (FDIC). An annual report is available to the public. Call reports require a written request or can be reviewed at the office.

West Virginia

Sharon G. Bias, Commissioner, West Virginia Division of Banking, State Capital Complex #3, Suite 311, 1900 Kanowha Blvd., E., Charleston, WV 25305-0240; 304-558-2294. Regulates: 167 banks, 15 industrial loans, 16 credit unions, 55 small loan companies, 12 mortgage companies. Audits are done once a year. All data files are confidential. Information from Call Reports and correspondence is available for public inspection at this office. A mailing list of all financial institutions is available for free. Some financial information and Call Reports are computerized and information is released upon request. An annual report is also available.

Wisconsin

Richard L. Dean, Office of the Commissioner of Banking, P.O. Box 7876, Madison, WI 53707; 608-266-1621. Regulates: finance companies, loan companies, insurance companies, adjustment services, and state chartered banks licensed as finance companies. All data files from an audit are confidential. Information available to the public includes complaints registered, rate charges and an annual report. A mailing list of all financial institutions is available for a fee. Some data is available in computer readable formats.

Wyoming

Sue E. Mecca, Bank Commissioner, Department of Audit, Herschler Bldg., 3rd Floor E, Cheyenne, WY 82002; 307-777-7797. Regulates: 34 state chartered banks, 40 state bank branches, 1 savings and loan, and 2 trust companies. Audits are done annually and data files are kept confidential. Information is sent to regulatory agencies and the Federal Deposit Insurance Corporation (FDIC). An annual report and balance sheet information are available for public inspection at this office. A mailing list of all state and national banks is available is available for $25. Call reports are available with a written request. Call report information is published in local newspapers.

Be patient. If any phone number is incorrect, call (area code) 555-1212 and request the new listing.

Commodities

See also Agriculture and Farming Chapter

* Commission-Registered Traders

Registration Unit
Commodity Futures Trading Commission
2033 K Street, NW, Room 701
Washington, DC 20581   202-418-5417

Futures Commission brokers, commodity trading advisors, commodity pool operators, and other companies and individuals involved in futures trading register with the Commodity Futures Trading Commission (CFTC). To determine is a specific company or individual is registered call the Registration Unit. For a directory listing all firms involved in futures trading contact the National Futures Association, P.O. Box 98383, Chicago, IL 60693-0001, Attention: Business Systems Group, 312-781-1300 or 800-621-3570. Send check or money order for $25 and include your telephone number on the payment.

* Commodities Futures Trading Reference Books

Library
Commodity Futures Trading Commission
2033 K Street, NW, 5th Floor
Washington, DC 20581   202-418-5255

A collection of commodity futures trading-related materials emphasizing law, economics, business, and commodities is maintained at the library. With approval and by pre-arranged appointment, limited public use of the facility is permitted. Contact the Library for details.

* Commodity Exchange Act Violations

Office of General Council
Commodity Futures Trading Commission
2033 K St. NW
Washington, DC 20581   202-418-5000

This office investigates alleged violations of the Commodity Exchange Act and Commodity Futures Trading Commission (CFTC) regulations. When a violation is found a complaint could be filed in the agency's administrative courts or in the U.S. District Courts. Alleged violations of the Commodity Exchange Act or of other Federal laws may be referred to the Justice Department for prosecution.

* Commodity Exchange Regulation

Division of Trading and Markets
Commodity Futures Trading Commission
2033 K St., NW, Room 640
Washington, DC 20581   202-418-5430

Regulation of the exchanges on which commodities futures are traded is the responsibility of this division. Approval of all futures contracts traded or exchanged must also be obtained from this office. For further information, contact the Division of Trading and Markets.

* Commodity Futures Trading Commission (CFTC) Regional and Sub-offices

Eastern Region
Commodity Futures Trading Commission (CFTC), One World Trade Center, Suite 3747, New York, NY 10048; 212-466-2061.

Central Region
Commodity Futures Trading Commission (CFTC), 300 South Riverside Plaza, Suite 1600 North, Chicago, IL 60606; 312-353-5990.

Minneapolis Region
Commodity Futures Trading Commission (CFTC), 510 Grain Exchange Bldg., Minneapolis, MN 55415. 612-370-3255.

Southwest Region
Commodity Futures Trading Commission (CFTC), 4900 Main St., Suite 721, Kansas City, MO 64112; 816-931-7600.

Western Region
Commodity Futures Trading Commission (CFTC), 10900 Wilshire Blvd., Suite 400, Los Angeles, CA 90024; 310-235-6783.

* Commodity Trading Complaints

Office of Proceedings
Complaint Section
Commodity Futures Trading Commission
2033 K St., NW
Washington, DC 20581   202-418-5250

This unit directs proceedings to determine if reparations are to be made to persons who claim damages as a result of violations of the Commodity Exchange Act. If you believe you may have been cheated or defrauded in trading transactions, the Commission should be advised. Staff here can also confirm if there are any pending or prior legal actions involving an individual or firm registered with the Commission.

* Company Information: FOIA Requests

Freedom of Information Act Office (FOIA)
Commodity Futures Trading Commission
2033 K St., NW, Room 211
Washington, DC 20581   202-418-5105

Information is collected by the Commission on futures commissions brokers, dealers, commodity futures exchanges, commodities trading advisors, and other individuals and companies involved in futures trading of commodities such as agricultural products, metals, and lumber. A Freedom of Information Act (FOIA) request must be filed to obtain information that may be disclosed from registration applications, hearing and appeal transcripts, and other records on specific individuals and firms. Contact the FOIA office listed for details.

* Futures Markets Publications and Reports

Office of Communication and Education Services
Commodity Futures Trading Commission (CFTC)
2033 K St., NW
Washington, DC 20581   202-418-5080

Information from the Commission's studies of the functioning of futures markets can be obtained from this office. Reports and publications about the Commission and explaining commodities futures trading include background on Commodity Futures Trading Commission (information provided when requested).

CFTC Annual Report
Economic Purposes of Futures Trading
Reading Commodity Futures Price Tables

Contact the office listed to obtain reports, publications, and information.

* Mineral Commodity Summaries 1989

Minerals Information Office
Bureau of Mines/U.S. Geological Survey
U.S. Department of the Interior
1849 C St., NW, MS 2647-MIB
Washington, DC 20240   202-208-5520

Mineral Commodity Summaries 1992 lists the statistics available for 90 commodities, including domestic production and uses; salient statistics - United States; recycling; import sources; tariff; depletion allowance; government stockpile; events and trends; world mine production, reserves and reserve base; world resources; and substitutes. The expert's name and phone number of each report is also listed. This publication is available for sale from the Government Printing Office, 202-512-1800.

Be patient. If any phone number is incorrect, call (area code) 555-1212 and request the new listing.

441

Investments and Financial Services

* Mineral Commodity Information

Minerals Information Office
U.S. Department of the Interior
1849 C St., NW, MS 2647-MIB
Washington, DC 20240 202-208-5520

The Minerals Information Office is staffed by mineral experts who distribute a wide variety of mineral-related information and publications to meet and support the needs of the public, as well as government agencies and the scientific and industrial sectors. The staff provides information on the most current as well as past published reports pertaining to minerals, mining, processing, and research, as well as updated listings of current reports.

* Mineral Deposits Database

Minerals Information Office
U.S. Department of the Interior
1849 C St., MS 2647-MIB
Washington, DC 20240 202-208-5520

The *Personal Computer Advanced Deposit Information Tracking System Mineral Deposit Data Base* contains information on 3,000 domestic and foreign (market economy countries) mining operations, including operation data (name, company, locations, etc.) and operation status (operation type, processing and milling methods, capacity, etc.). The database covers 34 critical and strategic commodities, representing those deposits most significant in terms of value and tonnage.

* Mineral Production and Consumption

Information and Analysis Division
Bureau of Mines
U.S. Department of the Interior
2401 E St., NW
Washington, DC 20241 202-634-7131

The Bureau of Mines collects information about minerals from U.S. mining companies and mineral processing plants. Mineral production and consumption is monitored throughout the world through contacts with foreign governments, U.S. embassies, international publications, and visits to mines overseas. The Bureau employs 11 state mineral specialists through cooperative data collection agreements with the states. Three regional field offices and nine research centers also gather information. The data is then made available to the public via reports, books, and computer disks.

* Minerals: Data, Industries, and Technology

Publication Distribution, Bureau of Mines
U.S. Department of the Interior
Cochrans Mills Rd.
P.O. Box 18070
Pittsburgh, PA 15236 412-892-4338

The Bureau of Mines publishes several reports of investigations and information circulars that are free of charge to those interested in mineral research. *Mineral Industry Surveys* are published monthly, quarterly, and annually, presenting data on various minerals and metals. Reprints from *Minerals Yearbook 1987* are available and report on the mineral industry in the United States and abroad. *Minerals Facts and Problems* covers the technology used in the extraction and processing of minerals.

* Minerals Yearbooks Bibliography

Superintendent of Documents
Government Printing Office 202-512-1800
Washington, DC 20402 Fax: 202-512-2250

Yearbooks on metals and minerals are listed, as well as reports on the domestic and international industry. Free.

* Monitoring Commodity Trading

Division of Economics and Analysis
Commodity Futures Trading Commission (CFTC)
2033 K St., NW
Washington, DC 20581 202-418-5260

Proposed futures trading contracts are reviewed for validity by this division. It also analyzes the economic implications of Commodity Futures Trading Commission (CFTC) regulations and policies and watchdogs trading to detect manipulations, price distortions, and congestion in the markets. For further details, contact the division listed.

* National Futures Association

National Futures Association (NFA)
200 West Madison St., #1600 312-781-1300
Chicago, IL 60606 800-676-4NFA

The Commodity Futures Trading Commission (CFTC) has delegated the authority for registering commodity future professionals to the National Futures Association (NFA), who will conduct a thorough background investigation. This is a self regulatory organization where you can obtain free information about commodity futures and option trading, or how to proceed if there has been any violations of the Commodity Exchange Act or the regulations of the CFTC.

* NYMEX Electronic Trading System

Commodity Futures Trading Commission (CFTC)
2033 K St. NW
Washington, DC 20561 202-418-5000

In June 1993, the commission approved the New York Mercantile Exchange's (NYMEX) ACCESS system for the trading of energy futures products available to U.S. and international traders. The system operates after regular New York trading hours. For more informaiton contact the Commodity Futures Trading Commission (CFTC).

Be patient. If any phone number is incorrect, call (area code) 555-1212 and request the new listing.

Taxes
Federal Tax Help

Federal Tax Help

Why pay money to expensive tax preparers, accountants, and attorneys when you can get better services and information directly from the government? The government has dozens of free tax help programs very few people know about. There is a special section at the end of this chapter for state tax assistance.

Interesting Facts

Gross internal revenue collections reached $1.01 trillion in 1989 (up 8.4%) and there were 199.6 million federal tax returns and supporting documents filed. IRS issued 82.6 million refunds totaling $93.6 billion, compared to $94.5 billion last year. Last year was the seventh year taxpayers were invited to make voluntary contributions to reduce the public debt. There were 529 contributions, totaling $204,000. For tax years beginning after 1990, unnecessary cosmetic surgery will not qualify as a deductible medical expense. Cosmetic surgery is any procedure that is directed at improving the patient's appearance and does not meaningfully promote the proper function of the body or prevent or treat illness or disease.

Taxpayers Affected by Operation Desert Shield

New Publication 945, *Tax Information for Those Affected by Operation Desert Shield*, contains answers to commonly asked questions that primarily apply to newly activated reservists, as well as all other active duty U.S. military personnel and their families, citizens who had been detained by Iraq, and citizens who had to leave the Middle East because of the adverse conditions. This publication covers many issues, such as available tax relief measures for suspending examinations or collection of back taxes, extending due dates for filing an income tax return, meeting the requirements for the foreign earned income exclusion, and seeking other tax assistance.

* Actuaries Enrollment Board

Joint Board for the Enrollment of Actuaries
Internal Revenue Service (IRS)
U.S. Department of the Treasury
Washington, DC 20220   202-376-1421

Individuals who wish to perform actuarial services must enroll with this Board within the IRS. The Board is also responsible for the supervision of actuaries and their enrollment revocation after fair hearings.

* Amending Your Tax Return

Service Center Directors
Deputy Commissioner, Operations
Internal Revenue Service (IRS)
1111 Constitution Ave, NW
Washington, DC 20224   202-622-4255

If you find that you did not report income on your tax form, did not claim deductions or credit you could have claimed, or you claimed deductions or credits that you should not have claimed, you can correct your return by filing a Form 1040X, Amended U.S. Individual Income Tax Return. Generally, this form must be filed within three years from the date of your original return or within two years from the date you paid your taxes, whichever is later. File Form 1040X with the IRS Service Center in your area, listed elsewhere in this book.

* Collection

Office of the Assistant Commissioner
Internal Revenue Service (IRS)
1111 Constitution Ave., NW, Room 7238
Washington, DC 20224   202-622-5430

Collection is responsible for securing delinquent Federal tax returns and for collecting taxes where the amount owed is not in dispute, but remains unpaid. The Service Center Collection Branch (SCCB) is Collection's first point of contact with taxpayers who are delinquent in filing returns and paying taxes. They send notices to taxpayers and act on the replies. The SCCB also reviews selected Forms W-4, Employee's Withholding Allowance Certificate, to determine whether employees have the correct amount of tax withheld from their wages and directs employers to increase the amount withheld when appropriate.

* Corporation Tax Statistics

Statistics of Income Division
Internal Revenue Service (IRS)
P.O. Box 2608
Washington, DC 20013-2608   202-874-0410

The following Statistics of Income reports and tapes can be purchased from the Statistics of Income Division. Prepayment is required, with checks made payable to the IRS Accounting section. These reports can also be purchased from the Superintendent of Documents, 202-512-1800.

Corporation Source Book, 1989, Publication 1053, $175. This 480-page document presents detailed income statement, balance sheet, tax and investment credit items by major and minor industries and size of total assets. A magnetic tape containing the tabular statistics for 1986 can be purchased for $1,500.

Partnership Source Book, 1957-1983, Publication 1289, $30. This 291-page document shows key partnership data for 1957 through 1983, at the minor, major and division industry levels. It includes a historical definition of terms section and a summary of legislative changes affecting the comparability of partnership data during that period. A magnetic tape containing the tabular statistics for partnerships can be purchased for $300 from the National Technical Information Service, Springfield, VA 22161.

Sole Proprietorship Source Book, 1957-1984, Publication 1323, $95. This source book is a companion to that for partnerships, described above. It is a 244-page document showing key proprietorship data for 1957 through 1984. Each page contains statistics for a particular industry. A magnetic tape containing the tabular statistics can be purchased for $245.

Studies of International Income and Taxes, 1979-1988, Publication 1267, $26. This report presents information from 13 Statistics of Income studies in the international area.

Statistics of Income, 1990, Individual Tax Returns, Publication 1304 (S/N 048-004-023-20-2). This report presents information on sources of income, exemptions, itemized deductions, and tax computations, with the data presented by size of adjusted gross income, and marital status. Current price is $10.

Statistics of Income, 1990, Corporation Income Tax Returns, Publication 16 (S/N 048-004-02316-4). This report presents information on receipts/deductions, net income, taxable income, income tax, tax credits, and assets/liabilities, with the data classified by industry, accounting period, size of total assets, and size of business receipts. Current price is $13.

Taxes

The Statistic of Income (SOI) Bulletin, Quarterly Publication 1136 (S/N 748-005-00000-5). Provides the earliest published annual financial statistics from the various types to tax and information returns filed with the Internal Revenue Service. The *Bulletin* also includes information from periodic or special analytical studies of particular interest to tax administrators. Historical data is provided for selected types of taxpayers, as well as state data and gross internal revenue collections. Current price is $23 annually or $6.50 for single copies.

Studies of Tax-Exempt Organizations, Publication 1416. This publication presents articles from *Statistics of Income* studies on tax-exempt organizations. The articles emphasize important issues within the non-profit sector, and also include several other articles previously unpublished in the *SOI Bulletin,* as well as papers published in proceedings of the American Statistical Association and the Independent Sector Research Forum. Topics features are non-profit charitable organizations (primarily charitable, educational, and health organizations), private foundations and charitable trusts, and unrelated business income of exempt organizations. Current price is $26.

* District Court and Claims Court

United States Claims Court
717 Madison Place NW
Washington, DC 20005   202-219-9657

Generally, the District Court and the Claims Court hear tax cases only after you have paid the tax and filed a claim for credit or refund. You may file a claim for a credit or refund if you think that the tax you paid is incorrect or excessive. If the claim is rejected, they will inform you unless you signed a Form 2297, Waiver of Statutory Notification of Claim Disallowance. If no action has taken place on a claim after 6 months from the date you filed it, you may then file suit for a refund. You must file suit for credit no later than 2 years after you have been informed that you were rejected or you file form 2297. For more information on filing a suit, write to the above address or the Clerk of the U.S. District Court listed below for your area.

United States District Courts

Alabama
Northern: 140 U.S. Courthouse, 1729 5th Ave. N, Birmingham, AL 35203
Middle: P.O. Box 711, Montgomery, AL 36101
Southern: Box 11, U.S. Courthouse, 113 St. Joseph St., Mobile, AL 36602

Alaska
222 W. 7th Ave., #4, Anchorage, AK 99513-7564

Arizona
Room 1400, U.S. Courthouse & Federal Bldg., 230 N. 1st Ave., Phoenix, AZ 85025

Arkansas
Eastern: P.O. Box 869, Little Rock, AR 72203-0869
Western: P.O. Box 1523, Fort Smith, AR 72902

California
Northern: P.O. Box 36060, 450 Golden Gate Ave., San Francisco, CA 94102
Eastern: 2546 U.S. Courthouse, 650 Capitol Mall, Sacramento, CA 95814
Central: 312 N. Spring St., Los Angeles, CA 90012
Southern: 940 Front St., San Diego, CA 92189

Colorado
Room C-145, U.S. Courthouse, 1929 Stout St., Denver, CO 80294

Connecticut
141 Church St., New Haven, CT 06510

Delaware
Lockbox 18, 844 King St., Wilmington, DE 19801

District of Columbia
U.S. Courthouse, 3rd & Constitution Ave. NW, Washington, DC 20001

Florida
Northern: 110 E. Part Ave., Tallahassee, FL 32301
Middle: P.O. Box 53558, Jacksonville, FL 32201-3558
Southern: 301 N. Miami Ave., Miami, FL 33128-7788

Georgia
Northern: 2211 U.S. Courthouse, 75 Spring St. SW, Atlanta, GA 30335
Middle: P.O. Box 128, Macon, GA 31202
Southern: P.O. Box 8286, Savannah, GA 31412

Hawaii
P.O. Box 50129, Honolulu, HI 96850

Idaho
550 W. Fort St., Box 039, Boise, ID 83724

Illinois
Northern: 219 S. Dearborn St., Chicago, IL 60604
Central: P.O. Box 315. Springfield, IL 62705
Southern: P.O. Box 249, 750 Missouri Ave., E St. Louis, IL 62202

Indiana
Northern: 102 Federal Bldg., 204S Main St., South Bend, IN 46601
Southern: Room 105, U.S. Courthouse, 46 E. Ohio St., Indianapolis, IN 46204

Iowa
Northern: 313 Federal Bldg. & U.S. Courthouse, 101 1st St., SE, Cedar Rapids, IA 52401
Southern: 200 U.S. Courthouse, E 1st St. SE, Des Moines, IA 50309

Kansas
204 U.S. Courthouse, 401 N. Market St., Wichita, KS 67202

Kentucky
Eastern: P.O. Box 741, Lexington, KY 40586
Western: 231 U.S. Courthouse, 601 W. Broadway, Louisville, KY 40202

Louisiana
Eastern: C-11 U.S. Courthouse, 500 Camp St., New Orleans, LA 70130
Middle: P.O. Box 2630, Baton Rouge, LA 70821
Western: 500 Fannin St., Room 106, Shreveport, LA 71101

Maine
P.O. Box 7505 DTS, Portland, ME 04112

Maryland
101 W. Lombard St., Baltimore, MD 21201

Massachusetts
Room 1515, John McCormick Post Office & Courthouse, Boston, MA 02108

Michigan
Eastern: Room 133, U.S. Courthouse, 231 W. Lafayette Blvd., Detroit, MI 48226
Western: 452 Federal Bldg., 110 Michigan St. NW, Grand Rapids, MI 49503

Minnesota
708 Federal Bldg., 316 N. Robert St., St. Paul, MN 55101

Mississippi
Northern: P.O. Box 727, Oxford, MS 38655
Southern: 245 E. Capitol St., Suite 416, Jackson, MS 39201

Missouri
Eastern: 1114 Market St., U.S. Court & Custom Bldg., St. Louis, MO 63101
Western: Room 201, U.S. Courthouse, 811 Grand Ave., Kansas City, MO 64106

Montana
5405 Federal Bldg., 316 N. 26th St., Billings, MT 59101

Nebraska
P.O. Box 129 DTS, Omaha, NE 68101

Nevada
300 Las Vegas Blvd. S, Las Vegas, NV 89101

New Hampshire
P.O. Box 1498, Concord, NH 03301

New Jersey
U.S. Post Office & Courthouse, Box 419, Newark, NJ 07102

New Mexico
P.O. Box 689, Albuquerque, NM 87103

New York
Northern: James T. Foley U.S. Courthouse, P.O. Box 1037, Albany, NY 12201
Southern: U.S. Courthouse, Foley Square, New York, NY 10007

Eastern: 225 Cadman Plaza E., Brooklyn, NY 11201
Western: 304 U.S. Courthouse, 68 Court St., Buffalo, NY 14202

North Carolina
Eastern: P.O. Box 25670, Raleigh, NC 27611
Middle: P.O. Box V-1, Greensboro, NC 27402
Western: 309 U.S. Courthouse, 100 Otis St., Asheville, NC 28801-2611

North Dakota
P.O. Box 687, Bismarck, ND 58502

Ohio
Northern: 102 U.S. Courthouse, 201 Superior Ave. NE, Cleveland, OH 44114
Southern: 260 U.S. Courthouse, 85 Marconi Blvd., Columbus, OH 43215

Oklahoma
Northern: 411 U.S. Courthouse, 333 W. 4th St., Tulsa, OK 74103
Eastern: P.O. Box 607, Muskogee, OK 74401
Western: 3210 U.S. Courthouse, 200 NW 4th St., Oklahoma City, OK 73102

Oregon
503 Gus J. Solomon U.S. Courthouse, 620 SW Main St., Portland, OR 97205

Pennsylvania
Eastern: 2609 U.S. Courthouse, Independence Mall St., 601 Market St., Philadelphia, PA 19106
Middle: P.O. Box 1148, Scranton, PA 18501
Western: P.O. Box 1805, Pittsburgh, PA 15230

Puerto Rico
P.O. Box 3671, San Juan, PR 00904

Rhode Island
119 Federal Bldg. & U.S. Courthouse, Providence, RI 02903

South Carolina
P.O. Box 867, Columbia, SC 29202

South Dakota
220 U.S. Courthouse & Federal Bldg., 400 S. Phillips Ave., Sioux Falls, SD 57102

Tennessee
Eastern: P.O. Box 2348, Knoxville, TN 37901
Middle: 800 U.S. Courthouse, 801 Broadway, Nashville, TN 37203
Western: 950 Federal Bldg., 167 N. Main St., Memphis, TN 38103

Texas
Northern: Room 14A20, U.S. Courthouse, 1100 Commerce St., Dallas, TX 75242-1496
Southern: P.O. Box 61010, Houston, TX 77208
Eastern: 309 Federal Bldg. & U.S. Courthouse, 211 W. Ferguson St., Tyler, TX 75702
Western: Hemisfair Plaza, 655 E. Durango Blvd., San Antonio, TX 78206

Utah
204 U.S. Courthouse, 350 S. Main St., Salt Lake City, UT 84101

Vermont
P.O. Box 945, Burlington, VT 05402

Virginia
Eastern: P.O. Box 21449, 200 S. Washington St., Alexandria, VA 22320
Western: P.O. Box 1234, Roanoke, VA 24006

Washington
Eastern: P.O. Box 1493, Spokane, WA 99210
Western: 308 U.S. Courthouse, 1010 5th Ave., Seattle, WA 98104

West Virginia
Northern: P.O. Box 1518, Elkins, WV 26241
Southern: P.O. Box 1493, Charleston, WV 25329

Wisconsin
Eastern: 362 U.S. Courthouse, 517 E. Wisconsin Ave., Milwaukee, WI 53202
Western: P.O. Box 432, Madison, WI 53701

Wyoming
P.O. Box 727, Cheyenne, WY 82001

* Earned Income Credit

Taxpayer Service Division
Internal Revenue Service (IRS)
1111 Constitution Ave., NW — 800-829-1040
Washington, DC 20224 — 202-874-1470

Low income taxpayers who keep a home for themselves and at least one child may claim the Earned Income Credit (EIC). Your earned income and adjusted gross income must each be less than $24,396. You may be entitled to a refundable credit of up to $2,528. Contact the toll-free hotline in your area for more information.

* Electronic Tax Filing

Electronic Filing Division
Internal Revenue Service (IRS)
1111 Constitution Ave., NW — 800-829-1040
Washington, DC 20224 — 202-927-2400

Electronic returns take a much shorter time to process because there are fewer steps in electronic processing, and that saves time. Electronic returns have a much higher accuracy rate than paper returns. This is because electronic returns are verified by electronic filing software before they are accepted. Usually, only people who expect a refund can file electronically, but this year, the service will conduct a pilot test for accepting and processing Balance Due returns. The test is limited to taxpayers who reside in the states of Georgia, Iowa, Indiana, Kentucky, Michigan, Ohio, Utah, Washington, and West Virginia. You must file you taxes electronically through a qualified electronic filer. This office can provide you with information on how to become an electronic filer, including the procedures, tests, and applications necessary. The following publications set the procedures for the electronic filing of tax year 1994 individual income tax returns and Direct Deposit. They also provide procedures for balance due returns.

1345 - *Procedures for Electronic Filing of Individual Income Tax Returns.*
1346 - *Electronic Return File Specifications and Record Layouts for Individual Income Tax Returns.*

* Employee Plans and Exempt Organizations

Exempt Organizations Technical Division
Internal Revenue Service (IRS)
U.S. Department of the Treasury
Washington, DC 20224 — 202-622-8100

The Employee Plans function administers the tax laws governing pension plans by issuing letters determining whether a plan qualifies under the law, examining returns to ensure that plans are complying with the law, and publishing rulings to clarify the law. Speakers address various practitioner groups across the country to highlight new Employee Plans developments and receive insights first-hand from practitioners. This office also handles exempt organizations, and administers the tax laws governing these organizations and private foundations. The IRS monitors whether sponsors of charitable fundraising events are providing accurate information on the extent to which contributions are deductible. The IRS educates the soliciting organizations and conducts a special examination program to decrease the abusive and misleading fundraising practices of some charities. Publication 1391, *Deductibility of Payments made to Charities Conducting Fundraising Events,* is part of an on-going educational program that includes speeches, taxpayer assistance workshops, and revisions to forms and publications. IRS has established a telephone hotline to help charities make a determination of the value of premiums offered in fundraising activities and to help charities answer questions from donors on the deductibility of contributions made. Charitable organizations engaging in misleading or abusive practices are referred for examination.

* Estate and Gift Tax

Office of Passthroughs and Special Industries
Internal Revenue Service (IRS)
1111 Constitution Ave., NW, Room 5427
Washington, DC 20224 — 202-622-3000

This office will help you on matters pertaining to the regulations of estate and gift tax. This office is most often used by lawyers who are helping people manage estates, but they will answer people's questions or direct them to appropriate sources for more information.

* Federal Tax Guide for Older Americans

Special Committee on Aging
U.S. Senate
Washington, DC 20510 — 202-224-5364

The *Federal Income Tax Guide for Older Americans* is a free publication, which

Be patient. If any phone number is incorrect, call (area code) 555-1212 and request the new listing.

445

presents an introduction to the basic provisions of the Tax code benefiting older Americans. It is designed to address the needs of older Americans with moderate income. In addition to emphasizing issues directly affecting senior citizens, the Tax Guide also discusses this year's tax forms to better help taxpayers fully understand the entire process. It also identifies numerous Internal Revenue service publications and prerecorded telephone messages which give more detailed information on the subjects discussed.

* Foreign Language Assistance in Tax Preparation

Taxpayer Services, International
Internal Revenue Service (IRS)
U.S. Department of the Treasury
950 L'Enfant Plaza
Washington, DC 20024   202-874-1470

Interpreters are available at the IRS in the major foreign languages to assist taxpayers who do not speak English. Written requests for help may be sent to the above office, and IRS interpreters will respond to the questions, but only in English. Sometimes the State Department assists in the interpretation of letters. Requests are received only for obtaining solutions to specific tax problems and not for the preparation of tax returns.

Volunteer Income Tax Assistance (VITA) centers in local area often have foreign interpreters if the population in that area warrants them. Contact your local IRS office in the white pages of your phone directory or your area's Taxpayer Education Coordinator, listed elsewhere in this book, for information.

Many of the IRS forms are also available in Spanish. They are:

1SP *Derechos del contribuyente (Your Rights as a Taxpayer), 179 Circular PR, Guia Contributiva Federal Para Patronos Puertoriquenos (Federal Tax Guide for Employers in Puerto Rico)*

556SP *Revision de las Declaraciones de Impuesto, Derecho de Apelacion y Reclamaciones de Reembolsos (Examination of Returns, Appeal Rights, and Claims for Refund)*

579SP *Como Preparar la Declaracion de Impuesto Federal (How to Prepare the Federal Income Tax Return)*

596SP *Credito por Ingroso del Trabajo*

594SP *Proceso de cobro (Deudas del impuesto por razon del empleo) (The Collection Process: Employment Tax Accounts)*

850 *English-Spanish Glossary of Words and Phrases Used in Publications Issued by the Internal Revenue Service.*

* Foreign Tax Credits

Assistant Commissioner (International)
U.S. Department of the Treasury
950 L'Enfant Plaza South, SW
Attn: IN:C:TPS   202-874-1460
Washington, DC 20024   Fax: 202-874-1752

If you need information or assistance in the guidelines for foreign tax credit allowed for income taxes paid to foreign governments, contact this office. Income in this situation is taxed by both the United States and the foreign country. Publication 514 from the IRS describes in detail the tax credit, who is eligible, and how to calculate the credit.

* Free Courses on How To Prepare Taxes

Volunteer and Education Branch
Taxpayer Service Division
Internal Revenue Service (IRS)
U.S. Department of the Treasury
1111 Constitution Ave., NW, Room 1046
Washington, DC 20224   202-283-0197

The Volunteer Income Tax Assistance (VITA) is a program within the IRS where training is provided to volunteers to help people prepare basic tax returns for older, handicapped and non-English speaking taxpayers. The volunteers serve in the community at neighborhood centers, libraries, churches and shopping malls. The IRS provides free instruction and materials and trains volunteers to prepare Forms 1040 EZ, 1040A, and the basic 1040. New volunteers generally receive four-to-five days instruction; experienced individuals, a one-to-two day refresher. There is also self-

instruction. Training is usually available December through January at convenient locations. In exchange for the free training, VITA asks that you spend several hours a week on VITA from January 1 through April 15. To join VITA in your area, just call the Taxpayer Education Coordinator at the number listed below.

Taxpayer Education Coordinators
General number; 800-829-1040

550 22nd St. S, Stop 117, Birmingham, AL 35233; 205-731-0403
949 E. 36th Ave., Anchorage, AK 99508-4328; 907-271-6231
210 E. Earil, Stop 6610-PX, Phoenix, AZ 85012-2623; 602-207-8618
700 W. Capitol, Stop 6030, Little Rock, AR 72201-3271; 501-324-5685
300 N. Los Angeles St., Room 5205, Los Angeles, CA 90012; 213-894-4574
1221 Broadway, 6th Floor, Oakland, CA 94612-1808; 510-637-2473
Chet Holifield Federal Bldg., P.O. Box 30212, Laguna Niguel, CA 92607-0210; 714-643-4060
P.O. Box 2900, Stop SA5650, Sacramento, CA 95812; 916-974-5088
P.O. Box 100, Stop HQ-6300, San Jose, CA 95113-2397; 408-291-7114
600 17th St., Stop 6610-DEN, Denver, CO 80202; 303-446-1660
135 High St., Stop 115, Hartford, CT 06103-1185; 203-240-4149
P.O. Box 28, Wilmington, DE 19899; 302-573-6270
31 Hopkins Plaza, Room 615A, Baltimore, MD 21201; 410-962-2222
400 W. Bay St., Stop 6450, Jacksonville, FL 32202-0045; 904-232-2514
One N. University Dr., Stop 6030, Bldg. A, Room 270, Ft. Lauderdale, FL 33324-2019; 305-424-2439
Peachtree Summit Bldg., 401 W. Peachtree St. NW, Room 526, Stop 902D, Atlanta, GA 30365; 404-331-3808
300 Ala Moana Blvd. #50089, Honolulu, HI 96850-4992; 808-541-3329
550 W. Fort St., Box 041, Boise, ID 83724; 208-354-9153
P.O. Box 1132, DPN 7-5, Chicago, IL 60604-1132; 312-886-4609
P.O. Box 1902, Stop 8, Springfield, IL 62794-9201; 217-627-6366
P.O. Box 44211, Stop 60, TX:ED, Indianapolis, IN 46244; 317-226-6543
210 Walnut St., Stop 30-2, Des Moines, IA 50309-2109; 515-284-4870
271 W. 3rd St., Stop 6610-WIC, Wichita, KS 67202; 316-352-7610
P.O. Box 1216, Stop 531, Louisville, KY 40201; 502-582-6259
Stop 21, 600 S. Maestro Pl., New Orleans, LA 70130; 504-558-3011
P.O. Box 787, Stop 6601, Augusta, ME 04302-0787; 207-622-8328
31 Hopkins Plaza, Room 615A, Baltimore, MD 02203; 410-962-2222
JFK Federal Bldg., P.O. Box 9088, Boston, MA 02203; 617-424-5310
P.O. Box 330500, Room 1196, Detroit, MI 48232-6500; 313-226-3674
316 N. Robert St., Stop 6500, St. Paul, MN 55101-1474; 612-290-3320
100 W. Capitol St., Room 101A, Stop 30, Jackson, MS 39269; 601-965-4142
P.O. Box 66784, Stop 612, St. Louis, MO 63166; 314-539-3660
Federal Bldg, 301 S. Park, Drawer 10016, Helena, MT 59626-0016; 406-449-5375
106 S. 15th, Stop 27, Omaha, NE 68102-1676; 402-221-3501
4750 W. Oakley Blvd., Las Vegas, NV 89102; 702-455-1029
80 Daniel St., Portsmouth, NH 03801; 603-433-0519
P.O. Box 5975, Edison, NJ 088128; 908-417-4075
517 Gold Ave. SW, Stop 6610-ALB, Albuquerque, NM 87102; 505-766-2537
P.O. Box 3036, Church St. Station, New York, NY 10008-3036; 212-264-3310
10 Metrotech Ctr., 625 Fulton St., Brooklyn, NY 11202-0013; 718-488-2908
Leo O'Brien Federal Bldg., Clinton & N. Pearl Sts., Room 421, Albany, NY 12207-2378; 518-472-3636
P.O. Box 606, Buffalo, NY 14225-0606; 716-686-4779
320 Federal Pl., Room 120, Greensboro, NC 27401; 919-378-2193
P.O. Box 2461, Fargo, ND 58108-2461; 701-239-5105
P.O. Box 3459, Cincinnati, OH 45201; 513-684-2828
P.O. Box 99184, Cleveland, OH 44199; 216-522-3414
55 N. Robinson, Stop 6610-OKC, Oklahoma City, OK 73102; 405-297-4125
P.O. Box 2709, Portland, OR 97208; 503-326-6565
600 Arch St., Room 6424, Philadelphia, PA 19106; 215-597-0512
P.O. Box 799, Room 1117, Pittsburgh, PA 15230-0799; 412-644-6504
P.O. Box 6627, Providence, RI 02940; 401-528-4276
Strom Thurmond Federal Bldg. 1835 Assembly St., MDP16, Columbia, SC 29201; 803-253-3031
P.O. Box 370, Aberdeen, SD 57402-0370; 605-226-7230
801 Broadway, MDP 46, Nashville, TN 37203-3836; 615-736-2280
300 E. 8th St., Stop 6610-AUS, Austin, TX 78701; 512-499-5439
8701 S. Gessner, Stop 6610HAL, Houston, TX 77074; 713-773-7070
1100 Commerce St., Stop 6610-DAL, Dallas, TX 75242; 214-767-1428
465 S. 400 E St., Stop 6610-SLC, Salt Lake City, UT 84111; 801-524-6095
Courthouse Plaza, 199 Main St., Burlington, VT 05401-8345; 802-860-2089
P.O. Box 10049, Room 5223, Richmond, VA 23240; 804-771-2289
915 Second Ave., MS-425, Seattle, WA 98174; 206-220-5776
P.O. Box 1138, Stop 2109, Parkersburg, WV 26102; 304-420-6612
M-132, 310 W. Wisconsin Ave., Milwaukee, WI 53203-2221; 414-297-3302
308 W. 21st St., Stop 6610-CHE, Cheyenne, WY 82001; 307-772-2325

Taxpayer Service Division, PDN Bldg., Room 902, Agana, Guam 96910;
617-472-7471
Mercantil Plaza Bldg., GF, Taxpayer Service Division Office GF-05, Avenida Ponce
De Leon, Hato Rey, PR 00918; 809-766-6305

* Free Legal Help if You Get Audited

Volunteer Assistance and Compliance Education Program
Internal Revenue Service (IRS)
U.S. Department of the Treasury
1111 Constitution Ave., NW, Room 1046   202-283-0197
Washington, DC 20224   Fax: 202-622-3190

Under this program, law and graduate accounting school students are given special
permission to practice before the IRS on behalf of taxpayers who cannot afford
professional help. Volunteers are needed to help with the clinic operations or to serve
as Student Tax Clinic Directors. Students work under the direction of their professors
to handle legal and technical problems. Your local taxpayer education coordinator
will inform you of tax clinics in your area.

* Free Tax Forms at Your Library

Volunteer Assistance and Compliance Education Program
Internal Revenue Service (IRS)
1111 Constitution Ave., NW, Room 1046   202-283-0197
Washington, DC 20224   Fax: 202-622-3190

The IRS supplies over 30,000 libraries, technical schools, prisons, and other facilities
with free tax forms, audiovisual aids, and reference materials. These facilities are in
need of volunteers to assist in distribution and use of these aids. Contact your local
library or center and volunteer to help.

* Future Tax Legislation

House Bill Status Office
Annex #2
H2696 Ford House Office Bldg.
Third and O Sts., SW
Washington, DC 20515   202-622-3700

The House Bill Status Office is responsible for developing IRS legislative proposals,
tracking pending legislation, analyzing and implementing new legislation, and
preparing responses to General Accounting Office reports.

For further information regarding tax laws that have been introduced, or for an
assessment of future laws, contact the following offices. Ask to speak with the
person monitoring changes in the tax provision you are calling about.

U.S. Department of the Treasury, Legislative Affairs, 15th and Pennsylvania, Ave.,
NW, Washington, DC 20224; 202-622-0576
Senate Committee on Finance, 205 Dirksen Senate Office Building, Washington,
DC 20510; 202-224-4515
House Committee on Ways and Means, 1102 Longworth House Office Building,
Washington, DC 20515; 202-225-3625
Joint Committee on Taxation, 205 Dirksen Senate Office Building, Washington,
DC 20510; 202-224-5561

* Historian

Historian
Internal Revenue Service (IRS)
1111 Constitution Ave., NW
Washington, DC 20224   202-622-3742

The IRS decision to create this position follows a growing trend in both the
government and corporate worlds to establish history offices, archives, and historic
preservation efforts. This new function will help the IRS move into the future with
an understanding and appreciation of its past. The historian will develop an archival
collection of the most important historical documents created by the IRS, will
research and write policy and management-related historical reports, prepare a full-
length history of taxation in the U.S., establish a collection of oral history interviews,
and assist IRS staff members in answering historical research questions.

* Hotline for Tax Aspects of Retirement Plans

Employee Plans Technical and Actuarial Division
Internal Revenue Service (IRS)
U.S. Department of the Treasury
Room 6550, CP:E:EP
1111 Constitution Ave., NW

Washington, DC 20224   Fax: 202-622-5797
                        Retirement and Pension: 202-622-6074/6075
                                        Actuarial: 202-622-6076

The above numbers are hotlines to attorneys within this division that are there to
discuss tax questions relating to retirement and pension plans, such as 401(k) and
501(c3). The hours are 1:30 to 4:00 p.m., Monday through Thursday.

* How the Public Rates the Internal Revenue Service

Public Affairs Office
Internal Revenue Service (IRS)
1111 Constitution Ave. NW
Washington, DC 20224   202-622-4010

Every three years, an independent company conducts a Public Opinion Survey to rate
the perception of the IRS in the eyes of the public. The findings of the latest survey
conducted are due to be released soon. Public Opinion Surveys is one of many
studies conducted by the Research Department. Other areas included, but are not
limited to, studies on alternative filing methods, identifying fraudulent returns, and
reducing the burden of paperwork for the taxpayer. If you are interested in keeping
up with the latest findings, you can subscribe to the *Internal Revenue Bulletin*. This
bulletin announces official IRS rulings, Treasury decisions, Executive orders,
legislation, and court decisions pertaining to Internal Revenue matters. To order the
Internal Revenue Bulletin, contact: Superintendent of Documents, P.O. Box 371954,
Pittsburgh, PA 15250-7954; 202-512-1800. To obtain copies of research studies,
contact the above office.

* How to Protect Older Americans From Overpayment

Special Committee on Aging
U.S. Senate
Washington, DC 20510   202-224-5364

This is a free information paper updated yearly, which is designed to assure that
older Americans claim every legitimate income tax deduction, exemption, and tax
credit. This publication is very easy to understand and provides many examples and
checklists. Also included is a section of income tax items which will change in the
following year.

* Individual Income Tax Statistics

Statistics of Income Division
Internal Revenue Service (IRS)
P.O. Box 2608
Washington, DC 20013-2608   202-874-0410

Statistics of Income, Individual Income Tax Returns, Publication 1304, is a report that
presents information on sources of income, exemptions, itemized deductions, and tax
computations, with the data presented by size of adjusted gross income and marital
status. This publication is available from the Superintendent of Documents,
Government Printing Office, Washington, DC 20402; 202-512-1800 (S/N
048-004-02296-6).

* Individual Tax Model

Statistics of Income Division
Internal Revenue Service (IRS)
U.S. Department of the Treasury
1111 Constitution Ave., NW
Attn: R:S:P
Washington, DC 20224   202-874-0700

State tax officials determine rate structure and revenue yields through the use of
Individual Tax Model. Public use tape files are available from the office above that
include this tax model.

* Information for Tax Practitioners

Forms Distribution Centers
Internal Revenue Service (IRS)
U.S. Department of the Treasury
P.O. Box 25866
Richmond, VA 23261-5074   800-829-3676

Tax practitioners can benefit from the following information made available to them
from the IRS. Publication 1045, *Information for Tax Practitioners*, contains orders
blanks for ordering bulk supplies of federal income tax forms. Also within the
publication is a form that allows one to be placed on a mailing list in his IRS district
to receive a tax practitioner's newsletter. Package X is also available to practitioners
with the most popular tax forms and instructions on how to prepare them.

Be patient. If any phone number is incorrect, call (area code) 555-1212 and request the new listing.

447

Taxes

* In-House IRS Audit Manuals

Freedom of Information Reading Room
Internal Revenue Service (IRS)
c/o Ben Franklin Station
P.O. Box 795   202-622-5164
Washington, DC 20044   Fax: 202-622-5165

Tax audit manuals use by IRS staff and other in-house manuals are available to the public. Contact the office above for arrangements to use particular materials. For copies of manuals and written requests, write to: Internal Revenue Service, c/o Ben Franklin Station, P.O. Box 388, Washington, DC 20044, Attn: Freedom of Information Request.

Available IRS Technical Manuals:
Organization and Staffing (1100), $36.45
Policies of the Internal Revenue Service (1218), $14.55
Delegation Orders (1229), $17.10
Internal Management Document System (1230), $21.90
Disclosure of Official Information (1272), $63.15
Travel (1763), $29.85
General (4000), $20.10
Income Tax Examinations (4200), $74.85
Tax Audit Guidelines for Internal Revenue Examiners (4231), $27.20
Techniques Handbook for Specialized Industries (4232)
    1. Insurance, $15.45
    2. Auto Dealers, $2.55
    3. Textiles, $4.80
    4. Timber, $6.15
    5. Brokerage Firms, $11.90
    6. Railroads, $13.65
    7. Construction, $4.65
    8. Oil and Gas, $47.85
    9. Financial Institution, $6.45
    10. Public Utilities, $10.05
    11. Barter Exchanges, -0-
Tax Audit Guidelines, Partnerships, Estates and Trusts, and Corporations (4233), $22.55
Techniques Handbook for In-Depth Examinations (4235), $25.65
Examination Tax Shelters (4236), $10.65
Report Writing Guide for Income Tax Examiners (4237), $21.30
Examination Techniques Handbook for Estate Tax Examiners (4350), $27.15
Handbook for Quality Review (4419), $11.40
Employment Tax Procedures (4600), $12.90
Excise Tax Procedure (4700), $17.55
Handbook for Examination Group Managers (4(10)20), $15.75
Classification (41(12)0), $8.10
General Procedural Guides (5100), $24.45
Collection Quality Review System (CQRS) (5190), $4.05
Delinquent Return Procedures (5200), $10.05
Balance Due Account Procedures (5300), $23.55
Service Center Collection Branch Procedures (5400), $93.90
Service Center Collection Branch Managers (5415), $9.90
Automated Collection Function Procedures (5500), $18.60
Automated Collection System Managers (5512), $21.30
Collection Field Function Techniques and Other Assignments (5600), $32.25
Employment Tax Examinations (5(10)00), $12.60
Collection Technical Review Handbook for Employment Tax Examination (5(10)20)), $2.25
Group Managers Handbook (5620)0), $8.40
Field Branch Chief's Handbook (5630)0), $3.75
Special Procedures (5700), $57
Special Procedures Function Managers (57(15)0), $3.90
Legal Reference Guide for Revenue Officers (57(16)0), $37.50
Records and Reports (5800), $9.60
Collection Reports for Field Managers (5890), $4.35
Collection Support Function (5900), $19.50
Taxpayer Service (6810), $51.45
Exempt Organizations (7751), $60.90
Private Foundations (7752), $40.05

Employee Plans Master File (7810), $10.50
Exempt Organizations Business Master File (7820), $26.70
Examination Procedures (7(10)00), $49.95
Employee Plans Examination Guidelines (7(10)54), $15
Exempt Organizations Exam. Guides Handbook (7(10)69), $13.80
Actuarial Guidelines (7(10)5(10)), $5.70
Appeals (Part VIII), $51
Handbook for Special Agents (9781), $84.15
Criminal Investigation (Part IX) $67.50
Employee Plans Training Program Phase I, Revised 10/87 (4210-01), $60.45
Employee Plans EP/EO CPE Operational Topics for 1989, Revised 12/88 (4213-002), $12.15
Employee Plans EP/EO CPE Technical Topics for 1989, Revised 12/88 (4213-003), $18.75
Employee Plans EP/EO CPE Technical Topics for 1989, Revised 3/89 (4213-005), $4.05
Employee Plans Training Program Phase II, Revised 01/87 (4220-01), $51.60
Exempt Organizations Continuing Professional Education Technical Instruction Program for 1986, Revised 01/86 (4277-20), $43.80
Exempt Organizations Continuing Professional Education Technical Instruction Program for 1987, Revised 01/87 (4277-25), $44.70
Exempt Organizations Continuing Professional Education Technical Instruction Program for 1988, Revised 01/88 (4277-28), $37.65
Exempt Organizations EP/EO CPE Operational Topics for 1989, Revised 01/89 (4277-31), $10.05
Exempt Organizations Continuing Professional Education Technical Instruction Program for 1989, Revised 01/89 (4277-32), $43.35
Exempt Organization Continuing Professional Education Technical Instruction Program for 1989 Index, Revised 01/89 (4277-33), $9
Exempt Organization Continuing Professional Education Technical Instruction Program for 1990, Revised 1/90 (4277-039), $68.85
Exempt Organization Continuing Professional Education Technical Instruction Program for 1990 Index, Revised 1/90 (4277-040), $6.60.
Employment Tax Examination (ETE) Support Operation Handbook (5(10)(30)0), $11.25
Offers in Compromise (57(10)0), $4.95
Collection Support Function Manager's Handbook (5918), $9.60
Penalties (Part XX), $39.15
Chief Counsel Directive Manuals
    Administrative (Part 30), $155.55
    Criminal Tax (Part 31), $48.00
    Disclosure Litigation (Part 32), $14.70
    General Legal Services (Part 33), $30.75
    General Litigation (Part 34), $46.20
    Tax Litigation (Part 35), $156.30
    Employee Plans and Exempt Organization Division (Part 36), $4.20
    Interpretive (Part 37), $8.25
    Legislation and Regulation Division (Part 38), $4.05
    Technical/Rulings (Part 39), $62.55
    Data Processing (Part 40), $10.80
    International (Part 42), $13.50
Employee Plans CPE Technical Topics for 1990, Revised 1/90 (4213-007), $52.80
Employee Plans CPE Technical Topics for 1990, Revised 1/90 (4213-009), $15.30
Employee Plans Phase II Examination Training Coursebook, Revised 1/87 (4215-01), $28.50
Update of Exempt Organizations Technical Topics for 1990, Revised 12/90 N/C
Exempt Organizations Continuing Professional Education Technical Instruction Program for 1992, Revised 8/91 (4277-41), $55.80
Exempt Organizations Continuing Professional Education Technical Instruction Program for 1992 Index, Revised 8/91 (4277-42), $7.05
Exempt Organizations Continuing Professional Education Technical Instruction Program for 1993, Revised 8/91 (4277-43), $79.95
Exempt Organizations Continuing Professional Education Technical Instruction Program for 1993 Index, Revised 9/92 (4277-44), $7.35
Exempt Organizations Continuing Professional Education Technical Instruction Program for 1994, Revised 9/93 (4277-45), $52.20
Exempt Organizations Continuing Professional Education Technical Instruction Program for 1994 Index, Revised 9/93 (4277-46), $8.10

* Internal Revenue Bulletin

Superintendent of Documents
Government Printing Office   202-512-1800
Washington, DC 20402   Fax: 202-512-2250

The *Internal Revenue Bulletin* announces official Internal Revenue Service rulings, Treasury decisions, Executive Orders, legislation, and court decisions pertaining to Internal Revenue matters. The price is $144 per year (S/N 748-004-00000-9). Twice yearly, the weekly issues of the *Internal Revenue Bulletin* are consolidated into the *Cumulative Bulletins* (Jan-June and July-Dec). These *Bulletins* are not included as part of this subscription, but are sold as separate subscriptions. The subject bibliography, *Internal Revenue Cumulative Bulletins*, lists the bulletins available, dating back to 1940. Prices range from $8 to $42, depending on the year.

* International Tax Assistance

Assistant Commissioner (International)
Internal Revenue Service (IRS)
950 L'Enfant Plaza, SW, CP:IN:D:CS:PAO
Washington, DC 20224   202-287-4311

The International Office plays the lead role in devising strategies to assure that worldwide revenues due the United States are assessed and collected. International maintains a high number of taxpayer service visits to U.S. embassies and consulates to help U.S. taxpayers living abroad and in U.S. territories and possessions. Year-round taxpayer assistance by IRS staff at 13 overseas posts is supplemented by these visits. International publicized worldwide undelivered refunds, attempting to reach 800 taxpayers owed over $1 million in refunds returned as undeliverable by the world's postal authorities. The specialists in this office will offer technical assistance concerning questions relating to foreign taxes and tax credits. Refer also to Publications 54, *Tax Guide for U.S. Citizens and Resident Aliens Abroad*, and 514, *Foreign Tax Credits for Individuals*. International's Office of International programs administers 35 income tax treaties, 16 estate tax treaties and 7 gift tax treaties worldwide. These treaties provide for relief from double taxation, exchanges of information, routine sharing of information, and simultaneous examinations. During the past year, this office successfully completed negotiations in 122 cases for U.S. taxpayers who requested relief from double taxation.

Overseas Posts:
Bonn: United States Embassy/IRS, Deichmanns Ave. 29, 53179 Bonn, Federal Republic of Germany; 49-228-339-2119, Fax: 49-228-339-2810
Caracas: United States Embassy, Avenida Principal Lo Floresta, Caracas, Venezeula; 58-2-285-4641, Fax: 58-2-285-4641
London: United States Embassy, 24/31 Grosvenor Square, London, England W1A-1AE; 44-71-408-8076/8077, Fax: 44-71-495-4224
Mexico City: United States Embassy-IRS, Apartado Postal 88-BIS, Delegacion Cuauhtemoc, 06500 Mexico, D.F., Mexico; 52-5-211-0042 ext. 3557 or 3559, Fax: 52-5-208-2494
Nassau: United States Embassy, P.O. Box N-8197, Nassau, Bahamas; 1-800-829-1040 or 809-766-5040
Ottawa: U.S. Internal Revenue Service, 60 Queen St., Suite 201, Ottawa, Ontario, Canada K1P5Y7; 613-563-1834, Fax: 613-230-1376
Paris: United States Consulate, 2 rue St. Florentin, 75001 Paris, France; 33-1-4296-1202
Riyadh: United States Embassy-IRS, P.O. Box 94309, Riyadh, 11693, Saudi Arabia; 966-1-488-3800 ext. 210, Fax: 966-1-488-7351
Rome: American Consulate/Rome, Via Veneto, 121, 2nd Floor, Rome, Italy 00187; 39-6-4674-2560, Fax: 39-6-4674-2223
Sao Paulo: American Consulate General, Rua Padre Joao Manoel, 933 01411 Sao Paulo, S.P. Brazil; 55-11-881-6511, ext. 287
Singapore: American Embassy, 30 Hill Street, Republic of Singapore 0617; 65-338-0251 ext. 247, Fax: 65-338-3205
Sydney: American Consulate General, IRS, Level 59, MLC Center, 19-29 Matin PL, Sydney, NSW 2000, Australia; 61-2-373-9194, Fax: 61-2-233-4445
Tokyo: United States Embassy, IRS, 10-5 Akasaka, 1-chome, Minato-ku, Tokyo 107, Japan; 81-3-3224-5466, Fax: 81-3-3224-5274

* IRS Assistance Through the Media

Media Relations Division
Internal Revenue Service (IRS)
U.S. Department of the Treasury
1111 Constitution Ave., NW
Washington, DC 20224   202-622-4000

To provide specialized tax information to targeted audiences, the IRS developed an alliance with various industry groups and Public Broadcasting Service stations to produce and market *Tax Tips on Tape*, a series of 27 videos. The programs were shown on 240 public broadcasting stations and coordinated with special Outreach Program events across the country. IRS also joined with Financial News Network to produce a weekly half-hour live show, *IRS Tax Beat*. Topics ranged from tax-exempt organizations to estate taxes and featured IRS executives and specialists answering call-in questions. As part of the continuing efforts to use the most efficient means

to distribute information, the IRS began a weekly satellite transmission of tax programs, which were made available to cable outlets and television stations free of charge. Watch for these broadcasts in your local listings.

* IRS Collection of Delinquent Child Support Payments

Chief Operations Officer
Internal Revenue Service (IRS)
U.S. Department of the Treasury
1111 Constitution Ave, NW
Washington, DC 20224   202-622-5430

If a taxpayer fails to make support payments to a child or spouse who receives public assistance, Congress requires the IRS to withhold all or part of the taxpayer's income tax refund to cover the delinquent payments. Since 1986, the IRS has also been required to apply individual income tax refunds to child support payments for individuals who are not on welfare and to non-tax debts owed to some Federal agencies, such as student loans, military enlistment bonuses, and home mortgage loans, etc. Through an agreement with the U.S. Department of Health and Human Services, IRS acts as a collection agent for the state welfare agencies in all child or spousal support cases. The refund amounts are used to reimburse the agencies for the support they furnish through Aid to Families with Dependent Children, or are turned over to the parents having custody of the child or children in non-welfare cases. Other agreements with the U.S. Departments of Housing and Urban Development, Agriculture, Energy, Interior, Education, Defense, Treasury, Justice, Health and Human Services, and the Veterans Affairs, Railroad Retirement Board and Small Business Administration require the IRS to act as a collection agent for delinquent non-tax Federal debts.

* IRS Collections and Returns

Office of the Assistant Commissioner
Internal Revenue Service (IRS)
U.S. Department of the Treasury
1111 Constitution Ave., NW
Washington, DC 20224   202-622-5430

This office is responsible for the processing of collection and returns within the IRS tax system. Statistics generated from this office are available in the *Commissioner's Annual Report*, available from the Government Printing Office, Washington, DC 20402, 202-512-1800, for $3.50 (S/N 048-004-02280-9).

* IRS Community Outreach Assistance

Volunteer Assistance and Compliance Education Program
Internal Revenue Service (IRS)
U.S. Department of the Treasury
1111 Constitution Ave., NW, Room 2706
Washington, DC 20224   202-283-0197

IRS employees and volunteers provide free tax help in coordination with local groups. The help is offered at places of business, community or neighborhood centers, libraries, colleges, and other popular locations. Within the Community Outreach program, line-by-line help with your income tax forms is provided. Tax information seminars are also held, including discussions, films or videotapes, and a question and answer period. The programs are aimed at particular interest groups, such as low-to-middle income people interested in preparing their own returns, or small business owners needing free tax assistance. Contact the taxpayer education coordinator in your area for additional information.

* IRS Criminal Investigation

Assistant Commissioner, Criminal Investigation
Internal Revenue Service (IRS)
U.S. Department of the Treasury
c/o Ben Franklin Station
Washington, DC 20044   202-622-6190

The mission of criminal investigation within the IRS is to encourage and achieve the highest possible level of voluntary compliance with the law by conducting investigations and recommending criminal prosecutions when warranted. Special agents target their efforts in the areas such as organized crime, narcotics trafficking, money laundering, questionable refund schemes, and tax shelters, of both domestic and international scope.

* IRS Private Letter Rulings and Information Letters

The Courier Desk
Internal Revenue Service (IRS)
U.S. Department of the Treasury

Taxes

1111 Constitution Ave., NW
Washington, DC 20224 — 202-622-6214

If your tax situation warrants special interpretation on a particular tax deduction you would like to take, you can ask the Internal Revenue Service (IRS) for a private letter ruling. The tax laws are applied to your case which can make this procedure time-consuming. To apply for a private-letter ruling, pertinent information must be sent, including names, addresses, taxpayer identification numbers, your IRS district office, a statement on why you qualify for the deduction, and legal documents pertaining to the case. Contact the above office on the procedure to follow. Someone from the IRS will be assigned to your case, and a notification will be sent to you on how to check the status of your ruling. Publication 91-1 explains the private letter ruling process. There is now a user fee, usually $2500, for each ruling.

Determination letters are also issued by the IRS to businesses and organizations concerning questions related to employee pension plans and tax-exempt status. The procedure for submitting information for a determination letter is similar to filing for a private-letter ruling; however, both the IRS district offices and the national office receive these requests and make the determinations.

General information letters are frequently issued by the IRS, and the request for the information is not as formal as the above mentioned letters. Simply write a letter or postcard to either the IRS district office in your area or to the national office with your question or situation on which you would like advice.

If making an inquiry to the national office, all of the above letters should be addressed to: Chief Counsel, Internal Revenue Service, Employee Plans, Rulings, Assistant Commissioner, Attn: E:ER:R, P.O. Box 14073, Ben Franklin Station, Washington, DC 20044 or Exempt Organization Rulings,, Internal Revenue Service, Assistant Commissioner (EP/EO), Attn: E:EO, P.O. Box 120, Ben Franklin Station, Washington, DC 20044.

* IRS Research Efforts

Research Division
Assistant Secretary for Tax Policy
U.S. Department of the Treasury
Washington, DC 20220 — 202-622-0120

Internal Revenue Service (IRS) research efforts emphasize voluntary compliance, trend identification, and analysis. The IRS published estimates and projections of gross income owed but not voluntarily paid for individuals and corporations for selected years from 1973 through 1992. An analysis is also being completed on the net tax gap, the amount of income tax owed but not paid either voluntarily or involuntarily.

One of the primary objectives is to provide high quality service to taxpayers. IRS began conducting taxpayer opinion surveys in its functions that have direct contact with taxpayers to get initial or baseline measurements of taxpayer perceptions about the quality level of IRS service. A report has also been released on a new method for estimating taxpayer paperwork burden associated with preparation, recordkeeping, obtaining and learning materials, and filing forms associated with tax preparation.

IRS completed a second major study of the effects of refund offsets for non-tax debts on subsequent taxpayer behavior. IRS learned that taxpayers are more likely to file balance-due returns or not to file in the subsequent year.

* IRS Service Centers

Service Center Directors
Deputy Commissioner, Operations
Internal Revenue Service (IRS)
U.S. Department of the Treasury
1111 Constitution Ave, NW
Washington, DC 20224 — 202-622-4255

The following is a listing of the Internal Revenue Service Centers where taxpayers must mail their tax forms. If an addressed envelope comes with your return, the IRS asks that you use it. If you do not have one, or if you have moved during the year, mail your return to the Internal Revenue Service Center for the place where you live. No street address is needed.

Service Center Offices:

Andover, MA	617-727-4392
Atlanta, GA	404-656-6286
Austin, TX	512-462-7025
Austin Compliance Center	512-326-0816
Brookhaven (Holtsville), NY	516-654-6886
Cincinnati, OH	606-292-5316

Fresno, CA	209-488-6437
Kansas City, MO	816-926-6828
Memphis, TN	901-365-5419
Ogden, UT	801-625-6374
Philadelphia, PA	215-969-2499

Regional Offices:

North Atlantic	212-264-0839
Mid-Atlantic	215-597-3991
Southeast	404-331-4506
Central	513-684-2587
Midwest	312-886-4291
Southwest	214-767-5762
Western	415-556-3035

* IRS Speakers and Customized Seminars

Volunteer Assistance and Compliance Education Program
Internal Revenue Service (IRS)
1111 Constitution Ave., NW
S.A.L. Bldg., Room 1046 — 202-283-0197
Washington, DC 20224 — 800-829-1040

The Internal Revenue Service (IRS) provides trained speakers for area civic organizations and other interested groups. Tax clinics are often organized for special interest groups. The IRS has also sponsored call-in radio programs where you may inquire about specific tax information. Contact the district offices of the IRS listed in this publication and inquire through the Public Affairs Director if these programs are of interest to you.

* IRS Special Enrollment Agents

Director of Practice
Internal Revenue Service (IRS)
U.S. Department of the Treasury
801 Market St., Suite 600
Washington, DC 20224 — 202-376-1418

The Internal Revenue Service (IRS) has designed a special enrollment of persons, other than attorneys and certified public accountants, who wish to represent clients before the IRS. This includes all matters connected with presentations to the Service, relating to a client's rights, privileges, and liabilities under laws or regulations administered by the Service. Such presentations include the preparation and filing of documents, all communications with the Service, and the representation of a client at conferences, hearings, and meetings. Candidates should be able to answer income tax accounting questions on the intermediate college course level. The following IRS publications, listed elsewhere in this book, will assist you in preparing for the examination:

17	*Your Federal Income Tax*
334	*Tax Guide for Small Business*
541	*Tax Information on Partnerships*
542	*Tax Information on Corporations*
553	*Highlights of the 1989 Changes*
560	*Self-Employed Retirement Plans*
589	*Tax Information on S Corporations*
590	*Individual Retirement Arrangements (IRAs)*

Answers to the previous year's examination may be obtained from the above address to assist you in preparing for the exam. Publication 1470, available from this office, includes an application for the test, as well as a copy of last year's exam. The two-day exam is given once a year in the fall.

* IRS Tax Compliance Program

Assistant Commissioner, Collection
Internal Revenue Service (IRS)
U.S. Department of the Treasury
1111 Constitution Ave., NW
Washington, DC 20224 — 202-622-5430

The Information Returns Program (IRP) is a largely computerized compliance program used by the Internal Revenue Service (IRS) to match third party information on items, such as wages, interest, dividends, and certain deductions, with the amounts reported by taxpayers on their income tax returns. The IRS also uses the information to identify people who are reported to have received income, but did not file returns. In 1988, the IRS sent out 3.8 million notices reflecting discrepancies, and 3 million notices were sent to taxpayers for failure to file a tax return based upon information returns filed.

* IRS Technical-Advice Memorandums

The Courier Desk
Internal Revenue Service (IRS)
U.S. Department of the Treasury
1111 Constitution Ave., NW
Washington, DC 20224   202-622-6214

If you are audited by the IRS and are in disagreement with the IRS agent over interpretation of a tax law, you can ask the agent to request a technical-advice memorandum for you. These memorandums must be requested through the IRS district offices. The national office then makes the final determination. Dollar amounts cannot be disputed through these memorandums, only the interpretation of the tax laws and procedures.

* IRS Walk-In Service Centers

Volunteer Assistance and Compliance Education Program
Internal Revenue Service (IRS)
U.S. Department of the Treasury
1111 Constitution Ave., NW, Room 1046
Washington, DC 20224   202-283-0197

Assisters are available in most IRS offices throughout the country to help you prepare your own return. In this way you will be given the opportunity to learn how to research and prepare your own tax return. An assister will "walk through" a return with you and a number of other taxpayers in a group setting. If you want help with your tax return, you should bring in your tax package, forms W-2 and 1099, and any other information (such as a copy of last year's return) that will help the assister to help you. At most IRS offices you can also get tax forms, publications, and help with questions about IRS notices or bills.

* Learn What's New in Taxes

Volunteer Assistance and Compliance Program
Internal Revenue Service (IRS)
U.S. Department of the Treasury
1111 Constitution Ave., NW, Room 1046
Washington, DC 20224   202-283-0197

Tax professionals can learn recent tax law changes at Practitioner Institutes, which will enhance the professional quality of the services they provide. These institutes are sponsored by qualified educational institutions, state and local governments, and professional and other non-profit organizations. Contact your local Taxpayer Education Coordinator regarding these institutes.

* Let the IRS Compute Your Taxes

District Offices
Internal Revenue Service (IRS)
U.S. Department of the Treasury
1111 Constitution Ave., NW   202-622-3190
Washington, DC 20224   800-829-1040

If you use Form 1040A to compute your taxes, the IRS will complete the calculation for your taxes. You must complete the tax return through Line 20. All income must be from wages and interest. Other minor stipulations also apply. Contact the above number for specific details on completing your taxes in this way.

* Money Waiting for You: Unclaimed Refunds

Department of Revenue
Income and Taxpayer Assistance
441 4th St., NW
Washington, DC 20001   202-726-6104

This office processes returned refund checks. After an attempt has been made by the Post Office to track the taxpayer fails, the IRS computer checks names against W2 forms, employer records and Social Security records for a correct address. Regional Offices use the media to advertise names of taxpayers who are due refunds. If after three years the IRS has been unsuccessful in finding the taxpayer, the money is deposited into an unclaimed refund account where it remains until it is claimed. Should a taxpayer discover at any time that they did not receive their refund they should contact the Internal Revenue Service Center where they filed their claim, or the office listed above.

* Obtaining Prior Year Tax Returns

Service Center Directors
Chief Operations Officer
Internal Revenue Service (IRS)
U.S. Department of the Treasury

1111 Constitution Ave., NW
Washington, DC 20224   202-622-4255

It is possible to obtain a copy of your prior year tax return by completing Form 4506, *Request for Copy of Tax Form*, and mailing it to the Service Center where you filed the return. The charge is $4.25 for each year's return and must accompany this request. If a taxpayer's authorized representative wishes to request a copy of a taxpayer's prior year return, he or she must attach a signed copy of Form 2848, *Power of Attorney and Declaration of Representative*, or other document authorizing him or her to act for the taxpayer. In lieu of Form 4506, you can send a written request to the Service Center including the following information: your name, your social security number, and if you filed a joint return, the name and social security number of your spouse, the form number, the tax period, and your current address. You must sign this request, and if a joint return was filed, only one signature is needed. Allow 45 days to process the request. However, you often only need certain information, such as the amount of your reported income, the number of your exemptions, and tax shown on the return. You can get this information free if you write or visit an IRS office or call the toll-free number for your area.

* Penalties and Interest

Volunteer Assistance and Compliance Education Program
1111 Constitution Ave., NW, Room 1046
Washington, DC 20224   202-283-0197

The law requires that IRS charge penalties for failure to file returns, late payments, payments with bad checks, negligence, false withholding statements, fraud, and other violations. The Penalty and Interest Notice Explanation (PINEX) notices are available upon request. These information notices show exactly how assessed penalties and interest have been computed on specific taxpayer accounts. The explanatory PINEX notices can be quickly computer-generated in response to taxpayer inquiries received by district offices and service centers. Taxpayer Service representatives are trained to answer taxpayer questions about these notices.

* Practitioner Services

Volunteer Assistance and Compliance Education Program
Taxpayer Service Division
Internal Revenue Service (IRS)
1111 Constitution Ave., NW
S.A.L. Bldg.
Washington, DC 20224   202-283-0197

Each District Office puts out a newsletter (the frequency varies) designed for practitioners that provides information on a wide variety of tax topics. The district offices also have practitioner hotlines, which can answer questions regarding account questions their clients have.

* Small Business Tax Education Course

Volunteer Assistance and Compliance Education Program
Taxpayer Service Division
Internal Revenue Service (IRS)
U.S. Department of the Treasury
1111 Constitution Ave., NW, Room 1046
Washington, DC 20224   202-283-0197

Approximately 1,000 junior colleges and universities are now offering a new course designed by the IRS for tax education of those in small businesses. Course materials are designed by the IRS, and the college may present the material as either a credit or non-credit course. Nine areas are covered in the course, including business assets; use of the home for business; employment taxes; excise taxes; starting a business and recordkeeping; *Schedules C (Profit or Loss from a Business), SE (Social Security Self-Employment Tax)*, and *1040-ES (Estimated Tax for Individuals)*; self-employment retirement plans; partnerships; and tip reporting and allocation rules. Contact a taxpayer education coordinator in your area, listed in this publication, for information on courses in your area.

* Statistics of Income Bulletin

Statistics of Income Division
Internal Revenue Service (IRS)
U.S. Department of the Treasury
P.O. Box 2608
Washington, DC 20013-2608   202-874-0410

The *Statistics of Income Bulletin* provides the earliest published annual financial statistics from the various types of tax and information returns filed with the Internal Revenue Service. The *Bulletin* also includes information from periodic or special analytical studies of particular interest to tax administrators. In addition, historical data is provided for selected types of taxpayers, as well as State data and gross internal revenue collections. The *SOI Bulletin* is published quarterly and is available from the Superintendent of Documents, Government Printing Office, Washington, DC 20402; 202-512-1800. The subscription service is $20 annually, $7.50 for single copies.

* Student Tax Clinics

Volunteer Assistance and Compliance Education Program
Internal Revenue Service (IRS)
111 Constitution Ave. NW, Room 7207   202-283-0197
Washington, DC 20224   Fax: 202-622-3190

Student Tax Clinics have been set up around the country to assist taxpayers who would not normally have the funds to obtain counsel when faced with a tax audit or examination. Some law and graduate accounting students are given special permission by the IRS Director of Practice to come before the IRS on behalf of taxpayers who can't afford professional assistance. Students work under the direction of their professors in handling legal/technical problems on a host of tax issues. If you are interested in starting a Student Tax Clinic or if you want general information on clinics in your area, you should contact the above office, or contact one of the current tax clinic participants listed below.

The American University: Washington College of Law, Washington, DC; 202-885-1520

Quinnipiac College: Bridgeport School of Law, Bridgeport, CT; 203-576-4073

Illinois Institute of Technology: Chicago-Kent College of Law, Chicago, IL; 312-906-5050

Widener University School of Law: Wilmington, DE; 302-477-2158

University of Denver College of Law: Graduate Tax Program, Denver, CO; 303-871-6239

Georgia State University: College of Law, Atlanta, GA; 404-651-2096

University of Illinois at Urbana-Champaign: Dept. of Accountancy, Champaign, IL; 217-333-4527

Loyola University of Chicago: School of Law, Chicago, IL; 312-915-7176

University of Minnesota Law School: Minneapolis, MN; 612-625-5515

University of Nebraska-Lincoln: College of Law, Lincoln, NE; 402-472-1246

University of New Mexico School of Law: Albuquerque, NM; 505-277-5265

University of North Texas: College of Business Administration, Denton, TX; 817-565-3097

San Jose State University: College of Business-Accounting & Finance, San Jose, CA; 408-924-3492

Southern Methodist University School of Law: Dallas, TX; 214-768-2562

Villanova University School of Law: Villanova, PA; 215-519-4123

* Tax Analysis

Assistant Secretary for Tax Policy
U.S. Department of the Treasury, Room 3108
Washington, DC 20220   202-622-0120

This departmental office within Treasury analyzes tax programs and legislation and looks for alternative programs depending on the current economic climate. Advisors are available in many areas, such as economic modeling, revenue estimating, international taxation, individual taxation, business taxation, and depreciation analysis.

* Tax Assistance for the Military

Taxpayer Services, International
Internal Revenue Service (IRS)
U.S. Department of the Treasury
950 L'Enfant Plaza
Washington, DC 20024   202-287-4311

The IRS sends trained instructors to military bases here and overseas to train personnel on tax procedures. Through the VITA program, these military personnel then organize internal training sessions to assist others in the preparation of their tax returns. Those chosen to be instructors often have experience in taxation or accounting. If your tax situation is complex, the Legal Assistance offices at military bases can assist you. United States embassies and consulates are also accessible for those in need of their services.

The following international telephone numbers are the local numbers of the 14 U.S. Embassies and consulates with full-time permanent staff from the IRS. Please check with your telephone company for any country or city codes required if you are outside the local dialing area. The Nassau and Ottawa numbers include the United States area codes.

Bonn, West Germany	339-2119
Caracas, Venezuela	285-4641
London, England	408-8076 or 408-8077
Mexico City, Mexico	525-211-0042, ext. 3559
Nassau, Bahamas	809-322-1181
Ottawa, Canada	613-238-5335
Paris, France	4296-1202
Riyadh, Saudi Arabia	488-3800, ext. 210
Rome, Italy	4674-2560
Sao Paulo, Brazil	881-6511, ext. 287
Singapore	338-0251, ext. 245
Sydney, Australia	261-9275
Tokyo, Japan	3224-5466

Publication 3, *Tax Information for Military Personnel*, may also be useful to you. Write to your area's IRS forms and publications distribution center, listed elsewhere, for a copy or call 800-424-3676.

* Tax Audits

Freedom of Information
Internal Revenue Service (IRS)
c/o Ben Franklin Station
P.O. Box 795
Washington, DC 20044   202-622-5164

If the IRS selects your return for examination, you may be asked to produce records such as canceled checks, receipts or other supporting documents to verify entries on your return. Not all examinations result in changes in tax liability. If the examination of your return shows that you overpaid your tax, you will receive a refund. If the examination of your return shows that you owe additional tax, payment is expected. If you don't agree with the Examiner's findings, you have the right to appeal them. During the examination process, you will be given information about your appeal rights. Publication 5, *Appeal Rights and Preparation of Protests for Unagreed Cases*, explains your appeal rights in detail and tells you exactly what to do if you want to appeal. You can appeal the findings of an examination with the IRS through their Appeals Office. Most differences can be settled through this appeals system without expensive and time-consuming court trials. If the matter cannot be settled to your satisfaction in appeals, you can take your case to court. Depending on whether you first pay the disputed tax, you can take your case to the U.S. Tax Court, the U.S. Claims Court, or your U.S. District Court. These courts are entirely independent of the IRS. As always, you can represent yourself or have someone admitted to practice before the court represent you. If you disagree about whether you owe additional tax, you generally have the right to take your case to the U.S. Tax Court if you have not yet paid the tax. Ordinarily, you have 90 days from the time the IRS mails you a formal notice telling you that you owe additional tax, to file a petition with the U.S. Tax Court. You can request simplified small tax case procedures if your case is $10,000 or less for any period or year. A case settled under these procedures cannot be appealed. If you have already paid the disputed tax in full, you may file a claim for a refund. If the IRS disallows the claim or you do not take action within 6 months, then you may take your case to the U.S. Claims Court or your U.S. District Court. If the court agrees with you on most issues in your case, and finds that the IRS position was largely unjustified, you may be able to recover some of your administrative and litigation costs. To do this, you must have used all the administrative remedies available to you within the IRS. This includes going through the Appeals system and giving the IRS all the information necessary to resolve the case. Publication 556, *Examination of Returns, Appeal Rights, and Claims for Refund*, will help you more fully understand your appeal rights.

Internal Revenue Service Regional Offices

Central Region: Disclosure Office, Internal Revenue Service, P.O. Box 1818, Cincinnati, OH 45201. Serves IN, KY, MI, OH, and WV.

Mid-Atlantic Region: EP/EO Division, Internal Revenue Service, Attn: Disclosure Asst., Customer Service Section, P.O. Box 13163, Baltimore, MD 21203. Serves: DE, DC, MD, NJ, PA, PR, VA and Virgin Islands.

Midwest Region: Disclosure Office, Internal Revenue Service, 230 S. Dearborn St., Room 2316, DPN 23-7, Chicago, IL 80604. Serves: IL, IA, MN, MO, MT, NE, ND, SD, and WI.

North-Atlantic Region: Disclosure Office, Internal Revenue Service, 35 Tillary St., Brooklyn, NY 11202. Serves: CT, ME, MA, NH, NY, RI, and VT.

Southeast Region: Disclosure Office, Internal Revenue Service, 401 W. Peachtree St. NW, Stop 602D, Room 926, Atlanta, GA 30365. Serves: AL, AR, FL, GA, LA, MS, NC, SC, and TN.

Southwest Region: Disclosure Office, Internal Revenue Service, 1100 Commerce St., Mail Stop 700 DAL, Dallas, TX 75242. Serves: AZ, CO, KS, NM, OK, TX, UT, and WY.

Western Region: Disclosure Office, Internal Revenue Service, 300 N. Los Angeles St., Room 5202, Los Angeles, CA 80012. Serves: AK, CA, HI, ID, NV, OR, and WA.

IRS Regional Directors of Appeals
Room 7514, 550 Main St., Cincinnati, OH 45202

841 Chestnut St., Philadelphia, PA 19107

230 N. Dearborn, 29th Fl., Room 2972, Chicago, IL 60604

90 Church St., New York, NY 10007

Room 625, 275 Peachtree St., NE, Atlanta, GA 30043

LB-70, Stop 8000 SWRO, 7839 Churchill Way, Dallas, TX 75251

1650 Mission St., 5th Fl., San Francisco, CA 94103

* Tax Counseling for the Elderly

Volunteer Assistance and Compliance Education Program
Taxpayer Service Division
Internal Revenue Service (IRS)
U.S. Department of the Treasury
1111 Constitution Ave., NW, Room 7207
Washington, DC 20224   202-622-3190

Tax Counseling for the Elderly (TCE) provides free tax help to people aged 60 or older, especially those who are disabled or who have special needs. Volunteers who provide tax counseling are often retired individuals who are associated with non-profit organizations that receive grants from the IRS. The grants are used to help pay out-of-pocket expenses for the volunteers to travel wherever there are elderly who need help, whether they are homebound, in retirement homes, or at special TCE sites. Sites are located conveniently in neighborhood centers, libraries, churches and other places in the community. Contact your local taxpayer education coordinator for programs in your area.

The following IRS Publications, available free from the IRS (800-TAX-FORM), may be useful for the elderly.

Publication 524, *Credit for the Elderly or the Disabled*
Publication 554, *Tax Information for Older Americans*

* Tax Court

United States Tax Court
400 Second St., NW
Washington, DC 20217   202-606-8754

If your taxes are delinquent, the Internal Revenue Service will issue you a delinquency notice, whether you are a consumer or a corporation. If you wish to contest the delinquency, a petition for a hearing can be filed with the U.S. Tax Court. This court is an independent court and not part of the IRS. The court's decision is final and cannot be appealed.

* Tax Data

Statistics of Income Division
Internal Revenue Service (IRS)
P.O. Box 2608
Washington, DC 20013-2608   202-874-0410

The Statistics of Income Division has Public Use Magnetic Tape Microdata Files from which specific information requests can be filled on a cost reimbursable basis. These files include individual income tax returns for 1978-1988. (Individual income tax returns for 1966-1988 are available from the Center for Electronic Records of the National Archives and Records Administration, Washington, DC, 20408.) Files containing more limited data for each State are also available for 1985. All of these files have been edited to protect the confidentiality of individual taxpayers. Private foundations for 1982, 1983 and 1985 and non-profit charitable organizations for 1983 and 1985 are also available. The individual private foundation and charitable organization files are the only microdata files that can be released to the public. This office also has Migration Data, with compilations showing migration patterns, from where to where, by State and county, based on year-to-year changes in the tax return address. Data are available for selected time periods (according to the years in which returns were filed) between 1978 and 1988 and include counts of the number of individual income tax returns and personal exemptions. In addition, county income totals are available for Income Years 1982 and 1984 through 1988.

* Tax Education for High School Students

Volunteer Assistance and Compliance Education Program
Internal Revenue Service (IRS)
U.S. Department of the Treasury
1111 Constitution Ave., NW, Room 1046
Washington, DC 20224   202-283-0197

The IRS sponsors an introductory tax education program, *Understanding Taxes*, for high school students. Since many of the students have part-time jobs, the material that is learned can be practiced immediately. Instructional materials include computer software and video programs. Volunteer instructors are those who enjoy teaching and helping others, and who are knowledgeable about taxation. Your local taxpayer education coordinator will assist you in organizing these courses.

* Tax Exempt Organizations

Exempt Organizations Technical Division
Internal Revenue Service (IRS)
U.S. Department of the Treasury
1111 Constitution Ave., NW, Room 6411
Washington, DC 20224   202-622-8100

This office within the IRS sets the qualifications of organizations seeking a tax exempt status. Compliance with the law is also monitored. For a listing of the names of exempt organizations, subscribe to *Cumulative List of Organizations*, as legislated through Section 170(c) of the Internal Revenue Code Pub. 78. The subscription is $48 annually and includes three cumulative quarterly supplements. Available from the Superintendent of Documents, P.O. Box 371954, Pittsburgh, PA 15250-7954; 202-512-1800, Fax: 202-512-2250.

* Tax Help for the Hearing Impaired

Taxpayer Services Division
Internal Revenue Service (IRS)
U.S. Department of the Treasury
1111 Constitution Ave, NW
Washington, DC 20224
Teletypewriter Number (TTN)   800-829-4059

Telephone tax service by way of a teletypewriter is available from the IRS to assist hearing impaired taxpayers. During the IRS filing season, the hours of operation are 8am to 6:45 pm EST. In the non-filing season, the hours are 8am to 4:30pm EST.

* Tax Help on Audio and Video Cassettes

Audio/Visual Branch
Public Affairs Division
Internal Revenue Service (IRS)
U.S. Department of the Treasury
1111 Constitution Ave., NW
Washington, DC 20224   202-622-7541

The IRS provides local libraries with audio cassettes and videocassettes, for loan to the public, on how to fill out Forms 1040EZ, 1040A, 1040, and Schedules A and B. These tax tapes contain simple, step-by-step instructions to the forms and tax tips. Contact this office or your local library for more information.

* Tax Information in Braille

National Library Service for the Blind and Physically Handicapped
1291 Taylor St., NW
Washington, DC 20542   202-707-5100
or

Visually Impaired Program
Braille Coordinator
Internal Revenue Service
1111 Constitution Ave.
S.A.L. Building
Washington, DC 20224   202-288-0686

IRS materials are available in Braille. They include Publications 17, *Your Federal Income Tax*, and 334, *Tax Guide for Small Business*, and Forms 1040, 1040A, and 1040EZ and instructions. They may be obtained at Regional Libraries for the Blind and Physically Handicapped. For a regional library in your area, contact the National Library Service for a listing.

Internal Revenue Service Libraries

Alabama
AL Regional Library for the Blind & Physically Handicapped, 6030 Monticello Dr., Montgomery, AL 6130; 205-277-7330

Library for the Blind & Handicapped, Public Library of Anniston and Calhoun County, P.O. Box 308, Anniston, AL 36202; 205-237-8501

Dept. for Blind & Physically Handicapped, Houston-Love Memorial Library, Dothan, AL 36302; 205-793-9767

Huntsville Subregional Library for the Blind & Physically Handicapped, P.O. Box 443, Huntsville, AL 35804; 205-532-5980/5981

Library & Resource Ctr. for Blind & Physically Handicapped, 705 S. St., Talladega, AL 35160; 205-761-3287/3288

Tuscaloosa Subregional Library for the Blind & Physically Handicapped, 1801 River Rd., Tuscaloosa, AL 35401; 205-345-3994

Alaska
Alaska State Library, Talking Book Center, 344 W. 3rd Ave., Suite 125, Anchorage, AK 99501; 907-272-3033

Arizona
Arizona State Braille and Talking Book Library, 1030 N. 32nd St., Phoenix, AZ 85008; 602-255-5578

Arkansas
Library for the Blind & Physically Handicapped, One Capitol Mall, Little Rock, AR 72201-1081; 501-682-1155

Library for Blind & Handicapped, NW, Ozarks Regional Library, 217 E. Dickson St, Fayetteville, AR 72701; 501-442-6253

Fort Smith Public Library for Blind and Handicapped, 61 S. 8th St., Fort Smith, AR 72901; 501-783-0229

Library for Blind & Physically Handicapped NE, Crowley Ridge Regional Library, 315 W. Oak, Jonesboro, AR 72401; 501-935-2114

Library for Blind & Handicapped, Southwest, CLOC Regional Library, P.O. Box 668, Magnolia, AR 71753; 501-234-1991

California (Southern)
Braille Institute Library Services, 741 N. Vermont Ave., Los Angeles, CA 90020; 203-660-3880

California (Northern)
Braille & Talking Book Library, CA State Library, 600 Broadway, Sacramento, CA 95818; 916-322-4090

Fresno County Free Library, Blind & Handicapped Services, 770 N. San Pablo, Fresno, CA 93728; 209-488-3217

Library for the Blind & Print Handicapped, 3150 Sacramento St., San Francisco, CA 94115-2090; 415-292-2022

Colorado
Colorado Talking Book Library, 180 Sheridan Blvd., Denver, CO 80226-8097; 303-727-9277

Connecticut
CT State Library, Library for Blind & Physically Handicapped, 198 West St., Rocky Hill, CT 06067; 203-566-2151

Delaware
Library for Blind & Physically Handicapped, 43 S. DuPont Hwy., Dover, DE 19901; 302-739-4748

District of Columbia
DC Regional Library for Blind & Physically Handicapped, 901 G St. NW, Room 215, Washington, DC 20001; 202-727-2142

Florida
FL Bureau of Library Services for Blind & Physically Handicapped, 420 Platt St., Daytona Beach, FL 32114-2804; 904-239-6000

Talking Book Service, Manatee County Public Library System, 1301 Barcarrota Blvd. W., Bradenton, FL 34205-7599; 813-749-7114

Brevard County Library System, Talking Books Library, 308 Forrest Ave., Cocoa, FL 32922-7781; 407-633-1810/1811

Broward County Talking Book Library, 100 S. Andrews Ave., Ft. Lauderdale, FL 33301; 305-357-7555/7413

Talking Book Library, Jacksonville Public Libraries, 1755 Edgewood Ave. W., Suite 1, Jacksonville, FL 32208-7206; 904-765-5588

Pinellas Talking Book Library for Blind & Physically Handicapped, 12345 Starkey Rd., Suite L, Largo, FL 34643; 813-538-9567

Talking Book Library of Dade/Monroe Counties, Miami-Dade Public Library System, 150 NE 79th St., Miami, FL 33138-4890; 305-751-8687

Orange County Library System, Talking Book Section, 101 E. Central Blvd., Orlando, FL 32801; 407-425-4694, exts. 421/422

W. Florida Regional Library, Subregional Talking Book Library, 200 W. Gregory St., Pensacola, FL 32501; 407-435-1760

Talking Books, Palm Beach County Library Annex, 7950 Central Industrial Dr., Riviera Beach, FL 33404-9947; 407-845-4600

Talking Book Library, Tampa-Hillsborough County Public Library System, 900 N. Ashley Dr., Tampa, FL 33602-3788; 813-273-3609

Georgia
Georgia Library for the Blind & Physically Handicapped, 1150 Murphy Ave. SW, Atlanta, GA 30310; 404-756-4619

Albany Library for the Blind & Handicapped, Dougherty County Public Library, 300 Pine Ave., Albany, GA 31701; 912-431-2920

Athens Talking Book Ctr., Athens-Clarke County Library, 2025 Baxter St., Athens, GA 30606; 706-613-3655

Talking Book Ctr., Augusta-Richmond County Public Library, 425 9th St., Augusta, GA 30901; 706-821-2625

Bainbridge Library for Blind & Physically Handicapped, SW Georgia Library, Shotwell & Monroe Sts., Bainbridge, GA 31717; 912-248-2680

Talking Book Ctr., Brunswick-Glynn County Regional Library, 208 Gloucester St., Brunswick, GA 31523; 912-267-1212

Library for Blind & Physically Handicapped, Talking Book Ctr., 1120 Bradley Dr., Columbus, GA 31906; 706-649-0780, ext. 22 or 23

Oconee Library, Library for Blind & Physically Handicapped, 801 Bellevue Ave., P.O. Box 100, Dublin, GA 31040; 912-275-5382

Chestatee Regional Library, Library for the Blind & Physically Handicapped, 127 N. Main St., Gainesville, VA 30501; 706-535-5738

La Fayette Subregional Library for the Blind & Physically Handicapped, 301 S. Duke St., La Fayette, GA 30728; 706-638-2992

Macon Library for Blind & Physically Handicapped, WA Memorial Library, 1180 Washington Ave., Macon, GA 31201; 912-744-0877

Rome Library for Blind & Physically Handicapped, Sara Hightower Regional Library, 205 Riverside Pkwy., Rome, GA 30161; 706-236-4618

Subregional Library for the Blind & Physically Handicapped, CEL Regional Library, 2002 Bull St., Savannah, GA 31499; 912-234-5127

Subregional Library for the Blind & Physically Handicapped, S GA Regional Library, 601 N. Lee St., Valdosta, GA 31601; 912-333-5210

Hawaii
HI State Library, Library for the Blind & Physically Handicapped, 402 Kapahulu Ave., Honolulu, HI 96815; 808-732-7767

Idaho
ID Regional Library, Library Service for the Blind & Physically Handicapped, 325 W. State St., Boise, ID 83702; 208-334-2117

Illinois
IL Regional Library for the Blind & Physically Handicapped, 1055 W. Roosevelt Rd., Chicago, IL 60608; 312-746-9310

Southern Illinois Talking Book Ctr., c/o Shawnee Library System, 511 Greenbriar Rd., Carterville, IL 62918; 618-985-8375

Chicago Public Library, Talking Book Ctr., 1055 W. Roosevelt Rd., Chicago, IL 60608; 312-746-9200

Talking Book Ctr. of NW Illinois, P.O. Box 125, Coal Valley, IL 61240; 309-799-3137

Voice of Vision, Talking Book Ctr., DuPage Library System, 127 S. 1st St., Geneva, IL 60134; 708-232-8457

Heart of Illinois Talking Book Ctr., IL Valley Library System, 845 Brenkman Dr., Pekin, IL 61554; 309-353-4110

River Road Talking Book Ctr., Great River Library System, 106 N. 5th, Quincy, IL 62301; 217-224-6619

Indiana
IN State Library, Special Services Division, 140 N. Senate Ave., Indianapolis, IN 46204; 317-232-3684

Bartholomew County Public Library, 5th at Lafayette, Columbus, IN 47201; 812-379-1277

Blind & Physically Handicapped Services, Elkhart Public Library, 300 S. 2nd, Elkhart, IN 46516-3184; 219-522-2665, ext. 46

Talking Books Service, Evansville-Vanderburgh County Public Library, 22 SE 5th St., Evansville, IN 47708; 812-428-8235

Readers' Services Dept., Allen County Public Library, P.O. Box 2270, Fort Wayne, IN 46801; 219-424-7241, ext. 2215

NW IN Library for Blind & Physically Handicapped, 1919 W. 81st Ave., Merrillville, IN 46410-5382; 219-769-3541, ext. 237

Iowa
Library for the Blind & Physically Handicapped, Iowa Dept. for the Blind, 524 4th St., Des Moines, IA 50309; 515-281-1333

Kansas
KS State Library, Kansas Talking Book Service, ESU Memorial Union, 1200 Commercial, Emporia, KS 66801; 316-343-7124

Talking Book Service, CKLS Headquarters, 1409 Williams, Great Bend, KS 67503; 316-792-2393, 316-792-5495

S. Central KS Library System, Talking Book Subregional, 901 N. Main, Hutchinson, KS 67501; 316-663-5441, ext. 7

Manhattan Public Library, Juliette & Poyntz, Manhattan, KS 66502; 913-776-4741

Talking Books, NW Kansas Library System, 2 Washington Sq., P.O. Box 446, Norton, KS 67654; 913-877-5148/5697

Talking Books, Topeka & Shawnee County Public Library, 1515 W. 10th St., Topeka, KS 66604; 913-233-2040

Wichita Public Library, Talking Books Dept., 223 S. Main, Wichita, KS 67602; 316-262-0611

Kentucky
KY Library for the Blind & Physically Handicapped, 300 Coffee Tree Rd., P.O. Box 818, Frankfort, KY 40602; 502-875-7000

Northern Kentucky Talking Book Library, 502 Scott St., Covington, KY 41011; 606-491-7610

Talking Book Library, Louisville Free Public Library, 301 W. York St., Louisville, KY 40203; 502-561-8625

Louisiana
LA State Library Section for the Blind & Physically Handicapped, 760 N. 3rd St., Baton Rouge, LA 70802; 504-342-4944/4943

Maine
Library Services for Blind & Physically Handicapped, ME State Library, State House Sta. 64, Augusta, ME 04333-0064; 207-287-5650

Maryland
MD State Library for the Blind & Physically Handicapped, 415 Park Ave., Baltimore, MD 21201-3603; 410-333-2668

Special Needs Library, Montgomery County Dept. of Public Libraries, 6400 Democracy Blvd., Bethesda, MD 20817; 301-897-2212

Talking Book Ctr., Prince George's County Memorial Library, 6530 Adelphi Rd., Hyattsville, MD 20782-2008; 301-779-2570

Massachusetts
Braille & Talking Book Library, Perkins School for the Blind, 175 N. Beacon St., Watertown, MA 02172; 617-972-7240

Talking Book Library, Worcester Public Library, 3 Salem Sq., Worcester, MA 01608-2074; 508-799-1730/1661

Michigan
Library of MI, Service for the Blind & Physically Handicapped, Box 3007, Lansing, MI 48909; 517-373-1590

Northland Library Cooperative, 316 E. Chisholm St., Alpena, MI 49707; 517-356-1622

Washtenaw County Library for the Blind & Physically Handicapped, P.O. box 8645, Ann Arbor, MI 48107; 313-971-6059

Macomb Library for the Blind & Physically Handicapped, 16480 Hall Rd., Clinton Township, MI 48038-1140; 313-286-1580

Oakland County Library for Blind & Physically Handicapped, Farmington Community Library, 32737 W. Twelve Mill Rd., Farmington Hills, MI 48334-3302; 313-553-0300

Mideastern MI Library Co-op, Library for the Blind & Physically Handicapped, G-4195 W. Pasadena Ave., Flint, MI 48504; 313-732-1120

Kent County Library for the Blind & Physically Handicapped, 775 Ball Ave. NE, Grand Rapids, MI 49503-1307; 616-774-3262

Upper Peninsual Library for the Blind & Physically Handicapped, 1615 Preque Isle Ave., Marquette, MI 49855; 906-228-7697

Muskegon County Library for the Blind & Physically Handicapped, 635 Ottawa St., Muskegon, MI 49442; 616-724-6257

Blue Water Library Federation, Blind & Physically Handicapped Library, 210 McMorran Blvd., Port Huron, MI 48060; 313-982-3600

Grand Traverse Area Library for the Blind & Physically Handicapped, 322 6th St., Traverse City, MI 49684; 616-922-4824

Wayne County Regional Library for the Blind & Physically Handicapped, 33030 Van Born Rd., Wayne, MI 48184; 313-274-2600

Downtown Detroit Subregional Library for Blind & Physically Handicapped, 121 Gratiot Ave., Detroit, MI 48226; 313-224-0580

Minnesota
MN Library for the Blind & Physically Handicapped, Academy for the Blind, Faribault, MN 55021; 507-332-3279

Mississippi
MS Library Commission, Talking Book & Braille Services, 5455 Executive Pl., Jackson, MS 39206; 601-354-7208

Missouri
Wolfner Library for the Blind & Physically Handicapped, P.O. Box 387, Jefferson City, MO 65102; 314-751-8720

Montana
MT State Library, Library for the Blind & Physically Handicapped, 1515 E. 6th Ave., Helena, MT 59620; 406-444-2064

Be patient. If any phone number is incorrect, call (area code) 555-1212 and request the new listing.

455

Taxes

Nebraska
NE Library Commission, Talking Book & Braille Service, The Atrium, 1200 N. St., Suite 120, Lincoln, NE 68508-2006; 402-471-2045

Nevada
Nevada State Library & Archives, Library for the Blind & Physically Handicapped, Capitol Complex, Carson City, NV 89701; 702-687-5154

Las Vegas-Clark County Library, Talking Book Program, 1401 E. Flamingo Rd., Las Vegas, NV 89119; 702-433-1925

New Hampshire
NH State Library, Division of Library Services to the Handicapped, 117 Pleasant St., Concord, NH 03301; 603-271-3429

New Jersey
NJ Library for the Blind & Handicapped, 2300 Stuyvesant Ave., CN 501, Trenton, NJ 08625-0501;609-292-6450

New Mexico
NM State Library, Talking Book Library, 325 Don Gaspar, Santa Fe, NM 87503; 505-827-3830

New York
NY State Library for the Blind & Visually Handicapped, Cultural Education Ctr., Empire State Plaza, Albany, NY 12230; 518-474-5935

Andrew Heiskell Library for Blind & Physically Handicapped, 40 W. 20th St., New York, NY 10011-4211; 212-206-5400, Fax: 212-206-5418

Talking Books Plus, Suffolk Cooperative Library System, 627 N. Sunrise Service Rd., Bellport, NY 11703; 516-286-1600/4685

Talking Books, Nassau Library System, 900 Jerusalem Ave., Uniondale, NY 11553; 516-579-8920

North Carolina
NC Library for Blind & Physically Handicapped, Dept. of Cultural Resources, 1811 Capital Blvd., Raleigh, NC 27635; 919-733-4376

North Dakota
Eligible readers of North Dakota receive library service from the regional library in Pierre, South Dakota

Ohio
Library for the Blind & Physically Handicapped, 800 Vine St., Library Sq., Cincinnati, OH 45202-2071; 513-369-6074/6075

Library for the Blind & Physically Handicapped, 325 Superior Ave. NW, Cleveland, OH 44114-1271; 216-623-2911

Oklahoma
OK Library for the Blind & Physically Handicapped, 300 NE 18th St., Oklahoma City, OK 73105; 405-521-3514/3833

Tulsa City-County Library System, Special Services, 1520 N. Hartford, Tulsa, OK 74106; 918-596-7920/7922

Oregon
OR State Library, Talking Book & Braille Services, State Library Bldg., Salem, OR 97310-0645; 503-378-3849

Pennsylvania
Library for Blind & Physically Handicapped, Free Library of Philadelphia, 919 Walnut St., Philadelphia, PA 19107; 215-925-3213

The Carnegie Library of Pittsburgh, The Leonard C. Staisey Bldg., 4724 Baum Blvd., Pittsburgh, PA 15213-1389; 412-687-2440

Puerto Rico
PR Regional Library for Blind & Physically Handicapped, 520 Ponce de Leon Ave., San Juan, PR 00901; 809-723-2519

Rhode Island
Library for Blind & Physically Handicapped, Dept. of State Library Services, 300 Richmond St., Providence, RI 02903-4222; 401-277-2726

South Carolina
SC State Library, Dept. for the Blind & Physically Handicapped, 301 Gervais St., P.O. Box 821, Columbia, SC 29202; 803-737-9970

South Dakota
SD Braille & Talking Book Library, State Library Bldg., 800 Governors Dr., Pierre, SD 57501-2294; 605-773-3514

Tennessee
TN Library for the Blind & Physically Handicapped, TN State Library & Archives, 403 7th Ave. N, Nashville, TN 37243-0313; 615-741-3915

Texas
Texas State Library, Talking Book Program, P.O. Box 12927, Austin, TX 78711; 512-463-5458

Utah
UT State Library Division, Program for Blind & Physically Handicapped, 2150 S. 300 W, Salt Lake City, UT 84115; 801-466-6363

Vermont
VT Dept. of Libraries, Special Services Unit, RD #4, Box 1879, Montpelier, VT 05602; 802-828-3273

Virginia
VA State Library for the Visually & Physically Handicapped, 1901 Roane St., Richmond, VA 23222-4826; 804-786-8016

Special Services, Fairfax County Public Library, 2501 Sherwood Hall Ln., Alexandria, VA 22306; 703-660-6943

Alexandria Library, Talking Book Service, 826 Slaters Ln., Alexandria, VA 22314; 703-838-4298

Talking Book Service, Arlington County Dept. of Libraries, 1015 N. Quincy St., Arlington, VA 22201; 703-358-6333

Central Rappahannock Regional Library, 1201 Caroline St., Fredericksburg, VA 22401; 703-372-1144

Hampton Subregional Library for the Blind & Physically Handicapped, 4207 Victoria Blvd., Hampton, VA 23669; 804-727-1900

Newport News Public Library System, 112 Main St., Newport News, VA 23601; 804-591-4855, 804-886-7999

Roanoke City Public Library, Outreach Services, Melrose Branch, 2607 Salem Turnpike NW, Roanoke, VA 24016; 703-981-2648

Talking Book Ctr., Staunton Public Library, 19 S. Market St., Staunton, VA 24401; 703-885-6215

Special Services Library, VA Beach Public Library, 930 Independence Blvd., Virginia Beach, VA 23455; 804-464-9175

Washington
Washington Library for the Blind & Physically Handicapped, 821 Lenora St., Seattle, WA 98129; 206-464-6930

West Virginia
WV Library Commission, Services for the Blind & Physically Handicapped, 1900 Kanawha Blvd., Charleston, WV 25305; 304-558-4061

Kanawha County Public Library, 123 Capitol St., Charleston, WV 25301; 304-343-4646, ext. 64

Cabell County Public Library, 455 9th St. Plaza, Huntington, WV 25701; 304-523-9451

Parkersburg & Wool County Public Library, 3100 Emerson Ave., Parkersburg, WV 26104-2414; 304-485-6564

WV School for the Blind Library, 301 E. Main St., Romney, WV 26757; 304-822-3521, ext. 218

Ohio County Public Library, Services for the Blind & Physically Handicapped, 52 16th St., Wheeling, WV 26003-3696; 304-232-0244

Wisconsin
WI Regional Library for the Blind & Physically Handicapped, 813 W. Wells St., Milwaukee, WI 53233-1436; 414-286-3045

Wyoming
Eligible readers of Wyoming receive library service from the regional library in Salt Lake City, Utah.

* Tax Matters Digest System

Superintendent of Documents
Government Printing Office   202-512-1800
Washington, DC 20402   Fax: 202-512-2250

The *Bulletin Index - Digest System* contains the *Finding List* and *Digests* of all permanent tax matters published in the Internal Revenue System. Each subscription service consists of a basic manual and cumulative supplements for an indefinite period.

Service No. 1 - Income Taxes, 1953-1987. ($42) (S/N 948-001-00000-4)
Service No. 2 - Estate and Gift Taxes, 1953-1986. ($17) (S/N 948-002-00000-1)
Service No. 3 - Employment Taxes, 1953-1986. ($17) (S/N 948-003-00000-7)
Service No. 4 - Excise Taxes, 1953-1986. ($17) (S/N 948-004-00000-3)

* Taxpayer Service

Director, Taxpayer Revenue Service
1111 Constitution Ave. NW, Room 7331
Washington, DC 20224   202-624-4224

The Taxpayer Service Division offers advisory services, counseling and training. The purpose is to give information and guidance on income tax matters. Apart from "800" numbers and information offices, IRS offers training for volunteer programs, films, seminars and other services. Special educational programs are available to assist small business, as well as elementary and secondary school teachers, adult education classes and colleges. Special procedures become effective for victims of natural disasters. Eligible applicants and beneficiaries are individuals with questions on tax returns, and groups interested in the tax system.

* Tax Returns Prepared Free for Low Income, Elderly and Handicapped

Volunteer Assistance and Compliance Education Program
Taxpayer Service Division
Internal Revenue Service (IRS)
U.S. Department of the Treasury
1111 Constitution Ave., NW, Room 7207
Washington, DC 20224   202-283-0197

The Volunteer Income Tax Assistance (VITA) Program offers free tax help to people who cannot afford professional assistance. Volunteers help prepare basic tax returns for older, handicapped, and non-English-speaking taxpayers. Assistance is provided in the community at libraries, schools, shopping malls, and at other convenient locations.

Volunteers may take part in various VITA program activities, such as directly preparing returns, teaching taxpayers to prepare their own returns, managing a VITA site, or arranging publicity. Volunteers generally include college students, law students, members of professional business and accounting organizations, and members of retirement, religious, military, and community groups. The IRS provides VITA training materials and instructors. Training is conducted at a time and location convenient to volunteers and instructors. Generally, these sessions are offered in December through January each year.

The emphasis in VITA is to teach taxpayers to complete their own tax returns. A volunteer's role becomes that of an instructor rather than a preparer. VITA volunteers will teach taxpayers to prepare their own Forms 1040EZ, 1040A, 1040, and W-4. Assistance with state and local returns can also be provided. If complicated questions or returns are introduced, professional assistance will be provided or the taxpayer will be referred to one of the IRS publications for guidance. Contact your local taxpayer education coordinator for additional information on programs in your district.

Contact your local library or IRS office for locations near you.

* Tax Workshops for Small Businesses

Volunteer Assistance and Compliance Education Program
Taxpayer Service Division
Internal Revenue Service (IRS)

U.S. Department of the Treasury
1111 Constitution Ave., NW
S.A.L. Building, Room 1046
Washington, DC 20224   202-283-0196

Small businesses usually need help getting started and taxes are one important aspect of successful entrepreneurship. Small Business Tax Workshops help people understand their federal tax obligations. Free workshops explain withholding tax responsibilities and the completion of employment tax returns. Contact the Taxpayer Education Coordinator in your area for information regarding the meeting time and place. The following IRS publications are particularly useful to small business and are free by calling the IRS at 800-TAX-FORM:

Publication 334, *Tax Guide for Small Business*
Publication 583, *Taxpayers Starting a Business*

* Taxpayer Publications

Taxpayer Services
Internal Revenue Service (IRS)
1111 Constitution Ave., NW
Washington, DC 20224   800-829-3676

The IRS publishes over 100 free taxpayer information publications on various subjects. One of these, Publication 910, *Guide to Free Tax Services*, is a catalog of the free services and publications they offer.

* The Buck Stops Here

Taxpayer Ombudsman, C:PRP
Internal Revenue Service (IRS)
U.S. Department of the Treasury
1111 Constitution Ave., NW
Washington, DC 20224   202-622-4300

A major goal of the Problem Resolution Program (PRP) is to solve tax problems that have not been resolved through normal procedures. PRP represents the interests and concerns of taxpayers within the IRS and seeks to prevent future problems by identifying the root causes of such problems. Each IRS district, service center and regional office has a Problem Resolution Officer (PRO). In resolving problems and protecting taxpayer rights, PROs have authority to intervene to assure IRS actions are correct and appropriate. Effective January 1, 1989, authority to issue Taxpayer Assistance Orders (TAOs) was granted to the Taxpayer Ombudsman. This authority was delegated to the Problem Resolution Officers, as field representatives of the Ombudsman. TAOs may be issued when, in the judgement of the Ombudsman or PRO, a taxpayer is suffering, or is about to suffer a significant hardship as a result of an IRS action or inaction. A TAO can order the function that is handling the taxpayer's case to take appropriate steps to relieve the hardship. The order can also suggest alternative actions to resolve the case. Requests for such relief may be made by taxpayers, their representatives, or by IRS employees on behalf of taxpayers. Contact the IRS toll-free information number regarding tax questions, and ask for Problem Resolution assistance.

Problem Resolution Centers

Alabama
500 22nd St. S, Birmingham, AL 35233, 205-731-1177

Alaska
949 E. 36th Ave., Anchorage, AK 99510, 907-271-6877

Arizona
210 E. Earil St., Phoenix, AZ 85012, 602-207-8250

Arkansas
700 W. Capital Ave., Little Rock, AR 72201, 501-324-6260

California
P.O. Box 30207, Laguna Niguel, CA 92607-0207, 714-643-4117
300 N. Los Angeles St., Los Angeles, CA 90012, 213-894-6111
4330 Watt Ave., North Highlands, CA 95660, 800-829-1040
1301 Clay St., #1540S, Oakland, CA 94612, 510-637-2703
55 S. Market St., Room 910, San Jose, CA 95113, 800-829-1040

Colorado
600 17th St., Denver, CO 80202-2490, 303-446-1012

Connecticut
135 High St., Hartford, CT 06103, 203-240-4179

Taxes

Delaware
409 Silverside Rd., Room 152, Wilmington, DE 19809, 302-791-4502

District of Columbia
31 Hopkins Plaza, Room 620A, Baltimore, MD 21201, 410-962-3324

Florida
1 N. University Dr., Plantation, FL 33324, 305-423-7677
400 W. Bay St., Jacksonville, FL 32202, 904-232-3440

Georgia
401 W. Peachtree St. NW, Atlanta, GA 30365, 404-331-5232

Hawaii
300 Ala Moana Blvd., Honolulu, HI 96850, 808-541-3300

Idaho
550 W. Fort St., Box 041, Boise, ID 83727, 208-334-1324

Illinois
230 S. Dearborn St., Room 3214, Chicago, IL 60604, 312-886-9183
320 W. Washington St., Springfield, IL 62701, 217-527-6332

Indiana
575 N. Pennsylvania St., Indianapolis, IN 46204, 317-226-6332

Iowa
210 Walnut St., Des Moines, IA 50309, 515-284-4780

Kansas
271 W. 3rd St. N, Wichita, KS 67202, 316-352-7506

Kentucky
601 W. Broadway, Louisville, KY 40201, 502-582-6030

Louisiana
600 S. Maestri Pl., New Orleans, LA 70130, 504-558-3001

Maine
220 Main Mall Rd., South Portland, ME 04106, 207-780-3309

Maryland
31 Hopkins Plaza, Room 620A, Baltimore, MD 21201, 410-962-3324

Massachusetts
JFK Bldg., Gov't Ctr. Plaza, Boston, MA 02203, 617-565-1857

Michigan
477 W. Michigan Ave., Detroit, MI 48226-2597, 313-226-4086

Minnesota
316 N. Robert St., Room 381, St. Paul, MN 55101, 612-290-3077

Mississippi
100 W. Capitol St., Stop 31, Jackson, MS 39269, 601-965-4800

Missouri
1222 Spruce St., St. Louis, MO 63103, 314-539-6770

Montana
Federal Bldg., 301 S. Park, Helena, MT 59626-0016, 406-449-5244

Nebraska
106 S. 15th St., Stop 2, Omaha, NE 68102, 402-221-4181

Nevada
4750 W. Oakey Blvd., Room 303, Las Vegas, NV 89102, 702-455-1099

New Hampshire
80 Daniel St., Portsmouth, NH 03801, 603-433-0571

New Jersey
970 Broad St., Newark, NJ 07102, 201-645-6698

New Mexico
517 Gold Ave. SW, Albuquerque, NM 87102, 800-829-1040

New York
Clinton Ave. & N. Pearl St., Albany, NY 12207, 518-472-4482
G.P.O. Box R, Brooklyn, NY 11201, 718-488-2029
111 W. Huron St., Buffalo, NY 14202, 716-846-4574
290 Broadway, New York, NY 10008, 212-436-1011

North Carolina
320 Federal Place, Room 125, Greensboro, NC 27401, 910-378-2180

North Dakota
657 2nd Ave. N, Fargo, ND 58107, 701-239-5141

Ohio
550 Main St., Cincinnati, OH 45202, 513-684-3094
1240 E. 9th St., Cleveland, OH 45202, 216-522-7134

Oklahoma
55 N. Robinson, Oklahoma City, OK 73102-9229, 405-297-4064

Oregon
1220 SW 3rd Ave., Room 681, Portland, OR 97208, 503-326-2333

Pennsylvania
600 Arch St., Room 7204, Philadelphia, PA 19106, 215-597-3377
1000 Liberty Ave., Room 1102, Pittsburgh, PA 15222, 412-644-5987

Rhode Island
380 Westminster St., Providence, RI 02903, 401-528-4492

South Carolina
1835 Assembly St., MDP 03, Columbia, SC 29201, 803-765-5939

South Dakota
115 4th Ave. SE, Aberdeen, SD 57401, 800-829-1040

Tennessee
801 Broadway, Stop 22, Nashville, TN 37203, 615-736-5219

Texas
300 E. 8th St., Stop 1005 AUS, Austin, TX 78701, 512-499-5875
1100 Commerce St., Dallas, TX 75242, 214-767-1289
1919 Smith St., Houston, TX 77002, 713-653-3660

Utah
465 S. 400 E, Salt Lake City, UT 84111, 801-524-6287

Vermont
199 Main St., Burlington, VT 05401, 802-860-2008

Virginia
400 N. 8th St., Richmond, VA 23240, 804-771-2643

Washington
915 Second Ave., Seattle, WA 98174, 206-220-6039

West Virginia
425 Juliana St., Parkersburg, WV 26101, 304-420-6616

Wisconsin
310 W. Wisconsin Ave., Milwaukee, WI 53202-2221, 414-297-3046

Wyoming
308 W. 21st St., Cheyenne, WY 82001, 307-772-2489

* Videos and Films on IRS Topics

Audio/Visual Branch
Public Affairs Division
Internal Revenue Service (IRS)
U.S. Department of the Treasury
1111 Constitution Ave., NW
Washington, DC 20224   202-622-7541

The IRS provides audio cassettes and video cassettes for loan to the public on how to fill out Forms 1040EX, 1040A, 1040, and schedules A and B. These tax tapes contain simple step-by-step instructions to the forms and tax tips. Other titles include:

Hey, We're Being Audited! - light-hearted film of an average family after being called in for an IRS tax audit.

A Sensible Approach for the Future of Your Business? - explains what electronic filing is, how to register with the IRS to offer electronic filing, and how it will benefit business.

You've Got To Do This - explains how electronic filing works and how you may get quick refunds.

Form 8300: Why You Should File - informs businesses about their reporting requirements to the IRS for cast transactions over $10,000.

A Video Guide to Taxes-1992 - quick update of tax law changes and general tax information for individual tax returns.

Por Que Nosotros, Los Garcia? - Spanish language film explains taxpayers' examination and appeal rights.

Por Que Los Impuestos? - reporter uncovers the history of taxation, how taxes are used, the rights and responsibilities of taxpayers, and the different kinds of IRS assistance available.

The IRS has distributed these tapes to many local libraries, as well as IRS district offices. Contact an IRS office near you for more information regarding these videos.

* Voicing Opinions of IRS Tax Laws

Secretary of the Treasury
U.S. Department of the Treasury
Room 3330
Washington, DC 20220   202-662-5000

or

Assistant Secretary for Tax Policy
U.S. Department of the Treasury
Room 3108
Washington, DC 20220   202-622-0120

If you have a personal recommendation for changing a federal tax law, you may send written comments to the address above. The letter must include the section within the Internal Revenue Code in which the portion of the law appears. Please send an original and eight copies of the correspondence.

If you wish to comment on how to improve a tax form or instruction booklet, you may address correspondence to the Chairman of the Tax Form Coordinating Committee, Internal Revenue Service, Room 5577, 1111 Constitution Ave. NW, Washington, DC 20224 or The Office of Management and Budget, 17th and Pennsylvania Ave. NW, Paperwork Reduction Project, Washington, DC 20503.

You may also want to contact your congressman or senator to draw attention to a particular issue. Their opinions and subsequent votes can indeed be influenced by hearing from a significant number or irate constituents. The Capitol Hill switchboard number is 202-224-3121. You may write to them at: The Honorable (your senator's name), U.S. Senate, Washington, DC 20515 or The Honorable (your representative's name), U.S. House of Representatives, Washington, DC 20515.

You can also write or call the House subcommittee, the Senate subcommittee and the Joint committee, (whose main task is reviewing tax laws and procedures) at : The Senate Committee on Finance, 205 Dirksen Senate Office Building, Washington, DC 20510, 202-224-4515; The Committee on Ways and Means, U.S. House of Representatives, 1102 Longworth House Office Building, Washington, DC 20515, 202-225-3625; and Joint Committee on Taxation, 204 Dirksen Building, Washington, DC 20515, 202-224-5561.

* Wage Reporting

Office of the Assistant Commissioner
Internal Revenue Service (IRS)
U.S. Department of the Treasury
1111 Constitution Ave., NW
Washington, DC 20224   202-622-5430

The combined annual wage reporting system was designed to assist employers in the reporting of taxes. For more assistance in this area, contact your local field office listed in your phone directory or the office above.

* Where To File: Mailing Address

If an addressed envelope came with your return, please use it. If you do not have one, or if you moved during the year, mail your return to the Internal Revenue Service Center for the place where you live. No street address is needed.

Florida, Georgia, South Carolina
Use this address: Atlanta, GA 39901

New Jersey, New York (New York City and counties of Nassau, Rockland, Suffolk, and Westchester)
Use this address: Holtsville, NY 00501

New York (all other counties), Connecticut, Maine, Massachusetts, New Hampshire, Rhode Island, Vermont
Use this address: Andover, MA 05501

Illinois, Iowa, Minnesota, Missouri, Wisconsin
Use this address: Kansas City, MO 64999

Delaware, District of Columbia, Maryland, Pennsylvania, Virginia
Use this address: Philadelphia, PA 19255

Indiana, Kentucky, Michigan, Ohio, West Virginia
Use this address: Cincinnati, OH 45999

Kansas, New Mexico, Oklahoma, Texas
Use this address: Austin, TX 73301

Alaska, Arizona, California (counties of Alpine, Amador, Butte, Calaveras, Colusa, Contra Costa, Del Norte, El Dorado, Glenn, Humboldt, Lake, Lassen, Mendocino, Modoc, Napa, Nevada, Placer, Plumas, Sacramento, San Joaquin, Shasta, Sierra, Siskiyou, Solano, Sonoma, Sutter, Tehama, Trinity, Yolo, and Yuba), Colorado, Idaho, Montana, Nebraska, Nevada, North Dakota, Oregon, South Dakota, Utah, Washington, Wyoming
Use this address: Ogden, UT 84201

California (all other counties), Hawaii
Use this address: Fresno, CA 93888

Alabama, Arkansas, Louisiana, Mississippi, North Carolina, Tennessee
Use this address: Memphis, TN 37501

American Samoa
Use this address: Philadelphia, PA 19255

Guam
Use this address: Commissioner of Revenue and Taxation
                                   855 West Marine Dr
                                   Agana, GU 96910

Puerto Rico (or if excluding income under section 933), Virgin Islands (Nonpermanent residents)
Use this address: Philadelphia, PA 19255

Virgin Islands (Permanent residents)
Use this address: V.I. Bureau of Internal Revenue
                                   Lockharts Garden No. 1A
                                   Charlotte Amalie,
                                   St. Thomas, VI 00802

Foreign country: U.S. citizens and those filing Form 2555 or Form 4563
Use this address: Philadelphia, PA 19255

All A.P.O. or F.P.O. addresses
Use this address: Philadelphia, PA 19255

Tax Hotlines

Toll-free telephone tax assistance is available in all 50 states, the District of Columbia, Puerto Rico, and the Virgin Islands. There is no long distance charge for your call. It is best to call early in the morning or later in the week for prompt service. The IRS offers these suggestions for using its services.

Call IRS With Your Tax Question:

If the instructions to the tax forms and our free tax publications have not answered your question, please call us Toll-Free, Monday through Friday, 7:30 am - 5:30 pm. Hours in Alaska and Hawaii may vary. Toll-Free is a telephone call for which you pay only local charges.

Choosing the Right Number:

Use only the number listed below for your area. Use a local city number only if it is not a long distance call for you. Please do not dial 1-800 when using a local city number.

Before You Call:

Remember that good communication is a two-way process. IRS representatives care about the quality of the service we provide to you, our customer. You can help us provide accurate, complete answers to your tax questions by having the following information available.

1. The tax form, schedule, or notice to which your question relates.
2. The facts about your particular situation (the answer to the same question often varies from one taxpayer to another because of differences in their age, income, whether they can be claimed as a dependent, etc.).
3. The name of any IRS publication or other source of information that you used to look for the answer.

Before You Hang Up:

If you do not fully understand the answer you receive, or you feel our representative may not fully understand your question, our representative needs to know this. He or she will be happy to take the additional time required to be sure we have answered your question fully and in the manner which is most helpful to you.

By law, you are responsible for paying your fair share of Federal income tax. If the IRS should make an error in answering your question, you are still responsible for the payment of the correct tax. Should this occur, however, you will not be charged any penalty. To make sure that IRS representatives give accurate and courteous answers, a second IRS representative sometimes listens in on telephone calls. No record is kept of any taxpayer's identity.

Alabama
800-829-1040

Alaska
Anchorage, 907-561-7484
Elsewhere, 800-829-1040

Arizona
Phoenix, 602-640-3900
Elsewhere, 800-829-1040

Arkansas
800-829-1040

California
Oakland, 510-839-1040
Elsewhere, 800-829-1040

Colorado
Denver, 303-825-7041
Elsewhere, 800-829-1040

Connecticut
800-829-1040

Delaware
800-829-1040

District of Columbia
800-829-1040

Florida
Jacksonville, 904-354-1760
Elsewhere, 800-829-1040

Georgia
Atlanta, 404-522-0050
Elsewhere, 800-829-1040

Hawaii
Oahu, 808-541-1040
Elsewhere, 800-829-1040

Idaho
800-829-1040

Illinois
Chicago, 312-435-1040
In area code 708, 312-435-1040
Elsewhere, 800-829-1040

Indiana
Indianapolis, 317-226-5477
Elsewhere, 800-829-1040

Iowa
Des Moines, 515-283-0523
Elsewhere, 800-829-1040

Kansas
800-829-1040

Kentucky
800-829-1040

Louisiana
800-829-1040

Maine
800-829-1040

Maryland
Baltimore, 410-962-2590
Elsewhere, 800-829-1040

Massachusetts
Boston, 617-536-1040
Elsewhere, 800-829-1040

Michigan
Detroit, 313-237-0800
Elsewhere, 800-829-1040

Minnesota
Minneapolis, 612-644-7515
St. Paul, 612-644-7515
Elsewhere, 800-829-1040

Mississippi
800-829-1040

Missouri
St. Louis, 316-342-1040
Elsewhere, 800-829-1040

Montana
800-829-1040

Nebraska
Omaha, 402-422-1500
Elsewhere, 800-829-1040

Nevada
800-829-1040

New Hampshire
800-829-1040

New Jersey
800-829-1040

New Mexico
800-829-1040

New York
Bronx, 212-488-9150
Brooklyn, 718-488-9150
Buffalo, 716-685-5432
Manhattan, 212-732-0100
Nassau, 516-222-1131
Queens, 212-488-9150
Staten Island, 718-488-9150
Suffolk, 516-724-5000
Elsewhere, 800-829-1040

North Carolina
800-829-1040

North Dakota
800-829-1040

Ohio
Cincinnati, 513-621-6281
Cleveland, 216-522-3000
Elsewhere, 800-829-1040

Oklahoma
800-829-1040

Oregon
Portland, 503-221-3960
Elsewhere, 800-829-1040

Pennsylvania
Philadelphia, 215-574-9900
Pittsburgh, 412-281-0112
Elsewhere, 800-829-1040

Puerto Rico
San Juan Metro area, 809-766-5040
Isla, 766-5549

Rhode Island
800-829-1040

South Carolina
800-829-1040

South Dakota
800-829-1040

Tennessee
Nashville, 615-259-4601
Elsewhere, 800-829-1040

Texas
Dallas, 214-742-2440
Houston, 713-541-0440
Elsewhere. 800-829-1040

Utah
800-829-1040

Vermont
800-829-1040

Virginia
Richmond, 804-649-2361
Elsewhere, 800-829-1040

Washington
Seattle, 206-442-1040
Elsewhere, 800-829-1040

West Virginia
800-829-1040

Wisconsin
Milwaukee, 414-271-3780
Elsewhere, 800-829-1040

Wyoming
800-829-1040

Telephone Assistance Services for Hearing Impaired Taxpayers Who Have Access to TDD Equipment

Hours of Operation:

8:00 am to 6:30 pm EST (January 1 - April 1)	9:00 am to 7:30 pm EDT (April 2 - April 17)
9:00 am to 5:30 pm EDT (April 18 to October 28)	8:00 am to 4:30 pm EST (October 29 to December 31)

All locations in U.S., including Alaska, Hawaii, Virgin Islands, and Puerto Rico   800-829-4059

Taxes

Recorded Messages

What is Tele-Tax?

Recorded Tax Information has about 140 topics of tax information that answer many Federal tax questions. You can hear up to three topics on each call you make.

Automated Refund Information is available so you can check the status of your refund.

To Call Tele-Tax Toll-Free, Use Only the Numbers Listed Below for Your Area

Long-distance charges apply if you call from outside the local dialing area of the numbers listed below. Do not dial "1-800" when using a local number. However, when dialing from an area that does not have a local number, be sure to dial "1-800" before calling the toll-free number. A complete list of these topics follows this section.

How Do I Use Tele-Tax?

Recorded Tax Information
Topic numbers are effective January 1, 1991. Push-button (tone signaling) service is available 24 hours a day, 7 days a week.
Rotary (dial)/Push-button (pulse dial) service is available Monday through Friday during regular office hours. (In Hawaii, from 6:30 am to 1:00 pm).
Select, by number, the topic you want to hear.
Have paper and pencil handy to take notes.
Call the appropriate phone number listed below. If you have a push-button (tone signaling) phone, immediately follow the recorded instructions. If you have a rotary (dial) or push-button (pulse dial) phone, wait for further recorded instructions.

Automated Refund Information
Be sure to have a copy of your tax return available since you will need to know the first social security number shown on your return, the filing status, and the exact amount of your refund.
Then, call the appropriate phone number listed below and follow the recorded instructions.
IRS updates refund information every 7 days. If you call to find out about the status of your refund and do not receive a refund mailing date, please wait 7 days before calling back.
Push-button (tone signaling) service is available Monday through Friday from 7:00 am to 11:30 pm. (Hours may vary in your area).
Rotary (dial)/push-button (pulse dial) service is available Monday through Friday during regular office hours. (In Hawaii, from 6:30 am to 1:00 pm.)

Alabama
800-829-4477

Alaska
800-829-4477

Arizona
Phoenix, 602-640-3933
Elsewhere, 800-829-4477

Arkansas
800-829-4477

California
Counties of Alpine, Amador, Butte, Calaveras, Colusa, Contra Costa, Del Norte, El Dorado, Glenn, Humboldt, Lake, Lassen, Marin, Mendocino, Modoc, Napa, Nevada, Placer, Plumas, Sacramento, San Joaquin, Shasta, Sierra, Siskiyou, Solano, Sonoma, Sutter, Tehama, Trinity, Yolo, Yuba, 800-829-4032
Oakland, 510-839-4245
Elsewhere, 800-829-4477

Colorado
Denver, 303-592-1118
Elsewhere, 800-829-4477

Connecticut
800-829-4477

Delaware
800-829-4477

District of Columbia
628-2929

Florida
800-829-4477

Georgia
Atlanta, 404-331-6572
Elsewhere, 800-829-4477

Hawaii
800-829-4477

Idaho
800-829-4477

Illinois
Chicago, 312-886-9614
In area code 708, 312-886-9614
Springfield, 312-789-0489
Elsewhere, 800-829-4477

Indiana
Indianapolis, 317-631-1010
Elsewhere, 800-829-4477

Iowa
Des Moines, 515-284-7454
Elsewhere, 800-829-4477

Kansas
800-829-4477

Kentucky
800-829-4477

Louisiana
800-829-4477

Be patient. If any phone number is incorrect, call (area code) 555-1212 and request the new listing.

Maine
800-829-4477

Maryland
Baltimore, 410-244-7306
Elsewhere, 800-829-4477

Massachusetts
Boston, 617-536-0709
Elsewhere, 800-829-4477

Michigan
Detroit, 313-961-4282
Elsewhere, 800-829-4477

Minnesota
St. Paul, 612-644-7748
Elsewhere, 800-829-4477

Mississippi
800-829-4477

Missouri
St. Louis, 316-241-4700
Elsewhere, 800-829-4477

Montana
800-829-4477

Nebraska
Omaha, 402-221-3324
Elsewhere, 800-829-4477

Nevada
800-829-4477

New Hampshire
800-829-4477

New Jersey
800-829-4477

New Mexico
800-829-4477

New York
Bronx, 212-488-8432
Brooklyn, 718-488-8432
Buffalo, 716-685-5533
Manhattan, 212-406-4080
Queens, 212-488-8432
Staten Island, 718-488-8432
Elsewhere, 800-829-4477

North Carolina
800-829-4477

North Dakota
800-829-4477

Ohio
Cincinnati, 513-421-0329
Cleveland, 216-522-3037
Elsewhere, 800-829-4477

Oklahoma
800-829-4477

Oregon
Portland, 503-294-5363
Elsewhere, 800-829-4477

Pennsylvania
Philadelphia, 215-627-1040
Pittsburgh, 412-261-1040
Elsewhere, 800-829-4477

Puerto Rico
800-829-4477

Rhode Island
800-829-4477

South Carolina
800-829-4477

South Dakota
800-829-4477

Tennessee
Nashville, 615-781-5040
Elsewhere, 800-829-4477

Texas
Dallas, 214-767-1792
Houston, 713-541-3400
Elsewhere, 800-829-4477

Utah
800-829-4477

Vermont
800-829-4477

Virginia
Richmond, 804-783-1569
Elsewhere, 800-829-4477

Washington
Seattle, 206-343-7221
Elsewhere, 800-829-4477

West Virginia
800-829-4477

Wisconsin
Milwaukee, 414-273-8100
Elsewhere, 800-829-4477

Wyoming
800-829-4477

Tele-Tax Topic Numbers and Subjects

IRS Help Available
101 IRS services--Volunteer tax assistance, toll-free telephone, walk-in assistance, and outreach programs
102 Tax assistance for individuals with disabilities and the hearing impaired
103 Small Business Tax Education Program (STEP)--Tax help for small businesses
104 Problem Resolution Program--Help for problem situations
105 Public Libraries: Tax information tapes & reproducible tax forms
911 Hardship assistance applications

IRS Procedures
151 Your appeal rights
152 Refunds--How long they should take
153 What to do if you haven't filed you tax return--nonfilers
154 Form W-2--What to do if not received
156 Copy of your tax return--How to get one
157 Change of address--How to notify IRS

Collection
201 The collection process
202 What to do if you can't pay your tax

Taxes

903 Federal employment taxes in Puerto Rico
904 Tax assistance for Puerto Rico residents

Other Tele-Tax Topics in Spanish

951 IRS services--Volunteer tax assistance, toll-free telephone, walk-in assistance, and outreach programs
952 Refunds--How long they should take
953 Forms and publications--How to order

954 Highlights of tax changes
955 Who must file?
956 Which form to use?
957 What is your filing status?
958 Social security & equivalent railroad retirement benefits
959 Earned income credit (EIC)
960 Advance earned income credit
961 Alien tax clearance

IRS Tax Forms

All Federal Income Tax Forms are listed in numerical order after this state-by-state roster. To order any of the IRS forms, publications and instruction packets which are listed in the next section, call the toll-free IRS hotline at 800-424-3676. To send for forms through the mail, write to the approriate state address below. Two copies of each form and one copy of each set of instructions will be sent.

Forms Distribution Centers

Alabama
P.O. Box 8903
Bloomington, IL 61703

Alaska
Rancho Cordova, CA 95743-0001

Arizona
Rancho Cordova, CA 95743-0001

Arkansas
P.O. Box 8903
Bloomington, IL 61703

California
Rancho Cordova, CA 95743-0001

Colorado
Rancho Cordova, CA 95743-0001

Connecticut
P.O. Box 85074
Richmond, VA 23261-5074

Delaware
P.O. Box 85074
Richmond, VA 23261-5074

District of Columbia
P.O. Box 85074
Richmond, VA 23261-5074

Florida
P.O. Box 85074
Richmond, VA 23261-5074

Georgia
P.O. Box 85074
Richmond, VA 23261-5074

Hawaii
Rancho Cordova, CA 95743-0001

Idaho
Rancho Cordova, CA 95743-0001

Illinois
P.O. Box 8903
Bloomington, IL 61703

Indiana
P.O. Box 8903
Bloomington, IL 61703

Iowa
P.O. Box 8903
Bloomington, IL 61703

Kansas
P.O. Box 8903
Bloomington, IL 61703

Kentucky
P.O. Box 8903
Bloomington, IL 61703

Louisiana
P.O. Box 8903
Bloomington, IL 61703

Maine
P.O. Box 85074
Richmond, VA 23261-5074

Maryland
P.O. Box 85074
Richmond, VA 23261-5074

Massachusetts
P.O. Box 85074
Richmond, VA 23261-5074

Michigan
P.O. Box 8903
Bloomington, IL 61703

Minnesota
P.O. Box 8903
Bloomington, IL 61703

Mississippi
P.O. Box 8903
Bloomington, IL 61703

Missouri
P.O. Box 8903
Bloomington, IL 61703

Montana
Rancho Cordova, CA 95743-0001

Nebraska
P.O. Box 8903
Bloomington, IL 61703

Nevada
Rancho Cordova, CA 95743-0001

New Hampshire
P.O. Box 85074
Richmond, VA 23261-5074

New Jersey
P.O. Box 85074
Richmond, VA 23261-5074

New Mexico
Rancho Cordova, CA 95743-0001

New York
P.O. Box 85074
Richmond, VA 23261-5074

North Carolina
P.O. Box 85074
Richmond, VA 23261-5074

North Dakota
P.O. Box 8903
Bloomington, IL 61703

Ohio
P.O. Box 8903
Bloomington, IL 61703

Oklahoma
P.O. Box 8903
Bloomington, IL 61703

Oregon
Rancho Cordova, CA 95743-0001

Pennsylvania
P.O. Box 85074
Richmond, VA 23261-5074

Puerto Rico
P.O. Box 85074
Richmond, VA 23261-5074

Rhode Island
P.O. Box 85074
Richmond, VA 23261-5074

South Carolina
P.O. Box 85074
Richmond, VA 23261-5074

South Dakota
P.O. Box 8903
Bloomington, IL 61703

Tennessee
P.O. Box 8903
Bloomington, IL 61703

Texas
P.O. Box 8903
Bloomington, IL 61703

Utah
Rancho Cordova, CA 95743-0001

Vermont
P.O. Box 85074
Richmond, VA 23261-5074

Virgin Islands
V.I. Bureau of Internal Revenue
Lockharts Garden No. 1A
Charlotte Amalie
St. Thomas, VI 00802

Virginia
P.O. Box 85074
Richmond, VA 23261-5074

Washington
Rancho Cordova, CA 95743-0001

West Virginia
P.O. Box 85074
Richmond, VA 23261-5074

Wisconsin
P.O. Box 8903
Bloomington, IL 61703

Wyoming
Rancho Cordova, CA 95743-0001

Foreign Addresses

Forms Distribution Center
P.O. Box 85074
Richmond, VA 23261-5074

Forms Distribution Center
Rancho Cordova, CA 95743-0001

Taxpayers with mailing addresses in foreign countries should send the order blank to either address. Send letter requests for other forms and publications to: Forms Distribution Center, P.O. Box 85074, Richmond, VA 23261-5074.

Numerical List of Federal Tax Return Forms and Related Forms

Timber/Forest Industries Schedules
Supplement to income tax return for taxpayers claiming a deduction for depletion of timber and for depreciation of plant and other timber improvements.
IT-IRC sec. 631; Regs. sec. 1.611-3: IT-IRC sec. 6012; Pub. 17

Package X
Informational Copies of Federal Tax Forms
A two-volume set of income tax and information return forms, substitute forms information, and other information needed by tax practitioners to service their clients.

CT-1
Employer's Annual Railroad Retirement and Unemployment Repayment Tax Return
Used to report employees' and employers' taxes under the RRTA and RURT.
Emp-IRC secs. 3201, 3202, 3221, 3321, 3322, and 6011; Regs. secs. 31.6011(a)-2, 31.6011(a)-3AT, and 31.6302(c)-2; Separate instructions

CT-2
Employee Representative's Quarterly Railroad Tax Return
Used to report employee representative's tax under the RRTA and RURT.
Emp-IRC secs. 3211, 3321, and 6011; Regs. secs. 31.6011(a)-2 and 31.6011(a)-3AT

W-2
Wage and Tax Statement (For Use in Cities and States Authorizing Combined Form)
Used to report wages, tips and other compensation, allocated tips, employee social security tax, income tax, state or city income tax withheld; and to support credit shown on individual income tax return.
Emp-IRC sec 6051; Regs secs 1.6041-2 and 31.6051-1; Circular E; Separate instructions

W-2AS
American Samoa Wage and Tax Statement
Used to report wages, tips, and other compensation, employee social security tax, Samoan income tax withheld, and to support credit shown on American Samoa individual income tax return.
Emp-IRC sec. 6051; Regs. sec. 31.6051-1, Circular SS

Be patient. If any phone number is incorrect, call (area code) 555-1212 and request the new listing.

467

Taxes

W-2cPR
Statement of Corrected Income and Tax Amounts
Used to correct previously filed Forms W-2, W-2P, W-2AS, W-2CNMI, W-2GU, and W-2VI. Emp-IRC sec. 6051; Reg. sec. 1.6041-2 and 31.6051-1

499R-2/W-2PR
Puerto Rico Withholding Statement
Used to report social security wages, tips, and social security tax withheld for employees in Puerto Rico. Emp-IRC sec. 6051; Regs. sec. 31.6051-1; Circular PR

W-2G
Statement for Recipients of Certain Gambling Winnings
Used to report gambling winnings and any taxes withheld.
IT-IRC sec 3402(q) and 6041; Temp Regs sec 7.6041-1 and Regs sec 31.3402(q)-1(f); See separate Instructions for Forms 1099, 1098, 5498, 1096, and W-2G.

W-2GU
Guam Wage and Tax Statement
Used to report wages, tips and other compensation, employee social security tax, Guam income tax withheld, and to support credit shown on individual income tax return. Emp-IRC sec. 6051; Regs. sec. 31.6051-1; Circular SS

W-2CNMI
Commonwealth of Northern Mariana Islands Wage and Tax Statement
Used to report wages, tips and other compensation, employee social security tax, CNMI income tax withheld, and to support credit shown on individual income tax return. Emp-IRC sec. 6051; Regs. sec. 31.6050-1; Circular SS

W-2VI
U.S. Virgin Islands Wage and Tax Statement
Used to report wages, tips and other compensation, employee social security tax, VI income tax withheld, and to support credit shown on individual income tax return. Emp-IRC sec. 6051; Regs. secs. 1.6041-2 and 31.6051-1; Circular SS

W-2P
Statement For Recipients of Annuities, Pensions, Retired Pay, or IRA Payments
Used to report periodic distributions from annuities, pensions, retirement pay, and payments from an IRA; Federal and state income tax withheld.
Emp-IRC sec. 3402(o); Regs. sec. 32.1-1; Circular E; Separate instructions

W-3
Transmittal of Income and Tax Statements
Used by employers and other payers to transmit Forms W-2 and W-2P to the Social Security Administration. Emp-IRC sec. 6011; Reg. sec. 31.6051-2

W-3c
Transmittal of Corrected Income and Tax Statements
Used by employers and other payers to transmit corrected income and tax statements (Forms W-2c). Emp-IRC sec. 6011; Reg. 31.6051-2

W-3PR
Transmittal of Withholding Statements
Used by employers to transmit Forms 499R-2/W-2PR.
Emp-IRC sec. 6011; Reg. sec. 31.6051-2; Circular PR

W-3SS
Transmittal of Wage and Tax Statements
Used by employers to transmit Forms W-2AS, W-2CNMI, W-2GU, and W-2VI. Emp-IRC sec. 6011; Reg. sec. 31.6051-2; Circular SS

W-4
Employee's Withholding Allowance Certificate
Completed by employee and given to employer so that proper amount of income tax can be withheld from wages. Also used by employee to claim exemption from withholding by certifying that he or she had no liability for income tax for preceding tax year and anticipates that no liability will be incurred for current tax year.
Emp-IRC secs. 3402(f), 3402(m) and 3402(n); Regs. secs. 31.3402(f)5)-1 and 31.3402(n)-1; Circular E

W-4P
Withholding Certificate for Pension or Annuity Payments
Used to figure amount of Federal income tax to withhold from periodic pension or annuity payments or to claim additional withholding or exemption from withholding for periodic or nonperiodic payments. Emp-IRC sec. 3405

W-4S
Request for Federal Income Tax Withholding from Sick Pay
Filed with a third party payer of sick pay to request Federal income tax withholding. Emp-IRC sec. 3402(o); Regs. sec. 31.3402(o)-3

W-5
Earned Income Credit Advance Payment Certificate
Used by employee to request employer to furnish advance payment of earned income credit with the employee's pay. IRC sec. 3507

W-8
Certificate of Foreign Status
Used by foreign persons to notify payers of interest, mortgage interest recipients, or middlemen, brokers, or barter exchanges not to withhold or report on payments of interest, or on broker transactions or barter exchanges.
IRC secs. 3406, 6042, 6044, 6045, and 6049

W-9
Request for Taxpayer Identification Number and Certification
Used by a person required to file certain information returns with IRS to obtain the correct taxpayer identification number (TIN) of the person for whom a return is filed. Also used to claim exemption from backup withholding and to certify that the person whose TIN is provided is not subject to backup withholding because of failure to report interest and dividends as income.

W-10
Dependent Care Provider's Identification and Certification
Used by taxpayers to certify that the name, address, and taxpayer identification number of their dependent care provider is correct. IRS secs. 21, 129, 501(c)3)

SS-4
Application for Employer Identification Number
Used by employers and other entities to apply for an identification number.
Emp-IRC Regs. sec. 31.6011(b)-1; Circulars A and E

SS-4 PR
Solicitud de Numero de Identificacion Patronal
Used by employers and other entities in Puerto Rico to apply for an identification number. A variation of Form SS-4.
Emp-IR Regs. sec. 31.6011(b)-1; Circular PR

SS-5
Application for a Social Security Card
Used by an individual to obtain a social security number and card.
Emp-IR Regs. sec. 31.6011(b)-2; Circulars A and E

SS-8
Information for Use in Determining Whether a Worker Is an Employee for Federal Employment Taxes and Income Tax Withholding
Used to furnish information about services of an individual, generally selected as representative of a class of workers, to get written determination on status.
Emp-IRC sec. 3121; Regs. sec. 31.3121(d)-1

SS-16
Certificate of Election of Coverage Under the Federal Insurance Contributions Act
Used by religious orders, whose members are required to take a vow of poverty, to elect social security coverage.
Emp-IRC sec. 3121(r); Regs. sec. 31.3121(r)-1

11-C
Occupational Tax and Registration Return for Wagering
Used to report taxes due under IRC sections 4401 and 4411, and as an application for registry and wagering activity. Upon approval of the return, the Service will issue a Special Tax Stamp.
Ex-IRC secs. 4411 and 4412; Regs. secs. 44.4412 and 44.4901

56
Notice Concerning Fiduciary Relationship
Used by persons to notify IRS that they are acting in fiduciary capacity for other persons.
IT-IRC sec. 6903; Regs. sec. 301.6903-1

637
Application for Registration
Used as an application and certificate; by manufacturers, refiners or importers who buy taxable articles tax-free for further manufacture of taxable articles, or for resale direct to a manufacturer for such purpose. The original of the application is validated and returned as the Certificate of Registry by the District Director.
Ex-IRC secs. 4052, 4064(b)(1)(c), 4101, 4221, and 4661; Regs. secs. 48.4101-1, 48.4222(a)-1, and 48.4222(d)-1

637A
Registration for Tax-Free Sales and Purchases of Fuel Used in Aircraft
Used to register for tax-free sales under IRC section 4041(c). Filed by a seller who is a manufacturer, producer, importer, wholesaler, Jobber, or retailer; or by a seller that is a commercial airline, nonprofit educational organization, or other exempt user that wishes to sell or purchase tax-free fuel for use in aircraft. The original of the application is validated by the District Director and returned as the Certificate of Registry.
Ex-IRC sec. 4041(c); Regs. sec. 48.4041-11

706
United States Estate (and Generation-Skipping Transfer) Tax Return
Used for the estate of a deceased United States resident or citizen.
E&G-IRC sec. 6018; Regs. sec. 20.6018-1; Separate instructions

706-A
United States Additional Estate Tax Return
Used to report recapture tax under special use valuation.
E&G-IRC sec. 2032A; Separate instructions

706CE
Certificate of Payment of Foreign Death Tax
Used to report credit against United States estate tax for estate inheritance, legacy, or succession tax paid to a foreign government.
E&G-IRC sec. 2014; Regs. sec. 20.2014-5

706GS(D)
Generation-Skipping Transfer Tax Return for Distributions
Used by distributees to report generation-skipping transfer tax on taxable distributions from trusts subject to the tax.
E&G-IRC sec. 2601; Temp Regs. sec. 26.2662-1(b)(1); Separate instructions

706GS(D-1)
Notification of Distribution from a Generation-Skipping Trust
Used by trustees to report certain information to distributees regarding taxable distributions from a trust subject to the generation-skipping transfer tax.
E&G-IRC sec. 2601; Temp. Regs. sec. 26.2662-1(b)(1)

706GS(T)
Generation-Skipping Transfer Tax Return for Terminations
Used by trustees to report generation-skipping transfer tax on taxable terminations of trusts subject to the tax.
E&G-IRC sec. 2601; Temp. Regs. sec. 26.2662-1(b)2); Separate instructions

706NA
United States Estate (and Generation-Skipping Transfer) Tax Return, Estate of nonresident not a citizen of the United States
Used for United States nonresident alien decedent's estate to be filed within 9 months after date of death.
E&G-IRC sec. 6018; Regs. sec. 20.6018-1(b); Separate instructions

706QDT
U.S. Estate Tax Return for Qualified Domestic Trusts
Used by trustee or designated filer to report estate tax on distribution from qualified domestic trust or on property in trust at death of surviving spouse.
E&G - IRC sec. 2056A, Separate instructions.

709
United States Gift (and Generation-Skipping Transfer) Tax Return
Used to report gifts of more than $10,000 (or, regardless of value, gifts of a future interest in property).
E&G-IRC sec. 6019; Regs. sec. 25.6019-1; Separate instructions

709-A
United States Short Form Gift Tax Return
Used to report gifts of more than $10,000 but less than $20,000 if the gifts are nontaxable by reason of gift splitting.
E&G-IRC secs. 6019, 6075; Regs. sec. 25.6019-1

712
Life Insurance Statement
Used with Form 706 or Form 709.
E&G-IRC secs 6001 and 6018; Regs secs 20.6001-1, 20.6018-4(d), 25.6001-1(b)

720
Quarterly Federal Excise Tax Return
Used to report excise taxes due from retailers and manufacturers on sale or manufacture of various articles; taxes on facilities and services; taxes on certain products and commodities (gasoline, coal, etc); windfall profits and Inland waterways taxes. Ex-IRC sec. 6011; Separate instructions

730
Tax on Wagering
Used to report taxes due under IRC section 4401.
Ex-IRC sec. 4401; Regs. sec. 44.6011(a)-1

843
Claim for Refund and Request for Abatement
Used to claim refund of taxes (other than income taxes) which were illegally, erroneously or excessively collected; or to claim amount paid for stamps unused or used in error or excess; and for a refund or abatement of interest or penalties assessed. Misc-IRC secs. 6402, 6404, 6511, 6404(e), and 6404(f); Regs. secs. 31.6413(c)-1, 301.6402-2, and 301.6404-1

851
Affiliations Schedule
Used with Form 1120 by parent corporation for affiliated corporations included in consolidated tax return. IT-IRC sec. 1502; Regs. sec. 1.1502-75(h)

872-C
Consent Fixing Period of Limitation Upon Assessment of Tax Under Section 4940 of the Internal Revenue Code
Used only with Form 1023, Application for Recognition of Exemption, by an organization described in Internal Revenue Code section 170(b)(1)(A)(vi) or section 509(a)2), to request the organization be treated as a publicly supported organization during an advance ruling period. IT-IRC sec. 6501(c)4)

926
Return by a Transferor of Property to a Foreign Corporation, Foreign Trust or Estate, or Foreign Partnership
Used to report transfers of property by a U.S. person to a foreign partnership, trust or estate, or corporation, and pay any excise tax due on the transfer.
IT-IRC sec. 1491; Regs. sec. 1.1491-2

Taxes

928
Fuel Bond
Used to post bond for excise tax on fuel.
Ex-IRC sec. 4101

940
Employer's Annual Federal Unemployment (FUTA) Tax Return
Used by employers to report Federal unemployment (FUTA) tax. Emp-IRC sec 6011; IRC Chapter 23; Regs sec 31.6011(a)-3; Circular E; Circular SS

940-EZ
Employer's Annual Federal Unemployment (FUTA) Tax Return
Used by employers to report Federal unemployment (FUTA) tax. This form is a simplified version of Form 940.
EMP-IRC sec. 6011; IRC Chapter 23; Regs. sec. 31.6011(a)-3; Circular E; Circular SS

940PR
Planilla Para La Declaracion Anual Del Patrono-La Contribucion Federal Para el Desempleo (FUTA)
Used by employers in Puerto Rico. A variation of Form 940.
Emp-IRC sec. 6011; IRC Chapter 23; Regs. sec. 31.6011(a)-3; Circular PR

941
Employer's Quarterly Federal Tax Return
Used by employer to report social security taxes and income taxes withheld, advance earned income credit (EIC), and back up withholding.
Emp-IRC secs. 3101, 3111, 3402, 3405 and 3406; Regs. secs. 31.6011(a)-1 and 31.6011(a)-4; Circular E

Sch. A (Form 941)
Record of Federal Backup Withholding Tax Liability
Used to report backup withholding liability when treated as a separate tax for depositing purposes.
Emp-IRC secs. 3406, 6302; Regs. secs. 31.6302 and 35a.9999-3

Schedule B (Form 941)
Employer Record of Federal Tax Liability
Used by employers required to deposit on a semiweekly basis to report employment tax liability.
Emp. - IRC sec. 6302(g).

Anexo B (Form 941-PR)
Registro Suplementario De La Obligacion Contributive
Federal Del Partono
Used by employers in Puerto Rico. A variation of Schedule B (Form 941).
Emp - IRC sec. 6302(g).

941c
Statement to Correct Information Previously Reported on the Employer's Federal Tax Return
Used by employers to correct wages, tips, and tax previously reported.
Emp-IRC secs. 6205 and 6402; Regs. secs. 31.6011(a)-1, 31.6205-1, and 31.6402(a)-2; Circulars A, E, and SS

941c PR
Planilla Para La Correccion De Informacion Facilitada Anteriormente En Complimiento Con La Ley Del Seguro Social
Used by employers in Puerto Rico. A variation of Form 941c.
Emp-IRC Chapter 21; Regs secs 31.6011(a)-1 and 31.6205-1, 31.6402(a)-2; Circular PR

941E
Quarterly Return of Withheld Federal Income Tax and Hospital Insurance (Medicare) Tax
Used by State and local government employers and by other organizations that are not liable for social security taxes. A variation of Form 941.
Emp-IRC secs. 3121(u) and 3402

941-M
Employer's Monthly Federal Tax Return
Used by employers to report withheld income tax and social security taxes (because they have not complied with the requirements for filing quarterly returns, or for paying or depositing taxes reported on quarterly returns).
Emp-IRC sec. 7512; Regs. sec. 31.6011(a)-5

941 PR
Planilla Para La Declaracion Trimestral Del Patrono-La Contribucion Federal al Seguro Social
Used by employers in Puerto Rico. A variation of Form 941.
Emp-IRC secs. 3101 and 3111; Regs. sec. 31.6011(a)-1; Circular PR

941SS
Employer's Quarterly Federal Tax Return
Used by employers in Virgin Islands, Guam, the Northern Mariana Islands, and American Samoa. A variation of Form 941.
Emp-IRC secs. 3101 and 3111; Regs. sec. 31.6011(a)-1; Circular SS

942
Employer's Quarterly Tax Return for Household Employees
Used by household employers quarterly to report social security and income taxes withheld from wages of household employees.
Emp-IRC secs. 3101 and 3111; Regs. sec. 31.6011(a)-1(a)(3)

942PR
Planilla Para La Declaracion Trimestral Del Patrono De Empleados Domesticos
Used by household employers in Puerto Rico to report social security taxes withheld from wages of household employees. A variation of Form 942.
Emp-IRC secs. 3101 and 3111; Regs. sec. 31.6011(a)-1(a)(3)

943
Employer's Annual Tax Return for Agricultural Employees
Used by Agricultural employers to report social security and income taxes withheld.
Emp-IRC secs. 3101, 3111 and 3402; Regs. sec. 31.6011(a)-1 and 31.6011(a)-4; Circular A

943A
Agricultural Employer's Record of Federal Tax Liability
Used by agricultural employers who have a tax liability of $3,000 or more during any month. Emp-IRC sec. 6302; Regs. sec. 6302(c)-1; Circular A

943 PR
Planilla Para La Declaracion Anual De La Contribucion Del Patrono De Empleados Agricolas
Used by agricultural employers in Puerto Rico. A variation of Form 943.
Emp-IRC secs 3101 and 3111; Regs sec 31.6011(a)-1, 31.6011(a)-4; Circular PR

943A-PR
Registro De La Obligacion Contributiva Del Patrono Agricola
Used by agricultural employers in Puerto Rico. A variation of Form 943A.
Emp-IRC sec. 6302; Regs. sec. 31.6302(c)-1; Circular PR

952
Consent to Fix Period of Limitation on Assessment of Income Taxes
Used when complete liquidation of a subsidiary is not accomplished within the tax year in which the first liquidating distribution is made. The receiving corporation is required to file this consent with its return for each tax year which falls wholly or partly within the period of liquidation. IT-IRC sec. 332; Regs. sec. 1.332-4

966
Corporate Dissolution or Liquidation
Used (under IRC section 6043(a)) by corporations within 30 days after adoption of resolution or plan of dissolution, or complete or partial liquidation. (An information return.)
IT-IRC sec. 6043(a)

Be patient. If any phone number is incorrect, call (area code) 555-1212 and request the new listing.

970
Application to Use LIFO Inventory Method
Used to change to the LIFO inventory method provided by section 472.
IT-IRC sec. 472; Regs. sec. 1.472-3

972
Consent of Shareholder to Include Specific Amount in Gross Income
Used by shareholders of a corporation who agree to include in their gross income for their taxable year a specific amount as a tax dividend.
IT-IRC sec. 565

973
Corporation Claim for Deduction for Consent Dividends
Used by corporations that claim a consent dividends deduction. Accompanied by filed consents of shareholders on Form 972. IT-IRC sec. 561

976
Claim for Deficiency Dividends Deduction by a Personal Holding Company, Regulated Investment Company, or Real Estate Investment Trust
Used by a personal holding company, regulated investment company, or real estate investment trust to claim a deficiency dividends deduction.
IT-IRC sec. 547 and 860; Regs. sec. 1.547-2(b)(2) and 1.860-2(b)(2)

982
Reduction of Tax Attributes Due to Discharge of Indebtedness
Used by a taxpayer who excludes from gross income under section 108 any amount of income attributable to discharge of indebtedness, in whole or in part, in the tax year, for which it is liable or subject. Also used as a consent of a corporation to adjustment of basis of its property under regulations prescribed under IRC section 1082(a)(2).
IT-IRC secs. 108, 1017, and 1082

990
Return of Organization Exempt From Income Tax (Except Private Foundation)
Used by organizations exempt under IRC section 501(a) and described in Code section 501(c), other than private foundations. (An information return.)
IT-IRC sec. 6033; Regs. sec. 1.6033-1(a)(2); Separate instructions

Sch. A (Form 990)
Organization Exempt Under 501 (c)(3) (Supplementary Information)
Used by organizations described in IRC section 501(c)(3) (other than private foundations filing Form 990-PF).
IT-IRC sec. 6033; Separate instructions

990-BL
Information and Initial Excise Tax Return for Black Lung Benefit Trusts and Certain Related Persons
Used by Black Lung Benefit Trusts exempt under Section 501(c)(21) as an information return. Also used by these trusts and certain related persons for attaching Schedule A (Form 990-BL) when taxes under sections 4951 or 4952 are due.
IT/EX-IRC sec. 501 (c)(21); Chapter 42; Separate instructions

990-C
Farmers' Cooperative Association Income Tax Return
Used by Farmers' Cooperative Marketing and Purchasing Association.
IT-IRC secs. 521, 1381, 1382, 1383, 1385, 1388, and 6012; Regs. secs. 1.522-1, 1.1381-1, 2, 1.1382-1, 2, 3, 4, 5, 6, 7, 1.1383-1, 1.1385-1, 1.388-1, and 1.6012-2(f); Separate instructions

990-EZ
Short Form Return of Organization Exempt Form Income Tax
Used by organizations of gross receipts less than $100,000 and total assets of less than $250,000 at end of year.
IT-IRC sec. 6033; Regs. sec. 1.6033-1(a)(2); Separate instructions

990-PF
Return of Private Foundation or Section 4947(a)(1)Trust Treated as a Private Foundation
Used by private foundations and Section 4947(a)(1)trusts. (An information return.)
IT/Ex-IRC sec. 6033; IRC Chapter 42; Separate instructions

990-T
Exempt Organization Business Income Tax Return
Used by exempt organization with unrelated business income (under IRC section 511).
IT-IRC secs. 511 and 6012; Regs. secs. 1.6012-2(e) and 1.6012-3(a)(5); Separate instructions

990-W
Estimated Tax on Unrelated Business Taxable Income for Tax-Exempt Organization
Used as a worksheet by tax-exempt trusts and tax-exempt corporations to figure their estimated tax liability. Tax-exempt trusts and corporations should keep it for their records. IT-IRC sec. 6154

1000
Ownership Certificate
Used by a citizen, resident individual, fiduciary, partnership, or nonresident partnership all of whose members are citizens or residents who have interest in bonds of a domestic or resident corporation (containing a tax-free covenant and issued before January 1, 1934). IT-IRC sec. 1461; Regs. sec. 1.1461-1(h)

1001
Ownership, Exemption, or Reduced Rate Certificate
Used by a nonresident alien individual or fiduciary, foreign partnership, foreign corporation or other foreign entity, nonresident foreign partnership composed in whole or in part of nonresident aliens (applies to IRC section 1451 only), or nonresident foreign corporation (applies to Code section 1451 only), receiving income subject to withholding under Code section 1441, 1442, or 1451. IT-IRC sec. 1461; Regs. sec. 1.1461-1(i)

Package 1023
Application for Recognition of Exemption Under Section 501(c)3-of the Internal Revenue Code
Used to apply for exemption under section 501(a) IRC as organizations described in section 501(c)3-(also sections 501(e) and (f)). Includes 3 copies of Form 872-C. IT-IRC sec. 501; Regs. sec. 1.501(a)-1(a)3)

Package 1024
Application for Recognition of Exemption Under Section 501(a) or Determination Under Section 120
Used by organizations to apply for exemption under IRC section 501(a) (as described in Code sections 501(c)2), 4), 5), 6), 7), 8), 9), (10), (12), (13), (15), (17), (19), 20) and 25). (Also used to apply for a determination as a qualified plan under section 120.) IT-IRC secs. 501, 120; Regs. sec. 1.501(a)-1(a)3)

1028
Application for Recognition of Exemption Under Section 521 of the Internal Revenue Code
Used by farmers, fruit growers, or similar associations to claim exemption under IRC section 521. IT-IRC sec. 521; Regs. sec. 1.521-1, Separate instructions

1040
U.S. Individual Income Tax Return
Used by citizens or residents of the United States to report income tax. (Also see Form 1040A, and 1040EZ.)
IT-IRC secs. 6012 and 6017; Regs. secs. 1.6012-1 and 1.6017-1; Pub. 17; Separate instructions

Sch. A (Form 1040)
Itemized Deductions
Used to report itemized deductions (medical and dental expense, taxes, contributions, interest, casualty and theft losses, moving expenses, miscellaneous deductions subject to the 2% AGI limit, and other miscellaneous deductions).
IT-IRC secs. 67, 163, 164, 165, 166, 170, 211, 212, 213, and 217; Pub. 17; See the separate instructions for Form 1040.

Be patient. If any phone number is incorrect, call (area code) 555-1212 and request the new listing.

471

Taxes

Sch. B (Form 1040)
Interest and Dividend Income
Used to list gross dividends received (if more than $400) and interest income (if more than $400), and to ask questions about foreign accounts and foreign trusts. IT-IRC secs. 6012, 61, and 116; Pub. 17; See the separate Instructions for Form 1040.

Sch. C (Form 1040)
Profit or Loss From Business
Used to figure profit or (loss) from business or professions.
IT-IRC sec. 6017; Regs. sec. 1.6017-1; Pubs. 17 and 334; See separate Instructions for Form 1040.

Sch. C-EZ (Form 1040)
Net Profit from Business
Used by individuals having gross receipts under $25,000 and expenses under $5,000. IT-IRC sec. 6017; Reg. sec. 1.6017-1.

Sch. D (Form 1040)
Capital Gains and Losses
Used to report details of gain (or loss) from sales or exchanges of capital assets; to figure capital loss carry-overs from 1989 to 1990, and to reconcile Forms 1099-B with tax return.
IT-IRC secs. 1202-1223, 6045; Pubs. 17 and 334; See the separate Instructions for Form 1040.

Sch. D-1 (Form 1040)
Continuation Sheet for Schedule D (Form 1040)
Used to attach to Schedule D (Form 1040) to list additional transactions in Parts 2a and 9a.

Sch. E (Form 1040)
Supplemental Income and Loss
Used to report income from rents, royalties, partnerships, S corporations, estates, trusts, REMICs, etc. IT-IRC secs. 6012 and 6017; Regs. secs. 1.6012-1 and 1.6017-1; Pub. 17; See the separate Instructions for Form 1040.

Sch. EIC (Form 1040 and 1040A)
Earned Income Credit
Used to figure the earned income credit and provide required identifying information for qualifying children.
IT-IRC sec. 32; PUB. 17 and 596.

Sch. F (Form 1040)
Profit or Loss from Farming
Used to figure profit or (loss) from farming.
IT-IRC sec. 6012; Regs. sec. 1.61-4; Pub. 225; See the separate Instructions for Form 1040.

Sch. R (Form 1040)
Credit for the Elderly or the Disabled
Used to figure credit for the elderly and for persons under 65 who retired on permanent and total disability and received taxable disability benefits.
IT-IRC sec. 22; Pub. 17 and 524; Separate instructions

Sch. SE (Form 1040)
Social Security Self-Employment Tax
Used to figure self-employment income and self-employment tax.
IT-IRC secs. 1401 and 1402; See the separate Instructions for Form 1040.

1040A
U.S. Individual Income Tax Return
Used by citizens and residents of the United States to report income tax. (Also see Form 1040 and 1040EZ.) IT-IRC sec. 6012; Regs. sec. 1.6012-1; Pub. 17; Separate instructions

Sch. 1 (Form 1040A)
Interest and Dividend Income for Form 1040A Filers
Part I is used by Form 1040A filers to report interest income (if more than $400) and for claiming the exclusion of interest from series EE U.S. savings bonds issued after 1989. Part II is used by Form 1040A filers to report dividends received (if more than $400).
IT-IRC sec. 61; PUB. 17.

Sch. 2 (Form 1040A)
Child and Dependent Care Expenses for Form 1040A Filers
Used by Form 1040A filers to figure the credit for child and dependent care expenses and/or the exclusion of employers-provided dependent care benefits.
IT-IRC secs. 21 and 129, Regs. sec. 1.44 A-1; PUB 17 and 503.

Sch. 3 (Form 1040A)
Credit for the Elderly or the Disabled for Form 1040A Filers
Used by Form 1040A filers to figure the credit for the elderly (age 65 or older) or the disabled (under 65 who retired on permanent disability and received taxable disability benefits).
IT-IRC sec. 22; PUB. 17 and 524; separate instructions.

1040C
U.S. Departing Alien Income Tax Return
Used by aliens who intend to depart from the U.S., to report income received, or expected to be received for the entire taxable year, determined as nearly as possible by the date of intended departure. (Also see Form 2063.)
IT-IRC sec. 6851; Regs. sec. 1.6851-2; Pub. 519; Separate instructions

1040-ES
Estimated Tax for Individuals
Used to pay income tax (including self-employment tax and alternative minimum tax) due (the tax that is more than the tax withheld from wages, salaries, and other payments for personal services). It is not required unless the total tax is more than withholding (if any) by $500 or more.
IT-IRC sec. 6654

1040-ES (Espanol)
Contribucion Federal Estimada Del Trabajo Por Cuenta Propia-Puerto Rico
Used in Puerto Rico. The payment vouchers are provided for payment of self-employment tax on a current basis.
IT-IRC sec. 6654

1040-ES (NR)
U.S. Estimated Tax for Nonresident Alien Individuals
Used by nonresident aliens to pay any income tax due in excess of the tax withheld. It is not required unless the total tax exceeds withholding (if any) by $500 or more.
IT-IRC sec. 6654

1040EZ
Income Tax Return for Single Filers With No Dependents
Used by citizens and residents of the United States to report income tax. (Also see Form 1040 and Form 1040A.)
IT-IRC sec. 6012; Reg. sec. 1.6012-1; Pub. 17; Separate instructions

1040NR
U.S. Nonresident Alien Income Tax Return
Used by all nonresident alien individuals, whether or not engaged in a trade or business within the United States, who file a U.S. tax return. Also used as required for filing nonresident alien fiduciary (estate and trusts) returns.
IT-IRC secs. 871 and 6012; Pub. 519; Separate instructions

1040 PR
Planilla Para La Declaracion De La Contribucion Federal Sobre El Trabajo Por Cuenta Propia-Puerto Rico
Used in Puerto Rico to compute self-employment tax in accordance with IRC Chapter 2 of Subtitle A, and to provide proper credit to taxpayer's social security account.
IT-IRC secs. 6017 and 7651; Regs. sec. 1.6017-1; Circular PR

1040SS
U.S. Self-Employment Tax Return-Virgin Islands, Guam, and American Samoa
Used to compute self-employment tax in accordance with IRC Chapter 2 of Subtitle A, and to provide proper credit to taxpayer's social security account.
IT-IRC secs. 6017 and 7651; Regs. sec. 1.6017-1; Circular SS

Be patient. If any phone number is incorrect, call (area code) 555-1212 and request the new listing.

1040X
Amended U.S. Individual Income Tax Return
Used to claim refund of income taxes, pay additional income taxes, or designate dollar(s) to a Presidential election campaign fund.
IT-IRC secs. 6402, 6404, 6511, and 6096; Separate instructions

1041
U.S. Fiduciary Income Tax Return
Used by a fiduciary of a domestic estate or domestic trust to report income tax. IT-IRC sec. 6012; Regs. secs. 1.671-4, 1.6012-3(a), and 1.6041-1; Separate instructions

Sch. D (Form 1041)
Capital Gains and Losses
Used to report details of gain (or loss) from sales or exchanges of capital assets.
IT-IRC sec. 6012; Regs. sec. 1.6012-3(a); Separate instructions

Sch. H (Form 1041)
Alternative Minimum Tax
Used by fiduciary of an estate or trust to compute the fiduciary's alternative minimum tax basis and to report any alternative minimum tax due.
IT-IRC secs. 55 through 59.

Sch. J. (Form 1041)
Information Return Trust Allocation of an Accumulation Distribution (IRC section 665)
Used by domestic complex trusts to report accumulation distributions. IT-IRC secs. 665, 666, and 667

Sch. K-1 (Form 1041)
Beneficiary's Share of Income, Deductions, Credits, etc.
Used to report each beneficiary's share of the income, deductions, credits, and distributable net alternative minimum taxable income form the estate or trust.
IT-IRC sec. 6012; Regs. secs. 1.6012-3(a)

1041-A
U.S. Information Return-Trust Accumulation of Charitable Amounts
Used by a trust that claims a contribution deduction under IRC section 642(c), or by a trust described in Code section 4947(a)2). (An information return.)
IT-IRC secs. 6034 and 6104; Regs. sec. 1.6034-1

1041-ES
Estimated Income Tax for Fiduciaries
Used to figure and pay estimated tax for fiduciaries. IT-IRC sec. 6654

1041-T
Allocation of Estimated Tax Payments to Beneficiaries
Used by a trust to make an election under section 643(g) to credit an overpayment of estimated tax to beneficiaries. IT-IRC sec. 643(g)

1042
Annual Withholding Tax Return for U.S. Source Income of Foreign Persons
Used by withholding agents to report tax withheld at source on certain income paid to nonresident aliens, foreign partnerships, or foreign corporations not engaged in a trade or business in the U.S. IT-IRC secs. 1441, 1442, and 1461; Regs. secs. 1.1441-1 and 1.1461-2(b); Separate instructions

1042S
Foreign Person's U.S. Source Income Subject to Withholding
Used by a withholding agent to report certain income and tax withheld at source for foreign payees. (An information return.)
IT-IRC sec. 1461; Regs. sec. 1.1461-2(c); Separate instructions

1045
Application for Tentative Refund
Used by taxpayers (other than corporations) to apply for a tentative refund from the carryback of a net operating loss, unused general business credit, or overpayment of tax due to a claim of right adjustment under section 1341(b)(1). T-IRC sec. 6411; Regs. sec. 1.6411-1

1065
U.S. Partnership Return of Income
Used by partnerships as an information return.
IT-IRC sec. 6031 and 6698; Regs. secs. 1.761-1(a), 1.6031-1, and 1.6033-1(a)5); Separate instructions

Sch. D (Form 1065)
Capital Gains and Losses
Used to show partnership's capital gains and losses. IT-IRC 6031

Sch. K-1 (Form 1065)
Partner's Share of Income, Credits, Deductions, Etc.
Used to show partner's share of income, credits, deductions, etc.
IT-IRC secs. 702 and 703; Separate instructions

1066
U.S. Real Estate Mortgage Investment Conduit Income Tax Return
Used to report income, deductions, gains and losses, and the tax on net income from prohibited transactions, of a real estate mortgage investment conduit.
IT-IRC secs. 860D and 860F(e); Separate instructions

Sch. Q (Form 1066)
Quarterly Notice to Residual Interest Holder of REMIC Taxable Income or Net Loss Allocation
Used to show residual interest holder's share of taxable income (or net loss), excess inclusion, and section 212 expenses. IT-IRC sec. 860G(c)

1078
Certificate of Alien Claiming Residence in the United States
Used by an alien claiming residence in the U.S., for income tax purposes. Filed with the withholding agent.
IT-IRC secs. 871 and 1441; Regs. secs. 1.1441-5 and 1.871-3,4

1096
Annual Summary and Transmittal of U.S. Information Returns
Used to summarize and transmit Forms W-2G, 1098, 1099-A, 1099-B, 1099-DIV, 1099-G, 1099-INT, 1099-MISC, 1099-OID, 1099-PATR, 1099-R, 1099-S, and 5498.
IT-IRC secs. 408(i), 6041, 6041A, 6042, 6043, 6044, 6045, 6047, 6049, 6050A, 6050B, 6050D, 6050E, 6050H, and 6050J

1098
Mortgage Interest Statement
Used to report $600 or more of mortgage interest from an individual in the course of a trade or business.
IT-IRC sec. 6050H; Regs. sec. 1.6050H-2; See the separate Instructions for Forms 1099, 1098, 5498, 1096, and W-2G

1099-A
Acquisition or Abandonment of Secured Property
Used by lenders to report acquisitions by such lenders or abandonments of property that secures a loan.
IT-IRC sec. 6050J; Temp. Regs. sec. 1.6050J-1T; See the separate Instructions for Forms 1099, 1098, 5498, 1096, and W-2G

1099-B
Proceeds From Broker and Barter Exchange Transactions
Used by a broker to report gross proceeds from the sale or redemption of securities, commodities or regulated futures contracts, or by a barter exchange to report the exchange of goods or services.
IT-IRC sec. 6045; Regs. sec. 1.6045-1; See the separate instructions for Forms 1099, 1098, 5498, 1096, and W-2G

1099-DIV
Dividends and Distributions
Used to report dividends and distributions. IT-IRC secs. 6042 and 6043; Regs. secs. 1.6042-2 and 1.6043-2; See the separate instructions for Forms 1099, 1098, 5498, 1096, and W-2G

Be patient. If any phone number is incorrect, call (area code) 555-1212 and request the new listing.

473

Taxes

1099-G
Certain Government Payments
Used to report government payments such as unemployment compensation, state and local income tax refunds, credits, or offsets, discharges of indebtedness by the Federal Government, taxable grants, and subsidy payments from the U.S. Department of Agriculture. IT-IRC secs. 6041, 6050B, 6050D, and 6050E; Regs. secs. 1.6041-1, 1.6050B-1, 1.6050D-1, and 1.6050E-1; See the separate Instructions for Forms 1099, 1098, 5498, 1096, and W-2G

1099-INT
Interest Income
Used to report interest income. IT-IRC secs. 6041 and 6049; Regs. secs. 1.6041-1, 1.6049-4, and Temp. Regs. sec. 1.6049-7T; See the separate Instructions for Forms 1099, 1098, 5498, 1096, and W-2G

1099-MISC
Miscellaneous Income
Used to report rents, royalties, prizes and awards, fishing boat proceeds, payments by health, accident and sickness insurers to physicians or other health service providers, fees, commissions or other compensation for services rendered in the course of the payer's business when the recipient is not treated as an employee, direct sales of $5,000 or more of consumer products for resale, substitute payments by brokers in lieu of dividends or tax-exempt interest, and crop insurance proceeds. IT-IRC secs. 6041, 6041A, 6045(d), and 6050A; Regs. secs. 1.6041-1, 1.6045-2, and 1.6050A-1; See separate Instructions for Forms 1099, 1098, 5498, 1096, and W-2G

1099-OID
Original Issue Discount
Used to report original issue discount. IT-IRC sec. 6049; Regs. sec. 1.6049-4; Temp. Regs. secs. 1.6049-4, 1.6049-5T, and 1.6049-7T; See the separate Instructions for Forms 1099, 1098, 5498, 1096, and W-2G

1099-PATR
Taxable Distributions Received From Cooperatives
Used to report patronage dividends. IT-IRC sec. 6044; Regs. sec. 1.6044-2; See the separate instructions for Forms 1099, 1098, 5498, 1096, and W-2G

1099-R
Distributions From Profit-Sharing, Retirement Plans, Individual Retirement Arrangements, Insurance Contracts, Etc.
Used to report total distributions from profit-sharing, retirement plans and individual retirement arrangements, and certain surrenders of insurance contracts. IT-IRC sec. 402, 408, and 6047; Temp Regs. sec. 35.3405-1; Regs. secs. 1.408-7 and 1.6047-1; See the separate Instructions for Forms 1099, 1098, 5498, 1096, and W-2G

1099-S
Proceeds From Real Estate Transactions
Used by the person required to report gross proceeds from real estate transactions. IT-IRC sec. 6045(e); Temp Regs. sec. 1.6045-3T; See the separate Instructions for Forms 1099, 1098, 5498, 1096, and W-2G

1116
Foreign Tax Credit (Individual, Fiduciary, or Nonresident Alien Individual)
Used to figure the foreign tax credit claimed for the amount of any income, war profits, and excess profits tax paid or accrued during the taxable year to any foreign country or U.S. possession. IT-IRC secs. 27, 901, and 904; Pub. 514; Separate instructions

1118
Foreign Tax Credit-Corporations
Used to support the amount of foreign tax credit claimed on corporation income tax returns. IT-IRC secs. 901 through 906; Separate instructions

I (Form 1118)
Reduction of Oil and Gas Extraction Taxes
Used to compute the section 907(a) reduction for a corporation that is claiming a foreign tax credit with respect to any income taxes paid, accrued, or deemed to have been paid during the tax year with respect to foreign oil and gas extraction income. IT-IRC sec. 907

Sch. J (Form 1118)
Separate Limitation Loss Allocations and Other Adjustments Necessary to Determine Numerators of Limitation Fractions, Year-End Recharacterization Balances and Overall Foreign Loss Account Balances
Used to show the adjustments to separate limitation income or losses in determining the numerators of the limitation fractions for each separate limitation; the year-end balances of separate limitation losses that were allocated among other separate limitations (in the current year or in prior years) that have yet to be recharacterized; and the balances in the overall foreign loss accounts at the beginning of the tax year, any adjustments to the account balances, and the balances, in the overall foreign loss accounts at the end of the tax year. IT-IRC sec. 904(f)

1120
U.S. Corporation Income Tax Return
Used by a corporation to report income tax. (Also see Form 1120-A.) IT-IRC sec. 6012; Regs. secs. 1.1502-75(h), and 1.6012-2; Separate instructions

Sch. D (Form 1120)
Capital Gains and Losses
Used with Forms 1120, 1120-A, 1120-DF, 1120-IC-DISC, 1120-F, 1120-FSC, 1120-H, 1120L, 1120-ND, 1120-PC, 1120-POL, 1120-REIT, 1120-RIC, 990-C and certain Forms 990-T to report details of gain (or loss) from sales or exchanges of capital assets, and to figure alternative tax. IT-IRC secs. 1201 and 1231

Sch. H (Form 1120)
Section 280H Limitation for a Personal Service Corporation (PSC)
Used by personal service corporations with the distribution requirements of section 280 and 444. IRS sec. 280H.

Sch. PH (Form 1120)
Computation of U.S. Personal Holding Company Tax
Used to figure personal holding company tax; filed with the income tax return of every personal holding company. IT-IRC secs. 541, 6012, and 6501(f); Separate instructions

1120-A
U.S. Corporation Short-Form Income Tax Return
Used by a corporation to report income tax. IT-IRC sec. 6012; Regs. sec. 1.6012-2; Separate instructions

1120-DF
U.S. Income Tax Return for Designated Settlement Funds (Under Section 468B)
Used by designated settlement funds to report contributions received, income earned, the administration expenses of operating the fund, and the tax on its investment income. IT-IRC secs. 468B and 6012; Separate instructions

1120F
U.S. Income Tax Return of a Foreign Corporation
Used by foreign corporations to report income tax. IT-IRC secs. 881, 882, 884, 887, and 6012; Separate instructions

1120-FSC
U.S. Income Tax Return of a Foreign Sales Corporation
Used by foreign sales corporations to report income tax. IT-IRC secs. 922, 6011(c), and 6012; Separate instructions

Sch. P (Form 1120-FSC)
Transfer Price or Commission
Used to compute transfer price or commission under IRC sections 925(a)(1) and 2). IT-IRC sec. 6011(c)

1120-H
U.S. Income Tax Return for Homeowners Associations
Used by homeowner associations to report income tax. (An annual return.) IT-IRC sec. 528 and Reg. sec. 1.528-8

Be patient. If any phone number is incorrect, call (area code) 555-1212 and request the new listing.

1120-IC-DISC
Interest Charge Domestic International Sales Corporation Return

Used by domestic corporations that make the election under IRC section 992(b) to be a domestic international sales corporation.
IT-IRC secs. 6011(c) and 6072(b); Separate instructions

Sch. K (Form 1120-IC-DISC)
Shareholder's Statement of IC-DISC Distributions

Used to report deemed and actual distributions from an IC-DISC to shareholders and to report deferred DISC income and certain other information to shareholders.
IT-IRC secs. 6011(c)

Sch. P (Form 1120-IC-DISC)
Inter-company Transfer Price or Commission

Used to compute inter-company transfer prices or commissions under IRC sections 994(a)(1) and (2). IT-IRC secs. 6011(c)

Sch. Q (Form 1120-IC-DISC)
Borrower's Certificate of Compliance with the Rules for Producer's Loans

Used by an IC-DISC to establish that the borrower is in compliance with the rules for producer's loans. IT-Regs. sec. 1.993-4(d)

1120L
U.S. Life Insurance Company Income Tax Return

Used by life insurance companies to report income tax.
IT-IRC secs. 801 and 6012; Reg. sec. 1.6012-2; Separate instructions

1120-ND
Return for Nuclear Decommissioning Funds and Certain Related Persons

Used by nuclear decommissioning funds to report income, expenses, transfers of funds to the public utility that created it and to figure the taxes on income plus penalty taxes on trustees and certain disqualified persons.
IT-IRC sec. 468A; Separate instructions

1120-PC
U.S. Property and Casualty Insurance Company Income Tax Return

Used by nonlife insurance companies to report income tax.
IT-IRC secs. 831 and 6012; Separate instructions

1120-POL
U.S. Income Tax Return for Certain Political Organizations

Used by certain political organizations to report income tax.
IT-IRC secs. 856 and 6012; Separate instructions

1120-REIT
U.S. Income Tax Return for Real Estate Investment Trusts

Used by real estate investment trusts to report income tax.
IT-IRC secs. 856 and 6012; Separate instructions

1120-RIC
U.S. Income Tax Return for Regulated Investment Companies

Used by regulated investment companies to report income tax.
IT-IRC secs. 851 and 6012; Separate instructions

1120S
U.S. Income Tax Return for an S Corporation

Used by S corporations that have made the election prescribed by IRC section 1362.
IT-IRC sec. 6037; IRC Subchapter S; Regs. sec. 1.6037-1; Separate instructions

Sch. D (Form 1120S)
Capital Gains and Losses and Built-in Gains

Used by S corporations that have made the election prescribed by IRC section 1362. Sch. D is used to report details of gains (and losses) from sales, exchanges or distribution of capital assets and to figure the tax imposed on certain capital gains and certain built-in gains.
IT-IRC secs. 1201 and 1231; and IRC Subchapter S; Separate instructions

Sch. K-1 (Form 1120S)
Shareholder's Share of Income, Credits, Deductions, Etc.

Used to show shareholder's share of income, credits, deductions, etc. A four-part assembly: A copy is filed with Form 1120S, a copy is for S corporation records, and a copy is given to each shareholder along with the separate instructions.
IT-IRC sec. 6037

1120-W
Corporation Estimated Tax

Used as a worksheet by corporations to figure estimated tax liability; not to be filed. Corporations should keep it for their records.
IT-IRC sec. 6655

1120X
Amended U.S. Corporation Income Tax Return

Used by corporations to amend a previously filed Form 1120 or Form 1120-A.
IT-Regs. sec. 301.6402-3

1122
Authorization and Consent of Subsidiary Corporation to be Included in a Consolidated Income Tax Return

Used as the authorization and consent of a subsidiary corporation to be included in a consolidated income tax return. IT-IRC sec. 1502; Regs. sec. 1.1502-75(h)

1128
Application for Change in Accounting Period

Used to obtain approval of a change, adoption or retention of an accounting period.
IT-IRC sec. 442; Regs. secs. 1.442-1(b) and 1.1502-76; Separate instructions

1138
Extension of Time for Payment of Taxes by a Corporation Expecting a Net Operating Loss Carryback

Used by a corporation expecting a net operating loss carryback to request an extension of time for payment of taxes.
IT-IRC sec. 6164

1139
Corporation Application for Tentative Refund

Used by corporations to apply for a tentative refund from the carryback of a net operating loss, net capital loss, unused general business credit, or overpayment of tax due to a claim or right adjustment under section 1341(b)(1).
IT-IRC sec. 6411

1310
Statement of Person Claiming Refund Due a Deceased Taxpayer

Used by claimant to secure payment of refund on behalf of a deceased taxpayer.
IT-IRC sec. 6402; Regs. sec. 301.6402-2(e); Pubs. 17 and 559

1363
Export Exemption Certificate

Used by shipper or other person to suspend liability for the payment of the tax for a period of 6 months from the date of shipment from the point of origin. The original is filed with the carrier at time of payment of the transportation charges and the duplicate is retained with the shipping papers for a period of 3 years from the last day of the month during which the shipment was made from the point of origin. May also be used as a blanket exemption certificate, with approval of District Director.
Ex-IRC secs. 4271 and 4272; Temp Regs. Part 154.2-1

2032
Contract Coverage Under Title II of the Social Security Act

Used to make an agreement pursuant to IRC section 3121(l).
Emp-IRC sec. 3121(l); Regs. sec. 36.3121(l)(1)-1

Be patient. If any phone number is incorrect, call (area code) 555-1212 and request the new listing.

475

Taxes

2063
U.S. Departing Alien Income Tax Statement
Used by a resident alien who has not received a termination assessment, or a nonresident alien who has no taxable income from United States sources.
IT-IRC sec. 6851(d); Regs. sec. 1.6851-2; Rev. Rul. 55-468; C.B.1955-2, 501; Pub. 519

2106
Employee Business Expenses
Used by employees to support deductions for business expenses.
IT-IRC secs. 62, 162, and 274; Instructions for Form 1040, Pub. 463; Separate instructions

2119
Sale of Your Home
Used by individuals who sold their principal residence whether or not they bought another one. Also used by individuals 55 or over who elect to exclude gain on the sale of their principal residence.
IT-IRC secs. 121 and 1034; Pub. 17; Separate instructions

2120
Multiple Support Declaration
Used as a statement disclaiming as an income tax exemption an individual to whose support the taxpayer and others have contributed.
IT-IRC sec. 152(c); Regs. sec. 1.152-3(c); Pub. 17

2210
Underpayment of Estimated Tax by Individuals and Fiduciaries
Used by individuals and fiduciaries to determine if they paid enough estimated tax. The form is also used to compute the penalty for underpayment of estimated tax.
IT-IRC sec. 6654; Regs. secs. 1.6654-1 and 1.6654-2; Separate instructions

2210F
Underpayment of Estimated Tax by Farmers and Fishermen
Used by qualified farmers and fishermen to determine if they paid enough estimated tax. Used only by individuals whose gross income from farming or fishing is at least two-thirds of their gross annual income. (All other individuals should use Form 2210.) The form is also used to compute the penalty for underpayment of estimated tax.
IT-IRC sec. 6654; Reg. secs. 1.6654-1 and 1.6654-2

2220
Underpayment of Estimated Tax by Corporations
Used by corporations to determine if they paid enough estimated tax. The form is also used to compute the penalty for underpayment of estimated tax.
IT-IRC sec. 6655; Separate instructions

2290
Heavy Vehicle Use Tax Return
Used to report tax due on use of any highway motor vehicle which falls within one of the categories shown in the tax computation schedule on the form or meets certain weight limitations.
Ex-IRC sec. 4481; Regs. sec. 41.6011(a)-1(a)

2350
Application for Extension of Time to File U.S. Income Tax Return
Used by U.S. citizens and certain resident aliens abroad, who expect to qualify for special tax treatment to obtain an extension of time for filing an income tax return.
IT-IRC secs. 911 and 6081; Regs. sec. temporary 5b.911-6(b), 1.911-7(c), and 1.6081-2; Pub. 54

2438
Regulated Investment Company Undistributed Capital Gains Tax Return
Used to report tax payable on or before 30th day after close of company's taxable year. A copy is filed with Form 1120-RIC. (An annual return.)
IT-IRC sec. 852(b)3; Regs. sec. 1.852-9

2439
Notice to Shareholder of Undistributed Long-Term Capital Gains
Used as an annual statement to be distributed to shareholders of a regulated investment company. (Copy to be attached to Form 1120-RIC.)
IT-IRC sec. 852(b)(3)(D)(i); Regs. sec. 1.852-9

2441
Child and Dependent Care Expenses
Used to figure the credit for child and dependent care expenses and/or the exclusion of employer-provided dependent care benefits. (To be attached to Form 1040.) IT-IRC sec. 21 and 129; Regs. sec. 1.44A-1; Pubs. 17 and 503

2553
Election by A Small Business Corporation
Used by qualifying small business corporations to make the election prescribed by IRC section 1362. IT-IRC sec. 1362; Separate instructions

2555
Foreign Earned Income
Used by U.S. citizens and resident aliens who qualify for the foreign earned income exclusion and/or the housing exclusion or deduction. (To be filed with Form 1040.) IT-IRC secs. 911 and 6012(c); Regs. secs. 1.911-1 and 1.6012-1; Pub. 54; Separate instructions

2555-EZ
Foreign Earned Income Exclusion
Used by citizens and resident aliens who qualify for the foreign earned income exclusion.
IT-IRC secs. 911 and 6012(c); Reg. secs. 1.911-1 and 1.6012-1; separate instructions.

2670
Credit or Refund-Exemption Certificate for Use by a Nonprofit Educational Organization
Used by certain nonprofit educational organizations to support a claim for credit or refund to the person who paid the manufacturers excise tax, or the exemption of these sales from the special fuels tax under IRC Chapter 31.
Ex-IRC secs. 4041, 4221, and 6416; Regs. sec. 48.4221-6

2688
Application for Additional Extension of Time To File U.S. Individual Income Tax Return
Used to apply for an extension of time to file Form 1040.
IT-IRC sec. 6081; Regs. sec. 1.6081-1(b)(5); T.D.6436

2758
Application for Extension of Time To File Certain Excise, Income, Information, and Other Returns
Used to apply for an extension of time to file Form 1041 and certain other returns. A separate Form 2758 must be filed for each return.
IT-IRC sec. 6081; Regs. sec. 1.6081-1(b)

2848
Power of Attorney and Declaration of Representative
Used as an authorization for one person to act for another in any tax matter (except alcohol and tobacco taxes and firearms activities).
IT-Title 26, CFR, Part 601; Separate instructions

3115
Application for Change in Accounting Method
Used to secure approval for change in accounting method.
IT-IRC sec. 446(e); Regs. sec. 1.446-1(e); Separate instructions

3206
Information Statement by United Kingdom Withholding Agents Paying Dividends From United States Corporations to Residents of the U.S. and Certain Treaty Countries
Used to report dividends paid by U.S. corporations to beneficial owners of dividends paid through United Kingdom Nominees. Used when the beneficial owners are residents of countries other than United Kingdom with which the U.S. has a tax

Be patient. If any phone number is incorrect, call (area code) 555-1212 and request the new listing.

treaty providing for reduced withholding rates on dividends.
IT secs. 7.507 and 7.508 of T.D. 5532

3468
Investment Credit
Used by individuals, estates, trusts, and corporations claiming an investment credit or business energy investment credit. Also see Form 3800.
IT-IRC secs. 38, 46, 47, 48, and 49; Separate instructions

3491
Consumer Cooperative Exemption Application
Used by certain consumer cooperatives that are primarily engaged in retail sales of goods or services generally for personal, living or family use to apply for exemption from filing Forms 1096 and 1099-PATR. IT-IRC sec. 6044(c); Regs. sec. 1.6044-4

3520
U.S. Information Return-Creation of or Transfers to Certain Foreign Trusts
Used by a grantor in the case of an inter vivos trust, a fiduciary of an estate in the case of a testamentary trust, or a transferor to report the creation of any foreign trust by a U.S. person or the transfer of any money or property to a foreign trust by a U.S. person.
IT-IRC sec. 6048; Regs. secs. 16.3-1 and 301.6048-1

3520-A
Annual Return of Foreign Trust with U.S. Beneficiaries
Used to report the operation of foreign trust that has U.S. beneficiaries.
IT-IRC sec. 6048

3800
General Business Credit
Used to summarize investment credit (Form 3468), jobs credit (Form 5884), credit for alcohol used as fuel (Form 6478), credit for increasing research activities (Form 6765), and low-income housing credit (Form 8586).
IT-IRC secs. 38 and 39; Separate instructions

3903
Moving Expenses
Used to support itemized deductions for expenses of travel, transportation and certain expenses attributable to disposition of an old residence and acquisition of a new residence for employees and self-employed individuals moving to a new job location.
IT-IRC sec. 217; Regs. sec. 1.217; Pub. 521; Separate instructions

3903F
Foreign Moving Expenses
Used by U.S. citizens or resident aliens moving to a new principal workplace outside the United States or its possessions.
IT-IRC 217(h); Pub. 521; Separate instructions

4029
Application for Exemption from Social Security Taxes and Waiver of Benefits
Used by members of qualified religious groups to claim exemption from social security taxes.
IT-IRC sec. 1402(g)

4070
Employee's Report of Tips to Employer
Used by employees to report tips to employers.
Emp-IRC sec. 3102(c); Regs. sec. 31.6053-1(b)(2)

4070-A
Employee's Daily Record of Tips
Used by employees to keep a daily record of tips received.
Emp-IRC sec. 3102(c); Regs. sec. 31.6053-4

4070PR
Informe al Patrono de Propinas Recibidas por el Empleado
Used by employees in Puerto Rico. A variation of Form 4070.
Emp-IRC sec. 3102(c); Regs. sec. 31.6053-1(b)(2)

4070A-PR
Registro Diario de Propinas Recibidas por el Empleado
Used by employees in Puerto Rico. A variation of Form 4070-A.
Emp-IRC sec. 3102(c); Regs. sec. 31.6053-4

4136
Credit for Federal Tax on Gasoline and Special Fuels
Used by individuals, estates, trusts, or corporations, including S corporations and domestic international sales corporations, to claim credit for Federal excise tax on the number of gallons of gasoline and special fuels used for business. Also used to claim the one-time credit allowed owners of qualified diesel-powered highway vehicles.
Ex-IRC secs. 34, 4041, 4081, 4091, 6420, 6421, and 6427

4137
Social Security Tax on Unreported Tip Income
Used by an employee who received tips subject to FICA tax but failed to report them to his or her employer.
IT/Emp-IRC sec. 3102; Regs. sec. 31.3102-3(d) and 31.6011(a)-1(d)

4224
Exemption From Withholding of Tax on Income Effectively Connected With the Conduct of a Trade or Business in the United States
Used to secure, at the time of payment, the benefit of exemption from withholding of the tax on certain income for nonresident alien individuals and fiduciaries, foreign partnerships, and foreign corporations.
IT-IRC secs. 1441 and 1442; Regs. sec. 1.1441-4

4255
Recapture of Investment Credit
Used by individuals, estates, trusts, or corporations to figure the increase in tax if regular or energy property was disposed of or ceased to qualify before the end of the property class life or life years used to figure the credit.
IT-IRC sec. 47

4361
Application for Exemption from Self-Employment Tax for Use by Ministers, Members of Religious Orders and Christian Science Practitioners
Used by members of qualified religious groups to claim exemption from tax on self-employment income.
IT-IRC sec. 1402(e)

4461
Application for Approval of Master or Prototype Defined Contribution Plan
Used by employers who want an opinion letter for approval of form of a master or prototype plan.
IT-IRC secs. 401(a), and 501(a)

4461-A
Application for Approval of Master or Prototype Defined Benefit Plan
Used by employers who want an opinion letter for approval of form of a master or prototype plan.
IT-IRC secs. 401(a) and 501(a)

4461-B
Application of Master or Prototype Plan, or Regional Prototype Plan Mass Submitter Adopting Sponsor
Used by mass submitters who want approval on a plan of adopting sponsoring organization or sponsor.
IT-IRC secs. 401(a) and 501(a)

4466
Corporation Application for Quick Refund of Overpayment of Estimated Tax
Used to apply for a "quick" refund of overpaid estimated tax. (Must be filed before the regular tax return is filed.)
IT-IRC sec. 6425; Regs. sec. 1.6425-1(b)

Be patient. If any phone number is incorrect, call (area code) 555-1212 and request the new listing.

477

4506

Request for Copy of Tax Form

Used by a taxpayer or authorized representative to request a copy of a tax return or Forms W-2 that were filed with the return. IT-Regs. sec. 601.702

4506-A

Request for Public-Inspection Copy of Exempt Organization Tax Form

Used by a third-party for a copy of an exempt organization tax form which may be inspected at an IRS office. IT-IRC sec. 6104(b)

4562

Depreciation and Amortization

Used by individuals, estates, trusts, partnerships, and corporations claiming depreciation and amortization. Also used to substantiate depreciation deductions for automobiles and other listed property. IT-IRC secs. 167, 168, 179 and 280F; Separate instructions

4563

Exclusion of Income for Bona Fide Residents of American Samoa

Used by bona fide residents of American Samoa to exclude income from sources in American Samoa, Guam, and the Commonwealth of the Northern Mariana Islands, to the extent specified in IRC section 931. IT-IRC sec. 931; Regs. sec. 1.931-1; Pub. 570

4626

Alternative Minimum Tax-Corporations

Used by corporations to figure their alternative minimum tax and their environmental tax. IT-IRC secs. 55, 56, 57, 58, 59, and 291; Separate instructions

4684

Casualties and Thefts

Used by all taxpayers to figure gains (or losses) resulting from casualties and thefts. IT-IRC sec. 165; Separate instructions

4720

Return of Certain Excise Taxes on Charities and Other Persons Under Chapters 41 and 42 of the Internal Revenue Code

Used by charities and other persons to compute certain excise taxes which may be due under IRC Chapters 41 and 42. Ex-IRC secs. 4911, 4912, 4941, 4942, 4943, 4944, 4945, and 4955; Separate instructions

4768

Application for Extension of Time To File U.S. Estate (and Generation-Skipping Transfer) Tax Return and/or Pay Estate (and Generation-Skipping Transfer) Tax(es)

Used to apply for estate tax extensions in certain cases. E&G-IRC secs. 6081 and 6161; Regs. sec. 20.6081-1 and 20.6161-1

4782

Employee Moving Expense Information

Used by employers to show the amount of any reimbursement or payment made to an employee, a third party for the employee's benefit, or the value of services furnished in-kind, for moving expenses during the calendar year. IT-IRC secs. 82 and 217; Regs. sec. 31.6051-1(e)

4789

Currency Transaction Report

Used by financial institutions to report deposit, withdrawal, exchange of currency, or other payment or transfer, by, through, or to such financial institution which involves currency transactions of more than $10,000. P.L.92-508; Treasury Regs. 31CFR103)

4797

Sales of Business Property

Used to report details of gain (or loss) from sales, exchanges, or involuntary conversions (from other than casualty and theft) of noncapital assets and involuntary conversions (other than casualty and theft) of capital assets, held in connection with a trade or business or a transaction entered into for profit. Also used to compute recapture amounts under sections 179 and 280F when the business use of section 179 or 280F property drops to 50% or less. IT-IRC secs. 1231, 1245, 1250, 1252, 1254, and 1255; IT-IRC secs. 1202, 1211, and 1212; Separate instructions

4835

Farm Rental Income and Expenses

Used by landowner (or sublessor) to report farm rental income based on crops or livestock produced by the tenant where the landowner (or sublessor) does not materially participate in the operation or management of the farm. (Also see Schedule F (Form 1040).) IT-IRC sec. 61

4868

Extension of Time to File U.S. Individual Income Tax Return

Used to apply for an automatic 4-month extension of time to file Form 1040. IT-IRC sec. 6081; Regs. sec. 1.6081-4; TD 7885

4876-A

Election To Be Treated as an Interest Charge DISC

Used by a qualifying corporation that wishes to be treated as an Interest Charge Domestic International Sales Corporation (Interest Charge DISC). IT-Regs. sec. 1.921

4952

Investment Interest Expense Deduction

Used by an individual, estate, or trust to figure the deduction limitation for interest expense on funds borrowed that is allocable to property held for investment. IT-IRC sec. 163(d)

4970

Tax on Accumulation Distribution of Trusts

Used by a beneficiary of a domestic or foreign trust to figure the tax attributable to an accumulation distribution. IT-IRC sec. 667

4972

Tax on Lump-Sum Distributions

Used to determine the income tax on the income portion of lump-sum distributions. IT-IRC sec. 402(e); Separate instructions

5074

Allocation of Individual Income Tax to Guam or the Commonwealth of the Northern Mariana Islands (CNMI)

Used as an attachment to Form 1040 filed by an individual who reports adjusted gross income of $50,000 or more, with gross income of $5,000 or more from Guam or CNMI sources. IT-IRC sec. 935; Regs. sec. 301.7654-1(d)

5213

Election to Postpone Determination as to Whether the Presumption that an Activity is Engaged in for Profit Applies

Used by individuals, trusts, estates, and S corporations to postpone a determination as to whether an activity is engaged in for profit. IT-IRC sec. 183(e)

5227

Split-Interest Trust Information Return

Used by section 4947(a)(2) trusts treated as private foundations. Ex-IRC sec. 6011; Separate instructions

5300

Application for Determination for Defined Benefit Plan

Used to request a determination letter as to the qualification of a defined benefit plan (other than a collectively-bargained plan). IT-IRC sec. 401(a); Separate instructions

5302
Employee Census
Used as a schedule of the 25 highest paid participants of a deferred compensation plan, which is attached to Forms 5300, 5301, 5303, and 5307 (where applicable). IT-IRC sec. 401(a)

5303
Application for Determination for Collectively-Bargained Plan
Used to request a determination letter as to the qualification of a collectively-bargained plan. Also used by multi-employer plans covered by PBGC insurance to request a determination letter regarding termination.
IT-IRC sec. 401(a); Separate instructions

5305
Individual Retirement Trust Account
Used as an agreement between an individual and the individual's trustee for the establishment of an individual retirement account. IT-IRC sec. 408(a)

5305-A
Individual Retirement Custodial Account
Used as an agreement between an individual and the individual's custodian for the establishment of an individual retirement account. IT-IRC sec. 408(a)

5305-SEP
Simplified Employee Pension-Individual Retirement Accounts Contribution Agreement
Used as an agreement between an employer and his or her employees to establish a Simplified Employee Pension. IT-IRC 408(k)

5305-A-SEP
Salary Reduction and Other Elective Simplified Employee Pension - Individual Retirement Accounts Contribution Agreement
Used as an agreement between an employer and his or her employees to establish a Simplified Employee Pension with an elective deferral.
IT-IRC sec. 408(k)(6)

5306
Application for Approval of Prototype or Employer Sponsored Individual Retirement Account
Used by banks, savings and loan associations, federally insured credit unions, and such other persons approved by the Internal Revenue Service to act as trustee or custodian, insurance companies, regulated investment companies and trade or professional societies or associations, to get the approval as to form of a trust or annuity contract which is to be used for individual retirement accounts or annuities. Also to be used by employees, labor unions and other employee associations that want approval of a trust which is to be used for individual retirement accounts. IT-IRC sec. 408(a), (b), or (c)

5306-SEP
Application for Approval of Prototype Simplified Employee Pension-SEP
Used by program sponsors who want to get IRS approval of their prototype simplified employee pension (SEP) agreements. IT-IRC sec. 408

5307
Application for Determination for Adopters of Master or Prototype, Regional Prototype or Volume Submitter Plans
Used to request a determination letter as to the qualification of any defined benefit or defined contribution plan (the form of which has been previously approved) other than a collectively bargained plan.
IT-IRC sec. 401(a); Separate instructions

5308
Request for Change in Plan/Trust Year
Used by employer or plan administrators to request approval of change in a plan year or a trust year.
IT-IRC sec. 412(c)(5), sec. 442

5309
Application for Determination of Employee Stock Ownership Plan
Used by corporate employers who wish to get a determination letter regarding the qualification of an Employee Stock Ownership Plan under IRC 409 or 4975(e)(7). IT-IRC 409-4975(e)(7)

5310
Application for Determination Upon Termination; Notice of Merger, Consolidation or Transfer of Plan Assets or Liabilities; Notice of Intent to Terminate
Used by an employer who wishes a determination letter as to the effect of termination of a plan on its prior qualification under IRC section 401(a); by every employer or plan administrator (if designated) for any plan merger or consolidation; or to give notice to PBGC of intent, for any transfer of plan assets or liabilities to another plan to terminate a defined benefit pension plan.
IT-IRC secs. 401(a), 6058(b), ERISA sec. 4041(a); Separate instructions

5310A
Notice of Merger, Consolidation or Transfer of Plan Liabilities
Used by every employer or plan administration for any plan merger, consolidation, or transfer of plan assets or liability required to be reported.
IT-IRC sec. 6058(b), 414(1), 401(a)(2); separate instructions.

5329
Return for Additional Taxes Attributable to Qualified Retirement Plans (Including IRAs), Annuities, and Modified Endowment Contracts
Used to report excise taxes or additional income tax owed in connection with individual retirement arrangements, annuities, and qualified retirement plans.
IT-IRC secs. 72, 4973, 4974, and 4980A; Separate instructions

5330
Return of Excise Taxes Related to Employee Benefits Plans
Used to report and pay the excise tax imposed by IRC section 4791 on a minimum funding deficiency, by Code section 4973(a)(2) on excess contributions to a section 403(b)(7)(A) custodial account, by section 4975 on prohibited transactions, by section 4976 on disqualified benefits from welfare plans, by 4977 on certain fringe benefits, and by 4978 on certain ESOP transactions.
Ex-IRC sec. 6011; Separate instructions

5452
Corporate Report of Nondividend Distributions
Used by corporations to report their nontaxable distributions.
IT-CFR 1.301-1, 1.316-1, 1.333-1, and 1.6042-2

5471
Information Return With Respect to a Foreign Corporation
Used by U.S. persons to report their activities with related foreign corporations.
IT-IRC secs. 951-972, 6035, 6038 and 6046; Separate instructions

Sch. M (Form 5471)
Foreign Corporation Controlled by a U.S. Person
Used by a U.S. person who controls a foreign corporation to report the activities between the U.S. person and the foreign corporation. IT-IRC sec. 6038

Sch. N (Form 5471)
Foreign Personal Holding Company
Used by officers, directors, and shareholders of foreign personal holding companies to report information concerning the foreign personal holding company. IT-IRC sec. 6035

Sch. O (Form 5471)
Organization or Reorganization of Foreign Corporation, and Acquisitions and Dispositions of its Stock
Used by U.S. persons to report acquisitions or dispositions of interests in foreign corporations. IT-IRC sec. 6046

Be patient. If any phone number is incorrect, call (area code) 555-1212 and request the new listing.

479

Taxes

5472
Information Return of a Foreign Owned Corporation
Used for reporting the activities between foreign owned corporations and persons related to transactions made by the corporations.
IT-IRC sec. 6038A

5498
Individual Retirement Arrangement Information
Used to report contributions to individual retirement arrangements (IRAs) and the value of the account.
IT-IRC sec. 408(i)(o); Prop. Regs. sec. 1.408-5; See the separate Instructions for Forms 1099, 1098, 5498, 1096, and W-2G

5500
Annual Return/Report of Employee Benefit Plan (with 100 or more participants)
Used to report on deferred compensation plans and welfare plans that have at least 100 participants.
IT-IRC sec. 6058(a); ERISA section 103; Separate instructions

Sch. A (Form 5500)
Insurance Information
Used as an attachment to Forms 5500, 5500-C, or 5500-R to report information about insurance contracts that are part of a qualified deferred compensation plan.
ERISA section 103(e)

Sch. B (Form 5500)
Actuarial Information
Used to report actuarial information for a defined benefit plan. (Attached to Forms 5500, 5500-C, or 5500-R.)
IT-IRC sec. 6059; ERISA section 103(a); Separate instructions

Sch. C (Form 5500)
Service Provider Information
Used as an attachment to Form 5500 to report information about service providers and trustees of qualified deferred compensation plans.
ERISA section 103.

Sch. F (Form 5500)
Fringe Benefit Annual Information Return
Used to report the annual information required by Code section 6039D(d) for plans described in section 120, 125, and 127.
IT-IRC sec. 6039D(d).

Sch. P (Form 5500)
Annual Return of Fiduciary of Employee Benefit Trust
Used as an annual return for employee benefit trusts which qualify under section 401(a) and are exempt from tax under section 501(a). (Attach to Forms 5500, 5500-C or 5500-R.) IT-IRC secs. 6033(a) and 6501(a)

Sch. SSA (Form 5500)
Annual Registration Statement Identifying Separated Participants with Deferred Vested Benefits
Used to list employees who separated from employment and have a deferred vested benefit in the employer's plan of deferred compensation. (Attached to Forms 5500, 5500-C, or 5500-R.) IT-IRC sec. 6057

5500-C/R
Return/Report of Employee Benefit Plan (with fewer than 100 participants)
Used to report on deferred compensation plans and welfare plans that have fewer than 100 participants.
IT-IRC sec. 6058(a); ERISA section 103; Separate instructions

5500EZ
Annual Return of One-Participant Owners and Their Spouses Pension Benefit Plan
Used to report on pension profit-sharing, etc. plans that cover only an individual or an individual and the individual's spouse who wholly own a business.
IT-IRC sec. 6058(a); Separate instructions

Sch. E (Form 5502)
ESOP Annual Information
Used to report an employee stock ownership plans which have an outstanding securities acquisition loan or corporation maintaining plan deducted dividends paid on its stock under Code section 404(k).
IT-IRC sec. 6047(e).

5558
Application for Extension of Time to File Certain Employee Plan Returns
Used to provide a means by which a person may request an extension of time to file Forms 5500, 5500-C, 5500-R, or 5330.

5578
Annual Certification of Racial Nondiscrimination for a Private School Exempt from Federal Income Tax
Used by certain organizations exempt or claiming to be exempt under IRC section 501(c)(3) and operating, supervising, or controlling a private school (or schools) to certify to a policy of racial nondiscrimination.
IT-IRC sec. 6001; Rev. Proc. 75-50, 1975-2; C.B.587

5712
Election to be Treated as a Possessions Corporation Under Section 936
Used by a corporation to elect to be treated as a possessions corporation for the tax credit allowed under IRC section 936. IT-IRC sec. 936(e)

5712-A
Cost Sharing or Profit Split Method Under Section 936(h)(5): Election and Verification
Used by a domestic corporation if it elects to compute its taxable income under either the cost sharing method or the profit split method. IT-IRC sec. 936(h)(5)

5713
International Boycott Report
Used by persons with operations in or related to any country associated in carrying out an international boycott.
IT-IRC sec. 999; Separate instructions

Sch. A (Form 5713)
Computation of the International Boycott Factor
Used by taxpayers in computing the loss of tax benefits under the international boycott factor method.
IT-IRC sec. 999

Sch. B (Form 5713)
Specifically Attributable Taxes and Income
Used by taxpayers in computing the loss of tax benefits under the specifically attributable taxes and income method.
IT-IRC sec. 999

Sch. C (Form 5713)
Tax Effect of the International Boycott Provisions
Used to summarize the loss of tax benefits resulting from the application of the international boycott provisions.
IT-IRC sec. 999

5735
Computation of Possessions Corporation Tax Credit Under Section 936
Used by qualified possessions corporations to compute credit allowed by IRC section 936.
IT-IRC sec. 936

Sch. P (Form 5735)
Allocation of Income and Expenses Under Section 936(h)(5)
Used by corporations that have elected the cost sharing or profit split method of computing taxable income. The form is attached to Form 5735.
IT-IRC sec. 935(h)(5)

5754
Statement By Person(s) Receiving Gambling Winnings
Used to list multiple winners of certain gambling proceeds.
IT-IRC sec. 3402(q); Regs. secs. 31.3402(q)-1(e) and 1.6011-3; See the separate Instructions for Forms 1099, 1098, 5498, 1096, and W-2G

5768
Election/Revocation of Election by an Eligible Section 501(c)3-Organization to Make Expenditures to Influence Legislation
Used by certain eligible IRC section 501(c)3-organizations to elect or revoke election to apply the lobbying expenditures provisions of code section 501(h).
IT-IRC secs. 501 and 4911

5884
Jobs Credit
Used by individuals, estates, trusts, and corporations claiming a jobs credit and any S corporation, partnership, estate or trust which apportion the jobs credit among their shareholders, partners, or beneficiaries. See also Form 3800.
IT-IRC secs. 38, 51, 52, and 53

6069
Return of Excise Tax on Excess Contributions to Black Lung Benefit Trust Under Section 4953 and Computation of Section 192 Deduction
Used by exempt Black Lung Benefit Trusts as a worksheet to determine deduction under section 192 and to report tax under section 4953.
IT/Ex-IRC secs. 192 and 4953

6088
Distributable Benefits from Employee Pension Benefit Plans
Used to report the 25 highest paid participants of a deferred compensation plan, which is attached to Form 5310. IT-IRC sec. 401(a)

6118
Credit for Income Tax Return Preparers
Used by income tax return preparers to file for refund of penalties paid.
IT-IRC sec. 6696

6177
General Assistance Program Determination
Used by a General Assistance Program of a state or political subdivision of a state in order to be designated as a Qualified General Assistance Program for purposes of certifying individual recipients of the program for the jobs credit.
IT-IRC sec. 51(d)(6)(B)

6197
Gas Guzzler Tax
Used by automobile manufacturers and importers to report the tax on "gas guzzler" types of automobiles. The form is filed as an attachment to Form 720.
Ex-IRC sec. 4064

6198
At-Risk Limitations
Used by individuals, partners, S corporation shareholders, and certain closely-held corporations to figure the overall profit (loss) from an at-risk activity for the tax year, the amount at-risk, and the deductible loss for the tax year.
IT-IRC sec. 465; Separate instructions

6199
Certification of Youth Participating in a Qualified Cooperative Education Program
Used by a qualified school to certify that a student meets the requirements of Sec. 51(d)8-as a member of a targeted group eligible for the jobs credit.
IT-IRC sec. 51

6251
Alternative Minimum Tax-Individuals
Used by individuals to figure their alternative minimum tax.
IT-IRC secs. 55, 56, 57, 58, and 59; Separate instructions

6252
Installment Sale Income
Used by taxpayers other than dealers, who sell real or personal property, and receive a payment in a tax year after the year of sale.
IT-IRC sec. 453; Pub. 537; Separate instructions

6406
Short Form Application for Determination for Amendment of Employee Benefit Plan
Used for amending a plan on which a favorable determination letter has been issued under ERISA.
IRC secs. 401(a) and 501(a); Separate instructions

6478
Credit for Alcohol Used as Fuel
Used by taxpayers to figure their credit for alcohol used as fuel. The credit is allowed for alcohol mixed with other fuels and for straight alcohol fuel. See also Form 3800. IT-IRC sec. 38 and 40

6497
Information Return of Nontaxable Energy Grants or Subsidized Energy Financing
Used by every person who administers a government program for a Federal, state, or local governmental entity or agent thereof, that provides grants or subsidized financing under programs a principal purpose of which is energy production or conservation if the grant or financing is not taxable to the recipient. IT-IRC sec. 6050D; Regs. sec. 1.6050D-1

6627
Environmental Taxes
Used to report environmental taxes on petroleum and certain chemicals.
Ex-IRC secs. 4611, 4661, and 4671

6765
Credit for Increasing Research Activities (or for claiming the orphan drug credit)
Used by individuals, estates, trusts, and corporations claiming a research credit for increasing the research activities of a trade or business. Also used to claim the orphan drug credit. See also Form 3800.
IT-IRC secs. 28 and 41; Separate instructions

6781
Gains and Losses From Section 1256 Contracts and Straddles
Used by all taxpayers that held section 1256 contracts or straddles during the tax year. IT-IRC secs. 1092 and 1256

7004
Application for Automatic Extension of Time to File Corporation Income Tax Return
Used by corporations and certain exempt organizations to request an automatic extension of 6 months to file corporate income tax return.
IT-IRC sec. 6081(b); Regs. sec. 1.6081-3

8023
Corporate Qualified Stock Purchase Election
Used by a purchasing corporation to elect section 338 treatment for the purchase of another corporation. IT-IRC sec. 338(g); Temp. Regs. sec. sf 338-1

8027
Employer's Annual Information Return of Tip Income and Allocated Tips
Used by large food or beverage employers to report each establishment's gross receipts, charge receipts and charge tips, and allocated tips of employees.
IT-IRC sec. 6053(c); Regs. sec. 31.6053-3; Separate instructions

8027-T
Transmittal of Employer's Annual Information Return of Tip Income and Allocated Tips
Used by large food or beverage employers with more than one establishment to transmit Forms 8027. IT-IRC sec. 6053(c); Regs. sec. 31.6053-3

Be patient. If any phone number is incorrect, call (area code) 555-1212 and request the new listing.

481

Taxes

8038
Information Return for Tax-Exempt Private Activity Bond Issues
Used by issuers of tax-exempt private activity bonds to provide IRS with information required by section 149(e).
IT-IRC sec. 149(e); Temp. Regs. sec. 1.149(e)-1T; Separate instructions

8038-G
Information Return for Tax-Exempt Governmental Bond Issues
Used by the issuers of tax-exempt governmental bonds (with issue prices of $100,000 or more) to provide IRS with information required by section 149(e).
IT-IRC sec. 149(e); Temp. Regs. sec. 1.149(e)-1T; Separate instructions

8038-GC
Consolidated Information Return for Small Tax-Exempt Governmental Bond Issues, Leases and Installment Sales
Used by the issuers of tax-exempt governmental bonds (with issue prices of less than $100,000) to provide IRS with information required by section 149(e).
IT-IRC sec. 149(e); Temp. Regs. sec. 1.149(e)-1T

8038-Q
Issuer's Information Return for Qualified Mortgage Bonds (QMBs) and Notice to Borrower of Potential Recapture
Used by issuers of qualified mortgage bonds to report information applicable to each federally-subsidized mortgage loan financed through the issuance of a bond. Also used to report information to the borrower regarding potential recapture of a federal mortgage subsidy upon early disposition of the mortgaged property.
IT-IRC sec. 143(m).

8038-T
Arbitrage Rebate and Penalty in Lieu of Arbitrage Rebate
Issuers of tax-exempt governmental bonds use Form 8038-T when paying to the United States the arbitrage rebate and the penalty in lieu of the rebate, etc., under section 143(g) and 148(f) and sections 103(c)(6)(D) and 103A(i)(4) of the Internal Revenue Code of 1954. IT-IRC secs. 143(g), 148(f).

8082
Notice of Inconsistent Treatment or Amended Return
Used by partners, S corporation shareholders and residual holders of an interest in a REMIC to report inconsistent treatment of partnership, S corporation or REMIC items or to report amendment of partnership, S corporation or REMIC items. Form 8082 is also used by the TMP (tax matters partner or tax matters person) to make an administrative adjustment request (AAR) on behalf of the partnership, S corporation, or REMIC. IT-IRC sec. 6222 and 6227(c); Separate instructions

8109
Federal Tax Deposit Coupon
Twenty-three preprinted deposit coupons for making deposits of Federal taxes (such as social security, Federal unemployment, and excise taxes) are contained in a coupon book. Instructions are in the coupon book, along with a reorder form (Form 8109A, FTD Reorder Form).
IT/Emp/Ex-IRC sec. 6302; Regs. secs. 1.6302-1, 1.6302-2, 31.6302(c)-1, 31.6302(c)-2, 31.6302(c)-3, 46.6302(c)-1, 48.6302(c)-1, 49.6302(c)-1, 51.4995-3, and 52.6302-1

8109-B
Federal Tax Deposit Coupon
An over-the-counter Federal tax deposit coupon for making Federal tax deposits when Form 8109 deposit coupons have been reordered but not yet received or when a new entity has received its employer identification number but has not yet received its initial order of Forms 8109.
IT/Emp/Ex-IRC sec. 6302; Regs. secs. 1.6302-1, 1.6302-2, 31.6302(c)-1, 31.6302(c)-2, 31.6302(c)-3, 46.6302(c)-1, 48.6302(c)-1, 49.6302(c)-1, 51.4995-3 and 52.6302-1

8233
Exemption From Withholding on Compensation for Independent Personal Services of a Nonresident Alien Individual
Used by nonresident alien individuals to claim exemption from withholding on compensation for independent personal services because of an income tax treaty or the personal exemption amount. Also used by nonresident alien students, teachers, and researchers to claim exemption from withholding under a U.S. tax treaty on compensation for services.
IT-IRC sec. 1441; Reg. sec. 1.1441-4

8264
Application for Registration of a Tax Shelter
Used by tax shelter organizers to register certain tax shelters with the IRS, for purposes of receiving a tax shelter registration number.
IT-IRC sec. 6111; Regs. secs. 301.6111-1T; Separate instructions

8271
Investor Reporting of Tax Shelter Registration Number
Used by persons who have purchased or otherwise acquired an interest in a tax shelter required to be registered to report the tax shelter registration number. Form is attached to any tax return on which a deduction, credit, loss, or other tax benefit is claimed, or any income reported, from a tax shelter required to be registered. IT-IRC. 6111; Regs. secs. 301.6111-1T

8274
Certification by Churches and Qualified Church-Controlled Organizations Electing Exemption from Employer Social Security Taxes
Used by churches and certain church-controlled organizations to elect exemption from social security taxes by certifying the organization is opposed to these taxes for religious purposes. Emp-IRC sec. 3121(w)

8275
Disclosure Statement Under Section 6661
Used to disclose items which could cause a substantial understatement of income and is filed to avoid the penalty imposed by section 6661; Separate instructions
PA-IRC sec. 6661; Regs. sec. 1.6661; Separate instructions

8275-R
Regulation Disclosure Statement
Used to disclose items to avoid portions of the accuracy-related penalties due to a position taken contrary to the regulations.
PA-IRC sec. 6662; Reg. sec. 1.6662-1 through 1.6662-5; separate instructions.

8279
Election To Be Treated as a FSC or as a Small FSC
Used by qualifying corporations that wish to be treated as a Foreign Sales Corporation (FSC) or Small Foreign Sales Corporation (Small FSC).
IT-IRC sec. 927

8281
Information Return for Publicly Offered Original Issue Discount Instruments
Used by issuers of publicly offered debt instruments having OID to provide the information required by section 1275(c).
IT-IRC sec. 1275(c); Temp. Regs. sec. 1.1275-3T

8282
Donee Information Return
Used by exempt organizations who sells, exchanges, transfers, or otherwise disposes of the charitable property within 2 years after the date of the receipt of the contribution. The return is filed with the IRS and a copy is given to the donor. IT-IRC sec. 6050L

8283
Noncash Charitable Contributions
Used by individuals, closely held corporations, personal service corporations, partnerships, and S corporations to report contributions of property other than cash in which the total claimed value of all property exceeds $500.
IT-IRC secs. 170; 1.170A-13 and 1.170A-13T; Separate instructions

8288
U.S. Withholding Tax Return for Dispositions by Foreign Persons of U.S. Real Property Interests
Used to transmit the withholding on the sale of U.S. real property by foreign persons. IT-IRC sec. 1445; Regs. secs. 1.1445-1 through 1.1445-7; Temp. Regs. secs. 1.1445-9T through 1.1445-11T

8288-A
Statement of Withholding on Dispositions by Foreign Persons of U.S. Real Property Interests
Anyone filing Form 8288 must attach copies A and B of Form 8288-A for each person subject to withholding. IT-IRC sec. 1445; Regs. secs. 1.1445-1 through 1.1445-7, Temp. Regs. secs. 1.1445-9T through 1.1445-11T

8288-B
Application for Withholding Certificate for Dispositions by Foreign Persons of U.S. Real Property Interests
Used to apply for a withholding certificate based upon certain criteria to reduce or eliminate withholding under section 1445.
IT-IRC sec. 1445; Regs. secs. 1.1445-3 and 1.1445-6 and Rev. Proc. 88-23

8300
Report of Cash Payments Over $10,000 Received in a Trade or Business
Used by a trade or business to report receipt of more than $10,000 cash in a transaction in the course of such trade or business.
IT-IRC sec. 6050l; Regs. 1.6050l-1

8308
Report of a Sale or Exchange of Certain Partnership Interests
Used by partnerships to report the sale or exchange of a partnership interest where a portion of any money or other property given in exchange for the interest is attributable to unrealized receivables or substantially appreciated inventory items (section 751(a) exchange). IT-IRC sec. 6050K

8328
Carryforward Election of Unused Private Activity Bond Volume Cap
Used by the issuing authority of tax-exempt private activity bonds to elect under section 146(f) to carryforward the unused volume cap for specific projects.
IT-IRC sec. 146(f)

8329
Lender's Information Return for Mortgage Credit Certificates
Used by lenders of certified indebtedness amounts to report information regarding the issuance of mortgage credit certificates under section 25.
IT-IRC sec. 25; Regs. sec. 1.25-8T

8330
Issuer's Quarterly Information Return for Mortgage Credit Certificates
Used by issuers of mortgage credit certificates to report information required under section 25. IT-IRC sec. 25; Regs. secs. 1.25-8T

8332
Release of Claim to Exemption for Child of Divorced or Separated Parents
Used to release claim to a child's exemption by a parent who has custody of his or her child and is given to the parent who will claim the exemption. The parent who claims the child's exemption attaches this form to his or her tax return.
IT-IRC sec. 152(e)(2); Temp. Regs. sec. 1.152-4T; Pub. 504

8362
Currency Transaction Reported by Casinos
Used by casinos licensed by a state or local government having annual gaming revenues in excess of $1 million to report each deposit, withdrawal, exchange of currency or gambling tokens or chips or other payment or transfer, by, through, or to such casino, involving currency of more than $10,000. P.L.91-508; Treasury Regs. secs. 31 CFR 103.22; 31 CFR 103.26; and 31 CFR 103.36

8390
Information Return for Determination of Life Insurance Company Earnings Rate Under Section 809
Used by certain life insurance companies to gather information to compute various earnings rates required by section 809.
IT-IRC sec. 809; Separate instructions

8396
Mortgage Interest Credit
Used by qualified mortgage credit certificate holders to figure their mortgage interest credit and any carryover to a subsequent year. IT-IRC sec. 25

8404
Computation of Interest Charge on DISC-Related Deferred Tax Liability
Used by shareholders of Interest Charge Domestic International Sales Corporations (IC-DISCs) to figure and report their interest on DISC-related deferred tax liability. ITC 995(f); Treasury Regs. 1.995(f)

8453
U.S. Individual Income Tax Declaration for Electronic Filing
Used by qualified filers who file Forms 1040 and certain related schedules, 1040A and 1040EZ via electronic transmission on magnetic media. These filers must file Form 8453 to transmit the individual taxpayer's and return preparer's signature(s) for the return. IT-IRC secs. 6012 and 6017

8453-E
Annual Return/Report of Employee Benefit Plan Magnetic Media/Electronic Filing
Used by qualified filers who file Forms 5500, 5500-C or 5500-R via electronic transmission. IT-IRC sec. 6058

8453-F
U.S. Fiduciary Income Tax Declaration for Magnetic Tape/Electronic Filing
Used by qualified filers who file Form 1041 and related schedules via electronic transmission.
IT-IRC sec. 6012

8453-P
U.S. Partnership Declaration for Magnetic Tape/Electronic Filing
Used by qualified filers who file Form 1065 and related schedules via electronic transmission.
IT-IRC sec. 6031

8582
Passive Activity Loss Limitations
Used by individuals, estates, and trusts to figure the amount of any passive activity loss for the current tax year for all activities and the amount of the passive activity loss allowed on their tax returns.
IT-IRC sec. 469; Separate instructions

8582-CR
Passive Activity Credit Limitations
Used by individuals, estates, and trusts to figure the amount of any passive activity credit for the current year and the amount allowed on their tax returns.
IT-IRC sec. 469; Separate instructions

8586
Low-Income Housing Credit
Used by owners of residential rental projects providing low-income housing to claim the low-income housing credit. IT-IRC sec. 42

8594
Asset Acquisition Statement
Used by the buyer and seller of assets used in a trade or business involving goodwill or a going concern value.
IT-IRC 1060, Temp. Regs. sec. 1.1060-1T

8606
Nondeductible IRA Contributions, IRA Basis, and Nontaxable IRA Distributions
Used by individuals to report the amount of IRA contributions they choose to be nondeductible and to figure their basis in their IRA(s) at the end of the calendar year and the nontaxable part of any distributions they received.
IT-IRC sec. 408(o)

Be patient. If any phone number is incorrect, call (area code) 555-1212 and request the new listing.

483

Taxes

8609
Low-Income Housing Credit Allocation Certification
Used by housing credit agencies to allocate a low-income housing credit dollar amount. Also, used by low-income housing building owners to make elections and certify certain necessary information. IT-IRC sec. 42

8610
Annual Low-Income Housing Credit Agencies Report
Used by housing credit agencies to transmit Forms 8609 and to report the dollar amount of housing credit allocations issued during the calendar year. IT-IRC sec. 42

8611
Recapture of Low-Income Housing Credit
Used by taxpayers to recapture low-income housing credit taken in a prior year because there is a decrease in the qualified basis of a residential low-income housing building from one year to the next.
IT-IRC sec. 42(j)

8612
Return of Excise Tax on Undistributed Income of Real Estate Investment Trusts
Used by real estate investment trusts to report the excise tax on undistributed income.
EX-IRC sec. 4981

8613
Return of Excise Tax on Undistributed Income of Regulated Investment Companies
Used by regulated investment companies to report the excise tax on undistributed income.
EX-IRC sec. 4982

8615
Computation of Tax for Children Under Age 14 Who Have Investment Income of More Than $1,000
Used to see if any of a child's investment income in excess of $1,000 is taxed at his or her parent's rate and, if so, to figure the child's tax.

8621
Return by a Shareholder of a Passive Foreign Investment Company or Qualified Electing Fund
Used by U.S. persons who own an interest in a foreign investment company to report elections, terminations of elections, and amounts to be included in gross income.
IT-IRC secs. 1291, 1293, and 1294

8645
Soil and Water Conservation Plan Certification
Used by taxpayers to certify that the plan under which they are claiming conservation expenses is an approved plan.
IT-IRC sec. 175(c)(3)

8656
Alternative Minimum Tax-Fiduciaries
Used by a fiduciary of an estate or trust to compute the alternative minimum taxable income, distributable net alternative minimum taxable income, and to report any alternative minimum tax due.
IT-IRC secs. 55 - 59; Separate instructions

8689
Allocation of Individual Income Tax to the Virgin Islands
Used as an attachment to Form 1040 filed by an individual who reports adjusted gross income from Virgin Islands sources.
IT-IRC sec. 932

8697
Interest Computation Under the Look-Back Method for Completed Long-Term Contracts
Used by taxpayers to figure the interest due or to be refunded under the look-back method of section 460(b)3-on certain long-term contracts entered into after February 28, 1986, that are accounted for under either the percentage of completion-capitalized cost method or the percentage of completion method.
IT-IRC secs. 460(a) and 460(b)(2)(B); Separate instructions

8703
Annual Certification by Operator of a Residential Rental Project
Used by operators of residential rental projects to provide annual information the IRS will use to determine whether the projects continue to meet the requirements of section 142(d). Operators indicate on the form the specific test the bond issuer elected for the project period and also indicate the percentage of low-income units in the residential rental project. IT-IRC secs. 142

8709
Exemption From Withholding on Investment Income of Foreign Governments
Used by foreign governments or international organizations to claim exemption from withholding under sections 1441 and 1442 on items of income qualifying for tax exemption under section 892.
IT-IRC secs. 892

8716
Election To Have a Tax Year Other Than a Required Tax Year
Used by partnerships, S corporations, and personal service corporations to elect to have a tax year other than a required tax year.
IT-IRC sec. 444

8717
User Fee for Employee Plan Determination Letter Request
Used by applicants for Employee Plan determination letters to transmit the appropriate user fee. Rev. Proc. 89-4, 1983-3 I.R.B. 18

8718
User Fee for Exempt Organization Determination Letter Request
Used by applicants for Exempt Organization determination letters to transmit the appropriate user fee.
Rev. Proc. 89-4. 1989-3 I.R.B. 18

8736
Application for Automatic Extension of Time to File Returns for a Partnership, a REMIC, or for Certain Trusts
Used to apply for an automatic three-month extension of time to file Form 1041 (trust), Form 1041S, or Form 1065.
IT-IRC sec. 6081; Regs. secs. 1.6081-2T and 1.6081-3T

8743
Information on Fuel Inventories and Sales
Used by refiners and importers to report information on fuel inventories and sales. The form is filed as an attachment to Form 720.
EX-IRC secs. 4041, 4081, and 4091

8800
Application for Additional Extension of Time to File Return for a U.S. Partnership, REMIC, or for Certain Trusts
Used to apply for an additional extension of up to three months of time to file Form 1041 (trust), Forms 1041S, or Form 1065. A separate Form 8800 must be filed for each return.
IT-IRC sec. 6081; Regs. secs. 1.6081-2T and 1.6081-3T

8801
Credit for Prior Year Minimum Tax
Used by taxpayers to figure the minimum tax credit allowed for tax year.
IT-IRC sec. 53; Separate instructions

8803
Limit on Alternative Minimum Tax For Children Under Age 14
Used by children under age 14 to see if the alternative minimum tax figured on Form 6251 can be reduced. IT-IRC sec. 59(j)

8804
Annual Return for Partnership Withholding Tax (Section 1446)
Used to report the total liability under section 1446 for the partnership's tax year. Form 8804 is also a transmittal form for Form 8805.
IT-IRC sec. 1446; Rev. Proc. 89-31; Separate instructions

8805
Foreign Partner's Information Statement of Section 1446 Withholding Tax
Used to show the amount of effectively connected taxable income and the tax payments allocable to the foreign partner for the partnership's tax year.
IT-IRC sec. 1446; Rev. Proc. 89-31; Separate instructions

8807
Computation of Certain Manufacturers and Retailers Excise Taxes
Used by manufacturers, producers, and importers to figure the tax on the sale of fishing equipment, bows and arrows, pistols and revolvers, firearms, and shells and cartridges. And, used by retailers to figure the excise tax on the sale of truck, trailer, and semitrailer chassis and bodies, and tractors. EX-IRC secs. 4161, 4181, and 4051

8809
Request for Extension of Time To File Information Returns
Used to request an extension of time to file Forms W-2, W-2G, W-2P, 1098, 1099, or 5498. PA-IRC sec. 6081; Regs. sec. 1.6081-1

8810
Corporate Passive Activity Loss and Credit Limitations
Used by closely held C corporations and personal service corporations that have passive activity losses and/or credits. IT-IRC sec. 469; Separate instructions

8811
Information Return for Real Estate Mortgage Investment Conduits (REMICs) and Issuers of Collateralized Debt Obligations
Used by REMICs and issuers of Collateralized Debt Obligations to report entity information needed to compile Publication 938, *Real Estate Mortgage Investment Conduit (REMIC) Reporting Information.*
IT-IRC secs. 860A-G and 1272(a)(6)(C)(ii)

8813
Partnership Withholding Tax Payment (Section 1446)
Used to make payment to the Internal Revenue Service of withholding tax under section 1446. Each payment of section 1446 taxes made during the partnership's tax year must be accompanied by Form 8813.
IT-IRC sec. 1446; Rev. Proc. 89-31; Separate instructions

8814
Parent's Election to Report Child's Interest and Dividends
Used by parents who elect to report the interest and dividends of their child under age 14 on their own tax return. The form is used to figure the amount of the child's income to report on the parent's return and the amount of additional tax that must be added to the parent's tax.
IT-IRC 1(i)(7)

8815
Exclusion of Interest From Series EE U.S. Savings Bonds Issued After 1989
Used by individuals who paid qualified higher education expenses and cashed series EE U.S. savings bonds during the year to figure the amount of bond interest that is exclusive from income.
IT-IRC sec. 135.

8816
Special Loss Discount Account and Special Estimated Tax Payments for Insurance Companies
Used by insurance companies that elect to take an additional deduction under section 847. IT-IRC sec. 847

8817
Allocation of Patronage and Nonpatronage Income and Dividends
Used by taxable farmers cooperatives to show income and deductions by patronage and nonpatronage sources.

8818
Optional Form to Record Redemption of Series EE U.S. Savings Bonds Issued After 1989
Used to keep a record of series EE bonds that were issued after 1989 and cashed in a year higher education expenses were paid. IRC sec. 135.

8819
Dollar Election Under Section 985
Used to make election to use U.S. dollar by U.S. and foreign business in countries whose currency is hyper-inflationary. IRC sec. 985

8821
Tax Information Authorization
Used as an authorization for an appointee to inspect and/or receive confidential tax information, but not to represent taxpayers. Do not use for alcohol and tobacco taxes and firearms activities.
IT-Title 26, CFR, Part 601

8822
Change of Address
Used to notify the Internal Revenue Service of a change of address.

8824
Like-Kind Exchanges
Used by taxpayers to report the exchange of like-kind property. Also used to report section 1043 dispositions.
IRC sec. 1031; separate instructions.

8825
Rental Real Estate Income and Expenses of a Partnership or an S Corporation
Used by partnerships and S Corporations to report income and deductible expenses from rental real estate activities.
IRC sec. 61

8826
Disable Access Credit
Used by an eligible business to claim the disabled access credit. The credit is a general business credit under section 38 and is figured under provisions of section 44. IT-IRC section 44.

8827
Credit for Prior Year Minimum Tax-Corporation
Used by a corporation to compute the minimum tax credit for alternative minimum tax incurred in prior tax years and any minimum tax credit carryforward that may be used in future years.
IT-IRC 53

8828
Recapture of Federal Mortgage Subsidy
Used by individuals to report recapture tax upon early disposition of a federally subsidized residence.
IT-IRC sec. 143(m)

8829
Expenses for Business Use of Your Home
Used by Sch. C (Form 1040) filers to figure the allowable expenses for business use of a home and to any carryover of amounts not deductible in the current year.
IT-IRC 280A

8830
Enhanced Oil Recovery Credit
Used to claim the enhanced oil recovery credit. The credit is a general business credit under section 38 and is figured under the provisions of section 43.
IT-IRC 43

Be patient. If any phone number is incorrect, call (area code) 555-1212 and request the new listing.

485

Taxes

8841
Deferral of Additional 1993 Taxes

8842
Election to Use Different Annualization Periods Under the Annualized Income Installment Method for Corporate Estimated Tax

8844
Empowerment Zone Employment Credit

8845
Indian Employment Credit

8846
Credit for Employer Social Security Taxes Paid on Certain Employee Cash Tips

8847
Credit for Contributions to Certain Community Development Corporations

TD F 90-22.1
Report of Foreign Bank and Financial Accounts
Used by individuals, trusts, partnerships or corporations having a financial interest in, or signature authority or other authority over, bank, securities, or other financial accounts in a foreign country, when the accounts were more than $10,000 in aggregate value at any time during the calendar year.
P.L.91-508; Treasury Regs. 31CFR103)

Free Tax Publications

The Internal Revenue Service publishes many free publications to help you "make your taxes less taxing." The publications listed in this section give general information about taxes for individuals, small businesses, farming, fishing, and recent tax law changes. (Forms and schedules related to the subject matter of each publication are indicated after each listing.) You may want to order one of these publications, and then, if you need more detailed information on any subject, order the specific publication about it.

IRS Forms and Publications Distribution

Taxpayer Services
Internal Revenue Service
U.S. Department of the Treasury
1111 Constitution Ave., NW, Room 2422
Washington, DC 20224   800-829-3676

Tax forms and publications can be obtained by calling the toll-free number. To send for forms through the mail, write to the state IRS address listed below. Two copies of each form and one copy of each set of instructions will be sent.

Alabama
P.O. Box 8903
Bloomington, IL 61703

Alaska
Rancho Cordova, CA 95743-0001

Arizona
Rancho Cordova, CA 95743-0001

Arkansas
P.O. Box 8903
Bloomington, IL 61703

California
Rancho Cordova, CA 95743-0001

Colorado
Rancho Cordova, CA 95743-0001

Connecticut
P.O. Box 85074
Richmond, VA 23261-5074

Delaware
P.O. Box 85074
Richmond, VA 23261-5074

District of Columbia
P.O. Box 85074
Richmond, VA 23261-5074

Florida
P.O. Box 85074
Richmond, VA 23261-5074

Georgia
P.O. Box 85074
Richmond, VA 23261-5074

Hawaii
Rancho Cordova, CA 95743-0001

Idaho
Rancho Cordova, CA 95743-0001

Illinois
P.O. Box 8903
Bloomington, IL 61703

Indiana
P.O. Box 8903
Bloomington, IL 61703

Iowa
P.O. Box 8903
Bloomington, IL 61703

Kansas
P.O. Box 8903
Bloomington, IL 61703

Kentucky
P.O. Box 8903
Bloomington, IL 61703

Louisiana
P.O. Box 8903
Bloomington, IL 61703

Maine
P.O. Box 85074
Richmond, VA 23261-5074

Maryland
P.O. Box 85074
Richmond, VA 23261-5074

Massachusetts
P.O. Box 85074
Richmond, VA 23261-5074

Michigan
P.O. Box 8903
Bloomington, IL 61703

Minnesota
P.O. Box 8903
Bloomington, IL 61703

Mississippi
P.O. Box 8903
Bloomington, IL 61703

Missouri
P.O. Box 8903
Bloomington, IL 61703

Montana
Rancho Cordova, CA 95743-0001

Be patient. If any phone number is incorrect, call (area code) 555-1212 and request the new listing.

Taxes

Nebraska
P.O. Box 8903
Bloomington, IL 61703

Nevada
Rancho Cordova, CA 95743-0001

New Hampshire
P.O. Box 85074
Richmond, VA 23261-5074

New Jersey
P.O. Box 85074
Richmond, VA 23261-5074

New Mexico
Rancho Cordova, CA 95743-0001

New York
P.O. Box 85074
Richmond, VA 23261-5074

North Carolina
P.O. Box 85074
Richmond, VA 23261-5074

North Dakota
P.O. Box 8903
Bloomington, IL 61703

Ohio
P.O. Box 8903
Bloomington, IL 61703

Oklahoma
P.O. Box 8903
Bloomington, IL 61703

Oregon
Rancho Cordova, CA 95743-0001

Pennsylvania
P.O. Box 85074
Richmond, VA 23261-5074

Puerto Rico
P.O. Box 85074
Richmond, VA 23261-5074

Rhode Island
P.O. Box 85074
Richmond, VA 23261-5074

South Carolina
P.O. Box 85074
Richmond, VA 23261-5074

South Dakota
P.O. Box 8903
Bloomington, IL 61703

Tennessee
P.O. Box 8903
Bloomington, IL 61703

Texas
P.O. Box 8903
Bloomington, IL 61703

Utah
Rancho Cordova, CA 95743-0001

Vermont
P.O. Box 85074
Richmond, VA 23261-5074

Virgin Islands
V.I. Bureau of Internal Revenue
Lockharts Garden No. 1A
Charlotte Amalie
St. Thomas, VI 00802

Virginia
P.O. Box 85074
Richmond, VA 23261-5074

Washington
Rancho Cordova, CA 95743-0001

West Virginia
P.O. Box 85074
Richmond, VA 23261-5074

Wisconsin
P.O. Box 8903
Bloomington, IL 61703

Wyoming
Rancho Cordova, CA 95743-0001

Foreign Addresses
Forms Distribution Center
P.O. Box 85074
Richmond, VA 23261

Forms Distribution Center
Rancho Cordova, CA 95743-0001

Taxpayers with mailing addresses in foreign countries should send requests or the order blank to whichever address is closer. Send letter requests for other forms and publications to: Forms Distribution Center, P.O. Box 85074, Richmond, VA 23261.

Free IRS Publications and Forms
The forms and schedules related to the subject matter of each publication are indicated after each listing.

1 Your Rights as a Taxpayer
To ensure that you always receive fair treatment in tax matters, you should know your rights. This publication clarifies your rights at each step in the tax process.

1SP Derechos del Contribuyente (Your Rights as a Taxpayer)
Spanish version of Publication 1.

3 Tax Information for Military Personnel
This publication gives information about the special tax situations of active members of the Armed Forces. It includes information on items that are includible in and excludable from gross income, alien status, dependency exemptions, sale of residence, itemized deductions, tax liability, and filing returns.
Forms 1040, 1040A, 1040EZ, 1040NR, 1040X, 1310, 2106, 2688, 2848, 3903, 3903F, 4868 and W-2.

4 Student's Guide to Federal Income Tax
This publication explains the federal tax laws that apply to high school and college students. It describes the student's responsibilities to file and pay taxes, how to file, and how to get help. Forms 1040EZ, W-2 and W-4.

17 Your Federal Income Tax for Individuals
This publication can help you prepare your individual tax return. It takes you through the individual tax return and explains the tax laws that cover salaries and wages, interest and dividends, rental income, gains and losses, adjustments to income (such as alimony, and IRA contributions), and itemized deductions.
Forms 1040, 1040A, 1040EZ, Schedules A, B, D, E, R, SE, Forms W-2, 2106, 2119, 2441, 3903.

Be patient. If any phone number is incorrect, call (area code) 555-1212 and request the new listing.

225 Farmer's Tax Guide

This publication explains the federal tax laws that apply to farming. It gives examples of typical farming situations and discusses the kinds of farm income you must report and the different deductions you can take. Schedules A, D, F, SE (Form 1040), and Forms 1040, 4136, 4255, 4562, 4684, 4797, 6251.

334 Tax Guide for Small Business

This book explains some federal tax laws that apply to businesses. It describes the four major forms of business organizations: sole proprietorship, partnership, corporation, and S corporation: and explains the tax responsibilities of each. Schedule C (Form 1040), Schedule K-1 (Form 1065 and 1120S), Forms 1065, 1120, 1120-A, 1120S, 4562.

595 Tax Guide for Commercial Fishermen

This publication will familiarize you with the federal tax laws as they apply to the fishing industry. It is intended for sole proprietors who use Schedule C (Form 1040) to report profit or loss from fishing. This guide does not cover corporations or partnerships. Schedule C (Form 1040), Forms 1099-MISC, 4562, 4797.

15 Circular E, Employer's Tax Guide

Every employer automatically receives this publication on its revision and every person who applies for an employer identification number receives a copy. Forms 940, 941, and 941E.

51 Circular A, Agricultural Employer's Tax Guide

Form 943.

54 Tax Guide for U.S. Citizens and Resident Aliens Abroad

This publication discusses the tax situations of U.S. citizens and resident aliens who live and work abroad. In particular, it explains the rules for excluding income and excluding or deducting certain housing costs. Answers are provided to questions that taxpayers abroad most often ask. Forms 2555, 1116, and 1040, Schedule SE (Form 1040).

80 Circular SS, Federal Tax Guide for Employers in the Virgin Islands, Guam, American Samoa, and the Commonwealth of the Northern Mariana Islands

Forms 940, 941SS, and 943.

179 Circular PR, Guia Contributiva Federal Para Patronos Puertorriquenos (Federal Tax Guide for Employers in Puerto Rico)

Forms W-3PR, 940PR, 941PR, 942PR, and 943PR.

349 Federal Highway Use Tax on Heavy Vehicles

This publication explains which trucks, truck-tractors, and buses are subject to the federal use tax on heavy highway motor vehicles, which is one source of funds for the national highway construction program. The tax is due from the person in whose name the vehicle is either registered or required to be registered. The publication tells how to figure and pay the tax due. Form 2290.

378 Fuel Tax Credits and Refunds

This publication explains the credit or refund allowed for the federal excise taxes paid on certain fuels, and the income tax credit available when alcohol is used as a fuel. Forms 843, 4136 and 6478.

448 Federal Estate and Gift Taxes

This publication explains federal estate and gift taxes. Forms 706 and 709.

463 Travel, Entertainment, and Gift Expenses

This publication explains what expenses you may deduct for business-related travel, meals, entertainment, and gifts and it discusses the reporting and recordkeeping requirements for these expenses. The publication also summarizes the deduction and substantiation rules for employees, self-employed persons (including independent contractors), and employers (including corporations and partnerships). Form 2106.

501 Exemptions, Standard Deduction, and Filing Information

This publication provides answers to some basic tax questions: who must file; what filing status to choose; how many exemptions to claim; and how to figure the amount of the standard deduction. It also covers rules for foster care providers. Form 2120 and 8332.

502 Medical and Dental Expenses

This publication tells you how to figure your deduction for medical and dental expenses. You may take this deduction only if you itemize your deductions on Schedule A (Form 1040).
Schedule A (Form 1040).

503 Child and Dependent Care Expenses

This publication explains the credit you may be able to take if you pay someone to care for your dependent who is under 13, your disabled dependent, or your disabled spouse. For purposes of the credit, "disabled" refers to a person physically or mentally unable to care for himself or herself. Schedule 1 (Form 1040A), and Form 2441.

504 Tax Information for Divorced or Separated Individuals

This publication explains tax rules of interest to divorced or separated individuals. It covers filing status, dependency exemptions, and the treatment of alimony and property settlements.

505 Tax Withholding and Estimated Tax

This publication explains the two methods of paying tax under our pay-as-you-go system. They are (1) Withholding. Your employer will withhold income tax from your pay. Tax is also withheld from certain other types of income. You can have more or less withheld, depending on your circumstances. (2) Estimated tax. If you do not pay your tax through withholding, or do not pay enough tax that way, you might have to pay estimated tax. Forms W-4, W-4P, W-4S, 1040-ES, 2210, and 2210F.

508 Educational Expenses

This publication explains what work-related educational expenses qualify for deduction, how to report your expenses and any reimbursement you receive, and which forms and schedules to use. Form 2106 and Schedule A (Form 1040).

509 Tax Calendars for 1995

510 Excise Taxes for 1995

This publication covers in detail the various federal excise taxes reported on Form 720. These include the following groupings: environmental taxes; facilities and service taxes on communication and air transportation; fuel taxes; manufacturers taxes; vaccines; and heavy trucks, trailers and tractors. In addition, it briefly describes other excise taxes and tells which forms to use in reporting and paying the taxes. Forms 720, 8743, and 8807.

513 Tax Information for Visitors to the United States

This publication briefly reviews the general requirements of U.S. income tax laws for foreign visitors. You may have to file a U.S. income tax return during your visit. Most visitors who come to the United States are not allowed to work in this country. Please check with the Immigration and Naturalization Service before you take a job. Forms 1040C, 1040NR, 2063, and 1040-ES (NR).

514 Foreign Tax Credit for Individuals

This publication may help you if you paid foreign income tax. You may be able to take a foreign tax credit or deduction to avoid the burden of double taxation. The publication explains which foreign taxes qualify and how to figure your credit or deduction. Form 1116.

515 Withholding of Tax on Nonresident Aliens and Foreign Corporations

This publication provides information for withholding agents who are required to withhold and report tax on payments to nonresident aliens and foreign corporations. Included are three tables listing U.S. tax treaties and some of the treaty provisions that provide for reduction of or exemption from withholding for certain types of income.
Forms 1042 and 1042S, 1001, 4224, 8233, 1078, 8288, 8288-B, 8804, 8805, 8288-A and W-8, 8813, and 8709.

516 Tax Information for U.S. Government Civilian Employees Stationed Abroad

This publication covers the tax treatment of allowances, reimbursements, and business expenses that U.S. government employees, including foreign service employees, are likely to receive or incur.

Be patient. If any phone number is incorrect, call (area code) 555-1212 and request the new listing.

489

Taxes

517 Social Security and Other Information for Members of the Clergy and Religious Workers

This publication discusses social security coverage and the self-employment tax for the clergy. It also tells you how, as a member of the clergy (minister, member of a religious order, or Christian Science practitioner), you may apply for an exemption from the self-employment tax that would otherwise be due for the services you perform in the exercise of your ministry. Net earnings from self-employment are explained and sample forms are shown.
Form 2106, Form 1040, Schedule SE (Form 1040), and Schedule C (Form 1040).

519 U.S. Tax Guide for Aliens

This comprehensive publication gives guidelines on how to determine your U.S. tax status and figure your U.S. tax.
Forms 1040, 1040C, 1040NR, 2063, and Schedule A (Form 1040).

520 Scholarships and Fellowships

This publication explains the tax laws that apply to U.S. citizens and resident aliens who study, teach or conduct research in the United States or abroad under scholarships and fellowship grants.

521 Moving Expenses

This publication explains how, if you changed job locations last year or started a new job, you may be able to deduct your moving expenses. You may qualify for a deduction whether you are self-employed or an employee. The expenses must be connected with starting work at your new job location. You must meet a distance test and a time test. You also may be able to deduct expenses of moving to the United States if you retire while living and working overseas or if you are a survivor or dependent of a person who died while living and working overseas.
Forms 3903, 3903F, 4782.

523 Tax Information on Selling Your Home

This publication explains how you report gain from selling your home, how you may postpone the tax on part or all of the gain, and how you may exclude part or all of the gain from your gross income if you are 55 or older. Form 2119.

524 Credit for the Elderly or the Disabled

This publication explains how to figure the credit for the elderly or the disabled. You may be able to claim this credit if you are 65 or older, or if you are retired on disability and were permanently and totally disabled when you retired. Figure the credit on Schedule R (Form 1040), Credit for the Elderly or the Disabled. To take the credit you must file a Form 1040.
Schedule R (Form 1040).

525 Taxable and Nontaxable Income

This publication discusses wages, salaries, fringe benefits, and other compensation received for services as an employee. In addition, it discusses items of miscellaneous taxable income as well as items that are exempt from tax.

526 Charitable Contributions

If you make a charitable contribution or gift to, or for the use of, a qualified organization, you may be able to claim a deduction on your tax return. This publication explains how the deduction is claimed, and the limits that apply.
Schedule A (Form 1040), Form 2106.

527 Residential Rental Property

This publication defines rental income, discusses rental expenses, and explains how to report them on your return. It also discusses casualty losses on rental property, passive activity limits, at-risk rules pertaining to rental property, and the sale of rental property.
Schedule E (Form 1040), and Forms 4562 and 4797.

529 Miscellaneous Deductions

This publication discusses expenses you generally may take as miscellaneous deductions on Schedule A (Form 1040), such as unreimbursed employee expenses and expenses of producing income. It does not discuss other itemized deductions, such as the ones for charitable contributions, moving expenses, interest, taxes, or medical and dental expenses.
Schedule A (Form 1040), Form 2106.

530 Tax Information for Homeowners (Including Owners of Condominiums and Cooperative Apartments)

This publication gives information about home ownership and federal taxes. It explains how to determine basis, how to treat settlement and closing costs, and how to treat repairs and improvements you make. The publication discusses itemized deductions for mortgage interest, real estate taxes, and casualty and theft losses. It also explains the mortgage interest credit.

531 Reporting Income From Tips

This publication gives advice about keeping track of cash and charge tips and explains that all tips received are subject to federal income tax. The publication also explains the rules about the information that employers must report to the Internal Revenue Service about their employees' tip income.
Forms 4070 and 4070A.

533 Self-Employment Tax

This publication explains the self-employment tax, which is a social security tax for people who work for themselves. It is similar to the social security tax withheld from the pay of wage earners.
Schedule SE (Form 1040).

534 Depreciation

This publication discusses the various methods of depreciation, including the modified accelerated cost recovery system (MACRS).
Form 4562.

535 Business Expenses

This publication discusses business expenses such as: fringe benefits; rent; interest; taxes; insurance; and employee benefit plans. It also outlines the choice to capitalize certain business expenses; discusses amortization and depletion; covers some business expenses that may be deductible in some circumstances and not deductible in others; and points out some expenses that are not deductible.

536 Net Operating Losses

537 Installment Sales

This publication discusses sales arrangements that provide for part or all of the selling price to be paid in a later year. These arrangements are "installment sales." If you finance the buyer's purchase of your property, instead of having the buyer get a loan or mortgage from a bank, you probably have an installment sale. Form 6252.

538 Accounting Periods and Methods

This publication explains which accounting periods and methods can be used for figuring federal taxes, and how to apply for approval to change from one period or method to another. Most individual taxpayers use the calendar year for their accounting period and the cash method of accounting. Forms 1128 and 3115.

541 Tax Information on Partnerships

Forms 1065 and Schedules D, K, and K-1 (Form 1065).

542 Tax Information on Corporations

Forms 1120 and 1120-A

544 Sales and Other Dispositions of Assets

This publication explains how to figure gain and loss on various transactions, such as trading or selling an asset used in a trade or business, and it explains the tax results of different types of gains and losses. Not all transactions result in taxable gains or deductible losses, and not all gains are taxed the same way.
Schedule D (Form 1040) and Form 4797.

547 Nonbusiness Disasters, Casualties, and Thefts

This publication explains when you can deduct a disaster, casualty, or theft loss. Casualties are events such as hurricanes, earthquakes, tornadoes, fire, floods, vandalism, loss of deposits in a bankrupt or insolvent financial institution, and car accidents. The publication also explains how to treat the reimbursement you receive from insurance or other sources. Form 4684.

550 Investment Income and Expenses

This publication explains which types of investment income are and are not taxable, when the income is taxed, and how to report it on your tax return. The publication discusses the treatment of tax shelters and investment-related expenses. The publication also explains how to figure your gain and loss when you sell or trade your investment property.
Forms 1099-INT and 1099-DIV, Schedules B and D (Form 1040).

551 Basis of Assets

This publication explains how to determine the basis of property. The basis of property you buy is usually its cost. If you received property in some other way, such as by gift or inheritance, you normally must use a basis other than cost.

Be patient. If any phone number is incorrect, call (area code) 555-1212 and request the new listing.

552 Recordkeeping for Individuals

This publication can help you decide what records to keep and how long to keep them for tax purposes. These records will help you prepare your income tax returns so that you will pay only your correct tax. If you keep a record of your expenses during the year, you may find that you can reduce your taxes by itemizing your deductions. Deductible expenses include medical and dental bills, interest, contributions, and taxes.

553 Highlights of 1994 Tax Changes

This publication discusses the more important changes in the tax rules brought about by recent legislation, rulings, and administrative decisions. It does not discuss all new tax rules or detail all changes. It highlights the important recent changes that taxpayers should know about when filing their 1989 tax forms and when planning for 1990.

554 Tax Information for Older Americans

This publication gives tax information of special interest to older Americans. An example takes you through completing a tax return and explains such items as the sale of a home, the credit for the elderly or the disabled, the supplemental Medicare premium, and pension and annuity income. The publication includes filled-in forms and schedules that show how these and other items are reported.
Schedules B, D, and R (Form 1040), and Forms 1040 and 2119.

555 Community Property and the Federal Income Tax

This publication may help married taxpayers who are domiciled in one of the following community property states: Arizona, California, Idaho, Louisiana, Nevada, New Mexico, Texas, Washington or Wisconsin. If you wish to file a separate tax return, you should understand how community property laws affect the way you figure your tax before completing your federal income tax return.

556 Examination of Returns, Appeal Rights, and Claims for Refund

This publication may be helpful if your return is examined by the Internal Revenue Service. It explains that returns are normally examined to verify the correctness of reported income, exemptions, or deductions, and it describes what appeal rights you have if you disagree with the results of the examination.
This publication also explains the procedures for the examination of items of partnership income, deduction, gain, loss, and credit. Information is given on how to file a claim for refund, the time for filing a claim for refund, and any limit on the amount of refund.
Forms 1040X and 1120X

556SP Revision de las Declaraciones de Impuesto, Derecho de Apelacion y Reclamaciones de Reembolsos (Examination of Returns, Appeal Rights, and Claims for Refund)

(Spanish version of Publication 556) Forms 1040X and 1120X

557 Tax-Exempt Status for Your Organization

This publication discusses how organizations become recognized as exempt from federal income tax under section 501(a) of the Internal Revenue Code. (These include organizations described in Code section 501(c).) The publication explains how to get a ruling or determination letter recognizing the exemption, and it gives other information that applies generally to all exempt organizations.
Forms 990, 990PF, 1023, and 1024.

559 Tax Information for Survivors, Executors, and Administrators

This publication can help you report and pay the proper federal income and estate taxes if you are responsible for settling a decedent's estate. The publication also answers many questions that a spouse or other survivor faces when a person dies.
Form 1040, Form 1041, Form 706, and Form 4810.

560 Self-Employed Retirement Plans

This publication discusses retirement plans for self-employed persons and certain partners in partnerships. These retirement plans are sometimes called Keogh plans or HR-10 plans.

561 Determining the Value of Donated Property

This publication can help donors and appraisers determine the value of property (other than cash) that is given to qualified organizations. It explains what kind of information you need to support a charitable deduction you claim on your return.
Form 8283.

564 Mutual Fund Distributions

This publication discusses the federal income tax treatment of distributions paid or allocated to you as an individual shareholder of a mutual fund. A comprehensive example shows distributions made by a mutual fund and an illustration of Form 1040. Forms 1040, Schedule B (Form 1040), and Form 1099-DIV.

570 Tax Guide for Individuals in U.S. Possessions

This publication is for individuals with income from American Samoa, Guam, the Commonwealth of the Northern Mariana Islands, Puerto Rico, and the U.S. Virgin Islands. Forms 4563, 5074, and 8689.

571 Tax-Sheltered Annuity Programs for Employees of Public Schools and Certain Tax-Exempt Organizations

This publication explains the rules concerning employers qualified to buy tax-sheltered annuities, eligible employees who may participate in the program, and the amounts that may be excluded from income. Form 5330.

575 Pension and Annuity Income (Including Simplified General Rule)

This publication explains how to report pension and annuity income on your federal income tax return. It also explains the special tax treatment for lump-sum distributions from pension, stock bonus, or profit-sharing plans.
Forms 1040, 1099-R and 4972.

578 Tax Information for Private Foundations and Foundation Managers

This publication covers tax matters of interest to private foundations and their managers, including the tax classification of the foundations, filing requirements, the tax on net investment income, and various excise taxes on transactions that violate the foundation rules. Form 990-F

579SP Como Preparar la Declaracion de Impuesto Federal (How to Prepare the Federal Income Tax Return)

Forms 1040, 1040A, 1040EZ.

583 Taxpayers Starting a Business

This publication shows sample records that a small business can use if it operates as a sole proprietorship. Records like these will help you prepare complete and accurate tax returns and make sure you pay only the tax you owe. This publication also discusses the taxpayer identification number businesses must use, information returns businesses may have to file, and the kinds of business taxes businesses may have to pay. Schedule C (Form 1040), and Form 4562.

584 Nonbusiness Disaster, Casualty, and Theft Loss Workbook

This workbook can help you to figure your loss from a disaster, casualty or theft. It will help you most if you list your possessions before any losses occur. The workbook has schedules to help you figure the loss on your home and its contents. There is also a schedule to help you figure the loss on your car, truck, or motorcycle.

584SP Registro de Perdidas Personales Causadas por Desastres, Hechos Fortuitos (Imprevistos) o Robos

Spanish version of Publication 584.

587 Business Use of Your Home

This publication can help you decide if you qualify to deduct certain expenses for using part of your home in your business. You must meet specific tests and your deduction is limited. Deductions for the business use of a home computer are also discussed. Schedule C (Form 1040), and Form 4562.

589 Tax Information on S Corporations

This publication discusses the way corporations are taxed under subchapter S of the Internal Revenue Code. In general, an "S" corporation does not pay tax on its income. Instead, it passes through its income and expenses to its shareholders, who then report them on their own tax returns.
Forms 1120S and Schedule K-1 (Form 1120S)

590 Individual Retirement Arrangements (IRAs)

This publication explains the rules for and the tax benefits of having an individual retirement arrangement (IRA). An IRA is a savings plan that lets you set aside money for your retirement. Generally, your contributions to an IRA are tax deductible in part or in full and the earnings in your IRA are not taxed until they are distributed to you. Forms 1040, 5329 and 8606.

Taxes

593 Tax Highlights for U.S. Citizens and Residents Going Abroad

This publication briefly reviews various U.S. tax provisions that apply to U.S. citizens or resident aliens who live or work abroad and expect to receive income from foreign sources.

594 Understanding The Collection Process (Employment Tax Accounts)

This booklet explains your rights and duties as a taxpayer who owes employer's quarterly federal taxes. It also explains how we fulfill the legal obligation of the Internal Revenue Service to collect these taxes. It is not intended as a precise and technical analysis of the law.

594SP Proceso de cobro (Deudas del impuesto por razon del empleo)

(Spanish version of Publication 594.)

595 Tax Guide for Commercial Fishermen

This publication is intended for sole proprietors who use Form 1040 (Schedule C) to report profit or loss from fishing. This publication does not cover corporations or partnerships. Forms 1040 (Schedule C), 1099-MISC, 4562, 4797.

596 Earned Income Credit

This publication discusses who may receive the earned income credit, and how to figure and claim the credit. It also discusses how to receive advance payments of the earned income credit. Forms W-5, 1040, and 1040A.

596SP Credito por Ingreso del Trabajo (Earned Income Credit)

Spanish version of Publication 596.

597 Information on the United States-Canada Income Tax Treaty

This publication reproduces the entire text of the U.S.-Canada income tax treaty, and also gives an explanation of provisions that often apply to U.S. citizens or residents who have Canadian source income. There is also a discussion that deals with certain tax problems that may be encountered by Canadian residents who temporarily work in the United States.

598 Tax on Unrelated Business Income of Exempt Organizations

This publication explains the unrelated business income tax provisions that apply to most tax-exempt organizations. An organization that regularly operates a trade or business that is not substantially related to its exempt purpose may be taxed on the income from this business. Generally, a tax-exempt organization with gross income of $1,000 or more from an unrelated trade or business must file a return. Form 990-T.

686 Certification for Reduced Tax Rates in Tax Treaty Countries

This publication explains how U.S. citizens, residents, and domestic corporations may certify to a foreign treaty country that they are entitled to treaty benefits.

721 Tax Guide to U.S. Civil Service Retirement Benefits

This publication explains how the federal income tax rules apply to the benefits that retired federal employees or their survivors receive under the U.S. Civil Service Retirement System or Federal Employees Retirement System. There is also information on estate taxes. Form 1040.

850 English-Spanish Glossary of Words and Phrases Used in Publications Issued by the Internal Revenue Service

901 U.S. Tax Treaties

This publication includes information about the reduced tax rates and exemptions from U.S. taxes provided under U.S. tax treaties with other countries. This publication is intended for residents of those countries who receive income from U.S. sources. Information for foreign workers and students is emphasized. Form 1040NR

904 Interrelated Computations for Estate and Gift Taxes

Forms 706 and 709.

907 Tax Highlights for Persons with Disabilities

This publication explains tax rules of interest to handicapped and disabled people and to taxpayers with disabled dependents. For example, you may be able to take a tax credit for certain disability payments, you may be able to deduct medical expenses, and you may be able to take a credit for expenses of care for disabled dependents. Schedule A (Form 1040), Schedule R (1040), and Form 2441.

908 Tax Information on Bankruptcy

This publication explains the income tax aspects of bankruptcy and discharge of debt for individuals and small businesses. Forms 982, 1040, 1041, 1120.

911 Tax Information for Direct Sellers

This publication may help you if you are a "direct seller," a person who sells consumer products to others on a person-to-person basis. Many direct sellers sell door-to-door, at sales parties, or by appointment in someone's home. Information on figuring your income from direct sales as well as the kinds of expenses you may be entitled to deduct is also provided. Schedules C and SE (Form 1040).

915 Social Security Benefits and Equivalent Railroad Retirement Benefits

This publication explains when you have to include part of your social security or equivalent railroad retirement benefits in income on Form 1040. It also explains how to figure the amount to include.
Forms SSA-1099 and RRB-1099, Social Security Benefits Worksheet, Notice 703, Forms SSA-1042S and RRB-1042S.

917 Business Use of a Car

This publication explains the expenses that you may deduct for the business use of your car. Car expenses that are deductible do not include the cost of commuting expenses (driving from your home to your workplace). The publication also discusses the taxability of the use of a car provided by an employer and rules on leasing a car for business. Form 2106

919 Is My Withholding Correct for 1995?

To help employees check their withholding, this publication has worksheets that will help them estimate both their 1995 tax and their total 1995 withholding. The employees can then compare the two amounts. The publication tells employees what to do if too much or too little tax is being withheld. Form W-4.

925 Passive Activity and At-Risk Rules

This publication covers the rules that limit passive activity losses and credits and the at-risk limits. Form 8582.

926 Employment Taxes for Household Employers

This publication shows how a household employer reports federal income tax withholding, social security (FICA), and unemployment taxes (FUTA). You may be a household employer if you have a babysitter, maid, or other employee who works in your house. The publication also shows what records you must keep.
Forms W-2, W-3, 940, 940EZ, and 942.

929 Tax Rules for Children and Dependents

This publication describes the tax law affecting certain children and dependents. No personal exemption is allowed to a taxpayer who can be claimed as a dependent by another taxpayer. The standard deduction for dependents may be limited. Minor children may have to pay tax at their parent's tax rate.
Form 8615, Form 8814, and Form 8803.

936 Home Mortgage Interest Deduction

This publication covers the rules governing the deduction of home mortgage interest if your acquisition cost exceeds $1 million ($500,000 if you are married filing separately) or your home equity debt exceeds $100,000 ($50,000 if you are married filing separately). Worksheets are provided to determine what interest expenses qualify as home mortgage interest.

937 Employment Taxes

The first part of this publication explains your responsibilities, if you have employees, to withhold federal income taxes and social security taxes (FICA) from their wages, and to pay social security taxes and federal unemployment taxes (FUTA). It also discusses the rules for advance payment of the earned income credit, and for reporting and allocating tips.

Be patient. If any phone number is incorrect, call (area code) 555-1212 and request the new listing.

The second part provides general information about the rules for reporting payments to nonemployees and transactions with other persons. It also provides information on taxpayer identification numbers, backup withholding, and penalties relating to information returns.
Forms W-2, W-2G, W-4, 940, 941, 1098, 1099 series, 4789, 5498, 8300, and 8308.

938 Real Estate Mortgage Investment Conduits (REMICS) Reporting Information (And Other Collateralized Debt Obligations (CDOs))

This new publication discusses reporting requirements for issuers of real estate mortgage investment conduits (REMICS) and collateralized debt obligations (CDOs). This publication also contains a directory of REMICS and CDOs to assist brokers and middlemen in fulfilling reporting requirements.

939 Pension General Rule (Nonsimplified Method)

This publication covers the nonsimplified General Rule for the taxation of pensions or annuities, which must be used if the Simplified General Rule is not applicable or is not chosen. For example, the nonsimplified method must be used for payments under commercial annuities. The publication also contains the necessary actuarial tables for this method.

945 Tax Information for Those Affected by Operation Desert Shield

This publication covers many issues, such as available tax relief measures for suspending examinations or collection of back taxes, extending due dates for filing an income tax return, meeting the requirements for the foreign earned income exclusion, and seeking other tax assistance. This publication applies to newly activated reservists, as well as all other active duty U.S. military personnel and their families, citizens who had been detained by Iraq, and citizens who had to leave the Middle East because of the adverse conditions.

946 How to Begin Depreciating your Property

Publication for people who are depreciating property for the first time.

947 Practice Before the IRS and Power of Attorney

This publication explains who can represent a taxpayer before the IRS and what forms or documents are used to authorize a person to represent a taxpayer. Forms 2848, and 8821.

950 Introduction to Estate and Gift Taxes

This publication outlines some of the topics covered in Publication 448, Federal Estate and Gift Taxes.

952 Sick Pay Reporting

This publication explains procedures for third-party insurers to report sick pay.

953 International Tax information for Businesses

Covers topics of interest to U.S. citizens and resident aliens with foreign investments and nonresident aliens who want to invest in U.S. businesses.

1004 Identification Numbers Under ERISA

1045 Information for Tax Practitioners

1212 List of Original Discount Instruments

This publication explains the tax treatment of original issue discount (OID). It describes how (1) Brokers and other middlemen, who may hold the debt instruments as nominees for the owners, should report OID to IRS and to the owners on Forms 1099-OID or 1099-INT, and (2) Owners of OID debt instruments should report OID on their income tax returns. The publication gives rules for figuring the discount amount to report each year, if required. It also gives tables showing OID amounts for certain publicly-traded OID debt instruments, including short-term U.S. Government securities.
Schedule B (Form 1040) and Forms 1099-OID and 1099-INT.

1244 Employee's Daily Record of Tips (Form 4070-A) and Employee's Report of Tips to Employer (Form 4070)

This publication explains how you must report tips if you are an employee who receives tips. Copies of the monthly tip report you must give your employer are included, as well as a daily list you can use for your own records.
Forms 4070 and 4070-A.

1542 Per Diem Rates

1544 Reporting Cash Payments of Over $10,000 (Received in a Trade or Business)

This new publication was developed to assist the government in the war against drugs. It contains information for filing Form 8300 and includes an example with a filled-in Form 8300.

1546 How to Use the Problem Resolution Programs of the IRS

State Tax Assistance

These state taxpayer service departments are the basic starting place for free assistance and guidance pertaining to your state taxes.

Alabama

Taxpayer Assistance
Alabama Income Tax Division
P.O. Box 327465
Montgomery, AL 36132-7465   205-242-2677

or

1021 Madison Ave.
Montgomery, AL 36132

Alaska

(No individual income tax; corporation tax only)
Alaska Department of Revenue
Income and Excise Audit Division
Attn: Corporations Unit
P.O. Box 11040
Juneau, AK 99811-0420   907-465-2370

Arizona

Personal Income Tax
Arizona Department of Revenue
P.O. Box 29002
Phoenix, AZ 85038

Corporation Tax
Arizona Department of Revenue
P.O. Box 29079
Phoenix, AZ 85038-9079
Information and fewer than 6 forms   602-255-3381

Arkansas

Arkansas Department of Finance Administration
Attn: Income Tax
P.O. Box 3628
Little Rock, AR 72203
General Information   501-682-1100
Refund Information   501-682-0200

California

Personal/Corporate
Franchise Tax Board
P.O. Box 942840   916-854-6500
Sacramento, CA 94240-0400   800-852-5711
Forms   800-338-0505
Hearing Impaired   800-822-6268

Colorado

Taxpayer Services
Department of Revenue
1375 Sherman Street
Denver, CO 80261
Personal   303-534-1209
Corporate   303-534-1209
Forms   303-534-1208

Connecticut

Department of Revenue Services
92 Farmington Avenue
Hartford, CT 06105

Information and Forms   800-382-9463
Information   203-566-8520
Forms   203-297-4753

Delaware

Delaware Division of Revenue
820 North French Street   800-292-7826
Wilmington, DE 19801   302-577-3300

Florida

Florida Taxpayer Assistance
5050 W. Tallahassee St.   800-352-3671
Tallahassee, FL 32399-0100   904-488-6800

Georgia

Income Tax Division
Atlanta, GA 30334
Information   404-656-6286
Forms   404-656-4293

Hawaii

Taxpayer Services Branch
Hawaii State Tax Collector
P.O. Box 259
Honolulu, HI 96809
Information   800-222-3229
Forms   808-587-7572/7573

Idaho

Idaho Department of Revenue and Taxation
P.O. Box 36
Boise, ID 83722
Taxpayer Assistance   208-334-7660
Forms and Refunds   208-334-7789

Illinois

Illinois Department of Revenue
P.O. Box 19015
Springfield, IL 62794-9015   217-785-6760
Information and Forms   217-785-7087

Indiana

Indiana Department of Revenue
Taxpayer Services Division
Government Center N.
Room N105
Indianapolis, IN 46204   317-232-2240
More than 10 forms   317-486-5103
Refunds   317-233-4018

Iowa

Iowa Department of Revenue and Finance
Taxpayer Service
Hoover State Office Building
Des Moines, IA 50319

Information and forms	515-218-3114
Bulk form orders	515-281-5370

Kansas

Kansas Department of Revenue
Box 12001
Topeka, KS 66612-2001

Information	913-296-0222

Kentucky

Kentucky Revenue Cabinet
Frankfort, KY 40618

Information	502-564-4580
Forms	502-564-3658

Louisiana

Louisiana Department of Revenue and Taxation
P.O. Box 201
Baton Rouge, LA 70821

Information	504-925-4611
Forms	504-925-7532

Maine

State of Maine
Department of Taxation
Station 24
Augusta, ME 04333

	207-626-8475
Information and Forms	800-773-7894

Maryland

Comptroller of the Treasury
Income Tax Information
301 W. Preston St.
Baltimore, MD 21201

	800-MD-TAXES
	410-974-3981

Massachusetts

Massachusetts Department of Revenue
Taxpayer Assistance
100 Cambridge Street
Boston, MA 02204

Attention: Correspondence Unit	617-727-4392

Michigan

Department of Treasury
430 West Allegan Street
Lansing, MI 48922

Information	800-487-7000
Forms	517-373-6598

Minnesota

Minnesota Taxpayer Assistance
10 River Park Plaza
St. Paul, MN 55146

Personal	800-652-9094
Personal	612-296-3781
Corporate	800-657-3777
Corporate	612-296-6181

Mississippi

Mississippi State Tax Commission
P.O. Box 1033
Jackson, MS 39215

	601-359-1141

Missouri

Taxpayer Assistance
Missouri Department of Revenue
P.O. Box 3300

Jefferson City, MO 65105-2200

Information (individual)	314-751-3505
Information (corporate)	314-751-4541
Forms	800-877-6881

Montana

Montana Department of Revenue
Income Tax Division
P.O. Box 5805
Helena, MT 59604

Personal	406-444-2837
Corporate	406-444-3388

Nebraska

Nebraska Department of Revenue
Taxpayer Assistance
P.O. Box 94818
Lincoln, NE 68509

Personal Information	402-471-5729
Corporate Information	800-742-7474
Forms	800-626-7899

Nevada

No Income Tax	702-687-4820

New Hampshire

No Income Tax	603-271-2191

New Jersey

New Jersey Division of Taxation
50 Barrack Street
CN 269
Trenton, NJ 08646

	800-323-4400
	609-588-2200

New Mexico

New Mexico Taxation and Revenue
P.O. Box 630
Santa Fe, NM 87509-0630

	505-827-0909

New York

New York State Department of Taxation and Finance
Taxpayer Assistance Bureau
State Campus
Bldg. #8, 9th Floor
Albany, NY 12227

General Information	518-438-8581 or 800-225-5829
Refund Information	518-438-6771 or 800-443-3200
Forms	518-438-1073 or 800-462-8100
All	518-438-6777

North Carolina

Information:
North Carolina Taxpayer Assistance
P.O. Box 25000
Raleigh, NC 27640

Refund Information:
North Carolina Department of Revenue
P.O. Box R
Raleigh, NC 27634

Information	919-733-4684 or 800-222-9965

North Dakota

Office of State Tax Commissioner
600 East Boulevard Avenue
Bismarck, ND 58505-0599

Individual	701-224-3450

Be patient. If any phone number is incorrect, call (area code) 555-1212 and request the new listing.

495

Taxes

Corporate	701-224-2014
Forms	701-224-3017

Ohio

Taxpayer Services
Ohio Department of Taxation
P.O. Box 2476
Columbus, Ohio 43266-0076

Information	614-846-6712
Forms	800-282-1782

Oklahoma

Oklahoma Tax Commission
2501 Lincoln Boulevard
Oklahoma City, OK 73194

	800-522-8165
Information	405-521-4321
Forms	405-521-3108

Oregon

Oregon Department of Revenue
Tax Help Section
955 Center Street, NE
Salem, OR 97310   503-378-4988

Pennsylvania

Personal:
Pennsylvania Department of Revenue
Taxpayer Services
4th and Walnut Sts.
Harrisburg, PA 17128-0101   717-787-8346

Corporate:
Pennsylvania Department of Revenue
Business Trust Fund Taxes
Department 280904
Harrisburg, PA 17128-0904   717-787-2416

Forms:
Pennsylvania Department of Revenue
2850 Turnpike and Middletown Industrial Pike   717-787-8094
Harrisburg, PA 17057-5492   800-362-2050

Rhode Island

Rhode Island Division of Taxation
1 Capitol Hill
Providence, RI 02908

Information	401-277-2905
Forms	401-277-3934

South Carolina

South Carolina Department of Revenue
P.O. Box 125
Columbia, SC 29214

Information	803-737-4709
Forms	803-737-5080

South Dakota

No Income Tax   605-773-3311

Tennessee

Tennessee Taxpayer Services
State Office Bldg., 3rd Floor
500 Deadrick St.
Nashville, TN 37242

Information	615-741-3581
Forms	615-741-2481

Texas

No Income Tax   512-463-4600

Utah

Utah State Tax Commission
160 East 3rd South
Salt Lake City, UT 84134   801-530-4848

Vermont

Personal/Corporate
Vermont Department of Taxes
Pavillion Office Building
109 State St.
Montpelier, VT 05602   802-828-2551
Taxpayer assistance   802-828-2865

Virginia

Virginia Department of Taxation
P.O. Box 1317
Richmond, VA 23210
* Place attention notation to what it concerns

Personal	804-367-8031
Corporate	804-367-8036
Forms	804-367-8055

Washington

No Income Tax
Department of Revenue
Taxpayer Information
P.O. Box 47478   206-753-5540
Olympia, WA 98504   800-233-6349

West Virginia

West Virginia Department of Revenue
P.O. Box 3784   800-982-8297
Charleston, WV 25337-3784   304-558-3333

Wisconsin

Taxpayer Services
Wisconsin Department of Revenue
P.O. Box 8906
Madison, WI 53708

Personal, information and forms	608-266-2486
Corporate, information and forms	608-266-2772
Bulk form orders	608-267-2025

Wyoming

No Income Tax
Department of Revenue
122 W. 25th St.
Cheyenne, WY 82001   307-777-7961

    Be patient. If any phone number is incorrect, call (area code) 555-1212 and request the new listing.

Health and Medicine
Clearinghouses and Starting Points

* *See also Consumer Power Chapter*
* *See also Careers and Workplace Chapter*
* *See also Drugs and Chemical Dependence Chapter*
* *See also Economics, Demographics, and Statistics Chapter*
* *See also Environment and Nature Chapter*
* *See also Experts Chapter*

Unlike any other chapter in this book, this chapter contains one information clearinghouse after another. Some of these national resource centers provide telephone help on many concerns; for example, the Family Life Information Exchange and Project Share. Other offices, like the Diabetic Information Clearinghouse, have a more concentrated focus. The Public Health Service of the U.S. Department of Health and Human Services is the primary arm of the federal government which disseminates information about promoting health and preventing disease. It sponsors the National Health Information Center which is accessible by a toll-free number. The Center will answer questions, send out medical journal abstracts, fact sheets and other materials, and refer callers to more specialized clearinghouses, government offices, city and county health departments, national associations, health advocacy groups, private organizations and foundations that focus on your health concern. Other government agencies, including the U.S. Department of Agriculture, the U.S. Environmental Protection Agency, and the Food and Drug Administration, also serve both as watchdogs and information providers on the safety of pharmaceuticals, drinking water, hazardous wastes, and food inspection.

Suppose your doctor has recommended a CAT scan or you've just gotten worrisome lab test results. Your first step is to call the National Health Information Center. The center can refer you to numerous organizations and one of the National Institutes of Health which specializes in this type of health problem. Do you have an appointment with a surgeon in a few weeks and want to be prepared to discuss the pros and cons of the operation? Look through this section for published resources, databases, medical libraries, and information clearinghouses that will give you powerful research tools. But, don't stop there. Consider contacting those universities and research centers identified in both the Medical Research Section as well as the Careers and Workplace Chapter, specifically the section titled Research Grants in Any Field, to learn about new experimental medical procedures, tests, and treatments. And, don't forget the hundreds of medical specialists whose phone numbers are listed in the Experts Chapter.

* Access to All Medical and Scientific Studies

National Library of Medicine
8600 Rockville Pike
Bethesda, MD 20894   301-496-6308

The National Library of Medicine (NLM) is the world's largest research library in a single scientific and professional field. The collection today stands at five million books, journals, technical reports, manuscripts, microfilms, and pictorial materials. The Library may be used by health professionals and health science students, and books and journals may also be requested on interlibrary loan (there is a fee for loan transactions). The Library's computer-based Medical Literature Analysis and Retrieval System (MEDLARS) has bibliographic access to the NLM's vast store of biomedical information. All of the MEDLARS databases are available through NLM's online network of more than 100,000 institutions and individuals. NLM charges a user fee for access to the system. The Regional Medical Library Program is intended to provide health science practitioners, investigators, and educators convenient access to health care and biomedical information resources. The Regional Libraries provide reference service, referral service, and online access to MEDLARS.

* Adolescent Health

National Maternal and Child Health Clearinghouse
2070 Chain Bridge Rd.
Vienna, VA 22182   703-821-8955

Needs Assessment and Beyond: 1991 State Adolescent Health Coordinator Conference Proceeding is one of the publications available free of charge from the clearinghouse.

* AIDS Information Clearinghouse

National AIDS Clearinghouse (NAC)   800-458-5231
P.O. Box 6003   301-217-0023

Rockville, MD 20849-6003   Fax: 301-738-6616
                                  TDD: 800-243-0023

The Center for Disease Control (CDC) National AIDS Clearinghouse (NAC) provides timely, accurate, and relevant information about HIV and AIDS. All of the Clearinghouse's services are designed to facilitate the sharing of resources and information about education and prevention, published materials, and research findings, as well as new about AIDS-related trends. The Clearinghouse offers comprehensive reference and referral services; distributes HIV/AIDS education and prevention materials; maintains a variety of databases on HIV/AIDS-related resources and services; offers bilingual reference specialists to talk to Spanish speaking callers; provides CDC NAC Online, an electronic bulletin board; provides DCD Business and Labor Resource Service; manages the AIDS Clinical Trials Information Service; operates the HIV/AIDS Treatment Information Service; and provides technical assistance services. The Clearinghouse distributes more than 300 different publication, educational materials, and scientific reports including brochures, posters, public service announcements, articles from CDC's *Morbidity and Mortality Weekly Report* series, HIV/AIDS Surveillance Reports and videotapes. Most items have a unit price to cover shipping and handling costs, while some are free of charge. The Clearinghouse published the *Catalog of HIV and AIDS Education and Prevention Materials*, which contains descriptions of, and ordering information for, the items from the Clearinghouse. There is no charge for the catalog.

* Alcohol and Drug Information Center

National Clearinghouse for Alcohol and Drug Information
P.O. Box 2345   800-729-6686
Rockville, MD 20847-2345   TDD: 800-487-4889

This clearinghouse makes referrals to local AA chapters and other self-help organizations as well as national associations as well as providing callers with materials about preventing or curing substance abuse.

Health and Medicine

* Almanac to National Institutes of Health

Division of Public Information
National Institutes of Health
Building 31, Room 2B03
Bethesda, MD 20892   301-496-4143

Published annually, the *NIH Almanac* (#94-5) presents pertinent facts about the National Institutes of Health (NIH). All the various institutes are listed, including information about their respective research and staffs. Historical data about NIH, as well as tables describing appropriations, staff and facilities, are also included. Information regarding lectures, Nobel Laureates, and the field units can also be found in this free sourcebook. Free database searches, publications and videos are available.

* America's Health Advisor: Surgeon General

Surgeon General
200 Independence Ave., SW, Room 716-G
Washington, DC 20201   202-690-6467

The Surgeon General provides leadership and direction for the Public Health Service (PHS) Commissioned Corps. He serves as principal federal health advisor to the nation on public health matters and serves as the focal point for dialogue with professional societies, representing PHS at national and international meetings. The Surgeon General releases many reports such as *Smoking and Health* and *Healthy People*, and issues warnings to the public on health hazards. The Surgeon General also reviews plans for transportation, open testing, and disposal of lethal chemicals and biological agents.

* Arthritis Clearinghouse

National Arthritis and Musculoskeletal and Skin Diseases (NIAMS)
1 AMS Circle   301-495-4484
Bethesda, MD 20892-3675   Fax: 301-587-4352
                                                 TDD: 301-565-2966

This clearinghouse responds to requests for information on arthritis, and musculoskeletal and skin diseases from health professionals and the general public. The National Arthritis and Musculoskeletal and Skin Diseases (NIAMS) Clearinghouse uses the online database CHID (Combined Health Information Database) from which they can reference health information. They can provide you with many brochures, reports, information packages, and other publications, along with a free publications listing. Publications available include:

Acne (AR-80)
Arthritis (AR-27)
Arthritis in Children (AR-163)
Arthritis and Diet (AR-046)
Hip Replacement (AR-149)
Knee Replacement (AR-102)
Neck and Cervical Pain (AR-147)
Psoriasis (AR-97)
Psoriatic Arthritis (AR-123)
Scoliosis in Adults (AR-94)
Scoliosis in Children (AR-131)
Sun and Skin (AR-153)
Sweating Disorders (AR-77)

* Asthma Clearinghouse

National Heart, Lung, and Blood Institute
National Asthma Education Program
P.O. Box 30105   301-251-1222
Bethesda, MD 20824-0105   Fax: 301-251-1223

The Asthma Clearinghouse provides publications, reports, resources, and referrals to experts in the field of asthma. One report, the *Expert Panel Report: Guidelines for the Diagnosis and Management of Asthma*, (55-3042A) explains the diagnosis, therapy, and other considerations for those that suffer from asthma. They can answer your questions or can direct you to those that can. Contact the Clearinghouse for more information. Other free publications include:

General Public
Check Your Asthma "I.Q." - true-or-false quiz. (92-1128)
Facts About Asthma - presents basic information on asthma. (90-2339)

Professionals
**Air Power* - basics of asthma management in four 1-hour sessions for children ages 9-13 and their parents. (PB95-217287, $27)
**Air Wise* - one-on-one sessions for hard to manage children. (PB95-217345, $36.50)
**Living With Asthma, Parts 1 and 2* - teaches children to deal independently with their health problem. (PB85-217352, $98)

**Open Airways* - seven sessions for inner-city children ages 4-14 and their parents and is designed for low-income, low-education families. (PB95-217279, $52)

**Available from: National Technical Information Service, 5285 Port Royal Rd., Springfield, VA 22161; 800-553-NTIS.

* Asthma Educational Materials

National Asthma Education and Prevention Program (NAEPP)
National Heart, Lung, and Blood Institute Information Center
P.O. Box 30105   301-251-1222
Bethesda, MD 20824-0105   Fax: 301-251-1223

The National Heart, Lung, and Blood Institute (NHLBI) is a collaboration of more than 20 professional, patient, and voluntary organizations. These groups are working together to raise awareness that asthma is a serious chronic disease and to educate the public, patients, and professionals about its symptoms, diagnosis, and management. Some of the educational materials available from the Information Center are:

General Public/Patient Materials:
Check Your Asthma I.Q. contains a quiz that gives general information on asthma in a true-false format. (92-1128)
Datos Sobre of Asma Spanish translation of *Facts About Asthma* (92-0734)
Facts About Asthma. This pamphlet presents the basic facts about asthma and includes suggestions for avoiding and lessening asthma episodes.
Your Asthma Can Be Controlled: Expect Nothing Less. This pamphlet shows asthma patients how to become active partners with their doctors. (92-2665)

Professional Materials:
Asthma Management Kit for Clinicians. This kit provides valuable information and materials to teach patients to manage their asthma. It includes the following: *Teach Your Patients About Asthma; Your Asthma Can Be Controlled, Expect Nothing Less; Partners in Asthma Management: Together, We Can Control Your Asthma; Check Your Asthma I.Q.;* and *Statement on Technical Standards for Peak Flow Meters*. (92-2113)

Asthma Management Kit for Emergency Departments. This kit provides information for emergency departments located in urban and rural settings that serve minority patients. (94-2992)

Asthma Statistics: Data Fact Sheet. Designed to communicate the magnitude and impact of this chronic health condition.

Expert Panel Report: Guidelines for the Diagnosis and Management of Asthma-Executive Summary. Provides information on mild, moderate, and severe asthma and includes details on home and hospital treatment (55-3042A)

Teaching Manual:
Asthma Awareness Curriculum for the Elementary Classroom. The goal of this curriculum is to help students understand, accept, and help their classmates with asthma. (93-2894)

Posters:
It's Like Drowning on Dry Land (55-600)
Kids Have a Lot of Energy. Some of Them Need it Just to Breathe (55-603)
Your Students With Asthma Can Be Winners, Too (55-504)
Partners in Asthma Management: Together, We Can Control Your Asthma (55-560)
Que Se Parece a un Catarrh, Suena Como un Catarrh, y Se Siente Como un Catarrh, Pero No Lo Es? (55-668)

* Biotechnology Information Center

National Agriculture Library Building
10301 Baltimore Blvd.   301-504-5340
Beltsville, MD 20705-2351   Fax: 301-504-7098

This Information Center covers genetic engineering and recombinant DNA techniques, tissue culture of plant and animal systems, single cell protein, immobilized enzymes, embryo transplants, and much more. They have access to a database, bibliographies, and other publications. Contact this Center for more information.

* Blood Resource

National Heart, Lung, and Blood Institute
National Blood Resource Education Program
P.O. Box 30105   301-251-1222
Bethesda, MD 20824-0105   Fax: 301-251-1223

This program was established to ensure an adequate supply of safe blood and blood components to meet the Nation's needs and to ensure that blood and blood components are transfused only when therapeutically appropriate. This Program helps health professional understand the risks and benefits of blood transfusions, and ensures that patients receive appropriate information regarding transfusions. They also work to increase awareness that donating blood is a safe process. Contact this office for more information regarding blood donations and transfusions. Free publications include:

General Public

Check Your Blood "I.Q." - true-false quiz designed to educate public about blood donation and transfusion. (92-2991)
Your Operation- Your Blood - describes autologous transfusion options. (92-2967)

Professionals

Management and Therapy of Sickle Cell Disease - a consensus guide in treating patients with sickle cell disease.
Transfusion Alert: Use of Autologous Blood - discusses preoperative autologous blood donation, perioperative blood salvage, and acute normovolemic hemodilution. (94-3038)

* Cancer Hotline

Cancer Information Service
National Cancer Institute
Building 31, Room 10A24
9000 Rockville Pike
Bethesda, MD 20892-2580   800-4-CANCER

The Cancer Information Service assists cancer patients, families, and medical personnel on all aspects of cancer. They have information on treatment, rehab, and detection, as well as on financial assistance. Through their databases (see Automated Information Systems-Cancer), they have access to current research and physician referrals. Pamphlets, reports, and assistance in locating community resources is also available.

* Cancer Information Regional Offices

Cancer Information Service
National Cancer Institute
Building 31, Room 10A24
9000 Rockville Pike
Bethesda, MD 20892-2580   800-4-CANCER

The National Cancer Institute has set up offices across the U.S. through which they route the Cancer Information Service calls for those particular areas. These offices offer the same services as the Cancer Information Service (see above). Calls will automatically be routed to your local cancer information specialist.

* Centers for Disease Control Fax Information Service

Centers for Disease Control (CDC)
1600 Clifton Rd. NE
Atlanta, GA 30333   404-639-3534

The Centers for Disease Control and Prevention provides a Fax Information Service that operates 24 hours a day, 7 days a week. To use the service call 404-332-4565 and follow the voice prompts. You can receive a directory of documents available on various subjects. The current directory includes:

000002 Childhood Immunizations
000003 Infection Control
000004 Disease Directory
000005 International Travelers Health Requirements
000006 National Institute of Occupational Safety and Health (NIOSH) Information
000007 Biosafety Information
000008 Smoking and Health Information
000010 Injury Prevention and Control
000011 Agency for Toxic Substances and Disease Registry Information

Information Specifically for Health-care Providers
000102 Immunization Information
000103 ACIP Immunization Recommendations

* Cheap Health Publications

R. Woods, Consumer Information Center-6A
P.O. Box 100
Pueblo, CO 81002   719-948-4000

The Consumer Information Center has many free or inexpensive publications dealing with a variety of health topics from various Federal Agencies. A new Consumer Information Catalog comes out each quarter. Write or call for your free copy. The following publications are available:

Aspirin: A New Look at an Old Drug. 534C (free)
Buying Medicine? Help Protect Yourself Against Tampering. 534C (free)
Cancer Tests You Should Know About: A Guide for People 65 and Over. 536C (free)
Choosing Medical Treatment. 537C (free)
Chronic Fatigue Syndrome. 323C (.50)
Decoding the Cosmetic Label. 527C (free)
Depo-Provera. (contraceptive injections) 538C (free)
Dizziness. 126C ($1.25)
Don't Lose Sight of Glaucoma. 324C (.50)
Eye Wear. 322C (.50)
FDA Consumer. 251C ($15 for 10 issues)
FDA Guide to Nonprescription Pain Relievers. 539C (free)
Getting Fit Your Way. 121C ($3.25)
Guide to Choosing a Nursing Home. 528 C (free)
Headaches. 127C ($2)
"Health Tan" A Fast Fading Myth. 529C (free)
Hocus-Pocus as Applied to Arthritis. 540C (free)
Kids' Vaccinations Get a Little Easier. 541C (free)
Making It Easier to Read Prescriptions. 542C (free)
Mammography Facilities Must Meet Quality Standards. 543C (free)
Menopause. 122C ($3.25)
Personal Health Guide. 123C ($1)
Prescriptions to Help Smokers Quit. 544C (free)
Progress in Blood Supply Safety. 530C (free)
Prostate Cancer. 547C (free)
Questions to Ask Your Doctor Before You Have Surgery. 124C ($1)
Silicone Breast Implants. 531C (free)
So You Have High Blood Cholesterol. 128C ($1.75)
Steroid Substitutes. 545C (free)
The Sun, UV, and You. 532C (free)
Unproven Medical Treatments Lure Elderly. 546C (free)
Understanding Urinary Tract Infections. 326C ($1)
Varicose Vein Treatments. 327C (.50)
Walking for Exercise and Pleasure. 124C ($1)
When the Spine Curves. 548C (free)
Why Do You Smoke? 533C (free)

* Child Abuse and Neglect Clearinghouse

National Center on Child Abuse and Neglect   800-FYI-3366
P.O. Box 1182   703-385-7565
Washington, DC 20013   Fax: 703-385-3206

The Center on Child Abuse and Neglect (NCCAN) oversees federal child abuse and neglect efforts and allocates child maltreatment funds appropriated by Congress. NCCAN is responsible for: conducting research on the causes, prevention, and treatment of child abuse and neglect; collection, analyzing, and disseminating information to professionals concerned with child abuse and neglect; increasing public awareness of the problems of child maltreatment; and assisting states and communities in developing programs related to the prevention, identification and treatment of child abuse and neglect. Services and publications available include:

Research:
Child Maltreatment 1993: Reports from the States to the national Center on Child Abuse and Neglect. #21-10058, free
Child Sexual Abuse Prevention Programs - Do They Work? #20-10079, $1.
A Nation's Shame: Fatal Child Abuse and Neglect in the United States #20-10077, free

Public Awareness:
Catalog of Videotapes and Other Media on Child Abuse and Neglect #25-01001, $6
"Working Together" Poster, #23-02013, free
Child Abuse and Neglect: A Shared Community Concern. #92-30531, free
Child Abuse and Neglect Thesaurus-1995. #25-01018, $27

NCCAN Programs:
Compendium of Discretionary Grants: Fiscal Years 1975-1993. #06-50006, $52
Profiles of Research Grants Funded by NCCAN 1990-1994. #08-70006, $5

Networking:
Consortium of Clearinghouses on Child Abuse and Neglect. #21-10025, free
Organizations Concerned With Child Abuse and Neglect Issues. #44-00002, $8

Health and Medicine

Computerized Services:
CANnet (Child Abuse and Neglect Network. To receive user ID, password and users guide, call 800-FYI-3366
Child Abuse and Neglect CD-ROM (call for details to order)

Training Support:
Supervision Child Protective Services Caseworkers. #20-10059, free
Protection Children in Substance-Abuse Families. #20-10060, free
Database Products categories include: (priced from $3 to $6)
- Types of Abuse
- Causes of Abuse
- Cultural and Ethnic Factors
- Effects of Abuse
- Sexual Abuse
- Disabilities
- Legal Issues and Services

* Child Health and Development

Office of Research Reporting
National Institute of Child Health and Human Development
Building 31, Room 2A-32
31 Center Dr., MSC 2425
Bethesda, MD 20892-2425   301-496-5133

This Institute disseminates information on fetal, maternal and child development, as well as materials on reproductive biology, contraception, mental retardation, and a host of other related fields. Some of the publications include:

Facts About Childhood Hyperactivity
Facts About Down Syndrome
Facts About Dyslexia
Facts About Dysmenorrhea and Premenstrual Syndrome
Facts About Endometriosis
Facts About Oral Contraceptives
Facts About Precocious Puberty
Facts About Premature birth
Facts About Vasectomy Safety
Pregnancy Basics
Understanding Gestational Diabetes
Cesarean Childbirth
Learning Disabilities: A Report to the U.S. Congress
Centers of Excellence: The Mental Retardation Centers

* Child Health USA

Superintendent of Documents
Government Printing Office (GPO)   202-512-1800
Washington, DC 20402   Fax: 202-512-2250

Child Health USA presents information on the health of children in various developmental stages. It measures children's health accordance with the World Health Organization's vision of the well-being of children. It's divided into four sections: population characteristics; health status; health services and utilization; and state-specific data. The order number is 017-091-00244-4, and costs $2.50.

* Combined Health Information Database (CHID)

CDP Online
Attn: CHID Database
333 Seventh Ave.   800-950-2045
New York, NY 10001   212-563-3006

The Combined Health Information Database (CHID) is a computerized bibliographic database developed and managed by health-related agencies of the Federal Government that collect health information, health education and promotion materials, and other health resources. It contains references to health information and health education resources. CHID is intended to serve health professionals, health educators, patients, and the public. The database is available at most medical schools, universities, hospitals and public libraries. Individuals or companies may also subscribe directly to CDP Online. A billing subscription and password are needed to access CHID. Currently there are 25 subfiles on CHID, with more than 109,000 abstracted items. The subfiles are:

AIDS in Education
Alzheimer's Disease
Arthritis and Musculoskeletal and Skin Disease
Asthma Education
Blood Resources
Cancer Patient Education
Cancer Prevention and Control
Cholesterol, High Blood Pressure and Smoking Education
Comprehensive School Health
Deafness and Other Communication Disorders
Diabetes
Digestive Disease
Disease Prevention/Health Promotion
Epilepsy Prevention and Control
Eye Health Education
Health Promotion and Education
Heart Attach
Kidney and Urologic Diseases
Maternal and Child Health
Medical Genetics and Rare Disorders
Oral Health
Post-Traumatic Stress Disorder
Prenatal Smoking Cessation
VA Patient Health Education
Weight Control

* Communicative and Learning Disabilities

Office of Special Education and Rehabilitation Services
U.S. Department of Education
330 C St., SW, Room 3132   202-205-8241
Washington, DC 20202-2524   TDD: 202-205-8723

This office promotes improved and expanded rehabilitation services for deaf, hard of hearing, speech impaired, and language disordered individuals. As the liaison to national organizations and agencies concerned with deafness and communicative disorders, this office provides the following services: 1) they develop policies and standards for state rehabilitation agencies' work with these clients; 2) they review services to these clients by the agencies; 3) they provide technical assistance to Rehabilitation Services Administration staff; and 4) they provide information on the State-Federal rehabilitation program for communicatively impaired persons to public and private agencies, consumers and the general public.

* Consumer Affairs Center

Director of Information
Office of Consumer Affairs
U.S. Department of Health and Human Services
5600 Fishers Lane, Room 16-75
Rockville, MD 20857   301-443-5006

This bureau coordinates new consumer programs, promotes improved consumer education, and serves as the catalyst for new laws and regulations protecting the interests of American health care consumers. It publishes a useful catalog titled *Consumer's Resource Handbook* which is available free from the Consumer Information Center, P.O. Box 100, Dept. 635H, Pueblo, CO 81009. This office can refer you to the appropriate office or agency for answers to your questions.

* Deafness Clearinghouse

National Institute on Deafness and Other
  Communication Disorders Clearinghouse (NIDCD)
NIDCD Clearinghouse
1 Communication Ave.   800-241-1044
Baltimore, MD 20892   TDD: 800-241-1055

The National Institute on Deafness and Other Communication Disorders (NIDCD) has established a national clearinghouse of information and resources on the normal and disordered mechanisms of hearing, balance, smell, taste, voice, speech, and language. The Clearinghouse collects information on these seven research areas and disseminates it to health professional, patients, industry, and the public. They have access to the Combined Health Information Database (CHID), and have an extensive list of publications, including fact sheets, bibliographies, information packets, catalogs, and directories of information sources. They also publish an biannual newsletter. One of their newest directories is a directory of associations and organizations with an interest in deafness and other communication disorders. Contact the clearinghouse for more information.

* Dental Research

National Institute of Dental Research (NIDR)
National Institutes of Health
Bldg. 31, Room 2C-27
31 Center Dr., MSC 2290

Bethesda, MD 20892-2290   301-496-6621

The National Institute of Dental Research (NIDR) conducts research into the causes, prevention, diagnosis, and treatment of oral and dental diseases and conditions. They can answer questions regarding current research, and have publications, posters, and reports on a variety of dental topics. Some of the publications cover canker sores, fluoride treatment, periodontal disease, and tooth decay.

* Diabetes Information Clearinghouse

National Diabetes Information Clearinghouse (NDIC)
1 Information Way   301-654-3327
Bethesda, MD 20892-3560   Fax: 301-907-8906

The National Diabetes Information Clearinghouse (NDIC) responds to requests for information about diabetes and its complications and distributes information appropriate to health professionals, people with diabetes and their families, and the general public. They have many publications and bibliographies, as well as *Diabetes Dateline*, a free quarterly current awareness newsletter that features news about diabetes research, upcoming meetings and events, and new publications. NDIC uses the online database CHID (Combined Health Information Database) from which they can reference health information. Contact this office for a free listing of their publications or further information.

* Digestive Diseases Information Clearinghouse

National Digestive Diseases Information
  Clearinghouse (NDDIC)
2 Information Way   301-654-3810
Bethesda, MD 20892-3570   Fax: 301-907-8906

The National Digestive Diseases Information Clearinghouse (NDDIC) responds to requests for information about digestive diseases and distributes information to health professionals, people with digestive diseases, and the general public. They have many publications, as well as a news bulletin. NDDIC uses the online database CHID (Combined Health Information Database) from which they can access health information and organizations. Contact this office for a free listing of publications.

* Disease Information

Centers for Disease Control (CDC)
Information Resources Management Office
Mail Stop C-15
1600 Clifton Rd., NE
Atlanta, GA 30333   404-332-4555

The Centers for Disease Control (CDC) and the Agency for Toxic Substances and Disease Registry have developed a Voice Information System and Fax Service that allows anyone using a touchtone phone, to obtain prerecorded information on particular health issue. The materials include information about certain diseases or health areas, symptoms and prevention methods, immunization requirements, current statistics, recent disease outbreak, and available printed materials. Currently information is available on AIDS, Chronic fatigue syndrome, cytomegalovirus, encephalitis, enteric diseases, Epstein-Barr, hepatitis, Lyme disease, malaria, rabies, Vaccine-preventable disease, and yellow fever. The most complex system is for international travelers' health. The system can also transfer the caller to a public health professional for additional information. The system is available 24 hours a day, although the health professionals are available Monday-Friday 8-4:30.

* Documents on Health Programs

General Accounting Office (GAO)
P.O. Box 6015   202-512-6000
Gaithersburg, MD 20884-6015   Fax: 301-258-4066
    TDD: 301-413-0006
    Internet: info@www.gao.gov

GAO Reports: Health, Education, Employment, Social Security, Welfare, and Veterans Issues is a 42 page document available from the General Accounting Office (GAO) Document Distribution Center (GAO/HEHS-95-58W). This booklet lists GAO documents on government programs related to health, education, employment, social security, welfare, and veterans issues, which are primarily run by the Departments of Health and Human Services, labor, Education, and Veterans Affairs. One section identifies reports and testimony issued during the past month and summarizes key products. Another section lists all documents published during the past year, organized chronologically by subject. Order forms are included. A single copy of this document is free of charge, $2.00 each additional copy. Orders for 100 documents ore more to be delivered to one address are discounted 25 percent. A check or money order made out to the Superintendent of Documents should accompany orders when necessary.

* Eye and Vision Clearinghouse

National Eye Institute (NEI)
Publications Distribution Center
National Institute of Health
2020 Vision Place
Bethesda, MD 20892   301-496-5248

The National Eye Institute (NEI) conducts, fosters and supports basic and applied research, including clinical trials, related to the cause, natural history, prevention, diagnosis, and treatment of disorders of the eye and visual system. Several brochures and reports are available for the general public and health professionals on a wide variety of related topics.

* Food Additives, RX and Medical Devices Consumer Info

Office of Public Affairs
Food and Drug Administration (FDA)
5600 Fishers Lane, HFE88
Rockville, MD 20857   301-443-3170

The Food and Drug Administration (FDA) distributes many brochures and publications which cover a variety of topics, such as cosmetics, drugs, and foods. This office will gladly send you publications on topics that interest you. The *FDA Consumer*, which contains the latest developments at FDA, can be ordered for $12 per year from the Superintendent of Documents, Government Printing Office, Washington DC 20402, 202-512-1800.

* General Medical Sciences

Office of Research Reports
National Institute of General Medical Sciences (NIGMS)
National Institutes of Health (NIH)
45 Center Dr., MSC 6200   301-496-7301
Bethesda, MD 20892-6200   Fax: 301-402-0224

The National Institute of General Medical Sciences (NIGMS) has five main program areas, all of which fund grants for research projects and research training. They are: Cellular and Molecular Basis of Disease, Genetics, Pharmacology and Biorelated Chemistry, Biophysics and Physiological Sciences, and Minority Opportunities in Research. The Institute has no laboratories on the National Institutes of Health (NIH) campus, although it does sponsor a small training program in which scientists work in selected laboratories of other NIH components. With the exception of this intramural activity, the research and research training NIGMS supports takes place at universities, medical schools, hospitals, and research institutions throughout the country and abroad. The publication *The National Institute of General Medical Sciences* (94-455) is a comprehensive guide to Institute programs, mechanisms of research training and grant support, structure, and history. A publications list is also available.

* Health and Science Journals: Computerized Databases

MEDLARS Management Section
National Library of Medicine (NLM)
8600 Rockville Pike   800-638-8480
Bethesda, MD 20894   301-496-0822

MEDLARS (MEDical Literature Analysis and Retrieval System) is the computerized system of databases and databanks offered by the National Library of Medicine (NLM). A person can search the computer files either to produce a list of publications (bibliographic, citations) or to retrieve factual information on a specific question. MEDLARS databases are used by universities, medical schools, hospitals, government agencies, commercial and non-profit organizations, and private individuals. MEDLARS comprises two computer sub-systems, ELHILL and TOXNET, on which reside over 40 online databases containing about 18 million references.

ELHILL databases provide online access to information on a wide range of subjects relating to biomedicine. ELHILL databases are:

MEDLINE: is NLM's premier bibliographic database covering the fields of medicine, nursing, dentistry, veterinary medicine, and the pre-clinical sciences. The file contains about 7.8 million records.

CATLINE: 730,000 references to books and serials cataloged at NLM.

SERLINE: contains bibliographic serial titles. This file contains about 84,000 records.

AVLINE: Citations to 27,000 audiovisual teaching packages covering subject areas in the health sciences.

AIDSLINE: Bibliographic file of published literature on AIDS, focusing on the clinical and research aspects of the disease.

AIDSDRUGS: a dictionary of chemical and biological agents currently being evaluated in the AIDS clinical trials.

AIDSTRIALS: clinical trials of substances being tested for use against AIDS, HIV infection, and AIDS related opportunistic diseases.

HISTLINE: 115,000 citations to monographs, journal articles, symposia, congresses, and similar composite publications as published annually in the Bibliography of the History of Medicine.

TOXLINE: Bibliographic references covering pharmacological, biochemical, physiological, environmental, and toxicological effects of drugs and other chemicals. The file contains about 2 million records.

CHEMLINE: An online chemical dictionary with over 1,250,000 records.

HEALTH: Contains 740,000 references to literature on health planning, organization, financing, management, and manpower.

CANCERLIT: 1,000,000 references dealing with various aspects of cancer.

PDQ: Provides state-of-the-art cancer treatment and referral information.

DIRLINE: A directory of organizations providing information in specific subject areas.

SIDILINE: Contains current month's input to MEDLINE.

BIOETHICSLINE: Contains citations to documents which discuss ethical and related public policy questions arising in health care or biomedical research.

POPLINE: Provides bibliographic citations to literature on population and family planning.

DOCUSER: Contains descriptive information about libraries and other organizations which use NLM's interlibrary loan services.

NAME AUTHORITY FILE: List of over 549,000 personal names, corporate names, and decisions on how monographic series are classed.

MeSH VOCABULARY FILE: Information on 18,000 medical subject headings and 50,000 chemical substances used for indexing and retrieving references.

BIOTECHSEEK: contains bibliographic citations from 31 selectively indexed biotechnology journals not covered in MEDLINE.

HSTAR: contains journal articles, government and technical reports, letters, books, and book chapters.

TOXLIT: contains bibliographic citations on toxicological, pharmacological, biochemical, and physiological effects of drugs and other chemicals.

TOXNET (TOXicology data NETwork) is a computerized collection of files on toxicology, hazardous chemicals and related areas.

TOXNET contains the following files:

DART: Subject coverage is Teratology. Developmental and reproductive toxicology. Coverage is from 1989 - present.

EMIC: contains references to chemical, biological, and physical agents that have been tested for genotoxic activity.

EMICBACK: contains bibliographic citations on the subject of Teratology. Developmental and reproductive toxicology. Coverage is from 1950-1989.

GENE-TOX: is a multi-phase effort to review and evaluated the existing literature and assay systems available in the field of genetic toxicology.

IRIS: contains factual coverage on the subject of potentially toxic chemicals.

TRI: annual estimated releases of toxic chemicals to the environment, amounts transferred to waste sites, and source reduction and recycling data.

TRIFACTS: covers health, ecological effects, safety, and handling information for most of the chemicals listed in the TRI files.

HSDB: Contains toxicological information strengthened with additional data related to the environment, emergency situations, and regulatory issues.

CCRIS: Contains evaluated data and information derived from both short- and long-term bioassays on 1200 chemical substances.

RTECS: Contains basic acute and chronic toxicity data on more than 92,000 potentially toxic chemicals.

The National Library of Medicine has developed GRATEFUL MED which is software program that allows you to track down information in the NLM databases via a personal computer. GRATEFUL MED is available for both IBM and Macintosh computers for only $29.95. For more information about GRATEFUL MED call 800-638-8480.

* Health Assessments of Hazardous Substances

Agency for Toxic Substances and Disease Registry
1600 Clifton Rd., NE, MSE-32
Atlanta, GA 30333   404-639-0600

The Division of Health Assessment and Consultation conducts health assessments, which are written evaluations of the public health impact of hazardous substances that have been released into the environment in a specific geographic area. The general public can request that a health assessment be conducted. This Division also sponsors Citizens' Roundtables, designed to provide communities with the opportunity to express their needs and concerns. This Division also develops, implements and evaluates simulated emergencies involving hazardous substances.

* Health Care Delivery

Bureau of Primary Health Care
Health Resources and Services Administration
4350 East West Hwy.
Bethesda, MD 20814   301-594-4110

The Bureau of Primary Health Care helps assure that health care services are provided to medically underserved populations and to persons with special health care needs. The Bureau serves as a national focus for the development of primary health care delivery capacity, and for placement of health care professionals in Health Professional Shortage Areas to promote sustained sources of health services. Support for primary health care is provided primarily through Community Health Centers, Migrant Health Centers, Service for Special Populations, Services for Residents of Public Housing and the national Health Service Corps. For more information on these programs contact the office listed above.

* Health Care Highlights

National Technical Information Service (NTIS)   800-553-6847
5285 Port Royal Road   703-487-4650
Springfield, VA 22161   Fax: 703-321-8547
                                                TDD: 703-487-4639

The National Technical Information Service (NTIS) *Highlights* keep you informed of new government technologies and thousands of research and development activities. They provide an easy way to find out about more than 700 government market studies, research results, and scientific reviews. The catalog features many of the more than 1,600 titles added to the NTIS collection each week and is divided into at least 10 sub-categories for quick referencing. The catalog (#PR-745CAU) is free of charge.

* Health Data and Indexes

Clearinghouse on Health Indexes
Division of Analysis
National Center for Health Statistics
3700 East-West Highway, Room 2-27
Hyattsville, MD 20782   301-436-7035

This clearinghouse maintains a database which purports to reflect the health status of an individual or defined group. This data are designed to help planners, researchers, and administrators develop and improve health programs and strategies.

* Health Education on Toxic Substances

Agency for Toxic Substances and Disease Registry
1600 Clifton Rd., NE

Atlanta, GA 30333   404-639-0730

The Division of Health Education provides health professionals with appropriate educational materials on the health effects and medical surveillance of persons exposed to hazardous substances. Target audiences include medical associations, academic medical centers, medical schools, and schools of public health. A series of self-instructional documents called *Case Studies in Environmental Medicine* are published by this Division. Contact this office for more information.

* Healthfinder Series:
Child Health to Long-term Care

Office of Disease Prevention and Health Promotion (ODPHP)
National Health Information Center
P.O. Box 1133   800-336-4797
Washington, DC 20013-1133   301-565-4167 (in Maryland)

Healthfinder is a series of publications, each on a specific health topic. Each issue includes some general information, a list of publications available, and resources relevant to the topic. Health topics include long-term care, minority health, and federal health information centers, clearinghouses and toll-free numbers for health information.

* Health Hotlines

Specialized Information Services
National Library of Medicine (NLM)
8600 Rockville Pike
Bethesda, MD 20894   301-496-6308

Health Hotlines is a compilation of organizations with toll-free telephone numbers. Most are listed in DIRLINE, the National Library of Medicine's (NLM) Directory of Information Resources OnLINE. DIRLINE is an online database containing information on approximately 17,000 organizations. These organizations will provide information services directly to requestors. This free 85 page book lists organizations alphabetically, and by health topic, in English and in Spanish.

* Health Profession Videotapes

Division of Disadvantaged Assistance
Bureau of Health Professions
5600 Fishers Lane, Room 8-20
Rockville, MD 20857   301-443-3843

The Bureau of Health Professions has produced fourteen videos appropriate for recruitment of minorities and disadvantaged students into the health professions. The minority focus includes Blacks, American Indians, Alaskan Natives, and Hispanics, and covers a wide variety of medical professions. Contact the Bureau for more information regarding these free videos.

* Health Reports

U.S. General Accounting office (GAO)
P.O. Box 6015   202-512-6000
Gaithersburg, MD 20884-6015   Fax: 301-258-4066
    TDD: 301-413-0006
    Internet: info@www.gao.gov

Copies of reports and testimony conducted by the General Accounting Office (GAO) are available from the Document Distribution Center. The first copy of each document is free. Additional copies are $2 each. Orders should be sent to the address above, accompanied by a check or money order made out to the Superintendent of Documents, when necessary. Orders for 100 or more copies to be mailed to a single address are discounted 25 percent. Some of the reports available include:

FDA Drug Approval: Review Time Has Decreased in Recent Years, 44 pages, order #GAO/PEMD-96-1
Medical Devices: FDA Review Time 87 pages, order #GAO/PEMD-96-2
Medicare Managed Care: Growing Enrollment Adds Urgency to Fixing HMO Payment Problem, 28 pages, order #GAO/HEHS-96-21
Pharmacy Benefit Managers: Early Results on Ventures With Drug Manufacturers, 30 pages, order #GAO/HEHS-96-45
Health Care Task Force: Governmentwide Costs, 10 pages, order #GAO/GGD-96-45R
Ryan White Care Act of 1990: Opportunities to Enhance Funding Equity, 65 pages, order #GAO/HEHS-96-26
Medicare: Enrollment Growth and Payment Practices for Kidney Dialysis Services, 17 pages, order #GAO/HEHS-96-33
Fraud and Abuse: Medicare Continues to Be Vulnerable to Exploitation by Unscrupulous Providers, Testimony, 16 pages, order #GAO/HEHS-96-7
Medicare Transaction System: Strengthened Management and Sound Development Approach Critical to Success, Testimony, 15 pgs., order #GAO-T-AIMD-96-12

VA Health Care: Effects of Facility Realignment on Construction Needs Are Unknown, 42 pages, order #GAO/HEHS-96-19

* Health Resource Guide

National Heart, Lung, and Blood Institute (NHLBI)
Information Center
P.O. Box 30105   301-251-1222
Bethesda, MD 20824-0105   Fax: 301-251-1223

The National Heart, Lung, and Blood Institute (NHLBI) sponsored educational programs that transfer new scientific technologies for cardiovascular disease risk reduction from research to community settings. These cooperative programs are multidisciplinary (including biomedical science, health communications, health education, clinical practice, and community development) as well as multilateral (combining government, voluntary, and private-sector efforts). The educational materials were developed in the education programs and initiatives of the NHBLI that support health professionals in the efforts to improve the health of the general public. The NHLBI catalog provides information about more than 150 publications, posters, and other educational materials available from the NHBLI. Included among these materials is information on cardiovascular (high blood pressure, cholesterol, obesity, and heart attack), pulmonary (asthma, other pulmonary diseases, and sleep disorders), and blood diseases and resources. Also included is a section on minority programs, a calendar of national health observances, as well as a variety of indexes. There are also publication lists of items available from the Government Printing Office and the National Technical Information Service.

* Health Services Publications Catalog

Office of Public Affairs
Health Resources and Services Administration (HRSA)
5600 Fishers Lane, Room 1445
Rockville, MD 20857   301-443-2086

The Health Resources and Services Administration (HRSA) offers a free catalog, *Current Publications*, which lists all the publications films, and videos produced by HRSA's three bureaus: Bureau of Health Care Delivery and Assistance, Bureau of Maternal and Child Health and Resources Development and Bureau of Health Professions. Also available is *HRSA: A Profile*, describing HRSA Bureaus, projects, issues, and initiatives.

* Health Studies of Toxic Substances

Agency for Toxic Substances and Disease Registry
1600 Clifton Rd., NE (E-60)
Atlanta, GA 30333   404-630-0500

The Division of Health Studies conducts health studies which evaluate the heath effects of human exposure to hazardous substances. This Division maintains the National Exposure Registry is comprised of chemical-specific subregistries designed to aid in assessing the long-term health consequences of low-level, long-term exposures to hazardous chemicals identifies at Superfund sites. A National Disease Registry is in the works.

* Healthy People

Office of Disease Prevention and Health Promotion (ODPHP)
National Health Information Center
P.O. Box 1133   800-336-4797
Washington, DC 20013-1133   301-565-4167

Healthy People 2000: National Health Promotion and Disease Prevention Objectives (B0024, $4) is a report which sets national goals for the decade to increase the span of healthy life for Americans, reduce health disparities, and achieve access to preventive services for all Americans. Goals are supported by 300 specific health objectives, in 22 priority areas, to be achieved by the year 2000.

Healthy People 2000: Midcourse Review and Revisions (B0053, $5). Reviews the progress toward the three goals of Healthy People 2000. The report includes a chapter on state and consortium organization action. A Summary List of Objectives reflects new objectives, new special population targets, revised language, and new targets.

Healthy People 2000: Face Sheet (B0034, free). Describes the Healthy People 2000 initiative and highlights key activities and publications.

Health People: The Surgeon General's Report on Health Promotion and Disease Prevention (F0005, $3). Sets out a national program for improving the health of Americans and lists five public health goals that are measurable and achievable.

Be patient. If any phone number is incorrect, call (area code) 555-1212 and request the new listing.

503

Health and Medicine

Health People 2000: Turning Commitment Into Action (B0049, $1). Provides new and continuing members of the Healthy People 2000 Consortium with activity ideas for embracing the Healthy People 2000 objectives.

* Healthy People 2000: Resource Lists

Office of Disease Prevention and Health Promotion
National Health Information Center
P.O. Box 1133   800-336-4797
Washington, DC 20013-1133   301-565-4167

This provides sources of Information related to each of the 22 priority areas. Each 2-page list offers a summary of the objectives and federal, private, state, and local resources. Each resource list is $1, or $3 for the full set.

The areas are:
Physical Activity and Fitness (B0001)
Nutrition (B0002)
Tobacco (B0003)
Alcohol and Other Drugs (B0004)
Family Planning (B0005)
Mental Health and Mental Disorders (B0006)
Violent and Abusive Behavior (B0007)
Educational and Community-Based Programs (B0008)
Unintentional Injuries (B0009)
Occupational Safety and Health (B0010)
Environmental Health (B0011)
Food and Drug Safety (B0012)
Oral Health (B0013)
Maternal and Infant Health (B0014)
Heart Disease and Stroke (B0015)
Cancer (B0016)
Diabetes and Chronic Disabling Conditions (B0017)
HIV Infection (B0018)
Sexually Transmitted Diseases (B0019)
Immunization and Infectious Diseases (B0020)
Clinical Preventive Services (B0021)
Surveillance and Data Systems (B0022)
Full Set (B0023)

* Healthy Start

Healthy Start Program Office
Health Resources and Services Administration
5600 Fishers Lane, Room 11A05
Rockville, MD 20857   301-443-0543

The Healthy Start Program is a Presidential initiative to reduce infant mortality through additional support for comprehensive service delivery in 15 high-risk communities, with the goal of reducing infant mortality by 50% over five years. The Office has put together an information packet, which includes some background information and a listing of grantees (including a breakdown of features and contact people).

* Heart Health Information Line

National Heart, Lung, and Blood Institute (NHLBI)
Information Center
P.O. Box 30105
Bethesda, MD 20824-0105   800-575-WELL

The Information Line on Heart Health gives recorded messages in English and Spanish about how to prevent and treat high blood pressure and high blood cholesterol. It is part of a nationwide campaign to help Americans reduce the risk of heart disease and stroke. Publications cannot be ordered from this number. For publications call 301-251-1222.

* Heart, Lung, and Blood Disease Clearinghouse

National Heart, Lung and Blood Institute
Building 31, Room 4A-21
3100 Center Dr., MSC 2840
Bethesda, MD 20892-2840   301-496-4236

The Institute oversees the scientific investigation, prevention, and control of heart, blood vessel, lung, and blood diseases. The program emphasizes education concerning these diseases through a more rapid transfer of information into the mainstream of clinical medicine and personal health practices. Many publications are available for professionals and the general public on a wide variety of topics.

* Home Health Care and Hospice Resources

Office of Disease Prevention and Health Promotion (ODPHP)
National Health Information Center
P.O. Box 1133   800-336-4797
Washington, DC 20013-1133   301-565-4167 in MD

In its series called "Healthfinder", the center publishes an 8-page bulletin titled *Long Term Care* (A0028, $1) which lists organizations, self-help and support groups, as well as books about home care for the chronically or terminally ill or the disabled child or aging parent. Suggested resources for preparing for death such as living wills and organ or tissue donation are included in this "Healthfinder."

* Injury Information Clearinghouse

National Injury Information Clearinghouse
Consumer Product Safety Commission
5401 Westbard Avenue, Room 625   301-504-0424
Washington, DC 20207   Fax: 301-504-0124

This clearinghouse gathers, investigates, analyzes, and disseminates injury data relating to the causes and prevention of death, injury, and illness associated with consumer products. Use this information center to tap into the National Electronic Injury Surveillance System (NEISS) which selected hospital emergency rooms contribute case reports on product-related injuries.

* Laser Surgery Referral Network

Office of Disease Prevention and Health Promotion (ODPHP)
National Health Information Center
P.O. Box 1133   800-336-4797
Washington, DC 20013-1133   301-565-4167 in DC

This center can provide you with names of organizations and agencies involved with laser surgery, which can then refer you to experts in the field.

* Lead Poisoning Prevention

National Maternal and Child Health Clearinghouse
2070 Chain Bridge Rd.
Vienna, VA 22182   703-821-8955

Manual for the Identification and Abatement of Environmental Lead Hazards, is a free publication available from the clearinghouse.

* Medical Films and Videos

National Library of Medicine (NLM)
8600 Rockville Pike
Bethesda, MD 20894   800-272-4787

The National Library of Medicine's (NLM) audiovisual collection consists of approximately 24,000 titles in a variety of formats including videocassettes, audiocassettes, 16mm films, filmstrips and slides, and some 3,000 audiovisuals of historical interest. Most audiovisuals are in core biomedical subjects and are in English. The audiovisual titles in the NLM collection are available online through AVLINE, and in printed catalogue form in the NLM Audiovisuals Catalog. AVLINE is one of a number of databases on NLM's MEDLARS computer system. MEDLARS is accessed by universities, medical schools, hospitals, government agencies, and private individuals. Audiovisuals may be borrowed through the interlibrary loan service by requesting items through your local libraries. Libraries should send requests to local sources, and send requests to NLM only for those titles not held in their regions. Contact NLM for more information regarding their audiovisual services and their catalog.

* Medicine for the Public

Office of Clinical Center Communications
National Institutes of Health
Building 10, Room 1C255
Bethesda, MD 20892   301-496-2563

The Clinical Center has developed a *Medicine for the Public* series which is designed to provide information to facilitate intelligent decisions, and includes free booklets and videotapes on a variety of topics. The booklets include:

Allergic Diseases
Alzheimer's Disease
Behavior Patterns and Health
Brain in Aging and Dementia
Cancer Treatment
Chronic Fatigue Syndrome
Diabetes in Adults

Drugs and the Brain
Food and Allergy Intolerances
Genetics of Cancer
Herpes
Hyperactivity
Multiple Sclerosis
Osteoporosis
Radiation Risks and Radiation Therapy
Risks of Heart Disease
Sickle Cell Anemia
Stroke Update
Sexually Transmitted Diseases

* Mental Health Clearinghouse

National Institute of Mental Health (NIMH)   301-443-4513
5600 Fishers Lane, Room 7C-02   Fax: 301-443-0008
Rockville, MD 20857   TDD: 301-443-8431

The National Institute of Mental Health (NIMH) conducts research on mental disorders and mental health services, distributes information, conducts demonstration programs for the prevention, treatment, and rehabilitation of the mentally ill. Research focuses on the biological, psychological, epidemiological, and social science aspects of mental health and illness. NIMH collaborates with other organizations to promote effective mental health programs and provides technical assistance.

* Mental Retardation

President's Committee on Mental Retardation
330 Independence Ave., SW, Room 5325
Washington, DC 20201   202-619-0634

More than six million Americans of all ages experience mental retardation. The President's Committee on Mental Retardation was established to focus on a single area of national concern- mental retardation. Some of the areas covered include full citizenship, prevention, family and community services, and public awareness. The Committee also conducts public forums and publishes numerous documents in the field.

* Minorities and Blacks Health Coordinator

Office of Minority Health
U.S. Department of Health and Human Services
Rockwall II Bldg.
5600 Fishers Lane   301-443-5224
Rockville, MD 20857   Fax: 301-443-8280

This office monitors community-based projects designed to reduce over 60,000 excess deaths each year among minority Americans and develops recommendations for health strategies and research on risk factors affecting these populations.

* Minority Health Care

Office of Disease Prevention and Health Promotion (ODPHP)
National Health Information Center
P.O. Box 1133   800-336-4797
Washington, DC 20013-1133   301-565-4167

Minority Health Care is part of the Healthfinder series, and is designed as a resource list of materials that can be used in support of the health education process. Providing information about the symptoms of diseases, the link between lifestyle and diseases, and the importance of early detection and treatment is a necessary component of any health communication program. The *Healthfinder* includes materials aimed specifically at minority audiences, with some in other languages. They cover the six minority health areas and AIDS (A0025, $1).

* Minority Health Clearinghouse

Office of Minority Health Resource Center (OMH)   800-444-6472
P.O. Box 37337   Fax: 301-589-0884
Washington, DC 20013   TDD: 301-589-0951

The Office of Minority Health (OMH) mission is to improve the health status of Asians, Pacific Islanders, Blacks, Hispanics, and Native Americans. Major activities include the dissemination of accurate and timely information regarding health care issues and status through conferences and workshops, awarding of grants for innovative community health strategies developed by minority coalitions, and research on risk factors affecting minority health. The Resource Center has information on minority health-related data and information resources available at the Federal, State, and local levels and provides assistance and information to people interested in minority health and minority health programs. A strategy guide was

developed on methods of achieving the minority health goals. They have prepared "Closing the Gap," a series of fact sheets on the priority areas that describe the extent to which specific minority groups are affected, detail avenues for prevention, and offer resources for additional information. They have a database of minority health-related publications, organizations and programs that concentrate on minority health. The Resource Persons Network consists of more than 2200 physicians, nurses, social workers, and health educators who provide expert technical assistance to minority community-based organizations, voluntary groups, and individuals needing assistance. Publications available include:

Pocket Guide to Minority Health Resources
Closing the Gap Newsletter
Child Health Guide
Health Education

* National Health Information Center

Office of Disease Prevention and Health Promotion (ODPHP)
National Health Information Center
P.O. Box 1133   301-565-4167 in MD
Washington, DC 20013-1133   800-336-4797

This center should be the initial phone call because it can direct you to more specialized clearinghouses as well as health organizations and foundations. The National Health Information Center, through its resource files and database (DIRLINE), responds to questions regarding health concerns and can send publications, bibliographies, and other material. A library focusing on health topics is open to the public, and the Center also produces many different directories, and resource guides, which are available for a minimal cost. A publications catalog is free of charge. Two of the publications include a list of Selected Federal Health Information Clearinghouses and Information Centers and Toll-free Numbers for Health Information.

* Native Americans Health Services

Indian Health Service
Office of Communications
5600 Fishers Lane, Room 6-35
Rockville, MD 20857   301-443-3593

The goal of the Indian Health Service (IHS) is to raise the health level of American Indians and Alaskan Natives to the highest possible level. IHS accomplishes this by providing a comprehensive health services delivery system, which includes hospital and ambulatory medical care, preventive and rehabilitative services, and community environmental health programs, among them the construction of water and sanitation facilities for more than one million American Indians and Alaskan Natives. The program offers maximum opportunity for tribal involvement in developing these and other programs to meet their health needs. IHS operates 43 hospitals, 71 health centers, and more than 100 smaller health stations and satellite clinics. Indian tribes may contract with IHS to operate their own health care facilities and programs.

* Neighborhood Medical Libraries Throughout the U.S.

The national network of libraries of medicine will automatically direct your call to the medical library near you by dialing 800-338-7658.

Middle Atlantic Regional Medical Library Program, The New York Academy of Medicine, 1216 Fifth Ave., New York, NY 10029; 212-876-8763, Fax: 212-534-7042. States served: Delaware, New Jersey, New York, and Pennsylvania.

South Atlantic Regional Medical Library Service, University of Maryland Health Sciences Library, 111 South Greene St., Baltimore, MD 21201-1583; 310-706-2855, Fax: 410-706-0099. States served: Alabama, Florida, Georgia, Maryland, Mississippi, North Carolina, South Carolina, Tennessee, Virginia, West Virginia, District of Columbia, and Virgin Islands.

Greater Midwest Regional Medical Library Network, University of Illinois at Chicago, Library of Health Sciences, (M/C 763), 1750 W. Polk St., Chicago, IL 60612-7223; 312-996-2464, Fax: 312-996-2226. States served: Iowa, Illinois, Indiana, Kentucky, Michigan, Minnesota, North Dakota, Ohio, South Dakota, and Wisconsin.

Midcontinental Regional Medical Library Program, University of Nebraska, Medical Center Leon S. McGoogan Library of Medicine, 600 S. 42nd St., Omaha, NE 68198-6706; 402-559-4326, Fax: 402-559-5482. States served: Colorado, Kansas, Missouri, Nebraska, Utah, and Wyoming.

Pacific Northwest Regional Health Sciences Library Service, Health Sciences Library and Information Center, University of Washington, Box 357155, Seattle, WA 98195-

Health and Medicine

7155; 206-543-8262, Fax: 206-543-2469. States served: Alaska, Idaho, Montana, Oregon, and Washington.

Pacific Southwest Regional Medical Library Service, Louise Darling Biomedical Library, University of California, 12-077 Center for Health Sciences, Los Angeles, CA 90095-1798; 310-825-1200, Fax: 310-825-5389. States served: Arizona, California, Hawaii, Nevada, and U.S. Territories in the Pacific Basin.

South Central Regional Medical Library Service, Houston Academy of Medicine, Texas Medical Center Library, 1133 M.D. Anderson Blvd., Houston, TX 77030-2809; 713-790-7053, Fax: 713-790-7030. States served: Arkansas, Louisiana, New Mexico, Oklahoma, and Texas.

New England Regional Medical Library, University of Connecticut Health Center, Lyman Maynard Stowe Library, 263 Farmington Ave., Farmington, CT 06034-4003; 203-679-4500, Fax: 203-679-1305. States served: Connecticut, Maine, Massachusetts, New Hampshire, Rhode Island, and Vermont.

* Nursing Research

National Institute for Nursing Research
National Institutes of Health
Bldg. 31, Room 5B13
31 Center Dr., MSC 2178
Bethesda, MD 20892-2178   301-496-0207

This Center supports research and research training related to promoting health and preventing disease, understanding and mitigating the effects of acute and chronic illnesses and disabilities, and improving patient care as well as the environment in which it is delivered.

* Occupational Health Clearinghouse

Technical Information Branch
National Institute for Occupational Safety and Health Information
4676 Columbia Parkway, Mail Stop C-13
Cincinnati, OH 45226-1998
Technical Info: 800-35-NIOSH; 513-533-8328
                                              Fax: 513-533-8573
Library: 513-533-8321

This center serves as a clearinghouse on occupational health, hazardous substances, and safety. Much of their information is available through interlibrary loans and online databases.

* Organ Transplantation

Division of Organ Transplantation
Bureau of Health Resources Development
Health Resources and Services Administration
5600 Fishers Lane, Room 11A-22
Rockville, MD 20857   301-443-7577

This Division conducts a program to foster relationships with public and private organizations to promote the concepts of organ donation and transplantation. The program provides information to professional associations, health providers, consumers and insurers, medical societies, State health departments, and the general public. The Program also supports the National Organ Procurement and Transplantation Network, designed to ensure equitable distribution of available organs to patients and transplant centers, and a Scientific Registry of demographic and clinical information on transplant recipients. An annual report, information on the Transplantation Network, a fact sheet on organ transplantation, and a Q&A publication are available.

* Practitioner Helpline

Bureau of Health Professions
Health Resources and Services Administration
P.O. Box 10832   800-767-6732
Chantilly, VA 22021   Fax: 703-802-4109

The National Practitioners Data Bank (NPDB) is a federally sponsored data bank containing information on all disciplinary actions and malpractice claims or actions against licensed health practitioners. The purpose of the NPDB is to contribute to the improvement of the quality of health care by restricting the ability of incompetent and unethical practitioners to move from State to State without disclosure or discovery of their previous poor performance. Insurance companies and other entities must report to the NPDB any payment they make on medical malpractice actions or claims. State medical and dental boards must report any disciplinary actions taken. Health Care entities must report decisions which adversely affect, for more than 30

days, the clinical privileges of the physician or dentist. Professional societies must report adverse actions regarding membership of physicians and dentists. This information is available to State licensing agencies, hospitals, and health care entities.

* Primary Care Information

Project Director
National Clearinghouse for Primary Care Information
2070 Chain Bridge Rd., Suite 450
Vienna, VA 22182   703-821-8955, x248

This center distributes materials on ambulatory care, financial management, primary health care, medical personnel and services primarily to health professionals as well as publications on community health centers, migrant health centers, childhood injury prevention efforts, clinical care and many other health concerns.

* Publications

Office of Disease Prevention and Health Promotion (ODPHP)
National Health Information Center
P.O. Box 1133   800-336-4797
Washington, DC 20013-1133   301-565-4167 in MD

The Office of Disease Prevention and Health Promotion (ODPHP) of the U.S. Public Health Service makes available single copies free of *Publications List* with an order form which describes publications under categories such as: Community Health Promotion; School Health; Worksite Health Promotion; Nutrition; Public Health Initiatives; Clinical Preventive Services; and Electronic Publications.

* Publications from all NIH Institutes

Public Information Division
National Institute of Health (NIH)
Bldg. 31, Room 2B03
Bethesda, MD 20892   301-496-4143

The *NIH Publications List* (#94-7) is a free catalog which lists the publications available from each of the Institutes, as well as their addresses and phone numbers.

* Rehabilitation and Prosthetics

National Center for Medical Rehabilitation Research
Executive Bldg., Room 2A03
6100 Executive Blvd., MSC 7510
Bethesda, MD 20892-7510   301-402-2242

This new Center will support and conduct research in restoring, replacing, or improving functional capability lost as a consequence of injury, disease, or congenital disorder; support research training programs; and foster research in assistive devices such as prosthetics and orthotics. Currently the Center is assessing the current status of medical rehabilitation, identifying medical rehabilitation research issues and opportunities, and recommending program priorities.

* Rehabilitation Resource Center

National Rehabilitation Information Center
8455 Colesville Road, Suite 935   301-588-9284 (MD only)
Silver Spring, MD 20910-3319   800-346-2742 (voice and TDD)
                                             Fax: 301-587-1967

This clearinghouse provides information on disability-related research, resources, and products for independent living as well as facts sheets, resource guides, and research and technical publications, newsletter, and a data base.

* Research Resources

Office of Science and Health Reports
National Center for Research Resources
National Institutes of Health
1 Rockledge Center
6705 Rockledge Dr.
Bethesda, MD 20892   301-435-0888

The National Center for Research Resources provides to scientists the resources and services essential to studies of the treatment, cure and prevention of human diseases. It awards grants to develop and maintain shared research resources, and maintains General Clinical Research Centers where scientist study patients in order to diagnose and treat disease. Its Animal Resources Program supports a variety of animal research facilities and resources. They publish several research resources directories and guidelines, as well as information regarding the research centers. Some of their publications include:

Research Resources Reporter - monthly newsletter.

NCRR Program Highlights - annual report.

NCRR General Clinical Research Centers Directory - contains information about the centers, staffs, resources and major areas of investigation.

NCRR Biomedical Research Technology Resources Directory - lists resource center, staffs, resources, and major areas of investigation.

NCRR Resources for Comparative Biomedical Research Directory - contains information about specialized animal research and supply facilities, staffs, types of resources, and major areas of research.

* School Health

Office of Disease Prevention and Health Promotion (ODPHP)
National Health Information Center
P.O. Box 1133   800-336-4797
Washington, DC 20013-1133   301-565-4167
The Clearinghouse has many publications dealing with health issues in schools, including the following:

Healthy Schools: A Directory of Federal Activities Related to Health Promotion through the Schools (S0018, $4) - presents information on activities of all Federal departments including contact information and brief program descriptions.

Evaluating Educational Outcomes of School Health Programs (S0020, $3) - provides an overview of eight general types of school health intervention, reviews measures of school performances and primary data sources, and describes three major evaluation design options.

School Health - Findings From Evaluated Programs (S0019, $3) - presents a sampling of school health programs that have been evaluated.

How Healthy Is Your School? ($12)- provides blueprint for assessing, planning, and implementing quality school health services, environment, and health education programs.

Promoting Health Education in Schools: Problems and Solutions ($13.95)- presents an informative overview of the critical issues involved in providing health education and health promotion through the schools.

* Sleep Disorders

National Heart, Lung, and Blood Institute Information Center
P.O. Box 30105   301-251-1222
Bethesda, MD 20824-0105   Fax: 251-1223
The Center on Sleep Disorders Research seeks to improve the health of Americans by supporting and conducting research, scientist training, and education about sleep disorders. It is also responsible for coordinating sleep research activities with other federal agencies and with public and non-profit organizations. Material available from the Center include:

Breathing Disorders During Sleep. This booklet reviews some of the more than 70 sleep-related breathing disorders and the associated health effects, such as high blood pressure, irregular heart rhythm, and heart attack. (94-2966)

National Center on Sleep Disorders Research. This brochure describes the mission and goals of the national center, created to foster research on disorders such as sleep apnea, narcolepsy, and insomnia. (55-613)

Strategy Development Workshop on Sleep Education-Summary Report. This report summarizes presentations made at a two day workshop held in June 1994. (95-3800)

* Spanish Language Health Information Materials

Office of Disease Prevention and Health Promotion (ODPHP)
National Health Information Center
P.O. Box 1133   800-336-4797
Washington, DC 20013-1133   301-565-4167
Spanish Language Health Information Materials (A0011, $1) is part of the Healthfinder series and is a guide to a number of public and private agencies and organizations that produce or distribute free or low-cost Spanish language health promotion materials. Entries are arranged alphabetically by health topics.

* Speech and Language Disorders Clearinghouse

National Institute on Deafness and
Other Communicative Disorders
National Institutes of Health (NIH)   301-496-7243
Building 31, Room 3C-35   Fax: 301-402-0018
Bethesda, MD 20892   TDD: 301-402-0252
This Institute funds intramural and extramural research on communicative disorders. Brochures and reports are available for professionals and the general public, covering a wide range of related topics.

* Sports Medicine and Orthopedics Clearinghouse

Musculoskeletal Diseases Program
National Institute of Arthritis and Musculoskeletal
and Skin Diseases   301-495-4484
1 AMS Circle   Fax: 301-587-4352
Bethesda, MD 20205   TDD: 301-565-2966
This program focuses on orthopedic research, which includes sports medicine, growth and development of bone and bone cells, as well as head injury. Staff can answer questions regarding current research and treatment issues. Brochures and pamphlets are available through the National Institute of Arthritis and Musculoskeletal and Skin Diseases.

* Stroke and Brain Disorders Resource Center

National Institute of Neurological Disorders
and Stroke (NINDS)
National Institutes of Health   800-352-9424
P.O. Box 5801   301-496-5751
Bethesda, MD 20892   Fax: 301-402-2186
The National Institute of Neurological Disorders and Stroke (NINDS) conducts and guides research on the causes, prevention, diagnosis, and treatment of fundamental neurological disorders and stroke and trauma. The Institute gives grants for extramural research, as well as providing fellowships. Other areas of research include cerebral palsy, autism, dyslexia, multiple sclerosis, Parkinson's and Huntington's diseases, and epilepsy. Brochures and pamphlets are available.

* Technology Assessment Reports

National Technical Information Service
U.S. Department of Commerce   800-553-6847
5285 Port Royal Rd.   703-487-4650
Springfield, VA 22161   Fax: 703-321-8547
                                                       TDD: 703-487-4639
These publications from the former Office of Technology Assessment (OTA) are available through the National Technical Information Service (NTIS). To find out correct ordering information and prices, along with brief summaries of the following studies, contact NTIS.

The Office of Technology Assessment (OTA) published hundreds of reports dealing with health topics. These titles include:
AIDS and Health Insurance: An OTA Survey PB88-170204
Artificial Insemination: Practicing in the United States PB89-139903
Confused Minds, Burdened Families: Finding Help for People With Alzheimer's and Other Dementias PB85-204451
Contact Lenses PB85-204451
How Effective is AIDS Education PB88-243530
Indian Health Care PB86-206091
Losing a Million Minds: Confronting the Tragedy of Alzheimer's Disease and Other Dementias PB87-183752
Neonatal Intensive Care for Low Birthweight Infants: Costs and Effectiveness PB88-158902
Passive Smoking in the Workplace: Selected Issues PB86-217627
Preventing Illness and Injury in the Workplace PB86-115334
Reproductive Health Hazards in the Workplace PB86-185030
Technology and Aging in America PB86-116514
The Use of Preventive Services by the Elderly PB91-192880
Unconventional Cancer Treatments PB91-104893

Biological Applications
Alternatives to Animal Use In Research, Testing, and Education PB88-183134
Artificial Insemination: Practice in the United States PB89-139903
Assessment of Technologies for Determining Cancer Risk From the Environment PB81-235400

Health and Medicine

* Toll-Free Health Hotlines

ADCARE Hospital Helpline
800-ALCOHOL

Aerobics and Fitness Foundation of America
800-YOUR-BODY; 800-446-2322

Agency for Health Care Policy and Research Clearinghouse
800-358-9295

AIDS Clinical Trials Information Service
800-874-2572
800-243-7012 TDD

Al-Anon Family Group Headquarters
800-356-9996

Alcohol and Drug Helpline
800-821-4357

Alzheimer's Association
800-272-3900

Alzheimer's Association Information Referral Service
800-621-0379

Alzheimer's Disease Education and Referral Center
800-438-4380

AMC Cancer Information Hotline
800-525-3777

American Academy of Allergy and Immunology
800-822-2762

American Academy of Husband-Coached Childbirth
800-4A-BIRTH

American Association of Kidney Patients
800-749-2257

American Board of Medical Specialties
800-776-2378

American Cancer Society Response Line
800-227-2345

American Council of the Blind
800-424-8666

American Council on Alcoholism
800-527-5344

American Diabetes Association
800-232-3472; 800-DIABETES

American Dietetic Association's Consumer Nutrition Hotline
800-366-1655

American Foundation for the Blind
800-232-5463

American Foundation for Urologic Disease
800-242-2383

American Heart Association
800-242-8721

American Heart Association Stroke Connection
800-553-6321

American Institute for Cancer Research
800-843-8114

American Kidney Fund
800-638-8299

American Leprosy Missions (Hansen's Disease)
800-543-3131

American Liver Foundation
800-223-0179

American Lupus Society, The
800-331-1802

American Paralysis Association
800-225-0292

American Parkinson's Disease Association
800-223-2732

American SIDS Institute
800-232-7437
800-847-7437

American Society for Dermatologic Surgery, Inc.
800-441-2737

American Society of Plastic Reconstructive Surgeons, Inc.
800-635-0635

American Speech-Language-Hearing Association
800-638-8255

American Trauma Society
800-556-7890

Amyotrophic Lateral Sclerosis Association
800-782-4747

Ankylosing Spondylitis Association
800-777-8189

Arthritis Foundation Information Hotline
800-283-7800

ASPO/Lamaze
800-368-4404

Asthma and Allergy Foundation of America
800-7-ASTHMA

Asthma Information Line
800-822-2762

Batten Disease Support
800-448-4570

Bethany Christian Services
800-238-4269

Blind Children's Center
800-222-3566
800-222-3567

Boys Town National Hotline
800-448-3000
800-448-1833 TDD

Cancer Information Service
800-4-CANCER

Centers for Disease Control (CDC) National AIDS Clearinghouse
800-458-5231
800-243-7012 TDD

Centers for Disease Control (CDC) National AIDS Hotline
800-342-2467
800-344-7432
800-243-7889 TDD

Centers for Disease Control (CDC) National STD Hotline
800-227-8922

Chemtrec Non-Emergency Services Hotline
800-262-8200

Child Find of America, Inc.
800-426-5678
800-292-9688

CHILDHELP/IOF Foresters National Child Abuse Hotline
800-4-A-CHILD
800-2-A-CHILD TDD

Children's Hospice International
800-242-4453

Cleft Palate Foundation
800-242-5338

Cooley's Anemia Foundation
800-522-7222

Covenant House Nineline
800-999-9999
800-999-9915 TDD

Cornelia de Lange Syndrome Foundation
800-223-8255

Crohn's and Colitis Foundation of America, Inc.
800-932-2423

Crohn's Foundation
800-343-3637

CSAP Drug-Free Workplace Helpline
800-843-4971

CSAP's National Clearinghouse for Alcohol and Drug Information
800-729-6686; 800-487-4889 TTY/TDD

CSAT's National Drug Information Treatment and Referral Hotline
800-662-HELP (English)
800-66-AYUDA (Spanish)
800-228-0427 TDD

Cystic Fibrosis Foundation
800-344-4823

Deafness Research Foundation
800-535-3323

Depression Awareness, Recognition, and Treatment (D/ART)
800-421-4211

Dial A Hearing Screening Test
800-222-3277

Ear Foundation at Baptist Hospital, The
800-545-4327

Endometriosis Association
800-992-3636

Epilepsy Foundation of America
800-332-1000

Facial Plastic Surgery Information Service
800-332-3223

Family Violence Prevention Fund
800-313-1310

Food Labeling Hotline, Meat and Poultry Hotline
800-535-4555

Grief Recovery Hotline
800-445-4808

Guide Dog Foundation for the Blind, Inc.
800-548-4337

Handicapped Media, Inc.
800-321-8708 Voice/TDD

Health Insurance Association of America
800-635-1271

Health Resource Center
800-544-3284

Hear Now
800-648-4327 Voice/TDD

Hearing HelpLine
800-EAR-WELL

Hill-Burton Hospital Free Care
800-638-0742; 800-492-0359

Histiocytosis Association
800-548-2758

Hospice Education Institute "Hospice Link"
800-331-1620

Be patient. If any phone number is incorrect, call (area code) 555-1212 and request the new listing.

509

Housing and Urban Development User
800-245-2691

HUD Drug Information and Strategy Clearinghouse
800-578-3472

Human Growth Foundation
800-451-6434

Huntington's Disease Society of America
800-345-4372

Impotence Information Center
800-843-4315
800-543-9632

Indoor Air Quality Information Clearinghouse
800-438-4318

Internal Revenue Service for TDD Users
800-829-4059 TDD

International Childbirth Education Association
800-624-4934

International Childbirth Education Association
800-624-4934

International Hearing Society
800-521-5247

Job Accommodation Network
800-ADA-WORK
800-526-7234 Voice TDD

John Tracy Clinic
800-522-4582

Joseph and Rose Kennedy Institute of Ethics
800-633-3849

"Just Say No" International
800-258-2766

Juvenile Diabetes Foundation International Hotline
800-223-1138

La Leche League International
800-LA-LECHE

Liberty Godparent Home
800-542-4453

Lighthouse National Center for Vision and Aging, The
800-334-5497

Living Bank, The
800-528-2971

Louisiana Center for the Blind
800-234-4166

Lung Line National Jewish Center for Immunology and Respiratory Medicine
800-222-5864; 800-552-LUNG (LUNG FACTS)

Lupus Foundation of America
800-558-0121

MedicAlert Foundation
800-432-5378

Medical Rehabilitation Education Foundation
800-GET-REHAB

Medicare Telephone Hotline
800-638-6833

Meniere's Network
800-545-4327

Modern Talking Picture Service, Inc. Captioned Films/Videos
800-237-6213

Myasthenia Gravis Foundation
800-541-5454

National Adoption Center
800-TO-ADOPT

National Association for the Education of Young Children
800-424-2460

National Association for Parents of the Visually Impaired
800-562-6265

National Audiovisual Center
800-788-6282

National Center for Sight
800-221-3004

National Center for Stuttering
800-221-2483

National Center for Youth with Disabilities
800-333-6293

National Child Safety Council Childwatch
800-222-1464

National Clearinghouse on Child Abuse and Neglect Information
800-394-3366

National Clearinghouse on Family Support and Children's Mental Health
800-628-1696

National Cocaine Hotline
800-262-2463

National Council on Aging
800-424-9046

National Council on Alcoholism and Drug Dependence, Inc.
800-622-2255

National Criminal Justice Reference Service
800-851-3420

National Dairy Council
800-426-8271

National Down Syndrome Society Hotline
800-221-4602

National Easter Seal Society
800-221-6847

Be patient. If any phone number is incorrect, call (area code) 555-1212 and request the new listing.

National Eye Care Project Helpline
800-222-EYES

National Eye Research Foundation
800-621-2258

National Eye Research Foundation's Memorial Eye Clinic, The
800-621-2258

National Federation of the Blind: Job Opportunities for the Blind
800-638-7518

National Fire Protection Association
800-344-3555

National Foundation for Depressive Illness
800-248-4344

National Headache Foundation
800-843-2256

National Head Injury Foundation Family Helpline
800-444-6443

National Health Information Center
800-336-4797

National Hearing Aid Helpline
800-521-5247

National Highway Traffic Safety Administration Auto Safety Hotline
800-424-9393

National Hotline for Missing Children
800-843-5678

National Information Center for Children and Youth With Disabilities
800-695-0285

National Information Clearinghouse for Infants With Disabilities and Life Threatening Conditions
800-922-9234 ext. 201

National Information Center for Orphan Drugs and Rare Diseases
800-300-7469

National Information System for Health Related Services
800-922-9234

National Information system for Vietnam Veterans and their Families
800-922-9234 ext. 401 Voice/TDD

National Indian AIDS Hotline
800-283-2437

National Institute for Occupational Safety and Health Technical Information Branch
800-356-4674

National Institute on Aging Information Center
800-222-2225

National Institute on Deafness and Other Communication Disorders Information Clearinghouse
800-241-1044; 800-241-1055 TT

National Insurance Consumer Helpline
800-942-4242

National Kidney Foundation
800-622-9010

National Lead Information Hotline (EPA)
800-532-3394

National Lead Information Hotline
800-LEAD-FYI (Hotline)
800-424-LEAD (Clearinghouse)
800-526-5456 TDD

National Library of Medicine
800-272-4787

National Library Service for the Blind and Physically Handicapped
800-424-8567

National Lymphedema Network
800-541-3259

National Marrow Donor Program
800-MARROW-2

National Mental Health Association
800-969-6642

National Mental Health Fund Directory
800-433-5959

National Multiple Sclerosis Society
800-FIGHT-MS

National Neurofibromatosis Foundation
800-323-7938

National Organization for Rare Disorders
800-999-6673

National Parkinson Foundation, Inc.
800-327-4545; 800-433-7022

National Pesticide Telecommunications Network
800-858-7378

National Radon Hotline (EPA)
800-SOS-RADON

National Rehabilitation Information Center
800-346-2742

National Resource Center on Child Abuse and Neglect
800-227-5242

National Resource Center on Homelessness and Mental Illness
800-444-7415

National Retinitis Pigmentosa Foundation
800-638-2300

National Reye's Syndrome Foundation
800-233-7393

Health and Medicine

National Runaway Switchboard
800-621-4000
800-621-0394 TDD

National Safety Council
800-621-7619

National Spinal Cord Injury Association
800-962-9629

National Spinal Cord Injury Hotline
800-526-3456

National Stroke Association
800-STROKES

National Tuberous Sclerosis Association
800-225-6872

National Youth Crisis Hotline
800-448-4663

Office of Minority Health Resource Center
800-444-6472

Orton Dyslexia Society, The
800-222-3123

Panic Disorder Information Line
800-64-PANIC

Parkinson's Educational Program
800-344-7872

Planned Parenthood
800-230-PLAN; 800-669-0156

PMS Access
800-222-4767

Prevent Blindness Center for Sight
800-331-2020

Project Inform HIV/AIDS Treatment Hotline
800-822-7422

Public Health Service AIDS Information Hotline
800-32-AIDS
800-344-7432 (Spanish)

Radon Hotline
800-SOS-RADON
800-526-5456 TDD

Recording for the Blind
800-221-4792

RP Foundation Fighting Blindness
800-683-5555
800-683-551 TDD

Runaway Hotline
800-231-6946

Rural Information Center Health Service
800-633-7701

Safe Drinking Water Hotline
800-426-4791

Sarcoidosis Family Aid and Research Foundation
800-223-6429

Seafood Hotline
800-FDA-4010

Shriners Hospital Referral Line
800-237-5055

Sickle Cell Disease Association of America, Inc.
800-421-8453

SIDS Alliance
800-221-7437

Simon Foundation for Continence, The
800-237-4666

Spina Bifida Information and Referral
800-621-3141

Spondylitis Association of America
800-777-8189

Sturge-Weber Disease Foundation
800-627-5482

Stuttering Foundation of America
800-992-9392

Target Resource Center
800-366-6667

Teen HIV Hotline
(operated by teens, Fri & Sat, 6pm-12am)
800-440-8336(TEEN)

Tele-Consumer Hotline
800-332-1124

Terri Gotthelf Lupus Research Institute
800-82-LUPUS

Tourette Syndrome Association, Inc.
800-237-0717

Tripod Grapevine
800-352-8888 Voice/TDD
800-287-4763 Voice/TDD

United Cerebral Palsy Association
800-872-5827

United Network for Organ Sharing
800-243-6667
800-24-DONOR

United Organ Donor Hotline
800-24-DONOR

United Scleroderma Foundation
800-722-HOPE

U.S. Coast Guard Boating Safety Hotline
800-368-5647

U.S. Consumer Product Safety Commission Hotline
800-638-2772
800-638-8270 TDD

U.S. Department of Health and Human Services (DHHS) Inspector General's Hotline
800-368-5779

Be patient. If any phone number is incorrect, call (area code) 555-1212 and request the new listing.

USP Practitioners Reporting Network
800-4-USP-PRM; 800-23-ERROR
800-638-6725

VD Hotline (Operation Venus)
800-227-8922

Women's Sports Foundation
800-227-3988

YMCA of the USA
800-872-9622

Y-ME National Organization for Breast Cancer Information Support Program
800-221-2141

* Toxic Substances

Agency for Toxic Substances and Disease Registry
1600 Clifton Rd., NE, E60
Atlanta, GA 30333   404-639-6000

The Division of Toxicology identifies priority hazardous substances, develops toxicological profiles, and implements health effects research. You can listen to various recorded messages concerning ongoing research 24 hours a day, 7 days a week. To speak to an information specialist during business hours, follow the voice prompts.

* Tracer Bulletins: Asthma to Edible Wild Plants

Science and Technology Division
Reference Section
Library of Congress
Washington, DC 20540   202-707-5580

Informal series of reference guides are issued free from the Science and Technology Division under the general title, *LC Science Tracer Bullet*. These guides are designed to help readers locate published material on subjects about which they have only general knowledge. New titles in the series are announced in the weekly Library of Congress *Information Bulletin* that is distributed to many libraries including the following health-related Tracer Bulletins:

81-3	*Alcoholism*
81-17	*Epilepsy*
82-1	*Food Additives*
82-9	*Sickle Cell Anemia*
83-1	*Biofeedback*
83-6	*Mental Retardation*
85-6	*Acupuncture*
85-8	*Anorexia Nervosa/Bulimia*
85-10	*Rose Culture*
85-11	*Acquired Immune Deficiency Syndrome (AIDS)*
86-6	*Diabetes Mellitus*
86-8	*Indoor Air Pollution*
87-1	*Asbestos*
87-2	*Alzheimer's Disease*
87-6	*Stress: Physiological and Psychological Aspects*
87-7	*Osteoporosis*
89-5	*Human Diet and Nutrition*
89-7	*Allergy and Asthma*
90-10	*The Brain: An Overview*
91-3	*Dyslexia*
91-7	*Breast Cancer*
91-8	*Medicinal Plants*
91-9	*AIDS*
91-11	*Chemical Exposures: Toxicology, Safety, and Risk Assessment*
94-5	*Pesticides in Food*
94-6	*Speech Recognition and Processing*

* Women's Health Resources

Office of Disease Prevention and Health Promotion (ODPHP)
National Health Information Center
P.O. Box 1133   800-336-4797
Washington, DC 20013-1133   301-565-4167 in MD

The Public Health Service (PHS) Action Plan for Women's Health (F0025, $3) provides a comprehensive framework for improving the status of women's health in the areas of research, prevention, treatment, service, information, education and policy. The Plan identifies specific goals and action steps being pursued by the Public Health Service (PHS) agencies and offices in an effort to meet the priority health needs of women across age, biological, and sociocultural contexts. The *1991 Progress Review* (F0026, $3) is also available.

Healthy Lifestyle and Physical Fitness

Health professionals, community health centers, organizations, businesses, and individuals all can take advantage of the multitude of resources available to promote good health and prevent disease. Several federal agencies and departments, as well as numerous national organizations, offer bulletins, reference manuals, publications and expertise to encourage maintaining a healthy lifestyle and proper medical care. The National Health Information Center, a clearinghouse sponsored by the U.S. government, can direct you to a helpful agency such as the President's Council on Physical Fitness as well as to private organizations.

* Behavior Patterns and Health
Office of Clinical Center Communications
National Institutes of Health
Building 10, Room 1C255   301-496-2563
Bethesda, MD 20892   Fax: 301-402-2984
A 36-page report titled *Behavior Patterns and Health* (No. 85-2682) discusses the scientific evidence linking behavior to disease and suggests ways to reduce the risks of heart attack, lung cancer, and stroke by changing our lifestyle.

* Cancer Prevention Awareness
Office of Cancer Communications
National Cancer Institute
Building 31, Room 10A-16
31 Center Dr., MSC 2580
Bethesda, MD 20892-2580   800-4-CANCER
Over 70 programs are described in this free *Cancer Prevention Resource Directory* which gives names, addresses, and telephone numbers of many national associations and health departments which encourage cancer prevention activities. Single copies of this manual are available free.

* Cancer: Testicular Self-Exam
Office of Communications
National Cancer Institute
Building 31, Room 10A16
31 Center Dr., MSC 2580   800-4-CANCER
Bethesda, MD 20892-2580   301-496-5583
A free pamphlet, *Testicular Self-Examination* (No. 92-2636), provides information about risks and symptoms of testicular cancer and suggestions effective self-examinations.

* Children: Risk Factors
National Technical Information Service (NTIS)
U.S. Department of Commerce
5285 Port Royal Road   800-553-6847
Springfield, VA 22162   703-487-4650
This Center offers research findings including *Determinants of Children's Health* (NTIS PB-80-163603, $48) which summarizes six closely related studies on the determinants of child health, with particular emphasis on home and local environmental factors, parents' schooling, and family income.

* Elderly and Exercise
National Institute on Aging
Information Center
P.O. Box 8057   800-222-2225
Gaithersburg, MD 20898-8057   TDD: 800-222-4225
Don't Take It Easy - Exercise! is a free two-page fact sheet which suggests ways for older Americans to remain active and healthy.

* Exercise and Arthritis
National Arthritis and Musculoskeletal and Skin Diseases
   Information Clearinghouse   301-495-4484
1 AMS Circle   Fax: 301-587-4352
Bethesda, MD 20892-3675   TDD: 301-565-2966
A 20-page resource catalog titled *Exercise and Arthritis: An Annotated Bibliography, 1995* contains 37 references with abstracts, books, reports, and audiovisuals along with resources for developing an aquatic exercise regime, a home maintenance program, and exercises specifically for children.

* Exercise and Physical Fitness Programs
President's Council on Physical Fitness and Sports
701 Pennsylvania Ave., NW, Suite 250
Washington, DC 20004   202-272-3421
This executive branch office provides free single copies of many of its publications and publishes a quarterly magazine.

* Exercising Your Heart
National Heart, Lung, and Blood Institute (NHLBI)
Information Center
P.O. Box 30105   301-251-1222
Bethesda, MD 20824-0105   Fax: 301-251-1223
Single copies are available at no charge on the following publications: *Exercise and Your Heart* (No. 93-1677), *NHLBI Facts About Exercise: How To Get Started*, and *Check Your Physical Activity and Heart Disease I.Q.* (95-3795).

* Family Relationships and Lifecycles
Rural Information Center
U.S. Department of Agriculture   800-633-7701
10301 Baltimore Blvd.   301-504-5372
Beltsville, MD 20705-2351   Fax: 301-504-5181
This center answers questions about families throughout the lifecycle, from marital relationships and childbearing families to empty nest families and retirement, and deals with matters concerning social environment and family economics education.

* Federal Health Information Catalog
Office of Disease Prevention and Health Promotion (ODPHP)
National Health Information Center
P.O. Box 1133   800-336-4797
Washington, DC 20013-1133   301-565-4167 (in MD)
Health Information Resources in the Federal Government (F004) identifies Federal agencies and projects that can provide information to health professionals and the general public. It includes major services and activities, publications and databases. Check with the Center to learn about the latest edition. A $2 fee covers the handling for this catalog. This information is also available on the Internet at Gopher.11odphp. oash.dhhs.gov:70/00%5codphp%5gopher.lst.

* Fitness Fundamentals
Superintendent of Documents
Government Printing Office (GPO)   202-512-1800
Washington, DC 20402   Fax: 202-512-2250
Fitness Fundamentals: Guidelines for Personal Exercise Programs provides basic information needed to begin and maintain a personal physical fitness program. It is intended for the average healthy adult. Order #017-001-00453-7, cost $25.

* Genetic Screening in the Workplace

National Technical Information Service
U.S. Department of Commerce   800-553-6847
5285 Port Royal Rd.   703-487-4650
Springfield, VA 22161   Fax: 703-321-8547
       TDD: 703-487-4639

The former Office of Technology Assessment (OTA) studied the state-of-the-art technologies used by employers for genetic screening and monitoring, which includes a survey of the 500 largest U.S. industries, to largest utilities, and 11 major unions to determine the current nature and extent of employer testing. They also examined the impact of genetic testing; relevant ethical issues; and legal issues, including employment discrimination. The report, *Genetic Monitoring and Screening in the Workplace*, is now available from the National Technical Information Service.

* Getting Fit

Superintendent of Documents
Government Printing Office (GPO)   202-512-1800
Washington, DC 20402   Fax: 202-512-2250

Getting Fit Your Way, A Self-Paced Fitness Guide provides information on the development and maintenance of a total physical fitness program. Also included is information on how to quit smoking, lose weight, and develop strength. Order #008-020-01182-7, price $3.25.

* Health Observances

Office of Disease Prevention and Health Promotion (ODPHP)
National Health Information Center
P.O. Box 1133   800-336-4797
Washington, DC 20013-1133   301-565-4167

National Health Observances (A006, $2) are special months, weeks, or days devoted to promoting particular health concerns. This Healthfinder lists selected health observances for the year. Health professionals, teachers, and community groups can use these special events to launch health promotion activities, stimulate awareness of health risks, or focus on disease eradication. Materials available from sponsoring organizations range from a single flyer to packets of promotional materials.

* Health Promotion in the Workplace

Office of Disease Prevention and Health Promotion (ODPHP)
Information Center
P.O. Box 1133   800-336-4797
Washington, DC 20013-1133   301-565-4167

As a policy arm of the Public Health Service, this office works on developing policies for the Year 2000 objectives for health promotion. Their Preventive Services Task Force is developing recommendations for clinical practice, in addition to a worksite Health Promotion Task Force and a Nutrition Branch. This office also operates the Health Promotion Clearinghouse which offers many publications.

* Health Promotion Project Funding

Office of Disease Prevention and Health Promotion (ODPHP)
National Health Information Center
P.O. Box 1133   800-336-4797
Washington, DC 20013-1133   301-565-4167 in MD

The guide, *Locating Resources for Healthy People 2000 Health Promotion Projects*, (Z001, #2) is designed to assist newcomers on their search for health promotion funding by introducing them to the major tasks involved and information services available. This publication is divided into four major sections. Section I discusses basic principles of fundseeking. Sections II and III discuss where and how to look for health promotion funds, focusing on both private and public sectors. Major foundations and Federal agencies interested in health promotion, as well as local sources are listed. Section IV lists resources — organizations, foundations, publications, and databases — that can be useful to those seeking funds. Also included is an appendix, which includes a glossary, a list of acronyms, a bibliography, and a sample grant application form.

* Healthy Teeth

National Institute of Dental Research
National Institutes of Health (NIH)
Building 31, Room 2C35
31 Center Dr., MSC 2290
Bethesda, MD 20892   301-496-6621

The mission of the National Institute of Dental Research (NIDR) is to support studies to establish the causes, develop better treatments, and ultimately find ways to prevent or substantially lower the risk of developing oral disease. NIDR has extramural and intramural research programs, and supports the Epidemiology and Oral Disease Prevention Program, which sponsors studies of oral disease and engages in controlled clinical trials of potential preventive agents. NIDR grants fellowships and career development awards and sponsors many conferences and workshops. They distribute a wide range of brochures, reports, and posters for both the general public and professionals (many of which are also in Spanish). Some of the topics covered are tooth decay, fluoride use, and the oral health of U.S. adults.

* Immunizations and Disease Prevention

Office of Consumer Affairs
Public Inquiries
Food and Drug Administration
5600 Fishers Lane (HFE-88)
Rockville, MD 20857   301-443-3170

This office has many free publications pertaining to vaccinations including *New Vaccine Protects Against Serious "Day Care" Disease, Shots Adults Shouldn't Do Without, Vaccines: Precious Ounces of Prevention*, and *Whooping Cough Still threatens U.S. Children*. If your questions cannot be answered here, you can be transferred to a specialist in the Office of Biologics.

* Lifestyle and Occupational Health Risk Scorecard

Health Risk Appraisal Activity
Centers for Disease Control
1600 Clifton Rd., NE
Atlanta, GA 30333   404-639-3311

The Health Risk Appraisal Activity program works to develop computerized health risk appraisals (HRA); to provide technical assistance in their use through state and regional contacts; and to distribute general background information on HRAs. Current activities include supporting the development of a state-of-the-art, public domain HRA at the Carter Center, Emory University; integrating occupational risk appraisal with lifestyle risk appraisal; evaluating the effect on communities of HRA use; and supporting the development of HRA programs for specific populations.

* Mental Retardation Prevention

President's Committee on Mental Retardation
330 Independence Avenue SW
Room 4061
Washington, DC 20201   202-619-0634

A Guide for State Planning for the *Prevention of Mental Retardation and Related Developmental Disabilities* is a resource tool not intended solely for state-level health planners but also for city and county health departments, advocacy groups, organizations and others. Single copies of this 20-page manual are available free.

* Physical Fitness

President's Council on Physical Fitness and Sports
701 Pennsylvania Ave., NW
Suite 250   202-272-3421
Washington, DC 20004   Fax: 202-504-2064

The President's Council on Physical Fitness and Sports was established to serve as a catalyst to promote, encourage and motivate the development of physical fitness and sports programs for all Americans. These programs help focus public awareness on the importance of staying physically active by encouraging schools, business and industry, government, recreation agencies, sports and youth-serving organizations to step up their emphasis on developing and maintaining physical fitness and sports programs.

* Physical Fitness Awards for Adults

President's Council on Physical Fitness and Sports
701 Pennsylvania Ave., NW, Suite 250   202-272-3421/3431
Washington, DC 20004   Fax: 202-504-2064

The Presidential Sports Award recognizes adult participation in a regular program of exercise. Men and women 10 years of age and older can qualify for the award in one or more of 58 different sports and fitness activities. Specific requirements for each activity have been established for a four-month period. Upon meeting the qualifying standards, participants receive a personalized Presidential certificate of achievement and a sports award lapel pin. The Amateur Athletic Union administers the program.

For additional information and logs contact: Jean Ann Ruppel, AAU, Lake Buena Vista, FL 32830-1000, 407-363-6170.

* Physical Fitness Awards for Youngsters

President's Council on Physical Fitness and Sports
701 Pennsylvania Ave., NW, Suite 250
Washington, DC 20004   202-272-3421/3431

The President's Council on Physical Fitness and Sports conducts a fitness assessment and recognition program for young people ages 6-17. This program is offered through the school system. Contact this office for more information and a list of their publications.

* Preventive Health National Programs

Centers for Disease Control
1600 Clifton Rd., NE
Atlanta, GA 30333   404-639-3311

This center plans, directs, and coordinates national programs of assistance involving preventive health services to State and local health agencies. The Center for Disease Control (CDC) provides leadership to the health community, especially State and local agencies, in the development and implementation of improved preventive health services programs. It assists States and localities in specifying major health problems in the community and formulating intervention strategies, and through grants, assists them in establishing and maintaining prevention and control programs directed toward health problems. Some of the preventive health services covered include dental disease, immunizations, sexually transmitted diseases, and tuberculosis.

* Rural Health Care

National Technical Information Service
U.S. Department of Commerce   800-553-6847
5285 Port Royal Rd.   703-487-4650
Springfield, VA 22181   Fax: 703-321-8547
                                   TDD: 703-487-4639

The former Office of Technology Assessment (OTA) reviewed and evaluated past and current rural health care efforts; examining how medical technologies have been and might be diffused into rural areas; and identifying policies that might improve the quality, affordability, and accessibility of rural health care. *Defining Rural Areas: Impact on Health Care Policy and Research* is the resulting publication. The report is now available from the National Technical Information Service, order #PB89-224646.

* Surgeon General's Reports on Health Promotion

Office of Disease Prevention and Health Promotion (ODPHP)
Health Information Center
P. O. Box 1133   800-336-4797
Washington, DC 20013-1133   301-565-4167 in MD

The nation's priorities are outlined in a 177-page report titled *Healthy People: The Surgeon General's Report on Health Promotion and Disease Prevention* (F0005, $3). It sets out a program for improving the health of Americans and lists five public health goals that are measurable and achievable.

* Walking for Exercise and Pleasure

Superintendent of Documents
Government Printing Office (GPO)   202-512-1800
Washington, DC 20402   Fax: 202-512-2250

This book provides information on the importance of walking as a form of exercise. It explains how walking provides exercise to people of all ages; how walking contributes to fitness; what to wear; warm-up and conditioning exercises; and how far and how fast to walk. Order #017-001-11447-2, $1.

* Worksite Health Promotion

Office of Disease Prevention and Health Promotion (ODPHP)
Health Information Center
P. O. Box 1133   800-336-4797
Washington, DC 20013-1133   301-565-4167 in MD

The Clearinghouse has the following publications dealing with worksite health promotion programs:

Healthy Worksites: Directory of Federal Initiatives in Worksite Health Promotion (W0019, $3). A compilation of projects and research sponsored by the Federal Government to stimulate and improve worksite health promotion in public and private sectors. Includes agency contacts, brief project descriptions, and available resources.

Health Promotion Goes to Work (W0021, $5). Produced on behalf of the National Coordinating Committee on Worksite Health Promotion, this compendium presents examples of worksite health programs with documented results.

Summary Report of the 1992 National Survey of Worksite Health Promotion Activities (W0020, $2). Measures the growth of worksite health promotion activities since the first national survey in 1985. A major focus of the survey was to assess progress toward worksite objectives in Healthy People 2000.

Worksite Nutrition: A Decision Maker's Guide (U00100, #2). Presents rationale for implementing nutrition programs in the workplace and describes what resources employers need to conduct worksite nutrition programs.

Worksite Nutrition: A Guide to Planning, Implementation, and Evaluation (U0010, $2). Update of *Worksite Nutrition: A Decision Maker's Guide*. Describes how to initiate, design, operate, and evaluate worksite nutrition programs. Profiles numerous worksite programs in corporations and in government agencies.

* Worksite Safety and Health

National Institute for Occupational Safety and Health (NIOSH)
4676 Columbia Parkway
Mail Stop C-13   800-35-NIOSH
Cincinnati, OH 45226-1998   Fax: 513-533-8513

Healthy People 2000: National Health Promotion and Disease Prevention Objectives - Occupational Safety and Health is a free publication which is part of Healthy People 2000. It includes over 15 objectives for health promotion and disease prevention related to occupational safety and health.

Food Facts, Nutrition, and Diets

* See also Consumer Chapter
* See also Agriculture and Farming; Food Quality and Distribution Chapter

Menu plans and recipes,as well as very technical information about the nutritional value of every conceivable food product, is available for the asking. Surplus commodities and donations to non-profits are contained here as well as in the Government Auctions and Surplus Property Chapter. Surveys of food expenditures and eating habits as well as eating disorders are just a phone call away.

* Agricola Database
Reference Branch
National Agricultural Library, Room 301
U.S. Department of Agriculture
Beltsville, MD 20705   301-504-5204
A computerized database called AGRICOLA contains information primarily on the agricultural sciences but includes a substantial number of citations to nutrition literature such as journal articles, government reports, serials, monographs, and pamphlets. The print counterpart to this online database is titled *Food and Nutrition Bibliography*. The database is accessible through DIALOG.

* Anorexia Nervosa and Bulimia
National Institute of Child Health and Human Development
National Institutes of Health (NIH)
Building 31, Room 2A-32
31 Center Dr., MSC 2425
Bethesda, MD 20892-2425   301-496-5133
Facts About Anorexia Nervosa explains the causes, symptoms and treatments for anorexia and bulimia as well as ongoing research efforts at the National Institutes of Health (NIH). This 8-page pamphlet is available free.

* Basic Four Food Groups: Dietary Guidelines
Office of Disease Prevention and Health Promotion (ODPHP)
Health Information Center
P.O. Box 1133   800-336-4797
Washington, DC 20013-1133   301-565-4167 in MD
Dietary Guidelines for Americans (U0003, $1). Presents seven guidelines for improved food habits for healthy Americans ages 2 years and older. Discusses fat, fruits, vegetables, grains and complex carbohydrates, fiber, sugar, sodium, alcohol, maintaining healthy weight, and eating a variety of foods. This is also for sale in packages of 100 by the Government Printing Office, 202-512-1800, S/N 001-000-04561-0, for $44. It is also available electronically at gopher.//odphp.oash.dhhs.gov:70/00%5codphp%5GOPHER.LST.

* Calcium and Other Special Needs of Women
Office of Public Affairs
Food and Drug Administration
5600 Fishers Lane, HFE88
Rockville, MD 20857   301-443-3170
Several publications are available free which address the special nutrition needs of females including *Please Pass That Woman Some More Calcium and Iron* (No. 85-2198), *Osteoporosis: Calcium, and Estrogens*, and *The Nutritional Gender Gap at the Dinner Table*.

* Cancer Prevention and Nutrition
Office of Cancer Communications
National Cancer Institute
Building 31, Room 10A-16
31 Center Dr., MSC 2580
Bethesda, MD 20892-2580   800-4-CANCER
This institute offers the latest findings and scientific studies about nutrition and cancer including a free 51-page pamphlet titled *Diet, Nutrition and Cancer Prevention: A Guide to Food Choices* (No. 85-2711) which describes what is known about the interrelationships of diet and certain cancers.

* Cellulite Removal Gimmicks
Office of Public Affairs
Food and Drug Administration
5600 Fishers Lane, HFE88
Rockville, MD 20857   301-443-3170
The Food and Drug Administration (FDA) monitors many weight loss related-products and warns consumers about gimmicks sold which promise to get rid of fat on the hips and thighs.

* Cheap Nutrition Publications
R. Woods
Consumer Information Center-6A
P.O. Box 100
Pueblo, CO 81002
The Consumer Information Catalog is a catalog of free and low-cost federal publications of consumer interest. A new catalog is published quarterly, and is available free of charge. You can request a free catalog by calling 719-948-4000. The publications dealing with nutrition include:

Eating Defensively: Food Safety Advice for People with AIDS 518C (free)
Eating for Life. 118C ($1)
Food Allergies: Rare but Risky. 519C (free)
Food Label Close-Up. 520C (free)
The Food Label, The Pyramid and You. 119C (free)
A Fresh Look at Food Preservatives. 521C (free)
Help in Preventing Heart Disease. 522C (free)
How to Buy Dairy Products. 316C (free)
How to Buy Fruits and Vegetables:
    How to Buy Canned & Frozen Fruits. 317C (.50)
    How to Buy Canned & Frozen Vegetables. 318C (.50)
    How to Buy Fresh Vegetables. 320C (.50)
How to Buy Meat. 321C (.50)
Quick Consumer Guide to Safe Food Handling. 523C (free)
Scouting for Sodium: The New Food Label. 524C (free)
Should You Go On A Diet? 525C (free)
Talking About Turkey: How to Buy, Store, Thaw, Stuff, and Prepare Your Holiday Turkey. 526C (free)
Thrifty Meals for Two. 120C ($2.50)

* Cholesterol Facts
National Cholesterol Education Program
National Heart, Lung, and Blood Institute
P.O. Box 30105   301-251-1222
Bethesda, MD 20824-0501   Fax: 301-251-1223
The Cholesterol Information Center has specialists on staff and provides printed information on cholesterol, diet, and high blood pressure to the public and health professionals. Some of the brochures which they distribute includes *NHLBI Facts About Blood Cholesterol* (#94-2696).

* Community Nutrition Services
National Clearinghouse for Primary Care Information
2070 Chain Bridge Rd.
Vienna, VA 22182   703-821-8955, x248
This center offers manuals for community health centers, primary care providers, home health services, HMOs, and outpatient clinics on approaches for a nutrition

program, such as counseling and referral. Single copies of a 96-page *Guide for Developing Nutrition Services in Community Health Programs* is available free.

* Dietary Analysis for the Individual

National Technical Information Service (NTIS)
U.S. Department of Commerce
5285 Port Royal Rd.   800-553-6847
Springfield, VA 22261   703-487-4650

The National Technical Information Service (NTIS) sells a simple software program for IBM PC-compatible computers which will give you a dietary analysis of the foods you eat in a meal or for each day. Just by entering the names of the foods you have eaten, this program, developed by the U.S. Department of Agriculture's Human Nutrition Information Service, will give you nutrient data information, calories, and recommended daily allowances on over 850 foods. The Dietary Analysis Program software is available for $60, order #PB90-504101.

* Dietary Essentials

Grand Forks Human Nutrition Research Center
P.O. Box 9034
University Station
Grand Forks, ND 58202-9034   701-795-8456

This center focuses on defining human requirements for trace elements and the physiological and biochemical factors which influence those requirements.

* Dietary Guidelines

Superintendent of Documents
Government Printing Office   202-512-1800
Washington, DC 20402   Fax: 202-512-2250

The Government Printing Office has several publications designed to improve your eating habits. They include the following:

Shopping for Food and Making Meals in Minutes Using the Dietary Guidelines - describes quick meal hints, tips on reading food labels, an aisle-by-aisle shopping guide, and 18 timesaving recipe ideas (S/N 001-000-04529-6, $3).

Preparing Foods and Planning Menus Using the Dietary Guidelines - contains tips for cooking with less sugar, fat, and sodium; a daily guide to food choices; making the menu fit the family; and 10 recipe ideas (S/N 001-000-04527-0, $2.50).

Eating Better When Eating Out Using the Dietary Guidelines - discusses ordering foods "your way," how to read menus, and fact and fiction about fast foods (S/N 001-000-04530-0, $1.50).

* Dietary Guidelines for Americans

Superintendent of Documents
Government Printing Office (GPO)   202-512-1800
Washington, DC 20402   Fax: 202-512-2250

This is a colorful poster depicting nutritious foods and listing the seven basic principles for a healthful diet. Their are nutrition tips, a nutrition quiz, and a list of additional Agriculture Department publications. Order #001-000-04531-8, cost is $3.75.

* Drugs and Food Interactions

Office of Public Affairs
Food and Drug Administration
5600 Fishers Lane, HFE88
Rockville, MD 20857   301-443-3170

A free report titled *Food and Drug Interactions* (No. OMB89-3023) explains why some foods and medicines may interfere with each other, and suggests ways to avoid the problem.

* Eating Better When Eating Out Using the Dietary Guidelines

Superintendent of Documents
Government Printing Office (GPO)   202-512-1800
Washington, DC 20402   Fax: 202-512-2250

This book contains information on ordering foods "your way"; menu reading clues; and fact and fiction about fast foods. The order number is 001-000-14530-0, the cost is $1.50.

* Eating Disorders

Office of Public Affairs
Food and Drug Administration
5600 Fishers Lane, HFE88
Rockville, MD 20857   301-443-3170

Bulimia and anorexia nervosa are discussed in a short pamphlet, *Eating Disorders: When Thinness Becomes an Obsession* and *Eating Disorders Require Medical Attention*. These are available free of charge.

* Eating Habits National Survey

Division of Health Examination Statistics
National Center for Health Statistics
6525 Belcrest Rd.
Hyattsville, MD 20782   301-436-7068

This division collects data on health-related matters and administers the National Health and Nutrition Survey, which assesses the health and nutritional status of the general population through direct physical examination.

* Elderly and Menu Ideas

National Institute on Aging
Information Center   800-222-2225
P.O. Box 8057   Fax: 301-589-3014
Gaithersburg, MD 20898-8057   TDD: 800-222-4225

The Institute makes available free several "Age Pages" which offer tips for seniors including *Food: Staying Healthy After 65, Be Sensible About Salt, Hints for Shopping, Cooking and Enjoying Meals*, and *Dietary Supplements: More Is Not Always Better*.

* Emergency Food Assistance Program

Public Information Staff
Food and Consumer Service
U.S. Department of Agriculture (USDA)
3101 Park Center Dr.   703-305-2286
Alexandria, VA 22302   Fax: 703-305-1117

The Program gives needy Americans USDA-donated foods for household use. The foods are free, but recipients must meet the program eligibility criteria set by the states. Local agencies usually, food banks, shelters and soup kitchens, are designed by the states to distribute the food.

* Fad Diets and Diet Books

Office of Public Affairs
Food and Drug Administration
5600 Fishers Lane, HFE88
Rockville, MD 20857   301-443-3170

Facts About Weight Loss: Products and Programs (No. 92-1189) reviews and evaluates some of the popular diet programs and products.

* Fast Foods and Nutrition

Office of Public Affairs
Food and Drug Administration
5600 Fishers Lane, HFE88
Rockville, MD 20857   301-443-3170

A free pamphlet titled *What About Nutrients In Fast Foods?* examines the pros and cons of "fast foods" and analyses the nutritional value of various menus.

* Fiber and Roughage

Office of Public Affairs
Food and Drug Administration
5600 Fishers Lane, HFE88
Rockville, MD 20857   301-443-3170

Single copies of the booklet, *Fiber: Something Healthy to Chew On* (No. 91-2206) discusses the role of fiber in nutrition.

* Food and Nutrition Service Publications

Food and Nutrition Service (FNS)
Public Information Office
U.S. Department of Agriculture
Public Affairs Staff

3101 Park Center Dr.
Alexandria, VA 22302   703-305-2554
The Food and Nutrition Service (FNS) publishes a variety of brochures explaining the various food assistance programs it operates both for those eligible for the programs and for those who administer them. Programs include the Child Nutrition Program; Food Distribution Program; Women, Infants, and Children (WIC) Program; Food Stamp Program; and various nutrition education materials. Requests for the Publications List are available from the above office, or from the Food and Nutrition Service Regional Offices listed below. Most publications are available free; those for sale are sold through the Government Printing Office.

* Food and Nutrition Services Regional Offices
Contact the regional office nearest you for getting answers to questions over the phone as well as data and information materials.

Northeast Region, 10 Causeway St., Room 501, Boston, MA 02222-1069; 617-565-6370.

Southeast Region, 77 Forsyth St. SW, Suite 112, Atlanta, GA 30302; 404-730-2565.

Southwest Region, 1100 Commerce St., Room 5-C-30, Dallas, TX 75242-9980; 214-767-0222.

Western Region, 550 Kearny St., Room 400, San Francisco, CA 94108-2518; 415-705-1310.

Mid-Atlantic Region, Mercer Corporate Park, 300 Corporate Blvd., Robbinsville, NJ 08691-1578; 609-259-5025.

Midwest Region, 77 W. Jackson Blvd., Suite 2002, Chicago, IL 60604-3507; 312-353-6664.

Northwest Region, 1244 Speer Blvd., Denver, CO 80204; 303-844-0300.

* Food Assistance to the Poor
Food and Consumer Service (FCS)
Public Information Office
3101 Park Center Dr.
Park Office Center Bldg.
Alexandria, VA 22302   703-305-2554
The Food and Consumer Service (FCS) administers many federal-state programs to provide food assistance to those in need. The agency cooperates with state and local welfare agencies to administer the Food Stamp Program, which enables low-income families to purchase a greater variety of food to improve their diets. Additional agency programs help reduce agricultural surpluses by providing commodities and other foodstuffs to schools and other institutions for their use in special nutrition programs. These programs are designed to help needy children achieve nutritionally balanced diets. The Special Supplemental Food Program for Women, Infants, and Children (WIC) provides specific nutritious food supplements to pregnant and nursing women, as well as to children up to 5 years of age who are found to be "at nutritional risk" because of poor diet or low income. The Food Distribution Program donates food to various outlets: schools, charitable institutions, nutrition programs for the elderly, summer camps, disaster relief agencies, and programs for needy families on some Indian reservations. A publications list is available.

* Food Consumption Research
Agricultural Research Service
U.S. Department of Agriculture
4700 River Rd.
Riverdale, MD 20737   301-734-5619
Data have been collected and is being compiled for the *1987-88 Nationwide Food Consumption Survey* (NFCS 1987-88). This survey, conducted every 10 years, provides comprehensive information on the consumption of foods and nutrients and on the dietary status of U.S. households and individuals. For a summary of survey results, contact the above office.

* Food Contamination Inspection
Center for Food Safety and Applied Nutrition
Food and Drug Administration
200 C Street, SW, Room 6815
Washington, DC 20204   202-205-5277
The Center for Food Safety and Applied Nutrition conducts research and develops

standards on the composition, quality, nutrition, and safety of food, food additives, colors, and cosmetics. The Center has cooperative arrangements with industries, such as milk and shellfish, where representatives from FDA, the state, and the industry meet to develop model codes and standards for the food product. The Center is responsible for food labeling, requiring ingredients to be listed in order of composition, as well as other nutritional information, such as fat and sodium content. They regulate the infant formula industry, ensuring that basic nutrients be included in the formula. The Center also administers a program of sampling food for possible contamination. Radiation from the Chernobyl accident and the Chilean Grape embargo are two recent examples studied under this program.

* Food Expenditures and Consumer Attitudes
Food and Consumer Economics Division
Economics Research Service
1301 New York Ave., NW
Washington, DC 20005-4788   202-219-0880
Studies and expertise on such topics as the convenience food market, food purchases away from home, the fast food industry, the relationship between consumer attitudes about nutrition and actual food expenditures, and the economic effects of food safety regulations are available from this office.

* Food Preparation and Refrigeration
Office of Public Affairs
Food and Drug Administration
5600 Fishers Lane, HFE88
Rockville, MD 20857   301-443-3170
Goce De Buena Salud! Aeoreja Los Alimentos (No. 92-2234S) is available only in Spanish and recommends proper food preparation and refrigeration of various types of foods and also discusses some common foodborne organisms.

* Food Review
Superintendent of Documents
Government Printing Office (GPO)   202-512-1800
Washington, DC 20402   Fax: 512-2250
Food Review, a subscription issued triannually, offers the latest developments in food prices, product safety, nutrition programs, consumption patterns, and marketing. Subscriptions are accepted for one or two years. The order number is 701-036-00000-0, and costs $8.50.

* Food Safety and Additives Info
Office of Public Affairs
Food and Drug Administration (FDA)
5600 Fishers Lane, HFE88
Rockville, MD 20857   301-443-3170
The Food and Drug Administration (FDA) distributes many brochures and publications including *Food Additives* (No. OM90-3016), *The Food Label Close-Up* (No. 15-2283), and *Genetically Engineered Foods: Fears and Facts*. The *FDA Consumer*, which contains the latest developments at FDA, can be ordered for $12 per year from the Superintendent of Documents, Government Printing Office, Washington DC 20402, 202-512-1800.

* Food Safety and Inspection
Office of Public Awareness
Food Safety and Inspection Service
U.S. Department of Agriculture
14th and Independence Ave., SW, Room 2925S
Washington, DC 20205   800-535-4555
This office inspects and analyzes domestic and imported meat and poultry and establishes standards for processed meat and poultry products. Questions can be answered about the proper handling, preparation, and refrigeration, food poisoning, and food labeling.

* Food Tampering and Foreign Objects
Emergency Services
Food and Drug Administration (FDA)
5600 Fishers Lane
HFC-162, Room 1362
Rockville, MD 20857   301-443-1240
If you find foreign objects or evidence of tampering with any food, drug (both human and animal), or cosmetic, you should report it to the Food and Drug

Administration. This office deals with consumer complaints and recalls. You can also report the tampering to any of the FDA regional offices.

* Free Food for Non-Profit Institutions

Food Distribution Program
Food and Consumer Service
U.S. Department of Agriculture (USDA)
3101 Park Center Dr., Room 502
Alexandria, VA 22302   703-305-2286

Thousands of charitable institutions throughout the country rely on foods donated by the U.S. Department of Agriculture (USDA) to help provide meals to needy people. These charitable groups range from churches operating community kitchens for the homeless and destitute, to orphanages and homes for the elderly. Other eligible groups include meals-on-wheels programs, soup kitchens, temporary shelters, correctional institutions offering rehabilitative activities, group homes for the mentally retarded, and hospitals that offer general and long-term care. To be eligible, charitable institutions must be nonprofit and serve meals on a regular basis. They may be either public or non-profit private institutions that have federal tax-exempt status.

* Government Dietary Guidelines

Center for Nutrition Policy and Promotion
U.S. Department of Agriculture
1120 20th St., NW, Suite 200
Washington, DC 20036   202-418-3139

The Center for Nutrition Policy and Promotion (CNPP) has developed seven basic eating principals, the Dietary Guidelines, that encourage variety, balance, moderation in food consumption. The first two guidelines recommend people eat a variety of foods that provide enough essential nutrients and calories to maintain a desirable weight; the other five suggest eating an adequate amount of starch and fiber and avoiding too much fat, sugar, sodium, and alcohol. Contact CNPP for a series of seven bulletins outlining the program. To order publications, call 202-606-8000.

* Health Promotion and Nutrition

Office of Disease Prevention and Health Promotion (ODPHP)
Health Information Center
P.O. Box 1133   800-336-4797
Washington, DC 20013-1133   301-565-4167

As a policy arm of the Public Health Service, this office works on developing policies for the Year 2000 objectives for health promotion. Their Preventive Services Task Force is developing recommendations for clinical practice, in addition to a worksite Health Promotion Task Force and a Nutrition Branch. This office also operates the Health Promotion Clearinghouse which offers many publications.

* Healthy Heart Menus

National Heart, Lung, and Blood Institute
Information Center
National Institutes of Health (NIH)
P.O. Box 30105   301-251-1222
Bethesda, MD 20824-0105   Fax: 301-251-1223

Stay Young at Heart Recipe Cards (55-648) is a recipe booklet that will convince you that it's easy to cook in a heart-healthy way and the results can be delicious. These recipes came from three sources: *Play Your Cards Right...Stay Young at Heart*, a nutrition education program developed by the National Heart, Lung, and Blood Institute (NHLBI); *Down Home Healthy* (94-3408), a cookbook and guide developed by the National Cancer Institute, the NHLBI, and Project Lean; and recipes from the American Heart Association. Other publications available include:

Eat Right to Help Lower Your High Blood Pressure (55-3289)
Eat Right to Lower Your High Blood Cholesterol (55-2920)
Eating With Your Heart in Mind (for 7-10 year olds) (92-3100)
Heart Health...Your Choice (for 11-14 year olds) (92-3101)
Hearty Habits: Don't Eat Your Heart Out (15-18 year olds) (93-3102)
Parents Guide: Cholesterol in Children, Healthy Eating is a Family Affair (92-3099)
Step by Step: Eating to Lower Your High Blood Cholesterol (55-2973)

* Healthy Menus

Food and Nutrition Information Center
U.S. Department of Agriculture
National Agricultural Library, Room 304
Beltsville, MD 20705   703-305-2556

Cartoons fill the pages of this booklet titled *Eating For Better Health* which contains

nutrition and weight loss information as well as inexpensive recipes and menus. Other information and scientific findings are available from this agency.

* Low-Income Families and Nutrition Awareness

Food and Consumer Information Center
National Agricultural Library Building
10301 Baltimore Blvd.
Beltsville, MD 20705-2351   301-504-5719

The Idea Book: Sharing Nutrition Education Experiences (H234) is designed for WIC (Women, Infants, and Children) nutrition educators and contains chapters covering motivation, planning, lesson plans, etc. This 89-page resource is available on loan from the Center and also is available through interlibrary loan.

* Malnutrition and Nutrition Research

Western Human Nutrition Research Center
P.O. Box 29997
Presidio of San Francisco
San Francisco, CA 94129   415-556-9699

This center develops improved methods for monitoring and evaluating nutritional status and investigates factors that lead to malnutrition. It also conducts studies on human nutritional requirements.

* Nutrient Data Tapes

National Technical Information Service
U.S. Department of Commerce
5285 Port Royal Rd.   800-553-6847
Springfield, VA 22261   703-487-4650

The Human Nutrition Information Service (HNIS) collects and publishes information on disc and magnetic tape on the nutritive composition of foods. The agency gathers data from the scientific literature and from government, university, and food industry laboratories and directs laboratory studies to produce information. HNIS also compiles information on yield and nutrient retention of food items at different stages in production. Complete ordering information is available from the above address. See Human Nutrition Information Service Reports to order print versions of this information.

* Nutrient Values and Food Groups

Center for Nutrition Policy and Promotion
U.S. Department of Agriculture
1120 20th St., NW, Suite 200
Washington, DC 20036   202-418-3139

This office shares its research in nutritive value of foods and of the nutritional adequacy of diets and food supplies. It also maintains the Nutrient Data Bank which contains surveys and data on the nutrient values in foods and descriptions of foods. Various consumer materials are available as well as a publications list, including over 20 publications on the nutrient composition of foods. The Center for Nutrition Policy and Promotion (CNPP) has several publications dealing with dietary guidelines for Americans, which are seven basic principles for developing and maintaining a healthier diet and are the basis for all Federal nutrition information and education programs for healthy Americans. To order publications, call 202-606-8000. Some of the publications available include:

Nutrition and Your Health: Dietary Guidelines for Americans (free, also in Spanish)
Dietary Guidelines and Your Diet ($4.50)
Preparing Foods and Planning Menus Using the Dietary Guidelines ($2.50)
Making Bag Lunches, Snacks, and Desserts Using the Dietary Guidelines ($2.50)
Shopping for Food and Making Meals in Minutes Using the Dietary Guidelines ($3)
Eating Better When Eating Out Using the Dietary Guidelines ($1.50)
Calories and Weight: The USDA Pocket Guide ($1.75)
Nutritive Value of Foods ($3.75)
Your Money's Worth in Foods ($2.25)
The Sodium Content of Your Food ($2.25)
Thrifty Meals for Two: Making Your Food Dollars Count ($2.50)
Cooking for People with Food Allergies ($1.50)
Good Sources of Nutrients ($5)

* Nutrition Education

Public Information Staff
Food and Consumer Service

U.S. Department of Agriculture
3101 Park Center Dr.   703-305-2286
Alexandria; VA 22303   Fax: 703-305-1117

The Nutrition Education Training Program is currently the only national school-based nutrition education and training program. It seeks to build good food habits by teaching the fundamentals of nutrition to children, educators, and food service personnel. Some of the things the program supports is development of national nutrition education and training programs for pre-school and school-aged children; development of print and video nutrition education and training materials; analysis and assessment of existing school meal patterns, development of new menus and recipes; training and assistance for local school food service operators; and incentives for schools to comply with the Dietary Guidelines.

* Nutrition Labels and U.S. RDA

Office of Public Affairs
Food and Drug Administration
5600 Fishers Lane, HFE88
Rockville, MD 20857   301-443-3170

A short fact sheet titled *Nutrition Labels and U.S. RDA* explains the evolution of the Recommended Daily Allowances (RDAs) and the intention of nutritional labeling information.

* Nutrition Needs of Mothers and Infants

Children's Nutrition Research Center
at Baylor College of Medicine
1100 Bates St.
Houston, TX 77030   713-798-7000

This center focuses on determining the unique nutrient needs of pregnant and lactating women, and of children from conception through early years of development.

* Nutrition Program for the Elderly

Public Information Staff
Food and Consumer Service
U.S. Department of Agriculture
3101 Park Center Dr.   703-305-2286
Alexandria, VA 22302   Fax: 703-305-1117

The Nutrition Program for the Elderly (NPE) helps provide elderly persons with nutritionally sound meals through meals-on-wheels programs or in senior citizen centers and similar settings. The NPE is administered by the U.S. Department of Health and Human Services (DHHS), but receives commodity foods and financial support from the U.S. Department of Agriculture (USDA). Under the Older Americans Act of 1965, USDA contributes commodity foods and/or cash to DHHS programs for the elderly. People age 60 or older and their spouses, regardless of age, are eligible for NPE benefits. Indian tribal organizations may select an age below 60 for defining an "older" person for their tribes. There is no income requirement to receive meals under NPE. Each recipient can contribute as much as he or she wishes toward the cost of the meal, but meals are free to those who cannot make any contribution.

* Nutrition: Technical Assistance

National Center for Chronic Disease Prevention and Health Promotion
Centers for Disease Control
1600 Clifton Rd., NW   404-639-3311
Atlanta, GA 30333   404-639-3534

Through its divisions — chronic disease control, community intervention, health education, nutrition, and reproductive health — this center offers technical assistance and expertise in these categories, as well as in health promotion and health education. Primary recipients of technical assistance are official state and local health agencies, schools, and health care delivery settings. The Center maintains a database of health education programs and methods in schools and rural and urban communities, which is part of the Combined Health Information Database (CHID).

* Nutritionally-Related Chronic Diseases

Beltsville Human Nutrition Research Center
Bldg. 308, Room 223
U.S. Department of Agriculture
ARS - BHNRC
10300 Baltimore Ave.
Beltsville, MD 20705   301-504-8157

This center conducts research on nutrient composition and nutritional qualities of food; performs studies on energy metabolism and nutritional requirements; and develops dietary strategies that can delay the onset of nutritionally-related chronic diseases.

* Nutri-Topics

Food and Nutrition Information Center
U.S. Department of Agriculture
National Agricultural Library, Room 304
10301 Baltimore Blvd.   301-504-5719
Beltsville, MD 20705   Fax: 301-504-6409

Nutri-Topics are free brief reading lists designed to help locate information or resources on a given topic. They are available as separate lists of resources appropriate for one or more user levels: consumer, educator, and health professional. Included are print materials and lists of contacts for further information. Many publications are available on disk (provided by the customer) or electronically, including the Forum Bulletin Board at 301-504-6510/6511. Topics include:

Adolescent Pregnancy and Nutrition
Anorexia Nervosa and Bulimia
Children's Literature on Food and Nutrition
Diet and Cancer
Food Composition
Nutrition and Cardiovascular Disease
Nutrition and Diabetes
Nutrition and the Elderly
Nutrition During Pregnancy
Sensible Nutrition
Sports Nutrition
Vegetarian Nutrition
Weight Control

Quick Biographies are lists of current references on a given topic. The topics covered include:

Adult/Patient Nutrition Education Materials
Childhood Obesity and Cardiovascular Disease
Cultural Perspectives on Food and Nutrition
Fish Oil: Role of Omega-3s in Health and Nutrition
Food Service: Printed Materials and Audiovisuals
Infant Nutrition
Nutrient Composition of Selected Grains as Food
Nutrition and AIDS
Nutrition and the Elderly
Nutrition Education Materials and Audiovisuals: Grades Preschool-6
Nutrition Education Printed Materials and Audiovisuals: Grades 7-12
Pesticide Residues in Food

* Obesity Education Initiative

National Heart, Lung, and Blood Institute Information Center
P.O. Box 30105   301-251-1222
Bethesda, MD 20824-0105   Fax: 301-251-1223

The National Heart, Lung, and Blood Institute (NHLBI) is responding to the increased concern about the impact of overweight and obesity on coronary heart disease and related risk factors, including high blood pressure and high blood cholesterol. The goal of the Obesity Education Initiative is to encourage the adoption of heart-healthy eating patterns and physical activity habits that will help to prevent or reduce the prevalence of overweight and obesity and their related risk factors. Materials available include:

Check Your Weight and Heart Disease I.Q. This 11 question true-false quiz addresses the independent relationship of obesity and overweight to coronary heart disease. (93-3034)

Exercise and Your Heart: A Guide to Physical Activity. This booklet provides up-to-date information on the effects of physical activity on the heart. (93-1677)

Check Your Physical Activity and Heart Disease I.Q. This 12 question true-false quiz addresses the relationship of physical activity to heart health. (95-3795)

Strategy Development Workshop for Public Education on Weight and Obesity-Summary Report. This report highlights panel presentations on the epidemiology of obesity and cardiovascular presentations on the epidemiology of obesity and cardiovascular disease, strategies for obesity prevention, issues in educating the public about weight and obesity, and communication strategies for educating the public. (95-3314)

Be patient. If any phone number is incorrect, call (area code) 555-1212 and request the new listing.

521

Health and Medicine

* Older Adults and Nutrition

Human Nutrition Research Center on
Aging at Tufts University
711 Washington, St.
Boston, MA 02111   617-556-3330

This center researches the special nutritional needs of persons as they age, with a view toward enhancing the quality of later life through improved nutrition and health.

* Organic and Natural Foods

Office of Public Affairs
Food and Drug Administration
5600 Fishers Lane, HFE88
Rockville, MD 20857   301-443-3170

A short pamphlet titled *The Confusing World of Health Foods* provides general information about foods sold as health foods and about such terms as "organic". *The Consumer's Guide to Food Labels* translates the nutrition information which appears on food labels.

* Pesticide Residues

Pesticide Information Network
Office of Pesticide Programs
U.S. Environmental Protection Agency
401 M St. SW, Mail Code 7507C   703-305-7499
Washington, DC 20460   Fax: 703-305-6309

The Pesticide Information Network (PIN) provides a contact directory, pesticide applicator training bibliography, pesticide monitoring inventory, pesticide environmental fate and effects data summaries, and current regulatory information on pesticides in special review, canceled or suspended pesticides, and restricted use product information. PIN services as a mechanism for collecting and disseminating pesticide information and provides a source of expertise for pesticide related activities. Currently the system contains the following files: Chemical Index, Pesticide Monitoring Inventory, Restricted use Products, Pesticide Applicator Training, Environmental Fate and Effects Data Summaries, Regulatory Information, and Contact Directory. To access the system dial 703-305-5919; for technical assistance call 703-305-5919.

* Pick Your Own Fruits and Vegetables

Contact your local USDA Extension Service agent

Many farmers allow consumers to pick produce directly from their fields at substantial savings.

* Saccharin, Cyclamate and Aspartame

Office of Public Affairs
Food and Drug Administration (FDA)
5600 Fishers Lane, HFE88
Rockville, MD 20857   301-443-3170

The Food and Drug Administration (FDA) offers information on food additives including free pamphlets such as *Sweetness Minus Calories = Controversy* which gives the legal and scientific histories of these sugar substitutes and other sweeteners.

* Salt and Low-Sodium Diets

Office of Public Affairs
Food and Drug Administration
5600 Fishers Lane, HFE88
Rockville, MD 20857   301-443-3170

Free pamphlets about consumption of salt in one's daily diet are available, including *A Word About Low-Sodium Diets* which suggests ways consumers can lower sodium intake and lists foods that are naturally low in sodium. A slide set titled "Good Sense About Sodium" (also available in Spanish), is obtainable through Consumer Affairs Officers in FDA district offices.

* Vitamins and Recommended Dietary Allowances

Office of Public Affairs
Food and Drug Administration
5600 Fishers Lane, HFE88
Rockville, MD 20857   301-443-3170

Single copies are available free of the government's recommended dietary allowances in a pamphlet titled *Some Facts and Myths of Vitamins*.

* Worksite Nutrition Programs

Office of Disease Prevention and Health Promotion (ODPHP)
Health Information Center
P.O. Box 1133   800-336-4797
Washington, DC 20013-1133   301-565-4167 in MD

The Information Center has the following publications available concerning worksite nutrition:

Healthy Worksites: Directory of Federal Initiatives in Worksite Health Promotion (W0019, $3) A compilation of projects and research sponsored by the federal government to stimulate and improve worksite health promotion in public and private sectors. Includes agency contacts, brief project descriptions, and available resources.

Health Promotion Goes to Work (W0021, $5) Produced on behalf of the National Coordinating Committee on Worksite Health Promotion, this compendium presents examples of worksite health programs with documented results.

Summary Report of the 1992 National Survey of Worksite Health Promotion Activities (W0020, $2) Measures the growth of worksite health promotion activities since the first national survey in 1985. A major focus of the survey was to assess progress toward worksite objectives in Healthy People 2000.

Worksite Nutrition: A Decision Maker's Guide (U00100, $2) Presents rationale for implementing nutrition programs in the workplace and describes what resources employers need to conduct worksite nutrition programs.

Worksite Nutrition: A Guide to Planning, Implementation, and Evaluation (U0010, $2) Update of *Worksite Nutrition: A Decision Maker's Guide*. Describes how to initiate, design, operate, and evaluate worksite nutrition programs. Profiles numerous worksite programs in corporations and in government agencies.

Contraception and Pregnancy

Several government-sponsored clearinghouses listed below, such as the National Center for Maternal and Child Health and the Family Life Information Exchange, offer materials published by both federal and state health agencies as well as private organizations such as the March of Dimes Birth Defects Foundation. These information centers work in close coordination with many government and private groups and research hubs so they are in a position to refer callers to experts and organizations who can answer questions and concerns.

* Adolescent Pregnancy
National Maternal and Child Health Clearinghouse
2070 Chain Bridge Rd.
Vienna, VA 22182   703-821-8955
This Clearinghouse has free publications focusing on adolescent pregnancy concerns, including *Healthy Foods, Healthy Baby.*

* Adolescent Pregnancy Programs
Population Affairs
Office of Adolescent Pregnancy Programs
U.S. Department of Health and Human Services
East West Towers, Suite 200W
4350 East West Hwy
Bethesda, MD 20814   301-594-4004
This office promotes adoption as an alternative to early parenting and focuses on teenagers under 18 years of age. Pregnancy prevention strategies and information resources are coordinated by this office.

* Birth Control Methods
National Institute of Child Health and Human Development
National Institutes of Health (NIH)
Building 31, Room 2A32
31 Center Dr., MSC 2425
Bethesda, MD 20892-2425   301-496-5133
The National Institute of Child Health and Human Development distributes pamphlets and reports on the various methods of contraception, as well as medical updates on the risks and/or effectiveness of new forms of birth control. The 19-page booklet, *Facts About Oral Contraceptives*, is available free.

* Birth Defects and Developmental Disabilities Research
Birth Defects and Developmental Disabilities Division
National Center For Environmental Health
  and Injury Control
Centers for Disease Control
1600 Clifton Rd., NE   404-639-3311
Atlanta, GA 30333   404-639-3534
Birth defects are the leading cause of infant mortality in the U.S., accounting for more than 20% of the infant deaths each year. This division conducts surveillance on birth defects and developmental disabilities, and assists states with programs to prevent both. They examine data to identify new risk factors for birth defects and developmental disabilities. They are now beginning to focus on three specific disease areas: spina bifida, fetal alcohol syndrome, and mild mental retardation, because research suggests that these diseases can be prevented. An annual program summary, and a bibliography of the division research reports are available.

* Breastfeeding Information
National Maternal and Child Health Clearinghouse
2070 Chain Bridge Rd.
Vienna, VA 22182   703-821-8955
This Clearinghouse has several free publications dealing with breastfeeding, including:

Breastfeeding Is Good for You, and Also for Your Baby, in Spanish (information card)

Connections: Government and Private Sector Sharing to Improve Breastfeeding Rates.
Nutrition during Lactation
Surgeon General's Workshop on Breastfeeding and Human Lactation - covers the physiology of breastfeeding, the unique values of human milk, current trends, and cultural factors relating to breastfeeding.

* Cesarean Childbirth
National Institute of Child Health and Human Development
National Institutes of Health (NIH)
Building 31, Room 2A32
31 Center Dr., MSC 2425
Bethesda, MD 20892-2425   301-496-5133
This institute can provide data and medical information about this health issue. A 13-page booklet, *Facts About Cesarean Childbirth* discusses cesarean delivery, types of incisions, current thinking about repeat cesarean, and the pros and cons of this method of birth.

* Child Health Info for Prospective and New Parents
National Center for Education in Maternal
  and Child Health (NCEMCH)
2000 15th St. North, Suite 701   703-524-7802
Arlington, VA 22201-2617   Fax: 703-524-9335
The Center responds to information requests from prospective and new parents, consumers, and professionals. This clearinghouse provides technical assistance, and develops educational and reference materials. The NCEMCH Resource Center contains professional literature, patient education materials, curricula, audiovisuals, and information about organizations and programs. Major content areas include pregnancy, child and adolescent health, and human genetics.

* Cigarettes and the Unborn
Office on Smoking and Health
Centers for Disease Control
Mail Stop K-50
4770 Buford Hwy, NE
Atlanta, GA 30341-3724   770-488-5705
This Office can provide you with information on smoking as it effects pregnancy and newborns. Some of the free pamphlets available include *Is Your Baby Smoking?* which explains the dangers of passive smoke on the baby; and "Pregnant? That's Two Good Reasons to Quit Smoking" which highlights the dangers of smoking to the fetus (available in English and Spanish).

* Condoms and Effectiveness of Other Contraception
Center for Population Research
Contraception Evaluation Branch
6100 Executive Blvd., Room 8B07
Bethesda, MD 20892   301-496-4924
The Contraception Evaluation Branch designs and supports a program of studies to clarify the safety and effectiveness of fertility control. They also provide on-going surveillance of the effectiveness of fertility regulating products and surgical procedures. A major emphasis now is to demonstrate the degree to which barrier contraceptives reduce the risk of sexually transmitted diseases, including AIDS. Staff can refer you to researchers examining a particular birth control method, with most of their research being published in journals.

Health and Medicine

* Comparing Contraceptives

Office of Consumer Affairs
Food and Drug Administration
Public Inquiries
5600 Fishers Lane (HFE-88)
Rockville, MD 20857   301-443-3170
This agency publishes *Choosing A Contraceptive* (No. 94-1213), which discusses the possible side effects and effectiveness of nine different types of birth control and also contains a chart.

* Dental Care for Your Babe

Public Information and Reports Branch
National Institute of Dental Research (NIDR)
Bldg. 31, Room 2C35
31 Center Dr., MSC 2290   301-496-4261
Bethesda, MD 20892-2290   Fax: 301-496-9988
The National Institute of Dental Research (NIDR) provides information on proper oral hygiene for infants. Two of the free health promotion items available are a pamphlet titled *A Healthy Mouth for Your Baby* (23A) and a *Prevent Baby Bottle Tooth Decay* bookmark (also available in Spanish, 3F).

* Diabetes and Pregnancy

Office of Research Reports
National Institute of Child Health and Human Development
National Institutes of Health
Building 31, Room 2A20
31 Center Dr., MSC 2420
Bethesda, MD 20892-2420   301-496-5133
Understanding Gestational Diabetes: A Practical Guide to a Healthy Pregnancy (91-2788) addresses questions about diet, exercise, measurement of blood sugar levels, and general medical and obstetric care of women with gestational diabetes. It answers such questions as: Will my baby have diabetes?, What can I do to control gestational diabetes?, and Will I have diabetes in the future? This is a free booklet.

* Down's Syndrome Information

Office of Research Reports
National Institute of Child Health and Human Development
National Institutes of Health (NIH)
Building 31, Room 2A32
31 Center Dr., MSC 2420
Bethesda, MD 20892-2420   301-496-5133
Facts About Down's Syndrome and *Facts About Down's Syndrome for Women Over 35* (No. 82-536), discuss genetic counseling, and the outlook for a child born with Down's syndrome. This institute can provide more technical and statistical information about this birth defect.

* Drinking When Pregnant

National Clearinghouse for Alcohol and Drug Information
P.O. Box 2345   800-729-6686
Rockville, MD 20847-2345   301-468-2600
                                          TDD: 800-487-4889
The Clearinghouse has several free publications dealing with drinking and drug use during pregnancy. Some of the titles include:

Alcohol, Tobacco, and Other Drugs May Harm the Unborn - presents the most recent finding of basic research and clinical studies (PH291).

Drug Abuse and Pregnancy - provides an overview of the scope of the problem and effects of maternal drug use on the mother, fetus, and infant (CAP33).

How To Take Care of Your Baby Before Birth - a low-literacy brochure aimed at pregnant women that describes what they should and should not do during their pregnancy, emphasizing a no use of alcohol and other drugs message (PH239, also in Spanish).

An Inner Voice Tells You Not to Drink or Use Other Drugs - poster depicts an artistic rendition of a pregnant American Indian Woman (AV161).

Prenatal Drug Exposure: Kinetics and Dynamics - NIDA Research Monograph 60 - presents research studies on the effects of maternal use of dugs on the fetus (M60).

Prevention Resource Guide: Pregnant/Postpartum Women and Their Infants - Resource Guide targets pregnant and postpartum women, women between the ages of 15-44, counselors, health care providers, and prevention program planners. It provides a high-demand, comprehensive resource for information concerning alcohol and other drug prevention among pregnant and postpartum women and their infants (MS420).

Women and Drug Use - discussion of women and drugs.

* Drugs (Legal and Illegal) and Pregnancy

Office of Consumer Affairs
Food and Drug Administration
Public Inquiries
5600 Fishers Lane (HFE-88)
Rockville, MD 20857   301-443-3170
Single copies are available free of *Drugs and Pregnancy*, (No. 90-3174), which explains how medications, drugs, alcohol and tobacco are shared with the unborn baby. Other related hazards to the fetus are also discussed.

* Eating for Two

Office of Consumer Affairs
Food and Drug Administration
Public Inquiries
5600 Fishers Lane (HFE-88)
Rockville, MD 20857   301-443-3170
A free booklet, *All About Eating for Two* discusses how pregnancy and breastfeeding affect a woman's nutritional needs.

* Fetal and Newborn Development and Child Health

Center for Research on Mothers and Children
National Institute of Child Health and Human Development
National Institutes of Health
Executive Bldg., Room 4B05
6100 Executive Blvd., MSC 7510
Bethesda, MD 20892-7510   301-496-5097
The National Institute of Child Health and Human Development (NICHHD) conducts and supports research on the reproductive, developmental, and behavioral process that determine the health of children, adults, families, and populations. Research for mothers, children, and families is designed to advance knowledge of fetal development, pregnancy, and birth; to identify the prerequisites of optional growth through infancy to adulthood; and to contribute to the prevention and treatment of mental retardation.

* Genetics

National Maternal and Child Health Clearinghouse
2070 Chain Bridge Rd.
Vienna, VA 22182   703-821-8955
This Clearinghouse has several free publications dealing with genetics. Some of the titles include: *Genetics: Abstract of Active Projects FY 1991*, *Genetics Support Groups* ($10), and *Resources for Clergy in Human Genetic Problems*.

* Genetics Research

Office of Research Reports
National Institute of General Medical Sciences (NIGMS)
National Institutes of Health
45 Center Dr., MSC 6200   301-496-7301
Bethesda, MD 20892-6200   Fax: 301-402-0224
The National Institute of General Medical Sciences (NIGMS) supports research and research training in the basic biomedical sciences that form the foundation needed to make advances in the understanding of disease. Research focuses on the cellular basis of disease, genetics, pharmacological sciences, physiology and biomedical engineering. For instance, they look at how DNA is replicated or how drugs are metabolized in your body. They have brochures and reports for the general public and professionals on such topics as medicines and genetic diseases.

* Gynecological Health

Office of Disease Prevention and Health Promotion (ODPHP)
National Health Information Center
P.O. Box 1133   800-336-4797
Washington, DC 20013   301-565-4167 in MD
The Information Center can provide you with names of organizations and agencies involved with gynecology, which can then refer you to experts in the field.

* Healthy Mothers, Healthy Babies

Office of Public Affairs
Health Resources and Services Administration
5600 Fishers Lane, Room 1445
Rockville, MD 20857   301-443-2086

The Health Resources and Services Administration (HRSA) offers a free catalog, *Current Publications*, which lists all the publications, films, and videos produced by HRSA's three bureaus: Bureau of Health Care Delivery and Assistance, Bureau of Maternal and Child Health and Resources Development, and Bureau of Health Professions.

* Immunizations

National Immunization Program
Centers for Disease Control
1600 Clifton Rd., NE
Atlanta, GA 30333   800-SHOT

Information on childhood or adult immunizations or specific vaccines is available by fax, mail, or recorded messages. An operator is available during business hours to answer other questions you might have.

* Infants at Risk

National Center for Clinical Infant Programs
2000 14th St.
Arlington, VA 22201   703-528-4300

The Center supports professional initiatives in infant health, mental health and development. Project Zero to Three, funded by the Bureau of Maternal and Child Health and Resources Development, focuses on infants who are disabled or at risk. Publications are available on clinical issues targeted at disciplines concerned with infants, toddlers, and their families. To order publications, call 800-544-0155.

* Infertility and Population Research

Reproductive Sciences Branch
Center for Population Research
6100 Executive Blvd., Room 603
Bethesda, MD 20892   301-496-6515

The Reproductive Sciences Branch supports basic research in reproductive sciences, such as the alleviation of human infertility, curing human reproductive diseases and disorders, development of healthy embryos, and the discovery of safe methods of contraception. Institutional Programs in Reproductive Sciences Research awards grants to leading institutions in the U.S. to help them to establish Program Projects and Research Centers to support research on reproductive sciences. They also support postdoctoral fellowships, institutional training grants, and other awards to facilitate the development and maintenance of reproductive sciences research programs. This Branch also organizes workshops and symposiums in the U.S. and abroad on various topics in the reproductive sciences.

* Infertility and Treatments

Office of Consumer Affairs
Food and Drug Administration
Public Inquiries
5600 Fishers Lane (HFE-88)
Rockville, MD 20857   301-443-3170

Single copies are available free of the two-page pamphlet, *Infertility and How It's Treated.*

* Maternal and Child Health Clearinghouse

National Maternal and Child Health Clearinghouse
2070 Chain Bridge Rd., Suite 450
Vienna, VA 22182   703-821-8955

This clearinghouse is a centralized source of materials and information in the areas of maternal and child health. The clearinghouse responds to inquiries, and distributes publications, bibliographies, and referral lists.

* Norplant

Center for Drug Evaluation and Research
Food and Drug Administration
5600 Fishers Lane, HFD W01
Rockville, MD 20857   301-594-6740

This Center can provide you with free reports and information regarding the new contraception called Norplant. Reports include information on patient labeling, prescribing, usage, warnings, and Food and Drug Administration (FDA) statements regarding Norplant. The Contraceptive Development Branch of the Center for Population Research is beginning to conduct research regarding who chooses to use Norplant, and who chooses to discontinue it. They can be contacted at 6100 Executive Blvd., Bethesda, MD 20892; 301-496-1661.

* Nutrition During Pregnancy

National Maternal and Child Health Clearinghouse
2070 Chain Bridge Rd., Suite 450
Vienna, VA 22182   703-821-8955

Healthy Foods, Healthy Babies summarizes the nutritional recommendations during pregnancy.

* Nutrition in Early Childhood

National Maternal and Child Health Clearinghouse
2070 Chain Bridge Rd., Suite 450
Vienna, VA 22182   703-821-8955

This Clearinghouse has two free publications concerned with childhood nutrition. *Nutritional Disorders of Children: Prevention, Screening, and Follow-up*, and *Nutrition Resources for Early Childhood - Resource Guide*, which is an annotated list of current nutrition education publication for children ages 1-5 years, their parents, caregivers, and teachers.

* Pediatric and Maternal AIDS

Pediatric, Adolescent, and Maternal AIDS Branch
National Institute of Child Health and Human Development
National Institutes of Health
Bldg. 6100, Room 4B11, MSC 7510
9000 Rockville Pike
Bethesda, MD 20892-7510   301-496-7339

This new Branch conducts research on AIDS and AIDS related viruses in pregnant women, mothers, infants, children, adolescents and the family unit as a whole and works towards providing a more precise understanding of the modes of transmission. This Branch strives to address areas which are unique to the maternal-child dyad, to the at-risk and infected adolescent, and to groups traditionally of special concern to pediatricians (hemophiliac children). A report to Council is available describing research efforts and goals. This office can provide you with current research, refer you to experts or provide you with information regarding clinical trials.

* Population Research: Fertility, Contraception

Center for Population Research (CPR)
6100 Executive Blvd.
Bethesda, MD 20892   301-496-1101

The Center for Population Research (CPR), as part of the National Institute of Child Health and Human Development, is responsible for the extramural effort in population research. It funds research through grants and contracts for studies on fertility, contraception, and population structure and change. The Inter-agency Committee on Population Research, a committee of Federal Agencies, facilitates the exchange of information on population research, which includes producing two free publications: *The Inventory and Analysis of Federal Population Research* which lists all the federally supported population research projects; and *The Inventory of Private Agency Population Research* which lists research projects by private organizations. CPR also advances international cooperation in population research and collaborates with the World Health Organization regarding the development of safe methods of contraception.

* Pregnancy and Infancy Resources

Pregnancy and Perinatology Branch
National Institute of Child Health and Human Development
NRCHD/CRMC/PP
6100 Executive Blvd., MSC 7510
Bethesda, MD 20892-7510   301-496-5575

Information on pregnancy, birth, and infant development and disorders is available through the Pregnancy and Perinatology Branch. They have brochures, pamphlets, reports, and information on current research. The research in this branch focuses on high-risk pregnancies, fetal pathophysiology, premature birth and labor, disorders of the newborn, sudden infant death syndrome, and AIDS. A report to Council is available which describes the research conducted.

Health and Medicine

* Pregnancy Basics

National Institutes of Child Health and Human Development
National Institutes of Health
Building 31, Room 2A32
31 Center Dr., MSC 2425
Bethesda, MD 20892-2425   301-496-5133

Pregnancy Basics: What you need to know and do to have a good healthy baby is a free booklet which examines weight gain, vitamins, nutrition, exercise, smoking, drinking, drugs, and X-rays.

* Pregnancy-Related Deaths Investigation

Center for Chronic Disease Prevention and Health Promotion
Centers for Disease Control
1600 Clifton Rd, NE   404-639-3311
Atlanta, GA 30333   404-639-3534

The National Maternal Mortality Surveillance System is maintained as an avenue for reporting pregnancy-related deaths in the United States. All reported deaths are investigated, and a liaison has been established with local and national organizations of obstetricians and gynecologists to improve obstetric practices.

* Premature Birth

National Institute of Child Health and Human Development
National Institutes of Health
31 Center Dr., MSC 2425
Bethesda, MD 20892-2425   301-496-5133

This institute has much information about premature labor and birth including two free booklets: *Little Babies Born Too Soon, Born Too Small* and *Facts About Premature Birth*.

* Prenatal Care

National Maternal and Child Health Clearinghouse
2070 Chain Bridge Rd., Suite 450
Vienna, VA 22182   703-821-8955

Baby on the Way Basics is a free publication available from the clearinghouse concerning prenatal care.

* Prenatal Care: Technical Assistance

National Center for Chronic Disease Prevention and Health Promotion
Centers for Disease Control (CDC)
1600 Clifton Rd., NW   404-639-3311
Atlanta, GA 30333   404-639-3534

This Centers for Disease Control (CDC) center offers technical assistance and expertise on reproductive health as well as in health promotion and health education. Primary recipients of technical assistance are official state and local health agencies, schools, and health care delivery settings. The Center maintains a database of health education programs and methods in schools and rural and urban communities, which is part of the Combined Health Information Database (CHID).

* Sonograms and Its Effects on Pregnancy

Office of Research Reporting
National Institute of Child Health and
 Human Development (NICHHD)
Building 31, Room 2A-32
31 Center Dr., MSC 2425
Bethesda, MD 20892-2425   301-496-5133

This office distributes a 1984 NICHHD conference report entitled, *Diagnostic Ultrasound Imaging in Pregnancy*, which discusses the biophysics and bioeffects of sonograms, clinical applications, epidemiological studies, and the psychological, legal, and ethical dimensions of ultrasound imaging. A brief pamphlet, *The Unknowns of Ultrasound* (No. 83-8201) is also available free.

* Sudden Infant Death Syndrome (SIDS)

National Sudden Infant Death Syndrome Clearinghouse
2070 Chain Bridge Rd., Suite 450
Vienna, VA 22182   703-821-8955

This clearinghouse was established to provide information and educational materials on SIDS, apnea, and other related issues. The staff responds to information requests from professionals, families with SIDS-related deaths, and the general public by sending written materials and making referrals. The clearinghouse maintains a library of reference materials and mailing lists of state programs, groups, and individuals concerned with SIDS. Their many publications include bibliographies on SIDS and self-help support groups, a publications catalogue, and a newsletter. The free publications include:

Crib Death - explains SIDS in easy to read booklet form.

Directory of State Title V Maternal and Child Health Directors and SIDS Program Coordinators - lists MCH directors and SIDS coordinators by state; Federal and Federally supported programs; and private SIDS and SIDS-related programs.

Examination of the SIDS Infant: Investigative and Autopsy Protocols - reports the results of a 1975 national conference.

Fact Sheet: Facts about Apnea and Other Apparent Life-Threatening Events.

Fact Sheet: Grief of Children - discusses some of the common expressions of children's grief and offers way in which adults can help during the grieving process.

Fact Sheet: Parents and The Grieving Process - defines grief, presents common reactions and emotions expressed by people who are bereaved, and highlights the process by which resolution and recovery may be achieved.

Fact Sheet: SIDS Information for the EMT - provides suggestions for first response of EMTs and others at the time of sudden infant death.

Fact Sheet: What Is SIDS? - provides basic facts about SIDS and discusses reactions of the surviving family members and ways they can be helped.

FDA Safety Alert: Important Tips for Apnea Monitor Users - lists important tips to help parents and caregivers understand the limitations of infant apnea monitors and offers guidelines for their proper use.

A Guide to Resources in Perinatal Bereavement - offers selected resources for professionals working with parents who have lost a child.

Infantile Apnea and Home Monitoring-Consensus Statement - Statement form the October 1986 National Institutes of Health Consensus Development Conference on Infantile Apnea and Home Monitoring.

Information Exchange - Quarterly newsletter of SIDS Clearinghouse.

Joint Hearing on SIDS Before the Committees on Post Office and Civil Service, Committee on Energy and Commerce, and the Select Committee on Children, Youth, and Families, 99th Congress - Testimony to bring the issue of SIDS into the public domain, to generate support for educating the public and professionals about SIDS, and to encourage further research.

Los Hechos Sobre El Sindrome De La Muerte Infantil Repentina - Spanish translation of a basic brochure containing information about SIDS.

Muerte En La Cuna - Spanish translation of Crib Death.

Nosology Guideline - supplement to the medical examiner's cause-of-death coding manual describing death certificate coding information for SIDS.

Sudden Infant Death Syndrome and Other Infant Losses Among Adolescent Parents: An Annotated Bibliography and Resource Guide - presents an overview of adolescent bereavement, abstract of articles, and resources for adolescents.

Sudden Unexplained Infant Death 1970-1975: An Evolution of Understanding - examines changes in understanding of sudden, unexpected, and unexplained infant death.

Talking to Children About Death - booklet helps prepare parents and other adults to talk to children about death.

* Teenage Pregnancy Prevention Grants

Office of Population Affairs
Adolescent Pregnancy Programs
East West Towers, Suite 200W
4350 East West Hwy.
Bethesda, MD 20814   301-594-4004

This office awards grants to private and public non-profit organizations to establish and operate voluntary family planning services. The Adolescent Family Life Program supports research projects and innovative family-centered, community-based demonstration projects to provide either care or prevention services for adolescents and their families.

* Toxoplasmosis and Birth Defects

National Institute of Allergy and Infectious Diseases
National Institutes of Health
Building 31, Room 7A-50
31 Center Drive, MSC 2520
Bethesda, MD 20892-2520   301-496-5717

Information on toxoplasmosis discussing the hazards to the fetus of the toxoplasma parasites and suggesting precautions to prevent the disease is available free from the institute.

* Workplace Hazards: Fetal Development and Pregnancy

National Institute for Occupational Safety
and Health (NIOSH)
4676 Columbia Parkway
Cincinnati, OH 45226   800-356-4674

The National Institute of Occupational Safety and Health (NIOSH) is responsible for conducting research to make the nation's workplaces healthier and safer by responding to urgent requests for assistance from employers, employees, and their representatives where imminent hazards are suspected. They conduct inspections, laboratory and epidemiologic research, publish their findings, and make recommendations for improved working conditions to regulatory agencies. NIOSH trains occupational health and safety workers and communicates research results to those concerned.

Stress, Mental Illness, and Family Violence

The National Institute of Mental Health of the National Institutes of Health is a useful starting place for discovering other information resources. Local and state chapters of the National Mental Health Association provide assistance to the mentally ill and their families, and provide help to school systems and local governments. Many county and state governments offer counseling and other services.

* Adolescent Violence and Death

National Technical Information Service
U.S. Department of Commerce
5285 Port Royal Rd.
Springfield, VA 22161   703-487-4650

Focal Points provides information on violence as a public health problem, particularly in the area of reducing the deaths of those in the 15-24 age group. Stress reduction and other programs that prevent violence are described. This publication (Order No. PB84-158385) is available for $12.50.

* Anger and Aggression

Public Inquiries Branch
National Institute of Mental Health   301-443-4513
5600 Fishers Lane, Room 7C-02   Fax: 301-443-0008
Rockville, MD 20857   TDD: 301-443-8431

This Institute publishes several free pamphlets including *Plain Talk About Adolescence* (#ADM-85-1965)

* Attention Deficit Hyperactivity Disorder

Superintendent of Documents
Government Printing Office (GPO)   202-512-1800
Washington, DC 20402   Fax: 202-512-2250

This book offers up-to-date information on attention deficit disorders and the role of the National Institute of Mental Health sponsored research in discovering underlying causes and effective treatments. It describes treatment options, strategies for coping, and sources of information and support. The book tells what it is like to have Attention Deficit Hyperactivity Disorder (ADHD) through the stories of fictional characters who are representative of people who show symptoms of ADHD. The order number is 017-024-01543-1 and costs $39.

* Biofeedback and Stress Reduction

Public Inquiries Branch
National Institute of Mental Health   301-443-4513
5600 Fishers Lane, Room 7C-02   Fax: 301-443-0008
Rockville, MD 20857   TDD: 301-443-8431

Plain Talk About Handling Stress discusses the stages of physical and mental stress, describes the symptoms and offers suggestions for stress reduction. This is available free from the Institute, as is *Plain Talk About the Art of Relaxation*.

* Child Abuse and Neglect Clearinghouse

Clearinghouse on Child Abuse and Neglect Information
P.O. Box 1182
Washington, DC 20013-1182   800-FYI-3366

The Clearinghouse on Child Abuse and Neglect Information is a major resource for both professionals and the general public interested in child maltreatment issues. Publications distributed include bibliographies, training materials, and research reviews. The clearinghouse maintains a database (Dialogue File 64) from which they can retrieve information on specific topics. Contact this office for a free listing of their publications and other resources.

* Child Abuse Prevention Programs

Clearinghouse on Child Abuse and Neglect
Administration for Children, Youth, and Families
P.O. Box 1182

Washington, DC 20013   800-FYI-3366

The National Center on Child Abuse and Neglect (NCCAN) awards grants to states for a variety of programs dealing with child abuse and neglect; conducts research into the causes, prevention, and treatment of child abuse and neglect; funds demonstration programs to identify the best means of preventing maltreatment and treating troubled families; and funds the development and implementation of training programs. It distributes information through the Clearinghouse on Child Abuse and Neglect Information.

* Child Abuse Resources for Professionals

National Resource Center on Child Abuse and Neglect   303-792-9900
63 Inverness Dr. East   Fax: 303-792-5333
Englewood, CO 80112-5117   Information Service: 800-227-5242

Information specialists are trained and have access to the most current resources in the area of child abuse and neglect. Information dissemination activities include teleconferences that address critical issues, information papers, and a national conference calendar which is distributed in the American Humane Association's quarterly publication, *Protection Children*. The Center conducts special events and provides training opportunities at major conferences, provides technical assistance and consultation to both public and private agencies, assists in identifying model programs and best practices throughout the country, and provides a wide variety of resources and services to improve the capacities of public and private agencies to respond effectively to the problem of child abuse and neglect.

* Child Abuse Signs and Symptoms

Clearinghouse on Child Abuse and Neglect Information
P.O. Box 1182
Washington, DC 20013-1182   800-FYI-3366

Child Abuse and Neglect: An Informed Approach To A Shared Concern is a free pamphlet providing information about detecting child abuse and how to obtain help.

* Child Adoption, Foster Care and Welfare

Children's Bureau
Administration for Children, Youth, and Families
Office of Human Development Services
330 C St., SW
Washington, DC 20201   202-205-8618

The Children's Bureau funds a range of state-run programs combatting child abuse and neglect, strengthening foster care and adoption services, and supporting other child welfare services.

* Child Sexual Abuse Info Center

National Resource Center on Child Sexual Abuse (NRCCSA)
Information Service   800-543-7006
2204 Whitesburg Dr., Suite 200   205-534-6868
Huntsville, AL 35801   Fax: 205-534-6883

The National Resource Center on Child Sexual Abuse (NRCCSA) is an information, training, and technical assistance center designed for all professionals working in the field of child sexual abuse. They provide an array of services to help professionals better to investigate and manage child sexual victimization cases. The Information Service handles requests for information, and for a quarterly publication, *NRCCSA News*, which offers information, updates, and new developments on child abuse. This office also sponsors comprehensive training with national experts and leading professionals. Single copies of bibliographies and information papers are available free of charge. Some of the publications available include:

Think Tank Reports ($15 each)

Allegations of Sexual Abuse in Child Custody and Visitation Situations
Child Protective Services: A System in Crisis
A Judicial Response to Child Sexual Abuse
Enhancing Child Sexual Abuse Services to Minority Cultures
Investigation of Ritualistic Abuse Allegations
Sibling Incest
Professionals and Volunteers with a History of Abuse
Traditional Native American Healing and Child Sexual Abuse
A Coordinated Community Approach to Child Sexual Abuse: Assessing a Model
Responding to Sexual Abuse of Children with Disabilities: Prevention, Intervention, and Treatment

Building Blocks - history of National Children's Advocacy Center and explanation of current procedures ($12).

Best Practices: A Guidebook to Establishing a Children's Advocacy Center Program - designed to provide technical assistance ($50).

For information on training resources, call 800-239-9939.

* Child Victimization and Exploitation

Juvenile Justice Clearinghouse   800-638-8736
P.O. Box 6000   Fax: 301-251-5212
Rockville, MD 20850   Internet: look@ncjrs.aspensys.com

The Juvenile Justice Clearinghouse is the Office of Juvenile Justice and Delinquency Preventions link to juvenile justice professionals and policymakers. The clearinghouse produces and distributes publications, prepares customized responses to information requests, and provides referrals.

* Children of Alcoholic Families

National Clearinghouse on Alcohol Information
PO Box 2345   800-729-6686
Rockville, MD 20852-2345   301-468-2600
    Fax: 301-468-6433
    TDD: 800-487-4889

The clearinghouse can provide you with information on alcohol abuse in the form of pamphlets, fact sheets, booklets, posters, and videos. Information is targeted at all age groups.

* Community Mental Health Help

Consumer Information Center
Dept. Z
Pueblo, CO 81009

A Consumer's Guide to Mental Health Services describes the services available from community mental health centers, details different kinds of therapy and mental health professionals, and provides a list of warning signals and tells what to do in a crisis situation. This 21-page booklet is available free.

* Crisis Counseling Grants and Materials

Emergency Services Branch
National Institute of Mental Health
5600 Fishers Lane, Room 11C25   301-443-4735
Rockville, MD 20857   Fax: 301-443-8040

The Emergency Services Branch oversees three programs: 1) The Emergency Research Program studies the psychosocial response to mass emergencies; 2) The Crisis Counseling Program administers crisis counseling grants to states in which there has been a Presidentially-declared disaster; 3) The Emergency Preparedness Program plans for alcohol, drug abuse, and mental health disaster-related services nationwide. The program provides technical assistance and public education materials to states and local agencies in times of emergencies, and has three publications designed for non-mental health emergency workers (police, fire, emergency medical personnel) which focus on mental health issues. The following free publications are available:

Crisis Intervention Programs for Disaster Victims in Smaller Communities
Disaster Work and Mental Health: Prevention and Control of Stress Among Workers
Field Manual for Human Service Workers in Major Disasters
Human Problems in Major Disasters: A Training Curriculum for Emergency Medical Personnel
Innovations in Mental Health Services to Disaster Victims

Manual for Child Health Workers in Major Disasters
Prevention and Control of Stress Among Emergency Workers: A Pamphlet for Team Managers
Prevention and Control of Stress Among Emergency Workers: A Pamphlet for Workers
Role Stressors and Supports for Emergency Workers
Training Manual for Human Service Workers in Major Disasters

* Death and Grieving

National Sudden Infant Death Syndrome Resource Center
2070 Chain Bridge Rd., Suite 450
Vienna, VA 22182   703-821-8955

The Grief of Children discusses some of the ways that children express grief and that adults can help. Two other short pamphlets available free are *Parents and the Grieving Process* and *Talking to Children About Death*.

* Depression: Diagnosis and Treatments

National Institute of Mental Health (NIMH)
5600 Fishers Lane, Room 7C-02   301-443-4515
Rockville, MD 20857   Fax: 301-443-0008
    TDD: 301-443-8431

The National Institute of Mental Health (NIMH) conducts research on depression and other mental disorders, distributes information, conducts demonstration programs for the prevention, treatment, and rehabilitation of the mentally ill. A major media campaign on depression, called Project D/ART (Depression/Awareness, Recognition, Treatment), has been developed by NIMH in collaboration with other organizations to provide information on symptoms, causes, and treatments of various depressive disorders. Many publications and reports are available on various topics for professionals and the general public. Some of the publications available include:

Bipolar Disorder (93-3679)
D/ART Fact Sheet (ADM 92-1680)
Depressive Illnesses: Treatments Bring New Hope (93-3612)
Helpful Facts About Depressive Disorders (ADM 92-1536)
Helping the Depressed Person Get Treatment (ADM 90-1675)
If You're Over 65 and Feeling Depressed...Treatment Brings New Hope (ADM 90-1653)
Let's Talk About Depression (ADM 91-1695)
Plain Talk About Depression (NIH 94-3561)
What to do When A Friend is Depressed: A Guide for Teenagers (94-3824)
Depression: What You Need to Know (94-3808)
Important Information About D/ART and Depression (ADM 91-1873)

* Depression in the Workplace

Information Resources and Inquiries Branch
National Institute of Mental Health   301-443-4513
5600 Fishers Lane, Room 7C-02   Fax: 301-443-0008
Rockville, MD 20857   TDD: 301-443-8431

The National Worksite Programs aims to reduce direct and indirect costs of depression in the workplace by education corporate executives, managers, employees, and families about symptoms of depression and about effective, available treatments. Publications available are *What To Do When an Employee Is Depressed: A Guide for Supervisors*, a 6-panel brochure that will enable an employer to recognize the symptoms of depression in an employee and offers suggestions on what to say to encourage him or her to seek help (ADM 91-1792); and *Managing Depression in the Workplace*, a useful pocket folder that contains information on the Depression/ Awareness, Recognition, Treatment (D/ART) Program. (ADM 91-1793). A poster for National Worksite Program is available in 2 sizes 16 1/2 and 22 (sent folded), ADM 91-1871, and 8 1/2 x 11, ADM 91-1872, is also available.

* Elderly Alcohol Abuse

Information Center
National Institute on Aging
P.O. Box 8057   800-222-2225
Gaithersburg, MD 20898-8057   Fax: 800-222-4225

Aging and Alcohol Abuse is a one-page information sheet available free from the National Institute on Aging.

* Family Adjustment and Crisis

Rural Information Center
U.S. Department of Agriculture

National Agricultural Library Building
10301 Baltimore Blvd.
Beltsville, MD 20705

800-633-7701
301-504-5372
Fax: 301-504-5181

This Center has information for the public on family adjustment to change and management of stress, as well as family and individual anxieties concerning transition, family support networks, and economical and social change. Publications for professionals include *Special Reference Briefs* on critical aspects and stages of family life.

* Free Mental Health Publications

S. James
Consumer Information Center-6A
P.O. Box 100
Pueblo, CO 81002

The Consumer Information Catalog is a catalog of free and low-cost federal publications of consumer interest. A new catalog is published each quarter, and is available free of charge. You can request your free catalog by calling 719-948-4000. The publications they have available dealing with mental health include:

Anxiety Disorders 549C (free)
Bipolar Disorder (Manic Depressive Illness) 550C (free)
Depression 551C (free)
Eating Disorders 552C (free)
Handling Stress 553C (free)
Obsessive-Compulsive Disorder 554C (free)
Panic Disorder 555C (free)
Schizophrenia: Questions and Answers 556C (free)
Wife Abuse 557C (free)

* Mental Health Databases

National Institute of Mental Health
5600 Fishers Lane, Room 7C-02
Rockville, MD 20857

301-443-4515
Fax: 301-443-0008
TDD: 301-443-8431

This Institute maintains databases which index and abstract documents from the worldwide literature pertaining to mental health. In addition to scientific journals, there are references to audiovisuals, dissertations, government documents and reports. Mental Health Abstracts is available on DIALOG, 800-334-2564.

* Mental Health Directory

Superintendent of Documents
Government Printing Office
Washington, DC 20402

202-512-1800
Fax: 202-512-2250

Mental Health Directory 1990 is a comprehensive listing, by State, of outpatient mental health clinics, psychiatric hospitals, Veterans Administration medical centers, residential treatment centers for emotionally disturbed children, mental health day/night facilities, community mental health centers, and general hospitals with separate psychiatric services (017-024-01419-2, $23).

* Mental Health Fax Service

Information Resources and Inquiries Branch
National Institute of Mental Health (NIMH)
5600 Fishers Lane, Room 7C-02
Rockville, MD 20857

301-443-4513
Fax: 301-443-0008
TDD: 301-443-8431

The National Institute of Mental Health provides a fax on demand system that will deliver documents directly to your fax machine 24 hours a day, 7 days a week. You can request a table of contents listing all publications available. Documents are available from the Division of Neuroscience and Behavioral Science, the Division of Clinical and Treatment Research, the Division of Epidemiology and Services Research, the Office on AIDS. Prevalence of Mental Disorders Data, Aging Materials, general publications, program announcements, and general information. You must call from the handset of your fax machine to use this free service. Follow the voice prompts to receive the documents you want. NIMH documents and other information is also available on the Internet at http://www.nimh.nih.gov/outline/nimhmenu.htm.

* Mental Health Publications

National Institute of Mental Health (NIMH)
5600 Fishers Lane, Room 7C-02
Rockville, MD 20857

301-443-4515
Fax: 301-443-0008
TDD: 301-443-8431

The National Institute of Mental Health (NIMH) has a catalogue of free publications

available dealing with a wide range of mental health issues. Some of the general publications available include:

A Consumer's Guide to Mental Health Services
Obsessive-Compulsive Disorder: Useful Information from the NIMH
Plain Talk About Aging
Plain Talk About Handling Stress
Plain Talk About Physical Fitness and Mental Health
Plain Talk About Mutual Help Groups
Plain Talk About the Art of Relaxation
Plain Talk About Wife Abuse
Useful Information on Paranoia
Useful Information on Sleep Disorders
You Are Not Alone: Facts About Mental Health and Mental Illness
Information Packet on Use of Mental Health Services by Children and Adolescents
National Plan for Research on Child and Adolescent Mental Disorders
Working Bibliography on Behavioral and Emotional Disorders and Assessment Instruments in Mental Retardation
Caring for People with Severe Mental Disorders: A National Plan of Research to Improve Services

Subscriptions

SAMHSA News ($9.50/yr) - Monthly newsletter of the Substance Abuse and Mental Health Services Administration which provides coverage of events, research findings, budget, legislation, etc. (S/N 717-002-00000-8)

Psychopharmacology Bulletin ($8/yr) - disseminates research findings in this country and abroad. Issued quarterly. (S/N 717-020-00000-6).

Both subscriptions available from: Superintendent of Documents, Government Printing Office, Washington, DC 20402; 202-512-1800.

* Mental Health Videos

National Institute of Mental Health (NIMH)
Technical Services Branch
5600 Fishers Lane, Room 7-89
Rockville, MD 20857

301-443-4183

The National Institute of Mental Health (NIMH) maintains a collection of videotapes, including public service announcements, If you want to order audiovisual materials, include in your order a blank videocassette with enough minutes on it to tape the materials you request.

Just Like You and Me (32 minutes) - features former mental patients who have made transition from hospitalization back to the community through the Transitional Employment Program.

Making the Numbers Work for You (35 minutes) - points out the need for timely, accurate statistical information from each State. Such information assists the Federal Government to compile figures on the needs and opportunities in promoting better mental health.

More Than A Grant (19 minutes) - describes some of the institute's programs and should encourage Historically Black Colleges and Universities faculties and students to explore ways of obtaining support for research projects in the field of mental health.

More Than A Passing Acquaintance (24 minutes) - story of how one community support program meets the challenge in providing services and opportunities for person who have made the transition from hospitalization back into the community.

Windows Into the Brain (19 minutes) - tells the story of three decades of scientific advances in brain imaging techniques.

Public Service Announcements (60 second and 30 second) - developed as part of the Anti-Stigma campaign, these announcements describe why people should not be "labeled" as former mental patients.

* Mental Illness and Attitudes

National Institute of Mental Health (NIMH)
5600 Fishers Lane, Room 7C-02
Rockville, MD 20857

301-443-4515
Fax: 301-443-0008
TDD: 301-443-8431

The National Institute of Mental Health (NIMH) has several free publications dealing with the stigma of mental illness and attitudes towards it. Some of the publications include:

Affirmative Action to Employ Mentally Restored People
Eight Questions Employers Ask About Hiring the Mentally Restored
Managing Depression in the Workplace
Plain Talk About the Stigma of Mental Illness
The 14 Worst Myths About Recovered Mental Patients
The Mentally Restored and Work: A Successful Partnership
Understanding Panic Disorder
You Are Not Alone: Facts About Mental Health and Mental Illness

* Mental Illness and Medications

National Institute of Mental Health	301-443-4515
5600 Fishers Lane, Room 7C-02	Fax: 301-443-0008
Rockville, MD 20857	TDD: 301-443-8431

Medications for Mental Illness: What You Should Know About the Drugs Doctors Prescribe for Anxiety, Depression, Schizophrenia and Other Mental Disorders (ADM 92-1509) is a free booklet designed to help people understand how and why drugs can be used as part of the treatment for mental health problems. It includes questions you should ask your doctor, and provides information on different classes of drugs, and things needing special consideration.

* Mental Retardation Research and Clearinghouse

Mental Retardation and Disabilities Branch
National Institute of Child Health and Human Development
Executive Plaza North, Room 631
6130 Executive Blvd.
Bethesda, MD 20897   301-496-1383

The Mental Retardation Research Centers are designed to further the understanding, treatment, and prevention of mental retardation. They are a combination of organized research and medical service programs, bringing the mentally retarded in contact with medical and behavioral specialists. The Centers offer programs to train medical students and postdoctoral fellows. Contact this office for a list of the Centers and information on current research.

* Mental Retardation Services

President's Committee on Mental Retardation
330 Independence Ave., SW, Room 5325
Washington, DC 20201   202-619-0634

The President's Committee on Mental Retardation has information on prevention of biomedical and environmental causes of retardation, and family and community support services. Materials are also available on the legal rights of the mentally retarded and employment programs.

* National Plan for Research on Child and Adolescent Mental Disorders

Superintendent of Documents	
Government Printing Office (GPO)	202-512-1800
Washington, DC 20402	Fax: 202-512-2250

This book addresses the status of research concerning mental disorders in young Americans and the steps that must be taken to improve the diagnosis, treatment, and prevention of mental illness. Order #017-024-01395-1, cost $4.25.

* Obsessive Compulsive Disorder

Information Resources and Inquiries Branch	
National Institute of Mental Health	301-443-4513
5600 Fishers Lane, Room 7C-02	Fax: 301-443-0008
Rockville, MD 20857	TDD: 301-443-8431

This booklet discusses the diagnosis of obsessive-compulsive (OCD) and its prevalence among both children and adults. It describes types of treatment, both pharmacotherapy and behavioral therapy. Sources of information for both the individual who has Obsessive Compulsive Disorder (OCD) and family are also included. Order #NIH 93-3611.

* Panic Disorder Education Program

Information Resources and Inquiries Branch	800-64-PANIC
National Institute of Mental Health	301-443-4513
5600 Fishers Lane, Room 7C-02	Fax: 301-443-0008
Rockville, MD 20857	TDD: 301-443-8431

Panic disorder, a condition in which a person has unexpected and repeated episodes of intense fear accompanied by multiple physical symptoms, is a serious mental health problem in this country. Effective treatments are available and offer hope to the more than 3 million Americans who suffer from the disorder during their lifetimes. The following are publications used in the national Panic Disorder Education Program:

Getting Treatment for Panic Disorder (NIH 94-3641) Written for patients, families, and friends, this pamphlet helps the reader identify the symptoms of panic disorder and emphasizes the importance of seeking treatment. Getting the correct diagnosis and the right treatment is essential to recovery as is enlisting the help of support groups and other self-help resources.

Panic Disorder (NIH 93-3508) Written for the public, this flyer contains a description of panic disorder and its symptoms, describes treatment methods, encourages people with the symptoms to seek treatment, and lists further sources of information. Also available in Spanish.

Panic Disorder Poster (OM-OO-4112) Useful for clinic settings and for advertising panic disorder educational seminars, this 4-color poster emphasizes that panic disorder is treatable. At the bottom of the poster is a perforated, 4" blank section for use in advertising local meetings or treatment services.

Panic Disorder in the Medical Setting (NIH 94-3482) A helpful guide for primary care physicians, clinicians, and mental health professionals in recognizing and treating panic disorder in patients and in identifying those who need a psychiatric consultation or referral.

Panic Disorder: Somatization, Medical Utilization, and Treatment, the American Journal of Medicine, 1992 (OM-00-4082) The goal of this supplement is to provide the primary care physician with knowledge of medical symptoms that are strongly associated with panic disorder and the state of research on current effective treatments.

Panic Disorder Fact Sheet (OM-00-4079) Statistics on the prevalence, diagnosis, and treatment of panic disorder, and comorbidity with other disorders.

Panic Disorder Referral List (OM-00-4098) A list of organizations that provide guidance about locating mental health treatment professionals, self-help groups and other resources for people with panic disorder.

Panic Disorder Resource List (OM-00-4078) A list of books, pamphlets, scientific articles, and videotapes available from several sources.

Panic Disorder Treatment and Referral: Information for Health Care Professionals (NIH 94-3642) This publication, intended to provide information on panic disorder to health care professionals, stresses that proper diagnosis is vital in the treatment of panic disorder.

Understanding Panic Disorder (NIH 03-3509) This booklet offers hope to those who suffer from panic disorder. It includes a description of the symptoms of the illness, its causes and available treatment options, successful coping strategies, how and where to find help, and a listing of sources for additional information and referral.

* Runaway and Homeless Youth Shelters

Division of Runaway Youth Programs
Administration for Children, Youth and Families
330 C St., SW
Washington, DC 20201   202-205-8102

The Division of Runaway Youth Programs provides federal grants to states, communities, and public and private organizations to establish and operate runaway and homeless youth shelters. This year's budget is for $26 million. An annual report is available which lists all the grantees.

* Runaway Hotline for Parents and Youngsters

800-621-4000

The National Runaway Hotline provides information and resources to parents and runaways. It will deliver messages to parents from their children and offer advice to runaways regarding places to go for help. The Hotline operates 24 hours a day, and all information is confidential.

* Schizophrenia

Information Resources and Inquiries Branch	
National Institute of Mental Health (NIMH)	301-443-4515
5600 Fishers Lane, Room 7C-02	Fax: 301-443-0008

Rockville, MD 20857 TDD: 301-443-8431

The National Institute of Mental Health (NIMH) supports research on the causes and new treatments of schizophrenia. They have produced several free publications dealing with schizophrenia, including:

A National Plan for Schizophrenia Research: Panel Recommendations
A National Plan for Schizophrenia Research: Report of the National Advisory Mental Health Council
Schizophrenia: Questions and Answers
Special Report: Schizophrenia 1987

Schizophrenia Bulletin (four issues, $18/yr) - publishes articles on all facets of schizophrenia research and treatment (available from: Superintendent of Documents, Government Printing Office, Washington, DC 20402; 202-512-1800).

* Schizophrenia Research

Schizophrenia Research Branch
Division of Clinical Research
National Institute of Mental Health
Parklawn Building, Room 10C-16
5600 Fishers Lane
Rockville, MD 20857 301-443-3524

This research bureau has news of the latest medical research into schizophrenia, however, access to this information is limited to mental health professionals and researchers.

* State Mental Institutions Survey

Surveys and Reports Branch
National Institute of Mental Health
Parklawn Building, Room 18C-07
5600 Fishers Lane
Rockville, MD 20857 301-443-3343

This office has data on mental health facilities and generates the annual Census of State Mental Health Hospitals, which provides characteristics of patients.

* Stress Management Publications

National Technical Information Service
U.S. Department of Commerce 800-553-6847
5285 Port Royal Rd. 703-487-4650
Springfield, VA 22161 Fax: 703-321-8547

An Evaluation Handbook for Health Education Programs in Stress Management (Order No. PB84-171735; $66) gives information on how to examine and evaluate stress management programs.

AIDS, Cancer, and Other Diseases

Many of the offices and publications listed here will direct you to numerous non-profit and private organizations which also offer information and expertise. The National Health Information Center, for example, suggests interested individuals contact the American Red Cross for a series of brochures on the *Latest Facts About AIDS* which are produced jointly with the U.S. Public Health Service. Similarly, the National Cancer Institute will refer callers to such national groups as the American Lung Association and the American Heart Association.

* Acne and Skin Disease Prevention and Treatment

National Institute of Arthritis and Musculoskeletal
and Skin Diseases (NIAMS)
National Institutes of Health 301-495-4484
1 AMS Circle .... Fax: 301-587-4352
Bethesda, MD 20892-3675 .... TDD: 301-565-2966

The National Institute of Arthritis and Musculoskeletal and Skin Diseases (NIAMS) conducts and supports basic and clinical research concerning the causes, prevention, diagnosis, and treatment of a large number of diseases, including acne and skin problems. Reports and brochures for professionals and the general public are available, along with an information specialist who can provide in-depth information on a variety of related topics.

* AIDS (Acquired Immune Deficiency Syndrome) Hotline

National AIDS Clearinghouse (NAC)
P.O. Box 6003
Rockville, MD 20849-6003
AIDS Hotline 800-342-2437
800-344-7432 (Servicia en Espanol)
800-243-7889 (TTY Deaf Access)

The Center for Disease Control (CDC) National AIDS Hotline provides accurate, up-to-date, confidential information about HIV and AIDS to callers 24 hours a day, 7 days a week, 365 days a year. Hotline Information Specialists provide details about HIV transmission, testing, counseling, and prevention. In addition callers can get printed materials on HIV and AIDS as well as referrals to local programs that provide health care, legal, and support services.

* AIDS and Criminal Justice Workers

National Criminal Justice Reference Service
U.S. Department of Justice
P.O. Box 6000 800-851-3420
Rockville, MD 20850 301-251-5500

The National Criminal Justice Reference Service is the only centralized source of information on how AIDS affects criminal justice professionals and their work. Staff specialists with a broad knowledge of AIDS issues are available to answer questions, make referrals, and suggest publications pertaining to AIDS as it relates to the criminal justice system.

* AIDS and Dentistry

Dental Disease Prevention Activity
Center for Prevention Services
Centers for Disease Control
1600 Clifton Road NE 404-639-3311
Atlanta, GA 30333 404-639-3534

Preventing the Transmission of Hepatitis B, AIDS, and Herpes in Dentistry offers 13 pages of advice on preventive measures for dental health care workers to minimize their risk of the transmission of these diseases to themselves, their families, and patients. Single copies are free.

* AIDS and Runaways

Research and Program Development Division
Office of Juvenile Justice and Delinquency Prevention
U.S. Department of Justice
633 Indiana Ave., NW

Washington, DC 20531 202-307-0586

Often runaways resort to supporting themselves through prostitution and selling illegal drugs, which they frequently use as well. Young people who engage in sexual activity with multiple partners and use intravenous drugs place themselves at great risk of contracting AIDS and spreading the disease to others. The Runaways Risk Reduction Project is documenting the obstacles faced by programs serving this population; the project is also identifying the most promising prevention and intervention strategies at each stage of contact with youth: outreach, crisis intervention, intermediate care, transitional living, and aftercare.

* AIDS and the Workplace

National AIDS Information Clearinghouse 800-458-5231
P.O. Box 6003 301-217-0023
Rockville, MD 20849-6003 .... Fax: 301-738-6616
TDD: 800-243-7012

The National AIDS Information Clearinghouse has just established a special resources center for businesses, called Business Response to AIDS Resource Services. They have information on workplace policy, as well as materials kits for employers, CEOs, managers and shop stewards. These kits will contain brochures, fact sheets, labor issues, and other helpful information (the CEOs kits will contain a video). This service can also refer you to resources in your State and locality, as well as nationally. Contact the number listed above for more information on there free services.

* AIDS Clinical Trials

National AIDS Information Clearinghouse 800-458-5231
P.O. Box 6003 301-217-0023
Rockville, MD 20849-6003 .... Fax: 301-738-6616
TDD: 800-243-7012

The AIDS Clinical Trials Information Services puts callers in touch with experienced health specialists who provide information about AIDS clinical trials. These specialists access a database featuring up-to-date, accurate information on AIDS studies currently underway. The Service's health specialists are available to answer questions from individuals infected with HIV and their families, as well as from health professionals. They provide information on the purpose of the study, studies that are open, study locations, eligibility requirements and exclusion criteria, and names and telephone numbers of contact persons. They provide information on what Clinical Trials are, and distribute two publications, *AIDS/HIV Clinical Trial Handbook*, and *AIDS/HIV Treatment Directory*, for the American Foundation for AIDS Research.

* AIDS Films and Videos

National AIDS Information Clearinghouse 800-458-5231
P.O. Box 6003 301-217-0023
Rockville, MD 20849-6003 .... Fax: 301-738-6616
TDD: 800-243-7012

The National AIDS Information Clearinghouse has access to information on over 300 AIDS films and videotapes, and can provide you with a printout of films and videos designed to target a specific audience, ranging from teenagers to physicians. Each listing includes information on the producer, year, source, audience, and availability, as well as an abstract. Contact the Clearinghouse for more information.

* AIDS Parent Guide

National AIDS Information Clearinghouse 800-458-5231
P.O. Box 6003 301-217-0023

Be patient. If any phone number is incorrect, call (area code) 555-1212 and request the new listing.

533

Health and Medicine

Rockville, MD 20849-6003
Fax: 301-738-6616
TDD: 800-243-7012

AIDS Prevention Guide is written for parents and other adults concerned about young people. It provides ideas to help adults start a conversation about AIDS. It presents the facts about AIDS - geared to elementary and junior and senior high school students - and offers common questions and accurate answers. It includes handouts for young people aged 10 to 20 years.

* AIDS Prevention Community Planning Groups

National AIDS Clearinghouse (NAC) 301-217-0023
P.O. Box 6003 Fax: 301-738-6616
Rockville, MD 20849-6003 800-458-5231
TDD: 800-243-7012

The Clearinghouse staff provides technical assistance to HIV/AIDS program managers, members of Centers for Disease Control's (CDC) HIV Prevention Community Planning groups, and other working in the field by providing links to local organizations and key materials to aid in assessing community needs, and implementing and evaluation prevention programs; identifying hard-to-find prevention materials targeting racial and ethnic populations; offering training in accessing CDC NAC ONLINE and other HIV/AIDS-related online and Internet services; and assisting community-based organizations and libraries in organizing HIV/AIDS information collections. For more information on technical assistance services speak with a reference specialist.

* AIDS Prevention National Clearinghouse

National AIDS Clearinghouse (NAC) 800-458-5231
P.O. Box 6003 301-217-0023
Rockville, MD 20849-6003 Fax: 301-738-6616
TDD: 800-243-0023

The Center for Disease Control (CDC) National AIDS Clearinghouse (NAC) provides timely, accurate, and relevant information about HIV and AIDS. All of the Clearinghouse's services are designed to facilitate the sharing of resources and information about education and prevention, published materials, and research findings, as well as news about AIDS-related trends. The Clearinghouse offers comprehensive reference and referral services; distributes HIV/AIDS education and prevention materials; maintains a variety of databases on HIV/AIDS-related resources and services; offers bilingual reference specialists to talk to Spanish speaking callers; provides CDC NAC ONLINE, an electronic bulletin board; provides CDC Business and Labor Resource Service; manages the AIDS Clinical Trials Information Service; operates the HIV/AIDS Treatment Information Service; and provides technical assistance services. The Clearinghouse distributes more than 300 different publications, educational materials, and scientific reports including brochures, posters, public service announcements, articles from CDC/s Morbidity and Mortality Weekly Report series, HIV/AIDS Surveillance Reports and videotapes. Most items have a unit price to cover shipping and handling costs, while some are free of charge. The Clearinghouse published the Catalog of HIV and AIDS Education and Prevention Materials, which contains descriptions of, and ordering information for, the items from the Clearinghouse. There is no charge for the catalog.

* AIDS Reference and Referral Services

National AIDS Clearinghouse (NAC) 800-458-5231
P.O. Box 6003 301-217-0023
Rockville, MD 20849-6003 Fax: 301-738-6616
TDD: 800-243-7012

Reference specialists provide a link between Clearinghouse users and an extensive collection of HIV information sources. They help requestors define their information needs and use computerized databases as well as other sources to answer their questions. NAC databases used are:

Resources and Services Database with descriptions of more than 19,000 organizations that provide HIV and AIDS prevention, education, health care, and social services.
Education Materials Database contains information about hard to find educational materials. The collection includes descriptions of more than 14,000 brochures, manuals, posters, teaching guides, audio and videotapes, and reports.
AIDS Daily Summary Database has abstracts of HIV/AIDS related articles from major newspapers, wire services, medical journals, and news magazines. The Funding Database contains information on funding sources of community-based HIV/AIDS service organizations.
Comprehensive School Health Education Database has descriptions of resource materials to teach children and young adults about HIV/AIDS
Conference Database has information on upcoming international, national, state, and local HIV/AIDS-related meetings, seminars, and workshops.

CDC Morbidity and Mortality Weekly Report (MMWR) Database has all HIV/AIDS related articles issued in the MMWR series.
Federal Information Database contains information on federal press releases and statements on HIV/AIDS.
Periodicals Database has bibliographic information on HIV/AIDS-related newsletters and journals.

* AIDS Research Worldwide

National Institute of Allergy and
Infectious Diseases (NIAID)
National Institutes of Health
Building 31, Room 7A50
31 Center Dr., MSC 2520
Bethesda, MD 20892 301-496-5717

The National Institute of Allergy and Infectious Diseases (NIAID) conducts and supports research to study the causes of allergic, immunologic, and infectious diseases, and to develop better means of preventing, diagnosing, and treating illness. Some of the studies look at the role of the immune system in chronic diseases, such as arthritis, and at disorders of the immune system, as in asthma. NIAID has become the lead component at NIH for coordinating and conducting AIDS research. Brochures and reports are available on a wide variety of topics. Some of the publications available include:

NIAID AIDS Research
Where do AIDS Drugs Come From?
NIAID AIDS Research: Opportunistic Infections
AIDS Clinical Trials: Talking It Over

* AIDS Resource Center

National AIDS Clearinghouse
P.O. Box 6003
Rockville, MD 20849-6003 800-458-5231

In the Resource Center, visitors can examine all items listed in the Clearinghouse's databases. Materials cover a wide range of AIDS-related subjects: counseling and support groups, drug therapy and other treatments, HIV-prevention education, insurance, AIDS in the workplace, legal issues, and special populations. The collection includes reference sources, brochures, posters, audiocassettes, and videotapes. The Center also houses a unique collection of 400 HIV/AIDS newsletters produced by community-based organizations, State and local government agencies, and national associations. For more information or to make an appointment, call the Clearinghouse and ask to speak with the Librarian. To visit the resource center in Atlanta, GA, call 404-982-0353.

* AIDS: Surgeon General's Report

National AIDS Information Clearinghouse 800-458-5231
P.O. Box 6003 301-217-0023
Rockville, MD 20849-6003 Fax: 301-738-6616
TDD: 800-243-7012

This detailed report titled *Surgeon General's Report on Acquired Immune Deficiency Syndrome* discusses the facts about this disease, how it is transmitted, the relative risks of infection, and how to protect yourself against the disease. The order number is .0539 (in Spanish 0589).

* AIDS Telecommunication Services

National AIDS Clearinghouse (NAC) 800-458-5231
P.O. Box 6003 301-217-0023
Rockville, MD 20849-6003 Fax: 301-738-6616
TDD: 800-243-7012

NAC ONLINE:
The Clearinghouse provides NAC ONLINE, a computerized information network, that gives people a direct link to clearinghouse information. Users can read the AIDS Daily Summary, search the Clearinghouse databases, download and print information, send and receive electronic mail, participate in interactive forums. and order publications. To obtain an online registration form, set your modem to dial 1-800-851-7245, with setting at nor parity, 8 databits, and 1 stop bit. Follow steps to fill out the online registration form and a representative will contact you within 48 hours.

NAC Fax Service:
The Clearinghouse offers a 24-hour fax-on-demand service for people who have access to a fax machine or a computer with an internal fax. To use NAC Fax dial the main Clearinghouse number 1-800-458-5231 on a touchtone phone. Follow the directions and prompts to reach the fax service.

Internet Services:

NAC World Wide Web site contains information about Clearinghouse services and how to access them at http://cdcnac.aspensys.com:86

NAC Gopher provides a simple menu that enables users to find a wide variety of documents on HIV and AIDS at Gopher: cdcnac.aspensys.com:72

AIDS News Listserv sends HIV/AIDS related news-including the AIDS Daily Summary-to subscribers at listserv@cdcnac.aspensys.com

The File Transfer Protocol site allows users to download current information on HIV/AIDS without an individual password at ftp://cdcnac.aspensys.com/pub/cdcnac

The Internet mailbox allows users to submit questions about Clearinghouse services and orders for free publications at aidsinfo@cdcnac.aspensys.com

* AIDS Treatment Information Service

National AIDS Clearinghouse (NAC)	301-217-0023
P.O. Box 6003	Fax: 301-738-6616
Rockville, MD 20849-6003	800-448-0440
	TDD: 800-243-7012

The HIV/AIDS Treatment Information Service (ATIS) is a toll-free reference service for health care and service providers as well as for people living with HIV infection who want to know about federally approved HIV/AIDS treatment options. ATIS is staffed by reference specialists who are health care professionals. Reference specialists use the National Library of Medicine database of HIV/AIDS treatment guidelines to answer questions.

* AIDS Videotapes

National AIDS Clearinghouse (NAC)	800-458-5231
P.O. Box 6003	301-217-0023
Rockville, MD 20849-6003	Fax: 301-738-6616
	TDD: 800-243-0023

Videos available from the Clearinghouse include:

America Responds to AIDS Public Service Announcements: It's Your Move, Prevent AIDS. This contains nine television public service announcements and three radio spots in Spanish and English. Limit one copy free, #V046.

Business Responds to AIDS/CDC National Teleconference. This 90 minute tape contains the CDC National Teleconference that launched the Business Responds to AIDS Program. There is testimony from more than 50 participants on such topics as policy making, training, education, community service, volunteerism, and prevention. Order #V047, cost is $12. *Teleconference Highlights* is an 18 minute video containing excerpts from the Teleconference. Limit one copy free, #V310.

"I Have AIDS" - A Teenager's Story. Basic information about HIV transmission and prevention for children, adolescents, and their families is presented in this videorecording produced by the Children's Television Workshop. It tells the story of Ryan White, a 16 year old hemophiliac infected with HIV prior to testing of the nation's blood supply. Order #V467, price is $12.

Song of Superman. This videotape uses an allegory based on a Superman story to illustrate the difficulties faced by an adolescent with hemophilia as he tries to tell his girlfriend that he is living with HIV infection. Limit one copy free.

AIDS Health Fraud. This videorecording, produced by the Food and Drug Administration, presents information about some of the fraudulent treatments offered to persons with HIV and AIDS. Order #V595, cost is $12.

Eating Defensively: Food Safety Advice for Persons with AIDS. Produced by the Food and Drug Administration and the Center for Disease Control and Prevention, this 15 minute tape alerts individuals with AIDS to their increased risk of contracting foodborne illnesses and suggests ways to lower these risks. Order #V466, cost is $12.

* Allergies and Infectious Diseases Research

National Institute of Allergy and Infectious Diseases (NIAID)
National Institutes of Health
Building 31, Room 7A50
31 Center Dr., MSC 2520
Bethesda, MD 20892-2520   301-496-5717

The National Institute of Allergy and Infectious Diseases (NIAID) conducts and supports research to study the causes of allergic, immunologic, and infectious diseases, and to develop better means of preventing, diagnosing, and treating illness. Some of the studies look at the role of the immune system in chronic diseases, such as arthritis, and at disorders of the immune system, as in asthma. NIAID has become the lead component at NIH for coordinating and conducting AIDS research. Brochures and reports are available on a wide variety of topics.

* Allergies: Dust and Drugs to Pollen

National Institute of Allergy and Infectious Diseases
National Institutes of Health
Building 31, Room 7A50
31 Center Dr., MSC 2520
Bethesda, MD 20892   301-496-5717

This institute offers publications that answer many general questions about allergies and offer information on their symptoms, prevention, diagnosis, and treatment. They offer single copies free of the following publications: *Drug Allergy, Allergic Diseases: Medicine for the Public* and *The Immune System: How it Works.*

* Allergies: Home, School, and Work

National Audiovisual Center
8700 Edgeworth Drive
Capitol Heights, MD 20743   301-763-1896

A slide set, "Coping With Your Allergies At Home, At School, and on the Job", is available for $45, which includes 40 color slides, an audiocassette, and a 13-page script and study guide, order # AVA 092095500.

* Alzheimer's and Dementia

Office of Clinical Center Communications
Warren G. Magnuson Clinical Center
NIH, Building 10, Room 1C255
Bethesda, MD 20892   301-496-2563

The Brain in "Aging" and Dementia (No. 83-2625) discusses brain anatomy and physiology, the normal process of brain aging, and senility. Vascular dementia and Alzheimer's disease are described as well as research on the causes and treatment.

* Alzheimer's Fact Sheet

Alzheimer's Disease Education and Referral Center	800-438-4380
P.O. Box 8250	301-495-3311
Silver Spring, MD 20907-8250	Fax: 301-495-3334

The *Alzheimer's Fact Sheet* addresses fundamental issues related to the causes, symptoms, and treatment of this disease as well as research efforts surrounding it.

* Alzheimer's: Long-Term Care

National Technical Information Service (NTIS)	
U.S. Department of Commerce	
5285 Port Royal Rd.	800-553-6847
Springfield, VA 22161	703-487-4650

The former Office of Technology Assessment (OTA) assessed existing methods of locating and arranging health and long-term care services for Alzheimer's and dementia patients. The study identified methods that are successful in some communities and may serve as models for others. *Losing a Million Minds: Confronting the Tragedy of Alzheimer's Disease and Other Dementias* is the resulting publication. It is now available from the National Technical Information Service, order #PB87-183752.

* Amyotrophic Lateral Sclerosis

National Institute of Neurological Disorders and Stroke	
National Institutes of Health	800-352-9424
P.O. Box 5801	301-496-5751
Bethesda, MD 20824	Fax: 301-402-2186

This institute offers information on neurological and communicative disorders including a free 26-page pamphlet titled *Amyotrophic Lateral Sclerosis* which discusses the physiology and symptoms of this progressively crippling and fatal disease.

* Apnea and SIDS

National Sudden Infant Death Syndrome Clearinghouse	
2070 Chain Bridge Rd., Suite 450	703-821-8955
Vienna, VA 22182	Fax: 703-821-2098

Be patient. If any phone number is incorrect, call (area code) 555-1212 and request the new listing.

535

Health and Medicine

This clearinghouse can provide many materials about infantile apnea, sudden infant death syndrome (SIDS), crib death including *Current Research in Sudden Infant Death* and *SIDS Information for the EMT*.

* Arteriosclerosis

National Heart, Lung, and Blood Institute
Information Center
P.O. Box 30105   301-251-1222
Bethesda, MD 20824-0105   Fax: 301-251-1223

Cardiovascular diseases including arteriosclerosis are studied by this institute. Free pamphlets are available on a variety of heart problems.

* Arthritis Information Clearinghouse

National Arthritis and Musculoskeletal
and Skin Disease Information Clearinghouse   301-495-4484
1 AMS Circle   Fax: 301-587-4352
Bethesda, MD 20892   TDD: 301-565-2966

This clearinghouse makes available many publications and offers telephone assistance. Information packages are available on: *Arthritis in Children* (AR 463), *Arthritis and Diet* (AR-46), *Arthritis and Exercise* (AR-103), and *Arthritis* (AR-27). Other topics available include *Eczema* (AR-68), *Hip Replacement*, (AR-149), *Neck and Cervical Pain* (AR-147), *Psoriasis* (AR-97), *Hair Loss in Women* (AR-157), and *Back Pain* (AR-78).

* Arthritis, Lyme and Other Musculoskeletal Diseases

National Institute of Arthritis and Musculoskeletal
and Skin Diseases (NIAMS) Clearinghouse
National Institutes of Health   301-495-4484
1 AMS Circle   Fax: 301-587-4352
Bethesda, MD 20892-3675   TDD: 301-565-2966

The National Institute of Arthritis and Musculoskeletal and Skin Diseases (NIAMS) conducts and supports basic and clinical research concerning the causes, prevention, diagnosis, and treatment of a large number of diverse diseases, including arthritis, muscle diseases, Lyme disease, and acne. They fund Multipurpose Arthritis Centers which conduct research on various types of arthritis. Reports and brochures for professionals and the general public are available, along with an information specialist who can provide in-depth information on a variety of related topics. Contact this office for a free listing of the Arthritis Centers or for more information.

Information Packages:
Juvenile Arthritis (AR-112)
Avascular Necrosis (AR-150)
Gout (AR-99)
Osteoarthritis (AR-73)
Osteomyelitis (AR-06)
Scoliosis in Adults (AR-94)
Scoliosis in Children (AR-131)
Vitiligo (AR-05)

Public/Patient Education Materials
Living With Epidermolysis Bullosa (AR-19)
Lyme Disease: The Facts, The Challenge (AR-20)
What Black Women Should Know About Lupus, 8 page booklet (AR-132), large type
    (132L0, braille (132B, audiotape (132A)
What Black Women Should Know About Lupus, 76 page kit (AR-138)

NIAMS Research Conference Reports:
Arthritis, Rheumatic Diseases, and Related Disorders 1993 (AR-160)
Conference on Sports Injuries in Youth: Surveillance Strategies, Executive Summary
    (AR-155)
Conference on Sports Injuries in Youth: Surveillance Strategies, Proceedings
    (AR-154)
Sunlight, Ultraviolet Radiation and the Skin (AR-72)

Annotated Bibliographies:
Lupus: Patient Education Materials, 1990 (AR-51)
Lupus: Professional Education Materials, 1990 (AR-52)
Scleroderma, 1992 (AR-140)
Spanish Language Materials for Patients, 1991 (AR-60)

Combined Health Information Database (CHID):
CHID Fact Sheet (AR-100)
CHID Search Reference Guide and CHID Work List (AR-106, $15)

Information on NIAMS:
NIAMS Extramural Research Program (AR-111)
NIAMS Fact Sheet (AR-119)
NIAMS Intramural Research Program (AR-110)
Grant Mechanisms for Extramural Support of Research, Research Training, and Research Career Development (AR-198)

* Asthma and Other Respiratory Disorders

National Institute of Allergy and Infectious Diseases
National Institutes of Health
Building 31, Room 7A50
31 Center Dr., MSC 2520
Bethesda, MD 20892-2520   301-496-5717

A free brochure describes the triggers of asthma attacks and treatment and research on this respiratory disorder. This institute can offer information on sinusitis, tuberculosis and other respiratory problems.

* Blindness and Vision Problems

National Eye Institute (NEI)
Building 31, Room 6A32
31 Center Dr., MSC 2510
Bethesda, MD 20892-2510   301-496-5248

The National Eye Institute (NEI) conducts, fosters and supports basic and applied research, including clinical trials, related to the cause, natural history, prevention, diagnosis, and treatment of disorders of the eye and visual system. Several brochures and reports are available for the general public and health professionals on a wide variety of related topics as well as more specific concerns such as *Diabetes and Your Eyes*.

* Blood Donation

Office of Consumer Affairs
Food and Drug Administration
5600 Fishers Lane, HFE-88
Rockville, MD 20857   301-443-3170

Who Donates Better Blood For You Than You? is a free pamphlet which discusses the advantages of donating blood for yourself before undergoing surgery.

* Bone and Orthopedics Research

National Institute of Arthritis and Musculoskeletal
and Skin Diseases   301-495-4484
1 AMS Circle   Fax: 301-587-4352
Bethesda, MD 20892-3675   TDD: 301-565-2966

This institute focuses on orthopedic research, which includes sports medicine, growth and development of bone and bone cells, as well as head injury. Staff can answer questions regarding current research and treatment issues and brochures and pamphlets are available through the National Institute of Arthritis and Musculoskeletal and Skin Diseases.

* Bowel Disease and Syndrome

National Digestive Diseases Information Clearinghouse
2 Information Way   301-654-3810
Bethesda, MD 20892-3570   Fax: 301-907-8906

This clearinghouse offers information and publications which compare inflammatory bowel disease and irritable bowel syndrome.

* Brain and Spinal Cord Tumors

National Institute of Neurological Disorders and Stroke
National Institutes of Health
9000 Rockville Pike
Building 31, Room 8A06
Bethesda, MD 20892   301-496-4697

Brain and Spinal Cord Tumors: Hope Through Research explains types of tumors, warning symptoms, and treatment including chemotherapy. This is a central information starting place for information on the brain and spine.

* Breast Cancer Prevention and Treatment Clearinghouse

Cancer Information Service (CIS)
National Cancer Institute

Be patient. If any phone number is incorrect, call (area code) 555-1212 and request the new listing.

Building 31, Room 10A16
31 Center Dr., MSC 2580
Bethesda, MD 20892-2580   800-4-CANCER

Contact the Cancer Information Service (CIS) for pamphlets, medical updates, organizations, and support groups dealing with breast cancer. *Breast Cancer: We're Making Progress Every Day* summarizes the latest information about breast cancer including surgery, breast reconstruction, and rehabilitation. Single copies of this 12-page pamphlet are available free. *Breast Cancer: What You Should Know* discusses X-ray mammography and other breast cancer screening methods.

* Breast Exams

Office of Cancer Communications
Bldg. 31, Room 10A16
31 Center Dr., MSC 2580
Bethesda, MD 20892-2580   800-4-CANCER

Chances Are You Need a Mammogram is a question and answer guide for older women on why and how to get regular mammograms and clinical breast exams.

* Breast Exams and Breast Lumps

Cancer Information Service
National Cancer Institute
Building 31, Room 10A16
31 Center Dr., MSC 2580
Bethesda, MD 20892-2580   800-4-CANCER

The booklet, *Understanding Breast Cancer: A Health Guide for All Women* (94-3536, 56 pages) explains how to evaluate breast lumps and other normal breasts changes that often occur and are confused with breast cancer. It recommends regular screening mammography beginning at age 50. A breast exam by the doctor as part of a woman's annual checkup, and monthly breast self-examinations for early detection of breast cancer.

* Breast Implants

Information Request Service
Center for Devices and Radiological Health
Food and Drug Administration (FDA)
Rockville, MD 20857   301-443-4190

The Food and Drug Administration (FDA) has put together an information packet to answer questions regarding breast implants. It answers questions regarding the FDA's moratorium on silicone gel-filled breast implants, as well as providing general information on breast implants and who to contact for more information.

* Cancer and Afro-Americans

Cancer Information Service
National Cancer Institute
Building 31, Room 10A16
31 Center Dr., MSC 2580
Bethesda, MD 20892-2580   800-4-CANCER

The 12-page pamphlet, *Get a New Attitude About Cancer: A Guide for Black Americans* (93-3412) encourages all black adults to get regular checkups from their doctors, to avoid smoking, and to eat less fat and more fruits and vegetables. It informs them of the specific cancers that are the leading cause of death for black men and women.

* Cancer-Causing Products

Clearinghouse of Occupational Safety
and Health Information
National Institute of Occupational Safety and Health (NIOSH)
4676 Columbia Pkwy.   513-533-8326
Cincinnati, OH 45226   800-35-NIOSH

The National Institute of Occupational Safety and Health (NIOSH) distributes a publication that lists the trade name products containing one or more of 16 carcinogens (substances for which evidence indicates a causal relationship between exposure to that substance and cancer). They can also provide you with other reports and information on carcinogens.

* Cancer: Chemotherapy, Radiation, Surgery

Office of Clinical Center Communications
National Institute of Health
Building 10, Room 1C255
Bethesda, MD 20892   301-496-2563

This clinical center which experiments with unproven therapies on cancer patients shares its findings and offers several relevant publications including *Cancer Treatment* (No. 84-1807) and *Radiation Risks and Radiation Therapy* (No. 83-2367).

* Cancer Clearinghouse: AZT to Radon

Office of Cancer Communications
National Cancer Institute (NCI)
Building 31, Room 10A16
31 Center Dr., MSC 2580   800-4-CANCER
Bethesda, MD 20892-2580   301-496-5583

The National Cancer Institute's (NCI) overall mission is to conduct and support research, training, health information distribution, and other programs with respect to the cause, diagnosis, prevention, and treatment of cancer, and the continuing care of cancer patients and their families. Some of their current research is looking at Azidothymidine (AZT) in relation to AIDS, and the possible link between radon and lung cancer risk. NCI supports an information and education center, an International Cancer Research Databank, as well as national cancer research and demonstration centers.

* Cancer Detection and Diagnostic Imaging

Diagnostic Imaging Research Branch
Radiation Research Program
National Cancer Institute
6130 Executive Blvd., Room 800   301-496-9531
Rockville, MD 20892   Fax: 301-480-5785

The Diagnostic Imaging Program supports and administers grants and contracts for extramural research in the field of diagnostic imaging. The staff can also answer your questions regarding this medical technology.

* CancerFax

Office of Communications
National Cancer Institute
Bldg. 31, Room 10A-16
31 Center Dr., MSC 2580   CancerFax: 301-402-5874
Bethesda, MD 20892-2580   For assistance: 800-624-7890

CancerFax allows you to obtain information from the National Cancer Institute (NCI) on your fax machine. You can request information summaries from the NCI's PDQ database. NCI fact sheets on various cancer topics, citations and abstracts on selected topics from the CANCERLIT database, press releases, bulletins, and publications. Selected information is also available in Spanish. You must call from the handset of a fax machine. CancerFax operates 24 hours a day, 7 days a week. The Contents List changes monthly as new information is included. Follow the voice prompts to receive a list of documents available.

* Cancer Information Regional Offices

Cancer Information Service
National Cancer Institute
Building 31, Room 10A16
31 Center Dr., MSC 2580
Bethesda, MD 20892-2580   800-4-CANCER

The National Cancer Institute has set up offices across the U.S. through which they route the Cancer Information Service calls. Your call will automatically be routed to a cancer specialist in your area.

* Cancer Journal

National Cancer Institute
Information Associates Program
9030 Old Georgetown Rd.   800-624-7890
Bethesda, MD 20814   301-496-7600

The Journal of the National Cancer Institute covers basic and clinical oncology. Published twice monthly, it contains peer-reviewed scientific articles and reports, reviews of technical areas and issues, commentaries and editorials, and a news section. Also included are book reviews and listings, upcoming events, employment opportunities, and grants and fellowships. The cost is $100 per year. For back issues, contact the Government Printing Office at 202-512-1800.

* Cancer Literature: Bulletins and Bibliographies

Superintendent of Documents
Government Printing Office   202-512-1800
Washington, DC 20402   Fax: 202-512-2250

Oncology Overviews are specialized bibliographies with abstracts, each referencing

Be patient. If any phone number is incorrect, call (area code) 555-1212 and request the new listing.

537

Health and Medicine

up to 500 recent publications. Some of the abstracts include editorial commentary which provides historical background and current research directions. Cost varies between $6.50-$10, depending upon topic. *Recent Reviews* are fully indexed and categorized collections of abstracts of 250-400 reviewed articles published during the year. The three volumes cover cancer diagnosis and treatment, carcinogenesis and cancer virology, immunology and biology. Cost varies between $4-$22 per volume.

* Cancer Pamphlets and Publications List
Cancer Information Service
National Cancer Institute
Building 31, Room 10A16
31 Center Dr., MSC 2580
Bethesda, MD 20892-2580   800-4-CANCER
The National Cancer Institute has over one hundred publications available to the general public and health professionals (many are also in Spanish). Topics range from information on smoking to radiation therapy. Contact this office for a list of publications.

* Cancer Prevention Awareness
Office of Cancer Communications
National Cancer Institute
Building 31, Room 10A16
31 Center Dr., MSC 2580
Bethesda, MD 20892-2580   800-4-CANCER
The National Cancer Institute launched the Cancer Prevention Awareness Program which is a national public education effort aimed at reducing the cancer morality rate by 50 percent by the year 2000. The Program provides information through mass media and intermediary organizations to improve public knowledge and attitudes related to cancer and its prevention, and encourages individuals to adopt lifestyles which reduce their risk of developing cancer. NCI is collaborating with Giant Food Inc., a supermarket chain, in a consumer education program entitled "Eat for Health." The study is designed to inform consumers about nutrition, health promotion, and cancer risk reduction, and to test the effectiveness of supermarket nutrition education programs. One of the free pamphlets titled *Everything Doesn't Cause Cancer* (No. 84-2039) answers some common questions about the causes and prevention of cancer as well as methods for testing chemicals and test results. *Good News, Better News, Best News: Cancer Prevention* (No. 84-2671) discusses avoidable cancer risks and gives steps that one can take every day to prevent it.

* Cancer Q & A International Clearinghouse
Service Desk
International Cancer Information Center
National Cancer Institute, NIH
Building 82, Room 103
Bethesda, MD 20892   301-496-7403
The International Cancer Information Center develops and applies state-of-the-art technology to collect the results of the latest information on cancer research, diagnosis, and treatment. Distributed through online databases, technical journals, and specialized publications (see Cancer Journal and Literature), the information services provide a resource to the most recent cancer information available. Updated monthly, the databases include PDQ and CLINPROT. PDQ's database includes a file that summarizes the most current approaches to cancer treatment, a file of research treatment protocols that are open to patient entry, and a directory of physicians who provide cancer treatment, and health care organizations the have programs of cancer care. CANCERLIT is a comprehensive bibliographic database containing over 650,000 citations and abstracts of published cancer literature. CLINPROT database provides detailed summaries of about 1500 active, experimental cancer therapy protocols from the U.S. and other countries.

* Cancer Research on Causes and Biology
Frederick Cancer Research Facility
P.O. Box B
Frederick, MD 21701   301-846-5096
The Frederick Cancer Research Facility, as part of the National Cancer Institute, (NCI) is the leading center for cancer research. They support research on the causes and biology of cancer, the regulation of given expression, and chemical carcinogenesis. All research information is distributed through NCI.

* Cancer: Spanish Publications
Office of Communications
National Cancer Institute

Building 31, Room 10A16
31 Center Dr., MSC 2580
Bethesda, MD 20892-2580   800-4-CANCER
The institute has numerous pamphlets published in Spanish that are available free including: *Datos Y Consejus Para Dejar De Fumar* (94-3405S). This bilingual pamphlet describes the health risks of smoking and how to quit. *Rompa Con el Vicio Una Guia Para Dejar De Fumar* (94-001) is a self-help smoking cessation booklet prepared specifically for Spanish speaking Americans.

* Cancer: Speakers
Office of Communications
National Cancer Institute
Building 31, Room 10A16
31 Center Dr., MSC 2580
Bethesda, MD 20892-2580   800-4-CANCER
This office can give you information on speakers who are available to talk on a variety of topics to the general public, as well as health professionals. The topics can range from current research to environmental risks. Contact this office for more information on scheduling.

* Cancer Unconventional Treatments
National Technical Information Service
U.S. Department of Commerce
5285 Port Royal Rd.   800-553-6847
Springfield, VA 22161   703-487-4650
The former Office of Technology Assessment (OTA) worked on a study that summarizes available information on the major types of unconventional cancer treatments; describes the legal constraints on their availability; and examines the potential for evaluating these new treatments for safety and effectiveness. The title of the resulting publication is *Unconventional Cancer Treatments*. It is now available from the National Technical Information Service, order #PB91-104893.

* Cancer: Videotapes
National Audiovisual Center
8700 Edgeworth Drive
Capitol Heights, MD 20743   800-788-6282
Several videos can be purchased including "Cancer and the Environment" which looks at such factors as chemical and industrial pollution, auto emissions, diet, estrogen, and tobacco. "Cancer: What Is It?" provides an overview of cancer and compares the behavior of malignant cells with normal cells. A 27-minute video, "Control and Prevention of Malignant Melanoma: A Program for Melanoma-Prone Families" discusses danger signs, skin self-examination, and prevention techniques of this potentially fatal skin cancer.

* Cerebral Palsy
National Institute of Neurological Disorders and Stroke
National Institutes of Health   800-352-9424
P.O. Box 5801   301-496-5751
Bethesda, MD 20824   Fax: 301-402-2186
This center for medical research has information about the latest developments on this disease as well as a free 26-page pamphlet titled *Cerebral Palsy: Hope Through Research* (No. 84-158).

* Children and Mental Health
National Institute of Mental Health (NIMH)
5600 Fishers Lane, Room 7C02   301-443-4515
Rockville, MD 20857   Fax: 301-443-0008
                    TDD: 301-443-8431
The National Institute of Mental Health (NIMH) has several publications which deal with mental health in children. These publications are available at no charge. Titles include:

Attention Deficit Hyperactivity Disorder (NIH-94-3571)
Eating Disorders (NIH-93-3477)
Learning Disabilities (NIH-93-3611)
Obsessive Compulsive Disorder (94-3755)
Plain Talk About Adolescence (ADM 85-1065)
Plain Talk About Dealing With the Angry Child (ADM 92-0781)
Pre-Term Babies (ADM 80-0972)
What To Do When a Friend is Depressed: Guide for Students (94-3824)

* Children with AIDS

National Maternal and Child Health Clearinghouse
2070 Chain Bridge Rd., Suite 450
Vienna, VA 22182   703-821-8955

How Can I Tell You? is a free publication from the clearinghouse concerning AIDS and children.

* Cholesterol and Coronary Heart Disease

National Cholesterol Education Program
National Heart, Lung, and Blood Institute
P.O. Box 30105   301-251-1222
Bethesda, MD 20824-0105   Fax: 301-251-1223

This clearinghouse of the National Heart, Lung and Blood Institute (NHLBI) works to inform the public about cardiovascular disease. One of many publications available free is *NHLBI Facts About Blood Cholesterol* (No. 90-2696). The Program works to increase the general public's awareness about the importance of having their blood cholesterol levels checked, knowing what their cholesterol levels are, and taking steps to lower elevated levels. The Program also develops materials for the worksite and the schools. Some of the free publications include:

General Public

Parents' Guide, Cholesterol in Children, Healthy Eating is a Family Affair. Designed for parents who want to encourage heart-healthy eating patterns in their families. (92-3099)

Eating With Your Heart in Mind (7 to 10 year olds). Hands-on activities such as word games and puzzles teach children about eating right and exercise. (92-3100)

Heart Health...Your Choice (11 to 14 year olds). Hands-on activities help this age group learn appropriate lifestyle changes to reduce high blood cholesterol.

Hearty habits, Don't Eat Your Heart Out (15 to 18 year olds). Interactive materials focus on getting teen involved in changing their eating habits and making appropriate lifestyle changes to reduce high blood cholesterol. (93-3102)

Step-by-Step: Eating to Lower Your High Blood Cholesterol. Contains general rules about diets, physical activity, and weight loss to lower blood cholesterol.

Stay Young at Heart Recipe Cards. The recipes in this booklet will convince you that it's easy to cook in a heart-healthy way. (55-648)

Facts About...Blood Cholesterol - Q&A on lowering high blood cholesterol. (94-2696)

Eating to Lower Your High Blood Cholesterol - how-to booklet gives all the information needed to change eating habits and lower high blood cholesterol. (92-2972)

So You Have High Blood Cholesterol - easy to read pamphlet designed for patients diagnosed as having high blood cholesterol. (93-2922)

Professionals

Cholesterol Lowering in the Management of Coronary Heart Disease videotape. This professional education video presents an expert review of research findings that demonstrate the benefits of reducing lipids in patients with coronary heart disease. (55-657)

Recommendations for Improving Cholesterol Management. Provides guidelines and recommendations to help implement the standardization of laboratory measurement.

Report of the Expert Panel on Population Strategies for Blood Cholesterol Reduction - reviews the scientific base for making recommendation to the general public. (90-3047)

Highlights of the NCEP Report on Blood Cholesterol Levels in Children and Adolescents - presents an overview of the recommendation in the Report. (91-2731)

* Chronic Disease Prevention

Center for Chronic Disease Prevention
and Health Promotion (CCDPHP)
Centers for Disease Control (CDC)
1600 Clifton Rd., NE   404-639-3534
Atlanta, GA 30333   404-639-3311

Begun in 1988, this center was established in the belief that more emphasis was needed on chronic disease prevention if CDC was to accomplish its mission of preventing unnecessary illness, disability, and death. CCDPHP stresses translating research findings into effective community-based programs, strengthening the delivery of preventive health services, and designing programs to meet the needs of minority groups. Units within the center cover smoking and health, nutrition, school health, chronic disease control, reproductive health, diabetes, and surveillance and analysis. The center works with State health departments on breast cancer control projects that promote screening mammography, advanced training for technicians, equipment testing, and peer review. The Preventive Health and Health Services Block Grant helps fund states' efforts to combat chronic diseases and to offer health education. Some interventions are designed to serve the dual purpose of meeting local health needs and providing a model for other programs. The Center has established a newsletter, *Chronic Disease Notes and Reports,* to provide a regular forum for communication.

* Chronic Fatigue Syndrome

National Institute of Allergy and
   Infectious Diseases
National Institutes of Health
Building 31, Room 7A51
31 Center Dr., MSC 2520
Bethesda, MD 20892-2520   301-496-5717

Chronic Fatigue Syndrome (CFS) is a fatigue that comes on suddenly and is relentless or relapsing, causing debilitating tiredness or easy fatigability in someone who has no apparent reason for feeling this way. National Institute of Allergy and Infectious Diseases (NIAID) has publications which explain CFS, including current research, treatment, and causes. They also have compiled a list of support groups and resources, as well as other relevant articles. *Chronic Fatigue Syndrome,* part of the Medicine for the Layman Series, describes possible causes and treatment for CFS, and is available free from: Clinical Center Communications, National Institutes of Health, Building 10, Room 1C255, Bethesda, MD 20892; 301-496-2563. The Centers for Disease Control also offers a background article and provides information about CDC research, including surveillance of community health department to determine the incidence of CFS and studies of blood samples from CFS patients to detect evidence of viral infection. For more information contact, Centers for Disease Control, Division of Viral Diseases, Bldg. 6, Room 120, Atlanta, GA 30333; 404-639-3534.

* Chronic Pain Research and Therapies

National Institute of Neurological Disorders and Stroke
National Institutes of Health
P.O. Box 5801   800-352-9424
Bethesda, MD 20824   301-496-5751

This Institute conducts research on persistent pain and various therapies including drugs, acupuncture, surgery, electrical stimulation, and also psychological techniques.

* Cirrhosis of the Liver

National Digestive Diseases Information Clearinghouse
2 Information Way   301-654-3810
Bethesda, MD 20892-3750   Fax: 301-907-8906

A free four-page pamphlet titled *Cirrhosis of the Liver* (No. 92-1134) explains preventive measures including alcohol abstinence and other causes, symptoms, diagnosis and treatment.

* Colon Colitis, Diverticulitis, and Cancer

Office of Consumer Affairs, Public Inquiries
Food and Drug Administration
5600 Fishers Lane (HFE-88)
Rockville, MD 20857   301-443-3170

The Food and Drug Administration (FDA) can provide information on how the colon works and is the site of many problems such as colon colitis, diverticulitis, and cancer.

* Condoms and Sexually Transmitted Diseases

National Clearinghouse for Primary Care Information
2070 Chain Bridge Rd.
Vienna, VA 22182   703-821-8955

Condoms and Sexually Transmitted Diseases... Especially AIDS is an easily understood brochure which answers 17 frequently asked questions about purchasing and using condoms. Facts about sexually transmitted diseases are listed.

Be patient. If any phone number is incorrect, call (area code) 555-1212 and request the new listing.

539

Health and Medicine

* Cooley's Anemia

National Heart, Lung, and Blood Institute
Information Center
P.O. Box 30105   301-251-1222
Bethesda, MD 20824-0105   Fax: 301-251-1223

This Institute offers information on many aspects of cardiovascular disease including a free pamphlet titled *Cooley's Anemia: Prevention Through Understanding* which discusses prevention through testing and genetic counseling.

* Crohn's Disease

National Digestive Diseases Information
   Clearinghouse
2 Information Way   301-654-3810
Bethesda, MD 20892-3570   Fax: 301-907-8906

Information about ulcerative colitis and Crohn's Disease, clinical symptoms, epidemiological patterns, treatment strategies and experimental therapies are provided by this clearinghouse.

* Dementia Disorders

National Institute of Neurological Disorders and Stroke
National Institutes of Health   800-352-9424
P.O. Box 5801   301-496-5751
Bethesda, MD 20824   Fax: 301-402-2186

Alzheimer's Disease: A Scientific Guide for Health Practitioners (No. 84-2251) is a booklet which describes Alzheimer's, possible causes of the disease, diagnosis and treatment.

* Depression: Diagnosis and Treatments

National Institute of Mental Health (NIMH)
Alcohol, Drug Abuse and Mental Health Administration
5600 Fishers Lane, Room 15C05
Rockville, MD 20857   301-443-4515

The National Institute of Mental Health (NIMH) conducts research on depression and other mental disorders, distributes information, conducts demonstration programs for the prevention, treatment, and rehabilitation of the mentally ill. A major media campaign on depression, called Project D/ART (Depression/Awareness, Recognition, Treatment), is being developed by NIMH in collaboration with other organizations to provide information on symptoms, causes, and treatments of various depressive disorders. Many publications and reports are available on various topics for professionals and the general public.

* Diabetes Control Programs

Division of Diabetes Translation
Office of Chronic Disease
Prevention and Health Promotion
Centers for Disease Control (CDC)
1600 Clifton Rd., EO8
Atlanta, GA 30333   770-488-5000

This division has cooperative agreements with 30 states to establish Diabetes Control Programs. Through each state's health department, with the Center for Disease Control providing matching funds, these programs are designed for complications specific interventions for diabetics. They examine for eye disease and make appropriate referrals, as well as assist with diabetic pregnancy and lower limb circulation problems. Contact this office for referral to local states of for more information.

* Diabetes Information Center

National Diabetes Information Clearinghouse (NDIC)
1 Information Way   301-654-3327
Bethesda, MD 20892-3560   Fax: 301-907-8906

The National Diabetes Information Clearinghouse (NDIC) responds to requests for information about diabetes and its complications and distributes information appropriate to health professionals, people with diabetes and their families, and the general public. They have many publications and bibliographies, as well as *Diabetes Dateline*, a free quarterly current awareness newsletter that features news about diabetes research, upcoming meetings and events, and new publications. NDIC uses the online database CHID (Combined Health Information Database) from which they can reference health information. Some other publications include:

Public and Patient Education Materials:
Dental Tips for Diabetics (DM-16)

The Diabetes Dictionary (DM-84)
Diabetic Retinopathy (DM-20)
End Stage Renal Disease: Choosing a Treatment That's Right For You (DM-130)
Insulin-Dependent Diabetes (DM-51)
Noninsulin-Dependent Diabetes (DM-81)
Periodontal Disease and Diabetes, A Guide for Patients (DM-21)
Pregnancy and Diabetes (DM-12)
Understanding Gestational Diabetes (DM-12)

Professional Materials
Diabetes Control and Complications Trial (DCCT) Slide Set, (DM-137, $18 per set)
Detection and Prevention of Periodontal Disease in Diabetes (DM-17)
Diabetes Dateline (DM-105)
Diabetes in America, Diabetes Data Compiled 1984 (DM-96)
Diabetes in Hispanic Americans: Current Research and Education Programs (DM-148)
Diabetes in Native Americans: The Eastern Tribes (DM-164)
Diabetes Special Report (DM-13)
Patient Education Fact Sheets (DM-129)

Catalogs and Guides
Combined Health Information Database (CHID) Fact Sheet (CM-70)
Directory of Diabetes Organizations (DM-128)
NDIC Brochure (DM-32)

Fact Sheets
Diabetes in Blacks (DM-113)
Diabetes in Hispanics (DM-114)
Diabetes Education (DM-115)
Diabetic Neuropathy (DM-116)
Diabetes Overview (DM-119)
Diabetes Statistics (DM-163)
Hypoglycemia (DM-167)
Kidney Disease of Diabetes (DM-168)

* Diabetes Information Reprints

National Diabetes Information
   Clearinghouse (NDIC)
1 Information Way   301-654-3327
Bethesda, MD 20892-3560   Fax: 301-907-8906

Reprints are copies of journal articles about the Diabetes Control and Complications Trial (DCCT) and other National Institute of Diabetes and Digestive and Kidney Diseases (NIDDK) research programs. The following is a list of articles currently available:

Effects of Age, Duration and Treatment of Insulin-Dependent Diabetes Mellitus on Residual B-cell Function: Observation During Eligibility Testing for DCCT (R-21)
Color Photography vs. Fluorescein Angiography in the Detection of Diabetic Retinopathy in the DCCT (R-22)
Sounding Board: Are Continuing Studies of Metabolic Control and Microvascular Complication in Insulin-Dependent Diabetes Mellitus Justified? (R-23)
Factors in Development of Neuropathy: Baseline Analysis of Neuropathy in Feasibility Phase of DCCT (R-24)
Feasibility of Centralized Measurements of Glycated Hemoglobin in the DCCT: a Multi-center Study (R-25)
Weight Gain Associated with Intensive Therapy in the DCCT (R-26)
Reliability and Validity of a Diabetes Quality-of-Life Measure for the DCCT (R-28)
DCCT Update (R-29)
Epidemiology of Severe Hypoglycemia in the DCCT (R-31)
Baseline Analysis of Renal Function in the DCCT (R-33)
Survey of Physician Practice Behaviors Related to Diabetes Mellitus in the United States (R-34)
The Effect of Intensive Treatment of Diabetes on the Development and Progression of Long-Term Complications of Insulin-Dependent Diabetes Mellitus (R-35)

* Diarrhea Prevention and Control

National Digestive Diseases Information Clearinghouse
2 Information Way   301-654-3810
Bethesda, MD 20892-3750   Fax: 301-907-8906

This clearinghouse offers information on this digestive tract disorder including information packets such as *Diarrhea in Adults* (DD-140) and *Diarrhea in Children* (DD-141).

Be patient. If any phone number is incorrect, call (area code) 555-1212 and request the new listing.

* Digestive Health and Disease Clearinghouse

National Digestive Diseases Information Clearinghouse (NDDIC)
2 Information Way   301-654-3810
Bethesda, MD 20892-3570   Fax: 301-907-8906

National Digestive Diseases Information Clearinghouse (NDDIC) responds to requests for information about digestive diseases and distributes information to health professionals, people with digestive diseases, and the general public. They have many publications, as well as a news bulletin. NDDIC uses the online database CHID (Combined Health Information Database) from which they can access health information and organizations. Some of their free publications include:

Age Page: Digestive Dos and Don'ts (DD-05)
Digestive Disease Statistics (DD-118)
Facts and Fallacies About Digestive Diseases (DD-02)
Your Digestive System and How It Works (DD-03)
Age Page: Constipation (DD-36)
Smoking and Your Digestive System (DD-52)
Harmful Effects of Medicines on the Adult Digestive System (DD-116)

Fact Sheets
Irritable Bowel Syndrome (DD-14)
Ulcerative Colitis (DD-15)
Diverticulosis and Diverticulitis (DD-27)
Bleeding In the Digestive Tract (DD-29)
Gas in the Digestive Tract (DD-30)
Hiatal Hernia and Heartburn (DD-160)
Constipation (D-35)
Lactose Intolerance (DD-48)
Hemorrhoids (DD-59)
Stomach and Duodenal Ulcers (DD-161)
Pancreatitis (DD-71)
Cirrhosis of the Liver (DD-73)
Gallstones (DD-97)

Information Packets
Crohn's Disease and Ulcerative Colitis (DD-103)
Hepatitis B (DD-110)
Hepatitis C (DD-111)
Irritable Bowel Syndrome (DD-103)
Celiac Disease (DD-112)
Gastritis (DD-113)
Abdominal Pain (DD-151)
Digestive Diseases - General Information (DD-123)

Catalogues and Guides
Digestive Diseases Organizations: For Patients (DD-05)
Digestive Diseases Organizations: Professional (DD-06)
NDDIC Brochure (DD-22)
DD Notes (DD-32)
CHID Fact Sheet (DD-33)
Therapeutic Endoscopy and Bleeding Ulcers (DD-41)
Research Opportunities and Programs in the Division of Digestive Diseases and Nutrition 1994 (DD-95)

* Dyslexia and Other Learning Disorders

Human Learning and Behavior Branch
National Institute of Child Health and Human Development
National Institutes of Health
Bldg. 6100, Room 4B05
Bethesda, MD 20892   301-496-6591

The Human Learning and Behavior Branch is concerned with the development of human behavior, from infancy, through childhood and adolescence, into early maturity. Studies are supported in developmental psychobiology, behavioral pediatrics, cognitive and communicative processes, social and affective development, and health related behaviors, as well as learning disabilities, dyslexia and language disorders. For information regarding current research and publications, contact the office listed above.

* Eye Research Experiments Nationwide

National Eye Institute
Publications Distribution Center
National Institute of Health
2020 Vision Place
Bethesda, MD 20892   301-492-5248

Intended for the practitioner, *Clinical Trials Supported by the National Eye Institute* briefly describes 20 ongoing research studies. Included is the current status of the study, the results, any publications that result from the studies, as well as a list of the participating clinical centers.

* Gallstone Disease

National Digestive Diseases Information Clearinghouse
2 Information Way   301-654-3810
Bethesda, MD 20892-3570   Fax: 301-907-8906

Questions about surgery and complications as well as the reasons for the formation of gallstones are addressed in this free 4-page pamphlet titled *Gallstone Disease*.

* Head Injury

National Institute of Arthritis and Musculoskeletal
and Skin Diseases   301-496-4484
1 AMC Circle   Fax: 301-587-4352
Bethesda, MD 20892-3675   TDD: 301-565-2966

This program focuses on orthopedic research, which includes sports medicine, growth and development of bone and bone cells, as well as head injury. Staff can answer questions regarding current research and treatment issues. Brochures and pamphlets are available through the National Institute of Arthritis and Musculoskeletal and Skin Diseases.

* Head Trauma and Rehab

National Institute of Neurological Disorders and Stroke
National Institutes of Health
P.O. Box 5801   800-352-9424
Bethesda, MD 20892   301-496-5751

Head Injury: Hope through Research (No. 84-2478) discusses ways to prevent head injuries and the resulting damage from different types of injuries, as well as rehabilitation techniques.

* Health Programs and Services

Information is available at all state public health offices.

Alabama
State Health Officer
Alabama Department of Public Health
610 E. Patton
Montgomery, AL 36111   334-613-5200

Alaska
Division of Public Health
Alaska Department of Health and Social Services
P.O. Box 110610
Juneau, AK 99811-0610   907-586-1877

Arizona
Public Information Office
Arizona Department of Health Services
1740 W. Adams
Phoenix, AZ 85007   602-542-1216

Arkansas
Department of Health Protection and Services
Arkansas Department of Health
4815 W. Markham
Little Rock, AR 77205-3689   501-661-2417

California
Health Section
Department of Health Services
714 P St., Room 499
P.O. Box 942732
Sacramento, CA 95814   916-657-1425

Colorado
Cardiovascular Disease Control Program
Division of Prevention Programs
Colorado Department of Health
4300 Cherry Creek Dr., South
Denver, CO 80222   303-692-2500

Connecticut
Public Health and Addiction Services
Connecticut Department of Health Services
150 Washington St.
Hartford, CT 06106   203-566-2038

Delaware
Division of Public Health
Department of Health and Social Services
P.O. Box 637
Dover, DE 19903   302-739-4701

District of Columbia
Prevention Health Services Administration
DC Commission of Public Health
1660 L St., NW
Washington, DC 20036   202-673-6741

Florida
Health Program Office
Florida Department of Health and Rehabilitative Services
1317 Winewood Blvd.
Tallahassee, FL 32399-0700   904-487-2705

Georgia
Division of Human Resources
Georgia Department of Human Resources
2 Peachtree St., 7th Floor
Atlanta, GA 30303   404-657-2702

Hawaii
Chief
Health Promotion and Disease Prevention
Hawaii State Department of Health
1250 Punchbowl St.
Honolulu, HI 96813   808-586-4438

Idaho
Bureau of Preventive Health
Division of Health
Idaho Department of Health and Welfare
450 W. State St., 10th Floor
Boise, ID 83720   208-334-5500

Illinois
Community Chronic Disease Programs Section
Division of Chronic Diseases
Illinois Department of Public Health
535 W. Jefferson St.
Springfield, IL 62761   217-782-4977

Indiana
Local Health Support
Indiana State Board of Health
1330 W. Michigan St.
P.O. Box 1964
Indianapolis, IN 46206   317-633-8451

Iowa
Director
Iowa Department of Public Health
Nutrition Bureau
Lucas State Office Building
Des Moines, IA 50319   515-281-5605

Kansas
Division of Health
Health and Environment Department
Landon State Office Building
Room 620
Topeka, KS 66612   913-296-1086

Kentucky
Department for Health Services
Cabinet of Human Resources
275 E. Main St.
Frankfort, KY 40621   502-564-4990

Louisiana
Louisiana Department of Health and Hospitals
Office of Public Health
P.O. Box 3214
New Orleans, LA 70160   504-342-8094

Maine
Health and Social Services
Maine Department of Human Services
State House Station 11
Augusta, ME 04333   207-624-5335

Maryland
Public Health Services
Maryland Department of Health and Mental Hygiene
201 W. Preston St.
Baltimore, MD 21201   301-225-6525

Massachusetts
Commissioners Office
Massachusetts Department of Public Health
150 Tremont St.
Boston, MA 02111   617-727-0201

Michigan
Center for Health Promotion
Michigan Department of Public Health
3500 N. Logan St.
P.O. Box 30195
Lansing, MI 48909   517-335-8368

Minnesota
Commissioners Office
Minnesota Department of Health
717 S.E. Delaware St.
P.O. Box 9441
Minneapolis, MN 55440   612-623-5460

Mississippi
State Health Office
Mississippi Department of Health
P.O. Box 1700
Jackson, MS 39215   601-960-7634

Missouri
Public Information Office
Missouri Department of Health
P.O. Box 570
Jefferson City, MO 65102   314-751-6062

Montana
Health Services Division
Montana Department of Health
Cogswell Building, Room C108
Helena, MT 59620   406-444-4473

Nebraska
Health Promotion and Education
Nebraska Department of Health
301 Centennial Mall S.
P. O. Box 95007
Lincoln, NE 68509   402-471-2101

Nevada
State Health Officer
Nevada State Health Division
505 E. King St., Room 201
Carson City, NV 89710   702-687-4740

New Hampshire
Division of Public Health Services
New Hampshire Division of Public Health Services
115 Pleasant St., Annex Bldg. 1
Concord, NH 03301   603-271-4505

New Jersey
Division of Epidemiology and Environmental,
Occupational, and Health Services

New Jersey State Department of Health
CN #360
Trenton, NJ 08625   609-588-7465

New Mexico
Public Health Division
New Mexico Health Department
1190 St. Francis Dr.
Santa Fe, NM 87502-6110   505-827-2389

New York
Public Affairs
New York State Department of Health
Corning Tower
Empire State Plaza
Albany, NY 12237   518-474-7354

North Carolina
Adult Health Promotion
North Carolina Department of Environment, Health, and Natural Resources
P.O. Box 2091
1330 St. Mary St.
Raleigh, NC 27611-7687   919-715-3158

North Dakota
State Health Officer
North Dakota State Department of Health
600 E. Boulevard Ave.
Bismarck, ND 58505   701-328-2372

Ohio
Director's Office
Ohio Department of Health
246 N. High St.
Columbus, OH 43266   614-466-2253

Oklahoma
Health Promotion and Policy
Health Education and Information Services
Oklahoma State Department of Health
1000 NE 10th St.
P.O. Box 53551
Oklahoma City, OK 73152   405-271-5601

Oregon
Health Policy Office
State of Oregon Department of Human Resources
800 NE Oregon St.
#23, Suite 640
Portland, OR 97232   503-731-4091

Pennsylvania
Health Promotion
Pennsylvania Department of Health
P.O. Box 90
Harrisburg, PA 17108   717-787-9857

Rhode Island
Health Promotion
Rhode Island Department of Health
3 Capitol Hill
Providence, RI 02908-5097   401-277-2553

South Carolina
Health Services Office
South Carolina Department of Health
and Environmental Control
2600 Bull St.
Columbia, SC 29201   803-737-3900

South Dakota
Health and Medical Services
South Dakota Department of Health
523 E. Capitol
Pierre, SD 57501-3185   605-773-3361

Tennessee
Health Services Bureau

Tennessee Department of Health and Environment
312 8th Ave. North, 12th Floor
Nashville, TN 37247-4501   615-741-7305

Texas
Public Information Officer
Texas Department of Health
1100 W. 49th St.
Austin, TX 78756-3199   512-458-7400

Utah
Human Services Department
Utah Department of Health
P.O. Box 45500
Salt Lake City, UT 84145-0500   801-538-3998

Vermont
Health Promotion
Vermont Department of Health
P.O. Box 70
Burlington, VT 05402   802-863-7280

Virginia
Public Health Programs
Virginia Department of Health
1500 E. Main St.
P.O. Box 2448
Richmond, VA 23218   804-786-3561

Washington
Community and Family Health Services
Department of Social and Health Services
P.O. Box 47890
Olympia, WA 98504-7800   360-753-7021

West Virginia
Public Health Bureau
West Virginia Department of Health and Human Resources
State Capitol Complex
Bldg. 3, Room 518
Charleston, WV 25305-0501   304-553-2971

Wisconsin
Health Division
Wisconsin Department of Health and Social Services
P.O. Box 7850
Madison, WI 53707-7850   608-266-1511

Wyoming
Public Health Division
Wyoming Department of Health and Medical Services
Hathaway Building, 4th Floor
Cheyenne, WY 82002-0710   307-777-6186

* Heart Attacks

National Heart, Lung, and Blood Institute
Information Center
P.O. Box 30105   301-251-1222
Bethesda, MD 20824-0105   Fax: 301-251-1223

The National Heart Attack Alert Program (NHAAP) aims to reduce death, including sudden death, and disability from heart attacks through faster identification and treatment of individuals with heart attack symptoms and signs. The NHAAP, along with 39 major health organizations and Federal agencies, is working to reduce the time lag between the first recognition of a heart attack and definitive treatment by education health care professionals, prehospital providers/emergency medical services (EMS) personnel, patients and their families, and the general public to identify manifestations of an acute myocardial infarction (AMI) and to take immediate action. There are numerous publications available from the Information Center including:

General Public Patient Materials:
The Healthy Heart Handbook for Women (92-2720) answers many questions about women and cardiovascular disease and provides self-help strategies for controlling risk factors.

Women's Fact Sheets. These reproducible fact sheets on women and heart disease are taken from the *Healthy Heart Handbook for Women*.
Facts About...

Be patient. If any phone number is incorrect, call (area code) 555-1212 and request the new listing.

543

Heart Disease and Women: Are You at Risk? (94-3654)

Heart Disease and Women: Self-Help Strategies for a Healthy Heart-Preventing and Controlling High Blood Pressure (94-3655)

Heart Disease and Women: Self-Help Strategies for a Healthy Heart-Getting Physical (94-3656)

Heart Disease and Women: Self-Help Strategies for a Healthy Heart-Kicking the Smoking Habit (94-3657)

Heart Disease and Women: Self-Help Strategies for a Healthy Heart-Reducing High Blood Pressure (94-3658)

Heart Disease and Women: So You Have Heart Disease (95-2645)

Exercise Your Healthy Heart I.Q. (92-2724) This brochure uses a true-false format to educate readers about heart disease.

Exercise and Your Heart: A Guide to Physical Activity (93-3795) A 12 question true-false quiz addresses the relationship of physical activity to heart health.

The Human Heart-A Living Pump (95-1058) This booklet describes how the heart functions as a pump for the body's blood.

Professional Materials:
Patient/Bystander Recognition and Action: Rapid Identification and Treatment of Acute Myocardial Infarction (93-3303)

9-1-1: Rapid Identification and Treatment of Acute Myocardial Infarction (94-3302)

Emergency Medical Dispatching: Rapid Identification and Treatment of Acute Myocardial Infarction (94-3287)

Staffing and Equipping Emergency Medical Services Systems: Rapid Identification and Treatment of Acute Myocardial Infarction (93-3304)

Emergency Department: Rapid Identification and Treatment of Patients with Acute Myocardial Infarction (93-3278)

Action Alerts: These one page highlights on rapid identification and treatment of individuals with symptoms and signs of an acute myocardial infarction:
Patient/Bystander (55-623)
9-1-1- (55-624)
Emergency Medical Dispatching (55-625)
Staffing and Equipment (55-626)
Emergency Department (55-627)

* Heart Disease: Diagnosis and Treatment

Office of Clinical Center Communications
National Institutes of Health (NIH)
Building 10, Room 1C255
9000 Rockville Pike
Bethesda, MD 20892   301-496-2563

A free pamphlet, *Risk of Heart Disease*, discusses new findings in clinical cardiology, new techniques to diagnose abnormalities in the pumping function of the heart, and new concepts in treating people who come to the hospital with an acute heart attack.

* Heart Disease Videotapes

National Audiovisual Center
8700 Edgeworth Drive
Capitol Heights, MD 20743   800-788-6282

Several videos can be purchased from the Center including "Cholesterol, Diet and Heart Disease", "Heart Attacks", and "Coronary Heart Disease: Roles of Surgery and Balloon Dilatation".

* Hepatitis

National Digestive Diseases Information Clearinghouse
2 Information Way
Bethesda, MD 20892-3570   301-654-3810

The following information packets include materials such as fact sheets, reprints of articles and literature searches from the Combined Health Information Database (CHID) which provide additional sources of information.

Hepatitis B (DD-110)
Hepatitis C (DD-111)

* Herpes Type II

National Institute of Allergy
and Infectious Diseases
National Institutes of Health
Building 31, Room 7A50
31 Center Dr., MSC 2520
Bethesda, MD 20892-2520   301-496-5717

This institute offers information and various publications on sexually transmitted diseases including *Genital Herpes* which is also available in Spanish, and *Sexually Transmitted Diseases* (STDs).

* High Blood Pressure

National Heart, Lung, and Blood Institute
High Blood Pressure Information Center
P.O. Box 30105   301-251-1222
Bethesda, MD 20824-0105   Fax: 301-251-1223

The National High Blood Pressure Education Program (NHBPEP) works to reduce death and disability related to high blood pressure and encourages program activities to prevent high blood pressure. It develops and disseminates educational materials, supports mass media campaigns, and provides technical support to regional, state, and community health programs. In addition the NHBPEP develops national guidelines for professionals and communities. Since the start of the Program public behavior has changed: more people are seeing their doctors for high blood pressure. In the past two decades, stroke and heart attack deaths have decreased by half. High Blood Pressure Education Month is celebrated annually in May. Single copies of publications for the general public, patients and professionals are available from the Information Center. These include:

Patient Education Booklets:
Eat Right to Help Lower Your High Blood Pressure. This easy to read (fifth grade level) conversational text brochure is presented in large type with illustrations. (550-3289)

High Blood Pressure: Treat it for Life. This booklet provides information on what high blood pressure is and how it can be treated and controlled. (94-3312)

The Sports Guide: NHLBI Planning Guide for Cardiovascular Disease Risk Reduction Projects at Sporting Events. This planning guide was developed to bring cardiovascular disease education and health promotion programs to sporting events on the professional, college, or high school level. (95-3802)

General Public/Patient Materials:
High Blood Pressure: A Common But Controllable Disorder. Age Page. This fact sheet presents information about high blood pressure and gives some facts about treatment. (55-486)

Stroke: Prevention and Treatment. Age Page. This fact sheet defines and describes stroke diagnosis, treatment, prevention, and rehabilitation. (55-487)

Fact About How to Prevent High Blood Pressure. This fact sheet explains what high blood pressure is, who is at risk, and what can be done to help prevent high blood pressure. (94-3281)

Check Your High Blood Pressure I.Q. This quiz tests your knowledge of high blood pressure prevention. (94-3671)

High Blood Pressure & What You Can Do About It. A concise explanation of high blood pressure and some of the causes and cures. (55-222A)

Professional Materials:
High Blood Pressure Prevention Infographs. One page with camera-ready layouts that advertise the primary prevention message and the 1-800-GET-WELL telephone number. (55-669)

Churches as an Avenue to High Blood Pressure Control. This guide is designed to help churches and other places of worship in establishing high blood pressure programs in their communities. (92-2715)

The Physicians Guide: Improving Adherence Among Hypertensive Patients. This guide presents ways physicians can improve patient education, adherence to treatment, and control of high blood pressure. (55-250)

The Stroke Belt: Stroke Mortality by Race and Sex. Data Fact Sheet. Stroke mortality rates differ substantially by state, and 11 states with the highest age-adjusted rates have been identified as "The Stroke Belt". (55-356)

Working Group Report on Ambulatory Blood Pressure Monitoring. This report examines the state of the technology of ambulatory blood pressure monitoring. (92-3028)

Working Group on Hypertension in the Elderly. This report presents the recommendations of the NHBPEP's Working Group on Hypertension in the Elderly. (94-3527)

Working Group Report on the Heart in Hypertension. This report reviews the adaptation of the heart to pressure overload due to hypertension and the resulting complications. (91-3033)

Prevalence of Hypertension in the U.S. Adult Population. Contains data on the prevalence of hypertension and mean arterial pressures by age, race, and gender. (55-681)

* Homeless Council

Interagency Council on the Homeless
451 Seventh St., SW, Suite 7274
Washington, DC 20410   202-708-1480

The Council was created by the Stewart B. McKinney Homeless Assistance Act to provide Federal leadership in the development of urgently needed assistance to protect and improve the lives and safety of homeless persons. The Council is comprised of 17 Federal agencies with jurisdiction over various aspects of Federal homelessness efforts. The Council provides technical assistance and publishes information concerning McKinney and other Federal homeless assistance programs in the Council Communique (a free, bi-monthly newsletter), funding bulletins, an annual report, and periodic legislative updates. The Council maintains a list of official state contacts for homeless issues.

* Homeless Mentally Ill Programs

Center for Mental Health Services
Homeless Programs Branch
Substance Abuse and Mental Health Services Administration
Walter Leginski, Ph.D., Chief   301-443-3706
5600 Fishers Land, Room 11C-05   Fax: 301-443-0541
Rockville, MD 20857   TDD: 301-443-9006

The Center for Mental Health Services, of the Substance Abuse and Mental Health Services Administration, is the Federal agency concerned with the prevention and treatment of mental illness and the promotion of mental health. The Homeless Programs Branch administers three programs supported by McKinney Act funds: (1) the Projects for Assistance in Transition from Homelessness (PATH) Formula Grant Program providing funds to 50 states, DC and five U.S. territories to support service delivery for homeless persons with mental illnesses, who may also have substance use disorders; (2) the Access to Community Care and Effective Services and Supports (ACCESS) Program which funds nine states to implement and evaluate a variety of innovative approaches that will integrate service delivery systems for homeless persons with serious mental illnesses, and (3) the CSAT/CMHS Dual Diagnosis Treatment Demonstration Program, a collaborative demonstration program with the Center for Substance Abuse Treatment evaluating the effectiveness of treatment models for homeless persons with co-occurring disorders. The Branch also provides professional leadership for collaborative intergovernmental initiatives designed to assist persons with mental illnesses who are homeless. In addition, the Branch supports a contract for the national Resource Center on Homelessness and Mental Illness.

* Homeless Veterans

Homeless Chronically Mentally Ill Veterans Program
Veterans Benefits Administration
U.S. Department of Veterans Affairs
810 Vermont Ave., NW 205-5
Washington, DC 20420   202-273-6771

The Homeless Chronically Mentally Ill Veterans Program provides outreach, VA case management services, and psychiatric residential treatment for homeless mentally ill veterans, when appropriate, in community-based facilities. A total of 45 sites in 26 states and the District of Columbia provide an integrated network of treatment programs for homeless veterans with chronic mental illness. The VA developed the Domiciliary Care for Homeless Veterans Program to address the unmet clinical needs of homeless veterans. More than 90% of the veterans served by this program, which operates in 27 sites, have psychiatric illness of alcohol or other drug dependency problems. Services include outreach and referral, screening and assessment, medical and psychiatric evaluation, treatment and rehabilitation, and post-discharge community support. Staff help veterans secure employment and housing.

* Homelessness

National Resource on Homelessness and Mental Illness
Policy Research Associates, Inc.
Deborah L. Dennis, Director   800-444-7415
262 Delaware Ave.   Fax: 518-439-7612
Delmar, NY 12054   E-mail: nrc3 pra@aol.com

The National Resource Center on Homelessness and Mental Illness, operated by Policy Research Associates under contract to the Center for Mental Health Services (CMHS), provides technical assistance and comprehensive information concerning the treatment, services and housing needs of homeless persons with severe mental illnesses. The Resource Center provides technical assistance to CMHS grantees; provides or arranges technical assistance on the development of housing for special needs populations; maintains an extensive bibliographic database of published and unpublished materials; develops workshops and substantive papers on the coordination of services and housing for homeless persons with mental illnesses; responds to requests for information; and publishes *Access*, a free, regular information update that features reports on research, program development, and public and private initiatives concerning homeless people with serious mental illnesses.

* Huntington's Disease Research Center

Department of Medical Genetics
Indiana University Medical School
Medical Research Building
975 W. Walnut St.
Indianapolis, IN 46202-5251   317-274-2245

The National Institutes of Health and Indiana University Medical Center, Indianapolis, maintain a roster of Huntington's Disease patients and families. Each of the families complete a family history questionnaire, and the statistics are used for research. IUMC also acts as a broker between families and researchers, who can request subjects for a particular project from IUMC's database of patients and families.

* Infectious Diseases

National Institute of Allergy and Infectious Diseases
National Institutes of Health
Building 31, Room 7A50
31 Center Dr., MSC 2520
Bethesda, MD 20892-2520   301-496-5717

This institute offers many publications and expertise about diarrhea, bacterial meningitis, the common cold, mononucleosis, herpes, rabies, Rocky Mountain Spotted Fever, schistosomiasis, and other infectious diseases. *The Immune System: How It Works* is a free report that discusses antigens, the immune system, disorders (including AIDS), the immunology of transplants, and new diagnostic methods.

* Infectious Diseases

Center for Infectious Diseases (CID)
Centers for Disease Control
1600 Clifton Rd., NE
Atlanta, GA 30333   404-639-3534

The Center for Infectious Diseases (CID) surveys AIDS cases, epidemiologic studies, laboratory investigations, prevention strategies, and technology transfer concerning the HIV infection. They also examine vaccines and other strategies against bacterial, viral, and parasitic pathogens, such as rabies, hepatitis B, Hemophilis influenzae b, and malaria. They also develop and evaluate prevention and control methods for foodborne pathogens, such as Salmonella. This office can refer you to publications and researchers concerning your particular topic of interest.

* Kidney and Urological Diseases

National Kidney and Urological Diseases
Information Clearinghouse
3 Information Way   800-891-5390
Bethesda, MD 20892-3580   301-654-4415

This clearinghouse responds to inquiries regarding kidney and urological diseases. They can access the CHID (Combined Health Information Database) database to get further information. They have pamphlets, brochures, and reports for the public and professionals, and can refer people to voluntary and professional organizations. The free publications they have available include:

Booklets:
Understanding Urinary Tract Infections - patient and public education booklet. (KU-03)

Prevention and Treatment of Kidney Stones - describes diagnosis, treatment, and types of urinary incontinence. (KU-04)

Urinary Incontinence - describes diagnosis, treatment, and types of urinary incontinence. (KU-06)

National Kidney and Urologic Diseases Information Clearinghouse brochure. (KU-08)

Combined Health Information Database - describes subfiles in the database. (KU-15)

National Kidney and Urologic Diseases Information Clearinghouse Thesaurus - searching tool for the subfile on CHID. (KU-16); brochure (KU-08)

Directory of Kidney and Urologic Disease-Related Organizations - lists professional, patient, and voluntary organizations. (KU-19)

Prostate Enlargement: Benign Prostatic Hyperplasia - gives basic information about the prostate gland and prostate enlargement. (KU-22)

Urinary Incontinence in Adults - summary statement of NIH Consensus Development Conference. (KU-55)

End-Stage Renal Disease: Choosing a Treatment That's Right for You (KU-50)

Interstitial Cystitis, describes the causes, symptoms, diagnosis, and treatment of interstitial cystitis (IC). Defines nonulcerative and ulcerative IC. Provides information on special concerns for patients and current research. (KU-72)

KU Notes, published twice a year, this features news about special events, patient and professional meetings, and publications (KU-17)

Fact Sheets:
Age Page: Prostate Problems, describes common prostate problems such as prostatitis, benign prostatic hyperplasia, and prostate cancer. (KU-07)
Age Page: Urinary Incontinence, describes diagnosis, treatment, and types of urinary incontinence. (KU-06)
Peyronie's Disease, describes the physical origin, various types, and treatment of this condition. (KU-91)

Information Packets:
The following comprehensive packets include materials such as fact sheets, reprints of articles, and literature searches from the Combined Health Information Database (CHID) that provide other sources of information.
Alport Syndrome (KU-67)
Amyloidosis and Kidney Disease (KU-73)
Childhood Nephrotic Syndrome (KU-59)
Cystinuria and Cystine Stones (KU-90)
Enuresis (Bedwetting) (KU-62)
Focal Glomerulosclerosis (KU-69)
General Information Packet (KU-47)
Glomerulonephritis (KU-48)
Hematuria (KU-85)
Hemolytic Uremic Syndrome (KU-60)
IgA Nephropathy (KU-61)
Impotence (KU-53)
Kidney Disease and Black Americans (KU-65)
Lupus Nephritis (KU-86)
Medullary Sponge Kidney (KU-84)
Membranoproliferative Glomerulonephritis (KU-92)
Polycystic Kidney Disease (KU-64)
Prostatitis (KU-52)
Urinary Incontinence (KU-55)
Urinary Reflux Disorders in Children (KU-70)
Urinary Tract Infections in Women (KU-66)

Searches-On-File:
These literature searches address specific topics related to kidney and urologic diseases. They include references from the kidney and urologic diseases subfile of the CHID database. An order form (KU-05L) needs to be requested.

* Kidney Stones
Kidney and Urologic Diseases Information Clearinghouse
3 Information Way
Bethesda, MD 20892-3580   301-654-4415

This institute offers several publications free including: *Kidney Stones in Adults* (KU-04), an 18-page patient and public education booklet which describes causes, symptoms, diagnosis, and treatment of kidney and urinary tract stones.

* Lead Poisoning
Lead Poisoning Prevention Branch
National Center for Environmental Health and Injury Control
Centers for Disease Control (CDC)
1600 Clifton Rd., NE
Atlanta, GA 3033   404-488-7330
Childhood lead poisoning is one of the most common pediatric health problems in the United States today, and it is entirely preventable. New data indicate significant adverse effects of lead exposure in children at blood lead levels previously believed to be safe. For more information on lead poisoning, and a free copy of Centers for Disease Control's *Preventing Lead Poisoning in Young Children*, contact the office listed above.

* Lead Studies
Agency for Toxic Substances and Disease Registry
1600 Clifton Rd., NE
Atlanta, GA 30333   404-639-6300
The Agency for Toxic Substances and Disease Registry (ATSDR) has developed a Lead Initiative to evaluate completed health assessments for sites that have lead as a contaminant of concern. This project stems from a report, *The Nature and Extent of Lead Poisoning in Children in the United States*, published by ATSDR. The goal of this project is to prevent lead toxicity in young children who are exposed to lead released from Superfund sites and facilities.

* Leprosy: Free Treatment
Gillis W. Long Hansen's Disease Center
5445 Point Claire Rd.
Carville, LA 70721   504-642-4706
The Gillis W. Long Hansen's Disease Center primarily provides Hansen's Disease (leprosy) patients a place to receive a complete evaluation and treatment. Any person with a confirmed diagnosis of leprosy is eligible for admission. The Center conducts an extensive patient care and rehabilitation program, as well as research, training and education activities.

* Medical Devices Information
Information Request Service
Center for Devices and Radiological Health
5600 Fishers Lane, HFZ-210
Rockville, MD 20857   301-443-4190
The Consumer Affairs Office can provide you with a publication list which contains information on a wide variety of medical and consumer products. Topics covered include: AIDS, air cleaners, apnea monitors, blankets, condoms, contraception, cordless phones, dental, dialysis, ECT, endometriosis, eyes, fluorescent lamps, gastric bubble, hair removal, handicapped, health fraud, hearing, home test kits, hyperthermia, investigational, lasers, mammography, medical devices, mercury vapor lamps, microwaves, MRI, nuclear medicine, osteoporosis, pacemakers, pain relief, product problem reporting program, scoliosis, silicone/collagen, sunlamps, sunscreens, tanning, toxic shock syndrome and tampons, ultraviolet radiation, ultrasound, video display terminals, and x-rays.

* Mitral Valve Prolapse
National Heart, Lung, and Blood Institute (NHLBI) Information Center
National Institutes of Health
P.O. Box 30105   301-251-1222
Bethesda, MD 20824-0105   Fax: 301-251-1223
This institute offers much information to enhance the public's understanding of cardiovascular disease and prevention. One of its free publications is *NHLBI Facts About...Mitral Valve Prolapse*.

* Nerve Regeneration and Brain Transplants
National Technical Information Service
U.S. Department of Commerce   800-553-6847
5285 Port Royal Rd.   703-487-4650
Springfield, VA 22161   Fax: 703-321-8547
Advances in neuroscience research have enormous potential to improve the lives of millions of Americans. The former Office of Technology Assessment (OTA) studied

the following neuroscience-associated topics: neural transplants and nerve regeneration, including related ethical and legal issues; biological rhythms and shift work; neurotoxicity testing by private and public organizations; and biochemical bases of mental illness. The resulting publication is titled *Impacts of Neuroscience*. It is now available from the National Technical Information Service, order #PB84-196716.

* Parkinson's Disease

National Institute of Neurological Disorders and Stroke
National Institutes of Health   800-352-9424
P.O. Box 5801   301-496-5751
Bethesda, MD 20824   Fax: 301-402-2186

Parkinson's Disease: Hope Through Research outlines the possible causes and treatments for Parkinson's disease and summarizes both research efforts and therapies.

* Periodontal Gum Disease

Public Information
National Institute of Dental Research
Bldg. 31, Room 2C35
31 Center Dr., MSC 2290   301-496-4261
Bethesda, MD 20892-2290   Fax: 301-496-9988

The National Institute of Health provides this information service on periodontal gum disease and other tooth care topics. The staff can answer general questions and have a variety of publications and posters available for the public and health professionals. (Those seeking information on special care topics such as oral health and diabetes or cancer will be directed to the national Oral Health Information Clearinghouse at 301-402-7345. The following is a sample of the type of information available from this office. (Some publications and posters are also available in Spanish.)

General Information:
The National Institute of Dental Research (1X)
Dental Sciences-Dental Health (13A)

Health Promotion Pamphlets:
Fluoride to Protect the Teeth of Adults (20A)
Seal Out Dental Decay (4A)
Snack Smart for Healthy Teeth (7A)
A Healthy Mouth for Your Baby (23A)
RX for Sound Teeth - Brushing and Flossing (2A)
What You Need to Know About Periodontal (Gum) Disease (6A)
Fever Blisters and Canker Sores (1A)

Materials for Health Professionals:
NIDR Division of Intramural Research (3X)
Proceedings--Effects and Side Effects of Dental Restorative Materials (Advances in Dental Research, Sept. 1992, Volume 6 (6B)
Workshop on Methods for Assessing Fluoride Accumulation and Effects in the Body (33B)

Research Training for Health Professionals:
Dentist Scientist Award (7X)
Opportunities for Minorities in Oral Health Research (9X)

Posters:
Weekly Fluoride Rinses for a Healthy Smile (8D)
Fluorides Aren't Just for Kids (11D)
Sealants and Fluorides: A Winning Combination for Tooth Protection (16D)
Read This Label: Your Baby's Teeth Depend On It.

* Rare Diseases and Orphan Drugs Clearinghouse

National Organization for Rare Disorders (NORD)
Office of Orphan Products Development
5600 Fishers Lane, Room 873   301-827-3666
Rockville, MD 20857   Fax: 301-443-4915

This center (NORD) responds to inquiries on diseases with a prevalence of 200,000 or fewer cases in the United States. This clearinghouse, sponsored by the Food and Drug Administration, also gathers and disseminates information on medicines not widely researched or available.

* Rheumatic Disease

National Institute of Arthritis and
Musculoskeletal Diseases (NIAMS)   301-495-4484

1 AMS Circle   Fax: 301-587-4352
Bethesda, MD 20892-3675   TDD: 301-565-2966

The National Institute of Arthritis and Musculoskeletal and Skin Diseases (NIAMS) has research and conference reports on arthritis, rheumatic diseases, and related disorders for 1993 (AR 160), 1992 (AR 141), and 1991 (AR 126).

* Sexually Transmitted Diseases Resource Center
     800-227-8922

The Sexually Transmitted Diseases Hotline provides information and referrals for treatment of sexually transmitted diseases. They can refer callers to clinics, support groups, and other services, and offer brochures and pamphlets. Their hours are 8 am to 8 pm (Pacific Standard Time).

* Sickle Cell Disease

National Heart, Lung, and Blood Institute Information Center
P.O. Box 30105   301-251-1222
Bethesda, MD 20824-0105   Fax: 301-251-1223

Management and Therapy of Sickle Cell Disease presents articles on the treatment and management of sickle cell diseases. It covers laboratory diagnosis and newborn screening, sickle cell trait, nursing management, and psychosocial management. It serves as a working document for clinicians and physicians who may see only a limited number of patients with sickle cell disorder (92-2117, 51 pgs).

* Sickle Cell Disease in Newborns

Agency for Health Care Policy and Research
AHCPR Publications Clearinghouse
P.O. Box 8547
Silver Spring, MD 20907   800-358-9295

Sickle Cell Disease in Newborns and Infants: A Parent's Guide (93-0564) describes types of sickle cell disease, kinds of problems a baby may have, causes, and ways to get help. It includes a list of common terms used by doctors when talking about the disease.

* Skin Diseases

National Arthritis and Musculoskeletal
and Skin Disease Information Clearinghouse   301-495-4484
1 AMS Circle   Fax: 301-587-4352
Bethesda, MD 20892-3675   TDD: 301-565-2966

Living with Epidermolysis Bullosa (AR-13), and *What You Should Know About Vitiligo* (AR-05) are a sampling of materials available free from this clearinghouse.

* Spina Bifida

National Institute of Neurological Disorders and Stroke
National Institutes of Health
P.O. Box 5801   800-352-9424
Bethesda, MD 20824   301-496-5751

Spina Bifida: Hope through Research (No. 86-309) discusses the prevailing views about the causes, diagnosis, and medical care of this congenital spinal cord defect.

* Spinal Cord Injury

National Institute of Neurological Disorders and Stroke
National Institutes of Health   800-352-9424
P.O. Box 5801   301-496-5751
Bethesda, MD 20824   Fax: 301-402-2186

This institute offers information about the causes, implications,and outlook for spinal cord injuries and drug therapy, neural prostheses, and rehabilitation.

* Spinal Cord Injury

National Rehabilitation Information Center (NARIC)
8455 Colesville, Rd, Suite 935   301-588-9284
Silver Spring, MD 20910-3319   800-346-2742 (Voice and TDD)
     Fax: 301-587-1967
     BBS: 301-589-3563

The National Rehabilitation Information Center (NARIC) has put together a free resource guide for people with spinal cord injury (SCI) and their families. Included in the guide is information about SCI-related magazines and newsletters you can read for knowledge and enjoyment; SCI organizations that assist people with SCI from point of injury onward, and organizations that focus on specific aspects of SCI; SCI

Be patient. If any phone number is incorrect, call (area code) 555-1212 and request the new listing.

547

Health and Medicine

membership organizations, and the names and addresses of their chapters; and a short listing of some of the documents available from the NARIC library that discuss topics of interest of people with SCI.

* Stroke and Brain Disorders Resource Center

National Institute of Neurological Disorders and Stroke (NINDS)
National Institutes of Health   800-352-9424
P.O. Box 5801   301-496-5751
Bethesda, MD 20824   Fax: 301-402-2186

The National Institute of Neurological Disorders and Stroke (NINDS) conducts and guides research on the causes, prevention, diagnosis, and treatment of fundamental neurological disorders and stroke and trauma. The Institute gives grants for extramural research, as well as providing fellowships. Other areas of research include cerebral palsy, autism, dyslexia, multiple sclerosis, Parkinson's and Huntington's diseases, and epilepsy. Brochures and pamphlets available free include: *Preventing Stroke*, and *Stroke Risk Factors and Warning Signs* (bookmark).

* Stroke: Prevention and Treatment

National Heart, Lung, and Blood Institute
Information Center
P.O. Box 30105   301-251-1222
Bethesda, MD 20824-0105   Fax: 301-251-1223

This fact sheet defines and describes stroke diagnosis, treatment, prevention, and rehabilitation. Written for the elderly in cooperation with the National Institute on Aging, it is applicable to other populations as well (55-487).

* Tooth Decay Prevention and Treatment

Dental Disease Prevention Activity
Centers for Disease Control
1600 Clifton Rd., NE   404-639-3311
Atlanta, GA 30333   404-639-3534

The Dental Disease Prevention Activity is a resource for information on prevention activities in the field of dental health. It can provide you with information on fluoridation, periodontal disease, and baby-bottle tooth decay. A list of educational materials is also available including the following free publications: *Fluoridation...Nature's Way To Prevent Tooth Decay* (No. 81-8321) and *Fluoridation is for Everyone* (No. 77-8334).

* Topics in Diabetes

National Diabetes Information Clearinghouse (NDIC)
1 Information Way   301-654-3327
Bethesda, MD 20892-3560   Fax: 301-907-8906

As one of its services, the National Diabetes Information Clearinghouse (NDIC) collects information about educational materials, products, and other resources used in managing diabetes. The clearinghouse indexes these resources on a computer-based system called the Combined Health Information Database (CHID). The database can be searched for resources on a specific topic and generate a list of materials. The listing may included journal articles, books, pamphlets, audiovisuals, teaching aids, and diabetes products on the topic. The search provides information about the author or producer, obtaining the items, and the contents. NDIC has prepared literature searches on certain topics. The searches are updated at least once a year and are free

of charge. If you need information about an area of diabetes that is not on the following list, you may request a customized search. Topics currently available are:

Gestational Diabetes (LS-01)
Diabetes in Children and Young Adults: Material for Lay People (LS-02)
Teaching Guides for Diabetes Education (LS-03)
Computer Programs for Diabetes Management (LS-04)
Diabetes Educational Materials in Spanish and Other Languages (LS-05)
Diabetes and Aging: Diagnosis and Therapy (LS-07)
Diabetes Educational Materials for Adults With Limited Reading Skills (LS-08)
Materials and Aids for Visually Impaired People With Diabetes (LS-09)
Diet and Nutrition: Guides, Manuals, Fact Sheets, and Cookbooks for People With Diabetes (LS-10)
Diabetes in Children and Young Adults: Materials for Health Professionals (LS-11)
Sports, Exercise, and Diabetes (LS-12)
Diet and Nutrition and Diabetes: Materials for Professionals (LS-13)
Diabetes and Kidney Disease: Patient Materials (LS-14)
Diabetes and Kidney Disease: Professional Materials (LS-15)
Foot Care and Diabetes (LS-16)

* Toxic Shock Syndrome

Office of Consumer Affairs
Public Inquiries
Food and Drug Administration
5600 Fishers Lane (HFE-88)
Rockville, MD 20857   301-443-3170

A short brochure titled *Toxic Shock Syndrome and Tampons* (No. 85-4169) explains the symptoms and causes of this syndrome.

* Traumatic Brain Injury

National Rehabilitation Information Center (NARIC)
8455 Colesville, Rd, Suite 935   301-588-9284
Silver Spring, MD 20910-3319   800-346-2742 (Voice and TDD)
                                      Fax: 301-587-1967
                                      BBS: 301-589-3563

The National Rehabilitation Information Center (NARIC) has put together a free resource guide for people with traumatic brain injury and their families. This guide has information regarding national organizations, associations, and programs; support groups and state associations of the National Head Injury Foundation, periodicals, catalogs, directories and other sourcebooks, information resources, regional medical libraries, and rehabilitation research and training centers, and lists of books and articles in the NARIC collection that may be of interest to the newly injured person of family member.

* Ulcers: Gastric and Duodenal

National Digestive Diseases Information Clearinghouse
2 Information Way   301-654-3810
Bethesda, MD 20892-3570   Fax: 301-907-8906

This clearinghouse can offer information on this disease and makes available free single copies of some publications. *Stomach and Duodenal Ulcers* (DD-161) is a fact sheet presenting causes, symptoms, prevalence, diagnosis, complications, and treatments.

Cigarettes and Chewing Tobacco

* Chewing Tobacco

Office of Cancer Communications
National Institute of Cancer
Building 31, Room 10A16
31 Center Dr., MSC 2580
Bethesda, MD 20892-2580   800-4-CANCER

Chew or Snuff is Real Bad Stuff (91-2976). This brochure, designed for seventh and eight graders, describes the health and social effects of using smokeless tobacco products. When fully opened, the brochure can be used as a poster.

* Cholesterol and Smoking Connection

Office of Cancer Communications
Building 31-A, Room 4A-16
31 Center Dr., MSC 2580
Bethesda, MD 20892-2580   800-4-CANCER

This center maintains a database and materials on blood cholesterol and smoking geared to the public, health professionals and issues pertaining to the workplace.

* Cigarettes: Self Test for Smokers

Office of Cancer Communications
National Cancer Institute
Building 31-A, Room 4A46
31 Center Dr., MSC 2580
Bethesda, MD 20892-2580   800-4-CANCER

Why Do You Smoke? (92-1822) is a brochure which contains a self-test to determine why people smoke and suggests alternatives and substitutes that can help them quit.

* Clearing the Air

Office of Cancer Communications
National Cancer Institute (NCI)
Building 31, Room 10A-16
31 Center Dr., MSC 2580
Bethesda, MD 20892-2580   800-4-CANCER

Clearing the Air: A Guide to Quitting Smoking (No. 94-1647) suggests various approaches to quit smoking. This 32 page pamphlet is also available in Spanish. Single copies are available free.

* Helping Smokers to Quit

Office of Cancer Communications
National Cancer Institute (NCI)
Building 31, Room 10A-16
31 Center Dr., MSC 2580
Bethesda, MD 20892-2580   800-4-CANCER

The National Cancer Institute (NCI) can provide you with free publications to assist smokers in the efforts to quit. Some of the publications include:

How To Help Your Patients Stop Smoking: A National Cancer Institute Manual for Physicians
How To Help Your Patients Stop Using Tobacco: A National Cancer Institute Manual For The Oral Health Team
Pharmacists Helping Smokers Quit Kit
Quit for Good Kit - packet designed for health professionals to assist their smoking patients to quit.

* No Smoking in Schools

Office of Cancer Communications
National Cancer Institute (NCI)
Building 31, Room 10A-16
31 Center Dr., MSC 2580
Bethesda, MD 20892-2580   800-4-CANCER

School Programs to Prevent Smoking: The National Cancer Institute Guide to Strategies That Succeed is designed to assist administrators in developing a successful no smoking policy in schools.

* School Programs to Prevent Smoking

Office of Cancer Communications
National Institute of Cancer
Building 31, Room 10A16
31 Center Dr., MSC 2580
Bethesda, MD 208-2-2580   800-4-CANCER

The School Programs to Prevent Smoking: The National Cancer Institute Guide to Strategies That Succeed (90-500) is a 24 page guide that outlines eight essential elements of a successful school-based smoking prevention program based on National Cancer Institute (NCI) research. It includes a list of available curriculum resources and selected references.

* Secondhand Smoke

Office of Cancer Communications
National Institute of Cancer
Building 31, Room 10A16
31 Center Dr., MSC 2580
Bethesda, MD 20892-2580   800-4-CANCER

I Mind Very Much If You Smoke (93-3544). This pamphlet explains that secondhand smoke can be a health hazard. It informs the public that secondhand smoke has been classified as a carcinogen by the Environmental Protection Agency.

* Smokeless Tobacco and Dangers of Chewing

Dental Disease Prevention Activity
Centers for Disease Control
1600 Clifton Road NE
Atlanta, GA 30333   404-639-3534

Smokeless Tobacco Education Resources is an annotated list which includes educational materials on snuff and chewing tobacco available from federal, state and local agencies and from private sources. This 6-page bibliography is free.

* Smoking and Health

Office on Smoking and Health
Centers for Disease Control
4707 Buford Hwy, NE
Mail Stop K-50
Atlanta, GA 30333   770-488-5705

The following are free publications dealing with smoking and health.

At A Glance - The Health Benefits Of Smoking Cessation: A Report Of the Surgeon General is a pamphlet highlighting the benefits of quitting smoking.

Smoking And Health: A National Status Report is a report to Congress discussing the status of smoking programs in the Nation.

Bibliography on Smoking and Health is a compilation of 1989 scientific information on tobacco and tobacco use.

* Smoking and Health Information Fax Service

Office on Smoking and Health
Centers for Disease Control
Mail Stop K-50
4770 Buford Hwy. NE
Atlanta, GA 30341-3724   404-488-5705

The Centers for Disease Control and Prevention provides a fax information service which is available 24 hours a day, 7 days a week. To use the service dial 404-332-4565 and follow the voice prompts and request document number 000008 to receive a directory of publications that are available concerning smoking and health.

* Smoking Cessation and Cancer Prevention

Office of Cancer Communications
National Cancer Institute (NCI)

Building 31, Room 10A-16
31 Center Dr., MSC 2580
Bethesda, MD 20892-2580   800-4-CANCER

The National Cancer Institute carries out a multi-disciplinary program in smoking and tobacco research and control through the Smoking, Tobacco and Cancer Program. It conducts research in epidemiology and carcinogenesis and carry out interventions to reduce smoking and tobacco use. The program is now supporting large-scale intervention trials in eight areas, some of which are adolescent smoking prevention, mass media approach to smoking prevention, and cessation and smoking among minorities. NCI has begun a multicenter Community Intervention Trial for Smoking Cessation (COMMIT) to test strategies to produce long-term cessation among all cigarette smokers within a community, with particular emphasis on heavy smokers. One of their many publications includes *Smoking Programs for Youth* which describes activities that can be pursued through schools and community groups.

* Smoking Cessation Guides for Professionals

Office of Cancer Communications
National Institute of Cancer
Building 31, Room 10A16
31 Center Dr., MSC 2580
Bethesda, MD 20892-2580   800-4-CANCER

How to Help Your Patients Stop Smoking: A National Cancer Institute Manual for Physicians (92-3064). This is a step-by-step, 77 page handbook for instituting smoking cessation techniques in medical practices. The manual, with resource lists and tear-out materials, is based on the results of NCI clinical trials. It includes a special section, Clinical Intervention to Prevent Tobacco Use by Children and Adolescents. (The Cancer Information Service has lists of health professionals in each state who have been approved by NCI as trainers). Other publications for professionals include: *How to Help Your Patients Stop Using Tobacco, A National Cancer Institute Manual for the Oral Health Team* (92-3191) and *Pharmacists Helping Smokers Quit.*

* Smoking Cessation Methods

Office of Cancer Communications
National Institute of Cancer
Building 31, Room 10A16
31 Center Dr., MSC 2580
Bethesda, MD 20892-2580   800-4-CANCER

Smoking Facts and Quitting Tips (94-3405). This booklet encourages smokers to make changes in everyday behavior that are necessary to quit smoking successfully. It provides practical suggestions to help distract a person from smoking; it encourages smokers that try to quit and fail, to try again.

* Smoking in the Workplace

Office of Cancer Communications
National Cancer Institute (NCI)
Building 31, Room 10A16
31 Center Dr., MSC 2580
Bethesda, MD 20892-2580   800-4-CANCER

The National Cancer Institute (NCI) has put together a smoking policy package which examines the various questions and issues regarding smoking in the workplace. This information is free for the asking.

* Smoking Risks and Prevention Clearinghouse

Information Center
National Heart, Lung, and Blood Institute
P.O. Box 30105   301-251-1222
Bethesda, MD 20824-0105   Fax: 301-251-1223

The National Heart, Lung, and Blood Institute sponsors a Smoking Education Information Center which provides services to health professionals and the general public on smoking issues. They provide pamphlets, fact sheets, posters, and other publications, as well as information in response to inquiries. The center can access information on the Combined Health Information Database (CHID). A library and reading room are open to the public, and librarians are available to assist you. Some of the publications available include:

Check Your Smoking IQ (91-3031)
Nurses: Help Your Patients Stop Smoking (92-2962)
Reducing the Risk of Second-Hand Smoke (55-569)

* Smoking Technical Information Center

Office on Smoking and Health
Centers for Disease Control
4707 Buford Hwy, NE
Mail Stop K-50
Atlanta, GA 30333   404-488-5705

This office offers bibliographic and reference services to researchers through its Technical Information Center (TIC). The TIC publishes and distributes a number of titles in the field of smoking and health, and through its database can provide you with further bibliographic information. TIC's Smoking Studies Section designs and conducts national surveys on smoking behavior, attitude, knowledge, and beliefs regarding tobacco use. Visitors may use the collection between 8:30 am and 5:00 pm EST (call ahead), but reference services are also provided by phone. A free publications listing is also available. The free publications include:

Public Information:
African Americans and Smoking: At a Glance
Pathways to Freedom
Smoking Tobacco: An International Perspective
Smoking Tobacco and Health: A Fact Book
Tobacco Control Information Sources

Cessation:
Clearing the Air
Good News for Smokers 50 and Older
Health Benefits of Smoking Cessation: At a Glance
Out of the Ashes

Environmental Tobacco Smoke:
It's Time to Stop Being a Passive Victim (English and Spanish)
Reducing the Health Risks of Secondhand Smoke
Respiratory Health Effects of Passive Smoking: Fact Sheet

Youth:
SGR Kids Magazine
SGR Kids Magazine - Leaders Guide
Spit Tobacco and Youth

Pregnancy and Infants:
Is Your Baby Smoking? (English and Spanish)
Pregnant? That's Two Good Reasons to Quit (Poster in English or Spanish)

Technical and Professional Information:
Bibliography on Smoking and Health 1991
Environmental Tobacco Smoke in the Workplace: A Selected Bibliography
JAMA Trends
Inspector General's Report on Minors Access to Cigarettes
Making Smoking Prevention a Reality
Smoking Status of High School Seniors

The Office on Smoking and Health also has a series of Morbidity and Mortality Weekly Report Articles and Summaries of the Surgeon General's Reports.

* Stop Smoking Posters

Office of Smoking and Health
Technical Information Center
Centers for Disease Control
4707 Buford Hwy, NE
Mail Stop K-50
Atlanta, GA 30341-3724   770-488-5705

The top half of the "Fashion's In/Smoking's Out" poster features color snapshots of trendy items that are "in" among young teenagers. The lower half of the poster pictures an ashtray filled with cigarette butts and the word "out" in large bold print. Other posters available include "Pregnant? That's Two Good Reasons To Quit Smoking" (available in Spanish) and "Heart Tug".

Fashion's In/Smoking Out
Performance Edge
Butt Out
History Posters:
   Alexander
   Columbus
   Ross

* Stop Smoking: State and Local Programs

Office on Smoking and Health
Technical Information Center
Centers for Disease Control
4707 Buford Hwy, NE
Mail Stop K-50
Atlanta, GA 30341-3724   770-488-5705

Tobacco Control Information Sources is a listing of government agencies and nonprofit organizations that provide information about smoking and health topics (1993, 4 pages).

* Teaching Materials

National Technical Information Service
U.S. Department of Commerce
5285 Port Royal Rd.   800-553-6847
Springfield, VA 22161   703-487-4650

I Don't! I Won't Chew Tobacco Curriculum Kit contains teacher's flip chart and manual, and comic books and stickers for students. It is geared for grades K-3 and cost $40 (PB90-780677).

Aging and America's Elderly

With the dramatic demographic changes occurring, a wider array of government agencies and private organizations are focusing on some aspect of the "graying of America". This section introduces a sampling of resources available which target the special health needs and problems that go hand-in-hand with the aging process. Also, don't overlook the House and Senate Aging Committees because they study many health issues.

* Accidental Hypothermia

National Institute on Aging Information Center
P.O. Box 8057   800-222-2225
Gaithersburg, MD 20898-8057   Fax: 301-589-3014
                                       TDD: 800-222-4225

A free 12-page booklet, *A Winter Hazard for Older People: Accidental Hypothermia* warns elderly persons to protect themselves against a progressive drop in deep body temperature that can be fatal if not detected in time and properly treated.

* Age Pages: Info on Health Concerns

National Institute on Aging Information Center
P.O. Box 8057   800-222-2225
Gaithersburg, MD 20898-8057   Fax: 301-589-3014
                                       TDD: 800-222-4225

This NIH Institute publishes dozens of fact sheets, printed on two sides in large type, for the lay audience. This series is termed "Age Pages" and a list for most of the fact sheets titled *Age Page Compilation*, is available free. Some of the "Age Pages" which are free include: *Be Sensible About Salt; Can Life Be Extended?; Considering Surgery?; Health Quackery; Hints for Shopping, Cooking and Enjoying Meals; Osteoporosis: The Bone Thinner; Prostate Problems; Safety Belt Sense; Senility: Myth or Madness?; Sexuality in Later Life; Stroke;* and *Urinary Incontinence*.

* Aging Administration

Administration on Aging
U.S. Department of Health and Human Services
330 Independence Ave., SW, Room 4661
Washington, DC 20201   202-401-4634

Administration On Aging's primary goals are to support a national network of State and area agencies on aging and Indian tribes in their efforts to reach out to older persons residing in communities; develop and oversee a comprehensive and coordinated system of supportive services and opportunities to meet the social and human service needs of the elderly; and service as an advocate on behalf of older people. AoA supports improvements in quality of life and services for older people through research and training grants. Results of these studies are made available to the public.

* Aging Issues

General Accounting Office
P.O. Box 6015
Gaithersburg, MD 20884-6015   202-512-6000

Aging Issues is a free report which is a compilation of all 1991 reports and ongoing work conducted by General Accounting Office (GAO) regarding older Americans. It covers a broad range of issues, including federal government activities in health care, housing, income security, and social and community services. This compilation provides a summary of reports for the given year.

* Aging Magazine

Administration on Aging
U.S. Department of Health and Human Services
Room 4643
330 Independence Ave., SW
Washington, DC 20201   202-619-1352

Aging Magazine, published quarterly for $6.50 per year, focuses on innovative programs and book reviews in the field of aging. This publication is primarily designed for professionals and service providers for the elderly.

* Alzheimer's Clearinghouse

Alzheimer's Disease Education and Referral Center
P.O. Box 8250   800-438-4380
Silver Spring, MD 20907-8250   Fax: 301-495-3334

The National Institute on Aging established the Alzheimer's Disease Education and Referral Center as part of a broad program to conduct research and distribute information about Alzheimer's disease. Services include: information and referral on research efforts, diagnosis and treatment issues, and services to patients and family members, including referrals to resources at the national and state levels; distributes brochures, factsheets publication and reports; maintains the Alzheimer's disease subfile on the online Combined Health Information Database; develops collaborative relationships with Federal and state agencies with an interest in Alzheimer's disease; and maintains a library which includes books, reprints, and reference works, as well as videotapes. The publications are free and include;

General Information Packet on Alzheimer's Disease
Alzheimer's Disease: Q&A
Differential Diagnosis of Dementing Diseases
Age Page - Confusion and Memory Loss in Old Age
Alzheimer's Disease Centers Program
Special Reports on Alzheimer's Disease
Fact Sheet: Alzheimer's Disease Database
ADEAR Center Brochure
Report of the DHHS Advisory Panel on Alzheimer's Disease
Family Reading List: Caring for Memory-Impaired Elders

* Alzheimer's Disease Educational Videos

Alzheimer's Disease Education and Referral Center (ADEAR)
P.O. Box 8250
Silver Spring, MD 20907-8250   800-438-4380

Three versions of a videotaped education program featuring African-American patients and family members, physicians, clergy, and other professionals are available from the ADEAR Center. The videotapes were produced by the Outreach Center at the University of Pittsburgh Alzheimer's Disease Center as part of a program to develop culturally-diverse educational materials on Alzheimer's disease. Although the videotapes share footage, each has been tailored to meet the information needs and time requirements of different audiences. These videotapes are intended for use by medical personnel, professional caregivers, and ministers.

Understanding Alzheimer's Disease (31:05 minutes) Topics include normal age-related memory changes, co-morbidity of Alzheimer's disease and hypertension, patients' changing needs, and the need to overcome prejudices about aging and provide quality services to all clients. Item #A-18, $20.

Memories of Love: Caring for the Caregiver (15:50 minutes). A multidisciplinary panel describes caregiver support options, such as respite and day care and family members discuss the effect of Alzheimer's disease on their lives. Item #A-19, $15.

Memories of Love: Families Caring (34:25 minutes). Family members of African-American patients share their personal experiences and recognizing the initial symptoms of the disease and coping with the disease's impact on their lives. Item #A-20, $20.

* Alzheimer's Research

National Institute of Mental Health (NIMH)
5600 Fishers Lane, Room 7C02   301-443-4515
Rockville, MD 20857   Fax: 301-443-0008
                                      TDD: 301-443-8431

Be patient. If any phone number is incorrect, call (area code) 555-1212 and request the new listing.

The National Institute of Mental Health (NIMH) supports intramural research on the causes and new treatment of Alzheimer's Disease. Some of the free publications available include:

Alzheimer's Disease (NIH 94-3676)
Report of the Advisory Panel on Alzheimer's Disease, 1988-1989 (ADM 89-1644)
Second Report of the Advisory Panel on Alzheimer's Disease, 1990 (ADM 91-1791)
Third Report of the Advisory Panel on Alzheimer's Disease, 1991 (ADM 92-1917)
Fourth Report of the Advisory Panel on Alzheimer's Disease, 1992 (ADM 93-3520

* Alzheimer's Treatment

Superintendent of Documents
Government Printing Office   202-512-1800
Washington, DC 20402   Fax: 202-512-2250

Alzheimer's Disease (017-024-01493-1, $50) defines Alzheimer's disease and then discusses its diagnosis, treatment, and the search for the causes of the disease. Includes a glossary. Sold in packages of 50 only.

* Brain and Dementia

Office of Clinical Center Communications
National Institutes of Health (NIH)
Building 10, Room 1C255
9000 Rockville Pike
Bethesda, MD 20892   301-496-2563

The Brain in "Aging" and Dementia (No. 83-2625) discusses brain anatomy and physiology, the normal process of brain aging, and senility. Vascular dementia and Alzheimer's disease are described as well as research on the causes and treatment.

* Brittle Bones

Osteoporosis and Related Bone Disease   800-624-BONE
National Resource Center   202-223-0344
1150 17th St., NW, Suite 500   Fax: 202-223-2237
Washington, DC 20036-4603   TDD: 202-466-4315

The center has information on diseases of the bone and other related metabolic bone diseases free of charge.

* Cataracts and Glaucoma

National Eye Institute (NEI)
Publications Distribution Center
National Institutes of Health
2020 Vision Place
Bethesda, MD 20892-3655   301-496-5248

The National Eye Institute (NEI) conducts research aimed at the prevention and nonsurgical treatment of cataracts. They also support research to understand the basis of optic nerve damage in glaucoma and at preventing loss of vision. They have publications on these topics and can answer your questions regarding current research.

* Depression: Getting Treatment

National Institute of Mental Health
5600 Fishers Lane, Room 7C02   301-443-4513
Rockville, MD 20857   Fax: 301-443-0008
                                     TDD: 301-443-8431

Helping the Depressed Person Get Treatment (ADM 90-1675) was written in response to requests from concerned family members and friends for help in convincing the depressed person to seek treatment.

* Depression in the Elderly

National Institute of Mental Health
5600 Fishers Lane, Room 7C02   301-443-4515
Rockville, MD 20857   Fax: 301-443-0008
                                     TDD: 301-443-8431

If You're Over 65 and Feeling Depressed...Treatment Brings New Hope (ADM 90-1653) is a free publication, which explains depression, provides a depression checklist, and describes causes and treatment for depression.

* Eating for the Elderly

National Clearinghouse for Primary Care Information
8201 Greensboro Dr., Suite 600
McLean, VA 22102   703-821-8955

Easy Eating for Well-Seasoned Adults is a free collection of recipes submitted by older adults. It provides an excellent resource for older adult health center clients.

* Geriatrics Career Training and Education Grants

Administration on Aging
Office of Program Development
330 Independence Ave., SW, Room 4661
Washington, DC 20201   202-619-0641

The Administration on Aging funds continuing education programs in the field of aging by giving grants to institutions of higher education and professional organizations. For a list of these institutions and organizations, contact this office.

* Geriatric Education Centers

Bureau of Health Professions
Health Resources and Services Administration (HRSA)
5600 Fishers Lane, Room 81-03
Rockville, MD 20857   301-443-6887

The Health Resources and Services Administration (HRSA) is supporting Geriatric Education Centers to facilitate the training of health professions faculty, students, and practitioners within specific geographical areas. These centers provide a nationwide network offering education and training opportunities for health professionals, including physicians, nurses, dentists, social workers, pharmacists, occupational therapists, physical therapists, optometrist, podiatrists, dieticians, health administrators, clinical psychologists, and other allied and public health personnel. The centers also develop new curricula, training materials, and clinical training sites. There are currently 33 centers. A 3 day "Geriatric Training Curriculum for Public Health Professionals" has been developed, and is intended to be a training resource useful in employment and educational settings, state and local governments, community-based organizations, and academic programs. A listing of the centers is available, as is information and publications available from each center.

* Gerontology Research: Physical, Mental, Emotional Changes

Gerontology Research Center
Francis Scott Key Medical Center
4940 Eastern Ave.
Baltimore, MD 21224   410-558-8114

The bulk of the National Institute on Aging intramural research is conducted at the Gerontology Research Center. In 1958 the Center began the Baltimore Longitudinal Study of Aging which involves 1,000 men and women, who, every two years, spend 2 1/2 days undergoing rigorous testing of their physical, mental, and emotional functions. The Center has laboratories to investigate a broad spectrum of human functions. They, as well as NIA, offer a wide range of pamphlets and reports on aging for professionals and the general public.

* Glaucoma Treatment

National Eye Institute (NEI)
NEI Publications Distribution Center
2020 Vision Place
Bethesda, MD 20892-3655   301-496-5248

A free pamphlet, *Don't Lose Sight of Glaucoma* (No. 80-3105) discusses the control of glaucoma with drugs and surgery.

* Healthy Older People: Exercise, Nutrition, Medicines

National Institute on Aging Information Center
P.O. Box 8057   800-222-2225
Gaithersburg, MD 20898-8057   TDD: 800-222-4225

The National Institute on Aging offers free information on health and aging. *Don't Take It Easy-Exercise!*, *Medicines: Use Them Safely*, and *Hints for Shopping, Cooking, and Enjoying Meals* are just a few of the many topics in the Age Pages series of publications. You can request them by subject or you can receive the entire set.

* Hearing Aids

Information Request Service
Food and Drug Administration (FDA)
5600 Fishers Lane
Rockville, MD 20857   301-443-4190

Contact this office for the free Food and Drug Administration (FDA) publication, *Facts about Hearing and Hearing Aids* and other information about these medical devices. This free pamphlet discusses the causes of and treatment for hearing loss and the selection, use, and care of hearing aids. When you call, press #2, then #6 to leave your mailing address, and information will be sent to you.

* Long-Term Care

Office of Disease Prevention and Health Promotion (ODPHP)
Health Information Center
P.O. Box 1133   800-336-4797
Washington, DC 20013-1133   301-565-4167

In its series called "Healthfinder", this clearinghouse publishes *Long-Term Care* (A0028, $1) which explains issues and concerns regarding long-term care, as well as a list of publications and audiovisuals available from government agencies, community organizations, foundations and many other health groups.

* Medicare Claims

Attn: Larry Beasley
Health Care Financing Administration
Room 577, East High Rise Building
6325 Security Boulevard
Baltimore, MD 21207 (Written requests only)

A free 8-page pamphlet, *How To Fill Out A Medicare Claim Form*, provides a step by step explanation of how to fill out this basic form in order to get reimbursed for medical bills.

* Medicare Handbook, 1995

Superintendent of Documents
Government Printing Office   202-512-1800
Washington, DC 20402   Fax: 202-512-2250

As a result of the repeal of the Medicare Catastrophic Coverage Act of 1988, benefits for hospital, skilled nursing care, and hospice services under Medicare are different from those that were available in 1989. *The Medicare Handbook, 1995* describes Medicare benefits available and premium, deductible, and coinsurance amounts that will have to be paid this year (S/N 017-060-00579-3, $4).

* Medicare Health Insurance

Medicare Hotline
Health Care Financing Administration
P.O. Box 340   800-638-6833
Columbia, MD 21045   800-492-6603 in MD
or
Local Social Security Office

Several handy pamphlets are available free from local Social Security offices including *A Brief Explanation of Medicare* and *A Guide to Health Insurance for People with Medicare*. Both of these publications discuss what Medicare does and does not cover and discusses Medi-gap and other supplementary private health insurance plans.

* Medicare Hotline

Health Care Financing Administration
P.O. Box 340   800-638-6833
Columbia, MD 21045   in MD 800-492-6603

The Medicare Hotline operates from 8 am to 8 pm EST, Monday through Friday. Specialists can provide information on topics including: Medicare coverage of mammograms, information on your claim, general information about Medicare, special benefit programs, and health maintenance organizations (HMOs).

* Medicare Videotapes

National Audiovisual Center
8700 Edgeworth Drive
Capitol Heights, MD 20743   800-788-6282

Several videotapes are sold by the Audiovisual Center including: "Medicare Magazine"; "Mr. Medicare" and "One Measure of Freedom." "Meet Medicare" is an audiocassette which can also be purchased.

* Medicine for the Public

Office of Clinical Center Communications
National Institutes of Health
Building 10, Room 1C255
Bethesda, MD 20892   301-496-2563

The Clinical Center has developed a *Medicine for the Public* series to educate consumers, allowing them to make informed medical decisions. Free booklets and videos are available on a variety of topics. Those related to the elderly include:
Arthritis
Alzheimer's
Brain in Aging and Dementia
Cancer Treatment
Chronic Fatigue Syndrome
Food Allergy and Intolerances
Hyperactivity
Multiple Sclerosis
Osteoporosis
Sickle Cell Anemia
Stroke Update

* Older Americans Policies and Programs Review

Federal Council on the Aging
Room 4280, Cohen Building
330 Independence Ave., SW
Washington, DC 202021   202-619-2451

The Federal Council on the Aging reviews and evaluates Federal aging policies and programs for the purpose of appraising their value and their impact on the lives of older Americans. They serve as spokesperson on behalf of older Americans by making recommendations about Federal policies and programs. They inform the public about the problems and needs of the aging by collecting and distributing information, conducting or commissioning studies, and publishing their results and issuing reports. The Council provides public forums for discussing problems by sponsoring conferences, workshops, and other meetings.

* Osteoporosis and Related Bone Diseases

Osteoporosis and Related Bone Diseases (ORBD)
National Resource Center (NRC)   800-624-BONE
1150 17th St. NW, Suite 500   202-223-0344
Washington, DC 20036-4603   Fax: 202-223-2237
                                             TDD: 202-466-4315

The Osteoporosis and Related Bone Diseases National Resource Center (ORBD-NRC) provides patients, health professionals, and the public with an important link to resources and information on metabolic bone diseases. The Center collects information on materials, programs, and support services on metabolic bone diseases and disseminates this information widely through publication, online services, professional and patient meetings, and general media outreach. In addition, its extensive database provides individuals with answers to their questions or refers them to sources of additional information. Publications available include:

Fact Sheets:
Fast Facts on Osteoporosis
The Diagnosis
What Is Bone?
Bone Basics for Kids
Bone Basics for Teens
Bone Basics for Midlife Women
Bone Basics for Older Women and Men
Bone Basics for Men of All Ages
Exercise for Your Bone Health
Calcium: Important at Every Age
Osteoporosis Coping With the Pain
Fall Prevention
Wrist Fractures
After the Vertebral Fracture
Recovery from Hip Fracture
Asian American Women and Osteoporosis

Public/Patient Information Packets;
Osteoporosis
Osteoporosis and Men
Osteoporosis and Older Persons
Osteoporosis and Youth
Exercise
Nutrition
Calcium

Related Bone Disease:
Paget's Disease
Osteogenesis Imperfecta
Primary Hyperparathyroidism
Fibrous Dysplasia

* Paget's Bone Disease

Osteoporosis and Related Bone Diseases
National Resource Center   800-624-BONE
1150 17th St., NW, Suite 500   202-223-0344
Washington, DC 20036-4603   Fax: 202-223-2237
           TDD: 202-466-4315

The center can provide you with current information on Paget's Disease free of charge.

* Positive Approach to Aging

National Institute of Mental Health
Public Inquiries Branch   301-443-4513
5600 Fishers Lane, Room 7C02   Fax: 301-443-0008
Rockville, MD 20857   TDD: 301-443-8431

A free four-page pamphlet, *Plain Talk About Aging*, describes the experience of growing old and suggests ways to plan carefully in order to have aging be a positive experience.

* Research on Aging

National Institute on Aging
National Institutes of Health
Bldg. 31, Room 5C27
Bethesda, MD 20892   301-496-1752

The National Institute on Aging (NIA) has responsibility for biomedical, social, and behavioral research and training related to the aging process and diseases and other special problems and needs of the aged. NIA continues to work on the Baltimore Longitudinal Study of Aging, which has followed the same 650 men since 1958 to measure the changes with age. NIA encourages and supports research on aging at universities, hospital, medical centers, and other organizations. Funds are made available for these investigations through a variety of grant and contract mechanisms. To receive publications, contact the clearinghouse at 800-222-2225.

* Rheumatic Disease

National Institute of Arthritis and Musculoskeletal
   and Skin Diseases   301-495-4484
1 AMS Circle   Fax: 301-587-4352
Bethesda, MD 20892-3675   TDD: 301-565-2966

The clearinghouse distributes an information package on *Rheumatic Arthritis* (AR-13). Information packages are 27-30 pages which list other organizations and support groups, fact sheets giving an overview of causes and treatment, a glossary of wording used, and articles on treatment and research.

* Sexuality in Later Life

National Institute on Aging Information Center
P.O. Box 8057   800-222-2225
Silver Spring, MD 20910   Fax: 800-222-4225

This double-sided fact sheet titled *Sexuality in Later Life* is one of many "Age Pages" available free from the center.

* Smoking and the Elderly

Office on Smoking and Health
Centers for Disease Control
4770 Buford Hwy, NE
Mail Stop K-50
Atlanta, GA 30341-3724   770-488-5705

Good News for Smokers 50 and Older is a free fact sheet for older smokers outlining the health benefits of quitting smoking at any age.

* Vision Impairment

National Eye Institute
Publications Distribution Center
2020 Vision Place
Bethesda, MD 20892-3655   301-496-5248

Age-Related Macular Degeneration explains how the eye works and how the degeneration occurs with the aging process. It tells how patients can check their own eyes and describes laser photocoagulation for treating this disease. Single copies available free. Also available are publications on cataracts and glaucoma.

* Volunteering

AmeriCorps
Corporation for National Service
1201 New York Ave., NW   800-424-8867
Washington, DC 20525   202-606-5000

AmeriCorps supports the development of creative, effective, and lasting solutions to the challenges of crime, hunger, poverty, illiteracy, drug abuse, and homelessness. AmeriCorps opens up rewarding opportunities for volunteers from all age groups and backgrounds to help their communities. The programs designed for older volunteers include the Foster Grandparents Program, Retired Senior Volunteer Program, and the Senior Companion Program. For more information about these programs contact the office listed above.

State Agencies on Aging

The offices listed in this section coordinate services for older Americans. They provide information on services, programs, and opportunities for these consumers and can refer you to local agencies.

Alabama
Martha Murphbeck
Executive Director
Commission on Aging
RSA Plaza, Suite 470   334-242-5743
770 Washington Ave.   800-243-5463 (AL)
Montgomery, AL 36130   Fax: 334-242-5594

Alaska
Ms. Connie Sipe
Division of Senior Services
Department of Administration
3601 C St., #380   907-563-5654
Anchorage, AK 99503   Fax: 907-562-0156

American Samoa
Tauala Luavasa, Director
Territorial Administration on Aging
Government of American Samoa
Pago Pago, AS 96799   011 684-633-1252

Arizona
Henry Blanco, Acting Director
Aging and Adult Administration
Department of Economic Security
1789 W. Jefferson, #950A   602-542-4446
Phoenix, AZ 85007   Fax: 602-542-6575

Arkansas
Mr. Herb Sanderson, Director
Division of Aging and Adult Services
Department of Human Services   501-682-2441
P.O. Box 1437, Slot 1412   800-482-8049 (AR)
Little Rock, AR 72201   Fax: 501-682-8155

California
Dixon Arnett, Director   916-322-5290
Department of Aging   916-323-8913 (TDD)
1600 K St.   800-231-4024 (CA)
Sacramento, CA 95814   Fax: 916-324-1903

Colorado
Rita Barreras, Director
Division of Aging and Adult Services
Colorado Department of Social Services
110 16th St., 2nd Floor   303-620-4147
Denver, CO 80203-1714   Fax: 303-620-4189

Connecticut
Christine Lewis
Director of Community Services
Department of Social Services
Elderly Services Division   203-424-5281
25 Sigourney St., 10th Floor   800-443-9946 (CT)
Hartford, CT 06106-5033   Fax: 203-424-4966

Be patient. If any phone number is incorrect, call (area code) 555-1212 and request the new listing.

555

Health and Medicine

Delaware
Ms. Eleanor Cain, Director
Department of Health and Social Services
Division of Services for Aging and
  Adults with Physical Disabilities — 302-577-4791
1901 North DuPont Highway — 800-223-9074 (DE)
New Castle, DE 19720 — Fax: 302-577-4793

District Of Columbia
Jearline Williams
Executive Director
DC Office on Aging
One Judiciary Square
441 4th St., NW, 9th Floor — 202-724-5622
Washington, DC 20001 — Fax: 202-724-4979

Florida
Bentley Lipscomb, Secretary
Department of Elder Affairs
Building B, Suite 152
4040 Esplanade Way — 904-414-2000
Tallahassee, FL 32399 — Fax: 904-414-2002

Georgia
Judy Hagebak
Office of Aging
#2 Peachtree St., NE, 18th Floor — 404-657-5258
Atlanta, GA 30303 — Fax: 404-657-5285

Guam
Florence P. Shimizu
Acting Administrator
Division of Senior Citizens
Department of Public Health and Social Services
Government of Guam
P.O. Box 2816
Agana, GU 96910 — 011 671-734-4361

Hawaii
Marilyn Seely
Executive Office on Aging — 808-586-0100
335 Merchant St., Room 241 — 800-468-4644 (HI)
Honolulu, HI 96813 — Fax: 808-586-0185

Idaho
Jessie Berain
Director, Idaho Office on Aging
Statehouse, Room 108 — 208-334-3833
Boise, ID 83720 — Fax: 208-334-3033

Illinois
Maralee Lindley
Department of Aging — 217-785-2870
421 East Capitol Ave. — 800-252-8966 (IL/TDD)
Springfield, IL 62701 — Fax: 217-785-4477

Indiana
Ms. Geneva Shedd, Director
Aging/In-Home Services
Department of Human Services — 317-232-7020
402 W. Washington St., #E-431 — 800-622-4972 (IN)
Indianapolis, IN 46207-7083 — Fax: 317-232-7867

Iowa
Ms. Betty Grandquist
Executive Director
Department of Elder Affairs — 515-281-5187
914 Grand Ave., Suite 236 — 800-532-3213 (IA)
Des Moines, IA 50319 — Fax: 515-281-4036

Kansas
Thelma Hunter Gordon, Director
Department on Aging
Docking State Office Building
Room 122 South — 913-296-4986
915 Southwest Harrison St. — 800-432-3535 (KS)
Topeka, KS 66612-1500 — Fax: 913-296-0256

Kentucky
S. Jack Williams, Director
Division of Aging Services
Cabinet for Human Resources — 502-564-6930
275 East Main St. — 800-372-2991 (KY)
6th Floor West — 800-372-2973 (TDD in KY)
Frankfort, KY 40621 — Fax: 502-564-4595

Louisiana
Robert Fontenot
Governors Office of Elder Affairs
P.O. Box 80374
4550 N. Blvd., 2nd Floor — 504-925-1700
Baton Rouge, LA 70890 — Fax: 504-925-1749

Maine
Ms. Christine Gianopoulos
Director
Bureau of Elder and Adult Service
State House, Station #11 — 207-624-5335
Augusta, ME 04333 — Fax: 207-624-5361

Mariana Islands
Joe C. Leon Guerrero, Director
CNMI Office on Aging, DC & CA
P.O. Box 2178 — 670-234-6011/6696
Saipan, MP 96950 — Fax: 670-234-2565

Maryland
Sue Ward
Office on Aging — 410-225-1100
301 West Preston St. — 410-383-7555 (TDD)
State Office Bldg., Room 1004 — 800-243-3425 (MD)
Baltimore, MD 21201 — Fax: 410-333-7943

Massachusetts
Mr. Franklin Ollivierre, Secretary
Executive Office of Elder Affairs — 617-727-7750
1 Ashburton Pl., 5th Floor — 800-882-2003 (in MA)
Boston, MA 02111 — 800-872-0166 (TDD in MA)
Fax: 617-727-6944
800-922-2275 (voice/TDD in MA - Elder Abuse Hotline)

Michigan
Diane Braunstein, Director
Office of Services to the Aging
P.O. Box 30026 — 517-373-8230
Lansing, MI 48909 — Fax: 517-373-4092

Minnesota
Jim Varpness
Executive Director
Minnesota Board on Aging — 612-296-2770
444 Lafayette Rd. — 800-652-9747 (MN)
St. Paul, MN 55155-3843 — Fax: 612-297-7855

Mississippi
Eddie Anderson
Director, Council on Aging
Division of Aging and Adult Services — 601-359-4929
750 N. State St. — 800-345-6347 (MS)
Jackson, MS 39203 — Fax: 601-359-4370

Missouri
Gregg Vadner, Director
Department of Social Services
Division of Aging
P.O. Box 1337
615 Howerton Court — 314-751-3082
Jefferson City, MO 65102-1337 — 800-392-0210 (MO)

Montana
Charles Rehbein, Coordinator
Governor's Office on Aging
State Capitol Bldg. — 406-444-3111
Capitol Station, Room 219 — 800-322-2272 (MT)
Helena, MT 59620 — Fax: 406-444-5529

Nebraska
Dennis Loose, Director
Nebraska Department on Aging
301 Centennial Mall South
P.O. Box 95044   402-471-2306
Lincoln, NE 68509   Fax: 402-471-4619

Nevada
Ms. Suzanne Ernst, Administrator
Division for Aging Services
Department of Human Resources
340 North 11th St.   702-486-3545
Las Vegas, NV 89158   Fax: 702-486-3572

New Hampshire
Ronald Adcock, Director
Division of Elderly and Adult Services
State Office Park South   603-271-4680
115 Pleasant St., Annex Bldg. #1   800-351-1888 (NH)
Concord, NH 03301-3843   Fax: 603-271-4643

New Jersey
Ruth Reader, Director
Division on Aging
Department of Community Affairs
101 South Broad St., CN 807   609-984-6693
Trenton, NJ 08625-0807   800-792-8820 (NJ)

New Mexico
Ms. Michelle Lujan Grisham
Director, State Agency on Aging
224 East Palace Ave., 4th Floor   505-827-7640 (voice/TDD)
La Villa Rivera Bldg.   800-432-2080 (NM)
Santa Fe, NM 87501   Fax: 505-827-7649

New York
Walter Hoefer
Office for the Aging
New York State Plaza   518-474-4425
Agency Building 2, ESP   800-342-9871 (NY)
Albany, NY 12223   Fax: 518-474-1398

North Carolina
Ms. Bonnie Cramer, Director
Division of Aging
Department of Human Resources
Caller Box No. 2953   919-733-3983
693 Palmer Dr.   800-662-7030 (voice/TDD in NC)
Raleigh, NC 27626-0531   Fax: 919-733-0443

North Dakota
Linda Wright, Director
Aging Services
Department of Human Service
P.O. Box 7070, Northbrook Shopping Center
North Washington St.   701-328-2577
600 East Boulevard   800-472-2622 (ND)
Bismarck, ND 58507-7070   Fax: 701-328-5466

Ohio
Ms. Judith Brachman, Director
Ohio Department of Aging   614-466-5500
50 West Broad St., 9th Floor   Fax: 614-466-5741
Columbus, OH 43266-0501   614-466-6191 (TDD)
                      800-282-1206 (OH-nursing home information)

Oklahoma
Mr. Roy Keen
Division Administrator
Aging Services Division
312 NE 28th St.
P.O. Box 25352   405-521-2327
Oklahoma City, OK 73125   405-521-2827 (TDD)

Oregon
Roger Auebach, Administrator
Senior and Disabled Services Division

Department of Human Resources   503-945-5811
500 Summer St., NE, 2nd Floor   800-232-3020 (voice/TDD in OR)
Salem, OR 97310-0105   Fax: 503-373-7823

Pennsylvania
Richard Browdie, Secretary
Department of Aging
MSS Office Bldg.
400 Market St., 7th Floor   717-783-1550
Harrisburg, PA 17101-2301   Fax: 717-783-6842

Puerto Rico
Ruby Rodriquez
Executive Director
Office of Elder Affairs
Corbain Plaza Stop 23
Ponce De Leon Ave., #1603
U.M. Office C   809-721-5710
San Ture, PR 00908   Fax: 809-721-6510

Republic of Palau
Lillian Nakamura, Director
Agency on Aging
P.O. Box 100
Koror, PW 96940

Rhode Island
Barbara Ruffino, Director   401-277-2858
Department of Elderly Affairs   401-277-2880 (voice/TDD)
160 Pine St.   800-322-2880 (RI)
Providence, RI 02903-3708   Fax: 401-277-1490

South Carolina
Constance Rinehart, Director
Division on Aging
Office of the Governor   803-737-7500
202 Arbor Lake Dr., #301   800-868-9095
Columbia, SC 29223   Fax: 803-737-7501

South Dakota
Ms. Gail Ferris, Executive Director
Office of Adult Services and Aging
700 Governors Dr.   605-773-3656
Pierre, SD 57501   Fax: 605-773-4855

Tennessee
Ms. Emily Wiseman, Executive Director
Commission on Aging
Andrew Jackson Bldg.
500 Deaderick Bldg., 9th Floor   615-741-2056
Nashville, TN 37243-0860   Fax: 615-741-3309

Texas
Mary Sapp
Executive Director
Texas Department on Aging
P.O. Box 12786, Capitol Station   512-444-2727 (voice/TDD)
1949 1H 35, South   800-252-9240 (TX)
Austin, TX 78741-3702   Fax: 512-440-5290

Utah
Helen Goddard, Director
Division of Aging and Adult Services
Department of Social Services
P.O. Box 45500
120 North 200 West   801-538-3910
Salt Lake City, UT 84145-0500   Fax: 801-538-4395

Vermont
Mr. Lawrence Crist, Commissioner
Department of Aging and Disabilities
103 South Main St.   802-241-2400 (voice/TDD)
Waterbury, VT 05676   Fax: 802-241-2325

Virgin Islands
Bernice Hall, Administrator
Senior Citizen Affairs

Health and Medicine

Department of Human Services
#19 Estate Diamond Fredericksted
St. Croix, VI 00840   809-772-4950, ext. 46

Virginia
Ms. Thelma Bland, Commissioner
Department for the Aging
700 Centre, 10th Floor   804-225-2271 (voice/TDD)
700 East Franklin St.   800-552-4464 (VA)
Richmond, VA 23219-2327   Fax: 804-371-8381
                                       800-552-3402 (VA Ombudsman Hotline)

Washington
Mr. Charles Reed Assistant Secretary
Aging and Adult Services Administration   360-586-3768
P.O. Box 45050   800-422-3263 (WA)
Olympia, WA 98504-5050   Fax: 360-586-5874

West Virginia
Dr. David Brown, Interim Executive Director
Department of Health and Human Resources
Commission on Aging
State Capitol, Holly Grove   304-558-3317
Charleston, WV 25305   Fax: 304-558-0004

Wisconsin
Ms. Donna McDowell, Director
Bureau on Aging
217 S. Hamilton St., Suite 300   608-266-2536
Madison, WI 53707   Fax: 608-267-3203

Wyoming
Deborah Fleming, Director
Commission on Aging   307-777-7986
Hathaway Building, Room 139   800-442-2766 (WY)
Cheyenne, WY 82002-0710   Fax: 307-777-5340

Resources for the Disabled

* See also Law and Social Justice Chapter

* AHCPR InstantFax

Division of Communications
Agency for Health Care Policy and Research (AHCPR)
Executive Office Center, Suite 501
2101 East Jefferson St.
Rockville, MD 20852   301-594-2800

The Agency for Health Care Policy and Research (AHCPR) InstantFAX is a quick way to obtain documents and publications developed by the AHCPR. The system allows you to request information about other products and services from AHCPR, including new publications available from the AHCPR Clearinghouse. You have to have access to a fax machine with a handset to use InstantFAX, which operates 24 hours a day, 7 days a week. The AHCPR InstantFAX Contents List is updated as new publications become available. To receive a Contents List by fax just follow the voice prompts when you cal. For more information about InstantFAX call 301-594-1364 ext. 159. To order documents from the Clearinghouse call 800-358-9295.

* Associations and Foundations Resource List

Office of Disease Prevention and Health Promotion (ODPHP)
National Health Information Center
P.O. Box 1133   800-336-4797
Washington, DC 20013-1133   301-565-4167 (in MD)

Health Information Resources in the Federal Government (F0004, $3) describes selected federal and federally sponsored health information resources. It directs the user to a central information source.

* Benefits and Services for the Disabled

Superintendent of Documents
Government Printing Office (GPO)   202-512-1800
Washington, DC 20402   Fax: 202-512-2250

The Pocket Guide to Federal Help for Individuals With Disabilities was written for people with disabilities, their families, and service providers. It contains information on government-wide benefits and services for which individuals with disabilities may be eligible.

* Braille Books and Computers for Blind

American Printing House for the Blind
1839 Frankfurt Ave.
Louisville, KY 40206   502-895-2405

The American Printing House for the Blind produces a variety of material for the blind, including books, textbooks, and music in Braille, large type and talking books, flexible records, and cassettes. They also have computer hardware and software and free catalogs both in print and Braille.

* Captioned Movies and Videos for the Hearing Impaired

National Institute on Deafness and Other
Communications Disorders Clearinghouse
1 Communication Way   800-241-1044
Bethesda, MD 20892-3456   TDD: 800-241-1055

The clearinghouse can search their databases and send you information on where you can find close-captioned videos and films for the hearing impaired.

* Clearinghouse on the Disabled

Clearinghouse on the Disabled
Switzer Building, Room 3132
330 C Street SW   202-205-8723
Washington, DC 20202-2524   202-205-8241

This center, sponsored by the U.S. Department of Health and Human Services, responds to inquiries by referrals to organizations that supply information to and about disabled individuals. This government clearinghouse also provides material on federal benefits, funding, and legislation for the disabled.

* Communicative and Deafness Disorders Rehabilitation

Office of Deafness and Communicative Disorders
Rehabilitation Services Administration
330 C St., SW, Room 3030
Washington, DC 20201-2531

The goal of this branch is to promote improved and expanded rehabilitation services for deaf, hard of hearing, speech impaired, and language disordered individuals. This office, as the liaison to national organizations and agencies concerned with deafness and communicative disorders, provide the following services: 1) they develop policies and standards for state rehabilitation agencies' work with these clients; 2) they review services to these clients by the agencies; and 3) they provide technical assistance to Rehabilitation Services Administration staff.

* Compliance Policy Guides

Division of Small Manufacturers Assistance (HFZ-220)
Center for Devices and Radiological Health
Food and Drug Administration
1350 Piccard Drive
Rockville, MD 20850-4307   Fax Service: 800-899-0381

The Center for Devices and Radiological Health (CDRH) Facts-on-Demand is an automated system that allows anyone access to CDRH information, 24 hours a day, 7 days a week by calling from a touch-tone telephone. Follow the voice prompts to request the Division of Small Manufacturers Assistance (DSMA) Facts Index. Document topics available include: Center and Office Director Letters, Committee/Panel Information, Compliance Policy Guides, Compliance Programs, Foreign Relations, Instructions and Indexes, MDR Policies and Guidelines, Manufacturer Assistance, and ODE/Blue Book documents.

* Council on Disability

National Council on Disability
1331 F St., NW
Suite 1050   202-272-2004
Washington, DC 20004   TDD: 202-272-2074

The fifteen Council members appointed by the President and confirmed by Congress review all laws, programs, and policies of the Federal Government that affect individuals with disabilities. The council then makes recommendations to the President, Congress, and Federal agencies on these issues. In addition, the council is studying the availability of health insurance coverage for persons with disabilities and sponsors conferences for families caring for the disabled. They publish *FOCUS*, a quarterly newsletter, an annual report, and *Education of Students with Disabilities: Where Do We Stand?*

* Deafness Clearinghouse

National Institute on Deafness and Other Communication
Disorders Clearinghouse (NIDCD)
1 Communication Way   800-241-1044
Bethesda, MD 20892-3456   TDD: 800-241-1055

The National Institute on Deafness and Other Communication Disorders (NIDCD) has established a national clearinghouse of information and resources on the normal and disordered mechanisms of hearing, balance, smell, taste, voice, speech, and language. The Clearinghouse collects information on these seven research areas and disseminates it to health professional, patients, industry, and the public. They have access to the Combined Health Information Database (CHID), and have an extensive list of publications, including fact sheets, bibliographies, information packets, catalogs, and directories of information sources. They also publish an biannual newsletter. One of their newest directories is a directory of associations and organizations with an interest in deafness and other communication disorders. Contact the clearinghouse for more information.

* Development Disabilities and Mental Retardation Research

Office of Research Reporting
National Institute of Child Health and Human Development
National Institutes of Health (NIH)
Building 31, Room 2A-32
31 Center Dr., MSC 2425
Bethesda, MD 20892-2425   301-496-5133

This National Institutes of Health (NIH) department can share scientific research and consumer information about various development disabilities, birth defects and related issues.

* Developmental Disabilities Resource Center

National Information System for Health Related Services
Center for Developmental Disabilities
Benson Building, First Floor   800-922-9234
Columbia, SC 29208   800-922-1107 in SC

This clearinghouse offers information and makes referrals for parents and professionals concerned with children ages 0-21 with development disabilities or special health care needs. It also can identify federal, state and non-profit agencies in every state in the country.

* Disabled and Gifted Children

ERIC Clearinghouse on Disabled and
   Gifted Children   800-328-0272
1920 Association Dr.   703-264-9474
Reston, VA 22091-1589   TDD: 703-264-9449

ERIC (Educational Resources Information Center) is a federally funded information system, and has a database of over 400,0000 journal annotations and 300,000 education related documents abstracts. ERIC is also a source of publication about all aspects of education. ERIC Clearinghouse on Disabled and Gifted Children gathers and disseminated educational information on all disabilities and giftedness across all age levels. They have publications, digests (2-4 page summaries of current topics), Research Briefs, Issue Briefs, Directories of currently funded research, topical INFO packets and Flyer Files, as well as a catalog of products and services available to the Special Educator. They also have database searches and reprints. For more information contact the Clearinghouse.

* Disabled Rehabilitation Resources

Superintendent of Documents
Government Printing Office   202-512-1800
Washington, DC 20402   Fax: 202-512-2250

Designed for professionals and consumer groups, *The American Rehabilitation*, a quarterly publication from the Rehabilitation Services Administration, comments on all aspects of life for disabled individuals and brings program, treatment, news, and legislative and technical matters of interest. It is sold by subscription for $9 per year, order #767-002-00000-1. Single copy price is $3.75.

* Disabilities Information Clearinghouse

Clearinghouse on Disability Information Program
Information and Coordination Staff
U.S Department of Education
Room 3132, Mary Switzer Building   202-205-8723
Washington, DC 20202-2524   202-205-8241

This Clearinghouse responds to inquiries, provides referrals, and disseminates information about services for individuals with disabilities at the national, state, and local levels. Information is especially strong in the areas of Federal funding for programs services individuals with disabilities, Federal legislation affecting the disability community, and Federal programs benefiting people with disabilities. The following publications are available free:

OSERS News in Print - newsletter focusing on Office of Special Education and Rehabilitative Services programs, innovative research, and topical information.

A Summary of Existing Legislation Affecting Persons with Disabilities.

A Pocket Guide to Federal Help for Individuals with Disabilities.

* Employment of the Disabled

President's Committee on Employment of People with Disabilities
1331 F St., NW, Suite 300   202-376-6200
Washington, DC 20004   TDD: 202-376-6205

This committee provides information, training and technical assistance to America's business leaders, organized labor, rehabilitation and other service providers, advocacy organizations, families and individuals with disabilities. *Worklife* is a quarterly magazine with information that is vital to both employers and persons with disabilities seeking employment. A monthly newsletter, *Tips and Trends*, keeps people informed of meetings, happenings, and new developments. The Job Accommodation Network, 800-526-7234, is a resource and consultation service to help firms make individualized accommodations for employees with disabilities. They offer technical help for specific accommodation solutions. The Committee has other helpful free publications available dealing with disabilities.

* Free Library Services for Physically Handicapped

National Library Service for the Blind and Physically Handicapped
Library of Congress   800-424-8567
Washington, DC 20542   202-707-5100
                                           Fax: 202-707-0712
                                           TDD: 800-424-9100

This center works through local and regional libraries to provide free library service to persons unable to read or use standard printed materials because of visual or physical impairment. A bibliography of Braille and recorded materials on health topics is available as well as *Talking Book Topics*.

* Infants with Disabilities Clearinghouse

National Information Clearinghouse for Infants with Disabilities
   and Life-Threatening Conditions
Center for Developmental Disabilities
University of South Carolina
School of Medicine   800-922-9234
Columbia, SC 29208   800-922-1107 in SC

This resource center offers help on legal and advocacy issues, financial assistance, community services, parent support and parent education, child protective services, home health services and other assistance to parents and professionals concerned about infants with disabilities.

* Learning Disabilities Clearinghouse

National Information Center for Children and
   Youth with Disabilities   800-695-0285 (voice and TDD)
P.O. Box 1492   202-884-8200
Washington, DC 20013-1492   Fax: 202-884-8441

This clearinghouse helps parents of handicapped children, disabled adults, and professionals locate services for the handicapped and information on learning disabilities. Newsletters, parent guides, and other helpful publications are available at no charge.

* Parents of Disabled Referral Center

National Information Center for Children and
   Youth with Disabilities   800-695-0285 (voice and TDD)
P.O. Box 1492   202-884-8200
Washington, DC 20013-1492   Fax: 202-884-8441

This clearinghouse helps parents of disabled children, disabled adults locate services and parent support groups. It also focuses on the needs of rural areas, culturally diverse populations, and severely disabled people. This center also provides information on vocational/transitional issues, special education, and legal rights and advocacy. It provides fact sheets on specific disabilities including autism, cerebral palsy, hearing impairments, Down's syndrome, epilepsy, learning disabilities, mental retardation, physical disabilities, speech and language impairments, spina bifida, visual impairments. They have materials designed especially for parents including:

Parents' Guide to Accessing Programs for Infants, Toddlers, Preschoolers with Disabilities (Ages 0-5)
Resources for Adults with Disabilities
Paying the Medical Bills
A Parent's Guide: Accessing the ERIC Resource Collection
A Parent's Guide to Doctors, Disabilities, and the Family
A Parent's Guide: Planning a Move; Mapping Your Strategy
A Parent's Guide: Special Education and Related Services: Communicating Through Letter Writing

They also have listings of National Resources, as well as State Resources and National Toll Free Numbers.

* Rehabilitation Clearinghouse and Databases

National Rehabilitation Information Center (NARIC)
8455 Colesville Road, Suite 935   301-588-9284 (MD only)
Silver Spring, MD 20910-3319   800-346-2742 (voice and TDD)
                                                              Fax: 301-587-1967

This clearinghouse provides information on disability-related research, resources, and products for independent living. It provides fact sheets, resource guides, and technical publications. It produces two bibliographic databases, ABLEDATA and REHABDATA which cover rehabilitation products and technical aids for disabled persons along with generic and brand names, manufacturers, distributors, uses, and costs. To access this information on the NARIC bulletin board, call 301-589-3563. The publications available include:

NARIC Guide to Resources for the Americans with Disabilities Act ($5)
REHABDATA Thesaurus ($25)
Guide to Periodicals in Disability and Rehabilitation ($15)
Directory of National Information Sources on Disabilities ($10)
NARIC Quarterly Newsletter
Resource Guides:
   Traumatic Brain Injury
   Spinal Cord Injury
NARIC Mailing List ($50/1000 labels)
REHABDATA Database on Disk ($50)
NARIC Calendar of Events (free)
Disability Statistic Report (free)

* Rehabilitation Research and Development

Director
National Institute on Disability and Rehabilitation Research
U.S. Department of Education
Mary E. Switzer Building
330 C Street SW   202-205-8723
Washington, DC 20202-8133   202-205-8241

This institute disseminates information concerning developments in rehabilitation procedures, methods, and devices for people of all ages with physical and mental handicaps, especially those who are severely disabled. Statistical data on disabilities and research funding information are also available. A program directory is available which includes information on projects funded for the year.

* Special Health Care Needs

National Maternal and Child Health Clearinghouse
2070 Chain Bridge Rd.
Vienna, VA 22182   703-821-8955

The Clearinghouse has an extensive list of free publications concerned with children with special health care needs. Two of the publications are resource guides: *Project Spoon: Special Programs of Oral Nutrition for Children with Special Needs* and *The Medical Home and Early Intervention - Linking Services for Children with Special Needs.*

* Speech and Language Disorders Clearinghouse

National Institute on Deafness and
Other Communicative Disorders
Information Clearinghouse
1 Communication Way   800-241-1044
Bethesda, MD 20892-3456   TDD: 800-241-1055

This Institute at the National Institutes of Health funds intramural and extramural research on communicative disorders. Brochures and reports are available for professionals and the general public, covering a wide range of related topics.

* TDD Directory

S. James
Consumer Information Center - 6A
P.O. Box 100
Pueblo, CO 81002

Office of Regional Liaison
General Services Administration
18th and F St., NW   202-501-1937
Washington, DC 20405   TDD: 202-501-2860

The U.S. Government TDD Directory lists federal agencies with Telecommunications Devices for the Deaf and how to reach hearing or speech-impaired federal employees if you don't use a TDD. This publication is free.

* Telephone Hotlines

The following clearinghouses are equipped to send information, make referrals to organizations as well as state and federal government agencies, and also provide telephone information.

Clearinghouse on the Handicapped   404-639-3534

Coordinating Council for the Handicapped   312-939-3513

Family Resource Center   800-952-4199

Information Center for Individuals
   with Disabilities   617-727-5540

March of Dimes Birth Defects Foundation   914-428-7100

National Center for Youth with Disabilities   800-333-NCYD

National Information Clearinghouse for Infants with Disabilities
   and Life-Threatening Conditions   800-922-9234

National Institute on Disability
   and Rehabilitation Research   202-205-8241

National Information System for Health
   Related Services   800-922-9234

National Rehabilitation Information Center   800-346-2742

Medical Devices, RX, and Surgery

Contemplating a new treatment for back pain, wondering about donating blood, considering elective surgery? There are many specialists and agencies available to offer their expert opinions to help you make informed decisions with your medical team. A few phone calls can boost your ability to weigh the pros and cons of various medical tests and procedures and learn about the reputation of a hospital or health clinic. Several agencies can provide the latest information on specific medications, their generic equivalents and other therapeutic drugs. Even offices that are established to collect and disseminate data for health professionals on adverse drug reactions and experimental drugs can be accessible to individual consumers.

* Anesthesia and Therapeutic Drug Findings

Office of Research Reports
National Institute of General Medical Sciences (NIGMS)
45 Center Dr., MSC 6200   301-496-7301
Bethesda, MD 20892-6200   Fax: 301-402-0224

The National Institute of General Medical Sciences (NIGMS) This program supports research aimed at providing an improved understanding of biological phenomena and related chemical and molecular processes involved in the actions of therapeutic drugs, anesthetic agents, and their metabolites. This program supports research ranging from synthetic chemistry and basic biological and biochemical studies in molecular pharmacology to comparative studies in cell cultures and laboratory animals, as well as controlled clinical investigations in patients and normal volunteers. Grants are available. There are research reports available containing highlights of recent research advances by NIGMS grantees. The *NIGMS Division of Grant Award Mechanisms* contains the names, addresses, and phone numbers of contact persons.

* Approval of All New Drugs

Center for Drug Evaluation and Research
Food and Drug Administration (FDA)
HFD 100, Room 14B45
5600 Fishers Lane
Rockville, MD 20857   301-827-2522

or

Office of Consumer Affairs
Food and Drug Administration
HFE 88, 5600 Fishers Lane
Rockville, MD 20857   301-443-3170

The Center for Drug Evaluation and Research develops policy with regard to the safety, effectiveness, and labeling of all drug products and evaluates new drug applications. It develops and implements standards for the safety and effectiveness of all over-the-counter drugs. It also conducts research and develops scientific standards on the composition, quality, safety, and effectiveness of drugs. A list of guidelines is available to help manufacturers comply with the requirements of the regulations. The staff will respond to requests from information regarding the laws, regulations, policies, and functions of the Food and Drug Administration (FDA) as it pertains to drugs. Many FDA Consumer Report articles, as well as an FDA Consumer Special Report on drugs, are available to the public.

* Blood Banks and Supply

Information Center
National Heart, Lung, and Blood Institute (NHLBI)
Blood Resource Education Program
P.O. Box 30105   301-251-1222
Bethesda, MD 20824-0105   Fax: 301-251-1223

The Blood Resource Education Program, supported by the National Heart, Lung, and Blood Institute, is designed to assure accessibility of an adequate supply of high-quality blood and blood products through studies of resource management, the establishment of a national blood data system, and recommendations concerning the structure and function of the national blood resource system. Contact this office for more information regarding the nation's blood supply.

* Brand Name Drug Directory

Superintendent of Documents
Government Printing Office   202-512-1800

Washington, DC 20402   Fax: 202-512-2250

The subscription service, *Approved Drug Products With Therapeutic Equivalence Evaluations*, consists of a basic manual and supplementary material for an indeterminate period. Lists current marketed prescription drug products that have been approved on the basis of their safety and effectiveness by the Food and Drug Administration. In addition, it contains therapeutic equivalence evaluations for multiple source drug products which are intended to promote public education in the area of drug product selection, to foster containment of health costs, and to serve state health agencies in the administration of their drug product selection laws. Order #917-021-00000-7, $55.

* CAT Scans and Safety of Other Technology

Office of Health Technology Assessment
Agency for Health Care Policy and Research
2101 E. Jefferson St., Suite 309
Rockville, MD 20852   301-594-4023

National Technical Information Service
5285 Port Royal Rd.
Springfield, VA 22161   703-487-4650

This office advises the Secretary of Health and Human Services regarding health care technology issues and makes recommendations with respect to whether specific health care technologies should be reimbursable under federally-financed health programs. The office also considers the safety and effectiveness of the technology. Impending assessments are announced in the Federal Register, and input is sought from appropriate Federal agencies. The final reports are made available to the public through the National Technical Information Service. Reports and abstracts published by the Office of Health Technology Assessment are available individually or in annual volume compilations. For copies of assessments or ordering information call: Agency for Health Care Policy and Research, P.O. Box 8547, Silver Spring, MD 20907-8547; 800-358-9295.

* Construction of Hospitals and Health Facilities

Loan Division
Health Resources and Services Administration
5600 Fishers Lane, Room 11-A17
Rockville, MD 20857   301-443-5317

This office serves as the federal focus for examining capital and financial issues involved in health facilities, and administering insured and guaranteed loan programs for health facilities to determine compliance with assurances made during application for federal construction assistance. Materials are available on a variety of topics, including capital formation in health care facilities and cost containment in hospitals through energy conservation.

* Drug Evaluation and Research Documents

Center for Drug Evaluation and Research (CDER)
Division of Communications Management, HFD-210
MetroPark North, Building 1, Suite 151
Rockville, MD 20857   Fax Service: 800-342-2722

CDER Fax on Demand Service operates 24 hours a day, 7 days a week. To receive an Index of Available Documents follow the voice prompts when you call. Documents are currently available on: Drug Approval Process, Generic Bioequivalence Guidances, CDER Publications, Generic Labeling Guidances, Over the Counter Drug Issues, and Press Releases. For more information call 301-594-1012.

* Drug Reactions and Pharmaceutical News
Drug Bulletin
Food and Drug Administration
HFI 42, 5600 Fishers Lane
Rockville, MD 20857   301-443-3220

Published on an as-needed basis, the *Drug Bulletin* is free to professionals and the general public interested in learning the latest developments in the drug field, such drug reactions and new medical devices.

* Effective Health Care
Dr. D. Kamerow
Office of the Forum for Quality and Effectiveness in Health Care
Agency for Health Care Policy and Research
Willco Bldg., Suite 310
6000 Executive Blvd.
Rockville, MD 20852   301-594-4015

The Office of the Forum for Quality and Effectiveness in Health Care promotes the quality, appropriateness, and effectiveness of health care by facilitating the development of clinically relevant guidelines for specific conditions and treatments. Health care providers, educators, and consumers may use these guidelines to help determine how to prevent, diagnose, treat, and manage health conditions most effectively. Panels for seven conditions and treatments are meeting to produce the first group of guidelines. The seven conditions for guidelines are pressure sore management, depression treated in outpatient community-based settings, urinary incontinence, cataracts in otherwise healthy eyes, sickle cell anemia management, and benign prostatic hypertrophy. For more information contact the office listed above.

* Electrical Stimulation Medical Devices
Electrophysics Branch
Center for Devices and Radiological Health
12721 Twinbrook Parkway
Rockville, MD 20857   301-443-3840

The Electrophysics Branch of conducts research on medical devices involving electrical stimulation to evaluate and examine their safety at the cellular level. They also examine the calibration of microwave ovens. The staff can respond to written requests for information.

* Experimental Drugs for Cancer Treatment
Developmental Therapeutics Program
National Cancer Institute (NCI)
Executive Plaza North, Room 818   301-496-8780
Bethesda, MD 20892   Fax: 301-496-8333

The National Cancer Institute distributes two pharmaceutical publications free of charge: 1) NCI Investigational Drugs (94-2141) is an annual publication which encompasses most of the drugs in clinical trial under NCI auspices. It provides necessary product information to health care providers who utilize investigational drug products. 2) NCI Investigational Drugs-Chemical Information (86-2654) is designed to provide selected relevant chemical and physical data to investigators involved in various multi-disciplinary studies of drugs which were developed or are being developed by the Developmental Therapeutics Program. The staff is also available to answer your questions related to pharmaceuticals.

* Fraudulent Medical Devices
Public Inquiries
Food and Drug Administration
5600 Fishers Lane, HFE 88
Rockville, MD 20857   301-443-3170

The Food and Drug Administration does not have the authority to regulate all medical products but it monitors the marketplace and publishes several pamphlets designed to help consumers spot bogus remedies for arthritis, cancer and medical devices including *An FDA Guide to Choosing Medical Treatments* (95-1223).

* Freedom on Information: Medical Devices
Device Monitoring Branch
Bureau of Medical Devices
Freedom of Information
5600 Fishers Lane, HFI 35
Rockville, MD 20857   301-443-1813

The Bureau of Medical Devices reviews medical devices for particular specialties (neurology, cardiovascular, ophthalmic, radiology), and then compiles the reactions and malfunctions into a computer database. Through a Freedom of Information request, you can receive information regarding a specific medical device.

* Health Care Policy Research Publications
AHCPR Clearinghouse
Agency for Health Care Policy and Research (AHCPR)
P.O. Box 8547
Silver Spring, MD 20907-8547   800-358-9295

The Center links the Agency for Health Care Policy and Research (AHCPR) with the health services community and the general public, and disseminates a wide variety of AHCPR publications, including intramural and extramural studies, technology assessments, conference proceedings, and research bibliographies. AHCPR's monthly newsletter, Research Activities, summarizes the findings of studies and announces publication of new research resources materials and upcoming conferences. A catalog of publications is available.

* Health Services Cost
Center for Cost and Financing Studies
Agency for Health Care Policy and Research
2101 E. Jefferson, Suite 500
Rockville, MD 20852   301-594-1400

The Center focuses on the effects of market forces on the costs and performance of the health care system; the impact of technology on the quality of care; and the content, attributes and practices of primary care. Current research in investigating health care services for people with HIV or AIDS; the health of low-income groups; the elderly; delivery of health services in rural areas; conditions common to primary care; technology assessment; and medical liability. The Division of Cost and Finance studies the economic problems involved in making more cost-effective decisions in the health care sector, productivity in health care, and the effect of third-party reimbursement. They study alternative delivery systems such as health maintenance organizations. For more information, contact the office listed above.

* Hospital Patients Complaints
Division of Facility Compliance and Recovery
Health Resources and Services Administration
5600 Fishers Lane, Room 7-31   800-638-0742
Rockville, MD 20857   800-492-0359 (in MD)

This division answers questions on the Hill-Burton Free Health Care Program and responds to patient complaints on Hill-Burton facilities via a toll-free hotline. They also maintain an in-house database on Hill-Burton facilities.

* Hospital Procedures and Discharge National Survey
Division of Health Care Statistics
National Center for Health Statistics (NCHS)
6525 Belcrest Rd.
Hyattsville, MD 20782   301-436-8522

This division has three branches which conduct research on long-term, hospital, and ambulatory care.

* Hospitalization and Treatment at Government's Expense
Patient Referral
The Clinical Center Communications
National Institutes of Health
Building 10, Room 1C255
10 Center Dr., MSC 1170
Bethesda, MD 20892-1170   301-496-4891

The Clinical Center, as part of the National Institutes of Health, is specially designed to place patient care facilities close to research laboratories to promote the quick transfer of new scientific findings to the treatment of patients. Institutes admit to their units only those patients (upon referral by personal physicians) who have the precise kind or stage of illness under investigation by scientist-clinicians. Contact the Clinic with questions regarding current research.

* Hospitals Providing Free Care
Division of Facility Compliance and Recovery
Health Resources and Services Administration
5600 Fishers Lane, Room 7-31   800-638-0742
Rockville, MD 20857   800-492-0359 (in MD)

This hotline is a service of the Bureau of Resources Development, U.S. Department of Health and Human Services. It distributes information on applying for Hill-Burton assistance, which provides free or low-cost health care. They can answer questions regarding eligibility guidelines and facilities obligated to provide medical services.

Health and Medicine

* Inventions and New Medical Treatments

Office of Medical Applications of Research (OMAR)
National Institutes of Health
Federal Bldg., Room 618
Bethesda, MD 20892　　　　　　　　　　301-496-1143

The Office of Medical Applications of Research (OMAR) is the focal point within the National Institutes of Health (NIH) for technology assessment and transfer activities. These activities are aimed at facilitating the transfer of results of publicly-funded biomedical research into clinical applications and evaluating these research findings for safety and effectiveness. OMAR co-sponsors Consensus Development Conferences which bring together representatives from various fields to assess the clinical applications of specific medical technologies, and then develop a consensus statement. Past topics include cesarean childbirth and Reye's Syndrome. OMAR also administers the National Institutes of Health patent program, which promotes the transfer and commercialization of federally funded inventions by the private sector. OMAR disseminates information on new treatment methods and new technology.

* Laser Surgery Information

Consumer Information Center
Pueblo, CO 81009

The Food and Drug Administration's (FDA) publication entitled *The Surgeon's Newest Scalpel is a Laser*, is designed for the general public and explains the medical applications of the laser and how it works.

* Laser Surgery Referral Network

Office of Disease Prevention and Health Promotion (ODPHP)
National Health Information Center
P.O. Box 1133　　　　　　　　　　　　301-565-4167
Washington, DC 20013-1133　　　　　　　800-336-4797

This center can provide you with names of organizations and agencies involved with laser surgery, which can then refer you to experts in the field.

* Lower-Cost Generic Drugs Information

Superintendent of Documents
Government Printing Office　　　　　　202-512-1800
Washington, DC 20402　　　　　　Fax: 202-512-2250

The publication, *Approved Drug Product with Therapeutic Equivalent Evaluation*, is designed for public education of prescription drugs and lower-cost substitutes in an effort to help the public and health care agencies control health care costs. The publication is sold by subscription from the Government Printing Office, order #917-021-00000-7, $55.

* Medical Data

Office of Scientific Affairs
Agency for Health Care Policy and Research
2101 E. Jefferson St., Suite 400
Rockville, MD 20852　　　　　　　　　301-594-1398

The Office of Science and Data Development is responsible for increasing the quality and quantity of data available for health services research, specifically for Medical Treatment Effectiveness Program and patient outcomes research. There are many sources of data on the care provided to patients. However, the usefulness of those data for outcomes research may be limited by lack of access to the data and lack of comparability and uniformity among data bases. The Office investigates the feasibility of linking research-related data from different sources to improve the quality and quantity of data available for research. The Office develops uniform definition of data, especially data and describe patient clinical and functional status, common reporting formats and linkages for those data. The Office evaluates existing data bases, their quality, and their availability, and then disseminates these findings. Contact the office listed above for more information.

* Medical Devices: Technical Assistance for Small Businesses

Division of Small Manufacturer's Assistance
Center for Devices and Radiological Health
Food and Drug Administration (FDA)
5600 Fishers Lane, HF2-220
Rockville, MD 20857　　　　　　　　　301-443-6597

The Food and Drug Administration (FDA) provides information to small businesses regarding device regulations and what is needed to get approval. The FDA often holds meetings and workshops to offer further assistance. The handbook, *A Small Business Guide to FDA*, explains how the FDA works and the approval process. This Center provides copies of device regulations and FDA documents, as well as guidelines and aids that simplify manufacturer requirements. The *SMA MEMO* contains articles and tips on medical device regulations and reports on Center activities.

* Medical Devices Updates

Center for Devices and Radiological Health
Food and Drug Administration
5600 Fishers Lane
Rockville, MD 20857　　　　　　　　　301-443-4690

This center conducts research relating to medical devices, reviews and evaluates medical devices approval application, and develops regulations relating to these devices. They publish two bulletins, the *Medical Devices Bulletin* and the *Radiological Health Bulletin*, both of which cover safety alerts, upcoming research, meetings, and new Food and Drug Administration (FDA) regulations. These bulletins are designed for the medical industry community. To order the bulletins, write the center or call the editors. Radiological Health Bulletin Editor: 301-443-5860; Medical Devices Bulletin Editor: 301-594-4754.

* Medical Effectiveness

Center for Outcomes Effectiveness Research
Agency for Health Care Policy and Research
2101 E. Jefferson St., Suite 605
Rockville, MD 20852　　　　　　　　　301-594-1485

The Center for Medical Effectiveness Research has primary responsibility for the health services research supported by grants and contracts under the Medical Treatment Effectiveness Program (MEDTEP). The goal of MEDTEP activities is improved effectiveness of clinical practice. The Center concentrates on studies of specific clinical conditions for which alternative treatments are widely used and for which data are available or can be readily developed. Conditions are emphasized that affect large numbers of people, involve relatively expensive treatment, and are priorities in the Medicare program. Patient Outcomes Research Team (PORT) projects focus on variations in clinical practice and outcomes for a particular medical condition. Each PORT project is designed to identify and analyze the outcomes and costs of alternative practice patterns for a specific condition, determine the best strategy for treatment or clinical management, and develop and test methods for reducing inappropriate variations. Contact the office listed above for more information.

* Medical Expenditures

Center for Cost and Financing Studies
Agency for Health Care Policy and Research
2101 E. Jefferson St., Suite 500
Rockville, MD 20857　　　　　　　　　301-594-1400

The National Medical Expenditure Survey was designed to meet the need for analyzing how Americans use medical services, what they pay for care, and how these expenditures are finances. A publications list is available which lists the publications from the Survey. For more information, contact the Office listed above.

* Medicines Affected by Age, Genes, and Diet

Office of Research Reports
National Institute of General Medical Sciences (NIGMS)
National Institute of Health (NIH)
45 Center Dr., MSC 6200　　　　　　　301-496-7301
Bethesda, MD 20892-6200　　　　　Fax: 301-402-0224

Today's pharmacologists are combining the techniques of genetic engineering and structural biology with such areas of science as biochemistry and natural product chemistry to design drugs that will treat disorders more efficiently and with fewer side effects. *Medicines By Design* (93-474) describes the history of pharmacology as well as some of the latest research developments in the field.

* Medicines and the Elderly

National Institute on Aging
Information Center
P.O. Box 8057　　　　　　　　　　　800-222-2225
Gaithersburg, MD 20898-8057　　　Fax: 800-222-4225

Medicines: Use Them Safely is a free brochure which includes questions to ask your doctor, a listing of what to do and what not to do concerning taking your medication, and lists other sources of information.

* Medicines: Bad Reactions and Complaints

Practitioner Reporting System
Food and Drug Administration
12601 Twinbrook Parkway   800-638-6725
Rockville, MD 20852   301-881-0256 (in MD)

The Practitioner Reporting System offers a service for health professionals to report problems with drugs or medical devices. A copy of the report goes to the manufacturer, as well as to the Food and Drug Administration.

* Orphan Drugs and Rare Diseases

National Organization for Rare Disorders
Office of Orphan Product Development
5600 Fishers Lane, Room 873   301-827-3666
Rockville, MD 20857   Fax: 301-443-4915

The National Organization for Rare Disorders (NORD), a component of the National Health Information Center, can answer questions on rare diseases and on orphan drugs. The Center is a service of the Office of Disease Prevention and Health Promotion (ODPHP), the U.S. Department of Health and Human Services (DHHS), and is sponsored by the Orphan Products Development Board of the Food and Drug Administration. A directory of organizations and educational materials is available from the National Technical Information Service (NTIS), 5285 Port Royal Rd., Springfield, VA 22161; 703-487-4650.

* Over-the-Counter Drugs and RX Consumer Info

Office of Public Affairs
Food and Drug Administration
5600 Fishers Lane
HFE 88
Rockville, MD 20857   301-443-3170

The Food and Drug Administration (FDA) distributes many brochures and publications which cover a variety of topics, such as drugs, cosmetics, and foods safety and additives. This office will gladly send publications on topics that interest you. The *FDA Consumer*, which contains the latest developments at FDA, can be ordered for $12 per year from the Superintendent of Documents, Government Printing Office, Washington DC 20402, 202-512-1800.

* Over-the-Counter and RX Drugs Safety

Center for Drug Evaluation and Research
Food and Drug Administration
5600 Fishers Lane, HFD 560
Rockville, MD 20857   301-827-2241
or
Office of Consumer Affairs
Food and Drug Administration
HFE 88, 5600 Fishers Lane
Rockville, MD 20857   301-443-3170

The Center for Drug Evaluation and Research develops policy with regard to the safety, effectiveness, and labeling of all drug products and evaluates new drug applications. It develops and implements standards for the safety and effectiveness of all over-the-counter drugs. It also conducts research and develops scientific standards on the composition, quality, safety, and effectiveness of drugs. A list of guidelines is available to help manufacturers comply with the requirements of the regulations. The staff will respond to requests from information regarding the laws, regulations, policies, and functions of the Food and Drug Administration (FDA) as it pertains to drugs. Many FDA Consumer Report articles, as well as an FDA Consumer Special Report on drugs, are available to the public.

* Pharmaceutical Companies Intelligence

Drug Listing Branch
Food and Drug Administration
5600 Fishers Lane, HFD 058
Rockville, MD 20857   301-594-1086

This Food and Drug Administration office compiles many different types of drug-related lists, which can be obtained by writing the Freedom of Information Office listed below. Available lists include drug establishments, private label distributors, prescription drug establishments, over-the-counter and bulk drugs, drug products, and import products. The fee varies, depending upon the list. Freedom of Information, Food and Drug Administration (FDA), 5600 Fishers Lane, HFI 35, Rockville, MD 20857, 301-443-6310.

* Pharmaceutical Exports and Mislabeling

National Technical Information Service
U.S. Department of Commerce   800-553-6847
5285 Port Royal Rd.   703-487-4650
Springfield, VA 22161   Fax: 703-321-8547

The U.S. pharmaceutical industry is a major supplier of pharmaceuticals to developing countries, but the industry has been criticized for mislabeling certain drugs sold in those countries. The Office of Technology Assessment studied whether inappropriate labeling is occurring today to allow health workers in those developing countries to use drugs safely and effectively. The resulting publication is titled *Drug Labeling in Developing Countries*. It is available from the National Technical Information Service, order #PB93-163343.

* Pharmacology Experiments and Research

Pharmacological and Physiological Sciences Branch
National Institute of General Medical Sciences
45 Center Dr., MSC 6200
Bethesda, MD 20892-6200   301-594-3827

This branch supports research aimed at providing an improved understanding of biological phenomena and related chemical and molecular processes involved in the actions of therapeutic drugs, anesthetic agents, and their metabolites. This program supports research ranging from synthetic chemistry and basic biological and biochemical studies in molecular pharmacology to comparative studies in cell cultures and laboratory animals, as well as controlled clinical investigations in patients and normal volunteers. Grants are available, including pre- and postdoctoral fellowships. For information on grant programs or for publications available from this branch, call the Office of Research Reports at 301-496-7301.

* Radiation Dose Information

Radiopharmaceutical Internal Dose Information Center
P.O. Box 117
Oak Ridge Associated Universities
Oak Ridge, TN 37831-0117   615-576-3450

This center primarily serves researchers at government agencies and nuclear medicine centers as well as private physicians having questions about internal radiation dose calculations, especially those involving radiopharmaceuticals.

* Radiation Safety Alerts

Medical Devices and Radiation
Food and Drug Administration
5600 Fishers Lane
Rockville, MD 20857   301-443-4690

This center conducts research relating to medical devices, reviews and evaluates medical devices approval application, and develops regulations relating to these devices. They publish two bulletins, the *Medical Devices Bulletin* and the *Radiological Health Bulletin*, both of which cover safety alerts, upcoming research, meetings, and new FDA regulations. These bulletins are designed for the medical industry community. To order the bulletins, write the center or call the editors. Radiological Health Bulletin Editor: 301-443-5860; Medical Devices Bulletin Editor: 301-594-4754

* Tranquilizer Warnings

Office of Public Affairs
Food and Drug Administration
5600 Fishers Lane, HFE88
Rockville, MD 20857   301-443-3170

Learning more about the medications your doctor prescribes will increase your health, safety, and well being. The Food and Drug Administration can provide information about drugs and their side effects.

* X-rays and Safety

Office of Consumer Affairs
Food and Drug Administration
Public Inquiries
5600 Fishers Lane
Rockville, MD 20857   301-443-3170

Several free pamphlets on radiation are available including: *Primer on Radiation* (No. 79-8099); *Seeking the Safest X-ray Picture* (No. 79-8091); *X-ray Record Card* (No. 80-8024); and *X-rays: Get the Picture on Protection* (No. 80-8088).

Chemicals, Toxins, and Other Health Hazards

* See also Careers and Workplace Chapter
* See also Environment and Nature Chapter

Online databases can be accessed to obtain the latest information on potential health hazards as well as known carcinogens and other dangerous chemicals and substances. In addition, several directories and printouts are available to determine environmental risks to our health in the home, school, and at work.

* Access to Computerized Toxicology Databases

Toxicology Information Program (TIP)
National Library of Medicine
8600 Rockville Pike
Bethesda, MD 20894   301-496-6308

The Toxicology Information Program (TIP) was established to provide national access to information on toxicology. The program is charged with setting up computerized databases of information from the literature of toxicology and from the files of both governmental and non-governmental organizations. Among the databases are TOXLINE (Toxicology Information Online) and CHEMLINE, a chemical dictionary file. TIP implemented the TOXNET (Toxicology Data Network) system of toxicologically-oriented data banks, including the HSDB (Hazardous Substances Data Bank), which is useful in chemical emergency response. TIP also supports the Toxicology Information Response Center, which provides reference services to the scientific community.

* Birth Defects and Cancer: Harmful Chemicals

Public Affairs Office
National Institute of Environmental Health Sciences
National Institutes of Health (NIH)
P.O. Box 12233, B2-05
Research Triangle Park, NC 27709   919-541-3665

This National Institutes of Health (NIH) institute can share the latest scientific findings on cancer-causing agents.

* Chemicals, Pesticides and Prevention

National Center for Environmental Health and Injury Control
Centers for Disease Control
1600 Clifton Road, F29   404-639-3311
Atlanta, GA 30333   404-639-3534

This center offers free publications on such topics as injury prevention, recreational safety, rodent control, and toxic agent control. You may request a copy of their publications list.

* Dangerous Exposure to Toxins: Experiments

Clinical Biochemistry Branch
Division of Environmental Health Laboratory Sciences
Centers for Disease Control (CDC)
1600 Clifton Rd.   404-639-3311
Atlanta, GA 30333   404-639-3534

This research branch of the Centers for Disease Control (CDC) develops, validates and applies laboratory technology which improves the detection, treatment, and prevention of human toxicant exposures and resulting adverse health effects. Contact this office for more information regarding toxicant exposures.

* Environmental Toxicology Training and Research

Office of Communications
National Institute of Environmental Health Sciences
National Institutes of Health
P.O. Box 12233
Research Triangle Park, NC 27709   919-541-3345

The National Institute of Environmental Health Sciences supports the National Toxicology Program, as well as research on how living organisms react and adapt to the environment. Some of the research encompasses neuroscience, biophysics, and genetics. They offer training programs for scientists and cooperate with many international organizations.

* Harmful Environment Factors

Office of Communications
National Institute of Environmental Health Sciences (NIEHS)
P.O. Box 12233
Research Triangle Park, NC 27709   919-541-3345

The National Institute of Environmental Health Sciences supports and conducts research focusing on the interaction between humans and potentially toxic agents in their environment. The research concentrates on recognizing, identifying and investigating environmental factors that may be harmful and quantifying those factors. NIEHS research also focuses on developing an understanding of the mechanisms of action of toxic agents on biological systems. Information based on research is transmitted to regulatory agencies, other government agencies, the Congress, industry and the public.

* Latest Findings about Toxics

National Toxicology Program
National Institute of Environmental Health Sciences
A-301
P.O. Box 12233
Research Triangle, NC 27709   919-541-0530

The National Toxicology Program's main objectives are to increase the depth of knowledge about the toxicology of chemicals, to evaluate the full range of toxic effects of chemicals, to develop and validate new more effective and efficient assays for toxicity, and to distribute toxicological information resulting from its studies. The *Environmental Health Perspectives* is a scientific journal on the biological effects of environmental agents and the mechanisms through which these agents interact with living systems. The journal can be ordered from Superintendent of Documents, U.S. Government Printing Office, Washington, DC 20402, 202-512-1800. For more information on the Journal, call 919-541-3406.

* Lead-Based Paint

Reference Supervisor
HUD User
Box 280   800-245-2691
Germantown, MD 20874   301-251-5154 in DC

This computer-based information service offer personalized literature searches by reference staff on such concerns about housing safety and lead-based paint.

* On-the-Job Hazards: Registry of 40,000 Chemicals

Toxicological Information Program
Specialized Information Services
National Library of Medicine
8600 Rockville Pike
Bethesda, MD 20894   301-496-1131

The Registry of Toxic Effects of Chemical Substances (RTECS) is a database of toxicological information compiled, maintained and updated by the National Institute for Occupational Safety and Health. The RTECS now lists over 40,000 chemicals and the concentrations at which toxicity is known to occur. The printed version is available from Superintendent of Documents, Government Printing Office, Washington, DC 20402, 202-512-1800. The magnetic computer tape is available from National Technical Information Service, 5285 Port Royal Road, Springfield, VA 22161, 703-487-4650. The on-line database is available from RTECS, Toxicological Information Program, Specialized Information Services, National Library of Medicine, Bethesda, MD 20894, 301-496-1131. For additional information, contact: The Editor, RTECS, 4676 Columbia Parkway, Cincinnati, OH 45226, 513-533-8317.

* Risk Reduction of Toxic Chemicals Exposures

National Center for Toxicological Research
3900 NCTR Road
Jefferson, AR 72079   501-543-7000

This center focuses on the need for increased research to develop better ways of assessing the risk of toxic chemicals to humans, and to help reduce those risks. This center also provides the Food and Drug Administration (FDA) and other regulatory agencies with the knowledge to make regulatory decisions concerning toxic substances. Research is undertaken by a variety of disciplines, including biochemical and comparative toxicology.

* Toxic and Pesticide Information Hotline

National Pesticide Telecommunications Network   800-858-7378

This service of the U.S. Environmental Protection Agency and Texas Tech University is open 24 hours, 7 days a week. It responds to non-emergency questions about the effects of pesticides, toxicology and symptoms, environmental effects, disposal and cleanup, and safe use of pesticides.

* Toxicological Information Program

Specialized Information Services
National Library of Medicine
8600 Rockville Pike
Bethesda, MD 20894   301-496-1131

The Registry of Toxic Effects of Chemical Substances (RTECS) is a database of toxicological information compiled, maintained and updated by the National Institute for Occupational Safety and Health. The RTECS now lists over 40,000 chemicals and the concentrations at which toxicity is known to occur. The printed version is available from Superintendent of Documents, Government Printing Office, Washington, DC 20402, 202-512-1800. The magnetic computer tape is available from National Technical Information Service, 5285 Port Royal Road, Springfield, VA 22161, 703-487-4650. The on-line database is available from RTECS, Toxicological Information Program, Specialized Information Services, National Library of Medicine, Bethesda, MD 20894, 301-496-1131. For additional information, contact: The Editor, RTECS, 4676 Columbia Parkway, Cincinnati, OH 45226, 513-533-8317.

* Workplace Hazards Detection

National Institute for Occupational Safety and Health (NIOSH)
4676 Columbia Parkway
Cincinnati, OH 45226   800-356-4674

The National Institute of Occupational Safety and Health (NIOSH) is responsible for conducting research to make the nation's workplaces healthier and safer by responding to urgent requests for assistance from employers, employees, and their representatives where imminent hazards are suspected. They conduct inspections, laboratory and epidemiologic research, publish their findings, and make recommendations for improved working conditions to regulatory agencies. NIOSH trains occupational health and safety workers and communicates research results to those concerned.

Medical Research: Clues and Answers

Knowledge about breakthroughs in medical research is not confined to the scientific community. Anyone should look upon organizations and centers engaged in clinical studies and experiments as important information resources to learn about the latest theories which explain the complexities of medicine and health.

* Applications and Answers about NIH Grants

Division of Research Grants (DRG)
National Institutes of Health
6701 Rockledge Dr.
Rockledge 2 Bldg.
Bethesda, MD 20892   301-435-1111

The Division of Research Grants provides for review of National Institutes of Health grant applications. They collect, store, analyze, and evaluate management and program data needed in the administration of extramural programs. This office disseminated information on the various extramural programs and now have the information on the DRG online system. For guidelines and proposal application, contact this office.

* Biomedical Computing, Engineering and Technologies

Marjorie Tingle
Biomedical Research Technology Program
Westwood Building, Room 8A11
National Institutes of Health (NIH)
Rockledge 2 Bldg.
6701 Rockledge Dr.
Bethesda, MD 20892   301-435-0772

The National Institutes of Health's (NIH) Biomedical Research Technology Program focuses on biomedical computing, biomedical engineering, and technologies for the study of bimolecular and cellular structure and function. Most of the Program's budget is directed to the support of research center grants. Grants are also available for projects of advanced technology related to biomedical research. The research centers are open to outside investigators. Contact this office for a free *Biomedical Research Technology Resources Directory* or grant applications.

* Biophysics and Cell Biology Research

Division of Cell Biology and Biophysics
National Institute of General Medical Sciences
National Institutes of Health
45 Center Dr., MSC 6200
Bethesda, MD 20892-6200   301-594-0828

This division supports research on the assembly, structure, and function of cellular components using biochemical, biophysical, chemical, genetic, and mathematical methods. The goal of their research is to understand cellular components and how they interact to maintain the function of the cell and the organism. Major areas of research by this division are: analytical and separation techniques, bioengineering; biomedical instrumentation; cell organization, motility, and division; lipid biochemistry, membrane structure and function; molecular biophysics; spectroscopic techniques; and structural biology. To order publications available from this division call the Office of Research Reports at 301-496-7301.

* Biosafety in Microbiological and Biomedical Laboratories

Superintendent of Documents
Government Printing Office (GPO)   202-512-1800
Washington, DC 20402   Fax: 202-512-2250

This indispensable resource from the U.S. Public Health Service guides the directors of microbiology laboratories in the containment of infectious agents. Describes specific combinations of microbiological practices, laboratory facilities, and safety equipment, and recommends their use in four categories (called biosafety levels) of laboratory operation involving selected agents infectious to humans. Also recommends standard practices for four biosafety levels in laboratories using experimental animals. Explains risk assessment and summarizes six types of infectious agents. Order #017-040-00523-7, cost $6.

* Birth Control: Researching New Contraceptive Methods

Contraception Development Branch
EPN 600, 6100 Executive Blvd.
Rockville, MD 20892   301-496-1661

The Contraception Development Branch supports research on the development of new fertility regulating methods with emphasis on improving both effectiveness and acceptability. Some of the research focuses on biological evaluation of new compounds, development of improved vaginal and uterine contraception based on chemical or physical methods, and clinical trials of sex steroids. They collaborate with other national and international organizations, such as The World Health Organization and the Population Council and its International Committee for Contraceptive Research. This Branch also holds workshops on various topics.

* Blood and Biological Products Standards

Center for Biologics Evaluation and Research
Food and Drug Administration
1401 Rockville Pike, Suite 200N
Rockville, MD 20852   301-827-0377

The Center for Biologics Evaluation and Research, a regulatory agency for biological products, and conducts research related to the development, manufacture, testing, and use of both new and old biological products. It also conducts research on the preparation, preservation, and safety of blood and blood products. The Center cooperates with other agencies, organizations, universities and, scientists regarding biological products. The information they have is technical in nature.

* Brain Tissue Banks for Neurological and Psychiatric Diseases Research

Dr. Edward D. Bird
Professor of Neuropathology
Mclean Hospital
115 Mill St.
Belmont, MA 02178   617-855-3426

Human Specimen Bank
Dr. Wallace W. Tourtellotte
Chief of Neurology Service
V.A.- Wadsworth Medical Center
Building 212, Room 31
Los Angeles, CA 90073   310-268-3536

The National Institute of Mental Health and National Institute of Neurological Disorders and Stroke support the Brain Tissue Bank at the Mclean Hospital, Belmont, MA. Both Institutes also support the Human Specimen Bank at the V.A.-Wadsworth Medical Center, Los Angeles, California. These tissue banking resource collects brain tissues obtained at autopsy, blood serum, and spinal fluid, stores them cryogenically and in formalin, and distributes these materials to research scientists.

* Catalog of Cell Lines

Office of Research Reports
National Institute of General Medical Sciences (NIGMS)
National Institute of Health (NIH)
45 Center Dr., MSC 6200   301-496-7301
Bethesda, MD 20892-6200   Fax: 301-402-0224

The *1994-1995 Catalog of Cell Lines: NIGMS Human Genetic Mutant Cell Repository* (#94-2011) catalogs for scientists the nearly 5,300 cell lines and 275 DNA samples banked at the NIGMS Human Genetic Mutant Cell Repository at the Coriell Institute for Medical Research in Camden, NJ. Cultures are taken from people with genetic disorders and chromosomal abnormalities, as well as from apparently normal individuals for use as controls.

* Computer-Assisted Medical Instruction R&D

Lister Hill Center for Biomedical Communications
8600 Rockville Pike
Bethesda, MD 20894   301-496-4441

This center is responsible for conducting research and development in computer-assisted instruction, distributed information systems, artificial intelligence and expert systems, and electronic document storage and retrieval. The Center's programs cover six areas: communications engineering, information technology, computer science, audiovisual program development, educational technology, and training and consultation. A publications list is available.

* Genetic Disorders

Office of Research Reports
National Institute of General Medical Sciences (NIGMS)
National Institute of Health (NIH)
45 Center Dr., MSC 6200   301-496-7301
Bethesda, MD 20892-6200   Fax: 301-402-0224

New gene-splicing technology is helping researchers diagnose and treat genetic disorders. *The New Human Genetics: How Gene Splicing Helps Researchers Fight Inherited Disease* (84-662) describes basic genetic processes and also explains how these processes can go awry in causing disease.

* Genetics and Developmental Biology Research

Division of Genetics and Developmental Biology
National Institute of General Medical Sciences
National Institutes of Health
45 Center Dr., MSC 6200
Bethesda, MD 20892-6200   301-594-0943

This division focuses on gaining a better understanding of the fundamental processes and mechanisms of inheritance and development. Projects supported by this division, which make use almost exclusively of model systems, provide the foundation for the design of better methods to diagnose, treat, cure, and prevent genetic diseases in humans. The division supports research in the following major areas: cell growth and differentiation; chromosome organization and mechanics; control of gene expression; developmental genetics and cell biology; extrachromosomal inheritance; human medical genetics; mechanisms of mutagenesis; molecular immunobiology; neurogenetics and the genetics of behavior; population genetics; and replication, recombination, and repair of genes. To order publications available from this division, or obtain information on grant programs, call the Office of Research Reports at 301-496-7301.

* Grants from National Institutes of Health

Office of Grants Inquiries
National Institutes of Health (NIH)
Rockledge 2 Bldg.
6701 Rockledge Dr.
Bethesda, MD 20892   301-435-0714

This office can answer your questions regarding policies, applications, procedures, and other information concerning National Institutes of Health (NIH) grants.

* Health Sciences International Collaboration

Fogarty International Center (FIC)
for Advanced Studies in Health Sciences
National Institutes of Health
Building 31, Room B2C08
31 Center Dr., MSC 2220
Bethesda, MD 20892-2220   301-496-2075

This international research center assembles scientists and others in the biomedical, behavioral and related fields for discussion, study, and research relating to the international development of the health science. It also sponsors research programs, conferences, and seminars to further international cooperation and collaboration in the life sciences. FIC oversees the Scholars-in-Residence program and awards fellowships to foreign scientists. Publications are available covering international health care concerns.

* Heart and Lung Transplants

National Heart, Lung, and Blood Institute
National Institutes of Health
Building 31, Room 4A21
31 Center Dr., MSC 284
Bethesda, MD 20892-2840   301-496-4236

This Institute is involved with both intra- and extramural, experimental research regarding transplantation of the heart and lungs. Current research focuses on immune modulation and organ rejection, as well as on long-term preservation of the heart to allow for transplantation. The staff can refer you to current researchers, and can send you brochures and reports on this procedure.

* Laboratory Animals for Medical Research

Veterinary Resources Program
National Center for Research Resources
National Institutes of Health
Bldg. G, 9000 Rockville Pike
Bethesda, MD 20892   301-496-2527

The Animal Resources Program helps meet the needs of biomedical researchers for high quality, disease-free animals and specialized animal research facilities. The program supports, via grants and contracts, primate research centers and their field stations, primate breeding and supply projects, animal diagnostic laboratories, and a variety of other research projects. The program comprises three subprograms: The Regional Primate Research Centers, Laboratory Animal Sciences, and Biological Models and Materials Resources. Contact this office for more information and a free directory which informs researchers of the resources provided and how to access them.

* Mental Health Grants for Hispanic and Other Minorities

Associate Director for Special Populations
National Institute of Mental Health
5600 Fishers Lane, Room 17-C14
Rockville, MD 20857   301-443-2847

The Minority Group Mental Health Program has two funding components. 1) It funds research and development centers to provide minorities (Hispanic, Asia and Native Americans) an opportunity to conduct research on specific minority concerns. And 2) It funds minority students through the MARC, Minority Fellowship, and Minority Institution Research Development Programs, which are designed to give minorities grants for mental health research.

* Minority Opportunities in Research

National Institute of General Medical Sciences
National Institutes of Health
Bldg. 31, Room 4A52   301-496-7301
Bethesda, MD 20892   Fax: 301-402-0224

This division serves as the focal point for Institute efforts to increase the number of minority biomedical scientists. Its components include the Minority Access to Research Careers Branch, which supports research training at institutions with substantial minority enrollments, and the Minority Biomedical Research Support Branch, which supports research projects at minority institutions. The division administers the Bridges to the Future Program which enhances the transition between institutions that grant associate degrees and those that grant baccalaureate degrees, as well as between master's and Ph.D. granting institutions. It also administers a program of individual predoctoral fellowship awards for minority students.

* Neurophysiology and Computer Systems

Research Services Branch
National Institute of Mental Health
Building 36, Room 2A03
Bethesda, MD 20892   301-496-4957

The scientists and engineers of this research branch of National Institute of Mental Health (NIMH) develop experimental design, data processing, and computer programs to help with research in neurophysiology, neurogenetics, and neurochemistry. The researchers can provide consultation in statistical analysis and experimental design, along with information on image processing programs which are available to the public.

* Ongoing NIH Scientific Research Database

Advanced Technology Branch
Division of Research Grants
National Institutes of Health
Rockledge 2 Bldg.
6701 Rockledge Dr., Room 3210
Bethesda, MD 20892   301-435-0716

The Computer Retrieval of Information on Scientific Projects (CRISPS) system is designed to provide scientific and associated grant identification information on research currently being done at the National Institute of Health.

Health and Medicine

* Pharmacology, Physiology, and Biological Chemistry Research

Division of Pharmacology, Physiology, and Biological Chemistry
National Institute of General Medical Sciences
National Institutes of Health
45 Center Dr., MSC 6200
Bethesda, MD 20892-6200   301-594-3827

This division attempts to integrate the investigational approaches of the disciplines of chemistry, biochemistry, physiology, and pharmacology into a molecular-level understanding of fundamental biological processes, and to uncover avenues for their control. Goals of supported research include an improved understanding of drug action, new methods and targets for drug discovery, advances in natural products synthesis, and enhanced understanding of biological catalysis, and a greater knowledge of metabolic control mechanisms and fundamental physiological processes. Research funded by the division also fosters the integration and application of physiological and biochemical research in addressing certain clinical issues and problems, such as drug interactions, mechanisms of anesthesia, and those that occur as a result of trauma and brain injury. To order publications available from this division, or obtain grant program information, call the Office of Research Reports, 301-496-7301.

* Research Money: Comprehensive List of Grantees

Carolyn Stelle
Health-Related Research and Development
Office of Extramural Research Programs
Rockledge 2 Bldg.
6701 Rockledge Dr.
Bethesda, MD 20892   301-435-0997

This office can answer your questions regarding grants and contracts and direct you to the appropriate office for your research needs. This office also formulates grant award policies and procedures. The *Research Awards Index* is no longer available in paper copy. You must access this information on the Internet at http://www.nih.gov.

* Researching Health Risks

Superintendent of Documents
Government Printing Office (GPO)   202-512-1800
Washington, DC 20402   Fax: 202-512-2250

This study from the Office of Technology Assessment analyzes the methods used by federally supported agencies to evaluate and estimate the health risks associated with toxic substances. It examines whether research is adequately supported and managed; identifies the available resources; analyzes research priorities, trends, and gaps; and discusses the impact of research on regulatory decisions. It also describes the prospects for the future, including promising research areas. Order #053-003-01360-6, cost $13.

* Therapies and Vaccines

Office of Research Reports
National Institute of General Medical Sciences (NIGMS)
National Institute of Health (NIH)
45 Center Dr., MSC 6200   301-496-7301
Bethesda, MD 20892-6200   Fax: 301-402-0224

The Structures of Life: Discovering the Molecular Shapes That Determine Health or Disease (91-2778) describes the latest research in the fast-moving field of structural biology, which aims to explain the activity of biologically important molecules in terms of their structure and to use this knowledge to design new therapies or vaccines.

Health Care Costs and Services

Health policy and the health care delivery systems are evaluated and reassessed every day. Numerous sources for data and statistics are readily available which can help reveal information on particular medical procedures, hospitals and other aspects of health care.

* Births, Abortions, Deaths Statistics

Division of Vital Statistics
National Center for Health Statistics
6525 Belcrest Rd.
Hyattsville, MD 20782   301-436-8952
This division collects data on births, deaths, abortions, marriages, and divorces, and produces annual data for the U.S., states, countries, and local areas.

* Community Health Services for Homeless, Migrant Farmworkers and Other Populations

Division of Programs for Special Populations
Bureau of Primary Health Care
Health Resources and Services Administration
West Tower Bldg., 9th Floor
435 East West Hwy.
Bethesda, MD 20814   301-594-4110
The Bureau of Primary Health Care focuses nationally on efforts to ensure the availability and delivery of health care services in health manpower shortage areas, to medically underserved populations, and to special services populations, such as migrants or the homeless. The Bureau provides project grants to community-based organizations to meet the health needs of the undeserved or special needs populations.

* Cost of Health Care: Statistics

Office of Public Affairs
Health Care Financing Administration
6325 Security Blvd.
364 East Highrise Bldg.
Baltimore, MD 21207   410-786-3000
or
Office of Public Inquiries
Social Security Administration
1-A-2 Gwynn Oak Ave.
6401 Security Blvd.
Baltimore, MD 21235   410-965-7700
These offices collect statistics regarding health, health care, and health care financing. They compile and distribute data on a wide variety of topics, such as spending on health care services, the age of recipients of services, and health problems.

* Cost of Medicaid and Medicare

Health Care Financing Administration (HCFA)
6325 Security Blvd.
364 East Highrise Bldg.
Baltimore, MD 21207   410-786-3689
This office compiles statistics on Medicaid, health coverage for low-income, and Medicare, health coverage for the elderly. The data are broken down many ways such as populations, expenditures, and utilization. Each year they publish a Health Care Financing Administration (HCFA) statistics booklet which provides significant summary information about health expenditures and HCFA programs.

* Cradle to Grave Health Statistics

National Center for Health Care Statistics
Data Dissemination Branch
6525 Belcrest Rd.
Hyattsville, MD 20782   301-436-8500
The National Center for Health Statistics (NCHS) is the Federal Government's

principal vital and health statistics agency. It collects, analyzes, and distributes data, conducts research in statistical and survey methodology, and provides technical assistance in the U.S., foreign countries, and for other organizations. They conducted several population-based surveys, such as the National Health Interview Survey and the National Health and Nutrition Examination Survey; and several record-based surveys, such as the National Hospital Discharge Survey and The National Nursing Home Survey. NCHS cooperates with states and other countries to improve the quality and availability of data. A central component of NCHS is to distribute its data, which is done through a series of publications, public use data files, and unpublished tabulations, as well as through journals, conferences, and workshops.

* Doctor Visits National Survey

Division of Health and Nutrition Examination Statistics
National Center for Health Statistics
6525 Belcrest
Hyattsville, MD 20782   301-436-7068
This division collects data on health-related matters and administers the National Health and Nutrition Survey, which assesses the health and nutritional status of the general population through direct physical examination.

* Federal Health Policy Evaluations

U.S. Department of Health and Human Services
Office of the Assistant Secretary for Planning and Evaluation
Policy Information Center
Room 438-F, Hubert H. Humphrey Bldg.
200 Independence Avenue SW   202-690-6445
Washington, DC 20201   Fax: 202-401-6228
The Policy Information Center (PIC) is a centralized source of information on in-process, completed, and ongoing health and human services evaluations; short-term evaluative research; and policy-oriented projects conducted by the U.S. Department of Health and Human Services (HHS) as well as by other federal departments, agencies, and the private sector. This information may be accessed in person, via the PIC Online databases system, or via the Internet (http://www.os.dhhs.gov or gopher://gopher.os.dhhs.gov). Requests for searches of the system may be made by mail, phone, or fax. The staff can also supply single copies of Executive Summaries and final reports as resources permit, or provide information on the availability of final reports from other sources, such as the National Technical Information Service, 703-487-4650.

* Health Care Delivery and Health Professions

Office of Public Affairs
Maternal and Child Health Bureau
Health Resources and Services Administration
5600 Fishers Lane, Room 1443
Rockville, MD 20857   301-443-2086
The Health Resources and Services Administration (HRSA) offers a free catalog, Current Publications, which lists all the publications films, and videos produced by HRSA's three bureaus: Bureau of Health Care Delivery and Assistance, Bureau of Maternal and Child Health and Resources Development and Bureau of Health Professions.

* Illness and Wellness Status of 50,000 Families

Division of Health Interview Statistics
National Center for Health Statistics
6525 Belcrest Rd., Room 850
Hyattsville, MD 20782   301-436-7085
This division administers the National Health Interview Survey, which is the

principal source of information on the health, illness, and disability status of non-institutionalized population. The survey focuses on current health topics and is conducted continually in 50,000 households.

* Government Health Programs Report Card

U.S. Department of Health and Human Services
Office of the Assistant Secretary for Planning and Evaluation
Policy Information Center
Room 438-F, Hubert H. Humphrey Bldg.
200 Independence Ave., SW   202-690-6445
Washington, DC 20201   Fax: 202-401-6228

The Policy Information Center (PIC) is a centralized source of information on in-process, completed, and ongoing health and human services evaluations; short-term evaluative research; and policy-oriented projects conducted by the U.S. Department of Health and Human Services (HHS) as well as by other federal departments, agencies, and the private sector. This information may be accessed in person, via the PIC Online databases system, or via the Internet (http://www.os.dhhs.gov or gopher://gopher.os.dhhs.gov). Requests for searches of the system may be made by mail, phone, or fax. The staff can also supply single copies of *Executive Summaries* and final reports as resources permit, or provide information on the availability of final reports from other sources, such as the National Technical Information Service, 703-487-4650.

* Grants for Health Promotion Projects

Office of Disease Prevention and Health Promotion (ODPHP)
National Health Information Center
P.O. Box 1133   800-336-4797
Washington, DC 20013-1133   301-565-4167 (in MD)

The guide, *Locating Resources for Healthy People 2000 Health Promotion Projects*, (20001, $2) is designed to assist newcomers on their search for health promotion funding by introducing them to the major tasks involved and information services available. This publication is divided into four major sections. Section I discusses basic principles of fundseeking. Sections II and III discuss where and how to look for health promotion funds, focusing on both private and public sectors. Major foundations and Federal agencies interested in health promotion, as well as local sources are listed. Section IV lists resources--organizations, foundations, publications, and databases--that can be useful to those seeking funds. Also included is an appendix, which includes a glossary, a list of acronyms, a bibliography, and a sample grant application form.

* Marriage and Divorce Statistics

Division of Vital Statistics
National Center for Health Statistics
6525 Belcrest Rd.
Hyattsville, MD 20782   301-436-8952

This division collects data on the number of marriages and divorces as well as statistics of births, abortions, and deaths. It produces annual data for the U.S., states, countries, and local areas. To request publications, call 301-436-8500.

* Medical Services and Personnel Shortages

National Clearinghouse for Primary Care Information
2070 Chain Bridge Rd.
Vienna, VA 22182   703-821-8955

This clearinghouse provides information services to support the planning, development, and delivery of ambulatory health care to urban and rural areas where shortages of medical personnel and services exist. Its primary audience is health care providers who work in community health centers. They have a list of publications

and can make referrals to other health-related organizations. This clearinghouse also publishes a newsletter, *Primary Care Perspectives*.

* Nurses, Doctors, and Services Availability

Division of Programs for Special Populations
Bureau of Primary Health Care
Health Resources and Services Administration
West Tower Bldg., 9th Floor
435 East West Hwy.
Bethesda, MD 20814   301-594-4110

The Bureau of Primary Health Care focuses nationally on efforts to ensure the availability and delivery of health care services in health manpower shortage areas, to medically underserved populations, and to special services populations. It also administers the National Health Service Corps Program which recruits health care practitioners and places them in areas having shortages of people trained in health-related fields.

* Planned Approach to Community Health (PATCH) Program

Center for Chronic Disease Prevention
 and Health Promotion (CCDPHP)
Centers for Disease Control
1600 Clifton Rd., NE   404-639-3311
Atlanta, GA 30333   404-639-3534

The Center for Chronic Disease Prevention and Health Promotion (CCDPHP) staff work with State and local health departments and community members to organize local intervention programs. The center provides materials and technical assistance, and the communities invest their time and resources and make the program work. Programs have focused on cholesterol screening and nutrition, smoking cessation, alcohol misuse, and prevention of injuries from falls. The PATCH program also conducts international training conferences.

* Prepaid Medicare Health Care

Office of managed Care
Medicare Payment and Audit
Health Care Financing Administration
7500 Security Blvd.
S3-21-17
Baltimore, MD 21244-1800   410-786-4287

This office offers materials on health maintenance organizations (HMOs), specifically the capitation concept under Medicare designed to control health costs. Since this bureau monitors qualified plans, it can serve as an information resource on Medicare prepaid health care plans.

* World Health Policies

Office of International Health (OIH)
U.S. Department of Health and Human Services
5600 Fishers Lane, Room 18-75
Rockville, MD 20857   301-443-1774

This office supports the Assistant Secretary for Health in developing policy, and also coordinates activities of the Public Health Service in the field of international health. It works closely with the World Health Organization and other international organizations and oversees PHS participation in over 25 bi-national health agreements. The Office of International Health (OIH) will respond to questions regarding U.S. participation in international health agreements and programs. A publications list is available.

Drugs and Chemical Dependence
General Sources

* See also Education Chapter
* See also Health and Medicine Chapter
* See also Law and Social Justice Chapter
* See also Information from Lawmakers Chapter

This chapter includes information sources which deal primarily with alcohol and illegal drugs. The first section identifies several different government agencies, private organizations, clearinghouses, and databases which track chemical dependence in the U.S., as well as international trends. Drug-related crime, traffic accidents, and other statistics are also included. The Education and Prevention Section offers all sorts of publications and audiovisuals for teachers, counselors, health professionals, parents, and students. Comic books and coloring books for youngsters also are noted, as well as free posters which carry the drug-free message. Many organizations experimenting with different strategies for prevention and detection of drug abuse in schools, communities and workplaces are listed. Under the Treatment and Rehabilitation section you'll find several resources which can provide you with counseling, referrals, and printed materials on the problems of addiction. Al-Anon Family Group Headquarters, for example, with its round-the-clock toll-free number, offers help to families dealing with alcoholism. The Psychiatric Institute runs the National Cocaine Hotline and answers questions and provides referrals to drug rehab centers. Both the National Health Information Center and the National Clearinghouse on Alcohol and Drug Information are excellent places to learn about the array of private resources, new organizations, hotlines, and self-help programs for those who need them. Dozens of federal and state government law enforcement agencies, as well as those involved with international drug trafficking enforcement and prosecution, are listed in the last section of this chapter.

* Academic Institutions and Strategies for Substance Prevention

Office for Substance and Alcohol Abuse (OSAP)
5600 Fishers Lane
Rockville, MD 20847-2345   301-443-6480

Single publications are free of charge, including a publications catalog. Many are available in Spanish. Examples are: *Alcohol Practices, Policies, and Potentials of American Colleges and Universities: A White Paper* (CS02) and *Strategies for Preventing Alcohol and Other Drug Problems on College Campuses: Program Administrators Guide* (CS03). Both of these are designed to help colleges deal with alcohol and drugs on campuses.

* Alcohol and AIDS

National Clearinghouse for Alcohol and Drug Information
P.O. Box 2345
Rockville, MD 20847   301-468-2600

The following are available publications that are free:

Preventing HIV Infection Among Youth (BK193)

NIDA-Capsule: Facts Supporting NIDA's Drug Abuse and AIDS Prevention Campaign for Teens (CP36). This pamphlet explains how alcohol can change a person's judgement about having unsafe sex.

* Alcohol, Drug Abuse and Mental Health Administration

Alcohol, Drug Abuse and Mental Health
  Administration (ADAMHA)
5600 Fishers Lane
Rockville, MD 20857   301-443-8956

ADAMHA conducts and supports research on the biological, psychological, behavioral and epidemiological aspects of alcoholism, drug abuse, and mental health and illness; supports the training of scientists to conduct research in the alcoholism, drug abuse and mental heath fields; gathers and analyzes data about the extent of alcohol, drug abuse and mental health problems and the national response to these needs; encourages groups to facilitate and expand programs for the prevention and treatment; and provides information on alcoholism, drug abuse, and mental health to the public and to the scientific community. A new pamphlet is available: *Update September 1992*, and will be sent upon request.

* Alcoholism and Health Insurance Coverage

National Institute on Alcohol Abuse and Alcoholism (NIAAA)
Parklawn Building
5600 Fishers Lane, Room 16C141
Rockville, MD 20857   301-443-3860

The NIAAA looks at trends relating to treatment of alcoholism and insurance financing issues. It advocates adequate health insurance coverage for alcoholism treatment, and conducts studies on this topic, which are available to the public. Call the Clearinghouse at 800-729-6686. Catalog is free upon request.

* Alcohol in the Workplace

National Clearinghouse
P.O. Box 2345
Rockville, MD 20847-2345   301-468-2600

An Employers Guide to Dealing with Substance Abuse (PHD543), *Research on Drugs and the Workplace* (CAP24), and *Workers at Risk: Drugs and Alcohol on the Job* (PHD521) discuss all aspects of alcohol and the workplace. These are available free, as well as a catalog of other publications.

* Alcoholism Magazine for Professionals

Superintendent of Documents
U.S. Government Printing Office
Washington, DC 20402   202-512-1800

Alcohol Health and Research World, a magazine published quarterly and available for $11 per year, provides professionals with information regarding current research, prevention, and treatment of alcoholism, and includes comment and opinion section, along with information about upcoming events.

* American Alliance for Rights and Responsibilities

AARR
Suite 1112, 1725 K St. NW
Washington, DC 20006   202-785-7844

This is a national non-profit membership organization which is trying to help restore civic duty to the American public. It is working on drug and alcohol abuse and the rights and responsibilities of families. Publications are available free. One of them is *The Winnable War: A Community Guide to Eradicating Street Drug Markets*.

Drugs and Chemical Dependence

* Alcohol Resources and Bibliographies

National Clearinghouse for Alcohol Information
P.O. Box 2345   800-729-6686
Rockville, MD 20847-2345   301-468-2600

Single copies of each of these resource bulletins are available free: *Self Help Groups for Professionals and Special Populations* (No. MS330); *Publishers of Books on Alcohol Topics* (No. MS313); *What You Can do About Drug Use in America* (PHD587); *You Can Help Your Community Get Rid of Drugs* (PHD577); *Training Drug Treatment Staff in the Age of Aids.* You can also order the latest copy of their catalog. The following Prevention Resource Guides are available free, and contain facts, figures, resources, and other information relevant to the specific guide:

Prevention Resource Guide: American Indians/Native Alaskans
Prevention Resource Guide: Asian and Pacific Islander Americans
Prevention Resource Guide: Children of Alcoholics
Prevention Resource Guide: College Youth
Prevention Resource Guide: Elementary Youth
Prevention Resource Guide: Pregnant/Postpartum Women and Their Infants
Prevention Resource Guide: Preschool Children
Prevention Resource Guide: Rural Communities
Prevention Resource Guide: Secondary School Students

* Alcohol and Drug Awareness

National Clearinghouse for Alcohol and Drug Information
P.O. Box 2345
Rockville, MD 20847-2345   301-468-2600

RADAR (The regional alcohol and drug awareness resource) network provides information centers across the country and in Canada. These centers provide the public with a variety of local services. State and Canadian locations are available through this office.

* Alcoholism and Pregnancy

National Clearinghouse
P.O. Box 2345
Rockville, MD 20847-2345   301-468-2600

These are two publications available on what happens when you drink when you are pregnant: *How to Take Care of Your Baby Before Birth* (PH239), *Alcohol Alert #13: Fetal Alcohol Syndrome* (PH297), and *Alcohol, Tobacco, and Other Drugs May Harm the Unborn* (PH291) are excellent sources on fetal risk of abnormalities. Also discussed are complications in labor and custodial rights after birth.

* Careers in Psychological and Epidemiological Aspects of Chemical Dependence

Chemical Dependence
National Institute on Drug Abuse (NIDA)
5600 Fishers Lane
Rockville, MD 20857   301-443-6480

It also supports research training of individuals and institutions who are training individuals in the biological and psychological sciences and epidemiological aspects of drug abuse to enable them to pursue careers in research. For free information call the National Clearinghouse, 301-468-2600.

* Children of Alcoholics

National Clearinghouse for Alcohol Information
P.O. Box 2345   800-729-6686
Rockville, MD 20852   301-468-2600

Prevention Resource Guide: Children of Alcoholics (MS417) and *Alcohol Alert #9: Children of Alcoholics: Are They Different?* (PH288) are two free publications. *The Typical Alcoholic American* (AV195) is a poster that is of particular interest to children of alcoholics.

* Cocaine: Pharmacology, Prevention, and Treatment

National Clearinghouse for Alcohol and
Drug Information
P.O. Box 2345   800-729-6686
Rockville, MD 20852   301-468-2600

These publications are available from the Clearinghouse:

Crack Cocaine: A Challenge for Prevention. OSAP Prevention, Monograph
9 (1991)

The Epidemiology of Cocaine Use and Abuse. NIDA Research, Monograph
110 (1991)
Cocaine Abuse (CAP05)
Cocaine Freebase (CAP05)
Use and Consequences of Cocaine (CAP07)

* Community Action Against Addiction

National Clearinghouse on Alcohol and Drug Information
P.O. Box 2345   800-729-6686
Rockville, MD 20892   301-468-2600

The Clearinghouse has many free publications dealing with drug abuse and the community. Some of the titles include:

Citizen's Alcohol and Other Drug Prevention Directory. Resources for Getting Involved.
Connections.
The Door to Recovery: Community Drug Abuse Treatment.
The Fact Is...Communications Programs Can Help to Prevent Alcohol and Other Drug Problems.
Communities Creating Change: 1990 Exemplary Alcohol and Other Drug Prevention Programs.
Evaluating Faculty Development and Clinical Training Programs in Substance Abuse: A Guidebook.
Handbook for Evaluating Drug and Alcohol Prevention Programs.
How to Start and Run an Alcohol and Other Drug Information Center: A Guide.
Little League Drug Education Program (video).
Making Health Communication Programs Work: A Planner's Guide.
Message and Material Review Process.
Parent Training Is Prevention.
Prevention Plus II: Tools for Creating and Sustaining a Drug-Free Community.
Turning Awareness Into Action.
What You Can Do About Drug Use in America.
Prevention: From Knowledge to Action.
The Primary Prevention of Alcohol Problems: A Critical Review of the Research Literature.
The Fact Is...Resources Are Available for Disabled Persons With Alcohol and Other Drug Problems.
The Fact Is...Reaching Hispanic/Latino Audiences Requires Cultural Sensitivity.
Safer Streets Ahead.
Substance Abuse Prevention Within Inner-City Communities.
Surgeon General's Workshop on Drunk Driving Proceedings.
Surgeon General's Workshop on Drunk Driving: Background Papers.
The Fact Is...Training Is Available for Professionals in the Field of Alcohol and Other Drug Abuse.
Twenty Exemplary Prevention Programs: Helping Communities to Help Themselves.
The Fact Is...You Can Effectively Launch Media Campaigns.
The Fact Is...You Can Start a Student Assistance Program.
Youth at High Risk for Substance Abuse.
A Community Solution, Drug Abuse Treatment.
Overcoming Barriers to Drug Abuse Treatment in the Community.

* Community Prevention and Education Grants

ACTION
Drug Alliance Office
1100 Vermont Ave., NW, Suite 8200
Washington, DC 20525   202-606-5212

ACTION supports community-based prevention and education efforts with grants, contracts, conferences, and technical assistance. Nonprofit organizations and state and local governments are eligible to receive grants from ACTION. An announcement is made in the Federal Register regarding the type of activities that the ACTION grant is available for and organizations are encouraged to apply. ACTION also maintains a mailing list which sends copies of the notices appearing in the Federal Register directly to those on the list. To get the name of your organization on this list, call the number above.

* Community Volunteer Service Programs

ACTION
Drug Alliance Office
1100 Vermont Ave., NW, Suite 8200
Washington, DC 20525   202-606-5212

ACTION is the principal agency in the Federal Government for administering volunteer service programs. Many of the various components of ACTION, such as

Foster Grandparents and VISTA, are involved in community drug abuse education, prevention or treatment programs. The Drug Alliance Office coordinates the agency's drug abuse activities, awards grants that strengthen and expand local volunteer activities combatting illegal drug use among youth and the misuse of prescription and over-the-counter drugs by the elderly, provides training and technical assistance, and conducts public awareness and education efforts.

* Driving-While-Intoxicated Statistics

Transportation Department
National Highway Traffic Safety Administration
400 7th Street SW
Washington, DC 20590   202-366-0123
The National Center tabulates data on highway traffic accidents and maintains statistics on accidents and fatalities due to alcohol or drug use. They have extensive data on drunk driving, seat belts and alcohol, as well as much more.
One free information pamphlet is *Drunk Driving Facts*.

* Drug Abuse and AIDS

National Clearinghouse for Alcohol and Drug Information
P.O. Box 2345
Rockville, MD 20852   800-729-6686
Publications available on Drug Abuse and Aids include:
Drug Abuse and AIDS (CAP04)
How Getting High Can Get You AIDS (PHD573)
Training Drug Treatment Staff in the Age of AIDS (PHD571).

Posters available include:
AIDS. Another Way Drugs Can Kill (AV187). This poster explains the drugs/sex/AIDS connection. It includes a quiz on drugs and AIDS.
Fatal Accident (AV60). This poster shows how drugs can cause two kinds of car "accidents", crashes and HIV/AIDS transmissions.

* Drug Abuse and AIDS Helpline

National Institute of Drug Abuse (NIDA)   800-662-HELP
The National Institute of Drug Abuse (NIDA) Helpline provides general phone information on drug abuse and on AIDS as it relates to intravenous drug users. This hotline offers referrals to drug rehab centers. Hours: 9 a.m. - 3 a.m. Monday through Friday; 12 p.m. - 3 a.m. on weekends.

* Drug Abuse and Pregnancy

National Clearinghouse for Alcohol and Drug Information
P.O. Box 2345
Rockville, MD 20852   800-729-6686
Publications about pregnant women and drug abuse include:

Guess Who Else Can Get AIDS If You Shoot Drugs? Your Baby (AVD23)
How to Take Care of Your Baby Before Birth (PH239)
Drug Abuse and Pregnancy (CAP33)
Alcohol, Tobacco, and Other Drugs May Harm the Unborn (PH291).

* Drug Abuse Research

National Institute on Drug Abuse (NIDA)
5600 Fishers Lane
Rockville, MD 20857   301-443-6480
NIDA conducts and supports research on the biological, psychological, psychosocial, and epidemiological aspects of drug abuse. It also collaborates with and provides technical assistance to State drug abuse authorities, and encourages State and community efforts in planning, establishing, maintaining, coordinating, and evaluating more effective drug abuse programs.

* Drug Dependent Youth and Jobs

Office of Juvenile Justice and Delinquency Prevention
U.S. Department of Justice
633 Indiana Ave., NW
Washington, DC 20531   202-307-5940
Drug-dependent youth who receive vocational rehabilitation services present unique challenges to State vocational rehabilitation service delivery systems. An interagency agreement (with the U.S. Department of Education) enables State vocational rehabilitation agencies to receive training through the development, implementation, and evaluation of a comprehensive drug rehabilitation training and information

program. The ultimate goal of this program is to secure employment for eligible youth ages 14-18 who have been drug dependent.

* Drug Rehabilitation Services

Office of Public Affairs
Administration for Children and Families (ACE)
902 9th and D Sts.
Washington, DC 20047   202-673-3331
This office provides leadership and direction to human services programs for the elderly, children and youth, families, Native Americans, persons living in rural areas, and handicapped persons. HDS administers rehabilitation services for these groups.

* Drugs and the Workplace

National Clearinghouse for Alcohol and Drug Information
P.O. Box 2345
Rockville, MD 20852   800-729-6686
These publications are available through the Clearinghouse Catalog:

An Employer's Guide to Dealing with Substance Abuse (PHD5430)
How Drug Abuse Takes Profit out of Business, How Drug Treatment Helps Put It Back (PHD574).

* Drug-Related Highway Accidents Research

National Highway Traffic Safety Administration (NHTSA)
400 Seventh St., SW
Washington, DC 20590   202-366-9550
NHTSA is the Federal focal point for the national effort to eliminate driving while intoxicated,, including research on drug-related highway problems. Call 202-366-9588 for free information.

* Drug Reports

General Accounting Office (GAO)
P.O. Box 6015
Gaithersburg, MD 20877   202-275-6241
The GAO conducts reports on various topics including various issues regarding drugs. *Nonprescription Drugs: Over the Counter and Underemphasized* examines the FDA's procedures for approving and monitoring over-the-counter drugs in order to identify potential vulnerabilities in the procedures that could result in the approval and marketing of unsafe and ineffective drugs. *Adolescent Drug Use Prevention: Common Features of Promising Community Programs* examines the design, implementation, and results of promising comprehensive, community-based drug use prevention programs for young adolescents, regardless of their funding sources. These reports are free.

* Drug Testing to Identify High-Risk Youths

Office of Juvenile Justice and Delinquency Prevention (OJJDP)
Office of Justice Programs
U.S. Department of Justice
633 Indiana Ave., NW
Washington, DC 20531   202-307-0751
The OJJDP funds programs such as Urine Testing of Juvenile Detainees to Identify High-Risk Youths, and Drug Testing Guidelines for Juvenile Justice agencies. Program goals include developing a comprehensive drug identification, screening, and testing program to be included in training curriculums for juvenile justice policymakers, administrators, and direct service professionals. Call 1-800-638-8736 for free information.

* Effective Anti-Drug Strategies

Office of Juvenile Justice and Delinquency Prevention (OJJDP)
U.S. Department of Justice
633 Indiana Ave., NW
Washington, DC 20531   202-307-5914
To effectively combat youth drug and alcohol abuse and coordinated juvenile substance abuse prevention and treatment programs, further knowledge must be gained on strategies and approaches that communities are using nationwide. OJJDP funded the Introduction of Effective Systemwide Strategies To Combat Youth Drug and Alcohol Abuse project to help communities assess their resources and capabilities, and use a coordinated systemwide approach to address drug- and alcohol-related problems. A three-volume assessment report was produced containing a review of literature, information describing 10 promising approaches, and a model for community action against drug and alcohol abuse.

Drugs and Chemical Dependence

* Effective Parenting Skills with High-Risk Youth

Office of Juvenile Justice and Delinquency Prevention (OJJDP)
Office of Justice Programs
U.S. Department of Justice
633 Indiana Ave., NW   800-638-8736
Washington, DC 20531   202-307-0751

The purpose of Identification and Transfer of Effective Juvenile Justice Projects and Services: Effective Parenting Strategies for Families of High Risk Youth is to reduce delinquency and drug abuse in youth by providing community agencies with information and skills to implement special programs for families of high-risk youth. This project currently is assessing existing family-oriented programs that have demonstrated success in decreasing delinquency, drug use, or associated risk factors.

* Employee Assistance for Drug and Alcohol Abuse

National Clearinghouse for Alcohol and Drug Information
P.O. Box 2345
Rockville, MD 20852   800-729-6686

The Fact Is...Employee Assistance Contacts Are Available In Every State is a free publication, which explains that an Employee Assistance Program is a professional assessment/referral and/or short term counseling service for motivating and helping employees with alcohol, drug, or mental health problems to seek and accept appropriate help. EAPs are particularly concerned with problems that adversely affect job performance. These programs can serve as part of a comprehensive approach to combat alcohol and other drug abuse in the workplace. The following is a list of State EAP contacts who are available for providing technical assistance to private sector CEOs, managers, supervisors, and union representatives who are establishing or managing employee assistance programs.

Alabama
Phillip Johnson
Alabama Department of Mental Health
P.O. Box 3710
Montgomery, AL 36193   205-271-9285

Alaska
Matthew Feliz/George Mundel
Office of Alcoholism and Drug Abuse
Department of Health and Social Services
BY H-05-F   907-586-6201 (Juneau)
Juneau, AK 99811   907-561-4213 (Anchorage)

Arizona
Russ Binicki
Maricopa County EAP
Luhrs Building.
11 W. Jefferson, Suite 14
Phoenix, AZ 85003   602-261-7030

Arkansas
Ray Stephens
Assistant Deputy Director
Office on Alcohol and Drug Abuse Prevention
400 Donaghey Plaza North
P.O. Box 1437
7th and Main St.
Little Rock, AR 72203   501-682-6652

California
Cliff Coleman
Department of Alcohol and Drug Programs
111 Capitol Mall
Sacramento, CA 95814   916-323-1860

Colorado
Ed Kraft
OPC Position
Alcohol and Drug Abuse Division
Department of Health
4210 East 11th Ave.
Denver, CO 80220   303-331-8201

Connecticut
Margaret Perla
Deputy Director
Connecticut Alcohol and Drug Abuse Commission
999 Asylum Ave.
Hartford, CT 06105   203-566-3075

Delaware
Paul Poplawski
Division of Alcoholism, Drug Abuse, and Mental Health
1901 North Dupont Highway
New Castle, DE 19720   302-421-6109

District Of Columbia
Charles W. Avery
Office of Health Planning and Development
Commission of Public Health
425 Eye St., NW, Room 3210
Washington, DC 20001   202-724-5637

Florida
Linda Lewis
HRS-Department of Personnel Management
1317 Winewood Blvd.
Building 3, Room 216
Tallahassee, FL 32399   904-488-0900

Georgia
Ed Pierce
Substance Abuse Service
878 Peachtree St., NE
Suite 319
Atlanta, GA 30309   404-728-4033

Hawaii
John McCarthy
Department of Health
c/o Alcohol and Drug Abuse Branch
P.O. Box 3378
Honolulu, HI 96801   808-548-4280

Idaho
Tina Klampt
Substance Abuse Program
Department of Health and Welfare
450 West State St.
Boise, ID 83720   208-334-5935

Illinois
Marie Apke
State of Illinois Center
100 West Randolph, Suite 3-300
Chicago, IL 60601   312-917-6983

Indiana
Johnie Underwood, Director
Division of Addiction Services
Department of Mental Health
117 E. Washington St.
Indianapolis, IN 46204   317-232-7816

Iowa
Janet Zwick, Director
Iowa Division of Substance Abuse and Health Promotions
Lucas State Office Building
321 E. Twelfth St.
Des Moines, IA 50319   515-281-8021

Kansas
Suzanne Milburn
Health and Environment
Landon State Office Building
10th Floor
900 Southwest Jackson St.
Topeka, KS 66620   913-296-1224

Kentucky
Michael Townsend
Substance Abuse Division
275 East Main St.
Frankfort, KY 40621   502-564-2880

    Be patient. If any phone number is incorrect, call (area code) 555-1212 and request the new listing.

Louisiana
Sanford Hawkins
Office of Prevention and Recovery
2744B Wooddale Blvd.
Baton Rouge, LA 70805 504-922-0728

Maine
Kevin Parker, Director
State Employee Assistance Program
P.O. Box 112
Hallowell, ME 04347 207-289-5752

Maryland
Sharon Dow
Alcohol and Drug Abuse Administration
201 West Preston St., 4th Floor
Baltimore, MD 21201 301-225-6548

Massachusetts
David Mulligan
Division of Alcoholism and Drugs
150 Tremont St., 6th Floor
Boston, MA 02111 617-727-8614

Michigan
Barry Mintzes
Programs Administrator, OSAS-MDPH
3423 North Logan
P.O. Box 30195
Lansing, MI 48909 517-335-8810

Minnesota
Keith Tweenen
Summit Bank Building, Suite 200
205 Aurora Ave.
St. Paul, MN 55103 612-296-0765

Mississippi
Anne Robertson, Director
Division of Alcohol and Drug Abuse
Department of Mental Health
1500 Woolfolk Building
Jackson, MS 39201 601-359-1297

Missouri
Lois Olson, Director
Division of Alcohol and Drug Abuse
Department of Mental Health
1915 South Ridge Dr.
P.O. Box 687
Jefferson City, MO 65102 314-751-4942

Montana
Daryl Bruno, Alcohol and Drug Abuse Division
Department of Institutions
1539 11th Ave.
Helena, MT 59620 406-444-2827

Nebraska
Malcolm Herd
Division of Alcoholism and Drug Abuse
Department of Public Institutions
P.O. Box 94728
Lincoln, NE 68509 402-471-2851, ext. 5583

Nevada
Sharyn Peal
Bureau of Alcohol and Drug Abuse
505 East King St., Room 500
Carson City, NV 89710 702-885-4790

New Hampshire
Carol Gregory
Employee Assistance Program
Health and Human Services Building
6 Hazen Dr.
Concord, NH 03301 603-271-4628

New Jersey
Larry Ganges/ Mark Brown
Department of Health
129 East Hanover St., CN 362
Trenton, NJ 08625 609-292-0729

New Mexico
Carol Ross, Director
New Mexico State EAP
825 Topeka St.
Santa Fe, NM 87501 505-827-9920

New York
Dan Forget
Bureau of Occupational Industrial Services
New York Division of Alcoholism and Alcohol Abuse
194 Washington Ave.
Albany, NY 12210 518-474-6422

Jim Sipe
Program Manager
State EAP
Governor's Office of Employee Relations
1 Commerce Plaza
Suite 706
Albany, NY 12260 518-473-3414

North Carolina
Roy Sonovick
Alcohol and Drug Abuse
Department of Human Services
State Capitol Building
Bismarck, ND 58505 701-224-2769

Ohio
Phil Flench
Industrial Commission of Ohio
4th Floor
246 North High St.
Columbus, OH 43215 614-644-8968

Oklahoma
Steve West
Alcohol and Drug Abuse Division
Department of Mental Health
p.O. Box 53277, Capitol Station
Oklahoma City, OK 73152 405-271-7474

Oregon
Jeffrey N. Kushner
Office of Alcohol and Drug Abuse Programs
1178 Chemeketa St., NE
Salem, OR 97310 503-378-2163

Pennsylvania
Jeff Johnston, Director
Bureau of Program Services
H&W Building, Room 929
P.O. Box 90
Harrisburg, PA 17109 717-783-8200

Puerto Rico
Isabel Sullveres de Martinez
Employee Assistance Program Department of Service Against Addiction
Box 21414
Rio Piedras Station
Rio Piedras, PR 00928 809-758-7330

Rhode Island
Robert MacDonald
Rhode Island Employee Assistance Program
33 College Hill Rd.
Warwick, RI 02886 401-828-9560

South Carolina
Robert R. Charles
South Carolina Commission on Alcohol and Drug Abuse

Drugs and Chemical Dependence

3700 Forest Dr.
Suite 300
Columbia, SC 29204 803-734-9547

South Dakota
Barry Pillen, EAP Coordinator
Division of Alcohol and Drug Abuse
Joe Foss Building
523 East Capital
Pierre, SD 57501 605-773-3123

Tennessee
Carole M. Boone, Ed.D.
Doctors Building, 4th Floor
706 Church St.
Nashville, TN 37219 615-741-1925

Texas
Robby Duffield
Commission on Alcohol and Drug Abuse
1705 Guadalupe St.
Austin, TX 78701 512-463-5510

Utah
Jeano Campanaro
Department of Social Services
Human Resources/Organizational Development
120 North, 200 West, Human Resources
3rd. Floor
Salt Lake City, UT 84103 801-538-4216

Vermont
Buell Mitchell and John Taylor
EAP Coordinators
Office of Alcohol and Drug Abuse Programs
103 South Main St.
Waterbury, VT 05676 802-241-2170

Virginia
Wayne Thacker
Division of Mental Health/Mental Retardation/Substance Abuse Services
109 Governor St.
Richmond, VA 23219 804-786-3906

Washington
Dwight Bond
907 North West Ballard Way
Seattle, WA 98107 206-545-7782

West Virginia
Jack Clohan/Gary Koontz
Department of Health and Human Services
Division of Alcohol and Drug Abuse
State Office Complex, Building 3
1800 Washington St., E
Room 402
Charleston, WV 25305 304-348-2276

Wisconsin
Steve Ojibway
Department of Health and Social Services
P.O. Box 7851
1 West Wilson St., Room 434
Madison, WI 53707 608-267-9281

Wyoming
Jean DeFratis, Director
Alcohol and Drug Abuse Programs
Hathaway Building
Cheyenne, WY 82002 307-777-7115, ext. 7118

* Gangs and Drugs

Office of Juvenile Justice and Delinquency Prevention
U.S. Department of Justice
633 Indiana Ave., NW
Washington, DC 20531 202-307-5940

A crucial issue in addressing gang and drug problems is the need for close cooperation and sharing of information among all key juvenile justice policymakers within a jurisdiction. The Gang and Drug POLICY Training Program provides assistance to personnel from all arenas of the local juvenile justice system in confronting drug activity by gangs. The objectives of this training program are to present to key policymakers a cooperative interagency process that leads to improved public and private gang and drug prevention, intervention, and suppression strategies.

* Homelessness and Alcohol and Drug Abuse

Homeless Demonstration and Evaluation Branch
National Institute on Alcohol Abuse and Alcoholism
5600 Fishers Lane
Room 13C-02
Rockville, MD 20857 301-443-9334

This Branch supports a variety of contracts and cooperative agreements, including a research demonstration program authorized by the Stewart B. McKinney Homeless Assistance Act. The research demonstration program contributes to scientific knowledge regarding effective interventions for homeless individuals with alcohol and other drug problems. The HDEB also supports technical assistance papers on the housing and service needs of this population. Information about the research demonstration program and other documents about homelessness, alcohol and other drug problems are available through the National Clearinghouse for Alcohol and Drug Information (800-729-6686).

* House of Representatives Narcotics Committee

U.S. Congress
House Select Committee on Narcotics Abuse and Control
Ford House Office Building
Washington, DC 20515 202-226-3040

This special committee investigates drug abuse, conducts hearings in Washington and throughout the country, and publishes numerous studies which are available to the public. The caller must request specific information for specific hearings.

* Illegal Drug Use in Youth

Office of Juvenile Justice and Delinquency Prevention
P. O. Box 6000
Rockville, MD 20850 800-638-8736

The Coordinating Council is a group of 16 Federal agencies who held a workshop to develop interagency initiatives to combat the juvenile drug problem. *The 1990 Action Plan to Prevent Illegal Drug Use Among High-Risk Youth* provides details of the 19 interagency projects. They also produced *Juvenile Alcohol and Other Drug Abuse: A Guide to Federal Initiatives for Prevention, Treatment, and Control* which will serve as a resource for State, local, and private agencies and individuals working to combat juvenile drug and alcohol abuse.

* Indian Housing Programs

Headstart Public and Indian Housing Program
U.S. Department of Housing and Urban Development
451 7th Street, SW
Room 4112
Washington, DC 20410 202-708-4214

This non-profit organization provides information for establishing child day care centers.

* Innovative Approaches in Criminal Justice

National Institute of Justice
U.S. Department of Justice
P.O. Box 6000 800-851-3420
Rockville, MD 20850 301-251-5500

National Institute of Justice (NIJ) publishes:

A Criminal Justice System Strategy for Treating Cocaine-Heroin Abusing Offenders in Custody

Issues and Practices in Criminal Justice

Arresting the Demand for Drugs; Characteristics of Different Types of Drug Involved Offenders.

Searching for Answers: Second Annual Evaluation Report on Drugs and Crime, Report to the President, the Attorney General, and the Congress

A Comparison of Urinalysis Technologies for Drug Testing in Criminal Justice Drug Use Forecasting

Mandatory and Random Drug Testing in the Honolulu Police Department

Prison Programs for Drug-Involved Offenders

Be patient. If any phone number is incorrect, call (area code) 555-1212 and request the new listing.

Urine Testing of Detained Juveniles To Identify High-Risk Youth
In-Prison Programs for Drug-Involved Offenders
Multijurisdictional Drug Law Enforcement Strategies: Reducing Supply and
Demand

* International Criminal Justice Clearinghouse

National Institute of Justice
U.S. Department of Justice
633 Indiana Ave., NW
Washington, DC 20531   202-307-0751

The Institute operates an international information center, the National Criminal Justice Reference Service. Subscribers receive the bimonthly *NIJ Reports*, which includes feature articles on major research developments and abstracts of the latest additions to the NCJRS database, which now numbers more than 100,000 documents.

* Juvenile Justice Clearinghouse

Office of Juvenile Justice and Delinquency Prevention (OJJDP)
P.O. Box 6000
Rockville, MD 20850   800-638-8736

Publications, research findings, and program evaluations are available as well as specific services including database searches, referrals, conference support, and other juvenile justice products. Free publications dealing with juveniles and alcohol and drug use include:

OJJDP Update on Statistics: *Juvenile Court Drug and Alcohol Cases: 1985-1988.*
OJJDP Update on Programs: *Drug Recognition Techniques for Juvenile Justice*
Professionals.
OJJDP Update on Statistics: *Growth In Minority Detentions Attributed to Drug*
Law Violators.
1990 Action Plan to Prevent Illegal Drug Use Among High-Risk Youth.
Juvenile Alcohol and Other Drug Abuse: A Guide to Federal Initiatives for
Prevention, Treatment, and Control.

* Local Drug Treatment Centers Incentives

Susan Lachter David or Audrey Yorrell
National Institute on Drug Abuse
5600 Fishers Lane
Room 10a-39
Rockville, MD 20857   301-443-1124

Overcoming Barriers to Drug Abuse Treatment in the Community is a flexible education model for use by communities which have funding and want to establish drug treatment facilities. This model is used in communities to educate people about drug treatment with the goal of countering resistance to the establishment of new treatment facilities. Materials are available to help local providers site facilities (How-to Resource Manual and Media package), as well as materials to assist communities groups in educating the public (Resource manual and media materials). These materials are free. This Office can also provide technical assistance.

* "McGruff" Crime Prevention Campaign

Bureau of Justice Assistance
U.S. Department of Justice
633 Indiana Ave., NW
Washington, DC 20531   202-307-0751

National Crime Prevention (McGruff) Campaign, supported by BJA, develops and disseminates crime prevention materials, provides technical assistance and training, and operates a clearinghouse for information on crime prevention programs, publications, and workshops.

* Mental Health and Chemical Dependence

National Institute of Mental Health (NIMH)
5600 Fishers Lane
Rockville, MD 20857   301-443-3877/4513

NIMH supports research on the relationships between mental health and drug or alcohol abuse.

* Minorities and Prevention Grants

Attie Key
Minority Substance Abuse Prevention
U.S. Department of Health and Human Services
Security Lane, Rockwall II

Rockville, MD 20857   301-443-0365

This government agencies awards grants for minority substance abuse prevention programs.

* Mutual-Help Groups

National Clearinghouse for Alcohol and Drug Information
P.O. Box 2345
Rockville, MD 20852   800-729-6686

The Fact Is...There Are Specialized Mutual-Help Groups For Those With Alcohol and Drug Problems (MS330) is a free publication which discusses self-help groups that have emerged in response to special concerns expressed by those seeking recovery for alcohol and other drug problem. The publication lists the self-help groups, providing general information about the group and a central phone number.

* Narcotic Drugs and Psychotropic Substances

International Regulations
Food and Drug Administration (FDA)
5600 Fishers Lane
Rockville, MD 20857   301-443-4480

FDA works with the DEA as a drug regulatory agency. Together, they are responsible for working with the international community (the U.N. and WHO) to ensure appropriate scheduling of narcotic drugs and psychotropic substances.

* National Criminal Survey and Other Statistics

Bureau of Justice Statistics
U.S. Department of Justice
633 Indiana Ave., NW
Washington, DC 20531   202-307-0751

The Bureau of Justice Statistics (BJS) maintains statistics about crime, its perpetrators and victims, and the operation of the criminal justice system at the Federal, State and local level. The National Institute of Justice sponsors research on crime and its control and is a central federal resource for information on innovative approaches in criminal justice. BJS publishes *Report to the Nation on Crime and Justice: Second Edition, Profile of State Prison Inmates, 1986, Drug Law Violators, 1980-86: Federal Offenses and Offenders, Drug Use and Crime: State Prison Inmate Survey, 1986, and Survey of Youth in Custody, 1987.*

* National Drug Enforcement Data Clearinghouse

Drugs and Crime Data Center and Clearinghouse
Bureau of Justice Statistics
U.S. Department of Justice
633 Indiana Ave., NW
Washington, DC 20531   202-307-0751

This clearinghouse gathers existing data on drugs and the justice system, identifies drug enforcement data gaps, and prepares special reports and tabulations of existing drug data. The clearinghouse will respond to your requests for drugs and crime data, let you know about new drugs and crime data reports, send you reports on drugs and crime, conduct special bibliographic searches for you, refer you to data on epidemiology, prevention and treatment of substance abuse, publish special reports, and prepare a comprehensive, concise report. Some of the reports available include:

BJS Sourcebook of Criminal Justice Statistics
Drugs and Crime Facts, 1990
Felony Case Processing in State Courts, 1986
Profile of Felons Convicted in State Courts, 1986
Felony Defendants in Large Urban Counties, 1988
Federal Criminal Case Process, 1980-87
Violent State Prisoners and Their Victims
State Drug Resources: A National Directory
Federal Drug Data for National Policy
Drugs and Crime Facts, 1989
Catalog of Selected Federal Publications On Illegal Drug and Alcohol Abuse

* President's Drug Czar

Office of National Drug Control Policy
Executive Office of the President
Washington, DC 20500   202-467-9800

The President's White House staff, specifically the Drug Policy Office, focuses on proposed legislation and other efforts in the "War on Drugs." The written information includes: *Understanding Drug Treatment, National Drug Control Safety,* and monthly bulletins. A free annual report is available, titled *National Drug Control*

Drugs and Chemical Dependence

Strategy: A Nation Responds to Drug Use. It sets forth a unified attack against illegal drugs. It examines, goals, objectives, current use, treatment, organizations, suppliers, recommendations, and much more. Call for your free copy.

* Prevention, Intervention and Treatment for Juveniles

Office of Juvenile Justice and Delinquency Prevention (OJJDP)
Office of Justice Programs
U.S. Department of Justice
633 Indiana Ave., NW
Washington, DC 20531   202-307-0751
Joint projects between The Research and Program Development Division and the Special Emphasis Division of OJJDP include:

Promising Approaches for the Prevention, Intervention, and Treatment of Illegal Drug and Alcohol Use Among Juveniles is designed to help communities with high rates of adolescent drug and alcohol abuse. The project will identify and review promising juvenile drug programs, develop and test program prototypes and provide training.

* Public Health Services and Resources

Health Resources and Services Administration (HRSA)
5600 Fishers Lane
Rockville, MD 20857   301-443-2086
HRSA has leadership responsibility in the Public Health Service for general health services and resource issues relating to access, equity, quality and cost of care. This treatment includes AIDS patients as well as drug or alcohol dependent persons.

* Public Housing Drug Strategy Clearinghouse

Drug Information and Strategy Clearinghouse
U.S. Department of Housing and Urban Development (HUD)
P.O. Box 6424
Rockville, MD 20850   800-955-2232
Sponsored by HUD, the clearinghouse provides housing officials, residents, and community leaders with information and assistance on drug abuse prevention and drug trafficking control techniques. They have created a database containing information on improving resident screening procedures, strengthening eviction policies, increasing cooperation with local law enforcement, implementing drug tip hotlines, forming resident patrols, starting child care centers, and organizing drug education/prevention activities. The clearinghouse also provides information packages, resource lists, HUD regulations, referrals, and a newsletter, Home Front. A community guide called *The Winnable War: A Community Guide to Eradicating Street Drug Markets,* is also available. The clearinghouse assists PHAs and IHAs applying for PHDEP grant funds. Publications include:

Funding Resource List
Information Resources List
State Contact List
Model Programs Information Package
Grantsmanship Information Package
Needs Assessment Information Package
Risk Factor Approach to Drug Abuse Prevention Programs
Drugs in Housing: What Managers Can Do
Drug Information and Strategy Clearinghouse Brochure
Home Front

* Public Housing Modernization Anti-Drug Project

Bill Flood and Janice Rattley
U.S. Department of Housing and Urban Development
Room 4122
7th and D Sts.
Washington, DC 20047   202-708-1422
The Comprehensive Improvement Assistance Program provides incentives for comprehensive modernization improvements, some of which may serve to prevent drug activity.

* Public Housing Resident Management Grants

U.S. Department of Housing and Urban Development (HUD)
820 1st St. NE
Washington, DC 20002   202-275-7965
This HUD program funds the establishment of resident management groups in public housing.

* Senate Committee

U.S. Senate
Subcommittee on Children
Committee on Labor and Human Resources
Washington, DC 20510   202-224-5630
This is one of several subcommittees in the U.S. Senate which focus on some aspect of chemical dependence.

* State Drug Abuse Authorities

The following is a list of the drug abuse agencies in each state responsible for drug abuse prevention and treatment services:

Department of Health and Social Services
Office of Alcoholism and Drug Abuse
P.O. Box 110607
Juneau, AK 99811-0607   907-586-6201

Department of Mental Health Community Programs
Div. of Mental Illness and Substance Abuse
200 Interstate Park Dr.
P.O. Box 3710
Montgomery, AL 36109   205-271-9209

Arkansas Office of Alcohol and Drug Abuse Prevention
P.O. Box 329
Little Rock, AR 72203
Director   501-371-2603
Program Implementation Development   501-371-2604

Arizona Department of Health Services
Office of Community Behavioral Health
1740 W. Adam
Phoenix, AZ 85007   602-220-6506

Department of Alcohol and Drug Abuse
1700 K St.
Sacramento, CA 95814   916-445-0834

Colorado Department of Health
Alcohol and Drug Abuse Division
4210 E. 11th Ave.
Denver, CO 80220   303-331-8201

Connecticut Alcohol and Drug Abuse Commission
999 Asylum Ave.
Hartford, CT 06105   203-566-4145

Department of Human Services
Office of Health Planning and Development
1660 L St. NW, Suite 1117
Washington, DC 20036   202-673-7481

Bureau of Alcoholism and Drug Abuse
1901 N. Dupont Hwy.
New Castle, DE 19720   302-577-4460

Department of Health and Rehabilitative Services
Alcohol and Drug Abuse Program
1317 Winewood Blvd.
Tallahassee, FL 32301   904-488-8304

Georgia Department of Human Resources
Div. of Mental Health and Mental Retardation
Alcohol and Drug Section
878 Peachtree St., NE, Suite 319
Atlanta, GA 30309   404-894-4200

Government of Guam
Dept. of Mental Health and Substance Abuse
P.O. Box 9400
Tamuning, GU 96931   671-646-9260

Department of Health
Mental Health Div.
Alcohol and Drug Abuse Branch

1270 Emma St.
Queen Emma Building, Room 706
Honolulu, HI 96813   808-586-4007

Iowa Department of Public Health
Div. of Substance Abuse and Health Promotion
321 E. 12th St.
Lucas State Office Bldg., Fourth Floor
Des Moines, IA 50319   515-281-4417

Department of Health and Welfare
Bureau of Substance Abuse and Social Services
450 W. State, 3rd Floor
Boise, ID 83720-5450   208-334-5935

Illinois Department of Alcoholism and Substance Abuse
100 W. Randolph St., Suite 5-600
Chicago, IL 60601   312-814-3840

State of Indiana Department of Mental Health
Division of Addiction Services
402 W. Washington St., Room 353
Indianapolis, IN 46204   317-232-7837

Alcohol and Drug Abuse Services
300 S.W. Oakley
Biddle Bldg., 6th Floor
Topeka, KS 66606   913-296-3925

Department for Mental Health/Mental Retardation Services
Div. of Substance Abuse
275 E. Main St.
Health Services Bldg, 1st Floor
Frankfort, KY 40621   502-564-2880

Office of Prevention and Recovery from Alcohol and Drug Abuse
1201 Capitol Access Rd.
P.O. Box 3868
Baton Rouge, LA 70821   504-342-9352

Massachusetts Divisions of Substance Abuse Services
150 Tremont St.
Boston, MA 02111   617-727-1960

Alcohol and Drug Abuse Administration
201 W. Preston St.
Herbert O'Conor Bldg.
Baltimore, MD 21201   410-225-6910

Office of Alcohol and Drug Abuse Prevention
Bureau of Rehabilitation
State House
Station 11
Augusta, ME 04333   207-287-2781

Michigan Department of Public Health
Office of Substance Abuse Services
3423 N. Logan St.
P.O. Box 30195
Lansing, MI 48909   517-335-8810

Department of Human Services
Chemical Dependency Program Division
444 Lafayette Road
Space Center Bldg., 2nd Floor
St. Paul, MN 55155-3823   612-296-4610

Mental Health Department
Alcohol and Drug Abuse Services
239 N. Lamar Street
Jackson, MS 39201   601-359-1288

Missouri Department of Mental Health
Div. of Alcohol and Drug Abuse
1706 E. Elm St.
P.O. Box 687
Jefferson City, MO 65102   314-751-4942

State of Montana Department of Institutions
Alcohol and Drug Abuse Div.
1539 11th Ave.
Helena, MT 59620   406-444-4927

Division of Mental Health/Mental Retardation Services
Alcohol and Drug Abuse Section
325 N. Salisbury St.
Albemarle Bldg., Room 1168
Raleigh, NC 27603   919-733-4670

North Dakota Department of Human Services
Division of Alcoholism and Drug Abuse
State Capitol/Judicial Wing
1839 E. Capitol Ave.
Bismarck, ND 58501   701-224-2769

Nebraska Department of Public Institutions
Div. of Alcoholism and Drug Abuse
P.O. Box 94728
Lincoln, NE 68509-4728   402-471-2851 or 5583

New Hampshire Office of Alcohol and Drug Abuse Prevention
State Office Park
105 Pleasant St.
Concord, NH 03301   603-271-6100

Alcoholism, Drug Abuse and Addiction Services Division
129 E. Hanover St.
CN 362
Trenton, NJ 08625   609-292-0362

Behavioral Health Services Division
Substance Abuse Bureau
1190 St. Francis Dr.
P.O. Box 968
Santa Fe, NM 87502   505-827-2601

Department of Human Resources
Bureau of Alcohol and Drug Abuse
505 E. King St.
Carson City, NV 89710   702-687-4790

Office of Alcoholism and Substance Abuse Services (OASAS)
Executive Park South, Box 8200
Albany, NY 12203   518-457-7629

Alcohol and Drug Abuse
181 Washington Blvd.
Columbus, OH 43215   614-645-7306

Oklahoma Department of Mental Health
Alcohol and Drug Programs
1200 NE 13th St.
P.O. Box 53277
Oklahoma City, OK 73152-3277   405-271-8653

Office of Alcohol and Drug Abuse Programs
1178 Chemeketa NE
Salem, OR 97310   503-378-2163

Pennsylvania Department of Health
Drug and Alcohol Programs
Commonwealth and Forster Sts.
P.O. Box 90
Harrisburg, PA 17108   717-787-9857

Puerto Rico Department of Addiction Control Services
P.O. Box 21414
Rio Piedras, PR 00928   809-764-3795

Department of Mental Health/
Mental Retardation and Hospitals
Division of Substance Abuse
Substance Abuse Administration Bldg.
P.O. Box 20363
Cranston, RI 02920   401-464-2091

Be patient. If any phone number is incorrect, call (area code) 555-1212 and request the new listing.

581

Drugs and Chemical Dependence

South Carolina Commission on Alcohol and Drug Abuse
3700 Forest Dr.
Landmark East, Suite 300
Columbia, SC 29204 — 803-734-9520

South Dakota Division of Alcohol and Drug Abuse
Hill View Plaza
500 E. Capital
Pierre, SD 57501 — 605-773-3123

Tennessee Department of Mental Health/Mental Retardation
Alcohol and Drug Abuse Services
255 Court of Hull Building
Nashville, TN 37247 — 615-741-1921

Department of Health Services
P.O. Box 409CK
HICOM
Saipan, Mariana Islands, TT 96950 — 670-234-8950

Texas Commission on Alcohol and Drug Abuse
1720 Brazof St.
Austin, TX 78701 — 512-867-8700

Utah State Division of Alcoholism and Drugs
120 N. 200 West
4th Floor
Salt Lake City, UT 84103 — 801-538-3939

Virginia Department of Mental Health/Mental Retardation
Office of Substance Abuse Services
109 Governor St.
P.O. Box 1797
Richmond, VA 23214 — 804-786-3906

Virgin Islands Division of Mental Health
St. Thomas, VI 00801 — 809-775-3302

Office of Alcohol and Drug Abuse Programs
103 S. Main St.
State Office Bldg.
Waterbury, VT 05676 — 802-241-2170

Washington Department of Social and Health Services
Bureau of Alcoholism and Substance Abuse
7th Ave. SE, Building C, Room 4408
Olympia, WA 98504-5330 — 206-438-8200

Office of Alcohol and Other Drug Abuse
1 W. Wilson St.
P.O. Box 7851
Madison, WI 53707 — 608-266-3442

Department of Health
Div. of Alcoholism and Drug Abuse
State Capital Complex
Building 6, Room 738
Charleston, WV 25305 — 304-558-2276

Alcohol and Drug Abuse Programs
Hathaway Bldg.
Room 451, 4th Floor
Cheyenne, WY 82003-0480 — 307-777-7116

* Steroids Abuse

Drug Planning and Outreach Staff
Office of Elementary and Secondary Education
400 Maryland Ave. SW
Washington, DC 20202-6123 — 202-401-3030
This office provides materials to schools and communities in developing a comprehensive program to prevent the use of alcohol and other drugs. Revised recently to include statistics and information on alcohol, tobacco, and steroids.

Steroids Mean Trouble (AVD16). A poster which shows a football player with facts about steroids.

Anabolic Steroids: A Threat to Body and Mind (PHD561) Reports on steroid abuse in the United States, most users being under age 18

Anabolic Steroid Abuse. NIDA Research Monograph 102 (M102) is a 248 page publication which discusses the abuse of steroids, as well as the history and development of this drug.

* TeamSpirit

Pacific Institute for Research and Evaluation
7315 Wisconsin Ave., Number 900 East
Bethesda, MD 20814
TeamSpirit is designed to empower high school youth to take an active role in preventing drug and alcohol use and impaired driving by their peers. It is based on the belief that youth can become a potent force in combating substance abuse among their peers. The TeamSpirit model consists of two phases: a residential leadership training conference at which youth develop action plans for local program activities, and the delivery of extensive technical assistance and support services to nurture individual school and community team activities. This program is sponsored by the Office of Juvenile Justice and Delinquency Prevention of the U.S. Department of Justice 202-307-5914.

* Toll-free Hotlines
Here are some of the primary hotlines:

* Child Help - National Child Abuse Hotline — 800-422-4453
A recorded phone system directs you to the pertinent area of information that you desire. Information can be received. A list of booklets, pamphlets, etc. are read through the system. The price and address is given for you to mail the information.

* Cocaine Helpline — 800-944-4860

* Humanistic Foundation — 800-999-4572
800-944-4860
This is a national 24 hour service which provides a recorded phone system to help you with various psychological problems. The menu includes depression, anxiety, AIDS, drug and chemical dependence. There is also health care information. Referrals to other agencies and services are given as they apply to your problem.

* Just Say No Foundation — 800-258-2766
A person will answer the phone if you call Monday through Friday between 7AM-5PM Pacific time. He or she will answer your questions and send you free information.

* CDC National AIDS Clearinghouse — 800-458-5231
This is a national service which operates Monday through Friday from 9AM-7PM. During these hours you can get information sent to you from the phone system or speak to a counselor. During off hours you can receive information only. It also speaks in Spanish.

* CDC National AIDS Hotline — 800-342-2437
This service is available 24 hours a day, 7 days a week. A person will answer the phone and answer questions about AIDS, give counseling, refer you to a support group, or help you in whatever way is possible.

* MADD - Mothers Against Drunk Driving — 800-438-6233
This is the national headquarters in Texas. Most states have their own 800 number and offices. They are there Monday through Friday from 8:30-5:00 Central time. On off hours there is an answering service. Some great pamphlets you can receive free are *One Drink Can Be Too Many* and *Every Drop Counts* which both explain how just one alcoholic drink can affect your driving ability and increase your risk of being in a car crash. Other booklets will tell you exactly what MADD is, programs in your area, statistics, and legislative goals. This is a reliable service available by phone.

* National Council of Child Abuse and Family Violence — 800-222-2000
This Monday-Friday, 8AM-5PM Pacific time service will answer your questions concerning referrals, services, etc. by phone or mail. On off days there is a recording telling you the days and hours to reach them. You can receive information by mail or phone on child abuse, family violence, and child sexual abuse. Printed information gives you current support programs and prevention/treatment programs.

* National Institute on Drug Abuse — 800-662-HELP
This service operates Monday through Friday, 9AM-3AM, and weekends, 12PM-3AM. You will be referred to appropriate agencies and sources in your area. They

Be patient. If any phone number is incorrect, call (area code) 555-1212 and request the new listing.

will direct you to information in your area and give you numbers to call. There is often a long wait to speak with someone.

* National Runaway Switchboard and Suicide Hotline   800-621-4000
                                        Hearing Impaired-TDD 800-621-0394
This national hotline is open 24 hours per day, 365 days a year. The services it can provide are crisis intervention, referrals and youth advocacy. A pamphlet is available which explains the service and gives advice for parents of runaways.

* National Sexually Transmitted Disease Hotline   800-227-8922
This service operates Monday through Friday, 8AM-11PM Eastern time. During off hours a recording will tell you the hours to call back. If you call during their hours of operation, a person will answer information on the phone, provide counseling and give you referrals. They will send you free information on specific diseases.

* Parents Anonymous National Office   800-421-0353
This non-profit service operates Monday through Friday, 8AM-4:30PM Pacific time. You will receive referrals to services in your state. During off hours you are directed to free support groups in the LA area.

* National Council on Alcoholism and Drug Dependence   800-322-2255
This recording operates Monday through Friday, 24 hours per day. You give it your zip code and receive local offices. You can also give it your name and number to get free information. The recording reassures you that your call is kept confidential.

* TARGET National Resource Bank   800-366-6667
This national service is located in Kansas City, Missouri. During off hours you can leave a message or call 800-999-9999 which is an emergency service. During their hours of operation, you can receive information on drugs. You can also receive a catalog with different sources on information on alcohol, tobacco, and other drugs.

* Emergency Service Hotline   800-999-9999
This is a 24 hour per day, Monday through Friday emergency service. It is available for runaways, pregnant women who need help, and those who need help with drug and/or alcohol related problems in an emergency situation.

* Workplace and Drug and Alcohol Use
National Clearinghouse for Alcohol and Drug Information
P.O. Box 2345
Rockville, MD 20852   800-729-6686
The Clearinghouse has several free publications and videos dealing with drugs and the workplace. Some of the titles include:

AIDS/HIV Infection and the Workplace: NIDA Workgroup Report
Assessment of Laboratory Quality in Urine Drug Testing.
Comprehensive Procedures for Drug Testing in the Workplace.
Drug Abuse Curriculum for Employee Assistance Program Professionals.
Drug Abuse in the Workplace Videotape Series.
Drug-Free Federal Workplace: Executive Order 12564 of September 15, 1988.
Drug-Free Workplace Requirements; Notice and Interim Final Rules.
Drugs in the Workplace, Research and Evaluation Data.
The Fact is...Employee Assistance Contacts Are Available in Every State.
An Employer's Guide to Dealing with Substance Abuse.
Listing of Drug Testing Laboratories Certified by the U.S. Department of Health and Human Services
Mandatory Guidelines for Federal Drug Testing.
Mandatory Guidelines for Federal Workplace Drug Testing Programs; Final Guidelines.
Model Plan for a Comprehensive Drug-Free Workplace Program.
NIDA Capsule: Resources to Address Drugs in the Workplace.
NIDA's Drug-Free Workplace Helpline.
Public Law 100-690. Subtitle D-Drug-Free Workplace Act of 1988.
Drug-Free Workplace Act.
Research on Drugs and the Workplace.
Technical, Scientific, and Procedural Issues of Employee Drug Testing.
What Works: Workplaces Without Drugs.
Workers at Risk: Drugs and Alcohol on the Job.

Education and Prevention

* Academic Institutions and Educational Resources

National Clearinghouse for Alcohol and Drug Information
Office for Substance and Alcohol Prevention (OSAP)
P.O. Box 2345
Rockville, MD 20847   301-468-2600

Single copies of publications are sent free of charge and a publications catalog is available. Examples include the *Directory of Academic Institutions and Organizations: Drug, Alcohol, and Employee Assistance Program Educational Resources,* which include educational opportunities on subjects relevant to employee assistance, covering academic institutions, national organizations, and State alcohol and drug abuse agencies.

* ACTION Drug Abuse Prevention Nationwide

ACTION
Drug Alliance Office
1100 Vermont Avenue NW   800-424-8867
Washington, DC 20525   202-606-4902

ACTION sponsors educational prevention programs in the community geared to youth drug abuse prevention. The Regional Offices are:

Region I
10 Causeway Street, Room #473, Boston, MA 02222; 617-565-7000. Services Connecticut, Maine, Massachusetts, New Hampshire, Vermont and Rhode Island.

Region II
6 World Trade Center, Room 758, New York, NY 10048-0206; 212-466-3858. Services New Jersey, New York, Puerto Rico and the Virgin Islands.

Region III
U.S. Customs House, 2nd and Chestnut Sts., Room 108, Philadelphia, PA 19106-2912; 215-597-3495. Services Kentucky, Maryland, Delaware, Ohio, Pennsylvania, Virginia, West Virginia and Washington, DC.

Region IV
101 Marietta St., NW, Suite 1003, Atlanta, GA 30323-2301; 404-331-2058. Services Alabama, Florida, Georgia, Mississippi, North Carolina, South Carolina and Tennessee.

Region V
175 West Jackson Blvd., Suite 1207, Chicago, IL 60604-3964; 312-353-5107. Services Illinois, Indiana, Iowa, Michigan, Minnesota and Wisconsin.

Region VI
1100 Commerce, Room 6B11, Dallas, TX 75242-9494; 214-767-9494. Services Arkansas, Kansas, Louisiana, Missouri, New Mexico, Oklahoma and Texas

Region VIII (There is no Region VII)
Executive Tower Bldg., Suite 2930, 1405 Curtis St., Denver, CO 80202; 303-844-2671. Services Colorado, Wyoming, Montana, Nebraska, North Dakota, South Dakota and Utah.

Region IX
211 Main St., Room 530, San Francisco, CA 94105-1914; 415-744-3016. Services Arizona, California, Hawaii, Nevada.

Region X
915 Second Avenue, Suite 3190 Federal Office Building, Seattle, WA 98174-1103; 206-553-4975. Services Alaska, Idaho, Oregon and Washington.

* Adolescent Peer Pressure and Prevention Study

National Clearinghouse for Alcohol and Drug Information
P.O. Box 2345   800-729-6686
Rockville, MD 20852   301-468-2600

The Clearinghouse has several free publications, posters, and videos dealing with teenagers and drug use. Some of the titles include:

The Adolescent Assessment/Referral System Manual.
Preventing Adolescent Drug Use: From Theory to Practice.
Prevention Resource Guide: Secondary School Students.
Facts About Teenagers and Drug Abuse.
High School Senior Drug Use: 1975-1990.
News Release: High School Senior Drug Use, 1990.
Steroids Mean Trouble (poster).
Alcohol and Youth: Fact Sheet.
Treatment for Adolescent Substance Abusers.
Adolescent Drug Abuse: Analyses of Treatment Research - NIDA Research Monograph.
Quick List: 10 Steps to Help Your Child Say No (PH230) is a poster that parents can use to help their child stay away from drugs.
Too Many Young People Drink and Know Too Little About the Consequences (PH305) provides answers to questions such as why teenagers drink, and why young drinkers turn to drugs; as well as up to date statistics about teenagers and drugs.

* After-School High Risk Youth

Federal Bureau of Investigation (FBI)
9th St. and Pennsylvania Ave., NW
Washington, DC 20535   202-324-2080

High Risk Youth Program is an FBI effort to establish an after school drug abuse prevention program in conjunction with the Office of Juvenile Justice and Delinquency Prevention (OJJDP), and the Boys and Girls Clubs of America. This program targets high risk youth in the area of drug prevention and education. The program goal is to channel the energies of youth into positive activities which will prepare them to live a drug free life. Activities will be developed which teach or reinforce youth life skills (self esteem, decision making, etc.), drug education, and drug refusal skills. This information will also be incorporated into existing programs, such as vocational training. Information on the High Risk Youth Program can be obtained from your local chapter of Boys and Girls Clubs of America.

* AIDS and IV Drug Users Educational Materials

Office of Substance Abuse Prevention (OSAP)
National Institute on Alcohol Abuse and Alcoholism
5600 Fishers Lane
Rockville, MD 20857   301-443-3860

OSAP, in cooperation with the Centers for Disease Control, develops educational materials to reduce the risks of AIDS among IV drug users. Publications to call and request are: *Psychological, Neurological, and Substance Aspects of AIDS* (OMOO-4044) and *When Someone Close Has AIDS: Acquired Immunodeficiency Syndrome* (ADM89-1515).

* Alcohol Abuse, Prevention and Education

National Clearinghouse for Alcohol Information
P.O. Box 2345   800-729-6686
Rockville, MD 20847   301-468-2600

The National Clearinghouse for Alcohol and Drug Information (NCADI) is a centralized source for information about the causes and treatment of alcoholism and other drug addiction. They have the latest research results, articles, videos and other print materials. A sampling of free fact sheets available includes: *Alcohol and Safety* (No. MS 311), *Legal Drinking Age Summary 1986* (No. MS308); *Treatment for Alcohol Problems: How to Find Help* (No. MS 299); *Sex-Related Alcohol Effects* (No. MS 247); *Prevention of Alcohol Problems* (No. MS 305). For a $15 annual handling fee, the bimonthly bulletin, *Prevention Pipeline,* can be sent to keep you informed of the latest research, programs, or events. NCADI offers technical support to organizations through use of resource lists, direct mail and materials, as well as outreach to groups.

* Americans For a Drug Free America

Federal Bureau of Investigation (FBI)
9th St. and Pennsylvania Ave., NW

Washington, DC 20536   202-324-3000

This booklet is available through the Federal Bureau of Investigation (FBI). It discusses the widespread drug abuse in our country. It explains different kinds of drugs, as well as the problems that are the result of them, such as suicide, child abuse, and other violence.

* Anti-Drug Effort in Workplace

Occupational Safety and Health Administration (OSHA)
200 Constitution Ave., NW
Washington, DC 20210   202-523-7162

The Occupational Safety and Health Administration (OSHA) aids the anti-drug effort by ensuring safe and healthful working conditions in the Nation's 4.5 million workplaces.

* Audiovisuals Videotapes Center

Drug Planning and Outreach Staff
Office of Elementary and Secondary Education
400 Maryland Ave., SW
Washington, DC 20202-6123   202-401-3030

During 1987, awards were made to develop and distribute audiovisual materials to elementary and secondary schools for drug abuse education and prevention activities. These materials are close-captioned videotapes with brief teacher guides. Copies of the tapes have been sent to all the Nation's school districts and are also available from the National Clearinghouse for Alcohol and Drug Information (301-468-2600), the National Audio-Visual Center (301-763-1896), and from each of the Regional Centers (Eileen Nicosia, 202-732-2311).

* Close-Captioned Hearing Impaired Videos

Office of Public Affairs
U.S. Department of Education
400 Maryland Ave., SW
Washington, DC 20202   202-401-3030

Eight productions, close-captioned for the hearing impaired, have been designed to inform students, attending kindergarten through 12th grade, about the dangers of drug use in an engaging and entertaining manner. Contact this office for further information on borrowing or purchasing these videos. Will send information upon request.

* College and University Drug-Free Network

Vonnie Clement
Office of Educational Research and Improvement (OERI)
555 NJ Ave., Room 5026
Washington, DC 20208-5644   202-401-3030

The Office of Educational Research and Improvement (OERI) continues to support development of a national network of colleges committed to eliminating drug and alcohol abuse on their campuses. Initial networking efforts focused on four year residential colleges so that information on comparable problems could be shared; however, the focus has expanded to address the concerns of the two-year degree student and the commuter population. Over 1300 colleges and universities have joined the Network. They have the following publications: *Network Directory*; a collection of presentations titled *Approaches to Drug Abuse Prevention at Colleges and Universities*; *Network Update* newsletter; *What Works: Schools Without Drugs*; *A Guide for College Presidents and Governing Boards*; and *Success Stories From Drug-Free Schools*.

* College Students and Drug Use

National Clearinghouse for Alcohol and Drug Information
P.O. Box 2345
Rockville, MD 20852   800-729-6686

The National Clearinghouse for Alcohol and Drug Information has several free publications, dealing with alcohol and drug use and college students. Some of the titles include:

Alcohol Practices, Policies, and Potentials of American Colleges and Universities: A White Paper.
Strategies for Preventing Alcohol and Other Drug Problems on College Campuses: Faculty Members' Handbook.
Strategies for Preventing Alcohol and Other Drug Problems on College Campuses: Program Administrators' Handbook.
Prevention Resource Guide: College Youth.

* Community Involvement with Workplace Drug Abuse Video

National Audiovisual Center
Customer Service Section
8700 Edgeworth Drive
Capitol Heights, MD 20743-3701   301-763-1896

National Clearinghouse for Alcohol and Drug Information
P.O. Box 2345   800-729-6686
Rockville, MD 20847   301-468-8200

Finding Solutions portrays drug abuse in the workplace as a community-wide problem; thus the solutions offered through education and prevention are presented as personal, workplace, and community responsibilities. Specific emphasis is placed on the need to effectively deliver accurate and credible information to the workforce, to promote workplace peer involvement and build community partnerships. It is available for sale and rental.

* Community Prevention and Education Grants

ACTION
Drug Alliance Office
1100 Vermont Ave., NW   800-424-8867
Washington, DC 20525   202-606-4920

ACTION supports community-based prevention and education efforts with grants, contracts, conferences, and technical assistance. Nonprofit organizations and state and local governments are eligible to receive grants from ACTION. An announcement is made in the Federal Register regarding the type of activities that the ACTION grant is available for and organizations are encouraged to apply. ACTION also maintains a mailing list which sends copies of the notices appearing in the *Federal Register* directly to those on the list. To get the name of your organization on this list, call the number above.

* Don't Drink Posters

National Clearinghouse for Alcohol and Drug Information
P.O. Box 2345   800-729-6686
Rockville, MD 20847   301-468-2600

Single copies of these posters are free from the National Clearinghouse for Alcohol and Drug Information:

The Herschel Walker Poster. (AVD45)
An Inner Voice Tells You Not to Drink or Use Other Drugs (AV161)
The Typical Alcoholic American (AV195)

* Drug Abuse Curricula

National Clearinghouse for Alcohol and Drug Information
P.O. Box 2345
Rockville, MD 20852   800-729-6686

The Office of Educational Research and Improvement of the U.S. Department of Education has developed several publications dealing with substance abuse curriculum. *Learning to Live Drug Free: A Curriculum Model for Prevention* provides a framework for classroom-based prevention efforts in kindergarten through grade 12. The model includes lessons, activities, background for teachers and suggestions for involving parents and the community in drug prevention. *Drug Abuse Curricula Criteria* is a guide to help schools and school district staff select and implement substance abuse curricula in elementary and secondary schools. Other publications developed by NCADI include *The National Commission on Drug-Free Schools: Final Report* which outlines goals for achieving drug-free schools by the year 2000. *Performance Edge Kit* is for teenagers and focuses on the effects smoking and drinking have on physical performance (includes video, magazine, poster and guide for coaches and teachers). *Teaching About Substance Abuse: A Resource Manual for Faculty Development* includes materials, information and resources to assist faculty members to learn more about alcohol and other drug abuse. Other publications include:

The Fact is...The Use of Steroids in Sports Can Be Dangerous.
The Fact Is...You Can Prevent Alcohol and Other Drug Problems Among Elementary School Children.
The Fact Is...You Can Prevent Alcohol and Other Drug Use Among Secondary High School Students.
The Fact Is...You can Start a Student Assistance Program.
What Works: Schools Without Drugs.

Be patient. If any phone number is incorrect, call (area code) 555-1212 and request the new listing.

585

Drugs and Chemical Dependence

* Drug Abuse Publications and Coloring Books

Office of Public Affairs
Drug Enforcement Administration
U.S. Department of Justice
1405 I Street, NW
Washington, DC 20537   202-307-7977

Soozie and Katy is a coloring and activity book for youngsters that describes the appropriate use of legal drugs and the dangers accompanying misuse of medicines. Other free publications include:

Drugs of Abuse - a reference for a consensus of current scientific findings.
Time to Focus On The User.
Anabolic Steroids and You.
DEA's Demand Reduction Program.
No Magic Bullet: A Look at Drug Legalization.
Pumping Trouble; The Problem of Steroid Use.
Guidelines for a Drug Free Workplace.
Drug Abuse Prevention for Explorers: A Guidebook.
Healthy Bodies Don't Need Drugs!
Coca Cultivation and Cocaine Processing: An Overview.

* Drug Abuse Posters

National Clearinghouse for Alcohol and Drug Information
P.O. Box 2345   800-729-6686
Rockville, MD 20847   301-468-2600

The clearinghouse has the following free posters dealing with drug abuse as well as AIDS and drugs:

AIDS. Another Way Drugs Can Kill
Drug Busters. Don't Let Drugs Win
Get Your Kids Addicted to Something That Costs Just 35 Cents an Ounce - (books)
Get Your Kids Hooked on Something Before Someone Else Does
Guess Who Else Can Get AIDS If you Shoot Drugs/ Your Baby Can
Guia Practica: 10 pasos que ayudan a sus hijos a decir "No"
The Herschel Walker Poster
If You Ever Shot Drugs, Get Tested Before you Get Pregnant
An Inner Voice Tells You Not to Drink or Use Other Drugs Poster
The Jets poster
Live the Dream, Say No To Alcohol and Drug Abuse Poster
A Man Who Shoots Up Can Be Very Giving. He Can Give You and Your Baby AIDS
McGruff: Say 'No' to Crack and Other Drugs
Most Babies with AIDS Are Born to Mothers of Fathers Who Have Shot Drugs
Performance Edge Poster
Quick List: Ten Steps to Help Your Child Say "No"
Steroids Mean Trouble Poster
Stopping Teenage Drug Abuse Will Take Two Generations
Studies Prove Children Can't Smoke Pot While Swimming Underwater
When You Share Needles You Could Be Shooting Up AIDS Poster

* Drug Abuse Resistance Education Project

Federal Bureau of Investigation
9th St. and Pennsylvania Ave., NW
Washington, DC 20535   202-324-2080

Drug Abuse Resistance Education (DARE) targets children before they are likely to experiment with drugs, alcohol, and tobacco. This approach attempts to prevent drug use and to reduce drug trafficking by eliminating the demand for drugs. Veteran uniformed law enforcement officers are trained to teach a structured curriculum in school classrooms, an effort that also enhances the image of police officers within the community.

* Drug and Substance Abuse Prevention

National Clearinghouse for Alcohol and Drug Information
P.O. Box 2345   800-729-6686
Rockville, MD 20847   301-468-2600

The office, created by the Anti-Drug Abuse Act, promotes and distributes prevention materials (posters, kits, resource lists) throughout the country. It develops materials and distributes information from its database on prevention, intervention, and treatment for a wide variety of audiences. OSAP supports community-based prevention programs through grant programs and on-site consultation, as well as the National Clearinghouse for Alcohol and Drug Information.

* Drug Alliance Coalitions and Networks Grants

ACTION
Drug Alliance Office
1100 Vermont Ave., NW   800-424-8867
Washington, DC 20525   202-606-4902

ACTION awards grants to develop coalitions and partnerships working together to prevent and combat chemical dependence at the community level.

* Drug Experts International Speakers Bureau

U.S. Information Agency (USIA)
301 Fourth St., SW
Washington, DC 20547   202-619-4700

USIA provides public affairs support through its posts in U.S. embassies in countries where illicit drug production and/or trafficking has been identified as a priority issue. USIA selects key people in the international drug field for professional exchange programs in the U.S.; and schedules seminars, conferences, and other activities for U.S. specialists in drug-related fields before selected audiences in key countries.

* Drug-Free School Recognition Program

James Better
Office of Educational Research and Improvement
U.S. Department of Education
555 NJ Ave.
Washington, DC 20208   202-708-5366

Under the Drug-Free School Recognition Program, applications from nominated schools are reviewed by experts in the area of drug and alcohol prevention. The schools or programs selected for recognition are honored at ceremonies in Washington, DC.

* Drug-Free Schools and Communities Coordination

Office of Substance Abuse Prevention (OSAP)
National Institute on Alcohol Abuse and Alcoholism
5600 Fishers Lane
Rockville, MD 20857   301-443-3860

OSAP conducts training, technical assistance, data collection, and evaluation activities of programs supported under the Drug Free Schools and Communities Act of 1986. It also supports the development of model, innovative, community-based programs to discourage alcohol and drug abuse among young people.

* Drug-Free Schools Manual

Information Office
U.S. Department of Education
555 New Jersey Avenue, NW   800-624-0100
Washington, DC 20208   202-659-4854

Schools Without Drugs suggests ways that students, parents, schools and communities can fight drugs and describes working programs. This free 87-page booklet also discusses legal issues faced by educational institutions. It also explains how different drugs are used, what they look like and the physical side effects that a user experiences.

* Drug-Free Workplace Helpline

National Information on Drug Abuse (NIDA)   800-843-4971
        301-443-6780 (in MD)

The Workplace Helpline answers questions and provides technical assistance to business, industry, and unions about developing and implementing comprehensive drug-free workplace programs. Corporate executive officers, managers, and union representatives are encouraged to call for assistance. The Helpline provides telephone consultation, resource referrals, networking services, and publications to assist in planning, policy development, and program implementation. They have a four-part videotape series for loan on drugs in the workplace. The hotline operates from 9 am to 8 pm EST (Monday-Friday).

* Drug Information for Community Groups

ACTION
1100 Vermont Ave., NW   800-424-8867
Washington, DC 20525   202-606-4902

Some of the publications currently available include: *Meeting the Challenge*, a guide for service clubs; *Take Action Against Drug Abuse: How To Start A Volunteer Anti-Drug Program in Your Community*; *Just Say No Guide for Older American Volunteers.*

* Drugs At Work Videotapes

Employee and Employer Versions
National Audiovisual Center
Customer Service Section
8700 Edgeworth Drive
Capitol Heights, MD 20743-3701   301-763-1896

National Clearinghouse for Alcohol and Drug Information
P.O. Box 2345   800-729-6686
Rockville, MD 20852   301-468-2600

"Drugs at Work" is a 23 minute educational documentary which describes costs of drug use for the workplace, the individual, and the public; and examines action being taken by government and private companies. Interviews with drug users who have sought treatment and with experts on drugs in the workplace are included; and government and industry representatives describe federal and corporate programs currently underway. This video is available in both employer and employee versions. It is available for sale and rental.

* Drugs: Fact Sheets

National Clearinghouse for Alcohol and Drug Information
P.O. Box 2345   800-729-6686
Rockville, MD 20852   301-468-2600

The clearinghouse offers a series of fact sheets giving basic information about the psychological and physiological effects of various drugs. Single copies of these booklets are available free; many are printed in Spanish:

Alcohol Alert #7, Alcohol Use and Abuse: Where Do the Numbers Come From?
   (PH278)
Drug Abuse Statistics, 1990 Population Estimates (CAP22)

* Drunk Driving Films and Videotapes

National Audiovisual Center
8700 Edgeworth Drive
Capitol Heights, MD 20743-3701   301-763-1896

The National Audiovisual Center sells several videotapes: "Under The Influence" and "Until I Get Caught." "Spirits of America," available for rent and sale, deals with issues, attitudes and standards of American drinking patterns and the historical and cultural aspects associated with them.

* Effective School Programs Newsletter

Drug Planning and Outreach Staff
Office of Elementary and Secondary Education
400 Maryland Ave. SW
Washington, DC 20202-6123   202-401-3030

Challenge Newsletter: bi-monthly, highlights successful programs, provides the latest research on effective prevention measures, and answers questions about school-based efforts. The newsletter is distributed to superintendents, principals, and parent groups across the country. Contact Charlotte Gillespie, 202-401-3030.

* Elementary School Drug Prevention Videos

National Audiovisual Center
8700 Edgeworth Drive
Capitol Heights, MD 20743   800-638-1300

The following drug prevention videos are available for loan through one of the above Regional Centers or the National Clearinghouse:

The Drug Avengers. Ten 5-minute animated adventures that urge caution about ingesting unfamiliar substances; encourages students to trust their instincts when they think something is wrong; and show that drugs make things worse, not better. Grades 1-6.

Fast Forward Future. A magical device allows youngsters to peer into the future and see on a TV screen what will happen if they use drugs and what will happen if they remain drug free. Grades 1-6.

Straight Up. A fantasy adventure that features information on the effects of drugs, developing refusal skills, building self-esteem, and resisting peer pressure. Grades 4-6.

Additional videos to purchase for Drug Abuse Prevention:
Straight At Ya'. Kirk Cameron talks with students about peer pressure and drugs. Grades 7-9.

Lookin' Good. Shows kids how to build a peer support group to resist drugs. Grades 7-9.

Downfall: Sports and Drugs. Shows athletes who took drugs, mainly steroids, and how their careers suffered. Grades 7-12.

Hard Facts. Three stories about drugs in high school. Grades 10-12.

Private Victories. Four stories on how drugs affect different aspects of a person's life. Grades 10-12.

* Elementary School Education Resources

National Clearinghouse for Alcohol and Drug Information
P.O. Box 2345   800-729-6686
Rockville, MD 20852   301-468-2600

Learning to Live Drug Free: A Curriculum Model for Prevention (BKD51) and *Performance Edge Kit* (PEO1-4) are teaching aids for kindergarten through grade 12.

* Employee Assistance Programs Videotape

National Audiovisual Center
Customer Service Section
8700 Edgeworth Drive
Capitol Heights, MD 20743-3701   301-763-1896

National Clearinghouse for Alcohol and Drug Information
P.O. Box 2345   800-729-6686
Rockville, MD 20852   301-468-8200

Getting Help presents detailed information about the use of Employee Assistance Programs (EAPs) in addressing drug use in the workplace. The film describes the value of EAPs to employees and employers through comments by business, labor, and government leaders, and EAP professionals; presentation of three model programs; and EAP client interviews. It encourages employers to consider EAPs as a tool in combatting drugs at work, and provides employees with reassuring information about the confidentiality and effectiveness of an EAP program. This video is available in both employer and employee versions. It is available for sale and rental.

* Ethnic Minorities and Alcoholism and Drug Prevention

National Clearinghouse on Alcohol Information
P.O. Box 2345   800-729-6686
Rockville, MD 20852   301-468-2600

Substance Abuse Among Blacks in the U.S. (CAP34)
Substance Abuse Among Hispanic Americans. (CAP30)
Minority Substance Abuse Prevention Project: Ad Hoc Task Force General Recommendations (RPO705)

The Clearinghouse catalog has other sources about this subject.

* FBI Substance Abuse Prevention Education

Federal Bureau of Investigation (FBI)
9th St. and Pennsylvania Ave., NW
Washington, DC 20535   202-324-2080

Each FBI field office has a Special Agent Drug Demand Reduction Coordinator who provides substance abuse prevention education to youth between the ages of 5 and 18 years. The FBI Coordinator gets involved in existing drug prevention initiatives in schools and may also assist in implementing new programs. The Research/Drug Demand Reduction Unit has the following free publications available:

Americans for a Drug-Free America.
Children and Drugs: What Can A Parent Do?
Captain America Goes to War Against Drugs (Marvel Comics).
Archie and His Pals In..The Peer Helping Program!
Drugs In The Workplace.

* Federal Employees Drug-Free Workplace Effort

Office of Personnel Management
1900 E St., NW
Washington, DC 20415   202-606-2424

The Office of Personnel Management (OPM) administers a merit system for Federal employment that includes recruiting, examining, training and promoting people on the basis of their knowledge and skills. The Office's role is to ensure that the Federal Government provides an array of personnel services to applicants and employees.

Drugs and Chemical Dependence

This office, with the U.S. Department of Health and Human Services, has developed drug-free workplace plans for Federal agencies.

* Handbooks: Schools Without Drugs

Drug Planning and Outreach Staff
Office of Elementary and Secondary Education
400 Maryland Ave., SW
Washington, DC 20202-6123   202-401-3030

This office provides materials to schools and communities in developing a comprehensive program to prevent the use of alcohol and other drugs. Revised recently to include statistics and information on alcohol, tobacco, and steroids. *Growing Up Drug Free: A Parent's Guide to Prevention*, a handbook for parents to help families take an active role in drug prevention before a problem occurs. Copies are available free of charge. Call 800-624-0100 or in the Washington metropolitan area call 202-401-3030. Books also can be ordered from the National Clearinghouse for Alcohol and Drug Information.

* Hawaiian Natives Education Program Grants

Drug Planning and Outreach Staff
Office of Elementary and Secondary Education
400 Maryland Ave., SW
Washington, DC 20202-6123   202-401-3030

Organizations, primarily those that serve and represent Hawaiian natives, can receive funds for drug prevention and education activities. Contact Allen King, 202-401-1599.

* High School Drug Prevention Videos

National Audiovisual Center
8700 Edgeworth Drive
Capitol Heights, MD 20743   800-638-1300

Hard Facts About Alcohol, Marijuana, and Crack. Offers factual information about the dangers of drug use in a series of dramatic vignettes.

Speak Up, Speak Out: Learning to Say No to Drugs. Gives students specific techniques they can use to resist peer pressure and say no to drug use.

Dare to be Different. Uses the friendship of two athletes in their last year of high school to illustrate the importance of goals and values in resisting pressures to use drugs.

Downfall: Sports and Drugs. Shows how drugs affect athletic performance and examines the consequences of drug use, including steroid use, on every aspect of an athlete's life - career, family, friends, sense of accomplishment, and self-esteem.

Private Victories. Illustrates the effects of drug and alcohol use on students and the value of positive peer influences in resisting peer pressure to use drugs.

* High School Student Attitudes and Trends

National Clearinghouse for Alcohol
 and Drug Information
P.O. Box 2345
Rockville, MD 20852   301-468-2600

High School Senior Drug Use: 1975-1990 provides tables on the prevalence and incidence of drug use among students (free).

* Indian Elementary and Secondary School Children

Drug Planning and Outreach Staff
Office of Elementary and Secondary Education
400 Maryland Ave., SW
Washington, DC 20202-6123   202-401-3030

Programs for Indian Youth: Anti-alcohol and drug abuse education and prevention services will be provided to Indian children attending elementary and secondary schools on reservations which are operated by the Bureau of Indian Affairs. Contact Allen King, 202-401-1599.

* Indian Tribes and Tribal Schools Education

Bureau of Indian Affairs (BIA)
U.S. Department of Interior
Washington, DC 20240   202-208-3710

The BIA funds drug education and prevention efforts aimed at American Indian youth as well as tribes and tribal schools. The purpose of the program is to heighten awareness of problems of alcohol and drug abuse among American Indians and to make BIA-funded schools drug-free. BIA also administers a program for Indian children on reservations who attend elementary and secondary schools through a memorandum of agreement with the U.S. Department of Education.

* Junior High School Drug Prevention Videos

National Audiovisual Center
8700 Edgeworth Drive
Capitol Heights, MD 20743   800-638-1300

The following drug prevention videos are available for loan through one of the above Regional Centers or the National Clearinghouse:

Straight at Ya. Tips on peer pressure, saying no and building self-esteem.

Lookin' Good. A two-part series based on actual incidents that convey the dangers of drug use and promote the use of peer support groups.

* Law Enforcement Officials Speakers Bureau

Executive Office for United States Attorneys
U.S. Department of Justice
Tenth Street and Pennsylvania Avenue NW
Washington, DC 20530   202-514-2121

The Department of Justice drug education effort emphasizes the importance of citizen involvement and the participation of local business and industry, law enforcement officials and schools. Public service announcements, lectures, and speeches by US Attorneys on the drug issue and prevention, are common.

* On-the-Job Drug Testing Videos

National Audiovisual Center
Customer Service Section
8700 Edgeworth Drive
Capitol Heights, MD 20743-3701   301-763-1896

National Clearinghouse for Alcohol and Drug Information
P.O. Box 2345
Rockville, MD 20852   800-729-6686
                               301-468-8200

Drug Testing: Handle with Care describes the options available in designing a drug testing component as part of a comprehensive drug-free workplace program. Procedures addressing the needs of both the employer and the employee, to ensure the accuracy and reliability of test results, for specimen collection and laboratory analysis, and a discussion of the critical role of the Medical Review Officer (MRO) are highlighted. Case studies of public/private, unionized/nonunionized work environments with testing components are presented. This video is available in both employer and employee versions. It is available for sale and rental.

* Parent Group Grants

ACTION
Drug Alliance Office
1100 Vermont Ave., NW
Suite 8300   800-424-8867
Washington, DC 20525   202-606-4902

The Drug Alliance Grants from ACTION are intended to strengthen and expand the efforts of community-based volunteer groups working to prevent drug abuse. These grants support innovative volunteer projects including organization of parent groups.

* Parent Guides for Alcohol and Drug Information

National Clearinghouse for Alcohol and Drug Information
P.O. Box 2345
Rockville, MD 20852   800-729-6686

The clearinghouse has the following free publications available, dealing with drug and alcohol use:

Growing Up Drug Free: A Parent's Guide to Prevention.
Guia Practica: 10 pasos que ayudan a sus hijos a decir "No" (Quick List: 10 Steps to Helps Your Child Say "No").
Parent Training Is Prevention.
Pointers for Parents Card.
Quick List: 10 Steps to Help Your Child Say "No".
10 Steps to Help Your Child Say "No". A Parent's Guide.

* Positive Peer Prevention Youth Groups Funding

Drug Alliance Office
ACTION
1100 Vermont Ave., NW, Suite 8200   800-424-8867
Washington, DC 20525   202-606-4902

Drug Alliance Grants from ACTION have supported positive peer prevention activities for youth; the development of technical assistance materials; organization of youth groups.

* Postsecondary Education and Prevention Grants

Drug Planning and Outreach Staff
Office of Elementary and Secondary Education
400 Maryland Ave., SW
Washington, DC 20202-6123   202-401-3030

Grants for Institutions of Higher Education (IHEs): This program is divided between two groups. First, the Fund for the Improvement of Postsecondary Education has awarded 297 grants since fiscal year 1987 to institutions of higher education to develop and operate drug education and prevention programs. Second, the Drug-Free Schools and Communities Staff in the Office of Elementary and Secondary Education (OESE) has awarded 138 grants to support preservice or inservice personnel training or demonstration programs in drug and alcohol abuse education and prevention for use in elementary and secondary schools. Discretionary grant program.

* Prevention Programs That Work

National Clearinghouse for Alcohol and Drug Information
P.O. Box 2345   800-729-6686
Rockville, MD 20852   301-468-2600

Single copies are free: *How to Start and Run an Alcohol and Other Drug Information Center: A Guide* (BK169).

* Public Service Announcements Available

National Institute on Drug Abuse (NIDA)
5600 Fishers La.
Rockville, MD 20857   301-443-1124

Radio, print and television public service announcements are available through NIDA which focus on high school and college students on crack and cocaine and a specially designed message for family members of cocaine users. NIDA also offers two booklets *Cocaine/Crack. The Big Lie*, and *When Cocaine Affects Someone You Love*, designed for family members of cocaine users.

* RADAR: Alcohol and Drug Awareness Centers

National Clearinghouse for Alcohol and Drug Information (NCADI)
P.O. Box 2345   800-729-6686
Rockville, MD 20852   301-468-2600

NCADI works with and through Regional Alcohol and Drug Awareness Resource (RADAR) Network Centers located in almost every state. NCADI and the RADAR Network have become the national resource system for information on the latest research results, popular press and scholarly journal articles, videos, prevention curricula, print materials, and program descriptions. Most of the materials are provided free.

* Respect for Laws and Legal System Curricula

Office of Juvenile Justice and Delinquency Prevention (OJJDP)
U.S. Department of Justice
633 Indiana Ave., NW
Washington, DC 20531   202-307-0751

Law-Related Education (LRE) is a program of instruction designed to provide students with a conceptual as well as a practical understanding of the law and legal processes. Its goal is to equip students with knowledge of both their rights and responsibilities under the law and to foster law-abiding behavior and respect for law enforcement and the justice system. In addition, law student chapters of LRE in 10 states are initiating LRE substance abuse prevention programs in their areas. (TDTAD)

* Roles and Responsibilities for a Drug Free School and Community

National Commission on Drug Free Schools
U.S. Department of Education

400 Maryland Ave. SW
Washington, DC 20201-0110   202-401-1599

This is a large poster with different aspects of drug awareness and prevention. The chart shows how students, families, the media, businesses, etc. deal with drug problems and prevention.

* Satellite Broadcasting on Chemical Dependence

U.S. Information Agency (USIA)
301 Fourth St., SW
Washington, DC 20547   202-619-4700

The U.S. Information Agency (USIA) uses satellite broadcasting and the full range of its communications resources, including the Voice of America, a world-wide press service and television production, to carry its message to foreign audiences. It also supports local programs by acquiring and adapting U.S. materials on drug abuse prevention and control for overseas use.

* School and Community Grants

Drug Planning and Outreach Staff
Office of Elementary and Secondary Education
400 Maryland Ave., SW
Washington, DC 20202-6123   202-401-3030

State and Local Grants Program: This is a formula grant program which allocates funds to States based on school-age enrollment. Funds are to be used for anti-drug abuse efforts in schools and community-based organizations. Contact Allen King, 202-401-1599.

* Safe Schools Program

National Institute of Justice
633 Indiana Ave. NW, Room 805
Washington, DC 20531   202-514-6235

This program assists school administrators in developing and maintaining safe environments.

* Spanish Drug Abuse Information Hotline

For Spanish speaking callers: 800-66-AYUNDA

The National Drug Abuse Information and Treatment Hotline helps drug users find and use local treatment programs, and acquaints those affected by the drug use of a significant other with much needed support groups and/or services. Referrals are also made to local crisis or information hotlines and support groups. Many pamphlets and brochures on a variety of drug topics are available. The hotline is in service 9 am to 3 am EST (Monday-Friday) and 12 pm to 3 am EST (Saturday-Sunday).

* Substance Abuse Counselors and Health Professionals

Office of Substance Abuse Prevention (OSAP)
National Institute on Alcohol Abuse and Alcoholism
5600 Fishers Lane
Rockville, MD 20857   301-443-0365

OSAP supports clinical training programs for substance abuse counselors and other health professionals involved in drug abuse education, prevention, and intervention.

* TARGET: Health Lifestyles for High School Students

National Federation of State High School Associations
P.O. Box 20626   800-366-6667
Kansas City, MO 64195   816-464-5400

The TARGET service is designed to cultivate healthy lifestyles among America's youth. The program offers workshops, training seminars, and an information bank on chemical use and prevention. It has a computerized referral service for substance abuse literature and prevention programs. A catalog is available with pamphlets, posters, videos, and course guides for teachers about steroids, crack, and alcohol as well as tobacco. Other information includes monthly newsletters and other publications.

* Teenagers and Alcoholism

National Clearinghouse for Alcohol and Drug Information
P.O. Box 2345
Rockville, MD 20847   301-468-2600

This clearinghouse provides many materials geared to adolescents including:

Drugs and Chemical Dependence

Too Many Young People Drink and Know Too Little About the Consequences (PH305) answers questions about frequency among teen drinking
Prevention Resource Guide: Impaired Driving (MS434) is a 20 page booklet that gives information about the effects of impaired driving
Safer Streets Ahead (PH292) discusses drinking and driving.

* Teachers, Counselors and Educational Personnel Training

Drug Planning and Outreach Staff
Office of Elementary and Secondary Education
400 Maryland Ave., SW
Washington, DC 20202-6123   202-401-3030

Educational Personnel Training Program is a discretionary grant program designed to provide financial assistance to State educational agencies, local educational agencies, and institutions of higher education for programs and activities used to train teachers, administrators, guidance counselors, and other educational personnel on drug and alcohol abuse education and prevention. Contact Allen King, 202-401-1599.

* U.S. Department of Education Regional Centers

Drug Planning and Outreach Staff
Office of Elementary and Secondary Education
400 Maryland Ave., SW
Washington, DC 20202-6123   202-401-3030

Regional Centers are authorized to: 1) train school teams to assess and combat drug and alcohol abuse problems, 2) assist State educational agencies in coordinating and strengthening alcohol and drug abuse education and prevention programs, 3) assist local educational agencies and institutions of higher education in developing training programs for educational personnel, and 4) evaluate and disseminate information on effective substance abuse, education prevention programs and strategies.

Northeast
12 Overton Ave., Sayville, NY 11782-0403; 516-589-7022. Serving: Connecticut, Delaware, Maine, Maryland, Massachusetts, New Hampshire, New Jersey, New York, Ohio, Pennsylvania, Rhode Island, and Vermont.

Midwest
1900 Spring Rd., Oak Brook, IL 60521; 708-571-4710. Serving: Indiana, Illinois, Iowa, Michigan, Minnesota, Missouri, Nebraska, North Dakota, South Dakota, and Wisconsin.

Southeast
Spencerian Office Plaza, University of Louisville, Louisville, KY 40292; 502-588-0052. Serving: Alabama, District of Columbia, Florida, Georgia, Kentucky, North Carolina, South Carolina, Tennessee, Virginia, West Virginia, Virgin Islands, and Puerto Rico.

Southwest
555 Constitution Ave., Norman, OK 73037; 405-325-1454, or 800-234-7972 (outside Oklahoma). Serving: Arizona, Arkansas, Colorado, Kansas, Louisiana, Mississippi, New Mexico, Oklahoma, Texas and Utah.

Western
101 SW Main St., Suite 500, Portland, OR 97204; 503-275-9480, or 800-547-6339 (outside Oregon). Serving: Alaska, California, Hawaii, Idaho, Montana, Nevada, Oregon, Washington, Wyoming, American Samoa, Guam, Northern Mariana Islands, and Republic of Palau.

* Women and Alcoholism

National Clearinghouse for Alcohol and Drug Information
P.O. Box 2345   800-729-6686
Rockville, MD 20852   301-468-2600

Information geared for women is available through the Clearinghouse. Some examples of their latest publications are:

Alcohol Alert #10- Alcohol and Women (PH290) examines physical and emotional side effects on women, as well as prevention and treatment.
Prevention Resource Guide: Women (MS433)
Prevention Resource Guide: Pregnant/Postpartum Women and Their Infants (MS420)
The Fact is...Education Can Help Prevent AIDS and Drug Abuse Among Women (MS395).

* Workplace Drug Awareness

American Council For Drug Education
204 Monroe St.
Rockville, MD 20850

A catalog is available with pamphlets and posters designed to give employers and employees information about drugs in the workplace.

* Workplace Initiatives Research Grants

Grants Management Office
National Institute on Drug Abuse (NIDA)
Room 10-25, 5600 Fishers Lane
Rockville, MD 20857   301-443-6480

NIDA supports research on the prevalence, impact, and treatment of drug abuse in the workplace through its research grant programs. Information on the grant application process can be obtained from Information and consultation on specific research topics can be obtained from the Office of Workplace Initiatives, NIDA, Room 10-A-53, 5600 Fishers Lane, Rockville, MD 20857.

* Young Athletes and Drug Prevention

Drug Enforcement Administration (DEA)
U.S. Department of Justice
700 Army Navy Dr.
Arlington, VA 22202   202-307-1000

Team Up for Drug Prevention With America's Young Athletes is a free booklet for coaches that includes information about alcohol and other drugs, reasons why athletes use drugs, suggested activities for coaches, a prevention program, a survey for athletes and coaches, and sample letters to parents.

Be patient. If any phone number is incorrect, call (area code) 555-1212 and request the new listing.

Treatment and Rehabilitation

* Alaskan Natives Prevention and Treatment Services

Indian Health Service
U.S. Department of Health and Human Services
5600 Fishers Lane
Rockville, MD 20857   301-443-1087

The Indian Health Service (IHS) coordinates agency resources and services for alcohol and drug abuse prevention, intervention, treatment and aftercare of American Indians as well as Alaska Natives with opportunity for maximum tribal involvement in developing and managing programs to meet their health needs.

* Drug and Alcohol Treatment for Disabled

Social Security Administration (SSA)   800-722-1213
6401 Security Blvd.   800-325-0778 for hearing impaired
Baltimore, MD 21235   301-965-7700

The SSA administers a national program of contributory social insurance, and provides extensive services for the disabled, including drug and alcohol treatment.

* Drug Abusers Treatment and Rehab Advocacy

National Institute on Drug Abuse (NIDA)
5600 Fishers Lane
Rockville, MD 20857   301-443-6480

NIDA encourages other Federal agencies, national, foreign, State and local organizations, hospitals and volunteer groups to enable them to facilitate and extend programs for the prevention of drug abuse, and for the care, treatment and rehabilitation of drug abusers.

* Drug and Alcohol Treatment Referrals

National Clearinghouse for Alcohol and Drug Information
Box 2345
Rockville, MD 20852   800-729-6686

The National Directory of Drug Abuse and Alcoholism Treatment and Prevention Programs is a free directory published by the National Institute on Alcohol Abuse and Alcoholism and the National Institute on Drug Abuse. It contains referral information about treatment and prevention programs (408 pp.).

* Drug Rehabilitation Services

Office For Children and Families (ACYF)
U.S. Department of Health and Human Services
200 Independence Ave., SW
Washington, DC 20201   202-205-8347

This office provides leadership and direction to human services programs for the elderly, children and youth, families, Native Americans, persons living in rural areas, and handicapped persons. ACYF administers rehabilitation services for these groups.

* Family-Based Approach and Adolescent Drug Treatment

National Clearinghouse for Alcohol and Drug Information
P.O. Box 2345   800-729-6686
Rockville, MD 20852   301-468-2600

Single copies of publications are sent free of charge and a publications catalog is available, including *Adolescent Drug Abuse: Analyses of Treatment Research*, which assesses the adolescent drug user and offers theories, techniques, and findings about treatment and prevention. It also discusses family-based approaches.

* Federal Employees with HIV/AIDS

Office of Personnel Management (OPM)
1900 E St., NW
Washington, DC 20415   202-606-2424

OPM has also developed guidelines for the Federal government in dealing with employees with HIV/AIDS.

* Local Drug Treatment Centers Incentives

Susan David or
Audrey Yowell
National Institute on Drug Abuse
5600 Fishers Lane, Room 10A-39
Rockville, MD 20857   301-443-1124

Overcoming Barriers to Drug Abuse Treatment in the Community is a flexible education model for use by communities which have funding and want to establish drug treatment facilities. This model is used in communities to educate people about drug treatment with the goal of countering resistance to the establishment of new treatment facilities. Materials are available to help local providers site facilities (How-to resource Manual and Media package), as well as materials to assist communities groups in educating the public (Resource manual and media materials). These materials are free. This Office can also provide technical assistance.

* Local Treatment Program Referrals

National Institute on Drug Abuse   800-662-HELP

This program provides drug related information to the general public, helps drug users find and use local treatment programs, and acquaints those affected by the drug use of a significant other with much needed support groups and/or services. Referrals are also made to local crisis or information hotlines and support groups, such as Cocaine Anonymous and Narcotics Anonymous. They provide many pamphlets and brochures on a variety of drug topics. The hotline is in service 9am to 3am EST (Monday-Friday) and 12pm to 3am EST (Sat.-Sun.).

* Methadone and Anti-Addiction Drugs

Food and Drug Administration (FDA)
5600 Fishers Lane
Rockville, MD 20857   301-295-8029

The Food and Drug Administration's (FDA) activities are directed toward protecting the health of the Nation against impure and unsafe foods, drugs, and cosmetics, and other potential hazards. The FDA directs educational efforts at the proper use of prescription and over-the-counter drugs. FDA is also responsible for the regulatory restrictions on the dispensing of drugs for treatment, including methadone to treat opiate addiction.

* Native Americans Intervention and Treatment

Bureau of Indian Affairs (BIA)
U.S. Department of Interior
Washington, DC 20240   202-208-3710

Through an agreement between Bureau of Indian Affairs (BIA) and the Indian Health Service, these organizations coordinate agency resources and services for alcohol and drug abuse prevention, intervention, treatment and aftercare of American Indians.

* Substance Abuse Treatment and Rehab

Health Care Financing Administration (HCFA)
200 Independence Ave., SW
Washington, DC 20201   202-690-6113

The financing of the national drug abuse treatment rehabilitation and prevention programs has been a joint effort of Federal and state government and the private sector. Medicare and medicaid will not pay for certain types of treatment for alcohol and/or drug dependency.

* Veterans Alcohol Dependent Treatment Programs

U.S. Department of Veterans Affairs
810 Vermont Ave., NW
Washington, DC 20420   202-233-4000

The Veteran's Administration offers treatment to veterans for alcohol and drug abuse. The Veteran's Administration currently operates 149 alcohol dependent treatment programs nationwide which provide diagnosis and treatment on both an inpatient and an outpatient basis.

Drugs and Chemical Dependence

* Veteran's Drug and Alcohol Treatment

U.S. Department of Veterans Affairs
810 Vermont Ave., NW
Washington, DC 20420   202-233-4000

The Veteran's Administration operates diverse programs to benefit veterans and members of their families. These benefits include education and rehabilitation, including drug or alcohol treatment. Call or write for booklet describing benefits available for veterans and their dependents.

* Veteran's Drug Abusers Halfway Houses and VA Hospitals

U.S. Department of Veterans Affairs
810 Vermont Ave., NW
Washington, DC 20420   202-233-4000

Additionally, the Veteran's Administration (VA) operates 52 specialized drug dependence programs which offer care and treatment for drug abusers in VA hospitals. They also have many contracts with half-way houses in local communities to place veterans with either alcohol or drug dependencies. Information on any of these programs can be obtained by contacting the Veteran's Administration office nearest you.

* Veteran's Hospitals Substance Abuse Research

U.S. Department of Veterans Affairs
810 Vermont Ave., NW
Washington, DC 20420   202-233-4000

The Veteran's Administration conducts extensive research in the field of substance abuse in the 172 VA hospitals nationwide. They also opened the Clinical Alcoholism Research Center in San Diego in 1985. No grants for research are offered by the Veteran's Administration in the field of alcohol and drug abuse.

* Veteran's Outpatient Treatment

U.S. Department of Veterans Affairs
810 Vermont Ave., NW
Washington, DC 20420   202-233-4000

After hospitalization for alcohol or drug treatment, veterans may be eligible for outpatient care, or may be authorized to continue treatment or rehabilitation in facilities such as halfway houses or therapeutic communities at the expense of the Department of Veterans Affairs.

* VA Medical Centers Inpatient and Outpatient Care

U.S. Department of Veterans Affairs
810 Vermont Ave., NW
Washington, DC 20420   202-233-4000

Patients may be admitted to any VA medical center for inpatient care. However, there are specialized VA Alcohol Dependence Treatment Programs and Drug Dependence Treatment Programs for inpatient and/or outpatient care in VA medical centers in the following states:

A denotes Alcoholism Program
D denotes Drug Dependence Program
A & D denote both Alcohol and Drug Dependence Programs

Alabama
700 S. 19th St., Birmingham, AL 35233 (A); 205-933-8101
Loop Rd., Tuscaloosa, AL 35404 (A); 205-554-2000
Tuskegee, AL 36803; 205-727-0550

Alaska
2925 DeBanrd, Anchorage, AK 99508-2989; 907-257-4700

Arizona
7th St. and Indian School Rd., Phoenix, AZ 85012 (A); 602-277-5551
500 Hwy. 89 N., Prescott, AZ 86313 (A); 602-445-4860
3601 6th Ave., Tucson, AZ 85723 (A & D); 602-792-1450

Arkansas
4300 W. 7th St., Little Rock, AR 72205 (A & D); 501-661-1202

California
2615 E. Clinton Ave., Fresno, CA 93703 (A); 209-225-5323
11201 Benton St., Loma Linda, CA 92357 (A); 714-825-7084
5901 E. 7th St., Long Beach, CA 90822 (A & D); 213-494-2611

11301 Wilshire Blvd., West Los Angeles, CA 90073 (A & D); 213-478-3711
425 S. Hill St., Los Angeles, CA 90013 (A & D); 213-894-3902
150 Muir Rd., Martinez, CA 94553 (A & D); 415-372-2000
3801 Miranda Ave., Palo Alto, CA 94304 (A & D); 415-493-5000
3350 LaJolla Village Dr., San Diego, CA 92161 (A & D); 619-552-8585
4150 Clement St., San Francisco, CA 94121 (A & D); 415-221-4810
16111 Plummer St., Sepulveda, CA 91343 (A & D); 818-895-9346
125 N. Jackson St., San Jose, CA 95116; 408-275-7600
4951 Arroyo Rd., Livermore, CA 94550; 415-447-2560

Colorado
1055 Clermont St., Denver, CO 80220 (A & D); 303-393-2882
Hwy. 183 off Hwy. 50, Fort Lyon, CO 81038 (A); 303-456-1260
2121 North Ave., Grand Junction, CO 81501; 303-242-0731

Connecticut
W. Spring St., West Haven, CT 06516 (A); 203-932-5711
555 Willard Ave., Newington, CT 06111 (A & D); 203-666-6951

Delaware
1601 Kirkwood Hwy., Wilmington, DE 19805; 302-994-2511

District of Columbia
50 Irving St., NW, Washington, DC 20422 (A & D); 202-745-8000

Florida
1000 Bay Pines Blvd., N. Bay Pines, FL 33504 (A); 813-398-6661
Archer Rd., Gainesville, FL 32602 (A); 904-374-6089
1201 N.W. 16th St., Miami, FL 33125 (A & D); 305-324-4455
801 S. Marion St., Lake City, FL 32055; 904-755-3016
13000 Bruce B. Downs Blvd., Tampa, FL 33612; 813-972-2000

Georgia
1670 Clairmont Rd., Atlanta (Decatur), GA 30033 (A & D); 404-321-6111
1 Freedom Way, Augusta, GA 30910 (A); 706-733-0188
1826 Veterans Blvd., Dublin GA 31021; 912-272-1210

Hawaii
300 Ala Moana Blvd., Honolulu, HI 96850; 808-541-1600

Idaho
500 W. Fort St., Boise, ID 83702; 208-336-5100

Illinois
820 S. Damen Ave., Chicago, IL 60680 (A & D); 312-666-6500
1900 E. Main St., Danville, IL 61832 (A); 217-442-8000
Roosevelt Rd. and 5th Ave., Hines, IL 60141 (A & D); 708-343-7200
333 E. Huron St., North Chicago, IL 60611 (A & D); 312-943-6600
2401 W. Main St., Marion, IL 62959 (A & D); 618-997-5311

Indiana
1481 W. 10th St., Indianapolis, IN 46202 (A & D); 317-635-7401
E. 38th St., Marion, IN 46952 (A); 317-674-3321
2121 Lake Ave., Fort Wayne, IN 46805; 219-436-5431

Iowa
30th and Euclid, Des Moines, IA 50310 (A); 515-271-5805
1515 W. Pleasant St., Knoxville, IA 50138; 515-842-3101

Kansas
4101 S. 4th St. Trafficway, Leavenworth, KS 66048 (A); 913-682-2000
2200 Gage Blvd., Topeka, KS 66622 (A); 913-272-3111
5500 E. Kellogg, Wichita, KS 67218; 316-685-2221

Kentucky
Leestown Rd., Lexington, KY 40511 (A); 606-233-4511
800 Zorn Ave., Louisville, KY 40206; 502-895-3401

Louisiana
1601 Perdido St., New Orleans, LA 70146 (A & D); 504-568-0811
510 E. Stoner Ave., Shreveport, LA 71101 (A); 318-424-6012
Shreveport Highway, Alexandria, LA 71301 (A & D); 318-473-0010

Maine
Rt. 17, Togus, ME 04330 (A); 207-623-8411

Be patient. If any phone number is incorrect, call (area code) 555-1212 and request the new listing.

Maryland
3900 Loch Raven Blvd., Baltimore, MD 21218 (A & D); 301-467-9932
31 Hopkins Plaza, Baltimore, MD 21201; 301-467-9932
9600 North Point Rd., Fort Howard, MD 21052; 410-477-1800
Perry Point, MD 21902 (A & D); 410-642-2411

Massachusetts
200 Springs Rd., Bedford, MA 01730 (A & D); 617-275-7500
150 S. Huntington Ave., Boston, MA 02130 (A & D); 617-232-9500
940 Belmont St., Brockton, MA 02401 (A); 508-583-4500
421 N. Main, Northampton, MA 01060 (A); 413-584-4040

Michigan
Southfield and Outer Dr., Allen Park, MI 48101 (A & D); 313-562-6000
5500 Armstrong Rd., Battle Creek, MI 49015 (A & D); 616-966-5600
H Street, Iron Mountain, MI 49801 (A & D); 906-774-3300
2215 Fuller Rd., Ann Arbor, MI 48105 (A & D); 313-769-7100

Minnesota
One Veterans Dr., Minneapolis, MN 55417 (A & D); 612-725-2000
8th St., St. Cloud, MN 56303 (A); 612-255-6395

Mississippi
400 Veterans Ave., Biloxi, MS 39531 (A); 601-388-5541
1500 E. Woodrow Wilson Dr., Jackson, MS 39216 (A); 601-362-4471

Missouri
I 270, St. Louis, MO 63125 (A & D); 314-894-6653
4801 Linwood Blvd., Kansas City, MO 64128; 816-861-4700
800 Hospital St., Columbia, MO 65201; 314-443-2511
1500 N. Westwood Blvd. Poplar Bluff, MO 63901; 314-686-4151

Montana
William St., Fort Harrison, MT 59636 (A & D); 406-442-6410

Nebraska
2201 N. Broad Well, Grand Island, NE 68803 (A & D); 308-382-3660
600 S. 70th St., Lincoln, NE 68510 (A); 402-489-3802
4101 Woolworth Ave., Omaha, NE 68105 (A); 402-346-8800

Nevada
1000 Locust St., Reno, NV 89520 (A & D); 702-786-7200
1703 W. Charleston Blvd., Las Vegas, NV 89102; 702-385-3700

New Hampshire
718 Smyth Rd., Manchester, NH 03104 (A); 603-624-4366

New Jersey
Tremont Ave., East Orange, NJ 07019 (A & D); 201-676-1000
Knoll Croft Rd., Lyons, NJ 07939 (A); 201-647-0180

New Mexico
2100 Ridgecrest Dr., SE, Albuquerque, NM 87108 (A); 505-265-1711

New York
113 Holland Ave., Albany, NY 12208 (A & D); 518-462-3311
130 W. Kingsbridge Rd., Bronx, NY 10468 (A & D); 212-584-9000
800 Poly Place, Brooklyn, NY 11209 (A & D); 718-630-3500
3495 Bailey Ave., Buffalo, NY 14215 (A & D); 716-834-9200
Fort Hill Ave., Canandaigua, NY 14424 (A); 716-394-2000
Old Albany Post Rd., Montrose, NY 10548 (A & D); 914-737-4400
1st Ave. at E. 24th St., New York, NY 10010 (D); 212-686-7500
Middleville Rd., North Port, NY 11678; 516-261-4400
100 State St., Rochester, NY 14614; 716-263-6710
800 Irving Ave., Syracuse, NY 13210 (A & D); 315-476-7461
Bath, NY 14810; 607-776-2111

North Carolina
1601 Brenner Ave., Salisbury, NC 28144 (A); 704-638-9000
508 Fulton St., Durham, NC 27705; 919-286-0411
2300 Ramsey St., Fayetteville, NC 28301; 919-488-2120
1100 Tunnel Rd., Asheville, NC 28805 (A & D); 704-298-7911

North Dakota
2101 Elm St., Fargo, ND 58102; 701-232-3241

Ohio
3200 Vine St., Cincinnati, OH 45220 (A & D); 513-861-3100
1000 Brecksville Rd., Brecksville, OH 44141 (A & D); 216-526-3030
17273 State Route 104, Chillicothe, OH 45601; 614-773-1141
4100 W. 3rd St., Dayton, OH 45428; 513-268-6511
2090 Kenny Rd., Columbus, OH 43221; 614-469-5916
10701 East Blvd., Cleveland, OH 44106 (A); 216-791-3800

Oklahoma
921 N.E. 13th St., Oklahoma City, OK 73104 (A & D); 405-270-0501
635 W. 11th St., Tulsa, OK 74127 (D); 918-581-7161

Oregon
New Garden Valley Blvd., Roseburg, OR 97470 (A); 503-440-1000
Hwy. 62, White City, OR 97503 (A); 503-826-2111
3710 SW US Veterans Hospital Rd., Portland, OR 97207 (A & D); 503-257-2500

Pennsylvania
Blackhorse Rd., Coatesville, PA 19320 (A & D); 215-384-7711
University and Woodland Ave., Philadelphia, PA 19104 (A & D); 215-823-5809
Highland Dr., Pittsburgh, PA 15206 (A); 412-363-4900
1111 East End Blvd., Wilkes-Barre, PA 18711; 717-824-3521
1700 S. Lincoln Ave., Lebanon, PA 17042; 717-272-6621
325 New Castle Rd., Butler, PA 16001; 412-287-4781

Puerto Rico
GPO Box 5800, San Juan, PR 00927 (A & D), 809-758-7575

Rhode Island
Davis Park, Providence, RI 02908 (A & D); 401-273-7100

South Carolina
109 Bee St., Charleston, SC 29401 (A); 803-577-5011
Garners Ferry Rd., Columbia, SC 29209 (A); 803-774-4000

South Dakota
I 90/Hwy. 34, Fort Meade, SD 57741 (A); 605-347-2511
5th St., Hot Springs, SD 57747 (A); 605-745-2000
601 S. Cliff Ave., Suite C, Sioux Falls, SD 57117 (A & D); 605-336-3230

Tennessee
1030 Jefferson Ave., Memphis, TN 38104 (A & D); 901-523-8990
Sidney and Lamont St., Johnson City, Mountain Home, TN 37684 (A); 615-926-1171
3400 Lebanon Rd., Murfreesboro, TN 37129 (A); 615-893-1360
1310 24th Ave. S, Nashville, TN 37212; 615-327-4751

Texas
2400 Gregg St., Big Spring, TX 79720 (A); 915-263-7361
4500 S. Lancaster Rd., Dallas, TX 75216 (A & D); 214-376-5451
2002 Holcombe Blvd., Houston, TX 77030 (A & D); 713-791-1414
7400 Merton Minter Blvd., San Antonio, TX 78284 (A); 512-617-5300
1901 S. First, Temple, TX 76504 (A); 817-778-4811
Memorial Dr., Waco, TX 76711 (A); 803-752-6581
5919 Brook Hollow Dr., El Paso, TX 79925 (A & D); 915-540-7892
1201 E. Ninth St., Bonham, TX 75418 (A & D); 903-583-2111
3600 Memorial Blvd. Kerrville, TX 78028 (A & D); 512-896-2020
6010 Amarillo Blvd., West, Amarillo, TX 79106 (A & D); 806-355-9703

Utah
500 Foothill Blvd., Salt Lake City, UT 84148 (A & D); 801-582-1565

Vermont
N. Hartland Rd., White River Junction, VT 05001 (A); 802-295-9363

Virginia
Emancipation Dr., Hampton, VA 23667 (A); 804-722-9961
1201 Broadrock Rd., Richmond, VA 23249 (D); 804-230-0001
1970 Roanoke Blvd., Salem, VA 24153 (A); 703-982-2585

Washington
Gravely Lake Dr. and Veterans Dr., American Lake, Tacoma, WA 98493 (A & D); 206-582-8440
1660 S. Columbian Way, Seattle, WA 98108 (A & D); 206-762-1010
77 Wainwright Dr., Walla Walla, WA 99362 (A & D); 509-525-5200
North 4815 Assembly St., Spokane, WA 99208 (A & D); 509-328-4521

Be patient. If any phone number is incorrect, call (area code) 555-1212 and request the new listing.

593

Drugs and Chemical Dependence

West Virginia
Rt 9, Martinsburg, WV 25410 (A); 304-263-0811
Milford/Chestnut Sts., Clarksburg, WV 26301 (A & D); 304-623-3461

Wisconsin
County Trunk E., Tomah, WI 54660 (A); 608-372-3971

5000 W. National Ave., Milwaukee, WI 53295 (A & D); 414-384-2000
2500 Overlook Terrace, Madison, WI 53705 (A & D); 608-256-1901

Wyoming
Fort Rd., Sheridan, WY 82801 (A); 307-672-3473
2360 E. Pershing Blvd., Cheyenne, WY 82001 (A & D); 307-778-7550

Be patient. If any phone number is incorrect, call (area code) 555-1212 and request the new listing.

Law Enforcement and Prosecution

* Airborne Drug Smugglers Interdiction

Federal Aviation Administration (FAA)
800 Independence Ave., SW
Washington, DC 20591   202-267-3484

The Federal Aviation Administration (FAA) assists the anti-drug effort in pinpointing and intercepting airborne drug smugglers by enhanced use of radar, posting aircraft lookouts and tracking the movement of suspect aircraft through air traffic control centers.

* Campaign Against Marijuana Planting

Bureau of Land Management (BLM)
U.S. Department of Interior
Washington, DC 20240   202-208-5717

The Campaign Against Marijuana Planting (CAMP) attempts to eliminate the planting of marijuana on public land as well as drug labs that are operated on public land. Information should be called in to either your local office of the Bureau of Land Management (BLM), local officials in your area, or the national office listed above.

* Chronic Juvenile Offenders, Victimization of Children

Office of Juvenile Justice and
Delinquency Prevention
U.S. Department of Justice
633 Indiana Ave., NW
Washington, DC 20531   202-724-7782

The Special Emphasis Division provides technical assistance for Federal, State and local governments, as well as for public and private agencies and individuals in planning, establishing, funding, operating, or evaluating juvenile delinquency prevention programs.

* Counternarcotics Intelligence Center

Central Intelligence Agency (CIA)
McLean, VA   703-482-1100

The DCI Counterintelligence Center at the Central Intelligence Agency (CIA) headquarters pools intelligence information to help in the search of drug traffickers, in conjunction with Federal Bureau of Investigation (FBI), Drug Enforcement Agency (DEA), and other government agencies. The DCI Counternarcotics Center includes representatives from the intelligence community including DEA, FBI, Customs, Coast Guard, NSA and DOD. The Center combines CIA and operations officers who have full access to intelligence on international drug trafficking. Its mission is to use intelligence better to help the policy community address the national security problems caused by narcotics and to help the U.S. government fight international narcotics trafficking.

* Court Security

U.S. Marshals Service
U.S. Department of Justice
Washington, DC 20531   202-307-9100

The Service protects members of the Federal judiciary and court facilities against all forms of terrorism and violent tactics which are routinely encountered. Cases generating broad media and public interest, as well as violent threats to the presiding trial judge, will intensify as law enforcement agencies focus on dangerous drug related investigations.

* Crime Victimization and Compensation

Office for Victims of Crime (OVC)
U.S. Department of Justice
633 Indiana Ave., NW
Washington, DC 20531   202-514-6444

This national office provides technical assistance and grants to states to enhance victim compensation and assistance programs.

* Criminal Justice Database and Reference Service

National Criminal Justice Reference Service
P.O. Box 6000   800-851-3420
Rockville, MD 20850   301-251-5000

The National Criminal Justice Reference System is a computerized database of more than 90,000 criminal-justice-related information sources. Information specialists are available to search the database or to use other research techniques to answer questions.

* Customs Service Air and Marine Interdiction Efforts

U.S. Customs Service (USCS)
1301 Constitution Ave., NW
Washington, DC 20229   202-927-6724

The Service is responsible for the processing and regulation of people, carriers, cargo, currency and mail which pass into and out of the United States. Customs has developed innovative inspection, air and marine interdiction programs and works closely with DEA in the development of intelligence and other cooperative drug enforcement efforts.

* Diplomatic Initiatives on Crop Control and Interdiction

Bureau of International Narcotics Matters
U.S. Department of State
2201 C St., NW
Washington, DC 20520   202-647-8464

The Bureau of International Narcotics Matters (INM) has overall responsibility for international drug policy development, program management, and diplomatic initiatives. Its major programs are concerned with bi- and multi-lateral assistance for crop control, interdiction, and related enforcement activities in producer and transit nations. INM also provides narcotics-related development assistance, technical assistance for demand reduction programs, and training for foreign personnel in narcotics enforcement and related procedures to strengthen interdiction and enforcement efforts.

* Drivers Under-the-Influence Detection

National Highway Traffic Safety Administration
400 Seventh St., SW
Washington, DC 20590   202-366-0123

The Drug Recognition Program is a program being conducted by the National Highway Traffic Safety Administration (NHTSA) and the Bureau of Justice Assistance. It is a means of improving enforcement of drug-impaired driving violations. The program trains police officers as Drug Recognition Experts (DREs), enabling the officers to develop skills in evaluating the drivers condition and securing evidence for conviction. Site selection criteria for this program are outline in a monograph available from the above address.

* Drug Dealer Evictions from Public Housing

U.S. Department of Housing and Urban Development (HUD)
451 Seventh Ave., SW
Washington, DC 20410   202-708-1422

The Department of Housing and Urban Development (HUD) is working with the Attorney General, and the Secretary of HHS as well as local public housing authorities, State and Federal law enforcement officers, and local agencies to achieve drug-free public housing.

* Drug-Free Federal Prisons

Bureau of Prisons
320 First St., NW
Washington, DC 20534   202-514-2000

The Bureau of Prisons provides psychological and drug abuse treatment services and places increased emphasis creating drug-free prisons so as to break the link between drug use and crime.

Drugs and Chemical Dependence

* Drug Labs on Public Lands Investigations

Bureau of Land Management (BLM)
U.S. Department of Interior
Washington, DC 20240   202-208-5717

The Campaign Against Marijuana Planting (CAMP) attempts to eliminate the planting of marijuana on public land as well as drug labs that are operated on public land. Information about brochures regarding the Bureau's efforts are available as well as copies of the annual report are available through the Washington, DC office.

* Drug-Related Crime Data

Data Center and Clearinghouse for Drugs and Crime
1600 Research Boulevard
Rockville, MD 20850   800-666-3332

Drug enforcement data, information on drug trafficking and illicit drug-related aspects of crime are available from this clearinghouse.

* Drug Seizures and Prosecution

Drug Enforcement Administration (DEA)
U.S. Department of Justice
1405 I St., NW
Washington, DC 20537   202-401-7834

DEA investigates and prosecutes suspects connected with illicit drug trafficking. It regulates the legitimate manufacture and distribution of controlled substances. It maintains statistics regarding all Federal illicit drug seizures. It trains narcotics officers in other Federal, State, and local agencies as well as foreign police. DEA operates the El Paso Intelligence Center (EPIC), 24 hour daily national center for operational drug enforcement information. The regional offices are:

Atlanta
Richard B. Russell Federal Building, 75 Spring St. SW, Room 740, Atlanta, GA 30303; 404-331-4401

Boston
Room G-64 JFK Federal Building, Boston, MA 02203; 617-565-2800

Chicago
500 Dirksen Federal Building, 219 S. Dearborn St., Chicago, IL 60604 312-353-7875

Dallas
1880 Regal Row, Dallas, TX 75235; 214-767-7151

Denver
721 19th St., Room 316, Denver, CO 80201; 303-844-3951

Detroit
357 Federal Building, 231 W. Lafayette, Detroit, MI 48226; 313-226-7290

Houston
333 W. Loop North, Suite 300, Houston, TX 77024; 713-681-1771

Los Angeles
350 S. Figueroa St., Suite 800, Los Angeles, CA 90071; 213-894-2650

Miami
8400 NW 53rd St., Miami, FL 33166; 305-591-4870

Newark
806 Federal Office Building, Newark, NJ 07102; 201-645-6060

New Orleans
1661 Canal St., Suite 2200, New Orleans, LA 70112; 504-589-3894

New York
555 W. 57th St., Suite 1900, New York, NY 10019; 212-399-5151

Philadelphia
10224 William J. Green Federal Building, Philadelphia, PA 19106; 215-597-9530

Phoenix
One N. First St., Suite 201, Phoenix, AZ 85004; 602-261-4866

San Diego
402 W. 35th St., National City, CA 92050; 619-585-4200

San Francisco
450 Golden Gate Ave., Room 12215, P.O. Box 36035, San Francisco, CA 94102; 415-556-6771

Seattle
220 W. Mercer, Suite 301, Seattle, WA 98119; 206-442-5443

St. Louis
7911 Forsythe Blvd., Suite 500, United Missouri Bank Bldg. St. Louis, MO 63015; 314-425-3241

Washington, DC
400 Sixth St., SW, Room 2558, Washington, DC 20024; 202-724-7834

* Drugs-in-the Workplace

Federal Bureau of Investigation
U.S. Department of Justice
9th St. and Pennsylvania Ave., NW
Washington, DC 20535   202-324-3000

Each of the 58 Federal Bureau of Investigation (FBI) field offices have a Special Agent Drug Demand Reduction Coordinator to the FBI's drugs-in-the-workplace efforts. The FBI coordinator may assist drug prevention efforts, for example, educational programs; employee assistance programs; supervisory training; and drug testing.

* Drug Smuggling Hotline

Interdiction Committee
U.S. Customs Service
U.S. Department of the Treasury
1301 Constitution Ave., NW
Washington, DC 20229   800-BE-ALERT

The Zero Tolerance program helps you notify authorities if you witness drug smuggling activities in your area. By calling the number above, authorities will be contacted, and the network will contact your local federal officials.

* Drug Sniffing Dogs

Canine Training Center
U.S. Customs Service
U.S. Department of the Treasury
HCR Box 7
Front Royal, VA 22630   202-566-8188

The Customs Canine Enforcement Training Center is about 70 miles west of Washington, DC, in Front Royal, VA. The dogs and officers are trained by Customs canine enforcement officers with professional experience in the field. The dogs are taught to detect concealed narcotics and dangerous drugs, while the officer is instructed in law enforcement and in detecting the dog's alert signals when contraband is discovered. Dogs are obtained from animal shelters around the country or from individual owners. Canine enforcement teams assigned to seaports and airports alternate between examining aircraft, vessels, baggage, cargo, and mail. Teams stationed at land border crossings devote their time to examining vehicles and merchandise entering the United States.

* Extraditions

U.S. Marshals Service
U.S. Department of Justice
600 Army Navy Dr.
Arlington, VA 22202   202-307-9100

The Marshals Service acts as the government's arm for reaching out and returning fugitives to the United States to face charges and put an end to their illegal activities.

* FBI Special Agent Drug Demand Reduction

Federal Bureau of Investigation (FBI)
9th St. and Pennsylvania Ave., NW
Washington, DC 20535   202-324-3000

The primary responsibility of the FBI is its cooperative efforts with the Drug Enforcement Agency to investigate drug matters and drug trafficking involvement by organized crime. The FBI conducts court authorized electronic surveillance and drug-related financial and public corruption investigations. Each of the 56 FBI field offices have a Special Agent (SA) Drug Demand Reduction Coordinator to carry forward the FBI's Drug Demand Reduction Program and the FBI's drugs-in-the-workplace efforts. These FBI Drug Demand Reduction Coordinators are also listed in the Experts Chapter.

Be patient. If any phone number is incorrect, call (area code) 555-1212 and request the new listing.

F.B.I. SA James Caverly
U.S. Post Office and Courthouse
5th Floor, 45 Broadway
Albany, NY 12201-1219
518-465-7551

F.B.I. SA James Garay
301 Grand Ave., NE
Albuquerque, NM 87192
505-247-1555

F.B.I. SA Billy G. Andrews
Suite 6
222 W. 7th Ave.
Anchorage, AK 99513-7598
907-276-4441

F.B.I. SA Frank Pickens
2635 Century Center Parkway
Atlanta, GA 30345
404-679-9000

F.B.I. SA Joseph Monroe
7142 Ambassador Rd.
Baltimore, MD 21207
301-265-8080

(2) F.B.I. SA Ashley C. Curry and G. Wray Morse
Room 1400
2121 Building
Birmingham, AL 35203
205-252-7705

F.B.I. SA Matthew J. Cronin
J.F.K. Federal Office Bldg.
Boston, MA 02203
617-742-5533

F.B.I. SA Bernard Walsh
Room 1400
Federal Office Bldg.
111 W. Huron St.
Buffalo, NY 14202
716-856-7800

F.B.I. SA Gerard D. Sullivan
6010 Kenley Lane
Charlotte, NC 28217
704-529-1030

F.B.I. SA Terri Beck
Room 905
E.M. Dirksen Federal Office Bldg.
219 S. Dearborn St.
Chicago, IL 60604
312-431-1333

F.B.I. SA David L. Lichtenfeld
Room 9023
Federal Office Bldg.
550 Main St.
Cincinnati, OH 45202
513-421-4310

F.B.I. SA Robert L. Hawk
Room 3005
Federal Office Bldg.
1240 E. 9th St.
Cleveland, OH 44199
216-522-1400

F.B.I. SA James H. Davis
Suite 1357
Strom Thurmond Federal Bldg.
1835 Assembly St.
Columbia, SC 29201
803-254-3011

F.B.I. SA Thomas Westberg
Suite 300
1801 N. Lamar
Dallas, TX 75202
214-720-2200

F.B.I. SA Alison King
Room 1823
Federal Office Bldg.
Denver, CO 80202
303-629-7171

F.B.I. SA Henry W. Glaspie, III
P.V. McNamara Federal Office Bldg.
477 Michigan Ave.
Detroit, MI 48226
313-965-2323

F.B.I. SA Hector Armijo
Suite C-600
700 E. San Antonio Ave.
El Paso, TX 79901
915-533-7451

F.B.I. SA Vincent John McNally
Room 4307
Kalanianaole Federal Office Bldg.
300 Ala Moana Blvd.
Honolulu, HI 96850
808-521-1411

F.B.I. SA Charles Kearney, Jr.
Suite 200
2500 East T.C. Jester
Houston, TX 77008
713-868-2266

F.B.I. SA Walter L. Setmeyer, Jr.
Room 679
Federal Office Bldg.
575 N. Pennsylvania St.
Indianapolis, IN 46204
317-639-3301

F.B.I. SA Laura Lee Henry
Suite 1553
Federal Office Bldg.
100 W. Capitol St.
Jackson, MS 39269
601-948-5000

F.B.I. SA James Stanton
4th Floor Oaks V
7820 Arlington Expressway
Jacksonville, FL 32211
904-721-1211

F.B.I. SA Dennis J. Glenn
Room 300
U.S. Courthouse
Kansas City, MO 64106
816-221-6100

F.B.I. SA A. Wayne Baker
6th Floor
710 Locust St.
Knoxville, TN 37901
615-544-0751

F.B.I. SA Debbie Calhoun
700 E. Charleston Blvd.
Las Vegas, NV 89104
702-385-1281

F.B.I. SA Phyllis Cournan
Suite 200
2 Financial Centre

Be patient. If any phone number is incorrect, call (area code) 555-1212 and request the new listing.

597

10825 Financial Pkwy.
Little Rock, AR 72201
501-221-9100

F.B.I. SA Brent Braun
Federal Office Bldg.
11000 Wilshire Blvd.
Los Angeles, CA 90024
213-477-6565

F.B.I. SA William S. Cheek, Jr.
Room 500, Federal Office Bldg.
600 Martin Luther King Pl.
Louisville, KY 40202
502-583-3941

F.B.I. SA Joseph F. DeBiaggio
Room 841
Clifford Davis Federal Office Bldg.
167 N. Main St.
Memphis, TN 38103
901-525-7373

F.B.I. SA Gordon McNeill
16320 NW Second Ave.
N. Miami Beach, FL 33169
305-944-9101

F.B.I. SA Dale G. Mueller
Room 700
Federal Office Bldg. and
 U.S. Courthouse
517 E. Wisconsin Ave.
Milwaukee, WI 53202
414-276-4684

F.B.I. SA Dag Sohlberg
5-1100, 111 Washington Ave. S,
Minneapolis, MN 55401
612-376-3200

F.B.I. SA David A. Chaney
One St. Louis Centre
1 St. Louis St.
Mobile, AL 36602
205-438-3674

F.B.I. SA James Kyle
Gateway 1, Market St.
Newark, NJ 07102
201-622-5613

F.B.I. SA Joseph W. Butchka
Federal Office Bldg.
150 Court St.
New Haven, CT 06510
203-777-6311

F.B.I. SA Ronald R. Travis
Suite 2200, 1250 Poydras St.
New Orleans, LA 70112
504-522-4671

F.B.I. SA Louis Stith
26 Federal Plaza
New York, NY 10278
212-553-2700

F.B.I. SA Joseph G. O'Brien
Room 839, 200 Granby St.
Norfolk, VA 23510
804-623-3111

F.B.I. SA Dan L. Vogel
Suite 1600, 50 Penn Plaza
Oklahoma City, OK 73118
405-842-7471

F.B.I. SA Jim W. Isom
Room 7401
Federal Office Bldg. and
 U.S. Courthouse
215 N. 17th St.
Omaha, NE 68102
402-348-1210

F.B.I. SA James T. McAleer
William J. Green, Jr. Federal
Federal Office Bldg.
600 Arch St.
Philadelphia, PA 19106
215-629-0800

F.B.I. SA John J. Callahan
Suite 400
210 E. Indiaola
Phoenix, AZ 85012
602-279-5511

F.B.I. SA David J. Kwait
Room 1300
Federal Office Bldg.
1000 Liberty Ave.
Pittsburgh, PA 15222
412-471-2000

F.B.I. SA C. Ronald J. Makinson
Crown Plaza Bldg.
1500 SW 1st Ave.
Portland, OR 97201
503-224-4181

F.B.I. SA Wayne Smith
111 Greencourt Rd.
Richmond, VA 23228
804-261-1044

F.B.I. SA Thomas P. Griffin
Federal Office Bldg.
2800 Cottage Way
Sacramento, CA 95825
916-481-9110

F.B.I. SA John M. Mauzey
Room 2704
Federal Office Bldg.
1520 Market St.
St. Louis, MO 63103
314-241-5357

F.B.I. SA E. Ronald J. Van Vranken
Room 3203
Federal Office Bldg.
125 S. State St.
Salt Lake City, UT 84138
801-355-7521

F.B.I. SA April Hall
Room 433
Old Post Office Bldg.
615 E. Houston
San Antonio, TX 78205
512-225-6741

F.B.I. SA Ronald G. Orrantia
Room 6S-31
Federal Office Bldg.
880 Front St.
San Diego, CA 92188
619-231-1122

F.B.I. SA Thomas Anderson
450 Golden Gate Ave.
San Francisco, CA 94102
415-553-7400

F.B.I. SA Jesus Marti
Room 526
U.S. Courthouse and Federal
 Office Bldg.
Hato Rey, PR 00918
809-754-6000

F.B.I. SA Richard Thurston
Room 710, Federal Office Bldg.
915 Second Ave.
Seattle, WA 98174
206-622-0460

F.B.I. SA DeWayne Wright
400 W. Monroe St., Suite 400
Springfield, IL 62704
217-522-9675

F.B.I. SA Maria Vazquez
Room 610
Federal Office Bldg.
500 Zack St.
Tampa, FL 33602
813-228-7661

F.B.I. SA Samuel Feemster
Washington Metropolitan Field Office
1900 Half St.
Washington, DC 20535
202-324-3000

* Federal Prosecutors

Executive Office for United States Attorneys
U.S. Department of Justice
Tenth Street and Pennsylvania Avenue NW
Washington, DC 20530   202-514-2000

The U.S. Attorneys conduct the prosecution in Federal court of drug trafficking and connected illegal activities. They provide coordination of major drug investigations to ensure that the court cases produced will be successfully prosecuted.

* Federal and Local Law Enforcement Prosecutors Coordination

Executive Office for United States Attorneys
U.S. Department of Justice
Tenth Street and Constitution Avenue NW
Washington, DC 20530   202-514-2000

Established Law Enforcement Coordinating Committees (LECCs) are composed of the heads of Federal, state and local law enforcement and prosecutorial agencies who collectively assess the crime problems in each district and determine how best to use available resources to attach those problems. Cross-designation of local prosecutors as Federal prosecutors is now a frequent occurrence in cooperative investigations and prosecutions.

* Firearms and Drug Trafficking

Bureau of Alcohol, Tobacco, and Firearms (ATF)
650 Massachusetts Ave., NW
Washington, DC 20226   202-927-7777

ATF is pursuing drug-related violations of Federal law concerning firearms, destructive devices and explosives. ATF's resources include undercover agents, national response bomb scene investigation teams, an international firearms identification and tracking system, a worldwide explosives incident data bank and tracking capability, auditors, and agents with experience in investigating complex RICO and conspiracy cases.

* Forest Service Anonymous Witness Reporting System

U.S. Forest Service
701-RP-E
P.O. Box 96090
Washington, DC 20090   800-782-7463

"Forest Service National Anonymous Witness Reporting System" is toll free nationwide "hotline" telephone number for the purpose of receiving confidential information related to drug and other criminal law violations occurring in the National Forest System, and providing this information to key contacts in the Forest Service. Rewards of up to $5000 may be given witnesses who report information leading to the seizure of controlled substances and/or for apprehension of suspects.

* Fugitive Apprehension

U.S. Marshals Service
U.S. Department of Justice
600 Army Navy Dr.
Arlington, VA 22202   202-307-9100

As the U.S. Department of Justice agency with primary investigative responsibility for most Federal fugitives, the Marshals Service devotes considerable resources toward apprehending those fugitives with drug-related charges and backgrounds. The Drug Enforcement Administration has transferred all its fugitive cases to the Service.

* Grants for Public Agencies and Non-Profits

Bureau of Justice Assistance
U.S. Department of Justice
633 Indiana Ave., NW
Washington, DC 20531   202-514-6278

The Bureau of Justice Assistance has a Discretionary Grant Program which provides assistance to public agencies and private nonprofit organizations for: 1) demonstration programs that, in view of previous research or experience, are likely to be successful in more than one jurisdiction. 2) Educational and training programs for criminal justice personnel and technical assistance to States and units of local government. 3) Projects that are national or multistate in scope, and that address the 18 authorized purposes of the Anti-Drug Abuse Act of 1986.

* Herbicides for Narcotic Plants International Eradication

USDA Agricultural Research Service (ARS)
Building 302
BARC-E
10300 Baltimore Ave.
Beltsville, MD 20705-2350   301-504-9403

ARS works with the State Department's Bureau of International Narcotics Matters and the Drug Enforcement Agency to determine the efficacy as well as the environmental impact of using herbicides in eradicating narcotic plants. The Agricultural Attaches posted in some drug producing countries are involved directly with local narcotic plant eradication programs.

* High-Level Drug Traffickers

Narcotics and Dangerous Drugs Section
Criminal Division
U.S. Department of Justice
700 Army Navy Drive
Arlington, VA 22202   202-307-4132

This section investigates and prosecutes high-level drug traffickers and members of criminal organizations involved in the importation, manufacture, shipment or distribution of illicit narcotics and dangerous drugs, with particular emphasis on litigation attacking the financial bases of those criminal organizations.

* Highway Safety and Enforcement Nationwide

National Highway Traffic Safety Administration (NHTSA)
400 Seventh St., SW
Washington, DC 20590   202-366-9550

The Drug Recognition Program is a program being conducted by National Highway Traffic Safety Administration (NHTSA) and the Bureau of Justice Assistance. It is a means of improving enforcement of drug-impaired driving violations. The program trains police officers as Drug Recognition Experts (DREs), enabling the officers to develop skills in evaluating the drivers condition and securing evidence for conviction. The Governors' Highway Safety Representatives and Coordinators may be contacted for those who are interested in exploring the possibilities of implementing this program.

Alabama
Representative: Gene Anderson, Director, Dept. of Economic and Community Affairs, 401 Adams Ave., P.O. Box 5690, Montgomery, AL 36103-5690; 205-242-8672
Coordinator: Kater Williams and James Quinn, Highway and Traffic Safety, Law Enforcement and Planning Division, 401 Adams Ave., P.O. Box 5690, Montgomery, AL 36103-5690; 205-242-5897

Be patient. If any phone number is incorrect, call (area code) 555-1212 and request the new listing.

599

Drugs and Chemical Dependence

Alaska

Representative and Coordinator: Gayle Horetski, Director, Highway Safety and Planning Agency, Department of Public Safety, 450 Whittier St., P.O. Box N, Juneau, AK 99811; 907-465-4322

Arizona

Representative: R.J. "Rick" Ayers, Office of Highway Safety, 3010 N. Second St., Suite 105, Phoenix, AZ 85012; 602-223-2359

Coordinator: Howard Adams, Office of Highway Safety, 3010 N. Second St., Suite 105, Phoenix, AZ 85012; 602-223-2359

Arkansas

Representative: Maurice Smith, Director, Arkansas State Highway and Transportation Department, P.O. Box 2261, Little Rock, AK 72203, 501-569-2648

Coordinator: Mike Selig, Manager, Traffic Safety Division; 501-569-2231

California

Representative: Peter O'Rourke, Director, Office of Traffic Safety, Business and Transportation Agency, 700 Franklin Blvd., Suite 330, Sacramento, CA 95823; 916-445-0527

Coordinator: Ray Biancalana, Office of Traffic Safety, Business and Transportation Agency, 700 Franklin Blvd., Suite 330, Sacramento, CA 95823; 916-445-0527

Colorado

Representative: Dr. A. Ray Chamberlain, 303-757-9201

Coordinator: John Conger, Director, Division of Highway Safety, 4201 E. Arkansas Ave., Denver, CO 80222; 303-757-9440

Connecticut

Representative and Coordinator: Susan C. Maloney, Governor's Representative, Bureau of Highways, 24 Wolcott Hill Road, P.O. Box Drawer A, Wethersfield, CT 06109; 203-666-4343

Delaware

Representative: Colonel Clifford M. Graviet, Rt. 13, P.O. Box 430, Dover, DE 19901; 302-739-5911

Coordinator: Lt. Paul Stafford, Rt. 13, P.O. Box 430, Dover, DE 19901; 302-739-5613

District of Columbia

Representative: Esther Hager Francis, Director, Department of Public Works, 2000 14th St., NW, 6th Floor, Washington, DC 20009; 202-939-8000

Coordinator: Carole A. Lewis, Highway Safety Program; 202-939-8018

Florida

Representative: Frank Carlile, Department of Transportation, 605 Suwanne St., MS-57, Tallahassee, FL 32399-0450; 904-922-5820

Coordinator: Billy G. Morris, Department of Transportation, 605 Suwanne St., MS-53; 904-488-3546

Georgia

Representative and Coordinator: Dr. Thomas L. Coleman, Governor's Office of Highway Safety, 100 Peachtree St., Suite 2000, Atlanta, GA 30303; 404-656-6996

Hawaii

Representative: Rex D. Johnson, Department of Transportation, 869 Punchbowl St., Honolulu, HI 96813; 808-587-2150

Coordinator: Lawrence Hao, Director, Motor Vehicle Safety Office, 1505 Dillingham Blvd., Room 214, Honolulu, HI 96817; 808-832-5820

Idaho

Representative: Marc Johnson, Governor's Highway Safety Representative, Governor's Office, State House Mail, Boise, ID, 208-344-2100

Coordinator: Marie Bishop, Transportation Department, P.O. Box 7129, 3311 W. State St., Boise ID; 208-334-8101

Illinois

Representative: Melvin H. Smith, Division of Traffic Safety, Department of Transportation, P.O. Box 19245, 3215 Executive Park Dr., Springfield, IL 62794; 217-782-4972

Coordinator: Larry Wort, Bureau of Safety Programs; 217-782-4974

Indiana

Representative: Bobby Small, State House, Room 206, Indianapolis, Indiana 46204; 317-232-2588

Coordinator: J. Thomas Koutsoumpas, Director, Office of Traffic Safety, ISTA Building, Suite 330, 150 West Market, Indianapolis, Indiana 46204; 317-232-4220

Iowa

Representative: Paul H. Wieck, Iowa Department of Public Safety, Wallace State Office Bldg., Des Moines, IA 50319; 515-281-5104

Coordinator: J. Michael Laski, Governor's Traffic Safety Bureau; 515-281-8400

Kansas

Representative: Michael Johnston, Department of Transportation, Docking St. Office Building, 7th Floor, Topeka, KS 66612; 913-296-3461

Coordinator: Rosalie Thornburgh, Transportation Safety Administrator; 913-296-3756

Kentucky

Representative: Billy G. Wellman, State Police Headquarters, 919 Versailles Rd., Frankfort, KY 40601-9980; 502-695-6300

Coordinator: David H. Salyers, Highway Safety Standards Branch; 502-695-6356

Louisiana

Representative: Betty Theis, Highway Safety Commission, P.O. Box 66336, Baton Rouge, LA 70896; 504-925-6991

Coordinator: Sue Dixon 504-925-6846

Maine

Representative and Coordinator: Richard Perkins, Department of Public Safety, 36 Hospital St., Augusta, ME 04330; 207-582-8776

Maryland

Representative: O. James Lighthizer, Secretary of Transportation, P.O. Box 8755, BWI International Airport, Baltimore, MD 21240-0755; 410-859-7397

Coordinator: Dennis Atkins, Division of Transportation Safety; 410-584-7697

Massachusetts

Representative and Coordinator: Nancy J. Luther, Governor's Highway Safety Bureau, 100 Cambridge Street, Room 2104, Boston, MA 02202; 617-727-5073

Michigan

Representative and Coordinator: Thomas Krycinski, Office of Highway Safety Planning, 300 S. Washington Square, Suite 300, Lansing, MI 48913; 517-334-5210

Minnesota

Representative: Thomas Frost, Department of Public Safety, Transportation Bldg., St. Paul, MN 55155; 612-296-6642

Coordinator: Thomas A. Boerner, Director of Traffic Safety; 612-296-3804

Mississippi

Representative and Coordinator: Donald O'Cain, 301 W. Pearl St., Jackson, MI 39203-3085; 601-949-2225

Missouri

Representative: Arvid E. West, Jr., Department of Public Safety, P.O. Box 104808, 311 Ellis Boulevard, Jefferson City, Missouri 65101-4808; 314-751-7643

Coordinator: Richard Echols, Deputy Director; 314-751-4161

Montana

Representative and Coordinator: Albert E. Goke, Highway Traffic Safety Division, Department of Justice, 303 N. Roberts, Helena, MT 59620; 406-444-3412

Nebraska

Representative: Jack C. Conrad, Department of Motor Vehicles, P.O. Box 94612, Lincoln, NE 68509; 402-471-2281

Coordinator: Fred E. Zwonechek, Highway Safety Program Office, State House Station 94612; 402-471-2515

Nevada

Representative: James P. Weller, Department of Motor Vehicles, 555 Wright Way, Carson City, NV 89711-0990; 702-687-5375

Coordinator: Marlen Schultz, Traffic Safety Division; 702-687-5720

New Hampshire

Representative and Coordinator: John B. McDuffee, Highway Safety Agency, 117 Manchester St., Concord, NH 03301; 603-271-2131

New Jersey

Representative and Coordinator: James Arena, Office of Highway Traffic Safety, Department of Law and Public Safety, CN048, Trenton, NJ 08625; 609-588-3750

New Mexico

Representative: Louis J. Medrano, Highway and Transportation Dept., P.O. Box 1149, Santa Fe, NM 87504-1149; 505-827-5109

Coordinator: John D. Fenner, Traffic Safety Bureau; 505-827-0427

Be patient. If any phone number is incorrect, call (area code) 555-1212 and request the new listing.

New York
Representative: Patricia B. Adduci, Department of Motor Vehicles, Empire State Plaza, Swan St. Bldg., Albany, NY 12228; 508-474-0841
Coordinator: William G. Rourke, Traffic Safety Committee; 518-474-3135

North Carolina
Representative and Coordinator: Paul B. Jones, Governor's Highway Safety Program, 215 E. Lane St., Raleigh, NC 27601; 919-733-3083

North Dakota
Representative: Richard J. Backes, Director, Highway Department, 608 E. Boulevard Ave., Bismarck, ND 58505-0178; 701-224-2581
Coordinator: Mylo J. Hehloff, Driver License and Traffic Safety; 701-224-2600

Ohio
Representative: Charles Shipley, Department of Highway Safety, P.O. Box 7167, Columbus, OH 42366-0563; 614-466-3383
Coordinator: Laura Ludwig, Office of the Governor's, Highway Safety Representative; 614-466-3250

Oklahoma
Representative and Coordinator: Dr. Tim W. Mauldin, Jr., Highway Safety Office, 3223 N. Lincoln, Oklahoma City, OK 73105; 405-521-3314

Oregon
Representative: Donald E. Forbes, Oregon Traffic Safety Commission, 135 Transportation Bldg., Salem, OR 97310; 503-378-6388
Coordinator: Edward Marqes, 503-378-3669

Pennsylvania
Representative: Mario D. Pirritano, Deputy Secretary for Safety Administration, 1200 Transportation and Safety Building, Harrisburg, PA 17120; 717-787-3928
Coordinator: Thomas E. Bryer, Center for Highway Safety, 215 Transportation and Safety Bldg; 717-787-7350

Puerto Rico
Representative: Dr. Hermenegildo Ortiz-Quinones, Secretary of Transportation and Public Works, Box 41269, Minillas Station, Santurce, PR 00940; 809-726-6670
Coordinator: Lenidas Ramirez, Traffic Safety Commission, Box 41289, Minillas Station; 809-723-3590

Rhode Island
Representative: Daniel P. Fanning, Department of Transportation, State Office Bldg., Smith St., Providence, RI 02903; 401-277-2481
Coordinator: Edward J. Walsh, Gov's Office of Highway Safety, 345 Harris Ave., Providence, RI 02909; 401-277-3024

South Carolina
Representative and Coordinator: Perry Brown, Office of Highway Safety Programs, 1205 Pendleton Street, Room 453, Columbia, SC 29201; 803-734-0421

South Dakota
Representative: Jeff Stingley, Department of Commerce and Regulation, 910 E. Sioux Ave., Pierre, SD 57501; 605-773-3178
Coordinator: Jeff Holden, State and Community Programs, Dept. of Commerce and Regulation, 118 West Capitol Avenue, Pierre, SD 57501; 605-773-3675

Tennessee
Representative: James Evans, Department of Transportation, 505 Deaderick St., Suite 700, Nashville, TN 37243-0341; 615-741-2848
Coordinator: Clarence Elkins, Governor's Highway Safety Program; 615-741-2589

Texas
Representative: Arnold W. Oliver, State Dept. of Highways and Public Transportation, 125 E. 11 St., Austin, TX 78701; 512-465-6751
Coordinator: Gary Trietsch, Traffic Safety Section (D-18STO); 512-465-6751

Utah
Representative: D. Douglas Bodrero, Department of Public Safety, 4501 S. 2700 West, Salt Lake City, UT 84119; 801-965-4463
Coordinator: Dick Howard, Highway Safety Division; 801-965-4409

Vermont
Representative: Michael D. Griffes, Secretary of Transportation, 133 State St., Montpelier, VT 05603-001; 802-828-2011
Coordinator: Jean Johnson, Exec. Asst. to the Secretary of Transportation, Vermont Highway Safety Program; 802-828-2665

Virginia
Representative: Donald E. Williams, Department of Motor Vehicles, P.O. Box 27412, Richmond, VA 23269; 804-357-6602
Coordinator: William Leighty, Deputy Commissioner for Transportation Safety; 804-357-6614

Washington
Representative: Chuck Hayes, Traffic Safety Commission, 1000 S. Cherry St., MS/PD-11, Olympia, WA 98504; 206-753-6197
Coordinator: Steve Lind, Traffic Safety Commission; 206-753-6197

West Virginia
Representative: James Albert, Criminal Justice and Highway Safety Office, 1204 Kanawha Blvd., Charleston, WV 25301; 304-558-8814
Coordinator: James R. Grate

Wisconsin
Representative: Charles Thompson, Department of Transportation, Office of Highway Safety, P.O. Box 7910, 4802 Sheboygan Ave., Madison, WI 53707; 608-266-1113
Coordinator: David Manning; 608-267-3710

Wyoming
Representative: Donald G. Pruter, State Highway Safety Engineer, Wyoming Highway Safety Department, P.O. Box 1708, Cheyenne, WY 82002-9019; 307-777-4450

Virgin Islands
Representative and Coordinator: Enrique Richards, Lagoon St. Complex, Frediksted, St. Croix, Virgin Islands 08840; 809-772-5820

* Immigration and Naturalization Service (INS)
Immigration and Naturalization Service
425 I St., NW
Washington, DC 20536   202-514-2000
The Immigration and Naturalization Service (INS) is responsible for control of illegal entry of persons along our borders, and assists in apprehending smugglers. The Border Patrol is active in drug abuse education and prevention, conducting demonstrations with "drug sniffing dogs" in classrooms and providing drug education information to students.

* Interagency Law Enforcement Training Center
Federal Law Enforcement Training Center
Glynco, GA 31524   912-267-2100
The Center is the interagency training facility serving 63 Federal law enforcement organizations. The major training effort is in the area of basic programs to teach common areas of law enforcement skills to police and investigative personnel. The Center offers selective, highly specialized training programs to State and local officers.

* International Fugitives and International Police
International Criminal Police Organization
U.S. National Central Bureau
Washington, DC 20530   202-272-8383
This Bureau serves as the communications link among more than 20,000 state and local law enforcement organizations and as the U.S. liaison to INTERPOL. It investigates large-scale narcotics offenses and apprehends international fugitives often involving arrests and extraditions to the countries where the crimes were committed.

* Justice Department Anti-Drug Coordination
Office of Justice Programs (OJP)
U.S. Department of Justice
633 Indiana Ave., NW
Washington, DC 20531   202-307-5933
This office is responsible for policy coordination and general management responsibilities for five OJP bureaus or offices. The Bureau of Justice Assistance (BJA) offers technical assistance to State and local units of government to control crime and drug abuse and to improve the criminal justice system. The Bureau of Justice Statistics (BJS) maintains statistics about crime, its perpetrators and victims, and the operation of the criminal justice system at the Federal, State and local level. The Office of Juvenile Justice and Delinquency Prevention attempts to prevent drug abuse among youth at high risk. The Office for Victims of Crime oversees the Crime Victims Fund which is money comes from fines of Federal criminals. These funds

Drugs and Chemical Dependence

are made available to each State, the District of Columbia, and six Territories to support expanded and improved State victim assistance and compensation programs. The National Victims Resource Center maintains a data base that describes more than 2,000 victim assistance and family violence programs throughout the country.

* Juvenile Delinquency National Trends

Office of Juvenile Justice and Delinquency Prevention (OJJDP)
Office of Justice Programs, U.S. Department of Justice
633 Indiana Ave., NW
Washington, DC 20531   202-307-0751

The Research and Program Development Division sponsors research on national trends in juvenile delinquency and serious juvenile crime, prevention strategies, and the juvenile justice system.

* Juvenile Justice Professionals Training

Office of Juvenile Justice and Delinquency Prevention (OJJDP)
Office of Justice Programs, U.S. Department of Justice
633 Indiana Ave., NW
Washington, DC 20531   202-307-0751

The Training, Dissemination, and Technical Assistance Division (TDTAD) is responsible for programs that train personnel who work with juvenile offenders and their families.

* Law Enforcement Explorer Programs

Office of Juvenile Justice and Delinquency Prevention (OJJDP)
Office of Justice Programs, U.S. Department of Justice
633 Indiana Ave., NW
Washington, DC 20531   202-307-0751

The Training, Dissemination, and Technical Assistance Division (TDTAD) oversees the Exploring Careers in Law Enforcement and Criminal Justice. About 42,000 youths, both male and female, are involved in Law Enforcement Explorer programs, which recently initiated an anti-substance abuse program.

* Law Enforcement Policy Resource Center

Law Enforcement Policy Resource Center
U.S. Department of Justice
633 Indiana Ave., NW
Washington, DC 20531   202-307-5933

The Center develops model policies for law enforcement agencies, as well as program briefs and model legislation regarding issues of interest to law enforcement policy makers.

* Mafia and Organized Crime Investigations

U.S. Marshals Service
U.S. Department of Justice
600 Army Navy Drive
Arlington VA 22202   202-307-9100

The Marshals Service is a charter member of the Organized Crime Drug Enforcement (OCDE) Task Force with full-time investigators assigned to all 13 task force locations.

* Maritime Drug Smuggling Interdiction

U.S. Coast Guard (USCG)
2100 Second St., SW
Washington, DC 20593   202-267-2229

The Coast Guard is the only Federal agency with jurisdiction on the high seas as well as territorial waters and has greatly expanded efforts directed against maritime drug smugglers. USCG ships, boats, planes and helicopters conduct routine drug law enforcement patrols and special operations through the maritime arena. Coast Guard emphasis is on detecting and boarding vessels smuggling illicit drugs while still in transit to the United States. In support of its expansive role in interdiction, the Coast Guard maintains an extensive intelligence organization with heavy emphasis on drug trafficking.

* Military Drug Testing Program

Health Affairs
U.S. Department of Defense
Washington, DC OSD 20301-1155   703-545-6700

Health Affairs is responsible for drug testing programs for the military services. It is also responsible for conducting periodic surveys of illegal drug use among the military.

* Money Laundering Investigations

Internal Revenue Service (IRS)
U.S. Department of Treasury
1111 Constitution Ave., NW
Washington, DC 20224   800-829-1040

The Internal Revenue Service (IRS) supports drug law enforcement by pursuing income tax violations and money laundering related to the financial aspects of illegal drug trafficking. IRS agents trace the movement of funds to document the acquisition of forfeitable assets by drug traffickers. Using search warrants, IRS seizes various financial reports, including travel records, money orders, and cashier check receipts, which can reveal the concealment or illegal transfer of financial assets. The information gained through the warrants can lead to assets seizable under statutory forfeiture provisions.

* Narcotics Cultivation in Developing Countries

Agency for International Development
320 21st St., NW
Washington, DC 20523   202-647-4000

The Agency for International Development (AID) works with the International Narcotics Matters Bureau at the U.S. Department of State in designing and implementing foreign assistance programs related directly and indirectly to drug problems in developing nations. AID assistance is particularly focused on rural development programs in traditional growing regions. The alternative agricultural and other economic pursuits made possible by AID funds are, in many countries, the key to gaining their cooperation towards eliminating cultivation of illicit narcotics.

* Narcotics Identification Manual

Superintendent of Documents
Government Printing Office
Washington, DC 20402   202-512-1800

The manual, *Narcotics Identification Manual*, provides descriptions and color photographs to help you identify narcotics, depressants, stimulants, cannabis, hallucinogens, and crack. Included is a chart listing controlled substances, their uses, and effects. This manual sells for $4.25 (S/N 048-002-00101-0).

* Narcotic Plants Detection and Eradication

National Park Service
U.S. Department of Interior
Washington, DC   202-619-7222

The Service is responsible for enforcing the laws on Federal lands which prohibit cultivation of narcotic plants.

* National Forests Marijuana Eradication Program

U.S. Forest Service
14th St. and Independence Ave., SW
Washington, DC 20250   202-205-1760

The Forest Service assists the Drug Enforcement Agency in the national Domestic Marijuana Eradication and Suppression Program which promotes information sharing and provides training, equipment, investigative and aircraft support to state and local enforcement officers. Some 150 special agents are involved in the Forest Service's Law Enforcement Staff, which consists of 650 armed, uniformed law enforcement officers, who since passage of National Forest Drug Control Act in 1986, have authority under Title 21 arrest drug traffickers and producers.

* National Victims Resource Center

Office for Victims of Crime (OVC)
U.S. Department of Justice
633 Indiana Ave., NW
Washington, DC 20531   202-307-5983

A National Victims Resource Center at the National Criminal Justice Reference Service that provides victim-related publications, statistics, research, program referrals, and other information from its computerized data base. The Center collects and maintains information on programs throughout the United States that provide services to victims, on State victim/witness programs that receive funds under VOCA, and on Federal victim/witness programs.

Be patient. If any phone number is incorrect, call (area code) 555-1212 and request the new listing.

* NOAA Drug Interdiction Efforts

National Oceanic and Atmospheric Administration (NOAA)
U.S. Department of Commerce
Washington, DC 20230   202-377-8090

Through the course of their regular activities, the National Oceanic and Atmospheric Administration (NOAA) provides detection assistance for drug interdiction efforts.

* On-the-Job Drug Testing Videos

National Audiovisual Center
Customer Service Section
8700 Edgeworth Drive
Capitol Heights, MD 20743-3701   301-763-1896

National Clearinghouse for Alcohol and Drug Information
P.O. Box 2345
Rockville, MD 20847   301-468-8200

Drug Testing: Handle with Care describes the options available in designing a drug testing component as part of a comprehensive drug-free workplace program. Procedures addressing the needs of both the employer and the employee to ensure the accuracy and reliability of test results, for specimen collection and laboratory analysis, and a discussion of the critical role of the Medical Review Officer (MRO) are highlighted. Case studies of public/private, and unionized/nonunionized work environments with testing components are presented. This video is available in both employer and employee versions for sale and rental.

* Parole and Recidivism Rate

U.S. Parole Commission
5550 Friendship Blvd.
Chevy Chase, MD 20815   301-492-5990

The Parole Commission is investigating ways in which they may help break the link between crime and drug use in hopes of both reducing drug use and crime, but also of reducing the recidivism rate.

* Pentagon Drug Policy and Enforcement

U.S. Department of Defense
Office of Drug Policy and Enforcement
Washington, DC 20301-1155   703-545-6700

Drug policy and enforcement, including coordination of all the Department of Defense (DOD) activities related to Federal drug abuse eradication; provision of Department resources and support to other agencies for drug law enforcement efforts; military and civilian drug testing policy; advice and assistance to the Secretary of Defense and other officials of the Department on anti-drug abuse aspects of departmental policy, plans and programs.

* Public Lands Special Drug Agents

Bureau of Land Management (BLM)
U.S. Department of Interior
Washington, DC 20240   202-208-5717

The Special Agents of the Bureau of Land Management (BLM) are responsible for enforcing Federal laws and regulations relating to the public lands and resources. This includes conducting criminal investigations and the ability to arrest violators. State Offices include:

Alaska
222 W. 7th Ave., #13, Anchorage, AK 99513-7599, Ed Spang, State Director 907-271-5076; David Vickery, Public Affairs, 907-271-5555

Arizona
3707 N. 7th St., P.O. Box 16563, Phoenix, AZ 85011, Les Rosenkrance, State Director, 602-640-5501; Joanie Redfield, Public Affairs, 602-640-5504

BIFC
Boise Interagency Fire Center, 3905 Vista Ave., Boise, ID 83705, Jack Wilson, BLM Director, 208-389-2446; Arnold Hartigan, Public Affairs, 208-389-2457

California
2800 Cottage Way, E-2841, Sacramento, CA 95825, Ed Hastey, State Director, 916-978-4743; Tony Staed, Public Affairs, 916-978-4746

Colorado
2850 Youngfield St., Lakewood, CO 80215-7076, Bob Moore, State Director, 303-239-3700; Marta Witt, Public Affairs, 303-239-3667

Eastern States
7450 Boston Blvd., Springfield, VA 22153, Denise Meridith, State Director, 703-440-1700; Terry Lewis, Public Affairs, 703-440-1713

Idaho
3380 Americana Terrace, Boise, ID 83706, Del Vail, State Director, 208-384-3001; Jack Sept, Public Affairs, 208-384-3014

Montana
222 N. 32nd St., P.O. Box 36800, Billings, MT 59107, Bob Lawton, State Director, 406-255-2904; Trudie Olson, Public Affairs, 406-255-2913

Nevada
850 Harvard Way, P.O. Box 12000, Reno, NV 89520-0006, Billy Templeton, State Director, 702-785-6590; Robert Stewart, Public Affairs, 702-785-6586

New Mexico
1474 Rodeo Rd., P.O. Box 27115, Santa Fe, NM 87505-7115, Larry Woodard, State Director, 505-438-7501; Lee Keesling, Public Affairs, 505-438-7514

Oregon
1300 N.E. 44th Ave., P.O. Box 2965, Portland OR 97213, Dean Bibles, State Director, 503-280-7024; Lauri Hennessey, Public Affairs, 503-280-7287

PTC
Phoenix Training Center, 5050 N. 19th Ave., Suite 300, Phoenix, AR 85015, Lynn Engdahl, Manager, 602-640-2651

Utah
324 South State St., CFS Finance Center Bldg., Suite 301, Salt Lake City, UT 84111-2303, James M. Parker, State Director, 801-539-4010; Jerry Meredith, Public Affairs, 801-539-4021

Wyoming
2515 Warren Ave., P.O. Box 1828, Cheyenne, WY 82001, Ray Brubaker, State Director, 307-775-6001; Jay Guerin, Public Affairs, 307-775-6011

* Public Housing Drug Eradication Grants

Howard Mortman
U.S. Department of Housing and Urban Development
Room 4114, P.O. Box 6424
Rockville, MD 20850   202-708-1197

HUD's Public Housing Drug Elimination Program - grant program for community-wide drug prevention programs

* Prisoner Detention and Transportation System

U.S. Marshals Service
U.S. Department of Justice
600 Army Navy Drive
Arlington, VA 22202   202-307-9100

All persons arrested and detained by order of the Federal courts for prosecution on violations of Federal laws are placed into the custody of the Marshals Service. The Service's National Prisoner Transportation System is continually required to provide extraordinary security for the movement of major drug dealers to and from scheduled court appearances.

* Prisoners, Paroles, Sentencing Data

Data Center and Clearinghouse for Drugs and Crime
Office of Justice Programs, U.S. Department of Justice
633 Indiana Ave., NW   800-666-3332
Washington, DC 20531   202-724-7782

The Data Center and Clearinghouse for Drugs and Crime was established by Justice Department's Bureau of Justice Statistics and the Bureau of Justice Assistance to provide access to existing data on drug law enforcement and the justice system's treatment of drug offenders and nondrug offenders who are drug users. They will send a free 1992 directory. Free publications include:

Order Number / Title and Release Date
86223   Prisoners and Alcohol - 1/83
87575   Prisoners and Drugs - 3/83
87068   Report to the Nation - 1st Edition - 83
96501   Examining Recidivism - 85
96132   Pretrial Release and Misconduct - 1/85

Be patient. If any phone number is incorrect, call (area code) 555-1212 and request the new listing.

603

Drugs and Chemical Dependence

97681	Felony Sentencing in 18 Local Jurisdictions - 5/85
99175	Jail Inmates, 1983 - 11/85
100582	Prison Admissions and Releases, 1983 - 86
101043	Sentencing and Time Served - 87
104916	Recidivism of Young Parolees - 5/87
105506	Report to the Nation - 2nd Edition - 88
105743	Sentencing Outcomes in 28 Felony Courts, 1985 - 87
108544	Time Served in Prison and on Parole, 1984 - 12/87
109686	Tracking Offenders, 1984 - 1/88
109926	Profile of State Prison Inmates - 1/88
109929	Pretrial Release and Detention: The Bail Reform Act of 1984 - 2/88
109945	Drunk Driving - 88
110643	Bureau of Justice Statistics Data Report 1987 - 88
111612	Sourcebook of Criminal Justice Statistics, 1987 - 88
111763	Drug Law Violators 1980-1986 - 6/88
111940	Drug Use and Crime - 7/88
113365	Survey of Youth in Custody - 9/88
114746	The Redesigned National Crime Survey: Selected New Data - 1/89
115210	Felony Sentences in State Courts, 1986 - 2/89
115749	Bureau of Justice Statistics Annual Report 1988 - 89
116261	Recidivism of Prisoners Released in 1983 - 3/89
116262	Bureau of Justice Statistics Data Report 1988 - 89
116315	Prisoners in 1988 - 4/89
118311	Federal Criminal Cases, 1980-87 - 7/89
94073	Drug Use and Pretrial Crime in the District of Columbia - 6/84
96668	Probing the Links Between Drugs and Crime - 2/85
98259	Use of Forfeiture Sanctions in Drug Cases - 85
98902	Interpol: Global Help in Fight Against Drugs - 9/85
100737	Drinking and Crime - 86
100741	Heroin - 87
100756	Project DARE: Teaching Kids to Say "No" - 3/86
102632	Employee Drug Testing Policies in Police Departments - 10/86
102668	Drugs and Crime: Controlling Use and Reducing Risk through Testing - 11/86
104555	Drug Trafficking - 87
104556	Drug Testing - 87
104557	Drug Education - 87
104865	Controlling Drug Abuse and Crime: A Research Update - 3/87
106992	Drugs and Crime: Current Federal Research - 8/88
107272	Drug Use Forecasting: New York 1984-1986 - 87
108560	Characteristics of Different Types of Drug Involved Offenders - 88
109957	Attorney General Announces NIJ DUF - 3/88
110423	Drug Use Forecasting Packet - 11/86
113915	A Criminal Justice System Strategy for Treating Cocaine-Heroin Abusing Offenders in Custody - 3/88
114730	Identifying Drug Users and Monitoring Them During Conditional Release - 2/88
115403	Street Level Drug Enforcement - 9/88
117999	In-Prison Programs for Drug-Involved Offenders - 7/89
106663	Intensive Supervision Probation and Parole - 88
113110	Reducing Crime by Reducing Drug Abuse - 6/88
114801	Implementing Project Dare: Drug Abuse Resistance Education - 6/88
116317	Drug Control and System Improvement Discretionary Grant Program - 1/89
116322	TASC: Implementing the Model - 9/88
116323	Treatment Alternatives to Street Crime - 1/88
117432	Drug Recognition Program - 89
117435	Report on Drug Control, 1988 - 89
118317	Estimating the Costs of Drug Testing - Pretrial Testing Program - 6/89
115416	Urinalysis as Part of a Treatment Alternatives to Street Crime Program - 7/88
999092	Data Center and Clearinghouse for Drugs and Crime brochure
999100	Drugs and Crime rolodex card

* Rewards for Information on Drug Traffickers Tax Evasion

Internal Revenue Service (IRS)
U.S. Department of Treasury
1111 Constitution Ave., NW
Washington, DC 20224   800-829-1040

Individuals who have information regarding drug traffickers that is of a financial nature can contact the Internal Revenue Service. If the information leads to a successful trial and unpaid taxes are received by the Internal Revenue Service, the informant is eligible to receive a reward (if the information given to the IRS was not obtainable elsewhere and was instrumental in the conviction). The reward varies and is based upon a percentage of assets retrieved. This is not an anonymous information tip system or reward system, but the IRS maintains that confidentiality is strictly enforced.

* Seized and Forfeited Assets

U.S. Marshals Service
U.S. Department of Justice
600 Army Navy Drive
Arlington, VA 22202   202-307-9100

The Marshal Service is responsible for the centralized management of the National Asset Seizure and Forfeiture Fund which includes uniform management procedures in the care, maintenance and disposal of seized and forfeited assets.

* U.S. Secret Service Involvement

U.S. Secret Service (USSS)
1800 G St., NW
Washington, DC 20223   202-435-7575

The USSS is involved in drug law enforcement investigations as a result of their following responsibilities including: any offense against the laws of the U.S. relating to currency, coins, obligations, and securities of the U.S. or of foreign governments; forgery and fraudulent negotiation or redemption of Federal Government checks, bonds, and other obligations or securities of the U.S.; offenders of laws pertaining to electronic funds transfer frauds, credit and debit card frauds, false identification documents or devices, computer access fraud, and U.S. Department of Agriculture food coupons, including authority to participate cares.

* Witness Security Protection

U.S. Marshals Service
U.S. Department of Justice
600 Army Navy Drive
Arlington, VA 22202   202-307-9100

The Federal Government's witness security program entails relocation, identity change and a range of other sophisticated services, including personal protection, in order for witnesses to contribute important testimony in drug court cases.

Be patient. If any phone number is incorrect, call (area code) 555-1212 and request the new listing.

Law and Social Justice
General Sources

* See also Careers and Workplace; Research Grants in Every Field Chapter
* See also Your Community; Money for Communities and Non-Profits Chapter
* See also Government Financial Help for Individuals Chapter
* See also Health and Medicine Chapter; Stress, Mental Illness and Family Violence Chapter
* See also Drug and Chemical Dependence Chapter
* See also Patents, Trademarks and Copyrights Chapter

The U.S. Department of Justice is the most well-known law enforcement organization of the federal government, particularly with the much-publicized activities of the Antitrust Division, the FBI and the Drug Enforcement Agency. The department is the central collector of local and state crime statistics. Also housed within this large department is the Immigration and Naturalization Service. But there are many other resources including state and federal agencies which provide free legal assistance.

* Adjudication, Arrests and National Statistics

Bureau of Justice Statistics
U.S. Department of Justice
633 Indiana Ave., NW
Washington, DC 20531   202-307-0765

The U.S. is one of only a few developed countries that has no national court statistics. There are police statistics compiled annually that show the number of persons arrested in the U.S., and there are national prison statistics compiled annually on the number sent to prison. But there are no nationwide statistics that show what happens between arrest and imprisonment. The BJS National Judicial Reporting Program is a statistical series designed to close this gap in American criminal justice statistics. This program will make it possible to answer numerous questions about felony courts that cannot now be answered, such as:

Nationwide, how many persons were convicted of felonies last year?
How many convicted felons received a jury trial?
What percent of convicted felons were sentenced to prison?
What was the average prison sentence for drug trafficking?

Contact this office to find out more information about the status and availability of new national adjudication statistics.

* Administrative Law and Government Procedures

Administrative Conference of the United States
1220 L St., NW, Suite 500
Washington, DC 20037   202-254-7020

This government think tank explores ways to improve federal agencies administer regulations, entitlements, and other programs. The Conference studies adjudication, administrative law, governmental processes, judicial review, regulation, and rulemaking. It publishes *1988 Annual Report* and their newsletter, *Administrative Conference News*, which are available free to the public. Also available is the *Administrative Conference of the United States: A Bibliography 1968-1986.*

* AIDS and the Law

National Institute of Justice (NIJ)
NCJRS, Box 6000
Dept. AID   800-851-3420
Rockville, MD 20850   301-251-5500 in DC

NIJ has the following publications and others on AIDS and legal issues available. Many of the documents are free of charge, while others are available for a modest fee. When ordering or inquiring about an NIJ publication, refer to its NCJ number.

HIV Infection and AIDS: Are You at Risk? 1992
AIDS and the Law Enforcement Officer (RIA). 1987, 6 pp. (NCJ 107541).
Voluntary HIV Counseling and Testing: Facts, Issues, and Answers, 1991.
The Cause, Transmission, and Incidence of AIDS (AIDS Bulletin). 1987, 4 pp.
(NCJ 106678).
AIDS Prevention Guide 1991.
Update on AIDS in Prisons and Jails 1991.
AIDS in Probation and Parole 1989.

* Antitrust Violations and Company Investigations

Legal Policy
Antitrust Division
U.S. Department of Justice
10th St. and Constitution Ave. NW
Room 3233
Washington, DC 20530   202-514-2512

A total case history of all antitrust investigations is available to the public. If you wish to know if a particular company is being, or ever has been, investigated for antitrust violations, and what the formal complaints were, you are welcome to thumb through the files. In addition, these files can tell you what types of violations have been investigated and what rulings have been brought down in each case. A complete transcript of pleadings, depositions, and summaries of legal procedures in all cases are available. These files are an invaluable source of legal history and precedents, and a perfect guide to business practices. For a photocopy of any portion of the Antitrust Case files, contact the Legal Procedure Unit at the above address.

* Antitrust Enforcement and the Consumer

Public Affairs
Antitrust Division
U.S. Department of Justice
10th St. and Constitution Ave., NW
Room 3107
Washington, DC 20530   202-324-2464

The free publication, *Antitrust Enforcement and the Consumer*, details general information on the how antitrust law helps the consumer, as well as specific descriptions of the Sherman and Clayton Acts, various cases the Justice Department has prosecuted and an explanation of how these violators cheated the consumer. The pamphlet also includes the addresses of all of the regional Antitrust Division offices and all of the Federal Trade Commission's regional offices throughout the country.

* Antitrust and Export Trading

Foreign Commerce Section
Antitrust Division
U.S. Department of Justice
10th St. and Constitution Ave., NW
Room 3264
Washington, DC 20530   202-514-2464

The United States' policy on foreign trade is developed and preserved by this office. Their staff and files are an incomparable source of information for anyone interested in United States trade and commerce, or the effect of foreign markets on our economy. Investors and bond salesmen, bankers and businessmen-- anyone who needs up-to-the-minute knowledge, even high-school students reporting on inflation-- should start here. Congressmen are constantly in touch with the Foreign Commerce Section before voting on trade bills. Rising politicians who want to stand on their economic platform get their data here; voters should, too. In addition, this Section administers the Export Trading Act and works with the Commerce Department to issue all Export Trading Certificates.

Law and Social Justice

* Antitrust Law and Joint Research Ventures

Superintendent of Documents
U.S. Government Printing Office
Washington, DC 20402   202-512-1800

The publication, *Antitrust Guide Concerning Research Joint Ventures*, describes the ways that corporate cooperation on research (joint ventures) can be pursued without violating antitrust laws. The *Guide* is available for $5.50 from the Government Printing Office.

* Arson, Burglary, and Other Crime Trends

Uniform Crime Reporting Section
Federal Bureau of Investigation
U.S. Department of Justice
9th and Pennsylvania Ave., NW, GRB
Washington, DC 20535   202-324-2614

Crime in the United States, an annual report taken from over 17,000 law enforcement agencies and 98% of the country, is the ultimate information source on crime. Breaking crime down into 8 basic categories (arson, larceny, burglary, aggravated assault, forgery fraud, drugs, prostitution, gambling) the report gives an exact reading of the criminal trends in our country. It lists the crime rates by state, in rural and urban areas, by gender, race, and age. Police find it an invaluable source for crime analysis and lean on it heavily when projecting the year's budget or discussing allocation of manpower. Public policy makers refer to it when debating new programs or community services. This report is fundamental for making better laws, for helping sociologists chart trends, for journalists writing articles. It can even tell prospective homebuyers how safe their future neighborhood will be. The report includes complete listings of types of weapons used in crimes, motives, victim/offender relationships. Anything you could ever want to know about crime in this country is in this report.

* Arson Control and Clearinghouse

U.S. Fire Administration
16825 South Seton Ave.
Emmitsburg, MD 21727   301-447-1122

The Arson Resource Center is available to help answer your questions and locate resources related to arson. It was established several years ago by the U.S. Fire Administration (USFA), and has developed an impressive collection of arson-related materials. Federal Emergency Management Agency (FEMA) personnel and NETC students can borrow materials from the Center, and books and research reports are available to the general public through area libraries (interlibrary loan). Audio-visual and general references are stored in the Center for in-house use. The following publications and source materials on arson are available from the USFA free of charge:

Arson Resource Directory (#5-0087)
Rural Arson Control (#5-0110)
Establishing an Arson Strike Force (#5-0111)
Arson Prosecution: Issues and Strategies
America Burning Revisited
Fire and Arson Investigator's Field Index Directory

* Arson Incidents National Database

Arson Information Management Systems (AIMS)
Office of Fire Prevention and Arson Control
U.S. Fire Administration
16825 South Seton Ave.
Emmitsburg, MD 21727   301-447-1200

The Arson Information Management Systems (AIMS) is a computerized database for the recording of data from reported arson cases, and used to facilitate analysis of such data for use by investigators, emergency personnel, law enforcers, and others. For more information on AIMS, contact the office above.

* Arson Prevention Traveling Exhibit

Office of Fire Prevention and Arson Control
Federal Emergency Management Agency
16825 South Seton Ave.
Emmitsburg, MD 21727   301-447-1200

Arson Trailers tour the country to provide technical and educational assistance to State, local, and national fire service and community groups. Their public educations demonstrations include fire safety issues, local fire problems, and smoke detector usage and maintenance.

* Art Theft FBI Database

Laboratory Division
Federal Bureau of Investigation
U.S. Department of Justice
9th St. and Pennsylvania Ave., NW
Washington, DC 20535   202-324-4545

The *National Stolen Art File* is a database which lists all currently missing works of art reported as stolen from either public or private collections in the United States. Contact this office for obtaining information from the file.

* Attorney Training

Attorney General's Advocacy Institute
Executive Office for US Attorneys
U.S. Department of Justice
10th St. and Constitution Ave., NW
Room 1342
Washington, DC 20530   202-514-2121

The Advocacy Institute trains Assistant U.S. Attorneys and all U.S. Department of Justice attorneys in trial advocacy. The Institute offers courses on civil, criminal and appellate advocacy, and seminars on such specialized topics as white-collar crime, narcotics, conspiracy, environmental litigation, bankruptcy, land condemnations, public corruption and fraud, civil rights, witness security, and computer fraud.

* Child Abuse Prosecution

National Center for the Prosecution of Child Abuse
1033 N. Fairfax St., Suite 200
Alexandria, VA 22314   703-739-0321

The National Center for the Prosecution of Child Abuse provides technical assistance, training, and clearinghouse services to improve the investigation and prosecution of child abuse cases and the procedures for dealing with children who have been victims of physical and sexual abuse. It is designed to help prosecutors dealing with the particular complexities of child abuse cases to safeguard child victims against further trauma during a criminal justice process designed for adults. The Center has produced a manual on the investigation and prosecution of child abuse cases. Contact this Center for more information.

* Child Victimization and the Law

National Institute of Justice (NIJ)
NCJRS, Box 6000
Dept. AID   800-851-3420
Rockville, MD 20850   301-251-5500 in DC

NIJ has the following publications and others on child victimization and the law. Many of the documents are free of charge, while others are available for a modest fee. When ordering or inquiring about an NIJ publication, refer to its NCJ number.

Guardians Ad Litem in the Criminal Courts. 1988, 64 pp. (NCJ 110006).
Prosecution of Child Sexual Abuse: Innovations in Practice (RIB). 1985, 7 pp. (NCJ 99317).
Prosecuting Child Sexual Abuse: New Approaches (RIA). 1985, 5 pp. (NCJ 102994).
Using Dolls to Interview Child Victims: Legal Concerns and Procedures (RIA). 1988, 6 pp. (NCJ 108470).
When the Victim Is a Child. 1985, 134 pp. (NCJ 97664).

* Cities in Schools: Truancy, Dropouts, Violence

Office of Juvenile Justice and Delinquency Prevention
U.S. Department of Justice
633 Indiana Ave., NW
Washington, DC 20531   202-307-0751

Cities in Schools, a public-private partnership that addresses the problems of dropouts and school violence, is designed to reduce school absenteeism and dropout rates by coordinating services for at-risk youngsters. Five regional offices help serve the 26 operating programs throughout the country and assist other local communities to initiate new Cities in Schools programs.

* Coast Guard Law Books

Law Library
U.S. Coast Guard
U.S. Department of Transportation
2100 2nd St., SW, Room 4407
Washington, DC 20593-0001   202-267-2536

This library supports the Coast Guard's enforcement division. Books housed here cover case law, statutory law, and other reference works specific to the Coast Guard's role as enforcer of Federal laws on the high seas and U.S. waters. The library is open to the public.

* Coast Guard Law Enforcement Planning

Planning Branch
Research and Development Staff
Office of Engineering and Development
U.S. Coast Guard
U.S. Department of Transportation
2100 2nd St., SW, Room 6208
Washington, DC 20593-0001   202-267-1030

Information can be obtained here about research conducted by the Coast Guard in support of its operations and responsibilities. Areas of study include ice operations, ocean dumping, law enforcement, environmental protection, port safety and security, navigation aids, search and rescue procedures, recreational boating, energy, and advanced marine vehicles. For referral to specific personnel working in these areas, contact the Planning Branch.

* Company Antitrust Compliance or Violation

Antitrust Division
U.S. Department of Justice
10th St. and Constitution Ave., NW
Room 3233
Washington, DC 20530   202-633-2481

Under the Business Review procedure, any firm may submit a proposed business activity to the Antitrust Division and receive a statement as to whether the Division would challenge the action as a violation of the federal antitrust laws. In addition, you can obtain copies of all such letters and replies in the *Digest of Business Reviews*, an annual publication of the U.S. Department of Justice. The indexes to the *Digest*, updated yearly, allow easy research of all the letters issued since 1968 according to topic, commodity, or service involved, and name of the requesting party. The *Digest*, annual supplements, and revised indexes are available from the Legal Procedure Unit.

* Conservation Law Enforcement Training

Law Enforcement Division
U.S. Fish and Wildlife Service
4401 N. Fairfax Dr. Room 500
Arlington, VA 22203   703-358-1949

Through this division, state conservation officers are trained in the area of criminal law as it applies to the enforcement of wildlife protection.

* Consumer Antitrust Complaint

Litigation Section
Antitrust Division
U.S. Department of Justice
10th St. and Constitution Ave. NW
Room 910
Washington, DC 20530   202-514-2464

If you wish to register a consumer complaint, call the Litigation Section of the Antitrust Division. The Litigation Section can tell you exactly who to get in touch with to lodge your complaint. They can also tell you if litigation is called for and are responsible for bringing such litigation to bear.

* Corrections and Prisons Clearinghouse

National Institute of Corrections
Bureau of Prisons
U.S. Department of Justice
320 1st St., NW
Washington, DC 20534   202-307-1304

This office provides several types of technical assistance to correctional agencies and institutes themselves. They can offer advice on managerial procedures or suggest security improvements. Agencies can seek the NIC's help for any nature of problem they may be having with policy and procedure. If an institution has had a rash of successful escapes, they will send people to investigate the problem and suggest potential solutions. The NIC also trains some state and local managerial or executive officials. Anyone interested in a career in corrections management should also contact them.

* Crime Insurance for Homeowners and Business

Federal Crime Insurance
P.O. Box 6301   800-638-8780
Rockville, MD 20850   301-251-1660 in DC

The Federal Crime Insurance Program is a federally subsidized program sponsored by the Federal Emergency Management Administration for homeowners and commercial businesses to insure against burglary and robbery. To find out if your state is eligible and for further information, contact the office above. Those living in Maryland outside DC should call collect: 301-251-1660.

* Crime Victims Publications

National Victims Resource Center (NVRC)
Box 6000-AIQ   800-627-6872
Rockville, MD 20850   301-251-5525 in DC area

The following crime victim-related publications are available free of charge from NVRC:

Crime of Rape
Domestic Violence
Drunk Driving
Economic Cost of Crime
Elderly Victims
Handgun Crime Victims
Hate Crimes
Missing, Abducted, Runaway, and Thrownaway Children in America
Neighborhood Safety
Police and Child Abuse
Risk of Violent Crimes
Robbery Victims
Sexual Assault: An Overview
Teenage Victims
Violence in Schools
Violent Crime By Strangers and Non-strangers
Violent Crime Trends

* Criminal Justice Bibliographies

National Criminal Justice Reference Service (NCJRS)
National Institute of Justice (NIJ)
U.S. Department of Justice
Box 6000   800-851-3420
Rockville, MD 20850   301-251-5500

The NCJRS acts as an international clearinghouse and reference center on subjects as diverse as Affirmative Action and Jail-Based Inmate Programs. The NCJRS has a bibliography of hundreds of publications. Contact the NCJRS Distribution Service at the above address, or contact the National Institute of Justice, 633 Indiana Ave., NW, Washington, DC 20531; 202-724-2956.

* Criminal Justice Database

National Crime Information Center
Technical Services Division
Federal Bureau of Investigation
JEH Bldg. NW
Washington, DC 20535   202-324-2711

On written request, the National Crime Information Center can provide you with information, on-line, concerning wanted persons, missing persons, stolen property, and computerized criminal histories. Searches and printouts are free.

* Criminal Justice Research

Office of Communication and Research Utilization
National Institute of Justice (NIJ)
U.S. Department of Justice
633 Indiana Ave. NW
Washington, DC 20531   202-514-6203

The National Institute of Justice has experts on nearly every field of criminal justice to help you find whatever information you're looking for. If you'd like to set up a Neighborhood Watch in your area, talk to Richard Titus or Lois Mock at 202-724-7684. Do you want to know about environmental security? The NIJ has a specialist for you. Child abuse, DWI's, incidents of family violence, drug prevention education? They have an expert. The NIJ even has a specialist who can tell you anything you want to know about insanity as a defense in a criminal case.

Law and Social Justice

* Criminal Justice: Schools, TV, Families

National Institute of Justice (NIJ)
NCJRS, Box 6000
Dept. AID   800-851-3420
Rockville, MD 20850   301-251-5500 in DC

NIJ has these and other videos and publications on crime and the law. Many of the documents are free of charge, while others are available for a modest fee. When ordering or inquiring about an NIJ publication, refer to its NCJ number.

Biology and Crime (Crime File videotape). 1985 (NCJ 97216).
Crime and Mental Disorder (RIB). 1984, 6 pp. (NCJ 94074).
Families and Crime (Crime File videotape). 1986 (NCJ 104208).
The Nature and Patterns of American Homicide. 1985, 73 pp. (NCJ 97964).
Safer Schools--Better Students (videotape). 1985 (NCJ 98687).
TV and Violence (Crime File videotape). 1985 (NCJ 97234).
Acquaintance Rape: The Hidden Crime. 1991, 423 pp. (NCJ 132446).
Crimes of the Middle Classes: White-Collar Offenders in the Federal Courts. 1991, 229 pp. (NCJ 132842).

* DNA Fingerprinting

National Institute of Justice (NIJ)
U.S. Department of Justice
Box 6000
Rockville, MD 20850   301-251-5500

NIJ-funded research has produced a new technique for identifying a criminal suspect by analyzing DNA in hair, blood, and other body fluids. The FBI is currently using this technology, which is expected to dramatically increase success in investigating violent crimes such as rape and murder. Another important breakthrough has shown that it is possible to determine blood group types from bone fragments left at the scene of a crime or accident. The research is working on a reliable procedure for grouping ABO antigens in bone. This research will eventually expand into testing for DNA in skeletal remains. Contact NIJ for more information on this new technology.

* Domestic Violence Resource Center

National Victims Resource Center
Box 6000-AIQ   800-627-6872
Rockville, MD 20850   301-251-5525 in DC

The National Victims Resource Center works as an information clearinghouse for the U.S. Department of Justice's Office of Victims of Crime. Family violence experts can assist callers in finding shelters for beaten women or local support groups. The NVRC also distributes a wide array of free publications. They also administer a library of more than 7,000 victim-related books and articles covering child physical and sexual abuse, victims services, domestic violence, victim-witness programs, and violent crime.

* Drug Abuse Warning Network (DAWN)

National Institute on Drug Abuse (NIDA)
5600 Fishers Lane
Rockville, Md 20857   301-443-6504

For those who want to understand and evaluate the scope and magnitude of drug abuse in the United States, this network is an invaluable information source. Whether you are a local public administrator considering programs, a reporter on the heels of a story, or just a concerned parent, the Drug Abuse Warning Network can provide you with needed information. More than 900 hospital emergency rooms and medical examiner facilities supply data to the program. DAWN identifies drugs currently in vogue, determines existing patterns and profiles of abuse/abuser in Standard Metropolitan Statistical Areas, monitors systemwide abuse trends, detects new abuse entities and polydrug combinations, and provides data needed for rational control and scheduling of drugs being abused. It is the full-information source on the drug problem in America.

* Drug Testing and the Law

National Institute of Justice (NIJ)
NCJRS, Box 6000
Dept. AID   800-851-3420
Rockville, MD 20850   301-251-5500 in DC

NIJ has these and other videos and publications on drug testing and the law. Many of the documents are free of charge, while others are available for a modest fee. When ordering or inquiring about an NIJ publication, refer to its NCJ number.

Drug Surveillance Through Urinalysis (videotape). 1986 (NCJ 100130). VHS, Beta, or 3/4-inch.

Drug Testing (Crime File videotape). 1986 (NCJ 104213). VHS, Beta, or 3/4-inch.
Drug Testing (Crime File study guide). 1986, 4 pp. (NCJ 104556).
Drugs and Crime: Controlling Use and Reducing Risk Through Testing (RIA). 1986, 6 pp. (NCJ 102668).
Police Drug Testing. 1987, 109 pp. (NCJ 105191).
Testing to Detect Drug Abuse (TAP publication). 1986, 2 pp. (NCJ 104282).

* Ethnic Tensions Resolution and Assistance

Community Relations Service (CRS)
U.S. Department of Justice
5550 Friendship Boulevard
Suite 300
Chevy Chase, MD 20815   301-492-5929

If your community is being torn apart by ethnic disputes or police-citizen conflicts, you may need help from this special service, set up by the Civil Rights Act of 1964. The Community Relations Service exists to resolve such disputes. The agency provides direct conciliation and mediation assistance to communities to facilitate the peaceful, voluntary resolution of racial and ethnic disputes or conflicts, and the peaceful co-existence of police and citizens' groups in the rapidly changing neighborhoods of today's cities. The CRS regularly provides conferences, training workshops, and publications to any and all communities in an attempt to forestall such disputes. However, when tensions do break out, the CRS will initiate whatever steps are necessary to begin making progress toward bringing about a resolution. They normally begin with extensive informal discussions with public or police officials and local community leaders, but if the agency and the parties determine that formal negotiations offer the best hope for a settlement, the agency arranges and mediates the negotiations.

* Explosives and Firearms Tracing Guidebook

Distribution Center
Bureau of Alcohol, Tobacco, and Firearms
U.S. Department of the Treasury
7943 Angus Ct.
Springfield, VA 22153   703-455-7801

The free book, *Firearms and Explosives Tracing Guidebook* is designed to assist law enforcement officials in preparing trace requests and determining whether or not firearms or explosives can be traced. Additional materials relating to firearms and explosives identification are included as a reference guide.

* FBI Academy and Careers

Federal Bureau of Investigation
Washington Metropolitan Field Office
Washington, DC 20535   202-324-3000

Federal Bureau of Investigation Academy
Quantico, VA 22135   703-640-6131

If you're interested in making a career out of the FBI, here's your chance. Contact the Academy or the FBI directly to obtain information on agent, special agent, or nonagent and managerial positions.

* Federal Law Enforcement Training

Federal Law Enforcement Training Center
U.S. Department of the Treasury
Glynco, GA 31524   912-267-2100

Federal Law Enforcement Training Center
Office of Artesia and Marana Operation
U.S. Department of the Treasury
1300 West Richey St.
Artesia, NM 88210   505-748-8000

The Centers above are the Federal Government's principal resources for conducting interagency law enforcement training. There are 62 Federal organizations that participate in training at Glynco. Since many individual agencies conduct very specific advanced programs for their own employees, approximately 20 participating organizations have training offices at Glynco, GA, or at the facilities at Marana, AZ and Artesia, NM.

Basic training programs provide training to entry-level Federal uniformed officers in basic law enforcement skills, such as firearms, arrest techniques, principles of law, and driver training. Programs include Immigration and Naturalization Service's Detention Officer Training, U.S. Customs Service Inspector Training, Basic Law

Enforcement for Land Management Agencies, Basic Law Enforcement for Indian Police, Border Patrol Training, and Park Police Training, among others. Examples of advanced training for experienced law enforcement officers include Officer Safety and Survival Training, Antiterrorism Management and Contingency Training, National Wildfire Investigation Training, White Collar Crime Training, and Marine Law Enforcement.

* Firearms: State Laws and Published Ordinances

Distribution Center
Bureau of Alcohol, Tobacco, and Firearms
U.S. Department of the Treasury
7943 Angus Ct.
Springfield, VA 22153   703-455-7801

The free book, *Firearms: State Laws and Published Ordinances*, outlines the state and local laws and ordinances for firearms of all states, commonwealths, and possessions of the United States. A ready reference table for use with the publication lists key elements of state laws, such as purchaser waiting period, purchaser requirements, license/permit to purchase, license as dealer manufacturer, licensee record-keeping requirements, and local government limits, and where they can be located in the laws and ordinances. State attorneys are also listed if you have state-related questions or problems regarding firearms.

* Forensics Computerized Database

Laboratory Division
Federal Bureau of Investigation
U.S. Department of Justice
9th St. and Pennsylvania Ave., NW
Washington, DC 20535   202-324-4545

The Forensics Information System is computerized database used to identify all types of forensic evidence. It includes a Rifling Characteristics File which can identify the manufacturer and type of weapon that may have been used to fire a bullet. Other files can be used to identify tire tracks or shoe prints left at the scene of a crime.

* Funding for Criminal Justice Research

Office on Justice Programs
U.S. Department of Justice
633 Indiana Ave. NW
Room 900
Washington, DC 20531   202-307-0652

Anyone interested in conducting advanced research in any Criminal Justice related fields can apply for funding from this office. Past projects to receive support from this office include studies investigating the impact of the latest technologies on conviction rates.

* Guns and Criminals Videos and Publications

National Institute of Justice (NIJ)
NCJRS, Box 6000
Dept. AID   800-851-3420
Rockville, MD 20850   301-251-5500 in DC

NIJ has these and other videos and publications on weapons, crime, and the law. Many of the documents are free of charge, while others are available for a modest fee. When ordering or inquiring about an NIJ publication, refer to its NCJ number.

The Armed Criminal in America (RIB). 1986, 5 pp. (NCJ 102827).
The Armed Criminal in America: A Survey of Incarcerated Felons. 1985, 52 pp. (NCJ 97099).
Gun Control (Crime File videotape). 1985 (NCJ 97224). VHS, Beta, 3/4-inch.
Gun Control (Crime File study guide). 1985, 4 pp. (NCJ 100740).

* Guns and Firearms Tracing Center

National Tracing Center
Bureau of Alcohol, Tobacco, and Firearms
U.S. Department of the Treasury
3361-F 75th Ave.
Landover, MD 20785   800-424-5057

The National Tracing Center provides firearms tracing services to duly authorized law enforcement agencies in the United States and those in many foreign countries. Tracing is the systematic tracking of firearms from manufacturer to purchaser (and/or possessor) for the purpose of aiding law enforcement in identifying suspects involved in criminal violations, establishing stolen status, and proving ownership.
24 Hour Number: 301-436-8159

Out of Business Records: 800-424-8201
Special Agent in Charge: 301-436-8230

* Habitual Juvenile Offenders

Office of Juvenile Justice and Delinquency Prevention
U.S. Department of Justice
633 Indiana Ave., NW
Washington, DC 20531   202-307-5914

The Serious Habitual Juvenile Offenders Comprehensive Action Program is providing intensive training and technical assistance to 20 communities to help their juvenile justice systems more efficiently identify, adjudicate, supervise, and incarcerate serious habitual juvenile offenders. Contact this office for more information on this program and how its successes might be applied to other communities.

* Heroin Situation Indicators

Office of Intelligence
Drug Enforcement Administration
U.S. Department of Justice
1405 Eye St., NW, Room 1013
Washington, DC 20537   202-307-1000

A retail and wholesale heroin price/purity index is available based upon data from the analysis of drug evidence samples submitted to the Drug Enforcement Administration. In addition, reports are available on heroin-related emergency room admissions and deaths from 21 major metropolitan areas scattered throughout the country. These reports are published on a quarterly basis.

* High Seas Law Enforcement

Navigation Safety and Waterway Services
U.S. Coast Guard
U.S. Department of Transportation
2100 2nd St., SW, Room 3110
Washington, DC 20593-0001   202-267-2267

As the primary maritime law enforcement agency for the U.S., the Coast Guard enforces Federal laws, treaties, and international agreements to which the U.S. is a party. The Coast Guard may conduct investigations when violations are suspected, such as smuggling, drug trafficking, or polluting. Empowered to board and inspect vessels routinely as well, the Guard also conducts :"suspicionless" boardings to prevent violations. To report suspicious or questionable activity on boats, or to complain about an improperly conducted boarding, call the Boating Safety Hotline, 800-368-5647; or 202-267-0780 in DC, or contact your local Coast Guard commander. The office listed above can provide you with information about the Coast Guard's law enforcement role and the National Narcotics Border Interdiction System, which coordinates multi-agency and international operations with other countries to suppress narcotics trafficking.

* Hypnosis: Forensic Tool

National Victims Resource Center
Box 6000-AIQ   800-627-6872
Rockville, MD 20850   301-251-5525 in DC area

Contact this Center for the free publication, *Forensic Use of Hypnosis*, which details how evidence revealed through hypnosis is used in court cases.

* Identifying Victims of Catastrophic Accidents

FBI Disaster Squad
Laboratory Division
Federal Bureau of Investigation
U.S. Department of Justice
J. Edgar Hoover Bldg., Room 11255
Washington, DC 20537   202-324-4410

The Disaster Squad is expert at identifying victims of catastrophic accidents. Government agencies rely upon them whenever victim identification is a problem. For local law enforcement, private investigators, transportation companies, or even families of the missing, the Disaster Squad can make a thorough analysis through fingerprints, dental records, and other physical evidence, and lay the mystery to rest. Contact this office for more information on the Squads services.

* Inmate Locator Line

Public Information
Bureau of Prisons
U.S. Department of Justice

Law and Social Justice

320 1st St., NW, Room 640
Washington, DC 20536   202-307-3198
A special phone service hotline is available for people trying to locate family
members or loved ones believed to be incarcerated in local, state, or federal
correctional institutions. Call the Inmate Locater Line: 202-724-3126 between 10
a.m. and 4:30 p.m. EST.

* Inside the FBI

Office of Public Affairs and Congressional Services
Federal Bureau of Investigation
U.S. Department of Justice
J. Edgar Hoover Bldg., Room 7116
Washington, DC 20535   202-324-5352
If you have a group planning on visiting Washington, DC, and would like to make
the FBI Headquarters a part of that trip, contact the Office of Public Affairs. Guided
tours are offered Mondays through Fridays (except holidays) from 9:00 a.m. to 4:00
p.m. No appointments are necessary for groups numbering fifteen or less.

* Jail Overcrowding

National Institute of Justice (NIJ)
NCJRS, Box 6000
Dept. AID   800-851-3420
Rockville, MD 20850   301-251-5500 in DC
NIJ has videos and publications on prison and jail overcrowding. Many of the
documents are free of charge, while others are available for a modest fee. When
ordering or inquiring about an NIJ publication, refer to its NCJ number.

* Juvenile Delinquency Risk Factors

Office of Juvenile Justice and Delinquency Prevention
Research and Program Development Division
U.S. Department of Justice
633 Indiana Ave., NW
Washington, DC 20531   202-307-5929
This research division assesses a wide range of risk factors faced by children between
the ages of six and 17. Researchers are looking beyond established delinquency
correlates--such as age, race, and sex--to investigate more practical factors, such as
personality characteristics, drug use, family relationships, school experience, the
community environment, peer/gang associations, and juvenile justice sanctions.
Contact this division for more information on this research.

* Juvenile Drug Abuse Risk Factors

Office of Juvenile Justice and Delinquency Prevention
Research and Program Development Division
U.S. Department of Justice
633 Indiana Ave., NW
Washington, DC 20531   202-724-7560
This division has researched drug use among juveniles to develop information on
high-risk factors for drug use among youth, and on the effectiveness of interventions
for preventing or controlling illegal drug use. These studies include recommendations
for promising prevention and rehabilitation strategies. Contact this division for more
information.

* Law Enforcement Officers: Deaths and Assaults

Uniform Crime Reporting Section
Federal Bureau of Investigation (FBI)
U.S. Department of Justice
9th and Pennsylvania Ave., NW, GRB
Washington, DC 20535   202-324-2614
The publication, *Law Enforcement Officers Killed or Assaulted*, is available from the
FBI Crime Reporting Section in three yearly forms: the six-month report, preliminary
annual, and annual. Write to the above address for a free copy.

* Law Enforcement Training for State and Local Officers

Federal Law Enforcement Training Center (FLETC)
U.S. Department of the Treasury
Glynco, GA 31524   912-267-2100
FLETC's Office of State and Local Law Enforcement conducts over 25 specialized
programs both at Glynco and at various sites around the country. Some of these
programs include: Child Abuse and Exploitation Investigative Techniques, Managing
Juvenile Operations, Schools Are For Effective Police Operations Leading to

Improved Children and Youth Services, Cargo Theft Investigations, Fraud and
Financial Investigations, Hazardous Waste Investigations, Prison/Jail Crisis Response
Training, Criminal Investigations in an Automated Environment, Fugitive
Investigations Training, Advanced Arson for Profit Investigations, and Narcotics
Officer Training.

* Lie Detector Tests: Reliability

National Institute of Justice (NIJ)
U.S. Department of Justice
Box 6000
Rockville, MD 20850   800-851-3420
To investigate the validity of polygraph examinations in criminal investigations, an
NIJ study compared the accuracy of human examiners to that of a computer program
in assessing the truth of answers to specific questions. The computer program was
found to be just as reliable as that of the human examiners. Contact this Institute for
more information on this study and the use of polygraphs in criminal justice.

* Maximum Speed Limit Enforcement

Police Traffic Services Division
Office of Enforcement and Emergency Services
Traffic Safety Programs
National Highway Traffic Safety Administration
U.S. Department of Transportation
400 7th Street, SW, Room 6124
Washington, DC 20590   202-366-5440
The National Maximum Speed Limit is 65 miles per hour on certain interstate
highways. This office processes annual certifications of maximum speed limit
enforcement programs throughout the U.S. and assists states in developing and
improving enforcement efforts.

* Missing and Exploited Children Clearinghouse

National Center for Missing and Exploited Children
Publications Department
2101 Wilson Blvd. Suite 550
Arlington, VA 22201-3052   703-235-3900
This Center serves as a clearinghouse of information on missing or exploited
children; provides technical assistance to citizens and law-enforcement agencies;
offers training programs to law-enforcement and social service professionals;
distributes photos and descriptions of missing children nationwide; coordinates child
protection efforts with the private sector; networks with nonprofit organizations and
state clearinghouses; and provides information on effective state legislation to ensure
the protection of children. The following publications are available free of charge:

Books:
Child Molesters: A Behavioral Analysis
Child Sex Rings: A Behavioral Analysis
Children Traumatized in Sex Rings
Interviewing Child Victims of Sexual Exploitation
Nonprofit Service Provider's Handbook
Parental Kidnapping
Selected State Legislation
Youth at Risk

Brochures:
Child Protection
Child Protection Priorities
For Camp Counselors
Just in Case...You are Considering Daycare
Just in Case...You Are Considering Family Separation
Just in Case...You Are Dealing with Grief Following the Loss of a Child
Just in Case...You Are Using the Federal Parent Locator Service
Just in Case...You Need a Babysitter
Just in Case...Your Child Is a Runaway
Just in Case...Your Child is Testifying in Court
Just in Case...Your Child is the Victim of Sexual Abuse or Exploitation
Just in Case...Your Child Is Missing

* National Emergencies

FEMA
P.O. Box 70274
Washington, DC 20024   202-646-2500
Federal Emergency Management Agency (FEMA) is part of our government which

deals with planning for and/or coordinating relief in various national emergencies. FEMA plans for nuclear attacks, security emergencies, disaster recovery aid, and helps to coordinate food, shelter, and financial aid in the event of any natural or manmade disasters. There are ten regional offices across the country. They are:

Region I - 442 J.W. McCormack, POCH, Boston, MA 02109; 617-223-9540
Region II - 26 Federal Plaza, N.Y.C., NY 10278; 212-264-8980
Region III - 105 S. 7th St., Philadelphia, PA 19106; 215-597-9416
Region IV - 1371 Peachtree St. N.E., Suite 700, Atlanta, GA 30309; 404-347-2400
Region V - 175 W. Jackson Blvd., 4th Floor, Chicago, IL 60604; 312-431-5501
Region VI - Federal Regional Center, Room 206, Denton, TX 76201;
    807-898-9104
Region VII - 911 Walnut St., Room 300, Kansas City, MO 64106; 816-374-5912
Region VIII - Federal Regional Center, Building 710, Box 25267, Denver, CO
    80225-0267; 303-235-4811
Region IX - Building 105, Presidio of San Francisco, San Francisco, CA 94129
    415-923-7100
Region X - Federal Region Center, 130 228th St., S.W., Bothell, WA 98021-9796
    206-487-4604

* Neighborhood Crime Comparison Information

Uniform Crime Reporting Section
Federal Bureau of Investigation
U.S. Department of Justice
9th and Pennsylvania Ave., NW, GRB
Washington, DC 20535   202-324-2614

If you'd like to know how safe your prospective new neighborhood is, contact the Uniform Crime Reporting Section. This annual report, *Crime In the United States* contains an exact reading of the crime rates of any city in America (down to the types of crimes committed most frequently in which neighborhoods). Also, local police departments of most major cities have neighborhood crime reports available and will actually rate the safety factor of your new address for you.

* Neighborhood Safety Videos and Publications

National Institute of Justice (NIJ)
NCJRS
Box 6000
Dept. AID   800-851-3420
Rockville, MD 20850   301-251-5500 in DC

NIJ has these and other publications and videos on crime prevention and the law. Many of the documents are free of charge, while others are available for a modest fee. When ordering or inquiring about an NIJ publication, refer to its NCJ number.

Crime Stoppers: A National Evaluation (RIB). 1986, 5 pp. (NCJ 102292).
The Growing Role of Private Security (RIB). 1984, 5 pp. (NCJ 94703).
Guardian Angels: An Assessment of Citizen Response to Crime: Executive Summary. 1986, 31 pp. (NCJ 1009111).
Improving the Use and Effectiveness of Neighborhood Watch Programs (RIA). 1988, 4 pp. (NCJ 108618).
Neighborhood Safety (Crime file videotape). 1985 (NCJ 97227). VHS, Beta, or 3/4-inch.
Taking a Bite Out of Crime: The Impact of a Mass Media Crime Prevention Campaign. 1984, 78 pp. (NCJ 93350).

* Neighborhood Watch Programs

National Crime Prevention Council
17 K St. N.W.
2nd Floor
Washington, DC 20036   202-466-NCPC

If you're interested in starting a Neighborhood Watch Program in your town, or want to know how you can make yours better, contact the Neighborhood Watch Specialists at the National Institute of Justice. They will be glad to help you make your neighborhood a safer place.

* New Federal Laws

Office of the Federal Register
National Archives and Records Administration
8th St. and Pennsylvania Ave., NW, Room 8401
Washington, DC 20408   202-523-5230

This office receives all the laws enacted by Congress for publication in the *Federal Register* and can provide information regarding these laws. They also publish *United States at Large*, a compilation of laws enacted during a particular year.

* Odometer Tampering

Odometer Fraud Staff
Office of Chief Counsel
National Highway Traffic Safety Administration (NHTSA)
U.S. Department of Transportation
400 7th Street, SW, Room 5219
Washington, DC 20590   202-366-9511

Federal law requires that the seller of a car sign a disclosure statement that the mileage on the odometer is accurate and has not been rolled back. NHTSA enforces the odometer law via inspections and criminal charges. Information on odometer tampering is also available from the Auto Safety Hotline: 800-424-9393.

* Police-Citizen Conflict Resolution

Community Relations Service (CRS)
U.S. Department of Justice
5550 Friendship Blvd., Suite 300
Chevy Chase, MD 20815   301-492-5929

The agency provides direct conciliation and mediation assistance to communities to facilitate the peaceful, voluntary resolution of racial and ethnic disputes or conflicts, and the peaceful co-existence of police and citizens' groups in the rapidly changing neighborhoods of today's cities. They normally begin with extensive informal discussions with public or police officials and local community leaders, but if the agency and the parties determine that formal negotiations offer the best hope for a settlement, the agency arranges and mediates the negotiations.

* Police Use of Deadly Force

Community Relations Service
5550 Friendship Blvd., Room 330
Chevy Chase, MD 20815   301-492-5929

There has been a steady increase in cases of community disruption due to minority groups' belief that the police have used deadly force--or a severe degree of non-lethal force-- when it was unwarranted. Two booklets, *Police Use of Deadly Force*, and *Principles of Good Policing*, provides information that will be useful to citizens and police looking for constructive alternatives to continued hostility and suspicion.

* Prisons and Correctional Institutions Clearinghouse

National Institute of Corrections Information Center
Bureau of Prisons
U.S. Department of Justice
1860 Industrial Circle, Suite A
Long Mont, CO 80501   303-682-0213

This center is the complete source of information on correctional institutions. They have the data to answer any and all questions. Public policy makers who are considering the economics and potential benefits of a proposed new prison would be wise to get in touch with the NIC, as would construction companies thinking of making a bid on a new site. Politicians, correctional officials, reporters, or even inmates who want to investigate possible reforms should contact this office.

* Prisons: History, Statistics

Public Affairs
Bureau of Prisons
U.S. Department of Justice
320 1st St., NW, Room 640
Washington, DC 20536   202-307-3198

The Bureau of Prisons has many publications available to the public. They release an annual *State of the Bureau* report, as well as publications describing new and existing facilities, a history of the development of the federal bureau, and an annual statistical report of the Nation's correctional facilities.

* Protection of the President

Personnel Division
U.S. Secret Service
U.S. Department of the Treasury
1800 G St., NW
Washington, DC 20223   202-435-5800

Protection is the key mission of the Uniformed Division of the Secret Service. They are responsible for the White House Complex; the Main Treasury Building and Annex and other Presidential offices; the President and immediate family; the official residence of the Vice President and his immediate family; and foreign diplomatic missions as prescribed by statute.

Law and Social Justice

* Racial Disputes Resolution
Community Relations Service (CRS)
U.S. Department of Justice
5550 Friendship Blvd., Suite 300
Chevy Chase, MD 20815   301-492-5929

If your community is being torn apart by ethnic disputes or police-citizen conflicts, you may need help from this special service, set up by the Civil Rights Act of 1964. The Community Relations Service exists to resolve such disputes. The agency provides direct conciliation and mediation assistance to communities to facilitate the peaceful, voluntary resolution of racial and ethnic disputes or conflicts, and the peaceful co-existence of police and citizens' groups in the rapidly changing neighborhoods of today's cities. The CRS regularly provides conferences, training workshops, and publications to any and all communities in an attempt to forestall such disputes. However, when tensions do break out, the CRS will initiate whatever steps are necessary to begin making progress toward bringing about a resolution. They normally begin with extensive informal discussions with public or police officials and local community leaders, but if the agency and the parties determine that formal negotiations offer the best hope for a settlement, the agency arranges and mediates the negotiations.

* Recidivism Statistics
Bureau of Justice Statistics
U.S. Department of Justice
633 Indiana Ave., NW
Washington, DC 20531   202-307-0765

The National Recidivism Data Base links Bureau of Justice Statistics corrections data with state and FBI criminal history information to derive representative samples of individuals released from State prisons, follow these samples for several years, and produce estimates on the incidence, prevalence, and seriousness of later arrests and dispositions. For information on available statistics on prison recidivism, contact this office.

* RX Drug and Controlled Substances Registration
Registration Section
Office of Compliance and Regulatory Affairs
Drug Enforcement Administration
U.S. Department of Justice
666 11th St., NW, Room 920
Washington, DC 20001   202-307-1000

Information is available about registration under the Controlled Substances Act. Every person who manufactures, distributes, or dispenses any controlled substance, or who proposes to engage in the manufacture, distribution, or dispensing of any controlled substance, must register annually with the Registration Branch of the DEA. The names of all registrants are available to the public, as well as a schedule of all controlled substances. In addition, the DEA will investigate any registrant to ensure that they are accountable for the controlled substances handled if presented with requests or evidence which would seem to warrant such investigation.

* Secret Service Special Agents
Personnel Division
U.S. Secret Service
U.S. Department of the Treasury
1800 G St., NW
Washington, DC 20223   202-435-5800

Special agents for the Secret Service are charged with two missions: protection and investigation. In addition to those protected by the Uniformed Division, the Special Agents guard former Presidents and their spouses, children of former Presidents, visiting heads of foreign states and governments and their spouses, and major Presidential and Vice Presidential candidates. Counterfeiting, forgery, and fraud investigations are also performed by Special Agents. Candidates interested in applying may contact local Secret Service field offices.

* Settlement of Claims Against the Government
Claims Group General Government Division
General Accounting Office (GAO)
441 G St., NW
Washington, DC 20548   202-275-3102

In addition to helping settle claims of one government agency against another, this GAO office also settles claims by and against the United States. Claims may involve individuals, businesses, or foreign, state, and municipal governments. Claims are settled by GAO when the departments and agencies have not been given specific authority to handle their own claims and when they involve 1) doubtful questions of law or fact; 2) appeals of agency actions; 3) certain debts which agencies are unable to collect; and 4) waivers of certain erroneous payments for pay. Contact GAO for more information.

* Stolen Pharmaceuticals and Other Drug Theft Office of Intelligence
Drug Enforcement Administration (DEA)
U.S. Department of Justice
1405 Eye St., NW, Room 1013
Washington, DC 20537   202-307-1000

All legal drug handlers registered with the Drug Enforcement Administration are required to report thefts or losses on controlled substances. Stolen supplies from legitimate drug handlers comprise a substantial portion of the illicit drug distribution network. The DEA has a fully updated list of all reports of drug theft. For information contact the Office of Intelligence at the above address or phone number.

* Supreme Court Library
Supreme Court of the United States Library
1 1st St., NE
Washington, DC 20543   202-479-3175

A complete working collection of American, English, and Canadian statutes, records and briefs dating back to 1832 are contained in this library. Historical and constitutional documents along with the federal tax laws and legislative histories of selected federal acts are also available here. The library is open to the public, Monday through Friday, 9am-4:15pm, to use the records and briefs department.

* U.S. Park Police
National Capital Region
National Park Service
U.S. Department of the Interior
1100 Ohio Dr., SW
Washington, DC 20242   202-208-4747

The U.S. Park Police have the same authority and powers as the Washington, DC metropolitan police. They also act as hosts to park visitors.

* Victimization Statistics
National Victims Resource Center
Box 6000-AIQ   800-627-6872
Rockville, MD 20850   301-251-5525 in DC

This Center can provide you with nationwide statistics on the victims of crime.

* Violent Criminal Behavior
National Institute of Justice (NIJ)
U.S. Department of Justice
Box 6000
Rockville, MD 20850   301-251-5500

NIJ research has examined the relation between early child abuse, neglect, and subsequent violent criminal behavior. Criminal records of substantiated cases of individuals abused as children were compared with criminal records of a matched group of non-abused individuals. The results to date suggest that those who were abused as children did commit more violent offenses as adults than those not abused as children. Contact this office for more information on this topic.

* Whistleblower Hotlines and Government Inspector Generals
Many federal departments and agencies have hotlines, some toll-free numbers, into the office of the Inspector General. The responsibility of the IG is chiefly an in-house auditor looking for fraud, mismanagement, and government waste. These whistleblower hotlines exist to encourage federal employees, state employees, contractors, and citizens to report any allegations.

U.S. Department of Agriculture
Office of Inspector General
P.O. Box 23399 800-424-9121
Washington, DC 20026 202-727-2540

U.S. Department of the Army
The Pentagon 800-572-9000
Washington, DC 20310 703-545-6700

U.S. Department of Commerce
14th and Constitution Ave., NW
Room 7898-C 800-424-5197
Washington, DC 20230 202-377-2495

U.S. Department of Defense
Defense Hotline
The Pentagon 800-424-9098
Washington, DC 20301-1900 703-545-6700

U.S. Department of Education
Inspector General Hotline
P.O. Box 23458 800-647-8733
Washington, DC 20026 202-205-5770

U.S. Department of Energy
1000 Independence Ave., SW
Room 5DO39, Forrestal Building
Washington, DC 20585 202-586-5000

U.S. Department of Health and Human Services
OIG Hotline
P.O. Box 17303 800-368-5779
Baltimore, MD 21203-7303 202-619-0257

U.S. Department of Housing and Urban Development
451 7th St., SW, Room 8254
Washington, DC 20410 202-708-1422

U.S. Department of the Interior
18th and C Sts., NW, Room 5359 800-424-5081
Washington, DC 20240 202-208-3424

U.S. Department of Justice
Office of Professional Responsibility
10th and Constitution Ave., NW, Room 4304 800-869-4999
Washington, DC 20530 202-514-3435

U.S. Department of Labor
200 Constitution Ave., NW
Room S1303 800-424-5409
Washington, DC 20210 202-357-0227

U.S. Department of State
2201 C St., NW
New State Building, Room 6821
Washington, DC 20520 202-647-3320

U.S. Department of Transportation
400 7th St., NW, Room 9210 800-424-9071
Washington, DC 20590 202-366-1461

U.S. Department of Treasury
15th and Pennsylvania Ave., NW, Room 2412 800-826-0407
Washington, DC 20220 202-622-1090

U.S. Department of Veterans Affairs
1425 K St., NW
McPherson Building, Room 1100
Washington, DC 20420 202-233-5394

Environmental Protection Agency
401 M St., SW
Room 307 NE Mall 800-424-4000
Washington, DC 20460 202-260-4977

Federal Bureau of Investigation
Inspections Division
Washington, DC 20535 202-324-2901

General Accounting Office
441 G St., NW 202-272-5557
Washington, DC 20548 800-424-5454

General Services Administration
18th and F Sts., NW, Room 5340 800-424-5210
Washington, DC 20405 202-501-0450

Merit Systems Protection Board
Office of the Special Counsel
1120 Vermont Ave., NW, Suite 1100 800-872-9855
Washington, DC 20005 202-653-9125

National Aeronautics and Space Administration
Inspector General
P.O. Box 23089
L'Enfant Station 800-424-9183
Washington, DC 20026 202-755-3402

Office of Personnel Management
1900 E St., NW, Room 6831
Washington, DC 20415 202-606-1200

Railroad Retirement Board
Office of Inspector General
Office of Investigation
844 N. Rush St., Room 450 800-772-4258
Chicago, IL 60611 312-751-4336

Small Business Administration
1441 L St., NW, Room 203
Washington, DC 20416 202-653-7557

Tennessee Valley Authority
400 West Summit Hill Drive 800-323-3835
Knoxville, TN 37902 615-632-3550

U.S. Agency for International Development
21st and Virginia Ave.
Room 5644, New State Building
Washington, DC 20523 202-647-7844

U.S. Information Agency
Donohoe Building, Room 1100
400 6th St., SW
Washington, DC 20547 202-401-7931

* World's Largest Law Library

Law Library
Library of Congress
Washington, DC 20540   202-707-5079

As the world's largest and most comprehensive library of foreign, international, and comparative law, the Law Library provides information for all known legal systems including common law, civil law, Roman law, canon law, Chinese law, Jewish and Islamic law, and ancient and medieval law. Specialists with knowledge of more than fifty languages provide reference and research service in all known legal systems. U.S. legislative documents housed here include the *Congressional Record* (and its predecessors), the serial set, a nearly complete set of bills and resolutions, current documents, committee prints, reports, hearings, etc. plus a complete set of U.S. Supreme Court records and briefs and collections of U.S. Court of Appeals records and briefs. The law library has only two divisions:

Western Law Division
United States, Australia, Canada, Great Britain, India, New Zealand, Pakistan, certain other countries of the British Commonwealth and their dependent territories, Eire, Spain and Portugal, Latin America, Puerto Rico, the Philippines, and Spanish- and Portuguese-language states of Africa: 202-707-5077.

Eastern Law Division
Nations of Europe and their possessions, except Spain and Portugal, nations of East and Southeast Asia including China, Indonesia, Japan, Korea, Thailand, and former British and French possessions in the area, Middle Eastern countries, including the Arab states, Turkey, Iran, and Afghanistan, and all African countries except Spanish- and Portuguese-language states and possessions: 202-707-5085.

Courts and Legal Help

* Administration of U.S. Courts

Administrative Office of the United States Courts
1 Columbus Circle, N.E.
Washington, DC 20002   202-273-3000

This Office is responsible for supervision of administrative matters in all courts except the Supreme Court, supervising accounts and practices of the Federal probation offices, certain administrative matters within the Bankruptcy court, and exercises general supervision over administrative matters in offices of the United States magistrates. Information may be obtained from the following offices:

Bankruptcy Division: 202-273-1900
Court Administration Division: 202-273-1530
Defender Services Division: 202-273-1670
General Counsel: 202-273-1100
Magistrates Division: 202-273-1830
Personnel Division: 202-273-2777
Probation Division: 202-273-1600
Human Resources 202-273-1200

* Arbitrators and Mediators

Federal Mediation and Conciliation Service (FMCS)
2100 K St., NW
Washington, DC 20427   202-653-5300

Through its regional offices and suboffices, FMCS assists federal agencies, private sector employers, and labor organizations in resolving labor-management disputes. When there is no local or state resource available, the parties involved may contact the regional FMCS office to be assigned a qualified mediator or arbitrator, on call 24 hours a day. Upon request, mediators will assist the parties in resolving disputes, and arbitrators will make a final decision. Technical assistance includes training for one or both parties in developing constructive methods of dispute resolution, help in forming committees, and collective bargaining workshops. Contact your local FMCS office for any of these services.

* Bankruptcy Clearinghouse

Administrative Office of the United States Courts
Bankruptcy Division
1 Columbus Circle N.E.
Washington, DC 20002   202-273-1900

Since the Administrative Office has general supervision for the bankruptcy courts, information on bankruptcy forms, fees, and explanations of the Bankruptcy Act is available.

* Bench Book for District Court Judges

Information Service Division
Federal Judicial Center
1 Columbus Circle NE
Washington, DC 20002   202-273-4153

The *Bench Book for United States District Court Judges* is available to judicial personnel only. This book contains statutes, suggestions, recommendations, and reference materials for judicial proceedings. The book is prepared by the Judicial Center from the guidance of experienced district judges.

* Civil and Criminal District Court Procedures

Superintendent of Documents
Government Printing Office
Washington, DC 20402   202-512-1800

Rules of Civil Procedure for the United States District Courts, With Forms. Contains the Rules of Civil Procedure for United States District Courts as promulgated and amended by the Supreme Court to October 1, 1977. $3.75

Federal Rules of Evidence. Sets forth Rules of Evidence for use in proceedings in the courts of the United States and before United States magistrates. $1.75

Federal Rules of Appellate Procedure. Contains the Federal Rules of Appellate Procedure as promulgates and amended by the United States Supreme Court to October 1, 1979, along with the forms adopted by the Court. $2

A publications catalog is available free upon request.

* Constitution and Supreme Court Decisions

Supreme Court of the United States
1 1st St., NE
Washington, DC 20543   202-252-3000

The *Constitution of the United States of America: Analysis and Interpretation* includes the text of the Constitution, along with its amendments prefacing annotations of the Supreme Court decisions that are relevant to the way the Constitution is interpreted. The cost is $70 and is available from the Superintendent of Documents, Government Printing Office, Washington, DC 20402; 202-512-1800.

* Disabled and Handicapped Persons: Legal Aid

National Association of Protection and Advocacy System (NAPAS)
220 Eye Street, NW
Suite 150
Washington, DC 20002   202-408-9514

Every state and the territories provide legal assistance for the handicapped and developmentally disabled. This national organization also coordinates state agencies for the mentally ill and client assistance program. NAPAS publishes a newsletter titled *Annual Report.* The following is a list of the state protection and advocacy agencies for those with developmental disabilities.

Alabama Disabilities Advocacy Program 205-348-4928
Alaska Advocacy Services 800-478-1234
    907-344-1002
American Samoa Client Assistance P&A Program 684-633-2441
Arizona Center for Law in the Public Interest 602-274-6287
Arkansas Advocacy Services 501-324-9215
    800-482-1174
California Protection and Advocacy Inc. 800-776-5746
    916-488-9950
    818-546-1631
    510-839-0811
Colorado Legal Center 303-722-0300
Connecticut Office of P&A 800-842-7303
    203-297-4300
    203-566-2101
Delaware Disabilities Law Program 302-856-0038
    302-764-2400
District of Columbia Information, Protection, and Advocacy ... 202-727-0977
    202-966-8081
Florida Advocacy Center for Persons with Disabilities 904-488-9071
    800-342-0823
Georgia Advocacy Office, Inc. 800-282-4538
    404-885-1234
Guam Advocacy Office 671-646-9026
Hawaii Protection and Advocacy Agency 808-949-2922
Idaho's Coalition of Advocates for the Disabled 208-336-5353
Illinois Protection and Advocacy Inc. 312-341-0022
    217-782-5374
Indiana Advocacy Services 800-622-4845
    317-232-1150
Iowa Protection and Advocacy Service, Inc. 515-278-2502
Kansas Advocacy and Protection Services 800-432-8276
    913-776-1541
Kentucky Office for Public Advocacy Division 800-372-2988
    502-564-2967
Louisiana Advocacy Center for the Elderly and Disabled 800-662-7705
    504-5522-2337
Maine Advocacy Services 800-452-1948
    207-377-6202

Maryland Disability Law Center 800-233-7201
　　　　　　　　　　　　　　　　　　　　　　　　　410-333-7251
Massachusetts Disability Law Center 617-723-8455
Michigan Protection and Advocacy Service 517-487-1755
Minnesota Legal Aid Society of Minneapolis 612-332-1441
Mississippi Protection and Advocacy System 601-981-8207
Missouri Protection and Advocacy System 800-392-8667
　　　　　　　　　　　　　　　　　　　　　　　　　314-893-3333
Montana Advocacy Program 800-245-4743
　　　　　　　　　　　　　　　　　　　　　　　　　406-444-3889
Nebraska Advocacy Services 402-474-3183
Nevada Office of Protection and Advocacy 800-992-5715
　　　　　　　　　　　　　　　　　　　　　　　　　702-575-5912
New Hampshire Disabilities Rights Center 603-228-0432
New Jersey Office of Advocacy 800-792-8600
　　　　　　　　　　　　　　　　　　　　　　　　　609-292-9742
New Mexico Protection and Advocacy System 800-432-4682
　　　　　　　　　　　　　　　　　　　　　　　　　505-256-3100
New York Commission on Quality of Care for the
　Mentally Disabled 518-473-7378
North Carolina Governor's Advocacy Council for Persons
　with Disabilities 919-733-9250
North Dakota Protection and Advocacy Project 800-474-2670
　　　　　　　　　　　　　　　　　　　　　　　　　701-224-2972
Northern Mariana Islands Catholic Social Services 670-234-6981
Ohio Legal Rights Service 800-282-9181
　　　　　　　　　　　　　　　　　　　　　　　　　614-466-7264
Oklahoma Protection and Advocacy Agency 918-664-5883
Oregon Advocacy Center 503-243-2081
Pennsylvania Protection and Advocacy 800-692-7443
　　　　　　　　　　　　　　　　　　　　　　　　　412-363-7223
. . . . 215-557-7112
Puerto Rico Governor's Office Ombudsman for the Disabled . . . 809-766-2333
Rhode Island Protection and Advocacy System 401-831-3150
South Carolina Protection and Advocacy System 800-922-5225
　　　　　　　　　　　　　　　　　　　　　　　　　803-782-0639
South Dakota Advocacy Project, Inc. 800-658-4782
　　　　　　　　　　　　　　　　　　　　　　　　　605-224-8294
Tennessee E.A.C.H. Inc. 800-342-1660
　　　　　　　　　　　　　　　　　　　　　　　　　615-298-1080
Texas Advocacy, Inc. 800-252-9108
　　　　　　　　　　　　　　　　　　　　　　　　　512-454-4816
Utah Legal Center for the Handicapped 800-662-9080
　　　　　　　　　　　　　　　　　　　　　　　　　801-363-1347
Vermont Developmental Disability Law Project 802-863-2881
Virginia Department for Rights of the Disabled 800-552-3962
　　　　　　　　　　　　　　　　　　　　　　　　　804-225-2042
Virgin Islands Committee on Advocacy for the
　Developmentally Disabled 809-772-1200
Washington Protection and Advocacy System 206-324-1521
West Virginia Advocates 800-950-5250
　　　　　　　　　　　　　　　　　　　　　　　　　304-346-0847
Wisconsin Coalition for Advocacy 608-267-0214
Wyoming Protection and Advocacy System 800-624-7648
　　　　　　　　　　　　　　　　　　　　　　　　　307-638-7668

* Disaster Victims Legal Services
Federal Emergency Management Agency (FEMA)
P.O. Box 70274
Washington, DC 20024　　　　　　　　　　　202-646-2500
The *Manual for Disaster Legal Services* has been prepared by FEMA and the Young Lawyers Division (YLD) of the American Bar Association. Its purpose is to orient new and potential volunteers to the FEMA-YLD Program for offering legal services to victims following major disasters. In order to facilitate this orientation, the *Manual* emphasizes schematic diagram, paraphrases statutes and regulations, and simplifies many issues relating to the program.

* Federal Courts Office Procedure
Judicial Center
1 Columbus Circle, N.E.
Washington, DC 20002　　　　　　　　　　　202-273-4153
Office procedures relating to organization and process of the federal courts is defined in a free handbook available only to certain judicial personnel from this office.

* Federal Courts Report
Administrative Office of the United States Courts
811 Vermont Ave., NW
Washington, DC 20544　　　　　　　　　　　202-273-3000
The business of all the federal courts (except the United States Court of Military Appeals and United States Tax Courts) is included in the *Reports of the Proceedings of the Judicial Conference of the United States*, 1991. It is available for $13 from the Superintendent of Documents, Government Printing Office, Washington, DC 20402; 202-512-1800.

* Federal Judicial Resource Center
Federal Judicial Center
1 Columbus Circle N.E.
Washington, DC 20002　　　　　　　　　　　202-273-4153
The subjects in this service cover civil and criminal procedure, constitutional law and probabilities, and court management. Material on all areas of the federal judicial administration can be obtained by writing the Federal Judicial Center.

* Federal Magistrates
Administrative Office of the United States Courts
Magistrates Division
1 Columbus Circle N.E.
Washington, DC 20002　　　　　　　　　　　202-273-1830
Information and statistics on the offices of the United States magistrates is provided annually to Congress and can be obtained by contacting this Administrative Office of the United States Courts, Magistrates Division.

* Federal Public Defenders
Administrative Office of the United States Courts
1 Columbus Circle N.E.
Washington, DC 20002　　　　　　　　　　　202-273-3000
Under the Criminal Justice Act, the *Federal Public Defenders and Federal Community Defender Organizations by the Districts Courts* is made available to the public. *Annual Reports* are provided by Defender organizations listing their activities.

* Foreigners Visiting Judicial Branch
Federal Judicial Center
Information Services Division
1 Columbus Circle N.E.
Washington, DC 20002　　　　　　　　　　　202-273-4153
Arrangements for official visitors from abroad, along with conducting briefings and assembling materials are conducted in this division.

* Judicial Branch Answer Desk
Federal Judicial Center
Dolly Madison House
1 Columbus Circle N.E.
Washington, DC 20002　　　　　　　　　　　202-273-4153
Call this center to determine how this branch of government can help you or can refer you to the appropriate office, agency, or court.

* Judicial Conference Update
Federal Judicial Center
Center Information Services Office
1 Columbus Circle N.E.
Washington, DC 20002　　　　　　　　　　　202-273-4153
The Third Branch is a monthly bulletin that reports to the federal judicial community and other parties on the endeavors of the Judicial Conference. It also provides a monthly update of changes in federal judicial personnel.

* Judicial Education and Training
Federal Judicial Center
1 Columbus Circle, NE
Washington, DC 20002　　　　　　　　　　　202-273-4153
This Center provides continuing education for federal judicial personnel. It also conducts research, development, and training for the judicial system.

Law and Social Justice

* Judicial Research Reports

Federal Judicial Center
1 Columbus Circle, NE
Washington, DC 20002   202-273-4153
Research reports, staff papers, manuals, handbooks, and catalogs are publications that are available containing the results of research and analysis done for or by the Center. A publications catalog and other information can be obtained from the Federal Judicial Center.

* Law School Free Legal Clinics

Office of Public Affairs
Legal Services Corporation
750 1st St., NE, 11th Floor
Washington, DC 20002   202-336-8896
The Law School Clinic Program is an additional source of legal assistance for the poor. A significant achievement of these clinics is their ability to educate students in substantive and procedural law, while providing a service to clients in their local communities.

* Legal Aid and Services Clearinghouse

National Clearinghouse on Legal Services
407 S. Dearborn St.
Chicago, IL 60605   312-939-3830
As a grantee of the Legal Services Corporation (LSC), this clearinghouse conducts research on computerized databases for LSC funded organizations. They maintain a brief bank and publish two newsletters each month with information on legal briefs. Copies of the briefs are free to LSC organizations, and for a slight fee to the public. Each month they publish *Clearinghouse Review*, which contains relevant articles and briefs (free to LSC organizations, a yearly fee to all others). The clearinghouse also has manuals on public law.

* Legal Services and Problems

Office of Public Affairs
Legal Services Corporation
750 1st St. NE, 11th Floor
Washington, DC 20002   202-336-8896
If you are in need of legal services, the Office of Public Affairs can direct you to the Legal Services Corporation (LSC) field office that serves your area. If you feel that you are eligible for services but are denied by the field office, LSC's Public Affairs Office will help you have your complaints investigated.

* Legal Services Corporation Grantees and Contracts

Office of Field Services
Legal Services Corporation
750 1st St. NE, 11th Floor
Washington, DC 20002   202-336-8800
A Fact Book, published yearly by the Legal Services Corporation (LSC) for $30, contains information regarding LSC funding data, program expenditures, and program characteristics, as well as information on national support centers and program services to clients. The Corporation's objective in compiling and issuing this *Fact Book* is to provide a complete and objective profile of legal services programs, which can serve as a reliable reference tool for policy decision-making and further quantitative analysis. A directory of the Legal Services Corporation's contract and grantee agencies is available for $8.

* Legal Services Corporation Opinions

General Counsel's Office
Legal Services Corporation
750 1st St. NE
Washington, DC 20002   202-336-8800
This office contains the final opinions, briefs, and orders for all cases adjudicated by Legal Services Corporation. All of these documents can be examined during business hours.

* Legal Services Corporation Newsletter

Legal Services Corporation
750 1st St. NE.
Washington, DC 20002   202-336-8800

Legal Services Board is a quarterly publication which contains information on Legal Services Corporation (LSC) regulations and activities, as well as articles by Board members. Information is also included on LSC funded organizations.

* Legal Services National Support Centers

Office of Public Affairs
Legal Services Corporation
750 1st St. NE
Washington, DC 20002   202-336-8896
The Legal Services Corporation currently funds sixteen National Support Centers that specialize in various aspects of "poverty law" or in the problems of particular classes of individuals, such as migrants or the elderly. The centers produce publications and provide information relating to their respective areas. In addition they lobby Congress and federal agencies and monitor legislation and regulations of interest to their purported constituencies. The Support Centers, however, provide little or no actual representation of poor clients. Contact this office for more information regarding the individual Support Centers and their areas of interest.

* Mediation Board Publications

Office of Executive Secretary
National Mediation Board
1301 K St., NW,
Washington, DC 20572   202-523-5920
There are three annual subscription mailing lists available from the National Mediation Board. Costs may be reduced or waived when it is in the public interest to do so.

Subscription List #1, $175: *Annual Reports of the NMB; Certifications and Dismissals; Determination of Craft or Class; Findings Upon Investigation; Emergency Board Reports.*

Subscription List #2, $ 50: *Annual Reports of the NMB; Emergency Board Reports; Determination of Craft or Class.*

Subscription List #3, $ 35: *The Representation Manual and Amendments.*

* Mediation Cases

Legal Services Office
Federal Mediation and Conciliation Service (FMCS)
2100 K St., NW, Room 712
Washington, DC 20427   202-653-5305
This office represents the Federal Mediation and Conciliation Service (FMCS) in legal cases. In unusually complex and technical mediation efforts, Legal Services staff participate as part of the mediation team. Contact this office for more information on labor-management conciliation cases.

* Mediation National Board Freedom of Information

National Mediation Board
1301 K St., NW
Washington, DC 20572   202-523-5996
This office handles Freedom of Information Act requests regarding the National Mediation Board.

* Native Americans with Disabilities Legal Aid

Native American DNA-People's Legal Services
P.O. Box 306
Window Rock, AZ 86515   602-871-4151
This advocacy group provides legal help to Indians with handicaps and developmental disabilities.

* Probation Practices

Administrative Office of the United States Courts
Probation Division
Washington, DC 20002   202-273-1600
The quarterly journal, *Federal Probation*, contains correctional philosophy and practices. The Administrative Office supervises the accounts and practices of the federal probation offices. Contact this office to obtain a copy.

* Public Defenders of U.S. Courts

Administrative Office of the United States Courts
1 Columbus Circle NW
Washington, DC 20002   202-273-3000

Under the Criminal Justice Act, the *Federal Public Defenders and Federal Community Defender Organizations by the Districts Courts* is made available to the public. *Annual Reports* are provided by Defender organizations listing their activities.

* State Justice Free Newsletter

State Justice Institute News
120 South Fairfax St.
Alexandria, VA 22314   703-684-6100

This free quarterly newsletter, *State Justice Institute News*, provides information about State Justice Institute (SJI) grant programs, upcoming conferences, and the grant application process.

* State Justice Grant Categories

State Justice Institute
120 South Fairfax St.
Alexandria, VA 22314   703-684-6100

The State Justice Institute provides grants, contracts and cooperative agreements to State courts and organizations that can help improve the judicial administration of the State courts. To accomplish this goal, the Institute funds education projects in five categories: 1) Programs of proven merit which support established, exemplary, direct training to State trial and appellate court judges and other court personnel; 2) State initiatives which support state-based training projects developed or endorsed by the State courts for the benefit of judges and other court personnel in a particular state. This would include pre-bench orientation, development of bench books and model plans for career-long education for the judiciary; 3) National and regional training programs which fund projects addressing SJI Special Interest categories, which include seminars on topics that transcend state lines, regional training programs sponsored by national organizations, or specialized training programs for trial court judges; 4) Technical assistance which provides coordination, support services, information distribution, and other activities necessary for the development of effective education programs for judges, such as the development of educational curriculum or distribution of information about continuing judicial education programs; 5) Conferences which fund regional or national conferences that address topics of major concern to state judiciary.

* Supreme Court Document Copies

Library
Supreme Court of the United States
1 1st St., NE
Washington, DC 20543   202-479-3175

Supreme Court documents may be copied at the Library, Supreme Court of the United States, or by mail at the cost of $.10 per page by contacting the Photoduplication Service, Library of Congress, Washington, DC 20540; 202-479-3011.

* Supreme Court Information

Supreme Court
Clerk's Office
1 1st St., NE
Washington, DC 20543   202-479-3011

The status of pending cases, docket sheet information, and admissions to the Supreme Court bar can be obtained from the Clerk's Office. This office also distributes court opinions.

* Supreme Court Publications

Supreme Court of the United States
Information
Supreme Court Building
1 1st St., NE
Washington, DC 20543   202-479-3000

Individual Slip Opinions include all of the Supreme Court's opinions as announced from the bench. They are issued periodically and cost $140 a term of Court. *Preliminary Prints* (advance parts) are official United States Reports containing all the opinions with syllabi, indices, tables of cases, and other editorial additions. They are issued periodically and cost $56 a term of Court.

* Supreme Court Records

Supreme Court
Clerk's Office
1 1st St., NE
Washington, DC 20543   202-479-3011

Supreme Court records are housed in over 20 regional depositories. Contact this office for a list of their locations.

* Tax Court Decisions

United States Tax Court
400 2nd St., NW
Washington, DC 20217   202-376-2754

United States Tax Court Reports contain a consolidation of the tax decisions for a month. The yearly subscription cost is $26 and is available from the Superintendent of Documents, Government Printing Office, Washington, DC 20402; 202-512-1800.

* Tribal Courts for Native Americans

Office of Tribal Services
Bureau of Indian Affairs
U.S. Department of the Interior
18th and C Sts., NW
Washington, DC 20240   202-208-3710

This office serves as a cross between the Health and Human Services, Labor, Justice, and Housing and Urban Development Departments for the Indian population. The needy are paid welfare subsidies and provided job training. This office also operates 19 special federal courts and funds 127 tribal courts, along with administering the police force for Indian reservations, and a rehabilitation program for Indian homes.

Law and Social Justice

Immigration and Naturalization

* "Ask Immigration" Center

Central Office
Immigration and Naturalization Service (INS)
425 I Street, NW
Washington, DC 20536   202-514-4316

The "Ask Immigration" telephone service system provides pre-recorded information on a wide range of immigration- and citizenship-related topics. This Service is available 24 hours a day, 7 days a week. If you are calling from a location outside the local calling area of the INS office, you will be charged long distance telephone costs. Immigration Information Officers are available to provide personal assistance at the local INS offices listed below during different times of the day. To find out the exact times such assistance is available and the regular business hours for each office, listen carefully to the initial answer message when you call the office in your area and follow the instructions provided. If all you need is an INS form and want it mailed to your address, the initial message will tell you which number on your telephone to press. Leave your name, address, INS form(s) needed, and/or information materials you require. For the Immigration Service to respond promptly to your request, be sure to state your name clearly, spelling it if necessary, and provide your current, complete address. After calling the appropriate state INS office (refer to separate listing of INS state offices), enter one of the number codes below which corresponds to the information about immigration and naturalization that you need.

Information About INS, Special Policies and How to Report Illegal Aliens:
101 the Immigration and Naturalization Service
102 how to report aliens illegally in the U.S. and companies that hire them
103 PRC Nationals
104 the INS Outreach Program
105 where to mail applications
106 reporting your change of address to INS
107 how to obtain copies of documents
108 immigrant visa availability list
109 filing Appeals and Motions

Information About Legalization and Employer Sanctions:
201 who is eligible for legalization
202 employer sanctions
203 family fairness program for legalized aliens
204 anti-discrimination protection under immigration law
205 how to apply for permanent resident status if you resided in the U.S. since January 1972
206 special agricultural worker program
207 systematic alien verification for entitlements program

Information About Immigrant Visas, Adoptions, Asylum and Permanent Residency:
301 filing petition to sponsor an immediate relative
302 filing petitions to sponsor prospective immigrant employees
303 how an alien in the U.S. may request to change their status to become a permanent resident
304 when a U.S. citizen marries a foreign national outside the U.S.A.
305 how to file a joint petition for a spouse to remove conditional basis of permanent resident status
306 immigration benefits for adoption before 16th birthday
307 orphan petitions
308 application for asylum in the U.S.A.
309 permanent residence for recipients of approved asylum applications

Information About Obtaining or Replacing an Alien Residency (or Green) Card:
401 how to obtain an alien residency card
402 applying for a replacement alien residency card
403 if you never received your alien residency card

Information About Temporary Nonimmigrant Visas and Status:
501 nonimmigrant or temporary visas
502 how to request an extension of temporary stay
503 change of status from one nonimmigrant classification to another for work purposes

504 applying for a replacement I-94 arrival-departure document
505 temporary visitors' visa
506 a fiance/fiancee visa
507 requirements for classification as a nonimmigrant temporary worker or trainee H-1, H-2 and H-3
508 requirements for classification as a J-1 nonimmigrant exchange alien
509 L-1 visa status for intracompany transfers
510 requirements for classification as an E-1 or E-2 nonimmigrant treaty trader or investor

Information About Foreign Student Visas:
601 permission to go to school
602 student visa extension
603 permission for foreign student to work
604 visas for spouse and dependent children of foreign students
606 how to maintain your student status

Permission For Travel Outside the United States:
701 departure from the U.S.A. by permanent residents
702 student travel outside the U.S.A.
703 travel authorization for refugees - refugee travel documents
704 how to request emergency travel
705 travel by an alien whose application for permanent resident status is still pending

Information About Citizenship and Naturalization:
801 citizenship and naturalization requirements
802 citizenship for children born outside the U.S.
803 naturalization bases upon military service
804 derivative citizenship for children of U.S. citizens
805 residency requirements for naturalization
806 how to file for naturalization in behalf of a child
807 replacement of certification of citizenship or naturalization
808 how to renounce or forfeit U.S. citizenship

* Citizenship Education Videos

Immigration and Naturalization Service (INS)
U.S. Department of Justice
425 Eye St., NW
Room 7228
Washington, DC 20536   202-514-4316

Schools, community service organizations, churches, or others who wish to run citizenship education programs may borrow any of the several videocassettes available from the INS free of charge. The INS currently has twelve videocassettes available covering topics ranging from a focus on specific articles of the Constitution to the story of the American Flag, from an examination of the electoral process to biographies of George Washington and Abraham Lincoln. All videocassettes will be shipped postage free. A complete list of the available videocassettes and a synopsis of each can also be obtained by writing or calling the INS. In addition, a series of textbooks are available for school districts wishing to include citizenship education in their curriculum. These textbooks come in elementary or secondary reading levels.

* Employers Hotline on Immigrant Employees

Immigration and Naturalization Service (INS)
U.S. Department of Justice
425 Eye St., NW
Room 7116
Washington, DC 20536   202-514-4316

If you are unsure how the Immigration Reform and Control Act affects you as employer, call this number. Information is available in both English and Spanish, on employee and employer responsibilities and punishments. You can also receive information on legalization requirements and other general information. It will tell you exactly what your responsibilities are both to those workers who are eligible for legalization and those who are not, as well as explain your rights as an employer.

Be patient. If any phone number is incorrect, call (area code) 555-1212 and request the new listing.

* Farmworkers: English and Spanish Immigration Information

Immigration and Naturalization Service (INS)
U.S. Department of Justice
425 Eye St., NW
Room 7116
Washington, DC 20536   202-514-4316

If you are unsure how the Immigration Reform and Control Act affects you as a farmworker, call this number. It contains important information, in both English and Spanish, on employee and employer responsibilities and punishments. It can tell you whether or not your employer has treated you fairly and what you can do about it. You can also receive information on alien benefits, legalization requirements, and other general information.

* Immigration and Naturalization State Offices

Each of these state offices operate "Ask Immigration". In addition to these tape recorded messages, staff is available to provide information and send literature in response to telephone requests.

Alaska
Anchorage: 907-343-7820

Arizona
Phoenix: 602-379-3122
Tucson: 602-670-6229

California
Fresno: 209-487-5091
Los Angeles: 213-894-2119
Sacramento: 916-551-2785
San Diego: 619-557-5570
San Francisco: 415-705-4411
San Jose: 408-291-7876

Colorado
Denver: 303-371-3041

Connecticut
Hartford: 203-240-3171

District of Columbia
Washington, (Arlington, VA): 703-307-1501
Washington, (INS Central Office): 202-514-4316

Florida
Jacksonville: 904-791-2624
Miami: 305-536-5741
Tampa: 813-228-2131

Georgia
Atlanta: 404-331-5158

Hawaii
Honolulu: 808-541-1379

Illinois
Chicago: 312-353-7334

Indiana
Indianapolis: 317-331-6009

Kentucky
Louisville: 502-582-6375

Louisiana
New Orleans: 504-589-6533

Maine
Portland: 207-780-3352

Maryland
Baltimore: 301-962-2065

Massachusetts
Boston: 617-565-3879

Michigan
Detroit: 313-226-3240

Minnesota
St. Paul: 612-854-7754

Missouri
Kansas City: 816-891-0603
St. Louis: 314-539-2532

Montana
Helena: 406-449-5288

Nebraska
Omaha: 402-697-9155

Nevada
Las Vegas: 702-384-3696
Reno: 702-784-5427

New Jersey
Newark: 201-645-4400

New Mexico
Albuquerque: 505-766-2378

New York
Albany: 518-472-4621
Buffalo: 716-849-6760
New York: 212-206-6500

North Carolina
Charlotte: 704-523-1704

Ohio
Cincinnati: 513-684-3781
Cleveland: 216-522-4770

Oklahoma
Oklahoma City: 405-231-4121

Oregon
Portland: 503-326-3006

Pennsylvania
Philadelphia: 215-597-3961
Pittsburgh: 412-644-3356

Puerto Rico
San Juan: 809-766-5280

Tennessee
Memphis: 901-544-3301

Texas
Dallas: 214-655-5384
El Paso: 915-532-0273
Harlingen: 512-425-7333
Houston: 713-847-7900
San Antonio: 512-229-6350

Utah
Salt Lake City: 801-524-5771

Virginia
Norfolk: 804-441-3081

Washington
Seattle: 206-442-5956
Spokane: 509-353-2129

* Political Asylum

Office of Asylum Affairs
Bureau of Human Rights and
Humanitarian Affairs
U.S. Department of State

Be patient. If any phone number is incorrect, call (area code) 555-1212 and request the new listing.

619

Law and Social Justice

SA-17, Room 520
Washington, DC 20520   202-326-6110

This office handles the U.S. Department of State's responsibilities regarding political asylum by providing advisory opinions on the cases to the Immigration and Naturalization Service.

* Work Permits for Foreigners

Labor Certification Division
Employment and Training Administration
U.S. Department of Labor
200 Constitution Ave., NW, Room N4456
Washington, DC 20210   202-535-0163

If an employer wishes to hire foreign workers, he must first obtain a foreign labor certificate, which is a statement from the U.S. Department of Labor stating that there is no U.S. citizen available to fill the job. The Department investigates to make sure the wages and working conditions of the foreign workers will not seriously affect U.S. workers. An employer applies for a foreign labor certificate through the local state employment service office, which then conducts a job hunt before sending the application form to the area regional office for approval or disapproval.

Be patient. If any phone number is incorrect, call (area code) 555-1212 and request the new listing.

Discrimination and Civil Rights

* *See also Health and Medicine Chapter; Handicapped/Disabled Resources*
* *See also Information from Lawmakers Chapter*

* Advocates for the Handicapped Clearinghouse
National Information Center for Handicapped
Children and Youth
P.O. Box 1492   703-893-6061
Washington, DC 20013   800-999-5599
This clearinghouse helps parents of handicapped children, disabled adults, and professionals locate services for the handicapped and information on disabilities.

* Affirmative Action and Hiring the Handicapped
Office of Federal Compliance Programs
Employment Standards Administration
U.S. Department of Labor
200 Constitution Ave., NW, Room C3325
Washington, DC 20210   202-523-9475
The Rehabilitation Act of 1973 prohibits most employers doing business with the federal government from discriminating in employment against handicapped persons. Employers with contracts in excess of $2,500 must take affirmative action to hire and promote qualified handicapped persons.

* Age Discrimination
U.S. Equal Employment Opportunity Commission (EEOC)
1400 L Street, NW   800-669-3362
Washington, DC 20005   202-663-4264
Persons 40 years of age or older are protected by the Age Discrimination in Employment Act, which prohibits arbitrary age discrimination in hiring, discharge, pay, promotions, fringe benefits, and other aspects of employment. Retaliation against a person who files a charge of age discrimination, participates in an investigation, or opposes an unlawful practice is also illegal. Contact this office for their free fact sheet and more information on age discrimination.

* Alaskan Natives
Office of Public Affairs
Bureau of Indian Affairs
U.S. Department of the Interior
18th and C Sts., NW
Washington, DC 20240   202-208-3710
Some free publications available from the Bureau of Indian Affairs Public Affairs office. Due to the limited supply and small staff, only one copy of each publication may be requested:

Federal Acknowledgment Process
Alaska Natives
American Indian and Alaskan Native Education
Bureau of Indian Affairs Social Services Program
1980 Census Count of American Indians
Employment with BIA
Housing Program for Indians
List of Tribal Entities Recognized and Eligible to Receive Services from the U.S. Bureau of Indian Affairs Federal/Indian Relationship

* American Indians Rights
Office of Public Affairs
Bureau of Indian Affairs
U.S. Department of the Interior
18th and C Sts., NW
Washington, DC 20240   202-208-3710
The free booklet, *American Indians Today: Answers to Your Questions, 1991,* contains useful information on the Native American Indians and their relationship to

the Bureau of Indian Affairs. Programs within the Bureau, including education, health services, and housing are briefly outlined and contain recent statistics. Many questions are answered within the booklet, including the rights of the Indians to own land and have their own governments. A map locates the Indian lands and communities, showing Federal and State Indian Reservations and other Indian groups. An excellent bibliography, prepared by the Smithsonian Institution, is included. It will also provide sources for audio-visual materials.

* Asian Americans and Immigrants Discrimination
U.S. Commission on Civil Rights
Clearinghouse Division, Room 700
1121 Vermont Ave., NW
Washington, DC 20425   202-376-8105
The Commission on Civil Rights is a primary source for civil rights laws and regulations. Numerous publications are available at no charge from the Commission on Civil Rights and they may also be available at depository libraries including:

Recent Activities Against Citizens and Residents of Asian Descent. Discusses historical discrimination against Asian immigrants and Asian Americans, factors in anti-Asian activity, and specific incidents since 1920 of violence, harassment, and intimidation against persons of Asian descent.

* Business EEOC Assistance Program
Office of Program Operations
U.S. Equal Employment Opportunity Commission (EEOC)
1400 L Street, NW   800-669-3362
Washington, DC 20005   202-663-4264
The Equal Employment Opportunity Commission (EEOC) offers access to equal employment information and provides educational and technical assistance to small and mid-size employers and unions regarding their rights and obligations under federal laws prohibiting discrimination in the workplace. The program stresses such topics as sex and discrimination, sexual harassment, employee selection procedures, recordkeeping requirements, and layoffs. Contact this office for more information on assistance programs.

* Civil Rights Commission Clearinghouse
Robert S. Rankin Civil Rights Library
U.S. Commission on Civil Rights
1121 Vermont Ave., NW, Room 709
Washington, DC 20425   202-376-8810
The Civil Rights Memorial Library, located at the Civil Rights Commission's headquarters in Washington, DC, is a clearinghouse of civil rights information and contains 50,000 reference works, including 400 civil rights and minority issues journals, periodicals, legal journals, 3,500 reels of microfilm, and a comprehensive collection of reports, transcripts, and civil rights texts. It also maintains two online database systems: Ohio College Library Center (OCLC), and Dialog.

* Civil Rights Commission Regional Offices

Eastern Regional Division, 1121 Vermont Ave., NW, Washington, DC 20425; 202-523-5264

Central Regional Division, Old Federal Office Building, 911 Walnut Street, Room 3103, Kansas City, MO 64106; 816-374-5253

Western Regional Division, 3660 Wilshire Boulevard, Suite 810, Los Angeles, CA 90010; 213-894-3437

Law and Social Justice

* Civil Rights Complaints

U.S. Commission on Civil Rights
Complaint Referral
1121 Vermont Ave., NW
Washington, DC 20425   202-376-8376

Contact this office or a regional office of the CCR if you have complaints about discrimination and/or the abuse of civil rights.

* Civil Rights Directories and Publications

U.S. Commission on Civil Rights
Clearinghouse Division, Room 700
1121 Vermont Ave., NW
Washington, DC 20425   202-376-8105

The following publications are a sampling of those available at no charge from the Commission on Civil Rights. These publications are designed to provide reliable information about civil rights problems and about the laws, procedures, and approaches available for resolving them. A complete *Catalog of Publications* is available free of charge, and those publications that are out of print may be available at depository libraries across the U.S.

Civil Rights Directory. Lists private and public individuals and organizations concerned with civil rights at local, State, Federal, and national levels.

The Economic Progress of Black Men in America. Examines earnings and employment of black men from 1940 to 1980, sources of the earning gap with white men and effects of civil rights policies.

Police Practices and the Preservation of Civil Rights. A statement expressing concern that violation of civil rights by some police officers is a serious national problem. Includes recommendations for remedy.

* Civil Rights Enforcement

Civil Rights Division
U.S. Department of Justice
10th St. and Constitution Ave., NW
Room 5643
Washington, DC 20530   202-514-2007

If you have any questions as to the enforcement of 1964 Civil Rights Act, contact the Civil Rights Division. Information on the history of Civil Rights enforcement, as well as actual case history may be obtained by calling or writing the above address. Note: This office will not have information on the Civil Rights movement or on Dr. Martin Luther King, Jr., except insofar as they pertain to federal investigations or prosecutions.

* Civil Rights Hearings

U.S. Commission on Civil Rights
Clearinghouse Division, Room 700
1121 Vermont Ave., NW
Washington, DC 20425   202-376-8376

Transcripts of discussions at conferences, consultations sponsored by the Commission on Civil Rights, and testimony at Commission hearings are available to the public. Commission hearings focus government and public attention on civil rights problems and examine the manner in which Federal authorities discharge their civil rights responsibilities.

* Civil Rights: Proposed Legislation

U.S. Commission on Civil Rights
Office of Staff Director
1121 Vermont Ave., NW
Washington, DC 20425   202-523-5571

This office can provide you with current information on civil rights legislation and other relevant issues of civil rights law.

* Civil Rights Updates and Newsletter

U.S. Commission on Civil Rights
1121 Vermont Ave., NW
Washington, DC 20425   202-376-8177

Update, a monthly summary of the Civil Rights Commission's projects and activities, is available to the public free of charge. Another free publication, *Perspectives*, is published quarterly to provide varied views and information on civil rights issues.

* Employment Discrimination and Affirmative Action

Equal Opportunity Programs Staff
Justice Management Division
U.S. Department of Justice
10th St. and Constitution Ave., NW
Room 1230
Washington, DC 20530   202-514-6734

Do you feel you've been unjustly discriminated against in the workplace? Contact this office and the U.S. Department of Justice will tell you exactly how the annual affirmative action plan affects equal employment opportunity.

* Employment Discrimination: Filing A Complaint

U.S. Equal Employment Opportunity Commission (EEOC)
1400 L Street, NW
Washington, DC 20005   800-669-3362

If you believe you have been discriminated against by an employer, labor union, or employment agency when applying for a job or on the job because of race, color, sex, religion, national origin, or age, you may file a charge of discrimination with the EEOC. Charges may be filed in person, by mail, or telephone by contacting the nearest EEOC field office or the national office listed above.

* Equal Employment Opportunity Hotline

U.S. Equal Employment Opportunity Commission (EEOC)
1400 L Street, NW   800-669-3362
Washington, DC 20005   202-663-4264

This toll-free hotline receives and investigates employment discrimination charges against private employers and state and local governments. The EEOC Attorney-of-the-Day can offer telephone guidance to callers with their questions about alleged discrimination.

* Equal Employment Opportunity Offices Nationwide

Albuquerque Area Office, 505 Marquette, NW, Suite 900, Albuquerque, NM 87102-2189, 505-766-2061

Atlanta District Office, 75 Piedmont Avenue, NE, Suite 1100, Atlanta, GA 30335; 404-331-6093

Baltimore District Office, 111 Market Place, Suite 4000, Baltimore, MD 21202; 301-962-3932

Birmingham District Office, 2121 Eighth Avenue, North, Suite 824, Birmingham, AL 35203; 205-731-0082

Boston Area Office, 1 Congress St., Boston, MA 02114; 617-565-3200

Buffalo Local Office, 28 Church Street, Room 301, Buffalo, NY 14202; 716-846-4441

Charlotte District Office, 5500 Central Avenue, Charlotte, NC 28212; 704-567-7100

Chicago District Office, 536 South Clark Street, Room 930-A Chicago, IL 60605; 312-353-2713

Cincinnati Area Office, The Ameritrust Building, 525 Vine St., Suite 801, Cincinnati, OH 45202; 513-684-2851

Cleveland District Office, 1375 Euclid Avenue, Room 600, Cleveland, OH 44115; 216-522-2001

Dallas District Office, 8303 Elmbrook Drive, Dallas, TX 75247; 214-767-7015

Denver District Office, 1845 Sherman Street, 2nd Floor, Denver, CO 80203; 303-866-1300

Detroit District Office, 477 Michigan Avenue, Room 1540, Detroit, MI 48226; 313-226-7636

El Paso Area Office, The Commons Building C., 4171 N.Mesa St., Suite 103, El Paso, TX 79901; 915-534-6550

Fresno Local Office, 1313 P Street, Suite 103, Fresno, CA 93721; 209-487-5793

Be patient. If any phone number is incorrect, call (area code) 555-1212 and request the new listing.

Greensboro Local Office, 324 West Market Street, Room B-27, P.O. Box 3363, Greensboro, NC 27401; 919-333-5174

Greenville Local Office, 15 S. Main St., Suite 530, Greenville, SC 29601; 803-241-4400

Honolulu Local Office, 677 Ala Moana Blvd., Suite 404, P.O. Box 50082, Honolulu, HI 96813; 808-541-3120

Houston District Office, 1919 Smith St., 7th Floor, Houston, TX 77002; 713-653-3320

Indianapolis District Office, 46 East Ohio Street, Room 456, Indianapolis, IN 46204; 317-226-7212

Jackson Area Office, 207 W. Amite St., Jackson, MS 39201; 601-965-4537

Kansas City Area Office, 911 Walnut, 10th Floor , Kansas City, MO 64106; 816-426-5773

Little Rock Area Office, 320 West Capitol Avenue, Suite 621, Little Rock, AR 72201; 501-378-5060

Los Angeles District Office, 3660 Wilshire Boulevard, 5th Floor, Los Angeles, CA 90010; 213-251-7278

Louisville Area Office, 600 Martin Luther King Jr. Place, Room 268, Louisville, KY 40202; 502-582-6082

Memphis District Office, 1407 Union Avenue, Suite 621, Memphis, TN 38104; 901-722-2617

Miami District Office, Federal Building, One Northeast First Street, 6th Floor, Miami, FL 33132; 305-536-4491

Milwaukee District Office, 310 West Wisconsin Avenue, Suite 800, Milwaukee, WI 53203; 414-297-1111

Minneapolis Local Office, 220 Second Street South, Room 108, Minneapolis MN 55401-2141; 612-370-3330

Nashville Area Office, 50 Vantage Way, Suite 202, Nashville, TN 37228; 615-736-5820

Newark Area Office, 60 Park Place, Room 301, Newark, NJ 07102; 201-645-6383

New Orleans District Office, 701 Loyola Avenue, Suite 600, New Orleans, LA 70113; 504-589-2329

New York District Office, 90 Church Street, Room 1501, New York, NY 10007; 212-264-7161

Norfolk Area Office, 252 Monticello Ave., 1st Floor, Norfolk, VA 23510; 804-441-3470

Oakland Local Office; 1333 Broadway, Room 430, Oakland, CA 94612; 415-273-7588

Oklahoma Area Office, 531 Couch Drive, Oklahoma City, OK 73102; 405-231-4911

Philadelphia District Office, 1421 Cherry Street, 10th Floor, Philadelphia, PA 19102; 215-592-9350

Phoenix District Office, 4520 N. Central Avenue, Suite 300, Phoenix, AZ 85012-1848; 602-640-5000

Pittsburgh Area Office, 1000 Liberty Ave., Room 2038 A, Pittsburgh, PA 15222, 412-644-3444

Raleigh Area Office, 1309 Annapolis Dr., Raleigh, NC 27608; 919-856-4064

Richmond Area Office, 3600 W. Broad St., Room 229, Richmond, VA 23240; 804-771-2692

San Antonio District Office, 5410 Fredericksburg Road, Suite 200, San Antonio, TX 78229; 512-229-4810

San Diego Local Office, 401 B St., Suite 1550, San Diego, CA 92101; 619-557-7235

San Francisco District Office, 901 Market Street, Suite 500, San Francisco, CA 94103; 415-744-6500

San Jose Local Office, 96 N. 3rd St., Suite 200, San Jose, CA 95112; 408-291-7352

Savannah Local Office, 10 Whitaker Street, Suite B, Savannah, GA 31401; 912-944-4234

Seattle District Office, 2815 Second Avenue, Suite 500, Seattle, WA 98121; 206-553-0968

St. Louis District Office, 625 N. Euclid Street, 5th Floor, St. Louis, MO 63108; 314-425-6585

Tampa Area Office, 501 E. Polk St., Suite 1020, Tampa, FL 33602; 813-228-2310

Washington Field Office, 1400 L St. NW, Suite 200, Washington, DC 20005; 202-663-4264

* Equal Opportunity and Non-Discrimination

Information Handling and Support Facilities
General Accounting Office
P.O. Box 6015
Gaithersburg, MD 20877   202-275-6241

A Compilation of Federal Laws and Executive Orders for Nondiscrimination and Equal Opportunity Programs (#HRD-78-138) is a free 72-page book that can help companies avoid employment discrimination problems. It cites 87 laws and orders relating to equal rights in employment practices, as well as in the provision of services. Each citation briefly describes the law or order, identifies what type of discrimination it prohibits and to whom it applies, and which agencies enforce it.

* Equal Work Equal Pay

U.S. Equal Employment Opportunity Commission (EEOC)
1400 L Street, NW   800-669-3362
Washington, DC 20005   202-663-4264

Women and men who perform substantially equal work in the same establishment are covered by the Equal Pay Act, which prohibits employers from discriminating in pay because of sex and from reducing the wages of either sex to comply with the law. A violation may exist where a different wage is paid to a predecessor or successor employee of the opposite sex. Retaliation against a person who files a charge of equal pay discrimination, participates in an investigation, or opposes an unlawful employment practice also is illegal. Contact this office for a free fact sheet or to file a complaint.

* Fair Housing Local and State Agencies

U.S. Commission on Civil Rights
Clearinghouse Division, Room 700
1121 Vermont Ave., NW
Washington, DC 20425   202-376-8105

The Commission is a primary source for civil rights laws and regulations. Numerous publications are available at no charge from the Commission on Civil Rights and they may also be available at depository libraries including:

Directory of State and Local Fair Housing Agencies. For 91 State and local governmental agencies, describes classes protected under the pertinent fair housing law and unlawful discriminatory housing practices.

* Housing Discrimination

Housing and Civil Enforcement Section
Civil Rights Division
U.S. Department of Justice
10th St. and Constitution Ave., NW, Room 7525
Washington, DC 20530   202-514-2007

If you feel you've been denied housing due to racial, sexual, or religious discrimination, contact the Housing and Civil Enforcement Section of the U.S. Department of Justice. Their advisers can tell you if and what action is warranted in your case, and they can also refer you to local agencies for the help you need. This office is also responsible for bringing civil actions in federal courts whenever there is reasonable cause to believe that a person or group is denying housing unjustly due to discrimination.

Law and Social Justice

* Minorities and Women: Last Hired, First Fired

U.S. Commission on Civil Rights
Clearinghouse Division
Room 700, 1121 Vermont Ave., NW
Washington, DC 20425   202-376-8105

The Commission is a primary source for civil rights laws and regulations. Numerous publications are available at no charge from the Commission on Civil Rights and they may also be available at depository libraries including:

Last Hired, First Fired: Layoffs and Civil Rights. Examines the effects of seniority as applied to layoffs of minority and female workers.

* Minority Hiring Statistics

U.S. Equal Employment Opportunity Commission (EEOC)
Survey Division, 9th Floor
1400 L Street, NW
Washington, DC 20005   202-363-4948

EEOC compiles minority employment statistics for the following groups: private employment; unions; state and local governments; elementary and secondary education; health services; clericals; service-oriented industries; and skilled and craft industries. The database is searchable by occupation, industry, and region--state, county, or city. Searches and printouts are available free of charge. A publications catalog is free upon request.

* Native Americans with Disabilities Legal Aid

Native American DNA-People's Legal Services
P.O. Box 306
Window Rock, AZ 86515   602-871-4151

This advocacy group provides legal help to Indians with handicaps and developmental disabilities.

* Native Americans Rights

Office of Public Affairs
Bureau of Indian Affairs
U.S. Department of the Interior
18th and C Sts., NW
Washington, DC 20240   202-208-3710

The free booklet, *American Indians Today: Answers to Your Questions, 1988*, contains useful information on the Native American Indians and their relationship to the Bureau of Indian Affairs. Programs within the Bureau, including education, health services, and housing are briefly outlined and contain recent statistics. Many questions are answered within the booklet, including the rights of the Indians to own land and have their own governments. A map locates the Indian lands and communities, showing Federal and State Indian Reservations and other Indian groups. An excellent bibliography, prepared by the Smithsonian Institution, is included.

* Pregnancy Discrimination

U.S. Equal Employment Opportunity Commission (EEOC)
1400 L Street, NW   800-669-3362
Washington, DC 20005   202-663-4264

Discrimination on the basis of pregnancy, childbirth, or related medical conditions constitutes unlawful sex discrimination. Women affect by pregnancy or related conditions must be treated in the same manner as other applicants or employees with similar abilities or limitations. Contact EEOC for more information on hiring, pregnancy and maternity leave, child care, health insurance, fringe benefits, and filing charges of discrimination.

* Religious Discrimination

U.S. Commission on Civil Rights
Clearinghouse Division, Room 700
1121 Vermont Ave., NW
Washington, DC 20425   202-376-8105

The Commission is a primary source for civil rights laws and regulations. Numerous publications are available at no charge from the Commission on Civil Rights and they may also be available at depository libraries including:

Religion in the Constitution: A Delicate Balance. Addresses the issues of religious discrimination.

* School Desegregation and Textbooks

U.S. Commission on Civil Rights
Clearinghouse Division, Room 700
1121 Vermont Ave., NW
Washington, DC 20425   202-376-8105

The Commission is a primary source for civil rights laws and regulations. Numerous publications are available at no charge from the Commission on Civil Rights and they may also be available at depository libraries including:

Fair Textbooks: A Resource Guide. Lists materials aimed at reducing biases in textbooks, organizations, publishers, and their guidelines.

New Evidence on School Desegregation. This report analyzes data from 125 school districts for 1967 to 1985 to see the extent of racial imbalance in schools.

* Sex Discrimination and Filing Complaints

U.S. Commission on Civil Rights
Clearinghouse Division, Room 700
1121 Vermont Ave., NW
Washington, DC 20425   202-376-8105

The Commission is a primary source for civil rights laws and regulations. Numerous publications are available at no charge from the Commission on Civil Rights and they may also be available at depository libraries including:

Guide to Federal Laws and Regulations Prohibiting Sex Discrimination. Summarizes Federal laws, policies, and regulations banning sex discrimination and tells how to file complaints.

* Voting Rights

U.S. Commission on Civil Rights
Clearinghouse Division, Room 700
1121 Vermont Ave., NW
Washington, DC 20425   202-376-8105

The Commission is a primary source for civil rights laws and regulations. Numerous publications are available at no charge from the Commission on Civil Rights and they may also be available at depository libraries including:

Citizen's Guide to Understanding the Voting Rights Act. Explains the provisions of the 1965 Voting Rights Act, and how individuals may make complaints and comments.

The Voting Rights Act: Unfulfilled Goals. An evaluation of the status of minority voting rights in jurisdictions covered by the original provision of the 1965 act.

Information on People, Companies, and Mailing Lists
Who Owes Money to Whom

Any public or private company, organization, and for that matter, individual, that borrows money and offers an asset as collateral, must file with the state at the Office of Uniform Commercial Code (UCC). A filing is made for each loan and each of the documents is available to the public. To obtain these documents is a two-step process. The first step is to request a search to see if there are any filings for a certain company. The fee for such a search usually is under $10. You will next want to request copies of each of these documents. The cost for each document averages only a few dollars. This Office of Uniform Commercial Code is part of the state government and usually is located near or in the same office as the Office of Corporations which falls under the Secretary of State.

The initial search of records will provide:

- the number of listings under one name;
- the file number for each of the listings;
- the date and time of filing; and
- the name and address of the debtor.

Each UCC filing will disclose:

- a description of the asset placed as collateral; and
- the name and address of the secured party.

This disclosure not only provides insights into the financial security of an individual or organization, but it can also give a picture of their assets. Remember, this information is available on any public or private company or individual. The next time your brother-in-law asks you for money for a new business venture, it probably is worth the investment of a few dollars for a UCC search to see whether your relative owes money to others.

Most states will ask if you would like certified or non-certified information. Certification means that they will stand by the accuracy of the information if it is used in a court or other legal proceeding. For most cases, business researchers will not need the extra procedure of certification.

Farm Loan Filings

The Food and Security Act of 1986 is a law that involves filings on crop and livestock loans. Not all states have adopted this law. However, those which have must set up an automated central filing system under the Office of Uniform Commercial Code. Many states have not adopted the law because of the expense involved in setting up the system. Under this system the office must be able to provide information on filings in 24 hours. The purpose of the system is to notify those who purchase crops from growers if the farmer has already offered that crop as collateral.

UCC Request Forms

Some states provide you with current information about recent filings over the telephone, but others will only accept your request on a standard UCC Form. Still others will respond if you send your request in writing but will give you a discount if your query is on an official UCC Form. Most states use UCC Form 11 for requesting information. Copies of UCC Forms for all 50 states are available by calling Forms, Inc. (800-854-1080). The cost for forms is as follows: 5 or less, $1 each; 6-49, $.75 each; 50-99, $.65 each; 100 and over, $.55 each.

Online Access

With online capabilities you can usually search by such categories as: personal or commercial debtor, type of amendments, name of secured party, name of assigned party, and type of collateral. The following states offer online access to their files: Alabama, Colorado, Florida, Illinois, Iowa, Kansas, Massachusetts, Mississippi, Montana, New Mexico, Nebraska, Oregon, Pennsylvania, South Carolina, South Dakota, Texas, Utah, Vermont, Washington, and Wyoming.

Exceptions

Louisiana is the only state that has not adopted the Uniform Commercial Code. Some parishes (counties) require filings. In Georgia these filings are maintained by the Clerk of the Superior Court.

Uniform Commercial Code Offices

Alabama

Uniform Commercial Code Division, Secretary of State, 4121 Carmichael Rd. Suite 200, Montgomery, AL 36106; 205-242-5231 (mailing address: P.O. Box 5616, Montgomery, AL 36103). Searches: Requests must be submitted in writing. The charge is $5 for name searches submitted on Alabama Form UCC-11, $7 for searches submitted by letter and $1 for each additional listing. Copies of Documents: Available for $1 per page. Farm Filings: Call 205-242-5231. List of new farm filings published every month. Regular printed listing is $25 per year for each collateral code. Microfiche listing is $15 per year for each collateral code. Online Access: Pilot Dial Up Program. Free. Does not show collateral. Contact: Robina Jenkins, 205-242-5136.

Alaska

Uniform Commercial Code Division, Central Filing System, 3601 C St., Suite 1140-A, Anchorage, AK 99503; 907-762-2104. Searches: Requests must be submitted in writing on an Alaska Form UCC-11. The charge is $15 per listing for copy search, $5 for information search. Information search only states whether an encumbrance exists and when it was filed. Copies of Documents: Available for $15 for all documents in a file (includes search fee.). File does not include lapsed documents. Farm Filings: Maintained by the District Recorder's Office.

Be patient. If any phone number is incorrect, call (area code) 555-1212 and request the new listing.

625

Information on People, Companies, and Mailing Lists

Arizona

Uniform Commercial Code Department, Secretary of State, 7th Floor, 1700 W. Washington, Phoenix, AZ 85007; 602-542-6178. Searches: Requests must be submitted in writing on Arizona Form UCC-3 or UCC-11. The charge is $6 per name plus 50 cents per listing for copying fee. Fees must be paid in advance. Send blank check with stated limit or $6 and they will call you with the additional amount for copies. When they receive it they will release the documents. Copies of Documents: Available for 50 cents a page. Farm Filings: Maintained by the County Recorder.

Arkansas

Uniform Commercial Code, Secretary of State, State Capitol Building, Room 25, Little Rock, AR 72201; 501-682-5078. Searches: Requests must be submitted in writing in a letter or on a Arkansas Form UCC-11. The charge is $5 per debtor name. Copies of Documents: Available for $5 for the first three pages. Each additional page is $1. They will bill you for copies. Farm Filings: Maintained in this office. Same price and search request structure.

California

Uniform Commercial Code Division, Secretary of State, P.O. Box 1738, Sacramento, CA 95812 (street address: 1230 J Street, Sacramento, CA 95814); 916-445-8061. Searches: Request must be submitted in writing in a letter, on a California Form UCC-3 or Form UCC-11. Charge is $11 per name. One name per request only. For $30 a one name search will be conducted and all documents copied. Additional charges will be billed by invoice. Copies of Documents: Available for $1 for the first page and 50 cents for every additional page. All documents are certified. For additional gold seal certification, or to certify a file number, the fee is an additional $5. Farm Filings: If you do not find them at the state level, remember some are filed with the county government (there is no standard procedure in California).

Colorado

Uniform Commercial Code Division, Secretary of State, 1560 Broadway, Suite 200, Denver, CO 80202; 303-894-2200. Searches: A telephone information searches of two debtor's names (last four filings of each) is available at no cost. These searches are not certified. Written requests must be on a Form UCC-11 or it will not be processed. They prefer you send no money in and let them bill you. The charge is $25 for a search of one debtor name. A computer printout will be sent to verify the search if you do not want a copy search. Copies of Documents: Available for $1.25 per page. Farm Filings: Maintained at the County Court Recorder. Online Access: Call Patti Webb at 303-894-2200 ext. 300 for information on orientation classes for new accounts. They offer several subscription packages: 3 months for $300, or 1 year for $1000 with 15 minute access time each call; 1 year for $5000 with private telephone number, and 1 year for $10,000 with direct computer hookup, which allows user to connect as many as 8 computer terminals to the system.

Connecticut

Uniform Commercial Code Division, Secretary of State, 30 Trinity St., Hartford, CT 06106; 203-566-4021. Searches: Request must be submitted in writing. The charge is $18 for requests submitted on a Connecticut Form UCC-11, and $22 for requests submitted by letter. Copies of Documents: The charge for the first three pages is $5, each additional page is $3. Farm Filings: Maintained in this office. Use Connecticut Form UCC-a.

Delaware

Uniform Commercial Code Section, P.O. Box 793, John G. Townsend Building, Dover, DE 19903 (Street Address: Federal and Duke of York Street, Dover, DE 19901); 302-739-4279 (Choose 8 for UCC recorded message, choose 0 for a UCC service representative). Searches: Requests must be submitted in writing on UCC-11 Form. $10 per each debtor's name search. Copies of Documents: Available for $2 per page, $5 minimum. They will bill you. Farm Filings: Maintained by this office. This office is in the middle of being computerized. A list of new filings in a particular category can be provided upon special request.

District of Columbia

Recorder of Deeds, 515 D Street NW, Washington, DC 20001; 202-727-5374. Searches: Requests must be submitted in writing. No special form is required. The charge is $30 for each secured party. Must be paid in advance. Copies of Documents: Available for $2.25 per page, plus $2.25 for certification. Farm Filings: Maintained in this office. This office is computerized.

Florida

Uniform Commercial Code Division, Department of State, P.O. Box 5588, Tallahassee, FL 32314 (Street Address: 409 Gaines Street, Tallahassee, FL 32301); 904-487-6845. Searches: 904-487-6063. For printed verification, a written request must be submitted on Florida Form UCC-11. Copies of Documents: Available for $20 per name. Farm Filings: Filings maintained by the County Circuit Court. Online Access: UCC Division, 409 E. Gaines St., Tallahassee, FL 32399; 904-487-6866. Write or call this office and they will send you an information booklet that describes the service they have available through CompuServe, 800-848-8199. The cost for online service is $24 per hour, plus $2 per month flat fee and other small fees charged by CompuServe.

Georgia

The State of Georgia does not maintain Uniform Commercial Code Filings. Contact the Clerk of Superior Court at the County level for these filings.

Hawaii

Uniform Commercial Code, Bureau of Conveyance, P.O. Box 2867, Honolulu, HI 96803; 808-587-0121. Searches: Requests must be submitted in writing on a Hawaii Form UCC-3 or any state's UCC-11. The search charge is $25 per debtor name, plus an additional 50 cents per listing. They will call you if there will be more charges for additional names found. Copies of Documents: Available for 50 cents per page. Farm Filings: Maintained by this office. Online Access: No.

Idaho

Secretary of State, Uniform Commercial Code Division, State House, Boise, ID 83720; 208-334-3191. Searches: Information may be requested by phone or in writing. The charge is $13 for phone requests and for written requests. An additional $1 is charged if the request is not submitted on an Idaho UCC-4 Form. Charge for written requests submitted on UCC Form is $12. Copies of Documents: The charge for copying all documents involved in a search is $1. Farm Filings: A 24-hour Expedite Service is available for these filings. The charge is $17 for info search and $23 for copies. Online Access: Hopefully will be available in the future.

Illinois

Uniform Commercial Code Division, Secretary of State, Centennial Building, Room 30, 2nd and Edwards Street, Springfield, IL 62756; 217-782-7518. Searches: All requests must be in writing. Requests on non-standard forms will not be processed. Requests submitted on a Illinois Form UCC-11.7 are $10. Copies of Documents: The charge is 50 cents per page. Farm Filings: If you do not find them at the state level, remember, some are filed with the county government. (There is no standard procedure in Illinois.) Payment for searches and copies may be charged to VISA or Master Charge. Microfilm: Copies of all documents filed within the month are available on a subscription basis for $250 per month. Daily Computer Printout Listing: Available for $250 per month. Online Access: For information write the above office, or contact: Louise Blakley, 217-785-2235. A brochure explaining the system will be sent to you.

Indiana

Uniform Commercial Code Division, Secretary of State, 302 West Washington Street, Room E 018, Indianapolis, IN 46204; 317-232-6393. Searches: All searches must be requested in writing. An Indiana Form UCC-11 is preferred. The charge is $1 per debtor's name, 50 cents for each filing, and 50 cents per statement on the listing. All requests for searches received by Federal Express or Express Mail with return envelope are given priority. Copies of Documents: The charge is 50 cents per page and $1 for certification. Farm Filings: If incorporated they are filed both at this office and the county recorder where the land is located. If the farm is not incorporated, the filing is placed at the county recorder's office only. Online Access: Not available. This office has one of the quickest turnaround times in the nation but is not computerized.

Iowa

Uniform Commercial Code Division, Secretary of State, Second Floor, Hoover Building, Des Moines, IA 50319; 515-281-5204. Searches: Information may be requested by phone if you already have an established account, or in writing. The cost of a phone search is $5, plus $1 for a printout. The charge for a non-standard request is $6 and $5 for a request submitted on an Iowa Form UCC-11. Copies of Documents: The fee is $1 for each copy requested. All copies of liens are certified. Farm Filings: Maintained by this office. (Monthly updating may be obtained from Iowa Public Record Service, 515-223-1153.) Online Access: Available. Contact Allen Welsh, 515-281-8363. Cost is $150 per year, 30 cents per minute, plus telephone charges for dialup program.

Kansas

Uniform Commercial Code Division, Secretary of State, Second Floor, State Capitol, Topeka, KS 66612; 913-296-3650. Searches: Phone requests are accepted with VISA or MC or from those holding a prepaid account with the UCC. The charge for phone requests is $15 per name for verbal information and $5 for an order. The charge for written requests is $5. If staffing permits, all requests are filled within 24 hours. Copies of Documents: The charge is $1 per page. There is no additional charge for certification of name searches. They are always sent out certified. For file number searches, certification must be requested. Fee is 50 cents. Farm Filings: This office has handled farm filings since 1984. Filings prior to that year are maintained by the County Register of Deeds. Online Access: Available from Kansas Information Network with imaging capacity. Contact: Cathy. Other: Microfilm cost $25 per roll plus $7.50 for postage and handling, for up to 50 rolls. Total file has 42 rolls. New rolls, 4-5 monthly can be sent. Magnetic Tape: Master file costs $2,000. Updates are $15 weekly or $75 monthly.

Kentucky

Uniform Commercial Code Division, Office of Secretary of State, State Capitol Bldg., Capitol Avenue, Frankfort, KY 40601; 502-564-2848 Ext. 441. Searches: All searches of UCC filings must be conducted in person by requester or by outside agencies. Law firms or Kentucky Lender's Assistance, 606-278-6586 may do it for you. In addition to their fee, the UCC charges 10 cents per page for plain copies; $5 for certification and 50 cents for every page thereafter. Farm Filings: Filings are maintained by the County Circuit Court. Online Access: No.

Louisiana

The state of Louisiana has not adopted the Uniform Commercial Code. Filings may be maintained at the Parish (county) level.

Maine

Uniform Commercial Code Division, Secretary of State, State House Station 101, Augusta, ME 04333; 207-287-4177. Searches: All requests must be submitted in writing in a letter or on a Form UCC-11. State whether plain or certified copies are desired. Cost is $2 per page plus $10 for certification. Will bill. For expedited service an additional $5 fee guarantees a 24 hour turnaround time. Farm Filings: Maintained by this office. Online Access: No.

Maryland

Uniform Commercial Code Division, State Department of Assessments and Taxation, 301 West Preston Street, Baltimore, MD 21201; 410-225-1340. Searches: The State of Maryland does not conduct searches. They will provide a list of title companies that do provide that service. Some are: Hylinf Infoquest, 410-728-4990 and Harbor City Research, 301-539-0400. Copies cost $1 per page. Cost to certify a document is $6. Farm Filings: Maintained by this office. Online Access: No.

Massachusetts

Uniform Commercial Code Division, Secretary of State, Room 1711, 1 Ashburton Place, Boston, MA 02108; 617-727-2860. Searches: Requests must be submitted in writing on a Form UCC-11 (any state's form is acceptable). The charge is $5 for an information computer printout and $10 for computer printout with face page and up to 15 pages. They will call you if pages exceed this limit. All fees must be paid in advance. Requests sent Aby Federal Express or Express Mail will be sent out same way with Air Bill, but all requests are processed in order received. No expediting service available. Copies of Documents: Charge is $2 per page and $3 for certification. Farm Filings: Maintained in Town Clerk's Office. Online Access: Available for $149 per year plus 40 cents per minute. Also carried by commercial services. Contact Richard Shipley, 617-729-5412.

Michigan

Uniform Commercial Code Section, P.O. Box 30197, Lansing, MI 48909-7697 (Mailing Address: 7064 Crowner Dr., Lansing, MI 48909); 517-322-1495. Searches: Telephone requests are handled on an expedite basis for already established accounts. The charge is an additional $25. You must have an account number with the UCC Section to obtain this service. The charge for requests submitted on non-standard forms are $6. Requests submitted on a Michigan Form UCC-11 is $3. Requests sent out by Federal Express or Express Mail are given priority, but all requests are processed in the order received. Copies of Documents: The charge is $1 per page and $1 for certification. Farm Filings: Filings are maintained by the County Recorder of Deeds. Online Access: No. Other: Microfilm available in contract basis for $50 per month. Format is not computer indexed. Write above address for details and contract.

Minnesota

Uniform Commercial Code Division, Secretary of State, 180 State Office Building, St. Paul, MN 55155; 612-296-2434. Searches: Requests must be submitted in writing and include a SASE. The charge for a request submitted on a Minnesota Form UCC-11 is $11. The charge for a request submitted on a non- standard form is $14. These charges include information on 5 listings and/or 5 copies. You will be billed if there are additional copies in excess of five. The charge for additional listings is 50 cents/listing. Copies of Documents: Available for 50 cents/page. Charge for certified copies is a $5 plus 50 cents for each page. Farm Filings: Available from the County Recorder of Deeds unless the debtor is a non-resident or a corporation and then they are filed with the UCC Division.

Mississippi

Uniform Commercial Code Division, Secretary of State, 202 N. Congress St., #601, Jackson, MS 39201; 601-359-1614. Searches: Phone information is available at no cost. Information available by phone is: approximate number of filings, secured party, file numbers, and date and time of filing. The charge for written requests submitted on Mississippi Form UCC-11 is $5. The charge for written requests submitted on non-standard forms is $10. Copies of Documents: Available for $2 a pages. Send initial $5 or $10 fee only. They will bill you for the exact amount of copies made. Farm Filings: Farm Filings are maintained by the above office. Other: Master list of all farm registrations available for $2040. Master list by type is $500 per crop. Online Access: Contact Cheryl Crawford, 601-359-1548. The cost is $250 per month plus 50 cents per transaction with minimum of 100 transactions. Service will be available as of 1/92. Will display name, address and collateral. Complete file microfilm available for $50 per roll.

Missouri

Uniform Commercial Code Division, Secretary of State, P.O. Box 1159, Jefferson City, MO 65102; 314-751-2360. Searches: Information searches will be given over the phone. These searches are not certified and are free of charge. (This service is not available on Mondays or on the day after a holiday.) The charge for written requests is $8. Copies of Documents: Available for $8 per listing. The $8 fee covers the first 10 pages. Additional pages are available for 50 cents each. Farm Filings: Maintained by the County Recorder.

Montana

Uniform Commercial Code Bureau, Secretary of State, Capitol Station, Helena, MT 59620; 406-444-3665, Fax: 406-444-3926. Searches: Requests for searches will be accepted by phone. The charge if you have a prepaid account is $7, the same as for a written request. There are no restrictions on form in which you put written requests. Searches are conducted the day of the request for a $5 fee. Regular requests processed in 48 hours. Copies of Documents: Available for 50 cents a page. The charge for certification is $2. Farm Filings: Maintained in this office. For total listing of crop you are interested in, fill out a Buyer's Registration Form for crops you want on the list. Results can be done on paper or microfiche. Service is done on a cost recovery basis. Online Access: Contact Florence, 406-444-3665. She will send you an information brochure. The charge is $25 per month for unlimited use. Printed copies cost 50 cents each and are statutorily accepted documents.

Nebraska

Uniform Commercial Code Division, P.O. Box 95104, 301 Centennial Mall S., Lincoln, NE 68509; 402-471-4080. Searches: The charge for requests by phone is $1 per debtor's name. No verification is sent unless requested. If requested the charge for the printout is $3. The charge for written requests is $3. A computer printout containing a list of the filings is sent to the requester. Copies of Documents: Available for 50 cents per page. They will bill. Farm Filings: Maintained by the county government, but the above office will hooked up to all 93 countries and will do a search for you. The county will bill you directly for its service. Magnetic Tape: Available to large companies for $250 per month. Online Access: Available. Charge is $2 per inquiry. Contact Debbie Pester.

Nevada

Uniform Commercial Code Division, Secretary of State, Capitol Complex, Carson City, NV 89710; 702-687-5298. Searches: Only written requests for information will be accepted. The charge is $6 for a request submitted on a Nevada Form UCC-3, Form UCC-11 or any type of letter. For an additional $10 your request will be expedited. This fee must be paid with a separate check. Copies of Documents: Available for $1 per page and an additional $6 for certified copies. Farm Filings: Maintained at the office of the County Recorder. Online Access: No.

New Hampshire

Uniform Commercial Code Division, Secretary of State, State House, Room 204, Concord, NH 03301; 603-271-3276 or 271-3277. Searches: Requests must be submitted in writing by letter or on a Form UCC-11, and must contain a SASE in which requested documents will be mailed. Requests will not be processed without an enclosed SASE. The charge for a request submitted on a New Hampshire Form UCC-11 is $5. The charge for a request submitted on a letter or non-standard form is $7. Copies of Documents: Available for 75 cents per file. Farm Filings: Maintained by this office. Microfiche: Available from New England Micrographics. Contact Nick Brattan, 603-625-1171. Online Access: No. This office is not computerized.

New Jersey

Uniform Commercial Code Division, State Department, State Capitol Building, CN303, Trenton, NJ 08625; 609-530-6426. Searches: Requests must be submitted in writing with the exact name and address of debtor or on a New Jersey Form UCC-11

Be patient. If any phone number is incorrect, call (area code) 555-1212 and request the new listing.

627

Information on People, Companies, and Mailing Lists

or a security agreement signed by the debtor. Payment must accompany request unless a prepaid UCC account, Visa or MasterCard is used. Request may be faxed to 609-530-0688. The charge is $25. Document is certified. Expedite Service is available for $5. The requester pays the express mail expense. Copies of Documents: Available for $1 per page. Farm Filings: Maintained by the county and the state. At the county level you will want to check with the County Recorder. Online Access: No.

New Mexico

Uniform Commercial Code Division, Bureau of Operations, Secretary of State, Executive Legislative Building, Room 400, Santa Fe, NM 87503; 505-827-3600. Searches: Certification is $8. Copies cost $1 per page. The State of New Mexico does not do searches, but they will provide you with a list of abstract companies that are authorized to do so. Call Bureau of Operations for list, 505-827-3608. Farm Filings: This office located at the same address with conduct a search for an Agricultural Eddective Financing Statement for $15. Contact Ben Vegil, 505-827-3609. They will follow-up the verbal report with a written statement. Online Access: Available through local services: Federal Abstracts, 505-982-5537, Lawyer's Title, 505-988-2333 and Capitol Documents, 505-984-2696. Also available from Dun and Bradstreet.

New York

Uniform Commercial Code Division, Secretary of State, P.O. Box 7021, Albany, NY 12225; 518-474-4763. Searches: Requests must be submitted in writing. For requests submitted on a New York Form UCC-11 the charge is $7. For requests submitted on non-standard forms the charge is $12. Copies of Documents: Available for $1.50 per page. Farm Filings: Maintained by both the state and the County Recorder. Online Access: No. Other: Microfiche available for $300 per month. Contact Virginia Cellery at 518-432-2733.

North Carolina

Uniform Commercial Code Division, Secretary of State, 300 N. Salisbury St., Raleigh, NC 27611; 919-733-4205. Searches: Requests must be submitted in writing. Signature for the requester is required, therefore make request on Form UCC-11 or North Carolina Form UCC-11. The charge is $8 per name. Search fee must be sent with request. All requests are handled within 24 hours of receipt. Copies of Documents: Available for $1 per page. Will bill. Farm Filings: Maintained by this office and County Recorder. Online Access: No, but will be available in the future. Other: Microfilm can be purchased for $50 per roll. New monthly listings generate about 2 rolls per month. Contact Judy Chapman.

North Dakota

Uniform Commercial Code Division, Secretary of State, Main Capitol Building, 600 Boulevard Avenue East, Bismarck, ND 58505; 701-224-3662. Searches: Requests may be phoned in or be submitted in writing preferably on a North Dakota UCC-11. Letters and nonstandard forms also accepted. The charge is $5. Copies of Documents: Available for $5 for the first three pages and $1 a page for additional pages. Farm Filings: The Central Notice staff will take requests for searches over the phone for crop and livestock filings. The charge is the same as above. Written requests are the same as stated above. Farm equipment and real estate filings are optional and were maintained by the state or the County Register of Deeds until 1/92. As of 1/92 the UCC and County Register of Deeds were hooked up to the same system. Online Access: No, but will be available in the future.

Ohio

Uniform Commercial Code Division, Secretary of State, 30 E. Broad Street, 14th Floor, Columbus, OH 43266-0418; 614-466-9316. Searches: Phone requests for information are not certified and are free of charge. Call 614-466-3623/3126. Limit is 3 requests per phone call. Written requests may be submitted on a non-standard letter form, Form UCC-11 or on an Ohio Form UCC-11. The charge is $9. It takes 6 months for these searches to be conducted. Expedite service is available for an additional $9. These requests are processed in 5 working days. Copies of Documents: Available for $1 per page. Farm Filings: Maintained by the County Recorder. Online Access: No.

Oklahoma

Uniform Commercial Code Office, Oklahoma County Clerk, 320 Robert S. Kerr, Room 105, Oklahoma City, OK 73102; 405-278-1521. Searches: Requests must be submitted in writing. The charge is $5. Copies of Documents: Available for $1 per page. Send $5 search fee with request. They will bill you for copies and call if amount is over $25. The charge for certification is $1. Farm Filings: Maintained by Secretary of State's Office, 405-521-2474. Online Access: No.

Oregon

Uniform Commercial Code Division, Secretary of State, 255 Capitol St., NE, Salem, OR 97310; 503-986-2200. Searches: Requests must be phoned in using Visa or

MasterCard, charged to an established prepaid UCC account or submitted in writing by letter, or on Form UCC-11 or preferably on a Oregon Form UCC-25R. The charge is $5 per debtor's name. Copies of Documents: Available for $1 per page. Farm Filings: Maintained by this office. The charge for a search is $5 per name. Monthly reports by agricultural product code are available on microfilm or paper copy. For microfilm contact Micelle. Cost is $10 per reel weekly. Online Access: Available for $25 per month, plus 20 cents a minute for online use. Contact Michelle. Commercially available from Prentice Hall, 800-452-7856.

Pennsylvania

Uniform Commercial Code Division, Corporation Bureau, State Department, 308 N. Office Building, Harrisburg, PA 17120; 717-787-8712. Searches: Requests for searches must be paid in advance by check or money order only and submitted in writing on a Pennsylvania Form UCC-11. The charge is $12 per name search. $28 to certify. Must may in advance by check or money order. Copies of Documents: Available for $2 per page. Farm Filings: Maintained by this office. Online Access: Information America, 404-892-1800.

Rhode Island

Uniform Commercial Code Division, Secretary of State, 100 North Main Street, Providence, RI 02903; 401-277-2521. Searches: Requests must be submitted in writing. Same charge for request in letter form or on Form UCC-11. Call for number of pages. Requests will not be processed without payment in full. The charge is $5. Copies of Documents: Available for 50 cents per copy. Farm Filings: Maintained by the City Recorder of Deeds. Online Access: No.

South Carolina

Uniform Commercial Code Division, Secretary of State, P.O. Box 11350, Columbia, SC 29211; 803-734-2175. Searches: Requests must be submitted in writing on Form UCC-11, or preferably South Carolina Form UCC-4. Letters are not accepted. The charge is $5 per debtor name. No priority or expediting service. All requests are done in the order received. Copies of Documents: Available for $2 for the first page, $1 for each page thereafter. Farm Filings: Maintained by County Recorder. Online Access: $70 monthly. Other: Microfilm from Archives is purchased by Dun and Bradstreet and may be purchased from the UCC division directly. Contact Thresha Southerland, 803-734-2176. One tape costs $50.

South Dakota

Central Filing System, Secretary of State, 500 E. Capitol, Pierre, SD 57501; 605-773-4422. Searches: Telephone information provided for no charge. Requests for searches are accepted from those with prepaid deposit accounts. Written requests are accepted on any UCC standard request form. The charge is $4. Fee for certification is $5. Copies of Documents: Available for 50 cents per page. They will bill you. Farm Filings: Maintained by this office. Online access at no charge is available. Online Access: Available by subscription. The system can be used by those with IBM compatible computers and Hayes compatible modems. Cost is $240 per year for 200 transactions and 10 cents per transaction thereafter.

Tennessee

Uniform Commercial Code Section, Secretary of State, J.K. Polk Bldg., 505 Deaderick St., Suite 1800, Nashville, TN 37219; 615-741-3276. Searches: Requests must be submitted in writing, preferably on a Tennessee Form UCC-11. Indicate if you want information or information plus copies. The charge is $10 even if the search shows no listing. Send the $10 fee with request. Copies of Documents: Available for $1 per copy. Do not send money with request. They will bill you. Requests sent with Express Mail envelopes will be sent the next day. All other requests take 3-4 days to process. Farm Filings: Maintained by this office and County Recorder. It is necessary to check with both offices. Online Access: No.

Texas

Uniform Commercial Code, Secretary of State, P.O. Box 13193, Austin, TX 78711-3193; 512-475-2705. Searches: The charge for a search requested by phone is $25. The charge for written requests submitted on Texas Form UCC-11 is $10. May Fax: 512-475-2812. The charge for written requests submitted on a letterhead or non-standard form is $25. Copies of Documents: Available for $1.50 per page with a $5 minimum charge. The charge for certification is an additional $5. Farm Filings: Maintained by the above office. Online Access: Available by Dialup Service. Cost is $3 per search, deducted from prepaid account. Contact Tina Whiteley, 512-475-2700.

Utah

Uniform Commercial Code Division, Business Regulation Dept., 300 South St., Second Floor, Salt Lake City, UT 84110; 801-530-6020. Searches: Written request may be on letter, UCC-11 or Utah Form UCC-2. The charge is $10 per debtor name.

Be patient. If any phone number is incorrect, call (area code) 555-1212 and request the new listing.

Copies of Documents: Available for 30 cents per page. Will bill. Certification: No additional charge. Document already certified. Farm Filings: Central Filings maintained these files. Phone requests are accepted. The charge is $10. Online Access: Available through Data-Share program on a subscription basis. The charge is $10 per month plus 10 cents per minute and telephone charges. Contact Mary Ann Saddler or Ted Wiggin at 801-530-6643.

Vermont

Uniform Commercial Code, Secretary of State, Montpelier, VT 05609 (Regular mail to: 109 State Street, Montpelier, VT 05609-1104; Fed Ex to: 94 Main Street, Montpelier, VT 05609); 802-828-2388. Searches: Requests for searches may be phoned in or submitted in writing, They will bill for phone requests. The charge is $5 per debtor name, plus 50 cents for an information sheet containing debtor's name, secured party, file number, and date and time filed. Copies of Documents: Available for $2 for 5" x 8" or $5 for 8 1/2" x 11" copies. Certification fee is $5. Farm Filings: Central Filings Section maintains these files. Contact the above address. The charges for searches is the same. Online Access: $10/month, $.10/minute.

Virginia

Uniform Commercial Code Division, State Corporation Commission, P.O. Box 1197, Richmond, VA 23209 (Street Address: 1220 Bank Street, Richmond, VA 23209); 804-786-3689. Searches: Requests for searches must be submitted in writing in a letter or Form UCC-11. The charge is $6 per debtor name. Copies of Documents: Available for $1 per page. There is an additional charge of $6 for certification. Farm Filings: Maintained by this office and the County Recorder. Online Access: No.

Washington

Uniform Commercial Code Division, Department of Licensing, 405 Black Lake Blvd., Olympia, WA 98502 (Mailing Address: PO Box 9660, Olympia, WA 98507); 206-753-2523. Searches: Requests must be submitted in writing. Indicate if you want information or information and copies. The charge is $7 for all the listings of one debtor. Copies of Documents: Available for $12. This includes search fee, plus

copies of all documents for one debtor. Farm Filings: Maintained in this office. Microfilm: Copies of each days filings are available for $6.50 per day plus shipping and handling fees. Online Access: Contact Darla Gehrke at 206-752-2523 for information on how to set up a prepaid account. Monthly minimum deposit is $200 from which $1 per minute online time and other fees are deducted.

West Virginia

Uniform Commercial Code Division, Secretary of State, 1900 Kanawha, Bldg. 1, Room 131W, Charleston, WV 25305-0770; 304-345-4000. Searches: Phone requests for information are accepted. The charge is $5. They will bill you. Written requests are preferred. The charge is $3 if Form UCC-11 is used, $5 for all others. Copies of Documents: Available for 50 cents per page. The charge for certification is $5. Farm Filings: Maintained by this office. Online Access: No.

Wisconsin

Uniform Commercial Code Division, Secretary of State, 30 West Mifflin St., Madison, WI 53703 (Mailing Address: P.O. Box 7847, Madison, WI 53707); 608-266-3087. Searches: Phone requests for information are accepted. The charge is $5 per filing. The charge for written requests is $5 per debtor name. Copies of Documents: Available for $1 per document. Certification certificate must be requested in writing and is an additional 50 cents. Farm Filings: Maintained by the County Register of Deeds. Other: Microfiche is available on a monthly basis. Contact Bonnie Fredrick at 608-266-3087.

Wyoming

Uniform Commercial Code, Secretary of State, State Capitol Building, Cheyenne, WY 82002; 307-777-5372. Searches: Phone requests for information are accepted for 2 debtor names. Requests may be Faxed to 307-777-5339. The charge is $5 for each name. The charge for written requests is the same. Copies of Documents: Available for 50 cents per page. Farm Filings: Maintained by this office and the County Recorder. Check both. Online Access: Available for $50 per month, plus telephone charges and usage fee. Minimum usage fee is $26 per month. Contact Jeanie Sawyer.

Be patient. If any phone number is incorrect, call (area code) 555-1212 and request the new listing.

629

Professional People and Local Businesses

State Licensing Offices

Buried within each state government are several, and sometimes dozens, of offices where individuals as well as business establishments must register in order to perform certain types of services and commercial activities. State laws require accountants, architects, concert promoters, employment agencies, podiatrists and numerous other professionals to register. The data derived from these regulatory boards provide unique opportunities for researchers and marketing executives to obtain demographic data, mailing lists and even competitive information.

Mailing Lists

Mailing lists offer the biggest potential from these offices. The unusual as well as the mundane are available in a variety of formats. Many of these lists are not accessible commercially, but you can get them from the states inexpensively and usually without restrictions. In other words, you can purchase a state list once, and use it over and over again. Commercial list brokers will never let you do this. Here is a sampling of available mailing lists:

- 1 cent per name for all dentists in Kentucky;
- Free directory of real estate agents in Arizona;
- $40 for a list of all nurses in Colorado;
- A mailing list of all contractors in Arkansas for $10;
- 2 cents per name for all swimming pool dealers in Florida;
- A listing of librarians in Georgia;
- 4 cents a name for all the psychologists in California;
- $100 for a computer tape of all accountants in Florida;
- $1.45 per 1,000 names for all medical practices in Illinois;
- Free list of all attorneys in Maine.

Almost every state provides mailing labels in the form of cheshire or pressure sensitive labels. In many cases, the charge is nominal.

Common Lists and Specialized Rosters

Every state maintains a variety of standard rosters. Some states keep as few as 20 lists and others have over 100. Names of licensed professionals and business establishments available from most every state include:

- medical professionals
- accountants
- real estate agents and brokers
- veterinarians
- barbers
- insurance agents
- architects
- nursing homes
- cosmetologists
- hearing aid dealers
- social workers
- lawyers

After reviewing the rundown of all 50 states and District of Columbia licensing boards, you will be amazed at the variety of lists that are within easy reach. In most cases you can obtain printouts for such licensed services as:

- burglar alarm contractors in Maine
- tow truck operations in Minnesota
- hat cleaners in Ohio
- ski areas in Michigan
- day care centers in New York
- security guards in New Hampshire
- outfitters in Colorado

Computer Tapes and Diskettes: Selections and Sorting Options

Many states can provide the information on magnetic tape and some are beginning to offer data on IBM PC compatible diskettes. Almost every state will allow you to select names by zip code or county whether the licensee is active or inactive. Some states will allow you to select certain demographic characteristics, such as years of formal education.

Markets and Demographics

With a little creativity and resourcefulness, the information at licensing boards can provide pertinent clues in formulating a market profile. For example, you can determine:

- which counties have the highest concentration of psychologists;
- what is the average number of years of schooling for real estate agents in certain zip codes;
- which zip codes have experienced the fastest growth for accountants for the past 10 years;
- the number of out-of-state licensed paralegals;
- which counties have the most podiatrists or veterinarians
- how many insurance agents there are in a given county.

Some states have the capability of performing historical analysis, while others will supply you with the raw data.

Competitive Intelligence

Depending upon the type of business you are investigating, pertinent competitive information may be ferreted from state licensing boards. For example, if you are a dentist, mobile home dealer, nursing home administrator or real estate broker, you could plot how many competitors you are up against in a given zip code or county. Or, you may be able to determine how many opticians work for an eye care chain, or tax consultants for a given tax preparer.

Organization of Licensing Boards

Approximately half of the states have a central office which is responsible for all licensed professions. For such states it is a relatively easy process to obtain information because it is all generated from a single source. However, the other states make this task difficult. Typically, each separate independent board maintains information for one profession. The only connection these agencies have to the state government is that their board members are appointed by the governor.

States With Restrictions

Some states have restrictions on the use of their lists of licensed professionals. California, District of Columbia, Hawaii, Louisiana, New Hampshire, North Dakota, and Oklahoma do not release information. Alabama and North Carolina will only release the number of professionals, not their names. Minnesota will only release information if action has been taken against a professional or business. And in Iowa, Montana, New York, and Rhode Island, the data may not be used for commercial purposes.

State Licensing Boards

Besides issuing licenses to professionals so they can do business, the following offices act as consumer watchdogs to make sure that those with licenses do business fairly and ethically. Not only will these offices investigate complaints against licensed professionals, they also have the ability to revoke or suspend the licenses if the professional repeatedly acts unprofessionally or unethically. Each state listing includes the professionals licensed in that state, including health professionals, along with their different licensing offices where noted.

Alabama
State Occupational Information Coordinating Community (SOICC), 401 Adams Ave., P.O. Box 5690, Montgomery, AL 36103-5690; 205-242-2990. Licensing boards and professions: accountants, aircraft personnel, architects, auctioneers, audiologists, speech pathologists, bar pilots, water transportation personnel, boxer and wrestler trainers, classroom teachers, coal mine foremen/mine electricians, cosmetologists, counselors, dentists, dental hygienists, chiropractors, doctors of medicine, physician's assistants, surgeon's assistants, school bus drivers, embalmer/funeral directors, engineer-in-training and professional engineers, land surveyors, fire fighters, foresters, general contractors, hearing aid specialists, heating and air conditioning contractors, insurance agents, interior designers, landscape architects, landscape horticulturist/planters, lawyers, pest control operators and fumigators, tree surgeons, law enforcement personnel, nurses, nursing home administrators, optometrists, pharmacists, physical therapists, physical therapist assistants, plumbers, podiatrists, polygraph examiners, psychologists, real estate brokers, security salespersons, social workers, veterinarians.

Alaska
Division of Occupational Licensing, Department of Commerce and Economic Development, State of Alaska, P.O. Box 110806, Juneau, AK 99811-0806; 907-465-2534. Licensing boards and professions: architects, engineers, land surveyors, audiologists, barbers and hairdressers, chiropractors, collection agencies, construction contractors, concert promoters, dental professionals, dispensing opticians, electrical administrators, geologists, guides, hearing aid dealers, marine pilots, physicians, morticians, naturopaths, nursing, nursing home administrators, optometrists, pharmacists, physical therapists, psychologists, public accountants, veterinarians.

Arizona
Arizona Department of Revenue, 1600 West Monroe, Phoenix, AZ 85007; 602-542-4576. Licensing boards and professions: pharmacists, physical therapists, podiatrists, psychologists, chiropractors, dentists, teachers, homeopathic specialists, veterinarians, medical examiners, radiologic technicians, naturopathic physicians, nurses, opticians, optometrists, osteopaths, barbers, cosmetologists, real estate brokers, contractors, technical registrars, insurance agents, physician assistants, nursing care administrators.

Arkansas
Governor's Office, State Capitol Building, Little Rock, AR 72201; 501-682-2345. Licensing boards and professions: architects, abstracters, accountants, barber examiners, funeral directors, contractors, cosmetologists, dental examiners, electricians, speech pathologists, audiologists, nurses, pharmacists, real estate brokers, veterinary engineers, land surveyors, athletic trainers, chiropractors, collection agencies, counselors, embalmers, foresters, landscape architects, manufactured home builders, physicians, opticians, optometrists, podiatrists, psychologists, sanitarians, social workers, soil classifiers, therapy technologists.

California
State of California, Department of Consumer Affairs, 400 R Street, Sacramento, CA 95814; 916-323-2191, or 800-344-9940 (toll-free in CA). Licensing boards professions: professional engineers, cosmetologists, fabric care technicians, physical therapists, medical quality assurance, physician's assistants, chiropractors, acupuncture specialists, accountants, psychologists, registered nurses, pharmacists, architects, funeral directors, embalmers, landscape architects, veterinarians, animal health technicians, home Furnishings decorators, collection and investigative agents, dentists, dental auxiliaries, barbers, behavioral scientists, optometrists, shorthand reporters, structural pest control operators, athletic trainers, vocational nurses, psychiatric technicians, osteopaths, electronic repair dealers, personnel services, geologists and geophysicists, dispensing opticians/contact lens examiners, respiratory care specialists, nursing home administrators, podiatrists, hearing aid dispensers, speech pathologists, audiologists, tax preparers.

Colorado
Department of Regulatory Agencies, State Services Building, 1560 Broadway, Suite 1550, Denver, CO 80202; 303-894-7855. Licensing Board/Professions: accountants, architects, barbers, cosmetologists, chiropractors, dentists, electricians, engineers, hearing aid dealers, insurance agents, land surveyors, mobile home dealers, nurses, nursing home administrators, optometrists, outfitters, pharmacists and pharmacies, physical therapists, physicians, plumbers, psychologists, realtors, ski lift operators, social workers, veterinarians.

Connecticut
Occupational Licensing Division, Department of Consumer Products, 165 Capitol Avenue, Hartford, CT 06106; 203-566-1107, or 800-842-2649 (toll-free in CT). Licensed Occupations: electricians, plumbers, heating and cooling specialists, well drillers, elevator installers, home improvement contractors, arborists, TV and radio repair specialists. Licensed Health Professions: Department of Health Services, 150 Washington St., Hartford, CT 06106; 203-566-7398. Physicians, dentists, optometrists, osteopaths, naturopaths, homeopaths, chiropractors, psychologists, registered nurses, licensed practical nurses, dental hygienists, registered physical therapists, hypertrichologists, audiologists, speech pathologists, podiatrists, hairdressers, barbers, embalmers, funeral directors, sewer installers/ cleaners, registered sanitarians, nursing home administrators, hearing aid dealers, opticians, veterinarians, occupational therapists. Other Licensed Professions: Contact Professional Licensing Division, 165 Capitol Avenue, Room G1, Hartford, CT 06106, 203-566-1814: architects, landscape architects, engineers, engineers-in-training, land surveyors, pharmacists, patent medicine distributors, mobile manufactured home parks.

Delaware
Division of Professional Regulation, P.O. Box 1401, O'Neil Building, Dover, DE 19903; 302-739-4522. Complaints in writing only. Licensed Professionals: architects, accountants, landscape architects, cosmetologists, barbers, podiatrists, chiropractors, dentists, electricians, adult entertainment, physicians, nurses, real estate brokers, land surveyors, private employment agencies, athletic (wrestling and boxing), deadly weapons dealers, nursing home administrators, funeral directors, social workers, speech pathologists, hearing aid dealers, audiologists, psychologists, veterinarians, optometrists, occupational therapists, pharmacists, river boat pilots.

District of Columbia
Department of Consumer and Regulatory Affairs, 614 H Street NW, Room 108, Washington, DC 20001; 202-727-7080. Licensing Board/Professions: accountants, architects, barbers, cosmetologists, dentists, dieticians, electricians, funeral directors,

physicians, nurses, nursing home administrators, occupational therapists, optometrists, pharmacists, physical therapists, plumbers, podiatrists, engineers, psychologists, real estate agents, refrigeration and air conditioning specialists, social workers, steam and other operating engineers, veterinarians.

Florida

Florida Department of Professional Regulation, 1940 N. Monroe St., Tallahassee, FL 32399-075; 904-488-6602. Licensing boards and professions: accountants, architects, barbers, chiropractors, cosmetologists, dentists, dispensing opticians, electrical contractors, professional engineers and land surveyors, landscape architects, funeral directors and embalmers, medical examiners, hearing aid dispensers, naturopathics, nursing home administrators, nurses, optometrists, osteopaths, pharmacists, pilot commissioners, podiatrists, psychologists, real estate brokers, veterinarians, acupuncture technicians, radiological health technicians, laboratory services, entomology specialists, emergency medical personnel.

Georgia

Examining Board Division, Secretary of State, 166 Pryor Street, SW, Atlanta, GA 30303; 404-656-3900. Licensing boards and professions: accountants, architects, athletic trainers, auctioneers, barbers, chiropractors, construction industry, cosmetologists, professional counselors, social workers, marriage and family therapists, dietitians, dentists, engineers, land surveyors, foresters, funeral directors/embalmers, geologists, hearing aid dealers and dispensers, landscape architects, librarians, physicians, nurses, nursing home administrators, occupational therapists, dispensing opticians, optometrists, pharmacists, physical therapists, podiatrists, polygraph testers, practical nurses, private detectives and security agencies, psychologists, recreation specialists, sanitarians, speech pathologists, audiologists, used car dealers, used motor vehicle dismantlers, rebuilders, and salvage dealers, veterinarians, water and wastewater treatment plant operators and laboratory analysts.

Hawaii

Office of the Director, Department of Commerce and Consumer Affairs, P.O. Box 3469, Honolulu, HI 96801; 808-586-2850. Licensing boards and professions: accountants, acupuncture specialists, barbers, boxers, chiropractors, contractors, cosmetologists, dental examiners, detectives and guards, electricians and plumbers, elevator mechanics, engineers, architects, land surveyors, landscape architects, hearing aid dealers and fitters, massage specialists, physicians, motor vehicle Industry, motor vehicle repair technicians, naturopaths, nurses, nursing home administrators, dispensing opticians, optometrists, osteopaths, pest control operators, pharmacists, physical therapists, psychologists, real estate brokers, speech pathologists, audiologists, veterinarians, embalmers/funeral directors, collection agencies, commercial employment agencies, mortgage and collection servicing agents, mortgage brokers and solicitors, port pilots, time sharing and travel agents.

Idaho

State of Idaho, Department of Self-Governing Agencies, Bureau of Occupational Licenses, Owyhee Plaza, 1109 Main, #220, Boise, ID 83702; 208-334-3233. Licensing boards and professions: accountants, athletic directors, bartenders, engineers, land surveyors, dentists, geologists, physicians, architects, barbers, chiropractors, cosmetologists, counselors, dentists, environmental health specialists, hearing aid dealers and fitters, landscape architects, morticians, nursing home administrators, optometrists, podiatrists, psychologists, social workers, outfitters and guides, pharmacists, public works contractors, real estate brokers.

Illinois

State of Illinois, Department of Professional Regulations, 320 W. Washington, Third Floor, Springfield, IL 62786; 217-785-0800. Licensed professions: athletic trainers, architects, barbers, cosmetologists, chiropractors, collection agencies, controlled substance specialists, dentists and dental auxiliaries, polygraph testers, detectives, embalmers, funeral directors, land sales, land surveyors, physicians, nurses, nursing home administrators, occupational therapists, optometrists, pharmacists, physical therapists, podiatrists, boxing and wrestling, engineers, psychologists, accountants, real estate brokers and salespersons, roofing contractors, shorthand reporters, social workers, structural engineers, veterinarians.

Indiana

Indiana Professional Licensing Agency, Indiana Government Center S., 302 W. Washington Street, Room E-034, Indianapolis, IN 46204; 317-232-3997. Licensing boards and professions: accountants, architects, auctioneers, barbers, beauticians, boxers, engineers and land surveyors, funeral directors, plumbers, real estate agents, TV-radio and watch repair technicians. Licensed health professionals: Indiana Health Professional Bureau, One America Square #1020, Indianapolis, IN 46282; 317-232-2960 for the following medical specialties: chiropractors, dentists, health facility administrators, nurses, optometrists, pharmacists, sanitarians, speech pathologists, audiologists, psychologists, veterinarians, hearing aid dealers, podiatrists, physical therapists.

Iowa

Bureau of Professional Licensing, Iowa Department of Health, Lucas State Office Building, Des Moines, IA 50319; 515-281-4401. Licensed professionals: dietitians, funeral directors and embalmers, hearing aid dealers, nursing home administrators, optometrists, ophthalmology dispensers, podiatrists, psychologists, physical and occupational therapists, occupational therapist assistants, social workers, speech pathologists and audiologists, respiratory care therapists, barbers, cosmetologists, chiropractors, nurses, physicians, dentists, pharmacists, veterinarians. Other licensed professionals: Professional Licensing Regulation Division, Department of Commerce, 1918 SE Hulsizer, Ankeny, IA 50021; 515-281-7400: accountants, engineers and land surveyors, landscape architects, architects, real estate agents.

Kansas

Secretary of State, State Capitol, 2nd Floor, Topeka, KS 66612; 913-296-3489. Licensing boards: abstracters, accountants, adult home administrators, operating engineers, plumbers and pipefitters, carpenters, electrical workers, attorneys, barbers, cosmetologists, court reporters, dentists and dental auxiliaries, educators, emergency medical services, healing arts specialists, hearing aid dispensers, insurance agents, land surveyors, embalmers/funeral directors, nurses, optometrists, pharmacists, physical therapists, podiatrists, private schools, real estate agents, engineers, architects, landscape architects, veterinarians.

Kentucky

Division of Occupations and Professions, P.O. Box 456, Frankfort, KY 40602-0456; 502-564-3296. Licensing boards and professions: hearing aid dealers, nurses, private schools, psychologists, social workers, speech and audiologists. Other licensed professionals: Kentucky Occupational Information Coordinating Committee, 275 E. Main St., Two Center, Frankfort, KY 40621; 502-564-4258: accountants, agriculture specialists, architects, auctioneers, bar examiners, chiropractors, dentists, hairdressers, cosmetologists, emergency medical technicians Services, radiation and product safety specialists, insurance agents, medical licensure supervisors, natural resources and environmental protection specialists, nursing home administrators, ophthalmic dispensers, optometric examiners, pharmacists, physical therapists, podiatrists, polygraph examiners, professional engineers and land surveyors, real estate agents, veterinarians.

Louisiana

Department of Economic Development, 101 France St., (P.O. Box 94185), Baton Rouge, LA 70802; 504-342-3000. Licensing boards and professions: acupuncture assistants, adoption agencies, adult day care administrators, agricultural consultants, alcoholic beverages solicitors, ambulatory surgical centers, arborists, archaeological investigators, architects, auctioneers, barbers, beauticians, bedding and furniture upholsterers, beer distributors, blind business enterprise operators, blood alcohol analysts, embalmers/funeral directors, accountants, shorthand reporters, chiropractors, pesticide applicators, driving school instructors, sewage/construction contractors, cotton buyers, waste-salvage oil operators, cut flower dealers, dairy product retailers, day care centers, fuels dealers, dentists, drug manufacturers, egg marketers, electrolysis technicians, embalmers, emergency medical technicians, employment service agencies, family support counselors, grain dealers, hearing aid dealers, hemodialysis clinics, home health centers, horticulturists, independent laboratories, sewage system installers, insurance, landscape architects, nurses, lime manufacturers, liquefied gas distributors, livestock dealers, maternity homes, mental and substance abuse clinics, midwives, nursing home administrators, nursery stock dealers, occupational therapists, optometrists, pesticide dealers, pharmacists, physical therapists, physicians, physicians, plant breeders, plumbers, podiatrists, solid waste processors, seafood distributors, psychologists, radiation therapists, radio and television repair technicians, radiologic technologists, real estate brokers, sanitarians, social workers, speech pathologists and audiologists, veterinarians, voice stress analysts.

Maine

Department of Professional and Financial Regulation, State House Station 35, Augusta, ME 04333; 207-582-8700. Licensing boards and professions: veterinarians, itinerant vendors, consumer credit protection services, insurance agents, athletic trainers, real estate agents, geologists and soil scientists, solar energy auditors, hearing aid dealers and fitters, accountants, arborists, barbers, commercial drivers, education instructors, speech pathologists and audiologists, auctioneers, electricians, funeral directors, foresters, dietitians, nursing home administrators, oil and solid fuel installers, substance abuse counselors, mobile home parks, river pilots, physical therapists, plumbers, psychologists, social workers, radiological technicians, occupational therapists, respiratory care therapists, nurses, dentists, chiropractors, osteopaths, podiatrists, physicians, engineers, attorneys.

Maryland

Division of Maryland Occupational and Professional Licensing, 501 St. Paul Pl., 9th Floor, Baltimore, MD 21202; 410-333-6209. Licensed professionals: architects, master electricians, engineers, foresters, hearing aid dealers, landscape architects, pilots, plumbers, land surveyors, public accountants, second hand dealers, precious metal and gem dealers, pawnbrokers, real estate agents and brokers, home improvement contractors, barbers and cosmetologists. Referral to the licensing agency for collection agencies, mortgage brokers and insurance agents can be provided by the office listed above. Other licensed professions: Boards and Commissions, Department of Health and Dental Hygiene, 4201 Patterson Ave., Baltimore, MD 21215; 410-764-4747: audiologists, chiropractors, dentists, dietitians, electrologists, medical examiners, morticians, nurses, nursing home administrators, optometrists, occupational therapists, pharmacists, physical therapists, podiatrists, professional counselors, psychologists, environmental sanitarians, speech pathologists, social workers, well drillers, water work and waste system operators.

Massachusetts

Division of Registration, 100 Cambridge St., Boston, MA 02202; 617-727-3074. Licensing boards and professions: electrologists, gas fitters, hairdressers, health officers, landscape architects, licensed practical nurses, nursing home administrators, optometrists, physician's assistants, podiatrists, pharmacists, plumbers, psychologists, real estate brokers, registered nurses, sanitarians, speech pathologists, audiologists, social workers, tv-repair technicians, physical therapists, occupational therapists, athletic trainers, architects, barbers, barber shops, certified public accountants, chiropractors, dental hygienists, dentists, dispensing opticians, pharmacies, electricians, embalmers, engineers, veterinarians, cosmetologists, and real estate appraisers.

Michigan

Michigan Department of License and Regulation, P.O. Box 30018, Lansing, MI 48909; 517-373-1870. Licensing board and professions: accountants, architects, barbers, athletic control (wrestlers and boxers), builders, carnival amusement rides, cosmetologists.

Minnesota

Office of Consumer Services, Office of Attorney General, 1400 NCL Tower, 445 Minnesota Street, St. Paul, MN 55101; 612-296-2331. Licensing boards and professions: abstracters, accountants, adjusters, alarm and communications contractors, architects, assessors, attorneys, auctioneers, bailbondsmen, barbers, beauticians, boiler operators, boxing related occupations, brokers, building officials, burglar installers, chiropractors, clergy, cosmetologists, dentists, dental assistants, dental hygienists, private detectives, electricians, energy auditors, engineers, financial counselors/financial planners, funeral directors/embalmers/morticians, hearing aid dispensers, insurance agents, investment advisors, landscape architects, land surveyors, midwives, notary publics, nursing home administrators, optometrists, osteopathic physicians, pawnbrokers, peace officers, pharmacists, physical therapists, physicians, surgeons, physician's assistants, high pressure pipefitters, plumbers, podiatrists, practical nurses, precious metal dealers, process servers, psychologists, real estate brokers, registered nurses, rehabilitation consultants, sanitarians, securities brokers, tax preparers, teachers, tow truck operators, transient merchants, veterinarians, water conditioning contractors and installers, water and waste treatment operators, water well contractors/explorers/engineers. Information will be released only if action has been taken against a professional or business.

Mississippi

Secretary of State, P.O. Box 136, Jackson, MS 39205; 601-359-3123. Licensing boards and professions: agricultural aviation pilots, architects, landscape architects, athletic trainers, funeral directors, chiropractors, dentists, physicians, nurses, nursing home administrators, optometrists, pharmacists, physical therapists, psychologists, veterinarians, barbers, cosmetologists, engineers and land surveyors, foresters, polygraph examiners, public accountants, public contractors, real estate agents, accountants, lawyers, dental hygienists, audiologists, embalmers, professional counselors, and speech pathologists.

Missouri

Division of Professional Registration, Department of Economic Development, 3605 Missouri Blvd., Jefferson City, MO 65109; 314-751-0293. Licensing boards and professions: accountants, architects/engineers/land surveyors, athletic trainers, barbers, chiropractors, cosmetologists, professional counselors, dentists, embalmers/funeral directors, healing arts specialists, employment agencies, hearing aid dealers/fitters, nurses, optometrists, podiatrists, pharmacists, real estate agents, veterinarians, insurance agents, nursing home administrators, lawyers, dental hygienists, physicians, physical therapists, speech pathologists and audiologists, psychologists.

Montana

Professional and Occupational Licensing, Business Regulation, Department of Commerce, 111 N. Jackson St., Helena, MT 59620; 406-444-3737. Licensing boards and professions: accountants, acupuncturists, architects, athletic trainers, barbers, beer distributors, chiropractors, cosmetologists, dental hygienists, dentists, denturists,

electricians, electrologists, employment Agencies, engineers and land surveyors, hearing aid dispensers, insurance, landscape architects, lawyers, librarians, medical doctors, morticians, nurses, nursing home administrators, occupational therapists, operating engineers(boiler), optometrists, osteopathic physicians, pawnbrokers, physical therapists, plumbers, podiatrists, polygraph examiners, private investigators, psychologists, contractors, radiologic technologists, real estate brokers and salesmen, sanitarians, securities brokers and salesmen, social workers and counselors, speech pathologists and audiologists, taxidermists, tourist campground and trailer courts, veterinarians, water well drillers.

Nebraska

Bureau of Examining Boards, Nebraska Department of Health, P.O. Box 95007, Lincoln, NE 68509; 402-471-2115. Licensing boards and health professions: athletic trainers, advanced emergency medical technicians, audiologist/speech pathologists, cosmetologists, chiropractors, dentists/dental hygienists, embalmers/funeral directors, hearing aid dealers and fitters, pharmacists, podiatrists, optometrists, physical therapists, nurses, nursing home administrators, massage specialists, occupational therapists, professional counselors, psychologists, respiratory care specialists, social workers, sanitarians, veterinarians. For other licensing boards and professions, contact the NE state operator at 402-471-2311 to be connected with the board that licenses the following professions: accountants, engineers/architects, barbers, abstracters, appraisers, land surveyors, landscape architects.

Nevada

State of Nevada Executive Chamber, Capitol Complex, 1 E. Liberty Street, #311, Reno, NV 89501; 702-786-0231. Licensing boards and professions: accountants, architects, athletic trainers, audiologists and speech pathologists, barbers, chiropractors, contractors, cosmetologists, dentists, engineers and land surveyors, funeral directors and embalmers, hearing aid specialists, homeopaths, landscape architects, liquefied petroleum gas distributors, marriage and family counselors, physicians, naturopathic healing arts specialists, nurses, dispensing opticians, optometrists, oriental medicine, osteopaths, pharmacists, physical therapists, podiatrists, private investigators, psychologists, shorthand reporters, taxicab drivers, veterinarians.

New Hampshire

SOICC of New Hampshire, 64 B Old Sun Cook Rd., Concord, NH 03301; 603-228-9500. Licensing boards and professions: accountants, emergency medical technicians, engineers/architects/land surveyors, attorneys, auctioneers, insurance (bailbondsmen), barbers, cosmetologists, chiropractors, court reporters, dentists, drivers education Instructors, electricians, funeral directors/embalmers, engineers, physicians, private security guards, lobbyists, nurses, nursing home administrators, occupational therapists, optometrists, psychologists, pesticide control operators, pharmacists, plumbers, podiatrists, real estate agents, teacher agents, veterinarians, water supply and pollution control operators.

New Jersey

Director, Centralized Licensing for the Licensing Boards, Division of Consumer Affairs, 140 E. Front Street, Trenton, NJ 08625; 609-826-7150. Licensing boards and professions: accountants, architects, barbers, beauticians, dentists, electrical contractors, marriage counselors, plumbers, morticians, nurses, ophthalmic dispensing technicians, optometrists, pharmacists, physical therapists, professional engineers and landscape surveyors, professional planners, psychological examiners, shorthand reporters, veterinarians, public movers and warehousemen, acupuncture specialists, landscape architects, athletic trainers, hearing aid dispensers, chiropractors, opthomologists.

New Mexico

Regulation and Licensing Department, 725 St. Michael's Drive, P.O. Box 25101, Santa Fe, NM 87504; 505-827-7000. Licensing boards and professions: accountants, architects, athletic promoters, barbers, chiropractors, cosmetologists, dentists, engineers and land surveyors, landscape architects, physicians, nurses, nursing home administrators, occupational therapists, optometrists, osteopaths, pharmacists, physical therapists, podiatrists, polygraphers, private investigators, psychologists, realtors, thanatopractice, veterinarians.

New York

New York State Education Department, Division of Professional Licensing, Cultural Education Center, Empire State Plaza, Albany, NY 12230; 518-474-3852, or 800-342-3729 (toll-free in NY). Licensed professionals: acupuncturists, architects, audiologists, certified shorthand reporters, chiropractors, dentists, landscape architects, land surveyors, massage therapists, physicians, osteopaths, nurses, occupational therapists, ophthalmic dispensers, optometrists, pharmacists, physical therapists, podiatrists, engineers, psychologists, public accountants, social workers, speech pathologists, veterinarians.

Information on People, Companies, and Mailing Lists

North Carolina

North Carolina Center for Public Policy Research, P.O. Box 430, Raleigh, NC 27602; 919-832-2839. Licensing boards and professions: architects, auctioneers, barbers, boiler operators, accountants, chiropractors, cosmetologists, registered counselors, dental, electrical contractors, foresters, general contractors, hearing aid dealers and fitters, landscape architects, landscape contractors, marital and family therapists, physicians, navigators and pilots, morticians, nurses, nursing home administrators, opticians, optometrists, osteopaths, pesticide operators, pharmacists, physical therapists, plumbers and heating specialists, podiatrists, practicing psychologists, private protective services, professional engineers and land surveyors, public librarians, real estate, refrigeration technicians, sanitarians, social workers, speech and language pathologists, structural pest control operators, veterinarians, waste water treatment operators, water treatment facility operators.

North Dakota

North Dakota Legislative Council Library, 600 East Boulevard Avenue, Bismarck, ND 58505; 701-224-2916. Licensing boards and professions: abstracters, accountants, architects, athletic trainers, audiologists and speech pathologists, barbers, chiropractors, cosmetologists, dentists, dietitians, electricians, embalmers, emergency medical services, engineers and land surveyors, hearing aid dealers and fitters, massage therapists, physicians, nurses, nursing home administrators, occupational therapists, optometrists, pharmacists, physical therapists, plumbers, podiatrists, private investigators, private police security, psychologists, real estate agents, respiratory care specialists, social workers, soil classifiers, veterinarians, water well contractors.

Ohio

State of Ohio, Department of Administrative Services, Division of Computer Services, 30 East Broad St., 40th Floor, Columbus, OH 43215-0409; 614-466-2000. Licensed professionals: wholesale distributors of dangerous drugs, terminal distributors of dangerous drugs, pharmacists, accountants, barbers, barber shops, beauty shops, managing cosmetologists, cosmetologists, manicurists, architects, landscape architects, practical nurses, registered nurses, surveyors, engineers, surveyors, dentists, dental hygienists, osteopaths, physicians, podiatrists, chiropractors, midwives, embalmers, funeral directors, embalmer and funeral directors, hat cleaners, dry cleaners, public employment agencies, auctioneers, private investigators, auctioneers.

Oklahoma

Governor's Office, State Capitol, Oklahoma City, OK 73105; 405-521-2342 or State Information Operator, 405-521-2011. Licensing board and professions: accountants, real estate agents, physicians, foresters, medico-legals, nursing homes, nurses, optometrists, osteopaths, physicians, pharmacists, polygraph examiners, psychologists, shorthand reporters, social workers, speech pathologists, veterinarians, landscape architects, architects, chiropractors, cosmetologists, dentists, embalmers and funeral directors. For other licensed professionals, contact Occupational Licensing, OK State Health Department, 1000 North East, 10th Street, Oklahoma City, OK 73117; 405-271-5217: barbers, hearing aid dealers, electricians, water and waste treatment plant operators.

Oregon

Department of Economic Development, Small Business Advocates, 595 Cottage St. NE, Salem, OR 97310; 800-547-7842 or 800-233-3306 (toll-free in OR). Licensing boards and professions: accountants, architects, barbers and hairdressers, builders, contractors, collection agencies, debt consolidators, geologists, landscape architects, landscape contractors, and TV/radio service dealers, engineering examiners, fire marshals, insurance agents, maritime pilots, real estate agents, tax practitioners.

Pennsylvania

Bureau of Professional and Occupational Affairs, 618 Transportation and Safety Building, Harrisburg, PA 17120-2649; 717-787-8503, or 800-822-2113 (toll-free in PA). Licensing boards and professions: accountants, architects, auctioneers, barbers, cosmetology, funeral directors, landscape architects, professional engineers, real estate agents. For licensed health professions, contact Bureau of Professional and Occupational Affairs, Secretary of State, 618 Transportation and Safety Building, Harrisburg, PA 17120; 717-783-1400: dentists, physicians, nurses, nursing home administrators, occupational therapists, optometrists, osteopaths, pharmacists, physical therapists, podiatrists, psychologists, speech-language and hearing specialists, veterinarians, navigators.

Rhode Island

Rhode Island Occupational Information Coordinating Commission, 22 Hayes Street, Providence, RI 02908; 401-272-0830. Licensing boards and professions: nurses aides, psychologists, respiratory therapists, sanitarians, speech pathologists, veterinarians, physical therapists, plumbers, podiatrists, prosthetists, nurses, nursing home administrators, occupational therapists, opticians, optometrists, osteopaths, physician

assistants, embalmers/funeral directors, hairdressers, cosmetologists, manicurists, massage therapists, physicians, midwives, acupuncturists, athletic trainers, audiologists, barbers, barber shops, chiropractors, dentists, dental hygienists, electrologist, architects, coastal resource management, engineers and land surveyors.

South Carolina

South Carolina State Library, 1500 Senate St., Columbia, SC 29201; 803-734-8666. Licensing boards and professions: accountants, architects, auctioneers, barbers, morticians, chiropractors, contractors, cosmetologists, dentists, engineers, environmental systems (well diggers), foresters, funeral services, landscape architects, physicians, nurses, nursing home administrators, occupational therapists, opticians, optometrists, pharmacists, physical therapists, professional counselors, marriage and family therapists, psychologists, real estate agents, sanitarians, home builder, social workers, speech pathologist/audiologists, veterinarians, athletic trainers (boxing and wrestling), geologists.

South Dakota

Department of Commerce and Regulation, 500 E. Capitol Ave., Pierre, SD 57501-5070; 605-773-3178. South Dakota Medical and Osteopath Examiners, 1323 S. Minnesota Avenue, Sioux Falls, SD 57105; 605-336-1965. Licensing boards and professions: physicians, osteopaths, physician's assistants, physical therapists, medical corporations, emergency technicians, abstracters, accountants, barbers, chiropractors, cosmetologists, electricians, engineers/architects, funeral directors, hearing aid dispensers, medical/osteopaths, nurses, nursing home administrators, optometrists, pharmacists, plumbers, podiatrists, psychologists, real estate agents, social workers, veterinarians.

Tennessee

Division of Regulatory Boards, Department of Commerce and Insurance, 500 James Robertson Parkway, Nashville, TN 37243; 615-741-3449. Licensing boards and professions: accountants, architects and engineers, auctioneers, barbers, collection services, contractors, cosmetologists, funeral directors and embalmers, land surveyors, motor vehicle salesmen and dealers, personnel recruiters, pharmacists, polygraph examiners, real estate. For other licensed health professionals, contact Division of Health Related Professions, Department of Health and Environment, 283 or 287 Plus Park Blvd Complex, Nashville, TN 37247-1010; 615-367-6220: dentists, dental hygienists, podiatrists, physicians, physician's assistants, osteopaths, optometrists, veterinarians, nursing home administrators, dispensing opticians, chiropractors, social workers, hearing aid dispensers, registered professional environmentalists, marital and family counselors, speech pathology/audiologists, occupational and physical therapists, x-ray technicians, registered nurses, licensed practical nurses.

Texas

Texas Department of Commerce, 410 E. 5th Street, P.O. Box 12047, Austin, TX 78711-2728; 512-320-0110, or 800-888-0511 (toll-free in TX). Licensing boards and professions: accountants, architects, barbers, cosmetologists, morticians, educators, public safety, chiropractors, psychologists, dentists, real estate agents, engineers, veterinarians, insurance agents, land surveyors, landscape architects, fitting and dispensing of hearing aids, private investigators and private security agencies, polygraph, Vocational nurses, nursing home administrators, physicians, optometrists, structural pest control operators, pharmacists, physical therapists, plumbers, podiatrists, professional counselors, dietitians, speech-language pathology and audiology.

Utah

Division of Occupational and Professional Licensing, Department of Business Regulation, Heber M. Wells Building, 160 East 300 South, P.O. Box 45805, Salt Lake City, UT 84145-0805; 801-530-6628. Licensing boards and professions: accountants, architects, barbers, cosmetologists, electrologists, chiropractors, podiatrists, dentists, dental hygienists, embalmers, funeral directors, pre-need sellers, engineers, land surveyors, physicians, surgeons, Naturopaths, registered nurses, licensed practical nurses, nurse midwives, nurse anesthetists, nurse specialists, prescriptive practice specialist, IV therapists, optometrists, osteopaths, pharmacists, pharmacies, manufacturing pharmacies, shorthand reporters, veterinarians, health facility administrators, sanitarians, morticians, physical therapists, psychologists, clinical social workers, conduct research on controlled substance, marriage and family therapists, master therapeutic recreational specialists, speech pathologists, audiologists, occupational therapists, hearing aid specialists, massage therapists, massage establishments, acupuncture practitioners, physician assistants, dieticians, contractors.

Vermont

Division of Licensing and Registration, Secretary of State, Pavilion Office Building, Montpelier, VT 05609; 802-828-2363. Licensing boards and professions: accountants, architects, barbers, boxing control, chiropractors, cosmetologists, dentists, engineers, funeral directors/embalmers, land surveyors, medical board (physicians, podiatrists,

Be patient. If any phone number is incorrect, call (area code) 555-1212 and request the new listing.

real estate brokers, veterinarians, physical therapists, social workers, physician assistants, motor vehicle racing, nurses, nursing home administrators, opticians, optometrists, osteopaths, pharmacies, pharmacist, psychologists, private detectives, security Guards, radiological technicians.

Virginia

Virginia Department of Commerce, 3600 W. Broad St., Richmond, VA 23230; 804-367-8500. Licensed professions: accountants, architects, auctioneers, audiologists, barbers, boxers, contractors, commercial driver training schools, employment agencies, professional engineers, geologists, hairdressers, harbor pilots, hearing aid dealers and fitters, landscape architects, nursing home administrators, librarians, opticians, polygraph examiners, private security services, real estate brokers, speech pathologists, land surveyors, water and wastewater works operators, wrestlers. For licensed health professions, contact receptionist, Health Professionals: 804-662-9900. The office listed above can provide you with phone numbers for the following licensing boards: dentists, funeral directors/embalmers, physicians, medical/legal assistants, nurses, optometrists, pharmacists, psychologists, professional counselors, social workers, veterinarians.

Washington

Department of Health, P.O. Box 47860, Olympia, WA 98504-7860; 206-586-4561. Licensed professions: acupuncturists, auctioneers, architects, barbers, camp club registration/salespersons, chiropractors, cosmetology schools/ instructors, cosmetologists, manicurists, collection agencies, debt adjusters/agencies, dentists, dental hygienists, drugless therapeutic-naturopaths, employment agencies/managers, professional engineers, engineers-in-training, land surveyors, engineering corporations/partnerships, escrow officers/agents, firearms dealers, embalmers, apprentice embalmers, funeral directors, funeral establishments, hearing aid dispensers/trainees, land development registration, landscape architects, massage operators, midwives, notary publics, nursing home administrators, occularists, occupational therapists, dispensing opticians, optometrists, osteopaths, osteopathic physician/ surgeon, osteopathic physician assistants, physicians, surgeons, physician's assistants, limited physician, podiatrists, practical nurses, psychologists, physical therapists, real estate (brokers, salespersons, corporations, partnerships, branch offices), land development representatives, registered nurses, timeshare registration and salespersons, veterinarians, animal technicians.

West Virginia

Administrative Law Division, Secretary of State, State Capitol, Charleston, WV 25305; 304-558-6000. Licensing boards and professions: accountants, architects, barbers, beauticians, chiropractors, dentists, and dental hygienists, embalmers and funeral directors, engineers, foresters, hearing-aid dealers, landscape architects, land surveyors, law examiners, physicians, practical nurses, registered nurses, nursing home administrators, occupational therapists, optometrists, osteopaths, pharmacists, physical therapists, psychologists, radiologic technicians, real estate agents, sanitarians, state water resources, veterinarians.

Wisconsin

Department of Regulation and Licensing, P.O. Box 8935, Madison, WI 53708; 608-266-7482. Licensed professions: accountants, animal technicians, architects, architects, engineers, barbers, bingo organizations, morticians, chiropractors, cosmetologists, distributors of dangerous drugs, dental hygienists, dentists, interior designers, private detectives, drug manufacturers, electrologists, professional engineers, funeral directors, hearing aid dealers/fitters, land surveyors, manicurists, physicians, surgeons, nurse midwives, registered nurses, licensed practical nurses, nursing home administrators, optometrists, pharmacists, physical therapists, physician's assistants, podiatrists, psychologists, raffle organizations, real estate brokers, beauty salons, electrolysis salons, veterinarians.

Wyoming

Governor's Office, State Capitol, Cheyenne, WY 82002; 307-777-7434. Licensing boards and professions: funeral directors and embalmers, health service administrators, buyers and purchasing agents, shorthand reporters, medical record technicians, accountants and auditors, claims adjusters, appraisers, engineers, architects, surveyors, interior designers and decorators, medical laboratory workers, dental laboratory technicians, opticians, radiological technicians, respiratory technicians, quality control inspectors, security salespeople, insurance agents, real estate agents, physicians, physician's assistants, chiropractors, pharmacists, occupational therapists, activity therapists, physical therapists, speech pathologist and audiologist, veterinarian, optometrist, dietitians, dentists, dental hygienists, registered nurses, licensed practical nurses, emergency medical technicians, nurse's aides, medical assistants, counselors, lawyers, legal assistants, cosmetologists and barbers.

Driver's Licenses and Motor Vehicles

State Division of Motor Vehicles

Mailing lists galore and plentiful market research data derived from state motor vehicle departments offer the potential for increasing your bottom line. Did you ever want to know how many 40-year old males in Boston wear contact lenses, or perhaps obtain the names and addresses of all Arizonians who own Cadillacs? Well, it is within the realm of possibility.

Believe it or not, those long lines that drive us crazy when registering a car or renewing a driver's license have a bright side. Each person in line turns over to the state a wealth of information about him or herself. This data -- name, address, age, physical characteristics, and buying patterns -- are the stuff of which customer lists, market studies, and demographic analyses are made. While states charge you for this information, it will cost a fraction of what you would spend if you hired some sharp marketing consultant to unearth the data.

Take the example of my friend, Ron, a mechanic for expensive foreign cars in Wilmington, Delaware. One day Ron got tired of watching his boss laugh all the way to the bank and decided he wanted to open a shop of his own. Through the state he was able to obtain printouts of all owners of Audis, BMWs, and Mercedes in his area. Armed with this information, Ron ultimately was able to obtain a small business loan, open a shop, and now is making more than I'd care to admit.

Many states maintain files not only on autos, but also on boats and recreational vehicles. This data can be of further help in targeting potential customers. It doesn't take business brilliance to deduce that a person living in Palm Beach, who owns several high-ticket imported cars and has a 37-foot Hatteras yacht, is a potential customer for a home security company.

Many states will sort through their driver's license database by age and sex for an additional charge and provide a listing, for example, of all females between the ages of 18 and 45 years living in a particular district. If you are launching a magazine aimed at working women, this is priceless marketing intelligence. The same holds true for older persons who have special senior citizen identifiers and for young males who are eligible for the Selective Service.

This data is used in countless ways by researchers for compiling statistics on health issues, and of course, used by the government for manufacturer recalls or warranty programs, and emission studies. Insurance companies, financial institutions, and other businesses thrive on this cross-sectioning of the body public.

Information derived from a state's automobile owner registration master file is usually available in two formats -- magnetic tape or computer printouts. Most states prefer sending you a tape for larger files, while printouts are allowed for shorter sorts. In addition, some states offer mailing labels for an additional charge.

The most likely sorting options include: an entire state file; all vehicles within a county; vehicle type (2-door, 4-door, 4-wheel drive) by state or county; and vehicle make or year by state or county.

Driver's license information can usually be extracted to provide: name and license number (only); name, license number, and address; and a variety of other factors regarding age or sex. All states charge for this information, usually per 1,000 entries plus a set-up fee, but the potential for increasing your profits by using this valuable data will far outweigh the costs.

There are a few states which do not release this data for commercial purposes. These are Alabama, Connecticut, Georgia, Hawaii, Indiana, Kansas, New Jersey, New Mexico, New York, Oklahoma, Pennsylvania, Rhode Island, and South Dakota. Arkansas, California, Montana, Nebraska, North Carolina, Utah, Virginia are the states which will not divulge driver's license information, but will turn over vehicle registration files. Wyoming will give you driver's license information, but will not turn over vehicle registration files. That leaves 29 states which are wide open.

Motor Vehicle Offices

Alabama

Drivers: Alabama Department of Public Safety, Drivers License Division, P.O. Box 1471, Montgomery, AL 36272; 205-242-4400. This data is not released for commercial purposes. Individuals can retrieve information. A form is required and it must be notarized. The cost is $5.75 per request.

Registration: Alabama Department of Revenue, Motor Vehicle Division, P.O. Box 327640, Montgomery, AL 36312-7630; 205-242-9000. This data is not released for commercial purposes. Individuals can retrieve information. A form is required. The cost is $15 per individual record.

Arizona

Drivers: Arizona Motor Vehicles Division, 1801 W. Jefferson St., Phoenix, AZ 85007; 602-255-7567. This data is not available for commercial purposes. Individuals can retrieve information. Request must be in writing with complete name, license number and date of birth. The cost is $3 for a 39 month check, $5 for a 5 year check.

Registration: Arizona Motor Vehicles Division, 1801 W. Jefferson St., Room 230M, Phoenix, AZ 85007; 602-255-7567. Database: Arizona Owners - contains owner's name and address plus make, model, year, tag and license numbers for 1,655,833 cars and 875,000 other vehicles. Services: A mailing list is available for $3,500, or a computer tape can be purchased and data sorted by name and address. Tape cost is $30 per 1,000 names received.

Arkansas

Drivers: Arkansas Office of Motor Vehicle Registration, P.O. Box 1272, Little Rock, AR 72203; 501-682-7060. Services: license information is protected under the Privacy Act. A release must be signed by a driver before that data can be released. Ths cost is $1 per request.

Registration: Arkansas Office of Motor Vehicle Registration, P.O. Box 1272, Little Rock, AR 72203; 501-682-7060. Database: Arkansas Automobile Owners - contains owner's name and address plus make, model, year and license number for over 15 million automobiles and approximately 300,000 million other vehicles including motorcycles and boats. Services: No data tapes are released. Records are open for public inspection at the office only.

California

Drivers: Department of Motor Vehicles, P.O. Box 944247, Sacramento, CA 94269; 916-657-6555. This data is not released for commercial purposes. Individuals can retrieve information. You must use a form or request in writing with the person's name and date of birth or license number. The cost is $5 per request, and $20 for documents.

Registration: Department of Motor Vehicles, P.O. Box 944240, MS-D-146, Sacramento, CA 94244-2470. Database: California Automobile Owners - contains owner's name and address as well as make, model, year, tag and license numbers of 16.5 million automobiles and 631,000 motorcycles. Services: This file must be purchased in its entirety (i.e., information of all motorcycles and registration records for automobiles) The cost is approximately $100 per 1,000 names.

Colorado

Drivers: Colorado Motor Vehicle Division, Traffic Records, 140 W. 6th Ave., #104, Denver, CO 80204; 303-572-5601. Database: Colorado Drivers - contains name, address, license number of 3,167,570 drivers. It is available in two files: provisional and adult permits. Services: One time single run only of name, address and license number is available. The cost is $35 per 1,000 names with a $1,000 minimum plus $5 set-up fee.

Registration: Colorado Motor Vehicle Division, Traffic Records, 140 W. 6th Ave., #103, Denver, CO 80204; 303-623-9463. Database: Colorado Owners - contains name and address only. Services: One time single run of name, address and license number only. The cost is $25 per 1,000 names with a $1,000 minimum.

Connecticut

Drivers and Registration: Connecticut State Department of Motor Vehicles, 60 State Street, Wethersfield, CT 06109; 203-566-3830. This data is not released for commercial purposes. Individuals can retrieve information. A form is required. The cost is $4.50 per request.

Delaware

Drivers: Delaware Motor Vehicles Division, P.O. Box 698, Dover, DE 19903; 302-739-4461. Database: Delaware Drivers - provides name, address, height, weight and other drivers license information except hair color of 494,035 drivers. Services: Some ready-made programs available. Any additional programming requires additional charges. Prices are available upon request.

Registration: Delaware Motor Vehicle Division, P.O. Box 698, Dover DE 19903; 302-739-4461. Database: Delaware Owners - provides owner's name and address along with make, model, year, title number, and expiration date of 580,849 registered cars, motorcycles or trucks. Services: A data tape can be purchased with sorting of reportable variables for $375 plus $11 per 1,000 names.

District of Columbia

Drivers: District of Columbia, Department of Public Works Information Office, 301 C St., NW, Room 1025, Washington, DC 20001; 202-727-6761. Database: District of Columbia Drivers - contains name, address, suspensions, sex, height, weight, type of permit, license number, expiration dates, and restrictions of 800,000 drivers. Services: Computer tapes and printouts available. Data can be sorted by categories but not recommended. Cost is $1,700.

Registration: District of Columbia, Department of Public Works Information Office, 301 C St., NW, Room 1025, Washington, DC 20001; 202-727-1159. Database: District of Columbia Owners - contains owner's name, address, make, model, year, tag number, and registration number of 263,290 vehicles. Services: Computer tape is available. The data can be sorted. The cost varies depending on the information requested.

Florida

Drivers: Florida Highway Safety and Motor Vehicles Department, Neil Kirkman Building, Tallahassee, FL 32301; 904-488-6710. Database: Florida Drivers - contains name, address, and date of birth of over 12 million drivers. Services: No sorting is available. A computer tape or printout can be obtained for $.45 per second.

Registration: Florida Highway Safety and Motor Vehicles Department, Neil Kirkman Building, Tallahassee, FL 32301; 904-488-6710. Database: Florida Automobile Owners - provides owner's name and address plus make, model, year, tag number and class code for 7 million cars and 5 million other vehicles. Services: No sorting is available. The data is available on a computer tape or printout. Cost is $1.60 per second.

Georgia

Drivers: Motor Vehicle Records, 959 E. Confederate Ave., Atlanta, GA 30316; 404-624-7487. Data is not released.

Registration: Motor Vehicle Division, Trinity Washington Bldg., Atlanta, GA 30334; 404-656-4156. This data is not released for commercial purposes. Individuals can request information, but must appear in person with identification and state reasons for the request. The cost depends on the information requested or the circumstances.

Hawaii

Drivers and Registration: Division of Motor Vehicles and Licenses, 2455 S. Beretainia St., Honolulu, HI 96814; 808-973-2700. Data is not released.

Idaho

Drivers: Idaho Transportation Department, Economics and Research Section, P.O. Box 7129, Boise, ID 83707-1129; 208-334-8741. Database: Idaho Drivers - provides name, address, sex, date of birth, license type, expiration date, and county of residence of approximately 1,000,000 drivers. Services: Data may be selected by sex, age or range of ages, and county of residence. The cost is $75 plus computer charges (this varies depending on size of the file, sorts, etc.) and shipping charges.

Registration: Idaho Transportation Department, Economics and Research Section, P.O. Box 7129, Boise, ID 83707-1129; 208-334-8741. Database: Idaho Owners - provides registered owner, address, make, model, year, issue and expiration dates of approximately 1,300,000 records. Services: Data can be selected by registration type, and/or county of residence. The cost is $75 plus computer charges (varies depending on the size of the file, sorts, etc.) and shipping charges. Computer tape or printouts are available.

Illinois

Drivers: Illinois Secretary of State, Drivers Services Division, 2701 S. Dirksen Parkway, Springfield, IL 62723; 217-782-1978. Database: Illinois Drivers - contains name, address, sex, make, model, and year of over 6 million passenger cars and over 2 million other vehicles. Services: Data can be sorted by various categories and provided on a computer tape for $200 plus $20 per 1,000 names, or on a printout for $.50 per page (15,000 names or less).

Registration: Illinois Secretary of State, Centennial Building, Room 114, Springfield, IL 62756; 217-782-0029. Database: Illinois Automobile Owners - provides owner's name and address, make, model and year of over 6 million passenger cars and over 2 million other vehicles. Services: Complete records are available. Data can be sorted by various categories. Computer tapes available for $200 plus $20 per 1,000; computer printouts for $.50 per page (15,000 names or less).

Indiana

Drivers and Registration: Indiana Bureau of Motor Vehicles, 100 N. Senate Ave., Indianapolis, IN 46204; 317-232-2798. This data is not released for commercial purposes. Individuals can request information. The request must be in writing. The cost is $4 per request.

Iowa

Drivers: Iowa Department of Transportation, Drivers Services, Lucas State Office Building, Des Moines, IA 50319; 515-244-8725. Database: Iowa Drivers - provides name, address, date of birth, height, weight, restrictions, issue and expiration dates, license number, and restrictions of 2.5 million drivers. Services: Data is listed in order by license number. Data cannot be sorted. Computer tapes are available for $370 (tapes must be provided by requester).

Registration: Iowa Department of Transportation, Office of Vehicle Registration, P.O. Box 9204, Des Moines, IA 50306-9204; 515-237-3182. Database: Iowa Automobile Owners - provides complete description of vehicle for 4.2 million cars and other vehicles. Services: Data tapes available for $.39 per thousand names plus $14 for each tape, computer time charge for sorts and a $20 set up fee.

Be patient. If any phone number is incorrect, call (area code) 555-1212 and request the new listing.

637

Information on People, Companies, and Mailing Lists

Kansas

Drivers: Topeka Drivers License Bureau, 37th and Burlingame, Topeka, KS 66609; 913-266-7380. This data is not released for commercial purposes. Individuals can request information, but must appear in person and have the name and date of birth or license number of the person to be searched. The cost is $3.50 per request.

Registration: Topeka Drivers License Bureau, 37th and Burlingame, Topeka, KS 66609; 913-266-3621. This data is not released for commercial purposes. Individuals can request information, but must appear in person and have the name and date of birth or registration number. The cost is $3.50 per request.

Kentucky

Drivers: Kentucky Transportation Cabinet, Division of Driver Licenses, State Office Bldg., 501 High St., Frankfort, KY 40622; 502-564-4864. Database: Kentucky Drivers - provides name, address, and date of birth of over 2.4 million drivers. Services: Data can be sorted by various categories. Computer tapes or printouts are available for $.01 per name plus $510 for programming and computer costs.

Registration: Kentucky Transportation Cabinet, Division of Motor Vehicle Licenses, State Office Building, Room 205, Frankfort, KY 40622; 502-564-5301. Database: Kentucky Automobile Owners - provides owner's name and address along with make, model and year for over 2 million vehicles. Services: Data can be sorted by various categories. Computer tapes and printouts available for $.02 per name plus programming costs ($510). Mailing labels can be purchased for $3.50 per 1,000 plus programming costs.

Louisiana

Drivers: Louisiana Department of Public Safety and Corrections, P.O. Box 66614, Baton Rouge, LA 70896; 504-925-6146. Database: Louisiana Drivers - provides name, address, height, weight, sex, date of birth of 2.7 million drivers. Services: Computer tapes and printouts are available. Data can be sorted by variables. Cost is $.03 per name plus $500.

Registration: Louisiana Department of Public Safety and Corrections, P.O. Box 66614, Baton Rouge, LA 70896; 504-925-6146. Database: Louisiana Owners - provides owner's name, address, make, model and year, date of acquisition, color, new or used for 4.5 million vehicles. Services: Computer tapes and printouts are available for $.03 per record and $500.

Maine

Drivers: Maine Motor Vehicle Division, 101 Hospital Street, Station 29, Augusta, ME 04333; 207-287-5553. Database: Maine Drivers - provides name, address, date of birth, and sex of 800,000 drivers. Services: Data available on computer tape or printouts Mailing labels are available for an extra charge. The cost depends on the type of search and the amount of time involved.

Registration: Maine Motor Vehicle Division, 101 Hospital Street, Station 29, Augusta, ME 04333; 207-287-5553. Database: Maine Automobile Owners - contains owner's name and address, date of birth as well as make, model, year, identification number for 700,000 registered vehicles. Services: Data can be sorted by variables and can be purchased on computer tape, printouts or mailing labels. Cost available on request.

Maryland

Drivers: Maryland Motor Vehicle Administration, 6601 Ritchie Highway, Room 200, Glen Burnie, MD 21062; 410-768-7665. Database: Maryland Drivers - contains name, address, date of birth, height, weight, and identification number of over 2 million drivers. Services: Data can be sorted by variables and is available on computer tape for $500 (non-refundable).

Registration: Maryland Motor Vehicle Administration, 6601 Ritchie Highway, Room 200, Glen Burnie, MD 21062; 410-768-7665. Database: Maryland Automobile Owners - provides owner's name and address along with make, manufacturer, and year for nearly 3 million passenger cars and 3 million other vehicles. Some insurance information is included such as company and policy number. The cost is available upon request.

Massachusetts

Drivers: Massachusetts Registry of Motor Vehicles, 100 Nashua Street, Boston, MA 02114; 617-727-3716. Database: Massachusetts Automobile Drivers - provides name, address, and Social Security number of 4 million drivers. Services: Data can be sorted by all variables except sex. The cost is $1,000 for the first 1,000 names and

$40 per 1,000 records thereafter. Data is available on computer tape or printout (for less than 30,000 names).

Registration: Massachusetts Registry of Motor Vehicles, 100 Nashua Street, Boston, MA 02114; 617-727-3716. Database: Massachusetts Automobile Owners - contains owner's name and address along with make, model and year of 5 million vehicles. Services: Sorting of data is available, for instance, by particular insurance company the owner carries. The cost is $1,000 for the first 1,000 names and $40 per 1,000 records thereafter. Data is available on computer tape or printout (for less than 30,000 names).

Michigan

Drivers: Michigan Systems Programming Division, 7064 Crowners Drive, Lansing, MI 48918; 517-322-1624. Database: Michigan Drivers - provides names, address, date of birth, and sex of 6,447,174 drivers. Services: Data may be selected by sex, date of birth, county, state, city, and zip code at a cost of $64 per 1,000 names versus $16 per 1,000 names unsorted. There is a $500 minimum charge. Data can be purchased on computer tape or printout. It is also available in limited amount on disk. The cost is available upon request.

Registration: Michigan Department of State, Data Processing Division, 7064 Crowners Drive, Lansing, MI 48918; 517-322-1584. Database: Michigan Automobile Owners - provides owner's name and address with year, license number, make and model of 5,234,916 passenger cars and 2,261,688 other vehicles. Services: The cost for sorting is $64 per 1,000 names versus $16 per 1,000 unsorted names. There is a $500 minimum charge. Data can be purchased on computer tape or printout. The cost is available upon request.

Minnesota

Drivers: Minnesota Department of Public Safety, Driver/Vehicle Services Division, Transportation Building, 395 John Ireland Blvd., St. Paul, MN 55155; 612-297-2442. Database: Minnesota Drivers - provides name, address, and sex of 3.3 million drivers. Services: Data can be sorted; there is an extra fee if more information is required. Data is available on printout or computer tape or mailing labels for $8 to $10 per name with a $500 minimum. Custom programming cost varies depending on complexity of request.

Registration: Minnesota Department of Public Safety, Driver/Vehicle Services Division, Transportation Building, 395 John Ireland Blvd., St. Paul, MN 55155; 612-297-2442. Database: Minnesota Automobile Owners - contains owner's name and address along with make, model and year for 3.2 million cars and 2.1 million other vehicles. Services: Certain data can be sorted. Data is available on computer tape or printout. There is a $500 minimum plus $8 per 1,000 names.

Mississippi

Drivers: Mississippi Department of Public Safety/Data Processing, P.O. Box 958, Jackson, MS 39205; 601-987-1212. Database: Mississippi Drivers - contains name, address, date of birth, race and sex of over 1,924,696 drivers. Services: Data cannot be sorted. The entire file must be purchased for $250 plus $20 per reel.

Registration: Mississippi State Tax Commission Network, P.O. Box 960, Room 220, Jackson, MS 39205; 601-359-1117. Database: Mississippi Automobile Owners - provides a complete file, including owner's name and address, make, model, year of 1.6 million registered vehicles. Services: Data can be sorted and made available on computer tape or printout. Cost varies according to the search done. Mailing labels are available for an extra charge.

Missouri

Drivers: Missouri Department of Revenue, Information Services Bureau, P.O. Box 41, Jefferson City, MO 65105; 314-751-4600. Database: Missouri Drivers - contains name, address, sex, date of birth, height, weight, eye color, restrictions, license number, class, and county of 3.4 million drivers. Services: Data available on computer tape or printouts for $.18 per 50,000 records. Process fee is $85.26 and programming fee is $28.75 per hour. Mailing labels available for an extra charge ($2 per 1,000).

Registration: Missouri Department of Revenue, Information Services Bureau, P.O. Box 41, Jefferson City, MO 65105; 314-751-5486. Database: Missouri Owners - provides name and address of registered owners plus make, model, year, number of cylinders, type of fuel, license number, license expiration date, and year for over 4.2 million cars and 3.4 million other vehicles. Services: Data available on computer tape or printout. Cost: $.18 per 50,000 records. Process fee is $85.26 and programming fee is $28.75 per hour. Mailing labels available for an extra fee of $2 per 1,000.

Montana

Drivers: Drivers Services, 303 North Roberts, Helena, MT 59620; 406-444-3275. Data is not released.

Registration: Montana Motor Vehicle Division, 925 Main St., Deer Lodge, MT 59722; 406-846-1423. Database: Montana Automobile Owners - provides owner's name and address along with year, make, model, body, color, serial number, second owner for over one million registered vehicles. Services: Data available on computer tape and printout. The cost is $300 for the first 10,000 names and $30 per 1,000 names thereafter on tape or disk. Cost for each additional 1,000 names on printout is $40.

Nebraska

Drivers: Nebraska Department of Motor Vehicles, P.O. Box 94789, Lincoln, NE 68509; 402-471-3909. This data is not released for commercial purposes. Individuals can request information. The request must be made in writing or in person. The cost is $2 per request.

Registration: Nebraska Department of Motor Vehicles, P.O. Box 94789, Lincoln, NE 69509; 402-471-3909. Database: Nebraska Automobile Owners - provides listing by make, model, and year which includes owner's name and address for 856,000 passenger cars and 650,000 other vehicles. Services: Data can be provided on computer tape and printout for $12 per 1,000 with a $500 minimum.

Nevada

Drivers: Nevada Department of Motor Vehicles, 555 Wright Way, Carson City, NV 89711; 702-687-5505. Database: Nevada Drivers - provides name, address, date of birth, height, weight, for more than one million drivers. Services: Data can be sorted by county, zip code, date of birth and make of car. Data available on computer tape or printout (up to 1,000,000 names). Mailing labels available for an extra fee. Cost is $2,500 for the entire file or $15 per 1,000 for a partial listing. This data is not released to individuals.

Registration: Nevada Department of Motor Vehicles, 555 Wright Way, Carson City, NV 89711; 702-687-5505. Database: Nevada Owenrs - provides owner's name, address along with make, model and year for one million registered vehicles. Data may be selected by county, zip code and make of car. Services: Computer tape is available for $2,500 or portions prorated $15 per thousand. A printout is available for up to 1,000,000 records. Data is also available on mailing labels. (Prices are subject to change.) This data is not released to individuals.

New Hampshire

Drivers: New Hampshire Department of Safety, Data Processing, 10 Hazen Drive, Concord, NH 03305; 603-271-2314. Database: New Hampshire Drivers - consists of name, address, physical characteristics, Social Security number, class of license, issue and expiration date, and restriction of 843,000 drivers. Services: Data can be sorted by sex or age. Data provided on computer tape or printout. Prices vary, depending on data requested and size of the file.

Registration: New Hampshire Department of Safety, Data Processing, 10 Hazen Drive, Concord, NH 03305; 603-271-2314. Database: New Hampshire Owners - contains owner's name and address along with make, model and year for 815,628 passenger cars and 517,606 other vehicles. Services: Data can be sorted by zip code, model or make. Data available on computer tape or printout (extra charge). Fees vary depending on request. Entire file available on microfiche for $50.

New Jersey

Drivers and Registration: Motor Vehicle Services, Certified Information Unit, CN142, Trenton, NJ 08666; 609-292-4102. This data is not released for commercial purposes. Individuals can request information. The request must be in writing. The cost is $5 for certified copy, $4 for non-certified copy.

New Mexico

Drivers and Registration: New Mexico Taxation and Revenue Department, Motor Vehicle Division, P.O. Box 1028, Santa Fe, NM 87504-1028; 505-827-2294. Data is not released.

New York

Drivers: New York State Department of Motor Vehicles, Data Preparation, Empire State Plaza, Albany, NY 12202; 518-473-5595. This data is not released for commercial purposes. Individuals can request information. The request must be in writing. The cost is $5 per request.

Registration: State Department of Motor Vehicles, Empire State Plaza, P.O. Box 2650, Room 433, Albany, NY 12202; 518-473-5595. This data is not released for commercial purposes. Individuals can request information. The request must be in writing. The cost is $5 per request.

North Carolina

Drivers: Transportation Data Service Center, Century Center, Building B, 1020 Birchridge Rd., Raleigh, NC 27610; 919-250-4204. This data is not released for commercial purposes. Individuals can request information, but you must appear in person. The cost is $5 for a 3-year search.

Registration: Transportation Data Service Center, Century Center, Bldg. B, 1020 Birchridge Rd., Raleigh, NC 27610; 919-250-4204. Database: North Carolina Automobile Owners - provides owner's name and address, second owner's name, make, model, year, plate classification, license number and weight of vehicle for 5.5 million registered vehicles. Services: Data can be sorted by model, year, make, county, zip code and other variables. Cost is $250 for the first 5,000 records and $20 per 1,000 records thereafter.

North Dakota

Drivers: North Dakota Drivers License and Traffic Safety Division, 608 East Boulevard Avenue, Bismarck, ND 58505-0700; 701-224-2601. Database: North Dakota Drivers - provides name, address, date of birth, and license number of 450,000 drivers. Services: Special sort/extraction is available. The cost is $9 per 1,000 names with a $250 minimum. Mailing labels are also available for an extra fee.

Registration: North Dakota Department of Transportation, Motor Vehicle Service Division, 608 E. Boulevard, Bismarck, ND 58505; 701-224-2725. Database: North Dakota Automobile Owners - contains owner's name and address along with make, model and year of 369,010 passenger cars and 391,968 other vehicles. Services: Data can be sorted by variables and provided on computer printout tape for $50 plus $40 per 1,000 names. Mailing labels available for an extra fee.

Ohio

Drivers: Ohio Bureau of Motor Vehicles, Data Services, P.O. Box 16520, Columbus, OH 43266-0020; 614-752-7695. Database: Ohio Drivers - includes name, address, sex, date of birth, height, weight, hair color, eye color, zip code, and some restrictions for over 7.4 million registered drivers. Services: Data can be sorted by variables. Data is available on computer tape for $.75 per record. Mailing labels are $.08 each.

Registration: Ohio Bureau of Motor Vehicles, Data Services, P.O. Box 16520, Columbus, OH 43266-0020; 614-752-7695. Database: Ohio Automobile Owners - provides owner's name, address, make, model, year, license number, and expiration date for over 9 million registered vehicles. Services: Data can be sorted by variables. Available on computer tape or printout at $.75 per record. Mailing labels provided for $.08 each.

Oklahoma

Drivers and Registration: Oklahoma Tax Commission, Motor Vehicle Division, 2501 N. Lincoln Blvd., Oklahoma City, OK 73194; 405-521-3217. Data tapes are not sold. Individual records can be requested for $1 each. The request must be made in writing.

Oregon

Drivers: Oregon Department of Transportation, Motor Vehicle Division, 1905 Lana Ave., NE, Salem, OR 97314; 503-945-5259. Database: Oregon Drivers - contains name, address, sex, age, and date of birth for over 2 million drivers. Services: Data can be sorted and provided on computer tape for $180 or printout for $180 for full file.

Registration: Oregon Department of Transportation, Motor Vehicle Division, 1905 Lana Ave., NE, Salem, OR 97314; 503-945-5259. Database: Oregon Automobile Owners - contains owner's name and address along with make, model and year for over two million registered vehicles. Services: Data can be selected by variables. Data is also available on computer tape or printout for $180.

Information on People, Companies, and Mailing Lists

Pennsylvania

Drivers and Registration: Bureau of Drivers License Information, Box 58691, Harrisburg, PA 17106; 717-787-2158. This data is not released for commercial purposes. Individuals can request information using a form or written request. The cost is $5 for a 3-year search or $10 for a 10-year certified search.

Rhode Island

Drivers and Registration: Department of Motor Vehicles, State Office Building, Providence, RI 02903; 401-277-2064. This data is not released for commercial purposes. Individuals can request information. The request must be in writing. The cost is $10 per request.

South Carolina

Drivers: South Carolina Highway Department, Public Transportation, P.O. Box 1498, Columbia, SC 29216-0028; 803-251-2940. Database: South Carolina Drivers - provides name, address, date of birth, license number, and restrictions for 1.8 million drivers. Services: Data may be sorted by last name, zip code, tag number as well as automobile and/or motorcycles for 100,000 records. Computer tapes or printouts are available for $1,200.

Registration: South Carolina Highway Department, Public Transportation, P.O. Box 1498, Columbia, SC 29216-0028; 803-251-2940. Database: South Carolina Automobile Owners - contains name and address of 700,000 registered vehicles along with make, year and serial number. Services: Data may be sorted by last name, county, city, state, insurance information and tag number as well as automobile and/or motorcycles. Requests must be in writing. Prices are available upon written request.

South Dakota

Drivers and Registration: Division of Motor Vehicles, 118 W. Capitol St., Pierre, SD 57501; 605-773-3545. Data is not released.

Tennessee

Drivers: Department of Safety Information System, 150 Forter Ave., Nashville, TN 37210; 615-251-5322. Database: Tennessee Drivers - contains name, address, date of birth, sex and physical characteristics of approximately 3.5 million drivers. Services: Data can be sorted by category. Computer tapes, printouts and mailing labels are available for a minimum $500 plus $.10 per record.

Registration: Department of Safety Information Systems, 150 Forter Ave., Nashville, TN 37210; 615-741-3945. Database: Tennessee Automobile Owners - contains owner's name, address, model, make, year and tag number of approximately 4 million vehicles. Services: Computer tapes, printouts and mailing labels available for $300 minimum, plus $100 set up fee plus $20.05 per 1,000 names. (Prices subject to change.)

Texas

Drivers: Texas Department of Public Safety, Attn: L.I. and V.I., P.O. Box 4087, Austin, TX 78773; 512-465-2000. Database: Texas Drivers - provides name, address, date of birth, and license number for over 1.3 million drivers. Services: Data can be sorted by category. Data provided on computer tape for $30,000 for the entire file, or $2.25 per 1,000.

Registration: Texas Department of Transportation, Division of Motor Vehicles, 40th and Jackson, Austin, TX 78779-0001; 512-465-7531. Database: Texas Automobile Owners - contains owner's name and address along with make, model, year, previous owner, and lien holder for 14 million vehicles. Services: Sorting is not available. Data available on computer tape for $4,000 plus $.30 per 1,000 written records.

Utah

Drivers: Department of Public Safety, Drivers License Division, 4501 S. 2700 West, 3rd Floor, P.O. Box 30560, Salt Lake City, UT 84130-0560; 801-965-4437. This data is not released for commercial purposes. Individuals can request information. The request must be in writing. The cost is $3 per request.

Registration: Utah State Tax Commission, Data Processing, 160 E. 300 South St., Salt Lake City, UT 84134; 801-538-8309. Database: Utah Automobile Owners - provides owner's name and address along with make, model and year for 1.9 million vehicles. Services: Data can be sorted and made available on computer tape for $300 to $400.

Vermont

Drivers: Vermont Department of Motor Vehicles, 120 State St., Montpelier, VT 05603; 802-828-2020. Database: Vermont Drivers - contains name, address, physical characteristics, license number and date of birth for 427,512 drivers. Services: Full identification must be provided in order to obtain information (company or corporation). Cost is $4 for each record up to 4 records.

Registration: Vermont Department of Motor Vehicles, 120 State Street, Montpelier, VT 05603; 802-828-2020. Database: Vermont Automobile Owners - provides owner's name and address along with make, model and year for 327,016 passenger cars and 207,684 other vehicles. Services: Must provide vehicle identification to obtain information. Cost is $4 for each record.

Virginia

Drivers: Dealer and Information, P.O. Box 7412, Richmond, VA 23269; 804-367-0538. Data is not released.

Registration: Dealer and Information, P.O. Box 7412, Richmond, VA 23269,; 804-367-0538. Services: If you provide the license number or registration number, they will provide the information. Initial fee of $3,000 plus $5 per record.

Washington

Drivers: Department of Licensing, Highways/Licensing Building, P.O. Box 3090, Olympia, WA 98507; 206-753-6961. Database: Washington Drivers - provides name, date of birth and address of registered drivers. Services: Sorting is available. A written request is required and an agreement must be signed. Each program is custom made. The charge is $3,680 plus tax.

Registration: Department of Licensing, Highways/Licenses Building, Olympia, WA 98507; 206-753-6950. Database: Washington Automobile Owners - contains owner's name, address, make, model, year and class of vehicle. Services: Data can be sorted alphabetically by owner's name, address, make, model, year and class of vehicle. It can be sorted alphabetically by owner's name, state or county. A written request is required and an agreement must be signed. Each program is custom made. The charge is $3,680 plus tax. This data is not released to individuals.

West Virginia

Drivers: West Virginia Dept. of Motor Vehicles, Bldg. #3, Room 113, Charleston, WV 25317; 304-558-2723. Database: West Virginia Drivers - provides name, address, height, weight, race, sex, and date of birth for 1.4 million drivers. Services: Data can be sorted and provided on computer tape or printout. Cost is $5,040.

Registration: West Virginia Department of Motor Vehicles, Bldg. #3, Room 113, Charleston, WV 25317; 304-558-2723. Database: West Virginia Automobile Owners - contains owner's name and address along with make, model and year of 1.4 million passenger cars and 246,000 other vehicles. Services: Data can be sorted and provided on computer tape or printout for $5,040.

Wisconsin

Drivers: Wisconsin Department of Transportation, 4802 Sheybogan Ave., P.O. Box 7918, Madison, WI 53711; 608-266-2353. Database: Wisconsin Drivers - provides an alphabetical list of name, address, date of birth, sex and drivers record for 4.5 million drivers. Services: Data available on computer tape for $2,200.

Registration: Wisconsin Department of Transportation, 4802 Sheybogan Ave., P.O. Box 7911, Madison, WI 53707-7911; 608-266-2353. Database: Wisconsin Owners - provides owner's name and address plus make, model and year of 2.3 million passenger cars and 1.7 million other vehicles. Services: Data cannot be sorted. Entire file must be purchased on computer tape for $2,200.

Wyoming

Drivers: Wyoming Department of Transportation, Attn: Driver Control, P.O. Box 1708, Cheyenne, WY 82003; 307-777-4710. Database: Wyoming Drivers - provides name, address, date of birth, Social Security number, status, expiration, and issuance date for 500,000 drivers. Services: Cost for magnetic tape: $1 per record with a $100 minimum. All requests must be approved by the Commission. This data is not released to individuals.

Registration: Wyoming Department of Transportation, Licensing Station, 5300 Bishop Blvd., Cheyenne, WY 82009; 307-777-4810. Data is not released.

Be patient. If any phone number is incorrect, call (area code) 555-1212 and request the new listing.

Other Info Sources on People

Here are trail guides for genealogy research as well as all the major federal government sources for locating individuals. Also refer to the other sections in this chapter, specifically Who Owes Money to Whom and Driver's Licenses and Motor Vehicles which identify other sources for gathering information on the family clan or next door neighbors.

* Army Active Personnel Locator
U.S. Department of the Army
Worldwide Locator, EREC   800-444-3333
Ft. Benjamin Harrison, IN 46249-5301   317-542-4211
To locate a missing relative in the active army, contact this service. There is a small fee for the search.

* Army Discharged Personnel Locator Service
National Personnel Records Center
9700 Page Blvd.
St. Louis, MO 63132-5200   314-538-4201
To locate a relative or friend who is has been discharged from the Army, or who is deceased, contact the above office. The locator service's records go back to 1912; you may be able to find out what your great, great grandfather did in the Army. There is a small fee for the search.

* Army Personnel Locator
U.S. Army Worldwide Locator, ELREC
Fort Benjamin Harrison, IN 46249   317-542-4211 (recording)
To locate a long lost relative who is still on active duty in the Army, contact this office by letter. There is a small fee for their services. The telephone recording will give you information on the procedure and the data they need from you to initiate their search.

* Army Reserve and Retiree Locator
Army Reserve Personnel Center
U.S. Department of the Army
9700 Page Blvd.
St. Louis, MO 63132-5200   314-538-3828
To locate a missing relative in the Army reserve (who is not assigned to a unit), or to locate a living Army retiree, contact this office. There is a small fee.

* Biographical Directory of the U.S. Congress 1774-1989
Superintendent of Documents
Government Printing Office
Washington, DC 20402   202-512-1800
The Biographical Directory of the U.S. Congress 1774-1989, contains authoritative biographies of the more than 11,000 men and women who have served in the U.S. Congress from 1789 to 1989, and in the Continental Congress between 1774 and 1789. Many features include a listing of all chairmen of standing committees, all major formal leadership positions, bibliographic citations, and major revisions of political party affiliations reflecting the latest scholarship. You'll also find complete rosters of State congressional delegations for the First through 100th Congresses. This bicentennial edition is the most comprehensive *Biographical Directory of the United States Congress* ever issued. The latest edition published at the beginning of the 101st Congress is available through the Government Printing Office for $82.

* Congressional Directory
Superintendent of Documents
Government Printing Office
Washington, DC 20402   202-512-1800
The *Congressional Directory* has been the official handbook for the Congress since 1821 and is also widely used by Federal agency officials and the general public. Its contents include lists of addresses, rooms, and phone numbers of Members, biographical sketches of Members, Capitol officers and officials, committees, departments, and information on diplomatic offices and statistics. It also includes lists of members of the press admitted to the House and Senate galleries. The *1991-1992 Official Congressional Directory of the 101st Congress* is available for $16 in paperback, $20 in hardback, and $27 for a hardback copy with a thumb index.

* Family and Military Genealogy
Military Reference Branch
National Archives and Records Administration
8th St. and Pennsylvania Ave., NW
Washington, DC 20408   202-501-5385
The National Archives and Records Administration holds military service records and veterans' benefits records (pensions and bounty-land application files) for service performed from the Revolution (1775) through the early 20th century. The Archives does not have Confederate pension records, which were authorized by some southern states. To order photocopies of military service records, you must use National Archives Trust Fund Form 80 and submit a separate form for each file requested. You can obtain copies of this form and additional information about military service records from the Reference Services Branch at 202-523-3218. Your order must contain the following information: soldier's full name; period/war in which he/she served; state from which he/she served; branch of service; and whether the service was with the Union or Confederate forces.

* Federal Campaign Finance Law Complaints
Federal Election Commission
999 E Street, NW   800-424-9530
Washington, DC 20463   202-219-3420
If you believe a violation of the Federal campaign finance law has taken place, you may file a complaint with the Federal Election Commission (FEC). Send the Commission a letter explaining why you believe the law may have been violated, describe the specific facts and circumstances, and name the individuals or organizations responsible. The letter must be sworn to, signed, and notarized. Complaints of alleged violations receive case numbers and are called MURs, Matters Under Review.

* Federal Elections Clearinghouse
Federal Election Commission
999 E Street, NW
Washington, DC 20463   202-219-3670
The Election Clearinghouse assists election officials and the general public by responding to inquiries concerning the electoral process, publishing research, and conducting workshops on all matters related to Federal election administration.

* Federal Elections Library
Federal Election Commission (FEC) Library
999 E Street, NW, Room 801
Washington, DC 20463   202-219-3312
The Federal Election Commission (FEC) Library's collection includes basic legal research tools and materials dealing with political campaign finance, corporate and labor political activity, and campaign finance reform. The Library staff prepares indexes to Advisory Opinions and Matters Under Review (MURs), as well as a *Campaign Finance and Federal Election Law Bibliography*, which are available for purchase from the FEC's Public Records Office.

* Federal Employees' Personnel Records
National Personnel Records Center
National Archives and Records Administration
111 Winnebago Street

Be patient. If any phone number is incorrect, call (area code) 555-1212 and request the new listing.

641

Information on People, Companies, and Mailing Lists

St. Louis, MO 63118   314-219-3312

Federal employees' personnel records are transferred and stored in the National Personnel Records Center. The Center can answer questions regarding the information available, and can provide copies of documents. Contact the Center for more information.

* Financial Disclosure Database on Federal Candidates

Federal Election Commission (FEC)
Data Systems Development Division
999 E Street, NW
Washington, DC 20463   202-219-4140

The Federal Election Commission (FEC) maintains a computer database of information from all reports filed by political committees, individuals, and other entities since 1972. The data is sorted into indexes which permit a detailed analysis of campaign finance activity and, additionally, provide a tool for monitoring contribution limitations. The data can be searched by specific candidate or contributor. By contacting this office, individuals can have searches done on twenty names or less free. For searches of more than 20 names, cost varies depending on computer time needed.

* Genealogy Reference

Main Reading Room
Library of Congress
Washington, DC 20540   202-707-5521

Located on the first floor of the Thomas Jefferson Building, the main reading room contains material on American history, economics, fiction, language and literature, political science, government documents, and sociology. A reference collection for these materials is also housed there. These reading rooms are not equipped to answer reference questions over the telephone, but will provide information on their collections, hours of operation, and the like.
Local History and Genealogy, 202-707-5537.

* Genealogy Research

Reference Services Branch
8th St. and Pennsylvania Ave., NW, Room 205
Washington, DC 20408   202-501-5400

Using Records in the National Archives for Genealogical Research is a free, 25-page brochure which explains a little about genealogical research in general, and then outlines the genealogical records in the National Archives. It includes the necessary information in order to research your request.

Guide to Genealogical Research in the National Archives is available for $25 and contains information about individuals whose names appear in census records, military service and pension files, ship passenger and arrival lists, land records, and many other types of records. This Guide shows how to tap this rich resource, explaining what types of records are preserved in the National Archives and what specific information about individuals is included in each type of record. For more information on genealogical research, contact the Reference Services Branch.

* Genealogical Workshops

Education Branch
National Archives and Records Administration
8th St. and Pennsylvania Ave., NW, Room 505
Washington, DC 20408   202-724-0456

Genealogical workshops are offered quite frequently by the Education Branch of the National Archives. The topics covered include census records, passenger lists, naturalization records, military service records, as well as many other genealogical topics. Each workshop lasts three hours and costs $10. Call or write for a complete workshop schedule.

* Historical Documentary Editions 1988

National Historical Publications and Records Commission
National Archives and Records Administration
8th St. and Pennsylvania Ave., NW, Room 300
Washington, DC 20408   202-501-5605

This free catalog lists and describes all the documentary editions supported by the Commission with funds or by formal endorsement. These editions represent a major, long-term effort to make the nation's important documents widely available for study and research. Each title includes a brief description, as well as ordering information.

* Inmate Locator Line

Public Information, Bureau of Prisons
U.S. Department of Justice
320 1st St., NW, Room 640
Washington, DC 20536   202-307-3198

A special phone service hotline is available for people trying to locate family members or loved ones believed to be incarcerated in local, state, or federal correctional institutions. Call the Inmate Locator Line: 202-724-3126 between 10 a.m. and 4:30 p.m. EST.

* Military and Civilian Employment Records

National Personnel Center
9700 Page Blvd.
St. Louis, MO 63232   314-538-5201

This Center holds both military and civilian Federal personnel records dating from 1900 to the present. The Center prefers written requests for reference assistance.

* Military Pension Genealogy Searches

General Reference Branch
National Archives and Records Administration
Washington, DC 20408   202-501-5430

This office holds military service and pension records of people who served prior to 1900. The office accepts written requests only. Ask for *Form NATF 80*.

* Military Records 19th Century On

Suitland Reference Branch
National Archives and Records Administration
Washington, DC 20409   202-763-7410

This office holds historical material, including Land Office records, military personnel records dating prior to 1900, State Department personnel overseas post records since 1935, the Japanese war relocation records, records of the U.S. military government of Germany and Japan, as well as records of all military actions dating from the Revolutionary War through 1963. The office provides reference assistance in locating historical material, and will accept reference questions both in writing and by phone.

* Military Reference

Office of the National Archives
National Archives and Records Administration
8th St. and Pennsylvania Ave., NW, Room 13W
Washington, DC 20408   202-501-5385

The Military Reference Branch maintains records of military personnel separated from the U.S. Air Force, Army, Coast Guard, Marine Corps, Navy, Confederate States, volunteers, as well as veterans records. The publication, *Military Service Records in the National Archives of the United States*, provides a detailed list of the holdings and pertinent details about the records.

* Military Service Genealogy Searches

General Reference Branch
National Archives and Records Administration
Washington, DC 20408   202-501-5430

This office holds military service and pension records of people who served prior to 1900. The office accepts written requests only. Ask for *Form NATF 80*.

* National Driver Register

National Driver Register (NTS-24)
Traffic Safety Programs
National Highway Traffic Safety Administration
U.S. Department of Transportation
400 7th Street, SW, Room 5119
Washington, DC 20590   202-366-4800

The *National Driver Register* is a central, computerized index of state records on drivers whose operator licenses have been revoked, denied, or suspended for more than 6 months. Data includes name, birthdate, height, weight, eye color, date and reason for action, and date of reinstatement. Applications for driver licenses are routinely checked against the register, and states exchange information via an electronic system.

* Personal Census Records Service

The Census History Staff
Data User Services Division
Bureau of the Census
U.S. Department of Commerce
Washington, DC 20233   301-763-7936

The Bureau of the Census employs a staff to search the Federal censuses of population from 1900 on, stored at Pittsburgh, Kansas, and provide, for a fee, official transcripts of personal data from these records to individuals who lack other birth or citizenship documents. Government agencies and employers often accept these transcripts as evidence of age and place of birth for obtaining employment, social security benefits, old age assistance, passports, naturalization papers, or delayed birth certificates, and for other purposes. The personal information recorded in these censuses may be furnished only upon the written request of the named individual or his or her legal representative. Application forms, with detailed information, can be obtained by contacting either office above.

* Photographs of Every Member of Congress

Superintendent of Documents
Government Printing Office
Washington, DC 20402   202-512-1800

The *Congressional Pictorial Directory* contains photographs of the President, Vice President, members of the Senate and House, Officers of the Senate and House, Officials of the Capitol, and a list of the Senate delegations and an alphabetical list of senators and representatives. The paperback edition is $4.24, and the hardback copy is $14.

* Presidential Political Appointments: The "Plum" Book

Senate Government Affairs Committee
Dirksen Office Building, Room S-340
Washington, DC 20510   202-224-3791

Superintendent of Documents
Government Printing Office
Washington, DC 20402   202-512-1800

U.S. Policy and Supporting Positions, more commonly known as the *Plum Book*, lists some 3,000 political appointment jobs and describes the type of appointment, tenure, grade, and salary. It is available for sale from the Superintendent of Documents for $14 per copy.

* Prisoners of War and Reclassification

U.S. Department of Defense
Force Management and Personnel
The Pentagon, Room 3E767
Washington, DC 20301-4000   703-695-7402

For information on conscientious objectors and POW's, including reclassification and discharge data, contact the above office.

* Prisoner-of-War Records

Military Services Branch
National Archives and Records Administration
8th St. and Pennsylvania Ave., NW, Room 13W
Washington, DC 20408   202-501-5385

This Branch has information regarding Prisoner-of-War records through the Civil War, and can also direct you to the proper office for information regarding prisoners-of-war through the Vietnam War.

* Salaries and Expenses of Congressmen, Congresswomen, and Their Employees

House Document Room
H-226 Capitol Bldg.
Washington, DC 20515   202-225-3456

The *Report of the Clerk of the House* includes the salaries of House members' staffs, committee staffs, and House officers and employees. This quarterly report includes a listing of House expenditures.

* Salaries and Expenses of U.S. Senators and Their Staff

Senate Document Room
B-04 Senate Hart Office Building
Washington, DC 20510   202-224-7860

The biannual *Report of the Secretary of the Senate* lists Senate expenditures and details the salaries of senators' staff, members, committee staff members, and officers and employees of the Senate.

* Selective Service Registration Status

Registration Information Office
P.O. Box 4638
North Suburban, IL 60197-4638   708-688-6888

If you have any questions regarding an individual's status and the requirement to register, call or write this office.

* Ship Passenger Arrival Lists

Reference Services Branch
National Archives and Records Administration
8th St. and Pennsylvania Ave., NW
Washington, DC 20408   202-501-5400

The National Archives compiles ship passenger arrival records dating from 1820 for most east and gulf coast ports, a few lists dating from 1800 for Philadelphia, and from the 1890's for San Francisco and Seattle. Archives staff can conduct searches if you know the full name of the passenger, the port of entry, and the approximate date of arrival.

* State Access to Financial Disclosure Database

Federal Election Commission
Public Records Office
999 E Street, NW
Washington, DC 20463   202-219-4140

Under the State Access Program, individuals and organizations in 15 states now have immediate online access to several standard Federal Election Commission (FEC) computer indexes which provide descriptive information on all registered political committees, the total receipts and disbursements of committees, and a listing of all PAC contributions to federal candidates. Participating states with operational terminals within their State Election Offices include: Arizona, Colorado, Connecticut, Georgia, Illinois, Iowa, Massachusetts, Michigan, New Jersey, New Mexico, Ohio, Tennessee, Vermont, Washington, and Wisconsin.

* State Election Finance Records

Federal Election Commission (FEC)
Public Records Office
999 E Street, NW   202-219-3420
Washington, DC 20463   800-424-9530

Researchers can obtain campaign finance reports from the records office in each state. Contact this Federal Election Commission office to order a list of the names, addresses, and phone numbers of national and state disclosure offices.

* Vietnam Casualty Computer Printout

Center for Electronic Records
National Archives and Records Administration
Washington, DC 20408   202-501-5575

This office holds all Federal records on computer disk, which include all recent Department of Defense records and the casualty lists from the Vietnam War. Copies may be purchased.

Information on Any Company

When many researchers are doing investigations on companies they often rely only on two major information sources:

Public Companies =   U.S. Securities and
                      Exchange Commission
                      Filings

Privately Held
Companies =   Dun & Bradstreet Reports

Although many people still depend heavily on the Securities and Exchange Commission (SEC) and Dun & Bradstreet (D & B), these two resources have severe limitations. The Securities and Exchange Commission has information on approximately only 10,000 public companies in the United States. However, according to the IRS and the U.S. Bureau of the Census (both agencies count differently), there are between 5,000,000 and 12,000,000 companies in the country. So you can see that the SEC represents only a small fraction of the universe. Also, if you are interested in a division or a subsidiary of a public corporation and that division does not represent a substantial portion of the company's business, there will be no information on their activities on file at the SEC. This means that for thousands of corporate divisions and subsidiaries, it is necessary to look beyond the SEC.

D & B Won't Jail You for Not Telling the Truth but the Government Will

The problems with Dun & Bradstreet reports are more significant than the shortcomings of company filings at the SEC. The main drawback is that D & B reports have been established primarily for credit purposes and are supposed to indicate the company's ability to pay its bills. Therefore, you will find information from current creditors about whether a business is late in its payments, which may or may not be a useful barometer to evaluate the company.

If there is additional financial information in these reports, you should also be aware of who in the company provides D & B with information and their motives. The information contained in these reports does not carry the legal weight of the company information registered with the Securities and Exchange Commission. If a company lies about any of the information it turns over to the SEC, a corporate officer could wind up in jail. Dun & Bradstreet, however, collects its information by telephoning a company and asking it to provide certain information voluntarily. The company is under no obligation to comply and, equally important, is under no obligation to D & B to be honest. Unlike the government, Dun & Bradstreet cannot prosecute.

If a competitor or someone was interested in acquiring Information USA, Inc., for example, the first likely step would be to obtain any financial data about this privately held company. In this hypothetical case, Information USA, Inc. might be interested in such a sale or perhaps want to impress the competition.

Consequently, the information supplied to Dun & Bradstreet most likely would be the sanitized version which I would want outsiders to see. My only dilemma would be in remembering what half truths we told D & B last year so that our track record would appear consistent. However, Information USA, Inc. would not, and does not, play such games with its financial information filed with the Maryland Secretary of State.

This is why resourceful researchers are starting to appreciate the value of the thousands of non-traditional information sources such as public documents and industry experts.

Starting at the Securities and Exchange Commission

First find out whether the company you are gathering intelligence about is a public corporation. If it is, you should get your hands on copies of the company's Securities and Exchange Commission (SEC) filings. The fastest way to make this determination is to call:

Disclosure Inc.
5161 River Road Building 60
Bethesda, MD 20816
301-951-1300
800-638-8241

The price depends on which document you wish to have retrieved. The range is between $18 to $38 per document. If the company in question files with the Securities and Exchange Commission, the least you should do is to obtain a copy of the Annual Report, known as 10-K. This disclosure form will give you the most current description of the company's activities along with their annual financial statement.

Financial Statements in Addition to the Annual Report

In addition to the 10-K you may also want to see the company's most current financial statements by obtaining copies of all 10-Q's filed since their last 10-K. 10-Q's are basically quarterly financial statements which will bring you up-to-date since the last annual report.

The two other documents which may be of immediate interest are the 8-K's and the Annual Report to Stockholders. An 8-K will disclose any major developments that have occurred since the last annual report, such as information about a takeover or major lawsuit. The Annual Report to Stockholders, the glossy quasi-public relations tool that is sent to all those who own stock in the company, can provide another component in assembling a company's profile. The most interesting item in this report, which is not included in the 10-K Annual Report, is the message from the president. This message often provides insights about the company's future plans.

Obtaining Copies of SEC Documents

The fastest way to get Securities and Exchange Commission (SEC) documents is through one of the many document retrieval companies which provide this service. In addition to the firm mentioned above, other companies that specialize in quickly obtaining corporate SEC filings include:

1) FACS Info Service, Inc.
   157 Fisher Avenue
   Eastchester, NY 10709
   914-779-6900
   Fax: 914-779-7038

2) Federal Document Retrieval, Inc. (Disclosure)
   SEC Building
   601 Indiana Ave., 8th Floor
   Washington, DC 20001
   202-347-2824

3) Research Information Services
   717 D Street, NW
   Washington, DC 20004
   202-737-7111
   Fax: 202-737-3324

4) Prentice Hall Legal and Financial Services
   1090 Vermont Ave., NW, Suite 430
   Washington, DC 20005
   202-408-3120
   Fax: 202-408-3142

5) Washington Service Bureau
   655 15th Street NW, Room 275
   Washington, DC 20005
   202-508-0600
   Fax: 202-508-0694

6) Washington Document Service
   400 7th Street NW, Suite 300
   Washington, DC 20001
   202-628-5200
   Fax: 202-626-7628

7) Vickers Stock Research Corp.
   600 S Street NW, Suite 504
   Washington, DC 20004
   202-626-4951

You can also go to one of the four major Securities and Exchange Commission Document Rooms to see any public filing. These reference rooms are located in Washington, DC, New York City, Chicago, and Los Angeles.

If the company headquarters or main office is located in the area served either by the Atlanta, Boston, Denver, Fort Worth, or Seattle regional offices, the 10-K and other documents can be examined at the appropriate SEC office. For the exact location of any of the regional offices mentioned contact:

Office of Public Affairs
U.S. Securities and Exchange Commission
450 5th Street NW, Stop 1-2

Washington, DC 20549
202-942-0020

One way to obtain free copies of these reports is to call the company and tell them you are a potential investor. Many public corporations are set up to respond to these inquiry.

Before you order any of these SEC filings, it is wise to ask for the total number of pages contained in each of the documents you want to obtain. Most of these document retrieval firms charge by the page, and no doubt, you don't want to be surprised if a company's amendment to its 10-K happens to run 500 pages in length.

Once you have obtained the SEC documents you can then explore the additional sources described below.

Clues at the State Level About Privately Held Companies Plus Divisions and Subsidiaries of Public Corporations

The following sources are designed primarily to help you gather information on privately held companies or those divisions and subsidiaries of public corporations which are not contained in documents filed with the U.S. Securities and Exchange Commission. However, the sources described here will enhance your work in collecting data on all types of companies. If the company in question is not publicly owned, the next step is to turn your attention to the appropriate state government offices. All companies doing business in any state leave a trail of documentation there. The number of documents and the amount of detail vary widely depending upon the state regulations and the type of company.

One of the main reasons you should begin your search with the state government is that it may take longer to retrieve the information from the state offices than from other checkpoints which are described in this Section.

Puzzling Together Bits of Information

Remember that only the U.S. Securities and Exchange Commission documents provide you with information on your competitor or acquisition candidate. All other government documents are generated to comply with some law or policy, such as pollution control, consumer protection, or tax collection. Because of this, government bureaucrats who collect and analyze these documents have no idea just how valuable the information can be to you. Do not expect that the data contained in other government documents will be presented in a way that automatically will suit your particular needs. Furthermore, no single document will provide all the information about a corporate entity that you are seeking.

The strategy is to get any information you can because each piece might contribute to your overall information mosaic. Although a full profit and loss statement will be out of reach, the office of uniform commercial code can tell you to whom the company owes money and provide a description of the corporation's assets. The state office of corporations may not give you the total sales figure, but if the company's headquarter is out of state, it may tell you the corporation's total sales in that state and what percentage

Be patient. If any phone number is incorrect, call (area code) 555-1212 and request the new listing.

645

Information on People, Companies, and Mailing Lists

this is of its total. With a little bit of algebra you can estimate the total sales.

If it were as easy as making one phone call and getting complete financial information on any company, everyone would be doing it. Your competitive advantage lies in getting information that other people don't know about, or are too lazy to get.

In the event you intend to dig around at the state level, the following three offices are a must. They offer the biggest potential for the least amount of effort:

1) Office of Corporations

Every corporation, whether it is headquartered or has an office in a state, must file some information with a state agency. The corporations division or office of corporations usually is part of the office of the Secretary of State. When a company incorporates or sets up an office in the state, it must file incorporation papers, or something similar. This provides, at a minimum, the nature of the business, the names and addresses of officers and agents, and the amount of capital stock in the company. In addition to this registration, every company must file some kind of annual report. These annual reports may or may not contain financial data. Some states require sales figures, and others ask just for asset figures.

2) Office of Uniform Commercial Code

Any organization, and for that matter, any individual, which borrows money and offers an asset as collateral, must file within the state at the office of uniform commercial code. A filing is made for each loan and each of the documents is available to the public. To obtain these documents is a two step process. First, one must request a search to see if there are any filings for a certain company. The fee for a search is usually under $10. Such a search will identify the number of documents filed against the company. You then will have to request copies of each of these documents. The cost for each document averages only a few dollars. This office of uniform commercial code usually is located in, or near to, the same office of corporations.

3) State Securities Office

The U.S. Securities and Exchange Commission in Washington, DC regulates only those corporations which sell stock in their company across state lines. There is another universe of corporations which sells stock in their companies only within state lines. For such stock offerings, complete financial information is filed with the state securities regulator. These documents are similar to a those filed at the U.S. Securities and Exchange Commission. But, remember, that the documents vary from one state to the next and, equally important, the requirement of filing an annual report differs from state to state. Usually a telephone call to the office in charge can tell you whether a particular company has ever offered stock intrastate. If so, you are then in a position of getting copies of these filings. Usually the Secretary of State's office can refer you to the state's securities regulator.

Finding the Right State Office

Because of the multitude of differences between the 50 state governments, expect to make half a dozen calls before you locate the right office. Several starting places are described below with the simplest ones listed first.

1) State Government Operator

The AT&T information operator can give you the telephone number for the state government operator, and then in turn you can ask for the phone number of the specific government office.

2) State Department of Commerce

Now that every state is aggressively trying to get companies to expand or relocate to their state, these departments can serve as excellent starting points, because they are familiar with other government offices which regulate business. Many times these departments have established a "one-stop office" with a separate staff on call to help a business find whatever information it needs.

3) State Capital Library

By asking the state government operator to connect you to the state capital library, a reference librarian can identify the state agency which can best respond to your queries.

4) Directories

If you intend to dig around various state government offices on more than just an infrequent basis, you might consider purchasing a state government directory. Usually the state office of Administrative Services will sell you a directory, or you might want to contact the state bookstore. If you want to purchase a directory that covers all 50 states, consider:

State Executive Directory
Carroll Publishing Company
1058 Thomas Jefferson Street NW
Washington, DC 20007
202-333-8620
(Price is $135 per year plus shipping and handling.)

Tracking the Trail of Company Information in Other State Offices

The three offices described earlier are only the starting places for information on companies. There are dozens of other state agencies that are brimming with valuable bits of data about individual corporations; however, these sources require a bit more care because they can be used only under certain circumstances or require extra resourcefulness.

1) Utility and Cable TV Regulators

Utility companies are heavily regulated by state agencies, and as a result, there is a lot of financial and operational information that is accessible. Most people know that gas and electric companies fall into this category, but you may not be aware that this also applies to water companies, bus companies, rail systems, telephone companies, telecommunication companies, and cable TV operators.

2) Other State Regulators

State government is very similar to the federal government in that its function is to regulate many of the activities of the business community. In those states where state laws and enforcement are very effective, Uncle Sam relies on those states to enforce the federal laws. For example, the U.S. Food and Drug Administration will use the records from the state of New Jersey for information on pharmaceutical manufacturers instead of sending out its own team of federal data collectors. The U.S. Environmental Protection Administration will use state records in those states that have strict environmental statutes rather than using its own resources.

3) Financial Institutions
Banks, savings and loans, credit unions and other financial institutions all file information with the state bank regulator. Many of these organizations are also regulated by federal agencies so what you get from the state office often will be a copy of the form filed with the federal government.

4) Environment Regulators
Almost every state has an office which regulates pollutants in the air, water and ground. Such departments are similar to the U.S. Environmental Protection Agency in Washington, DC and monitor whether any new or old business is polluting the environment. If the company you are investigating has plans to build a new plant in the state, get ready to collect some valuable information. Before construction can begin, the company must file information with the state environmental protection agency. These documents will detail the size of the plant, what kind of equipment it will use, and how much this equipment will be used. With such information, other manufacturers in the same business can tell exactly what the capacity and estimated volume of the plant will be. Sometimes there will be three separate offices with authority over air, water or solid waste. Each will collect basically the same information, and they can be used, one against each other, to ensure that you get all the information you need.

5) Department of Commerce/Economic Development
As mentioned earlier, each state is now actively trying to attract and develop business development within the state. The state's office of economic development or department of commerce is normally charged with this responsibility. To attract business to the state, this agency has to know all about existing business throughout the state, which all translates into who is doing what, how successful they are, and how large the company is. At a minimum, the economic development office can probably provide you with information on the number of employees for a given company. They will also be aware what other government offices in the state keep records about the industry or company which interests you. The experts at this state agency are similar to the 100 industry analysts at the U.S. Department of Commerce and can serve as excellent resources for collecting government information on an industry.

6) State Government Contractors
Although many states are not accustomed to sharing information with researchers, you should be able to obtain details about any purchase the state makes. If the company in question sells to the state, you should get copies of their contracts. Just like the federal government which makes all this procurement information available, the state which spends public funds guarantees that the public has a right to know how the money is being spent. You may have to enforce your rights under the state law which is equivalent to the federal Freedom of Information Act.

7) Minority and Small Business
Many states maintain special offices which track minority firms and other small companies. These offices can be helpful by identifying these businesses and may also be able to tell you the size or products of a given business. The small business office and possibly a separate minority business division normally fall under the state department of commerce.

8) Attorney General
The state Attorney General's office is the primary consumer advocate for the state against fraudulent practices by businesses operating within the state. So, if the company you are investigating is selling consumer services or products, it would be worth the effort to check with this office. In some states the attorney generals have begun to concentrate on certain areas. For example, the office in Denver specializes in gathering information on companies selling energy saving devices, and the one in New York investigates companies with computerized databases which provide scholarship information.

9) Food and Drug Companies
Any company which produces, manufactures or imports either food or drug products is likely to come under the jurisdiction of the state food and drug agency. This office makes routine inspections of facilities and the reports are generally accessible; however, a Freedom of Information Act request is sometimes necessary.

County and Local Sources

County and local sources can prove to be the biggest bucket of worms as far as information sources go. Unlike state government offices where there are 50 varieties to choose from, there are over 5,000 different jurisdictions at the local level. Here are some basic checkpoints that can enhance your information gathering efforts.

Local Newspapers: Business Editors

The local newspaper can provide the best leads for anything you are investigating at the local level. It is perhaps the best source mentioned in this book. A well placed telephone call to the business editor or the managing editor, if there is not a business section, can prove to be most useful. In smaller towns, and even in suburbs of larger cities where there are suburban newspapers, a local business generates a good deal of news. A local reporter often knows the company like no one else in the country. The company executives usually are more open with the local media because they like to show off about how big they are, how much the company is growing, etc. A reporter is also likely to know company employees who can corroborate or refute the executive's remarks.

Ask the local newspaper if you can get copies of all articles written about the company in question. After you review them, call the reporter to see what additional information may be stored in his or her head.

Other Checkpoints

It is worth fishing for information in a number of other places, including agencies and private organizations.

1) Chamber of Commerce
Talking to someone on the research staff or the librarian can help you identify sources within the community about a company. A friendly conversation with Chamber executives can also provide insight into a company's financial position and strategies.

Information on People, Companies, and Mailing Lists

2) Local Development Authority

Many local communities, counties, and regional areas have established development authorities to attract business and industry to their area. They operate pretty much the same as the state department of economic development described above, and as a result, collect a large amount of data about the businesses in their area.

3) Local Courts

Civil and criminal court actions can provide excellent source material for company investigations. Perdue Chicken Company, a private corporation in Maryland, revealed its annual sales figures while fighting Virginia sales tax in the courts. A recent search revealed four financial-related suits filed against a large privately held political campaign fund raising firm in McLean, Virginia. If you are not in close proximity to the court, it may be worthwhile to hire a local freelance reporter or researcher. In most jurisdictions there are chronological indexes of both civil and criminal cases which are kept by the clerk of the court. These indexes record all charges or complaints made, the names of the defendants and plaintiffs in the event of civil cases, the date of the filing, the case number, and the disposition if one has been reached. Armed with the case number you can request to see the case files from the clerk.

Company Information at the Office of Federal Regulators

The federal offices identified in the preceding section on market studies are also excellent sources for information on companies. Industry specialists within the federal government are likely to have information on companies or can refer you to other sources which may have just the information you need.

The 26 government agencies listed here are those that are involved with regulating industries and/or the companies within those industries. The information held at each federal office varies from agency to agency; however, most of the offices maintain financial or other information that most researchers would consider sensitive.

Airlines, Air Freight Carriers, and Air Taxis
Office of Community and Consumer Affairs
U.S. Department of Transportation
400 7th Street SW, Room 10405
Washington, DC 20590   202-366-2220/5957

Airports
Airport Section
National Flight Data Center, Room 634
Federal Aviation Administration, ATM-612
800 Independence Avenue SW
Washington, DC 20591   202-267-9311

Bank Holding Companies and State Members of the Federal Reserve System
Freedom of Information Act Office
Board of Governors of the Federal Reserve System
20th St. and Constitution Ave. NW, Room B1122
Washington, DC 20551   202-452-3684

Banks, National
Communications Division
Comptroller of the Currency
250 E St., SW
Washington, DC 20219   202-874-4700

Barge and Vessel Operators
Financial Analysis, Tariffs
Federal Maritime Commission
800 N. Capitol St., NW
Washington, DC 20573   202-523-5876

Cable Television System Operators
Cable TV Branch
Federal Communications Commission
1919 M Street NW, Room 416
Washington, DC 20554   202-416-0856

Colleges, Universities, Vocational Schools, and Public Schools
Office of Educational Research and Improvement
U.S. Department of Education
555 New Jersey NW, Room 600
Washington, DC 20208-5530   202-219-2050

Commodity Trading Advisors
National Futures Association
200 W. Madison St., Suite 1600
Chicago, IL 60606-3447   800-621-3570
Attn: Compliance Dept.   Fax: 312-781-1467

Consumer Products
Consumer Protection Division
U.S. Consumer Product Safety Commission
200 St. Paul Place
Baltimore, MD 21202   410-528-8662

Electric and Gas Utilities and Gas Pipeline Companies
Federal Energy Regulatory Commission
825 North Capitol Street NE, Room 9204
Washington, DC 20426   202-208-0200

Exporting Companies
Office of Export Trading Companies Affairs
U.S. Department of Commerce
14th and Constitution Avenue, Room 1800
Washington, DC 20230   202-482-5131

Federal Land Bank and Production Credit Associations
Farm Credit Administration
1501 Farm Credit Drive
McLean, VA 22102-5090   703-883-4000

Foreign Corporations
World Traders Data Report
U.S. Department of Commerce
Washington, DC 20230   202-482-4204

Government Contractors
Federal Procurement Data Center
General Services Administration
7th and D Streets, SW, Room 5652
Washington, DC 20407   202-401-1529

Hospitals and Nursing Homes
National Center for Health Statistics
6525 Belcrest Rd.
Hyattsville, MD 20782   301-436-8500

Land Developers
Office of Interstate Land Registration
U.S. Department of Housing and Urban Development
451 7th Street SW, Room 6262
Washington, DC 20410   202-708-0502

Mining Companies
Mine Safety and Health Administration
U.S. Department of Labor
4015 Wilson Boulevard
Arlington, VA 22203   703-235-1452

Be patient. If any phone number is incorrect, call (area code) 555-1212 and request the new listing.

Non-Profit Institutions
U.S. Internal Revenue Service
Freedom of Information Reading Room
1111 Constitution Ave. NW, Room 1563
P.O. Box 388, Ben Franklin Station
Washington, DC 20044   202-622-5164

Nuclear Power Plants
Director, Office of Nuclear Reactor Regulation
U.S. Nuclear Regulatory Commission   301-415-7163
Washington, DC 20555   301-492-7000

Pension Plans
Division of Inquiries and Technical Assistance
Office of Pension and Welfare Benefits Programs
U.S. Department of Labor
200 Constitution Avenue NW, Room N5658
Washington, DC 20210   202-219-8233

Pharmaceutical, Cosmetic and Food Companies
Associate Commissioner for Regulatory Affairs
U.S. Food and Drug Administration
5600 Fishers Lane, Room 14-90
Rockville, MD 20857   301-443-1594

Pesticide and Chemical Manufacturers
U.S. Environmental Protection Agency
Office of Pesticides and Toxic Substances
401 M Street, SW (7101)
Washington, DC 20460   202-260-2902

Radio and Television Stations
Mass Media Bureau
Federal Communications Commission
1919 M Street NW, Room 302
Washington, DC 20554   202-632-6485

Railroads, Trucking Companies, Bus Lines, Freight Forwarders, Water Carriers, Oil Pipelines, Transportation Brokers, Express Agencies
U.S. Interstate Commerce Commission
12th and Constitution Avenue NW, Room 4419
Washington, DC 20423   202-927-7119

Savings and Loan Associations
Office of Thrift Supervision
1700 G Street NW
Washington, DC 20552   202-906-6000

Telephone Companies, Overseas Telegraph Companies, Microwave Companies, Public Land and Mobile Service
Common Carrier Bureau
Federal Communications Commission
1919 M Street NW, Room 500
Washington, DC 20554   202-632-6910

Suppliers and Other Industry Sources

If all of the above sources fail to provide information you need on a given company, your last resort is to go directly into the industry and try to extract the information by talking with insiders.

Although your telephone is an essential and perhaps the best research tool, there are two other reference sources that will help you track down industry specialists:

1) **Trade Associations** are identified in *Encyclopedia of Associations* - (Gale Research Inc., Book Tower, 835 Penobscot Building, Detroit, MI 48277, 313-961-2242, 800-877-4253. For prepaid order, mail check for $395 for 1994 edition, $415 for 1995 edition to P.O. Box 71701, Chicago, IL 60694-1701);

2) **100 Industry Analysts** at the U.S. Department of Commerce. Government Industry Analysts who cover industries such as athletic goods, dairy products or truck trailers.

Your first step is to begin casting around for someone in the industry who knows about the company in question. When hunting for an expert, it is essential that you remain determined and optimistic about eventually finding one or several individuals who will be "information jackpots."

People who know their industry will be able to give you the details you need about any company (i.e., its size, sales, profitability, market strategies). These sources probably will not be able to give you the precise figure that is on the balance sheet or profit and loss statement, but they will offer a very educated guess which is likely to be within 10 to 20% of the exact figure. And usually this estimate is good enough for anyone to work with.

The real trick is finding the right people -- the ones who know. Talk to them and get them to share their knowledge with you.

Where Else to Look for Industry Experts

Industry experts are not concentrated in Washington, DC but are located all over the world, so you need to exercise some common sense to figure out where to find them. Here are some general guidelines.

1) **Industry Observers**
These are specialists on staff at trade associations, think tanks, and at the U.S. Department of Commerce and other government agencies. Anyone who concentrates on an industry has familiarity with the companies that comprise that industry.

2) **Trade Magazines**
You will find that there is at least one magazine which reports on every industry. The editors and reporters of these trade publications are also well acquainted with individual companies.

3) **Suppliers**
Most industries have major suppliers which must know about the industry they service and the companies within that industry. For example, the tire manufacturers anticipate every move among auto makers well before any other outsiders. Suppliers also have to know the volume of every manufacturer to whom they sell their product because of the obvious repercussions on the supplier's business. Every company is like this, even Information USA, Inc. We are basically a publisher, and if you talk to our printers, you would get a pretty good picture of exactly what we are doing.

Company Case Studies and Databases

1) **Company Case Studies For As Little As $2 Each**
Case studies of major and minor companies, as well as subsidiaries of public companies, can provide valuable competitive intelligence. These cases are identified in an $10 publication titled *Catalog of Teaching Materials*.

Information on People, Companies, and Mailing Lists

HBS Publications Division
Operations Department
Boston, MA 02163
617-495-6117; 617-495-6006
Fax: 617-495-6985

2) Government and Commercial Databases

ABI/Inform, Disclosure, and Management Contents are just a few of the online databases which provide quick access to information about all types of companies. Additional leads for gathering information about companies can be derived from diverse databases maintained by the U.S. government, many of which are identified in the *Federal Data Base Finder* (Information USA, Inc.).

Complete Financials on Franchising Companies

Franchising companies, whether public or privately held, must file detailed financial information in 14 different states. These state statutes create excellent opportunities for gathering competitive and marketing data as outlined below.

Inside Information

If the company of interest is a franchise organization, a great deal of financial information for their average franchisee is available in addition to their corporate profit and loss statements and balance sheets. A typical table of contents for a filing includes:

* biographical information on persons affiliated with the franchisor
* litigation
* bankruptcy
* franchisees' initial franchise fee or other initial payment
* other recurring or isolated fees and payments
* the franchisee's initial investment
* obligations of the franchisee to purchase or lease from designated sources
* obligations of the franchisee to purchase or lease in accordance with specifications or from approved suppliers
* financing arrangements
* obligations of the franchisor: other supervision, assistance or services
* territorial rights
* trademarks, service marks, trade names, logotypes and commercial symbols
* patents and copyrights
* obligation of the franchisee to participate in the actual operation of the franchise business
* restrictions on goods and services offered by the franchisee
* term, renewal, termination, repurchase, modification, assignment and related information
* agreements with public figures
* actual, average, projected or forecasted franchisee sales, profits and earnings
* information regarding franchises of the franchisor
* financial statements
* contracts
* standard operating statements
* list of operational franchisees
* estimate of additional franchised stores
* company-owned stores
* estimate of additional company-owned stores
* copies of contracts and agreements

Market Information and Franchising Trends

The franchise information packets often include information on the results of their market studies which establish the need for their product or service. These can provide valuable market information as well as forecasts for potential markets. Is the ice cream boom over? A quick check into Ben and Jerry's forecast for future stores will give you a clue of what the experts think.

Franchise companies are often the first to jump into current trends and fads in the U.S., for example, ice cream shops and diet centers. You can get an instant snapshot of such a trend by reviewing the marketing section of a franchise agreement.

Career Opportunities

If you ever wondered how much it would cost to open up your own bookstore, restaurant, video store, or most any other kind of venture, you can get all the facts and figures you need without paying a high-priced consultant or tipping your hand to your current employer. Just take a look at a franchise agreement from someone in a similar line of business. You can even discover the expected salary level.

New Business for Suppliers

If you are looking to sell napkins, Orange Julius or computer services to Snelling & Snelling, their franchise statements will disclose what kind of agreements they currently have with similar suppliers.

State Checkpoints for Franchising Intelligence

To obtain franchise agreements from the 14 states that require such disclosure, simply call one or more of the offices listed below and ask if a specific company has filed. Copies of the documentation are normally sent in the mail with a copying charge of $.10 to $.50 per page.

California
Department of Corporations, 1115 11th Street, Sacramento, 95814, 916-445-7205. Fee is 30 cents per page. Send blank check stating $25 limit. They will call with price for orders exceeding that amount.

Hawaii
Department of Commerce and Consumer Affairs, Business Registration Department, 1010 Richards Street, Honolulu, 96813, P.O. Box 40, Honolulu, 96810, 808-586-2730. Fee is 25 cents per page.

Illinois
Franchise Division, Office of Attorney General, 500 South Second Street, Springfield, 62704, 217-782-1090. Charge is a $40 flat fee per company franchise.

Indiana
Franchise Division, Secretary of State, 302 West Washington Street, Room E-111, Indianapolis, 46204, 317-232-0735. Fee is 10 cents per page plus handling charges.

Be patient. If any phone number is incorrect, call (area code) 555-1212 and request the new listing.

Maryland

Assistant Attorney General, Maryland Division of Securities, 200 St. Paul Place, 21st Floor, Baltimore, 21202-2020, 410-576-6360. Maryland does not make copies. Suggests contacting Documents-To-Go, 800-879-4949.

Minnesota

Minnesota Department of Commerce, Enforcement Division, 133 East Seventh Street, St. Paul, 55101, 612-296-2594. Contact Ann Hagestad at 612-296-6328. Fee is 50 cents per page.

New York

Bureau of Investor and Protection Securities, New York State Department of Law, 120 Broadway, New York, 10271, 212-341-2200. Fee is 25 cents per page.

North Dakota

Franchise Examiner, North Dakota Securities Commission, 600 East Blvd., Fifth Floor, Bismarck, 58505, 701-224-2910. Documents are open for the public to inspect and copy, but this office does not provide copies as a service.

Oregon

Department of Insurance and Finance, Corporate Securities Section, Division of Finance and Corporate Securities, 21 Labor and Industries Bldg., Salem, 97310, 503-378-4387. Oregon does not keep franchise documents on file.

Rhode Island

Securities Section, Securities Division, 233 Richmond Street, Suite 232, Providence, 02903-4237, 401-277-3048. Special request form must be used. Fee is 15 cents per page copy and $15 an hour per search time.

South Dakota

Franchise Administrator, Division of Securities, State Capitol, Pierre, 57501, 605-773-4013. Fee is 50 cents per sheet.

Virginia

Franchise Section, Division of Securities and Retail Franchising, 1300 E. Main Street, Richmond, 23219, 804-371-9276. Fee is $.50 per page.

Washington

Department of Licensing, Securities Division, 405 Black Lake Blvd., SW, Olympia, 98507-9033, 206-753-6928. No charge for orders under 30 pages, then 10 cents for each page thereafter, plus tax.

Wisconsin

Franchise Investment Division, Wisconsin Securities Commission, PO Box 1768, 101 East Wilson Street, Madison, 53701, 608-266-3414/3364. Wisconsin does not provide copies of franchise agreements. One must come in person or hire private service.

Be patient. If any phone number is incorrect, call (area code) 555-1212 and request the new listing.

651

Companies in Your State

State documents on 9,000,000 public and private companies have hit the computer age. Thirty states already offer online access to their files and others intend to follow suit within the next year. Computerized records are such a major issue with state officials who administer corporate division offices that they have placed online access on their annual convention agenda. Furthermore, 27 states will make their complete files available on magnetic tape, and, I should say, at bargain prices. And if you are not computerized, all but a few states offer free telephone research services. Here are a dozen ways to ferret out current information on companies:

- a list of companies by SIC code within a given state or county
- names and addresses of a company's officers and directors
- a list of all new companies incorporated in a given week or month
- the location of any company with a single phone call
- a mailing list of 300,000 companies for $100
- the availability of a given company name
- a complete list of non-profit organizations
- a list of companies by city, zip, date of incorporation, or size of capital stock
- a mailing list of limited partnerships
- a listing of companies on which a given individual is an officer or board member
- a listing of trademarks for a given state
- which companies in a given state are subsidiaries of a given company

Financial Data and
Other Documents on File

Although there are variations, almost all states maintain the following documents for every company doing business in their state: Certificate of Good Standing; Articles of Incorporation; Reinstated Articles of Incorporation; Articles of Amendment; Articles of Merger; Articles of Correction; Articles of Dissolution; Certificate of Incorporation; Certificate of Authority; and Annual Report (which contains list of officers and directors).

All states require corporations to file the original Articles of Incorporation, a yearly annual report and amendments to the Articles of Incorporation. Clerks can provide you with certifications of good standing stating that the corporation has complied with the regulation to file a yearly annual report. A certificate of good standing does not assure financial stability, and is only a statement that the corporation has abided by the law. You may obtain a statement of name availability if you are searching for a name for your new corporation. Most states require prepayment for copies of documents. You can mail them a blank check stipulating the amount not to exceed a certain amount. You may want to call the phone information number for details before sending in your written request.

Only a few states require financial information in their annual reports. However, every state requires companies to list the value of the capital stock in their Articles of Incorporation. Some states, such as Massachusetts used to require financial data in the past, so it may be useful to request annual reports of previous years.

Data on Six Different Types of Companies

The types of companies required to file documents with the state include: Domestic Companies (those incorporated within the state), Foreign Companies (those incorporated in another state, but doing business in the state), Partnerships, Limited Partnerships, Non-Profit Organizations, Business Names (incorporated and non-incorporated firms). It should be emphasized here that all public and private companies as well as subsidiaries of public corporations are required to reveal this information.

Company Information Available in Numerous Formats

Each state provides information about corporations in some or all of the following formats:

1) Telephone, Mail and Walk-In Services:
Telephone information lines have been established in all but one state to respond to inquiries regarding the status of a specific corporation. New Jersey and North Dakota charge for phone service. The NJ Expedite Service allows you to receive information over the phone and charge the cost of the service to your credit card. Another option for New Jersey company information is to have it sent via Western Union's electronic mail service.

Telephone operators can verify corporate names, identify the resident agent and his address, the date of incorporation, the type of corporation (foreign, domestic, etc.), and the amount of capital stock. Often these operators can either take your request for documents on file pertaining to a corporation or they can refer you to the appropriate number. Names of officers and directors are never given over the phone. This information is usually contained in a company's annual report, copies of which can be requested by phone or letter.

These state telephone lines tend to be quite busy. It is not unusual for the larger offices of a corporation to answer over 1,200 inquiries a day. Persistence and patience are essential on your part. Requests for copies of documents usually require prepayment. You can mail them a blank check stipulating the amount not to exceed a certain amount. You may want to call the phone information number for details before sending in your written request.

Walk-in service, with access to all documents, is an option in every state. However, if you do not want to do the research yourself, almost every state can suggest private firms which will obtain the pertinent data for you.

2) Mailing Labels:

The following six states will print mailing labels of companies on file: Arizona, Idaho, Maine, New Mexico, Mississippi, and Nebraska. However, over half the states will sell you a computer tape of their files, from which mailing labels can be generated easily by a good mailhouse or service bureau.

3) Computer Tape Files:

Currently 27 states will provide you with magnetic tapes of their corporate files. The cost is very reasonable, and in many cases the state will require the user to supply blank tapes.

4) Custom Services:

Many of the states provide custom services with outputs ranging from computer printouts and magnetic tape files to statistical tables. Such services are a valuable way to obtain specific listings of corporations such all non-profit corporations or all companies within a given SIC code. Most states that offer this option compute cost by figuring time, programming time, and printing expense.

5) New Companies:

Almost all of the states offer some type of periodic listing of newly formed companies. As a rule, these can be purchased on a daily, weekly, or monthly subscription basis.

6) Microfiche and Microfilm:

Eleven of the states will also sell you copies of their documents on microfiche or microfilm at a nominal fee.

7) Online Access:

As mentioned earlier, thirty states now provide online access to their files, and other states are in the active planning stages. The states currently with online systems include:

Alabama, Alaska, Arizona, Arkansas, Colorado, Florida, Georgia, Hawaii, Idaho, Illinois, Indiana, Iowa, Kansas, Louisiana, Massachusetts, Michigan, Minnesota, Mississippi, Missouri, Nevada, New Mexico, North Carolina, Oklahoma, Pennsylvania, South Carolina, Texas, Utah, Virginia, and Vermont.

State Corporation Divisions

Alabama

Division of Corporation, Secretary of State, 4121 Carmichael Road, Montgomery, AL 36106 or P.O. Box 5616, Montgomery, AL 36103-5616, 205-242-5324; Selected Publications: *Guide to Incorporation*. Phone Information: 205-242-5324. Office is not completely computerized yet, but can do word search or partial name search by officer, incorporator, or serving agent. Copies of Documents on File: Available by written request for $1 per page plus $5 for certified copies. Mailing Labels: No. Magnetic Tape: No. Microfiche: No. New Corporate Listings: No. Custom Searches: Can do word search or partial name search. Online Access: Yes. Dial-up Program available. No fee for this pilot program. Contact Robina Jenkins, 205-242-5974. This office is in the process of being computerized. When fully on computer access, fee for online service may be charged. Number of Active Corporations on File: Figures not available.

Alaska

State of Alaska, Division of Banking, Securities and Corporation, Corporation Section, P.O. Box 110808, Juneau, AK 99811-0808, 907-465-2530. Selected Publications: *Establishing Business in Alaska* ($3), from State of Alaska, Division of Economic Development, P.O. Box 110808, Juneau, AK 99811-0808. Phone Information: 907-465-2530. Copies of Documents on File: Complete corporate record (Articles of Incorporation, annual report, amendments, etc.). Certified copies cost $20, list of Officers and Directors cost $1, Certificate of Status cost $25. Mailing Labels: No. Magnetic Tape: IBM- compatible. Copy of complete master file,

excluding Officers and Directors is priced at $100. Hard copy directory is $65. Weekly supplements are an additional $5. Requester must supply blank tape. Microfiche: Yes. Complete file for $6. New Corporate Listings: No. Custom Searches: Available directly from them soon. Online Access: Yes. Contact Mike Monagle, 907-465-2530. Other: Printouts are available by corporation, SIC code, and zip code for $25 per list. Number of Active Corporations on File: 23,000.

Arizona

Arizona Corporations Division, Records Division, Secretary of State, 1200 W. Washington, Phoenix, AZ 85007 or P.O. Box 6019, Phoenix, AZ 85005, 602-542-3026. Selected Publications: Sample packet with forms and statutes mailed for $4. Guideline booklets will be available soon. Phone Information: 602-542-3026. Copies of Documents on File: Cost 50 cents per page, $5 for certified copies. Mailing Labels: No. Magnetic Tape: Master File $400, issued monthly. Requester must supply blank tape. Microfiche: All corporations statewide $75. New Corporate Listing: Monthly Listing of New Domestic Companies for $200 plus $200 for new foreign listings. Custom Searches: No. Can search by title or cross-reference by statutory agent only. Online Access: Yes. Available through Information America (800-235-4008), Dunn and Bradstreet and other commercial services. Number of Corporations on File: 100,000.

Arkansas

Secretary of State, Corporations Division, State Capitol Building, Room 058, Little Rock, AR 72201, 501-682-5151. Selected Publications: *Corporate Guide*. Phone Information: 501-682-5151. Copies of Documents on File: Call 501-371-3431 for copies at 50 cents a page plus $5 for certified copies. Mailing Labels: No. Magnetic Tape: Master file 2 cents per name. Microfiche: No. New Corporate Listing: Statistics only. Custom Searches: Categories include foreign, domestic, profit, and non-profit corporations. Cost: 2 cents per name, 50 cents per page. Online Access: Contact Philip Hoots at 501-682-3411. Number of Active Corporations on File: 1000,000.

California

Corporations, Supervisor of Records, Secretary of State, 1230 J Street Sacramento, CA 95814, 916-324-1485. Selected Publications: *Corporations Checklist Booklet*. Request must be in writing and cost is $5. Phone Information: Name Availability at 916-322-2387, Forms and Samples at 916-445-0620. Copies of Documents on File: Cost is $1 for first page, 50 cents for each additional page plus $5 for certified copies (written requests only). You must pay in advance or send check stating limit. Mailing Labels: No. Magnetic Tape: Yes. You must supply the tapes or be charged $24 for tape. Charges for making 22 tapes is $300. Contact Kevin Tibown. Categories: Active $521; Active Stock $427; Active Non-Stock $150; Active Non-Stock by Classification $150 per tape. Microfiche: No. Custom Searches: Computer generated listing of Active Stock ($17,030), Active Non-Stock ($422), Active Non-Stock by Classification $150 per list. Contact: Patricia Gastelum, Management Services Division, Information Systems Section, 1230 J Street, Suite 242, Sacramento, CA 95814, 916-322-0418. All orders must be submitted in writing. Basic cost of magnetic tape copy is $1.02 per 1,000 names. Basic cost of same run, for custom search, printed on paper, is $4.13 per 1,000 names. $150 minimum is applied to both. Online Access: No. Number of Corporations on File: 1,050,000.

Colorado

Corporate Division, Secretary of State, 1560 Broadway, Suite 200, Denver, CO 80202, 303-894-2251. Selected Publications: *Corporate Guide*. Copies of Documents on File: Cost is $1 a page, plus $5 for certification. Mailing Labels: No. Magnetic Tape: Available for $500 for complete set of five. Tapes must be purchased individually. Categories: Foreign and Domestic. Microfiche: Available at $1 a sheet (includes Summary of Master Computer File, total of 60-75 sheets - must be purchased in its entirety). New Corporate Listings: Reporting Service costs $200 a year. Weekly List of New Corporations. Written requests only. Custom Searches: Yes. Categories: Foreign and Domestic available on a cost recovery basis. The minimum fee is $50. Online Access: Available. Contact Patty Webb, 303-894-2200, ext. 300. Fee is $300 for 3 months or $1,000 per year. Number of Corporations on File: 235,000.

Connecticut

Office of Secretary of State, Division of Corporations, 30 Trinity Street, Hartford, CT 06106, 203-566-2448. Selected Publications: None, but to get a copy of *The Connecticut Law Book*, call 203-458-8000 or 203-741-3027. Phone Information: 203-566-8570. Copies of Documents on File: Fees are $20 for plain copy, $25 for certified. Written requests only. Mailing Labels: No. Magnetic Tape: Copy of master file $110. Requester must provide tapes. Microfiche: No. New Corporate Listing: No. Custom Searches: No. Online Access: Not at this time, but Southern New England Telephone (SNET) is working on a pilot program which should be available soon. Number of Corporations on File: 325,000.

Be patient. If any phone number is incorrect, call (area code) 555-1212 and request the new listing.

653

Information on People, Companies, and Mailing Lists

Delaware

Delaware Department of State, Division of Corporations, Secretary of State, P.O. Box 898, Dover, DE 19903, 302-739-3073. Selected Publications: *Incorporating in Delaware*. Phone Information: 302-739-3073. Copies of Documents on File: Available at $1 per page plus $20 for certification, $100 for long forms of good standing. Contains all documents on the corporation. Requests may be faxed to 302-739-3812, but written requests are preferred. Requests must be paid for in advance. Call for number of pages. Documents filed prior to 1983 are not on computer and must be requested in writing. They offer Corporate Expedited Services (same day or 24-hour service) to file or retrieve certified documents. Additional fee is $20. You can pay by MasterCard or Visa and it is sent by Federal Express. Mailing Labels: No. Magnetic Tape: No. Microfiche: No. New Corporate Listings: Monthly New Corporation Listing. Fees are $10 per month which can be paid in advance for 6 months or a year. Contact Karen Scaggs. Custom Searches: Yes. Categories include foreign and domestic which are available on cost recovery basis. For manual search of foreign corporations, the fee is $30. Online Access: Not available. Number of Active Corporations on File: 212,000.

District of Columbia

Corporations Division, Consumer and Regulatory Affairs, 614 H Street, N.W., Room 407, Washington, DC 20001, 202-727-7278. Selected Publications: *Guideline and Instruction Sheet for Profit, Non-Profit, Foreign, or Domestic*. Phone Information: 202-727-7283. Copies of Documents on File: Available for $5 each (all copies certified). Mailing Labels: Will be available in near future. Profit and non-profit lists updated quarterly. Magnetic Tape: No. Microfiche: No. New Corporate Listings No. Custom Searches: Computer searches on agents are available. Online Access: Possibly available in 1993. Number of Active Corporations on File: 40,000.

Florida

Division of Corporations, Secretary of State, PO Box 6327, Tallahassee, FL 32314, 904-487-6000. Selected Publications: *Copy of the Law Chapter 607* (corporate law). Forms included. (Publications on laws of non-profit corporations and limited partnerships also available.) Phone Information: 904-488-9000. Limit of up to 3 inquiries per call. No charge to receive hard copy of microfiche on the corporations. Copy of Documents on File: Available at $1 per page if you do it yourself. Written requests must be paid for advance: $1 for non-certified annual report; $10 for plain copy of complete file; $52.50 for any certified document including complete file. Microfiche: Yes. Contact Frank Reinhart or Ed Bagnell at Anacomp, 813-289-1608. Categories: Officers and Directors, Registered Agents and Domestic Corporations $250; Foreign, Non-Profit $85, Limited Partnerships $50, Trademarks $75 (addresses are included). Magnetic Tape: No. New Corporate Listings: No. Custom Searches: No. Online Access: Available on CompuServe, 800-848-8199. Address written request to Attn: Public Access, Division of Corporations, 904-487-6866. Ask for a CompuServe Intro-Pak. Charge for connect time is $24 per hour, plus $12.50 per hour additional corporate access fee. Both are prorated by time used. CompuServe can be contacted directly at South Eastern Information Systems, P.O. Box 6867, Tallahassee, FL 32314, Attn: Keith Meyer, 904-656-4500. As of February, 1992, Anacomp will handle. Contact Eileen Self, 904-487-6073 for service. Number of Active Corporations on File: 691,000.

Georgia

Division of Business Services and Regulation, Secretary of State, Suite 306, West Tower #2, Martin Luther King Drive, S.E., Atlanta, GA 30334, 404-656-2185. Selected Publications: None, but information package sent upon request. Phone Information: 404-656-2817. Copies of Documents on File: Available for at least a minimum of $10 and all copies certified. Bills will be sent for orders over $10. Mailing Labels: No. Magnetic Tape: Master file available for $600 a month if you supply the tape. Add $18 if they supply tape. Microfiche: No. New Corporate Listings: Quarterly Listing of New Corporations on magnetic tape. There are three lists which include Fulton County, the remainder of the state and foreign. Cost is $25 each. Send written requests to James Gullion. Custom Searches: No. Online Access: Available by subscription through Information America at 404-892-1800. Connect fee is $50. Access time is 55 cents per minute. Monthly service charge is $25-$55 per month depending on size of the firm. Number of Active Corporations on File: 200,000

Hawaii

Business Registration Division, Department of Commerce and Consumer Affairs, 1010 Richards Street, PO Box 40, Honolulu, HI 96810, 808-586-2727. Selected Publications: None. Phone Information: 808-586-2727. Copies of Documents on File: Available at 25 cents per page, plus 10 cents per page for certified copies. Expedited service available for $10 fee plus 25 cents per sheet, plus $1 per page. Mailing Labels: No. Magnetic Tape: No. Microfiche: No. New Corporate Listing: Weekly printout available but only for walk-ins. Custom Searches: No. Online Access: Available through FYI for no charge. Call 808-536-7133 (direct access number) or 808-586-1919. Number of Active Corporations on File: 45,000.

Idaho

Corporate Division, Secretary of State, Room 203, Statehouse, Boise, ID 83720, 208-334-2300. Selected Publications: *Idaho Corporation Law*. Phone Information: 208-334-2300. Copies of Documents on File: Available at 25 cents per page, $2 for certified copies. Mailing Labels: Very flexible and may be combined with custom search. Fee is $10 for computer base, 25 cents for first 100 pages, 10 cents for next 500 pages, and 5 cents per page thereafter. Magnetic Tape: Available for $20 per tape if you supply the tape. They will supply diskette for additional $10. Microfiche: Available for $10, 50 cents for each additional copy of same. Custom Searches: Available on basis of serving agent, profit, non-profit, type, status, state and jurisdiction. Very flexible. Same prices and categories apply to labels, microfiche and custom search. You supply the tapes or they will at cost. Contact Everett Wholers. New Corporate Listing: No, but published weekly in *The Idaho Business Review*. Online Access: Available through Data Share Program. Fee is $150 per year plus $18 per hour plus telephone line charges. Number of Active Corporations on File: 30,000.

Illinois

Corporations Division, Centennial Building, Room 328, Springfield, IL 62756, 217-782-6961. Selected Publications: *Guide for Organizing (Domestic, Non-profit, or Foreign)*. Phone Information: 217-782-7880. Copies of Documents on File: Available at $5 per page up to first 10 pages; 50 cents for each page thereafter. Fee is $10 for first 10 certified copies; 50 cents for each page thereafter. Mailing Labels: No. Magnetic Tape: Yes. Categories: Domestic and Foreign cost $1,500; Not-for-Profit cost $1,500. You must supply tape. Microfiche: Only condominiums list available for $150. New Corporate Listings: Daily list of newly formed corporations costs $318 per year; Monthly List priced at $180 per year. Custom Searches: No. Other: Certified List of Domestic and Foreign Corporations (Address of Resident Agent included) costs $38 for two volume set. Online Access: Available from Mead Data Central (LEXIS), 9393 Springboro Pike, P.O. Box 933, Dayton, OH 45401, Contact: Diane Fisher at 800-227-4908, ext. 6382. Cost is $500 per month. Number of Active Corporations on File: 240,000.

Indiana

Office of Corporation, Secretary of State, Room E018, 302 West Washington Street, Indianapolis, IN 46204, 317-232-6582. Selected Publications: *Indiana Corporation Guide*. Phone Information: 317-232-6576. Copies of Documents on File: Available at $1 per page and $15 to certify. May pay in advance or be billed. Mailing Labels: No. Magnetic Tape: No. Microfiche: No. New Corporate Listings: Daily Listing is published monthly for $20 a month. Custom Searches: No. Online Access: Available. Tapes made into computer database by Mead Data (LEXIS) at 800-634-9738 and by Information America 800-235-4008. Contact Bob Gardner at 317-232-6691. Number of Active Corporations on File: 200,000.

Iowa

Corporate Division, Secretary of State, Hoover State Office Building, Des Moines, IA 50319, 515-281-5204. Selected Publications: *Iowa Profit Corporations*. Phone Information: 515-281-5204. Copies of Documents on File: Available at $1 per page; certified copies cost $5. Mailing Labels: No. Magnetic Tape: Master file costs $165; detailed domestic profit $415; domestic non-profit $160 and requester must supply tape. Microfiche: No. New Corporate Listings: No. Custom Searches: Searches by Chapters of Incorporation (profit, non-profit, etc.) and or. Cost determined at time of request. Online Access: Available through Dial Up Program. Contact Allen Welsh at 515-281-8363. Cost is $150 per year, 30 cents per minute plus telephone charges. Number of Active Corporations on File: 97,000.

Kansas

Corporate Division, Secretary of State, Capitol Building, Second Floor, Topeka, KS 66612, 913-296-4564. Selected Publications: None. Will send out forms with instruction sheets. Phone Information: 913-296-4564. Copies of Documents on File: Available at 50 cents per page plus $7.50 for certified copies (written requests only). Must be paid for in advance. Mailing Labels: No. Magnetic Tape: Available. Master file costs $2,000. Microfiche: No. Other: Microfilm is available for $25 a roll plus $7.50 postage for up to 50 rolls. Master File on magnetic tape will be needed to use. Contact Cathy Martin. New Corporate Listings: No. Custom Searches: No. May be available in the future. Online Access: Available through Info Network Kansas, 913-296-5143. Number of Active Corporations on File: 66,000.

Kentucky

Corporate Division, Secretary of State, Room 154, Capitol Building, Frankfort, KY 40601, 502-564-2848. Selected Publications: *Rules and Laws Manual* ($8). Phone Information: 502-564-7336. Copies of Documents on File: Mail in request with payment. Call 502-564-7330 to obtain number of copies in advance. Cost is $1 per page; $5 plus $.50 per page for certified copies. Mailing Label: No. Magnetic Tape: Available for $250. Tape contains all profit and non-profit corporations on file. Microfiche: No. New Corporate Listings: Available for $50 a month. Custom Searches: No. Online Access: No, but is being considered. Number of Active Corporations on File: 80,000.

Louisiana

Corporate Division, Secretary of State, 3851 Essen Lane, Baton Rouge, LA 70809, 504-925-4704. Selected Publications: *Corporate Law Book* ($6). Phone Information: 504-925-4704. Copies of Documents on File: Available starting at $10 for certified articles. Cost for total file is $20. Mailing Label: No. Magnetic Tape: Available in the future. Microfiche: No. New Corporate Listing: Weekly Newsletter at no charge. (Requester must supply large pre-addressed envelope). Custom Searches: No. Online Access: Dial Up Access, 504-922-1475. Number of Active Corporations on File: 120,000.

Maine

Information and Report Section, Bureau of Corporations, Secretary of State, State House Station 101, Augusta, ME 04333, 207-287-4195. Selected Publications: *Guide to Completing Forms of Incorporation* (Blue Guide). Phone Information: 207-287-4195. Copies of Documents on File: Available for $2 per page, plus $5 for certified copies. Mailing Labels: No. Magnetic tape: No, but hope to have it in the near future. Contact Rebecca Wyke at 207-287-6308. Microfiche: No. New Corporate Listings: Monthly Corporations Listing costs $10. Contact Betsy at 207-289-4183. Custom Searches: No, but hope to have it in near future. Online Access: No. Number of Active Corporations on File: 40,000.

Maryland

Corporate Charter Division, Department of Assessments and Taxation, 301 W. Preston Street, Baltimore, Maryland 21201, 410-225-1330. Selected Publications: *Guide to Corporations*. Phone Information: 410-225-1330. Copies of Documents on File: Available for $1 per page, plus $6 for certified copies for walk-ins. If they make copy there is a $20 expediting fee. Mailing Labels: No. Magnetic Tape: Available for $250 weekly. Infrequent requests cost $425. Microfiche: No. New Corporate Listings: Monthly Corporate Computer Printout costs $25 a month. Custom Searches: Not at this time. Online Access: Hope to have in near future. Number of Active Corporations on File: 300,000.

Massachusetts

Corporate Division, Secretary of State, 1 Ashburton Place, Boston, MA 02108, 617-727-2850. Selected Publications: *Organizing a Business Corporation, Organizing a Non-Profit Corporation, When You Need Information About Corporations in Massachusetts, Choose a Name for Your Business, Compendium of Corporate Law* ($15). Phone Information: 617-727-2850. Copies of Documents on File: Available for 20 cents per page (send a minimum of 80 cents), $12 for certified copies. Mailing Labels: No. Magnetic Tape: Cost is $300 for copy of master file and record layout. Requester must supply tapes. Microfiche: No. New Corporate Listings: Semi-monthly Filings cost $15; Quarterly Filings cost $50; bi-weekly printout cost $15. Custom Searches: Available on a cost recovery basis. Online Access: Direct Access program. Cost is $149 annually. Connect time is 40 cents per minute. Number of Corporations on File: 375,000.

Michigan

Corporation Division, Corporation and Securities Bureau, Michigan Department of Commerce, PO Box 30054, 6546 Mercantile, Lansing, MI, 48909, 517-334-6302. Selected Publications: None. Phone Information: 517-334-6311. Copies of Documents on File: Available at a minimum of $6 for 6 pages or less, $1 for each page thereafter. Certified copies cost $10. (Request a price list.) Mailing Labels: No. Magnetic Tape: No. Microfiche: Available for $145. New Corporate Listings: Monthly Listing costs $90 per month. Custom Searches: No. Online Access: Available through Information America, 800-235-4008 or Mead Data, 313-259-1156. Number of Corporations on File: 251,000.

Minnesota

Corporate Division, Secretary of State, 180 State Office Building, St. Paul, MN 55155, 612-296-2803. Selected Publications: *Guide to Starting a Business in Minnesota*. Phone Information: 612-296-2803. Copies of Documents on File: Available for $3 per document, $8 for certified copies. Mailing Labels: Yes. Categories: Domestic, Limited Partnerships, Non-profits, Foreign, Foreign Limited, Foreign Non-profits, Trademarks, Business Trusts. Cost determined at time of request. Magnetic Tape: No. Microfiche: Available documents on file (Articles of Incorporation, annual reports, amendments) cost 21 cents sheet plus filing or retrieval fees. Paper copy of microfiche is $6 per corporation for complete file. $3 for articles of incorporation. New Corporate Listings: Daily Log costs 25 cents per page. Custom Searches: Available on a cost recovery basis. Categories same as for mailing labels. Online Access: Direct Access available for $50 annually plus transaction charge of $1 to $4. Number of Corporations on File: 194,500.

Mississippi

Office of Corporations, Secretary of State, PO Box 136, Jackson, MS 39205, 601-359-1350 or mailing address: 202 N. Congress, Suite 601, Jackson, MS 39201.

Selected Publications: None. Phone Information: 601-359-1627. Copies of Documents on File: Available at $1 per page plus $10 for certified copies. Mailing Labels: No. Magnetic Tape: Available for $200 for set of 2. You are to supply tapes. Microfiche: No. New Corporate Listings: Monthly Listing costs $25. Custom Searches: Available to limited extent. Printout costs $2 per page. Online Access: Yes. $250 sign-up fee, plus flat monthly fee. $50 is monthly minimum for first 100 transactions. Contact Sheryl Crawford at 601-359-1548. Number of Active Corporations on File: 80,000. This office has converted to an automated system with advanced search capabilities.

Missouri

Corporate Division, Secretary of State, 301 High Street, PO Box 77, Jefferson City, MO 65102, 314-751-4194. Selected Publications: *Corporation Handbook*. Phone Information: 314-751-4153. Copies of Documents on File: Available at 50 cents per page plus $5 for certified copies. Send in written requests and they will bill. Mailing Labels: No. Magnetic Tape: Cost is between $100 and $200 for copy of master file. Contact Sara Welch at 314-751-5832. Microfiche: No. New Corporate Listings: Not usually, but can be set up on special request. Custom Searches: No. Online Access: Available through Mead Data Central (LEXIS), 9393 Springboro Pike, PO Box 933, Dayton, OH 45401, 513-865-6800; Prentice-Hall, Dunn and Bradstreet or Information America. Direct Dial Up access is available through the State Access Center. Contact John Bluma at 314-751-4780 or Sara Welch at 314-751-5832. Number of Active Corporations on File: 140,000.

Montana

Corporate Department, Secretary of State, Capitol Station, Helena, MT 59620, 406-444-3665. Selected Publications: None. Phone Information: 406-444-3665. Copies of Documents on File: Available for 50 cents per page; $2 for certification. Mailing Labels: No. Magnetic Tape: No. Microfiche: No. New Corporate Listings: No. Custom Searches: No, but can search by name of corporation only. Online Access: No. Number of Active Corporations on File: 33,000.

Nebraska

Corporate Division, Secretary of State, State Capitol, Lincoln, NE 68509, 402-471-4079. Selected Publications: None. Phone Information: 402-471-4079. Copies of Documents on File: Available for $1 per page, $10 for certified copies. Will bill for requests under $50. Mailing Labels: Available on a cost recovery basis. Can do for entire data base only. Contact Mr. Englert at 402-471-2554. Magnetic Tape: Available on a cost recovery basis. Also contact Mr. Englert. Microfiche: No. New Corporate Listings: Available upon request. Will set up for number of issues customer requests. $100 per issuance. Custom Searches: No. Online Access: No. Number of Active Corporations on File: 50,000

Nevada

Office of Corporations, Secretary of State, Capitol Complex, Carson City, NV 89710, 702-687-5203. Selected Publications: *Guidelines*. Phone Information: Corporate Status call 702-687-5105. Copies of Documents on File: Available for $1 per page, $10 for certified copies. Written request only, prepayment required (send a blank check stating limit). Mailing Labels: No. Magnetic Tape: Copy of master file available. Corporations takes 2 tapes which requester supplies. Cost per tape is $25. Microfiche: No. New Corporate Listings: Monthly Listing of New Corporations costs $25 a month. Custom Searches: Yes. Searches may be done by location of resident agent and other ways. Cost determined at time of request. Other: A three volume listing of corporations on file, in the "Alpha Listing", is published twice a year which includes names of active and inactive corporations but not addresses. Cost for set is $25. Contact Cindy Woodgate. Online Access: Dial Up Direct Access through subscription service. Your computer needs a communication pack and you must set up trust account from which $24.50 per hour, prorated by actual minutes used, will be deducted. For ID number and password, contact Cindy Woodgate. Number of Active Corporations on File: 60,000.

New Hampshire

Corporate Division, Secretary of State, State House, Room 204, Concord, NH 03301, 603-271-3244. Selected Publications: *How to Start a Business, New Hampshire Corporate Law*. Phone Information: 603-271-3246. Copies of Documents on File: Available for $1 per page, plus $5 for certified copies. Mailing Labels: No. Magnetic Tape: No. Microfiche: Complete listing of all registrations. No breakdown by type of entity (updated monthly). Annual Subscription costs $200. New Corporate Listings: Monthly Subscriber List costs $15 plus postage. Custom Searches: No. Other: Booklet listing all non-profit corporations is available for $45. Online Access: No. Number of Active Corporations on File: 33,000.

New Jersey

Commercial Recording Division, Secretary of State, 820 Bear Tavern Road, West Trenton, NJ 08628, (Mailing address: CN 308), 609-530-6400. Selected Publications: *Corporate Filing Packet*. Phone Information: General Information call 609-530-6405; Forms call 609-292-0013; Expedite Service call 609-984-7107. There is a charge for

Be patient. If any phone number is incorrect, call (area code) 555-1212 and request the new listing.

655

Information on People, Companies, and Mailing Lists

standard information, $5 look-up fee for each request plus $10 expedite fee. User may use VISA or Master Charge for payment. Answers available by phone, mail or Western Union Electronic Mail. Requests and answering copies may be done through Fax at 609-530-6433. Copies of Documents on File: Available for $10 plus $15 for certified copies. Mailing Labels: No. Magnetic Tape: No. Microfiche: No. New Corporate Listings: Monthly List of Corporations costs $100 per month. Custom Searches: Numerous search capabilities are available. Each request is reviewed on individual basis. Requester is billed for computer time. Online Access: No. Number of Active Corporations on File: 436,314.

New Mexico

State Corporation Commission, PO Drawer 1269, Santa Fe, NM 87504-1269, 505-827-4502. Selected Publications: None. Phone Information: 505-827-4504. Copies of Documents on File: Available for $1 per page, minimum $10, plus additional $25 for certified copies. Mailing Labels: No. Magnetic Tape: No. Microfiche: No. New Corporate Listings: Yes. Monthly listings available. Requester must send manilla self-addressed envelope. Online Access: Available through New Mexico Technet, 4100 Osuna N.E., Albuquerque, NM 87109, 505-345-6555. You may also pay the same charge as the State by purchasing it directly from the Corporation Division. They will bill you for usage monthly. Contact Mr. Salinas at 505-827-4502. Custom Searches: Yes. Categories: Corporate Name, Domestic or Foreign, Profit or Non-profit, Date of Incorporation, Active or Inactive, Identification Number, Amount of Capital Stock, Authorized Stock, Instrument file, Principal Office Address, Officers and Directors Names (includes addresses, Social Security numbers and titles), Name of Incorporators, Registered Agent and Office, Good Standing Status, Parent/Subsidiary Information. Call or put request in writing. Only a limited number of custom searches can be performed each month. Number of Active Corporations on File: over 100,000.

New York

New York State, Department of State, Division of Corporations, 162 Washington Avenue, Albany, NY 12231, 518-474-6200. Selected Publications: *Extract of Laws for Incorporating*. Phone Information: 518-474-6200. Copies of Documents on File: Available for $5 per document, $10 for certified copies. Mailing Labels: No. Magnetic Tape: No. Microfiche: No. New Corporate Listing: Report of Corporations is printed daily and mailed out every other day. It is available by subscription only for $125 per year, $75 for 6 months or $40 for 3 months. Online Access: Available in the near future. Number of Corporations on File: 1,200,000.

North Carolina

Division of Corporation, Secretary of State, 300 N. Salisbury Street, Raleigh, NC 27603-5909, 919-733-4201. Selected Publications: *North Carolina Business Corporation Guidelines, North Carolina's Non-profit Corporation Handbook*. Phone Information: 919-733-4201. Copies of Documents on File: Available for $1 per page, $5 for certified copies. Mailing Labels: No. Magnetic Tape: Available on cost recovery basis. To make a request, write Bonnie Elek. Categories: All active corporations, foreign, domestic, non-profit, and profit. Microfiche: No. New Corporate Listings: Available for $20 per month and issued in hard copy only. Custom Searches: Yes. Categories: Type of Corporation, Professional Corporations, Insurance Corporations, Banks, and Savings and Loans. Not available for the type of business a corporation conducts. This may be available in the future. Online Access: Available. Number of Active Corporations on File: 180,000.

North Dakota

Corporation Division, Secretary of State, Capitol Building, 600 East Boulevard Avenue, Bismarck, ND 58505, 701-224-2905. Selected Publications: *North Dakota Business Corporation Act Statute*, $3. Phone Information: 701-224-4284. Copies of Documents on File: Search of records cost $5, four pages for $1, $10 for certified copies. Written or phone requests accepted. Requester will be billed for phone orders. Mailing Labels: No. Magnetic Tape: No. Microfiche: No. New Corporate Listings: Monthly Corporation List costs $10 per month. Custom Searches: No. Online Access: No, but may be available in the future. Number of Active Corporations on File: 22,500.

Ohio

Corporation Division, Secretary of State, 30 East Broad Street, 14th Floor, Columbus, OH 43266-0418, 614-466-3910. Selected Publications: *Corporate Checklist*. Phone Information: Corporate Status call 614-466-3910; Name Availability call 614-466-0590. Copies of Documents on File: Contact 614-466-1776. Available for $1 per page, $5 for certified copies. Mailing Labels: No. Magnetic Tape: Available for $125 for 6,250 corporation names, thereafter the cost is 2 cents per corporate name with a maximum of 25,000 names. Microfiche: No. New Corporate Listing: Call 614-466-8464. Weekly County-Wide Listing costs 25 cents per page, Weekly Statewide Listing costs 10 cents per page ($45 a month). Custom Searches: Yes. Categories: location (county), Foreign, Domestic, Profit, Non-Profit. Price

structure is same as for Magnetic tape. Online Access: No. Number of Active Corporations on File: 400,000.

Oklahoma

Corporations, Secretary of State, 101 State Capitol Building, Oklahoma City, OK 73105, 405-521-3911. Selected Publications: *Forms and Procedures to Incorporate*. Phone Information: 900-820-2424 for record search. Charge is $3 per call. Copies of Documents on File: Available for $1 per page, $5 for certified copies. Mailing Labels: No. Magnetic Tape: $5 per tape which is supplied by requester. Microfiche: No. New Corporate Listings: Monthly Charter List costs $150 a month, plus Amendments $250 a month plus postage. Custom Searches: No. Online Access: Contact Beverly Curry at Information Systems, 404-892-1800. They purchase magnetic tape of Division's master file weekly to make a database which is complete except for new names. Number of Corporations on File (Active and Inactive): 224,159.

Oregon

Corporation Division, Department of Commerce, 255 Capitol St., NE, Suite 151, Salem, OR 97310-1327, 503-986-2200. Selected Publications: None. Phone Information: 503-986-2200. Copies of Documents on File: Available for $5 for all documents in a corporation's file except annual report. Annual reports are an additional $5. Certification fee is $15. Mailing Labels: No. Magnetic Tape: Complete master file costs $200. Requester must provide tape. Microfiche: No. New Corporate Listings: Statistical Report of New Corporations is available for $15 per monthly issue, $150 per year. Custom Searches: Yes. Numerous categories with a minimum charge of $50. Online Access: Yes. Charges include $50 for hookup, $50 monthly fee, plus telephone charges and prorated computer time with a minimum $10 charge. Total minimum monthly cost is $80. Cost of average user is $100 per month. Mead Data, Information America and Dunn and Bradstreet also have database. Number of Active Corporations on File: 73,000.

Pennsylvania

Corporation Bureau, 308 N. Office Building, Harrisburg, PA 17120, 717-787-1997. Selected Publications: *Corporate Guide* (currently under revision). Phone Information: 717-787-1057. Copies of Documents on File: Available for $2 per page, $12 search fee, $28 for certified copies. Mailing Labels: No. Magnetic Tape: Copy of master file available for $900 per tape, Requester must supply 11 blank tapes. Microfiche: No. New Corporate Listings: County or area listing available for 25 cents per name. Custom Searches: Yes. Categories: Non-Profit, Domestic, Foreign, county location, Limited Partnerships, Fictitious name, Trademarks, Foreign Non-profits, Cooperatives, Professional Corporations 25 cents per name). Online Access: Available from Information America at 404-892-1800; Prentice-Hall, Legal and Financial Services at 518-458-8111; or Mead Data Central at 513-865-6800. Number of Corporations on File: 616,000.

Rhode Island

Corporations Division, Secretary of State, 100 North Main Street, Providence, RI 02903, 401-277-3040. Selected Publications: Instruction sheet, *The Rhode Island Law Book* ($10). Phone Information: 401-277-3040. Staff will look up two corporations per call. Copies of Documents on File: Available for 50 cents per page, $5 for certified sheet. Mailing Labels: No. Magnetic Tape: Available for $250 per tape. Requester supplies tape. They will put their database on disc. You supply 5 1/4 disc, MAG high density. Printouts cost 50 cents per page. There approximately 11 names per page. Microfiche: No. New Corporate Listings: Not usually provided. New corporate listings are published weekly in *The Providence Journal*, Sunday Business Section. Send a letter requesting weekly printouts. Custom Searches: No. Online Access: No. Number of Active Corporations on File: 90,000.

South Carolina

Division of Corporations, Secretary of State, PO Box 11350, Columbia, SC 29211, 803-734-2158. Selected Publications: None. Phone Information: 803-734-2158. Copies of Documents on File: Available for $1 for first page, 50 cents thereafter. $2 for plain charter and $4 for certified charter. Amendments are $1 per page thereafter and it costs $2 for certification. Mailing Labels: No. Magnetic Tape: No. Microfiche: No. New Corporate Listing: Special request only; contact Amy Hoskin at 803-734-2159. Custom Searches: No. Online Access: Yes. Available for $70 per month. Contact Bob Knight, Deputy Secretary. Number of Active Corporations on File: 250,000.

South Dakota

Corporate Division, Secretary of State, 500 East Capitol, Pierre, SD 57501, 605-773-4845. Selected Publications: None. Phone Information: 605-773-4845. Copies of Documents on File: Available for 50 cents per page plus $5 for certification. Mailing Labels: No. Magnetic Tape: No. Microfiche: No. New Corporate Listings: No. Custom Searches: No. Online Access: No. Number of Active Corporations on File: 30,000.

Tennessee

Office of Secretary of State, Services Division, Suite 1800, James K. Polk Building, Nashville, TN 37243-0306, 615-741-2286. Select Publications: None. Phone Information: 615-741-2286. Copies of Documents on File: Certified copies only are available for $10. Mailing Labels No. Magnetic Tape: Yes. Categories: All Corporations on file, Foreign, Domestic, Profit, Non-Profit, Banks, Credit Unions, Cooperative Associations. Charge of an additional $2 for each tape supplied. Cost, done on a cost recovery basis, is determined at time of request. Contact Mr. Thompson at 615-741-0584. Microfiche: No. New Corporate Listings: Monthly New Corporation Listing on a cost recovery basis of 25 cents per page, 8 names per page. Call 615-741-1111. Custom Searches: Yes. Categories: Same as for magnetic tape. Cost is same as for New Corporate Listing. Contact Mr. Thompson at 615-741-0584. Online Access: No. Number of Active Corporations on File: 100,000.

Texas

Corporation Section, Statute Filing Division, Secretary of State, PO Box 13697, Austin, TX 78711, 512-463-5586. Selected Publications: *Filing Guide to Corporations*. (Written requests only for a $15 fee.) Phone Information: 512-463-5555. Copies of Documents on File: Available for 85 cents for first page, 15 cents for each additional page. Certification is $5 plus $1 for each additional page. Invoices are sent for order not in excess of $100. Mailing Labels: No. Magnetic Tape: No. Microfiche: Names of officers and directors available. Cost determined at time of request. New Corporate Listings: Weekly Charter Update costs $27.50 per week. Custom Searches: No. Online Access: Available through Information America 404-892-1800. Contact Linda Gordon at 713-751-7900. Number of Active Corporations on File: 400,000.

Utah

Corporations and UCC, Division of Business Regulations, P.O. Box 45801, 160 East 300 South Street, Second Floor, Salt Lake City, UT 84145-0801, 801-530-4849. Selected Publications: *Going into Business, Doing Business in Utah, A Guide to Business Information*. Phone Information: 801-530-4849. Copies of Documents on File: Available for 30 cents a page plus $10 for certified copies. Mailing Labels: No. Magnetic Tape: Yes. Categories: Profit, Non-Profit, Foreign, Domestic. Cost includes computer time and programming fee. Microfiche: No. New Corporate Listing: Weekly New Corporation List 30 cents per page, New Doing Business As (DBA) List 30 cents per page. Custom Searches: Yes. Categories: Same as for Magnetic tape. Cost includes printing charge of 30 cents per page plus computer time and programming fee. Online Access: Available for $10 per month, 10 cents per minute. Contact Mya Eddy at 801-530-6643 about Data Share. Number of Active Corporations on File: 40,000.

Vermont

Corporate Division, Secretary of State, 109 State Street, Montpelier, VT 05602-2710, 802-828-2386. Selected Publications: *Doing Business in Vermont*. Phone Information: 802-828-2386. Copies of Documents on File: Available for $1 per page, $5 for certified copies. Send the $5 certification fee in advance. They will bill you for the copies. Mailing Labels: No. Magnetic Tape: Diskettes available for $6 to $10 plus 1 cent per name. Entire database costs $250. Microfiche: No. New Corporate Listings: Yes. Monthly New Corporations and Trade names on diskette cost $6 plus 1 cent per name. Total cost is never more than $15. Out-of-State Corporations, $50 for complete list. Custom Searches: Yes. Categories: Foreign, Domestic, Non-profits, by date of registration. Cost is 1 cent per name plus $6 to run list. Online Access: $10 per month, $.10 per minute. Contact: Betty Poulin. Number of Active Corporations on File: 24,000.

Virginia

Clerk of Commission, State Corporation Commission, Secretary of State, P.O. Box 1197, Richmond, VA 23209 (Street Address: 1220 Bank Street, Richmond, VA 23219), 804-786-3672, Fax: 804-371-0118. Selected Publications: *Business Registration Guide*. Phone Information: 804-786-3733. Copies of Documents on File: Available for $1 per page, $3 for certified copies. Mailing Labels: No. Magnetic Tape: Possibly in the future. Microfiche: No. New Corporate Listings: No. Custom Searches: Yes. Categories: Foreign, Domestic, Non-profit, Professional corporation, Non-Stock, Public Service, Cooperatives. Available on a cost recovery basis. Online Access: Available. Contact Betty Williams at 804-786-6703. Available free while in pilot stage, then available on cost recovery basis. Number of Active Corporations on File: 160,000.

Washington

Corporate Division, Secretary of State, 2nd Floor Republic Bldg., 505 Union Ave, Mail Stop PM-21, Olympia, WA 98504, 206-753-7115. Selected Publications: *None*. Phone Information: 206-753-7115. Copies of Documents on File: Call 206-586-2061 to leave recorded message for document orders. Fees are $1 for the first page and 20 cents thereafter. Certification is $10. Mailing Labels: No. Magnetic Tape: No. Microfiche: Cost is $10 a month per set. New Corporate Listings: No except for statistical sheet. Custom Searches: No. Online Access: No. Number of Active Corporations on File: 145,000. This office is not computerized.

West Virginia

Corporate Division, Secretary of State, Room 139 West, State Capitol, Charleston, WV 25305, 304-342-8000. Selected Publications: *The Corporate Filings Requirements*. Phone Information: 304-342-8000. Copies of Documents on File: Available for 50 cents per page, $10 for certified copies. Mailing Labels: No. Magnetic Tape: No. Microfiche: No. New Corporate Listing: Monthly Report costs $5 a month or $50 per year. Custom Searches: Yes. Cost is $1 for first hour and $5 for every hour thereafter, prorated. Online Access: No. Number of Active Corporations on File: 39,000.

Wisconsin

Corporate Division, Secretary of State, PO Box 7846, Madison, WI 53707; Street address: 30 W. Mifflin St., 9th Floor, Madison, WI 53703, 608-266-3590. Selected Publications: *Chapter 180 Statutes Book ($5)*. Phone Information: 608-266-3590, Fax: 608-267-6813. Copies of Documents on File: For simple copy request must be in writing. Fee is $2. Faxed copies are 50 cents per page. Requests for certified copies may be phoned in. Fee is $10. Mailing Labels: No. Magnetic Tape: Available for $175. Address inquiries to Molly O'Connell. Microfiche: Yes. Monthly New Corporations costs $11 per month. New Corporate Listing: Yes (see microfiche entry). Minimum cost is $10 per week. Custom Searches: No. Online Access: No. Number of Active Corporations on File: 176,000.

Wyoming

Corporate Division, Secretary of State, State of Wyoming, Capitol Building, Cheyenne, WY 82002, 307-777-7311; Fax: 307-777-5339. Selected Publications: *Wyoming Business Corporation Act ($3)*. Phone Information: 307-777-7311. Copies of Documents on File: Available for 50 cents for first 10 pages then 15 cents per page, $3 for certified copies. Mailing Labels: No. Magnetic Tape: Yes. Categories: Trademarks, New Domestic, New Foreign. $18.76 per tape, customer must provide tape. Information cannot be used for solicitation. Submit written request with letter of purpose. Microfiche: Available for foreign and nonprofit corporations for $15. New Corporate Listings: Yes. $100 in state, $150 out of state. Also, you may be put on mailing list for weekly press release that appears in local journals, Business Section. Custom Searches: Yes. Categories: Trademarks 25 cents per name and address, New Domestic $120 or $80 if in-state request, New Foreign $120 or $80 if instate request. Limited capacity for other types of searches. Information cannot be used for solicitation. Submit written request with letter of purpose. Listing of all active profit corporation can be purchased for $25. Online Access: Will soon be available. Contact Jeanie Sawyer, 307-777-5334. Number of Active Corporations on File: 28,000.

Be patient. If any phone number is incorrect, call (area code) 555-1212 and request the new listing.

657

State Company Directories

Market Info, Mailing Lists, Databases Available from State Company Directories

Would you like to know what kind of computing systems and software 24,000 manufacturing firms in California use? Or where to find out what materials 7,000 manufacturers in North Carolina need for their manufacturing processes? Or which of 2,700 manufacturers in Nevada have contracts with the federal government? You can get quick answers to these questions and more in the state directories of manufacturing companies.

These directories contain valuable information concerning what products are bought, sold, and distributed in each state. At the very least, each directory lists the companies' names, addresses, phone numbers, products, and SIC codes, and is cross-referenced by company name, location, and SIC code/product. So, if you want to find out which companies in Tennessee manufacture a certain type of electronic component and where they are located, all you have to do is look it up in the product index. If you want to find out what manufacturing firms are operating in a certain town or county, the geographic index will tell you. These directories can be invaluable for targeting new market areas, monitoring industry trends, developing more effective mailing lists, and much more.

The majority of these directories are put out by the individual state's Chamber of Commerce or Department of Economic Development, while private publishing firms compile and distribute the rest. The price and sophistication of these directories vary widely from state to state. While some, like Montana's, may offer only the basic information mentioned above, others, like the Illinois directory, will also include key personnel, CEO, parent company, employment figures, import/export market, computer system used, and more. Prices range from $5 for Wyoming's directory, all the way to $165 for California's directory. Most of the prices listed below include shipping and handling, and state sales tax where applicable.

Many of these directories are also available in database formats and differ widely in cost. While there are some real bargains, such as Rhode Island's directory of 2,600 firms on diskette for $50, some, like Texas's of 18,000 firms, will cost you $1,000. Before ordering any of these databases, make sure that the software is compatible with your own system. Mailing labels are available for many of the directories, and many states allow you to choose the companies you want for your mailing list on a cost per label basis.

List of State Company Directories

Alabama

Alabama Development Office, Research Division, State Capitol, 135 S. Union Street, Montgomery, AL 36130; 205-242-0400. $55. Listing of 6,500 companies includes name, address, phone, CEO, year established, employee figures, product lines, parent company, import/export, and SIC code. Cross-referenced by company name, location, product, parent company, international trade, and SIC code. Available on diskette. There is a $35 set up fee plus $.09 for each record. Entire state would be $600.

Alaska

Alaska Center for International Business, University of Alaska, 3211 Providence, Suite 203, Anchorage, AK 99508; 907-786-4300. *The Alaska Trade Directory*, a listing of 150 Alaska companies and industries that import or export, includes name, address, phone, CEO, key personnel, market area, product/service, and SIC code. Cross-referenced by company name and product/SIC code. Prices available on request.

Arizona

Phoenix Chamber of Commerce, Bank One Plaza, 201 N. Central, Suite 2700, Phoenix, AZ 85073; 602-254-5521. $75. Listing of 5,000 companies includes name, address, phone, CEO, employee figures, market area, products, and SIC code. Cross-referenced by company name, location, market area, and products/SIC code. Diskette format, $403.

Arkansas

Arkansas Industrial Development Foundation, P.O. Box 1784, Little Rock, AR 72203; 501-682-1121. $50. Listing of 2,500 companies includes name, address, phone, contact person, parent company, products, and SIC code. Cross-referenced by company name, location, and product/SIC code.

California

Database Publishing Company, 523 Superior Avenue, Newport Beach, CA 92663; 800-888-8434. $165. Listing of 24,000 companies includes name, address, phone, CEO, key personnel, sales volume, year established, parent company, products, computer brand used, import/export, employee figures, and SIC code. Cross-referenced by company name, location, products, and SIC code. Available on diskette for $975, book included.

Colorado

Business Research Division, University of Colorado, Campus Box 420, Boulder, CO 80309; 303-492-8227. $75. Listing of 4,700 companies includes name, address, phone, employee figures, market area, CEO, products, and SIC code. Cross-referenced by company name, location, and SIC code. Available in database format for $395. Mailing labels: $275/set. Prices may vary.

Connecticut

Connecticut Labor Department, Employment Security Division, Attn: Business Management, 200 Folly Brook Boulevard, Weathersfield, CT 06109; 203-566-3470. $24. The 1984 directory of 4,000 companies includes name, address, products, and SIC code. Cross-referenced by company name, location, products, and SIC codes. A quarterly updated listing is available for $7/year.

MacRae's Industrial Directories, 817 Broadway, 3rd Floor, New York, NY 10003; 800-622-7237. $129.50. Listing of 8,200 CT manufacturing firms includes name, address, phone, parent company, key personnel, employee figures, size, products, and SIC code. Cross-referenced by company name, location, and SIC code.

Delaware

Delaware State Chamber of Commerce, 1201 N. Orange Street, P.O. Box 671, Wilmington, DE 19899; 302-655-7221. $45 for state Chamber members; $55 for non-members. The directory of commerce and industry, listing over 5,600 companies, includes name, address, phone, CEO, employee figures, products/ services, and SIC code. Cross-referenced by company name, location, and SIC code. Mailing labels: 25 cents/company.

Florida

Harris Publishing Company, 2057 Aurora Road, Twinsburg, OH 44087; 800-888-5900. $85. Listing of over 9,000 companies includes name, address, phone, CEO, employee figures, products, import/export, and SIC code. Cross-referenced by company name, location, and SIC code. Available on diskette, $325. Mailing labels: 10 cents per company, $150 per 1,000 names, 1,000 minimum.

Georgia

Georgia Department of Industry and Trade, Directory Section, P.O. Box 56706, Atlanta, GA 30343; 404-656-3619. $55. Listing of 8,000 companies includes name, address, phone, market area, parent company, key personnel, employee figures, year established, products, and SIC code. Cross-referenced by company name, location and SIC code.

Hawaii

Chamber of Commerce of Hawaii, 735 Bishop St., Honolulu, HI 96813; 808-522-8800. $45. The current edition of over 150 companies includes name, address, phone, contact person, product, and SIC code. Cross-referenced by company name, location, and SIC code.

Idaho

Center for Business Development and Research, University of ID, Moscow, ID 83844-3227; 208-885-6611. The new directory of over 1,300 manufacturers will include name address, phone, CEO, product/service, contact person, import/ export, employee figures, and SIC code. Cross-referenced by company name, location, and SIC code. Diskette: PC compatible, cost available upon request.

Illinois

Harris Publishing Company, 2057 Aurora Road, Twinsburg, OH 44087; 800-321-9136. $145. Listing of over 20,000 companies includes name, address, phone, CEO, employee figures, computer brand used, year established, sales volume, product, and SIC code. Cross-referenced by company name, location, product, and SIC code. Diskette format, containing 9,000 companies with 20 or more employees, available for $325.

Indiana

Harris Publishing Company, 2057 Aurora Road, Twinsburg OH 44087; 800-321-9136. $98. Listing of over 8,000 companies includes name, address, phone, CEO, employee figures, year established, annual sales, computer brand used, products, and SIC code. Cross-referenced by company name, location, product, and SIC code. Diskette format, containing 6,000 companies with 10 or more employees, available for $295.

Iowa

Iowa Department of Economic Development, Research Section, 200 E. Grand Ave., Des Moines, IA 50309; 515-281-3925. $67. Listing of over 5,000 companies includes name, address, phone, CEO, purchasing agent, parent company, employee figures, product, and SIC code. Cross-referenced by company name, location, product, and SIC code. Available on diskette, $299. Contact Harris Publishing, 2057 Aurora Road, Twinsburg, Oh 44087; 800-888-5900.

Kansas

Kansas Department of Commerce, 700 SW Harrison Street, Suite 1300, Topeka, KS 66603-3712; 913-296-3481. $40. Listing of 4,000 companies includes name, address, phone, contact person, parent company, employee figures, product, and SIC code. Cross-referenced by company name, location, product, and SIC code. Diskettes will be available in 1994.

Kentucky

Department of Economic Development, Maps and Publications, 133 Holmes Street, Frankfort, KY 40601; 502-564-4715. $30. Listing of 3,600 companies includes name, address, phone, CEO, year established, employee figures, products, and SIC code. Cross-referenced by company name, location, and SIC code.

Louisiana

Department of Economic Development, Commerce and Industry, P.O. Box 94185, Baton Rouge, LA 70804-9185; 504-342-5361. $55. Listing of 3,000 companies includes name, address, phone, CEO, purchasing agent, marketing area, import/export, products, and SIC code. Cross-referenced by company name, location, and SIC code. Database price available on request.

Maine

Maine Manufacturing Directory, Tower Publishing Company, 34 Diamond St., P.O. Box 7220, Portland, ME 04112; 800-431-2665 in-state; 207-774-5361 out-of-state. $42.50. Listing of 2,200 companies includes name, address, phone, three contact persons, employee figures, gross sales, product, and SIC code. Cross-referenced by company name, location, and SIC code. Mailing labels: $55 for first 1,000, then 5 cents each. Diskettes, $225.

Maryland

Harris Publishing Company, 2057 Aurora Rd., Twinsburg, OH 44087; 800-888-5900. $62. Listing of 2,500 companies includes name, address, phone, employee figures, year established, annual sales, products, key personnel, and SIC code. Divided into sections by company name, location, industry, import/ export, products, and SIC code. Mailing labels: $75 per 1,000 names, minimum charge $150. Diskette available for $249.

Massachusetts

George D. Hall Publishing Company, 50 Congress Street, Boston, MA 02109; 617-523-3745. $67.95 in-state; $56.95 out-of-state. Listing of 7,400 companies includes name, address, phone, CEO, sales volume, employee figures, products, and SIC code. Cross-referenced by company name, location, and product. Database format on diskette for any 3,000 companies available for $400. Mailing labels $225 minimum per 3,000; 6 cents/name.

Michigan

Harris Publishing Company, 2057 Aurora Road, Twinsburg, OH 44087; 800-321-9136. $145. Listing of 14,000 companies includes name, address, phone, CEO, employee figures, computer brands used, year established, products, and SIC code. Cross-referenced by company name, location, product, and SIC code. Diskette format, containing 7,000 companies with 20 or more employees, available for $325.

Minnesota

National Information Systems, 4401 West 76th Street, Edina, MN 55435; 612-893-8308. $83.49. Listing of 9,000 companies includes name, address, phone, contact person, employee figures, sales volume, year established, products, and SIC code. Cross-referenced by company name, location, and product/SIC code.

Mississippi

Mississippi Department of Economic and Community Development, 1400 Walter Sillers Bldg., P.O. Box 849, Jackson, MS 39205; 601-359-3448. $50. Listing of 2,600 companies includes name, address, phone, CEO, key personnel, employee figures, parent company, products, international trade, and SIC code. Cross-referenced by company name, location, product, and SIC code. Available on diskette for $400, and $200 for yearly update.

Missouri

Harris Publishing Company, 2057 Aurora Road, Twinsburg, OH 44087; 800-321-9136. $97. Listing of 8,000 companies includes name, address, phone, CEO, employee figures, computer brand used, year established, product, and SIC code. Cross-referenced by company name, location, product, and SIC code. Diskette format, containing 4,800 companies with 10 or more employees, available for $299.

Montana

Department of Commerce, Business Assistance Division, 1424 9th Avenue, Helena, MT 59620; 406-444-3923. $20. Listing of 2,500 companies includes name, address, phone, owner, size classification, products, and SIC code. Cross-referenced by company name, location, product, and SIC code.

Nebraska

Nebraska Department of Economic Development, P.O. Box 94666, Lincoln, NE 68509; 402-471-3784. $40. Listing of 1,849 companies includes name, address, phone, CEO, parent company, employee figures, import/export, products, and SIC code. Cross-referenced by company name, location, and product/SIC code. Available on IBM compatible diskette for $150.

Nevada

Gold Hill Publishing Company, P.O. Drawer F, Virginia City, NV 89440; 702-847-0222. $109. Listing of 6,530 companies includes name, address, phone, parent company, CEO, key personnel, Fax #, square footage occupied, sales volume, products, import/ export, federal contracts, year established, years in NV, products, and SIC code. Cross-referenced by company name, location, and product/SIC code. Available on diskette for $400.

New Hampshire

Department of Resources and Economic Development, Industrial Development Office, 172 Pembroke Road, P.O. Box 1856, Concord NH 03302-1856; 603-271-2591. $47.50. Listing of 4,800 companies includes name, address, phone, CEO, ranking officers, year established, sales volume, import/export, products, and SIC code. Cross-referenced by company name, location, and product/SIC code. Available on IBM compatible diskette for $250/set of 4 + $4.74 postage and handling. To order, call Tower Publications, 800-969-8693.

New Jersey

Commerce Register, Inc., 190 Godwin Avenue, Midland Park, NJ 07432; 800-221-2172. $98.05. Listing of 11,000 companies includes name, address, phone, key personnel, sales volume, products, employee figures, square footage and acreage occupied, year established, SIC code, and bank, accountants, and law firms used. Cross-referenced by company name, location, and product/SIC code. Available on diskette for $155 minimum charge, depending on number of listings ordered.

Be patient. If any phone number is incorrect, call (area code) 555-1212 and request the new listing.

659

Information on People, Companies, and Mailing Lists

New Mexico

Department of Economic Development, Joseph M. Montoya Bldg, 1100 St. Francis Dr., Santa Fe, NM 87503; 505-827-0300. $25. Listing of 1,800 companies includes name, address, phone, CEO, employee figures, products/ services, and SIC code. Cross-referenced by company name, location, and product/SIC code.

New York

MacRAE's Industrial Directories, 817 Broadway, 3rd Floor, New York, NY 10003; 800-622-7237. $135. Listing of 12,000 companies includes name, address, phone, key personnel, size classification, products, location, and SIC code. Diskette price, $400.

North Carolina

North Carolina Business Industry, Dept. D, P.O. Box 25249, Raleigh, NC 27611; 919-733-4151. $52.50. The new edition of 7,000 companies includes name, address, phone, CEO, year established, employee figures, parent company, import/export, product, and purchasing and product SIC codes. Cross-referenced by company name, location, parent company, product, products purchased, and import/export capabilities. Available on IBM magnetic tape database format for $1,000.

North Dakota

North Dakota Department of Economic Development and Finance, 1833 E. Bismarck Express, Bismarck, ND 58504; 701-224-2810. $50. Listing of over 600 companies includes name, address, phone, contact person, employee figures, products, and SIC code. Cross-referenced by company name, location, and product/SIC code. Diskette price $50.

Ohio

Harris Publishing Company, 2057 Aurora Road, Twinsburg, OH 44087; 800-321-9136. $145. Listing of 18,000 companies includes name, address, phone, CEO, employee figures, year established, annual sales, computer brand used, products, and SIC code. Cross-referenced by company name, location, product, and SIC code. Diskette format, containing 8,700 companies with 20 or more employees, available for $325.

Oklahoma

Oklahoma Department of Commerce, P.O. Box 26980, Marketing Division, Oklahoma City, OK 73126-0980; 405-843-9770, ext. 207. $40. Listing of 4,500 companies includes name, address, phone, owner's name, employee figures, product, and SIC code. Cross-referenced by company name, location, product, and SIC code.

Oregon

Oregon Economic Development Department, 775 Summer Street, NE, Salem, OR 97310; 503-986-0123. $75. Listing of 7,500 companies includes name, address, phone, employee figures, parent company, CEO, import/export, products, and SIC code. Cross-referenced by company name, product, and SIC code. Available in database formats and mailing labels at variable cost.

Pennsylvania

Harris Publishing Company, 2057 Aurora Road, Twinsburg, OH 44087; 800-321-9136. $145. Listing of 18,000 companies includes name, address, phone, CEO, employee figures, computer brand used, year established, products, and SIC code. Cross-referenced by company name, location, product, and SIC code. IBM compatible diskette format, containing 8,800 companies with 20 or more employees, available for $325.

Rhode Island

Department of Economic Development, Research Division, 7 Jackson Walkway, Providence, RI 02903; 401-277-2601. $10 for RI residents; $30 for non-residents. Listing of 2,600 companies includes name, address, phone, CEO, employee figures, parent company, products, and SIC code. Cross-referenced by company name, location, and SIC code. Available on IBM or MacIntosh compatible diskette for $50. Mailing labels: 5 cents per name.

South Carolina

State Development Board, P.O. Box 927, Columbia, SC 29202; 803-737-0400. Attn: Industrial Directory sales. $60. Listing of 3,200 companies includes name, address, phone, CEO, geographical location, purchasing agent, employee figures, product line, parent company, and SIC code. Cross-referenced by company name, location, product, and SIC code. Available on IBM compatible diskette for $500. Mailing labels: $50 set up fee, 10 cents per label.

South Dakota

Governor's Office of State Economic Development, Capitol Lake Plaza, Pierre, SD 57501; 605-773-5032. $35. Listing of 1,000 companies includes name, address,

phone number, trade name, county, fax number, marketing area, employee figures, CEO, purchasing agent, sales manager, products, and SIC code. Cross-referenced by company name, location, and SIC code. Mailing labels: $35/set.

Tennessee

M. Lee Smith Publishers and Printers, P.O. Box 198867, Arcade Station, Nashville, TN 37219; 615-242-7395. $68 in-state; $65 out-of-state. Listing of 5,300 companies includes name, address, phone, parent company, key personnel, employee figures, marketing area, computer brand used, products, and SIC code. Available in database format, magnetic tape or diskette: $100 conversion fee, then $250 per 1,000 chosen. Mailing labels: $90/ 1,000. Diskette cost: $395. Diskette and book cost: $345.

Texas

University of Texas, Bureau of Business Research, P.O. Box 7459, Austin, TX 78713-7459; 512-471-1616. $130. Two volume directory of 18,000 companies includes name, address, phone, key personnel, year established, sales volume, employee figures, market area, import/export, products, and SIC code. Volume 1 lists companies by name; volume 2 lists companies by product/SIC code. Available on diskette from $300 per section, or $1000 for entire state listing, 18,000 companies.

Utah

Utah Department of Community and Economic Development, 324 S. State St., Suite 500, Salt Lake City, UT 84111; 801-538-8700. $26. Listing of 2,600 companies includes name, address, phone, employee figures, products, and SIC code. Cross-referenced by company name and SIC code. Available in dBase 3 database format, high or low density diskettes. Prices may vary.

Vermont

Vermont Business Magazine, 2 Church Street, Burlington, VT 05401; 802-863-8038. $10 plus tax in-state; $15 out of state. Listing of 2,500 companies includes name, address, phone, geographical listing, plant location, CEO, parent company products trade names, products exported, employee figures, retail/mail order/or wholesale distribution, and SIC code. Cross-referenced by company name, location, and product/SIC code. Available on diskette for $300.

Virginia

Virginia Chamber of Commerce, 9 South 5th Street, Richmond, VA 23219; 804-644-1607. $78.38 in-state; $75 out-of-state. Listing of 4,000 companies includes name, address, phone, CEO, employee figures parent company, products, and SIC code. Cross-referenced by product, SIC code, county, and city. Available in ASCII and ABCDIC magnetic tape database formats for $225. Mailing labels vary in price.

Washington

Database Publishing Company, 523 Superior Ave., Newport Beach, CA 92663; 800-888-8434. $99. Listing of 4,100 companies includes name, address, phone, CEO, key personnel, sales volume, year established, parent company, products, computer brand used, employee figures, import/export, product, and SIC code. Cross-referenced by company name, location, products, and SIC code. Diskette available for $395. Mailing labels, $65/1,000.

West Virginia

Harris Publishing Company, 2057 Aurora Rd., Twinsburg, OH 44087; 800-321-9136. $49. Listing of 1,200 companies includes name, address, phone, CEO, employee figures, computer brand used, year established, products, and SIC code. Cross-referenced by company name, location, product, and SIC code. Diskette price, $249.

Wisconsin

WMC Service Corporation, P.O. Box 352, 501 East Washington Street, Madison, WI 53701-0352; 608-258-3400. $89.68/member, $131.88/non-member. Listing of 9,000 companies includes name, address, phone, CEO, year established, computer brand used, employee figures, parent company, Fax #, import/export, out-of-state affiliates, products, and SIC code. Cross-referenced by company name, location, product, and SIC code. Available on IBM compatible diskette $300/member, $450/non-member.

Wyoming

Department of Commerce, Division of Economic and Community Development, Barrett Bldg. 4 North, Cheyenne, WY 82002; 307-777-7284. $5 in-state, $15 out-of-state. Listing of 250 companies includes name, address, phone, CEO, market area, employee figures, product, and SIC code. Cross-referenced by company name, location, and SIC code. Diskette price $5 in-state, $15 out-of-state.

Be patient. If any phone number is incorrect, call (area code) 555-1212 and request the new listing.

State Securities and Stockbrokers

State Securities Offices Offer Company Information, Mailing List of Brokers and More

The offices of state security regulators offer financial data on thousands of companies which are not required to file with the U.S. Securities and Exchange Commission as well as the names, addresses, financial data, and consumer information on thousands of stockbrokers and broker-dealers.

State regulation of the sale of securities in the U.S. began in 1911 when the Kansas legislature passed the first securities law. North Carolina enacted a law the same year; Arizona and Louisiana did so in 1912. By 1919, 32 states had followed suit. Now, all states and the federal government have laws regulating the sale of corporate securities, bonds, investment contracts and stocks.

The reason for these laws is simple enough: they protect the public, unfamiliar with the intricacies of investing, against deceitful promoters and their often worthless stocks. This is the same type of function that the U.S. Securities and Exchange Commission performs in Washington, DC. The United States covers companies trading stocks across state boundaries, and the states cover companies trading stocks within their state. The laws — called Blue Sky laws — prevent speculative schemes "which have no more basis than so many feet of blue sky," according to the Commerce Clearing House Blue Sky Law Reports.

The Blue Sky Law is usually administered by each state's Securities Commission or Securities Division. Securities to be sold within a state must register with this office. If the issuer is a corporation, for example, it must submit the following information:

- articles of incorporation
- purpose of proposed business
- names and addresses of officers and directors
- qualifications and business history of applicant
- detailed financial data

Each state, however, has numerous exemptions. Securities issued by national banks, savings and loan associations, non-profit organizations, public utilities, and railroads are usually exempt from the Blue Sky laws, as are securities listed on the stock exchange, those issued by companies registered with the U.S. Securities and Exchange Commission, and those issued by foreign governments with which the U.S. has diplomatic relations.

Securities offices also require broker-dealer firms, the agents (or sales representatives), and investments advisers wanting to work in the state to file applications.

Agents wanting to work in one or more states now apply for registration by filing with National Association of Securities Dealers' Central Registration Depository (CRD). To keep the CRD current, agents must submit all pertinent employment and application changes. All state securities offices are hooked up to the CRD through computer terminals and use them to monitor agents registered or applying to register in their jurisdictions as well as any complaints filed against individuals.

Most states will also use the system for registration of broker-dealer firms. Information kept in the repository will include registration applications, amendments to applications, complaints on file, and so forth. The purpose is to reduce the amount of paperwork for the states and to promote more uniformity.

The system is not set to accept broker-dealers' audited financial statements or annual reports so applicants will have to continue to file in the states requiring them. The broker-dealer phase of the CRD is now in operation. Several states are now trying to determine what, if any, information they will require broker- dealers to file with their securities divisions. Most of those states that have made a decision said they will continue to require annual financial reports to be filed with their offices.

Below are the names, addresses and telephone numbers for the state securities offices. Most of these offices will routinely provide information over the phone on whether specific companies, agents, or broker-dealers are registered in their states. Requests for more detailed information may have to be submitted in writing.

Securities Offices

Alabama
Securities Commission, 770 Washington Ave., Suite 570, Montgomery, AL 36130; 205-242-2984.

Alaska
Division of Banking, Securities and Corporations, Department of Commerce and Economic Development, State Office Building #94, P.O. Box 110807, Juneau, AK 99811-0807; 907-465-2521.

Arizona
Securities Division, Arizona Corporation Commission, 1200 West Washington St., Suite 201, Phoenix, AZ 85007; 602-542-4242.

Arkansas
Securities Department, Heritage West Building, Third Floor, 201 East Markham, Little Rock, AR 72201; 501-324-9260.

California
Securities Regulation Division, Department of Corporations, 3700 Wilshire Blvd., 6th Floor, Los Angeles, CA 90010; 213-736-2741.

Colorado
Division of Securities, Department of Regulatory Agencies, 1580 Lincoln, Suite 420, Denver, CO 80203; 303-894-2320.

Connecticut
Securities and Business Investments Division, Department of Banking, Securities and Business, 44 Capitol Ave., Hartford, CT 06106; 203-566-4560.

Delaware
Division of Securities, Dept. of Justice, 8th Floor, Civil Division, 820 N. French St., Wilmington, DE 19801; 302-577-2515.

Information on People, Companies, and Mailing Lists

District of Columbia
Division of Securities, DC Public Service Commission, 450 5th St., NW, Suite 821, Washington, DC 20001; 202-626-5105.

Florida
Division of Securities and Investor Protection, Department of Banking and Finance, Office of Comptroller, The Capitol, LL-22, Tallahassee, FL 32399-0350; 904-488-9805.

Georgia
Business Services and Regulations, Office of Secretary of State, Suite 315 West Tower, Two Martin Luther King Dr., Atlanta, GA 30334; 404-656-2894.

Hawaii
Business Registration Division, Department of Commerce and Consumer Affairs, 1010 Richards St., PO Box 40, Honolulu, HI 96810; 808-586-2737.

Idaho
Securities Bureau, Department of Finance, 700 West State St., Boise, ID 83720-2700; 208-334-3684.

Illinois
Securities Department, Office of Secretary of State, 900 South Spring St., Springfield, IL 62704; 217-782-2256.

Indiana
Securities Division, Office of Secretary of State, 302 W. Washington, Room E-111, Indianapolis, IN 46204; 317-232-6681.

Iowa
Securities Bureau, Office of Commissioner of Insurance, Lucas State Office Bldg., 2nd Floor, Des Moines, IA 50319; 515-281-4441.

Kansas
Office of Securities Commissioner, 618 S. Kansas, 2nd Floor, Topeka, KS 66603-3804; 913-296-3307.

Kentucky
Division of Securities, Department of Financial Institutions, 477 Versailles Rd., Frankfort, KY 40601; 502-564-3390.

Louisiana
Securities Commission, 1100 Paydras Street, Suite #2250, New Orleans, LA 70163; 504-568-5515.

Maine
Securities Division, Bureau of Banking, Department of Professional and Financial Regulation, State House Station 121, Augusta, ME 04333; 207-582-8760.

Maryland
Division of Securities, Office of Attorney General, 200 St. Paul Place, 21st Floor, Baltimore, MD 21202-2020; 410-576-6360.

Massachusetts
Securities Division, Department of Secretary of State, 1719 John W. McCormack Bldg., One Ashburton Place, Boston, MA 02108; 617-727-3548.

Michigan
Corporation and Securities Bureau, Department of Commerce, 6546 Merchantile Way, Lansing, MI 48909; 517-334-6200.

Minnesota
Registration and Licensing Division, Department of Commerce, 133 East 7th Street, St. Paul, MN 55101; 612-296-4026.

Mississippi
Securities Division, Office of Secretary of State, P.O. Box 136, Jackson, MS 39205; 601-359-1350.

Missouri
Office of Secretary of State, 600 West Main, Jefferson City, MO 65101; 314-751-4136.

Montana
Securities Department, State Auditor's Office, 126 North Sanders, Room 270, Helena, MT 59620; 406-444-2040.

Nebraska
Bureau of Securities, Department of Banking and Finance, 1200 N Street, The Atrium #311, Lincoln, NE 68508; 402-471-3445.

Nevada
Securities Division, Office of Secretary of State, 1771 E. Flamingo Rd., Suite 212-B, Las Vegas, NV 89158; 702-486-6440.

New Hampshire
Department of State, Bureau of Securities Regulation, State House, Room 204, Concord, NH 03301-4989; 603-271-1463.

New Jersey
Bureau of Securities, 153 Halsey Street, 6th Floor, Newark, NJ 07101; 201-504-3600.

New Mexico
Securities Division, Regulation and Licensing Department, 725 St. Michaels Dr., P.O. Box 25101, Santa Fe, NM 87501; 505-827-7140.

New York
Bureau of Investor Protection and Securities, Department of Law, 120 Broadway, 23rd Fl., New York, NY 10271; 212-416-8200.

North Carolina
Securities Division, Department of State, 300 N Salisbury St., Suite 1000, Raleigh, NC 27603; 919-733-3924.

North Dakota
Office of Securities Commission, 600 E. Boulevard, 5th Floor, Bismarck, ND 58505; 701-224-3924.

Ohio
Division of Securities, Department of Commerce, 77 South High St, 22nd Fl., Columbus, OH 43266-0548; 614-644-7381.

Oklahoma
Department of Securities, 2401 North Lincoln Blvd., 4th Fl., Oklahoma City, OK 73152; 405-235-0230.

Oregon
Division of Finance and Corporate Securities, Department of Insurance and Finance, 21 Labor and Industries Bldg., Salem, OR 97310; 503-378-4387.

Pennsylvania
Securities Commission, Division of Licensing and Compliance, 1010 North Seventh St., 2nd Floor, Harrisburg, PA 17102-1410; 717-787-8061.

Rhode Island
Securities Division, Department of Business Regulation, 233 Richmond St., #232, Providence, RI 02903-4232; 401-277-3049.

South Carolina
Securities Division, Department of State, 1205 Pendelton St., #501, Columbia, SC 29201; 803-734-1087.

South Dakota
Division of Securities, Department of Commerce and Regulation, 118 W. Capitol, Pierre, SD 57501-2017; 605-773-4823.

Tennessee
Division of Securities, Department of Commerce and Securities, Volunteer Plaza, Suite 680, 500 James Robinson Pkwy., Nashville, TN 37243; 615-741-3187.

Texas
State Securities Board, 221 W. 6th Street, Suite 700, Austin, TX 78701; 512-474-2233.

Be patient. If any phone number is incorrect, call (area code) 555-1212 and request the new listing.

Utah

Securities Division, Department of Business Regulation, P.O. Box 45808, Salt Lake City, UT 84145-0808; 801-530-6600.

Vermont

Securities Division, Department of Banking & Insurance, 89 Main Street, Drawer 20, Montpelier, VT 05600-3101; 802-828-3420.

Virginia

Division of Securities and Retail Franchising, State Corporation Commission, PO Box 1197, Richmond, VA 23209; 804-371-9051.

Washington

Securities Division, Department of Licensing, PO Box 9033, 405 Black Lake Blvd., SW, 2nd Floor, Olympia, WA 98507-9033; 206-753-6928.

West Virginia

Securities Division, State Auditor's Office, Room W-118, State Capitol, Charleston, WV 25305; 304-558-2257.

Wisconsin

Office of Commissioner of Securities, 101 East Wilson St., P.O. Box 1768, Madison, WI 53701; 608-266-3431.

Wyoming

Securities Division, Office of the Secretary of State, Capitol Building, Cheyenne, WY 82002; 307-777-7370.

Be patient. If any phone number is incorrect, call (area code) 555-1212 and request the new listing.

663

Food and Drug Companies

If you are seeking information on sanitation or safety conditions at a particular restaurant, fast food franchise, or meat packing facility and don't want to wade through masses of information maintained by the federal government, you can always start at the state level. All state departments of health have a division that oversees the inspection and certification of food processing, storing, and serving facilities in the state.

This information might be valuable if you were interested in buying into a facility or if you have a new product that you want to market in a specific area, say sanitation shields for salad bars. Conversely, having state records can add weight to your argument if you want to close an offensive facility down, such as a slaughterhouse or noisy neighborhood bar.

Among the types of facilities most state offices regulate are:

- food processing plants
- food storage facilities
- non-alcoholic bottling plants
- public accommodations (AL)
- vending machines (CT)
- school lunch programs (NH)
- bed and breakfast facilities (NH)
- wineries (OR)

License and inspection forms are a matter of public record in most states and may be obtained by submitting a Freedom of Information Act (FOI) request. The license form will include the address of the facility, the owner's name, and the number of people employed at the facility. Inspection forms provide information on:

- structure of facility
- construction of equipment
- condition of equipment
- sanitation procedures
- how products are handled
- type of labeling
- type of packaging
- safety violations

State offices responsible for regulating the manufacture, distribution, and sale of drugs can provide computer listings of the facilities that they license and inspect.

The types of facilities most often regulated are:

- pharmacies
- drug manufacturers
- drug wholesalers
- medical device manufacturers
- research institutions using controlled substances or hazardous materials

Food and Drug Offices

Alabama

Department of Public Health, Division of Environmental Health, 515 W. Jeff Davis Ave., Montgomery, AL 36104; 205-263-6671. This agency acts as a consultative agency and oversees the inspections of food plants and warehouses. Most of their inspections are done at the county level. The Environmental Health Division inspects and certifies all aspects of environmental health including food processing, storing and serving facilities; sanitation procedures, and safety violations. They have computerized their inspection and licensing data and will provide free printouts upon request. Licensing and inspections forms are also available through the department's legal office.

Alabama State Board of Pharmacy, 1 Perimeter Park South, Suite 425 South, Birmingham, AL 35243; 205-967-0130. This agency licenses and inspects all state pharmacies, drug manufacturers and drug wholesalers. Application and inspection records are confidential. Some of the information has been computerized and a computer listing and mailing labels are available only if the information is to be used for continuing education purposes. A mailing list of state pharmacists is $84 and a list of pharmacies costs $25.

Alaska

Department of Environmental Conservation, Division of Environmental Health, 410 Willobough Ave., Suite 105, Juneau, AK 99801-1795; 907-465-5280. This agency licenses and inspects restaurants, food processors, storage facilities, public accommodations, and bottling companies. Some information is stored on the computer and is available upon request. Lists of businesses are provided upon request at no charge.

Department of Commerce and Economic Development, Division of Occupational Licensing, P.O. Box D-LIC, Juneau, AK 99811. 907-465-2534. This department licenses and inspects pharmacies, drug manufacturers and wholesalers.

Arizona

State Department of Health Services, Food Protection and Institutional Sanitation Section, 3008 N. 3rd St., Suite 207, Phoenix, AZ 85012; 602-230-5912. Most inspections and permits are issued on the county level. This office inspects institutions contracted by the FDA and includes wholesale food manufacturers. The county is responsible for retail food and food processors. A mailing list is available for those places it inspects (around 100). Prices vary according to the nature of the request.

State Board of Pharmacy, 5060 N. 19th Ave. Suite 101, Phoenix, AZ 85015; 602-255-5125. The State Board of Pharmacy licenses and inspects pharmacies, drug wholesalers and manufacturers. Inspection reports are available to the public. Information can be retrieved and a computer printout provided. A mailing list is available and can be sorted in any form needed.

Arkansas

Environmental Health Protection, Department of Health, Division of Sanitation Services, 4815 West Markham, Little Rock, AR 72205; 501-661-2171. This department provides management to county agencies for inspection of retail food operations. The state is responsible for inspecting canning plants, bottling plants and manufactured milk plants. It has a contract with FDA to inspect their inventories. Individuals can receive a listing of selected facilities and inspection reports upon completion of a Freedom of Information request. Listings are $.25 per page.

Board of Pharmacy, 320 W. Capitol, Suite 802, Little Rock, AR 72201; 501-324-9200. This agency inspects and licenses retail and hospital pharmacies, wholesale drug distributors, and medical device manufacturers. Computer listings and mailing labels are available upon written request. Application forms are public information. Computer listings of pharmacists are $75. A listing of pharmacies is $55. A complete set of pharmacy mailing labels is $75. Labels for pharmacists cost $100.

California

State Department of Health Section, Food and Drug Branch, 601 N. 7th St., Sacramento, CA 95814; 916-445-2263. This agency licenses and inspects food processing, packaging and storage facilities; bottled water plants, cold storage facilities, shellfish processors, frozen food lockers, water vending machines, drug and medical device manufacturers, and water haulers. Ceramic tableware manufacturers must register with the agency so that they can collect tableware samples for safety testing. Information from application forms is generally available unless the firm is under current investigation for possible violations of the law that could result in civil or criminal investigation. Licensing programs are on a database but the agency's ability to generate specific reports varies considerably depending upon the request. Computer printouts are $.25 per page. If a legal review is required before data are released, there is an extra charge. Mailing labels are available for some programs. Fees vary according to the scope of the request.

State Board of Pharmacy, 400 R St., Suite 4070, Sacramento, CA 95814; 916-323-7018. This agency licenses and inspects pharmacies and drug wholesalers. A mailing list of the entire file is available. The list can be sorted by county, zip code. The minimum order for mailing labels or printed lists is $100.

Colorado

Colorado Department of Health, Division of Consumer Protection, 4300 Cherry Creek Drive South, Denver, CO 80222-1530; 303-692-2000. This office inspects restaurants, retail markets, food processing plants and food warehouses, dairy farms and milk plants, schools, child care centers licensed by social services, summer camps and group homes, hotels and motels on complaint, campgrounds, and corrections facilities. It also inspects drug manufacturers, wholesalers and medical device manufacturers.

Board of Pharmacy, 1560 Broadway, Suite 1310, Denver, CO 80202-5146; 303-894-7750. The Board of Pharmacy licenses pharmacists and inspects and licenses state pharmacies. The office provides mailing lists and labels of both pharmacies and pharmacists. Costs range from $113 to $130. Requests must be placed in writing and be accompanied by a check.

Connecticut

State Department of Consumer Protection, Food Division, State Office Building, 165 Capitol Ave., Room 167, Hartford, CT 06106; 203-566-3388. This department licenses non-alcoholic beverage manufacturers including bottled water; bakeries, frozen dessert manufacturers, vending machines, and apple juice ciders. It inspects all food warehouses plus those listed above. Information from application forms is public. The office provides listings of licensed establishments. Information will soon be computerized. Lists of licensed plants are free.

State Department of Consumer Protection, Division of Drug Control, State Office Building, 165 Capitol Ave., Hartford, CT 06106; 203-566-4490. This agency licenses and inspects drug manufacturers and wholesalers. They oversee the inspection and regulation of retail pharmacies, hospitals, nursing homes, public and private clinics, and on a limited basis, dentists, physicians, nurses and veterinarians. Mailing lists are not provided but routine inspection reports can be obtained.

Professional Licensing Division, Division of Consumer Protection, Commission of Pharmacy, State Office Building, 165 Capitol Ave., Hartford, CT 06106; 203-566-4832. This agency inspects pharmacies, pharmacists and convenience stores. Requests must be made in writing and approved by the Board. Lists can be sorted into alphabetical, numerical or zip code order. Mailing labels cost $50, printouts cost $40.

Delaware

State Department of Public Health, Office of Food and Milk Protection, P.O. Box 637, Jesse Cooper Building, Dover, DE 19903; 302-739-3841. This agency inspects and licenses milk processors, restaurants, water distribution systems, dairy farms, and non-alcoholic bottling centers. Most inspections are done at the county level. They do not oversee wholesale food processor plants since this is regulated by the USDA. A listing of licensed facilities can be obtained at $.25 per page.

State Department of Health and Social Services, Division of Narcotics and Dangerous Drugs, Delaware Board of Pharmacy, Jesse Cooper Building, P.O Box 637, Room 205, Dover, DE 19903, 302-739-4798. This agency regulates any facility in which drugs are prescribed, dispensed and stored and runs routine compliance inspections. They oversee the inspection and regulation of retail pharmacies, hospitals, nursing homes, public and private clinics, and on a limited basis, dentists, physicians, and veterinarians. Their data has been computerized and a mailing list of pharmacists and pharmacies is available for $25. The office also responds to consumer complaints against pharmacies and physicians that prescribe controlled drugs.

District of Columbia

Department of Consumer Regulatory Affairs, Business Regulations Administration, Food Protection Branch, 614 H Street, NW, Room 616, Washington, DC 20001; 202-

727-7250. This agency inspects and licenses approximately 1,800 District restaurants and all food processing, packaging and storage facilities. A listing of licensed restaurants is available upon request. Costs of listings vary and are based upon the amount of computer time needed to complete the request.

Board of Pharmacy, Department of Consumer and Regulatory Affairs, Pharmaceutical, Radiological and Medical Devices Control Division, Room 1016, 614 H Street, NW, Washington, DC 20001; 202-727-7223. This office licenses all pharmacies, drug manufacturers and wholesalers in the District of Columbia and oversees the regulation of radiological and medical devices. A computer listing of regulated agencies is available upon written request. Fees for services vary according to the complexity of the request.

Florida

State Department of Agriculture and Consumer Services, Bureau of Food Grade and Standards, Lab Complex M-A, 3125 Conner Blvd., Tallahassee, FL 32399; 904-488-3951. This bureau oversees the inspection and certification of over 22,000 food storing and serving facilities and certain food processing plants. This includes food processors, distributors, and retail stores. They do not, however, inspect meat and poultry facilities. The office provides a listing of licensed facilities at $.25 per page. Mailing labels are not available.

State Department of Health and Rehabilitative Services, Pharmacy Program Office, 2633 Mahan Dr., Tallahassee, FL 32308 ; 904-487-1257. This department licenses and inspects retail pharmacies, prescription drug wholesalers and manufacturers; cosmetic manufacturers, device manufacturers, compressed medical gas distributors and wholesalers; and medical oxygen retail establishments. The office all inspects consumer complaints lodged against physicians, pharmacies or clinics. A listing of facilities that have obtained permits is available, free of charge. License application forms are available to the public.

Georgia

Department of Agriculture, Consumer Protection Field Forces Division, 19 Martin Luther King Jr. Drive, Atlanta, GA 30334; 404-656-3627. This department licenses and inspects food processors, producers, distributors and warehouses; grocery stores, wholesale seafood dealers, soft drink and bottled water manufacturers, and bedding manufacturers. This office does not routinely provide mailing lists of inspected facilities. However, the Georgia Department of Industry Trade and Tourism publishes a yearly *Georgia Manufacturing Directory* which lists information on over 9,300 manufacturing plants. For ordering information, call 404-656-3619.

State Drugs and Narcotics Agency, Board of Pharmacy, 166 Pryor St. S.W., Atlanta, GA 30303; 404-656-3912. This agency licenses and inspects pharmacies, drug manufacturers, and wholesalers. A mailing list of licensed facilities is available for $170. Requests should be in writing, and checks may be made out to the Board of Pharmacy. The board also provides license application information.

Hawaii

State Department of Health, Kinau Hale Building, 1250 Punchbowl St., P.O. Box 3378, Honolulu, HI 96801; 808-586-4725. This agency is divided into a number of sections. None offer mailing lists. The Food Products Section inspects for misbranded and adulterated products and medical devices. The Consumer Products Section licenses and inspects food processors, warehouses, manufacturers and bottling plants. The Food Contamination Section oversees pesticides, frozen desserts, and monitors lead content in tableware. Inspection reports are available upon request.

Dept. of Commerce and Consumer Affairs, State Board of Pharmacy, 1010 Richards St., P.O. Box 3469, Honolulu, HI 96801; 808-586-2698. This agency inspects and licenses pharmacies and pharmacists. A roster of pharmacies sorted alphabetically is $12.75. Requests should be made in writing and accompanied by a check made out to the Department of Commerce.

Food and Drug Administration, P.O. Box 50061, Honolulu, HI 96810; 808-541-2661. This office licenses and inspects drug manufacturers, processors, re-labelers, packagers and wholesalers once a year. For information concerning a particular company, write a letter with your specific question to the Office of Legal Affairs at the address listed above.

Idaho

State Department of Health and Welfare, Food Protection Program, Bureau of Communicable Disease Prevention, Division of Health, H&W, 450 W. State St., Boise, ID 83720; 208-334-5938. This agency consults with local health departments and monitors their performances. Inspections are done at the local level. The State Food Program Coordinator can answer general questions about an establishment or will find out specific information upon request.

Information on People, Companies, and Mailing Lists

Board of Pharmacy, 280 N. 8th, St., Suite 20450, Boise, ID 83720; 208-334-2356. This agency licenses and inspects drug manufacturers, wholesalers, distributors, re-packers and non-pharmacy outlets. Mailing lists and labels are available. A listing of licensed pharmacies is $10 and pharmacists is $20. Mailing labels are provided at the same price. Lists can be sorted by zip code order or by type of facility.

Illinois

Department of Public Health, Division of Food, Drugs and Devices, 525 W. Jefferson St., Springfield, IL 62761; 217-785-2439. There is no licensing program in Illinois. This office inspects: bottling plants, candy and cookie manufacturers, bakeries, warehouses, food processors and dairy manufacturing plants. This office also inspects drug manufacturers and medical device manufacturers. Computer listings of inspected facilities are available for $.25 per page. Inspection forms, including a description summary, are also available for $.10 per page upon written request.

State Board of Pharmacy, Office of Drug Compliance, 100 W. Randolph, Suite 9-300, Chicago, IL 60601; 312-814-4573. This agency licenses and inspects pharmacies, drug manufacturers, wholesalers and distributors of controlled substances. Computer printouts of pharmacies and pharmacists are $58.90, each. If you provide your own mailing labels they will print the information on them for the price quoted above. Labels must be three columns across, and 4 by 1 and 7/16 inches in size.

Indiana

State Board of Health, Divisions of Retail and Manufactured Foods, 1330 West Michigan St., P.O. Box 1964, Room 136 Indianapolis, IN 46206; 317-633-0360. This agency is divided into two divisions, retail foods and manufactured foods. The manufactured foods division licenses and inspects wholesale food processors, bottling plants, warehouses, and manufacturers. The retail foods division inspects state facilities such as the State Fair and local health departments. It also handles consumer complaints. Mailing lists are not available for commercial purposes.

State Board of Pharmacy, 402 W. Washington St, Room 041, Indianapolis, IN 46204; 317-232-2960. In addition to inspecting pharmacies, this agency licenses pharmacists, and wholesale legend drug distributors. Under a separate division it also licenses optometrists who wish to prescribe legend drugs. The agency also contains a controlled substance advisory committee that licenses anyone who manufactures, distributes or performs research with controlled substances. Mailing lists and labels are both available. There is a base fee of $20 per listing and an additional few cents per mailing label. Individuals must first complete an application and information is released at the agency's discretion.

Iowa

State Department of Inspections and Appeals, 2nd Floor, Lucas Building, Des Moines, IA 50319; 515-281-6538. This agency licenses and inspects all food related businesses, motels and hotels. They inspect but do not license barbers and cosmetologists. Computer listings are available for $12 per listing. Files are sorted by zip code and type of facility.

Board of Pharmacy, 1209 East Court, Des Moines, IA 50319; 515-281-5944. This agency licenses and inspects pharmacies, drug manufacturers and distributors. Mailing lists are available. The minimum order is $20, and sorting is available by several categories. Mailing labels are also available. Requests must be made in writing. Once the agency has received your request they will forward the information to you along with an invoice.

Kansas

State Department of Health and Environment, Division of Health, Food Service, Drug and Lodging Section, 109 SW 9th St., Suite 604, Topeka, KS 66612-1271; 913-296-1500. This agency licenses all food services, and inspects food and drug manufacturers, bakeries, bottling plants and warehouses. It also handles customer complaints. The agency no longer provides mailing lists or labels to the general public. However, the Department of Health and Environment publishes a newsletter which includes information about the Division of Health, Food Service.

Board of Pharmacy, Landon State Office Building, 900 Jackson St., Room 513, Topeka, KS 66612; 913-296-4056. The Board of Pharmacy licenses and inspects pharmacies, distributors, retail dealers, analytical laboratories for controlled substances, and research institutions using controlled substances. Before a mailing list is released, the board must give its approval and an Open Records Act application must be completed.

Kentucky

Cabinet for Human Resources, Division of Local Health, 275 East Main St., Frankfort, KY 40621; 502-564-3722. This agency licenses and inspects food service

establishments, retail food markets, vending machines, bottling companies, frozen food lockers, shellfish re-packers, food salvage dealers, food processing plants and food warehouses. Copies of information can be obtained for $.25 per page. Computer research time requires an additional fee.

Board of Pharmacy, 1228 U.S. 127 South, Frankfort, KY 40601; 502-564-3833. This agency licenses and inspects drug manufacturers, wholesalers, pharmacies, and grants licenses to pharmacists and pharmacy interns. Listings and self-adhering mailing labels of pharmacists and pharmacies are provided. Information is available in zip code, county or alphabetical order. A listing of licensed pharmacists is $50, a listing of pharmacies, $35. Checks may be made out to the Kentucky State Treasurer's Office and mailed to the above address. Orders may take up to two weeks to complete.

Louisiana

State Department of Health and Human Resources, Food and Drug Control Unit, 325 Loyola Avenue, P.O. Box 60630, New Orleans, 70160; 504-568-5402. This agency licenses and inspects warehouses, manufacturers, distributors and re-packers. Computer lists are available, but are not released for commercial purposes. To receive a listing send a written request to William Swiler, Program Manager, at the address listed above. Be very specific concerning the purpose of your request. Once the office has received your letter they will inform you of costs.

Board of Pharmacy, 5615 Corporate Blvd., #8, Baton Rouge, LA 70808-2537; 504-925-6496. This agency licenses pharmacists and licenses and inspects pharmacies and manufacturers. Approved requests for mailing labels are provided through the Louisiana Pharmacists Association. There is a base charge of $210 for the service and $.10 per label. Call 504-767-7115 for details.

Maine

State Department of Agriculture, Division of Regulations, State House Station 28, Augusta, ME 04333; 207-289-3841. This department licenses and inspects food processors, bakeries, bottling plants, warehouses, mobile vendors and retail stores. Computer listings are available for $1 per sheet. Sorting can only be done by type of facility.

Board of Pharmacy, State House Station 35, Augusta, ME 04333; 207-783-9769. This agency licenses and inspects pharmacies, drug manufacturers and drug wholesalers. Mailing lists are available for $20. Mailing labels are available for $30.

Maryland

Department of Health and Mental Hygiene, Division of Food Control, 4201 Patterson Ave., Baltimore, MD 21215; 410-764-3539. This agency acts as a consultant to counties for their inspection programs, and provides back-up support and guidance. It inspects and licenses all wholesale food facilities. This includes warehouses, food processors, and distributors. Computer listings of licensed facilities are available upon written request.

Department of Health and Mental Hygiene, Drug Control Division, 4201 Patterson Ave., Baltimore, MD 21215; 410-764-2890. This division licenses pharmacies and drug manufacturers. It also inspects wholesale pharmacies and does field work inspection for the Board of Pharmacy. The division enforces state drug law enforcement of controlled substances, prescription and non-prescription drugs. Application information is open to the public for review. Copies and mailing labels of licensed facilities are available.

Massachusetts

Department of Public Health, Division of Food and Drugs, 305 South St., Jamaica Plain, MA 02130; 617-522-3700. This department licenses and inspects food processors, warehouses, bottled water plants, bakeries, and distributors. Computer listings can be generated upon written request. There is a charge of $.20 per page plus $6 for staff computer time.

State Board of Pharmacy, State Office Building, Government Center, 100 Cambridge St., Boston, MA 02202; 617-727-7390. This agency licenses pharmacists, pharmacies and wholesalers. A mailing list, labels or magnetic tape can be purchased, sorted by zip code or alphabetical order. A written request is required. A mailing list of pharmacies is $120. A listing of pharmacists is $320. Information on mailing labels and computer tape costs $200 for the first 1,000 names and $50 for each additional name.

Michigan

Department of Agriculture, Food Division, P.O. Box 30017, Lansing, MI 48909; 517-373-1060. This office licenses and inspects food processors, canners, distributors, warehouses and grocery stores. Computer listings are available, the charge is based on the size of the run. The file can be sorted by county, region, zip code or

Be patient. If any phone number is incorrect, call (area code) 555-1212 and request the new listing.

alphabetical order. Requests for information should be made in writing. The office will then forward you the mailing list along with an invoice.

Office of Health Services, Board of Pharmacy, P.O. Box 30018, Lansing, MI 48909; 517-373-0620, 335-0918. This agency licenses pharmacists, and licenses and inspects pharmacies, drug manufacturers, wholesalers, and distributors. It also deals with consumer complaints lodged against health professionals. Computer lists can be generated for $.20 per page with a $20 minimum.

Minnesota

Department of Agriculture, Food Inspection Department, 90 W. Plato Blvd., St. Paul, MN 55107; 612-296-1592. This agency licenses and inspects food manufacturers, processors, wholesalers, warehouses, and retail stores. For mailing list information contact the Minnesota Trade Office at 612-297-4222.

Board of Pharmacy, 2700 University Ave. West, #107, St. Paul, MN 55114-1079; 612-642-0541. The Board of Pharmacy licenses and inspects drug manufacturers, wholesalers, and pharmacies. Mailing lists and labels are available through the State of Minnesota Mailing List Service at 612-297-2552. Information from application forms is available to the public.

Mississippi

State Department of Health, Division of Sanitation, P.O. Box 1700, Jackson, MS 39215-1700; 601-960-7689. This agency licenses and inspects bottling plants, warehouses and waste water installers. Permits are issued to food service establishments, recreational vehicle parks, and milk plants. Computer lists are available for a fee. Send a written request to the Office of Public Records, Health Communications, Public Relations Division at the above address.

State Board of Pharmacy, Suite D, C & F Plaza, 2310 Hwy. 80 West, Jackson, MS 39204; 601-354-6750. This office licenses and inspects drug manufacturers, wholesalers and pharmacies for instate registrants, only. It also licenses pharmacists. A computer listing of licensed pharmacists is $125. A listing of pharmacies is $100. Information is also available on peel-off labels. A listing of pharmacies is $150, a listing of pharmacists costs $200.

Missouri

State Department of Health, Bureau of Community Sanitation, P.O. Box 570, 1730 Elm St., Jefferson City, MO 65102; 314-751-6400. This agency licenses frozen dessert manufacturers and distributors, non-alcoholic bottlers, manufacturers and distributors, hotels and motels. It also inspects retail food establishments, food plants and warehouses. Frozen desserts and hotel and motels have been computerized. The cost is $.15 per page plus $2.50 for shipping and handling.

State Board of Pharmacy, P.O. Box 625, Jefferson City, MO 65102; 314-751-0091. This agency licenses pharmacists in addition to licensing and inspecting drug wholesalers and distributors. Mailing lists for licensed pharmacists are $15. Mailing labels for licensed pharmacists are $45. Labels for licensed pharmacies are $25. Lists may be sorted by type or by zip code.

Montana

State Department of Health and Environmental Sciences, Food and Consumer Safety Bureau, Cogswell Building, Helena, MT 59620; 406-444-2408. This agency licenses and inspects food warehouses, manufacturers, packagers and processors. Mailing lists are available on a limited basis. Costs vary from $5 to $20, dependent upon the size of the request.

State Board of Pharmacy, 111 N. Last Chance Gulch, Helena, MT 59620; 406-444-3737. The Board of Pharmacy licenses pharmacists and licenses and inspects drug wholesalers and manufacturers. Mailing lists are only available for continuing education purposes. Records can, however, be inspected on site.

Nebraska

State Department of Agriculture, Dairy and Foods, 301 Centennial Mall South, PO Box 95064, Lincoln, 68509; 402-471-2536. The food division of this agency licenses and inspects food manufacturers, processors, restaurants, retail stores and warehouses. The dairy division licenses and inspects dairy producers and plants. Files are open to the public but the only way to obtain a listing is to visit the office and hand copy the information. No information is released for commercial purposes.

Bureau of Examining Boards, State Department of Health, 301 Centennial Mall South, P.O. Box 95007, Lincoln, NE 68509; 402-471-2115. This office licenses pharmacies and all health-related professions. Wholesalers and distributors are licensed only in-state. Listings can be sorted into hospital or community pharmacies. Fees vary according to the complexity of the request.

Nevada

State Department of Human Resources, Bureau of Health Protection Services, 505 East King St., Room 103, Carson City, NV 89710; 702-687-4750. This agency licenses all food establishments, processors and manufacturers. All application information is available to the public. The agency is in the process of setting up computer databases. Prices will vary according to the complexity of the request. This department also licenses and inspects drug manufacturers. There are so few that a hand written list can be obtained. All financial information is confidential.

State Board of Pharmacy, 1201 Terminal Way, Suite 212, Reno, NV 89502; 702-322-0691. The Board of Pharmacy licenses pharmacists and licenses and inspects drug wholesalers, manufacturers and pharmacies. Computer listings and mailing labels are available. Mailing lists of pharmacies and pharmacists are $10, each. Sets of mailing labels are $40, each.

New Hampshire

State Department of Health and Welfare, Division of Public and Health Services, Bureau of Food Protection, Health and Welfare Building, 6 Hazen Drive, Concord, NH 03301-6527; 603-271-4589. New Hampshire does not inspect food processors or warehouses. It licenses restaurants, grocery stores, school lunch programs, hotels, motels, and snack bars. Individuals interested in a particular file must first place their request in writing to the director. Lists of inspected facilities are free and also available upon written request.

State Board of Pharmacy, Health and Welfare Building, 57 Regional Dr., Concord, NH 03301; 603-271-2350. The commission oversees the licensing and inspection of retail pharmacies, wholesalers, distributors and manufacturers of prescription drugs, and health clinics. It also enforces compliance standards at hospitals, nursing homes, and public and private clinics. It also makes required visits to dentists, physicians, and veterinarians to ensure that compliance standards are maintained. Computer lists of licensed pharmacists are available for $150. Mailing labels cost $200.

New Jersey

State Health Department, Consumer Health Services, Food and Milk Program, 3635 Quaker Bridge Road, Trenton, NJ 08625; 609-984-1370. This department licenses and inspects all food and cosmetic wholesalers, processors and distributors, plus frozen desserts and milk plants. Computer listings are available from $40 to $50, dependent upon the size of the request.

State Department of Health, Office of Drug Control, CN-367, Trenton, NJ 08625-0367; 609-984-1308. This agency licenses and inspects drug manufacturers and packagers, and licenses all medical practitioners, except chiropractors. Directories of all manufacturers and distributors are available for $37.75 each.

Board of Pharmacy, P.O. Box 45013, 1100 Raymond Blvd., Newark, NJ 07101; 201-504-6450. This office licenses and inspects pharmacies and licenses pharmacists. Mailing lists and labels are available. Fees vary according to the size of the request.

New Mexico

State Department of Health and Environment, Environmental Improvement Division, 4131 Montgomery Ave. N.E., Santa Fe, NM 87109; 505-827-2850. This agency licenses dairy farms and restaurants only. A listing of licensed dairy farms is $25. A separate division inspects food processors, warehouses and bottling plants. Mailing lists are available; costs vary according to the complexity of the request.

State Board of Pharmacy, 1650 University NE, Suite 400 B, Albuquerque, NM 87102; 505-841-9102. This agency oversees the inspection and regulation of retail pharmacies, hospitals, nursing homes, public and private clinics, drug manufacturers and wholesalers. They also license medical professionals who deal with controlled substances such as pharmacists, physicians and veterinarians. A computer listing of pharmacists or pharmacies is available. The cost is $.10 per name or company.

New York

State Department of Agriculture and Markets, Division of Food Inspection Services, One Winners Circle, Albany, NY 12235; 518-457-4492. This agency licenses and inspects refrigerated warehouses, salvagers, distributors, and food processing plants including over 16,000 groceries. Requests for information should be placed in writing to: Gerald Moore, Freedom of Information Officer, at the address listed above. Include the purpose of your request and be as specific as possible, There is a charge of $.25 per page for information that runs over one hundred pages.

Board of Pharmacy, Cultural Education Center, Room 3035, Albany, NY 12230; 518-474-3848. This office licenses and registers pharmacies, manufacturers, distributors, wholesalers and re-packagers. Computer listings and magnetic tapes are available with a written request. You must include the purpose of your request in your letter. Once the office has received you request it will send you an application form and list of fees.

Be patient. If any phone number is incorrect, call (area code) 555-1212 and request the new listing.

667

Information on People, Companies, and Mailing Lists

North Carolina

State Department of Agriculture, Food and Drug Protection Division, 4000 Reedy Creek Rd., Raleigh, NC 27607; 919-733-7366. Under a contract with FDA, this office licenses and inspects wholesale food manufacturers, warehouses, bottling plants, bakeries, and prescription drug wholesale manufacturers. Computer listings are available and can be sorted by type of industry. There is a flat fee of $15 plus $.05 per page. Listings include: name of firm, address, city, zip and phone number. Some inspection reports are available through the Public Records Act.

Board of Pharmacy, P.O. Box 459, Carrboro, NC 27510-0459; 919-942-4454. This office licenses and inspects pharmacies. Computer lists and mailing labels are available upon written request. The cost of all state registered pharmacies is $74.94. The cost for a listing of licensed pharmacists is $180.18. If you wish a list of those pharmacists that reside in the state, the cost is $150.86.

North Dakota

Department of Health and Consolidated Laboratories, Division of Consumer Protection, 2635 E. Main St., P.O. Box 937, Bismarck, ND 58502-0937; 701-221-6147. This agency licenses and inspects retail food establishments, bed and breakfast facilities, vending operations, bottling plants and ice manufacturers. They are under contract with FDA to inspect food warehouses and processors. Computer listings are $.25 per page. A complete listing costs approximately $100.

State Board of Pharmacy, P.O. Box 1354, Bismarck, ND 58502; 701-258-1535. This agency licenses pharmacists and licenses and inspects all pharmacies and wholesale drug manufacturers. Mailing labels and lists of pharmacists in charge and pharmacies are available for $20 each. Information from application forms is public.

Ohio

Department of Agriculture, Division of Foods, Dairies and Drugs, 8995 E. Main St., Reynoldsburg, OH 43068; 614-866-6361. This department licenses and inspects food processors, cold storage warehouses, grocery stores, frozen food storage facilities, canneries, syrups and extracts, frozen desserts, bottling plants, and wholesale and home bakeries. Computer listings can be generated, sorted by county or commodity. A listing of frozen desserts and bakeries is $30, each. The remaining lists are $10, each.

State Board of Pharmacy, 77 South High St., Columbus, OH 43266-0320; 614-466-4143. This agency licenses pharmacists and licenses and inspects retail and wholesale pharmacies, drug distributors, and industrial first aid rooms. Mailing lists and labels of pharmacies and pharmacists are available. They can be sorted by county, type of license, or zip code. Fees for printed materials are $.07 per record. Mailing labels cost $.10 per record. Requests for information should be in writing and accompanied by a check.

Oklahoma

State Department of Health, Food Protection Service, 1000 N.E. 10th St. Oklahoma City, OK 73117-1299; 405-271-5243. This department licenses and inspects bottling plants, food processors, manufacturers and wholesalers. Computer listings are available at $10 per listing. Requests must be made in writing. Send a letter of intent to Richard Barnes at the address listed above.

State Board of Pharmacy, 4545 Lincoln Blvd., Suite 112, Oklahoma City, OK 73105; 405-521-3815. The Board of Pharmacy licenses and inspects pharmacies, wholesalers, manufacturers and packagers. A mailing list of pharmacies is $200. A list of pharmacists is $400. Requests must be made in writing and include a letter of intent.

Oregon

Department of Agriculture, Food and Dairy Division, 635 Capitol St., N.E., Salem, OR 97310; 503-378-3790. This agency licenses and inspects food processors, retail stores, bakeries, food storage warehouses, bottling plants, retail meat facilities and dairies. Computer listings and mailing labels are available and can be sorted by type of facility. Fees are $.05 per name. A minimum order of $25 is required.

Board of Pharmacy, 800 N.E. Oregon St., #9, Portland, OR 97232; 503-731-4032. The Board of Pharmacy licenses pharmacists and interns and licenses and inspects drug manufacturers, pharmacies, wholesalers, and retail outlets with over the counter drugs. Listings are $75, each. Mailing labels are $80 per set.

Pennsylvania

State Department of Agriculture, Bureau of Food Safety and Laboratory Services, 2301 N. Cameron St., Harrisburg, PA 17110-9408; 717-787-4315. This agency licenses and inspects bakeries, bottling plants and warehouses, and issues non-alcoholic drink licenses. Mailings lists are available. Costs vary according to the size of the list.

State Department of Health, Drug Registration Section, Division of Drugs, Devices and Cosmetics, P.O. Box 90, Harrisburg, PA 17108-0090; 717-787-2307. This agency licenses and inspects drug, cosmetic and device manufacturers. It does not normally issue computer listings.

Board of Pharmacy, P.O. Box 2649, Harrisburg, PA 17105; 717-783-7157. This agency licenses and inspects pharmacies. Computer listings are available. There is a charge of $.005 per name plus a $71 service fee.

Rhode Island

State Department of Health, Division of Food Protection, Room 203, Canon Bldg., 3 Capitol Hill, Providence, RI 02908-5097; 401-277-2750. Licenses and inspects food processors, wholesalers and food service establishments, dairies, vending machines and warehouses. Computer listings are available and range between $10 to $90, depending upon the complexity of the request. Interested individuals must first file a release of information request form.

State Department of Health, Division of Drug Control, 304 Cannon Bldg. 3 Capitol Hill, Providence, RI 02908. 401-277-2837. The Division of Drug Control licenses and inspects drug manufacturers, wholesalers, retailers, pharmacies, and some devices and cosmetics. A list of pharmacies costs $42. Interested individuals must first file a release of information request form.

South Carolina

Department of Health and Environmental Control, Division of Dairy Foods and Bottling Plants, 2600 Bull St., Columbia, SC 29201; 803-734-4970. This agency inspects soft drink bottling plants and dairy farms. Computer listings and mailing labels are available. The cost is $10 per listing plus a $3.50 set up charge for sorting the file.

Department of Agriculture, Laboratory Division, 1101 William St., P.O. Box 11280, Columbia, SC 29211; 803-737-2070. This agency inspects non-meat manufacturers such as bakeries and warehouses. A computer listing is provided free of charge.

State Board of Pharmaceutical Examiners, 1026 Sumter St., P.O. Box 11927, Columbia, SC 29211; 803-734-1010. This office licenses both pharmacists and pharmacies. Files are open to the public. Computer lists and mailing labels are available. Mailing lists cost $.01 per name, plus postage. Mailing labels are $.04 per name, postage, and $6 for staff computer time. Place your requests in writing to the address listed above.

South Dakota

Department of Agriculture, Division of Regulatory Services, Anderson Building, 445 East Capitol, Pierre, SD 57501; 605-773-3724. This agency inspects milk plants, pesticide producers, fertilizer producers and nurseries. Mailing lists are available and cost between $10 and $50.

State Board of Pharmacy, P.O. Box 518, Pierre, SD 57501; 605-224-2338. The Board of Pharmacy licenses both pharmacists and pharmacies. A mailing list of pharmacies is $15, pharmacists cost $25. Mailing labels are also available in each category for an additional $5. Requests must be placed in writing.

Tennessee

State Department of Agriculture, Division of Quality and Standards, Ellington Agricultural Center, Melrose Station, P.O. Box 40627, Nashville, TN 37204; 615-360-0150. The Food and Drug Administration maintains all information and inspection files on retail food stores, warehouses, processors, bottling plants, bakeries, grain elevators, and produce warehouses. Data on retail foods stores has been computerized. Requests for information must first be placed in writing to the director's office. The cost of a listing is dependent upon the information requested.

Board of Pharmacy, 500 James Robertson Parkway, 2nd Floor, Nashville, TN 37243-1149; 615-741-2718. This office licenses and inspects drug wholesalers, distributors, manufacturers, and pharmacies. Computer listings of pharmacies and pharmacists are $100, each. Mailing labels are $50 extra. Listings can be sorted by zip code, county or alphabetical order.

Texas

Department of Health, Division of Food and Drugs, 1100 W. 49th St., Austin, TX 78756; 512-458-7248. This agency licenses and inspects food manufacturers, bottling plants, bakeries, and retail food markets. Computer listings can be generated and information can be sorted by county or zip code order. Computer listings are $.05 per page and mailing labels, $.01 each. Faxes are $.17 per minute. Information is also available on diskette or magnetic tape. For detailed requests there is a charge of $16.50 for professional time and $8.50 for clerical support staff time. Inspection form information must be requested under the Freedom of Information Act.

State Board of Pharmacy, 8505 Cross Park Drive, Suite 110, Austin, TX 78754; 512-832-0661. This agency licenses pharmacists and licenses and inspects pharmacies. Computer lists and labels are available. Sorting is possible, the cost varies according to the size of the request. Fees range from $10 to $40.

Utah

Department of Agriculture, Division of Food and Dairy, 350 N. Redwood Road, Salt Lake City, UT 84116; 801-538-7124. This agency licenses and inspects food manufacturers, processors, retail stores and warehouses. Computer listings can be generated for $5 and sorted into broad categories such as zip code and type of facility. A written request is required.

Division of Occupational Licensing, Board of Pharmacy, Heber Wells Building, 160 East 300 South, Salt Lake City, UT 84145; 801-530-6628. The Board of Pharmacy licenses pharmacists and licenses and inspects pharmacies, wholesalers, and manufacturers. Computer listings of pharmacies and pharmacists are $40, each. Mailing labels are also available. Information can be transferred onto disk, but the individual must provide the disk, himself. Information requests should be placed in writing and include disk specifications.

Vermont

Department of Health and Human Services, Environmental Health Division, P.O. Box 70, 60 Main St., Burlington, VT 05402; 802-863-7220. This department licenses and inspects bakeries, restaurants, delis, mobil food units, and food and lodging establishments. The agency inspects the following on a complaint basis only: bottling plants, warehouses and food processors. Computer lists can be generated, there is a minimum charge of $5 with an additional cost of $.04 per page.

State Department of Agriculture, Dairy Division, 120 State Street, Montpelier, VT 05620-2901; 802-828-2433. The Dairy Division licenses and inspects dairy farms, milk plants, dairy processors, warehouses (dairy) retail stores. Computer lists can be generated upon request. The agency does not provide a list of dairy farmers but does distribute free lists of licensed firms or establishments. A separate division licenses and inspects the plant industry. A free listing of licensed plant nurseries is available upon request.

State Board of Pharmacy, c/o Secretary of State, Office of Prof Regulation, 109 State St., Montpelier, VT 05609-1106; 802-828-2875. This agency licenses pharmacists and inspects and licenses pharmacies and drug wholesalers. Listings of pharmacists are available at $.03 per name. Lists are also available on mailing labels at $.04 per name and on diskettes for $.01 per name. There is a $5 handling fee involved for each list. Data can be sorted alphabetically or by zip code.

Virginia

State Department of Agriculture, Bureau of Food Inspection, 1100 Bank St., P.O. Box 1163, Richmond, VA 23209; 804-786-3520. This bureau inspects food processors, warehouses, storage plants and retail food establishments such as grocery stores. Restaurants are inspected through another agency. Information is available on a firm's inspection history. Computer listings can be generated for a processing fee.

State Board of Pharmacy, 1601 Rolling Hills Dr., Richmond, VA 23229; 804-662-9911. This agency licenses and inspects pharmacies, drug manufacturers, wholesalers and any company handling controlled substances. For a listing, the request must be made in writing. Lists can be sorted by zip code, alphabetically or license number order. Mailing labels can also be ordered. There is a $45 minimum fee. All licensure information is confidential.

Washington

State Dept of Agriculture, Food Safety and Animal Health Division, P.O. Box 42576, Olympia, WA 98504-2576; 206-902-1876. This agency inspects and licenses in-state food processors and warehouses. It does not release listings for commercial use.

Board of Pharmacy, P.O. Box 47863, Olympia, WA 98504-7863; 206-753-6834. The Board of Pharmacy licenses and inspects pharmacies, drug wholesalers and manufacturers and animal shelters. A computer list or mailing labels may be obtained through a written request. The cost is $.25 per page.

West Virginia

State Health Department, Environmental Health Services, Sanitation Department, 815 Quarrier St., Suite 418, Charleston, WV 25301; 304-558-2981. This agency licenses and inspects primarily interstate commerce facilities such as food processors, bakeries, canneries, candy manufacturers and bottling plants. A mailing list of licensed facilities is provided, free of cost.

State Board of Pharmacy, 236 Capitol St., Charleston, WV 25301 304-558-0558. The Board of Pharmacy licenses pharmacists and licenses and inspects pharmacies, drug distributors and manufacturers. Computer printouts or labels are available. Data can be sorted alphabetically or by zip code order. Computer printouts are free. Mailing labels of pharmacies are $50. Labels for pharmacists cost $100.

Wisconsin

Department of Agriculture, Trade and Consumer Protection, Food Division, 801 West Badger Road, Madison, WI 53708; 608-266-7240. This department licenses and inspects food processors, warehouses, bottling plants, dairy farms and bakeries. Computer lists are available for some types of establishments. There is a processing fee. Sorting is available to a limited extent. Individuals seeking mailing lists can call the open records request line at 608-266-7210 for further information.

State Department of Regulation and Licensing, P.O. Box 8935, Madison, WI 53708; 608-266-2112. The Board of Pharmacy licenses pharmacists and licenses and inspects pharmacies, manufacturers, and distributors. Computer listings and labels are available from the Renewal Document Processing Center 608-266-0627. A listing of pharmacies is $21.20. A listing of pharmacists is $29. Mailing labels are available to state agencies, only.

Wyoming

Department of Agriculture, Food and Drug Section, 2219 Carey Ave. Cheyenne, WY 82002; 307-777-6587. This agency licenses and inspects food processors, warehouses and distributors, dairy farms, and meat plants. Restaurants are licensed through another agency. Listings of licensed facilities may be obtained for $.20 per page, with a $5 minimum required.

State Board of Pharmacy, 1720 South Poplar St., #5, Casper, WY 82601; 307-234-0294. This agency licenses pharmacists and licenses and inspects pharmacies and hospitals with retail licenses. A listing of pharmacies is available for $10 as long as it is not used for advertising purposes. Requests should be made in writing.

Utility Companies

A consulting firm in New Jersey was interested in working out a deal between an electrical company that needed extra power to meet increasing consumer demands, and some private companies that had the ability to generate and sell their extra power. By determining the power needs and financial resources of the utility company, the consulting firm could then match them up with the appropriate power sources in private industry, and along the way save the public utility company millions of dollars by not having to build expensive new power plants of their own. But how did this consulting firm discover the operational and financial background of the electric company to draw up their proposals? The State Utility Regulatory Commission was their source.

If a company provides a service that its state considers a public utility, it must, at the very least, provide detailed financial statements and annual reports to the state's Utility Regulatory Commission (URC). The URC's role is to ensure that utility companies follow the state operating guidelines and make their annual findings available to the public.

The one thing you can count on about utility regulation commissions across the U.S. is that they are all different. The utilities they regulate, the information they gather, and the way they are set up all vary from state to state. For example, Tennessee regulates the standard utilities--transportation, water and sewer, electricity, gas, and telephone--South Dakota regulates all of these along with warehouses and elevators. And while Hawaii will provide you with monthly financial and annual reports, Vermont will give you all that plus a company's tariff information, informal complaints, and special contracts, along with the state regulatory commission's proceedings reports.

Many state utility regulatory commissions have different divisions for each type of utility. Telecommunications, for example, generally include the following divisions: local and long distance telephone, radio common carriers, re-sellers, cable television, and coin operated pay telephones. Fixed utilities often include gas, electricity, water, sewer, and refuse. Many states, like Utah and Pennsylvania, also have transportation divisions that regulate trucking, railroads, taxicabs, buses, and so forth. Some states regulate utilities not regulated in other states, such as cotton gins in Oklahoma, and elevators in South Dakota.

Information in the Public Utility Commission (PUC) files is meant for and mostly used by consumers--whether individual or commercial--for the purposes of estimating and comparing costs. However, the financial information kept on file at commissions contains a wealth of information invaluable to the entrepreneur. In many states, utilities file reports on sales volume, details on revenues raised and customer base, balance sheets, and service reliability and responsiveness. All of this is important for targeting your competition, and developing market studies, mailing lists, and much more. Most state commissions have this information on file in hard copy, but some have begun transferring it into computer formats and will do customized searches based on your specific needs.

Utility Commissions

Alabama
Wallace Tidmore, Secretary of the Commission, Public Service Commission, Box 991, Montgomery, AL 36101-0991; 205-242-5218. Utilities regulated include: Local and long distance telephone, radio common carriers and re-sellers, coined operated telephones; some gas, electric and water (investor owned); transportation (rail, buses, taxis, trucks); gas pipeline (for safety only). Examples of Information on file include annual reports and other financial information including current operating charges and changes in rates. Format of Files and Costs: Hard copy, but efforts to automate are underway. No charge for simple requests; charges on a cost recovery basis for extensive searches. The office provides a listing of regulated companies at no cost. Publications include their free *1991 Annual Report* which includes information on the transportation, telecommunications and energy departments.

Alaska
Ray Wipperman, Public Utilities Commission, 1016 W. 6th Ave., Ste. 400, Anchorage, AK 99501; 907-276-6222. Utilities regulated include: telephone, radio common carriers, some cable television, electricity, gas, water, sewer, steam, garbage, and refuse. Examples of information on file include: fully regulated companies file tariff and financial information. Cost for duplicating information is $.25 per page. A listing of regulated companies is available for $5. A report entitled *Notices*, published twice weekly, lists public notices on tariff filings, etc. It is available through subscription at $40 per year. Another publication, *Order List*, published weekly, lists all orders issued. It is available at $25 per year.

Arizona
Carmine Madrid, Docket Control Center, Arizona Corporation Commission, 1200 W. Washington Street, Phoenix, AZ 85007; 602-542-4251. Utilities regulated include: water, sewer, irrigation, gas, electricity, and telephone. Examples of Information kept on file includes: annual reports; applications called Certificates of Convenience and Necessity, which cover changes in rates; current operating tariffs, and service reliability reports. The staff will make hard copies or copies of microfilm for $.50 per page. The charge is $.10 per page if the requestor comes in to the office to make copies, himself. A listing of regulated companies is available at $.50 per page. Other publications include: *Hearing Notices*, which lists dates and times and specific information about hearings and the *Hearing Calendar* which lists weekly dates and times of hearings. Both are available at $.50 per page.

Arkansas
Jan Sanders, Secretary, Public Service Commission, P.O. Box 400, Little Rock, AR 72203-0400; 501-682-2051. This office regulates: electricity, telephone, gas, and water. Information on file includes: annual reports, complaints, rate and tariff information, and service reliability. Hard copy and older records are on microfilm. Costs are $.25 per page for duplicating. The office will also fax information to you for $3 for the first page and $2 for each additional page. Microfiche is $.25 per page. A 16-page listing of the companies regulated is also available at $.25 per page. The commission also publishes two weekly reports: the *Daily Log*, an agenda of the commission, and *Pending Rate Cases*, which lists upcoming rate hearings. Both are available for $.10 per page.

California
Office of the Director, Public Utilities Commission, Consumer Affairs Branch, 505 Van Ness Ave., San Francisco, CA 94102; 415-557-0647. Utilities regulated include: Local and long distance telephone, telegraph, mobile telephone, cellular telephone facilities and re-sellers, gas, electricity, water, steam, gas pipeline, sewer, and transportation. Examples of information on file: Annual Reports, applications, case files (orders, pleadings, correspondence, exhibits, transcripts) tariff information. The staff will make copies of requested information for $.20 per page. They will also provide listings of regulated companies. Lists are arranged by the type of company, and prices vary for from $1 to $10. For information contact the Documents Section at 415-703-1713. Other publications available include: *Agendas for Meetings*, $75 per year; *Daily Calendar* $125 per year; *Bi-Weekly Calendar*, $50 per year; and the *Transportation Calendar*, $75 per year. The first copy of the *Annual Report*, is free. Each additional copy is $10.

Colorado

Information Center, Public Utilities Commission, Department of Regulatory Agencies, 1580 Logan St., Office Level 2, Denver, CO 80203; 303-894-2000. Utilities regulated include: water and electricity (investor owned), gas (distribution companies only and inspection of new pipeline), telecommunications (all local and long distance only in Colorado), and transportation (taxis and hauling for hire). Examples of Information on file: annual reports, current operating tariffs, changes in rates, and all pending commission actions. Files are microfilmed as the arrive. The office provides hard copies and microfilmed copies at $.20 per printed page. Customized computer searches are available on a cost recovery basis. The office also maintains mailing lists of all active carriers, common and deregulated carriers with state depositories. The *Weekly Agenda* is available at $.20 per page through the Executive Secretary, at the above address.

Connecticut

Barney Spector, Director, Consumer Services Division, Public Utility Control, 1 Central Park Plaza, New Britain, CT 06051; 203-827-2622. Utilities regulated include electricity, gas, water, local and cellular telephone, and cable television. Information on file includes annual reports, customer complaints, financial information, service reliability on cable companies, and changes in rates for all utilities except cable television. Hard copy files are available for $.50 per page. Listings of regulated companies are also available for $.50 per page.

Delaware

Melinda S. Carl, Public Information Officer, Public Service Commission, 1560 South Dupont Highway, P.O. Box 457, Dover, DE 19903-0457; 302-739-4333. Utilities regulated include: Electricity, telephone and water. The commission issues franchises for cable television, and handles disputes concerning new car franchises. Information on file includes: quarterly financial reports, new service or elimination of existing service, rate changes, and issuance of stock. Information, whether on hard copy or microfilm, is $.25 per page. The office also provides a listing of regulated companies, free of charge. Other publications include the yearly *Meeting Agenda* and *Monthly Calendar*, both $18.

District of Columbia

Office of the Secretary, Service Commission, 450 5th Street, N.W., Suite 800, Washington, DC 20001; 202-626-5100. Utilities regulated include: electricity, gas, local telephone, stock broker securities, and coin operated telephones. Examples of information on file include annual reports, other periodic accounting information, service reliability reports, changes in rates, and new tariffs or amendments. The office provides hard copy files at $.15 per sheet plus some computerized records. They also provide a listing of regulated companies, free of charge. Publications include an *Annual Report*, and the *Utility Bulletin*, their quarterly newsletter.

Florida

Steve Tribble, Director of Records and Reporting, Public Service Commission, 101 E. Gaines Street, Tallahassee, FL 32399-0850; 904-488-7238. The commission oversees the intrastate operations of investor-owned utilities -- electric, gas, water and waste water, and telecommunications. It does not regulate publicly-owned, municipal, or cooperative utilities. Information on file includes: monthly general operating reports, earnings, current operating tariffs, rate changes, and complaints. Copies of information and a listing of regulated companies is available at $1 per page. The commission publishes *From the PSC Agenda*, a monthly consumer publication which is distributed to consumer organizations throughout the state, as well as to members of the media, legislators, and city and county government officials.

Georgia

Executive Director's Office, Public Service Commission, 244 Washington St., S.W. Atlanta, GA 30334; 404-656-4501. Utilities regulated include: local telephone, electric, gas, radio common carriers, and transportation. Information on file includes: annual reports, changes in names, rates or management; current operating tariffs, and service reliability. Copies of information are provided at $.25 per page. The office also provides a listing of all companies by type at $.25 per page. An *Annual Report* is also available.

Hawaii

Norman Lee, Chief Engineer, Public Utilities Commission, 465 S. King St., Kekuanaoa Building, Room 103, Honolulu, HI 96813; 808-586-2020. Utilities regulated include: local and cellular telephone, radio common carriers, electricity, gas, water, sewer, trucking, and intra-state transportation. Information on file includes: monthly financial and annual reports. The commission will make hard copies of information for individuals at $.25 per page plus postage. A listing of regulated companies is also $.25 per page.

Idaho

Commission Secretary, Public Utilities Commission, State House, Boise, Idaho 83720; 208-334-0338. Utilities regulated include telephone, gas, electricity, water, and trucking. The office keeps information of file such as applications for rate increases, financial statements, changes in rates and current operating tariffs. Information has not been computerized. The cost of receiving hard copy of information is $.05 per page. The office can provide a list of regulated companies, free of charge. Other publications include an *Annual Report* and monthly *Summary List of Cases*. Both are free to the public.

Illinois

Chief Clerk's Office, Public Utilities Commission, 527 E. Capitol Avenue, P.O. Box 19280, Springfield, IL 62794-9280; 217-782-7434. Utilities regulated include: local and long distance telephone, radio common carriers, customer-owned pay telephones, gas, electricity, water and sewer, gas pipeline, railroad, bus, towing and tractor-trailer haulers. This office keeps files on annual reports, service reliability, all tariff information, and general financial information. There is a $.05 per page copying charge. Publications include the *Annual Report*, which is divided into two parts: public utilities and telecommunication. Each section is available for $10. The office does publish a directory of regulated companies.

Indiana

Public Information Office, Utility Regulatory Commission, Indiana Government Center South, 302 West Washington Street, Suite E-306, Indianapolis, IN 46204; 317-232-2715. Regulated utilities include: local telephone, WATS re-sellers, telephone cooperatives, inter-exchange carriers, radio common carriers, gas, gas transportation companies, electricity, steam, water, and sewer. Information on file includes: rates and charges, tariffs, financial reports, and changes in rates. Hard copies of information are $.15 per page. The office provides a listing of regulated companies, free of charge. The office also publishes an *Annual Report*.

Iowa

Iowa State Utilities Board, Department of Commerce, Utilities Division, Lucas State Office Building, 5th Floor, Des Moines, IA 50319; 515-281-5979. Utilities regulated include: local and long distance telephone, telegraph, investor-owned gas and electricity. The office keeps records of annual reports, financial information, changes in rates and current operating tariffs. There is a $.50 charge for the first three pages of information. Each following page is $.15. A listing of regulated companies is provided at $.50 per page. Their *Annual Report* includes filings and description of proceedings.

Kansas

Director of Public Affairs, Corporation Commission, Utilities Division, 1500 S.W. Arrowhead Rd., Topeka, KS 66604-4027; 913-271-3140. Utilities regulated include: local and long distance telephone, electricity, gas and water, and transportation. Examples of information on file include: annual reports, records of proceedings, current operating tariffs, and rate changes. Information is provided on hard copy. For information between 1-10 pages, the cost is $.10 per copy. Costs decrease as the number of pages increases. Microfilm copies are available at $.25 per page. There is also an additional cost for postage in both cases. The office provides a listing of regulated companies, but the caller must certify that the list will not be used for solicitation purposes.

Kentucky

Public Service Commission, 730 Schenkel Lane, Box 615, Frankfort, KY 40601; 502-564-3940. This office regulates local and long distance telephone, WATS re-sellers, radio common carriers, cellular telephone, electricity, gas, water, sewage, and coin operated telephones. Annual reports, tariffs, and applications for changes are all kept on file. There is a charge of $.10 a page for printed copies of information and $.50 for older information on microfilm. Postage is extra. A listing of regulated companies is free. Publications include a monthly *Public Service Commission Update Listing* which lists all cases filed, hearings, and decisions. It is available for an annual fee of $63.60.

Louisiana

Secretary of the Commission, Public Service Commission, One American Place, Suite 1630, Baton Rouge, LA 70825; 504-342-4416. This office regulates: local, long distance, and cellular telephone; long distance facility-based carriers, electricity, gas, water, sewage, and transportation. Information on file includes: current operating tariffs, financial information, rate changes and service reliability reports. A listing of regulated companies is available free. Copies of information are provided at $.25 per page. Transcription hearings are $1 per page.

Be patient. If any phone number is incorrect, call (area code) 555-1212 and request the new listing.

671

Information on People, Companies, and Mailing Lists

Maine

Mary Broad, Public Utilities Commission, 242 State Street, Station 18, Augusta, ME 04333-0018; 207-289-3831. Regulated utilities include local exchange telephone, re-sellers, electricity, gas, and water. Annual reports, financial statements, and transfer of stock or rate changes are all kept on file. Hard copies of information are provided at $.20 per page. The office provides a listing of regulated companies, free of charge. Other publications available include: *Monthly Docket*, $10 semiannually; *Weekly Agenda*, $12 semiannually; and copies of all orders and decisions, $73 semiannually.

Maryland

Director of Consumer Assistance and Public Affairs, Public Service Commission, The American Building, 231 E. Baltimore St., Baltimore, MD 21202; 301-333-6028. Utilities regulated include: gas, electricity, and some privately owned water and sewer companies. The office provides financial information, annual reports, rate changes and tariff information. Information is provided on hard copy. The office charges $.20 per page plus postage. A listing of regulated companies is also available at $.20 per page. The state's transportation division regulates trucking, buses and taxi cabs.

Massachusetts

Secretary of the Department of Public Utilities, Department of Public Utilities, Leverett Saltonstall Building, Government Center, 100 Cambridge St., 12th Floor, Boston, MA 02202; 617-727-3500. Utilities regulated include: trucks, buses, and railroad; gas, water and voluntary holding companies for electricity, telecommunications, and pipeline engineering and safety. Examples of information on file include: annual reports and financial statements, service reliability reports, tariff information and rate changes. Information is provided on hard copy at $.20 per page. A listing of regulated companies is available at $.10 per page. Their last annual report was published in 1989.

Michigan

Executive Secretary, Public Service Commission of the Department of Commerce, P.O. Box 30221, Lansing, MI 48909; 517-334-6445. Utilities regulated include: local and long distance telephone, electricity, gas and water, and transportation. This office keeps records on tariffs, annual reports, audit information, and filings to the commission. Hard copies of information and microfilm are $.05 per page. There is an additional charge for research services. A listing of regulated companies is provided, also at $.05 per page. Individuals may subscribe to listings of orders, agendas, and minutes; fees vary. Their *Annual Report* is free.

Minnesota

Department of Public Service, Public Utilities Commission, 780 American Center Building, 150 E. Kellogg Blvd., St. Paul, MN 55101; 612-296-7124. The commission regulates: local and inter-LATA telephone, pay telephone, electricity, and gas. Information on file includes: annual financial reports, current operating tariffs, and case files. The staff will provide hard copies of information at $.25 per page. A listing of regulated companies is also available at $.25 per page. The Commission also publishes a *Biennial Report* and summary of hearings.

Mississippi

Public Service Commission, P.O. Box 1174, Jackson, MS 39215-1174; 601-961-5400. Utilities regulated include: land-line telephone, radio common carriers, some personal paging systems, WATS re-sellers, interstate telephone, electricity, gas, water, and sewer. Annual reports, tariffs, financial information, and proceedings before the commission are all on file. Information provided on hard copy is $.50 per page. A case-tracking system was implemented in 1990 and is now being expanded. The commission provides a listing of regulated companies at $.50 per page.

Missouri

Secretary of the Commission, Public Service Commission, P.O. Box 360, Jefferson City, MO 65102; 314-751-7494. The commission regulates: local telephone, inter-exchange facility-based carriers, inter-exchange re-sellers, pay telephones, and privately owned electricity, gas, water, and sewer companies. Information on file includes: applications, financial information, complaints, annual reports, current operating tariffs and rate changes. Information is available on hard copy and some records are computerized. The office can perform some custom searches; charges vary. Copying costs are $.30 per page and $1 for certified copies. Transcripts are $.25 per page. The office also provides a listing of regulated companies, free of charge. Other publications include: the weekly *Tariff Filing Docket*, which lists tariff matters. This is available for $24 per year. The commission also publishes a free *Weekly Docket* which lists upcoming hearings.

Montana

Public Service Commission, 1701 Prospect Ave., Helena, MT 59620-2601; 406-444-6199. The utilities regulated by the commission include: local and long distance telephone, electricity, water and sewer, gas, and intra-state oil pipeline. Information on file includes annual reports, special reports, rules, regulations, rate increases and current operating tariffs. Information is available both on hard copy and microfilm. The charge is $.30 per page if the staff does the research, and $.15 per page if the requestor does the research. The commission also provides a listing of regulated companies, free of charge.

Nebraska

Public Service Commission, 300 the Atrium, 1200 N St., P.O. Box 94927, Lincoln, NE 68509; 402-471-3101. Utilities regulated include: local and long-distance telephone and motor carriers, and railroads to some extent. Information on file includes: annual reports, financial information, tariffs, and proceedings of hearings. The office charges $.25 per page for copying information. Transcripts of hearings are $.50 per page. A listing of regulated companies is available, free of charge. Other publications include their free annual *Legislative Report*.

Nevada

Public Information Officer, Public Service Commission, Capitol Complex, 727 Fairview Drive, Carson City, NV 89710; 702-687-6082. Utilities regulated include: electricity, gas, telephone, water and sewer, various motor carriers, and railroad transportation. Examples of information on file include: annual reports, insurance and operating certificates, current operating tariffs and rate changes. The commission provides copies of microfilmed and printed information for $.25 per page. It also provides a listing of regulated companies sorted alphabetically and by utility at no charge. Other free publications include a *Biennial Report and Transportation Quarterly Newsletter*.

New Hampshire

Executive Director, Public Utilities Commission, 8 Old Suncook Rd., Concord, NH 03301; 603-271-2431. Utilities regulated include: gas, electricity, telephone, sewer, water, and steam. Examples of information on file include: service reliability, financial information, records of responsiveness and responsibility, tariff information, and changes in rates. Information printouts are $.50 per page. A listing of regulated companies is also available at $.50 per page. The office also publishes a *Biennial Report for the Legislature*.

New Jersey

Sharon Schulman, Director of Public Information, Board of Public Regulatory Commissioners, CN 350, Trenton, NJ 08625; 609-777-3303. Utilities regulated include: electricity, gas, water, sewer, cable television, and telephone. Examples of information on file include: tariff information, annual reports on revenue, expenses, and capitalization. Information on hard copy is $1 per page. Annual reports are computerized. A listing of regulated companies is available at $1 per page. Other publications available include: *Case File Report*, published weekly. The cost is $120 per year. A bi-monthly report of the commission's agenda is also available.

New Mexico

Records Office, Public Service Commission, 224 E. Palace Ave., Santa Fe, NM 87501-2013; 505-827-6940. Utilities regulated include: Gas, electricity, water, and sewer. Examples of information on file include: tariffs, annual reports, and hearing proceedings. Information is available on hard copy or microfilm. A listing of regulated companies is available at $.15 per page.

New York

Central Files, Public Service Commission, 3 Empire State Plaza, Albany, NY 12223; 518-474-7080. This office regulates private and some state utilities including: water, gas, electricity, and telephone. The office keeps annual reports, financial statements, performance material, rate changes, and current operating tariffs on file. Copies of information can be obtained at $.25 per page. Requests must be of a reasonable size. Older records are on microfilm. The office provides a list of regulated companies, free of charge. Other publications include: *Financial Statistics of Major Utilities*, $10; *Public Service Commission Reports*, $125; and *The Weekly Bulletin*, $20.

North Carolina

Chief Clerk's Office, Utilities Commission, Box 29510, Raleigh, NC 27626-0510; 919-733-0839. Utilities regulated include: electricity, telephone, gas, water, and sewer, transportation, and radio common carriers. The office keeps records of annual reports, applications, rates, current operating tariffs and comments from orders issued. Hard copies of information are $.20/page. Transcriptions of testimony is $1/page. The office will also provide a listing of regulated companies at $.20 per page. Other publications available include: *North Carolina Public Utilities Law Book--Rules and Regulations*, $30, and *Orders and Decisions*, $60.

North Dakota

Secretary of the Commission, Public Service Commission, 12th Floor, State Capitol, Bismark, ND 58505; 701-224-2400. The commission regulates: electricity, gas, telephone, and transportation. Information on file includes annual reports, financial information, current operating tariffs, and rate case information. The staff will provide hard copy and microfilm information. The first ten pages copied are free, additional copies are $.10 per page. There are also additional charges if research is performed.

Ohio

Fiscal Office, Public Utilities Commission, 180 E. Broad St., Columbus, OH 43266-0573; 614-466-3016. Utilities regulated include: heating and cooling through pipes or tubing, inter-urban railroad, water transportation through pipelines, sewage, electricity, natural gas, railroad, water works, and telephone. Annual reports, current operating tariffs, and rate changes are on file. Hard copies of information are $1 for the first page and $.10 for each subsequent page. Copies of microfilm are $.35 per page. The office does provide a listing of regulated companies, also at $.35 per page. Other publications available include: the *Commission Meeting Agenda, Commission Rules and Regulations and the Yearly Calendar*, all available through subscription.

Oklahoma

Office Manager, Oklahoma Corporation Commission, Public Utilities Division, Room 500, Jim Thorpe Office Building, Oklahoma City, OK 73105; 405-521-3908. The commission regulates utilities divisions including: electricity, gas, telephone, water, and cotton gins. Information on file includes all information connected with case hearings or filing, current operating tariffs, annual reports, audit reports, and applications. Copies of information can be obtained for $.25 per page or $10 per document. The office also provides a listing of regulated companies that is available for $.25 per page. Each utility division has recodified their rules and regulations. These are available in separate reports for $10 each. An *Annual Report* is also available.

Oregon

Public Information Office, Public Utilities Commission, 550 Capitol St., NE., Salem, OR 97310-1380; 503-378-5849. The commission regulates investor owned utilities including: gas, water, electricity and telephone; trucking, and railroad safety. Examples of information on file include: financial and operational information, current operating tariffs, rate changes and service reliability. The staff will copy information for $.25 for the first 10 pages and $.10 per each additional page. The commission also provides a free listing of regulated companies. Other free publications available include: general information pamphlets, fax sheets, and a public involvement guide.

Pennsylvania

Public Utilities Commission, P.O. Box 3265, Harrisburg, PA 17105-3265; 717-783-1740. The commission regulates gas, electricity, water, sewer, communications, and transportation utilities. Information on file includes: annual reports, updated tariff information, rate changes, financial information and other periodic reports. The office provides hard copies of records at $.75 per page. Records are computerized and customized searches are available on a limited basis. The office will also provide you with a listing of regulated companies at $.75 per page.

Rhode Island

Commission Clerk's Office, Public Utilities Commission, 100 Orange St., Providence, RI 02903; 401-277-3500. Utilities regulated include: gas, electricity, telephone, water, sewer, cable television, and trucking. Information on file includes: annual reports, materials from rate hearings, rate changes, current operating tariffs and complaints. Individuals can receive hard copies of information at $.25 per page.

South Carolina

Executive Director, Public Service Commission, 111 Doctor's Circle, P.O. Drawer 11649, Columbia, SC 29211; 803-737-5135. This office regulates gas, electricity, telecommunications, water and waste water, and transportation. Records on file include: quarterly financial reports, rate-of-return, sales, cost information, rate changes, and current operating tariffs. Hard copies of information are $.25 per page. Regulated companies are listed within the commission's *Annual Report*, which is $5. The office also publishes *Rules and Regulations*, which is also $5.

South Dakota

Public Utilities Commission, 500 E. Capital Avenue, Pierre, SD 57501; 605-773-3201. The commission regulates telephone, electricity, and gas utilities; transportation, warehouses, and elevators. Information on file includes: current operating tariffs, rate changes and various financial information. The staff will copy requested information at $.25 per page. A listing of regulated companies is available

at no charge. Other free publications include an *Annual Report.* and various consumer guide pamphlets such as *Energy Efficient Appliances, Rate Changes, Lower Phone Bills Made Easy*, and *Pulling the Plug*.

Tennessee

Public Utilities Commission, 460 James Robertson Pky., Nashville, TN 37243-0505; 615-741-2125. Utilities regulated include: transportation, water/sewer, electricity, gas, and telephone. Information on file includes: annual reports, rate and tariff information, ad valorem tax reports, financial records, and service reliability reports. The staff will provide hard copies of information at $.25 per page. Copies of microfilm are $2.50 per page or $1.50 per page if the customer does the work, himself. Transcripts are $1.50 per page. Customized searches are available with an additional charge for computer time. The office also provides a free listing of regulated companies. Other publications include a free *Annual Report* and *Agenda of Cases*.

Texas

Public Utility Commission, 7800 Shoal Creek Blvd., Austin, TX 78757; 512-458-0100. The commission regulates the following utilities: electricity, local telephone, and AT&T long distance telephone. Examples of information on file include: annual reports, financial information, tariff information, and transcripts of commission hearings. The office provides information on both hard copy and microfilm. The staff will copy up to 50 pages of information for free. The cost is $.85 for the following page and $.15 for each additional page. The office also provides a listing of regulated companies for $5, each. Other publications available include: news releases, new filings, and agendas. The office also provides annual reports for the electric and telephone divisions. They are sold for $10 each. *Substantive Rules* is a loose-leaf edition of all rules issued by the commission and is available for $25 per year.

Utah

Public Service Commission, 160 East 300 South, Salt Lake City, UT 84111; 801-530-6716. Utilities regulated include: electricity, gas, water, transportation (including trucking and railroad), telephone, and steam heat companies. Annual reports, complaints, petitions, and requests for agency action are kept on file. Hard copy and microfilm for older records are available for $.50 per page. A listing of regulated companies is available at no charge. An *Annual Report* is also available, free of charge.

Vermont

Public Service Board, 120 State St., Montpelier, VT 05620-2701; 802-828-2358. Utilities regulated include: gas, electricity, telephone, water, and cable television. The office has information on file including: proceedings, tariff information, annual reports, informal complaints, rate changes, and special contracts. Information on hard copy and microfilm are available for $.10 per page. They will also provide a listing of regulated companies, free of charge. Other publications include *Board Decisions*, which is available through a monthly subscription. Specific information can be obtained at $.10 per page.

Virginia

Division of Energy Regulation, State Corporation Commission, P.O. Box 1197, Richmond, VA 23209; 804-786-3611. The commission regulates electricity, gas, water, and sewer. Telephone is regulated by the communications division. Examples of information on file include: financial information, transmission applications, and annual operating reports that include credit information, sales volumes and operating expenses. Individuals can receive information on hard copy for $2 for the first two pages and $.50 for each additional page. An *Annual Report* is also available. The price of the report is dependent upon production costs and varies.

Washington

Public Utilities and Transportation Commission, P.O. Box 47250, 1300 S. Evergreen Park Dr. SW, Olympia, WA 98504-7250; 206-753-6423. Utilities regulated include: electricity, telephone, telecommunications, water, gas, and transportation. Balance sheets and annual reports are kept on file. Copies of information is available at $.20 per page. A free listing of regulated companies is available upon completion of a public request form. Individuals may subscribe to reports such as the *Transportation Docket*, at $43.16 per year and the *Utilities Docket* at $77.69 per year.

West Virginia

Public Service Commission, P.O. Box 812, Charleston, WV 25323; 304-340-0300. Utilities regulated include: telecommunications, gas, water, sewer, railroad, electricity, gas pipelines, and motor carriers. Information on file includes: annual reports, financial statements, current operating tariffs, service reliability, rate changes and sales volumes. Copied and microfilmed information is available at $.20 per page.

Be patient. If any phone number is incorrect, call (area code) 555-1212 and request the new listing.

673

Information on People, Companies, and Mailing Lists

Wisconsin

Public Service Commission, P.O. Box 7854, Madison, WI 53707-7854; 608-267-7915. Utilities regulated include: gas, electricity, telephone, water, and sewer. The commission keeps annual reports, tariffs, rate changes and regulations on file. Copies of information and a listing of regulated companies can be obtained at $.15 per page. Each utility publishes an annual report. The same copying charges apply as listed above.

Wyoming

Public Service Commission, Herschler Building, 700 W. 21st St., Cheyenne, WY 82002; 307-777-7427. Utilities regulated include: electricity, gas, pipelines, telephone, telegraph, radio common carriers, water, railroad, and motor carriers. Information on file includes: rates, conditions of service, contracts, and financial conditions. A directory of regulated companies is $2. A report, *Rules and Regulations*, is $5.

Be patient. If any phone number is incorrect, call (area code) 555-1212 and request the new listing.

Weights and Measures

Looking for a mailing list of all delicatessens in the state? This office is likely to have it for you. The same is true for any other organization which uses a scale for commercial purposes, including gas stations, pharmacies, and dairies.

Every time you buy a half pound of corned beef or gas up the car, you rely on the accuracy of the scale behind the counter or meter on the pump. These and thousands of other measuring devices are used with confidence every day by businesses and consumers, most never questioning the accuracy of the information. Who then is charged with making sure a pound is a pound and an inch an inch?

All commercial measuring devices are regularly inspected by agents of your state office of weights and measures. In addition, such offices are the official keepers of state standards of mass, length, and volume traceable to those maintained by the National Institute of Standards and Technology (formerly the National Bureau of Standards).

These offices are staffed by professionals who can answer questions as simple a child's homework assignment or as complicated as determining the best method of sale for a particular commodity. Many types of businesses rely on the expertise of these offices: defense industries, scale companies, and store-front businesses such as fabric shops, railroads, feed stores, and so on.

In general, most agents of a state office of weights and measures conduct on-site inspections of equipment at commercial businesses and manufacturing plants, ensuring that measuring devices are being used correctly and are being maintained so as to ensure their accuracy. Investigators also inspect scales used to weigh trucks and other vehicles used for transporting goods from factory or farm to market. Among the measuring devices inspected on a regular basis are: gasoline and air pumps, gas storage tanks, dairies, truck scales, pharmacy scales, and those used by commercial businesses.

The offices also field and investigate numerous complaints, most questioning the accuracy of fuel pumps. State agents also enforce standards of the Fair Packaging and Labeling Act. This law, passed by Congress in 1966, standardized the packaging and labeling of products so that they are packaged in containers of approximate similar size and labeled so as not to mislead.

Virtually every commercial transaction involves the use of weights and measures, so the state files are extensive. Given the number of transactions, even a slight measurement error can add up to thousands of dollars. Most state offices will provide business addresses and the type and capacity of measuring devices owned by companies on their files.

The following is a listing of state offices of weights and measures.

Weights and Measures Offices

Alabama
Weights and Measures Division, Alabama Department of Agriculture and Industry, P.O. Box 3336, Montgomery, AL 36109-0336; 205-242-2613. This agency will provide listings of licensed warehouses, free of charge. The listings are categorized by type, and include cotton gins, and cattle and grain warehouses.

Alaska
Division of Measurement Standards, 12050 Industrial Way, Huffman Business Park, Business Park Building, 99515; 907-345-7750. No listings of inspected businesses are provided.

Arizona
Jeffrey Gonscher, Deputy Chief, Arizona Weights and Measures Division, 1951 W. North Lane, Phoenix, AZ 85021; 602-255-5211. A computer listing of licensed businesses is $48. Requests must be in writing.

Arkansas
Acting Director, James Michael Hile, Bureau of Standards, Division of Weights and Measures, 4608 West 61st Street, Little Rock, AR 72209; 501-562-7605. A listing of licensed scale operators is available. The division also prints an annual report. Both publications are free.

California
Darrell A. Guensler, Acting Assistant Director, Division of Measurement Standards, California Department of Food and Agriculture, 8500 Fruitridge Rd., Sacramento, CA 95826; 916-366-5119. No listings of inspected businesses are provided.

Colorado
David Wallace, Chief, Measurement Standard Securities, Department of Agriculture, 3125 Wyandot, Denver, CO 80211; 303-866-2845. No listings of inspected businesses are provided.

Connecticut
Department of Consumer Protection, State Office Building, Room G17, 165 Capitol Ave., Hartford, CT 06106; 203-566-5230. This office inspects commercial and industrial scales, licenses retail gas stations and oversees motor fuel registration. They will release a listing of licensed businesses. Prices vary, according to the length of the list.

Delaware
Eugene Keeley, Supervisor, Office of Weights and Measures, Department of Agriculture, 2320 South Dupont Hwy., Dover, DE 19901; 302-739-4811. No listings of inspected businesses are provided.

District of Columbia
Department of Consumer and Regulatory Affairs, Weights, Measures and Markets Division, 1110 U. St., SE, Washington, DC 20020; 202-767-7923. No listings of inspected businesses are provided.

Florida
Maxwell Gray, Chief, Bureau of Weights and Measures, Department of Agriculture and Consumer Services, 3125 Conner Blvd., Lab 2, Tallahassee, FL 32399-1650; 904-488-9140. This office will provide lists of tests reports. Costs vary according to the size of the request.

Georgia
Martin Coile, Director, Weights and Measures Laboratory, Atlanta Farmers Market, 16 Forest Parkway, Forest Park GA 30050; 404-363-7685. Licensed scale companies are available for a nominal fee.

Hawaii
George E. Mattimore, Administrator, Measurement Standards, Department of Agriculture, 725 Ilelo St., Honolulu, HI 96813; 808-586-0886. Licensed scale companies are provided free to the public.

Be patient. If any phone number is incorrect, call (area code) 555-1212 and request the new listing.

675

Information on People, Companies, and Mailing Lists

Idaho
Glen Jex, Chief, Bureau of Weights and Measures, Department of Agriculture, 2216 Kellogg Lane, Boise, ID 83712; 208-334-2345. Individual test reports of specific companies can be obtained. There is no charge involved.

Illinois
Rebecca Doyle, Weights and Measures Program Manager, Bureau of Product Inspection and Standards, Department of Agriculture, P.O. Box 19281, 801 Sangamon Ave., Springfield, IL 62794-9281; 217-782-3817. Lists of licensed or inspected businesses are released at the discretion of the agency's Freedom of Information Act officer. Put requests for information in writing, be as specific as possible, and include the purpose of your request. The agency will then respond with a decision and cost of the list.

Indiana
Sharon Rhoades, Director of Weights and Measures, State Board of Health, 1330 West Michigan St., Indianapolis, IN 46206; 317-633-0350. No listings of inspected businesses are provided.

Iowa
Gerald Bane, Supervisor, Weights and Measures Division, Department of Agriculture and Land Stewardship, Henry A. Wallace Building, Des Moines, IA 50319; 515-281-5794. This office will provide a listings of inspected and licensed businesses. There is a $12 set-up fee and additional charge of $.01 per line. Information provided through the basis list includes the company's license, county and location. A master list is also available with more detailed information.

Kansas
Larry Woodson, Division of Inspections, Kansas State Board of Agriculture, 7th Fl, 901 S. Kansas Ave, Topeka, KS 66612-1272; 913-296-3511. This agency will release certain business addresses of companies that they keep on file. Individuals must place their request in writing and then complete an open records request form certifying that the information they obtain will not be used for commercial gain. Once approved, lists of information is $.35 per page.

Kentucky
Danny Willis, Director, Division of Weights and Measures, Department of Agriculture, 106 West Second St., Frankfort, KY 40601; 502-564-4870. Copies of individual company inspection reports are filed by county and are $.10 per page. Requests must be made in writing.

Louisiana
Ronald Harold, Director, Louisiana Weights and Measures, Department of Agriculture, P.O. Box 3098, Baton Rouge, LA 70821; 504-925-3780. No listings of inspected businesses are provided.

Maine
Clayton F. Davis, Director, Agriculture Inspections Division, Division of Regulation, Stationhouse 28, Augusta, ME 04333; 207-289-3841. At the present time Maine is not computerized and does not release listings of licensed businesses.

Maryland
Louis Straub, Chief, Weights and Measures Section, Department of Agriculture, 50 Harry S. Truman Parkway, Annapolis, MD 21401; 410-841-5790. No listings of inspected businesses are provided.

Massachusetts
Steven Berard, Supervising Inspector, Massachusetts Division of Standards, One Ashburton Place, Room 1115, Boston, MA 02108; 617-727-3480. This agency provides printouts of various licensed business including: gas stations, body shops with repair licenses, indoor vendors and auctioneers. Lists are $25, each. Please make your request in writing and include a check made out to the Commonwealth of Massachusetts.

Michigan
Edward Heffron, Chief, Food Division, Department of Agriculture, 611 W. Ottawa, Box 30017, Lansing, MI 48909; 517-373-1060. Individuals can receive printouts of licensed businesses for $.04 per page plus a base rate of $17.98 per hour. Lists are sorted by county.

Minnesota
Michael Blacik, Director, Division of Weights and Measures, State of Minnesota, Department of Public Service, 2277 Highway 36, St. Paul, MN 55113; 612-639-4010. No listings of inspected businesses are provided.

Mississippi
William P. Eldridge, Director, Weights and Measures Division, Mississippi Department of Agriculture and Commerce, 1603 Walter Sillers Building, P.O. Box 1609, Jackson, MS 39215-1609; 601-354-7077. No listings of inspected businesses are provided.

Missouri
Lester Barrows, Director, Weights and Measures Division, Department of Agriculture, P.O. Box 630, Jefferson City, MO 65102; 314-751-4278. This agency provides various computer listings of businesses sorted by category. Requests should be in writing. Costs vary depending upon the type of information requested.

Montana
Jim Kimball, Division Chief, Bureau of Weights and Measures, Department of Commerce, Capitol Station, Helena, MT 59620; 406-444-3164. No listings of inspected businesses are provided.

Nebraska
Steven A. Malone, Director, Division of Weights and Measures, Department of Agriculture, State Office Building, 301 Centennial Mall South, Lincoln, NE 68509; 402-471-4292. No listings of inspected businesses are provided.

Nevada
William McCrea, Chief Deputy State Sealer, Bureau of Weights and Measures, Department of Agriculture, P.O. Box 11100, Reno, NV 89510-1100; 702-688-1166. This agency will provide listings of inspected businesses on file. Costs range from $60 to $100.

New Hampshire
Mike Grenier, Director, Bureau of Weights and Measures, Department of Agriculture, P.O Box 2042, Concord, NH 03302-2042; 603-271-3700. No business listings are provided.

New Jersey
William J. Wolfe, State Superintendent, State Office of Weights and Measures, 1261 Rts. 1 ad 9 South, Evenel, NJ 07701; 908-815-4840. No business listings are provided.

New Mexico
Gary D. West, Chief, Standards and Consumer Services, Department of Agriculture, Department 3170, P.O. Box 30005, Las Cruces, NM 88003; 505-646-1616. No business listings are provided.

New York
John J. Bartfai, Director, Bureau of Weights and Measures, Department of Agriculture, Building 7-A State Campus 1220 Washington Ave., Albany, NY 12235; 518-457-3452. No business listings are provided.

North Carolina
David N. Smith, Director, Consumer Standards Division, Department of Agriculture, P.O. Box 27647, Raleigh, NC 27611; 919-733-3313. Listings of registered scale technicians such as petroleum dispensers or gasoline station owners are available for $10, each. The agency is working on a listing of licensed businesses and will provide you with their most up-to-date copy upon request. Requests should be placed in writing and be accompanied by a check made out to the North Carolina Department of Agriculture.

North Dakota
Al Moch, Director, North Dakota Public Service Commission, Department of Weights and Measures, State Capitol, 12th Floor, Bismarck, ND 58505; 701-224-2400. The agency does not provide listings on a regular basis,

Ohio
John J. Steinberger, Jr., Chief, Division of Weights and Measures, Ohio Department of Agriculture, 8995 East Main St., Reynoldsburg, OH 43068; 614-866-6361. This agency does provide a listing of businesses licensed through their office. The cost is $.25 per page.

Oklahoma
Charles Carter, Program Administrator, Bureau of Standards, Oklahoma Department of Agriculture, 2800 North Lincoln Blvd., Oklahoma City, OK 73105-4298; 405-521-3864, Ext 261. Listings of licensed scale companies and standard labeling rules and regulations are provided, free of charge.

Be patient. If any phone number is incorrect, call (area code) 555-1212 and request the new listing.

Oregon
Kendrick J. Simila, Administrator, Measures Standard Division, Dept. of Agriculture, 635 Capitol St., NE, Salem, OR 97310-0110; 503-378-3792. The agency will provide a listing of licensed businesses. There is a $25 minimum charge.

Pennsylvania
Neil Cashman, Director, Bureau of Standard Weights and Measures, Department of Agriculture, 2301 North Cameron St., Harrisburg, PA 17110; 717-787-6772. Listings of businesses are not provided.

Rhode Island
Lynda Agresti Maurer, Sealer of Weights and Measures, Department of Labor, Division of Professional Regulations, 220 Elmwood Ave., Providence, RI 02907; 401-457-1863. Listings of businesses are not provided.

South Carolina
Carol Fulmer, Director, Weights and Measures, Department of Agriculture, P.O. Box 11280, Consumer Services Division, Columbia, SC 29211; 803-734-2210. This office does maintain a listing of registered businesses. Although prices vary, lists are at least $1 per page.

South Dakota
Mike Kumm, Director, Division of Consumer Inspection, Office of Weights and Measures, 118 West Capitol Ave., Pierre, SD 57501; 605-773-3697. Listings of businesses are not provided.

Tennessee
Bob Williams, Administrator, Director, Weights and Measures, Department of Agriculture, Box 40627, Nashville, TN 37204; 615-360-0159. Listings of businesses are not provided.

Texas
Ed Price, Supervisor of Weights and Measures, Department of Agriculture, Box 12847, Stephen F. Austin Bldg., Austin, TX 78711; 512-463-7530. This agency supplies listings of inspected businesses sorted by category. Requests should be placed in writing. The cost is $.05 per name for the first 1,000 and $.05 for every name thereafter.

Utah
Edison J. Stephens, Deputy Commissioner, Division of Weights and Measures, State Department of Agriculture, 350 North Redwood Road, Salt Lake City, UT 84116; 801-538-7159. All licensed businesses must register with the state's corporation office. Information is kept on a city by city basis and listings of licensed businesses are not normally released.

Vermont
Bruce Martell, Director, Division of Weights and Measures and Retail Inspection, Department of Agriculture, Food and Markets, Consumer Assurance Section, 120 State St., Montpelier, VT 05620-2901; 802-828-2436. This office can supply individuals with copies of retail outlets. Copies of information are $.08 per page. Requests should be placed in writing.

Virginia
Kermit Spruill, Director, Weights and Measures Section, Department of Agriculture and Consumer Services, 1100 Banks St., Room 402, Richmond, VA 23209; 804-786-2476. Business listings are not provided.

Washington
Mike Willis, Assistant Supervisor, Department of Agriculture, Office of Weights and Measures, Consumer and Producer Protection Division, P.O. Box 42560, Olympia, WA 93504; 206-753-5042. Business listings are not provided.

West Virginia
Stephen L. Casto, Director, Division of Weights and Measures, Department of Labor, 570 W. McCorkle Ave., St. Albans, WV 25177; 304-727-5781. Business listings are not provided.

Wisconsin
Alan Porter, Program Manager, Bureau of Weights and Measures, Wisconsin Department of Agriculture, Trade and Consumer Protection, Box 8911, Madison, WI 53708; 608-266-2295. Business listings are not provided.

Wyoming
Jim Bigelow, Manager, Consumer/Compliance Division, Department of Agriculture, 2219 Carey Ave., Cheyenne, WY 82002; 307-777-6591. This office will provide a listing of licensed businesses at $.10 per page.

Information on People, Companies, and Mailing Lists

Insurance Companies and Salesmen

An insurance company wants to compare their rates to those of their competitors. A software company with a new time saving product needs the names of all the 1,500 insurance companies in Minnesota for a mailing list. Someone shopping for auto insurance wants to see sample policies from five different insurance companies in her area before she makes a final decision. A prospective insurance buyer wants to know how many complaints have been lodged against a certain company before he signs on the dotted line. All of this information and more can be found at the State Insurance Offices.

Although the kinds of information available at each of these offices varies from state to state, all except Colorado and Hawaii have listings of the insurance companies in their state, and only nine states--Arkansas, Georgia, Hawaii, Louisiana, Maryland, Montana, New York, Texas, and Washington--do not compile comprehensive listings of the in-state insurance agents. About thirty states will provide you with these listings in the form of a computer printout and/or mailing labels. California, Indiana, and Kansas also offer these listings on computer tape or diskettes.

Most state offices also handle consumer complaints and make their findings available to the public. Illinois, for example, not only compiles a "Complaint Rating List" that will tell you the number of complaints filed against a company, they also calculate "Complaint Ratios," which show the number of complaints versus the amount of insurance a company writes. If a company writes 100 policies and has 20 complaints, chances are you shouldn't buy a policy from them. But these "Complaint Ratios" can also be used by insurance companies to find out which of their competitors' policies produce the highest number of complaints. This is invaluable information for a company that plans to sell a new type of policy and wants a market study.

When a company wants to sell certain commercial or personal lines of insurance, they must file the policy forms and endorsements at the state office. Individuals can request copies of these policies before they make a purchase to compare rates from one company to another. Some states, in fact, publish *Premium Comparison Manuals* for personal auto and homeowner's policies. For the rate charts listed in these manuals, each insurance company must take the same policy situation, such as a three bedroom house or a twenty-seven year-old driver, and prepare a rate estimate for an insurance policy.

Some state offices also require insurance companies to file their *Rate Manuals* which show their brokers how to estimate their company's insurance premiums. These are valuable sources of information for both the consumer and competitor. And if you are interested in looking into a company's history--when it was first licensed, owners and former owners--many state offices can furnish you with that information, too.

Insurance Divisions

Alabama
Insurance Department, 135 S. Union St., Montgomery, AL 36130; 205-269-3550. Insurance Companies Documents on File: Available for $1 a page plus mailing costs from Blue Print Services, P.O. Box 1383, Montgomery, AL 36109; 205-263-4865. Listing of Insurance Companies: *Annual Report* (List of all licensed insurance companies) is available at no charge. Number of Licensed Insurance Companies: 1,300. Licensed Agents. Listing of Agents: Published yearly and available at no cost. Listing does not contain addresses. Number of Licensed Agents: Available for a fee.

Alaska
Insurance Division, Department of Commerce and Economic Development, PO Box 110805, Juneau, AK 99811-0805; 907-465-2515. Insurance Companies Documents on File: Cost recovery basis. Listing of Insurance Companies: Available for $25. Number of Licensed Insurance Companies: 1,058. Licensed Agents. List of Agents: Available for $25. Number of Agents: 4,800.

Arizona
Insurance Department, 3030 N. 3rd Street, Suite 1100, Phoenix, AZ 85014; 602-255-5367. Insurance Companies Documents on File: Available for 50 cents per page. Requests must be submitted in writing. Listing of Insurance Companies: Contained in *Annual Report*, which is published yearly. Cost is $16.50. Prepayment required, 602-255-5605. Number of Licensed Insurance Companies: 2,540. Licensed Agents. List of Agents: A computer printout is available by line of insurance. Cost is 3 cents a name. Average cost is $400. 602-255-5605. Number of Agents: 60,000.

Arkansas
Insurance Department, 1123 S. University, STE-400, Little Rock, AR 72204; 501-686-2900. Insurance Companies Documents on File: Available for $1 a page. Licensed Agents. List of Agents: Not Available. Number of Agents: 31,000.

California
Insurance Department, Business, Transportation and Housing Agency, 3450 Wilshire Blvd, Los Angeles, CA 90010; 213-736-3582, 800-927-4357 (in state) Insurance Companies Documents on File: Annual/Quarterly Statements are available to public at a cost of 50 cents per page plus sales tax up to four pages, then an outside copy service must be brought in. There is a one dollar fee per document certification. Listing of Insurance Companies: Lists are available, either in printout format (Cheshire labels) or magnetic tape format. Cost for list of all admitted companies is $40. Other lists, including breakdowns of different classes of insurance carriers or license types are also available at prices ranging from approximately $350 to $800. Interested parties should contact the Department's Electronic Data Processing Bureau, at 916-323-5171 to request an order form. Number of Licensed Insurance Companies: 1,344. Licensed Agents. List of Agents: Available by calling 916-322-3555. Number of Agents: 110,000. Send written request to: Dept. of Insurance, Attn: Lucy Chavez, 700 L. St., 3rd Floor, Sacramento, CA 95140. Fee: $1,067 + postage and handling.

Colorado
Insurance Division, 1560 Broadway, Suite 850, Denver, CO 80202; 303-894-7499. Insurance Companies Documents on File: Available to the public for 25 cents per page or $6.50 for each list sorted by line of Insurance, but a visit to the office is necessary. Listing of Insurance Companies: A current listing is not available. Number of Licensed Companies: 1,786. Licensed Agents. List of Agents: Available by calling 303-894-7495. Lists are sorted by line of insurance and the cost is $100 a list. Number of Agents: 38,000.

Connecticut
Insurance Department, 153 Market St., Hartford, CT 06103; 203-297-3800. Insurance Companies Documents on File: A visit to the office is necessary to copy documents. Listing of Insurance Companies: List is printed twice a year and is available for $10.75. All requests must be submitted in writing and be prepaid. Number of Licensed Companies: 1,000. Licensed Agents. List of Agents: Lists are available by calling 203-297-3841. Lists are sorted by authority, company, and locality. Cost of each list is $318. Number of Agents: Not available.

Delaware

Insurance Department, 841 Silver Lake Blvd, Dover, DE 19901; 302-739-4251. Insurance Companies Documents on File: Documents are available. Cost is 25 cents per page or $15.50 for listing. Listing of Insurance Companies: Cheshire or pressure sensitive labels are available for $75. Computer printouts are available on a cost recovery basis. Number of Insurance Companies: 1,400. Licensed Agents. List of Agents: Available by contacting 302-739-4251. Number of Agents: 8,000.

District of Columbia

Insurance Administration, Dept. of Consumer and Regulatory Affairs Dept., P.O. Box 37200, Washington, DC 20013-7200; 202-727-8000. Insurance Companies Documents on File: Documents may be reviewed and copied in the office. Listing of Insurance Companies: A free listing is available. Number of Insurance Companies: Not available. Licensed Agents. List of Agents: No listing available. Number of Licensed Agents: Not available. All requests must be in writing.

Florida

Dept of Insurance Agents and Agent Licensing, 200 E. Gaines, Tallahassee, FL 32399-0300; 904-922-3100. Insurance Companies Documents on File: Copies are available for 50 cents per page and $5 for certified copies. Listing of Insurance Companies: Complimentary copy of *Year List of All Insurance Companies Licensed to Do Business in State of Florida* available upon written request. *Annual Report* also contains listing. Number of Insurance Companies: 1,800. Licensed Agents. List of Agents: List is sorted by type of insurance. They categorize 5 types of adjusters. Computer printouts are available on a cost recovery basis, as are magnetic tape formats and gummed labels. Number of Agents: 169,458.

Georgia

Insurance Commissioner, #2 Martin Luther King Dr., 7th Floor, W. Tower, Atlanta, GA 30334; 404-656-2056. Insurance Companies Documents on File: Annual Statements are available. Listing of Insurance Companies: Computer printouts are available for $30. Number of Insurance Companies: 1,500. Licensed Agents. List of Agents: No list available, 404-656-2100. Number of Agents: 48,000.

Hawaii

Commerce and Consumer Affairs Department, Insurance Division, 250 S. King St., Honolulu, HI 96813; 808-586-2790. Insurance Companies Documents on File: Available for 25 cents per page. List of Insurance Companies: *Commissioner Report* available free of charge. Number of Insurance Companies: 760. Licensed Agents. List of Agents: None available. Number of Agents: 9,670. 808-586-2788.

Idaho

Insurance Department, 500 S. 10th, Boise, ID 83720; 208-334-2250. Insurance Companies Documents on File: Available for 50 cents per page. Listing of Insurance Companies: Company Listing available for $7.50. This order must be prepaid. Number of Insurance Companies: 1,500. Licensed Agents, 208-334-4339. List of Agents: Computer printout available for a fee. Pressure Sensitive labels available for a fee. List and labels can be sorted by line of insurance or ZIP code. Number of Agents: 11,500.

Illinois

Insurance Department, 320 W. Washington St., 4th Floor, Springfield, IL 62767; 217-782-4515. Insurance Companies Documents on File: Available for $1 a page. Listing of Insurance Companies: Annual Statement available quarterly. Computer Information, 217-782-3045: Printout available for $100. Magnetic tape or diskette available for $100. Requester must supply tape or diskette. Pressure sensitive labels can be run on a cost recovery basis if requester supplies labels. Cheshire labels also available on a cost recovery basis, you supply the labels. All computer runs are in ZIP code order. Number of Insurance Companies: 1,813. Licensed Agents. List of Agents: 217-782-3045. Computer printouts available for $100. Magnetic tape or diskette available for $600. Requester must supply tape or diskette. Cheshire labels available for $1,000. All computer runs are in ZIP code order. Number of Agents: 80,000.

Indiana

Insurance Department, 311 W. Washington St., Suite 300, Indianapolis, IN 46204; 317-232-2405. Phone Information: 317-232-2392. Documents on File: Available for 25 cents per page. Listing of Insurance Companies: Monthly computer run available for $25. This listing contains name of company, address, phone number, and type of insurance. Computer generated labels and listings on magnetic tape or diskette will be available in the near future. Number of Insurance Companies: 1,700, 317-232-2410. Licensed Agents. List of Agents: Computer listing will be available in near future. Diskette available for a fee. Number of Agents: 97,000.

Iowa

Commerce Department, Insurance Division, Lucas State Office Building, Des Moines, IA 50319; 515-281-4033. Insurance Companies Documents on File: Documents can be reviewed in the office and may be copied for a minimal charge. Listing of Insurance Companies: Available for $5. Number of Insurance Companies: 1,487. Licensed Agents, 515-281-4039. List of Agents: Computer printout available on a cost recovery basis. Pressure sensitive labels available on a cost recovery basis. Customized listing or labels may be sorted by type of insurance, ZIP Code, county, or company. Number of Agents: 32,170.

Kansas

Kansas Insurance Department, 420 S. West 9th St, Topeka, KS 66612; 913-296-3071. Insurance Companies Documents on File: Documents can be copied on a cost recovery basis. Listing of Insurance Companies: Kansas Insurance Company Directory available free of charge. Listing available on magnetic tape if requester supplies the tape. (Kansas forbids use of public information for solicitation purposes.) Number of Insurance Companies: 1,200. Licensed Agents. List of Agents: Customized lists of agents by company, line of business or location are available on a cost recovery basis, 913-296-7861. Number of Agents: 24,500.

Kentucky

Department of Insurance, PO Box 517, Frankfort, KY 40602; 502-564-3630. Insurance Companies Documents on File: 502-564-6081. Call and then submit written request and prepayment. Annual statements, copies 50 cents per page. Listing of Insurance Companies: Directory available for $150. Pressure sensitive labels available for $150. Number of Insurance Companies: 1,438. Licensed Agents, 502-564-6004. List of Agents: Computer printouts are available in many formats but due to computer limitations no listing of all agents is available. The following listings are available for $5 each: ZIP Code, Company Name, and Lines of Insurance. Number of Agents: 31,340.

Louisiana

Insurance Department, PO Box 94214, Baton Rouge, LA 70804-9214; 504-342-5900. Insurance Companies Documents on File: A written request must be submitted for all documents. All documents are available for 25 cents per page, complete list for $31.25. Listing of Insurance Companies: Report of the Commissioners of Insurance is available at no charge. It contains name, address and telephone number of all insurance companies. Number of Insurance Companies: 2,358. Licensed Agents. List of Agents: No list of agents is available. Names may be obtained by visiting the office. Number of Agents: 70,000. 504-342-3565.

Maine

Bureau of Insurance and Financial Regulations Dept., State House #34, Augusta, ME 04333; 207-582-8707. Insurance Companies Documents on File: Documents will be copied as staffing permits on a cost recovery basis. Listing of Insurance Companies: written request required. Computer printout available on a cost recovery basis. Printouts can be sorted by ZIP code, alphabetical, county, or type of insurance. Pressure sensitive labels available for 4 cents a name. Number of Insurance Companies: 800. Licensed Agents. List of Agents: Computer printout available on a cost recovery basis. Pressure sensitive labels available for 4 cents a name. Number of Agents: 9,000.

Maryland

Insurance Division, Licensing and Regulation Department, 501 St. Paul PL. Baltimore, MD 21202; 301-333-6300. Insurance Companies Documents on File: Available for $1 per page. Listing of Insurance Companies: Not Available, 301-333-6192. Number of Insurance Companies: 1,884. Licensed Agents, 301-333-4074. List of Agents: No listing available. Number of Agents: 75,000.

Massachusetts

Commonwealth of Massachusetts, Division of Insurance, 280 Friend St., Boston, MA 02114; 617-727-5503. Insurance Companies Documents on File: Copies of documents may be obtained on a cost recovery basis. Listing of Insurance Companies: Computer printout available for a fee. Number of Insurance Companies: 900. Licensed Agents, 617-727-7189 ext. 350. List of Agents: Not available. Number of Agents: 60,000.

Michigan

Insurance Bureau, Dept. of Commerce, PO Box 30220, Lansing, MI 48909; 517-373-9273. Insurance Companies Documents on File: Office will copy up to 14 pages free, over 15 pages documents are copies on a cost recovery basis. Listing of Insurance Companies: Computer printouts available for 20 cents per page, written request only! Number of Insurance Companies: 110. Licensed Agents. List of Agents: Written request only. Number of Agents: 60,000. 517-373-0234.

Be patient. If any phone number is incorrect, call (area code) 555-1212 and request the new listing.

679

Information on People, Companies, and Mailing Lists

Minnesota

Insurance Division, Minnesota Department of Commerce, 133 E. 7th St., St. Paul, MN 55101; 612-296-6319. Insurance Companies Documents on File: Copies available for 50 cents per page. Listing of Insurance Companies: Minnesota Book Store, 117 University Avenue, St. Paul, MN 55155; 612-297-3000. Photocopied listing available for $25 plus tax and handling cost. Mailing list office, Debbie Sabota 612-297-2552. Number of Insurance Companies: 1,500. Licensed Agents. List of Agents: Contact Mailing List Office listed above. Number of Agents: 38,000-40,000.

Mississippi

Insurance Department, PO Box 79, Jackson, MS 39205; 601-359-3576. Insurance Company Documents on File: Copies of documents available on a cost recovery basis if staffing permits. Listing of Insurance Companies: Company book available with written request. Pressure sensitive labels available for $360. Number of Insurance Companies: 17,000. Licensed Agents. List of Agents: Available from the Mississippi Association of Life Underwriters, P.O. Box 13649, Jackson, MS 39236; 601-981-1522. Labels, printouts or tapes available for a fee. Number of Agents: 16,000.

Missouri

Missouri Dept. of Insurance, Regulatory Agencies, PO Box 690, 301 W. High, Room 630, Jefferson City, MO 65102; 314-751-2562. Insurance Companies Documents on File: A Book of documents available for $10. Listing of Insurance Companies: Computer printout and pressure sensitive labels available on a cost recovery basis. Number of Insurance Companies: 1,200. Licensed Agents. List of Agents: Computer printout and pressure sensitive labels available on a cost recovery basis. Number of Agents: 64,000.

Montana

Insurance Commissioner, PO Box 4009, Helena, MT 59604-4009; 406-444-2040. Insurance Companies Documents on File: Documents can be copied for 50 cents per pages as staffing permits. Listing of Insurance Companies: Computer printout available for $6 plus postage, (1990 latest listing). Number of Insurance Companies: 1,400. Licensed Agents. List of Agents: No listing available. Names may be viewed by visiting the office. Number of Agents: 8,310.

Nebraska

Insurance Department, Terminal Bldg, 941 O Street, Suite 1400, Lincoln, NE 68508; 402-471-2201. Insurance Companies Documents on File: Available for 50 cents per page. Listing of Insurance Companies: Computer printouts, pressure sensitive labels, or magnetic tape can be obtained for $50. Computerized information can be sorted by ZIP code, alphabetical, or by line of insurance. Summary of Insurance Business is available annually for $20. It lists amount of premiums each company collects and the volume of business. Number of Licensed Insurance Companies: 16,500. Licensed Agents. List of Agents: Computer printouts, pressure sensitive labels or magnetic tape are available for $150. Computerized information can be sorted by ZIP code, alphabetical, or by line of insurance. Number of Agents: 22,000.

Nevada

Department of Insurance, Commerce Department, 1665 Hot Spring Rd., Suite 152, Carson City, NV 89710; 702-687-4270. Insurance Companies Documents on File: Available for 50 cents per page or $45 for a list. Listing of Insurance Companies: Computer printouts, Cheshire and pressure sensitive labels and diskettes available on a cost recovery basis. Computerized information can be sorted by ZIP code, alphabetical, or city. Number of Insurance Companies: 2,000. Licensed Agents. List of Agents: Same as for insurance companies. Number of Agents: 18,000.

New Hampshire

Insurance Department, 169 Manchester St., Concord, NH 03301; 603-271-2261. Insurance Companies Documents on File: Documents may be viewed by visiting the above office. List of Insurance Companies: A printout titled Licensed Companies is available on a cost recovery basis. Number of Insurance Companies: 900. Licensed Agents. List of Agents: Laser printout $50. Number of Agents: 3,500.

New Jersey

Department of Insurance, 20 W. State St, CN 325, Trenton, NJ 08625; 609-292-5371. Insurance Company Documents on File: Free. Listing of Insurance Company: Commissioners Annual Report contains a listing of insurance companies. Number of Insurance Companies: 1,500. Licensed Agents. List of Agents: 609-292-4390. List is available on a cost recovery basis. Number of Agents: Not available. For a list of agents, send written request to State of New Jersey, 20 W. State St., CN 327, Trenton, NJ 08625.

New Mexico

Insurance Division, Corporation Commission, 500 Old Santa Fe Trail, Santa Fe, NM 87501-1269; 505-827-4542. Insurance Companies Documents on File: Documents will be copied on a cost recovery basis. Listing of Insurance Companies: Directory of Insurance Companies available free of charge. Number of Insurance Companies: 1,500. Licensed Agents. List of Agents: Computer printout available for $400, 505-827-4549 (Licensing). Pressure sensitive labels available for $200. Number of Agents: 10,000.

New York

Insurance Department, Empire State Plaza, Building 1, Albany, NY 12257; 518-474-6615. Insurance Companies Documents on File: Available for 50 cents per page. Listing of Insurance Companies: 518-474-7159. Directory of Licensed Insurance Companies available for $1, (Out of state only). Number of Insurance Companies: 1,000. Licensed Agents. List of Agents: requests in writing only. Number of Agents: 40,000. 518-474-6620 ext. 30.

North Carolina

Insurance Department, Box 26387, 430 N. Salisbury St., Raleigh, NC 27611; 919-733-5633. Insurance Companies Documents on File: Available for 50 cents per page. Average cost is $10. Listing of Insurance Companies: Computer printout is available for $5. Number of Insurance Companies: 1,069. Licensed Agents, 919-733-7487. List of Agents: Available for $175 for the first 5,000 names, for every additional 1,000 the cost is $7. Lists may be sorted by company, line of insurance, resident or nonresident, and ZIP. Number of Agents: 70,000.

North Dakota

Insurance Department, Capitol Building, 600 E. Blvd., 5th Floor, Bismarck, ND 58505; 701-224-2440. Insurance Companies Documents on File: Available for 20 cents per page. Listing of Insurance Companies: Computer printout is available for $20 or 2 cents per name. Pressure sensitive labels are available for $100. Number of Insurance Companies: 1,300. Licensed Agents. List of Agents: Pressure sensitive labels and computer printout are available for $20 plus 2 cents a name. List may be sorted by resident or nonresident and line of insurance. Number of Agents: 10,000.

Ohio

Insurance Department, 2100 Stella Court, Columbus, OH 43266-0566; 614-644-2658. Insurance Companies Documents on File: Available for 50 cents per page. Listing of Insurance Companies: Authorized list of Insurance Companies is available free of charge. This list contains names only. Computer printouts, pressure sensitive labels and magnetic tape are available on a cost recovery basis. Lists can be sorted by types of insurance, foreign or domestic, ZIP Code, and city. All requests must be submitted in writing. Number of licensed insurance companies: 1,665. Licensed Agents. List of Agents: Computer printout and pressure sensitive labels are available on a cost recovery basis. Number of Agents: 54,000.

Oklahoma

Insurance Department, 1901 N. Walnut, Oklahoma City, OK 73152-3408; 405-521-3966. Insurance Companies Documents on File. Listing of Insurance Companies: Annual Report and Directory is available free with written request. Computer printouts and pressure sensitive labels available on a cost recovery basis. Magnetic tape available for $25 plus 1 cent per record. Lists may be sorted by line of insurance or ZIP code. Licensed Agents. List of Agents: Computer printouts and pressure sensitive labels available on a cost recovery basis for $200. Number of Agents: 17,000. 405-521-3916.

Oregon

Department of Insurance and Finance, Insurance Division, 440 Labor and Industrial Bldg., Salem, OR 97310; 503-378-4271. Insurance Companies Documents on File: Available for 50 cents per page. Listing of Insurance Companies: Directory available for $2.50. Number of Insurance Companies: 1,500. Licensed Agents. List of Agents: Computer printout is available for $25. Pressure sensitive labels are available for $50. Number of Agents: 19,000.

Pennsylvania

Insurance Department, 1311 Strawberry Square, Harrisburg, PA 17120; 717-787-2735. Insurance Companies Documents on File: Available for 25 cents per page. Listing of Insurance Companies: Listing is available for $20. Number of Insurance Companies: 1,500. Licensed Agents. List of Agents: 717-787-3840, Not available. Number of Agents: 190,000.

Rhode Island

Insurance Division, Business Regulations Department, 233 Richmond St., Providence, RI 02903; 401-277-2223. Insurance Companies Documents on File: Available for 20 cents per page. Average cost is $32. Listing of Insurance Companies: Annual Report is available for $15. It contains names and addresses of all insurance companies. Number of Insurance Companies: 900. Licensed Agents. List of Agents: Available on a cost recovery basis with written request. Number of Agents: 25,000.

South Carolina

Insurance Department, P.O. Box 100105, Columbia, SC 29202-3105; 803-737-6120. Insurance Companies Documents on File: Available by written request for $25. Listing of Insurance Companies: Master list of all licensed companies is available for $5. Pressure sensitive labels are available on a cost recovery label. Number of Insurance Companies: 1,420. Licensed Agents, 803-737-6095. List of Agents: Listing available for 3 cents per name. Pressure sensitive labels are available for 6 cents per label. Number of Agents: 45,000.

South Dakota

Insurance Division, Commerce and Regulations Department, 500 East Capitol, Pierre, SD 57501; 605-773-3563. Insurance Companies Documents on File: Available for 75 cents per page. Listing of Insurance Companies: Computer printout and pressure sensitive labels are available for $25. Number of Insurance Companies: 1,464. Licensed Agents. List of Agents: Computer printouts are available for $200. Pressure sensitive labels are available for $200. Number of Agents: Not available. 605-773-3513.

Tennessee

Commerce and Insurance Department, 500 James Robertson Pkwy, Volunteer Plaza, Nashville, TN 37243; 615-741-1692. Insurance Companies Documents on File: All documents may be viewed in the office. Listing of Insurance Companies: Quarterly listing of companies available for free. The listing contains addresses, type of insurance, and ZIP code. Number of Insurance Companies: 1,574. Licensed Agents. List of Agents: List may be copied in the office. Number of Agents: 83,000.

Texas

Texas Dept of Insurance, 333 Guadalope, Austin, TX 78701-1998; 512-463-6425. Insurance Companies Documents on File: Available for 50 cents per page. Listing of Insurance Companies: Computer printout available for $37.80. Send written request to Texas Dept. of Insurance Publications, PO Box 149104 #999, Austin, TX 78714. Licensed Agents. List of Agents: Available for a fee. Number of Agents: 150,000, 512-322-4105.

Utah

Insurance Department, 3110 State Office Bldg., Salt Lake City, UT 84114; 801-538-3800. Insurance Companies Documents on File: Available for 25 cents per page. Listing of Insurance Companies: Computer printouts are available for $1 a sheet. Average cost is $50. Pressure sensitive labels are available for $10 per page. Average cost is $140. Number of Insurance Companies: 1,500. Licensed Agents. List of Agents: Written request for pressure sensitive labels are available for $350 or $1 per page. 801-538-3855. Number of Agents: 16,500.

Vermont

Department of Banking and Insurance, 89 Main St, Montpelier, VT 05602; 802-828-3301. Insurance Companies Documents on File: Documents may be viewed in the office. Annual report is free. Listing of Insurance Companies: Available free of charge. Number of Insurance Companies: 1,000. Licensed Agents. List of Agents: Computer printouts, mailing labels and magnetic tape available on a cost recovery basis. Number of Agents: 7,200.

Virginia

Insurance Bureau, State Corporation Commission, 1220 Bank St., P.O. Box 1197, Richmond, VA 23219; 804-786-3741. Insurance Companies Documents on File: Available for $1 for first page, 50 cents each page after. Listing of Insurance Companies: Available free of charge. Number of Insurance Companies: 1,700. Licensed Agents. List of Agents: Available by company. Not available at Bureau. Number of Agents: Not available.

Washington

Insurance Commissioner, Insurance Building, PO Box 40255, Olympia, WA 98504; 206-753-2418. Insurance Companies Documents on File: Documents available for $10. Listing of Insurance Companies: Available on a cost recovery basis. Number of Insurance Companies: 1,500. Licensed Agents. List of Agents: No list available. The state law forbids the use of names for commercial purposes. Number of Agents: Not available.

West Virginia

Insurance Department, 2100 Washington St East, Charleston, WV 25305; 304-348-2100. Insurance Companies Documents on File: Available for 50 cents per page. Listing of Insurance Companies: Commissioners Annual Report contains names and addresses. It is available for $10. Number of Insurance Companies: 1,000. Licensed Agents, 304-348-3386. List of Agents: Written request required. Computer printout available for $60. Pressure sensitive labels available for $60. Number of Agents: 20,000.

Wisconsin

Insurance Commission, P.O. Box 7573, Madison, WI 53707-7873; 608-267-9456. Insurance Companies Documents on File: Available for 20 cents per page. Listing of Insurance Companies: Computer printout available for $50. Listing can be searched by ZIP code, county, line of insurance, company, and resident or nonresident. Licensed Agents, 608-266-8699. List of Agents: Available for $50. It can be searched by ZIP code, county, line of insurance, company and resident or nonresident. Number of Agents: 50,000.

Wyoming

Insurance Department, 122 West 25th Street, Cheyenne, WY 82002-0440; 307-777-7401. Insurance Companies Documents on File: Available for $1 per page plus postage. Average cost $100. Listing of Insurance Companies: Computer printouts available for $50. Number of Insurance Companies: 970. Licensed Agents, 307-777-7319. List of Agents: Computer printout is available for $50. Number of Agents: 3,100.

Be patient. If any phone number is incorrect, call (area code) 555-1212 and request the new listing.

681

Federal Mailing Lists

Listed below are a number of mailing lists available from the federal government. This does not represent all available mailing lists, but only the more popular ones. Remember that anywhere the government collects names and addresses, that information theoretically is available to the public. Keep this in mind as you review the other chapters in this book.

At the end of each description below is a vendor code. A listing of the complete name and address for vendor codes is at the end of the mailing list descriptions.

Abstract Newsletter Subscribers
Contains 14,000 subscribers to the National Technical Information service newsletter service which covers the most recent research findings in 26 areas of industrial, technological, and sociological interest. Format: Off-line; Price: $100/per thousand names; Vendor: NTIS.

Agexporter (formerly Foreign Agriculture)
A monthly magazine targeted at business firms selling United States farm products overseas. Provides timely information on overseas trade opportunities, including reports on marketing activities and how-to's of agricultural exporting. List ID: FA-2E; 460 paid subscribers; Vendor: GPO.

Airman's Information Manual
Subscription provides the fundamentals required in order to fly in the United States National Airspace System. It also contains items of interest to pilots concerning health and medical facts, factors affecting flight safety, a pilot/controller glossary of terms used in the Air Traffic Control System, and information on safety, accident and hazard reporting. List ID: BFAP-2D; 9,134 paid subscribers; Vendor: GPO.

Alcohol Health and Research World
Presents current research findings; prevention, treatment, and training program descriptions; and observations with opinions from those working at the base level to provide services to persons affected by alcohol-related problems. List ID: AHRW-2Q; 5,932 paid subscribers; Vendor: GPO.

Area Wage Survey
These bulletins report on earnings in 70 major metropolitan areas for occupations common to a wide variety of establishments, including office clerical, professional and technical, maintenance, custodial, and material movement occupations. List ID: AWS-2B; 327 paid subscribers; Vendor: GPO.

Business America, The Magazine of International Trade
A biweekly publication designed to help American exporters penetrate overseas markets by providing them with timely information on opportunities for trade and methods of doing business in foreign countries. List ID: CRTD-2E; 4,632 paid subscribers; Vendor: GPO.

Branch Office Deposits
The Office of Thrift Supervision contains street addresses for home offices and branch offices of 3,196 FSLIC insured institutions. Zip codes are not included. Format: Tape; Price: $150; Vendor: FHLBB.

Business Conditions Digest
Prepared in the Statistical Indicators Division of the Bureau of Economic Analysis, the Digest presents almost 500 economic indicators in a form convenient for analysis with different approaches to the study of current business conditions and prospects (e.g., the national income model, the leading indicators, and anticipations and intentions), as well as for analysts who use combinations of these approaches. List ID: BCD-2G; 4,123 paid subscribers; Vendor: GPO.

Cancergrams
Current awareness bulletins in numerous cancer-related subject areas; Vendor: GPO.

Catalog of Federal Domestic Assistance
A Government-wide summary of financial and nonfinancial Federal programs, projects, services, and activities that provide assistance or benefits to the American public administered by departments and establishments of the Federal Government.

Describes the type of assistance available and the eligibility requirements for the particular assistance being sought, with guidance on how to apply. Also intended to improve coordination and communication between the Federal Government and State and local governments. List ID: COF89-1X; 4,456 paid subscribers; Vendor: GPO.

Census and You (formerly Data User News)
A monthly newsletter for users of Census Bureau statistics, which gives up-to-date information on Bureau programs, products and services and the latest news about demographic and economic data. List ID: DUN-2G; 2,941 paid subscribers; Vendor: GPO.

Census and You Mailing List (formerly Data User News)
Listing of the 394 free subscribers to the *Data User News*, which contains news highlights of current products available from the U.S. Bureau of the Census. Format: Tape; Price: $10; Vendor: CENSUS.

Children Today
Reports on Federal, State, and local services for children, child development, health and welfare laws, and other news pertinent to child welfare in the United States. List ID: CT-2S; 5,201 paid subscribers; Vendor: GPO.

Commerce Business Daily: Synopsis of United States Government Proposed Procurement, Sales, and Contract Awards
The Synopsis is of particular value to firms interested in bidding on U.S. Government purchases, surplus property offered for sale, or in seeking subcontract opportunities from prime contractors. It lists current information received daily from military and civilian procurement offices. List ID: COBD-2P; 42,106 paid subscribers; Vendor: GPO.

Commercial Info Management (CIMS)
CIMS is a decentralized database of the U.S. Dept. of Commerce that matches subscribing U.S. firms with foreign companies and governments interested in purchasing U.S. goods and services. Information connecting buyers and sellers is transmitted via telecommunications between U.S. posts in foreign counties and District Offices in the U.S. District Offices maintain data on the size, products and export capabilities of companies in their area. Format: Off-line; Price: $500 for entire list; Vendor: COMMERCE.

Committee on Scientific and Technical Information
List of individuals who have requested copies of the index by 22 major categories of National Technical Information Service reports that were developed and endorsed by the Committee on Scientific and Technical Information. Format: Off-line; Price: $100/per thousand; Vendor: NTIS.

Congressional Record
A verbatim report on Congressional debates and other proceedings.
List ID: CR-3A; 1,698 paid subscribers.
List ID: CRM-3A (Microfiche); 70 paid subscribers; Vendor: GPO.

Consumer Directory - Catalog
CERN-II is a directory of more than 2,000 organizations involved in consumer education or protection. Groups listed range from government agencies to university programs at the national, state, or local level. Retrieval information includes: address, phone number, contact person, type of organization (25 categories), staff size, funding, subject areas covered, etc. Format: Off-line; Price: Free; Vendor: GSA-CIC.

Cumulative List of Organizations
Lists contributions of organizations which are deductible under Section 170(c) of the Internal Revenue Code of 1954. List ID: CL-1L; 5,075 paid subscribers; Vendor: GPO.

Current Housing Reports
H-111. Housing Vacancies. Quarterly reports and an annual issue which give percent distributions of rental vacancies and homeowner vacancies, by facilities, number of rooms, monthly rent asked and sales price asked, etc., compared with same quarter of previous year.
H-121. Housing characteristics. Occasional reports of data for the country as a whole and for regions on selected characteristics of housing. List ID: CHR-2Q; 211 paid subscribers; Vendor: GPO.

Current Wage Development
Presents wage and benefit changes that result from collective bargaining settlements and unilateral management decisions. Also includes statistical summaries and special reports on wage trends. List ID: CWD-2M; 650 paid subscribers; Vendor: GPO.

Customs Bulletin and Decisions
Contains regulations, rulings, decisions, and notices concerning Customs and related matters of the United States Court of Appeals for the Federal Circuit and the United States Court of International Trade.
List ID: CB-2E; 1,041 paid subscribers; Vendor: GPO.

Customs Regulations of the United States
Contains regulations made and published for the purpose of carrying out customs laws administered by the United States Customs Service.
List ID: CRUS-1F; 3,710 paid subscribers; Vendor: GPO.

DOD FAR Supplement
This U.S. Department of Defense supplement to the Federal Acquisition Regulation contains guidelines on the provisions, clauses, and cost principles authorized for DOD contracts, as well as procedures and actions necessary for awarding and administering the contracts.
List ID: DFARS-1A; 4,806 paid subscribers; Vendor: GPO.

Domestic Mail Manual
Designed to assist Postal Service customers in obtaining maximum benefits from domestic postal services. It includes applicable regulations and information about rates and postage, classes of mail, special services, wrapping and mailing requirements, and collection and delivery services.
List ID: DOM-2S; 8,631 paid subscribers; Vendor: GPO.

Economic Indicators
Gives pertinent economic information on prices, wages, production, business activity, purchasing power, credit, money and Federal finance.
List ID: ECIN-2G; 4,766 paid subscribers; Vendor: GPO.

Education Statistics Mailing List
Contains over 5,000 people who requested material from the National Center for Education Statistics. Format: Tape; Price: See Vendor; Vendor: NCES.

EIA Publication New Releases (DOE-EIA-0204)
Contains 14 categories of users of U.S. Energy Department's Energy Information Administration publications with approximately 13,000 names.
Format: Off-line; Price: Cost Recovery; Vendor: EIA.

Employment and Earnings
Current data on employment, hours, and earnings for the United States as a whole, for States, and for more than 200 local areas.
List ID: EMEA-2M; 3,485 paid subscribers; Vendor: GPO.

Export Administration Regulations
Subscription service consists of a compilation of official regulations and policies governing the export licensing of commodities and technical data.
List ID: EAR88-1A; 8,385 paid subscribers; Vendor: GPO.

FAA Aviation News
Designed to help airmen become safer pilots, this publication gives updates and major Federal Aviation Administration rule changes and proposed Changes, as well as refresher information on flight rules, maintenance airworthiness, avionics, accident analysis, and other related topics. Covers all types of aircraft, including helicopters, balloons, gliders, antique, sport and experimental.
List ID: FAN-2D; 15,032 paid subscribers; Vendor: GPO.

FDA Consumer
Covers information written especially for consumers about Food and Drug Administration regulatory and scientific decisions, and about the safe use of products regulated by FDA. List ID: FDAP-2G; 23,942 paid subscribers; Vendor: GPO.

Federal Acquisition Regulations
The Federal Acquisition Regulation (FAR) is the primary regulation used by Federal Executive Branch agencies purchasing supplies and services.
List ID: FEACR-1A; 13,757 paid subscribers; Vendor: GPO.

The Federal Labor-Management and Employee Relations Consultant
Presents current information in the field of labor-management and employee relations. List ID: FLMC-2G; 365 paid subscribers; Vendor: GPO.

Federal Procurement Data Center
This database contains two million records pertaining to federal procurement actions from 1979 to present. Information is on contracts totaling $25,000 or more and also includes the purchasing or contracting office, date of award, principal place of performance and dollars obligated. Format: Tape, hard copy, gummed labels, microfiche; Price: variable; Vendor: FPDC.

Federal Register
Provides a uniform system for making available to the public regulations and legal notices issued by Federal agencies. These include Presidential proclamations and Executive orders and Federal agency documents having general applicability and legal effect, documents required to be published by Act of Congress and other Federal agency documents of public interest.
List ID: FR-3A; 17,085 paid subscribers; Vendor: GPO.
List ID: MFFR-3A Microfiche; 1,129 paid subscribers.

Federal Trainer
Contains news and features pertaining to programs for training Federal employees.
List ID: FEDT-2Q; 164 paid subscribers; Vendor: GPO.

Fishery Bulletin
Publishes original research papers, and occasionally, reviews of topical interest, in the broad discipline of fishery science. Research fields of particular interest are ecology, oceanography, and limnology; mariculture; ocean pollution; physiology, behavior and taxonomy of marine organisms, particularly fishes; technology; gear development; and economics.
List ID: FB-2D; 214 paid subscribers; Vendor: GPO.

Foreign Economic Trends and Their Implications for the United States
Includes key economic indicators, a brief summary of the state of the economy of the subject country, the current situation and economic trends, industrial report, agricultural report, foreign trade situation, living costs, monetary situation, and conclusions and implications for the United States.
List ID: ECTR-2B; 845 paid subscribers; Vendor: GPO.

Foreign Traders Index (FTI)
A directory of manufacturers, service organizations, agent representatives, retailers, wholesalers, distributors and cooperatives in 130 countries outside the U.S. Data are maintained by the International Trade Administration at the U.S. Department of Commerce. It provides the nature of business, name of officers, size, employees and establishment date. FTI is restricted to U.S. use. It is current for 5 years and is updated quarterly. Format: Tape, hard copy, gummed labels; Price: Varies, 25 cents/per name; Vendor: ITA.

Foreign Trade Reports FT990
Highlights of United States export and import trade.
List ID: FT990-2M; 380 paid subscribers; Vendor: GPO.

FSS Agency Rehabilitation
The General Services Administration sells this mailing list which totals some 1,000 addresses. Format: Tape; Price: $50/per reel; Vendor: GSA-MLIC.

FSS Excess Property
The General Services Administration sells this mailing list which totals some 2,000 addresses. Format: Tape; Price: $50/per reel; Vendor: GSA-MLIC.

FSS Publications
The General Services Administration sells this mailing list which totals 47,000 addresses. Format: Tape; Price: $50/per reel; Vendor: GSA-MLIC.

Be patient. If any phone number is incorrect, call (area code) 555-1212 and request the new listing.

683

Information on People, Companies, and Mailing Lists

FSS Procurement Bidders

The General Services Administration sells this mailing list which totals some 47,000 addresses. Format: Tape; Price: $50/per reel; Vendor: GSA-MLIC.

FSS Property Rehabilitation

The General Services Administration sells this mailing list which totals some 1,000 addresses. Format: Tape; Price: $50/per reel; Vendor: GSA-MLIC.

FSS Surplus Personal Property Zone (Regions 4 & 5)

Some 24,000 addresses comprise this General Services Administration mailing list. Surplus property auctioned by the federal government consists of hand and machine tools, office machines and supplies, furniture, hardware, motor vehicles, confiscated boats, airplanes and construction equipment. Format: Tape; Price: $50/per reel; Vendor: GSA-MLIC.

FSS Surplus Personal Property Zone (Regions 6 & 7)

Some 9,000 addresses comprise this General Services Administration mailing list. Surplus property auctioned by the federal government consists of hand and machine tools, office machines and supplies, furniture, hardware, motor vehicles, confiscated boats, airplanes and construction equipment.
Format: Tape; Price: $50/per reel; Vendor: GSA-MLIC.

FSS Surplus Personal Property Zone (Regions 8 - 10)

Some 38,000 addresses comprise this General Services Administration mailing list. Surplus property auctioned by the federal government consists of hand and machine tools, office machines and supplies, furniture, hardware, motor vehicles, confiscated boats, airplanes and construction equipment.
Format: Tape; Price: $50/per reel; Vendor: GSA-MLIC.

FSS Surplus Personal Property Defaulted Bidders

Some 4,000 addresses comprise this General Services Administration mailing list. Surplus property auctioned by the federal government consists of hand and machine tools, office machines and supplies, furniture, hardware, motor vehicles, confiscated boats, airplanes and construction equipment.
Format: Tape; Price: $50/per reel; Vendor: GSA-MLIC.

FSS Surplus Personal Property Zone (Regions 1, 2, 3)

Some 19,000 addresses comprise this General Services Administration mailing list. Surplus property auctioned by the federal government consists of hand and machine tools, office machines and supplies, furniture, hardware, motor vehicles, confiscated boats, airplanes and construction equipment.
Format: Tape; Price: $50/per reel; Vendor: GSA-MLIC.

Futures All Firm Directory

The National Future Association directory contains an alphabetical listing of the four categories of futures traders: Commodity Trading Advisors, Commodity Pool Operators, Futures Commission Merchants, and Introducing Brokers. Includes addresses and phone numbers. Format: Off-line; Price: $10-$25; Vendor: NFA.

Government Unit Name and Address File

Contains names, addresses, and geographic codes of local governments in the census for the years ending in 2 and 7.
Format: Tape; Price: $140/per reel; Vendor: CENSUS 2.

GPO Sales Publications Reference File

A guide to current publications offered for sale by the Superintendent of Documents arranged by GPO stock numbers; Superintendent of Documents classification numbers; and alphabetically by subjects, titles, agency series and report numbers, key words and phrases, and personal authors.
List ID: PRF-2N; 441 paid subscribers; Vendor: GPO.

GSA Rocky Mountain Bulletin

The General Services Administration sells this mailing list which totals some 3,000 addresses.
Format: Tape; Price: $50/per reel; Vendor: GSA-MLIC.

General Services Administration Training (Classes)

The GSA sells this mailing list which totals some 26,000 names and addresses.
Format: Tape; Price: $50/per reel; Vendor: GSA-MLIC.

Harmonized Tariff Schedules of the U.S. Annotated

For use in classifying imported merchandise for rate of duty and statistical purposes.
List ID: TSA88-1A; 9,673 paid subscribers; Vendor: GPO.

Humanities

Published by the National Endowment for the Humanities, this publication describes the NEH program, projects, and issues in the humanities. Gives recent grants, deadlines, and useful information for applicants seeking funds.
List ID: NR-2N; 3,671 paid subscribers; Vendor: GPO.

ICC Interstate Carrier Listing

Provides names, addresses, phone number, and motor carrier number of 51,000 active motor carriers. Types of carriers included in file are: railroads, trucking co., bus lines, freight forwarders, water carriers, property brokers, rate bureaus, and private carriers.
Format: Tape $45, Hard copy $100; Price: Cost recovery; Vendor: ICC.

ICD-9-CM International Classification of Diseases, 9th Revision, Clinical Modification, 3rd Edition:

Volumes 1 and 2; 47,684 paid subscribers; List ID: ICDP-1C.
Volume 3, Procedures Tabular List and Alphabetic Index; 108 paid subscribers; List ID: ICDH-1C.

Internal Revenue Bulletin

Announces official Internal Revenue Service rulings, Treasury Decisions, Executive Orders, legislation, and court decisions pertaining to internal revenue matters. List ID: IRB-2E; 5,027 paid subscribers; Vendor: GPO.

International Flight Information Manual

Primarily designed as a preflight and planning guide for use by United States non-scheduled operators, business and private aviators contemplating flights outside of the United States.
List ID: IFM89-1F; 1,016 paid subscribers; Vendor: GPO.

International Mail Manual

List ID: IMM-2S; 4,603 paid subscribers; Vendor: GPO.

Journal of the National Cancer Institute

An up-to-the-minute, reliable and comprehensive source of critical news and information on the latest developments in cancer research and treatment, including: prevention, clinical trials, immunology, molecular and tumor cell biology, biochemistry, carcinogenesis, epidemiology, biological response modifiers, cancer control, drug development, pharmacology, and many other fields. List ID: JNCI-2E; 2,232 paid subscribers; Vendor: GPO.

Lists of Parties Excluded from Federal Procurement or Nonprocurement Programs

List ID: CLDSC-2M; 959 paid subscribers; Vendor: GPO.

Management

Focuses attention on important developments in the Office of Personnel Management.
List ID: CSJ-2Q; 1,793 paid subscribers; Vendor: GPO.

Manual on Uniform Traffic Control Devices for Streets and Highways

This manual provides detailed uniform standards for all signs, markings and devices placed on, over, or adjacent to a street or highway. Included are general specifications of sizes, shapes and colors, as well as sections on guide signs, pavement markings, traffic control signals, and islands. List ID: N-523-2A; 6,415 paid subscribers; Vendor: GPO.

Marine Fisheries Review

A review of developments and news of the fishery industries prepared in the National Marine Fisheries Service, United States Department of Commerce. List ID: MFR-2M; 177 paid subscribers; Vendor: GPO.

Master Cross Reference List

Part I, Logistics Reference No. to NSN; 379 paid subscribers; List ID: MCR01-2Q
Part II, NIIN to Logistics Reference No.; 463 paid subscribers; List ID: MCR02-2Q
Part III, FSCM and Logistics Reference to NSN; 212 paid subscribers; List ID: MCR03-2Q; Vendor: GPO

Monthly Catalog of United States Government Publications

Lists the publications printed and processed during each month. It includes the

publications sold by the Superintendent of Documents, those for official use, and those sent to Depository Libraries.
List ID: MC89-1F; 1,242 paid subscribers; Vendor: GPO.

Monthly Energy Review
Illustrates current and historical statistics on United States production, storage, imports and consumption of petroleum, natural gas, and coal.
List ID: MER-2B; 1,273 paid subscribers; Vendor: GPO.

Monthly Labor Review
Includes articles on labor force, wages, prices, productivity, economic growth, and occupational injuries and illnesses. Regular features include a review of developments in industrial relations, book reviews, and current labor statistics.
List ID: MLR-2D; 6,976 paid subscribers; Vendor: GPO.

National Library of Medicine Audiovisuals Catalog
List ID: MAC89-1S; 251 paid subscribers; Vendor: GPO.

Nuclear Safety
Through this periodical the Energy Department provides concise and authoritative evaluation of scientific and technological developments relating to nuclear safety as they emerge from atomic research and development programs. List ID: NS-2N; 535 paid subscribers; Vendor: GPO.

Occupational Outlook Quarterly
A periodical to help young people, employment planners, and guidance counselors keep abreast of current occupational and employment developments. List ID: OOQ-2R; 22,730 paid subscribers; Vendor: GPO.

OSHA Standards and Regulations
Volume I, General Industry Standards and Interpretations; 5,056 paid
subscribers; List ID: OSH01-1A
Volume II, Maritime Standards; 1,380 paid subscribers; List ID: OSH02-1A Volume III, Construction Industry Standards and Interpretations; 4,579 paid
subscribers; List ID: OSH03-1A
Volume IV, Other Regulations and Procedures; 1,631 paid subscribers; List ID:
OSH04-1A
Volume V, Field Operations Manual; 1,029 paid subscribers; List ID: OSH05-1A
Volume VI, Industrial Hygiene Technical Manual; 1,102 paid subscribers; List
ID: OSH06-1A; Vendor: GPO

Official Gazette of the United States Patent and Trademark Office: Patents
Contains the patents, Patent Office notices, and designs issued each week.
List ID: OG-2D; 2,313 paid subscribers; Vendor: GPO.

Official Gazette of the United States Patent and Trademark Office: Trademarks
Contains Trademarks, Trademark Notices, Marks Published for Opposition, Trademark Registrations Issued, and Index of Registrants.
List ID: OGT-2D; 1,565 paid subscribers; Vendor: GPO.

Official Summary of Security Transactions and Holdings
Contains securities holdings figures showing owners, relationships to issues, amounts of securities bought or sold by each owner, their individual holdings at the end of the reported month, and types of securities. List ID: OSST-2G; 916 paid subscribers; Vendor: GPO.

Postal Bulletin
Contains current orders, instructions and information relating to the United States Postal Service, and Commemorative Stamp Posters. List ID: POB-2E; 3,062 paid subscribers; Vendor: GPO.

Resources in Education
List ID: RIE-2M; 933 paid subscribers; Vendor: GPO.

Schedule B: Statistical Classification of Domestic and Foreign Commodities Exported from the United States
Contains approximately 40,007 digit commodity classifications, based on the organization framework of the Tariff Schedules of the United States, Annotated, to be used by shippers in reporting export shipments from the United States and for use in compiling official statistics on exports of merchandise from the United States. List ID: SCHB-1A; 28,436 paid subscribers; Vendor: GPO.

Schizophrenia Bulletin
Facilitates the dissemination and exchange of information about schizophrenia and provides abstracts of the recent literature on the subject.
List ID: SB-2Q; 2,160 paid subscribers; Vendor: GPO.

SEC Monthly Statistical Review
Includes statistical summaries of new securities, securities sales, common stock prices, stock transactions, and other phases of securities exchange.
List ID: STBU-2M; 375 paid subscribers; Vendor: GPO.

Survey of Current Business
Gives information on trends in industry, the business situation, outlook, and other points pertinent to the business world.
List ID: SCUB-2D; 7.031 paid subscribers; Vendor: GPO.

Vendor List

The following is an alphabetical listing of government agencies according to their vendor symbols noted above.

CENSUS
Customer Service, Census Bureau
Data Services Division
Washington, DC 20233
301-763-4100

COMMERCE
U.S. Department of Commerce
World Traders Data Reports Section
14th St. and Constitution Ave., NW
Washington, DC 20230
202-482-4204

EIA
Energy Information Administration
Freedom of Information Office
U.S. Department of Energy
1000 Independence Ave., SW, 1G051
Washington, DC 20462
202-586-5955

FPDC
Federal Procurement Data Center
7th and D St., SW, Room 5652
Washington, DC 20407
202-401-1529

GSA-CIC
Consumer Information Center
General Services Administration
Room G142/18th and F St., NW
Washington, DC 20405
202-501-1794

GSA-MLIC
GSA/BSC
819 Taylor St., Room 11A05
Ft. Worth, TX 76102
817-334-3284

GPO
Superintendent of Documents
U.S. Government Printing Office
Washington, DC 20401
202-512-1800
Prices and Selections:
Cheshire labels: $85 per 1,000
minimum list user charge of $300 per order
Pressure sensitive labels: $5.30 per 1,000
Key coding (up to 5 digits): $2 per 1,000
No geographic selections available. No foreign lists available.
Shipping charges: $10 to $15.

Be patient. If any phone number is incorrect, call (area code) 555-1212 and request the new listing.

685

Information on People, Companies, and Mailing Lists

ICC

Interstate Commerce Commission
Section of System Development
12th and Constitution, NW, #1349
Washington, DC 20423
202-275-7682

IRS

Internal Revenue Service Headquarters
U.S. Department of the Treasury
1111 Constitution Ave., NW
Washington, DC 20224
202-566-4743

ITA

International Trade Administration or
District Office
U.S. Department of Commerce
Washington, DC 20230
202-482-3808

MINING

Mining Information Division
Mine Safety and Health Administration
P.O. Box 2537
Denver, CO 80225
303-231-5475

NCES

National Center for Education Statistics/
Data Systems Branch
555 New Jersey Ave., NW, #300
Washington, DC 20208
202-357-6651

NFA

National Future Association
200 West Madison
Chicago, IL 60606
312-781-1300

NTIS

National Technical Information Service
5285 Port Royal Road
Springfield, VA 22161
703-487-4812

OTS

Office of Thrift Supervision
1700 G St., NW
Washington, DC 20552
202-906-5900

Be patient. If any phone number is incorrect, call (area code) 555-1212 and request the new listing.

Government Auctions and Surplus Property

Whether you're looking for a good bargain on equipment to furnish your home office, or whether you're interested in a low overhead business of buying government property and reselling it, all you need is here. Year round, the federal government offers hundreds of millions of dollars worth of property and goods — from animals to real estate — at remarkable prices. The Customs Service sells seized property — jewelry, camera, rugs — anything brought in from another country. The Internal Revenue Service (IRS) auctions off everything imaginable — boats, cars, businesses. The U.S. Postal Service sells unclaimed merchandise, including lots of books.

There is one story to inspire: a New Yorker bought surplus parachutes from the Pentagon and became a supplier selling clothesline cord. If you are looking for a business, try the Small Business Administration, which sells equipment and businesses it has acquired through foreclosure. Want a good deal on a house? U.S. Department of Housing and Urban Development offers repossessed homes — sometimes for practically nothing — on government foreclosures. There are also many people who go to the U.S. Postal Service auctions and buy bin loads of videos, CDs, and other goodies, and make nice money reselling them at flea markets.

Very few people know about these unique bargains because the federal government doesn't advertise them. Described below are 30 of Uncle Sam's Red Tag Specials. Contact the appropriate offices for more information. And remember, if you don't find what you want, stay at it. This is ongoing, and new merchandise and property are coming in all the time.

* Burros and Horses: Bureau of Land Management

Nevada State Office
Bureau of Land Management
U.S. Department of the Interior
850 Harvard Way   702-785-6400
Reno, NV 89520-0006   Fax: 702-673-6010

Or contact your local Bureau of Land Management office. The "Adopt-a-Horse" program is aimed at keeping wild herds at in the West at manageable levels, and allows individuals around the country to purchase a wild horse for $125 or a burro for $75. The animals usually have their shots. Aside from the purchase price you only need pay for shipping. If you live west of the Mississippi, call the Program Office above to find out which of the 12 adoption satellites are nearest you. Representatives of the BLM travel around the country, so you don't have to travel to Wyoming to participate. The only qualifications for adoption are that you have appropriate facilities to house the animal, that you are of legal age in your state, and that you have no record of offenses against animals. The horses and burros may not be used for any exploitative purposes such as rodeos or races, nor may they be re-sold. Upon adoption, you sign an agreement to that effect, and no title of ownership is given until one year after an adoption. Animals are usually from two to six years in age, and must be trained. The offices listed above have a brochure called *So You'd Like to Adopt a Wild Horse or Burro* on the "Adopt-a-Horse" program that gives more details.

Alaska
Alaska State Office, 222 W. 7th Ave., #13, Anchorage, AK 99513-7599; 907-271-5555.

Arizona
Phoenix District Office, 2015 W. Deer Valley Rd., Phoenix, AZ 85027; 602-780-8090.
Kingman Resource Area, 602-757-3161.

California
California State Office, Federal Building, Room E-2807, 2800 Cottage Way, Sacramento, CA 95825-1889; 916-979-2800.
Bakersfield District Office, 805-391-6049.
Ridgecrest, CA, 619-446-6064.
Susanville District Office, 916-257-5381.

Colorado
Canon City District Office, 3170 E. Main St., Canon City, CO 81212; 303-275-0631.

Idaho
Boise District Office, 3948 Development Ave., Boise, ID 83705-5389; 208-384-3300.

Montana, North Dakota, South Dakota
Montana State Office, 2222 N. 32nd St., Billings, MT 59107-6800; 406-255-2925.

Nevada
National Wild Horse and Burro Center, Palomino Valley, P.O. Box 3270, Sparks, NV 89432; 702-475-2222.

New Mexico, Kansas, Oklahoma, Texas
Oklahoma Resource Area, 221 N. Service Rd., Moore, OK 73160-4946; 405-794-9624.

Oregon, Washington
Burns District Office, HC74-12533, Highway 20 West, Hines, OR 97738; 503-573-4400.

Utah
Salt Lake City District Office, 2370 South 2300 West, Salt Lake City, UT 84119; 801-977-4300.

Wyoming, Nebraska
Rock Springs District Office, P.O. Box 1869, Highway 191 North, Rock Springs, WY 82902-1869; 307-382-5350.
Elm Creek, NE, 308-856-4498.

AL, AR, FL, GA, KY, LA, MS, NC, SC, TN, VA
Jackson District Office, 411 Briarwood Dr., Suite 404, Jackson, MS 39206; 601-977-5430.
Cross Plains, TN, 615-654-2180.

CT, DE, DC, IL, IN, IA, ME, MD, MA, MI, MN, MO, NH, NJ, NY, OH, PA, RI, VT, WV, WI
Milwaukee District Office, 310 W. Wisconsin Ave., Suite 225, Milwaukee, WI 53203.

* Christmas Trees, Seedling, Wooden Poles and Posts: Bureau of Land Management

U.S. Department of the Interior
Bureau of Land Management
Division of Forestry
1849 C Street, NW
Washington, DC 20240   202-653-8864

or

U.S. Forest Service (USDA)   202-208-3435
    202-205-1389

Government Auctions and Surplus Property

Contact your local Bureau of Land Management (BLM), U.S. Department of Interior. In the 11 Western states, the Bureau of Land Management has a program for obtaining low-cost Christmas trees from Federal lands. By contacting your local BLM office, you may obtain a permit for a nominal fee (usually $10) to cut a tree for your own use. You will be given a map with directions as to which are permissible areas for tree-cutting. Non-profit organizations may also qualify. Non-profit may get free use permits and cut larger amounts. Trees must be for their own use and may not be resold at fundraisers.

In addition, under the Minor Forest Products program, you may collect or cut specified small trees for use as poles or posts; or, you may obtain cactus or plant seedlings from areas of natural growth where there are abundant supplies -- again at a very low cost. These items are free for non-profit organizations for their own use. Permits for commercial usage may also be available. Cost depends on market value. Below are the addresses and phone numbers of Regional Bureau of Land Management Offices.

Alaska
222 W. 7th Ave. #13, Anchorage, AK 99513-5076; 907-271-5555.

Arizona
3707 N. 7th St., P.O. Box 16563, Phoenix, AZ 85011; 602-640-0504.

California
2800 Cottage Way, E-2841, Sacramento, CA 95825; 916-978-2835.

Colorado
2850 Youngfield St., Lakewood, CO 80215-7076; 303-239-3670.

Eastern States
7450 Ballston Blvd., Springfield, VA 22153; 703-440-1713.

Idaho
3380 Americana Terrace, Boise, ID 83706; 208-384-3014.

Montana
Granite Tower, 222 N. 32nd St., P.O. Box 36800, Billings, MT 59107-6800; 406-255-2913.

Nevada
850 Harvard Way, Reno, NV 89520-0006; 702-785-6586.

New Mexico
1474 Rodeo Road, P.O. Box 27115, Santa Fe, NM 87502-0115; 505-438-7514.

Oregon
1515 SW 5th Ave., P.O. Box 2965, Portland, OR 97208-2965; 503-952-6027.

Utah
324 South State Street, Suite 301, P.O. Box 45155, Salt Lake City, UT 84145-0155; 801-539-4021.

Wyoming
5353 Yellowstone Rd., P.O. Box 1828, Cheyenne, WY 82009; 307-775-6011.

* Federal Depository Insurance Corporation (FDIC)

Federal Depository Insurance Corporation
550 17th St. NW
Washington, DC 20429   202-393-8400
or
Office of Liquidations
1776 F Street NW
Washington, DC 20429   202-898-7343

The FDIC sells at auctions the furnishings and equipment of failed commercial banks. Consult the blue pages in your phone directory for the regional FDIC office nearest you. Each regional office handles their own personal property disposal. Professional auctioneers are contracted to auction off the accumulation of desks, calculators, chairs, computers and other furnishings that banks normally have. These auctions will be advertised in the auction section or classifieds of local newspapers.

The FDIC also holds open for offers costly commercial property and real estate. For a full catalog of these listings across the country, which also includes homes over $250,000 call 1-800-445-3683. They will send *The Liquidation Book* which is the marketing list that is most current. All the property the FDIC has to sell is in this book, but if you are interested in bidding on a house under $250,000, it is wise to ask them for the phone number of the FDIC sales office in your area that is in

charge of selling them, and then contact them directly. About 97 percent of the listings in it are commercial offerings such as hotels, offices, and industries. Sales of commercial real estate are advertised nationally by the FDIC in such papers as *The Wall Street Journal*. Call for information on how to be placed on a mailing list.

* FHA Money May Be Waiting for You

Support Service Center
P.O. Box 23699
Washington, DC 20026-3699
HUD Locator   1-800-697-6967
    202-708-1422

If you or someone in your family has successfully paid off a mortgage on a house, there may be money waiting for you at the U.S. Department of Housing and Urban Development (HUD). HUD oversees the Federal Housing Administration (FHA) which insures mortgages that your bank lends to house buyers. Each year FHA predicts how many people will default on their loans, and based on that prediction, they calibrate how much mortgage insurance home buyers will pay during that year. If it turns out that there are fewer loan defaults than FHA predicted, those borrowers that have continued to pay their mortgages have what are called "Mutual Mortgage Dividend" checks coming to them upon completion of the loan agreement. Call 703-235-8117 if you think you are due a one time mortgage insurance premium refund or a distributive share.

Another way you may qualify for an FHA insurance refund is to have taken out, say, a 30 year mortgage and paid the entire FHA insurance premium up front instead of in installments over the entire period of the loan. If you have completed the loan agreement in less than 30 years, you may have money coming back to you since you didn't use the insurance for the entire 30 years you've already paid for. In most cases, though, you have to carry a loan for at least 7 years to qualify for a dividend, and the longer you have a loan, the more likely it is that you will qualify for a dividend check.

In these cases where you prepay all of your mortgage insurance premium up front, your bank should let you know that you may eventually be eligible for a mutual mortgage refund upon fulfillment of the loan agreement. Also, after you have paid off your loan, your bank should notify HUD, who in turn should notify you if you have any refund coming, usually within six months. However, if HUD cannot locate you, they will add your name to a list of other individuals who cannot be located but have HUD money coming to them.

Through the Freedom of Information Act many individuals have gotten their hands on copies of this list from HUD and gone around the country tracking down the people and charging them fees to recover this HUD money. Depending on the size of the original loan, your dividend refund could be several thousand dollars, and since some of these "bounty hunters" may ask for up to 50% of the refund just for making a phone call that you could make yourself, you could be losing out on a substantial sum of money by letting them do it. In fact, all you have to do to get the same list the bounty hunters are using is to call 703-235-8117. The staff will mail to you an "information package" which contains the names of all the mortgagors in the state in which you reside (or request the list for), forms and basic information you would need to apply for a refund.

If you feel you may have money coming to you, or if a member of your family who took out a mortgage is now deceased and you are an heir, try to locate the original loan contract number, and then make a few calls. To apply for a refund you will need the loan number and FHA case number, which you can find on the Recorded Deed of Purchase, kept at your local county courthouse.

* Firewood: U.S. Forest Service

U.S. Forest Service
Timber Management
U.S. Department of Agriculture
14th & Independence Ave. SW
Box 96090
Washington, DC 20090-6090
Operations and Technology Information   202-205-0855/0893

Contact your nearest National Forest Office (listed below) to find out about the firewood program and to learn which national forest is near you. Also, ask these regional offices about firewood from state forestry organizations and private timber companies. Ask about availability of firewood before you make the trip. In any National Forest, you may pick up downed or dead wood for firewood for a nominal charge of $5 per cord, $10 minimum fee, after requesting a permit from the Forest of your choice. You may phone to request the permit, and must have it in your possession while collecting the wood. The Forest Service allows you to gather 2-10 cords worth of wood. Six cords are equal to 12 pick-up truck loads. Wood may not be collected for commercial purposes. All permits to cut wood are issued locally, so you must purchase permits directly from the district ranger. Regional offices do not sell permits.

Northern Region I
Federal Building, 200 East Broadway St., P.O. Box 7669, Missoula, MT 59807; 406-329-3316. Includes Northern Idaho and Montana.

Rocky Mountain Region II
740 Simms Ave., P.O. Box 25127, Lakewood, CO 80225; 303-275-5350. Includes Colorado, Nebraska, South Dakota, Eastern Wyoming.

Southwestern Region III
Federal Building, 517 Gold Ave. S.W., Albuquerque, NM 87102; 505-842-3306. Includes New Mexico, Arizona.

Intermountain Region IV
Federal Building, 324 25th St., Ogden, UT 84401; 801-625-5605. Includes Southern Idaho, Nevada, Utah, and Western Wyoming.

Pacific Southwest Region V
630 Sansome St., San Francisco, CA 94111; 415-705-2870. Includes California, Hawaii, Guam, Trust Territories of the Pacific Islands.

Pacific Northwest Region VI
333 SW First Avenue, P.O. Box 3623, Portland, OR 97208-3623; 503-326-3626. Includes Oregon and Washington. (Mt. Hood is the most popular national forest and may be sold out of permits. Call them in advance at 503-666-0700. Try also the state and private timber units at 503-326-2727 or the U.S. Forest Service at 503-326-2877 or 503-326-2957.)

Southern Region VIII
1720 Peachtree Rd. N.W., Atlanta, GA 30367; 404-347-4177. Includes Alabama, Arkansas, Florida, Georgia, Kentucky, Louisiana, Mississippi, North Carolina, Puerto Rico and the Virgin Islands, South Carolina, Tennessee, Texas, Virginia.

Eastern Region IX
310 West Wisconsin Ave., Room 500, Milwaukee, WI 53203; 414-297-3600. Includes Illinois, Indiana, Ohio, Michigan, Minnesota, Missouri, New Hampshire, Maine, Pennsylvania, Vermont, West Virginia, Wisconsin, and Fingerlakes section of New York.

Alaskan Region X
Federal Office Building, 709 West Ninth St., P.O. Box 21628, Juneau, AK 99802-1628; 907-586-8863. Abundance of wood results in extensive free-use permits.

* Homes: Department of Agriculture
Rural Housing and Community Development Service
14th & Independence Ave., SW
Room 5334-S
Washington, DC 20250   202-720-1474/1577

Contact your local Rural Housing and Community Development Service (formerly Farmers Home Administration FmHA) Office. There are 1900 around the country. The Rural Housing and Community Development Service, part of the Department of Agriculture, makes low-interest loans available to qualified applicants to purchase homes or farms in rural areas (among other things). Rural settings are small towns with a population under 10,000. Check to see if the locale you are interested in qualifies. Sometimes areas of up to 25,000 in population are approved. Rural Housing and Community Development Service (RHCDS) is also charged with disposing of properties that are foreclosed. First, they make any necessary repairs to the properties, then offer them for sale to people who have the same qualifications as those applying for RHCDS loans (based on income, credit worthiness and other criteria). Eligible applicants also qualify to purchase the properties at special low RHCDS interest rates (as low as 1%). If no eligible applicants purchase a property, it is then put up for sale to the general public at competitive prices. If the property is not sold within 10 days, it may be reduced by 10%. Sales to the general public may be through RHCDS offices or through private real estate brokers. RHCDS "eligible applicants" must reside on the property purchased; but if no such eligible buyers are available, other buyers may use it for investment or rental purposes. A separate program applies for farms. This program is designed to serve people of modest income and good credit who don't have enough to make a down payment on a home. Credit evaluation is done on the most recent 12 months. Bankruptcy is not looked at after 36 months. The current loan budget is one-third of what is was in the 70's. This program is being changed to eventually act as insurers to guarantee loans

from professional lenders. Applicants may work in a city if their home is rural. The address and telephone number for your local county office may be obtained by calling or writing the applicable state office listed below.

Alabama
Rural Housing and Community Development Service, Sterling Center, Office Building, 4121 Carmichael Rd., Suite 601, Montgomery, Al 36106-3683; 205-279-3400.

Alaska
Rural Housing and Community Development Service, 634 S. Bailey, Suite 103, Palmer, AK 99645; 907-745-2176.

Arizona
Rural Housing and Community Development Service, Phoenix Corporate Center, 3003 N. Central Ave., Suite 900, Phoenix, AZ 85012; 602-280-8700.

Arkansas
Rural Housing and Community Development Service, P.O. Box 2778, 700 W. Capitol, Little Rock, AR 72203; 501-324-6281.

California
Rural Housing and Community Development Service, 194 W. Main St., Suite F, Woodland, CA 95695-2915; 916-668-2000.

Colorado
Rural Housing and Community Development Service, 655 Parfet St., Room E100, Lakewood, CO 80215; 303-236-2801.

Delaware, Maryland
Rural Housing and Community Development Service, P.O. Box 400, 4611 S. DuPont Hwy., Camden, DE 19934-9998; 302-697-4300.

Florida
Rural Housing and Community Development Service, P.O. Box 147010, 4440 NW 25th Pl., Gainesville, FL 32614-7010; 904-338-3400.

Georgia
Rural Housing and Community Development Service, Stephens Federal Bldg., 355 E. Hancock Ave., Athens, GA 30610; 706-546-2162.

Hawaii
Rural Housing and Community Development Service, Federal Bldg., Room 311, 154 Waianuenue Ave., Hilo, HI 96720; 808-933-3000.

Idaho
Rural Housing and Community Development Service, 3232 Elder St., Boise, ID 83705; 208-334-1301.

Illinois
Rural Housing and Community Development Service, Illini Plaza, Suite 103, 1817 S. Neil St., Champaign, IL 61820; 217-398-5235.

Indiana
Rural Housing and Community Development Service, 5975 Lakeside Blvd., Indianapolis, IN 46278; 317-290-3100.

Iowa
Rural Housing and Community Development Service, 873 Federal Blvd., 210 Walnut St., Des Moines, IA 50309; 515-284-4663.

Kansas
Rural Housing and Community Development Service, P.O. Box 4653, 1200 SW Executive Dr., Topeka, KS 66604; 913-271-2700.

Kentucky
Rural Housing and Community Development Service, 771 Corporate Dr., Suite 200, Lexington, KY 40503; 606-224-7300.

Louisiana
Rural Housing and Community Development Service, 3727 Government St., Alexandria, LA 71302; 318-473-7920.

Maine
Rural Housing and Community Development Service, P.O. Box 405, 444 Stillwater Ave., Suite 2, Bangor, ME 04402-0405; 207-990-9106.

Be patient. If any phone number is incorrect, call (area code) 555-1212 and request the new listing.

689

Government Auctions and Surplus Property

Massachusetts, Connecticut, Rhode Island
Rural Housing and Community Development Service, 451 West Street, Amherst, MA 01002; 413-253-4300.

Michigan
Rural Housing and Community Development Service, 3001 Coolidge Rd., Room 200, East Lansing, MI 48823; 517-337-6635.

Minnesota
Rural Housing and Community Development Service, 410 Farm Credit Service Bldg., 375 Jackson St., St. Paul, MN 55101-1853; 612-290-3842.

Mississippi
Rural Housing and Community Development Service, Federal Bldg., Suite 831, 100 W. Capitol St., Jackson, MS 39269; 601-965-4316.

Missouri
Rural Housing and Community Development Service, Parkdade Center, Suite 235, 601 Business Loop 70 West, Columbia, MO 65203; 314-876-0976.

Montana
Rural Housing and Community Development Service, Unit 1, Suite B, 900 Technology Blvd., Bozeman, MT 59715; 406-585-2580.

Nebraska
Rural Housing and Community Development Service, Federal Building, Room 308, 100 Centennial Mall N, Lincoln, NE 68508; 402-437-5551.

Nevada
Rural Housing and Community Development Service, 1390 S. Curry St., Carson City, NV 89703-5405; 702-887-1222.

New Jersey
Rural Housing and Community Development Service, Tarnsfield Plaza, Suite 22, 790 Woodlane Rd., Mt. Holly, NJ 08060; 609-265-3600.

New Mexico
Rural Housing and Community Development Service, Federal Building, Room 3414, 517 Gold Ave., SW, Albuquerque, NM 87102; 505-766-2462.

New York
Rural Housing and Community Development Service, The Galleries of Syracuse, 441 S. Salina St., Suite 357, Syracuse, NY 13202; 315-477-6400.

North Carolina
Rural Housing and Community Development Service, 4405 Bland Rd., Suite 260, Raleigh, NC 27609; 919-790-2731.

North Dakota
Rural Housing and Community Development Service, Federal Bldg., Room 208, 220 E. Rosser, P.O. Box 1737, Bismarck, ND 58502; 701-250-4781.

Ohio
Rural Housing and Community Development Service, Federal Bldg., Room 507, 200 N. High St., Columbus, OH 43215; 614-469-5606.

Oklahoma
Rural Housing and Community Development Service, 100 USDA, Suite 108, Stillwater, OK 74074; 405-742-1000.

Oregon
Rural Housing and Community Development Service, 101 SW Main, Suite 1410, Portland, OR 97204; 503-414-3300.

Pennsylvania
Rural Housing and Community Development Service, One Credit Union Place, Suite 330, Harrisburg, PA 17110-2996; 717-782-4476.

Puerto Rico
Rural Housing and Community Development Service, New San Juan Office Bldg., Room 01, 159 Carlos E. Chardon St., Hato Rey, PR 00918-5481; 809-766-5095.

South Carolina
Rural Housing and Community Development Service, Strom Thurmond Federal Bldg., Room 1007, 1835 Assembly St., Columbia, SC 29201; 803-765-5163.

South Dakota
Rural Housing and Community Development Service, Federal Bldg., Room 308, 200 Fourth St., SW, Huron, SD 57350; 605-352-1100.

Tennessee
Rural Housing and Community Development Service, 3322 West End Ave., Suite 300, Nashville, TN 37203-1071; 615-783-1300.

Texas
Rural Housing and Community Development Service, Federal Bldg., Suite 102, 101 South Main, Temple, TX 76501; 817-774-1301.

Utah
Rural Housing and Community Development Service, Wallace F. Bennett Federal Bldg., 125 S. State St., Room 5438, Salt Lake City, UT 84138; 801-524-4063.

Vermont, New Hampshire, Virgin Islands
Rural Housing and Community Development Service, City Center, 3rd Floor, 89 Main St., Montpelier, VT 05602; 802-828-6002.

Virginia
Rural Housing and Community Development Service, Culpeper Bldg., Suite 238, 1606 Santa Rosa Rd., Richmond, VA 23229; 804-287-1550.

Washington
Rural Housing and Community Development Service, Federal Bldg., Room 319, 301 Yakima St., P.O. Box 2427, Wenatchee, WA 98807; 509-664-0240.

West Virginia
Rural Housing and Community Development Service, 75 High St., Morgantown, WV 26505-7500; 304-291-4791.

Wisconsin
Rural Housing and Community Development Service, 4949 Kirschling Ct., Stevens Point, WI 54481; 715-345-7600.

Wyoming
Rural Housing and Community Development Service, Federal Bldg., Room 1005, 100 East B, P.O. Box 820, Casper, WY 82602; 307-261-5271.

* Homes: Department of Housing and Urban Development

Property Disposition Division
U.S. Department of Housing and Urban Development (HUD)
451 7th St. SW, Room 9172

Washington, DC 20410-4000	202-708-0740
HUD Locator	202-708-1422
Multi-Family Property Dispositions	202-708-3343
Single-Family Property Dispositions	202-708-0740

HUD homes are properties HUD owns as a result of paying the balance on foreclosed FHA insured home mortgages. Any qualified buyer can purchase a HUD home. Generally, your monthly mortgage payment should be no more than 29% of your monthly gross income. Many HUD homes require only a 3% down payment. You can move into some HUD homes with a $100 down payment. HUD will pay the real estate brokers commission up to the standard 6% of the sales price. HUD may also pay your closing costs. HUD homes are priced at fair market value. Consult your local newspapers for HUD listings; or, your regional HUD office, listed below; or, the real estate broker of your choice.

HUD's Property Disposition facilities are located within state offices and various coordinator's offices around the country. Contact your state office for details (see listing below). Frequently, HUD will advertise upcoming auctions of foreclosed properties in a local newspaper. The properties may be apartments, condominiums, or various kinds of single-family homes. The condition of these properties varies widely, including some that are little more than shells; and that, of course, affects the price. Some may be located in less than desirable neighborhoods; but others may end up being bargains, either as investments or personal residences. Bids are placed through private real estate brokers, who then submit them to HUD. Some offers for HUD homes are made to the seller and there may be negotiations. Offers for other HUD homes are done by bids placed during an "Offer Period." If you bid the full asking price, it may be accepted immediately. Otherwise, all the bids are opened at the close of the "Offer Period." The highest bidder wins. Contact the participating broker of your choice to show you the property and submit your bid. HUD broker contracted services are free to prospective buyers. Earnest money is a flat scaled fee ranging from $500-$2000 and must accompany the bid. Bidders must furnish their own financing. HUD stresses that properties sell "as is," so HUD will not make any repairs. It is up to a potential buyer to determine the value and condition, although the listings will state major problems.

Newspaper ads list houses that will be available for the next ten days, as well as others that did not sell in previous auctions. Listings include addresses, number of bedrooms and bathrooms, and suggested prices. Remember that HUD contracts are binding and non-negotiable: once your bid has won, there's no turning back. For a step by step buying guide to purchasing HUD owned homes, call the HUD Homeline, 1-800-767-4483, and request the brochure, *A Home of Your Own*. To learn about other programs at HUD that may be useful to you, call 202-708-0685.

Alabama
Heager Hill, State Coordinator, HUD-Alabama State Office, Beacon Ridge Tower, Suite 300, 600 Beacon Parkway West, Birmingham, AL 35209-3144; 205-290-7617.

Arizona
Terry Goddard, State Coordinator, HUD-Arizona State Office, Two Arizona Center, 400 N. 5th St., Suite 1600, Phoenix, AZ 85004-2361; 602-379-4434.

Arkansas
Bobbie J. (BJ) McCoy, Acting State Coordinator, HUD-Arkansas State Office, TCBY Tower, Suite 900, 425 W. Capitol Ave., Little Rock, AR 72201-3488; 501-324-5401.

Alaska
Arlene Patton, State Coordinator, HUD-Alaska State Office, University Plaza Bldg., 949 E. 36th Ave., Suite 401, Anchorage, AK 99508-4135; 907-271-4170.

California
Arthur Agnos, Secretary's Representative, HUD-California State Office, Philip Burton Federal Bldg. and U.S. Courthouse, 450 Golden Gate Ave., P.O. Box 36003, San Francisco, CA 94102-3448; 415-556-4752.

Colorado
Anthony Hernandez, Secretary's Representative, HUD-Colorado State Office, 633 17th St., Denver, CO 80202-3607; 303-672-5448, ext. 1487.

Connecticut
Robert S. Donovan, Acting State Coordinator, HUD-Connecticut State Office, 330 Main St., Hartford, CT 06106-1860; 203-240-4523.

Delaware
David Sharbaugh, Acting State Coordinator, HUD-Delaware State Office, 824 Market St., Suite 850, Wilmington, DE 19801-3016; 302-573-6258.

District of Columbia
Jessica Franklin, State Coordinator, HUD-District of Columbia Office, Union Center Plaza, Phase II, 820 First St., NE, Suite 300, Washington, DC 20002-4205; 202-275-9206.

Florida
Jose Cintron, State Coordinator, Gables One Tower, 1320 S. Dixie Hwy., Coral Gables, FL 33146-2911; 305-662-4510.

Georgia
Davey L. Gibson, Secretary's Representative, HUD-Georgia State Office, Richard B. Russell Federal Bldg., 75 Spring St., SW, Atlanta, GA 30303-3388; 404-331-5136.

Hawaii
Gordon Y. Furutani, State Coordinator, HUD-Hawaii State Office, Seven Waterfront Plaza, 500 Ala Moana Blvd., Suite 500, Honolulu, HI 96813-4918; 808-522-8175.

Idaho
Gary Gillespie, Acting State Coordinator, HUD-Idaho State Office, Park IV, 800 Park Blvd., Suite 220, Boise, ID 83712-7743; 208-334-1991.

Illinois
Edwin Eisendrath, Secretary's Representative, HUD-Illinois State Office, Ralph Metcalfe Federal Bldg., 77 W. Jackson Blvd., Chicago, IL 60604-3507; 312-353-5680.

Indiana
William Shaw, State Coordinator, HUD-Indiana State Office, 151 N. Delaware St., Indianapolis, IN 46204-2526; 317-226-7606.

Iowa
William McNarney, State Coordinator, HUD-Iowa State Office, Federal Bldg., 210 Walnut St., Room 239, Des Moines, IA 50309-2155; 515-284-4512.

Kansas
Joseph O'Hern, Secretary's Representative, HUD-Kansas-Missouri State Office, Gateway Tower II, 400 State Ave., Room 200, Kansas City, KS 66101-2406; 913-551-5462.

Kentucky
State Coordinator, HUD-Kentucky State Office, 601 W. Broadway, P.O. Box 1044, Louisville, KY 40201-1044; 502-595-3607.

Louisiana
Jason Gamlin, State Coordinator, HUD-Louisiana State Office, Hale Boggs Federal Bldg., 9th Floor, 501 Magazine St., New Orleans, LA 70130-3099; 504-589-7200.

Maine
Richard Young, Acting State Coordinator, HUD-Maine State Office, 99 Franklin St., Bangor, ME 04401-4925; 207-945-0467.

Maryland
Harold Young, Acting State Coordinator, HUD-Maryland State Office, City Crescent Bldg., 10 S. Howard St., 5th Floor, Baltimore, MD 21201-2505; 410-962-2520.

Massachusetts
Mary Lou Crane, Secretary's Representative, HUD-Massachusetts State Office, Thomas P. O'Neill, Jr. Federal Building, 10 Causeway St., Room 375, Boston, MA 02222-1092; 617-565-5236.

Michigan
Regina F. Solomon, State Coordinator, HUD-Michigan State Office, Patrick V. McNamara Federal Bldg., 477 Michigan Ave., Detroit, MI 48226-2592; 313-226-7900.

Minnesota
Thomas Feeney, State Coordinator, HUD-Minnesota State Office, 220 Second St., South, Minneapolis, MN 55401-2195; 612-370-3288.

Mississippi
Thomas Cooper, Acting State Coordinator, HUD-Mississippi State Office, Dr. AH McCoy Federal Bldg., 100 W. Capitol St., Room 910, Jackson, MS 39269-1096; 601-965-4738.

Montana
Richard Brink, State Coordinator, HUD-Montana State Office, Federal Office Bldg., Drawer 10095, 301 South Park, Room 340, Helena, MT 59626-0095; 406-449-5707.

Nebraska
Terry Gratz, State Coordinator, HUD-Nebraska State Office, Executive Tower Centre,, 10909 Mill Valley Rd., Omaha, NE 68154-3955; 402-492-3101.

Nevada
Paul Pradia, State Coordinator, HUD-Nevada State Office, Atrium Bldg., 333 N. Rancho Dr., Suite 700, Las Vegas, NV 89106-3714; 702-388-6500.

New Hampshire
David B. Harrity, State Coordinator, HUD-New Hampshire State Office, Norris Cotton Federal Bldg., 275 Chestnut St., Manchester, NH 03103-2487; 603-666-7681.

New Jersey
Diane Johnson, State Coordinator, HUD-New Jersey State Office, One Newark Center, 13th Floor, Newark, NJ 07102-5260; 201-622-7900, ext. 3102.

New Mexico
Michael R. Griego, State Coordinator, HUD-New Mexico State Office, 625 Truman St., NE, Albuquerque, NM 87110-6443; 505-262-6463.

New York
Diane Johnson, Acting Secretary's Representative, HUD-New York State Office, 26 Federal Plaza, New York, NY 10278-0068; 212-264-8068.

North Carolina
James Blackmon, State Coordinator, HUD-North Carolina State Office, Koger Bldg., 2306 W. Meadowview Rd., Greensboro, NC 27407-3707; 919-547-4001.

North Dakota
Keith Elliot, Acting State Coordinator, HUD-North Dakota State Office, Federal Bldg., 657 2nd Ave., North, P.O. Box 2483, Fargo, ND 58108-2483; 701-239-5136.

Ohio
Deborah C. Williams, State Coordinator, HUD-Ohio State Office, 200 N. High St., Columbus, OH 43215-2499; 614-469-7345.

Oklahoma
Katie Worsham, Acting State Coordinator, HUD-Oklahoma State Office, 500 Main St., Oklahoma City, OK 73102; 405-553-7400.

Oregon
Mark Pavolka, Acting State Coordinator, HUD-Oregon State Office, 400 SW 6th Ave., Suite 700, Portland, OR 97204-1632; 503-326-2561.

Pennsylvania
Karen A. Miller, Secretary's Representative, HUD-Pennsylvania State Office, The Wanamaker Bldg., 100 Penn Square East, Philadelphia, PA 19107-3390; 215-656-0600.

Puerto Rico
Maria Teresa Pombo, Acting State Coordinator, HUD-Caribbean Office, New San Juan Office Bldg., 159 Carlos E. Chardon Ave., San Juan, PR 00918-1804; 809-766-6121.

Rhode Island
Nancy Smith, State Coordinator, HUD-Rhode Island State Office, 10 Weybosset St., 6th Floor, Providence, RI 02903-3234; 401-528-5230.

South Carolina
Choice Edwards, State Coordinator, HUD-South Carolina State Office, Strom Thurmond Federal Bldg., 1835 Assembly St., Columbia, SC 29201-2480; 803-765-5592.

South Dakota
Dwight Peterson, State Coordinator, HUD-South Dakota State Office, 2400 West 49th St., Suite I-201, Sioux Falls, SD 57105-6558; 605-330-4223.

Tennessee
Ginger Van Ness, State Coordinator, HUD-Tennessee State Office, 251 Cumberland Bend Dr., Suite 200, Nashville, TN 37228-1803; 615-736-5213.

Texas
Stephen Weatherford, Secretary's Representative, HUD-Texas State Office, 1600 Throckmorton, P.O. Box 2905, Fort Worth, TX 76113-2905; 817-885-5401.

Utah
John Milchick, State Coordinator, HUD-Utah State Office, 257 Tower, 257 East 200 South, Suite 550, Salt Lake City, UT 84111-2048; 801-524-5241.

Vermont
William Peters, Acting State Coordinator, HUD-Vermont State Office, Federal Building, 11 Elmwood Ave., Room 244, P.O. Box 879, Burlington, VT 05402-0879; 802-951-6290.

Virginia
Mary Ann Wilson, State Coordinator, HUD-Virginia State Office, The 3600 Centre, 3600 West Broad St., P.O. Box 90331, Richmond, VA 23230-0331; 804-278-4507.

Washington
Bob Santos, Secretary's Representative, HUD-Washington State Office, Seattle Federal Office Bldg., 909 First Ave., Suite 200, Seattle, WA 98104-1000; 206-220-5101.

West Virginia
Fred Roncaglione, State Coordinator, HUD-West Virginia State Office, 405 Capitol St., Suite 708, Charleston, WV 25301-1795; 304-347-7036.

Wisconsin
Delbert F. Reynolds, State Coordinator, HUD-Wisconsin State Office, Henry S. Reuss Federal Plaza, 310 W. Wisconsin Ave., Suite 1380, Milwaukee, WI 53203-2289; 612-370-3288.

Wyoming
William Garrett, Acting State Coordinator, HUD-Wyoming State Office, 4225 Federal Office Bldg., 100 East B St., P.O. Box 120, Casper, WY 82602-1918; 307-261-5252.

* Homes: H.O.P.E. 3

U.S. Department of Housing and Urban Development
Office of Community Planning and Development
Office of Affordable Housing Programs
451 7th St., SW
Washington, DC 20410-7000
202-708-0324

The HUD Urban Homesteading Program has been replaced by the HOPE 3 Program. It is designed to provide homeownership for low income families and individuals. The funds will be distributed to the 10 HUD regions and awarded to local governments and non-profit organizations on a competitive bidding basis. It will generally provide down payment assistance for groups to acquire or rehabilitate affordable low income housing. Call your regional HUD office to find out who has been awarded grants, and then contact them directly to see what is available.

You qualify for housing help through HOPE 3 under the Low Income Family Housing Act if you are a first time homebuyer and are below 80% of the median income in your area. You may also qualify if you have not owned a home in 3 years. You must also meet the affordability criteria -- which requires that the cost of principal interest, taxes and insurance for the home comes to no more than 30% of your income. Since the program is new, the quality of public dissemination of information about these programs remains to be seen. These programs are instituted to help you, so don't be afraid to be persistent in asking for information about what HOPE 3 programs are available in your area from the Community Planning and Development Office at the Field or Regional HUD office nearest you.

To find out what the programs will provide and how to apply for a grant, contact John Garrity, DHUD, Office of Urban Rehabilitation, Room 7158, 451 Seventh Street, SW, Washington, DC 20410-7000, 202-708-0324 or look up the Monday, February 4, 1991 issue of the *Federal Register*, Part X, DHUD, 24 CFR Subtitle A called *HOPE for Homeownership for Single Family Homes Program; Notice of Program Guidelines*.

* Homes: Veterans Administration

U.S. Veterans Administration (VA)
1120 Vermont Ave., NW
Washington, DC 20420   202-418-4270

Contact the local Veterans Administration Office in your state, or a real estate broker. Watch newspaper ads in local papers for listings of foreclosed properties. The "For Sale" signs on VA foreclosed properties are distinctive. The National Veterans Administration office in Washington, DC is not directly involved in handling the sales; for any inquiries you will be referred to a real estate broker or local VA office.

The Veterans Administration sells foreclosed properties through private real estate brokers. Properties are frequently advertised in local newspapers, giving information such as address, number of bedrooms and bathrooms, particular defects in the property, and price. Almost any real estate agent can show you the property. No broker has an exclusive listing for any of these properties. Local VA offices are the best source of information on the procedures involved in purchasing these properties. Regional offices publish lists of foreclosed properties with descriptions in multiple listing code and phone numbers to call about the property. In some cases, they will also directly send you lists of properties currently available in your area. These offices will mail out a list each time you write in a request, but unless you are a broker, they will not send the list for foreclosures to you on a monthly basis. You can, however, have the agent of your choice put on the mailing list. Others will not mail lists to you, but allow you to pick up the list from their office and/or will refer you to a broker. In either case, you must go through an agent to purchase the house, since they have the keys to the premises, and the process is very much like a regular real estate transaction. The listing has the price on it the VA wants. It will also state if the VA is willing to entertain a lower price. Houses come "as is" with no guarantees, so it is important to inspect them carefully. Some are located in less than desirable neighborhoods, but there are bargains to be had as well. For the most part VA financed homes are mainstream suburban, not inner city. They are often found in neighborhoods located in economically hard hit areas -- such as the Southwest. Prices may drop on homes that are not sold in a certain period of time. VA financing is possible. Also, if you plan on VA financing, in cases of a tie, the other bidder gets priority for cash offers (pre-approved financing through a commercial lender.) You must state at the time of the bid whether you intend to use VA financing or have found your own.

There are two basic avenues to arrange financing. You can be pre-qualified by lenders and then go shopping. More commonly, the real estate broker you are working with will tell you what is available in the mortgage market. The usual way it works is that you find a broker, find a house, bid on it, wind the bid and then the broker helps you to find financing.

If you should win a bid on a VA foreclosed home but be unable to procure financing, some regional offices will put the home up for bid again. Others hold backup offers and will contact the next highest bidder if the original successful bidder is unable to complete the purchase. Most listings offer to sell financing at the current rate of interest for GI loans, even if the buyer is not a GI. A purchaser who is a GI can get these rates without using his GI benefits. Call the office listed above if you have questions. They will direct you to the appropriate department of your regional office. If you are a GI and wish to find out about a Certificate of Eligibility, whereby you can purchase a home worth up to $203,000 without a down payment, call 202-418-4270, ext. 3308 or your regional office. To discuss VA loan qualifications generally, call 202-827-1000 or your regional office.

Purchase is done through a sealed bidding process. Earnest money requirements are 1 percent of the purchase price, and are nonrefundable if the bid is accepted. This is a salvage program designed to recover what it can of the cost to the VA for purchasing the property, within a reasonable amount of time after foreclosure -- usually around 6 months.

* Miscellaneous Property: U.S. Customs Service

E.G.& G. Dynatrend
Attn: PAL
2300 Clarendon Blvd., Suite 705   703-351-7887
Arlington, VA 22201   703-351-7880

E.G.& G. Dynatrend, under contract with the U.S. Customs Service, auctions forfeited and confiscated general merchandise, including vehicles, on a nationwide basis. Items include everything from vessels--both pleasure and commercial--to aircraft, machinery, clothes (in both commercial and individual quantities), jewelry, household goods, precious stones, liquor, furniture, high technology equipment, and infrequently, real estate. Public auctions and sealed and open bid methods are all used. Items are sold only by lot and number of items in a lot vary from one to many. You must bid on the entire lot.

The U.S. Customs Public Auction Line is 703-351-7887. Call it to subscribe to the mailing list of locations and dates of sales, to obtain general information about the custom sales program, dates of sales in your region or information about real estate sales. For $50 dollars per year you can subscribe to a mailing list of items to be auctioned nationwide; or you may subscribe to a list limited to one region of the country for $25. You will then receive fliers with descriptions of items available in upcoming auctions. There are two regions: states east of the Mississippi River, and states west of the Mississippi River. Send your name, address, telephone number, and a money order to the above address. Allow six to eight weeks for the first flier to arrive. The fliers will then arrive three weeks prior to the viewing period and will tell you when and where the items are available for inspection and details of auction procedures. Catalogs are also available a week before the sale with additional details. For sealed bids, a deposit in cashier's check for the total bid must be submitted along with the bid. Make the cashier's check payable to U.S. Customs Service/E.G.& G. Dynatrend, Agent. Indicate sale number on cashier's check and outside on the envelope.

U.S. Customs auctions are held every nine weeks in the following eight cities: Los Angeles, CA; Laredo, TX; Nogales, AZ; Miami, FL; Edinburg, TX; Houston, TX; Chula Vista, CA (San Diego, CA area); El Paso, TX; and Yuma, AZ. Other auctions are scheduled at different times at various other cities also.

* Miscellaneous Property: U.S. Department of Defense

The Defense Reutilization Marketing Service (DRMS)
Federal Center
74 N. Washington   616-961-7014
Battle Creek, MI 49017-3092   1-800-GOVT-BUY

Imagine what kinds of items are used, then discarded, by a government department as big as the Defense Department: literally everything from recyclable scrap materials and weapons accessories, to airplanes, ships, trains, and motor vehicles; to wood and metalworking machinery, agricultural equipment, construction equipment, communications equipment and medical, dental and veterinary supplies. Not to forget photographic equipment, chemical products, office machines, food preparation and serving equipment, musical instruments, textiles, furs, tents, flags, and sometimes live animals such as goats and horses. No activated items with military applications are included. Neither are real estate or confiscated items such as sports cars or luxury goods.

Goods sold are either surplus or not usable by other government agencies. First priority is given to designated groups which qualify for donations. The rest is then put up for public sale. By contacting the Defense Reutilization Marketing Service at the above address or telephone, you can receive a booklet called *How to Buy Surplus*

Personal Property which explains what Department of Defense has for sale and how to bid for it. The Defense Department also lists notices of Sealed Bid property sales in the *Commerce Business Daily*, available from the Superintendent of Documents, Government Printing Office, Washington, DC 20402-9325; 202-512-1800.

Sales are conducted by regional Defense Reutilization and Marketing Region (DRMR) sales offices which coordinate sales in their geographical area. Listed below are addresses and telephone numbers of the regional offices, which can direct you further as to exactly where items are physically sold. Local sales are by auction, spot bid, or on a retail basis. Auctions are held where there are relatively small quantities of a variety of items. Spot bids are made through forms submitted in the course of a sale - usually when the property is something with a high demand or interest. The retail sales offer small quantities at fixed, market-level prices. There are 180 retail sales outlets, on military bases.

Large quantities of goods are usually sold by sealed bid, which you submit by mail, along with a deposit, on a form you obtain in a catalog which describes the items. (You receive the catalogs once you are on the mailing list). Recyclable materials are sold through the Resource Recovery Recycling Program or through the Hazardous Property Program. Call the above listed number for further details. You can be put on a mailing list to receive advance notice of DOD sales in your region, but if you don't make any bids after two notifications it will probably be removed unless you make an additional request to remain on the list. You can also be placed on a National Bidders List for sales throughout the country by contacting 1-800-222-DRMS. People under age 18 and members of the U.S. Armed Forces, including civilian employees, are not eligible to participate in these sales. This 800 number can also direct you to the retail sales outlet nearest you, and can give you other information on DRMS sales, including how to obtain a catalog.

Following are the Defense Reutilization and Marketing sales offices:

DRMR: Columbus, P.O. Box 500, Blacklick, OH 43004-0500, 614-692-2114. This region includes: MN, WI, MI, IA, NE, KS, MO, IL, IN, OH, WV, VA, DE, NJ, PA, MD, CT, NY, RI, MA, ME, VT, NH, and District of Columbia

DRMR: Memphis, 2163 Airways Blvd., Memphis, TN 38114-0716, 901-775-4554. This region includes: TX, OK, AR, LA, MS, AL, TN, KY, GA, FL, SC, NC.

DRMR: Ogden, 500 W. 12 St., Building 2A1, Ogden, UT 84407-5001, 801-777-6557. This region includes: ND, SD, MT, WY, ID, UT, CO, AZ, NM, WA, OR, NV, CA.

You can also take advantage of DOD sales if you live outside the United States. The DOD booklet, *How to Buy Surplus Personal Property*, lists addresses for various regions in Europe and the Pacific.

* Miscellaneous Property: General Services Administration Property

Personal Property Sales Center
U.S. General Services Administration
1941 Jefferson Davis Hwy.
Arlington, VA 22202   703-305-7814/7240

Contact your local General Services Administration (GSA) office listed below. The GSA disposes of surplus property for most of the government agencies, and has items ranging from vehicles and scrap metals, to office furniture, office and industrial equipment, data processing equipment, boats, medical equipment, waste paper and computers; as well as aircraft, railroad equipment, agricultural equipment, textiles, food waste, photographic equipment, jewelry, watches, and clothing.

Some regional offices have no mailing list. Instead, there is a number they will give you to call that is a recorded message of all upcoming events. It will give the time, date, and location of the auction and type, such as warehouse, vehicles or office furniture. Other regions allow you to have your name placed on a mailing list to receive advance notices of auctions at no cost. Catalogs list the specific items and their condition. Sales are conducted as regular auctions, spot auctions (where bids are submitted on-the-spot in writing) and by sealed bid (written on a form and mailed in). For auctions and spot bids, you will have two days prior to the sale to view and inspect property, and one week prior for sealed bids. For sealed bid items you receive a catalog, once your are on the mailing list, describing the merchandise. If your region does not have a mailing list, you may pick up catalogs at the office or the sale. Announcements come out as property is accumulated, with March to October being the busiest period. The highest bidder wins in all cases.

Prices may range from way below wholesale for some items to close-to-market prices for others, especially automobiles and boats. Cars tend to be common American-made brands, such as Tempos, Citations, and Reliances. Cars are auctioned when they are three years old or have reached 60,000 miles, whichever occurs first, and are usually sold at a fair market price. Seized cars may be newer and of a foreign make. A Mercedes-Benz was recently sold at a National Capitol Region auction. Payment may be by cash, cashier's checks, money orders, traveler's checks, government, or credit union checks; but any personal or business checks must be accompanied by an Informal Bank Letter guaranteeing payment. Full payment must be made by the following day, and bidders are responsible for removal of all property. To bid in GSA auctions, you must register at the site and obtain a bidder number. Once you are on the bidders mailing list, you must bid at least once while receiving five mailings or your name will be removed from the list. Then you must contact the appropriate office again to continue receiving mailings.

Some listings for a GSA sale in Bismarck, North Dakota included the following items: miscellaneous kitchen equipment, meat slicers, coffee makers, cameras, film, binoculars, screens, paper, postage meter, nuts and bolts, typewriters, lettering set, mailboxes, lamps, and a streetlight.

For information about GSA auctions in your area, contact one of the regional offices listed below:

National Capitol Region (Washington DC and vicinity)
6808 Loisdale Rd., Building A, Springfield, VA 22150; 703-557-7785, or 703-557-7796, for a recording.

Region I (Boston)
GSA, Surplus Sales Branch, 10 Causeway St., Room 1079, Boston, MA, 02109; 617-565-7326, Auction Hotline Recording, 617-565-6045 or 800-755-1946.

Region II (New York)
GSA Surplus Sales Branch, 26 Federal Plaza, Room 20-116, New York, NY, 10078; 212-264-4824, or 212-264-4823, for a recording.

Region III (Philadelphia)
GSA Surplus Sales Branch, P.O. Box 40657, Philadelphia, PA 19107-3396; 215-656-3939 or 215-656-3400 for a recording.

Region IV (Atlanta)
GSA Surplus Sales Branch, Attn: 4PR, 401 West Peachtree St., Room 3015, Atlanta, GA 30365-2550; 404-331-0972, recording 404-331-5133 or 800-473-7836.

Region V (Chicago)
230 S. Dearborn St., Chicago, IL 60604; 312-353-6061 office, 800-755-1946 or 312-353-0246 hotline for a recorded announcement.

Region VI (Kansas)
GSA Surplus Sales Branch (6FB), 4400 College Blvd., Suite 175, Overland Park, KS 66211; 816-823-3700.

Region VII (Ft. Worth)
GSA Surplus Sales Branch (2PR), 819 Taylor St., Room 9A33, Ft. Worth, TX 76102-6105; 817-334-2352 or 800-833-4317, 817-334-2331 for a recorded announcement.

Region VIII (Denver)
GSA Surplus Sales Branch (7FBP-8), Denver Federal Center, Building 41, Room 253, P.O. Box 22506-DSC, Denver, CO 80225-0506; 303-236-7705 for recording or 303-236-7702.

Region IX (San Francisco)
GSA Surplus Sales Section 9PR, 525 Market St., 5th Floor, San Francisco, CA 94105; 415-744-5245 or 800-676-SALE for catalogs or mailing lists.

Region X (Washington)
GSA Surplus Sales Branch GSA Center (9PR-F), 400 15th St., SW, Room 1138, Auburn, WA 98001-6599; 206-931-7566 for a recording or 206-931-7547.

* Miscellaneous Property: Internal Revenue Service
Office of Special Procedures
Internal Revenue Service (IRS)
U.S. Department of the Treasury
1111 Constitution Ave., NW
Washington, DC 20224   202-622-6938
No information concerning auctions is available from this office. Contact your local district office to see if they maintain a mailing list to receive information on upcoming auctions. If not, this information can be found in your local newspaper.

Check the classified section for a listing of IRS seized property to be sold. The listing will give phone number and details. The property sold by the IRS is seized from delinquent taxpayers rather than being used or surplus government property. Many kinds of merchandise are put up for auction, including real estate, vehicles, and office and industrial equipment. Sales are by both sealed bids and public auction. Regarding property sales, the IRS warns that land may still be redeemed by the original owner up to 180 days AFTER you, the bidder, purchase it at an auction; and therefore no deed is issued until this time period has elapsed. Buildings on land being sold by the IRS are NOT open for inspection by a potential buyer unless permission is granted by the taxpayer/owner.

Payment may be by cash, certified check, cashier's check, or money order. In some cases, full payment is required the day of the sale. Otherwise, a 20% downpayment (or $200, whichever is greater) is needed to hold the property, with the balance due at a specified time from the date of the sale, not to exceed one month.

* Miscellaneous Property: U.S. Marshals Service
U.S. Marshals Service
Seized Assets Division
U.S. Department of Justice
600 Army-Navy Drive
Arlington, VA 22202   202-307-9237
Contact your local Sunday newspaper for auction notices in the legal section, or the nearest U.S. Marshals Office under U.S. Department of Justice. Usually the Marshals Office is located in the Federal Building of a city. The U.S. Marshals Service or a contracted commercial sales or auction service may handle disposal of the property. Sales are always listed every third Wednesday in *USA Today* newspaper.

In 1991, the Drug Enforcement Agency managed 1.4 billion dollars worth of property from convicted drug dealers. The U.S. Marshals Service, which holds crime-related property accumulated in Federal drug-related and other confiscations, auctions much of this off to the public through 94 offices around the country. Items sold include everything from entire working businesses, to cars, houses, copiers, jewelry, rare coin and stamp collections, apartment complexes, and restaurants. The government is not giving these properties away by any means, but bargains are possible as well as opportunities to purchase some exotic goodies. Confiscated viable businesses are managed by the Service until the time of the auction in order to keep up or increase the businesses' value.

Auctions are not scheduled regularly, but occur when items accumulate. Auctions may be conducted by private auctioneers or the Marshals Service itself. No mailing list is kept to notify you individually, and there is no national listing of items, since new properties are seized daily and adjudication of drug-related cases may take years. Payment at these auctions is by cash, certified check, or special arrangements when large amounts of money are involved. One note, the Marshals Service checks out people paying for large items with cash to make sure the government is not re-selling things to drug dealers. The Marshals Service also auctions off property seized by the Drug Enforcement Agency and the Federal Bureau of Investigation.

* Miscellaneous Property: U.S. Postal Service
Claims and Inquiry Office
U.S. Postal Service
475 L'Enfant Plaza, S.W.
Washington, DC 20260-0001   202-636-1500
Vehicle Management Facility   202-832-0176
Contact the Mail Recovery Centers listed below for undeliverable goods; or your local Postmaster for Vehicle Maintenance Facilities and surplus property auctions. To receive advance notice of the auctions you can write to a Mail Recovery Center and request that your name be put on the auction sales mailing list. To be on all of them, you must write to each one separately. Usually 10 days before the auction, you will be notified by postcard of the time, date and place. Viewing inspections are usually held 2 hours before the auction begins.

The Postal Service holds auctions of unclaimed merchandise which includes a wide range of property -- from electronic and household items -- to clothes, jewelry, linens, toys, all types of equipment, and lots of books. Sales are handled through the Mail Recovery Centers throughout the country listed below. However, any high value items such as art works, are sold at the New York auction. Contact your local Postmaster to ask about their auctions of surplus property and used vehicles. There are 225 post office vehicle maintenance facilities throughout the country. Their addresses and phone numbers are all listed at the back of the Zip Code Directory kept at post offices. The used vehicle sales can be good bargains, since the vehicles are somewhat fixed up, painted, and occasionally in good condition. Some jeeps, for instance, may sell for between $1200 and $1500. Recently a man bought 15 jeeps for $100 each at auction. Vehicles that do not sell off the storage lot are auctioned. Sometimes cars such as Pintos can be picked up for as little as $750. The sales conducted by the 225 Vehicle Maintenance Facilities around the country are usually fixed price sales, but 5 or 6 times per year auctions have been held at larger cities.

The mail recovery items are usually sold in lots of similar goods, with the volume or quantity varying widely. Prices depend on what the goods are and the number of people bidding at a particular auction. There may be a minimum bid required, such as $20; and often cash is the only acceptable payment. Bidders are responsible for removing the items purchased.

A flier for a Postal Service auction of unclaimed and damaged merchandise in St. Paul, Minnesota advised that only those already on an established check register may pay by check; otherwise, cash is required. It also advised that potential bidders to bring their own containers -- boxes, crates, and bags -- for packing. The Postal Service in San Francisco, California, announced that books, jewelry, sound recordings, speakers, and cabinets, as well as miscellaneous merchandise would be available.

Eastern Region
U.S. Postal Service Mail Recovery Center, Room 531 A, 2970 Market St., Philadelphia, PA 19104-9652; 215-895-8140 (auction information and number to call to be notified by postcard of next upcoming auction). Includes Pennsylvania, Southern New Jersey, Maryland, Delaware, Ohio, Kentucky, Indiana, Virginia, West Virginia, North Carolina, and South Carolina.

Central Region
U.S. Postal Service Mail Recovery Center, 180 E. Kellogg St., Room 932, St. Paul, MN 55101-9607; 612-293-3083. Includes Minnesota, Michigan, Wisconsin, North Dakota, South Dakota, Nebraska, Iowa, Illinois, Northern New Jersey, New Hampshire, Maine, Vermont, Rhode Island, Massachusetts, Kansas, Missouri, Connecticut, and New York.

Southern Region
U.S. Postal Service Mail Recovery Center, 730 Great Southwest Parkway, Atlanta, GA 30336-2496; 404-344-1625. Includes Georgia, Florida, Louisiana, Tennessee, Arkansas, Mississippi, Oklahoma, part of Texas, Alabama, Mississippi, Virgin Islands, and Puerto Rico.

Western Region
U.S. Postal Service Mail Recovery Center, 390 Main St., 4th Floor, San Francisco, CA 94105-9602; 415-543-1826. Auctions are held at 228 Harrison St., San Francisco, CA. Includes: Alaska, Oregon, Idaho, California, Washington, Nevada, Utah, Arizona, New Mexico, part of Texas, Hawaii, Wyoming, Colorado, Montana, Guam, and Samoa.

* Natural Resources Sales Assistance
Office of Liquidations
Small Business Administration (SBA)
409 Third Street SW, 8th Floor   1-800-827-5722
Washington, DC 20416   202-205-6500
The federal government sells surplus property and natural resources, such as timber. SBA works with government agencies which are selling the property and resources to assure that small businesses have an opportunity to buy a fair share of them. Occasionally natural resources that the federal government is releasing on the market are made available. Small fuel companies and producers may get the option to buy their fair share of federal government coal leases. The royalty oil program enables small and independent refineries to buy oil at valuations set by the federal government - which is in excess of spot market prices. Agricultural leases may be had for land on which to graze cattle or grow crops. This SBA program is designed to ensure that small businesses get their fair share of real and personal federal property put on the market. Don't expect bargains. To find out what SBA Natural Resources Sales Assistance programs are in your area, contact your nearest SBA office. For information on other SBA services, call 1-800-827-5722 (recorded listing from which you can order brochures.)

* Real Estate: General Services Administration
Property Sales
General Services Administration (GSA)
Office of Real Estate Sales
Washington, DC 20406   1-800-GSA-1313
Call this toll-free number for national listing of properties and to receive a booklet describing the GSA real estate program. Then contact local GSA office for the area you are interested in. You can also obtain the list by calling the Property Disposal

Division, 202-501-0067. The phone number of the local GSA office to contact will be provided on the list that is mailed to you free of charge upon request. If you have a computer equipped with a modem, you can access the Federal Real Estate Bulletin Board for information on real estate sales. Set you communications software to 8 data bits, no parity, and 1 stop bit. Dial 800-776-7872 or 202-501-6510.

* Real Estate: Small Business Administration (SBA)
U.S. Small Business Administration
Portfolio Management Division
409 Third Street, SW
Washington, DC 20416   202-205-6481
Recording from which to order brochures 1-800-827-5722
Contact your local SBA office located in 10 Regional Offices around the country, or any of the 68 District Offices. SBA does not maintain a mailing list. No district or regional SBA office is aware of what the other offices are offering. The SBA auctions off properties of people who have defaulted on home loan payments in SBA-sponsored programs. Listings of auctions are printed in local newspapers, usually in the Sunday edition in the classified section. Merchandise is identified as SBA property and sold by brokers, none of whom have the exclusive listing, or by private auctioneers. The auctioneers are chosen on a rotating basis. SBA attempts to sell to the highest bidder, but may reject a winning bid if too low. Sales are infrequent. Do not expect bargains. Items sold range from office furniture and equipment to buildings or entire bakeries, drycleaners, or other businesses. There may be parts or whole businesses available. The auctioneer may have an entire auction of SBA items, or a mixture of things from various sources. You may request to bid by sealed bid if you desire; and a deposit is required. Payment is by cash or certified check. If you are interested in certain categories of merchandise, you might want to be placed on the mailing list of one or more auctioneers who specialize in that particular type of item, such as farm equipment, for example. Since the SBA is often the guarantor of bank loans, SBA auctions are relatively infrequent and bargains are not easy to find. SBA Regional Offices follow:

Dallas: 8625 King George Dr., Dallas, TX 75235-3391; 214-767-7633

Kansas City: 328 8th St., Suite 307, Kansas City, MO 64105; 816-374-6380

Denver: 633 17th St., 7th Floor, Denver, CO 80202; 303-294-7186

San Francisco: 71 Stevenson St., 20th Floor, San Francisco, CA 94105-2939; 415-744-6402

Seattle: 1200 6th Ave., Suite 1805, Seattle, WA 98101-1128; 206-553-5676

Boston: 10 Causway, Room 812, Boston, MA 02222-1093; 617-565-8415

New York: 26 Federal Plaza, Room 3108, New York, NY 10278; 212-264-1450

King of Prussia: 475 Allendale Rd., Suite 201, King of Prussia, PA 19406; 610-962-3700

Atlanta: 1375 Peachtree St. N.E., 5th Floor, Atlanta, GA 30367-8102; 404-347-2797

Chicago: 300 South Riverside Plaza, Suite 1975 South, Chicago,IL 60606-6617; 312-353-5000

* Ships: Maritime Administration
U.S. Department of Transportation
Office of Ship Operations
Maritime Administration
400 7th St., SW, Room 7324
Washington, DC 20590   202-366-5111
When the government decides that a merchant ship is no longer needed or useable, it may put that ship up for sale by auction, through a sealed bid procedure. A ten percent deposit is required. It is sold to the highest bidder for its scrap value. Contact the above address to be put on the auction mailing list. When ships are available, you will receive descriptions of the ships and information on the bidding procedure.

* Timber Sales for Small Business
Government Contracting
Small Business Administration (SBA)
409 3rd St., SW, #8800
Washington, DC 20416   202-205-6470
The U.S. Government regularly sells timber from the federal forests managed by the

U.S. Forest Service, Department of Agriculture, and the Bureau of Land Management, Department of Interior. On occasion, timber also is sold from federally-owned forests which are under the supervision of the Department of Defense, the Department of Energy, and the Tennessee Valley Authority, and the Department of the Interior. The SBA and these agencies work together to ensure full opportunity for concerns to bid on federal timber sales. SBA and the sales agencies jointly set aside timber sales for bidding by small concerns when it appears that, under open sales, small business would not obtain a fair share at reasonable prices. Contact your local SBA office for further specific information. It is listed in the blue pages of the telephone directory.

Donations to Non-Profit Organizations

* Art Exhibits

Smithsonian Institution
1100 Jefferson Dr., SW
Room 3146   202-357-3168
Washington, DC 20560   Fax: 202-357-4324

The Smithsonian can bring art to you, whether you live in a major metropolitan area or a rural one. The Smithsonian Institute Traveling Exhibition Service (SITES) sponsors approximately 65 different exhibits at any given time in museums and other locations around the country. The participation fee will range from $100 to $100,000. The exhibitions range from popular culture, to fine arts, photography, science, historical exhibits, or topics of interest to children. The collections are from other museums and institutions, and are most frequently sent to other museums, libraries, historic homes, or even schools and community centers. More than half the locations are in rural settings. SITES estimates that more than 11 million people view the exhibits it circulates in this program. The bigger exhibits that require special security arrangements go only to museums equipped to handle them. If interested, call the above number for the SITES *Updates* catalog.

* Books

Library of Congress
Exchange and Gift Division
1st and C Street, SE
Washington, DC 20540-4280   202-707-9511/9512

Government agencies, educational institutions, and other non-profit organizations may qualify to obtain free books from the U.S. Library of Congress. The books are largely technical and legal works, but from time to time contains entire collections from military installation lending libraries that have been closed. There is no way to tell what books will be available. Stock is constantly changing. Books are first offered on a competitive bidding basis. If they are not sold, they become available on a donation bidding basis. Commercial book dealers may compete in this bidding against non-profit organizations. The proceeds sustain the Book Preservation Program. Someone from the organization must choose which books are desired. He or she must have a letter from the organization or appropriate Congressional representative stating that the person it selected to choose the books acts for a non-profit organization. The Library will ship the books UPS at the organization's expense or the organization may supply the Library with pre-addressed franking labels. Congressional offices will help educational institutions such as universities and schools obtain these labels. Non-profit organizations may submit bids to purchase books. The Library will contact the organization if the bid is unacceptably low and give the bidder one chance to raise it. There is no limit on the number of books a group may order.

* Department of Housing and Urban Development (HUD)

HUD Library and Information Service
451 7th Street SW
Room 814
Washington, DC 20743

To find out about the over 100 programs HUD offers to assist low and moderate income housing groups and individuals, obtain *Programs of HUD* by calling 202-708-1420.

* Food and Surplus Commodities

USDA Food Distribution Programs
or Food Distribution Division
Food and Nutrition Service
3101 Park Center Drive, Room 503
Alexandria, VA 22302   703-305-2680

Non-profit groups with tax-exempt status may apply for surplus commodities held by the Agriculture Department, such as grain (usually flour), oils, and sometimes milk and cheese. The large quantities of surplus cheese and milk that existed a couple of years ago are largely depleted. The items available depend somewhat on which foods are currently in surplus. Contact your state distribution agency, frequently the state Department of Agriculture, Department of Education, or Administrative Services, or the above address.

* Foreign Gifts

General Services Administration
Crystal Mall Building #4
1941 Jefferson Davis Highway, Room 800
Washington, DC 20406   703-308-0745

Non-Presidential gifts worth over $200 from foreign countries to U.S. government agencies or their representatives may be displayed by the recipient in his government office, then purchased by him at an officially assessed value. If the gift is not purchased, it may end up in a State Surplus Property office, where the general public can get a chance to buy it. Watches and jewelry are commonly available, along with books, sculptures, and various artifacts. But the souvenir from Anwar Sadat to Jimmy Carter during the Middle East peace talks goes to the U.S. Archives and possibly later to the Jimmy Carter Library.

When gifts are reported to the GSA, they first go through the federal screening cycle. Federal agencies have the first chance to purchase items at retail value price. If none exercise that option, the recipient may purchase the item. If the item remains unsold, it enters the donation screening cycle. It may then be used for display purposes at state agencies such as libraries or museums. After that, it may be sold to the public at auction. At public auction, anyone can purchase the item. Non-profits have no special footing. Items are disposed of by GSA in basically the same way as other surplus and excess property.

Items desired by non-profit organizations should be requested through your local Surplus Property Office, which can then contact the GSA about a donation. You can find a list of foreign gifts given to government agencies published yearly in the *Federal Register*, State Department, Chief of Protocol, Washington, DC, 202-647-4169.

* Housing for the Homeless

Judy Breitman
Chief, Real Property Branch
Division of Health Facilities Planning
ORM/OM
U.S. Department of Health and Human Services
Parklawn Building, Room 17A-10
5600 Fishers Lane   301-443-2265
Rockville, MD 20857   Fax: 301-443-0084

The above will send you a helpful brochure entitled *Obtaining Federal Property for the Homeless: Questions and Answers About Federal Property Programs*. If you are part of a non-profit organization ministering to the homeless, the government is currently taking applications for eligible groups to receive excess or unused federal buildings or land for homeless people. The property is leased or deeded over. To find out what properties are available call the 24 hour hotline, 1-800-927-7588. Every Friday, *The Federal Register* (available from libraries or by subscription) will list which federal properties are available and where. The applying organization has 60 days after notice of property availability is published to submit a written expression of interest. It will then be sent an application packet and have 90 days after that to apply for the property. Criteria is outlined in *The Federal Register*. If you think your organization may qualify, call Public Health Service, 301-443-2265.

* Interagency Council on the Homeless

Office of Special Needs Assistance Programs
U.S. Department of Housing and Urban Development
451 Seventh Street, SW, Room 7262
Washington, DC 20410   202-708-1480

This is a coordinating counsel of 16 different federal agencies, headed by the HUD Secretary. It works with state and local governments and private organizations on homeless-related efforts. Call for information on homeless activities. For information on financing rehabilitation or support services, contact HUD's Office of Special Needs Assistance Program at 202-708-4300.

Title V of the McKinney Act is the "Federal Surplus Property Program." You can call 1-800-927-7588 to get answers about the Title V Program and properties 24 hours per day. Under this program, federally owned surplus or unused property may

Be patient. If any phone number is incorrect, call (area code) 555-1212 and request the new listing.

697

Government Auctions and Surplus Property

be deeded, leased or made available on an interim basis at no cost to homeless providers such as states, local governments and non-profit organizations. To find out about eligible properties, ask to be put on the mailing list that tells you of properties in your area as they are published by contacting your nearest field HUD office.

* Miscellaneous Property

Director, Property Management Division
Office of Transportation and Property Management
Federal Supply Service
Washington, DC 20406   703-308-0745

Or contact your local State Office of Surplus Property. The General Services Administration (GSA) will donate items it handles to qualifying non-profit organizations which request it. Items are "as is" and range from tools, office machines, supplies and furniture, clothes, hardware, medical supplies to cars, boats, and planes. Your State Agency for Surplus Property, also called Office of Purchasing, Property Control, or General Services, makes the determination whether your group qualifies, then contacts the GSA to obtain it. There may be a charge of 2% of the value and a fee for handling and service. Groups eligible can include public agencies, and non-profit educational, public health, elderly, or homeless organizations.

* Tools for Schools

Federal Surplus Warehouse
1910 Darbytown Rd.
Richmond, VA 23231   804-236-3665

Qualifying nonprofit organizations and educational institutions can receive surplus federal property. Items available depend on what is in the warehouse at the time, which ranges from office furniture to industrial equipment. A completed application must first be submitted and approved. There are some stipulations, including a service charge based on the value of the merchandise. Contact this office for more information and an application.

* Travel Aboard an Icebreaker

Ice Operations Division
U.S. Coast Guard Headquarters
2100 2nd Street, SW
Washington, DC 20593   202-267-1450

The Coast Guard does not evaluates scientific projects to determine if they qualify. The group that qualifies as a primary user, because it is willing to pay for fuel and part of maintenance and helicopter costs on resupply trips, may send a scientist they select to ride along with one of the two Coast Guard Icebreakers that travel to the Arctic and Antarctica. At present, the National Science Foundation (4201 Wilson Blvd., Arlington, VA 22230, 703-306-1070) is the primary user. Other interested parties who wish to send scientists or observers, such as scientific or environmental groups must obtain the consent of the primary user for that trip. Most travelers are sponsored by government or educational organizations, but the Coast Guard is interested in any appropriate, professional project and will consider other applications as well. They can also be flexible on their itinerary to accommodate projects. Sometimes scientists on short missions may travel at no cost. In addition, special expeditions are commissioned, such as the one in 1992 by the U.S. Geological Survey. If interested, contact the primary user.

State Government Auctions

The following is a descriptive listing of state government offices which offer auctions or donations of surplus property.

Alabama

Alabama Surplus Property, P.O. Box 210487, Montgomery, AL 36121, 334-277-5866. Alabama auctions off a variety of items about three times per year, including office equipment, heavy machinery (such as milling machines and drill presses), and vehicles, including cars, trucks, boats, and tractors. Trailers, medical equipment, tires, dossiers, and lathes are also sold. The state advertises upcoming auctions in the classified section of local newspapers. Upon written request made to the above address, you can be put on a mailing list. You will then be notified 2 or 3 weeks in advance of each upcoming auction, but you won't receive a list of items. Lists of items can be picked up at the above office 2 days before the auction. Payment can be by cash, cashier's check, or personal check with a bank letter of credit. Items are available for viewing two days prior to the auction. No bids by mail.

Alaska

Surplus Property Management Office, 2400 Viking Dr., Anchorage, AK 99501, 907-279-0596. The Juno office is 907-465-2172. Call it for general information and mailing list information. Alaska's Division of General Services and Supply sells surplus office equipment, including furniture and typewriters, every Wednesday from 8:30 am to 3:30 pm in a garage sale fashion with prices marked for each item. For items costing over $1000, cash or cashiers checks are required. Vehicles, at various locations throughout the state, are sold during sealed bid or outcry auctions twice a year, in the spring and fall. Payment is by cashiers check after you have been notified of your winning bid.

Arizona

Office of Surplus Property, 1537 W. Jackson St., Phoenix, AZ 85007, 602-542-5701. About three times per year, usually in January, May, and September, Arizona auctions off everything from vehicles to miscellaneous office equipment and computers. Items are sold by lots rather than individually; and prices, especially cars, can be below blue book price, depending upon opening bids. Vehicles range from empty frames to Jaguars. A mailing list is maintained. You can have it sent to you for no charge. Individual cities and county governments in Arizona also hold their own surplus auctions.

Arkansas

State Marketing and Redistribution Office, 6620 Young Rd., Little Rock, AR 72209, 501-565-8645. Arkansas conducts both sealed bid and retail, fixed price sales of surplus items. On Wednesdays, between 7:30 am and 3:00 pm, buyers may view and purchase items, which include office machines, tables, and tires, valued at under $500. Larger, more valuable items, including vehicles, medical equipment, mobile homes, and machine shop and automotive supplies, are sold by sealed bid. You can have your name placed on the mailing list for various categories such as computers, autos and miscellaneous equipment. You must bid three times to keep your name on the mailing list. The state also conducts sealed bids by mail. The bid fee is $1. No personal checks are accepted for sealed bids. All items are sold "as is," with no refunds or guarantees implied or stated.

California

State of California, Office of Fleet Administration, 1421 Richards Blvd., Sacramento, CA 95814, 916-327-9196 (recorded message), 916-327-2085.. Once a month on Wednesdays, the General Services Department of the state holds open bid auctions at Sacramento or Los Angeles State Garages of surplus automobiles previously owned by state agencies. Vehicles can be viewed from 8:30 am to 9:30 am. The auction begins at 9:30 am. Vehicles may include sedans, cargo and passenger vans, pick-ups (mostly American-made). Auctions are occasionally advertised in the newspapers. Minimum bid prices are set for exceptionally nice cars. Only state agency vehicles are sold. Payment is by cash, cashiers check, or certified check. Successful bidders have up to five working days to pay for and pick up the cars (the following Friday). Out-of-state checks are frowned upon. Prices vary greatly, and some vehicles have required minimum bids.

California Highway Patrol, Used Vehicle Sales Office, 3300 Reed Ave., W. Sacramento, CA 95605, 916-371-2270. Minimum bids are stated on a recorded telephone message (916-371-2284). The auction is by sealed bids which are opened at 3:00 pm daily; winners may be present or notified by telephone. Payment is by cashiers check, certified check, or, money order only -- no personal checks or cash accepted. Bids may be submitted and inspection is available between 8:00 am and 3:00 pm.

Colorado

Department of Correctional Industries, State Surplus Agency, 4200 Garfield Street, Denver, CO 80216, 303-321-4012. Several times a year, Colorado auctions off its surplus property, including motor vehicles. Auctions are pre-announced in newspaper ads, and a mailing list is also maintained. To be put on the mailing list, call the above number. The auctions of state property are held the third Thursday of every month. If you are on the mailing list, you will receive a notice the weekend before the auction with a brief description of the items. Non-profit organizations have first choice of state surplus items, which can include typewriters, desks, computers, file cabinets, hospital beds, and much more. Payment may be made by cash, money order or personal checks with two IDs.

Connecticut

60 State St. Rear, Wethersfield, CT 06109, 203-566-7018, or 203-566-7190. Items vary from day to day. Vehicles are auctioned separately 8 or 9 times per year, with ads in the 4 largest newspapers and on 2 radio stations giving advance notice. There is no mailing list. These auctions are usually on the second Saturday of the month. Vehicles may be viewed one hour prior to the auction. Buyers may also purchase a brochure with vehicle descriptions when they pay the $3 registration fee. You may go Monday-Friday, noon to 3:45 to view and purchase smaller items in their warehouse.

Delaware

Division of Purchasing Surplus Property, P.O. Box 299, Delaware City, DE 19706, 302-834-4550. Twice a year, in May and in September, Delaware publicly auctions off vehicles, office furniture, and other surplus or used property. Vehicles include school buses, paddle boats, vans, pick-up trucks, heavy equipment, and sedans. Prices depend on the condition of the item and how many people are bidding for it. Vehicles may be inspected prior to the auction. You may get on a mailing list to be advised of upcoming auctions. A flyer with information and conditions of payment will be sent to you.

District of Columbia

District of Columbia Dept. of Public Works, 5001 Shepard Parkway, SW, Washington, DC 20032, 202-645-4227. DC holds vehicle auctions every 1st and 3rd Tuesday of every month. Vehicles include cars, trucks, buses, ambulances, and boats. Inspection and viewing is available at 7:00 am, one hour prior to the 8:00 am open bid auction. $100 cash must be paid to attend the auction. Prices and conditions of vehicles vary greatly. No mailing list is kept. Auctions are posted 45 days in advance in the *Washington Times*. A $100 cash entry fee must be paid to attend an auction. This fee will be credited toward the purchase price, and is refunded if no car is purchased. Cars must be paid for in full at the auction by certified or cashier's check. Twice a year confiscated bikes and property found inside of cars go to auction.

Florida

Department of Management Services, Division of Motor Pool Bureau of Motor Vehicles, 813B Lake Bradford Rd., Tallahassee, FL 32304, 904-488-5178. Approximately once per month, somewhere in Florida, items are auctioned for the state. Descriptive information and viewing schedules are published in newspapers. Surplus items, including motorcars, heavy equipment and boats are sold. Automobile auctions take place anywhere from 7 to 15 times per year, with dates set 4 to 6 weeks in advance at various auction locations throughout the state. The auctions are advertised. Some industrial equipment is also included, along with various kinds of used and confiscated vans, trucks, and cars. Pleasure and fishing boats are also auctioned. Items may be viewed prior to the auction. Call 800-342-2666 (in state) to be placed on a mailing list.

Be patient. If any phone number is incorrect, call (area code) 555-1212 and request the new listing.

699

Government Auctions and Surplus Property

Georgia

State of Georgia, Dept. of Administrative Services, Purchasing Division, Surplus Property Services, 1050 Murphy Ave., SW, Atlanta, GA 30310, 404-756-4800. Georgia auctions vehicles, including sedans, wagons, trucks, vans, buses, and cement mixers. The state also auctions shop equipment, generators, typewriters, copiers, computers, tape recorders, and other office equipment, as well as audio-visual equipment, cameras, electronic equipment, and air conditioners. They keep a mailing list and also advertise the auctions in local newspapers. Merchandise may be inspected by pre-registered bidders two days before an auction. Vehicles may be started up, but not driven. For auctions, items are payable with cash only. Items must be paid for on the day of sale. Auctions are held every three months at different locations.

Hawaii

State Government Stock Control Department, 808-735-0348/0349. Hawaii does not conduct surplus sales at the state level. Federal public auctions are held by the Defense Reutilization Marketing Office, 808-474-2238.

Idaho

Division of Purchasing, 208-327-7465. In 1991 the Idaho state legislature dissolved centralized public auctions. Each state agency now holds its own auction or has a commercial auctioneer handle its surplus. If an agency decides to auction cars through sealed bids, it must advertise in 3 newspapers for 10 days. To find out if, when, and what an agency is disposing of through auction, contact that agency directly.

Illinois

Central Management Services, Division of Property Control, 1912 South 10 1/2 St., Springfield, IL 62707, 217-785-6903. Two or three times per year this office auctions vehicles and property. Auctions are held at the address listed above. Auctions are always held on Saturdays. Property includes office equipment, desks, chairs, typewriters, restaurant equipment, calculators, cameras, refrigerators, and filing cabinets. Scrap metal and equipment not easily moved are sold by sealed bid. The office maintains a mailing list which costs $20/year to subscribe. Notices of auctions and bids are mailed out 3 weeks prior to the auction. The auctions are also advertised in advance in local newspapers. All the cars auctioned have a minimum mileage of 75,000 miles and were driven by state employees. Prices vary widely, but below-market prices are available. Illinois auctions off vehicles by open bid auctions. (Confiscated cars are sold at federal auctions and may present greater possibility for a bargain.) Payment is made by cash, cashiers or certified check, or personal check with bank letter.

Indiana

State Surplus Property Section, 229 W. New York St., Indianapolis, IN 46202, 317-232-0134, warehouse; 317-232-1365, office. Indiana holds auctions as items accumulate through open cry auctions to the highest bidder. During the summer months, the state sells surplus from the Department of Transportation and the Department of Natural Resources. A mailing list is maintained. Auctions are advertised the first Thursday of every month in the *Indianapolis Star*. The auction date and selected auctioneer changes every year during July. Call the above office in May to obtain the new schedule. Sealed bids must contain 100% deposit. Payment is by cash, certified check, cashiers check, or money order. No personal checks or letters of credit are accepted. Items vary and are all state surplus.

Iowa

Department of Natural Resources, Wallace State Office Bldg., Des Moines, IA 50319, 515-281-5145. The Department of Natural Resources holds an auction when and if a sufficient number of items have accumulated, on the second Saturday of every May. Items disposed of include boats, fishing rods, tackle boxes, guns, and other fishing and hunting equipment, as well as office equipment. Payment is by cash or check with appropriate identification. There is no mailing list, but auctions are advertised in local newspapers.

Vehicle Dispatchers Garage, 301 E. 7th, Des Moines, IA 50319, 515-281-5121. The Vehicle Dispatchers Garage holds auctions, if there is sufficient accumulation, three to four times per year at 9:00 am on Saturdays. The state disposes of approximately 500 vehicles yearly through these auctions. They mostly sell patrol cars, pickups and trucks. All have at least 81,000 miles of travel on them, and prices vary widely. A deposit of $200 is required on the day of the sale, with full payment due by the following Wednesday. Payment may be made by cash or check with an accompanying letter of credit guaranteeing payment by the issuing institution. Viewing is possible Friday all day and Saturday morning prior to the sale. There is a mailing list. Auctions are advertised in the local papers.

Kansas

Kansas State Surplus Property, P.O. Box 19226, Topeka, KS 66619-0226, 913-296-2334, Fax: 913-296-7427. The State Surplus Property office sells sedans, snow plows, and everything they have, from staples to bulldozers. Property is first offered to other state agencies at set prices for 30 days. Whatever is left over is opened to public sale at the same prices. Prices tend to be competitive. Items are sold at set prices, with a catalog available containing descriptions of items and where they are located. Confiscated vehicles are not sold to the public. They are disposed of by county courthouses, usually to county agencies. To obtain copies of catalogs describing sealed bid items, write to the above address. It will be sent to you for 6 months, after which time your name will be purged unless you re-request it.

Kentucky

Kentucky Office of Surplus Property, 514 Barrett Ave., Frankfort, KY 40601, 502-564-4836. Kentucky holds public auctions on Saturdays every two or three months. Items may include vehicles, desks, chairs, calculators, typewriters, file cabinets, tape recorders, electronic equipment, couches, beds, and lawnmowers, to name a few. Merchandise may be viewed the day before an auction. The office maintains a mailing list and also advertises upcoming auctions in local newspapers two to three weeks before the sale. Some items are auctioned by sealed bids. Property is payable by cash, certified check, or money order.

Louisiana

Division of Administration, Louisiana Property Assistance Agency, P.O. Box 94095, 1059 Brickyard Lane, Baton Rouge, LA 70804-9095, 504-342-6849. Public auctions are held on the second Saturday of every month at 9:00 am at 1502 North 17th St. Items may be viewed at the warehouse from 8:00 am to 4:30 pm the week before. Property sold ranges from medical and office equipment, to boats, shop equipment, typewriters, file cabinets, pinball machines, bicycles, televisions, adding machines, and chairs, and vehicles. All items are sold "as is" and "where is." Payment is required in full the day of the auctions, but no personal or company checks are accepted. In addition, all merchandise must be removed within five days after the sale. Auctions are conducted by a different auctioneer each year, depending on who wins the bid for the annual contract.

Maine

Office of Surplus Property, Station 95, Augusta, ME 04333, 207-287-5750. Five or six times per year, Maine publicly auctions off vehicles on the grounds of the Augusta Mental Health Institute. You must register to be able to bid. Vehicles may include police cruisers, pick-up trucks, snowmobiles, lawn mowers, and heavy equipment, such as large trucks, graders, and backhoes. Inspection is allowed between 7:30 am and 10:00 am the day of the auctions, which are always held on Saturdays. The impound yard opens at 7:00 am. Vehicles may be started up but not driven. Personal checks (local banks only), money orders, certified checks, and cash are all accepted. Exact date, place, and time of auctions are announced in local newspapers, but there is no mailing list. Payment is due for both vehicles and other items the day of the auction or sale.

Maryland

Maryland State Agency for Surplus Property, P.O. Box 122, 8037 Brock Bridge Rd., Jessup, MD 20794, 410-799-0440. Office furniture and the like are sold or donated to non-profit organizations or state agencies, and vehicles are sold to dealers only. The state maintains a warehouse for surplus property at the above address. After a certain length of time, items that do not go to non-profits or state agencies become available to the public at set prices at its retail store. Checks are acceptable up to $500.

Massachusetts

Massachusetts State Purchasing Agency, Department of Procurement and General Services, Surplus Property, One Ashburton Place, Room 1017, Boston, MA 02108, 617-727-7500. About six times per year, Massachusetts holds public auctions of surplus property. Bidders must register in the morning by filling out a card. The State Purchasing Agency places ads in The Boston Globe on the Sunday and Wednesday prior to each of the auctions, which are normally held on Saturdays. Vehicles are usually auctioned after about 60 or so accumulate. Vehicles sold include sedans, wagons, vans, and pick-ups with an average age of 7 years. The average car has over 100,000 miles. Conditions range from good to junk. Viewing is available the day before the auction from 9:00 am to 4:00 pm. Purchases are "as is". No start-ups allowed. The state does not auction other surplus property, in general, but occasionally special auctions are held for boats, parts from the Department of Public Works, and most recently, helicopters.

Michigan

State of Michigan, Department of Management and Budget, State Surplus Property, P.O. Box 30026, 12 Martin Luther King Blvd., Lansing, MI 48913, 517-335-8444. The state auctions off all kinds of office furniture, household goods, machinery,

Be patient. If any phone number is incorrect, call (area code) 555-1212 and request the new listing.

livestock, and vehicles, such as sedans, buses, trucks, and boats. Auctions are held at different locations for different categories of property. The State Surplus Property Office sends out yearly calendars with auction dates and information. Contact them at the above address to have it sent to you. Double check dates because additions or changes may occur. Auctions are also published in the local newspapers. Payment may be made by cash or check and should include the 6% state sales tax. No refunds are made. Inspections of merchandise are available either the day before from 8:00 am to 3:00 pm or the morning of an auction from 8:00 am to 9:30 am. Vehicles may be started but not driven. Auctions begin at 10:00 am. Items must be paid in full on the day of sale by cash or in state check. Buyer has 3 working days to remove the property.

Minnesota

Minnesota Surplus Operations Office, 5420 Highway 8, New Brighton, MN 55112, 612-639-4022; Hotline: 612-296-1056. The hotline is updated with any changes in the auction schedule. Minnesota holds about 15 auctions per year at different locations around the state. They sell vehicles such as old patrol cars, passenger cars, trucks, vans, and trucks, as well as heavy machinery, boats, snowmobiles and outboard motors. The state also auctions off furniture, office equipment, kitchen equipment, tools, and confiscated items such as vehicles, computers, jewelry, car stereos and radios, and other personal effects. Many of these items are sold under market price. You may be put on a mailing list to receive a calendar for the schedule of upcoming auctions for the year. Auctions are advertised in the locale where they occur by radio, TV, and in Minneapolis and St. Paul newspapers. Inspection of property is held from 8:00 am to 9:30 am, an hour and a half before the auction begins; and payment is by personal check for in-state residents, cash, or money order.

Mississippi

Department of Public Safety, Support Services, P.O. Box 958, Jackson, MS 39205, 601-987-1500. The state cars that are auctioned are mostly patrol cars, and only occasionally vans and other types of vehicles. State cars are usually wrecked or old. Most have at least 100,000 miles on them. Recent average prices have ranged from $1200 to $1500. The state is keeping cars longer, so less are being sold. These agency cars and others from the Department of Wildlife and Fisheries, military bases, Narcotics Division, and U.S. Marshal's Office -- which includes confiscated cars -- are auctioned the first Tuesday of every month by Mid South Auctions, 6655 N. State St., Jackson, MS 39213, 601-956-2700. Call to be put on the mailing list. Many car dealers as well as the public attend these auctions, so prices are competitive. Bargains are still possible. Payment must be in cash or cashiers check -- no personal checks. The balance is due the day of the auction. Cars are available a few days before the auction.

Missouri

State Of Missouri, Surplus Property Office, Materials Management Section, P.O. Drawer 1310, 117 N. Riverside Dr., Jefferson City, MO 65102, 314-751-3415. At various times throughout the year, Missouri holds regular public auctions every 6-8 weeks, as well as sealed bid auctions of merchandise located at various places in the state. The wide range of items include clothing, office equipment and vehicles. No confiscated or seized vehicles or other items are sold. You can be put on a mailing list to receive notices of upcoming auctions, plus they are advertised in local newspapers. For regular auctions, inspection is available the day before or on the day of the auction; and sealed bid items may be viewed two or three days before the deadline. Items may be sold by lot or individually. Payment may be made by cash or personal check.

Montana

Property and Supply Bureau, 930 Lyndale Ave., Helena, MT 59620-0137, 406-444-4514. Montana holds a vehicle auction once a year, of about 300 state vehicles. Contact the above to get on the mailing list. The auctions are by open cry and sealed bid. All items are from state surplus; nothing is seized or confiscated. These auctions are advertised in local newspapers prior to the auction. In addition, the state offers other property for sale each month on the second Friday of the month at set prices. The sales include items such as office supplies, computers, chairs, tables, and vehicles including trucks, vans, sedans, highway patrol cars, and more. Payment can be by cash, certified or business check, or bank check.

Nebraska

Nebraska Office of Administrative Services, Material Division, Surplus Property, P.O. Box 94901, Lincoln, NE 68509, 402-479-4890. Three or four times a year, Nebraska auctions off office furniture, computers, couches, and more. Separate auctions are held for vehicles and heavy equipment -- also about three or four times per year. Auctions are advertised in newspapers and on radio, and a mailing list is also kept. Sealed bids for property such as scrap iron, wrecked vehicles, guard posts, and tires are taken. Items are available for viewing two days prior to the auctions, which are held on Saturdays at 5001 S. 14th St. All items are sold "as is". Payment, which can be made by cash or check, must be in full on the day of the auction.

Nevada

Nevada Purchasing Division, Kinkead Bldg., Room 304 Capitol Complex, 209 E. Muzzer, Carson City, NV 89710, 702-687-4070. The sales and auction are located at the warehouse at 2250 Barnett Way, Reno, NV 89512. About once a year, Nevada holds a sale on the second Saturday in August of such items as calculators, desks, cabinets, tables and chairs. Office equipment is released for sale to the public at a set price. The sale is held to clear the warehouse, and is on a first come, first serve basis, with minimum prices to cover service and handling marked on the property. Very few vehicles are confiscated. Most are surplus turned in by other state agencies for resale. Vehicles and motorcycles are auctioned. Public auctions are not served by mailing lists but are advertised in the newspapers. You can be put on a mailing list to receive notice of sealed bid sales of 19 categories of merchandise, including heavy equipment, boats, and planes. Once you have requested to place your name on the mailing list, if you do not subsequently bid on two consecutive occasions, it will be removed. Payment is by cash or local check with proper I.D. No out of state checks accepted. For vehicles, you can put down a 5% deposit with 5 days to complete payment. The county, city and University of Nevada also advertise and hold public auctions.

New Hampshire

Office of Surplus Property 78 Regional Dr., Building 3, Concord, NH 03301, 603-271-2126. New Hampshire holds two auctions per year of vehicles and other equipment, such as office furniture and machines, and refrigerators. Vehicles, which include cruisers, pickups, vans, and sometimes confiscated vehicles may be viewed the day before the auction, while other merchandise can be viewed on the same day just before the auction. Vehicles may be started but not driven. A mailing list is maintained, and ads are also placed in local newspapers prior to the auctions. Acceptable payment includes cash and certified funds.

New Jersey

New Jersey Purchase and Property Distribution Center, CN-234, Trenton, NJ 08625-0234, 609-530-3300. New Jersey auctions used state vehicles such as vans, various types of compacts, and occasionally boats, buses and heavy equipment. Frequency of auctions depends on availability which currently averages once per month. Vehicles may be inspected and started up the day before the auction from 9:00 am to 3:00 pm. Payment is by cash, money order, or certified check. No personal checks. A 10% deposit is required to hold a vehicle. The successful bidder has 7 calendar days to complete payment and remove the vehicle by Friday. If an item is left after that, even if paid in full, a $20 per day storage fee is charged. After one week, the vehicle is forfeited. To be advised of auctions, put your name on the mailing list by writing the address above. Phone calls are not accepted. A recent vehicle auction in New Jersey offered a variety of Dodge and Chevy vehicles, ages ranging from three to thirteen years, with mileages from 50,000 to 130,000. Other surplus items are not put up for public auction, but are offered to other state agencies.

New Mexico

New Mexico Highway and Transportation Department, SB-2, 7315 Cerrillos Road, P.O. Box 1149, Santa Fe, NM 87504-1149, 505-827-5580. About once a year, on the last Saturday of September, New Mexico auctions off vehicles, including sedans, loaders, backhoes, snow removal equipment, pick-ups, vans, four-wheel drives, and tractors. They have some office equipment as well. The items come from state agencies. You may place your name on a mailing list to receive the exact date of the auction and descriptions of merchandise up for bidding. A public entity auction is held first. The published list of items to be publicly auctioned consists of what is left over. Everything is open auction; there are no sealed bids. Items may be inspected the day before the auction. Payment is by cash, checks with proper I.D., money orders, or cashier's checks. No credit cards.

Department of Public Safety, State Police Division, Attn: Major W.D. Morrow, P.O. Box 1628, Santa Fe, NM 87504; 505-827-9001. The above holds a public auction on the second Saturday in July at 4491 Cerrillos Road. Write the office above to be put on the mailing list. It is also advertised in local newspapers. Items sold include everything from calculators to cars. They come from seizures and surplus from other agencies. The vehicles may be viewed and started up the Friday before the auction. Payment may be by cash, money order, cashier's check or personal check with bank letter of guarantee.

New York

State of New York Office of General Service, Bureau of Surplus Property, Building #18, W.A. Harriman State Office Building Campus, Albany, NY 12226, 518-457-6335. The Office of General Services holds auctions continuously in locations around the state. The items are so numerous that the state finds it necessary to sell them by category. You can designate which categories you are interested in on the mailing list application. Items are sold as they become available. Sales are advertised one week in advance in local newspapers. These items include surplus and used office equipment, scrap material, agricultural items (even unborn cows). Most categories

Be patient. If any phone number is incorrect, call (area code) 555-1212 and request the new listing.

701

such as medical, photographic, institutional and maintenance equipment are sold through sealed bids, usually in lots of varying size. To participate in a sealed bid, you place your name on a mailing list for items in seven different categories, then make your bid by mail. Send the sealed bids to Bureau of Surplus Property Distribution, Building 18, State Office Building, Albany, NY 12226. The highest bidder wins and is notified by mail. Mailings give as much information as possible about the items being auctioned; but state officials stress that merchandise is sold "as is" and "where is". They advise viewing property in person before making a bid. A ten percent deposit is required with each sealed bid. Vehicles are sold by public auction and may include cars, trucks, buses, tractors, bulldozers, mowers, compressors, plows, sanders, and other highway maintenance and construction equipment. Large items are sold individually, and smaller equipment, such as chain saws, is more likely to be sold in lots. These auctions take place about 55 times per year. It is always possible that enough surplus may not accumulate to warrant an auction. The state warns that just because an auction is scheduled is no guarantee that it will occur. Payment may be made by certified check or cash. A ten percent deposit will hold a vehicle until the end of the day.

North Carolina

State Surplus Property, P.O. Box 33900, Raleigh, NC 27636-3900, 919-733-3889. North Carolina sells through sealed bids surplus state merchandise including vehicles and office equipment every Tuesday. Office equipment includes furniture, typewriters, desks, and chairs. For a fee of $15 you can be placed on a mailing list to receive weekly advisories of what is for auction, with a description of the item and its condition. Otherwise, if you visit the warehouse in person, you can pick up free samples of bid listings and look at lists of prices that items sold for in previous auctions. The warehouse is located on Highway 54 - Old Chapel Hill Road. Payment is by money order or certified check, and you have 15 days to pay for your merchandise and 15 days to pick it up. Items may be inspected two weeks before an auction from Monday to Friday between 8:00 am and 5:00 pm. On Tuesdays, the warehouse is closed between 1:00 pm and 3:00 pm when the bids are opened and the public is then invited to attend. The state may reject bids that are too low. Vehicles vary greatly in type and condition.

North Dakota

Surplus Property Office, P.O. Box 7293, Bismarck, ND 58507, 701-328-2273. Once a year, usually in August or September, the Office of Surplus Property auctions through open bidding surplus office furniture and equipment, as well as vehicles and scrap materials. The auction is advertised the two days before and merchandise may be viewed the morning of the auction. The auction is held at Igo Industrial Park. Cash, cashiers checks, or money orders are acceptable forms of payment. Personal or business checks are accepted only with a bank letter of credit.

Ohio

Office of State and Federal Surplus Property, 4200 Surface Road, Columbus, OH 43228, 614-466-5052. Ohio holds public auctions and sealed bid sales on a wide range of office machines and equipment, and furniture. There are no sealed bids on vehicles. No mailing list is maintained. Call or write for the information. When you attend an auction, you can fill out a label that will be used to notify you of the next auction. Vehicle auctions are held three to four times a year, depending on the amount accumulated. Inspections are available the day before. Vehicles may include sedans, trucks, vans, 4x4s, boats, mowers, tractors, and chain saws. No seized or confiscated items are sold. At the time of the auction, a 25% downpayment is required, with the balance due by the following Monday (auctions are held on Saturdays). For the sealed bid auctions, payment must be by money order or certified check.

Oklahoma

Central Purchasing, Dept. Central Services, B-4, State Capitol, Oklahoma City, OK 73105, 405-521-3046; general information only for public auctions, 405-521-3835; for general information and information on sealed bids, 405-521-2110. Oklahoma auctions vehicles as they accumulate. Vehicles often have from 80,000 to 120,000 miles on them and it is rare for a car to be rated as fair -- which means it is in running condition. They are usually bought by wholesalers. State agency cars are commonly sold, but occasionally seized or confiscated cars are sold. Agencies most likely to have auctions are: Department of Human Services (occasionally vehicles and other items, but they usually take their cars to public auctions); Wildlife Department (vehicles); Department of Public Safety (vehicles); and the Department of Transportation (vehicles). The Department of Transportation has four auctions per year. Vehicles are usually not in good condition. The state advises that you contact each agency separately for details. The auctions are not always advertised in newspapers, but some agencies, such as the Department of Transportation (405-521-2550) have mailing lists.

Oregon

Department of General Services, Surplus Property, 1655 Salem Industrial Drive NE, Salem, OR 97310, 503-378-4714 (Salem area). Oregon auctions both vehicles and

other equipment, such as office furniture. Merchandise may include snow plows, horse trailers, computer equipment, desks, chairs, tires or shop equipment. Some items are in excellent condition, and bargains may be found. Items come from state agency surplus and confiscations. On rare occasions exotic items such as a Porsche and hot tub have been sold. Public sales are held every Friday at set prices. Sealed bid sales are held separately. The frequency of auctions depends on the amount of items to be disposed. The numbers of vehicles for sale is increasing. Cars are also sold every week at set prices. For info call the 24 hour information line that is always kept current, 503-373-1392, ext. 400. Ads are also placed on radio and in local newspapers in the areas where the auction will be held, giving the date and location of the auction. The procedure is to register and obtain a bidder number, which you hold up when you are making a bid. The forms may be obtained at the auction site. At the same time as you register, you must show some form of identification. The conditions and terms of sale are always listed. At the public sales if you pay by Mastercard or Visa, title is immediately released. You can also pay 10% down at the auction site and pay the balance at the office with Mastercard or Visa in 3 days. A mailing list is maintained.

Pennsylvania

General Services Department, Bureau of Vehicle Management, P.O. Box 1365, 2221 Forster Street, Harrisburg, PA 17105, 717-783-3132. About 10 times per year, depending on the number of cars accumulated, the DGS auctions off all kinds of vehicles. Many have mileages under 100,000, and ages commonly range from 1979 to 1986. There are about 200 cars at each auction. They are mostly used state agency cars that have been replaced, but up to 3 seized cars are also sold each year. An inspection period begins two weeks before an auction on Monday through Friday from 9:00 am to 5:00 pm at the storage facility located at 22nd & Forster Sts. in Harrisburg. Inspection period ends 2 days before the auctions. Each car has a form detailing its condition. It will state if the car must be towed. All cars are sold "as is". Cars are started up the day of the auction, which is open cry. If you request an application, you may have your name put on a mailing list for advance advisories of auctions for a period of six months. A $100 deposit is required (cash only) if you win a bid, with full payment due within five working days by cashier's check, certified check, or postal money order. No personal or company checks accepted.

Bureau of Supplies and Surplus, Department of General Services, P.O. Box 1365, 2221 Forster Street, Harrisburg, PA 17105, 717-787-4083. The Bureau of Supplies and Surplus of the General Services Department sells such items as mainframe computers and off-loading equipment, office furniture and machines, including typewriters, desks, chairs, sectional furniture, filing cabinets, copy machines, dictaphones, and calculators. This merchandise is first offered to other state agencies, then municipalities, and is then put up for public sale after five days. There is no mailing list for notification of upcoming auctions, but ads are placed in the local newspapers in the area where an auction will be held and in the *Pennsylvania Bulletin*. Property is sold at set prices. You may call to find out what items are currently for sale, or visit the warehouse which sells mostly office equipment such as computers, desks, chairs and file cabinets, between 10:00 am and 2:45 pm Monday through Friday.

Rhode Island

Department of Administration, Division of Purchase, 1 Capitol Hill, Providence, RI 02908, 401-277-2375. Rhode Island's Division of Purchase auctions off its surplus vehicles and office equipment, as well as other items, through sealed bid to a list of buyers who are usually in the business. Most of the cars sold have no plates and must be towed. They are sold primarily to wholesalers. Office equipment and supplies are primarily sold to suppliers. If the state ever does hold a public auction, it advertises two or three times in the local papers.

South Carolina

Surplus Property Office, Division of General Services, 1441 Boston Avenue, West Columbia, SC 29170, 803-822-5490. South Carolina sells items ranging from vehicles to office and heavy equipment. Property is collected in monthly cycles and offered first to state agencies before being put up for sale to the public. No mailing list is kept for it, but you can visit the warehouse on 1441 Boston Ave., in West Columbia, which is open between 8:00 am and 4:30 pm Monday through Friday. Prices are tagged; there is no auction. Every 6 to 8 weeks, the General Services Division holds public auctions of items by lot for State, Federal, and Wildlife Department property. A mailing list is kept for advance advisories and property descriptions. There is a $15 fee, payable by check or money order, to receive the mailings annually. Items can be inspected two days prior to the sale. You are advised to make notes of the numbers of property you are interested in, then to check back to inquire if it is still available, since state agencies have first choice.

South Carolina Public Transportation Department, 1500 Shop Road, P.O. Box 191, Columbia SC 29202, 803-737-6635, for general information; 803-737-1488, for mailing list. About every five weeks, the South Carolina Department of Public Transportation holds auctions of its used and surplus vehicles, which include everything from patrol cars, trucks, and passenger cars, to highway equipment. To have your name put on a mailing list of upcoming auctions, call the number above. Payment is by cash, check or money order. Banking information will be requested for personal checks. Vehicles may be viewed from 9:00 am to 4:30 pm on the Tuesday before the auctions, which are always held on Wednesdays at 10 am. Vehicles are also available for viewing the day of the auction from 8 am - 10 am. You may start up the cars. The bidding is open. Usually about 100 cars are sold at each auction.

South Dakota
Bureau of Administration, State Property Management, 500 E. Capital, Pierre, SD 57501-3221, 605-773-4935. Twice a year, in the spring and fall, the Department of Transportation holds on its premises public auctions for office equipment and vehicles, including pick-ups. Most vehicles have over 85,000 miles on them and sell for well under market price. The cars usually sell for under $5000. Most are surplus or have been replaced at state agencies. A few are from seizures or confiscation. You may visually inspect the vehicles prior to the auction, but you may not enter them. However, during the auction, the vehicles are started and demonstrated. Auctions and special sales are located wherever the most property has accumulated in the state. Call or write the above office to have your name put on the mailing list. There is no charge. Terms are up to the auctioneer. Title is released only after checks clear, or immediately if accompanied by a bank letter.

Tennessee
Department of General Services Property Utilization, 6500 Centennial Boulevard, Nashville, TN 37243-0543, 615-741-1711. Tennessee auctions surplus vehicles, and machinery of various kinds -- milling machines, lathes, welders, and metal working equipment. The vehicles are of all types, including dump trucks, pick-ups, sedans, and station wagons. Auctions are held in Jackson, Dandridge, Nashville, and Chattanooga when property accumulates. A mailing list is kept, and auctions are advertised in local newspapers. Items are available for inspection the day before the auction. Keys are in the car, and start ups are allowed. Register at no charge the morning of the auction. Payment can be in cash, cashier's checks, or certified check. The state also conducts sealed bids usually 12 times a year and most commonly on office furniture.

Texas
General Services Commission, P.O. Box 13047, Austin, TX 78711-3047, 512-463-3445. Every two months, Texas auctions off vehicles, office furniture and machines, and highway equipment. You must apply to be put on the mailing list, which will give you a brief description of items available at the next auction (call 512-463-3416). It will also tell you the location of the auction, which changes often. You may call the agency selling the property to arrange to inspect it; however, merchandise that is on site is available for inspection two hours before the auction. Items are mostly used state property, although some is confiscated as well. You must register to bid beforehand. Most registrations take place the day of the auction, beginning at 7:00 am. Payment on a winning bid is due at the end of the auction. Cash, cashiers check, certified check, money order, bank draft with Letter of Credit, or personal or company check with Letter of Credit are acceptable forms of payment. Items sold on site must be removed the day of the sale. For off-site items, 30 days are usually allowed for removal. Texas also holds sealed bid auctions, where you make a bid by mail. First, you indicate what category of property you are interested in, and they will send you bid forms and descriptions of items in that category. Sealed bid participants are notified by letter if winning bids and the exact amount due. Deposits for non-winners are returned. Also, each of the Texas state agencies hold local sales, for which each has its own mailing list and advertises in the local papers.

Utah
Utah State Surplus Office, 522 South 700 West, Salt Lake City, UT 84104, 801-533-5885. Utah auctions vehicles and office furniture, as well as heavy equipment, whenever property accumulates. Most items are sold by public auction, although sealed bid auctions are sometimes held as well. Mail-in bids are accepted if you can't attend in person. A 10% deposit is required. It is refunded unless you win the bid. Most of the public auctions are held in Salt Lake City at the address above, although some are occasionally held in other parts of the state. You may request your name be put on a mailing list to receive advance notice of auctions and a description of the items. Auctions are usually held on Saturdays. Property may be viewed the Thursday and Friday prior to an auction. Acceptable forms of payment are cash, cashier's check, and personal checks up to $100 with two forms of I.D. Checks over $100 must have a letter of guarantee from the bank. No business checks are accepted. Items must be removed and payments must be made in full on the day of the auction.

Vermont
Vermont Central Surplus Property Agency, RD #2, Box 520, Montpelier, VT 05602, 802-828-3394. Vermont sells low-priced surplus office furniture and machines on retail basis between 8:00 am and 4:00 pm Tuesday-Friday at the warehouse on Barre Montpelier Rd. Items include desks, chairs, file cabinets, and book shelves. Twice a year, vehicles, which may include police cruisers, dump trucks, and pick-ups, are sold by public auction, on a Saturday in late May and September. A mailing list is kept to advise you in advance of upcoming auctions. To have your name placed on it, contact the auctioneer. Local newspapers also advertise them. Vehicles may be inspected the Friday before an auction. The auctions are open bid, "as is", and "where is". There are no hold backs. The highest bid, even if it is far below market value, will take the item. A 25% deposit is due the day of the sale. The balance is due in 2 days, by the following Tuesday by 3:00 pm. Payment is up to the auctioneer, a private contractor. Usually, checks must be bank-certified, and a deposit is required to hold any vehicle not paid for in full the day of the auction.

Virginia
State Surplus Property, P.O. Box 1199, Richmond, VA 23209, 804-236-3666. Virginia auctions everything but land. It sells vehicles, office equipment and furniture, computers, tractors, bulldozers, dump trucks, pick-ups, and vans. Some of the cars are in good condition. Scrap metal, tires, and batteries are sold separately. Auctions may be held on any day of the week except Sunday. Sales are by both public auction and sealed bid. Agencies have the discretion to decide which way their surplus is sold. There may be sealed bid offerings every week, and as many as two auctions per week. Twice a year there are auctions for cars only. The rest are mixed. Items are occasionally seized, such as jewelry. Auction sites are at various locations around the state. You may call or write to place your name on a mailing list for both public auctions and sealed bid auctions. For sealed bid, there are usually 100 to 200 items available. Inspections are encouraged. They are allowed the day before the auction and again for a couple of hours on the day of the auction. For sealed bid items, you may call for more details on the items offered for sale or to make an appointment to inspect the items.

Washington
Office of Commodity Redistribution, 2805 C St. S.W., Building 5, Door 49, Auburn, WA 98001-7401, 206-931-3931, Fax: 206-931-3946. Washington holds auctions of used state vehicles, conducts "silent bids" (auctions where the bids are written rather than spoken), and also sells surplus materials by sealed bid (bids are placed through the mail) via catalogs. The vehicles are auctioned five times a year and include all kinds of used state conveyances, from patrol cars, to trucks and passenger cars, most having over 100,000 miles. There are few new luxury or confiscated type vehicles. The "silent bids" are held once a month, and include large quantities of office furniture sold by the pallet, with the exception of typewriters, which are sold individually. You may visit the warehouse to inspect the items beforehand. Payment may be made by cashiers check, money order, or cash, but no personal checks. For the sealed bids, you may request a catalog of merchandise, which includes everything from vehicles, to scrap material, office equipment, computers, clothes, cleaning fluids, tools, and pumps. Periodically the store at the central warehouse is open to the public where items may be purchased at set prices for cash. For any of these sales, you may request to be put on the mailing list at the address above.

West Virginia
West Virginia State Agency Surplus Property, 2700 Charles Ave., Dunbar, WV 25064, 304-766-2626. Contact the above to be put on the mailing list. Statewide sealed bids have a separate mailing list you must specifically request. For sealed bids, prospective buyers can inspect only by going to the site. Each month, West Virginia auctions such items as chairs, desks, telephones, computers, typewriters, office equipment and furniture, and other miscellaneous property, as well as vehicles. They are all auctioned at the same auction. The vehicles are in varying conditions. The auctions are always held on a Saturday. Inspection is available the week before the auction from 8:30 am to 4:30 pm. On auction day, the gate opens at 9:00 am. Miscellaneous property is sold until 12:00 noon. Then all the cars are sold. If time allows, any remaining miscellaneous property is auctioned. Payment may be by personal check, business check, or certified check, but no cash. Payment is due in full the same day. For sealed bids, payment is due 7-10 days after a bid has won.

Wisconsin
Wisconsin Department of Administration, P.O. Box 7880, Madison, WI 53707, 608-266-8024. The Department of Administration holds vehicle auctions approximately eight times a year -- usually with around 100 vehicles, including passenger vehicles, vans, trucks, and station wagons, all of different makes and models. Most are in running condition. Cars that need towing are rare and clearly designated. The vehicles are usually at least four years old, or have at least 70,000 miles on them. The auctions begin on Saturday at 10:00 am. Cars may be inspected the Friday before from 1:00 pm to 6:00 pm. The public may also inspect and start up the cars from 8:00 am to 10:00 am on the morning of the auction. Cars may be started but not driven. You may have your name placed on a mailing list for advance notice of auctions; however, the auctions are also advertised in local newspapers. There are no sealed bids. Payment is by cash, personal check, cashiers check, or money order. No credit cards. The full amount is due the day of the auction. Occasionally, if the auctioneer is consulted at pre-registration, a small delay for bank loan arrangements are pre-approved so that the prospective buyer can bid.

Be patient. If any phone number is incorrect, call (area code) 555-1212 and request the new listing.

703

Government Auctions and Surplus Property

Wyoming

State Motor Pool, 723 West 19th Street, Cheyenne, WY 82002, 307-777-7247. Although it first donates most of its surplus property to other state agencies, Wyoming does auction its remaining surplus vehicles, which may include pick-ups, vans, sedans, and jeeps, and also tires. Although most have high mileage -- from 80,000 to 100,000 miles, the majority are dependable vehicles. You can have your name placed on a mailing list to receive advance notices of auctions, which are held when items accumulate. On the average, two or three auctions are held each year. The state also advertises in local newspapers. Inspection of the vehicles is available between 3:00 pm and 5:00 pm the Friday before the auction, which is usually held on Saturdays and begins at 10:00 am. No start ups are allowed. Anything known to be wrong with the car will be on the list handed out at the auction, or sent if you are on the mailing list. Payment depends on the auctioneer who is a private contractor. Usually, cash or check with proper I.D. are acceptable. Some cars go for well below market value, but others may bid up in price, depending on the mood of the crowd.

Be patient. If any phone number is incorrect, call (area code) 555-1212 and request the new listing.

Unclaimed Money

In the United States today, experts believe that about $5 billion in unclaimed money is collecting dust in state Abandoned Property offices. Some of the monetary items that end up in a state's possessions after being declared abandoned by the holding institution include:

- forgotten bank accounts
- uncashed stock dividends
- insurance payments
- safe deposit boxes
- utility deposits
- travelers checks
- money orders

People move away, lose track of investments, or die, and the accounts or funds, after a set amount of time -- frequently five years -- are reported to the state Treasurer's Escheats, Comptroller's, or Revenue office. The state then tries to track down the owners and return the money.

If you think financial property may be held by your state, the first step is to contact the appropriate office (a state by state list follows) to find out whether your name is listed. Or, in the case of the estate of a deceased person, the listing would be under his/her name. You will then fill out a claim form which you must return together with the required identification or proof of ownership. Requirements for proving ownership may vary according to the amount of the claim and the complications involved, but frequently states will ask for such things as copies of driver's licenses, social security numbers, and bank account numbers and passbooks. Most require that the information be notarized. A few states have limitations on how long they keep abandoned property before turning it over to state coffers, but most keep it indefinitely. Some also pay interest on the money if the property was originally interest-bearing.

Honest Finders vs. Vultures

The states currently owe money from abandoned property to an estimated one in ten people in the country, according to attorney David Epstein. But many states do not have the resources to investigate every case, and do little more than advertise names of owners in local newspapers. The resulting gap is sometimes filled by professional "finders" or "heir searchers" who find the owners themselves and charge a fee or commission in exchange for returning it. They can obtain lists, legally in most cases but sometimes surreptitiously, of the names of the owners from the state offices, then conduct their own search. Some finders have charged commissions of 60% to 100%. The price of one finders fee in a past Colorado case was 30% of the dividends and all the shares of stock! Finders can, however, perform a valuable service by reuniting people with money that would have been lost to them forever. Because of cases where these finders have charged excessive fees to people for returning their own money, and because of the strain their demands have put on some already

over-burdened state offices, the finders have a shady reputation in some quarters. One state office, for example, refers to them as "bounty hunters," and another calls them "vultures." Many state offices feel that the finders infringe on the owner's right to have their money returned with no charge involved, which is the goal of the state.

The National Association of Abandoned Property Administrators says that since the states never find 100% of the owners, there is a place for honest finders. For example, if a state is unable to locate the owner of a sizable property that he didn't even know about, and a finder does the job, then a service has been performed. Many states, such as Texas, limit the amount of commission a finder may charge; and others have confidentiality laws that prevent them from aiding finders in any way.

One of the biggest obstacles states face is obtaining the cooperation of the banks, insurance companies, and other institutions in reporting properties to them. Despite laws that govern how a holding institution should deal with dormant accounts, they are often low priority items in a business. A state must sometimes work hard to convince them that it is best qualified to return the money. Some states are passing laws that would penalize lax holding companies by charging them a fee.

With billions of dollars in property sitting around out there, clearly many people have an interest in what happens to it. Finders, keepers, states and businesses all have something at stake, and the losers will be those who fail to take advantage of the services that the states offer.

State Listing of Unclaimed Property Offices

Alabama
Department of Revenue and Unclaimed Property, 50 Ripley Street, Room 1116, Montgomery, AL 36104, or P.O. Box 327580, Montgomery, AL 36132-7580; 334-242-9614. Alabama sends notices to the last known addresses of people whose unclaimed property has reverted to the Department of Revenue. The state also advertises in local newspapers twice a year for two consecutive weeks - in a total of 63 different publications. In Alabama only owners, heirs or those possessing power of attorney will receive the property once it has been rightfully claimed. It usually takes at least three weeks for the claimant to receive his money once the claim has been approved. The state has no statute of limitations on how long it can hold unclaimed property.

Alaska
Alaska Department of Revenue, Income and Excise Audit Division, Unclaimed Property Section, P.O. Box 110420, Juneau, AK 99801; 907-465-4653. Alaska publishes names of unclaimed property owners once a year in the three major newspapers, sends the information to state legislators, and contacts local news services in order to try to find the owners. They have a three person office, and the person in charge of refunds also makes efforts to investigate the whereabouts of owners. There is no full time locator. Alaska is currently holding an estimated 4.4 million dollars worth of unclaimed property.

Arizona
Arizona Department of Revenue, Unclaimed Property, 1600 West Monroe, Room 610, Phoenix, AZ 85007; 602-542-3908. Twice a year the state runs advertisements in local newspapers with the names of people who have unclaimed property. They

Be patient. If any phone number is incorrect, call (area code) 555-1212 and request the new listing.

705

will also send letters to the last known address. Claimants need three pieces of I.D. to identify themselves as the rightful owners. In the case of an estate or property of a deceased person, a copy of the will and death certificate is also required. The cumulative number of people who once had, or still do have unclaimed property in Arizona is over 170,000.

Arkansas

Auditor of the State, Unclaimed Property Division, 103 W. Capitol, Suite 805, Little Rock, AR 72201; 501-324-9670. Arkansas publishes the names of owners yearly in local newspapers once a week for two consecutive weeks. It also sends letters to the last known address of each person. Since 1988 the state has held "The Great Arkansas Treasure Hunt " which featured TV spots in an effort to locate owners. This year out of a total of $1,666,802 in unclaimed property, the state paid out $632,428. Arkansas is one of the few states where the unclaimed property reverts to a general fund after three years in the Unclaimed Property Office. This does not mean the money escheats to the state, but once the money goes into the fund, the owner must go to the State Claims Commissioner to claim it. The state will deal only with the actual owner of the property and not with other parties, including those endowed with power of attorney unless it is court ordered. Finders are restricted to a ten per-cent commission of the total retrieved. Refunds are usually sent out within about two weeks of approval.

California

Bureau of Unclaimed Property, P.O. Box 942850, Sacramento, CA 94250-5873; 916-323-2827, toll free 800-992-4647 (CA only). In California the law requires the state to advertise unclaimed properties. They no longer publish advertisements by name, but they run block ads in all major neewspapers once a year. A person inquiring about abandoned property in California can get an instant answer by phone from the Office's computer. However, they still need to fill out a claim form and show proof of identity such as birth certificate and social security card once they have determined that the property they are looking for is in the hands of the state. There are hundreds of finders in California trying to get a piece of the considerable action in a state with over 2.5 million unclaimed properties worth 1.7 billion dollars. They can come to the state's office or a public library and look up information on microfiche, but are limited to a ten per cent commission. Also, the state will only make checks out amounting to 10 percent for a finder, while sending the remaining 90 percent directly to the owner.

Colorado

Colorado State Treasurer, Division of Unclaimed Property, 1560 Broadway, Suite 1225, Denver, CO 80202; 303-894-2449. Colorado has no statute of limitations on unclaimed property. Once a year in March, the state places the names of owners whose accounts they received the previous year in local newspapers. Colorado will deal only with owners. Finders may obtain a list of property owners for $120 in the office or $125 by mail, but no research is available to them. The list has 60,000 names on it. The Unclaimed Property Office will only send checks directly to owners. Returns usually go out within four to six weeks of approval. Colorado, like other states, also stipulates that no owner is obligated to pay a finder a commission until the funds have been held by the state for 24 months or longer. The state will not go through an intermediary. Claim forms are only sent to owners. The state currently holds 200,000 names on file of unclaimed property owners.

Connecticut

Treasury Department, 55 Elm St., Hartford, CT 06106; 203-566-5516. Accounts bearing interest are paid a 4 percent interest. Connecticut lists names of owners in local newspapers every quarter, rotating through two of the eight counties. The state has about 185 million dollars that is currently unclaimed - approximately 800,000 owners. This office is currently getting onto computer. Returns are made out to owners only. Finders are not allowed if the claim is under two years old. After two years, finders are limited to a 10% commission.

Delaware

Delaware State Escheator, Abandoned Property Division, P.O. Box 8931, Wilmington, DE 19899; If you have a claim, write to Delaware State Escheator, P.O. Box 1039, Boston, MA 02103-1039; 302-577-3349. Delaware requires different kinds of proof of ownership, depending on the kind or amount of the claim. After approval, a return is usually mailed out in about six to eight weeks. The state publishes names of owners in local newspapers and occasionally takes the lists to state fairs. On average, Delaware receives 20,000 items per year. Delaware will send returns in joint names of finder and owner.

District of Columbia

Office of the Controller, Room 408, 415 12th St., NW, Washington, DC 20004; 202-727-0063. The District of Columbia requires the usual proof of ownership, plus social security numbers to identify owners. They get out the returns in about four to six weeks. DC places advertisements in newspapers in August and February, as well

as sending out letters to owners. They do not have a locating unit. The District of Columbia currently holds $11 million in unclaimed property. In 1991 two million dollars of unclaimed property has been returned. Finders are limited to 10% commission. Finders must wait until the District government has held an account for seven months before they can contract to recover it, and must have documentation and a contract that proves they have authority to act on behalf of the owner. The check is issued in the owner's name, but is sent to the address requested.

Florida

Office of Comptroller, Division of Finance, Abandoned Property Section, Talla-hassee, FL 32399-0350; 904-488-5381. Florida deals with owners and other parties, but finders must be licensed private investigators. Claims are advertised in newspapers. Claims may be viewed on microfiche in the office. Lists of items are sold for $30. Returns are made out only to owners or investigators. They currently have about 141 million dollars worth of unclaimed property. There is no limit to the amount of commission finders may collect.

Georgia

Georgia Department of Revenue, Unclaimed Property Office, 270 Washington Street, Room 405, Atlanta, GA 30334; 404-656-4244. Georgia is in the process of upgrading its office and soon hopes to speed up its return time on claims. Claimants may write, telephone, or come in and view lists on microfiche at the Georgia Department of Archives, 404-656-2393 in order to determine if they have property in the office. The next step is to fill out a claim form and return it with the necessary documentation and proof of identity. Checks are then sent out within a month. The office now has 7 employees. As part of its upgrading, the Georgia office also has more resources to locate owners, through records searches and outreach programs at state public events and placing lists in state Tax Commissioners' offices. They also place advertisements in 159 county newspapers and on television. Georgia holds property in perpetuity and does not pay interest. If you call to inquire about unclaimed property you may have coming to you, the office will check its records. However, nothing has been updated since 1992 on either microfiche or computer. If you think your claim originated after 1992, you must contact the holder directly to get the needed information. The office is currently holding about 50,000 names on file - a total of $157 million dating from 1973. However, they are also holding some safe deposit box items that date back to the 1800s. Finders are not dealt with. Checks are issued only to owners. Finders must wait for 24 months until they can contract to recover claims and they may charge no more than a 10% commission.

Hawaii

Director of Finance, State of Hawaii, Unclaimed Property Section, P.O. Box 150, Honolulu, HI 96810; 808-586-1589. Hawaii lists property owners names in local papers and attempts to locate people by phone. As of June 30, 1995, the state had about 41 million dollars worth of unclaimed property - approximately 282,000 names. No interest is paid on accounts. The amounts range from a few cents to hundreds of thousands of dollars. Accumulation began in 1974. As of September 30, 1991, Hawaii is holding 21 million dollars of unclaimed property. Hawaii does deal with finders, in providing lists of owners names, etc, but the state will send out checks only to owners. People inquiring about unclaimed property may do so by phone. Records are kept on microfiche. Commission of finders is limited to 20%.

Idaho

Ms. Mary Weirick, State Tax Commission, Unclaimed Property Division, P.O. Box 36, Boise, ID 83722-2240; 208-334-7623. Idaho publishes a list of names once a year in local newspapers, and puts circular inserts in all state and senior citizens papers. It advertises on 2 radio stations and 3 television stations. In addition, some local radio stations announce 25 names per day on weekdays. Also, they now have a full-time locator in the office to find potential owners. Idaho is currently holding approximately 11 million dollars in cash, 125,000 stock shares, 80,000 individual accounts, and thousands of safety deposit boxes. Property must be held for two years by the state before a commission may be charged. After that, checks may be mailed to finders, but they will be made out to the owner.

Illinois

Department of Financial Institutions, Unclaimed Property Division, P.O. Box 19495, Springfield, IL 62794-9495. Illinois requests that inquiries to the office be in writing to facilitate their research. With sufficient detail, the search takes 3 to 4 weeks. Claim analysis takes 6 to 8 weeks. After approval, returns usually take about three months. The state advertises the names of owners twice a year in the newspapers of the county of each owner's last known address. They currently have over 3.6 million names. Since 1961 over 656 million dollars have accumulated. Finders must be licensed detectives and are required to send the contract with the owners to the state office for approval. Items must be held by the state 2 years before finders make a contract on it. As of August 1990, finders are limited to a 10% commission. Checks are sent to owners only.

Indiana

Office of Attorney General Pamela Carter, Unclaimed Property Division, 219 State House, Indianapolis, IN 46204-2794; 317-232-6348. Indiana has a statute of limitations of 25 years before unclaimed property reverts to the Common School Building Fund. After reversion, the property can no longer be claimed. The first time this will occur is in 1993. After approval, returns take about six to eight weeks. The whole claim process takes about 3 months. The state runs newspaper advertisements as well as television spots and a cable show called *Consumer Corner* in an effort to find owners. Finders must submit the contract with the owners for approval by the state, and checks are sent directly to the owners. Also, finders are limited to 10% commission and may collect nothing on items held for less than 24 months by the state.

Iowa

Great Iowa Treasure Hunt, Treasurer's Office, Hoover Building, State Capitol Complex, Des Moines, IA 50319; 515-281-5540/5366. You may write or call this office to see if you have unclaimed property. They will look it up on their computers. Iowa publishes owners' names in local newspapers twice a year, and has representatives at the State and County Fairs to disseminate information. Big books are brought and people can look through them. They use radio and TV advertisements for larger claims - $100 and over. Iowa currently has close to 200,000 unclaimed properties. The office takes about two weeks to make the returns once the claim is approved. Finders must be private investigators. They may use the office's microfiche, but no lists are sold to them. Their commission is limited to 15 percent.

Kansas

State Treasurer's Office, Unclaimed Property Division, 900 Southwest Jackson, Suite 201, Topeka, KS 66612-1235; 913-296-3171, or toll free 800-432-0386 (KS only). Kansas will take phone or written inquiries about lost properties. They pay owners directly. Currently the unclaimed properties in the state are worth $60 million. The Treasurer's office makes attempts by mail and through public gatherings such as booths at state fairs to find owners. About 45 percent of properties are recovered. Finders commissions are limited to 15 percent and contracts for items held by the state for less than two years are not valid.

Kentucky

Kentucky Treasurers Department, Unclaimed Property Branch, Suite 183, Capitol Annex, Frankfort, KY 40601; 502-564-6823. Kentucky successfully processes 250-300 claims per year. They place advertisements in local newspapers, produce press releases, and run radio, television announcements, and at state fairs in attempts to locate owners. In addition, they try to find people by mail. Kentucky requests all inquiries to be in writing. In the past, they have even discovered people attempting fraud by using fake letterhead. One man claimed to be Thomas Edison's heir and owed $25,000. Finders need a power of attorney or other legal document. Returns are issued to owners and sent to the address requested. The office says they hope to see new legislation soon to control finders' fees.

Louisiana

Louisiana Department of Revenue and Taxation, Unclaimed Property Section, P.O. Box 91010, Baton Rouge, LA 70823-9010; 504-925-7425. Louisiana holds unclaimed items into perpetuity. It holds about 100 million dollars in unclaimed funds. About 3500 items are successfully united with owners each year. To research records, call the office to make an appointment. You can take the whole day to view printouts. Printouts are not for sale. Claims are advertised in newspapers and letters are sent to last known address. Finders must wait two years before making contracts on items over $50. Finders commission is limited to 10 percent. The office has a locator program. Once a claim is approved, the check will be issued within 90 days.

Maine

Treasurer's Department, Abandoned Property Division, 39 State House, Augusta, ME 04333-0039; 207-289-2771. Maine accepts either phone or written inquiries, and will have a return in about a month from approval, although stock returns take longer. There is about a two month backlog in running computer searches. Since 1979, there has been no statute of limitation on the length of time, and the office will hold funds in perpetuity. The state currently holds about 14 million dollars worth of unclaimed property from 4000 holders and 20,000 owners. Finders cannot collect commissions on properties held less than two years. After that they are limited to 15% for items over $50. After three years, finders fees may exceed 15% for items over $50. Maine uses advertising, personal letters, and booths at fairs to try to locate owners. The office has had good results in locating people. Maine pays interest that item earned at the time it was turned over to the state for up to 10 years. The office has hired a national firm to locate property. Also, state legislators are given lists of constituents in zip codes which they represent, and the legislators' offices attempt to locate those who have unclaimed property.

Maryland

Comptroller of the Treasury, Unclaimed Property Section, 301 West Preston St., Baltimore, MD 21201; 410-225-1700. Maryland has no statute of limitations governing the length of time property is held. Maryland advertises in the jurisdiction of the last known address twice a year and mails notices to the last known address. It also advertises on radio and television, and disseminates information at state fairs. The office has been in existence since 1966 and deals with both finders and owners. Claim forms must be signed by the owner if possible. Only owners may ask for claim forms. Finders cannot, even if they have a contract. Payment is made only to the claimant. As of July 1, 1991, finders need not be paid on items held by the state for less than 2 years. No limits are placed on the amount of commission finders may charge after the two years elapses.

Massachusetts

Commonwealth of Massachusetts, Treasury Department, Unclaimed Property Division, One Ashburton Place, Room 1207, Boston, MA 02108; 617-367-3900. Massachusetts, whose office has been in existence since 1955, pays interest to owners on interest-earning property. The state holds 47,000 items. They publish names in local newspapers every year to try to locate owners. Safety deposit boxes held more than 7 years are sold at auction. Once ownership has been established, the office pays returns in about four to six weeks. The state does not give returns to finders, but sells microfiche to finders for $25. There is a 10 percent cap on finders fees.

Michigan

Michigan Department of the Treasury, Abandoned and Unclaimed Property Division, Lansing, MI 48922; 517-335-4327. Michigan has a statute of limitations of seven years after abandonment for amounts under $50. Michigan is a custodial state. Lists of items are advertised in each county after they go through probate. Since 1988 listings have been put on computer. Prior to 1988, unless you know the holder, it is difficult to trace a claim. Approximately 68 million dollars worth of property is being held. They get the returns out within several weeks. Finders must have a contract if they charge more than 5 percent commission. Finders need a private detective's license. The office makes out checks only to owners or heirs. Third parties are never issued checks even if they have power of attorney.

Minnesota

Minnesota Department of Commerce, Office of Unclaimed Property, 133 East 7th Street, St. Paul, MN 55101-2362; 612-296-2568, toll free 800-652-9747 within the state but outside Minneapolis/St.Paul area. Minnesota has about 150,000 properties currently unclaimed. Inquiries may be made by phone or in writing, and specific documentation will be required. Normally 10 - 12 weeks are needed to process returns. Lists are advertised in newspapers. Searchers can collect for owners if proper documents are presented, but there is a 10 % limit on commissions unless there is a prior agreement between the owner and the searcher. Finders may not enforce contracts for locating items that have been held by the state for less than one year.

Mississippi

Mississippi Treasurer's Office, Unclaimed Property Division, P.O. Box 138, Jackson, MS 39205; 601-359-3600. Mississippi pays interest on accounts - 5% on interest-bearing accounts and 1% on everything else. They currently hold $5.4 million in unclaimed funds. Holding period, called dormancy, is 5 years. After that time, the holding company must turn the property over to the state. The state sets a limit of 10% commission for finders, but expects new legislation to restrict that amount further. The state is required by law to publish the names of all owners every third year with items worth $100 or more. It usually takes 30 to 60 days for returns to be processed, if all the information has been properly supplied by the claimant.

Missouri

State Treasurers Office, Unclaimed Property, Box 1272, Jefferson City, MO 65102; 314-751-0840. Missouri pays interest on interest-bearing accounts; and finders are limited to a 20% fee. The office tries to locate owners through advertising twice per year in news publications, mailing postcards to last known addresses, and some searches, but they do not have investigative capability.

Montana

State Of Montana, Department of Revenue, Abandoned Property Section, Mitchell Bldg., Helena, MT 59620; 406-444-2425. Montana's two-person office cannot conduct extensive investigations to find property owners, but are exceptionally dedicated to finding owners and have an excellent return rate. They can access state's income tax records and drivers license records for addresses. They will soon be able to access the Federal Deed Check. This office has a refund rate of 33 percent. In 1990 it took in $1.5 million and refunded one-half million dollars. Items over $100 are advertised in the county of the person's last known address. There are currently between 70 and 100 thousand accounts unclaimed. Returns are made to finders with legal contracts or power of attorney. There are no limits on finders.

Be patient. If any phone number is incorrect, call (area code) 555-1212 and request the new listing.

707

Government Auctions and Surplus Property

Nebraska

Nebraska State Treasurer's Office, Property Capitol Building, P.O. Box 94788, Lincoln, NE 68509; 402-471-2455. Nebraska publishes the names of property owners in local newspapers, sends out letters, and conducts research in an effort to locate the rightful owners. It does not pay interest on accounts. The office will deal with owners only and issues checks to them alone. For the first 90 days during which property is held by the state, finders may not charge more than 10 percent commission. After that there is no limit.

Nevada

State of Nevada, Department of Business and Industry, Unclaimed Property Division, 2501 E. Sahara Ave., Suite 304, Las Vegas, NV 89104; 702-486-4140/3000, or toll free 800-521-0019 (NV only). Nevada currently has about 80 thousand unclaimed properties, the vast majority of which are under $500. The current unclaimed amount, which the state holds in perpetuity, is $29 million. This 18 person office is on computer. They prefer anyone wishing to make an inquiry to call this office. No interest is paid on interest bearing accounts. The state allows finders to make claims after the state has tried for two years to locate the rightful owner. Computer printouts of lists can be viewed by researchers at the office, but they are not for sale. The finders are then limited to ten percent commission, and the checks are sent only to the owner. Nevada advertises in local papers and on television and radio as part of its efforts to locate the owners.

New Hampshire

New Hampshire State Treasurer's Office, Abandoned Property Division, 25 Capitol St., State House Annex Room 205, Concord, NH 03301; 603-271-2619. People can come to the office and look at the books. Not all listings are on the computer. After advertising an abandoned property for two years in a statewide newspaper and sending a letter to the last known address, New Hampshire can go to court and have the account escheated to the county involved, with 15% going to a general State Treasurer's fund. After the two year period, the owner needs a special bill in the state legislature to retrieve his money. The State advertises once again in the newspaper prior to escheatment, and they research large accounts. New Hampshire does not recognize finders; any agreement between a finder and owner is unenforceable for 24 months after a property is turned over to the state, and then the escheatment process takes over.

New Jersey

Department of Treasurer, Unclaimed Property, CN-214, Trenton, NJ 08646; 609-292-9200. All requests must be in writing. No information on claims is given out by phone. New Jersey will not supply lists of owners' names to finders. They pay interest on interest bearing accounts as of April 14, 1989, and are a custodial state. Their efforts to find owners consist mostly of running newspaper advertisements. The state of New Jersey does not deal with finders.

New Mexico

New Mexico Taxation and Revenue Department, P.O. Box 25123, Santa Fe, NM 87504-5123; 505-827-0767. New Mexico puts funds from unclaimed property in a special account in the General Fund, but it is still accessible to owners who make a claim. Objects such as those found in safe deposit boxes can be auctioned when they are turned over to the state, after 3 years. So far that has never happened, but it may in the future. The state currently holds 200,000 names on cards, which date back to 1959, and more than 70,000 names on computer, which date from March 1989 when the office was automated. Approximately 4 million dollars worth of properties are added every year. The state advertises owners' names statewide and sends letters to the last known addresses. Finders are subject to a gross receipts tax, but there is no limit on the commission they may charge. As of November 1, 1991, no finders may contract on items held by the state for less than two years.

New York

Administrator, Office of Unclaimed Funds, Alfred E. Smith Bldg., 9th Floor, Albany, NY 12236; 518-474-4038, toll free 800-221-9311 (NY only). New York State Comptroller, H. Carl McCall, encourages everyone to call New York's Unclaimed Funds Hotline to find out immediately if any of their funds have been turned over to the state. To obtain a refund, claimants will need to provide proof of identification and seom documentation, which will vary for different kinds of funds. No particular application is needed, just proof that the funds belong to the claimant. Interest is paid for the first five years on interest bearing funds, and the interest rate is adjusted quarterly by the NYS Department of Taxation and Finance. There are currently 11 million unclaimed accounts, amounting to voer $3.4 billion dollars. New York is very active in its efforts to find the owners of these funds. Besides periodically sending out letters, they hav a mobile outreach program, where office personnel travel to various locations with computerized information and visit senior citizen centers, malls, fairs, etc. They say taht these efforts have been very successful in locating owners. The state also cooperates with asset finders to locate owners. By law, finder fees are limited to 15% of the funds recovered; however, people are advised to deal directly with the state to reclaim their funds, free of charge.

North Carolina

Administrator, Escheat and Abandoned Property Section, Department of State Treasurer, 325 N. Salisbury St., Raleigh, NC 27603-1385; 919-733-6876. In North Carolina, the Abandoned Property Section can return funds in less than two weeks in uncomplicated situations. By law, they must send lists of owners names to clerks of the State Supreme Court in each county. Although not required, they give lists to local newspapers. They also use computer matches with the Department of Motor Vehicles and Department of Revenue, and they have a locator unit as well. As of June 30, 1995, the balance of abandoned monies was over $126 million. In 1990 they took in over ten million dollars worth. Finders must be licensed private investigators or detectives and licenses may not be transferred from state to state. Finders must state their fees in a contract with the owner. Commissions are limited to 25%.

North Dakota

North Dakota Unclaimed Property Division, 918 East Divide Ave., Suite 410, P.O. Box 5523, Bismarck, ND 58502; 701-328-2805. North Dakota publicizes abandoned properties in local newspapers, radio, television, through mailings to last known addresses, and booths at the State Fair. They accept inquiries by phone or mail, and then require claim forms to be filled out with appropriate documents attached. Once approved, returns usually take about two weeks. The state sends checks only to owners and has a two-year waiting period before finders can contract on a property. Finders' fees are limited to 25% of the total amount. Interest earned by abandoned properties goes to a common school fund.

Ohio

Chief, Division of Unclaimed Funds, Department of Commerce, 77 South High Street, 20th Floor, Columbus, OH 43266-0545; 614-466-4433. In Ohio, the published lists of owners' names includes a coupon in the larger newspapers that they can fill out to expedite their claim. Returns could take from eight weeks to three months, depending on the complications involved. Ohio also has an outreach program where the office sends representatives to state and county fairs, shopping malls and other public events. This includes visiting sites of the Governor's "Regional Cabinet Day" program where he picks a town to spend the day in to conduct business. The state currently has 1.5 million accounts worth 130 million dollars. They pay interest on accounts held since before July 26, 1991, but pay interest only until July 26, 1991. There is a 5 percent processing fee for payment of claims. Ohio is unusual in that the Unclaimed Funds Division operates on the money it is holding, at no cost to the government. The state's Department of Development also uses unclaimed funds to guarantee loans that stimulate economic development. In addition, the original holding institutions in Ohio are only required to turn 10% of the unclaimed funds over to the state, and they use the money to invest at market value. The holding company may retain the other 90 percent and invest it in secured stock in the name of the State of Ohio. The claimant still receives the full amount owed to him. The Ohio office must hold funds for two years before finders can make contracts on them, and their fees are restricted to 10%. Checks are paid to owners only unless another party has the power of attorney.

Oklahoma

Oklahoma Tax Commission, Unclaimed Property Section, 2501 Lincoln Blvd., Oklahoma City, OK 73194-0010; 405-521-4275. Oklahoma is a custodial state and keeps unclaimed properties in perpetuity. Requests about claims must be in writing. State does not pay interest on interest-bearing accounts. The state currently holds $75 million worth of these monies. Approximately $20 million has been returned to owners. They publicize names in local newspapers twice a year and intend to have a locator service in the near future. If a finder has a power of attorney, he can submit a claim and there is a 25 percent limit on the amount of commission he can charge.

Oregon

Oregon Division of State Lands, 775 Summer Street NE, Salem, OR 97310; 503-378-3805. Oregon will hold unclaimed property indefinitely while it is invested in the School District Fund. From the time property is reported by a holding company as unclaimed until the time it is advertised and remitted to the state, which is about 6 months duration, information about it is not public information. Inquiries during that time must be directed to the holding company. Interest earned also goes to the Fund. There is $46 million worth of unclaimed property belonging to 120,000 persons. No interest is paid on interest-bearing accounts. The state sends letters to the last known addresses of owners and advertises in local newspapers. They publish an information brochure for consumers explaining the procedures involved for claiming abandoned property. They also publish an information packet for researchers who want to find claims as a business. State emphasizes to owners that it will do the search for them. The state sends checks jointly to finders and owners and there are currently no restrictions on the amount of commission finders may charge.

Pennsylvania

State Treasury Office of Unclaimed Property, Attn: Research Department, P.O. Box 1837, Harrisburg, PA 17105-1837; 717-772-2722 or toll free 800-222-2046 (PA

Be patient. If any phone number is incorrect, call (area code) 555-1212 and request the new listing.

only). Procedures and proof required to reclaim property depend on the type and size of the property, and whether the claimant is the owner, heir or estate. The state holds the property in perpetuity. Pennsylvania checks its list of names against state tax records to help locate people and sends out notices for amounts over $100. They send letters to the last known address. The state also lists the names of owners in local newspapers, and passes lists on to General Assembly members. In addition, they have an outreach program that travels to public functions, such as the governor's "Capitol for the Day" program, around the state looking for owners, and they have found one in five people on their list in this manner. In Pennsylvania there are no restrictions on finders. However, before claim forms are sent to finders, they must have a notarized power of attorney. There is a recording on the phone line while on hold which warns people against dealing with finders until contacting the Office of Unclaimed Property.

Rhode Island

State Of Rhode Island, Unclaimed Property Division, 40 Fountain St., Providence, RI 02903; 401-277-6505. Rhode Island takes about three to four weeks to return lost funds once the claim is made. People with more recent claims may call the state office to find out immediately from the computerized listing if they actually have money there. Older claims take a day to research. No dollar amounts are given out. They must then follow up with the proper identification. The state pays simple interest - 2.25% on interest-bearing accounts. Holders are required to notify owners that the property is being turned over to the state before they do so. They send out letters to the last known addresses of owners, and place advertisements in all the state newspapers. They also have an outreach program, where representatives of the Unclaimed Property Office travel to public functions around the state to try to locate people. The state says this program has been very effective. In March of 1988 Rhode Island advertised six thousand names of property owners and was able to locate half of them. Finders are on their own here - they receive no help from the state, nor are there restrictions on the fees they may charge. Finders' contracts are null and void if item has been in state custody for under 24 months. Finders may view microfiche of names at the State House, but no amounts are given. There is no microfiche at the Fountain St. address.

South Carolina

South Carolina Department of Revenue, Abandoned Property Division, P.O. Box 125, Columbia, SC 29214; 803-737-4771. In South Carolina, a claimant looking for lost property can go to the holding institution - that is, the original business where the account or money was located - within the first sixty days after his funds have been declared abandoned. Then, he must look for them in the state office. Make an appointment. The hours are 9:00 am to 11:00 am and 2:30 pm to 4:30 pm weekdays. The information is kept on microfiche. Twice a year the office runs advertisements in county newspapers, with names of people known to have lived in each county. They also travel to the State Fair in October, as well as mail letters to the last known addresses. South Carolina currently holds $38 million in abandoned property, representing 383,000 accounts. In 1989, lists of owners' names were made available to the public for the first time, but the office will not duplicate or mail copies. Finders fees have also been limited to 15%, and the finder must be a licensed private investigator. The state now mandates it must hold a property for two years before a finder can contract to recover it.

South Dakota

Abandoned Property, State Treasurer's Office, 500 East Capitol, Pierre, SD 57501; 605-773-3378. Inquiries may be by phone or in writing to the office, which can do an immediate computer search to determine if a claimant's property is being held there. South Dakota has, after returns taken out, 8 million dollars of unclaimed property that has accumulated since the inception of the program. The accounts belong to about 15,000 people. Then, the claimant must submit whatever proof is required and complete the necessary paperwork. South Dakota has a successful outreach program that travels to state and county fairs with a specially-made list of names that is posted so the public may easily read it. In the past two years, they have tripled their refunds as a result of the program. In addition, the office lists names in local newspapers. Finders are limited to 25% commission and the office pays returns directly to owners only. No lists of names are made available for heir-finding purposes, although anyone who wants to see the names may come to the office by appointment only.

Tennessee

State of Tennessee, Unclaimed Property Division, Andrew Jackson State Office Bldg., 11th floor, Nashville, TN 37243-0242; 615-741-6499. In Tennessee the Unclaimed Property Division pays only to original owner or estates in the case of money belonging to a deceased person. In all cases, they require suitable proof identification such as proof of address, social security number, etc. Returns take approximately three weeks. Interest is paid only if the original holder paid it as well. Tennessee advertises names of owners in local newspapers, sends letters to last known addresses, matches its list with other state agencies, and searches current

telephone directories in an effort to locate owners. Further efforts, such as consulting credit bureaus, may be made in cases of large accounts. The office currently holds $46 million worth of property. Finders must make appointments with the office to view lists of names, and they are frequently booked a week in advance. The records viewed at the office are on microfiche and can be purchased for $30. Any contract made between a finder and owner must be approved by the state; and contracts are only valid after the state has held the property for one year. Finders are restricted to 10% commission or $50, whichever is greater.

Texas

Unclaimed Money Fund, P.O. Box 12019, State Treasurer's Office, Austin, TX 78711; 512-463-6000, or toll free 800-321-CASH (TX only). This office has a full-time locator and aggressively pursues search for owners. Texas claimants follow procedures similar to those in most states - that is, filling out claim forms, providing notarized documentation of ownership, and submitting driver's license or social security numbers. Returns take about 90 days to process. The state advertises names in local newspapers, on radio and television, and sends notices to the last known address of the owner. Holding companies also return many items. The state currently holds $870 million in unclaimed property. No interest on interest-bearing accounts is paid. Finders are limited to 10% commission; and the Treasurer's office advises people who have been contacted by a finder to check with them first before paying someone a fee to return their money. Half of the money never claimed in Texas goes to a Foundation School Fund, and the other half goes to the State general revenue. However, the money is always available to the rightful owner and claimants can retrieve their funds at any time.

Utah

Utah Unclaimed Property Division, 341 South Main Street, 5th Floor, Salt Lake City, UT 84111; 801-533-4101. The state advertises one time in the paper names they received in the past year and publicizes on radio and television. They also run a booth at the State Fair and maintain a locator in the office. The state has over 250,000 unclaimed properties worth over $30 million at the present time. Searchers or finders can apply with a valid power of attorney and checks are issued either to owners or those with power of attorney. No agreement between owners and fee-finders is enforceable until the state has held the property for two years.

Vermont

State Treasurer's Office, Unclaimed Property Division, 133 State St., Montpelier, VT 05633-6200; 802-828-2301. Vermont sends out letters to owners of property worth $25 or more. If the amount is over $50, the state runs advertisements in local newspapers for two consecutive weeks. They have no other investigative capability due to the very small size of the office. Books are open to the public view at the office. Vermont currently holds 32,000 properties. Finders can only contract with owners after the state has held a property for twelve months.

Virginia

Department of the Treasury, Division of Unclaimed Property, P.O. Box 2478, Richmond, VA 23207; 804-225-2393, or toll free 800-468-1088 (VA only). Virginia requires a claimant to submit proof of whatever information the state received from the holder. For example, someone claiming money in a savings account would have to produce a passbook or other proof of ownership of that account. In most cases, returns are made within two months. The state pays interest if the original holder was also paying it. There is a 5 % limit. In Virginia , unclaimed property information is classified as confidential, so the state cannot release information to finders. The public is not invited to look at the office's records. Private agreements between finders and owners are limited to a 10% commission for the finder. In addition, the property must be held for 36 months before such a contract is recognized. Approximately one million names are currently on file with the abandoned property office.

Washington

State of Washington Department of Revenue, Unclaimed Property Section, P.O. Box 448, Olympia, WA 98507; 360-586-2736. Washington has an automated system that enables the office to respond immediately to inquiries about unclaimed property. Their list dates back to 1955. The office attends county and state fairs, malls, and other public locations to locate owners. The state also has a system called WIN (Washington Information Network), in which people living in Washington may access the lists through ATM machines if they believe they have a claim. The machine dispenses a slip of paper which they may fill out and return with proper identification and documentation. The staff now has two full time locators. From July 1, 1994 to June 30, 1995, they paid out $6,300,151 in claims. In November 1995 alone, they received over 65,000 calls. The staff searches telephone books. One found the owner of $149,000 by looking in the telephone directory. She had not even known the money was owed to her. They also place advertisements once a year for two consecutive weeks in 39 county newspapers. Efforts to advertise through the broadcast media have been very successful. A recent television show brought 250

Be patient. If any phone number is incorrect, call (area code) 555-1212 and request the new listing.

709

calls. Washington pays interest if an account was previously an interest-bearing bank and CD account, and continues to pay the same rate of interest for up to 10 years. The state currently holds about $200 million in unclaimed property, from about 900,000 owners. Washington is one of the most restrictive states for finders, limiting them to 5% commission and subjecting them to the confidentiality law which limits what information the office can reveal about abandoned property owners. As a result, they say they have few problems with heir-finding.

West Virginia

Treasurer of the State, Unclaimed Property Division, Bldg. 1, Suite E145, State Capital, Charleston, WV 25305; 304-343-4000. West Virginia is currently holding 12 million dollars in unclaimed funds for some 120,000 accounts. No interest is paid on interest-bearing accounts. West Virginia has a five-person office for unclaimed property, so the efforts they can make to locate owners are minimal, and returns may take some time. By law, however, the state must advertise the names in local newspapers, and send notices to the last known address within 10 days. There are no regulations on finders, but the office does not supply lists of names. Finders can view the names by visiting the office, but no information except names and addresses is released unless an owner has authorized it.

Wisconsin

Office of the State Treasurer, Unclaimed Property Division, P.O. Box 2114, Madison, WI 53701-2114; 608-267-7977. The Wisconsin office prefers written inquiries about lost properties, including as accurate a description as possible. Once a claim is approved by the Unclaimed Property Division and the Attorney General's office, returns are made within six to eight weeks. The state pays interest if the account was interest-bearing in the first place. For properties over $50, Wisconsin runs newspaper advertisements listing the names of owners. The office is able to perform only limited research. They search current telephone directories, and try to check social security numbers with the Department of Revenue. The state holds $32 million of unclaimed property. Finders are limited to 20% commission as of May 1988. They may purchase a list of names and view the records in the office, but checks are made out only in the names of the owners.

Wyoming

Unclaimed Property Division, Wyoming State Treasury Office, 1222 W. 25th St., 1st Floor, West Herschler Bldg., Cheyenne, WY 82002; 307-777-5590. In March, 1993, Wyoming became the last state to pass Uniform Unclaimed Property Laws, which bring them in line with other states. The state currently holds 6.5 million dollars in unclaimed property. Properties are held until claimed. They require identification and other proof of ownership which varies depending on the property being claimed. Returns usually take 4 - 6 weeks. Finders can come into the office to view the list of names and there are no restrictions on the amount of commission they may charge. However, finders have no access to property until the account has been held by the state for two years. The state will deal with finders, but payment will only be made to owners.

Small Business and Entrepreneuring
Federal Starting Places

* See also Information on People, Companies, and Mailing Lists Chapter
* See also Business and Industry Chapter
* See also Selling to the Government Chapter
* See also Selling Overseas: International Trade Chapter
* See also Economics, Demographics, and Statistics Chapter
* See also Patents, Trademarks, and Copyrights Chapter

Here you will discover that the U.S. Small Business Administration is not the only federal agency that provides financial and managerial assistance to small businesses and entrepreneurs. For example, trade remedy relief is the responsibility of the U.S. International Trade Commission and the National Science Foundation offers small firms R&D opportunities. After you become more familiar with the Answer Desk, incubator programs, FTC rules, certified lenders, and other federal help, you may want to move on to the next section, State Starting Places and Money. You'll probably find a lot of help close by in the state capital and in other major metropolitan areas besides Washington, DC. State governments are increasingly responsive to small business and offer many services.

* Advocacy and Small Business
Office of Advocacy
U.S. Small Business Administration (SBA)
409 3rd Street, SW, Suite 7800
7th Floor
Washington, DC 20416   202-205-6533

As the watchdog for small business within the federal government, this office carries out the following: researching the effect of federal laws, programs, regulation, and taxation on small business and making recommendations to federal agencies for appropriate adjustments to meet the needs of small business; conducting economic studies and statistical research into matters affecting small business and evaluating future opportunities, problems, and needs of small business; and serving as a conduit through which small business can make suggestions and comment on policy. Available for sale from the U.S. Government Printing Office, *The State of Small Business: A Report of the President*, contains the most current information on small business performance in the economy. Also issued from this office is the *Small Business Advocate*, a monthly newsletter that reports on small business issues and actions of the Office of Advocacy. It is available through Advocacy's Office of Information by calling 202-205-6531. For more information contact the office above.

* Answer Desk
U.S. Small Business Administration
409 3rd Street, SW, 5th Floor   800-827-5722
Washington, DC 20416   202-205-7701

The Small Business Answer Desk helps callers with questions on how to start and manage a business, where to get financing, and other information needed to operate and expand a business. This toll-free hotline is provided by the Small Business Administration's (SBA) Office of Advocacy and operates from 8:30 a.m. to 5:00 p.m. EST, Monday through Friday. Contact the Answer Desk for a free copy of the *Small Business Directory*, a listing of SBA publications and products.

* Broadcast Entrepreneurs: Purchasing and Technical Assistance
Consumer Assistance and Small Business Division
Office of Public Affairs
Federal Communications Commission
1919 M Street, NW, Room 254
Washington, DC 20554   202-418-0200

The Consumer Assistance and Small Business (CASB) Division will provide you with personal assistance in locating information concerning Federal Communications Commission (FCC) rules, policies, procedures, and guidance concerning participation in FCC rulemaking proceedings. In addition, this office provides specialized to assistance to those interested in becoming involved in the small business telecommunications industry. They will walk you through the purchasing procedures, identify resources for financial and technical assistance, and perform license status checks for applicants. The Public Affairs office also coordinates broadcast ownership

workshops, which cover these topic and more, every year across the country. Contact CASB for more information.

* Business Assistance--Directory of Federal and State
National Technical Information Service
U.S. Department of Commerce
5285 Port Royal Rd.
Springfield, VA 22161   703-487-4650

The *Directory of Federal and State Business Assistance* describes more than 180 Federal and 500 state programs. Each entry gives a summary of the service offered, a telephone number and address, and eligibility requirements if any. These programs are designed to help new and growing companies compete more effectively in domestic and international markets. Uses of this directory can include how to get funding for a company's research and development; where to get mail lists of potential overseas business buyers; who provides venture money; and what Federal and state contacts offer free management consulting. Contact the Sales Desk to place an order or request the free information brochure, *PR-801*.

* Business Assistance Newsletter
Public Affairs
Minority Business Development Agency
14th and Constitution Ave. NW, Room 6707
Washington, DC 20230   202-482-4547

Call this office for a copy of the brochure *Q&A: Most Frequently Asked Questions and Answers About Minority Business Development Agency*.

* Business Loans from the SBA
Contact your local SBA office or the Small Business Answer Desk listed in this Section.

The Small Business Administration (SBA) offers two basic types of business loans: guaranteed loans which are made by private lenders, usually banks, and guaranteed up to 90 percent by SBA; and SBA direct loans which are available only to applicants unable to secure an SBA guaranteed loan. *Business Loans from the SBA* is a brochure available from your SBA office which gives information on these two types of loans, how to apply for a loan, terms of loans, collateral, eligibility requirements, and general size standards.

* Capital Formation for Small Businesses
The Office of Small Business Policy
Division of Corporation Finance
U.S. Securities and Exchange Commission (SEC)
450 5th St., NW
Washington, DC 20549   202-942-2950

The Securities and Exchange Commission's (SEC) main responsibility under the

Small Business and Entrepreneuring

securities laws is to protect investors and to make sure the capital markets operate fairly and orderly. However, the Commission is careful not to let its regulations impair capital formation by small businesses. Therefore, the SEC has taken a number of steps to help small businesses raise capital and to ease the burden of undue regulations under the federal securities laws. The Commission is continually examining other ways to meet these goals. For more information, contact this office.

* Coal Operator Assistance

Small Coal Operator Assistance
Land Resources
Natural Resources Management
Resource and Development
Tennessee Valley Authority (TVA)
17 Ridgeway Rd.
Norris, TN 37828   615-632-1750

To ensure more competition and reasonable prices, the Tennessee Valley Authority (TVA) reserves a portion of its coal purchases for small producers. In addition, the TVA provides mining and reclamation technical assistance to small coal producers. The program is also involved in non-coal mineral abandoned mine reclamation. The percentage of contracts awarded to coal suppliers is evaluated based on the capability of the company to comply with TVA's mine reclamation programs.

* Contract Loans

Contact your local SBA office or the Small Business Answer Desk listed in this section.

The Contract Loan Program (COL) is a short term line of credit, without a revolving feature. It is available under the SBA's guaranty loan program solely to finance the estimated cost of labor and material needed to perform on a specific contract. Detailed information can be obtained from the SBA office in your area.

* Definition of a Small Business

Contact your local SBA office or the Small Business Answer Desk listed in this section.

The Small Business Administration (SBA) generally defines a small business as one which is independently owned and operated and is not dominant in its field. Most small, independent businesses or individuals starting a business are eligible for SBA assistance. To be eligible for SBA loans and other assistance, a business must meet a size standard set by the SBA. Specific size standard information is available through any SBA office around the country.

* Development Company Loans

Contact your local SBA office or the Small Business Answer Desk listed in this section.

Development Company Loans are made to development organizations approved by the Small Business Administration (SBA) for the purpose of fostering economic growth in rural and urban areas. Growth is measured primarily by job creation and retention. Loan proceeds are used by development companies to assist small business concerns with plant acquisition, construction, conversion, or expansion, including the acquisition of machinery and equipment. Contact the nearest SBA office for more information on these loans.

* Disaster Assistance

Contact your local SBA office or the Small Business Answer Desk listed in this section.

Natural disasters, such as hurricanes, floods, tornados, and earthquakes, often cause hardship to business and individuals. When the U.S. President or SBA Administrator declares a specific area to be a disaster area, two types of loans are offered by the SBA: Physical Disaster Loans and Economic Injury Disaster Loans. To obtain the pamphlets *Disaster Loans for Homes and Personal Property, Economic Injury Disaster Loans for Small Businesses,* and *Physical Disaster Business Loans,* or for more information about disaster loans, contact your local SBA office.

* Economic Database

Office of Economic Research
Office of Advocacy
U.S. Small Business Administration
409 3rd Street, SW, 5th Floor, Room 5500
Washington, DC 20416   202-205-6530

The Office of Economic Research provides data to the research community for analyzing cause and effect relationships of small business problems and progress. Contact this office for information on accessing the database files.

* Environmental Protection Agency Small Business Ombudsman

Small Business Ombudsman
Environmental Protection Agency (EPA)
401 M Street SW, 1230C
Washington, DC 20460   703-305-5938

The Small Business Ombudsman in the EPA Office of the Administrator provides various services to help small business comply with EPA regulations. The Ombudsman serves as information services and advocate for small business interests in the regulatory development process. It helps these small businesses with their individual problems.

* EPA-Help Hotline for Small Business

Environmental Protection Agency
401 M Street SW   800-368-5888
Washington, DC 20460   202-260-2090

The Small Business Hotline is an EPA-based hotline that gives advice and information to small businesses on complying with EPA regulations. It deals with problems encountered by small-quantity generators of hazardous waste and other small businesses with environmental concerns.

* Expanding SBA Services to Business

Office of Business, Initiative, Education, and Training (BIET)
U.S. Small Business Administration (SBA)
409 3rd St., SW, Room 6400
Washington, DC 20460   202-205-6665

The main focus of this office is enlarging the capability of the Small Business Administration (SBA) to provide valuable services to small businesses through cooperative, jointly-sponsored activities with the private sector, particularly at reduced cost. Some of the ways the private sector helps SBA in delivering these services is by co-sponsoring management training programs (courses, conferences, clinics, seminars, and workshops), providing speakers, panelists, and moderators for training programs, and offering one-on-one counseling to small business persons. For additional information on this program, contact your SBA office or the office above.

* Facts About Small Businesses

Office of Public Communications
U.S. Small Business Administration
409 3rd St., SW, Room 7600   202-205-6740
Washington, DC 20416   Fax: 202-205-6913

Call or fax a request to the office above to obtain any of the following fact sheets:

Contract Loan Program
Handicapped Assistance Loans
Small Business Institute Program
Loans to Small General Contractors
Management and Technical Assistance 7(j) Program
Surety Bond Guarantee Program
Secondary Market Program - Fact Sheet for Lenders
Section 504 - Certified Development Company Program
Small Business Solar Energy and Conservation Loan Program
Interest Rate Policy
Facts About Certified and Preferred Lender Programs
Facts about Small Business
International Trade Assistance
Small Business Development Centers
Private Sector Initiatives Program
Guaranteed Loans to Employee Trusts

* Small Business Administration Field Offices

The Small Business Administration (SBA) field offices are comprised of regional offices (RO), district offices (DO), branch offices (BO), post-of-duty offices (POD), and disaster area offices (DAO). The regional offices are located in 10 major cities around the country and each directs a number of district offices within the region. Regional offices do not make individual loans or offer specific assistance to individuals or companies. District offices are the real contact point for small businesses needing information or assistance. Each district office is staffed by a team of experts in the lending, procurement, and management assistance areas who have the responsibility to consider loan applications, to offer individual management assistance, and to coordinate other small business services. Branch offices and post-of-duty offices have a smaller staff than district offices and are not quite as full-serviced. Disaster area offices are located in four cities around the country and each provides disaster assistance for their individual regions to small business owners.

Region 1

Augusta
40 Western Ave., Room 512, Augusta, ME 04330; 207-622-8378; Fax 207-622-8277

Boston
155 Federal St., 9th Floor, Boston, MA 02110; 617-451-2023; Fax 617-424-5485

Boston
10 Causeway St., Room 265, Boston, MA 02222-1093; 617-565-5590; Fax 617-565-5598

Concord
143 N. Main St., Suite 202, Concord, NH 03301; 603-225-1400; Fax 603-225-1409

Hartford
330 Main St., 2nd Floor, Hartford, CT 06106; 203-240-4700; Fax 203-240-4659

Montpelier
87 State St., Room 205, Montpelier, VT 05602; 802-828-4422; Fax 802-828-4485

Providence
380 Westminster Mall, 5th Floor, Providence, RI 02903; 401-528-4561; Fax 401-528-4539

Springfield
1550 Main St., Room 212, Springfield, MA 01103; 413-785-0268; Fax 413-785-0267

Region 2

Albany
Corner of Clinton and Pearl, Suite 815, Albany, NY 12207; 518-472-6300; Fax 518-472-7138

Buffalo
111 W. Huron St., Room 1311, Buffalo, NY 14202; 716-846-4301; Fax 716-846-4418

Camden
2600 Mt. Ephrain Ave., Camden, NJ 08104; 609-757-5183; Fax 609-757-5335

Elmira
333 E. Water St., 4th Floor, Elmira, NY 14901; 607-734-8130; Fax 607-733-4656

Hato Rey
Carlos Chardon Ave., Suite 691, Hato Rey, PR 00918; 809-766-5572; Fax 809-766-5309

Melville
35 Pinelawn Rd., Suite 207W, Melville, NY 11747; 516-454-0750; Fax 516-454-0769

New York
26 Federal Plaza, Suite 31-08, New York, NY 10278; 212-264-1450; Fax 212-264-0900

New York
26 Federal Plaza, Suite 31-00, New York, NY 10278; 212-264-2454; Fax 212-264-4963

Newark
60 Park Place, 4th Floor, Newark, NJ 07102; 201-645-2434; Fax 201-645-6265

Rochester
100 State St., Suite 410, Rochester, NY 14614; 716-263-6700; Fax 716-263-3146

Syracuse
100 S. Clinton St., Suite 1071, Syracuse, NY 13260; 315-423-5383; Fax 315-423-5370

Region 3

Baltimore
10 S. Howard St., Suite 6220, Baltimore, MD 21201-2525; 410-962-4392; Fax 410-962-1805

Charleston
550 Eagan St., Room 309, Charleston, WV 25301; 304-347-5220; Fax 304-347-5350

Clarksburg
168 W. Main St., 5th Floor, Clarksburg, WV 26301; 304-623-5631; Fax 304-623-0023

Harrisburg
100 Chestnut St., Room 309, Harrisburg, PA 17101; 717-782-3840; Fax 717-782-4839

King of Prussia
475 Allendale Rd., Suite 201, King of Prussia, PA 19406; 215-962-3700; Fax 215-962-3743

King of Prussia
475 Allendale Rd., Suite 201, King of Prussia, PA 19406; 215-962-3800; Fax 215-962-3795

Pittsburgh
960 Penn Ave., 5th Floor, Pittsburgh, PA 15222; 412-644-2780; Fax 412-644-5446

Richmond
400 N. 8th St., Room 3015, Richmond, VA 23240; 804-771-2400; Fax 804-771-8018

Washington
1110 Vermont Ave., NW, Suite 900, Washington, DC 20036; 202-606-4000; Fax 202-606-4225

Wilkes-Barre
20 N. Pennsylvania Ave., Room 2327, Wilkes-Barre, PA 18701-3589; 717-826-6497; Fax 717-826-6287

Wilmington
920 N. King St., Suite 412, Wilmington, DE 19801; 302-573-6295; Fax 302-573-6060

Region 4

Atlanta
1375 Peachtree St., NE, 5th Floor, Atlanta, GA 30367-8102; 404-347-2797; Fax 404-347-2355

Atlanta
1720 Peachtree Rd., NW, 6th Floor, Atlanta, GA 30309; 404-347-4749; Fax 404-347-4745

Birmingham
2121 8th Ave., N., Suite 200, Birmingham, AL 35203-2398; 205-731-1344; Fax 205-731-1404

Charlotte
200 N. College St., Suite A2015, Charlotte, NC 28202-2137; 704-344-6563; Fax 704-344-6769

Columbia
1835 Assembly St., Room 358, Columbia, SC 29201; 803-765-5377; Fax 803-765-5962

Coral Gables
1320 S. Dixie Hwy, Suite 501, Coral Gables, FL 33146-2911; 305-536-5521; Fax 305-536-5058

Gulfport
One Hancock Plaza, Suite 1001, Gulfport, MS 39501-7758; 601-863-4449; Fax 601-864-0179

Jackson
101 W. Capitol St., Suite 400, Jackson, MS 39201; 601-965-4378; Fax 601-965-4294

Jacksonville
7825 Baymeadows Way, Suite 100-B, Jacksonville, FL 32256-7504; 904-443-1900; Fax 904-443-1980

Louisville
600 Dr. Martin Luther King Place, Room 188, Louisville, KY 40202; 502-582-5971; Fax 502-582-5009

Nashville
50 Vantage Way, Suite 201, Nashville, TN 37228-1500; 615-736-5881; Fax 615-736-7232

Be patient. If any phone number is incorrect, call (area code) 555-1212 and request the new listing.

713

Tampa
501 E. Polk St., Ste. 104, Tampa, FL 33602-3945; 813-228-2594; Fax 813-228-2111

Region 5
Chicago
300 S. Riverside Plaza, Suite 1975 S, Chicago, IL 60606-6617; 312-353-5000; Fax 312-353-3426

Chicago
500 W. Madison St., Suite 1250, Chicago, IL 60661-2511; 312-353-4528; Fax 312-886-5108

Cincinnati
525 Vine Street, Suite 870, Cincinnati, OH 45202; 513-684-2814; Fax 513-684-3251

Cleveland
1111 Superior Ave., Suite 630, Cleveland, OH 44114-2507; 216-522-4180; Fax 216-522-2038

Columbus
2 Nationwide Plaza, Suite 1400, Columbus, OH 43215-2592; 614-469-6860; Fax 614-469-2391

Detroit
477 Michigan Ave., Room 515, Detroit, MI 48226; 313-226-6075; Fax 313-226-4769

Indianapolis
429 N. Pennsylvania St., Suite 100, Indianapolis, IN 46204-1873; 317-226-7272; Fax 317-226-7259

Madison
212 E. Washington Ave., Room 213, Madison, WI 53703; 608-264-5261; Fax 608-264-5541

Marquette
228 W. Washington, Suite 11, Marquette, MI 49885; 906-225-1108; Fax 906-225-1109

Minneapolis
100 N. 6th St., Suite 610, Minneapolis, MN 55403-1563; 612-370-2324; Fax 612-370-2303

Milwaukee
310 W. Wisconsin Ave., Suite 400, Milwaukee, WI 53203; 414-297-3941; Fax 414-297-1377

Springfield
511 W. Capitol St., Suite 302, Springfield, IL 62704; 217-492-4416; Fax 217-492-4867

Region 6
Albuquerque
625 Silver Ave., SW, Suite 320, Albuquerque, NM 87102; 505-766-1870; Fax 505-766-1057

Austin
300 East 8th Street, Room 967, Austin, TX 78701; 512-482-5288; Fax 512-482-5290

Corpus Christi
606 N. Carancahua, Suite 1200, Corpus Christi, TX 78476; 512-888-3331; Fax 512-888-3418

Dallas
8625 King George Dr., Bldg. C, Dallas, TX 75235-3391; 214-767-7633; Fax 214-767-7870

El Paso
10737 Gateway W., Suite 320, El Paso, TX 79935; 915-540-5676; Fax 915-540-5636

Ft. Worth
4300 Amon Carter Blvd., Suite 114, Ft. Worth, TX 76155; 817-885-6500 Fax 817-885-6516

Harlingen
222 E. Van Buren St., Room 500, Harlingen, TX 78550-6855; 210-427-8533; Fax 210-427-8537

Houston
9301 Southwest Freeway, Suite 550, Houston, TX 77074-1591; 713-773-6500; Fax 713-773-6550

Little Rock
2120 Riverfront Dr., Suite 100, Little Rock, AR 72202; 501-324-5871; Fax 501-324-5199

Lubbock
1611 Tenth St., Suite 200, Lubbock, TX 79401-2693; 806-743-7462; Fax 806-743-7487

Marshall
505 East Travis, Room 112, Marshall, TX 75670; 903-935-5257; Fax 903-935-1248

New Orleans
365 Canal St., Suite 2250, New Orleans, LA 70130; 504-589-6685; Fax 504-589-2339

Oklahoma City
200 NW 5th St., Suite 670, Oklahoma City, OK 73102; 405-231-5521; Fax 405-231-4876

San Antonio
727 E. Durango Blvd., Room A-527, San Antonio, TX 78206-1204; 210-229-5900; Fax 210-229-5937

Shreveport
401 Edwards St., Room 916, Shreveport, LA 71101-5523; 318-676-3196; Fax 318-676-3214

Region 7
Cedar Rapids
215 4th Ave., SE, Suite 200, Cedar Rapids, IA 52401-1806; 319-362-6405; Fax 319-362-7861

Des Moines
210 Walnut St., Room 749, Des Moines, IA 50309; 515-284-4422; Fax 515-284-4572

Kansas City
911 Walnut St., 13th Floor, Kansas City, MO 64106; 816-426-3210; Fax 816-426-5559

Kansas City
323 W. 8th St., Suite 501, Kansas City, MO 64105; 816-374-6708; Fax 816-374-6759

Omaha
11145 Mill Valley Rd., Omaha, NE 68154; 402-221-4691; Fax 402-221-3680

Springfield
620 S. Glenstone St., Suite 110, Springfield, MO 65802-3200; 417-864-7670; Fax 417-864-4108

St. Louis
815 Olive St., Room 242, St. Louis, MO 63101; 314-539-6600; Fax 314-539-3785

Wichita
100 E. English St., Suite 510, Wichita, KS 67202; 316-269-6616; Fax 316-269-6499

Region 8
Casper
100 East B St., Room 4001, Casper, WY 82602-2839; 307-261-5761; Fax 307-261-5499

Denver
633 17th St., 7th Floor,, Denver, CO 80202; 303-294-7186; Fax 303-294-7153

Denver
721 19th St., Room 426, Denver, CO 80202-2599; 303-844-3984; Fax 303-844-6468

Fargo
657 Second Ave. N, Room 219, Fargo, ND 58108-3086; 701-239-5131; Fax 701-239-5645

Helena
301 S. Park, Room 334, Helena, MT 59626; 406-449-5381; Fax 406-449-5474

Salt Lake City
125 S. State St., Room 2237, Salt Lake City, UT 84138-1195; 801-524-5804; Fax 801-524-4160

Sioux Falls
110 S. Phillips Ave., Suite 200, Sioux Falls, SD 57102-1109; 605-330-4231; Fax 605-330-4215

Region 9
Fresno
2719 North Air Fresno Dr., Suite 107, Fresno, CA 93727-1547; 209-487-5189; Fax 209-487-5636

Glendale
330 N. Brand Blvd., Suite 1200, Glendale, CA 91203-2304; 818-552-3210; Fax 818-552-3260

Honolulu
300 Ala Moana Blvd., Room 2213, Honolulu, HI 96850-4981; 808-541-2990; Fax 808-541-2976

Las Vegas
301 E. Stewart St., Room 301, Las Vegas, NV 89125-2527; 702-388-6611; Fax 702-388-6469

Phoenix
2828 N. Central Ave., Suite 800, Phoenix, AZ 85004-1093; 602-640-2316; Fax 602-640-2360

Reno
50 S. Virginia St., Room 238, Reno, NV 89505-3216; 702-784-5268

Sacramento
660 J St., Room 215, Sacramento, CA 95814-2413; 916-498-6410; Fax 916-498-6422

San Diego
550 W. C St., Suite 550, San Diego, CA 92188-3340; 619-557-7250; Fax 619-557-5894

San Francisco
211 Main St., 4th Floor, San Francisco, CA 94105-1988; 415-744-6820; Fax 415-744-6812

San Francisco
71 Stevenson St., 20th Floor, San Francisco, CA 94105-2939; 415-744-6404; Fax 415-744-6435

Santa Ana
901 W. Civic Center Dr., Suite 160, Santa Ana, CA 92703-2352; 714-836-2494; Fax 714-836-2528

Tucson
300 W. Congress St., Box FB 33, Room 7-H, Tucson, AZ 85701-1319; 602-670-4759; Fax 602-670-4763

Ventura
6477 Telephone Rd., Suite 10, Ventura, CA 93003-4459, 805-642-1866, Fax 805-642-9538

Region 10
Anchorage
222 W. 8th Ave., Room A36, Anchorage, AK 99513-7559; 901-271-4022, Fax 907-271-4545

Boise
1020 Main St., Suite 290, Boise, ID 83702-5745; 208-334-1696, Fax 208-334-9353

Portland
222 SW Columbia St., Suite 500, Portland, OR 97201-6695; 503-326-2682, Fax 503-326-2808

Seattle
2601 Fourth Ave., Suite 440, Seattle, WA 98121-1273; 206-553-5676, Fax 206-553-4155

Seattle
915 Second Ave., Room 1792, Seattle, WA 98174-1088; 206-220-6520, Fax 206-220-6570

Spokane
W. 601 First Ave., 10th Floor, Spokane, WA 99204-0317; 509-353-2800, Fax 509-353-2829

Disaster Area Offices

Atlanta
One Baltimore Place, Suite 300, Atlanta, GA 30308; 404-347-3771, Fax 404-347-4183

Niagara Falls
360 Rainbow Blvd S., 3rd Floor, Niagara Falls, NY 14303-1192; 716-282-4612; Fax 716-282-1472

Ft. Worth
4400 Amon Carter Blvd., Suite 102, Ft. Worth, TX 76155; 817-885-7600, Fax 817-885-7616

Sacramento
1825 Bell St., Suite 208, Sacramento, CA 95825; 916-566-7248, Fax 916-566-7280

* Films on Small Business
National Technical Information Services
U.S. Department of Commerce
5285 Port Royal Rd.   800-553-6847
Springfield, VA 22161   703-487-4650
A number of films on small business topics are available for sale and sometimes for rental purposes. *The Media Resource Catalog* contains a list of the titles. To obtain the free catalog, contact this office.

* Financial Management and Your Business
Superintendent of Documents
U.S. Government Printing Office
Washington, DC 20402   202-512-1800
Financial Management: How to Make a Go of Your Business ($2.50, S/N 045-00000-233-1) contains information required to familiarize the small business owner/manager with the basic concepts of financial management. Tips on financial planning, cash-flow management, forecasting and obtaining capital, and other topics are covered.

* Food and Drug Small Business Assistance
Small Business Coordinator
Food and Drug Administration (FDA)
5600 Fishers Lane
Room 1372, HFZ-220
Rockville, MD 20857   301-443-6597
The Food and Drug Administration (FDA) has established the Division of Small Manufactures Assistance to help small companies learn about and comply with FDA regulations. This office can explain FDA procedures and provide assistance in dealing with the FDA. For a free copy of *A Small Business Guide to FDA* or more information contact this office.

* Franchise and Business Opportunities Rules
Federal Trade Commission (FTC)
Marketing Practices
6th and Pennsylvania Ave., NW
Washington, DC 20580   202-326-3128
Under the Federal Trade Commission's (FTC) Franchise and Business Opportunities Rule, sellers of franchises and business opportunities are required to give prospective buyers a disclosure document containing specific information about the franchise and any earning claims. For more information on this regulation, contact this office or your regional FTC.

Small Business and Entrepreneuring

* Incubators

Business Initiative, Education and Training
U.S. Small Business Administration (SBA)
409 3rd Street, SW
6th Floor
Washington, DC 20416   202-205-6665

A small business incubator is a flexible method of encouraging the development of new businesses and fostering local economic development. Incubators are facilities in which a number of new and growing businesses operate under one roof with affordable rents, sharing services and equipment, and having equal access to a wide range of professional, technical, and financial programs. For more information, contact your nearest Small Business Administration office or the office listed above.

* Indian Business Development

Bureau of Indian Affairs
U.S. Department of the Interior
1849 C St., NW
Washington, DC 20240   202-208-5326

Indian tribes and small businesses may receive technical assistance and financial backing through this office. Contact this office for the free booklet entitled *Bureau of Indian Affairs Economic Development*.

* International Visitors Program

International Visitors Liaison
U.S. Small Business Administration (SBA)
409 3rd St., SW
Washington, DC 20416   202-205-6770

The growing influx of foreign visitors to the Small Business Administration (SBA) reflects the growing world-wide interest in small business and the appreciation of small business contributions to national economies. SBA personnel are pleased to meet with government officials, embassy personnel, private sector individuals, educators, students, and other interested parties. Program policies, administration, and operational aspects can be shared through consultation, observation, and briefing sessions. If you are interested in attending a half-day, full-day, or two-day session, contact this office.

* Lenders Programs

Office of Financial Institutions
U.S. Small Business Administration
409 3rd St., SW
Washington, DC 20416   202-205-6510

Under the Certified Lenders Program, the lenders, acting under Small Business Administration (SBA) supervision, handle much of the necessary paperwork and review client financial status - thereby speeding up loan processing and freeing SBA personnel for other assistance to small businesses. Under SBA's Preferred Lenders Program, the lenders handle all loan paperwork, processing, and servicing. For more detailed information, contact the SBA office in your area or the office above.

* Lending and Bonding for Minority Business

Minority Business Resource Center (MBRC)
Small and Disadvantaged Business Utilization (SDBU)
Director of Civil Rights
Office of the Secretary of Transportation
U.S. Department of Transportation
400 7th Street, SW, Room 9414
Washington, DC 20590   202-366-2852

This office offers short-term lending and bonding assistance to small businesses in the transportation industry. The Short-term Lending Program offers loans at prime interest rates, while the Bonding Assistance Program enables small firms to obtain bonding in support of transportation-related contracts. Entrepreneurs can contact MBRC for information and certification details.

* Management and Technical Assistance

Office of Minority Small Business and Capital Ownership
U.S. Small Business Administration
409 3rd St., SW
Washington, DC 20416   202-205-6555

The Small Business Administration (SBA) initiates, organizes, and maintains a management counseling service for small firms in the 8(a) program. Under this authority, SBA places grants, agreements, and contracts with qualified individuals, profit-making firms, state and local governments, educational institutions, and some non-profit organizations to furnish management and technical aid to SBA clients and other eligible small firms. Some of the services performed are accounting, marketing, engineering, and bookkeeping. Eligible recipients of development assistance are generally firms in SBA's 8(a) contracting program, socially or economically disadvantaged individuals, or small firms located in areas of high concentration of unemployed and low-income individuals. If you are interested in providing technical or management assistance to eligible small firms, contact the office above. If you are interested in receiving technical or management assistance, contact the SBA field office in your area.

* Medical Devices: Technical Assistance for Small Businesses

Division of Small Manufacturer's Assistance
Center for Devices and Radiological Health
Food and Drug Administration (FDA)
5600 Fishers Lane, HFZ-220
Rockville, MD 20857   301-443-6597

The Food and Drug Administration (FDA) provides information to small businesses regarding device regulations and what is needed to get approval. The FDA often holds meetings and workshops to offer further assistance. The handbook, *A Small Business Guide to FDA*, explains how the FDA works and the approval process. This Center provides copies of device regulations and FDA documents, as well as guidelines and aids that simplify manufacturer requirements. The *SMA MEMO* contains articles and tips on medical device regulations and reports on Center activities.

* Minority Business Development Centers

Public Affairs
Minority Business Development Agency (MBDA)
U.S. Department of Commerce
14th St. and Constitution Ave. NW, Room 6707
Washington, DC 20230   202-482-4547

The Minority Business Development Agency (MBDA) funds a nationwide network of 100 Minority Business Development Centers--in large minority population areas-- to help minority-owned firms needing assistance in counseling, accounting, administration, business planning, inventory control, negotiations, referrals, networking, construction, and marketing. The MBDC offers entrepreneurs managerial and technical assistance for bonding, bidding, estimating, financing, procurement, international trade, franchising, acquisitions, mergers, joint ventures, and leverage buyouts. The MBDC provides vital business information from corporations, trade associations, export management companies, and federal, state, and local government agencies. The MBDC also identifies minority-owned firms for contract opportunities with state and local government agencies, and private institutions. Business referral services are provided free. The MBDCs, however, generally charge nominal fees for specific management and technical assistance services.

* Minority Business Program Development

Office of Program Development
Minority Business Development Agency
U.S. Department of Commerce
14th St. and Constitution Ave., NW, Room 5096
Washington, DC 20230   202-482-4547

The office is responsible for designing and developing all Minority Business Development Agency (MBDA) programs, and identifying private and public sector resources in connection with the delivery of direct and indirect assistance to develop the minority business community. The Private Sector Division develops programs to encourage the creation and growth of business opportunities within the private sector by providing funding to business and trade associations, foundations, corporations, financial and education institutions, and other private sector organizations. The Public Sector Division is responsible for program development, oversight, and implementation of Federal, state, and local programs that impact on minority business enterprise.

* Minority Business Purchasing

National Minority Supplier Development Council
15 W. 39th St., 9th Floor
New York, NY 10018   212-944-2430

The National Minority Supplier Development Council works with 47 Councils throughout the U.S. to promote the use of minority-owned firms. They assist firms in developing and marketing their capabilities, and acts as a liaison between minority companies and companies who wish to purchase their products or services. Contact the Council for more information.

* Minority Business Regional Assistance
Public Affairs
Minority Business Development Agency
U.S. Department of Commerce
14th St. and Constitution Ave. NW, Room 6707
Washington, DC 20230   202-482-4547
The Minority Business Development Agency conducts most of its activities through its five Regional Offices and three District Offices:

Regional Offices:
Atlanta
401 W. Peachtree St., NW, Suite 1930, Atlanta, GA 30308-3516; 404-730-3300

Chicago
55 East Monroe St., Suite 1440, Chicago, IL 60603; 312-353-0182

Dallas
1100 Commerce St., Room 7B23, Dallas, TX 75242; 214-767-8001

New York
26 Federal Plaza, Room 37-20, New York, NY 10278; 212-264-3262

San Francisco
221 Main St., Room 1280, San Francisco, CA 94105; 415-744-3001

District Offices:
Boston
Room 418, 10 Causeway St., Boston, MA 02222; 617-565-6850

Elmonte
9660 Flair Dr., Suite 455, Elmonte, CA 91731; 818-453-8636

Miami
Room 1314, Box 25, 51 SW., 1st Ave., Miami, FL 33130; 305-536-5054

Philadelphia
Room 10128, 600 Arch St., Philadelphia, PA 19106; 215-597-9236

* Minority Business Week
Minority Enterprise Development Week
Minority Business Development Agency
U.S. Department of Commerce
14th St. and Constitution Ave., NW, Room 6713
Washington, DC 20230   202-501-4693
Minority Enterprise Development Week (MED Week) is an annual celebration to honor the contributions of minority entrepreneurs and those individuals and organizations who actively support minority business development. It is celebrated the first full week in October, and includes workshops, seminars, an Awards Gala, as well as a Marketplace where public and private sector buyers meet with minority vendors.

* Minority Research
Research Division
Minority Business Development Agency
U.S. Department of Commerce
14th St. and Constitution Ave., NW, Room 5701
Washington, DC 20230   202-482-4671
This Division conducts research on minority businesses and issues related to them. A complete listing of research studies is available for free by contacting this office.

* Minority Small Business
Contact your local SBA office or the Small Business Answer Desk listed in this section.
Members of minority groups who own or are interested in owning small businesses are eligible for all Small Business Administration (SBA) programs. In addition, SBA offers special programs to assist members of minority groups who want to start small businesses or expand existing ones. Contact your SBA office for information.

* Money, Management, and Marketing
Office of Public Communications
U.S. Small Business Administration (SBA)

409 3rd St., SW, Room 7600
Washington, DC 20416   202-205-6740
Focus on the Facts is a series of information sheets issued by the Small Business Administration (SBA) which includes those listed below. To obtain copies, contact the office above.

How to Raise Money for a Small Business (#1)
How to Start a Small Business (#2)
Planning...The Most Important Ingredient (#3)
Knowing Your Market (#4)
Information...The Key to Success (#5)
How to Price Your Products and Services (#6)
Opportunities in Exporting (#7)
How to Start a Home-Based Business (#8)

* Patent Licensing Opportunities
U.S. Government Printing Office
Superintendent of Documents
Washington, DC 20402   202-512-1800
Government patents resulting from research discoveries are available for licensing to U.S. companies and citizens. Licenses are offered on a non-exclusive, exclusive, and co-exclusive basis. Non-exclusive licenses are generally granted when no large investment to market a product is expected. Exclusive and co-exclusive licenses are granted when substantial investment is required. Fees for licenses are negotiable. Lists of such patents are made available each week by the Government Printing Office in the form of the *Patent Official Gazette*. Subscriptions or single copies are available from the above address or phone number. The cost is $617 per year or $41 per single weekly issue.

* Publications on Small Business
U.S. Small Business Administration (SBA) Publications
P.O. Box 46521
Denver, CO 80201
The Small Business Administration (SBA) has a collection of over 100 business booklets which are sold for a nominal fee (most are under $2). These publications address the most important business topics and answer the questions most asked by prospective and existing business owners. The topics include financial management, management and planning, marketing, personnel management, and new products, ideas, and inventions. Some of the booklets are listed below. A free *Resource Directory for Small Business Management* and order forms can be received by contacting your local SBA office or by calling the Small Business Answer Desk at 1-800-368-5855. To order any of the publications below send your request to the Denver, Colorado address in this listing.

Emerging Business Series
Transferring Management/Family Business ($3)
Marketing Strategies for Growing Business ($3)
Management Issues for Growing Business ($3)
Human Resource for Growing Business ($3)
Audit Checklist for Growing Business ($3)
Strategic Planning for Growing Business ($3)
Financial Management for Growing Business ($3)

Financial Management
ABCs of Borrowing ($2)
Elementos Basicos Para Pedir Dinero Prestado ($2)
Understanding Cash Flow ($2)
A Venture Capital Primer for Small Business ($2)
Budgeting in a Small Service Firm ($2)
Recordkeeping in a Small Business ($2)
Pricing Your Products and Services Profitably ($2)
Financing for Small Business ($2)

Management and Planning
Problems in Managing a Family-Owned Business ($2)
Business Plan for Small Manufacturers ($2)
Business Plan for Small Construction Firms ($2)
Planning and Goal Setting for Small Business ($2)
Business Plan for Retailers ($2)
Business Plan for Small Service Firms ($2)
Checklist for Going into Business ($2)
How to Get Started With a Small Business Computer ($2)
The Business Plan For Home-based Business ($2)
How to Buy or Sell a Business ($2)

Small Business and Entrepreneuring

Developing a Strategic Business Plan ($2)
Inventory Management ($2)
Selecting the Legal Structure for your Business ($2)
Evaluating Franchise Opportunities ($2)
Small Business Risk Management Guide ($2)
Child Day-Care Services ($3)
Handbook for Small Business ($3)
How to Write a Business Plan ($3)

Marketing
Creative Selling: The Competitive Edge ($2)
Marketing for Small Business: An Overview ($2)
Researching Your Market ($2)
Selling by Mail Order ($2)
Advertising ($2)

Products/Ideas/Inventions
Ideas Into Dollars ($2)
Avoiding Patent, Trademark, and Copyright Problems ($2)

Personnel Management
Employees: How to Find and Pay Them ($2)

* Research and Development

Office of Technology (SBIR)
409 Third St., SW (6470)
Washington, DC 20416   202-205-6450
This office offers information and guidance on SBIR programs and research opportunities for small firms involved in research and technology.

* Research and Development Funding for Small Business

National Technical Information Service
U.S. Department of Commerce
5285 Port Royal Rd.
Springfield, VA 22161   703-487-4650
The *Small Business Guide to Federal Research and Development Funding Opportunities* provides you with direct contacts to U.S. Government offices that contract out research and development work. It is written for smaller businesses with strong scientific and technical competence that want to do research and development work with the government. Highlighted is the Small Business Innovation Research (SBIR) Program. This program requires agencies to set aside a portion of the R&D awards for small businesses. This guide gives you steps to obtaining Federal R&D funding, an overview of Federal laboratory research efforts, criteria companies must meet, and certain laws and regulations that affect small business participation. Contact the Sales Desk to place your order or request the free information brochure, *PR-801*.

* Research Studies in Small Business

Office of Economic Research
Office of Advocacy
U.S. Small Business Administration
409 3rd St., SW, 5th Floor
Washington, DC   202-205-6530
The Office of Advocacy conducts and coordinates applied research in a variety of areas important to small business to promote policies that strengthen the performance of American small business. *The Catalog of Completed Research Studies* is a listing of SBA contracted research studies completed between 1978 and 1994, with over 500 studies covering a broad scope of small business topics and issues, including studies on finance and credit, capital formation, taxes and regulation, government competition and procurement, job creation, innovation, and women and minority business ownership. Contact the office above to obtain this catalog.

* Seasonal Line of Credit

Contact your local SBA office or the Small Business Answer Desk listed in this section.
The Seasonal Line of Credit program is a short-term loan available under the Small Business Administration's (SBA) guaranty program to finance an increase in the trading assets (receivables and inventory) of eligible small businesses arising from a seasonal upswing in business. For additional information on this program, contact the nearest SBA office in your area.

* Section 8(a) Program

Contact your local SBA office or the Small Business Answer Desk listed in this section.
Through the 8(a) Program, small companies owned by socially and economically disadvantaged persons can obtain federal government contracts and other assistance in developing their business. Under the 8(a) Program, the Small Business Administration (SBA) acts as the prime contractor and enters into all types of federal government contracts (including, but not limited to, supply, services, construction, research and development) with other government departments and agencies, and negotiates subcontracts for small companies in the 8(a) Program. Contact your SBA office for more information.

* Securities and Exchange Commission (SEC) Policy

The Office of Small Business Policy
Division of Corporation Finance
U.S. Securities and Exchange Commission (SEC)
450 5th St., NW
Washington, DC 20549   202-942-2950
This office directs the Securities and Exchange Commission's (SEC) small business rulemaking goals, reviews and comments on the impact the SEC rule proposals have on small issuers, and serves as a liaison with Congressional committees, government agencies, and other groups concerned with small business. Information on security laws that pertain to small business offerings may be obtained from this office.

* Service Corps of Retired Executives Association (SCORE)

Service Corps of Retired Executives Association
409 Third St., SW, 4th Floor   800-634-0245
Washington, DC 20009   202-205-6762
The Service Corps of Retired Executives Association (SCORE) is an independent, voluntary, non-profit association funded almost exclusively by the Small Business Administration (SBA). It is made up of over 13,000 men and women from all walks of business management, many of whom are retired, who volunteer their services to small businesses seeking managerial assistance. SCORE volunteers work in each district and their services are free. They provide small-business community assistance in the form of one-on-one and team counseling and nominal-fee workshops. SCORE is developing special programs geared especially for women. Call their toll-free number (800-634-0245) for the location of the SCORE office in your district. Some are located in Small Business Administration (SBA) offices.

* Small Business and the Securities and Exchange Commission (SEC)

Publications Section
Printing Branch
U.S. Securities and Exchange Commission (SEC)
450 5th St., NW (3C-38)
Washington, DC 20549   202-942-4040
The free booklet, *Q&A: Small Business and the SEC*, discusses capital formation and the federal securities laws and is designed to help you understand some of the basis, necessary requirements that apply when you wish to raise capital by selling securities. It answers such questions as:

What are the federal securities laws?
Is any special help available for a small business that wants to sell its securities?
Should my company "go public"?
How does my small business "go public"?
If my company becomes "public," what are its disclosure obligations?
Are there legal ways to sell securities without registering with the SEC?
Are there state law requirements in addition to those under the federal securities laws? and
Where can I go for more information?

* Small Business Development Centers (SBDCs)

Contact your local SBA office or the Small Business Answer Desk listed in this section.
Small Business Development Centers are located in 46 states, the District of Columbia, Puerto Rico, and the Virgin Islands. These centers provide quality assistance, counseling, and training to prospective and existing business owners. They also provide managerial and technical help, research studies, and other types of specialized assistance.

Be patient. If any phone number is incorrect, call (area code) 555-1212 and request the new listing.

* Small Business Innovation Research (SBIR) Program

Office of Technology
U.S. Small Business Administration
409 Third St., SW (6470)
Washington, DC 20416   202-205-6450

The Small Business Innovation Research (SBIR) Program came into existence with the enactment of the Small Business Innovation Development Act of 1982. Under SBIR, agencies of the federal government with the largest research and development budgets are mandated to set aside a legislated percentage each year for the competitive award of SBIR funding agreements to qualified high technology small business concerns. The Small Business Administration (SBA) was designated as the federal agency having unilateral authority and responsibility for coordinating and monitoring the government-wide activities of the SBIR program and reporting on its results annually to Congress. In line with this responsibility, SBA compiles the *SBIR Pre-Solicitation Announcement* (PA) quarterly. The *PA* contains pertinent information on the program and specific data on upcoming SBIR solicitations. The data is not published, but is available on the Internet. To obtain information on the *SBIR Pre-Solicitation Announcement*, call the office above.

* Small Business Institutes (SBIs)

Contact your local SBA Office or the Small Business Answer Desk listed in this section.

Small Business Institutes (SBIs) are organized through the Small Business Administration (SBA) on almost 500 college campuses and universities around the nation. The institutes are staffed by senior business administration students and their faculty advisors and offer free guidance and assistance to troubled small firms. Contact your local SBA district office to obtain the name and telephone number of the SBI nearest you.

* Small Business Investment Companies (SBICs)

Financial Assistance
U.S. Small Business Administration
409 3rd St., SW, Room 8300
Washington, DC 20416   202-205-6570

The Small Business Administration (SBA) licenses, regulates, and provides financial assistance to privately owned and operated Small Business Investment Companies (SBICs). Their major function is to make "venture" or "risk" investments by supplying equity capital and extending unsecured loans and loans not fully collateralized to small enterprises which meet their investment criteria. The Small Business Administration also licenses a specialized type of Small Business Investment Company (SBIC) solely to help small businesses owned and managed by socially or economically disadvantaged persons. This type of SBIC is a Section 301(d) SBIC, formerly referred to as a MESBIC (Minority Enterprise SBIC). For more information or to obtain the free brochure, *Small Business Investment Companies: The SBIC Program*, contact the office above.

* Solar Energy and Conservation Loans

Contact your local SBA office or the Small Business Answer Desk listed in this section.

Financial assistance is provided to small business concerns engaged in the engineering, manufacturing, distributing, marketing, installing, or servicing of energy measures designed to conserve the Nation's energy resources. Detailed information can be obtained from the Small Business Administration office in your area.

* Surety Bonds

Contact your local SBA office or the Small Business Answer Desk listed in this section.

Through its Surety Bond Guarantee Program, the Small Business Administration (SBA) helps to make the bonding process accessible to small and emerging contractors, including minorities who find bonding unavailable to them. The SBA is authorized to guarantee to a qualified surety up to 90 percent of losses incurred under bid, payment, or performance bonds issued to contractors on contracts valued up to $1.25 million. These contracts may be for construction, supplies, manufacturing, or services provided by either a prime or subcontractor for government or non-government work. This program is administered through SBA's 10 regional offices and participating surety companies and agents throughout the nation.

* Trade Remedy Assistance for Small Businesses

The Trade Remedy Assistance Office
U.S. International Trade Commission (ITC)
500 E St., SW, Room 601
Washington, DC 20436   202-205-2200

Small businesses are often adversely affected by U.S. trade laws, which may allow foreign products to flood the U.S. market and unfairly compete with U.S. businesses which sell similar products. The International Trade Commission (ITC), however, provides technical assistance under U.S. trade remedy laws to eligible small businesses which have experienced such effects. To qualify, businesses must have neither adequate resources nor the financial ability to obtain qualified outside assistance. ITC staff is available to meet with eligible small businesses to discuss the petition process and to help organize and assemble relevant background material. The office has assisted eligible small businesses at the preinstitution stage in analyzing their trade-related problems and deciding which statutes may offer relief. Technical assistance may include the review of initial drafts submitted by the eligible small business and advice on additions, deletions, and possible alternative presentations, leading to the final preparation of the petition for filing with the ITC. Such assistance also includes discussion of relevant ITC precedents and publications.

* Transportation Small Business Assistance

Public Assistance Office
Interstate Commerce Commission
12th St. and Constitution Ave., NW
Washington, DC 20423   202-927-7597

The Commission maintains a Public Assistance Office to help the small business owner or transportation firm in such matters as how to file protests on rates, how to file new operating authority or extensions, or how to get adequate service where there is none.

* Veterans Assistance

Contact your local SBA office or the Small Business Answer Desk listed in this section.

The Small Business Administration (SBA) makes special efforts to help veterans get into business or expand existing veteran-owned small firms. Acting on its own or with the help of veterans organizations, the SBA sponsors special business training workshops for veterans. The SBA also sponsors special computer-based training and long-term entrepreneurial programs for veterans. Each SBA office has a veterans affairs specialist to help give veterans special consideration with loans, training, and/or procurement. The *Veterans Handbook*, which outlines the Agency's special consideration programs for veterans, is also available from SBA offices.

* Vietnam-Era and Disabled Veterans Loans

Contact your local SBA office or the Small Business Answer Desk listed in this section.

Under a special appropriation, funds are available for direct loans to disabled and Vietnam-era veterans. These loans can be made only when financing is not available from other sources on reasonable terms. These loans may be made to establish a small firm or assist in the operation or expansion of an existing business. The administrative ceiling on these loans is $150,000. While all qualified veterans receive special consideration in connection with applications for SBA assistance, most loans are made by financial institutions and many are guaranteed by SBA. When a guaranteed loan or other reasonable credit is available, the SBA cannot make a direct loan.

* Women's Business Ownership

Office of Women's Business Ownership
U.S. Small Business Administration
409 3rd St., SW
Washington, DC 20416   202-205-6673

This office was formed to implement a national policy to support women entrepreneurs. Its primary functions include developing and coordinating a national program to increase the number and success of women-owned businesses while making maximum use of existing government and private sector resources; researching and evaluating the special programmatic needs of current or potential women business owners, and develop and test ways of meeting them; working with federal, state, and local governments to ensure that they consider women's business ownership in their program areas.

State Starting Places for Money

Who Can Use State Money?

All states require that funds be used solely by state residents. But that shouldn't limit you to exploring possibilities only in the state in which you currently reside. If you reside in Maine, but Massachusetts agrees to give you $100,000 to start your own business, it would be worth your while to consider moving to Massachusetts. Shop around for the best deal.

Types Of State Money And Help Available

Each state has different kinds and amounts of money and assistance programs available, but these sources of financial and counseling help are constantly being changed. What may not be available this year may very well be available next. Therefore, in the course of your exploration, you might want to check in with the people who operate the business "hotlines" to discover if anything new has been added to the states' offerings.

Described below are the major kinds of programs which are offered by most of the states.

Information

Hotlines or One-Stop Shops are available in many states through a toll-free number that hooks you up with someone who will either tell you what you need to know or refer you to someone who can. These hotlines are invaluable -- offering information on everything from business permit regulations to obscure financing programs. Most states also offer some kind of booklet that tells you to how to start-up a business in that state. Ask for it. It will probably be free.

Small Business Advocates operate in all fifty states and are part of a national organization (the National Association of State Small Business Advocates) devoted to helping small business people function efficiently with their state governments. They are a good source for help in cutting through bureaucratic red tape.

Funding Programs

Free Money can come in the form of grants, and works the same as free money from the federal government. You do not have to pay it back.

Loans from state governments work in the same way as those from the federal government — they are given directly to entrepreneurs. Loans are usually at interest rates below the rates charged at commercial institutions and are also set aside for those companies which have trouble getting a loan elsewhere. This makes them an ideal source for riskier kinds of ventures.

Loan Guarantees are similar to those offered by the federal government. For this program, the state government will go to the bank with you and co-sign your loan. This, too, is ideal for high risk ventures which normally would not get a loan.

Interest Subsidies On Loans is a unique concept not used by the federal government. In this case, the state will subsidize the interest rate the bank is charging you. For example, if the bank gives you a loan for $50,000 at 10 percent per year interest, your interest payments will be $5,000 per year. With an interest subsidy you might pay only $2,500 since the state will pay the other half. This is like getting the loan at 5 percent instead of 10 percent.

Industrial Revenue Bonds Or General Obligation Bonds are a type of financing that can be used to purchase only fixed assets, such as a factory or equipment. In the case of Industrial Revenue Bonds the state will raise money from the general public to buy your equipment. Because the state acts as the middleman, the people who lend you the money do not have to pay federal taxes on the interest they charge you. As a result, you get the money cheaper because they get a tax break. If the state issues General Obligation Bonds to buy your equipment, the arrangement will be similar to that for an Industrial Revenue Bond except that the state promises to repay the loan if you cannot.

Matching Grants supplement and abet federal grant programs. These kinds of grants could make an under-capitalized project go forward. Awards usually hinge on the usefulness of the project to its surrounding locality.

Loans To Agricultural Businesses are offered in states with large rural, farming populations. They are available solely to farmers and/or agribusiness entrepreneurs.

Loans To Exporters are available in some states as a kind of gap financing to cover the expenses involved in fulfilling a contract.

Energy Conservation Loans are made to small businesses to finance the installation of energy-saving equipment or devices.

Special Regional Loans are ear-marked for specific areas in a state that may have been hard hit economically or suffer from under-development. If you live in one of these regions, you may be eligible for special funds.

High Tech Loans help fledgling companies develop or introduce new products into the marketplace.

Loans To Inventors help the entrepreneur develop or market new products.

Local Government Loans are used for start-up and expansion of businesses within the designated locality.

Childcare Facilities Loans help businesses establish on-site daycare facilities.

Loans To Women And/Or Minorities are available in almost every state from funds specifically reserved for economically disadvantaged groups.

Many federally funded programs are administered by state governments. Among them are the following programs:

The SBA 7(A) Guaranteed and *Direct Loan* program can guarantee up to 90 percent of a loan made through a private lender (up to $750,000), or make direct loans of up to $150,000.

The SBA 504 establishes Certified Development Companies whose debentures are guaranteed by the SBA. Equity participation of the borrower must be at least 10 percent, private financing 60 percent and CDC participation at a maximum of 40 percent, up to $750,000.

Small Business Innovative Research Grants (SBIR) award between $20,000 to $50,000 to entrepreneurs to support six months of research on a technical innovation. They are then eligible for up to $500,000 to develop the innovation.

Small Business Investment Companies (SBIC) license, regulate and provide financial assistance in the form of equity financing, long-term loans, and management services.

Community Development Block Grants are available to cities and counties for the commercial rehabilitation of existing buildings or structures used for business, commercial, or industrial purposes. Grants of up to $500,000 can be made. Every $15,000 of grant funds invested must create at least one full-time job, and at least 51 percent of the jobs created must be for low and moderate income families.

Farmers Home Administration (FmHA) Emergency Disaster Loans are available in counties where natural disaster has substantially affected farming, ranching or aquaculture production.

FmHA Farm Loan Guarantees are made to family farmers and ranchers to enable them to obtain funds from private lenders. Funds must be used for farm ownership, improvements, and operating purposes.

FmHA Farm Operating Loans to meet operating expenses, finance recreational and nonagricultural enterprises, to add to family income, and to pay for mandated safety and pollution control changes are available at variable interest rates. Limits are $200,000 for an insured farm operating loan and $400,000 for a guaranteed loan.

FmHA Farm Ownership Loans can be used for a wide range of farm improvement projects. Limits are $200,000 for an insured loan and $300,000 for a guaranteed loan.

FmHA Soil And Water Loans must be used by individual farmers and ranchers to develop, conserve, and properly use their land and water resources and to help abate pollution. Interest rates are variable; each loan must be secured by real estate.

FmHA Youth Project Loans enable young people to borrow for income-producing projects sponsored by a school or 4H club.

Assistance Programs

Management Training is offered by many states in subjects ranging from bookkeeping to energy conservation.

Business Consulting is offered on almost any subject. Small Business Development Centers are the best source for this kind of assistance.

Market Studies to help you sell your goods or services within or outside the state are offered by many states. They all also have State Data Centers which not only collect demographic and other information about markets within the state, but also have access to federal data which can pinpoint national markets. Many states also provide the services of graduate business students at local universities to do the legwork and analysis for you.

Business Site Selection is done by specialists in every state who will identify the best place to locate a business.

Licensing, Regulation, And Permits information is available from most states through "one-stop shop" centers by calling a toll-free number. There you'll get help in finding your way through the confusion of registering a new business.

Employee Training Programs offer on-site training and continuing education opportunities.

Research And Development assistance for entrepreneurs is a form of assistance that is rapidly increasing as more and more states try to attract high technology-related companies. Many states are even setting up clearing-houses so that small businesses can have one place to turn to find expertise throughout a statewide university system.

Procurement Programs have been established in some states to help you sell products to state, federal, and local governments.

Export Assistance is offered to identify overseas markets. Some states even have overseas offices to drum up business prospects for you.

Assistance In Finding Funding is offered in every state, particularly through regional Small Business Development Centers. They will not only identify funding sources in the state and federal governments but will also lead you through the complicated application process.

Special Help For Minorities And Women is available in almost every state to help boost the participation of women and minorities in small business ventures. They offer special funding programs and, often, one-on-one counseling to assure a start-up success.

Venture Capital Networking is achieved through computer databases that hook up entrepreneurs and venture capitalists. This service is usually free of charge. In fact, the demand for small business investment opportunities is so great that some states require the investor to pay to be listed.

Small Business and Entrepreneuring

Inventors Associations have been established to encourage and assist inventors in developing and patenting their products.

Annual Governors' Conferences give small business people the chance to air their problems with representatives from state agencies and the legislature.

Small Business Development Centers (SBDCs), funded jointly by the federal and state governments, are usually associated with the state university system. SBDCs are a god-send to small business people. They will not only help you figure out if your business project is feasible, but also help you draw up a sensible business plan, apply for funding, and check in with you frequently once your business is up and running to make sure it stays that way.

Tourism programs are prominent in states whose revenues are heavily dependent on the tourist trade. They are specifically aimed at businesses in the tourist industries.

Small Business Institutes at local colleges use senior level business students as consultants to help develop business plans or plan expansions.

Technology Assistance Centers help high tech companies and entrepreneurs establish new businesses and plan business expansions.

On-Site Energy Audits are offered free of charge by many states to help control energy costs and improve energy efficiency for small businesses. Some states also conduct workshops to encourage energy conservation measures.

Minority Business Development Centers offer a wide range of services from initial counseling on how to start a business to more complex issues of planning and growth.

Business Information Centers (BICs) provide the latest in high-tech hardware, software, and telecommunications to help small businesses get started. BIC is a place where business owners and aspiring business owners can go to use hardware/software, hard copy books, and publications to plan their business, expand an existing business, or venture into new business areas. Also, on-site counseling is available.

U.S. Small Business Administration (SBA) Programs

The SBA offices listed under each state can provide you with detailed information on the following programs:

Small Business Innovative Research Grants (SBIR): Phase I awards between $20,000 to $50,000 to entrepreneurs to support six months of research on a technical innovation. Phase II grants are an additional $500,000 for development. Private sector investment funds must follow.

International Trade Loans: Guaranteed long-term loans through private lenders to develop or expand export markets, or to recover from the effects of import competition. Maximum guaranteed loan is $1,000,000 for fixed assets and an additional $250,000 for working capital and/or export revolving line of credit.

Contract Loan: Short-term loans are available to small businesses to finance the costs of labor and materials on contracts for which the proceeds are assignable. Program guarantees up to 90 percent of loans not in excess of $750,000. Qualifying small businesses must be in business for at least 12 calendar months prior to the date of the loan application.

General Contractor Loans: Small general construction contractors may obtain short-term loans or loan guarantees for residential or commercial construction or rehabilitation of property to be sold. The SBA will guarantee up to 90 percent of qualifying loans made by private lenders up to a maximum of $750,000. Direct loans can be up to $150,000.

7(a) Loan Guaranty Program: This program is used to fund the varied long-term needs of small businesses. It is designed to promote small business formation and growth by guaranteeing long-term loans to qualified firms. Can guarantee up to $750,000, generally between 70%-90% of the loan value, at an interest rate not to exceed 2.75 over the prime lending rate. Maturities are up to 10 years for working capital; up to 25 years for fixed assets.

7(a) Loan Guaranty Program
Low Documentation Loan Program (LowDoc): Purpose is to reduce the paperwork involved in loan requests of $100,000 or less. A one-page application is used and it relies on the strength of the individual applicant's character and credit history.

7(a) Loan Guaranty Program
GreenLine Program: Intended to finance short-term, working-capital needs of small businesses. Loan advances are usually made against a borrower's certified level of inventory and accounts payable.

7(a) Loan Guaranty Program
Vietnam-Era and Disabled Veteran Loan Program: Assists disabled veterans of any era who can't secure business financing from private sector or other guaranty loan sources. Veterans can apply for loans to establish a small business or expand an existing small business. The maximum is $150,000.

7(a) Loan Guaranty Program
Handicapped Assistance Loans: Assists individuals with disabilities and public/private nonprofit organizations for the employment of the handicapped. Financing is available for starting/acquiring or operating a small business. There are 2 programs of assistance: HAL-1 and HAL-2.

> *HAL-1:* Financial assistance is available to state and federal-chartered organizations that operate in the interest of disabled individuals. Applicants must provide evidence that the business is operated in the interest of handicapped individuals.

> *HAL-2:* Financial assistance is provided to handicapped persons who provide evidence that their business is a for-profit operation, qualifies as a small business, is 100% owned by 1 or more handicapped individuals, and the handicapped owner(s) must actively participate in managing the business.

7(a) Loan Guaranty Program
Women's Prequalification Loan Program: Provides women business owners a pre-authorized loan guaranty commitment. It provides a quick response to loan requests of $250,000 or less.

Be patient. If any phone number is incorrect, call (area code) 555-1212 and request the new listing.

7(a) Loan Guaranty Program
Secondary Market: Lenders who hold business loans guaranteed by the SBA may improve profitability and liquidity by selling the guaranteed portions of those loans in the secondary market. Banks, savings and loan companies/ credit unions and pension funds, and insurance companies are frequent buyers.

8(a) Participant Loan Programs:
Makes financial assistance available to 8(a) certified firms. Applicants must be participants in the 8(a) Program and eligible for contractual assistance. Loans can be made directly or through lending institutions under the agency's immediate participation or guaranty programs. Loans may be used for facilities/equipment or working capital.

7(m) MicroLoan Demonstration Program:
Aimed at small businesses needing small-scale financing/technical assistance for start-up or expansion. Short-term loans of up to $25,000 are made to small businesses for the purchase of machinery and equipment, furniture and fixtures, inventory, supplies and working capital.

502 Local Development Company Program:
Provides long-term, fixed asset financing through certified development companies. Proceeds are provided as follows: 50% by an unguaranteed bank loan, 40% by an SBA guaranteed debenture, 10% by the small business customer. The maximum SBA debenture is $1 million.

504 Certified Development Company Program:
Provides long-term, fixed asset financing through certified development companies. Proceeds are provided as follows: 50% by an unguaranteed bank loan, 40% by an SBA guaranteed debenture, 10% by the small business customer. The maximum SBA debenture is $1 million.

Surety Bond Program
Prior Approval Program: Aimed at small construction/service contractors; surety/insurance companies; minority/women's groups; federal/state agencies; state insurance depts.; federal/state and other procurement officials.

Surety Bond Program
Preferred Surety Bond (PSB) Program: Aimed at small construction and service contractors; surety/insurance companies; minority and women's groups; federal/state agencies; state insurance depts.; federal and state and other procurement officials. The decision to issue a surety bond guarantee is made by participating sureties. There are participating sureties authorized by SBA to issue/monitor and service bonds without prior SBA approval. SBA guarantees surety bonds for construction, service/supply contracts up to $1.25 million.

Export Working Capital Program (EWCP):
Replaces the Export Revolving Line of Credit Program. EWCP will allow up to a 90% guarantee on private-sector loans of up to $750,000 for working capital. Loans can be for single or multiple export sales and can be extended for pre-shipment working capital and post-shipment exposure coverage.

Disaster Assistance Loan Program:
A disaster-assistance loan program for nonagricultural victims. Eligibility is based on financial criteria. Interest rates fluctuate according to statutory formulas. There is a lower rate available to applicants without credit available elsewhere, not to exceed 4%, and a higher interest rate for those with credit available elsewhere, not to exceed 8%.

Disaster Assistance to Businesses
Loans for Physical Damage: Available to qualified businesses for uninsured losses up to $1.5 million for businesses of any size to repair/replace business property to pre-disaster conditions. Loans may be used to replace/repair equipment, fixtures, inventory, and leasehold improvements.

Disaster Assistance to Businesses
Economic Injury Disaster Loan (EIDL): For businesses that sustain economic injury as a result of a disaster. Working capital loans are made to help businesses pay ordinary/necessary expenses which would have been payable barring disaster. Maximum loan amounts is $1.5 million EIDL and physical damage loans combined unless the business meets the criteria for major source of employment.

Disaster Assistance to Businesses
Loan for Major Source of Employment (MSE): For business, large and small, and nonprofit organizations. The $1.5 million limit may be waived for businesses that employ 250 or more in an affected area.

Disaster Assistance to Individual Homeowners and Renters:
Real Property: Loans available to qualified homeowner/renter applicants for uninsured losses up to $200,000 to repair/restore a primary residence to pre-disaster condition. Homeowners may apply for an additional 20% for disaster mitigation. This is a long-term program for individual disaster losses.

Disaster Assistance to Individuals Homeowners and Renters:
Personal Property: Loans available to qualified homeowner/renter applicants for uninsured losses up to $40,000 to repair/replace personal property such as clothing, furniture, cars, etc.

Government Contracting
Certificate of Competency: Helps small businesses to receive government contracts by providing an appeal process to low-bidder businesses denied government contracts by contracting officers for perceived lack of ability to satisfactorily perform.

Government Contracting
Prime Contract: Program increases small business opportunities in the federal acquisition process through initiation of small business set-asides, identification of new small business sources, counseling small businesses on how to do business with the federal government, and assessment of compliance with the Small Business Act through surveillance reviews.

Government Contracting
Breakout Program: Promotes/influences and enhances the break-out of historically sole-source items for full and open competition in order to effect significant savings to the federal government.

Government Contracting
Natural Resources Sales Assistance Program:
> **Timber Sales:** Set-aside program maintains small businesses in the forest products industry by providing them with preferential bidding opportunities for purchasing timber offered by the federal government. Joint operation of the SBA and federal timber-selling agencies throughout the U.S.

National Small Business Tree Planting Program: Allocates grants to the states/trust territories for the purpose of contracting with small businesses to plant trees on land owned and controlled by state/local governments. Federal dollars are matched by community funds.

Government Contracting

Procurement Automated Source System (PASS): A computerized data base of small businesses nationwide which are interested in federal procurement opportunities. Information on each company includes a summary of capabilities, ownership and qualifications.

Small Business Technology Transfer Program (STTR) Pilot Program: This is similar in philosophy and objectives to the SBIR program. It has a requirement that the small firm competing for the Small Business Technology Transfer Program (STTR) Research and Development (R&D) project must collaborate with a nonprofit research institution. This is a joint venture project from the initial bid submission to project completion. Available to small high-tech R&D firms.

State Starting Places

Alabama

General Information

Sherman Shores, Alabama Development Office, 401 Adams Ave. #600, Montgomery, AL 36130; 205-242-0400, Fax: 205-242-0486. Answers general inquiries about Alabama's programs. *Small Business is Big Business in Alabama* is a free packet with information on assistance programs, sources of financing, a licensing handbook, and tips on preparing business and financial plans.

Small Business Advocate, c/o Alabama Development Office, 401 Adams Ave. #600, Montgomery, AL 36130; 205-242-0400, Fax: 205-242-0486. Assistance in cutting bureaucratic red tape. Information and expertise in dealing with state, federal and local agencies.

Small Business Development Centers

The following offices offer free and fee-based services to new and expanding businesses:

Lead Center: Office of State Director, Alabama Small Business Development Consortium, University of Alabama at Birmingham, 1717 11th Ave. South, Suite 419, Birmingham, AL 35294-7645; 205-934-7260, Fax: 205-934-7645.

Auburn: Auburn University, Small Business Development Ctr., College of Business, Auburn, AL 36849, 205-844-4220.

Birmingham: University of Alabama at Birmingham, Small Business Development Center, 1601 11th Ave. S., Birmingham, AL 35294-2060, 205-934-6760.

Birmingham: Alabama Small Business Procurement System, University of Alabama at Birmingham, Small Business Development Center, 1717 11th Ave. South, Suite 419, Birmingham, AL 35294-4410, 205-934-7260.

Florence: University of North Alabama, Small Business Development Center, P.O. Box 5248, Keller Hall, School of Business, Florence, AL 35632-0001, 205-760-4629.

Huntsville: North East Alabama Regional Small Business Development Center, Alabama A&M University and University of Alabama in Huntsville, 225 Church St., NW, Huntsville, AL 35804-0343, 205-535-2061.

Jacksonville: Jacksonville State University, SBDC, 114 Merrill Hall, Jacksonville, AL 36265, 205-782-5271.

Livingston: Livingston University, Small Business Development Center, 212 Wallace Hall, Livingston, AL 35470, 205-652-9661, ext. 439.

Mobile: University of South Alabama, SBDC, 8 College of Business, Mobile, AL 36688, 334-460-6004.

Montgomery: Alabama State University, SBDC, 915 S. Jackson St., Montgomery, AL 36195, 334-269-1102.

Troy: Troy State University, Small Business Development Ctr., 102 Bibb Graves, Troy, AL 36082-0001, 334-670-3771.

Tuscaloosa: Alabama International Trade Center, University of Alabama, 250 Bidgood Hall, Tuscaloosa, AL 35487-0396, 205-348-7621.

Tuscaloosa: University of Alabama, SBDC, 250 Bidgood Hall, Tuscaloosa, AL 35487-0397, 205-348-7011.

Alaska

General Information

Division of Economic Development, Alaska Department of Commerce and Economic Development (DCED), P.O. Box 110804, Juneau, AK 99811-0804; 907-465-2018; or 3601 C St. #724, Anchorage, AK 99503; 907-563-2165. Answers general inquiries. A free booklet, *Establishing a Business in Alaska*, provides information on assistance programs, licensing requirements, taxation, labor laws, financial assistance programs, and state sources of information.

Small Business Advocate, Division of Economic Development, Alaska Department of Commerce and Economic Development (DCED), P.O. Box 110804, Juneau, AK 99811-0804; 907-465-2018 (Juneau). Assistance in cutting bureaucratic red tape. Information and expertise in dealing with state, federal, and local agencies.

Business Development Information Network (BDIN), Division of Economic Development, Alaska Department of Commerce and Economic Development (DCED), P.O. Box 110804, Juneau, AK 99811-0804; 907-465-2017. Alaska Biz Link Computer: 907-272-7524. One-stop clearinghouse/marketing center for inter-state and intra-state businesses and corporations wishing to start, expand or relocate business operations into or within the state. Answer questions, provide information, technical assistance, referrals, and access to all state publications related to establishing, relocating, or expanding a business.

Department of Commerce and Economic Development (DCED), Division of Economic Development, 3601 C St., Anchorage, AK 99503; 907-563-2165. Small Business Counseling Centers: Provide general assistance to small businesses such as business and finance plan development, marketing advice, etc.

Small Business Development Centers

The following offices offer free and fee-based services to new and expanding businesses:

Lead Center: Jan Fredericks, University of Alaska, Small Business Development Center, 430 West 7th Avenue, Suite 110, Anchorage, AK 99501; 907-274-7232, Fax: 907-274-9524, Outside Anchorage: 800-478-7232.

Anchorage: University of Alaska-Anchorage SBDC, 430 West 7th Ave., Suite 110, Anchorage, AK 99501, 907-274-7232; Fax: 907-274-9524; outside Anchorage: 800-478-7232.

Fairbanks: University of Alaska-Fairbanks, SBDC, 510 Fifth Ave., Suite 101, Fairbanks, AK 99701, 907-456-1701; Fax: 907-456-1942; outside Fairbanks: 800-478-1701.

Juneau: Southeast Alaska Small Business Development Center, 400 Willow St., Juneau, AK 99801, 907-463-3789; Fax: 907-463-3929.

Wasilla: Matanuska-Susitna Borough, Small Business Development Center, 1801 Parks Highway, #C-18, Wasilla, AK 99654, 907-373-7232; Fax: 907-373-2560.

Arizona

General Information

Arizona Office of Economic Development, Department of Commerce, 3800 N. Central, #1500, Phoenix, AZ 85012; 602-280-1300. State Small Business Advocate: Assistance in cutting bureaucratic red tape. Information and expertise in dealing with state, federal, and local agencies.

Arizona Business Connection, Arizona Office of Economic Development, Department of Commerce, 3800 N. Central, #1500, Phoenix, AZ 85012; 602-280-1480.

Business Development Division, Arizona Office of Economic Development, Dept. of Commerce, 3800 N. Central, #1500, Phoenix, AZ 85012; 1-800-528-8421.

Small Business Assistance Center, Arizona Office of Economic Development, Department of Commerce, 3800 N. Central, #1500, Phoenix, AZ 85012; 1-800-524-5684. This office provides information on licenses, applications, permits and any other requirements for small businesses. A customized packet containing the forms needed for starting a business, information on taxes and government regulations is available. Assistance with site selection, procurement of raw materials, financing sources, government agencies and programs referral is also provided. Speakers will be provided on request.

Small Business Development Centers

The following offices offer free and fee-based services to new and expanding businesses:

Lead Center: Arizona Small Business Development Center, 9215 N. Black Canyon Highway, Phoenix, AZ 85021; 602-943-9818, Fax: 602-943-3716.

Flagstaff: Coconino County Community College, SBDC, 3000 N. 4th St., Suite 25, Flagstaff, AZ 86004, 602-526-5072; Fax: 602-526-8693; 1-800-350-7122.

Holbrook: Northland Pioneer College, Small Business Development Center, P.O. Box 610, Holbrook, AZ 86025, 602-537-2976; Fax: 602-524-2227.

Kingman: Mojave Community College, Small Business Development Center, 1971 Jagerson Ave., Kingman, AZ 86401, 602-757-0894; Fax: 602-787-0836.

Phoenix: Rio Salado Community College, Small Business Development Center, 301 West Roosevelt, Suite B, Phoenix, AZ 85003, 602-238-9603; Fax: 602-340-1627.

Phoenix: Gateway Community College, Small Business Development Center, 108 N. 40th St., Phoenix, AZ 85034, 602-392-5223; Fax: 602-392-5329.

Prescott: Yavapal College, Small Business Development Center, 1100 E. Sheldon St., Prescott, AZ 86301, 602-778-3088; Fax: 602-778-3109.

Sierra Vista: Cochise College, SBDC, 901 N. Colombo, Room 411, Sierra Vista, AZ 85635, 602-459-9778; Fax: 602-459-9737; 1-800-966-7943, ext. 778.

Thatcher: Eastern Arizona College, Small Business Development Center, 622 College Ave., Thatcher, AZ 85552-0769, 602-428-8590; Fax: 602-428-8462.

Tucson: Pima Community College, Small Business Development Center, 4903 E. Broadway, Suite 101, Tucson, AZ 85709, 602-748-4906; Fax: 602-748-4585.

Yuma: Arizona Western College, Small Business Development Center, 281 W. 24th St., #152 Century Plaza, Yuma, AZ 85364, 602-341-1650; Fax: 602-726-2636.

Arkansas

General Information

Small Business Clearinghouse, Arkansas Industrial Development Commission, One State Capitol Mall, Little Rock, AR 72201; 501-682-1121, Fax: 501-682-7341. Counseling and referral service to serve small business and potential entrepreneurs, including invention assistance, reference catalog, printed materials, assistance programs evaluations.

Coordinator, Small Business Programs, Arkansas Industrial Development Commission, One State Capitol Mall, Room 4C300, Little Rock, AR 72201; 501-682-5275. Small Business Advocate: Assistance in cutting bureaucratic red tape. Information and expertise in dealing with state, federal, and local agencies.

Small Business Development Centers

The following offices offer free and fee-based services to new and expanding businesses:

Lead Center: Arkansas Small Business Development Center, University of Arkansas at Little Rock, Little Rock Technology Center Building, 100 S. Main, Suite 401, Little Rock, AR 72201; 501-324-9043, Fax: 501-324-9049.

Arkadelphia: Henderson State University, Small Business Development Center, P.O. Box 7624, Arkadelphia, AR 71923, 501-246-5511, ext. 327.

Fayetteville: University of Arkansas at Fayetteville, Small Business Development Center, College of Business - BA 117, Fayetteville, AR 72701, 501-575-5148.

Jonesboro: Arkansas State University, Small Business Development Center, P.O. Drawer 2650, Jonesboro, AR 72467, 501-972-3517.

California

General Information

Office of Small Business, California Department of Commerce, 801 K St., Suite 1700, Sacramento, CA 95814; 916-324-1295. Offers workshops, seminars, individual counseling, and publications.

Enterprise Zone, California Department of Commerce, 801 K St., Suite 1700, Sacramento, CA 95814; 916-324-8211.

Main Street Development, California Department of Commerce, 801 K St., Suite 1700, Sacramento, CA 95814; 916-322-3520. Provides case studies, handbooks, slide presentations, on-site training workshops, and seminars on a wide range of topics, including downtown revitalization, industrial development, streamlining the local permit process, and financing.

Small Business Advocate, 801 K St., #1700, Sacramento, CA 95814; 916-322-6108, 916-327-HELP. Provides assistance in cutting bureaucratic red tape and information and expertise in dealing with state, federal, and local agencies.

California Commission for Economic Development, Office of the Lieutenant Governor, State Capitol, Room 1028, Sacramento, CA 95814; 916-445-8994. Publishes *Doing Business in California: A Guide for Establishing Business*. Cost: $3.00.

Small Business Development Centers

The following offices offer free and fee-based services to new and expanding businesses:

Lead Center: California Small Business Development Center, California Department of Commerce, Office of Small Business, 801 K Street, Suite 1700, Sacramento, CA 95814; 916-324-5068, Fax: 916-322-5084.

Aptos: Central Coast Small Business Assistance Center, 6500 Soquel Dr., Aptos, CA 95003, 408-479-6136; Fax: 408-479-5743.

Auburn: Sierra College, Small Business Development Center, 560 Wall St., Suite J, Auburn, CA 95603, 916-885-5488; Fax: 916-823-4704.

Bakersfield: Weill Institute, Small Business Development Center, 1330 22nd St., Bakersfield, CA 93301, 805-322-5881; Fax: 805-322-5663.

Chico: Butte College, Tri-County Small Business Development Center, 260 Cohasset Ave., Chico, CA 95926, 916-895-9017; Fax: 916-895-9099.

Chula Vista: Southwestern College, Small Business Development Center and International Trade Center, 900 Otay Lakes Rd., Bldg. 1600, Chula Vista, CA 91910, 619-482-6393; Fax: 619-482-6402.

Clearlake: Satellite Operation, Small Business Development Center, Hilltop Professional Ctr., Suite 205, Box 4550, Clearlake, CA 95422, 707-996-3440; Fax: 707-995-3605.

Crescent City: North Coast Small Business Development Center, 779 9th St., Crescent City, CA 95531, 707-464-2168; Fax: 707-465-6008.

Eureka: North Coast Satellite Center, 408 7th St., Suite "E", Eureka, CA 95501, 707-445-9720; Fax: 707-445-9652.

Fresno: Central California Small Business Development Center, 1999 Tuolumine St., Suite 650, Fresno, CA 93721, 209-237-0660; Fax: 209-237-1417.

Gilroy: Gavilan College, Small Business Development Center, 7436 Monterey St., Gilroy, CA 95020, 408-847-0373; Fax: 408-847-0393.

Small Business and Entrepreneuring

Irvine: Accelerate Technology Small Business Development Center, Graduate School of Management, Room 230, University of California, Irvine, CA 92717-3125, 714-856-8366; Fax: 714-725-2978.

La Jolla: Greater San Diego Chamber of Commerce, Small Business Development Center, 4275 Executive Square, Suite 920, La Jolla, CA 92037, 619-453-9388; Fax: 619-450-1997.

Los Angeles: Export Small Business Development Center of Southern California, 110 E. 9th, Suite 669, Los Angeles, CA 90079, 213-892-1111; Fax: 213-892-8232.

Merced: Satellite Operation, Small Business Development Center, 1632 N. St., Merced, CA 95340, 209-385-7312; Fax: 209-383-4959.

Modesto: Valley Sierra Small Business Development Center, 1012 11th St., Suite 300, Modesto, CA 95354, 209-521-6177; Fax: 209-521-9373.

Napa: Napa Valley College, Small Business Development Center, 1556 First St., Suite 103, Napa, CA 94559, 707-253-3210; Fax: 707-253-3068.

Oakland: East Bay Small Business Development Center, 2201 Broadway, Suite 701, Oakland, CA 94612, 510-893-4114; Fax: 510-893-5532.

Oxnard: Satellite Operation, Small Business Development Center, 300 Esplanade Dr., Suite 1010, Oxnard, CA 93030, 805-981-4633; Fax: 805-988-1862.

Pomona: Eastern Los Angeles County Small Business Development Center, 363 S. Park Ave., Pomona, CA 91766, 909-629-2297; Fax: 909-629-8310.

Riverside: Inland Empire Small Business Development Center, 2002 Iowa Ave., Suite 110, Riverside, CA 92507, 714-781-2345; Fax: 714-781-2345.

Sacramento: Greater Sacramento Small Business Development Center, 1787 Tribute Rd., Suite A, Sacramento, CA 95815, 916-263-6580; Fax: 916-263-6571.

San Jose: Silicon Valley - San Mateo County, Small Business Development Center, 111 North Market Street, Suite 150, San Jose, CA 95113, 408-298-7694; Fax: 408-971-0680.

San Mateo: San Mateo County Satellite Center, Bayshore Corporate Center, 1730 S. Amphlett Blvd., Ste. 208, San Mateo, CA 94402, 415-358-0271; Fax: 415-358-9450.

Santa Ana: Rancho Santiago Small Business Development Center, 901 East Santa Ana Boulevard, Suite 108, Santa Ana, CA 92701, 714-647-1172; Fax: 714-835-9008.

Santa Rosa: Redwood Empire, Small Business Development Center, 520 Mendocino Ave., Suite 210, Santa Rosa, CA 95401, 707-524-1770; Fax: 707-524-1772.

Stockton: San Joaquin Delta College, Small Business Development Center, 814 N. Hunter, Stockton, CA 95202, 209-474-5089; Fax: 209-263-6571.

Suisun: Solano County Small Business Development Center, 320 Campus Lane, Suisun, CA 94585, 707-864-3382; Fax: 707-864-3386.

Torrance: Southwest Los Angeles County Small Business Development Ctr., 21221 Western Ave., Suite 110, Torrance, CA 90501, 310-782-3861; Fax: 310-782-8607.

Van Nuys: Northern Los Angeles Small Business Development Center, 14540 Victory Blvd, Suite #206, Van Nuys, CA 91411, 818-373-7092; Fax: 818-373-7740.

Visalia: Satellite Operation, Central California SBDC, 430 W. Caldwell, Suite D, Visalia, CA 93277, 209-625-3051/3052; Fax: 209-625-3053.

Colorado

General Information

Office of Business Development, 1625 Broadway, Suite 1710, Denver, CO 80202; 303-892-3840, Fax: 303-892-3848, Hotline: 1-800-592-5920 in Colorado. Provides information and assistance to local economic development organizations, assists in retaining and expanding existing businesses, and responds to out-of-state inquiries concerning expanding or relocating in Colorado. The booklet, *A Capital Venture*, lists sources and contacts for venture capital and is available from the above office.

Small Business Advocate, Office of Business Development, 1625 Broadway, Suite 1710, Denver, CO 80202; 303-892-3840, Fax: 303-892-3848, Hotline: 1-800-592-5920 in Colorado. Provides assistance in cutting bureaucratic red tape and information and expertise in dealing with state, federal, and local agencies.

Colorado Office of Small Business, Office of Business Development, 1625 Broadway, Suite 1710, Denver, CO 80202; 303-892-3840, Fax: 303-892-3848, Hotline: 1-800-592-5920 in Colorado. Offers information, assistance and referrals for Colorado's small business owners and operators. The Small Business Hotline provides access to the Colorado Business Clearinghouse, a computerized database that contains information on over 2,000 business resources.

Small Business Development Centers

The following offices offer free and fee-based services to new and expanding businesses:

Lead Center: Colorado Small Business Development Center, Office of Economic Development, 1625 Broadway, Suite 1710, Denver, CO 80202; 303-892-3809, 303-892-3840, Fax: 303-892-3848.

Alamosa: Adams State College, Small Business Development Center, Alamosa, CO 81102, 719-589-7372; Fax: 719-589-7522.

Aurora: Community College of Aurora, Small Business Development Center, 16000 East Centretech Parkway, #A201, Aurora, CO 80011-9036, 719-341-4849.

Canon City: Canon City (Satellite) Small Business Development Center, 402 Valley Rd., Canon City, CO 81212, 719-442-1475.

Colorado Springs: Pikes Peak Community College/Colorado Springs Chamber of Commerce, Small Business Development Center, P.O. Drawer B, Colorado Springs, CO 80901-3002, 719-471-4836.

Craig: Colorado Northwestern Community College, Small Business Development Center, 50 Spruce Drive, Craig, CO 81625, 303-824-7078; Fax: 303-824-3527.

Delta: Delta Montrose Vocational School, Small Business Development Center, 1765 US Hwy 50, Delta, CO 81416, 303-874-8772; Fax: 303-874-8796.

Denver: Community College of Denver/ Denver Chamber of Commerce, Small Business Development Center, 1445 Market St., Denver, CO 80202, 303-620-8076; Fax: 303-534-3200.

Durango: Fort Lewis College, Small Business Development Center, Miller Student Center, Room 108, Durango, CO 81301, 303-247-9634; Fax: 303-247-7620.

Fort Collins: Fort Collins (Satellite), P.O. Box 2397, Fort Collins, CO 80522, 303-226-0881.

Fort Morgan: Morgan Community College, Small Business Development Center, 300 Main St., Fort Morgan, CO 80701, 303-867-4424; Fax: 303-867-7580.

Grand Junction: Mesa State College, Small Business Development Center, 304 W. Main St., Grand Junction, CO 81505-1606, 303-243-5242.

Greeley: Aims Community College/Greeley and Weld Chamber of Commerce, Small Business Development Center, 1407 8th Ave., Greeley, CO 80631, 303-352-3661; Fax: 303-352-3572.

Lakewood: Red Rocks Community College, Small Business Development Center, 13300 West 6th Avenue, Lakewood, CO 80401-5398, 303-987-0710; Fax: 303-969-8039.

Lamar: Lamar Community College, Small Business Development Center, 2400 S. Main, Lamar, CO 81052, 719-336-8141; Fax: 719-336-2448.

Littleton: Arapaho Community College/South Metro Chamber of Commerce, Small Business Development Center, 7901 S. Park Plaza, Suite 110, Littleton, CO 80120, 303-795-5855; Fax: 303-795-7520.

Pueblo: Pueblo Community College, Small Business Development Center, 900 West Orman Ave., Pueblo, CO 81004, 719-549-3224; Fax: 719-546-2413.

Stratton: Stratton (Satellite) Small Business Development Center, P.O. Box 28, Stratton, CO 80836, 719-348-5596; Fax: 719-348-5887.

Trinidad: Trinidad State Junior College, Small Business Development Center, 600 Prospect St., Davis Building, Trinidad, CO 81082, 719-846-5645.

Be patient. If any phone number is incorrect, call (area code) 555-1212 and request the new listing.

Westminister: Front Range Community College, Small Business Development Center, 3645 West 112th Avenue, Westminister, CO 80030, 303-460-1032; Fax: 303-466-1623.

Connecticut

General Information

Office of Small Business Services, Department of Economic Development, 865 Brooks St., Rocky Hill, CT 06067; 203-258-4270. Offers a One Stop Licensing Center for call-in or drop-in service. Publishes *Starting a Business*, a free booklet for ready reference to state licensing laws.

Small Business Advocate, Office of Small Business Services, Department of Economic Development, 865 Brooks St., Rocky Hill, CT 06067; 203-258-4270. Provides assistance in cutting bureaucratic red tape, and information and expertise in dealing with state, federal, and local agencies.

Small Business Development Centers

The following offices offer free and fee-based services to new and expanding businesses:

Lead Center: Connecticut Small Business Development Center, University of Connecticut, School of Business Administration, Box U-41, Room 422, 368 Fairfield Rd., Storrs, CT 06268; 203-486-4135, Fax: 203-486-1576.

Bridgeport: Business Regional B.C., Small Business Development Center, 10 Middle St., 14th Floor, Bridgeport, CT 06604-4229, 203-335-3800; Fax: 203-366-9105.

Bridgeport: University of Bridgeport, Small Business Development Center, 141 Linden Avenue, Bridgeport, CT 06601, 203-576-4538.

Danielson: Quinebaug Valley Community College, SBDC, 742 Upper Maple Street, Danielson, CT 06239-1440, 203-774-1133; Fax: 203-774-7768.

Hartford: University of Connecticut/MBA, Small Business Development Center, 1800 Asylum Ave., West Hartford, CT 06117, 203-241-4986; Fax: 203-241-4907.

Groton: University of Connecticut, Small Business Development Center, Administration Building, Room 313, 1084 Shennecossett Rd., Groton, CT 06340-6097, 203-449-1188; Fax: 203-445-3415.

Middletown: Middlesex County Chamber of Commerce, Small Business Development Center, 393 Main St., Middletown, CT 06457, 203-344-2158; Fax: 203-346-1043.

New Haven: Greater New Haven Chamber of Commerce, Small Business Development Center, 195 Church St., New Haven, CT 06506, 203-773-0782; Fax: 203-787-6730.

Stamford: Southwestern Area Commerce and Industry Association (SACIA), Small Business Development Center, One Landmark Square, Stamford, CT 06901, 203-359-3220; Fax: 203-967-8294.

Waterbury: Greater Waterbury Chamber of Commerce, Small Business Development Center, 83 Bank St., Waterbury, CT 06702, 203-757-0701; Fax: 203-756-3507.

Willmantic: Eastern Connecticut State University, Small Business Development Center, 83 Windham St., Willmantic, CT 06226-2295, 203-456-5349; Fax: 203-456-5670.

Delaware

General Information

John S. Riley, Delaware Development Office, 99 Kings Highway, P.O. Box 1401, Dover, DE 19903; 302-739-4271. Offers referrals to appropriate state agencies and other organizations. Free tabloid, *Small Business Start-Up Guide*, is available.

Small Business Advocate, Delaware Development Office, 99 Kings Highway, P.O. Box 1401, Dover, DE 19903; 302-739-4271. Provides assistance in cutting bureaucratic red tape, and information and expertise in dealing with state, federal, and local agencies.

Small Business Development Centers

The following offices offer free and fee-based services to new and expanding businesses:

Lead Center: Delaware Small Business Development Center, University of Delaware, Purnell Hall, Suite 005, Newark, DE 19716; 302-831-1555, Fax: 302-831-1423.

City of Wilmington: Wilmington Economic Development Corporation, 605A Market Street Mall, Wilmington, DE 19801; 302-571-9088.

New Castle County: New Castle County Economic Development Corporation, First Federal Plaza, Suite 536, Wilmington, DE 19801; 302-656-5050.

Sussex County: Sussex County Department of Economic Development, P.O. Box 589, 11 South Race Street, Georgetown, DE 19947; 302-855-7770; Fax: 302-855-7773.

District of Columbia

General Information

Office of Business and Economic Development, 717 14th St., NW, 10th Floor, Washington, DC 20005; 202-727-6600. Offers a wide range of technical and financial assistance programs.

Small Business Development Centers

The following offices offer free and fee-based services to new and expanding businesses:

Lead Center: District of Columbia Small Business Development Center, Howard University, 6th and Fairmont St., NW, Room 128, Washington, DC 20059; 202-806-1550, Fax: 202-806-1777.

Arlington: Marymount University, Small Business Development Center, Office of Continuing Education, 2807 N. Glebe Rd., Arlington, VA 22207-4299, 703-522-5600.

College Park: University of Maryland (UMCP), Small Business Development Center, College of Business and Management, Tydings Hall, College Park, MD 20742, 301-405-2144.

Landover: National Business League of Southern Maryland, Inc., Small Business Development Center, 1400 McCormick Drive, Landover, MD 20785, 301-883-6491.

Washington: Galludet University, Small Business Development Center, Management Institute, 800 Florida Avenue, NE, Washington, DC 20002-3625, 202-651-5312.

Washington: George Washington University, Small Business Development Center, National Law Center, 720 20th St., NW, Suite SL-101B, Washington, DC 20052, 202-994-7463.

Florida

General Information

Business Services Section, Bureau of Business Assistance, Department of Commerce, 107 W. Gains St., Collins Building, Room 443, Tallahassee, FL 32399-2000; 904-488-9357, 1-800-342-0771 in Florida. Offers information and referral services for current and potential small business owners. Also serves as ombudsman to small businesses to help resolve problems being experienced with state agencies. They also sponsor workshops and business forums and an annual Small Business Development Workshop that brings together local, state, and federal agency representatives. Distributes and publishes the *Florida New Business Guide Checklist* for small businesses.

Bureau of Industry Development, Department of Commerce, 107 W. Gains St., Collins Building, Room 443, Tallahassee, FL 32399-2000; 904-488-9360. Provides assistance in obtaining labor, financing, zoning permits, and licenses, meeting regulations, and coordinating between state and local government. Assists businesses in locating hard-to-find suppliers of products or services. In addition, assists in several areas to manufacturing companies experiencing problems in staying in business.

Small Business and Entrepreneuring

These centers provide assistance with Department of Defense procurement who continuously search for suppliers for its vast array of needs and offer many business opportunities for competent suppliers.

Lead Center: Florida Small Business Development Center Network, University of West Florida, Downtown Center, 19 W. Garden St., Suite 366, Pensacola, FL 32561; 904-444-2060, Fax: 904-474-2092.

AltaMonte Springs: Seminole Community College, Small Business Development Center, Seminole Chamber of Commerce, P.O. Box 150784, AltaMonte Springs, FL 32715-0784, 407-834-4404.

Boca Raton: Florida Atlantic University, Small Business Development Center, Building T-9, P.O. Box 3091, Boca Raton, FL 33431, 407-362-5620.

Cocoa: Brevard Community College, Small Business Development Center, 1519 Clearlake Rd., Cocoa, FL 32922, 407-951-1060, ext. 2045.

Dania: Small Business Development Center, 46 SW 1st Ave., Dania, FL 33304, 305-987-0100.

Deland: Stetson University, Small Business Development Center, School of Business Administration, P.O. Box 8417, Deland, FL 32720, 904-822-7326.

Fort Lauderdale: Small Business Development Center, Florida Atlantic University, Commercial Campus, 1515 West Commercial Blvd., Room 11, Fort Lauderdale, FL 33309, 305-771-6520.

Fort Pierce: Indian River Community College, Small Business Development Center, 3209 Virginia Avenue, Room 114, Fort Pierce, FL 34981-5599, 407-468-4756.

Fort Myers: University of South Florida, Small Business Development Center, Sabal Hall, Rooms 219 and 220, 8111 College Parkway, Fort Myers, FL 33919, 813-489-4140.

Fort Walton Beach: University of West Florida, Fort Walton Beach Center, Small Business Development Center, 414 Mary Esther Cutoff, Fort Walton Beach, FL 32548, 904-244-1036.

Gainesville: Small Business Development Center, 214 W. University Ave., P.O. Box 2518, Gainesville, FL 32601, 904-377-5621.

Gainesville: FSBDC Product Innovation Program, Florida Product Innovation Center, 2622 NW 43rd St., Suite B-3, Gainesville, FL 32606, 904-334-1680.

Jacksonville: University of North Florida, Small Business Development Center, College of Business, 4567 St. John's Bluff Rd., S., Jacksonville, FL 32216, 904-646-2476.

Lynn Haven: Gulf Coast Community College, Small Business Development Center, 2500 Minnesota Ave., Lynn Haven, FL 32444, 904-271-1108.

Miami: Florida International University, Small Business Development Center, Trailer MO1, Tamiami Campus, Miami, FL 33199, 305-348-2272.

Ocala: Small Business Development Center, 110 East Silver Springs Blvd., P.O. Box 1210, Ocala, FL 32670, 904-629-8051.

Orlando: University of Central Florida, Small Business Development Center, P.O. Box 161530, Orlando, FL 32816, 407-823-5554.

Pensacola: University of West Florida, Small Business Development Center, Building 8, 11000 University Parkway, Pensacola, FL 32514, 904-474-2908.

St. Petersburg: University of South Florida, St. Petersburg Campus, Small Business Development Center, 830 First St. S., Room 113, St. Petersburg, FL 33701, 813-893-9529.

Sarasota: Small Business Development Center, 5700 N. Tamiami Trail, Sarasota, FL 33580, 813-359-4292.

Tallahassee: Florida A & M University, Small Business Development Center, 1157 Tennessee St., Tallahassee, FL 32308, 904-599-3407.

Tampa: University of South Florida, Small Business Development Center, College of Business Administration, 4202 Minnesota Ave., BSN 3403, Tampa, FL 32444, 813-974-4274.

West Palm Beach: Small Business Development Center, Prospect Place, Suite 123, 3111 S. Dixie Highway, West Palm Beach, FL 33405, 407-837-5311.

Georgia

General Information

Georgia Department of Community Affairs, 1200 Equitable Building, 100 Peachtree Street, Atlanta, GA 30303; 404-656-2900, 404-656-6200. Provides information on financing programs and other services offered by the state government.

Georgia Chamber of Commerce, 233 Peachtree Street, #200, Atlanta, GA 30303; 404-223-2271. Information and referral for federal and state labor laws, publications, seminars, workshops, state legislation. The Business Council is a clearinghouse for information and makes referrals to the Georgia Department of Labor, the Georgia Department of Industry and Trade, and other agencies. The council often acts as a liaison between businesses and local chambers of commerce. The lobbying group is for members only.

Minority and Small Business Affairs, Department of Administrative Services, West Floyd Blvd., Room 1620, 200 Piedmont Avenue Southeast, Atlanta, GA 30334; 404-656-6315. Assistance in cutting bureaucratic red tape. Information and expertise in dealing with state, federal, and local agencies.

Small Business Development Centers

The following offices offer free and fee-based services to new and expanding businesses:

Lead Center: Georgia Small Business Development Center, University of Georgia, Chicopee Complex, 1180 East Broad Street, Athens, GA 30602; 706-542-5780, Fax: 706-542-6776.

Albany: Small Business Development Center, Southwest Georgia District, Business and Technology Center, 230 S. Jackson Street, 3rd Floor, Suite 333, Albany, GA 31701, 912-430-4303; Fax: 912-430-3933.

Athens: Small Business Development Center, University of Georgia, Chicopee Complex, 1180 E. Broad St., Athens, GA 30602, 706-542-7436; Fax: 706-542-6776.

Atlanta: Morris Brown College, Small Business Development Center, 634 Martin Luther King Jr. Dr., NW, Atlanta, GA 30314, 404-220-0201; Fax: 404-220-0236.

Atlanta: Georgia State University, Small Business Development Center, Box 874, University Plaza, Atlanta, GA 30303-3083, 706-651-3550; Fax: 706-651-1035.

Augusta: Small Business Development Center, 1061 Katherine Street, Augusta, GA 30910, 706-737-1790; Fax: 706-731-7937.

Brunswick: Small Business Development Center, 1107 Fountain Lake Drive, Brunswick, GA 31525, 912-264-7343; Fax: 912-262-3095.

Columbus: Small Business Development Center, 928 45th St. North Bldg., Room 523, Columbus, GA 31902, 706-649-7433; Fax: 706-649-1928.

Decatur: DeKalb Chamber of Commerce, Small Business Development Center, 750 Commerce Drive, Decatur, GA 30030, 404-378-8000; Fax: 404-378-3397.

Gainesville: Small Business Development Center, 456 Jesse Jewel Parkway, Suite 302, Gainesville, GA 30501, 706-531-5881; Fax: 706-531-5684.

Lawrenceville: Gwinnett Technical Institute, Small Business Development Center, 1250 Atkinson Road, Lawrenceville, GA 30246, 404-339-2287; Fax: 404-339-2329.

Macon: Small Business Development Center, P.O. Box 13212, Macon, GA 91208-3212, 912-751-6592.

Marietta: Kennesaw State College, SBDC, P.O. Box 444, Marietta, GA 30061, 404-423-6450; Fax: 404-423-6564.

Morrow: Clayton State College, Small Business Development Center, P.O. Box 285, Morrow, GA 30260, 404-961-3440; Fax: 404-961-3428.

Be patient. If any phone number is incorrect, call (area code) 555-1212 and request the new listing.

Rome: Floyd College, SBDC, P.O. Box 1664, Rome, GA 30162, 706-295-6326; Fax: 706-295-5732.

Savannah: Small Business Development Center, 450 Mall Blvd., Suite H, Savannah, GA 31405, 912-356-2755; Fax: 912-353-3033.

Statesboro: Small Business Development Center, Landrum Center, Box 6156, Statesboro, GA 30460, 912-681-5194; Fax: 912-681-0648.

Valdosta: Small Business Development Center, Valdosta Area Office, Baytree West Professional Offices, Suite 9, Baytree Rd., Valdosta, GA 31602, 912-245-3738; Fax: 912-245-3741.

Warner Robins: Middle Georgia Technical Institute, SBDC, 151 Asigian Blvd., Warner Robins, GA 31088, 912-953-9356; Fax: 912-953-9376.

Hawaii

General Information

Small Business Information Service, Department of Business and Economic Development and Tourism, P.O. Box 2359, Honolulu, HI 96804; 808-586-2600. Assists both new and existing businesses with information on government permit and license requirements, government procurement, sources of alternative financing, marketing, preparing a business plan, and available entrepreneurship training programs.

Small Business Advocate, Small Business Information Service, Department of Business and Economic Development and Tourism, P.O. Box 2359, Honolulu, HI 96804; 808-586-2600. Assistance in cutting bureaucratic red tape. Information and expertise in dealing with state, federal, and local agencies.

Small Business Development Centers

The following offices offer free and fee-based services to new and expanding businesses:

Lead Center: Hawaii Small Business Development Center, University of Hawaii at Hilo, 200 W. Kawili St., Hilo, HI 96720-4091; 808-933-3515, Fax: 808-933-3683.

Hilo: Small Business Development Center - Big Island, University of Hawaii at Hilo, 523 W. Lanikaula Street, Hilo, HI 96720-4091, 808-933-3515.

Lihue: Small Business Development Center - Kauai, Kauai Community College, 3-1901 Kaumualii Highway, Lihue, HI 96766-9591, 808-246-1748.

Kihei: Small Business Development Center - Maui, Maui Research and Technology Center, 590 Lipoa Parkway, Kihei, HI 96753, 808-875-2402.

Honolulu: Small Business Development Center - Oahu, Business Action Center, 1130 N. Merchant St., Suite 1030, Honolulu, HI 96817, 808-522-8131.

Idaho

General Information

Small Business Advocate, Idaho Department of Commerce, Economic Development Division, P.O. Box 83720, Boise, ID 83720-0093; 208-334-2470, Fax: 208-334-2631. Assistance in cutting bureaucratic red tape. Information and expertise in dealing with state, federal, and local agencies.

Small Business Development Centers

The following offices offer free and fee-based services to new and expanding businesses:

Lead Center: Idaho Small Business Development Center, Boise State University, College of Business, 1910 University Drive, Boise, ID 83706-9987; 208-385-1640, Fax: 208-385-3877.

Idaho Falls: Idaho State University, Small Business Development Center, 2300 North Yellowstone, Idaho Falls, ID 83401, 208-523-1087; Fax: 208-523-1049.

Lewiston: Lewis-Clark State College, Small Business Development Center, 500 8th Avenue, Lewiston, ID 83501, 208-799-2465; Fax: 208-799-2831.

McCall: Boise Satellite Office, SBDC, Boise State Univ., College of Business, 415 Railroad, McCall, ID 83638, 208-634-2883.

Nampa: Boise Satellite Office, SBDC, Boise State Univ., College of Business, Canyon County Center, 2407 Caldwell Blvd., Nampa, ID 83651, 208-467-5707, ext. 4728.

Pocatello: Idaho State University, Small Business Development Center, 1651 Alvin Ricken Dr., Pocatello, ID 83201, 208-232-4921; Fax: 208-233-0268; 1-800-232-4921.

Post Falls: North Idaho College, Small Business Development Center, 525 W. Clearwater Loop, Post Falls, ID 83854, 208-769-3296.

Twin Falls: College of Southern Idaho, Small Business Development Center, Region IV, 315 Falls Ave., Twin Falls, ID 83303, 208-733-9554, ext. 2477; Fax: 208-734-6592.

Illinois

General Information

Small Business Advocate, Illinois Department of Commerce and Community Affairs, James R. Thompson Center, 100 West Randolph Street, Suite 3-400, Chicago, IL 60601; 312-814-6648. Assistance in cutting bureaucratic red tape. Information and expertise in dealing with state, federal, and local agencies. Targets business populations such as minorities, women, start-ups and home based enterprises, providing, or referring to the appropriate technical, management and/or financial assistance program.

Small Business Development Centers

The following offices offer free and fee-based services to new and expanding businesses:

Lead Center: Illinois Small Business Development Center Network, Dept. of Commerce and Community Affairs, 620 East Adams Street, 6th Floor, Springfield, IL 62701; 217-524-5856, Fax: 217-785-6328.

Aurora: Waubonsee Community College/ Aurora Campus, Small Business Development Center, 5 East Galena Blvd., Aurora, IL 60506, 708-892-3334, Ext. 139; Fax: 708-892-3374.

Carbondale: Southern Illinois University/Carbondale, Small Business Development Center, Carbondale, IL 62901, 618-536-2424; Fax: 618-453-5040.

Centralia: Kaskaskia College (Satellite), Small Business Development Center, Shattuc Road, Centralia, IL 62801, 618-532-2049; Fax: 618-532-4983.

Chicago: Back of the Yards Neighborhood Council (Sub-Center), Small Business Development Center, 1751 West 47th Street, Chicago, IL 60609, 312-523-4419; Fax: 312254-3525.

Chicago: Greater North Pulaski Economic Development Corp., Small Business Development Center, 4054 West North Avenue, Chicago, IL 60639, 312-384-2262, Fax: 312-384-3850.

Chicago: Women's Business Development Center, Small Business Development Center, 8 South Michigan, Suite 400, Chicago, IL 60603, 312-853-3477; Fax: 312-853-0145.

Chicago: Olive-Harvey College, Small Business Development Center, 10001 South Woodlawn Drive, Chicago, IL 60628, 312-468-8700; Fax: 312-468-8086.

Chicago: Industrial Council of NW Chicago, Small Business Development Center, 2023 West Carroll, Chicago, IL 60612, 312-421-3941; Fax: 312-421-1871.

Chicago: Latin American Chamber of Commerce, Small Business Development Center, 539 North Kedzie, Suite 11, Chicago, IL 60647, 312-252-5211; Fax: 312-252-7065.

Chicago: Eighteenth Street Development Corp., Small Business Development Center, 1839 South Carpenter, Chicago, IL 60608, 312-733-2287; Fax: 312-733-7512.

Chicago: Loop Small Business Development Center, DCCA, State of Illinois Ctr., 100 W. Randolph, Suite 3-400, Chicago, IL 60601, 312-814-6111; Fax: 312-814-2807.

Be patient. If any phone number is incorrect, call (area code) 555-1212 and request the new listing.

729

Crystal Lake: McHenry County College, Small Business Development Center, 8900 U.S. Highway 14, Crystal Lake, IL 60012-2761, 815-455-6098; Fax: 815-455-3999.

Danville: Danville Area Community College, Small Business Development Center, 28 West North Street, Danville, IL 61832, 217-442-7232; Fax: 217-442-6228.

DeKalb: Northern Illinois University, Small Business Development Center, Department of Management, 305 East Locust, DeKalb, IL 60115, 815-753-1403; Fax: 815-753-2305.

Dixon: Sauk Valley College, SBDC, 173 Illinois Route #2, Dixon, IL 61021-9110, 815-288-5605; Fax: 815-288-5958.

Edwardsville: Southern Illinois University/Edwardsville, SBDC, Campus Box 1107, Edwardsville, IL 62026, 618-692-2929; Fax: 618-692-2647.

Elgin: Elgin Community College, SBDC, 1700 Spartan Drive, Elgin, IL 60115, 708-697-1000, ext. 7923; Fax: 708-888-7995.

Evanston: Evanston Business and Technology Center, Small Business Development Center, 1840 Oak Ave., Evanston, IL 60201, 708-866-1841; Fax: 708-866-1808.

Freeport: Highland Community College (Satellite), Small Business Development Center, 2998 West Pearl City, Freeport, IL 61032-9341, 815-232-1362; Fax: 815-235-6130.

Glen Ellyn: College of DuPage, Small Business Development Center, 22nd and Lambert Road, Glen Ellyn, IL 60137, 708-858-2800, ext. 2771.

Grayslake: College of Lake County, SBDC, 19351 West Washington Street, Grayslake, IL 60030, 708-223-3633, 708-223-3612; Fax: 708-223-9371.

Harrisburg: Southeastern Illinois College (Satellite), 325 Poplar, Suite A, Harrisburg, IL 62946, 618-252-5001; Fax: 618-252-0210.

Ina: Rend Lake College, SBDC, Route #1, Ina, IL 62846, 618-437-5321, ext. 335.

Joliet: Joliet Junior College, SBDC, Renaissance Center, Room 319, 214 North Ottawa Street, Joliet, IL 60431, 815-727-6544, Ext. 1313; Fax: 815-722-1895.

Kankakee: Kankakee Community College, SBDC, Box 888, River Road, Kankakee, IL 60901, 815-933-0376; Fax: 815-933-0380.

Macomb: Western Illinois University, SBDC, 216 Seal Hall, Macomb, IL 61455, 309-298-2211; Fax: 309-298-2520.

Mattoon: Lake Land College, Small Business Development Center, South Route #45, Mattoon, IL 61938-9366, 217-235-3131; Fax: 217-258-6459.

East Moline: Black Hawk College, Small Business Development Center, 301 42nd Ave, East Moline, IL 61244, 309-752-9759, 309-752-0262; Fax: 309-755-9847.

Monmouth: Maple City Business and Technology (Satellite), Small Business Development Center, 620 South Main Street, Monmouth, IL 61462, 309-734-4664; Fax: 309-734-8579.

Oglesby: Illinois Valley Community College, Small Business Development Center, Building 11, Route 1, Oglesby, IL 61348, 815-223-1740; Fax: 815-224-3033.

Olney: Illinois Eastern Community College, Small Business Development Center, 233 East Chestnut, Olney, IL 62450, 618-395-3011; Fax: 618-395-1922.

Palos Hills: Moraine Valley College, Small Business Development Center, 10900 South 88th Avenue, Palos Hills, IL 60465, 708-974-5468; Fax: 708-974-0078.

Peoria: Bradley University, Small Business Development Center, 141 North Jobst Hall, 1st Floor, Peoria, IL 61625, 309-677-2992; Fax: 309-677-3386.

Rockford: Rock Valley College, Small Business Development Center, 1220 Rock Street, Rockford, IL 61102, 815-968-4087; Fax: 815-968-4157.

Springfield: Lincoln Land Community College, Small Business Development Center, 200 West Washington, Springfield, IL 62701, 217-524-3060; Fax: 217-782-1106.

East St. Louis: East St. Louis, DCCA, State Office Building, 10 Collinsville, East St. Louis, IL 62201, 618-583-2272; Fax: 618-588-2274.

Ullin: Shawnee College (Satellite), Small Business Development Center, Shawnee College Road, Ullin, IL 62992, 618-634-9618; Fax: 618-634-9028.

University Park: Governor's State University, Small Business Development Center, University Park, IL 60466, 708-534-4929; Fax: 708-534-8457.

Indiana

General Information

Small Business Advocate, Small Business Administration, 429 N. Pennsylvania #100, Indianapolis, IN 46204-1873; 317-226-7272, Fax: 317-226-7259. Assistance in cutting bureaucratic red tape. Information and expertise in dealing with state, federal, and local agencies.

Small Business Development Centers

The following offices offer free and fee-based services to new and expanding businesses:

Lead Center: Indiana Small Business Development Center, Economic Development Council, One North Capitol, Suite 420, Indianapolis, IN 46204; 317-264-6871, Fax: 317-264-3102.

Bloomington: Greater Bloomington Chamber of Commerce, Small Business Development Center, 116 W. 6th Street, Bloomington, IN 47404, 812-339-8937.

Columbus: Columbus Enterprise Development Center, Inc., Small Business Development Center, 4920 North Warren Drive, Columbus, IN 47203, 812-372-6480; Fax: 812-372-0228.

Evansville: Evansville Chamber of Commerce, Small Business Development Center, 100 NW Second Street, Suite 200, Evansville, IN 47708, 812-425-7232.

Fort Wayne: Northeast Indiana Business Assistance Corporation, Small Business Development Center, 1830 West Third Street, Fort Wayne, IN 46803, 219-426-0040.

Jeffersonville: Hoosier Valley Economic Opportunity Corporation, Small Business Development Center, 1613 E. 8th Street, Jeffersonville, IN 47130, 812-288-6451.

Indianapolis: Indiana University, Small Business Development Center, 342 Senate Ave., Indianapolis, IN 46204, 317-261-3030.

Kokomo: Kokomo-Howard County Chamber of Commerce, Small Business Development Center, P.O. Box 731, Kokomo, IN 46903, 317-457-5301.

Lafayette: Greater Lafayette Progress, Inc., Small Business Development Center, 122 N. Third, Lafayette, IN 47901, 317-742-2394.

Madison: Madison Area Chamber of Commerce, Small Business Development Center, 301 East Main Street, Madison, IN 47250, 812-265-3127.

Muncie: Muncie-Delaware County Chamber, Small Business Development Center, 401 South High Street, Muncie, IN 47308, 317-284-8144; Fax: 317-741-5489.

Portage: Northwest Indiana Forum, Inc., Small Business Development Center, 6100 Southport Rd., Portage, IN 46410, 219-762-1696.

Richmond: Richmond Area Chamber of Commerce, Small Business Development Center, 33 South 7th Street, Richmond, IN 47374, 317-962-2887.

South Bend: South Bend Chamber of Commerce, Small Business Development Center, 300 North Michigan Street, South Bend, IN 46601, 219-282-4350.

Terre Haute: Indiana State University, Small Business Development Center, School of Business, Terre Haute, IN 47809, 812-237-7676.

Iowa

General Information

Iowa Department of Economic Development, 200 East Grand Avenue, Des Moines, IA 50309; 515-242-4700.

Small Business Advocate, Small Business Division, Iowa Department of Economic Development, 200 East Grand Avenue, Des Moines, IA 50309; 515-242-4899. Assistance in cutting bureaucratic red tape. Information and expertise in dealing with state, federal, and local agencies.

Small Business Development Centers

The following offices offer free and fee-based services to new and expanding businesses:

Lead Center: Iowa Small Business Development Center, Iowa State University, College of Business Administration, Chamblynn Building, 137 Lynn Avenue, Ames, IA 50010; 515-292-6351, Fax: 515-292-0020.

Ames: Iowa State University, ISU Small Business Development Center, 137 Lynn Avenue, Ames, IA 50014, 515-292-6351; Fax: 515-292-0020.

Ames: ISU Small Business Development Center, ISU Ames Branch, 111 Lynn Avenue, Ames, IA 50014, 515-292-6355; Fax: 515-292-0020.

Audubon: ISU Small Business Development Ctr., ISU Audubon Branch, Circle West Incubator, P.O. Box 204, Audubon, IA 50025, 712-563-2623; Fax: 712-563-2301.

Cedar Falls: University of Northern Iowa, Small Business Development Center, Suite 5, Business Bldg, Cedar Falls, IA 50614-0120, 319-273-2696; Fax: 319-273-6830.

Council Bluffs: Iowa Western Community College, SBDC, 2700 College Road, Box 4C, Council Bluffs, IA 51502, 712-325-3260; Fax: 712-325-3424.

Creston: Southwestern Community College, Small Business Development Center, 1501 West Townline, Creston, IA 50801, 515-782-4161; Fax: 515-782-4164.

Davenport: Eastern Iowa Community College District, Small Business Development Center, 304 W. Second St., Davenport, IA 52801, 319-322-4499; Fax: 319-322-8241.

Des Moines: Drake University, Small Business Development Center, Drake Business Center, Des Moines, IA 50311-4505, 515-271-2655; Fax: 515-271-4540.

Dubuque: Dubuque Area Chamber of Commerce, Northeast Iowa Small Business Development Center, 770 Town Clock Plaza, Dubuque, IA 52001, 319-588-3350; Fax: 319-557-1591.

Iowa City: University of Iowa, Oakdale Campus, Small Business Development Center, 108 Pappajohn Business Adm. Bldg., Suite 5160, Iowa City, IA 52242, 319-335-3742; Fax: 319-335-1956.

Marion: Kirkwood Community College, Small Business Development Center, 2901 Tenth Avenue, Marion, IA 52302, 319-377-8256; Fax: 319-377-5667.

Mason City: North Iowa Area Community College, Small Business Development Center, 500 College Dr., Mason City, IA 50401, 515-421-4342; Fax: 515-424-2011.

Ottumwa: Indian Hills Community College, Small Business Development Center, 525 Grandview Avenue, Ottumwa, IA 52501, 515-683-5127; Fax: 515-683-5263.

Sioux City: Western Iowa Tech Community College, Small Business Development Center, 4647 Stone Ave., Bldg. B, Sioux City, IA 51102, 712-274-6418; Fax: 712-274-6429.

Spencer: Iowa Lakes Community College, Small Business Development Center, Gateway North Shopping Center, Highway 71 North, Spencer, IA 51301, 712-262-4213; Fax: 712-262-4047.

West Burlington: Southeastern Community College, Small Business Development Center, Drawer F, West Burlington, IA 52655, 319-752-2731, ext. 103; Fax: 319-752-4957.

Kansas

General Information

First-Stop Clearinghouse, Existing Industry Development Division, Kansas Department of Commerce and Housing, 700 SW Harrison Street, #1300, Topeka, KS 66603-3712; 913-296-5298. A One-Stop Clearinghouse for general information. Also provides necessary state applications required by agencies which license, regulate and tax business, and furnishes information about starting or expanding a business.

Small Business Development Centers

The following offices offer free and fee-based services to new and expanding businesses:

Lead Center: Kansas Small Business Development Center, Wichita State University, 1845 Fairmount, Wichita, KS 67260-0148; 316-689-3193, Fax: 316-689-3647.

Atchison: Benedictine College, Small Business Development Center, 1020 N 2nd St, Atchison, KS 66002, 913-367-5340, ext. 2425; Fax: 913-367-6102.

Augusta: Butler County Community College, Small Business Development Center, 600 Walnut, Augusta, KS 67010, 316-775-1124; Fax: 316-775-1370.

Chanute: Neosho County Community College, Small Business Development Center, 1000 S Allen, Chanute, KS 66720, 316-431-2820, ext 219; Fax: 316-431-0082.

Coffeyville: Coffeyville Community College, Small Business Development Center, 11th and Willow Sts., Coffeyville, KS 67337-5064, 316-252-7007; Fax: 316-252-7098.

Colby: Colby Community College, SBDC, 1255 South Range, Colby, KS 67701, 913-462-3984, ext. 239; Fax: 913-462-8315.

Concordia: Cloud County Community College, SBDC, 2221 Campus Drive, P.O. Box 1002, Concordia, KS 66901, 913-243-1435; Fax: 913-243-1459.

Dodge City: Dodge City Community College, Small Business Development Center, 2501 North 14th Avenue, Dodge City, KS 67801, 316-227-9247, ext. 247; Fax: 316-227-9200.

Emporia: Emporia State University, Small Business Development Center, 207 Cremer Hall, Emporia, KS 66801, 316-342-7162; Fax: 316-341-5418.

Fort Scott: Fort Scott Community College, Small Business Development Center, 32108 S Horton, Fort Scott, KS 66701, 316-223-2700; Fax: 316-223-6530.

Garden City: Garden City Community College, Small Business Development Center, 801 Campus Drive, Garden City, KS 67846, 316-276-9632; Fax: 316-276-9630.

Hays: Fort Hays State University, Small Business Development Center, 1301 Pine, Hays, KS 67601, 913-628-5340; Fax: 913-628-1471.

Hutchinson: Hutchinson Community College, Small Business Development Center, 815 N. Walnut, #225, Hutchinson, KS 67501, 316-665-4950; Fax: 316-665-8354.

Independence: Independence Community College, SBDC, College Ave. and Brookside, Box 708, Independence, KS 67301, 316-331-4100; Fax: 316-331-5344.

Iola: Allen County Community College, T.B.D., Small Business Development Center, 1801 N. Cottonwood, Iola, KS 66749, 316-365-5116; Fax: 316-365-3284.

Lawrence: University of Kansas, SBDC, 734 Vermont, Suite 104, Lawrence, KS 66044, 913-843-8844; Fax: 913-865-4400.

Liberal: Seward County Community College, Small Business Development Center, 1801 North Kansas, Liberal, KS 67905, 316-629-2650, ext. 148; Fax: 316-624-0637.

Manhattan: Kansas State University, Small Business Development Center, 2323 Anderson Ave., Suite 100, Manhattan, KS 66502-2947, 913-532-5529; Fax: 913-532-5827.

Ottawa: Ottawa University, Small Business Development Center, College Avenue, Box 70, Ottawa, KS 66067, 913-242-5200, ext. 5457; Fax: 913-242-7429.

Overland Park: Johnson County Community College, Small Business Development Center, CEC Bldg., Room 223, Overland Park, KS 66210-1299, 913-469-3878; Fax: 913-469-4415.

Parsons: Labette Community College, Small Business Development Center, 200 S. 14th, Parsons, KS 67357, 316-421-6700; Fax: 316-421-0921.

Pittsburgh: Pittsburgh State University, Small Business Development Center, Shirk Hall, Pittsburgh, KS 66762, 316-235-4920; Fax: 316-232-6440.

Pratt: Pratt Community College, Small Business Development Center, Hwy. 61, Pratt, KS 67124, 316-672-5641; Fax: 316-672-5288.

Be patient. If any phone number is incorrect, call (area code) 555-1212 and request the new listing.

731

Small Business and Entrepreneuring

Salina: KSU-Salina College of Technology, Small Business Development Center, 2409 Scanlan Avenue, Salina, KS 67401, 913-826-2622,; Fax: 913-826-2936.

Topeka: Washburn University, Small Business Development Center, 101 Henderson Learning Center, Topeka, KS 66621, 913-231-1010, ext. 1305; Fax: 913-231-1063.

Wichita: Wichita State University, Small Business Development Center, Brennan Hall, 1845 Fairmount, Wichita, KS 67208, 316-689-3193; Fax: 316-689-3647.

Kentucky

General Information

Kentucky Business Information Clearinghouse, Business Information Clearinghouse, Cabinet of Economic Development, Department of Existing Business and Industry, 2200 Capital Plaza Tower, Frankfort, KY 40601; 502-564-4252, 1-800-242-1545 in Kentucky. Provides a centralized information source. Handles requests for business licensing and permit information, assembles customized application and information packets for business proposals, referrals to other state, federal and local government agencies, and problems with government red tape.

Small Business Advocate, Small Business Division, Cabinet of Economic Development, Department of Existing Business and Industry, 2200 Capital Plaza Tower, Frankfort, KY 40601; 502-564-4252, 1-800-242-1545 in Kentucky. Assistance in cutting bureaucratic red tape. Information and expertise in dealing with state, federal, and local agencies.

Division of Research and Planning, Cabinet of Economic Development, Department of Existing Business and Industry, 2200 Capital Plaza Tower, Frankfort, KY 40601; 502-564-4886. A list of business development publications are available through this office. There is a charge for some.

Small Business Development Centers

The following offices offer free and fee-based services to new and expanding businesses:

Lead Center: Kentucky Small Business Development Center, University of Kentucky, Center for Business Development, College of Business and Economics, 205 Business and Economics Building, Lexington, KY 40506-0034; 606-257-7668, Fax: 606-258-1907.

Ashland: Ashland Small Business Development Center, Boyd-Greenup County Chamber of Commerce Building, P.O. Box 830, 207 15th Street, Ashland, KY 41105-0830, 606-329-8011; Fax: 606-325-4607.

Bowling Green: Western Kentucky University, Bowling Green Small Business Development Center, 245 Grise Hall, Bowling Green, KY 42101, 502-745-2901; Fax: 502-745-2902.

Cumberland: Southeast Community College, Small Business Development Center, Room 113, Chrisman Hall, Cumberland, KY 40823, 606-589-4514; Fax: 606-589-4941.

Elizabethtown: Elizabethtown Small Business Development Center, 238 West Dixie Avenue, Elizabethtown, KY 42701, 502-765-6737; Fax: 502-765-6737.

Highland Heights: Northern Kentucky University, North Kentucky Small Business Development Center, BEP Center, Room 463, Highland Heights, KY 41099-0506, 606-572-6524; Fax: 606-572-5566.

Hopkinsville: Hopkinsville Small Business Development Center, 300 Hammond Drive, Hopkinsville, KY 42240, 502-886-8666; Fax: 502-886-3211.

Lexington: University of Kentucky, Small Business Development Center, College of Business and Economics, 205 Business and Economics Building, Lexington, KY 40506-0034, 606-257-7666; Fax: 606-258-1907.

Louisville: Bellarmine College, Small Business Development Center, School of Business, 2001 Newburg Road, Louisville, KY 40205-0671, 502-452-8282; Fax: 502-452-8288.

Louisville: University of Louisville, SBDC, Center for Entrepreneurship and Technology, Room 122, Burhans Hall, Louisville, KY 40292, 502-588-7854; Fax: 502-588-8573.

Morehead: Morehead State University, Small Business Development Center, 207 Downing Hall, Morehead, KY 40351, 606-783-2895; Fax: 606-783-2678.

Murray: Murray State University, West Kentucky Small Business Development Center, College of Business and Public Affairs, Murray, KY 42071, 502-762-2856; Fax: 502-762-3049.

Owensboro: Owensboro Small Business Development Center, 3860 U.S. Highway 60 West, Owensboro, KY 42301, 502-926-8085; Fax: 502-684-0714.

Pikeville: Pikeville Small Business Development Center, 222 Hatcher Court, Pikeville, KY 41501, 606-432-5848.

Somerset: Eastern Kentucky University, Small Business Development Center, 107 West Mt. Vernon Street, Somerset, KY 42501, 606-678-5520; Fax: 606-678-8349.

Louisiana

General Information

Louisiana Department of Economic Development, 101 France Street, Suite 115, P.O. Box 94185, Baton Rouge, LA 70804-9185; 504-342-3000.

Small Business Advocate, Community Development Division, Louisiana Department of Commerce and Industry, P.O. Box 94185, Baton Rouge, LA 70804-9184; 504-342-3000. Assistance in cutting bureaucratic red tape. Information and expertise in dealing with state, federal, and local agencies.

Small Business Development Centers

The following offices offer free and fee-based services to new and expanding businesses:

Lead Center: Louisiana Small Business Development Center, Northeast Louisiana University, Adm. 2-57, Monroe, LA 71209; 318-342-5506, Fax: 318-342-5510.

Alexandria: Small Business Development Center, 5212 Rue Verdun, Alexandria, LA 71306, 318-484-2123.

Baton Rouge: Capital Small Business Development Center, 9613 Interline Avenue, Baton Rouge, LA 70809, 504-922-0998.

Hammond: Southeastern Louisiana University, Small Business Development Center, Box 522, SLU Station, Hammond, LA 70402, 504-549-3831; Fax: 504-549-2127.

Lafayette: University of Southwestern Louisiana, Arcadiana SBDC, Box 43732, Lafayette, LA 70504, 318-262-5344; Fax: 318-262-5296.

Lake Charles: McNeese State University, Small Business Development Center, College of Business Administration, Lake Charles, LA 70609, 318-475-5529; Fax: 318-475-5529.

Monroe: Northeast Louisiana University, College of Business Administration, Monroe, LA 71209, 318-342-1224; Fax: 318-352-5506.

Monroe: Northeast Louisiana University, Small Business Development Center, Louisiana Electronic Assistance Program, College of Business Administration, Monroe, LA 71209, 318-342-1215; Fax: 318-342-1209.

Monroe: Northeast Louisiana University, Small Business Development Center, Adm. 2-57, Monroe, LA 71209, 318-342-5506; Fax: 318-342-5510.

Natchitoches: Northwestern State University, Small Business Development Center, College of Business Administration, Natchitoches, LA 71497, 318-357-5611; Fax: 318-357-6810.

New Orleans: University of New Orleans, Small Business Development Center, Louisiana International Trade, 2 Canal St., New Orleans, LA 70148, 504-568-8222.

New Orleans: Loyola University, Small Business Development Center, Box 134, New Orleans, LA 70118, 504-865-3474; Fax: 504-865-3347.

New Orleans: Southern University, Small Business Development Center, College of Business Administration, New Orleans, LA 70126, 504-286-5308; Fax: 504-286-5306 (call first).

New Orleans: University of New Orleans, SBDC, Lakefront Campus, College of Business Administration, New Orleans, LA 70148, 504-539-9292.

Ruston: Louisiana Tech University, Small Business Development Center, Box 10318, Tech Station, Ruston, LA 71271-0046, 318-257-3537; Fax: 318-257-3356.

Shreveport: Louisiana State University at Shreveport, Small Business Development Center, College of Business Administration, 1 University Place, Shreveport, LA 71115, 318-797-5144; Fax: 318-797-5156.

Thibodaux: Nicholls State University, Small Business Development Center, P.O. Box 2015, Thibodaux, LA 70310, 504-448-4242; Fax: 504-448-4922.

Maine

General Information

Business Answers/Small Business Advocate, Department of Economic and Community Development, 219 Capital St., State House Station #130, Augusta, ME 04333; 207-624-6800, Fax: 207-287-2861. Serves as a central clearinghouse of information regarding business assistance programs and services available to state businesses.

Small Business Development Centers

The following offices offer free and fee-based services to new and expanding businesses:

Lead Center: Maine Small Business Development Ctr, University of Southern Maine, 96 Falmouth St., Portland, ME 04103-9989; 207-780-4420, Fax: 207-780-4810.

Auburn: Androscoggin Valley Council of Governments, Small Business Development Center, 125 Manley Rd., Auburn, ME 04210, 207-783-9186; Fax: 207-783-5211.

Bangor: Eastern Maine Development Corporation, Small Business Development Center, P.O. Box 2579, Bangor, ME 04401, 207-942-6389; Fax: 207-942-3548.

Caribou: Northern Maine Regional Planning Commission, Small Business Development Center, P.O. Box 779, 2 Main Street, Caribou, ME 04736, 207-498-8736; Fax: 207-493-3108.

Sanford: Southern Maine Regional Planning Commission, Small Business Development Center, Box Q, 255 Main Street, Sanford, ME 04073, 207-324-0316; Fax: 207-324-2958.

Wiscasset: Coastal Enterprises, Inc., Small Business Development Center, Walter Street, Box 268, Wiscasset, ME 04578, 207-882-7552; Fax: 207-882-7308.

Maryland

General Information

Maryland Business Assistance Center, 217 East Redwood Street, 10th Floor, Baltimore, MD 21202; 301-333-6975. A direct link to state services including public financing, facility location, state-funded employee training, government procurement assistance, help with licensing and permit processing, and information on starting a business.

Small Business Advocate, Department of Economic and Employment Development, 30 Hudson Street, Annapolis, MD 21401; 301-974-7942. Assistance in cutting bureaucratic red tape. Information and expertise in dealing with state, federal, and local agencies.

Small Business Development Centers

The following offices offer free and fee-based services to new and expanding businesses:

Lead Center: Small Business Development Center, 1420 N. Charles St., Baltimore, MD 21201; 410-837-4141, Fax: 410-837-4151.

Annapolis: Anne Arundel Office of Economic Development, Small Business Development Center, 2660 Riva Rd., Annapolis, MD 21401, 410-224-4205; Fax: 410-222-7415.

Baltimore: Business Resource Center, Small Business Development Center, 3 W. Baltimore St., Baltimore, MD 21202, 410-605-0990; Fax: 410-605-0995.

Bel Air: Harford County Economic Development Office, Small Business Development Ctr., 220 S. Main St., Bel Air, MD 21014, 410-893-3837; Fax: 410-879-8043.

College Park: Manufacturing and Technology, Small Business Development Center, Dingman Center for Entrepreneurship, College of Business and Management, University of Maryland, College Park, MD 20742, 301-405-2144; Fax: 301-314-9152.

Columbia: Howard County Economic Development Office, Small Business Development Center, 6751 Gateway Drive, Columbia, MD 21043, 410-290-0066; Fax: 410-313-2662.

Cumberland: Western Region Small Business Development Center, 3 Commerce Drive, Cumberland, MD 21502, 301-724-6716; Fax: 301-777-7504.

Elkton: Cecil Community College, Eastern Region Small Business Development Center, 135 E. Main St., Elkton, MD 21921.

Glen Burnie: Arundel Center N, Small Business Development Center, 101 Crain Highway NW, Room 110B, Glen Burnie, MD 21601, 410-766-1910; Fax: 410-766-1911.

Landover: Suburban Washington Small Business Development Center, 1400 McCormick Dr., Suite 282, Landover, MD 20785, 301-883-6491; Fax: 301-883-6479.

Salisbury: Eastern Shore Small Business Development Center SubCenter, Salisbury State University, Perdue School of Business, 1101 Canden Ave., Salisbury, MD 21801, 410-546-4325; Fax: 410-548-5389.

Towson: Baltimore County Chamber of Commerce, Small Business Development Center, 102 W. Pennsylvania Ave., Towson, MD 21204, 410-832-5866; Fax: 410-821-9901.

Waldorf: Charles Community College, Southern Region Small Business Development Center, 235 Smallwood Village Center, Waldorf, MD 20601, 301-932-4155; Fax: 301-645-9082.

Westminster: Carroll County Economic Development, Small Business Development Center, 125 North Court Street, Room 103, Westminster, MD 21157, 410-857-8166; Fax: 410-848-0003.

Massachusetts

General Information

Massachusetts Office of Business Development, 1 Ashburton Place, 21st Floor, Boston, MA 02108; 617-727-3221. Operates the *SPIRIT* Business Line, a toll-free, direct hot-line service to answer business-related questions.

Small Business Development Centers

The following offices offer free and fee-based services to new and expanding businesses:

Lead Center: Massachusetts Small Business Development Center, University of Massachusetts, 205 School of Management, Amherst, MA 01003; 413-545-6301, Fax: 413-545-1273.

Boston: University of Massachusetts at Amherst, Minority Business Assistance Center, 250 Stuart Street, 5th Floor, Boston, MA 02116, 617-287-7750; Fax: 617-426-7854.

Chestnut Hill: Boston College, Metropolitan Regional Small Business Development Center, 96 College Road - Rahner House, Chestnut Hill, MA 02167, 617-552-4091; Fax: 617-552-2730.

Chestnut Hill: Boston College, Capital Formation Service/East, Small Business Development Center, 96 College Road - Rahner House, Chestnut Hill, MA 02167, 617-552-4091; Fax: 617-552-2730.

Fall River: University of Massachusetts at Dartmouth, Southeastern Massachusetts Regional Small Business Development Center, 200 Pocasset Street, P.O. Box 2785, Fall River, MA 02722, 508-673-9783; Fax: 508-674-1929.

Small Business and Entrepreneuring

Salem: Salem State College, North Shore Regional Small Business Development Center, 197 Essex Street, Salem, MA 01970, 508-741-6343; Fax: 508-741-6345.

Springfield: University of Massachusetts, Western Massachusetts Regional Small Business Development Center, 101 State Street, Suite #424, Springfield, MA 01103, 413-737-6712; Fax: 413-737-2312.

Worcester: Clark University, Central Massachusetts Regional Small Business Development Center, 950 Main Street, Worcester, MA 01610, 508-793-7615; Fax: 508-793-8890.

Michigan

General Information

Michigan Business Ombudsman, P.O. Box 30107, 525 W. Ottawa, 5th Floor Law Bldg., Lansing, MI 48909; 517-373-6241, 1-800-232-2727 in Michigan. Acts as a mediator in resolving regulatory disputes between business and the various state departments and also provides consultation and referral services. The ombudsman also serves as a "one-stop" center for business permits.

Small Business Advocate, Michigan Department of Commerce, P.O. Box 30004, Lansing, MI 48909; 517-373-1820. Assistance in cutting bureaucratic red tape. Information and expertise in dealing with state, federal and local agencies.

Small Business Development Centers

The following offices offer free and fee-based services to new and expanding businesses:

Lead Center: Michigan Small Business Development Center, 2727 Second Avenue, Detroit, MI 48201; 313-964-1798, Fax: 313-577-4222.

Allendale: Ottawa County Economic Development Office, Inc., SBDC, 6676 Lake Michigan Drive, Allendale, MI 49401, 616-892-4120; Fax: 616-895-6670.

Ann Arbor: Merra Specialty Business Development Center, SBDC, 2200 Commonwealth, Suite 230, Ann Arbor, MI 48105, 313-930-0034; Fax: 313-663-6622.

Bad Axe: Huron County Economic Development Corporation (Satellite), SBDC, Huron County building, Room 303, Bad Axe, MI 48413, 517-269-6431; Fax: 517-269-7221.

Battle Creek: Kellogg Community College, Small Business Development Center, 450 North Avenue, Battle Creek, MI 49017-3397, 616-965-3023; 1-800-955-4KCC; Fax: 616-965-4133.

Benton Harbor: Lake Michigan College, Small Business Development Center, Corporate and Community Services, 2755 E. Napier, Benton Harbor, MI 49022-1899, 616-927-3571, ext. 247; Fax: 616-927-4491.

Big Rapids: Ferris State University, Small Business Development Center, Alumni 226, 901 S. State Street, Big Rapids, MI 49307, 616-592-3553; Fax: 616-592-3539.

Cadillac: Wexfor-Missaukee Business Development Center (Satellite), 117 W. Cass Street, Suite 1, Cadillac, MI 49601-0026, 616-775-9776; Fax: 616-775-1440.

Caro: Tuscola County Economic Development Corporation, Small Business Development Center, 1184 Cleaver Road, Suite 800, Caro, MI 48723, 517-673-2849; Fax: 517-673-2517.

Detroit: NILAC-Marygrove College, Small Business Development Center, 8425 West McNichols, Detroit, MI 48221, 313-945-2159; Fax: 313-864-6670.

Detroit: Wayne State University, Small Business Development Center, School of Business Administration, 2727 Second Avenue, Detroit, MI 48201, 313-577-4850; Fax: 313-577-8933.

Detroit: Comerica Small Business Development Center, 8300 Van Dyke, Detroit, MI 48213, 313-571-1040.

East Lansing: Michigan State University, International Business Development Center, 6 Kellogg Center, East Lansing, MI 48824-1022, 517-353-4336; Fax: 517-336-1009; 1-800-852-5727.

Escanaba: 1st Step, Inc., Small Business Development Center, 2415 14th Avenue, South, Escanaba, MI 49829, 906-786-9234; Fax: 906-786-4442.

Flint: Genesee Economic Area Revitalization, Inc. (Satellite), Small Business Development Center, 412 S. Saginaw Street, Flint, MI 48502, 313-238-7803; Fax: 313-238-7866.

Grand Rapids: Grand Rapids Community College, SBDC, Applied Technology Ctr., 151 Fountain NE, Grand Rapids, MI 49503, 616-771-3600; Fax: 616-771-3605.

Hart: Oceana Economic Development Corporation (Satellite), Small Business Development Center, P.O. Box 168, Hart, MI 49420-0168, 616-873-7141; Fax: 616-873-3710.

Houghton: Michigan Technological University, Small Business Development Center, Bureau of Industrial Development, 1400 Townsend Drive, Houghton, MI 49931, 906-487-2470; Fax: 906-487-2858.

Howell: Livingston County Business Development Center, 404 E. Grand River, Howell, MI 48843, 517-546-4020; Fax: 517-546-4115.

Kalamazoo: Kalamazoo College, SBDC, Stryker Center for Management Studies, 1327 Academy Street, Kalamazoo, MI 49007, 616-383-8602; Fax: 616-383-5663.

Lansing: Lansing Community College, Small Business Development Center, P.O. Box 40010, Lansing, MI 48901, 517-483-1921; Fax: 517-483-9616.

Lapeer: Lapeer Development Corporation (Satellite), 449 McCormick Drive, Lapeer, MI 48446, 313-667-0080; Fax: 313-667-3541.

Marlette: Thumb Area Community Growth Alliance, Small Business Development Center, 3270 Wilson Street, Marlette, MI 48453, 517-635-3561; Fax: 517-635-2230.

Marquette: Northern Economic Initiative Corporation, Small Business Development Center, 1009 West Ridge Street, Marquette, MI 49855, 906-228-5571; Fax: 906-228-5572.

Mt. Clemens: Macomb County Business Assistance Network, 115 South Groesbeck Highway, Mt. Clemens, MI 48043, 313-469-5118; Fax: 313-469-6787,

Mt. Pleasant: Central Michigan University, Small Business Development Ctr., 256 Applied Business Studies Complex, Mt. Pleasant, MI 48859, 517-774-3270; Fax: 517-774-2372.

Muskegon: Muskegon Economic Growth Alliance, Small Business Development Center, 349 West Webster Avenue, Suite 104, P.O. Box 1087, Muskegon, MI 49443-1087, 616-722-3751; Fax: 616-728-7251.

Peck: Sanilac County Economic Growth (Satellite), 175 East Aitken Road, Peck, MI 48466, 313-648-4311; Fax: 313-648-4617.

Port Huron: St. Claire County Community College, SBDC, 323 Erie Street, P.O. Box 5015, Port Huron, MI 48061-5015, 313-984-3881, ext. 457; Fax: 313-984-2852.

Saginaw: Saginaw Future, Inc., Small Business Development Center, 301 East Genesee, Fourth Floor, Saginaw, MI 48607, 517-754-8222; Fax: 517-754-1715.

Scottville: West Shore Community College (Satellite), Business and Industrial Development, 3000 North Stiles Road, Scottville, MI 49454-0277, 616-845-6211; Fax: 616-845-0207.

Sidney: Montcalm Community College (Satellite), 2800 College Drive SW, Sidney, MI 48885, 517-328-2111; Fax: 517-328-2950.

Sterling Heights: Sterling Heights Area Chamber of Commerce (Satellite), 12900 Paul, Suite 110, Sterling Heights, MI 48313, 313-731-5400.

Traverse City: Northwestern Michigan College, Center for Business and Industry, 1701 East Front Street, Traverse City, MI 49684, 616-922-1105.

Traverse City: Travers Bay Economic Development Corporation, Traverse City Small Business Development Center, 202 East Grandview Parkway, P.O. Box 387, Traverse City, MI 49685-0387, 616-946-1596; Fax: 616-946-2565.

Traverse City: Greater Northwest Regional CDC, 2200 Dendrinos Drive, Traverse City, MI 49685-0506, 616-929-5000.

Be patient. If any phone number is incorrect, call (area code) 555-1212 and request the new listing.

Traverse City: Traverse City Area Chamber of Commerce BDC, 202 E. Grandview Parkway, P.O. Box 387, Traverse City, MI 49685-0387, 616-947-5075.

Troy: Walsh/O.C.C. Business Enterprise Development Center, 340 E. Big Beaver, Suite 100, Troy, MI 48083, 313-689-4094; Fax: 313-689-4398.

University Center: Saginaw Valley State University (Satellite), Business and Industrial Development Institute, 2250 Pierce Road, University Center, MI 48710, 517-790-4000; Fax: 517-790-1314.

Minnesota

General Information

Small Business Assistance, Minnesota Small Business Assistance Office, 900 American Center Building, 150 East Kellogg Boulevard, St. Paul, MN 55101; 612-296-5005, Hotline: 1-800-657-3858. Provides accurate, timely and comprehensive information and assistance to businesses in all areas of start up, operation, and expansion. Referrals to other state agencies.

Small Business Advocate, Minnesota Small Business Assistance Office, 900 American Center Building, 150 East Kellogg Boulevard, St. Paul, MN 55101; 612-296-5005, Hotline: 1-800-657-3858. Assistance in cutting bureaucratic red tape. Information and expertise in dealing with state, federal and local agencies.

Small Business Development Centers

The following offices offer free and fee-based services to new and expanding businesses:

Lead Center: Minnesota Small Business Development Center, Department of Trade and Economic Development, 550 Metro Square, 121 7th Place E., St. Paul, MN 55101; 612-297-5773, Fax: 612-296-1290.

Bemidji: Customized Training Center, Small Business Development Center, Bemidji Technical College, 905 Grant Avenue, SE, Bemidji, MN 56601, 218-755-4286; Fax: 218-755-4289.

Bloomington: Normandale Community College, Small Business Development Center, 9700 France Avenue South, Bloomington, MN 55431, 612-832-6560.

Brainerd: Brainerd Technical College, Small Business Development Center, 300 Quince Street, Brainerd, MN 56401, 218-828-5302; Fax: 218-828-5340.

Duluth: University of Minnesota at Duluth, Small Business Development Center, 10 University Drive, 150 SBE, Duluth, MN 55812, 218-726-8758.

Grand Rapids: Itasca Development Corporation, Grand Rapids Small Business Development Center, 19 NE Third Street, Grand Rapids, MN 55744, 218-327-2241; Fax: 218-327-2242.

Hibbing: Hibbing Community College, Small Business Development Center, 1515 East 25th Street, Hibbing, MN 55746, 218-262-6703.

International Falls: Small Business Development Center, Rainy River Community College, 1501 Hwy 71, International Falls, MN 56649, 218-285-2255; Fax: 218-285-2239.

Mankato: Mankato State University, Small Business Development Center, P.O. Box 3367, 410 Jackson St., Mankato, MN 56001, 507-387-5643.

Marshall: Southwest State University, Small Business Development Center, ST #105, Marshall, MN 56258, 507-537-7386; Fax: 507-537-6094.

Minneapolis: Minnesota Project Innovation, Small Business Development Center, Suite 410, 111 Third Avenue South, Minneapolis, MN 55401, 612-338-3280; Fax: 612-338-3483.

Minneapolis: SBDC, University of St. Thomas, 1000 LaSalle Ave., Suite MPL100, Minneapolis, MN 55403, 612-962-4500; Fax: 612-962-4410.

Moorhead: Moorhead State University, Small Business Development Center, 1104 7th Ave.S, MSU Box 303, Moorhead, MN 56560, 218-223-2280.

Owatonna: SBDC, Owatonna Incubator, Inc., P.O. Box 505, 560 Dunnell Dr., Suite #203, Owatonna, MN 55060, 507-451-0517; Fax: 507-455-2788.

Pine City: Pine Technical College, Small Business Development Center, 1100 4th St., Pine City, MN 55063, 612-629-7340.

Plymouth: SBDC, Hennepin Technical College, 1820 N. Xenium Lane, Plymouth, MN 55441, 612-550-7218; Fax: 612-550-7272.

Red Wing: Red Wing Technical Institute, Small Business Development Center, 2000 Pottery Place Dr., Suite 339, Red Wing, MN 55066, 612-388-4079.

Rochester: Rochester Community College, Small Business Development Center, 851 30th Avenue, SE, Rochester, MN 55904, 507-285-7536.

Rosemount: Dakota County Technical Institute, Small Business Development Center, 1300 145th Street East, Rosemount, MN 55068, 612-423-8262.

Rushford: SBDC, SE Minnesota Development Corp., P.O. Box 684, 111 W. Jessie St., Rushford, MN 55971, 507-864-7557; Fax: 507-864-2091.

St. Cloud: St. Cloud State University, Small Business Development Center, Business Resource Center, 4191 2nd St. S, St. Cloud, MN 56301, 612-255-4842.

Virginia: Minnesota Technology Inc., Small Business Development Center, Olcott Plaza, 820 N.9th St., Virginia, MN 55792, 218-741-4251.

Wadena: Wadena Technical College, Small Business Development Center, 222 Second Street, SE, Wadena, MN 56482, 218-631-1502; Fax: 218-631-2396.

White Bear Lake: North/East Metro Technical College, Small Business Development Center, 3500 Century Ave. N, Suite 200D, White Bear Lake, MN 55110, 612-779-5764.

Mississippi

General Information

Small Business Advocate, Mississippi Department of Economic and Community Development, P.O. Box 849, 1200 Walter Sillers Building, Jackson, MS 39205; 601-359-3552. Assistance in cutting bureaucratic red tape. Information and expertise in dealing with state, federal and local agencies. Assistance also available from Small Business Development Centers.

Small Business Development Centers

The following offices offer free and fee-based services to new and expanding businesses:

Lead Center: Mississippi Small Business Development Center, University of Mississippi, Old Chemistry Building, Suite 216, University, MS 38677; 601-232-5001, Fax: 601-232-5650.

Booneville: Northeast Mississippi Community College, Small Business Development Center, Cunningham Blvd., Holliday Hall, 2nd Floor, Booneville, MS 38829, 601-728-7751, ext. 317; Fax: 601-728-1165.

Cleveland: Delta State University, Small Business Development Ctr., P.O. Box 3235 DSU, Cleveland, MS 38733, 601-846-4236; Fax: 601-846-4235.

Decatur: East Central Comm. College SBDC, Broad St., P.O. Box 129, Decatur, MS 39327, 601-635-2111; Fax: 601-635-2150.

Ellisville: Jones Jr College SBDC, 900 Court St., Ellisville, MS 39437, 601-477-4165; Fax: 601-477-4166.

Gautier: Mississippi Gulf Coast Community College Small Business Development Center, Jackson County Campus, P.O. Box 100, Gautier, MS 39553, 601-497-9595; Fax: 601-497-9604.

Greenville: Delta Community College, Small Business Development Center, P.O. Box 5607, Greenville, MS 38704-5607, 601-378-8183; Fax: 601-378-5349.

Gulfport: MS Contract Procurement Center, SBDC, 3015 12th St., P.O. Box 610, Gulfport, MS 39502-0610, 601-864-2961; Fax: 601-864-2969.

Hattiesburg: Pearl River Community College, Small Business Development Center, 5448 U.S. Highway 49 South, Hattiesburg, MS 39401, 601-544-0030; Fax: 601-544-0032.

Itta Bena: Mississippi Valley State University SBDC, MS Valley State University, Itta Bena, MS 38941, 601-254-3601; Fax: 601-254-6704.

Jackson: Jackson State University, SBDC, Suite A1, Jackson Enterprise Center, 931 Highway 80 West, Jackson, MS 39204, 601-968-2795; Fax: 601-968-2796.

Long Beach: University of Southern Mississippi, SBDC, 136 Beach Park Place, Long Beach, MS 39560, 601-865-4578; Fax: 601-865-4581.

Lorman: Alcorn State University SBDC, P.O. Box 90, Lorman, MS 39095-9402, 601-877-6684; Fax: 601-877-6256.

Meridian: Meridian Community College, Small Business Development Center, 910 Highway 19 North, Meridian, MS 39307, 601-482-7445; Fax: 601-482-5803.

Mississippi State: Mississippi State University, Small Business Development Center, P.O. Drawer 5288, Mississippi State, MS 39762, 601-325-8684; Fax: 601-325-4016.

Natchez: Copiah-Lincoln Community College, SBDC, 823 Hwy. 61 North, Natchez, MS 39120, 601-445-5254.

Raymond: Hinds Community College, SBDC, International Trade Center, P.O. Box 1170, Raymond, MS 39154, 601-857-3536; Fax: 601-857-3535.

Ridgeland: Holmes Comm. College SBDC, 412 West Ridgeland Ave., Ridgeland, MS 39159, 601-853-0827; Fax: 601-853-0844.

Southaven: Northwest MS Comm. College SBDC, Desoto Center, 8700 Northwest Dr., Southaven, MS 38671, 601-342-1570; Fax: 601-342-5686.

Summit: Southwest MS Comm. College SBDC, College Dr., Summit, MS 39666, 601-276-3890; Fax: 601-276-3867.

Tupelo: Itawamba Community College, Small Business Development Ctr., 653 Eason Blvd., Tupelo, MS 38801, 601-680-8515; Fax: 601-680-8547.

University: University of Mississippi, Small Business Development Center, Old Chemistry Bldg., Suite 216, University, MS 38677, 601-234-2021; Fax: 601-232-5650.

Missouri

General Information

Missouri Business Assistance Center, Department of Economic Development, P.O. Box 118, Jefferson City, MO 65102; 314-751-4241. First-Stop Shop: 1-800-523-1434. The First-Stop Shop number for Missouri residents serves to link business owners and state government and provides information on state rules, regulations, licenses, and permits. The Business Assistance Center provides information and technical assistance to start-up and existing businesses on available state and federal programs.

Federal Information Center, Federal Building, 601 East 12th Street, Kansas City, MO 64106; 1-800-392-7711 in Missouri. Offers information regarding Missouri programs for business people.

Small Business Advocate, Department of Economic Development, P.O. Box 118, Jefferson City, MO 65102; 1-800-523-1434. Assistance in cutting bureaucratic red tape. Information and expertise in dealing with state, federal, and local agencies.

Small Business Development Centers

The following offices offer free and fee-based services to new and expanding businesses:

Lead Center: Missouri Small Business Development Center, University of Missouri, Suite 300, University Place, Columbia, MO 65211; 314-882-0344, Fax: 314-884-4297.

Camdenton: Camden County Extension Center, Small Business Development Center, 113 Kansas, P.O. Box 1405, Camdenton, MO 65020, 314-346-2644; Fax: 314-346-2694.

Cape Girardeau: Southwest Missouri State University, Small Business Development Center, 222 N. Pacific, Cape Girardeau, MO 63701, 314-290-5965; Fax: 314-290-5651.

Chillicothe: Livingston County Extension Center, Small Business Development Center, 3rd Floor Library, 450 Locust, Chillicothe, MO 64601, 816-646-0811.

Chillicothe: Small Business Development Center, Chillicothe City Hall, 715 Washington Street, Chillicothe, MO 64601-2229, 816-646-6920; Fax: 816-646-6811.

Clayton: St. Louis County Extension Center, Small Business Development Center, 121 South Meramac, Suite 501, Clayton, MO 63105, 314-889-2911; Fax: 314-854-6147.

Columbia: Boone County Extension Center, Small Business Development Center, 1012 North Highway UU, Columbia, MO 65205, 314-445-9792; Fax: 314-445-9807.

Columbia: State Marketing Specialist, Small Business Development Center, 300 University Place, Columbia, MO 65211, 314-882-2595; Fax: 314-884-4297.

Columbia: University Extension, Small Business Development Center, 821 Clark Hall, Columbia, MO 65211, 314-882-4142; Fax: 314-882-2595.

Columbia: University of Missouri at Columbia, Small Business Development Center, 1800 University Place, Columbia, MO 65211, 314-882-7096; Fax: 314-882-6156.

Forsyth: Taney County Extension Center, Small Business Development Center, P.O. Box 218, Forsyth, MO 65653, 417-546-2371; Fax: 417-546-2981.

Hannibal: Hannibal Satellite Center, Small Business Development Center, Hannibal, MO 63401, 816-385-6550; Fax: 816-385-6568.

Hillsboro: Jefferson County Extension Center, Small Business Development Center, Courthouse, #203, 725 Maple St., Hillsboro, MO 63050, 314-789-5391; Fax: 314-789-5059.

Independence: Jackson County Extension Center, Small Business Development Center, 1507 S. Noland Rd., Independence, MO 64055-1307, 816-252-5051; Fax: 816-252-5575.

Jackson: Cape Girardeau County Extension Center, Small Business Development Center, P.O. Box 408, 815 Highway 25S, Jackson, MO 63755, 314-243-3581; Fax: 314-243-1606.

Jefferson City: Cole County Extension Center, Small Business Development Center, 2436 Tanner Bridge Rd., Jefferson City, MO 65101, 314-634-2824; Fax: 314-634-5463.

Joplin: Missouri Southern State College, Small Business Development Center, 107 Mathews Hall, Joplin, MO 64801-1595, 417-625-9313; Fax: 417-625-9782.

Kansas City: Rockhurst College, Small Business Development Center, 1100 Rockhurst Road, Kansas City, MO 64110-2599, 816-926-4572; Fax: 816-926-4646.

Kansas City: Western Region, University of Missouri-Kansas City, Small Business Development Center, 5110 Cherry St., Kansas City, MO 64110, 816-235-2891; Fax: 816-235-2947.

Kansas City: Jackson County Extension Center, Small Business Development Center, 1901 NE 48th, Kansas City, MO 65118, 816-792-7760; Fax: 816-792-7779.

Kirksville: Northeast Missouri State University, Small Business Development Center, 207 East Patterson, Kirksville, MO 63501, 816-785-4307; Fax: 816-785-4357.

Macon: Thomas Hill Enterprise Center, Small Business Development Center, P.O. Box 246, Macon, MO 63552, 816-385-6550; Fax: 816-385-6568.

Maryville: Northwest Missouri State University, Small Business Development Center, 423 North Market Street, Maryville, MO 64468, 816-646-6920; Fax: 816-646-6811.

Mexico: Audrain County Extension Center, Small Business Development Center, 101 N. Jefferson, 4th Floor Courthouse, Mexico, MO 65265, 314-581-3231; Fax: 314-581-3232.

Moberly: Randolph County Extension Center, Small Business Development Center, 417 E. Urbandale, Moberly, MO 65270, 816-263-3534; Fax: 816-263-1874.

Park Hills: Small Business Development Center, Mineral Area College, P.O. Box 1000, Park Hills, MO 63601-1000, 314-431-4593, ext. 283; Fax: 314-431-2144.

Poplar Bluff: Three Rivers Community College, Small Business Development Center, Business Incubator Building, 3019 Fair Street, Poplar Bluff, MO 63901, 314-686-3499; Fax: 314-686-5467.

Potosi: Washington County Extension Center, Small Business Development Center, 102 N. Missouri, Potosi, MO 63664, 314-438-2671; Fax: 314-438-2079.

Rolla: MO Enterprise Business Assistance Center, Small Business Development Center, 800 W. 14th St., Suite 111, Rolla, MO 65401, 314-364-8570; Fax: 314-364-6323.

Rolla: Phelps County Extension Center, SBDC, Courthouse, 200 N. Main, P.O. Box 725, Rolla, MO 65401, 314-364-3147; Fax: 314-364-0436.

Rolla: Center for Technology Transfer and Economic Development, University of Missouri at Rolla, Room 104, Nagogami Terrace, Rolla, MO 65401-0249, 314-341-4559; Fax: 314-341-6495.

Sedalia: Pettis County Extension Center, Small Business Development Center, 1012 A Thompson Blvd., Sedalia, MO 65301, 816-827-0591; Fax: 816-826-8599.

Springfield: Green County Extension Center, SBDC, 833 Boonville Ave., Springfield, MO 65802, 417-862-9284; Fax: 417-868-4175.

Springfield: Southwest Missouri State University, Small Business Development Center, Center for Business Research, 901 S. National, Springfield, MO 65804-0089, 417-836-5685; Fax: 417-836-7666.

St. Joseph: Buchanan County Extension Center, SBDC, 4125 Mitchell Ave., Box 7077, St. Joseph, MO 64507, 816-279-1691; Fax: 816-279-3982.

St. Louis: St. Louis County Extension Center, 207 Marillac, UMSI, 8001 Nttl. Bridge Rd, St. Louis, MO 63042, 314-731-3533; Fax: 314-731-0523.

St. Louis: St. Louis University, Small Business Development Center, 3750 Lindell Boulevard, St. Louis, MO 63108, 314-534-7232; Fax: 314-534-7023.

St. Peters: St. Charles County Extension Center, SBDC, 260 Brown Rd., St. Peters, MO 63376, 314-970-3000.

Union: Franklin County Extension Center, SBDC, 414 E. Main, P.O. Box 71, Union, MO 63084, 314-583-5141; Fax: 314-583-3500.

Warrensburg: Central Missouri State University, Center for Technology, Grinstead #75, Warrensburg, MO 64093-5037, 816-543-4402; Fax: 816-747-1653.

Warrensburg: Central Missouri State, Small Business Development Center, Grinstead #609, Warrensburg, MO 64093-5037, 816-543-4402; Fax: 816-543-8159.

West Plains: Howell County Extension Center, SBDC, 217 S. Aid Ave., West Plains, MO 65775, 417-256-2391; Fax: 417-256-8569.

Montana

General Information

Business Assistance Division, Department of Commerce, 1424 Ninth Avenue, Helena, MT 59620; 406-444-3923. *A Guide to Montana's Economic Development Assistance Program*, which lists state and federal agencies and other sources of business assistance is available at no charge.

Business Development Division, Department of Commerce, 1424 Ninth Avenue, Helena, MT 59620; 406-444-4780. Publications printed and on disk are available at a fee. Available are *Montana Exporters Guide*, *Montana Consumer Products Buyers Director*, *Montana Manufacturers Director*, *Business Planning Guide*.

Business Information System (BIS), On Line Electronic Bulletin Board, Department of Commerce, 1424 Ninth Avenue, Helena, MT 59620; 404-444-4780. The electronic bulletin board is accessible free of charge to anyone with a personal computer communications software and modem. The BIS posts a variety of economic, demographic and business data, including state government bid solicitations, export trade opportunity leads from U.S. Dept. of Commerce, and population, income and employment statistics for Montana cities and counties.

Small Business Advocacy and Licensing, Department of Commerce, 1424 Ninth Avenue, Helena, MT 59620; 1-800-221-8015 in Montana. Assistance in cutting bureaucratic red tape. Information and expertise in dealing with state, federal, and local agencies, licensing and permit questions.

Small Business Development Centers

The following offices offer free and fee-based services to new and expanding businesses:

Lead Center: Montana Small Business Development Center, Department of Commerce, 1424 Ninth Avenue, Helena, MT 59620; 406-444-4780, Fax: 406-444-1872.

Billings: Billings Area Business Incubator, Small Business Development Center, 2722 3rd Avenue, Suite 300 W., Billings, MT 59101, 406-256-6875; Fax: 406-256-6877.

Bozeman: Bozeman Human Resources Development Council, Small Business Development Center, 215 Mendenhall, Bozeman, MT 59715, 406-587-3113; Fax: 406-587-9565.

Butte: Butte REDI, Small Business Development Center, 305 W. Mercury Street, Suite 211, Butte, MT 59701, 406-782-7333; Fax: 406-782-9675.

Haver: Haver Small Business Development Center, Bear Paw Development Corporation, P.O. Box 1549, Haver, MT 59501, 406-265-9226; Fax: 406-265-5602.

Kalispell: Flathead Valley Community College, Small Business Development Center, 777 Grandview Drive, Kalispell, MT 59901, 406-756-3833; Fax: 406-786-3815.

Missoula: Missoula Incubator, Small Business Development Center, 127 N. Higgins, 3rd Floor, Missoula, MT 59802, 406-278-9234; Fax: 406-721-4584.

Sidney: Sidney Small Business Development Center, 123 W. Main, Sidney, MT 59270, 406-482-5024; Fax: 406-482-5306.

Nebraska

General Information

One-Stop Business Assistance Program, Department of Economic Development, P.O. Box 94666, 301 Centennial Mall South, Lincoln, NE 68509-4666; 402-471-3782, 1-800-426-6505 in Nebraska, Fax: 402-471-3778. Provides assistance on identifying marketing and finance information; business information and research, regulations, licenses, fees, and other state requirements for business operation. searches, and business counseling.

Existing Business Division, Department of Economic Development, P.O. Box 94666, 301 Centennial Mall South, Lincoln, NE 68509-4666; 402-471-3782, 1-800-426-6505 in Nebraska, Fax: 402-471-3778. Offers technical assistance to small businesses and acts as a clearinghouse for information on other state services. Activities include acting as a link between business and government contracts, promoting exports of Nebraska products to foreign markets, maintaining a job training liaison to coordinate labor training with industrial location and expansion, maintaining business finance consultants in outreach offices, and providing information on federal programs such as Community Development Block Grants, SBA loans, and FmHA Business and Industry loans.

Small Business Advocate, Department of Economic Development, P.O. Box 94666, 301 Centennial Mall South, Lincoln, NE 68509-4666; 402-471-3782, 1-800-426-6505 in Nebraska, Fax: 402-471-3778. Assistance in cutting bureaucratic red tape. Information and expertise in dealing with state, federal, and local agencies.

Small Business Development Centers

The following offices offer free and fee-based services to new and expanding businesses:

Lead Center: Nebraska Small Business Development Center, Omaha Business and Technical Center, 2505 North 24th Street, Suite 101, Omaha, NE 68110; 402-595-3511.

Chadron: Chadron State College, Small Business Development Center, Administration Building, Chadron, NE 69337, 308-432-6282.

Kearney: University of Nebraska at Kearney, Small Business Development Center, Welch Hall, 19th and College Drive, Kearney, NE 68849, 308-234-8344.

Be patient. If any phone number is incorrect, call (area code) 555-1212 and request the new listing.

737

Lincoln: University of Nebraska at Lincoln, Small Business Development Center, Cornhusker Bank Bldg., 11th and Cornhusker Hwy., Suite 302, Lincoln, NE 68521, 402-472-3358.

North Platte: Mid-Plains Community College, Small Business Development Center, 416 North Jeffers, Room 26, North Platte, NE 69101, 308-534-5115.

Omaha: University of Nebraska at Omaha, SBDC, Peter Keiwit Conference Center, 1313 Farnam, Suite 132, Omaha, NE 68182, 402-595-2381.

Peru: Peru State College, Small Business Development Center, T.J. Majors Building, Room 248, Peru, NE 68421, 402-872-2274.

Scottsbluff: Small Business Development Center, Nebraska Public Power Building, 1721 Broadway, Room 400, Scottsbluff, NE 69361, 308-635-7513.

Wayne: Wayne State College, Small Business Development Center, Connell Hall, Wayne, NE 68787, 402-375-7575.

Nevada

General Information

State of Nevada Commission on Economic Development, Capitol Complex, Carson City, NV 89710; 702-687-4325, Fax: 702-687-4450. Publishes a pamphlet, *Business Assistance*. Acts as a clearinghouse for information and technical assistance. Operates several business assistance programs and performs advertising and public relations activities on behalf of Nevada business. Maintains a computerized inventory of available manufacturing and warehousing buildings, land and corporate office space, customized site selection.

Small Business Advocate, Nevada Office of Community Services, 400 W. King, Suite 400, Carson City, NV 89710; 702-687-4990. Assistance in cutting bureaucratic red tape. Information and expertise in dealing with state, federal, and local agencies.

Small Business Development Centers

The following offices offer free and fee-based services to new and expanding businesses:

Lead Center: Nevada Small Business Development Center, University of Nevada at Reno, College of Business Administration, Room 411, Reno, NV 89577-0100; 702-784-1717, Fax: 702-784-4305.

Elko: Northern Nevada Community College, Small Business Development Center, 901 Elm Street, Elko, NV 89801, 702-738-8493.

Las Vegas: University of Nevada at Las Vegas, SBDC, College of Business and Economics, 4505 Maryland Parkway, Las Vegas, NV 89154, 702-739-0852.

New Hampshire

General Information

Small Business Advocate, Office of Business and Industrial Development, Director, Division of Economic Development, 172 Pembroke Road, P.O. Box 856, Concord, NH 03302-0856; 603-271-2591. Assistance in cutting bureaucratic red tape. Information and expertise in dealing with state, federal, and local agencies.

Office of Business and Industrial Development, Division of Economic Development, P.O. Box 856, Concord, NH 03302-0856; 603-271-2591, Fax: 603-271-2629. Provides assistance and publications designed to support and promote business and industry in the state. Information in areas such as licensing and permits, financial counseling, marketing, and exporting, labor markets, economic and demographic statistics, and site location information.

Small Business Development Centers

The following offices offer free consulting and information referral services. Nominal fees are charged for most training programs.

Lead Center: New Hampshire Small Business Development Center, University of New Hampshire, 108 McConnell Hall, Durham, NH 03824; 603-862-2200, Fax: 603-862-4876.

Durham: Office of Economic Initiatives, Heidelberg Harris Building, Technology Drive, Durham, NH 03824, 603-862-0710.

Durham: Small Business Development Center, Heidelberg Harris Building, 125 Technology Drive, Durham, NH 03824, 603-862-0700; Fax: 603-862-0701.

Keene: Keene State College, Small Business Development Center, Blake House, Keene, NH 03431, 603-358-2602; Fax: 603-358-3612.

Littleton: Small Business Development Center, P.O. Box 786, Littleton, NH 03561, 603-444-1053.

Manchester: Small Business Development Center, 1000 Elm Street, 8th Floor, Manchester, NH 03101, 603-624-2000; Fax: 603-627-4410.

Plymouth: Plymouth State College, Small Business Development Center, Hyde Hall, Plymouth, NH 03264, 603-535-2523; Fax: 603-535-2611.

Nashua: Center for Economic Development, Small Business Development Center, 188 Main Street, Nashua, NH 03062, 603-886-1233; Fax: 603-886-1164.

New Jersey

General Information

Office of Small Business Assistance, Department of Commerce and Economic Development, 20 West State, CN 835, Trenton, NJ 08625; 609-292-3860. Advice on expansion and business start-ups, and marketing and procurement assistance are some of the services available to small businesses. The office also offers seminars throughout the state as part of its outreach program.

Small Business Advocate, Office of Business Advocacy, Department of Commerce and Economic Development, 20 West State Street, CN 823, Trenton, NJ 08625; 609-292-0700. Assistance in cutting bureaucratic red tape. Information and expertise in dealing with state, federal, and local agencies.

Small Business Development Centers

The following offices offer free and fee-based services to new and expanding businesses:

Lead Center: New Jersey Small Business Development Center, Rutgers Graduate School of Management, University Heights, 180 University Avenue, Newark, NJ 07102; 201-648-5950, Fax: 201-648-1110.

Atlantic City: Small Business Development Center, Greater Atlantic City Chamber of Commerce, 1301 Atlantic Avenue, Atlantic City, NJ 08401, 609-345-5600; Fax: 609-345-4524.

Camden: Rutgers - The State University Of New Jersey at Camden, Small Business Development Center, Business and Science Building, 2nd Floor, Camden, NJ 08102, 609-225-6221; Fax: 609-225-6231.

Jersey City: Hudson County Community College, 900 Bergen Ave., Jersey City, NJ 07093.

Lincroft: Brookdale Community College, Small Business Development Center, Newman Springs Road, Lincroft, NJ 07738, 908-842-8685; Fax: 908-842-0203.

New Brunswick: County of Middlesex, Department of Industrial and Economic Development, 150 Neilson St., New Brunswick, NJ 08901, 908-745-5836.

Newark: Rutgers - The State University of New Jersey at Camden, Small Business Development Center, University Heights, 180 University Ave., 3rd Floor, Newark, NJ 07102, 201-648-5950; Fax: 201-648-1110.

Paramus: Bergen Community College, Small Business Development Center, 400 Paramus Road, 3rd Floor, Room A328, Paramus, NJ 07652, 201-447-7841.

Trenton: Mercer County Community College, Small Business Development Center, P.O. Box B, Trenton, NJ 08690, 609-586-4800; Fax: 609-890-6338.

Trenton: Mercer County Community College, Small Business Development Center, James Kerney Campus, N. Broad and Academy Sts., Trenton, NJ 08608, 609-586-4800, ext. 688.

Union: Kean College of New Jersey, Small Business Development Center, East Campus, Room 242, Union, NJ 07083, 908-527-2946; Fax: 908-527-2960.

Washington: Warren County Community College, Small Business Development Center, Route 57 West, Box 55A, Washington, NJ 07882-9605, 201-689-9620.

West New York: Hudson County Community College, 6501 Polk St., 3rd Fl., West New York, NJ 07306.

New Mexico

General Information

One-Stop Shop, Office of Enterprise Development, Department of Economic Development and Tourism, Joseph Montoya Building, 1100 St. Francis Drive, P.O. Box 20003, Santa Fe, NM 87503; 505-827-0300, Fax: 505-827-0407, Modem: 1-800-827-0285. Provides business with a computer system that displays New Mexico's regulatory framework for firms considering relocation or expansion of their manufacturing operations. It consists of the following on-line computer data: Regulatory Environment Bulletin Board (REBB), financial resources, county profiles, site and building locations, directory of New Mexico manufacturers as well as licensing, permitting and taxation procedures.

Small Business Advocate, Department of Economic Development and Tourism, Joseph Montoya Building, 1100 St. Francis Drive, P.O. Box 20003, Santa Fe, NM 87503; 505-827-0300, Fax: 505-827-0407. Assistance in cutting bureaucratic red tape. Information and expertise in dealing with state, federal, and local agencies.

Small Business Development Centers

The following offices offer free and fee-based services to new and expanding businesses:

Lead Center: New Mexico Small Business Development Center, Santa Fe Community College, P.O. Box 4187, Santa Fe, NM 87502-4187; 505-438-1362, Fax: 505-438-1237.

Alamogordo: New Mexico State University at Alamogordo, Small Business Development Center, 1000 Madison, Alamogordo, NM 87310, 505-434-5272.

Albuquerque: Albuquerque Technical Vocational Institute, Small Business Development Center, 525 Buena Vista SE, Albuquerque, NM 87106, 505-224-4246.

Carlsbad: New Mexico State University at Carlsbad, Small Business Development Center, 301 South Canal, P.O. Box 1090, Carlsbad, NM 88220, 505-887-6562.

Clovis: Clovis Community College, Small Business Development Center, 417 Schepps Blvd., Clovis, NM 88101, 505-769-4136.

Espanola: Northern New Mexico Community College, Small Business Development Center, 1002 N. Onate Street, Espanola, NM 87532, 505-753-7141.

Farmington: San Juan College, Small Business Development Center, 203 West Main, Farmington, NM 87401, 505-326-4321.

Gallup: University of New Mexico at Gallup, Small Business Development Center, P.O. Box 1395, Gallup, NM 87305, 505-722-2220.

Grants: New Mexico State University at Grants, Small Business Development Center, 709 E. Roosevelt Ave., Grants, NM 87020, 505-287-8821.

Hobbs: New Mexico Junior College, Small Business Development Center, 5317 Lovington Highway, Hobbs, NM 88240, 505-392-4510.

Las Cruces: Dona Ana Branch Community College, Small Business Development Center, Box 30001, Department 3DA, Las Cruces, NM 88003-0001, 505-527-7566.

Las Vegas: Luna Vocational Technical Institute, Small Business Development Center, Luna Camp, P.O. Drawer K. Las Vegas, NM 88701, 505-454-2595.

Los Alamos: University of New Mexico at Los Alamos, SBDC, P.O. Box 715, Los Alamos, NM 87544, 505-662-0001.

Los Lunas: University of New Mexico at Valencia, Small Business Development Center, 280 La Entrada, Los Lunas, NM 87031, 505-865-9596, ext. 317.

Roswell: Eastern New Mexico University at Roswell, SBDC, P.O. Box 6000, Roswell, NM 88201-6000, 505-624-7133.

Santa Fe: Santa Fe Community College, Small Business Development Center, South Richards Avenue, P.O. Box 4187, Santa Fe, NM 87502-4187, 505-438-1343.

Silver City: Western New Mexico University, Southwest Small Business Development Center, Glazer Hall, Continuing Education Department, P.O. Box 2672, Silver City, NM 88062, 505-538-6320.

Tucumcari: Tucumcari Area Vocational School, Small Business Development Center, 824 W. Hines, P.O. Box 1143, Tucumcari, NM 88401, 505-461-4413.

New York

General Information

Small Business Division, Department of Economic Development, One Commerce Plaza, Albany, NY 12245; 518-474-7756.

Business Opportunity Center, Small Business Division, Department of Economic Development, 1515 Broadway, New York, NY 10036; 212-827-6150, 1-800-STATE NY, 1-800-782-8369. A special service that offers fast, up-to-date information on the State's economic development programs and can help in make contact with appropriate agencies in such areas as financing, job training, technical assistance, etc.

Small Business Advocate, Small Business Division, Department of Economic Development, 1515 Broadway, New York, NY 10036; 212-827-6150. Information and expertise in dealing with state, federal, and local agencies.

Small Business Development Centers

The following offices offer free and fee-based services to new and expanding businesses:

Lead Center: New York Small Business Development Ctr., State University of New York, State University Plaza, S-523, Albany, NY 12246; 518-443-5398, 1-800-732-7232, Fax: 518-465-4992.

Albany: State University of New York at Albany (SUNY), Small Business Development Center, Draper Hall, 107, 135 Western Ave., Albany, NY 12222, 518-442-5577; Fax: 518-442-5582.

Albany: The National SBDC Research Network, State University of New York, State University Plaza, 85277, Albany, NY 12246, 518-443-5265; Fax: 518-443-5275.

Binghamton: SUNY at Binghamton, Small Business Development Center, P.O. Box 6000, Vestal Parkway East, Binghamton, NY 13902-6000, 607-777-4024; Fax: 607-777-4029.

Brockport: Small Business Development Center, 74 North Main Street, Brockport, NY 14420, 716-637-6660; Fax: 716-637-2102.

Bronx: Bronx Community College, SBDC, McCracken Hall, Room 14, West 181st St. and University Ave., Bronx, NY 10453, 718-220-6464; Fax: 718-563-3572.

Brooklyn: Kingsborough Community College, 2001 Oriental Blvd., Bldg. Tr Room 4204, Manhattan Beach, Brooklyn, NY 11235, 718-368-4619; Fax: 718-368-4629.

Brooklyn: Downtown Outreach Center, SBDC, 111 Livingston St., Room 208, Brooklyn, NY 11201, 718-596-7081; Fax: 718-596-6989.

Buffalo: State University College at Buffalo, Small Business Development Center, 1300 Elmwood Avenue, BA 117, Buffalo, NY 14222, 716-878-4030; Fax: 716-878-4067.

Cobleskill: Cobleskill Outreach Center, SBDC, SUNY Cobleskill, Warner Hall, Room 218, Cobleskill, NY 12043, 518-234-5528; Fax: 518-234-5292.

Corning: Corning Community College, Small Business Development Center, 24 Denison Parkway West, Corning, NY 14830, 607-962-9461; Fax: 607-936-6642.

Dobbs Ferry: Mercy College, Small Business Development Center, Westchester Outreach Center, Mercy College, 555 Broadway, Dobbs Ferry, NY 10522, 914-674-7845, ext. 485; Fax: 914-693-4996.

Be patient. If any phone number is incorrect, call (area code) 555-1212 and request the new listing.

739

Farmingdale: SUNY College of Technology at Farmingdale, Small Business Development Center, Campus Commons, Farmingdale, NY 11735, 516-420-2765; Fax: 516-293-5343.

Fishkill: Marist College, Small Business Development Center, Fishkill Extension Center, 2600 Route 9, Unit 90, Fishkill, NY 12524-2001, 914-897-2607/2608/2609; Fax: 914-897-4653.

Geneseo: SUNY Geneseo, Small Business Development Center, 1 College Circle, Geneseo, NY 14454-1485, 716-245-5429; Fax: 716-245-5430.

Geneva: Geneva Outreach Center, Small Business Development Center at Geneva, 122 N. Genesee St., Geneva, NY 14456, 315-781-1253.

Hempstead: EOC Hempstead Outreach Center, SBDC, 269 Fulton Ave., Hempstead, NY 11550, 516-564-8672/1895; Fax: 516-481-4938.

Jamaica: York College, Small Business Development Center, Science Building, Room 107, The City University of New York, Jamaica, NY 11451, 718-262-2880; Fax: 718-262-2881.

Jamestown: Jamestown Community College, Small Business Development Center, P.O. Box 20, Jamestown, NY 14702-0020, 716-665-5754, 1-800-522-7232; Fax: 716-665-6733.

Kingston: Kingston SBDC, 649 Ulster Ave., Kingston, NY 12401, 914-339-1322; Fax: 914-339-1631.

New York: Harlem Outreach Center, SBDC, 163 W. 125th St., Room 1307, New York, NY 10027, 212-865-4299/4399; Fax: 212-865-0622.

New York: East Harlem Outreach Center, SBDC, 145 E 116th St., 3rd Floor, New York, NY 10029, 212-534-2729/4526; Fax: 212-410-1359.

New York: Midtown Outreach Center, SBDC, Baruch College, 360 Park Ave. South, Room 1101, New York, NY 10010, 212-802-6620; Fax: 212-802-6613.

New York: Pace University, SBDC, Pace Plaza, New York, NY 10038, 212-346-1899; Fax: 212-346-1613.

Oswego: SUNY at Oswego, SBDC, Operation Oswego County, 44 W. Bridge St., Oswego, NY 13126, 315-343-1545; Fax: 315-343-1546.

Plattsburgh: Clinton Community College, SBDC, Lake Shore Rd., Suite 9 South, 136 Clinton Point Dr., Plattsburgh, NY 12901, 518-562-4260; Fax: 518-563-9759.

Riverhead: Riverhead Outreach Center, Small Business Development Center, Suffolk County Community College, Riverhead, NY 11901, 516-369-1409/1507; Fax: 516-369-3255.

Rochester: Small Business Development Center-SUNY Brockport, Temple Bldg., 14 Franklin St., Suite 200 Rochester, NY 14604, 716-232-7310.

Sanborn: Niagara County Community College at Sanborn, Small Business Development Center, 3111 Saunders Settlement Road, Sanborn, NY 14132, 716-693-1910; Fax: 716-731-3595.

Southampton: Southampton Outreach Center, SBDC, Long Island University at Southampton, Abney Peak, Montauk Highway, Southampton, NY 11968, 516-287-0059/0071; Fax: 516-287-8287.

Staten Island: The College of Staten Island, SBDC, Sunnyside Campus, Room B140, 715 Ocean Terrace, Staten Island, NY 10301, 718-390-7645; Fax: 718-876-9378.

Stony Brook: SUNY at Stony Brook, Small Business Development Center, Harriman Hall, Room 109, Stony Brook, NY 11794, 516-632-9070; Fax: 516-632-7176.

Suffern: Rockland Community College at Suffern, Small Business Development Center, 145 College Road, Suffern, NY 10901, 914-356-0370; Fax: 914-356-0381.

Syracuse: Onondaga Community College at Syracuse, Small Business Development Center, Excell Bldg., Room 108, Route 173, Syracuse, NY 13215, 315-492-3029; Fax: 315-492-3704.

Troy: Manufacturing Technology Center, SBDC, New York Manufacturing Partnership, 385 Jordan Rd., Troy, NY 12180-8347, 518-286-1014. Fax: 518-286-1006.

Utica: SUNY College of Technology at Utica/Rome, Small Business Development Center, P.O. Box 3050, Utica, NY 13504-3050, 315-792-7546; Fax: 315-792-7554.

Watertown: Jefferson Community College, Small Business Development Center, Watertown, NY 13601, 315-782-9262; Fax: 315-782-0901.

White Plains: The Small Business Resource Center, Small Business Development Center, 222 Bloomingdale Road, 3rd Floor, White Plains, NY 10605-1500, 914-644-4116; Fax: 914-644-2184.

North Carolina

General Information

North Carolina Department of Economic and Community Development, Business Industrial Development, 430 North Salisbury Street, Raleigh, NC 27603; 919-733-4151. Coordinates state small business assistance programs and financing. Includes pooled industrial revenue bonds, a certified SBA Development Company, and a long-term, fixed-rate financing program. Also provides information and referral services to small firms and prospective entrepreneurs and acts as advocate for the state's small business community.

Small Business Advocate, North Carolina Department of Economic and Community Development, Business Industrial Development, 430 North Salisbury Street, Raleigh, NC 27603; 919-571-4154. Assistance in cutting bureaucratic red tape. Information and expertise in dealing with state, federal, and local agencies.

Business License Information Office, N.C. Department of the Secretary of State, 301 West Jones Street, Raleigh, NC 27603; 919-733-0641, 1-800-228-8443 in NC. A central information source offering prompt, individualized assistance to new and existing businesses to secure the necessary State issued licenses, permits, and/or authorizations in order to operate a business in the State. Acts as an advocate for regulatory reform.

Small Business Development Centers

The following offices offer free and fee-based services to new and expanding businesses:

Lead Center: North Carolina Small Business Development Center, University of North Carolina, 4509 Creedmoor Road, Suite 201, Raleigh, NC 27612; 919-571-4154, Fax: 919-571-4161.

Asheville: Asheville Office, Small Business Development Center, 34 Wall St., Suite 707, Public Services Bldg., Asheville, NC 28805, 704-251-6025.

Boone: Appalachian State University, SBDC, Northwestern Region, Walker College of Business, Boone, NC, 28608, 704-262-2492; Fax: 704-262-2027.

Chapel Hill: Small Business Development Center, Central Carolina Region, 608 Airport Road, Suite B, Chapel Hill, NC 27514, 919-962-0389; Fax: 919-962-0389.

Charlotte: Small Business Development Center, Southern Piedmont Region, The Ben Craig Center, 8701 Mallard Creek Road, Charlotte, NC 28262, 704-548-1090; Fax: 704-548-9050.

Cullowhee: Small Business Development Center, Center for Improving Mountain Living, Western Carolina University, Cullowhee, NC 28723, 704-227-7494; Fax: 704-227-7422.

Elizabeth City: Elizabeth City State University, Small Business Development Center, Northeastern Region, P.O. Box 874, Elizabeth City, NC 27909, 919-335-3247; Fax: 919-335-3648.

Fayetteville: Fayetteville State University, Small Business Development Center, Cape Fear Region, Continuing Education Center, P.O. Box 1334, Fayetteville, NC 28302, 919-486-1727; Fax: 919-486-1949.

Greensboro: North Carolina A&T University/CH Moore Agricultural Research Center, Small Business Development Center, Box D-22, Greensboro, NC 27411, 910-334-7005; Fax: 910-334-7073.

Greenville: East Carolina University, Small Business Development Center, Eastern Region, 300 E. 1st St., Willis Bldg., Greenville, NC, 27858-4353, 919-757-6157; Fax: 919-757-6992.

Hickory: Catawba Valley Region, Small Business Development Center, 514 Hwy 321, Suite A, Hickory, NC 28601, 704-345-1110; Fax: 704-326-9117.

Pembroke: Pembroke State University, Office of Economic Development and SBTDC, Pembroke, NC 28372, 910-521-6603; Fax: 910-521-6550.

Raleigh: MCI Small Business Resource Center, 800 1/2 S. Salisbury St., Raleigh, NC 27601, 919-715-0520; Fax: 919-715-0518.

Rocky Mount: NC Wesleyan College, Small Business Development Center, 3400 N. Wesleyan Blvd., Rocky Mount, NC 27804, 919-985-5130; Fax: 919-977-3701.

Wilmington: University of North Carolina at Wilmington, SBDC, Southeastern Region, Room 131, Cameron Hall, 601 South College Road, Wilmington, NC 28403, 919-395-3744; Fax: 919-395-3815; Fax: 910-350-3990.

Winston-Salem: Winston-Salem University, SBDC, Northern Piedmont Region, P.O. Box 13025, Winston-Salem, NC 27110, 919-750-2030; Fax: 919-750-2031.

North Dakota

General Information

Center for Innovation and Business Development, Box 8103, University Station, University of North Dakota, Grand Forks, ND 58202; 701-777-3132. The *Business Plan* and *Marketing Plan* workbooks are step-by-step guides, with optional software, to writing your own business and marketing plans. They are targeted to new manufacturing ventures producing new products or technology, but the guides can also be relevant to many entrepreneurs, academics, and business professionals. The workbooks are $30 each; with software $79.

Small Business Advocate, North Dakota Economic Finance Corp., 1833 E. Bismarck Expressway, Bismarck, ND 58504; 701-221-5300, Fax: 701-221-5320. Assistance in cutting bureaucratic red tape. Information and expertise in dealing with state, federal, and local agencies.

Small Business Development Centers

The following offices offer free and fee-based services to new and expanding businesses:

Lead Center: North Dakota Small Business Development Center, University of North Dakota, 118 Gamble Hall, Box 7308, Grand Forks, ND 58202; 701-777-3700, Fax: 701-777-3225.

Bismarck: Small Business Development Center, Bismarck Regional Center, 400 East Broadway, Suite 416, Bismarck, ND 58501, 701-223-8583; Fax: 701-255-7228.

Devils Lake: Devils Lake Outreach Center, Small Business Development Center, 417 5th Street, Devils Lake, ND 58301, 800-445-7232.

Dickinson: Small Business Development Center, Dickinson Regional Center, 314 3rd Avenue West, Drawer L, Dickinson, ND 58602, 701-227-2096; Fax: 701-225-5116.

Fargo: Small Business Development Center, Fargo Regional Center, 417 Main Avenue, Fargo, ND 58103, 701-237-0986; Fax: 701-235-6706.

Grafton: Grafton Outreach Center, Red River Regional Planning Council, Small Business Development Center, P.O. Box 633, Grafton, ND 58237, 800-445-7232.

Grand Forks: Small Business Development Center, Grand Forks Regional Center, The Hemp Center, 1407 24th Avenue S., Suite 201, Grand Forks, ND 58201, 701-772-8502; Fax: 701-775-2772.

Jamestown: Jamestown Outreach Center, Small Business Development Center, 210 10th St. SE, Box 1530, Jamestown, ND 58402, 701-252-9243; Fax: 701-251-2488/ 252-4837.

Minot: Minot Outreach Center, SBDC, 4215 E. Burdick Expy. Minot, ND 58701, 701-839-6641; Fax: 701-838-8955.

Minot: Small Business Development Center, Minot Regional Center, 1020 20th Ave. Southwest, P.O. Box 940, Minot, ND 58702, 701-852-8861; Fax: 701-838-2488.

Williston: Williston Outreach Ctr., Tri-County Economic Development Assn., SBDC, Box 2047, Williston, ND 58801, 800-445-7232.

Ohio

General Information

One-Stop Business Permit Center, Ohio Department of Development, P.O. Box 1001, Columbus, OH 43266-0101; 614-644-8748, 1-800-848-1300. Provides new entrepreneurs with licensing and permit information, and acts as an advocate for licensing and permit problems. Directs you to proper area for technical, financial and management resources.

Small Business Advocate, Small And Developing Business Division, Ohio Department of Development, 77 S. High Street, P.O. Box 1001, Columbus, OH 43266-0101; 614-466-2718. Assistance in cutting bureaucratic red tape. Information and expertise in dealing with state, federal, and local agencies.

Small Business Development Centers

The following offices offer free and fee-based services to new and expanding businesses:

Lead Center: Ohio Small Business Development Center, Department of Development, State Office Tower, P.O. Box 1001, Columbus, OH 43226-0101; 614-466-2480, Fax: 614-466-0829.

Akron: Small Business Development Center, Akron Regional Development Board, One Cascade Plaza, 8th Floor, Akron, OH 44308, 216-379-3170; Fax: 216-379-3164.

Athens: Ohio University, Small Business Development Center, Innovation Center, 20 E. Circle Dr., Athens, OH 45701, 614-593-1797; Fax: 614-593-1795.

Athens: Athens Small Business Center, Inc., 900 East State Street, Athens OH 45701, 614-592-1188.

Bowling Green: Wood County Small Business Development Center, WSOS Community Action Commission, Inc., P.O. Box 539, 121 E. Wooster St., Bowling Green, OH 43402, 419-352-3817; Fax: 419-353-3291.

Canton: Small Business Development Center, Greater Stark Development Board, 6000 Frank Ave. NW, Canton, OH 44704, 216-379-3170; Fax: 216-379-3164.

Celina: Wright State University, Lake Campus, Small Business Development Center, 7600 State Route 703, Celina, OH 45882, 419-586-0355; Fax: 419-586-0358.

Cincinnati: Cincinnati Small Business Development Center, IAMS Research Park, MC189, 1111 Edison Avenue, Cincinnati, OH 45216-2265, 513-948-2082; Fax: 513-948-2007.

Cincinnati: Clemont County Chamber of Commerce, Small Business Development Center, 4440 Glen Este-Withamsville Road, Cincinnati, OH, 513-753-7141; Fax: 513-753-7146.

Cincinnati: Cincinnati Minority Business Assistance Corporation, University of Cincinnati, Small Business Development Center, 2900 Reading Rd., Box 210167, Cincinnati, OH 45237-2810, 513-556-1922; Fax: 513-556-0097.

Cleveland: Northern Ohio Mfg. Small Business Development Center, Prospect Pk. Bldg., 4600 Prospect Ave., Cleveland, OH 44103-4314, 216-432-5364; Fax: 216-361-2900.

Cleveland: Women's Business Development Center of Cleveland, 601 Lakeside Ave., Cleveland, OH 44114, 216-654-4162; Fax: 216-664-3002.

Cleveland: Greater Cleveland Growth Association, Small Business Development Center, 200 Tower City Center, 50 Public Square, Cleveland, OH 44113-2291, 216-621-3300; Fax: 216-621-4617.

Columbus: Columbus Small Business Development Center, Columbus Area Chamber of Commerce, 37 North High Street, Columbus, OH 43215, 614-225-6082; Fax: 614-469-8250.

Columbus: Ohio Dept. of Development, Ohio Women's Business Resource Network, Small Business Development Center, 77 S. High St., 28th Floor, Columbus, OH 43266-0101, 800-849-1300, ext. 6-2682; Fax: 614-466-0829.

Coshocton: Coshocton Area Chamber of Commerce, Small Business Development Center, 124 Chestnut Street, Coshocton, OH 43812, 614-622-5411; Fax: 614-622-9902.

Be patient. If any phone number is incorrect, call (area code) 555-1212 and request the new listing.

741

Dayton: Dayton Area Chamber of Commerce, Small Business Development Center, Chamber Plaza, 5th and Main Streets, Dayton, OH 45402-2400, 513-226-8239; Fax: 513-226-8254.

Dayton: Dayton Satellite, Center for Small Business Assistance, College of Business, 310 Rike Hall, Dayton, OH 45433, 513-873-3503; Fax: 523-873-3545.

Dayton: Microenterprise Development Program, Small Business Development Center, 1152 W. Third St., Dayton, OH 45407, 513-222-0065; Fax: 513-222-8658.

Dayton: City of Dayton MCBAP, Small Business Development Center, 1116 W. Stewart St., Dayton, OH 45408, 513-223-2164; Fax: 513-223-8495.

Dayton: Central State University, Miami Valley OPTA Outreach Center, Small Business Development Center, 100 Jenkins Hall, Dayton, OH 45384, 513-376-6514; Fax: 513-376-6598.

Defiance: Northwest Small Business Development Center, 1935 E. Second St., Suite D, Defiance, OH 43512, 419-784-3777; Fax: 419-782-4649.

Fremont: North Central Small Business Development Center, Fremont Office, Terra Technical College, 1220 Cedar Street, Fremont, OH 43420, 419-332-1002; Fax: 419-334-2300.

Hillsboro: Enterprise Center Small Business Development Center, 129 E. Main St., Hillsboro, OH 45132, 513-393-9599; Fax: 513-393-8159.

Jefferson: Ashtabula County Economic Development Council, Inc., Small Business Development Center, 36 West Walnut Street, Jefferson, OH 44047, 216-576-9134; Fax: 216-576-5003.

Kent: Kent Regional Business Alliance Small Business Development Center, Kent State Univ. Partnership, College of Business Admin., Room 302, Kent, OH 44242, 216-672-2750; Fax: 216-672-2448.

Kettering: EMTEC/Small Business Development Center, Southern Area Mfg. Small Business Development Center, 2171 Research Park, Kettering, OH 45420, 513-259-1361; Fax: 513-259-1303.

Lima: Lima Technical College, Small Business Development Center, 545 West Market Street, Suite 305, Lima, OH 45801, 419-229-5320; Fax: 419-229-5424.

Lorain: Lorain County Chamber of Commerce, Small Business Development Center, 6100 S. Broadway, Lorain, OH 44053, 216-246-2833; Fax: 216-246-4050.

Mansfield: Mid-Ohio Small Business Development Center, 246 E. 4th St., P.O. Box 44901, Mansfield, OH 44902, 800-366-7232; Fax: 419-522-6811.

Marietta: Marietta College, Small Business Development Center, 213 4th St., Marietta, OH 45750, 614-376-4832; Fax: 614-376-4801.

Marion: Marion Small Business Development Center, Marion Area Chamber of Commerce, 206 S. Prospect Street, Marion, OH 43302, 614-382-0181.

Mentor: Lakeland Community College, Lake County Economic Development Center, Small Business Development Center, Mentor, OH 44080, 216-951-1290; Fax: 216-951-7336.

New Philadelphia: Tuscarawas Chamber of Commerce, Small Business Development Center, 330 University Drive, NE, New Philadelphia, OH 44663, 216-339-3391; Fax: 216-339-2637.

Oxford: Miami University Small Business Development Center, Dept. of Decision Sciences, 336 Upham Hall, Oxford, OH 44045, 513-529-4841; Fax: 513-529-1469.

Piqua: Upper Valley Joint Vocational School, Small Business Development Center, 8811 Career Drive, North County Road 25A, Piqua, OH 45356, 513-778-8419; Fax: 513-778-9237.

Portsmouth: Portsmouth Area Chamber of Commerce, Small Business Development Center, 1206 Weller St., P.O. Box 1757, Portsmouth, OH 45662, 614-354-2833; Fax: 614-353-2695.

Shaker Heights: Western Reserve Minority Chamber of Commerce, Small Business Development Center, 20475 Farnsleigh, Shaker Heights, OH 44122, 216-283-4700; Fax: 216-283-5006.

Southpoint: Lawrence County Chamber of Commerce, Small Business Development Center, U.S. Route 52 and Solida Road, P.O. Box 488, Southpoint, OH 45680, 614-894-3838; Fax: 614-894-3836.

Springfield: Springfield Small Business Development Center, INC., 300 E. Auburn Ave., Springfield, OH 45505, 513-322-7821; Fax: 513-322-7874.

St. Clairsville: Department of Development of the CIC of Belmont County, Small Business Development Center, St. Clairsville Office, 100 East Main Street, St. Clairsville, OH 43950, 614-695-9678; Fax: 614-695-1536.

Steubenville: Greater Steubenville Chamber of Commerce, Small Business Development Center, 630 Market Street, P.O. Box 278, Steubenville, OH 43952, 614-282-6226; Fax: 614-282-6285.

Toledo: Toledo MCBAP, Economic Opportunity Planning Association, Small Business Development Center, 505 Hamilton St., Toledo, OH 43602, 419-242-7304; Fax: 419-242-8263.

Toledo: Northwest Ohio Women's Business Entrepreneurial Network, Small Business Development Center, Toledo Regional Growth Partnership, 300 Madison Ave., Toledo, OH 43604, 419-252-2700; Fax: 419-252-2724.

Youngstown: Youngstown State University, Cushwa Center for Industrial Development, Small Business Development Center, 410 Wick Ave., Youngstown, OH 44555, 216-742-3495; Fax: 216-742-3784.

Zanesville: Zanesville Area Chamber of Commerce, Small Business Development Center, 217 N. Fifth St., Zanesville, OH 43701, 614-452-4868; Fax: 614-454-2963.

Oklahoma

General Information

Teamwork Oklahoma, P.O. Box 26980, Oklahoma City, OK 73126-0980; 405-843-9770, Fax: 405-841-5199, 1-800-879-6552. A business referral service that acquaints business persons or potential business person with the many financial and consulting services available in Oklahoma.

Small Business Advocate, Oklahoma Department of Commerce, P.O. Box 26980, Oklahoma City, OK 73126-0980; 405-841-5236, Fax: 405-841-5199. Assistance in cutting bureaucratic red tape. Information and expertise in dealing with state, federal, and local agencies.

Small Business Development Centers

The following offices offer free and fee-based services to new and expanding businesses:

Lead Center: Oklahoma Small Business Development Center Network, Southeastern Oklahoma State University, 517 University, Durant, OK 74701; 405-924-0277, 1-800-522-6154, Fax: 405-924-7471.

Ada: East Central State University, Small Business Development Center, 1036 East 10th, Ada, OK 74820, 405-436-3190; Fax: 405-436-3190.

Alva: Northwestern State University, Small Business Development Center, 709 Oklahoma Blvd., Alva, OK 73717, 405-327-0560; Fax: 405-327-8608.

Durant: Southeastern State University, Small Business Development Center, 517 University, Durant, OK 74701, 405-924-0277; Fax: 405-920-7471.

Enid: Phillips University, Enid Satellite Center, 100 South University Avenue, Enid, OK 73701, 405-242-7989; Fax: 405-237-1607.

Langston: Langston University, Minority Assistance Center, Hwy. 33 East, Langston, OK 73050, 405-466-3256; Fax: 405-466-3381.

Lawton: Lawton Satellite Center, Small Business Development Center, American National Bank Building, 601 SW "D", Suite 209, Lawton, OK 73501, 405-248-4946.

Miami: Miami Satellite, 215 I St. NE, Miami, OK 74354, 918-540-0575; Fax: 918-540-0575.

Midwest City: Rose State College, Procurement Specialty Center, 6420 Southeast 15th Street, Midwest City, OK 73110, 405-733-7348; Fax: 405-733-7495.

Oklahoma City: University of Central Oklahoma, SBDC, 621 N. Robinson, Suite 372, Oklahoma City, OK 73102, 405-232-1968; Fax: 405-232-1967.

Poteau: Carl Albert Junior College, Poteau Satellite Center, SBDC, 1507 South McKenna, Poteau, OK 74953, 918-647-4019; Fax: 918-647-1218.

Tahlequah: Northeastern State University, Small Business Development Center, Tahlequah, OK 74464, 918-458-0802; Fax: 918-458-2105.

Tulsa: Tulsa Satellite Center, State Office Building, 440 South Houston, Suite 507, Tulsa, OK 74107, 918-581-2502; Fax: 918-581-2745.

Weatherford: Southwestern State University, Small Business Development Center, 100 Campus Drive, Weatherford, OK 73096, 405-774-1040; Fax: 405-774-7091.

Oregon

General Information

Business Development Division, Department of Economic Development, 775 Summer Street NE, Salem, OR 97310; 503-373-1225. Provides information to business investors on land, buildings, financing, and other relevant issues. Provides consulting services for manufacturing and processing companies with problems. Supports local economic development organizations in expansion efforts. Manages the Oregon Enterprize Zone program which offers property tax relief incentives in 30 specified regions, and a computer-based inventory of available industrial sites and buildings in the state. The Division maintains regional offices in six locations around the state.

Small Business Program, Department of Economic Development, 775 Summer Street NE, Salem, OR 97310; 503-373-1241, Hotline: 1-800-442-8275 in Oregon. Assistance in cutting bureaucratic red tape. Information and expertise in dealing with state, federal, and local agencies.

Small Business Development Centers

The following offices offer free and fee-based services to new and expanding businesses:

Lead Center: Oregon Small Business Development Center, 44 W. Broadway, Suite 501, Eugene, OR 97401-3021; 503-726-2250, Fax: 503-345-6006.

Albany: Linn-Benton Community College, Small Business Development Center, 6500 S.W. Pacific Boulevard, Albany, OR 97321, 503-967-6112; Fax: 503-967-6550.

Ashland: Southern Oregon State College, Small Business Development Center, Regional Service Institute, Ashland, OR 97520, 503-482-5838, Fax: 503-482-5838.

Bend: Central Oregon Community College, Small Business Development Center, 2600 N.W. College Way, Bend, OR 97701, 503-383-7290; Fax: 503-383-7503.

Coos Bay: Southwestern Oregon Community College, Small Business Development Center, 340 Central, Coos Bay, OR 97420, 503-269-0123; Fax: 503-269-0323.

Eugene: Lane Community College, Small Business Development Center, 1059 Willamette Street, Eugene, OR 97401, 503-726-2255; Fax: 503-686-0096.

Grants Pass: Rogue Community College, Small Business Development Center, 214 SW 4th St., Grants Pass, OR 97526, 503-471-3515.

Gresham: Mount Hood Community College, Small Business Development Center, 323 NE Roberts Street, Gresham, OR 97030, 503-667-7658, Fax: 503-666-1140.

Klamath Falls: Oregon Institute of Technology, Small Business Development Center, 3201 Campus Drive, South 314, Klamath Falls, OR 97601, 503-885-1760; Fax: 503-885-1855.

Lincoln City: Oregon Coast Community College Service District, Small Business Development Center, 4157 NW Highway 101, Suite 123, Lincoln City, OR 97367, 503-994-4166; Fax: 503-996-4958.

Medford: Small Business Development Center, 229 N. Bartlett, Medford, OR 97501, 503-772-3478; Fax: 503-776-2224.

Milwaukie: Clackamas Community College, Small Business Development Center, 7616 S.E. Harmony Road, Milwaukie, OR 97222, 503-656-4447; Fax: 503-652-0389.

Ontario: Treasure Valley Community College, Small Business Development Center, 88 S.W. Third Avenue, Ontario, OR 97914, 503-889-2617, Fax: 503-889-8331.

Pendleton: Blue Mountain Community College, Small Business Development Center, 37 S.E. Dorion, Pendleton, OR 97801, 503-276-6233.

Portland: Portland Community College, Small Business Development Center, 123 N.W. 2nd Avenue, Suite 321, Portland, OR 97209, 503-273-2828; Fax: 503-294-0725.

Portland: Small Business International Trade Program, 121 S.W. Salmon Street, Suite 210, Portland, OR 97204, 503-274-7482, Fax: 503-228-6350.

Rosenburg: Umpqua Community College, Small Business Development Center, 744 S.E. Rose, Rosenburg, OR 97470, 503-672-2535; Fax: 503-672-3679.

Salem: Chemeketa Community College, Small Business Development Center, 365 Ferry Street S.E., Salem, OR 97301, 503-399-5181; Fax: 503-581-6017.

Seaside: Clatsop Community College, Small Business Development Center, 1761 N. Holladay, Seaside, OR 97138, 503-738-3347.

The Dalles: Columbia Gorge Community College, Small Business Development Center, 400 E. Scenic Dr., Suite 257, The Dalles, OR 97058, 503-298-3118, Fax: 503-298-3119.

Tillamook: Tillamook Bay Community College Service District, Small Business Development Center, 401 B Main St., Tillamook, OR 97141, 503-842-2551; Fax: 503-842-2555.

Pennsylvania

General Information

Bureau of Small Business Appalachian Development, 461 Forum Building, Harrisburg, PA 17120; 717-783-5700. Acts as a clearinghouse to assist small business in finding resources and services available in the state.

Business Resource Network, Office Of Enterprise Development, 461 Forum Building, Harrisburg, PA 17120; 717-783-5700. Assists with coordinating and expediting the necessary permits for start-up, expansion, or relocation of job creating opportunities. Publishes and distributed booklets on how to plan and start a business and on resources available to small business. Interacts with other state agencies to insure a timely response to the small business person.

Small Business Advocate, Office Of Enterprise Development, 461 Forum Building, Harrisburg, PA 17120; 717-783-5700. Assistance in cutting bureaucratic red tape. Information and expertise in dealing with state, federal, and local agencies.

Small Business Development Centers

The following offices offer free and fee-based services to new and expanding businesses:

Lead Center: Pennsylvania Small Business Development Center, University of Pennsylvania, The Wharton School, 444 Vance Hall, Philadelphia, PA 19104-6374; 215-898-1219, Fax: 215-573-2135.

Aliquippa: Beaver Valley Technology Center, Small Business Development Center, 300 Main Ave., W. Aliquippa Business and Technology Ctr., Aliquippa, PA 15001, 412-378-7422.

Bethlehem: Lehigh University, Small Business Development Center, Rauch Business Center #37, Bethlehem, PA 18015, 215-758-3980; Fax: 215-758-5205.

California: California University, SBDC, Mon Valley Renaissance Center, Box 62, California, PA 15419, 412-938-5938.

Clarion: Clarion University of Pennsylvania, Small Business Development Center, Dana Still Building, Clarion, PA 16214, 814-226-2060; Fax: 814-226-2636.

Erie: Gannon University, SBDC, Carlisle Building, 3rd Floor, Erie, PA 16541, 814-871-7714; Fax: 814-871-7383.

Exton: West Chester University, Small Business Development Center, Suite 201, 930 East Lancaster Ave., Exton, PA 19341, 215-363-5175.

Be patient. If any phone number is incorrect, call (area code) 555-1212 and request the new listing.

743

Harrisburg: Kutztown University, Small Business Development Center, University Center, 2986 N. 2nd St., Harrisburg, PA 17110, 717-233-3120.

Huntingdon: Juniata College, Business Outreach Center, Small Business Development Center, 1700 Moore St., Huntingdon, PA 16652, 814-643-4310, ext. 633.

Indiana: Indiana University of Pennsylvania, Small Business Development Center, 202 McElhaney Hall, Indiana, PA 15705, 412-357-2179.

Latrobe: St. Vincent College, Small Business Development Center, Alfred Hall, 4th Floor, Latrobe, PA 15650, 412-537-4572; Fax: 412-537-0919.

Lewisburg: Bucknell University, Small Business Development Center, Dana Engineering Building, Lewisburg, PA 17837, 717-524-1249; Fax: 717-524-1768.

Loretto: St. Francis College, Small Business Development Center, Business Resource Center, Loretto, PA 15940, 814-472-3200; Fax: 814-472-3202.

Mansfield: Mansfield Univ., Northern Tier Small Business Assistance Center, Rural Services Institute, Mansfield, PA 16933, 717-662-4972.

Philadelphia: Drexel University, Small Business Development Center, Department of Management, College of Business, Academic Building, Philadelphia, PA 19104, 215-895-2122.

Philadelphia: Temple University, Small Business Development Center, Room 6, Speakman Hall, 006-00, Philadelphia, PA 19122, 215-204-7282.

Philadelphia: LaSalle University, Small Business Development Center, 20th St. and Olney Ave., Philadelphia, PA 19141, 215-951-1416.

Philadelphia: University of Pennsylvania, Small Business Development Center, The Wharton School, 409 Vance Hall, Philadelphia, PA 19104-6357, 215-898-4861; Fax: 215-898-1299.

Pittsburgh: Duquesne University, Small Business Development Center, Rockwell Hall-Room 10 Concourse, 600 Forbes Avenue, Pittsburgh, PA 15282, 412-434-6233; Fax: 412-434-5072.

Pittsburgh: University Small Business Development Center, Room 343 Mervis Hall, Pittsburgh, PA 15260, 412-648-1544; Fax: 412-648-1693.

Scranton: University of Scranton, Small Business Development Center, St. Thomas Hall, Room 588, Scranton, PA 18510, 717-941-7588; Fax: 717-941-4053.

Villanova: Villanova University, Small Business Development Center, Management Dept., Ithan and Lancaster Aves., Villanova, PA 19085, 215-645-4382.

Washington: Washington and Jefferson College, Small Business Development Center, Center for Economic Development, Department of Economics and Business, Washington, PA 15301, 412-222-4400.

Wilkes-Barre: Wilkes College, Small Business Development Center, Hollenback Hall, 192 South Franklin Street, Wilkes-Barre, PA 18766, 717-824-4651, ext. 4340.

Rhode Island

General Information

Small Business Advocate, Good Neighbor Alliance Corp., 15 Messenger Drive, Warwick, RI 02888; 401-467-2880. Assistance in cutting bureaucratic red tape. Information and expertise in dealing with state, federal, and local agencies.

Business Action Center, Rhode Island Department of Economic Development (RIDED), 7 Jackson Walkway, Providence, RI 02903; 401-277-2601. One-stop problem-solving center which provides assistance and information businesses throughout the state. Guarantees an answer to each caller within two working days.

Small Business Development Centers

The following offices offer free and fee-based services to new and expanding businesses:

Lead Center: Rhode Island Small Business Development Center, Bryant College, 1150 Douglas Pike, Smithfield, RI 02917; 401-232-6111, Fax: 401-232-6416.

Newport: Salve Regina University, SBDC, Miley Hall, Room 006, Newport, RI 02840, 401-849-6900; Fax: 401-847-0372.

North Kingstown: Rhode Island Small Business Development Center, Quonset P/D Industrial Park, 35 Belver Ave., Room 217, North Kingstown, RI 02852, 401-294-1228/1227; Fax: 401-294-6897.

Providence: Rhode Island SBDC, CCRI-Providence Campus, One Hilton St., Providence, RI 02905, 401-455-6088; Fax: 401-455-6047.

Providence: Bryant College, Small Business Development Center, 7 Jackson Walkway, Providence, RI 02903, 401-831-1330; Fax: 401-454-2819.

Providence: Rhode Island Small Business Development Center, Providence Campus, One Hilton Street, Providence, RI 02905, 401-455-6042; Fax: 401-455-6047.

South Carolina

General Information

Enterprise Development Department, South Carolina State Development Board, P.O. Box 927, Columbia, SC 29202; 803-737-0400. This department stimulates the formation and growth of new businesses. It provides a network of services for development of business plans, offers assistance to small businesses on individual problems, and establishes a regional network for women-owned businesses. Technical assessments are available as well as educational and training programs and financial and marketing assistance.

Small Business Advocate, Industry-Business and Community Services, South Carolina State Development Board, P.O. Box 927, Columbia, SC 29202; 803-734-1400. Provides assistance in cutting bureaucratic red tape, as well as information and expertise in dealing with state, federal, and local agencies.

Small Business Development Centers

The following offices offer free and fee-based services to new and expanding businesses:

Lead Center: South Carolina Small Business Development Center, University of South Carolina, College of Business Administration, Columbia, SC 29208; 803-777-4907, Fax: 803-777-4403.

Alkan: University of South Carolina, Alkan Office, Small Business Development Center, 171 University Pkwy., Suite 100, School of Business, Alkan, SC 29801, 803-641-3646.

Beaufort: University of South Carolina at Beaufort, Small Business Development Center, 801 Carterat Street, Beaufort, SC 29902, 803-521-4143; Fax: 803-521-4198.

Charleston: Charleston SBDC, 901 E. Bay St., Suite 539, P.O. Box 20339, Charleston, SC 29413-0339, 803-727-2020; Fax: 803-727-2013.

Clemson: Clemson University, Small Business Development Center, 425 Sirrine Hall, Clemson, SC 29634-1392, 803-656-3227; Fax: 803-656-4869.

Columbia: University of South Carolina, USC Regional Small Business Development Center, College of Business Administration, Columbia, SC 29208, 803-777-5118; Fax: 803-777-4403.

Conway: Coastal Carolina, Small Business Development Center, School of Business Administration, Conway, SC 29526, 803-349-2170; Fax: 803-349-2445.

Florence: Florence Darlington Technical College, Small Business Development Center, P.O. Box 100548, Florence, SC 29501-0548, 803-661-8256; Fax: 803-661-8041.

Greenville: Greenville Chamber of Commerce, Small Business Development Center, 24 Cleveland St., Greenville, SC 29606, 803-239-3753; Fax: 803-282-8549.

Greenwood: Upper Savannah Council of Governments, Small Business Development Center, SBDC Exchange Building, 222 Phoenix Street, P.O. Box 1366, Greenwood, SC 29648, 803-227-6110; Fax: 803-229-1869.

Hilton Head: University of South Carolina at Hilton Head, Small Business Development Center, Suite 300, Kiawah Bldg., 10 Office Park Road, Hilton Head, SC 29928, 803-785-3995; Fax: 803-777-0333.

Orangeburg: South Carolina State College, Small Business Development Center, School of Business, 300 College Ave., Orangeburg, SC 29117, 803-536-8445; Fax: 803-536-8066.

Rock Hill: Winthrop University, Small Business Development Center, 119 Thurmond Building, Rock Hill SC 29733, 803-323-2283, Fax: 803-323-3960.

Spartanburg: Spartanburg Chamber of Commerce, SBDC, P.O. Box 1636, 105 N. Pine St., Spartanburg, SC 29304, 803-594-5080; Fax: 803-594-5055.

South Dakota

General Information

Small Business Advocate, Governor's Office of Economic Development, 711 East Wells Avenue, Pierre, SD 57501-3369; 1-800-872-6190, 605-773-5032. Assistance in cutting bureaucratic red tape. Information and expertise in dealing with state, federal, and local agencies.

Small Business Development Centers

The following offices offer free and fee-based services to new and expanding businesses:

Lead Center: South Dakota Small Business Development Center, University of South Dakota, 414 East Clark, Vermillion, SD 57069-2390; 605-677-5549, Fax: 605-677-5272.

Aberdeen: Small Business Development Center, 226 Citizens Building, Aberdeen, SD 57401, 605-662-2252.

Pierre: Small Business Development Center, 105 South Euclid, Suite C, Pierre, SD 57501, 605-773-5941.

Rapid City: Small Business Development Center, 444 Mount Rushmore Road, Rapid City, SD 57709, 605-394-5311.

Sioux Falls: Small Business Development Center, 200 North Phillips, L103, Sioux Falls, SD 57102, 605-330-5756.

Tennessee

General Information

Office of Small Business, Department of Economic and Community Development, Rachel Jackson State Office Building, 320 Sixth Avenue North, Nashville, TN 37243-0405; 615-741-2626. Serves as an advocate for the small business community. Acts as a clearinghouse on programs and projects in both the public and private sectors that assist small business.

Small Business Advocate, Office of Small Business, Department of Economic and Community Development, Rachel Jackson State Office Building, 320 Sixth Avenue North, Nashville, TN 37243-0405; 615-741-2626. Assistance in cutting bureaucratic red tape. Information and expertise in dealing with state, federal, and local agencies.

Small Business Development Centers

The following offices offer free and fee-based services to new and expanding businesses:

Lead Center: Tennessee Small Business Development Center, Memphis State University, South Campus (Getwell Road), Building #1, Memphis, TN 38152; 901-678-2500, Fax: 901-678-4072.

Chattanooga: Chattanooga State Technical Community College, Small Business Development Center, 4501 Amnicola Highway, Chattanooga, TN 37406-1097, 615-697-4410; Fax: 615-698-5653.

Chattanooga: Southeast Tennessee Development District, Small Business Development Center, 25 Cherokee Blvd., Chattanooga, TN 37405, 615-266-5781; Fax: 615-267-7705.

Clarksville: Austin Peay State University, Small Business Development Center, College of Business, Clarksville, TN 37044-0001, 615-648-7764; Fax: 615-648-7475.

Cleveland: Cleveland State Community College, SBDC, Business and Technology, P.O. Box 3570, Cleveland, TN 37320-3570, 615-478-6247; Fax: 615-478-6251.

Columbia: Small Business Development Center, Memorial Building, Room 205, 308 West 7th Street, Columbia, TN 38401, 615-388-5674.

Cookeville: Tennessee Technological University, Small Business Development Center, College of Business Administration, P.O. Box 5023, Cookeville, TN 38505-0001, 615-372-3648; Fax: 615-372-6112.

Dyersburg: Dyersburg Community College, Small Business Development Center, P.O. Box 648, Dyersburg, TN 38024, 901-286-3200; Fax: 901-286-3201.

Hartsville: Four Lakes Regional Industrial Development Authority, Small Business Development Center, P.O. Box 63, Hartsville, TN 37074-0063, 615-374-9521; Fax: 615-374-4608.

Jackson: Jackson State Community College, Small Business Development Center, 2046 North Parkway Street, Jackson, TN 38310-3797, 901-424-5389; Fax: 901-425-2647.

Johnson City: East Tennessee State University, SBDC, College of Business, P.O. Box 70, 698A, Johnson City, TN 37614-0698, 615-929-5630; Fax: 615-929-5274.

Knoxville: Pellissippi State Technical Community College, SBDC, P.O. Box 22990, Knoxville, TN 37933-0990, 615-694-6660; Fax: 615-694-6583.

Knoxville: International Trade Center, 301 E. Church Avenue, Knoxville, TN 37915, 615-637-4283.

Memphis: Memphis State University, Small Business Development Center, 320 South Dudley Street, Memphis, TN 38104-3206, 901-527-1041; Fax: 901-527-1047.

Memphis: Memphis State University, Small Business Development Center, International Trade Center, Memphis, TN 38152, 901-678-4174; Fax: 901-678-4072.

Morristown: Walters State Community College, Small Business Development Center, Business/Industrial Services, 500 S. Davy Crockett Parkway, Morristown, TN 37813-688, 615-587-9722; Fax: 615-586-1918.

Murfreesboro: Middle Tennessee State University, Small Business Development Center, School of Business, P.O. Box 487, Murfreesboro, TN 37132, 615-898-2745; Fax: 615-898-5538.

Nashville: Tennessee State University, Small Business Development Center, School of Business, 330 10th Avenue North, Nashville, TN 37203-3401, 615-251-1178; Fax: 615-251-1178 (call first).

Texas

General Information

Texas Department of Commerce, Small Business Division, P.O. Box 12728, Austin, TX 78711; 512-472-5059, 1-800-888-0511. Provides business counseling for both new and established firms. Helps firms locate capital, state procurement opportunities, state certification program for minority and women-owned businesses, and resources for management and technical assistance. An Office of Business Permit Assistance serves as a clearinghouse for permit-related information throughout the state and refers applicants to appropriate agencies for permit and regulatory needs. Publications available containing information and resources for start-up and existing businesses.

Small Business Advocate, Texas Department of Commerce, Small Business Division, P.O. Box 12728, Austin, TX 78711; 512-472-5059, 1-800-888-0511. Assistance in cutting bureaucratic red tape. Information and expertise in dealing with state, federal, and local agencies.

Small Business Development Centers

The following offices offer free and fee-based services to new and expanding businesses:

Lead Center: North Texas Small Business Development Center, Dallas County Community College, 1402 Corinth Street, Dallas, TX 75215; 214-565-5835, Fax: 214-565-5857.

Be patient. If any phone number is incorrect, call (area code) 555-1212 and request the new listing.

745

Small Business and Entrepreneuring

Lead Center: Houston Small Business Development Center, University of Houston, 1100 Louisiana, Suite 500, Houston, TX 77002; 713-752-8444, Fax: 713-752-8484.

Lead Center: Northwest Texas Small Business Development Center, Center for Innovation, 2579 South Loop 289, Suite 114, Lubbock, TX 79423; 806-745-3973, Fax: 806-745-6207.

Lead Center: South Texas Border Small Business Development Center, University of Texas at San Antonio, 801 S. Bowie, San Antonio, TX 78205; 210-558-2450.

Abilene: Abilene Christian University, Caruth Small Business Development Center, College of Business Administration, ACU Station, Box 8307, Abilene, TX 79699, 915-674-2776; Fax: 915-674-2507.

Alvin: Alvin Community College, Small Business Development Center, 3110 Mustang Road, Alvin, TX 77511-4898, 713-338-4686; Fax: 713-388-4903.

Amarillo: West Texas State University, Panhandle Small Business Development Center, T. Boone Pickens School of Business, 1800 South Washington, Suite 110, Amarillo, TX 79102, 806-372-5151.

Athens: Trinity Valley Small Business Development Center, 500 South Prairieville, Athens, TX 75751, 903-675-7403; Fax: 903-675-6316.

Austin: Austin Small Business Development Center, 221 South IH 35, Suite 103, Austin, TX 78741, 512-326-2256; Fax: 512-447-9825.

Baytown: Lee College, SBDC, P.O. Box 818, Baytown, TX 77522-4703, 713-425-6309; Fax: 713-425-6307.

Beaumont: John Gray Institute/Lamar University, Small Business Development Center, 855 Florida Ave., Beaumont, TX 77705, 409-880-2367; Fax: 409-880-2201; 1-800-722-3443.

Bonham: Bonham Small Business Development Center (Satellite), Sam Raybourn Center, Bonham, TX 75418, 903-583-4811.

Brenham: Blinn College, Small Business Development Center, 902 College Ave., Brenham, TX 77833, 409-830-4137; Fax: 409-830-4116.

Bryan: Bryan/College Station Chamber of Commerce, Small Business Development Ctr., P.O. Box 3695, Bryan, TX 77806, 409-260-5222.

Corpus Christi: Corpus Christi Chamber of Commerce, Small Business Development Center, 1201 North Shoreline, Corpus Christi, TX 78403, 512-882-6161; Fax: 512-888-5627.

Corsicana: Navarro Small Business Development Center, 120 North 12th Street, Corsicana, TX 75110, 903-874-0658; Fax: 903-874-4187.

Dallas: International Business Center, 2050 Stemmons Freeway, World Trade Center, Suite #150, P.O. Box 58299, Dallas, TX 75258, 214-653-1777; Fax: 214-748-5774.

Denison: Grayson Small Business Development Center, 6101 Grayson Drive, Denison, TX 75020, 903-786-3551; Fax: 903-463-5284.

Denton: Denton Small Business Development Center (Satellite), P.O. Drawer P, Denton, TX 76202, 817-382-7151; Fax: 817-382-0040.

DeSoto: Best Southwest Small Business Development Center, 1001 N. Beckley, Suite 606D, DeSoto, TX 75115, 214-228-3783.

Edinburg: University of Texas/Pan American, Small Business Development Center, 1201 West University Drive, Edinburg, TX 78539-2999, 512-381-3361; Fax: 512-381-2322.

El Paso: El Paso Community College, Small Business Development Center, 103 Montana Avenue, Room 202, El Paso, TX 79902-3929, 915-534-3410; Fax: 915-534-3420.

Fort Worth: Tarrant Small Business Development Center, 1500 Houston Street, Room 163, 7917 Highway 80 West, Fort Worth, TX 76102, 817-244-7158; Fax: 817-877-9295.

Gainesville: Cooke Small Business Development Center, 1525 West California, Gainesville, TX 76240, 817-665-4785; Fax: 817-668-6049.

Galveston: Galveston College, Small Business Development Center, 4015 Avenue Q, Galveston, TX 77550, 409-740-7380; Fax: 409-740-7381.

Hillsboro: Hillsboro Small Business Development Center (Satellite), SOS Building, P.O. Box 619, Hillsboro, TX 76645, 817-582-2555, ext. 282.

Houston: North Harris Community College District, SBDC, 250 N. Sam Houston Parkway, Houston, TX 77060, 713-591-9320; Fax: 713-591-3513; 1-800-443-SBDC.

Huntsville: Sam Houston State University, SBDC, College of Business Administration, P.O. Box 2058, Huntsville, TX 77341, 409-294-3737; Fax: 409-294-3612.

Kingsville: Kingsville Chamber of Commerce, Small Business Development Center, 635 East King, Kingsville, TX 78363, 512-595-5088; Fax: 512-592-0866.

Lake Jackson: Brazosport College, SBDC, 500 College Drive, Lake Jackson, TX 77566, 409-266-3380.

Laredo: Laredo Development Foundation, SBDC, 616 Leal Street, Laredo, TX 78041, 512-722-0563.

Longview: Kilgore College, Small Business Development Center, 300 South High, Longview, TX 75601, 903-757-5857; Fax: 903-753-7920.

Lubbock: Texas Tech University, SBDC, Center for Innovation, 2579 South Loop 289, Suite 114, Lubbock, TX 79423, 806-745-1637; Fax: 806-745-6207.

Lufkin: Angelina Community College, SBDC, P.O. Box 1768, Lufkin, TX 75902, 409-639-1887; Fax: 409-639-4299.

Mt. Pleasant: Northeast Texarkana Small Business Development Center, P.O. Box 1307, Mt. Pleasant, TX 75455, 214-572-1911; Fax: 903-572-6712.

Odessa: University of Texas/Permian Basin, Small Business Development Center, 4901 East University, Odessa, TX 79762, 915-563-0400; Fax: 915-561-5534.

Paris: Paris Small Business Development Center, 2400 Clarksville Street, Paris, TX 75460, 214-784-1802; Fax: 903-784-1801.

Plano: Collin County Small Business Development Center, Plano Market Square, 1717 East Spring Creek Parkway, #109, Plano, TX 75074, 214-881-0506; Fax: 214-423-3956.

San Angelo: Angelo State University, Small Business Development Center, 2610 West Avenue N, Campus Box 10910, San Angelo, TX 76909, 915-942-2119; Fax: 915-942-2038.

San Antonio: UTSA, International Small Business Development Center, 801 S. Bowie, San Antonio, TX 78205, 512-227-2997; Fax: 512-222-9834.

Stafford: Houston Community College System, Small Business Development Center, 13600 Murphy Road, Stafford, TX 77477, 713-499-4870; Fax: 713-499-8194.

Stephenville: Tarleton State University, Small Business Development Center, Box T-158, Stephenville, TX 76402, 817-968-9330; Fax: 817-968-9329.

Texas City: College of the Mainland, Small Business Development Center, 8419 Emmett F. Lowry Expressway, Texas City, TX 77591, 409-938-7578; Fax: 409-935-5816.

Tyler: Tyler Small Business Development Center, 1530 South SW Loop 323, Suite 100, Tyler, TX 75701, 903-510-2975; Fax: 903-510-2978.

Victoria: University of Houston-Victoria, Small Business Development Center, 700 Main Center, Suite 102, Victoria, TX 77901, 512-575-8944; Fax: 512-575-8852.

Waco: McLennan Small Business Development Center, 4601 North 19th Street, Waco, TX 76708, 817-750-3600; Fax: 817-756-0776.

Wharton: Wharton County Junior College, Small Business Development Center, Administration Building, Room 102, 911 Boling Highway, Wharton, TX 77488-0080, 409-532-0604; Fax: 409-532-2201.

Wichita Fall: Midwestern State University, Small Business Development Center, Division of Business, 3400 Taft Blvd., Wichita Falls, TX 76308, 817-696-6738; Fax: 817-689-4374.

Utah

General Information

One-Stop Service Center, State Tax Commission, Heber M. Wells Building, First Floor, 160 East 300 South, Salt Lake City, UT 84134; 801-530-4848 (recording). You can register a business name, file Articles of Incorporation, obtain application for State Sales Tax License and State and Federal Tax Identification Numbers, file a Status Report with the Department of Employment Security, and apply for State Workers' Compensation Insurance. A *Going Into Business Workbook* is also available which includes all the forms and instructions necessary to do any of these activities.

Small Business Advocate, Utah Small Business Development Center, 102 W. 500 South, Suite 315, Salt Lake City, UT 84101-2315; 801-581-7905. Assistance in cutting bureaucratic red tape. Information and expertise in dealing with state, federal, and local agencies.

Small Business Development Centers

The following offices offer free and fee-based services to new and expanding businesses:

Lead Center: Utah Small Business Development Center, University of Utah, 102 West 500 South, Suite 315, Salt Lake City, UT 84101; 801-581-7905, Fax: 801-581-7814.

Cedar City: Southern Utah University, Small Business Development Center, 351 West Center, Cedar City, UT 84720, 801-586-5400; Fax: 801-586-5493.

Ephraim: Snow College, Small Business Development Center, 345 West 100 North, Ephraim, UT 84627, 801-283-4021; 801-283-6890; Fax: 801-283-6913.

Logan: Utah State University, Small Business Development Center, East Campus Building, Logan, UT 84322-8330, 801-797-2277; Fax: 801-797-3317.

Ogden: Weber State University, Small Business Development Center, College of Business and Economics, Ogden, UT 84408-3806, 801-626-7232; Fax: 801-626-7423.

Price: College of Eastern Utah, Small Business Development Center, 451 East 400 North, Price, UT 84501, 801-637-1995; Fax: 801-637-4102.

Orem/Provo: Utah State College, Small Business Development Center, School of Management, 800 W. 200 S, Orem, UT 84058, 801-222-8230; Fax: 801-225-1128.

Roosevelt: Uintah Basin Applied Technology Center, Small Business Development Center, 1100 East Lagoon, P.O. Box 124-5, Roosevelt, UT 84066, 801-722-4523; Fax: 801-722-5804.

St. George: Dixie College, Small Business Development Center, 225 South 700 East, St. George, UT 84770, 801-673-4811 ext 353; Fax: 801-673-8552.

Vermont

General Information

Vermont Economic Development Department, 109 State St, 4th Floor, Montpelier, VT 05609; 802-828-3221, 1-800-622-4553 in Vermont, Fax: 802-828-3258.

Small Business Advocate, Vermont Agency of Development and Community Affairs, 109 State Street, Montpelier, VT 05609; 802-828-3211. Assistance in cutting bureaucratic red tape. Information and expertise in dealing with state, federal, and local agencies.

Small Business Development Centers

The following offices offer free and fee-based services to new and expanding businesses:

Lead Center: Vermont Small Business Development Center, Vermont Tech. College, P.O. Box 422, Randolph, VT 05060-0422; 802-464-7232, Fax: 802-728-3026.

Burlington: Northwestern Vermont Small Business Development Center, 60 Main St, Suite 101, P.O. Box 786-GBIC, Burlington, VT 05402-0786, 802-658-9228; Fax: 802-860-1899.

Rutland: Southwestern Vermont Small Business Development Center, 256 N. Main St., REDC, Rutland, VT 05701-2413, 802-773-9147; Fax: 802-773-2772.

Springfield: Southeastern Vermont Small Business Development Center, Clinton Square-SRDC, P.O. Box 58, Springfield, VT 05156-0058, 802-885-2071; Fax: 802-885-3027.

St. Johnsbury: Northeastern Vermont Small Business Development Center, 44 Main St.,-NVDA, P.O. Box 640, St. Johnsbury, VT 05819-0640, 802-748-5181; Fax: 802-748-1223.

White River Jct: Central Vermont Small Business Development Center, P.O. Box 246, White River Jct., VT 05001, 802-295-3710; Fax: 802-295-3779.

Virginia

General Information

Department of Economic Development, Office of Small Business, P.O. Box 798, Richmond, VA 23206-0798; 804-371-8252. Helps new or expanding business by answering questions about licensing, taxes, regulations, assistance programs, etc. The office can also locate sources of information in other state agencies, and it also can identify sources of help for business planning, management, exporting, and financing.

Small Business Advocate, Department of Economic Development, Office of Small Business, P.O. Box 798, Richmond, VA 23206-0798; 804-371-8252. Assistance in cutting bureaucratic red tape. Information and expertise in dealing with state, federal, and local agencies.

Virginia Employment Commission Economic Information Services Division, 703 E. Main St., P.O. Box 1358, Richmond, VA 23211; 804-786-3047. Publishes the *Virginia Business Resource Directory*, a comprehensive source of information on every aspect of doing business in the state, from business planning, management and personnel issues to sources of finance, marketing assistance, and regulations and licenses.

Small Business Development Centers

The following offices offer free and fee-based services to new and expanding businesses:

Lead Center: Virginia Small Business Development Center, P.O. Box 798, Richmond, VA 23206-0798; 804-371-8253, Fax: 804-225-3384.

Abingdon: VA Highland Community College, Small Business Development Center, P.O. Box 828, Abingdon, VA 24212, 703-964-7345; Fax: 703-964-9307.

Arlington: George Mason University/Arlington Campus, Small Business Development Center, 3401 N. Fairfax Dr., Arlington, VA 22201, 703-993-8129; Fax: 703-993-8130.

Big Stone Gap: Mt. Empire Community College, Southwest Small Business Development Center, Drawer 700, Route 23, Big Stone Gap, VA 24219, 703-523-6529; Fax: 703-523-4130.

Blacksburg: Western Virginia Small Business Development Center Consortium, VPI and SU, Economic Development Assistance Center, 404 Clay Street, Blacksburg, VA 24061-0539, 703-231-5278; Fax: 703-231-8850.

Blacksburg: New River Valley Small Business Development Center, 234 Donaldson Brown Center, Virginia Tech., Blacksburg, VA 24061-0539, 703-231-5278/231-4004; Fax: 703-231-8850.

Charlottesville: Central Virginia Small Business Development Center, 918 Emmet Street North, Suite 200, Charlottesville, VA 22903, 804-295-8198, Fax: 804-295-7066.

Fairfax: Northern Virginia Small Business Development Center, 4260 Chainbridge Road, Suite A-1, Fairfax, VA 22030, 703-993-2131; Fax: 703-993-2126.

Farmville: Longwood College, 515 Main St., Small Business Development Center, Farmville, VA 24592, 804-395-2086, Fax: 804-395-2359.

Fredericksburg: Rappahannock Region SBDC, 1301 College Ave., Seacobeck Hall, Fredericksburg, VA 22401, 703-899-4076.

Be patient. If any phone number is incorrect, call (area code) 555-1212 and request the new listing.

747

Small Business and Entrepreneuring

Harrisonburg: James Madison University, Small Business Development Center, College of Business Building, Room 523, Harrisonburg, VA 22807, 703-568-3227; Fax: 703-568-3399.

Lynchburg: Lynchburg Regional Small Business Development Center, 147 Mill Ridge Road, Lynchburg, VA 24502, 804-582-6170; Fax: 804-582-6106.

Manassas: Small Business Development Center, Dr. William E.S. Flory, 10311 Sudley Manor Drive, Manassas, VA 22110, 703-335-2500; Fax: 703-335-1700.

Middletown: Lord Fairfax Community College, Small Business Development Center, P.O. Box 47, Middletown, VA 22645, 703-869-6649; Fax: 703-869-7881.

Norfolk: Hampton Roads Inc., Small Business Development Center, P.O. Box 327, 420 Bank Street, Norfolk, VA 23501, 804-622-6414; Fax: 804-622-5563.

Richlands: Southwest Virginia Community College, Small Business Development Center, P.O. Box SVCC, Richlands, VA 24641, 703-964-7345; Fax: 703-964-9307.

Richmond: Capital Area Small Business Development Center, 403 East Grace Street, Richmond, VA 23219, 804-648-7838; Fax: 804-648-7849.

Roanoke: The Blue Ridge Small Business Development Center, 310 First Street, Southwest Mezzanine, Roanoke, VA 24011, 703-983-0717; Fax: 703-983-0723.

South Boston: South Boston Small Business Development Center, P.O. Box 1116, 515 Broad Street, South Boston, VA 24596, 804-575-0044, Fax: 804-572-4087.

Sterling: Loudoun County Small Business Development Center, 21515 Ridgetop Circle, Suite 220, Sterling, VA 22170, 703-430-7222; Fax: 703-430-9562.

Warsaw: Warsaw Small Business Development Center, P.O. Box 490, 106 W. Richmond Rd., Warsaw, VA 22572, 804-333-0286, 804-333-0183, 800-524-8915; Fax: 804-333-0187.

Wytheville: Wytheville Community College, Small Business Development Center, 1000 E. Main Street, Wytheville, VA 24382, 703-228-5541, ext 314; Fax: 703-228-2541.

Washington

General Information

Business Assistance Center, Department of Trade and Economic Development, 2001 6th Avenue, Suite 2600, Seattle, WA 98121; 206-464-7350, 1-800-237-1233 in Washington. Services available are a Business Assistance Hotline, an Ombudsperson to assist with business/government dilemmas, a variety of publications, and an Electronic Bulletin Board, 206-441-5472, for quick computer access to business information.

Small Business Advocates, Washington State Business Assistance Center, 919 Lakeridge Way, Southwest, Suite A, Olympia, WA 98502; 206-753-5632. Assistance in cutting bureaucratic red tape. Information and expertise in dealing with state, federal, and local agencies.

Small Business Development Centers

The following offices offer free and fee-based services to new and expanding businesses:

Lead Center: Washington Small Business Development Center, Washington State University, 245 Todd Hall, Pullman, WA 99164-4727; 509-335-1576, Fax: 509-335-0949.

Aberdeen: Grays Harbor College, Small Business Development Center, 1602 Edward P. Smith Drive, Aberdeen, WA 98520, 206-532-9020.

Bellevue: Bellevue Community College, Small Business Development Center, 3000 Landerholm Circle, Bellevue, WA 98009, 206-641-2265; Fax: 206-453-3032.

Bellingham: Western Washington University, Small Business Development Center, College of Business and Economics, 415 Park Hall, Bellingham, WA 98225, 206-676-3899; Fax: 509-647-4844.

Centralia: Centralia Community College, Small Business Development Center, 600 West Locust Street, Centralia, WA 98531, 206-736-9391; Fax: 206-753-3404.

Everett: Edmonds Community College, Small Business Development Center, 917 134th Street, SW, Everett, WA 98204, 206-745-0430; Fax: 206-745-5563.

Moses Lake: Big Bend Community College, Small Business Development Center, 7662 Chanute St., Bldg. 1500, Moses Lake, WA 98837-3299, 509-762-6239; Fax: 509-762-6329.

Mt. Vernon: Skagit Valley College, Small Business Development Center, 2405 College Way, Mt. Vernon, WA 98273, 206-428-1282; Fax: 206-428-1186.

Olympia: South Puget Sound Community College, Small Business Development Center, 2011 Mottman Road SW, Olympia, WA 98501, 206-754-7711; Fax: 206-586-6054.

Omak: Wenatchee Valley College, Small Business Development Center, P.O. Box 1042, Omak, WA 98841, 509-826-5107; Fax: 509-826-4604.

Pasco: Columbia Basin College, Small Business Development Center, 2600 North 20th, Pasco, WA 99301, 509-547-0511; Fax: 509-546-0401.

Seattle: South Seattle Community College, Small Business Development Center, 6000 16th Avenue, SW, Seattle, WA 98106, 206-764-5339; Fax: 206-764-5393.

Seattle: Washington State University at Seattle, Small Business Development Center, 2001 Sixth Avenue, Suite 2608, Seattle, WA 98121-2518, 206-464-5450.

Seattle: North Seattle Community College, Small Business Development Center, International Trade Institute, 9600 College Way North, Seattle, WA 98103, 206-527-3732; Fax: 206-527-3734.

Spokane: Community College of Spokane, Small Business Development Center, West 601 First, Spokane, WA 99204, 509-459-3741; Fax: 509-459-3433.

Tacoma: Washington State University at Tacoma, Small Business Development Center, 950 Pacific Avenue, Suite 300, Box 1933, Tacoma, WA 98401-1933, 206-272-7232; Fax: 206-597-7305.

Tacoma: Pierce College, Small Business Development Center, 9401 Farwest Drive, SW, Tacoma, WA 98498, 206-964-6776; Fax: 206-964-6746.

Vancouver: Columbia River Economic Development Council, SBDC, 100 E. Columbia Way, Vancouver, WA 98660-3156, 206-693-2555; Fax: 206-694-9927.

Wenatchee: Wenatchee Valley College, Small Business Development Center, 1300 Fifth Street, Wenatchee, WA 98801, 509-662-1651; Fax: 206-764-5393.

Yakima: Yakima Valley Community College, Small Business Development Center, P.O. Box 1647, Yakima, WA 98907, 509-575-2284; Fax: 509-575-2461.

West Virginia

General Information

Small Business Development Center, 1115 Virginia Street E, Charleston, WV 25301; 304-558-2960. Acts as a one-stop resource center for information and assistance in filing state and federal forms and coordinates assistance programs with other agencies.

Small Business Advocate, Small Business Development Center, 1115 Virginia Street E, Charleston, WV 25301; 304-558-2960. Assistance in cutting bureaucratic red tape. Information and expertise in dealing with state, federal, and local agencies.

Small Business Development Centers

The following offices offer free and fee-based services to new and expanding businesses:

Lead Center: West Virginia Small Business Development Center, West Virginia Development Office, 950 Kanawha Blvd., Charleston, WV 25301; 304-558-2960, Fax: 304-558-0127.

Athens: Concord College, Small Business Development Center, Box D-125, Athens, WV 24712, 304-384-5103.

Fairmont: Fairmont State College, Small Business Development Center, Fairmont, WV 26554, 304-367-4125.

Huntington: Marshall University, Small Business Development Center, 1050 Fourth Avenue, Huntington, WV 25755, 304-696-6789.

Montgomery: West Virginia Institute of Technology, Small Business Development Center, Room 102, Engineering Building, Montgomery, WV 25136, 304-442-5501.

Morgantown: West Virginia University, Small Business Development Center, P.O. Box 6025, Morgantown, WV 26506, 304-293-5839.

Parkersburg: West Virginia University at Parkersburg, Small Business Development Center, Route 5, Box 167-A, Parkersburg, WV 26101, 304-424-8277.

Shepherdstown: Shepherd College, Small Business Development Center, 120 North Princess Street, Shepherdstown, WV 25443, 304-876-5261.

Wheeling: West Virginia Northern Community College, Small Business Development Center, College Square, Wheeling, WV 26003, 304-233-5900; ext. 206.

Wisconsin

General Information

One-Stop Business Hotline, Permit Information Center, Department of Development, P.O. Box 7970, Madison, WI 53707; 608-266-1018, Fax: 608-267-2829, 1-800-HELP-BUS. Coordinates state regulatory and business development needs by providing information on permit requirements, expedition of permit issuance, monitoring of a permit's progress in the bureaucracy, and recommending improvements in the permit process.

Small Business Ombudsman Program, Department of Development, P.O. Box 7970, Madison, WI 53707; 608-266-1018, Fax: 608-267-2829. Provides information and referral to new businesses regarding government regulations, management assistance and financing.

Small Business Advocate, Bureau of Advocacy, Department of Development, P.O. Box 7970, Madison, WI 53707; 608-266-1018. Assistance in cutting bureaucratic red tape. Information and expertise in dealing with state, federal, and local agencies.

Small Business Development Centers

The following offices offer free and fee-based services to new and expanding businesses:

Lead Center: Wisconsin Small Business Development Center, University of Wisconsin, 432 N. Lake Street, Room 423, Madison, WI 53706; 608-263-7794, Fax: 608-262-3878.

Eau Claire: University of Wisconsin at Eau Claire, Small Business Development Center, Schneider Hall, #113, Eau Claire, WI 54701, 715-836-5637.

Green Bay: University of Wisconsin at Green Bay, Small Business Development Center, 460 Wood Hall, Green Bay, WI 54302, 414-465-2089.

La Crosse: University of Wisconsin at LaCrosse, Small Business Development Center, School of Business, 323 N. Hall, La Crosse, WI 54601, 608-785-8782.

Madison: University of Wisconsin at Madison, Small Business Development Center, 3260 Grainger Hall, Madison, WI 53715, 608-263-2221.

Milwaukee: University of Wisconsin at Milwaukee, Small Business Development Center, 929 North Sixth Street, Milwaukee, WI 53203, 414-227-3240.

Oshkosh: University of Wisconsin at Oshkosh, Small Business Development Center, 157 Clow Faculty, Oshkosh, WI 54901, 414-424-1453.

Stevens Point: University of Wisconsin at Stevens Point, Small Business Development Center, Main Building, Stevens Point, WI 54481, 715-346-2004.

Superior: University of Wisconsin at Superior, Small Business Development Center, 29 Sundquist Hall, Superior, WI 54880, 715-394-8351.

Whitewater: University of Wisconsin at Whitewater, Small Business Development Center, 2000 Carlson Building, Whitewater, WI 53190, 414-472-3217.

Wyoming

General Information

Division of Economic and Community Development, Department of Commerce, Barrett Building, 4th Floor North, Cheyenne, WY 82002; 307-777-7284, Fax: 307-777-5840, 1-800-262-3425. Provides information on Wyoming's favorable tax structure and corporation laws.

Business Permit Coordinator (Small Business Advocate), Division of Economic and Community Development, Department of Commerce, Barrett Building, 4th Floor North, Cheyenne, WY 82002; 307-777-7284, Fax: 307-777-5840, 1-800-262-3425. Assistance in cutting bureaucratic red tape. Information and expertise in dealing with state, federal, and local agencies. Publishes a comprehensive guide to permits and licensing.

Small Business Reports, Business Development Officer, Division of Economic and Community Development, Department of Commerce, Barrett Building, 4th Floor North, Cheyenne, WY 82002; 307-777-7284, Fax: 307-777-5840, 1-800-262-3425. Designed to help small businesses deal with basic business issues.

Small Business Development Centers

The following offices offer free and fee-based services to new and expanding businesses:

Lead Center: Wyoming Small Business Development Center, 111 West 2nd Street, Suite 416, Casper, WY 82601; 800-348-5207, 307-234-6683, Fax: 307-577-7014.

Cheyenne: Laramie County Community College, Small Business Development Center, 1400 East College Drive, Cheyenne, WY 82007, 307-632-6141, 800-348-5208; Fax: 307-632-6061.

Laramie: University of Wyoming, Small Business Development Center, P.O. Box 3620, University Station, Laramie, WY 82071, 307-766-3050, 800-348-5194; Fax: 307-766-3406.

Powell: Northwest Community College, Small Business Development Center, John DeWitt Student Center, Powell, WY 82435, 307-754-6067, 800-348-5203; Fax: 307-754-6069.

Rock Springs: Wyoming Small Business Development Center, P.O. Box 1168, Rock Springs, WY 82902, 307-352-6894, 800-348-5205; Fax: 307-352-6876.

Federal Money for Business

* See also Careers and Workplace; Research Grants in Every Field

The following is a description of the federal funds available to small businesses, entrepreneurs, inventors, and researchers. This information is derived from the *Catalog of Federal Domestic Assistance* which is published by the U.S. Government Printing Office in Washington, DC. The number next to the title description is the official reference for this federal program. Contact the office listed below the caption for further details. The following is a description of the terms used for the types of assistance available:

Loans: money lent by a federal agency for a specific period of time and with a reasonable expectation of repayment. Loans may or may not require payment of interest.

Loan Guarantees: programs in which federal agencies agree to pay back part or all of a loan to a private lender if the borrower defaults.

Grants: money given by federal agencies for a fixed period of time and which does not have to be repaid.

Direct Payments: funds provided by federal agencies to individuals, private firms, and institutions. The use of direct payments may be "specified" to perform a particular service or for "unrestricted" use.

Insurance: coverage under specific programs to assure reimbursement for losses sustained. Insurance may be provided by federal agencies or through insurance companies and may or may not require the payment of premiums.

* Grants to Producers of Honey, Cotton, Rice, Soybeans, Canole, Flaxseed, Mustard Seed, Rapeseed, Safflower, Sunflower Seed, Feed Grains, Wheat, Rye, Peanuts, Tobacco, and Dairy Products.

(10.051 Commodity Loans and Purchases)
Cotton, Grain and Rice Price Support Division
Agricultural Stabilization and Conservation Service
U.S. Department of Agriculture
P.O. Box 2415
Washington, DC 20013   202-720-7641

Objectives: To improve and stabilize farm income, to assist in bringing about a better balance between supply and demand of the commodities, and to assist farmers in the orderly marketing of their crops. Types of assistance: direct payments with unrestricted use; direct loans. Estimate of annual funds available: Commodity purchases: $1,096,976,000; Loans: $8,336,213,000.

* Grants to Producers of Cotton

(10.052 Cotton Production Stabilization)
Deputy Administrator
Policy Analysis
Agricultural Stabilization and Conservation Service
P.O. Box 2415
U.S. Department of Agriculture
Washington, DC 20013   202-720-7583

Objectives: To assure adequate production for domestic and foreign demand for fiber, to protect income for farmers, to take into account federal costs, to enhance the competitiveness of U.S. cotton for domestic mill use and export, and to conserve our natural resources. Types of assistance: direct payments with unrestricted use. Estimate of annual funds available: Direct cash and certificate payments: $363,054,000.

* Grants to Dairy Farmers Whose Milk Is Contaminated Because of Pesticides

(10.053 Dairy Indemnity Program)
Emergency Operations and Livestock Program Division
Agricultural Stabilization and Conservation Service
U.S. Department of Agriculture

P.O. Box 2415
Washington, DC 20013   202-720-7673

Objectives: To protect dairy farmers and manufacturers of dairy products who through no fault of their own, are directed to remove their milk or dairy products from commercial markets because of contamination from pesticides which have been approved for use by the federal government. Dairy farmers can also be indemnified because of contamination with chemicals or toxic substances, nuclear radiation or fallout. Types of assistance: direct payments with unrestricted use. Estimate of annual funds available: Direct payments: $200,000.

* Grants to Producers of Corn, Sorghum, Barley, Oats, and Rye

(10.055 Feed Grain Production Stabilization)
Deputy Administrator
Policy Analysis
Agricultural Stabilization and Conservation Service
U.S. Department of Agriculture
P.O. Box 2415
Washington, DC 20013   202-720-4418

Objectives: To assure adequate production for domestic and foreign demand, to protect income for farmers, to take into account federal costs, to enhance the competitiveness of United States exports, to combat inflation, to conserve our natural resources, and to comply with statutory requirements. Types of assistance: direct payments with unrestricted use. Estimate of annual funds available: Direct cash and certificate payments: $2,017,300,000.

* Grants to Producers of Wheat

(10.058 Wheat Production Stabilization)
Deputy Administrator
Policy Analysis
Agricultural Stabilization and Conservation Service
U.S. Department of Agriculture
P.O. Box 2415
Washington, DC 20013   202-720-4418

Types of assistance: direct payments with unrestricted use. Estimate of annual funds available: Direct cash and certificate payments: $1,969,000,000.

* Grants to Producers of Wool and Mohair

(10.059 National Wool Act Payments)
Manager, Federal Crop Insurance Corporation
U.S. Department of Agriculture
2101 L Street NW, Suite 500
Washington, DC 20250
Mailing address:
Federal Crop Insurance Corporation
U.S. Department of Agriculture
Washington, DC 20250   202-254-8460

Objectives: To encourage continued domestic production of wool at prices fair to both producers and consumers in a manner which will assure a viable domestic wool industry in the future. Types of assistance: direct payments with unrestricted use. Estimate of annual funds available: Total indemnities: $979,412,000; Premium subsidy to farmers through direct writings and reinsured companies: $109,800,000.

* Grants to Producers of Rice

(10.065 Rice Production Stabilization)
Deputy Administrator
Policy Analysis
Agricultural Stabilization and Conservation Service
U.S. Department of Agriculture
P.O. Box 2415
Washington, DC 20013   202-720-7923

Objectives: To assure adequate production for domestic and foreign demand, to protect income for farmers, to take into account federal costs, to enhance the competitiveness of U.S. exports, and to conserve our natural resources. Types of assistance: direct payments with unrestricted use. Estimate of annual funds available: Direct cash and certificate payments: $844,500,000.

* Grants to Feed Livestock in an Emergency

(10.066 Emergency Livestock Assistance)
Emergency Operations and Livestock Programs Division
Agricultural Stabilization and Conservation Service
U.S. Department of Agriculture
P.O. Box 2415
Washington, DC 20013   202-720-5621

Objectives: To provide emergency feed assistance to eligible livestock owners, in a state, county, or area approved by the Executive Vice President, CCC, where because of disease, insect infestation, flood, drought, fire, hurricane, earthquake, hail storm, hot weather, cold weather, freeze, snow, ice, and winterkill, or other natural disaster, a livestock emergency has been determined to exist. These programs also provide feed assistance to eligible livestock owners for the preservation and maintenance of livestock in any county contiguous to a county where a livestock emergency has been determined to exist. Types of assistance: direct payments with unrestricted use. Estimate of annual funds available: Direct cash payments: $80,000,000.

* Grants to Producers of Grain

(10.067 Grain Reserve Program)
Manager
Federal Crop Insurance Corporation
U.S. Department of Agriculture
2101 L Street NW, Suite 500
Washington, DC 20250
Mailing address:
Federal Crop Insurance Corporation
U.S. Department of Agriculture
Washington, DC 20250   202-254-8460

Objectives: To insulate sufficient quantities of grain from the market to increase price to farmers. To improve and stabilize farm income and to assist farmers in the orderly marketing of their crops. Types of assistance: direct payments with unrestricted use. Estimate of annual funds available: Total indemnities: $979,412,000; Premium subsidy to farmers through direct writings and reinsured companies: $227,026,000.

* Money to Run an Agriculture Related Business, Recreation Related Business or Teenage Business

(10.406 Farm Operating Loans)
Director
Farm Credit Programs Loan Making Division
Consolidated Farm Service Agency
U.S. Department of Agriculture

Washington, DC 20250   202-720-1632

Objectives: To enable operators of not larger than family farms through the extension of credit and supervisory assistance, to make efficient use of their land, labor, and other resources. Types of assistance: direct loans; guaranteed/insured loans. Estimate of annual funds available: Direct Loans: $500,000,000; Guaranteed Loans: $1,735,000,000.

* Money to Farmers, Ranchers, and Aquaculture Businesses

(10.407 Farm Ownership Loans)
Administrator
Farmers Home Administration
U.S. Department of Agriculture
Washington, DC 20250   202-720-1632

Objectives: To assist eligible farmers, ranchers, and aquaculture operators, including farming cooperatives, corporations, partnerships, and joint operations, through the extension of credit and supervisory assistance to: Become owner-operators of not larger than family farms; make efficient use of the land, labor, and other resources; carry on sound and successful farming operations; and enable farm families to have a reasonable standard of living. Types of assistance: direct loans; guaranteed/ insured loans. Estimate of annual funds available: Direct Loans: $78,081,000; Guaranteed Loans: $540,674,000.

* Loans to Family Farms That Can't Get Credit

(10.437 Interest Assistance Program)
FmHA County Supervisor in the county where the proposed farming operation will be located
or
FmHA
U.S. Department of Agriculture
Washington, DC 20250

Objectives: To aid not larger than family sized farms in obtaining credit when they are temporarily unable to project a positive cash flow without a reduction in the interest rate. Types of assistance: guaranteed/insured loans. Estimate of annual funds available: Subsidized Guaranteed Loans: $230,000,000.

* Premium Subsidies to Agriculture

(10.450 Crop Insurance)
Manager
Federal Crop Insurance Corporation
U.S. Department of Agriculture
2101 L Street NW, Suite 500
Washington, DC 20250
Mailing address:
Federal Crop Insurance Corporation
U.S. Department of Agriculture
Washington, DC 20250   202-254-8460

Objectives: To promote the national welfare by improving the economic stability of agriculture through a sound system of crop insurance and providing the means for the research and experience helpful in devising and establishing such insurance. Types of assistance: insurance. Estimate of annual funds available: Total Indemnities: $1,435,921,000. Premium Subsidy: $690,094,000.

* Grants to Market Food Related Products Overseas

(10.600 Foreign Agricultural Market Development and Promotion)
Assistant Administrator
Commodity and Marketing Programs
Foreign Agricultural Service
U.S. Department of Agriculture
Washington, DC 20250   202-720-2705

Objectives: To create, expand, and maintain markets abroad for U.S. agricultural commodities. Types of assistance: direct payments for specified use (cooperative agreements). Estimate of annual funds available: Direct payments: $20,000,000 in 1995.

* Grants to Sell Food Related Products Overseas

(10.601 Market Promotion Program)
Assistant Administrator
Commodity and Marketing Programs
Foreign Agricultural Service
U.S. Department of Agriculture

Washington DC 20250   202-720-2705
Objectives: To encourage the development, maintenance, and expansion of commercial export markets for U.S. agricultural commodities through cost-share assistance to eligible trade organizations that implement a foreign market development program. Priority for assistance is provided for agricultural commodities or products in the case of an unfair trade practice. Funding of the program is accomplished through the issuance by the Commodity Credit Corporation (CCC) of a dollar check to reimburse participants for activities authorized by a specific project agreement. Types of assistance: direct payments for specified use (cooperative agreements). Estimate of annual funds available: Direct payments: $75,000,000.

* Money to Local Communities Near National Forests to Help Businesses Grow or Expand

(10.670 National Forest-Dependent Rural Communities)
Deputy Chief
State and Private Forestry
Forest Service
U.S. Department of Agriculture
P.O. Box 96090
Washington, DC 20090-6090   202-205-1394
Objectives: Provide accelerated assistance to communities faced with acute economic problems associated with federal or private sector land management decisions and policies or that are located in or near a national forest and are economically dependent upon forest resources. Aid is extended to these communities to help them to diversify their economic base and to improve the economic, social, and environmental well-being of rural areas. Types of assistance: project grants; direct loans; use of property, facilities, and equipment; training. Estimate of annual funds available: $4,900,000 in 1995.

* Loans to Non-Profits to Lend Money to New Businesses

(10.767 Intermediary Relending Program)
Rural Business and Cooperative Development Service
Room 6321, South Agriculture Building
Washington, DC 20250-0700   202-690-4100
Objectives: To finance business facilities and community development. Types of assistance: direct loans. Estimate of annual funds available: Loans: $88,038,000.

* Loans to Businesses in Small Towns

(10.768 Business and Industrial Loans)
Administrator
Rural Business and Cooperative Development Service
U.S. Department of Agriculture
Washington, DC 20250-0700   202-690-1553
Objectives: To assist public, private, or cooperative organizations (profit or non-profit), Indian tribes or individuals in rural areas to obtain quality loans for the purpose of improving, developing or financing business, industry, and employment and improving the economic and environmental climate in rural communities including pollution abatement and control. Types of assistance: guaranteed/insured loans. Estimate of annual funds available: Guaranteed Loans: $500,000,000.

* Grants to Non-Profits to Lend Money to New Businesses

(10.769 Rural Development Grants)
Director
Community Facilities Loan Division
Rural Business and Cooperative Development Service
U.S. Department of Agriculture
Washington, DC 20250   202-720-1490
Objectives: To facilitate the development of small and emerging private business, industry, and related employment for improving the economy in rural communities. Types of assistance: project grants. Estimate of annual funds available: Grants: $45,500,000.

* Loans to Companies That Provide Electricity to Small Towns

(10.850 Rural Electrification Loans and Loan Guarantees)
Administrator
Rural Electrification Administration
U.S. Department of Agriculture

Washington, DC 20250-1500   202-720-9540
Objectives: To assure that people in eligible rural areas have access to electric services comparable in reliability and quality to the rest of the Nation. Types of assistance: direct loans. Estimate of annual funds available: Direct Loans: $725,000,000; Guaranteed Loans: $275,000,000.

* Loans to Companies That Provide Telephone Service to Small Towns

(10.851 Rural Telephone Loans and Loan Guarantees)
Administrator
Rural Utilities Services
U.S. Department of Agriculture
Washington, DC 20250   202-720-9540
Objectives: To assure that people in eligible rural areas have access to telephone service comparable in reliability and quality to the rest of the Nation. Types of assistance: direct loans. Estimate of annual funds available: Direct Loans: $236,000,000; Guaranteed Loans: $120,000,000.

* Extra Loans to Companies That Provide Telephone Service to Small Towns

(10.852 Rural Telephone Bank Loans)
Administrator
Rural Utilities Services
U.S. Department of Agriculture
Washington, DC 20250   202-720-9540
Objectives: To provide supplemental financing to extend and improve telephone service in rural areas. Types of assistance: direct loans. Estimate of annual funds available: Direct Loans: $175,000,000.

* Grants and Loans to Telephone Companies That Then Provide Financing to Small Businesses

(10.854 Rural Economic Development Loans and Grants)
Administrator
Rural Utilities Service
U.S. Department of Agriculture
Washington, DC 20250   202-720-9552
Objectives: To promote rural economic development and job creation projects, including funding for project feasibility studies, start-up costs, incubator projects, and other reasonable expenses for the purpose of fostering rural development. Types of assistance: direct loans; project grants. Estimate of annual funds available: Loans/Grants: $13,025,000 in 1995.

* Free Plants to Nurseries

(10.905 Plant Materials for Conservation)
Deputy Chief For Technology
Soil Conservation Service
U.S. Department of Agriculture
P.O. Box 2890
Washington, DC 20013   202-720-3905
Objectives: To assemble, evaluate, select, release, and introduce into commerce, and promote the use of new and improved plant materials for soil, water, and related resource conservation and environmental improvement programs. Types of assistance: provision of specialized services. Estimate of annual funds available: Salaries and expenses: $8,745,000.

* Grants to Communities That Provide Money And Help to Small Business Incubators

(11.300 Economic Development-Grants for Public Works and Development Facilities)
David L. McIlwain, Director
Public Works Division
Economic Development Administration
Room H7326
Herbert C. Hoover Building
U.S. Department of Commerce
Washington, DC 20230   202-482-5265
Objectives: To promote long-term economic development and assist in the construction of public works and development facilities needed to initiate and encourage the creation or retention of permanent jobs in the private sector in areas

experiencing severe economic distress. Types of assistance: project grants. Estimate of annual funds available: Grants: $195,000,000.

* Grants to Communities to Help Small Businesses Start or Expand

(11.302 Economic Development Support for Planning Organizations)
Luis F. Bueso
Director Planning Division
Economic Development Administration
Room H7319, Herbert C. Hoover Building
Washington, DC 20230   202-482-2873

Objectives: To assist in providing administrative aid to multi-county districts, redevelopment areas and Indian tribes to establish and maintain economic development planning and implementation capability and thereby promote effective utilization of resources in the creation of full-time permanent jobs for the unemployed and the underemployed in areas of high distress. Types of assistance: project grants. Estimate of annual funds available: Grants: $21,484,000.

* Grants to Communities That Help Finance New or Old Businesses Due to New Military Base Closings

(11.307 Special Economic Development and Adjustment Assistance Program-Sudden and Severe Economic Dislocation (SSED) and Long-Term Economic Deterioration (LTED))
David F. Witschi, Director
Economic Adjustment Division
Economic Development Administration
Room H7327, Herbert C. Hoover Building
U.S. Department of Commerce
Washington DC 20230   202-482-2659

Objectives: To assist state and local areas develop and/or implement strategies designed to address adjustment problems resulting from sudden and severe economic dislocation such as plant closings, military base closures and defense contract cutbacks (SSED), or from long-term economic deterioration in the area's economy (LTED). Types of assistance: project grants. Estimate of annual funds available: Grants: $165,000,000.

* Grants to Fishermen Hurt by Oil and Gas Drilling on the Outer Continental Shelf

(11.408 Fishermen's Contingency Fund)
Chief
Financial Services Division
National Marine Fisheries Service
1315 East West Highway
Silver Spring, MD 20910   301-713-2396

Objectives: To compensate U.S. commercial fishermen for damage/loss of fishing gear and 50 percent of resulting economic loss due to oil and gas related activities in any area of the Outer Continental Shelf. Types of assistance: direct payments with unrestricted use. Estimate of annual funds available: Direct payments: $625,000.

* Grants to Fishermen Hurt by Foreign Fishing Vessels

(11.409 Fishing Vessel and Gear Damage Compensation Fund)
Chief
Financial Services Division
Attn: National Marine Fisheries Service
U.S. Department of Commerce
1315 East-West Highway
Silver Spring, MD 20910   301-713-2396

Objectives: To compensate U.S. fishermen for the loss, damage, or destruction of their vessels by foreign fishing vessels and their gear by any vessel. Types of assistance: direct payments with unrestricted use. Estimate of annual funds available: Direct payments: $1,000,000.

* Grants to Develop New Technologies for Your Business

(11.612 Advanced Technology Program)
Mr. George Uriano, Director
Advanced Technology Program
National Institute of Standards and Technology
Gaithersburg, MD 20899   301-975-5187

To receive application kits:

Ms. Gail Killen   301-975-2636

Objectives: To assist U.S. businesses in creating and applying pre-competitive generic technology and research results necessary to: (1) commercialize significant new discoveries and technologies rapidly, and (2) refine manufacturing technologies. The ultimate objective is to improve U.S. industry competitiveness. Types of assistance: project grants (cooperative agreements). Estimate of annual funds available: Grants and Cooperative Agreements: $417,105,000 in 1995.

* Grants to Organizations That Help Minorities Start Their Own Businesses

(11.800 Minority Business Development Centers)
Assistant Director
Office of Operations
Room 5063, Minority Business Development Agency
U.S. Department of Commerce
14th and Constitution Avenue, NW.
Washington, DC 20230   202-482-2366

Objectives: To provide business development services for a minimal fee to minority firms and individuals interested in entering, expanding, or improving their efforts in the marketplace. Minority business development center operators provide a wide range of services to clients, from initial consultations to the identification and resolution of specific business problems. Types of assistance: project grants. Estimate of annual funds available: Grants: $23,924,000.

* Grants to Organizations That Help American Indians Start Their Own Businesses

(11.801 American Indian Program)
Assistant Director
Office of Operations, Room 5063
Minority Business Development Agency
U.S. Department of Commerce
14th and Constitution Avenue, NW
Washington, DC 20230   202-482-2366

Objectives: To provide business development service to American Indians interested in entering, expanding, or improving their efforts in the marketplace. To help American Indian business development centers and American Indian business consultants to provide a wide range of services to American Indian clients, from initial consultation to the identification and resolution of specific business problems. Types of assistance: project grants. Estimate of annual funds available: Grants: $1,906,500.

* Grants to Help Minority Businesses Enter New Markets

(11.802 Minority Business Resource Development)
Ms. Theresa Speake
Assistant Director for Program Development
Room 5096, Minority Business Development Agency
U.S. Department of Commerce
14th and Constitution Avenue, NW
Washington, DC 20230   202-482-5770

Objectives: The resource development activity provides for the indirect business assistance program conducted by MBDA. These programs encourage minority business development by identifying and developing private markets and capital sources; decreasing minority dependence on government programs; expanding business information and business services through trade associations; promoting and supporting the mobilization of resources of federal agencies and state and local governments at the local level; and assisting minorities in entering new and growing markets. Types of assistance: project grants (cooperative agreements). Estimate of annual funds available: Grants: $2,202,000 in 1995.

* Grants to Organizations That Will Help You Sell to the Department of Defense

(12.002 Procurement Technical Assistance For Business Firms)
Defense Logistics Agency
Cameron Station
Office of Small and Disadvantaged Business
  Utilization (DLA-U), Room 4B130
Alexandria, VA 22304-6100   202-274-6471

Objectives: To assist eligible entities in the payment of the costs of establishing new Procurement Technical Assistance (PTA) Programs and maintaining existing PTA Programs. Types of assistance: project grants (cooperative agreements). Estimate of annual funds available: Cooperative Agreements: $12,000,000 in 1995.

Small Business and Entrepreneuring

* Loans to Start a Business on an Indian Reservation

(15.124 Indian Loans - Economic Development)
Director, Office of Economic Development
Bureau of Indian Affairs
1849 and C Street, NW, Room 4060
Washington, DC 20240   202-208-5324
Contact: Jerry Folsom

Objectives: To provide assistance to Indians, Alaska Natives, tribes, and Indian organizations to obtain financing from private and governmental sources which serve other citizens. When otherwise unavailable, financial assistance through the Bureau is provided eligible applicants for any purpose that will promote the economic development of a Federal Indian Reservation. Types of assistance: direct loans; guaranteed/insured loans; provision of specialized services. Estimate of annual funds available: Total Funds: $29,791,000.

* Grants to Start Indian-Owned Businesses

(15.145 Indian Grants - Economic Development)
Jerry Folsom, Office of Economic Development
Bureau of Indian Affairs
1849 C Street, NW, Room 4060
Washington, DC 20240   202-208-5324

Objectives: To provide seed money to attract financing from other sources for developing Indian owned businesses; to improve Indian reservation economies by providing employment and goods and services where they are now deficient. Types of assistance: project grants; direct payments for specified use. Estimate of annual funds available: Grants: $3,900,000.

* Grants to Small Coal Mine Operators to Clean Up Their Mess

(15.250 Regulation of Surface Coal Mining and Surface Effects of Underground Coal Mining)
Arthur Abbs, Chief
Division of Regulatory Programs
Office of Surface Mining Reclamation and Enforcement
U.S. Department of the Interior
1951 Constitution Ave., NW
Washington, DC 20240   202-208-2651

Objectives: To protect society and the environment from the adverse effects of surface coal mining operations consistent with assuring the coal supply essential to the Nation's energy requirements. Types of assistance: project grants; direct payments for specified use. Estimate of annual funds available: $51,661,000. (Includes all cooperative agreements and State Grants except SOAP grants.) Small Operator Assistance: $1,760,000.

* Grants to Environmental Engineering Companies to Help the Environment

(15.503 Small Reclamation Projects)
Dick L. Porter, Chief
Contracts and Repayment Division
Bureau of Reclamation
U.S. Department of the Interior
Washington, DC 20240   202-208-3014
or
Ron Willhite, Loan Program Coordinator
Resources Management
Bureau of Reclamation
U.S. Department of the Interior
Denver, CO 80225   303-236-8410

Objectives: To encourage state and local participation in the development of projects under federal reclamation laws, with emphasis on rehabilitation and betterment of existing projects for the purposes of significant conservation of water, energy, the environment, water quality control and to provide for federal assistance in the development of similar projects located in the 17 western most contiguous states and Hawaii. Types of assistance: direct loans; project grants. Estimate of annual funds available: Grants and loans: $3,000,000; Salaries and expenses: $600,000.

* Money to Help Start a Business in the Virgin Islands

(15.875 Economic and Political Development of the Territories and the Trust Territory of the Pacific Islands)
Assistant Secretary
Office of Territorial and International Affairs

U.S. Department of the Interior
Washington, DC 20240   202-208-4822

Objectives: To promote the economic, social, and political development of the territories, leading toward greater self-government for each of them. Types of assistance: project grants. Estimate of annual funds available: Grants: $74,110,000.

* Money to Fishermen Who Have Their Boats Seized by a Foreign Government

(19.204 Fishermen's Guaranty Fund)
Mr. Stetson Tinkham
Office of Fisheries Affairs
Bureau of Oceans and International Environmental and Scientific Affairs
Room 5806, U.S. Department of State
Washington, DC 20520-7818   202-647-2009

Objectives: To provide for reimbursement of losses incurred as a result of the seizure of a U.S. commercial fishing vessel by a foreign country on the basis of rights or claims in territorial waters or on the high seas which are not recognized by the United States. Effective November 28, 1990, the United States acknowledges the authority of coastal states to manage highly migratory species, thus reducing the basis for valid claims under the Fishermen's Protective Act. Types of assistance: insurance. Estimate of annual funds available: Reimbursement of Losses: $186,000.

* Grants to Build an Airport

(20.106 Airport Improvement Program)
Federal Aviation Administration
Office of Airport Planning and Programming
Airports Financial Assistance Division, APP-500
800 Independence Avenue, SW
Washington, DC 20591   202-267-3831

Objectives: To assist sponsors, owners, or operators of public-use airports in the development of a nationwide system of airports adequate to meet the needs of civil aeronautics. Types of assistance: project grants; advisory services and counseling. Estimate of annual funds available: Grants: $1,500,000,000.

* Grants to Bus Companies

(20.509 Public Transportation for Nonurbanized Areas)
Federal Transit Administration
Office of Grants Management
Office of Capital and Formula Assistance
400 Seventh Street, SW
Washington, DC 20590   202-366-2053

Objectives: To improve, initiate, or continue public transportation service in nonurbanized areas by providing financial assistance for the acquisition, construction, and improvement of facilities and equipment and the payment of operating expenses by operating contract, lease, or otherwise. Also to provide technical assistance for rural transportation. Types of assistance: formula grants. Estimate of annual funds available: Grants: $158,831,000. The RTAP was fully funded under the new transit planning and research program. The estimated obligations for FY 1994 and 1995 included $4.6 Million for RTAP.

* Grants to Become a Women-Owned Transportation Related Company

(20.511 Human Resource Programs)
Director, Office of Civil Rights
Federal Transit Administration
U.S. Department of Transportation
400 Seventh Street, SW, Room 7412
Washington, DC 20590   202-366-4018

Objectives: To provide financial assistance for national and local programs that address human resource needs as they apply to public transportation activities particularly in furtherance of minority and female needs. Types of assistance: project grants (cooperative agreements); dissemination of technical information. Estimate of annual funds available: Grants, Cooperative Agreements: $1,189,000.

* Grants to U.S. Shipping Companies That Have to Pay Their Employees Higher Salaries Than Foreign Shipping Companies

(20.804 Operating Differential Subsidies)
Associate Administrator for Maritime Aids

Maritime Administration
U.S. Department of Transportation
400 Seventh Street, SW
Washington, DC 20590   202-366-0364
Objectives: To promote development and maintenance of the U.S. Merchant Marine by granting financial aid to equalize cost of operating a U.S. flag ship with cost of operating a competitive foreign flag ship. Types of assistance: direct payments for specified use. Estimate of annual funds available: $214,356,000.

* Money for Airlines to Fly to Small Towns and Make a Profit

(20.901 Payments for Essential Air Services)
Director, Office of Aviation Analysis, P-50
U.S. Department of Transportation
400 Seventh Street, SW
Washington, DC 20590   202-366-1030
Objectives: To assure that air transportation is provided to eligible communities by subsidizing air carriers when necessary to provide service. Types of assistance: direct payments for specified use. Estimate of annual funds available: Direct payments to air carriers: $25,600,000.

* Grants to Women-Owned Businesses in Transportation

(20.902 Student Training and Education Program)
Office of Small and Disadvantaged Business Utilization, S-40
Office of the Secretary
400 Seventh Street, SW
Washington, DC 20590   202-366-1930
Objectives: To support Historically Black Colleges and Universities (HBCUs) in advancing the development of potential by providing quality education to minority students. This project will strengthen HBCU efforts to promote the full diversification of the work force by implementing programs and developing curriculums dedicated to providing a continuous pool of individuals to occupy professional and management positions in the Nation's work force, including minority, women-owned and disadvantaged business enterprises (DBEs). This project will provide opportunities for DBEs to enhance their knowledge and skills in the field of transportation and their involvement with the HBCUs and minority students. Types of assistance: project grants. Estimate of annual funds available: Grants: $800,000.

* Grants to Women-Owned Businesses to Help Get Contracts from the Department of Transportation

(20.903 Support Mechanisms for Disadvantaged Businesses)
Office of Small and Disadvantaged Business
  Utilization, S-40
Office of the Secretary
400 Seventh Street, SW
Washington, DC 20590   202-366-1930
Objectives: To develop support mechanisms, including liaison and assistance programs, that will enable Disadvantaged Business Enterprises (DBEs) to take advantage of transportation-related contracts. Recipients will provide a communications link between the Department of Transportation; its grantees, recipients, contractors, subcontractors; and minority, women-owned and disadvantaged business enterprises in order to increase their participation in existing DOT programs and to provide more DBEs with DOT contracting opportunities. Types of assistance: project grants (cooperative agreements). Estimate of annual funds available: Grants: $1,000,000 in 1995.

* Loans to Start a Credit Union

(44.002 Community Development Revolving Loan Program for Credit Unions)
Mr. Ron Lewandowski
Community Development Revolving Loan Program for Credit Unions
National Credit Union Administration
1775 Duke St.
Alexandria, VA 22314   202-518-6490
Objectives: To support community based credit unions in their efforts to: (1) stimulate economic development activities (in the community they service), which result in increased income, ownership, and employment opportunities for low-income residents; and (2) to provide basic financial and related services to residents of their communities. Types of assistance: direct loans. Estimate of annual funds available: Direct Loans: $1,800,000.

* Grants to Publish Books for a Limited Audience

(45.132 Promotion of the Humanities-Subventions)
Division of Research Programs
Subventions, Room 318
National Endowment for the Humanities
Washington, DC 20506   202-606-8207
Objectives: To ensure through grants to publishing entities the dissemination of works of scholarly distinction in the humanities. Types of assistance: project grants. Estimate of annual funds available: Grants: $5,720,000. (Note: In FY 1994 the budgets for the following programs were combined into one: 45.146, Editions; 45.147, Translations; and 45.132, Subventions. The program is called Scholarly Publications and is comprised of the three funding categories, Editions, Translations, and Subventions.

* Money if Your Business Was Hurt by a Natural Disaster or Drought

(59.002 Economic Injury Disaster Loans)
Office of Disaster Assistance
Small Business Administration
409 3rd Street, SW
Washington, DC 20416   202-205-6734
Objectives: To assist business concerns suffering economic injury as a result of certain Presidential, SBA, and/or Department of Agriculture declared disasters. Types of assistance: direct loans; guaranteed/insured loans (including immediate participation loans). Estimate of annual funds available: $76,563,000.

* Money for Small Businesses Owned by Low-Income People in Areas of High Unemployment

(59.003 Loans for Small Businesses)
Director, Loan Policy and Procedures Branch
Small Business Administration
409 Third Street, SW
Washington, DC 20416   202-205-6570
Objectives: To provide direct loans to small businesses owned by low-income persons or located in any area having a high percentage of unemployment, or having a high percentage of low income individuals. (Guaranteed Loans, including Immediate Participation Loans are provided under program 59.012.) Types of assistance: direct loans; advisory services and counseling. Estimate of annual funds available: Loans: $8,502,000.

* Money for Businesses Hurt by Physical Disaster or Drought

(59.008 Physical Disaster Loans)
Office of Disaster Assistance
Small Business Administration
409 3rd Street, SW
Washington, DC 20416   202-205-6734
Objectives: To provide loans to the victims of designated physical-type disasters for uninsured losses. Types of assistance: direct loans; guaranteed/insured loans (including immediate participation loans). Estimate of annual funds available: Loans: $411,627,000.

* Money to Start a Venture Capital Company

(59.011 Small Business Investment Companies)
Director, Office of Investments
Investment Division
Small Business Administration
409 Third Street, SW
Washington, DC 20416   202-205-6510
Objectives: To establish privately owned and managed investment companies, which are licensed and regulated by the U.S. Small Business Administration; to provide equity capital and long term loan funds to small businesses; and to provide advisory services to small businesses. Types of assistance: direct loans; guaranteed/ insured loans; advisory services and counseling. Estimate of annual funds available: Direct Loans: $15,000,000; Guarantees: $665,210,000.

* Up to $750,000 to Start Your Own Business

(59.012 Small Business Loans)
Director, Loan Policy and Procedures Branch
Small Business Administration

409 Third Street, SW

Washington, DC 20416   202-205-6570

Objectives: To provide guaranteed loans to small businesses which are unable to obtain financing in the private credit marketplace, but can demonstrate an ability to repay loans granted. Guaranteed loans to low-income business owners or businesses located in areas of high unemployment, non-profit sheltered workshops and other similar organizations which produce goods or services; to small businesses being established, acquired or owned by handicapped individuals; and to enable small businesses to manufacture, design, market, install, or service specific energy measures. Types of assistance: guaranteed/insured loans (including immediate participation loans). Estimate of annual funds available: Loans: $8,994,000,000.

* Loans to Local Organizations That Finance Small Businesses

(59.013 Local Development Company Loans)
Office of Rural Affairs and Economic Development
Small Business Administration
409 3rd Street, SW
Washington, DC 20416   202-205-6485

Objectives: To make federal loans to local development companies to provide long-term financing to small business concerns located in their areas. Local development companies are corporations chartered for the purpose of promoting economic growth within specific areas. Types of assistance: guaranteed/insured loans. Estimate of annual funds available: Loans: $50,316,000.

* Help for Contractors and Others to Get Bonded to Obtain Contracts

(59.016 Bond Guarantees for Surety Companies)
Dorothy Kleeschulte, Assistant Administrator
Office of Surety Guarantees
Small Business Administration
409 3rd Street, SW
Washington, DC 20416   202-205-6540

Objectives: To guarantee surety bonds issued by commercial surety companies for small contractors unable to obtain a bond without a guarantee. Guarantees are for up to 90 percent of the total amount of bond. Types of assistance: insurance (guaranteed surety bonds). Estimate of annual funds available: Bond-guarantees SBA shares to surety companies: $1,555,076,000.

* Low Interest Loans for Persons with Disabilities to Start a Business

(59.021 Handicapped Assistance Loans)
Director, Loan Policy and Procedures Branch
Small Business Administration
409 Third Street, SW
Washington, DC 20416   202-205-6570

Objectives: To provide direct loans for non-profit sheltered workshops and other similar organizations that produce goods and services; and to assist in the establishment, acquisition, or operation of a small business owned by handicapped individuals. (Guaranteed Loans, including Immediate Participation Loans, are provided under program 59.012.) Types of assistance: direct loans. Estimate of annual funds available: Direct Loans: $9,553,000.

* Loans to Veterans to Start a Business

(59.038 Veterans Loan Program)
Director, Loan Policy and Procedures Branch
Small Business Administration
409 Third Street, SW
Washington, DC 20416   202-205-6570

Objectives: To provide loans to small businesses owned by Vietnam-era and disabled veterans. Types of assistance: direct loans. Estimate of annual funds available: Loans: $12,000,000.

* Money to Local Organizations to Finance Small Businesses

(59.041 Certified Development Company Loans [504 Loans])
Office of Rural Affairs and Economic Development
Small Business Administration
409 3rd Street SW
Washington, DC 20416   202-205-6485

Objectives: To assist small business concerns by providing long-term fixed rate financing for fixed assets through the sale of debentures to private investors. Types of assistance: guaranteed/insured loans. Estimate of annual funds available: Guaranteed Loans: $2,078,571,000.

* Loans to Minority Businesses That Want to Do Business with the Government

(59.042 Business Loans for 8(a) Program Participants)
Director, Loan Policy and Procedures Branch
Small Business Administration
409 Third Street, SW
Washington, DC 20416   202-205-6570

Objectives: To provide direct and guaranteed loans to small business contractors receiving assistance under the subsection 7(j) 10 and section 8(a) of the Small Business Act (15 U.S.C. 636 (a)), who are unable to obtain financing on reasonable terms in the private credit marketplace, but can demonstrate an ability to repay loans granted. Terms not to exceed 25 years. Types of assistance: direct loans; guaranteed/insured loans (including immediate participation loans). Estimate of annual funds available: Direct Loans: $4,989,000.

* Grants to Local Organizations That Help Women Start Their Own Businesses

(59.043 Women's Business Ownership Assistance)
Harriet Fredman
Office of Women's Business Ownership
Small Business Administration
409 3rd Street, SW
Washington, DC 20416   202-205-6673

Objectives: To promote the legitimate interest of small business concerns owned and controlled by women and to remove, in so far as possible, the discriminatory barriers that are encountered by women in accessing capital and other factors of production. Types of assistance: project grants (cooperative agreements or contracts). Estimate of annual funds available: Cooperative Agreements: $4,000,000.

* Grants to Local Organizations That Help Veterans Start Their Own Businesses

(59.044 Veterans Entrepreneurial Training and Counseling)
Reginald Teamer or William Truitt
Office of Veteran Affairs
Small Business Administration
6th Floor, 409 3rd Street, SW
Washington, DC 20416   202-205-6773

Objectives: To design, develop, administer, and evaluate an entrepreneurial and procurement training and counseling program for U.S. veterans. Types of assistance: project grants (cooperative agreements). Estimate of annual funds available: Grants: $445,000.

* Grants to Small Businesses That Want to Plant Trees on Government Land

(59.045 Natural Resource Development)
William F. Berry
Office of Procurement Assistance
Small Business Administration
409 3rd St., SW
Washington, DC 20416   202-205-6470

Objectives: To make grants to states to contract with small business concerns to plant trees on state or local government owned land. Types of assistance: project grants. Estimate of annual funds available: Grants: $18,000,000.

* Money to Local Organizations to Provide Micro-Loans

(59.046 Microloan Demonstration Program)
SBA Central Office
Office of Financial Assistance   202-205-6570
or write to:
Office of Financing
Loan Policy and Procedures Branch
Small Business Administration
409 Third Street SW, Eighth Floor
Washington, DC 20416

Objectives: To assist women, low-income, and minority entrepreneurs, business owners, and other individuals possessing the capability to operate successful business concerns and business concerns in areas suffering from lack of credit due to economic downturn through the establishment of the Microloan Demonstration Program. Under the program the Small Business Administration (SBA) will make loans to private, non-profit and quasi-governmental organizations (intermediaries) which will, in turn, make loans in amounts up to $25,000 to start up, newly established, or growing concerns for the provision of working capital or the acquisition of materials, supplies, or equipment. Types of assistance: formula grants; project grants; direct loans. Estimate of annual funds available: Loans: $65,016,000.

* Money for Disabled Veterans to Start New Businesses

(64.116 Vocational Rehabilitation for Disabled Veterans)
Central Office
U.S. Department of Veterans Affairs
Washington, DC 20420

Objectives: To provide all services and assistance necessary to enable service-disabled veterans and service persons hospitalized pending discharge to achieve maximum independence in daily living and, to the maximum extent feasible, to become employable and to obtain and maintain suitable employment. Types of assistance: direct payments with unrestricted use; direct payments for specified use; direct loans; advisory services and counseling. Estimate of annual funds available: Direct payments: $279,840,000; Loan advances: $1,964,000.

* Help for Retired Military to Start a Business

(64.123 Vocational Training for Certain Veterans Receiving
VA Pension)
Central Office
U.S. Department of Veterans Affairs
Washington, DC 20420

Objectives: To assist new pension recipients to resume and maintain gainful employment by providing vocational training and other services. Types of assistance: direct payments for specified use; advisory services and counseling. Estimate of annual funds available: $1,280,000.

* Money to Invest in Companies Overseas

(70.002 Foreign Investment Guaranties)
Information Officer
Overseas Private Investment Corporation
1100 New York Ave., NW
Washington, DC 20527   202-336-8799

Objectives: To guarantee loans and other investments made by eligible U.S. investors in friendly developing countries and emerging economies throughout the world, thereby assisting development goals and improving U.S. global competitiveness, creating American jobs and increasing U.S. exports. Types of assistance: guaranteed/insured loans; direct loans. Estimate of annual funds available: Loan Guaranties: $500,000,000.

* Insurance Against Your Business in Another Country Being Hurt by Foreign Politics

(70.003 Foreign Investment Insurance)
Information Officer
Overseas Private Investment Corporation
1100 New York Ave., NW
Washington, DC 20527   202-336-8799

Objectives: To insure investments of eligible U.S. investors in developing friendly countries and areas, against the risks of inconvertibility, expropriation, war, revolution and insurrection, certain types of civil strife, and business interruption. Special programs to insure contractors and exporters against arbitrary drawings of letters of credit posted as bid, performance or advance payment guaranties, energy exploration and development, leasing operations. Types of assistance: insurance. Estimate of annual funds available: Insurance: $5,000,000; Contracts Issued: $3,600,000,000.

* Free Patent Rights to Government Discoverers of Energy Saving Ideas

(81.003 Granting of Patent Licenses)
Robert J. Marchick
Office of the Assistant General Counsel for Patents

U.S. Department of Energy
Washington, DC 20585   202-586-2802

Objectives: To encourage widespread utilization of inventions covered by Department of Energy (DOE) owned patents. Types of assistance: dissemination of technical information. Estimate of annual funds available: (Salaries) Not identifiable.

* Money to Work on an Energy-Related Invention

(81.036 Energy-Related Inventions)
George Lewett, Director
Office of Technology Evaluation and Assessment
National Institute of Standards and Technology
Gaithersburg, MD 20899   301-975-5500

or

Terry Levinson
Inventions and Innovation Division
Energy-Related Inventions Programs (CE-521)
U.S. Department of Energy
1000 Independence Avenue, SW
Washington, DC 20585   202-586-1479

Objectives: To encourage innovation in developing non-nuclear energy technology by providing assistance to individual and small business companies in the development of promising energy-related inventions. Types of assistance: project grants; use of property, facilities, and equipment; advisory services and counseling; dissemination of technical information. Estimate of annual funds available: Grants: $5,700,000.

* Grants to Local Organizations That Help Women and Minorities Get Department of Energy Contracts

(81.082 Management and Technical Assistance for Minority Business
Enterprises)
Sterling Nichols
Office of Minority Economic Impact
U.S. Department of Energy
Forrestal Building, Room 5B-110, MI-1
Washington, DC 20585   202-586-1594

Objectives: (1) To support increased participation of minority, and women-owned and operated business enterprises (MBE's); (2) to develop energy-related minority business assistance programs and public/private partnerships to provide technical assistance to MBE's; (3) to transfer applicable technology from national federal laboratories to MBE's; and (4) to increase the Department of Energy's (DOE) high technology research and development contracting activities. Types of assistance: advisory services and counseling. Estimate of annual funds available: Contracts and Grants: $382,000.

* Grants to Develop Energy Saving Products

(81.086 Conservation Research and Development)
Barbara Twigg
Office of Management and Resources
Conservation and Renewable Energy
Washington, DC 20585   202-586-8714

Objectives: To conduct a balanced long-term research effort in the areas of buildings, industry, transportation. Grants will be offered to develop and transfer to the non-federal sector various energy conservation technologies. Types of assistance: project grants. Estimate of annual funds available: Grants: $3,700,000.

* Grants to Work on Solar Energy Products

(81.087 Renewable Energy Research and Development)
Barbara Twigg
Office of Management and Resources
U.S. Department of Energy
Washington, DC 20585   202-586-8714

Objectives: To conduct balanced research and development efforts in the following energy technologies; solar buildings, photovoltaics, solar thermal, biomass, alcohol fuels, urban waste, wind, and geothermal. Grants will be offered to develop and transfer to the nonfederal sector various renewable energy technologies. Types of assistance: project grants. Estimate of annual funds available: Grants: $2,100,000.

* Grants to Develop Uses of Fossil Fuels

(81.089 Fossil Energy Research and Development)
Mr. Dwight Mottet
Fossil Energy Program, FE-122

U.S. Department of Energy
Germantown, MD 20545   301-903-2787
Objectives: The mission of the Fossil Energy (FE) Research and Development program is to promote the development and use of environmentally and economically superior technologies for supply, conversion, delivery and utilization of fossil fuels. These activities will involve cooperation with industry, DOE Laboratories, universities, and states. Success in this mission will benefit the Nation through lower energy costs, reduced environmental impact, increased technology exports, and reduced dependence on insecure energy sources. Types of assistance: project grants; project grants (cooperative agreements). Estimate of annual funds available: Grants and cooperative agreements: $86,064,000.

* Grants to Small Businesses to Develop Energy Information Databases

(81.091 Socioeconomic and Demographic Research, Data and Other Information)
Georgia R. Johnson
U.S. Department of Energy
Forrestal Building
Room 5B-110
Washington, DC 20585   202-586-1593
Objectives: (1) To provide financial support for developing and enhancing socioeconomic and demographic research, data, and other information which would help to determine minority energy consumption and usage patterns; (2) to evaluate the percentage of disposable income spent by minorities on energy compared to national usage patterns; (3) to develop policy analysis and economic indicators relating to the Department of Energy's (DOE) policies and programs and for use in the development of assessments for legislative and regulatory actions of DOE and other federal and state agencies; (4) to develop appropriate technical information to assist minority educational institutions and minority businesses; and (5) develop technical information on energy conservation and related efficiency options. Types of assistance: project grants. Estimate of annual funds available: Grants: $780,000.

* Grants to Figure Out How to Make Money Out of Department of Energy Information and Discoveries

(81.103 Technology Integration)
C. Sink
Office of Technology Development, EM-52
Environmental Restoration and Waste Management
Washington, DC 20545   301-903-7928
Objectives: To transfer technologies/information from the U.S. Department of Energy (DOE) to industry, universities, other federal agencies and vice versa, to develop public participation in the nation's environmental, technological needs, and to develop public/private partnership with companies of all sizes. Types of assistance: project grants (cooperative agreements). Estimate of annual funds available: $13,100,000.

* Grants to Work with Local Schools to Train Your Workers

(84.228 Educational Partnerships)
Educational Networks Division
Room 502, 555 New Jersey Avenue, NW
Washington, DC 20208-5644   202-219-2116
Objectives: To encourage the creation of alliances between public elementary and secondary schools or institutions of higher education and the private sector in order to: (1) Apply the resources of the private and non-profit sectors of the community to the needs of elementary and secondary schools or institutions of higher education in that community to encourage excellence in education; (2) encourage businesses to work with educationally disadvantaged students and with gifted students; (3) apply the resources of communities for the improvement of elementary and secondary education or higher education; and (4) enrich the career awareness of secondary or postsecondary school students and provide exposures to the work of the private sector. Types of assistance: project grants; project grants (contracts). Estimate of annual funds available: Grants: $4,135,564.

* Grants to Businesses That Employ People with Disabilities

(84.234 Projects with Industry)
Dr. Thomas E. Finch
Rehabilitation Services Administration
Office of Assistant Secretary for Special Education and Rehabilitation Services
U.S. Department of Education
Washington, DC 20202   202-205-9796
Objectives: To create and expand job and career opportunities for individuals with disabilities in the competitive labor market, to provide appropriate placement resources by engaging private industry in training and placement. Types of assistance: project grants; project grants (cooperative agreements). Estimate of annual funds available: (Grants) $22,071,000.

* Grants to Local Organizations to Improve the Literacy of Commercial Drivers of Local Businesses

(84.247 Commercial Drivers Education)
Paul Geib, Division of National Programs
Office of the Assistant Secretary for Vocational and Adult Education
U.S. Department of Education
400 Maryland Avenue, SW
Washington, DC 20202-7242   202-205-5864
or

Carroll F. Towey
Division of Adult Education and Literacy
Office of the Assistant Secretary for Vocational and Adult Education
400 Maryland Avenue, SW
Washington, DC 20202-7320   202-205-9791
Objectives: To establish and operate adult education programs that increase the literacy skills of eligible commercial drivers to successfully complete the knowledge test requirements under the Commercial Motor Vehicle Safety Act of 1986. Types of assistance: project grants. Estimate of annual funds available: Grants: $340,000.

Franchising: How to Select the Best Opportunity

Franchising could be for you, according to a study conducted by Arthur Andersen & Company of 366 franchise companies in 60 industries reported that nearly 86% of all franchise operations opened in the previous five years were still under the same ownership; only 3% of these businesses were no longer in business. The U.S. Commerce Department reports that from 1971 to 1987, less than 5% of franchises were terminated on an annual basis. In contrast, a study conducted by the U.S. Small Business Administration from 1978 to 1988 found 62.2% of all new businesses were dissolved within the first six years of their operation, due to failure, bankruptcy, retirement, or other reasons. While we are sure you are beginning to entertain the idea of owning a new business, franchising is not risk free and needs to be entered into with a degree of caution. Therefore, you need to take measures to protect yourself. The following organizations and publications will help you find the right franchise for you.

Organizations

Federal Trade Commission (FTC)
Bureau of Consumer Protection
Division of Marketing Practices
Pennsylvania Avenue at 6th Street, NW
Washington, DC 20580
202-326-3128

Buying a franchise or a business opportunity may be appealing if you want to be your own boss, but have limited capital and business experience. However, without carefully investigating a business before you purchase, you may make a serious mistake. It is important to find out if a particular business is right for you and if it has the potential to yield the financial return you expect. A Federal Trade Commission (FTC) rule requires that franchise and business opportunity sellers provide certain information to help you in your decision. Under the FTC rule, a franchise or business opportunity seller must give you a detailed disclosure document at least ten business days before you pay any money or legally commit yourself to a purchase. This document gives 20 important items of information about the business, including: the names, addresses, and telephone numbers of other purchasers; the fully-audited financial statement of the seller; the background and experience of the business's key executives; the cost required to start and maintain the business; and the responsibilities you and the seller will have to each other once you buy. The disclosure document is a valuable tool that not only helps you obtain information about a proposed business, but assists you in comparing it with other businesses. If you are not given a disclosure document, ask why you did not receive one. Some franchise or business opportunity sellers may not be required to give you a disclosure document. If any franchise or business opportunity says it is not covered by the rule, you may want to verify it with the FTC, an attorney, or a business advisor. Even if the business is not required to give the document, you still may want to ask for the data to help you make an informed investment decision.

Some Important Advice from the FTC:

1.   Study the disclosure document and proposed contracts carefully.

2.   Talk to current owners. Ask them how the information in the disclosure document matches their experiences with the company. Visit the franchises to be sure they really exist. One group you should interview is those who have been in business less than a year. Ask about the company's training program. Find out how long it took to break even and if the company's estimate of operating and working capital was accurate. The second group should be those in business for six years. Find out what kind of deal they got for the franchise and compare it to yours. There are strains in every franchise marriage. Find out what they are. Some franchises hire their own accountants to double check the franchises' accounting. When mistakes are made, it is often attributed to the franchise.

3.   Investigate earnings claims. Earnings claims are only estimates. The FTC rule requires companies to have in writing the facts on which they base their earnings claims. Make sure you understand the basis for a seller's earnings claims.

4.   Shop around: compare franchises with other available business opportunities. You may discover that other companies offer benefits not available from the first company you considered. The *Franchise Opportunities Handbook*, which is published annually by the Department of Commerce, describes thousands of companies that offer franchises. Contact other companies and ask for their disclosure documents. Then you can compare offerings.

5.   Listen carefully to the sales presentation. Some sales tactics should signal caution. A seller with a good offer does not have to use pressure.

6.   Get the seller's promises in writing. Any important promises you get from a salesperson should be written into the contract you sign.

7.   Consider getting professional advice. You may want to get a lawyer, an accountant, or a business advisor to read the disclosure document and proposed contract to counsel you and help you get the best deal.

Although the FTC cannot resolve individual disputes, information about your experiences and concerns is vital to the enforcement of the Franchise and Business Opportunities Rule. The time to protect yourself is before you buy rather than after. Only fifteen states give you private rights to sue, and there is often a limited ability to recover. A franchiser knows your financial situation, and can often outwait you. Many franchise owners have no money left to hire a lawyer to try to recoup their losses. The FTC has two phone numbers of places you can call to ask for assistance. The Franchise Complaint Line, 202-326-2128, is staffed by a duty attorney and takes complaints about franchisers or disclosure requirements. The second number is:

FTC Franchise Rule Information Hotline   202-326-3220
Information on Federal Disclosure Requirements for Franchise and Business Opportunities ext.2

Information on Disclosure Statements for Specific Franchise and Business Opportunity Companies ext.3

Information on Complaints on File Against a Particular Franchise or Business Opportunity Venture ext.4

To Speak to an Attorney . . . . ext. 5

The following publications are available from the Federal Trade Commission Headquarters, 6th and Pennsylvania Ave., NW, Washington, DC 20850; 202-326-2502 voice/TDD:

Franchise and Business Opportunities -- a four-page guide about what to consider before buying a franchise.

The Franchise and Business Rule: Questions and Answers -- a one-page summary of the disclosure rule and penalties for infractions by the franchiser.

Franchise Rule Summary -- a seven-page, detailed technical explanation of the federal disclosure rule, which requires franchisers to furnish a document (with information on twenty topics) to the potential franchisee before a sale. This includes an explanation and description of the Uniform Franchise Offering Circular (UFOC) required in fourteen states.

State Agencies Administering Franchise Disclosure Laws

California (filing required)
Franchise Division, Department of Corporations, 1115 11th St., Sacramento, CA 95814; 916-445-7205.

Hawaii (filing required)
Franchise and Securities Division, State Department of Commerce, P.O. Box 40, Honolulu, HI 96813; 808-586-2722.

Illinois (filing required)
Franchise Division, Office of Attorney General, 500 South Second Street, Springfield, IL 62706; 217-782-4465.

Indiana (filing required)
Franchise Division, Office of Secretary of State, One N. Capitol St., Suite 560, Indianapolis, IN 46204; 317-232-6576.

Maryland (filing required)
Franchise Office, Division of Securities, 200 St. Paul Place, 20th Floor, Baltimore, MD 21202; 301-576-6360.

Michigan (notice required)
Antitrust and Franchise Unit, Office of Attorney General, 670 Law Building, Lansing, MI 48913; 517-373-7117.

Minnesota (filing required)
Franchise Division, Department of Commerce, 133 East Seventh St., St. Paul, MN 55101; 612-296-6328.

New York (filing required)
Franchise and Securities Division, State Department of Law, 120 Broadway, 23rd Floor, New York, NY 10271; 212-416-8211.

North Dakota (filing required)
Franchise Division, Office of Securities Commission, 600 East Boulevard, 5th Floor, Bismarck, ND 58505; 701-224-4712.

Oregon (no filing)
Corporate Securities Section, Dept. of Insurance and Finance, Labor and Industries Bldg., Salem, OR 97310; 503-378-4387.

Rhode Island (filing required)
Franchise Office, Division of Securities, 233 Richmond St., Suite 232, Providence, RI 02903; 401-277-3048.

South Dakota (filing required)
Franchise Office, Division of Securities, 910 E. Sioux Ave., Pierre, SD 57501; 605-773-4013.

Virginia (filing required)
Franchise Office, State Corporation Commission, 1300 E. Main St., Richmond, VA 23219; 804-371-9276.

Washington (filing required)
Franchise Office, Business License Services, State Securities Division, P.O. Box 648, Olympia, WA 98504; 206-753-6928.

Wisconsin (filing required)
Franchise Office, Wisconsin Securities Commission, P.O. Box 1768, Madison, WI 53701; 608-266-3364.

State Offices Administering Business Opportunity Disclosure Laws

California (filing required)
Consumer Law Section, Attorney General's Office, 1515 K St., Sacramento, CA 92101; 916-445-9555.

Connecticut (filing required)
Department of Banking, Securities Division, 44 Capitol Avenue, Hartford, CT 06106; 203-566-4560 ext. 8322.

Florida (filing required)
Department of Agriculture and Consumer Services, Room 110, Mayo Building, Tallahassee, FL 32301; 904-488-2221, 800-342-2176 (in-state only).

Georgia (no filing required)
Office of Consumer Affairs, No. 2 Martin Luther King Dr., Plaza Level, East Tower, Atlanta, GA 30334; 404-656-3790.

Indiana (filing required)
Consumer Protection Division, Attorney General's Office, 219 State House, Indianapolis, IN 46204; 317-232-6331.

Iowa (filing required)
Securities Bureau, Second Floor, Lucas State Office Building, Des Moines, IA 50319; 515-281-4441.

Kentucky (filing required)
Attorney General's Office, Consumer Protection Division, 209 St. Clair, Frankfort, KY 40601; 502-573-2200.

Louisiana (bond filing required)
Office of the Attorney General, Consumer Protection Division, 2610-A Woodale Blvd., Baton Rouge, LA 70804; 504-342-7900.

Maine (filing required)
Banking Bureau, Securities Division, State House, Station 121, Augusta, ME 04333; 207-582-8760.

Maryland (filing required)
Attorney General's Office, Securities Division, 200 St. Paul Pl., 20th Floor, Baltimore, MD 21202; 301-576-6360.

Michigan (notice required)
Consumer Protection Division, Department of the Attorney General, 670 Law Building, Lansing, MI 48913; 517-373-7117.

Minnesota (filing required)
Department of Commerce, Registration Division, 133 East 7th Street, St. Paul, MN 5501; 612-296-6328.

Nebraska (filing required)
Department of Banking and Finance, P.O. Box 95006, Lincoln, NE 68509; 402-471-2171, 402-471-3445.

New Hampshire (filing required)
Attorney General's Office, Consumer Protection Division, State House Annex, Concord, NH 03301; 603-271-3641.

North Carolina (filing required)
Department of Justice, Consumer Protection Division, P.O. Box 629, Raleigh, NC 27602; 919-733-3924.

Ohio (no filing required)
Attorney General's Office, Consumer Fraud and Crime Section, 25th Floor, State Office Tower, 30 East Broad Street, Columbus, OH 43266-0410; 614-466-8831, 800-282-0515 (in-state only).

Oklahoma (filing required)
Department of Securities, P.O. Box 53959, Oklahoma City, OK 73152; 405-235-0230.

South Carolina (filing required)
Secretary of State's Office, P.O. Box 11350, Columbia, SC 29211; 803-734-2169.

South Dakota (filing required)
Division of Securities, 910 E. Sioux Avenue, Pierre, SD 57501.

Texas (filing required)
Secretary of State's Office, Statutory Documents Section, P.O. Box 13563, Austin, TX 78711; 512-475-1769.

Utah (filing required)
Consumer Protection Division, 160 East 300 South, Salt Lake City, UT 84111; 801-530-6601.

Virginia (no filing required)
Consumer Affairs Office, 101 North 8th Street, Richmond, VA 23219; 804-786-0594, 800-451-1525 (in-state only).

Washington (filing required)
Department of Financial Institutions, Securities Division, P.O. Box 9033, Olympia, WA 98507-9033; 206-753-6928.

Publications

International Franchise Association (IFA)
1350 New York Avenue, NW
Washington, DC 20005
John Reynolds, Public Relations Officer   202-628-8000
Founded in 1960, the International Franchise Association (IFA) has more than 600 franchiser members, including thirty-five overseas. IFA members are accepted into the organization only after meeting stringent requirements regarding number of franchises, length of time in business, and financial stability. The IFA offers about twenty-five educational conferences and seminars yearly, including an annual convention and a legal symposium. There is a program on financing and venture capital designed to bring together franchisers and franchisees. Each year the association also sponsors several trade shows, open to the public, so that franchisers may attract potential franchisees. There is a library, and in the near future the Franchise Edge Data Base should be available for $49.95 offering informative information on 5,000 franchises. Information will also be available through Prodigy in the near future. For more information about Prodigy, call Scott Lehr at 202-662-0785. Ms. Holly Perkins, Public Relations Officer, will answer inquiries from the public and make referrals for speakers, courses, and resources on franchising.

The International Franchise Association publishes the following publications, which you can order by phone: 1-800-543-1038. For quick response regarding general information, membership information, educational programs, major conferences, international information, and CFE certification, you may contact the International Franchise Association's Fax-On-Demand Information Line at 202-628-3132.

To Help You Buy a Franchise
Answers to the 21 Most Commonly Asked Questions - $3
College of Franchise Knowledge - $49.95
50 Best Low-Investment,...Franchises - $12.95
Financing Your Franchise - $ 18.95
Franchise Bible - $ 19.95
Franchise Opportunities Guide - $ 15.00
The Franchise Survival Guide - $ 24.95
The Franchises: Dollars & Sense - $ 45.95
Franchising: The Inside Story - $ 20.00
Investigate Before Investing - $ 6.00
Tips and Traps When Buying a Franchise - $ 14.95

For Franchisees
Public Relations for the Franchisee - $ 21.00
Running a Successful Franchise - $ 29.95

To Help You Franchise Your Business
Between the Bumpa's - $ 22.50
Blueprint For Franchising A Business - $ 35.00
Complete Guide to Franchising in Canada - $ 30.00
Financial Strategies... - $ 25.00
The Franchise Option
    Hardcover - $ 30.00
    Softcover - $ 24.00
Franchising & Licensing - $ 32.00
Franchising in Europe - $ 28.50
Franchising--The How-To-Book - $ 12.50
The Guide to Franchising - $ 28.50
How To Be A Franchisor - $ 8.00

Small Business and Entrepreneuring

How To Franchise Internationally - $ 30.00
Restaurant Franchising - $ 46.95
Target Success - $ 5.95

For Franchisors
Franchise Relations Handbook - $ 35.00
Franchising: The Business Strategy... - $ 19.95
The Franchising Handbook - $ 75.00
How To Organize a Franchisee Advisory Council -
$ 10.00
Multiple-Unit Franchising - $ 27.50
Wealth Within Reach - $ 20.00

Legal Information
Covenants Against Competition - $125.00
The Franchise Industry - $ 40.00
Franchise Legal Digest - $195.00
Franchise Sales Compliance Guide - $225.00
Franchising: Accounting, Auditing, Tax... - $ 95.00
Franchising Law: Practice & Forms - $335.00
International Franchising - $95.00

Audiocassettes, Videotapes, Disks
The Franchise Edge (Computer Disk) - $ 50.00
Franchising: A World of Opportunity (VHS) - $145.00
*Franchising: How To Be In Business For Yourself, Not
By Yourself* (VHS) - $ 49.95
How To Make Franchising Work For You (Audio) -
$ 35.00
IFA: A World Of Difference - $ 20.00
The National Franchise Mediation... (VHS) - $ 60.00
The New Entrepreneur (Audio) - $ 49.95
The New UFOC Guidelines (VHS) - $145.00
Opportunities In Franchising (Audio) - $ 35.00

Target Success (Audio set and workbook) - $ 39.95
Using The Media To Generate Leads (Audio) - $ 35.00

Reference Materials
Franchising in the Economy: 1991-1993 - $ 25.00
Franchisor/Franchisee Relations Survey - $ 5.00
The Future of Franchising... - $ 10.00
Glossary of Franchising Terms - $ 4.00
International Franchising: Selection... - $100.00
National Franchise Owner Study (Gallup) - $ 10.00
Franchising World magazine (price includes postage)
Domestic - $ 12.00
Canadian - $ 20.00
Foreign - $ 39.00

Minority Business Development Agency
Department of Commerce
14th and Constitution Ave, NW
Washington, DC 20230   202-377-3237
The Minority Business Development Agency (MBDA) can
provide information to all businesses, not just minority-owned
businesses, regarding franchising. They are the publishers of
Franchise Opportunities Handbook. A bible of franchising
information, this 336 page directory has thousands of detailed
listings of companies, facts about the franchising industry,
guidance for investing in a franchise, resource listings of helpful
agencies and organizations, and a bibliography. The cost is
$21.00; U.S. Government Printing Office, Superintendent of
Documents, Washington, DC 20420; 202-512-1800. MBDA has
several other free publications to assist people who are interested
in learning more about franchising. They also answer questions
regarding FTC rules, major growth areas, how does a franchise
chain start, where do franchise sales come from, and other general
questions.

Top 30 Fastest Growing Franchise Companies

1. 7-Eleven Convenience Stores
2. Subway
3. Snap-On Tools
4. Matco Tools
5. McDonald's
6. Chem Dry Carpet Cleaning
7. Little Caesars Pizza
8. Burger King Corporation
9. Coverall North America Inc.
10. Mail Boxes Etc.
11. CleaNet USA Etc.
12. Jani-King
13. Dunkin' Donuts
14. Coldwell Banker Res. Affil., Inc.
15. Jazzercise Inc.
16. Tower Cleaning Systems
17. Miracle Ear
18. Play It Again Sports
19. GNC Franchising Inc.
20. Super 8 Motels Inc.
21. Choice Hotels International
22. Jackson Hewitt Tax Services
23. Blimpie Corporation
24. Re/Max International
25. O.P.E.N. Cleaning Systems
26. Decorating Den
27. Baskin-Robbins USA Co.
28. Holiday Inn Worldwide
29. Superglass Windshield Repair
30. Hardee's

Did You Know?...

According to the International Franchise Association:

- A new franchise opens every 8 minutes of each business day.

- 1 of every 12 businesses is a franchise.

- By the year 2000 total franchise sales could reach $1 trillion dollars.

- Franchise sales account for 40.9% of all retail sales.

- In 1992, franchise chains created approximately 21,000 new business format franchises. In contrast, more than 220,000 new businesses failed last year, resulting in over 400,000 job losses.

- According to a 1991 Gallup Poll an overwhelming 94% of franchise owners say that they are successful. Seventy-five percent of franchise owners would do it again while, only 39% of Americans would repeat their job or business.

- Based on the Gallup Poll survey, the average total investment cost, including fees and any additional expenses, was $147,570. Fifty-six percent reported total investment cost under $100,000 while 26% reported total investment cost over $100,000.

- Based on the Gallup Poll survey, the average gross income before taxes of franchisees is $124,290. Forty-nine percent reported gross income of less than $100,000 and 37% reported gross income of more than $100,000.

Be patient. If any phone number is incorrect, call (area code) 555-1212 and request the new listing.

Business and Industry
General Sources

* *See also Law and Social Justice Chapter*
* *See also Small Business and Entrepreneuring Chapter*
* *See also Selling Overseas: International Trade Chapter*
* *See also Science and Technology Chapter*
* *See also Energy Chapter*
* *See also Experts Chapter*

This chapter covers big business and major industries in the U.S., such as telecommunications, mining, transportation, railroads, and shipping. Because businesses in these industries are regulated by the federal government, a significant amount of revealing information about them is often available to the public, including financial reports, safety records, business volumes, and violations of industry regulations. But you'll also find other important sources on consumer relations, hiring incentives, child care, and even help in converting your business to the metric system.

This introductory section lists general sources of information on major industries with a particular stress on sources for finding company information collected by the U.S. government.

* Airline Data

Office of Airline Statistics
Research and Special Programs Administration
U.S. Department of Transportation
400 7th Street, SW, Room 4125
Washington, DC 20590   202-366-9059

The Aviation Information Management (AIM) program collects information on the financial operations of air carriers. Government, industry, and the general public may access this information. Database functions are housed at the Transportation Systems Center (see entry) but this office can serve as liaison for access to air carrier reports and data requiring DOT approval for release.

* Alcohol Production Regulations

Wine and Beer Branch
Office of Compliance Operations
Bureau of Alcohol, Tobacco, and Firearms
U.S. Department of the Treasury
650 Massachusetts Ave., NW
Washington, DC 20226   202-927-8230

Distilled Spirit and Tobacco Branch
Office of Compliance Operations
Bureau of Alcohol, Tobacco, and Firearms
U.S. Department of the Treasury
650 Massachusetts Ave., NW
Washington, DC 20226   202-927-8210

These offices regulate basic permit requirements under the Federal Alcohol Administration, as well as the use, bulk sales, bottling, labeling, and advertising of wine, beer, and distilled spirits. Regulations for the sale and production of distilled spirits are also outlined in the booklet, *Laws and Regulations under the Federal Alcohol Administration Act*, available from the Bureau's Distribution Center at 7943 Angus Ct., Springfield, VA 22153.

* Alcohol, Tobacco, and Firearms Regulation Research

National Laboratory Center
Bureau of Alcohol, Tobacco, and Firearms
U.S. Department of the Treasury
1401 Research Blvd.
Rockville, MD 20850   301-294-0410

Laboratory services for the Bureau are conducted at the National Laboratory Center in Rockville, MD, and at regional locations in Atlanta, GA, and San Francisco, CA, in the areas of compliance and law enforcement. All alcohol-containing products sold in the United States and imported to this country are analyzed at these laboratories, and tobacco products are examined for tax classification. Specialists also investigate firearms, explosives, and arson evidence at the forensic labs. Crime lab scientists are also trained at this facility.

* Alcohol, Tobacco, and Firearms Regulations Update

Wine and Beer Branch
Bureau of Alcohol, Tobacco, and Firearms
U.S. Department of the Treasury
650 Massachusetts Ave., NW
Washington, DC 20226   202-927-8230

In April and October, this office publishes the *Unified Agenda* in the *Federal Register*. The *Agenda* outlines regulations that have been issued, are being proposed, or are being reviewed within a six month period by the entire Bureau to give the public ample notice of all regulatory activities. Contact this office for additional information.

* Alcohol, Tobacco, and Firearms Statistics

Public Affairs Branch
Office of Congressional and Media Affairs
Bureau of Alcohol, Tobacco, and Firearms
U.S. Department of the Treasury
650 Massachusetts Ave., NW
Washington, DC 20226   202-927-8500

The free booklet, *Ready Reference Statistics*, outlines the Bureau's statistical activities. Alcohol statistics include moonshine seizures; beer, wine, and distilled spirits production; the number of licensees and permittees; and federal excise tax rates. The U.S. viticulture areas (areas where wine may be produced) are also listed. The tobacco section outlines production and tax rates. The booklet also includes the number of domestic, imported, and exported manufacturers of firearms by type, as well as a listing of the number of registered weapons by state and type.

* Alcohol Trade Laws

Alcohol Import-Export Branch
Office of Industry Compliance
Bureau of Alcohol, Tobacco, and Firearms
U.S. Department of the Treasury
650 Massachusetts Ave., NW
Washington, DC 20226   202-927-8110

The Trade Affairs Branch informs industry of the provisions of the Federal Alcohol Administration Act, as well as issues of product compliance, permits applications, and Bureau opinions relating to the Act.

* Annual Report of Interstate Transportation Companies

Bureau of Accounts' Public Reference Room
Interstate Commerce Commission (ICC)
12th St. and Constitution Ave., NW, Room 3378
Washington, DC 20403   202-927-7119

Annual reports of companies regulated by the ICC contain revealing information concerning those companies, including annual income, balance sheets, expenses, types of equipment owned, and much more. These documents may be examined by the public in the Reference Room from 8:30 a.m. to 5:00 p.m. weekdays, and photocopies of these reports, at a cost of $.60 per page, with a $3 minimum charge per order, may be obtained by writing the Office of the Secretary, Room 2215, ICC, Washington, DC, 20423.

* Bureau of Alcohol, Tobacco, and Firearms Publications

Distribution Center
Bureau of Alcohol, Tobacco, and Firearms
U.S. Department of the Treasury
7943 Angus Ct.
Springfield, VA 22153   703-455-7801
The following is a sampling of free publications from the ATF Distribution Center:

Index of Materials Required by the Freedom of Information Act
Public Use Forms
Information to Claimants
Distilled Spirits for Fuel Use
Payment of Tax by Electronic Fund Transfer
Importation of Distilled Spirits, Wines, and Beer
Beverage Distilled Spirits Plants and Breweries Authorized to Operate
Bonded Wineries and Bonded Wine Cellars Authorized to Operate
Information for Specially Denatured Spirits Applicants
Information for Tax-Free Alcohol Applicants
Distribution and Use of Denatured Alcohol/Rum and formulas for Denatured Alcohol/Rum
Liquor Laws and Regulations for Retail Dealers
Instructions - Application for FAA Act Basic Permits: Wholesalers and Importers
Firearms Curios and Relics List
Federal Firearms Licensee Information
Importation of Arms, Ammunition, and Implements of War
Bomb Threats and Physical Security Planning

* Business Assistance Service

Office of Business Liaison
U.S. Department of Commerce
14th St. and Constitution Ave., NW, Room 5898C
Washington, DC 20230   202-377-3176
The Business Assistance Service provides information and guidance on programs throughout the Federal Government. The Service can answer such questions as:

How can I sell my products or services to the Federal Government?
Where do I find overseas buyers?
Where can I get Federal business loans?

The Business Assistance staff maintains a network of interagency contacts so that they can quickly provide you with current information on a wide range of subjects. People with specific questions about government programs can also find the answers by contacting the Business Assistance staff.

* Business and Transport Records

National Archives and Records Administration
Center for Electronic Records
Washington, DC 20408   202-501-5579
The National Archives Center for Electronic Records maintains several databases of interest to the business researcher. The standard charge for a copy of an electronic dataset on magnetic tape is $90. Photocopies of documents cost $.25 per page; microfiche costs $1.25 per fiche. Transfer of information onto CD-Rom or floppy disks is generally not available. Agencies with records available include: Civil Aeronautics Board; U.S. Department of Labor; Minerals Management Service; Bureau of Mines; National Oceans and Atmospheric Administration; President's Commission on the Coal Industry 1978-1980; U.S. Railway Association; U.S. Department of Transportation General Records; and U.S. Department of Transportation Research and Special Programs Administration. Call for more information and for a printout of the specific records available.

* Business Briefings and Speakers

Office of Business Liaison
U.S. Department of Commerce

14th St. and Constitution Ave., NW, Room 5898C
Washington, DC 20230   202-377-3176
This office has an Outreach Program which organizes a series of briefings for the business community. These briefings serve a dual purpose of promoting the Department's activities to business and allowing Commerce officials to be familiar with business perspectives. The briefings are free and are held in Washington, DC. Speaking requests from business organizations are also routinely handled through this office. Sending Commerce officials across the country, promoting Departmental programs, and listening to concerns of business allows OBL to extend its outreach.

* Business Community Representation

Chamber of Commerce of the United States
1615 H St., NW
Washington, DC 20062   202-659-6000
The Chamber of Commerce is generally regarded as the spokesgroup for United States business. It is the world's largest business federation composed of more than 180,000 companies plus several thousand other organizations such as local and state chambers of commerce and trade and professional associations. It has an environmental department. Publications: *Nation's Business, The Business Advocate.*

* Business Radio Services

Licensing Division
Federal Communications Commission
1270 Fairfield Rd
Gettysburg, PA 17326   717-337-1212
The FCC authorizes and licenses all Business Radio Services used in commercial activity. Over 640,000 businesses in the U.S., from mail couriers to exterminators to plumbers, use radio services as part of their operations and must be licensed by the FCC. Updated daily, these files are available on database and can be accessed through SAFE, or at an access terminal by visiting the FCC office in person.

* Business Reference Service

Library
U.S. Department of Commerce
14th St. and Constitution Ave., NW
Washington, DC 20230   202-377-5511
The U.S. Department of Commerce's Library is open to the public, 1:00 p.m. to 4 p.m., Monday through Friday. Their collection is business oriented, and the staff is available to direct you to appropriate resources.

* Business Services Directory

Office of Business Liaison
U.S. Department of Commerce
14th St. and Constitution Ave., NW, Room 5898C
Washington, DC 20230   202-377-3176
The *Business Services Directory* gives you a brief description of all the programs of the U.S. Department of Commerce, including phone numbers, and is used by the business community to find sources of information within the Department. Those in business can see the activities of the various programs and how they relate to their particular business. This free directory is available from the office listed above.

* Census Information on Business

Bureau of the Census
U.S. Department of Commerce
Washington, DC 20233   301-763-4040
The U.S. Bureau of the Census collects a vast amount of information on business. *The Factfinder for the Nation* series summarizes reports and their availability by subject area. CFF-5 lists reference sources for Census Data and is a good place to begin your research. Factfinders related to business are the following:

CFF-6 Housing Statistics - June 1991
CFF-9 Construction Statistics - September 1989
CFF-10 Retail Trade Statistics - May 1989
CFF-11 Wholesale Trade Statistics - May 1989
CFF-12 Statistics on Service Industries - July 1989
CFF-13 Transportation Statistics - September 1989
CFF-15 Statistics on Manufacturing - March 1990
CFF-16 Statistics on Mineral Industries - February 1990
CFF-20 Energy and Related Statistics - September 1991

Census Fact Finders are available for a nominal fee, usually $.25 or $.30 per copy.

Business and Industry

* Census Statistics Business Experts

Bureau of the Census
U.S. Department of Commerce
Washington, DC 20233   301-763-4100

The Telephone Contact List at the Bureau of the Census can put you in touch with a census expert studying business (or other) issues. It is available free.

* Commerce Libraries

Library
U.S. Department of Commerce
14th St. and Constitution Ave., NW
Washington, DC 20230   202-377-5511

Many libraries within the U.S. Department of Commerce are open to the public and have collections specific to the concerns of the various Bureaus. You can contact the libraries directly regarding hours of operations, and questions on various topics:

NOAA

Library and Information Services, National Oceanic and Atmospheric Administration, 6009 Executive Blvd., Rockville, MD 20852; 301-443-8330

NIST

Research Information Center, National Institute of Standards and Technology, Administration Bldg. 101, Room E106, Gaithersburg, MD 20899; 301-975-3052

Patent and Trademark Office

Scientific Library, Patent and Trademark Office, 2021 Jefferson Davis Hwy., Arlington, VA 22202; 703-557-2955

Census Bureau

Library, Bureau of the Census, Federal Office Bldg. No. 3, Room 2455, Washington DC 20233; 301-763-5042

* Commercial and Industrial Conservation

Distributer and Marketing Services
Tennessee Valley Authority (TVA)
Power, 1101 Market St.
4S136X Missionary Ridge Pl.
Chattanooga, TN 37402   615-751-5103

The TVA offers businesses, industries, and other nonresidential power users free, in-depth energy conservation audits upon request, with loans available for those businesses and industries which carry out measures recommended in the audits. The program assists with water heating, space heating, and air conditioning as end uses. Contact this office for more information on energy audits and conservation.

* Communications and Information Policy

Public Information
National Telecommunications and
Information Administration
U.S. Department of Commerce
14th St. and Constitution Ave., NW, Room 4898
Washington, DC 20230   202-377-1551

The National Telecommunications and Information Administration's policy recommendations affect the nation's economic and technological advancement in the telecommunications industry. This includes common carrier, telephone, broadcast, and satellite communications systems. It is involved with regulatory changes that have led to increased competition in common carrier operations and the growing overlap between telecommunications and computers. In the information field, NTIA focuses attention on issues of privacy and security and the impact of U.S. and international privacy legislation on the flow of electronic data across national boundaries. Contact this office for more information.

* Communications Industry Analysis

Federal Communications Commission (FCC)
Public Reference Room
1919 M Street, NW, Room 537
Washington, DC 20554   202-632-0745

Documents on File: Reports required by FCC Rules and Regulations, Administrative Reports, Annual Reports to Stockholders, FCC Form 492, Rate of Return Report, Statistics of Communications Common Carriers, Quarterly Operating Data of Telephone and Telegraph Carriers, Switched Access Reports, Equal Access Implementation Reports, NECA - Pool Results, Local Exchange Rates, Monthly Bypass Request Report - AT&T, Lifeline Link-Up Reports, IAD Reports, General

Reference Material from Sources. Hours of Operation: Monday through Friday, 9:00 a.m. to 1:00 p.m., 2:00 p.m. to 5:00.

* Consumer Affairs

Office of Consumer Affairs (OCA)
U.S. Department of Commerce
14th St. and Constitution Ave., NW, Room 5718
Washington, DC 20230   202-377-5001

The office provides advice and technical assistance to businesses on problems and issues of concern to consumers. Through cooperative projects among businesses, consumers, and local and state governments, this office works to improve companies' customer relations and the quality of goods and services. OCA also helps businesses deal with customer concerns about advertising, warranties, complaint-handling, credit, and products safety, as well as helping them establish ways to involve consumers in the development of product safety and performance standards. OCA also mediates between consumers and businesses on complaints and inquiries, helping businesses to reach equitable resolutions to such complaints.

* Consumer Information and Complaint Centers

The Interstate Commerce Commission has three regional offices which serve a variety of functions, one of which is to answer inquiries and assist the public with concerns regarding interstate bus, trucking, and railroad companies. The most frequent calls involve moving companies.

Eastern

Interstate Commerce Commission, 3535 Market St., Room 16400, Philadelphia, PA 19104; 215-596-4040. States served: AL, CT, DE, DC, FL, GA, KY, MA, MD, ME, MS, OH, PA, NC, NH, NJ, NY, RI, SC, TN, VA, VT, WV.

Central

Interstate Commerce Commission, Xerox Center, 55 West Monroe Street, Suite 570, Chicago, IL 60603; 312-353-6204. States served: AR, IA, IL, IN, KS, LA, MI, MO, MN, NE, ND, OK, SD, TX, WI.

Western

Interstate Commerce Commission, 211 Maine St., Suite 500, San Francisco, CA 94105; 415-774-6520. States served: AK, AZ, CA, CO, ID, MT, NV, NM, OR, UT, WA, WY.

Questions can also be directed to the ICC office in Washington DC, at 202-927-7597.

* Consumer Rule Guides for Businesses

Federal Trade Commission
Public Reference Branch, Room 130
6th and Pennsylvania Ave., NW
Washington, DC 20580   202-326-2222

The FTC publishes the following guides for businesses to help them comply with the most current consumer trade rules and regulations, on everything from offering layaways to the Federal warranty law.

Business Guide to the Federal Trade Commission's Mail Order Rule
Businessperson's Guide to Federal Warranty Law
Direct Marketer's Guide to Labeling Requirements Under the Textile and Wool Acts
Complying with the Credit Practices Rule
Guides for the Jewelry Industry
Handling Customer Complaint: In-House and Third-Party Strategies
How to Write Readable Credit Forms
Offering Layaways
Payments and Services
Rules and Regulations Under the Hobby Protection Act
Textile and Wool Acts
Writing a Care Label: How to Comply with the Amended Care Labeling Rule
Writing Readable Warranties

* Donations to the Peace Corps

Peace Corps
1990 K St., NW
Washington, DC 20526   202-606-3063

The Peace Corps offers corporations donate materials if a need for them materials exists. Contact this office for more information on the donation process.

Be patient. If any phone number is incorrect, call (area code) 555-1212 and request the new listing.

* Economic Studies of Transit Industry

Industry, Economics and Finance Division (P-37)
Office of Economics
Policy and International Affairs
Office of the Secretary of Transportation
U.S. Department of Transportation
400 7th Street, SW, Room 10223
Washington, DC 20590   202-366-5412

Financial and economic studies of the transportation industry are prepared by this office. Air transportation is emphasized, but other modes are also evaluated. Report topics include mergers, regional marketing studies, gross receipts at airports, and intelligent vehicle highway systems. Contact this office to determine if a study has been prepared on your subject.

* Explosives: Laws and Regulations

Distribution Center
Bureau of Alcohol, Tobacco, and Firearms (ATF)
U.S. Department of the Treasury
7943 Angus Ct.
Springfield, VA 22153   703-455-7801

ATF laws and regulations for firearms are described in the free book, *ATF: Explosives Law and Regulations*. Commerce in explosives is highlighted, describing licenses and permits, business conduct, records and reports, storage, exemptions, and unlawful acts. The impact of the regulations on the fireworks industry is also discussed.

* Federal Maritime Commission

Federal Maritime Commission
1100 L Street NW
Washington, DC 20573   202-523-5725

Established in 1961, the Federal Maritime Commission (FMC) monitors relationships among carriers and also ensures that individual carriers fairly treat shippers and other members of the shipping public. The commission consists of 5 full time commissioners appointed by the President, with no more than 3 from the same political party, serving 5 year terms. The FMC has 230 full time equivalent positions and an appropriated budget of $15,452,000.

* Gifts-in-Kind Program

Office of Private Sector Development
Peace Corps
1990 K St., NW
Washington, DC 20526   202-606-3063

The Peace Corps allows corporations to donate materials if a need for them materials exists. Contact this office for more information on the donation process.

* Highway Contractors and Subcontractors

Office of Civil Rights (HCR-1)
Federal Highway Administration (FHWA)
U.S. Department of Transportation
400 7th St., SW
Washington, DC 20590   202-366-0693

This office monitors compliance with civil rights laws by requiring contractors and subcontractors of Federal highway projects to submit employment data. Equal opportunity issues are also addressed in the Disadvantaged Business Enterprise Program, which awards contracts and subcontract commitments to small and minority businesses, and in the Federal Highway Administration's (FHWA) Historically Black Colleges and Universities Programs. Data from contractor filings and a list of contractors and subcontractors, by state or county, are available from this office. You can also obtain a copy of *FHWA's Historically Black Colleges and Universities Programs*, a publication with details about those programs.

* Hiring Incentives for Employers of Veterans

Assistant Secretary for Veterans
Employment and Training
U.S. Department of Labor
200 Constitution Ave., NW, Room S1313
Washington, DC 20210   202-523-9116

As a hiring incentive, the Veterans Administration will pay an employer half of a Veteran's entry wages up to $10,000 for up to nine months or fifteen months for a veteran with a disability rating of 30% or more. A veteran must have served during the Korean Conflict or the Vietnam Era, and have been unemployed for 10 to 15 weeks. Employers must certify that they intend to hire the veteran upon completion of training. Adequate training facilities must be available; wages and benefits must be no less than those normally paid; and training cannot be for a position for which the Veteran already qualifies. Veterans and employers alike must apply for certification with any local job service office or VA Regional Office.

* Infrastructure Technologies

Office of Technology Assessment (OTA)
600 Pennsylvania Ave., SE
Washington, DC 20510   202-228-6939

Public works infrastructure, which includes roads, bridges, sewers, etc., provides essential services--moving people and goods, supplying water, and disposing of waste. And there is little disagreement about the urgency of repair, maintenance, or new construction of these vital systems. The Office of Technology Assessment (OTA) is currently studying how technological, institutional, and financial alternatives could be combined to meet the challenges posed by infrastructure needs that might be required in the Federal role. Contact Edith Page, the project director, for more information.

* International Trade Administration Publications

International Trade Administration (ITA)
U.S. Department of Commerce
14th St. and Constitution Ave., NW
Washington, DC 20230   202-377-5487

The International Trade Administration (ITA) of the U.S. Department of Commerce produces numerous publications on U.S. business, particularly related to exports and foreign domestic competition in the U.S. Publications are available from ITA, NTIS, and GPO. Contact ITA for a free publications list.

* Interstate Commerce Commission

Interstate Commerce Commission (ICC)
12th St. and Constitution Ave., NW
Washington, DC 20423   202-927-7597

The Interstate Commerce Commission was created as an independent regulatory agency by act of February 4, 1887 to regulate commerce. ICC's responsibilities include regulation of carriers engaged in transportation in interstate commerce and in foreign commerce to the extent that it takes place within the U.S. Surface transportation under the Commission's jurisdiction includes railroads, trucking companies, bus lines, freight forwarders, water carriers, transportation brokers, and a coal slurry pipeline. The regulatory laws vary depending on the type of transportation; however, they generally involve certification of carriers seeking to provide transportation for the public, rates, adequacy of service, purchases, and mergers. The Commission assures that the carriers it regulates will provide the public with rates and services that are fair and reasonable.

* ICC Library

Interstate Commerce Commission (ICC)
12th St. and Constitution Ave., NW, Room 3392
Washington, DC 20423   202-927-5642

The Interstate Commerce Commission's library is open to the public, and its collection focuses on transportation and transportation law. You must sign in with the building guard before going up to the library.

* Long Distance Carrier Information

Industry Analysis
Federal Communications Commission
Public Reference Room
1919 M Street, NW, Room 537
Washington, DC 20554   202-632-0745

The Industry Analysis division compiles information on market share for all long distance carriers whose total toll service revenue is $100 million or greater. The Downtown Copy Center has a report entitled the *Long Distance Market Share Report*, detailing this information.

* Major Developments in U.S. Shipping Trade

Federal Maritime Commission (FMC)
1100 L Street, NW
Washington, DC 20573   202-523-5725

The Federal Maritime Commission continually monitors developments in the major shipping markets around the world. Information on rates, capacity, and international

Business and Industry

agreements is compiled. The FMC also has information on developments with respect to the major carriers. The FMC breaks its analysis down in the following geographic manner: Transatlantic, Mediterranean, Africa, Transpacific, Latin America and the Caribbean, and the Middle East.

* Maritime Administration Activities and Statistics

MARAD - Public Affairs
U.S. Department of Transportation
400 7th Street, SW, Room 7219
Washington, DC 20590   202-366-5807

MARAD's annual report is an excellent place to begin your search for information on U.S. maritime activities and statistics. The report includes a profile of the U.S. Merchant Fleet, U.S. Department of Defense Cargo programs, information on maritime labor and training, and a report on maritime agreements recently concluded between the U.S. and foreign nations. Statistics include listings for worldwide ship deliveries, Federal Ship financing guarantee program, U.S. Oceangoing Merchant Marine, major world merchant fleets, U.S. Great Lakes Merchant Fleet, the National Defense Reserve Fleet, and maritime subsidy outlays. The report is available free upon request.

* Maritime Commerce Financial Analysis

Bureau of Domestic Regulation
Federal Maritime Commission
1100 L Street, NW
Washington, DC 20573   202-523-5796

The Bureau of Domestic Regulation provides accounting and financial expertise to help ensure the reasonableness of rates for the transportation of cargo and other services provided by common carriers in the domestic offshore waterborne commerce of the U.S. The Bureau also provides technical assistance to other activities within the Commission.

* Metals and Mining Producers

American Mining Congress (AMC)
1920 N St., NW, Suite 300
Washington, DC 20036   202-861-2800

The American Mining Congress (AMC) is an industry association of producers of metals, coal industrial and agricultural minerals; manufacturers of mining and mineral processing machinery, equipment and supplies; and mining engineering firms. AMC publishes the *American Mining Congress Journal*, a monthly journal which focuses on mining issues and policy and is available for $30 per year. AMC can also put you in touch with members who can provide you with detailed information on most aspects of the mining industry.

* Metric Conversion Assistance

National Institute of Standards and Technology
Office of Metric Programs
U.S. Department of Commerce
Building 411, Room A146
Gaithersburg, MD, 20899   301-975-3689

This office coordinates Federal metric transition to promote consistency in agency plans, policies, and practices. It identifies and helps remove barriers that inhibit or block metric transition in federal, state, or local rules, standards and codes, or regulations. It also provides technical and general information about the metric system and its use to businesses, educators, the news media, and the general public. There are several free brochures and pamphlets available from the Office explaining the metric system and metric conversions.

* Mine Maps/Mine Companies Property Ownership

Division of Program Information and Analysis
Bureau of Mines
U.S. Department of the Interior
810 7th St., NW
Washington, DC 20241   202-501-9650

Valuable information is available from the mine maps available through the mine map repositories of the Office of Surface Mining Reclamation and Enforcement. Mine and company names, water sources, property ownership of adjoining companies and towns, latitudes and longitudes, coal outcrop seam designations, openings and emergency exits of mines, and gas and power lines are some of the topics covered. This information can be useful to local developers, engineering firms, and energy interests, as well as private citizens.

* Minerals: Data, Industries, and Technology

Publication Distribution
Bureau of Mines
U.S. Department of the Interior
Cochrans Mills Rd.
P.O. Box 18070
Pittsburgh, PA 15236   412-892-4338

The Bureau of Mines publishes several reports of investigations and information circulars that are free of charge to those interested in mineral research. *Mineral Industry Surveys* are published monthly, quarterly, and annually, presenting data on various minerals and metals. Reprints from *Minerals Yearbook 1987* are available and report on the mineral industry in the United States and abroad. If documents are unavailable here, they will refer you to the appropriate headquarters office.

* Multinational Corporations in Mining

Office of Mineral Commodities
Bureau of Mines
U.S. Department of the Interior
810 7th St., NW
Washington, DC 20241   202-501-9449

An expert in the office of mineral commodities, Mr. Balazik, can discuss the results of a major study he did for the Bureau of Mines on Multinational Corporations in the mining industry. He examined both U.S. ownership and interest in foreign mining operations as well as foreign ownership and interest in American mining operations. The information presented in the study is based on a review of over 2200 mineral properties operated by more than 400 companies in 80 countries. The study has not yet been published, but Mr. Balazik will share the results of his study and can aid you in your research in this area.

* National Association of Manufacturers

National Association of Manufacturers (NAM)
1331 Pennsylvania Ave., NW, Suite 1500
North Lobby
Washington, DC 20004   202-637-3000

The National Association of Manufacturers is a voice for industry at the national level. Members are manufacturing companies from throughout the United States. Publications: *PAC Manager*, published monthly.

* National Telecommunications

National Telecommunications and Information Administration
U.S. Department of Commerce
14th St. and Constitution Ave., NW
Room 4898
Washington, DC 20230   202-377-1551

This Administration's broad goals include formulating policies to support the development and growth of telecommunications, information and related industries, furthering the efficient development and use of telecommunications and information services, providing policy and management for Federal use of the electromagnetic spectrum, and providing telecommunications facilities grants to public service users. NTIA employs approximately 300 people and has an annual budget of $35,104,000.

* Ocean Commerce Statistics and Information

Bureau of Economic Analysis
Federal Maritime Commission
1100 L Street, NW
Washington, DC 20573   202-523-5870

The Bureau of Economic Analysis provides economic, statistical and financial analysis for the Commission. The Bureau assists in the development of long-range plans for the commission and enhances the agencies responsiveness to new developments and trends in U.S. ocean commerce and the liner shipping industry.

* On-Site Child Care

Women's Bureau
U.S. Department of Labor
200 Constitution Ave., NW, Room S3309
Washington, DC 20210   202-523-6652

The free publication, *Employers and Child Care: Benefiting Work and Family*, is designed for employers and employees concerned with developing programs and policies to assist in quality and cost-efficient child care programs while parents are at work. Created to help in a vast array of situations, it provides guidance to those who wish to improve employee productivity and business' ability to recruit and retain the best workers. It is designed for people who are concerned about fulfilling two essential and often conflicting responsibilities--working and caring for their families.

* Private Sector Initiatives in Mass Transit

Office of Private Sector Initiatives (UBP-30)
Office of Budget and Policy
Federal Mass Transit Administration
U.S. Department of Transportation
400 7th St., SW, Room 9300
Washington, DC 20590   202-366-1666

This office encourages private sector involvement in mass transit throughout the United States. Specifically, they work through the following four areas:

Competitive Contracting: Local transit authorities are encouraged to open the provisioning of services up to private sector competition.

Entrepreneurial Services: Groups in the private sector are encouraged to start self-sustaining transit services (such as taxi and bus) in cooperation with local transit authorities.

Joint Development: Federal assistance is available to help plan public/private sector joint ventures at transit facilities.

Demand Management Program: Federal funds are available to encourage local employers and merchants to develop techniques to help manage transportation and mobility problems in their areas.

* Pulp and Paper Industry

Technical Association of the Pulp and Paper Industry (TAPPI)
Box 105113   800-332-8636
Atlanta, GA 30348   404-446-1400

The Technical Association of the Pulp and Paper Industry consists of individual professionals working in pulp, paper, packaging, converting and non-wovens industries. Publications: *TAPPI Journal*.

* Rail Industry Conditions

Office of Industry, Finance and Operations (RRP-11)
Federal Railroad Administration
U.S. Department of Transportation
400 7th Street, SW, Room 8302
Washington, DC 20590   202-366-0386

This office serves as the principal advisory element in assessing the financial and operating condition of the railroad industry, with special emphasis on carriers in marginal or bankrupt financial condition. This office also administers programs to improve railroad labor/management relations and monitors disputes under the Railway Labor Act.

* Railroad Industry Analysis

Office of External Affairs
Interstate Commerce Commission (ICC)
12th Street and Constitution Ave., NW
Washington, DC 20423   202-927-5737

The ICC Annual Report contains a detailed analysis of current developments in the Rail industry falling under their jurisdiction including financial conditions, reorganizations, mergers and acquisitions, labor issues, abandonments, rates, freight service, and passenger service.

* Science and Technical Business References

Science and Technology Division
Reference Section
Library of Congress
Washington, DC 20540   202-707-5580

Informal series of reference guides are issued free from the Science and Technology Division under the general title, *LC Science Tracer Bullet*. These guides are designed to help readers locate published material on subjects about which they have only general knowledge. New titles in the series are announced in the weekly Library of Congress *Information Bulletin* that is distributed to many libraries including:

80-3 Automotive Electronics
80-6 Lasers and Their Applications

80-19 Industrial Robots
81-9 Cable Television (Cable TV)
82-5 Jet Engines and Jet Aircraft
84-7 Biotechnology
87-9 Microcomputers
87-12 Optical Disc Technology

* Space Management Research

Office of Planning
Public Buildings Service
General Services Administration
18th and F Sts., NW
Washington, DC 20405   202-501-0638

Information on space management research studies which emphasize efficiency and cost productiveness can be obtained by contacting this office.

* Statistics Reports

Publications
Office of the Secretary
Interstate Commerce Commission
12th St. and Constitution Ave., NW
Washington, DC 20423   202-927-5930

This office compiles and publishes statistics on the various modes of transportation.

Annual
Transport Statistics in the United States. Detailed data on traffic, operations, equipment, finances, and employment for carriers subject to the Interstate Commerce Act.

A-300 Wage Statistics of Class I Freight Railroads in the United States-Calendar Year. Number of employees, service hours, and compensation by occupational group: Executive, Officials, and Staff Assistants; Professional and Administrative; Maintenance-of-Way and Structures; Maintenance of Equipment and Stores, etc.

Quarterly
Large Class I Motor Carriers of Property Selected Earnings Data. Operating revenues, net carrier operating income, net income, revenue tons hauled, operating ratio and rate of return.

Class I Freight Railroads Selected Earnings Data. Railway operating revenues, net railway operating income, income before extraordinary items, net income, revenue ton-miles of freight, and rate of return.

Large Class I Motor Carriers of Passengers Selected Earnings Data. Operating revenues, net carrier operating income, net income, revenue passengers carried, operating ratio, and rate of return.

Large Class I Household Goods Carriers Selected Earnings Data. Operating revenues, net carrier operating income, net income, revenue tons hauled, operating ratio and rate of return.

Monthly
M-350 Preliminary Report of Railroad Employment, Class I Line-Haul Railroads. Number of employees at middle of month, group totals.

* Tax Credits for Employers of Targeted Groups

Employment and Training Administration
U.S. Department of Labor
200 Constitution Ave., NW, Room S2322
Washington, DC 20210   202-523-6871

The Targeted Jobs Tax Credit Program offers employers a credit against their tax liability for hiring individuals from nine target groups that have traditionally had difficulty obtaining and holding jobs. Groups include disadvantaged youths, the handicapped, disadvantaged veterans, ex-offenders, and recipients of state and federal assistance. An employer must request certification for the individual prior to starting work. The credit applies only to employees hired into a business or trade. For more information contact your local Employment Service offices or your local Internal Revenue Service office.

* Transport Statistics in the United States

Publications
Interstate Commerce Commission

Business and Industry

12th St. and Constitution Ave., NW
Washington, DC 20423   202-927-5930
This is an annual report which contains statistics of railroads and motor carriers. It includes a complete breakdown of finances, expenses and equipment, as well as service statistics. The tables are compiled from reports filed with the Commission by railroads and motor carriers.

* Trucking Company Analysis
Office of External Affairs
Interstate Commerce Commission (ICC)
12th Street and Constitution Ave., NW
Washington, DC 20423   202-927-5737
The *ICC Annual Report* contains a detailed analysis of the developments in the

trucking industry falling under ICC jurisdiction. The 1990 Report discusses the financial condition of the industry, mergers, rates, operating rights, safety, and insurance issues. The report is available free from the ICC.

* Updates on Industry
Industrial Reports and Studies
U.S. Department of Commerce
14th St. and Constitution Ave., NW
Washington, DC 20230   202-377-4356
The U.S. Department of Commerce publishes a massive yearly study on some 350 U.S. industries entitled the *U.S. Industrial Outlook*. Included in this study are analyses of the aviation, maritime, and railroad industries. It is available from the Government Printing Office, 202-512-1800 for $38.

Airlines

The Federal Aviation Administration, an arm of the U.S. Department of Transportation, is the central locus of information on aviation in the U.S. Government. Other sources of information include the Aviation Office within the Office of the Secretary of Transportation and the National Transportation Safety Board.

* Air Carrier Market Data and Statistics

Public Reference Room
Research and Special Programs Administration
U.S. Department of Transportation
400 7th Street, SW, Room 4201
Washington, DC 20590   202-366-4888

Start with this office for market data, financial information, and traffic statistics on air carrier passenger and cargo operations. Information is compiled by DOT from schedules that air carriers file, and some data is stored in a computerized database. For the publication, *Air Carrier Traffic Statistics*, contact the Transportation Systems Center in Cambridge. (See that entry.)

* Air Traffic Management

Office of Air Traffic Management
Federal Aviation Administration (FAA)
U.S. Department of Transportation
800 Independence Ave., SW, Room 400E
Washington, DC 20591   202-267-9155

This office establishes and oversees policies for civilian and military air traffic management. It also operates the FAA national and international flight information and cartographic program and coordinates U.S. policies and procedures related to international air traffic.

* Air Traffic Plans and Requirements

Air Traffic Plans and Requirements
Federal Aviation Administration (FAA)
U.S. Department of Transportation
800 Independence Ave., SW
Room 400 East
Washington, DC 20591   202-267-3136

The air traffic control system tracks flights automatically and tags each one with a small block of information written electronically on the radar scope used by air traffic controllers. The data block includes aircraft identity, altitude and ground speed, and transponder code. Contact this office for more information.

* Air Traffic System Errors

Quality Assurance Division
Air Traffic Services
Federal Aviation Administration (FAA)
U.S. Department of Transportation
800 Independence Ave., SW, Room 416
Washington, DC 20591   202-267-9205

All system errors are logged on a central file chronologically by region. The file consists of reports identifying anything wrong in the air traffic service terminal. Contact this FAA office for more information on system errors.

* Air Travel - General Information

Office of Public Affairs
Federal Aviation Administration (FAA)
U.S. Department of Transportation
800 Independence Ave., SW, Room 907B
Washington, DC 20591   202-267-3481

The FAA can provide you with information on many aspects of air travel. Popular publications include:

Fly Rights: A Guide to Air Travel in the U.S.
Air Travel for the Handicapped.
Child/Infant Safety Seats Recommended for Use in Aircraft.
Air Travel for Your Dog or Cat.
How Safe is Flying?

Alert: FAA Security Tips for Air Travelers.
Caution: Shipping Hazardous Materials by Air.

* Air Travelers' Rights and Complaints

Consumer Affairs Division
Intergovernmental and Consumer Affairs
Governmental Affairs
Office of the Secretary of Transportation
U.S. Department of Transportation
400 7th Street, SW
Washington, DC 20590   202-366-2220

If your problem cannot be resolved directly with the airline, contact this office for information on air travelers' rights and for assistance in resolving problems with airlines and charter flights. Complaints about delayed or canceled flights, reservations, lost baggage, smoking, refunds, and overbooking can also be handled here.

* Aircraft Accident Data: U.S. Air Carrier Operations

National Technical Information Services
5285 Port Royal Road
Springfield, VA 22161

The *Annual Review of Aircraft Accident Data: U.S. Air Carrier Operations* contains statistical tabulations of data compiled from reports of accidents involving revenue operations of U.S. air carriers in a particular calendar year. The report is divided into sections according to the Part of the Code of Federal Regulations under which the aircraft were flown when the accidents occurred (14 CFR Part 121 or 14 CFR Part 135). The Part 135 section is further divided into scheduled and non-scheduled operations. Information provided within each section includes a list of accidents, tabulations of injuries, types of accidents, accident causes and related factors, and accident rates. Comparisons are made of data for the given year to averages of accident data for several prior years. The publication is available for a fee from the office above. Call 703-487-4650 for single copies and microfiche; or 703-487-4630 for an annual subscription.

* Aircraft Accident Investigations

Biomedical and Behavioral Science Division
Office of Aviation Medicine
Federal Aviation Administration (FAA)
U.S. Department of Transportation
800 Independence Ave., SW, Room 400 East
Washington, DC 20591   202-366-6910

This office analyses medical data associated with victims of aviation accidents.

* Aircraft Accident Prevention

Accident Prevention Staff
General Aviation Division
Flight Standards Service
Federal Aviation Administration (FAA)
U.S. Department of Transportation
800 Independence Ave., SW, Room 2322
Washington, DC 20591   202-366-6321

The staff provides national guidance and policy on accident prevention in general aviation. This office supports 9 regional offices and 78 field offices. For information on available publications, tapes, slides, seminars, and speakers, contact the office at the above address or contact your local field office. General publications available from this office include the following:

The Accident Prevention Program   FAA P 8740-8
Safe Flying for Agricultural Aviation   FAA P 8740-42
Notices to Airmen   FAA P 8740-54

Be patient. If any phone number is incorrect, call (area code) 555-1212 and request the new listing.

771

Business and Industry

* Aircraft Accident Reports

Accident/Incident Analysis Branch
Air Traffic Service
Federal Aviation Administration (FAA)
U.S. Department of Transportation
800 Independence Ave., SW, Room 417D
Washington, DC 20591   202-267-9612

Accidents and incidents involving aircraft are documented in a central file maintained by this FAA branch. Contact this office for more information on the information in these files.

* Aircraft Accidents

Safety Analysis Division
Office of Aviation Safety
Federal Aviation Administration (FAA)
U.S. Department of Transportation
800 Independence Ave., SW, Room 2221A
Washington, DC 20591   202-366-6003

The division can provide you with information on general aviation accidents and near mid-air collisions. The Office keeps statistics on operational errors, deviations, pilot errors, accidents, and near mid air collisions.

* Aircraft Accident Statistics

Safety Data Branch
Information Management
National Field Office
Federal Aviation Administration (FAA)
U.S. Department of Transportation
P.O. Box 25082, AVN-124
Oklahoma City, OK 73125   405-680-6420

The FAA maintains statistics on the following: general aviation accident information; incidents (little damage or minor injury) of both air carrier and general aviation; service difficulty reports; and enforcement data and violations. Contact this office for more information.

* Aircraft Certification Service

Administrator for Regulation and Certification
Federal Aviation Administration (FAA)
800 Independence Ave SW, Room 300W
Washington DC 20591   202-267-7270

The certification of airworthiness goes to the heart of aviation safety. Certification occurs at three stages: the design of the aircraft; the production of the aircraft; and the operation of the aircraft. For information and a copy of a booklet on the Aircraft Certification Service, contact the above office.

* Aircraft Flight Data and Voice Recorders Investigations

Engineering Services Division
Bureau of Technology
National Transportation Safety Board (NTSB)
800 Independence Avenue, SW, Room 826
Washington, DC 20594   202-382-6686

For information on aircraft flight data and voice recorders examined by the NTSB, contact the office above.

* Aircraft Maintenance Data

Maintenance Analysis Center Section
AVN-140
Federal Aviation Administration (FAA)

U.S. Department of Transportation
Aeronautical Center
P.O. Box 25082
Oklahoma City, OK 73125   405-680-6495

Information and statistics are available regarding aircraft include maintenance surveillance, mechanical interruptions, and inflight mechanical problems.

* Aircraft Noise

Noise Abatement Division
Office of Environment and Energy
Federal Aviation Administration (FAA)
U.S. Department of Transportation
800 Independence Ave., SW, Room 432
Washington, DC 20591   202-267-3699

This FAA division conducts research on reducing noise levels of new aircraft, and retrofitting older aircraft to reduce noise levels. Contact this office for recent noise Advisory Circulars that certify the noise levels for aircraft under Federal Aviation Regulation 36. Ask for Advisory Circulars 36-1E; 36-2C; and 36-2F.

* Aircraft Standards and Statistics Data Base

Management Standards and Statistics Division
Federal Aviation Administration (FAA)
AMS-400
U.S. Department of Transportation
800 Independence Ave., SW
Washington, DC 20591   202-267-8063

The FAA maintains several computerized data files on a variety of aviation-related subjects such as: aviation safety, air traffic, aviation schools, commercial and government ownership and operation of aircraft, aircraft repair stations, FAA facilities, and procurement. While the FAA does not conduct searches of these files for anyone outside the agency, they will copy any file you designate onto a blank tape that you provide for $38.

* Airline Antitrust Violations

Aviation Analysis
Federal Aviation Administration (FAA)
U.S. Department of Transportation
800 Independence Ave., SW, Room 10223
Washington, DC 20591   202-267-4382

The office investigates airline mergers and interlocks, unfair methods of competition among carriers, and also determines antitrust immunity. Contact this FAA office for more information on airline antitrust issues.

* Airline Data

Office of Airline Statistics
Research and Special Programs Administration
U.S. Department of Transportation (DOT)
400 7th Street, SW, Room 4125
Washington, DC 20590   202-366-9059

The Aviation Information Management (AIM) program collects information on the financial operations of air carriers. Government, industry, and the general public may access this information. Database functions are housed at the Transportation Systems Center (see entry) but this office can serve as liaison for access to air carrier reports and data requiring DOT approval for release.

* Airline Passenger Safety

Community and Consumer Liaison Division
Office of Public Affairs
Federal Aviation Administration (FAA)
U.S. Department of Transportation
800 Independence Ave., SW
Washington, DC 20591   202-267-3481

Airline passengers who have inquiries or complaints regarding airplane safety should contact this office.

* Airlines General Inquiries

Office of Public Affairs
Federal Aviation Administration (FAA)
U.S. Department of Transportation
800 Independence Ave., SW

Washington, DC 20591   202-267-3481

Questions and information requests about the aviation industry can be directed to this FAA office.

* Airline Transportation Data Files

Center for Electronic Records
National Archives and Records Administration
8th St. and Pennsylvania Ave., NW, Room 20E
Washington, DC 20408   202-523-3267

This center has information regarding airline transportation from the U.S. Department of Transportation and the Civil Aeronautics Board. Contact the Center for a detailed listing of the data available and the fees for retrieval.

* Airmen and Aircraft Registry

Airmen and Aircraft Registry
Federal Aviation Administration (FAA)
U.S. Department of Transportation
Mike Monroney Aeronautical Center
P.O. Box 25082
Oklahoma, OK 73125   405-680-4331

The FAA keeps permanent records on all U.S. civil aircraft and airmen (students, private, commercial and airline transport). The Registry also issues and monitors certificates to air carrier personnel involved in international civil aviation. Contact this office for information on these records, along with the registration records of all civil aircraft.

* Airport Capacity

Office of Systems Capacity and Requirements
Airport Capacity Planning and Development
Federal Aviation Administration (FAA)
U.S. Department of Transportation
800 Independence Ave., SW, Room 723
Washington, DC 20591   202-267-7425

This office is involved in a variety of programs to increase the capacity of the national air system through programs of improved airport and air routes design; improved procedures that allow planes to fly in closer proximity more safely; and developing new technology in areas such as radar precision. This office's work is detailed in the Aviation System Capacity Plan, which publishes statistics and outlines FAA programs in capacity expansion.

* Airport Hubs

Office of Aviation Policy and Plans
Forecast Branch
Federal Aviation Administration (FAA)
U.S. Department of Transportation
800 Independence Ave.,SW, Room 935F
Washington, DC 20591   202-267-3355

The Office of Aviation Policy and Plans analyzes activity at different airport hubs around the country. There are currently 25 large hubs, encompassing 40 carrier airports, in the U.S. There are reports on all the major hubs in the U.S. Contact this office for more information. Recent reports focus on:

Washington/Baltimore Hub	October 1991
Denver Hub/Colorado Airports	October 1990
Miami/ Ft. Lauderdale (update)	December 1990
Nashville, Tn.	September 1989
Dayton, Ohio.	September 1989
Cincinnati, Ohio.	September 1989
Raleigh/Durham, N.C.	June 1989
Atlanta (update)	June 1989

* Airport Security

Airport Security Program
Civil Aviation Security Service
Federal Aviation Administration (FAA)
U.S. Department of Transportation
800 Independence Ave., SW, Room 319
Washington, DC 20591   202-267-9863

The FAA ensures the presence of law enforcement in U.S. airports, and approves the security programs of all airports under FAR 107. It also certifies walk-through detection devices.

* Airport Safety and Facilities

Airport Safety Data Branch
Federal Aviation Administration (FAA)
U.S. Department of Transportation
800 Independence Ave., SW, Room 616A
Washington, DC 20591   202-267-8730

This office collects data on airport services, schedules, runway layouts, and lighting. The data is published in the *Airport Facility Directory*. Information is available to the public, but requestors are limited to two facility inquiries per request. Those wishing to do large scale research may make an appointment and go to the Airport Safety Data Branch and use the files. The information is also available on magnetic disk. For further information, contact the Branch.

* Airport Standards

Design and Operational Criteria Division
Office of Airport Standards
Federal Aviation Administration (FAA)
U.S. Department of Transportation
800 Independence Ave., SW, Room 614
Washington, DC 20591   202-267-3446

This office can provide you with information on standards required for constructing and operating airports. Such standards include size, length, separation between runways, snow and ice control, and crash and fire rescue equipment. Contact this office for more information.

* Airway Facilities

Associate Administrator for Airway Facilities
Planning Branch
Federal Aviation Administration (FAA)
U.S. Department of Transportation
800 Independence Ave., SW, Room 731
Washington, DC 20591   202-267-7304

This office is responsible for the establishment, installation and maintenance of the infrastructural facilities such as radars, communications, and navigation aids in the National Aerospace System.

* Annual Review of Aircraft Accidents

National Technical Information Services
5285 Port Royal Road
Springfield, VA 22161   703-557-4650

The *Annual Review of Aircraft Accident Data: U.S. General Aviation* contains statistical tabulations of data compiled from reports of accidents involving U.S. general aviation aircraft in a particular calendar year. The report is divided into sections according to the type of aircraft and also according to the purpose for which aircraft was being used at the time of an accident. Within each section, tabulations provide data describing the types, causes, and circumstances of accidents. Accident rates (total and fatal) are provided, as are comparisons of the data of the given year to averages of accident data for several prior years. This publication is available from the office above. Call 703-487-4650 for single copies and microfiche; or 703-487-4630 for an annual subscription.

* Aviation Accident Prevention

Flight Standards Service
Accident Prevention Program
Federal Aviation Administration (FAA)
U.S. Department of Transportation
800 Independence Ave.,SW, Room 2232
Washington, DC 20591   202-267-6321

The Accident Prevention Program has a variety of publications on aircraft safety. All are free and can be obtained by contacting the above office.

The Accident Prevention Program.	*FAA P 8740-8*
Safe Flying for Agricultural Aviation.	*FAA P 8740-42*
Notices to Airmen.	*FAA P 8740-54*
Weight and Balance: An Important Safety Consideration for Pilots.	*FAA P 8740-5*
Pilot Prerogatives.	*FAA P 8740-17*
Dead Reckoning Navigation.	*FAA P 8740-22*
Always Leave Yourself an Out.	*FAA P 8740-25*
Using the System.	*FAA P 8740-32*
The Propwatchers Guide.	*FAA P 8740-37*
Radio Communications.	*FAA P 8740-47*
How to Avoid a Mid-Air Collision.	*FAA P 8740-51*

Be patient. If any phone number is incorrect, call (area code) 555-1212 and request the new listing.

773

Business and Industry

* Aviation Equipment Specifications

Engineering and Specifications Division
Office of Airport Standards
Federal Aviation Administration (FAA)
U.S. Department of Transportation
800 Independence Ave., SW, Room 614
Washington, DC 20591   202-267-3826

This office can supply you with information on specifications for the manufacturing and installation of such aviation equipment as visual aides associated with aircraft landing and taxiing, runway lights, approach lights, beacons, and so forth.

* Aviation Forecasts

Aviation Forecasts Branch
Office of Aviation Policy
Federal Aviation Administration (FAA)
U.S. Department of Transportation
800 Independence Ave., SW, Room 935F
Washington, DC 20591   202-267-3103

This Branch is responsible for forecasting aviation activity for the United States. Data collected include the number of landings, takeoffs, aircraft, enplanements, and deplanements.

The following publications are available through this office, free of charge, depending on availability; otherwise you will be referred to the Government Printing Office, where they can be purchased:

Federal Aviation Administration Aviation Forecast. This microfiche provides 12-year projections on all aspects of aviation, including total aircraft, total airborne, statute miles of U.S. air carriers, hours flown in general aviation, and fuel consumed.

Terminal Area Forecasts. This microfiche provides 10-year projections on 400 specific airports including in-plane passengers, and operations of air carriers.

North Atlantic Forecast. This report contains short, medium, and long-term forecasts of air traffic over the North Atlantic and between North America and the Caribbean area for the periods 1991-1996, 2000, 2005 and 2010. Annual forecasts are provided for total passengers and aircraft movements.

Sixteenth Annual FAA Aviation Forecast Conference Proceedings. This report discusses a variety of forecast related issues including the outlook for Hubbing, Education and Noise, and financing issues in the aviation industry.

Forecasting Civil Aviation Activity: Methods and Approaches.

FAA Flight Service Station Facility Level Forecast: Fiscal Years 1992-2002.

* Aviation History

Agency Historian
Office of Public Affairs
Federal Aviation Administration (FAA)
U.S. Department of Transportation
800 Independence Ave., SW, Room 907A
Washington, DC 20591   202-267-3478

This office can provide you with the facts on the history of American aviation as well as a five page brief on the history of the Federal Aviation Administration (FAA). A list of FAA historical works is also available from this office. Books can be purchased from the Government Printing Office (GPO), 202-512-1800. Additional information on aviation or FAA history can also be obtained at the FAA library, which is open to the public.

* Aviation Medicine

Biomedical and Behavioral Science Division
Office of Aviation Administration
Federal Aviation Administration (FAA)
U.S. Department of Transportation
800 Independence Ave., SW, Room 2338C
Washington, DC 20591   202-366-6910

The FAA conducts aeromedical research on in the following areas:

- **Psychology:** evaluates spatial disorientation and visual perception in the aviation environment;
- **Physiology:** performance and health of aircrew and air traffic controllers under diverse environmental conditions;

- **Toxicology:** toxic hazards such as pesticides used in aerial application, products of combustion and ionizing radiation from air shipment of radioactive cargo in the high-altitude environment;
- **Protection and survival:** studies of techniques for lessening or preventing crash injuries, developing concepts and evaluating survival equipment used under adverse physical conditions, establishing human physical limitations of civil aviation operations, and evaluating emergency procedures for downed aircraft.

* Aviation News

FAA General Aviation News
General Aviation and Commercial Division
Flight Standards Service, AFS-800
Federal Aviation Administration (FAA)
U.S. Department of Transportation
800 Independence Ave., SW, Room 325
Washington, DC 20591   202-267-8212

The bimonthly publication, *Aviation News,* is a safety magazine for general aviation pilots (for more information about content, contact the above office). It is available for $13 per year from the Government Printing Office, Superintendent of Documents, Washington, DC 20402; 202-512-1800.

* Aviation Policy

Information Systems Branch
Policy Analysis Division, APO-130
Office of Aviation Policy and Plans
Federal Aviation Administration (FAA)
U.S. Department of Transportation
800 Independence Ave., SW, Room 937C
Washington, DC 20591   202-267-3350

Reports and other data are generated by approximately 18 databases to aid in aviation policy decisions on such matters as the activities of airlines, seat belt configurations, and the number of airports in the United States.

* Aviation Procedures Periodicals

Superintendent of Documents
U.S. Government Printing Office (GPO)
Washington DC 20402   202-512-1800

The following two periodicals from GPO contain the current internal directives of the Federal Aviation Administration:

Flight Services Handbook. Describes the procedures and terms used by personnel providing assistance and communications services ($46/subscription, #950-032-00000-6).

Data Communications Handbook. Describes teletypewriter operating procedures, applicable international teletypewriter procedures, and continuous U.S. Service weather schedules ($34/subscription, #950-004-00000-2).

* Aviation Publications

U.S Department of Transportation
M-443.2
Washington, DC 20590

Write to the above address to order free copies of the annual *Guide to Federal Aviation Administration Publications* (FAA-APA-PG-11). For approval of more that 10 copies, write to: Federal Aviation Administration, U.S. Department of Transportation, 800 Independence Ave., SW, APA-230, Washington, DC 20591. Many of the publications listed are free.

* Aviation Research and Development Efforts

System Research and Development
Federal Aviation Administration (FAA)
U.S. Department of Transportation, Room 500W
800 Independence Ave., SW
Washington, DC 20591   202-267-8183

This office directs, coordinates, and controls the FAA's Research, Engineering, and Development efforts aimed at bringing new into the National Aerospace System.

* Aviation Safety

Assistant Administrator for Aviation Safety
Federal Aviation Administration (FAA)
U.S. Department of Transportation

Be patient. If any phone number is incorrect, call (area code) 555-1212 and request the new listing.

800 Independence Ave., SW, Room 1000E
Washington, DC 20591   202-267-9613
The Assistant Administrator is involved in all aspects of aviation safety. The Office reviews and recommends safety programs for the FAA and the aviation community. It also initiates special safety reviews and maintains reports on safety data.

* Aviation Standards

Assistant Administrator for Aviation Standards
Mike Monroney Aeronautical Center
P.O. Box 25082
Oklahoma City, OK 73125   405-680-3306
This office promotes flight safety, develops flight procedures, oversees the management of the airman and aircraft registry, provides for the operation and maintenance of FAA aircraft, and investigates aircraft accidents and incidents.

* Aviation Statistics--General

Information Analysis Branch
Management Standards and Statistics Division
Office of Information Technology
Federal Aviation Administration (FAA)
U.S. Department of Transportation
800 Independence Ave., SW, Room 607
Washington, DC 20591   202-267-8063
Historical and current aviation statistics are available on such subjects as: air traffic activities, number of aircraft, flying hours, pilots, and passengers. For a listing of available publications, contact the above office.

* Balloon Safety

Flight Standards Service
Accident Prevention Program
Federal Aviation Administration (FAA)
U.S. Department of Transportation
800 Independence Ave., SW, Room 2322
Washington, DC 20591   202-267-6321
The FAA publishes the following booklets on balloon safety: *Powerlines and Thunderstorms-Balloon Safety,* and *False Lift, Shears, and Rotors - Balloon Safety.* They are available free from the Accident Prevention program.

* Bird Strikes

Airport Safety Data Group
Office of Airport Standards
Federal Aviation Administration (FAA)
U.S. Department of Transportation
800 Independence Ave., SW, Room 615
Washington, DC 20591   202-267-8792
Birds being accidentally sucked into jet engines is a serious aviation hazard. Contact this office for information on where bird strikes occur.

* Careers in Aviation

Office of Public Affairs
Aviation Education Program
Federal Aviation Program
U.S. Department of Transportation
800 Independence Ave., SW, Room 907F
Washington, DC 20591   202-267-3476
Federal, state, and local government agencies are a major source of aviation jobs. The FAA publishes a booklet entitled *Aviation Careers Series* which details a variety of careers in the aviation field. It is available free.

* Commuter and Air Taxi Services

Commuter and Air Taxi Branch
Air Carrier Division
Office of Flight Operations
Federal Aviation Administration (FAA)
U.S. Department of Transportation
800 Independence Ave., SW, Room 306A
Washington, DC 20591   202-267-8086
Contact this office for information regarding policy, regulations, and directives for commuter and air taxi aircraft. A list is available of air taxi operators and commercial operators of small aircraft.

* Consumer Complaints

Community and Consumer Liaison Division
Office of Public Affairs
Federal Aviation Administration (FAA)
U.S. Department of Transportation
800 Independence Ave., SW
Washington, DC 20591   202-267-3481
Complaints involving such aviation issues as safety, noise, pesticide spraying, or broken seat belts can be directed to this office.

* Consumer Rights on Airlines

Government Printing Office (GPO)
Superintendent of Documents
Washington DC 20402   202-512-1800
Fly Rights is an easy-to-read booklet that explains the rights and responsibilities of air travellers. It is available at nominal cost from the Government Printing Office.

* Educational Resources in Aviation

Aviation Education Officer
Federal Aviation Administration (FAA)
U.S. Department of Transportation
800 Independence Ave., SW
Washington, DC 20591   202-267-3469
The Federal Aviation Administration's (FAA) Aviation Education Program offers volunteer assistance to the nation's schools through the following programs: career guidance; tours of airports, control towers, and other facilities; classroom lectures and demonstrations; aviation safety information; aviation education resource materials; computerized clearinghouse of aviation and space information; aviation science instruction programs for home/school computers; "Partnerships-in-Education" activities; and teachers' workshops. Write to the above office for more information.

* Essential Air Passenger Service

Aviation Analysis
Federal Aviation Administration (FAA)
U.S. Department of Transportation
800 Independence Ave., SW, Room 5100
Washington, DC 20591   202-267-5903
This office guarantees that certain cities will be served by airlines. It also represents community views. Contact this office for information on airport service.

* Essential Air Service

Office of Aviation Analysis
Policy and International Affairs
Office of the Secretary of Transportation
U.S. Department of Transportation
400 7th Street, SW, Room 6401
Washington, DC 20590   202-366-5903
The Departments's Essential Air Service Program ensures that certain cities will be served by air transportation. The program establishes subsidy levels, selects carriers, processes applications to change service levels, and reviews fitness of carriers. Contact the office listed for information about this program.

* Experimental Aircraft Association (EAA)

EAA Aviation Center
P.O. Box 3086
Oshkosh, WI 54903-3086   800-322-2412
The Experimental Aircraft Association (EAA) brings together aircraft and aviation enthusiasts from around the country for air shows and activities. It also represents member interests in Washington DC with the Federal Aviation Administration (FAA) and promotes safety and education in aviation. It currently has 700 chapters nationwide.

* Federal Aviation Administration Academy

Federal Aviation Administration (FAA)
U.S. Department of Transportation
P.O. Box 25082, AAC-900
Oklahoma, OK 73125   405-680-6900
The Academy is the principal source of technical information on U.S. civil aviation. It conducts training for FAA personnel through resident or correspondence courses

Be patient. If any phone number is incorrect, call (area code) 555-1212 and request the new listing.

775

Business and Industry

and occasional on-site training. Air traffic training is available for specialists who man the FAA airport traffic control towers, air route traffic control center, and flight service stations. Electronic training is also available for engineers and technicians who install and maintain navigation and traffic control communications facilities. Initial and recurrent training is also conducted for air carrier and general operations inspectors. The Academy provides air navigation facilities and flight procedures analysis to flight inspection personnel.

* Federal Aviation Administration Directives

Office of Public Affairs
Document Inspection Facility
Federal Aviation Administration (FAA)
U.S. Department of Transportation
800 Independence Ave., SW, Room 907
Washington, DC 20591   202-267-3883

Requests for copies of the FAA Directives list should be sent here.

* Films and Videos on Aviation

Public Inquiry Center
Federal Aviation Administration (FAA)
U.S. Department of Transportation, APA-230
Washington, DC 20591   202-267-3481

The Federal Aviation Administration (FAA) has a free catalog of films and videos useful both for experienced aviators as well as the general public. They describe the kinds of programs and measures that can be taken collectively to increase the safety, capacity, and efficiency of the U.S. national airspace system--in areas ranging from air traffic control to aeromedical research, meteorology, and safety. Most of the titles listed in the catalog are available in both 16mm film and 1/2" VHS videocassette. There is no charge for borrowing these FAA titles, and no admission may be charged to any audiences viewing the programs. These titles may also be purchased. For a copy of the *FAA Film/Video Catalog*, contact this office. The following is a list of some of the titles available.

Where Airports Begin.	*#11106*
Looking Up to Your Aviation Career.	*#10314*
Area Navigation.	*#11114*
Flight 52.	*#11127*
Aeromedical Factors.	*#19981*
Medical Facts for Pilots.	*#11138*
Dusk to Dawn.	*#11124*
Mountain Flying.	*#11140*
Overwater Flying.	*#11141*
Path to Safety.	*#11142*

* Financial Analysis of Airline Industry

Aviation Analysis
Office of the Secretary of Transportation
U.S. Department of Transportation
800 Independence Ave., SW, Room 5100
Washington, DC 20591   202-267-5903

Financial studies and evaluations of the air transportation industry are available on such subjects as profit margin trends, aircraft cost and performance, domestic jet trends, fuel trends, carrier lenders, passenger yield, used aircraft sales, aircraft seating trends, and airline employment.

* Flight Instruction

General Aviation Manufactures Association
1400 K. St. NW, Suite 801
Washington, DC 20005   202-393-1500

This association publishes a pamphlet entitled *Learning to Fly* that discusses the basics of flying and the first steps on where to go for flying lessons.

* Flight Procedures

Flight Procedures Branch
Federal Aviation Administration (FAA)
U.S. Department of Transportation
P.O. Box 25082
AVN-220900
Oklahoma, OK 73125   405-680-3382

The branch develops and maintains instrument flight procedures.

* Flight Standards

Flight Procedures Standards Branch
Federal Aviation Administration (FAA)
800 Independence Ave., SW, Room 305C
Washington, DC 20591   202-267-8277

Along with the Flight procedures branch in Oklahoma, the Flight Standards Branch plays a key role in developing flight procedures and overseeing flight inspectors.

* General Inquiries

Office of Public Affairs
Federal Aviation Administration (FAA)
U.S. Department of Transportation
800 Independence Ave., SW
Washington, DC 20591   202-267-3481

The stating place for any information on airlines, airports and aircraft.

* Human Factors: Aviation Research

Civil Aeromedical Institute (CAMI)
Federal Aviation Administration (FAA)
U.S. Department of Transportation
Mike Monroney Aeronautical Center
P.O. Box 25082
Oklahoma, OK 73125   405-680-4806

CAMI conducts research to identify human factor causes of aircraft accidents, prevent future accidents, and make accidents that do occur more survivable. Contact this Institute for more information on this research.

* International Air Transportation

Office of International Aviation
Policy and International Affairs
Office of the Secretary of Transportation
U.S. Department of Transportation
400 7th Street, SW, Room 6402
Washington, DC 20590   202-366-2423

This office studies and develops U.S. policy with regard to international aviation. It ensures cooperation between U.S. and foreign-flag airlines and negotiates air service agreements with other countries.

* International Aviation

Bureau of Economic and Business Affairs
U.S. Department of State
2201 C St., NW, Room 5531
Washington, DC 20520   202-647-7973

In handling all international aviation negotiations and agreements, this office works on expanding aviation markets overseas, aviation security, and other issues relating to international aviation, such as assisting airlines in operating overseas and monitors agreements thereof. Information is available on these topics.

* International Aviation Assistance

Office of International Aviation
International Operations Organization Division
Federal Aviation Administration (FAA)
800 Independence Ave., SW, Room 1027
Washington, DC 20591   202-267-3230

This office handles affairs concerning both international organizations and international assistance for foreign aviation systems. This office works with FAA technical offices on political and bureaucratic aspects of aviation policy with foreign nations. It also works with nations who request assistance for developing aviation infrastructure and training programs.

* Light Twin Engine Aircraft

Flight Standards Service
Accident Prevention Program
Federal Aviation Administration (FAA)
U.S. Department of Transportation
800 Independence Ave., SW, Room 2322
Washington, DC 20591   202-267-6321

The FAA publication *Flying Light Twins Safely* discusses safety with respect to light twin engine aircraft. It is available free.

Be patient. If any phone number is incorrect, call (area code) 555-1212 and request the new listing.

* Medical Certification of Airmen

Civil Aeromedical Institute (CAMI)
Federal Aviation Administration (FAA)
U.S. Department of Transportation
Mike Monroney Aeronautical Center
P.O. Box 25082
Oklahoma, OK 73125   405-680-4806

The Civil Aeromedical Institute (CAMI) operates a program for the medical certification of airmen, and educates pilots and physicians in matters related to aviation safety. It is also responsible for developing and producing brochures, slides, and training films for distribution to aviation groups and organizations. Contact CAMI for more information on certification or these education programs.

* National Aerospace System Development

Assistant Administrator for NAS Development
Federal Aviation Administration (FAA)
U.S. Department of Transportation
800 Independence Ave., SW, Room 800W
Washington, DC 20591   202-267-3555

This office directs Federal Aviation Administration's (FAA) requisition, engineering and management activities for National Aerospace System (NAS) Planning Programs associated with the next generation of communications, navigational, surveillance, and weather systems.

* National Airport System Plan

Office of Airport Planning and Programming
National Planning Division
Federal Aviation Administration (FAA)
U.S. Department of Transportation
800 Independence Ave., SW, Room 615C
Washington, DC 20591   202-267-3451

Contact this office for statistical information on the National Airport System.

* National Flight Data

National Flight Data Center
Airspace--Rules and Aeronautical Information Division
Air Traffic Service
Federal Aviation Administration (FAA)
U.S. Department of Transportation
800 Independence Ave., SW, Room 634
Washington, DC 20591   202-267-9311

This Center can provide you with information on all civilian airports (and those military airports with joint usage), navigation aids, and procedures for the national airspace system. The Center also maintains a database which contains such items as the latitude and longitude of airports, airport runways, records of obstruction to air navigation, flight planning information, bearing and distance information, and records of hazards to air navigation.

* Pilot's Aeromedical Standards

Medical Specialties Division
Office of Aviation Medicine
Federal Aviation Administration (FAA)
U.S. Department of Transportation
800 Independence Ave., SW, Room 322
Washington, DC 20591   202-267-3535

Contact this Federal Aviation Administration (FAA) division for information on policy, regulations, and standards for medical certificates required for a pilot's license.

* Pilot Judgement and Accident Prevention

Flight Standards Service
Accident Prevention Program
Federal Aviation Administration (FAA)
U.S. Department of Transportation
800 Independence Ave., SW, Room 2322
Washington, DC 20591   202-267-6321

Most aircraft accidents occur due to human error rather than mechanical malfunction. The Federal Aviation Administration (FAA) Accident Prevention Program publishes several pamphlets on both common judgement errors and medical problems that can lead to accidents. The following are available free by contacting the above office.

Human Behavior: The No. 1 Cause of Accidents.	*FAA P 8740-38*
What's an Accident Prevention Counselor?	*FAA P 8740-43*
Medical Facts for Pilots.	*FAA P 8740-41*
Introduction to Pilot Judgement.	*FAA P 8740-53*
Impossible Turn.	*FAA P 8740-44*
Proficiency and the Private Pilot.	*FAA P 8740-36*
Pilot Vision.	
Disorientation.	
Beyond the Medical.	
Alcohol and Flying Don't Mix!	

* Pilot Schools

U.S. Government Printing Office (GPO)
Superintendent of Documents
Washington DC 20402   202-512-1800

The *List of Certified Pilot Schools* provides you with an up-to-date directory of pilot training schools in the U.S. It is available for $1.75 from the Government Printing Office (GPO), order #050-007-00763-9.

* Radio Frequency Systems Compatibility

Spectrum Engineering Division
Systems Research and Development Service
Federal Aviation Administration (FAA)
U.S. Department of Transportation
800 Independence Ave., SW, Room 714
Washington, DC 20591   202-267-9710

The Federal Aviation Administration (FAA) ensures that radio systems have frequencies on which to operate that are compatible with other frequencies. Work is also done in conjunction with international organizations on plans for future radio systems.

* Regulatory Standards for Aviation

Regulatory Standards and Compliance
Federal Aviation Administration (FAA)
U.S. Department of Transportation
800 Independence Ave, SW, Room 1040
Washington, DC 20591   202-267-3330

This office provides guidance relating to flight standards, aircraft certification, aircraft programs, aviation medicine, aviation security, aircraft accident investigations, airman and aircraft registry, and rulemaking.

* Relocation Assistance Near Airports

Community and Environmental Needs Division
Office of Airport Planning and Programming
Federal Aviation Administration (FAA)
U.S. Department of Transportation
800 Independence Ave., SW, Room 615B
Washington, DC 20591   202-267-3263

The division assists airport owners involved with airport development projects provide uniform and equitable treatment of persons displaced from their homes and businesses due to federal or federally-assisted programs. Assistance is also available on environmental impact and noise.

* Safety and Aircraft Mechanical Systems.

Flight Standards Service
Accident Prevention Program
Federal Aviation Administration (FAA)
U.S. Department of Transportation
800 Independence Ave., SW, Room 2322
Washington, DC 20591   202-267-6321

Aircraft maintenance and performance are vital parts of aviation safety. The accident prevention program publishes a series of booklets in these areas. They are available free upon request.

Maintenance Aspects of Owning Your Own Airplane	*FAA P 8740-15A*
Meet Your Aircraft	*FAA P 8740-29*
Engine Operation for Pilots	*FAA P 8740-13*
The Silent Enemy: Pneumatic System Malfunction	*FAA P 8740-52*
All About Fuel	*FAA P 8740-35A*
Time in Your Tanks	*FAA P 8740-3*

Business and Industry

* Security

Civil Aviation Security Service (ACS 400)
Federal Aviation Administration (FAA)
U.S. Department of Transportation
800 Independence Ave., SW, Room 320
Washington, DC 20591   202-267-9075

The office is a source of information and expertise on the following airport security issues: domestic and foreign aircraft hijacking; bomb threats at airports and on airplanes; compliance and enforcement of regulations; prevention of attempts; explosives and explosive devices found at airports and on airplanes; international crimes involving civil aviation; information on numbers of people screened, numbers of weapons found, and weapon detection devices.

* Small Business Procurement

Small Business Specialist Procurement Division
AAC-70A
Federal Aviation Administration (FAA)
U.S. Department of Transportation
Mike Monroney Aeronautical Center
P.O. Box 25082
Oklahoma, OK 73125   405-680-7702

The office provides FAA contracting and procurement support for spare parts, modifications and service contracts for the fleet of aircraft, and their air navigation and communication gear operated by the FAA.

* Standards and Statistics Data Base

Management Standards and Statistics Division
Federal Aviation Administration (FAA)
AMS-400
U.S. Department of Transportation
800 Independence Ave., SW, Room 606A
Washington, DC 20591   202-267-8063

The FAA maintains several computerized data files on a variety of aviation-related subjects such as: aviation safety, air traffic, aviation schools, commercial and government ownership and operation of aircraft, aircraft repair stations, FAA facilities, and procurement. While the FAA does not conduct searches of these files for anyone outside the agency, they will copy any file you designate onto a blank tape that you provide for $38.

* Takeoff and Landing Safely

Flight Standards Service
Accident Prevention Program
Federal Aviation Administration (FAA)
U.S. Department of Transportation
800 Independence Ave., SW, Room 2322

Washington, DC 20591   202-267-6321

Many air accidents occur during takeoff or landing. The Federal Aviation Administration (FAA) publishes a series of booklets discussing takeoff and landing safety. The following are available free from the FAA.

Planning Your Takeoff	*FAA P 8740-23*
Preventing Accidents During Aircraft Ground Operations	*FAA P 8740-20*
On Landings Parts I-III	*FAA P 8740-4-50*
Aviation Safety: The Runway Incursion Problem	

* Tariffs and Routes

Aviation Analysis
Federal Aviation Administration (FAA)
U.S. Department of Transportation
800 Independence Ave., SW, Room 10223
Washington, DC 20591   202-267-4382

Contact this office for information regarding carriers' passenger and cargo operations.

* Unauthorized Low Flying Aircraft

Office of Public Affairs
Federal Aviation Administration (FAA)
U.S. Department of Transportation
800 Independence Ave., SW, Room 907B
Washington, DC 20591   202-267-3481

Aircraft flying excessively low are not just a bother, but a threat to public safety. The Federal Aviation Administration (FAA) enforces regulations against unauthorized low flying aircraft. For information, contact the FAA and ask for the publication *How You Can Help FAA Identify Unauthorized Low Flying Aircraft.*

* Weather Factors and Flight Safety

Flight Standards Service
Accident Prevention Program
Federal Aviation Administration (FAA)
U.S. Department of Transportation
800 Independence Ave., SW, Room 2322
Washington, DC 20591   202-267-6321

Changes in weather patterns as well as the normal weather patterns at different points in the year pose significant hazards to pilots. The Accident Prevention Program publishes several pamphlets on flying in difficult weather. They are available free.

Density Altitude	*FAA P 8740-02*
Thunderstorms - Don't Flirt...Skirt em.	*FAA P 8740-12*
Wind Shear.	*FAA P 8740-40*
Tips on Winter Flying.	*FAA P 8740-24*
How to Obtain a Good Weather Briefing.	*FAA P 8740-30B*

Communications

Given its importance to society, the Communications industry is among the most regulated of all industries by the Federal government. The two principal government entities charged with monitoring and regulating the Communications industry are the Federal Communications Commission (FCC) and the National Telecommunications and Information Administration, an arm of the U.S. Department of Commerce. You will find the FCC particularly helpful in locating information. The listings below cover a wide range of communications media including radio, television, cable television, microwave transmissions, long distance telephone service, pay per call (900) services, and political broadcasting.

* Amateur Radio Operators

National Technical Information Service (NTIS)
5285 Port Royal Road
Springfield, VA 22161   703-487-4808

A database of all the Federal Communications Commission's licensed amateur radio operators is available through the National Technical Information Service (NTIS). This magnetic tape file contains records on over 450,000 operators, including names, addresses, ages, station locations, and other licensing information. This Amateur Radio Service Master File (PB 83-220-889), available for $625 (6,250 BPI) or for $825 (BPI), is updated weekly.

* Amateur Radio Services

Consumer Assistance Branch
Federal Communications Commission (FCC)
1270 Fairfield Road
Gettysburg, PA 17326   717-337-1212

The Federal Communications Commission's (FCC) Amateur Radio Services is comprised of three parts--amateur Service, amateur-satellite service, and Radio Amateur Civil Emergency Radio (RACES). During times of national crises, licensed amateur stations can assist local governments in coordinating emergency efforts. Those interested in becoming a licensed ARS operator must take a qualifying exam. Over 450,000 licensed individuals in the U.S. are ARS members.

* Applications and Publications

Services and Supply Branch
Federal Communications Commission (FCC)
1919 M Street, NW, Room B-10
Washington, DC 20554   202-632-7272

This office will provide you with any Federal Communications Commission (FCC) licensing application forms, construction permits, and instructional publications on how to conform with FCC guidelines.

* Auxiliary Services Branch

Federal Communications Commission (FCC)
2025 M Street, NW, Room 7310
Washington, DC 20554   202-632-6485

Documents on File: FM Booster Stations, International, Intercity Relays, Remote Pickups, Translator Relays, Studio Transmitter Link, and so on. Hours of Operation: Monday through Friday, 1:00 p.m. to 5:00 p.m.

* Broadcast Ownership Reference Room

Federal Communications Commission (FCC)
1919 M Street, NW, Room 234
Washington, DC 20554   202-632-6993

Documents on File: Commercial and Non-Commercial Ownership Reports for Station AM, FM, and TV, Contract Files, and Network Affiliation Agreements. Information in these files includes lists of broadcast owners, directors, shares of stock sold, shareholders, media interests held by broadcasters outside their own station in areas such as newspapers. The *Ownership Report* is available from the Reference Room and details this information. Hours of Operation: Monday through Friday, 9:00am to 4:30pm.

* Broadcast Regulations

Mass Media Bureau
Federal Communications Commission (FCC)
1919 M Street, NW, Room 314
Washington, DC 20554   202-632-6460

The Mass Media Bureau has three major responsibilities: 1) regulating AM, FM, and television broadcast stations and related facilities; 2) administering and enforcing cable TV rules; and 3) licensing private microwave radio facilities used by cable systems. The Bureau also processes applications for licenses or other filings, analyzes complaints, and conducts investigations.

* Broadcast Violations

Field Operations Bureau
Federal Communications Commission (FCC)
1919 M Street, NW, Room 725
Washington, DC 20554   202-632-1940

FOB is the FCC's primary point of contact with the public. Field office personnel nationwide interact with consumers, radio communications users, and the telecommunications industry through enforcement and public service activities. The Field Operations Bureau detects violations of radio regulations, monitors transmissions, inspects stations, investigates complaints of radio interference, and issues violations notices. It also examines and licenses radio operators; processes applications for painting, lighting, and placing antenna towers; and furnishes direction-finding aids for ships and aircraft in distress. The bureau maintains over 30 field offices across the country.

* Business Radio Services

Licensing Division
Federal Communications Commission (FCC)
1270 Fairfield Rd
Gettysburg, PA 17326   717-337-1212

The FCC authorizes and licenses all Business Radio Services used in commercial activity. Over 640,000 businesses in the U.S., from mail couriers to exterminators to plumbers, use radio services as part of their operations and must be licensed by the FCC. Updated daily, these files are available on database and can be accessed through SAFE, or at an access terminal by visiting the FCC office in person.

* Cable Television

Federal Communications Commission (FCC)
File Room Number 2
1919 M Street, NW, Room 248
Washington, DC 20554   202-632-6993

Documents on File: FCC Form 325 Schedule 2, Physical System Data, Reference to files that are filed by county, state, and/or operator legal name. Hours of Operation: Monday through Friday, 9:00am to 4:30pm.

* Cable Television

Federal Communications Commission (FCC)
File Room Number 1
1919 M Street, NW, Room 244
Washington, DC 20554   202-632-6993

Documents on File: Correspondence Files, FCC Form 325 Schedule 1, Community

Business and Industry

Unit Data, 76.12 Registration (letter), 76.400 Ownership Change (Letters), Cable Antenna Relay Services (CARS), Cable Show Cause Orders, (CSC) Files, Cable Special Relief (CSR), and Cross-Ownership Files. Hours of Operation: Monday through Friday, 9:00am to 4:30pm.

* Cellular Reference Room

Federal Communications Commission (FCC)
1919 M Street, NW, Room 209
Washington DC 20554   202-632-6400
Documents on File: Pending Cellular Applications, Petitions. Hours of Operation: Tuesday, Thursday, and Friday, 1:00pm to 4:00pm.

* Common Carrier Bureau Reference and File Rooms

Federal Communications Commission (FCC)
Accounting and Audits Division
Public Reference Room
2000 L Street, NW, Room 812
Washington, DC 20554   202-634-1861
Documents on File: Accounts and Subaccounts, Continuing Property Records, Disposition Units, Pension Filings, Official Correspondence, Computer II Public Files, Depreciation Rates, Filings, Docket 86-111 Implementation Filings, Contracts between Carriers, and Affiliations Waiver Requests dealing with Accounting and Reporting. Hours of Operation: Monday through Friday, 9:00am to 4:00pm.

* Common Carrier Regulations

Common Carrier Bureau
Federal Communications Commission (FCC)
1919 M Street, NW, Room 500
Washington, DC 20554   202-632-6910
This office regulates wire and radio communications common carriers--paging, digital electronic message service, point-to-point microwave, multipoint distribution service, rural radio, cellular radio, offshore radio, international fixed radio, international fixed public radio, telephone, telegraph, and satellite companies. It also processes applications for licenses or other filings, analyzes related complaints, and conducts investigations into common carrier-related problems.

* Communications and Information Policy

Public Information
National Telecommunications and Information Administration
U.S. Department of Commerce
14th St. and Constitution Ave., NW, Room 4898
Washington, DC 20230   202-377-1551
The National Telecommunications and Information Administration's policy recommendations affect the nation's economic and technological advancement in the telecommunications industry. This includes common carrier, telephone, broadcast, and satellite communications systems. It is involved with regulatory changes that have led to increased competition in common carrier operations and the growing overlap between telecommunications and computers. In the information field, NTIA focuses attention on issues of privacy and security and the impact of U.S. and international privacy legislation on the flow of electronic data across national boundaries. Contact this office for more information.

* Communications Networks and New Technologies

Office of Technology Assessment (OTA)
600 Pennsylvania Ave., SE
Washington, DC 20510   202-228-6774
Recent advances in information storage and transmission technologies, occurring in a new deregulated and intensely competitive economic climate, are rapidly changing the Nation's communication networks. OTA is studying the role of the Federal government in this area, along with how to coordinate them, resolve potential conflicts between them, and examine new communication systems abroad and their potential relationships to the U.S. systems. Contact Linda Garcia, the project director, for more information.

* Communications Treaties

Federal Communications Commission (FCC)
Treaty Library
2025 M Street, NW, Room 7112
Washington, DC 20554   202-632-7025
Documents available include: International Telecommunications Union Publications

including International Telecommunications Convention, Radio Convention, Radio Regulations, List of Addresses of Administrations, etc., Final Acts of ITU Conferences, CCIR and CCITT Reports and Recommendations, International Frequency Assignments and specialized lists including the international frequency list, list of Coast Stations, list of Ship Stations, IFRB Weekly Circular with Annexed Special Sections, Canadian Frequency Assignment List. Hours of operation: Monday through Friday, 7:00am to 3:30pm.

* Consumer Complaints: Television, Broadcast Radio

Mass Media Division
Complaints and Investigations Branch
Federal Communications Commission (FCC)
2025 M Street, NW, Room 8210
Washington, DC 20554   202-632-7048
This office handles consumer complaints involving commercial, non-commercial and cable TV, and broadcast radio. These complaints generally involve transmission interference problems, complaints about indecent language, and commercial sponsorship regulations. Complaints about billing, programming, and scheduling are handled by the local governments and stations themselves.

* Database Search Service

ATA Services Inc.
2200 Mill Rd.
Alexandria, VA 22314   703-838-1901
The FCC has contracted ATA to provide the public with a search and retrieval service for all information contained in the FCC database files. For example, they could give you the names of all the businesses within a 70 mile radius of Washington, DC, that use mobile radios in their operations, or even equal opportunity employment statistics for TV stations in Dallas, Texas. They provide on-line access to the databases for $54 per hour, and or they will do customized searches for $55 per hour plus the cost of materials. ATA has on-line FCC information on the following areas: Private Radio Land/Mobile Licenses; Common Carrier Land/Mobile Licenses; Common Carrier Multipoint Distribution Service Licenses; Common Carrier Cellular Licenses; Pending Data on Applications for these licenses; Telephone Interconnection Data; Private Radio Bureau Administrative Tracking Information for - Aviation Ground - Marine Coast - Private Microwave. Data is available on computer tape, floppy disks, paper, and mailing labels. For a complete description of the FCC's databases and costs of searches, contact ATA.

* Domestic Facilities Division

Federal Communications Commission (FCC)
Public Reference Room
2025 M Street, NW, Room 6220
Washington, DC 20554   202-634-1860
Documents on File: *Point to Point Microwave, Digital Electronic Message Services, Multi-Point Distribution Services, Space Stations, Section 214,* and *Equipment Registration.* Hours of Operation: Monday through Thursday, 8:30am to 12:30pm, 1:30pm to 3:00pm.

* Domestic Telecommunication Policy Development

Office of Policy Analysis and Development (OPAD)
National Telecommunications and Information Administration
U.S. Department of Commerce
14th Street and Constitution Ave. NW, Room 4725
Washington, DC 20230   202-377-1880
OPAD develops policy recommendations on the introduction of competition into, and the deregulation of, the telecommunications industries, information service, radio and television broadcasting, and Cable TV. OPAD also administers NTIA's Minority Telecommunications Development Program (MTDP), which promotes minority ownership participation in the telecommunications industry.

* Electric Borrowers Operations Database

Public Information Office
Rural Electrification Administration
U.S. Department of Agriculture
Washington, DC 20250   202-720-9560
The Rural Electrification Administration (REA) Database contains financial and statistical information about the operations of approximately 2,160 REA electric and telephone borrowers individually and as a group. The following information can be retrieved about each borrower: outstanding loans, REA debit service repayments, balance sheet items, revenue and expense items, operating statements, and sales

statistics. REA maintains a variety of files containing information, ranging from loan statistics to accounting data. Searches and printouts are available free of charge. Tapes can be purchased for a cost-recovery fee, and hard copy reports are also available.

* Electronic Equipment Authorization

Equipment Authorization Branch
Federal Communications Commission (FCC)
7435 Oakland Mills Road
Columbia, MD 21046   410-725-1585

All electronic equipment must be approved by the FCC before it is marketed in or imported into the U.S. The FCC's equipment authorization program also includes procedures for approving telephone equipment connected to public telephone network and for advance approval of over-the-air subscription (pay) TV systems before their authorization for use. The FCC also maintains and constantly updates a database of the equipment it authorizes. For more information on equipment application guidelines and regulations, contact EAB.

* Enforcement

Common Carrier Bureau
Federal Communications Commission (FCC)
2025 M Street, NW, Room 6202
Washington, DC 20554   202-632-7553

This office handles consumer complaints involving communications services provided by interstate common carriers, which include voice, record, data, video and facsimile transmissions via wire, microwave, satellite, radio marine cable, optical fiber, and other facilities. The majority of complaints generally concern a carrier's rates or practices or the accuracy of a service charge or billing practice. Contact this office for more information on lodging a complaint.

* Enforcement Reference Room

Federal Communications Commission (FCC)
2025 M Street, NW, Room 8210
Washington, DC 20554   202-632-6968

Documents on File: *Station Complaint Files, Congressional Correspondence, Files, and Network Correspondence Files.* Hours of Operation: Monday through Friday, 9:00am to 5:00pm.

* Equal Employment Opportunity

Federal Communications Commission (FCC)
2025 M Street, NW, Room 7218
Washington, DC 20554   202-632-6968

Documents on File: *FCC Form 395 Reports* (Broadcast Stations and Cable Employment Units), *Submissions that Cable Companies File in the Certification Process, Labor Force Statistics, Correspondence to and from Broadcast Stations and Cable Employment Units, and Cable Certification Process Results.* Hours of Operations: Monday through Friday, 8:00am to 4:30pm.

* Emergency Broadcast System

Federal Communications Commission (FCC)
1919 M Street, NW, Room 840
Washington, DC 20554   202-632-3906

The Emergency Broadcast System (EBS) was originally developed to be used by the President in times of national crisis or war. EBS may now also be used by state and local officials in all 50 states, the District of Columbia, Puerto Rico, the Virgin Islands, American Samoa, and Guam to disseminate warning and instructions to the public in situations threatening life and property. Nationally, the EBS, which can be activated only by the White House, is designed to enable the President to speak to the nation within 10 minutes of his request. This office can also provide you with documents on the history of the EBS. Contact this office for more information.

* Evolution of Broadcasting

Federal Communications Commission (FCC)
Consumer Assistance and Small Business Division
Office of Public Affairs
1919 M Street, NW, Room 254
Washington, DC 20554   202-632-7000

The FCC publishes several packets detailing the evolution of television, cable television, and radio broadcasting. These information packets also discuss the evolution of the rules governing mass media.

* Experimental Radio Service

Frequency Liaison Branch
Federal Communications Commission (FCC)
1919 M Street, NW, Room 7326
Washington, DC 20554   202-653-8141

The Federal Communications Commission's (FCC) Experimental Radio Service permits the public to experiment with new uses of radio frequencies. Individuals or manufacturers wishing to conduct research involving radiowave propagation equipment must be licensed by the FCC. For more information on the application procedures or on the database maintained on all experimental radio licenses granted, contact this office.

* Fairness/Political Programming Branch

Federal Communications Commission (FCC)
2025 M Street, NW, Room 8202
Washington, DC 20554   202-632-6968

Documents on File: *Correspondence and Rulings on Fairness/Political Programming Complaints.* Hours of Operation: Monday through Friday, 8:00am to 5:30pm. In early 1992, the Federal Communications Commission (FCC) released a new report on the Codification of the Commissions Political Programming Policies - MM Docket 91-168, detailing FCC rules and policies with respect to political programming.

* FCC Information Bulletins and Fact Sheets

Federal Communications Commission (FCC)
Consumer Assistance and Small Business Division
Office of Public Affairs
1919 M Street, NW, Room 254
Washington, DC 20554   202-632-7000

If you are looking for general information about communications issues or background material about the Federal Communications Commission (FCC), you may want to obtain copies of the following bulletins from this office. Single copies only are supplied free of charge.

Bulletins:
How to Apply for a Broadcast Station
Mass Media Services
The FCC in Brief
Radio Stations and Other Lists
Private Radio Services
Evolution of Wire and Radio Communications
Station Identification and Call Signs
Frequency Allocation
Memo to All Young People Interested in Radio
Cable Television
Field Operation Bureau

Fact Sheets:
Low Power Television (LPTV)
Multipoint Distribution Service (MDS)
Instructional Television Fixed Service (ITFS)
Direct Broadcast Service (DBS)
Cellular Radio
Satellite Program Scrambling
Indecency/Obscenity
Exparte'
Dial-a-Porn
FCC Fee Information
Specialized Mobile Radio Service (SMRS)

* FCC Library

1919 M Street NW
Room 639
Washington, DC 20554   202-632-7100

Documents available include the following: *Code of Federal Regulations Title 47, Telecommunications 1938-1988, FCC Annual Reports, FCC Federal Court Briefs,* selected *FCC Records, FCC Reports* - first and second series, *Federal Radio Commission Annual Reports, Pike and Fischer Radio Regulations* - first and second series, and the *Radio Act of 1927* and the *Communication Act of 1934* as well as other proposed and/or enacted legislation pertaining to communications, telecommunications, broadcasting, administrative procedures, and independent agency regulations. Two collections that may be of particular interest to telecommunications researchers are the collection of cross indexed legislative histories which date back

Business and Industry

to the early beginnings of communication law and the wide range of scholarly periodicals (some 250) on communications.

* FCC Mass Media Bureau Reference and File Sources

Federal Communications Commission (FCC)
Mass Media
Pubic Reference Room
1919 M Street, NW, Room 239
Washington, DC 20554   202-632-6485

Documents on File: Station License Files, New Applications, Assignments and Transfers, Engineering Files, Construction Permits, LPTV, and ITFS. Hours of Operation: Monday through Friday, 9:00am to 5:30pm.

* FCC News Releases Recording

Federal Communications Commission (FCC)
News Media Division
Office of Public Affairs
1919 M Street, NW
Washington, DC 20554   202-632-0002

The Office of Public Affairs' recorded message will provide information on the latest news releases concerning the Federal Communications Commission and the telecommunications industry.

* FCC Open Meetings

Federal Communications Commission (FCC)
Office of Public Affairs
1919 M Street, NW, Room 856
Washington, DC 20554   202-632-7000

The general public is welcome to attend and observe all Commission meetings, except when the Commission finds that the public interest requires otherwise. This office can provide you with the free brochure, *A Guide To Open Meetings*, which outlines how FCC meetings work and where to obtain information on their findings.

* FCC Record of Actions

U.S. Government Printing Office
Superintendent of Documents
Washington, DC 20402   202-512-1800

The *FCC Record* provides a comprehensive, timely, and cost-effective source of FCC actions, including all texts released to the public daily through the FCC Office of Public Affairs. It contains a table of contents, a popular name case table, table of docket numbers, DA and FCC numbers, a list of cases by locale, and an alphabetical subject index. In addition, the *FCC Record* contains some public notices, speeches, and staff papers, and is available every two weeks through the GPO at an annual subscription rate.

* FCC Research and Copy Service

Federal Communications Commission (FCC)
1919 M Street, Room 246
Washington, DC 20037   202-857-3815

Any documents on file at the FCC's library or reference rooms listed below can be researched and copied for you for a fee by DCC, Inc. ITS charges $22 per hour for research, and $.08 per page for photocopying. Documents located in the Private Radio Licensing Division must be ordered from ITS, Inc., 1270 Fairfield Road, Gettysburg, PA 17325; 717-337-1433.

* FCC Rules and Regulations

U.S. Government Printing Office
Superintendent of Documents
Washington, DC 20402   202-512-1800

The volumes of *FCC Rules and Regulations* must be purchased from the Government Printing Office (GPO), rather directly from the Federal Communications Commission (FCC). In addition to the FCC Rules, the GPO has available for purchase the following publications and documents often requested by customers:

Communications Act of 1934 (including amendments)
Volumes of FCC Reports and Decisions
FCC Annual Reports
Federal Register
Code of Federal Regulations

* FCC Rules On-line

Federal Communications Commission (FCC)
1919 M Street, NW, Room 230
Washington, DC 20554   202-632-4128

By visiting the FCC in person can you have the most up-to-date information on the complete FCC rules and regulations through the Automated FCC Rules Reference System. This system provides the only on-line computer access to FCC rules and regulations, and can be accessed free of charge at designated computer terminals at the FCC.

* FCC Telephone Directory

Downtown Copy Center
1114 21st Street, NW
Washington, DC 20036   202-452-1422

Issued on a quarterly basis, the FCC's telephone directory is available for $2.50 by mail or $1 if you pick it up in person. This directory can be a very useful research tool not only because it includes FCC telephone and room numbers of staff members, but also because it contains functional listings which identify key telephone numbers by subject areas.

* Federal Communications Commission Reference Room

Dockets Reference Room
1919 M Street, NW, Room 239
Washington, DC 20554   202-632-6410

The Dockets Reference Room maintains files on all rulemaking proceedings, docket files, transcripts of hearing proceedings, decisions, briefs, depositions, interrogatories, and ex parte comments. If you cannot visit the docket room in person, the FCC's copying service, ITS, Inc., will reproduce any documents you wish and send them to you for a fee.

* Federal Telecommunications Resource

Interdepartment Radio Advisory Committee (IRAC)
National Telecommunications and Information Administration
14th St. and Constitution Ave., NW, Room 1605
Washington, DC 20230   202-377-0319

Radio frequency spectrum management is the concern of NTIA's Office of Spectrum Management (OSM). By statute, NTIA manages the Federal government's use of the radio spectrum, while the Federal Communications Commission is responsible for non-Federal usage. OSM processes nearly 100,000 frequency assignment actions every year. It chairs and provides administrative and analytic support to the Interdepartment Radio Advisory Committee (IRAC). The IRAC is the central advisory body to NTIA regarding Federal Government radio spectrum management and use. When calling, ask for the Report of IRAC January 1, 1990 - June 30, 1990 and July 1990 - June 1991. These reports detail IRAC activities over the last few years as well as providing valuable background information.

* Foreign Press and Radio Translations

Foreign Broadcast Information Service
National Technical Information Service
U.S. Department of Commerce
5282 Port Royal Rd.
Springfield, VA 22161   703-487-4630

The subscription, *Foreign Press and Radio Translations*, provides a daily (paper copy) or weekly (microfiche copy) publication featuring news accounts, commentaries, and government statements from foreign broadcasts, press agency transmissions, newspapers, and periodicals published in the previous 48 to 72 hours. The selections available are the following:

People's Republic of China
Eastern Europe
Central Eurasia
East Asia
Near East and South Asia
Latin America
Western Europe
Sub Saharan Africa

The paper copy is available for $525 annually, and the microfiche copy for $230. Costs per category decline if more than one is ordered. Contact the Subscription Department to place an order or request a free information brochure *PR-376*.

* Formal Complaints and Investigations

Federal Communications Commission (FCC)
2025 M Street, NW, Room 6206
Washington, DC 20554   202-632-4890

Documents on File: Formal Complaints and Related Pleadings, Interlocking Directorate Reports and Applications, Pole Attachment Complaints and Related Pleadings, Pole Attachment State Certifications, Enforcement Proceedings which include: mergers, acquisitions, and transfers of control files. Hours of Operation: Monday through Friday, 9:00am to 5:00pm.

* Freedom of Information Act Requests

FCC Managing Director
1919 M Street, Room 852
Washington, DC 20554   202-632-6390

FOIA requests for FCC materials should be submitted in writing to this office.

* Frequency Allocations History

Federal Communications Commission (FCC)
2025 M Street, NW, Room 7102
Washington, DC 20554   202-632-7025

This office has files of notices and orders dealing with Frequency allocations proceedings available in chronological order.

* History of FCC Rules

Publications Branch
1919 M Street, NW, Room 224
Washington, DC 20554   202-632-6410

Files in this Branch contain information on the history of FCC rules. It is open weekdays from 8am to 5:30pm.

* Industry Analysis

Federal Communications Commission (FCC)
Public Reference Room
1919 M Street, NW, Room 537
Washington, DC 20554   202-632-0745

Documents on File: Reports required by FCC Rules and Regulations, Administrative Reports, Annual Reports to Stockholders, FCC Form 492, Rate of Return Report, Statistics of Communications Common Carriers, Quarterly Operating Data of Telephone and Telegraph Carriers, Switched Access Reports, Equal Access Implementation Reports, NECA - Pool Results, Local Exchange Rates, Monthly Bypass Request Report - AT&T, Lifeline Link-Up Reports, IAD Reports, General Reference Material from Sources. Hours of Operation: Monday through Friday, 9:00am to 1:00pm, 2:00pm to 5:00pm.

* Informal Complaints and Public Inquiries Branch

Federal Communications Commission (FCC)
2025 M Street, NW, Room 6202
Washington, DC 20554   202-632-4890

Documents on File: Informal Written Telephone Related Complaints and Public Information. Hours of Operation: Monday through Friday, 8:00am to 5:00pm.

* Instructional Television Fixed Service (ITFS)

Federal Communications Commission (FCC)
Consumer Assistance and Small Business Division
Office of Public Affairs
1919 M Street, NW, Room 254
Washington, DC 20554   202-632-7000

ITFS was created over 20 years ago to provide in school instructional/cultural programming in accredited educational institutions. It can only be received using a special receiving antenna. Recent rule changes allow a licensee to air non ITFS programming using excess channel capacity or lease time to third parties on a profit making basis. A Fact Sheet on ITFS available from the FCC explains rules and procedures for applying for an ITFS station.

* Interference Complaints

FOB Public Contact Branch
Federal Communications Commission (FCC)
1919 M Street, NW, Room 725

Washington, DC 20554   202-634-1940

Interference happens when radio signals are picked up by consumer electronic products, most often TVs, VCRs, Hi Fi equipment, electronic organs and cordless telephones. *Something About Interference* and the *Interference Handbook* are two publications free from the FCC on interference problems. Complaints about interference and requests for free publications can be directed to the local FCC office in your area or to the FOB Public Contact Branch.

* International Broadcasting Service

Federal Communications Commission (FCC)
2025 M Street, NW, Room 8120-A
Washington, DC 20554   202-254-3394

The IBS sets aside a portion of the radio spectrum for stations wishing to broadcast to foreign countries. Currently, IBS regulates 18 such stations, most of which are religious-oriented. Additionally, IBS negotiates telecommunications agreements with foreign countries. Contact this office for more information.

* International Communications

Bureau of International Communications
and Information Policy
U.S. Department of State
2201 C St., NW, Room 6317
Washington, DC 20520   202-647-8345

As the principal advisor to the Secretary of State on international telecommunications policy issues affecting U.S. foreign policy and national security, this bureau coordinates with other U.S. Government agencies and the private sector in formulating and implementing international policies relating to communications and information technologies. CIP provides guidance and instructions to U.S. representatives to such international organizations as the International Telecommunications Satellite Organization, the International Maritime Satellite Organization, The Information, Computers, and Communications Policy Committee of the Organization for Economic Cooperation and Development, and the International Telecommunication Union. Through bilateral negotiations and multilateral programs, CIP promotes the principles of free enterprise and the free flow of communication.

* International Communications Regulation

Federal Communications Commission (FCC)
International Facilities Division
1919 M Street, NW, Room 533
Washington, DC 20554   202-632-7834

Documents on File: *International Microwave Point-to-Point Files, International Fixed Radiotelephone Files, International Fixed Radiotelegraph Files, International Space Station Files, Recognized Private Operating Agency Files, Uniform Settlement Policy Files, Submarine Cable Landing License Files, International Earth Station Files, Transborder Earth Station Files, Section 214, INTELSAT, and Comsat Documents, Rulemakings, Rulings, Assignments of Licenses, Transfer of Control, and Temporary Authorities.* Hours of Operation: Monday through Friday, 8:00am to 1:00pm, 2:00pm to 5:00pm.

* International Telecommunications

Office of International Affairs (OIA)
National Telecommunications and Information Administration
14th St., NW, Room 4090
Washington, DC 20230   202-377-1304

This office is responsible for developing International Communications policy. OIA works to minimize unnecessary Federal and foreign government interference in the efficient functioning of international telecommunications markets. It also seeks to identify and, where feasible, lessen foreign obstacles to U.S. trade in telecommunications and information services and products. To do this, OIA assesses the communications policies of other nations and cooperates with the State Department in preparing U.S. positions before various international forums, such as the International Telecommunication Union and the Organization for Economic Cooperation and Development. Also, OIA reviews a wide rage of issues pertinent to regulatory and legislative proceedings. Contact this office for more information on international communications.

* Legislative Affairs

Office of Legislative Affairs
Federal Communications Commission (FCC)
1919 M Street, NW, Room 808

Washington, DC 20554   202-632-6405

If you have questions concerning congressional testimony, current bills, or other legislative matters related to the FCC, this office has two attorneys on staff who specialize in mass media and common carrier law to answer your questions.

* Litigation Against the FCC

Litigation Division File Room
1919 M Street, NW, Room 609-C
Washington, DC 20554   202-632-7112

Documents on file include all case files of actions that have been brought against the FCC; computer listings of case histories including: lists of pending cases, background histories of cases, status of cases, deadlines for submission of briefs, etc. Hours of operation: Monday through Friday, 10:00am to 12:00pm and 3:00pm to 4:00pm.

* Live TV Coverage of the FCC

The Capitol Connection
George Mason University, Kelly Drive
Fairfax, VA 22030-4444   703-993-3100

For residents of the Washington DC area, the Capitol Connection can provide live coverage of FCC open meetings via microwave transmissions. The service costs $795 annually. In the future, FCC meeting coverage may be available nationwide via the use of satellite transmissions. Call for more information.

* Long Distance Carrier Information

Industry Analysis
Federal Communications Commission (FCC)
Public Reference Room
1919 M Street, NW, Room 537
Washington, DC 20554   202-632-0745

The Industry Analysis division compiles information on market share for all long distance carriers whose total toll service revenue is $100 million or greater. The Downtown Copy Center has a report entitled the *Long Distance Market Share Report*, detailing this information.

* Low Power Television (LPTV)

Federal Communications Commission (FCC)
Consumer Assistance and Small Business Division
Office of Public Affairs
1919 M Street, NW, Room 254
Washington, DC 20554   202-632-7000

Established in 1982, LPTV was intended to provide opportunities for locally oriented television service in small rural communities, and in industrial communities in larger urban areas. LPTV presents a less expensive and very flexible means of delivering programming tailored to the interests of viewers in small localized areas. Today there are approximately 800 stations in 550 towns in the Continental U.S. The FCC can provide you with an information packet on LPT that includes information on starting an LPTV station.

* Marine Radio Services

Aviation and Marine Branch
Federal Communications Commission (FCC)
2025 M Street, NW, Room 5114
Washington, DC 20554   202-632-7175

The FCC regulates the Marine Radio Services for the safety and operational communications of non-federal maritime activities, including U.S. vessels that traverse international waters and land stations in the Maritime Mobile Radio Service. This office also regulates the Aviation Radio Services for nongovernment use of radio for aeronautical radionavigation, search and rescue, and other safety operations.

* Master Frequency File Database

Frequency Liaison Office
Federal Communications Commission (FCC)
2025 M Street, NW, Room 7326
Washington, DC 20554   202-653-8141

The Master Frequency File contains information on the identification, location, and technical characteristics of almost 900,000 radio and television broadcast stations, satellite stations, land mobile and microwave stations, and all other types of radio frequency transmitters. Information on each facility includes name of owner, mailing address, height of transmitting towers, power, frequency, number of mobile units, and much more. This file is available for sale from NTIS on microfiche or magnetic

tape, or specialized searches can be arranged through ATA Services Inc., 2200 Mill Rd., Alexandria, VA 22314; 703-838-1901.

* Mobile Services Division

Federal Communications Commission (FCC)
Public Reference Room
1919 M Street, NW, Room 628
Washington, DC 20554   202-632-6400

Documents on File: *Station Files, Maps, Diagrams, Petitions, Co-Channel Searches and Background Material Pending Files, and Cellular Granted Station Files*. Hours of Operation: Monday through Thursday, 8:00am to 12:00pm.

* Multipoint Distribution Service

Federal Communications Commission (FCC)
Consumer Assistance and Small Business Division
Office of Public Affairs
1919 M Street, NW, Room 254
Washington, DC 20554   202-632-7000

Multipoint Distribution Service (MDS) programming is unlike conventional broadcasts in that it is designed to reach only those who subscribe to the service by obtaining a special receiving antenna capable of receiving special microwave frequencies. Operators can choose to be common or non-common carriers. While originally thought to be an effective medium for business data transmission, it has become popular for transmitting entertainment programming. Information on licensing and filing is available from the FCC.

* National Telecommunications

National Telecommunications and Information Administration
U.S. Department of Commerce
14th St. and Constitution Ave., NW, Room 4898
Washington, DC 20230   202-377-1551

This Administration's broad goals include formulating policies to support the development and growth of telecommunications, information and related industries, furthering the efficient development and use of telecommunications and information services, providing policy and management for Federal use of the electromagnetic spectrum, and providing telecommunications facilities grants to public service users. NTIA employs approximately 300 people and has an annual budget of $35,104,000.

* Pay Per Call (900) Services

Common Carrier Bureau
Enforcement Division
Federal Communications Commission (FCC)
2025 M Street, NW, Room 6202
Washington, DC 20554   202-632-7553

The FCC adopted rules governing interstate pay per call (900) services effective December 2, 1991. These rules require information providers to disclose the cost of the call and describe the service being provided, giving the caller the opportunity to hang up before charges are assessed. The rules also require local telephone companies to offer blocking of 900 services to all subscribers where technically feasible and one-time free blocking of 900 services to residential subscribers. The Enforcement Division can furnish you with complete information on FCC rules governing 900 number telephone services. The Division also logs complaints on these services.

* Policy and Program Planning

Federal Communications Commission (FCC)
1919 M Street, NW, Room 544
Washington, DC 20554   202-632-9342

Documents on File: *Petitions in Non-Docketed Proceedings, Comments and Replies in Non-Docketed Proceedings, Applications for Review, Petitions for Declaratory Rulings/Comments and Replies, Petitions for Waiver/Comments and Replies, CEI Plans/Comments and Replies*. Hours of Operation: Monday through Friday, 9:00am to 5:30pm.

* Political Programming Rules

Political Programming
Federal Communications Commission (FCC)
2025 M Street, NW, Room 8202
Washington, DC 20554   202-632-7586

This office can answer questions concerning political programming rules and

Communications

regulations. For example, if a station lets a legally qualified candidate for public office use its broadcast facilities, it must give "equal opportunities" to other candidates for the same office. This office can also tell you about programming costs for political candidates, who are all entitled to "lowest unit charges" for use of broadcast or cable TV facilities during 45 days preceding a primary and 60 days preceding a general election. Contact this office for more information.

* Private Radio Reference Room
Federal Communications Commission (FCC)
1270 Fairfield Road
Gettysburg, PA 17325   717-337-1311
Documents on File: *Land Mobile and GMRS Applications, Microwave Applications, Aviation Ground Applications, Marine Coast Applications, all Dismissals, Copies of Special Temporary Authorities (STA) or Transfers of Control.* Hours of Operation: Monday through Friday, 8:00am to 4:30pm.

* Private Radio Licensing
Licensing Division
Federal Communications Commission (FCC)
1270 Fairfield Road
Gettysburg, PA 17325   717-337-1212
For information on the status of any pending applications for FCC private radio licenses, contact this office.

* Private Radio Regulations
Private Radio Bureau
Federal Communications Commission (FCC)
2025 M Street, NW, Room 5002
Washington, DC 20554   202-632-6940
This office regulates radio stations serving the communications needs of businesses, individuals, nonprofit organizations, and state and local governments, including the following uses: private land mobile, private operational fixed microwave, aviation, marine, personal, amateur, and disaster. It also compiles applications for licenses for processing in Gettysburg, analyzes complaints, and conducts investigations.

* Public Access Link (PAL)
Equipment Authorization Branch
Federal Communications Commission (FCC)
7435 Oakland Mill Road
Columbia, MD 21046   410-725-1585
The Public Access Link (PAL) provides computerized information on the status of pending applications and technical information on granted authorizations. The system remains on-line continuously, providing a twenty-hour service to the public. You can also access the Federal Communications Commission (FCC) "Bulletin Board" of recent Commission actions which might impact on the equipment authorization program, a list of testing laboratories which have filed required information with the FCC, and grantee and manufacturer codes assigned for equipment identification. For direct, on-line hook-up with your modem, call 301-725-1072.

* Public Service Workshops and Seminars
Federal Communications Commission (FCC)
1919 M Street, NW, Room 725
Washington, DC 20554   202-634-1940
The Federal Communications Commission (FCC) conducts free seminars and workshops across the country to help the public identify and resolve telecommunications-related interference problems. For example, the FCC will train TV service technicians, telephone companies and manufacturers, and power company technicians how to eliminate interference in consumer-related products and services. Also, the FCC will conduct seminars by special request from any group which needs help addressing interference-related problems. Examples of special requests include Cable television companies, Taxi Cab Associations, and hospital paging users. These services are handled through the field offices and coordinated by the regional offices. For more information on having a seminar address your group, contact your local FCC office or contact the above office for information and the number of your local office.

* Public Service Reference
Federal Communications Commission (FCC)
1919 M Street, NW, Room 728
Washington, DC 20554   202-632-7240

Documents on File: *Commercial Radio Operator Application Files* and *Bulletins Concerning Radio Operator Matters.*

* Public Telecommunications Facilities Program (PTFP)
Office of Telecommunications Applications
National Telecommunications and Information Administration
14th Street and Constitution Ave, NW, Room 4625
Washington, DC 20230   202-377-1835
The PTFP expands and improves the public telecommunications services of the U.S. by providing grants for the dissemination of equipment. The major objective of the PTFP is to extend the delivery of quality public telecommunication services to unserved areas of the U.S. The PTFP concentrates mostly on TV and radio services. Recent rule changes have created a new subcategory to provide satellite downlinks at public radio and TV stations that would bring nationally distributed programming to a geographic area for the first time. Contact the above office for information on and applications for PTFP grants.

* Purchasing and Technical Assistance for Broadcast Entrepreneurs
Consumer Assistance and Small Business Division (CASB)
Office of Public Affairs
Federal Communications Commission (FCC)
1919 M St., NW, Room 254
Washington, DC 20554   202-632-7000
The CASB Division will provide you with personal assistance in locating information concerning FCC rules, policies, procedures, and guidance concerning participation in FCC rulemaking proceedings. In addition, this office provides specialized to assistance to those interested in becoming involved in the small business telecommunications industry. They will walk you through the purchasing procedures, identify resources for financial and technical assistance, and perform license status checks for applicants. The Public Affairs office also coordinates broadcast ownership workshops, which cover these topic and more, every year across the country. Contact CASB for more information.

* Radio-Frequency (RF) Radiation
Office of Engineering and Technology
Federal Communications Commission (FCC)
2025 M Street, NW, Room 7130
Washington, DC 20554   202-653-8169
Every transmitting device emits Radio Frequency (RF) radiation, and levels which exceed FCC standards can be a serious health risk. If you have questions about RF radiation in your community or workplace, contact the FCC for a free consumer information package on RF radiation, along with technical surveys and investigations of certain transmitters across the country. In particular ask for the publication *Questions and Answers about Biological Effects and Potential Hazards of Radiofrequency Radiation, OET Bulletin No. 56.* It is available free upon request.

* Rulemaking Changes at the FCC
The Secretary
Federal Communications Commission (FCC)
1919 M Street, NW, Room 222
Washington, DC 20554   202-632-6410
The FCC is interested in any experiences, judgments, or insights you might have that would shed light on issues and questions raised in an inquiry or rulemaking. To obtain guidelines on how to submit your ideas on any FCC rulemaking changes, contact this office.

* Spectrum Management
Office of Spectrum Management
National Telecommunications and Information Administration
U.S. Department of Commerce
14th Street and Constitution Ave, NW, Room 4099
Washington, DC 20230   202-377-1850
OSM is charged with developing and implementing policies and procedures regarding the use of the radio frequency spectrum. By statute, NTIA manages the Federal Governments use of the spectrum, while the FCC manages all non-Federal spectrum usage. OSM also chairs the Interdepartmental Radio Advisory Committee. OSM plays an important role in the preparations for the many conferences and meetings of the International Telecommunications Union (ITU), and chairs the Frequency Management Advisory Council - which provides advice on spectrum allocation and assignment matters.

Business and Industry

* Tariff Legal Documents

Federal Communications Commission (FCC)
1919 M Street, NW, Room 518
Washington, DC 20554   202-632-6387

Documents on File: *Notices of Proposed Rulemakings, Petitions against Tariffs* (including comments and replies), *Petitions for Reconsideration* (including comments and replies), *Access Tariffs, Petitions dealing with Access Tariff, Applications for Review* (comments and replies).

* Tariff Review Public Reference Room

Federal Communications Commission (FCC)
1919 M Street, NW, Room 513
Washington, DC 20554   202-632-6387

Documents on File: *Multipoint Distribution Service (MDS), American Telephone and Telegraph Company, Access Service Tariffs by Bell Operating Companies, National Exchange Carrier Association, and Independent Telephone Companies, Western Union Telegraph Company, International Record Carriers, and other Overseas Carriers, Specialized Common Carriers, Satellite Carriers, Microwave Carriers, Maritime Carriers, Facilities for CATV and Wide Spectrum Service, and Mobile Radiotelephone Service.* Hours of Operation: Monday through Friday, 1:30pm to 4:30pm.

* Tax Breaks for Broadcasting Entrepreneurs

Consumer Assistance and Small Business Division
Office of Public Affairs
Federal Communications Commission (FCC)
1919 M Street, NW, Room 254
Washington, DC 20554   202-632-7260

If an owner of a broadcast or cable facility sells that station to a minority-owned purchaser, the FCC can permit the seller to defer the payment of capital gains tax, generally for 2 to 3 years. The FCC defines minority-ownership as consisting in excess of 50 per cent of controlling interest. Also, shareholders in a minority-controlled broadcast or cable entity are eligible for tax certificates upon the sale of their shares, provided that their interest was acquired to assist in the financing of the acquisition of the facility. The FCC may also issue tax certificates in transfers to limited partnerships where the general partner is a minority individual and owns more than 20 per cent interest in the broadcast or cable facility. For more information, contact CASB.

* Telecommunications Expertise for Public Service Groups

Public Telecommunications Facilities Program
National Telecommunications and Information Administration
U.S. Department of Commerce
14th St. and Constitution Ave., NW, Room 4625
Washington, DC 20230   202-377-5802

By identifying public service telecommunications needs, NTIA assists schools, hospitals, libraries, policy, fire departments, and government agencies in using advanced telecommunications systems and technology to achieve their goals.

* Telecommunications Publications

Publications Information
National Telecommunications and Information Administration
U.S. Department of Commerce
14th St. and Constitution Ave., NW, Room 4625
Washington, DC 20230   202-377-5802

A catalog is available which lists all the reports available from NTIA. Most are technical research studies, but several deal with communications policies and standards. In 1988, NTIA issued *TELECOM 2000*, the first comprehensive review and analysis of U.S. telecommunications policy in 20 years, as well as a number of reports regarding new computer-related communications and information services, expansion of broad-band and cable television systems, and customer options, high-definition television, and other topics.

* Telecommunications Research

Institute for Telecommunications Sciences (ITS)
National Telecommunications and Information Administration
U.S. Department of Commerce
325 Broadway
Boulder, CO 80303   303-497-3572

As the chief research and engineering arm of the National Telecommunications and Information Administration (NTIA), the Institute for Telecommunication Sciences supports Administration Telecommunication objectives such as enhanced domestic competition, improved foreign trade opportunities for U.S. telecommunication firms, and more efficient and effective use of the radio frequency spectrum. ITS also serves as a principal Federal resource for assistance in solving problems of other Federal agencies, state and local governments, private corporations and associations, and international organizations. ITS conducts research in spectrum use analysis, telecommunication standards development, telecommunication systems performance, telecommunication systems planning and applied research. The *Annual Technical Progress Report* describes in more detail the research conducted, as well as listing the publications available.

* Telephone Utility Systems

Assistant Administrator--Telephone
Rural Electrification Administration
U.S. Department of Agriculture (USDA)
Room 4056 South Building
Washington, DC 20250   202-720-0715

The USDA lends money to approximately 1,000 rural telephone companies and maintains a staff knowledgeable in both operations and equipment. Consumer Complaints: Telephones, Faxes.

* Transcripts of FCC Hearings

Capitol Hill Reporting, Inc.
1825 K Street, NW, Suite 1122
Washington, DC 20006   202-466-9500

Transcripts of hearings, FCC Official Court Reporting Service, and Transcripts of Court hearings may be obtained by contacting this office.

* Unauthorized Long Distance Carrier Switch

News Media Division
Federal Communications Commission (FCC)
1919 M Street NW
Washington, DC 20554   202-632-5050

Long distance carriers may not switch you from one company to another without your explicit consent. The News Media Division can provide you with information on what steps long distance carriers must take in order to switch customers from one carrier to another. The Division also outlines consumer rights with respect to long distance carrier choice. *FCC Report DC-2016* outlines FCC rules and actions with regard to unauthorized switches. It is available free upon request from the above office.

* Video/Audio Tape Recordings of FCC Open Meetings

CLI Productions Inc.
4320 Hamilton Street, Suite 102
Hyattsville, MD 20871   301-864-6333

Video and audio tape recordings of Commission open meetings, official sessions, and FCC tutorials, are available to the public only from a this private contractor on a fee basis. Customers may buy blank tapes from this office or provide their own. Videotapes can be 3/4 inch U-Matic or 1/2 inch VHS, audio tapes C-90 (45 minutes per side) cassettes. Customers should be prepared to provide date of meetings, and, when appropriate, agenda number, unless they want this office to perform a search for a fee.

Be patient. If any phone number is incorrect, call (area code) 555-1212 and request the new listing.

Shipping and Fishing

As an island nation of continental proportions, shipping is vital to the economic well being and national security of the United States. Within the U.S. Department of Transportation, the Coast Guard and the Maritime Administration ensure set and enforce regulations for maritime safety. The Maritime Administration also monitors other aspects of shipping and marine affairs. An independent government agency, the Federal Maritime Commission, monitors private shipping, ensuring compliance by foreign and domestic shippers with U.S. shipping laws.

Fish are important both as a food source and as a part of our environment. Within the U.S. government, the Department of Commerce's, National Oceans and Atmospheric Administration monitors fish catches off the coasts of the U.S. to ensure compliance with catch limits and to monitor fish stocks off the coasts of the U.S.

* Aids to Navigation

Office of Navigation Safety and Waterways Services
U.S. Coast Guard
U.S. Department of Transportation
2100 2nd St., SW, Room 1116
Washington, DC 20593-0001   202-267-1965

The Coast Guard maintains aids to navigation such as lighthouses and lights, buoys, beacons, fog signals, and long-range radionavigation aids like LORAN-C and OMEGA. The aids are established to assist navigators in plotting safe courses on waters under U.S. jurisdiction and in certain international areas. The seven volumes of *Light Lists*, which detail the navigation aids in seven geographic areas, are available at varying cost from the Superintendent of Documents, Government Printing Office (GPO), Washington, DC 20402; 202-512-1800. The *LORAN-C User Handbook*, which explains the radionavigation system and how to use it, is also available from GPO for $4.75.

* Anti-Rebate Certification Program

Bureau of Domestic Regulation
Federal Maritime Commission
1100 L Street, NW
Washington, DC 20573   202-523-5796

The Commission ensures that foreign commercial shippers so not receive a rebate from their countries on shipments to the U.S. Shippers not certifying their compliance with U.S. anti-rebate regulations may be assessed a civil penalty of $5,000 per day for each day the violation continues. For information on anti-rebate actions, contact the above office.

* Automated Electronic System for Ocean Pollution

Ocean Pollution Data and Information Services
Central Coordination and Referral Office
National Oceanographic Data Center
National Oceanic and Atmospheric Administration
1825 Connecticut Ave, NW
Washington, DC 20235   202-606-4539

The Automated Electronic System for Ocean Pollution (AESOP) is a newly developed software application created at OPDIN for making access to its ocean and Great Lakes databases quick and easy. The system contains the following: summaries of federal projects and programs - organized by department and abstracts contain project summaries; guide to marine pollution related data; handbook of federal systems and services related to marine pollution control; and marine, Great Lakes, and Arctic pollution related literature - containing several thousand citations and updated regularly.

* Boating Correspondence Course

U.S. Government Bookstore
World Savings Building
720 N. Main St.
Pueblo, CO 81003   719-544-3142

Designed for boaters who can't attend a boating class, *The Skipper's Course* covers basic navigation, legal requirements, anchoring, weather, emergency procedures, boat handling, and safety. A certificate of completion is awarded. Stock No: 050012002258. Price: $6.50.

* Bridges Over Navigable Waters

Bridge Administration Division
Office of Navigation Safety and Waterways Services
U.S. Coast Guard
U.S. Department of Transportation
2100 2nd St., SW, Room 1408
Washington, DC 20593-0001   202-267-0368

Bridges and causeways spanning navigable waterways in the U.S. are subject to Coast Guard safety regulations concerning their construction, operation, and maintenance. This office oversees bridge engineering and issues permits. For further details, contact the division listed above.

* Capital Construction Fund

Office of Maritime Aids
Maritime Administration
U.S. Department of Transportation
400 7th Street SW, Room 8126
Washington, DC 20590   202-366-0364

The Capital Construction Fund assists operators in accumulating capital to build, acquire, and reconstruct vessels through the deferral of Federal Income Taxes on certain deposits, as defined in Section 607 of the Merchant Marine Act of 1936. Any U.S. citizen owning or leasing an eligible vessel may enter into an agreement with the Maritime Administration to obtain tax-deferral privileges on deposits placed in the fund. Call MARAD for details.

* Cargo Preference Programs

Office of Market Development
Maritime Administration
U.S. Department of Transportation
400 7th Street, SW, Room 7209
Washington, DC 20590   202-366-5517

MARAD is the central authority overseeing U.S. cargo preference programs. U.S. law requires that 50% of U.S. foreign assistance deliveries and Department of Defense shipments be carried on U.S. flag vessels. For more information on this program, contact MARAD.

* Certificates of Documentation for Vessels

Vessel Documentation Branch
Merchant Vessel Inspection and Documentation Division
Office of Marine Safety, Security, and Environmental Protection
U.S. Coast Guard
U.S. Department of Transportation
2100 2nd St., SW, Room 1312
Washington, DC 20593-0001   202-267-1492

Most commercial vessels of 5 or more net tons used on U.S. waters must be documented. Commercial vessels engaged in foreign trade and recreational boats of that size, may be documented at the option of the owner. Also, undocumented vessels equipped with propulsion machinery are required to be numbered by their individual states. Lending institutions regard a documented vessel to be a more secure form of collateral, thus making bank financing easier to obtain. Considered a form of international registration, the *Certificate of Documentation* may also make customs entry and clearance easier in foreign ports. The initial documentation fee is about

$100. *Certificates of Documentation* are issued by the Coast Guard at documentation offices around the U.S. The office listed above can provide you with the address of the one nearest you.

* Coast Guard Courses and Textbooks

Coast Guard Auxiliary National Board, Inc.
9949 Watson Industrial Park
St. Louis, MO 63126   800-336-BOAT

The following are textbooks used in Coast Guard Auxiliary public education courses. They can be ordered by writing to the above address, or you can get each textbook by taking the course of the same title through the Coast Guard. To find out where courses are offered near you, call the Courseline at 800-336-BOAT; or 800-245-BOAT in VA.

Boating Skills and Seamanship. Boating laws and regulations, boat handling, and navigation ($8).
Sailing and Seamanship. Same basic text as above, geared to sailboats ($8).
Advanced Coastal Piloting. How to read charts, plot courses, predict tides, and use navigation aids ($8).

* Coast Guard Regulations

Marine Safety Council
U.S. Coast Guard
U.S. Department of Transportation
2100 2nd St., SW, Room 3600
Washington, DC 20593-0001   202-267-1477

Rules and regulations proposed by the Coast Guard are taken under consideration and studied by this Council. Hearings are held at Coast Guard headquarters in DC and at other locations around the country. Announcements appear Monday through Friday in the *Federal Register*. For further information, contact the Council.

* Coast Guard Rescue Service

SAR Database Manager
Search and Rescue Division
Office of Navigation Safety and Waterways Services
U.S. Coast Guard
U.S. Department of Transportation
2100 2nd St., SW, Room 1422
Washington, DC 20593-0001   202-267-1054

The Search and Rescue (SAR) program maintains a comprehensive system of resources to save lives and prevent personal injury and property damage on the navigable waters of the United States. This system includes rescue vessels, aircraft, and communication facilities. A cooperative international distress response system is also maintained for incidents on the high seas. For more information about the Guard's SAR program, contact the branch listed above.

* Coast Guard Reserve

Office of Readiness and Reserve
U.S. Coast Guard
U.S. Department of Transportation
2100 2nd St., SW, Room 5101   202-267-2350

In time of war or national emergency, the Coast Guard Reserve provides trained individuals and units for active duty. The Reserve also assists the Guard in peacetime missions during domestic emergencies and peak operations. The *Coast Guard Reservist Magazine*, available free from the office listed above, provides bimonthly news and human interest stories about Coast Guard Reservists and their activities.

* Coastal Zone Management

Office of Ocean and Coastal Resource Management
National Ocean Service
National Oceanic and Atmospheric Administration
U.S. Department of Commerce
1825 Connecticut Ave., NW, Room 724
Washington, DC 20235   202-606-4158

To balance the needs for preserving and developing the resources in the U.S. coastal zone, the National Ocean Service, through its Office of Ocean and Coastal Resource Management, provides the coordination and expertise at the Federal level needed for effective management of these coastal resources. NOS has begun to expand the technical assistance provided to States and territories, emphasizing special area management planning, coastal hazards mitigation, cost-effective coastal management, and the simplification of permit processes for coastal activities. Ask for Technical Bulletins 101-104, which detail activities in Coastal Zone Management and Environmental Protection.

* Commercial Fisheries Clearinghouse

Public Affairs
National Marine Fisheries Service
National Oceanic and Atmospheric Administration
U.S. Department of Commerce
1335 East-West Hwy.
Silver Spring, MD 20910   301-713-2370

The National Marine Fisheries Service (NMFS) manages the country's stocks of saltwater fish and shellfish for both commercial and recreational interests. NMFS administers and enforces the Magnuson Fishery Conservation and Management Act to assure that fishing stays within sound biological limits, and that U.S. commercial and recreational fishermen have the opportunity to harvest all the available fish within these limits. Several hundred Fisheries Service scientists conduct research relating to these management responsibilities in science and research centers in 15 states and the District of Columbia. Many of these laboratories have evolved a major field of interest, and have special knowledge of the fish in their geographical area that leads to predictions of abundance, economic forecasts, and direct assistance to sport fishermen and commercial fishing businesses. Each of the science and research centers of the National Marine Fisheries Service has their own area of expertise and knowledge of the fish in their area. Contact them directly regarding questions or publications requests.

* Commercial Vessel Inspections

Merchant Vessel Inspection and Documentation Division
Office of Marine Safety, Security, and
    Environmental Protection
U.S. Coast Guard
U.S. Department of Transportation
2100 2nd St., SW, Room 1400
Washington, DC 20593-0001   202-267-2978

The Coast Guard administers and enforces safety standards for the design, construction, equipment, and maintenance of commercial vessels and offshore structures on the Outer Continental Shelf. Foreign vessels subject to U.S. jurisdiction must also meet the required standards. Boardings are conducted to detect and prevent violations. Safety regulations cover such ship characteristics as hull structure, watertight integrity, fire safety, and navigation instrumentation. Records, mostly computerized, are kept on these inspections at district Coast Guard offices. For general information or referral to a records inspection facility near you, contact the division listed.

* Crew Certification

Licensing and Evaluation Branch
Merchant Vessel Personnel Division
Office of Marine Safety, Security, and
    Environmental Protection
U.S. Coast Guard
U.S. Department of Transportation
2100 2nd St., SW, Room 1210
Washington, DC 20593-0001   202-267-0218

To ensure that vessels are safely and sufficiently crewed with properly trained personnel, the Coast Guard develops safe manning standards for commercial vessels and administers a system for evaluation and licensing. Crew requirements on a vessel depend on factors such as route, tonnage, horsepower, and type of trade. The rules and regulations for licensing are included in the *Code of Federal Regulations*, Title 46, parts 10-14. Licensing and exams are given in applicable professional fields at regional examination centers around the country. Contact your local Coast Guard office or the branch listed above for referral to the center nearest you.

* Current Fisheries Statistics Series

Fisheries Statistics Division
National Marine Fisheries Service
National Oceans and Atmospheric Administration
U.S. Department of Commerce
1335 East-West Highway
Silver Spring, MD 20910   301-427-2328

The Current Fisheries Statistics (CFS) series are statistical bulletins on marine recreational fishing, commercial fishing, and on the manufacture and commerce of fishery products. For further information, or to order these bulletins, contact the above office.

* Enforcement of Shipping Law

Bureau of Hearing Counsel/Bureau of Investigation
Federal Maritime Commission
1100 L Street, NW
Washington, DC 20573   202-523-5783/523-5860

Under the 1984 Shipping Act, the commission has put more emphasis on enforcement activities. Through the Transpacific malpractice program, the commission seeks compliance with the 1984 Act and seeks to establish an equitable trade environment for carriers, shippers, and middlemen participating in the transpacific trades.

* Environmental Impact Statements

Office of Ship Operations
Maritime Administration
U.S. Department of Transportation
400 7th Street SW
Washington, DC 20590   202-366-5737

MARAD participates in international conferences on environmental issues and also develops environmental impact statements on the construction and operation of vessels, training in marine pollution abatement, and projects to producer safer more efficient vessels and operating methods.

* Federal Maritime Commission

1100 L Street, NW
Washington DC 20573   202-523-5725

Established in 1961, the Federal Maritime Commission (FMC) monitors relationships among carriers and also ensures that individual carriers fairly treat shippers and other members of the shipping public. The commission consists of 5 full time commissioners appointed by the President, with no more than 3 from the same political party, serving 5 year terms. The FMC has 230 full time equivalent positions and an appropriated budget of $15,452,000.

* Federal Maritime Commission (FMC) - District Offices

1100 L Street, NW
Washington, DC 20573   202-523-5725

FMC District Offices represent the Commission in their jurisdictions, provide liaison between the Commission and the maritime industry and the shipping public, collects and analyzes intelligence of regulatory significance, and assesses industry wide conditions for the Commission. District offices are located in the following cities:

New York 212-264-1425
New Orleans 504-589-6662
San Francisco 415-744-7016
Puerto Rico 809-766-5581
Los Angeles 213-514-6127
Miami 305-536-6963
Houston 713-229-2841

* Federal Maritime Commission - Special Docket Decisions

Office of Administrative Law Judges
Federal Maritime Commission
1100 L Street, NW
Washington, DC 20573   202-523-5750

This office has information on a variety of special docket cases that have come before the Commission.

* Fish Exports

Office of Trade and Industry Services
National Marine Fisheries Service
National Oceanic and Atmospheric Administration
U.S. Department of Commerce
1335 East-West Hwy., Room 6212
Silver Spring, MD 20910   301-713-2379

This office assists seafood exporters by providing trade leads, conducting sales missions, doing market studies, and organizing "how to export" seminars. It helps industry by improving their access to markets in other countries. The Service provides inspection services for fishery commodities for export and issues official U.S. Government certificates attesting to the findings. Statistics on Fish exports can be found in the book *Fisheries of the United States* (see listing below).

* Fisheries Technical Reports

Scientific Publications Office
National Marine Fisheries Service
National Oceanic and Atmospheric Administration
U.S. Department of Commerce
7600 Sand Point Way N.E.
Seattle, WA 98115   206-526-6107

This office prepares the following scientific and technical publications having to do with fisheries:

Fishery Bulletin. Publishes original research reports and technical notes on investigations in fishery science, engineering, and economics. Quarterly, $24 per year.

Marine Fisheries Review. Publishes review articles, original research reports, significant progress reports, technical notes, and new articles on fisheries science, engineering, and economics, commercial and recreational fisheries, marine mammal studies, and foreign fisheries developments. Quarterly, $7 per year.

NOAA Technical Reports. Publishes scientific investigations that document long-term continuing programs of NMFS, technical papers of general interest intended to aid conservation and management, as well as many other topic areas. Indexes are available. Issued irregularly, price varies.

* Fishery Products Grading and Inspection

Utilization Research and Services
National Marine Fisheries Service
National Oceanic and Atmospheric Administration
U.S. Department of Commerce
1335 East-West Hwy., Room 6142
Silver Spring, MD 20910   301-713-2355

The National Marine Fisheries Service conducts a voluntary seafood inspection program on a fee-for-service bases. A wide range of inspection services are available to any interested party, including harvesters, processors, food-service distributors, and importers and exporters. These services include vessel and plant sanitation inspection, product evaluation (in-plant and warehouse lot), product specification review, label review, laboratory analyses (microbiological tests, chemical contaminant/indices of decomposition, species identification), training, and education and information. This office has a great deal of information concerning inspections, grading of products, and regulations. They also publish a document listing fishery products that have been produced in fish establishments approved by the National Marine Fisheries Service.

* Fisheries of the United States

Office of Research and Environmental Information
National Marine Fisheries Service
National Oceanic and Atmospheric Administration
U.S. Department of Commerce
1335 East-West Hwy., Room 8313
Silver Spring, MD 20910   301-713-2328

This publication is prepared by the Fisheries Statistics Division, and includes information on U.S. commercial fishery landings, U.S. exclusive economic zone catches, world fisheries, imports and exports, U.S. supply, and per capita fish consumption. It is an invaluable source of statistics on fishing and fishing related activities. This publication is available through Superintendent of Documents, Government Printing Office, Washington, DC 20402; 202-512-1800, cost $6.50.

* Fisheries Publications

National Technical Information Service (NTIS)
5285 Port Royal Road   800-553-6847
Springfield, VA 22161   703-487-4650

The National Marine Fisheries Service has made many of its technical reports available through NTIS. Subject areas include: Commercial fisheries, Fisheries of the United States (issues published from 1939 on), State Landings, Processed Fishery Products Annual Summary (issues published from 1979 on), Marine Recreational Fishing Statistics Survey (1979 on), as well as other publications. Publications list can be obtained from the annual publications *Fisheries of the United States*, which is available from NTIS or GPO, 202-512-1800.

* Fisheries Research

Office of Research and Environmental Information
National Marine Fisheries Service (NMFS)
National Oceanic and Atmospheric Administration
U.S. Department of Commerce

1335 East-West Hwy., Room 6310
Silver Spring, MD 20910   301-713-2367
Contact this office for information regarding fisheries research. Topics covered include acid rain and pollution, aquaculture information, diseases of fish, ecology and fish recruitment, fishing methods, and resource abundance. Fisheries research is also undertaken at the NMFS regional offices, which can be contacted directly.

North East Region 508-281-9250
South East Region 813-893-3141
North West Region 206-526-6150
South West Region 213-548-2575
Alaska 907-586-7221

* Fisheries - Oceanography Research

Oceanic and Atmospheric Research
National Oceanic and Atmospheric Administration
U.S. Department of Commerce
1335 East-West Hwy., Room 6310
Silver Spring, MD 20910   301-713-2463
This research, conducted jointly with the National Marine Fisheries Service, seeks to improve understanding of the effects of atmospheric and oceanic variations on fish and shellfish.

* Fishery Statistics

Office of Research and Environmental Information
National Marine Fisheries Service
National Oceanic and Atmospheric Administration
U.S. Department of Commerce
1335 East-West Hwy., Room 8313
Silver Spring, MD 20910   301-713-2328
The Fisheries Statistics Division publishes statistical bulletins on marine recreational fishing and commercial fishing, and on the manufacture and commerce of fishery products. Annual publications available from this office include:

Marine Recreational Fishery Statistics
Frozen Fishery Products
Processed Fishery Products
Imports and Exports of Fishery Products
Fish Meal and Oil

* Fisheries Trade and Industry Services

Office of Trade and Industry Services
National Marine Fisheries Service
National Oceanic and Atmospheric Administration
U.S. Department of Commerce
1335 East-West Hwy.
Silver Spring, MD 20910   301-713-2351
This office conducts activities designed to improve the competitiveness of the U.S. fishing industry in domestic and world markets and to enhance the safety and quality of U.S. seafood products. Programs include identification of industry trade issues and problems; financial assistance in the form of loan guarantees, insurance programs, a capital construction fund, and research and development grants; administration of fishery marketing councils; administration of inspection and grading programs; and research and development of product safety, quality and use.

* Fishing Multi-Lateral Agreements

Bureau of Oceans and International Environmental
and Scientific Affairs
U.S. Department of State
2201 C St., NW, Room 5806
Washington, DC 20520   202-647-2335
This office negotiates fishing agreements with countries who want to fish within the U.S. economic zone, along with agreements with countries within whose zone the U.S. would like to fish. They are also responsible for multi-lateral agreements dealing with fishing on the high seas, with particular attention to conservation issues. Information is available on these agreements and on fishery concerns in general.

* Fishing Vessels International Claims

Assistant Legal Advisor for International Claims
Office of the Legal Advisor
U.S. Department of State

2201 C St., NW
Washington, DC 20520   202-632-7810
The Fishermen's Protective Act provides for reimbursement for financial loss to owners of vessels registered in the United States for fines paid to secure the release of vessels seized for operation in waters not recognized as territorial waters by the United States. No registration or payment of premiums is required prior to the seizure in order to qualify for reimbursement.

* Foreign Fish Catches

Office of International Affairs
National Marine Fisheries Service
National Oceanic and Atmospheric Administration
U.S. Department of Commerce
1335 East-West Hwy. , Room 7624
Silver Spring, MD 20910   301-427-2272
For information regarding foreign fishing catches (allocations) or foreign fisheries in general contact the Office of International Affairs.

* Freight Forwarders

Bureau of Domestic Regulation
Federal Maritime Commission
1100 L Street, NW
Washington, DC 20573   202-523-5796
Ocean freight forwarders serve export shippers by arranging for the ocean transportation of cargo by common carriers, and by handling the paperwork, legal requirements, safety requirements and other incidentals related to the shipment of cargo. The Commission is vested with the authority for the licensing and regulation for independent ocean freight forwarders. The Commission also maintains surety bonds on file for freight forwarders.

* Habitat Conservation

National Marine Fisheries Service
National Oceanic and Atmospheric Administration
U.S. Department of Commerce
1335 East-West Hwy., Room 6212
Silver Spring, MD 20910   301-713-2325
The Habitat Conservation Program helps minimize losses and degradation in areas where fish and shellfish grow and live by working with other federal and state agencies involved in development projects. It also helps the regional offices incorporate habitat considerations into their management plans.

* High Seas Law Enforcement

Operational Law Enforcement Division
Office of Law Enforcement and Defense Operations
U.S. Coast Guard
U.S. Department of Transportation
2100 2nd St., SW, Room 3110
Washington, DC 20593-0001   202-267-1890
As the primary maritime law enforcement agency for the U.S., the Coast Guard enforces Federal laws, treaties, and international agreements to which the U.S. is a party. The Coast Guard may conduct investigations when violations are suspected, such as smuggling, drug trafficking, or polluting. Empowered to board and inspect vessels routinely as well, the Guard also conducts :"suspicionless" boardings to prevent violations. To report suspicious or questionable activity on boats, or to complain about an improperly conducted boarding, call the Boating Safety Hotline, 800-368-5647; or 202-267-0780 in DC, or contact your local Coast Guard commander. The office listed above can provide you with information about the Coast Guard's law enforcement role and the National Narcotics Border Interdiction System, which coordinates multi-agency and international operations with other countries to suppress narcotics trafficking.

* Impact of Human Activities on Marine Life

Office of Oceanic and Atmospheric Research
National Oceanic and Atmospheric Administration
U.S. Department of Commerce
1335 East-West Hwy., Room 6212
Silver Spring, MD 20910   301-713-2463
The Marine Assessment Program determines the ecological impacts of human activities, such as coastal power generation, fishing, mining, and waste disposal. Scientists conduct theoretical and laboratory experiments of chemical and dynamical processes in the deep oceans as well as in the Great Lakes estuaries.

* International Marine Environmental Efforts

Environmental Coordination Branch
Marine Environmental Response Division
Office of Marine, Safety, Security, and Environmental Protection
U.S. Coast Guard
U.S. Department of Transportation
2100 2nd St., SW, Room 1202
Washington, DC 20593-0001   202-267-0421

Information is available here on the Coast Guard's role in international marine environmental efforts, such as representation in the U.N. International Maritime Consultative Organization. For further information on cooperative environmental efforts, contact the branch listed.

* International Maritime Activities

Office of International Activities
Maritime Administration
U.S. Department of Transportation
400 7th Street, SW, Room 7119
Washington, DC 20590   202-366-5773

This office plans and coordinates MARAD participation in international activities as well as keeping track of external developments affecting U.S. shipping interests. Specific activities include information collection, analyses, contract negotiations, promotional programs and the development of contacts between U.S. and foreign governments/foreign maritime industry representatives.

* Joint Seafood Inspection Program

National Marine Fisheries Service
Industry and Consumer Liaison Branch
National Oceanic and Atmospheric Administration (NOAA)
1335 East West Highway
Silver Spring, MD 20910   301-713-2355

The Food and Drug Administration and NOAA are designing and pilot testing a new joint seafood inspection program based on the Hazard Analysis Critical Control Point (HACCP) concept. The final program will be a voluntary fee-for-service inspection program. The basic tenet of HACCP is the identification of critical control points, the establishment of controls for those points, and the continuous monitoring of these areas to prevent problems before they begin. For information on the progress of the pilot programs, contact Lu Cano of NOAA at the above number.

* Major Developments in U.S. Shipping Trade

Federal Maritime Commission (FMC)
1100 L Street, NW
Washington, DC 20573   202-523-5725

The Federal Maritime Commission continually monitors developments in the major shipping markets around the world. Information on rates, capacity, and international agreements is compiled. The FMC also has information on developments with respect to the major carriers. The FMC breaks its analysis down in the following geographic manner: Transatlantic, Mediterranean, Africa, Transpacific, Latin America and the Caribbean, and the Middle East.

* Marine Advisory Service

National Sea-Grant College Program
National Oceanic and Atmospheric Administration
U.S. Department of Commerce
1335 East-West Hwy.
Silver Spring, MD 20910   202-377-8090

Operated through the Sea-Grant Colleges, the marine advisory service consists of agents and specialists who are experts in areas such as seafood technology, marine economics, coastal engineering, commercial fishing, recreation, and communications. These specialists provide a link between the people who live and work in coastal areas and researchers in the universities. They sponsor workshops, conferences, and seminars on marine issues for the public and representatives of industry and government agencies. They talk to high school science classes, as well as publish bulletins, fact sheets, newsletters, technical papers, and audio-visual materials concerning marine affairs. The following is a list of Sea-Grant Colleges, and people you can contact for more information.

Sea Grant Colleges

Alabama
See Mississippi

Alaska
Alaska Sea Grant College Program
University of Alaska Fairbanks
138 Irving II
Fairbanks, AK 99775-5040   907-474-7086

Arizona
Environmental Research Laboratory
University of Arizona
2601 E. Airport Drive
Tucson, AZ 85706-6985   602-741-1990

California
California Sea Grant
University of California/San Diego
9500 Gilman Drive
La Jolla, CA 92093-0232   619-534-4444

Sea Grant Program
University of Southern California
University Park
Los Angeles, CA 90089-1231   213-740-1961

Connecticut
Connecticut Sea Grant
Marine Sciences Institute
University of Connecticut
Building 24
Avery Point
Groton, CT 06340   203-445-8664

Delaware
University of Delaware Sea Grant
Marine Communications Office
263 E. Main Street
Newark, DE 19716   302-831-8083

Florida
Florida Sea Grant
Building 803
University of Florida
Gainesville, FL 32611-0341   904-392-2802

Georgia
Georgia Sea Grant
Ecology Building
University of Georgia
Athens, GA 30602   404-542-7671

Hawaii
University of Hawaii
Sea Grant College Program
1000 Pope Road
MSB 200
Honolulu, HI 96822   808-956-7410

Illinois
Illinois-Indiana Sea Grant
University of Illinois
65 Mumford Hall
1301 W. Gregory Drive
Urbana, IL 61801   217-333-9448

Indiana
See Illinois

Louisiana
Louisiana Sea Grant
Center for Wetland Resources
Louisiana State University
Baton Rouge, LA 70803   504-388-6449

Maine
Maine Sea Grant Communications
30 Coburn Hall
University of Maine
Orono, ME 04469   207-581-1440

Be patient. If any phone number is incorrect, call (area code) 555-1212 and request the new listing.

791

Marine Law Institute
University of Maine School of Law
246 Deering Avenue
Portland, ME 04102   207-780-4474

Maryland
Maryland Sea Grant
1123 Taliaferro Hall
University of Maryland
College Park, MD 20742   301-405-6371

National Sea Grant College Program
NOAA, SSMB-1/5206
1335 East-West Hwy.
Silver Spring, MD 20910   301-713-2431

Massachusetts
MIT Sea Grant
Building E-38, Room 300
Massachusetts Inst. of Technology
292 Main Street
Cambridge, MA 02139   617-253-7041

Sea Grant Program
Woods Hole Oceanographic Institution
Woods Hole, MA 02543   508-548-1400

Michigan
Michigan Sea Grant Publications
University of Michigan
2200 Bonisteel Blvd.
Ann Arbor, MI 48109-2099   313-764-1138

Minnesota
Minnesota Sea Grant
University of Minnesota
1518 Cleveland Ave. N, Room 302
St. Paul, MN 55108   612-625-9288

Mississippi
Mississippi-Alabama Sea Grant Consortium
P.O. Box 7000
Ocean Springs, MS 39564-7000   601-875-9341

New Hampshire
New Hampshire Sea Grant
Kingman Farm
University of New Hampshire
Durham, NH 03824   603-749-1565

New Jersey
Sea Grant Program
New Jersey Marine Sciences Consortium
Building No. 22
Fort Hancock, NJ 07732   908-872-1300

New York
New York Sea Grant Institute
Dutchess Hall Room 137
SUNY at Stony Brook
Stony Brook, NY 11794-5001   516-632-6905

North Carolina
North Carolina Sea Grant
North Carolina State University
Box 8605
Raleigh, NC 27695   919-515-2454

Ohio
Ohio Sea Grant
Ohio State University
1314 Kinnear Road
Columbus, OH 43212   614-292-8949

Oklahoma
Department of Chemistry
Attn. F. Schmitz

University of Oklahoma
620 Parrington Oval, Room 208
Norman, OK 73019   405-325-5581

Oregon
National Coastal Resources Research and Development Inst.
528 SW Mill, Suite 222
P.O. Box 751
Portland, OR 97207   503-725-5725

Oregon Sea Grant
Oregon State University
AdS 402
Corvallis, OR 97331-2134   503-737-2716

Publications Orders
Agricultural Communications
Oregon State University
AdS 422
Corvallis, OR 97331-2119   503-737-2513

Puerto Rico
Puerto Rico Sea Grant Program
Communications Office
RUM-UPR P.O. Box 5000
Mayaguez, PR 00709-5000   809-834-4726

Rhode Island
National Sea Grant Depository
Pell Library Building
Bay Campus
University of Rhode Island
Narragansett, RI 02882   401-792-6114

Rhode Island Sea Grant
Publications Unit
University of Rhode Island
Bay Campus
Narragansett, RI 02882-1197   401-792-6842

South Carolina
South Carolina Sea Grant Consortium
287 Meeting Street
Charleston, SC 29401   803-727-2078

Texas
Texas Sea Grant
Texas A&M-Galveston
P.O. Box 1675
Galveston, TX 77553-1675   409-762-9800

Virginia
Virginia Sea Grant
Madison House
University of Virginia
170 Rugby Road
Charlottesville, VA 22903   804-924-5965

Washington
Washington Sea Grant, HG-30
University of Washington
3716 Brooklyn Avenue, NE
Seattle, WA 98105   206-543-6600

Wisconsin
Sea Grant Institute
University of Wisconsin
1800 University Avenue
Madison, WI 53705   608-263-3259

* Marine Environmental Reports
Coastal Monitoring and Bioeffects Division
National Oceanic and Atmospheric Administration (NOAA)
Washington Science Center, Building 5
6010 Executive Blvd., Room 320
Rockville, MD 20852   301-713-2465

Under the National Status and Trends Program, NOAA produced some 63 papers and reports in 1991 dealing with a wide range of Marine environmental issues and their impact on Marine life. A list of these reports is available from NOAA at the above number. Specific questions on marine pollution research at NOAA can be directed to Dr. Andrew Robertson, Dr. Douglas Wolfe, or Dr. Thomas O'Connor.

* Marine Terminal Activities

Bureau of Domestic Regulation
Federal Maritime Commission
1100 L Street, NW
Washington, DC 20573   202-523-5796

The Commission is responsible for the review and processing of certain agreements and tariffs related to the Marine terminal industry under the 1984 and 1916 Acts.

* Marine Environmental Information

Pollution Response Branch
Marine Environmental Response Division
Office of Marine Safety, Security, and Environmental Protection
U.S. Coast Guard
U.S. Department of Transportation
2100 2nd St., SW, Room 2104   202-267-0518
Washington, DC 20593-0001   202-267-2611

This office responds to requests for marine environmental protection information from Congress and other federal agencies, state agencies, schools, industries, and the general public. Data is available on laws relating to the protection of the marine environment, incidents involving releases of oil or other hazardous substances, and federally funded spill response operations. Currently the Division is working on new regulations regarding dumping in the Caribbean.

* Marine Mammals Protection Enforcement

Office of Protected Resources
National Marine Fisheries Service
National Oceanic and Atmospheric Administration
U.S. Department of Commerce
1335 East-West Hwy.
Silver Spring, MD 20910   301-713-2322

The Marine Mammal Protection Act commits the United States to long-term management and research programs to conserve and protect these animals. Marine mammals may be taken for scientific research, public display, and incidentally to commercial fishing. The National Marine Fisheries Service grants or denies requests for exemptions, issues permits, carries out research and management programs, enforces the Act, participates in international programs, and issues rules and regulations to carry out its mission to conserve and protect marine mammals. An annual report is available for the Office of Protected Resources, which gives detailed information regarding the activities of the Office. This office can also provide you with copies of the Act, and two publications: *Handbook for the Determination of Adverse Human-Marine Mammal Interaction from Necropsies*, and *Proceedings of the Workshop to Review and Evaluate Whale Watching Programs and Management Needs*. The report *Marine Mammal Strandings in the U.S.*, *NMFS report 98*, January 1991, is available from National Technical Information Service 703-487-4650. Each regional office also puts out a report on stranded mammals (see Fisheries Research for their phone numbers.)

* Marine Pollutants

Office of Oceanography and Marine Assessments
National Ocean Service
National Oceanic and Atmospheric Administration
U.S. Department of Commerce
6001 Executive Blvd.
Rockville, MD 20852   301-443-8487

This office surveys and monitors the oceans, U.S. coastal waters and the Great Lakes to produce data and information products that are critically important for offshore oil and gas exploration, dredging operations, coastal and offshore construction, sea floor mining, waste disposal management, and for protecting the marine environment from the adverse effects of ocean and coastal pollution.

* Mariners Weather Log

National Oceanographic Data Center
National Oceanic and Atmospheric Administration
Universal Building Room 412
Washington, DC 20235   202-606-4561

The Mariners Weather Log is a unique source of information on marine weather and climate and their effects on operations at sea. Published quarterly by the National Oceanographic Data Center, the *Mariners Weather Log* provides comprehensive coverage of major storms of the North Atlantic and North Pacific, reports and annual summaries on tropical cyclones, information on the National Weather Service's Marine Observation Program, selected shipboard gale and wave observations, and general articles about weather and climate, hazards and safety precautions, and related marine lore. An annual subscription is available for $8 from the Superintendent of Documents, Government Printing Office, Washington, DC 20402; 202-512-1800.

* Marine Debris

National Ocean Service
Office of Ocean and Coastal Resource Management
National Oceanic and Atmospheric Administration (NOAA)
1825 Connecticut Ave., NW, Room 724
Washington, DC 20235   202-606-4158

There has been an explosion of plastic pollution in the world's oceans and waterways in the last 20 years. One survey stated that some 58% of fishermen had incurred costs due to damage caused by plastic debris. Ingestion and entanglement due to plastics cause the death of an estimated 100,000 marine mammals each year. The NOAA technical assistance bulletin *Marine Debris: Status Report and Bibliography* (number 104) documents the problem, discusses innovative solutions now being undertaken in several states, and contains detailed reference bibliographies on beach cleanups, entanglement, plastic article debris, and regulations on pollution. It is available free upon request.

* Marine Recreational Fishing Publications

Fisheries Statistics Division
National Marine Fisheries Service
National Oceans and Atmospheric Administration
U.S. Department of Commerce
1335 East-West Highway
Silver Spring, Md 20910   301-427-2328

The National Marine Fisheries Service publishes the following regional fishing reports. They are available from the above office. Marine Recreational Fishing Statistics Survey:

Atlantic and Gulf Coasts, 1987-1989, CFS #8904
Pacific Coast, 1986, CFS #8393
Atlantic and Gulf Coasts, 1986, CFS #8392
Atlantic and Gulf Coasts, 1983-1984, CFS #8326
Pacific Coast, 1983-1984, CFS #8325
Pacific Coast, 1981-1982, CFS #8323
Atlantic and Gulf Coasts, 1979 (revised) - 1980, CFS #8322
Atlantic and Gulf Coasts, 1979-1980, CFS #8321

* Marine Technology

Library, Coast Guard Research and Development Center
U.S. Coast Guard
U.S. Department of Transportation
Avery Point
Groton, CT 06340-6096   203-441-2648

Marine research is conducted here in areas such as ice technology, navigation instrumentation technology, ocean dumping surveillance, pollution, search and rescue techniques, and marine fire and safety technology. This library is a good starting point for obtaining specific information about what research is done by the Center and for referrals to appropriate experts.

* Marine Technology Society

1828 L St NW, Suite 906
Washington, DC 20036   202-775-5966

This non-profit organization is dedicated to providing information about marine science and engineering. It is divided into 14 geographical sections in the U.S. and Canada, and each section holds monthly meetings, at which brief technical presentations are given. The Society has 31 professional committees that sponsor technical conferences, workshops, and short courses that are open to members and nonmembers. The staff can provide you with technical information and referrals. The Society publishes the *Journal of the Marine Technology Society*, a quarterly publication that presents technical activities of the Society, papers, conferences summaries, book reviews, and so on. It is available free of charge to members and for $5 for nonmembers.

Business and Industry

* Maritime Administration Activities and Statistics

MARAD - Public Affairs
U.S. Department of Transportation
400 7th Street SW, Room 7219
Washington, DC 20590   202-366-5807

MARAD's annual report is an excellent place to begin your search for information on U.S. maritime activities and statistics. The report includes a profile of the U.S. Merchant Fleet, Department of Defense Cargo programs, information on maritime labor and training, and a report on maritime agreements recently concluded between the U.S. and foreign nations. Statistics include listings for worldwide ship deliveries, Federal Ship financing guarantee program, U.S. Oceangoing Merchant Marine, major world merchant fleets, U.S. Great Lakes Merchant Fleet, the National Defense Reserve Fleet, and maritime subsidy outlays. The report is available free upon request.

* Maritime Administration Publications

MARAD - Public Affairs
U.S. Department of Transportation
400 7th Street SW, Room 7219
Washington, DC 20590   202-366-5807

MARAD publishes a booklet containing a listing of all MARAD publications. Some MARAD publications are free and others are available for sale through the Government Printing Office (GPO), 202-512-1800, or National Technical Information Service (NTIS), 703-487-4650. The catalogue is available free from the above address.

* Maritime Affairs

Bureau of Economic and Business Affairs
Office of Maritime and Land Transport
U.S. Department of State
2021 C St., NW, Room 5828
Washington, DC 20520   202-647-5840

This office is involved with all matters concerning maritime affairs, including unions, shipping regulations, the exporting and importing of cargo, and rights of passage. They also take part in the negotiations and agreements on these issues and monitor them to make sure the agreements are followed.

* Maritime Commerce Financial Analysis

Bureau of Domestic Regulation
Federal Maritime Commission
1100 L Street, NW
Washington, DC 20573   202-523-5796

The Bureau of Domestic Regulation provides accounting and financial expertise to help ensure the reasonableness of rates for the transportation of cargo and other services provided by common carriers in the domestic offshore waterborne commerce of the U.S. The Bureau also provides technical assistance to other activities within the Commission.

* Maritime Complaints

Office of Informal Inquiries and Complaints
Federal Maritime Commission
1100 L Street, NW
Washington, DC 20573   202-523-5807

This office coordinates the informal complaint handling system throughout the Federal Maritime Commission. The Office is also responsible for the initial adjudication of reparation claims for less than $10,000 that are filed by shippers against common carriers by water engaged in the foreign and domestic offshore commerce of the U.S. The office supplies copies of procedures, dockets, and other information on complaints to the public.

* Maritime Information FOIA Requests

Office of the Secretary
Federal Maritime Commission
1100 L Street, NW
Washington, DC 20573   202-523-5911

Among the Secretary's responsibilities are administering Freedom of Information (FOIA), Government in the Sunshine, and Privacy Acts. Requests for information under these Acts should be directed to the Secretary's office.

* Maritime and Shipping Tariffs

Bureau of Tariffs, Certification and Licensing
Federal Maritime Commission
1100 L Street, NW
Washington, DC 20573   202-523-5796

The 1916 and 1984 Shipping Acts require that common carriers by water file and keep open to public inspection their tariffs. The 1984 Act additionally requires that service contracts be filed and that their essential terms be made available to the public in tariff format. At the end of 1990 there were some 5757 tariffs on file. The Commission is currently working on an automatic tariff filing and information system. Information on tariffs is available to the public. Call for more information.

* Maritime Legal Cases and Petitions

Office of the General Counsel
Federal Maritime Commission
1100 L Street, NW
Washington, DC 20573   202-523-5740

The General Counsel provides legal counsel to the Commission. This counsel includes reviewing for legal sufficiency staff recommendations for commission action, drafting proposed rules to implement Commission policies, and preparing final decisions, orders and regulations for Commission ratification. The Office has information on a variety of recent cases and petitions brought before the Commission.

* Maritime Technology

Office of Technology Assessment
Maritime Administration
U.S. Department of Transportation
400 7th Street SW, Room 7328
Washington, DC 20590   202-366-1925

This office conducts technology assessment activities related to the development and use of waterborne transportation systems with application in such areas as cargo handling, fleet productivity, military sealift, port activities, trade and intermodal transportation support. It additionally serves as the focal point of maritime technological expertise within the U.S. Department of Transportation.

* Maritime Trade Statistics

Trade Analysis Division (MAR-570)
Office of Trade and Analysis and Insurance
Maritime Administration
U.S. Department of Transportation
400 7th Street, SW
Washington, DC 20590   202-366-2282

Records on federally subsidized shipping companies are maintained by this Division. Information includes vessel name, port dates, and crew costs. The public can visit the document inspection room or write for information.

* Market Development for U.S. Shipping

Office of Market Development
Maritime Administration
U.S. Department of Transportation
400 7th Street, SW, Room 7209
Washington, DC 20590   202-366-5517

MARAD conducts programs designed to increase U.S. flag participation in the nation's overseas commerce. Contact this office for information on programs.

* Monitoring the 1984 Shipping Act

Bureau of Trade Monitoring
Federal Maritime Commission
1100 L Street, NW
Washington, DC 20573   202-523-5787

The Bureau of Trade Monitoring has produced a number of reports and studies relating to the 1984 Shipping Act. These include: an economic analysis of the impact of the Commissions Transatlantic Enforcement Initiative; a report on the issues surrounding the application of terminal handling charges; a profile of the North Europe trade routes; an extensive profile of the carrier services in the transpacific trade routes; the monitoring of the agreement activity in the Venezuelan trade; a report on the carryings of a controlled carrier service patterns and vessel utilization in the U.S. trades; a report on the carryings of a controlled carrier to and from U.S. Gulf ports; a report on Freight All Kinds rates and the potential abuse by controlled carriers; a report on potential trade restrictions by the Ivory Coast; and a report on trade information on carriers serving the Middle East. Contact the Trade Monitoring Bureau for information on these and other reports.

* Nautical Charts

Chart Distribution Branch
National Ocean Service
National Oceanic and Atmospheric Administration
U.S. Department of Commerce
6501 Lafayette Blvd.
Riverdale, MD 20737 301-436-6990

The National Ocean Service produces approximately 1,000 nautical charts for navigation in U.S. estuarine waters and navigable inland waterways, the Great Lakes, and the 2 1/2 million square miles of coastal waters of the United States and its possessions. National Oceanic and Atmospheric Administration (NOAA) *Chart and Map Catalogs* describe nautical charts which are listed in a series of four catalogs, one for each region of the U.S. ocean and coastal waters. NOAA bathymetric maps and special purpose charts are listed in a single catalog. A sixth catalog is a guide to NOAA nautical products and services. The catalogs contain a brief description of each nautical chart, bathymetric map, special purpose chart, and chart-related publication produced by the NOS. They also include the price of the chart of publication, other information needed to select and order nautical charting products, and a list of NOAA chart sales facilities and authorized commercial chart sales agents. Contact this office for your free catalogs.

* Ocean Commerce Statistics and Information

Bureau of Economic Analysis
Federal Maritime Commission
1100 L Street, NW
Washington, DC 20573 202-523-5870

The Bureau of Economic Analysis provides economic, statistical and financial analysis for the Commission. The Bureau assists in the development of long-range plans for the commission and enhances the agencies responsiveness to new developments and trends in U.S. ocean commerce and the liner shipping industry.

* Ocean Common Carrier Investigations

Bureau of Investigation
Federal Maritime Commission
1100 L Street, NW
Washington, DC 20573 202-523-5860

The Bureau of Investigations monitors the activities of, and conducts investigations of alleged violations by, ocean common carriers, non-vessel operating common carriers, freight forwarders, shippers, ports and terminals, and other persons to ensure compliance with the statutes and regulations issued by the commission. The Bureau maintains a staff of 48 personnel located in Washington DC, Houston, Los Angeles, Miami, New Orleans, New York, San Francisco, and Puerto Rico. District offices also provide a liaison between the Commission, industry, and the shipping public. Investigations focus on the following areas: illegal rebates by carriers; misdescriptions and misdeclarations of cargo by shippers, carriers, consignees and other persons; activities of ocean common carriers which may be in violation of the Shipping Acts; failure by carriers to charge rates in effect and on file with the Commission; and operating as an ocean freight forwarder without a license issued by the Commission or contrary to statute or regulation.

* Oceanboard Liner Cargo

Federal Maritime Commission
1100 L Street, NW
Washington, DC 20573 202-523-5725

Section 10002(g)(1) of the Omnibus Trade and Competition Act of 1988 requires the Commission to include in its annual report to Congress a listing of the 20 foreign countries which generated the largest volume of bilateral oceanboard liner cargo with the U.S. for the most recent calendar year available. The Annual Report is available from the FMC at the above listed number.

* Oceanographic Data and Publications

National Oceanic and Atmospheric Administration
U.S. Department of Commerce
1825 Connecticut Ave., NW
Washington, DC 20235 202-606-4561

The National Oceanographic Data Center has a free publications list which includes technical reports and bulletins, as well has a variety of data reports pertaining to oceanographic research.

* Oceanographic Information

National Oceanographic Data Center
National Environmental Satellite, Data and Information Service
National Oceanic and Atmospheric Administration
U.S. Department of Commerce
1825 Connecticut Ave., NW
Washington, DC 20235 202-606-4561

The National Oceanographic Data Center provides global coverage of oceanographic data and services. NODC's databases cover physical and chemical properties of the world's oceans, seas, and estuaries, plus information on selected continental shelf and coastal waters. Researchers using NODC data range from industrial scientists through local, state, and national government investigators, to university or academic personnel. Information is available in various forms: publications, computer plots, computer printouts, magnetic tapes and floppy disks. NODC publishes a *Users Guide*, which describes the data and products services available. Simple questions usually can be answered without charge by telephone or mail, but more complicated ones requiring research or computer processing usually carry a fee. The fees range upward from a base of $49 per floppy disk to $110 per reel of magnetic tape. Publications available from NODC include *Newsletter on Oceanography*, the *Earth System Monitor*, published quarterly, and the *Environmental Information Bulletin*, published 4-6 times annually.

* Oceanographic Corps Jobs

Commission Personnel Division, NOAA Corps
National Oceanic and Atmospheric Administration (NOAA)
U.S. Department of Commerce
11400 Rockville Pike
Rockville, MD 20852 301-443-8984

The NOAA Corps is the uniformed service of the U.S. Department of Commerce responsible for operating and managing NOAA's fleet of hydrographic, oceanographic, and fisheries-research ships and for supporting NOAA scientific programs. Engineering, computer science, mathematics, and science baccalaureate or higher degree graduates are sought for positions in the Corps.

* Ocean Pollution Information Network

Ocean Pollution Data and
 Information Network/CCRO
National Oceanographic Data Center
National Oceanic and Atmospheric Administration
1825 Connecticut Ave., NW
Washington, DC 20235 202-606-4539

The Ocean Pollution Data and Information Network facilitates user access to ocean pollution data and information generated by 11 participating Federal departments and agencies. OPDIN provides a wide range of products and services to researchers, managers, and others who need data and information about ocean pollution. OPDIN is managed by the Central Coordination and Referral Office (CCRO). The CCRO maintains a directory of Federal ocean pollution data and information systems and services, lists of ocean pollution scientists and managers and their fields of expertise, and annually-updated catalogs of Federal marine pollution research, development, and monitoring projects. The CCRO also provides information and advice about ocean pollution data management and processing, as well as copies of catalogs, directories, technical reports, data inventories, and data products.

* Oil and Chemical Spills Hotline

National Response Center (NRC)
Marine Environmental Response Division
Office of Marine Safety, Security, and Environmental Protection
U.S. Coast Guard
U.S. Department of Transportation
2100 2nd St., SW, Room 2611 800-424-8802
Washington, DC 20593 202-267-2188

The NRC receives reports of oil and hazardous substance spills, investigates incidents, initiates civil penalty actions, monitors cleanups, and coordinates federally funded spill response operations. NRC's National Strike Force assists federal coordinators on the scene in responding to pollution accidents. For further details, or to report information, contact the Center toll-free.

* Panama Canal Dredging Division

Engineering and Construction Bureau
Dredging Division
c/o Panama Canal Commission
Unit 2300

Business and Industry

APO AA 34011   011 507-56-6232

The Dredging Division is responsible for maintenance and construction dredging; slide removal; inspection and maintenance of the Atlantic breakwater; operation and maintenance of navigational aids; the detection, containment, recovery, and disposal of oil pollution in Canal operating areas; and the removal and control of aquatic weeds through the use of chemical and biological means. For more information on the dredging operations, contact this office.

* Panama Canal Economic and Market Research

Economic Research and Market Development Division
The Office of Executive Planning
c/o Panama Canal Commission
Unit 2300
APO AA 34011   011 507-52-7806

As an agency of the U.S. Government, the Panama Canal Commission has a legal obligation to operate on a break-even basis, recovering all costs of operating, maintaining, and improving the Canal through tolls revenue. The agency tries to have a high standard of service at the lowest possible cost. As a reflection of this, toll rates have gone up only four times since the Canal opened in 1914. Operating costs are very carefully controlled so that it provides an economic advantage to world trade on many routes. Even if other world trade routes may be shorter in distance, the Canal remains competitive because of its reliable, cost-effective service. For more information on operating costs, contact this office.

* Panama Canal Environmental Safeguards

Sanitation Branch
General Services Bureau
Panama Canal Commission
Unit 2300
APO AA 34011   011 507-52-3464

The Sanitation Branch carries out measures to control disease carrying organisms and environmental sanitation measures essential to maintaining a high standard of public health which can be enjoyed by Panama Canal Commission employees and their families. There is an effort to control insect vector and vermin by nonchemical methods. For more information, contact the above office.

* Panama Canal General Information

Office of the Secretary
Panama Canal Commission
2000 L Street, NW
Room 550
Washington, DC 20036-4996   202-634-6441

This office is a good place to start in acquiring general information on the Canal. It can also supply you with information related to transiting the Canal.

* Panama Canal Logistical Support

Office of Logistical Support
General Services Bureau
Panama Canal Commission
4400 Dauphine St.
New Orleans, LA 70146-6800   504-948-5299

The Logistical Support Division provides centralized procurement, inventory management, warehousing, distribution, contract administration, and supply and property disposal support to Canal operations. For more information, contact this office.

* Panama Canal Publications and Audiovisuals

The Office of Public Affairs
c/o Panama Canal Commission
Unit 2300
APO AA 34011   507-52-3165

The Office of Public Affairs has available various publications including the *Panama Canal 75th Anniversary Commemorative Album* and *The Panama Canal Spillway* as well as press releases, brochures, and other matters of related interest are distributed to the work force and the public at large. A broad range of photographic and audio-visual support services were created as well. A limited number of projection prints are available for loan to individuals and groups interested in the canal and its operation. All films are 16mm color and sound. Individuals may obtain video tapes of all subjects by submitting a blank tape in the desired format and the payment of a transfer charge. Some examples of the available films for general audiences are as follows:

The Task That Never Ends. 1984. Depicts the on going job of maintaining and improving the channel of the Panama Canal, widening, deepening and straightening the water route.

The Vital Link. 1986. Depicts the role of the Panama Canal in world commerce with a layman's introduction to the people and methods of Canal operations. Details of lockages, traffic control, and communications at the crossroads of the world.

1986 Landslide. 1987. Shows the resumption of the Cucaracha Slide in October, 1986. Measures taken to maintain Canal traffic while the obstruction was removed and remedial actions taken.

Some examples of the available films of special interest to engineers and mechanical craftsmen include the following:

Locks Overhaul - Strut Arms. 1981. A detailed description of strut arm removal prior to gate or bullwheel removal and replacement.

Locks Overhaul - Bullwheels. 1982. A detailed description of bullwheel removal and replacement.

There are also films of special interest to canal operating personnel. Films are available in both Spanish and English. For a complete listing of films produced by the Panama Canal Commission, contact the above office.

* Panama Canal Traffic Data

Economic Research and Market Development Division
The Office of Executive Planning
c/o Panama Canal Commission
Unit 2300
APO AA 34011   011 507-52-7961

The Panama Canal is a vital link in the world transportation chain. A large share of world trade passes through the Canal over any of the world's major trade routes. In 1988, 156.5 million long tons of cargo moved through the Canal aboard 12,318 oceangoing vessels. More than 690,962 vessels have crossed the waterway, carrying more than 4 billion long tons of the world's goods from one ocean to the other. For more information or compilations of Canal traffic data, contact this office.

* Panama Canal Transit

Canal Operations Unit
c/o Panama Canal Commission
Unit 2300
APO AA 34011   011 507-52-4211

This office can provide information for those considering taking a boat or ship through the canal.

* Panama Canal Vessel Emergency Response Management

Marine Director
Marine Bureau
c/o Panama Canal Commission
Unit 2300
APO AA 34011   011 507-52-4500

For information on marine operations including inspections, piloting, locks, traffic management, canal services, marine safety, canal operations and maritime training, contact this Bureau. The Commission's marine risk management team is devoted to the prevention of and response to accidents involving vessels carrying hazardous cargoes. The team consists of an experienced fireman, a licensed marine engineer, a safety generalist, an experienced chemist, and lead by an experienced active duty U.S. Coast Guard officer. This team is also responsible for updating the Commission's Vessel Emergency Response Plan and in conducting vessel emergency training exercises.

* Passenger Safety Certification

Bureau of Domestic Regulation
Federal Maritime Commission
1100 L Street, NW
Washington, DC 20573   202-523-5796

Owners, charters, and operators of American and foreign vessels having berth or stateroom accommodations for fifty or more passengers and embarking passengers at U.S. ports must establish financial responsibility to meet any liability incurred for death or injury to passengers on voyages to or from U.S. ports and to indemnify passengers for non-performance of transportation to which they would be entitled under ticket contracts. Call this office for more information.

* Port Development

Office of Port Development
Maritime Administration
U.S. Department of Transportation
400 7th Street, SW
Washington, DC 20590   202-366-4357

As part of its marketing program, the Maritime Administration (MARAD) actively promotes the improvement of the national port facilities and advanced intermodal transportation systems. MARAD advises and assists port communities in promoting advanced, highly efficient marine terminal and intermodal operations to speed the flow of cargo. MARAD also conducts research to help ports update facilities, services, and equipment. Recent port studies include:

Report to Congress on the Status of U.S. Public Ports - 1988-89.
Water Transportation and Ports.
Changing Directions for Traditional Ports.

These are available free from MARAD.

* Port Regulations

Port Safety and Security Division
Office of Marine Safety, Security, and
  Environmental Protection
U.S. Coast Guard
U.S. Department of Transportation
2100 2nd St., SW, Room 1104
Washington, DC 20593-0001   202-267-0489

Coast Guard Captains of the Port enforce rules and regulations concerning the safety and security of ports and the anchorage and movement of vessels. This includes supervising cargo transfers and storage; conducting harbor patrols and facility inspections; establishing security zones; and surveying to prevent water pollution. The Division also administers a licensing and registration program for deepwater ports transferring oil from tankers to shore via pipelines. For information on regulations and operations, contact the division listed.

* Protection of Ships From Seizure

Assistant Legal Advisor for International Claims
Office of the Legal Advisor
U.S. Department of State
2201 C St., NW
Washington, DC 20520   202-632-7810

The Fishermen's Protective Act provides for reimbursement for financial loss to owners of vessels registered in the United States for fines paid to secure the release of vessels seized for operation in waters not recognized as territorial waters by the United States. No registration or payment of premiums is required prior to the seizure in order to qualify for reimbursement.

* Ready Reserve Fleet

Division of Reserve Fleet
Maritime Administration
U.S. Department of Transportation
400 7th Street SW, Room 2117
Washington, DC 20590   202-366-5776

MARAD maintains an inactive reserve of over 300 ships in the National Defense Reserve Fleet as a source of vessels available for the U.S. government in the event of an emergency. The Ready Reserve Force is a portion of the NDRF and can be activated in 5-20 days. MARAD activated some 78 ships during Operation Desert Shield/Storm.

* Saint Lawrence Seaway Statistics

Office of Trade and Traffic Development
Saint Lawrence Seaway Development Corporation
400 7th Street, SW, Room 5424
Washington, DC 20590   202-366-0091

This office keeps statistics on traffic in the Great Lakes/Seaway system. Data is recorded on the number of vessels and their size, type, cargo, and nationality. Cargo vessel statistics are published in the *Annual Traffic Report in the Saint Lawrence Seaway.*

* Saint Lawrence Seaway Publications

Public Affairs Office
Saint Lawrence Seaway Development Corporation
U.S. Department of Transportation
180 Andrews Street
Massena, NY 13662-1763   315-764-3232

Free publications about the Seaway are available by contacting this office. Some of the titles available include the following:

Annual Traffic Report in the Saint Lawrence Seaway. Cargo vessel statistics for traffic between Montreal and Lake Erie.

Pleasure Craft Guide: The Seaway. Information on boating in the St. Lawrence River.

The Saint Lawrence Seaway. General and historical information in French and English, including port data, schedules, and tourist information.

The Saint Lawrence Seaway Annual Report.

Seaway Regulations. Includes regulations and toll schedule, operating manual, and chart booklet.

* Sea Grant Abstracts

National Sea Grant Depository
Pell Library Building
The University of Rhode Island
Narragansett Bay Campus
Narragansett, RI 02882-1197   401-792-6114

Sea Grant Abstracts cites, on a quarterly basis, the majority of the literature which is received by the National Sea Grant Depository. This literature covers pure and applied science, engineering, business management, shipping and navigation, fisheries, wetlands management, law and policy, economics, and education. Each reference contains a short abstract, a bibliographic reference, and information for obtaining the document. Back issues are also available.

* Sea-Grant Colleges

Office of Oceanic Research Programs
National Oceanic and Atmospheric Administration
U.S. Department of Commerce
1335 East-West Hwy.
Silver Spring, MD 20910   301-713-2465

The National Sea Grant College Program is a national network of over 300 colleges, universities, research institutions, and consortia working in partnership with industry and the federal government to support Great Lakes and marine research, education, and extension services. This program provides support for institutions engaged in comprehensive marine research, education, and advisory service programs, supports individual projects in marine research and development, and sponsors education of ocean scientists and engineers, marine technicians, and other specialists at selected colleges and universities.

* Sea Grant Depository

National Sea Grant Depository
Pell Library Building
University of Rhode Island, Bay Campus
Narragansett, RI 02882   401-792-6114

The National Sea Grant Depository is a clearinghouse for all Sea Grant publications. The scope of the collection includes a wide variety of marine topics, such as oceanography, marine education, aquaculture, fisheries, coastal zone management, recreation, and law. The collection includes journal reprints, technical and advisory reports, books, manuals, directories, annual reports, conference proceedings, and newsletters. The Depository Database includes some 22,000 citations. The Depository provides reference and online search services, and welcomes telephone, mail and inter-library loan requests. The Depository will loan documents, but does not distribute the publications (they refer you to the authors). There is a loan limit of 10 documents per request. To be sure that your request for materials is not returned, the library urges people to state clearly that you wish to borrow materials.

* Ship Construction

Office of Ship Construction (MAR-720)
Maritime Administration
U.S. Department of Transportation

Be patient. If any phone number is incorrect, call (area code) 555-1212 and request the new listing.

797

Business and Industry

400 7th Street, SW, Room 6422
Washington, DC 20590   202-366-1880
Contact this office for information on the cost of and market for shipbuilding. The difference between the cost of constructing ships here and abroad are also examined.

* Ship Mortgage Guarantees

Office of Ship Operations
Maritime Administration
U.S. Department of Transportation
400 7th Street, SW, Room 8122
Washington, DC 20590   202-366-5744
Through the Merchant Marine Act of 1936, MARAD guarantees commercially placed construction loans and ship mortgages on vessels built in the U.S. for operation on domestic or foreign trade routes. Qualified applicants can obtain long term financing on favorable terms. Contact MARAD for details.

* Shipping Analysis

Office of Domestic Shipping
Maritime Administration
U.S. Department of Transportation
400 7th Street, SW
Washington, DC 20590   202-366-5123
The Maritime Administration promotes U.S. domestic shipping services through analysis of the domestic fleet, its markets, the commodities it moves, and its modal competition. Information compiled or maintained by this office is available to the maritime community.

* Shipping Service Contract Regulation

Bureau of Domestic Regulation
Federal Maritime Commission
1100 L Street, NW
Washington, DC 20573   202-523-5796
Shippers must file service contracts with the Commission. The Commission ensures that service contracts filed with it meet the necessary statutory and regulatory requirements. The Commission does not accept service contracts which fail to contain mutually binding service and cargo commitments, or which contain meaningless liquidated damages provisions. Contact the Commission to find out shippers requirements with respect to service contracts under the 1984 Shipping Act.

* Small Passenger Vessel Safety

Marine Inspection Office
Your Local Coast Guard Office
Most small passenger vessels (less than 100 tons and carrying more than 6 people) are required to adhere to certain Coast Guard safety regulations. These include having a safety orientation procedure for passengers (announcement or placard), posting of emergency instructions, a life preserver for every person on board, and a Coast Guard safety certification. Marine Inspection Offices around the country issue the certificates. To find an Inspection Office near you, or to report a violation or complaint, call the Boating Safety Hotline 800-368-5647; or 202-267-0780 in DC.

* Sockeye Odyssey and Other Films

National Oceanic and Atmospheric Administration (NOAA)
U.S. Department of Commerce
14th St. and Pennsylvania Ave., NW, Room 6013
Washington, DC 20230   202-377-8090
A brochure is available which lists motion picture films produced by the National Oceanic and Atmospheric Administration. Most NOAA productions are available in both motion picture and video formats. Unless noted, these films are not available directly from NOAA. To borrow prints without charge, except for return postage, write to: Modern Talking Pictures, 6000 Park Street North, St., Petersburg, FL 33709. These films are heavily booked, so you must send your request as early as possible. The following is a list of their titles:

Sockeye Odyssey
The Awesome Power
The Great American Fish Story
The Great American Fish Story- The West
The Great American Fish Story- The Northeast
The Great American Fish Story- The South
The Great American Fish Story- The Lakes and Rivers

Down to the Monitor
Estuary
*FAMOUS- Boundary of Creation**
*Give Me The Tides**
Global Weather Experiment
*Longlines: An Undersea Investigation**
NOAA Corps- The Seventh Service
Trashing The Oceans

*Available directly from NOAA. Contact the office listed above for a free catalog.

* Trade Monitoring

Bureau of Trade Monitoring
Federal Maritime Commission
1100 L Street, NW
Washington, DC 20573   202-523-5787
The Bureau's major program activities include: administering comprehensive trade monitoring programs to identify and track relevant competitive, commercial, and economic activity in each major U.S. trade in order to keep the Commission and its staff appraised of current trade conditions, emerging trends and regulatory needs impacting on waterborne liner transportation. Other monitoring duties include: systematic surveillance of carrier activity and processing and analysis of agreements involving common carriers.

* Updates for Mariners

District Commander
Your local Coast Guard Office
The free *Local Notice to Mariners* is issued weekly by each Coast Guard District. Intended for small craft owners, it advises you of changes in the status of aids to navigation (buoys, radiobeacons, etc.); chart updates; drawbridge operations; and safety warnings for particular areas. This *Local Notice* often includes temporary changes not included in the Defense Mapping Agency's *Notice to Mariners*. To order a subscription for the *Local Notice*, send a written request to the District Commander of your local Coast Guard office. For referral to the correct address, call the Boating Safety Hotine 800-368-5647; or 202-267-0780 in DC.

* U.S. Living Marine Resources

National Marine Fisheries Service
Office of Predictions and Analysis
National Oceanic and Atmospheric Administration
1335 East West Highway
Silver Spring, MD 20910   301-713-2363
In 1991 the NMFS published the first annual report *Our Living Oceans*, a comprehensive report on the status of U.S. living marine resources. The study contains status reports on many U.S. coastal fish stocks and regional reports detailing fisheries in the Northeast, Atlantic, Gulf of Mexico, Southeast, Pacific Coast, and Alaskan waters. The report is available in limited supply from the above office and is sold by GPO (202-512-1800), S/N #0030200161-1, $6.

* U.S. Merchant Marine Academy

U.S. Merchant Marine Academy
Maritime Administration
U.S. Department of Transportation-Kings Point
Long Island, NY 11024   516-773-5000
Future merchant marine officers are trained here in navigation instrumentation, ship maneuvering, ship management, and communications. The Academy also administers a Federal assistance program for maritime academies in California, Maine, Massachusetts, Michigan, New York, and Texas.

* Vessel Operating Aid

Office of Maritime Aids
Maritime Administration
U.S. Department of Transportation
400 7th Street, SW
Washington, DC 20590   202-366-0364
The Maritime Administration pays a subsidy to U.S. Shipping companies to offset the higher cost of operating under U.S. flags. To qualify for the subsidy, a vessel operator must be a U.S. citizen who owns or leases ships to compete in foreign trade. Operators must additionally be fiscally sound and agree to make their ships available to the government in the event of a military emergency. Call or write MARAD for more information.

* War Risk Insurance for Ships

Marine Insurance Division
Office of Trade and Analysis and Insurance
Maritime Administration
U.S. Department of Transportation
400 7th Street, SW, Room 8121
Washington, DC 20590   202-366-4161

The War Risk Insurance Program insures operators and seamen against losses from hostile action if commercial insurance is not available to them. The program covers loss of life and materials due to war or nuclear detonation.

* Waterways Traffic Regulation

Commander G-NSP
Vessel Traffic Services Branch
Office of Navigation Safety and Waterways Services
U.S. Coast Guard
U.S. Department of Transportation
2100 2nd St., SW, Room 3202
Washington, DC 20593-0001   202-267-1539

To ensure the safe and orderly passage of vessels, cargo, and people, Vessel Traffic Services in major ports oversee the movement of vessels and install necessary safety equipment. Traffic is monitored closely during hazardous conditions and bad weather. To locate the Vessel Traffic Service nearest you, contact the branch listed above or your local Coast Guard office.

Be patient. If any phone number is incorrect, call (area code) 555-1212 and request the new listing.

799

Mining

Given the central importance of minerals to the modern economy, the Federal government closely monitors the position of the U.S. with respect to key minerals. The central locus of information in the U.S. government on mine and mineral related matters is the U.S. Department of the Interior's Bureau of Mines. Another good source of information is the U.S. Geological Survey. With the creation of the U.S. Department of Energy in 1977, many policy decisions on the mining of energy producing materials such as coal and uranium and on the drilling for oil and natural gas moved largely to Energy. The Office of Surface Mining and Reclamation in the U.S. Department of the Interior can provide you with information on surface mining for coal and environmental reclamation.

* Abandoned Mine Land Reclamation

Office of Surface Mining Reclamation and Enforcement
U.S. Department of the Interior
1951 Constitution Ave., NW
Washington, DC 20240   202-208-5365

The surface mining law requires that operators pay a reclamation fee for each ton of coal produced. These fees are deposited with the U.S. Treasury in a fund called the Abandoned Mine Reclamation Fund and are used to reclaim sites that were mined and left unreclaimed before the surface mining law was enacted in 1977. Fifty percent of the fees collected in a state that has approved reclamation and regulatory programs is returned to that state for use in its reclamation program. The other fifty percent is the Federal share. This portion is used by the Office of Surface Mining Reclamation and Enforcement to address public health and safety emergencies caused by past mining practices, and to fund high-priority reclamation projects in non-program states. The Office of Surface Mining also publishes a booklet entitled *Abandoned Mine Reclamation: Ten Years of Progress*, which details the progress of the program. To obtain your state contact for the abandoned mine land reclamation program and for a copy of the *Abandoned Mine Reclamation* booklet, contact the office above.

* Bureau of Land Management: Mineral Publications

Bureau of Land Management (BLM)
U.S. Department of the Interior
18th and C Streets, NW
Washington, DC 20240   202-208-3435

The BLM has several free publications dealing with mining and minerals. The following is a partial list of publications.

Energy and Mineral Resources on Public Lands
Mining Claims and Sites on Public Domain Lands
Federal Coal Management Report
Mineral Revenues: The 1989 Report on Receipts from Federal and Indian Lands

* Bureau of Mines Educational Publications

Office of Public Affairs
Bureau of Mines
U.S. Department of the Interior
810 7th St., NW
Washington, DC 20241   202-501-9650

The Bureau of Mines outreach efforts are targeted at both school age children as well as adults. For elementary school children, the Bureau of Mines materials package includes a coloring book entitled *Minerals and You*. A three part package consisting of an introductory mineral information text, a coloring book, and a booklet of teacher-student activities. For adults, the Bureau of Mines publishes a 70 page book entitled *Minerals in 1991*, which profiles 34 minerals and discusses the importance of minerals to the U.S. economy.

* Bureau of Mines Field Facilities

Bureau of Mines
U.S. Department of the Interior
810 7th St., NW
Washington, DC 20241   202-501-9650

Alabama
Tuscaloosa Research Center, University of Alabama Campus, P.O. Box L, Tuscaloosa, AL 35486; 205-759-9474

Alaska
Alaska Field Operations Center, 3301 C St., Suite 325, Anchorage, AK 99501; 907-271-2454

Colorado
Intermountain Field Operations Center, P.O. Box 25086, Building 20, Denver Federal Center, Denver, CO 80225; 303-236-0421

Minerals Availability Field Office, Building 20, Denver Federal Center, Denver, CO 80225; 303-236-5200

Denver Research Center, P.O. Box 25086, Building 20, Denver Federal Center, Denver, CO 80225; 303-236-0697

Minnesota
Twin Cities Research Center, 5629 Minnehaha Ave. S., Minneapolis, MN 55417; 612-725-4610

Missouri
Rolla Research Center, P.O. Box 280, 1300 Bishop Ave., Rolla, MO 65401; 314-364-3169

Nevada
Reno Research Center, 1605 Evans Ave., Reno, NV 89512; 702-334-6610

Oregon
Research Center, 1450 Queen Ave., SW, Albany, OR 97321; 503-967-5893

Pennsylvania
Pittsburgh Research Center, Cochrans Mill Rd, P.O. Box 18070, Pittsburgh, PA 15236; 412-892-6601

Texas
Helium Field Operations, 1100 South Fillmore, Amarillo, TX 79101; 806-376-2602

Utah
Salt Lake City Research Center, 729 Arapeen Dr., Salt Lake City, UT 84108; 801-524-6100

Washington
Spokane Research Center, E 315 Montgomery Ave., Spokane, WA 99207; 509-484-1610
Western Field Operations Center, E. 360 Third Ave., Spokane, WA 99202; 509-353-2712

* Bureau of Mines Programs

Office of Public Affairs
Bureau of Mines
810 7th Street, NW
Washington, DC 20241   202-501-9650

The Bureau of Mines publishes the booklet *The Minerals Source*, which discusses different programs os the Bureau of Mines. It is available free from the public affairs office.

* Bureau of Mines Publications

Superintendent of Documents
Government Printing Office
Washington, DC 20420   202-512-1800

Publications of the Bureau of Mines in an annotated bibliography of new publications by the Bureau of Mines. Included in this monthly flyer are listings of free publications, open file reports, and outside publications available concerning the mineral industry. The annual subscription price is $19, and the single copy price is $1.75 (S/N 724-004-00000-8).

* Bureau of Mines State Activities Directory

Chief, Office of State Activities
Bureau of Mines
U.S. Department of the Interior
810 7th St., NW
Washington, DC 20241   202-501-9650

The following offices are sources of information on state mineral activity:

Alaska

Regional Office of State Activities, Bureau of Mines, U.S. Department of the Interior, P.O. Box 20550, Juneau, AK 99802-0550; 907-364-2111

Denver

Regional Office of State Activities, Bureau of Mines, U.S. Department of the Interior, Denver Federal Center, Bldg. #20, P.O. Box 25086, Denver, CO 80225-0086; 303-236-0435

Pittsburgh

Regional Office of State Activities, Bureau of Mines, U.S. Department of the Interior, Cochrans Mill Rd., P.O. Box 18070, Pittsburgh, PA 15236-0070; 412-892-6601

Reno

Regional Office of State Activities, Bureau of Mines, U.S. Department of the Interior, Reno Research Center, 1605 Evans Ave., Reno, NV 89512-2295; 702-334-6610

Spokane

Regional Office of State Activities, Bureau of Mines, U.S. Department of the Interior, E. 360 Third Ave., Spokane, WA 99202-1413; 509-353-2720

Tuscaloosa

Regional Office of State Activities, Bureau of Mines, U.S. Department of the Interior, University of Alabama Campus, P.O. Box L, University, AL 35486-9777; 205-759-9465; 205-759-9466

Tucson

Regional Office of State Activities, Bureau of Mines, U.S. Department of the Interior, 210 E. 7th St., Tucson, AZ 85705-8454; 602-629-5111

Twin Cities

Regional Office of State Activities, Bureau of Mines, U.S. Department of the Interior, 5629 Minnehaha Ave., S., Minneapolis, MN 55417-3099; 612-725-4534; 612-725-4535

* Bureau of Reclamation Regional Offices

Bureau of Mines
U.S. Department of Interior
18th and C Sts, NW
Washington, DC 20240   202-208-4662

Here are the regional offices which enforce strip mining and reclamation laws; also listed are the Headquarters contacts for these regions:

Lower Colorado Region

Box 61470, Boulder City, NV 89006; 702-293-8420; DC contact 202-208-6269

Mid-Pacific Region

2800 Cottage Way, Sacramento, CA 95825; 916-978-4919; DC contact 202-208-6274

Pacific Northwest Region

Box 043, 550 W. Fort St., Boise, ID 83724; 208-334-1938; DC contact 202-208-6271

Upper Colorado Region

Box 11568, 125 S. State St., Salt Lake City, UT 84147; 801-524-6477; DC contact 202-208-6751

Great Plains Region

Box 36900, 316 N. 26th St., Billings, MT 59107; 406-657-6218; DC contact 202-208-6267

Contact headquarters for information and addresses for international project/overseas offices in Brazil, Egypt, Guam, Pakistan, Saudi Arabia, and Saipan.

* Byproduct Metals Study

Research Division, Bureau of Mines
U.S. Department of the Interior
810 7th St., NW
Washington, DC 20241   202-501-9290

A new study, *Byproduct Output from Domestic Primary Copper, Lead, and Zinc Industries*, examined the collective role of byproducts with regard to the economics of mineral production, and their individual significance in terms of dollar values, end uses and strategic considerations. The study also analyzes circumstances that have affected the competitiveness and structure of the copper, lead, and zinc industries and the factors that impact byproduct availability, including production capacity at domestic smelters and refineries, process technology, changing sources and composition of ores, foreign ownership, and byproduct demand and price. Call or write for information on obtaining the study.

* Census of Minerals Industries Bibliography

Superintendent of Documents
Government Printing Office
Washington, DC 20402   202-512-1800

The Census of Mineral Industries, 1987, Geographic Series is featured in this bibliography, as well as the *Industry Series* subscription service.

* Claims on Federal Lands

Energy and Mineral Resources
Bureau of Land Management
U.S. Department of the Interior
18th and C Sts., NW
Washington, DC 20240   202-208-4201

The brochure, *Staking a Mining Claim on Federal Lands*, describes the procedure you would follow to stake a mining claim on public lands. Claims are granted to individuals for particular pieces of land, valuable for specific mineral deposits. Questions concerning the definition of a mining claim and the technicalities of recording and maintaining mining claims are also covered.

* Coal Ash Producers

American Coal Ash Association (ACAA)
1913 Eye St., NW, 6th Floor
Washington, DC 20006   202-659-2303

ACAA has been representing producers and marketers of coal combustion products (some 68 at present) as well as coal companies and suppliers of ash-related equipment and services as a "resource conservation and recovery" association since 1968. ACAA's technology development program attempts to protect and increase the use of coal ash by developing a technological base for coal ash as a commercially viable and environmentally sound alternative to virgin materials. The ACAA also collects information for members and end users of coal ash. Contact ACAA for more information.

* Coal Mining and Environmental Protection

Office of Public Affairs
Office of Surface Mining Reclamation and Enforcement
1951 Constitution Avenue, NW
Washington, DC 20240   202-208-2553

This office works to protect people and the environment from the side-effects of coal mining, while continuing to regulate coal mining. Lands that were affected by past coal mining operations must be repaired if left unreclaimed or abandoned. Technical assistance is provided to states so that they can perform their responsibilities under the surface mining law. State personnel are trained in the technical aspects of surface mining, such as soil compaction, revegetation, and groundwater hydrology, so that they can better enforce regulations.

Business and Industry

* Coal Mining Research

Bureau of Mines
Research Division
U.S. Department of the Interior
810 7th St., NW
Washington, DC 20241   202-501-9274

The Bureau of Mines is currently researching and evaluating a system for teleoperated highwall coal mining. Teleoperations for mining is computer based, remote control of mining machinery from a protected operator compartment located distantly from the mine site, so that sensory information about the mining operation cannot be obtained directly. Video, sound, and other relevant data are gathered through sensors and transmitted electronically to the operators location. This technology offers the possibility to dramatically increase worker safety. For more information, contact the research division.

* Critical Minerals Assessment

Bureau of Mines
Research Division
U.S. Department of the Interior
810 7th St., NW
Washington, DC 20241   202-501-9274

The Bureau evaluates and catalogues potential mineral resources, especially those on federal land, to assist lawmakers and land use managers in making decisions. It has also been a major participant in a joint task force investigating placer resources in the U.S. Exclusive Economic Zone off the coast of Oregon.

* Deep Seabed Mining

Ocean Minerals and Energy Division
National Ocean Service
National Oceanic and Atmospheric Administration
U.S. Department of Commerce
1825 Connecticut Ave., NW
Washington, DC 20235   202-606-4121

Extensive information is available on deep seabed mining, which includes the annual report to Congress and an updated environmental assessment of NOAA deep seabed mining licensees' exploration plans. The Office's current focus is on exploration for Manganese nodules on the ocean floor. No mining permits for Manganese nodules on the ocean floor have been issued. This office can provide you with information regarding the research conducted concerning the environmental impact of the mining, as well as information on the regulations and licenses. The *1989* and *1991 Annual Reports to Congress* are excellent places to begin your information search. They are available free.

* Energy and Mineral Resources

Office of Energy and Marine Geology
U.S. Geological Survey
National Center, MS 915
Reston, VA 22092   703-648-6472

Investigations of the nature, extent, and origin of the Nation's coal, oil and gas, oil shale, uranium, and geothermal resources are basic to this office's research efforts. Acquired data are placed in computerized databases, such as the National Coal Resources Data System.

* Environmental Mining Research

Environmental Technology Division
Bureau of Mines
U.S. Department of the Interior
810 7th St., NW
Washington, DC 20241   202-501-9271

Researchers at the Bureau of Mines are working on low-cost ways to deal with the problem of acid drainage at abandoned mines. They are developing computer programs to predict potential drainage at new mines. The Bureau's environmental research also addresses the problem of solid waste disposal and soil and water contaminated by metals. Technologies are developed that will reduce or remove the threats that these wastes pose.

* Films on the Mining Industry

Office of Technology Transfer
Bureau of Mines
U.S. Department of the Interior
810 7th Street, NW
Washington, DC 20241   202-501-9652

This office publishes a listing of films and videos on topics related to the mineral industry. Topics include safer coal mining equipment, mine shaft smoke and fire protection system, and a retractable diamond bit system for core drilling, among others. All of the films and videos may be purchased or can be borrowed free of charge.

* Gold Prospecting

Publications Department
Bureau of Mines
U.S. Department of the Interior
810 7th Street., NW
Washington, DC 20241   202-208-9650

The publications department of the Bureau of Mines distributes the free booklet, *How To Mine and Prospect for Gold*. The booklet is no longer in print, but the Bureau of Mines can send you a photocopy. It is *Information Circular 8517*.

* Indian Lands and Minerals

Office of Trust and Economic Development
Bureau of Indian Affairs
U.S. Department of the Interior
18th and C Sts., NW
Washington, DC 20240   202-208-5831

This office manages some 53 million acres of land held in trust by the United States for Indians. Tribes are helped in protecting their lands and in developing their forest, water, mineral, and energy resources.

* International Mineral Data

Superintendent of Documents
Government Printing Office
Washington, DC 20402   202-512-1800

The *Minerals Yearbook, 1985: Volume 111 (Area Reports: International)* contains the latest available mineral data from more than 150 foreign countries and discusses the importance of minerals to the economies of these nations. It reviews the international minerals industry in general and its relationship to the world economy. 1987 (S/N 024-004-02179-9, $36).

* International Minerals Research

Information and Analysis Division
Bureau of Mines
U.S. Department of the Interior
810 7th St., NW
Washington, DC 20241   202-501-9660

The Bureau of Mines continually assesses the world mineral situation as it impacts the United States. The U.S. Department of State regional resource officers report regularly from 10 major minerals - and mineral producing countries: Australia, Belgium, Brazil, Chile, India, Indonesia, Japan, Mexico, South Africa, and Venezuela. As part of its China studies program, the bureau in 1990 published *The Iron and Steel Industry of China.* The Bureau of Mines also closely coordinates with the United States Trade Representative on trade matters, particularly relating to Canada, Mexico, and the European Community.

* Land Management Annual Report

Bureau of Land Management (BLM)
U.S. Department of the Interior
18th and C Streets, NW
Washington, DC 20240   202-208-3435

The Bureau of Land Management (BLM) *Annual Report* contains information on current BLM programs in the areas of land and mineral management. The 1989-1992 BLM report contains an excellent discussion of surface mining management initiatives. The report is available free from BLM.

* Materials Research: Wear and Corrosion

Research Division
Bureau of Mines
U.S. Department of the Interior
810 7th St., NW
Washington, DC 20241   202-501-9290

Advanced materials research is being conducted to eliminate wear and corrosion within the minerals industry through the use of ceramics, high-performance plastics, high-tech metals and alloys, and composites. Bureau scientists are also developing new coatings to protect equipment from the heat, corrosive chemicals, and abrasive materials found in mills, smelters, refineries, and furnaces.

* Metals and Mining Producers

American Mining Congress (AMC)
1920 N St., NW, Suite 300
Washington, DC 20036 202-861-2800

The American Mining Congress is an industry association of producers of metals, coal industrial and agricultural minerals; manufacturers of mining and mineral processing machinery, equipment and supplies; and mining engineering firms. AMC publishes the *American Mining Congress Journal*, a monthly journal which focuses on mining issues and policy and is available for $30 per year. AMC can also put you in touch with members who can provide you with detailed information on most aspects of the mining industry.

* Mine Map Repositories

Office of Public Affairs
Bureau of Mines
U.S. Department of the Interior
810 7th Street, NW
Washington, DC 20241 202-501-9650

The Mine Map Repositories were established in 1970 and are responsible for collecting and archiving mine maps both east and west of the Mississippi River and in Alaska. The brochure, *Mine Map Repositories*, provides information and statistics on the mine map repository facilities of the Office of Surface Mining Reclamation and Enforcement. The five repositories are listed with their addresses and phone numbers. They are located in Pittsburgh, PA, Wilkes-Barre, PA, Denver, CO, Spokane, WA, and Juneau, AK.

* Mine Maps/Mine Companies Property Ownership

Division of Program Information and Analysis
Bureau of Mines
U.S. Department of the Interior
810 7th St., NW
Washington, DC 20241 202-501-9650

Valuable information is available from the mine maps available through the mine map repositories of the Office of Surface Mining Reclamation and Enforcement. Mine and company names, water sources, property ownership of adjoining companies and towns, latitudes and longitudes, coal outcrop seam designations, openings and emergency exits of mines, and gas and power lines are some of the topics covered. This information can be useful to local developers, engineering firms, and energy interests, as well as private citizens.

* Mine Safety

Health, Safety, and Mining Technology
Bureau of Mines
U.S. Department of the Interior
810 7th St., NW
Washington, DC 20241 202-501-9321

The Bureau is studying ways to improve mine safety and to eliminate the health risks of mining. One of the areas of emphasis is finding ways to reduce a miner's exposure to respirable dust, which causes black lung and other respiratory diseases. Studies in safety precautions help companies build more stable mines with better roof support systems and more efficiently detect flammable gases and ignition sources. Research on automation and robotics to do the more hazardous jobs is also being done.

* Mine Safety and Health Administration (MSHA)

Office of Public Affairs
U.S. Department of Labor
4015 Wilson Blvd., Room 601
Arlington, VA 22203 703-235-1452

The Labor Department's Mine Safety and Health Administration (MSHA) helps to reduce deaths, injuries and illnesses in the nations mines with a variety of activities and programs. The agency develops and enforces safety and health rules applying to all U.S. mines, helps mine operators who have special compliance problems, and makes available technical, educational and other types of assistance. MSHA's authority derives from the 1977 Federal Mine Safety and Health Act. The Office of Public Affairs can provide you with information on MSHA programs including: injury statistics; safety, health, and education training enforcement; technical

assistance; and legislation. MSHA has technical support offices in Pittsburgh and Denver.

* Mineral Commodity Information

Minerals Information Office
Bureau of Mines
U.S. Geological Survey
U.S. Department of the Interior
18th and C Sts.
MS 2647-MIB, Room 2647
Washington, DC 20240 202-208-5520

The Minerals Information Office is staffed by mineral experts who distribute a wide variety of mineral-related information and publications to meet and support the needs of the public, as well as government agencies and the scientific and industrial sectors. The staff provides information on the most current as well as past published reports pertaining to minerals, mining, processing, and research, as well as updated listings of current reports.

* Mineral Commodity Summaries 1992

Minerals Information Office
Bureau of Mines
U.S. Geological Survey
U.S. Department of the Interior
18th and C Sts.
MS 2647-MIB, Room 2647
Washington, DC 20240 202-208-5520

Mineral Commodity Summaries 1992 lists the statistics available for 82 commodities, including domestic production and uses; salient statistics - United States; recycling; import sources; tariff; depletion allowance; government stockpile; events and trends; world mine production, reserves and reserve base; world resources; and substitutes. The expert's name and phone number of each report is also listed.

* Mineral Deposits Database

Minerals Information Office
Bureau of Mines
U.S. Geological Survey
U.S. Department of the Interior
18th and C Sts.
MS 2647-MIB, Room 2647
Washington, DC 20240 202-208-5520

The Bureau of Mines has three mining databases. The *Personal Computer Advanced Deposit Information Tracking System Mineral Deposit Data Base* contains information on 3,000 domestic and foreign (market economy countries) mining operations, including operation data (name, company, locations, etc.) and operation status (operation type, processing and milling methods, capacity, etc.). The database covers 34 critical and strategic commodities, representing those deposits most significant in terms of value and tonnage. The *Automated Minerals Information System (AMIS)* is an integrated system that includes information on mineral production, capacity, consumption, industrial stocks, imports, exports, reserves and recycled materials. Information on personal computer access for AMIS is available at 202-501-9750. The *Minerals Industry Locator System (MILS)* contains nearly 200,000 records of mineral occurrences, identified and described in terms of geographic, geologic, ownership, and production information. Call for information on accessing these databases.

* Mineral Deposits Distribution

Mineral Resources
Geologic Inquiries
U.S. Geological Survey
907 National Center
Reston, VA 22092 703-648-4383

The U.S. Geological Survey assesses the distribution of the mineral resources of the United States, especially strategic and critical commodities, and studies the processes that control the occurrence of mineral deposits. New techniques and methods useful in the search for these resources are continually being developed.

* Mineral Policy Analysis

Policy Analysis
Information and Analysis Division
Bureau of Mines
U.S. Department of the Interior

810 7th St., NW
Washington, DC 20241   202-501-9734
Bureau economists prepare special studies that analyze issues involving minerals in the United States. An ongoing assessment of the Nation's "mineral position" is conducted. Specialists examine factors that affect the competitiveness of the U.S. mineral industry and its contribution to the Nation's economy. Environmental regulations are also evaluated as to their impact on U.S. mineral production.

* Mineral Position of the United States

Bureau of Mines
U.S. Department of the Interior
810 7th St., NW
Washington, DC 20241   202-501-9650
The Mineral Position of the United States is an annual report published by the U.S. Department of the Interior under the Mining and Minerals Policy Act of 1970. It contains a detailed analysis and statistics for key mineral industries such as steel, copper, aluminum, and gold as well as discussing government initiatives related to mineral issues. These initiatives include new programs as well as international agreements that influence the U.S. mineral position. The final section of the report discusses research and new technologies in the mineral industry. The 1988 edition of the report is the latest available. It is free from the public affairs office.

* Mineral Processing Research

Minerals and Materials Science
Bureau of Mines
U.S. Department of the Interior
810 7th St., NW
Washington, DC 20241   202-501-9274
This office looks for ways to improve mineral processing operations by cutting costs and recovering more minerals contained in ores. A variety of processing methods are studied, including crushing, grinding, flotation, smelting, solvent extraction, and leaching. Their research also includes long-range efforts to apply high technology to mineral processing.

* Mineral Production and Consumption

Information and Analysis Division
Bureau of Mines
U.S. Department of the Interior
810 7th St., NW
Washington, DC 20241   202-501-9365
The Bureau of Mines collects information about minerals from U.S. mining companies and mineral processing plants. Mineral production and consumption is monitored throughout the world through contacts with foreign governments, U.S. embassies, international publications, and visits to mines overseas. The Bureau employs 11 state mineral specialists through cooperative data collection agreements with the states. Three regional field offices and nine research centers also gather information. The data is then made available to the public via reports, books, and computer disks.

* Mineral Resource Films

Audiovisual Library
Office of Public Affairs
Bureau of Mines
U.S. Department of the Interior
810 7th St., NW
Washington, DC 20241   202-501-9652
This office's brochure, *Mineral Resource Films*, lists information on borrowing and scheduling films and videocassettes, along with National distribution centers. Films available cover such topics as copper, cast iron, silver, mine fire control, the minerals challenge, wealth out of waste, tungsten, lead, boron, chromium, gold, and platinum. Recently released titles include *Out of the Rock*, *Call me Can*, and *Aluminum Recycling*.

* Mineral Resources

Mineral Resources
Geologic Inquiries
U.S. Geological Survey
907 National Center
Reston, VA 22092   703-648-4383
The U.S. Geological Survey assesses the distribution of the mineral resources of the United States, especially strategic and critical commodities, and studies the processes that control the occurrence of mineral deposits. New techniques and methods useful in the search for these resources are continually being developed.

* Mineral Technology Transfer

Office of Technology Transfer
Bureau of Mines
U.S. Department of the Interior
810 7th St., NW
Washington, DC 20241   202-501-9306
The Bureau of Mines supports an active technology and information transfer program. The objective of the program is to encourage the use by the minerals industry of valuable research and minerals data. Industry is kept informed of developments though exhibits, briefing, seminars, special workshops, patent licenses, films, and *Technology News*. Call for more information.

* Minerals and Mining Bibliography

Superintendent of Documents
Government Printing Office (GPO)
Washington, DC 20402   202-512-1800
This bibliography features Bureau of Mines publications and mineral industry publications. Books describing the coal mining industry, gold availability, and the wilderness mineral potential are included. Also featured is the *Bureau of Mines List of Publications and Articles*: 1985-1989 SP-391. List number at the Government Printing Office (GPO) - 024-004-02218-3.

* Minerals: Data, Industries, and Technology

Publication Distribution
Bureau of Mines
U.S. Department of the Interior
Cochrans Mills Rd.
P.O. Box 18070
Pittsburgh, PA 15236   412-892-4338
The Bureau of Mines publishes several reports of investigations and information circulars that are free of charge to those interested in mineral research. *Mineral Industry Surveys* are published monthly, quarterly, and annually, presenting data on various minerals and metals. Reprints from *Minerals Yearbook 1987* are available and report on the mineral industry in the United States and abroad. If documents are unavailable here, they will refer you to the appropriate headquarters office.

* Minerals Management Service Field Offices

Bureau of Mines
U.S. Department of Interior
1951 Constitution Avenue, NW
Washington, DC 20240   202-208-4662
U.S. Department of Interior has the following regional offices:

Atlantic Region
381 Elden St., Suite 1109, Herndon, VA 22070-4817; 703-787-1113

Alaska Region
949 E. 36th Ave., Suite 604, Anchorage, AK 99508-4302; 907-261-4070

Gulf of Mexico Region
1201 Elmwood Park Blvd., New Orleans, LA 70123-2394; 504-736-2595

Pacific Region
1340 W. 6th St., Los Angeles, CA 90017; 213-894-3389

Rocky Mountains
Royalty Management Program Accounting Center and Central Service Center, 6th Ave. and Kipling St., Bldg. 85, Lakewood, CO 80225; 303-231-3162

* Minerals of Critical and Strategic Importance

Research Division
Bureau of Mines
U.S. Department of the Interior
810 7th St., NW
Washington, DC 20241   202-501-9290
An emphasis within the Bureau of Mines' Research Division is reducing the Nation's dependence on imports for certain minerals that have key defense and industrial applications. The Bureau is developing ways to recover strategic and critical minerals

from mineral processing wastes and to recycle these minerals. Key minerals of this type include cobalt, chromium, manganese, and platinum.

* Minerals on Federal Lands
Bureau of Land Management (BLM)
U.S. Department of the Interior
18th and C Streets NW
Washington, DC 20240 — 202-208-4537

The Bureau of Land Management (BLM) regulates and manages the exploration, development and extraction of minerals and energy sources on Federal Land and Native American lands in coordination with other Federal, State, and Local agencies. Its role is to balance the need for these resources while ensuring protection of the environment.

* Minerals on Public Lands - Statistics
Bureau of Land Management (BLM)
U.S. Department of the Interior
18th and C Streets, NW
Washington, DC 20240 — 202-208-3435

The Bureau of Land Management (BLM) publication *Public Land Statistics 1990*, includes statistics on oil, gas, coal and other minerals on public lands. It is available free from BLM.

* Minerals Research
Research Division
Bureau of Mines
U.S. Department of the Interior
810 7th St., NW
Washington, DC 20241-0001 — 202-501-9290

Research is being conducted here to find cheaper, more efficient ways of mining and processing minerals. Robotics and advanced automation is also being researched for use in mining operations. Immediate problems in the industry are also studied, such as improvement of equipment and procedures.

* Minerals Today
Bureau of Mines
U.S. Department of the Interior
810 7th St., NW
Washington, DC 20241 — 202-501-9650

In 1990 the Bureau of Mines launched a new bimonthly magazine entitled *Minerals Today*. The magazine covers the latest developments, trends, and issues related to minerals and materials. The regular feature "Mineral Indicators" helps industry analysts track the flow of minerals by presenting statistics on production, supplies, and consumption. Call the public affairs office for ordering information.

* Minerals Yearbooks Bibliography
Superintendent of Documents
Government Printing Office
Washington, DC 20402 — 202-512-1800

Yearbooks on metals and minerals are listed, as well as reports on the domestic and international industry. Free.

* Mines Library
Bureau of Mines
U.S. Department of the Interior
810 7th St., NW,
Washington, DC 20241 — 202-501-9756

The Bureau of Mines' Library contains a wealth of technical information involving the mineral industry. Reference librarians are available to answer questions by phone or mail. Topics include state and county mineral data, mineral supply and demand analysis, congressional reports pertaining to minerals, oil and gas reports, and market studies. Free mineral publications published by the Bureau of Mines are also available. The hours of the library are 7:45 a.m. to 4:15 p.m., Monday through Friday.

* Mines Technology Transfer
Office of Technology Transfer
Bureau of Mines

U.S. Department of the Interior
810 7th St., NW
Washington, DC 20241 — 202-501-9323

The Technology Transfer Group distributes information on mining industry issues in many ways. *Technology Transfer* is a newsletter announcing the latest technology and research in mining. Free conferences are also held around the country on a variety of topics, such as advanced materials research and new technology for minerals. To be placed on the mailing list, contact the office above.

* Mining Research Update
Public Affairs
Bureau of Mines
U.S. Department of the Interior
810 7th St., NW
Washington, DC 20241 — 202-501-9323

The Bureau of Mines publication *Research 91* is an invaluable source of information on the latest Bureau of Mines research work. The publication highlights the latest developments in research, as well as updating program information. It also has a reference bibliography on all aspects of mining. It is available free from the Bureau of Mines.

* Multinational Corporations in Mining
Office of Mineral Commodities
Bureau of Mines
U.S. Department of the Interior
810 7th St., NW
Washington, DC 20241 — 202-501-9449

An expert in the office of mineral commodities, Mr. Balazik, can discuss the results of a major study he did for the Bureau of Mines on Multinational Corporations in the Mining industry. He examined both U.S. ownership and interest in foreign mining operations as well as foreign ownership and interest in American mining operations. The information presented in the study is based on a review of over 2200 mineral properties operated by more than 400 companies in 80 countries. The study has not yet been published, but Mr. Balazik will share the results of his study and can aid you in your research in this area.

* Offshore Geologic Resources
Geologic Inquiries
U.S. Geological Survey
907 National Center
Reston, VA 22092 — 703-648-4383

Using remotely sensed data, including sidescan sonar and other geophysical surveys, and direct sampling, the U.S. Geological Survey (USGS) studies the geology and assesses the potential mineral and energy resources of the continental margins and the Exclusive Economic Zone of the United States (200 miles from the coastline) and its territories. Also identified are geologic features that must be considered in the selection of sites for offshore drilling platforms and pipelines.

* Offshore Minerals Leasing and Management
Offshore Minerals Management
Mineral Management Service
U.S. Department of the Interior
18th and C Sts., NW
Washington, DC 20240 — 202-208-3530

The Mineral Management Service leases the rights to explore and develop oil and gas on Federal lands of the continental shelf. The "shelf" is made up of the submerged offshore areas lying seaward of the territorial sea to a depth of 200 meters (656 feet) and beyond that area to that depth which allows for mineral exploration. The brochure, *Leasing Energy Resources on the Outer Continental Shelf*, explains the leasing procedure and gives a history of the program.

* Onshore Minerals Leases
Bureau of Land Management (BLM)
U.S. Department of the Interior
18th and C Streets, NW
Washington, DC 20240 — 202-208-4636

The Bureau of Land Management (BLM) leases and sells onshore minerals. Its responsibilities include land use planning; issuance of leases; reworking and annual filing of mines claims; review of plans for exploration and development; and inspection, enforcement and productive verification of leases and mining operators to ensure compliance with approved claims.

Business and Industry

* Regulatory Projects Coordination

Office of Regulatory Projects Coordination
Bureau of Mines
U.S. Department of the Interior
810 7th St., NW
Washington, DC 20241 202-501-9732

This office serves as a focal point in the bureau, identifying, monitoring, and assessing the impact of regulations as well as evolving regulatory issues of vital concern to the minerals industry. At present, the Office's primary concern remains the regulation of mining and mineral processing solid wastes. This office is a good source for conservation and environmental information on the mining industry.

* Surface Coal Mining Reclamation

Office of Surface Mining, Public Affairs
1951 Constitution Ave, NW
Washington, DC 20420 202-208-2553

While surface mining for coal is less costly than underground mining, it is also more destructive to the environment. In 1977 Congress passed the Surface Mining Control and Reclamation Act (SMCRA) to coordinate the Federal and State efforts to prevent further environmental destruction from surface mining. The law mandated an environmental protection program to establish standards and procedures for approving permits and inspecting current surface coal mining and reclamation operations. It also established a reclamation program for abandoned mine lands, funded by fees that operators pay on each ton of coal mined, to reclaim land and water resources adversely affected by pre-Act coal mining. *Surface Coal Mining Reclamation: 10 Years of Programs*, 1977-1987 is a report detailing progress under the SMCRA. Also available is *Abandoned Mine Reclamation: 10 Years of Progress*, which describes programs in abandoned mine reclamation under SMCRA. Both are available free.

* Steel Research

Bureau of Mines
Research Division
U.S. Department of the Interior
810 7th St., NW
Washington, DC 20241 202-501-9274

The Bureau of Mines is working on research in the area of powder metallurgy which offers the potential for producing steel with 2 to 4 times greater tensile strength and higher temperature resistance than conventional steel. For information on this program, contact the research division.

* Strip Mining and Reclamation

Office of Public Affairs
Office of Surface Mining Reclamation and Enforcement
U.S. Department of Interior
1951 Constitution Avenue, NW
Washington, DC 20240 202-208-2553

This office works to protect people and the environment from the side-effects of coal mining, while continuing to regulate coal mining. Lands that were affected by past coal mining operations must be repaired if left unreclaimed or abandoned. Technical assistance is provided to states so that they can perform their responsibilities under the surface mining law. State personnel are trained in the technical aspects of surface mining, such as soil compaction, revegetation, and groundwater hydrology, so that they can better enforce regulations.

* Strip Mining Enforcement Offices

Office of Surface Mining Reclamation and Enforcement
U.S. Department of Interior
1951 Constitution Avenue, NW
Washington, DC 20240 202-208-2553

Albuquerque
625 Silver Ave., SW, Suite 310, Albuquerque, NM 87102; 505-766-1486

Appalachia
1300 New Circle Rd, Lexington, KY 40504; 606-233-2792

Ashland
Federal Bldg., Room 120, 1430 Greenup Ave., Ashland, KY 41101; 606-324-2828

Beckley
101 Harper Park Dr., Beckley, WV 25801; 304-255-5265

Birmingham
135 Gemeni Circle, Suite 215, Homewood, AL 35209; 205-290-7282

Big Stone Gap
P.O. Box 1216, Big Stone Gap, VA 24219; 703-523-4303

Casper
Federal Bldg., 100 East B St., Room 2128, Casper, WY 82601-1918; 307-261-5776

Columbus
2242 S. Hamilton Rd., Columbus, OH 43232; 614-866-0578

Chattanooga
900 Georgia Ave., Room 30, Chattanooga, TN 37402; 615-752-5175

Charleston
603 Morris St., Charleston, WV 25301; 304-347-7158

Denver
Bldg. 20, Room B2015, P.O. Box 25065, Denver CO 80225; 303-236-0331

Eastern
Ten Parkway Center, Pittsburgh, PA 15220; 412-937-2828

Harrisburg
Harrisburg Transportation Ctr., Third Fl., Suite 3C, 4th and Market Sts., Harrisburg, PA 17101; 717-782-4036

Hazard
516 Village Lane, Hazard, KY 41701; 606-439-5843

Indianapolis
Minton-Capehart Federal Bldg., 575 N. Penn St., Room 301, Indianapolis, IN 46204; 371-226-6700

Johnstown
Penn Traffic Bldg., Room 20, 319 Washington St., Johnstown, PA 15901; 814-533-4223

Kansas City
934 Wynadotte St., Room 500, Kansas City, MO 64105; 816-374-6405

Knoxville
530 Gay St., Suite 500, Knoxville, TN 37902; 615-673-4504

Lexington
340 Legion Dr., Suite 28, Lexington, KY 40504; 606-233-2494

London
P.O. Box 1048, London, KY 40741; 606-878-6440

Madisonville
100 YMCA Drive, Madisonville, KY 42431; 502-825-4500

Morgantown
P.O. Box 886, Morgantown, WVA 26505; 304-291-4004

Norris
P.O. Box 179, Norris, TN 37828; 615-632-1730

Olympia
Columbia Commons, 3773 C Martin Way East, Suite 104, Olympia, WA 98506; 206-753-9538

Pikesville
Division of Audit Management, First National Bank, Room 608B, 334 Main St., Pikesville, KY 41505; 606-432-4123

Prestonburgh
P.O. Box 306, 2664 West Mountain Parkway, West Prestonburg, KY 41668; 606-866-1391

Springfield
509 West Capitol Avenue, 2nd Fl., Springfield IL 62701; 217-492-4495

Tulsa
5100 East Skelley Dr., Suite 550, Tulsa, OK 74135; 918-581-6430

Wilkes-Barre

20 N. Penn. Ave., Suite 3323, Wilkes-Barre, PA 18701; 717-826-6333

Western

1020 15th St., 2nd Fl., Brooks Towers, Denver, CO 80202; 303-844-2459

* Surface Mining Information and Programs

Office of Public Affairs
Office of Surface Mining Reclamation and Enforcement
U.S. Department of Interior
1951 Constitution Avenue, NW
Washington, DC 20240   202-208-2553

The Office of Surface Mining *Annual Report* details OSM activities under the Surface Mining Control and Reclamation Act of 1977. The report discusses Regulatory enforcement of the SMCRA and aspects of the Abandoned Mine Land Program. It is available free from the Office of Public Affairs at OSM.

* U.S. Geological Survey History

U.S. Geological Survey
Public Affairs Office
12201 Sunrise Valley Drive
Reston, VA 22092   703-648-4660

The *U.S. Geological Survey 1879-1989* gives an overview of the history of U.S. Geological Survey (USGS) and its role in the development of public land, Federal science and mineral resources in the U.S. It is available free.

* U.S. Geological Survey Reports

U.S. Geological Survey (USGS)
Public Affairs Office
12201 Sunrise Valley Drive
Reston, VA 22092   703-648-4660

The U.S. Geological Survey (USGS) publishes reports on minerals, geography and cartography, water resources, and geology. The public affairs office has an index available of current reports and their availability.

Be patient. If any phone number is incorrect, call (area code) 555-1212 and request the new listing.

807

General Transportation

The section details general sources of information on transportation with particular emphasis on safety related issues. The key government agencies dealing with transportation safety is the National Transportation Safety Board, which investigates all major transportation accidents. Within the U.S. Department of Transportation one finds safety offices in each of the major Administrations. In addition to these programs, the DOT National Highway Traffic Safety Administration works to promote automobile and highway safety.

* Accident Briefs (Non-major Accident Reports)

Public Inquiries Section
National Transportation Safety Board (NTSB)
490 L'Enfant Plaza East, SW
Washington, DC 20594   202-382-6735

Reports of accidents in brief or summary format are issued for all aviation accidents and for all non-major railroad, highway, pipeline, and marine accidents investigated by or for the National Transportation Safety Board (NTSB), for which probable cause is determined. The accident reports are issued in a publication containing up to 200 individual reports, which identify the facts, conditions, circumstances, and probable cause for each accident. The publication may include other statistical data such as tabulations by type of accident, phase of operation, casual factors, and injuries. For information on ordering these publications, which are available for a fee, contact the office above.

* Accident Investigations

Office of Aviation Safety
National Transportation Safety Board (NTSB)
490 L'Enfant Plaza East, SW
Washington, DC 20594   202-382-6610

Office of Surface Transportation Safety
National Transportation Safety Board (NTSB)
490 L'Enfant Plaza East, SW
Washington, DC 20594   202-382-6800

The Bureaus of Accident Investigation and Field Operations investigate or cause to be investigated all aviation and selected surface transportation accidents and incidents; develop proposed probable cause(s) of accidents; formulate recommendations to minimize their recurrence; and prepare detailed reports for use by other government agencies, the Congress, the transportation industry, and the traveling public. The Bureau of Accident Investigation manages the investigations of major transportation accidents--those accidents for which multi-disciplinary teams (go-teams) are sent to the accident site. The Bureau of Field Operations manages the investigations of the smaller-scale accidents that are usually investigated by one person from the Safety Board. For more information, contact the appropriate office listed above.

* Accident Reports (Major)

Public Inquiries Section
National Transportation Safety Board (NTSB)
490 L'Enfant Plaza East, SW
Washington, DC 20594   202-382-6735

Detailed narrative reports which contain the facts, conditions, circumstances, analysis, conclusions, and probable cause of major aviation, railroad, highway, pipeline, and marine accident investigations are issued for all accidents which resulted in a major investigation. Major accident reports are issued irregularly and are available for a fee from the National Technical Information Service (NTIS). For information on ordering, contact the office above.

* Alaska Pipeline

Alaska Natural Gas Pipeline Project
Office of Pipeline Safety
Research and Special Programs Administration
U.S. Department of Transportation
400 7th Street, SW
Washington, DC 20590   202-366-4556

Contact this office for information about the plans, programs, policies, and regulation concerning the Alaska pipeline.

* Alternative Fuels Initiative

Office of Engineering
Federal Transportation Administration (FTA)
400 7th St., SW, Room 6431
Washington, DC 20590   202-366-0090

Since 1988, the Federal Transportation Administration's (FTA) Office of Engineering has been involved in the effort to replace today's conventional fuels with cleaner-burning alternative fuels, such as methanol, ethanol, and compressed natural gas. For more information, contact the office at the above address.

* Appealing Transportation Licensing Decisions

Office of Administrative Law Judges
National Transportation Safety Board (NTSB)
490 L'Enfant Plaza East, SW
Washington, DC 20594   202-382-0650

This office provides the initial forum for the review of appeals from the suspension, amendment, modification, revocation, or denial of any operation certificate or license issued by the Secretary of Transportation under the Federal Aviation Act of 1958. The primary purpose of this function is to assure fair and impartial review when appeals are taken from safety enforcement certificate actions by the Administrator of the Federal Aviation Administration against airmen or certificate holders or from denials of pilot applications for airman medical certificates. For more information on the process involved, contact the office above.

* Automobile Fuel Economy

Motor Vehicle Requirements Division
Office of Market Incentives
Rulemaking
National Highway Traffic Safety Administration (NHTSA)
U.S. Department of Transportation
400 7th Street, SW, Room 5320
Washington, DC 20590   202-366-0846

The National Highway Traffic Safety Administration (NHTSA) issues fuel economy standards and collects information on the technological and economic capabilities of automobile manufacturers to maximize fuel efficiency. Contact this office for information and referrals.

* Auto Safety Hotline

Office of Defects Investigation (NEF-10)
National Highway Traffic Safety Administration
U.S. Department of Transportation
400 7th Street, SW
Room 5326   800-424-9393
Washington, DC 20590   202-366-0123

This toll-free hotline is accessible in all 50 states, Puerto Rico, and the Virgin Islands. Consumers may call to report automobile safety problems or to request information on recalls, defects, investigations, child safety seats, tires, drunk driving, crash test results, seat belts, air bags, odometer tampering, and other related topics. Staff will also make referrals to state and other agencies. Also ask about the New Car Assessment Program (NCAP), which provides comparable data on the frontal crashworthiness of selected new vehicles.

* Aviation Accident Data on Computer Tape

Analysis and Data Division
National Transportation Safety Board (NTSB)
490 L'Enfant Plaza East, SW
Washington, DC 20594   202-382-6672

Computerized tapes containing public data on aircraft accidents are available. Contact the office above for information on ordering the tapes.

* Aviation Accident Investigation

Office of Aviation Safety
National Transportation Safety Board (NTSB)
490 L'Enfant Plaza East, SW
Washington, DC 20594   202-382-6610

The National Transportation Safety Board (NTSB)investigates all air carrier accidents, all in flight collisions, fatal general aviation accidents, and all air taxi/commuter accidents. The Board also participates in the investigation of major airline crashes overseas involving American carriers and US manufactured airliners. The Board also takes a broader approach in investigating accidents in order to improve preventive measures. The Office produces accident reports, recommendation letters on prevention, and statistical summaries. Call for information.

* Census Statistics in Transportation

Bureau of the Census
U.S. Department of Commerce
Washington, DC 20223   301-763-7039

Surveys of the transportation industry are currently taken at 5 year intervals in years ending in the number "2" or "7." The 1987 Census of Transportation included a *Truck Industry and Use Survey*, which reported on the characteristics and operational use of truck resources and other than those of the Federal, State, or local governments; ambulance; buses; motor homes; and off highway vehicles. The Census also included a *Census of Selected Transportation Industries*, which covered a wide range of industries and services. *Factfinder CFF-13* lists data available on the transportation industry. It is available from customer services at the Census Bureau for $.25.

* Certificate and License Appeals

Office of Administrative Law Judges
National Transportation Safety Board (NTSB)
490 L'Enfant Plaza East, SW
Washington, DC 20594   202-382-0650

The Safety Board serves as the "court of appeals" for any airman or mariner whenever certificate action is taken by the Federal Aviation Administrator or the U.S. Coast Guard Commandant. The Board's administrative law judges hear, consider, and issue initial decisions on appeals from Federal Aviation Administration (FAA) certificate actions taken under Section 602(b), 609 and 501(c) of the Federal Aviation Act of 1958, as amended. Judges' decisions may be appealed to the five-member Board by the airman or Federal Aviation Administration (FAA). The Board's review of the appeal encompasses the transcripts of the proceeding, the judge's decision, and appeal briefs submitted by the parties. For more information, contact the office above.

* Consumer Liaison

Office of Public Interest Groups
Intergovernmental and Consumer Affairs
Governmental Affairs
Office of the Secretary of Transportation
U.S. Department of Transportation
400 7th Street, SW
Washington, DC 20590   202-366-1524

This office acts as a liaison between Congress, state and local governments, business and industry, and public interest groups to ensure that their needs are considered when Department policy decisions are made. Public and private organizations can contact this office to communicate needs and comment on Department of Transportation (DOT) programs and regulations.

* Current Department of Transportation Programs

Office of Public Affairs (A-30)
Office of the Secretary of Transportation
U.S. Department of Transportation
400 7th Street, SW, Room 10413
Washington, DC 20590   202-366-5580

The U.S. Department of Transportation *Annual Report* is an excellent place to find information on current United States transportation programs. Included in the report is a summary of program initiatives as well as a breakdown by specific administrations such as Federal Highway Administration, Federal Aviation Administration, Federal Railroad Administration, and Maritime Administration. Also included are summary statistics for transportation programs. It is available free from the public affairs office.

* Economic Analysis of Transportation Policy

Office of Economics (P-30)
Policy and International Affairs
Office of the Secretary of Transportation
U.S. Department of Transportation
400 7th Street, SW, Room 10305
Washington, DC 20590   202-366-4416

Staff in this office analyze transportation policy issues to assess their economic and institutional implications. Studies focus on energy and environmental concerns, safety, the handicapped, user charges, and Federal assistance. Contact this office to determine what reports are available and how to obtain them.

* Economic Studies of Transit Industry

Industry, Economics and Finance Division (P-37)
Office of Economics
Policy and International Affairs
Office of the Secretary of Transportation
U.S. Department of Transportation
400 7th Street, SW, Room 10223
Washington, DC 20590   202-366-5412

Financial and economic studies of the transportation industry are prepared by this office. Air transportation is emphasized, but other modes are also evaluated. Report topics include mergers, regional marketing studies, gross receipts at airports, and intelligent vehicle highway systems. Contact this office to determine if a study has been prepared on your subject.

* Employment in Transportation

Central Employment Office (M18.1)
Office of Personnel
U.S. Department of Transportation
400 7th St., SW, Room 9113
Washington, DC 20590   202-366-9417

Employment inquiries for positions in Washington, DC, should be submitted to this office. Regional and district offices handle employment in their areas. Civil Service positions include air traffic controller; electronics maintenance technicians; civil, aeronautical, automotive, electronic, and highway engineers; and administrative, management, and clerical positions.

* Environmental Policies

Office of Transportation Regulatory Affairs (P-14)
Environmental Policy Division
U.S. Department of Transportation
400 7th Street, SW, Room 9217
Washington, DC 20590   202-366-4366

The National Environmental Policy Act (NEPA) requires all federal agencies to assess thoroughly the environmental consequences of any major federal action, either directly or through financial assistance, before an action decision can be taken. This office can provide you with a list of internal directives and documentation on the various Department of Transportation component Administration's procedures for considering environmental impacts. Call for information.

* Federal Transportation Administration (FTA)

U.S. Department of Transportation
400 7th St., SW
Washington, DC 20590   202-366-4040

The Federal Transportation Administration (FTA) assists in the development of improved mass transportation facilities, equipment, techniques, and methods; encourages the planning and establishment of area-wide urban mass transportation systems; and provides assistance to state and local governments in financing such systems.

* Federal Transportation Administration Research

Manager, UMTRIS
Transportation Research Board

Business and Industry

National Research Council
2101 Constitution Ave., NW
Washington, DC 20418   202-334-2995

The Federal Transportation Administration Research Information Service is a computerized database on worldwide transportation research. Administered by the Transportation Research Board (TRB), it covers all phases of conventional, new, and automated public transportation. The Urban Mass Transit Research Information System (UMTRIS) features database storage/retrieval of abstracts of technical papers, journal articles, research reports, computer program descriptions, and statistical sources, as well as state-of-the-art bibliographies. Descriptions of ongoing research, especially that sponsored by FTA, are also included. UMTRIS offers the public nearly 20,000 information references to ongoing and completed research activities, and adds 2,000 new references annually to the database. In addition to serving as the central source of technical information to the public and private sectors, UMTRIS also serves as an institutional memory for FTA projects and project reports. The database can be searched online by any computer with a modem through DIALOG Information Services File 63. UMTRIS is supported by a National Network of Transportation Libraries (18), and they serve both as repositories that house and make FTA documents available to the general public, as well as document delivery centers that provide UMTRIS users with full text copies of citations retrieved from the database.

* Freedom of Information

Freedom of Information Act (FOIA) Division (C-12)
Office of the General Counsel
Office of the Secretary of Transportation
U.S. Department of Transportation (DOT)
400 7th Street, SW, Room 5432
Washington, DC 20590   202-366-4542

Inspection of some Department of Transportation (DOT) documents which have proprietary information may require formal Freedom of Information Act (FOIA) requests. Each administration within DOT has a FOIA office. The central office listed here can supply you with addressees and contacts for submittal of FOIA requests.

* Handicapped Assistance and Mass Transit

Office of Research, Training,
 and Rural Transportation (UTS-30)
Federal Transportation Administration (FTA)
400 7th St., SW, Room 6102
Washington, DC 20590   202-366-4995

The Federal Transportation Administration (FTA) is involved in a Congressionally-mandated project with the National Easter Seals Committee to study accessibility problems faced by the handicapped who use mass transit. The office runs a series of demonstrations on improved arrangements to help the handicapped.

* Hazardous Material Transportation Accidents

Information Systems Division (DHM-63)
Office of Hazardous Materials Transportation
Research and Special Programs Administration
U.S. Department of Transportation
400 7th Street, SW, Room 8108
Washington, DC 20590   202-366-4555

This division collects and analyzes accident data from transporters of hazardous materials by highway, rail, air, and water and from container manufacturers. Information stored in the database includes the hazardous material involved, transporter name and mode, packaging used, cause of accident, and results. Contact the above office for searches. There may be a charge.

* Highway Accident Investigation

Office of Surface Transportation Safety
Highway Division
National Transportation Safety Board (NTSB)
490 L'Enfant Plaza, SW
Washington, DC 20594   202-382-6850

The National Transportation Safety Board (NTSB) investigates highway accidents involving issues of wide-ranging safety significance, specifically: all accidents that involve the collapse of a highway bridge structure, accidents that involve a fatality on a public transportation vehicle; and grade crossing accidents that involve collisions between trains and public transportation vehicles or hazardous materials vehicles. The Board also makes recommendations to the U.S. Department of Transportation and local agencies on highway safety issues. Statistical data is available from the National

Highway Traffic Safety Administration in the U.S. Department of Transportation, 202-366-0123.

* Lending and Bonding for Small Business

Minority Business Resource Center (MRBC) (S-44)
Small and Disadvantaged Business Utilization (SDBU)
Director of Civil Rights
Office of the Secretary of Transportation
U.S. Department of Transportation
400 7th Street, SW, Room 9410
Washington, DC 20590   202-366-2852

This office offers short-term lending and bonding assistance to small businesses in the transportation industry. The Short-term Lending Program offers loans at prime interest rates, while the Bonding Assistance Program enables small firms to obtain bonding in support of transportation-related contracts. Entrepreneurs can contact MBRC for information and certification details.

* Marine Accidents

Office of Surface Transportation Safety
Marine Division
National Transportation Safety Board (NTSB)
490 L'Enfant Plaza, SW
Washington, DC 20594   202-382-6862

The Board investigates all major maritime accidents that occur in navigable waters of the U.S. In addition, it investigates major maritime accidents that involve US merchant vessels in international waters and accidents involving US public vessels and non-public vessels. Under the Board's criteria, a major maritime accident is one that involves the loss of six or more lives, the loss of a self propelled vessel of over 100 gross tons, property damage at more than $500,000, or an accident involving a serious threat from hazardous materials.

* Mass Transit Program Evaluation

Program Evaluation Division
Federal Transportation Administration (FTA)
U.S. Department of Transportation
400 7th St., SW, Room 9306
Washington, DC 20590   202-366-1727

This office can provide you with information on its recent and on-going evaluations of projects and programs implemented by the Federal Transportation Administration (FTA). For information on earlier evaluations, refer to Urban Mass Transit Research Information System (UMTRIS) (see separate listing).

* NTSB Annual Report to Congress

Public Inquiries Section
National Transportation Safety Board (NTSB)
490 L'Enfant Plaza East, SW
Washington, DC 20594   202-382-6735

NTSB's Annual Report to the U.S. Congress details the major activities of the National Transportation Safety Board (NTSB) aviation, railroad, highway, pipeline, and marine safety during the previous calendar year. The biennial additions also include an appraisal, evaluation, and review, and recommendations for legislative and administrative action and change, with respect to transportation safety. It is available free from the office above.

* NTSB Directives

Public Inquiries Section
National Transportation Safety Board (NTSB)
490 L'Enfant Plaza East, SW
Washington, DC 20594   202-382-6735

NTSB Directives is a manual of orders and notices, which identify the National Transportation Safety Board (NTSB) organization, policies, and procedures. The directives are updated as NTSB organization, policies, and procedures change. They are available for a fee from the office above.

* NTSB General Information

Public Inquiries Section
National Transportation Safety Board (NTSB)
490 L'Enfant Plaza East, SW
Washington, DC 20594   202-382-6735

The pamphlet, The National Transportation Safety Board, provides you with general information on the mission and responsibilities of the National Transportation Safety Board (NTSB) and how it accomplishes these responsibilities. The Board is the chief government investigator of transportation accidents. It is available free from the office above.

* NTSB Regional Offices

Office of Government and Public Affairs
National Transportation Safety Board (NTSB)
490 L'Enfant Plaza East, SW
Washington, DC 20594   202-382-6600

To obtain the addresses and telephone numbers of National Transportation Safety Board's (NTSB) ten regional offices located around the country, contact the office above.

* Pipeline Safety

Office of Pipeline Safety (OPS) (DPS-35)
Research and Special Programs Administration
U.S. Department of Transportation
400 7th Street, SW
Washington, DC 20590   202-366-4572

OPS establishes and enforces safety standards for the transportation of gas and other hazardous materials by pipeline. A computerized reporting system is maintained to collect and analyze accident and incident data from pipeline operators. Accident reports include the operator's name, the hazardous material involved, description of the accident, and results. For database searches, contact the office listed. There may be a charge.

* Private Sector Initiatives in Mass Transit

Office of Private Sector Initiatives (UBP-30)
Office of Budget and Policy
Federal Transportation Administration (FTA)
U.S. Department of Transportation
400 7th St., SW, Room 9300
Washington, DC 20590   202-366-1666

This office encourages private sector involvement in mass transit throughout the United States. Specifically, they work through the following four areas:

Competitive Contracting: Local transit authorities are encouraged to open the provisioning of services up to private sector competition.

Entrepreneurial Services: Groups in the private sector are encouraged to start self-sustaining transit services (such as taxi and bus) in cooperation with local transit authorities.

Joint Development: Federal assistance is available to help plan public/private sector joint ventures at transit facilities.

Demand Management Program: Federal funds are available to encourage local employers and merchants to develop techniques to help manage transportation and mobility problems in their areas.

* Public Docket

Public Inquiries Section
National Transportation Safety Board (NTSB)
490 L'Enfant Plaza East, SW
Washington, DC 20594   202-382-6735

The Safety Board's Public Inquiries Section maintains a public docket at the Board's headquarters in Washington, DC. The docket contains the records of all Board investigations, all safety recommendations, and all safety enforcement proceedings. These records are available to the public and may be reviewed or duplicated for public use.

* Public Hearings on Accidents

Public Inquiries Section
National Transportation Safety Board (NTSB)
490 L'Enfant Plaza East, SW
Washington, DC 20594   202-382-6735

Following an accident, the Board may decide to hold a public hearing to collect added information and to air in a public forum the issues involved in an accident. Contact the office above for more information on obtaining accident reports from the hearings.

* Public Private Transportation Network

8737 Colesville Road
Suite 1100
Silver Spring, Maryland 20910   800-522-7786

The Transit Information Exchange is a free technical assistance program sponsored by the Federal Transit Administration. PPTN assists public transit agencies, private transit operators, federal state and local officials and others seeking guidance on transportation issues especially concerning identification and fostering of public/private partnerships. Assistance includes site visits by a network of industry professionals; speakers and facilitators for seminars, conferences, and workshops; and a library of technical assistance materials.

* Railroad Accidents

Office of Surface Transportation Safety
Railroad Division
National Transportation Safety Board (NTSB)
490 L'Enfant Plaza East, SW
Washington, DC 20594   202-382-6843

The Board places special emphasis on train accidents that involve the travelling public, such as rail rapid transit accidents. The Board's criteria for a railroad accident investigation include any accident in which damage exceeds $150,000. Safety studies in the rail mode have included such areas as the carriage of hazardous materials and track maintenance.

* Regulations of the NTSB

Public Inquiries Section
National Transportation Safety Board (NTSB)
490 L'Enfant Plaza East, SW
Washington, DC 20594   202-382-6735

Regulations of the NTSB are published in the *Federal Register* and codified in the *Code of Federal Regulations*, Chapter VIII, Title 49 - Transportation. These regulations are issued irregularly as procedures change. They are available free from the office above. Contact the office above for information on ordering the regulations.

* Research Abstracts

Manager, UMTRIS
Transportation Research Board
National Research Council
2101 Constitution Ave., NW
Washington, DC 20418   202-334-2995

Twice annually the Urban Mass Transit Research Information System (UMTRIS) publishes the *Urban Transportation Abstracts* which provide all the new references added to the it transportation research database during the preceding six months. Each issue is divided into five sections: *Abstracts of Reports and Journal Articles, Summaries of New and Ongoing Research, Source Index, Author/Investigator Index,* and *Retrieval Term Index.* Summer and winter issues can be purchased individually, or through an annual subscription fee of $72.

* Research Bibliography Services

Manager, UMTRIS
Transportation Research Board
National Research Council
2101 Constitution Ave., NW
Washington, DC 20418   202-334-2995

Urban Mass Transit Research Information System provides computerized, online responses to transit inquiries. A computer-generated bibliography, including abstract of articles, reports, and summaries of new and ongoing research, can be created for almost any subject related to mass transportation. UMTRIS is now providing a new, low-cost extension to its online capability. The Data Base is accessible through Dialog and costs $45 per hour on line. Because transportation professionals are often interested in the same current problems, UMTRIS has made available, at a nominal fee, copies of the database literature searches that have been recently completed and may be of interest to other professionals.

* Safety Institute

Transportation Safety Institute (DTI-1)
Research and Special Programs Administration
U.S. Department of Transportation
6500 South MacArthur Blvd.
Oklahoma City, OK 73125   405-680-3153

Be patient. If any phone number is incorrect, call (area code) 555-1212 and request the new listing.

811

Business and Industry

The Institute supports the Department's efforts to reduce transportation accidents. It develops and conducts training programs for Federal, state, and local governments; industry; and foreign personnel. Courses are offered in aviation, highway, marine, pipeline, and railroad safety; materials analysis; transportation security; and other subjects.

* Safety Monitoring of the Trucking Industry

Motor Carrier Information and Analysis (HIA-10)
Office of Motor Carriers
Federal Highway Administration (FHWA)
U.S. Department of Transportation
400 7th St., SW, Room 3104
Washington, DC 20590   202-366-4023

The Federal Highway Administration (FHWA) motor carrier programs address licensing interstate and intrastate commercial truck and bus drivers and enforce uniform safety regulations for commercial motor vehicles and their cargo. Driver and vehicle tests and inspections are designed to determine safety performance on the road, and follow-up reviews are conducted when problem areas are identified. The Cargo Security Program regulates the movement of dangerous cargoes on the Nation's highways. This includes hazardous wastes, explosives, flammables, and other volatile materials. Permits are issued to regulate packaging, labeling and transporting of these materials. The transport of migrant workers is also regulated.

Carrier data by state can be obtained from the office listed above. Some information in printout form is available on a cost basis, with price varying according to the information requested. Driver and vehicle tests and inspections are conducted in the field by Motor Carrier Safety and Field Operations, Office of Motor Carriers, Federal Highway Administration (FHWA), U.S. Department of Transportation (DOT), 400 7th St., SW, Room 3408, Washington, DC 20590; 202-366-2952.

* Safety Publications

Public Inquiries Section
National Transportation Safety Board (NTSB)
490 L'Enfant Plaza East, SW
Washington, DC 20594   202-382-6735

The Safety Board makes public all of its actions and decisions in the form of accident reports, special studies, statistical reviews, safety recommendation and press releases. Details on available publications can be obtained by writing to the office above.

* Safety Recommendations

Public Inquiries Section
National Transportation Safety Board (NTSB)
490 L'Enfant Plaza East, SW
Washington, DC 20594   202-382-6735

Safety Recommendations are issued by the National Transportation Safety Board as a result of the investigation of transportation accidents and other safety problems. Recommendations usually identify a specific problem uncovered during an investigation of an accident or other safety problems and specify how to correct the situation. Such recommendations are directed to the organization best able to act on the problem, whether it is private or public. These recommendations are issued when a problem is identified, and are distributed individually and in a monthly publication. Contact the office above for information on ordering the recommendations.

* Speeches of the NTSB Members of the Board

Public Inquiries Section
National Transportation Safety Board (NTSB)
490 L'Enfant Plaza East, SW
Washington, DC 20594   202-382-6735

The Members of the Board are frequently asked to speak before Congressional Committees and state, local, and private organizations. Their prepared statements enunciate the National Transportation Safety Board's (NTSB) positions on transportation issues. The topics of these statements vary depending on the organization before which they are speaking. Speech texts are issued irregularly. They are available free from the office above. When ordering, specify the date of the speaking engagement and the committee or organization before which the speech was made.

* Spill Maps

Public Inquiries Section
National Transportation Safety Board (NTSB)

490 L'Enfant Plaza East, SW
Washington, DC 20594   202-382-6735

Spill maps are developed on selected transportation accidents involving hazardous materials. The maps identify how the hazardous materials spread based on environment in the subject accident. Spill maps are issued irregularly. They are available free from the office above until limited supplies are exhausted. For information on ordering the maps, contact the office above.

* State Motor Vehicle Inspections

Records and Motor Vehicle Services Division (NTS-43)
National Highway Traffic Safety Administration (NHTSA)
U.S. Department of Transportation
400 7th Street, SW
Washington, DC 20590   202-366-2676

NHTSA's Motor Vehicle Inspection Program is aimed at providing car owners with preventative information on what repairs are needed to achieve greater safety, lower pollution, and better mileage. The annual *Study of the State Motor Vehicle Inspection Program* is available from this office.

* Surface Transportation Information

Office of Surface Transportation Safety
National Transportation Safety Board (NTSB)
490 L'Enfant Plaza East, SW
Washington, DC 20594   202-382-6800

This Office conducts accident investigations for a variety of surface transportation modes, including highway, railroad, marine, and pipeline. contact the above number for information about reports, statistics, and recent and ongoing investigations.

* Technical Transportation Information

Technology Sharing Program (DRT-1)
Office of Research and Technology
Research and Special Programs Administration (RSPA)
U.S. Department of Transportation
400 7th Street, SW
Washington, DC 20590-0001   202-366-4208

The RSPA develops and coordinates a comprehensive transportation information service. Contact this office for referrals and details on DOT programs, projects, contacts, available technical information on transportation-related topics. Technological areas include energy, security, emergency preparedness, and safety. Publications are available in the following areas: General Information, transit, commuter/travel demand, Highways and street maintenance, Rural Transportation, Energy, Hazardous Materials, Taxi/Personalized Transportation, Disadvantaged (Handicapped and Specialized Transportation), Water Marine, and Safety. Publications are obtained by returning an order form specifying which publications lists you would like to be on.

* Technology Exchange Programs

International Cooperative Division and Secretariat (P-25)
Office of International Transportation and Trade
Office of the Secretary of Transportation
U.S. Department of Transportation (DOT)
400 7th Street, SW
Washington, DC 20590   202-366-4398

DOT participates in a number of cooperative programs with other countries to exchange mutually beneficial transportation research data and state-of-the-art technical information. Areas of exchange include highway technology; ports and inland waterways; railway technology; and search and rescue operations. Contact this office for information about these programs.

* Transit Environments

Environment Division
Policy and International Affairs
Office of the Secretary of Transportation
U.S. Department of Transportation
400 7th Street, SW, Room 9217
Washington, DC 20590   202-366-4366

This is the DOT contact point for environmental issues. Staff can provide you with information and referrals on such subjects as highway beautification, transportation architecture, bicycle paths, historic preservation activities, wetlands laws and environmental impact statements. Office activities are governed in large part by the requirements of the National Environmental Policy Act.

Be patient. If any phone number is incorrect, call (area code) 555-1212 and request the new listing.

* Transportation Library

Library (M-493)
Office of the Secretary of Transportation
U.S. Department of Transportation
400 7th Street, SW, Room 2200
Washington, DC 20590   202-366-0736

An extensive collection of literature on all aspects of transportation is housed here. Reading rooms are also available in regional offices around the country. Contact the specific administration of interest. Law Library: 202-366-0749.

* Transportation of Hazardous Materials

Office of Hazardous Materials Transportation
Research and Special Programs Administration
U.S. Department of Transportation
400 7th Street, SW
Washington, DC 20590-0001   202-366-2301

This office can provide you with information on the transportation of hazardous materials by highway, rail air, and water. Data is collected directly from industry and also via compliance inspections by field staff. The quarterly *Hazardous Material Newsletter* is available free from the office above.

* Transportation Systems Center

Technical Information Center-Library
Transportation Systems Center (TSC)
Research and Special Programs Administration
U.S. Department of Transportation (DOT)
Kendall Square, 55 Broadway
Cambridge, MA 02142   617-494-2306

The Transportation Systems Center (TSC) is the U.S. Department of Transportation's (DOT) multimodal research and analysis center to address national transportation and logistics issues. With contractual participation by industry and academia, it conducts technical, socio-economic, and human-factor studies on which the Department's transportation policy decisions are based. Areas of research include safety, security, transportation infrastructure, system modernization, and information technology relevant to transportation system operations. Research covers highways, rail, air, and water. The Center maintains statistics and a transportation information database which include information on aviation safety and statistical references on rail transport. The Center will provide copies of reports if they are available. New reports are listed in the acquisitions list that is published monthly. If reports are unavailable for the Center, NTIS retains copies for sale. Contact the center for more information.

* University Research on Transportation

Office of University Research (P-34)
Policy and International Affairs
Office of the Secretary of Transportation
U.S. Department of Transportation
400 7th Street, SW
Washington, DC 20590   202-366-0190

Grants are made to institutions of higher learning to establish and administer transportation research centers. Issues for study are determined by the Department. This office can provide you with a list of universities that receive federal money for this purpose.

* Vehicle Manufacturer Safety Compliance

Vehicle Manufacturer Safety Compliance (NEF-30)
Enforcement
National Highway Traffic Safety Administration
U.S. Department of Transportation
400 7th Street, SW
Washington, DC 20590   202-366-2832

To ensure that foreign and domestic vehicle and equipment manufacturers comply with federal motor vehicle safety standards, this office performs compliance testing, inspections, and investigations involving about 150 performance requirements and nearly 3000 equipment items.

* Vehicle Research and Testing

Vehicle Research and Test Center
Research and Development
National Highway Traffic Safety Administration (NHTSA)
U.S. Department of Transportation
P.O. BOX 37
East Liberty, OH 43319   513-466-4521

NHTSA evaluates the effectiveness of Federal Motor Vehicle Safety Standards. This engineering facility performs tests to obtain basic data used to establish standards for safety and fuel efficiency of motor vehicles.

Highways, Waterways, and Railways

The U.S. Department of Transportation's Federal Highway Administration, Federal Railroad Administration, Federal Transportation Administration, and Research and Special Programs Administration are the loci of highway and railroad expertise in the U.S. government. The Interstate Commerce Commission is an excellent source of information on road and rail transportation companies.

* AMTRAK: National Railroad Passenger Corporation

AMTRAK
60 Massachusetts Ave., NE
Washington, DC 20002   202-906-3000

AMTRAK was created in 1970 to provide a balanced national transportation system by developing, operating, and improving U.S. intercity rail passenger service.

* AMTRAK Financial and Operating Statistics

AMTRAK
Office of Public Affairs
60 Massachusetts Ave., NE
Washington, DC 20002   202-906-3860

No rail passenger system in the world makes a profit; therefore, AMTRAK does require government assistance in the form of an annual appropriation. However, AMTRAK has made significant progress in reducing its dependence on federal support while at the same time improving the quality of service. *The Annual Report* provides operating statistics and financial statements, which cover operations, cashflows, and changes in capitalization.

* AMTRAK Passenger Services

AMTRAK
60 Massachusetts Ave., NE
Washington, DC 20002   202-906-2733

The Passenger Services Department handles all of the onboard service aspects of AMTRAK, including all of its employees across the country.

* AMTRAK Customer Relations

AMTRAK
60 Massachusetts Ave., NE
Washington, DC 20002   202-906-2121

You may call or write the Customer Relations Office concerning any comments or problems with AMTRAK service. Please include your ticket receipt and dates of travel to help with the resolution of your problem.

* AMTRAK Tickets or Travel Information

AMTRAK
60 Massachusetts Ave., NE
Washington, DC 20002   800-USA-RAIL

For information regarding tickets or travel on AMTRAK, call 1-800-USA-RAIL. AMTRAK also publishes a travel planner which provides travel tips and services, as well as a listing of AMTRAK's vacation packages.

* Annual Report of Interstate Transportation Companies

Bureau of Accounts' Public Reference Room
Interstate Commerce Commission (ICC)
12th St. and Constitution Ave., NW
Room 3378
Washington, DC 20403   202-927-7119

Annual reports of companies regulated by the Interstate Commerce Commission (ICC) contain revealing information concerning those companies, including annual income, balance sheets, expenses, types of equipment owned, and much more. These documents may be examined by the public in the Reference Room from 8:30 a.m. to 5:00 p.m. weekdays, and photocopies of these reports, at a cost of $.60 per page, with a $3 minimum charge per order, may be obtained by writing the Office of the Secretary, Room 2215, ICC, Washington, DC, 20423.

* Applications of Motor Carriers

Motor and Rail Docket File
Office of the Secretary
Interstate Commerce Commission (ICC)
12th St. and Constitution Ave., NW
Room 1221
Washington, DC 20423   202-927-7510

As required by the Motor Carrier Act, all motor carriers must be willing to give a copy of its application package to anyone willing to pay the $10 fee. These packages include information on the type of authority requested from the Interstate Commerce Commission (ICC), the type of business run by the applicant, a history of the applicant's business, and more. Contact this office for more information on examining these applications.

* Assistance to Foreign Highways

International Highway Programs (HPI-10)
Associate Administrator for Policy
Federal Highway Administration (FHWA)
U.S. Department of Transportation (DOT)
400 7th St., SW
Washington, DC 20590   202-366-9632

The Federal Highway Administration (FHWA) administers programs which provide assistance and advice to foreign governments engaged in highway engineering and administration. Projects have included technical assistance in fabricating bridge segments, value engineering skills, development of transportation systems, materials testing, quality control, and skid testing. Through the International Visitors Program, highway specialists from over 40 countries receive training. Countries that have participated include China, Indonesia, Haiti, Kuwait, Dubai, and Saudi Arabia. Two publications available from this office are *World of Technology for Sharing* and *Highway Community on the Occasion of the 18th World Road Congress*.

* Automobile Safety Investigation Reports

Office of Public and Consumer Affairs (NOA-40)
National Highway Traffic Safety Administration
U.S. Department of Transportation (DOT)
400 7th Street, SW
Washington, DC 20590   202-366-5971

The Office of public affairs has available and posts monthly notices on ongoing defects investigations, recall notices, and the results of completed defects investigations. They are available free from the above listed office.

* Automobile Sales Statistics

Transportation Branch
U.S. International Trade Commission (ITC)
500 E St., SW
Washington, DC 20436   202-205-3392

Under Section 302 of the Tariff Act of 1930, the International Trade Commission (ITC) publishes a monthly report on select economic indicators for the United States automobile industry. *USITC publication 2485* (February 1992) details sales and inventory figures for United States producers, comparing selected months in 1991 and 1990, and also lists import figures for November and December 1991. It is available free.

* Automotive Trade Statistics

Machinery and Transportation Equipment Branch
Machinery and Equipment Division
Office of Industries
U.S. International Trade Commission (ITC)
500 E St., SW, Room 500
Washington, DC 20436   202-205-3380

At the request of the House Ways and Means Committee, this office publishes a monthly newsletter on automobile trade and industry which includes many current statistics of interest. The *ITC Annual Report* also lists ongoing investigations with respect to trade in automobiles. It is available from the International Trade Commission (ITC), 202-205-2000.

* Bridges Over Navigable Waters

Bridge Administration Division (G-NBR)
Office of Navigation Safety and Waterways Services
U.S. Coast Guard
U.S. Department of Transportation (DOT)
2100 2nd St., SW, Room 1408
Washington, DC 20593-0001   202-267-0368

Bridges and causeways spanning navigable waterways in the U.S. are subject to Coast Guard safety regulations concerning their construction, operation, and maintenance. This office oversees bridge engineering and issues permits. For further details, contact the division listed above.

* Bus Transportation

Office of External Affairs
Interstate Commerce Commission (ICC)
12th Street and Constitution Ave, NW
Washington, DC 20423   202-927-5737

Part of the *ICC Annual Report* analyzes the Bus transport industry. The report is available free from the Interstate Commerce Commission.

* Consumer Assistance

Office of Compliance and Consumer Assistance
Interstate Commerce Commission (ICC)
12th Street and Constitution Ave, NW
Room 4412
Washington, DC 20423   202-927-5500

This office monitors the activities of Interstate Commerce Commission (ICC) regulated companies, ensuring compliance with ICC rules and assisting the public in the resolution of complaints against ICC regulated companies.

* Cargo Insurance

Office of the Secretary
Interstate Commerce Commission (ICC)
12th St. and Constitution Ave., NW
Room 2215
Washington, DC 20423   202-927-5480

All motor common carriers of property and freight forwarders are required to maintain cargo insurance for the protection of the shipping public. Under this protection, the insurance company is directly liable to a shipper or consignee for any cargo claim for which the motor carrier or freight forwarder may be legally liable. No limitations in the policy itself, such as deductibles, may be used as a defense by the insurance companies against claims filed under this Commission's prescribed cargo endorsements. Railroads are not required to maintain cargo insurance. The name of the insurance company may be obtained by writing the Office of the Secretary.

* Civil Emergency Preparedness - Railroads

Office of Policy (RRP-8)
Defense and Special Programs Staff
Federal Railroad Administration (FRA)
U.S. Department of Transportation (DOT)
400 7th Street, SW, Room 8307
Washington, DC 20590   202-366-8307

This Office directs the Federal Railroad Administration (FRA) Emergency Preparedness Program in fulfillment of FRA and Department of Transportation (DOT) Federal Emergency Management Agency requirements. It also identifies and analyzes rail industry capabilities in support of national security, defense, and emergency response needs.

* Commission Reports and Orders Certification

Public Records Room
Interstate Commerce Commission (ICC)
12th Street and Constitution Ave, NW, 2115
Washington, DC 20423   202-927-5710

All Commission Reports and Orders are available to the public at a slight cost ($.60 per page) and can be received by contacting the Public Records Room.

* Computerized Data Base of Railroads

Office of Transportation Analysis
Interstate Commerce Commission (ICC)
12th St. and Constitution Ave., NW, Room 3219
Washington, DC 20423   202-927-6203

The Office of Transportation Analysis maintains a computerized data base of railroad contract summaries, which include shipper names on agricultural commodities.

* Consumer Information Brochures

Office of Public and Consumer Affairs (NOA-40)
National Highway Traffic Safety Administration (NHTSA)
U.S. Department of Transportation, Room 5232
400 7th Street, SW
Washington, DC 20590   202-366-5971

The National Highway Traffic Safety Administration (NHTSA) issues a series of consumer fact sheets on an assortment of safety related and other questions. Fact sheets available include:

Insurance Discounts
School Bus Safety
Traffic Tips for Older Drivers
Transporting Your Child Safely
Auto Safety Defects and Recalls
Brakes
Buckle Up in the Back Seat
Motorcycle Safety Helmets
Safety Belts - Proper Use
Utility Vehicles

* Crashworthiness

Office of Crashworthiness Research (NRD-10)
Research and Development
National Highway Traffic Safety Administration
U.S. Department of Transportation (DOT)
400 7th Street, SW
Washington, DC 20590   202-366-4862

Research is conducted on vehicle crashworthiness and crash avoidance. To determine how drivers and passengers fare in head-on collisions, information is collected on seat belts, air bags, child safety restraints, motorcycle helmets, fuel systems, rearview mirrors, tires, door locks, seats, bumpers, and school busses. The annual publication, *Federal Motor Vehicle Safety Standards and Regulations*, is available for $82 from the Government Printing Office. Superintendent of Documents, Washington, DC 20402; 202-512-1800. New Car Assessment Program information on selected models is available from the Auto Safety Hotline: 800-424-9393.

* Diesel Fuel Recording

Interstate Commerce Commission (ICC)
12th St. and Constitution Ave., NW
Washington, DC 20423   202-927-6237

This recording states the average diesel fuel price each week after a survey is taken of fuel stations across the country.

* Driver and Pedestrian Research

Office of Driver and Pedestrian Research (NRD-40)
Research and Development
National Highway Traffic Safety Administration
U.S. Department of Transportation (DOT)
400 7th Street, SW
Washington, DC 20590   202-366-9591

This office studies factors affecting the safety of drivers and pedestrians. Research areas include determining the causes of unsafe driving and developing counter-measures; the effectiveness of vehicle occupant safety restraints; the effect of alcohol and drugs; the safety concerns of bicycles, motorcycles, and mopeds; driver license standards; and young drivers. This office can refer you to staff researching the topic of your interest.

* Funded Traffic Safety Projects

Evaluation Staff (NTS-02.1)
Traffic Safety Programs
National Highway Traffic Safety Administration
U.S. Department of Transportation (DOT)
400 7th Street, SW
Washington, DC 20590   202-366-2752

Once known as the National Project Reporting System, funded project information collected by this office from each state is stored in a database. Projects are funded in areas such as occupant safety and alcohol. Findings are assembled annually in a published report providing an overview of the projects, their status, and how funding is apportioned, such as amounts to each project and within each project, amount to education, to enforcement, and to other areas. Contact the Evaluation Staff for details.

* Hazardous Material Transportation Accidents

Information Systems Division (DHM-63)
Office of Hazardous Materials Transportation
Research and Special Programs Administration
U.S. Department of Transportation (DOT)
400 7th Street, SW, Room 8112
Washington, DC 20590   202-366-4555

This division collects and analyzes accident data from transporters of hazardous materials by highway, rail, air, and water and from container manufacturers. Information stored in the database includes the hazardous material involved, transporter name and mode, packaging used, cause of accident, and results. Contact the above office for searches. There may be a charge.

* Highway Beautification

Environment Division
Policy and International Affairs
Office of the Secretary of Transportation
U.S. Department of Transportation (DOT)
400 7th Street, SW, Room 9217
Washington, DC 20590   202-366-4366

This is the Department of Transportation (DOT) contact point for environmental issues. Staff can provide you with information and referrals on such subjects as highway beautification, transportation architecture, bicycle paths, historic preservation activities, and environmental impact statements.

* Highway Construction Accident Prevention

Office of Highway Safety (HHS-21)
Associate Administrator for Safety and Operations
Federal Highway Administration (FHWA)
U.S. Department of Transportation (DOT)
400 7th St., SW
Washington, DC 20590   202-366-2177

Highway construction safety programs are funded to remove, relocate, or shield roadside obstacles; to identify and correct hazards at railroad crossings; and to improve signing, pavement markings, and signalization. For information and referral, contact the Office of Highway Safety. The following publications are also available from this office:

Highway Safety Improvement Programs, Annual Report
Status Report of Federal Funds Used for Highway Safety Programs.

Several other reports prepared by this office are available from National Technical Information Service, 5285 Port Royal Road, Springfield, VA 22161; 703-487-4650. A sampling of titles follows:

Inexpensive Accident Countermeasures at Narrow Bridges
Legibility and Driver Response to Selected Lane and Road Closure Barricades
Re-Evaluation of Traffic Control at Non-Signalized Intersections
Rollover Potential of Vehicles on Embankments, Sideslopes, and Other Roadside Features; Railroad-Highway Grade Crossing Signal Visibility Improvement Program, Final Report
Studies of the Road Marking Code
Constant Warning Time Devices for Railroad-Highway Crossings: Technical Summary

* Highway Contractors and Subcontractors

Office of Civil Rights (HCR-1)
Federal Highway Administration (FHWA)
U.S. Department of Transportation (DOT)
400 7th St., SW
Washington, DC 20590   202-366-0693

This office monitors compliance with civil rights laws by requiring contractors and subcontractors of Federal highway projects to submit employment data. Equal opportunity issues are also addressed in the Disadvantaged Business Enterprise Program, which awards contracts and subcontract commitments to small and minority businesses, and in FHWA's Historically Black Colleges and Universities Programs. Data from contractor filings and a list of contractors and subcontractors, by state or county, are available from this office. You can also obtain a copy of *FHWA's Historically Black Colleges and Universities Programs*, a publication with details about those programs.

* Highway Environment

Environmental Operations Division (HEP-1)
Office of Environment and Planning
Federal Highway Administration (FHWA)
U.S. Department of Transportation (DOT)
400 7th St., SW
Washington, DC 20590   202-366-0106

FHWA assesses environmental impact so that highways are located, constructed, and designed in cooperation with environmental concerns. Water and air quality, noise abatement, vegetation management, corrosion control, and preserving wildlife are some of the factors considered. For more information on FHWA efforts in these areas, contact the office listed above.

* Highway Information

Office of Highway Information Management
40 7th Street, SW
Washington, DC 20590   202-366-0160

The Office of Highway Management puts out reports on many aspects of highway travel, highway accident statistics, and vehicle operating costs. Reports available include:

Highway Taxes and Fees, How They Are Collected and Distributed - 1991
Monthly Motor Fuel Reported by States
A Guide to Reporting Highway Statistics
Highway Performance Monitoring System Field Manual-1990
Toll Facilities in the United States - 1991
Fatal and Injury Accident Rates on Federal-aid and Other Highway Systems - 1990
Summary and Recommendations of the Workshop on National Urban Congestion Monitoring - September 1990
Traffic Volume Trends
Speed Monitoring Summary
Traffic Monitoring Guide
Highway Statistics
Selected Highway Statistics and Charts - 1990
Our Nation's Highways - Selected Facts and Figures - 1990
Drivers Licenses - 1990
Nationwide Personal Transportation Study - 1991
Driver License Administration Requirements and Fees - 1990
Road User and Property Taxes on Selected Vehicles - 1987
Cost of Owning and Operating Vehicles and Vans - 1992

* Highway Programs Updates

Office of Public Affairs (A-30)
U.S. Department of Transportation (DOT), Room 10413
400 7th Street, SW
Washington, DC 20590   202-366-5580

The U.S. Department of Transportation *Annual Report* has information on current DOT and Federal Highway Administration programs for highways. The report highlights FHWA accomplishments in the areas of safety, environment, Federal lands projects, motor carrier programs, and international highway assistance. The report also discusses FHA activities in the areas of pavement and bridge management. The report is free from the office of public affairs.

* Highway Publications

Office of Public Affairs (HPA-1)
Federal Highway Administration (FHWA)

U.S. Department of Transportation (DOT)
400 7th St., SW
Washington, DC 20590 202-366-0660

The *FHWA Publications Index*, free from Public Affairs, is a useful guide to current reports, manuals, and summaries generated by programs of the Federal Highway Administration. The *Index* provides contact addresses and telephone numbers for obtaining the publications from offices within FHWA or from NTIS and GPO. The titles listed below are available directly from Public Affairs:

Motor Carrier Activities of the FHWA
U.S. Highways
Commercial Motor Vehicle Safety Act of 1986
FHWA News
The Single License Requirement for Truck and Bus Drivers

* Highway R&D Programs/Publications

Federal Highway Administration (FHWA) (HRD-11)
Office of Research and Development
Turner-Fairbank Highway Research Center
6300 Georgetown Pike
McLean, VA 22101-2144 703-285-2144

The Office of Research, Development and Technology Annual Report details research activities at the Turner-Fairbank Highway Research Center. The report also contains a detailed list of publications. Some categories of publications include: R&D reports; Technology Sharing Reports; Implementation Packages; Rural Technical Reports; Training Materials; TFHRC Update; NCP Progress Report; Technical Summaries; and Public Roads: A Journal of Highway Research and Development.

* Highway Reports List

Federal Highway Administration (FHWA) (HRD-11)
Office of Research and Development
Turner-Fairbank Highway Research Center
6300 Georgetown Pike
McLean, VA 22101-2144 703-285-2144

This office can provide you with a computer runout of all reports, videos, and films produced by the FHWA. Not all items are available. Call the above number for the list or for information on specific publications.

* Highways Research Center

Technical Information Center-Library
Transportation Systems Center (TSC)
Research and Special Programs Administration
U.S. Department of Transportation (DOT)
Kendall Square, 55 Broadway
Cambridge, MA 02142 617-494-2306

TSC is the DOT's multimodal research and analysis center to address national transportation and logistics issues. With contractual participation by industry and academia, it conducts technical, socio-economic, and human-factor studies on which the Department's transportation policy decisions are based. Areas of research include safety, security, transportation infrastructure, system modernization, and information technology relevant to transportation system operations. Research covers highways, rail, air, and water. The Center maintains statistics and a transportation information database. There is no central point for distribution of reports, publications, data tapes, and other information available from the Center, so contact the Library above for referral to the appropriate source within the Center for the information you need.

* Highway Statistics

Office of Highway Information Management (HPM-1)
Associate Administrator for Policy
Federal Highway Administration (FHWA)
U.S. Department of Transportation (DOT)
400 7th St., SW, Room 3306
Washington, DC 20590 202-366-0180

This office is the centralized source for highway statistics compiled by FHWA. The *Highway Statistics Summary*, updated every ten years, summarizes historical information on the Nation's highway system, its users, and Federal, State, and local highway funding. You can also obtain statistics and information on personal, regional, and national travel trends; fuel usage and taxes; road user and motor vehicle taxes; toll bridges, roads, tunnels, and ferries in the U.S.; traffic volume; driver licenses; and yearly statistical summaries. Contact this office to be added to the mailing list for a free subscription to *Monthly Motor Fuels Reported by State*, which indicates trends in gasoline sales.

* Highway Traffic Safety Records

Technical Reference Division (NAD-52)
Office of Administrative Operations
National Highway Traffic Safety Administration
U.S. Department of Transportation (DOT)
400 7th Street, SW
Washington, DC 20590 202-366-2768

NHTSA reports and records are available for public inspection at this location, and database searches can be requested for a fee. Holdings include vehicle research and test reports; investigation reports on accidents and defects; recall information; compliance reports; consumer complaints; consumer advisories; filmed records of research and tests; NHTSA *Technical Reports*; engineering specifications; and certification information. Both light and heavy highway vehicles are covered. Call ahead to ensure that the records you need will be on hand.

* Intermodal Surface Transportation Efficiency Act

Office of Public Affairs (A-30)
Federal Highway Administration (FHWA)
U.S. Department of Transportation (DOT)
400 7th St., SW
Washington, DC 20590 202-366-5580

On December 18, 1991 President Bush signed the Intermodal Surface Transportation Efficiency Act of 1991, providing authorizations for highways, highway safety, and mass transportation for the next six years. Total funding of about $155 billion will be available from FY 1992 - FY 1997. The Office of the Secretary of Transportation published a booklet outlining the provisions of the Act, including tables containing programmatic authorization amounts. The booklet, entitled *Intermodal Transportation Efficiency Act of 1991 - A Summary*, is free from the Office of Public Affairs.

* International Motor Vehicles Standards Harmonization

Director of International Harmonization (NOA-5)
National Highway Traffic Safety Administration
U.S. Department of Transportation (DOT)
400 7th Street, SW
Washington, DC 20590 202-366-2114

The Director formulates strategies for dealing with issues arising from the agencies program for harmonization of US motor vehicle safety standards and regulations with those of foreign countries. This office also contributes to policy guidance used by US negotiators at international standards conferences.

* Interstate Commerce Commission (ICC)

Interstate Commerce Commission
12th St. and Constitution Ave., NW
Washington, DC 20423 202-927-7597

The Interstate Commerce Commission was created as an independent regulatory agency by act of February 4, 1887 to regulate commerce. ICC's responsibilities include regulation of carriers engaged in transportation in interstate commerce and in foreign commerce to the extent that it takes place within the U.S. Surface transportation under the Commission's jurisdiction includes railroads, trucking companies, bus lines, freight forwarders, water carriers, transportation brokers, and a coal slurry pipeline. The regulatory laws vary depending on the type of transportation; however, they generally involve certification of carriers seeking to provide transportation for the public, rates, adequacy of service, purchases, and mergers. The Commission assures that the carriers it regulates will provide the public with rates and services that are fair and reasonable.

* Interstate Commerce Commission Register

Superintendent of Documents
Government Printing Office
Washington, DC 20402 202-512-1800

The *ICC Register* is a daily summary of motor carrier applications and of decisions and notices issued by the ICC. Subscription information is available from the Government Printing Office.

* Interstate Commerce Publications

Office of External Affairs
Interstate Commerce Commission (ICC)
12th St. and Constitution Ave., NW, Room 4111
Washington, DC 20423 202-927-5737

The *ICC Annual Report* contains a complete list of publications, including explanatory material on the operation and activities of the ICC and on special consumer-related fields, such as household goods movements and small shipments, is available. Most of the publications are available directly from the offices that publish them or from the Government Printing Office.

* Interstate Commerce Rules Enforcement

Office of External Affairs
Interstate Commerce Commission (ICC)
12th Street and Constitution Ave, NW
Washington, DC 20423   202-927-5540

The Interstate Commerce Commission (ICC) vigorously enforces rules with respect to motor carrier safety and financial responsibility under the Interstate Commerce Act. Particular commission activities have focused on ensuring that: household good transportation companies abide by applicable regulations; owner operator transportation companies do not violate regulations with respect to tariffs; and transport companies operate safely and with the proper insurance. Recent ICC enforcement activities are documented in the *Annual Report*. Complaints can be filed with the Compliance and Consumer Assistance Office.

* Interstate Commerce Speakers

Office of Government and Public Affairs
Interstate Commerce Commission (ICC)
12th St. and Constitution Ave., NW
Room 4111
Washington, DC 20423   202-927-5737

Speakers are available to discuss subjects relating to the Commission's organization, operations, procedures, and regulations.

* Legal Assistance

Office of the Secretary
Interstate Commerce Commission (ICC)
12th St. and Constitution Ave., NW
Room 2215
Washington, DC 20423   202-927-7428

To assist claimants in disputes, the Commission requires all motor carriers to designate an agent for service of legal process in each state into or through which they operate. The name of this process agent may be obtained by writing to the Office of the Secretary.

* Magnetic Levitation/High Speed Rail

Office of Railroad Development (RDV-7)
Federal Railroad Administration
U.S. Department of Transportation (DOT)
400 7th St., SW, Room 5106
Washington, DC 20590   202-366-6593

This office plans, develops and demonstrates technology toward the application and use of magnetic levitation (Maglev) and high speed transportation systems. This office maintains program documentation and status reports on Maglev and high speed technology programs.

* Mass Transportation Abstracts

Federal Transportation Administration (FTA)
Office of Technology Assistance and Safety
U.S. Department of Transportation (DOT)
400 7th Street, SW, Room 6100
Washington, DC 20590   202-366-4995

The Federal Transportation Administration publishes a *Compendium of Technical Report Abstracts* that provide bibliographic information and abstracts for recently available FTAC (formerly Urban Mass Transportation Administration) - sponsored research project reports. All abstracts are logged in the transportation database (UMTRIS) and are also available online (Dialog file 63) to users of Dialog Information Services, Palo Alto, California. Research reports are available either from NTIS or FTA regional offices. Call for information and to order the Compendium.

* Maximum Speed Limit

Police Traffic Services Division (NTS-41)
Office of Enforcement and Emergency Services
Traffic Safety Programs
National Highway Traffic Safety Administration
U.S. Department of Transportation (DOT)

400 7th Street, SW, Room 5119
Washington, DC 20590   202-366-4295

The National Maximum Speed Limit is 65 miles per hour on certain interstate highways. This office processes annual certifications of maximum speed limit enforcement programs throughout the U.S. and assists states in developing and improving enforcement efforts.

* Minority Contracts for Rail Revitalization

Office of Civil Rights (ROA-10)
Federal Railroad Administration
U.S. Department of Transportation (DOT)
400 7th Street, SW, Room 8314
Washington, DC 20590   202-366-9753

The Office of Civil Rights designs, plans, and implements programs to encourage, promote, and assist minority enterprises to secure contracts and subcontracts with recipients of Federal assistance related to revitalizing the nations railroads. It also serves as the focal point/liaison with the Black Colleges Program and the Office of the Secretary of Transportation's Office of Small and Disadvantaged Business Utilization.

* Mobility Manager Technologies

Technology Sharing Program DRT-1MM
Research and Special Programs Administration
U.S. Department of Transportation (DOT)
400 7th St, SW
Washington, DC 20590   202-366-4208

The Department of Transportation (DOT) is conducting ongoing research into new technologies for local transportation organization. Electronic technologies now make possible mobility manager systems that allow people to plan trips and actually make reservations from a single point of contact. The report *Mobility Management and Market Oriented Local Transportation* (DOT-T-92-07) describes the concept and its operation in detail, explores how the service would work in practice, and sets forth criteria for continuing demonstrations. Single copies are available at no charge.

* Motor and Rail Dockets

Office of the Secretary
Motor and Rail Docket File Room
Interstate Commerce Commission (ICC)
12th St. and Constitution Ave., NW, Room 1221
Washington, DC 20423   202-927-5710

All the Commission's decisions and other legal documents are available for public inspection in the Office of the Secretary.

* Motor Vehicle Standards Enforcement

Office of Enforcement (NEF-01)
National Highway Traffic Safety Administration
U.S. Department of Transportation (DOT)
400 7th Street, SW, Room 5321
Washington, DC 20590   202-366-9700

This Office ensures manufacturer compliance with Federal Laws regarding vehicle safety, fuel economy, theft prevention, damageability, consumer information and odometer fraud. Non compliance and defect recalls are also enforced by this office. It also supports an auto-safety hotline (800-424-9323) for consumer complaints about vehicle safety related defects.

* NHTSA Congressional Liaison

Director for Intergovernmental Affairs (NOA-1)
National Highway Traffic Safety Administration (NHTSA)
U.S. Department of Transportation (DOT)
400 7th Street, SW
Washington, DC 20590   202-366-2105

This office provides a communications link between the National Highway Traffic Safety Administration (NHTSA) and Congress, ensuring Congress understands NHTSA programs and in turn assuring that NHTSA understands Congressional concerns in the areas of highway safety and standards.

* National Driver Register

National Driver Register (NTS-24)
Traffic Safety Programs
National Highway Traffic Safety Administration

U.S. Department of Transportation (DOT)
400 7th Street, SW, Room 6124
Washington, DC 20590 202-366-4800

The *National Driver Register* is a central, computerized index of state records on drivers whose operator licenses have been revoked, denied, or suspended for more than 6 months. Data includes name, birthdate, height, weight, eye color, date and reason for action, and date of reinstatement. Applications for driver licenses are routinely checked against the register, and states exchange information via an electronic system.

* National Highway Traffic Safety Administration

National Highway Traffic Safety Administration (NHTSA)
U.S. Department of Transportation (DOT)
400 7th Street, SW
Washington, DC 20590 202-366-0123

The National Highway Traffic Safety Administration (NHTSA) supports the U.S. Department of Transportation with programs to reduce automobile fuel consumption and motor vehicle crashes with resulting deaths, injuries, and economic losses, and to safeguard the public through regulation, research, information and education on motor vehicles. NHTSA concentrates on developing highway safety programs and monitoring compliance by auto manufacturers with fuel and safety standards. NHTSA has 10 regional offices. The General information number listed above can provide you with the phone number and address of the regional office for your state.

* Northeast Corridor Rail Project

Public Affairs (ROA-30)
Federal Railroad Administration
U.S. Department of Transportation (DOT)
400 7th St., SW, Room 8125
Washington, DC 20590 202-366-0881

Now in its final stages, the project is a major track upgrading on AMTRAK's main line from Washington, DC to Boston. The goal of the upgrading is to produce the best high-speed passenger railroad in the United States. This office can be contacted for information regarding current progress.

* Occupants Displaced by Highway Construction

Office of Right-of-Way (HRW-22)
Federal Highway Administration (FHWA)
U.S. Department of Transportation (DOT)
400 7th St., SW, Room 3219
Washington, DC 20590 202-366-2028

This office administers the Federal Highway Administration's (FHWA) lead role in implementing the Uniform Relocation Assistance and Real Property Acquisition Policies Act. When Federally funded highway construction projects involve displacing residents from acquired property, this Act sets policies for purchase of the land and relocating the people on it. The publication, *Your Rights and Benefits as Displaced Under the Federal Relocation Assistance Program*, is available from this office.

* Pedestrian Safety

Geometric and Roadside Design Branch (HGN-14)
Office of Engineering Program Development
Federal Highway Administration (FHWA)
U.S. Department of Transportation (DOT)
400 7th St., SW, Room 3128
Washington, DC 20590 202-366-1312

Highway design and roadside facilities are studied by this office to determine their impact on pedestrians and bicyclists. The publication, *Pedestrian and Bicycle Facilities*, provides you with information about the roadside designs and structures used in safety-related applications.

* Pedestrian Safety Programs

Federal Highway Administration (FHWA) (HSR-1)
Office of Safety and Traffic Operations R&D
Turner-Fairbank Highway Research Center
6300 Georgetown Pike
McLean, VA 22101-2144 703-285-2054

The Federal Highway Administration and the National Highway Traffic Safety Administration jointly fund the Walk Alert program, which focuses on engineering, education, and enforcement to improve pedestrian safety.

* Public Tariff File

Tariff Examining Branch
Bureau of Traffic
Interstate Commerce Commission (ICC)
12th St. and Constitution Ave., NW, Room 4360
Washington, DC 20423 202-927-5648

The Bureau of Traffic monitors tariff publication, filing, and interpretation, and suspends any unreasonable or unlawful tariffs before they become effective. The tariffs are available for public inspection by contacting the Tariff Examining Branch.

* Rail and Service Abandonments

Office of Transportation Analysis
Interstate Commerce Commission (ICC)
12th St. and Constitution Ave., NW, Room 3100
Washington, DC 20423 202-927-6203

No line of railroad may be abandoned and no rail service discontinued unless the Commission has a certificate of public convenience and necessity authorizing the abandonment or discontinuance. The Notice of Intent must be filed with the Commission at least 15 days, but not more than 30 days, prior to the filing of the abandonment application. The public may become a party to this proceeding by filing a protest, which the Commission will then investigate. For more information, contact the Office of Transportation Analysis.

* Rail Freight Carrier Assistance

Freight Assistance Division
Office of Railroad Development (RDV-11)
Federal Railroad Administration
U.S. Department of Transportation (DOT)
400 7th St., SW, Room 5411
Washington, DC 20590 202-366-9657

This office implements and administers Federal programs of financial and technical assistance to rail roads. It also evaluates requests for financial and technical assistance.

* Rail Industry Conditions

Office of Industry, Finance and Operations (RRP-11)
Federal Railroad Administration
U.S. Department of Transportation (DOT)
400 7th Street, SW, Room 8302
Washington, DC 20590 202-366-0386

This office serves as the principal advisory element in assessing the financial and operating condition of the railroad industry, with special emphasis on carriers in marginal or bankrupt financial condition. This office also administers programs to improve railroad labor/management relations and monitors disputes under the Railway Labor Act.

* Rail Transit Safety

Office of Safety (UTS-30)
Federal Transportation Administration (FTA)
400 7th St., SW, Room 6432
Washington, DC 20590 202-366-2896

The Federal Transportation Administration's (FTA) rapid- and light-rail transit safety system is made up of the following aspects: 1) Safety Information--Reporting and Analysis System--developing a new rapid rail transit accident/incident reporting system; 2) System Safety--disseminating pertinent information to individuals working in the field of mass transit; 3) Drug and Alcohol Abuse information; and 4) Information on State Transit Programs.

* Railroad Accidents

System Support Division
Safety, RRS 22
Federal Railroad Administration
U.S. Department of Transportation (DOT)
400 7th St., NW, Room 8301
Washington, DC 20590 202-366-2760

The division maintains data accessible to the public regarding railroad accidents on a computer database, as well as in the following free publications:

Accident-Incident Bulletin (annual)
Railroad Highway Crossing Accident-Incident and Inventory Bulletin
Summary of Accidents Investigated by the Federal Railroad Administration (1987)

Be patient. If any phone number is incorrect, call (area code) 555-1212 and request the new listing.

819

Business and Industry

Railroad Employee Fatalities Investigated by the Federal Railroad Administration (quarterly)

Railroad Accident Investigation Reports (National Transportation Safety Board)

* Railroad Freight and Operations

Office of Policy Systems
Federal Railroad Administration
U.S. Department of Transportation (DOT)
400 7th Street, SW, RRP-20
Washington, DC 20590   202-366-2920

This office studies the use of freight cars, accounting and financial systems of railroads, coal rates, grain transportation, and mergers. Available for purchase is the yearly series *Carload Waybill Statistics (Report TD1)*, a compilation of rail freight statistics calculated annually showing traffic flows by commodity across broad geographic areas (including from Canada). You can order this report through the National Technical Information Service, or contact the above office for more information. *Freight Commodity Statistics* is available for purchase from the Association of American Railroads, and contact the above office for more information. The public use computer tape of the *Carload Waybill Sample* is available for purchase from ALK Associates, Inc., 1000 Herrontown Rd., Princeton, NJ 08540. Attn: Database Mgr.

* Railroad Industry Analysis

Office of External Affairs
Interstate Commerce Commission (ICC)
12th Street and Constitution Ave, NW
Washington, DC 20423   202-927-5737

The Interstate Commerce Commission (ICC) *Annual Report* contains a detailed analysis of current developments in the Rail industry falling under their jurisdiction including financial conditions, reorganizations, mergers and acquisitions, labor issues, abandonments, rates, freight service, and passenger service.

* Railroad Information

Public Affairs (ROA-30)
Federal Railroad Administration (FRA)
U.S. Department of Transportation (DOT)
400 7th St., SW, Room 8125
Washington, DC 20590   202-366-0881

Contact the Public Affairs for additional information on Federal Railroad Administration (FRA) programs, publications, and activities.

* Railroad Reports

Reports Branch (RRS-22.1)
Federal Railroad Administration
U.S. Department of Transportation (DOT)
400 7th St., SW, Room 8301
Washington, DC 20590   202-366-2760

This office prepares Accident Investigation Reports and Employee Fatality Reports for publication and distribution. It also administers and processes Freedom of Information Act requests on matters pertaining to railroad safety.

* Railroad Research and Development

Office of Research and Development (RDV-30)
Federal Railroad Administration
U.S. Department of Transportation (DOT)
400 7th St., SW, Room 5420
Washington, DC 20590   202-366-0453

Call this office for information on the latest trends in railway technology and thinking. Topics include developments to improve track and track bed structures; work to reduce the effects of accidents involving tank cars carrying hazardous materials; efforts to gain a better understanding of equipment failures; development of less expensive and more effective grade crossing techniques; and research into human factors in train operation.

* Railroad Safety

Office of Safety (RRS-20)
Federal Railroad Administration
U.S. Department of Transportation (DOT)
400 7th St., SW, Room 8314
Washington, DC 20590   202-366-0521

This office inspects tracks, equipment, signals, and general railroad operations. It investigates accidents and complaints, and makes routine investigations. The office has jurisdiction over such areas as locomotives, signals, safety appliances, power brakes, hours of service, transportation of explosives; and human factors in rail operations. The free publication, *Safety Report*, lists federal government actions to improve railroad safety. It includes statistical compilations of accidents; incident reports, federal safety regulations, orders and standards issues by the Federal Railroad Administration; evaluation of the degree of their observance; summary of outstanding problems; analysis and evaluation of research and related activities; a list of completed or pending judicial actions for the enforcement of any safety rules, regulations, orders, or standards issued; and recommendations for additional legislation. The publication is available by contacting Public Affairs, Federal Railroad Administration, U.S. Department of Transportation, 400 7th St., SW, Room 3413, Washington, DC 20590; 202-366-0881.

* Railway Hazardous Materials Transport

Hazardous Materials Division (RRS-12)
Federal Railroad Administration (FRA)
U.S. Department of Transportation (DOT)
400 7th Street, SW, Room 8326
Washington, DC 20590   202-366-0495

This office develops, reviews, analyzes, and prepares Department of Transportation (DOT) exemptions to the hazardous materials regulations covering such items as package design, specifications and operating requirements for the Federal Railroad Administration (FRA). This office coordinates its programs with the other DOT offices handling hazardous materials transport regulations.

* Railway Regulatory Analysis

Regulatory Analysis Division (RRP-31)
Federal Railroad Administration
U.S. Department of Transportation (DOT)
400 7th Street, SW, Room 8302J
Washington, DC 20590   202-366-0344

This office assesses the effects of proposed legislative and administrative changes to the rail regulatory system and evaluates the impact on railroads and shippers of changes implemented by Congress or the Interstate Commerce Commission.

* Rates and Charges

Bureau of Traffic
Rates and Informal Cases Section
Interstate Commerce Commission (ICC)
12th St. and Constitution Ave., NW, Room 4310
Washington, DC 20423   202-927-5180

A tariff is a schedule of rates and charges, and each carrier must file a copy with the Interstate Commerce Commission (ICC). If you have a complaint with a company regarding the charges, contact the Bureau of Traffic for assistance. They may be able to help resolve the matter quickly.

* Road Signs

Traffic Control Development Applications Division (HHS-32)
Traffic Control Systems, Traffic Operations Division
Office of Highway Safety
Federal Highway Administration (FHWA)
U.S. Department of Transportation (DOT)
400 7th St., SW
Washington, DC 20590   202-366-2187

Efforts by this division improve the effectiveness and uniformity of such traffic control devices as road signs, signal lamps, and highway markings throughout the country. Standards are developed for designing signs and using other traffic control devices. The meanings of road signs and markings are described in *Road Symbol Signs*, which can be obtained by contacting the office listed above. Two other publications on the subject, listed below, are available from the Superintendent of Documents, Government Printing Office, Washington, DC 20402; 202-512-1800:

Manual on Uniform Traffic Control Devices, ($22)
Standard Highway Signs Book, ($30)

* Rural Technical Assistance Program

Federal Highway Administration (FHWA) (HHI-20)
Office of Research and Development
Turner-Fairbank Highway Research Center

6300 Georgetown Pike
McLean, VA 22101-2144   703-285-2770

The Rural Technical Assistance Program (RTAP) is managed by the National Highway Institute, the technical training arm of the Federal Highway Administration (FHWA). The RTAP provides direct technical assistance to those transportation agencies responsible for constructing or maintaining rural roads and local streets. Assistance is generated through RTAP's three supportive services: local technology transfer centers; a national clearinghouse for technical resources; and national technical projects. Contact the Turner-Fairbank center for more information.

* Special Permission Authority

Special Permission Board
Bureau of Traffic
Interstate Commerce Commission (ICC)
12th St. and Constitution Ave., NW
Room 4338
Washington, DC 20423   202-927-7348

Companies must give the Interstate Commerce Commission (ICC) one day's notice for new or reduced rates and five to seven working days for increased rates or fares. You must contact the Special Permission Board to shorten the time period.

* Traffic Accident Data

Information Management and Analysis
Office of Highway Safety (HHS-12)
Federal Highway Administration (FHWA)
U.S. Department of Transportation (DOT)
400 7th St., SW
Washington, DC 20590   202-366-2159

Statistics are kept here on fatal and injury accident rates for the Nation's highways. The office accepts inquiries for specific topics of interest as well as copies of publications that contain fatality and injury data. The Office does not maintain a publications list, but will assist you in finding the information you need. The office can also transfer data onto magnetic tape. Call or write this office to request the data you need.

* Tariff Instructional Manual

Tariff Section
Bureau of Traffic
Interstate Commerce Commission (ICC)
12th St. and Constitution Ave., NW
Room 4363A
Washington, DC 20423   202-927-5150

The *Tariff Instructional Manual* is intended as a guide for carriers wishing to publish their own tariffs. It includes only the essentials and will require some adjustment to meet individual needs. This outlines the rules and regulations and offers several examples. They also include information on frequent problems and define some of the terms used in the tariff application.

* Traffic Safety Programs

Office of Traffic Safety Programs (NTS-01)
National Highway Traffic Safety Administration
U.S. Department of Transportation (DOT)
400 7th Street, SW, Room 5125
Washington, DC 20590   202-366-1755

This office develops national goals and objectives with respect to highway safety as well as evaluating both in place and proposed state highway safety programs. It also manages national programs dealing with drunk and drugged driving, use of safety belts and child safety seats, automatic crash protection, police traffic services, emergency medical services, traffic records, pedestrian safety, and motorcycle safety.

* Transportation of Hazardous Materials

Office of Hazardous Materials Transportation (DHM-50)
Research and Special Programs Administration
U.S. Department of Transportation (DOT)
400 7th Street, SW
Washington, DC 20590-0001   202-366-4465

This office can provide you with information on the transportation of hazardous materials by highway, rail air, and water. Data is collected directly from industry and also via compliance inspections by field staff. The quarterly *Hazardous Material Newsletter* is available free from the office above.

* Transportation Safety Institute

Transportation Safety Institute (DTI-1)
Research and Special Programs Administration
U.S. Department of Transportation (DOT)
6500 South MacArthur Blvd.
Oklahoma City, OK 73125   405-680-3153

The Institute supports the Department's efforts to reduce transportation accidents. It develops and conducts training programs for Federal, state, and local governments; industry; and foreign personnel. Courses are offered in aviation, highway, marine, pipeline, and railroad safety; materials analysis; transportation security; and other subjects.

* Transport Statistics in the United States

Publications
Interstate Commerce Commission (ICC)
12th St. and Constitution Ave., NW
Washington, DC 20423   202-927-5930

This is an annual report which contains statistics of railroads and motor carriers. It includes a complete breakdown of finances, expenses and equipment, as well as service statistics. The tables are compiled from reports filed with the Commission by railroads and motor carriers.

* Transportation Statistics Compilation

Office of Economics
Interstate Commerce Commission (ICC)
12th Street and Constitution Ave, NW
Washington, DC 20423   202-927-5156

This office conducts economic and statistical analyses of the transportation industry for the Interstate Commerce Commission (ICC). It compiles and publishes transport statistics and cost studies. Contact the Office of Economic for more specific information and requests.

* Transportation Technical Reports Bibliography

Research and Special Programs Administration
John A. Volpe Transportation System Center
U.S. Department of Transportation (DOT)
Cambridge, MA 02142   617-494-2306

The Bibliography lists reports released by the Volpe National Transportation System Center from january 1980 to December 1990. Reports are listed by sponsoring agency and are indexed by author, title, subject, report number and performing organization. The bibliography includes reports from all of the component administrations of the U.S. Department of Transportation. It is available free from the Center.

* Trucking Company Analysis

Office of External Affairs
Interstate Commerce Commission (ICC)
12th Street and Constitution Ave, NW
Washington, DC 20423   202-927-5737

The *ICC Annual Report* contains a detailed analysis of the developments in the trucking industry falling under ICC jurisdiction. The 1990 Report discusses the financial condition of the industry, mergers, rates, operating rights, safety, and insurance issues. The report is available free from the Interstate Commerce Commission.

* Updates on Federal Railroad Administration Programs

Office of Public Affairs (A-30)
U.S. Department of Transportation (DOT)
400 7th Street, SW, Room 10413
Washington, DC 20590   202-366-5580

The U.S. Department of Transportation Annual Report has information on current rail programs. The 1990 report highlights programs in the areas of rail safety, deregulation, labor/management disputes, services restructuring, magnetic levitation and high speed rail. The report is free from the office of public affairs.

* Updates on Traffic Programs

Office of Public Affairs (A-30)
U.S. Department of Transportation (DOT), Room 10413
400 7th Street, SW

Business and Industry

Washington, DC 20590   202-366-5580

The U.S. Department of Transportation *Annual Report* lists the latest activities of the National Highway Traffic Safety Administration (NHTSA). Included are accident statistics, recent research on motor vehicle safety, and report summaries on highway safety. Recent litigation involving NHTSA is also outlined. The report is available free from the Office of Public Affairs.

* Vehicle Import Investigations

International Trade Commission (ITC)
500 E Street, SW
Washington, DC 20436   202-205-1807

The International Trade Commission (ITC) investigates matters pertaining to domestic industry injury from imports and unfair trade practices. It's reports are available to the public. Reports are free from the ITC. Reports pertaining to auto imports include:

Rules of Origin Related to NAFTA and the North American Automotive Industry - USITC 2460.
All Terrain Vehicles (Japan) USITC 2071 and USITC 2163.
Automotive Glass (Mexico) USITC 2299.

The Reports Index for all *ITC Reports* is USITC 2484.

* Vehicle Performance Standards

Office of Rulemaking (NRM-1)
National Highway Traffic Safety Administration
U.S. Department of Transportation (DOT)
400 7th Street, SW
Washington, DC 20590   202-366-1810

This office develops and promulgates rules dealing with crash protection, crash survivability, crash avoidance, fuel economy, and theft protection of motor vehicles. It also directs programs relating to bumper standards, safety performance standards, tire standards, and other equipment standards. The Office also develops consumer information on crash protection and survivability characteristics for new and used motor vehicles and equipment.

* Waterways Traffic Regulation

Commander G-NSP
Vessel Traffic Services Branch
Office of Navigation Safety and Waterways Services
U.S. Coast Guard
U.S. Department of Transportation (DOT)
2100 2nd St., SW, Room 3202
Washington, DC 20593-0001   202-267-1539

To ensure the safe and orderly passage of vessels, cargo, and people, Vessel Traffic Services in major ports oversee the movement of vessels and install necessary safety equipment. Traffic is monitored closely during hazardous conditions and bad weather. To locate the Vessel Traffic Service nearest you, contact the branch listed above or your local Coast Guard office.

Be patient. If any phone number is incorrect, call (area code) 555-1212 and request the new listing.

Selling to the Government
Government Contracts

If you produce a product or service, you've probably always wondered how you could offer what you produce to the biggest client in the world — the federal government. Have you thought of the government as being a "closed shop" and too difficult to penetrate? Well, I'm happy to say that you're entirely wrong on that score. The federal government spends over $180 billion each year on products ranging from toilet paper to paper clips and writes millions of dollars in contracts for services like advertising, consulting, and printing. Most Americans believe that a majority of those federal purchasing contracts have been eliminated over the last few years, but that's simply not true — they've just been replaced with new contracts that are looking for the same kinds of goods and services. Last year the government took action (either initiating or modifying) on over 350,000 different contracts. They buy these goods and services from someone, so why shouldn't that someone be you? To be successful doing business with the government, you need to learn to speak "governmenteze" to get your company into the purchasing loop, and I can show you how to accomplish that in just a few easy steps.

Step 1

Each department within the federal government has a procurement office that buys whatever the department needs. Most of these offices have put together their own *Doing Business With the Department of* _____ publication, which usually explains procurement policies, procedures, and programs. This booklet also contains a list of procurement offices, contact people, subcontracting opportunities, and a solicitation mailing list. Within each department is also an Office of Small and Disadvantaged Business Utilization, whose sole purpose is to push the interests of the small business, and to make sure these companies get their fair share of the government contracts. Another resource is your local Small Business Administration Office which should have a listing of U.S. Government Procurement Offices in your state.

Step 2

Once you have familiarized yourself with the process, you need to find out who is buying what from whom and how much, as well as who wants what when. There are three ways to get this important information.

A. Daily Procurement News
Each weekday, the *Commerce Business Daily* (CBD) gives a complete listing of products and services (that cost over $25,000) wanted by the U.S. government — products and services that your business may be selling. Each listing includes the following: the product or service, along with a short description; name and address of the agency; deadline for proposals or bids; phone number to request specifications; and the solicitation number of the product or service needed. Many business concerns, including small businesses, incorporate CBD review into their government marketing activities. To obtain a $208/year subscription, contact: Superintendent of Documents, U.S. Government Printing Office, Washington, DC 20402; 202-512-1800.

B. Federal Data Systems Division (FDSD)
This Center distributes consolidated information about federal purchases, including research and development. FDSD can tell you how much the federal government spent last quarter on products and services, which agencies made those purchases, and who the contractors were that did business with the government. FDSD summarizes this information through two types of reports: The FDSD standard report and the FDSD special report. The standard report is a free, quarterly compilation containing statistical procurement information in "snapshot" form for over 60 federal agencies, as well as several charts, graphs, and tables which compare procurement activities by state, major product and service codes, method of procurement, and contractors. The report also includes quarterly and year-to-year breakdowns of amounts and percentages spent on small, women-owned, and minority businesses. Special reports are prepared upon request for a fee, based on computer and labor costs. They are tailored to the specific categories, which can be cross-tabulated in numerous ways. A special report can help you analyze government procurement and data trends, identify competitors, and locate federal markets for individual products or services. Your Congressman may have access to the Federal Procurement Database from his/her office in Washington, which you may be able to use for free. For more information, contact: Federal Data Systems Division, General Services Administration, 7th and D St., SW, Room 5652, Washington, DC 20407; 202-401-1529.

C. Other Contracts
For contracts under $25,000, you need to be placed on a department's list for solicitation bids on those contracts. The mailing list forms are available through the Procurement Office, the Office of Small and Disadvantaged Business Utilization, or your local Small Business Association office. Last year 18.7 billion dollars was spent on these "small" purchases, so these contracts are not to be overlooked.

Step 3: Subcontracting Opportunities

All of the federal procurement offices or Offices of Small and Disadvantaged Business Utilization (SDBU) can provide you with information regarding subcontracting. Many of the departments' prime contracts require that the prime contractor maximize small business subcontracting opportunities. Many prime contractors produce special publications which can be helpful to those interested in subcontracting. The SDBU Office can provide you with more information on the subcontracting process, along with a directory of prime contractors. Another good source for

Selling to the Government

subcontract assistance is your local Small Business Administration (SBA) office, 1-800-827-5722. SBA develops subcontracting opportunities for small business by maintaining close contact with large business prime contractors and referring qualified small firms to them. The SBA has developed agreements and close working relationships with hundreds of prime contractors who cooperate by offering small firms the opportunity to compete for their subcontracts. In addition, to complete SBA's compliance responsibilities, commercial market representatives monitor prime contractors in order to assess their compliance with laws governing subcontracting opportunities for small businesses.

Step 4: Small Business Administration's 8(a) Program

Are you a socially or economically disadvantaged person who has a business? This group includes, but is not limited to, Black Americans, Hispanic Americans, Native Americans, Asian Pacific Americans, and Subcontinent Asian Americans. Socially and economically disadvantaged individuals represent a significant percentage of U.S. citizens, yet account for a disproportionately small percentage of total U.S. business revenues. The 8(a) program assists firms to participate in the business sector and to become independently competitive in the marketplace. SBA may provide participating firms with procurement, marketing, financial, management, or other technical assistance. A Business Opportunity Specialist will be assigned to each firm that participates, and is responsible for providing the firm with access to assistance that can help the firm fulfill its business goals. SBA undertakes an extensive effort to provide government contracting opportunities to participating businesses. SBA has the Procurement Automated Source System (PASS) which places your company's capabilities online so that they may be available to government agencies and major corporations when they request potential bidders for contracts and subcontracts. To apply for the 8(a) program, you must attend an interview session with an official in the SBA field office in your area. For more information, contact your local Small Business Administration Office, or you can call 1-800-827-5722 for the SBA office nearest you.

Step 5: Bond

A Surety bond is often a prerequisite for government and private sector contracts. This is particularly true when the contract involves construction. In order for the company to qualify for an SBA Guarantee Bond, they must make the bonding company aware of their capabilities based on past contract performance and meeting of financial obligations. SBA can assist firms in obtaining surety bonding for contracts that do not exceed $1,250,000. SBA is authorized, when appropriate circumstances occur, to guarantee as much as 90 percent of losses suffered by a surety resulting from a breach of terms of a bond.

Step 6: Publications

The Government Printing Office has several publications for sale which explain the world of government contracts. For ordering information, contact: Superintendent of Documents, Government Printing Office, Washington, DC 20402; 202-512-1800.

* *U.S. Government Purchasing and Sales Directory* ($23): The Directory is an alphabetical listing of the products and services bought by the military departments, and a separate listing of the civilian agencies. The Directory also includes an explanation of the ways in which the SBA can help a business obtain government prime contracts and subcontracts, data on government sales of surplus property, and comprehensive descriptions of the scope of the government market for research and development.

* *Guide to the Preparation of Offers for Selling to the Military* ($4.75)

* *Small Business Specialists* ($3.75)

* *Small Business Subcontracting Directory* ($7.00): designed to aid small businesses interested in subcontracting opportunities within the Department of Defense (DOD). The guide is arranged alphabetically by state and includes the name and address of each current DOD prime contractor as well as the product or service being provided to DOD.

* *Women Business Owners; Selling to the Federal Government* ($3.75)

* *Selling to the Military,* ($8.00)

Step 7: What is GSA?

General Services Administration (GSA) is the Government's business agent. On an annual budget of less than half a billion dollars, it directs and coordinates nearly $8 billion a year worth of purchases, sales, and services. Its source of supply is private enterprise, and its clients are all branches of the federal government. GSA plans and manages leasing, purchase, or construction of office buildings, laboratories, and warehouses; buys and delivers nearly $4 billion worth of goods and services; negotiates the prices and terms for an additional $2.3 billion worth of direct business between federal groups and private industry; sets and interprets the rules for federal travel and negotiates reduced fares and lodging rates for federal travelers; and manages a 92,000 vehicle fleet with a cumulative yearly mileage of over 1 billion. For a copy of *Doing Business With GSA, GSA's Annual Report*, or other information regarding GSA, contact: Office of Publication, General Services Administration, 18th and F Streets, NW, Washington, DC 20405; 202-501-1235. For information on GSA's architect and engineer services, such as who is eligible for GSA professional services contracts, how to find out about potential GSA projects, what types of contracts are available, and where and how to apply, contact: Office of Design and Construction, GSA, 18th and F Streets, NW, Washington, DC 20405; 202-501-1888. Information on specifications and standards of the federal government is contained in a booklet, *Guide to Specifications and Standards*, which is available free from Specifications Sections, General Services Administration, 470 E L'Enfant Plaza, SW, Suite 8100, Washington, DC 20407; 202-755-0325.

Step 8: Bid and Contract Protests

The General Accounting Office (GAO) resolves disputes between agencies and bidders for government contracts, including grantee

Be patient. If any phone number is incorrect, call (area code) 555-1212 and request the new listing.

award actions. The free publication, *Bid Protests at GAO; A DescriptiveGuide*, contains information on GAO's procedures for determining legal questions arising from the awarding of government contracts. Contact Information Handling and Support Facilities, General Accounting Office, Gaithersburg, MD 20877; 202-275-6241. For Contract Appeals, the GSA Board of Contract Appeals works to resolve disputes arising out of contracts with GSA, the Departments of Treasury, Education, Commerce, and other independent government agencies. The Board also hears and decides bid protests arising out of government-wide automated data processing (ADP) procurements. A contractor may elect to use either the GSA Board or the General Accounting Office for resolution of an ADP bid protest. Contractors may elect to have

their appeals processed under the Board's accelerated procedures if the claim is $50,000 or less, or under the small claims procedure if the claim is $10,000 or less. Contractors may also request that a hearing be held at a location convenient to them. With the exception of small claims decisions, contractors can appeal adverse Board decisions to the U.S. Court of Appeals for the Federal Circuit. For more information, contact: Board of Contract Appeals, General Services Administration, 18th and F Streets, NW, Washington, DC 20405; 202-501-0720. There are other Contract Appeals Boards for other departments. One of the last paragraphs in your government contract should specify which Board you are to go to if a problem arises.

Free Local Help:
The Best Place to Start to Sell to the Government

Within each state there are offices that can help you get started in the federal procurement process. As was stated previously, your local Small Business Administration (SBA) office is a good resource. In addition to their other services, the SBA can provide you with a list of Federal Procurement Offices based in your state, so you can visit them in person. Another place to turn is your local Small Business Development Center (look under Economic Development in your phone book). These offices are funded jointly by federal and state governments, and are usually associated with the state university system. They are aware of the federal procurement process, and can help you draw up a sensible business plan.

Some states have established programs to assist businesses in the federal procurement process for all departments in the government. These programs are designed to help businesses learn about the bidding process, the resources available, and provide information on how the procurement system operates. They can match the product or service you are selling with the appropriate agency, and then help you market your product. Several programs have online bid matching services, whereby if a solicitation appears in the *Commerce Business Daily* that matches what your company markets, then the program will contact you to start the bid process. They can then request the appropriate documents, and assist you in achieving your goal. These Procurement Assistance Offices (PAOs) are partially funded by the Department of Defense to assist businesses with Defense Procurement. For a current listing of PAOs contact:

Defense Logistics Agency
Office of Small and Disadvantaged Utilization
Bldg. 4, Cameron Station
Room 4B110
Alexandria, VA 22304-6100
703-274-6471

Let Your Congressman Help You

Are you trying to market a new product to a department of the federal government? Need to know where to try to sell your wares? Is there some problem with your bid? Your Congressman can be of assistance. Because they want business in their state to boom, they will make an effort to assist companies in obtaining federal contracts. Frequently they will write a letter to accompany your bid, or if you are trying to market a new product, they will write a letter to the procurement office requesting that they review your product. Your Congressman can also be your personal troubleshooter. If there is some problem with your bid, your Congressman can assist you in determining and resolving the problem, and can provide you with information on the status of your bid. Look in the blue pages of your phone book for your Senators' or Representatives' phone numbers, or call them in Washington at 202-224-3121.

Small Business Set-Asides

The Small Business Administration (SBA) encourages government purchasing agencies to set aside suitable government purchases for exclusive small business competition. A purchase which is restricted to small business bidders is identified by a set aside clause in the invitation for bids or request for proposals. There is no overall listing of procurements which are, or have been, set aside for small business. A small business learns which purchases are reserved for small business by getting listed on bidders' lists. It also can help keep itself informed of set aside opportunities by referring to the *Commerce Business Daily*. Your local SBA office can provide you with more information on set asides, as can the Procurement Assistance Offices listed at the end of this section. You can locate your nearest SBA office by calling 1-800-827-5722.

Veterans Assistance

Each Small Business Administration District Office has a Veterans Affairs Officer which can assist veteran-owned businesses in obtaining government contracts. Although there is no such thing as veterans set aside contracts, the Veterans Administration does make an effort to fill its contracts using veteran-owned businesses. Contact your local SBA office for more information.

Woman-Owned Business Assistance

There are over 3.7 million women-owned businesses in the United States, and the number is growing each year. Current government policy requires federal contracting officers to increase their purchases from women-owned businesses. Although the women-owned firms will receive more opportunities to bid, they still must be the lowest responsive and responsible bidder to win the contract. To assist these businesses, each SBA district office has a Women's Business Representative, who can provide you with information regarding government programs. Most of the offices hold a *Selling to the Federal Government* seminar, which is designed to educate the business owner on the ins and outs of government procurement. There is also a helpful publication, *Women Business Owners: Selling to the Federal Government*, which provides information on procurement opportunities available. Contact your local SBA office or your Procurement Assistance Office (listed below) for more information.

Minority and Labor Surplus Area Assistance

Are you a socially or economically disadvantaged person who has a business? This group includes, but is not limited to, Black Americans, Hispanic Americans, Native Americans, Asian Pacific

Americans, and Subcontinent Asian Americans. Socially and economically disadvantaged individuals represent a significant percentage of U.S. citizens yet account for a disproportionately small percentage of total U.S. business revenues. The 8(a) program assists firms to participate in the business sector and to become independently competitive in the marketplace. SBA may provide participating firms with procurement, marketing, financial, management, or other technical assistance. A Business Opportunity Specialist will be assigned to each firm that participates, and is responsible for providing the firm with access to assistance that can help the firm fulfill its business goals.

SBA undertakes an extensive effort to provide government contracting opportunities to participating businesses. SBA has the Procurement Automated Source System (PASS) which places your company's capabilities online so that they may be available to government agencies and major corporations when they request potential bidders for contracts and subcontracts. To apply for the 8(a) program, you must attend an interview session with an official in the SBA field office in your area. Some areas of the country have been determined to be labor surplus areas, which means there is a high rate of unemployment. Your local SBA office can tell you if you live in such an area, as some contracts are set asides for labor surplus areas. For more information, contact your local Small Business Administration office (call 1-800-827-5722 for the SBA office nearest you), or call the Procurement Assistance Office in your state (listed below.)

Federal Procurement Assistance Offices

Alabama
University of Alabama at Birmingham, Alabama Small Business Development Consortium, 1717 11th Ave. S., Suite 419, Birmingham, AL 35294; 205-934-7260, Fax: 205-934-7645.

Alaska
University of Alaska/Anchorage, Small Business Development Center, 430 W. Seventh Ave., Suite 110, Anchorage, AK 99501; 907-274-7232, Fax: 907-274-9524.

Arizona
APTAN, Inc., 360 N. Hayden Rd., Scottsdale, AZ 85257; 602-945-5452, Fax: 602-970-6355.

National Center for American Indians Enterprise Development, National Center Headquarters, 953 E. Juanita Ave., Mesa, AZ 85204; 602-831-7524, Fax: 602-491-1332.

Arkansas
Board of Trustees, University of Arkansas, College of Business Administration/ESC, 120 Ozark Hall, Fayetteville, AR 72701; 501-337-5358, Fax: 501-337-5045.

California
c/o AMD, Procurement Assistance Center, m/s 31, 901 Thompson Place, P.O. Box 3453, Sunnyvale, CA 94088-3453; 408-739-6283.

Business Innovation Center, San Diego Incubator Corp., 3350 Market St., San Diego, CA 92102; 619-685-2949, Fax: 619-531-8829.

Merced County Office of Economic and Strategic Development, Contract Procurement Center, Karen Prentiss, 1632 N St., Merced, CA 95340; 209-385-7312, Fax: 209-383-4959.

Colorado
Office of Business Development, Governor's Office, 1625 Broadway, Suite 1710, Denver, CO 80202; 303-620-8082, Fax: 303-892-3848.

Connecticut
SEATECH, 1084 Shennecossett Rd., Gorton, CT 06340; 203-449-8777, Fax: 203-449-9463.

Delaware
Delaware State College, Dept. of Economics and Business, Dr. Winston Awadzi, 1200 N. Dupont Hwy., Dover, DE 19901; 302-739-5146, Fax: 302-739-3517.

Florida
University of West Florida, Florida Procurement Technical Assistance Program, 11000 University Parkway, Pensacola, FL 32514; 904-444-2066, Fax: 904-444-2070.

Georgia
Columbus College, Division of Continuing Education, 1 Arsenal Pl., 901 Front Ave., Columbus, GA 31901; 706-649-1092, Fax: 706-649-1094.

Georgia Tech Research Corporation, Economic Development Institute, 400 10th St., Atlanta, GA 30332-0420; 404-894-6121, Fax: 404-853-9172.

Hawaii
State of Hawaii, Department of Business, Economic Development and Tourism, Mr. Larry Nelson, P.O. Box 2359, Honolulu, HI 96813; 808-586-2598, Fax: 808-587-2777.

Idaho
State of Idaho, Mr. Larry Demirelli, Department of Commerce, 700 W. State St., Boise, ID 83720; 208-334-2470, Fax: 208-334-2631.

Illinois
Black Hawk College District 503, 6600 34th Ave., Moline, IL 61268; 309-755-2200, Fax: 309-755-9847.

Latin American Chamber of Commerce, The Chicago PAC, 2539 N. Kedzie Ave., Suite 11, Chicago, IL 60647; 312-252-5211, Fax: 312-252-7065.

State of Illinois, Department of Commerce and Community Affairs, 620 East Adams, 6th Floor, Springfield, IL 62701; 217-785-6310, Fax: 217-785-6328.

Indiana
Indiana Institute for New Business Ventures, Government Marketing Assistance Group, One North Capitol, Suite 1240, Indianapolis, IN 46204-2026; 317-264-5600, Fax: 317-264-2806.

Partners in Contracting Corp., PTA CTR, 200 Russell St., Suite 200E, Hammond, IN 46320; 219-932-7811, Fax: 219-932-5612.

Iowa
State of Iowa, Iowa Department of Economic Development, 200 E. Grand Ave., Des Moines, IA 50309; 515-242-4888, Fax: 515-242-4893.

Kentucky
Kentucky Cabinet for Economic Development, Department of Community Development, 500 Mero St., Capital Plaza Tower, 22nd Floor, Frankfort, KY 40601; 1-800-838-3266, Fax: 502-564-3250.

Louisiana
Jefferson Parish Economic Development Commission, The Bid Center, Ms. Phyllis McLaren, 1221 Elmwood Park Blvd., Suite 405, Harahan, LA 70123; 504-736-6550, Fax: 504-763-6554.

Louisiana Productivity Center/USL, Procurement Technical Assistance Network, P.O. Box 44172, 241 E. Lewis St., Lafayette, LA 70504-4172; 318-231-6767, Fax: 318-262-5472.

Northwest Louisiana Government Procurement Center, Greater Shreveport Economic Development, P.O. Box 20074, 400 Edwards St., Shreveport, LA 71120-0074; 318-677-2530, Fax: 318-677-2534.

Maine
Eastern Maine Development Corporation, Market Development Center, One Cumberland Place, Suite 300, Bangor, ME 04401; 207-942-6389, 1-800-339-6389 (ME), 1-800-955-6549, Fax: 207-942-3548.

Maryland
Morgan State University, School of Business and Mgmt., Dr. Otis Thomas, Cold Spring Lane and Hillen Road, Baltimore, MD 21239; 410-319-3861, Fax: 410-319-3532.

Be patient. If any phone number is incorrect, call (area code) 555-1212 and request the new listing.

827

Tri-County Council for Western Maryland Inc., 111 S. George St., Cumberland, MD 21502; 301-777-2158, Fax: 301-777-2495.

Massachusetts
Commonwealth of Massachusetts, MA Office of Business Development, 1 Ashburton Place, 21st Floor, Boston, MA 02108; 508-657-8600, Fax: 508-657-0185.

Michigan
Genesee County Metropolitan Planning Commission, Procurement Technical Assistance Program, 1101 Beach St., Flint, MI 48502; 810-257-3010, Fax: 810-257-3185.

Jackson Alliance for Business Development, PTA Center, 133 W. Michigan Ave., Jackson, MI 49201; 517-788-4455, Fax: 517-788-4337.

Kalamazoo County CGA, Inc., Government Contracting Office, Ms. Sandra Ledbetter, 100 W. Michigan, Suite 294, Kalamazoo, MI 49007; 616-342-0000, Fax: 616-343-1151.

Downriver Community Conference, Economic Development Department, 15100 Northline, Southgate, MI 48195; 313-281-0700, Fax: 313-281-3418.

Northeast Michigan Consortium, 320 State St., P.O. Box 711, Onaway, MI 49765; 517-733-8548, Fax: 517-733-8069.

Northwest Michigan Council of Governments, Procurement Technical Assistance Center, Mr. James F. Haslinger, P.O. Box 506, Traverse City, MI 49685-0506; 616-929-5036, Fax: 616-929-5012.

Saginaw Future, Inc., Contract Procurement Office, 301 E. Genessee, 3rd Floor, Saginaw, MI 48607; 517-754-8222, Fax: 517-754-1715.

Schoolcraft College, Ms. Judi Zima, 18600 Haggerty Rd., Livonia, MI 48152-2696; 313-462-4438, Fax: 313-462-4439.

Thumb Area Consortium/Growth Alliance, Local Procurement Office, 3270 Wilson St., Marlette, MI 48453; 517-635-3561, Fax: 517-635-2230.

Warren, Center Line, Sterling Heights Chamber of Commerce, Ms. Janet E. Masi, 30500 Van Dyke Ave., Suite 118, Warren, MI 48093-2178; 810-751-3939, Fax: 810-751-3995.

West Central Michigan Employment and Training Consortium, Procurement Tech. Assistance, Mr. John Calabrese, 110 Elm St., Big Rapids, MI 49307; 616-796-4891, Fax: 616-796-8316.

Minnesota
Minnesota Project Innovation, Govt. Marketing Assistance, Mill Place, 111 3rd Ave., S, Suite 100, Minneapolis, MN 55401-2554; 612-341-0641, Fax: 612-338-3483.

Mississippi
Mississippi Contract Procurement Center, 3015 12th St., Gulfport, MS 39502; 601-864-2961, Fax: 601-864-2969.

Missouri
Curators of the University of Missouri, University Extension, 310 Jesse Hall, Columbia, MO 65211; 314-882-0344, Fax: 314-884-4297.

Missouri Southern State College, 3950 E. Newman Rd., Joplin, MO 64801-1595; 417-625-9313, Fax: 417-625-9782.

Montana
Montana Tradeport Authority, James F. Ouldhouse, 2722 3rd Ave., N., Suite 300 West, Billings, MT 59101; 406-256-6871, Fax: 406-256-6877.

High Plains Development Authority Inc., 2800 Terminal Dr., Suite 209, P.O. Box 2568, Great Falls, MT 59404; 406-454-1934, Fax: 406-454-2995.

Procurement Technical Institute, Greg Depuydt, 305 W. Mercury, Butte, MT 59701; 406-723-4061, Fax: 406-723-5345.

Nebraska
Nebraska Department of Economic Development, Existing Business Assistance Division, 301 Centennial Mall So., P.O. Box 94666, Lincoln, NE 68509-4666; 308-535-8213, Fax: 308-535-8175.

Nevada
State of Nevada, Commission on Economic Development, Mr. Ray Horner, Capitol Complex, Carson City, NV 89710; 702-687-4325, Fax: 702-687-4450.

New Hampshire
Office of Business and Industrial Development, P.O. Box 1856, 172 Pembroke Rd., Concord, NH 03302-1856; 603-271-2591, Fax: 603-271-2629.

New Jersey
New Jersey Institute of Technology, Procurement Technical Assistance Center, Mr. John McKenna, 240 Martin Luther King Blvd., Newark, NJ 07102; 201-596-3105, Fax: 201-596-5806.

Union County PTA Center, 1085 Morris Ave., Suite 531, Liberty Hall, Union, NJ 07083; 908-527-1166, Fax: 908-527-1207.

New Mexico
State of New Mexico, Procurement Assistance Program, 1100 St. Francis Dr., Room 2006, Santa Fe, NM 87503; 505-827-0425, Fax: 505-827-0499.

New York
Cattaraugus County, Department of Economic Development and Tourism, 303 Court St., Little Valley, NY 14755; 716-938-9111, Fax: 716-938-9438.

Long Island Development Corporation, Procurement Technical Assistance Program, 255 Glen Cove Rd., Carle Place, NY 11514; 516-741-5690, Fax: 516-741-5851.

New York City Department of Business Services, Procurement Outreach Program, 110 William St., New York, NY 10038; 212-513-6472, Fax: 212-618-8987.

Rockland Economic Development Corporation, Procurement Division, 1 Blue Hill Plaza, Suite 812, Pearl River, NY 10965; 914-735-7040, Fax: 914-735-5736.

South Bronx Overall Economic Development Corporation, 370 East 149th St., Bronx, NY 10455; 718-292-3113, Fax: 718-292-3115.

State University of New York, Office of Research and Sponsored Prog., P.O. Box 6000, Binghamton, NY 13902; 607-777-2718, Fax: 607-777-2022.

North Carolina
University of North Carolina at Chapel Hill, Small Business and Technology Development Center, Bynum Hall, Chapel Hill, NC 27599; 919-571-4154, Fax: 919-571-4161.

North Dakota
University of North Dakota, North Dakota Small Business Development Center, Department of Grants and Contracts, P.O. Box 8164, Grand Forks, ND 58202; 701-237-9678, Fax: 701-235-6706.

Ohio
Central State University, Ohio Procurement and Technical Assistance Ctr., Wilberforce, OH 45384; 513-376-6514.

Columbus Area Chamber of Commerce, Central Ohio Government Marketing Assistance Program, 37 N. High St., Columbus, OH 43215; 614-225-6952, Fax: 614-469-8250.

Community Improvement Corporation of Lake County, Northeast Ohio Government Contract Assistance Center, 7750 Clocktower Dr., Mentor, OH 44060; 216-951-8488, Fax: 216-951-7336.

Greater Cleveland Government Business Program, 200 Tower City Center, 50 Public Square, Cleveland, OH 44113; 216-621-3300, Fax: 216-621-6013.

Lawrence Economic Development Corporation, Outreach Center, 101 Sand and Solida Rd., P.O. Box 488, South Point, OH 45680; 614-894-3838, Fax: 614-894-3836.

Mahoning Valley Economic Development Corp., Mahoning Valley Technical Procurement Center, Stephen J. Danyi, 4319 Belmont Ave., Youngstown, OH 44505; 216-759-3668, Fax: 216-759-3680.

Terra Technical College, North Central Ohio Procurement Technical Assistance Program, 1220 Cedar St., Fremont, OH 43420; 419-332-1002.

University of Cincinnati, CECE-Extension Unit Small Business Ctr., Ms. Nancy Rogers, 1111 Edison Dr., IAMS Bldg., Cincinnati, OH 45216; 513-948-2083, Fax: 513-948-2007.

Oklahoma

Oklahoma Department of Vocational-Technical Education, Business Assistance and Development Division, 1500 W. Seventh Ave., Stillwater, OK 74074-4364; 405-743-5574, Fax: 405-743-6821.

Tribal Government Institute, 111 N. Peters, Suite 400, Norman, OK 73069; 405-329-5542, Fax: 405-329-5543.

Oregon

Organization for Economic Initiatives, Government Contract Acquisition Program, 99 W. 10th Ave., Eugene, OR 97401; 503-344-3537, Fax: 503-687-4899.

Pennsylvania

Chester County Department of Commerce, Office of Economic Development, 117 W. Gay St., West Chester, PA 19380; 610-436-3337, Fax: 610-436-3110.

Economic Development Council of Northeastern Pennsylvania, Local Development District, 1151 Oak St., Pittston, PA 18640; 717-655-5581, Fax: 717-654-5137.

Government Contracting Assistance, Slippery Rock University, Economic and Community Development Center, Slippery Rock, PA 16057-1326; 412-738-2346.

Indiana University of Pennsylvania, Dr. Robert Camp, Robertshaw Center, 650 S. 13th St., Suite 303, Indiana, PA 15705; 412-357-7824, Fax: 412-357-3082.

Johnstown Area Regional Industries, Defense Procurement Assistance Center, 111 Market St., Johnstown, PA 15901; 814-535-8675, Fax: 814-535-8677.

Kutztown University, Small Business Development Center, University Center, 2986 N. 2nd St., Harrisburg, PA 17110; 717-233-3120.

Lehigh University, Rach Business Center #37, 412 S. New St., Bethlehem, PA 18015; 215-758-3980.

Mon Valley Renaissance, California University of Pennsylvania, 250 University Ave., California, PA 15419; 412-938-5881, Fax: 412-938-4575.

Montgomery County Department of Commerce and Economic Development, #3 Stony Creek Office Center, West Marshall Street, Norristown, PA 19404; 215-278-5950.

North Central Pennsylvania Regional Planning and Development Commission, 651 Montmorenci Ave., Ridgway, PA 15853; 814-772-3162, Fax: 814-772-7045.

Northern Tier Regional Planning and Development Commission, 507 Main St., Towanda, PA 18848; 717-265-9103, Fax: 717-265-7585.

Northwest Pennsylvania Regional Planning and Development Commission, 614 Eleventh St., Franklin, PA 16323; 814-437-3024, Fax: 814-432-3002.

Private Industry Council of Westmoreland/ Fayette, Inc., Procurement Assistance Center, 531 S. Main St., Greensburg, PA 15601; 412-836-2600, Fax: 412-836-8058.

SEDA - Council of Governments, RD 1, Timberhaven, Lewisburg, PA 17837; 717-524-4491, Fax: 717-524-9190.

South Western Pennsylvania Regional Development Council, The Waterfront, 200 First Ave., Pittsburgh, PA 15222-1573; 412-391-5590, Fax: 412-391-9160.

Southern Alleghenies Planning and Development Commission, 541 58th St., Altoona, PA 16602; 814-949-6528, Fax: 814-949-6505.

Temple University, Room 6, Speakman Hall, Philadelphia, PA 19122; 215-787-5893.

Trustees University of Pennsylvania, SE-PA PTAP, 3733 Spruce St., Vance Hall, Philadelphia, PA 19104-6374; 215-898-1219, Fax: 215-573-2135.

Puerto Rico

Commonwealth of Puerto Rico (FOMENTO), Economic Development Administration, Mr. Pedro J. Acevedo, 355 Roosevelt Ave., Hato Rey, PR 00918; 809-752-6861, Fax: 809-751-6239.

Rhode Island

Rhode Island Department of Economic Development, Business Development Office, 7 Jackson Walkway, Providence, RI 02903; 401-277-2601, Fax: 401-277-2102.

South Carolina

University of South Carolina, College of Business Administration, Small Business Development Center, Columbia, SC 29208; 803-777-4907, Fax: 803-777-4403.

South Dakota

South Dakota Procurement Technical Assistance Center, School of Business, 414 E. Clark, Vermillion, SD 57069; 605-330-6191, Fax: 605-330-6231.

Tennessee

University of Tennessee, Center for Industrial Services, Mr. T.C. Parsons, 226 Capitol Boulevard Bldg., Suite 606, Nashville, TN 37219-1804; 615-532-8657, Fax: 615-532-4937.

Texas

Angelina College, Defense PTA Center, P.O. Box 1768, Lufkin, TX 75902; 409-639-3678, Fax: 409-639-3863.

El Paso Community College, P.O. Box 20500, El Paso, TX 79998; 915-534-3405, Fax: 915-534-3420.

Northeast Texas Community College, East Texas Procurement Technical Assistance Program, P.O. Box 1307, Mt. Pleasant, TX 75455; 903-572-1911, Fax: 903-572-0598.

Panhandle Regional Planning Commission, Economic Development Unit, P.O. Box 9257, Amarillo, TX 79105-9257; 806-372-3381, Fax: 806-373-3268.

San Antonio Procurement Outreach Center, Department of Economic and Employment Development, Ms. Rosalie O. Manzano, P.O. Box 839966, San Antonio, TX 78283; 210-554-7133, Fax: 210-554-7160.

Small Business Development Center, Chamber of Commerce, 101 N. Shoreline, Corpus Christi, TX 78401; 512-882-6161, Fax: 512-888-5627.

Texas Technical University, College of Business Administration, 2579 S. Loop 289, Lubbock, TX 79423; 806-745-1637, Fax: 806-745-6207.

University of Houston/TIPS, Texas Information Procurement Service, 1100 Louisiana, Houston, TX 77204; 713-752-8477, Fax: 713-756-1515.

University of Texas at Arlington, Automaton and Robotics Research Institute, P.O. Box 19125, Arlington, TX 76019; 817-794-5978, Fax: 817-794-5952.

University of Texas at Brownsville, Office of President, 80 Fort Brown, Brownsville, TX 78520; 210-544-8812, Fax: 210-548-5627.

Utah

Utah Department of Community and Economic Development, Utah Procurement Outreach Program, 324 S. State St., Suite 504, Salt Lake City, UT 84111; 801-538-8791, Fax: 801-538-8825.

Vermont

State of Vermont, Agency of Development and Community Affairs, 109 State St., Montpelier, VT 05609; 802-828-3221, Fax: 802-828-3258.

Virginia

Crater Planning District Commission, The Procurement Assistance Center, 1964 Wakefield St., P.O. Box 1808, Petersburg, VA 23805; 804-861-1667, Fax: 804-732-8972.

George Mason University, Entrepreneurship Center, 4400 University Dr., Fairfax, VA 22030; 703-993-8300, Fax: 703-330-5891.

Southwest Virginia Community College, Procurement Technical Center, Ms. Maxine B. Rogers, P.O. Box SVCC, Richlands, VA 24641; 703-964-7334, Fax: 703-964-9307.

Washington

Economic Development Council of Snohomish County, 917 134th St. SW, Everett, WA 98204; 206-743-4567, Fax: 206-745-5563.

Be patient. If any phone number is incorrect, call (area code) 555-1212 and request the new listing.

829

Selling to the Government

Spokane Area Economic Development Council, P.O. Box 203, 221 N. Wall, Suite 310, Spokane, WA 99210-0203; 509-624-9285, Fax: 509-624-3759.

Economic Development Council of Kitsap County, 4841 Auto Center Way, Suite 204, Bremerton, WA 98312; 206-643-0102, Fax: 206-643-6673.

West Virginia

Mid-Ohio Valley Regional Council, Procurement Technical Assistance Center, P.O. Box 247, Parkersburg, WV 26105; 304-295-8714, Fax: 304-295-7681.

Regional Contracting Assistance Center, Inc., Mr. Mick Walker, 1116 Smith St., Suite 202, Charleston, WV 25301; 304-344-2546, Fax: 304-344-2574.

Wisconsin

Procurement Institute, Inc., 840 Lake Ave., Racine, WI 53403; 414-632-6321, Fax: 414-632-7157.

Madison Area Technical College, Small Business Assistance Center, 211 N. Carroll St., Madison, WI 53703; 608-258-2330, Fax: 608-258-2329.

Government Buys Bright Ideas From Inventors:
Small Business Innovative Research Programs (SBIR)

The Small Business Innovative Research Program (SBIR) stimulates technological innovation, encourages small science and technology-based firms to participate in government-funded research, and provides incentives for converting research results into commercial applications. The program is designed to stimulate technological innovation in this country by providing qualified U.S. small business concerns with competitive opportunities to propose innovative concepts to meet the research and development needs of the federal government. Eleven federal agencies with research and development budgets greater than $100 million are required by law to participate: The Departments of Defense, Health and Human Services, Energy, Agriculture, Commerce, Transportation, and Education; the National Aeronautics and Space Administration; the National Science Foundation; the Nuclear Regulatory Commission; and the Environmental Protection Agency.

Businesses of 500 or fewer employees that are organized for profit are eligible to compete for SBIR funding. Non-profit organizations and foreign-owned firms are not eligible to receive awards, and the research must be carried out in the U.S. All areas of research and development solicit for proposals, and the 1995 budget for SBIR is $900 million. There are three phases of the program: Phase I determines whether the research idea, often on high-risk advanced concepts, is technically feasible, whether the firm can do high quality research, and whether sufficient progress has been made to justify a larger Phase II effort. This phase is usually funded for 6 months with awards up to $50,000. Phase II is the principal research effort, and is usually limited to a maximum of $500,000 for up to two years. The third phase, which is to pursue potential commercial applications of the research funded under the first two phases, is supported solely by non-federal funding, usually from third party, venture capital, or large industrial firms. SBIR is one of the most competitive research and development programs in government. About one proposal out of ten received is funded in Phase I. Generally, about half of these receive support in Phase II. Solicitations for proposals are released once a year (in a few cases twice a year). To assist the small business community in its SBIR efforts, the U.S. Small Business Administration publishes the Pre-Solicitation Announcement (PSA) in December, March, June, and September of each year. Every issue of the PSA contains pertinent information on the SBIR Program along with details on SBIR solicitations that are about to be released. This publication eliminates the need for small business concerns to track the activities of all of the federal agencies participating in the SBIR Program. In recognition of the difficulties encountered by many small firms in their efforts to locate sources of funding essential to finalization of their innovative products, SBA has developed the Commercialization Matching System. This system contains information on all SBIR awardees, as well as financing sources that have indicated an interest in investing in SBIR innovations. Firms interested in obtaining more information on the SBIR Program or receiving the PSA, should contact the Office of Technology, Small Business Administration, 409 3rd St., SW, MC/6470, Washington, DC 20416, 202-205-6450.

SBIR representatives listed below can answer questions and send you materials about their agency's SBIR plans and funding:

Department of Agriculture
Dr. Charles F. Cleland, Director, SBIR Program, U.S. Department of Agriculture, Small Business Association, 409 Third St., SW, 8th Floor, Washington, DC 20416; 202-205-7777.

Department of Defense
Mr. Robert Wrenn, SBIR Program Manager, OSD/SADBU, U.S. Department of Defense, The Pentagon, Room 2A340, Washington, DC 20301-3061; 703-697-1481.

Department of Education
Mr. John Christensen, SBIR Program Coordinator, U.S. Department of Education, 555 New Jersey Ave., NW, Room 602D, Washington, DC 20208; 202-219-2050.

Department of Energy
Dr. Samuel J. Barish, SBIR Program Manager, ER-16, U.S. Department of Energy, Washington, DC 20585; 301-903-3054.

Department of Health and Human Services
Mr. Veri Zanders, SBIR Program Manager, Office of the Secretary, U.S. Department of Health and Human Services, Washington, DC 20201; 202-690-7300.

Department of Transportation
Dr. George Kobatch, DOT SBIR Program Director, DTS-22, Research and Special Program Administration, Volpe National Transportation Systems Center, U.S. Department of Transportation, 55 Broadway, Kendall Square, Cambridge, MA 02142-1093; 617-494-2051.

Environmental Protection Agency
Mr. Donald F. Carey, SBIR Program Manager, Research Grants Staff (8701), Office of Research and Development, U.S. Environmental Protection Agency, 401 M St., SW, Washington, DC 20460; 202-260-7899.

National Aeronautics and Space Administration
Mr. Harry Johnson, Manager, SBIR Office, Code CR, National Aeronautics and Space Administration Headquarters, 300 E St., SW, Washington, DC 20546-0001; 202-358-0691.

National Science Foundation
Mr. Roland Tibbetts, Mr. Ritchie Coryell, Mr. Daryl G. Gorman, Mr. Charles Hauer, Dr. Sara Nerlove, SBIR Program Managers, National Science Foundation, 4201 Wilson Boulevard, Room 590, Arlington, VA 22230; 703-306-1391.

Nuclear Regulatory Commission
Ms. Marianne M. Riggs, SBIR Program Representative, Financial Management, Procurement, and Administrative Staff, Nuclear Regulatory Commission, Washington, DC 20555; 301-415-5822.

State Procurement Offices

Have you ever wondered where the government buys all of the products that it works with each day? Well, they buy from small businesses just like yours that produce products such as:

- work clothing
- office supplies
- cleaning equipment
- miscellaneous vehicles
- medical supplies and equipment

Imagine what your bottom line could look like each year if you won just ONE lucrative government contract that would provide your business with a secure income! It might even buy you the freedom to pursue other clients that you wouldn't have the time or money to go after otherwise.

The following offices are starting places for finding out who in the state government will purchase your products or services.

State Procurement Offices

Alabama
Finance Department, Purchasing Division, 11 S. Union, Room 200, Montgomery, AL 36130; 205-242-7250.

Alaska
State of Alaska, Department of Administration, Division of General Services and Supply, P.O. Box 110210, Juneau, AK 99811-0210; 907-465-2253.

Arizona
State Purchasing, Executive Tower, Suite 101, 1700 W. Washington, Phoenix, AZ 85007; 602-542-5511.

Arkansas
Office of State Purchasing, P.O. Box 2940, Little Rock, AR 72203; 501-324-9312.

California
Office of Procurement, Department of General Services, 1823 14th St., Sacramento, CA 95814; 916-445-6942.

Colorado
Division of Purchasing, 225 E. 16th Ave., Suite 900, Denver, CO 80203; 303 866-6100.

Connecticut
State of Connecticut, Department of Administrative Services, Bureau of Purchases, 460 Silver St., Middletown, CT 06457; 203-638-3280.

Delaware
Purchasing Division, Purchasing Bldg., P.O. Box 299, Delaware City, DE 19706; 302-834-4550.

District of Columbia
Department of Administrative Services, 441 4th St. NW, Room 710, Washington, DC 20001; 202-727-0171.

Florida
General Service Department, Division of Purchasing, Knight Bldg., 2737 Centerview Dr., 2nd Floor, Tallahassee, FL 32399-0950; 904-488-8440.

Georgia
Administrative Services Department, 200 Piedmont Ave., Room 1308 SE, Atlanta, GA 30334; 404-656-3240.

Hawaii
Purchasing Branch, Purchasing and Supply Division, Department of Accounting and General Services, Room 416, 1151 Punch Bowl, Honolulu, HI 96813; 808- 586-0575.

Idaho
Division of Purchasing, Administration Department, 5569 Kendall, State House Mall, Boise, ID 83720; 208-327-7465.

Illinois
Department of Central Management Services, Procurement Services, 801 Stratton Bldg., Springfield, IL 62706; 217-782-2301.

Indiana
Department of Administration, Procurement Division, 402 W. Washington St., Room W-468, Indianapolis, IN 46204; 317-232-3032.

Iowa
State of Iowa, Department of General Services, Purchasing Division, Hoover State Office Building, Des Moines, IA 50319; 515-281-3089.

Kansas
Division of Purchasing, Room 102 North, Landon State Office Building, 900 SW Jackson St., Topeka, KS 66612; 913-296-2376.

Kentucky
Purchases, Department of Finance, Room 367, Capital Annex, Frankfort, KY 40601; 502-564-4510.

Louisiana
State Purchasing Office, Division of Administration, P.O. Box 94095, Baton Rouge, LA 70804-9095; 504-342-8010.

Maine
Bureau of Purchases, State House Station #9, Augusta, ME 04333; 207-287-3521.

Maryland
Purchasing Bureau, 301 W. Preston St., Mezzanine, Room M8, Baltimore, MD 21201; 410-225-4620.

Massachusetts
Purchasing Agent Division, One Ashburton Place, Room 1017, Boston, MA 02108; 617-727-7500.

Michigan
Office of Purchasing, Mason Bldg., P.O. Box 30026, Lansing, MI 48909, or 530 W. Ellegan, 48933; 517-373-0330.

Minnesota
State of Minnesota, 112 Administration Bldg., 50 Sherburne Ave., St. Paul, MN 55155; 612-296-6152.

Mississippi
Office of Purchasing and Travel, 1504 Sillers Bldg., 550 High St., Suite 1504, Jackson, MS 39201; 601-359-3409.

Missouri
State of Missouri, Division of Purchasing, P.O. Box 809, Jefferson City, MO 65102; 314-751-3273.

State Procurement Offices

Montana
Department of Administration, Procurement Printing Division, 165 Mitchell Bldg., Helena, MT 59620-0135; 406-444-2575.

Nebraska
State Purchasing, Material Division, 301 Centennial Mall S., P.O. Box 94847, Lincoln, NE 68509; 402-471-2401.

Nevada
Nevada State Purchasing Division, 209 E. Musser St., Room 304, Blasdel Bldg., Carson City, NV 89710; 702-687-4070.

New Hampshire
Plant and Property Management, 25 Capitol St., State House Annex, Room 102, Concord, NH 03301; 603-271-2201.

New Jersey
Division of Purchase and Property, CN-039, Trenton, NJ 08625; 609-292-4886.

New Mexico
State Purchasing Division, 1100 St. Frances Dr., Joseph Montoya Bldg., Room 2016, Santa Fe, NM 87503; 505-827-0472.

New York
Division of Purchasing, Corning Tower, Empire State Plaza, 38th Floor, Albany, NY 12242; 518-474-3695.

North Carolina
Department of Administration, Division of Purchase and Contract, 116 W. Jones St., Raleigh, NC 27603-8002; 919-733-3581.

North Dakota
Central Services Division of State Purchasing, Purchasing, 600 E Blvd., I Wing, Bismarck, ND 58505-0420; 701-224-2683.

Ohio
State Purchasing, 4200 Surface Rd., Columbus, OH 43228-1395; 614-466-5090.

Oklahoma
Office of Public Affairs, Central Purchasing Division, Room B4, State Capital Bldg., Oklahoma City, OK 73105; 405-521-2110.

Oregon
General Services, Purchasing, 1225 Ferry St., Salem, OR 97310; 503-378-4643.

Pennsylvania
Procurement Department Secretary, N. Office Bldg., Room 414, Commonwealth and North St., Harrisburg, PA 17125; 717-787-5295.

Rhode Island
Department of Administration, Purchases Office, One Capital Hill, Providence, RI 02908-5855; 401-277-2317.

South Carolina
Materials Management Office, General Service Budget and Control Board, 1201 Main St., Suite 600, Columbia, SC 29201; 803-737-0600.

South Dakota
Division of Purchasing, 118 W. Capitol Ave., Pierre, SD 57501; 605-773-3405.

Tennessee
Purchasing Division, C2-211, Central Services Bldg., Nashville, TN 37219; 615-741-1035.

Texas
State Purchasing and General Services Commission, P.O. Box 13047, Austin, TX 78711; 512-463-3445.

Utah
Purchasing Division, Department of Administrative Services, State Office Bldg., Room 3150, Salt Lake City, UT 84114; 801-538-3026.

Vermont
Purchasing Division, 128 State St., Drawer 33, Montpelier, VT 05633-7501; 802-828-2211.

Virginia
Department of General Services, Purchasing Division, P.O. Box 1199, Richmond, VA 23209; 804-786-3172.

Washington
Office of State Procurement, 216 GA Building, P.O. Box 41017, Olympia, WA 98504-1017; 206-753-6461.

West Virginia
Department of Administration, Purchasing Section, Room E102, Building One, 1900 Kanawha Blvd. E, Charleston, WV 25305-0110; 304-558-2306.

Wisconsin
Division of State Agency Services, Bureau of Procurement, 101 E. Wilson, 6th Floor, P.O. Box 7867, Madison, WI 53707-7867; 608-266-2605.

Wyoming
Department of Administration, Procurement Services, 2001 Capitol Ave., Cheyenne, WY 82002; 307-777-7253.

Be patient. If any phone number is incorrect, call (area code) 555-1212 and request the new listing.

833

Selling Overseas:
International Trade

If you've found that the domestic market for your product or service is dwindling, it's time to consider broadening your sales base by selling overseas. Hey, it's not as complicated as you might think. There is a lot of information available to us in this country about other countries that isn't even available in that particular country. In other words, we have access to things like marketing trend reports on countries like Turkey that business people in Turkey can't even get hold of! Important expertise and assistance for new and more experienced exporters continue to increase at both the federal and state level.

That widget that you invented in your garage so many years ago is now found in every hardware store in this country — why shouldn't it be in every French hardware store? Or the line of stationery that sold so well for you in this country could definitely be a hit in British stores that specialize in selling fine writing papers. So how do you go about finding what countries are open to certain imports and what their specific requirements are? If you're smart, you go to the best source around — the government — and make it work for you.

Polypropylene In Countries
That Don't Even Count People

A few years ago a Fortune 500 company asked us to identify the consumption of polypropylene resin for 15 lesser developed countries. It was a project they had been working on without success for close to a year. After telexing all over the world and contacting every domestic expert imaginable, we too came up empty handed. The basic problem was that we were dealing with countries that didn't even count people, let alone polypropylene resin.

Our savior was a woman at the U.S. Commerce Department named Maureen Ruffin, who was in charge of the World Trade Reference Room. Ms. Ruffin and her colleagues collect the official import/export statistical documents for every country in the world as soon as they are released by the originating countries. Although the data are much more current and more detailed than those published by such international organizations as the United Nations, the publications available at this federal reference room are printed in the language of origin. Because none of the 15 subject countries manufacture polypropylene resin, Ms. Ruffin showed us how to get the figures by identifying those countries which produce polypropylene and counting up how much each of them exported to the countries in question. To help us even further, she also provided us with free in-house translators to help us understand the foreign documents.

Exporter's Hotline

The Trade Promotion Coordinating Committee has established this comprehensive "one-stop shop" for information on U.S. Government programs and activities that support exporting efforts.

This hotline is staffed by trade specialists who can provide information on seminars and conferences, overseas buyers and representatives, overseas events, export financing, technical assistance, and export counseling. They also have access to the National Trade Data Bank.

Trade Information Center
U.S. Department of Commerce
Washington, DC 20230
800-USA-TRADE; 202-482-0543
Fax: 202-482-4473
TDD: 800-833-8723

Country Experts

If you are looking for information on a market, company or most any other aspect of commercial life in a particular country, your best point of departure is to contact the appropriate country desk officer at the U.S. Department of Commerce. These experts often have the information you need right at their fingertips or they can refer you to other country specialists that can help you.

U.S. and Foreign Commercial Services (FCS)
International Trade Administration
U.S. Department of Commerce, Room 2810
Washington, DC 20230   202-482-6220

All the Department of Commerce/US & FCS field offices around the country are listed later in this chapter. (You will also find a separate roster of international trade offices maintained by the states.)

ITA Country Desk Officers

A

ASEAN	Karen Goddin	202-482-3877	2032
Afghanistan	Tim Gilman	202-482-2954	2308
Albania	EEBIC	202-482-2645	7412
Algeria	Claude Clement	202-482-5545	2033
Angola	Finn Holm-Olsen	202-482-4228	3317
Anguilla	Michelle Brooks	202-482-2527	2039
Antigua/			
Barbuda	Michelle Brooks	202-482-2527	2039
Argentina	Randy Mye	202-482-1548	3021
Aruba	Michelle Brooks	202-482-2527	2039
Australia	Gary Bouck	202-482-4958	2036
Austria	Philip Combs	202-482-2920	3039
Armenia	BISNIS	202-482-4655	7413
Azerbaijan	Mark Siegelman	202-482-5680	7413

B

Bahamas	Mark Siegelman	202-482-5680	2039
Bahrain	Claude Clement		
	/Chris Carone	202-482-1860	2029B

Balkan States	EEBIC	202-482-2645	7412
Bangladesh	John Simmons	202-482-2954	2308
Barbados	Michelle Brooks	202-482-2527	2039
Belgium	Simon Bensimon	202-482-5401	3039
Belize	Michelle Brooks	202-482-2527	2039
Benin	Debra Henke	202-482-5149	3317
Bhutan	Tim Gilman	202-482-2954	2308
Bolivia	Rebecca Hunt	202-482-2521	2037
Botswana	Finn Holm-Olsen	202-482-4228	3317
Brazil	Horace Jennings	202-482-3871	3019
Brunei	Raphael Cung	202-482-4958	2036
Bulgaria	EEBIC	202-482-2645	7412
Burkina Faso	Philip Michelini	202-482-4388	3317
Burma	Gary Bouck	202-482-4958	2306
Burundi	Philip Michelini	202-482-4388	3317
Belarus	BISNIS	202-482-4655	7413

C

Cambodia	Gary Bouck	202-482-4958	2036
Cameroon	Debra Henke	202-482-5149	3317
Canada	Kathy Klein	202-482-3103	3033
Cape Verde	Philip Michelini	202-482-4388	3317
Caymans	Mark Siegelman	202-482-5680	2039
Central Africa Republic	Philip Michelini	202-482-4388	3317
Chad	Philip Michelini	202-482-4388	3317
Chile	Roger Turner	202-482-1495	3021
Columbia	Paul Moore	202-482-1659	2037
Comoros	Chandra Watkins	202-482-4564	3317
Congo	Debra Henke	202-482-5419	3317
Costa Rica	Mark Siegelman	202-482-5680	2039
Cuba	Mark Siegelman	202-482-5680	2039
Cyprus	Ann Corro	202-482-3945	3042
Czech Republic	EEBIC	202-482-2645	7412
Cote d'Ivoire	Philip Michelini	202-482-4388	3317

D

D'Jibouti	Chandra Watkins	202-482-4564	3317
Denmark	James Devlin	202-482-3254	3037
Dominica	Michelle Brooks	202-482-2527	2039
Dominican Republic	Mark Siegelman	202-482-5680	2039

E

E. Caribbean	Michelle Brooks	202-482-2527	3021
Ecuador	Paul Moore	202-482-1659	2037
Egypt	Thomas Sams /Corey Wright	202-482-1860	2029B
El Salvador	Helen Lee	202-482-2528	2039
Equatorial Guinea	Philip Michelini	202-482-4388	3317
Ethiopia	Chandra Watkins	202-482-4564	3317
European Community	Charles Ludolph	202-482-5276	3036

F

Finland	James Devlin	202-482-3254	3037
France	Elena Mikalis	202-482-6008	3042

G

Gabon	Debra Henke	202-482-5149	3321
Gambia	Philip Michelini	202-482-4388	3317
Germany	Brenda Fisher	202-482-2435	3409
Germany	John Larsen	202-482-2434	3409
Ghana	Debra Henke	202-482-5149	3321
Greece	Ann Corro	202-482-3945	3042
Grenada	Michelle Brooks	202-482-2527	2039
Guatemala	Helen Lee	202-482-2528	2039
Guinea	Philip Michelini	202-482-4388	3317
Guinea-Bissau	Philip Michelini	202-482-4388	3317
Guyana	Michelle Brooks	202-482-2527	2039

H

Haiti	Mark Siegelman	202-482-5680	2039
	Helen Lee	202-482-2528	2039
Hong Kong	Sheila Baker	202-482-3932	2317
Hungary	EEBIC	202-482-2645	7412

I

Iceland	James Devlin	202-482-3254	3037
India	John Simmons /John Crown /Tim Gilman	202-482-2954	2308
Indonesia	Karen Goddin	202-482-3877	2036
Iran	Paul Thanos	202-482-1860	2029B
Iraq	Thomas Sams	202-482-1860	2029B
Ireland	Boyce Fitzpatrick	202-482-2177	3045
Israel	Paul Thanos	202-482-1860	2029B
Italy	Boyce Fitzpatrick	202-482-2177	3045

J

Jamaica	Mark Siegelman	202-482-5680	2039
Japan	Ed Leslie /Cynthia Cambell /Eric Kennedy	202-482-2425	2320
Jordan	Paul Thanos	202-482-1860	2029B

K

Kenya	Chandra Watkins	202-482-4564	3317
Korea	Jeffrey Donius /Dan Duvall /William Golike	202-482-4390	2327
Kuwait	Corey Wright /Thomas Sams	202-482-5506	2033
Kazakhstan	BISNIS	202-482-4655	7413
Krygyz Republic	BISNIS	202-482-4655	7413

L

Laos	Hong-Phong B. Pho	202-482-4958	2036
Lebanon	Corey Wright /Thomas Sams	202-482-1860	2029B
Lesotho	Finn Holm-Olsen	202-482-4228	3317
Liberia	Philip Michelini	202-482-4388	3317
Libya	Claude Clement	202-482-5545	2033
Luxembourg	Simon Bensimon	202-482-5401	3039
Lativa	EEBIC	202-482-2645	7412
Lithuania	EEBIC	202-482-2645	7412

M

Macau	Sheila Baker	202-482-3932	2317
Madagascar	Chandra Watkins	202-482-4564	3317
Malawi	Finn Holm-Olsen	202-482-4228	3317
Malaysia	Raphael Cung	202-482-4958	2036
Maldives	John Simmons	202-482-2954	2308

Be patient. If any phone number is incorrect, call (area code) 555-1212 and request the new listing.

835

Mali	Philip Michelini	202-482-4388	3317
Malta	Robert McLaughlin	202-482-3748	3045
Mauritana	Philip Michelini	202-482-4388	3317
Mauritius	Chandra Watkins	202-482-4564	3321
Mexico	Shawn Ricks	202-482-0300	3022
Mongolia	Sheila Baker	202-482-3932	2317
Montserrat	Michelle Brooks	202-482-2527	2039
Morocco	Claude Clement	202-482-5545	2033
Mozambique	Finn Holm-Olsen	202-482-4228	3317
Moldova	BISNIS	202-482-4655	7413

N

Namibia	Finn Holm-Olsen	202-482-4228	3317
Nepal	Tim Gilman	202-482-2954	2308
Netherlands	Simon Bensimon	202-482-5401	3039
Netherlands Antilles	Michelle Brooks	202-482-2527	2039
New Zealand	Gary Bouck	202-482-4958	2036
Nicaragua	Mark Siegelman	202-482-5680	2039
Niger	Philip Michelini	202-482-4388	3317
Nigeria	Debra Henke	202-482-5149	3317
Norway	James Devlin	202-482-4414	3037

O

Oman	Paul Thanos	202-482-1860	2029B

P

Pacific Islands	Gary Bouck	202-482-4958	2036
Pakistan	Tim Gilman	202-482-2954	2308
Panama	Helen Lee	202-482-2527	3021
Paraguay	Randy Mye	202-482-1548	2039
People/China	Cheryl McQueen /Laura McCall	202-482-3583	2317
Peru	Rebecca Hunt	202-482-2521	2037
Philippines	Ed Oliver	202-482-3875	2036
Poland	EEBIC	202-482-2645	7412
Portugal	Mary Beth Double	202-482-4508	3045

Q

Qatar	Paul Thanos	202-482-1860	2029B

R

Romania	EEBIC	202-482-2645	7412
Russia	BISNIS	202-482-4655	7413
Rwanda	Philip Michelini	202-482-4388	3317

S

Sao Tome & Principe	Debra Henke	202-482-4228	3317
Saudi Arabia	Chris Cerone /Claude Clement	202-482-5545	2033
Senegal	Philip Michelini	202-482-4388	3317
Seychelles	Chandra Watkins	202-482-4564	3317
Sierra Leone	Philip Michelini	202-482-4388	3317
Singapore	Raphael Cung	202-482-4988	2036
Somalia	Chandra Watkins	202-482-4564	3317
South Africa	Emily Solomon	202-482-5148	3317
Spain	Mary Beth Double	202-482-4508	3045
Sri Lanka	John Simmons	202-482-2954	2308
St. Bartholomy	Michelle Brooks	202-482-2527	2039
St. Kitts-Nevis	Michelle Brooks	202-482-2527	2039
St. Lucia	Michelle Brooks	202-482-2527	2039
St. Martin	Michelle Brooks	202-482-2527	2039

St. Vincent Grenadines	Michelle Brooks	202-482-2527	3021
Sudan	Chandra Watkins	202-482-4564	3317
Suriname	Michelle Brooks	202-482-2527	3021
Swaziland	Finn Holm-Olsen	202-482-5148	3317
Sweden	James Devlin	202-482-4414	3037
Switzerland	Philip Combs	202-482-2920	3039
Syria	Corey Wright /Thomas Sams	202-482-2515	2039
Slovak Republic	EEBIC	202-482-2645	7413

T

Taiwan	Rbert Chu /Dan Duvall /Paul Carroll	202-482-4390	2327
Tanzania	Vacant	202-482-4228	3317
Thailand	Jean Kelly	202-482-3875	2032
Togo	Debra Henke	202-482-5149	3317
Trinidad/ Tobago	Michelle Brooks	202-482-2527	2039
Tunisia	Corey Wright /Thomas Sams	202-482-1860	2029B
Turkey	Ann Corro	202-482-3945	3042
Turks & Caicos Islands	Mark Siegelman	202-482-5680	2039

U

Uganda	Chandra Watkins	202-482-4564	3317
United Arab Emirates	Claude Clement	202-482-5545	2033
United Kingdom	Robert McLaughlin	202-482-3748	3045
Uruguay	Roger Turner	202-482-1495	3021

V

Venezuela	Laura Zieger Hatfield	202-482-4303	2037
Vietnam	Hong-Phong B. Pho	202-482-4958	2036
Virgin Islands (UK)	Michelle Brooks	202-482-2527	2039

Y

Yemen, Rep of	Paul Thanos	202-482-1860	2029B

Z

Zaire	Philip Michelini	202-482-4388	3317
Zambia	Finn Holm-Olsen	202-482-4228	3317
Zimbabwe	Finn Holm-Olsen	202-482-4228	3317

State Department Country Experts

If you need information that is primarily political, economic or cultural in nature, direct your questions first to the State Department Country Desk Officers. An operator at the number listed below can direct you to the appropriate desk officer.

U.S. Department of State
2201 C Street, NW
Washington, DC 20520
202-647-6575

Foreign Specialists
At Other Government Agencies

The following is a listing by subject area of other departments within the federal government which maintain country experts who are available to help the public:

1) **Mineral Resources:**
Bureau of Mines, U.S. Department of Interior, Division of International Minerals, 810 7th St. NW, Washington, DC 20241-0002, 202-501-9666.

2) **Foreign Agriculture:**
Foreign Agriculture Service, Agriculture and Trade Analysis Division, U.S. Department of Agriculture, Room 732, 1301 New York Ave., NW, Washington, DC 20005, 202-219-0700.

Food Safety and Inspection Service, International Programs, U.S. Dept. of Agriculture, Room 341-E, 14th and Independence Ave., SW, Washington, DC 20250-3700, 202-720-3473.

Animal and Plant Health Inspection Service, Import-Export, U.S. Department of Agriculture, 6505 Bellcrest Rd., Hyattsville, MD 20782, 301-436-8590.

Food Transportation, International Transportation Branch, U.S. Department of Agriculture, Room 1217 South Building, Washington, DC 20250, 202-690-1320.

3) **Energy Resources:**
Office of Export Assistance, U.S. Department of Energy, 1000 Independence Ave., SW, Washington, DC 20585, 202-586-7997.

Office of Fossil Energy, U.S. Dept. of Energy, 1000 Independence Ave., SW, Washington, DC 20585, 202-586-7297.

4) **Economic Assistance to Foreign Countries:**
Business Office, U.S. Agency for International Development, 320 21st St. NW, Washington, DC 20523, 703-875-1551.

5) **Information Programs and Cultural Exchange:**
U.S. Information Agency, 301 4th St. SW, Washington, DC 20547, 202-619-4700.

6) **Seafood Certificates:**
Inspection Certificates for Seafood Exports, National Oceanic and Atmospheric Administration, 1315 East-West Highway, Room 12554, Silver Spring, MD 20910, 301-713-2355.

7) **Metric:**
Office of Metric Programs, National Institute of Standards and Technology, Building 411, Room A146, Gaithersburg, MD 20899, 301-975-3690.

8) **Telecommunications Information:**
Bureau of International Communications and Information Policy, U.S. Department of State, Washington, DC 20520, 202-647-5231.

9) **Fisheries:**
Office of Trade and Industry Services, Fisheries Promotion and Trade Matters, National Marine Fisheries Service, 1315 East-West Highway, Silver Spring, MD 20910, 301-713-2379.

Fax Directory of
Overseas Commercial Counselors

You can just say, "FAX IT", if you are looking for a market study, a client or any other piece of information in a given country and want the information as quickly as possible. Listed below are the fax numbers of the commercial officers who work at U.S. Embassies around the world. These officers are available to assist U.S. businesses succeed in selling their products overseas.

Algeria:
Algiers — 011-213-2-69-18-63
Argentina:
Buenos Aires — 011-54-1777-0673
Australia:
Sydney — 011-61-2-221-0576
Brisbane — 011-61-7-832-6247
Melbourne — 011-61-3-510-4660
Perth — 011-61-9-231-9444
Austria:
Vienna — 011-43-1310-6917
Barbados:
Bridgetown — 1-809-431-0179
Belgium:
Brussels (Emb) — 011-32-2-512-6653
Brussels (EC) — 011-32-2-513-1228
Antwerp — 011-32-03-542-6567
Brazil:
Brasilia — 011-55-61-225-9136
Belo Horizonte — 011-55-31-335-3054
Rio de Janeiro — 011-55-21-240-9738
Sao Paulo — 011-55-11-853-2744
Cameroon:
Yaounde — 011-237-23-07-53
Canada:
Ottawa — 1-613-233-8511
Calgary — 1-403-264-6630
Halifax — 1-902-423-6861
Montreal — 1-514-398-0711
Toronto — 1-416-595-5466
Vancouver — 1-604-687-6095
China:
Beijing — 011-86-1-532-3297
Guangzhou — 011-86-20-666-6409
Shanghai — 011-86-21-433-1576
Shenyang — 011-86-24-282-0074
Columbia:
Bogata — 011-57-1-285-7945
Costa Rica:
San Jose — 011-506-231-4783
Cote D'Ivoire:
Abidjan — 011-225-22-32-59
African Dev Bk — 011-225-22-2437
Czech Republic:
Prague — 011-42-2-2421-4465
Denmark:
Copenhagen — 011-45-31-42-01-75
Dominican Republic:
Santo Domingo — 1-809-688-4838
Ecuador:
Quito — 011-593-2-504-550
Guayaquil — 011-593-4-324-558

Be patient. If any phone number is incorrect, call (area code) 555-1212 and request the new listing.

837

Selling Overseas

Egypt:		**Malaysia:**	
Cairo	011-20-2-355-8368	Kuala Lumpur	011-60-3-242-1866
Finland:		**Mexico:**	
Helsinki	011-358-0-635-332	Mexico City	011-52-5-207-8938
France:		Mexico City	
Paris(EMB)	011-33-1-4266-4827	(Trade Center)	011-52-5-566-1115
Paris (ORCD)	011-33-1-4524-7410	Guadalajara	011-52-36-26-6549
Bordeaux	011-33-56-51-60-42	Monterrey	011-52-83-45-7748
Lyon	011-33-1-4266-4827	**Morocco:**	
Marseille	011-33-91-550-947	Casablanca	011-212-22-02-59
Nice	011-33-16-9387-0738	Rabat	011-212-7-656-51
Strasbourg	011-33-88-24-0695	**Netherlands:**	
Germany:		The Hague	011-31-70-363-29-85
Bonn	011-49-228-334-649	Amsterdam	011-31-20-5755-350
Berlin	011-49-30-238-6290	**Nigeria:**	
Dusseldorf	011-49-211-594-897	Lagos	011-234-1-261-9856
Frankfurt	011-49-69-748-204	**Norway:**	
Hamburg	011-49-40-410-6598	Oslo	011-47-2243-07-77
Munich	011-49-89-285-261	**Pakistan:**	
Stuttgart	011-49-711-236-4350	Karachi	011-92-21-568-3089
Greece:		**Panama:**	
Athens	011-30-1-721-8660	Panama	011-507-27-1713
Guatemala:		**Peru:**	
Guatemala	011-502-2-317-373	Lima	011-51-14-33-4887
Honduras:		**Philippines:**	
Teguicigalpa	011-504-38-2888	Manila	011-63-2-818-2684
Hong Kong:		Asian Dev Bank	011-63-2-632-4003
Hong Kong	011-852-845-9800	**Poland:**	
Hungary:		Warsaw	011-48-22-21-63-27
Budapest	011-36-1-142-2529	**Portugal:**	
India:		Lisbon	011-351-1-726-9109
New Delhi	011-91-11-687-2391	Oporto	011-351-2-600-2737
Bombay	011-91-22-262-3850	**Romania:**	
Calcutta	011-91-33-242-2335	Bucharest	011-40-1610-5316
Madras	011-91-44-825-0240	**Russia:**	
Indonesia:		Moscow	011-7-095-230-2101
Jakarta	011-62-21-385-1632	**Saudi Arabia:**	
Medan	011-62-61-518-711	Riyadh	011-966-1-488-3237
Surabaya	011-62-31-574-492	Dhahran	011-966-3-891-8332
Iraq:		Jeddah	011-966-2-665-8106
Baghdad	011-964-1-718-9297	**Singapore:**	
Ireland:		Singapore	011-65-338-4550
Dublin	011-353-1-682-840	**South Africa:**	
Israel:		Johannesburg	011-27-11-331-6178
Tel Aviv	011-972-3-663-449	Cape Town	011-27-21-254-151
Italy:		**Spain:**	
Rome	011-39-6-4674-2113	Madrid	011-34-1-575-8655
Florence	011-39-55-283-780	Barcelona	011-34-3-205-7705
Milan	011-39-2-481-4161	**Sweden:**	
Naples	011-39-81-761-1869	Stockholm	011-46-8-661-1964
Jamaica:		**Switzerland:**	
Kingston	1-809-926-6743	Bern	011-41-31-357-7336
Japan:		Geneva(GATT)	011-41-22-749-4885
Tokyo	011-81-3-589-4235	Zurich	011-41-1-382-2655
Tokyo (TradeCtr)	011-81-3-987-2447	**Taiwan:**	
Fukuoka	011-81-9-271-3922	Taipei	011-886-2-757-7162
Osaka-Kobe	011-81-6-361-5978	Kaohsiung	011-886-7-223-8237
Sapporo	011-81-11-643-0911	**Thailand:**	
Kenya:		Bangkok	011-66-2-255-2915
Nairobi	011-254-2-216-648	**Trinidad & Tobago:**	
Korea:		Port-of-Spain	1-809-628-5462
Seoul	011-82-2-738-8845	**Turkey:**	
Kuwait:		Ankara	011-90-312-467-1366
Kuwait	011-965-244-2855		

838   *Be patient. If any phone number is incorrect, call (area code) 555-1212 and request the new listing.*

Istanbul	011-90-212-252-2417
United Arab Emirates:	
Adu Dhabi	011-971-2-331-374
Dubai	011-971-4-313-131
United Kingdom:	
London	011-44-71-491-4022
U.S.S.R.:	
Moscow	011-7-095-230-2101
Venezuela:	
Caracas	011-58-2-285-0336
Yugoslavia:	
Belgrade	011-38-11-645-096
Zagreb	011-38-41-440-235

Money for Selling Overseas

1) State Government Money Programs:

Some state government economic development programs offer special help for those who need financial assistance in selling overseas. See the section presented later in this chapter entitled *State Government Assistance To Exporters.*

2) Export-Import Bank Financing:

The Export-Import Bank facilitates and aids in the financing of exports of United States goods and services. Its programs include short-term, medium-term, and long-term credits, small business support, financial guarantees, and insurance. In addition, it sponsors conferences on small business exporting, maintains credit information on thousands of foreign firms, supports feasibility studies of overseas programs, and offers export and small business finance counseling. To receive *Marketing News* Fact Sheets, or the *Eximbank Export Credit Insurance* booklet, or the Eximbank's *Program Selection Guide,* contact: Export-Import Bank, 811 Vermont Ave. NW, Washington, DC 20571, 202-565-3901, 1-800-565-EXIM.

3) Small Business Administration (SBA) Export Loans:

This agency makes loans and loan guarantees to small business concerns as well as to small business investment companies, including those which sell overseas. It also offers technical assistance, counseling, training, management assistance, and information resources, including some excellent publications to small and minority businesses in export operations. Contact your local or regional SBA office listed in the blue pages of your telephone book under Small Business Administration, or Small Business Administration, Office of International Trade, 409 3rd St., SW, Washington, DC 20416, 202-205-6720.

4) Overseas Private Investment Corporation (OPIC):

This agency provides marketing, insurance, and financial assistance to American companies investing in 118 countries and 16 geographic regions. Its programs include direct loans, loan guarantees, and political risk insurance. OPIC also sponsors seminars for investment executives as well as conducts investment missions to developing countries. The Investor Services Division offers a computer service to assist investors in identifying investment opportunities worldwide. A modest fee is charged for this service and it is also available through the Lexis/Nexis computer network. Specific Info-Kits are available identifying basic economic, business, and political information for each of the countries covered. In addition, it operates:

Program Information Hotline
Overseas Private Investment Corporation
1100 New York Ave., NW
Washington, DC 20527
202-336-8799 (Hotline)
202-336-8400 (General Information)
202-457-7128 (Investor Services Division)
202-336-8636 (Public Affairs)
202-336-8680 (Press Information)
202-408-5155 (Fax)

5) Agency for International Development (AID):

AID offers a variety of loan and financing guarantee programs for projects in developing countries that have a substantial developmental impact or for the exportation of manufactured goods to AID-assisted developing countries. Some investment opportunities are region specific, which include the Association of Southeast Asian National, the Philippines, and Africa. For more information contact the Office of Investment, Agency for International Development, 515 22nd St. NW, Room 301, Washington, DC 20523-0231, 202-663-2280.

6) Grants to Train Local Personnel

The Trade and Development Agency has the authority to offer grants in support of short-listed companies on a transaction specific basis. These are usually in the form of grants to cover the cost of training local personnel by the company on the installation, operation, and maintenance of equipment specific to bid the proposal. Contact: Carol Stillwell, 703-875-4357; Fax: 703-875-4009.

7) Consortia of American Businesses in Eastern Europe (CABEE):

CABEE provides grant funds to trade organizations to defray the costs of opening, staffing, and operating U.S. consortia offices in Eastern Europe. The CABEE grant program initially began operations in Poland, the Czech Republic, Slovikia, and Hungary, targeting five industry sectors: agribusiness/agriculture, construction/housing, energy, environment, and telecommunications. Contact: CABEE, Department of Commerce, 14th and Constitution Avenue, Washington, DC 20230, 202-482-5004.

8) Consortia of American Businesses in the Newly Independent States (CABNIS):

This program was modeled after CABEE and stimulates U.S. business in the Newly Independent States (NIS) and assist the region in its move toward privatization. CABNIS is providing grant funds to nonprofit organizations to defray the costs of opening, staffing, and operating U.S. consortia offices in the NIS. Contact: CABNIS, Department of Commerce, 14th and Constitution Avenue, Washington, DC 20230, 202-482-5004.

Marketing Data, Custom Studies, and Company Information

Further information on any of the following services and products can be obtained by contacting a U.S. Department of Commerce/ US & FCS field office listed later in this chapter, or by contacting the US & FCS at: United States and Foreign Commercial Services, U.S. Department of Commerce, Room 3810, HCH Building, 14th and Constitution Ave., NW, Washington, DC 20230, 202-482-4767 or call 1-800-USA-TRADE.

Be patient. If any phone number is incorrect, call (area code) 555-1212 and request the new listing.

839

Selling Overseas

1) International Industry Experts:
A separate Office of Trade Development at the Commerce Department handles special marketing and company problems for specific industries. Experts are available in the following international market sectors:

Aerospace:	202-482-2835
Automotive and Consumer Goods:	202-482-0823
Basic Industries:	202-482-5023
Capital Goods and International Construction:	202-482-5023
Science and Electronics:	202-482-3548
Telecommunications:	202-482-4466
Service:	202-482-5261
Textiles and Apparel:	202-482-3737

You can also talk to industry desk officers at the Department of Commerce. They can provide information on the competitive strengths of U.S. industries in foreign markets from abrasives to yogurt. They are listed in the "Experts" section at the end of this book and have "COMMERCE" after their name. You can call the Department of Commerce at 202-482-2000 (main office) or 1-800-872-8723 (trade information) to locate specific industry analysts.

2) Trade Lists:
Directories of overseas customers for U.S. exports in selected industries and countries: They contain the names and product lines of foreign distributors, agents, manufacturers, wholesalers, retailers, and other purchasers. They also provide the name and title of key officials as well as telex and cable numbers, and company size data. Prices range up to $40 for a list of a category.

3) Country Trade Statistics:
The Export and Import Trade Database maintains worldwide export and import statistics tracked by mode of transportation and port of entry or exit. Customized tabulation and reports can be prepared to user specifications. Prices begin at $25 and vary depending on job size. Contact: Trade Data Services Branch at 301-457-2311.

4) Demographic and Social Information:
The Center for International Research compiles and maintains up to date global demographic and social information for all countries in its International Data Base (IDB). Printed tables are available on selected subjects for selected countries can be purchased for a minimum of $75. Contact: Systems Analysis and Programming Staff, 301-457-1403.

5) Customized Export Mailing Lists:
Selected lists of foreign companies in particular industries, countries, and types of business can be requested by a client. Gummed labels are also available. Prices start at $35.

6) World Traders Data Reports:
Background reports are available on individual firms containing information about each firm's business activities, its standing in the local business community, its creditworthiness, and overall reliability and suitability as a trade contact for exporters. The price is $100 per report.

7) Agent Distributor Service (ADS):
This is a customized search for interested and qualified foreign representatives on behalf of an American client. U.S. commercial officers overseas conduct the search and prepare a report identifying up to six foreign prospects which have personally examined the U.S. firm's product literature and have expressed interest in representing the firm. A fee of $250 per country is charged.

8) New Product Information Service:
This service is designed to help American companies publicize the availability of new U.S. products in foreign markets and simultaneously test market interest in these products. Product information which meets the criteria is distributed worldwide through Commercial News USA and Voice of America broadcasts. A fee is charged for participation.

9) Customized Market Studies:
At a cost of $800 to $13,500 per country per product, these studies are called "Comparison Shopping Service". They are conducted by the U.S. Embassy foreign commercial attaches and can target information on quite specific marketing questions such as:

- Does the product have sales potential in the country?
- Who is the supplier for a comparable product locally?
- What is the going price for a comparable product in this country?
- What is the usual sales channel for getting this type of product into the market?
- What are the competitive factors that most influence purchases of these products in the market (i.e., price, credit, quality, delivery, service, promotion, brand)?
- What is the best way to get sales exposure in the market for this type of product?
- Are there any significant impediments to selling this type of product?
- Who might be interested and qualified to represent or purchase this company's products?
- If a licensing or joint venture strategy seems desirable for this market, who might be an interested and qualified partner for the U.S. company?

10) Special Opportunities in the Caribbean Basin and Latin America:
Under the Caribbean Economic Recovery Act of 1983, the government has established special incentives for American firms wishing to do business with Latin American and Caribbean Basin companies. Seminars, workshops, business development missions, business counseling, as well as marketing and competitive information are available.

Latin America/Caribbean Business Development Center
U.S. Department of Commerce
Washington, DC 20230
202-482-0841
Fax: 202-482-2218

11) New Markets in Eastern European Countries
The Eastern Europe Business Information Center is stocked with a wide range of publications on doing business in Eastern Europe. These include lists of potential partners, investment regulations, priority industry sectors, and notices of upcoming seminars, conferences, and trade promotion events. The center also serves as a referral point for programs of voluntary assistance to the region.

Eastern Europe Business Information Center
U.S. Department of Commerce
Washington, DC 20230
202-482-2645
Fax: 202-482-4473

12) Exporting to Japan: Japan Export Information Center (JEIC)

The Japan Export Information Center (JEIC) provides business counseling services and accurate information on exporting to Japan. The JEIC is the point of contact for information on business in Japan, market entry alternatives, market information and research, product standards and testing, tariffs, and non-tariff barriers. The center maintains a commercial library and participates in seminars on various aspects of Japanese business. Contact: Japan Export Information Center, (202) 482-2425; Fax: (202) 482-0469.

13) Office of Export Trading Company Affairs

The Office of Export Trading Company offers various information as well as promoting the use of export trading companies and export management companies; offers information and counseling to businesses and trading associations regarding the export industry; and administers the Export Trade Certificate of Review program which provides exporters with an antitrust "insurance policy" intended to foster joint export activities where economies of scale and risk diversification are achieved. Contact: Office of Export Trading Company Affairs, 202-482-5131; Fax: 202-482-1790.

14) U.S.-Asia Environmental Partnership

US-AEP is a comprehensive service to help U.S. environmental exporters enter markets in the Asia/Pacific region. It is a coalition of public, private and non-governmental organizations which promotes environmental protection and sustainable development in 34 nations in the Asia/Pacific area. Contact: 1-800-USA-TRADE or 202-482-0543; Fax: 202-482-4473.

15) Business Information Service for the Newly Independent States (BISNIS)

BISNIS provides "one stop shopping" for U.S. firms interested in doing business in the Newly Independent States (NIS) of the former Soviet Union. Information is available on commercial opportunities in the NIS, sources of financing, up to date lists of trade contacts as well as on U.S. Government programs supporting trade and investment in the region. BISNIS publishes a monthly bulletin with information on upcoming trade promotion events, practical advice on doing business with NIS and other topics. Contact: BISNIS, 202-482-4655; Fax: 202-482-2293.

16) Technical Assistance with Transportation Concerns

The Department of Transportation provides technical assistance to developing countries on a wide range of problems in the areas of transportation policy, highways, aviation, rail and ports. It also supports AID in the foreign aid development program. Contact: Bernestine Allen, International Transportation and Trade, 202-366-4398; Fax: 202-366-7417; Herbert Baschner, Federal Aviation Administration, 202-267-3173; Fax: 202-267-5306; John Cutrell, Federal Highway Administration, 202-366-0111; Fax: 202-366-9626; Ted Krohn, Federal Railroad Administration, 202-366-0555; Fax: 202-366-7688; James Treichel, Maritime Administration, 202-366-5773; Fax: 202-366-3746.

17) "Doing Business"

The "Doing Business" television program is a half-hour long monthly televised business program sent by satellite to more than 100 countries highlighting innovation and excellence in U.S. business. The program consists of segments on new products, services, and processes of interest to overseas buyers and promising research. Contact: Paul Vamvas, Worldnet Television, 202-501-8450; Fax: 202-501-6689.

18) Japan's Official Development Assistance Program:

This program is the central source for information about how to access procurement through Japan's foreign aid program. Contact: Robert Lurensky, Office of Energy, Environment and Infrastructure, 202-482-4002, Fax: 202-482-0136; Elizabeth Johns, Office of Japan Trade Policy, 202-482-1820; Fax: 202-482-0469.

19) Environmental Technology Network for Asia (ETNA):

ETNA matches environmental trade leads sent from U.S.-Asia Environmental Partnership (USAEP) Technology Representatives located in 9 Asian countries with appropriate U.S. environmental firms and trade associations that are registered with ETNA's environmental trade opportunities database. U.S. environmental firms receive the trade leads by Broadcast Fax system within 48 hours of leads being identified and entered electronically from Asia. Contact: 202-663-2674; Fax: 202-663-2760.

20) Automated Trade Locator Assistance System:

The SBAtlas is a market research tool which provides free of charge two types of reports: product- specific and country-specific. The product report ranks the top 35 import and export market for a particular good or service. The country report identifies the top 20 products most frequently traded in a target market. Contact: SBAtlas is available through SBA district offices, Service Corps of Retired Executives (SCORE) office, and Small Business Development Centers, to get the address and phone number to the nearest office call 1-800-U-ASK-SBA.

21) Export Contact List Service (ECLS):

This database retrieval service provides U.S. exporters with names, addresses, products, sizes and other relevant information on foreign firms interested in importing U.S. goods and services. Similar information is also available on U.S. exporters to foreign firms seeking suppliers from the U.S. Names are collected and maintained by Commerce district offices and commercial officers at foreign posts. Contact your nearest district Commerce office located in this book or call 1-800-USA-TRADE.

Trade Fairs and Missions

Trade fairs, exhibitions, trade missions, overseas trade seminars, and other promotional events and services are sponsored by the Export Promotion Services Group, U.S. and Foreign Commercial Services, U.S. Department of Commerce, 14th and E Streets, NW, Room 2810, Washington, DC 20230, 202-482-6220. This office or one of its field offices which are listed later in this chapter can provide additional details on these activities.

1) Industry-Organized, Government-Approved Trade Missions:

Such missions are organized by trade associations, local Chambers of Commerce, state trade development agencies, and similar trade-oriented groups that enjoy U.S. Department of Commerce support.

Be patient. If any phone number is incorrect, call (area code) 555-1212 and request the new listing.

841

2) Catalog Exhibitions:
Such exhibitions feature displays of U.S. product catalogs, sales brochures, and other graphic sales materials at American embassies and consulates or in conjunction with trade shows. A Department of Commerce specialist assists in the exhibition. Call 202-482-3973; Fax: 202-482-2716.

3) Video Catalog:
This catalog is designed to showcase American products via video tape presentation. This permits actual product demonstrations giving the foreign buyer an opportunity to view applications of American products. Federal specialists participate in these sessions. Call 202-482-3973; Fax: 202-482-0115.

4) U.S. Specialized Trade Missions:
These missions are distinct from those mentioned above since the U.S. Department of Commerce plans the visits and accompanies the delegation. They are designed to sell American goods and services as well as establish agents or representation abroad. The Department of Commerce provides marketing information, advanced planning, publicity, and trip organization. Call 1-800-USA-TRADE.

5) U.S. Seminar Missions:
The objective here is to promote exports and help foreign representation for American exporters. However, unlike trade missions, these are designed to facilitate the sales of state-of-the-art products and technology. This type of mission is a one to two day "seminar" during which team members discuss technology subjects followed by private, sales-oriented appointments. Call 1-800-USA-TRADE.

6) Matchmaker Trade Delegations:
These Department of Commerce-recruited and planned missions are designed to introduce new-to-export or new-to-market businesses to prospective agents and distributors overseas. Trade Specialists from Commerce evaluate the potential firm's products, find and screen contacts, and handle logistics. This is followed by an intensive trip filled with meetings and prospective clients and in-depth briefings on the economic and business climate of the countries visited. Call Office of Export Promotion Services, 202-482-3119; Fax: 202-482-0178.

7) Investment Missions:
These events are held in developing countries offering excellent investment opportunities for U.S. firms. Missions introduce U.S. business executives to key business leaders, potential joint venture partners, and senior foreign government officials in the host country. Call Investment Missions, 202-336-8799; Fax: 202-408-5155.

8) Foreign Buyer Program:
This program supports major domestic trade shows featuring products and services of U.S. industries with high export potential. Government officials recruit on a worldwide basis qualified buyers to attend the shows. Call Export Promotion Services, 202-482-0481; Fax: 202-482-0115.

9) Trade Fairs, Solo Exhibitions, and Trade Center Shows:
The Department of Commerce organizes a wide variety of special exhibitions. These events range from solo exhibitions representing U.S. firms exclusively at trade centers overseas to U.S. pavilions in the largest international exhibitions. Call 1-800-USA-TRADE.

10) Agent/Distributor Service (ADS):
Looking for overseas representatives to expand your business and boost your export sales? Commerce will locate, screen, and assess agents, distributors, representatives, and other foreign partners for your business. Call 1-800-USA-TRADE.

11) Trade Opportunities Program (TOP):
The Trade Opportunities Program (TOP) provides companies with current sales leads from international firms seeking to buy or represent their products or services. TOP leads are printed daily in leading commercial newspapers and are also distributed electronically via the U.S. Department of Commerce Economic Bulletin Board. Call 202-482-1986; Fax: 202-482-2164.

12) Travel and Tourism:
The U.S. Travel and Tourism Administration (USTTA) promotes export earnings through trade in tourism. USTTA stimulates demand for travel to the United States; encourages and facilitates promotion in international travel markets by U.S. travel industry concerns; works to increase the number of new-to-market travel businesses participating in the export market; forms cooperative marketing opportunities for private industry and regional, state, and local government; provides timely data; and helps to remove government-imposed travel barriers. Call 202-482-4904, 202-482-4752; Fax: 202-482-2887.

13) Gold Key Service:
This customized service is aimed at U.S. firms which are planning to visit a country. Offered by many overseas posts, it combines several services such as market orientation briefings, market research, introductions to potential partners, and interpreters for meetings, assistance in developing a sound market strategy, and an effective followup plan. Call 1-800-USA-TRADE.

Special Programs for Agricultural Products

The following programs are specifically aimed at those who wish to sell agricultural products overseas. Agricultural exporters should also be sure not to limit themselves only to programs under this heading. Programs listed under other headings can also be used for agricultural products.

1) Office Space for Agricultural Exporters:
The Foreign Agriculture Service (FAS) maintains overseas agricultural trade offices to help exporters of U.S. farm and forest products in key overseas markets. The facilities vary depending on local conditions, but may include a trade library, conference rooms, office space, and kitchens for preparing product samples. Contact: Foreign Agriculture Service, U.S. Department of Agriculture, 14th and Independence Ave. SW, Washington, DC 20250, 202-720-9509; Fax: 202-690-4374.

2) Research Services:
The Agricultural Research Service provides exporters with information, research, and consultants on a wide array of topics including shipping, storage, insect control, pesticide residues, and market disorders. Contact: Agricultural and Trade Analysis Division, U.S. Department of Agriculture, 14th and Independence Avenue, SW, Washington, DC 20250, 202-219-0700; Fax: 202-219-0759.

3) Foreign Market Information:

A special office serves as a single contact point within the Foreign Agriculture Service for agricultural exporters seeking foreign market information. The office also counsels firms which believe they have been injured by unfair trade practices. Contact: Trade Assistance and Promotion Office, U.S. Department of Agriculture, 14th and Independence Avenue, SW, Washington, DC 20250, 202-720-7420; Fax: 202-720-3229.

4) Export Connections:

The AgExport Action Kit provides information which can help put U.S. exporters in touch quickly and directly with foreign importers of food and agricultural products. The services include trade leads, a *Buyer Alert* newsletter, foreign buyer lists, and U.S. supplier lists. All services are free. Contact: AgExport Connections, U.S. Department of Agriculture, Washington, DC 20250, 202-720-7103; Fax: 202-690-4374.

5) Country Market Profiles:

Country-specific two to four page descriptions are available for 40 overseas markets for high value agricultural products. They provide market overview, market trends, and information on the U.S. market position, the competition, and general labeling and licensing requirements. Contact: Country Market Profiles, FAS Information Division, U.S. Department of Agriculture, Washington, DC 20250, 202-720-7420; Fax: 202-720-3229.

Export Regulations, Licensing, and Product Standards

Talk to ELVIS — Bureau of Export Administration (BXA)

BXA is responsible for controlling exports for reasons of national security, foreign policy, and short supply. Licenses on controlled exports are issued, and seminars on U.S. export regulations are held domestically and overseas.

Export license applications may be submitted and issued through computer via the Export License Application and Information Network (ELAIN). The System for Tracking Export License Application (STELA) provides instant status updates on license applications by the use of a touch-tone phone.

The Export Licensing Voice Information (ELVIS) is an automated attendant that offers a range of licensing information and emergency handling procedures. Callers may order forms and publications or subscribe to the *Office of Export Licensing (OEL) Insider Newsletter*, which provides regulatory updates. While using ELVIS, a caller has the option of speaking to a consultant.

Office of Export Licensing	202-482-4811
	Fax: 202-482-3322
ELAIN	202-482-4811
STELA	202-482-2752
ELVIS	202-482-4811

The National Institute of Standards and Technology provides a free service which will identify standards for selling any product to any country in the world. This federal agency will tell you what the standard is for a given product or suggest where you can obtain an official copy of the standard.

National Center for Standards and Certification
National Institute of Standards and Technology
Building 411, Room A163
Gaithersburg, MD 20899   301-975-4040

Cheap Office and Conference Space Overseas

If you are travelling overseas on a business trip, you may want to look into renting office space and other services through the American Embassy. Depending on the country and the space available, the embassy can provide temporary office space for as low as $25 per day, along with translation services, printing, and other services. Meeting rooms, seminar or convention space along with promotion services, mailings, freight handling, and even catering may be available in many countries. Contact the Department of Commerce/US & FCS field office which is listed later in this chapter, or the appropriate country desk officer at the U.S. Department of Commerce in Washington, DC.

Other Services, Resources, and Databases

The following is a description of some of the additional services and information sources that can be useful to anyone investigating overseas markets:

1) World Import/Export Statistics:

For the latest information on any product imported to or exported from any foreign country, contact: Foreign and U.S. Trade Reference Room, U.S. Department of Commerce, Room 2233, Washington, DC 20230, 202-482-4855.

2) Help in Selling to Developing Nations:

The U.S. Agency For International Development (AID) provides information to U.S. suppliers, particularly small, independent enterprises, regarding purchases to be financed with AID funds. U.S. small businesses can obtain special counseling and related services in order to furnish equipment, materials, and services to AID-financed projects. AID sponsors Development Technologies Exhibitions, where technical firms in the U.S. are matched up with those in lesser developed countries for the purpose of forming joint ventures or exploring licensing possibilities. AID provides loans and grants to finance consulting services that support project activities related to areas such as agriculture, rural development, health, and housing. Contact: Office of Business Relations, U.S. Agency for International Development, State Annex 14, Room 1200A, 320 21st St., NW, Washington, DC 20523, 703-875-1551.

3) Foreign Demographic Profiles:

The Government Printing office has a publication called the CIA *World Factbook*. Produced annually, this publication provides country-by-country data on demographics, economy, communications, and defense. The cost is $29 (GPO: 041-015-00173-6). Order by contacting Superintendent of Documents, Government Printing Office, Washington, DC 20402; 202-512-1800.

4) Help With Selling Commodities Abroad:

The Foreign Agricultural Service is charged with maintaining and expanding export sales of U.S. agricultural commodities and products. Staff can provide information on foreign agricultural production, trade and consumption, marketing research including areas of demand for specific commodities in foreign countries, and analyses of foreign competition in agricultural areas. Other services include financing opportunities, contributing to export promotion costs, and testing market assistance. This office also handles U.S. representation to foreign governments and participates in formal trade negotiations. Contact: Foreign Agricultural Service, U.S. Department of Agriculture, 14th and Independence Ave., S.W., Room 4647, South Building, Washington, DC 20250, 202-720-7420.

5) International Prices:

Export price indexes for both detailed and aggregate product groups are available on a monthly basis. Price trends comparisons of U.S. exports with those of Japan and Germany are also available. Contact: International Prices Division, Bureau of Labor Statistics, U.S. Department of Labor, 2nd Massachusetts Ave., NE, Room 3955, Washington, DC 20212, 202-606-7100.

6) Identifying Overseas Opportunities:

The International Trade Administration (ITA) of the Commerce Department assists American exporters in locating and gaining access to foreign markets. It furnishes information on overseas markets available for U.S. products and services, requirements which must be fulfilled, economic conditions in foreign countries, foreign market and investment opportunities, etc. Operations are divided into four major areas:

- **International Economic Policy:** promotes U.S. exports geographically by helping American businesses market products in various locations abroad and by solving the trade and investment problems they encounter. This office is staffed by Country Desk Officers knowledgeable in marketing and business practices for almost every country in the world. Contact: Office of International Economic Policy, ITA, U.S. Department of Commerce, Washington, DC 20230, 202-482-3022.

- **Export Administration:** supervises the enforcement provisions of the Export Administration Act, and administers the Foreign Trade Zone Program. Personnel in its export enforcement and its administration, policy, and regulations offices can offer technical advice and legal interpretations of the various export legislation which affect American businesses. Assistance in complying with export controls can be obtained directly from the Exporter Counseling Division within the Bureau of Export Administration (BXA) Office of Export Licensing in Washington, DC, 202-482-4811.

  BXA also has four field offices that specialize in counseling on export controls and regulations:

Western Regional Office	714-660-0144
Northern California	
Branch Office	408-748-7450
Southern Branch Office	714-660-0144
New England Office	603-598-4300

- **Trade Development:** advises businesses on trade and investment issues, and promotes U.S. exports by industry or product classifications. Offices offer assistance and information on export counseling, statistics and trade data, licensing, trading companies, and other services. Contact: Office of Trade Development, ITA, U.S. Department of Commerce, Washington, DC 20230, 202-482-1461; Fax: 202-482-5697.

- **U.S. and Foreign Commercial Service:** provides information on government programs to American businesses, and uncovers trade opportunities for U.S. exporters. They also locate representatives and agents for American firms, assist U.S. executives in all phases of their exporting, and help enforce export controls and regulations. They operate through 47 district offices located in major U.S. cities and in 124 posts in 69 foreign countries. In addition, a valued asset of the U.S. and Foreign Commercial Services is a group of about 525 foreign nationals, usually natives of the foreign country, who are employed in the U.S. embassy or consulate and bring with them a wealth of personal understanding of local market conditions and business practices. U.S. exporters usually tap into these services by contacting the Department of Commerce/US & FCS field office in their state (listed later in this chapter), or Office of U.S. and Foreign Commercial Service, U.S. Department of Commerce, Washington, DC 20230; 1-800-USA-TRADE.

Or contact regional directors at:

Africa, Near East and Southeast Asia	202-482-4925
East Asia and Pacific	202-482-5251
Europe	202-482-5638
Western Hemisphere	202-482-5324
Japan	202-482-4527
FAX (Europe and Western Hemisphere)	202-482-3159
FAX (All others)	202-482-5179

7) Latest News on Foreign Opportunities:

In addition to technical reports on foreign research and development, National Technical Information Service sells foreign market airgrams and foreign press and radio translations. A free video is available explaining NTIS services. Contact: National Technical Information Service, U.S. Department of Commerce, 5285 Port Royal Rd., Springfield, VA 22161, 703-487-4650.

8) Planning Services for U.S. Exporters:

In its effort to promote economic development in Third World countries, the Trade and Development Program finances planning services for development projects leading to the export of U.S. goods and services. A free pamphlet is available that describes the planning services offered by the Trade and Development Program. To obtain a copy, contact: U.S. Trade and Development Program, Department of State, Room 309 SA-16, Washington, DC 20523-1602, 703-875-4357.

9) Terrorism Abroad:

Assistance is available to companies doing business abroad to assess current security conditions and risk in certain cities and countries which may pose a threat. Contact: Overseas Security Advisory Council (OSAC), U.S. Department of State, Washington, DC 20522-1003, 202-663-0533.

10) Trade Remedy Assistance Center:

The Center provides information on remedies available under the Trade Remedy Law. It also offers technical assistance to eligible small businesses to enable them to bring cases to the International Trade Commission. Contact: ITC Trade Remedy Assistance Center, U.S. International Trade Commission, 500 E St. SW, Washington, DC 20436, 202-205-2200.

11) International Expertise:
Staff in the following offices will prove helpful as information sources regarding the international scope of their respective subject areas:

Economics:
International Investment, Bureau of Economic Analysis, U.S. Department of Commerce, 1441 L St., NW, Washington, DC 20230, 202-606-9800.

Productivity and Technology Statistics:
Bureau of Labor Statistics, U.S. Department of Labor, 2 Massachusetts Ave., NE, #2150, Washington, DC 20212, 202-606-5600.

Investments and Other Monetary Matters:
Office of Assistant Secretary for International Affairs, U.S. Department of the Treasury, Room 3430, Washington, DC 20220, 202-622-0060.

European Lifestyles:
European Community Information Service, 2100 M St. NW, 7th Floor, Washington, DC 20037, 202-862-9500.

Population:
Barbara Boyle Torrey, Chief, Center for International Research, Bureau of Census, U.S. Department of Commerce, Room 205, Washington Plaza, Washington, DC 20233, 301-457-1403.

Population Reference Bureau, Inc., 1875 Connecticut Ave., NW, #520, Washington, DC 20009, 202-483-1100.

Country Development:
Inter-American Development Bank, 1300 NY Ave., NW, Washington, DC 20577, 202-623-1000.

International Monetary Fund, 700 19th St. NW, Washington, DC 20431, 202-623-7000.

World Bank, 1818 H St. NW, Washington, DC 20433, 202-477-1234.

12) National Trade Data Bank (NTDB):
This is a "one-stop" source for export promotion and international trade data collected by 17 U.S. government agencies. Updated each month and released on CD-ROM, the Data Bank enables a user with an IBM-compatible personal computer equipped with a CD-ROM reader to access over 100,00 trade documents. It contains the latest Census data on U.S. imports and exports by commodity and country; the complete Central Intelligence Agency (CIA) *World Factbook*; current market research reports compiled by the U.S. and Foreign and Commercial Service; the complete Foreign Traders Index which has over 60,000 names and addresses of individuals and firms abroad interested in importing U.S. products; and many other data services. It is available for free at over 900 Federal Depository Libraries and can be purchased for $35 per disc or $360 for a 12-month subscription. Contact: Economics and Statistics Administration, U.S. Department of Commerce, Washington, DC 20230, 202-482-1986; Fax: 202-482-2164.

13) Global Demographics:
The Center for International Research at the Department of Commerce compiles and maintains up-to-date global demographic and social information for all countries in its International Data Base, which is accessible to U.S. companies seeking to identify potential markets overseas. Contact Systems Analysis and Programming Staff, 301-457-1403.

14) International Energy Database:
The Office of Fossil Energy forwards prospective energy-related leads to the Agency for International Development (AID) for inclusion in its growing trade opportunities database in an effort to reach an extended audience seeking energy-related trade opportunities. For more information on the Fossil Energy-AID Database contact: The Office of Fossil Energy, U.S. Department of Energy, 1000 Independence Ave. SW, Washington, DC 20585, 202-586-9680.

15) Product Info on 25 World Markets:
The Small Business Administration has an Export Information System (XIS), which are data reports providing specific product or service information on the top 25 world markets and market growth trends for the past five years. Contact: Office of International Trade, Small Business Administration, 409 Third St. SW, Washington, DC 20416, 202-205-6766.

16) Online Economic Bulletin Board (EBB):
This computer-based electronic bulletin board, is an online source for trade leads as well as the latest statistical releases from the Bureau of Census, the Bureau of Economic Analysis, the Bureau of Labor Statistics, the Federal Reserve Board, and other federal agencies. Subscribers pay an annual fee, plus cost per minute. Contact: EBB, Office of Business Analysis, U.S. Department of Commerce, Washington, DC 20230, 202-482-1986.

Now use your fax machine to get the latest economic, financial, and trade news available from the U.S. government. Just dial 1-900-786-2329 from your fax machine's touchtone telephone and follow the simple voice instructions. EBB/FAX™ stores the complete text of many government press releases and information files. The cost for this service is 65¢ per minute. Charges will appear on your regular phone bill and there are no registration fees. The list of files is updated every business day and the service is available 24 hours a day, 7 days a week.

17) Free Legal Assistance:
The Export Legal Assistance Network (ELAN) is a nationwide group of attorneys with experience in international trade who provide free initial consultations to small businesses on export related matters. Contact: Export Legal Assistance Network, Small Business Administration, 409 Third St. SW, Washington, DC 20416, 202-778-3080; Fax: 202-778-3063.

18) Global Learning:
U.S. Department of Education, Business and International Education Programs. The business and international education program is designed to engage U.S. schools of business language and area programs, international study programs, public and private sector organizations, and U.S. businesses in a mutually productive relationship which will benefit the Nation's future economic interest. Approximately $2.3 million annually is available to assist U.S. institutions of higher education to promote the Nation's capacity for international understanding. Typical

grantee activities include executive seminars, case studies, and export skill workshops. For more information contact: Center for International Education, U.S. Department of Education, 600 Independence Avenue, SW, Washington, DC 20202; 202-401-9798.

19) Export Counseling — SCORE, ACE:

The Small Business Administration can provide export counseling to small business exporters by retired and active business executives. Members of the Service Corps of Retired Executives (SCORE) and the Active Corps of Executives (ACE), with years of practical experience in international trade, assist small firms in evaluating their export potential and developing and implementing basic export marketing plans. For more information, contact your local Small Business Administration (SBA) office listed in the government pages of your telephone book, or National SCORE Office, 1825 Connecticut Ave., NW, Suite 503, Washington, DC 20009; 800-634-0245; Fax: 202-705-7636.

20) Department of Energy — Office of International Affairs and Energy Emergencies:

The Department of Energy (DOE) promotes U.S. exports of energy goods, services, and technology primarily through participation in The Committee on Renewable Energy Commerce and Trade, and The Coal and Clean Technology Export Program. The following is a list of the Department of Energy's programs and the corresponding telephone numbers to call for more information.

Committee on Renewable Energy Commerce and Trade (CORECT): Through the concept of "one-stop shopping" potential exporters can receive comprehensive advice on potential markets, financing and information on export guidelines. Call the Office of Conservation and Renewable Energy, 202-586-8302; Fax: 202-586-1605.

Coal and Technology Export Program (CTEP): The Coal and Technology Export Program (CTEP) serves as a reservoir for international information on U.S. coal and coal technologies, as the Department of Energy's intradepartmental coordinator, and as the USG inter-agency liaison for coal companies and technology firms. Call 202-586-7297.

The Export Assistance Initiative: This entity in the Bureau of International Affairs has been designed to help identify overseas opportunities for U.S. companies, identify and attempt to alleviate discriminatory trade barriers, and identify possible financing alternatives for U.S. companies. Call 202-586-1189.

21) Fax Retrieval Systems

A number of offices offer documents on demand, delivered directly to a fax machine 24 hours a day. These automated systems each have a menu of available documents which can be sent to a fax machine by dialing from a touch-tone phone and following directions. Below is a list of offices who offer this program:

Uruguay Round Hotline: This Fax retrieval system is located at the Trade Information Center and has information on the GATT agreement. Document #1000 is the menu of available information packets; 1-800-872-8723.

Eastern European Business Information Center (EEBIC): This Fax system has 5 main menus. Menu document #1000 has export and financing information. Document #2000 has a menu of documents relating to export and investment opportunities and upcoming trade events. A listing of Eastern European country information is available on menu document #3000. Document menus #4000 and #5000 have information on the *Eastern Europe Business Bulletin*, and the *Eastern Europe Looks For Partners* publications; 202-482-5745.

Business Information Service for the Newly Independent States: There are 3 menus available through BISNIS. Menu number 1, document #0001 has trade and investment opportunities and trade promotion information. Menu number 2, document #0002 has industry and country specific information, and financing alternatives. Menu number 3, document #0003, has information on BISNIS publications; 202-482-3145.

Office of Mexico: The main menu for Mexico is document #0101. There is also a menu of labeling and standards requirements (document #8404). Information on documents relating to the certificate of origin and rules of origin under NAFTA is document #5000. A complete NAFTA tariff schedule is on document #6000; 202-482-4464.

Office of Canada: The main menu for Canada is document #0100. The number for the Canadian tariff schedule listed by Harmonized System tariff classification is document #0220; 202-482-3101.

Office of the Pacific Basin: The menu for the Pacific Basin system is document #1000. A listing of documents regarding Vietnam are available by requesting document #8600; 202-482-3875 or 202-482-3646.

Office of Africa, Near East, and South Asia: A list of documents covering the nations of the Near East is document #0100. Africa is #3000 and South Asian countries is #4000; 202-482-1064.

Overseas Private Investment Corporation: This system has information on OPIC project finance and political risk insurance programs; 202-336-8700.

22) International Visitors Program

Foreign individuals or groups are brought to the U.S. for about one month. The programs feature visits by business leaders and foreign government officials who have the opportunity to meet with their U.S. counterparts. Contact: William Codus, Office of Education/Voluntary Visitors, U.S. Information Agency, 202-619-5217; Fax: 202-205-0792.

Read All About It: Helpful Publications

Basic Guide to Exporting:
This publication outlines the sequence of steps necessary to determine whether to, and how to, use foreign markets as a source of profits. It describes the various problems which confront smaller firms engaged in, or seeking to enter, international trade, as well as the types of assistance available. It also provides a guide to appraising the sales

potential of foreign markets and to understanding the requirements of local business practices and procedures in overseas markets. The booklet is available for $9.50 (GPO: 003-009-00604-0) from: Superintendent of Documents, U.S. Government Printing Office, Washington, DC 20402, 202-512-1800.

Exporter's Guide to Federal Resources for Small Business:

This free booklet describes the types of assistance available for small businesses interested in international trade opportunities. It is available from any of the Small Business Administration field offices or by contacting: Office of International Trade, U.S. Small Business Administration, 409 3rd St., SW, 6th Floor, Washington, DC 20416, 202-205-6720.

Commercial News USA:

This publication describes a free export promotion service that will publicize the availability of your new product to foreign markets, and test foreign market interest in your new product. There is a small fee. Contact: Marketing Programs Section, Room 2106, U.S. Department of Commerce, Washington, DC 20230, 202-482-4918.

Export Programs: A Business Directory of U.S. Government Resources:

This guide provides an overview of U.S. government export assistance programs and contact points for further information and expertise in utilizing these programs. Contact: Trade Information Center, U.S. Department of Commerce, Washington, DC 20230, 1-800-872-8723.

Business America:

The principal Commerce department publication for presenting domestic and international business news. Each monthly issue includes a "how to" article for new exporters, discussion of U.S. trade policy, news of government actions that may affect trade, a calendar of upcoming trade shows, exhibits, fairs, and seminars. The annual subscription is $32 (GPO: 703-011-0000-4-W). Contact: Superintendent of Documents, Government Printing Office, Washington, DC 20402, 202-512-1800.

Key Officers of Foreign Service Posts: A Guide for Business Representatives:

Lists the names of key State and Commerce officers at U.S. embassies and consulates. Cost is $3.75 per copy. Contact: Superintendent of Documents, Government Printing Office, Washington, DC 20402, 202-512-1800.

Export Trading Company (ETC) Guidebook:

This Guidebook is intended to assist those who are considering starting or expanding exporting through the various forms of an ETC. The Guidebook will also facilitate your review of the ETC Act and export trading options and serve as a planning tool for your business by showing you what it takes to export profitably and how to start doing it. Cost is $11 (GPO: 003-009-00523-0). Contact: Superintendent of Documents, Government Printing Office, Washington, DC 20402, 202-512-1800.

Foreign Labor Trends:

Published by the Department of Labor, these are a series of reports, issued annually, that describe and analyze labor trends in more than 70 countries. The reports, which are prepared by the American Embassy in each country, cover labor-management relations, trade unions, employment and unemployment, wages and working conditions, labor and government, international labor activities, and other significant developments. Contact: Office of Foreign Relations, Room S 5006, 200 Constitution Ave., NW, Washington, DC 20210, 202-523-6257, 202-219-6257.

ABC's of Exporting:

This is a special issue of Business America which takes you step by step through the exporting process. It explains the federal agencies and how they can help, as well as providing a directory of export sources. This publication is free and is available by contacting: Trade Information Center, U.S. Department of Commerce, Washington, DC 20230, 1-800-872-8723.

Ag Exporter:

Monthly magazine published by the U.S. Department of Agriculture's Foreign Agricultural Service (FAS). The annual subscription cost is $17 (GPO: 701-027-00000-1). Contact: Superintendent of Documents, Government Printing Office, Washington, DC 20402; 202-512-1800.

AID Procurement Information Bulletin:

This publication advertises notices of intended procurement of AID-financed commodities. The subscription cost is free. Contact: USAID's Office of Small and Disadvantaged Business Utilization/ Minority Resource Center, Washington, DC 20523-1414; 703-875-1551.

The Government Printing Office (GPO) has many titles to choose from. For a listing, contact the GPO (listed below) by mail, or phone and ask for the Foreign Trade and Tariff Subject Bibliography (SB-123; 021-123-00405-1).

Government Printing Office
Superintendent of Documents
Washington, DC 20402
202-512-1800

U.S. Department of Commerce/ US & FCS Field Offices

Trade experts at these 64 offices advise companies on foreign markets.

Alabama
Birmingham: 950 22nd St., N, Room 707, 35203, 205-731-1331; Fax: 205-731-0076.

Alaska
Anchorage: 4201 Tudor Center Dr., World Trade Center, Suite 319, 99508-5916, 907-271-6237; Fax: 907-271-6242.

Arizona
Phoenix: 2901 North Central Ave., Phoenix Plaza, Suite 970, 85012, 602-640-2513; Fax: 602-640-2518.

Arkansas
Little Rock: 425 West Capitol Ave., TCBY Tower Building, Suite 700, 72201, 501-324-5794; Fax: 501-324-7380.

Be patient. If any phone number is incorrect, call (area code) 555-1212 and request the new listing.

847

Selling Overseas

California

Los Angeles: 11000 Wilshire Blvd., Room 9200, 90024, 310-575-7104; Fax: 310-575-7220.

Long Beach: One World Trade Center, Suite 1670, 90831, 310-980-4550; Fax: 310-980-4561.

Newport Beach: 3300 Irvine Ave., Suite 305, 92660, 714-660-1688; Fax: 714-660-8039.

San Diego: 6363 Greenwich Drive, 92122, 619-557-5395; Fax: 619-557-6176.

San Francisco: 250 Montgomery St., 14th Floor, 94104, 415-705-2300; Fax: 415-705-2297.

Santa Clara: 5201 Great America Pkwy., Techmart Building, Suite 456, 95054, 408-970-4610; Fax: 408-970-4618.

Colorado

Denver: 1625 Broadway, Suite 680, 80202, 303-844-6623; Fax: 303-844-5651.

Connecticut

Hartford: 450 Main St., Room 610-B, 06103, 203-240-3530; Fax: 203-240-3473.

District of Columbia

Served by Baltimore, MD, U.S. Export Assistance Center.

Delaware

Served by Philadelphia, PA, District Office.

Florida

Miami: 5600 Northwest 36th St., Trade Port Building, 6th Floor, 33166, 305-526-7425; Fax: 305-526-7434.

Clearwater: 128 North Osceola Ave., 34615, 813-461-0011; Fax 813-449-2889.

Tallahassee: 107 W. Gaines St., Collins Bldg., Room 366G, 32399, 904-488-6469; Fax: 904-487-1407.

Georgia

Atlanta: 4360 Chamber-Dunwoody Road, Suite 310, 30341, 404-452-9101; Fax: 404-452-9105.

Savannah: 120 Barnard St., A-107, 31401, 912-652-4204; Fax: 912-652-4241.

Hawaii

Honolulu: 300 Ala Moana Blvd., Room 4106, Box 50026, 96850, 808-541-1782; Fax: 808-541-3435.

Idaho

Boise: 700 W. State St., Box 83720, Boise, 83720, 208-334-3857; Fax: 208-334-2361.

Illinois

Chicago: 55 W. Monroe, Xerox Center Suite 2440, 60603, 312-353-8040; Fax: 312-353-8120.

Rockford: 515 N. Court St., 61110-0247, 815-987-4347; Fax: 815-987-8122.

Indiana

Indianapolis: 11405 N. Pennsylvania St., Penwood One, Suite 106, Carmel, IN 46032, 317-582-2300; Fax: 317-582-2301.

Iowa

Des Moines: 210 Walnut St., Room 817, 50309, 515-284-4222; Fax: 515-284-4021.

Kansas

Wichita: 151 North Volutsia, 67214-4695, 316-269-6160; Fax: 316-683-7326.

Kentucky

Louisville: 601 W. Broadway, Room 636B, 40202, 502-582-5066; Fax: 502-582-6573.

Louisiana

New Orleans: 501 Magazine St., Hale Boggs Federal Building, Room 1043, 70130, 504-589-6546; Fax: 504-589-2337.

Maine

Augusta: 187 State St., Suite 59, 04333, 207-622-8249; Fax: 207-626-9156.

Maryland

Baltimore: 401 East Pratt St., World Trade Center, Suite 2432, 21202, 410-962-4539; Fax: 410-962-4529.

Massachusetts

Boston: World Trade Center, Suite 307, 02210, 617-424-5950; Fax: 617-424-5992.

Michigan

Detroit: 477 Michigan Ave., 1140 McNamara Bldg., 48226, 313-226-3650; Fax: 313-226-3657.

Grand Rapids: 300 Monroe NW, Room 408, 49503, 616-456-2411; Fax: 616-456-2695.

Minnesota

Minneapolis: 110 S. 4th St., Room 108, 55401, 612-348-1638; Fax: 612-348-1650.

Mississippi

Jackson: 201 W. Capitol St., Suite 310, 39201-2005, 601-965-4388, Fax: 601-965-5386.

Missouri

St. Louis: 8182 Maryland Ave., Suite 303, 63105, 314-425-3302; Fax: 314-425-3381.

Kansas City: 601 E. 12th St., Room 635, 64106, 816-426-3141; Fax: 816-426-3140.

Montana

Served by Boise, Idaho, Branch Office.

Nebraska

Omaha: 11133 O St., 68137, 402-221-3664; Fax: 402-221-3668.

Nevada

Reno: 1755 E. Plumb Lane, #152, 89502, 702-784-5203; Fax: 702-784-5343.

New Hampshire

Portsmouth (Boston, Massachusetts, District Office): 601 Spaulding Turnpike, Suite 29, 03801-2833, 603-334-6074; Fax: 603-334-6110.

New Jersey

Trenton: 3131 Princeton Pike Building 6, Suite 100, 08648, 609-989-2100; Fax: 609-989-2395.

New Mexico

Santa Fe: c/o Department of Economic Development, 1100 St. Francis Dr., 87503, 505-827-0350; Fax: 505-827-0263.

New York

Buffalo: 111 W. Huron St., Room 1312, Federal Building, 14202, 716-846-4191; Fax: 716-846-5290.

Rochester: 111 East Ave., 14604, 716-263-6480; Fax: 716-325-6505.

New York: 26 Federal Plaza, Room 3718, 10278, 212-264-0634; Fax: 212-264-1356.

North Carolina

Greensboro: 400 W. Market St., Suite 400, 27401, 919-333-5345; Fax: 919-333-5158.

North Dakota

Served by Minneapolis, Minnesota, District Office.

Ohio

Cincinnati: 9504 Federal Building, 550 Main St., 45202, 513-684-2944; Fax: 513-684-3200.

Cleveland: 600 Superior Ave., Bank One Center, Suite 700, 44114, 216-522-4750; Fax: 216-522-2235.

Oklahoma

Oklahoma City: 6601 Broadway Extension, Room 200, 73116, 405-231-5302; Fax: 405-841-5245.

Tulsa: 440 S. Houston St., Suite 505, 74127, 918-581-7650; Fax: 918-581-2844.

Oregon

Portland: Suite 242, One World Trade Center, 121 SW Salmon St., 97204, 503-326-3001; Fax: 503-326-6351.

Pennsylvania

Philadelphia: 660 American Ave., Suite 201, King of Prussia, PA 19406, 215-962-4980; Fax: 215-962-4989.

Pittsburgh: 1000 Liberty Ave., Room 2002, 15222, 412-644-2850; Fax: 412-644-4875.

Be patient. If any phone number is incorrect, call (area code) 555-1212 and request the new listing.

Puerto Rico

San Juan: Room G-55 Federal Building, Chardon Ave. 00918, 809-766-5555; Fax: 809-766-5692.

Rhode Island

Providence: 7 Jackson Walkway, 02903, 401-528-5104; Fax: 401-528-5067.

South Carolina

Columbia: 1835 Assembly St., Suite 172, 29201, 803-765-5345; Fax: 803-253-3614.
Charleston: c/o Trident Technical College, Box 118067, CE-P, 66 Columbus St., 29423, 803-727-4051; Fax: 803-727-4052.

South Dakota

Served by Omaha, Nebraska, District Office.

Tennessee

Nashville: 404 James Robertson Pkwy., Suite 114, 37219, 615-736-5161; Fax: 615-736-2454.
Memphis: 22 N. Front St., Suite 200, 38103, 901-544-4137; Fax: 901-575-3510.

Texas

Dallas: 2050 N. Stemmons Freeway, Suite 170, Box 58130, 75258, 214-767-0542; Fax: 214-767-8240.
Austin: 410 E. 5th St., Suite 414A, Box 12728, 78711, 512-482-5939; Fax: 512-482-5940.
Houston: 1 Allen Center, Suite 1160, 500 Dallas 77002, 713-229-2578; Fax: 713-229-2203.

Utah

Salt Lake City: Suite 105, 324 S. State St., 84111, 801-524-5116; Fax: 801-524-5886.

Vermont

Montpelier: 109 State St., 4th Floor, 05609, 802-828-4508; Fax: 802-828-3258.

Virginia

Richmond: 704 E. Franklin St., 700 Center, Suite 550, 23219 804-771-2246; Fax: 804-771-2390.

Washington

Seattle: 3131 Elliott Ave., Suite 290, 98121, 206-553-5615; Fax: 206-553-7253.
Tri Cities: 320 N. Johnson St., Suite 350, Kennewick, WA 99336, 509-735-2751; Fax: 509-735-9385.

West Virginia

Charleston: 405 Capitol St., Suite 807, 25301, 304-347-5123; Fax: 304-347-5408.

Wisconsin

Milwaukee: 517 E. Wisconsin Ave., Room 596, 53202, 414-297-3473; Fax: 414-297-3470.

Wyoming

Served by Denver, Colorado, District Office.

State Government Assistance to Exporters

Last year state governments spent approximately $40,000,000 to help companies in their state sell goods and services overseas. This figure increased almost 50% over the previous two years. During the same period of time, federal monies devoted to maximizing companies' export capabilities remained virtually constant. This is another indicator of how the states are fertile sources of information and expertise for large and small businesses.

The underlying mission of these offices is to create jobs within their state. Usually their approach is to help companies develop overseas marketing strategies or to offer incentives to foreign companies to invest in their state. The major state trade development programs and services are outlined below.

1) **Marketing Research and Company Intelligence:**
All of the states can provide some degree of overseas marketing information. The level of detail will depend upon the resources of the state. Thirty-five states (except for California, Hawaii, Idaho, Kansas, Maryland, Minnesota, Nebraska, Nevada, New Jersey, New York, South Dakota, Texas, Washington, West Virginia, and Wyoming) say they will do customized market studies for companies. Such studies are free or available for a small fee. For example, the Commonwealth of Virginia will do an in-depth market study for a company and charge $1,000. They estimate similar surveys done by the private sector cost up to $20,000. Virginia relies on MBA students and professors within the state university system who get credit for working on such projects.

Even if a state does not perform customized studies, the trade office within a Department of Economic Development will prove to be an ideal starting place for marketing information. Some states which do not undertake comprehensive studies for prospective exporters will do a limited amount of research for free. These offices can also point to outside sources as well as the notable resources at the federal level which may be able to assist. And those states with offices overseas also can contact these foreign posts to identify sources in other countries. Moreover, many of the offices have people who travel abroad frequently for companies and also work with other exporters. Such bureaucrats can be invaluable for identifying the exact source for obtaining particular market or company intelligence.

2) **Company and Industry Directories:**
Many states publish directories which are helpful to both exporters and researchers. Some states publish export/import directories which show which companies in the state are exporters and what they sell as well as which are importers and what they buy. Because many of the trade offices are also interested in foreign investment within their state, many publish directories or other reference sources disclosing which companies in their state are foreign owned, and by whom. Other state publications may include export service directories which list organizations providing services to exporters such as banks, freight forwarders, translators, and world trade organizations. Some also publish agribusiness exporter directories, which identify agricultural-related companies involved in exporting.

3) **Free Newsletters:**
All but four states (i.e., Florida, Kentucky, Ohio, and North Carolina) generate international newsletters or publish a special section within a general newsletter on items of interest to those selling overseas. These newsletters are normally free and cover topics like new trade leads, new rules and regulations for exports, and details about upcoming overseas trade shows. Such newsletters can also be a source for mailing lists for those whose clients include exporters. We haven't specifically investigated the availability of such lists, but remember that all states have a law comparable to the federal Freedom of Information Act which allows public access to government data.

4) **Overseas Contacts:**
Finding a foreign buyer or an agent/distributor for a company is one of the primary functions of these state offices. How they do this varies from state to state. Many sponsor trade fairs and seminars overseas to attract potential buyers to products produced in their state. The more aggressive trade promotion offices may organize trade missions and escort a number of companies

overseas and personally help them look for buyers or agents. Many will distribute a company's sales brochures and other literature to potential buyers around the world through their overseas offices. Some states work with the federal government and explore general trade leads and then try to match buyers with sellers. Others will cultivate potential clients in a given country and contact each directly.

5) Export Marketing Seminars:
Many of the states conduct free or modestly priced seminars to introduce companies to selling overseas. Some of the courses are held in conjunction with the regional International Trade Administration office of the U.S. Commerce Department. The course may be general in nature, for example, *The Basics of Exporting*, or focused on specific topics such as *International Market Research Techniques, Letters of Credit, Export Financing*, or *How to do Business with Israel*.

6) State Grants and Loans for Exporters:
Many states offer financial assistance for those wishing to export. Some states even provide grants (money you do not have to pay back) to those firms which cannot afford to participate in a trade mission or trade fair. This means that they provide money to those companies which are just trying to develop a customer base overseas. More typically the state will help with the financing of a sale through state-sponsored loans and loan guarantees, or assistance in identifying and applying for federal or commercial export financing.

7) Trade Leads Databases:
Because these offices provide mostly services, there are not many opportunities for them to develop databases. However, their trade leads program is one area where a number of offices have computerized their information. These databases consist of the names and addresses along with some background information on those overseas companies which are actively searching or might be interested in doing business with companies within the state. The number of leads in such a system could range from several hundred to five or ten thousand. None of these states seem to have made such information available on machine readable formats to those outside the office. But, in light of state Freedom of Information statutes, it may be worth making a formal inquiry if you have an interest. The states which have computerized their trade leads include: Alabama, Arkansas, Arizona, California, Colorado, Connecticut, Delaware, Florida, Georgia, Hawaii, Illinois, Indiana, Iowa, Maine, Michigan, Maryland, Minnesota, Mississippi, Missouri, Nebraska, New Jersey, New York, North Carolina, North Dakota, Ohio, Oklahoma, Oregon, New Hampshire, Pennsylvania, Puerto Rico, Rhode Island, South Dakota, Tennessee, Texas, Utah, Virginia, Washington, West Virginia, and Wisconsin.

State International Trade Offices

The foreign cities in parentheses after the telephone number are those locations where the state maintains a trade office.

Alabama
International Development and Trade Division, Alabama Development Office, State Capitol, Montgomery, AL 36130, 205-242-0400, 800-248-0033; Fax: 205-242-0486 (Hanover, **Germany**; Seoul, **Korea**; Tokyo, **Japan**).

Alaska
International Trade Director, Office of International Trade, Dept. of Commerce and Economic Development, 3601 C St., Suite 798, Anchorage, AK 99503, 907-561-5585; Fax: 907-561-4557 (Tokyo, **Japan**; Seoul, **Korea**; Taipei, **Taiwan**).

Arizona
International Trade, Department of Commerce, 3800 N. Central, 15th Floor, Phoenix, AZ 85012, 602-280-1371; Fax: 602-280-1305 (Mexico City, **Mexico**; Tokyo, **Japan**; Taipei, **Taiwan**).

Arkansas
International Marketing, Arkansas Industrial Commission, One State Capitol Mall, Little Rock, AR 72201, 501-682-7690; Fax: 501-324-9856 (Brussels, **Belgium**; Tokyo, **Japan**; Taipei, **Taiwan**; Mexico City, **Mexico**).

California
California State World Trade Commission, 801 K St., Suite 1700, Sacramento, CA 95814, 916-324-5511; Fax: 916-324-5791 (Tokyo, **Japan**; London, **England**; Hong Kong; Frankfurt, **Germany**; Mexico City, **Mexico**; Taipei, **Taiwan**; Israel).

Export Development Office, 107 S. Broadway, Room 8039, Los Angeles, CA 90012, 310-590-5965.

Colorado
International Trade Office, Department of Commerce and Development, 1625 Broadway, Suite 680, Denver, CO 80202, 303-892-3850; Fax: 303-892-3820 (Tokyo, **Japan**; Seoul, **Korea**; London, **England**; Mexico City, **Mexico**).

Connecticut
International Division, Department of Economic Development, 865 Brook St., Rocky Hill, CT 06067, 203-258-4256; Fax: 203-529-0535 (Tokyo, **Japan**; Taipei, **Taiwan**; Hong Kong; Mexico City, **Mexico**).

Delaware
Delaware Development Office, International Trade Section, 820 French St., Carvel State Building, 3rd Floor, Wilmington, DE 19801, 302-577-6262; Fax: 302-577-3302.

District of Columbia
D.C. Office of International Business, 717 14th St., 11th Floor, NW, Washington, DC 20005, 202-727-1576; Fax: 202-727-1588.

Florida
Florida Department of Commerce, 366 Collins Building, Tallahassee, FL 32399-2000, 904-488-6124; Fax: 904-487-1407 (Toronto, **Canada**; Taipei, **Taiwan**; Seoul, **Korea**; Frankfurt, **Germany**; Tokyo, **Japan**; London, **England**; Sao Paulo, **Brazil**; Mexico City, **Mexico**).

Georgia
Department of Industry, Trade and Tourism, Suite 1100, 285 Peachtree Center Ave., Atlanta, GA 30303, 404-656-3545; Fax: 404-651-6505 (Brussels, **Belgium**; Tokyo, **Japan**; Toronto, **Canada**; Seoul, **Korea**; Mexico City, **Mexico**).

Hawaii
International Services Branch, Department of Business and Economic Development, P.O. Box 2359, Honolulu, HI 96804, 808-587-2797; Fax: 808-587-2790.

Idaho
Economic Development, Department of Commerce, 700 W. State St., Boise, ID 83720, 208-334-2470; Fax: 208-334-2783.

Illinois
International Business Division, Illinois Department of Commerce and Community Affairs, 100 W. Randolph St., Suite 3-400, Chicago, IL 60601, 312-814-7164; Fax: 312-814-6581 (Brussels, **Belgium**; Hong Kong; Tokyo, **Japan**; Warsaw, **Poland**; Mexico City, **Mexico**; Budapest, **Hungary**).

Illinois Export Council, 333 N. Michigan Ave., Chicago, IL 60601, 312-236-2162; Fax: 312-236-4625.

Indiana
International Trade Division, Department of Commerce, One North Capitol, Suite 700, Indianapolis, IN 46204, 317-232-3527; Fax 317-232-4146 (Tokyo, **Japan**; Mexico City, **Mexico**; Toronto, **Canada**; Taipei, **Taiwan**; Beijing, **China**; Seoul, **Korea**; Netherlands).

Iowa
International Marketing Division, Iowa Dept. of Economic Development, 200 East Grand Ave., Des Moines, IA 50309, 515-242-4743; Fax: 515-242-4918 (Frankfurt, **Germany**; Tokyo, **Japan**).

Kansas
Kansas Department of Commerce, 700 SW Harrison St., Suite 1300, Topeka, KS 66603, 913-296-4027; Fax: 913-296-5055 (Tokyo, **Japan**; Brussels, **Belgium**).

Kentucky
International Trade, Kentucky Office of Economic Development, 500 O St., #2300, Capitol Plaza, Frankfort, KY 40601, 502-564-7670; Fax 502-564-3256 (Tokyo, **Japan**; Brussels, **Belgium**).

Louisiana
Office of International Trade, P.O. Box 94185, Baton Rouge, LA 70804-9185, 504-342-4319; Fax: 504-342-5389 (Mexico City, **Mexico**; Taipei, **Taiwan**; **Netherlands**).

Maine
International and Economic Trade, Maine World Trade Commission, State House, Station 59, Augusta, ME 04333, 207-287-2656; Fax: 207-622-0234.

Maryland
Maryland International Division, World Trade Center, 401 East Pratt St., 7th Floor, Baltimore, MD 21202, 410-333-4295; Fax: 410-333-4302 (Brussels, **Belgium**; Yokohama, **Japan**; **Hong Kong**; Taipei, **Taiwan**).

Massachusetts
Office of International Trade and Investment, 100 Cambridge St., Room 1302, Boston, MA 02202, 617-367-1830; Fax: 617-227-3488 (Berlin, **Germany**).

Michigan
International Trade Division, International Trade Authority, Michigan Department of Commerce, P.O. Box 30105, Lansing, MI 48909, 517-373-1054; Fax: 517-335-2521 (Toronto, **Canada**; Hong Kong; Brussels, **Belgium**; Tokyo, **Japan**).

Minnesota
Minnesota Trade Office, 1000 World Trade Center, 30 E. 7th St., St. Paul, 55101, 612-297-4222; Fax: 612-296-3555 (Oslo, **Norway**; Stockholm, **Sweden**).

Mississippi
Department of Economic and Community Development, P.O. Box 849, Jackson, MI 39205, 601-359-6672; Fax: 601-359-3605 (Seoul, **Korea**; Tokyo, **Japan**; Hong Kong; Frankfort, **Germany**; Taipei, **Taiwan**).

Missouri
International Trade, Department of Economic Development, P.O. Box 118, Jefferson City, MO 65102, 314-751-4855; Fax: 314-751-7384 (Tokyo, **Japan**; Dusseldorf, **Germany**; Seoul, **Korea**; Taipei, **Taiwan**; Guadalajara, **Mexico**).

Montana
International Trade Office, Montana Department of Commerce, 1424 9th Ave., Helena, MT 59620, 406-444-3494; Fax: 406-444-2903 (Taipei, **Taiwan**; Kumamoto, **Japan**).

Nebraska
Department of Economic Development, 301 Centennial Mall South, P.O. Box 94666, Lincoln, NE 68509, 402-471-3111; Fax: 402-471-3778.

Nevada
Commission of Economic Development, Capital Complex, Carson, NV 89710, 702-687-4325; Fax: 702-787-4450.

New Hampshire
Office of International Commerce, Department of Resources and Economic Development, 601 Spaulding Turnpike, Suite 29, Portsmouth, NH 03801, 603-334-6074; Fax: 603-334-6110.

New Jersey
Division of International Trade, Department of Commerce and Economic Development, 28 West State St., 8th Floor, Trenton, NJ 08625, 609-633-3606; Fax: 609-633-3675 (Tokyo, **Japan**; London, **England**).

New Mexico
Trade Division, Economic Development, 1100 St. Francis Dr., Joseph Montoya Building, Santa Fe, NM 87503, 505-827-0307; Fax: 505-827-0263 (Mexico City, **Mexico**).

New York
International Division, Department of Commerce, 1515 Broadway, 51st Floor, New York Department of Economic Development, New York, NY 10036, 212-827-6100; Fax: 212-827-6279 (Tokyo, **Japan**; Wiesbaden, **Germany**; London, **England**; Milan, **Italy**; Ontario and Montreal, **Canada**; Hong Kong; Frankfurt, **Germany**).

North Carolina
International Division, Dept. of Commerce, 430 N. Salisbury St., Raleigh, NC 27611, 919-733-7193; Fax: 919-733-0110 (Dusseldorf, **Germany**; Hong Kong; Tokyo, **Japan**).

North Dakota
International Trade Specialist, Department of International Trade and Finance, 1833 E. Bismarck Expressway, Bismarck, ND 58504, 701-224-2810; Fax: 701-328-5320.

Ohio
International Trade Division, Department of Development, 77 S. High St., P.O. Box 1001, Columbus, OH 43216, 614-466-5017; 614-463-1540 (Brussels, **Belgium**; Tokyo, **Japan**; Hong Kong, Toronto, **Canada**).

Oklahoma
International Trade Division, Oklahoma Dept. of Commerce, 6601 Broadway Extension, Oklahoma City, OK 73116, 405-841-5220; Fax: 405-841-5245 (Frankfort, **Germany**; Seoul, **Korea**; Mexico City, **Mexico**; **Singapore**).

Oregon
International Trade Division, Oregon Economic Development Dept., #1 World Trade Center, Suite 300, 121 Salmon St., Portland, OR 97204, 503-229-5625; Fax: 503-222-5050 (Tokyo, **Japan**; Seoul, **Korea**; Taipei, **Taiwan**).

Pennsylvania
Dept. of Commerce, Office of International Trade, 464 Forum Building, Harrisburg, PA 17120, 717-783-5107; Fax: 717-234-4560 (Frankfurt, **Germany**; Tokyo, **Japan**; Brussels, **Belgium**; Toronto, **Canada**).

Puerto Rico
P.R. Dept. of Commerce, P.O. Box 4275, San Juan, PR 00936, 809-721-3290; Fax: 809-722-8477.

Rhode Island
International Trade Office, Department of Economic Development, 7 Jackson Walkway, Providence, RI 02903, 401-277-2601; Fax: 401-277-2102 (Mexico City, **Mexico**).

South Carolina
International Business Development, South Carolina State Department of Commerce, P.O. Box 927, Columbia, SC 29202, 803-737-0400; Fax: 803-737-0418 (Tokyo, **Japan**; Frankfort, **Germany**; Seoul **Korea**; **United Kingdom**).

South Dakota
South Dakota International Trade Center, Capitol Lake Plaza, Pierre, SD 57501, 605-773-5032.

Tennessee
Export Promotion Office, Department of Economic and Community Development, Rachel Jackson Building, 7th Floor, Nashville, TN 37219, 615-741-5870; Fax: 615-741-5829.

Texas
International Business Development Dept., Texas Department of Commerce, P.O. Box 12728, Austin, TX 78711, 512-320-0110; Fax: 512-320-9424 (Mexico City, **Mexico**; Frankfurt, **Germany**; Tokyo, **Japan**; Taipei, **Taiwan**).

Utah
Export Development Committee, Economic and Industrial Development Division, 324 S. State St., Salt Lake City, UT 84111, 801-538-3631 (Tokyo, **Japan**).

Selling Overseas

Vermont
International Business, Dept. of Economic Development, 109 State St., Montpelier, VT 05602, 802-828-3221; Fax: 802-828-3258.

Virginia
International Trade and Investment, 2 James Center, P.O. Box 798, Richmond, VA 23206, 804-371-8100; Fax: 804-371-8860 (Tokyo, **Japan**; Brussels, **Belgium**).

Washington
Domestic and International Trade Division, Department of Trade and Economic Development, 2001 Sixth Ave, 26th Floor, Seattle, WA 98121, 206-464-7143; Fax: 206-464-7222 (Tokyo, **Japan**; **Canada**).

West Virginia
West Virginia Development Office, Capitol Complex Bldg. 6, Room 525, Charleston, WV 25305, 304-558-2234; Fax: 304-558-1189 (Tokyo, **Japan**).

Wisconsin
Bureau of International Business Development, Department of Development, 123 W. Washington Ave., Madison, WI 53702, 608-266-1767; Fax: 608-266-5551 (Frankfurt, **Germany**; **Hong Kong**; Mexico City, **Mexico**; Toronto, **Canada**; Tokyo, **Japan**; Seoul, **Korea**; **South Korea**).

Wyoming
International Trade Division, Department of Commerce, 2301 Central Avenue, Cheyenne, WY 82002, 307-777-6412; Fax: 307-777-5840.

Overseas Travel: Business or Pleasure

The following sources and services will be helpful to anyone who is on business or vacation in any foreign country:

1) Arts America:
The U.S. Information Agency assists qualified artists and performers in arranging private tours overseas. Its aim is to present a balanced portrayal of the American scene. Some of the past activities have included a major exhibition of American crafts shown in China, a modern dance company in the USSR, Spain, and Portugal, and a jazz ensemble in Nigeria, Senegal and Kenya. Contact: Program Manager, Office of the Arts in America, United States Information Agency, 301 4th St. SW, Room 568, Washington, DC 20547, 202-619-4779.

2) Travel Overseas on Government Expense:
The U.S. Speakers program will pay experts, who can contribute to foreign societies' understanding of the United States, to travel abroad and participate in seminars, colloquia, or symposia. Subjects relevant to the program include economics, international political relations, U.S. social and political processes, arts and humanities, and science and technology. To see if you qualify contact: U.S. Speakers, Office of Program Coordination and Development, U.S. Information Agency, 301 4th St. SW, Room 550, Washington, DC 20547, 202-619-4764.

3) Citizens Arrested Overseas:
The Arrest Unit at the State Department monitors arrests and trials to see that American citizens are not abused; acts as a liaison with family and friends in the United States; sends money or messages with written consent of arrestee; offers lists of lawyers; will forward money from the United States to detainee; tries to assure that your rights under local laws are observed. The Emergency Medical and Dietary Assistance Program includes such services as providing vitamin supplements when necessary; granting emergency transfer for emergency medical care; and short-term feeding of two or three meals a day when arrestee is detained without funds to buy his or her own meals. Contact:

Arrests Unit, Citizens Emergency Center, Overseas Citizens Service, Bureau of Consular Affairs, U.S. Department of State, 2201 C St. NW, Room 4811, Washington, DC 20520, 202-647-5225.

4) Citizens Emergency Center:
Emergency telephone assistance is available to United States citizens abroad under the following circumstances:

Arrests: 202-647-5225 (see details above)

Deaths: 202-647-5225; notification of interested parties in the United States of the death abroad of American citizens; assistance in the arrangements for disposition of remains.

Financial Assistance: 202-647-5225; repatriation of destitute nationals, coordination of medical evacuation of non-official nationals from abroad; transmission of private funds in emergencies to destitute United States nationals abroad when commercial banking facilities are unavailable (all costs must be reimbursed).

Shipping and Seamen: 202-647-5225; protection of American vessels and seamen.

Welfare and Whereabouts: 202-647-5225; search for nonofficial United States nationals who have not been heard from for an undue length of time and/or about whom there is special concern; transmission of emergency messages to United States nationals abroad. For other help contact: Overseas Citizen Services, Bureau of Consular Affairs, U.S. Department of State, 2201 C St. NW, Washington, DC 20520, 202-647-5225.

5) Country Information Studies:
For someone who wants more than what the typical travel books tell about a specific country, this series of books deals with more in-depth knowledge of the country being visited. Each book describes the origins and traditions of the people and their social and national attitudes, as well as the economics, military, political and social systems. For a more complete listing of this series and price information, contact: Superintendent of Documents, U.S. Government Printing Office, Washington, DC 20402, 202-512-1800.

6) Foreign Country Background Notes:
Background Notes on the Countries of the World is a series of short, factual pamphlets with information on the country's land, people, history, government, political conditions, economy, foreign relations, and U.S. foreign policy. Each pamphlet also includes a factual profile, brief travel notes, a country map, and a reading list. Contact: Public Affairs Bureau, U.S. Department of State, Room 4827A, 2201 C St. NW, Washington, DC 20520, 202-647-2518 for a free copy of *Background Notes* for the countries you plan to visit. This material is also available from the: Superintendent of Documents, U.S. Government Printing Office, Washington, DC 20402, 202-512-1800. Single copies cost from $1.50 to $56 for a set.

7) Foreign Language Materials:
The Defense Language Institute Foreign Language Center (DLIFC) has an academic library with holdings of over 100,000 books and periodicals in 50 different foreign languages. These

Be patient. If any phone number is incorrect, call (area code) 555-1212 and request the new listing.

materials are available through the national interlibrary loan program which can be arranged through your local librarian.

8) Foreign Language Training:

The Foreign Service Institute is an in-house educational institution for foreign service officers, members of their families and employees of other government agencies. It provides special training in 50 foreign languages. Its instructional materials, including books and tapes, are designed to teach modern foreign languages. Instruction books must be purchased from Superintendent of Documents, U.S. Government Printing Office, Washington, DC 20402, 202-512-1800. Tapes must be purchased from the National Audiovisual Center, National Archive, NTIS, Springfield, VA 22161, 1-800-788-6282 or 703-487-8400.

9) Free Booklets for Travelers:

The following booklets and guides are available free of charge:

Travel Information: Your Trip Abroad:

Contains basic information such as how to apply for a passport, customs tips, lodging information, and how American consular officers can help you in an emergency. Contact: Publications Distribution, Bureau of Public Affairs,

U.S. Department of State, 2201 C St. NW, Room 5815A, Washington, DC 20520, 202-647-9859.

Customs Information:

Provides information about custom regulations both when returning to the U.S. as well as what to expect when traveling to different parts of the world. Contact: Customs Office, P.O. Box 7118, Washington, DC 20044.

Visa Requirements of Foreign Governments:

Lists entry requirements of U.S. citizens traveling as tourists, and where and how to apply for visas and tourist cards. Contact: Passport Services, Bureau of Consular Affairs, U.S. Department of State, 1425 K St. NW, Room G-62, Washington, DC 20524, 202-647-0518.

10) Passport Information:

A recorded telephone message provides general information on what is needed when applying for a U.S. passport. Call 202-647-0518. U.S. citizens and nationals can apply for passports at all passport agencies as well as those post offices and federal and state courts authorized to accept passport applications.

Economics, Demographics, and Statistics
General Sources

* See also Information on People, Companies, and Mailing Lists Chapter
* See also Current Events and Homework Chapter
* See also Experts Chapter

During a recent hearing on Capitol Hill, a congressman asked a Bureau of the Census official why so much money needs to be spent collecting census data when all the information is contained in the popular paperback, *Information Please Almanac*. Of course, all this information comes from the Census Bureau which conducts surveys and the decennial census. This attitude is typical of those who have no idea that the U.S. Government is the largest producer of data in the world, and that anyone else selling it is probably getting it from Uncle Sam. The major publication which identifies many of the statistical sources from the federal government is the *Statistical Abstract of the U.S.* Be sure you look through the Experts Chapter where thousands of data experts are listed by name and telephone number. Most Census information is available on the World Wide Web at http://www.census.gov.

* 1990 Census Block-Numbered Maps
Customer Services Branch
Data User Services Division
Bureau of the Census
Washington, DC 20233   301-457-4100
The 1990 census block-numbered map series includes county-wide maps prepared on the smallest possible number of map sheets at the maximum practical scale. The 1992 map series depicts each county (or county equivalent) on one or more map sheets--depending on the areal size and shape of the county, the number of blocks in the county, and the density of the block pattern--that will allow displaying all block numbers and feature identifiers, as well as show the county boundary and the (MCDs)/(CCDs), places, and census tracts/BNAs in the county. Each county consists of one or more parent sheets at a single scale, plus insets of densely settled geographic areas as required. As a result, the maps for counties could be at different scales. Insets will be single sheets at a larger scale. In densely developed areas where an inset will not fit on one sheet, multiple-sheet insets are used. An index showing the map sheet and inset coverage are included. The standard sheet size for all maps is 36" x 42" with a maximum 32" x 32" map display area. Data users must purchase these maps from the Census Bureau; they will not be printed and sold through the Government Printing Office (GPO) as in 1980. The maps will be produced by map plotting equipment on paper by Census Bureau staff. There is a charge of $5 per map sheet and $25 processing fee per order.

* 1990 Tabulation and Publication Report
Customer Services Branch
Data User Services Division
Bureau of the Census
Washington, DC 20233   301-457-4100
The *1990 Census of Population and Housing Tabulation and Publication Program* report describes the 1990 census tabulation and publication program for the 50 states and the District of Columbia. While it is impossible to anticipate all user needs in a changing environment, the Census Bureau designed the 1990 census tabulation and publication program to meet a variety of data needs for different segments of the data user community. Highlights in the report include information on questionnaire content, sample design and disclosure avoidance, dissemination media, map products, data products, custom data products, how to obtain 1990 census data products, and a dictionary of geographic terms. For further information about the report, or to order a free copy, contact the Customer Services Branch. For more information about the tabulation and publication program, contact the Data Products Branch, Decennial Planning Division, Census Bureau, Washington, DC 20233; 301-457-3946.

* X-11.2 and X-11.2Q Seasonal Adjustments
Customer Services (Diskettes)
Data User Services Division
Bureau of the Census
Washington, DC 20233   301-457-4100
Two improved versions of the Census-developed X-11 and 11.Q seasonal adjustment software programs are now available which adjust series that range from 3 to 30

years. They are based on the ratio-to-moving average method which provides a moving average and includes trend-cycle curves, ratios of trend-cycle estimates, and estimates of seasonal factors from those ratios. The X-11.2 program adjusts monthly series with a variety of options for adjusting special characteristics. It provides substantial practical flexibility with respect to the kinds of series that can be adjusted. Included in the package are trading and holiday routines, diagnostic plots for output, and a table of the final combined adjustment. The adjusted data can be output to a pre-specified file. The X-11.2Q program adjusts quarterly series and follows the same basic procedures as the X-11.2 program. The trading day and holiday routines are not included, and some options differ somewhat. To request a data diskette, contact Customer Services and they will mail ordering information to you for the diskette files of interest to you.

* Agriculture, Economic, and Government Areas
Data User Services Division
Customer Services
Bureau of the Census
U.S. Department of Commerce
Washington, DC 20233   301-457-4100
The following agriculture, economic, and government areas statistical publications are free from this office.

Guide to the 1992 Census of Agriculture and Related Statistics
A Review of the 1992 Census of Agriculture
Guide to the 1992 Economic Censuses and Related Statistics
An Overview of the 1992 Economic Censuses is free from the Bureau of the Census
Guide to Service Industry Statistics and Related Data

* American Housing Survey 1993 on CD-ROM
Customer Services
Data User Services Division
Bureau of the Census
Washington, DC 20233   301-457-4100
The *American Housing Survey* (AHS) is the largest regular national sample survey that describes people and their homes in the United States. It is sponsored by the U.S. Department of Housing and Urban Development (HUD) and conducted by the Census Bureau which uses interviews to gather information on approximately 42,000 individual housing units and the households that occupy them. The 1993 Core file is in both ASCII SDF (flat) file and SAS formats (PC SAS Version 6.03). The files are microdata files containing the results of each individual interview in the national survey. The technical documentation that comes with the disc is very detailed. It sells for $150; the technical documentation alone is $40. For a brochure containing additional ordering information, contact Customer Services.

* Approved Recurring Reports Bulletin
Office of Records Management
Services (045A4)

U.S. Department of Veterans Affairs
Washington, DC 20420   202-565-8272

The *Approved Recurring Reports Bulletin* includes a list of reports which have been cleared by the Reporting Policy and Review Service for data collection or have been discontinued since the last printed issue. Contact the office above to obtain a copy.

* Automated Geographic Support System

Chief
Geography Division
Bureau of the Census
Washington, DC 20233-7400   301-457-1132

This interagency project was created to produce geographic products for the 1990 census. The geographic component of the new generation of computer-based approaches for taking the 1990 census is called the TIGER System (Topologically Integrated Geographic Encoding and Referencing System). The TIGER File provides geographic products and services from the 1990 decennial census from a totally automated single source. This means that all mapping and geoprocessing would be in complete agreement. In conjunction with the U.S. Geological Survey, the Geography Division developed a computer-readable map file for the whole United States, providing the most complete and accurate set of maps ever prepared for the U.S.--and the first from a computer file. The TIGER System is used to produce publication quality maps on high precision computer-driven map production devices to accompany the data files for the census bureau's 1990 decennial publication programs. For detailed information on the TIGER System, ask for the *Tiger Tales Presentation* from your regional Census office or the office listed above.

* Automated Management Information System

Office of Information Management Services (045A4)
U.S. Department of Veterans Affairs
801 I St., NW
Washington, DC 20420   202-565-8208

The Automated Management Information System (AMIS) is an agency-wide system designed to meet the U.S. Department of Veterans Affairs' statistical reporting needs. Contact the office above for further information.

* Bureau of the Census

Bureau of the Census
U.S. Department of Commerce
Washington, DC 20233   301-457-2794

The Bureau of the Census takes a census of the U.S. population every 10 years, and they keep the information collected from individual persons, households, or establishments strictly confidential and use it only for statistical purposes. The agency collects, tabulates, and publishes a wide variety of statistical data about the people and the economy of the U.S. These data are utilized by the Congress, the executive branch, and by the public generally in the development and evaluation of economic and social programs. Its principal functions include: 1) decennial censuses of population and housing, 2) quinquennial censuses of agriculture, state and local governments, manufacturers, mineral industries, distributive trades, construction industries, and transportation, 3) current surveys that provide information on many of the subjects covered in the censuses at monthly, quarterly, annual, or other intervals, 4) compilation of current statistics on U.S. foreign trade, including data on imports, exports, and shipping, 5) special censuses at the request and expense of states and local government units, 6) publication of estimates and projections of the population, 7) current data on population and housing characteristics; and 8) current reports on manufacturing, retail and wholesale trade, services, construction, imports and exports, state and local government finances and employment, and other subjects.

April 1, 1990, marked 200 years of census taking in America. A national census has been taken every ten years in the United States since 1790. Mandated by the U.S. Constitution, the decennial census was the basis for determining how many seats each state filled in the House of Representatives. The census provides important social and economic information about our people and our nation. Many federal, state, and local government programs, private corporations, and community agencies use census data. Each census portrays America, and over the years the census has revealed a great deal about how our country has changed as we have grown from a young agrarian nation of about 4 million people clustered along the Eastern seaboard to a complex post-industrial society of nearly 250 million spread across the continent and beyond. Techniques for taking the census have steadily improved over the past two centuries. The 1990 Census relied heavily on computerization in field operations, processing, geography, data tabulations, and products. The 1990 Census was the most accurate census in U.S. history. Issues such as census undercount and the homeless population were important factors taken into consideration.

* Business Economics - Publications and Databases

Public Information
Bureau of Economic Analysis (BEA)
U.S. Department of Commerce
1401 K St., NW, Room 713
Washington DC 20230   202-606-9900

A User's Guide to BEA Information contains program descriptions and entries for specific products and services, including publications, computer tapes, diskettes, and other information services. The first, general section of the *Guide* describes the products and services that cut across the range of the Bureau of Economic Analysis' (BEA) work. The following sections describe the products and services related to BEA's four program areas: national economics, regional economics, international economics, and other tools for measuring, analyzing, and forecasting. Some highlights include the following:

Survey of Current Business. A monthly journal containing estimates and analyses of U.S. economic activity. Includes the *Business Situation*, a review of current economic developments and articles pertaining to the national, regional, and international economic accounts and related topics ($41 per year). This survey has incorporated information that used to be published in the *Business Conditions Digest*.

Gross State Product, Annual Estimates, 1977-1989-. These estimates are the counterpart of gross domestic product and provide the most comprehensive measure of State production now available. The estimates are for the 50 States, nine BEA regions, and the United States, and for 61 industries. The DOS version is available for $20, and the Windows version for $40. Call 202-606-3700.

* Business and Industry Data Centers

Data User Services Division
Customer Services
Bureau of the Census
U.S. Department of Commerce
Washington, DC 20233   301-457-4100

The Census Bureau has established four Business and Industry Data Centers as economic counterparts to the network of State Data Centers. Contact this office for a free listing.

* Census Bureau Library

Library, Bureau of the Census
U.S. Department of Commerce
Washington, DC 20233   301-457-2511

The Census Bureau Library collection contains general statistical information, population areas statistics, demographics, migration, foreign country censuses, and the complete collection of census publications. It is open to the public, and photocopying equipment is available.

* Census Bureau's Online Data System

Customer Services
Data User Services Division
Bureau of the Census
Washington, DC 20233   301-457-4100

CENDATA is the Census Bureau's online service, available commercially for access from remote terminals or microcomputers, that carries selected current data, press releases, and publication lists from Bureau programs. If you need the most recent population estimates for states, counties, incorporated places, and selected towns and townships use CENDATA. CompuServe and DIALOG, information service companies, are offering CENDATA to their customers. Contact this office for more information about CENDATA content and on-line services, or call CompuServe: 800-848-8199; or DIALOG Information Services: 800-334-2564.

* Census CD-ROM Products

Customer Services
Data User Services Division
Bureau of the Census
Washington, DC 20233   301-457-4100

The Census Bureau continues to produce its popular large data files in CD-ROM format. CD-ROM products include:

1992-93 County Business Patterns
1994 County and City Data Book
1992 Census of Agriculture
1994 Tiger/Line Extract Files
1990 Census of Population and Housing

Economics, Demographics, and Statistics

* Census Data Diskettes

Customer Services (Diskettes)
Data User Services Division
Bureau of the Census
Washington, DC 20233   301-457-4100

The data diskettes are available from the Bureau of the Census. These files are generated on an IBM Personal Computer and can be used with compatible microcomputers using the PC DOS 3.0 or higher operating systems. Contact this office for a complete listing of those available.

* Census Data on CD-ROM

Customer Services
Data User Services Division
Bureau of the Census
Washington, DC 20233   301-457-4100

The Census Bureau now makes several of its large databases available in microcomputer format. To use Compact Disc - Read Only Memory (CD-ROM) you will need a personal computer, a CD-ROM reader, and the appropriate CD-ROM software for your system. The discs are standard 4 3/4" size and are compatible with all CD-ROM readers. If you are interested in learning more about the software and hardware requirements of CD-ROM technology, request an Information Packet from this office. To demonstrate CD-ROM products, Census Bureau analysts have written various software programs for public access. The software is available to users from the an electronic bulletin board accessed by modem on 301-763-1663.

* Census Depository Libraries

Data User Services Division
Customer Services
Bureau of the Census
U.S. Department of Commerce
Washington, DC 20233   301-457-4100

There are nearly 1,500 Government and Census depository libraries; these include large public and university libraries that will have census reports in their reference collections. The holdings in the Census Bureau's library are complete. To contact the library, call 301-457-2511. A listing entitled *Government and Census Depository Libraries Holding Census Bureau Reports* is free from the Census Bureau.

* Census/Equal Employment Opportunity Special File

Customer Services Branch
Data User Services Division
Bureau of the Census
Washington, DC 20233   301-457-4100

This special computer tape file provides sample census data to support affirmative action planning for equal employment opportunity. The file contains tabulations showing detailed occupations and educational attainment data by age. These data are cross tabulated by sex, Hispanic origin, and race. Data are provided for all counties, MSAs, and places of 50,000 or more inhabitants. For more information on this special computer tape file, contact this office.

* Census Newsletter

Superintendent of Documents
Government Printing Office   202-512-1800
Washington, DC 20402   Fax: 202-512-2250

Census and You brings you the latest news about Census Bureau products and programs. This monthly newsletter cuts through the complexities of Government statistical programs and tells you where to find the statistics you need on the latest trends in various areas, what products fit your needs, how to get in touch with the experts, where to turn locally for information, and what programs the Census Bureau is planning now and how to be sure your views are heard. It is available from the Government Printing Office for $21, S/N 703-022-00000-6.

* Census of Agriculture Diskettes

Customer Services (Diskettes)
Data User Services Division
Bureau of the Census
Washington, DC 20233   301-457-4100

These diskettes include data from the *1987 Census of Agriculture Advance Reports* for each State and each county with ten or more farms. County and State data items include: farms by size, land use, value of agricultural products sold, selected expense items, operator characteristics, major livestock and poultry inventories and sales, and selected crops by State. The *1987 Census of Agriculture Preliminary Reports* for each State is available for all states.

* Census Products and Services

Data User Services Division
Customer Services
Bureau of the Census
U.S. Department of Commerce
Washington, DC 20233   301-457-4100

The *Census Catalog and Guide 1992* is a one-stop guide that tells you where to look for every Census Bureau data product and service. In it you'll find information on every report, microfiche, computer tape, floppy disk, and map issued, 1980-1991; explanations of the censuses and surveys of business, manufacturing, and population-- plus all the others; and lists of over 5,000 sources of assistance--Census Bureau specialists, other Federal statistical offices, State and local agencies, and private companies. There also is a nationwide list of Government and Census depository libraries. The book sells for $17. To fax orders or inquiries, dial 202-512-2250. International customers should add 25% to the cost.

* Census Regional Offices

The regional offices of the Census Bureau play a vital role in the work of the Census Bureau. They offer educational, inquiry, and reference services to federal, state, and local government agencies; minority organizations; businesses; libraries; educational institutions; community service organizations; the media; and the general public. Information services specialists in the offices assist data users across the country by furnishing information about Census Bureau reports and tape files, and making presentations at workshops and conferences. The Information Services Program staff in all 12 offices can help:

Atlanta
101 Marietta St., NE, Suite 3200, Atlanta, GA 30303-2700; 404-730-3833

Boston
2 Copley Place, Suite 201, Boston, MA 02117-9108; 617-424-0510

Charlotte
901 Center Park Dr., Charlotte, NC 28217-2935; 704-344-6144

Chicago
2255 Enterprise Dr., Suite 5501, Westchester, IL 60154-5800; 708-562-1723

Dallas
6303 Harry Hines Blvd., Suite 210 E, Dallas, TX 75235; 214-767-7105

Denver
6900 W. Jefferson, P.O. Box 272020, Denver, CO 80227-9020; 303-969-7750

Detroit
27300 W. 11 Mile Rd., Suite 200, South Field, MI 48034; 313-259-1875

Kansas City
Gateway Tower II, Suite 600, 400 State Ave., Kansas City, KS 66101-2410; 913-551-6711

Los Angeles
15350 Sherman Way, Suite 300, Van Nuys, CA 91406-4224; 818-904-6339

New York
Federal Office Building, Room 37-130, 26 Federal Plaza, New York, NY 10278-0044; 212-264-4730

Philadelphia
105 South 7th Street, 1st Floor, Philadelphia, PA 19106-3395; 215-597-8313

Seattle
101 Stewart St., Suite 500, Seattle, WA 98101-1098; 206-728-5314

* Census Reports

Data User Services Division
Customer Services
Bureau of the Census
U.S. Department of Commerce

Washington, DC 20233   301-457-4100

The Bureau publishes a number of guides, catalogs, indexes, Factfinders, and other user aids. Most of these materials are available for reference as well as purchase; some are free. Printed reports for the individual economic censuses usually consist of separate series for industries, geographic areas, subjects, and special reports. Some of the series are designated as preliminary and will appear several months before corresponding final reports. Preliminary reports have limited detail, however, and their figures are subject to change in the final reports. Copies of printed reports can also be obtained on microfiche.

* Census Schedules Available to the Public

National Archives and Records Service
Reference Services Branch
7th and Pennsylvania Avenue, NW
Washington, DC 20408   202-501-5400

The United States population census records contain a wealth of information about people. They are useful in learning about one's ancestors and about local social and economic conditions at various times in history. Microfilm copies of the original population schedules, form 1790 through 1920 are open to the public at the National Archives and its regional center and at many libraries in various parts of the United States. Most now have facilities for making paper copies from the microfilm.

* Census Statistical Areas Committees

Census statistical areas committees consist of local data users with an interest in the census statistical areas programs. These committees exist in all metropolitan statistical areas and some other counties. The committee memberships represent the data users within the community by including planners, representatives from the business community, government agencies, the media, minority organizations, and neighborhood associations. The local census statistical areas committees play an important part in defining geographic statistical areas. The committees recommend or approve the boundaries for statistical reporting units. Each local committee selects a census statistical areas key person as a liaison between the Bureau of the Census and the committee for these programs. For the key person in your area, contact the Census Bureau regional office nearest you.

* Census Telephone Contacts

Data User Services Division
Customer Services
Bureau of the Census
U.S. Department of Commerce
Washington, DC 20233   301-457-4100

Telephone Contacts for Data Users is free from the Census Bureau.

* Census Tract/Block Numbering Area Outline Maps

Customer Services Branch
Data User Services Division
Bureau of the Census
Washington, DC 20233   301-457-4100

These maps show census tract/block numbering area boundaries and numbers and the features and feature names underlying these boundaries (for example, the boundaries and names of counties, county subdivisions, and places). The scale of the maps are determined such that the number of map sheets for each area are minimal, but vary by area. For densely settled areas, where the census tract/block numbering area numbers and boundary features cannot be shown, the Census Bureau issues insets at a larger scale. These maps are available in both electrostatic plotter version and a printed version. Data users who do not wish to wait for the printed maps can purchase these maps from the Census Bureau for a fee. Data users who want printed maps can purchase the printed maps from the Superintendent of Documents.

* Clearinghouse for Census Data Services

Customer Services Branch
Data User Services Division
Bureau of the Census
Washington, DC 20233   301-457-4100

The National Clearinghouse for Census Data Services is a referral service for users needing special assistance in obtaining and using statistical data and related products prepared by the Census Bureau. Organizations registered with the Clearinghouse offer assistance ranging from informational services, such as seminars or workshops, to technical services such as providing tape copies or performing geocoding. A list is available.

* Compensation and Working Conditions

Superintendent of Documents
Government Printing Office
Washington, DC 20402   202-512-1800

Each monthly issue of *Compensation and Working Conditions* includes selected wage and benefit changes, work stoppages, major agreements that expire during the next month, calendar of features, and statistics on compensation changes. The cost is $23 per year (S/N 729-003-00000-0) or $4.75 per single edition. For more information on this data, contact Office of Compensation and Working Conditions, Bureau of Labor Statistics, U.S. Department of Labor, #2 Massachusetts Ave., NE, Room 4160, Washington, DC, 20212; 202-606-6220.

* Consultation Over the Telephone

Data User Services Division
Customer Services
Bureau of the Census
U.S. Department of Commerce
Washington, DC 20233

Subject-matter specialists from all areas of the Census Bureau may be consulted by telephone. For detailed statistical information route calls as follows:

Government, Commerce, and Industry

Agriculture Data: 301-763-1113
Business Data:
  Retail 301-457-2687
  Wholesale 301-457-2625
Construction Statistics 301-457-4680
Foreign Trade Data 301-457-3041
State Exports 301-457-2227
Government Data 301-457-1486
Industry Data 301-457-4817
Manufacturers Data 301-457-4769

Population, Housing, and Income

Housing Data 301-763-8553
International Statistics 301-457-1403
Population Data 301-457-2422
Special Demographic Studies 301-457-2422

* Consumer Expenditure and Family Budgets

Consumer Expenditure Surveys Division
Office of Prices and Living Conditions
Bureau of Labor Statistics (BLS)
U.S. Department of Labor
#2 Massachusetts Ave., NE
Washington, DC 20212   202-606-6872

The *Consumer Expenditure Studies*, a continuing annual survey of consumer expenditures and income, is the basic source of data for the revision of items and weights in the market basket of consumer purchases to be priced for the Consumer Price Index. Selected data is classified by income class, family size, and other demographic and economic characteristics of consumer units. Coverage includes the urban population of the U.S. through 1983, and the total population in 1984 and after.

* Consumer Price Index on Computer Diskette

BLS Office of Publications
U.S. Department of Labor
441 G St., NW, Room 2831A
Washington, DC 20212   202-606-7000

Computer diskettes offer an easy-to-use way to manipulate data for economists, other social scientists, researchers, managers, and policy makers with an interest in measuring employment, prices, productivity, injuries and illnesses, and wages. BLS diskette users need an IBM-compatible microcomputer and Lotus 1-2-3 Version 2. Each diskette contains the named data series and a brief technical description that highlights regular revisions, if any, and typical uses for statistics. A flyer is available which describes the diskettes available and their cost.

* Consumer Price Index Within 24 hours

National Technical Information Service
U.S. Department of Commerce
5285 Port Royal Road

Be patient. If any phone number is incorrect, call (area code) 555-1212 and request the new listing.

857

Springfield, VA 22161   703-487-4630

A Consumer Price Index (CPI) data summary is available by mailgram within 24 hours of the CPI release. It provides unadjusted and seasonally adjusted U.S. City average data for all urban consumers and for urban wage earners and clerical workers. The cost of this service is $190 per year.

* Consumer Prices

Division of Consumer Prices
Bureau of Labor Statistics
U.S. Department of Labor
#2 Massachusetts Ave., NE
Room 3615
Washington, DC 20212-0001   202-606-7000

The Labor Department measures consumer price changes for a predetermined market basket of consumer goods and services for two population groups: all urban consumers, and urban wage earners and clerical workers. The fixed market basket includes items representing all goods and services purchased for everyday living by all urban residents. Monthly and bimonthly indexes are available for various geographic regions.

* Consumer Purchasing Power Index

Superintendent of Documents
Government Printing Office
Washington, DC 20402   202-512-1800

Each monthly issue of the *Consumer Price Index Detailed Report* provides a comprehensive summary of price movements for the month, plus statistical tables, charts, and technical notes. The report covers two indexes, the Consumer Price Index for All Urban Consumers, and the Consumer Price Index for Wage Earners and Clerical Workers. The indexes reflect data for the U.S. city average and selected areas. An annual subscription is available for $24 (S/N 729-002-00000-3). A single issue costs $7.50.

* Cost-Reimbursable Surveys from Census

Special Census Staff
Demographic Surveys Division
Bureau of the Census
U.S. Department of Commerce
Federal Bldg. 3, Room 3319
Washington, DC 20233   301-457-3801

Upon request the Census Bureau conducts cost-reimbursable surveys and special studies for federal agencies on such topics as employment, health, housing, crime, and consumer expenditures. It also performs similar work for educational institutions, qualified private organizations, and takes special censuses requested by local governments needing up-to-date census figures. Contact this division for more information.

* County and City Data Book

Superintendent of Documents
Government Printing Office   202-512-1800
Washington, DC 20402-9325   Fax: 202-512-2250

The *County and City Data Book* is your one-stop, official source for county and city data. You can profile or compare thousands of cities and counties. It gives you quick access to comprehensive data including maps for each state highlighting metropolitan counties and cities with 25,000 or more inhabitants. It answers these questions:

What percentage of your county's population is made up of persons 65 years old and over?
Which county in your state experienced the largest increase in business establishments?
How many building permits authorized new housing in your city?

The subjects covered include agriculture, bank deposits, business, climate, crime, electric bills, employment, government finances, health care, housing, personal income, population, poverty, vital statistics, and many more. The book sells for $40, S/N 003-024-08753-7. International customers should add 25% to the cost.

* County and City Data Books: 1983, 1988, and 1994

Customer Services (Diskettes)
Data User Services Division
Bureau of the Census
Washington, DC 20233   301-457-4100

The 1988 and 1983 files provide a compendia of data from the *1994 Census of Population and Housing*, the *1992 Economic Census*, the *1987 Census of Agriculture*, and other data from a variety of federal government, private agency, and national association sources. Some data items included are vital statistics, government employment, climate, and social security.

* County Business Patterns on Diskette

Customer Services (Diskettes)
Data User Services Division
Bureau of the Census
Washington, DC 20233   301-457-4100

Data on diskette are available annually for every U.S. county--1983 to 1989--and show number of establishments, employment, and payroll, for industries in the Standard Industrial Classification (SIC) levels: two-digit State and county level, 2-, 3-, and 4-digit at U.S. level. Software is not provided.

* County Subdivision Maps

Customer Services Branch
Data User Services Division
Bureau of the Census
Washington, DC 20233   301-457-4100

These maps show the names and boundaries of all counties (or county equivalent) and subdivisions in each State, as well as all places for which the Census Bureau tabulates data for the 1990 census. They also depict American Indian reservations, including off-reservation trust lands, tribal jurisdiction statistical areas in Oklahoma, tribal designated statistical areas, Alaska Native Regional Corporations, and Alaska Native village statistical areas. All boundaries are as of January 1, 1990. Both electrostatically plotted (computer-generated) and printed maps are available. The plotted maps are made to order and sold separately from the data products. The electrostatic plotter paper sheet size is generally 36" x 42" with the largest size being 36" x 48" long. The number of map sheets for each area varies, depending on coverage type, size, scale and population density. The printed reports can be purchased through the Superintendent of Documents, Government Printing Office, Washington, DC 20402-9325; 202-512-1800.

* County-to-County Migration

Customer Services Branch
Data User Services Division
Bureau of the Census
Washington, DC 20233   301-457-4100

Computer files are issued by state, providing summary records for all intrastate county-to-county migration streams and significant interstate county-to-county migration streams. Each record includes codes for the geographic area of origin, codes for the geographic area of destination, and selected characteristics of the persons who made up the migration stream. For more information on these special computer tape files, contact this Census office.

* Current Economic Data

Data User Services Division
Customer Services
Bureau of the Census
U.S. Department of Commerce
Washington, DC 20233   301-457-4100

The Census Bureau's integrated program of current surveys produced data supporting key indicators of monthly economic performance and quarterly GNP calculations covering most goods producing sectors. The Bureau has taken steps to improve and expand its economic products and services in a number of areas. The Bureau improved current merchandise trade data by re-instituting seasonal adjustments of monthly imports and exports, generating new tabulations of state-of-shipment for exports, providing monthly graphic information on trade performance, and publishing data for imports (c.i.f. basis) and imports (customs basis) simultaneously. Contact this office for more information the economic data products from Census.

* Current Employment Analyses

Office of Employment and Unemployment Statistics
Bureau of Labor Statistics
U.S. Department of Labor
#2 Massachusetts Ave., NE
Room 4675
Washington, DC 20212   202-606-6378

Labor force statistics from the *Current Population Survey* provide a comprehensive body of information on the employment and unemployment experience of the nation's population, classified by age, sex, race, and a variety of other characteristics. The data is published in a variety of sources, including the monthly news release, *The Employment Situation*, and the monthly periodical, *Employment and Earnings*. Data uses include economic indicators, measure of potential labor supply, and evaluation of wage rates and earnings trends for specific demographic groups.

* Detailed Census Information

For detailed information about the contents of specific censuses, programs, or publications, contact the following offices:

General Trade

Retail Trade	301-457-2687
Wholesale Trade	301-457-2725
Service Industries	301-457-2689
Transportation	301-457-2777
Establishment Data	301-763-7596
Truck, commodity surveys	301-457-2797

Manufacturers

Electrical and Trnasportation	301-457-4817
Chemicals and Wood Products	301-457-4810
Food, Textiles and Apparel	301-457-4651
Construction Industries	301-457-4680
Metals and Industrial Machinery	301-457-4755

Minority- and Women-Owned

Businesses	301-763-5726
Enterprise Statistics	301-763-7174
Puerto Rico and other U.S. possessions	301-763-8564

* Economic Bulletin Board

Office of Business Analysis
U.S. Department of Commerce
14th St. and Constitution Ave., NW
Room 4887
Washington, DC 20230   202-482-1986

The Economic Bulletin Board is a one-stop source for current economic information. It has the latest releases from the Bureau of Economic Analysis, the Bureau of the Census, the Bureau of Labor Statistics and other Federal agencies. The Bulletin Board includes summaries of economic news from the U.S. Department of Commerce, economic indicators, gross national product, Consumer Price Index, and special economic studies and reports, as well as listings of new publications and databases. The Bulletin Board is available 24 hours a day. Contact the office listed above for more information regarding the Bulletin Board and subscription fees.

* Economic Data

Center for Electronic Records
National Archives and Records Administration
8th St. and Pennsylvania Ave., NW
Room 18E
Washington, DC 20408   202-501-5400

The Center has a vast amount of economic data from various government agencies, such as the Bureau of Economic Analysis, Agencies for Economic Opportunity and Legal Services, Economic Stabilization Programs, Economics, Statistics, and Cooperative Service, and the Bureau of the Census. Contact this office for a complete listing of information available from each agency.

* Economic Indicators

Public Information
Bureau of Economic Analysis (BEA)
U.S. Department of Commerce
Washington DC 20230   202-606-9900

The Bureau of Economic Analysis can provide you with basic information on such key issues as economic growth, inflation, regional development, and the Nation's role in the world economy. BEA's current national, regional, and international estimates usually appear first in news releases. The information is available to the general public in three forms: on recorded telephone messages, online through the Economic Bulletin Board, and in *BEA Reports*. The recorded messages are available 24 hours a day for several days following release. The usual time of release (eastern standard time) and the telephone numbers to call are as follows:

Composite Index Indicators: The message is updated weekly, usually on Monday, to include recently available component data. Release time: 8:30 a.m. Call 202-339-0345.

Gross National Product. Release time: 8:30 a.m. Call 202-606-9700.

Personal Income and Outlays. Release time: 10:00 a.m. Call 202-606-5360.

Merchandise Trade, Balance of Payments Basis or U.S. International Transactions. Release time: 10:00 a.m. Call 202-606-9545.

News releases are available on the Economic Bulletin Board shortly after their release. Selected estimates and articles are also available. The Bulletin Board is available by subscription from the U.S. Department of Commerce, STAT USA, Room H-4885, Washington DC 20230; 202-482-1986. The *BEA Reports* present information contained in BEA news releases and are mailed the day after estimates are released. An annual subscription can be ordered from the Bureau. Contact the Public Information Office listed above for more information and a list of release dates for BEA estimates.

* Economic Census in the U.S.

Data User Services Division
Customer Services
Bureau of the Census
U.S. Department of Commerce
Washington, DC 20233   301-457-4100

Taken every 5 years, the economic censuses include the manufacturing, service, construction, and mineral industries; retail and wholesale trade; transportation; agriculture; and governments. For more information on the censuses of the U.S. economy, contact this office.

* Economic Monitoring

The Office of Economic Analysis
U.S. Securities and Exchange Commission (SEC)
450 5th St., NW, Room 11118
Washington, DC 20549   202-942-8020

The SEC's Office of Economic Analysis deals with the economic and practical issues that affect the Commission's regulatory activities. To accomplish this, it builds and maintains different computer databases, designs programs to access data, and develops and tests research methods. The staff looks at how market regulations affect issuers, broker-dealers, investors, and the economy in general. The office also closely watches the national market structure and regulation changes that affect the ability of small businesses to raise capital. Significant developments in the marketplace are analyzed, as are new trends in the securities market and new types of securities. Results of the studies are occasionally published with the Commission's approval. For more information on current and past studies, contact this office.

* Economic Policy Development

U.S. Department of Commerce
14th St. and Constitution Ave., NW, Room 4855
Washington DC 20230   202-482-1405

Economic Affairs analyzes economic developments, develops economic policy options and oversees the collection and distribution of a major share of federal government economic and business developments; promotes efforts to improve productivity; and analyzes supply and demand for strategic materials.

* Economic Reports

What follows is a list of the Federal Reserve Banks across the U.S., along with their free consumer publications available:

Board of Governors of the Federal Reserve System
Publication Services, MS-127
20th St. and C Streets, NW
Washington, DC 20551   202-452-3244

Consumer Handbook on Adjustable Rate Mortgages. Explains adjustable rate mortgages and some of the risks and advantages.
Consumer Handbook to Credit Protection Laws. Tells how consumer credit laws can help in shopping for and applying for credit and in keeping a good credit record.
Consumer's Guide to Mortgage Settlement Costs. Explains the mortgage closing process.
Consumer's Guide to Mortgage Lock-Ins. Describes various aspects of mortgage lock-ins.

Economics, Demographics, and Statistics

Consumer's Guide to Mortgage Refinancing. Discusses the process and some of the risks and advantages to mortgage refinancing.

Federal Reserve Glossary. Defines many of the terms used in monetary policy and in bank supervision.

Guide to Business Credit for Women, Minorities and Small Businesses. Advises consumers of their rights under the Act when applying for a business loans and helps consumers prepare effective loan presentations.

How to File a Consumer Credit Complaint. Tells how to file a complaint against a bank.

Federal Reserve Bank of Atlanta
  Public Information Department
  104 Marietta St. NW
  Atlanta, GA 30303-2713   404-521-8500

Economic Review. A bimonthly publication presenting new research and articles on the economy of the Southeast.

Federal Reserve Bank of Boston
  Bank and Public Services Department
  Office of Public and Community Affairs
  600 Atlantic Ave., P.O. Box 2076
  Boston, MA 02106-2076   617-973-3459

Checkpoints. Explains how to write, deposit, and cash checks; also available in Spanish and Portuguese.

Consumer Education Catalog. Lists consumer education materials published by the System.

New England Economic Indicators. Quarterly report of statistical data for the nation and New England states.

New England Economic Review. Publishes articles of broad economic interest six times a year.

Federal Reserve Bank of Chicago
  Public Information Center
  230 S. LaSalle St.
  P.O. Box 834
  Chicago, IL 60690   312-322-5111

Economic Perspectives. Bimonthly publication on banking, business, and agriculture.

Agriculture Letter. Monthly publication on agricultural conditions for the five states of the 7th Federal Reserve District.

Fedwire. Monthly publication on current Federal Reserve automated services such as electronic payment and automated clearinghouses.

Federal Reserve Bank of Cleveland
  Public Information Department
  P.O. Box 6387
  Cleveland, OH 44101-1387   216-579-2047

Economic Review. Quarterly publication featuring monetary, economic, and banking topics of district and national interest.

Economic Trends (Chartbook). Tracks latest economic statistics and briefly discusses the current economy.

Economic Commentary. Bimonthly newsletter that highlights a current banking or economic issue.

Federal Reserve Bank of Dallas
  Public Affairs Department
  2200 N. Pearl
  Dallas, TX 75201-2272   214-922-5270

Economic Review. Bimonthly publication of articles on economic and financial topics.

Federal Reserve Bank of Kansas City
  Public Affairs Department
  925 Grand Blvd.
  Kansas City, MO 64198-0001   816-881-2402

Economic Review. Discusses a variety of economic and financial topics; 4 issues per year.

Federal Reserve Bank of Minneapolis
  Public Affairs
  P.O. Box 291
  250 Marquette Ave.
  Minneapolis, MN 55480-291   612-340-2446.

Agricultural Credit Conditions. Quarterly survey of district farm economy.

Fedgazette: This quarterly newspaper includes articles, editorials and statistics on the district economy.

Quarterly Review. Includes feature articles on the district economy.

Federal Reserve Bank of New York
  Public Information Department
  33 Liberty Street
  New York, NY 10045   212-720-6134

Consumer Credit Regulators (Fedpoints 17). Reviews the responsibilities of the 12 Federal organizations charged with administering consumer regulations.

Economic Policy Review. Reports on business activities and the money and bond markets.

Federal Reserve Bank of Philadelphia
  Public Information Department
  10 Independence Mall
  Philadelphia, PA 19106   215-574-6115

Business Outlook Survey. Reports on manufacturing in the district and provides forecasts for the next six months; monthly.

Business Review. Bimonthly articles for readers with a general interest in economics.

Buying Treasury Securities. Provides basic information on investing in Treasury bills, notes, and bonds.

Electronic Banking for Today's Consumer. Explains electronic services such as ATMs, direct deposit, bill-paying services, and point-of-sale terminals, as well as consumer projections of Regulation E.

Fair Debt Collection Practices Act. Summarizes the main provisions of the Act.

How the New Equal Credit Opportunity Act Affects You. Outlines the Act's main provisions for consumers.

Plastic Fraud: Getting a Handle on Debit and Credit Cards. Discusses consumer awareness concerning credit and debit card fraud and the regulations protecting consumers.

Quarterly Regional Economic Report. Analyzes the economy of the district.

Your Credit Rating. Describes the importance of credit histories and consumers' rights when using credit, including ways to correct records.

How to Establish and Use Credit. Guidelines on obtaining credit and using it wisely.

Frauds and Scams. Tips on how to avoid telephone and mail fraud.

Federal Reserve Bank of Richmond
  Public Affairs
  P.O. Box 27622
  Richmond, VA 23261   804-697-8000

Cross Sections. Quarterly reviews of business and economic developments.

Federal Reserve Bank of St. Louis
  Public Information Office
  P.O. Box 442
  St. Louis, MO 63166   314-444-8444

Regional Economist. Quarterly summary of national and district businesses and agricultural developments.

Annual U.S. Economic Data. Provides selected economic statistics.

Review. Examines national and international economic developments; analyzes various sectors of the district; ten issues per year.

Federal Reserve Bank of San Francisco
  Public Information Department
  P.O. Box 7702
  MS 1110
  San Francisco, CA 94120   415-974-2163

Give Yourself Credit. Guides the consumer through various credit protection laws.

Economic Review. Discusses selected economic, banking, and financial topics; quarterly.

* Economic Studies
  The Office of Economic Analysis
  U.S. Securities and Exchange Commission
  450 5th St., NW, Room 11118
  Washington, DC 20549   202-942-8020

The following are just a few of the many economic studies that are available from the SEC. Contact this office to obtain one of the following or a complete listing of all the reports available:

Spillover Effects of Shelf Registration

Transcript of Proceedings in the Matter of: Economic Forum on Tender Offers

Institutional Ownership and Long-Term Investments

The Economics of Any-or-All, Partial, and Two-Tier Tender Offers

Shark Repellents and Stock Prices: The Effects of Anti-takeover Amendments Since 1980

Do Bad Bidders Become Good Targets?

* Economists: Regional, National, International

Public Information
Bureau of Economic Analysis
U.S. Department of Commerce
1401 K St., NW
Washington DC 20230   202-606-9900

The Bureau can provide you with an extensive list of telephone numbers of economists who can be contacted for information pertaining to their area of expertise. The list includes a wide rage of economic issues within national, regional, and international economics.

* Education-Related Surveys

Data User Services Division
Customer Services
Bureau of the Census
U.S. Department of Commerce
Washington, DC 20233   301-457-4100

In the educational field, a set of surveys provide information about principals and teachers, teacher supply and demand, staffing patterns, working conditions in the schools, policies of schools and school districts, and other data. Contact this office for more information on educational surveys.

* Elderly Statistics

Data User Services Division
Customer Services
Bureau of the Census
U.S. Department of Commerce
Washington, DC 20233   301-457-4100

The Census Bureau, playing a major role in collecting, publishing, and distributing statistics on the older population, is cosponsor of the Federal Interagency Forum on Aging-Related Statistics, as are the National Institute on Aging and the National Center for Health Statistics. Contact this office for more information on available statistics.

* Employment Projections

Office of Employment Projections
Bureau of Labor Statistics
U.S. Department of Labor
#2 Massachusetts Ave., NE
Room 2135
Washington, DC 20212   202-606-5700

Projections of U.S. economic growth and industry employment provides a framework for studying the factors affecting long-range economic growth. Data available include projections of total gross national product (GNP), demand and income composition of GNP, and aggregate components of demand specified by 160 industry groups under alternative assumptions for basic economic variables and government economic policies. Reference period for projections is for approximately 10 years ahead.

* Employment and Unemployment: Monthly Data and Estimates

Office of Employment and Unemployment Statistics
Bureau of Labor Statistics
#2 Massachusetts Ave., NE
Room 4675
Washington, DC 20212   202-606-6378

This office collects, analyzes, and publishes detailed industry data on employment, wages, hours, and earnings of workers on payrolls of non-agricultural business establishments. It also publishes monthly estimates of state and local area unemployment for use by federal agencies in allocating funds as required by various federal laws. In addition, the office provides current data on occupational employment for most industries for economic analysis and for vocational guidance and education planning.

* Exhibits and Conventions at Census

User Training
Bureau of the Census
U.S. Department of Commerce
Washington, DC 20233   301-457-1350

For information on exhibits and conventions, contact this office.

* Factfinder for the Nation

Customer Services Branch
Data User Services Division
Bureau of the Census
Washington, DC 20233   301-457-4100

The U.S. Bureau of the Census Factfinder for the Nation describes, in a series of reports, the range of Census Bureau materials available on a given subject and suggests some of their uses. Factfinders are published on an irregular basis as topical brochures that may be used individually, in groupings of related topics, or as a complete series:

No. 1. *Statistics on Race and Ethnicity*. 4 pp. 1981. 6 pp. 1991. .40.
No. 2. *Availability of Census Records About Individuals*. 4 pp. 1989. .25.
No. 3. *Agricultural Statistics*. 4 pp. 1989. 4 pp. .25
No. 4. *History and Organization*. 12 pp. 1989 .40.
No. 5. *Reference Sources*. 12 pp. 19892 .40.
No. 6. *Housing Statistics*. 4 pp. 1991 .40.
No. 7. *Population Statistics*. 4 pp. 1991. .40.
No. 8. *Census Geography--Concepts and Products*. 8 pp. 1991. .40.
No. 9. *Construction Statistics*. 4 pp. 1989. .25.
No. 10. *Retail Trade Statistics*. 4 pp. 1989. .25.
No. 11. *Wholesale Trade Statistics*. 4 pp.. 1989. .25.
No. 12. *Statistics on Service Industries*. 4 pp. 1995. .25.
No. 13. *Transportation Statistics*. 4 pp. 1989. .25.
No. 14. *Foreign Trade Statistics*. 4 pp. 1990. 4 pp. .25.
No. 15. *Statistics on Manufacturers*. 8 pp. 1990. .30.
No. 16. *Statistics on Mineral Industries*. 4 pp. 1990. .25.
No. 17. *Statistics on Governments*. 4 pp. 1990. .25.
No. 18. *Census Bureau Programs and Products*. 24 pp. 1990. $1.
No. 19. *Enterprise Statistics*. 4 pp. 1991. .25.
No. 20. *Energy and Related Statistics*. 4 pp. 1991. 4 pp. .25.
No. 21. *International Programs*. 4 pp. 1991. .25.
No. 22. *Data for Communities*. 12 pp. 1992. .40.

These *Factfinders* are available from Customer Services. A 25% discount is available on orders of 100 copies or more sent to a single address.

* Federal Budget: Economic Impact

Publications Office
Congressional Budget Office (CBO)
Ford House Office Building, Room 413
Second and D Streets, SW
Washington, DC 20515   202-226-2809

All information published by CBO is available to the public in print form only. Most analysis results in publications, but there are also working papers and memoranda available. Among the major on-going publications at CBO are the following:

Annual Report to Congress is done in two parts:
Part I: *Economic and Budget Outlook*, which has baseline budget projections.
Part II: *Reducing the Deficit, Spending and Revenue Options*.

Bill Cost Estimates. CBO prepares cost estimates for nearly every public bill reported by Congressional committees and shows how these legislative proposals would affect spending or revenues over the next five years.

Analysis of the President's Budgetary Proposal. CBO publishes an analysis of the President's annual budget that examines the scope and impact of the Administration's revenue and spending proposals.

The Sequestration Report. This biannual advisory report provides CBO's economic assumptions of real economic growth, estimates budget base levels according to current spending and taxing law and the effects on deficit targets, and calculates the amount of money to be sequestered to eliminate any excess.

* Federal Economic Policy

Office of the Assistant Secretary
of the Treasury for Economic Policy
U.S. Department of the Treasury
1500 Pennsylvania Ave., NW
Washington, DC 20220   202-622-2200

Under the Secretary of the Treasury, this office recommends economic policy and formulates policies that have general significance for the nation's economy.

Economics, Demographics, and Statistics

* Finding and Using the Data

Census Office of Public Affairs
U.S. Department of Commerce
Public Affairs Office, (2705-3)
Washington, DC 20233   301-457-4040

Census Bureau products are available in a variety of places. Libraries across the country have printed reports, and an increasing number have microfiche. Current publications are kept for reference and order at the 12 Bureau of the Census regional offices and the 47 U.S. Department of Commerce district offices. Summary-tape, public-use microdata, and geographic reference files, and flexible diskettes, as well as those microfiche (including recent out-of-print reports), maps, and publications not sold by the Government Printing Office (GPO) can be ordered from the Census Bureau. Help is also available through the Bureau's national headquarters. Copies of products and materials generally can be purchased from the Census office above or from the Superintendent of Documents, U.S. Government Printing Office, Washington, DC 20402; 202-512-1800.

* Fiscal and Federal Budget Alternatives

Publications Office
Congressional Budget Office (CBO)
Ford House Office Building, Room 413
Second and D Streets, SW
Washington, DC 20515   202-226-2809

The Congressional Budget Office (CBO) has published thousands of papers since its inception in 1974, and all are available to the general public. These reports are written to provide Congress with budget-related information and with analyses of alternative fiscal, budgetary, and programmatic policies. A listing of all CBO publications is available from the CBO Publications Office. All publications are available from that office, and many are available from GPO. CBO studies fall into categories including U.S. economy and fiscal policy; federal budget; commerce, industry, and trade; social programs; national security; and government operations. Congressional Office Division, U.S. Government Printing Office, Washington, DC 20402; 202-512-1800.

* Financial Statistics

Division of Research and Statistics
Federal Reserve System, Room B3048
20th St. and Constitution Ave., NW
Washington, DC 20551   202-452-3301

Economic and financial information is available on such topics as government finances, business conditions, wages, prices, and productivity. A variety of reports and studies are published regularly. Contact this office or any Federal Reserve Bank for more information on available financial statistics.

* Foreign Investment Statistics

International Investment Division
Bureau of Economic Analysis (BEA)
U.S. Department of Commerce
1441 L St., NW (BE 49)
Washington DC 20005   202-606-5577

The Bureau of Economic Analysis's (BEA) international economics program encompasses international transactions accounts (balance of payments) and the direct investment estimates. The international transactions accounts, which measure U.S. transactions with foreign countries, include merchandise trade, trade in services, the current-account balance, and capital transactions. The direct investment estimates cover estimates of U.S. direct investment abroad and foreign direct investment in the United States, income and other flows associated with these investments, and other aspects of the operations of multinational enterprises. Contact this office for further information on direct investment and international services.

* Foreign Money Markets

Foreign Exchange and Gold Operations
U.S. Department of the Treasury
1500 Pennsylvania Ave., NW, Room 2409
Washington, DC 20220   202-622-2650

This office monitors the foreign money markets for the U.S. Department of the Treasury. Contact them for more information.

* Foreign Portfolio Investment

Office of Foreign Investment Studies
U.S. Department of the Treasury

1500 Pennsylvania, Ave., NW
Room 5438
Washington, DC 20220   202-622-2240

Once every five years, this office conducts a survey of foreign portfolio investment within the United States. The last survey was conducted in 1994.

* General Accounting Office

General Accounting Office (GAO)
P.O. Box 6015
Gaithersburg, MD 20884   202-512-6000

The General Accounting Office (GAO) assists the Congress, its committees, and its members in carrying out their legislative and oversight responsibilities; carries out legal, accounting, auditing, and claims settlement functions of federal government programs and operations; and makes recommendations designed to provide for more efficient and effective government operations.

* General Accounting Office Annual Report

Information Handling and Support Facilities
General Accounting Office
P.O. Box 6015
Gaithersburg, MD 20877   202-512-6000

The General Accounting Office's (GAO) *Annual Report to Congress* highlights its efforts for the present fiscal year. It contains budget information, a list of recommendations to Congress, and a catalog of Audit Reports issued during the fiscal year. As with most GAO publications, the annual report is available free of charge for the first copy ordered (thereafter, $2 per copy).

* General Accounting Office Reports

Information Handling and Support Facilities
General Accounting Office
P.O. Box 6015
Gaithersburg, MD 20877   202-512-6000

Each month the Comptroller General sends a list of General Accounting Office (GAO) reports and testimony issued or released during the previous month to Congress, its committees, and its members. Up to one copy of each GAO report is provided free of charge, and $2 is charged for each additional copy.

* Geography of the Census

Data User Services Division
Customer Services
Bureau of the Census
U.S. Department of Commerce
Washington, DC 20233   301-457-4100

The Bureau collects and publishes data for two kinds of geographical areas:

Governmental
-the United States, Puerto Rico, and outlying areas under U.S. sovereignty or jurisdiction
-States, counties, and county equivalents
-incorporated places (e.g., cities, villages) and minor civil divisions (MC's) of counties (such as townships)
-congressional districts and election precincts
-American Indian reservations and Alaska Native villages

Statistical
-four census regions (Northeast, South, Midwest, and West) and nine census divisions, all of which are groupings of States
-Metropolitan areas
-census country divisions in States where minor civil division boundaries are not satisfactory for statistical purposes
-census designated places
-urbanized areas
-census tracts and block numbering areas averaging about 4,000 people
-census blocks--generally equivalent to city blocks
-enumeration districts--census administrative areas, averaging around 700 inhabitants, where block statistics are not available
-block groups--counterparts to enumeration districts, averaging 900 population, in areas with census blocks
-Neighborhoods--subareas locally defined by participants in the Bureau's Neighborhood Statistics Program
-ZIP Codes--Postal Service administrative areas independent of either governmental or other statistical areas.

In the census of retail trade, the Bureau publishes data for central business districts (CAD's) and major retail centers outside CAD's; in the census of governments, for school districts and other special districts; and in foreign trade and international research, for countries and world areas. Generally, survey data are published only for the larger areas, such as the U.S., its regions, and some States, while census data are made available for smaller areas as well. Contact this office for more information on Census geography.

* Government Auditing Standards

Superintendent of Documents
Government Printing Office
Washington, DC 20548   202-512-1800

The *Yellow Book--Government Auditing Standards* (S/N 020-000-00265-4, $4) carries standards for audits of government organizations, programs, activities and functions; and of government money received by contractors, non-profit organizations, and other non-government organizations. The standards are to be followed by auditors and audit organizations where regulated by law, regulation agreement, or policy. The statements pertain to the auditors' professional quality, quality of audit effort, and the character of professional and meaningful audit reports.

* Government Income and Expenses: Monthly

Superintendent of Documents
Government Printing Office
Washington, DC 20402   202-512-1800

For monthly information on the U.S. Government's monthly income and expenses, subscribe to the publication, *Monthly Treasury Statement of Receipts and Outlays of the United States Government*. The annual price is $36 (S/N 748-009-00000-1).

* Government Transactions

Government Division
Bureau of Economic Analysis
U.S. Department of Commerce
1441 L St., NW
Washington DC 20230   202-606-9900

The Bureau of Economic Analysis's (BEA) national economics program encompasses the government transactions on a national income and product accounting basis, which include estimates of government receipts, expenditures, and surplus of deficit. The estimates are prepared separately for Federal and for State and local governments. Contact the office listed above for further information.

* Homeless Statistics

Population Division
U.S. Bureau of the Census
U.S. Department of Commerce
Room 2375
Washington, DC 20233   301-457-2422

As part of the 1990 Census the Census Bureau made special efforts to include homeless persons in census counts and to meet public demand for information about homeless persons. The Census Bureau used two operations designed to count the homeless. A "shelter and street night" count took place that counted people in hotels and motels identified beforehand as shelters for the homeless, or that cost $12 or less per night. It also included "emergency" shelters and open locations in the streets, parks, and other areas not intended for habitation. Contact this office for a fact sheet of their study.

* Hours and Earnings Monthly Survey

Office of Employment
Bureau of Labor Statistics
U.S. Department of Labor
#2 Massachusetts Ave., NE, Room 4860
Washington, DC 20212   202-606-6555

A monthly survey provides hours and earnings data collected from payroll records of business establishments. The data available includes gross hours and earnings of production or non-supervisory workers in a variety of industries, and overtime hours in manufacturing industries. The data are published in a variety of sources, and are used as economic indicators, wage negotiations, and economic research and planning.

* Income and Program Participation Survey

Data User Services Division
Customer Services

Bureau of the Census
U.S. Department of Commerce
Washington, DC 20233   301-457-4100

New information on important aspects of household economic activity has continued to emerge from the *Survey of Income and Program Participation* (SIPP), including more detailed observations on income flows and frequency of participation in government assistance programs. Special reports issued from SIPP were *Who's Helping Out--Support Networks Among American Families*, and *Pensions: Worker Coverage and Retirement Income*. For information on these special reports, or questions about the *Survey of Income and Program Participation*, contact this office.

* Industry and Employment Projections

Office of Economic Growth and
Employment Projections
Bureau of Labor Statistics
U.S. Department of Labor
#2 Massachusetts Ave., NE
Room 2135
Washington, DC 20212   202-606-5730

State and area employment data classified by industry division, and gross weekly hours and earnings for production and related workers in manufacturing is available, as is other data, including demographic employment/unemployment, monthly labor force and unemployment, occupational employment, and area wage surveys.

* Industry-Occupation Employment Matrix

Office of Economic Growth and Employment Projections
Bureau of Labor Statistics
U.S. Department of Labor
#2 Massachusetts Ave., NE, #2135
Washington, DC 20212   202-606-5730

The National Industry-Occupation Employment Matrix provides detailed information on the distribution of occupational employment by industry. Coverage is for over 500 detailed occupations--wage and salary, self-employed, and unpaid family workers, and wage and salary workers only for over 240 detailed industries.

* Industry Productivity Measurements

Industry Productivity and Technology Studies
Office of Productivity and Technology
U.S. Department of Labor
#2 Massachusetts Ave., NE
Room 2150
Washington, DC 20212   202-606-5624

The Industry Productivity Measurement Program develops annual indexes of productivity for individual industries. Available data include annual indexes of output per employee hour, output per employee, output, employment, and employee hours, as well as annual indexes of industry multifactor productivity (labor and capital combined). Data are published in a variety of sources, including the annual bulletin, *Productivity Measures for Selected Industries*.

* Information Resources

Office of Information
U.S. Department of Veterans Affairs
810 Vermont Ave., NW, #600
Washington, DC 20420   202-273-5589

This office is the information management branch of the VA. This office is also responsible for VA-wide information resources management policy, and records management. Contact this office to request the publication, *Summary of Medical Programs*, which presents facility specific program data.

* Industry Wage Statistics

Office of Compensation and Working Conditions
Bureau of Labor Statistics
U.S. Department of Labor
#2 Massachusetts Ave., NE, Room 4160
Washington, DC 20212   202-606-6220

Data available from industry surveys include averages and distributions of straight-time earnings for representative occupations--nationwide, regions, selected areas--by size of establishment and other characteristics, depending on industry and how they were studied. Published in summaries and in *Industry Wage Surveys*, the data are useful for wage and salary administration, union contract negotiation, arbitration, and government policy considerations.

Economics, Demographics, and Statistics

* Information Services Specialists

Data User Services Division
Customer Services
Bureau of the Census
U.S. Department of Commerce
Washington, DC 20233   301-457-4100

Customer Services staff and subject specialists at Bureau headquarters, as well as information services specialists in its regional offices, are equipped to answer questions about census and survey data and provide personalized attention to your needs. To receive a telephone contact list, contact the office above.

* Interindustry Economics

Interindustry Economics Division (BE-51)
Bureau of Economic Analysis
U.S. Department of Commerce
1441 L St., NW
Washington DC 20230   202-606-5586

Input-output accounts for the United States show how industries interact--providing input to, and taking output from, each other--to produce the GNP. *Benchmark tables, based largely on the economic census, are prepared every 5 years. Annual tables are prepared using basically the same procedures as used for the benchmark tables, but with less comprehensive and less reliable source data. For more information contact the office listed above.

* Internal Auditing

Information Handling and Support Facilities
General Accounting Office
P.O. Box 6015
Gaithersburg, MD 20877   202-512-6000

The free book, *Accounting Principles and Standards for Federal Agencies* (#123095), provides guidance for internal auditing in federal agencies.

* International Comparisons of Productivity, Labor Costs, Economic Indicators, and Unemployment

International Training Division
Office of Productivity and Technology
Bureau of Labor Statistics
U.S. Department of Labor
#2 Massachusetts Ave., NE, Room 2150
Washington, DC 20210   202-606-5600

This office develops comparisons of productivity and labor costs to assess U.S. economic performance relative to other countries. Data available include indexes of output per employee hour, hourly compensation, and unit labor costs in manufacturing. The coverage includes 11 industrial countries plus regional groupings. Also available are data concerning labor force, employment, and unemployment for foreign countries, by selected characteristics, approximating U.S. concepts. This office also makes comparisons of prices, compensation costs, and other major economic indicators in industrial countries.

* International Energy Economic Research

Office of Middle East and Energy Policy
U.S. Department of the Treasury
1500 Pennsylvania Ave., NW, Room 5206
Washington, DC 20220   202-622-0174

This office under the Secretary of the Treasury studies international energy resources and technology and their impact on the United States' economy.

* International Finance

Division of International Finance
Federal Reserve System
20th St. and C St, NW, Room B1242C
Washington, DC 20551   202-452-3614

For information relating to foreign financial markets, international banking, U.S./international transactions, international development, world payments, and economic activity, contact this office.

* International Price Indexes: Export and Import

Office of Prices and Living Conditions
Bureau of Labor Statistics
CPI Information and Analysis Section

#2 Massachusetts Ave., NE, Room 3615
Washington, DC 20212   202-606-7000

This office measures change in the prices of commodities exported from and imported into the United States. Quarterly price indexes are available for all exported and imported items and major subgroups, such as food, beverages and tobacco, crude materials except fuels, animal and vegetable oils, fats and waxes, chemicals, manufactured goods, machinery and transport equipment, and miscellaneous manufactured articles.

* International Statistics

Data User Services Division
Customer Services
Bureau of the Census
U.S. Department of Commerce
Washington, DC 20233   301-763-4100

The Bureau published demographic statistics for the world's countries in cooperation with the Agency for International Development and also developed international data bases on AIDS, youth, and aging for developing countries. Also, the Census Bureau is assisting 25 countries in planning, conducting, or analyzing population censuses.

* International Visitors Program

International Visitors Program
Bureau of the Census
Public Information Office
U.S. Department of Commerce
Washington, DC 20233   301-457-1368

The International Visitors Program provides an opportunity for consultation with experts at the Census Bureau. Consultation sessions can last for a day to a week. Workstudy tours are also available, generally lasting two to six weeks. Statistical consultations are offered on surveys, data processing, and technical and analytical aspects of census and survey taking.

* Labor Statistics Availability

Division of Information Services
Bureau of Labor Statistics (BLS)
U.S. Department of Labor
#2 Massachusetts Ave., NE
Washington, DC 20212   202-606-7828

The Bureau of Labor Statistics (BLS) can provide you with a tentative release schedule for BLS major economic indicators. The schedule lists the information available (i.e., employment situation, consumer price index, productivity and costs, etc.), as well as the date and time of the information release. The *BLS Update* also contains the release dates for the quarter.

* Local Area Employment and Unemployment

Office of Employment and Unemployment Statistics
Bureau of Labor Statistics
U.S. Department of Labor
#2 Massachusetts Ave., NE, Room 4675
Washington, DC 20212   202-606-6378

This office provides labor force, employment, and unemployment data estimated by state employment security agencies. These data are used primarily to allocate federal funds to local jurisdiction. The coverage includes annual average data with demographic detail for 50 states, the District of Columbia, 30 large metropolitan areas, and 11 of their central cities, and monthly data to include 50 states, 330 areas, 3,100 counties, and 500 cities of 50,000 or more. The data are published in a variety of sources, including the annual bulletin, *Geographic Profile of Employment and Unemployment*, and the monthly periodical, *Employment and Earnings*.

* Longitudinal Employment Surveys

Office of Economic Research
Bureau of Labor Statistics
U.S. Department of Labor
#2 Massachusetts Ave., NE, Room 4945
Washington, DC 20212   202-606-7386

Every couple of years, this office updates *The National Longitudinal Surveys*, which study employment profiles of certain age groups. The groups include: young women who were 14-24 in 1968; mature women who were 30-44 in 1967; and youth who were 14-21 in 1979. Information available includes labor market activities, characteristics of jobs, earnings, unemployment, social and demographic characteristics, education, and training.

* Map Products from Census

Customer Services Branch
Data User Services Division
Bureau of the Census
Washington, DC 20233   301-457-4100

Superintendent of Documents
Government Printing Office
Washington, DC 20402-9325   202-512-1800

Each of the following map types are available for purchase separately. Listed are descriptions of the map products offered through the 1990 census program. This listing includes only those maps that are sold separately; it does not include maps that are prepared and included in the printed reports.

1) Count Block Map (1990): This is the most detailed of the series. It is county-based and contains block numbers and physical features, and the boundaries, names and codes for legal and statistical entities in the county. The scale varies by county and may include inset sheets.

2) P.L. 94-171 County Block Map: This is the same as the County Block Map described above and includes codes and boundaries of voting districts where these were delineated by states for the 1990 census.

3) Entity-Based County Block Map: The three series included in this category are: American Indian Area Block Map (1990); Alaska Native Area Block Map (1990); and Place Block Map (1990) -- for places in more than one county. The content is the same as the County Block Map. Scales are adjusted to focus on the subject entity.

4) Census Tract/Block Numbering Area Outline Map: This county-based map shows the boundaries and codes of census tracts or block numbering areas, the features and feature names underlying the boundaries, and the names and boundaries of counties, county subdivisions, places, and American Indian and Alaska Native areas. The scale varies by county and may include inset sheets.

5) Voting District Outline Map: This county-based map shows voting district boundaries, names, and codes; the features and feature names underlying the boundaries; and the names of counties, county subdivisions, places, and American Indian and Alaska Native areas. The scale varies by county and may include inset sheets.

6) County Subdivision Outline Map: This state-based map shows the boundaries and names of all counties and statistically equivalent areas, county subdivisions, places, and American and Alaska Native areas. The scale varies by state and may include inset sheets.

7) Urbanized Area Boundary Map: The urbanized area-based map shows 1990 urbanized area boundaries, the underlying features,and their names. It also shows the boundaries and names of states, American Indian and Alaska Native areas, counties, county subdivisions and places. The scale varies by urbanized area.

* Mapping Algorithms

Customer Services Branch
Data User Services Division
Bureau of the Census
Washington, DC 20233   301-457-4100

The Census Bureau is making the FORTRAN source code routines available that it used to produce TIGER maps on its Unisys 1100 Series mainframe computers, so that experienced FORTRAN systems analysts can learn how Census mapping algorithms work. However, the routines do not run on any computer system without extensive additional programming, and the Bureau will not support the routines, nor answer questions about them. If you would still like to obtain these algorithms to assist you in your own programming efforts, you can order them on computer tape together with documentation on the TIGER data structure for $600 from the office above.

* Market News Reports

Information Staff
Agricultural Marketing Service
U.S. Department of Agriculture
Room 3510, South Building
P.O. Box 96456
Washington, DC 20090-6456   202-720-8998

Skilled market reporters gather and document marketing information that is distributed quickly throughout the U.S. via telephone recorders, newspapers, radio, television, and in printed reports. The reports are available for seven commodities: dairy, tobacco, cotton, fruits and vegetables, livestock, grain, and poultry, and they contain information on supply and demand and shipping point reports that cover prices paid by types of sale. Much of the information is gathered and distributed by local field offices via satellite.

* Monetary Affairs

Bureau of Economic and Business Affairs
U.S. Department of State
21st and C Streets, NW
Room 6820
Washington, DC 20520   202-647-3105

This office evaluates foreign policy aspects of the functioning of the International Monetary System and examines international banking and taxation issues. A member of the Joint IMF-IBID, this office also conducts multilateral negotiations of rescheduling of foreign debts to the United States.

* National Income and Wealth Economics

National Income and Wealth Division
Bureau of Economic Analysis
U.S. Department of Commerce
1441 L St, NW (BE-54)
Washington DC 20230   202-606-9700

The national income and product accounts show the value and composition of the Nation's output and the distribution of incomes generated in its production. The accounts include estimates of gross national product (GNP), GNP price measures, the goods and services that make up GNP in current and constant dollars, national income, personal income, and corporate profits. Contact the office listed above for more information.

* New Census Materials

Data User Services Division
Customer Services
Bureau of the Census
U.S. Department of Commerce
Washington, DC 20233   301-457-4100

The *Monthly Product Announcement* is a free listing of every new report, computer tape, microfiche, and so forth, from the Census Bureau complete with price and ordering information, as it is issued. It is available from Customer Services office above.

* Online Economic Indicators

BLS Electronic News Releases Service
Bureau of Labor Statistics
U.S. Department of Labor
INC-Room 2860
#2 Massachusetts Ave., NE
Washington, DC 20212   202-606-7614

Economic indicators from the Bureau of Labor Statistics are available electronically at the time of their release. There is no charge for the data. Users pay only for the actual computer time used. Approximately 30 different releases a year are available online, including monthly releases on consumer and producer prices, earnings, employment and unemployment, as well as quarterly releases on productivity, employment costs, collective bargaining, and import and export price indexes.

* Policy and Procedures Manual

Information Handling and Support Facilities
General Accounting Office (GAO)
P.O. Box 6015
Gaithersburg, MD 20877   202-512-6000

The General Accounting Office (GAO) publishes the *Policy and Procedures Manual for Guidance of Federal Agencies*, the official medium through which the Comptroller announces principles, standards, and related requirements for accounting to be observed by the federal departments and agencies. Formation report forms designed by these agencies for the collection of information from the public are required to be cleared by GAO before they may be issued. The review and clearance functions are to ensure that information is obtained with minimum burden on those businesses required to provide the information, to eliminate duplicate data collection efforts, and to ensure that collected information is tabulated so as to maximize its usefulness.

Economics, Demographics, and Statistics

* Population and Housing 1990

Superintendent of Documents
Government Printing Office
Washington, DC 20402   202-512-1800

The Census Bureau provides the results of the 1990 census in various printed reports in different subject title series. The 1990 subject titles are *Census of Population and Housing* (1990 CPH), *Census of Population* (1990 CP) and *Census of Housing* (1990 CH). Most report series contain one report for each state, the District of Columbia and a United States Summary. They are available from the Government Printing Office.

* Population and Housing Statistics

Data User Services Division
Customer Services
Bureau of the Census
U.S. Department of Commerce
Washington, DC 20233   301-457-4100

The following population and housing publications are available free from Census: *Neighborhood Statistics From the 1990 Census*; and *Subject Index to Current Population Reports*.

* Population Survey

Data User Services Division
Customer Services
Bureau of the Census
U.S. Department of Commerce
Washington, DC 20233   301-457-4100

The *Current Population Survey* continues to generate the Nation's official measures of employment, unemployment, income, and poverty. Plans are in the works to redesign the survey early in the 1990s. The Bureau continues working with agencies sponsoring other recurring surveys on such topics as consumer expenditures, housing, crime, job training, and health, including the development of data on Acquired Immune Deficiency Syndrome (AIDS). For more information about the current population survey, contact this Census office.

* Prices and Living Conditions

Office of Prices and Living Conditions
Bureau of Labor Statistics
U.S. Department of Labor
#2 Massachusetts Ave., NE, Room 3615
Washington, DC 20212   202-606-7000

This office develops a wide variety of information on prices in retail and primary markets and conducts research to improve the measurement of price change. The program also includes Consumer Price Indexes, Producer Price Indexes, and export and import price indexes for U.S. foreign trade. The Bureau can also provide you with information on its studies of consumer expenditures, income assets, and liabilities of all U.S. families.

* Private Sector Productivity

Productivity Research Division
Office of Productivity and Technology
Bureau of Labor Statistics
U.S. Department of Labor
#2 Massachusetts Ave., NE, #2140
Washington, DC 20212   202-606-5606

This office develops measures for the business, non-farm business, and manufacturing sectors of the economy, as well as for nonfinancial corporations. Available information includes quarterly and annual levels, indexes, and percent changes for output per hour for all persons and related measures, such as unit labor cost, real and current dollar compensation per hour, and unit labor payments. Monthly employment and employee hour data are available.

* Producer Prices and Price Indexes

Office of Prices and Living Conditions
U.S. Department of Labor
#2 Massachusetts Ave., NE, Room 3615
Washington, DC 20212 202-606-7000

This office provides measures of changes in prices received by producers at the level of the first commercial transaction for many commodities and a few services. Price indexes are available for virtually all industries in the mining and manufacturing sectors. *Producer Price Indexes* is a monthly periodical, which includes a

comprehensive report on price movements for the month, plus regular tables and technical notes. A subscription is available for $35 per year (S/N 729-009-00000-8) or $14 per month from: Superintendent of Documents, Government Printing Office, Washington, DC 20402; 202-512-1800.

* Productivity and Technology Statistics

Office of Productivity and Technology Studies
Bureau of Labor Statistics
U.S. Department of Labor
#2 Massachusetts Ave., NE, Room 2140
Washington, DC 20210   202-606-5606

This office is responsible for three major research programs. The productivity program compiles and analyzes productivity and related statistics on the U.S. business economy and its major sectors, and on individual industries and government. The technological studies program investigates trends in technology and their impact on employment and productivity. And the international labor statistics program compiles and analyzes data on productivity and related factors in foreign countries for comparison with the U.S. experience.

* Productivity and Technology Trends

Office of Productivity and Technology
Bureau of Labor Statistics
U.S. Department of Labor
#2 Massachusetts Ave., NE, Room 2140
Washington, DC 20210   202-606-5606

To better understand the factors underlying productivity change, this office measures productivity trends in the economy, major sectors, industrial industries, and government. The staff also investigates and can provide you with information on the nature and effect of technological change within industries and across industry lines.

* Program Evaluation

Program Evaluation and Methodology Division
General Accounting Office
441 G St. NW, Room 4062
Washington, DC 20548   202-512-2900

This office evaluates the effectiveness of virtually any government program. These evaluations focus on both improving government, and introducing innovations in the evaluation of such programs. The Division encourages and maintains contacts with evaluation professionals in other federal agencies, universities, professional societies, and state and local governments, and fosters improved communication within the evaluation community. It makes available a series of papers introducing such topics as how to design program evaluations, and how to conduct survey questionnaires.

* Public Debt of the United States: Monthly

Superintendent of Documents
Government Printing Office
Washington, DC 20402   202-512-1800

For a monthly description of the public debt of the United States Government, subscribe to *Monthly Statement of the Public Debt of the United States*. The price is $37 (S/N 748-008-00000-4).

* Public-Use Microdata Sample for the Older Population

Customer Services Branch
Data User Services Division
Bureau of the Census
Washington, DC 20233   301-457-4100

The Census Bureau produces this product to meet the increasing demand for data on the older population. This file could be used to generate sufficient data, especially for the oldest age groups, to construct detailed cross tabulations by age, sex, race, and other characteristics. Contact this office for more information.

* Regional Economic Forecast

Regional Economic Analysis Division
Bureau of Economic Analysis (BEA)
U.S. Department of Commerce
1441 L St., NW (BE-61)
Washington DC 20005   202-606-3700

The Bureau of Economic Analysis's (BEA) regional economics program provides estimates, analyses, and projections by region, State, metropolitan statistical area, and county. Estimates of total and per capita personal income are used by the Federal government in formulas to distribute funds to States and local areas, by State and local governments for revenue projections, and by businesses in marketing and plant location studies. BEA also maintains econometric models to forecast annual changes in economic activity and to analyze the impacts of projects and programs. In conjunction with the projections work, BEA has developed estimates of gross state product. Contact this office for more information.

* Report Guidelines for GAO

Superintendent of Documents
General Accounting Office (GAO)
DHIS, P.O. Box 6015
Gaithersburg, MD 20877   202-512-6000

The *Checklist for Report Writers and Reviewers* (#091096) standardizes the report format and shows how it should be organized. It breaks a General Accounting Office (GAO) report down to its components--cover, transmittal letter, digest--and poses questions to use in judging how well each was written. The booklet includes reminders of GAO reporting policies, principles taught in Producing Organized Writing and Effective Reviewing (POWER), recurring reporting problems, and technical reporting requirements. Another publication, *From Auditing to Editing* (#095119), is a guide for teaching report writing. Each book is on microfiche and one copy per individual is available upon request.

* Resources, Community, and Economic Development

Resources, Community, and Economic Development Division
General Accounting Office (GAO)
441 G St. NW, Room 1842
Washington, DC 20548   202-512-3200

As with most sections of the General Accounting Office (GAO), this section does most of its work in the form of reports requested specifically by the Congress. However, the division does share its reports, testimony and studies with interested groups outside the government. This division coordinates GAO's work in the areas of food, domestic housing and community development, environmental protection, land use planning arrangement and control, transportation systems and policies, and water and water-related programs. The division also provides GAO audit coverage at the U.S. Departments of Agriculture, Commerce, Energy, Housing and Urban Development, Interior, and Transportation; the Army Corps of Engineers (civil function); the Environmental Protection Agency; the Small Business Administration; the Interstate Commerce, Federal Maritime and Federal Communications Commissions; the National Railroad Passenger Corporation (Amtrak); the Washington Metropolitan Area Transit Authority; the U.S. Railway Association; the Civil Aeronautics Board; the Federal Emergency Management Agency; and a variety of boards, commissions, and quasi-governmental entities.

* Revenue from Public Lands

Management Services
Bureau of Land Management
U.S. Department of the Interior
18th and C Sts., NW
Washington, DC 20240   202-452-7719

The Bureau of Land Management (BLM), Budget and Finance Division, is responsible for collecting and disbursing revenues and receipts from public lands. BLM is the fourth largest generator of revenues in the federal government, with approximately $133 million collected annually from a variety of sources, including timber sales, sale of public lands, grazing leases, right-of-way leases, permits, and mineral receipts.

* Seminars at the Census Bureau

User Training Branch
Data User Services Division
Bureau of the Census
U.S. Department of Commerce
Washington, DC 20233   301-457-1350

Seminars are available for librarians, government personnel, and for the general public to help you identify the types of statistical data available from Census and other Federal agencies as well as how to use these data. Seminars last from one-half day to four days, and there is a nominal fee. Current courses include:

Understanding Federal Statistics
Census Bureau Data on CD-ROM
In the Eye of the Tiger: Understanding and Using the TIGER System

From time to time the Bureau also trains people in preparing population projections and estimates, and on special topics. Contact the office above for information on fees and scheduling.

* Special Services of the Census

The Director
Bureau of the Census
Washington, DC 20233

The Bureau of the Census can provide you with special services on a cost-reimbursable basis, such as designing and carrying out sample surveys (including collecting data by mail or field enumeration), providing population estimates and projections, making special tabulations of data collected in censuses and surveys, and giving other technical assistance. The Bureau of the Census may act as consultant to or agent for groups on special statistical problems. Inquiries concerning special services should be addressed to the office above.

* Special Tabulations Program

Housing and Household Economic Statistics Division
Bureau of the Census
U.S. Department of Commerce
#307-I Iverson Mall
Washington, DC 20233   301-763-8553

This division handles specialized needs of the data user that are not met through the 1990 standard data products or the User-Defined Areas Program. Such needs include specialized cross tabulations, product formats, or geographic areas which require splitting blocks. The computer process for this program generally involves retabulating data from the confidential internal record files. The Census Bureau prepares these special tabulations on a user-fee basis. The Census Bureau provides free estimates of the cost and time required to produce a special tabulation. To obtain these estimates, the user must provide specific information on the proposed data content as well as the geographic areas. Contact this office for more information on available special services.

* State and Metropolitan Area Data Book

Superintendent of Documents
Government Printing Office   202-512-1800
Washington, DC 20402-9325   Fax: 202-512-2250

The *State and Metropolitan Area Data Book* contains statistics for states, metropolitan statistical areas, 738 component counties, and 510 central cities. You can use this edition to find the areas that are growing the fastest, with the highest median family income, or the most college graduates, to determine where your metro area ranks in amount of Federal contracts, retail sales, or service receipts, or to track past employment trends by industry between areas or patterns within an area. The book also contains explanatory notes, and source citations for finding additional information. The book sells for $26, S/N 003-024-07259-9. International customers should add 25% to the cost.

* State and Metropolitan Area Data Book 1991 on Diskettes

Customer Services (Diskettes)
Data User Services Division
Bureau of the Census
Washington, DC 20233   301-457-4100

These diskettes present selected data from the book. There are over 1,800 variables for states, about 300 for metropolitan areas and component counties, and over 80 for central cities. A wide variety of subject areas are included. Sources include the Bureau of the Census and several other national agencies both public and private. Note that free sampler diskettes previewing this product are available from Customer Services. To request a data diskette, contact Customer Services and they will mail ordering information to you for the diskette files of interest to you.

* State Data Centers

Data User Services Division
Customer Services
Bureau of the Census
U.S. Department of Commerce
Washington, DC 20233   301-457-1305

The Census Bureau began the State Data Center program to make statistical information more readily available to the public. There are State Data Centers (in almost all States, the District of Columbia, the Virgin Islands, and Puerto Rico) and private and public organizations registered with the Bureau's National Clearinghouse for Census Data Services located throughout the country. The Bureau furnishes data products, training in data access and use, technical assistance, and consultation to states. Listings of the centers are available upon request from the Census division listed above.

Economics, Demographics, and Statistics

* Statistical Abstract of the United States

Superintendent of Documents
Government Printing Office   202-512-1800
Washington, DC 20402-9325   Fax: 202-512-2250

The official *Statistical Abstract of the United States* is the one reference book to have in your home, office, school, or library. It is an extensive collection of statistics on social, economic and political subjects from over 200 sources. It includes source notes for each table and a guide to statistical publications for more information, a list of telephone contacts for key Federal statistical agencies, a special section on State rankings, a comprehensive index, many graphs and tables depicting analytical percents and rankings, and the latest available official data--quoted and used by experts in every field. The paper edition is $37, S/N 003-024-08787-1. The cloth edition is $42, S/N 003-024-08788-0. International customers should add 25% to the cost.

* Statistical Briefs

Data User Services Division
Customer Services
Bureau of the Census
U.S. Department of Commerce
Washington, DC 20233   301-457-4100

The Bureau produces the *Statistical Brief Series*--short, nontechnical presentations on such policy-related topics as child care, pension coverage, computer usage, consumer markets in China, and housing in selected metropolitan areas. Briefs are distributed to audiences ranging from Congress and government officials to the general public. Contact this office for more information.

* Statistical Methodology

Data User Services Division
Customer Services
Bureau of the Census
U.S. Department of Commerce
Washington, DC 20233   301-457-4100

Internationally recognized researchers have worked with Census Bureau specialists on a variety of statistical challenges. Studies included economic development in ghettos, undercount adjustment, value of fringe benefits, effect of income fluctuations on poverty rates, improving state-to-state migration estimates, and recalibration of earlier occupation and industrial classification to make them more compatible with 1990 census data. Contact this office for more information on these statistical studies.

* Statistics Services

Customer Services
Bureau of the Census
U.S. Department of Commerce
Washington, DC 20233   301-457-4100

Population, housing, business, agriculture, government finances, foreign trade--the Bureau of the Census gathers data on these and many other subjects. Do you need statistics like the following?

Which areas have the fastest growing populations?
What is the average value of houses in my neighborhood?
How do shoe sales in my area compare with sales in other parts of the country?
How many acres of wheat did farmers grow in my county?
How much money did my county government spend on road maintenance last year, and how did that compare with the neighboring counties?
How well do imports and exports balance in U.S. trade with the Mideast?

For more information on these and other statistics, contact this service division.

* Supplementary Reports

Customer Services Branch
Data User Services Division
Bureau of the Census
Washington, DC 20233   301-457-4100

Supplementary reports present special compilations of census data dealing with specific population and housing subjects as well as for sub-groups of the population. The types of reports vary from census to census. Some examples of supplementary reports include *Advance Estimates of Social, Economic, and Housing Characteristics*; *Social, Economic, and Housing Characteristics for Redefined Metropolitan Statistical Areas*; graphic chartbooks; thematic maps portraying 1990 census data; and an atlas of census maps that contain the printed publication maps. Contact this office for more information.

* Teaching Materials from Census

User Training Branch
Data User Services Division
Bureau of the Census
U.S. Department of Commerce
Washington, DC 20233   301-457-1350

CCSP Update keeps college instructors informed about new resources, teaching materials, and projects for students. It is available at no cost from the Census Bureau.

* Thematic Statistical Maps

Customer Services Branch
Data User Services Division
Bureau of the Census
Washington, DC 20233   301-457-4100

The maps, which the Census Bureau issues as part of the GE-50 map series, usually depict a wide variety of statistical topics. In the past, the Census Bureau issued these maps as a single sheet wall map. Similar maps also appeared in selected printed report series as page-size maps. For more information, contact this office.

* TIGER Database

U.S. Department of Commerce
Geography Division
Bureau of the Census
Washington, DC 20233

The TIGER database contains digital data for all 1990 census map features (such as roads, railroads, and rivers) and the associated collection geography (such as census tracts and blocks), political areas (such as cities and townships), feature names and classification codes, alternate feature names, 1980 and 1990 census geographic area codes, Federal Information Processing Standard codes, and within metropolitan areas, address ranges and ZIP Codes for streets. Contact this office for more information on the TIGER database.

* TIGER/Line Comments

State and Regional Programs Staff
Data User Services Division
Bureau of the Census
Washington, DC 20233

The Bureau of the Census would like to find out how you are using TIGER/Line data, especially your specific applications. Please send your comments to this address.

* TIGER/Line Files

Customer Services Branch
Data User Services Division
Bureau of the Census
Washington, DC 20233   301-457-4100

The TIGER database is not available to the public; however, TIGER/Line Files are. The TIGER/Line File is an extract of selected geographic and cartographic information from the TIGER database. The normal geographic coverage for a TIGER/Line File is a county. Each file contains appropriate census geographic area codes, latitude/longitude coordinates, the name and type of the feature, the relevant census feature class code identifying the feature segment by category and, for portions of metropolitan and highly populated areas, the address ranges and associated Zip Codes for each side of a street segment. The files can be combined to cover the whole nation. There are now two different sets of TIGER files: the 1992 version and the 1994 version. Contact this office for information. Prices are subject to change.

* TIGER System Information Assistance

Data Developments
Data User Services Division
Bureau of the Census
Washington, DC 20233   301-457-4100

Additional information about TIGER/Line and its various extracts, as well as training and technical assistance, are available from the Census Bureau, its regional offices or agencies participating in the State Data Center Program.

* Trade Product Classification

Data User Services Division
Customer Services
Bureau of the Census
U.S. Department of Commerce

Be patient. If any phone number is incorrect, call (area code) 555-1212 and request the new listing.

Washington, DC 20233   301-457-4100

The Census Bureau has prepared for implementation of the complex new Harmonized System of trade product classification. Meetings were held to inform exporters of the changes, and domestic product classifications were produced to support better analyses of production and trade flows. Researchers are studying the statutory request for constant-dollar information on U.S. merchandise trade. Contact this office for more information.

* Treasury Bulletin

Superintendent of Documents
Government Printing Office
Washington, DC 20402   202-512-1800

Treasury Bulletin is a quarterly synopsis of Treasury activities, covering financial operations, budget receipts and expenditures, debt operations, cash income and outgo, internal revenue collections, capital movements, yields of long-term bonds, ownership of Federal securities, and other Treasury activities. The annual subscription price is $31 (S/N 748-007-00000-8); the price per single copy is $11.

* Types of Data Files

Customer Services Branch
Data User Services Division
Bureau of the Census
Washington, DC 20233   301-457-4100

The Bureau of the Census gathers data on many subjects, but only a fraction of this information is published. To help meet needs not met by these regular publication sources, the Census Bureau maintains an extensive holding of data in computerized form. Almost 1,500 separate data files are available, the majority of which are products of the Bureau's regular data collection and tabulation programs. The types of files include:

Summary Data. Resemble information in published reports; however, data files are often more detailed and cover more geographic areas.

Public-Use Microdata Samples. Include records for unidentifiable individual observations--persons, households, and housing units in a form that protects the confidentiality of the responses, but allows users to design their own tabulations. The Census Bureau does limit the sample size and geographic identification on microdata files.

Geographic Reference Files. List geographic codes associated with specific areas; present computerized representations of maps; and relate various geographic concepts to Census Bureau geography.

Special Tabulations. Statistical information specially prepared by the Census Bureau at the request and expense of the user. These data are furnished on computer tape, printouts, or microfiche, and cannot be sold by the Census Bureau as a standard product for approximately 6 months after completion.

For a brief description of selected tape files and a list of files issued within the past five years showing the number of tape reels, price of technical documentation and references to the Data Development containing a more detailed file description, contact the office listed above.

* User-Defined Areas

Decennial Management Division/DPD
Bureau of the Census
Room 3554 (GOB-3)
U.S. Department of Commerce
Washington, DC 20233   301-457-3999

This program gives the Census Bureau a generalized capability to produce data based on locally specified geographic areas not available in census tabulations and publications. Through this program, participants are provided population and housing data for their specified area on a user-fee basis. The primary objective of the program is to process requests for data for specialized geography efficiently to ensure timely delivery of the program products for reasonable user fees. If you are interested in obtaining further information about the User-Defined Areas Program, contact the office above.

* Voting District Outline Maps

Customer Services Branch
Data User Services Division
Bureau of the Census

Washington, DC 20233   301-457-4100

The maps in this series show voting district numbers and boundaries as well as the underlying features such as roads, railroads, and rivers. They also show the boundaries and names of counties, county subdivisions, and places. The mapping unit is a county with a variable scale. The maps are created on demand are expensive to produce. These maps are produced using map plotting equipment on paper by Census Bureau staff. Contact this office for more information.

* Wage and Price Indexes on Computer Tape

Bureau of Labor Statistics (BLS)
U.S. Department of Labor
#2 Massachusetts Ave., NE
Washington, DC 20212   202-606-5888

The Bureau of Labor Statistics (BLS) major data series are available on magnetic tape. The standard format is 9-track, 6250 BPI. In addition to the data files listed, BLS makes some microdata tapes and also prepares customized data files on a cost-for-service basis. Available data files include consumer expenditures, consumer price index, export-import price indexes, and labor force, as well as many others. A brochure is available which describes the tapes, ordering information, and the cost of each tape.

* Wage Surveys: Area, Industry and White Collar Earnings

Office of Compensation and Working Conditions
Bureau of Labor Statistics
U.S. Department of Labor
#2 Massachusetts Ave., NE, Room 4160
Washington, DC 20212   202-606-6220

This office conducts three different types of wage surveys. The area and industry surveys provide annual data on averages and distributions of earnings for selected occupations in major industry groups in metropolitan areas. *The Professional, Administrative, Technical and Clerical Survey* has been revised. *The Occupational Compensation Survey*, as it is now known, resumed annual publication in 1993. The survey is used in the federal pay-setting process and provides data on salaries in white-collar occupations from a national sample of establishments.

* Women Worker Data

Office of Publications
Bureau of Labor Statistics
#2 Massachusetts Ave., NE
Room 2860
Washington, DC 20212   202-606-7828

This office publishes a wide array of information about women in the labor force. This information is presented to the public through a variety of publications, including news releases, periodicals, bulletins, reports, tapes, and diskettes. The pamphlet, *Women in the Work Force*, identifies the particular publications in which specific data services may be found, along with information on how to obtain BLS publications. The data includes information labor force status, employment, and unemployment, earnings and hours of work, education, occupational injuries and illness, and unpublished data.

* Workshops on Census Data

Data User Services Division
Customer Services
Bureau of the Census
U.S. Department of Commerce
Washington, DC 20233   301-457-4100

The Bureau conducts workshops for data users. For more information, contact the office above or the Data User Training Program at 301-457-1350.

* World Population Database

International Demographic Data Center
Information Resource Branch Program Center
Scuderi Building, Room 614
Camp Springs, MD 20748   301-457-1403

The World Population database contains population data for the overall world, its regions (i.e. Latin America, Asia, etc.) and 205 individual countries. Population statistics include total population, estimated projections, growth rate, migratory rate, and crude (number per 1,000) birth and death rates. Data is collected from a survey and is continuously updated. Contact this office for free searches and print-outs or to purchase diskettes.

Be patient. If any phone number is incorrect, call (area code) 555-1212 and request the new listing.

869

State Crime Statistics

* See also Law and Social Justice Chapter

You wouldn't put your kid in a day care center near an outdoor drug market or buy a fast-food franchise in an area where the crime rate is ten times the national average, but how can you stay away from such areas if the crime statistics aren't common knowledge? Among the largest databases maintained by states are those pertaining to crime and to law enforcement. These statistics provide a fairly accurate profile of how an area is affected by crime and how the police and the criminal justice system react.

The data are valuable for students and researchers, political aspirants, real estate companies, urban planners, journalists, private rehabilitation facilities, burglar alarm and security services firms, and, in particular, any business seeking a fairly safe place from which to operate.

Before drawing conclusions from state crime data, a number of factors should be considered, including:

* Strength of local police departments
* Economic profile
* Density and size of the area and surrounding communities
* Cultural factors such as education, recreation, ethnic makeup and religion
* attitudes of residents toward police, crime
* Policies and characteristics of other components in the law enforcement system
* Organization and cooperation of adjoining and overlapping police departments
* Membership and attitudes toward special police organizations
* Climate
* Standards of appointments to local police force
* Crime reporting practices
* Age makeup
* Voluntary reporting

Forty-nine states and the District of Columbia have a central collection agency for criminal statistical data. Most of them publish an annual report or a pamphlet summarizing crime in their state. These publications are available to the general public upon request. Only four states (Montana $4, North Carolina $15, Rhode Island $7, and Virginia $15) charge for these publications. While Idaho, Indiana, and Louisiana do not publish a compiled annual report, they do have computer printouts available.

Each agency's annual crime and delinquency report summarizes data pertaining to its own criminal justice system. Information is available on a state-wide and/or county-wide basis. Most reports are in the form of statistical tables with an introduction explaining how to use the information and a summary. Examples of the type of data available include:

* number of juveniles arrested in your state for possession of illegal drugs
* number of shoplifting convictions in your county

* incidents of white-collar crime in major metropolitan areas
* number of armed robberies
* aggravated assault
* forcible rape
* automobile theft
* arrests
* expenditures
* size of law enforcement personnel
* correctional offenses
* adult misdemeanor offenses
* adult probation
* juvenile probation

Other services include computer printouts, special reports, online databases, and transferring of information to diskette and magnetic tape. Most provide these services free or on a cost-recovery basis. Some agencies ask that you make requests in writing, especially if they are complex.

Nationwide information is available through the U.S. Department of Justice, Office of Justice Programs, Bureau of Justice Statistics Clearinghouse, P.O. Box 6000, Rockville, MD 20850; 800-732-3277 or 800-638-8736 for juvenile statistics. Their publications include the *Sourcebook*. The latest data release are available through their electronic bulletin board, 301-738-8895.

Another source of nationwide information is the Uniform Crime Reports, Criminal Justice Information Services Division, FBI/GRB, Washington, DC 20535. Publications include *Crime in the United States* ($24), *Law Enforcement Officers Killed and Assaulted, Hate Crime Statistics, Age-Specific Arrest Rates and Race-Specific Arrest Rates for Selected Offenses, Population-at-Risk Rates*, and *Selected Crime Indicators*. Requests for published and unpublished data; printouts, magnetic tapes, and book should call 202-324-5015. Requests regarding statistical models, special studies and analyses, crime forecasting, processing of summary and incident-based reports from data contributors, data processing, and data quality should call 202-324-3821.

The federal agencies listed above should prove quite helpful, especially for the state of Tennessee which is the only state that has no central collection agency.

List of State Crime Statistics Offices

Alabama

Criminal Justice Information Center, 770 Washington Ave., Suite 350, Montgomery, AL 36130; 205-242-4900. This division publishes the *Crime in Alabama Annual Report*. Computer printouts of selected data are provided if the information is readily available. Special statistical analysis of data not found in the annual report is also provided. There is no cost for these services.

Alaska

Department of Public Safety, Information Systems, Uniform Crime Reporting Section, 5700 E. Tudor Rd., Anchorage, AK 99507; 907-269-5703. The *Crime in Alaska Annual Report* is free. Computer printouts are not provided at this time.

Arizona

Department of Public Safety, Uniform Crime Reporting Section, P.O. Box 6638, Phoenix, AZ 85005; 602-223-2163. The department publishes the *Crime in Arizona Annual Report*. Computer printouts of selected data are provided at no charge.

Arkansas

Crime Information Center, Uniform Crime Reporting Section, 1 Capitol Mall, Room 4D 200, Little Rock, AR 72201; 501-682-2222. The Crime Information Center publishes an annual report entitled *A Public Opinion Report* from the Arkansas Crime Poll. Computer printouts of selected data are provided at no charge. Requests should be placed in writing and may be faxed to: 501-682-7444.

California

Department of Justice, Bureau of Criminal Statistics and Special Services, P.O. Box 903427, Sacramento, CA 94203-4270; 916-227-3460. Publications include the *Crime and Delinquency in California Report* and *Annual Criminal Justice Profile*, which are free upon request. Computer printouts are provided at $.30 per page. Requests for computer reports cost $150 per hour. Information is also available on diskette or magnetic tape. There is no additional charge for the software involved. Fees are based only on programming services.

Colorado

Department of Public Safety, Division of Criminal Justice, 700 Kipling St., Suite 1000 Denver, CO 80215; 303-239-4442. Publications include *Community Corrections Annual Report*. The office does not provide crime statistics printouts upon request.

Connecticut

Department of Public Safety, Department of State Police, Uniform Crime Reporting Program, Crimes Analysis Division, P.O. Box 2794, Middletown, CT 06457-9294; 203-685-8030. Publications include the *Annual Uniform Crime Report* and *Crime in Connecticut Quarterly Report*. Computer printouts of selected data are not available.

Delaware

Delaware State Police, State Bureau of Identification, P.O. Box 430, Dover, DE 19901; 302-739-5871. Publications and Services: This bureau publishes the *Crime in Delaware Annual Report* plus monthly computer printout reports of various statistics on the state and county level. Selected data runs are also available. Fees vary according to the complexity of the request.

District of Columbia

Metropolitan Police Department, Crime Research and Analysis Section (CRAS), Room 4156, 300 Indiana Ave., NW, Washington, DC 20001; 202-727-4100. Publications include the *Statistical Report of Crime Index Offenses and Arrests* which is published monthly and annually. Most computer printouts are provided free of charge.

Florida

Department of Law Enforcement, Uniform Crime Reporting Section, P.O. Box 1489, Tallahassee, FL 32302; 904-487-1179. This department publishes a four-page summary pamphlet of Florida crime statistics which is available at no cost. Computer printouts of selected data are available at no charge.

Georgia

Georgia Bureau of Investigation, Georgia Crime Information Center, P.O. Box 370748, Decatur, GA 30037; 404-244-2840. A four-page pamphlet with a breakdown of crime in Georgia is available free of charge. Computer printouts of selected data are also provided upon request, generally at no cost. On a case by case basis information can be transferred to magnetic tape and diskette.

Hawaii

Attorney Generals Office, Crime Prevention Division, Department of the Attorney General, Suite 701, 810 Richards St., Honolulu, HI 96813; 808-586-1416. A *Crime in Hawaii Annual Report* is published. Computer printouts of selected data are available depending upon the complexity of the request. Information is now available on diskette free of charge.

Idaho

Criminal Identification Bureau, Uniform Crime Reporting Program, Department of Law Enforcement, P.O. Box 700, Meridian, ID 83642; 208-884-7155. An annual *Uniform Crime Reporting Program Report* is available for free. Computer printouts of selected data are provided free upon request.

Illinois

Bureau of Identification, Illinois State Police, 726 South College St., Springfield, IL 62704; 217-782-8263. Publications include *Crime in Illinois*. The office will re-run

monthly special reports for individuals upon request. There is no charge for this service.

Indiana

Indiana State Police, Data Division, 100 Indiana Government Center North, 100 N. Senate, Indianapolis, IN 46204-2259; 317-232-8289. Although this office doesn't publish an annual report, it will provide individuals with computer printouts or copies of crime statistics. There is no charge involved in these instances. Data is also available on diskette or magnetic tape. Charges vary according to the complexity of the request. Detailed requests should be placed in writing.

Iowa

Department of Public Safety, Field Services Bureau, Third Floor, Wallace State Office Bldg., Des Moines, IA 50319; 515-281-8494. This department publishes the *Iowa Uniform Crime Annual Report*. Computer printouts are not available at this time although they are planning to expand their services in 1993.

Kansas

Statistical Analysis Center, Kansas Bureau of Investigation, 1620 Tyler, Topeka, KS 66612; 913-296-8200. The Statistical Analysis Center publishes the *Crime in Kansas Annual Report*. Occasionally low volume computer printouts are provided on selected data. In the near future, staff will transfer data to magnetic tape or diskettes that you provide.

Kentucky

State Police, Information Section. 1250 Louisville Road, Frankfort, KY 40601; 502-227-8700, ext. 359. Publications include the *Crime in Kentucky Annual Report* and *Traffic Accident Facts Report*. Computer printouts of selected data are available in special circumstances, depending upon the request. Most printouts are free.

Louisiana

Commission on Law Enforcement, Uniform Crime Reporting, 1885 Wooddale Blvd., Baton Rouge, LA 70806; 504-925-7526. Louisiana Uniform Crime Reporting staff does not publish an annual report, but computer printouts of crime statistics are available free of charge.

Maine

Dept. of Public Safety, Uniform Crime Reporting Division, 36 Hospital St., Station # 42, Augusta, ME 04333; 207-624-7004. Publications include the *Crime in Maine Annual Report*.

Maryland

Maryland State Police, Uniform Crime Reporting Unit, 1711 Belmont Ave., Baltimore, MD 21244, Attn. UCR; 410-298-3883. Publications include the annual *Crime in Maryland Report*. Computer printouts are not generally provided, but can be done upon special request.

Massachusetts

Massachusetts State Police, Crime Reporting Unit, 470 Worcester Rd., Farmingham, MA 01701; 508-820-2114. The Crime Reporting Unit publishes a *Massachusetts Uniform Crime Report* and a variety of special reports available upon request. They also do computer printouts and will transfer data to diskettes. Some additional information is available through an electronic bulletin at 508-820-2117.

Michigan

Uniform Crime Reporting Section, Michigan State Police, 7150 Harris Dr., Lansing, MI 48913; 517-322-1150. The Uniform Crime Reporting Division publishes an annual *Michigan Crime Report*, which is free upon request. Computer printouts of selected data are also free.

Minnesota

Department of Public Safety, Office of Information Systems, Suite 100H Town Square, 444 Cedar St., St. Paul, MN 55101-2156; 612-296-7589. Publications include an *Annual Report*. Computer printouts of selected data are provided at no charge if the information is readily available. Programmers will quote fees for complex requests requiring systems changes.

Mississippi

Department of Public Safety, P.O. Box 958, Jackson, MS 39205; 601-987-1212. Publications include an annual report. Mississippi does not have a central agency for collecting crime statistics. Each county or city has a department of safety that keeps individual records of criminal data. Computer printouts are not available. They are currently in the process of building an online database. Once this process is complete, computer printouts will be available.

Be patient. If any phone number is incorrect, call (area code) 555-1212 and request the new listing.

871

Economics, Demographics, and Statistics

Missouri

State Highway Patrol, Criminal Records Division, P.O. Box 568, Jefferson City, MO 65102; 314-526-6153. The *Missouri Crime Summary* is available free of charge upon request. No computer printouts are available.

Montana

Montana Board of Crime Control, 303 North Roberts, Helena, MT 59620; 406-444-3604. Publications available include the *Crimes of Montana Annual Report* which is $4. Computer printouts of selected data are provided upon written request.

Nebraska

Commission on Law Enforcement and Criminal Justice, 301 Centennial Mall South, P.O. Box 94946, Lincoln, NE 68509; 402-471-3982. The Commission publishes a *Crime In Nebraska Annual Report* which is free upon request. Computer printouts of selected data are available upon request.

Nevada

DMV and Public Safety, Uniform Crime Reporting, 555 Wrightway, Carson City, NV 89711; 702-687-5713. The Uniform Crime Reporting staff publishes a *Nevada Uniform Crime Report* annually. Computer printouts of selected data are available free of charge.

New Hampshire

Department of State Police, Uniform Crime Reports, 10 Hazen Drive, Concord, NH 03305; 603-271-2509. Publications include the *Crime Statistics In New Hampshire Annual Report*. Computer printouts of selected data are provided at no charge upon written request.

New Jersey

Department of Law and Public Safety, Division of State Police, Uniform Crime Reporting Unit, Box 7068, West Trenton, NJ 08628-0068; 609-882-2000, ext. 2392. The *Crime In New Jersey Report* is published annually. The office does not supply computer printouts of selected data.

New Mexico

Department of Corrections, Data Processing, P.O. Box 27116, Santa Fe, NM 87502-0116; 505-827-8655. Publications include an *Annual Report*. Computer printouts of selected data are available upon written request. Some fees may be involved.

New York

Statistical Services, New York State Division of Criminal Justice Services, 8th Floor, Executive Park Tower Bldg., Stuyvesant Plaza, Albany, NY 12203; 518-457-8381. This division publishes the *Crime and Justice Annual Report* which is free upon request. Computer printouts are available at no cost.

North Carolina

Division of Criminal Information, 407 N. Blount St., Raleigh, NC 27601; 919-733-3171. The *Crime in North Carolina Annual Statistics Report* is available for $15. Printouts of statistics already collected in their annual report are provided at no cost, if requests are reasonable. Individualized computer runs can also be performed but may become expensive. Costs vary according to the complexity of the request.

North Dakota

State Crime Bureau, Bureau of Criminal Investigation, P.O. Box 1054, Bismarck, ND 58502; 701-328-5500. Publications include an *Annual Report* which is free upon request. Computerized printouts of crime data are available. In most cases the cost is minimal. Detailed requests should be placed in writing. Information can also be transferred to computer diskette or magnetic tape if you supply the software, yourself.

Ohio

Governor's Office of Criminal Justice Services, Capitol Square, 400 E. Town St., Suite 120, Columbus, OH 43215-4242; 614-466-5126. One of the publications available through this office is *State of Crime*. The office does not provide computer printouts of selected data.

Oklahoma

Oklahoma State Bureau of Investigation, 6600 N. Harvey, Suite 300, Oklahoma City, OK 73116; 405-848-6724. The statistics unit publishes the *Crime in Oklahoma Annual Report*. Computer printouts of selected data are provided at no cost.

Oregon

State Executive, Law Enforcement Data System, 155 Cottage Street, NE, Salem, OR 97310; 503-378-3057. Publications and Services: This division publishes the *Criminal Offenses and Arrests Annual Report* which is available for $10, and quarterly reports which are available upon request. Computer services are not available, but standard output reports can be obtained upon request.

Pennsylvania

Commission on Crime and Delinquency, P.O. Box 1167, Harrisburg, PA 17108-1167; 717-787-5152. The *Commission on Crime and Delinquency Annual Report* is free upon request. Computer printouts of annual data are also provided at no charge.

Rhode Island

Rhode Island State Police, 311 Danielson Pike, North Scituate, RI 02857; 401-444-1120. The commission publishes the *Serious Crime in Rhode Island Annual Report* for $7. Computerized data is not available.

South Carolina

South Carolina Law Enforcement Division, Uniform Crime Reporting, 4400 Broad River Road Columbia, SC 29210; 803-737-9000. This division publishes the *Crime in South Carolina Annual Report* which is $5.75 per mailed copy and $3.75 if picked up. Computer printouts of selected data are provided. The cost varies and is based on the complexity of the request. Requests should be made in writing and as specific as possible. Direct inquiries to: Lt. Jerry Hamby, c/o SLED, UCR Dept., P.O. Box 21398, Columbia, SC 29221-1398. Certain data may be available on diskette or magnetic tape on a case by case basis.

South Dakota

Statistical Analysis Center, 500 E. Capitol St., Pierre, SD 57501; 605-773-6312 or 605-773-6310. Publications include a newsletter and annual and quarterly reports which are free upon request. Computerized printouts of selected crime data are available at no cost. Detailed requests should be placed in writing. Information can also be transferred to computer diskette or magnetic tape if you supply the software yourself.

Tennessee

The state of Tennessee does not have a central collection agency for criminal statistics. You will need to contact individual county and city law enforcement agencies. The federal agencies listed in the introduction to this chapter may be helpful, especially if you are out-of-state.

Texas

Department of Public Safety, Crime Records Services, Uniform Crime Reporting, Box 4143, Austin, TX 78765; 512-465-2000. Publications include the *Crime In Texas Annual Report*. Computer printouts of selected data are provided free, upon request.

Utah

Department of Public Safety, Bureau of Criminal Identification, 4501 South, 2700 West, Salt Lake City, UT 84119; 801-965-4566. Publications include the *Crime in Utah Annual Report* which is free upon request. Computer printouts of selected data are available, usually at no cost.

Vermont

Department of Public Safety, Vermont Criminal Information Center, P.O. Box 189, Waterbury VT 05676; 802-244-8727, ext. 5224. The Criminal Information Center publishes the *Vermont Annual Crime Report* which is free upon request. Computer printouts of selected data are not available.

Virginia

Department of State Police, Uniform Crime Reporting Section, P.O. Box 27472, Richmond, VA 23261; 804-674-2031. The *Crime in Virginia Annual Report* is available for $5. Computer printouts of selected data are provided on a cost recovery basis.

Washington

Washington Association of Sheriffs and Police Chiefs, P.O. Box 826, Olympia, WA 98507; 206-586-3221. This organization produces the *Crime in Washington State Annual Report*, which is free upon request. Information that is not included in the annual report but readily accessible in their data banks is available to the public upon request.

West Virginia

Department of Public Safety, Uniform Crime Reporting Division, 725 Jefferson Road, South Charleston, WV 25309; 304-746-2159. The UCR Division publishes a *Crime in West Virginia Annual Report*.

Be patient. If any phone number is incorrect, call (area code) 555-1212 and request the new listing.

Wisconsin

Office of Justice Assistance, Wisconsin Statistical Analysis Center, 222 State St., 2nd Floor, Madison, WI 53702; 608-266-3323. The Statistical Analysis Center publishes a free *Crime and Arrests Annual Report* which is available upon request. Computer printouts of selected data provided at no charge.

Wyoming

Criminal Justice Information Section, 316 W. 22nd St., Cheyenne, WY 82002; 307-777-7625. Publications include the *Uniform Crime Annual Report*. Computer printouts of selected data are provided at no charge. The office will supply special reports if the data requested is of the type they usually collect. These reports are usually in table or letter form. Services are free unless there is significant computer programming involved. Complex requests should be placed in writing.

Be patient. If any phone number is incorrect, call (area code) 555-1212 and request the new listing.

873

State Labor Offices

* See also Careers and Workplace Chapter

Labor market information departments are an overlooked resource within state governments. These little-known offices can provide current, customized data such as:

- which cities have the highest concentration of restaurants or credit agencies;
- how many Hispanic males were living in Bridgeport, Connecticut in 1987;
- which zip codes have the fastest growing population of working women in managerial positions;
- the name, address and size of each new business or business expansion in a given state;
- which U.S. counties offer the highest entry level salaries for market research analysts.

Two reasons for tapping state government labor offices for market and demographic data are that in most cases the information is free and less than one year old.

Sources of Data

The primary function of each state labor information office is to collect data in conjunction with the federal government in order to produce employment, unemployment, occupational and wage information. The most interesting data sources are state unemployment contribution forms filled out by every employer in the state. This form is filed quarterly revealing total wages and number of employees for companies by SIC code in each city and county.

In addition, each state compiles data showing future manpower needs within the state. By studying labor trends, economic conditions and school enrollments, these agencies project the future supply and demand for up to 1,000 different occupations. Many offices also supplement their information with data from the U.S. Bureau of Census as well as other state data collection agencies to provide additional studies and forecasts.

More Current than Federal Data

If you are a user of the Census Bureau's *County Business Patterns*, you are aware that the latest information available is nearly two years old. But, are you aware that right now you can obtain basically the same information from most states that was collected only six months ago? This information is 18 months more current than Census data? If you are looking for personal income figures by state, county or city, the latest available data from the federal government dates back two years. Moreover, the majority of personal income is made up of wage data which is available from most states much more recently.

Also remember that all data, such as state unemployment information, are passed on to the federal government for publication, but are available from state governments several weeks before being released from Washington.

State Data More Detailed, Cheaper and More Accessible than Federal Data

Unemployment rate data are released by the U.S. Bureau of Labor Statistics for approximately 150 major cities. However, the state of Connecticut alone can provide unemployment data for 169 cities. If you are looking for salary by type of occupation, the Bureau of the Census covers about 400 occupations in their data. But state governments will cover up to one thousand occupations based on data which can be up to three years more current.

Federal policies combined with the public's increased reliance on traditional federal data sources have caused many of major federal statistical agencies to increase prices and to decrease services. In contrast, using state labor information centers is like walking into virgin data territory. Almost everything is still free from these offices, and state employees are eager to do a lot of free research for those who call. In a conversation I had with the labor information office in Ohio, the director recounted how a local bank requested demographic data for a few dozen zip codes in a three state area. Not only did the state office assemble this information but also gave it to the bank on diskettes...all for free.

Multiple Uses of Labor Market Data

State labor data provide an endless array of uses, but here are some of the primary applications.

1) Marketing:

The marketing information available from the states is overwhelming. The data cover both the consumer and industrial markets. It can be used for determining your current market size as well as identifying new or emerging marketing opportunities. For example, you can find:

- monthly employment and average wages by SIC code, by county;
- annual employment for up to 1,000 occupations, by county, by SIC code;
- which counties have the highest concentration of hairdressers making over $20,000 per year;
- how many bartenders are working in a given city;
- how many hotels with fewer than 100 employees operate in a given city;
- what are the fastest growing jobs or industries in any county or city;
- one year projections (1987) of demographic data for each city and county; or
- five to ten year projections of industries and occupations by city and county.

Many labor market information centers also offer special market studies to cover specific industries which may be important within the state. You can get free studies covering the hospital industry, ski industry, finance industry and many high-tech related industries.

2) Company Information:

These offices can tell you how many companies in a given SIC code are located in any county or city. States also can provide the median salary and average starting salary for up to 1,000 different jobs, and can even tell you how many people are employed in all these companies by type of job. Many states keep information on any company which is a newcomer to the state or undertaking major business expansion. And, almost every state can give you the number of employees for any manufacturer in the state.

3) Business Location:

Whether you are establishing a new plant, a real estate business, or fast food franchise, these offices can help you locate the best location with regard to labor availability, customer availability and competition. The state labor experts can furnish specifics on how many college graduates, typists or computer programmers with three years of experience are looking for work in any given area. Or, how many are unemployed and looking for work, or how many are working for other companies in the area and their salaries. You can discover what wages are being paid by your competitors in the area for these jobs. Some states volunteer to provide information on union activity in any area. Some states can give you an indication of the work ethic of potential employees. Work ethic can be quantified by showing the number of days off taken by specific employees in certain industries. And if your customers are going to be consumers or businesses in the area, these labor market specialists can share estimates on your potential clientele.

4) Employee Development:

If you are worried about the availability of skilled employees for the future growth of your business, these offices can forecast for you the exact number of people who will be available from school training programs and other employers. This can help you determine if your business will have to move to another location or begin an in-house training program to ensure a plentiful supply of trained labor.

5) Labor Negotiations:

You can find out what the average entry wage for a typist is in your area or what the average fringe benefit package looks like for businesses in your industry. What is the maximum amount of days off allowed for sick leave in your industry? How many companies in your industry offer paid dental care? Answers to these, and other employee benefit questions, can be useful leverage in negotiating employee benefit packages.

6) Affirmative Action, EEOC and Government Contracts:

Organizations which have to comply with EEOC and affirmative action criteria can get all the data necessary from these offices. Labor force data for any area can pinpoint how many women, Hispanics, etc., are in the labor force for various occupations. Such data can be compared with a company's current employee demographics. This information can be useful when seeking government contracts. Also, remember that many government contracts are set aside for those companies in high unemployment areas. This data, too, can be obtained from these offices to see if you qualify.

7) Economic Analysis:

If you are interested in any local area economic forecasting or economic monitoring, this is an ideal place to start. All of these offices have monthly and quarterly newsletters which plot economic health down to the city and county level. If your business is dependent on the economic conditions of a specific region, state, city or county, this approach is an easy way to keep your finger on the pulse of what is happening.

8) Careers and Job Search:

An important function of each of these offices is to provide career and job counseling information. If you are looking for a job, each office has access to a state database which identifies available job openings throughout the state. They project which jobs will in demand in the next 10 to 20 years. And more importantly, the future supply is projected for these positions so that you can more easily spot important opportunities. Moreover, you can obtain the starting salaries and median wages for approximately 1,000 occupations in hundreds of industries. Many states give out free books designed for job seekers, as well as information on how to participate in training programs and vocational education opportunities.

9) Computer Formats and Special Services:

You must remember that no two states operate in the same manner or generate identical data. Although many offer the same reports, some may break down the data into 2-digit SIC codes and others into 4-digit SIC codes. What you must never forget is that although one state may NOT provide the data in the format you need, this does not rule out the possibility when dealing with other states. A few states now have their data online and more are beginning to offer diskettes and computer tapes. But if a state labor office says it does not provide computer readable formats, you may be able to convince them to let you be the first. These offices all seem to be very flexible and not heavily encumbered in bureaucracy.

Be sure to investigate any special services which may be offered by the state. Some offer free sources on how to interpret and use labor data and others provide customized affirmative action reports.

State Labor Offices

Alabama

Department of Industrial Relations, Research and Statistics Division, 649 Monroe St., Montgomery, AL 36130, 205-242-8855; Selected Publications: *Monthly Labor Market, Annual Average Labor Force, Occupational Trends.* Computer Readable Formats: No; Custom Research: Limited amount available free.

Alaska

Department of Labor, Research and Analysis, P.O. Box 25501, Juneau, AK 99802-5501, 907-465-4500; Selected Publications: *Economic Trends, Akcens Quarterly Newsletter, Career Guide, Industry-Occupation Outlook to 1994, Micro-Computer Occupational Information System (Micro-OIS), Wage Rates, Occupational Injury and Illness Information, Population Overview, Special Demographic Reports, Directory of Licensed Occupations, Residency Analysis of Alaska's Workers by Firm, Employment Insurance, Actuarial Study and Financial Handbook, State Salary Survey.* Computer Readable Formats: Limited availability; Custom Research: Limited amount available free.

Arizona

Department of Economic Security West, Research Administration, 1789 West Jefferson, Site Code 733A, Phoenix, AZ 85007, 602-542-3871; Selected Publications: *Arizona Economic Trends, Job Searchers Guide, Metro, Non-Metro Affirmative Action Planning Information, Applying for Government Jobs, Arizona Labor Market Newsletter, Arizona Occupational Employment Forecasts, Arizona Occupational*

Be patient. If any phone number is incorrect, call (area code) 555-1212 and request the new listing.

875

Economics, Demographics, and Statistics

Profiles, Employer Wage Survey, Helpful Hints for Job Seekers, Map of Major Employers. Charge for special projects; all shelf publications are free.

Arkansas

Employment Security Department, Labor Market Information Section, P.O. Box 2981, Little Rock, AR 72203, 501-682-3197; Selected Publications: *Annual Planning Information, Annual Report, Annual Report of the Employment Security Division, Arkansas Labor Force Statistics, Covered Employment and Earnings, Interface Supply and Demand, Statistical Review, Current Employment Developments, Monthly Employment Trends, Monthly County Labor Market Information, Directory of Licensed Occupations, Job Hunters Guide to AR, Occupational Trends, Staffing Patterns.* Computer Readable Formats: Occupational trends on disk; Custom Research: A limited amount is available free.

California

Employment Development Department, Labor Market Information Division, 7000 Franklin Blvd., #1100, Sacramento, CA 95823, 916-262-2237; Selected Publications: *Annual Planning Information, California Labor Market Bulletin, Labor Market Information for Affirmative Action Programs, Labor Market Conditions in California, California Occupational Guides, Projections of Employment By Industry and Occupation.* Computer Readable Formats: Limited; Custom Research: Most everything is free.

Colorado

Department of Labor and Employment, Labor Market Information Section, 393 S. Harland Street, Lakewood, CO 80226; 303-937-4935; Selected Publications: *Affirmative Action Packets, Annual Planning Information Report, Colorado Springs Labor Force, Employment and Wages Quarterly, Occupational Employment Outlook Projection, Job Bank Wage Listing, Occupational Employment in Selected Industries, Quarterly Occupational Supply/Demand Outlook, Pueblo Labor Force, Occupational Supply and Demand, Denver, Boulder, Front Range, Western Slope, Occupational Employment Survey Publishing, Employment Projections.* Computer Readable Formats: No; Custom Research: Free on a limited basis.

Connecticut

Department of Labor, Office of Research and Information, 200 Folly Brook Blvd, Wethersfield, CT 06109-1114, 203-566-3472; Selected Publications: *Annual Report of the Commission of the Labor in Economy Work Force and Training Needs in Connecticut, Planning for the Future Publishing, Work Place 2000, Labor Situation, Labor Force Data, Annual Planning Information, The Occupational Outlook, New Manufacturing Firms* ($7 per year fee), *Occupations in Demand, Labor Market Review, Occupational Projections and Training Data.* Computer Readable Formats; No: Custom Research: Free.

Delaware

Labor Department, Occupational and Labor Market Information Office, P.O. Box 9029, University Office Plaza, Newark, DE 19714, 302-368-6962; Selected Publications: *Delaware Annual Brief, Delaware Monthly Digest, Delaware Jobs to 2005* $7.50, *Delaware Career Compass, Career Guidance-High School Information on Job Growth, ES202 Series, Occupational Wage Data-Government and Educational Services* (three year cycle), *Delaware Labor Supply and Demand: Occupational and Industrial Projections.* Computer Readable Formats: Inquire requested; Custom Research: Limited amount available free.

District of Columbia

Employment Services Department, Labor Market Information, Room 201, 500 C St., NW, Washington, DC 20001, 202-724-7214; Selected Publications: *Area Labor Summary, Labor Market Information for Affirmative Action Programs, Directory of 200 Major Employers, Annual Population Estimates By Census Tract*; Computer Readable Formats: No; All shelf publications are free.

Florida

Department of Labor and Employment Security, Bureau of Labor Market Information, Suite 200, Hartman Building, 2012 Capital Circle, S.E., Tallahassee, FL 32399-2151, 904-488-1048; Selected Publications: *Affirmative Action Statistical Packets, Florida Employment Statistics, Florida Industry and Occupational Employment 1995, Florida Occupational Employment in Hospitals, Labor Force Summary, Labor Market Trends, Occupational Employment in Federal Government, Occupations Employment in the Finance, Insurance and Real Estate Industry, Occupational Employment in the Services Industry, Occupational Wage Surveys.* Computer Readable Formats: Bulletin board system for direct downloading.

Georgia

Department of Labor, Labor Information Systems, 148 International Blvd., NE, Atlanta, GA 30303, 404-656-3177; Selected Publications: *Area Labor Profiles,*

Civilian Labor Force Estimates, GA Employment and Earnings, GA Employment and Wages, GA Labor Market Trends, GA Occupational Employment, Civilian Labor Force Estimates, Data on Occupational Supply and Demand, Earnings by Industry and Area. Computer Readable Formats: No; Custom Research: Charge for Large projects, all others free.

Hawaii

Labor Market and Employment Services Branch, Labor and Industrial Relations Dept., 830 Punchbowl St., Research Division, Honolulu, HI 96813, 808-586-8999; Selected Publications: *Labor Shortages in Agriculture, Demand Occupations, Occupations in Communication Industry, Job Hunters's Guide, Selected Wage Information, Unemployment Insurance Fact Book, Licensed Occupations, Occupational Employment Statistics, Occupational Illness and Injuries, Wage Rate, Workers Compensation, Characteristics of the Insured Unemployed, Employment and Payrolls, Labor Area News, Labor Force Information for Affirmative Action Programs.* Computer Readable Formats: No; Custom Research: Free.

Idaho

Department of Employment, Research and Analysis Bureau, 317 Main St., Boise, ID 83735, (208) 334-6469; Selected Publications: *LMI Directory, Idaho Monthly Employment Newsletter, Labor Forces in Idaho, Basic Economic Data, Annual Demographics Report, Affirmative Action Statistics, Area Employment Newsletter, Employment and Wages by Industry in Idaho.* Most everything is free, Fee for larger projects.

Illinois

Employment Security Bureau, Research and Analysis, 401 South State St., Chicago, IL 60605, 312-793-2316; Selected Publications: *Country Labor Force Summary-2000, Labor Market Review, Illinois at Work, Affirmative Action Information, Occupational Employment Statistics, Occupational Projections, Wage Survey, Where Workers Work, Illinois Employment Industrial Summary.* Computer Readable Formats: No; Custom Research: Nominal fee.

Indiana

Employment Security Division, Labor Market Information, 10 N. Senate Ave., Indianapolis, IN 46209, 317-232-7701; Selected Publications: *Annual County Employment Patterns, Indiana Employment Review, Labor Force Estimates, Quarterly Covered Employment and Payrolls, Regional Economic Profiles, Occupational Employment Projections, Occupational Wage Surveys, Occupations In Demand, Hours and Earnings of Production Workers.* Computer Readable Formats: No; All shelf publications are free.

Iowa

Department of Employment Services, Labor Market Information Unit, 1000 E. Grand Ave., Des Moines, IA 50319, 515-281-8182; Selected Publications: *Condition of Employment Report/Analysis of the Iowa Market, Labor Market Information for Service Delivery Areas, State-Wide Wage Surveys, Labor Market Information for Affirmative Action Programs, Industry/Occupational Projections, Job Insurance Benefits, Iowa Occupational Planning Guide, Licensed Occupations, Labor Market Information Directory, Wages and Employment Covered by Employment Security, Affirmative Action Data for Iowa, Condition of Employment.* Computer Readable Formats: Electronic bulletin board; Custom Research: Free, nominal fee for larger projects.

Kansas

Department of Human Resources, Division of Employment and Training, Research and Analysis Section, 401 S.W. Topeka Blvd., Topeka, KS 66603, 913-296-5058; Selected Publications: *Occupational Staffing Patterns, Kansas Unemployment Insurance Claims, Monthly Labor Market Summary, Kansas Wage Survey, Affirmative Action Packet, Labor Market Review, Report on Employment-Hours and Earnings, Labor Force Estimates.* Computer Readable Formats: Limited; Custom Research: Charge for large projects, all others free.

Kentucky

Department for Employment Services, Research and Statistics, 275 E. Main St., CHR Bldg and Fl., Frankfort, KY 40601, 502-564-7976; Selected Publications: *Non-Agricultural Wage and Salary Employment, Kentucky Labor Market Newsletter, Estimate of Production Workers and Average Hours and Earnings, Labor Force Estimates, Occupational Outlook, Labor Area Summary, Labor Area Profile, Annual Planning Information, Affirmative Action, Labor Supply Estimates, Characteristics of Insured Unemployed, Average Covered Monthly Workers in Manufacturing by Industry Division and County, Total Wages by Industrial Division and County, Average Weekly Wages by Industrial Division and County.* Computer Readable Formats: No; Custom Research: Limited.

Louisiana

Department of Employment Security, Research and Statistics Unit, P.O. 94094, Baton Rouge, LA 70804-9094, 504-342-3141; Selected Publications: *Occupational Projections-1999-2000, Quarterly Employment and Wages, Annual Employment and Wages, Monthly Labor Market Information, Manpower for Affirmative Action, Annual Planning Report, Occupational Employment Statistics, Average Weekly Wage, LA Occupational Injuries and Illnesses*. Computer Readable Formats: Limited; Custom Research: Limited amount available free.

Maine

Bureau of Employment Security, Division of Economic Analysis and Research, 20 Union St., Augusta, ME 04330-6826, 207-287-2271; Selected Publications: *Labor Market Digest Monthly, Maine Occupational Staffing Patterns in Hospitals-Government-Manufacturing/ Nonmanufacturing-Trade, Careers In Maine Woods*. Computer Readable Formats: Yes; Custom Research: Charge for larger projects, all others free.

Maryland

Department of Human Resources, Research and Analysis, Employment and Training, 1100 N. Eutaw St., Baltimore, MD 21201, 410-333-5007; Selected Publications: *Affirmative Action Data, Maryland Occupational Industrial Outlook, Civilian Labor Force Employment and Unemployment by Place of Residence, Claims Processed for Unemployment Insurance Benefits, Occupations in Maryland, Current Employment Statistics, Employment and Payrolls Covered by the Unemployment Insurance Law of Maryland, Zoned Employment and Unemployment Statistics, Industries in Maryland, Highlights of Maryland's Population Projections, Maryland Rural Manpower Report, Occupational Wage Information, Year in Review, Population and Labor Force in Maryland, A Profile: Services Industry in Maryland 1980-Present*. Computer Readable Formats: No. Customer Research: Limited amount available free.

Massachusetts

Division of Employment Security, Massachusetts Employment and Training Center, 19 Saniford Street, Charles F. Hurley Building, Boston, MA 02114, 617-626-6003; Selected Publications: *Planning Data: Massachusetts, Employment and Wages, Massachusetts Employment Review* (monthly), *Careers and Training in Allied Health, Career Choices in a Changing Economy*. Computer Readable Formats: Limited amount available free; Publications free when available.

Michigan

Employment Security Commission, Bureau of Research and Statistics, 7310 Woodward Ave., Detroit, MI 48202, 313-876-5439; Selected Publications: *Affirmative Action Information Report, Annual Planning Information, Claims Counter, Covered Employment Statistics, Monthly Labor Market Review, Occupational Employment Statistics Survey Publications, Occupations in Education, Occupational Wage Information, Michigan Regulated and Trade Industries, Occupational Projections and Training Data, Michigan Occupation/Industry Outlook 2000, Michigan Metropolitan Areas Occupation/Industry Outlook 2000, Michigan Non-metropolitan Areas Occupation/Industry Outlook 2000, Michigan Occupational Supply/Demand Report, Occupational Projections and Training Information for Michigan-OPTIM, Civilian Labor Force, Employment and Unemployment Estimates, Employment Hours and Earnings Estimates, Unemployment Insurance Program Statistics, Employment Trends, Hours and Earnings Trends, Production Worker Employee Trends 1982 to Present*. Computer Readable Formats: Limited, electronic bulletin board; Custom Research: Limited amount available free.

Minnesota

Department of Jobs and Training, Research Office, 390 North Robert St., St. Paul MN 55101, 612-296-8716; Selected Publications: *Consumer Price Index, Career Bulletin, Employment Outlook by Region, Minnesota Wage Data by Industry and Area, Minnesota Employment Outlook to 1996, Minnesota Careers, MN Wage Data By Industry and Size of Firm, Employment and Wage Data By County, Minnesota Labor Market Review*. Computer Readable Format: Some data available via electronic bulletin board; Custom Research: Charge for large projects, all others free.

Mississippi

Employment Security Commission, Labor Market Information Department, P.O. Box 1699, Jackson, MS 39215-1699, 601-961-7424; Selected .PA Publications: *Guide to Labor Market Information, Annual Labor Force Averages, Annual Report, Employment and Job Openings 2005, Farm Income and Expenditures, Affirmative Action Programs, Monthly Labor Market Data, Labor Market Trends for Jackson Metro Area, Mississippi's Business Population, Occupational Employment and Job Openings by Unit of Analysis, Personal Income by Major Sources, Quarterly Labor Market Summary, Transfer Payments by Major Sources*. Computer Readable Formats: Yes, some publications available on diskettes; Customer Research: Limited amount available free.

Missouri

Division of Employment Security, Research and Analysis, P.O. Box 59, Jefferson City, MO 65104, 314-751-3602; Selected Publications: *Monthly Area Labor Trends, Labor Market Information for Affirmative Action Programs, Wages Paid in Selected Occupations, Employment Outlook*. Custom Research: Limited research available.

Montana

Department of Labor and Industry, Research and Analysis Bureau, P.O. Box 1728, Helena, MT 59624, 406-444-2430; Selected Publications: *Wage Surveys of the Private Sector, Wage Surveys of the Public Sector, Wage Surveys of Public Education, Quarterly Employment and Labor Force, Monthly Statistics in Brief, Annual Planning Information*. Computer Readable Formats: Forthcoming; Custom Research: Limited Amount available free.

Nebraska

Department of Labor, Labor Market Information, 550 South 16th St., Lincoln, NE 68509, 402-471-2600; Selected Publications: *Prairie/Farm and Ranch Profile, NE Labor Market Information Quarterly, Careers and Education in Nebraska, Monthly Labor Area Summary, Occupational Employment Statistics by Industry, Monthly Labor Force, Affirmative Action, Survey of Average Hourly Wage Rates, Occupational Newsletter*. Computer Readable Formats: No; Custom Research: Limited amount available for free.

Nevada

Employment Security Department, Employment Security Research Section, 500 E Third St., Carson City, NV 89713, 702-687-4550; Selected Publications: *Area Labor Review, Directory of Labor Market Information, Quarterly and Monthly Economic Update, Nevada Wage Survey, Occupational Projections, Job Finding Techniques*. Computer Readable Formats: Limited; Custom Research: Limited amount available free.

New Jersey

Labor Department, Labor Market Information Office, John Fitch Plaza CN056, Trenton, NJ 08625, 609-292-7376; Selected Publications: *Regional Labor Market Reviews, Regional Labor Market Newsletters, Compendium of New Jersey Wage Surveys, Employment and Economy Newsletter, Employment Trends, Economic Indicators Monthly*. Computer Readable Formats: Limited electronic bulletin board usage; Custom Research: Limited amount available free.

New Hampshire

Employment Security Department, Economic Analysis and Reports and Labor Market Information Bureau, 32 South Main St., Concord, NH 03301, 603-224-3311; Selected Publications: *Wage Survey, Vital Signs, Staffing Patterns in NH, Annual Report, Annual Planning Information, Annual Planning Information MSA's, Community Patterns NH, Economic Conditions, Employment and Wages by County, Employment and Wages MSA's, Employment and Wages by Planning Region, Fact Book: Cities and Towns, Firms By Size, Local Area Unemployment Statistics, NH Affirmative Action Data, NH Occupational Outlook 2005, Users Guide to Labor Market Information*. Computer Readable Formats: Call for availability and cost; Custom Research: Free.

New Mexico

Department of Employment Security, Economic Research and Analysis, P.O. Box 1928, Albuquerque, NM 87103, 505-841-8645; Selected Publications: *Covered Employment and Wages, Basic Concepts, Monthly Labor Market Review, Nonagricultural Wage and Salary Employment, Facts and Figures about New Mexico, Hours and Earnings Estimates, Albuquerque Small Employer Wage Survey, Jobs to 2000, Area Job Market Flyers, Large Employers in New Mexico by County*. Computer Readable Formats: Limited; Customer Research: Limited amount available for free.

New York

Department of Labor, Division of Research and Statistics, State Office Bldg. Campus #12, Albany, NY 12240, 518-457-3800; Selected Publications: *Statistics on Operations, Occupational Outlooks, Civilian Labor Force by Occupation, Selected Demographic Groups, Regular and Extended Benefits, State Unemployment Insurance, Collective Bargaining Settlements, Directory of Labor Unions and Employee Organizations in New York State Employment Review, Current Population Survey Data, Earnings and Hours in Selected Industries, The Job Seeker, Labor Area Summary Monthly Statistical Report, Labor Area Summary Quarterly Analytical Report, Labor Market Assessment: Occupational Supply and Demand, Occupational Brief, Occupational Projections, Occupational Employment Statistics, Occupational Guide, Occupational Needs, Occupation Licensed or Certified by New York State, Operations, Resident Employment Status of the Civilian Labor Force, Careers Exploration and Job Seeking, Total and Civilian Labor Force Summary, Selected*

Economics, Demographics, and Statistics

Demographic Groups - NYS, Counties and SMSA's, Selected Labor Research Reports, Apprentice Training Hours and Earnings, Insured Employment and Payrolls, Local Area Unemployment Statistics, Non-Agricultural Wage and Salary Employment, Unemployment Insurance Operating Statistics. Custom Research: Charge for large projects, all others free.

North Carolina

Employment Security Commission, Labor Market Information Division, P.O. Box 25903, Raleigh, NC 27611, 919-733-2936; Selected Publications: *Employment and Wages in NC Quarterly, Market Areas Newsletter, Past High School Intentions of NC Graduates by County, Occupational Trends: Year 2000: NC, NC Metro State Planning Regions A-F; G-L; M-R, NC Preliminary Civilian Labor Force Estimates, Active Job Applicants by County, Registered Applicants and Job Openings, Follow-Up Survey of NC High School Graduates by County, Wage Rates in Selected Occupations.* Computer Readable Formats: Forthcoming; Custom Research: Free, charge for larger projects.

North Dakota

Job Service, Research and Statistics, P.O. Box 5507, Bismarck, ND 58502, 701-224-3048; Selected Publications: *Occupational Supply/Demand Report, Employment and Wages, Monthly Labor Market Advisor, Occupations Wage Surveys and Benefits for Major Cities, Occupational Projections to 2000, Employment Surveys by Major City, Annual Planning Report.* Computer Readable Formats: No; Custom Research: Charge for large amounts, all others free.

Ohio

Bureau of Employment Services, Labor Market Information Division, 145 South Front St., Columbus, OH 43216, 614-466-4636; Selected Publications: *Employment and Unemployment Estimates, Covered Employment and Payroll, Trend Tables, Monthly Labor Market Review, County Labor Force Reports, Labor Force Estimates, Metropolitan Profile, Occupational Projections, Composition of Job Placements, Summary of Ohio Worker Training Program Activities.* Computer Readable Formats: Yes; Custom Research: Charge for large projects, all others free.

Oklahoma

Oklahoma Employment Security Commission, Economic Analysis, 2401 N. Lincoln Blvd., Oklahoma City, OK 73105, 405-557-7104; Selected Publications: *Labor Market Information, Manpower Information for Affirmative Action, Annual Report to the Governor, Handbook of Employment Statistics, County Employment and Wage Data, Occupational Wage Surveys.* Computer Readable Formats: Yes; Custom Research: Charge for large projects, all other free.

Oregon

Employment Division, Research and Statistics, 875 Union NE, Salem, OR 97311, 503-378-8656; Selected Publications: *Oregon Work Force at Risk, Dislocated Workers, Oregon Works, Affirmative Action Programs, Agricultural Employment, Average Weekly Earnings-Hours, Business and Employment Outlook, Monthly Local Labor Trends, Occupational Program Planning System, Oregon Wage Information.* Computer Readable Formats: No; Custom Research: Charge for large projects, all others free.

Pennsylvania

Department of Labor and Industry, Research and Statistics Division, 300 Capital Associates Bldg., Harrisburg, PA 17120-0034, 717-787-2114; Selected Publications: *Work Force 2000, Civilian Work Force Data by Labor Market Area of Residence, Annual Average Labor Force Data, Civilian Labor Force Series by Labor Market Area, PA Labor Market Areas Ranked on Basis of Rate of Unemployment, PA Unemployment Fact Sheet, Occupational Wage Surveys, Employment and Wages of Workers Covered by the PA Unemployment Compensation Law, Occupations Employment in Hospital Occupational Staffing Patterns for Selected Non-Manufacturing Industries, Affirmative Action Report, Labor Market Job Guides, PA's Microcomputer Occupational Information System* ($250); *Current Trends in Employment and Wages in PA Industries, PA Labor Force, Annual Planning Information Report, Hours and Earnings in Manufacturing and Selected Non-manufacturing Industries.* Computer Readable Formats: No; Custom Research: Charge for large projects, all others free.

Rhode Island

Department of Employment Security, Research and Statistics, 101 Friendship St., Providence, RI 02903, 401-277-3706; Selected Publications: *Occupational Projections 2000, Characteristics of Insured Unemployed, RI Employment Newsletter, Quarterly Labor Supply and Demand Report, Employment and Wages by City and Industry, Annual Planning Information, Manpower Information for Affirmative Action Programs, Employment In RI Hospitals.* Computer Readable Format: No; Custom Research: Free.

South Carolina

Employment Security Commission, Labor Market Information Division, P.O. Box 995, Columbia, SC 29202, 803-737-2660; Selected Publications: *Industrial Monographs, Wage Survey, Labor Market Review, Employment Trends, Occupational Projections 2005, Labor Force in Industry, Covered Employment and Wages in SC.* Computer Readable Formats: Limited; Custom Research: Charge for large projects, all others free.

South Dakota

Department of Labor, Labor Market Information Center, P.O. Box 4730, Aberdeen, SD 57402-4730, 605-622-2314; Selected Publications: *Labor Availability Studies, Labor Bulletin, Occupational Wage Information, Occupational Outlook Handbook, Employment and Earnings, Affirmative Action Package, Statewide Job Listings.* Computer Readable Formats: No; Custom Research: Limited amount available free.

Tennessee

Department of Employment Security, Research and Statistics Division, 11th Floor, James Robertson Parkway, Nashville, TN 37245-1040, 615-741-3639; Selected Publications: *Occupational Wage and Benefit Information, Minorities in Tennessee, Occupations in Demand, Licensed Occupations in Tennessee, Monthly Available Labor, Monthly Labor Force Summary, Commuting Patterns, Tennessee Employment Projections 2005, Tennessee Youth Report, Veterans in Tennessee, Women in the Labor Force, Tennessee High School Graduates.* Computer Readable Formats: Limited; Custom Research: Limited amount available free.

Texas

Texas Employment Commission, Economic Research and Analysis Dept., Room 208-T, TEC Building, Austin, TX 78778, 512-463-2616; Selected Publications: *Labor Force Estimates, Current Population Survey, Nonagricultural Wage and Salary Employment Estimates, Average Hours and Earnings Data, Employment and Wages by Industry and County, Affirmative Action Packets, Characteristics of the Insured Unemployed, Regional Reports, Labor Demand Projects by 2000, Occupational Employment Statistics.* Computer Readable Formats: Limited; Custom Research: Charge for large projects, all others free.

Utah

Utah Department of Employment Security, Labor Market Information Services, P.O. Box 45249, Salt Lake City, UT 84147, 801-536-7800; Selected Publications: *Annual Labor Market Report, Licensed Occupations in Utah, Utah Directory of Business and Industry.* Computer Readable Formats: On a limited basis. Custom Research: Free.

Vermont

Department of Employment and Training, Labor Market Information, P.O. Box 488, Montpelier, VT 05601, 802-229-0311; Selected Publications: *Occupation, Wage and Employment Survey, Job Openings, Affirmative Action Planning Data, Annual Planning Information, Combined Annual Report of DET and JTPA, Directory of Labor Market Information Employment and Earnings, Labor Market Area Bulletins, Vermont Labor Market, Employment and Wages Covered by Unemployment Insurance, Licensed Occupations in Vermont Mining and Quarrying, Construction, Unemployment Compensation Statistical Table, Vermont Economic and Demographic Profile Series.* Computer Readable Formats: No; Custom Research: Upon request, limited time available.

Virginia

Virginia Employment Commission, Labor Market and Demographics Analysis Section, P.O. Box 1358, Richmond, VA 23211, 804-786-8222; Selected Publications: *Guide to Establishing a Business, LMI Directory, Business Registration Guide, Work Force 2000, Labor Force by Sex and Minority Status, Commuting Patterns, Data on Public Schools, Economic Assumptions for the U.S. and VA, Economically Disadvantaged Data, Employment and Training Indicators, Employment and Wages in Establishments, Employment and Wages in VA, Monthly Labor Market Review, Wage Survey Selected Manufacturers Occupation, Licensed Occupations in VA, List of Employers By Size, State and County Veteran Population, Trends in Employment-Hours and Earnings, Quarterly Virginia Economic Indicators, Virginia Business Resource Directory.* Computer Readable Formats: ALICE (Virginia based only); Custom Research: Limited for nominal fee.

Washington

Employment Security Group, Labor Market and Economic Analysis Branch, 605 Woodland Square Loop S.E., Lacey, WA 98503, mailing address P.O. Box 9046, Olympia, WA 98507-9046, 206-438-4804; Selected Publications: *Washington Labor Market, LMI Review, Annual Demographic Information, Area Wage Survey, Employment and Payrolls in Washington, Occupational Profiles and Projections.* Computer Readable Formats: Some; Custom Research: Large projects are charged on a contract basis.

West Virginia

Employment Security Department, Labor and Economic Research, 112 California Ave., Charleston, WV 25305, 304-558-2660; Selected Publications: *Affirmative Action, West Virginia Women in the Labor Force, Annual Planning Information, Metropolitan Statistical Areas Annual Planning Information, Job Training Partnership Act, West Virginia County Profiles, WV Economic Summary, Employment and Earnings Trends, Insured Workers Summary, Occupational Projections, Veterans Report, Wage Survey, Directory of Publications, Licensed Occupations in West Virginia.* Computer Readable Formats: Forthcoming; Custom Research: Limited amount available free.

Wisconsin

Department of Industry, Labor and Human Relations, Employment and Training Library, P.O. Box 7944, Madison, WI 53707, 608-267-9613; Selected Publications:

LMI: A Reference Guide of WI Publications, Labor Market Planning Information, Taxes Due Covered by Wisconsin U.C. Law, Wisconsin Projections 1988-2000, Affirmative Action Data, Career Connection, Monthly Wisconsin Economic Indicators, Civilian Labor Force Estimates, Consumer Price Index, Employment and Wages, Wage Survey, Covered Employment By Size of Industry and County, Wisconsin Employment Picture, Wisconsin Works, Inform Bi-Monthly. Computer Readable Formats: Some; Custom Research: Charge for large projects.

Wyoming

Employment Security Commission, Research and Analysis, P.O. Box 2760, Casper, WY 82602, 307-265-6732; Selected Publications:*Manufacturing and Hospitals, Wyoming's Annual Planning Report, Wyoming's Covered Employment and Wage Data, Labor Force Trends, Affirmative Action Package.* Computer Readable Format: No; Custom Research: Limited amount available.

State Health Statistics

* See also Health and Medicine Chapter

Vital and Infectious Disease Statistics

The last few years have witnessed explosive growth in products and services aimed at the health-conscious baby-boomers and their aging parents. In order to market products and services, many businesses use state health statistics and records. State health data are used to great success by insurance companies, individual medical providers and doctor groups, private health care clinics and rehabilitative service centers, diet and natural food producers, pharmaceutical and cosmetic companies, and even publishers.

A state's health care registration system is often the best place to start researching specific health data for an entire state's population. In addition, each state makes available its annual health report in a number of formats.

Some insurance companies use this information to steer away from areas where cancer rates are too high or to zero in on areas where rates are lower than the national norm. Along this same line, a new doctor might search for an area where there is a greater demand for his or her specific medical expertise.

Exercise equipment manufacturers can use the data to target upscale, "yuppie" markets for their sales campaigns -- or identify clusters of older hospitals with on-site physical therapy facilities that might need new equipment. Other examples include:

- how many people have cancer, diabetes, or high blood pressure by zip code
- hospitals with CAT scans and other sophisticated medical equipment
- vaccination records to find which homes have babies, preschoolers, grade schoolers, etc.
- names, addresses and neighborhoods with the most senior citizens
- names and addresses of ambulatory care facilities and state-funded birth control/venereal disease counseling clinics
- neighborhoods not immediately serviced by existing drug stores

Data are collected and used to assess the current status of health and health care in a state and to help state officials better anticipate future health care needs and resources. In addition, the information provides baseline data for medical research, charts population shifts, and identifies specific groups, communities, neighborhoods, etc. for special state and federal health programs.

Annual reports, available from state vital statistics departments, contain information on births, deaths, marriages and divorces, with narrative and graphic highlights of emerging demographic and health issue trends.

Annual reports from a state's office of epidemiology contain specific data on the incidence of notifiable communicable diseases and related information reported by area physicians, hospitals and health clinics.

Computer printouts of selected data provide the most current health and health care information in detail, much of which does not make it into a state's annual reports. Data can be sorted and printed to assist individuals and businesses with statistical research projects. Most states are staffed with experts to help with individual research requests. Most offices prefer that information requests be placed in writing. State offices release aggregate data that includes no names or personal identifiers.

All states will provide computer printouts of selected data, at least on limited basis. In most instances, there is no charge for printouts. When requesting specific data not found in a state's annual report, place your information request in writing, be as specific as possible in what you are asking, and specify your computer system's requirements.

The following states provide information on magnetic tape or diskette. Fees vary from state to state depending upon the complexity of the request.

Magnetic tape: Alabama, Arizona, California, Colorado, Delaware, Florida, Georgia, Idaho, Illinois, Indiana, Kentucky, Maine, Maryland, Mississippi, Missouri, New Hampshire, New York, North Carolina, Oklahoma, Pennsylvania, South Carolina, South Dakota, Tennessee, Texas, Utah, Virginia, West Virginia, Washington, Wyoming

Diskette: Alabama, Alaska, Arizona, Arkansas, California, Colorado, Delaware, Florida, Georgia, Idaho, Illinois, Kentucky, Maine, Maryland, Minnesota, Mississippi, Missouri, Montana, Nebraska, New Hampshire, New Mexico, New York, North Carolina, Oklahoma, Oregon, Pennsylvania, South Carolina, South Dakota, Tennessee, Texas, Utah, Virginia, West Virginia, Wyoming

Offices for Vital and Infectious Disease Statistics

Alabama

Department of Public Health, Center for Health Statistics, P.O. Box 5625, Montgomery, AL 36103-5625; 334-613-5429. This office can provide computer printouts or data on diskettes or magnetic tape. Prices vary according to the number of years for which data are desired and the storage media. Current publications include: *Pregnancy Statistics, Mortality Statistics, Marriage and Divorce Statistics, County Profiles, Detailed Mortality Statistics, Teenage Birth Statistics,* and *Births by Residence and Occurrence.*

Bureau of Preventive Health Services, Epidemiology Division, Department of Health, 434 Monroe St., Montgomery, AL 36130-3017; 334-613-5347.. Publications include their annual report, *Notifiable Diseases in Alabama.* The office can supply limited computer printouts of selected aggregate data on communicable diseases.

Alaska

State Department of Health, Division of Public Health, Bureau of Vital Statistics, P.O. Box 110610, Juneau, AK 99811-0675; 907-465-3393. Publications include the *Vital Statistics Annual Report.* Information is available on computer printouts and on diskette on a limited basis. Fees vary according to the complexity of the request.

State Department of Health, Office of Epidemiology, P.O. Box 240249, Anchorage, AK 99811-0610; 907-561-4406. Publications include the *Epidemiology Bulletin*. Information is available on computer printouts, usually free of charge.

Arizona

Department of Health Services, Office of Vital Records, 2727 W. Glendale Ave., Phoenix, AZ 85051; 601-255-3260. Publications include *Abortion Surveillance Report*, *Accidental Deaths in Arizona*, and *Health Status and Vital Statistics*. The office provides aggregate data on computer printouts, free of charge. Special requests for selected data are handled on a limited basis. There is a minimum charge of $25 for computer programming time.

Department of Health Services, Office of Chronic Diseases, Epidemiology, 3815 N. Black Canyon Hwy., Phoenix, AZ 85015; 602-230-5886. Publications include *Communicable Diseases in Arizona*. This office provides computer printouts of selected data. If you send them a blank diskette they will transfer the information requested on to it, free of charge.

Arkansas

Department of Health, Office of Vital Records, State Health Building, 4815 W. Markham, Little Rock, AR 72205; 501-661-2336. This office publishes an *Annual Report*. Computer printouts are available for certain items for a processing fee. If you provide a diskette, the office will process it for you.

Department of Health, Division of Epidemiology, 4815 W. Markham, Little Rock, AR 72205; 501-661-2264. Publications include an *Annual Report*, *Annual Animal Morbidity Report*, and an *Annual Report for Communicable Diseases*. The office provides computer printouts of selected data, free of charge.

California

California Department of Health Data and Services, 714 P. St., Sacramento, CA 95814; 916-657-3057. Publications include: *Vital Statistics of California, General Fertility Rates and Age-Specific Live Births by Age of Mother, Suicides in California, Multiples Causes of Death*, and *California's Non-licensed Marriages -- A first Look at Their Characteristics*. Publication prices vary and a complete catalogue of titles can be obtained from this office. Specific computer searches are available. Information is provided on computer printout, diskette and magnetic tape. Fees vary according to the complexity of the request.

Colorado

Department of Health, Health Statistics Section, 4300 Cherry Creek Dr. South, Denver, CO 80222; 303-692-2248. Publications include the 400-page *Colorado Vital Statistics Report*. The office does provide specialized computer runs of extracted data at a minimum cost of $25. Computer printouts are provided, and information is distributed on diskette or magnetic tape.

Department of Health, Division of Disease Control and Environmental Epidemiology, 4300 Cherry Creek Dr., South, Denver, CO 80222; 303-692-2700. Publications include the bi-monthly *Colorado Disease Bulletin* which contains yearly totals of infectious diseases.

Connecticut

Department of Health Services, Vital Records Section, 150 Washington St., Hartford, CT 06106; 203-566-6545. Publications include an *Annual Report*. Computer printouts and machine readable forms are offered through this office for a fee.

Department of Health Services, Epidemiology Program, 150 Washington St., Hartford, CT 06106; 203-240-9284. Although this office provides information on infectious diseases such as hepatitis, separate statistics on AIDS, cancer and tuberculosis are handled through individual offices. There is no charge for computer printouts of statistical reports.

Delaware

Delaware Division of Public Health, Vital Statistics Office, P.O. Box 637, Dover, DE 19903; 302-739-4721. Publications include an *Annual Report*. Computer printouts and information on diskette and magnetic tape are generally provided free of charge.

Bureau of Disease Prevention, Division of Public Health, P.O. 637, Dover, DE 19903; 302-739-5617. This office's publications include a *Monthly Surveillance Report*. Computer printouts of data are generated, usually at no cost.

District of Columbia

Department of Human Services, Research and Statistics Division, 800 9th St., SW, Room 3007, Washington, DC 20024; 202-645-5889. Publications include the *Annual Report of Vital Statistics*. Statistical data tables are available on computer printout form.

Florida

Department of Health and Rehabilitative Services, Office of Public Health Statistics abd Program Assessment (HSI), 1317 Winewood Blvd., Tallahassee, FL 32399-0700; 904-487-1515. Publications include: *Outcome Indicators Workbook, County Quality Improvement Indicators* and *Years of Potential Life Lost*. Data reports are also available for over 300 indicators statewide and county by year (1961-1991) via an interactive data system - Public Health Indicators Data System. Routine reports are distributed at no charge.

Department of Health and Rehabilitative Services, Vital Records, 1317 Winewood Blvd. Tallahassee, FL 32399-0700; 904-359-6970. Publications include a *Monthly Report*, and *Florida Morbidity Statistics*. Computer printouts of selected data are provided on a limited basis.

Georgia

Department of Human Resources, Vital Records, 47 Trinity Ave., SW, Room 217-H, Atlanta, GA 30334; 404-656-4750. Publications include an *Annual Report*. Information requests must be made in writing. There is a $25 minimum charge for computer printouts of selected data. Information is available on diskette and on magnetic tape. Fees vary depending upon the scope of the project.

Department of Human Resources, Epidemiology Section, 2 Peachtree St. NE, Room 6.100, Atlanta, GA 30303; 404-656-5680. Publications include a *Communicable Disease Morbidity Annual Report* and *Annual Report*. Computer printouts on certain selected statistics are available.

Hawaii

Research and Statistics Office, State Department of Health, 1250 Punchbowl St., Honolulu, HI, 98613; 808-586-4526. Publications include the *1990 Statistical Report*, which is free. Computer printouts of information are available on a limited basis. Detailed information requests should be in writing. The office can retrieve some information from databases on tape but it depends on the time frame involved and the resources available. At present, there is no charge for computer printouts.

Department of Health, Epidemiology Branch, Kinau Hale Building, 1250 Punchbowl St., Room 107, Honolulu, HI 96813; 808-586-4586. Publications include *Communicable Disease Report* which is published bi-monthly.

Idaho

Department of Health and Welfare, Bureau of Vital Statistics, 450 W. State St., P.O. Box 83720, Boise, ID 83720-0036; 208-334-5976. Publications include an *Annual Report*. The office provides reports, free of charge, of existing data tables. Tables can also be placed on diskette for a fee of $25 to $50. There is a charge of $15 if computer programming runs over an hour. Records are legally confidential, so the use of magnetic tapes is possible only as long as data is not potentially identifying.

Department of Health and Welfare, Communicable Disease Prevention, 450 W. State St., P.O. Box 83720, Boise, ID 83720-0036; 208-334-5930. This office publishes a *Biweekly Disease Surveillance Report*. Computer printouts of information are available.

Illinois

Department of Public Health, Division of Vital Records, Division of Data Processing, 605 W. Jefferson, Springfield, IL 62761-5097; 217-782-6554. Publications include the *Vital Statistics Annual Report*. Computer printouts of selected data are copied at $.25 per page. Magnetic tapes of birth/death data are available for a fee. If you supply the office with a blank diskette they will transfer the information on to it for a fee.

Department of Public Health, Division of Infectious Diseases, 525 W. Jefferson, Springfield, IL 62761; 217-782-2016. Computer printouts are available through individual departments. You must fill out a data request form before information is released.

Economics, Demographics, and Statistics

Indiana

State Department of Health, Epidemiology Resource Center, Public Health Statistics, 1330 West Michigan St., P.O. Box 1964, Indianapolis, IN 46206-1964; 317-383-0695. Publications include *Indiana Abortion Report*, and *1990 Indiana County Population Estimates*. Computer printouts and tapes are available on a limited basis. Programming fees vary depending upon the complexity of the request. The office also publishes an annotated list of publications.

State Department of Health, Epidemiology Resource Center, 1330 West Michigan St., P.O. Box 1964, Indianapolis, IN 46206-1964; 317-383-6807. Publications include an *Annual Report* Computer printouts are provided, if data exists.

Iowa

Department of Public Health, Statistic Services, 321 E. 12th St., Lucas State Office Building, Des Moines, IA 50319-0075; 515-281-6762. Publications include a *Vital Statistics Annual Report*. This office provides yearly data tables. Information is available on computer printouts and fees vary according to the complexity of the request.

Department of Public Health, Epidemiology Section, Lucas State Office Building, Des Moines, IA 50319; 515-281-4941. Weekly health updates are available through this office.

Kansas

Department of Health and Environment, Office of Health Care Information, 109 SW 9th St., Mills Bldg., Suite 400A, Topeka, KS 66612; 913-296-0632. Publications include an *Annual Report*. This office will provide printouts of selected data. There is a fee for reports over 25 pages. Information is available on computer diskette and there is a fee which is dependent upon the amount of programming time involved.

Department of Health and Environment, Bureau of Disease Control, Suite 605, Mills Building, 109 S.W. 9th St., Topeka, KS 66612; 913-296-5586. Publications include their *Annual Report*. Computer printouts are available, free of charge.

Kentucky

Cabinet for Human Resources, Health Data Branch, 275 East Main St., Frankfort, KY 40621; 502-564-2757. Publications include an annual vital statistics report. Computer printouts of selected data are available at cost upon written request. Diskettes and magnetic tapes are available. The cost depends upon the scope of the request.

Cabinet for Health Services, Division of Epidemiology, 275 East Main St., Frankfort, KY 40621; 502-564-3418. Publications include monthly and year- end summary reports of specific diseases plus their *Monthly Epidemiologic Notes and Reports*. The office does provide computer printouts of selected data but information on diskette or magnetic tape is not available.

Louisiana

Department of Health and Human Resources, Public Health Statistics, P.O. Box 60630, New Orleans, LA 70160; 504-568-8353. This office publishes an *Annual Report*. Computer printouts are available, if the data is complete. There is no charge.

Department of Health and Human Resources, Office of Epidemiology, P.O. Box 60630, New Orleans, LA 70160; 504-568-5005. This office publishes an *Annual Report*. Computer printouts of data are provided free of charge.

Maine

Department of Human Services, Department of Vital Records, 221 State St., Augusta, ME 04333; 207-624-5445. Publications include the *1991 Annual Report of Vital Statistics* which is available at $10.50. This office will provide raw data via printouts, diskettes and magnetic tapes. There is a base fee of $27.50 per diskette and $52 per magnetic tape. All request should be in writing, and be as specific as possible regarding the data that you request and the requirements of your computer system. The office encourages callers to provide their own disk or magnetic tape when possible.

Bureau of Health, Division of Disease Control, State House Station 11, Augusta, ME 04333; 207-287-3591. Publications include the *Epigram* which is published every two months on topics of health concern to Maine residents. A limited amount of raw data can be provided to callers on computer printouts. All requests for detailed information should be in writing.

Maryland

Department of Health and Mental Hygiene, Division of Health Statistics, 201 West Preston St., Baltimore, MD 21201; 410-225-5950. Publications include the *Vital Statistics Preliminary Report*. Computer printouts of tables of selected data are provided. Requests for information should be in writing. Information is available on magnetic tape and diskette. Fees vary according to the amount of information requested.

Department of Health and Mental Hygiene, Communicable Diseases Surveillance, 201 West Preston St., 3rd Floor Baltimore, MD 21201; 410-225-6712. This office publishes an *Annual Report* that is free of charge.

Massachusetts

Department of Public Health, Division of Health Statistics and Research, 250 Washington St., Boxton, MA 02108; 617-624-6000. Publications include an *Annual Report*. Computer printouts of selected data are provided, free of charge.

Department of Public Health, Epidemiology Program, 305 South St., Jamaica Plains, MA 02130; 617-522-3700. Publications include fact sheets on various communicable diseases.

Michigan

Department of Public Health, Office of State Registrar, Center for Health Statistics, Statistical Services Section, P.O. Box 300195, Lansing, MI 48909; 517-335-8656. Publications include: *Health Statistics Pocket Guide, Abortions in Michigan, Cancer Incidence and Mortality, Michigan Perinatal Effectiveness Index, Infant and Maternal Health Statistics*, most of which are free. Requests for computer printouts should be placed in writing. There is a fee for services.

Department of Public Health, Division of Disease Surveillance, P.O. Box 30035, Lansing, MI 48909; 517-335-8050. Publications include weekly surveillance reports of communicable diseases. These are available for researchers.

Minnesota

State Health Department, Vital Records Services, 717 Delaware St., SE, P.O. Box 9441, Minneapolis, MN 55440; 612-623-5121. Publications include the *Annual Report of Health Statistics*. This office will provide you with selected tables from their annual report at no cost. The fees for information transferred to computer diskette would depend upon the complexity of the request.

State Health Department, Acute Epidemiology Department, 717 Delaware St., S.E., Minneapolis, MN 55440; 612-623-5414. Publications include various statistical reports on all reportable diseases. Computer printouts of summary data can be obtained from the Center for Health Statistics, described above.

Mississippi

Department of Health, Vital Records Division, Statistical Services, P.O. Box 1700, 2423 N. State St., Jackson, MS 39216; 601-960-7982. Publications include the *Annual Report*. Computer printouts of specific information require a written request. The office will provide photocopies of tables at no charge. If you furnish your own magnetic tape or computer diskette they will transfer information on to it for you.

Department of Health, Office of Epidemiology, P.O. Box 1700, Jackson, MS 39216; 601-960-7725. Publications include the *Mississippi Morbidity Report* which includes annual case tabulation. Aggregate data is available via computer printouts and diskettes.

Missouri

Department of Health, State Center for Health Statistics, P.O. Box 570, Jefferson City, MO 65102; 573-751-6400. Publications include the *Annual Report of Vital Statistics*. Requests for information should be in writing. Printouts of data, such as tables already printed in the annual report, are free of charge. A special computer run of a selected year of data is $48.50, including programming time and shipping and handling. Each additional year of data requested is $21. Information transferred to floppy disk costs $100. Information transferred to magnetic tape costs $250.

Department of Health, Office of Epidemiology, 1730 E. Elm St., P.O. Box 570, Jefferson City, MO 65102; 573-751-6128. Publications include the *1991 Annual Report* and the bi-monthly *Missouri Epidemiologist*. The office will distribute data information included in their Annual Report, free of charge.

Montana

Department of Public Health and Human Service, Vital Records Bureau, Helena, MT 59604; 406-444-2614. Publications include the *Vital Statistics Report* and *The Impact of Cancer in Montana*. Specific data can be provided on computer printout and diskette. Fees vary according to the complexity of the request and the amount of programming time involved.

Department of Public Health and Human Services, Epidemiology Section, Cogswell Building, Helena, MT 59620; 406-444-0274. Computer printouts of aggregate data are available on a limited basis.

Nebraska

Department of Health, Health Records, P.O. Box 95007, Lincoln, NE 68509-5007; 402-471-2871. Publications include the *Annual Report of Vital Statistics*. The Health Data and Statistical Research Department will help with statistical information on the phone as well as provide information on computer printout and diskette. The cost of computer time is $20 per hour. Requests for selected data should be made in writing. Be as specific as possible, including your computer system's requirements as well as diskette size and density.

Department of Health, Data Collection, P.O. Box 95007, Lincoln, NE 68509-5007; 402-471-7241. Publications include the *Nebraska Morbidity Report*. Computer printouts of data are available on a limited basis.

Nevada

Department of Human Resources, State Health Division, Office of Vital Records, 505 East King St., Room 102, Carson City, NV 89710; 702-687-4481. Publications include the *Annual Vital Statistics Report*. Computer printouts on selected data are available free of charge on a limited basis.

Department of Human Resources, State Health Division, Bureau of Disease Control, 505 East King St., Room 304 Carson City, NV 89710; 702-687-4800. This office provides various publications and information on communicable diseases.

New Hampshire

Department of Health and Welfare, Bureau of Vital Records and Health Statistics, Health and Human Services Building, 8 Hazen Drive, Concord, NH 03301; 603-271-4651. Publications include an *Annual Report*. Requests are for specific information are handled on a case by case basis. Fees vary according to the amount of computer programming involved. Computer printouts, diskettes and magnetic tapes are available.

Department of Health and Welfare, Bureau of Communicable Disease Control, Health and Human Services Building, 6 Hazen Dr., Concord, NH 03301-6527; 603-271-4477. Publications include several bimonthly bulletins. Computer printouts are available of selected data.

New Jersey

Department of Health, Bureau of Vital Statistics, CN 370, Trenton, NJ 08625; 609-292-4087. Publications include an *Annual Report*. Computer printouts are available for a fee.

Department of Health, Division of Epidemiology and Disease Control, University Office Plaza, CN 369, Trenton, NJ 08625; 609-588-7500. This office will answer specific questions over the phone, but does not provide computer printouts.

New Mexico

Department of Health and Environment, Office of Vital and Health Statistics, Public Health Division, 1190 St. Francis Dr., P.O. Box 26110, Santa Fe, NM 87503-6110; 505-827-2539. Publications include the *Annual Report*. Detailed requests for information not found in their annual report should be placed in writing. Information can be provided on diskette. Fees vary according to the complexity of the request.

Department of Health, Division of Epidemiology, 1190 St. Francis Dr., P.O. Box 26110, Santa Fe, NM 87502; 505-827-0006. Publications include their monthly *Epidemiology Report*. Requests for information not found in their monthly report should be placed in writing. If you provide them with a blank diskette they will download data on to it for you and omit any identifiers.

New York

Department of Health, Bureau of Biometrics, Empire State Plaza, Concourse Room C144, Albany, NY 12237-0044; 518-474-3189. Publications include the *Annual Report of Vital Statistics*. Requests for information should be placed in writing. Information that is readily available, such as tables printed in the Annual Report, are distributed at no cost. A specific data run of information is available for a fee. Some information is available on diskette and magnetic tape. Fees vary, according to the complexity of the request.

Department of Health, Bureau of Communicable Disease Control, Tower Bldg., Room 651, Empire State Plaza, Albany, NY 12237; 518-474-3187. Publications include the *Annual Report*. The office will run computer searches of aggregate data, depending upon the purpose of the request.

North Carolina

North Carolina Center for Health and Environmental Statistics, 225 N. McDowell St., P.O. Box 29538, Raleigh, NC 27603-5902; 919-733-3005. Publications include an *Annual Report* and *1990 Vital Statistics Report*, among others. Information requests should be in writing. If requesting a magnetic tape, be sure to include your system requirements. Computer printouts, diskettes, and magnetic tapes are provided on a limited basis. The charge for magnetic tapes is the cost of the tape and the computer time involved.

North Dakota

Department of Health, Administrative Services Section, 600 E. Boulevard Ave., Bismarck, ND 58505-0200; 701-328-2360. Publications include the *Vital Statistics Annual Report*. Computer searches and printouts are provided free of charge.

Department of Health, Division of Disease Control, 600 E. Boulevard Ave., Bismarck, ND 58505-0200; 701-328-2378. This office publishes a variety of publications on communicable diseases. Computer searches and printouts are not provided.

Ohio

Statistical Analysis Unit, Health Policy Data Center, Ohio Department of Health, P.O. Box 118, Columbus, OH 43266-0118, 614-644-7800. Publications include the *Annual Report of Vital Statistics* which is $9. The office also publishes a *Vital Statistics Summary Fact Sheet*, which is free. Special computer runs are $25 per data year. Extensive programming is extra, and the amount depends upon the complexity of the request. Information is provided via computer printouts.

Ohio Department of Health, Infectious Disease Unit, P.O. Box 118, Columbus, OH 43266-0118; 614-466-0265. Publications include the *Annual Summary of Infectious Diseases* which is available at no cost.

Oklahoma

Department of Health, Division of Data Management, 1000 NE 10th St., P.O. Box 53551, Oklahoma City, OK 73117; 405-271-4542. Publications include the *Annual Report of Vital Statistics*. Computer searches and printouts are provided, usually free of charge. If you supply your own magnetic tape or diskette, they will transfer information to it for you. Fees vary according to the complexity of the request. All information for specific data runs should be in writing. Be sure to include information describing your computer system's requirements.

Department of Health, Office of General Communicable Diseases-0305, 1000 NE 10th St., Oklahoma City, OK 73117-1299; 405-271-4060. Publications include a monthly *Epidemiological Bulletin* and *Epidemiologic Annual Summary of Communicable Diseases*. Computer searches and printouts are provided free. All requests for information should be submitted in writing at least two weeks before the data is needed. Fees vary according to the complexity of the request.

Oregon

State Health Division, Center for Health Statistics, P.O. Box 14050, Portland, OR 97293-0050; 503-731-4108. Publications include: *Oregon Vital Statistics*, and their newsletter, *Oregon Health Trends*. Information is available on computer printout and diskette. Fees vary according to the complexity of the request. Selected tables are available on the Internet at: gopher.or.gov.

State Health Division, Center for Disease Prevention and Epidemiology Control, P.O. Box 14450, Portland, OR 97293-0450; 503-731-4023. Publications include the *Current Disease Summary*, which is published every other week. This office is not equipped to provide printouts of selected data that do not already exist in published form.

Economics, Demographics, and Statistics

Pennsylvania

Department of Health, Health Statistics and Research, State Health Data Center, P.O. Box 90, Harrisburg, PA 17108; 717-783-2548. Publications include the *County Profile*, *Statistical News*, and *Pennsylvania Assessment - Healthy People 2000*. Computer searches and printout requests must be made in writing. Costs vary depending on request. Information on tape and disk is also available.

Department of Health, Division of Epidemiology, Health and Welfare Building, 7th and Forster Sts., P.O. Box 90, Harrisburg, PA 17108; 717-787-3350. Publications include an *Annual Report*. Computer searches and printouts are available, free of charge.

Rhode Island

Department of Health, Vital Records, 3 Capitol Hill, Room 101, Providence, RI 02908-5097; 401-277-2812. Publications include the *1992 Annual Report of Vital Statistics*. Printouts of information are available depending upon whether or not the data is available on computer. Requests for individualized reports must be made in writing. Fees vary and are based upon the amount of computer programming needed to fulfill a request.

Department of Health, Office of AIDS-Sexually Transmitted Diseases, 3 Capitol Hill, Room 105, Providence, RI 02908-5097; 401-277-2320. Publications include the bimonthly *Disease Bulletin*. This office does not provide selected data printouts.

South Carolina

Department of Health and Environmental Control, Office of Vital Records and Public Health Statistics, 2600 Bull St., Columbia, SC 29201; 803-734-4860. Publications include the *South Carolina Vital and Morbidity Report*. Computer searches, printouts, and information on diskette and magnetic tape are provided. Information requests should be in writing, be sure to specify your computer system requirements. Each request is evaluated individually. Although in-house printouts are free, individual requests for selected data require a fee based on the complexity of the request and computer time involved.

Department of Health and Environmental Control, Communicable Disease Control Section, Robert Mills Complex, Box 101106, Columbia, SC 29211; 803-737-4165. Publications include the *South Carolina Reportable Diseases Report*. Computer searches and printouts of information are provided. Requests for information should be in writing. Information on diskette is provided on a limited basis. Since patient data is confidential, aggregate data is releases without any personal identifiers.

South Dakota

South Dakota Department of Health, 445 E. Capitol Ave., Pierre, SD 57501-3185; 605-773-3361, Fax: 605-773-5683. Health Statistics or Communicable Disease groups. Publications include: *South Dakota Vital Statistics and Health Status*, *Health Behaviors of South Dakotans*, *South Dakota Medical Facilities Report*, *South Dakota Cancer Data Collection System Report*, and *South Dakota Health Check-Up*. Current prices can be quoted at the time of the request. Limited special requests are possible with a fee for programming time.

Tennessee

Department of Health, Health Statistics and Information, 426 5th Ave., North, 4th Floor, Cordell Hull Building, Nashville, TN 37247-5262; 615-741-1954. Publications include an *Annual Report of Vital Statistics*. There is also a series of four publications, *Tennessee's Health*, which gives a detailed health profile based on 1990 statistics. The series can be ordered in its entirety for $38. You can purchase the volumes separately, also. *Picture of the Present* is $8, *Picture of the Present, Part II*, $20, *Guidelines for Growth*, $5, and *Focus on the Future*, is also $5. Printouts are provided free of charge. The office will also download limited data to a magnetic tape or diskette at no charge, but you must supply them with the materials needed. All requests for information should be in writing, and be sure to include your computer system's specifications in your letter.

Texas

Department of Health, Bureau of Vital Statistics, Statistical Services Division, 1100 West 49th St., Austin, TX 78756; 512-458-7111. Publications include *1990 Texas Vital Statistics*. The office will provide information on computer printouts, diskettes and magnetic tapes. Printouts are available at $150 per hour, diskettes at approximately $25 per tape. Programming charges are $30 per hour.

Department of Health, Bureau of Disease Control and Epidemiology, 1100 West 49th St., Austin, TX 78756; 512-458-7268. Publications include their annual summary, *Reported Morbidity and Mortality in Texas*. Computer searches and printouts are provided at no cost.

Utah

Department of Health, Bureau of Vital Records, P.O. Box 142855, Salt Lake City, UT 84114-2855; 801-538-6105. Publications include the *Vital Statistics Report*. Information is provided via computer printouts, diskettes and magnetic tapes. The office does charge for the use of the computer and the information analysts's time. Fees vary according to the complexity of the request. If detailed information is required, requests should be made in writing. Be sue to include the specifications needed for diskettes or magnetic tapes.

Department of Health, Bureau of Epidemiology, P.O. Box 16660, Salt Lake City, UT 84116-0660; 801-538-6191. Publications include the monthly *Epidemiology Newsletter*. The Department of Health is the process of creating a centralized statistics center. This should be in full operation as of Fall, 1992.

Vermont

Department of Health and Human Services, Vital Records Statistics, P.O. Box 70, Burlington, VT 05402; 802-863-7275. Publications include the *Vital Statistics Report*. Computer searches and printouts are available through this office.

Department of Health and Human Services, Division of Epidemiology and Disease Prevention, P.O. Box 70, Burlington, VT 05402; 802-863-7240. Publications include the *Vermont Disease Control Bulletin* which is published bi-monthly. Reportable disease totals for the previous year are listed through this publication. The office releases county specific information.

Virginia

Department of Health, Center for Health Statistics, 109 Governors St., Room 308, Richmond, VA 23218-1000; 804-786-6206. Publications include: *Annual Reports* (the latest is for 1994), plus supplemental reports on *Teen Pregnancy* and *Maternal and Infant Health*. Cost is $10 per publication. Special analyses are available with fees varying according to the complexity of the search. Products are available in hard copy, diskettes, magnetic tapes, and electronically.

Department of Health, Office of Epidemiology, 1500 E. Main St., Room 113, P.O. Box 2448, Richmond, VA 23218; 804-786-6261. Publications include the monthly *Virginia Epidemiology Bulletin*. The office provides county specific information. No diskettes or magnetic tapes are available.

Washington

Department of Health, Center for Health Statistics, P.O. Box 47814, Olympia, WA 98504; 206-753-5936. Publications include a series of reports on vital statistics, *Selected Pregnancy Reports of Statistics for 1990*, Age Adjusted Death Rates for 1986-1989, and *Minority Health in Washington*. The office provides computer searches for selected data and computer printouts at the cost of reproduction.

West Virginia

State Health Department, Epidemiology and Health Promotion, Surveillance and Disease Control, State Capitol Complex, Charleston, WV 25305; 304-558-9100. Publications include the *Annual Report of Vital Statistics* and the *County Health Profile*. The office provides computer printouts of selected data, free of charge. Magnetic tapes and diskettes can be obtained on a limited basis for a fee.

Wisconsin

Department of Health and Social Services, Vital Statistics Department, 1 West Wilson St., Madison, WI 53701; 608-266-1939. Publications include the *Annual Report of Vital Statistics*. Information requests should be in writing. Computer printouts of selected data are provided at no cost.

Department of Health and Social Services, Community Communicable Disease Section, P.O. Box 309, Madison, WI 53701; 608-267-9003. Publications include the quarterly *Wisconsin Epidemiologic Bulletin*. Requests for information should be made in writing. Information is available on computer printout, free of cost.

Be patient. If any phone number is incorrect, call (area code) 555-1212 and request the new listing.

Wyoming

Department of Health, Division of Public Health, Preventive Medicine, Vital Records Services, Hathaway Building, Cheyenne, WY 82002; 307-777-7264. Publications include the *1993 Vital Statistics Report*. The office does provide computer searches and information is available on printouts, diskettes and magnetic tapes. There is a flat fee of $25 for computer searches. Diskettes and magnetic tapes require additional fees that vary with the complexity of the request.

Department of Health, Division of Public Health, Preventive Medicine, Hathaway Building, Cheyenne, WY 82002; 307-777-6004. Publications include the *Wyoming Epidemiology Bulletin* (307-777-7719). Basic information is provided on computer printouts. Detailed requests should be in writing.

Highway Accident Statistics

* See also Your Community Chapter
* See also Business and Industry Chapter

A car runs a red light and slams into your brand new Jeep Cherokee, doing $1,500 worth of damage. You shout, they shout, a police officer comes and files an accident report. Guess what? You've just become part of your state's traffic accident database. Not just your name, mind you, but every little detail about the accident will be entered into a computer file and stored for posterity -- or until someone asks the state for the information.

A state accident database is a file made up of reports completed by all law enforcement agencies which investigate accidents. While it might seem that this data should be confidential, it is freely available to engineers, lobbyists, courts, safety organizations, and such citizen-action groups as Mothers Against Drunk Drivers (MADD).

In most instances, the computerized system can be searched and printouts provided by a number of variables.

* The Human Element: driver sex, age, equipment used by age, charged driver violations, pedestrian age.

* Environmental Elements: accident type vs. highway conditions, traffic control vs. accident site, accident type vs. weather, and accident type vs. light conditions.

* Accident Characteristics: county, month of year, time of day, rural/urban road system, hit and run severity, holiday accidents, fatal accidents, alcohol involved, property damage, type of car, accidents caused by animals in the highway.

Our research indicates that state highway accident database searches can be tailored to individual requests within reason. In some states, state employees will perform computer searches and provide printouts--all free of charge. Other states charge up to $150 per hour or require a Freedom of Information Act request.

States that do not provide data searches and printouts are: Arkansas, Colorado, District of Columbia, Georgia, Minnesota, Mississippi, Ohio, West Virginia, Wisconsin.

A statewide accident summary and a breakdown of accident problems by specific areas can be obtained by contacting the state offices listed below.

Highway Department Offices

Alabama
Alabama Highway Department, Accident Identification and Surveillance Section, Traffic Engineering, 1409 Coliseum Blvd., Montgomery, AL 36130; 334-242-6128. A report, *Alabama Traffic Accident Facts*, is available to individuals at no cost. The accident database can be searched, sorted and a printout produced. This service is free unless it is to be used for legal purposes. In those instances there is a $100 fee per computer run.

Alaska
Department of Transportation and Public Facilities, 3132 Channel Drive, Juneau, AK 99801-7908; 907-465-2777. Publications include a free annual report. Accident database printouts are provided. If you supply your own computer disks the department will transfer data on to them at no additional charge.

Arizona
Arizona Department of Transportation, Traffic Records Unit, 1739 W. Jackson Ave., Phoenix, AZ 85007; 602-255-7724. Publications include the *Arizona Traffic Accident Summary*. The accident database can be searched, sorted and a printout provided at no charge.

Arkansas
Arkansas State Highway and Transportation Division, P.O. Box 2261, Little Rock, AR 72203; 501-569-2564. Publications include an annual *State Accident Data Report*. Information from accident databases is not released on a routine basis.

California
Department of Transportation, Caltrans, 1120 N. St., P.O. Box 1499, Room 4123, Sacramento, CA 95807; 916-654-2852. Publications include the annual *Accident Data on California Highways Report*. The accident database can be searched, sorted and a printout provided on a cost recovery basis.

Colorado
Department of Highways, Staff Traffic Division, 4201 E. Arkansas Ave., Room 172, Denver, CO 80222; 303-757-9271. This department's publications include: *Accidents by County*, and *Accidents by City*. Both are free. A report entitled, *Accidents by Rates*, is $5. The Department of Revenue issues standard summaries of motor vehicle reports for a nominal fee. Information from accident databases is not released as a general policy.

Connecticut
Department of Transportation, Planning Inventory and Data, Bureau of Policy and Planning, P.O. Box 317546, Newington, CT 06131; 860-594-2096. The accident database can be searched, sorted, and a printout provided at no cost to state and non-profit agencies. Others are charged a fee of $.50 per page. Requests should be in writing. Publications include a *Statewide Accident Summary* and *1989 Connecticut Accidents Facts Booklet* which are $5.30 each. Traffic accident surveillance reports are available on microfiche. There is a $.50 per page copying fee.

Delaware
State Police Headquarters, Delaware State Traffic Section, 3036 Upper King Rd., Dover, DE 19904; 302-739-4865. Publications include monthly and annual reports. The database can be searched, sorted, and a printout provided at no cost.

District of Columbia
DC Department of Public Works, Bureau of Traffic Services, 2000 14th St., NW, 7th Floor, Washington, DC 20009; 202-939-8098. No listings are provided on a regular basis. General questions are answered over the telephone.

Florida
Department of Highway Safety and Motor Vehicles, Office of Management and Planning, Statistics Division, 2900 Appalachia Parkway, Room A-430, Tallahassee, FL 32399; 904-488-3666. Publications include the *Florida Traffic Accident Facts Report* which is free upon request. The accident database can be searched, sorted, and a printout provided, usually free of charge. If the department must perform a mainframe computer search there is an additional charge.

Georgia
Department of Public Safety, Accident Reporting Section, P.O. Box 1456, Atlanta, GA 30371; 404-624-7660. Standard accident summaries and an annual report is free upon request. Copies of individual accident reports are also provided. The agency does not routinely provide computer printouts of accident data.

Hawaii

Department of Transportation, Traffic Branch, 869 Punchbowl Street, Room 120, Honolulu, HI 96813; 808-587-2171. Publications include *Major Traffic Accidents in Hawaii* which is available for $30. The accident database has information up to 1990. Printouts are available. Charges vary according to the complexity of the request.

Idaho

Office of Highway Safety, Idaho Transportation Department, P.O. Box 7129, Boise, ID 83707-1129; 208-334-8100. Publications include the *Idaho Traffic Accident Analysis*, which is free upon request. The accident database can be searched, sorted and a printout provided. A broad search of the data base is usually under $10, but fees vary depending upon the complexity of the request. A specific accident report is $4 plus tax and shipping.

Illinois

Department of Transportation, Division on Traffic Safety, 3215 Executive Park Dr., Springfield, IL 62764; 217-782-2575. Publications include an *Accident Facts Report*. The accident database can be searched, sorted and a printout provided at no cost.

Indiana

State Police Data Section, Indianapolis Government Center North, 100 N. Senate Ave., Indianapolis, IN 46204; 317-232-8289. Publications include monthly and annual summaries of motor vehicle traffic accidents. The accident database can be searched, sorted and a printout provided on a cost recovery basis. A written request is required.

Iowa

Iowa Department of Transportation, Driver Services, 100 Euclid Ave., State Office Building, Parkfair Mall, Des Moines, IA 50306; 515-244-8725. Publications include the *Accident Facts Report*. The accident database can be searched, sorted and a printout provided for a cost recovery fee.

Kansas

Department of Transportation, Office of Traffic Safety, 217 S.E. 4th St., 2nd Floor, Thatcher Building, Topeka, KS 66603-3504; 913-296-3756. Publications include the *Annual Summary of Accident Statistics*, *Kansas Traffic Accident Facts*, and an *Age, Alcohol and Traffic Accidents Report*. The accident database can be searched, sorted and a printout provided at no cost.

Kentucky

State Police, Records Center, 1250 Louisville Road, Frankfort, KY 40601; 502-227-8717. Publications include an *Accident Facts Book*. The accident database can be searched for records dating back to 1985, sorted, and a printout provided. A written request is required and there is a charge of $2 for the first 10 pages and $.10 for every following page.

Louisiana

Department of Public Safety and Corrections, Highway Safety Commission, P.O. Box 66336, 265 S. Foster Dr., Baton Rouge, LA 70896; 504-925-6991. This department publishes an annual *Louisiana Traffic Accident Report* which is free upon request. The accident database can be searched, sorted and a printout provided upon written request. Information not found in their annual report may require an additional charge.

Maine

Department of Highway Safety, 42 State House Station, Augusta, ME 04333; 207-624-8756. The accident database can be searched, sorted and a printout provided at no cost upon request.

Maryland

Ron Lips, State Highway Administration, Traffic Safety, 7491 Connelly Dr., Hannover, MD 21076; 410-787-5849. The staff will supply data tailored to individual needs within reasonable requests. There is normally no charge, but fees are based on the amount of data requested and staff time involved.

Massachusetts

Registry of Motor Vehicles, Accident Records, 1135 Tremont St., Boston, MA 02120; 617-351-9434. The accident database can be searched, sorted, and a printout provided in most cases. There is a fee for the data retrieval service. Requests should be in writing. Requests for an entire year's worth of data can be very expensive. A magnetic tape of 1991 accident report data costs $7,640.

Michigan

Michigan State Police, Office of Highway Safety Planning, 300 S. Washington

Square, Suite 300, Lansing, MI 48913; 517-334-5200. Publications include the annual *Traffic Accident Facts Book*. The department does provide computer printouts of selected data. Requests should be made in writing. Easily accessible information is provided at no cost. Detailed searches may require an additional fee.

Minnesota

Department of Public Safety, Office of Public Education, 444 Cedar St., Suite E, St. Paul, MN 55101; 612-296-6652. Publications include the *1991 Crash Facts Report*. This department does not provide accident database searches.

Mississippi

Department of Public Safety, Statistical Bureau, P.O. Box 958, Jackson, MS 39205; 601-987-1212. This department does not provide accident database searches. General questions are handled over the phone.

Missouri

State Highway Patrol, Traffic Division, P.O. Box 568, Jefferson City, MO 65102; 314-751-3313. Publications include the annual *Missouri Traffic Crashes Report*. The accident database can be searched, sorted and a printout provided upon special request. Fees vary and are based on a cost recovery basis.

Montana

Montana Highway Patrol, Records Bureau, 303 N. Roberts, Helena, MT 59601; 406-444-3278. Publications include their free *Annual Statistical Report*. The accident database can be searched, sorted and a printout provided at no cost.

Nebraska

Department of Roads, Highway Safety Bureau, Accident Records, P.O. Box 94669, Lincoln, NE 68509; 402-479-4645. Publications include the annual *Traffic Accident Facts Report*. The accident database can be searched, sorted and a printout provided, usually at no cost.

Nevada

Department of Transportation, Safety Engineering, 1263 S. Stewart St., Carson City, NV 89712; 702-687-3468. Publications include the annual *Nevada Traffic Accidents Report*. The accident database can be searched, sorted and a printout provided. There is a fee of $35 per hour for staff computer time unless the requestor is a non-profit or government agency.

New Hampshire

Department of Safety, Data Processing Division, 10 Hazen Drive, Concord, NH 03305; 603-271-2554. A *Fatal Accident Summary* is free to the public. The accident database can be searched, sorted and a printout provided for a fee of $.50 per page. Thirty-five accidents are listed per page.

New Jersey

Department of Transportation, Accident Statistics, 1035 Parkway Ave., CN 600, Trenton, NJ 08625; 609-530-8082. Publications include a *Fatal Statistics Report* and *Annual Report*. Both are free to the public. The accident database can be searched, sorted and a printout provided. Requests should be made in writing. There may be a fee depending upon the amount of computer programming time involved.

New Mexico

Highway and Transportation Department, Traffic Safety Bureau, P.O. Box 1149, Santa Fe, NM 87502; 505-827-0427. Publications include the annual *New Mexico Traffic and Crash Data Report*. The accident database can be searched, sorted and a printout provided at no cost. Requests for data not found in the annual report should be placed in writing.

New York

State Department of Motor Vehicles, Accident Safety Division, Empire State Plaza, Albany, NY 12228; 518-474-0679. Publications include an annual *Summary of Motor Vehicle Accidents Report*. The accident database can be searched, sorted and a printout provided. Fees vary according to the complexity of the request.

North Carolina

Division of Motor Vehicles, Collision Reports, 1100 New Bern Ave., Raleigh, NC 27697; 919-733-7250. Publications include a free report entitled *Traffic Accident Facts*. The accident database can be searched, sorted and a printout provided for a fee from: Highway Safety Research Center, 13040 1/2 E. Franklin St., CB 3430, UNC Campus, Chapel Hill, NC 27599; 919-962-2202.

North Dakota

State Highway Department, Drivers License and Traffic Safety Division, Accident

Be patient. If any phone number is incorrect, call (area code) 555-1212 and request the new listing.

887

Economics, Demographics, and Statistics

Records Section, 608 East Boulevard Ave., Bismarck, ND 58505; 701-328-2553. Publications include the *Annual Accident Facts Report*. The accident database can be searched, sorted and a printout provided. There is a $7 minimum charge.

Ohio

Department of Highway Safety, Public Information Office, 240 Parsons Ave. Columbus, OH 43266; 614-466-2550. The accident database can be searched, sorted and a printout provided to other government agencies. At the present time, individual requests are not handled on a regular basis. A 70-page publication entitled *Crash Facts Book* is available that is updated annually.

Oklahoma

Department of Public Safety, Accident Records Division, Box 11415, Oklahoma City, OK 73136; 405-425-2192. Publications include the annual *Oklahoma Traffic Accident Facts Report*, which is free. Computer printouts are available upon written request. Fees vary according to the complexity of the data search.

Oregon

Department of Transportation, Accident Data Unit, 555 13th St., NE, Salem, OR 97310; 503-986-4245. Publications include an *Oregon Accident Rate Table* which is $20. The accident database can be searched, sorted and a printout provided at no cost.

Pennsylvania

Department of Transportation, Center for Highway Safety, Safety Management, Room 216, Transportation and Safety Building, Harrisburg, PA 17120; 717-787-3393. This office publishes a free report entitled *Traffic Accident Facts and Statistics*. The accident database can be searched, sorted and a printout provided. Fees vary according to the scope of the request. All requests should be made in writing.

Rhode Island

Department of Transportation, Planning Section, Two Capitol Hill, Room 372, Providence, RI 02903; 401-277-2694. Standard tables of accident reports are published yearly and are available upon request. The accident database can be searched, sorted and a printout provided upon special, written request. Individuals must first complete an open records request. Costs vary according to the actual research and computer time involved.

South Carolina

Department of Highways, Safety Office, P.O. Box 191, Columbia, SC 29202; 803-737-1162. Publications include the *South Carolina Traffic Accidents Report* which is $3. The accident database can be searched, sorted and a printout provided. The minimum charge is $43.75.

South Dakota

Department of Transportation, Accident Records, 118 W. Capitol, Pierre, SD 57501; 605-773-3868. Publications include an annual *South Dakota Accident Facts Book*. Individuals can receive copies of individual accident reports for $4, each. Individual computer runs of selected data are provided generally at no cost.

Tennessee

Department of Safety, 1150 Foster Ave., Nashville, TN 37249-1000; 615-251-5220. Publications include a *1987 Accident Facts Book* and *1991 Annual Report*. The accident database can be searched, sorted and a printout provided. There is a minimum charge of $500.

Texas

Department of Public Safety, Statistical Services, Box 15999, Austin, TX 78761-1599; 512-424-2000. Publications include the *Motor Vehicle Traffic Accidents Report*, and a report entitled *A Look at DWI... Accidents, Victims, Arrests*. The accident database can be searched, sorted and a printout provided for a cost recovery fee.

Utah

Department of Transportation, Division of Traffic Safety, 4501 South, 2700 West, Salt Lake City, UT 84119; 801-965-4284. Publications include *Utah Annual Safety Report*. The accident database can be searched and printouts provided. Requests should be in writing and individuals must first complete a request form. Fees for computer printouts vary. Individuals may receive data within the last five years at a cost of $10 per year. Printouts of older data cost $15 per year.

Vermont

Agency for Transportation, Planning Division, 133 State St., Montpelier, VT 05633. 802-828-3960. Publications include an annual report. The accident database can be searched, sorted and printouts provided. Costs for individual searches vary depending upon the scope of the request. Requests should be made in writing to the attention of Jeff Squires.

Virginia

Department of Transportation, Traffic Engineering, 1401 E. Broad St., Richmond, VA 23219; 804-786-2969. Publications include an *Accident Summary Book*. The accident database can be searched, sorted and printouts provided upon special, written request. There may be a charge depending upon the complexity of the information requested.

Washington

Department of Transportation, Public Transportation Plan, Accident Data, 318 E. State Ave., Olympia, WA 98504-7300; 360-753-3211. Publications include the *Washington State Department of Transportation Highway Traffic Report*. The accident database can be searched, sorted and a printout provided. Normally, there is a charge of $20 to $25 per hour. Most requests usually require only one hour of staff time.

West Virginia

Department of Highways, Traffic Engineering Division, 1900 Kanawah Blvd., Capitol Complex, Building 5, Room A550, Charleston, WV 25305; 304-558-3063. Publications include the *West Virginia Accident Data Report* which is free. The accident database is not available to the general public.

Wisconsin

Department of Transportation, Bureau of Traffic Accidents, P.O. Box 7917, Madison, WI 53707; 608-266-8753. Publications include a report entitled *Wisconsin Traffic Crash Facts* which is free to the public. Computer printouts not normally available.

Wyoming

Highway Safety Branch, Wyoming Highway Department, P.O. Box 1708, Cheyenne, WY 82002; 307-777-4450. Publications include the *Wyoming Comprehensive Report on Traffic Accidents*. The accident database can be searched and printouts provided at no cost.

Be patient. If any phone number is incorrect, call (area code) 555-1212 and request the new listing.

State Data Centers

Approximately 1,300 organizations nationwide receive data from the U.S. Bureau of the Census and in turn disseminate the information to the public free of charge or on a cost recovery basis. These organizations are called state data centers and serve as ideal information sources for both local and national markets. The centers listed in this report are the major offices for each state. If you are looking for national markets, start with a center in your state. If you are searching for local market data, contact the center located in the relevant area.

Demographics and Target Market Identification

State data center offices are most frequently used for obtaining information on target markets. For instance, the Army and Navy used such services to identify which areas are populated with large numbers of teenagers in order to open recruiting offices and focus their advertising campaign. Avon door-to-door sales reps used state data center generated demographic maps to identify homes with highest potential. L.L. Bean relied on a center to determine large Hispanic populations for a special promotion of outdoor recreational products. These offices could provide current data including:

- The age distribution within a given county;
- Moving patterns for particular geographical areas;
- The number of wells and mobile homes in 85 counties;
- How many gravel pits in the state of Montana;
- Counties with the highest rate of illegitimate children;
- Analysis of why certain stores in an auto parts chain are doing better than others;
- Demographic profile of a person in need of child care;
- The top 25 markets by zip code;
- The number of male secretaries in a dozen contiguous counties.

Forecasting Future Markets

The biggest opportunities often lie in knowing the future of a market. Many of the state data centers have developed specific software for analyzing Census and other data to project growth of specific markets. Here is a sampling of what some centers can do:

- Population projections for every three years to the year 2020 (done by California center);
- State population changes by the year 2000;
- What year the white population will not be in the majority;
- The number of teenagers by the next century;
- Series of economic indicators for plotting future economic health in state (Oklahoma center provides such data).

Site Location

Another major area of interest is in providing information to companies considering relocating into a state. Because most states are aggressively trying to attract business, numerous customized services receive a high priority. Local centers can provide information such as the number of fast food restaurants in the area and the best location for another one. And some states, like Arkansas, have special site evaluation software which can manipulate Census data to show the demographic characteristics for market radiuses which are 2, 5 or 10 miles from a given site. Oklahoma and other states have free data sheets covering every community in their state which are loaded with specifics for choosing a location. Their reports contain data on:

- Distance from major cities
- Population: past and future
- Climate
- Municipal services
- Utilities
- Labor market analysis
- List of major manufacturers
- List of major employers
- Transportation
- Commercial services
- Major freight lines and truck terminals
- Educational facilities
- Financial institutions
- Tax structure
- Housing and churches
- Medical facilities
- Retail business in city
- Industrial financial assistance
- Water analysis report
- Recreational facilities
- Wholesale business in city
- Items deserving special consideration

Professional and Personal Relocation

The same services that are intended to help businesses relocate also can be useful to individuals and professionals. For example, if you are looking for a place to start an orthodontics practice, a local data center could determine which counties and cities have the most affluent families with young people -- a prime market for braces. Also, if you get an offer for a new job in another city, obtaining a data sheet on the local community like the one described above provides insight into the types of housing, schools, churches, and recreational facilities available.

Business Proposals Plus Loan and Grant Applications

If you are looking for money for either a grant, a loan or even venture money, data centers can provide the information needed

Be patient. If any phone number is incorrect, call (area code) 555-1212 and request the new listing.

889

for proposal writing. Grantors must have information such as what percent of people live below poverty line, and banks want to know current business patterns for a new enterprise when seeking a loan. These sorts of data can be obtained easily from these centers.

Level of Detail

Because the data centers use information from other sources in addition to the Bureau of Census, the level of detail will vary according to subject area as well as the state and office contacted. Much of the Census data can be provided at the state, county, city, census tract and block group level (which is normally even smaller than a zip code). Data according to zip code are also available for many categories of information. All states also have the public use micro data sample, which do not contain aggregate data, but actual questionnaire information filled out by respondents. They can be manipulated into any kind of special detail required.

Custom Work, Workshops and Other Services

A lot of work performed by the data centers is customized in nature. The organizations collect data from other federal and state sources to enhance their Census information. Many have arrangements with other state data centers to send any computer file needed to do special analysis. This is how local centers can provide national information or inter-market comparisons. Some centers will even perform custom census projects for clients, which means raw data collection for market research.

Free and low cost workshops about services and information opportunities are sponsored in some areas for potential users. These workshops are important at the local level because in the past they were readily available from the Bureau of Census, but recent budget cuts have reduced their frequency and increased their price. Because of the centers' familiarity of census data, these offices are excellent starting places for almost any information search.

Formats

Data centers offer some of the most sophisticated formats you are likely to find from public organizations. They all provide computer tapes, off-the-shelf reports, custom reports from computer analysis, and quick answers over the telephone. Most are also set up to provide custom analysis and/or raw data on computer diskettes, and some -- like Ohio -- have developed a PC database from which they can generate standard reports and download onto diskettes. Colorado and other states are beginning to make data accessible online.

Prices

Although the U.S. government provides most of the data to these centers, the feds do not interfere with fee schedules. Most offices try to give out information free, but some charge on a cost recovery basis. Some states do not charge for the first so many pages of a report but charge a nominal fee for additional pages. Some say they have a minimum fee of $20 for customized computer runs. It is interesting that these centers sell you computerized data cheaper than the U.S. Bureau of the Census in Washington. In contrast to the Bureau's fee of $140, Illinois and Georgia only charge $50 for a data tape file, and in Florida, the cost is $15 for a file.

In the dozens of interviews we conducted with these centers about the complicated market research reports they have provided to clients, the highest figure we found they ever charged was $2,000. That amount of money would buy virtually nothing from most marketing consultants.

State Data Centers

Below is a roster of data centers in all 50 states as well as the District of Columbia, Puerto Rico and Virgin Islands. Some of these Census Bureau information providers are based in state departments and agencies, universities, business colleges, and libraries. Each center listed below includes the name and phone number of the data expert.

Alabama
Center for Business and Economic Research, University of Alabama, P.O. Box 870221, Tuscaloosa, AL 34587-0221, Ms. Annette Walters, 205-348-6191.

Alabama Department of Economic and Community Affairs, Office of State Planning, P.O. Box 5690, 3465 Norman Bridge Road, Montgomery, AL 36103-5690, Mr. Parker Collins, 205-242-5493.

Alabama Public Library Service, 6030 Monticello Drive, Montgomery, AL 36130, Mr. Vince Thacker, 205-277-7330.

Alaska
Alaska State Data Center, Research and Analysis, Department of Labor, P.O. Box 25504, Juneau, AK 99802-5504, Ms. Kathryn Lizik, 907-465-6026.

Office of Management and Budget, Division of Policy, Pouch AD, Juneau, AK 99811, Mr. Jack Kreinheder, 907-465-3640.

Department of Education, Division of Libraries and Museums, Alaska State Library, Pouch G, Juneau, AK 99811, Ms. Patience Fredrickson, 907-465-2927.

Department of Community and Regional Affairs, Division of Municipal and Regional Assistance, P.O. Box BH, Juneau, AK 99811, Ms. Laura Walters, 907-465-4750.

Institute for Social and Economic Research, University of Alaska, 3211 Providence Drive, Anchorage, AK 99508, Mr. Jim Kerr, 907-786-7710.

Arizona
Arizona Department of Economic Security, Mail Code 045Z, 1789 West Jefferson Street, Phoenix, AZ 85007, Ms. Betty Jeffries, 602-542-5984.

Center for Business Research, College of Business Administration, Arizona State University, Tempe, AZ, 85287, Mr. Tom Rex, 602-965-3961.

College of Business Administration, Northern Arizona University, Box 15066, Flagstaff, AZ 86011, Ms. Linda Stratton, 602-523-7313.

Research Library, Department of Library, Archives, and Public Records, 1700 West Washington, 2nd Floor, Phoenix, AZ 85007, Ms. Janet Fisher, 602-542-3701.

Division of Economic and Business Research, College of Business and Public Administration, University of Arizona, Tucson, AZ 85721, Ms. Pia Montoya, 602-621-2155.

Arkansas

State Data Center, University of Arkansas-Little Rock, 2801 South University, Little Rock, AR 72204, Ms. Sarah Breshears, 501-569-8530.

Arkansas State Library, 1 Capitol Mall, Little Rock, AR 72201, Ms. Mary Honeycutt-Leckie, 501-682-2864.

Research and Analysis Section, Arkansas Employment Security Division, P.O. Box 2981, Little Rock, AR 72203, Mr. Coy Cozart, 501-682-3159.

California

State Census Data Center, Department of Finance, 915 L Street, Sacramento, CA 95814, Ms. Linda Gage, Director, 916-322-4651, Mr. Richard Lovelady, 916-323-4141.

Sacramento Area COG, 106 K Street, Suite 300, Sacramento, CA 95816, Mr. Bob Faseler, 916-457-2264.

Association of Bay Area Governments, Metro Center, 8th and Oak Streets, P.O. Box 2050, Oakland, CA 94604-2050, Ms. Patricia Perry, 510-464-7937.

Southern California Association of Governments, 818 West 7th Street, 12th Floor, Los Angeles, CA 90017, Mr. Javier Minjares, 213-236-1800.

San Diego Association of Governments, First Federal Plaza, 401 B Street, Suite 800, San Diego, CA 92101, Ms. Karen Lamphere, 619-236-5300.

State Data Center Program, University of California-Berkeley, 2538 Channing Way, Berkeley, CA 94720, Ms. Ilona Einowski/Fred Gey, 510-642-6571.

Association of Monterey Bay Area Governments, 445 Reservation Road, Suite G, P.O. Box 838, Marina, CA 93933, Mr. Steve Williams, 408-883-3750.

Colorado

Division of Local Government, Colorado Department of Local Affairs, 1313 Sherman Street, Room 521, Denver, CO 80203, Ms. Rebecca Picaso, 303-866-2156.

Business Research Division, Graduate School of Business Administration, University of Colorado-Boulder, Boulder, CO 80309, Ms. Ginny Hayden, 303-492-8227.

Natural Resources and Economics, Department of Agriculture, Colorado State University, Fort Collins, CO 80523, Ms. Sue Anderson, 303-491-5706.

Documents Department, The Libraries, Colorado State University, Fort Collins, CO 80523, Ms. Suzanne Taylor, 303-491-1880.

Connecticut

Policy Development and Planning Division, Connecticut Office of Policy and Management, 80 Washington Street, Hartford, CT 06106-4459, Mr. Bill Kraynak, 203-566-8285.

Government Documents, Connecticut State Library, 231 Capitol Avenue, Hartford, CT 06106, Mr. Albert Palko, 203-566-4971.

Connecticut Department of Economic Development, Research, Planning, and Information Systems, 865 Brook Street, Rocky Hill, CT 06067-3405, Mr. Jeff Blodgett, 203-258-4219.

Capitol Region Council of Governments, 221 Main Street, Hartford, CT 06106, Ms. Barbara MacFarland, 203-522-2217.

Delaware

Delaware Development Office, 99 Kings Highway, P.O. Box 1401, Dover, DE 19903, Ms. Judy McKinney-Cherry, 302-739-4271.

College of Urban Affairs and Public Policy, University of Delaware, Graham Hall, Room 286, Academy Street, Newark, DE 19716, Mr. Ed Ratledge, 302-831-8406.

District of Columbia

Data Services Division, Mayor's Office of Planning, Room 570, Presidential Bldg., 415 12th Street, NW, Washington, DC 20004, Mr. Gan Ahuja, 202-727-6533.

Metropolitan Washington Council of Governments, 777 North Capitol Street, NE, Suite 300, Washington, DC 20002-4201, Mr. Robert Griffith/Ms. Carol Huskey, 202-962-3200.

Florida

Florida State Data Center, Executive Office of the Governor, REA/OPB, The Capitol, Room 1604, Tallahassee, FL 32399-0001, Ms. Valerie Jugger, 904-487-2814.

Center for the Study of Population, Institute for Social Research, 654 Bellemy Building, R-93, Florida State University, Tallahassee, FL 32306-4063, Dr. Ike Eberstein, 904-644-1762.

State Library of Florida, R.A. Gray Building, Tallahassee, FL 32399-0250, Ms. Lisa Close, 904-487-2651.

Bureau of Economic Analysis, Florida Department of Commerce, 107 West Gaines Street, 315 Collins Building, Tallahassee, FL 32399-2000, Mr. Nick Leslie, 904-487-2971.

Georgia

Division of Demographic and Statistical Services, Georgia Office of Planning and Budget, 254 Washington Street, SW, Room 640, Atlanta, GA 30334, Ms. Marty Sik, 404-656-0911.

Data Services, University of Georgia Libraries, 6th Floor, Athens, GA 30602, Dr. Hortense Bates, 404-542-0727.

Georgia Department of Community Affairs, Office of Coordinated Planning, 100 Peachtree Street, NE #1200, Atlanta, GA 30303, Mr. Keith Nelms, 404-656-3879.

Guam

Guam Department of Commerce, 590 South Marine Drive, Suite 601, 6th Floor GITC Building, Tamuning, Guam 96911, Mr. Peter R. Barcinas, 671-646-5841.

Hawaii

Hawaii State Data Center, Department of Business, Economic Development, and Tourism, 220 S. King Street, Suite 400, Honolulu, HI 96813, Mailing Address: P.O. Box 2359, Honolulu, HI 96804, Ms. Jan Nakamoto, 808-586-2493.

Information and Communication Services Division, State Dept. of Budget and Finance, Kalanimoku Building, 1151 Punchbowl Street, Honolulu, HI 96813, Ms. Joy Toyama, 808-568-1940.

Idaho

Idaho Department of Commerce, 700 West State Street, Boise, ID 83720, Mr. Alan Porter, 208-334-2470.

Institutional Research, Room 319, Business Building, Boise State University, Boise, ID 83725, Mr. Don Canning, 208-385-1613.

The Idaho State Library, 325 West State Street, Boise, ID 83702, Ms. Stephanie Kukay, 208-334-2150.

Center for Business Research and Services, Campus Box 8450, Idaho State University, Pocatello, ID 83209, Dr. Paul Zelus, 208-236-3049.

Illinois

Illinois Bureau of the Budget, William Stratton Building, Room 605, Springfield, IL 62706, Ms. Suzanne Ebetsch, 217-782-1381.

Census and Data Users Services, Department 4690, Research Services Bldg., Suite A, 4950 Illinois State University, Normal, IL 61790-4950, Dr. Roy Treadway/Dr. Del Ervin, 309-438-5946.

Center for Governmental Studies, Northern Illinois University, Social Science Research Bldg., DeKalb, IL 60115, Ms. Ruth Anne Tobias/Ms. Charlene Ceci, 815-753-0922/0934.

Regional Research and Development Services, Southern Illinois University at Edwardsville, P.O. Box 1456, Edwardsville, IL 62026-1456, Mr. Charles Kofron, 618-692-2278.

Chicago Area Geographic Information Study, Department of Geography, M/C 092, 1007 W. Harrison St., Room 2102, University of Illinois at Chicago, Chicago, IL 60607-7138, Mr. Jim Bash, 312-996-5274.

Northeastern Illinois Planning Commission, Research Services Department, 222 S. Riverside Plaza, Suite 1800, Chicago, IL 60606-6097, Max Dieber/Mary Cele Smith, 312-454-0400.

Be patient. If any phone number is incorrect, call (area code) 555-1212 and request the new listing.

891

Economics, Demographics, and Statistics

Indiana

Indiana State Library, Indiana State Data Center, 140 North Senate Avenue, Indianapolis, IN 46204, Mr. Ray Ewick, Director/Mr. Laurence Hathaway, 317-232-3733.

Indiana Business Research Center, Indiana University, School of Business, Bloomington, IN 47405, Dr. Morton Marcus, 812-855-5507.

Indiana Business Research Center, 801 W. Michigan, B.S. 4015, Indianapolis, IN 46202-5151, Ms. Carol Rogers, 317-274-2205.

Research Division, Indiana Department of Commerce, 1 North Capitol, Suite 700, Indianapolis, IN 46204, Mr. Robert Lain, 317-232-8959.

Iowa

State Library of Iowa, East 12th and Grand, Des Moines, IA 50319, Ms. Beth Henning, 515-281-4350.

Center for Social and Behavioral Research, University of Northern Iowa, Cedar Falls, IA 50614, Dr. Robert Kramer, 319-273-2105.

Census Services, Iowa State University, 320 East Hall, Ames, IA 50011, Dr. Willis Goudy, 515-294-8337.

Iowa Social Science Institute, University of Iowa, 345 Shaeffer Hall, Iowa City, IA 52242, Ms. Joyce Baker, 319-335-2371.

Census Data Center, Dept. of Education, Grimes State Office Building, Des Moines, IA 50319, Mr. Steve Boal, 515-281-4730.

Kansas

State Library, Room 343-N, State Capitol Building, Topeka, KS 66612, Mr. Marc Galbraith, 913-296-3296.

Division of the Budget, Room 152-E, State Capitol Building, Topeka, KS 66612, 913-296-0025.

Institute for Public Policy and Business Research, 607 Blake Hall, The University of Kansas, Lawrence, KS 66045-2960, Ms. Thelma Helyar, 913-864-3123.

Center for Economic Development and Business Research, Box 48, Wichita State University, Wichita, KS 67208, Ms. Janet Nickel, 316-689-3225.

Population and Research Laboratory, Department of Sociology, Kansas State University, Manhattan, KS 66506, Dr. Leonard Bloomquist, 913-532-5984.

Kentucky

Center for Urban and Economic Research, College of Business and Public Administration, University of Louisville, Louisville, KY 40292, Mr. Ron Crouch, 502-852-7990.

Governor's Office of Policy and Management, Capitol Annex, Room 201, Frankfort, KY 40601, Mr. Mike Mullins, 502-564-7300.

State Library Division, Department for Libraries and Archives, 300 Coffeetree Road, P.O. Box 537, Frankfort, KY 40601, Ms. Brenda Fuller, 502-875-7000.

Louisiana

Office of Planning and Budget, Division of Administration, P.O. Box 94095, 1051 N. 3rd Street, Baton Rouge, LA 70804, Ms. Karen Paterson, 504-342-7410.

Division of Business and Economic Research, University of New Orleans, Lake Front, New Orleans, LA 70148, Mr. Vincent Maruggi, 504-286-6980.

Division of Business Research, Louisiana Tech Univ., P.O. Box 10318, Ruston, LA 71272, Dr. Edward O'Boyle, 318-257-3701.

Reference Department, Louisiana State Library, P.O. Box 131, Baton Rouge, LA 70821, Ms. Virginia Smith, 504-342-4920.

Center for Life Course and Population Studies, Department of Sociology, Room 126, Stubbs Hall, Louisiana State University, Baton Rouge, LA 70803-5411, Mr. Charles Tolbert, 504-388-5359.

Center for Business and Economic Research, Northeast Louisiana University, Monroe, LA 71209, Dr. Jerry Wall, 318-342-1215.

Maine

Division of Economic Analysis and Research, Maine Department of Labor, 20 Union Street, Augusta, ME 04330, Mr. Raynold Fongemie, Director, Ms. Jean Martin, 207-287-2271.

Maine State Library, State House Station 64, Augusta, ME 04333, Mr. Gary Nichols, 207-287-5600.

Maryland

Maryland Department of State Planning, 301 West Preston Street, Baltimore, MD 21201, Mr. Robert Dadd/Ms. Jane Traynham, 410-225-4450.

Computer Science Center, University of Maryland, College Park, MD 20742, Mr. John McNary, 301-405-3037.

Enoch Pratt Free Library, Resource Center, Maryland Room, 400 Cathedral Street, Baltimore, MD 21201, Mr. Jeff Korman, 410-396-1789.

Small Business Development Center, 217 E. Redwood St., 10th Floor, Baltimore, MD 21202, Mr. Michael E. Long, 410-333-6996.

Massachusetts

Massachusetts Institute for Social and Economic Research, 128 Thompson Hall, University of Massachusetts, Amherst, MA 01003, Dr. Stephen Coelen, Director, 413-545-3460, Ms. Valerie Conti, 413-545-0176.

Massachusetts Institute for Social and Economic Research, Box 219, Saltonstall State Office Building, Room 1103, Boston, MA 02133, Mr. William Murray, 617-727-4537.

Cape Cod Community Library, Library/Learning Resource Center, Route 132, West Barnstable, MA 02668, Ms. Jeanmarie Fraser, 508-362-8638.

University of Massachusetts, Documents Library, 100 Morrissey Blvd., Boston, MA 02125, Ms. Frances Schlisinger, 617-287-5935.

Michigan

Michigan Information Center, Department of Management and Budget, Office of Revenue and Tax Analysis, P.O. Box 30026, Lansing, MI 48909, Mr. Eric Swanson, 517-373-7910.

MIMIC/Center for Urban Studies, Wayne State University, Faculty/Administration Bldg., 656 W. Kirby, Detroit, MI 48202, Kurt Metzger, 313-577-8996.

The Library of Michigan, Government Documents Service, P.O. Box 30007, 717 W. Allegan St., Lansing, MI 48909, Ms. F. Anne Diamond, 517-373-0640.

Minnesota

State Demographer's Office, Minnesota Planning, 300 Centennial Office Building, 658 Cedar Street, St. Paul, MN 55155, Mr. David Birkholz, 612-296-2557, Mr. David Rademacher, 612-297-3255.

Metropolitan Council Research, 230 East 5th Street, St. Paul, MN 55101, Mr. Chuck Ballantine, 612-291-8140.

Interagency Resource and Information Center, Department of Education, 501 Capitol Square Building, St. Paul, MN 55101, Ms. Patricia Tupper, 612-296-6684.

Mississippi

Center for Population Studies, The University of Mississippi, Bondurant Bldg., Room 3W, University, MS 38677, Dr. Max Williams, Director/Ms. Rachel McNeely, Manager, 601-232-7288.

Governor's Office of Federal-State Programs, Department of Community Development, 301 West Pearl Street, Jackson, MS 39203-3096, Mr. Jim Catt, 601-949-2219.

Division of Research and Information Systems, Department of Economic and Community Development, 1200 Walter Sillas Building, P.O. Box 849, Jackson, MS 39205, Mr. Bill Rigby, 601-359-2674.

Missouri

Missouri State Library, 600 W. Main Street, P.O. Box 387, Jefferson City, MO 65102, Ms. Kate Graf, 314-751-1823.

Be patient. If any phone number is incorrect, call (area code) 555-1212 and request the new listing.

Missouri Small Business Development Centers, 300 University Place, Columbia, MO 65211, Terry Maynard, 314-882-0344.

Office of Administration, 124 Capitol Building, P.O. Box 809, Jefferson City, MO 65102, Mr. Ryan Burson, 314-751-2345.

Office of Computing, University of Missouri-St. Louis, 8001 Natural Bridge Road, Room 451 CCB, St. Louis, MO 63121, Dr. John Blodgett/Ms. Linda McDaniel, 314-553-6014.

Office of Social and Economic Data Analysis, University of Missouri-Columbia, 224 Lewis Hall, Columbia, MO 65211, Ms. Evelyn J. Cleveland, 314-882-7396.

Geographic Resources Center, University of Missouri-Columbia, 17 Stewart Hall, Columbia, MO 65211, Mr. Tim Haithcoat, 314-882-1404.

Montana
Census and Economic Information Center, Montana Department of Commerce, P.O. Box 200501, 1424 9th Avenue, Helena, MT 59620-0501, Ms. Patricia Roberts, 406-444-2896.

Montana State Library, 1515 East 6th Avenue, Capitol Station, Helena, MT 59620, Ms. Kathy Brown, 406-444-3004.

Bureau of Business and Economic Research, University of Montana, Missoula, MT 59812, Mr. Jim Sylvester, 406-243-5113.

Research and Analysis Bureau, Employment Policy Division, Montana Department of Labor and Industry, P.O. Box 1728, Helena, MT 59624, Ms. Cathy Shenkle, 406-444-2430.

Nebraska
Center for Public Affairs Research, Nebraska State Data Center, Peter Kiewit Conference Center, #232, University of Nebraska at Omaha, Omaha, NE 68182, Mr. Jerome Deichert, 402-595-2311/Mr. Tim Himberger, 402-554-4883.

Policy Research Office, P.O. Box 94601, State Capitol, Room 1319, Lincoln, NE 68509-4601, Ms. Prem L. Bansal, 402-471-2414.

Federal Documents Librarian, Nebraska Library Commission, The Atrium, 1200 North Street, Suite 120, Lincoln, NE 68508-2006, 402-471-2045.

The Central Data Processing Division, Dept. of Administration Services, 301 Centennial Mall S., Lower Level, P.O. Box 95045, Lincoln, NE 68509-5045, Mr. Jerry Douglas, 402-471-4862.

Nebraska Department of Labor, 550 S. 16th St., P.O. Box 94600, Lincoln, NE 68509-4600, Mr. Robert H. Shanahan, 402-471-2518.

Natural Resources Commission, 301 Centennial Mall South, P.O. Box 94876, Lincoln, NE 68509-4876, Mr. Mahendra Bansal, 402-471-2081.

Nevada
Nevada State Library, Capitol Complex, 100 Stewart Street, Carson City, NV 89710, Ms. Joan Kerschner/Ms. Patricia Deadder, 702-687-8327.

New Hampshire
Office of State Planning, 2-1/2 Beacon Street, Concord, NH 03301, Mr. Tom Duffy, 603-271-2155.

New Hampshire State Library, 20 Park Street, Concord, NH 03301-6303, Mr. John McCormick, 603-271-2060.

Office of Biometrics, University of New Hampshire, Pettee Hall, Durham, NH 03824, Mr. Owen Durgin, 603-862-3930.

New Jersey
New Jersey Department of Labor, Division of Labor Market and Demographic Research, CN 388-John Fitch Plaza, Trenton, NJ 08625-0388, Ms. Connie O. Hughes, Asst. Dir., 609-984-2593.

New Jersey State Library, U.S. Documents Office, 185 West State Street, CN 520, Trenton, NJ 08625-0520, Ms. Beverly Railsback, 609-292-6259.

CIT - Information Services, Princeton University, 87 Prospect Ave., Princeton, NJ 08544, Ms. Judith S. Rowe, 609-258-6052.

Center for Computer and Information Services, Rutgers University, CCIS-Hill Center, Busch Campus, P.O. Box 879, Piscataway, NJ 08854, Ms. Chris Jarocha-Ernst, 908-932-0265.

Rutgers University, Edward J. Bloustein School of Planning and Public Policy, Kilmer Campus, Lucy Stone Hall, B Wing, New Brunswick, NJ 08903, Dr. James Hughes, Assoc. Dean, 908-932-3822.

New Mexico
Economic Development Department, 1100 St. Francis Drive, Santa Fe, NM 87503, Ms. Laurie Moye, 505-827-0182.

New Mexico State Library, 325 Don Gaspar Avenue, P.O. Box 1629, Santa Fe, NM 87503, Ms. Laura Chaney, 505-827-3824.

Bureau of Business and Economic Research, University of New Mexico, 1920 Lomas NE, Albuquerque, NM 87131-6021, Mr. Kevin Kargacin, 505-277-6626, Mr. Bobby Leitch, 505-277-2216.

Department of Economics, New Mexico State Univ., Box 30001, Las Cruces, NM 88003, Dr. Kathleen Brook, 505-646-2112.

New York
Division of Policy and Research, Department of Economic Development, 1 Commerce Plaza, Room 905, 99 Washington Avenue, Albany, NY 12245, Mr. Robert Scardamalia, 518-474-1141.

Cornell University, CISER Data Archive, 201 Caldwell Hall, Ithaca, NY 14853, Ms. Ann Gray, 607-255-4801.

Nelson A. Rockefeller Institute of Government, 411 State Street, Albany, NY 12203, Michael Cooper, 518-443-5258.

New York State Library, 6th Floor, Cultural Education Center, Empire State Plaza, Albany, NY 12230, Ms. Mary Redmond, 518-474-3940.

Division of Equalization and Assessment, 16 Sheridan Avenue, Albany, NY 12210, Mr. Wilfred B. Pauquette, 518-474-6742.

North Carolina
North Carolina Office of State Planning, 116 West Jones Street, Raleigh, NC 27603-8003, Ms. Francine Stephenson, 919-733-3683.

Division of State Library, 109 East Jones Street, Raleigh, NC 27601-2807, Mr. Joel Sigmon, 919-733-3683.

Institute for Research in Social Science, University of North Carolina, Manning Hall CB 3355, Chapel Hill, NC 27599-3355, Mr. Ed Bachmann, 919-962-0512.

Center for Geographic Information, Office of State Planning, P.O. Box 27687, Raleigh, NC 27611, Ms. Karen Siderelis/Tim Johnson, 919-733-2090.

North Dakota
Department of Agricultural Economics, North Dakota State University, Morrill Hall, Room 224, P.O. Box 5636, Fargo, ND 58105, Dr. Richard Rathge, 701-237-8621.

Office of Intergovernment Assistance, State Capitol, 14th Floor, Bismarck, ND 58505, Mr. Jim Boyd, 701-224-2094.

Department of Geography, University of North Dakota, Grand Forks, ND 58202, Mohammad Hemmasi, 701-777-4246.

North Dakota State Library, Liberty Memorial Building, Capitol Grounds, Bismarck, ND 58505, Ms. Susan Pahlmeyer, 701-224-2490.

Northern Mariana Islands
Department of Commerce and Labor, Central Statistics Division, Saipan, Mariana Islands 96950, Mr. Juan Borja, 670-322-0874/0876.

Ohio
Ohio Data Users Center, Ohio Department of Development, P.O. Box 1001, 77 High Street, 27th Floor, Columbus, OH 43266-0101, Mr. Barry Bennett, 614-466-2115.

State Library of Ohio, 65 South Front Street, Columbus, OH 43215, Mr. Clyde Hordusky, 614-644-7051.

Be patient. If any phone number is incorrect, call (area code) 555-1212 and request the new listing.

893

Cleveland State University, Northern Ohio Data and Information Service/The Urban Center, 1737 East Euclid Avenue, Room 45, Cleveland, OH 44115-9239, Mr. Mark Salling, 216-687-2209.

Ohio State University Library/ Census Data Center, 126 Main Library, 1858 Neil Avenue Mall, Columbus, OH 43210, Mr. Brian Martin, 614-292-6175.

University of Cincinnati, Southwest Ohio Regional Data Center, Institute for Policy Research, Mail Loc. 132, Cincinnati, OH 45221, Mr. Mark Carrozza, 513-556-5082.

Oklahoma

Oklahoma State Data Center, Oklahoma Department of Commerce, 6601 Broadway Extension, (Mailing address) P.O. Box 26980, Oklahoma City, OK 73126-0980, Mr. Jeff Wallace, 405-841-5184.

Oklahoma Department of Libraries, 200 NE 18th Street, Oklahoma City, OK 73105, Mr. Steve Beleu, 405-521-2502.

Center for Economic and Management Research, The University of Oklahoma, 307 W. Brooks, Norman, OK 73019, Mr. John McCraw, 405-325-2931.

Oregon

Oregon State Library, State Library Building, Salem, OR 97310, Mr. Craig Smith, 503-378-4277.

Center for Population Research and Census, School of Urban and Public Affairs, Portland State University, P.O. Box 751, Portland, OR 97207-0751, Mr. Ed Shafer/Ms. Maria Wilson-Figueroa, 503-725-5159.

Oregon Housing and Community Services Department, 1600 State Street, Suite 100, Salem, OR 97310-0161, Mr. Mike Murphy, 503-378-4730.

Geographic Information Systems, Department of Energy Building, 625 Marion Street NE, Salem, OR 97310, Mr. Kenneth C. Yingling, 503-378-4036.

Pennsylvania

Pennsylvania State Data Center, Institute of State and Regional Affairs, Pennsylvania State University at Harrisburg, 777 W. Harrisburg Pike, Middletown, PA 17057, Mr. Michael Behney, 717-948-6336.

Pennsylvania State Library, Forum Building, Harrisburg, PA 17105, Mr. John Geschwindt, 717-787-2327.

Puerto Rico

Puerto Rico Planning Board, Minillas Government Center, North Bldg., Avenida De Diego, P.O. Box 41119, San Juan, PR 00940-9985, Sr. Jose Jiminez, 809-728-4430.

Departmento de Educacion, P.O. Box 759, Hato Rey, PR 00919, Sra. Carmen Martinez, Sra. Nayada Pratts, 809-724-1046.

Universidad Intermaericana, Recinto de Guayama, P.O. Box 1559, Guayama, PR 00785, Angel Rivera, 809-864-2222.

Rhode Island

United Way of Rhode Island, 229 Waterman Street, Providence, RI 02906, Ms. Jane Nugent, 401-521-9000.

Rhode Island Department of State Library Services, 300 Richmond Street, Providence, RI 02903, Mr. Frank Iacona, 401-277-2726.

Social Science Data Center, Brown University, P.O. Box 1916, Providence, RI 02912, Mr. James McNally, 401-863-3459.

Rhode Island Department of Administration, Office of Municipal Affairs, One Capitol Hill, Providence, RI 02908-5873, Mr. Paul Egan, 401-277-6493.

Office of Health Statistics, Rhode Island Department of Health, 3 Capitol Hill, Providence, RI 02908, Dr. Jay Buechner, 401-277-2550.

Rhode Island Department of Education, 22 Hayes Street, Providence, RI 02908, Mr. James P. Karon, 401-277-3126.

Rhode Island Department of Economic Development, 7 Jackson Walkway, Providence, RI 02903, Mr. Vincent Harrington, 401-277-2601.

South Carolina

Division of Research and Statistical Services, South Carolina Budget and Control Board, Rembert Dennis Bldg. Room 425, Columbia, SC 29201, Mr. Bobby Bowers/Mr. Mike Macfarlane, 803-734-3780.

South Carolina State Library, P.O. Box 11469, Columbia, SC 29211, Ms. Mary Bostick, 803-734-8666.

South Dakota

Business Research Bureau, School of Business, University of South Dakota, 414 East Clark, Vermillion, SD 57069, Ms. DeVee Dykstra, 605-677-5287.

Documents Department, South Dakota State Library, 800 Governors Drive, Pierre, SD 57501-2294, Ms. Cheri Adams, 605-773-3131.

Labor Market Information Center, South Dakota Department of Labor, 420 S. Roosevelt, Box 4730, Aberdeen, SD 57402-4730, Mr. Phillip George, 605-622-2314.

Office of Administration Services, South Dakota Department of Health, 445 E. Capitol Avenue, Pierre, SD 57501-3185, Mr. John Jones, 605-773-3693.

South Dakota State University, Rural Sociology Department, Scobey Hall 226, Box 504, Brookings, SD 57007, Mr. Jim Satterlee, 605-688-4132.

Tennessee

Tennessee State Planning Office, John Sevier State Office Bldg., 500 Charlotte Ave., Suite 307, Nashville, TN 37243-0001, Mr. Charles Brown, 615-741-1676.

Center for Business and Economic Research, College of Business Administration, University of Tennessee, Room 100, Glocker Hall, Knoxville, TN 37996-4170, Ms. Betty Vickers, 615-974-5441.

Texas

State Data Center, Texas Department of Commerce, 9th and Congress Streets, (Mailing address) P.O. Box 12728, Capitol Station, Austin, TX 78711, Ms. Susan Tully, 512-320-9667.

Department of Rural Sociology, Texas A & M University System, Special Services Building, College Station, TX 77843-2125, Dr. Steve Murdock, 409-845-5115/5332.

Texas Natural Resources Information System (TNRIS), P.O. Box 13231, Austin, TX 78711, Mr. Charles Palmer, 512-463-8399.

Texas State Library and Archive Commission, P.O. Box 12927, Capitol Station, Austin, TX 78711, Ms. Diana Houston, 512-463-5455.

Utah

Office of Planning and Budget, State Capitol, Room 116, Salt Lake City, UT 84114, Ms. Linda Smith, 801-538-1550, Ms. Kirin McInnis, 801-538-1036.

University of Utah, Bureau of Economic and Business Research, 401 KDGB, Salt Lake City, UT 84112, Mr. Frank Hachman, 801-581-3353.

Department of Community and Economic Development, 324 South State Street, Suite 500, Salt Lake City, UT 84111, Mr. Doug Jex, 801-538-8897.

Department of Employment Security, 140 East 300 South, P.O. Box 11249, Salt Lake City, UT 84147-0249, Mr. Ken Jensen, 801-536-7813.

Vermont

Office of Policy Research and Coordination, Pavilion Office Building, 109 State Street, Montpelier, VT 05609, Ms. Cynthia Clancy, 802-828-3326.

Center for Rural Studies, University of Vermont, 207 Morrill Hall, Burlington, VT 05405-0106, Mr. Kevin Wiberg, 802-656-3201.

Vermont Department of Libraries, 109 State Street, Montpelier, VT 05609-0601, Ms. Sybil McShane, 802-828-3261.

Vermont Travel Department, 134 State Street, Montpelier, VT 05609, 802-828-3217.

Virginia

Virginia Employment Commission, 703 East Main Street, Richmond, VA 23219, Mr. Dan Jones, 804-786-8308.

Center for Public Service, University of Virginia, 918 Emmet Street North, Suite 300, Charlottesville, VA 22903-3491, Dr. Michael Spar, 804-982-5585.

Virginia State Library, Documents Section, 11th Street at Capitol Square, Richmond, VA 23219-3491, Mr. William R. Chamberlin, 804-786-2303.

Virgin Islands

University of the Virgin Islands, Eastern Caribbean Center, No. 2 John Brewer's Bay, Charlotte Amalie, St. Thomas, VI 00802, Dr. Frank Mills, 809-776-9200.

Virgin Islands Department of Economic Development, P.O. Box 6400, Charlotte Amalie, St. Thomas, VI 00801, Mr. Dan Inveen, 809-774-8784.

Washington

Forecasting Division, Office of Financial Management, 450 Insurance Bldg., Box 43113, Olympia, WA 98504-3113, Mr. George Hough, 206-586-2504.

Puget Sound Council of Govts., 216 1st Avenue South, Seattle, WA 98104, Neil Kilgren, 206-464-5355.

Social Research Center, Department of Rural Sociology, Washington State University, Pullman, WA 99164-4006, Dr. Annabel Kirschner-Cook, 509-335-4519.

Department of Sociology, Demographic Research Laboratory, Western Washington University, Bellingham, WA 98225, Mr. Lucky Tedrow, Director, 206-650-3176.

Department of Employment Security, LMEA, P.O. Box 46000, Olympia, WA 98504-6000, Gary Bodeutsch, 206-438-4804.

CSSCR, University of Washington, 145 Savery Hall, DK 45, Seattle, WA 98195, Fred Nick, 206-543-8110.

West Virginia

West Virginia Development Office, Research and Strategic Planning Division, Capitol Complex, Building 6, Room 553, Charleston, WV 25305, Ms. Mary C. Harless, 304-558-4010.

Reference Library, West Virginia State Library Commission, Science and Cultural Center, Capitol Complex, Charleston, WV 25305, Ms. Karen Goff, 304-348-2045.

Office of Health Services Research, WVU Health Science Center, Medical Center Drive, P.O. Box 9145, Morgantown, WV 26506-9145, Mr. Alex Lubman, 304-293-1086.

The Center for Economic Research, West Virginia University, 323 Business and Economic Building, Morgantown, WV 26506-6025, Dr. Tom Witt, Director/Mr. Randy Childs, 304-293-7832.

Wisconsin

Department of Administration, Demographic Services Center, 101 E. Wilson Street, 6th Floor, P.O. Box 7868, Madison, WI 53707-7868, Ms. Nadene Roenspies/Mr. Robert Naylor, 608-266-1927.

Applied Population Laboratory, Department of Rural Sociology, University of Wisconsin, 1450 Linden Drive, Room 316, Madison, WI 53706, Mr. Michael Knight, 608-265-3044.

Wyoming

Survey Research Center, University of Wyoming, P.O. Box 3925, Laramie, WY 82071, Mr. G. Fred Doll, 307-766-2931.

Department of Administration and Information, Economic Analysis Division, Emerson Building 327E, Cheyenne, WY 82002-0060, Mr. Steve Furtney/Mr. Wenlin Liu, 307-777-7504.

Be patient. If any phone number is incorrect, call (area code) 555-1212 and request the new listing.

895

State Statistical Abstracts

For years researchers have been aware of the importance of keeping around the latest edition of the *Statistical Abstract of the United States* (available for $32 in paperback and $38 in hardback from Superintendent of Documents, U.S. Government Printing Office, P.O. Box 371954, Pittsburgh, PA 15250-7954, 202-512-1800). Now if you are interested in local or regional opportunities, trends, or markets, every state government offers their own *State Statistical Abstract* or something comparable. Most of the states produce their abstract on an annual basis.

Tables and graphs are used to illustrate the performance of the economy. Where comparisons can be made, state, regional, and national data can be compared. Market analysts, businesses and researchers will find the following kinds of information in a statistical abstract:

- how many of Fortune magazine's top 500 companies have manufacturing plants in the state;
- the number of jobs directly or indirectly related to exports;
- largest sources of personal income;
- number of people employed in agricultural/non-agricultural jobs;
- how a state ranks in population and land size;
- number of acres of forest land;
- number of airports, number privately owned;
- number of registered aircraft;
- changes in population-age distribution;
- percentage of 17- and 18 year olds graduating from high school;
- number of state universities, vocational schools;
- number of vehicle registrations;
- crime rates; and
- traffic fatalities.

Similar to the *Statistical Abstract of the U.S.* in providing important data in charts and tables, these state abstracts offer important leads to more detailed sources of information. Although the specific charts and tables may not offer the exact detail of data you require on a particular topic, they will identify the offices which generate this type of information. By contacting the specific office, you are likely to get the precise data you require. They can't publish everything they have in a single statistical abstract, but they can dig the information out of their files for you.

State Statistical Abstracts

Alabama
Alabama Department of Economic and Community Affairs, P.O. Box 25037, Montgomery, AL 36125-0347; 205-242-8672. Publication: *County Data Book* ($12).

Alaska
Alaska Department of Labor, Research and Analysis, P.O. Box 25501, Juneau, AK 99802; 907-465-4500, Publications: *Employment and Earnings Report, Statistical Quarterly* (free).

Arizona
Arizona Department of Economic Security Research Administration, P.O. Box 6123, Phoenix, AZ 85007; 602-542-3871. Publication: *Labor Market Information-Annual Planning Information* (free).

Arkansas
Arkansas Industrial Development Commission, 1 State Capitol Mall, Little Rock, AR 72201; 501-682-1121. Publication: *Arkansas Statistical Abstract 94'*.

California
Department of Finance, 915 L St., 8th Floor, Sacramento, CA 95814; 916-322-2263. Publication: *California Statistical Abstract* (free).

Colorado
State Planning and Budget, Room 114, 2000 E. Colfax St., Denver, CO 80203; 303-866-3386. Publication: *Economic Perspective* (free).

Connecticut
Office of Policy and Management, Budget and Financial Management Div., 80 Washington St., Hartford, CT 06106; 203-566-8342. Publication: *Economic Report of the Governor* (free).

Delaware
Delaware Economic Development Office, State of Delaware, Executive Dept., 99 Kings Highway, P.O. Box 1401, Dover, DE 19903; 302-739-4271. Publication: *Data Book 94'* ($25).

District of Columbia
Office of Policy and Program Evaluation, Room 208, District Building 1350, Pennsylvania Ave., NW, Washington, DC 20004; 202-727-6979. Publication: *Indices* ($21).

Florida
University Presses of Florida, 15 NW 15th St., Gainesville, FL 32611; 904-392-1351. Publication: *Florida Statistical Abstract* ($29.95), *A Statistical Abstract* ($10 or more).

Hawaii
State of Hawaii, Business and Economic Development, P.O. 2359, Honolulu, HI 96804, Attention: Library; 808-586-2424. Publication: *State of Hawaii Data Book* ($8).

Idaho
Secretary of State, P.O. Box 83720, Boise, ID 83720-0080; 208-334-2852. Publication: *Idaho Blue Book* ($10).

Illinois
University of Illinois, Bureau of Economic and Business Research, 1206 S. 6th St., 428 Commerce West, Champaign, IL 61820; 217-333-2330. Publication: *Illinois Statistical Abstract* ($40).

Indiana
Indiana University Press, 601 N. Morton St., Bloomington, IN 47404; 812-855-5507. Publication: *The Indiana Fact Book* ($39.95 plus $3 shipping and handling).

Iowa
Iowa Department of Economic Development, 200 East Grand Ave., Des Moines, IA 50309; 515-242-4700. Publication: *Statistical Profile of Iowa* (free).

Kansas
Department of Commerce and Housing, 700 SW Harrison St., Suite 100, Topeka, KS 66603-3712; 913-296-3481. Publication: *Kansas Facts and Statistics*.

Kentucky
Cabinet for Economic Development, 133 Holmes St. Frankfort, KY 40601; 502-564-4715. Publication: *Maine Statistical Summary* (free).

Maryland

Department of Economic and Employment Development, 217 East Redwood, 11th Floor, Baltimore, MD 21202; 410-333-6953. Publication: *Statistical Abstract* ($40).

Massachusetts

MISER/State Data Center, University of Massachusetts, 128 Thompson Hall, Amherst, MA 01003. Publication: *1990 Census of Population and Housing* (summary tape file #3) $15.

Michigan

University of Michigan Press, P.O. 1104, Ann Arbor, MI 48106; 313-764-4392. Publication: *Michigan Statistical Abstract* ($50).

Minnesota

Department of Trade and Economic Development, Business Division, St. Paul, MN 5501-2146; 612-297-2353. Publication: *Compare Minnesota* (free).

Mississippi

Mississippi State University, Business and Community Development Division, 500 Metro Square, 121 7th Place, East, Mississippi State, MS 39762; 601-325-3817. Publication: *Mississippi Statistical Abstract* ($35).

Missouri

University of Missouri, B&PA Research Center, 10 Professional Building, Columbia, MO 65211; 314-882-4805. Publication: *Statistical Abstract* ($25).

Montana

Department of Commerce, Census and Economic Information Center, 1424 9th Ave., Helena, MT 59620-0501. Publication: *County Data Base* ($20 for a complete copy or $4 per section).

Nebraska

Department of Economic Development, Research Division, P.O. Box 94666, Lincoln, NE 68509; 402-471-3111. Publication: *Nebraska Statistical Handbook* (approximately $12.50).

Nevada

Vital Statistics, 505 East King St., Carson City, NV 89710; 702-687-4480. Publication: *Statistical Abstract* (free).

New Jersey

New Jersey Department of Labor, Publication Unit, CN056, Trenton, NJ 08625-0056; 609-633-6434. Publication: *Monthly New Jersey Economic Indicators.*

New Mexico

Economic Development Department, 1100 St. Francis Drive, Santa Fe, NM 87503; 505-827-1734. Service: "One Stop Shop", an on-line database offering a variety of information, 1-800-283-2638 (free).

New York

Rockefeller Institute of Government, 411 State St., Albany, NY 12203-1003; 518-443-5522. Publication: *New York Statistical Yearbook* ($50 plus $4 shipping and handling).

North Carolina

State Planning Office, State Library, 116 W. Jones St., Raleigh, NC 27603; 919-733-3270. Publication: *North Carolina State Statistical Abstract* (1991 is the last hard copy available. This information is now on an on-line data base which can be accessed via LINK. The state library charges a $3.50 access fee plus .05 cents per page).

North Dakota

The Bureau of Business and Economic Research, College of Business and Public Administration, Box 8369, Univ. of North Dakota, Grand Forks, ND 58202; 701-777-3353. Publication: *North Dakota Statistical Abstract* ($4 to cover shipping and handling). The last edition is 1987; although there has been interest in an update, the funding has not been available.

Ohio

Ohio of Strategic Research, Ohio Department of Development, P.O. Box 1001, Columbus, OH 43216-1001; 1-800-848-1300 ext. 2116. Publication: *County Profiles* ($50).

Oklahoma

University of Oklahoma, CEMR (Center for Economic and Management Research), College of Business Administration, 307 W. Brooks St., Room 4, Norman OK 73019; 405-325-2931. Publication: *Statistical Abstract* ($22).

Oregon

Economic Development Department, 775 Summer St., Salem, OR 97310; 503-986-0118. Publication: *Oregon Economic Profile* ($3.50).

Pennsylvania

State Data Center, State University at Harrisburg, Capitol, Middletown, PA 17057. Publication: *Statistical Abstract* ($40).

Rhode Island

Department of Economic Development, 7 Jackson Walkway, Providence, RI 02903; 401-277-2601. Publication: *Annual Economic Trend Series* (free).

South Carolina

Division of Research and Statistical Services, 1000 Assembly St., Rembert C. Dennis Building, Suite 425, Columbia, SC 29201; 803-734-3793. Publication: *South Carolina Statistical Abstract* ($30 your choice of hard copy or disk).

South Dakota

Business Research Bureau, School of Business, The University of South Dakota, 414 East Clark St., Vermillion, SD 57069-2390; 605-677-5287. Publication: *South Dakota Community Abstract* ($25, 1993 available).

Tennessee

University of Tennessee, Center for Business and Economic Research, S. 100 Glocker Hall, College of Business Administration, Knoxville, TN 37996; 615-974-5441. Publication: *Tennessee State Statistical Abstract* ($36 plus shipping and handling).

Texas

Department of Commerce, Research and Planning Division, State Data Center, P.O. Box 12728, Austin, TX 78711; 512-463-1166. Publication: *The Texas Almanac* is available in bookstores.

Utah

Office of Planning and Budget, Room 116, State Capitol Building, Salt Lake City, UT 84114; 801-538-1027. Publication: *Economic Report to the Governor* ($15).

Vermont

Vermont Department of Employment and Training, Office of Labor Market Information, P.O. Box 488, Montpelier, VT 05601-0488; 802-828-4202. State labor market information publications are available upon request at no charge. Publications: *Annual Planning Information, Annual Report, Projections to 2000.*

Virginia

Cooper Center for Public Service, 918 Emmet North, Suite 300, Charlottesville, VA 22903; 804-982-5522. Publication: *Virginia Statistical Abstract* ($42.50 plus $4 shipping and handling).

Washington

Office of the Forecast Council, Evergreen Plaza, Room 300, Mail Stop 0912, Olympia, WA 98504; 206-586-6785. Publication: *Economic and Revenue Forecast for Washington State* ($4.50 per issue in state, $9 per issue out of state or you can subscribe annually for $18 and $36, respectively.

West Virginia

Chamber of Commerce, Research and Strategic Planning, P.O. Box 2789, Charleston, WV 25330; 304-342-1115.

Wisconsin

Wisconsin Department of Development, 123 West Washington Ave., P.O. Box 7970, Madison, WI 53707; 608-266-1018. Publications: *Biennial Report--Wisconsin Department of Development, Community Profiles* (Specify Community), *Wisconsin Economic Profile.*

Wyoming

Division of Economic Analysis, Room 327E, Emerson Building, Cheyenne, WY 82002-0060; 307-777-7504. Publications: *The Wyoming Data Handbook* (free), *The Equality State Almanac.*

Be patient. If any phone number is incorrect, call (area code) 555-1212 and request the new listing.

897

State Forecasting Centers

State planning offices can provide vast quantities of local market information, demographic data, and company intelligence--more than you would believe possible. Every state has a bureau equivalent to a planning office to assist the Governor in charting future economic change. Of course, the quantity of information varies from one state to the next as does the sophistication in methods of gathering and analyzing data. However, most information is generated to support decision making for policies and legislative initiatives which will affect the current and future status of the state economy. These blueprints for the future usually include plans for attracting new businesses and industries as well as improving the quality of housing, education and transportation.

It should be noted that there is a wide disparity in the research and strategic focus of these state planning offices. The position of this function within the state bureaucratic structure often provides clues about the scope of its mission. In most states this forecasting operation is housed in the Department of Economic Development or in a separate policy office under the Governor's office. However, in our survey of all fifty states, we discovered this crucial function in unexpected places. In South Carolina, for example, there is a special Commission on the Future within the Lieutenant Governor's office, and in Texas, a comparable office falls under the jurisdiction of the state comptroller.

Business Expansion and Economic Outlook

If you currently do business in a state or intend to establish a business there, it would be wise to learn about the Governor's long-term strategy. Keep in mind that no one is more concerned about the state's future than this elected official. If your company sells to farmers, inquire at the planning office about the Governor's agricultural policies. If your firm relies on high tech complementary business, see whether there is a plan to attract high tech companies. Or, if you are interested in consumer markets, be aware of demographic projections conducted by the planning agency for the state as well as for specific regions and counties. Many states appear to be charting future population patterns on a regular basis as is evident with the sampling of publications noted here.

Georgia: *Total Population: 1980, 1990; Projection 2000, 2010*
Nebraska: *Nebraska Statistical Handbook*
New Hampshire: *New Hampshire Population Projections*
New Jersey: *Annual Economic Forecast*
South Carolina: *Commission on the Future*
Utah: *Utah: 2000*

Demographics and Market Studies

Most of these offices are aware of the current demographic situation within their state. They also continually monitor the major industries in the state as well as emerging industries. Their data are usually derived from a combination of federal, state and locally generated information. Sometimes these offices are part of the state data center program run by the U.S. Bureau of the Census. Demographic studies as well as state statistical abstracts are readily available.

Arizona: *Community Profiles*
Minnesota: *Counties & Townships Demographics Estimates Survey*
North Dakota: *Demographics*
Oklahoma: *County Profiles*
Utah: *Utah Economic and Demographic Profiles*
Wisconsin: *Community Economic Profiles*

These state planning offices often produce in-depth market studies on diverse topics, for example:

Arizona: *Economic Impact Study of Major League Baseball Team on State of Arizona*
Michigan: *Michigan Products*
Missouri: *The Missouri Advantage for Plastics and Metal Industries*
Nebraska: *Profit Opportunities in Nebraska for Manufacturers of Pet Food*
New York: *Canadian Investment in Northern New York--Some Empirical Observations*

Company Information and Industry Directories

Many of these offices are responsible for maintaining information on the companies which are located within their state. It is not unusual for the state to collect the following data on every manufacturer and corporation:

- Name of company;
- Address and telephone number;
- Names of principal officers;
- Types of products or services produced;
- Number of employees; and
- Sales estimate.

You stand to learn more about a company, especially its financial picture, if the business in question received some type of economic assistance from the state. After all, once a company takes taxpayer money, the public has a right to know. There is a number of companies that fall into this category. We have received a list of over 100 firms which obtained financial assistance from Pennsylvania in a single year.

Other handy resources available from many state planning offices are company directories. Many of them concentrate on one industry sector.

Kansas: *Kansas Minority Business*
Montana: *The Montana Manufacturers Directory*

Oregon: *Directory of Oregon Wood Products Manufacturers*
South Dakota: *Directory of Manufacturers and Processors*
Wisconsin: *Business Help Directory*
Wyoming: *Directory of Manufacturing and Mining*

Databases and Special Services

Because these planning agencies share their forecasts and statistical data with other offices with the state government, often the data are readily available to the public, usually for free or on a cost recovery basis. Already many have established customized databases, some of which permit direct online access. Examples include:

- Delaware's online information available on real-estate and census;

- Florida's nine public access databases and customized research requests;

- Oklahoma's Oklahoma Resources Integrated General Information Network System; and

- Utah's OPB online database (current publications and census information).

State Planning Offices

The address and telephone numbers are included for the primary planning offices in each state as well as the District of Columbia. The publications listed with the office do not represent the entire universe of hardcopy data available. These titles are included only when the office is capable of providing us with a current listing. There are states which have publication, but do not have any sort of a catalog. For those states you must request data under specific topic headings.

Alabama
Alabama Department of Economic and Community Affairs, P.O. Box 25037, Montgomery, AL 36125-0347; 205-242-8672. Publication: *Annual Report*.

Alaska
State Planning Office, Division of Policy, Commerce and Economic Development, Office of Management and Budget, P.O. AM, Juneau, AK 99811; 907-465-2500.

Arizona
Arizona Department of Commerce, 3800 N. Central, Suite 1500, Phoenix, AZ 85012; 602-280-1300. *1994 Governor's Report on Affordable Housing, Arizona Federal Labor Standards Handbook, Arizona Housing Resource Directory, Arizona Housing Trust Fund Program Summary, Community Development Block Grant Procurement and Contracting Handbook, Community Development Block Grant Program Guide* ($5), *Comprehensive Housing Affordability Strategy FY 1994* ($10), *HOME Program Summary, Housing Rehabilitation Manual, Low Income Housing Tax Credit Allocation Plan, Office of Housing and Infrastructure Development Program Information, Twenty Questions About Community Development Block Grants, Economic Impact Study of Major League Baseball Team on State of Arizona* (Deloitte-Touche) ($20), *Business Assistance Center Promotional Brochure, Business Connection Information Packet, Guide to Establishing a Business in Arizona, Strategic Plan* (Volume 1) ($18), *Advisory/Expert Reports* (Volume II) ($70), *Townhall/Public Forum Reports* (Volume III) ($25), *Strategic Assessment* (Volume IV) ($20), *Strategic Assessment: Regional Data* (Volume V) ($15), *Strategic Framework* (Volume VI) ($10), a complete set of all six documents ($135), *GSPED Information Packets, GSPED News* (Newsletter), *Annual Report, The Arizona Advantage, Arizona Community Profiles* (by community, annual) (145 in all - $18 with binder - $15 without binder), *Arizona Growth Report, Relocation Information Packet, Student Facts Packet of Information Especially for Students, Arizona: Our*

Brand Means Business, Arizona Statistical Review, Doing Business in Indian Country, Arizona Directory of Exporters (annual) ($35 for book $100 for diskette), *Arizona Exports, Arizona High Technology Directory* (call the Kelland Corporation at 948-3198 - annual $55), *Arizona International Business Resource Guide* (annual $15), *Financial Resources for Business Development, Arizona State Clearinghouse Procedures, Federal Funding Guide* (bi-weekly), *Federal Grants and Contracts, Federal Monitor* (bi-monthly), *Local/State Funding Report, Reviewer Bi-Weekly, Arizona Economic Development Directory* (semi-annually $2.50), *Arizona Newsletter* (quarterly), *Board of Adjustment Handbook, Common Questions about Planning Newsletter* (quarterly), *Community Guide to Preparing a Housing Plan* ($9), *EconDB Newsletter* (quarterly), *Economic Development & Community Assessment Database* (EconDB) software available on disk in Windows and DOS version), *Facilitators Handbook* ($2), *General and Comprehensive Plan, Guidelines for Organizing a Chamber* ($8), *Guide to the Mainstreet Program* (annual), *The Lonely Guy's Handbook* (a compilation of handy material for new executive directors $10), *Planning and Developing Laws in Arizona, Planning and Zoning Handbook* ($25), *The Planning Commission Basics, A Planning Guide to Tourism Development for Rural Areas* ($3), *Public Meetings, Rural Resource Directory* ($3), *Town Hall Workbook* ($5), Film in Arizona Hotline, 602-280-1389, *Film in Arizona Products and Services Manual, Apartment Guide to Saving Energy and Money, "Arizona Build" 1992-93 Directory, Arizona Energy News* (quarterly), *Arizona Energy Patterns and Trends 1960-1990* ($3), *Arizona Quarterly Energy Data Report, Award-winning Energy Conscious Community Projects, Bright Ideas Series: Energy and the Environment/ Photovoltaic - Solar Energy/Recycling/Shading and Landscaping for Energy Efficiency/Solar Cookers, Consumer Rights, DriveWise, DriveWise Glove Compartment Card, Energy Checklist, Energy Checklist for Commercial Buildings, Energy Dollar Flow Analysis for the State of Arizona 1990, Energy Policy in Arizona: A Plan for Sustainable Development 1990, How to Reduce Your Energy Costs, Just Conserve It! Fact Sheets, Money, Energy and the Manufactured Home, Public Policy Update, Starting at Home: Recycling to Protect Our Environment, The Solar Electric Option* ($1), *Sunsmart: An Energy Handbook for Desert Dwellers, Your Guide to the Arizona Corporation Commission.*

Arkansas
Office of Industrial Development, State of Arkansas, #1 Capitol Mall, Little Rock, AR 72201; 501-682-1121. Publication: *Annual Report*.

California
Commission on Economic Development, State of California, State Capital, Room 1028, Sacramento, CA 95814; 916-324-5065. Publications: *Guide for Entrepreneurs, Department of Finance-Statistical Forecasting, Guide to Business Resources-The Climate's Right, Los Angeles-Economics, Trade and Commerce-Small Business Centers* (916-322-1394).

Colorado
Colorado Department of Personnel, 1313 Sherman St., Denver, CO 80203; 303-866-2321. Publication: *Stateline*. Other Services: Community Profiles Database, covering 63 counties and 260 municipalities. More information on demographics can be obtained from State of Colorado, Division of Local Government, Department of Local Affairs, Room 521, Denver, CO 80203; 303-866-2156.

Connecticut
Connecticut Department of Economic Development, Research Department, 865 Brook St., Rocky Hill, CT 06067; 203-258-4288. Publications: *Annual Report, Connecticut Economic Forecast, New England Economic Projections* (includes all 6 states).

Delaware
Delaware Economic Development Office, State of Delaware, Executive Department, 99 Kings Highway, P.O. Box 1401, Dover, DE 19903; 302-739-4271. Publications: *Data Book 94'* (will not be revised, $25), *Comparison of Estimated State and Local Family Tax Burdens, Small Business Start-Up Guide, Procurement Guide*. Call 302-739-4204 for a copy of the 3 year Capital Budget Plan. Other Services: Business Research Section maintains an extensive library of data resources and responds to requests for economic, demographic and travel information. Selective online access available to computerized real estate file. Online census information is available. A computerized hotel reservation system is also available.

District of Columbia
District of Columbia Office of Planning, 415 12th Street, NW, Washington, DC 20004; 202-727-6492. Publications: *Census Tract Map* (large $2), *Census Tract Map* (small $1), *STFI Census Data* (single ward, single tract or city $1.50/8 wards and city $10), *1990 Census Tract/Block Population and Housing Units Data Book* ($10), *1990 Census: Social, Economic and Housing Characteristics/ STF-3* (District of Columbia and each ward/book $30, set of tables for one indicator plus map $4),

Be patient. If any phone number is incorrect, call (area code) 555-1212 and request the new listing.

899

Economics, Demographics, and Statistics

Socio/Economic Indicators (book by census tract $15, set of tables for one indicator plus map $3), *Monograph 1 - Population and Housing Unit Changes 1980 to 1990* ($7.50), *Monograph 2 - Population, Household and Household Characteristics: 1990* ($12), *Monograph 3 - Senior Population 1990 Census* ($10), *Monograph 4 - Youth Population 1990 Census* ($10), *Monograph 5 - Hispanic Population 1990 Census* ($10), *District of Columbia Street Address Directory by Street, Census Tract and Ward* ($30), *Chinatown Design Guidelines Study/December 1989* ($5), *Comprehensive Plan Generalized Land Use Map 1* ($5), *Comprehensive Plan for the National Capital/District Elements* ($5), *D.C. Law 8-129 District of Columbia Comprehensive Plan Amendments Act of 1989* ($5), *Draft Ward Plan/by Ward January 1992* ($5), *Implementing the District Elements of the Comprehensive Plan for the National Capital Fiscal Years 1990-1991 Fifth Edition* ($15), *Comprehensive Plan Planning Report/August 1983* ($15), *A Living Downtown for Washington, D.C./April 1981* ($6), *Downtown D.C.: Recommendations for the Downtown Plan/Mayor's Downtown Committee - July 1982* ($9), Photocopies ($.10 per image).

Florida

Bureau of Economic Analysis, Florida Department of Commerce, Division of Economic Development, Tallahassee, FL 32399-2000; 904-487-2971. Publications: *Florida and the Other Forty-Nine, County Comparisons, Profile of the Florida Visitor.* A 5-year Agency Strategic Plan can be obtained by calling 904-487-2156. Special Services: Five public access databases and customized research requests; 904-488-4255.

Georgia

Office of Planning and Budget, Demographic and Statistical Services, 254 Washington St., SW, Atlanta, GA 30334-8500; 404-656-3820. Publications: *The Georgia State: Attachment A* - Population projections by age, sex, and race for 2000 for all Georgia counties, *Attachment B* - Population projections by age, sex, and race for 2010 for all Georgia, *Attachment C* - 1990 Census by age, sex and race for all Georgia counties, *Attachment 1* - Civilian Labor Force Estimates, Georgia Department of Labor (monthly, annually), *Attachment 2* - Total Population: 1980, 1990; Projections: 2000, 2010, *Attachment 3* - 1992 Population Estimates by County, U.S. Census Bureau, *Attachment 4* - Personal & Per Capita Income by County (1992) from "Survey of Current Business", BEA, *Attachment 5* - State Data Center Program, Georgia, U.S. address list, *Attachment 6* -1990 Census Population totals by county and incorporated place, *Attachment 7* - 1990 & 1980 Census counts and comparisons by county, *Attachment 8* - 1990 Census counts by race for Georgia cities, *Attachment 10* - Public Law 94-171 totals and age 18 and over by county, *Attachment 11* - 1990 and 1980 census counts and comparisons by place, *Attachment 12* - 1990 Census tract population by race, housing units by MSA, *Attachment 13* - 1990 Census counts by CCD, *Attachment 14* - 1990 Census STF 1A by county, MSA, and selected cities, *Attachment 15* - 1990 Census STF 1A, Tables 1-18 (in file cabinet), *Attachment 16* - 1990 Census STF 1A by age, race, sex, and Hispanic origin for Georgia counties, *Attachment 17* - 1980 and 1990 Census counts for all states, *Attachment 18* - 1990 PL94-171 Block data by county (in library), *Attachment 20* - 1990 Census STF 1A 15 page profile by state, county, MSA, RDC, place, census tract, *Attachment 21* - 1990 Census per capita income, median family income, median household income, *Attachment 22* - MSA Counties, 1993, *Attachment 23* - Poverty characteristics, 1990 Census, *Attachment 27* - "Georgia Descriptions in Data" order form, STF 1A, STF 3A order forms, *Attachment 28* - Georgia Population 1970, 1980, *Attachment 31* - Per capita income, 1979-92, BEA, *Attachment 34* - Provisional estimates of households for counties, July 1, 1988, *Attachment 38* - Housing units authorized by building permits, (monthly, annually), *Attachment 40* - County estimates for 1970 through 1980, *Attachment 41* - Population of Incorporated Places 1960-1080 from "Number of Inhabitants", *Attachment 42* - DEA Regional Economic Projections for MSAs (1990 & 2000) projected), *Attachment 44* - Regional Development Center contacts and map, executive directors, counties in each RDC, *Attachment 45* - Map of Georgia counties, MSAs, *Attachment 47* - BEA projections 2040.

Hawaii

Department of Business, Economic Development and Tourism, 220 S. King St., Honolulu, HI 96813; 808-586-2406. Publications: *Facts and Figures, State and Economic Report, Annual Report of Hawaii, Starting a Business in Hawaii.*

Idaho

Department of Commerce, Economic Development, Room 108, State Capital, Boise, ID 83720; 208-334-2470. Publications: *Economic Development Agenda, Operating a Business, Agencies That Help Businesses.*

Illinois

Illinois Department of Commerce dend Community Affairs, 620 East Adams St., Springfield, IL 62701; 217-782-3233. Publication: *Annual Report* (free).

Indiana

Indiana Economic Development Council, One North Capitol Ave., Suite 425, Indianapolis, IN 46204-2224; 317-631-0871, Fax: 317-231-7067. Publications: *Annual Report: Indiana Economic Development Council, Inc., An Assessment of Indiana's Competitive Position in Business Recruitment* ($1), *An Assessment of Indiana's Competitive Position in Business Recruitment* ($5), *Best Practice in Business Attraction and Indigenous Development* ($2.50), *Business Climate and Quality of Life in Indiana: Survey of Leading Hoosier Firms* ($2.50), *Building Foundations for Growth: Financing Infrastructure in Indiana During the 1990s* ($2.50), *Business Education Partnerships: How They Work in Indiana, The Corporation for Science and Technology 1982-1990: A Mid-Course Review of Indiana's Lead Technology Development Initiative of the 1980's* ($15), *Corporate Profile: Indiana Economic Development Council, Inc., A Discussion of Market-Based Approaches to Workforce Training in Indiana* ($4.50), *Economic Development* ($2.50), *The Employment Service Sector in Indiana: Key Strategic Issues for the '90s* ($4,50), *The Effectiveness of Tax Incentives in Economic Development* ($2.50), *Economic Development Program Profiles* ($10), *Finance "Tool Box" Reference Guide* ($10), *Food Processing Industries in Indiana* ($5), *Governor's Initiative in Economic Development* ($5), *Growing Indiana's Wood Products Industry: The Competitive Challenge* ($4), *Hoosier Horizons: 1992 Assessment of the Indiana Economy, Hoosier Horizons: 1992 Assessment of the Indiana Economy, Indiana Small Business Expansion Through Capital Availability* ($2), *Infrastructure Investment: A Key to Growth of the Hoosier Economy* ($2), *Investing IN Indiana* (free summary), *Investing IN Indiana 1994* ($20), *KREDA Update 1993* ($2.50), *Lifelines to Rural Indiana: The Role of Telecommunications in Rural Economic Development 1991*, (4.50), *The New Localism*, Entrepreneurial Economy Review 1991, *1994 Economic Report to the Governor: Changes and Challenges in Workforce Development, Urban Development*, Entrepreneurial Economy Review, *Rural Development: What is Known and Where Might We Go With It* ($2.50, *SWOT Analysis for Indiana's Strategic Economic Development Planning Process 1992* ($4.50), *Southern Indiana Grows 1993* ($2.50), *A Sector-Based Approach for Economic Development Indiana Business Review 1993* ($1), *Towards an Investment-Led Approach to Economic Development in the Midwest 1992* ($2.50).

Iowa

Iowa Dept. of Economic Development, 200 East Grand Ave., Des Moines, IA 50309; 515-242-4700. Publications: *Iowa Economic Forecast Quarterly, The Digest, Statistical Profile of Iowa.*

Kansas

Department of Commerce and Housing, 700 SW Harrison St., Suite 100, Topeka, KS 66603-3712; 913-296-3481. Publications: *Guide to Starting a Business in Kansas*, ("Steps to Success") 1991 edition $2.50), *Data for Site Selection* (Kansas Data Book $5), *Business Climate Review, Business Assistance Resource Directory* (1993 edition), *Kansas Minority Business Directory* (1994 edition), *Kansas Housing Services Directory* (1994 edition), *Directory of Kansas JobShops* (1988 edition), *Kansas Association Directory* (1991 edition), *Kansas International Trade Resource Directory* (1990 edition), *Kansas Companies Who Export Directory* (1992 edition), *Kansas Aerospace Directory* (1990 edition), *Kansas Agribusiness Directory* (1990 edition), *Kansas Facts and Stats, KDOC&H Annual Report, Trade Show Assistance Program, Workforce Training Programs, Kansas PRIDE Program Annual Report, Existing Industry Development, Community Development Information* (1993 edition), *Export Financing, Minority & Women-Owned Business, Venture Capital, Helping Kansas Companies, Kansas Housing, Kansas Housing Profile, Kansas Comprehensive Housing Affordability Strategy, Kansas Mortgage Savers Program, "Kansas!" Magazine, Stories with a Common Thread, Developing Kansas, Kansas Main Street, Kansas Pride Program* (bi-monthly newsletter), *Rooftops.*

Center for Economic Development and Business Research, 2nd Floor, Devlin Hall, W. Frank Barton School of Business, Wichita State University, Wichita, KS 67260-0121; 316-689-3225. Publications: *Business & Economic Report, Kansas Economic Indicators.*

The University of Kansas, Institute for Public Policy and Business Research, 607 Blake Hall, Lawrence, Kansas 66045-2960. Publication: *Kansas Business Review.*

Kentucky

Center for Business and Economic Research, 302 Mathews Building, University of Kentucky, Lexington, KY 40506-0047; 606-257-7675. Publication: *Annual Economic Report.*

Louisiana

State Planning Office, Division of Administration, 1051 North Riverside Mall, Baton Rouge, LA 70804; 504-342-7410.

Be patient. If any phone number is incorrect, call (area code) 555-1212 and request the new listing.

Maine

Department of Economic and Community Development, State House Station 59, Augusta, ME 04333; 207-287-2656. Also, Data Census Manager, 20 Union Street, Augusta, ME 04330-6827; 207-287-2271.

Maryland

Office of Research, Department of Economic and Employment Development, 217 E. Redwood Street, Baltimore, MD 21202; 410-333-6947, Publications: *The Economic Impact of Horseracing Industry on the Economy of Maryland, The Impact of Defense Spending on the Maryland Economy, The Impact of the Preakness Celebration '90 in Maryland, The Impact of the Christopher Columbus Center of Marine Research and Exploration, The Impact of the National Aquarium in Baltimore City, The Impact of Savage River State Forest in Maryland, The Economic and Fiscal Impacts of the US Canoe and Kayak Team Olympic Trials, The Economic and Fiscal Impacts from the Construction and Operations of the Oriole Park at Camden Yards, The Economic and Fiscal Impacts of Baltimore Orioles' 1992 Season In Maryland, 1992 Update--Christopher Columbus Center of Marine Research and Exploration, The Economic Impact of Baltimore Area Chemical Establishments, The Economic Impact of Maryland Insurance Industry, The Economic and Fiscal Impacts of Electric Vehicle Drivetrain Production in Maryland, The Economic and Fiscal Impacts of NIH in Maryland and the United States, Maryland Economic Outlook, Maryland International Business Report, Maryland Economic Indicators, Reports on Manufacturing, and Workers' Compensation.*

Massachusetts

Executive Office of Economic Affairs, One Ashburton Place, Room 2101, Boston, MA 02108; 617-727-1130.

Michigan

Michigan Jobs Commission, Customer Assistance and Research Services, 201 N. Washington Sq., Lansing, MI 48913; 517-373-4600. Publications: *Michigan: The Location of Choice, Welcome to Michigan, Michigan Overview, Michigan's Business Services, Michigan's Commitment to Advanced Technology, Michigan's Education System, Michigan's Energy Costa and Availability, Michigan's Labor Force Characteristics, Michigan's Strategic Access to Markets and Suppliers, Michigan's Transportation Infrastructure, Review of Michigan Taxes, A, Questions and Answers on Michigan's Single Business Tax, A Review of Michigan Taxes: The Impact of Proposal A, 16-State Tax Comparison Tables, Tax Comparison: Michigan Vs. Ontario, State Tax Comparison Services--Michigan vs. (any of the following) Arkansas, California, Connecticut, Florida, Georgia, Illinois, Indiana, Kentucky, Minnesota, Missouri, New Jersey, New York, North Carolina, Ohio, Pennsylvania, South Carolina, Tennessee, Texas, Wisconsin, Michigan and Ontario Industrial Comparison, D&B Top 100 Companies Based on Annual Sales, D&B Top 500 Companies Based on Annual Sales, Michigan Products, Economic Growth Report 1992, Economic Performance & Condition of Michigan's MSA's 1989, Employment Trends in Michigan's Large & Small Firms, Michigan Community Indicators-1991, Michigan Business Activity Quarterly Report, Michigan Economic Update, Michigan Economic News, Michigan Economy, Michigan Export Data, Michigan Gross State Product, Michigan's Rural Lower Peninsula, Michigan Personal Income Growth, Small Business Questions & Answers, University of Michigan Mid-Year Review & Economic Forecast for 1992 to 1994, Automotive Update, Electronic Component Industry Report, GM Willow Run Suppliers Survey Results, Michigan Office Furniture Industry, Michigan Plastics Industry Update, Michigan Service Industry, Michigan Manufacturing Statistics, State Manufacturing Statistics* for the following States: Arkansas, Georgia, Illinois, Indiana, Kentucky, Minnesota, Missouri, New York, North Carolina, Ohio, Pennsylvania, South Carolina, Tennessee, Texas and Wisconsin covering the following industries: Chemical Products, Electric/Electronic Equipment, Fabricated Metals, Food Products, Furniture, Instruments, Lumber/Wood, Machinery, Paper Products, Primary Metals, Printing/Publishing, Rubber & Plastics, Transportation Equipment, United States and Michigan Industry Profiles, Agriculture, Auto Parts, Financial Services & Insurance, Food Processing, High Technology, Machine Tool, Motor Vehicle, Pollution Control, Steel, United States and Michigan Industry Profiles, Biotech, Chemical & Allied Products, Medical Instruments, Office Furniture, Plastics, Service, Wholesale Trade.

Minnesota

Minnesota State Planning Agency, Office of Strategic and Long-Range Planning, 300 Centennial Building, 658 Cedar St., St. Paul, MN 55155; 612-296-3985. Publications: *A Cut Above: Criminal Justice Cost* (line item), *School Enrollment Growth* (line item), *Counties/Payroll and Employment Growth* (line item), *Welfare Migration* (line item), *Children's Services Report Card, Minnesota Milestones: 1993 Progress Report, A Cut Above: Minnesota's National Rankings, Tomorrow's Households: Trends and Issues, Children's Services Report Card* (online from DATANET), *Conversations About the Future* ($3), *Redefining Progress: Working Toward a Sustainable Future* ($15), *Troubling Perceptions: 1993 Minnesota Crime Survey, Minnesota's National Rankings, A Shared Vision--State Level Governance Options for Children and Family Services, Achieving Inclusive Policy Projects: A Guide to Success, Action for Children Listen '94 Brochure, Action for Children Kids Conference, Agency Style Guide, Budget 2001 Line Item Overall Design, Budget 2001: Government Salaries Line Item, Budget 2001: Welfare Migration Line Item, Child Poverty in Minnesota Population Note, Child Poverty in Minnesota: Trends and Issues, Children's Services Report Card* (available in hard-copy or online from DATANET), *Collaborative Grants Prevention and Intervention Funding Brochure Collaborative Grants Prevention and Intervention Manual, Counties and Townships Demographics Estimates Survey, Syberstate: Minnesota on the Information Superhighway, Doing Things Better--Innovation, Cooperation and Quality, EPPL-7 Licensing Brochure, Government Ethics Report, Growth Management Full Report--Phase 1, Kids Can't Wait Progress Report, Labor Force Projections* (Demography Series Report #4), *Media Mailing List/Faxing List, Minnesota Milestones Progress Report Card, Minnesota Planning Logo* (Electronic File), *MOAPPP Third Annual Conference--4/18, Narcotics Task Force Report, Redefining Progress: Working Toward a Sustainable Future, Tomorrow's Households: The Next 30 Years* (Demography Series Report #3), *Troubling Perceptions: 1993 Minnesota Crime Survey, Action for Children Newsletter* (monthly-fax), *EQB MONITOR* (bi-weekly newsletter), *Fresh Facts: Emerging Issues and Vital Trends* (6 times/year-fax), *MOAPP Monitor: Teen Pregnancy Prevention* (Quarterly newsletter), *Population Notes* (Newsletter), *A Changing Population: The Next 30 Years* (Demography Series Report #1), *A Question of Balance: Managing Growth and the Environment, District Data Book: Minnesota Legislative Districts 1993, Making the Connection: Linking Housing, Jobs and Transportation, Minnesota Gambling 1993, Minnesota Multi-jurisdictional Narcotic Task Force Program 1992 Report, Minnesota's Changing Counties: The Next 30 Years* (Demography Series Report #2), *Population and Household Estimates 1992* (Available on Diskette), *State of Diversity: A Plan of Action for Minnesota, State of Diversity Resource Guide, What Can I Do To Prevent Harm To Children.*

Mississippi

Department of Economic and Community, P.O. Box 849, Jackson, MS 39205; 601-359-3449. Publications: *Annual Report, Newsletter, Overview Brochure.*

Missouri

Department of Economic Development, State of Missouri, P.O. Box 118, 301 W. High, Room 770, Jefferson City, MO 65102-0118; 314-751-4241, 800-523-1434.

Community Development Block Grants (CDBG Program): 314-751-4146. Publications: *On the Block* (newsletter), *Community Development Block Grant Programs Annual Competition Guidelines and Application.*

Community Programs: 314-751-4849. Publications: *Awards in Review, Missouri Community Betterment, Surveying Community Attitudes, Elements of Economic Development, Role of the Economic Developer, Rural Communities Economic Assistance Application, Missouri Main Street Program Brochure, Main Street Missouri--The First Three Years, CDBG Downtown Revitalization Guidelines and Application, Community Solid Waste Management, Attracting New Enterprises, Assisting Local Enterprises, Creating New Enterprises, Capturing Outside Wealth, Capturing Local Wealth, Rural Economic and Community Development Catalog.*

Finance: 314-751-0717. Publications: *Action Fund Guidelines and Application, Industrial Infrastructure Guidelines and Application, Loan Guarantee Application (MEDEIB), Single Issue Tax Exempt IRB General Information and Application, Missouri Economic Development Export and Infrastructure Board (MEDEIB) Tax Credit Application, Spec Building Guidelines and Application, Neighborhood Improvement District, Finance Programs Available in Missouri.*

High Technology: 314-751-5095. Publications: *High Technology Companies in Missouri, Missouri Business Modernization and Technology Corporation Annual Report, Small Business Innovation Research (SBIR) Resource Guide, SBIR Program Brochures, Venture Capital Companies in Missouri.*

Business Development: 314-751-4999. Publications: *Missouri Export Credit Insurance, Missouri International Trade Directory, Export Development Office (EDO), Foreign Investment Directory, Joint Venture Opportunities, Department of Commerce Commercial News, United Kingdom Investment in Missouri, Canadian Investment in Missouri, Japanese Investment in Missouri, German Investment in Missouri, European Investment in Missouri.*

National: 314-751-9045. Publications: *The Missouri Advantage, Helping Missouri Business Prosper.*

Research and Planning: 314-751-3674. Publications: *Basics of Economic Development, Community Fact Book--A Guide for Missouri Communities, Community Profiles, DED Annual Report, Economic Development Laws, Executive Planning Summary, Language of Economic Development, Missouri Facts and Figures, Missouri Directory of Manufacturers* (this directory must be ordered from Harris Publishing Co., Twinsburg, Ohio 800-888-5900), *New and Expanding Industry*

Economics, Demographics, and Statistics

Annual Report, The Missouri Advantage for Automotive Industry, The Missouri Advantage for Communication Industry, The Missouri Advantage for Electronics, The Missouri Advantage for Food Industry, The Missouri Advantage for Office, Research, and Distribution Facilities, The Missouri Advantage for Plastics and Metals Industries.

Business Information Programs: 314-751-4982, 800-523-1434. Publications: *Starting a New Business in Missouri, MEDIS Quick Reference Manual, Missouri Product Finder Brochure and Registration Form, MEDIS Brochure, Industrial Land Site Registration Form, Industrial Building Registration Form, Home-based Business Literature, Demographics Book and Disk, Missouri Product Finder Directory, MBAC Card, MSCL Business Start-up Handouts, Publications and Brochures, Spec/Shell Building Survey.*

Tax Benefits: 314-751-6835. Publications: *New/Expanded Business Facility and Enterprise Zone Tax Benefits Application, Small Business Incubator Tax Credit Application, Neighborhood Assistance Program Tax Credit Application, Development and Reserve Fund; Export Finance; Infrastructure Fund Tax Credit Application, Seed Capital Tax Credit Application, Taxes--The Missouri Advantage, Nine Tax Benefit Programs--The Missouri Advantage, New/Expanded Business Facility and Enterprise Zone Tax Laws, Enterprise Zone Contact List, Enterprise Zone Map, Research Tax Credit Application* (effective 1/1/94).

Montana

Business Assistance Division, Department of Commerce, State of Montana, 1424 9th Ave., Helena, MT 59620; 406-444-3923. Publications: *The Montana Manufacturers Directory* ($25), *The Montana Exporters Guide, The Made in Montana Products Directory, The "Business Finance Under the Big Sky", The "Montana Statewide Training Calendar", SBDC Newsletter.*

Nebraska

Nebraska Department of Economic Development, 301 Centennial Mall South, P.O. Box 94666, Lincoln, NE 68509; 402-471-3111, 1-800-426-6505. Publications: *Nebraska Statistical Handbook* ($15), *Nebraska Directory of Manufacturers* ($50), *Nebraska Development News* (newsletter), *NCIP* (Nebraska Community Improvement Program, newsletter).

Nevada

Commission on Economic Development, State of Nevada, Capitol Complex, Carson City, NV 89710; 702-687-4325. Publications: *Focus 2000, Nevada Progress, Nevada Business Guide, Nevada Industrial Directory.*

New Hampshire

Office of State Planning, State of New Hampshire, Executive Dept., 2 1/2 Beacon St., Concord, NH 03301; 603-271-2155.

Data Management Publications: *Current Estimates and Trends in New Hampshire's Housing Supply, New Hampshire Population Projections-Total Population for Cities and Towns; 1990-2015* (five year increments), *OSP Program Handbook; 1993, 1993 Population Estimates of New Hampshire Cities and Towns, A BRIEF LOOK* (an introductory profile of state data, amenities and characteristics, 1993), *Full and Part-Time Employment by Major Industry for U.S., N.H. and N.H Counties 1986-1991, New Hampshire Population Projections for Counties by Age and Sex 1994, Selected Economic Characteristics of NH Municipalities, 1990 Census, Statistical Profile of NH 1970-1990.*

Policy and Administration Publications: *Federal Register Report, Annual Federal Assistance Report* (published twice monthly), *New Hampshire Intergovernmental Review Process* (annual), *Legislative Update* (weekly), *Legislative Session Final Report.*

GIS Publications: *NH GRANIT Data Catalog* (June 1993), *NH GRANIT Users Guide* (October 1992), *GIS Handbook for Municipalities* (August 1994).

Water Protection Assistance Program Publications: *Municipal Guide to Wetland Protection, A Summary of the Plan for the Squam Lakes Watershed* (1991), *Local Land Use Management Techniques for Water Resources Protection and Geographic Inventory Procedures* (January 1992), *Model Health Ordinances to Implement a Wellhead or Groundwater Protection Program, State Development Plan* (1994), *State Development Plan Economic Trends Analysis* (1994), *Model Shoreland Protection Ordinance* (April 1994).

Municipal and Regional Assistance Publications: *Planning and Land Use Regulation* (annual $5.25), *The Board of Adjustment in New Hampshire: A Handbook for Local Officials* (1994 $5), *Status of Municipal Planning and Land Use Regulations in New Hampshire* (annual 1994), *The Handbook of Subdivision Review* (1988 with 1994 amendments), *OSP Technical Bulletins 1-10.*

Recreation Planning Publications: *Municipal Recreation and Conservation Budget Survey* (1991), *Public Access Plan for New Hampshire's Lakes, Ponds, and Rivers* (1991), *Outdoor Recreation Action Program* (1990-1991), *New Hampshire Wetlands Priority Plan, 1994, New Hampshire Outdoors* (1994-1998 SCORP), *Land Protection and the Tax Advantages for New Hampshire Land Owners,* Second Edition (1987), *Land Protection for NH Communities and Conservation Organizations* (1985).

New Jersey

Office of Economic Analysis, State of New Jersey, 1 West State St., Trenton, NJ 08625; 609-292-2568. Publications: *Economic Report of the Governor-Annual, Economic Forecast-Annual.*

New Mexico

Economic Development Department, 1100 St. Francis Drive, Santa Fe, NM 87503; 505-827-1734. Service: "One Stop Shop", an online data base with various information (free).

New York

The Nelson A. Rockefeller Institute of Government, 411 State St., Albany, New York 12203-1003; 518-443-5522. Publications: *Rockefeller Institute Publications List, Attrition Versus Layoffs: How to Estimate the Costs of Holding Employees on Payroll When Savings are Needed* ($2), *Background Data on the Implementation of the 1985 Albany Strategic Plan: Task Force on Downtown, Government Finances and Services, Housing and Community Development, Business Opportunities and Employment* (free), *Building the Twentieth Century Public Works Machine* ($2), *Canadian Investment in New York State: Appalachia or a Haven for Foreign Investors?* ($3), *Canadian Investment in Northern New York: Some Empirical Observations* ($2), *Capital Cities: Challenges and Opportunities* ($5), *Case for Tax-Exempt Bond Financing of Mortgages: The Rich Get Richer But The Poor Get Houses* ($2), *Citizen Participation in Government Decision Making: The Toxic Waste Threat at Love Canal, Niagara Fall, New York* ($2), *Citizen Surveys as Citizen Participation Mechanisms, Development of Local Discretionary Authority* ($2), *Diagnosing and Planning for the Learning Disabled: The Relationship Between State Policies and Services* ($3), *Differences Among States in the Impact of the Recession* ($20), *Diversification Into Long Term Care: A New Opportunity for Hospitals?* ($2), *Economic Growth and Development on Long Island* ($2), *Economic Recovery of New York: When and How?* (free), *Economic Restructuring and the Politics of Land/Use Planning in NYC* ($2), *Expanding the Economic Pie* ($3), *Feasibility Study for Establishing a New York State Research and Development Center for Hazardous Waste Management* (Includes Executive Summary) ($10), *Federal Role in State Fiscal Stress* ($20), *Free Trade for New York: The Economic Impact of the Canada-US Free Trade Agreement on NYS* ($3), *Governing the Empire State: An Insider's Guide* ($9.95), *Governor and the Attorney General in New York* ($3), *Gubernatorial-Legislative Relations in New York State* ($2), *Hard Truths/Tough Choices: An Agenda for State and Local Reform* (call 518-443-5825), *Impact of State Human Resource Policy on New York's Economic Development* ($3), *Legislative Appropriation of Federal Grants in New York* ($2), *Legislative Initiative in Budgeting Reform: New York's Key Item Reporting Systems* ($5), *New York State Project 2000: Prevention Policies for At-Risk Children* (1989/$10), *New York State Project 2000: Report on Electricity* (1986/$10), *New York State Project: Report on Corrections and Criminal Justice* (1986/$10), *New York State Project 2000: Report on Economic Development* (1986/$10), *New York State Project 2000: Report on Economic Structure* (1986/$10), *New York State Project 2000: Report on Housing* (1988/$10), *New York State Project 2000: Report on Long-Term Care* (1986/$10), *New York State Project 2000: Report on Population* (1986/$10), *New York State Project 2000: Report on Science and Technology* (1986/$10), *New York State Project 2000: Report on Water Resources* (1986/$10), *North Country Successes: Case Studies of Successful Entrepreneurs in the ANCA Region* ($3), *Partnership to Progress, Realizing Albany's Future* ($5), *Perspectives on Budgeting in New York* ($3), *Probable Effects of Introducing a Sectional Fare System into the NYC Subway* ($2), *Profile of a Recession: The New York Experience in the Early 1990's* ($3), *Promotion, Policies and Programs* ($3), *Public Service and the Future* (free), *Reorganization of New York State Government in the Twentieth Century* ($2), *Report on the Local Government Restructuring Project of the Nelson A. Rockefeller Institute of Government* (free), *Rethinking State and Local Economic Development Strategies* (free), *Revenue Estimation in New York State: Technique, Politics, or Luck?* ($5), *Role of State Tax Incentives in Attracting and Retaining Business* ($3), *State Fiscal Briefs* (call for more information, $15 each), *Structural Changes, Employment and Pay Trends: Shaping Federal Staffing Issues in the New York Region* ($3), *Study of the Nonprofit Sector in New York State: Its Size, Nature and Economic Impact* ($15), *Technology and the Research Environment of the Future: The Impact of the Information Science Revolution on the Research Environment of the Future* ($3), *Toward a Better Partnership: the Nonprofit Sector and State Government in NYS* ($5), *Toward the Implementation of the 21 Alcoholic Beverage Law in NYS* ($5), *Toward Integrating the Electricity Production of Hydro Quebec and the NY Power Pool* ($2).

North Carolina

Business and Industry Development, 116 Jones St., Raleigh, NC 27603-8003; 919-733-4151. Publications: *Department of Commerce-Community Profiles, General Information Business Climate*.

North Dakota

North Dakota Research Department, Office of the Governor, Bismark, ND 58505; 701-328-5300. Publications: *Statistical Study-North Dakota University, Planning Report, Demographics, Directory of North Dakota Manufacturers*.

Ohio

State of Ohio, Department of Development, Office of Strategic Research, P.O. Box 1001, Columbus, OH 43216; 614-466-2116. Publication: *Annual Report*.

Oklahoma

Oklahoma Department of Commerce, Research and Planning Division, 6601 Broadway, P.O. Box 26980, Oklahoma City, OK 73126-0980; 405-843-9770, 800-879-6552. Publications: *Directory*.

Census/Data Center: 405-841-5184. Publications: *Demographic State of the State*. Services: Census data requests, census maps, demographic/population research, Geographic Information System (GIS). Oklahoma Resources Integrated General Information Network System is a free, online computerized bulletin board system; Oklahoma City calling area 325-5883, Washington, D.C. area 800-765-6552, out-of-state 405-325-5883 (ORIGINS), population projections/estimates, population requests, TIGER (Topologically Integrated Geographic Encoding and Referencing System (geographic digital database).

Data Management Team: 405-841-5183. Publications: *Community Profiles, County Profiles, Fortune 500 List* (Oklahoma), *Major Employers Report, Manufacturer's Directory, New and Expanded Manufacturers, Real Estate Database, State Data, Union Election Results*.

Economic Analysis Team: 405-841-5178. Publications: *Analysis of Capital Spending Plans, Annual MISER Census Export by State, Capital Investment Trends in Industry, Construction/Real Estate Reports, Consumer Price Index/Cost of Living, County Business Patterns, Economic Forecasts & Impact Analysis, Economic and Policy Research, Economic Trends, Federal Government Statistical Releases, Forecast Data, HUD Median Family Income, Income and Employment Data, Industry Reports, Micro IMPLAN* (software), *Oklahoma Business & Industry Survey, Quarterly Economic Indicators, Targeted Industries*.

Policy and Planning Team: 405-841-5148. Publications: *Business Plan/Program Performance, Oklahoma Futures, Planning Assistance, Policy Research and Analysis, Winning the Race to the Future-Oklahoma 2007, Building a Better Oklahoma* (5-year plan), *Strategic Economic Development Plan* (also known as The 5-Year Plan), *Current Realities*.

Oregon

Oregon Economic Development Department, 775 Summer St., NE, Salem, OR 97310; 503-373-1290 (contact this office unless another phone number is given). Publications: *A Summary of Oregon Taxes* (Oregon Department of Revenue), *Business Referral List* (Small Business Program, 503-373-1241), *Challenge the Future* (Key Industries Section, 503-378-2286), *Executive Summary, Oregon Travel and Tourism* (Tourism Division, 503-373-1270), *Job Training Partnership, Key Industry Profiles* (Key Industries Section, 503-378-2286), *The Official Oregon Travel Guide* (Tourism Division, 503-373-1270), *Oregon, Oregon Fact Sheets, Oregon Film & Video Industry Relocation Packet* (Film & Video Office, 503-373-1232), *Oregon Film Locations Brochure* (Film & Video Office, 503-373-1232), *Oregon Helping Oregon* (Key Industries Section, 503-378-2286), *Oregon's Largest Employers 1992, Regulatory Research Project: Gasoline Service Stations in Oregon* (Small Business Program, 503-373-1241), *A Plan for the Tourism Industry* (503-373-1270, $5), *Annual Economic Impact Report for Oregon Travel* (503-373-1270, $10), *Directory of Oregon Manufacturers* (printed version for $75 or diskette for $200), *Directory of Oregon Wood Products Manufacturer* ($25), *Doing Business in Oregon* (0-10 copies free, 11+ copies $1.50 each plus shipping and handling), *Economic Profile of Oregon* ($3.50), *Ad Conversion Studies* ($10), *Helping Oregon Export* ($10), *Oregon County Economic Indicators* ($3.50), *Oregon International Trade Directory, 1990-91* edition ($15), *Oregon Travel and Tourism Visitor Profile* ($15), *Travel Industry Employment in Oregon: 1991* ($10).

Pennsylvania

Pennsylvania Department of Commerce, 433 Forum Bldg., Harrisburg, PA 17120; 717-783-1132. Publication: *Leaders in Economic Development*.

South Carolina

Commission on the Future of South Carolina, Office of Lieutenant Governor, P.O. Box 142, Columbia, SC 29202; 803-734-2080.

South Dakota

Governor's Office of Economic Development, Capitol Lake Plaza, 711 Wells Ave., Pierre, SD 57501-3369; 605-773-5032. Publication: *Economic Development Programs of Manufacturers and Processors* ($45).

Tennessee

Department of Economic and Community Development, 32- Sixth Ave., North, Rachel Jackson Bldg., Nashville, TN 37219; 615-741-1888.

Texas

Comptroller of Public Accounts, LBJ State Office Building, Austin, TX 78774; 512-463-4000. Publications: *Annual Financial Report, 1988-1989 Biennial Revenue Estimate, 1988-1989 Biennial Budget Estimate, Taxes and Texas: A National Survey on Alternatives and Comparisons, Texas Fees-Putting a Price on State Services, Quarterly Survey of Business Expectations in Texas, Sales and Franchise Tax Exemptions, Decontrolling Natural Gas-The Impact on Texas Prices and Tax Revenue, The High Finance of Higher Education, The Petroleum Industry and the Texas Sales Tax*.

Utah

Governor's Office of Planning and Budget, 116 State Capitol, Salt Lake City, Utah 84114; 801-538-1027, Fax: 801-538-1547. Publications: *Executive Budget Recommendations, Budget Summary, Utah Data Guide Newsletter, Economic and Demographic Projections, Utah Economic and Demographic Profiles, Utah Demographic Report, 1990 Census Briefs, Utah Migration Database: Sources, Methods, Limitations and Analysis 1994, Utah State and Local Government Fiscal Impact Model Working Paper Series: 1994, Utah Local Government Fiscal Database: An overview and Evaluation, June 1994* ($10), *Utah Ski Data Base 1994, Utah in the Global Economy 1993, Utah State Senate Districts: Economic and Demographic Characteristics, Higher Education Enrollment in Utah: A Demographic Perspective of Growth, Rural Utah Tourism Report 1992, Tourism Infrastructure Inventories for Mountainland, Bear River, Central and Southeastern Multi-County District 1992, Utah's Defense Economy 1992, Environment and Development in Rural Utah 1992, Water Development in Utah 1992, Utah Ski Database 1991, Utah State and Local Government Fiscal Benefit-Cost Model* (1990), *Technical Report on the Economic Analysis of the Brighton Ski Area Master Plan* (1991), *Historic Analysis of Property Taxes* (1980 Update), *Impact of Lake Powell Tourism on State and Local Tax Revenues* (1989), *Analysis of Demand for Recreation Uses in the Wasatch Front Canyons* (1988), *Migration in Utah* (1988), *Historic Analysis of Public Education Expenditures* (1987), *Historic Analysis of Property Taxes* (1986), *Economic Issues of Wilderness* (1986), *The Impacts of the Gramm-Rudman-Hollings Deficit Reduction Act* (1986), *The Importance of the Agricultural Industry in Utah* (1984), *Social and Economic Impact Analysis: Utah-Southwestern Utah Coal Environmental Impact Statement* (1983), *The Economic Issues Surrounding the Vitro Remedial Action Alternatives* (1983), *Final Socio-economic Technical Report: Utah Basin Synfuels Development* (1983), *The Economic and Demographic Impacts of the Intermountain Power Project* (1982), *Utah: 2000* (1980), *Energy: 2000* (1980), *The Planning Project Newsletter, State Planning Report, Economic Report to the Governor* ($15), *State Economic Coordinating Committee, The Impact of Tax Limitation in Utah* (1987), *State Mandates Study, Utah Advisory Commission on Intergovernmental Relations, The First Four Years: July 1987 - June 1991, State of Utah Comprehensive Annual Financial Report, Going Into Business In Utah, Poverty in Utah* (1985), *Utah Directory of Business and Industry, Utah Export Directory, Utah Facts, Affirmative Action Information, Annual Report of Job Service Activities, Labor Market Information Reports, Occupations In Demand, Helpful Hints for Job Seekers, Utah Labor Market Report, Utah Job Outlook for Occupations, Utah Directory of Business and Industry, Employment & Wages - By Size of Firm* (1989), *Hard at Work: Women in the Utah Labor Force* (1989), *Licensed Occupations in Utah, Utah's Career Guide, Utah Workforce 2000, Utah's Labor Force Characteristics, Crime in Utah, Utah Marriage and Divorce, Utah Vital Statistics, Fall Enrollment Report of Utah School Districts, Data Book, Utah Energy Statistical Abstract, Annual Report, Statistical Study of Assessed Valuations, Utah Statistics of Income, Gross Taxable Retail Sales and Purchases, New Car and Truck Sales, Initial Tax Burdens on Business and Households in Ten Western States: 1984-1985, Utah Construction Report Newsletter, Statistical Abstract of Utah, Utah Economic and Business Review Newsletter, Research Briefs, Research Reports, Statistical Review of Government in Utah, State Local Government in Utah 1992, Regional Planning Projections, Surveillance of Land Use and Socio-economic Characteristics, Economic Outlook, Office of Job Training Career Decisions Survey, Panel Survey of Migration History and Intentions Among Utahns, Follow-up Survey of Utah Exporters to Pacific Rim Countries, Survey of Utah Farmers and Economic Effects of the 1988 Drought, Survey of the Canyon Master Plan, Survey of Salt Lake City Residents on Earthquake*

Be patient. If any phone number is incorrect, call (area code) 555-1212 and request the new listing.

903

Preparedness, Survey of Utah Exporters to Pacific Rim Countries, Omnibus Survey of Utah Households, Survey of University of Utah Students: Financing, Satisfaction, Plans for the Future, Time-Use Patterns Among One- and Two-Parent Households, School-Age Children's View of the Future, Survey of Utah Communities to Assess Impact of Changes in Long Distance Rates on Consumers, Survey of Utahns to Assess Attitudes About Wilderness Designations, Socio-demographic Survey of Residents in Southeastern Utah, Health Interview Survey of Utah, Panel Survey of Utah Households, Satisfaction with Primary Care in Rural Utah, Perceptions of the Quality of Life Among Elderly Viewed by the Elderly, by Adult Children of the Elderly, and by General Practitioners, Olympic Survey Results, Survey of Health Services Utilization Patterns and Mental Health Help-Seeking Behavior, Nuclear Waste Survey, Cost of Living Index, American Demographics magazine, *Business Economics - The Journal of the National Association of Business Economists, Economic Report of the President, John Naisbitt's Trend Letter, Salt Lake Area Keeping Score, State Bond Prospectuses, State Policy Data Book: 1985-1990, U.S.G.S. Topographical Maps, Utah Business* magazine, *Utah Spectrum, News on Multiple-Use Management* (BLM newsletter), *Western Blue Chip Economic Forecast* (Arizona State University). OPB Online Database provides current publications and Census information that can be downloaded to a personal computer. Call 801-538-1550 for more information.

Vermont

Office of Policy Research and Coordination, Pavillion Office Building, 109 State St., Montpelier, VT 05602; 802-828-3326. Services and Responsibilities: Monitor trends and anticipate the impact of evolving technologies such as telecommunications, provide staff for the Governor's Council of Economic Advisors, Data on Vermont's Economy.

Virginia

Governor's Office, Department of Economic Development, 901 East Byrd, Richmond, VA 23219; 804-371-8263.

Washington

Washington State, Community Trade and Economic Development, Office of Financial Management, 9th and Columbia Bldg., P.O. Box 48300, Olympia, WA 98504-8300; 306-753-5617. Publication: *1993 Washington State Data Book.*

West Virginia

Research and Strategic Planning, Department of Industrial and Community Development, 1900 Washington St., East Building 6, Room 904, Charleston, WV 25305; 304-558-4010.

Wisconsin

Wisconsin Department of Development, 123 West Washington Ave., P.O. Box 7970, Madison, WI 53707; 608-266-1018. Publications: *Business Tax Chronology, Business Help Directory, Biennial Report--Wisconsin Department of Development (DOD), Community Economic Profiles* (Specify Community), *Community Preparedness Manual, County Economic Profiles* (Specify Community), *Doing Business and Living in Wisconsin, Financing Alternatives* ($2), *Financial Resources Available to Wisconsin Businesses: A Quick Reference Guide, Going Into Business in Wisconsin: An Entrepreneur's Guide, High Technology Companies in Wisconsin* ($4), *Industrial Revenue Bond Report, Key Media Contracts* ($3.50), *Local Development Organizations, New Industries and Plant Expansions, Starting A Business? Here's Help!, Technical Resources Available to Wisconsin Businesses and Communities, Technology Resources Available to Wisconsin Businesses* ($3.50), *Wisconsin Economic Profile, Wisconsin Highway Map, Wisconsin: The Resourceful State, Worker's Compensation Insurance Rates: A Four-State Comparison.*

Wyoming

Economic Development and Stabilization Board, 2301 Central Ave., Barrett Building, 4th Floor North, Cheyenne, WY 82002; 307-777-7284. Publications: *Wyoming Directory of Manufacturing and Mining, Wyoming Financial Assistant Programs, Mineral Yearbook.*

International Relations and Defense
Foreign Policy

* See also Vacations and Business Travel Chapter
* See also Drugs and Chemical Dependence; Law Enforcement and Prosecution Chapter
* See also Law and Social Justice; Immigration and Naturalization Chapter
* See also Selling Overseas: International Trade Chapter
* See also Economics, Demographics, and Statistics Chapter
* See also Information from Lawmakers; Tracking Federal Legislation Chapter
* See also Current Events and Homework Chapter
* See also Experts Chapter

The U.S. Department of State, the Agency for International Development (AID), and nearly half a dozen other government agencies study the changing political, social, and economic situations in every region of the world. All this intelligence is spun off into studies and reports as well as informative and readable material such as the State Department's Dispatch. If you are considering travel abroad, information about a country's history and culture is readily available. Anyone doing research on any region of the world can benefit from using the historical resources available as well as the country desk officers who track daily developments abroad. International treaties, peace and conflict resolution, and international organizations such as the World Bank also erase boundaries for obtaining information about our increasingly inter-dependent world. International agreements from Law of the Sea to the Nuclear Test Ban Treaty are spelled out in materials that the average person can understand. You'll also find plenty of public information on weapons systems and other aspects of the U.S. military.

* Advisory Commission on Public Diplomacy
United States Advisory Commission on Public Diplomacy
United States Information Agency (USIA)
301 Fourth St., SW, Room 600
Washington, DC 20547   202-619-4457
The seven Presidentially-appointed Commissioners oversee the operations of the U.S. Information Agency (USIA) and make a yearly report of findings and recommendations to the President, Congress, the Secretary of State, the Director of USIA, and the American people. The free report is available from this office.

* African Countries and US Foreign Policy
Bureau for African Affairs
U.S. Department of State
2201 C St., NW, Room 3509
Washington, DC 20520   202-647-7371
This Bureau develops implementation of U.S. policy in 46 Sub-Sahara African countries. The Office advises the Secretary of State on foreign policy issues, especially those focusing on democracy, economics, and human rights. Information is available on each of the countries, including *Background Notes*, foreign economic trend reports, and GIST summaries.

* Agency for International Development Library
Development Information Center, Room 105 SA-18
Agency for International Development (AID)   Fax: 703-875-5269
Washington, DC 20523-1801   703-875-4818
The library collections include: reference collection of current and retrospective runs of the major Agency for International Development (AID) program documents and financial reports, such as *Congressional Presentations, Country Development Strategy Statements, Action Plans, Policy Papers, Current Technical Service Contracts and Grants,* and *U.S. Overseas Loans and Grants,* also the current *AID Handbook;* microfiche collection; historical off-site collection; Women in Development collection; current book collection of commercial publication, directories, yearbooks, and reports from other bilateral and international development agencies, private voluntary organizations, and research institutions which deal with current development issues. Access is through an online catalog. Although the library contains some information on development in general, most materials relate to AID-supported research and projects. The library holdings focus on those countries in which AID has or has had project or program activities, and on those subjects related to the Agency's work. If you are flexible about the countries and topics you are willing to investigate, you will have a much better chance of finding relevant

information. A list of countries with AID missions is available in AID's *Project History List,* by Country Name in a black binder located on the right as you enter the library.

* Agriculture Assistance
Office of Agriculture
Bureau for Research and Development
Room 409, SA-18
Agency for International Development (AID)
Washington, DC 20523-1809   202-663-2530
This office provides technical leadership in the broad range of activities related to international agriculture development. The focus of the Agency for International Development's (AID) agriculture, rural development, and nutrition program is to increase the incomes of the poor and expand the availability and consumption of food while maintaining the country's natural resource base. To obtain a copy of *A Program Guide to the Office of Agriculture, Bureau for Science and Technology,* contact this office.

* Agriculture Information
Office of Public Affairs
U.S. Department of Agriculture
Washington, DC 20250   202-720-7507
The U.S. Department of Agriculture (USDA) *Annual Report* and the annual *Fact Book of Agriculture* discuss important Agricultural foreign trade and policy developments. They are available free along with the *List of Available Publications,* which details USDA publications for sale. Publications include:

AIB 516 *Trade Liberalization in World Farm Markets,* 1987 p.ERS
    PB 87-190559-AS PC AO3 MF AO1.
FAER 227 *Exporting U.S. Food to Sweden, Norway, and Finland,* 1987 57 p.ERS
    PB 87-204582 PC AO5 MF AO1.

* Agricultural Policy
Economic Research Service
U.S. Department of Agriculture
1301 New York Ave., Room 208
Washington, DC 20005   202-219-0515
While agriculture makes up a very small part of the economies of the industrialized world, it has become a very large and contentious foreign policy issue for

industrialized nations, stalling trade negotiations and creating animosity. The Economic Research Service publishes a wealth of information for those interested in agricultural issues and foreign policy. Publications can be ordered toll free in the U.S. and Canada by calling 1-800-999-6779, elsewhere call 301-725-7937, and include:

Agricultural Outlook - the premier USDA agriculture magazine it presents long term analyses of such issues as U.S. agricultural policy, trade forecasts and export-market development, food safety, and the environment. 11 issues Order # AGO, cost - 1 yr, $26; 2 yrs, $51; 3 yrs, $75.

World Agriculture - deals with worldwide developments in agricultural markets and trade. It is based on research ongoing in ERS. quarterly, Order # WAS. 1 yr,$21; 2 yrs, $41; 3 yrs, $60.

Foreign Agricultural Trade of the United States - updates the quantity and value of U.S. farm exports and imports, plus price trends. It also tracks U.S. in relation to the world market. 4 issues plus 2 supplements. Order # FAT. 1 yr, $25; 2 yrs, $49; 3 yrs, $72.

* AID Information

Development Information Center
Research and Reference Services
Room 105 SA-18
Agency for International Development (AID)
Washington, DC 20523-1801   703-875-4818

Information about the structure and administration of the Agency for International Development (AID) is available from the series of *AID Handbooks* from the above reference section of the library. General information about AID's plans in a particular country can be found in the *Country Development Strategy Statements* (CDSSs) in the serials room. Also in the serials room are *Congressional Presentations* (CPs) and *Annual Budget Submissions* (ABSs), which contain financial information on AID projects. Information on all phases on AID projects is available in project documents (PDs).

* AID Magazine and Newsletter

Office of Publications
Agency for International Development (AID)
320 21st St., NW
Washington, DC 20523   202-647-4330

The Agency for International Development (AID) publishes a free quarterly newsletter, *AID Highlights*, which describes a different AID program in each issue. This publication is designed for those in the general public interested in Agency activities. *Frontlines* is a monthly newspaper, available to Agency staff and retirees that also highlights the current activities of the AID.

* AID Reference Services

Development Information Center
Room 105 SA-18
Agency for International Development (AID)
Washington, DC 20523-1801   703-875-4818

The library's holding of Agency for International Development (AID) documents catalogued since 1974 are available on microfiche and can be read on microfiche readers in the library. Hard copies or microfiche copies of documents can be ordered from AID's Document Information Services Clearinghouse in Arlington, Va. The library's historical (pre-1974) documents are stored off-site, but may be retrieved upon request at the reference desk (be sure to have a full citation and complete call number). For more information, contact the office above.

* AID Speakers Bureau

Office of Public Liaison
Bureau for External Affairs
Agency for International Development (AID)
320 21st St., NW, Room 4889
Washington, DC 20523   202-647-4213

Speakers within the Agency for International Development (AID) organization are available to address meetings and conferences. A wide variety of topics can be discussed, including women's issues, health, economic policy, agriculture, world hunger, and disaster relief. A letter must be sent to the office above outlining the format of the meeting, the number of people attending, the location of the meeting, and the subject of the presentation. A minimum of two weeks is needed to secure a speaker.

* Alien Registration Information

Central Office
Immigration and Naturalization Service
425 I Street, NW
Washington, DC 20536   202-307-1501

Publications and tape recorded messages about immigration are available from this central office. However, field offices operate in most states and these local phone numbers appear in the Law and Social Justice Chapter and, of course, are easy to obtain from the directory assistance operators. When calling the tape recorded telephone number listed above, enter one of the number codes below which corresponds to the information about immigration and naturalization that you need:

401 Permanent alien residency card
402 Applying for a replacement alien residency card (I-90)
403 If you never received your alien residency card (I-90)

* American and Foreign Teachers Exchange Program

Office of Academic Programs
United States Information Agency (USIA)
301 Fourth St., SW, Room 353
Washington, DC 20547   202-619-4555

The Advising, Teaching, and Specialized Programs Division serves overseas education advising centers, foreign exchange students in the U.S., and administers the International Student Exchange Program for one-to-one exchange of university students. Its Teacher Exchange Branch arranges one and two way exchanges of U.S. and foreign teachers, and summer seminars for U.S. teachers to study abroad. Free brochures and applications are available.

* American Books Overseas Distribution

Book Programs Division
Office of Cultural Centers and Resources
Bureau of Educational and Cultural Affairs
United States Information Agency (USIA)
301 Fourth St., SW, Room 320
Washington, DC 20547   202-619-4896

The U.S. Information Agency (USIA) helps in the translation, publication, and promotion of American books overseas. The Promotion Branch organizes traveling book exhibits and supports an American presence at international book fairs. The Field Operations Branch supports the translation and publication of a broad range of titles, mostly in the social sciences and humanities.

* American Business and AID Coordination

Office of Trade and Investment
Agency for International Development (AID)
320 21st St., NW, Room 3253
Washington, DC 20523   202-647-9100

This office assists, coordinates, and advises on the involvement of the U.S. business community with the Agency for International Development (AID) to achieve Agency objectives. Cooperative projects between AID and the U.S. business community within AID's guidelines are encouraged. Contact this office for more information. For regional information one can also contact the Development Center at the U.S. Department of Commerce at 202-377-0841.

* American Enterprise Institute

American Enterprise Institute
1150 17th St., NW
Washington, DC 20036   202-862-5800

The American Enterprise Institution (AEI) is an independent, non-partisan organization dedicated to the "maintenance of a free and prosperous economic order, a resolute national defense, and tradition-proven cultural and political values." AEI conducts research in three general areas: domestic and international economic policy; foreign and defense policy; and social and political studies. A free catalogue of AEI books and publications is available.

* American Experts Overseas Lecture Tour

Office of Program Coordination and Development
United States Information Agency (USIA)
301 Fourth St., SW, Room 550
Washington, DC 20547   202-619-4720

AmParts are experts in a field--usually economics, international affairs, literature, the arts, U.S. political and social processes, sports, science, or technology--sent abroad by the U.S. Information Agency (USIA) to meet with groups or individual professional counterparts. Recruited on the basis of requests of USIA staff in other countries, AmParts often engage in informal lecture/discussions with small groups, grant media interviews, or speak before larger audiences. Those interested in the American Participant program are invited to submit a brief letter indicating times of availability, along with a curriculum vitae and at least two lecture topics with brief talking points. A free brochure on the program is available from this office.

* American Foreign Policy Information Clearinghouse

Bureau of Public Affairs
U.S. Department of State
2201 C St., NW, Room 5819
Washington, DC 20520   202-647-6575 or 6576

The State Department in Washington, DC receives thousands of reports daily, and produces hundreds of publications, speeches, and conferences are produced each year. The Bureau of Public Affairs informs the American people on foreign policy and advises the Secretary of State on public opinion. To request information or express an opinion, contact the above office. If unable to answer an inquiry directly, staff will direct you to the appropriate source. This bureau issues various publications covering U.S. foreign relations, some of which are free. In 1991 the State Department phased out many of its publications including *Gist Series, Current Policy Series, Special Report Series, Selected Documents Series, Regional Briefs*, and the *Historical Issues Series*. The information in these documents can now be found in the new U.S. Department of State *Dispatch*. Contact the above office for further information.

* American Publications Translated and Distributed Worldwide

Superintendent of Documents
Government Printing Office (GPO)   202-512-1800
Washington, DC 20402   Fax: 202-512-2250

The United States Information Agency publishes many teaching materials, including books, maps, complete teaching modules, and 14 magazines in 20 languages. By law most U.S. Information Agency (USIA) publications may be distributed only in foreign countries. However, by congressional action, two magazines are available in the United States. *English Teaching Forum*, a quarterly for English teachers worldwide, is published by USIA's English Language Programs Division. *Problems of Communism* is a bi-monthly forum for American and foreign scholars discussing communist and socialist affairs. It is published in English and Spanish. Both these magazines are available through the Government Printing Office.

* American Schools and Hospitals Abroad

Bureau for Food and Humanitarian Assistance
Agency for International Development (AID), SA-8
Washington, DC 20523   703-351-0232

Each year this Bureau gives grants on a competitive basis to private, non-profit schools, hospitals, and libraries known for their excellence in demonstrating U.S. ideas and practices of education and medicine to citizens of other countries. Grant recipients must by U.S.-based, tax-exempt, private citizens' organizations which have founded and/or sponsor overseas institutions on a continuing basis. Eligible schools must be for secondary or higher level educations, while hospitals must conduct medical education and research. Grants are made to the U.S. sponsors for the exclusive benefit of the overseas institutions and customarily carry matching or cost-sharing provisions. Contact the office above for more information.

* American Studies for Foreigners

Division of Study of the U.S.
United States Information Agency (USIA)
301 Fourth St., SW, Room 256
Washington, DC 20547   202-619-4557

The Division for the Study of the U.S. promotes foreign education through conferences, seminars, exchange programs for foreign educators, grants, and development of school resource materials. The Academic Specialist Branch provides grants for American teachers to instruct their peers at foreign educational institutions. Contact this office for more information.

* Aquaculture and Fishing in Third World

Fisheries Specialist
Office of Programming and Training Support
Peace Corps, 1990 K St., NW
Washington, DC 20526   202-606-3402

In helping people help themselves, fishery specialists provide information and techniques to farmers and fishermen on stocking, managing, feeding, and harvesting fish.

* Arctic and Antarctic International Policy

Office of Oceans
Bureau of Oceans and International Environmental
and Scientific Affairs
U.S. Department of State
2201 C St., NW, Room 5801
Washington, DC 20520   202-647-3262

This office is concerned with all issues concerning the Arctic and Antarctic, including the environment and marine life, such as whales and seals. They are also closely involved with the many science stations located on the Antarctic.

* Artistic Ambassador Program

United States Information Agency (USIA)
301 4th St., SW, Room 216
Washington, DC 20547   202-619-5338

Begun in 1983, the Artistic Ambassador Program is designed to utilize the wealth of often undiscovered American musical talent to enhance the USIA mission of cross-cultural understanding. Musicians are sent on tours ranging from 4-6 weeks. Since the programs inception, 41 musical ambassadors have visited 79 nations. For information, contact the above office.

* Assistance to Foreign Highways

International Highway Programs (HPI-10)
Associate Administrator for Policy
Federal Highway Administration (FHWA)
U.S. Department of Transportation
400 7th St., SW
Washington, DC 20590   202-366-0111

The Federal Highway Administration (FHWA) administers programs which provide assistance and advice to foreign governments engaged in highway engineering and administration. Projects have included technical assistance in fabricating bridge segments, value engineering skills, development of transportation systems, materials testing, quality control, and skid testing. Through the International Visitors Program, highway specialists from over 40 countries receive training. Countries that have participated include China, Indonesia, Haiti, Kuwait, Dubai, and Saudi Arabia. Two publications available from this office are *World of Technology for Sharing* and *Highway Community on the Occasion of the 18th World Road Congress*.

* Balance of Payments Support

International Monetary Fund (IMF)
700 19th St., NW
Washington, DC 20431   202-623-7000

The International Monetary Fund's (IMF) primary purpose is to provide short term balance of payments assistance to members experiencing temporary difficulties. The Fund also operates a Compensatory Financing Facility to support members, particularly those producing primary products which suffer from fluctuations in export receipts. The Fund issues a broad range of studies, reports, and publications on its activities and related economic subjects.

* Bilateral and Multilateral International Aid Donors

International Donor Programs
Policy Office
Agency for International Development (AID)
320 21st St., NW, Room 3637
Washington, DC 20523   202-647-0600

This Bureau coordinates Agency for International Development (AID) policies and programs with other bilateral assistance donors, United Nations development organizations, and multilateral development banks. In close collaboration with State, Treasury, and other interested government agencies, the Bureau reviews programs, budgets, and staffing of the international development organizations. Recommendations are made on the U.S. Government's position regarding these matters, and guidance is provided to U.S. representatives to these organizations.

* Binational Libraries and Cultural Centers Worldwide

Library Programs Division
Bureau of Educational and Cultural Affairs

United States Information Agency (USIA)
301 Fourth St., SW, Room 314
Washington, DC 20547   202-619-4915
The U.S. Information Agency (USIA) maintains or supports libraries and reading rooms in 160 cities in 89 countries, as well as library programs at 111 binational centers in 17 countries. Collections focus on fostering foreign understanding of U.S. people, history, and culture. A bi-weekly bibliography, listing 80-100 titles on international relations and developments in the U.S., is one of many library services provided for the overseas posts, including reference and research assistance. More information on the program can be obtained in the Bowker Annual Library and Book Trade Information Manual, which can be found in many libraries.

* Black Medical Schools and International Development

Agency Center for University Cooperation
and Development
Bureau for Research and Development
Room 900, SA-38
Agency for International Development (AID)
Washington, DC 20523-3801   703-816-0295
The Agency for International Development (AID) has initiated a program to increase participation by historically black medical schools in AID-supported international activities. The program links each of four participating medical schools with a major U.S. School of Public Health that already has extensive overseas experience. Through a set of Joint Memoranda of Understanding (JMOU), program support grants have been awarded to the eight participating institutions to increase their capacity to provide technical assistance to AID field missions in implementing health, population, and nutrition policies and strategies. Contact this office for more information.

* Brookings Institution

Brookings Institution
1775 Massachusetts Ave., NW
Washington, DC 20036   202-797-6105
Brookings can be considered the "dean" of public policy/foreign policy think tanks in Washington. With 50 full time scholars and 200 staff assistants, the Institution pursues research in the areas of Economic Studies, Foreign Policy Studies, Governmental Studies, and Public Policy Education. Each research area is headed by a nationally renowned scholar. Contact Brookings for information on current research projects and for the latest catalogue of books.

* Business Development Teaching Overseas

Peace Corps
1990 K St., NW, 9th Floor
Washington, DC 20526   202-606-3412
Volunteers teach new ways of conducting business and trade by introducing basic accounting skills, administration, and marketing to farmers, fisherman, and village women.

* Caribbean and Latin America Field Project Histories

Inter-American Foundation
1515 Wilson Blvd.
Rosslyn, VA 22209   703-841-3830
The Inter-American Foundation (IAF) is compiling 267 project file-based histories and 13 field-based project histories which outline the background, results, and lessons learned of each of IAF's funded projects in Latin America and the Caribbean. These histories are valuable research tools for those interested in development efforts in these regions.

* Caribbean Basin Employment and Trade

Office of International Economic Affairs
Bureau of International Economic Affairs
U.S. Department of Labor
200 Constitution Ave., NW, Room S5355
Washington, DC 20210   202-523-7597
The annual report, *Trade and Employment Effects of the Caribbean Basin Economic Recovery Act (CBERA)*, describes the provisions included in the CBERA, along with the benefits they provide to beneficiary countries. It also analyzes changes in U.S. trade with CBERA countries, and looks at trends in U.S. employment in those industries which have undergone the most significant changes in trade flows. Contact this office for more information on the report.

* Carnegie Endowment for International Peace

2400 M St. NW
Washington, DC 20037   202-862-7900
Established in 1910 through a gift from Andrew Carnegie, the Endowment conducts programs of research, discussion, publication, and education in international affairs and American foreign policy. Special projects include the Middle East Arms Control Project; Immigration Policy Project; and the U.S.-Soviet Relations Study Group. For a list of current research projects and internship opportunities, contact the Endowment.

* Center for the Study of Foreign Affairs

Foreign Service Institute
1400 Key Blvd., Room 304
Arlington, VA 22209   703-875-5183
The Center for the Study of Foreign Affairs aims to enrich traditional Foreign Service training by keeping government officials in many agencies abreast of emerging foreign policy concepts. Its program of conferences, research, and publications combines new perspectives developed by private scholarship with the practical experience of foreign affairs personnel. The Center publishes full-length studies of various foreign policy issues in its *Study of Foreign Affairs series*, many of which are based on conferences and workshops held at the Center.

* Central and Eastern Europe Assistance Programs

Peace Corps
Eastern European Desk
1990 K St., NW, 9th Floor
Washington, DC 20526   202-606-3412
The revolutions of 1989 that swept the communists from power in Eastern Europe also swept in the Peace Corps for the first time since their creation in 1961. Peace Corps volunteers now serve in Poland, Czechoslovakia, Bulgaria, Romania, Yugoslavia, Albania, and in the former USSR. Initially, most volunteers taught english at the secondary school and university level. Plans are being developed for programs in Agriculture, Child Survival, Environmental Protection, and Small Business Development. Currently there are 461 volunteers in Eastern Europe. For background information on the current programs, contact the above office.

* Central Intelligence Agency Catalog of Maps and Publications

Public Affairs
Central Intelligence Agency (CIA)
Washington, DC 20505   703-351-2053
The CIA declassifies many of its maps which are available from the National Technical Information Service, 5285 Port Royal Road, Springfield, VA 22161 703-487-4650. The catalog, titled *CIA Maps and Publications Released to the Public*, is available free from the CIA. Some of the titles include *The Impact of Gorbachev's Policies on Soviet Economic Statistics* (NTIS SOV 88-10049); *Chiefs of State and Cabinet Members of Foreign Governments* (NTIS LDA-CS 88-001); *The World Factbook* (NTIS PB 88-928009) and *OECD Trade with the Middle East* (PB-91-928012).

* Central Intelligence Agency Information

Public Affairs
Central Intelligence Agency (CIA)   703-351-2053
Washington, DC 20505   703-482-7676
The Public Affairs office can provide declassified information and respond to inquiries.

* Central Intelligence Agency Reports Published Before 1980

Photoduplication Service
Library of Congress
Washington, DC 20540   202-707-9527
The Library of Congress distributes Central Intelligence Agency (CIA) reports that have been released to the public. These reports detail foreign government structures, trade news, economic conditions, and industrial development. Orders must be prepaid or charged to a standing account at the Library of Congress. For a nominal fee the projects unit for the CIA in the Photoduplication Service can also provide you with a list of CIA reports available. Reports can be purchased on microfilm for $.50 per exposure or $30 per reel. (Prices due to change)

* Child Survival Action Program

Office of Health
Bureau for Research and Development, Room 709, SA-18
Agency for International Development (AID)
Washington, DC 20523   703-875-4600

Each year, fourteen to fifteen million children in developing countries die of disease and malnutrition before they reach the age of five. In February 1985, the Agency for International Development (AID) demonstrated its commitment to helping these children by establishing the Child Survival Action Program (CSAP) to deliver simple, inexpensive, and proven technologies to save the lives of these children and to improve their prospects for a healthy future. AID's child survival strategy includes four basis interventions: oral rehydration therapy (ORT), immunization, birth spacing, and better infant and child nutrition. For information on CSAP, contact the office above.

* Child Survival in the Third World

Document Information Services Clearinghouse
1500 Wilson Blvd., Suite 1010
Arlington, VA 22209-2404   703-351-4006

The child health publications listed below can be viewed in the Library on microfiche, and paper copies may be obtained from the address above. Note that document identification call numbers follow the identification number. Their telefax number is 301-951-9624.

The AID Diarrheal Disease Control Strategy (Oral Rehydration Therapy and Related Interventions). Washington, DC; U.S. Agency for International Development, 1986. (616.3427.A288) (PN-AAX-052).

Birth Spacing and Child Survival. Maine, Deborah and Regina McNamara. Sponsored by the U.S. Agency for International Development, Bureau for Science and Technology, Office of Population, New York: Columbia University, Center for Population and Family Health, 1985. (613.94.M225) (PN-AAV-575).

Risks and the Road to Health. Galway, Katrina, Brent Wolff and Richard Sturgis. Sponsored by the U.S. Agency for International Development, Bureau for Science and Technology, Office of Population. Columbia, MD: Westinghouse Company, Institute for Resource Development, Inc. 1987. (362.19892.G183) (PN-AAX-157).

Child Survival Strategy, 1987-1990: Bureau for Africa, U.S. Agency for International Development. Washington, DC: U.S. Agency for International Development, Bureau for Africa, Office of Technical Resources, 1987. (613.0432.C536) (PD-AAU-969).

Health and Family Planning in Community-Based Distribution Programs. Mawer, Maria, Sandra Huffman, Deborah Cebula and Richard Osbor, eds. Sponsored by the U.S. Agency for International Development, Bureau for Science and Technology, Office of Population, Boulder, CO: Westview Press, 1985. (362.1.W356) (PN-AAT-004).

Immunizations. Primary Health Care Issues Series. Sabin, Edward and Wayne Stinson. Washington, D.C: American Public Health Association, 1981. (614.47.I33) (PN-AAJ-782).

* Childhood Communicable Disease Control

Health Programmer
Office of Programming and Training Coordination
Peace Corps
1990 K St., NW, 9th Floor
Washington, DC 20526   202-254-8400

The Peace Corps has developed child survival programs that train parents as well as children with curricula designed to teach better nursing skills, with an emphasis on vaccination.

* Citizenship and Naturalization

Central Office
Immigration and Naturalization Service
425 I Street, NW
Washington, DC 20536   202-307-1501

Publications and tape recorded messages about immigration are available from this central office. However, field offices operate in most states and these local phone numbers appear in the Law and Social Justice Chapter and, of course, are easy to obtain from the directory assistance operators. When calling the tape recorded telephone number listed above, enter one of the number codes below which corresponds to the information about immigration and naturalization that you need:

801 Citizenship and Naturalization requirements (N-400)
805 Residency requirements for naturalization
804 Derivative citizenship for children of U.S. citizens
802 Citizenship for children born outside the United States (N-600)
803 Naturalization based upon military service
807 Replacement of certificate of citizenship or naturalization (N-565)
806 How to file for naturalization on behalf of a child
808 To renounce or forfeit United States citizenship

* Commerce and Foreign Affairs

International Trade Administration
U.S. Department of Commerce
14th St. between E St. and Constitution Ave NW.
Washington, DC 20230   202-377-2000

In the post-Cold War international environment, trade and economic issues will take on increased foreign policy importance for the United States. The International Trade Administration is a good source of information on the political aspects of trade negotiations such as the Uruguay Round of multilateral trade negotiations. For further information, contact the International Trade Administration (ITA) at the number above and ask to speak to the officer for the country or region you are interested in.

* Conflict Resolution

U.S. Institute of Peace
1550 M St., NW, Suite 900
Washington, DC 20005   202-457-1700

The Jeanette Rankin library program supports the expansion of the Institute's and the nation's information resources on issues in the fields of peace and international conflict management. The Institute also conducts the annual National Peace Essay Contests for high school students, and has many television and other media projects on such subjects as the history of U.S.--USSR summitry and issues and ideas in peacemaking. Publications of the Institute include the biennial report; the bimonthly Journal which provides information on the Institute's programs and achievements and increases public knowledge of important projects and points of view; and *In Brief*, a new series highlighting results from Institute projects, as well as books and papers.

Institute reports available include the following:

Biennial Report of the United States Institute of Peace, 1989.
Contributions to the Study of Peacemaking: A Summary of Completed Grant Projects (12/90)
The Gulf Crisis: Finding A Peaceful Solution (1990).
Guide to Specialists (Institute fellow and staff areas of expertise, 1991-92).
Making Peace Among Arabs and Israelis: Lessons from Fifty Years of Negotiating Experience (1991).
Prospects for Conflict or Peace in Central and Eastern Europe (1990).

* Congress-Bundestag Youth Exchange Program

Youth Programs Division
United States Information Agency (USIA)
301 4th St., SW, Room 357
Washington, DC 20547   202-619-6299

Jointly funded by the United States Congress and the German Bundestag, this program is designed to strengthen ties between the two countries. The program provides full scholarships or a year of study, homestay, and work internships. The program serves approximately 800 American and German students each year, most of whom are in high school.

* Congressional Research Service (CRS)

Foreign Affairs and National Defense Division
Room 315
Library of Congress
Washington, DC 20540   202-707-5700

The Congressional Research Service (CRS) is an excellent source for foreign affairs information. The foreign affairs division has some 60 full time analysts writing and updating reports as well as answering special requests for Congress. Individual analysts are superb sources for information as they often follow issues for years. CRS reports are not normally available to the public, but can be obtained through your Congressman's or Senator's office. If you contact CRS directly, see if the report you are interested in has been inserted into the Congressional Record and/or a House or Senate report. A complete list of CRS reports has been reprinted in the Current Events and Homework section of this book.

* Cooperatives and Credit Unions

Office of Private and Voluntary Cooperation
Bureau for Food and Humanitarian Assistance, Room 712, SA-8
Agency for International Development (AID)
Washington, DC 20523   703-351-0211

U.S. cooperatives provide business services and outreach in cooperative development to underdeveloped countries for their U.S. membership. These organizations support the participation of rural and urban poor people in their countries' development. These organizations are not charitable or fund-raising groups and rely almost exclusively on AID funding for their international programs.

* Country and Territory Info Pamphlets

Superintendent of Documents
Government Printing Office   202-512-1800
Washington, DC 20402   Fax: 202-512-2250

Background Notes, a series of short, factual pamphlets about various countries and territories of the world, plus selected international organizations, contain up-to-date information on each country's people, culture, geography, history, government, political conditions, economy, defense, and foreign relations with other countries, including the United States. A reading list provides additional sources of information about the country, and travel notes, maps, and occasional photographs are often included. A complete set can be purchased from the Government Printing Office for $63.

* Country "Desks"

Country Desk Officers
U.S. Department of State
2201 C St., NW
Washington, DC 20520   202-647-4000

The State Department's Country Desk Officers are responsible for following all activities in their assigned countries, from the political, economic, and social perspectives. These officers are in contact with the embassies; deliver and receive documents from the embassies; and write reports on the current activities in the country. The officers can provide the most current information available about their country. Call the number above and ask for the country you wish to find information about. Also see the Expert Chapter for a complete roster giving the name and phone number of the country specialists.

* Country Intelligence and Research Coordination

U.S. Department of State
Bureau of Intelligence and Research
2201 C St., NW, Room 8732
Washington, DC 20520   202-647-2025

This bureau coordinates programs of intelligence, research, and analysis for the State Department and for other Federal agencies, and produces intelligence studies and current intelligence analyses essential to foreign policy determination and execution. The Office of Research maintains a liaison with cultural and educational institutions on a wide range of matters relating to Government contractual and private foreign affairs research.

* Cultural and Educational International Exchange

Office of Public Liaison
United States Information Agency (USIA)
301 Fourth St., SW, Room 602
Washington, DC 20547   202-619-2355

The U.S. Information Agency (USIA) distributes the free *Directory of Resources for Cultural and Educational Exchanges and U.S. Information*, a treasure trove of information on cultural and educational exchange programs in the U.S. The directory provides contacts and background information of government agencies and non-profit and private organizations which sponsor exchange programs.

* Development Aid Policy and Budget

Directorate of Finance Administration
Policy Office
Agency for International Development (AID)
320 21st St., NW, Room 3756
Washington, DC 20523   202-647-9110

The Agency for International Development's (AID) program and budget is formulated and revised as needed by the Bureau for Program and Policy Coordination. This Bureau presents the Agency's program to Congress, and reviews country program strategies and project proposals. The Bureau develops economic assistance policies, provides guidance on long-range program planning, economic analysis, sector assistance strategies, and project analysis and design.

* Development Assistance

World Bank
1818 H. Street, NW
Washington, DC 20433   202-473-5787

The World Bank is made up of three separate institutions - the International Bank for Reconstruction and Development (IBRD), The International Development Association (IDA), and the International Finance Corporation (IFC) - which share the common goal of helping to raise standards of living of the people in the developing countries by channelling financial resources from developed countries to the developing world. World Bank institutions support programs of technical assistance and research in support of its development goals.

* Development Fund for Africa

Bureau of African Affairs
Office of Development Policy
New State, Room 2495
Agency for International Development (AID)
Washington, DC 20523   202-647-3362

In 1987 Congress consolidated many of the aid programs to Sub-Saharan Africa into the Development Fund for Africa (DFA). The implementation of the DFA since its inception has been focused on helping African governments and people to achieve the goal of sustainable broad-based, market-oriented economic growth. Contact this office for the following reports: *The Development Fund for Africa* report, 1991; and *U.S. Assistance for Africa - The Development Fund for Africa (DFA): An Action Plan*, May 1989.

* Development Information System

Center for Development Information and Evaluation
Policy Coordination Office
Agency for International Development (AID)
Washington, DC 20523-1801   703-875-4818

This Center operates and maintains the Agency for International Development (AID) Development Information System (DIS), which provides online access to development assistance experience from almost 9,000 AID-funded projects and over 70,000 AID-generated technical, evaluation, and research reports. The *AID Technical Reports* is a monthly acquisitions list which presents citations recently added to the DIS of technical reports from Agency sponsored projects and activities. The *AID Project Descriptions* is a quarterly acquisitions list which presents abstracts of grant agreements, project design documents, and project identification documents recently added to the DIS. Citations are organized by sector and within sector by title. Contact the office above for further information.

Patrons outside the Washington metropolitan area may request searches of DIS by writing to AID, Development Information Center, Room 105, SA-18, Washington, DC 20523-1801. Include your return address and in 4-6 weeks you will receive a computer print-out listing projects, with descriptions, and document bibliographies. This search service is free. Patrons outside the Washington metropolitan area may request searches of DIS by writing to AID, Development Information Center, Room 105 SA-18, Washington, DC 20523-1801. Include your return address and in 4 to 6 weeks you will receive a computer print out listing projects, with descriptions, and document bibliographies. This search service is free.

* Diplomatic Archives in Foreign Countries

Office of the Historian
Bureau of Public Affairs
S A-1, Room 3100
U.S. Department of State
Washington, DC 20522   202-663-1122

The monograph, *Public Availability of Diplomatic Archives in Foreign Countries*, lists each country and its archival rules, requirements, and documents made available by contacting the Government Printing Office, Superintendent of Documents, Washington, DC, 20402-6518, 202-512-1800. A list of important published works on archival sources is also available.

* Drug War

Bureau of International Narcotics Matters
U.S. Department of State
2201 C St., NW, Room 7331

Washington, DC 20520   202-647-6936

To coordinate the worldwide effort to halt the production and flow of illegal drugs to the United States, this bureau works closely with foreign governments and international organizations. Under bilateral agreements and international treaties, it provides technical and material assistance to foreign governments for such programs as eradication of narcotics crops, destruction of illicit laboratories, and training of antinarcotics interdiction personnel. This office also produces the *International Narcotics Control Strategy Report*, which is available for purchase at the Government Printing Office, 202-512-1800.

* East Asia and Pacific Region Clearinghouse

Bureau of East Asia and Pacific Affairs
U.S. Department of State
Public Affairs, Room 5209
2201 C St., NW
Washington, DC 20520   202-647-2538

This Bureau is responsible for U.S. relations with the countries in East Asia and the Pacific, which include Australia, New Zealand, China, Indonesia, Malaysia, Brunei, Singapore, Japan, North and South Korea, Philippines, the Pacific Islands, Taiwan, Thailand, Burma, Vietnam, Laos, and Cambodia. This office advises the Secretary on foreign policy issues, especially those focusing on democracy, economics, and human rights.

* Economic and Social Conditions Worldwide

Center for Development Information and Evaluation
Agency for International Development (AID)
PPC/CDIE, SA-18
Washington, DC 20523-1802   703-875-4818

The Economic and Social Data System (ESDS) contains statistical information gathered from government agencies and organizations from around the world. Countries worldwide are characterized according to the Country's economy, financial situation, demographics, poverty indicators, labor force, social factors, and the levels of education, nutrition, health, and food. This database is for use by Agency for International Development (AID) employees and contractors only.

* Economic Development in the Third World

Office of Economic and Institutional Development
Bureau for Research and Development
Room 608, SA-18
Agency for International Development (AID)
Washington, DC 20523   703-875-4710

This office's goal is to create broadly based and sustainable economic growth and the active economic participation of the poor in underdeveloped countries. The staff of economists, anthropologists, and social and management scientists work on policy and institutional change and technology transfer in three key areas: employment and enterprise development; decentralization and public management; and natural resources and regional economic systems analysis and management. Contact this office for more information.

* Economic Development Projects Involving Women

Women in Development
Office of Training and Program Support
Peace Corps
1990 K St., NW
Washington, DC 20526   202-606-2366/4472

This office ensures that Peace Corps programs are designed to fully integrate women into the economic development process of their countries and communities. This office provides programming, training, and evaluation to the field workers. *The Exchange*, a quarterly newsletter, is published and distributed to 6,000 volunteers and staff in the field, with a focus on projects involving women.

* Economic Policy

Bureau of International Organization Affairs
U.S. Department of State
2201 C St., NW, Room 5328
Washington, DC 20520   202-647-8270

This office, as coordinator of U.S. economic policy within the United Nations, is responsible for the analysis and handling of international economic issues as they arise in international organizations, especially those in force in the U.N. system.

* Economic Support Fund

Office of Finance Administration and Budgeting
Bureau of Finance Administration
Agency for International Development (AID)
320 21st St., NW, Room 3847
Washington, DC 20523   202-647-6671

The Economic Support Fund (ESF) supports U.S. economic, political, and security interests and advances U.S. foreign policy objectives. The resources that ESF provides curb the spread of economic and political disruption and help friends and allies to deal with threats on their security and independence. ESF is flexible economic assistance provided on a grant or loan basis. It may be used to sustain economic activity to address basic development needs, or to improve the basic framework of the existing system. Additional information is available in the *AID Congressional Presentation Document*, which is available from the Office of Legislative Affairs, 202-647-8441.

* Education Development in Developing Countries

Office of Education
Bureau for Research and Development, SA-18 Room 609
Agency for International Development (AID)
Washington, DC 20523-1815   703-875-4700

This office helps developing countries more efficiently allocate and use of their education resources, especially at the primary school level. To improve the quality of education, the office also develops appropriate and effective teaching technologies. And by developing educational communications and social marketing systems, researchers help improve AID's health and agriculture extension services. Contact the office above for a portfolio directory of projects and for further information.

* Energy Assessments

Energy Assessments Division
Forrestal Bldg., Room 7G-076
U.S. Department of Energy
Washington, DC 20585   202-586-6140

This office develops strategic assessments on critical international energy issues including: world oil market conditions, petroleum stocks, natural gas security, electricity policy, and energy environmental concerns.

* Energy Development in Developing Countries

Office of Energy and Infrastructure
Bureau for Research and Development
Agency for International Development (AID)
SA-18, Room 508
Washington, DC 20523   703-875-4203

With the Agency for International Development's (AID) Missions and Regional Bureaus, this office helps assisted countries develop appropriate energy services. Program goals with respect to programs in Less Developed Countries include: increased consideration of environmental criteria in projects; increased technical efficiency and financial performance of energy systems; greater private enterprise involvement in energy development and management; and expanded use of sustainable indigenous energy resources. Office projects include: Energy Planning and Policy Development Project; Energy and Environmental Policy Planning Project; and Biomass Energy Systems and Technology Project (BEST). The *Program Plan*, available from the office above, explains the programs of this office in pursuit of that goal and how the Office is organized to implement those programs.

* Energy Emergencies

Office of Energy Emergencies Operations
Forrestal Bldg., Room 8F-073
U.S. Department of Energy
Washington, DC 20585   202-586-3271

This office is responsible for improving the Federal Government's ability to meet U.S. and allied energy requirements during catastrophic disasters.

* Energy Policy

Office for International Affairs and Energy Emergencies
Room 7C-016, Forrestal Building
U.S. Department of Energy
Washington, DC 20585   202-586-5800

The office of the Assistance Secretary for International Affairs and Energy Emergencies is responsible for developing and directing international energy policy, including the international component of overall energy policy, and for coordinating the Department's energy emergency preparedness planning, and the encouragement of free trade in energy resources, services, equipment, and technology.

* Energy Organizations

Office of International Energy Organizations and Policy Development
Forrestal Bldg., Room 7G-046
U.S. Department of Energy
Washington, DC 20585   202-586-6140

This office develops objectives, generic policy positions, specific policies with respect to individual foreign countries, and prepares briefing papers for all U.S. Government energy-related bilateral and multilateral Ministerial meetings.

* Energy Publications

AID Document Information Services Clearinghouse
1500 Wilson Blvd, Suite 1010
Arlington, VA 22209-2404   703-351-4006 ext. 9624

The following reports of the Office of Energy and Infrastructure, Bureau for Research and Development, can be obtained from the office above (the Document no. follows the Office of Energy Report no.):

New Direction for AID, Renewable Energy Activities. February 1988 (88-01; PN-ABB-532).
The AID Experience with Independent Power Generation. August 1988 (88-14; PN-ABB-535).
Private Sector Participation in the Energy/Power Sector of Jamaica, Sept. 1990 (PN-ABH-191)
Poland: An Energy and Environmental Overview, Oct. 1990 (PN-ABH-045).

* Farmer-to-Farmer Program

Agriculture Sector Specialist
Office of Training and Program Support
Peace Corps, 1990 K St., NW, 9th Floor
Washington, DC 20526   202-606-3412

Working in collaboration with the Agency for International Development (AID) and Volunteers in Overseas Cooperative Assistance (VOCA), the Peace Corps has added this program to its Agriculture Sector. This office provides specific short-term (30 to 120 days) technical assistance to countries whose requests are approved in such areas as dairy production, vegetable production, and vegetable handling.

* Federal Aviation Administration (FAA)

U.S. Department of Transportation
Washington, DC 20590   202-267-3883

The problems of aircraft hijacking and sabotage remain pressing concerns of the Federal Aviation Administration (FAA). The agencies response has included tightened airport security and the planned deployment of advanced explosive-detection systems around the world in coming years.

* Fishing Multi-Lateral Agreements

Bureau of Oceans and International Environmental
and Scientific Affairs
U.S. Department of State
2201 C St., NW, Room 5806
Washington, DC 20520   202-647-2335

This office negotiates fishing agreements with countries who want to fish within the U.S. economic zone, along with agreements with countries within whose zone the U.S. would like to fish. They are also responsible for multi-lateral agreements dealing with fishing on the high seas, with particular attention to conservation issues. Information is available on these agreements and on fishery concerns in general.

* Fishing Vessels International Claims

Assistant Legal Advisor for International Claims
Office of the Legal Advisor
U.S. Department of State
2201 C St., NW
Washington, DC 20520   202-632-7810

The Fishermen's Protective Act provides for reimbursement for financial loss to owners of vessels registered in the United States for fines paid to secure the release of vessels seized for operation in waters not recognized as territorial waters by the United States. No registration or payment of premiums is required prior to the seizure in order to qualify for reimbursement.

* Food for Peace Program

Bureau for Food and Humanitarian Assistance
Office of Food for Peace
Room 300, SA-8
Agency for International Development (AID)
Washington, DC 20523   703-351-0107

To obtain information on the Food for Peace Program, contact the office above. To receive a copy of the *Food for Peace 1988 Annual Report,* contact the Operations office 703-351-0112, or the U.S. Department of Agriculture.

* Foreign Affairs Education

Foreign Service Institute
1400 Key Boulevard SA-3
Arlington, VA 22209   703-235-8727

The Foreign Service Institute provides foreign affairs and language training for employees of the State Department and other government agencies involved with foreign affairs.

* Foreign Aid Development Reports

AID Document Information Services Clearinghouse
1500 Wilson Blvd, Suite 1010
Arlington, VA 22209-2404   703-351-4006 ext. 9624

The Agency for International Development's (AID) Center for Development Information and Evaluation (CDIE) produces an evaluation publications series includes a broad range of subjects of interest to those working in international development. The series comprises project impact evaluations, program evaluations, special studies, program design and evaluation methodology reports, and discussion papers. The *CDIE Evaluation Publications List* is arranged by general subject category and by type of report within each category or subcategory. Each document has an identification number and is available in hard copy or on microfiche. A partial list of the documents follows:

AID's Experience in Latin America and The Caribbean. May 1990, N. 69 (PN-AAX-232).
AID Assistance to Local Government: Experience and Issues. November 1983, No. 17 (PN-AAL-026).
Agricultural Policy Analysis and Planning: A Summary of Two Recent Analyses of AID-Supported Projects Worldwide. August 1988, No. 55 (PN-AAX-205).
Agricultural Research in Northeastern Thailand. May 1982, No. 34 (PN-AAJ-615).
An Evaluation of the African Emergency Food Assistance Program in Chad. 1984-1985, June 1987, No. 48 (PN-AAL-091).
Child Survival Programs in Egypt. Feb. 1990, No. 73 (PN-AAX-235).
Conducting Mini Surveys in Developing Countries. Dec. 1990, No. 15 (PN-AAX-249).
Development Assistance and Health Programs: Issues of Sustainability. October 1987, No. 23 (PN-AAL-097).
Natural Resource Management: AID's Experience in Nepal. Oct. 1990, No. 41 (PN-AAX-247).
Private Sector: Ideas and Opportunities -- A review of Basic Concepts and Selected Experience. June 1982, No. 14 (PN-AAJ-618).
Private Volunteer Organizations and the Promotion of Small-Scale Enterprise. July 1985, No. 27 (PN-AAL-055).
Promoting Trade and Investment in Constrained Environments: AID Experience in Latin America and the Caribbean. May 1990. No. 69 (PN-AAX-237).
Small Farmer Attitudes and Aspirations. May 1989, No. 26 (PN-AAX-217).
Terms of Endowment: A New AID Approach to Institutional Development. Dec. 1990, No. 3 (PN-ABG-001).
The Impact of Irrigation on Development: Issues for Comprehensive Evaluation Study. October 1980, No. 9 (PN-AAJ-208).
Reaching the Rural Poor: Indigenous Health Practitioners Are There Already. March 1979, No. 1 (PN-AAG-685).
Rural Development: Lessons From Experience -- Highlights of the Seminar Proceedings. January 1989, No. 25 (PN-AAX-214).
Strengthening the Agriculture Research Capacity of the Less Developed Countries: Lessons From AID Experience. September 1983, No. 10 (PN-AAL-020).
Study of Family Planning Program Effectiveness. April 1979, No. 5 (PN-AAG-672).
Universities for Development: Report of the Joint Indo-U.S. Impact Evaluation of the Indian Agricultural Universities. September 1988, No. 68 (PN-AAX-206).
Women in Development: AID's Experience, 1973-1985. Vol. I, Synthesis Paper, March 1987, No. 18 (PN-AAL-087).

For more information on ordering documents or to obtain the CDIE Evaluation Publications List, contact the clearinghouse listed above.

* Foreign Aid Projects Database

Development Information Center
Room 105 SA-18
Agency for International Development (AID)
Washington, DC 20523-1801   703-875-4818

The Development Information System (DIS) contains information on Agency for International Development (AID) projects, programs, policies, and research, as well as associated project, research, and technical documents. Anyone can search DIS databases through the easy-to-use Menu DOS system on the library's public computer terminal. Records can be located by subject, author, title, project number, date, project status, or bibliographic type (e.g. project paper, evaluation, research report). All of these fields can be combined during one search. The MenuDIS quick reference guide to the right of the terminal can help you with your search. For more information on the Agency for International Development's three main databases, "Document," "Project," and "Library Catalog," contact the office above.

* Foreign Assistance Funding

House Committee on Appropriations
Subcommittee on Foreign Operations
U.S. House of Representatives
H-218 Capitol Building
Washington, DC 20515   202-225-2041

In recent years, the House Appropriations Subcommittee on Foreign Operations has played a very important role in the allocation of American foreign assistance. Subcommittee hearings, reports, and markup bills provide a rich source of information on foreign assistance policy. For more information, contact the subcommittee. To order bills and reports, contact the House Documents room at 202-225-3456 and have the House Resolution or Public Law number ready. Prints are free if in stock.

* Foreign Attitudes of USA

Office of Research
United States Information Agency (USIA)
301 Fourth St., SW, Room 352
Washington, DC 20547   202-619-4965

Assessing foreign attitudes is one of the U.S. Information Agency's (USIA) prime responsibilities. A daily summary of worldwide media reaction to events of concern to the United States is used throughout the official diplomatic community. The research staff also amasses information for use by the White House, the U.S. Department of State, government agencies and U.S. Information Agency staff in assessing issues. Interested persons can obtain U.S. Information Agency research reports from depository libraries throughout the country. A list of these libraries is available.

* Foreign Disaster Assistance

Office of U.S. Foreign Disaster Assistance (OFDA)
Agency for International Development (AID)
320 21st St., NW, Room 1262A
Washington, DC 20523   202-647-8924

The office administers Agency for International Development's (AID) overseas disaster assistance program. The office involves other U.S. Government agencies, voluntary and international organizations, and the U.S. private sector to meet the demands of disaster relief, rehabilitation, preparedness, early warning, and mitigation in countries stricken or threatened by natural or man-made disasters, including earthquakes, floods, cyclones, volcanoes, accidents, and civil strife. The Office of U.S. Foreign Disaster Assistance (OFDA) provides technical assistance and training for the development of government disaster assistance programs, technology transfer for improved prediction and warning systems, and material and personnel resources for emergency relief and rehabilitation. An *Annual Report* detailing this office's activities is available by calling the above number.

* Foreign Economic Aid Projects

AID Document Information Services Clearinghouse
1500 Wilson Blvd
Suite 1010
Arlington, VA 22209-2404   703-351-4006 ext. 9624

Reports containing information on the Agency for International Development's (AID) projects may be obtained from the above facility for a minimal fee. One may also wish to subscribe to *Research and Development Abstracts* for a listing of available material for $10 per year.

* Foreign Economic Impact on U.S. Employment

Office of International Economic Affairs
Bureau of International Labor Affairs
200 Constitution Ave., NW, Room S5325
Washington, DC 20210   202-523-7597

The Labor Department's foreign economic research program evaluates the effects of foreign economic developments on the earnings and employment of U.S. workers. This includes quantitative analysis of the impact of policies on international trade, investment, and technology transfer. Often undertaken in response to congressionally-mandated studies or to requests from other executive branch agencies, research is conducted by staff economists and supplemented by outside research contractors. Studies undertaken during FY 1991 include: the effects of the Proposed North American Free Trade Area on U.S. workers; the implications for U.S. workers and the lessons on economic integration of EC 1992; and seventh annual report on the Caribbean Basin Economic Recovery Act. Studies are also released through the Labor Department's *Economic Discussion Paper* series. A complete list of the research is available by contacting this office.

* Foreign Language Training

Defense Language Institute
Foreign Language Center
AISO Library
Presidio of Monterey, CA 93944   408-647-5572

The Defense Language Institute is one of the world's largest language training centers. The holdings of its library--over 100,000 books in 50 languages--are available through a national inter-library loan program. The non-resident division offers foreign language courses for sale. A catalog of the languages available may be obtained for $5.25. Write or call for brochures on the Institute and information regarding inter-library loans.

* Foreign Policy and Energy

Office of International Affairs
Forrestal Bldg., Room 7C-034
U.S. Department of Energy
Washington, DC 20585   202-586-5918

This office is responsible for the development and conduct of international energy policy consistent with U.S. foreign policy objectives. It also promotes international energy research and development collaboration policy and the strengthening of the international nuclear non-proliferation regime.

* Foreign Policy Briefings and Speakers

Office of Public Liaison
Bureau of Public Affairs
2201 C St NW, Room 5831
U.S. Department of State
Washington, DC 20520   202-647-1710

Foreign policy briefings are arranged on request for interested groups to the extent that resources permit. These briefings can be on a variety of topics, such as foreign economic environment or human rights.

* Foreign Policy Public Forums

Office of Public Programs
Bureau of Public Affairs
U.S. Department of State
2201 C St., NW, Room 5831
Washington, DC 20520   202-647-1710

The State Department encourages public dialogue on foreign policy topics through nationwide public appearances by Department officials. The following is a list of public programs available:

Conferences - National foreign policy conferences are scheduled throughout the year for leaders from business, labor, government, and other organizations. Regional foreign policy conferences are held several times a year in major cities. These day-long meetings involve senior department officials, a variety of local co-sponsoring organizations, and flexible formats to encourage the free exchange of information and opinions.

Seminars - Foreign policy seminars attract 30 to 40 specialists from the private sector together with Department officials for informal discussions. The Bureau offers 1 or 2 day seminars for business executives and media representatives, emphasizing international economic and other foreign policy issues.

International Relations and Defense

Liaison with Nongovernmental Organizations - NGO liaison is initiated and maintained with national organizations interested in foreign policy issues. Briefings on these issues are organized for NGO leaders and staffers and other special interest groups.

* Foreign Press Centers

Washington Foreign Press Center
529 Fourteenth St., NW, Suite 898
Washington, DC 20045   202-724-1640

New York Foreign Press Center
110 E. 59th St.
New York, NY 10022   212-826-4722

Los Angeles Foreign Media Liaison Office
11000 Wilshire Blvd.
Los Angeles, CA 90024   310-575-7693

Press offices in Washington, DC, New York, and Los Angeles assist foreign journalists, resident and visiting, in acquiring press credentials and gaining access to newsmakers. Facilities at the Press Centers include Wire New Services, television monitors, copying machines, TV and Radio studios, and a conference facilities.

* Foreign Service Career Counseling

Personnel Office
Special Services Branch
United States Information Agency (USIA)
301 Fourth St., SW, Room 525
Washington, DC 20547   202-619-4695

Information on career opportunities for serving Foreign Service Officers is available from this office.

* Foreign Service Careers

Personnel Office
Special Recruitment Office
United States Information Agency (USIA)
301 Fourth St., SW, Room 518
Washington, DC 20547   202-619-4659

Information is available for those interested in taking the Foreign Service Exam. Call or write in August or September for a registration and sample Foreign Service exam test booklet.

* Foreign Studies of America and English

Division for the Study of the U.S.
Office of Academic Programs
Bureau of Educational and Cultural Affairs
United States Information Agency (USIA)
301 Fourth Street, SW
Room 256
Washington, DC 20547   202-619-4557

The U.S. Information Agency (USIA) supports academic programs for the study of America, as well as the study of the English language. It acts as liaison between American and foreign universities, academic associations, and scholars, and supports 200 cultural centers and binational centers in 100 countries for the study of the English language. It publishes teaching materials in many languages and numerous publications, including *English Teaching Forum*, a professional quarterly for English teachers worldwide. It also sponsors many seminars, institutes, study tours, exchange programs and curriculum support geared to the study of America in foreign countries.

* Forest Management and Education Worldwide

Natural Resources Sector
Office of Training and Programming Support
Peace Corps
1990 K St., NW
Washington, DC 20526   202-606-3412

Working in 38 countries, forestry specialists design and execute forest management plans designed to help combat the overcutting, droughts, and deserts that are beginning to threaten many tropical forests around the world. They also help establish nurseries, curricula in environmental education, and skills in tropical fruit cultivation.

* Forestry, Environment, and Natural Resources

Office of Environment and Natural Resources
Bureau for Research and Development, Room 509 SA-18
Agency for International Development (AID)
Washington, DC 20523-1812   703-875-4106

To maximize the amount of development that is sustainable, the Agency is working toward networking of worldwide development planning. This office's strategy includes providing technical assistance to government and non-government agencies working toward the development of national environmental policy and programs which will contribute to sustainable economic development; and to provide assistance in research and the transfer of appropriate technologies. For more information or to obtain the *User's Guide to the Office of Environment and Natural Resources*, contact the office above.

* Fulbright Foreign Policy Scholarships

Office of Academic Programs
600 Maryland Ave. SW
Washington, DC 20024   800-726-0479

This office develops and runs all academic programs of the U.S. Information Agency (USIA), including the best-known educational exchange, the Fulbright Scholarship program. About 5,000 Fulbright grants are awarded each year to American students, teachers, and scholars to work abroad and to foreign citizens to teach, study, and conduct research in the U.S. In addition to the Fulbright program, the Academic Exchange Programs Division of this office administers grants to private agencies conducting complementary programs to the Fulbright academic exchanges, and has responsibilities for foreign research centers, Fulbright commissions, and seminars for foreign Fulbright students. Contact this office for more information and application forms for the Fulbright program.

* Fulbright Teacher Exchange Program

Office of Academic Programs
600 Maryland Ave. SW
Washington, DC 20024   800-726-0479

Opportunities are available for elementary and secondary school teachers and administrators, and college faculty to attend seminary or teach in schools abroad. Grants in most cases include round trip transportation. Applications must be submitted by October 15 for the following summer or academic years' program. Contact the Office of Academic Programs for information/applications.

* General Accounting Office International Affairs Reports

General Accounting Office
P.O. Box 6015
Gaithersburg, MD 20877   202-275-6241

The General Accounting Office (GAO) publishes dozens of reports each year on different American programs overseas. These reports, as well as reports published in previous years, are available free by request from GAO, up to five copies. Collectively, these reports are a treasure trove of information on U.S. policy. In addition, this office can put you on the mailing list for the monthly index of reports.

* Geographic Boundaries and Disputes

Office of the Geographer
Bureau of Intelligence and Research
U.S. Department of State
2201 C St., NW, Room 8742
Washington, DC 20520   202-647-1205

This office distributes several publications which contain a variety of geographical information. Some of them include:

Geographic Notes. Contains brief analyses of current issues relevant to United States foreign policy. These analyses provide a geographical perspective on such foreign policy-related topics such as boundary, sovereignty, and territorial disputes. Subscriptions cost $8 per year and can be ordered from the above office or from the Government Printing Office; 202-512-1800.

International Boundary Studies. This is a series of specific boundary papers. Recent studies analyze developments in the borders between Iraq-Saudi Arabia, Iraq-Kuwait, and Argentina-Chile.

Cartoanalytic Briefs. These are occasionally published large thematic maps depicting developments in such regions as the former U.S.S.R. or Yugoslavia. They are available from the National Information Technical Service; 703-487-4650.

* Geographic Bureaus

Agency for International Development (AID)
320 21st St., NW
Washington, DC 20523

These Bureaus are the principal Agency for International Development (AID) line offices with responsibility for the planning, formulation, and management of United States economic development and/or supporting assistance programs in their respective areas overseas. An annual budget of proposed Bureau activities is submitted for approval, and a program and budget is presented to Congress through the Policy Coordination Office. The Bureaus also represent the agency before the press and public as required.

Bureau for Africa	202-647-7371
Bureau for Latin America and the Caribbean	202-647-8246
Bureau for Asia	202-647-7302
Bureau for Europe and the Near East	202-647-9119
Bureau for the Near East	202-647-0462

* Grants for International Research Development

Agency Center for University Cooperation and Development
Bureau of Research and Development, SA-38, Room 900
Agency for International Development (AID)
Washington, DC 20523-3801   703-816-0295

The Agency for International Development (AID) links the land grant universities with the historically black colleges and universities both in the United States and abroad in an effort of cooperation. Research grants, usually in the amount of $100,000, are given in the areas of health, agriculture, rural development and nutrition to historically black colleges and universities in 30 countries. The presidentially appointed Board for International Food and Agricultural Development formulates policy and projects to foster the working relationship of agricultural universities in AID programs. Research projects are listed in the *Commerce Business Daily* for which colleges and universities can compete. Unsolicited research proposals by individuals are also considered, but only a limited number are accepted. For information on the guidelines for these proposals, contact the above office.

* Health Assistance

World Health Organization (WHO)
525 23rd St. NW
Washington, DC 20037   202-861-3305

The World Health Organization (WHO) helps countries strengthen their health systems by building up services for the individual, family, and community; health institutions, referral systems; and the provision of essential drugs, other supplies and equipment. The organization promotes research on appropriate health technologies, and social and behavioral approaches that could lead to healthier lives in both the industrialized and developing societies. WHO has major programs to combat global diarrhoeal disease, smallpox, and river blindness. In addition, it has expanded the immunization program in recent years and hopes to protect all the worlds children in 1990 from diphtheria, pertussis, tetanus, measles, polio, and tuberculosis.

* Health Development

Office of Health
Bureau for Research and Development
Room 1200, SA-18
Agency for International Development (AID)
Washington, DC 20523   703-875-4600

This office serves as the Agency for International Development's (AID) principal source of technical expertise and assistance on international health issues and projects. Contact this office for more information, or to obtain a copy of the *Directory of the Office of Health, Bureau for Research and Development*.

* High Seas Law Enforcement

Operational Law Enforcement Division
Office of Law Enforcement and Defense Operations
U.S. Coast Guard
U.S. Department of Transportation
2100 2nd St., SW, Room 3110
Washington, DC 20593-0001   202-267-1890

As the primary maritime law enforcement agency for the U.S., the Coast Guard enforces Federal laws, treaties, and international agreements to which the U.S. is a party. The Coast Guard may conduct investigations when violations are suspected, such as smuggling, drug trafficking, or polluting. Empowered to board and inspect vessels routinely as well, the Guard also conducts :"suspicionless" boardings to prevent violations. To report suspicious or questionable activity on boats, or to complain about an improperly conducted boarding, call the Boating Safety Hotline, 800-368-5647; or 202-267-0780 in DC, or contact your local Coast Guard commander. The office listed above can provide you with information about the Coast Guard's law enforcement role and the National Narcotics Border Interdiction System, which coordinates multi-agency and international operations with other countries to suppress narcotics trafficking.

* Historian of the State Department

Bureau of Public Affairs
Columbia Plaza Office Building
2401 E St., NW, Room 3100
U.S. Department of State
Washington, DC 20522   202-663-1122

The office of the Historian has twin missions: to compile and publish the official diplomatic record of the United States in the series *Foreign Relations of the United States*; and to prepare policy-related historical research studies for the key officers of the U.S. Department of State. *Foreign Relations of the United States* is a multi-volume series in which the Historian's staff seeks, arranges, and edits principal papers which comprise the record of American foreign policy. Although principally based on State Department records, the series also is derived from White House files, the archives of other agencies, and, where relevant, papers and recollections of former officials. Resources and the pace at which the documents are declassified determine the rate at which the series is published. The office also publishes the *American Foreign Policy* series which contains texts of official messages, addresses, statements, reports, and communications which best convey the objectives of U.S. foreign policy. Microfiche supplements of documents are also available. These publications are available from the Government Printing Office.

* Historically Black Colleges and International Development Research

Agency Center for University Cooperation and Development
Bureau for Research and Development, Room 900, SA-38
Agency for International Development (AID)
Washington, DC 20523-3801   703-816-0295

The Agency for International Development's (AID) Historically Black Colleges and Universities (HBCUs) Research Program seeks to take advantage of the strong interest of HBCUs in development assistance activities. Through this program, AID hopes to involve researchers from HBCUs in the problems of developing countries. Inclusion in the research program is determined through an AID formal review process. Contact this office for more information.

* House Committee on Foreign Affairs

U.S. House of Representatives
2170 Rayburn House Office Building
Washington, DC 20515   202-225-5021

The House Foreign Affairs Committee is a rich source of information on most all aspects of American foreign policy. Committee hearings include testimony from Government experts, academics, think tanks, and interested private individuals. For committee hearings and reports, contact the above number or call the House Documents room at 202-225-3456. When calling the House Documents room, have the bill or Public Law number ready. Further information is available from the geographic subcommittees.

Subcommittees:

Africa	202-226-7807
Arms Control, International Security	202-225-8926
Asian and Pacific Affairs	202-226-7801
Europe and the Middle East	202-225-3345
Human Rights and International Organizations	202-226-7825
International Economic Policy	202-225-7820
International Operations	202-225-3324
Western Hemisphere	202-226-7812

* Housing in Developing Countries

Office of Housing and Urban Programs
Bureau for Private Enterprise
Agency for International Development (AID)
320 21st St., NW, Room 401, SA-2
Washington, DC 20523-0214   202-663-2530

This program facilitates private financing for shelter for lower income families in developing countries by guaranteeing repayment to U.S. lenders for projects requested by these countries. Innovative programs are financed, such as upgrading the provisions of sewerage, potable water, electricity, and home improvements. Basic urbanized lots are financed for the construction of family dwellings, and low-cost, expandable core housing units are made available. An Annual Report detailing office activities is available.

* Human Rights Violations Worldwide
U.S. Department of State
Bureau of Human Rights and Humanitarian Affairs
2201 C St., NW, Room 7802
Washington, DC 20520 202-647-1383

Country Reports on Human Rights in 1991 covers the human rights practices of all nations that receive U.S. foreign assistance, those nations that do not receive it but are members of the United Nations, and those few nations that are not members of the U.N. Each country's section begins with a brief description of the country, including information on political parties and security forces. It then is broken down into several area. The first deals with respect for human rights and includes information on political killings, disappearances, torture, and denial of public trial. Other sections include information on respect for civil liberties, such as freedom of speech, press and religion, respect for political rights and worker rights, as well as information on discrimination. This annual report can be purchased from the Government Printing Office, Superintendent of Documents, Washington, DC 20402; 202-512-1800.

* Immigrant Visas and Immigrant Status
Central Office
Immigration and Naturalization Service
425 I Street, NW
Washington, DC 20536 202-307-1501

Publications and tape recorded messages about immigration are available from this central office. However, field offices operate in most states and these local phone numbers appear in the Law and Social Justice Chapter and, of course, are easy to obtain from the directory assistance operators. When calling the tape recorded telephone number, 202-307-1501, enter one of the number codes below which corresponds to the information about immigration and naturalization that you need:

301 Filing petitions to obtain immediate relative status (I-130)
302 Filing petitions to sponsor prospective immigrant employee (I-140)
303 How an alien in the United States may request a change of status to permanent resident status (I-485)
304 When a United States citizen marries a foreign national outside the USA
506 Fiance/fiancee visa (I-129F)
305 How to file joint petitions for spouse to remove conditional basis of their permanent resident status (I-751)
307 Orphan petitions (I-600)
306 Immigration benefits for adoption before 16th birthday (I-130)
308 Application for asylum in the USA (I-589)
309 Permanent residence for beneficiaries of approved asylum applications

* Immigration Act of 1990
Central Office
Immigration and Naturalization Service
425 I Street, NW 800-755-0777
Washington, DC 20536 202-307-1501

On November 29, 1990 President Bush signed into law the Immigration Act of 1990. This resulted in major changes in immigration which affect immigrants and non-immigrants, Philippine WWII veterans desiring American citizenship, El Salvadorean nationals, and many others with immigration related concerns. One major provision offers Temporary Protective Status (TPS) to nationals of El Salvador. Call the toll-free number listed above to obtain up-to-the-minute information on Immigration Act regulations and procedures as they become finalized. To hear recorded messages detailing established Immigration and Naturalization Service (INS) regulations, contact the "Ask Immigration" system at 202-307-1501.

* Impact of Human Rights Activities on Foreign Policy
U.S. Department of State
Bureau of Human Rights and Humanitarian Affairs
2201 C St., NW, Room 7802
Washington, DC 20520 202-647-1383

This bureau ensures that consideration of human rights is a regular part of U.S. foreign policy decision-making, as expressed through direct contacts between the U.S. and individual countries, quiet diplomacy, and continuous public activity. In the

1970s, Congress passed a series of laws linking human rights conditions in specific countries to actions by the U.S. government, such as most-favored-nation tariff status, U.S. government credits guaranties, and economic and military assistance. Congress has mandated that this bureau submit an annual report reviewing human rights practices country by country.

* Intelligence: The Acme of Skill
Public Affairs
Central Intelligence Agency (CIA)
Washington, DC 20505 703-351-2053

Two free Central Intelligence Agency (CIA) brochures are available to the public include *Intelligence: The Acme of Skill*, and *The Factbook on Intelligence*. The Factbook contains background information on the Central Intelligence Agency as well as information on how to order CIA publications which are available to the public.

* Inter-American Affairs
Public Affairs
Bureau of Inter-American Affairs
U.S. Department of State
2201 C St., NW, Room 5913
Washington, DC 20520 202-647-472

This bureau prepared foreign policy documents relating to U.S. relations with all countries of the Western Hemisphere except Canada. The documents focus on issues revolving around democracy, human rights, economic policy, narcotics, and promotion of U.S. security and commercial interests.

* Inter-American Foundation Publications
Inter-American Foundation (IAF)
Publications Office
1515 Wilson Blvd.
Rosslyn, VA 22209 703-841-3821

Established in 1969 by Congress as an independent agency, the Inter-American Foundation makes grants to agricultural cooperatives, community associations, and small urban enterprises in Central and Latin America. The Inter-American Foundation also grants fellowships to University students from the Western Hemisphere. The following is a sampling of the free titles published in English, Spanish, and Portuguese.

The Inter-American Foundation and the Small- and Micro-Enterprise Sector
What to Think About Cooperatives: A Guide From Bolivia
In Support of Women: Ten Years of Funding by the Inter-American Foundation
A Review of the Inter-American Foundation's Support for Health Activities
Bottom-up Development in Haiti
The Inter-American Foundation in the Making
In Partnership with People: An Alternative Development Strategy
Grassroots Development
Inter-American Foundation Annual Report.
Direct to the Poor: An Anthology of articles from Grassroots Development.

* International Aid Public Information
Office of Public Inquiry
Bureau for External Affairs
Agency for International Development (AID)
320 21st St., NW
Washington, DC 20523 202-647-1850

For further information on the programs and projects within the Agency, contact the office above.

* International Aid Report to Congress
Office of Public Inquiry
Bureau for External Affairs
Agency for International Development (AID)
320 21st St., NW
Washington, DC 20523 202-647-1850

Congressional Presentation is a seven volume document that describes the Agency for International Development program of each developing country. Statistical information is included for present and prior years. Copies are available in limited supply from the above office and are also available for use at the Center for Development Information and Evaluation, 1601 N. Kent St., Room 105, Arlington, VA; 703-875-4818.

* International Air Transportation

Office of International Aviation
Policy and International Affairs
Office of the Secretary of Transportation
U.S. Department of Transportation
400 7th Street, SW, Room 6402
Washington, DC 20590   202-366-2423

This office studies and develops U.S. policy with regard to international aviation. It ensures cooperation between U.S. and foreign-flag airlines and negotiates air service agreements with other countries.

* International Conferences Coordination

Bureau of International Organization Affairs
U.S. Department of State
2201 C St., NW, Room 1517
Washington, DC 20520   202-647-6875

This office organizes over 700 intergovernmental conferences each year. They accredit all participating delegations and decide who represents the U.S. and what information is allowed to be shared.

* International Development Resource Materials

Development Information Center, Room 105 SA-18
Agency for International Development (AID)
Washington, DC 20535-1801   703-875-4818

The Agency for International Development (AID) Library also has a collection of non-AID materials. You can identify materials acquired after April 1984 using the on-line catalog in the Development Information System, and earlier acquisitions will be found in the card catalog.

* International Energy Analysis

Office of International Energy Analysis
Forrestal Bldg., Room 7G-090
U.S. Department of Energy (DOE)
Washington, DC 20585   202-586-5893

This office is responsible for monitoring and analyzing world energy market developments and the international political, economic and strategic factors that influence these developments; providing policy recommendations on international energy issues; and managing U.S./Department of Energy (DOE) participation in international energy related organizations.

* International Law Library

Law Library
Library of Congress
Washington, DC 20540   202-707-5073

As the world's largest and most comprehensive library of foreign, international, and comparative law, the Law Library provides information for all known legal systems including common law, civil law, Roman law, canon law, Chinese law, Jewish and Islamic law, and ancient and medieval law. Specialists with knowledge of more than fifty languages provide reference and research service in all known legal systems. U.S. legislative documents housed here include the *Congressional Record* (and its predecessors), the serial set, a nearly complete set of bills and resolutions, current documents, committee prints, reports, hearings, etc. plus a complete set of U.S. Supreme Court records and briefs and collections of U.S. Court of Appeals records and briefs. The law library has only two divisions:

Western Law Division
United States, Australia, Canada, Great Britain, India, New Zealand, Pakistan, certain other countries of the British Commonwealth and their dependent territories, Eire, Spain and Portugal, Latin America, Puerto Rico, the Philippines, and Spanish- and Portuguese-language states of Africa: 202-707-5077.

Eastern Law Division
Nations of Europe and their possessions, except Spain and Portugal, nations of East and Southeast Asia including China, Indonesia, japan, Korea, Thailand, and former British and French possessions in the area, Middle Eastern countries, including the Arab states, Turkey, Iran, and Afghanistan, and all African countries except Spanish- and Portuguese-language states and possessions: 202-707-5085.

* International Visitors Program

Bureau of Educational and Cultural Affairs
United States Information Agency (USIA)
301 Fourth St., SW, Room 255
Washington, DC 20547   202-619-5217

Some 2,600 foreign leaders from many fields are invited each year by the U.S. Information Agency (USIA) to meet with their counterparts in the United States, either joining group projects or an individually tailored program to learn about our society. Arrangements for visitors' programs are made by USIA, often with the cooperation of several private nonprofit organizations with support from the Agency. In addition to these visits, partially or wholly funded by USIA, another 2,000 Voluntary Visitors participate in similar programs, traveling at their own or their governments' expense.

* International Youth Exchange

The Bureau of Educational and Cultural Affairs
United States Information Agency (USIA)
301 Fourth St., SW, Room 357
Washington, DC 20547   202-619-6299

This office administers grants to non-profit organizations for international educational and cultural exchanges for youths 15 to 30 years of age. The principal objective of youth exchange programming is the promotion of better understanding of U.S. society among foreign youth. The program has stimulated over 22,000 exchanges since its inception in 1982. Organizations wishing to become sponsors, or individuals wishing to be put in contact with sponsoring organizations, can receive free information from this office.

* Japan-United States Friendship Commission

Japan-United States Friendship Commission
1120 Vermont Ave. NW
Washington, DC 20005   202-275-7712

The Commission was established in 1975 as an independent government agency to promote friendship and cultural understanding between the United States and Japan. The endowment fund contained some $14 million in 1990. The Commission funds five categories of projects: Japanese Study in American Education; American Studies in Japanese Education; Policy-oriented Research; Public Affairs/Education; and The Arts. To this end, it provided some $1.8 million and 240 million Yen in grants in FY 1990. Grant information and applications can be obtained from the above address.

* Junior Foreign Service Officer Trainee Program

Personnel Office
Special Recruitment Branch
United States Information Agency (USIA)
301 Fourth St., SW, Room 525
Washington, DC 20547   202-619-4667

Each December the Foreign Service Officer Examination is held at many locations in this country and overseas to screen candidates for the Junior Officer Trainee Program. Date, locations, and other information is available from this office.

* Latin American/Caribbean Foreign Assistance

Inter-American Foundation
Program Office
1515 Wilson Blvd.
Rosslyn, VA 22209   703-841-3855

The Inter-American Foundation (IAF) database monitors projects that receive IAF funding, and can be search by the following areas: type of project, urban/rural area, type of beneficiary, whether it generates income, and more. Contact this office for more information on the database or searching the files.

* Law of the Sea Treaty

Office of Oceans Law and Policy
Bureau of Oceans and International Environmental
 and Scientific Affairs
U.S. Department of State
2201 C St., NW, Room 5805A
Washington, DC 20520   202-647-9098

In working out policy regarding use of the world's oceans, this office monitors countries to see if they conform to the Law of the Sea Treaty, and negotiate U.S. policy regarding the Treaty. This is a large treaty with over 300 articles, dealing with such issues as uses of the outer continental shelf, pollution, fishing, use of Straits and territorial zones. As of early 1992 51 nations had ratified the treaty. The treaty comes into force when ratified by 60 countries. The United States has not signed the treaty due to concerns about the seabed mining article, but observes the provisions of the treaty as customary law.

International Relations and Defense

* Law Enforcement Overseas

Federal Bureau of Investigation (FBI)
10th and Pennsylvania Ave, NW
Washington, DC 20535   202-324-3000

While primarily a domestic law enforcement agency, the Federal Bureau of Investigation (FBI) does engage in some law enforcement activities overseas. The Bureau posts legal attaches in some American embassies overseas as well as maintaining liaison functions with foreign police forces. In certain areas, the United States maintains extraterritorial jurisdiction. For further information contact your local FBI office or the above number.

* Limited Resource Farming Projects

Agriculture Sector Specialist
Office of Training and Program Support
Peace Corps
1990 K St., NW, 9th Floor
Washington, DC 20526   202-606-3412

The Peace Corps' agricultural specialists provide personnel and services to 46 countries, and have recently become especially proficient in bee-keeping projects. They help teach and establish crop production techniques, basic production research, small animal husbandry, and are currently developing a project for iguana production in Honduras. This project, though, is only in the early planning stages and would not be implemented until the 1990s; it is being designed as a food resource and forest preservation program. They also work closely with volunteers in the U.S. and abroad to share culturally related information regarding such topics such as limited resource farming practices here and abroad.

* Marine Environmental Efforts

Environmental Coordination Branch
Marine Environmental Response Division
Office of Marine, Safety, Security,
    and Environmental Protection
U.S. Coast Guard
U.S. Department of Transportation
2100 2nd St., SW, Room 2100
Washington, DC 20593-0001   202-267-0421

Information is available here on the Coast Guard's role in international marine environmental efforts, such as representation in the U.N. International Maritime Consultative Organization. For further information on cooperative environmental efforts, contact the branch listed.

* Marine Science and International Policy

Office of Oceans and Fisheries Affairs
2201 C St., NW, Room 5801
U.S. Department of State
Washington, DC 20520   202-647-3262

This office handles international marine environment concerns, from the protection of whales to cleaning up oil spills, by negotiating bilateral and multilateral agreements.

* Maritime Boundaries

Office of Ocean Law and Policy
Bureau of Oceans and International Environmental
    and Scientific Affairs.
2201 C St., NW, Room 5805A
U.S. Department of State,
Washington, DC 20520   202-647-9098

This office tracks and analyzed national claims to maritime jurisdictions. It publishes *Limits in the Seas*, which details maritime boundaries. Contact the above office for more information.

* Maritime Organization

International Maritime Organization (IMO)
4 Albert Embankment
London SE1 7SR, England

The International Maritime Organization's (IMO) main objective is to facilitate co-operation among Governments on technical matters affecting international shipping and to ensure the highest standards of maritime safety, navigational efficiency, and prevention of maritime pollution of the sea. To these ends it prepares international conventions, recommendations, codes and other material on the technical aspects of shipping and related maritime matters.

* Maritime Trade Statistics

Trade Analysis Division (MAR-570)
Office of Trade and Analysis and Insurance
Maritime Administration
U.S. Department of Transportation
400 7th Street, SW
Washington, DC 20590   202-366-2282

Records on federally subsidized shipping companies are maintained by this Division. Information includes vessel name, port dates, and crew costs. The public can visit the document inspection room or write for information.

* Narcotics Cultivation Worldwide

Policy Coordination Office
Narcotics Coordinator
Agency for International Development (AID)
320 21st Street, NW
Washington, DC 20523   202-647-8383

The Agency for International Development (AID) in conjunction with other international agencies collects data about narcotics growing areas of the world and attempts channel economic development for narcotics producing areas into alternative crops and rural development. AID missions are involved in research for developing and testing alternative crops. Other agencies are responsible for the monitoring of enforcement and eradication of illegal narcotics cultivation.

* Natural Resources and the Environment

Document Information Services Clearinghouse
Agency for International Development (AID)
1500 Wilson Blvd., Suite 1010
Arlington, VA 22209-2404   703-351-4006

The following documents may be viewed in the Library on microfiche. Hard copies may be obtained from the address above. Note document identification numbers are included. Also, the Agency for International Development (AID) publishes a collection of *Country Environmental Profiles* which may assist persons doing research on the environmental issues of a specific country. A listing of these *Country Environmental Profiles* is available at the reference desk of the Library.

Arid and Semiarid Rangelands: Guidelines for Development.
    Handbook/Manual/Guide, 1987. PN-AAY-730.
Ecological Development in the Humid Topics: Guidelines for Planners. AID
    Supported Study by the Winrock International Institute of Agricultural
    Development, 1987. PN-ABB-421.
*Economics and Biological Diversity: Developing and Using Economic Incentives
    to Conserve Biological Resources.* AID Supported Study, Nov. 1988.
    PN-ABA-988 (Not available on microfiche).
Environment and Natural Resources. AID Policy Paper. Apr. 1988.
    PN-AAV-464.
Forest for the Trees: Government Policies and the Misuse of Forest Resources. AID
    Supported Study, May 1988. PN-ABB-973 (Not available on microfiche).
*Progress in Conserving Tropical Forests and Biological Diversity in Developing
    Countries: The 1987 Annual Report to Congress on the Implementation of
    Sections 118 and 119 of the Foreign Assistance Act, as amended.* AID
    Program Document, 27 June 1988. PN-AAY-764.
*Thailand Natural Resources Profile: Is the Resource Base for Thailand's
    Development Sustainable?* AID Environmental Assessment, Jan. 1987.
    PD-AAY-099.

* Near Eastern and South Asian Countries Update

Bureau of Near Eastern and South Asian Affairs
U.S. Department of State
2201 C St., NW, Room 6243
Washington, DC 20520   202-647-5151

This office develops United States foreign policy for the countries in North Africa, north of the Sahara, the Middle East, the Persian Gulf and West Asia. They follow political, social, and economic developments and prepare policy papers. Specialized offices and functions include the Special Envoy to the Afghan Resistance and the Office for Regional and Multilateral Force Observers Affairs. *Background Notes* and GIST summaries are available on the various countries, as well as foreign policy papers and speeches.

* Newspapers and Periodicals Worldwide

Library of Congress
Washington, DC 20540   202-707-5650

Hundreds of different newspapers and periodicals from all fifty states and countries around the world are available on microfilm for $30 for domestic and $35 for foreign publications. Subscriptions are available or single issues can be ordered. Orders must be prepaid or charged to a standing account at the Library of Congress.

* Nonimmigrant Visas and Nonimmigrant Status

Central Office, Immigration and Naturalization Service
425 I Street, NW
Washington, DC 20536   202-307-1501

Publications and tape recorded messages about immigration are available from this central office. However, field offices operate in most states and these local phone numbers appear in the Law and Social Justice Chapter and are easy to obtain from the directory assistance operators. When calling the tape recorded telephone number above, enter one of the number codes below which corresponds to the information about immigration and naturalization that you need:

501 Nonimmigrant or temporary visas
505 Temporary visitor's visa
502 How to request an extension of temporary stay (I-539)
504 Applying for a replacement arrival-departure document I-94 (I-102)
503 Change of status from one nonimmigrant classification to another nonimmigrant classification for purpose of work (I-506)
510 Requirements for classification as nonimmigrant treaty trader E-1 or treaty investor E-2.
508 Requirements for classification as nonimmigrant exchange alien J-1
507 Requirements for classification as nonimmigrant temporary workers H-1, H-2, and H-3, (I-129B)
509 Intracompany transfers L-1 (I-129L, I-129S)

* Non-Violent Conflict Resolution Grants

United States Institute of Peace
1550 M St., NW, Suite 900
Washington, DC 20005   202-457-1700

The Grants Program provides financial support to nonprofit organizations, official public institutions, and individuals to fund projects on various themes and topics of interest. Past projects have included the role of third-party negotiators in the resolution of regional conflicts, religious and ethical questions in war and peace, and the use of non-violent sanctions in confronting political violence. Call or write for more information regarding grant application procedures.

* Nuclear Non-Proliferation

Office of Nuclear Nonproliferation Policy
Forrestal Building, Room 7G-050
U.S. Department of Energy
Washington, DC 20585   202-586-6175

Implements U.S. Department of Energy non-proliferation programs and activities.

* Nutrition and Food Science

Office of Nutrition
Bureau for Research and Development, Suite 411, SA-18
Agency for International Development (AID)
Washington, DC 20523-1808   703-875-4003

This office's resources are invested at the "cutting edge" of nutrition science, food science, and technology and in creating mechanisms for adapting food and nutrition content to specific conditions and needs of host countries. As a result of these efforts, the Office has created programs in three major categories: child survival, household food security, and nutribusiness. The *1989 Interim Directory: Sustained Enhanced Nutritional Status for Everyone* (SENSE) will help you better understand this Bureau's nutrition programs. For more information on the Office of Nutrition, or to obtain a copy of the *Directory*, contact the office above.

* Nutrition and Health Education in Developing Countries

Health Programmer
Office of Training and Programming Support
Peace Corps
1990 K St., NW, 9th Floor
Washington, DC 20526   202-606-3412

Volunteers work to teach modern health-care techniques through programs on vaccination and hygiene and nursing. They design health curricula as well as teaching basic elements of nutrition.

* Opportunities for Women in Developing Countries

International Women's Program
Bureau of International Organization Affairs
U.S. Department of State
2201 C St., NW, Room 4334A
Washington, DC 20520   202-647-1155

Working through the United Nations Commission, this office strives to improve the lives of women in developing countries. Toward this end, this office develops and introduces resolutions to the U.N., and focuses on such issues as increasing literacy, equality in the law, and the availability of credit information.

* Organization of American States (OAS)

Documents Officer
Permanent Mission of the U.S.A. to the
  Organization of American States
U.S. Department of State
2201 C St., NW, Room 6489
Washington, DC 20520   202-647-8650

The Documents Officer can provide you with all reference documents and other general information concerning the Organization of American States.

* Organization of the U.S. State Department

Bureau of Public Affairs
U.S. Department of State
2201 C St., NW, Room 5819
Washington, DC 20520   202-647-6575

Department of State Today is a free publication which outlines the general organization of the State Department, including descriptions of the various Bureaus and their responsibilities. A list of public services is available, along with a section of charts, maps, and tables.

* Panama Canal Crisis Hotline

Office of the Ombudsman
Panama Canal Commission
Unit 2300
APO AA 34011   011 507-52-3305

The Office of the Ombudsman handles administrative problems, inefficiencies, and policy conflicts existing within the Panama Canal Commission and other US Government agencies on the Isthmus of Panama resulting from the Treaty. The office does its best to improve employee morale and their quality of life. Due to the recent political unrest in Panama, a "hotline" was established to help employees, dependents, area residents and others previously employed with U.S. Federal agencies on the Isthmus, work through their concerns and hardships. For more information, contact this office.

* Panama Canal Dredging Division

Engineering and Construction Bureau
Dredging Division
c/o Panama Canal Commission
Unit 2300
APO AA 34011   011 507-52-3305

The Dredging Division is responsible for maintenance and construction dredging; slide removal; inspection and maintenance of the Atlantic breakwater; operation and maintenance of navigational aids; the detection, containment, recovery, and disposal of oil pollution in Canal operating areas; and the removal and control of aquatic weeds through the use of chemical and biological means. For more information on the dredging operations, contact this office.

* Panama Canal Economic and Market Research

Economic Research and Market Development Division
The Office of Executive Planning
c/o Panama Canal Commission
Unit 2300
APO AA 34011   011 507-52-3305

As an agency of the U.S. Government, the Panama Canal Commission has a legal obligation to operate on a break-even basis, recovering all costs of operating, maintaining, and improving the Canal through tolls revenue. The agency tries to have a high standard of service at the lowest possible cost. As a reflection of this, toll rates have gone up only four times since the Canal opened in 1914. Operating costs are very carefully controlled so that it provides an economic advantage to world trade on many routes. Even if other world trade routes may be shorter in distance, the

Canal remains competitive because of its reliable, cost-effective service. For more information on operating costs, contact this office.

* Panama Canal Environmental Safeguards

Sanitation Branch, General Services Bureau
Panama Canal Commission
Unit 2300
APO AA 34011   011 507-52-3464

The Sanitation Branch carries out measures to control disease carrying organisms and environmental sanitation measures essential to maintaining a high standard of public health which can be enjoyed by Panama Canal Commission employees and their families. There is an effort to control insect vector and vermin by nonchemical methods. For more information, contact the above office.

* Panama Canal Logistical Support

Office of Logistical Support
General Services Bureau
Panama Canal Commission
4400 Dauphine St.
New Orleans, LA 70146-6800   504-948-5299

The Logistical Support Division provides centralized procurement, inventory management, warehousing, distribution, contract administration, and supply and property disposal support to Canal operations. For more information, contact this office.

* Panama Canal Publications and Audiovisuals

The Office of Public Affairs
c/o Panama Canal Commission
Unit 2300
APO AA 34011   507-52-3305

The Office of Public Affairs has available various publications including the *Panama Canal 75th Anniversary Commemorative Album* and *The Panama Canal Spillway* as well as press releases, brochures, and other matters of related interest are distributed to the work force and the public at large. A broad range of photographic and audio-visual support services were created as well. A limited number of projection prints are available for loan to individuals and groups interested in the canal and its operation. All films are 16mm color and sound. Individuals may obtain video tapes of all subjects by submitting a blank tape in the desired format and the payment of a transfer charge. Some examples of the available films for general audiences are as follows:

The Task That Never Ends. 1984. Depicts the on going job of maintaining and improving the channel of the Panama Canal, widening, deepening and straightening the water route.
The Vital Link. 1986. Depicts the role of the Panama Canal in world commerce with a layman's introduction to the people and methods of Canal operations. Details of lockages, traffic control, and communications at the crossroads of the world.
1986 Landslide. 1987. Shows the resumption of the Cucaracha Slide in October, 1986. Measures taken to maintain Canal traffic while the obstruction was removed and remedial actions taken.

Some examples of the available films of special interest to engineers and mechanical craftsmen include the following:

Locks Overhaul - Strut Arms. 1981. A detailed description of strut arm removal prior to gate or bullwheel removal and replacement.
Locks Overhaul - Bullwheels. 1982. A detailed description of bullwheel removal and replacement.

There are also films of special interest to canal operating personnel. Films are available in both Spanish and English. For a complete listing of films produced by the Panama Canal Commission, contact the above office.

* Panama Canal Traffic Data

Economic Research and Market Development Division
The Office of Executive Planning
c/o Panama Canal Commission
Unit 2300
APO AA 34011   011 507-52-3305

The Panama Canal is a vital link in the world transportation chain. A large share of world trade passes through the Canal over any of the world's major trade routes. In 1988, 156.5 million long tons of cargo moved through the Canal aboard 12,318 oceangoing vessels. More than 690,962 vessels have crossed the waterway, carrying more than 4 billion long tons of the world's goods from one ocean to the other. For more information or compilations of Canal traffic data, contact this office.

* Panama Canal Transit

Canal Operations Unit
c/o Panama Canal Commission
Unit 2300
APO AA 34011   011 507-52-3305

This office can provide information for those considering taking a boat or ship through the canal.

* Panama Canal Treaty Implementation

Office of the Secretary
Panama Canal Commission
2000 L St., NW, Room 550
Washington, DC 20036-4996   202-634-6441

On September 7, 1977, the United States and the Republic of Panama signed the Panama Canal Treaty of 1977. The Treaty provided for the establishment of the Panama Canal Commission on October 1, 1979, to assume certain operational responsibilities for the Canal until December 31, 1999. When the Treaty terminates on December 31, 1999, the Republic of Panama shall assume total responsibility for the management, operation, and maintenance of the Panama Canal, which shall be turned over in operating condition and free of liens and debts, except as the two parties may otherwise agree. Of the permanent current work force, 84 percent are Panamanians. **This office can also supply annual reports and a packet of general information on the Canal.** For more information, contact this office.

* Panama Canal Vessel Emergency Response Management

Marine Director
Marine Bureau
c/o Panama Canal Commission
Unit 2300
APO AA 34011   011 507-52-3305

For information on marine operations including inspections, piloting, locks, traffic management, canal services, marine safety, canal operations and maritime training, contact this Bureau. The Commission's marine risk management team is devoted to the prevention of and response to accidents involving vessels carrying hazardous cargoes. The team consists of an experienced fireman, a licensed marine engineer, a safety generalist, an experienced chemist, and lead by an experienced active duty U.S. Coast Guard officer. This team is also responsible for updating the Commission's Vessel Emergency Response Plan and in conducting vessel emergency training exercises.

* Peace and International Conflict Resolution Clearinghouse

Education and Public Information Program
United States Institute of Peace
1550 M St., NW, Suite 900
Washington, DC 20005   202-457-1700

The Jeanette Rankin library program supports the expansion of the Institute's and the nation's information resources on issues in the fields of peace and international conflict management. The Institute also conducts the annual *National Peace Essay Contests* for high school students, and has many television and other media projects on such subjects as the history of U.S.--USSR summitry and issues and ideas in peacemaking. Publications of the Institute include the biennial report; the bimonthly *Journal* which provides information on the Institute's programs and achievements and increases public knowledge of important projects and points of view; and *In Brief*, a new series highlighting results from Institute projects, as well as books and papers.

* Peace Corps Environment Education Curricula

Natural Resources Sector
Office of Training and Program Support
Peace Corps
1990 K St., NW
Washington, DC 20526   202-606-3412

In charge of the forestry sector, natural resources encompasses wildlife management, national parks management, soil conservation, and environmental education curricula.

* Peace Corps Reference Manuals

Information Collection and Exchange (ICE)
Office of Training and Program Support
Peace Corps
1990 K St., NW
Washington, DC 20526   202-606-3412

The Peace Corps publishes a number of handbooks and materials written by their experienced Peace Corps volunteers which are designed to assist new volunteers abroad:

Community Health Education in Developing Countries
Cooperatives
Disaster Procedures
Freshwater Fish Pond Culture and Management
A Glossary of Agricultural Terms
Health and Sanitation Lessons--Africa
Pesticide Safety
The Photonovel--A Tool for Development
Programming and Training for Small Farm Grain Storage
Self-Help Construction of One-Story Buildings
Water Purification, Distribution, and Sewage Disposal

* Peace Corps Regional Bureaus

Peace Corps
1900 K St., NW, 9th Floor
Washington, DC 20526   202-606-3412

The Peace Corps has regional bureaus for Asia, Africa, Interamerican Affairs, and Eastern Europe. These offices can answer questions about specific projects and countries. For further information call:

Africa Bureau 202-606-3181
Inter-American Bureau 202-606-3714
Eastern Europe 202-606-3606

* Political Asylum

Office of Asylum Affairs
Bureau of Human Rights and Humanitarian Affairs
U.S. Department of State
Washington, DC 20520   202-647-1383

This office handles the U.S. Department of State's responsibilities regarding political asylum by providing advisory opinions on the cases to the Immigration and Naturalization Service.

* Population Planning

Office of Population
Bureau for Research and Development, Room 811, SA-18
Agency for International Development (AID)
Washington, DC 20523-1819   703-875-4402

Here population projects are designed to strengthen Agency for International Development (AID) assistance to country family planning programs worldwide. The projects fall into two broad categories: those which support current family planning service delivery, and research to enhance future efforts in the population field. Contact the office above for more information.

* President's Eastern European Initiative

U.S. Information Agency (USIA)
301 4th St., Room 753
Washington, DC 20547   202-619-5066

Begun in 1989, the President's Eastern European Initiative (EEI) is designed to strengthen democratic values in the newly democratic Eastern European nations. The program is organized into four pillars: *The John Marshall Pillar:* emphasizing legislative and judicial reform; *The Noah Webster Pillar:* emphasizing English teaching; *The Alexander Hamilton Pillar:* emphasizing free enterprise; and *The Samuel Gompers Pillar:* emphasizing free trade unionism.

* Private Voluntary Organizations

Office of Private and Voluntary Cooperation
Bureau for Food and Humanitarian Assistance
Room 260, SA-8
U.S Agency for International Development (AID)
Washington, DC 20523   703-351-0201

The Agency for International Development (AID) has long recognized the important contribution made by private voluntary organizations (PVOs) to development efforts in the Third World. According to AID, PVOs are tax-exempt non-profit organizations which receive some portion of their annual revenue from the private sector (demonstrating their private nature) and receive voluntary contributions of money, staff time, or in-kind support from the general public (a demonstration of their voluntary nature). For information on AID available to PVOs, grants reserved for registered PVOs, and for general information including program descriptions and a breakdown of program funding, contact the office above. Also ask for a copy of *The AID-PVO Partnership: Sharing Goals and Resources in the Work of Development* and the *Voluntary Agencies Registered with AID (Volag) Report*.

* Problems of Communism and Socialism

Superintendent of Documents
Government Printing Office (GPO)   202-512-1800
Washington, DC 20402   Fax: 202-512-2250

The United States Information Agency publishes many teaching materials, including books, maps, complete teaching modules, and 14 magazines in 20 languages. By law most U.S. Information Agency (USIA) publications may be distributed only in foreign countries. However, by congressional action, two magazines are available in the United States. *English Teaching Forum*, a quarterly for English teachers worldwide, is published by USIA's English Language Programs Division. *Problems of Communism* is a bi-monthly forum for American and foreign scholars discussing communist and socialist affairs. It is published in English and Spanish. Both these magazines are available through the Government Printing Office.

* Radio Free Europe/Radio Liberty

Board for International Broadcasting
1201 Connecticut Avenue, NW, Suite 400
Washington, DC 20036   202-457-6900

The Board for International Broadcasting's annual reports, available free of charge to the public, cover Radio Free Europe's (RFE) and Radio Liberty's (RL) research, audience, technical facilities, future plans, and more. RFE's Research and Analysis Department (RAD) is the largest center in the West for research on Eastern Europe. RAD's analytical staff produce papers in English on a broad range of subjects, including the internal situations in the countries to which RFE broadcasts. Also available are situation and background reports, along with special publications covering timely topics in those countries. RL publications covering activities in the Soviet Union are also available, including research reports and bulletins, and press surveys and monitoring reports. Specific reports include the *Soviet/East European Report*, and the *RFE/RL Daily Report*. Contact this office for more information on how to order these research publications.

* Radio Free Europe/Radio Liberty Library

Reference Library
1775 Broadway
New York, NY 10019   212-397-5343

This library contains over 17,000 volumes, 3,000 reels of microfilm, 355 subscriptions to periodicals and newspapers in English, Russian, and other languages, and Radio Free Europe/Radio Liberty Archival Material.

* RAND

1700 Main St.
P.O. Box 2138
Santa Monica, CA 90406-2138   213-393-0411

RAND began as a research project sponsored by the United States Air Force with the Douglas Aircraft Corporation in 1946. While RAND is a private, non-profit institution, most of its research contracts were security oriented and sponsored by the Air Force and other government agencies. RAND operates three Federally Funded Research and Development Centers: Project AIR FORCE; the Arroyo Center; and the National Defense Research Institute. Today, while Defense and Foreign policy work still predominates, RAND does do some nondefense related research and has developed significant non-government support. For further information, a publications list, and a sample of the *RAND Research Review*, contact the above address.

* Refugee Resettlement and Asylum

Bureau of Refugee Programs
U.S. Department of State
2201 C St., NW, Room 5824
Washington, DC 20520   202-647-5767

At the center of a cooperative effort between the State Department, other

Government agencies, private voluntary organizations, and international agencies, this bureau provides assistance to refugees in countries of first asylum, and to implement the admission policies to the United States for refugee resettlement. Some of the programs for which this bureau is responsible include relief and repatriation of refugees, and the selection, processing, and training of refugees to be admitted to the United States.

* Refugees, Permanent Residents, Students, and Aliens Travel

Central Office
Immigration and Naturalization Service
425 I Street, NW
Washington, DC 20536   202-307-1501

Publications and tape recorded messages about immigration are available from this central office. However, field offices operate in most states and these local phone numbers appear in the Law and Social Justice Chapter and, of course, are easy to obtain from the directory assistance operators. When calling the tape recorded telephone number, above, enter one of the number codes below which corresponds to the information about immigration and naturalization that you need:

701 Departure from the USA by permanent residents: reentry permits (I-131)
703 Travel authorization for refugees: Refugee travel documents (I-570)
705 Travel by an alien whose application for permanent resident status is still pending
704 Emergency travel requests
702 Student travel outside the USA

* Resolution of Human Rights Violations

Bureau of International Organization Affairs
U.S. Department of State
2201 C St., NW, Room 4334A
Washington, DC 20520   202-647-2708

This office focuses on human rights issues within the United Nations, with the hope of improving the state of human rights in foreign countries. They also oversee U.N. human rights organizations and write U.S. government replies to accusations of U.S. human rights violations.

* Sahel Development Program

Office of West Africa and the Sahel
Bureau for Africa, Room 3491
Agency for International Development (AID)
Washington, DC 20523   202-647-5993

The Agency for International Development (AID) participates in a long-term program for the development of the Sahelian region of West Africa as part of the Development Fund for Africa. The objectives of the Sahel Development Program are to promote regional food self-reliance and self-sustaining economic growth. The program is coordinated, planned, and designed by the Club du Sahel, comprised of nine Sahel states: Mali, Chad, Niger, Burkina Fasco, Senegal, Mauritania, Cape Verde, the Gambia, and Guinea-Bissau; the United States; and over 20 participating governments and international organizations.

* Samantha Smith Memorial Exchange Program

Youth Programs Division
United States Information Agency (USIA)
301 4th St., SW, Room 357
Washington, DC 20547   202-619-6299

Private Organizations and schools are invited to submit proposals for grants in support of exchanges of young people under the age of 21 between the U.S. and the countries of Eastern Europe and the former Soviet Union.

* Science and Technology Development

Bureau for Research and Development, Room 4942
Agency for International Development (AID)
Washington, DC 20523-0057   202-647-1827

Multi-disciplinary science expertise from this office work closely with regional and field staffs, offering needed technical assistance, and serve as a link to U.S. and international development specialists. A major responsibility is to identify and support research having interregional or worldwide implications and research on the "cutting edge" of technology generation, such as biotechnology and the use of genetic engineering techniques. Contact this office for more information.

* Science Capacity-Building in Third World

Office of the Research Advisor
Agency for International Development (AID)
Room 320, SA-18
Washington, DC 20523-1818   703-875-4444

This office coordinates the more innovative and collaborative approaches to the problems and processes of development research, technology transfer, and related capacity-building programs and activities in the development of Third World countries. Scientific and technological needs and opportunities in developing countries are identified, and resources are found to meet those needs from the United States and foreign public and private sources. Effective communication is ensured between the United States scientific and technological capacities and the development programs in which the United States participates.

* Seabed Mining, Outer Continental Shelf and Other Ocean Policies

Office of Oceans Law and Policy
Bureau of Oceans and International Environmental
   and Scientific Affairs
U.S. Department of State
2201 C St., NW, Room 5805A
Washington, DC 20520   202-647-3262

This series of studies deals with a variety of topics concerning the seas, such as sea boundaries, straight baselines, and national maritime claims. Call or write for copies of specific studies and more information.

* Senate Foreign Relations Committee

Suite SD-419 Dirksen Senate Office Building
Washington, DC 20510   202-224-4651

The Senate Foreign Relations Committee (SFRC) reviews all aspects of American foreign relations. In particular, the SFRC is a good source for information on treaties, as it reviews them before they go to the full Senate for ratification.

* Small Business Contracts with AID

Office of Small and Disadvantaged Business Utilization
Agency for International Development (AID), SA-14
Washington, DC 20523-1414   703-875-1551

Information and other handout materials are provided for Agency for International Development (AID) procurement for small and disadvantaged businesses. A weekly bulletin is published that lists the current need of the agency. For a packet of information on the requirements for securing business with AID, write to the office above.

* State Department Speakers

Office of Public Programs
Bureau of Public Affairs
U.S. Department of State
2201 C St, NW, Room 5831
Washington, DC 20520   202-647-6575

Speaking engagements are arranged with organizations throughout the country. To make the best use of the speakers' time, the bureau normally tries to schedule other events during trips, such as media interviews, informal discussion with community leaders, and visits to academic institutions.

* State of World Peace Survey

United States Institute of Peace
1550 M St., NW
Washington, DC 20005   202-457-1700

The Institute has decided to undertake a task of presenting critical information on the state of peace worldwide to the American public and to the international community. A number of valuable studies are available in areas such as human rights and global ecology. The Institute's report will be a periodically updated survey seeking to identify trends, causes, and consequences of armed international conflict on a region-by-region basis. In addition, efforts will be made to standardize methods of statistical reporting on the state of world peace.

* Student Visa Information

Central Office
Immigration and Naturalization Service
425 I Street, NW

Washington, DC 20536   202-307-1501

Publications and tape recorded messages about immigration are available from this central office. However, field offices operate in most states and these local phone numbers appear in the Law and Social Justice Chapter and are easy to obtain from the directory assistance operators. When calling the tape recorded telephone number above, enter one of the number codes below which corresponds to the information about immigration and naturalization that you need:

601 Permission to go to school (I-20, I-134)
606 How to maintain your student status
604 Visas for spouse and dependent children of student
602 Student visa extension (I-538)
603 Permission to work (I-538)
605 F-1 Transfer to another school (I-538) and M-1 Transfer to another school (I-538)

* Teaching in the Third World
Education Sector
Office of Programming and Training Support
Peace Corps
1990 K St., NW
Washington, DC 20526   202-606-3412

Volunteers are trained to teach people of other cultures by experienced educators. Programs are planned here to fit the basic needs of the countries being served.

* Technology Transfer in the Third World
Office of the Science Advisor
Agency for International Development (AID)
Room 320, SA-18
Washington, DC 20523-1818   703-875-4444

This office responds to the interest of Congress in supporting innovative, collaborative approaches in Third World development research and technology transfer. A small, highly competitive research grant program funds the more experimental and less widely known technologies that might later be incorporated into AID's mainstream programs. This grant program is designed to encourage the involvement of scientists in the developing countries and seeks to support research that will lead to solutions to serious developing-country problems. Research Modules include: Biotechnology/Immunology; Chemistry for World Food Needs; Plant Biotechnology; and Global Climate Change. The office also helps support a National Academy of Sciences program to establish research networks among institutions in the developing countries that can identify underexploited resources of potential economic value. Contact the office above for more information.

* Trade Agreements
Developed Countries Trade Division
Bureau of Economic and Business Affairs
U.S. Department of State
2201 C St., NW, Room 3822
Washington, DC 20520   202-647-1162

In handling the U.S. relationship with developed countries regarding bilateral and multilateral trade agreements, this offices examine all aspects of trade, such as restrictions on exports, customs, and licensing requirements. Information is available on these agreements and other issues concerning trade with these developed countries.

* Trade-Related Employment Issues
U.S. Department of Labor
200 Constitution Ave., NW, Room S2235
Washington, DC 20210   202-523-6043

The Bureau of International Labor Affairs represents the U.S. Department of Labor in the development of international economic and trade policies that affect the welfare of U.S. workers. This role includes conducting research on trade-related employment issues, coordinating advice received from Labor Advisory Committees on Trade authorized by the Trade Agreements Act of 1979, and acting as a liaison between other federal departments, agencies, and organized labor. The Bureau is also a member of various interagency committees charged with trade policy functions, and continues to participate in the formulation of U.S. immigration policy. Contact this office for information on studies in progress.

* Training Engineers Overseas
Office of Programming and Training Support
Peace Corps, 1990 K St., NW

Washington, DC 20526   202-606-3398

Civil, mechanical, mining, environmental, and metallurgical engineers help train people to develop water, sanitation, and transportation systems, as well as building bridges and roads.

* Transportation Technology Exchange
International Cooperative Division and Secretariat (P-25)
Office of International Transportation and Trade
Office of the Secretary of Transportation
U.S. Department of Transportation (DOT)
400 7th Street, SW
Washington, DC 20590   202-366-4368

The Department of Transportation (DOT) participates in a number of cooperative programs with other countries to exchange mutually beneficial transportation research data and state-of-the-art technical information. Areas of exchange include highway technology; ports and inland waterways; railway technology; and search and rescue operations. China and the Soviet Union are among the countries participating. Contact this office for information about these programs.

* Travel Advisories and Alerts for Unstable Countries
Overseas Citizens Services
U.S. Department of State
2201 C St., NW, Room 4800
Washington, DC 20520   202-647-5225

This office can provide you with visa requirements for U.S. citizens wishing to travel to foreign countries. They stress that this information is subject to change and that definitive information regarding visas can come only from the foreign embassies. This taped message lists all the countries, their current visa requirements, travel advisories for the countries, and the embassies' phone numbers.

* Treaties and International Agreements
Office of Legal Advisor
U.S. Department of State
2201 C St., NW, Room 5420
Washington, DC 20520   202-647-2044

Information on treaties and international agreements to which the U.S. is a party is prepared by the Office of Legal Advisor. The following publications can be purchased from the Superintendent of Documents, Government Printing Office, Washington, DC 20402; 202-512-1800:

United States Treaties and Other International Agreements. This multivolume series presents the texts of all treaties and other international agreements of the U.S. entered into force since January 1, 1950. It contains the official, legal texts of agreements in their original languages, with English translations when necessary.
Treaties and Other International Agreements of the United States of America, 1776 - 1949. This contains the texts of bilateral, multilateral, and other international agreements entered into by the United States.
Treaties in Force. Lists the treaties and other international agreements in effect for the United States on record in the U.S. Department of State at the beginning of each year ($16).
Treaties and Other International Acts Series (TIAS). TIAS provides in pamphlet form the texts of treaties and international agreements to which the U.S. is a party. Purchase is by subscription or single copy ($89 per year).

* United Nations Documents and Reference
Bureau of International Organization Affairs
U.S. Department of State
2201 C St., NW, Room 3428
Washington, DC 20520   202-647-6878

This office performs general reference on United Nations matters for the State Department. There is limited availability for U.N. documents.

* United Nations Educational Scientific and Cultural Organizations (UNESCO)
UNESCO Affairs
Bureau of International Organization Affairs
U.S. Department of State
2201 C St., NW, Room 5331
Washington, DC 20520   202-647-6882

Although the United States withdrew from UNESCO in 1984, it still maintains a foreign service officer observes UNESCO and reports their activities to the State Department. This office can provide you with general information regarding UNESCO.

* United Nations Information

United Nations Association of the United States of America
1010 Vermont Ave., NW, Suite 904
Washington, DC 20005   202-347-5004

The Association provides information and educational services on the work of the U.N. and on other global issues for students, scholars, Congress, and the media. The United National Association of the United States of America (UNA-USA) also supports the model U.N. program in which some 60,000 high school and college students assume the role of diplomats and debate issues from the U.N. agenda. UNA-USA also publishes studies on the U.N., the environment, international economics, and the role of the U.S. in the United Nations. A list of publications with prices is available from the above office.

* United Nations Special Agencies

Office of Technical Specialized Agencies
Bureau of International Organization Affairs
U.S. Department of State
2201 C St., NW, Room 5331
Washington, DC 20520   202-647-2330

In overseeing U.S. relationships with United Nations technical and specialized organizations, this office is responsible for planning, coordinating, and implementing U.S. policy toward these organizations and other programs within the United Nations. They work closely with other offices, governmental agencies, and organizations.

* United States Coast Guard

U.S. Department of Transportation
Washington, DC 20590   202-267-1587

In the last several years, the Coast Guard has played a central role in the war against illicit drugs. The Coast Guard patrols the American shores, intercoastal waterways, rivers, and the Great Lakes.

* University Expertise in International Development

Agency Center for University Cooperation and Development
Bureau for Research and Development, Room 900, SA-38
Agency for International Development (AID)
Washington, DC 20523-3801   703-816-0295

U.S. universities are the primary centers which generate knowledge and the development of skills essential to the U.S. role in development assistance. The overseas missions of the Agency for International Development (AID) in particular need to be able to draw upon the scientific community in order to apply the most current technical expertise and judgment to mission plans and programs. In response to this need, AID has established a Joint Career Corps (JCC) to encourage certain exchanges of work assignments between university faculty and Agency staff. Candidates proposed by their universities must be tenured faculty, at least at the Associate Professor level, with established scientific reputations, leadership qualities, and the ability to provide both technical and policy related advice to missions and high-level host country officials. Contact this office for more information.

* Urban Development in Third World

Office of Housing and Urban Programs
Bureau for Private Enterprise
Agency for International Development (AID)
320 21st St., NW
Washington, DC 20523   202-663-2530

This office supports a program of research and technical assistance in urban development. New tools are developed and applied to the analysis of urban issues and urban investment strategies to strengthen their effectiveness.

* U.S. Exports to Developing Countries

Commercial, Legislative and Business Affairs
Bureau of Economic and Business Affairs
U.S. Department of State
2201 C St., NW, Room 6822
Washington, DC 20520   202-647-1942

This office acts as a clearinghouse within the State Department for general questions concerning international business exporting and U.S. Government programs to support U.S. business and exports. It also works with the U.S. Department of Commerce to support U.S. commercial assistants working in 140 U.S. embassies overseas.

* U.S. Foreign Policy Press Materials

Press and Publications Service
Bureau of Programs
United States Information Agency (USIA)
301 Fourth St., SW, Room 406
Washington, DC 20547   202-619-4265

The U.S. Information Agency (USIA) prints materials to project an accurate image of the United States and its foreign policy abroad. The Wireless File, a radioteletype network which now can also be accessed computer-to-computer, sends five regional transmissions of policy statements and interpretation each weekday. Each contains 20,000 to 30,000 words in English, but also includes Spanish, French, and Arabic portions, and is sent to U.S. personnel abroad for background information and to distribute to foreign opinion leaders and news media. The Express File transmits material from the Wireless directly into the news rooms of foreign media. This division also distributes articles, photographs, and Dateline America news-feature service. USIA also prints 14 magazines and commercial bulletins in 20 languages, mostly at foreign locations. Generally, they contain reprints from American periodicals for distribution abroad. Publications printed in Washington, DC, are *America Illustrated*, a monthly printed in Russian; *Topic*, published six times a year for sub-Saharan Africa, in English and French; *Dialogue*, a quarterly devoted to American culture and ideas, printed in English, French, and Spanish, as well as other translations put out by field posts; *Economic Impact*, an English and Spanish quarterly; *English Teaching Forum*, a quarterly for English teachers around the world; and *Problems of Communism*. The latter two are available in the United States through the Government Printing Office. Other magazines printed overseas are *al-Majal*, an Arabic monthly; *Span*, an English monthly published in India; and *Trends*, a Japanese bi-monthly. USIA also distributes pamphlets and leaflets in more than 100 countries.

* U.S. Information Agency Library

United States Information Agency (USIA)
301 Fourth St., SW, Room 135
Washington, DC 20547   202-619-5947

The Washington library of the U.S. Information Agency (USIA) houses a varied collection, including a Russian language section. Access is restricted: permission to use the library can be obtained through the Office of Congressional and Public Liaison, address above, Room 602, 202-619-4355.

* U.S. Representation at International Organizations

Bureau of International Organization Affairs
U.S. Department of State
2201 C St., NW, Room 6334
Washington, DC 20520   202-647-9490

This bureau explains the United States' foreign policy positions to other nations and does the day-in and day-out work of representing the U.S. and presenting U.S. policies at the United Nations. They work with many international organizations, such as the International Labor Organization, and take part in over 700 international conferences each year. Concerns include UN peace keeping operations in the Middle East, nuclear facility safeguards and refugee assistance.

* U.S. Role in United Nations

United States Mission to the United Nations
799 United Nations Plaza
New York, NY 10017   212-415-4404

This office can provide information regarding the activities and positions of U.S. representatives as well as the delegations of other countries at the United Nations. Specific areas reviewed include UN Peacekeeping Operations in the Middle East, nuclear facility safeguards, and refugee assistance. Specialized sections within the Mission include: the Economic and Social Affairs Section; the Legal Section; the Resources and Management Section; the Military Staff; and the Press/Publications Office.

* U.S.-Soviet Exchange Initiative

President's U.S.-Soviet Exchange Initiative
United States Information Agency (USIA)
301 Fourth St., SW, Room 751
Washington, DC 20547   202-619-4548

This office is implementing the General Exchanges Agreement signed by the U.S. and the Soviet Union in 1985 to resume academic, cultural, and performing artists exchanges, officially suspended since 1979. It is also charged with facilitating a new, extensive initiative to foster direct contact between their citizens, endorsed by the leaders of both countries. Presidents Bush and Gorbachev upgraded the program in June 1990, expanding exchanges of U.S. and Soviet undergraduates by 1000 in each direction. Guidance is provided to private-sector groups interested in establishing exchanges in the areas of performing arts, exhibitions, education, health, sports, television, film, youth, citizen and professional counterparts.

* Videos and Transcripts on the Persian Gulf Crisis

Center for Defense Information (CDI)
1500 Massachusetts Ave., NW
Washington, DC 20005   202-862-0700

The Center for Defense Information (CDI), an independent military affairs research organization, produces a weekly TV show, "America's Defense Monitor," which aired a series of three episodes dealing with the Persian Gulf Crisis. Copies of VHS tapes can be purchased from the above address for $65 plus $2 postage and handling. Or order transcripts of the episodes for $5 each, plus $2 postage and handling.

* Visa Information for Aliens

Visa Services, U.S. Department of State
Bureau of Consular Affairs
Columbia Plaza Office Building
2401 E St., NW, Room 1353
Washington, DC 20520   202-647-0510

This office provides visa information for citizens of foreign countries who wish to come to the United States for a temporary stay, such as for studies, tourism, or medical treatment. To obtain a visa you must contact the nearest American embassy or consulate. This office can direct you to the closest place, as well as inform you of documents necessary for the application process.

* Voice of America Facilities

Office of Engineering and Technical Operations
Voice of America (VOA)
United States Information Agency (USIA)
330 Independence Ave., SW, Room 3348
Washington, DC 20547   202-619-1060

The Voice of America (VOA) has a Master Control and Network Control Center in Washington, DC, facilities in New York City, Chicago, Los Angeles, and Miami, 107 transmitters worldwide, and 15 satellite circuits to use in reaching audiences all over the globe. A Satellite Interconnect System (SIS) is in the beginning phases of operation and will eventually improve reception of VOA broadcasts in many remote areas. The public can receive free of charge information on the technical operations of VOA, including a descriptive leaflet on SIS, a table of VOA relay stations, showing the locations, transmitters, power range, and area reached, and a frequency schedule.

* Voice of America International Broadcasting

Office of External Affairs
Voice of America (VOA)
United States Information Agency (USIA)
330 Independence Ave., SW, Room 3323
Washington, DC 20547   202-619-2538

On the air since 1942, the Voice of America (VOA) has built an audience of more than 127 million adults, listening to some 1200 hours of broadcasting a week in 43 languages. With 34 studios at headquarters in Washington, DC, three more in New York, one in Los Angeles, and one in Miami, VOA beams programs worldwide through a satellite network. VOA maintains news bureaus in 26 cities, and uses part-time correspondents in many countries to supplement its own staff. Radio Marti broadcasts seven days a week to Cuba, and a test of TV Marti has been funded. Information on the VOA and its program schedules is available. Forty-five-minute tours of VOA facilities are given weekdays, except holidays. Call for reservations.

* Voluntary Relief Organizations Reports

Bureau for Food and Humanitarian Assistance
Room 260, SA-8
Agency for International Development (AID)
Washington, DC 20523   703-351-0201

Voluntary Foreign Aid Programs: Report of American Voluntary Agencies Engaged in Overseas Relief and Development Registered with the Agency for International

Development describes the general nature of the work being carried out by the Private and Voluntary Organizations (PVOs) which are registered with the Agency for International Development (AID). Included is such information as a PVO's geographic focus and sectorial concentration, as well as summaries of support, revenue, and expenditures. Contact the office above to obtain a copy.

* War Risk Insurance for Ships

Marine Insurance Division
Office of Trade and Analysis and Insurance
Maritime Administration
U.S. Department of Transportation
400 7th Street, SW, Room 8121
Washington, DC 20590   202-366-4161

The War Risk Insurance Program insures operators and seamen against losses from hostile action if commercial insurance is not available to them. The program covers loss of life and materials due to war or nuclear detonation.

* Water and Sanitation Assistance and Training

Office of Training and Program Support
Peace Corps
1990 K St., NW
Washington, DC 20526   202-606-2174

This office works at encouraging and implementing better methods of sanitation and water purification.

* Weekly Updates on Foreign Policy

U.S. Department of State Dispatch
Office of Public Communication
Bureau of Public Affairs
Washington, DC 20520-6810   202-647-6317

The U.S. Department of State Dispatch chronicles U.S. foreign policy on a weekly basis. Containing original source material and indexed every six months (index is included in the subscription), *DISPATCH* incudes speeches and Congressional testimony; fact sheets on critical international issues and organizations; analyses of foreign policy; photographs; maps and profiles of countries in the news; updates on U.S. initiatives abroad; treaty actions and other foreign policy topics. Several subscription options are available: $75 per year 3rd Class Mail; $142, First Class; $93.75 foreign mail. Order from Superintendent of Documents, Government Printing Office, Washington, DC 20402-9371, 202-512-1800. Overnight delivery is available for $430 from National Technical Information Service, U.S. Department of Commerce, 5285 Port Royal Road, Springfield, VA 22161-2171, 703-487-4650 (Pub. No. PB90-923500ACT). For Electronic Subscriptions, contact the State Department's Computer Information Delivery Service (CID) at 703-802-5700.

* Who's Who in the Diplomatic Community

Bureau of Public Affairs
U.S. Department of State
2201 C St., NW, Room 5815A
Washington, DC 20520   202-647-6575

The Bureau of Public Affairs publishes a sales catalog, which lists their publications, as well as ordering information. The following publications are also available from the Superintendent of Documents, Government Printing Office (GPO), Washington, DC 20402; 202-512-1800. Documents can also often be obtained at a local GPO bookstore. Check for one in your area.

Diplomatic List ($4.50 per issue). Prepared quarterly, the Diplomatic List includes the names of the members of the diplomatic staffs of all missions and their spouses, as well as the addresses and phone numbers of the foreign missions.

Employees of Diplomatic Missions ($2.50 per issue). This quarterly publication lists all the members of the technical, administrative, and service staffs of more than 130 foreign missions. It gives the employee's name, function, and home address.

Key Officers of Foreign Service Posts ($1.75 per issue). Produced three times a year, this publication lists all key officers at Foreign Service posts whom business representatives would most likely need to contact. Addresses and phone numbers are included.

State Department Organizational Directory ($11). It includes detailed organizational listings of State, AID, ACDA, and the U.S. Information Agency, with titles, names, and phone numbers. There is a directory of services listing available services within the Department of State.

Update From State (free). A new bimonthly publication dedicated to informing the public about the policies, operations, and diplomatic efforts of the U.S. Department of State and the Foreign Service.

Be patient. If any phone number is incorrect, call (area code) 555-1212 and request the new listing.

925

* Women in Development Program

Development Information Center
Room 105, SA-18
Agency for International Development (AID)
Washington, DC 20523-1801   703-875-4818

Contact this Center for information on the Agency for International Development's (AID) Women in Development subject collection of papers and documents assembled and organized by the AID Women in Development Office. Access is through a handlist.

* Women Empowerment in Third World

Bureau of Research and Development
Agency for International Development (AID)
Room 714, SA-18
Washington, DC 20523   703-875-4474

Women in developing countries play a significant role in economic production, family support, and the overall development process of the national economies. Bilateral aid is therefore administered to give particular attention to the programs, projects, and activities that tend to integrate women and improve their status in these countries. Materials on experiences within this program are available through the Center for Development Information and Evaluation, 1601 N. Kent St., Room 105, Arlington, VA; 703-875-4818.

* Work Permits for Foreigners

Labor Certification Division
Employment Service
Employment and Training Administration
U.S. Department of Labor
200 Constitution Ave., NW, Room N4456

Washington, DC 20210   202-535-0163

If an employer wishes to hire foreign workers, he must first obtain a foreign labor certificate, which is a statement from the U.S. Department of Labor stating that there is no U.S. citizen available to fill the job. The Department investigates to make sure that the wages and working conditions of the foreign workers will not seriously affect the wages and working conditions of U.S. workers. An employer applies for a foreign labor certificate through the local state employment service office, which then conducts a job hunt before sending the application form to the area regional office for approval or disapproval.

* WORLDNET Radio and Television Satellite Network

Public Liaison
Television and Film Service
United States Information Agency (USIA)
601 D St., NW
Washington, DC 20547   202-501-7806

The first live global satellite television network, WORLDNET now reaches every continent, transmitting five days a week. Designed to link overseas posts and embassies with Washington and to provide news and feature programming for foreign broadcast media, WORLDNET allows the U.S. to explain our foreign policy with new immediacy and to act quickly in response to global events. "Dialogues" are an innovative way to demonstrate American press freedom by linking American newsmakers electronically with foreign journalists in unrehearsed, live "telepress conferences." The network utilizes Intelsat and regional satellites. Nearly 200 U.S. embassies, consulates, and cultural centers around the world are equipped with antennae to receive WORLDNET programming and distribute it to local broadcasters. Topics covered on WORLDNET include Arts and Literature, Business and Economics, Current Events, Entertainment, Sports, Environment, Language Instruction, Science, and American Society. A free brochure on WORLDNET is available. On August 22, 1988, RIAS-TV joined RIAS (Radio in the American Sector), a 40-year-old U.S.-German cooperative effort.

Arms Control and World Peace

In the United States, the Arms Control and Disarmament Agency (ACDA) coordinates the ongoing negotiations between the United States, Russia, and other nuclear powers to reduce their arsenals. This federal agency also takes the lead in other efforts to reduce the risk of war by, for example, verifying other countries' compliance with the Nuclear Non-Proliferation Treaty and other international agreements. Information about these developments as well as technical materials are identified here. Weapons sales to foreign governments, technology transfer, and treaties are also important elements of arms control. As Congressional approval is necessary for these actions, the foreign affairs and armed services committees as well as other congressional panels serve as additional information sources, often providing a different approach to the objectives of the President and the ACDA.

* Arms Control and Disarmament Agreements

Arms Control and Disarmament Agency (ACDA)
320 21st St., NW
Washington, DC 20451   202-647-4800

The 1990 edition of *Arms Control and Disarmament Agreements* contains all the texts and histories of all major arms control agreements to which the U.S. was a participant up through May 1988. The publication is for sale at the Government Printing Office, 202-512-1800, stock number 002000-00096-2. Cost is $15.

* Current and Future Negotiations

Bureau of Strategic and Nuclear Affairs
Arms Control and Disarmament Agency (ACDA)
320 21st St., NW
Washington, DC 20451   202-647-6566

This office coordinates with other agencies on research and policy studies to support the development of a comprehensive and effective arms control program. The Bureau also conducts external research on the technical and political implications of current and proposed negotiating options. This research supports implementation of existing agreements, ongoing negotiations, and planning for future negotiations.

* Defense Facts and Analyses

Center for Defense Information (CDI)
1500 Massachusetts Ave., NW
Washington, DC 20005   202-862-0700

In pursuit of its goal to lessen the possibility of nuclear war, the Center for Defense Information (CDI) analyzes military issues and collects information, facts, and statistics. The staff includes many former military officers and civilians trained in military analysis. CDI regularly presents information to the Pentagon, State Department, and Congress. This information is also made available to the public and the media through a variety of services and publications. Members of CDI's Military Advisory Council (MAC) are available to speak to civic, school and business groups. Contact the Center at the telephone number listed above.

* Defense Systems Impact on Arms Control

Defense Programs and Analysis
Bureau of Nuclear Non-Proliferation Policy
Arms Control and Disarmament Agency (ACDA)
320 21st St., NW
Washington, DC 20451   202-647-9610

Arms Control Impact Statement, an annual report to Congress, contains details on certain weapons systems and analyses on the impact that such systems have on arms control agreements, treaties, and negotiations. Those weapon systems include nuclear weapon-related programs, defense programs which exceed specified cost ceilings, and other technology and weapons systems which the Executive Branch certifies as having significant effects on arms control. Impact statements are intended to be of value to the executive branch, to the Congress, and to the general public in evaluating the arms control implications of the development of major U.S. nuclear and non-nuclear weapons systems. Impact statements are intended to enhance the likelihood that arms control considerations become and remain integral to the decision making process on major U.S. defense programs, and that ACDA be instrumental in the process. This office can provide further information in this

regard. Contact the public affairs office (202-647-4800) to obtain a copy of this annual publication.

* Diplomatic Coordination

Office of Public Affairs
Arms Control and Disarmament Agency (ACDA)
320 21st St., NW, Room 5843
Washington, DC 20451   202-647-9610

As part of an interagency public diplomacy group, this office prepares, coordinates, and publishes materials to support the Administration's conduct of public diplomacy activities. The Arms Control and Disarmament Agency (ACDA) also provides guidance on arms control matters to press spokesmen of other Federal agencies, assists in preparation of information for use abroad, conducts special programs and conferences for nongovernmental organizations and the news media, and conducts briefings for media representatives, visiting students, and scholars.

* Disarmament Activities and Documents

Superintendent of Documents
Government Printing Office   202-512-1800
Washington, DC 20402   Fax: 202-512-2250

Each volume of the Arms Control and Disarmament Agency's (ACDA) historical series, *Documents on Disarmament*, contains complete details on significant arms control and disarmament activities by printing the textual materials of treaties, agreements, laws, reports, statements, resolutions, communiques, proposals, declarations, and speeches of both U.S. and foreign origin.

* Economic Analysis of Arms Control Programs

Defense Programs and Analysis Division
Bureau of Nuclear Non-Proliferation Policy
Arms Control and Disarmament Agency (ACDA)
320 21st St., NW
Washington, DC 20451   202-647-9610

This division is responsible for the Agency's economic analysis of defense and arms control programs, and the analysis of weapons technology. Contact them for more information on these issues.

* Economic Impact of Arms Reduction Treaties

Office of Public Affairs
Arms Control and Disarmament Agency (ACDA)
320 21st St., NW, Room 5843
Washington, DC 20451   202-647-9610

Research relevant indirectly to negotiation support and directly to assessing the economic impact of treaties and agreements is an important part of the Arms Control and Disarmament Agency's (ACDA) activities. They analyze the economics of defense strategies, and are currently building data banks on worldwide defense and economic information. One of the objectives of arms control is the reduction of global military expenditures, and research in support of this objective includes analyses of the economic impact of the INF Treaty, defense spending and national budgets, and military procurement. ACDA economists review Russian and Eastern European countries' national accounts, and prepare an annual submission on U.S.

defense spending for the U.N. military expenditures reporting program. For questions regarding economics research, contact this office.

* Europe

Theater Affairs Division
Bureau of Strategic and Nuclear Affairs
Arms Control and Disarmament Agency (ACDA)
320 21st St. NW
Washington, DC 20451   202-647-9610

Europe is the most heavily militarized continent on the planet. Even in the post Cold-War era, the danger of conflict remains. The task of arms control in Europe is to reduce the danger of war. Contact this bureau for more information on European arms control programs.

* Foreign Military Sales

Defense Security Assistance Agency
Operations Directorate
The Pentagon, Room 4B740
Washington, DC 20301-2800   703-604-6513

This office administers the Foreign Military Sales (FMS) Program, which deals with U.S. government sales of defense articles and services to foreign governments. A free booklet containing information on the Program and the U.S. Defense Security Assistance Agency is available upon request.

* Foreign Weapon Sales Statistics

FMS Reports and Controls Division
Defense Security Assistance Agency
The Pentagon, Room 4B659
Washington, DC 20301-2800   703-604-6513

This office publishes a free annual publication, *Foreign Military Sales, Foreign Military Construction Sales, and Military Assistance Facts,* which contains information and detailed statistics on all grant programs, sales, and Federal financing of security assistance to foreign countries. Write or call for a copy.

* INF Treaty Q & A

Office of Public Affairs
Arms Control and Disarmament Agency (ACDA)
320 21st St., NW, Room 5834
Washington, DC 20451   202-647-9610

Understanding the INF Treaty reviews the post-World War II history leading up to the treaty, its negotiation, ratification, and implementation. This 36-page booklet provides the historical context to NATO's 1979 two-track decision, a history of the negotiations themselves, the ratification process that took place in both countries, an overview of the inspection and elimination procedures that are now being implemented, and an addendum that addresses may questions frequently asked about the INF Treaty.

* Legal Advice on Arms Control Treaties

The Office of the General Counsel
Arms Control and Disarmament Agency (ACDA)
320 21st St., NW
Washington, DC 20451   202-647-9610

This office is responsible for all matters of domestic and international law relevant to the Arms Control and Disarmament Agency's (ACDA) work. It provides advice and assistance in drafting and negotiating arms control treaties and agreements, and on questions regarding their approval by Congress, and their implementation, interpretation, ratification, and revision. Attorneys from the office also serve as legal advisers on U.S. arms control negotiating delegations. The office also handles the legal aspects of Agency policies and operations in the areas of personnel, ethics, security, patents, contracts, procurement, and fiscal and administrative matters.

* Military Equipment Export Licenses

Office of Defense Trade Controls
Bureau of Politico-Military Affairs
U.S. Department of State, SA-6
Washington, DC 20520   202-647-1256

Being responsible for the licensing and regulation of commercial exports of military equipment and services, this office develops policy guidance on munitions exports, and registers all U.S. exports of arms, ammunition, and implements of war.

* Multilateral Arms Control Negotiations

Bureau of Multilateral Affairs
Arms Control and Disarmament Agency (ACDA)
320 21st St. NW
Washington, DC 20451   202-647-9610

This office develops arms control policy, strategy, and tactics for ongoing multilateral arms control negotiations, and provides organizational support, delegation staffing, and Washington backstopping for multilateral negotiations, such as multilateral and bilateral chemical weapons negotiations and the First Committee of the United Nations General Assembly. Contact this bureau for more information relevant to multilateral affairs.

* Newsletter

Office of Public Affairs
Arms Control and Disarmament Agency (ACDA)
320 21st St., NW, Room 5832
Washington, DC 20451   202-647-9610

Arms Control Update, an eight-page, serially-published Arms Control and Disarmament Agency (ACDA) newsletter, reviews recent developments in arms control and contains excerpts from administration statements on U.S. arms control policy. Recent issues contain broad overviews of U.S. arms control activities and information about other, more in-depth, publications. Contact this office to receive a free subscription.

* Non-Proliferation Evaluation

International Nuclear Affairs Division
Bureau of Nuclear and Weapons Control
Arms Control and Disarmament Agency (ACDA)
320 21st St. NW
Washington, DC 20451   202-647-9610

This division provides advice, assessments, and policy recommendations on the international relations aspects of nonproliferation. It also assesses each proposed agreement for peaceful cooperation and provides ACDA views on U.S. nuclear export control issues.

* Non-Proliferation Policy

Office of Nuclear Non-Proliferation Policy
U.S. Department of Energy
Room 7G-050 Forrestal Bldg.
Washington, DC 20585   202-586-6175

This office implements U.S. Department of Energy programs and activities derived from formal international non-proliferation agreements.

* Nuclear Risk Reduction Center

Nuclear Risk Reduction Center
U.S. Department of State
2201 C St., NW, Room 7532
Washington, DC 20520   202-647-0025

The United States Nuclear Risk Reduction Center and its Soviet counterpart have been established to reduce the risk of conflict that might result from accident, misinterpretation, or miscalculation. The increasing complexity of arms control agreements associated with the end of the Cold War has led to the expansion of the centers.

* Nuclear Technologies

Nuclear Safeguards and Technology Division
Bureau of Nuclear Non-Proliferation Policy
Arms Control and Disarmament Agency (ACDA)
320 21st St. NW
Washington, DC 20451   202-647-9610

This division provides advice and policy recommendations on safeguard systems, nuclear fuel cycles, and the technology aspects of nonproliferation. It also assesses the safeguards and nonproliferation implications of emerging technologies. Contact this division for more information.

* Peace and International Conflict Grants

Jennings Randolph Program for International Peace
United States Institute of Peace
1550 M St., NW

Washington, DC 20005   202-457-1700

This Program provides fellowships to scholars and leaders in peace to undertake research and other appropriate forms of communication on issues of international peace and the management of international conflict. The Fellowship Program has three levels: Jennings Randolph Distinguished Fellows are individuals whose careers show extraordinary accomplishment concerning questions of international peace; United States Institute of Peace Fellows are individuals also of accomplishment, but of somewhat less eminence; and United States Institute of Peace Scholars are individuals working on doctoral dissertations in the field.

* Policy Coordination

Bureau of Strategic and Nuclear Affairs
Arms Control and Disarmament Agency (ACDA)
320 21st St. NW
Washington, DC 20451   202-647-9610

This office is responsible for U.S.-Soviet nuclear arms control. In coordination with other U.S. agencies, it develops U.S. nuclear arms control policies for Presidential approval, supports negotiations on nuclear arms control, and provides analytical support for these efforts. Its responsibilities also include consultation and coordination with allied and other foreign governments on U.S./Soviet arms control negotiations. This bureau maintains the official record of all relevant documents, speeches, significant comments, and general material related to bilateral arms control and negotiations.

* Politico-Military Considerations

Bureau of Politico-Military Affairs
U.S. Department of State
2201 C St., NW, Room 7321
Washington, DC 20520   202-647-1256

The bureau advises the Secretary of State on the military aspects of various foreign policy matters, such as arms control negotiations, regional security arrangements, security assistance, arms sales programs, and technology transfers. It has primary responsibility for coordinating U.S. arms sales, military assistance, and Economic Support Fund programs to other nations. With a role in ongoing arms control negotiations, the bureau prepares talks with the Russians and other powers on reduction of strategic nuclear weapons, defense and space issues, and nuclear testing. It also is involved in multilateral negotiations to ban chemical weapons and reduce conventional forces in Europe.

* Press Releases

Office of Public Affairs
Arms Control and Disarmament Agency (ACDA)
320 21st St., NW, Room 5843
Washington, DC 20451   202-647-9610

This office publishes and distributes a daily compilation of press clippings; dispatches a daily cable containing selected press releases on arms control to U.S. Diplomatic posts overseas; and supplies numerous updates of arms control topics in its *Issues Brief* series. Contact this office for more information on these news releases.

* Proposals in U.S. Congress

Office of Congressional Affairs
Arms Control and Disarmament Agency (ACDA)
320 21st St. NW
Washington, DC 20451   202-647-9610

This office responds to congressional interest in arms control and negotiations by arranging briefings and consultations between the Arms Control and Disarmament Agency (ACDA) officials and Members of Congress and staff; arranging arms control seminars for Congressional staff with ACDA officials and officials from other agencies; working with Congressional committee staffs in arranging hearings at which ACDA officials appear as witnesses; and distributing informational material on arms control issues to Members of Congress and their staffs. In response to requests from Senators and staff, this office provides information and coordinated briefings, seminars, and speakers.

* Proposed Arms and Technology Transfers

Arms Transfer Division
Bureau of Nuclear Non-Proliferation Policy
Arms Control and Disarmament Agency (ACDA)
320 21st St. NW
Washington, DC 20451   202-647-9610

This office assesses the arms control implications of proposed arms transfers and technology transfers, represents the Agency in the preparation of the Administration's annual security assistance programs, and participates in the implementation of the Missile Technology Control Regime. Contact this office for more information concerning arms transfer.

* Proposed Weapons Sales Analysis

Office of Security Assistance and Sales (OSAS)
Bureau of Politico-Military Affairs
U.S. Department of State
2201 C St., NW, Room 7424
Washington, DC 20520   202-647-9792

The Office of Security Assistance and Sales (OSAS) sets policy regarding transfer or sales of arms to foreign countries with respect to geographic regions and the technology allowed in the regions. They also deal with the transfer of arms regarding their purpose for use, as well as third country transfers, where a country who bought arms from the U.S. wants to sell these arms to another country. This office handles munitions control which concerns the licensing of items with military applications. Working closely with the U.S. Department of Defense on many of these areas, OSAS also helps in formulating the budget for military needs.

* Public Information on Arms Control Policies

Office of Public Affairs
Arms Control and Disarmament Agency (ACDA)
320 21st St., NW, Room 5834
Washington, DC 20451   202-647-9610

This office distributes and coordinates public information on arms control and disarmament. The staff works to ensure accurate and complete media coverage of U.S. arms control policies, and makes the public aware of arms control activities through speaking engagements and publications. This office also responds to information requests, and provides Agency leaders with advice on public perceptions of U.S. arms control policies.

* Safeguards and Arms Control Research

Office of Public Affairs
Arms Control and Disarmament Agency (ACDA)
320 21st St., NW, Room 5834
Washington, DC 20451   202-647-9610

The Arms Control and Disarmament Agency's (ACDA) sponsored external research covers a wide range of arms control issues, such as verification, nuclear safeguards, nuclear test ban monitoring, and crisis stability issues. Specific examples of projects include Retrieval of Public Statements on Verification, and a Computer Model for Simulating Conventional Warfare. Conferences and seminars on related issues are also arranged. Contact this office for more information on these projects and other on-going external research.

* Science, Technology, and Arms Control

Office of the Science Advisor
Arms Control and Disarmament Agency (ACDA)
320 21st St. NW
Washington, DC 20451   202-647-9610

This office, created by Congress as part of the 1990 ACDA authorization, will serve as the focal point within the Arms Control and Disarmament Agency (ACDA) and the U.S. government for matters of science and technology in arms control and for coordination of arms control verification research and development. The Chief Science advisor also serves as the chair of the ACDA Research Review Board, which recommends the research budget requirements and allocates ACDA external research funds. Contact this office for more information.

* Soviet Compliance with Arms Control Agreements

Office of Public Affairs
Arms Control and Disarmament Agency (ACDA)
320 21st St., NW, Room 5834
Washington, DC 20451   202-647-9610

The President's annual *Report on Soviet Noncompliance* to Congress presents in detail an evaluation of Soviet actions with respect to arms control obligations. Annually, the Arms Control and Disarmament Agency (ACDA) also prepares for the President to submit to the Congress the report, *Adherence to and Compliance with Agreements*. This report contains details of the process by which the U.S. Government ensures U.S. compliance with its arms control obligations, detailed responses to Soviet charges of U.S. noncompliance, and an evaluation of other nations' compliance with international arms control agreements.

Be patient. If any phone number is incorrect, call (area code) 555-1212 and request the new listing.

929

International Relations and Defense

* Speakers on Arms Control
Office of Public Affairs
Arms Control and Disarmament Agency (ACDA)
320 21st St., NW, Room 5834
Washington, DC 20451   202-647-9610

Officers of the U.S. Arms Control and Disarmament Agency will address audiences in all parts of the country if speaking engagements can be worked into their schedules.

* Status of Current Arms Control Activities
Office of Public Affairs
Arms Control and Disarmament Agency (ACDA)
320 21st St., NW, Room 5834
Washington, DC 20451   202-647-9610

Each year the President is required to send to the Congress an annual report on the activities of the Arms Control and Disarmament Agency (ACDA) and the nation's arms control agenda. The report includes a complete review of arms control and disarmament goals, research, and activities, as well as appraisals of the status and prospects of arms control negotiations and of arms control measures in effect. Contact this office of more information on this report.

* Treaty Verification Operations
Division of Verification
Bureau of Verification and Implementation
Arms Control and Disarmament Agency (ACDA)
320 21st St., NW
Washington, DC 20451   202-647-9610

The Arms Control and Disarmament Agency (ACDA) VAX computer helps evaluate and improve treaty verification procedures, assess treaty compliance, and verify provisions of proposed treaties, along with other facets of negotiation support. One of the VAX programs, for example, keeps track of all arms control-related external research conducted throughout the U.S. Government. All agencies are informed of on-going research to ensure that no duplication of work occurs. Contact this office for more information on computer aided research and arms control.

* Verification of Soviet Compliance
Bureau of Verification and Implementation
Arms Control and Disarmament Agency (ACDA)
320 21st St. NW
Washington, DC 20451   202-647-9610

This bureau provides a focal point within the Arms Control and Disarmament Agency (ACDA) and the U.S. Government for formulating U.S. arms control verification policy and for assessing Soviet compliance with arms control agreements.

* Weapons Reduction Research and Arms Control Options
Office of Public Affairs
Arms Control and Disarmament Agency (ACDA)
320 21st St., NW, Room 5834
Washington, DC 20451   202-647-9610

Research, both short-run and long-run, on all aspects of arms control and disarmament, is one of the Arms Control and Disarmament Agency's principal functions. While most research projects support the immediate requirements of ongoing negotiations, others have been directed toward the goal of a world free from war and the dangers of armaments. Over the years, the Arms Control and Disarmament Agency (ACDA) has accumulated a wealth of information on every conceivable aspect of arms control and disarmament. ACDA also coordinates research and studies by or for other government agencies, and analyzes selected defense programs for their arms control implications. Contact this office for information on specific research topics.

* World Peace Assessment
United States Institute of Peace
1550 M St., NW
Washington, DC 20005   202-457-1700

The Institute has decided to undertake a task of presenting critical information on the state of peace worldwide to the American public and to the international community. A number of valuable studies are available in areas such as human rights and global ecology. The Institute's report will be a periodically updated survey seeking to identify trends, causes, and consequences of armed international conflict on a region-by-region basis. In addition, efforts will be made to standardize methods of statistical reporting on the state of world peace.

* Worldwide Military Expenditures and Arms Transfers
Superintendent of Documents
Government Printing Office   202-512-1800
Washington, DC 20402   Fax: 202-512-2250

This annual publication provides a compilation of annual military and other relevant statistics for each of 145 countries over a decade, as well as essays on pertinent topics and special analyses. Military data include military spending, numbers of armed forces, and arms exports and imports in value and quantity terms. Comparative economic data include gross national product, central government expenditures, population, and total exports and imports. This publication also provides worldwide military and other relevant statistics for the period 1979-1986, as well as arms transfer data through 1987.

Military and National Security

* See also *Information from Lawmakers Chapter*
* See also *Selling to the Government Chapter*
* See also *Science and Technology Chapter*
* See also *Foreign Policy section at the beginning of this chapter*

The military-industrial complex is vast. Many of the research and development centers and laboratories identified below are useful information sources. Defense procurement and contracts are included here as well as in the *Selling to the Government* Chapter. Military installations, personnel, spending, and other dimensions to the armed forces are contained in this chapter. There are 108 House and Senate committees and subcommittees that not only oversee the Pentagon but also have the last word on the defense budget. Listings for them can be found here as well as in the *Information from Lawmakers* Chapter. Policy concerning weapons sales and technology transfer to foreign governments are also addressed in the preceding section on arms control and disarmament.

Main phone numbers and public affairs offices are good places to get started when seeking information. Military and National Security affairs are the preserve of the State and Defense Departments. The State Department's main switchboard number is 202-647-4000. The Defense Department's main switchboard number is 703-545-6700. In the State Department, the Bureau of Politico-Military Affairs is the main action bureau in military affairs. The Arms Control and Disarmament Agency also has good information resources. The Regional desks have information on their individual areas. The size of the Defense Department inevitably makes it more complicated. Good places to start hunting are the Office of the Secretary of Defense's public affairs office, and the individual services public affairs offices. When calling, explain what you need as clearly as possible. Given the overlapping jurisdictions in this area, expect to get mis-routed at least once. Hang in there and you'll get to where you need to go. Keep in mind that often times bureaucrats in these areas (and others as well) think in terms of people as often as issues, meaning that when you request information on some topic their first thought is "who do I know that handles that type of thing?" Calling is probably more effective than writing because you are more likely to get into the right network and therefore find the right person to answer your question.

* Aeromedical Research

Strughold Aeromedical Library
U.S. Department of the Air Force
Air Force School of Aerospace Medicine
Brooks Air Force Base, TX 78235-5031   512-536-3322
This library will provide inter-library loans, and can help you identify reports and refer you to the appropriate source. Strughold is linked to the OCLC and Doc Line systems (symbol TBM) and is located in the Amigos region of these systems.

* Aeronautical Systems Clearinghouse

Aeronautical Systems Division
Office of Public Affairs
U.S. Department of the Air Force
Wright-Patterson Air Force Base, OH 45433   513-255-3334
This office develops and acquires aeronautical systems, their components, and related aerospace equipment, including aircraft engines, airborne communications systems, special reconnaissance projects, and interpretation facilities. Fact sheets are available for each of the 200 programs administered by the agency. Write or call the above office for a free brochure describing the Division's mission.

* Aeronautics Research: Air Force

U.S. Department of the Air Force
Arnold Engineering Development Center
Air Force Systems Command
Arnold Air Force Base, TN 37389   615-455-2611
This center has test laboratories in which atmospheric conditions, orbital, space flight, and ballistic conditions can be simulated. A brochure on the base, its programs, and mission, along with fact sheets on technical subjects, including wind tunnels, aeropropulsion systems, and rocket test facilities can be obtained by writing or calling the above office.

* Aerospace Research Library

Information Management Division
National Air and Space Museum, Room 3100
Smithsonian Institute
Washington, DC 20560   202-357-3133
The Museum has a research library devoted to books and journals on aviation history, space exploration history, and science and technology in the fields of astronomy, astrophysics, engineering, geology, and space medicine. Appointments are strongly recommended as there is a limit of 5 researchers a day permitted due to limited staff resources. The library is open weekdays, 10am to 5pm.

* Aerospace Structures

Aerospace Structures Information
 and Analysis Center (ASIAC)
WL/FIBRA/ASIAC
Bldg. 45, Room 038
Wright-Patterson AFB, OH 45433   513-255-6688
This Center is a central point for the collection and distribution of aerospace structures information. It maintains a library of reports done by various government agencies, and can refer you to other libraries and sources. Requests for specific information are served for researchers or contractors with a "need to know" status. Write or call for *How to Get It: A Guide to Defense-related Information Sources* and a free brochure describing the Center, its services, and user eligibility.

* Aircraft Armament Research

U.S. Air Force Systems Command
Eglin Air Force Base, FL 32542   904-882-3931
This Command conducts research, development, testing, and evaluation of guns and other aircraft weapons, explosives, chemical-biological weapons, and missile systems. Other units based at or associated with Eglin include the Air Force Tactical Air Warfare Center, 33rd Tactical Fighter Wing, 919th Special Operations Group, 20th Surveillance Squadron, the 6th Ranger Training Battalion, and the Naval School,

Explosive Ordnance Disposal. The office will respond to requests for information on specific technical topics.

* Aircraft Test Flights

Air Force Flight Test Center
Public Affairs Office
Edwards Air Force Base, CA 93523-5000   805-277-3510

This office can supply you with fact sheets on all aircraft tested on its facilities, the history of the Test Center, significant historical events, biographies of famous people associated with the base, and tour information.

* Air Force Aeronautical Systems

U.S. Department of the Air Force
Aeronautical Systems Division
Public Affairs Office
Wright-Patterson Air Force Base, OH 45433   513-255-3334

The Public Affairs Office's brochure, *What's Happening at ASD*, lists the major programs in all the Aeronautical Systems Division (ASD) offices, the contractors involved, and the program status. Also available is a brochure describing the five laboratories which make up the Wright Research and Development Center: aeropropulsion and power, flight dynamics, materials, avionics, and electronic technology.

* Air Force Armament Museum

Air Force Armament Museum
Eglin Air Force Base, FL 32542   904-882-3931

The Armament museum at Eglin AFB is the only facility in the U.S. dedicated to the display of Air Force armament. The main attractions are the 18 aircraft on display including an SR-71 Blackbird, a B-17 Flying Fortress, and an F-4 Phantom. The indoor museum features many World War II and Korean War aircraft including a P-51 Mustang and a F-80 Shooting Star. The museum is open seven days a week, 9:30-4:30.

* Air Force Aviation History

U.S. Department of the Air Force
1352 AVSDOLD - Media Center
Air Force Central Visual Information Library
Norton Air Force Base, CA 92409-5996   714-382-2493

This library will loan copies from their collection, which includes visual productions of documentaries, training materials, the history of aviation, and W.W.II and Korean War produced by the Air Force. Written requests for information are preferred.

* Air Force Directives, Research and Development, Goals

U.S. Department of the Air Force
Air Force Information for Industry Office
5001 Eisenhower Ave.
Alexandria, VA 22333   202-247-5838

The Air Force Information for Industry Office offers information, assistance, and resources to aid potential contractors in doing business with the Air Force. You may write or call their office. The following are among the free publications available: *Air Force Logistics Needs, Mission Element Need Statements (MENS), Program Element Descriptive Summaries, Program Management Directive, R & D Planning Summaries, Technical Objective Documents, Technology Needs Documents*, and *Selling to the United States Air Force*.

* Air Force Historical Records

Air Force Historical Research Agency
HQUSAFHRC/HD
Maxwell Air Force BASE, AL 36112-6678   205-953-5342

This is the principal repository for Air Force historical records. It holds the most extensive collection of documentary source material on the history of U.S. military action, and has its own historical studies and oral histories collection. The Center is open to researchers, scholars, as well as the general public. The library operates on a non-circulating, research basis, ie. reference librarians take written requests for information and pull information for patrons. Inter-library loan is available for items it has duplicates of within its collection. Microfilm copies of records are available for $20 per roll; each roll contains 2000 frames. Hours of operation are Monday-Saturday, 8am-4:45pm.

* Air Force Historical Research Library

Secretary of the U.S. Air Force
Public Resource Library
The Pentagon, Room 5C945
Washington, DC 20330-1000   703-697-4100

The Resource Library is able to answer a broad range of Air Force related questions and has printed material available such as biographies of prominent Air Force generals, fact sheets on Air Force related topics (such as aircraft, weapons systems, missions), and "Speech Inserts" from key speeches by Air Force leadership. Contact this office for a catalogue of fact sheets.

* Air Force Housekeeping Programs

U.S. Air Force Engineering Agency
Morale, Welfare and Recreation
Public Affairs Office
Tyndall Air Force Base, FL 32403-6001   904-283-6476

This Center conducts research and forms Air Force policy for the managing of food services, laundry services, and billeting on Air Force bases worldwide. They can provide fact sheets on their programs and engineering activities.

* Air Force Information Fact Sheets

Secretary of the Air Force
Office of Public Affairs
Washington, DC 20330-1000   703-697-3329

The Air Force has fact sheets available on virtually all of its systems, bases, commands, services, and programs. Call or write for the master list. Fact sheets are available electronically via modem by dialing commercial 512-925-8608 and downloading from the AFNEWS T-COMM Bulletin Board.

* Air Force Military History

Office of Air Force History
Building 5681, Room 200
Bolling AFB, Washington, DC 20332-6098   202-767-0412

This office has a small library and archives on Air Force military history going back to the Civil War era, and is available to researchers and scholars. It has holdings on microfilm of the Air Force Historical Research Center in Alabama. Research is by appointment. Copies cost 7 cents, but the first 20 are free. It offers a brochure on Air Force research programs with opportunities for research fellowships. Also ask for a publications list, which contains titles on the air-force role in World Wars I and II, as well as Korea and Vietnam. The list contains prices and ordering information.

* Air Force Patents

The Judge Advocate General
Patents Division, AF/JACP
1900 Half St., SW
Washington, DC 20324-1000   202-475-1386

This office grants licenses for commercial use of government-owned patents. For information on the patents available, contact the above office.

* Air Force Procurement

U.S. Air Force
Air Force Information for Industry Office (AFIFIO)
5001 Eisenhower Ave.
Alexandria, VA 22333   202-247-5838

This office maintains a research and development, technical reading room open to DOD contractors, and will provide research and development planning and requirement documents to qualified users. A security clearance and, in the case of private firms, a government contract, is necessary to enter the reading room as most material is classified. The office can also give information on the Air Force Potential Contractors Program, which was instituted to facilitate technology transfer between the military and industry. Write or call for the free brochure explaining eligibility requirements and how to access the reading room, as well as how to enroll in the Potential Contractors Program and gain access to the Defense Technology Information Center.

* Air Force Research Grants

Office of Scientific Research
U.S. Air Force
Bolling Air Force Base

Washington, DC 20332   202-767-4910

This office accepts proposals for scientific research and requests for grants. Current research interests lie in the areas of Aerospace Sciences, Chemical and Materials Sciences, Physics and Electronics, Life and Environmental Sciences, and Mathematical and Computer Sciences. Write or call for copies of the *Research Interest* pamphlet, *Proposer's Guide*, *Grant Brochure* (which lists types of grants available), and technical brochures on Air Force research programs.

* Air Force Space and Missile Museum

U.S. Air Force
P.O. Box 893
Cape Canaveral, FL 32920-0893   407-853-3245

The Museum documents America's race to the Space Age. Exhibits include *Thor, Minuteman I, Polaris A-3,* and many other missiles presently or formerly in America's active arsenal. Within the Museum, the Center for Aerospace Technology contains documents and records which will enable scholars to analyze ballistic missile warfare ideas and technology. Call or write for more information.

* Air Force Special Missions

Headquarters, U.S. Air Force Reserve
Public Affairs Office
Robins Air Force Base, GA 31098   404-926-1113

Write for photographic reproductions of Air Force aircraft, including the one and only C130 spray mission airplane used for drug enforcement and control. The office also has fact sheets available containing little known but interesting data on other special missions of the Air Force Reserve, including the Central American support flights.

* Air Warfare and Missile Systems Research

U.S. Navy
Crane Division
Naval Surface Warfare Center
Public Affairs Office
Crane, IN 47522   812-854-1394

This Center conducts research and development, testing, and evaluation on air warfare and missile systems. Write or call for their free brochure containing vital statistics on the Center, its mission, and personnel, and which lists major contractors in the local area. Copies of technical reports may be ordered from the Center, a list of reports is also available.

* Aircraft Carriers

U.S. Department of the Navy
OP-553
Washington, DC 20350-2000   703-697-9360

The aircraft carrier is the centerpiece of the American Navy, capable of deploying airpower anywhere in the world. Carrier aircraft played an important role in the air war against Iraq in January-February 1991. For vital statistics on the carrier fleet, contact the above office.

* Airport Security: Hijacking, Bomb Threats

Civil Aviation Security Service (ACS 400)
Federal Aviation Administration (FAA)
U.S. Department of Transportation
800 Independence Ave., SW, Room 319
Washington, DC 20591   202-267-9075

The FAA ensures the presence of law enforcement in U.S. airports, and approves the security programs of all airports under FAR 107. It also certifies walk-through detection devices. The office is a source of information and expertise on the following airport security issues: domestic and foreign aircraft hijacking; bomb threats at airports and on airplanes; compliance and enforcement of regulations; prevention of attempts; explosives and explosive devices found at airports and on airplanes; international crimes involving civil aviation; information on numbers of people screened, numbers of weapons found, and weapon detection devices.

* American Military History 15th Century On

Army Military History Institute
Carlisle Barracks, PA 17013-5008   717-245-3611

The Institute collects original source material on American military history dating as far back as the 15th Century, and holds over one million catalogued items. The Institute provides research and reference assistance to researchers on site and by written and telephone request. The library does lend its materials through inter-library loan programs. No appointment is necessary for research. Photocopies are limited to 100 per year, with a cost of $3.50 for the first 6 copies (including service fee) and 10 cents per page thereafter. The library is open weekdays 8am to 4:30pm.

* Ammunition, Combat, Weapons Testing

U.S. Army
Public Affairs Office (AMSTE-PA)
Aberdeen Proving Ground, MD 21005   301-278-3840

This facility conducts research, development, and testing of weapons, systems, ammunition, and combat and support vehicles. Their pamphlet entitled *This is TECOM* explains the Command, its mission, organization, structure, history, and methods of testing. The booklet *Facts and Figures* provides statistics on property values, energy consumption, number of employees, and population figures. Both are free upon request.

* Army Active Personnel Locator

U.S. Department of the Army
Worldwide Locator, EREC
Ft. Benjamin Harrison, IN 46249-5301   317-542-4211

To locate a missing relative in the active army, contact the above office. There is a small fee for the search.

* Army Aircraft Worldwide

U.S. Department of the Army
Aviation Systems Command
Federal Center, 4300 Goodfellow Blvd.
St. Louis, MO 63120-1798   314-263-1164

This Command maintains all Army aircraft. It publishes a booklet entitled *AVSCOM - Worldwide*, containing facts and figures on troops, world locations, resources, and assets of the Command. To obtain a free copy, write or call the above office.

* Army and Navy Historic Photographs

Still Picture Branch
7th and Pennsylvania Ave., NW
National Archives and Records Administration
Washington, DC 20408   202-501-5455

This office holds photographs from all Federal agencies, including the historical Matthew Brady Civil War collection, and Army and Navy photographs from World War II. Copies may be obtained at cost.

* Army Budget and Forces

Community Relations Division
U.S. Army Public Affairs
The Pentagon, Room 2E631
Washington, DC 20310   703-695-5732

The Posture of the Army and the *Department of the Army Budget Estimates* is published each fiscal year and contains information on the status and direction of Army forces and the budget overview. The Fiscal Year 92/93 Posture Statement contains information on the Army's restructuring for the post Cold-War international security environment. Write or call to obtain a copy of the statement.

* Army Computer Procurement

Public Affairs Office
U.S. Army Information Systems Selection
and Acquisition Agency
2461 Eisenhower Ave.
Alexandria, VA 22331   703-325-9762

This office is responsible for the procurement of all Army computer systems. Write for its fact sheet which describes the agency's mission, philosophy, and procurement process.

* Army Corps of Engineers Historical References

U.S. Army Corps of Engineers
Attn: Office of History
Humphreys Engineering Center
Ft. Belvoir, VA 22060-5577   703-355-3554

This office will respond to reference inquiries regarding the history of the Army

Corps of Engineers. Permission is granted to serious researchers for the use of its archival library, which maintains historical documents dating from the beginning of the Corps. Historical studies analyze the role of the Corps in, among other things, the construction of Washington DC, Yellowstone park, the St. Lawrence Seaway, and the Mississippi River Basin. Recent information is available on the Corps' involvement in the 1989 Alaskan oil spill, the California earthquake, and Hurricane Hugo. The office publishes numerous books and reports and a free list of publications is available on request. The Center extends an open invitation for visitors to drop in.

* Army Discharged Personnel Locator Service

National Personnel Records Center
9700 Page Blvd.
St. Louis, MO 63132-5200   314-538-4261

To locate a relative or friend who is has been discharged from the Army, or who is deceased, contact the above office. The locator service's records go back to 1912; you may be able to find out what your great-great grandfather did in the Army. The above number leads to a recording with detailed information. All requests must be in writing. There is a small fee for the search.

* Army Engineers' Environmental Publications

U.S. Army Corps of Engineers
Public Affairs
20 Massachusetts Ave., NW
Washington, DC 20314   202-272-0011

The Corps offers free brochures on a wide variety of subjects, including archaeology, camping, environment, erosion control, flood control, flood plain management, history, safety, waste-water treatment and water supply. For a publications list, call or write the above office or call the publications office directly at 301-436-2065.

* Army Exploration Maps

Cartographic and Architectural Branch
National Archives and Records Administration
Washington, DC 20408   703-756-6700

This office provides reference service on maps and architectural drawings in its holdings, which include survey maps, early Army exploration maps of the Old West dating from 1860. This office has over 2 million maps and drawings. Call or write for assistance and specify area and time period you are interested in. For in person visits, the center is located at 841 S. Pickett St., Alexandria, Va. The Center is open daily from 8am to 4 pm. Do not send written requests to this address; use the above National Archives address.

* Army Historical Publications

U.S. Army Center for Military History
Federal Center SE./Navy Yard, Bldg 159
Washington, DC 20374-5088   202-475-2587

The Army Center for Military History publishes books, monographs and series on Army military related history. A small sampling of the selections include *The Military and the Media*, *The Final Years*, a series on the Korean War, the Vietnam era, and a series on World War II. Write or call to order their 50-page brochure listing over 200 publications. The center is open 7:30 am to 4 pm weekdays. Appointments are requested. Researchers may peruse the stacks themselves. Microfilm copies of documents are not for sale.

* Army Historical Research

U.S. Army Center of Military History
Historical Resources Branch
Federal Center SE./ Navy Yard, Bldg. 159
Washington, DC 20374-5088   202-475-2581

The Army Center of Military History maintains a library and archives which may be used by serious researchers. For information about use of the library and its holdings, write or call the above office.

* Army Information Technology Laboratory

U.S. Army Corps of Engineers
Waterways Experiment Station
Public Affairs Office
3909 Halls Ferry Road
Vicksburg, MS 39180-6199   601-634-2504

The Information Technology Laboratory (ITL) operates one of the Army's largest

computers and is also responsible for developing, managing and coordinating research and development projects in computer-aided interdisciplinary engineering areas; computer science; automation; visual information; etc. For more information, contact the Laboratory.

* Army Medical Library

Stimson Library
U.S. Department of the Army
Academy of Health Science
Building 2840, Room 106
Ft. Sam Houston, TX 78234-6100   512-221-6900

This library will provide inter-library loans, answer information requests, or give referrals to serious researchers. The collection is particularly good on physical therapy, health care administration, and materials on Army medical history.

* Army Medical Research

U.S. Department of the Army
Army Medical Research and Development Command
Attn: SGRD-PA
Fort Detrick
Frederick, MD 21702   301-663-2732

This Command conducts research and development in medical sciences, supplies, and equipment. Write or call for free copies of the brochure describing the Command, a quarterly newsletter, and the *Broad Agency Announcement* describing the research areas for which they solicit and instructions for submitting proposals.

* Army Patents

Intellectual Property Law Division
Patents, Copyrights and Trademarks Division
U.S. Army Legal Services Agency
5611 Columbia Pike, Room 332A
Falls Church, VA 22041-5013   703-756-2617

This office grants licenses for commercial use of government-owned patents. For information on the patents available and the cooperative research and development agreements with Army regional laboratories, contact the above office.

* Army Personnel Locator

U.S. Army Worldwide Locator
ELREC
Fort Benjamin Harrison, IN 46249   317-542-4211

To locate a long lost relative who is still on active duty in the Army, contact this office by letter. There is a small fee for their services ($3.50 in early 1992). The telephone recording will give you information on the procedure and the data they need from you to initiate their search.

* Army Procurement

U.S. Army
Technical Industrial Liaison Office (TILO)
5001 Eisenhower Ave.
Alexandria, VA 22333   202-274-8948

This office maintains a research and development, technical reading room open to DOD contractors, and will provide research and development planning and requirement documents to qualified users. Security clearance is required to enter the reading room. The office can also give information on the Army Potential Contractors Program, which was instituted to facilitate technology transfer between the military and industry. Write or call for the free brochure explaining eligibility requirements and how to access the reading room, as well as how to enroll in the Potential Contractors Program and gain access to the Defense Technology Information Center.

* Army Recruitment Audiovisuals

Army Recruiting Support Command
Cameron Station, Building 6
Alexandria, VA 22304   703-274-6670

Civic groups may request the Army's recruiting films for community fairs and youth events. The Army has a traveling slide projection show with short subject presentations on American history, the Federal government, development of the English language, Army basic training, and the Army nursing program. If interested in this service, contact your local Army recruiter for information and to request the Audiovisuals.

* Army Research Grants
U.S. Army Research Office
P.O. Box 12211
Research Triangle Park, NC 27709-2211   919-549-0641
This office considers requests for support of basic scientific research from educational institutions and nonprofit organizations. Army special research areas include the following: Young Investigator Program, Short Term Innovative Research Program, and the Research Instrumentation Program. The Army also has a strong interest in research conducted at Historically Black Colleges or Minority Institutions. Write or call for a free pamphlet entitled *Broad Agency Announcement*, which describes the type of research being solicited by the Army, how to fashion a proposal and how to apply for a grant.

* Army Research Labs, Speakers on Technology
U.S. Department of the Army
Army Research Laboratory
AMSLC-PA
2800 Powder Mill Rd.
Adelphi, MD 20783-1145   301-394-3590
This Command oversees the work of the seven major U.S. Army research laboratories. Laboratory work is done in the areas of advanced computing and electronics; battlefield environmental effects; materials and structures; power sources; signal processing; and survivability enhancement. A brochure on the laboratories' missions and programs is available, and the Command can provide public speakers for civic groups in the field of technology development. Write or call for information.

* Army Reserve and Retiree Locator
Army Reserve Personnel Center
U.S. Department of the Army
9700 Page Blvd.
St. Louis, MO 63132-5200   314-263-3901
To locate a missing relative in the Army reserve (who is not assigned to a unit), or to locate a living Army retiree, contact this office. Requests for information must be made in writing.

* Army Speakers Bureau
Community Relations Division
U.S. Army Public Affairs
The Pentagon, Room 2E631
Washington, DC 20310   703-697-2707
The Army supplies speakers on a wide range of subjects to civic groups across the country, including chaplains, doctors, and nutritionists. They have experts in their Wildlife and Environment Conservation Program and Drug and Alcohol Abuse Program who will speak to you about how to start and run your own community programs. Contact your nearest Army installation, or the above office, for a referral.

* Army Technology Transfer and Commercialization
U.S. Department of the Army
Army Research Office
P.O. Box 12211
Triangle Park, NC 27709-2211   919-549-0641
The Army Research Office sponsors programs to further technology development and technology transfer in the United States. Its Technology Transfer Program allows private industry to enter into patent agreements with the Army, making possible the commercialization of Army technological findings. Write or call for free brochures and information describing these programs.

* Army Weapons Systems and Prime Contractors
Superintendent of Documents
Government Printing Office   202-512-1800
Washington, DC 20402-6518   Fax: 202-512-2250
The U.S. Department of the Army publishes the *Army Weapons Systems Handbook*, which contains photographs and descriptions of the major weapons systems in the Army, their program status, and a list of the prime contractors involved. It also gives information on the Soviet counterparts. A copy can be ordered through the Government Printing Office for a moderate charge.

* Astronomy: Naval Observatory
Naval Observatory
34th and Massachusetts Ave.
Washington, DC 20392-5100   202-653-1513
Monday night tours are conducted at the Observatory; call for reservations. A tour brochure and fact sheets on topics such as telescopes, planetariums, and astronomy may be obtained by writing or calling the above office. (Note: The Observatory does not have a planetarium.)

* Atomic Era Veterans Hotline
Defense Nuclear Agency
Public Affairs Office
6801 Telegraph Rd.
Alexandria, VA 22310-3398   800-462-3683
This toll free number is for "atomic" era veterans and their families to call for information on whether he or she was exposed to dangerous radiation in the course of their military duty. Call or write for more information.

* Atmospheric Nuclear Test Era
Defense Nuclear Agency
Public Affairs Office
6801 Telegraph Rd.
Alexandria, VA 22310-3398   703-325-7095
The Agency maintains a public reading room holding information and historical documents pertaining to the atmospheric nuclear testing era. Appointments are required. This specific reading room is administered by the Nuclear Test Personnel Review Program of the U.S. Department of Defense.

* Aviation History
Information Management Division
National Air and Space Museum, Room 3100
Smithsonian Institute
Washington, DC 20560   202-357-3133
The Museum archives have photographs, manuscripts, and personal papers related to major figures in aviation history from the turn of the century to the present. Holdings include NASA "moon shots," and the official collection of Air Force photographs dating back from 1955 to the earliest days of aviation, including both World Wars and the Korean War. Write for their information brochure.

* Aviation Services
U.S. Army Aviation Systems Command
4300 Goodfellow Blvd.
Attn: AMSAV-Z
St. Louis, MO 63120-1798   314-263-1164
This Command is responsible for depot activities and services, serving all four branches of the military. The Command has a Speakers Bureau which responds to requests from civic organizations, of any age group, to speak on scientific and technological topics, as well as the varied personal hobbies of its members. Write or call for free brochures describing the Command's mission, programs, and functions.

* Ballistic Missiles Procurement
U.S. Department of the Army
Strategic Defense Command
Public Affairs Office
P.O. Box 1500
Huntsville, AL 35807-3801   205-955-3887
This Command conducts advanced research and development in the fields of radar, interceptors, optics, and other technical aspects of ballistic missile defense. It publishes fact sheets on the various research programs of the Command, and booklets entitled *Doing Business with the U.S. Army Strategic Defense Command* and *U.S. Army--First in Space and Strategic Defense*.

* Ballistic Research and Engineering
Ballistic Research Laboratories
314 Ryan Building
Aberdeen Proving Ground, MD 21005-5066   301-278-6954
This is an advanced technology laboratory conducting basic and applied research in mathematics, physics, chemistry, biophysics, and engineering related to defense ballistics. Write or call for more information.

International Relations and Defense

* Base Closures and Economic Impact

Office of Economic Adjustment
U.S. Department of Defense
400 Army Navy Drive, Suite 200
Arlington, VA 22202-1155   703-695-1800

With cutbacks in defense, the President and Congress established the Defense Base Closure and Realignment Commission to gather recommendations for streamlining the domestic military base structure. The Office of Economic Adjustment assists local communities, areas or states affected by U.S. Department of Defense actions, such as base closures, establishment of new installations, and cutbacks or expansion of activities. It publishes a number of free publications on these issues, including *Communities in Transition, Planning Civilian Reuse of Former Military Bases, Civilian Reuse of Former Military Bases*. The office also puts out additional information for Communities concerned about base closings. Write or call for more information.

* Bases Overseas

Foreign Military Rights Affairs
International Security Affairs
U.S. Department of Defense
The Pentagon, Room 4D830
Washington, DC 20301   703-695-6386

This office can supply you with information on the status of negotiations for U.S. bases in foreign countries. As much of this information is classified, you may also want to call the public affairs offices at the State and Defense departments.

* Biological Defense Research

U.S. Department of the Army
Dugway Proving Ground
Public Affairs Office STEDP-PA
Dugway, UT 84022-5000   801-831-2116

This facility conducts biological defense research and field and lab tests to evaluate chemical and radiological weapons and defense systems. This center also conducts Smoke Program training exercises in operating under conditions of battlefield obscurement. Dugway is aligned under the Army's Test and Evaluation Command at Aberdeen Proving Ground, MD. Its technical library can be made accessible to approved researchers; requests for technical reports are handled on a case by case basis. Write or call for a brochure describing the installation.

* Biological Research in Medical Defense

U.S. Army Medical Research Institute
for Infectious Diseases
Public Affairs Office
Fort Detrick, MD 21701   301-663-2285

This Institute conducts research on biological agents of military significance and development of vaccines, anti-toxins, toxoids and drugs for medical defense. Write or call for a free brochure on the Institute; copies of technical reports are also available.

* Burial of Veterans

Superintendent
Arlington National Cemetery
Arlington, VA 22211   703-695-3250

Many veterans are eligible to be buried or inurned at Arlington. As burial space is limited mainly to holders of the nations highest military decorations or 20 year or more veterans. Arlington constructed a Columbarium which opened in 1980. Any honorably discharged veteran and their spouse and dependent children can be inurned there. Write or call this office for information on eligibility requirements and procedures.

* Casualty Reporting: Army

Casualty Services Division
U.S. Department of the Army
Hoffman Building, Room 920
Alexandria, VA 22331   703-325-7990

The Casualty Services Division is responsible for the Army's casualty reporting and notification system worldwide, and provides a survivor and next-of-kin assistance program. The office is available for calls 24 hours a day, seven days a week. Army policy is that next of kin can be notified on injuries over the phone. Next of kin are notified of deaths in person. A free brochure is available explaining their procedures.

* Central Command

Public Affairs Office
McDill AFB, FL 33608   813-830-6393

The Central Command's responsibilities include, countries in Europe, Asia, and Africa. Included within its Area of Responsibility (AOR) is the volatile Persian Gulf region, which contains over 70% of the world's oil reserves. Senior command at Central Command (CENTCOM) rotates between an Army and Marine senior officer. American and allied forces during the Gulf War came under the CENTCOM command and its senior commander, U.S. Army General Schwarzkopf. This office is a good place to start searching for information on the Gulf War. Requests for Gulf War information should be made in writing.

* Ceramics and Metals Research

U.S. Department of the Army
Army Materials Technology Lab
Watertown, MA 02172-0001   617-923-5278

This Center specializes in research regarding metals and ceramics. Major programs currently include: the battle against *Corrosion*; *Advanced Armor*; *Structural Ceramics*; *Elastomers*; and *Composite Materials Hull*. The Lab's work has done much to improve the armors of American mechanized forces. It maintains a library open to approved researchers, and copies of technical reports are available upon request. Write or call for free brochures describing the Center, its mission, and programs.

* Chemical and Biological Weapons

U.S. Department of the Army
Public Affairs Office STEDP-PA
Dugway Proving Ground, UT 84022-5000   801-831-2116

This facility conducts biological defense research, and field and lab tests to evaluate chemical and radiological weapons and defense systems. A post guide, economic impact statement, and fact sheets on the history of the post, and its mission are available. Write or call for free copies.

* Chemical Defense, Bald Eagles and Peregrine Falcons

U.S. Department of the Army
Chemical Research Development
and Engineering Center
Aberdeen Proving Ground, MD 21010-5423   301-671-4345

While the Center's primary mission is concerned with research on chemical defensive material, the Center has become very involved in wildlife conservation programs because of its location on the Chesapeake Bay. The Center is especially experienced in a Bald Eagle program and a Peregrine Falcon program. Fact sheets on these and other wildlife issues may be obtained by writing or calling the above office.

* Chemical Defense Technologies

U.S. Army Medical Research
Institute of Chemical Defense
Attn: SGRD-UV-R
Aberdeen Proving Ground, MD 21010-5425   301-278-6954

This Institute conducts research, development, testing, and evaluation of medical/chemical defense technologies. Write or call for a free brochure describing the work of the Institute and a list of technical reports.

* Chemical Propulsion Resource Center

The Johns Hopkins University
Applied Physics Laboratory
Chemical Propulsion Information Agency (CPIA)
10630 Little Patuxent Parkway
Columbia, MD 21044-3200   410-992-7307

Chemical Propulsion Information Agency (CPIA) provides products, specialized reference service, database searches, and copies of technical reports on all areas of chemical propulsion. Publications include *The Chemical Propulsion Abstracts, The CPIA/M1 Rocket Motor Manual, the CPIA/M2 Solid Propellant Manual, the CPIA/M6 Airbreathing Propulsion Manual, The JANNAF Propulsion Meeting,* and *Selected Papers.* CPIA also puts out a monthly bulletin updating subscribers on its activities. Write or call for a free pamphlet explaining their services and how to become a subscriber. Note, however, that this service is primarily for Department of Defense contractors.

* Civil Air Patrol (CAP)

HQ Civil Air Patrol
U.S. Department of the Air Force
Office of Public Affairs
Maxwell AFB, AL 3611-5572   205-953-5463

The Civil Air Patrol has three main missions: 1) emergency services; 2) aerospace education; and 3) a cadet program for high school students. CAP has offices in all 50 states and in the District of Columbia. CAP flies most of the search and rescue hours requested by the Air Force. Write or call for a leaflet explaining the programs, the benefits of membership, and a list of CAP posts in your area.

* Civil Engineering and Construction Research

Naval Civil Engineering Laboratory
Naval Construction Battalion Center
U.S. Department of the Navy
Port Hueneme, CA 93043   805-982-1124

This Center is the principal research, development, test, and evaluation center for shore and sea-floor facilities and for support of Navy and Marine Corps construction forces. The Public Affairs Office of the Center has a brochure on the Laboratory's mission, programs, and personnel entitled *Tech Activities*. There are also two procurement offices located at the Center. Write or call the above office for further information.

* Civil War Photographs

Still Picture Branch
7th and Pennsylvania Ave. NW
National Archives and Records Administration
Washington, DC 20408   202-501-5455

The American Civil War was the first large scale conflict in history to be captured on film. The Still Picture Branch has the famous Brady collection of photos. The Collection includes photos of Army life, Generals in the field, Navies, battlefields, and famous figures from both the Blue and the Gray. Call or write for a list of the photos available.

* Coast Guard Reserve

Office of Readiness and Reserve
U.S. Coast Guard
U.S. Department of Transportation
2100 2nd St., SW, Room 5101
Washington, DC 20593-0001   202-267-2350

In time of war or national emergency, the Coast Guard Reserve provides trained individuals and units for active duty. The Reserve also assists the Guard in peacetime missions during domestic emergencies and peak operations. The *Coast Guard Reservist Magazine*, available free from the office listed above, provides bimonthly news and human interest stories about Coast Guard Reservists and their activities.

* Coastal Engineering Research Center (CERC)

U.S. Army Corp of Engineers
Waterways Experiment Station
Public Affairs Office
3909 Halls Ferry Road
Vicksburg, MS 39180-6199   601-634-2504

The Coastal Engineering Research Center (CERC) is the nations foremost research and development for coastal engineering. Research focuses on problems relating to shore and beach erosion control; flooding and storm protection; coastal dredging; and design, construction, and maintenance of coastal navigation. Contact WES for more information.

* Cold Environments Research

U.S. Army Corps of Engineers
Army Cold Regions Research and Engineering Laboratory
72 Lyme Rd.
Hanover, NH 03755-1290   603-646-4100

This Laboratory conducts research on living, working, traveling, building and military operations in cold environments. A Speakers Bureau will provide experts to speak before civic groups. The Laboratory also has an extensive library on cold regions research. The Library of Congress prepares the *Bibliography on Cold Regions Science and Technology*. Write or call for brochures explaining the mission and programs, accessing information from the library, and how to do business with the Laboratory.

* Communications and Electronic Government Contracts

U.S. Army Communications-Electronics Command
Ft. Monmouth, NJ 07703   908-532-1258

This Command is concerned with research, development and acquisition of communications tactical data, command and control systems, and the components and materials of electronic communications. Its Technical/Industrial Liaison and Special Projects Office will supply information and literature on Advance Planning Briefings for-Industry and how to do business with CECOM.

* Conscientious Objectors and Reclassification

U.S. Department of Defense
Force Management and Personnel
The Pentagon, Room 3E764
Washington, DC 20301-4000   703-695-7402

For information on conscientious objectors and prisoners of war, including reclassification and discharge data, contact the above office.

* Contracting with the Defense Logistic Agency

Public Affairs (DLA-B)
Defense Logistics Agency
Cameron Station
Alexandria, VA 22304-6100   703-274-6135

This office has information on all Defense Logistics Agency (DLA) business and activities, and a pamphlet on it mission, *The ABC's of DLA*. It also offers a *DLA Index to Publications*, a *DLA Index to Forms*, and the brochure, *An Identification of Commodities Purchased by the Defense Logistics Agency*.

* Contracting Research and Development with the Defense Department

Defense Technical Information Center (DTIC)
Attn: FDRB
Cameron Station
Alexandria, VA 22304-6145   202-274-6847

The Defense Technical Information Center (DTIC) is the clearinghouse for the U.S. Department of Defense's collection of scientific and technological research and development information. The booklet entitled *Registration and Certification for Scientific and Technical Services* will explain who is eligible to use the Center's services and how to register as a user. The manual also contains a list of contractors, their offices and phone numbers, and information on the potential contractor program. The *Handbook for Users* and the *Green and White* brochure (DTIC-BC-1) explain the two major databases available to contractors and potential contractors: one for completed research and technological reports and one for ongoing research and development information.

* Construction Productivity Partnership

U.S. Army Corps of Engineers
Public Affairs Office
20 Massachusetts Ave., NW
Washington, DC 20314-1000   202-272-0010

The Army Corps of Engineers sponsors the Construction Productivity Advancement Research Program (CPAR), in which the Corps joins in partnership with city government, public utilities, or private industry to fund research which will benefit the U.S. construction industry as a whole. Write or call for their booklet describing the program and participation guidelines.

* Contractors and Government Procurement

Defense Logistics Agency
Defense Contract Administration Service (DCAS)
Cameron Station
Alexandria, VA 22304-6100   703-274-6135

The nine regional offices of this Service provide post-award contract administration. Booklets are available which explain the services of the agency and the procedure for obtaining a government contract, and the staff will answer questions on current contractors and contracts. Contact your regional office or the above office to locate the office nearest you.

* Correcting Errors in Air Force Records

Air Force Board for the
Correction of Military Records
U.S. Department of the Air Force
The Pentagon, Room AFBCMR
Washington, DC 20330-1430   703-692-4726

This Board handles appeals for correction of Air Force military records containing errors or unjust information. Write or call for the appropriate application forms.

* Correcting Errors in Army Records

Army Board for Correction of
Military Records
U.S. Department of the Army
1914 Jefferson Davis Hwy.
CM4, 2nd Floor, Room 220
Arlington, VA 22202-4508   703-607-1601

This Board handles appeals for correction of Army military records containing errors or unjust information. Write or call for the appropriate application forms.

* Correcting Errors in Navy Records

Board for the Correction
of Naval Records
U.S. Department of the Navy
Arlington Navy Annex, Room 2432
Washington, DC 20370-5100   703-614-1765

This Board handles appeals for correction of Navy military records containing errors or unjust information. Write or call for the appropriate application forms.

* Critical and Strategic Mineral Commodities

Minerals Information Office
Bureau of Mines/U.S. Geological Survey
U.S. Department of the Interior
18th and C Sts., MS 2647-MIB
Room 2647
Washington, DC 20240   202-208-5512

The *Personal Computer Advanced Deposit Information Tracking System Mineral Deposit Data Base* contains information on 3,000 domestic and foreign (market economy countries) mining operations, including operation data (name, company, locations, etc.) and operation status (operation type, processing and milling methods, capacity, etc.). The database covers 34 critical and strategic commodities, representing those deposits most significant in terms of value and tonnage. This information is not printed, but visitors can look at it on the Minerals Information Office computer system or can request the information on disk from the Minerals Availability Branch.

* Defense Analysis

Center for Defense Information (CDI)
1500 Massachusetts Ave NW
Washington, DC 20005   202-862-0700

The *Defense Monitor*, published about 10 times per year, provides analyses, statistics, facts, quotes and information about military programs and spotlights military issues of national importance. Issues are available for $1 each (half price for 10 or more) from the above address. Some titles included are as follows:

The Stealth Bomber
U.S. Invasion of Iraq: Appraising the Option
Space Warfare: A New Cold War Battleground
Nuclear Bomb Factories: The Danger Within
What Should We Defend?
Defending the Environment? The Record of the U.S. Military

* Defense Budget and Military Spending Reports

National Technical Information Service
5285 Port Royal Rd.
Springfield, VA 22161   703-487-4650

The Service has both paper copy and microfiche copy of U.S. Department of Defense budget reports, including *Program Acquisition Costs by Weapons System*; *Construction Programs*; *Research, Development, Test and Evaluation Program*; and *Procurement Programs*. For price and ordering information, write or call the above office. The office is open weekdays 8:30 to 5:30.

* Defense Contractor Fraud Hotline

The Pentagon   703-693-5080
Washington, DC 20301-1900   800-424-9098

Call this number to report fraud or corruption by anyone working for a U.S. Department of Defense contractor. The Hotline people are eager to supply your office with posters, brochures, and wallet size cards displaying their number.

* Defense Data Worldwide Network

Ada Information Clearinghouse
c/o IIT Research Institute
4600 Forbes Blvd.
Lanham, MD 20706   703-685-1477

This organization supplies comprehensive services and information to Ada database users worldwide. It offers a free quarterly newsletter, a calendar of events, a list of resources for reusing the Ada code, information on how to access the *Defense Data Network*, a list of Ada compilers, a list of Ada serial publications, a list of classes and seminars, a free monthly handout on new products and tools for Ada, a catalog of college courses, and two bulletin boards with comprehensive Ada information. Call or write for an information packet explaining their services and resources.

* Defense Department General Information

Directorate for Public Communication
U.S. Department of Defense
The Pentagon, Room 2E777
Washington, DC 20301-1400   703-697-5737

This office answers general questions concerning the work of the U.S. Department of Defense, including defense spending and defense policy. Upon request, the office can supply copies of major speeches delivered by officials in the Office of the Secretary of Defense, reports issued by the Office, and fact sheets on defense issues. Speeches are referenced by date delivered. Write or call for more information.

* Defense Department Manpower Statistics

Washington Headquarter Services
Directorate for Information Operations and Reports
1215 Jefferson Davis Hwy., Suite 1204
Arlington, VA 22202-4302   703-746-0786

A free catalog is available which lists this office's publications covering DOD manpower statistics, including financial management data, logistic data, health care statistics, and prime contract award data. Write or call to order a copy.

* Defense Department Organization and Functions

Directorate for Organizational
and Management Planning
U.S. Department of Defense
The Pentagon, Room 3A326
Washington, DC 20301-1100   703-697-5737

This office publishes the *Defense Organizational and Functions Guidebook*, which outlines the functions of the major components of the U.S. Department of Defense. It contains a functional statement citing the pertinent charter and detailed information on the authority and responsibilities of each organization, including an organizational chart. To request a free copy, write or call the above office.

* Defense Department Publications List

Directorate for Public Communication
U.S. Department of Defense
The Pentagon, Room 2E777
Washington, DC 20301-1400   703-697-5737

The Directorate for Public Communication puts out a list of Defense Department publications available from the Department of Defense, National Technical Information Service (NTIS), or Government Printing Office (GPO). Call or write for the list. Publications include:

Allied Contributions to the Common Defense
Armed Forces Insignia Poster
Defense Industrial Base: Report to Congress
Defense Issues (speech texts)
Joint Military Net Assessment
National Security Strategy
Security Assistance Programs: Congressional Presentation Document
Military Forces in Transition (formerly Soviet Military Power)
Strategic Defense Initiative Annual Report

* Defense Energy Consumption

Defense Energy Policy Directorate
Office of the Assistant Secretary of Defense
DEF/P&L/L(EP), The Pentagon, Room 1D760
Washington, DC 20301-3000   703-697-5737

This office can provide you with wholesale petroleum data and facility energy consumption data. Inquiries will be answered on a cost recovery basis and should be made in writing.

* Defense Maps and Charts Toll-free Number

Defense Mapping Agency
Combat Support Center
Attn: Customer Assistance Office   800-826-0342
Washington, DC 20315-0010   301-227-2495

The Defense Mapping Agency makes available at cost a broad range of maps and charts. There are four categories available: aeronautical, topographic, hydrographic, and digital (lists those products available on magnetic tape). Each map costs $2.75 each.

* Defense Monthly Magazine

American Forces Information Service
1735 N. Lynn St.
Arlington, VA 22209   703-274-4847

The Information Service publishes *Defense 92*, a bi-monthly magazine devoted to defense issues and policy. You can order it through the Government Printing Office, Superintendent of Documents, Washington, DC 20402; 202-512-1800.

* Defense Technical Information and Referral Center

Defense Technical Information Center (DTIC)
Cameron Station
Alexandria, VA 22304-6145   202-274-7633

The Defense Technical Information Center (DTIC) maintains a *Referral Data Bank Directory* of major resource and holding centers in the U.S. Department of Defense. Write or call the above office for more information.

* Defense Videos

Center for Defense Information (CDI)
1500 Massachusetts Ave NW
Washington, DC 20005   202-862-0700

The Center for Defense Information's (CDI) weekly TV show, "America's Defense Monitor", covers military and international affairs and is available on VHS for $25 per episode plus $2 shipping and handling. Transcripts are $5 each plus $2 postage and handling. Contact the above listing for more information. Some of the titles available are as follows:

The Spread of Nuclear Weapons
Testing Nuclear Arms
The Face of the "Enemy"
The Stealth Bomber

* Desert Shield/Desert Storm - Air Force Role

Office of the Secretary of the Air Force
Public Affairs Office
Washington, DC 20330-1000   703-695-9664

The Air Force published several items documenting its role in the Gulf War. The August 1991 commemorative issue of *Airman*, the Magazine of the Air Force, has personal stories from airmen who took part in the conflict, including interviews with men who were taken prisoner in Iraq. Also ask for the Air Force White Paper and Backgrounder on the Gulf War, both of which provide analysis of the air campaign against Iraq and the performance of the many aircraft and air delivered munitions used in the conflict. All of these publications are free but availability may be limited.

* Desert Shield/Desert Storm - Army Role

Association of the United States Army
Institute for Land Warfare (ILW)
2425 Wilson Blvd.
Arlington, VA 22201-3385   703-841-4300

The Institute for Land Warfare (ILW) publishes numerous fact sheets and special reports on all aspects of land warfare. Reports on the Persian Gulf War include:

AUSA Background Brief, No. 30, Summary of Authorities Available to the President in Emergencies Short of Declared War - January 1991
AUSA Background Brief, No. 34, Army equipment performance in Operation Desert Storm - April 1991
Landpower Essay Series, No. 91-1, The Impact of Desert Storm and the Growing Soviet Military Dissatisfaction with Defense Doctrine, by MG Edward b. Atkeson, USA Retired, March 1991
Special Report - The U.S. Army in Operation Desert Storm - An Overview, June 1991
Landpower Essay Series, No.91-2, Desert Storm Fire Support - Classic Airland Battle Operations, by BG Paul F. Pearson, USA Retired, and General Glenn K. Otis, USA Retired, June 1991
Special Report - Operations Desert Shield and Desert Storm: The Logistics Perspective, September 1991
Defense Report 91-1, Victory in the Persian Gulf War -- Only America Could Do It, March 1991
Defense Report 91-2, How We Did It -- Smart Weapons Operated by Smart People, March 1991

* Desert Shield/Desert Storm - GAO Analyses

General Accounting Office (GAO)
National Security and International Affairs Division
Post Office Box 6015
Gaithersburg, MD 20877   202-275-6241

In the afterglow of the Persian Gulf War, the General Accounting Office has been studying logistical and equipment problems in order to improve military performance in future conflicts. Call for a complete list of reports.

Reports on the War include:
Operation Desert Storm: The Services Efforts to Provide Logistics Support for Selected Weapon Systems. GAO/NSIAD 91-321, Sept 26, 1991.
Operation Desert Storm: Army's Use of Water Purification Equipment. GAO/NSIAD 91-325, Sept. 26 1991.
Operation Desert Storm: Problems Encountered by Activated Reservists. GAO/NSIAD 91-290, Sept 27, 1991.

* Desert Shield/Desert Storm - Logistics

Military Traffic Management Command (MTMC)
5611 Columbia Pike
Falls Church, VA 22041-5050   703-756-1242

The Military Traffic Management Command (MTMC) has facts and figures on the astonishing logistical movements that made Desert Shield/Storm such a monumental and successful operation. Ask for the MTMC facts, which details the number of ships used and vehicles moved in the operation. It is available free upon request.

* Desert Shield/Desert Storm - Navy Role

U.S. Department of the Navy
Office of Information
Washington, DC 20350-1200   703-697-2904

The Navy has published several items highlighting Navy and Marine roles in the U.S. victory in the Gulf War. The Special Issue of the U.S. Navy official magazine *All Hands*, includes articles on Sealift, Marine combat engagements, and Navy Medicine in the Gulf. The Office of the Chief of Naval Operations has also published a book entitled *The United States Navy in Desert Shield/Desert Storm*. This book details the Navy and Marine role in the conflict and outlines lessons learned for the future. Both publications are available free to the public but supplies may be limited.

* Dictionary of Military Terms

Superintendent of Documents
Government Printing Office   202-512-1800
Washington, DC 20402-6518   Fax: 202-512-2250

The Joint Staff has published a comprehensive *Dictionary of Military and Associated Terms*, available for approximately $15. Contact the Government Printing Office for current price and ordering information.

* Doing Business with the Military

Director, Office of Small and
Disadvantaged Business Utilization
Undersecretary of Defense for Acquisition
The Pentagon, Room 2A340

International Relations and Defense

Washington, DC 20301   703-614-1151

This office has an information package on how to sell to the U.S. Department of Defense. It contains a booklet of rules and regulations in selling to the military, a booklet listing all the procurement offices worldwide, and a subcontracting directory.

* Electronic Warfare

U.S. Navy
Crane Division
Naval Surface Warfare Center
Public Affairs Office
Crane, IN 47522   812-854-1394

As the Gulf War vividly demonstrated, electronic warfare has become an indispensable part of modern combat. The Naval Surface Warfare Center engages in research in Microelectronic Technology, Microwave components, electronic warfare, and electronic module test and repair. Contact the above office for further information.

* Electromagnetic Technology

Directorate for Public Communication
U.S. Department of Defense
The Pentagon, Room 2E777
Washington, DC 20301-1400   703-697-5737

This office can provide you with general information about electromagnetic technology, including annual reports, newsletters and fact sheets, and will make referrals for you if you need more detailed information.

* Excavation and Dredging Regulation Regulatory Branch

U.S. Army Corps of Engineers
20 Massachusetts Ave., NW, Room 6235
Washington, DC 20314   202-272-0397

You must obtain a Corps permit if you plan to locate a structure, excavate, or discharge dredged or fill material in waters of the United States, including wetlands, or if you plan to transport dredged material for the purpose of dumping it into ocean waters. Contact the appropriate District Engineer office for current information and to apply for a permit. You may contact the above office for addresses and telephone numbers of the District offices.

* Federal Helium Stockpile

Helium Operations
Bureau of Mines
U.S. Department of the Interior
810 7th St, NW
Washington, DC 20241   202-501-9244

The Bureau of Mines' Federal Helium Program provides helium for the current and foreseeable needs of essential government activities and assists individual enterprises with the production and distribution of helium. Approximately 300 million cubic feet of helium is withdrawn annually from the Bureau's Cliffside Helium Storage Reservoir near Amarillo, Texas. After purification, this helium is distributed to federal agencies, the private helium industry, and to university and college research facilities.

* Federal Technological Resources Directory

National Technical Information Service
Springfield, VA 22161   703-487-4650

The *Directory of Federal Technological Resources* listing all federal resources for services, expertise, and facilities of interest to engineers, scientists, and technology-oriented businesses may be ordered from this service for a moderate charge.

* Film Footage

U.S. Department of Defense
Motion Media Records Center
Building 248
Norton Air Force Base, CA 92409   714-382-2307

This Center holds Army, Navy, and Marine Corps stock footage from 1964 to the present. Contact the National Archives for footage from prior years. They will assist researchers, educators, or commercial enterprises in locating specific scenes for a moderate fee. Write for their free brochure describing the holdings and how to access the Center.

* Flight Testing and Aerial Support Systems

Air Force Flight Test Center
Air Force Systems Command
U.S. Department of the Air Force
Edwards Air Force Base, CA 93523   805-277-3510

This Test Center conducts advanced development programs in flight testing and evaluation of new aircraft, rocket propulsion systems, aerial support systems (parachutes, delivery and recovery systems), and the training of research pilots. Its technical library may be made available for approved researchers. Fact sheets on the history, mission, aircraft, and space shuttle, as well as photographs of the base and aircraft are available at no charge upon request.

* Foreign Language Training

Defense Language Institute
Foreign Language Center, also Library
Non-Resident Division
Presidio of Monterey, CA 93944   408-647-5572

The Defense Language Institute is one of the world's largest language training centers. The holdings of its library--over 100,000 books in 50 languages--are available through a national inter-library loan program. The non-resident division offers foreign language courses for sale. A catalog of the languages available may be obtained for $5.25. Write or call for brochures on the Institute and information regarding inter-library loans.

* Foreign Military Sales

Defense Security Assistance Agency
The Pentagon, Room 4D720
Washington, DC 20301-2800   703-604-6513

This office administers the Foreign Military Financing Program (FMFP) Program, which deals with U.S. government sales of defense articles and services to foreign governments. A free booklet containing information on the Program and the U.S. Defense Security Assistance Agency is available upon request.

* Foreign Weapon Sales Statistics

FMS Reports and Controls Division
Defense Security Assistance Agency
The Pentagon, Room 4B659
Washington, DC 20301-2800   703-604-6513

This office publishes a free annual publication, *Foreign Military Sales, Foreign Military Construction Sales, and Military Assistance Facts*, which contains information and detailed statistics on all grant programs, sales, and Federal financing of security assistance to foreign countries. Write or call for a copy.

* Freedom of Information Access

Defense Intelligence Agency (DIA)
Attn: RTS-1B
Washington, DC 20340-3299   202-373-8361

For access to information held by the Defense Intelligence Agency and subject to the provisions of the Freedom of Information Act, contact this office. A brochure, *Brief History of DIA*, which gives information on the various functions and the mission of the agency is available upon request.

* Fuel Suppliers and Consumption in the Military

Public Affairs Office
Defense Fuel Supply Center
Defense Logistics Agency
Cameron Station
Alexandria, VA 22304-6160   703-274-6489

This office will supply information on almost anything you will want to know concerning fuel supply in the military. The staff will explain how to contract for the Strategic Petroleum Reserve, and how to request information under the Freedom of Information Act, such as statistics on fuel consumption patterns in the military and copies of current contracts with major suppliers. You may request a free copy of their *Fact Book*, which tells how much was spent on fuel throughout the U.S. Department of Defense, the sources of supply, and how the fuel was allocated. It includes line graphs and pie charts, with a national geographic distribution breakdown. This office also publishes the magazine *Fuel Line*, available by subscription.

* Genealogy Searches Military Service

General Reference Branch
National Archives and Records Administration
Washington, DC 20408   202-501-5402

This office holds military service and pension records of people who served prior to 1900. The office accepts written requests only. Ask for *Form NATF 80.*

* Geotechnical Research

U.S. Army Corps of Engineers
Waterways Experiment Station
3909 Halls Ferry Rd.
Vicksburg, MS 39180-6199   601-634-2504

A component of the Geotechnical Lab, the Pavements and Soil Trafficability Information Analysis Center (PSTIAC) provides products and specialized reference services to the public. The staff can be tasked to provide evaluative engineering and/or analytical service on pavements, trafficability, vehicle mobility, and terrain, primarily relevant to military needs. Database searches are performed on a cost recovery basis, and requests are approved on a case by case basis. The Station's library participates in the national inter-library loan system, and copies of technical reports are distributed on a first come, first served basis. (Reports are thereafter available from DTIC.) The Public Affairs Office can provide a summary of publications, fact sheets on the Center's programs, brochures on subject areas, and a comprehensive book entitled *Summary of Capabilities* describing the Center's work. Time on the Center's super computer is available for sale to academic researchers.

* Government Films, Videos, and Slides

National Audio-Visual Center
8700 Edgeworth Dr.
Capital Heights, MD 20743   301-763-1891

This is the sole source from which to purchase all U.S. government produced films, video tapes and slide sets. Write or call their office for a list of the specialty catalogs available; the catalogs are free, the products are for sale.

* Guided Missiles and Rocket Launching

Naval Ordnance Missile Test Facility
White Sands Missile Range, NM 88002   505-678-1134

This facility is used for the testing and evaluation of guided missiles, and endo- and exo-atmospheric research in rocket launching. Testing is conducted by the armed services, NASA, and private corporations. The Range also has a thriving wildlife reserve. Write or call for a free brochure detailing the type of research conducted on the facility and its range capabilities.

* High Seas Law Enforcement

Operational Law Enforcement Division
Office of Law Enforcement and Defense Operations
U.S. Coast Guard
U.S. Department of Transportation
2100 2nd St., SW, Room 3110
Washington, DC 20593-0001   202-267-1890

As the primary maritime law enforcement agency for the U.S., the Coast Guard enforces Federal laws, treaties, and international agreements to which the U.S. is a party. The Coast Guard may conduct investigations when violations are suspected, such as smuggling, drug trafficking, or polluting. Empowered to board and inspect vessels routinely as well, the Guard also conducts "suspicionless" boardings to prevent violations. To report suspicious or questionable activity on boats, or to complain about an improperly conducted boarding, call the Boating Safety Hotline, 800-368-5647; or 202-267-0780 in DC, or contact your local Coast Guard commander. The office listed above can provide you with information about the Coast Guard's law enforcement role and the National Narcotics Border Interdiction System, which coordinates multi-agency and international operations with other countries to suppress narcotics trafficking.

* History Museums in U.S. and Germany

U.S. Army Center of Military History
Pulaski Bldg.
Room 4124-C
Washington, DC 20314   202-272-0321

The Army Center of Military History administers 73 public museums throughout the U.S. and West Germany. Write or call the above office for a list of museum locations and collections.

* House of Representatives Hearings and Research

House Armed Services Committee
Suite 2120, Rayburn House Office Building
Washington, DC 20515   202-225-4151

The House Armed Services Committee concerns itself with defense, military personnel and installations, procurement, nuclear systems, research and development, seapower, and strategic and critical materials such as petroleum and Chromium. To be placed on the mailing list for hearing dates, call the above telephone number. Transcripts of committee hearings may be obtained directly from the committee or you may ask your representative for help. Copies of House bills and committee reports can also be obtained free of charge from the House Documents room 202-225-3456. Your Congressman can also obtain Congressional Research Reports on national defense issues for you. A list of reports is located in the back of this book.

* Installations Public Works Construction

U.S. Department of the Army
Public Affairs Office
Construction Engineering Research Laboratory
P.O. Box 4005
Champaign, IL 61824-4005   217-373-7216

This office has copies of technical reports on research related to the construction, operation, maintenance, and repair of public works facilities at military installations. For a free brochure detailing your nearest Construction Engineering Research Laboratory and where to obtain reports, contact this office.

* Joint Chiefs of Staff

Historical Division
Joint Chiefs of Staff
U.S. Department of Defense
The Pentagon, Room 1A-714
Washington, DC 20318-0400   703-697-3088

This office publishes a number of military history series and volumes, including *Joint Chiefs of Staff and National Policy (1945-1954)* and *The Chairmen of the Joint Chiefs of Staff,* discussing the evolution of the office and profiles of its chiefs and *The Organizational Development of the Joint Chiefs of Staff: 1942-1989.* Write or call the above office for the availability of the publications.
Publications are free but quantities are limited.

* Land and Aeronautical Target Survivability

Survivability/Vulnerability Information Analysis Center
2130 8th St., Bldg. 45
Wright-Patterson AFB, OH 45433   513-256-6880

SURVIAC maintains and operates a database of non-nuclear survivability/vulnerability data, information, methodologies, models, and analyses relating to U.S. and foreign land and aeronautical targets. The Center is a source for products, database searches, and technical reports offered on a cost recovery basis. Specialized reference services are available for questions that exceed the limits of resources available for an inquiry response. Requests must be relevant to SURVIAC's primary areas of interest and funded by the requestor. Contact SURVIAC to order services or obtain general information.

* Land Warfare

Association of the United States Army
Institute for Land Warfare
2425 Wilson Blvd.
Arlington, VA 22201-3385   703-841-4300

The Institute's mission is to inform national leaders and the American public about the nature of land warfare and the importance of the U.S. Army. The Institute for Land Warfare (ILW) publishes Defense Reports, Special Reports, Fact Sheets, and Background Briefs. For a list of publications, contact the above number.

* Largest Defense Contractors

Directorate for Information Operations and Reports
Washington Headquarters Services
1215 Jefferson Davis Hwy., Suite 1204
Arlington, VA 22202   703-746-0786

This office publishes such reports as *100 Companies Receiving the Largest Dollar Volume of Prime Contract Awards* and the *Atlas/Data Abstract for the United States and Selected Areas,* which contains a map showing all the military installations and a compendium of U.S. Department of Defense statistics for each state. Write or call for their free catalog list all their publications available through the Government Printing Office, 202-512-1800.

International Relations and Defense

* Laser Research
High Energy Laser Systems Test Facility
White Sands Missile Range
Public Affairs Office
New Mexico, NM 88802   505-678-1134

This Facility tests and evaluates high energy laser systems, subsystems and components. For information on tests and facilities, contact the above office.

* Lawrence Livermore Computer Facility
Visitors Center
Lawrence Livermore National Laboratory
Greenville Road
Livermore, CA 94550   510-422-9797

The National Laboratory conducts public tours of its computing center. You must, however, be 18 years of age or older. For information, contact the Visitors Center.

* Lawrence Livermore National Laboratory
Laboratory Communications and Public Information
Lawrence Livermore National Laboratory
7000 East Ave. (Mail Stop L-404)
Livermore, CA 94550   510-422-4599

The Laboratory maintains a library accessible to researchers able to demonstrate a "need to know." The collection includes reports, texts, and journals on biomedicine, physics, energy, and military weapons design. Their *Rainbow* brochure outlines the programs, functions, and mission of the laboratory, and *Science and Engineering on the Grand Scale* gives an overview of each laboratory department. Free booklets on a broad range of subjects are available, including physics, the national magnetic fusion energy computing center, biomedical cancer research, solar energy research, and history of the National Laboratory and its role in weapons research.

* Logistics Research
U.S. Army
Ordnance Center and School Library
(AMATSL-SE-LI)
Aberdeen Proving Ground, MD 21004   301-278-6954

The Center's school has several technical libraries devoted to military logistics, supply and maintenance, which are open to approved researchers. Part of the collection is closed. Materials are available through inter-library loan. For additional information on their holdings and accessibility, contact the above office.

* Marine Corps Historical Research and Internships
U.S. Marine Corps Historical Center
Building 58, Navy Yard
9th and M Sts., SE
Washington, DC 20374-0580   202-433-3840

The Historical Center encompasses a museum, library, archives, reference section, a world historical section, and a publishing department. The library is open to serious researchers. The Center sponsors an internship program whereby students may earn college credit for performing research work at the Center. Write or call for brochures describing both the museum and the library. A free publications catalog is also available.

* Marine Corps Information Clearinghouse
Marine Corps-Public Affairs
Headquarters, U.S. Marine Corps
Washington, DC 20380-0001   703-614-1492

This office publishes material describing Marine Corps programs, personnel, and budget. Publication indexes and checklists are also available for a small fee. Write for information.

* Medical History Research
National Museum of Health and Medicine
Building 54, South Wing
Walter Reed Army Medical Center
Washington, DC 20606-6000   202-576-2348

The museum maintains an archives and a behind-the-scenes collection available to serious researchers. Write or call for brochures and information on the collection and for information on the tax-exempt, non-profit foundation headed by Surgeon General Dr. Koop for a new national health museum.

* Medical Scholarships through the Air Force
U.S. Department of the Air Force
Headquarters, USAFRS/RSH   512-652-4334
Randolph Air Force Base, TX 78150-5421   800-531-5980

The Air Force offers Health Professions Scholarships in return for military service obligation. These scholarships are for those entering medical school. At the completion of medical school scholarship recipients can begin their obligation or file for a deferment in order to seek specialized training. Educational costs determine the length of service to the Air Force required. Contact the above office or call toll-free number for further information. Local Air Force recruiters also have information on this program.

* Microcomputers and Semiconductors
Reliability Analysis Center (RAC)
P.O. Box 4700
Rome, NY 13442-4700   315-739-7047

Evaluation engineering, analytical services, products, and specialized reference services are provided by RAC in the areas of microcircuits, semiconductors, nonelectric devices, and electronic modules. Reliability and maintainability data on planned and operational systems and equipment is stored in a database. A user's catalog, searches, and technical reports can be obtained on a cost recover basis. Searches cost $50 for two or more records found; there is generally no charge if less than two records are recovered. The Center does not release documents, but documents can be ordered from the Defense Technical Information Service in Alexandria, Va. 703-274-7633.

* Military Academies
Training and Education
Manpower, Installation and Logistics
U.S. Department of Defense
The Pentagon, Room 3B930
Washington, DC 20301   202-607-0512

To meet a portion of the long-range requirement for career military officers the U.S. Military Academy, U.S. Naval Academy, and the U.S. Air Force Academy were established. These schools offer curricula specifically designed to train students as professional officers. For more information on these academies, contact them at the following addresses:

U.S. Military Academy, West Point, NY 10996; 914-938-4011
U.S. Naval Academy, Annapolis, MD 21402; 301-267-4361
U.S. Air Force Academy, USAFA, CO 80840; 719-472-4050

* Military and Civilian Employment Records
National Personnel Center
9700 Page Blvd.
St. Louis, MO 63232   314-538-4261

This Center holds both military and civilian Federal personnel records dating from 1900 to the present. The Center prefers written requests for reference assistance.

* Military Archives
U.S. Department of Defense
Still Media Records Center, Code SSRC-PSa
Building 168 Naval Imaging Command
Anacostia Naval Station
Washington, DC 20374-1681   202-433-2166

This photographic archives/library maintains 100,000 photographs and a ready access slide file for all four branches of the military. Its holdings date from 1982 to the present (photographs prior to this have been transferred to the National Archives), and include pictures of ships, tanks, missiles, rockets, the Grenada invasion, and military exercises in Honduras. Research assistants are available to help patrons, and the Center will do research for fee of $5 for the first 15 minutes and $20 per hour after that. The Center is open 9am to 3 pm daily but access is by appointment only.

* Military Commands
Directorate for Public Communication
U.S. Department of Defense
The Pentagon, Room 2E777
Washington DC 20301-1400   703-697-5737

The United States military is organized into Specified and Unified Commands that combine forces from different services. Unified commands are organized on a regional basis. For information about the commands, contact the above number or contact the commands directly:

Atlantic Command	804-444-6294
Pacific Command	808-471-9779
Space Command	719-554-6889
Central Command	813-830-6393
European Command	011 49 711 680 8486 (Germany)
Southern Command	507-82-4278 (Panama)
Special Operations Command	813-830-4600
Strategic Air Command	402-294-4130
Forces Command	404-669-7301

* Military Photographs Prior to 1982

National Archives and Records Administration
Still Picture Branch
Washington, DC 20408   703-763-7410

The Archives contain photographic records for the armed services prior to 1982. Air Force records predating 1954 can be ordered from the National Air and Space Museum, Information Management Division, Smithsonian Institution, Washington, DC 20560.

* Military Records 19th Century On

Suitland Reference Branch
National Archives and Records Administration
Washington, DC 20409   703-763-7410

This office holds historical material, including Land Office records, State Department personnel overseas post records since 1935, the Japanese war relocation records, records of the U.S. military government of Germany and Japan, as well as records of all military actions from World War II through the Vietnam War. The office provides reference assistance in locating historical material, and will accept reference questions both in writing and by phone. The Library is open Monday through Saturday 8am to 4:15 pm. If requesting materials over the phone, the Library charges $6 minimum fee and 25 cents a page for any requests costing more than $6.

* Military Systems Reports and Audits

General Accounting Office (GAO)
Post Office Box 6015
Gaithersburg, MD 20877   202-275-6241

The National Security and International Affairs Division of the General Accounting Office (GAO) authored some 125 reports on defense and security matters in 1991. As GAO is the auditing agency of Congress, the reports are generally critical in nature, calling for reforms to improve program efficiency. Past year reports are also available. The first five copies of GAO reports are free. The following is a small sample of what's available.

Naval Aviation: The V-22 Osprey - Progress and Problems. GAO/NSIAD 91-45 October 12, 1991
Defense Reorganization: DOD's Efforts to Streamline the Special Operations Command. GAO/NSIAD 91-24BR November 23, 1991
Army Budget: Potential Reductions in Helicopter Programs. GAO/NSIAD 91-55BR December 5, 1991
Weapons Production: Impacts of Production Rate Changes on Aircraft Unit Costs. GAO/NSIAD 91-12 December 18, 1991
Antisubmarine Warfare: Tactical Surveillance Sonobuoy and Related Software Need to be Tested Together. GAO/NSIAD 91-41 January 9, 1991
Enlisted Force Management: Past Practices and Future Challenges. GAO/NSIAD 91-48 January 22, 1991
Battleships: Issues Arising from the Explosion Aboard the USS Iowa. GAO/NSIAD 91-4 January 4, 1991
Chemical Weapons: DOD's Successful Effort to Remove US Chemical Weapons from Germany. GAO/NSIAD 91-105 February 13, 1991

* Military Traffic Management

Military Traffic Management Command
U.S. Department of Army
5611 Columbia Pike
Falls Church, VA 22041-5050   703-756-1242

This Command manages all Department of Defense (DOD) freight and passenger movement in the United States, and all Army transport activities worldwide; however, the Command's expertise and responsibilities are considerably more complex and far-ranging. Upon request, this office will supply you with a 25-page brochure entitled *Ensuring Combat Power Gets to Its Place of Business*, an information brief on specific traffic management topics and projects, a copy of their *Traffic Management Progress Report* (published quarterly), a pamphlet on how to do business with the Command, and MTMC Facts, which outlines the structure of the command as well as providing statistics on the monumental logistics involved with Operations Desert Shield and Desert Storm. All are free of charge.

* Mine Sweeping and Other Naval Coastal Activities

Coastal Systems Station - Dahlgrin Division
Naval Surface Warfare Center
Panama City, FL 32407-5000   904-234-4083

The Center is involved in research and development in support of naval missions and operations in the coastal (Continental Shelf) regions, including mine sweeping, diving and salvage, and amphibious operations. Experts may be obtained from their Speakers Bureau to talk on naval research and development issues, and their office will make every effort to answer specific questions from serious researchers. Write or call for a brochure describing their work and programs, and for information on their Tour Program for civic groups.

* Mine Warfare

U.S. Department of the Navy
OP-744
Washington, DC 20350   703-694-7334

Both mine warfare and mine countermeasures are vital for controlling essential sea areas. In 1987 the U.S. commissioned the USS Avenger, the first new mine countermeasures ship to be built since the 1950s. The Navy is also currently working on the MHC-51 (Osprey) class mine hunter. For information on mine warfare, contact the above office.

* Missile and Space Launchers

HQ 20th USAF
Office of Public Affairs
Vandenberg Air Force Base, CA 93437-5000   805-866-3016

This center conducts developmental and operational testing of missile and space launchers. It is the only test launch facility in the U.S. for ICBMs, and the only facility to have launched test orbiters into polar orbit. The public is invited to its annual open house, held usually in the spring. Fact sheets on the base, its mission, programs, and history can be obtained by writing or calling the above office.

* Missile and Weapons Testing

Naval Air Weapons Station
Office of Public Affairs
Code 6033
Point Mugu, CA 93042-5011   805-989-8094

This Center tests and evaluates Naval weapons systems and devices and provides logistics and training support. Included are guided missiles, rockets, free-fall weapons, fire control and radar systems, drones and target drones, electronic devices, countermeasures equipment, test planning, simulations, and data collection. Reports are available only through Freedom of Information Act requests. For further details, contact Public Affairs.

* Missile Research

U.S. Army Missile Command
Redstone Arsenal, AL 35898   205-842-0560

This Command conducts research and development on rockets, guided missiles, air defense weapons systems, meteorology, missile launching, and associated equipment. Write or call for a free brochure on the Command and its history, which contains pictures and descriptions of virtually every missile the U.S. Army has ever used. Also ask for a pamphlet on how to do business with the Command. Copies of technical reports are also available upon request.

* Missile Testing Center

U.S. Department of the Army
Public Affairs Office, Building 122
White Sands Missile Range, NM 88002-5047   505-678-2101

This research and missile testing center invites the public to an open house twice a year, which includes a visit to the "Trinity Site" where the first atomic detonation took place. The center publishes a brochure and fact sheets on its history, mission, and wide range of programs. Facilities at White Sands are shared by the U.S. Naval Ordinance Missile Test Station, Atmospheric Sciences Laboratory, National Aeronautics and Space Administration, and the U.S. Army's Training and Doctrine Command's Analysis Command. The test range also functions as a wildlife preserve. Write or call for their free publications and information on open house days.

Be patient. If any phone number is incorrect, call (area code) 555-1212 and request the new listing.

943

* Museum of Health and Medicine

National Museum of Health and Medicine
Building 54, South Wing
Walter Reed Army Medical Center
Washington, DC 20606-6000   202-576-2348

The museum is open to the public every day of the week, and features exhibits illustrating health and disease in their social and historical contexts. You may see organ specimens dating from the Civil War, the bullet that killed President Lincoln, a famous collection of microscopes dating from their invention, and currently an "interactive" exhibit on AIDS and another on "Headache Art"--migraine sufferers' depiction on paper on what a migraine headache is like. Notable exhibits are "Living In a World With AIDS," and "The Patient is Abraham Lincoln" and "Substance Abuse Prevention." Call or write for more information. Write or call for a free brochure on the museum and its hours.

* National Air and Space Archives

Paul E. Garber Preservation
Restoration and Storage Facility
3904 Old Silver Hill Road, Bldg. 12
Suitland, MD 20746   301-238-3480

The National Air and Space Museum (NASM) library houses more than 35,000 books, 7000 bound journals as well as collections of microforms and other technical documents. The collection encompasses the history of aviation and space, flight technology, the aerospace industry, rocketry, earth and planetary sciences, and astronomy. The library hours are 8:30-4:30 weekdays. Appointments are necessary. Inquiries may be made by phone, fax, or mail. The staff will photocopy up to 25 documents while you wait. Larger orders are sent out to external vendors and then forwarded to researchers. Loans are not made to individuals.

* National Guard Bands

National Guard Bureau
Attn: NGB-PAC
4501 Ford Ave.
Alexandria, VA 22301-1457   703-695-0421

Local National Guard units provide bands, color guards, and flight demonstrations for community events upon request of civic groups. The Guard also sponsors annual open houses and conducts tours of the local bases. A Speakers Bureau will provide experts to speak on defense and local issues, and the Guard sponsors orientation trips for civic leaders. Call or write for more information on the Guard's varied community assistance programs, including the loan of equipment to civic groups.

* National Guard Posters and History

National Guard Bureau
Attn: PAH, The Pentagon
Washington, DC 20310-2500   703-695-0421

Posters and lithographs of historical events involving the Guard, which date from 1636 to the present, are available free of charge. This office will provide advice and help in obtaining information on specific Guard Units.

* National Guard Statistical Information

National Guard Bureau
NSB-PA, Room 23261, The Pentagon
Washington, DC 20310-2500   703-695-0421

The Guard publishes a brochure entitled *National Guard Updates* which discusses the Federal and State mission, force structure, overseas deployments, and personnel statistics, and an *Annual Review* of its work and accomplishments. Write or call for a free copy.

* National Security Research

The Rand Corporation
1700 Main Street
P.O. Box 2138
Santa Monica, CA 90407-2138   213-393-0411

The National Defense Research Institute conducts research in several areas of national security affairs. Contact RAND for a list of available publications.

* National Strategy

Directorate for Public Communications
Office of Assistant Secretary of Defense for Public Affairs
The Pentagon, Room 2E777

Washington, DC 20301   703-697-5737

This Public Affairs office will answer your general questions regarding American National Security Strategy. It can also provide you with the document *National Security Strategy of the United States*. This document, published annually, provides good insight into Administration thinking on security issues. Call or write for a copy.

* Naval Air Procurement

Naval Air Warfare Center
Aircraft Division
Public Affairs Division
Lakehurst, NJ 08733-5041   908-323-2620

This Center conducts research, development, testing, and evaluation of aircraft launching and landing equipment and airborne weapons systems. Write or call the Center for copies of a mission statement, historical background sheet, and information on contracting.

* Naval Avionics Development Center

U.S. Department of the Navy
Naval Air Warfare Center
Code 094, Small Business Office
Warminster, PA 18974   215-441-2456

This laboratory researches, develops, tests, and evaluates naval avionic systems. Write or call for their free pamphlet, *Doing Business with the Naval Air Development Center*.

* Naval Avionics Procurement

Naval Air Warfare Center
Aircraft Division
Public Affairs Office
6000 E. 21st St.
Indianapolis, IN 46219   317-353-4009

This Center conducts research and development on avionics and related equipment. Call or write for free brochures describing the Center, its programs, statistics on its employees, and a booklet on *How to Do Business with NAC*.

* Naval Construction Battalion Center

Commander Port Hueneme Division
Naval Surface Warfare Center
Port Hueneme, CA 93043   805-982-4493

This is the training center for the Navy's Construction Battalion (the "Seabees"). The Center has a base guide, a profile sheet giving statistical information on the base, and a brochure on the history of the Center, which was founded during W.W. II. They will accept written or phone requests for information.

* Naval Guided Weapons Systems

U.S. Department of the Navy
Public Affairs Office
Naval Surface Warfare Center
Port Hueneme, CA 93043-5007   805-982-7972

This Station conducts research and development, testing, and evaluation on ships' guided weapons systems. To obtain information about the station, its programs, and activities, write or call for the booklets, *PHDNSWC*, *Your Navy in Ventura County*, and a copy of their 25th anniversary magazine containing articles about the various departments.

* Naval Historical Research

Naval Historical Center
Washington Navy Yard
Washington, DC 20374   202-433-2210

The Navy Historical Center's research library and operational archives is open to private researchers. Its holdings include a still photographic collection of over 225,000 views and an art collection of over 8,000 pieces. Write or call for their free catalog of books in print, which includes an 8-volume series *Dictionary of American Naval Fighting Ships* and a 9-volume series *Naval Documents of the American Revolution*. Of current interest are *Origins of the Maritime Strategy* and *Power and Change: The Administrative History of the Chief of Naval Operations*, 1946-1989. Books may be ordered through the Government Printing Office, 202-512-1800. Center hours are 8:30 to 4:30 daily and no appointment is necessary. Parts of the library are classified.

* Naval Observatory Library

34th and Massachusetts Ave.
Washington, DC 20392-5100   202-653-1541

The Naval Observatory's research library is open to the public by appointment. Its holdings (over 75,000 volumes) include many rare books on astronomy as well as the current literature. A list of publications is available at no charge, which includes the *Astronomical Almanac*, the *Nautical Almanac*, the *Air Almanac*, the *Almanac for Computers*, *Astronomical Phenomena*, various periodicals, and reference materials. For publications call 202-653-1547.

* Naval Ordinance

Naval Ordinance Missile Test Station
Public Affairs Office
White Sands Missile Range
New Mexico, NM 88002   505-678-1134

The Naval Ordinance Missile Test Station (NOTMS) tests land based weapons and directed energy weapons as well as engaging in rocket launch support research. The Station is the only test station capable of firing all versions of the Standard Missile. For more information, contact the above office.

* Naval Patents

Deputy Counsel
Office of the Chief of Naval Research
(Intellectual Property)
800 N. Quincy St.
Arlington, VA 22217-5000   703-696-4000

This office grants licenses for commercial use of government-owned patents. For information on the patents available for licensing, contact the above office.

* Naval Reservists

Naval Reserve Recruiting Office
Naval Reserve Center
2600 Powder Mill Road
Adelphi, MD 20783-1198   301-394-2510

Naval Reservists are prepared for mobilization with equipment and training programs that parallel those of the regular Navy, including participation in fleet exercises. The Recruiting Office can provide information and brochures about the Reserve.

* Navy Band

U.S. Navy Band
Public Affairs Office
Washington Navy Yard
Washington, DC 20374-1052   202-433-2394

The U.S. Navy Concert Band and its specialty units--including the Commander's Trio, Windjammers, Tuba-Euphonium Quartet, Sea Chanters, Country Current, and the Commodores--are available to perform at community events nationwide. Units of the band perform a wide range of musical styles, from jazz, folk, and blue grass to classical chamber and cocktail music. Band bookings are done through the operations office, at 202-433-3676. Write or call for information on how to request the Band.

* Navy Budget and Forces Summary

Comptroller of the Navy, NCB33
Crystal City Mall, No. 2, Room 606
Statistical and Report Branch
Washington, DC 20350-1100   703-607-0875

This office publishes a *Budget and Forces Summary* covering the overall Navy budget for current and prior years, and a projection for the coming year. It contains a complete breakdown of Nay appropriations and is published annually, usually in mid April of each year. Write or call for a free copy.

* Navy Exchanges Procurement

Navy Resale and Services Support Office
Naval Station New York
Staten Island, NY 10305-5097   718-390-3700

This office handles procurement of resale merchandise for Navy exchanges and commissary stores. Write or call for the free *Guide for Doing Business with the Navy Resale System*.

* Navy Information Clearinghouse

U.S. Navy, Office of Information
The Pentagon
Washington, DC 20350-1200   703-695-6915

This office answers a broad range of general questions pertaining to Navy affairs. It can also supply a copy of the *Navy Fact File* containing general information on ships, aircraft and weapons systems, ship programs, and other statistics.

* Navy Medical Research

Naval Medical Research and Development Command
Attn: Code 40C
Bethesda, MD 20814   301-295-0325

This Command conducts research, development, testing, and evaluation in diving medicine, submarine medicine, aviation medicine, fleet health care, infectious diseases, and dental health. A list of their technical reports is available upon request.

* Navy Procurement

Navy Acquisition, Research and
 Development Information Center (NARDIC)
5001 Eisenhower Ave.
Alexandria, VA 22333   703-274-9315

This Center maintains a research and development, technical reading room open to DOD contractors, and will provide research and development planning and requirement documents to qualified users. The Center can also give information on the Navy Potential Contractors Program, which was instituted to facilitate technology transfer between the military and industry. Write or call for the free brochure explaining eligibility requirements and how to access the reading room, as well as how to enroll in the Potential Contractors Program and gain access to the Defense Technology Information Center.

* Navy Ship Historic Photographs and Drawings

Still Picture Branch
7th and Pennsylvania Ave., NW
National Archives and Records Administration
Washington, DC 20408   202-501-5455

The Still Picture Branch has drawings and photos of many Navy ships commissioned from the founding of the republic to the eve of World War II. The Collection includes: Thomas Birche's famous drawing of the battle between the USS Constitution (Old Ironsides) and the British Warship Guerriere in the War of 1812; a photo of the battleship Maine shortly before she mysteriously exploded in Havana harbor touching off the Spanish-American War; and the aircraft carrier Yorktown. 8x10 reproductions cost $6.25. Call or write for details.

* Navy Ship Historic Plans

Cartographic and Architectural Branch
National Archives and Records Administration
Washington, DC 20408   703-756-6700

This office compiles the plans of all U.S. Navy ships since the Navy was founded to 1939. If you make your request in writing, provide ship name and designation. The office will accept no more than three requests at a time. Cost for the service is $1.80 per print foot. The average request costs $5.40 - $7.20. Call or write for assistance.

* Night Vision Research

Office of Public Affairs
Night Vision and Electro-Optics Laboratories (NVEOL)
Fort Belvoir, VA 22060-5677   703-664-5151

The Night Vision and Electro-Optics Laboratories (NVEOL) conducts research and development into electro-optical low-energy lasers, all-weather systems, infrared, radiation, visionics, and image intensification. The laboratories provide the Army with equipment to enable it to carry out nocturnal operations efficiently. This office can offer information and referral on laboratory programs.

* North Atlantic Treaty Organization

Bureau of Public Affairs
Office of Public Communication
U.S. Department of State, Room 5815A
Washington, DC 20520-6816   202-647-6317

This office publishes the bimonthly magazine *NATO Review*, which contains timely articles on European defense issues as well as copies of recent unclassified Alliance documents. The magazine is free and can be ordered by contacting the above office.

* Nuclear Armaments Research

U.S. Army Armament Research and Development Command
U.S. Department of the Army - ARDEC
Picatinny Arsenal, NJ 07806-5000   201-724-6364

This Command conducts research, development, life-cycle engineering, and initial acquisition of various nuclear and non-nuclear weapons and ammunition. The Command accepts requests for information on specific technical topics on a case-by-case basis. Write or call for their information pamphlet and brochures on the research center and current programs.

* Nuclear Weapons Effects Testing

Field Command Defense Nuclear Agency
Defense Nuclear Agency
6801 Telegraph Road
Alexandria, VA 22310-3398   703-325-7095

This Command carries out much of the operational work done by the Defense Nuclear Agency (DNA) and maintains a liaison with the military services and is located in Kirtland Air Force Base, New Mexico. The Command is also responsible for operations and maintenance on Johnston Atoll. The mission of the DNA personnel on Johnston Atoll is to maintain facilities to resume nuclear tests in treaty prohibited environments, should this be required. This mission is specified in the legislation passed by Congress in ratifying the Limited Test Ban Treaty of 1963. For more information on the Field Command or Johnston Atoll, contact the DNA.

* Overseas Navy Exchanges

Navy Exchange Service Command
Naval Station New York
Staten Island, NY 10305-5097   718-390-3700

Overseas Navy exchanges in Guam, Hawaii, Italy, Japan, Spain, and the United Kingdom have independent purchasing authority for themselves and one or more branch exchanges. Those interested in selling to these exchanges can contact the Exchange Service Command for the addresses of the overseas exchanges, which may then be contacted directly.

* Pacific Fleet

United States Navy
Commander in Chief
U.S. Pacific Fleet
Public Affairs Office
Pearl Harbor, HI 96860-7000   808-471-9779

Based in Pearl Harbor, the Commander in Chief, U.S. Pacific Fleet command encompasses 102 million square miles of ocean, just over half of the earth's ocean area. Operational commands include the Seventh Fleet, Third Fleet, Task Force Fourteen, Task Force Twelve, Maritime Defense Zone, and Submarine Force Pacific.

* Patents Owned by Uncle Sam

National Technical Information Service
U.S. Department of Commerce
5285 Port Royal Rd.
Springfield, VA 22161   703-487-4650

This Service has a list of government patents available for licensing, as well as copies of all patents issued by the U.S. Patent Office. Call or write for ordering information.

* Pension Genealogy Searches

General Reference Branch
National Archives and Records Administration
Washington, DC 20408   202-501-5402

This office holds military service and pension records of people who served prior to 1900. The office accepts written requests only. Ask for Form NATF 80.

* Pentagon Products and Services

National Technical Information Service
U.S. Department of Commerce
5285 Port Royal Rd.

Springfield, VA 22161   703-487-4650

This agency collects and publishes the results all government-sponsored research carried out by corporations, universities, and government agencies. The Products and Services Catalog gives an overview of the agency's services, and describes by subject the reports, subscription newsletters, database and microfiche services available. The catalog is free; publications and services may be purchased at cost. Write or telephone the above office for more information.

* Persian Gulf Crisis - Videos and Transcripts

Center for Defense Information (CDI)
1500 Massachusetts Ave. NW
Washington, DC 20005   202-862-0700

The Center for Defense Information (CDI), an independent military affairs research organization, produces a weekly TV show, "America's Defense Monitor", which aired a three part series on the Persian Gulf Crisis. Copies on VHS tapes can be purchased from the above address for $65 plus $2 postage and handling. Or order transcripts of the episodes for $5 each, plus $2 postage and handling.

* Photographic Archives

Still Picture Branch (NNSP)
National Archives Records Administration
Seventh and Pennsylvania Ave., NW, Room 18N
Washington, DC 20408   202-523-3236

The archives holds the official photographic collection for the Army, Navy, and Marine Corps dating 1955 back to the founding of the country. Patrons can order photographic reproductions and posters for a small fee. Write or call for a price sheet, a "Select List" of period topics--including The Civil War, World War II, the Old West, the American Revolution, Indians, Navy Ships, and American Cities--and a catalog entitled War and Conflict.

* Photographic Archives of U.S. Military

U.S. Department of Defense
Still Media Records Center
Anacostia Naval Station
Building 168
Washington, DC 20374-1681   202-433-2168

This Center holds over one million negatives from all four military services, dating from the mid-1950s to present. Its archives are open to the public (appointments are preferred), and copies of negatives may be purchased. The Center maintains a research file by subject, and the staff will do research on a fee basis.

* Plastics and Adhesives Research

Plastics Technical Evaluation Center
U.S. Army Armament Research, Development
   and Engineering Center (ARDEC)
Building 355-N
Picatinny Arsenal, NJ 07806-5000   201-724-4222

Technical information related to plastics, adhesives, and organic matrix composites is generated, evaluated, stored, and distributed at this Center, with an emphasis on performance and properties. Computerized databases are maintained on the compatibility of polymers with propellants and explosives and on materials deterioration. The Center provides services on a fee basis, including consulting, state-of-the-art studies, handbooks, analysis, evaluation, and bibliographic and literature searches. To arrange for services or to get information, contact PLASTEC at the number listed above.

* Potential Military Contracts

Defense Advanced Projects Research Agency
3701 N. Fairfax Dr. Room 905
Arlington, VA 22203-1714   703-696-2402

This office will answer your general questions regarding the Defense Advanced Research Projects Agency (DARPA), which supports high-risk, high-payoff programs for research and technology development. Brochures available include the Defense Advanced Research Projects Agency updated annually, Information, Science and Technology Office Research Programs which lists current research programs, and the report, Strategic Computing: Seventh Annual Report November 1991. Technical program offices include the areas of Aerospace technology; Defense Sciences; Directed Energy; and Information Science and Technology. DARPA works closely with the Small Business Administration. All publications are free upon request, as well as press releases on major events sponsored by DARPA. Write or call also for their User's Guide for Potential Contractors.

* President's National Security Council
National Security Council (NSC)
Old Executive Office Building
17th St. and Pennsylvania Ave., NW
Washington, DC 20506   202-395-4974
The National Security Council (NSC) is responsible to assess and appraise the objectives, commitments, and risks of the United States in relation to our actual and potential military, economic, and political power, in the interest of national security, and to consider policies on matters of common interest to the department and agencies of the Government, and to make such recommendations and reports to the President as it deems appropriate or as the President may require. Council members are the President, the Vice President, the Secretary of State, and the Secretary of Defense, as prescribed by statute. The Chairman, Joint Chiefs of Staff, and the Director of Central Intelligence are statutory advisors. The Council's staff is headed by the Executive Secretary and provides day-to-day support for the President and his Assistant for National Security Affairs.

* Prisoners of War and Reclassification
U.S. Department of Defense
Force Management and Personnel
The Pentagon, Room 3E767
Washington, DC 20301-4000   703-695-7402
For information on conscientious objectors and POW's, including reclassification and discharge data, contact the above office.

* Radiobiology Research
Armed Forces Radiobiology Research Institute (AFRRI)
Defense Nuclear Agency
National Naval Medical Center
Bethesda, MD 20814   301-295-1330
The Institute conducts tours of the facility, and makes its library available to approved researchers. Armed Forced Radiobiology Research Institute (AFRRI) scientists conduct research on the biological effects of radiation and their relationship to national defense, space exploration and medical progress. Its *Annual Report* summarizes the current work being performed in radiobiological research, and a brochure explains the Institute and its various programs. To request literature, contact the AFRRI's parent institution, the Defense Nuclear Agency at 703-325-7306. Literature is free upon request.

* Relocation Assistance
Realty Services Division
Corps of Engineers Real Estate
U.S. Army Corps of Engineers
Attn: CERE-R
Washington, DC 20314-1000   202-272-0517
This office administers the Uniform Relocation Assistance Act for the U.S. Department of the Army. The Act provides benefits to landowners, tenants, businesses, and farmers who must move or must move property as a result of government acquisition of real property for Federal projects. Benefits include reimbursement for moving, costs, replacement housing, and direct losses. For further information, contact the Realty Services Division.

* Research and Development Standards for Military Contractors
Tri-Service Industry Information Center
5001 Eisenhower Ave.
Alexandria, VA 22333   703-274-8948
This office provides information on research and development, planning, and requirements information to suppliers of military equipment for the Army, Navy, and Air Force. To enter the research center, you must have a DOD contract and a personal security clearance. Write or call to obtain brochures on how to use the center and for its publications, including *Air Force Logistics Needs, Mission Element Need Statements (MENS), Program Element Descriptive Summaries, Program Management Directive, R&D Planning Summaries, Technical Objective Documents Technology Needs Documents*, and *Selling to the United States Air Force*.

* Retirement Home
Public Relations
U.S. Soldiers' and Airmen's Home
3700 North Capitol St., NW

Washington, DC 20317   202-722-3386
The Home was established for retired or discharged enlisted and warrant officer personnel, men and woman, who have served 20 years or more in the Army or Air Force; or who have a service-connected disability preventing them from earning a living; or who have served during periods of war and have a nonservice connected disability preventing their earning a livelihood. For general information and brochures, contact the office listed above. For admissions, call 202-722-3336. For information about the U.S. Soldiers' and Airmen's Home National Cemetery, contact the following address: 21 Harewood Road, NW, Washington, DC 20011; 202-695-3190.

* Revolutionary War Paintings and Drawings
Still Picture Branch
7th and Pennsylvania Ave. NW
National Archives and Records Administration
Washington, DC 20408   202-501-5455
The Still Picture Branch has reproduced hundreds of famous scenes from the Revolutionary War. Pictures include the battles of Lexington, Concord, and Bunker Hill; the signing of the Declaration of Independence; and the surrender of Cornwallis at Yorktown. Call or write for the list of pictures available and prices.

* ROTC: Reserve Officers Training Corps
Training and Education
Manpower, Installation and Logistics
U.S. Department of Defense
The Pentagon, Room 3B930
Washington, DC 20301   703-695-2618
The Reserve Officers Training Corps (ROTC) program is conducted at over 500 U.S. colleges and universities and is the single largest source of officers for the Armed Forces, both career and non-career. For further details about ROTC, contact the office listed above or contact the programs directly at the individual colleges and universities.

* Science and Engineering Army Apprenticeships
U.S. Department of the Army
Chemical Research Development
 and Engineering Center
Aberdeen Proving Ground, MD 21010-5423   301-278-6954
This Center sponsors a science and engineering apprenticeship program for high school students, summer "associateships" for high school faculty, and a faculty research and engineering program for university level scientists. The Center further welcomes requests from high schools for assistance with "Science Fairs" not only locally, but at the national and regional level.

* Science Fairs and Research Grants
U.S. Department of the Army
Army Research Office
P.O. Box 12211
Triangle Park, NC 27709-2211   919-549-0641
This office administers the nation-wide Science Fair program, which sponsors science competition at the high school level, and the Defense Research Initiative, which is a competitive grant program for government funding of university research. Write or call for free brochures and information describing these programs.

* Security Assistance/ Foreign Assistance Funding
Agency for International Development
Bureau for External Affairs
Office of Publications
320 21 St., NW
Washington DC 20523   202-647-4330
This office can provide you with statistics on American foreign assistance, which includes security assistance, broken down both by country and program. Copies of the statistical tables are free.

* Security Assistance Journal
Defense Institute for Security Assistance Management
DISAM Journal
Wright-Patterson AFB, OH 45433-5000   513-255-6688
The Institute publishes the *DISAM Journal*, a must for those interested in security assistance policy. The *Journal* analyzes management issues and programs as well as annual security assistance legislation in Congress. The *Journal* also reprints the

testimony of key Executive branch officials on security assistance. The *Journal* is published quarterly. Subscriptions cost $12 per year and can be ordered from the above office. The Institute also has a library specializing in security assistance matters.

* Security Assistance Policy

Defense Security Assistance Agency (DSSA)
The Pentagon 4B659
Washington DC 20301-2800   703-604-6513

Each February the State Department and the Defense Department jointly release the *Congressional Presentation Document for Security Assistance Programs*. This document, mandated by law, contains a complete list of security assistance programs descriptions as well as country by country breakdowns with discussion of current American security assistance programs in each country. The document also contains funding requests for the next fiscal year as well as final aid figures for the prior two fiscal years. The Document costs $25 and can be ordered from the Defense Security Assistance Agency (DSAA) at the above number.

* Selective Service Fact Sheets: Deferments, Exemptions, Etc.

Public Affairs
Selective Service System
1023 31st St., NW
Washington, DC 20435   202-724-0790

The Selective Service System provides free to the public fact sheets which contain information on certain aspects of the Selective Service System.

Address Verification Program
Aliens and Dual Nationals
Federal Student Aid, Job Training Benefits and Federal Employment
Postponements, Deferments, Exemptions
Selective Service and the Immigration Reform and Control Act of 1986
Alternative Service for Conscientious Objectors
Appeals Boards
Draft Cards

* Selective Service Regulations

Public Affairs, Selective Service System
1023 31st St., NW
Washington, DC 20435   202-724-0790

The documents listed below are usually available in the government documents section of major libraries:

Military Selective Service Act of June 24, 1948. This is the law under which the Selective Service System operates.
Code of Federal Regulations. Selective Service Regulations are contained within.

* Selective Service Registration: Induction, Claims, and Appeals

Public Affairs
Selective Service System
1023 31st St., NW
Washington, DC 20435   202-724-0790

The booklet, *Information for Registrants*, furnishes information about Selective Service responsibilities, and registrant rights and obligations. It also explains the induction, claims, and appeals process. To obtain a copy, contact this office.

* Selective Service Registration Status

Registration Information Office
P.O. Box 4638
North Suburban, IL 60197-4638   708-688-6888

If you have any questions regarding an individual's status and the requirement to register, call or write this office.

* Selective Services Semiannual Update

Public Affairs
Selective Service System
1023 31st St., NW
Washington, DC 20435   202-724-0790

Every six months, the Selective Service System publishes a summary of its program. Copies of the report can be obtained from this office.

* Selling to the Army: Commodity Commands

U.S. Army Materiel Command
Public Affairs
5001 Eisenhower Ave.
Alexandria, VA 22333   703-274-8010

The U.S. Army Materiel Command encompasses seven commodity commands which contract for both products and research and development. The Materiel Command buys everything the soldier uses, both personally and professionally. The commodity commands include the Armament, Munitions and Chemical Command; the Aviation Systems Command; the Communications-Electronics Command; the Laboratory Command (which contracts for research); the Missile Command; the Tank-Automotive Command; and the Troop Support Command (includes portable sanitary equipment, food, and uniforms). Call or write for a free brochure explaining what the Material Command encompasses.

* Selling to the Army: Small Business

U.S. Army Material Command
Small and Disadvantaged Business
Utilization Office
5001 Eisenhower Ave.
Alexandria, VA 22333   703-274-8185

A series of brochures is available for small and women-owned businesses on how to sell their products and services to the Army. *How to Do Business with AMC* lists the commodity commands and each Small Business Office at each command. *Selling to the Military*, *Small Business Specialists*, and *Small Business Subcontracting* all cover information on the application process through the U.S. Department of Defense. Also available are other free brochures explaining finance regulations for small businesses and how to prepare offers.

* Selling to the Military

Defense Logistics Agency
DFSC-DU
Cameron Station
Alexandria, VA 22304-6160   703-274-6135

The Department of Defense (DOD) contracts literally hundreds of billions of dollars worth of goods and services annually. Call and request the book *Selling to the Military*, and *Guide to the Preparation of Offers For Selling to the Military*, both musts for getting started in this area. The publications are free upon request.

* Selling to the Marine Corps

Commandant of the Marine Corps
Morale Welfare Recreation Support Center
3044 Catlin Ave
Quantico, VA 22134-5099   703-640-3800

This office supplies fact sheets listing Marine Corps installations worldwide and explaining how to sell to the military exchanges on those installations. Requests for information must be made in writing.

* Selling to Navy Exchanges

Navy Exchange Services Command
Naval Station - NY
Staten Island, NY 10305-5097   718-390-3841

This office supplies the brochure, *The Navy Resale System*, which explains how to sell to the Navy military exchanges. Call or write for a free copy.

* Small Business and Disadvantaged Procurement

Small Business Office
U.S. Department of Defense (DOD)
The Pentagon 2A340
OUSD(A)SADBU
Washington, DC 20301-3061   703-697-9383

This office will supply information and guidance to small and disadvantaged businesses. Free copies are available of a list of the 700 DOD procurement offices and a book listing the major prime DOD contractors and the products and services they provide. Write or call their office to get on the solicitors' mailing list.

* Small Business Pentagon Procurement Assistance

Small Business Office
Defense Fuel Supply Center
5010 Duke St.
Cameron Station, Building 8
Alexandria, VA 22304-6160   703-274-7428

This Small Business Office will refer potential contractors to the major buying centers within the Defense Logistics Agency for the commodity or service they wish to market. They have two standard brochures, *Selling to the Military* and *Guide to Preparation*. Write or call for free copies.

* Software Development and Technology

Data and Analysis Center for Software (DACS)
P.O. Box 120
Utica, NY 13503   315-336-0937

The Data and Analysis Center for Software (DACS) provides products and specialized reference services on software development and maintenance programs. Subsets of its database can be obtained on hard copy or magnetic tape. Database searches and copies of technical reports are furnished on a cost recovery basis. Write or call for a free products and services brochure containing ordering and price information.

* Solid State Laser Research

Documents Office
Naval Research Laboratory (NRL)
Code 4827, 4555 Overlook Ave., SW
Washington, DC 20375-5000   202-767-2949

The Laboratory conducts research on low- and medium-power solid state lasers and infrared detectors. Technical reports can be obtained on the research from National Technical Information Service, 5285 Port Royal Road, Springfield, VA 22161; 703-487-4650. A few are available from NRL directly. Contact the Documents Office for details.

* Space Command

HQ NORAD
Director Public Affairs
Peterson AFB, CO 80914   719-554-6889

This Command is in charge of America's early warning systems for detecting attacks launched against North America.

* Space and Missile Product Engineering

Office of Public Affairs
Western Space and Missile Center
U.S. Department of the Air Force
U.S. Department of Defense
Vandenberg AFB, CA 93437-6021   805-866-3016

Research, development, and product engineering in support of U.S. space and missile programs are conducted at this Center. Work focuses on radar, telemetry, electro-optics, communications range and mission control, weather timing, aircraft impact location, and data handling. Contact the Office of Public Affairs for information and referral.

* Space and Missile Test Range Research

45th Space Wing/ PA
Patrick Air Force Base, FL 32925   407-494-5933

This center conducts research and development activities in test range instrumentation and provides support for the Defense Department's missile and space programs. This involves radar, trajectory computers, tracking and target analysis, communications, timing and firing systems, telemetry, and data storage. For more information, contact research and development staff at the address listed above.

* Space Technology Research

U.S. Air Force Space Technology Center
Kirtland Air Force Base, NM 87117-6008   505-646-5354

This Center oversees the work of the three major Air Force research laboratories: the Weapons Laboratory at Kirtland; the Astronautics Laboratory at Edwards Air Force Base, California; and the Geophysics Laboratory at Hanscom Air Force Base, Massachusetts. Free fact sheets on all three labs and their programs are available from this Center, including fact sheets on the SDI program, the relay mirror experiment, the Alpha chemical laser experiment, "Brilliant Pebbles" research, optics research, microwaves, plasma physics, and nuclear weapons effects research. The Center offers a Speakers Bureau of experts and intern programs for outside researchers.

* Speakers Bureau: Chemical Weapons

U.S. Department of the Army
Chemical Research Development and Engineering Center
Aberdeen Proving Ground, MD 21010-5423   301-278-6954

While the Center's mission is to conduct research on chemical defense materials, it also provides a variety of programs involving the Center in the civic and scientific communities. Through its Speakers Bureau the Center will provide experts on scientific and technological topics. Write or call for a brochure explaining the laboratory, the Center's programs, and statistics on the post. Interested persons from the business and scientific community may call or write to be added to their mailing list for Advance Planning Briefings to Industry and notices of conferences and seminars.

* Special Forces

Special Operations Command (SOC)
Public Affairs Office
McDill AFB, FL 33608-6001   813-830-4600

The Special Operations Command (SOC) was formed in 1987 as a result of the Cohen-Nunn amendment to the National Defense Authorization Act of 1987. It currently has approximately 42,000 active, reserve, and national guard forces. Special forces throughout the military, including the Army Rangers, Navy SEALs, and the Air Force Special Tactic Units, come under this command.

* Specifications and Standards

Naval Publications and Printing Service
Standardization Documents Order Desk
700 Robins Ave. Bldg. 4D
Philadelphia, PA 19111-5094   215-697-2179

This Center is the Department of Defense's (DOD) distribution point for unclassified specifications and standards used to determine requirements for military procurement. Military personnel can obtain the *Index of Specifications and Standards* from this Center. The general public can obtain it from the Government Printing Office, Superintendent of Documents, Washington, DC 20402; 202-512-1800. Contact the Center for the following types of information:

Military specifications and standards
Federal specifications and standards
Qualified product lists
Military handbooks
Air Force-Navy aeronautical specifications and standards
Air Force specifications
Air Force specifications bulletins
Air Force-Navy aeronautical bulletins

* Star Wars and Advanced Defense Technology

Strategic Defense Initiative Organization (SDI)
The Pentagon
Washington, DC 20301-7100   703-695-8743

The Strategic Defense Initiative Organization (SDI) is responsible for overseeing development of the defensive system popularly known as Star Wars - a defensive system against enemy ballistic missiles. Under the authority and direction of the Secretary of Defense, SDI manages and directs research in advanced technology that will provide the technological basis for national defense decisions relating to nuclear ballistic missiles and defensive system. The agency utilizes the services of the military, the U.S. Department of Energy, private industry, and educational and research institutions. Some publications are available to the public from the above listed office, including *SDI's Annual Report to Congress* and various booklets about SDI activities. For further information, contact the above office.

* Star Wars and Other Defense Research Information

Office of Assistant Secretary of Defense
Public Affairs
Directorate for Defense Information
Pentagon 2E765
Washington, DC 20301-1400   703-695-8743

This office can supply you with fact sheets, press releases, and reports on defense programs such as Star Wars, the Department of Defense Laser and Space Program, and the Defense Advanced Research Projects Agency (DARPA) activities, and related Congressional activity. Staff can also direct you in making Freedom of Information Act (FOIA) requests for Defense contract information.

* Strategic Bomber Forces

Strategic Air Command, HQ/SAC/PA
901 SAC Blvd. Suite 1A1
Offutt AFB, NE 68113-5150   402-294-4130

This Command is headquarters for America's B-52, B-1 and B-2 strategic bomber forces, as well as America's arsenal of intercontinental missiles. The Strategic Air Command (SAC) also has bases at Beale AFB, California; Barksdale AFB, Louisiana; March AFB, California; and Vandenberg AFB; California. For more information on SAC, its forces and its mission, contact SAC at the above address.

* Strategic Defense Research

U.S. Army Strategic Defense Command
Public Affairs Office
P.O. Box 1500
Huntsville, AL 35807-3801   205-955-3887

The U.S. Army Strategic Defense Command conducts programs designed to defeat ballistic missile attacks at each phase of their trajectory. The program has recently been expanded to include Theater missile defense. Army programs work on developing technologies for Systems Analysis/ Battle Management as well as various types of energy weapons. In conjunction with the Strategic Defense Initiative, the Army is conducting programs on ground based interceptors and tracking. For information and fact sheets on individual programs, call or write to the Command.

* Surplus Property from Defense Department

Defense Reutilization and Marketing Service
Public Affairs Office
P.O. Box 1370
Battle Creek, MI 49016-1370   616-961-7331

This office manages and disposes of surplus property from all U.S. Department of Defense (DOD) agencies. Many items are for sale by public auction. Write or call for free pamphlets on how to buy DOD surplus property and applications for the national bidders mailing list. For local sales, contact the nearest DRMS office or the above office for a referral.

* Tactical Weapons: Database Searches for Contractors

GACIAC/IIT Research Institute   312-567-4519/4526
10 W. 35th St.   312-567-4564/4587
Chicago, IL 60616   312-567-4345

This organization offers user guides, a bi-monthly bulletin, and complex database searches on tactical weapons guidance and control, information, and analysis. Write or call for further information; requesters must be registered DOD contractors.

* Tanks and Armor Research

U.S. Army Tank Automotive Command
ATTN. AMSTA-CB
Warren, MI 48397-5000   313-574-5388

This Command conducts research into combat tactical and special purpose vehicles. Component programs involve engines, transmissions, suspensions, electrical and miscellaneous vehicular components. Call or write for more information.

* Technical Assistance to Foreign Countries

U.S. Army Corps of Engineers
Attn: CEMP-MG
20 Massachusetts Ave., NW
Washington, DC 20314-1000   202-272-0397

Through its Foreign Military Sales Program, the Army Corps of Engineers can provide a full range of services to foreign governments, including construction management, research and development, procurement, training, and engineering design. For information, contact the above office.

* Technical Exchange Between Government and Industry

Government Industry Data Exchange Program (GIDEP)
GIDEP Operations Center
Corona, CA 91720-5000   714-736-4677

The Government Industry Data Exchange Program (GIDEP) is a data exchange program between government and industry. Members have access to five databases, grouped by subject: Failure Experience; Engineering; Reliability, Maintainability and Quality; Metrology; and Value Engineering. In addition, GIDEP has a newsletter and an *Urgent Data Request System*. For a free information package on program services, membership, and application forms, write or call the above office.

* Technical Expertise at Federal Labs

Defense Technical Information Center
Cameron Station, DTIC-BC
Alexandria, VA 22304-6145   703-274-6434

The Defense Technical Information Center (DTIC) maintains a Domestic Technology Referral Database, supplying a broad referral to federal laboratories and their areas of expertise. The service is available to all legitimate requesters; the requester need not be a "registered user." Call or write for information.

* Technology Research Army Libraries

U.S. Army Materiel Command
Information Systems Command
Public Affairs Office
Timberlake, AZ   602-538-8609

Each Army Materiel Command installation has a technological library. It is usually possible to gain access to the library if you obtain prior approval. Contact your local AMC for information, or the above office for a referral to your closest installation.

* Technology Transfer and Systems Engineering

Director of Publications, DRI-P
Defense Systems Management College
Ft. Belvoir, VA 22060-5426   703-664-5082

This College publishes 28 books and a bi-monthly magazine entitled *Program Manager* (subscription, $7.50 per year). Titles include *Systems Engineering Management Guide* (a Government Printing Office all-time best-seller), *Cost Estimating, Subcontract Management Guide, Skill in Communications*, and *Program Office Guide to Technology Transfer*. All apply to acquisition and program management. Write for a free publications list explaining where to purchase them, stock numbers, and prices. Non-government employees must order publications through the Government Printing Office at 202-512-1800. The editor will also supply a sample copy of the *Program Manager* upon written request.

* Technology Transfer Competitiveness

Administrator
Federal Laboratory Consortium (FLC)
P.O. Box 545
Sequim, WA 98382   206-683-1005

The mission of the Consortium is to facilitate technology transfer among government, business, and academic entities in order to foster American economic and technological competitiveness. It sponsors conferences and seminars and publishes a free monthly newsletter (currently no charge). For very specific questions from bona fide researchers who find themselves at an impasse, the Consortium will conduct a database search to refer the inquirer to an appropriate lab. Write or call for a free general information packet explaining the organization, how to access its services, facilities available for testing, and examples of technology transfers. Also ask for the Consortium's newsletter *News Link*, which regularly provides updates on FLC activities. The FLC also has regional contacts:

Far West Region 619-553-2101
Midwest Region 513-255-2006
Northeast Region 609-484-6689
Mid-Atlantic Region 202-653-1442
Washington DC Rep 202-331-4220
Southeast Region 601-688-2042
Mid-Continental Region 501-541-4516

* Test Flight History

Air Force Flight Test Center
Air Force Systems Command
U.S. Department of the Air Force
Edwards Air Force Base, CA 93523   805-277-3510

The History Office on Edwards Air Force Base has an archival library of history documents about the base. Videotapes of historical events are also available for viewing on site. Call or write the above office for information on its holdings.

* Time: Naval Observatory's Atomic Clock
Atomic Clock
National Observatory
34th and Massachusetts Ave.
Washington, DC 20392-5100   202-653-1541
The Observatory's Master Clock is the source for all standard time in the United States. For the correct time, call the number above, or dial 1-900-410-TIME if you are outside of the DC area.

* Training Methods Speakers Bureau
U.S. Army Research Institute for
Behavioral and Social Sciences
5001 Eisenhower Ave., Room 6E06
Alexandria, VA 22333   703-274-8683
The Institute conducts research for the military on educational and training methods and organizational effectiveness. Requests may be made to its Speakers Bureau for experts in the field. Copies of its published reports may be obtained through the Defense Technology Information Center.

* Training Military Doctors
Uniformed Services University of Health Sciences
U.S. Department of Defense
4301 Jones Bridge Road, Room A1045
Bethesda, MD 20814   301-295-3101
Physicians for the military services and for the Public Health Service are educated at this institution. In addition to a school of medicine and graduate and continuing education programs, the university incorporates the Military Medical Education Institute which provides combat training for health care professionals in the military service. You can obtain information and brochures from the above address.

* Trinity Test Site
Public Affairs Office
White Sands Missile Range
New Mexico, NM 88002   505-678-1700
This was the site of the first Atomic test explosion, July 16, 1945. While the site still has trace radiation from the test, a short visit exposes one to no more radiation than many other activities undertaken in a typical year. Call the Range for more information on visiting Trinity.

* Underwater Defense Systems Research
Office of Public Affairs
Naval Underwater Systems Center
U.S. Department of the Navy
Newport Laboratory
Newport, RI 02840   401-841-2182
Underwater warfare systems and components, undersea surveillance systems, navigation systems, and related technologies are developed, tested, and analyzed at the Center. The Office of Public Affairs sometimes has publications on hand or can refer you to appropriate information sources within the Center.

* Vietnam Casualty Computer Printout
Center for Electronic Records
National Archives and Records Administration
Washington, DC 20408   202-501-5402
This office holds all Federal records on computer disk, which include all recent DOD records and the casualty lists from the Vietnam War. Copies may be purchased.

* Voluntary Draft and Selective Service Compliance
Selective Service System
1023 31st St., NW
Washington, DC 20435   202-724-0820
Applicants for Title IV federal student aid, Job Training Partnership Ace benefits, and those young men seeking employment with the federal government who are required to register must be in compliance with the registration requirement in order to be eligible for those programs. For more information, contact this office.

* Waterways and Wetlands Research and Development
Research and Development Division
U.S. Army Corps of Engineers
CERD-ZA
20 Massachusetts Ave NW
Washington, DC 20314-1000   202-272-0254
Contact this office for information and referral on Corps of Engineers research and development into reservoir water quality; coastal ecology; aquatic plant control; environmental impact of development projects; designing dams, locks, and other hydraulic structures for earthquakes; river ice and winter navigation; battlefield environment; Army installations; and combat engineering.

* Weapons Lab Super Computer Center
U.S. Air Force Super Computer Center
Kirtland Air Force Base, NM 87117-6008   505-646-5354
The Super Computer Center is administered by the Weapons Laboratory. Academic researchers sponsored by the U.S. Department of Defense may have access to the Cray 1 and Cray 2 super computer services and a bi-monthly newsletter. Write or call for their brochure on how to subscribe for time on the computer, eligibility for use, and prices.

* Weapons Museum
U.S. Army Ordnance Museum
Aberdeen Proving Ground
Aberdeen, MD 23005   301-278-6954
This museum holds the free world's largest collection of military weapons and paraphernalia, including captured W.W. II German V-2 rockets, the one and only atomic cannon, and handguns with curved barrels to shoot around corners. It's open to the public Tuesday through Sunday, and admission is free. You can also write for their pamphlet, *Welcome to the U.S. Army Ordnance Museum.*

Science and Technology
General Sources

* See also Economics, Demographics, and Statistics Chapter
* See also International Relations and Defense Chapter
* See also Patents, Trademarks and Copyrights Chapter
* See also Current Events and Homework Chapter
* See also Experts Chapter

Part of the reason we are suffering from an information explosion can be attributed to technology. About 90 percent of all scientific knowledge has been generated since 1950. And, according to the U.S. Department of Commerce, this knowledge is expected to double again in the next ten to fifteen years. Technology, once again, has recaptured the interest and investment of both American business and the public. In 1982, Time magazine selected the computer as its "Man of the Year." Continuing this trend, April 22-28, 1992 was designated National Science and Technology Week. In 1992 President Bush also launched his National Technology Initiative to increase U.S. strength in new technology. In line with this initiative, the National Institute of Standards and Technology held a special series of conferences on new technology throughout 1992.

This section will introduce you to the major sources of information about technology throughout the government, including those located at the National Technical Information Service (NTIS), the Science and Technology Reading Room at the Library of Congress, the Office of Technology Assessment, and the U.S. Department of Defense. Through these sources you'll find sources of information on everything from Alzheimer's disease and genetic fingerprinting to supercomputers and commercial biotechnology.

* 3 Million Science and Technical Books

Science and Technology Division
Library of Congress
Washington, DC 20540   202-707-5639

The Science and Technology collection contains more than 3 million scientific and technical books and pamphlets and 3 million technical reports, including those issued by the U.S. Department of Energy, National Aeronautics and Space Administration (NASA), the U.S. Department of Defense, and other government agencies. The collections, which are particularly strong in aeronautical materials, contain first editions of Copernicus and Newton and the personal papers of the Wright Brothers and Alexander Graham Bell. Computer terminals provide principal access to the collections. Special scientific finding aids, such as abstracting and indexing journals, are part of the division's reference collection. This Division also prepares an informal series of reference guides called Tracer Bullets, which are available free upon request. More extensive bibliographies are published from time to time.

* Agriculture Research Service (ARS) Programs

Information Staff
Beltsville Agricultural Research Center
Room 307A
10301 Baltimore Blvd
Beltsville, MD 20705-2350   301-504-6421

The Agriculture Research Service (ARS) of the U.S. Department of Agriculture (USDA) conducts research in several areas designed to increase the quality of American crops, livestock, and nutrition. ARS also conducts research designed to improve the competitiveness of U.S. agriculture on the world market. For more information on specific ARS programs, contact the information office listed above.

* Air Force Research Grants

Office of Scientific Research
U.S. Air Force, Bolling Air Force Base
Washington, DC 20332   202-767-4910

This office accepts proposals for scientific research and requests for grants. Current research interests lie in the areas of Aerospace Sciences, Chemical and Materials Sciences, Physics and Electronics, Life and Environmental Sciences, and Mathematical and Computer Sciences. Write or call for copies of the Research Interest pamphlet, the Proposer's Guide, the Grant Brochure (which lists the types of grants available), and technical brochures on Air Force research programs.

* American Association for the Advancement of Science

American Association for the Advancement of Science
1333 H Street, NW
Washington, DC 20005   202-326-6400

The largest scientific organization in the country with membership exceeding 136,000, this association was formed to promote increased public understanding of science and technology. Its activities are divided regionally and by field of interest, and it also sponsors international events such as its annual meeting which brings together scientists from all over the world. The Association can provide information about major scientific and technological issues, and staff will help you locate both specialists and printed materials. It publishes Science Magazine as well books about topics of immediate scientific interest, as well as directories and other materials of interest to its members.

* Association of Science-Technology Centers (ASTC)

Association of Science-Technology Centers
1025 Vermont Ave, NW, Suite 500   202-783-7200
Washington, DC 20005-3516   Fax: 202-783-7207

With over 400 members, this association of science museums and science/technology centers promotes public understanding of science and technology. It publishes a quarterly calendar of museum exhibits. The Association of Science-Technology Centers (ASTC) sponsors conferences which are open to the public. It sells surveys about computers, along with a bimonthly newsletter. Call for more information and for a publications list.

* Ballistic Research and Engineering

Ballistic Research Laboratories
314 Ryan Building
Aberdeen Proving Ground, MD 21005-5066   301-278-6954

This is an advanced technology laboratory conducting basic and applied research in mathematics, physics, chemistry, biophysics, and engineering related to defense ballistics. Write or call for more information.

* Basic Energy Sciences Research

Office of Basic Energy Sciences
Office of Energy Research
U.S. Department of Energy

19901 Germantown Rd.
Germantown, MD 20585   301-903-3081

The Basic Energy Sciences office supports some 1,400 research projects and is organized to manage research in five areas: Materials Science, Chemical Sciences, Engineering and Geosciences, Advanced Energy Projects, and Energy Biosciences.

Materials Research

This research seeks to mitigate unforeseen materials problems in advanced energy systems. The current emphasis of the program is on high temperature superconductivity, use of supercomputers in calculations and modeling of materials phenomena, polymer research, surfaces and interface research, and materials synthesis and processing science. [Contact at DOE: 301-903-3427.]

Chemical Sciences Research

This Chemical Sciences subprogram includes research that impacts such fields as photovoltaics, production of fuels and chemicals from coal, catalysis, nuclear waste separation, conversion of biomass into liquid fuels, separation of metals from low-grade mineral resources, combustion, and detection and measurement of harmful by products of energy processes.

Engineering and Geosciences

The objective of the engineering research program is to provide experimental tests of theories and models of processes needed for energy production facilities and for increased energy efficiency. The geosciences research is aimed at developing a quantitative, predictive understanding of the energy-related aspects of geological, geophysical and geochemical processes both in the earth and at the solar-terrestrial interface.

Applied Mathematical Sciences

This program supports research in mathematics and computer science required by DOE researchers.

Advanced Energy Projects

This program supports research that explores the feasibility of novel energy-related concepts evolving from basic research. Projects are supported typically for about three years, at which time it is expected that they will transferred to a technology program or private industry.

Energy Biosciences

This subprogram focuses on understanding the limits of productivity in green plants how plants adapt to suboptimal conditions of growth and the mechanisms of microbial conversion of various biomass forms. An integral part of the subprogram is the development of genetic information that may ultimately be used to produce new or improved microorganisms and plants to facilitate the production of fuels or petroleum-saving chemicals or to yield biotechnologies capable of conserving energy.

* Ceramics and Metals Research

U.S. Department of the Army
Army Materials Technology Lab
Ft. Dietrick, MA 02172   617-619-2736

This Center specializes in research regarding metals and ceramics. Major programs currently include: the battle against Corrosion; Advanced Armor; Structural Ceramics; Elastomers; and Composite Materials Hull. The Lab's work has done much to improve the armors of American mechanized forces. It maintains a library open to approved researchers, and copies of technical reports are available upon request. Write or call for free brochures describing the Center, its mission, and programs.

* Cold Environments Research

U.S. Army Corps of Engineers
Army Cold Regions Research and Engineering Laboratory
72 Lyme Rd.
Hanover, NH 03755-1290   603-646-4100

This Laboratory conducts research on living, working, traveling, building and military operations in cold environments. A Speakers Bureau will provide experts to speak before civic groups. The Laboratory also has an extensive library on cold regions research. The Library of Congress prepares the *Bibliography on Cold Regions Science and Technology*. Write or call for brochures explaining the mission and programs, accessing information from the library, and how to do business with the Laboratory.

* Computer Information/Research

National Technical Information Service (NTIS)
U.S. Department of Commerce
5285 Port Royal Rd.

Springfield, VA 22161   703-487-4650

The National Technical Information Service (NTIS) puts out the following reports related to computers and information systems:

American National Dictionary for Information Systems. Offers precise definitions of terms relating to information systems and services as the official source for U.S. Government contract terminology in this area. Price - $50.

Computer Viruses and Related Threats. Addresses the current problem of computer viruses, analyzing where they attack and why they are on the rise. Price - $17.

Federal Information Processing Standards (FIPS) Program. These standards serve as the official source within the Federal Government for information on the approval, implementation and maintenance of FIPS resulting from the provisions of Public Law 89-306. Call for prices.

POSIX Conformance Test Suite (PCTS). This program tests the conformance of computer operating system environments to the FIPS release 151, which defines the standard for functional interface between an operating environment and applications to promote applications portability. Price - $2,500.

* Computerized Data File Directory

Directory of Computerized Datafiles
National Technical Information Service
U.S. Department of Commerce
5285 Port Royal Rd.
Springfield, VA 22161   703-487-4650

The annual *Computerized Data File Directory* contains more than 1,300 source files for unique Federal numeric and text data. This publication offers its readers a single, convenient reference to important datafiles prepared by a variety of Federal agencies. The cost is $65. Call the Sales Desk to place an order or ask for a free information brochure *PR-629*.

* Computer Software Directory

Directory of Computer Software
National Technical Information Service
U.S. Department of Commerce
5285 Port Royal Rd.
Springfield, VA 22161   703-487-4650

The *Directory of Computer Software* contains detailed descriptions of software applications and tools. Information has been compiled in cooperation with hundreds of U.S. Government agencies. More than 1,700 programs are arranged under 21 subject headings. Full indexes by subject, hardware, language, and sponsoring agency are included. Agencies providing programs include the National Library of Medicine, Environmental Protection Agency, U.S. Department of Defense, the U.S. Department of Energy, plus many others. The cost is $65. Contact the Sales Desk of place an order or ask for a free information brochure *PR-261*.

* Critical Technologies

National Technical Information Service
U.S. Department of Commerce
5285 Port Royal Rd.
Springfield, VA 22161   703-487-4650

The President's Council on Competitiveness has examined America's declining position in the area of critical technologies and makes recommendations as to what the country must do to regain its position as world leader in this area. The cost of this report is $20. Order number is PB91-180281CAU.

* Defense Technical Information and Referral Center

Defense Technical Information Center (DTIC)
Cameron Station
Alexandria, VA 22304-6145   703-617-7931

The Defense Technical Information Center (DTIC) maintains a *Referral Data Bank Directory* of major resource and holding centers in the U.S. Department of Defense. Write or call the above office for more information.

* Digital Spatial Data and Mapping Software

U.S. Geological Survey
Reston-ESIC
507 National Center
Reston, VA 22092   703-648-4119

Be patient. If any phone number is incorrect, call (area code) 555-1212 and request the new listing.

953

Science and Technology

The U.S. Geological Survey's Earth Science Information Center (ESIC) now offers inventories of digital spatial data sets and cartographic applications software in two bound listings. These inventories provide up-to-date bibliographic descriptions of data sets and software available from federal, state, and local government agencies and the private sector.

Sources for Digital Spatial Data. Describes more than 500 data sets containing spatially referenced base or thematic categories of data. The data sets are indexed by geographic area of coverage and cross-indexed by type of data.

Sources for Software for Computer Mapping and Related Disciplines. Describes more than 700 subroutines, programs, and systems that can be used in geographic information systems, map and chart plotting and construction, image processing and analysis, surveying, photogrammetry, data modeling and analysis, coordinate conversion, and other applications. Each publication is $22.

* Digital Spatial Data Applications Cooperation

U.S. Geological Survey
Reston-ESIC
507 National Center
Reston, VA 22092 703-648-4119

If your organization is involved in digital spatial data applications, the Earth Science Information Center invites you to contribute information about your holdings. Your data and software may be valuable to other users.

* Earth System Data Directory

National Oceanographic Data Center
National Oceanic and Atmospheric Administration (NOAA)
NESDIS E/OCx7
Washington, DC 20235 202-673-5548

The National Oceanic and Atmospheric Administration (NOAA) Earth System Data Directory provides users with an online catalogue and index to data files and data sets held by elements of the National Oceanographic and Atmospheric Administration. Most entries at this time describe data held by NOAA's three national data centers, but the directory will become increasingly comprehensive as other NOAA offices add descriptions of their data holdings. The directory may be searched by scientific discipline, measured parameters, time period, geographic location, project, and other criteria. The directory was developed by the National Aeronautics and Space Administration (NASA). For more information, contact NOAA at the above listing.

* Electromagnetic Technology

Directorate for Public Communication
U.S. Department of Defense
The Pentagon
Room 2E777
Washington, DC 20301-1400 703-697-5737

This office can provide you with general information about electromagnetic technology, including annual reports, newsletters and fact sheets, and will make referrals for you if you need more detailed information.

* Emerging Technologies

National Technical Information Service
U.S. Department of Commerce
5285 Port Royal Rd.
Springfield, VA 22161 703-487-4650

This report identifies twelve technologies in four commercial areas that will create markets for an estimated $1 trillion in sales by the year 2000. The four commercial areas covered are: advanced materials; electronics and information systems, manufacturing systems, and life sciences applications. The cost of this document is $19, order number PB90-216557CAU.

* Energy Bioscience Research

Office of Energy Research
Energy Biosciences Division
U.S. Department of Energy
19901 Germantown Rd., Room G-34
Germantown, MD 20585 301-903-2873

This office funds fundamental research in the plant and microbial sciences that will underpin new biotechnologies related to energy matters.

* Energy Pollutants Health Research

Health Effects and Life Sciences Research Division
Office of Health and Environmental Research
U.S. Department of Energy
19901 Germantown Rd.
Germantown, MD 20585 301-903-5468

This Division conducts studies to characterize and develop a basis for understanding biological phenomena used in predicting human health effects from exposure to energy pollutants. It conducts fundamental research into structural, molecular, and cellular biology, and develops technologies and resources needed to characterize the molecular nature of the human genome.

* Energy Related Chemical Research

Office of Energy Research
Chemical Sciences Division
19901 Germantown Rd., Room G-34
Germantown, MD 20585 301-903-3427

This office funds and administers programs in energy-related chemical sciences research such as photochemistry, radiation chemistry, hot atom chemistry, chemical dynamics, theoretical chemistry, spectroscopy, and the physics of ions, atoms, and molecules. It also supports research in the area of chemical thermodynamics related to energy resources such as coal. Contact this office for more information on facilities available for researchers.

* Energy Science and Technology Database

National Technical Information Service
U.S. Department of Commerce
5285 Port Royal Rd.
Springfield, VA 22161 703-487-4650

The Energy Science and Technology Database (ESTD) is a multidisciplinary file containing two and a half million references to the world's scientific and energy related literature. In addition to nuclear science and technology and basic scientific studies in biology, chemistry, engineering, geology, physics, nuclear medicine, computers, and environment and pollution, it contains more than a million entries in areas not considered strictly energy fields, e.g. nuclear medicine computers, and mathematical models. Contact the National Technical Information Service (NTIS) for more information.

* Environmental Research Technology Transfer

Center for Environmental Research Information
Environmental Protection Agency (EPA)
26 West Martin Luther King Dr.
Cincinnati, OH 45263 513-569-7391

The Office of Research and Development of the Environmental Protection Agency (EPA) has centralized most of its information distribution and technology transfer activities in the Center for Environmental Research Information listed above. The Center for Environmental Research Information (CERI) also serves as a central point of distribution for the Office of Research and Development (ORD) research results and reports.

* European Technology in Computers, Telecommunications and Electronics

National Technical Information Service
U.S. Department of Commerce
5285 Port Royal Rd.
Springfield, VA 22161 703-487-4650

This report, prepared by the Department of the Navy, provides material important for those doing business in the areas of computers, telecommunications, and electronics. The report looks at the impact of microcomputers, distributed systems, supercomputers, and minicomputers are having on the European computer market. It also describes the European programs in the area of Integrated Services Digital Network. Cost is $19; order number PB90-215773CAU.

* Federal Laboratory Consortium (FLC)

FLC Management Support Office
224 W. Washington St., Suite 3
Sequim, WA 98382 360-683-1005

The Federal Laboratory Consortium (FLC) is a national network of 300 individuals from federal laboratories and centers across the country. Members are responsible for assessing the technologies developed at their facility and then passing that knowledge

Be patient. If any phone number is incorrect, call (area code) 555-1212 and request the new listing.

onto industry, government, and the general public. Through the FLC the public can gain access to all unclassified research conducted by the federal government. The FLC director can refer you to an FLC member in your specialty or geographical area. Its *Federal Laboratory Directory 1985* provides data on 388 federal laboratories with ten or more full-time professionals engaged in research and development. Information is provided about staff size, mission, and major scientific or testing equipment. The Directory can be obtained for free from the National Technical Information Service NTIS, 5285 Port Royal Rd., Springfield, VA 22161, 703-487-4650.

* Federal Research in Progress Database

National Technical Information Service
U.S. Department of Commerce
5285 Port Royal Rd.
Springfield, VA 22161   703-487-4650

The Federal Research in Progress (FEDRIP) database summarizes 120,000 U.S. Government funded research projects currently in progress. These summaries make it possible to determine progress in specific areas before technical reports or journal literature become available. The database content focuses on health, physical sciences, agriculture, engineering, and life sciences. Each listing describes a research project, its project, its objectives, and when available, preliminary findings. For a free brochure describing this service, contact the National Technical Information Service (NTIS) and ask for PR847/827.

* Fermi National Accelerator Laboratory

Public Information Office
P.O. Box 500
Batavia, IL 60510   312-840-3351

This laboratory was established in 1967 to explore the field of elementary particle physics so that the understanding of the basic structure of matter may be broadened. A related mission is the improvement of accelerator design that has resulted in numerous technological spinoffs: the development of various applications other than magnets for superconductivity; fast electronics and particle detector technology; and special computers and computer programs.

* Former Office of Technology Assessment (OTA) Publications and Reports

National Technical Information Service (NTIS)
U.S. Department of Commerce
5285 Port Royal Rd.
Springfield, VA 22161   703-487-4650

These publications from the former Office of Technology Assessment (OTA) are available through the National Technical Information Service.

Agriculture and Forestry

Agricultural Commodities as Industrial Raw Materials (F-476) PB91-198093
Agricultural Research and Technology Transfer Policies for the 1990s (F-448) PB90-219981
Assessing Biological Diversity in the United States: Data Considerations (BP-F-39) PB86-181989
An Assessment of the U.S. Food and Agricultural Research System (F-155) PB82-170572
Continuing the Commitment: Agricultural Development in the Sahel (F-308) PB87-117644
Drugs in Livestock Feed (F-91) PB-298450
Emerging Food Marketing Technologies (F-79) PB-291039
Enhancing the Quality of U.S. Grain for International Trade (F-399) PB89-187199
Environmental Contaminants in Food (F-103) PB80-153265
Food Information Systems (F-35) PB-258172
Grain Quality in International Trade: A Comparison of Major U.S. Competitors (F-402) PB89-187249
Impacts of Technology on U.S. Cropland and Rangeland Productivity (F-166) PB83-125013
Integrated Renewable Resource Management for U.S. Insular Area (F-325) PB87-205829
Nutrition Research Alternatives (F-74) PB-289825
Open Shelf-Life Dating of Food (F-94) PB80-101629
Perspectives on Federal Retail Food Grading (F-47) PB-273163
Pest Management Strategies in Crop Protection (F-98) PB80-120017
Plants: The Potential for Extracting Protein, Medicines, and Other Useful Chemicals (BP-F-23) PB84-114743
Sustaining Tropical Forest Resources: Reforestation of Degraded Lands (BP-F-18) PB84-104058

Sustaining Tropical Forest Resources: U.S. and International Institutions (BP-F-19) PB84-104041
Technologies To Benefit Agriculture and Wildlife (BP-F-34) PB85-239747
Technologies To Maintain Biological Diversity (F-330) PB87-207494
Technology, Public Policy, and the Changing Structure of American Agriculture (F-285) PB86-210374
Water-Related Technologies for Sustainable Agriculture in U.S. Arid/Semiarid Lands (F-212) PB84-172667
Water-Related Technologies for Sustainable Agriculture in U.S. Arid/Semiarid Lands: Selected Foreign Experience (BP-F-20) PB84-102912

Biological Applications

Alternatives to Animal Use In Research, Testing, and Education (BA-273) PB86-183134
Assessment of Technologies for Determining Cancer Risk From the Environment (H-138) PB81-235400
Biological Rhythms: Implications for the Worker (BA-463) PB92-117589
Biotechnology in a Global Economy (BA-494) PB92-115823
Commercial Biotechnology: An International Analysis (BA-218) PB84-173608
Genetic Monitoring and Screening in the Workplace (BA-455) PB91-105940
Humane Gene Therapy (BP-BA-32) PB85-206076
Identifying and Controlling Immunotoxic Substances (BP-BA-75) PB91-183145
Impacts of Applied Genetics: Micro-Organisms, Plants, and Animals (HR-132) PB81-206609
Impacts of Neuroscience (BP-BA-24) PB84-196716
Mapping Our Genes: Genome Projects - How Big, How Fast? (BA-373) PB88-212402
Medical Monitoring and Screening in the Workplace: Results of a Survey (BP-BA-67) PB92-117738
Neural Grafting: Repairing the Brain and Spinal Cord (BA-462) PB91-114249
Neurotoxicity: Identifying and Controlling the Poisons of the Nervous System (BA-436) PB90-252511
The Role of Genetic Testing in the Prevention of Occupational Disease (BA-194) PB83-233734
Status of Biomedical Research and Related Technology for Tropical Diseases (H-258) PB87-139614
Technologies for Detecting Heritable Mutations in Human Beings (H-298) PB87-140158

Defense

Adjusting to a New Security Environment: The Defense Technology and Industrial Base Challenge (BP-ISC-79) PB91-163261
Arming Our Allies: Cooperation and Competition in Defense Technology (ISC-449) PB90-254160
American Military Power: Future Needs and Future Choices (BP-ISC-80) PB92-157585
Anti-Satellite Weapons, Countermeasures, and Arms Control (ISC-281) PB86-182953
Arms Control in Space (BP-ISC-28) PB84-198209
Ballistic Missile Defense Technology (ISC-254) PB86-182961
Containment of Underground Nuclear Explosions (ISC-414) PB90-156183
Cooperative Aerial Surveillance in International Agreements (ISC-480) PB81-220020
Directed Energy Missile Defense in Space (BP-ISC-26) PB84-21011
The Effects of Nuclear War (NS-89) PB-296946
Global Arms Trade: Commerce in Advanced Military Technology and Weapons (ISC-460) PB91-212175
Holding the Edge: Maintaining the Defense Technology Base - 2 vols. (ISC 420 and 432) PB90-253345
Managing Research and Development for Cooperative Arms Control Monitoring Measures (ISC-488) PB91-197913
New Technologies for NATO: Implementing Follow-On Forces Attack (ISC-309) PB87-200267
Nuclear Proliferation and Safeguards (E-48) PB-275843
Redesigning Defense: Planning the Transition to the Future U.S. Defense Industrial Base (ISC-500) PB91-220012
Remote Sensing and the Private Sector: Issues for Discussion (TM-ISC-20) PB84-18077
SDI: Technology, Survivability, and Software (ISC-353) PB88-236245
Seismic Verification of Nuclear Testing Treaties (ISC-361) PB88-214853
Taggants in Explosives (ISC-116) PB80-192719
Technology Against Terrorism: The Federal Effort (ISC-481) PB92-152509
Technologies for NATO's Follow-On Forces Attack Concept (ISC-312) PB87-100343

Education and Training

Automation and the Workplace: Selected Labor, Education, and Training Issues (TM-CIT-25) PB83-191320

Be patient. If any phone number is incorrect, call (area code) 555-1212 and request the new listing.

955

Displaced Homemakers: Programs and Policy (ITE-292) PB86-206182

Educating Scientist and Engineers: Grade School to Grad School (SET-377) PB88-235973

Elementary and Secondary Education for Science and Engineering (TM-SET-41) PB89-139182

Higher Education for Science and Engineering (BP-SET-62) PB89-191290

Linking for Learning: A New Course for Education (SET-430) PB90-156969

Plant Closing: Advance Notice and Rapid Response (ITE-321) PB87-18212

Performance Standards for Secondary School Vocational Education (April 1989) PB89-195176

Power On! New Tools for Teaching and Learning (SET-379) PB89-114276

Technology and Structural Unemployment: Reemploying Displaced Adults (ITE-250) PB86-206174

The Use of Integrity Tests for Pre-Employment Screening (SET-442) PB91-107011

Worker Training: Competing in the New International Economy (ITE-457) PB91-106716

Energy and Mineral Resources

Application of Solar Technology to Today's Energy Needs (E-66) PB-283770

Conservation and Solar Energy Programs of the Department of Energy: A Critique (E-120) PB80-197759

Electric Power-Wheeling and Dealing: Technological Considerations for Increasing Competition (E-409) PB89-232748

Energy and Efficiency of Building in Cities (E-168) PB82-200346

Energy Efficiency in the Federal Government: Government by Good Example? (E-492) PB93-203750

Energy in Developing Countries (E-486) PB91-133694

Energy Technology Choices: Shaping our Future (E-493) PB91-220004

Energy Technology Transfer to China (TM-ICS-30) PB80-211477

Energy Use and the U.S. Economy (BP-E-57) PB90-254145

Gasohol (TM-E-1) PB80-105885

Increased Automobile Fuel Efficiency and Synthetic Fuels: Alternatives for Reducing Oil Imports (E-185) PB88-126094

Improving Automobile Fuel Economy: New Standards, New Approaches (E-504) PB92-115989

Industrial and Commercial Cogeneration (E-192) PB83-180547

Industrial Energy Use (E-198) PB83-240606

New Electric Power Technologies: Problems and Prospects for the 1990's (E-246) PB86-121746

Nuclear Power in an Age of Uncertainty (E-216) PB84-183953

Nuclear Powerplant Standardization: Light Water Reactors (E-134) PB81-213589

Physical Vulnerability of Electrical Systems to Natural Disasters and Sabotage (E-453) PB90-253287

Replacing Gasoline: Alternative Fuels for Light Duty Vehicles (E-364) PB91-104901

Residential Energy Conservation (E-92) PB-298410

Solar Power Satellite Systems (E-144) PB82-108846

Starpower: The U.S. and the International Quest for Fusion Energy (E-338) PB88-128731

Environment and Pollution

Acid Rain and Transported Air Pollutants: Implications for Public Policy (O-204) PB84-222967

Beneath the Bottom Line: Agricultural Approaches to Reduce Agrichemical Contaminants of Groundwater (F-418) PB91-129874

Catching Our Breath: Next Steps for Reducing Urban Ozone (O-412) PB90-130451

Changing By Degrees: Steps to Reduce Greenhouse Gases (O-482) PB91-163428

Complex Cleanup: The Environmental Legacy of Nuclear Weapons Production (O-484) PB91-143743

The Direct Use of Coal: Prospects and Problems of Production and Combustion (E-86) PB-295797

Environmental Protection in the Federal Coal Leasing Program (E-237) PB84-222413

From Pollution to Prevention: A Progress Report on Waste Reduction (ITE-347) PB87-208062

Habitability of the Love Canal Area: An Analysis of the Technical Basis for the Decision on the Habitability of the Emergency Declaration Area (TM-M-13) PB84-114917

Long Lived Legacy: Managing High Level and Transuranic Waste at the DOE Nuclear Weapons Complex (BP-O-83) PB91-186205

Marine Applications for Fuel Cell Technology (TM-O-37) PB86-183597

Nonnuclear Industrial Waste: Classifying for Hazards Management (TM-M-9) PB82-134305

Oil and Gas Technologies for the Arctic and Deepwater (O-270) PB86-119948

Oil Transportation by Tankers: An Analysis of Marine Pollution and Safety Measures (O-9) PB-244457

Protecting the Nation's Groundwater From Contamination (O-233) PB85-154201

Serious Reduction of Hazardous Waste (ITE-317) PB87-139622

Technologies and Management Strategies for Hazardous Waste Control (M-196) PB83-189241

Technologies for Prehistoric and Historic Preservation (E-319) PB87-222519

Technologies for the Preservation of Prehistoric and Historic Landscapes (BP-E-44) PB87-140166

Technologies for Reducing Dioxin in the Manufacture of Pulp and Paper PB89-223291

Technologies for Underwater Archaeology and Maritime Preservation (BP-E-37) PB88-142559

Technology and Oceanography: An Assessment of Federal Technologies for Oceanographic Research and Monitoring (O-141) PB82-101718

Urban Ozone and the Clean Air Act: Problems and Proposals for Change (Staff paper) PB88-205414

Wastes in Marine Environments (O-334) PB87-194585

Western Surface Mine Permitting and Reclamation (E-279) PB87-100350

Wetlands: Their Use and Regulation (O-206) PB84-175918

Health

Adolescent Health-Volume I: Summary and Policy Options (H-468) PB91-197921

Adolescent Health-Volume II: Background and the Effectiveness of Selected Prevention and Treatment Services (H-466) PB92-157577

Adolescent Health-Volume III: Crosscutting Issues in the Delivery of Health and Related Services (H-467) PB91-212183

Adolescent Health Insurance Status: Analyses of Trends in Coverage and Preliminary Estimates of the Effects of an Employer Mandate and Medicaid Expansion on the Uninsured (BP-H-56) PB90-116-66

Artificial Insemination: Practice in the United States (BP-BA-48) PB89-139903

Assessing the Efficacy and Safety of Medical Technologies (H-75) PB-286929

Assessment of Technologies for Determining Cancer Risks From the Environment (H-138) PB81-235400

Assistive Devices for Severe Speech Impairments (HCS-26) PB84-175371

Blood Policy and Technology (H-260) PB85-234870

Cancer Testing Technology and Saccharin (H-55) PB-273499

Children's Dental Services under the Medicaid Program (BP-H-78) PB91-106708

Confused Minds, Burdened Families: Finding Help for People with Alzheimer's and Other Dementias (BA-403) PB90-259540

Costs and Effectiveness of Screening for Cervical Cancer in the Elderly (Contractor Paper) PB90-166018

Children's Mental Health: Problems and Services (BP-H-33) PB87-207486

Costs and Effectiveness of Screening for Cholesterol in the Elderly (Contractor Paper) PB91-104877

Commercial Biotechnology: An International Analysis (BA-218) PB84-173608

Computer Technology in Medical Education and Assessment (BP-H-1) PB80-102528

Contact Lenses (HCS-31) PB85-204451

Cost-Effectiveness Analysis of Influenza Vaccine (H-152) PB82-178492

The Cost-Effectiveness of Digital Subtraction Angiography in the Diagnosis of Cerebrovascular Disease (HCS-34) PB85-241115

Defining Rural Areas: Impact on Health Care Policy and Research (July 1989) PB89-224646

Diagnostic Related Groups (DRGs) and the Medicare Program: Implications for Medical Technology (TM-H-17) PB84-111525

The Effectiveness of Costs of Alcoholism Treatment (HCS-22) PB83-192492

Effects of Federal Policies on Extracorporeal Shock Wave Lithotripsy (HCS-36) PB86-217999

Federal Policies and the Medical Devices Industry (H-229) PB85-199552

Forecasts of Physician Supply and Requirements (H-113) PB80-181670

Healthy Children: Investing in the Future (H-344) PB88-178454

Health Care in Rural America (H-434) PB91-104927

Hearing Impairment and Elderly People (BP-BA-30) PB86-218559

Hemodialysis Equipment (HCS-32) PB85-154553

Human Gene Therapy (BP-BA-32) PB85-206076

Identifying and Regulating Carcinogens (BP-H-42) PB88-136999

The Impacts of Neuroscience (BP-BA-24) PB84-196716

The Implications of Cost-Effectiveness Analysis of Medical Technology (H-126) PB80-216864

Indian Health Care (H-290) PB86-206091

Indian Adolescent Mental Health (H-446) PB90-254095

Infertility: Medical and Social Choices (BA-358) PB88-196464

Institutional Protocols for Decisions About Life-Sustaining Treatments (BA-389) PB89-138895

Intensive Care Units (ICU's) Clinical Outcomes, Costs, and Decisionmaking (HCS-28) PB85-145928

Life-Sustaining Technologies and the Elderly (BA-306) PB87-222527

Losing a Million Minds: Confronting the Tragedy of Alzheimer's Disease and Other Dementias (BA-323) PB87-183752

The Management of Health Care Technology in Ten Countries (BP-H-7) PB81-144628

Mandatory Passive Restraint Systems in Automobiles: Issues and Evidence (BP-H-15) PB83-159822

The Market of Wheelchairs: Innovation and Federal Policy (HCS-30) PB85-145944

Medical Technology and the Costs of the Medicare Program (H-227) PB85-146215

Medical Technology Under Proposals To Increase Competition in Health Care (H-190) PB83-164046

Medical Testing and Health Insurance (H-384) PB89-116958

Medicare's Prospective Payment System: Strategies for Evaluating Cost, Quality, and Medical Technology (H-262) PB86-184926

MEDLARS and Health Information Policy (TM-H-11) PB83-168658

Methodological Issues and Literature Review (BP-H-5) PB81-144602

Neonatal Intensive Care for Low Birthweight Infants: Costs and Effectiveness (HCS-38) PB88-158902

Nuclear Magnetic Resonance Imaging Technology: A Clinical, Industrial, and Policy Analysis (HCS-27) PB85-146207

Nurse Practitioners, Physician Assistants, and Certified Nurse-Midwives: A Policy Analysis (HCS-37) PB87-177465

Outpatient Immunosuppressive Drugs under Medicare (H-452) PB92-117720

Passive Smoking in the Workplace: Selected Issues (Staff Paper) PB86-217627

Payment for Physician Services: Strategies for Medicare (H-294) PB86-182011

Policy Implications of Medical Information Systems (H-56) PB-274857

Policy Implications of the Computed Tomography (CT) Scanner (H-72) PB-284872

Policy Implications of the Computed Tomography (CT) Scanner: An Update (BP-H-8) PB81-163917

Preventive Health Services for Medicare Beneficiaries: Policy and Research Issues (H-416) PB90-219999

Preventing Illness and Injury in the Workplace (H-256) PB86-115334

The Quality of Medical Care: Information for Consumers (H-386) PB89-102180

Reproductive Health Hazards in the Workplace (BA-266) PB86-185030

A Review of Selected Federal Vaccine and Immunization Policies Based on Case Studies of Pneumococcal Vaccine (H-96) PB80-116106

Recombinant Erythropoietin: Payment Options for Medicare (H-451) PB90-256124

The Role of Genetic Testing in the Prevention of Occupational Disease (BA-194) PB83-233734

Rural Emergency Medical Services (H-445) PB90-159047

The Safety, Efficacy, and Cost Effectiveness of Therapeutic Apheresis (HCS-23) PB84-114842

Screening for Open-Angle Glaucoma in the Elderly (Staff Paper) PB91-192872

Selected Telecommunication Devices for Hearing-Impaired Persons (BP-H-16) PB83-169293

Selected Topics in Federal Health Statistics (H-90) PB-298449

Status of Biomedical Research and Related Technology for Tropical Diseases (H-258) PB87-139614

Strategies for Medical Technology Assessment (H-181) PB83-113274

Technologies for Detecting Heritable Mutations in Human Beings (H-298) PB87-140158

Technology and Aging in America (BA-264) PB86-116514

Technology and Handicapped People (H-179) PB83-172056

Technology and Learning Disabilities (HCS-25) PB84-184043

Technology Dependent Children: Hospital v. Home Care (TM-H-38) PB87-194531

Technology Transfer at the National Institutes of Health (TM-H-10) PB82-202904

Update of Federal Activities Regarding the Use of Pneumococcal Vaccine (TM-H-23) PB85-128155

Unconventional Cancer Treatments (H-405) PB91-104893

Variations in Hospital Length of Stay: Their Relationship to Health Outcomes (HCS-24) PB84-111493

World Population and Fertility Planning Technologies: The Next 20 Years (HR-157) PB82-200338

Industry

AIDS and Health Insurance: An OTA Survey (Staff Paper) PB88-170204

An Assessment of Maritime Trade and Technology (O-220) PB84-177781

An Assessment of Technology for Local Development (B-129) PB81-189979

Automation and the Workplace: Selected Labor, Education, and Training Issues (TM-CIT-25) PB83-191320

Automation of America's Offices (CIT-287) PB86-185055

Benefits of Increased Use of Continuous Casting by the U.S. Steel Industry (TM-ISC-2) PB80-104907

Boston Elbow (HCS-29) PB85-145936

Census of State Government Initiatives for High-Technology Industrial Development (BP-STI-21) PB84-104033

Commercial Biotechnology: An International Analysis (BA-218) PB84-173608

Commercializing High-Temperature Superconductivity (ITE-388) PB88-246442

Competing economies: America, Europe, and the Pacific Rim (ITE-498) PB92-115757

Computer-Based National Information Systems: Information and Public Policy (CIT-146) PB82-126681

Computerized Manufacturing Automation: Employment, Education, and the Workplace (HCS-31) PB84-196500

Copyright and Home Copying PB90-151309

Displaced Homemakers: Programs and Policy (ITE-292) PB86-120276

Drug Labeling in Developing Countries PB93-163343

The Effectiveness and Costs of Alcoholism Treatment (HCS-22) PB83-192492

The Efficacy and Cost Effectiveness of Psychotherapy (BP-H-6) PB81-144610

Electric Power - Wheeling and Dealing: Technological Considerations for Increasing Competition (E-409) PB89-232748

Encouraging High-Technology Development (BP-STI-25) PB84-180181

Federal Policies and the Medical Devices Industry (H-229) PB85-199552

Gearing Up for Safety: Motor Carrier Safety in a Competitive Environment (SET-382) PB89-124796

Hemodialysis Equipment (HCS-32) PB85-154953

The Impact of Randomized Clinical Trials on Health Policy and Medical Practice (BP-H-22) PB84-114560

Impacts of Applied Genetics: Micro-Organisms, Plants, and Animals (HR-132) PB81-206609

Industrial and Commercial Cogeneration (E-192) PB83-180547

Industrial Energy Use (E-198) PB83-240606

Information Technology R&D: Critical Trends and Issues (CIT-268) PB85-245660

Informing the Nation: Federal Information Dissemination in an Electronic Age (CIT-396) PB83-114243

International Competition in Services: Banking, Building, Software, Know-How (ITE-328) PB84-170695

International Competitiveness in Electronics (ISC-200) PB87-212403

Making Things Better: Competing in Manufacturing (ITE-443) PB90-205469

Marine Applications for Fuel Cell Technology (TM-O-37) PB86-183597

The Market for Wheelchairs: Innovation and Federal Policy (HCS-30) PB85-145944

Medical Testing and Health Insurance (H-384) PB89-116958

Microelectronics R&D (BP-CIT-40) PB86-205200

New Developments in Biotechnology: U.S. Investment in Biotechnology (BA-360) PB88-246939

Nuclear Magnetic Resonance (NMR) Imaging Technology: A Clinical, Industrial, and Policy Analysis (O-270) PB85-146207

Paying the Bill: Manufacturing and America's Trade Deficit (ITE-390) PB88-229539

Plant Closing: Advance Notice and Rapid Response (ITE-321) PB87-118212

Policy Implications of the Computed Tomography (CT) Scanner (H-72) PB-274857

Policy Implications of the Computed Tomography (CT) Scanner: An Update (BP-H-8) PB-284872

Preventing Illness and Injury in the Workplace (H-256) PB86-115334

R&D in the Maritime Industry (BP-O-35) PB85-246932

Reproductive Health Hazards in the Workplace (BA-266) PB86-185030

Strategies for Medical Technology Assessment (H-181) PB83-113274

Technology and Steel Industry Competitiveness (M-122) PB80-208200

Technology and Structural Unemployment: Reemploying Displaced Adults (ITE-250) PB86-206174

Technology and the American Economic Transition (TET-283) PB88-214127

Technology and the Future of the U.S. Construction Industry PB86-209442

Technology, Innovation, and Regional Economic Development (STI-238) PB85-150894

U.S. Industrial Competitiveness: A Comparison of Steel, Electronics, and Automobiles (ISC-135) PB81-235749

The U.S. Textile and Apparel Industry: A Revolution in Progress (TET-332) PB87-196762

Wood Use: U.S. Competitiveness and Technology (ITE-210) PB84-109925

Information Technology and Services

An Assessment of Alternatives for a National Computerized Criminal History System (CIT-161) PB83-166678

An Assessment of Information System Capabilities Required To Support U.S. Materials Policy Decision (M-40) PB-273462

Automation and the Workplace: Selected Labor, Education, and Training Issues (TM-CIT-25) PB83-191320

Automation of America's Offices (CIT-287) PB86-185055

Big Picture: HDTV and High Resolution Systems (BP-CIT-64) PB90-256108

Biology, Medicine, and the Bill of Rights (CIT-371) PB89-136428

Book Preservation Technologies (O-375) PB88-212410

Computer Software and Intellectual Property (BP-CIT-61) PB90-220005

Costs and Effectiveness of Screening for Cervical Cancer in the Elderly (Contractor Paper) PB90-166018

Children's Mental Health: Problems and Services (BP-H-33) PB87-207486

Costs and Effectiveness of Screening for Cholesterol in the Elderly (Contractor Paper) PB89-224638

Computer-Based National Information Systems: Technology and Public Policy Issues (CIT-146) PB82-126681

Be patient. If any phone number is incorrect, call (area code) 555-1212 and request the new listing.

957

Science and Technology

Computerized Manufacturing Automation: Employment, Education, and the Workplace (CIT-235) PB84-196500

Copyright and Home Copying PB90-151309

Criminal Justice, New Technologies, and the Constitution (CIT-366) PB88-213921

Defending Secrets, Sharing Data: New Locks and Keys for Electronic Information (CIT-310) PB88-143185

Educating Scientists and Engineers: Grade School to Grad School (SET-377) PB86-235973

Electronic Delivery of Public Assistance Benefits: Technology Options and Policy Issues (BP-CIT-47) PB89-138911

Electronic Bulls and Bears: U.S. Securities Markets and Information Technology (CIT-469) PB91-106153

The Electronic Supervisor: New Technology, New Tensions (CIT-333) PB88-156351

Elementary and Secondary Education for Science and Engineering (TM-SET-41)

Helping America Compete: the Role of Federal Scientific and Technical Information (CIT-454) PB90-252537

Higher Education for Science and Engineering (BP-SET-52) PB89-191290

High Performance Computing and Networking for Science (BP-CIT-59) PB90-131228

Implications of Electronic Mail and Message Systems for the U.S. Postal Service (CIT-183) PB83-265017

The Information Context of Premanufacture Notices (BP-H-17) PB83-241059

Information Technology R&D: Critical Trends and Issues (CIT-268) PB85-245660

Informational Technology and Its Impact on American Education (CIT-187) PB83-174664

Informing the Nation: Federal Information Dissemination in an Electronic Age (CIT-396) PB89-114243

Intellectual Property Rights in an Age of Electronics and Information (CIT-302) PB87-100301

Medical Testing and Health Insurance (H-384) PB89-116958

MEDLARS and Health Information Policy (TM-H-11) PB83-168658

Patent-Term Extension and the Pharmaceutical Industry (CIT-143) PB82-100918

Payment for Physician Services: Strategies for Medicare (H-294) PB86-182011

Policy Implications of Medical Information Systems (H-56) PB81-163917

Power On! New Tools for Teaching and Learning (SET-379) PB89-114276

A Preliminary Assessments of the National Crime Information Center and the Computerized Criminal History System (I-80) PB-291845

The Quality of Medical Care: Information for Consumers (H-386) PB89-102180

Radiofrequency Use and Management: Impacts From the World Administrative Radio Conference of 1979 (CIT-163) PB82-177536

Review of Postal Automation Strategy: A Technical and Decision Analysis (TM-CIT-22) PB82-182609

Rural America at the Crossroads: Networking for the Future (TCT-471) PB91-198135

Science, Technology, and the Constitution (BP-CIT-43) PB88-142534

Science, Technology, and the First Amendment (CIT-369) PB88-166426

Scientific Validity of Polygraph Testing: A Research Review and Evaluation (TM-H-15) PB84-181411

Seeking Solutions: High Performance Computing for Science (BP-TCT-77) PB91-169763

Selected Electronic Funds Transfer Issues: Privacy, Security and Equity (BP-CIT-12) PB82-202532

Strategies for Medical Technology Assessment (H-181) PB83-113274

Technology and Structural Unemployment: Reemploying Displaced Adults (ITE-250) PB86-206174

Trading Around the Clock: Global Securities Markets and Information Technology (BP-CIT-66) PB90-252537

International Trade, Competition, and Cooperation

Arms Control in Space (BP-ISC-28) PB84-198209

Civilian Space Policy and Applications (STI-177) PB82 234444

Civilian Space Stations and U.S. Future in Space (STI-241) PB85-205391

Commercial Biotechnology: An International Analysis (BA-218) PB84-173608

Copper: Technology and Competitiveness (E-367) PB89-138887

Energy Technology Transfer to China (TM-ISC-30) PB86-113008

Enhancing Agriculture in Africa: A Role for Development Assistance (F-356) PB89-137087

Enhancing the Quality of U.S. Grain for International Trade (F-399) PB89-187199

Grain Quality in International Trade: A Comparison of Major U.S. Competitors (F-402) PB89-187249

International Competition in Services: Banking, Building, Software, Know-How (ITE-328) PB87-212403

International Competitiveness in Electronics (ISC-200) PB84-170695

Paying the Bill: Manufacturing and America's Trade Deficit (ITE-390) PB88-229539

Starpower: The U.S. and the International Quest for Fusion Energy (E-338) PB88-128731

Technology and East-West Trade (ISC-101) PB80-119381

Technology and East-West Trade: An Update (ISC-209) PB83-234955

Technology and Soviet Energy Availability (ISC-153) PB82-133455

Technology Transfer to China (ISC-340) PB87-223418

Technology Transfer to the Middle East (ISC-173) PB85-127744

Technology Transfer to the United States: The MIT-Japan Science and Technology Program (April 1989) PB89-224711

Trade in Services: Exports and Foreign Revenues (ITE-316) PB87-118204

UNISPACE '82: A Context for International Cooperation and Competition (TM-ISC-26) PB83-201848

U.S. - Soviet Cooperation in Space (TM-STI-27) PB86-114758

Oceans and Water Resources

An Assessment of Maritime Trade and Technology (O-220) PB84-177781

Bioremediation for Marine Oil Spills (BP-O-70) PB91-186197

The Border War on Drugs (TM-O-8) PB87-184172

Coal Exports and Port Development (TM-O-8) PB81-203358

Competition in Coastal Areas: An Evaluation of Foreign Maritime Activities in the 200 Mile EEZ (BP-O-55) PB89-224653

Coping With an Oiled Sea (P-O-63) PB90-219973

Costal Effects of Offshore Energy Systems (O-37) PB-274033

Establishing a 200-Mile Fisheries Zone (O-46) PB-273578

Issues in Medical Waste Management (BP-O-49) PB89-136410

Marine Applications for Fuel Cell Technology (TM-O-37) PB86-183597

Marine Minerals: Exploring Our New Ocean Frontier (O-342) PB87-217725

Ocean Incineration: Its Role in Managing Hazardous Waste (O-313) PB87-100327

Ocean Margin Drilling (TM-O-4) PB80-198302

Oil Transportation by Tankers: An Analysis of Marine Pollution and Safety Measures (O-9) PB-24457

Protecting the Nation's Groundwater From Contamination (O-233) PB85-154201

R&D in the Maritime Industry (BP-O-35) PB85-246932

Recent Developments in Ocean Thermal Energy (TM-O-3) PB80-20185

Technology and Oceanography: An Assessment of Federal Technologies for Oceanographic Research and Monitoring (O-141) PB82-101718

Transportation of Liquefied Natural Gas (O-53) PB-273486

Using Desalination Technologies for Water Treatment (BP-O-46) PB88-193354

Wastes in Marine Environments (O-334) PB87-194585

Wetlands: Their Use and Regulation (O-206) PB84-175918

Science and Technology, Research and Development

Advanced Materials by Design: New Structural Materials Technologies (E-351) PB88-243548

Alternatives to Animal Use in Research, Testing, and Education (BA-273) PB86-183134

Anti-Satellite Weapons, Countermeasures, and Arms Control (ISC-281) PB86-182953

Assessment of Technologies for Determining Cancer Risks From the Environment (H-138) PB81-235400

An Assessment of the United States Food and Agriculture Research System (F-155) PB82-170572

Ballistic Missile Defense Technology (ISC-254) PB86-182961

Biology, Medicine, and the Bill of Rights (CIT-371) PB89-136428

Blood Policy and Technology (H-260) PB85-234870

Book Preservation Technologies (O-375) PB88-212410

Cancer Testing Technology and Saccharin (H-55) PB-273499

Civilian Space Policy and Applications (STI-177) PB82-234444

Civilian Space Stations and U.S. Future in Space (STI-241) PB85-205391

Commercializing High-Temperature Superconductivity (ITE-388) PB88-246442

Criminal Justice, New Technologies, and the Constitution (CIT-366) PB88-213921

Demographic Trends and the Scientific and Engineering Work Force (TM-SET-35) PB86-206186

Elementary and Secondary Education for Science and Engineering (TM-SET-41) PB89-139182

Energy Technology Transfer to China (TM-ISC-30) PB91-220004

Federally Funded Research: Decisions for a Decade (SET-490) PB91-198101

Global Models, World Futures, and Public Policy (R-165) PB82-521299

Human Gene Therapy (BP-BA-32) PB85-206076

Identifying and Regulating Carcinogens (BP-H-42) PB88-136999

Impacts of Neuroscience (BP-BA-24) PB84-196716

Information Technology R&D: Critical Trends and Issues (CIT-268) PB85-245660

Microelectronics R&D (BP-CIT-40) PB86-205200

New Developments in Biotechnology: Field Testing Engineered Organisms: Genetic and Ecological Issues (BA-350) PB88-214101

New Developments in Biotechnology: Ownership of Human Tissues and Cells (BA-337) PB87-207537

New Developments in Biotechnology: Patenting Life (BA-370) PB89-196612

New Developments in Biotechnology: Public Perceptions of Biotechnology (BP-BA-45) PB87-207544

New Developments in Biotechnology: U.S. Investment in Biotechnology (BA-360) PB88-246939

New Structural Material Technologies: Opportunities for the Use of Advanced Ceramics and Composites (TM-E-32) PB87-118253

Patent-Term Extension and the Pharmaceutical Industry (CIT-143) PB82-100918

Power On! New Tools for Teaching and Learning (SET-379) PB89-114276

R&D in the Maritime Industry (BP-O-35) PB85-246932

The Regulatory Environment for Science (TM-SET-34) PB86-182003

Research Funding As An Investment: Can We Measure the Returns? (TM-SET-36) PB86-218278

Salyut: Soviet Steps Toward Permanent Human Presence in Space (TM-STI-14) PB84-181437

Science, Technology, and the Constitution (BP-CIT-43) PB88-213921

Science, Technology, and the First Amendment (CIT-369) PB88-166426

Scientific Validity of Polygraph Testing: A Research Review and Evaluation (TM-H-15) PB84-181411

SDI: Technology, Survivability, and Software (ISC-353) PB88-236245

Seismic Verification of Nuclear Test Ban Treaties (ISC-361) PB88-214853

Space Science Research in the United States (TM-STI-19) PB83-166512

Status of Biomedical Research and Related Technology for Tropical Diseases (H-258) PB87-139614

Technologies for Detecting Heritable Mutations in Human Beings (H-298) PB87-140158

Technology Transfer at the National Institutes of Health (TM-H-10) PB82-202904

Technology Transfer to China (ISC-340) PB87-223418

Space

Access to Space: the Future of U.S. Space Transportation Systems (ISC-415) PB90-253154

Affordable Spacecraft Design and Launch Alternatives (BP-ISC-60) PB90-203225

Anti-Satellite Weapons, Countermeasures, and Arms Control (ISC-281) PB86-182953

Arms Control in Space (BP-STI-28) PB84-198209

Ballistic Missile Defense Technology (ISC-254) PB86-182961

Civilian Space Policy and Applications (STI-177) PB82-234444

Civilian Space Stations and U.S. Future in Space (STI-241) PB85-205391

Commercial Newsgathering From Space (TM-ISC-40) PB87-235396

International Cooperation and Competition in Civilian Space Activities (ISC-239) PB87-136842

Launch Options for the Future: A Buyer's Guide (ISC-383) PB89-114208

Orbital Debris: A Space Environmental Problem (BP-ISC-72) PB91-114272

Reducing Launch Operations Costs: New Technologies and Practices (TM-ISC-28) PB89-136402

Round Trip to Orbit: Human Spaceflight Alternatives (ISC-419) PB89-224661

SDI: Technology, Survivability, and Software (ISC-353) PB88-236245

Seismic Verification of Nuclear Test Ban Treaties (ISC-361) PB88-214853

Solar Power Satellite Systems (E-144) PB82-108846

Space Science Research in the United States (TM-STI-19) PB83-166512

Space Stations and the Law: Selected Legal Issues (BP-ISC-41) PB87-118200

UNISPACE '82: A Context for International Cooperation and Competition (TM-ISC-26) PB83-201848

U.S. - Soviet Cooperation in Space (TM-STI-27) PB86-114758

Transportation

Airport and Air Traffic Control Systems (STI-175) PB82-207606

Airport System Development (STI-231) PB88-127793

Automated Guideway Transit: An Assessment of Personal Rapid Transit and Other New Systems (T-8) PB-244854

The Border War On Drugs (O-336) PB87-184172

Civilian Space Policy and Applications (STI-177) PB82-234444

Delivering the Goods: Public Works Technologies, Management, and Financing (SET-477) PB91-197939

The Direct Use of Coal: Prospects and Problems of Production and Combustion (E-86) PB-295797

Energy From Biological Processes (E-124) PB80-211477

An Evaluation of Railroad Safety (T-61) PB-281169

Gasohol (TM-E-1) PB80-105885

Gearing Up for Safety: Motor Carrier Safety in a Competitive Environment (SET-382) PB89-124796

Impact of Advanced Air Transport Technology: Pt.1-Advanced High-Speed Aircraft (T-112) PB80-153323

Impact of Advanced Air Transport Technology: Pt.2-Air Cargo (BP-T-10) PB80-153323

Impact of Advanced Air Transport Technology: Pt.3-Air Services to Small Communities (T-170) PB82-186800

Impact of Advanced Air Transport Technology: Pt.4-Financing and Program Alternatives for Advanced High-Speed Aircraft (BP-T-14) PB80-200504

Increased Automobile Fuel Efficiency and Synthetic Fuels: Alternatives for Reducing Oil Imports (E-185) PB83-126094

Launch Options for the Future: A Buyer's Guide (ISC-383) PB89-114268

Managing the Nation;s Commercial High-Level Radioactive Waste (O-171) PB86-116852

Moving Ahead: 1991 Surface Transportation Legislation (SET-496) PB91-212159

Oil Transportation by Tankers: An Analysis of Marine Pollution and Safety Measures (O-9) PB-244457

Rebuilding the Foundations: State and Local Public Works Financing and Management (SET-447) PB90-254152

Reducing Launch Operations Costs: New Technologies and Practices (TM-ISC-28) PB89-136402

Review of the FAA 1982 National Airspace System Plan (STI-176) PB83-102772

Safe Skies for Tomorrow: Aviation Safety in a Competitive Environment (SET-381) PB89-114318

Safer Skies with TCAS (Traffic Alert and Collision Avoidance System) (SET-432) PB89-169211

Strategic Materials: Technologies to Reduce U.S. Import Vulnerability (ITE-248) PB86-115376

A Technology Assessment of Coal Slurry Pipelines (E-60) PB-278675

Transportation of Hazardous Materials (SET-304) PB87-100319

Transportation of Hazardous Materials: State and Local Activities (SET-301) PB86-181971

U.S. Passenger Rail Technologies (STI-222) PB84-182609

Wastes in Marine Environments (O-334) PB87-194585

* Fusion Energy Research

Office of Fusion Energy
Office of Energy Research
U.S. Department of Energy
19901 Germantown Rd.
Germantown, MD 20874-1290   301-903-4941

Magnetic fusion is a long term energy option that could become a principal energy source in the next century. The role of the Federal government in magnetic fusion is to establish the scientific and technological base required for an assessment of the feasibility of magnetic fusion as an energy source. Four issues are currently at the forefront of magnetic fusion research: improving magnetic confinement systems; determining the properties of burning plasmas; developing economic and environmentally suitable materials fusion systems; and developing nuclear technologies that can be successfully integrated into advanced fusion systems. Contact this office for more information on the current status of magnetic fusion research.

* Geotechnical Research

U.S. Army Corps of Engineers
Waterways Experiment Station
3909 Halls Ferry Rd.
Vicksburg, MS 39180-6199   601-634-2504

A component of the Geotechnical Lab, the Pavements and Soil Trafficability Information Analysis Center (PSTIAC) provides products and specialized reference services to the public. The staff can be tasked to provide evaluative engineering and/or analytical service on pavements, trafficability, vehicle mobility, and terrain, primarily relevant to military needs. Database searches are performed on a cost recovery basis, and requests are approved on a case by case basis. The Station's library participates in the national inter-library loan system, and copies of technical reports are distributed on a first come, first served basis. (Reports are thereafter available from DTIC.) The Public Affairs Office can provide a summary of publications, fact sheets on the Center's programs, brochures on subject areas, and a comprehensive book entitled *Summary of Capabilities* describing the Center's work. Time on the Center's super computer is available for sale to academic researchers.

* Health and Environmental Research

Office of Health and Environmental Research
Office of Energy Research
U.S. Department of Energy
19901 Germantown Rd.
Germantown, MD 20874-1290   301-903-3251

The Office of Health and Environmental Research seeks to understand the long term health effects and environmental consequences of energy use and development. To this end, its program focus is on research in atmospheric, marine and terrestrial processes; molecular and subcellular mechanisms underlying human somatic and genetic processes and their responses to energy related environmental toxicants; nuclear medicine and epidemiology; and structural biology.

Science and Technology

* Health Services Research

Health Services Research (152)
5109 Leesburg Pike
Falls Church, VA 22041-3258   703-756-8215

The goal of this research is to improve the effectiveness and efficiency of the U.S. Department of Veterans Affairs health care delivery system. Health services researchers develop and distribute information designed to help clinicians, investigators, and administrators select medical interventions and administrative actions that are most appropriate to the Agency's mission: the provision of quality medical care services to the veteran patient.

* High Energy Physics Advisory Panel

U.S. Department of Energy
19901 Germantown Rd., Room G-48
Germantown, MD 20585   301-903-4140

This Advisory Panel provides guidance to the Secretary of Energy on high energy physics research program which encompasses the Superconducting Super Collider (SSC) activities. The panel, among other things, recommends changes in the program based on scientific and technological advances.

* High Energy and Nuclear Physics Program

Office of Energy Research
U.S. Department of Energy
19901 Germantown Rd.
Germantown, MD 20585   301-903-3713

The High Energy and Nuclear Physics Programs seek a deeper understanding of the nature of matter and energy and the basic forces that exist between the fundamental constituents of matter. The program focuses on obtaining an understanding of the ultimate structure of all matter and energy through the study of properties of elementary particles. This program is supported by three major research laboratories:

Fermi National Accelerator Laboratory - Batavia, Illinois.
The Tevatron, currently the worlds only superconducting proton synchrotron, is capable of accelerating particles to the highest energies available anywhere in the world.

Stanford Linear Accelerator Center - Menlo Park, CA.
The Stanford Linear Accelerator Center carries out experimental and theoretical research in high energy physics, and also developmental work in new techniques for particle acceleration and for experimental instrumentation. The Stanford Linear Collider project recently began and promises to be a major step toward reducing the cost of future high energy electron-positron colliders. It also gives U.S. physicists early access to the physics resulting from production of "Z" particles.

Brookhaven National Laboratory - Upton, NY.
The Alternating Gradient Synchrontron provides a facility for research using beams of protons, polarized protons, and various secondary particles, at energies up to 33 GeV. The main focus of the present research program using the proton primary beam are on studies of very rare decays of the K meson.

* Ice Navigational Technology

Planning Branch
Research and Development Staff
Office of Engineering and Development
U.S. Coast Guard
U.S. Department of Transportation
2100 2nd St., SW, Room 6208
Washington, DC 20593-0001   202-267-1030

Information can be obtained here about research conducted by the Coast Guard in support of its operations and responsibilities. Areas of study include ice operations, ocean dumping, law enforcement, environmental protection, port safety and security, navigation aids, search and rescue procedures, recreational boating, energy, and advanced marine vehicles. For referral to specific personnel working in these areas, contact the Planning Branch.

* Institute of Electrical and Electronics Engineers (IEEE)

IEEE Headquarters
345 East 47th Street
New York, NY 10017   212-705-8287

This large engineering society focuses on advancing the theory and practice of electrical engineering, electronics, computer engineering and computer science. The Institute of Electrical and Electronics Engineers (IEEE) consists of 30 technical societies corresponding to essentially every recognized discipline or interest area. There are, for example, societies for biomedical engineering, control systems, communications, and power engineering. The largest is the IEEE Computer Society. Staff at IEEE can respond to questions and refer you to members in regional chapters around the U.S. One of the organization's main functions is publishing technical literature, and presently it is credited with publishing 15% of the world's technical papers in the electrical and electronic fields. Each Society publishes one or more technical periodicals, usually called *Transactions* or *Journals*, which cover such fields as aerospace and electronic systems, electron devices, lightwave technology, microwave theory and techniques, and quantum electronics. The primary periodical is *IEEE Spectrum* which contains state-of-the-art news, reviews, and application articles of interest to many engineers and scientists. Call 212-705-7890 for information on technical activities; and 201-981-1393 for publications from the Piscataway, NJ, Service Center.

* Japanese Technology Evaluation Center

National Technical Information Service
U.S. Department of Commerce
5285 Port Royal Rd.
Springfield, VA 22161   703-487-4650

The Japanese Technology Evaluation Center issues a series of reports written by panels of U.S. industrial, government, and academic experts. These reports are definitive assessments of emerging Japanese efforts in selected high-technology areas. The JTEC evaluations provide technical input for those who make technology forecasts and competitive assessments and establish a direction for U.S. research and trade policies. The Center has numerous reports available. Call for a list of reports.

* Japanese Technical Resources

Directory of Japanese Technical Resources
National Technical Information Service
U.S. Department of Commerce
5285 Port Royal Rd.
Springfield, VA 22161   703-487-4650

The directory, *Japanese Technical Resources*, allows government, industry, and the academic community to find U.S. sources of Japanese high-technology information. It is divided into four parts: 1) an alphabetical list of commercial organizations that collect, abstract, translate, or distribute Japanese technical information; 2) a list of government agencies with programs and services involving Japanese technical information; 3) a list of libraries that have extensive holdings of Japanese technical information; and 4) a list of Japanese technical reports translated by the U.S. Government and available to the public. It is available for $36.

* Laser Research

High Energy Laser Systems Test Facility
White Sands Missile Range
Public Affairs Office
New Mexico, 88802   505-678-1134

This Facility tests and evaluates high energy laser systems, subsystems and components. For information on tests and facilities, contact the above office.

* Lawrence Berkeley Laboratory

Lawrence Berkeley Laboratory
1 Cyclotron Road
Berkeley, CA 94720   510-486-5771

The Lawrence Berkeley Laboratory (LBL) is managed by the University of California for the U.S. Department of Energy. The laboratory has more than 3,000 employees and an operating budget of more than $235 million. The laboratory conducts research in the following areas: acceleration and fusion research, energy and environment, cell and molecular biology, chemical biodynamics, earth sciences, chemical sciences, materials sciences, nuclear science, physics, research medicine and radiation biophysics, engineering, information and computing sciences, and environment, safety and health. The *LBL Research Review*, a quarterly publication, is a good way to keep up with current research activities at the laboratory. For more information on programs or to get a sample copy of the *LBL Research Review*, contact the above office.

* Materials Research: Wear and Corrosion

Research Division
Bureau of Mines
U.S. Department of the Interior
810 7th St., NW

Washington, DC 20241-0001   202-501-9274

Advanced materials research is being conducted to eliminate wear and corrosion within the minerals industry through the use of ceramics, high-performance plastics, high-tech metals and alloys, and composites. Bureau scientists are also developing new coatings to protect equipment from the heat, corrosive chemicals, and abrasive materials found in mills, smelters, refineries, and furnaces.

* Medical Research

Medical Research Service
Veterans Health Services and Research Administration
U.S. Department of Veterans Affairs
810 Vermont Ave., NW
Washington, DC 20420   202-576-3551

Veterans Administration (VA) efforts in this area fall into two broad categories: research on medical, dental, and psychiatric problems that are specific to the veteran population (spinal cord injury, Agent Orange, etc); and research on general health problems that are particularly prevalent among veterans (e.g., alcoholism, aging, and schizophrenia). Most of the investigators are VA clinicians and the close links between research and patient care functions give the research program a clinical orientation that is directly related to its goal of providing quality medical care to the veteran patient. For more information, contact the office above.

* Microcomputers and Semiconductors

Reliability Analysis Center (RAC)
P.O. Box 4700
Rome, NY 13440-8200   315-339-7054

Evaluation engineering, analytical services, products, and specialized reference services are provided by the Reliability Analysis Center (RAC) in the areas of microcircuits, semiconductors, nonelectric devices, and electronic modules. Reliability and maintainability data on planned and operational systems and equipment is stored in a database. A user's catalog, searches, and technical reports can be obtained on a cost recovery basis. Cost for searches depends on the search. The Center does not release documents, but documents can be ordered from the Defense Technical Information Service in Alexandria, VA; 703-274-7633, or they will refer you to the agency that does release these documents.

* Mines Technology Transfer

Office of Technology Transfer
Bureau of Mines
U.S. Department of the Interior
810 7th St., NW, MS 6201
Washington, DC 20241-0001   202-501-9323

The Technology Transfer Group distributes information on mining industry issues in many ways. *Technology Transfer* is a newsletter announcing the latest technology and research in mining. Free conferences are also held around the country on a variety of topics, such as advanced materials research and new technology for minerals. These conferences are announced through the newsletter *Technology Transfer Announcement*. To be placed on the mailing list, contact the office above.

* National Critical Technologies Panel Report

National Technical Information Service
U.S. Department of Commerce
5285 Port Royal Rd.
Springfield, VA 22161   703-487-4650

This report describes 22 technologies identified as critical to the economic prosperity and national defense of the United States. How the technologies were identified is described in the appendix. Some of the broad areas selected include materials, manufacturing, information and communications, biotechnology and life sciences, and energy and environment. Each of these areas is further broken down into specific technologies. The report costs $16. The order number is PB91-156869CAU.

* Night Vision Research

Office of Public Affairs
Night Vision and Electro-Optics
Laboratories (NVEOL)
Fort Belvoir, VA 22060-5806   703-704-2279

The Night Vision and Electro-Optics Laboratories (NVEOL) conducts research and development into electro-optical low-energy lasers, all-weather systems, infrared, radiation, visionics, and image intensification. The laboratories provide the Army with equipment to enable it to carry out nocturnal operations efficiently. This office can offer information and referral on laboratory programs.

* NTIS Alert on Computers

National Technical Information Service
U.S. Department of Commerce
5285 Port Royal Rd.
Springfield, VA 22161   703-487-4650

This bulletin describes new software and datafiles received by the Federal Computer Products Center. It also includes abstracts of Government research in computers and information technology, such as computer hardware; control systems and theory; information processing standards; information theory; and pattern recognition and image processing.

* NTIS Database Searches

Selected Research in Microfiche (SRIM)
National Technical Information Service
5285 Port Royal Rd.
Springfield, VA 22161   703-487-4650

Selected Research in Microfiche (SRIM) automatically provides selected technical reports as they are issued. Using SRIM, customers design (or select) their own subscription parameters, choosing from more than 350 subject topics. They then receive all reports that fall within their selections. Customers pay only $1.25 for each report they receive. Call SRIM Product Manager to start your subscription or request the free information brochure, *PR-271*.

* NTIS Foreign Technology Alert

National Technical Information Service
U.S. Department of Commerce
5285 Port Royal Rd.
Springfield, VA 22161   703-487-4650

This newsletter covers significant breakthroughs in foreign research and industrial technology. Coverage includes the areas of advanced microelectronics structural ceramics, superconductivity, and biotechnology. The subscription price for the *Alert* is $165 per year. A free brochure is available *(PR-842/827)* that describes the service.

* NTIS Index

National Technical Information Service (NTIS)
U.S. Department of Commerce
5285 Port Royal Rd.
Springfield, VA 22161   703-487-4650

NTIS Title Index is a microfiche list that provides an economical means of locating reports for sale from the National Technical Information Service (NTIS). It cites titles, order numbers, and prices of reports input into NTIS for a two-year period. A key-word-out-of-context title listing index is provided along with a personal author index and an order/report number index. The price for a two-year subscription is $400. Call the Sales Desk to place an order or request the free information brochure, *PR-567*.

* NTIS Products

National Technical Information Service
U.S. Department of Commerce
5285 Port Royal Rd.
Springfield, VA 22161   703-487-4650

The National Technical Information Service (NTIS) information products and services presented in this section give you ready access to the results of both U.S. and foreign government-sponsored research. The U.S. Government alone invests billions of dollars in research and development and engineering programs. Much of the resulting knowledge and technology is available through NTIS. And in the case of applied technology, this information can be of great value because it is not proprietary and may be used freely. The following newsletters are available through NTIS:

NTIS Alerts. These weekly bulletins present summaries of the most recent U.S. and foreign government research and development and engineering results. Prices range from $125-$175 depending upon subject area. For more information, request the free brochure, *PR-797*.

Computers, Control and Information Theory Abstract Newsletter. This bulletin provides early notice of new software and datafiles as they are received by the Federal Computer Products Center. It also includes abstracts of Government research in computers and information theory. A subscription is available for $150 per year. For more information, request the free brochure, *PR-797*.

Science and Technology

Tech Notes. This is a monthly service providing access to the Federal laboratory activities and resources. An NTIS Tech Notes subscription provides selected *Fact Sheets* on the latest U.S. government-developed technologies and know-how. This low-cost service provides concise, illustrated one page announcements describing new processes, instruments, materials, equipment, software, services, and techniques. Each month more than 100 fact sheets are arranged under twelve subject headings. A subscription is available for $157 per year. For more information request the free brochure, *PR-365.*

Government Reports Announcements and Index Journal. This journal is issued twice monthly for those who want to see all of the research and development and engineering results announced annually by NTIS. Its comprehensive coverage provides 2,500 results within each issue. Entries are arranged under 38 major subject headings and then further sorted within more than 350 subheadings. A subscription is available for $495 per year. For more information, request the free information brochure, *PR-195.*

* NTIS Product Services Catalog

National Technical Information Service
U.S. Department of Commerce
5285 Port Royal Rd.
Springfield, VA 22161   703-487-4650

NTIS Product Services Catalog describes the bulletins, journals, catalogs, and directories produced by the National Technical Information Service (NTIS) and available for sale. It also includes descriptions of more than eighty subscription items produced by other government agencies and made available from NTIS. Call for your free copy.

* Nuclear Physics/High Energy Research

Office of High Energy and Nuclear Physics
Office of Energy Research
19901 Germantown Rd.
Germantown, MD 20585   301-903-3613

This office establishes basic research policies for nuclear physics and high energy research and funds meritorious research programs at Federal laboratories, universities, and industrial institutions. It also provides scientific and technical knowledge for development of technology options and technology transfer of those projects which show promise of becoming important as energy technologies.

* Ocean Science Information Exchange

National Oceanographic Data Center
User Services Branch
National Oceanic and Atmospheric Administration (NOAA)
NESDIS E/OC21
Washington, DC 20235   202-673-5548

This is an experimental prototype system developed to provide frequent National Oceanographic Data Center (NODC) users with online access to information about its data sets and services. In addition to containing most of the information contained in the *NODC Users Guide*, it also contains modules that provide searchable inventories of some of NODC's major data files, as well as other useful features. Contact NODC for more information on this database.

* Plastics and Adhesives Research

Plastics Technical Evaluation Center
U.S. Army Armament Research, Development
  and Engineering Center (ARDEC)
Building 355-N
Picatinny Arsenal, NJ 07806-5000   201-724-4222

Technical information related to plastics, adhesives, and organic matrix composites is generated, evaluated, stored, and distributed at this Center, with an emphasis on performance and properties. Computerized databases are maintained on the compatibility of polymers with propellants and explosives and on materials deterioration. The Center provides services on a fee basis, including consulting, state-of-the-art studies, handbooks, analysis, evaluation, and bibliographic and literature searches. To arrange for services or to get information, contact PLASTEC at the number listed above.

* Science Information Tracer Bullets

Science and Technology Division
Reference Section
Library of Congress
Washington, DC 20540   202-707-5580

Informal series of reference guides are issued free from the Science and Technology Division under the general title, *LC Science Tracer Bullet*. These guides are designed to help readers locate published material on subjects about which they have only general knowledge by providing detailed bibliographies and search strategies for topics of interest. New titles in the series are announced in the weekly Library of Congress *Information Bulletin* that is distributed to many libraries. The following is a list of *Tracer Bullets* currently available:

TB No.	Title
80-1	*Green Revolution*
80-3	*Automotive Electronics*
80-4	*Aging*
80-5	*Low-Level Ionizing Radiation: Health Effects*
80-7	*Solar Energy*
80-8	*Electric and Hybrid Vehicles*
80-9	*Terminal Care*
80-10	*Infrared Applications*
80-11	*Drug Research on Human Subjects*
80-12	*Ocean Thermal Energy*
80-14	*Automotive Maintenance and Repair*
80-15	*The History of Psychology II*
80-16	*Synthetic Fuels*
80-18	*Health Foods*
80-19	*Industrial Robots*
81-2	*Medicinal Plants*
81-3	*Alcoholism*
81-5	*Wind Power*
81-9	*Cable Television (Cable TV)*
81-10	*Manned Space Flight*
81-11	*Mariculture*
81-13	*Wood As Fuel*
81-14	*Volcanoes*
81-15	*History of American Agriculture*
81-17	*Epilepsy*
82-1	*Food Additives*
82-3	*Earth Sheltered Buildings*
82-4	*Extraterrestrial Life*
82-5	*Jet Engines and Jet Aircraft*
82-6	*Biological Control of Insects*
82-8	*Chemical and Biological Warfare (CBW)*
82-9	*Sickle Cell Anemia*
83-1	*Biofeedback*
83-2	*Power Metallurgy*
83-3	*Hazardous Wastes (Non-nuclear)*
83-4	*Science Policy*
83-5	*Plant Exploration and Introduction*
83-6	*Mental Retardation*
83-8	*Women in the Sciences*
83-9	*Geothermal Energy*
83-10	*High Technology*
84-1	*Aquaculture*
84-3	*Japanese Science and Technology*
84-4	*Sharks*
84-5	*Scientific and Technical Libraries: Administration and Management*
84-7	*Biotechnology*
85-1	*Herbs and Herb Gardening*
85-2	*Landscape Gardening*
85-3	*Endangered Species (Animals)*
85-4	*Computer Security*
85-5	*Black Scientists*
85-6	*Acupuncture*
85-7	*CAD/CAM (Computer Aided Design/Computer Aided Manufacture)*
85-8	*Anorexia Nervosa/Bulimia*
85-10	*Rose Culture*
85-11	*Acquired Immune Deficiency Syndrome (AIDS)*
86-1	*Artificial Intelligence*
86-2	*Mars (Planet)*
86-3	*Jojoba and Other Oilseed Plants*
86-4	*Composite Materials*
86-5	*Electromagnetic Fields--Physiological and Health Effects*
86-6	*Diabetes Mellitus*
86-8	*Indoor Air Pollution*
86-10	*Career Opportunities in Science and Technology*
86-11	*Acid Rain*
87-1	*Asbestos*
87-2	*Alzheimer's Disease*

* Patent, Trademark, and Copyright Monitoring

Intellectual Property Owners, Inc.
1255 23rd St., NW, Washington, DC 20037; 202-466-2396. IPO is a nonprofit trade association representing people who own patents, trademarks, and copyrights. It gathers and disseminates information on legislative and regulatory matters, and monitors international events and intellectual property developments. It publishes the *IPO News* which keeps members up-to-date on developments in the field.

Patent Office Society
Commissioner of Patents and Trademarks, 2021 Jefferson Davis Highway, Crystal City, VA 22202; 703-415-0350. This professional society for patent examiners promotes the patent system to the general public. It publishes the *Journal of the Patent Office Society* and the *Official Gazette*. The *Official Gazette* is printed every Tuesday for those trying to secure patents. It can be purchased from the Government Printing Office, 202-512-1800.

Commissioner of Patents and Trademarks
Public Service Center, Office of Patents and Trademarks, 2021 Jefferson Davis Highway, Crystal City, VA 20231; 703-308-HELP or 703-557-4636. The Center publishes a newsletter that includes a listing of publications and brochures put out by the Patent and Trademark Office. The staff tries to answer all questions such as finding the right office or locating publications. Patent specifications and drawings, as well as trademarks, are $3 each. You must have the patent or trademark number.

Search Room--Patents
2021 Jefferson Davis Highway, Crystal City, VA 22202; 703-557-4636 for general information; 703-308-0808 for the Scientific Library. This service will search for any patent, and give the vendor's name, the issue date, and the title. You can also go in and search all patents in any field. The Scientific Library contains all U.S. and foreign patents and is open to the public.

Search Room--Trademarks
2021 Jefferson Davis Highway, Crystal City, VA 22202; 703-308-9800. To search a trademark, you must either go to this office or call the Trademark Library, which is open to the public.

Trademark Information Office
2021 Jefferson Davis Highway, Crystal City, VA 22202; 703-308-9000. This office will answer questions on different aspects of trademarks, and has a booklet describing trademarks and what the Patents and Trademarks Office does.

Copyright Office
Reference and Bibliographic Section, Library of Congress, Washington, DC 20559; 202-707-6850. This office will research the copyright you need and send you the information by mail. Requests must be in writing and you must specify exactly what it is you need to know.

United States Trademark Association
6 East 45th Street, New York, NY 10017; 212-986-5880. The United States Trademark Association (USTA) keeps abreast of all aspects of the trademark field. Forums, educational meetings and an annual meeting are held. It maintains a comprehensive library that offers access to source material on all aspects of trademarks. Publications include *The Trademark Reporter*, *The Executive Newsletter*, and over 50 bulletins which are published each year, reporting on general news, publications, and events related to trademark law, advertising, marketing, and design.

American Intellectual Property Law Association
2001 Jefferson Davis Highway, Suite 203, Arlington, VA 22202; 703-415-0780. The American Intellectual Property Law Association (AIPLA) tries to promote better understanding of the patent, trademark, and copyright systems. Its law library is open to the public which makes available a wide range of material on patents. Publications include *AIPLA Bulletin* ($40/year), *AIPLA Quarterly Journal* ($45/year), and *An Overview of Intellectual Property* ($.25/pamphlet).

* Publications Prepared by the Science and Technology Division

Science and Technology Division
Library of Congress
Washington, DC 20540   202-707-5655
The Library of Congress' Science and Technology Division recently released a report entitled *Fifty Years of Science*, which lists hundreds of publications produced by the Division over the past fifty years with abstracts. Contact the Division to obtain a copy of the list.

* Scientific and Technical Information

National Technical Information Service
U.S. Department of Commerce
5285 Port Royal Rd.
Springfield, VA 22161   703-487-4650
The U.S. government publishes a directory that provides an overview of Federal agencies' responsibilities in disseminating scientific and technical information originating with Federal research and development programs. It lists that major agencies involved and is a guide to comprehending the scope and relationships of Federal STI programs. It includes a table that shows the policy and operational roles of Federal agencies and their research and development budgets. Directory cost - $30. Order number PB91-180216CAU.

* Science and Technology Resources in U.S. Industry

National Technical Information Service
U.S. Department of Commerce
5285 Port Royal Rd.
Springfield, VA 22161   703-487-4650
The National Science Foundation has prepared a report that explores American industrial science and technological resources in terms of research and development activities, employment and use of scientists, engineers, and technicians. It examines how a country's competitive position is largely determined y its investment in human and capital resources dedicated to science and technology. Cost is $26; order number PB90-107194CAU.

Science and Technology

* Science Fairs and Research Grants

U.S. Department of the Army
Army Research Office
P.O. Box 12211
Triangle Park, NC 27709 919-549-0641

This office administers the nation-wide Science Fair program, which sponsors science competition at the high school level, and the Defense Research Initiative, which is a competitive grant program for government funding of university research. Write or call for free brochures and information describing these programs.

* Science Resources Center

National Science Resources Center
Smithsonian Institution
Arts and Industries Building, Room 1201
Washington, DC 20560 202-357-2555

The National Science Resources Center was established to improve the teaching of science and mathematics in the nation's schools. The NSRS has established a science and mathematics curriculum resource collection and database, developed and disseminates resources materials for science and mathematics teachers, and offers a program of outreach and leadership-development activities. One resource guide, *Science for Children: Resources for Teachers*, is a guide designed to help teachers and science educators identify teaching materials and resources that can be used to improve science teaching in elementary schools. Contact the Resource Center for more information.

* Standards for Industrial Engineering

Technical Reports Section
Science and Technology Division
Library of Congress
Washington, DC 20540 202-707-5655

The Standards Collection of the Science and Technology Division contains almost 500,000 items. In addition to the hundreds of organizations who have contributed to the collection, the *Technical Reports Section* holds a complete set of standards issued and sponsored by the American National Standards Institute (ANSI) as well as a complete set of U.S. Federal/Military and DOD adopted standards and specifications. The collection also includes a complete hardbound set of standards for the former Soviet Union, the Peoples Republic of China, and the Republic of South Africa. They are the only complete set of standards available to the public located in the U.S. For a list of the organizations whose standards are held by the Library of Congress, contact the Technical Reports Section at the above number.

* Superconducting Super Collider

Office of the Superconducting Super Collider
Office of Energy Research
U.S. Department of Energy
1000 Independence Ave., SW, Room 6E-034
Washington, DC 20585 202-586-7170

The Superconducting Super Collider (SSC) will be the worlds largest particle accelerator, with two rings of superconducting magnets in a 53-mile circumference race-track shaped tunnel. Continued progress in high-energy physics research in the late-1990s will require the study of collisions at energy levels that cannot be achieved with any accelerator now in operation. The total budget for the project is currently projected at $5.9 billion, with an expected completion around the year 1998. The site chosen for the Collider is located about 25 miles south of Dallas and 35 miles south-east of Fort Worth. For more information on the Collider, contact the above office.

* Superfund Technology

Center for Environmental Research Information
Environmental Protection Agency
26 West Martin Luther King Dr.
Cincinnati, OH 45263 513-569-7392

The Center for Environmental Research Information can provide you with the publication entitled *Compendium of Superfund Program Publications*, which details, among other things, the technologies used for the superfund cleanup programs of hazardous waste sites around the country.

* Technical Agriculture Resources

National Agricultural Library (NAL)
10301 Baltimore Blvd.
Beltsville, MD 20705 301-504-3755

The National Agricultural Library (NAL) provides comprehensive information services for the food and agricultural sciences through a variety of sources, which include bibliographies, personal reference services, loans, photocopies, and online data files. Services are provided to agricultural colleges, research institutions, government agencies, agricultural associations, industry, individual scientists, and the general public. The NAL cooperates with the Library of Congress and the National Library of Medicine to provide access to publications worldwide in the agricultural, chemical, and biological sciences. The NAL houses one of the largest collections in the free world on agricultural subjects - 2.3 million volumes and 26,000 periodicals - including biology, chemistry, nutrition, forestry, soil sciences, and much more.

* Technical Bibliographies

Published Searches
National Technical Information Service (NTIS)
U.S. Department of Commerce
5285 Port Royal Rd.
Springfield, VA 22161 703-487-4650

Published Searches contains bibliographies available on more than 3,000 topics from the National Technical Information Service (NTIS) and 23 international information sources. These specialized bibliographies are created not only from material announced by NTIS, but also from published scientific journal articles gathered from 23 other international information sources. Each bibliography is chosen for its current interest to a particular audience. Most titles are updated annually. For a copy of the *NTIS Published Search Master Catalog* listing more the 3,000 titles, contact NTIS and ask for *PR-186*.

* Technology Research Army Libraries

U.S. Army Materiel Command
Information Systems Command
Public Affairs Office
Timberlake, AZ 602-538-8609

Each Army Materiel Command (AMC) installation has a technological library. It is usually possible to gain access to the library if you obtain prior approval. Contact your local AMC for information, or the above office for a referral to your closest installation.

* Technology Assessment with Patents

Office of Documentation Information
Patent and Trademark Office
U.S. Department of Commerce
1921 Jefferson Davis Hwy., Room 304
Arlington, VA 22202 703-308-0808

The Technology Assessment and Forecast (TAF) Program's mission is to stimulate the use and enhance the usability of the more than 27 million documents which make the categorized U.S. patent file. The Patent and Trademark Office (PTO) has assembled the TAF database which covers all U.S. patents. The PTO extracts meaningful information about the U.S. patent file from the TAF database, analyzes the information, and makes it available in a variety of formats. Users of TAF information include patent attorneys, researchers, PTO employees and other government agencies. Patent information from the TAF database is distributed to users through publications, such as *Patent Profiles* and *Technology Assessment and Forecast Reports*, as well as through custom patent reports and statistical reports. Contact this office for more information on the TAF database, and ordering information for TAF publications.

* Technology Catalogs

National Technical Information Service
U.S. Department of Commerce
5285 Port Royal Rd.
Springfield, VA 22161 703-487-4650

Each of the *Federal Technology Catalogs: Guides to New and Practical Technologies* contains more than 1,000 summaries of selected processes, instruments, materials, equipment, software, services, and techniques. In conjunction with Federal agencies and their laboratories, key practical and applied results are screened for interest to U.S. engineers, research and development managers, and business planners. Most entries give a telephone contact for further detailed information or for specific technical discussion. Each catalog is subdivided into 23 subject headings making it easy to scan for exact references. Each entry includes full bibliographic information, full summaries, and how to obtain additional information. Catalogs are available for each year going back to 1981, and range in price from $27 to $36. Contact the Sales Desk to place an order or request the free information brochure, *PR-801*.

* Technology Commercialization

Office of Commercial Affairs (OCA)
Technology Administration
U.S. Department of Commerce
14th St. and Constitution Ave., NW
Washington, DC 20230   202-377-4743

This office works with industry to develop a consensus regarding technology opportunities and foreign competitive challenges. The Office of Commercial Affairs (OCA) facilitates cooperative joint ventures with U.S. industry in areas of research and technology development, and aims to improve the ability of U.S. industry to access federally-funded technology. This office also provides specific assistance in targeting and coordinating information activities in areas such as Japanese science and technology and metric conversion. Key activities include facilitating the adoption of flexible computer-integrated manufacturing by small- and medium-sized businesses by encouraging the establishment of private sector-funded joint centers and by working with other federal agencies and industry to remove barriers and create incentives. Contact this office for more information.

* Technology Exchange Programs

International Cooperative Division and Secretariat (P-25)
Office of International Transportation and Trade
Office of the Secretary of Transportation
U.S. Department of Transportation (DOT)
400 7th Street, SW
Washington, DC 20590   202-366-4368

The Department of Transportation (DOT) participates in a number of cooperative programs with other countries to exchange mutually beneficial transportation research data and state-of-the-art technical information. Areas of exchange include highway technology; ports and inland waterways; railway technology; and search and rescue operations. China and the Soviet Union are among the countries participating. Contact this office for information about these programs.

* Technology Policy

Office of Technology Policy (OTP)
Technology Administration
U.S. Department of Commerce
14th St. and Constitution Ave., NW
Washington, DC 20230   202-377-4743

This office analyzes and advocates the removal of technical and non-technical barriers to the commercialization of technology, including such macroeconomic policies as antitrust, trade, product liability, tax. regulatory, and intellectual property laws. The Office of Technology Policy (OTP) staff also evaluate civilian technology trends and commercial potential in the U.S., and assesses options for greater cooperation among industry, government, and academia. This office assists state, local, and regional organizations in their support of technology-oriented companies and institutions through a clearinghouse with information on the initiatives and experiences of these organizations to date. Contact this office for more information on technology policy.

* Technology, Productivity, and Innovation

Technology Administration
U.S. Department of Commerce
14th St. and Constitution Ave., NW
Washington, DC 20230   202-377-4743

This administration identifies opportunities or barriers affecting U.S. commercial innovation, quality, productivity, and manufacturing, and advocates Federal policies and programs to eliminate government-wide statutory, regulatory, or other barriers to the rapid commercialization of U.S. science and technology. The Technology Administration represents U.S. commercial interests in international science and technology agreements and forums, and promotes joint efforts involving business, industry, educational institutions, and state and local organizations to encourage technology commercialization.

* Technology Resources Directory

National Technical Information Service
U.S. Department of Commerce
5285 Port Royal Rd.
Springfield, VA 22161   703-487-4650

The *Directory of Federal Laboratory and Technology Resources* guides readers to hundreds of Federal agencies, laboratories, and engineering centers willing to share their expertise, equipment--and sometimes even their facilities--to aid in U.S. research efforts. The current edition contains detailed summaries of more than 1,000 unique resources, including descriptions of some 90 technical information centers. The name, address, and telephone number of a personal contact is listed for each entry, along with a detailed descriptive summary. The directory is available for $36. Contact the Sales Desk to place an order or to request the free information brochures, *PR-746* and *PR-801*.

* Technology Transfer in Agriculture

National Agriculture Library (NAL)
10301 Baltimore Blvd.
Beltsville, MD 20705-2351   301-504-3755

The TTIC works to convert agriculture related technology and innovations into practical commercial products. Increasing emphasis has been placed on technology transfer in recent years. A 1989 report *Technology Transfer: A Profile of Agency Activities in USDA*, details technology transfer activities in U.S. Department of Agriculture. Several projects are currently underway with respect to wood products. For more information, contact the TTIC.

* Technology Transfer Competitiveness

Technology Transfer Competitiveness
Administrator, Federal Laboratory Consortium
P.O. Box 545
Sequim, WA 98382   206-683-1828

The mission of the Consortium is to facilitate technology transfer among government, business, and academic entities in order to foster American economic and technological competitiveness. It sponsors conferences and seminars and publishes a free monthly newsletter (currently no charge). For very specific questions from bona fide researchers who find themselves at an impasse, the Consortium will conduct a database search to refer the inquirer to an appropriate lab. Write or call for a free general information packet explaining the organization, how to access its services, facilities available for testing, and examples of technology transfers.

* Technology Transfer and Systems Engineering

Director of Publications, DRI-P
Defense Systems Management College
Ft. Belvoir, VA 22060-5426   703-664-5082

This College publishes 28 books and a bi-monthly magazine entitled *Program Manager* (subscription, $7.50 per year). Titles include *Systems Engineering Management Guide* (a Government Printing Office (GPO) all-time best-seller), *Cost Estimating*, *Subcontract Management Guide*, *Skill in Communications*, and *Program Office Guide to Technology Transfer*. All apply to acquisition and program management. Write for a free publications list explaining where to purchase them, stock numbers, and prices. Non-government employees must order publications through GPO at 202-512-1800. The editor will also supply a sample copy of the *Program Manager* upon written request.

* U.S. Government Datafiles for Computers

National Technical Information Service
U.S. Department of Commerce
5285 Port Royal Rd.
Springfield, VA 22161   703-487-4650

The *Directory of U.S. Government Datafiles for Mainframe and Minicomputers* describes 1600 datafiles for unique Federal numeric and textual data. It offers a convenient reference to datafiles prepared by Federal agencies.

* U.S. Government Software

National Technical Information Service
U.S. Department of Commerce
5285 Port Royal Rd.
Springfield, VA 22161   703-487-4650

The U.S. Government publishes a directory of software for mainframes and microcomputers. It describes software applications and tools available from the National Technical Information Service (NTIS) for more than 2000 programs arranged under 21 subject headings. For a free brochure on the directory, ask for *PR-261/827*. Directory cost is $59; order number is PB92-100106CAU.

Aerospace Technology / Space Research

* Aeronautical Engineering

National Technical Information Service (NTIS)
U.S. Department of Commerce
5285 Port Royal Rd.
Springfield, VA 22161   703-487-4650

This publication is prepared monthly for joint use by National Aeronautics and Space Administration (NASA), the Federal Aviation Administration (FAA), and the scientific and technical community concerned with the field of aeronautical engineering. Each entry consists of a standard bibliographic citation and an abstract. This information includes a subject, personal author, and contract number.

* Aeronautical Systems Clearinghouse

Aeronautical Systems Division
Office of Public Affairs
U.S. Department of the Air Force
Wright-Patterson Air Force Base, OH 45433   513-255-3334

This office develops and acquires aeronautical systems, their components, and related aerospace equipment, including aircraft engines, airborne communications systems, special reconnaissance projects, and interpretation facilities. Fact sheets are available for each of the 200 programs administered by the agency. Write or call the above office for a free brochure describing the Division's mission.

* Aeronautics Research: Air Force

U.S. Department of the Air Force
Arnold Engineering Development Center
Air Force Systems Command
Arnold Air Force Base, TN 37389   615-454-5586

This center has test laboratories in which atmospheric conditions, orbital, space flight, and ballistic conditions can be simulated. A brochure on the base, its programs, and mission, along with fact sheets on technical subjects, including wind tunnels, aeropropulsion systems, and rocket test facilities can be obtained by writing or calling the above office.

* Aerospace Commercialization Agreements

National Aeronautical and Space Administration (NASA)
Office of Commercial Programs
Code C/PAO
Washington, DC 20546   202-358-2320

The National Aeronautics and Space Administration (NASA) uses a number of innovative and functional agreements which provide private industry with assistance, services, and facilities to help reduce the risks associated with their commercial space ventures. This family of agreements include:

Joint Endeavor Agreements (JEAs): Involving no exchange of funds between the National Aeronautics and Space Administration (NASA) and the private company, Joint Endeavor Agreements (JEAs) are designed to encourage early space ventures and demonstrate the use of space technology to meet marketplace needs. Private industry funds the experiments and NASA provides the transportation and other services.

Space Systems Development Agreements (SSDAs): Space Systems Development Agreements (SSDAs) provide industry with a deferred payment schedule for Shuttle launch services. This allows the entrepreneur to have a more favorable cash flow during a time when capital investment costs are typically the greatest.

Technical Exchange Agreements (TEAs): Technical Exchange Agreements (TEAs) are designed for companies interested in applying microgravity or other technologies to their commercial operations, but who are not yet ready to commit to a specific space flight experiment or venture. Under the agreement, National Aeronautics and Space Administration (NASA) and a company agree to exchange technical information and cooperate in the conduct and analysis of ground-based research programs. The company funds its own participation, while at the same time gaining direct access to and results from NASA facilities and research.

* Aerospace Commercialization Publications

Office of Commercial Programs
National Aeronautics and Space Administration (NASA)
Code C/PAO
Washington, DC 20546   202-358-2320

The following publications on the commercial applications of space are available from this office:

Spinoff: An illustrated summary of the National Aeronautics and Space Administration's (NASA) major aeronautical and space programs, their goals and directions, their contributions to American scientific and technological growth, and their potential for practical benefits in new products and processes.

Aerospace Spinoffs: Twenty-Five Years of Technology Transfer.

Commercial Use of Space: A New Economic Strength for America.

NASA Commercial Programs: A Progress Report 1990. The Progress reports detail the years activities and include such information as discussion of the latest commercial program development, discussions of technology transfer activities, and Small Business Innovation Research Awards.

* Aerospace Commercial Users Catalog

Commercial Development Division (Code CC)
Office of Commercial Programs
National Aeronautics and Space Administration (NASA)
Washington, DC 20546   202-358-2320

This catalog, *Accessing Space: A Catalog of Process Equipment, and Resources for Commercial Users*, provides a broad range of information for the commercial developer of space seeking to understand and experience the areas of microgravity research and remote sensing. This publication provides an inventory along with information about the equipment and facilities that are being used and developed for commercial space applications.

* Aerospace Research Library

Information Management Division
National Air and Space Museum, Room 3100
Smithsonian Institute
Washington, DC 20560   202-357-3133

The Museum has a research library devoted to books and journals on aviation history, space exploration history, and science and technology in the fields of astronomy, astrophysics, engineering, geology, and space medicine. Appointments are strongly recommended as there is a limit of 5 researchers a day permitted due to limited staff resources. The library is open weekdays, 10am to 5pm.

* Aerospace Structures

Aerospace Structures Information
and Analysis Center
U.S. Department of the Air Force
WRDC/FIBR
Wright-Patterson AFB, OH 45433   513-255-6688

This Center is a central point for the collection and distribution of aerospace structures information. It maintains a library of reports done by various government agencies, and can refer you to other libraries and sources. Requests for specific information are served for researchers or contractors with a "need to know" status. Write or call for *How to Get It: A Guide to Defense-related Information Sources* and a free brochure describing the Center, its services, and user eligibility.

* Aerospace Technology Briefs

Office of Commercial Programs
National Aeronautical and Space Administration (NASA)
Code C/PAO
Washington, DC 20546   202-358-2320

Be patient. If any phone number is incorrect, call (area code) 555-1212 and request the new listing.

Each issue of National Aeronautics and Space Administration's (NASA) *Tech Briefs* contains concise descriptions of newly developed products and processes arising from NASA research and development efforts, and identifies and highlights information on new aerospace technologies which appear to have potential non-aerospace uses. Once you've identified a specific technology you are interested in, you can request a *Technology Support Package*, which provides more detailed information. Contact this office to be put on the *Tech Briefs* mailing list.

* Air Force Aeronautical Systems

U.S. Department of the Air Force
Aeronautical Systems Division
Public Affairs Office
Wright-Patterson Air Force Base, OH 45433-6503   513-255-2725

The Public Affairs Office's brochure, *What's Happening at ASD*, lists the major programs in all the Aeronautical Systems Division offices, the contractors involved, and the program status. Also available is a brochure describing the five laboratories which make up the Wright Research and Development Center: aeropropulsion and power, flight dynamics, materials, avionics, and electronic technology.

* Ames Research Center

National Aeronautics and Space Administration (NASA)
Moffett, CA 94035   415-604-4044

Located in the heart of "Silicon Valley" at the southern end of San Francisco Bay, Ames specializes in scientific research, exploration, and applications aimed toward creating new technology for the Nation. The center's major program responsibilities are concentrated in computer science and applications, computational and experimental aerodynamics, flight simulation, flight research, hypersonic aircraft, rotorcraft and powered-lift technology, aeronautical and space human factors, life sciences, space sciences, solar system exploration, airborne science and applications, and infrared astronomy. The center also supports military programs, the Space Shuttle, and various civil aviation projects such as the National Aerospace Plane. The center's laboratories are equipped to study solar and geophysical phenomena, life evolution and life environmental factors, and to detect life on other planets.

* Army Information Technology Laboratory

U.S. Army Corps of Engineers
Waterways Experiment Station
Public Affairs Office
3909 Halls Ferry Road
Vicksburg, MS 39180-6199   601-634-2504

The Information Technology Laboratory (ITL) operates one of the Army's largest computers and is also responsible for developing, managing and coordinating research and development projects in computer-aided interdisciplinary engineering areas; computer science; automation; visual information; etc. For more information, contact the Laboratory.

* Army Medical Research

U.S. Department of the Army
Army Medical Research and Development Command
Attn: SGRD-PA
Fort Detrick
Frederick, MD 21702-5012   301-619-2736

This Command conducts research and development in medical sciences, supplies, and equipment. Write or call for free copies of the brochure describing the Command, a quarterly newsletter, and the *Broad Agency Announcement* describing the research areas for which they solicit and instructions for submitting proposals.

* Army Research Labs, Speakers on Technology

U.S. Department of the Army
Army Research Laboratory
AMSLC-PA
2800 Powder Mill Rd.
Adelphi, MD 20783-1197   301-394-3098

This Command oversees the work of the seven major U.S. Army research laboratories. Laboratory work is done in the areas of advanced computing and electronics; battlefield environmental effects; materials and structures; power sources; signal processing; and survivability enhancement. A brochure on the laboratories' missions and programs is available, and the Command can provide public speakers for civic groups in the field of technology development. Write or call for information.

* Army Technology Transfer and Commercialization

U.S. Department of the Army
Army Research Office
P.O. Box 12211
Triangle Park, NC 27709-2211   919-549-0641

The Army Research Office sponsors programs to further technology development and technology transfer in the United States. Its Technology Transfer Program allows private industry to enter into patent agreements with the Army, making possible the commercialization of Army technological findings. Write or call for free brochures and information describing these programs.

* Astronaut Candidates

Astronaut Selection Office, Mail Code AHX
National Aeronautics and Space Administration (NASA)
Johnson Space Center
Houston, TX 77058

National Aeronautics and Space Administration (NASA) accepts applications on a continuous basis and selects astronaut candidates as needed. Civilians and military personnel are considered for the one-year training program. Current regulations require that preference be given to U.S. citizens when they are available. Contact this office for more information on pilot astronaut or mission specialist opportunities.

* Automated Space Flight

Office of Space Science and Applications
National Aeronautics and Space Administration (NASA)
400 Maryland Avenue, SW
Washington, DC 20546   202-453-1547

The National Aeronautics and Space Administration (NASA) automated space flight program is directed toward scientific investigations of the solar system using ground-based, airborne, and space techniques, including rockets, Earth satellites, and deep space probes. This office oversees research and development activities leading to programs that demonstrate the application of space systems, space environment, and space-related or derived technology for the benefit of the world. These activities involve such disciplines as weather and climate, pollution monitoring, Earth resources survey, and Earth and ocean physics.

* Balloon Projects at NASA

Goddard Space Flight Center
Greenbelt, MD 20771   301-286-0828

Wallops manages and coordinates the National Aeronautics and Space Administration's (NASA) Scientific Balloon Projects using thin film, helium-filled balloons to provide approximately 45 scientific missions each year. When fully inflated, the balloons can expand to nearly 600 feet in diameter with a volume of more than 50 million cubic feet. Contact Wallops for more information.

* Big Bang Theory

Goddard Space Flight Center
Greenbelt, MD 20771   301-286-0828

The Cosmic Background Explorer (COBE), a spacecraft built at Goddard, has been deployed to test the "Big Bang" theory about the origins of our universe, and gain answers to such questions as, What started the formation of galaxies? What caused galaxies to be arranged in giant clusters? Results have begun to come in. Contact Goddard for more information concerning the project and its results.

* Bioserve ITA Materials Experiment

National Aeronautics and Space Administration (NASA)
Office of Commercial Programs
Code C/Room 1223 CG4
Washington, DC 20546   202-358-2320

Shuttle flights are increasingly used for scientific experimental research programs carried out by private companies in conjunction with the National Aeronautics and Space Administration (NASA). In July 1991, Instrumentation Technology Associates of Pennsylvania and BioServe Space Technologies of Colorado carried out a series of space experiments using a Materials Dispersion Apparatus developed by the companies. The objective of the experiments was to further obtain scientific and technical knowledge regarding the commercial potential of biomedical manufacturing processes and fluid science processing in the microgravity environment of space. In an experiment using the MDA, Urokinase crystals that take from 6 months to 3 years to grow on earth were grown in less than 7 days. Research on Urokinese may lead to significant progress in fighting cancer spreading and metastasis. The success in growing the crystals so quickly holds promise for future research in this area.

Be patient. If any phone number is incorrect, call (area code) 555-1212 and request the new listing.

967

Science and Technology

* Black Holes, Quasars, and Exploding Galaxies

Goddard Space Flight Center
Greenbelt, MD 20771   301-286-0828
The Gamma Ray Observatory (GRO) will try to study the processes that propel the energy-emitting objects of deep space: exploding galaxies, black holes, and quasars. One of the instruments used in this study is the Energetic Gamma-Ray Experiment Telescope. Contact Goddard for more information.

* Business in Space

Office of Commercial Programs
National Aeronautics and Space Administration (NASA)
400 Maryland Avenue, SW, Code C
Washington, DC 202546   202-358-2320
This office provides the focus within the National Aeronautics and Space Administration (NASA) for an agency-wide program to expand U.S. private sector investment and involvement in civil space activities. The office is responsible for programs actively supporting new, high technology commercial space ventures, the commercial application of existing aeronautics and space technology, and expanding commercial access to available NASA capabilities and services.

* Centers for the Commercial Development of Space

Office of Commercial Programs
Commercial Development Division
National Aeronautics and Space Administration (NASA)
Washington, DC 20546   202-358-2320
The National Aeronautics and Space Administration's (NASA) Centers for the Commercial Development of Space (CCDS) are non-profit consortia of industry, universities, and government which conduct space-based, high-technology research and development in specific areas ranging from materials processing to remote sensing. These CCDS serve as incubators for future commercial space ventures, enabling their industrial affiliates to explore the economic value of space in a program where financial and technical risks are shared. For more information on becoming an industrial affiliate, contact one of the following centers:

Space Automation and Robotics Center, P.O. Box 134001, Ann Arbor MI 48105; 313-994-1200.
The SPARC has three major focuses: 1. To develop Key Space Industrialization Enabling Technologies: Machine Vision and Sensing Systems, Robotics and Automated Manufacturing Concepts and Systems. 2. To develop commercial and technical plans as well as key components for space servicing applications: Design of Space Systems for Robotic Servicing, Space Services Technology, Tooling, and Systems. 3. To provide support for terrestrial Robotics and Automation applications: Servicing industrial systems, Robotics systems for operations in hazardous environments.

Wisconsin Center for Space Automation and Robotics (WCSAR), University of Wisconsin, Madison, 1357 University Avenue, Madison, WI 53715-1020; 608-262-5524.
The WCSAR was established in 1989 to conceive, demonstrate and stimulate commercialization of space and terrestrial technology in the areas of ASTROBOTICS, to enhance the ability of humans to perform functional tasks required to travel, explore, and live in space; ASTROCULTURE, to develop technologies for a bioregenerative life support system required for long duration space missions ad for the establishment of permanently manned space settlements; and ASTROFUEL, to demonstrate that the thermonuclear fuel, Helium-3 (He3), uniquely present on the moon, can be of critical importance to the economies and future energy supplies of the Earth and for development of technologies to recover minerals from the lunar regolith.

Center for Mapping, The Ohio State University, 1216 Kinnear Rd., Columbus, OH 43212; 614-292-6446.
This Center has four key objectives: timely collection of data that allows accurate location of surface features in terms of their geographical coordinates; merging these data; converting the data in useful information through the use of application and process models; and providing the information to those who need it.

ITD Space Remote Sensing Center, Building 1103, Suite 118, John Stennis Space Center, MS 39529; 601-688-2509.
The Space Remote Sensing Center (SRSC) is providing commercial technology applications development of satellite remote sensing, image processing, and geographic information systems.

Bioserve Space Technologies, University of Colorado-Boulder, Department of Aerospace Engineering Sciences, Campus Box 429, Boulder, CO 80309; 303-492-1411.

There are approximately 30 projects now underway in the different Bioserve locations. Projects fall under one of the following four general headings: Biomedical Isomorphism - the study of earthly disease disorders that may have space-borne counterparts that could facilitate study in both Space and on Earth; Controlled Ecological Life Support Systems (CELSS) - a system is being set up at the University of Colorado; Bioprocessing and Bioproduct Research - Biological self assembly processes are under active study; and Related Hardware Development Tasks - Bioserve is engaged in a range of projects to develop hardware for its research.

Center for Cell Research, Pennsylvania State University, 117 Research Rd., University Park, PA 16802; 814-865-2407.
The CCR focuses on commercial, product and process-oriented, biomedical/biotechnology projects in three main areas: physiological testing - using test animals and tissues in space research; bioseparations - this program offers American industry access to continuous flow electrophoresis and aqueous two phase partitioning in space; and illumination - this program seeks to develop photometric equipment for biological experiments.

Center for Macromolecular Crystallography, University of Alabama at Birmingham, Box 7, THT, UAB Station, Birmingham, AL 35294-0005; 205-934-5329.
This center specializes in space-grown crystals of biological materials which are identified by participating firms in pharmaceutical, biotechnology and chemical industries. Its goal is to develop the technology and applications for the space-based material processing of biological crystals.

Advanced Materials Center, Battelle, 505 King Ave, Columbus, OH 43201-2693; 614-424-6376.
The Advanced Materials CCDS conducts ground based research and microgravity flight experiments on advanced materials and processes, including polymers, industrial catalysts, electronic materials, metals, ceramics and superconductors.

Center for Commercial Crystal Growth in Space, Clarkson University, NASA Center for Crystal Growth, Clarkson University, Potsdam, NY 13699; 315-268-6446.
This center focuses on the following: developing commercial crystal growth in space by developing larger, more perfect unique crystals in the space environment; and a broad spectrum of crystal growth techniques, theoretical modelling, complementary thermophysical property measurement, and structural and electronic characterization.

Consortium for Materials Development in Space, University of Alabama at Huntsville, Research Institute Building, 4701 University Drive, Huntsville, AL 35899; 205-895-6620.
This center focuses on commercial materials development projects that benefit from the unique attributes of space. Principal activities include physical vapor transport growth of highly non-linear optical inorganic and organic crystals and thin films, surface coatings and surface particle inclusions by electrodeposition, material preparations and longevity in hyperthermal atomic oxygen, physical properties of immiscible polymers and unique polymer production, and powdered metal sintering.

Center for Space Power, Texas A&M University, 223 W.I.E.C., The Texas A&M University System, College Station, TX 77843; 409-845-8768.
CSP conducts research relevant to space power, and develops and demonstrates technology associated with the commercial use of space. Its goal is to demonstrate that providing power in space is an attractive commercial venture. The center supports a series of projects related to the production, storage and transmission of power.

CCDS Power and Advanced Electronics, Auburn University, Space Power Institute, Auburn, AL 36849-5320; 334-844-5894.
The overall objective of the center's efforts in space power is to identify critical technological impediments to the economic deployment of power systems in space, advance these technologies, and develop new products to meet power generation, storage, conditioning, and distribution needs.

Center for Materials and Space Structures, Case Western Reserve University, White Bldg, Room 219, 10900 Euclid Ave, Cleveland, OH 44106; 216-368-4203.
This center focuses on providing materials for space structures that are capable of being processes in space and capable of withstanding the space environment. Research projects will focus on the following six areas: Polymeric composites; Metallic composites; Ceramic composites; Organic coatings; and Metallic coatings.

Center for Satellite and Hybrid Communication Networks, University of Maryland Systems Research Center, A.V. Williams Bldg, College Park, MD 20742; 301-405-6606.
The focus of this center is space-based communications, especially in the context of hybrid networks which integrate terrestrial and extra-terrestrial communication technologies.

Be patient. If any phone number is incorrect, call (area code) 555-1212 and request the new listing.

Center for Space Communications Technology, Florida Atlantic University Research Corporation, Space Communications Technology Center, Florida Atlantic University, Boca Raton, FL 33431; 407-367-3411.
The mission of this center is to develop the commercial use of digital transmission techniques for transmitting video, audio and data to the earth by satellite.

* Challenger Center for Space Science Education

1029 N. Royal St.
Suite 300
Alexandria, VA 22314   703-683-9740

The Challenger Center, founded as a living memorial to the Challenger crew, plans to construct a series of simulated space environment centers linked to museums, science centers, and school districts throughout the world through a comprehensive, international endowment program. The first center, the Challenger Center Space-Life Station, will be build in the Washington, DC, area, and will serve as headquarters for the network. The Marsville project is the first project in the Center's Adventures in Exploration program. In it, students will be asked to create a new human world, a multi-national settlement on Mars. The program is currently being piloted at thirty sites nationally. An educator membership is available that includes a journal, newsletter, updates, and conference information. There will be 30 Challenger Learning Center Sites open by the end of 1992. Contact the center for information on sites in your area.

* Chemical Propulsion Resource Center

The Johns Hopkins University
Applied Physics Laboratory
Chemical Propulsion Information Agency (CPIA)
10630 Little Patuxent Parkway
Columbia, MD 21044-3200   410-992-7307

The Chemical Propulsion Information Agency (CPIA) provides products, specialized reference service, database searches, and copies of technical reports on all areas of chemical propulsion. Publications include *The Chemical Propulsion Abstracts*, *The CPIA/M1 Rocket Motor Manual*, the *CPIA/M2 Solid Propellant Manual*, the *CPIA/M6 Airbreathing Propulsion Manual*, *The JANNAF Propulsion Meeting*, and *Selected Papers*. CPIA also puts out a monthly bulletin updating subscribers on its activities. Write or call for a free pamphlet explaining their services and how to become a subscriber. Note, however, that this service is primarily for DOD contractors.

* Commercial Flight Program

Office of Commercial Programs
National Aeronautics and Space Administration (NASA)
Code C/PAO
Washington, DC 20546   202-358-2320

Under this program, businesses can gain access to NASA space capabilities and use the unique environment of space to conduct investigations that may lead to new, high-value products and technological advances. Certain portions of the Space Shuttle, Spacelab, and the Space Station Freedom payloads, for example, are being set aside for commercial uses.

* Commercial Payloads Video

Office of Commercial Programs
Commercial Development Division
National Aeronautics and Space Administration (NASA)
Washington, DC 20546   202-358-2320

The National Aeronautics and Space Administration's (NASA) Commercial Development Division is producing a videotape which shows how commercial payloads on spacecraft are developed, managed, and processed. The film is designed to provide viewers with a perspective on the basic flow of payload processing from concept, through ground processing, to post-mission analysis. It will be available through NASA's Headquarters, Centers for the Commercial Development of Space, and Field Centers.

* Commercial Programs Advisory Committee

National Aeronautics and Space Administration (NASA)
Office of Commercial Programs
Washington, DC 20546   202-358-2320

As a subcommittee of the NASA Advisory Council, the Commercial Programs Advisory Committee (CPAC) assists NASA by reviewing policies and programs, and recommending strategies to implement the national space policy goals to promote greater investment and participation by the U.S. private sector in America's civil space program. The Committee holds meetings that are open to the public. A free

brochure, *Charting the Course: U.S. Space Enterprise and Space Industrial Competitiveness*, which includes highlights of the Committee's findings, is available.

* Commercial Programs Newsletter

Office of Commercial Programs
National Aeronautics and Space Administration (NASA)
Code C/PAO
Washington, DC 20546   703-557-5609

The free bimonthly publication, *Office of Commercial Programs Newsletter*, covers the latest news related to the NASA's commercial programs, including new publications, projects, committee meetings, grants, congressional actions, and technology transfer. For more information on obtaining copies, contact this office.

* Competitive Contract Space Launches

National Aeronautics and Space Administration (NASA)
Office of Commercial Programs
Code C/Room 1223, CG4
Washington, DC 20546   202-358-2320

The Office of Commercial Programs (OCP) is sponsoring two sounding rocket series through a unique program developed with the consortium for Materials Development in Space (CDMS) based at the University of Alabama at Huntsville. The Sounding Rocket Program, initiated in 1988, acquires commercial suborbital launch services through competitive procurements and provides a range of early flight opportunities for various commercial payloads. The key element of the program is that the UAH CDMS seeks commercial launch services, specifying the requirements needed for the flight. The contractors then bid on the flights. The first series, named Consort, has had three successful flights in four attempts. The experiments vary according to flight.

* Crystal Growth in Space

National Aeronautics and Space Administration (NASA)
Office of Commercial Programs
Code C/Room 1223, CG4
Washington, DC 20546   202-358-2320

Protein crystal growth experiments have been conducted aboard 11 Shuttle flights over the past six years. The first four flights used hand held prototype equipment to test vapor diffusion technology. On the next four flights several protein crystals were produced by the vapor diffusion process within Refrigerator/Incubator Modules. Results from these experiments were encouraging and have led to two more flights in which crystals were grown using a new hardware configuration known as the Protein Crystallization Facility. The purpose of these experiments is to grow crystals that are larger and more pure than those which are produced on earth.

* Dryden Flight Research Facility

Ames Research Center
Hugh L. Dryden Flight Research Facility
P.O. Box 273
Edwards, CA 93523   805-258-3441

Located at in the Mojave Desert about 80 miles north of Los Angeles, California, Ames-Dryden has developed a unique and highly specialized capability for conducting flight research programs. The facility was actively involved in the Approach and Landing Tests of the Space Shuttle Orbiter Enterprise and continues to support Shuttle landings from space. Currently, Ames-Dryden is conducting research on the X-29 program in a variety of advanced aero technologies, including forward swept wings, aeroelastic tailoring, and thin supercritical wings.

* Dual Use Technology

Office of Commercial Programs
National Aeronautics and Space Administration (NASA)
Code C/PAO
Washington, DC 20546   202-358-2320

Through the Small Business Innovation Research Program, established by Congress in 1982, the National Aeronautics and Space Administration (NASA) has worked with hundreds of small businesses on developing technologies useful for both the space program and commercial uses. Spinoffs from technologies originally developed primarily for the space program have benefitted the following areas: food safety, structural analysis of items such as oil drilling platforms, X-ray imaging, ultrasonic maintenance, aircraft collision avoidance, fire protection, flight simulation, performance testing, lightning protection, transportation safety, automotive design, and health monitoring. This information is detailed in the NASA publication *Spinoffs 1991*, which is available free from the Office of Commercial Programs.

Be patient. If any phone number is incorrect, call (area code) 555-1212 and request the new listing.

969

Science and Technology

* Earth Observing System (EOS)

Goddard Space Flight Center

Greenbelt, MD 20771   301-286-0828

EOS, the Earth Observing System, is a planned NASA program for observing the Earth from space using unmanned platforms in conjunction with the Space Station. Its goal is to understand the Earth as an integrated system. The platform will be equipped with remote sensing instruments, and launched into polar orbit so that all parts of the globe can be viewed. Contact Goddard for more information.

* Electronic Still Camera Experiment

National Aeronautics and Space Administration (NASA)

Office of Commercial Programs

Code C/Room 1223, CG4

Washington, DC 20546   202-358-2320

The National Aeronautics and Space Administration (NASA), in conjunction with Autometric Inc. of Alexandria, VA, is evaluating and analyzing the commercial potential of a high-resolution Electronic Still Camera developed by the Johnson Space Center. Electronic still photography is a developing technology providing the means by which a hand-held camera electronically captures and produces a digital image with resolution approaching film quality. The image can be computer enhanced and/or downlink transmitted. This technology will greatly aid Space Shuttle and Space station capabilities in Earth observations and on-board photo documentation. During STS-42 mission, the Shuttle crew will operate the ESC. NASA will evaluate the results of this test after the mission.

* Fluid Experiment Apparatus

National Aeronautics and Space Administration (NASA)

Office of Commercial Programs

Code C/Room 1223, CG4

Washington, DC 20546   202-358-2320

The Fluid Experiment Apparatus (FEA) is a modular microgravity chemistry and physics laboratory used on the Space Shuttle for materials processing research. The FEA is used for the float-zone crystal growth process, which results in the production of pure crystals from samples. The project is being carried out in conjunction with Rockwell International.

* Goddard Space Flight Center

Goddard Space Flight Center

Greenbelt, MD 20771   301-286-0828

Located 10 miles northeast of Washington, DC, Goddard's research is centered in six space and Earth Science laboratories and in the management, development, and operation of several near-Earth space systems: The Hubble Space Telescope is an important astronomical telescope in space, studying the stars, planets, and interstellar space. The Upper Atmosphere Research Satellite will be launched to look back at Earth's atmosphere to help understand its composition and dynamics. As part of the Space Station program, Goddard will develop the detailed design, construction, and test and evaluation of the automated free-flying polar platform and provisions for instruments and payloads to be attached externally to the Space Station.

* HL-20 Space Launch System

Langley Research Center, MS 146

Hampton, VA 23665-5225   804-864-6005

For the past several years, the National Aeronautics and Space Administration (NASA) has been studying an enhanced lifting body candidate for manned orbital missions. The concept, designated HL-20, has been designed for low operations cost, improved flight safety, and conventional runway landings. The orbiter is designed to take crews but not bulky cargo into space and return. Notably, unlike the Space Shuttle, the HL-20 would not have a payload bay nor main engines. Its size, only 20% of the Shuttle, would reduce maintenance time on the ground, reducing cost. Contact Langley for information on the continuing research on the HL-20.

* Hubble Space Telescope

Goddard Space Flight Center

Greenbelt, MD 20771   301-286-0828

The Hubble Space Telescope is an important astronomical telescope in space. Its deployment in space allows Hubble to see things more clearly than its counterparts on earth, which have to look through the atmosphere into space. Its movements are controlled from Goddard's Space Telescope Operations Control Center, as the observatory's five scientific instruments study the stars, planets, and interstellar space. The Space Telescope Science Institute in Baltimore, Maryland, is analyzing much of the data generated from the Hubble Space Telescope.

* Jet Propulsion Laboratory

4800 Oak Grove Drive

MS 180-800C

Pasadena, CA 91109   818-354-4862

Located 20 miles northeast of Los Angeles, California, the Jet Propulsion Laboratory (JPL) is engaged in activities associated with deep space automated scientific missions--engineering subsystem and instrument development, and data reduction and analysis required in deep space flight. Current NASA flight projects under JPL include Voyager, Galileo, Magellan, and the Mars Observer. JPL also designs and tests flight systems, including complete spacecraft, and provides technical direction to contractor organizations. JPL also operates the worldwide deep space tracking and data acquisition network (DSN) and maintains a substantial technology program to support present and future NASA flight projects.

* Langley Research Center

Langley Research Center

Hampton, VA 23665-5225   804-864-6005

Located about 100 miles south of Washington, DC, Langley's primary mission is the research and development of advanced concepts and technology for future aircraft and spacecraft systems, with particular emphasis on environmental effects, performance, range, safety, and economy. Examples of this research are projects involving flight simulation, composite structural materials, and automatic flight control systems. Work is continuing in the development of technology for avionic systems for reliable operations in terminal areas of the future. Efforts continue to improve supersonic flight capabilities for both transport and military aircraft. The center also works with the general aviation industry to help solve problems concerning aircraft design and load requirements and to improve flight operations. Overall about 60% of the work done at Langley is related to Aeronautics, while 40% relates to the Space program. Langley's newest major project is developing technology for the National Aero-Space Plane.

* Manned Space Flight Research

Lyndon B. Johnson Space Center

Houston, TX 77058   713-483-3671

Located 20 miles southeast of downtown Houston, Texas, the Johnson Center is the National Aeronautics and Space Administration's (NASA) primary center for design, development, and testing of spacecraft and related systems for manned flight; selection and training of astronauts; planning and conducting manned missions; and extensive participation in the medical, engineering, and scientific experiments carried aboard space flights. Johnson has program management responsibility for the Space Shuttle program and the Space Station, along with the interfaces between the two. The Johnson Center also directs the operations of the White Sands Test Facility in Las Cruces, New Mexico, which supports the Space Shuttle propulsion system, power system, and materials testing.

* Marshall Space Flight Center

Marshall Space Flight Center

Huntsville, AL 35812   216-433-6043

Located in Huntsville, Alabama, the Marshall Center, along with being NASA's launch vehicle development center, manages projects involving scientific investigation and application of space technology to the solution of problems on Earth. The Center provides the Shuttle orbiter's engines, the external tank that carries liquid hydrogen and liquid oxygen for those engines, and the solid rocket boosters that assist in lifting the Shuttle orbiter from the launch pad. Marshall's Orbital Maneuvering Vehicle will be carried into orbit also by the Shuttle to perform a number of activities, including moving satellites from one orbit to another. Marshall will also design the living and working, laboratory, and life support modules for the Space Station, along with an environmental control system.

* Michoud Assembly Facility

NASA SA-39

P.O. Box 29300

New Orleans, LA 70189   504-257-2601

Located about 15 miles east of downtown New Orleans, Louisiana, Michoud's primary mission is the systems engineering, engineering design, manufacture, fabrication, and assembly for the Space Shuttle external tank.

* NASA Activities Newsletter

Superintendent of Documents

Government Printing Office

Washington, DC 20402   202-512-1800

Be patient. If any phone number is incorrect, call (area code) 555-1212 and request the new listing.

NASA Activities covers current agency highlights, including new programs and projects, personnel activities, field center news, relevant legislation, community activities, and more. It is available by subscription from GPO for $8 per year.

* NASA Formal Series Reports

National Technical Information Service
U.S. Department of Commerce
5285 Port Royal Rd.
Springfield, VA 22161   703-487-4650

Through the National Technical Information Service (NTIS) you can obtain full copies of scientific and technical reports produced by National Aeronautics and Space Administration (NASA). Original copies of these reports are sent to you as they are printed, even before they are announced to the general public by NASA. You can order reports under one of the ten following categories: Aeronautics, Astronautics, Chemistry and Materials, Engineering, Geosciences, Life Sciences, Mathematical and Computer Sciences, Physics, Social Sciences, and Space Sciences. Price per copy is $18.

* NASA Headquarters

NASA Headquarters
400 Maryland Avenue, SW
Washington, DC 20546   202-453-1000

The National Aeronautics and Space Administration (NASA) Headquarters manages the space flight centers, research centers, and other installations that make up the National Aeronautics and Space Administration. The staff at Headquarters determine the programs and projects; establish management policies, procedures, and performance criteria; evaluate progress; review and analyzes all phases of the aerospace program.

* NASA Magazine

Internal Communications
Code P-2
NASA Headquarters
Washington, DC 20546   202-453-8332

Founded in 1991, the *NASA Magazine* is a quarterly news and information publication detailing the latest goings on at the National Aeronautics and Space Administration (NASA) as well as containing interesting articles on topics related to Space research.

* NASA Monetary Awards for Inventions

Staff Director
Inventions and Contributions Board
National Aeronautics and Space Administration (NASA)
Washington, DC 20546   202-453-2890

The National Aeronautics and Space Administration (NASA) makes monetary awards to individuals or organizations for scientific or technical contributions which have been used and have proven to be of verifiable value to NASA. Many qualified contributions have been produced during the performance of contracts for NASA. Contact this office for information concerning the criteria for eligibility and the procedure for submitting an application for an award.

* NASA Patent Bibliography

National Technical Information Service
U.S. Department of Commerce
5285 Port Royal Road
Springfield, VA 22101   703-487-4650

The *NASA Patent Abstracts Bibliography*, a semiannual updated compendium of over 4,000 NASA patented inventions, is published as a service to companies, firms, and individuals seeking new licensable products for the commercial market. For convenience, each issue has a separately bound *Abstract Section* ($13.75 per issue) and *Index Section* ($29 per copy). The *Abstract Section* covers only the indicated 6 month period, while the *Index Section* is cumulative, covering all NASA-owned inventions announced since May 1969.

* NASA Procurement Report

National Aeronautics and Space Administration (NASA)
Office of Procurement
Central Promenade
425 L'Enfant Plaza SW
Washington, DC 20546   202-453-2130

The *NASA Semiannual Procurement Report* presents summary data on all National Aeronautics and Space Administration (NASA) procurement actions and detailed information on contracts, grants, agreements, and other procurements over $25,000 awarded by NASA during a six month period. Contact the office listed above for your free copy.

* NASA STAR Journal

National Technical Information Service
U.S. Department of Commerce
5285 Port Royal Rd.
Springfield, VA 22161   703-487-4650

The *NASA STAR Journal* is a microfiche copy of the National Aeronautics and Space Administration's (NASA) biweekly *STAR* journal, which indexes and abstracts all of NASA's research and development results, as well as other research and engineering related to aerodynamics and space. The price is $70 per year for 24 issues.

* NASA Technology Transfer Network

NASA Field Centers
Office of Commercial Programs
Technology Transfer Division, Code CU
Washington, DC 20546   202-358-2320

The following National Aeronautics and Space Administration (NASA) field centers can provide you with information on technology transfer activities and sources of information on NASA technical activities.

Ames Research Center
Office of Commercial and Community Programs, Mail Stop 223-3, Moffett Field CA 94035-1000; 415-604-4044.

Goddard Space Flight Center
Office of Commercial Programs, Technology Utilization Office, Mail Code 702, Greenbelt, MD 20771; 301-286-0828

Jet Propulsion Laboratory
NASA Resident Office, Mail Stop 180-801, 4800 Oak Grove Dr., Pasadena, CA 91109; 818-354-4862.

Johnson Space Center
Technology Utilization Office, Mail Code IC4, Houston, TX 77058; 713-483-3671.

Kennedy Space Center
Technology Utilization Office, Mail Stop PT-PAT-A, Kennedy Space Center, FL 32899; 407-867-3017.

Langley Research Center
Technology Utilization and Applications Office, Mail Stop 200, Hampton, VA 23665-5225; 804-864-6005.

Lewis Research Center
Technology Utilization Office, Mail Stop 7/3, 21000 Brookpark Rd., Cleveland, OH 44135; 216-433-5568.

Marshall Space Flight Center
Technology Utilization Office, Mail Code AT01, MSFC, AL 35812; 216-433-6043.

Stennis Space Center
Technology Utilization Office, Mail Code HA30, SSC, MS 39529-6000; 601-688-2509.

* National Aerospace Plane

Aerospace Plane Research and Development
Wright-Patterson Air Force Base
Dayton, OH 45433-6503   513-255-2725

The National Aerospace Plane, the X-30, capable of achieving low orbit but taking off and landing like a plane, could be one of the most significant technologies of the early 21st century. The National Aeronautics and Space Administration (NASA) program isn't geared to developing the Orient Express high speed airliner that President Reagan referred to in his 1986 State of the Union address. To achieve orbit, the plane must be able to accelerate to Mach 25, or 17,500 miles per hour. At the same time, it has to both be able to carry enough fuel to get to orbit but in a small enough container so the plane isn't too large. Currently there are several labs working on the project, with Wright-Patterson coordinating the research effort. Contact the above office for more information on the project.

Science and Technology

* National Space Council

Executive Office of the President
Washington, DC 20500   202-395-6175

Established by Executive Order 12675 in March 1989 under the Office of the Vice President, the National Space Council oversees the United States National Space Strategy. The five elements of this strategy are: transport - to develop U.S. space transport infrastructure and ability; exploration - to establish a permanent space station and study the possibility of a permanent Moon presence and a mission to Mars; solutions - to use Space technologies to solve problems here on Earth; opportunity - to foster economic well being on Earth; and freedom - so that space will be free for exploration and development. Contact the Space Council for more information on its activities and in particular for an annual report detailing its activities.

* National Space Technology Laboratories

Building 1100
Education and Productivity Office
Stennis Space Center
NSTL, MS 39529-6000   601-688-2739

Located near Bay St. Louis, Mississippi, NSTL's main mission is the support of Space Shuttle main engine and main orbiter propulsion system testing. NSTL is also a center of excellence in the area of remote sensing and is involved in Earth sciences programs of national and international significance, which are conducted at its Earth Resources Laboratory. NSTL also conducts data systems and commercial utilization studies in support of the Space Station.

* Oceans and Space

Goddard Space Flight Center
Greenbelt, MD 20771   301-286-0828

The National Aeronautics and Space Administration's (NASA) Laboratory for Oceans at Goddard works to expand the applications of space technology in oceanographic research by demonstrating new research uses of satellite data and initiating new flight instrument concepts for satellite flight missions.

* Ozone and Chlorofluorocarbons

Goddard Space Flight Center
Greenbelt, MD 20771   301-286-0828

Using such tools as Goddard's Total Ozone Mapping Spectrometer (TOMS) aboard the Nimbus-7 Spacecraft, NASA conducts research missions over Antarctica and Arctic regions to measure ozone, aerosol profiles, and other constituents of the atmosphere. Recent studies look at the relationship between fluorocarbons and ozone holes in the atmosphere. Contact Goddard for more information.

* Polymer Membrane Processing Experiments

National Aeronautics and Space Administration (NASA)
Office of Commercial Programs
Code C/Room 1223, CG4
Washington, DC 20546   202-358-2320

This experiment was sponsored by the Battelle Advanced Materials Center, a NASA Center for the Commercial Development of Space (CCDS), based in Columbus, Ohio. The objective of this payload was to investigate the physical and chemical processes that occur during the formation of polymer membranes in microgravity so that the improved technology base can be applied to commercial membrane processing techniques. Preliminary results from previous experiments indicate that membranes with significantly different porous qualities can be obtained in microgravity environments. Polymer membranes have been used by the separations industry for many years in such areas as water desalinization and kidney dialysis.

* Polymer Morphology Tests in Space

National Aeronautics and Space Administration (NASA)
Office of Commercial Programs
Code C/Room 1223, CG4
Washington, DC 20546   202-358-2320

As part of a joint endeavor agreement between NASA and 3M, a shuttle mission in November 1989 conducted the first real time study of microgravity on polymers as they change from solids to liquids and back to solids, using a Fourier Transform Infrared (FTIR) specrometor to gather data samples as the polymers underwent the melt processing.

* Private Investment in Space

Superintendent of Documents
U.S. Government Printing Office
Washington, DC 20402   202-512-1800

A recent Congressional Budget Office report entitled *Encouraging Private Investment in Space*, examines the current status of private investment in space activities in three areas: the provision of space launch services by large-capacity launch vehicles; the production of information based on data gathered by satellites through remote sensing; and the processing of materials in space, along with the provision of necessary orbital facilities.

* Propulsion Systems Research

NASA Lewis Research Center
21000 Brookpart Road
Cleveland, OH 44135   216-433-2899

Located about 20 miles southwest of Cleveland, Ohio, Lewis is NASA's leading center for research, technology, and development in aircraft propulsion, space propulsion, space power, and satellite communication. Lewis has the responsibility for developing the largest space power system ever designed to provide the electrical power necessary to accommodate the life support systems and research experiments to be conducted aboard the Space Station. In addition, Lewis will support the Station in other major areas, such as auxiliary propulsion systems and communications. This center is also working on materials and propulsion development for the National Aerospace Plane. Other facilities here include a zero-gravity drop tower, wind tunnels, space environment tanks, chemical rocket thrust stands, and chambers for testing jet engine efficiency and noise.

* Regional Technology Transfer Centers

Mid-Atlantic RTTC
NASA Industrial Applications Center, 823 William Pitt Union, Pittsburgh, PA 15260; 412-648-7000.

Far-West RTTC
Far West Technology Transfer Center, University of Southern California, 3716 South Hope Street, Los Angeles, CA 90007; 213-743-8988.

Northeast RTTC
Center for Technology Commercialization, Massachusetts Technology Park, 100 North Drive, Westborough, MA 01581; 508-870-0042.

Technology Applications Team
Research Triangle Institute, P.O. Box 12235, Research Triangle Park, NC 27709; 919-549-0671.

Southeast RTTC
Southern Technology Applications Center, One Progress Boulevard, Box 24, Alachua, FL 32615; 904-462-3913.

Mid-West RTTC
Battelle Memorial Institute, Great Lakes Industrial Technology Center, 25000 Great Northern Corporate Center, Suite 450, Cleveland, OH 44070; 216-734-0094.

Mid-Continent RTTC
Commercial Technology Services, Texas Engineering Experiment Station, The Texas A&M University System, 237 Wisenbaker Engineering Research Center, College Station, TX 77843-3401.

National Technology Transfer Center
Wheeling Jesuit College, 316 Washington Ave., Wheeling, WV 26003; 304-243-2455.

Technology Applications Center
University of New Mexico, Technology Applications Center, Albuquerque, NM 87131; 505-277-3622.

Center for Aerospace Information
PO Box 8757, Baltimore, MD 21240; 410-859-5300, x241.

Computer Software Management and Information Center
University of Georgia, 382 East Broad St., Athens, GA 30602; 404-542-3265.

Be patient. If any phone number is incorrect, call (area code) 555-1212 and request the new listing.

* Remote Sensing Systems Research

ITD Space Remote Sensing Center
Bldg. 1103, Suite 118
John Stennis Space Center, MS 39529   601-688-2509

The SRSC is providing commercial technology applications development of satellite remote sensing, image processing, and geographic information systems.

* Robot Space Retrieving Equipment

Goddard Space Flight Center
Greenbelt, MD 20771   301-286-0828

The National Aeronautics and Space Administration (NASA) is developing an autonomous free flying robot for retrieving equipment or a spacewalking astronaut drifting in separated flight near the Space Station. Recent test flights have been flown from the Space Shuttle's cargo bay. Contact Goddard for more information.

* Satellite-Aided Search and Rescue

Goddard Space Flight Center
Greenbelt, MD 20771   301-286-0828

In a cooperative project sponsored by the U.S., Canada, France, and the Soviet Union, NASA is working on a satellite system, SARSAT, that greatly reduces the time required to rescue air, sea, and other distress victims and to find victims which otherwise might not be found. Contact Goddard for more information.

* Satellite Repair in Space

Goddard Space Flight Center
Greenbelt, MD 20771   301-286-0828

The Satellite Servicing Project is working on ways to expand the operational life of satellites to be launched in the future. Not only does this project repair satellites, it also allow for planned routine maintenance calls in space which will maximize the longevity of the satellites and save money. Contact Goddard for more information.

* Spacecraft and Launch Vehicles

Office of Space Operations
National Aeronautics and Space Administration (NASA)
400 Maryland Avenue, SW, Code T
Washington, DC 20546   202-453-2019

This office tracks activities involving aeronautical research aircraft, space launch vehicles, and spacecraft. It also acquires and distributes technical and scientific data from these spacecraft. Contact this office for more information on this subject.

* Space Exploration

Office of Exploration
National Aeronautics and Space Administration (NASA)
400 Maryland Avenue, SW, Code Z
Washington, DC 20546   202-453-1000

The office develops long range plans for exploration and expansion of human presence beyond Earth into the solar system, along with a roadmap which provides opportunities and options leading to the commitment to national space exploration initiatives by 1992.

* Space Exploration Initiative

National Space Council
Executive Office of the President
Washington, DC 20500   202-395-6175

The National Space Council is involved with the planning for the Space Exploration Initiative. The goal of this initiative is to establish a permanent presence on the Moon and then use this base for robust exploration activities on Mars using both robotic and human missions.

* Space Flight History

Office of Space Flight
National Aeronautics and Space Administration (NASA)
400 Maryland Avenue, SW, Code M
Washington, DC 20546   202-453-1000

The publication *Space Flight: The First 30 Years*, details the history of the space program and includes information on the Mercury, Gemini, Apollo, Skylab and Space Shuttle missions. It is available free from this office.

* Space Launches

John F. Kennedy Space Center
Kennedy Space Center, FL 32899   407-867-3017

Located on the east coast of Florida, 150 miles south of Jacksonville, the Kennedy Space Center serves as the primary center within NASA for the test, checkout, and launch of space vehicles, which presently includes the launch of manned and unmanned vehicles at Kennedy, Cape Canaveral, and Vandenberg Air Force base in California. The Center is also responsible for the assembly, checkout, and launch of Space Shuttle vehicles and their payloads, landing operations, and the turn-around of Space shuttle orbiters between missions.

* Space Research and Technology

Office of Aeronautics and Space Technology (OAST)
National Aeronautics and Space Administration (NASA)
400 Maryland Avenue, SW, Code R
Washington, DC 20546   202-453-1000

This office plans, directs, executes, evaluates, documents, and distributes the results of NASA research and technology development programs. These programs are conducted primarily to demonstrate the feasibility of a concept, structure, or component system which may have general application to the nation's aeronautical and space objectives. For information on specific research programs, contact this NASA office.

* Space Shuttle and Spacelab

Office of Space Flight
National Aeronautics and Space Administration (NASA)
400 Maryland Avenue, SW, Code M
Washington, DC 20546   202-453-1000

To permit humans to explore space and perform missions which will lead to increased knowledge and the quality of life on Earth, this office directs the development of space transportation and the required supporting systems for humans to perform missions in space. One of the major program now underway is the Space Shuttle, and this office is responsible for scheduling Space Shuttle flights, including the Spacelab. This office also develops financial plans and pricing structures for these flights; provides services to users; manages expendable launch services and upper stages; and manages of NASA's advanced program activities.

* Space Shuttle Program Book

Superintendent of Documents
Government Printing Office (GPO)
Washington, DC 20402   202-512-1800

The NASA publication *Space Shuttle: The Renewed Promise*, discusses the changes made in the Shuttle program in the wake of the Challenger accident and the achievements of the program to date. Contact the Government Printing Office (GPO) for price and availability.

* Space Station

Office of Space Station
National Aeronautics and Space Administration (NASA)
600 Independence Avenue, SW, Code S
Washington, DC 20546   202-453-4164

This office manages and directs all aspects of NASA's Space Station program whose goal is to develop a permanently manned Space Station by the mid 1990s; to encourage other nations to participate in the Space Station program; and to promote private sector investment in space through enhanced space-based operational capabilities.

* Space Technology Research

U.S. Air Force Space Technology Center
Kirtland Air Force Base, NM 87117-6008   505-846-1911

This Center oversees the work of the three major Air Force research laboratories: the Weapons Laboratory at Kirtland; the Astronautics Laboratory at Edwards Air Force Base, California; and the Geophysics Laboratory at Hanscom Air Force Base, Massachusetts. Free fact sheets on all three labs and their programs are available from this Center, including fact sheets on the SDI program, the relay mirror experiment, the Alpha chemical laser experiment, "Brilliant Pebbles" research, optics research, microwaves, plasma physics, and nuclear weapons effects research. The Center offers a Speakers Bureau of experts and intern programs for outside researchers.

Science and Technology

* Space Telescope Science Institute (STSI)

Johns Hopkins Homewood Campus
Baltimore, MD 21218   301-338-4514

Located in Baltimore, Maryland, the Space Telescope Science Institute (STSI) plans and conducts science operations for the Edwin P. Hubble Space Telescope, a cooperative venture between NASA and the European Space Agency (ESA). Scheduled for launch aboard the Space shuttle, the telescope spacecraft will orbit the Earth at approximately 350 miles sending data and receiving commands through NASA's Tracking and Data Relay Satellite System.

* Space-Type Freeze-Dehydrated Foods

GEWA Visitor Center Gift Shop
Goddard Space Flight Center
Greenbelt, MD 20771   301-286-6476

The Gift Shop at Goddard sells samples of foods that astronauts eat during space flights. The food, however, is for sale only in the Gift Shop--no mail orders. Other companies that can provide you with information on space-type, freeze dried foods include the following: Spaceland Enterprises, Inc., 1970 Carroll Ave., San Francisco, CA 94124; and Sky-Lab Foods, Inc., 177 Lake Street, White Plains, NY 10604.

* Stars in the Sky

R. Woods
Consumer Information Center-2A
P.O. Box 100
Pueblo, CO 81002

The Consumer Information Catalogue has two inexpensive publications available dealing with stars. *A Look at the Planets* contains full-color photos and descriptions of the planets ($1), and *Stars in Your Eyes: A Guide to the Northern Skies* provides helpful hints on how to find the seven best know constellations ($1.50).

* Star Wars and Other Defense Research Information

Office of Assistant Secretary of Defense
Public Affairs
Directorate for Defense Information
Pentagon 2E765
Washington, DC 20301-1400   703-695-3886

This office can supply you with fact sheets, press releases, and reports on defense programs such as Star Wars, the DOD Laser and Space Program, and the Defense Advanced Research Projects Agency (DARPA) activities, and related Congressional activity. Staff can also direct you in making Freedom of Information Act (FOIA) requests for Defense contract information.

* Super-Maneuverable Jet Fighter

Ames Research Center
Hugh L. Dryden Flight Research Facility
P.O. Box 273
Edwards, CA 93523   805-258-8381

Ames-Dryden is testing a specially instrumented F-18 fighter jet to investigate high alpha or high angle of attack flight which may result in airplanes capable of "supermaneuvers." Contact Ames for more information.

* Technology Transfer Statistics

Office of Commercial Programs
National Aeronautical and Space Administration (NASA)
Washington, DC 20546   202-358-2320

The National Aeronautics and Space Administration (NASA) is currently studying the economic impact of their technology transfer programs in both the aerospace industry and the nation at large. When completed, the study will be available through this office. For more information on the study, contact this office.

* Technology Utilization Officers

Technology Utilization Division
NASA Scientific and Technical Information Facility
P.O. Box 8757
Baltimore, MD 21240

Within the NASA technology transfer network, Technology Utilization Officers (TUOs) are placed at each of NASA's field centers. They work with industry, providing information on new technologies developed at the center and matching and cross-correlating NASA technologies with industrial needs. They also provide a link

to NASA's engineers and scientists, who can help clients locate, adapt, and implement NASA technology. The following is a list of the NASA field centers and their technology utilization officers.

Ames Research Center, Mail Code 223-3, Moffett Field, CA 94035; 415-604-4044.
Goddard Space Flight Center, Mail Code 702, Greenbelt, MD 20771; 301-286-0828.
Lyndon B. Johnson Space Center, Mail Code EA4, NASA Road One, Houston, TX 77058; 713-483-3809
Langley Research Center, Mail Stop 139A, Hampton, VA 23665; 804-864-6005.
Marshall Space Flight Center, Code AT01, MSFC, AL 35812; 216-433-6043.
Lewis Research Center, Mail Stop 7-3, 21000 Brookpark Road, Cleveland, OH 44135; 216-433-5568.
Jet Propulsion Laboratory, Mail Stop 156-211, 4800 Oak Grove Drive, Pasadena, CA 91109; 818-354-4862.
National Space Technology Laboratories, Code GA-00, NSTL Station, MS 39529; 601-688-1929.
John F. Kennedy Space Center, Mail Stop PT-TPO-A, Kennedy Space Center, FL 32899; 407-867-3017.
NASA Resident Office-JPL, Mail Stop 180-801, 4800 Oak Grove Drive, Pasadena, CA 91109; 818-354-4849.

* Tethered Satellite System

Marshall Space Flight Center
Huntsville, AL 35812   216-433-6043

Marshall manages the Tethered Satellite System, expected to be in orbit by 1990, which will be carried by the Space Shuttle into space and suspended from the orbiter's cargo bay on a tether to study electrodynamic phenomena and the Earth's upper atmosphere for magnetospheric, atmospheric, and gravitational data.

* Tracking and Data Relay Satellite System

Goddard Space Flight Center
Greenbelt, MD 20771   301-286-0828

Voice and data transmissions between Earth and orbital regions are multiplying rapidly, and to accommodate this communications growth NASA is building a new Earth-to-orbit and orbit-to-Earth communications link called the Tracking and Data Relay Satellite System. When completed, TDRSS, along with two other communications satellites, will comprise NASA's Space Network, and will be one of the biggest advances in space communications technology to date. For more information, contact Goddard.

* Transonic Wind Tunnels

Langley Research Center
Hampton, VA 23665-5225   804-864-6005

Included in Langley's research labs are a variety of wind tunnels covering the entire Mach-number speed range. The National Transonic Facility is a new cryogenic wind tunnel providing a unique opportunity for conducting high Reynolds number research at subsonic and transonic speeds.

* Upper Atmosphere Research Satellite (UARS)

Goddard Space Flight Center
Greenbelt, MD 20771   301-286-0828

To investigate current upper atmospheric changes, the Upper Atmosphere Research Satellite (UARS) will provide for the first time the global data required in probing the chemistry, dynamics, and radiative inputs of the stratosphere and mesosphere. Contact Goddard for more information.

* Wallops Flight Facility

Goddard Space Flight Center
Wallops Island, VA 23337   804-824-1579

A part of Goddard Space Flight Center, Wallops manages and implements NASA's sounding rocket projects which use suborbital rocket vehicles to accommodate approximately 50 scientific missions each year. Approximately 100-150 rocket launches are conducted each year from the Wallops Island site. In cooperative and commercial projects, Wallops provides support which includes launching, tracking, aircraft flights, and data reduction, to various segments of the U.S. Department of Defense and commercial and educational ventures. Wallops also conducts Earth and ocean physics, ocean biological and atmospheric science field experiments; satellite correlative measurements; and developmental projects for new remote sensor systems.

Be patient. If any phone number is incorrect, call (area code) 555-1212 and request the new listing.

* X-Ray Astrophysics

Goddard Space Flight Center
Greenbelt, MD 20771   301-286-0828

When completed, NASA's X-ray Astrophysics Facility (AXAF) will permit astronomers to extend their observations of the cosmos beyond the normal visible band to the X-ray region of the spectrum, providing valuable new information on phenomena spanning our Milky Way galaxy and stretching to the farthest reaches of the known universe. Contact Goddard for more information.

Geology and Earth Science

* Do You Love GOLD?

USGS Book and Report Sales
P.O. Box 25425
Denver, CO 80225   303-202-4700

The U.S. Geological Survey has several free publications dealing with Gold.

Gold - discusses the nature of gold, its origins, and the geologic environments in which it is found.

Prospecting for Gold in the United States - describes various kinds of gold deposits and their locations.

Suggestions for Prospecting - compares modern prospecting techniques with those of earlier years.

* Drilling Core Library

Core Library
U.S. Geological Survey (USGS)
MS 975, Building 810
Box 25046, Federal Center
Denver, CO 80225-0046   303-202-4200

The U.S. Geological Survey (USGS) Core Library collects, stores, and makes available to the public valuable core material from boreholes drilled for oil and gas. The cores are collected from a variety of public and private sources, most of them being from the Rocky Mountain and the Great Plains regions. The cores are processed into core slabs, a more usable and easily archived form. You can examine the processed cores at the facility.

* Earth Science Bibliography

Superintendent of Documents
Government Printing Office
Washington, DC 20402   202-512-1800

Earthquake and volcano publications are listed in this bibliography. *Earthquakes and Volcanoes*, a bimonthly subscription service is featured at an annual cost of $6.50. The *Preliminary Determination of Epicenters* subscription service is listed at a yearly cost of $14. Space and satellite publications are also included. Free.

* Earth Science Data Directory

National Technical Information Service
U.S. Department of Commerce
5285 Port Royal Road
Springfield, VA 22161   703-487-4650

The *Earth Science Data Directory (ESDD)* is a comprehensive listing of available databases in earth sciences and natural resources. References include databases on global change, the *Arctic Environment Data Directory*, and geographic and socioeconomic databases. Contributors include governmental agencies, academic institutions, and the private sector. For more information on the database itself, contact the U.S. Geological Survey (USGS) at 703-648-7112.

* Earth Science Information Centers

Reston-ESIC
U.S. Geological Survey (USGS)
507 National Center
Reston, VA 22092   703-648-6045

The Earth Science Information Office operates a nationwide information and sales service for the results of earth science research, maps, and related products and publications. A network of Earth Science Information Centers (ESIC) provides information about geologic, hydrologic, topographic, and land-use maps; books and reports; aerial, satellite, and radar images and related products; earth science and map data in digital form and related applications software; and geodetic data. ESIC offices can take orders for such customized products as aerial photographs and orthophoto-quads, digital cartographic data, and geographic names gazetteers. These centers also function as over-the-counter dealers for USGS books and maps.

Anchorage

ESIC, U.S. Geological Survey, 4230 University Dr., Room 101, Anchorage, AK 99508-4664; 907-786-7011, Fax: 907-786-7050.

Lakewood

ESIC, U.S. Geological Survey, Box 25046, Bldg. 810, Denver, CO 80225-0046; 303-202-4200, Fax: 303-202-4188.

Menlo Park

ESIC, U.S. Geological Survey, Building 3, Room 3128, 345 Middlefield Rd., Menlo Park, CA 94025; 415-329-4309, Fax: 415-329-5130.

Reston

ESIC, U.S. Geological Survey, 507 National Center, Reston, VA 22092; 703-648-6045, Fax: 703-648-5548.

Rolla

ESIC, U.S. Geological Survey, 1400 Independence Rd., MS 231, Rolla, MO 65401; 314-341-0851, Fax: 314-341-9375.

Salt Lake City

ESIC, U.S. Geological Survey, 2222 West 2300 South, 2nd Floor, Salt Lake City, UT 84119; 801-975-3742, Fax: 801-975-3740.

Sioux Falls

ESIC U.S. Geological Survey, EROS Data Center, Sioux Falls, SD 57198; 605-594-6151, Fax: 605-594-6589

Spokane

ESIC, U.S. Geological Survey, U.S. Post Office Bldg., 904 W. Riverside Ave., Spokane, WA 99201; 509-353-2524, Fax: 509-353-2872.

Stennis Space Center

ESIC, U.S. Geological Survey, Bldg. 3101, Stennis Space Center, MS 39529; 601-688-3541, Fax: 601-688-2230.

Washington, DC

ESIC, U.S. Geological Survey, Department of the Interior Building, 1849 C St. NW, Room 2650, Washington, DC 20240; 202-208-4047, Fax: 202-208-6297.

* Earth Science Information Just a Phone Call Away

ESDD Project Manager
U.S. Geological Survey (USGS)
801 National Center
Reston, VA 22092   703-648-7112

The Earth Science Data Directory (ESDD) is a directory of earth-science databases that is administered by the U.S. Geological Survey (USGS). Between 400-600 references to data bases are being added annually. The referenced databases involve a wide range of earth science fields including geology, hydrology, cartography, and biology. Contact this office for more information.

* Earth Science Teaching Materials

Geologic Inquiries Group
U.S. Geological Survey (USGS)
907 National Center   703-648-4383
Reston, VA 22092   Fax: 703-648-6645

Packets of geological teaching aids for different grade levels and geographic location are available from the Geologic Inquiries Group and from the Earth Science Information Centers listed elsewhere in this book. These packets include lists of reference materials, various maps and map indexes, and a selection of general interest publications. Requests for teachers packets should be sent on school letterhead, indicating the grade level and subject of interest.

* Earthquake Information

General Inquiries Group
U.S. Geological Survey (USGS)
907 National Center
Reston, VA 22092   703-648-4383

The National Earthquake Information Center compiles, computes, and distributes digital and analog data on earthquakes that have occurred around the world. Using the Global Digital Seismic Network and other sources the Center compiles digital data on earthquakes measuring 5.5 or higher onto Event Tapes. For more information, contact the Center.

* Earthquake Safety

S. James
Consumer Information Center-2A
P.O. Box 100
Pueblo, CO 81002

Safety and Survival in an Earthquake explains actions you take before, during and after an earthquake which may save you and your family's lives. Learn what to do at home and in your community (146Y, $2).

* Energy Engineering and Geoscience Research

Office of Basic Energy Sciences
Engineering and Geosciences Division
U.S. Department of Energy
19901 Germantown Rd.
Germantown, MD 20585   301-903-5822

This Division supports the U.S. Department of Energy's central fundamental research activities in the engineering and geoscience disciplines conducted by universities, Federal Laboratories, and industrial firms throughout the U.S. Emphasis in geoscience research is given to the geophysics and geochemistry of rock/fluid systems.

* Energy Science Research

Office of Fusion Energy
19901 Germantown Rd.
Germantown, MD 20874   301-903-4941

The Lawrence Berkeley Laboratory (LBL) undertakes a wide ranging research program in Energy Sciences, which includes geology, chemistry, materials sciences, physics and engineering. LBL pursues basic research and seeks ways of practical application of the basic results. The work of this division of the Laboratory is designed to reflect Energy Department priorities in finding ways to explore and recover energy resources, as well as protecting people and the environment from possible hazards. Contact the above office for further information.

* Environmental Geology

Geologic Division
U.S. Geological Survey (USGS)
907 National Center
Reston, VA 22092   703-648-4383

The U.S. Geological Survey (USGS) conducts geologic mapping and gathers other basic information about the Nation's geologic framework and the processes that have shaped it. Scientists also determine the age and distribution of different types of rocks, climatic changes and their effect on land and water resources, and variations in the Earth's gravity and magnetic field.

* EROS Data Center

U.S. Geological Survey (USGS)
EROS Data Center
Sioux Falls, SD 57198-0001   605-594-6151

The EROS data center receives, processes, and distributes earth-image data acquired by satellite and aircraft and investigates new uses for such data. The Center also develops computerized land information systems and studies new ways of handling data and information. The EROS Data Center also sells high and low altitude photographs as well as photographs from NASA's manned spacecraft. In cooperation with the National Oceanic and Atmospheric Administration (NOAA), the Center also distributes LANDSAT data. Contact the center for more information.

* Field Record Collections

U.S. Geological Survey (USGS)
Building 810

Box 25046, Federal Center
Denver, CO 80225-0046   303-202-4200

The Field Records collection is the depository for the original materials produced by the U.S. Geological Survey (USGS) geologists during their field investigations. The collection consists primarily of materials on the U.S. and holdings consist of 15,600 notebooks, 2000 folders, 2400 map groups, and 60,000 aerial photographs. Contact the Denver office to inquire about specific records and the possibility of having them sent to a more convenient library for examination.

* Free Information on Earthquakes and Volcanoes

USGS Book and Report Sales
P.O. Box 25425
Denver, CO 80225   303-202-4700

The U.S. Geological Survey has the following free publications dealing with earthquakes and volcanoes:

Earthquakes - explains the nature and causes of earthquakes.

Safety and Survival in an Earthquake - describes the hazards posed by earthquakes and offers instructions for individual action before, during, and after a tremor.

The San Andreas Fault - describes the nature, behavior, and earthquake history of this major fault system.

Volcanoes - describes the principal types of volcanoes, different types of eruptions, associated volcanic phenomena, their geologic settings, and how volcanoes are monitored.

Volcanic Hazards of Mount Shasta, California - describes the kinds of volcanic activity that have occurred in the past, shows areas that could be affected in the future, and suggests ways of reducing the risks.

* Geodetic Information

National Geodetic Data Center
National Ocean Service
National Oceanic and Atmospheric Administration
U.S. Department of Commerce
11400 Rockville Pike
Rockville, MD 20852   301-443-8631

The National Geodetic Data Center (NGDC) collects, maintains, publishes, and distributes a complete range of information pertaining to the National Geodetic Reference System, including data on vertical and horizontal geodetic survey stations, geodetic control diagrams for the conterminous United States, Alaska, and Hawaii, gravity values for over 1 million points, calibration base line data, astronomic and Doppler satellite data, computer programs for geodetic applications, and geodetic publications and historical records. NGDC has catalogs available describing a variety of maps, slide sets, and educational tools which are appropriate for both technical and non-technical audiences. Data is broken down into ten categories: solid earth geophysics, earthquake seismology, geomagnetic survey data, marine geological data, marine geophysical data, solar-terrestrial data, solar activity data, geomagnetic variations data, ionospheric data and glaciology. Databases, bulletins, and reports are available within each category. A *Directory of Data Services* lists researchers who can be contacted for technical information about data and products.

* Geologic Names Committee

U.S. Geological Survey (USGS)
507 National Center
Reston, VA 22092   703-648-6045

The Geologic Names Committee defines and recommends policy and rules governing stratigraphic nomenclature and classification for the U.S. Geological Survey (USGS). *Stratigraphic Notes* is published to announce changes in official geologic names usage. Lexicons are compiled that show domestic geologic names usage, and a file is maintained of geologic names reserved future use.

* Geologic Inquiries

U.S. Geological Survey (USGS)
507 National Center
Reston, VA 22092   301-648-6045

To obtain technical information on such geologic topics as earthquakes and volcanoes, energy and mineral resources, the geology of specific areas, and geologic maps, contact this office.

Science and Technology

* Geologic Science

Office of Scientific Publications
Geologic Division
U.S. Geological Survey (USGS)
507 National Center
Reston, VA 22092   703-648-6045

This office reviews all scientific publications in the geologic field for scientific accuracy. Both internal and outside publications are analyzed. All must comply with the Geological Survey's standards.

* Geology Films

Visual Services
U.S. Geological Survey (USGS)
790 National Center
Reston, VA 22092   703-648-4379

The geology motion picture films are available on a free short-term loan to educational and scientific communities, professional and technical societies, civic and industrial groups, and other established organizations. Those marked by an asterisk should be borrowed from: Modern Talking Picture Service, 5000 Park St. North, St. Petersburg, FL 33709.

In The Beginning * - Upper Elementary, Junior High
When The Earth Moves * - College, State Agencies
1955 Eruption of Kilauea Volcano, Hawaiian Islands - Elementary
Inside Hawaiian Volcanoes * - Elementary
The Alaskan Earthquake, 1964 * - Elementary
John Wesley Powell: Canyon Geologist * - Junior High
Geology of the Berlize Barrier Reef - High School, College
The 1923 Surveying Expedition of the Colorado River in Arizona - Junior High
The Subject is Water * - High School
Flow in Alluvial Channels - College
The Sea River - High School
The Little Plover (River) Project, A Study in Sand Plains Hydrology - High School
The Water Below - Elementary
To Fill The Gap - Elementary
National Petroleum Reserve in Alaska - Junior High
Yakutat - High School

* Geology Information Centers

Public Inquiries Offices (PIO) are a network of earth-science information offices that are especially convenient for walk-in customers but also answer inquiries made by mail or telephone. In addition to assisting the public in the selection and ordering of all U.S. Geological Survey (USGS) products, the PIOs provide counter service for USGS topographic, geologic and water-resources maps and reports. The offices furnish information about the USGS and its programs and are a link to information held by State and other federal offices. PIOs distribute catalogs, circulars, indexes, and leaflets and provide bibliographic and geographic reference searches. Most PIOs (those not located near regional USGS centers) maintain libraries of USGS book reports and are regional depositories for Open-File Reports. Below are PIO locations, regions of specialization, addresses, and phone numbers:

Public Inquiries Office
U.S. Geological Survey (USGS)
4230 University Dr., Room 101
Anchorage, AK 99508-4664   907-786-7011
(Alaska)

Public Inquiries Office
U.S. Geological Survey (USGS)
Box 25046, Bldg. 810
Denver, CO 80225-0046   303-202-4200
(AK, AZ, CO, KS, MT, NE, ND, SD, UT, WY)

Public Inquiries Office
U.S. Geological Survey (USGS)
Building 3, Room 3128
Mail Stop 532
345 Middlefield Rd.
Menlo Park, CA 94025-3591   415-329-4309
(AK, AZ, CA, HI, ID, NV, OR, UT, WA)

Public Inquiries Office
U.S. Geological Survey (USGS)
907 National Center

Reston, VA 22092   703-648-4383
(all States)

Public Inquiries Office
U.S. Geological Survey (USGS)
2222 West 2300 South, 2nd Floor
Salt Lake City, UT 84119   801-975-3742
(AZ, CO, ID, NV, NM, UT, WY)

* Geology Publications

U.S. Geological Survey (USGS)
Distribution Support Section
417 National Center
Reston, VA 22092   703-648-5023

Write to the address listed above to get on the free mailing list for the monthly list of new publication of the U.S. Geological Survey (USGS). *Guide to Obtaining USGS Information* is a free publication which describes sources of USGS information and lists in tabular form USGS products and their sources. To receive your copy write: Books and Open File Reports Section, USGS, Federal Center, Box 25425, Denver, CO 80225.

* Geology Teacher Packets

Geologic Inquiries Group
U.S. Geological Survey (USGS)
907 National Center
Reston, VA 22092   703-648-4383

Packets of teaching aids, which differ according to subject, grade level, and geographic location, are available through the Geologic Inquiries Group (GIG). These packets include lists of reference materials, various maps and map indexes, and a selection of general interest publications. Requests for teachers packets should be sent on school letterhead to GIG, and should indicate the grade level and subject of interest. GIG compiles two packets; 1) "Selected Packet of Geologic Teaching Aids," for elementary- and secondary-school teachers of general science courses, and 2) "Teachers Packet of Geologic Materials," for Secondary-school and college teachers of earth-science courses.

* Geophysical and Solar-Terrestrial Information

National Geophysical Data Center (NGDC)
National Oceanic and Atmospheric Administration
U.S. Department of Commerce
325 Broadway
Boulder, CO 80303   303-497-6215

The National Geophysical Data Center (NGDC) combines in a single center all data activities in the fields of solid earth geophysics, marine geology and geophysics, and solar-terrestrial physics. NGDC produces numerous publications which catalog and document data. In addition, NGDC has available a variety of maps, slide sets, and educational tools which are appropriate for both technical and non-technical audiences.

Marine Data 303-497-6338
Land Data 303-497-6123
Seismological Data 303-497-6472

* Geoscience Research: Department of Energy

Office of Fossil Energy
Office of Communications
FE-5, Room 46-085
Forrestal Bldg.
Washington, DC 20585   202-586-6503

This office is the chief coordinator for geoscience programs of the U.S. Department of Energy. It also manages and directs the Hydrocarbon Geoscience Research Coordinating Committee activities, which includes as ex-officio members from the National Science Foundation, the U.S. Department of Interior's Geological Survey and Minerals Management Service.

* Geoscience Research - Grand Junction

Grand Junction Projects Office
P.O. Box 2567
Grand Junction, CO 81502   303-248-6000

The primary mission of the Grand Junctions projects office is to apply its project management, engineering, and geoscience capabilities to support national programs in environmental restoration, geoscience, and energy. Activities include: the Grand Junction Uranium Mill Tailings Remedial Action (UMTRA) vicinity properties project; the Monticello, Utah, mill site and vicinity properties project; the remediation of DOE's Grand Junction Projects Office; and the DOE-Wide Long Term Surveillance and Maintenance Program.

* Geology and Earth Science Libraries
The U.S. Geological Survey (USGS) library system is one of the largest earth science library systems in the world. Holdings include 1.1 million monographs and serials 385,000 maps; 355,000 pamphlets; and 340,000 reports and dissertations in microform. The libraries are open to the public and some materials may be available on inter-library loan.

Reston, VA
USGS Library, 950 National Center, Room 4-A-100, 12201 Sunrise Valley Dr., Reston, VA 22092; 703-648-4302.

Menlo Park, CA
USGS Library, Mail Stop 955, 345 Middlefield Road, Menlo Park, CA 94025; 415-329-5090.

Denver, CO
USGS Library, Mail Stop 914, Building 20, Box 25046, Federal Center, Denver, CO 80225; 303-236-1000.

Flagstaff, AZ
USGS Library, 2255 North Gemini Dr., Flagstaff, AZ 86001; 602-527-7009.

* International Geology
Geologic Division
U.S. Geological Survey (USGS)
507 National Center
Reston, VA 22092   703-648-6045
Through scientific cooperation and exchange programs, this office coordinates geologic activities and research with other countries, including developing nations.

* Landslide Information
Landslide Information Center
U.S. Geological Survey (USGS)
Box 25046, Bldg. 810
Denver, CO 80225-0046   303-236-1599
This center responds to inquiries on landslide research and maintains files of landslide documents, newspaper clippings, and photographs that may be examined or photocopied at the Center.

* Earthquakes and Other U.S. Geological Survey Publications
U.S. Geological Survey (USGS)
Book and Report Sales
Box 25425
Denver, CO 80225   303-202-4200
This is a listing of some of the general interest publications available through the U.S. Geological Survey. They are free unless otherwise indicated. Also ask about getting of the mailing list for new publications.

The Antarctic and its Geology
Earthquakes
Eruptions of Hawaiian Volcanoes: Past, Present and Future
Eruptions of Mount St. Helens: Past, Present, and Future
Geologic History of Cape Cod, Massachusetts
Geology of Caves
The Great Ice Age
The Interior of the Earth
Landforms of the United States
Marine Geology: Research Beneath the Sea
Our Changing Continent
Permafrost
Safety and Survival in an Earthquake
The San Andreas Fault
Volcanoes
Geysers
Natural Steam for Power

Elevations and Distances in the United States
Geologic Maps: Portraits of the Earth
Steps to the Moon
Tree Rings: Timekeepers of the Past

* Global Seismology
Branch of Global Seismology and Geomagnetism
U.S. Geological Survey (USGS)
Box 25046, Bldg. 810
Denver, CO 80225-0046   303-202-4200
Current and historical magnetic-declination information can be obtained from this Branch. Contact this office for further information.

* Mineral Information
Minerals Information Office
U.S. Department of the Interior
1849 C. St., NW, Room 2647
Washington, DC 20240   202-208-5512
The U.S. Department of the Interior can answer questions and provide you with information on minerals and mineral science. The Minerals Information Office can provide you with publications and database searches also.

* Rock Collecting
USGS Book and Report Sales
P.O. Box 25425
Denver, CO 80225   303-202-4200
Collecting Rocks is a free publication, which describes the origin of major rock types and how rocks can provide clues to the Earth's history. It includes suggestions for starting a rock collection, identifying specimens, and housing such a collection.

* State Geoscience Agencies
Many state geoscience agencies sell U.S. Geological Survey (USGS) products (book reports, maps, etc.) that pertain to their regions or states. Some state geoscience agencies are also affiliated with the National Cartographic Information Center. The U.S. Geological Survey (USGS) cooperates with state geoscience agencies in a variety of projects; publications resulting from these projects are commonly available from both organizations. In addition to selling USGS products, many state geoscience agencies allow the public to consult, but not borrow, these materials. Certain state geoscience agencies are also designated as depositories of specific USGS Open-File Reports.

Alabama
Geological Survey of Alabama, PO Box O, University Station, Tuscaloosa, AL 35486; 205-349-2852, Fax: 205-349-2861.

Alaska
Department of Geological and Geophysical Surveys, 794 University Ave., Fairbanks, AK 99709; 907-451-5005, Fax: 907-451-5050.

Arizona
Arizona Geological Survey, 845 North Park Avenue, Tucson, AZ 85719; 602-882-4795.

Arkansas
Arkansas Geological Survey, 3815 West Roosevelt Road, Little Rock, AR 72204; 501-324-9165.

California
California Division of Mines and Geology, 801 K St., MS 12-30, Sacramento, CA 95814; 916-445-1923, Fax: 916-445-5718.

Colorado
Colorado Geological Survey, 1313 Sherman Street, Room 715, Denver, CO 80203; 303-866-2611, Fax: 303-866-2115.

Connecticut
Department of Environmental Protection, 79 Elm St., Hartford, CT 06106; 203-566-3540.

Delaware
Delaware Geological Survey, University of Delaware, DGS Bldg., Newark, DE 19716; 302-831-2833, Fax: 302-831-3579.

Science and Technology

Florida
Florida Geological Survey, 903 West Tennessee Street, Tallahassee, FL 32304-7795; 904-488-4191, Fax: 904-488-8086.

Georgia
Georgia Geologic Survey, Room 400, 19 Martin Luther King Jr Drive, SW, Atlanta, GA 30334; 404-656-3214.

Hawaii
Department of Land and Natural Resources, Division of Water and Land Development, P.O. Box 373, Honolulu, HI 96809; 808-587-0230, Fax: 808-587-0293.

Idaho
Idaho Geological Survey, University of Idaho Campus, Morrill Hall, Room 332, Moscow, ID 83843; 208-885-7991, Fax: 208-885-5826.

Illinois
Illinois State Geological Survey, 615 East Peabody Dr., Room 121, Champaign, IL 61820; 217-333-5111, Fax: 217-244-7004.

Indiana
Indiana Geological Survey, Department of Natural Resources, 611 North Walnut Grove, Bloomington, IN 47405; 812-855-7636, Fax: 812-855-2862.

Iowa
Iowa Geological Survey, 109 Throwbridge Hall, Iowa City, IA 52242; 319-335-1575, Fax: 319-335-2754.

Kansas
Kansas Geological Survey, 1930 Constant Avenue, Campus West, The University of Kansas, Lawrence, KS 66046; 913-864-3965.

Kentucky
Kentucky Geological Survey, University of Kentucky, 228 Mining and Mineral Resources, Lexington, KY 40506; 606-257-5500.

Louisiana
Louisiana Geological Survey, Department of Natural Resources, Box G, University Station, Baton Rouge, LA 70893; 504-388-5320, Fax: 504-388-5328.

Maine
Maine Geological Survey, Department of Conservation, State House, Station 22, Augusta, ME 04333; 207-289-2801, Fax: 207-289-2353.

Maryland
Maryland Geological Survey, 2300 St. Paul St., Baltimore, MD 21218; 410-554-5500, Fax: 410-554-5502.

Massachusetts
Department of Environmental Quality Engineering, 100 Cambridge St., 20th Floor, Boston, MA 02202; 617-727-5830, Fax: 617-727-2754.

Michigan
Geological Survey Division, Michigan Department of Natural Resources, Steven T. Mason Building, PO Box 30028, Lansing, MI 48909; 517-334-6923, Fax: 517-334-6038.

Minnesota
Minnesota Geological Survey, 2642 University Ave., St. Paul, MN 55114-1057; 612-627-4780, Fax: 612-627-4778.

Mississippi
Department of Natural Resources, Bureau of Geology, PO Box 5348, Jackson, MS 39296; 601-354-6228, Fax: 601-354-6327.

Missouri
Department of Natural Resources, Division of Geology and Land Survey, P.O. Box 250, Rolla, MO 65401; 314-368-2101.

Montana
Montana Bureau of Mines and Geology, Montana College of Mineral Science and Technology, Butte, MT 59701; 406-496-4180, Fax: 406-496-4451.

Nebraska
Conservation and Survey Division, 113 Nebraska Hall, The University of Nebraska, Lincoln, NE 68588-0517; 402-472-3471, Fax: 402-472-2410.

Nevada
Nevada Bureau of Mines and Geology, University of Nevada, Reno, NV 89557-0088; 702-784-6691, Fax: 702-784-1709.

New Hampshire
New Hampshire Geological Survey, P.O. Box 2008, Concord, NH 03302-2008.

New Jersey
New Jersey Geological Survey, CN-427, Trenton, NJ 08625; 609-292-1185, Fax: 609-633-1004.

New Mexico
New Mexico Bureau of Mines and Mineral Resources, Campus Station, Socorro, NM 87801; 505-835-5420, Fax: 505-835-6333.

New York
New York State Geological Survey, 3136 Cultural Education Center, Albany, NY 12230; 518-474-5816, Fax: 518-473-8496.

North Carolina
North Carolina Geological Survey Section, PO Box 27687, Raleigh, NC 27611; 919-733-3833, Fax: 919-733-4407 or 919-733-2876.

North Dakota
North Dakota Geological Survey, University Station, 600 E. Blvd., Bismarck, ND 58205; 701-328-4109, Fax: 701-328-3682.

Ohio
Division of Geological Survey, 4383 Fountain Square, Building B, Columbus, OH 43224; 614-265-6576, Fax: 614-447-1918.

Oklahoma
Oklahoma Geological Survey, 100 E. Boyd, Room N-131, Norman, OK 73019; 405-325-3031, Fax: 405-325-7069.

Oregon
Department of Geology and Mineral Industries, 800 NE Oregon St., Portland, OR 97232; 503-731-4100, Fax: 503-731-4066.

Pennsylvania
Bureau of Topographic and Geologic Survey, P.O. Box 8453, Harrisburg, PA 17105; 717-787-2169, Fax: 717-783-7267.

Rhode Island
Department of Geology, 315 Green Hall, The University of Rhode Island, Kingston, RI 02881; 401-792-2265, Fax: 401-792-2190.

South Carolina
South Carolina Geological and Geodetic Survey, Harbison Forest Road, Columbia, SC 29210; 803-737-9440, Fax: 803-737-9487.

South Dakota
South Dakota Geological Survey Science Center, University of South Dakota, Vermillion, SD 57069; 605-677-5227, Fax: 605-677-5895.

Tennessee
Department of Conservation, Division of Geology, 401 Church St., Nashville, TN 37243; 615-532-1500, Fax: 615-532-0231.

Texas
Bureau of Economic Geology, The University of Texas at Austin, University Station, Box X, Austin, TX 78713-7508; 512-471-7721, Fax: 512-471-0140.

Utah
Utah Geological and Mineral Survey, 606 Black Hawk Way, Salt Lake City, UT 84108; 801-467-7970, Fax: 801-467-4070.

Vermont
Vermont Geological Survey, 103 South Main St., Center Building, Waterbury, VT 05676; 802-244-3601, Fax: 802-244-1102.

Virginia
Virginia Division of Mineral Resources, PO Box 3667, Charlottesville, VA 22903; 804-293-5121, Fax: 804-293-2239.

Washington
Division of Geology and Earth Resources, Department of Natural Resources, Olympia, WA 98504; 306-902-1450, Fax: 306-902-1785.

Be patient. If any phone number is incorrect, call (area code) 555-1212 and request the new listing.

West Virginia

West Virginia Geological Survey, P.O. Box 879, Morgantown, WV 26507; 304-594-2331, Fax: 304-594-2575.

Wisconsin

Wisconsin Geological and Natural History Survey, University of Wisconsin Extension, 3817 Mineral Point Rd., Madison, WI 53705; 608-262-1705, Fax: 608-262-8086.

Wyoming

Geological Survey of Wyoming, P.O. Box 3008, University Station, Laramie, WY 82071.

Puerto Rico

Servicio Geologico de Puerto Rico, Department of Consumer Affairs, P.O. Box 41059, Santurce, PR 00940; 809-721-0940.

* U.S. Geological Survey Regional Information Offices

For information, you can contact the office in your geographic area or contact the Reston, VA office or Washington, DC office, which handle all states.

Anchorage

Public Inquiries Office, U.S. Geological Survey, Room 101, 4230 University Dr., Anchorage, AK 99508-4664; 907-271-4320

Denver

Public Inquiries Office, U.S. Geological Survey, Federal Building, Room 169, 1961 Stout St., Denver, CO 80294; 303-844-4169

Los Angeles

Public Inquiries Office, U.S. Geological Survey, Federal Building, Room 7638, 300 N. Los Angeles St., Los Angeles, CA 90012; 213-894-2850

Menlo Park

Public Inquiries Office, U.S. Geological Survey, Building 3 (Stop 533), Room 3128, 345 Middlefield Rd., Menlo Park, CA 94025; 415-329-4390

Reston

Public Inquiries Office, U.S. Geological Survey, 503 National Center, Room IC402, 12201 Sunrise Valley Dr., Reston, VA 22092; 703-648-6892

Salt Lake City

Public Inquiries Office, U.S. Geological Survey, Federal Building, Room 8105, 125 South State St., Salt Lake City, UT 84138; 801-524-5652

Spokane

Public Inquiries Office, U.S. Geological Survey, U.S. Courthouse, Room 678, West 920 Riverside Ave., Spokane, WA 99201; 509-456-2524

Washington, DC

Public Inquiries Office, U.S. Geological Survey, Main Interior Building, 2600 Corridor, 18th and C Sts., NW, Washington, DC 20240; 202-343-8073

* Volcanoes and Earthquakes

Science and Technology Division
Reference Section
Library of Congress
Washington, DC 20540   202-707-5580

Informal series of reference guides are issued free from the Science and Technology Division under the general title, *LC Science Tracer Bullet*. These guides are designed to help readers locate published material on subjects about which they have only general knowledge. New titles in the series are announced in the weekly Library of Congress *Information Bulletin* that is distributed to many libraries. Two relevant *Tracer Bullets* currently available are: *TB 81-14 Volcanoes*, and *TB 89-8 Earthquakes and Earthquake Engineering*.

* Want to Learn About Earthquakes?

U.S. Geological Survey (USGS)
Box 25046, Bldg. 810
Denver, CO 80225-0046   303-202-4200

The National Earthquake Information Center (NEIC) compiles, computes, and distributes digital and analog data on earthquakes that have occurred around the world. NEIC routinely publishes earthquake data. The NEIC publications are the principal sources of current earthquake information for thousands of seismologists around the world for use in fundamental research and in the evaluation of earthquake hazards. Other publications include an annual *United States Earthquakes*, and state seismicity maps which are available to the public from the Geological Survey.

National Institute of Standards and Technology

A good idea often isn't good enough anymore. As U.S. firms have discovered in international markets, innovation by itself does not ensure commercial success. Unless a new technology is quickly translated into an efficiently manufactured, high-quality product, a faster-acting competitor is likely to capitalize on the advance and reap most of the market returns. The National Institute of Standards and Technology (NIST), formerly the National Bureau of Standards, as a world-class center for science and engineering research, is uniquely positioned to help U.S. firms strengthen their competitive performance.

NIST has been a valuable behind-the-scenes partner of industry and academia, providing the standards and measurement techniques that foster technological advance, domestic and international commerce, and, ultimately, economic progress. NIST is also responsible for speeding innovation and accelerating the adoption of new technologies and new ideas by U.S. companies. That's why about half of the organization's scientists and engineers focus their work on the fastest-moving and, perhaps, most commercially attractive areas of science: advanced materials, electronics, superconductivity, automation, computing, biotechnology, and thin-layer technology.

The National Institute of Standards and Technology provides advisory and consulting services to assist government and industry in the development of standards. As the national reference for physical measurement, NIST produces measurement standards data necessary to create, make, and sell U.S. products and services at home and abroad. Staff work with industry and consumers at every level. Generally, a staffer can lead you to major companies, research centers, experts, and literature. Listed below are the NIST laboratories and centers which can provide you with scientific and technological services as well as measurement, instrumentation and standards information.

* Advanced Measurement Techniques

Office of Physical Measurement Services
National Measurement Laboratory
National Institute of Standards and Technology (NIST)
B362 Physics Bldg
Gaithersburg, MD 20899   301-975-5727

The National Measurement Laboratory develops advanced measurement techniques for complex physical and chemical systems for use in areas such as chemical manufacturing, waste disposal, biotechnology, and environmental studies. Contact this office for more information.

* Alloys: New and Improved

Metallurgy Division
Institute for Materials Science and Engineering
National Institute of Standards and Technology (NIST)
Gaithersburg, MD 20899   301-975-5727

The Institute for Materials Science and Engineering explores and quantifies processing technologies to produce new and improved alloys. For more information, contact this division.

* Analytical Mass Spectrometry

Chemical Science and Technology Laboratory
National Institute of Standards and Technology (NIST)
Gaithersburg, MD 20899   301-975-4109

Analytical mass spectrometry has played a key role in industries, such as the semiconductor industry, that require accurate measurements of trace elements in raw materials, products, and product containers. The NIST inorganic mass spectrometry program is concerned with developing analytical capabilities for making highly accurate determinations of trace inorganics using stable isotope compositions, as well as highly accurate measurements of absolute isotopic compositions to redetermine atomic weights. Areas of research include instrumentation in thermal source, inductively coupled plasma source, and ionization and chemical separations at the trace level using chromatography and other techniques.

* Applications Portability Profile

Systems and Software Technology Division
National Computer Systems Laboratory
National Institute of Standards and Technology (NIST)
Gaithersburg, MD 20899   301-975-3290

The ability to move or port an application from one operating system environment to another is important for cost effective computing. The National Computer Systems Laboratory is working with users and industry to define and implement the Applications Portability Profile (APP), a group of standard elements, including database management, data interchange, network services, user interfaces, and programming services. Workshops for vendors and users are sponsored to explore common requirements for software portability, and to reach agreements on common ways to implement the standards that are being developed. Contact this office for more information on portability and workshops.

* Applied Mathematics

Computing and Applied Mathematics
National Institute of Standards and Technology (NIST)
Gaithersburg, MD 20899   301-975-3816

The Center for Applied Mathematics conducts research and supports NIST activities and other Federal agencies in selected fields of the mathematical and computer sciences. The Center also develops such mathematical tools as scientific software, statistical models and computational methods, mathematical handbooks, and manuals. Contact this office for more information.

* Atomic Mapping

Chemical Science and Technology
National Institute of Standards and Technology (NIST)
Gaithersburg, MD 20899   301-975-3463

The National Measurement Laboratory has developed a tool for "atomic mapping" of the magnetic characteristics of material surfaces. A boon to the $40 billion magnetic recording industry, the instrument will be produced commercially by a U.S. firm. Contact this Center for more information on atomic mapping.

* Atomic Scale Measuring Machine

Manufacturing Engineering Laboratory
National Institute of Standards and Technology (NIST)
Gaithersburg, MD 20899   301-975-3490

By the year 2001, uncertainty requirements for dimensional metrology of step heights, surface roughness, linewidth, and line spacing for the integrated circuit and optics industries will be 0.1nm to 1nm. Furthermore these uncertainties must be held over areas ranging from several square millimeters to fractions of a square meter. To address these needs, NIST is building the molecular measuring machine (M^3) It will be capable of positioning and measuring atomic-scale accuracies over an area of 25 square centimeters. The machine represents a combined effort of NIST and several universities, Watson Research Center, AT&T Bell Laboratories, and Zygo Corporation.

* Automated Manufacturing Data Handling

Automated Manufacturing Research Facility
Manufacturing Technology Centers Program
National Institute of Standards and Technology (NIST)
Gaithersburg, MD 20899   301-975-6100

In a very real sense, the cornerstone of the "factory of the future" will be information. The hardware of the facility--robots, machine tools and sensors--is very visible, but the ability to generate, store, retrieve, and transfer information accurately and on time will be just as important as any hardware. Special features of this unseen part of the Automated Manufacturing Research Facility include the use of distributed databases and a data communications system. Contact this facility for more information on the on-going data handling projects.

* Automated Manufacturing Data Preparation

Automated Manufacturing Research Facility
Manufacturing Technology Centers Program
National Institute of Standards and Technology (NIST)
Gaithersburg, MD 20899   301-975-6100

At the Automated Manufacturing Research Facility, research is underway to determine exactly what sorts of data are required by a factory's manufacturing and inspection systems, and how these data can be generated automatically by the various data preparation systems in use in the facility. Contact this facility for more information on this research.

* Bioanalytical Sensors

Chemical Science and Technology Laboratory
National Institute of Standards and Technology (NIST)
Gaithersburg, MD 20899   301-975-3130

Biosensors are a new generation of analytical devices with the potential for widespread use in biomedical and industrial monitoring applications. Biosensors will incorporate the latest advances in biotechnology to provide high specificity and sensitivity. The National Institute of Standards and Technology (NIST) is conducting research using a variety of optical techniques for detection and amplification of changes detected.

* Biotechnology Research

Chemical Science and Technology Laboratory
9600 Gudelsky Dr.
National Institute of Standards and Technology (NIST)
Rockville, MD 20850   301-738-6277

Working in several areas of DNA chemistry, NIST scientists are actively manipulating DNA to produce proteins, developing methods for measuring DNA damage on the molecular level, and developing methods for characterizing DNA, including profiling. NIST scientists are working on new methods for DNA profiling, ranging from developing well-characterized DNA fragment standards for restriction fragment length polymorphisms to performing research for rapid determination of DNA profiles y polymerase chain reaction amplification ad automated detection of fragments.

* Building Environment

Building Environment Division
National Institute of Standards and Technology (NIST)
Gaithersburg, MD 20899   301-975-5851

The Building Environment Division develops fundamental data, measurement techniques, test methods, and models for the design, construction, and operation of the building envelope and building mechanical and electrical systems. The division also develops software performance criteria, interface standards, and test methods needed to make effective use of modern computer-aided design hardware and software and database management systems within the disaggregated construction industry. Sample outputs for the division include testing and rating procedures and computer models for the performance of heating and air conditioning systems, predictive models for estimating peak heating/cooling requirements and annual building energy use, and indoor air quality, criteria for improving thermal performance of insulating materials, and criteria for measuring and improving the

lighting in buildings. The division also has computer aids to assist in formulating building standards and expert systems. Contact this office for more information.

* Building Materials Research

Building Materials Division
National Institute of Standards and Technology (NIST)
Gaithersburg, MD 20899   301-975-6706

The Building Materials Division conducts laboratory, field and analytical research and develops methods for evaluating the performance and durability of building materials and components. The division also develops chemical, physical, microstructural, and mechanical characterization procedures and mathematical methods for describing microstructures for building materials. Also, the division conducts voluntary laboratory inspection and proficiency sample programs to aid maintenance of quality in execution of standard tests on materials used in building and highway construction. Researchers at NIST are working to gain a better understanding of the lifespan of inorganic materials such as cement and concrete used in building. Artificial intelligence systems are being developed for optimizing the selection of materials and for diagnosing the causes of material degradation. Researchers are also looking into the lifespans of organic building materials such as protective coatings for steel, roofing materials, and asphalt. Contact this office for guidelines for selecting building materials, or for more information on the on-going research in building materials.

* Building Technology

Building Materials Division
National Institute of Standards and Technology (NIST)
Gaithersburg, MD 20899   301-975-6706

The Center for Building Technology is the national building research laboratory. It works cooperatively with other organizations, private and public, to improve building practices. It conducts laboratory, field, and analytical research. It develops technologies to predict, measure, and test the performance of building materials, components, systems, and practices. This knowledge is required for responsible and cost effective decisions in the building process and cannot be obtained through proprietary research and development. The Center provides technologies needed by the building community to achieve the benefits of advanced computation and automation. It does not distribute building standards or regulations, but its technologies are widely used in the building industry and adopted by governmental and private organizations which have standards and codes responsibilities. Contact this Center for more information.

* Building Technology Presentations and Symposia

Building Materials Division
National Institute of Standards and Technology (NIST)
Gaithersburg, MD 20899   301-975-6706

Staff at the Center for Building Technology make a number of presentations at professional societies and at technical meetings of building community organizations. Also, the center presents a monthly series of Building Technology Symposia, in cooperation with other organizations concerned with building research and practice. Contact this Center for further information.

* Calibration Services

Manufacturing Engineering Laboratory
National Institute of Standards and Technology (NIST)
Gaithersburg, MD 20899   301-975-3400

The Center for Manufacturing Engineering maintains the national standards for the length, force, and a number of subsidiary standards. It offers primary calibration services for these standards. Under unique circumstances, the Center accepts especially complex or sensitive measurement assignments of national significance. Contact this Center for more information.

* Center for Advanced Biotechnology Research

Center for Advanced Biotechnology Research
9600 Gudelsky Dr.
Rockville, MD 20850   301-738-6277

At this center, jointly established by the University of Maryland, Montgomery County, MD, and the National Institute of Standards and Technology (NIST), researchers study protein structure/function relationships. They are focusing on the measurement of protein structure by X-ray crystallography and nuclear magnetic resonance spectroscopy, and the manipulation of structure by molecular biological techniques including site-directed mutagenesis. Protein modeling and molecular dynamics and computational chemistry are used to understand protein structure to

Be patient. If any phone number is incorrect, call (area code) 555-1212 and request the new listing.

983

predict the effects of specific structural modifications on the properties of proteins and enzymes.

* Center for Analytical Chemistry Services

Chemical Science and Technology Laboratory
National Institute of Standards and Technology (NIST)
Gaithersburg, MD   301-975-4109

The availability of Center for Analytical Chemistry analytical expertise to other institutions is an important service function. In addition to service analyses, the Center is frequently called upon to consult or advise, to provide various metrological calibrations of a chemical nature on a wide variety of industrial and research materials, and to provide analytical services of a unique nature such as compositional mapping, depth profiling, or ultra-trace analysis. These services are available to private industry when the uniqueness of the Center capability has been demonstrated, and similar services are not available in the private sector. Contact this office for more information.

* Center for Analytical Chemistry Technical Activities

Center for Analytical Chemistry
National Institute of Standards and Technology (NIST)
Gaithersburg, MD 20899   301-975-4109

Center for Analytical Chemistry Technical Activities annual report summarizes the technical activities in the Inorganic Analytical Research Division, the Organic Analytical Research Division, and the Gas and Particulate Science Division. It also describes certain special activities in the Center, including quality assurance and voluntary standardization coordination. Contact this office for a free copy.

* Center for Manufacturing Engineering

Manufacturing Engineering Laboratory
National Institute of Standards and Technology (NIST)
Gaithersburg, MD 20899   301-975-3400

The Center for Manufacturing Engineering provides competence and develops technical data, findings, and standards in manufacturing engineering, mechanical metrology, automation, robotics, control technology, and precision mechanical engineering to support the discrete parts manufacturing industries. Contact this office for more information on the research and developments at the Center.

* Ceramic and Metal Powder Production

Office of Nondestructive Evaluation
Materials Science and Engineering Laboratory
National Institute of Standards and Technology (NIST)
Gaithersburg, MD 20899   301-975-6226

The *Nondestructive Evaluation Technical Activities 1989* annual report reviews the technical activities and developments at NIST, including ceramic and metal powder production and consolidation, formability of metals, composites processing and interfaces, and standards and methods. Also included are listings of the various seminars and invited talks which were presented in 1989. A listing of the Office's publications are also available.

* Ceramics Program

Ceramics Division
Institute for Materials Science and Engineering
National Institute of Standards and Technology (NIST)
Gaithersburg, MD 20899   301-975-5658

The Institute for Materials Science and Engineering conducts a high-tech ceramics program geared to help U.S. industry stay competitive in the worldwide race to expand production and application of these materials. Direct your inquiries to the above office.

* Chemical Engineering Center

Center for Chemical Engineering
National Institute of Standards and Technology (NIST)
325 Broadway
Boulder, CO 80303   303-497-3247

The Center for Chemical Engineering performs research in process metrology, thermophysical properties of fluids and solids, and unit operations and processes; provides measurement practices and standards, fundamental engineering data, calibration and measurement services, and engineering science for the chemical and related industries, academe, and Government.

* Chemical Engineering Separations

Chemical Science and Technology Laboratory
Division 832
National Institute of Standards and Technology (NIST)
Gaithersburg, MD 20899   301-975-3145

Separation and purification are critical steps in the manufacture of chemical products using existing and emerging process technologies, such as energy production or environmental protection. Separation processes affect both the economies of production and the fundamental ability to produce a product of desired form or purity. The National Institute of Standards and Technology (NIST) is creating an engineering science based on separations.

* Chemical Process Research

Chemical Process Metrology Division
Center for Chemical Engineering
National Institute of Standards and Technology (NIST)
Gaithersburg, MD 20899   301-975-5727

Research is on-going in the Chemical Process Metrology Division to develop measurement standards and provide measurement services for flow (volume and mass rates), liquid density, liquid volume, and humidity. Experimental and theoretical research is conducted to characterize fluid behavior.

* Chemical Reference Laboratory

Chemical Science and Technology Laboratory
National Institute of Standards and Technology (NIST)
Gaithersburg, MD 20899   301-975-3145

The National Measurement Laboratory serves as the nation's reference laboratory for the more than 250 million chemical composition measurements made each day in the United States for industrial process control, environmental protection, toxic substances control, and health services. Working with a U.S. firm, the National Measurement Laboratory designed a new instrument for more efficient and more accurate separation and analysis of chemical elements in a sample. Contact this Lab for more information.

* Chemical Research

Chemical Science and Technology Laboratory
National Institute of Standards and Technology (NIST)
Gaithersburg, MD 20899   301-975-3145

Current programs at the Center for Analytical Chemistry include the following: Clinical Standards, Environmental Standards, Metal Standards, Gas Standards, Biomaterial Standards, Acid Rain, Environmental Analysis, Particle Analysis, Specimen Banking, and Nutrient Analysis. Research interests include atom reservoirs, bioanalytical sensors, bioanalytical techniques, compositional mapping, electrochemical techniques, high resolution chromatography, laboratory automation, laser enhanced ionization in flames, and multicomponent analysis. Contact the Center for more information about research interests or its current programs.

* Commercialization of Advanced Technology

Manufacturing Technology Centers Program
Manufacturing Engineering Laboratory
National Institute of Standards and Technology (NIST)
Gaithersburg, MD 20899   301-975-3400

Through the Advanced Technology Program, NIST is directed to speed the commercialization of new technology and the development of new, generic manufacturing techniques. NIST may support or participate in research consortia to develop and test new equipment or production processes, provided that they are "generic" to a particular industry or group of industries. The program will be aimed at small- to mid-sized, high technology firms or consortia. The idea is to "leverage" the relatively small financial resources of NIST by using the Institute's support to encourage private investment in each project. For more information, contact this office.

* Computer and Telecommunications Standards Assistance

Information Systems Engineering Division
Computer Systems Laboratory
National Institute of Standards and Technology (NIST)
Gaithersburg, MD 20899   301-975-3262

The National Computer Systems Laboratory helps computer manufacturers, communications companies, and domestic and international standards-writing groups to produce and test standards for off-the-shelf compatibility of computer and related telecommunications systems. Contact this NIST division for more information.

* Computer Assistance for Organizations

Computer Systems Laboratory
National Institute of Standards and Technology (NIST)
Gaithersburg, MD 20899   301-975-2822

The National Computer Systems Laboratory works on techniques and tools to help organizations make effective use of computers and information technology, reduce training costs, and improve productivity. Contact this Lab for more information.

* Computer Information Technology

Computer Systems Laboratory
National Institute of Standards and Technology (NIST)
Gaithersburg, MD 20899   301-975-2822

Computers are indispensable tools of the Information Age. Current uses, however, tap neither the full potential of rapidly improving hardware and software, nor the growing opportunities arising from new telecommunications technology that can simultaneously transmit data, image, and voice signals. The National Computer Systems Laboratory (NCSL) is helping to ensure that the manufacturers and users of information technology will reap the anticipated benefits--better products, the growth of markets, and production applications of information technology. Beyond providing technical assistance, NCSL serves government and industry by developing standards, test methods, and computer security measures. It consists of the following divisions:

Information Systems Engineering Division, A266 Technology Bldg.; 301-975-3262

Systems and Software Technology Division, B266 Technology Bldg.; 301-975-3290

Computer Security Division, A216 Technology Bldg.; 301-975-2934

Systems and Network Architecture Division, B217 Technology Bldg.; 301-975-1233

Advanced Systems Division, A224 Technology Bldg.; 301-975-2904

* Computer Security Consulting

Computer Security Division
Computer Systems Laboratory
National Institute of Standards and Technology (NIST)
Gaithersburg, MD 20899   301-975-2934

The National Computer Systems Laboratory (NCSL) provides federal agencies with advice and assistance in computer security planning, training, and related activities. With the National Security Agency, NCSL reviews and comments on agency security plans for sensitive, unclassified systems. Regular workshops, meetings, and a national computer security conference comprise the ongoing program to facilitate the interchange of ideas, needs, guidance, and standards.

* Computer Systems Consulting

Computer Systems Laboratory
National Institute of Standards and Technology (NIST)
Gaithersburg, MD 20899   301-975-2822

The National Computer Systems Laboratory (NCSL) consults with federal agencies to solve technical problems. Carried out on a cost-reimbursable basis, projects are selected for their broad applicability to federal agency information processing and their contributions to NCSL programs. The professional staff is uniquely qualified to address technical problems in computer security, software engineering, advanced computer systems, database management and graphics systems, and distributed processing. For specific information on how NCSL's products, services, and expertise can help your organization, contact this laboratory.

* Cooperative Data Programs

Reference Center
Standard Reference Data
National Institute of Standards and Technology (NIST)
Gaithersburg, MD 20899   301-975-2002

The need for high quality data far exceeds the resources of the Standard Reference Data Program. as a result, NIST participates in numerous cooperative data projects which have been set up to meet the needs. In a typical project, the NIST technical centers work together with an outside group, such as a technical society, industry group, or government agency to develop databases. Contact this Center for more information.

* Cooperative Research with NIST Experts

Cooperative Research Program
National Institute of Standards and Technology (NIST)
Gaithersburg, MD 20899   301-975-3084

Researchers from industry and universities regularly work in NIST laboratories with Institute experts on projects of mutual interest. For example, engineers, machinists, and computer specialists from private companies, other government agencies, and universities have joined NIST researchers to develop the quality control techniques and the computer software interface standards needed for the automated factory of the future. For information on conducting cooperative research at the Institute write or call David Edgerly, or call the individual division listed previously that applies to your interests directly.

* Data Evaluation Centers

An important part of the National Standard Reference Data System is the data evaluation centers active in major areas of physics, chemistry, and materials science. These centers represent a long-term commitment to assessing and improving the quality of data in each area. Each of the centers maintains a close working relationship with other government agencies, private-sector organizations, and international groups active in its area. The centers welcome inquiries and opportunities for cooperative projects. The data centers are, unless otherwise indicated, located at the National Institute of Standards and Technology, Gaithersburg, MD 20899.

Chemistry
Chemical Kinetics Information Center, A147 Chemistry Building
Chemical Thermodynamics Data Center, A158 Chemistry Building
Fluids Mixtures Data Center, Mail Code 774.00, National Institute of Standards and Technology, Boulder, CO 80303
Ion Kinetics and Energetics Data Center, A147 Chemistry Building
Molten Salts Data Center, Rensselaer Polytechnic Institute, Department of Chemistry, Troy, NY 12181
Radiation Chemistry Data Center, University of Notre Dame, Radiation Laboratory, Notre Dame, IN 46556
Thermodynamics Research Center, Texas A&M University, College Station, TX 77843-3111

Materials Science
Alloy Phase Diagram Data Center, B150 Materials Building
Center for Information and Numerical Analysis and Synthesis, Purdue University, 2595 Yeager Road, West Lafayette, IN 47906
Corrosion Data Center, B259 Materials Building
Crystal Data Center, A207 Materials Building
Phase Diagrams for Ceramists Data Center, A229 Materials Building
Tribology Information Center, A247 Materials Building

Physics
Atomic Collision Cross Section Data Center, Joint Institute for Laboratory Astrophysics, University of Colorado, Boulder, CO 80309
Atomic Energy Levels Data Center, A167 Physics Building
Atomic Transition Probabilities Data Center, A267 Physics Building
Fundamental Constants Data Center, B258 Metrology Building
Molecular Spectra Data Center, B268 Physics Building
Photon and Charged-Particle Data Center, C311 Radiation Physics Building

* Dielectric Properties of Materials

Electronics and Electrical Engineering Laboratory
National Institute of Standards and Technology (NIST)
Gaithersburg, MD 20899   301-975-2220

Inadequate knowledge of the electromagnetic properties of materials inhibits development of new technologies, drives up the cost of systems and components, and may prevent achievement of optimal performance levels. A relatively new NIST program in materials is aimed at developing primary standards for measuring the dielectric materials of properties of materials used in electromagnetic applications.

* Dynamic Pressure and Temperature Research

Chemical Science and Technology Laboratory
B312 Physics
National Institute of Standards and Technology (NIST)
Gaithersburg, MD 20899   301-975-4814

U.S. industry increasingly relies on real-time monitoring of process parameters, particularly temperature and pressure, to produce efficiently a desired endproduct, to warrant safe operation and to assure equity in commerce. NIST has a research program and is developing a test facility to provide a reliable basis for the evolution and calibration of transducer dynamical response functions. This research seeks to develop a primary standard for dynamic temperature and pressure based on the fundamental properties of the molecular constituents of the dynamic system. Contact NIST for more information.

* Earthquake Safety

Building and Fire Research Laboratory
National Institute of Standards and Technology (NIST)
B250 Building Research Bldg
Gaithersburg, MD 20899   301-975-5900

The National Engineering Laboratory uses a specially designed computerized facility to test how full-scale bridge and building components would perform in earthquakes. Contact this Center for more information.

* Electromagnetic Interference and Compatibility

Electronics and Electrical Engineering Laboratory
Div. 813.03
National Institute of Standards and Technology (NIST)
Boulder, CO 80303-3328   303-497-3535

NIST researchers are engaged in a wide range of projects aimed at quantifying electromagnetic interference and electromagnetic compatibility. One thrust of NIST work is to develop measurement techniques and methodologies for measuring the emission of unintentional radiation from electronic devices. Another aspect under active investigation is the susceptibility of electronic equipment to such radiation. Success of this research should lead to the development of new standards which can be adopted both in the U.S. and internationally.

* Electromagnetic Technology/Magnetics

Electronics and Electrical Engineering Laboratory
Div. 814.05
National Institute of Standards and Technology (NIST)
325 Broadway
Boulder, CO 80303-3328   303-497-3535

NIST researchers characterize magnetic materials, such as ferromagnetic and magnetoresistive films, recording tapes and disks, ferromagnetic steels, very weakly magnetic alloys, amorphous ribbons, spin glasses, ferrites, and permanent magnets as a function of magnetic field and temperature. Attention in this work is given to calibration accuracy measurement precision and instrument development. The research done in this lab has applications in basic physics and in applied engineering.

* Electronic Information Retrieval Systems

Publications and Programs Inquiries Unit
National Institute of Standards and Technology (NIST)
Gaithersburg, MD 20889   301-975-3058

The National Institute of Standards and Technology (NIST) operates different electronic information retrieval systems and bulletin boards designed to encourage dissemination of information on a variety of topics. For assistance about information on programs not provided below, contact the NIST Publications and Programs Inquiries Unit at the number listed above or by email: inquiries@enh.nist.gov.

NIST Gopher Information Service

This is part of the Gopher system on the Internet which allows users to search through databases, using menus to locate materials of interest. The following is a partial listing of topics that are available: Guide to NIST; Guide to Mathematical Software (GAMS); computer security; Standard Reference Data Program; and NIST phone book and email directory. To access the NIST gopher via Internet:
- from remote log in, type "telnet gopher.nist.gov." At the log in prompt, type "gopher."
- from a gopher client, use the gopher server as "Gopherserver.nist.gov" with port 70.

Step Online Information Service (SOLIS)

SOLIS provides access to draft standards, supporting documents, and software that contribute to the Standard for Exchange of Product Model Data (STEP).
- Internet access: send an email message to "nptserver@cme.nist.gov". In the body of the message, type "help".
- Anonymous ftp: ftp ftp.cme.nist.gov, name: anonymous, password: <userid>, files to be downloaded are located at "cd.pub/step".

Weights and Measures Bulletin Board

This bulletin board provides information on certificates of conformance, software programs, publication lists, and contacts.
- Modem access: 301-869-1665 for 1200 baud (data bits: 8/no parity, stop bits: 1).

Computer Security Bulletin Board

This bulletin board provides information on computer viruses, software reviews, computer security alerts, and publications.
- Modem access: 301-948-5717 for 300, 1200, or 2400 baud; 301-948-5140 for 9600 baud (data bits: 8/no parity or 7/even parity, stop bits: 1).
- Internet access: telnet cs-bbs.ncsl.nist.gov or telnet 129.6.54.30. To download files, Internet users need to use ftp as follows: type "ftp csrc.nist.gov" or "ftp 129.6.54.11." Log in to account "anonymous" using your Internet address as the password. Computer security bulletin board files are located in directory bbs. Or, telnet to the NIST Gopher server. Type "telnet gopher.nist.gov."

Data Management Activities and Application Bulletin Board

This bulletin board provides information on activities of the NIST Information Systems Engineering Division, which develops standards and provides technical assistance to government and industry in data administration, data management, technology, computer graphics, and software standards validation.
- Modem access: 301-948-2048 for 2400 baud, 301-948-2059 for 300 or 1200 baud (data bits" 8/no parity or 7/even parity, stop bits: 1).

Fire Research Computer Bulletin Board

This bulletin board features fire computer programs developed by the Building and Fire Research Laboratory at NIST.
- Modem access: 301-990-2272 for 300, 1200, 2400, or 9600 baud (data bits: 8/no parity, stop bits: 1).

North American Integrated Services Digital Network (ISDN) Users Forum Bulletin Board

This bulletin board provides minutes from the North American ISDN Users' Forum, meeting dates and agendas, user applications, analyses, and profiles. When prompted for password, type "dialin".
- Modem access: 301-869-7281 for 1200 or 2400 baud (data bits: 8/no parity, stop bits: 1).
- Internet access: telnet 129.6.53.11.

* Electronic Publishing

Systems and Software Technology Division
Computer Systems Laboratory
National Institute of Standards and Technology (NIST)
B218, Technology Bldg.
Gaithersburg, MD 20899   301-975-3252

The National Computer Systems Laboratories' Electronic Publishing Laboratory assists federal agencies in the selection and use of publishing systems by demonstrating the capabilities and limitations of different publishing technologies. Laboratory demonstrations focus on electronic publishing and the role of standards in electronic document processing and interchange. To visit the laboratory, contact the office above.

* Electrical Metrology with Optical Sensors

Electronics and Electrical Engineering Laboratory
Room B344, Metrology Bldg
National Institute of Standards and Technology (NIST)
Gaithersburg, MD 20899   301-975-2418

Researchers at the National Institute of Standards and Technology (NIST) are developing electro-optical methods to measure electrical quantities and phenomena as part of a program to develop theory, methods, and physical standards for measuring electrical quantities in advanced high-voltage/high power systems.

* Electronics and Electrical Engineering

Electronics and Electrical Engineering Laboratory
B352 Metrology
National Institute of Standards and Technology (NIST)
Gaithersburg, MD 20899   301-975-4091

This Center conducts research and development in the field of electronic and electrical materials, devices, instruments, and systems. The Center develops engineering data, measurement methods, theory, physical standards, and associated technology, and provides technical services, national reference standards, and engineering measurement traceability for the benefit of government, industry, and the scientific community. Contact this office for more information.

* Emerging Technologies in Manufacturing Engineering

Manufacturing Engineering Laboratory
National Institute of Standards and Technology (NIST)

B326 Metrology Bldg.
Gaithersburg, MD 20899   301-975-3400

Emerging Technologies in Manufacturing Engineering is an internal report produced by the managers and staff of the Center for Manufacturing Engineering for planning purposes only. It represents their current best thinking about emerging technologies in manufacturing engineering, the impact these technologies will have on their programs, and the directions their programs will go if sufficient resources are available. The emerging technologies discussed are those that they believe will require increased support and leadership from CME in coming years. Contact this office for a free copy.

* Energy Efficient Chemical Separation

Chemical Engineering Science Division
Chemical Science and Technology Laboratory
National Institute of Standards and Technology (NIST)
325 Broadway
Boulder, CO 80303   303-497-2627

The Chemical Engineering Science Division creates mass transfer models and heat transfer codes for new, energy efficient separation concepts.

* Energy-Related Inventions Program

Office of Technology Evaluation and Assessment
Energy-Related Inventions
National Institute of Standards and Technology (NIST)
Gaithersburg, MD 20899   301-975-5500

The National Institute of Standards and Technology evaluates all promising non-nuclear energy-related inventions, particularly those submitted by independent inventors and small companies for the purpose of obtaining direct grants for their development from the U.S. Department of Energy. The Energy-Related Inventions Program provides an opportunity for inventors to obtain Federal assistance in developing and commercializing their inventions. For a leaflet answering questions about qualifying, the evaluation process, types of assistance, patent policy, and other frequently asked questions about the program; and to request an Evaluation Request Form, contact the office above.

* Fire Center Research Grants

Fire Science and Engineering
Building Fire and Research Laboratory
National Institute of Standards and Technology (NIST)
Gaithersburg, MD 20899   301-975-6864

The Center for Fire Research (CFR) awards, mostly to universities, about 25 research grants annually that are integrated with the in-house program by CFR technical monitors who have related project responsibilities. Contact this Center for more information on the research grants. FIREDOC is the automated database of the Fire Research Information Services bibliographic collection. The collection contains national and international fire research reports, books, journal articles and conference proceedings. FIREDOC contains the references and, if possible, abstract and keywords. The full text of the document is not included in the database. FIREDOC is available 23 hours per day, Monday through Friday. It is not available between 8:30 a.m. and 9:30 a.m. eastern time. On Saturdays and Sundays, it is available 24 hours per day. For detailed instructions on how to access the database and how to perform bibliographic searches, you can get the *FIREDOC User's Manual* for $11.95 from National Technical Information Service (NTIS), 5285 Port Royal Rd., Springfield, VA 22161; 703-487-4650. For additional information, call Nora Jason at the NIST office above.

* Fire Hazard Analysis

Building and Fire Research Laboratory
National Institute of Standards and Technology (NIST)
Gaithersburg, MD 20899   301-975-6879

The U.S. has one of the worst fire records in the industrialized world. NIST researchers are helping to reduce the losses and cost of fire protection by providing scientific and engineering bases needed by manufacturers and the fire protection community. The project relies on numerical and hand calculation methods as well as computer graphics and design techniques.

* Fire Measurement and Research Developments

Fire Science and Engineering
Building and Fire Research Laboratory
National Institute of Standards and Technology (NIST)
Gaithersburg, MD 20899   301-975-5900

Contact this division for information on studies which identify and measure potentially harmful combustion products and their effects on living organisms, and studies to develop less flammable furnishings.

* Fire Research and Consulting

Building and Fire Research Laboratory
National Institute of Standards and Technology (NIST)
Gaithersburg, MD 20899   301-975-6699

The Center for Fire Research (CFR) provides technical support to voluntary standards and codes groups, the engineering and design community, the building industry, fire services, and fire protection organizations. It also provides scientifically-based recommendations to other government agencies on fire-related issues. CFR also conducts fire research for private industry when CFR facilities or expertise are unique and when the requested research complements the on-going CFR program. Contact this Center for more information.

* Fire Research Center

Building and Fire Research Laboratory
National Institute of Standards and Technology (NIST)
Gaithersburg, MD 20899   301-975-5900

This Center performs and supports research to provide the scientific and technical basis for reducing fire losses and the cost of fire protection. The Center's technical promotes the development and widespread use of scientifically-based fire protection engineering practices, promote the continued advance in knowledge of the physics and chemistry behind actual fires, and maintain the technical capability for timely response to current fire problems. The Center maintains a definitive fire research information center for its use and as a resource for the fire community. The Center also manages a grants program for basic and applied fire research to complement in-house research. For more information, contact this Center.

* Fire Research Computer Bulletin Board

Building and Fire Research Laboratory
National Institute of Standards and Technology (NIST)
B218, Building Research Bldg
Gaithersburg, MD 20899   301-975-5852

The Center for Fire Research Computer Bulletin Board is a public access computer bulletin board featuring computer programs developed by the Center for Fire Research. The bulletin Board also contains information on FIREDOC and Center for Fire Research activities. You will find fire simulation programs developed at the Center, information on upcoming activities at the Center, including conferences, workshops and seminars, a listing of recent reports from the Center, and more. Contact this Center for more information on accessing the bulletin board.

* Fire Research Publications, 1987

National Technical Information Service
5825 Port Royal Rd
Springfield, VA 22161   703-487-4650

Interested in the combustion toxicity of various plastics? cigarette fire-safety? sprinklers? smoke control? soot formation? The NIST Center for Fire Research issued publications and articles on these topics and many others, all of which are compiled in the bibliography, *Fire Research Publications, 1987*. NIST conducts research on how fires start and spread and how they can be detected and suppressed. This research leads to realistic material test methods, cost-effective fire safety design concepts, and new methods of fire control and extinguishment. Copies are $14.95 prepaid through the office above.

* Fire Safety

Building and Fire Research Laboratory
National Institute of Standards and Technology (NIST)
A218 Building Research Bldg
Gaithersburg, MD 20899   301-975-6865

The National Engineering Laboratory develops computer-based models and engineering tools that predict fire and its effects for use by the fire protection and building communities in designing safer buildings. Contact this Center for more information.

* Fire Safety in Transportation Vehicles

Fire Science and Engineering
Building and Fire Research Laboratory
National Institute of Standards and Technology (NIST)

Science and Technology

Gaithersburg, MD 20899   301-975-6865

This division makes recommendations for upgrading fire safety of mass transportation vehicles such as subway cars and trains.

* Fire Science and Engineering

Fire Science and Engineering Division
Building and Fire Research Laboratory
National Institute of Standards and Technology (NIST)
Gaithersburg, MD 20899   301-975-6863

This Division develops new methods for determining fire hazard and risk and extends them into engineering practice. The division provides information and analytical methods for advancing the science of fire protection, develops comprehensive and user-friendly computer models of fire and its effects within complex structures, performs experiments and analysis on the growth and spread of fire on materials and within structures, and develops measurement techniques and analyses to study the dynamics of water in putting out fires. Sample outputs include a fire hazard assessment method that addresses smoke transport and the behavior and effects on people, a handbook of smoke control, an improved room fire growth computer model, and a salt water analog technique for determining the motion of smoke in complex structures. Contact this division for more information on fire science and engineering developments.

* Fire Sensing Research

Building and Fire Research Laboratory
National Institute of Standards and Technology (NIST)
Gaithersburg, MD 20899   301-975-6866

Researchers at the National Institute of Standards and Technology (NIST) are working on a new generation of fire detectors that will detect fires earlier and avoid the high current rate of false alarms generated by current sensing technologies.

* Fracture and Deformation Research

Materials Reliability Division
Institute for Materials Science and Engineering
National Institute of Standards and Technology (NIST)
Division 853.00
Boulder, CO 80303-3328   303-497-3268

Understanding how and why structural materials fail--the aim of the Materials Reliability Division--can yield enormous benefits. When used in the design and fabrication of structure, detailed, quantitative knowledge of the mechanics of fracture and deformation can improve safety and reliability, increase productivity, and even avert disaster, such as bridge collapses and railroad derailments that stem from stresses and flows in materials. The division's staff studies nonlinear fracture mechanics, arc physics, acoustoelasticity, the mechanics of composite materials, and the relationship between the structure, properties, and mechanical behavior of materials. Materials are examined over a wide range of temperatures. The division conducts studies for other government agencies and provides technical services to industry and public and private research institutions. For more information, contact this NIST division.

* Frequency, Time, and Phase Noise Measurement

Physics Laboratory
Division 847
National Institute of Standards and Technology (NIST)
Gaithersburg, MD 20899   301-975-4201

Advancements in communication and navigation systems require atomic oscillators with increased performance. NIST has several programs aimed at providing advanced frequency standards with the potential for benefitting commercial atomic standards. NIST has also begun a program to develop methods for measuring phase noise over a broad frequency range.

* Fuel Consumption Maximization

Chemical Science and Technology Laboratory
National Institute of Standards and Technology (NIST)
Gaithersburg, MD 20899   301-975-3145

NIST is working on research to help U.S. industry obtain maximum energy output from fuel consumption. The researchers are studying the dynamics of spray flames to investigate droplet vaporization, pyrolysis, combustion, and particulate formation processes and to delineate the effect of chemical and physical properties of fuels on the above processes. The research will lay the necessary groundwork for developing and validating spray combustion models.

* GATT Standards Code Activities of the National Bureau of Standards 1987

Office of Standards Code and Information
Administration Bldg
Gaithersburg, MD 20899   301-975-4029

GATT Standards Code Activities of the National Bureau of Standards 1987 is an annual report that describes the National Institute of Standards and Technology's (NIST) role over the past year as the official U.S. GATT (General Agreement on Tariffs and Trade) inquiry point for information on standards and certification activities that might significantly affect U.S. trade. The NIST effort included coordinating comments on proposed foreign regulations, translating of foreign texts, and operating the GATT "hotline" 301-975-4041, not toll free) that provides the latest information on foreign notifications from the GATT Secretariat in Geneva, Switzerland. The 1987 highlights were participation in the GATT Standards Code meeting on information exchange and the ISONET (International Organization for Standardization Information Network) workshop on international trade; publication of an introduction to standardization, certification, and laboratory accreditation; and background research for the Canadian Free Trade Agreement. Contact the office above to obtain a copy.

* Guest Researcher Opportunities in Building Technology

Building and Fire Research Laboratory
B222, Building Research Bldg
National Institute of Standards and Technology (NIST)
Gaithersburg, MD 20899   301-975-5900

The Center for Building Technology performs cooperative research with other organizations, private and public. There are many opportunities for engineers, scientists, and students from private and public organizations to participate in CBT research:

- Research Associates (from industry and academia),
- Guest Researchers (from U.S. and international organizations),
- Postdoctoral Research Associates (selected by National Academies),
- Engineers and Scientists from State and local governments,
- Visiting Scholars from universities, and
- Cooperative and Summer Students

Contact this office for more information on guest researcher opportunities.

* HAZARD I

National Technical Information Service
U.S. Department of Commerce
5825 Port Royal Rd.
Springfield, VA 22161   703-487-4650

Building and Fire Research Laboratory
Room A-247, Building 224
Gaithersburg, MD 20899   301-975-5900

HAZARD I is a method for predicting the hazards to the occupants of a building from a fire therein. Within prescribed limits, *HAZARD I* allows you to predict the outcome of a fire in a building populated by a representative set of occupants in terms of which persons successfully escape and which are killed, including the time, location, and likely cause of death for each. Specific applications vary, but some include material/product performance evaluation, fire reconstruction and litigation, evaluation of code changes or variances, fire department pre-planning, and extrapolation of fire test data to additional physical configurations. *HAZARD I* consists of a three volume report and a set of computer disks and costs $225 per copy from the National Fire Protection Association or the National Technical Information Service. Training programs are planned for a variety of target groups at the Center for Firesafety Studies. For more information, contact the Center for Fire Research.

* Hydrocarbon Engineering Properties

Office of Standard Reference Data
National Institute of Standards and Technology (NIST)
Gaithersburg, MD 20899   301-975-2208

A new database for calculating viscosity, density, and other important engineering property data of hydrocarbons--natural gas, petroleum, and organic materials, including mixtures of fluids--has been developed by National Institute of Standards and Technology (NIST). The "DDMIX" database was developed as part of a research project sponsored by an industry consortium of petroleum, chemical, and gas processing firms. Available on a floppy disk for personal computers, it provides rapid access to important information on the storage and transportation of fluids, and for the design of new chemical processes. Among other things, the program allows users to calculate quickly various thermodynamic and transport properties of fluid mixtures. To order the *DDMIX--Mixture Property Program (1988), NIST Standards Reference Database 14*, a floppy disk for personal computers for $400, contact the office above.

* Image Recognition
Computer Systems Laboratory
National Institute of Standards and Technology (NIST)
Gaithersburg, MD 20899   301-975-2080

Image-recognition research at NIST focuses on developing methods for evaluating image quality, compression efficiency, and image systems used in optical character recognition. The methods being developed are used for automated fingerprint recognition, automation of data entry from images of forms, and measurement of recognition systems on realistic applications.

* Industry Pollution Reduction
Chemical Science and Technology Laboratory
National Institute of Standards and Technology (NIST)
Gaithersburg, MD 20899   301-975-2610

The chemical and associated industries produce enormous amounts of byproducts. To avoid wasting industrial resources and polluting the environment, the impact of these byproducts must be minimized. The solution of the problem lies in the following: minimizing waste at the source by modifying industrial processes; recovering energy and chemicals for reuse; and converting pollutants to acceptable species. NIST is pursuing research in the area of thermal treatments, which seems to be the most promising approach to the problem. Contact NIST for information on facilities and current research.

* Industrial Quality Control
Office of Standard Reference Materials
National Measurement Laboratory
National Institute of Standards and Technology (NIST)
Gaithersburg, MD 20899   301-975-2016

The National Measurement Laboratory contributes to improved industrial quality control by developing Standard Reference Materials and calibrating equipment and devices. Contact this office for more information.

* Information Resource Dictionary System
Information Systems Engineering Division
Computer Systems Laboratory
National Institute of Standards and Technology (NIST)
Gaithersburg, MD 20899   301-975-2080

The Information Systems Engineering Laboratory research initiative resulted in the Information Resource Dictionary System (IRDS) standard and an IRDS prototype, a software system that records, stores, and processes information about an organization's data and data processing resources. The IRDS enables federal government users to improve productivity by identifying information resources that can be shared within an organization and between organizations. Contact this office for more information on IRDS and its uses.

* Information Services
Technology Services
Room A128, Administration Bldg
National Institute of Standards and Technology (NIST)
Gaithersburg, MD 20899   301-975-2790

The Office of Information Services maintains a comprehensive international collection of information in scientific disciplines such as metrology, mathematics, computer science, and materials science. The NIST staff participate in national and international publications and technical information networks and consortia, as well as a document exchange program to ensure that NIST publications are available to interested parties. An inquiries service assists the public in obtaining information about past and present NIST programs, projects, and publications.

* Information Systems Engineering Assistance
Information Systems Engineering Division
Computer Systems Laboratory
National Institute of Standards and Technology (NIST)
Gaithersburg, MD 20899   301-975-2080

The Information Systems Engineering Division supports standards development and provides technical assistance to government and industry in data administration; data

management; computer graphics; geographic information systems; standards validation; and programming language technologies. Contact this division for more information on available assistance.

* Information Technology Research
Information Systems Engineering Division
Computer Systems Laboratory
National Institute of Standards and Technology (NIST)
Gaithersburg, MD 20899   301-975-3262

The National Computer Systems Laboratory conducts research on parallel processing performance, speech recognition, and other rapidly evolving applications of information technology to provide a basis for standards development.

* Information Technology Standards
Information Systems Engineering Division
Computer Systems Laboratory
National Institute of Standards and Technology (NIST)
Gaithersburg, MD 20899   301-975-3262

The National Computer Systems Laboratory helps the information technology industry and users develop cost-effective national and international standards for open systems that erase incompatibility barriers and allow exchange of information between the systems of different manufacturers. Contact this division for more information.

* Integrated Services Digital Networks
Advanced Systems Division
Computer Systems Laboratory
National Institute of Standards and Technology (NIST)
Gaithersburg, MD 20899   301-975-2822

The National Computer Systems Laboratory (NSCL) investigates standards and develops conformance test methods for Integrated Services Digital Networks (ISDN), a new telecommunications technology that makes it possible to send and receive voice, data, and image signals simultaneously over digital telephone networks. Researchers in this area focus on the measurement capabilities and testbed facilities required to develop conformance tests and performance metrics for engineering ISDN standards. NCSL established the North American ISDN User's Forum to create a strong user voice in the implementation of ISDN. Contact this office for more information.

* Integrated-Circuit Test Structure Metrology
Electronics and Electrical Engineering Laboratory
Room B360
National Institute of Standards and Technology (NIST)
Gaithersburg, MD 20899   301-975-2070

Integrated-circuit (IC) test structures and test methods developed by NIST are used widely by the semiconductor industry and other government agencies. These devices can be used to evaluate manufacturing processes and equipment used to manufacture semiconductors and to test the reliability of the finished product. NIST engineers are investigating pattern recognition techniques for the rapid diagnosis of IC manufacturing processes and for establishing methods to determine the reliability of thin films used in state-of-the-art microcircuits.

* Intelligent Processing of Materials
Materials Science and Engineering Laboratory
National Institute of Standards and Technology (NIST)
Gaithersburg, MD 20899   301-975-5727

Advanced materials are capable of providing outstanding properties, but they generally require unusual processing operations and tend to be expensive. Intelligent processing offers the potential to design and produce materials with improved quality, reduced lead time, and increased production flexibility. Research sponsored by the Office of Intelligent Processing of Materials is directed to process models, sensors, and intelligent control systems.

* Laboratory Automation for Organic Analysis
Chemical Science and Technology Laboratory
National Institute of Standards and Technology (NIST)
Gaithersburg, MD 20899   301-975-3145

NIST has joined with industry and other government agencies in a cooperative project to develop automated analytical devices for organic analysis based on new chemistries and apparatus, as well as on laboratory robotic systems.

Be patient. If any phone number is incorrect, call (area code) 555-1212 and request the new listing.

989

Science and Technology

* Law Enforcement Standards Laboratory

Law Enforcement Standards Laboratory
National Institute of Standards and Technology (NIST)
Gaithersburg, MD 20899   301-975-2757

The Law Enforcement Standards Laboratory conducts research and provides technical services to the U.S. Department of Justice and State and local governments in support of law enforcement agencies. The division develops standards for police bullet-resistant equipment, handguns, shotguns, communications equipment, physical security equipment, tear gas devices, speed measuring devices, and evidential breath testers. The division also provides guides for selecting and applying commercial intrusion systems, facsimile equipment, and protective equipment. Technical reports on various related subjects such as handgun ammunition, blood/breath alcohol analysis, and arson investigation, are available. Contact this laboratory for more information.

* Low-Alloy Steel Calibration Standards

Office of Standard Reference Materials
National Institute of Standards and Technology (NIST)
Gaithersburg, MD 20899   301-975-2016

The National Institute of Standards and Technology (NIST) has developed a new graded series of seven low-alloy steel standards for calibrating optical emission and x-ray fluorescence spectrometers. Great care has been used in preparing these materials to obtain a high level of homogeneity to meet the demands of new, highly precise instruments used in the quality control of alloy materials. *Standard Reference Materials* (SRM's) 1761-1767, prepared in consultation with ASTM and industry, are available for $135 each in the form of disks approximately 34 mm in diameter and 19 mm thick. To obtain information on the certified values of each disk, or to order the new graded series of calibration standards, contact the office above.

* Low-Temperature Electronics

Electronics and Electrical Engineering Laboratory
Division 814.03
National Institute of Standards and Technology (NIST)
Boulder, CO 80303   303-497-3776

Cyrogenic, and especially superconducting electronics, provide remarkably high speed and sensitivity, coupled with exceptionally low power dissipation. The National Institute of Standards and Technology (NIST) has a complete facility for fabricating superconducting integrated circuits from conventional low-temperature superconductors and is developing a similar capability for high-temperature ceramic superconductors. NIST's work in this area has established numerous world performance records over the years with such devices as analogue-to-digital converters, samplers, electrometers, microwave and infrared detectors, lithographed antennas, and magnetic flux detectors using SQUIDs. NIST works closely with private industry in this area.

* Malcolm Baldrige National Quality Awards

National Institute of Standards and Technology (NIST)
Inquiries Unit
Administration Bldg
Gaithersburg, MD 20899   301-975-2758

A goal of the National Institute of Standards and Technology is to aid firms in building a competitive advantage. NIST manages the annual Malcolm Baldrige National Quality Awards to work towards this goal. Winning firms achieve continuous improvement in their manufacturing processes and final products. They, like formidable foreign competitors, have succeeded in meshing efficiency, flexibility, quality, and innovation in a single operation. Contact this office for more information on the awards.

* Manufacturing Engineering Publications

Manufacturing Engineering Laboratory
National Institute of Standards and Technology (NIST)
Technology Bldg
Gaithersburg, MD 20899   301-975-3400

The current edition of the *Publications of the Center for Manufacturing Engineering* covers the period January, 1978 through December, 1988. This listing reflects the diversity of scientific and technical problems which have been attacked over the past ten years in fulfillment of the Center's mission. Publications, indexed by subject area, cover research done by the Center in the areas of high precision dimensional measurement and precision engineering; robotics and intelligent machines; manufacturing data description, data administration, and information processing; and sensors for manufacturing processes. Contact this Center for a free copy.

* Manufacturing Engineering Research

Manufacturing Engineering Laboratory
Metrology Bldg
National Institute of Standards and Technology (NIST)
Gaithersburg, MD 20899   301-975-3400

The National Institute of Standards and Technology (NIST) is recognized as the Nation's finest general purpose scientific and engineering laboratory. The mission of the Center for Manufacturing Engineering is to bring the resources of this laboratory to bear on the standards and measurements problems associated with America's discrete parts manufacturing. In fulfillment of its mission, the Center conducts active programs of research in the areas of high precision dimensional measurement; sensing and measurement of force, sound, vibration, and surface finish characteristics; and application of advanced control and sensing techniques to automated machines, manufacturing systems, and robot manipulators. Contact this Center for more information on current research.

* Manufacturing Systems Integration

Manufacturing Engineering Laboratory
National Institute of Standards and Technology (NIST)
Gaithersburg, MD 20899   301-975-2298

Despite years of product development, truly modular, flexible, integrated manufacturing systems are still not prevalent in the U.S. Information sharing across engineering product management and control systems is still not possible. The National Institute of Standards and Technology (NIST) has begun a manufacturing systems integration project to develop a prototype environment for conducting integration experiments. NIST is working on this project with several major universities, auto companies, aerospace companies, and vendors. In a related project, NIST is researching the "process of design," with the hopes of creating a more integrated process rather than one-shot design programs.

* Manufacturing Technology Centers Program

Manufacturing Technology Centers Program
National Institute of Standards and Technology (NIST)
Gaithersburg, MD 20899   301-975-5020

To bring automated manufacturing technology to small- and mid-sized manufacturing firms, NIST has begun a manufacturing technology centers program. The program is designed to establish regional centers that will help these companies improve their technical capabilities and competitiveness. Their central activity is working hands-on with small and mid-size firms to 1) determine their particular technology needs; 2) develop a technology up-grade plan; 3) assist with business and financial planning to make the up-grade possible; and 4) help in the implementation of the new technology. The program will help to move new technology into the marketplace and will accelerate adoption of well-established "off-the-shelf" technologies to improve competitiveness of U.S.-based firms. The Centers invite inquiries from small and mid-sized manufacturers who want to find out more about their services. For more information about the program, or for phone numbers contact the above office or one of the following centers:

California Manufacturing Technology Center (MTC), Attn: John J. Chernesky, 13430 Hawthorne Blvd., Hawthorne, CA 90250; 310-355-3060.

Great Lakes Manufacturing Technology Center (MTC), Attn: George H. Sutherland, Prospect Park Bldg., 4600 Prospect Ave., Cleveland, OH 44105-4314; 216-432-5300.

Mid-America Manufacturing Technology Center (MTC), Attn: Paul E. Clay, Jr., 10561 Barkley, Suite 602, Overland Park, KS 66212; 913-649-4333.

Midwest Manufacturing Technology Center (MTC), Attn: Michael A. Taback, 2901 Hubbard Rd., Ann Arbor, MI 48105; 313-769-4377.

Northeast Manufacturing Technology Center (MTC), Attn: Mark Tebbano, 385 Jordan Rd., Troy, NY 12180-8347; 518-283-1010.

Southeast Manufacturing Technology Center (MTC), Attn: Jim Bishop, P.O. Box 1149, Columbia, SC 29202; 803-252-6976.

Upper Midwest Manufacturing Technology Center (MTC), Attn: Jan Pounds, 111 Third Ave., S., Suite 400, Minneapolis, MN 55401; 612-338-7722.

* Materials Science

Materials Science and Engineering Laboratory
National Institute of Standards and Technology (NIST)
Gaithersburg, MD 20899   301-975-5658

Be patient. If any phone number is incorrect, call (area code) 555-1212 and request the new listing.

Without new and better materials, technological progress would come to a halt. Increasingly, advances in fields ranging from electronics to construction depend on the mastery of an almost infinitesimally small domain, the arrangements of atoms and molecules that determine material properties. The Materials Science and Engineering Laboratory's (MSEL) research staff investigate all classes of advanced materials: ceramics, polymers, composites, and metallic alloys. The results are data, measurement tools, and services for understanding, improving, predicting, and controlling the processing and performance of materials. From autos to aerospace, improved materials are changing our lives. Car bodies and airplane parts are being made from polymer composites. Unconventional processing or synthesizing techniques are giving metal, ceramic, and polymer alloys increased strength or unusual properties. The laboratory consists of the following divisions:

Office of Intelligent Processing of Materials, B344 Materials Bldg; 301-975-5727
Ceramics Division, A256 Materials Bldg.; 301-975-6119
Fracture and Deformation Division, 430.0 NIST, Boulder, CO 80303; 303-497-3062
Polymers Division, A305 Polymer Bldg.; 301-975-6762
Metallurgy Division, B261 Materials Bldg.; 301-975-5963
Reactor Radiation Division, A106 Reactor Bldg.; 301-975-6210

* Materials Science and Engineering Laboratory Annual Report

Director, Materials Science and Engineering Laboratory
National Institute of Standards and Technology (NIST)
Gaithersburg, MD 20899   301-975-5658

The *Materials Science and Engineering Laboratory Annual Report* describes in detail the technical activities of each of the Laboratory's major units and is available on request from the Lab above.

* Mathematical Analysis

Mathematical Analysis Division
Computing and Applied Mathematics Laboratory
National Institute of Standards and Technology (NIST)
Gaithersburg, MD 20899   301-975-2732

The Mathematical Analysis Division provides consulting services in applied economics. The Division also performs research and collaborates in the application of mathematical analysis, mathematical modeling, and requisite computer-based methods to science and engineering. Contact this division for more information on the services offered, or the research conducted.

* Mathematical Software

Scientific Computing Division
Center for Applied Mathematics
National Engineering Laboratory
National Institute of Standards and Technology (NIST)
Gaithersburg, MD 20899   301-975-3834

The Center for Applied Mathematics puts out the *Guide to Available Mathematical Software*. Contact this office to obtain a copy.

* Measurement Technology

Office of Measurement Services
National Institute of Standards and Technology (NIST)
Gaithersburg, MD 20899   301-975-3143

The National Measurement Laboratory's researchers subscribe to the maxim: If a process cannot be measured or a product characterized, then it is not completely understood. Their work takes them to the frontiers of the physical and chemical sciences, the birthplace of many new technologies. And it takes them to the manufacturing floor, where their technical understanding is translated into sensors, analytical methods, and other tools required for efficient production of high-technology materials and products. NML also coordinates the U.S. measurement system with those of other nations, facilitating international trade. It consists of the following centers:

Center for Basic Standards, B160 Physics Bldg.; 301-975-4203
Center for Radiation Research, C229 Radiation Physics Bldg.; 301-975-6090
Center for Chemical Physics, A363 Physics Bldg.; 301-975-4500
Center for Analytical Chemistry, A309 Chemistry Bldg.; 301-975-3143
Office of Standard Reference Data, A323 Physics Bldg.; 301-975-2200
Office of Standard Reference Materials, B311 Chemistry Bldg.; 301-975-2012
Office of Physical Measurement Services, B362 Physics Bldg.; 301-975-2005

* Metals Quality and Cost

Metallurgy Division
Materials Science and Engineering Laboratory
National Institute of Standards and Technology (NIST)
Gaithersburg, MD 20899   301-975-5658

The Institute for Materials Science and Engineering works with the U.S. metals industry and other federal laboratories to develop and exploit technologies that will improve the quality and reduce the cost of domestic steel, aluminum, and other metals. For more information, contact this division.

* Metallurgy Process Control

Materials Science and Engineering Laboratory
National Institute of Standards and Technology (NIST)
Gaithersburg, MD 20899   301-975-5658

Special facilities at NIST enable researchers to develop advanced measurement methods and standards for application in process modeling and control for intelligent processing of materials. Measurement methods available include ultrasound, eddy currents, and acoustic emission. Coupled with state-of-the-art materials processing equipment and expertise these facilities offer a unique opportunity to ascertain feasibility and develop prototype specifications for a wide spectrum of sensor needs.

* Microwave/Millimeter-Wave Metrology

Electronics and Electrical Engineering Laboratory
National Institute of Standards and Technology (NIST)
Boulder, CO 80303   303-497-3066

Rapidly developing and expanding microwave technology requires research in advanced microwave measurements and standards. NIST researchers have developed highly accurate six-port techniques for automated measures of microwave power, attenuation, impedance, scattering parameters, and noise. They currently are developing greatly improved power and impedance standards and extending measurement services to cover millimeter waves and subminiature coaxial connectors.

* National Computer Systems Laboratory Newsletter

Computer Systems Laboratory
National Institute of Standards and Technology (NIST)
Gaithersburg, MD 20899   301-975-2822

Published every six weeks, the *National Computer Systems Laboratory Newsletter* includes information on conferences, Federal Information Processing Standards, and NCSL special publications. Contact this office for more information.

* National Engineering Laboratory

National Engineering Laboratory
National Institute of Standards and Technology (NIST)
Gaithersburg, MD 20899   301-975-2300

Scores of studies have emphasized the importance of manufacturing to the competitive position of U.S. industry. The National Engineering Laboratory researchers are making accelerated efforts to provide the measurements and technology U.S. firms need to compete in burgeoning markets for ever faster semiconductors and optical communications equipment. On NEL's agenda are safety, public health, and the environment, as reflected in studies of fire prevention, evaluations of alternatives to ozone-depleting chlorofluorocarbons, and research supporting development of effective building regulations. It consists of the following centers:

Center for Computing and Applied Mathematics, A438 Administration Bldg.; 301-975-2728
Center for Electronics and Electrical Engineering, B358 Metrology Bldg.; 301-975-2220
Center for Manufacturing Engineering, B322 Metrology Bldg.; 301-975-3400
Center for Building Technology, B250 Building Research Bldg.; 301-975-5900
Center for Fire Research, A247 Polymer Bldg.; 301-975-6850
Center for Chemical Engineering, 770.0, NIST, Boulder, CO 80303; 303-497-5108

* National Innovation Workshops

Office of Energy-Related Inventions
National Institute of Standards and Technology (NIST)
Gaithersburg, MD 20899   301-975-5500

The Office of Energy-Related Inventions conducts a series of National Innovation Workshops for inventors and small businesses. Contact this office for more information.

Science and Technology

* National Measurement Standards

Center for Basic Standards, B160 Physics Bldg
National Institute of Standards and Technology (NIST)
Gaithersburg, MD 20899   301-975-4023

The National Measurement Laboratory maintains and improves national standards for mass, length, time, temperature, and electric current. Inquiries should be directed to this Center.

* National Technical Information Service

National Technical Information Service
U.S. Department of Commerce
5825 Port Royal Rd.
Springfield, VA 22161   703-487-4650

The National Institute of Standards and Technology publications are sold by the National Technical Information Service. They can supply microfiche, or paper copy from microfiche, at any time. *Federal Information Processing Standards, NIST Interagency Reports* (a special series of interim or final reports on work performed by NIST for outside sponsors), and *Grant/Contract Reports* are available only from NTIS. Place orders on 800-336-4700. For more information call the office above.

* Network Management

Computer Systems Laboratory
B217 Technology Bldg
National Institute of Standards and Technology (NIST)
Gaithersburg, MD 20899   301-975-3669

NIST researchers are working with industry to establish a set of standards for exchanging network management information between heterogeneous management systems. Their goal is to establish a standard enabling integrated, interoperable, automated management of multivendor computer systems, routers, bridges, switches, multiplexors, modems, and provider services.

* Neutron-Scattering Experiments

Reactor Radiation Division
Institute for Materials Science and Engineering
National Institute of Standards and Technology (NIST)
A106, Reactor
Gaithersburg, MD 20899   301-975-6226

Neutron-scattering methods of research permit studies of bulk samples, often yielding information on submicroscopic materials behavior and structure that is unsurpassed in detail and accuracy. Division scientists are engaged in a broad research program aimed at understanding and measuring the structure and properties of virtually all classes of materials used by industry, including high-temperature superconductors, advanced ceramics, catalysts, artificially structured materials, hydrogen in metals, and others that hold promise for high-technology applications. They are also furthering the uses of neutron diffraction and radiography for nondestructive evaluation. Other activities include efforts to develop new instrumentation and to strengthen the theoretical foundation of neutron-scattering research. Contact the office above for information on free services, including descriptive literature, telephone or on-site descriptions of the facilities, and discussion of problems.

* NIST List of Publications by Subject Category

National Institute of Standards and Technology (NIST)
U.S. Department of Commerce
Publications and Program Inquiries
E128 Administration Bldg
Gaithersburg, MD 20899   301-975-3058

A complimentary abridged journal of research, the *NIST List of Publications by Subject Category* compiles the NIST publications that are available, along with ordering information. It also contains a listing of depository libraries and a listing of Dept. of Commerce District Offices, two other sources of NIST publications.

* NIST Nonperiodical Technical Publications

Superintendent of Documents
Government Printing Office
Washington, DC 20402   202-512-1800

The nonperiodical publications from the National Institute of Standards and Technology include:

Monographs. Major contributions to the technical literature on various subjects related to the Institute's scientific and technical activities.

Handbooks. Recommended codes of engineering and industrial practice (including safety codes) developed in cooperation with interested industries, professional organizations, and regulatory bodies.

Special Publications. Includes proceedings of conferences sponsored by NIST, NIST annual reports, and other special publications appropriate to this grouping such as wall charts, pocket cards, and bibliographies.

Applied Mathematics Series. Mathematical tables, manuals, and studies of special interest to physicists, engineers, chemists, biologists, mathematicians, computer programmers, and others engaged in scientific and technical work.

National Standard Reference Data Series. Provides quantitative data on the physical and chemical properties of materials, compiled from the world's literature and critically evaluated.

Building Science Series. Disseminates technical information developed at the Institute on building materials, components, systems, and whole structures. The series presents research results, test methods, and performance criteria related to the structural and environmental functions and the durability and safety characteristics of building elements and systems.

Technical Notes. Studies or reports which are complete in themselves but restrictive in their treatment of a subject. Analogous to monographs but not so comprehensive in scope or definitive in treatment of the subject area. Often serve as a vehicle for final reports of work performed at NIST under the sponsorship of other government agencies.

Voluntary Product Standards. Developed under procedures published by the U.S. Department of Commerce, these standards establish nationally recognized requirements for products, and provide all concerned interests with a basis for common understanding of the characteristics of the products. NIST administers this program as a supplement to the activities of the private sector standardizing organizations.

Consumer Information Series. Practical information, based on NIST research and experience, covering areas of interest to the consumer. Easily understandable language and illustrations provide useful background knowledge for shopping in today's technological marketplace.

Order the above NIST publications from the Government Printing Office (see the address listed above).

* NIST Research Reports

Public Information Division
National Institute of Standards and Technology (NIST)
A903 Administration Bldg
Gaithersburg, MD 20899   301-975-3058

NIST Research Reports is a special publication which includes a research update, a listing of new NIST publications, and a conference calendar. It also includes specific NIST research reports of general public interest. Contact this office to obtain a copy.

* Nondestructive Evaluation Research

Office of Intelligent Processing of Materials
Materials Science and Engineering Laboratory
National Institute of Standards and Technology (NIST)
B344, Materials Bldg
Gaithersburg, MD 20899   301-975-6227

Nondestructive evaluation (NDE) is concerned with inspecting structures and products such as nuclear reactors, aircraft, and pipelines--an essential component of safety programs. Researchers are also concerned with monitoring important properties and characteristics of materials while they are being processed. In this capacity, NDE provides the information necessary for guiding or controlling production processes, assuring uniform high-quality products, and reducing waste. Contact the office above for more information.

* Non-Energy Invention Assistance

Office of Non-Energy Inventions
National Engineering Laboratory
National Institute of Standards and Technology (NIST)
Gaithersburg, MD 20899   301-975-5504

The National Institute of Standards and Technology (NIST) is developing a new program to reach out to individuals. Any inventor will be able to submit an invention to NIST for evaluation, so long as it is non-nuclear. Drawing on a national network of science and engineering consultants, NIST--for *free*--will evaluate the technical feasibility and marketability of the invention: Will it work? Will anyone buy it? Recommendations for support will go elsewhere for marketing assistance or development grants. This program is not yet operational as it is awaiting congressional approval, but if you wish to submit a non-energy invention to the program, you may put your name on a waiting list. For more information, contact the office above.

* Oil Spill Cleanup

National Institute of Standards and Technology (NIST)
Gaithersburg, MD 20899   301-975-6668

In the wake of the Exxon Valdez accident and the Persian Gulf War, researchers have been searching for better ways to cleanup oil spills. One possible solution would be to burn the oil. Researchers at the National Institute of Standards and Technology (NIST) have developed methods for more accurately determining the airborne concentration of smoke particles billowing off major oil fires. Using this information, local authorities may decide that less environmental damage would be caused by burning the oil than by other cleanup options.

* Open Systems Interconnection Technology

Systems and Network Architecture Division
National Computer Systems Laboratory
National Institute of Standards and Technology (NIST)
Building 225
Gaithersburg, MD 20899   301-975-2822

The National Computer Systems Laboratory supports private industry and government through testing and standards implementation activities. For example, the Laboratory established OSINET, a cooperative government/ industry research network which tests commercial Open Systems Interconnection (OSI) technology products to see how well they operate together. Contact this division for more information about the program to advance the standards necessary for effective integrated network management.

* Optical Disk Media

Advanced Systems Division
National Computer Systems Laboratory
National Institute of Standards and Technology (NIST)
Building 225
Gaithersburg, MD 20899   301-975-2904

The National Computer Systems Laboratory is developing a testing methodology that predicts life expectancy of optical disk media. This research will assist government managers in planning how long information may safely be stored on these media. Contact this office for more information.

* Optical Electronics Research

Electronics and Electrical Engineering Laboratory
Div. 814.02
National Institute of Standards and Technology (NIST)
Boulder, CO 80303   303-497-5341

Researchers at the National Institute of Standards and Technology (NIST) are studying optical fiber measurements, optical communication device metrology, laser measurements, and optical fiber sensors. This research results in publication of new technology and measurement procedures and calibration services to support the laser and optical communications industries.

* Origins of Historical Artifacts

Materials Science and Engineering Laboratory
National Institute of Science and Technology (NIST)
B309 Materials Bldg
Gaithersburg, MD 20899   301-975-5658

In a remote Asian village, an archaeologist unearths a bronze art object. Though the object appears similar to many discovered in other excavations, a basic question must be answered before it can be catalogued or displayed in a museum: Where did it originate? More specifically, where did the raw materials come from that make up the object? One of the most useful techniques of tracing an ancient artifact or verifying the authenticity of a piece is lead isotope ratio analysis. Scientists at the National Institute of Standards and Technology are using the technique in collaboration with museum researchers who seek to pinpoint just where precious art pieces come from. For more information, contact this laboratory.

* Phase Diagram Databases

Institute for Materials Science and Engineering
National Institute of Standards and Technology (NIST)
Gaithersburg, MD 20899   301-975-5658

The Institute for Materials Science and Engineering works with professional societies to develop phase diagram databases that will help improve processing control and use of metals, ceramics, and polymers. For more information, contact this Institute.

* Photoduplicated Copies of NBS Publications

Photoduplication Service
Library of Congress
Washington, DC 20540   202-287-5640

Photoduplicated copies of many old National Bureau of Standards publications can be purchased from this Library of Congress service.

* Polymer Composites

Materials Science and Engineering Laboratory
National Institute of Standards and Technology (NIST)
Gaithersburg, MD 20899   301-975-6762

Researchers in industry, universities, and government are invited to participate in an NIST research program that addresses the most critical barriers in high-performance polymer composite processing which producers must overcome to meet increasing international competition. The U.S. market for high technology plastic products is expected to grow. The United States now has the technological lead in the use of high performance polymer composites in defense and aerospace applications. In high-volume mass markets, however, U.S. industries face intense competition. For more information, contact Donald L. Hunston at the above office.

* Polymer Science

Polymers Division
Materials Science and Engineering Laboratory
National Institute of Standards and Technology (NIST)
Gaithersburg, MD 20899   301-975-6762

The uses of polymers and polymer-based composites are virtually unlimited, and the materials are even displacing metals in many structural and high-performance applications, including automobiles and commercial and military aircraft. Advances in polymer science have paced important technological developments. The Polymers Division supports U.S. industries that produce, process, or use synthetic polymers. Its basic research programs are devoted to strengthening the scientific foundation that sustains continued advances in this important class of materials. These programs are designed according to the perceived needs of industry. The division is developing novel sensors for monitoring viscosity, flow, molecular orientation, and mixing. For more information on polymers research, contact this NIST division.

* Product Development Exchange Research

Manufacturing Engineering Laboratory
National Institute of Standards and Technology (NIST)
Gaithersburg, MD 20899   301-975-3400

Product data is an integral part of the information shared across computer applications and organizations forming a critical part of any integration scheme. Currently no commercial products exist that allow systems to share information in a standard way so as to be integrated. The Standard for the Exchange of Product Model Data (STEP) will help to alleviate the integration problem. NIST is also working on testing STEP, evaluating proposed standards with respect to applications.

* Protecting Computerized Information

Computer Security Division
Computer Systems Laboratory
National Institute of Standards and Technology (NIST)
Gaithersburg, MD 20899   301-975-2934

The National Computer Systems Laboratory develops standards and guidelines for protecting computerized information from threats of all kinds--operator error, power losses, natural disasters, and unauthorized users. Contact this division for more information.

* Quality Assurance

Building and Fire Research Laboratory
National Institute of Standards and Technology (NIST)
Building Research Laboratory
Gaithersburg, MD 20899   301-975-6850

Science and Technology

The Center for Building Technology provides a quality assurance program for over 1000 public and private construction materials testing laboratories nationwide that is relied upon by owners, designers, builders, and State and local governments responsible for buildings and transportation facilities. Contact this Center for more information on the Quality Assurance Program.

* Quality in Automation Program

Manufacturing Engineering Laboratory
B106 Sound
National Institute of Standards and Technology (NIST)
Gaithersburg, MD 20899   301-975-6618

This program is an effort to achieve higher part accuracy from existing discrete parts manufacturing equipment. A four layer closed loop control architecture has been proposed, and three layers are presently being implemented. The Real Time and Process Intermittent loops use algorithms to predict systematic errors and compensate for them in real time. The Post Process loop verifies the cutting process and is also a check for errors that evade the first two loops. NIST is also working on research in machine tool performance, based on the premise that errors in manufacturing are repeatable, and thus predictable and correctable. Working closely with academia and industry, this research should result in improved manufacturing quality in the future.

* Radiation Measurements

Center for Radiation Research
National Measurement Laboratory
National Institute of Standards and Technology (NIST)
Radiation Physics Bldg
Gaithersburg, MD 20899   301-975-5541

The National Measurement Laboratory designs dosimeters used to assure accurate measurement of radiation for diagnostic and therapeutic uses, personnel monitoring, and the production of materials. Contact this Center for more information on radiation measurement.

* Radiation Research

Center for Radiation Research
National Institute of Science and Technology (NIST)
Radiation Physics Bldg
Gaithersburg, MD 20899   301-975-5541

The Center for Radiation Research develops and maintains the scientific competencies and experimental facilities necessary to provide the Nation with a central basis for uniform physical measurements, measurement methodology, and measurement services in the areas of near infra-red radiation, optical radiation, ultraviolet radiation, and ionizing radiation; provides government, industry, and the academic community with essential calibrations for field radiation measurements needed in such applied areas as nuclear power, lighting, solar radiation processing, advanced laser development, and radiation protection for public safety; and carries out research in order to develop improved radiation standards, new radiation measurement technology, and improved understanding of atomic, molecular, and ionizing radiation processes, and to elucidate the interaction of radiation and particles with inanimate and biological materials. Contact this Center for a copy of the annual report summarizing the activities that were carried out in 1989, and listing publications, talks, and professional interactions.

* Research and Testing Facilities

National Institute of Standards and Technology (NIST)
U.S. Department of Commerce
E128 Administration Bldg
Gaithersburg, MD 20899   301-975-2758

The NIST has some of the premier research and testing facilities in the United States, several of which are unequaled anywhere in the world. To aid firms in building a competitive advantage, NIST makes available for cooperative and proprietary work its varied research and testing facilities at its headquarters in Gaithersburg, Maryland, and its site in Boulder, Colorado. To contact a facility, see the previous listing of centers and laboratories. The following is a listing of some of the special facilities that are available to conduct research at various centers and laboratories:

Chemical Science and Technology Laboratory

Research Reactor

NIST has a 20-megawatt research reactor used in materials research, molecular structure determination, and neutron activation analysis. This analysis is applicable to a wide variety of biomedical problems such as nutrition, the role of trace elements in human development, bioaccumulation, the role of trace elements in disease processes, investigations of metal-containing drugs, and utilization of cold neutrons.

Microprobe Facilities

The Center's microanalysis facilities are among the most advanced and complete in the world. Instruments include an analytical electron microscope, ion microprobe, secondary ion mass spectrometer, time of flight secondary ion mass spectrometer, laser microprobe mass analyzer, and a Raman microprobe. The latter two instruments provide molecular information from micro-regions and offer great potential in biomedical applications.

Trace Element Facilities

The Center for Analytical Chemistry has a wide variety of instruments used for the determination of trace element concentrations in virtually any matrix. These instruments include the following: atomic absorption spectrometer, spark atomic emission spectrometer, inductively coupled plasma spectrometer, dc plasma spectrometer, laser enhanced ionization spectrometer, spark source mass spectrometer, thermal ionization mass spectrometer, electrochemical analyzers, neutron activation analysis

Trace Organic Analysis

The Center performs basic and applied research in many areas of organic analysis. They have a variety of research instruments for this research.

Specimen Bank Research Facility

This facility contains separate clean areas for organic and inorganic sample preparation, biohazard hoods, cryogenic homogenization apparatus, and low temperature storage facilities. The specimen bank project is part of a multi-agency program in environmental monitoring and health research.

Ultrapure Reagents Facility

Modern trace analysis requires the use of high-purity reagents to minimize contamination problems commonly associated with measurements at parts-per-million and lower levels. A new reagents facility has been completed for the preparation of key trace analytical reagents.

Fluid Metering Research Facility

This facility combines primary calibration techniques with the capability to conduct detailed surveys of fluid velocity profiles in temperature controlled water flows using laser Doppler velocimetry (LDV). An industry - government consortium currently supports a research program on flowmeter installation effects, and the US Navy is sponsoring a series of tests to assess the performance of selected flow transfer standards in a range of non-ideal conditions. It is also used to generate critical databases to update the national standards on generic fluid metering topics.

Nitrogen Flow Measurement Facility

The facility is a mass-based reference system capable of both liquid and gas flow measurement. Well instrumented for temperature and pressure, the facility is adaptable and capable of a variety of piping arrangements. The Flow Facility can be used for testing a variety of flow measurement instrumentation, including flow meters, temperature sensors, pressure sensors, and densimeters.

Neutron Depth Profiling Facility

This facility uses a neutron beam for non-destructive evaluation of elemental depth distribution materials. Working with the Institute's 20MW nuclear reactor, researchers use the technique to provide concentration profiles for characterizing the near-surface regime of semiconductors, metals, glasses, and polymers to depths of several micrometers. With the neutron beam provided by the reactor, depth profiling can be carried out with sensitivities approaching 10^{13} atoms/cm^2.

Manufacturing Engineering Laboratory

Automated Manufacturing Research Facility

This facility is the major national laboratory for research in automated manufacturing. The facility provides a "test-bed" where researchers from NIST, industrial firms, universities, and other government agencies can work together on projects of mutual interest. Their research concentrates on the standards and measurement techniques required for successful automated manufacturing. The supporting technology for future computer integrated manufacturing systems are developed.

Computing and Applied Mathematics Laboratory

Consolidated Scientific Computing System

This major computation facility provides services through telecommunications links.

Evans and Sutherland PS-300 Dynamical Graphics System

This facility provides local display at video rates and includes 3-D perspective and orthographics projections, zoom, rotation and scaling on three axes, and variable-depth contrast. Transformed data may be transmitted back to the host computer after graphical treatment is completed. The system offers a "window" capability for difficult mathematical operations, such as the problem of visualizing a large data set at some intermediate stage of a large scale computation.

Raster Technologies ONE/380 Graphics System

This facility provides high resolution color raster images of three-dimensional objects or 24-bit color imaging data. The objects may be point clouds, wire frames, or solid objects with hidden surface removal, and lighting models for solid rendering. Local object manipulations include perspective or orthographic projections, translation, rotation, and scaling in three axes. All local operational parameters can be recovered by the host computer. High level graphics software available for major host computers at NIST supports this terminal. Applications include CAD/CAM rendering, four-dimensional data using color as the fourth dimension, and interaction with mathematical models through surface rendering.

Electronics and Electrical Engineering Laboratory

Data Converter Testing Facility

This facility offers regular calibration service for static parameters of high-accuracy A/D and D/A converters, particularly for linearity and differential linearity measurements. The facility also includes testing of data converters under certain dynamic conditions, e.g., settling time measurements and noise measurements.

High Voltage Measurement Facility

This facility provides tests at high voltages requiring accurate measurements and sensitive diagnostics. The equipment includes high-speed photographic equipment for electrical breakdown diagnostics, Kerr effect electro-optical equipment for space charge diagnostics, equipment for partial discharge measurements, and equipment for dielectric loss measurements. Additionally, precision dividers provide for high voltage measurements under steady-state and transient conditions.

Semiconductor Processing Facility

This facility occupies about 4,000 sq. ft. of space, half of it clean room space, and has the capability of state-of-the-art semiconductor processing for research applications. It produces specialized test specimens, experimental samples, customized device prototypes, and carefully prepared materials under extremely well-controlled and flexible conditions.

Antenna Scanning Facility

The planar, near-field antenna scanning range in Boulder, Colorado, represents the state-of-the-art in measurement accuracy for such facilities, utilizing a highly accurate verified technique. It can be used to characterize antennas of various types indoors, at lower cost, at high accuracies, and with more resultant information than that yielded by conventional outdoor antenna range techniques. It can also be used for measurements not possible inn other types of facilities. Using theory, new measurement techniques, and computer software, a laser interferometer controlled probe precisely scans the antenna under test to determine near-field antenna parameters which are then converted to the desired far-field characteristics.

Near Field Scanning Facility for Antenna Measurements

The automated facility is designed to measure the near-zone phase and amplitude distributions of the fields radiated from an antenna under test. Mathematical transformations are used to calculate the desired antenna characteristics. The facility has several applications. Its primary use is for determining the gain, pattern and polarization of antennas. Near-field data can also be used to compute near-field interactions of antennas and radiated field distributions in the near zone. Near-field scanning is also a valuable took for identifying problems and for achieving optimal performance of various types of antenna systems.

Electromagnetic Anechoic Chamber

The electromagnetic anechoic chamber is a facility for generating standard (known) electronic fields which are fundamental to the research, development, and evaluation of antennas field probes, and EM material properties.

Manufacturing Engineering Laboratory

Automated Manufacturing Research Facility

This facility is a research laboratory for study of the measurement and standards problems of the "factory of the future." An extensive network of computers makes up the real-time control, distributed data administration, and manufacturing engineering elements of the facility. Research is currently supported on sensors, real-time control, deterministic metrology, production management and scheduling, data administration, communications, and preparation of manufacturing data.

Acoustical Anechoic Chamber

This facility provides a free-field environment for research and calibrations on measurement of the directivity of sound sources and the directional response of microphones and sensor arrays.

Building and Fire Research Laboratory

Large Scale Structural Test Facility

This facility, with a 45 foot reaction wall and its 12-million pound capacity universal testing machine, is capable of testing large-scale structural components 60-feet in length. Specimens can also be subjected to lateral loading up to 1 million pounds. It is the largest facility of its kind in the free world.

Tri-Directional Structural Testing Facility

This facility is a unique computer-controlled apparatus capable of applying forces or displacements in three directions simultaneously to large-scale structural components and systems. This facility currently supports the National Institute of Standards and Technology's (NIST) research role in developing seismic design and construction standards for reducing the hazards of earthquakes.

Environmental Chambers

These facilities support development of thermal performance modeling techniques required for predicting human comfort, energy efficiency, and fire safety in buildings. The chambers can automatically control temperatures with automatic humidity control.

Calibrated Hot-Box Facility

This facility provides precise measurements of heat, air, and moisture transfer through full-scale building wall and roof sections including door and window openings. The facility can simulate worldwide climatic conditions through the use of temperature, humidity, and air control. The measurements provide the basis for standard measurement methods used in private laboratories.

Reverberation Chamber

This facility is used to develop sound pressure coefficients and to calibrate test equipment in other laboratories. The chamber supports research to define the acoustical parameters for building materials and spaces and to develop models and test methods for evaluating acoustical performance.

Construction Materials Reference Laboratories

In conjunction with other laboratories, this facility serves over 1,000 public and private laboratories nationwide by providing proficiency samples, inspections, and field test methods for cost effective quality assurance in materials.

Outdoor Energy Conservation Test Site

This facility includes a passive solar test house containing over 400 sensors and transducers for measuring the thermal performance of such solar features as clerestory windows, mass storage wall, and direct-gain cell. Six single-room test houses provide data on heat exchange. Other facilities study solar heat pumps and domestic hot water systems.

Image Analysis Laboratory

This facility has two special-purpose image analysis computers and cameras for obtaining images and converting them into digital form. The facility is used extensively in studies of materials degradation involving images from the scanning electron microscope or photographs of surfaces of full-scale structures.

Fire Test Building

This facility is designed for large scale fire experiments. Smoke abatement equipment permits large fires to be conducted safely without pollution of the environment. Some of the experimental capabilities are single room fire experiments; room-corridor fire experiments; rate of heat release (small to large scale including material samples, single items of furniture, full size rooms); fire endurance furnace with unique high rate of temperature increase capability; room-corridor smoke travel experiments; and two-story smoke travel experiments.

NIST Annex

This facility serves as a field station for experiments not readily accommodated in the main laboratories. Some of the experimental capabilities include multiroom single story structure for smoke movement studies; two story, four bay, steel frame structure for studies of steel framing movement and deflection and floor/ceiling performance with significant fire exposures; compartment fire facility for studying vent flows; sprinkler facility for droplet distribution studies; small scale gas-well simulation blow-out experiment; small scale aircraft cabin fire experiment.

Center for Fire Research Laboratory Facilities

The Center for Fire Research Laboratories' facilities include Lateral Ignition and

Be patient. If any phone number is incorrect, call (area code) 555-1212 and request the new listing.

995

Science and Technology

Flame Spread Test for wall materials; vertical flame heat transfer rig; salt water smoke movement analog facilities; Fire Simulation Laboratory with dedicated mini-computer and high resolution graphics capability; apparatus for combustion product toxicity studies; Fire Research Information Service--a library of over 30,000 fire research documents; droplet imaging system for size and velocity distribution measurements in sprays.

National Measurement Laboratory

Materials Science and Engineering Laboratory
The specialized facilities include an array of metals and ceramics laboratories for controlled materials synthesis and process; a 12-million-pound test rig for evaluating large-scale mechanical material properties; experimental stations for studying arc-welding processes; specialized small-angle and texture x-ray diffractometers particularly suited for polymer characterization; and a 20-megawatt reactor for neutron scattering experiments.

Metals Processing Laboratory
This NIST laboratory contains special facilities for the production of rapidly solidified alloys, including equipment for gas atomization and electrohydrodynamic atomization to produce rapidly solidified alloy powders, melt spinning to produce rapidly solidified alloy ribbons, and electron beam surface melting to produce rapidly solidified surface layers. These facilities are designed to produce alloy research samples that otherwise are difficult for users to obtain. Typically, industrial companies or universities send workers to NIST to participate in preparing alloys of special industrial and scientific interest for further analyses in their home laboratories and to collaborate NIST scientists in investigations of generic relationships between processing conditions and resulting alloy microstructures and their properties.

Polymer Composite Fabrication Facility
This facility permits the preparation of well-controlled polymer composite samples for scientific studies and the evaluation of results from NIST's processing science program in a realistic fabrication environment. This lab can be used for a variety of fiber related studies.

Powder Characterization and Processing Laboratory
This facility offers specialized instrumentation for measuring physical properties, phase composition, and surface chemical properties of powders. Facilities also exist for processing and synthesizing ultrapure powders. Some of this labs capabilities include: physical properties, surface, and interface chemistry measurements; phase composition research; solid state imaging, for the identification of impurities, chemical state, and composition; powder synthesis and colloidal suspensions.

Mechanical Behavior Laboratories
Mechanical property measurement facilities at NIST permit characterization of all mechanical properties over a wide range of force levels and temperatures. Facilities are available for outside sponsors and tests can be conducted at temperatures ranging from 4 degrees Kelvin to 2800 degrees Kelvin.

Small-Angle X-Ray Scattering Facility
Small angle x-ray scattering is a technique used to probe the structures of materials on the scale size of 0.1nm to 100nm. Materials exhibiting structure in this size range include polymers, biological macromolecules, ceramics, metals, and alloys. This technique is used to study molecular conformation, microphase domain structures, crystallization phenomena, network formation, craze initiation, void distribution, and other phenomena resulting from fluctuation in the electron density within a material.

Cold Neutron Research Facility
This facility is the nation's first for "cold Neutron" studies, filling a serious void in the nation's materials science and engineering research. The facility provides beams of deeply penetrating low-energy neutrons, essential for important experiments that are impractical or even impossible with conventional neutron sources. The facility is available to all U.S. users for the study of materials research, molecular structure determination, and neutron activation analysis.

Center for Chemical Engineering

Gas Flow Measurement Facility/Boulder
This facility measures the flow rate of gas on a mass basis. Gas flows through the meter to be tested and then is condensed by passing the gas through a cryogenic system and into a weigh tank. The time integrated mass flow rate passing through the test meter is the same as the mass accumulated in the weigh tank. This facility provides high accuracy and the only mass-based continuous gas flow measurement in the world.

Computer Systems Laboratory

CD-ROM Technology Evaluation Laboratory
The Compact Disk-Read Only Memory technology evaluation laboratory provides a site where Federal users can evaluate CD-ROM hardware and retrieval systems. More than 25 CD-ROM disks and 6 CD-ROM players have been installed; the National Computer Systems Laboratory solicited disk and equipment donations for the laboratory from the private sector. Other available CD-ROM databases include library catalogs, journal indexes, zip code directories, dictionaries, and product catalogs. CD-ROM drives and interfaces include systems manufactured by Phillips, Toshiba, Hitachi, and Sony.

Information Systems Engineering Facility
This facility consists of labs with computer hardware and software needed for research and development of standards, guidance to federal agencies, and validation tests. The following areas are included: graphics; programming languages; database management systems; distributed database management systems; object database management; data dictionary systems; data administration, especially database design; data interchange; knowledge-based and expert systems; and geographic information systems.

Computer and Network Security Facility.
The NIST computer and network security facility is used to improve the current security posture of federal computer and telecommunication systems ad to provide security for these systems as they migrate toward open system environments. Research done in the facility is aimed at applying methods to protect the secrecy and integrity of information in computer systems and data networks; evaluating personal identification and authentication techniques to control access to information resources; and developing computer and network security architectures to determine proper implementation of controls for integrity and confidentiality of information and authentication of users.

ISDN and Distributed Systems Facility
The NIST Integrated Services Digital Network (ISDN) and distributed systems facility provides laboratories for research and development, standards, and conformance testing in distributed computer systems and advanced computer communications, including ISDN and the fiber distributed data interface (FDDI). Significant research and development programs include open distributed systems, transaction processing, distributed multimedia, ISDN applications, ISDN conformance testing and broadband ISDN.

Physics Laboratory

Synchrotron Ultraviolet Radiation Facility-II
The SURF-II is a 300 MeV electron storage ring that radiates synchrotron radiation which is highly collimated, nearly linearly polarized, and of calculable intensity. It is well suited for studies in radiometry, atomic, molecular, bimolecular, and solid-state physics, surface and materials science, electro-optics, and surface chemistry and radiation effects on matter.

Low Background Infrared Radiation Facility
In this facility, radiant background noise levels less than a few nanowatts are attained in a large vacuum chamber by cooling internal cryoshields to temperatures less than 20K using a closed cycle helium refrigerator system. This unique facility can be used to measure total radiant power from sources such as cryogenic blackbodies. Ongoing improvements will allow measurement of spectral distribution of radiation from sources and characterization of infrared detectors and optical components.

Electronic Paramagnetic Resonance Facility
The National Institute of Standards and Technology (NIST) is leading a national and international effort in electron paramagnetic resonance dosimetry for measuring ionizing radiation. In the EPR experiment, irradiated materials are placed in a magnetic field and electron spin transitions are induced by an electromagnetic field of the appropriate frequency. This process is used as a non-destructive probe of the structure and concentration of paramagnetic centers. Industrial applications include radiation protection/accident dosimetry, for retrospective dose assessment of clothing or biological tissue; clinical radiology, ionizing radiation doses administered in cancer therapy can be measured for enteral beam therapy using dosimeters of crystalline alanine or validated for internally bone seeking radiopharmaceuticals using bone biopsies; industrial radiation processing, monitoring of radiation process meats, shellfish, and fruits using bone, shell, or seed.

Radiopharmaceutical Standardization Laboratory
Radioactivity measurements for diagnostic and therapeutic nuclear medicine in the U.S. are based on measurements at NIST. Recent development work has focused on therapeutic nuclides for nuclear medicine, radioimmunotherapy, and bone palliation.

Be patient. If any phone number is incorrect, call (area code) 555-1212 and request the new listing.

The lab provides calibration for gamma ray emitting radionuclides equipment for users requiring higher standards than can be attained using commercial equipment.

Magnetic Microstructure Measurement Facility
The magnetic microstructure of materials can be measured with very high spatial resolution by a technique called scanning electron microscopy with polarization analysis. This unique measurement facility can be used for research in magnetic thin films, high-coercivity magnetic materials, high density magnetic storage media, and other advanced magnetic materials.

* Research Associate Program
Office of Research and Technology Applications
National Institute of Standards and Technology (NIST)
Room A537, Administration Bldg
Gaithersburg, MD 20899   301-975-4016
The National Institute of Standards and Technology's Research Associate Program is an effective means for the transfer of technology, and in particular, measurement technology. The Program offers the opportunity to work under the supervision of and consult with NIST professionals of recognized stature in their fields, makes available the extensive laboratory and related facilities at NIST, and is an effective means of communicating industrial views and needs directly to NIST. Contact this office for more detailed information.

* Research of the National Institute of Standards and Technology (NIST)
Superintendent of Documents
Government Printing Office
Washington, DC 20402-9371   202-512-1800
For $27 a year, you can't afford not to know what's going on at the Nation's Measurement Science Laboratory. The *Journal of Research of the National Institute of Standards and Technology* brings you up-to-date scientific articles and information on NIST research and development in physics, chemistry, engineering, mathematics, and computer sciences. Papers cover a broad range of subjects, with major emphasis on measurement methodology and the basic technology underlying standardization. Also included from time to time are survey articles on topics closely related to the Institute's technical and scientific programs, cooperative research opportunities and grants, conference reports, and more. The journal is issued six times a year. Contact Government Printing Office (GPO) to subscribe.

* Robotics Demonstrations
Manufacturing Engineering Laboratory
National Institute of Standards and Technology (NIST)
Gaithersburg, MD 20899   301-975-3422
Demonstrations of robot-tended machining workstations, and inspection machines, as well as demonstrations of optical measurement of surface finish are presented for the public. To schedule a tour, contact this Center.

* Robot Systems Division
The Robot Systems Division
Manufacturing Engineering Laboratory
National Institute of Standards and Technology (NIST)
Gaithersburg, MD 20899   301-975-3418
The Robot Systems Division develops and maintains competence in robotics, real-time sensory interactive control technology, robot programming languages and standards, and interface standards for computer-integrated manufacturing systems and advanced robotic systems. The division conducts research into new techniques of sensing and control, sensory data processing, and uses databases, communications, world models, robot programming languages and techniques, interactive graphics for programming and intelligent, real-time control for industrial military, space, and construction applications. Work is on-going to develop experimental hardware and software, and measures of system performance for a wide variety of robot applications. Research in robot safety, robot assembly of parts, tools, and fixtures, and applications of intelligent control to military and industrial systems is performed. Contact this division for more information.

* Scientific Computer Users Newsletter
Computer Planning and Analysis
Center for Applied Mathematics
National Institute of Standards and Technology (NIST)
Gaithersburg, MD 20899   301-975-2733
The Office of Computer Planning and Analysis puts out a bi-monthly newsletter for scientific computer users. Contact this office for information on subscriptions.

* Scientific Computing Services
Scientific Computing Division
Computing and Applied Mathematics Laboratory
National Institute of Standards and Technology (NIST)
Gaithersburg, MD 20899   301-975-3834
The Scientific Computing Division provides consulting services; performs research, and collaborates in the application of computer science and technology to computation problems in physical science and engineering at NIST.

* Seismic Safety of Structures
Building and Fire Research Laboratory
National Institute of Standards and Technology (NIST)
Gaithersburg, MD 20899   301-975-6865
Under the National Earthquake Hazards Reduction Program, NIST does research and development work that is used in standards for seismic safety of structures. Research is underway to develop knowledge for design and construction standards for new and existing buildings as well as lifeline structures.

* Semiconductor Electronics
Electronics and Electrical Engineering Laboratory
National Institute of Standards and Technology (NIST)
Gaithersburg, MD 20899   301-975-2699
NIST conducts research in semi-conductor materials, processes, devices and integrated circuits to provide the necessary basis for understanding measurement-related requirements in semiconductor technology. As part of this program, NIST scientists are using electrical, optical, and X-ray methods to study the resistivity, dopant distribution, and concentration of electrically inactive impurities, such as carbon and oxygen in silicon. Other studies are looking at compound semiconductors for devices that need structures unable to be fabricated from silicon.

* Semiconductor Industry
Manufacturing Engineering Laboratory
National Institute of Standards and Technology (NIST)
Gaithersburg, MD 20899   301-975-2699
The National Engineering Laboratory (NEL) helps the semiconductor industry improve the quality, cost, and reliability of U.S. manufactured semiconductor devices through new measurement methods and calibration services. NEL is developing, with a major electronics firm, a computerized "expert" system to help process engineers pinpoint probable causes of errors in semiconductor manufacturing.

* Small Business Specialist
Small Business Specialist
National Institute of Standards and Technology (NIST)
U.S. Department of Commerce
Gaithersburg, MD 20899   301-975-6343
NIST's small business specialist is the contact for small businesses who wish to use the services of the National Institute of Standards and Technology.

* Small-Scale Advanced Manufacturing
Center for Manufacturing Engineering
National Engineering Laboratory
National Institute of Standards and Technology (NIST)
Gaithersburg, MD 20899   301-975-3400
Small job shops--operations with fewer than 50 employees--make up about 85 percent of U.S. metal fabrication facilities and account for about 75 percent of all U.S. metal fabrication. They are running substantially behind their overseas competitors in the use of modern technology. The National Institute of Standards and Technology is working to answer questions such as What modern technologies are commercially available, affordable, and useful to the small job shop? and What return on investment might be expected? To help answer these questions, NIST is using its own job shop to conduct an experiment in the practical implementation of computer-integrated manufacturing. Contact this Center for more information.

* Speech Recognition Research
National Computer Systems Laboratory
National Institute of Standards and Technology (NIST)
Gaithersburg, MD 20899   301-975-2935
Computers that understand spoken language and can carry on conversations with humans are a science fiction staple. But in reality, comprehending and responding to spoken language is a difficult process for most computers. Interactions between

Science and Technology

people and machines still are limited mostly to communicating through mechanical means such as a keyboard. NIST researchers are developing improved algorithms and software for phonetically-based recognition of speech and ways to measure the performance of automatic speech recognizes. Basic research as well as measurement methods are needed to advance the technology. For more information on speech recognition research, contact this laboratory.

* Speech Recognition Shared Databases
Computer Systems Laboratory
National Institute of Standards and Technology (NIST)
Gaithersburg, MD 20899   301-975-2935
Speech recognition databases are typically too large and costly for any one organization to develop. To improve the technology, the research community in this area relies heavily on shared uses of databases and standard test methodologies. Using CD-ROM technology, NIST in cooperation with the Defense Advanced Research Projects Agency, has distributed material to over 100 research organizations.

* Standards Certification Activities in the United States
Office of Standards Code and Information
Administration Bldg
Gaithersburg, MD 20899   301-975-4029
Certification programs, considered a vital link between product standards and actual products, have significant impact on the marketplace. *The ABC's of Certification Activities in the United States* describes the different types of programs or schemes used to produce written assurance that a product or service conforms to a standard or specification. A sequel to *The ABC's of Standards-Related Activities in the United States* (1987), the new report provides a further introduction to certification for those not familiar with this important standards-related activity. Included are descriptions of product quality; self certification; third-party certification; federal, state, international, and regional programs; choice of standards; certification methodology; and certification marks. The report also addresses some of the potential problems with certification programs. To obtain a copy send a self-addressed mailing label to Maureen A. Breitenberg at the above address.

* Standards for Federal Government Certification Programs
Superintendent of Documents
Government Printing Office
Washington, DC 20402-9371   202-512-1800
Federal Government Certification Programs is a guide for manufacturers, distributors, state and local government officials, importers, consumers, and others concerned with standards and procedures used in federal certification programs. It contains information on manufactured products, agricultural commodities, medical services--devices and drugs, defense procurement items, transportation, and the voluntary inspection and uniform grading of such food items as dairy products, meats, and produce. Each entry describes the scope and nature of the program, lists the testing and inspection practices, standards used, methods of identification and enforcement, reciprocal recognition or acceptance of certification, and a contact point in the federal agency. The updated directory is a joint effort by NIST and the U.S. Department of Agriculture.

* Standard Reference Data
Reference Center
Standard Reference Data
National Institute of Standards and Technology (NIST)
Gaithersburg, MD 20899   301-975-2200
The Standard Reference Data Program aims to provide reliable, well-documented data to scientists and engineers for use in technical decision making, research and development. Experts in the physical, chemical, and materials sciences critically evaluate data that result from experimental measurements, calculations, and theory. The evaluations are carried out through a network of data centers, projects, and cooperative programs that comprise the National Standard Reference Data System. Experienced researchers in each area assess the accuracy of the data reported in the literature, prepare compilations, and recommend best values. The outputs are widely distributed as publications and computer-readable databases. Some of the databases are also accessible via on-line data systems. For a free complete catalog of publications and databases, contact the office above.

* Standard Reference Data Grants
Reference Center
Standard Reference Data

National Institute of Standards and Technology (NIST)
Gaithersburg, MD 20899   301-975-2200
Each year, the Standard Reference Data Program, in cooperation with other government funding agencies, administers a grant program aimed at involving experts in universities, industry, and government in data evaluation projects. This competitive program focuses on high priority short-term projects within the overall chemistry, physics, and materials scope of the program. Contact this office for more information and application procedures.

* Standard Reference Materials Catalog
Office of Standard Reference Materials
National Institute of Science and Technology
Gaithersburg, MD 20899   301-975-2016
Nearly 1,000 Standard Reference Materials available from NIST are listed in the *NBS Standard Reference Materials Catalog 1988-89*. The materials, certified for specific chemical and physical properties, include cements, ores, metals, glass, plastics, food, and environmental and clinical items. The expanded list of nutrition and health standards includes materials to calibrate instruments to detect marijuana in a human urine sample and to improve the precision of tests for elevated levels of the enzyme aspartate aminotransferase (AST) to detect heart attacks. Two new micro-length standards also are listed. The first commercial space-made product, 10-Micrometer Polystyrene Spheres, is available on a glass slide to calibrate microscopes. The second commercial space-made product, 30 Micrometer Polystyrene Spheres, is a new measurement standard for powder manufacturers. Also available is a series of seven individual low-alloy steels widely used in industry. Contact the office above to obtain the catalog.

* Standard Technical Data
Office of Standard Reference Data
National Institute of Standards and Technology (NIST)
Gaithersburg, MD 20899   301-975-2200
The National Measurement Laboratory provides reliable technical data required by industry, government, and academia to increase the effectiveness of U.S. science and technology. For information on this data, contact this office.

* State Technology Programs Clearinghouse
Director
National Institute of Standards and Technology (NIST)
Manufacturing Technology Centers Program
Bldg. 220, Room B111
Gaithersburg, MD 20899   301-975-3414
This clearinghouse gathers and analyzes information on the many State and local technology development programs across the nation. The idea is to develop a central base of information on what programs are available, what has been tried, and what the results have been. The clearinghouse will be a resource for state and local governments when deciding on new technology policies. The information will be shared through workshops and other mechanisms. For more information, contact this office.

* Statistical Engineering Services
Statistical Engineering Division
Computing and Applied Mathematics Laboratory
Administration Bldg
National Institute of Standards and Technology (NIST)
Gaithersburg, MD 20899   301-975-2840
The Statistical Engineering Division provides consulting services in the application of mathematical statistics to physical science experiments and engineering tests. The division conducts studies of computational methods and prepares reports, manuals, handbooks, and tools for statistical computing. The outputs include the Handbook for Development and Implementation of Measurement Assurance Programs, and DATAPLOT computer software for data analysis and model building. Contact this division for more information.

* Structures Research
Structures Division
Building and Fire Research Laboratory
Building Research Bldg
National Institute of Standards and Technology (NIST)
Gaithersburg, MD 20899   301-975-5900
The Structures Division conducts laboratory, field, and analytical research in structural and earthquake engineering, investigates structural failures, characterizes normal and extreme loads on buildings occurring during construction and in service,

Be patient. If any phone number is incorrect, call (area code) 555-1212 and request the new listing.

develops design criteria for reduction of damage caused by natural hazards, and develops advanced computation methods for evaluating static and dynamic response of structures. Work is on-going to enhance building safety. Sample outputs include technical data and design criteria for loads on buildings and technical data for building performance in earthquakes. Contact this division for more information.

* Superconductor Measurements

Electronics and Electrical Engineering Laboratory
Division 814.05
National Institute of Standards and Technology (NIST)
Boulder, CO 80303   303-497-3785

Recent advances in superconductivity have resulted in a critical need for measurement technology to characterize the different types of superconductors, which now range from very fine filament alloy conductors to high-temperature ceramic superconductors. Active research programs at NIST involve measurement techniques for critical current, critical magnetic field, ac losses, magnetic hysterisis, and electron tunneling. Recent breakthroughs in conductivity between normal metals and high-temperature superconductors has been made, and a new reference manual for large currents is being prepared.

* Technology at a Glance

Public Affairs Division
Administration Bldg
National Institute of Standards and Technology (NIST)
Gaithersburg, MD 20899   301-975-3392

Technology at a Glance is a monthly publication published by NIST containing updates on current research activities and upcoming events sponsored by or coordinated by NIST. Contact NIST for copies of the latest issue and for subscription information.

* Technology Development and Small Business Innovation

Technology Services
Room A343 Physics Bldg
National Institute of Standards and Technology (NIST)
Gaithersburg, MD 20899   301-975-3084

One of NIST's most important jobs is to aid in the transfer of technology to American businesses. Staff members help members of the private sector to locate experts in NIST that can be of assistance to them. In a separate program, NIST evaluates proposals sent to the U.S. Department of Commerce for small business grants. Phase I awards receive $35,000 to support studies of technological feasibility. In Phase II, applicants may receive up to $200,000 to support development of promising technologies. Contact this office for more information on this program.

* Technology Extension Programs

Director
National Institute of Standards and Technology (NIST)
Manufacturing Technology Centers Program
Bldg. 220, Room B111
Gaithersburg, MD 20899   301-975-3414

The NIST is making efforts to forge new ties to the many State and local technology extension services that have been created throughout the country. NIST can establish cooperative agreements with state or local programs to develop programs that transfer federally developed technology to business within their area. State and local extension services typically emphasize business advice rather than dealing with sophisticated technology. Ties with NIST will help to coordinate the state and local extension services with federal technology transfer programs. Through workshops, seminars, and other mechanisms, NIST plans to help technology extension agents make the best use of federal resources.

* Technology Services

Technology Services
National Institute of Standards and Technology (NIST)
Gaithersburg, MD 20899   301-975-4500

For many U.S. businesses, the tools for building a competitive advantage already exist--in other firms, in university or federal laboratories, or even in off-the-shelf technology available from suppliers. The National Institute of Technology and Standard's industrial technology services, a still evolving array of outreach programs, aim to get the productivity-enhancing equipment and methods to the companies that need them. Technology Services provides technical support, and in some cases financial assistance, to U.S. industry, especially small and medium-sized businesses, to facilitate the commercialization of products based on new scientific discoveries.

Among the services are:

- Providing technical support and financial assistance to regional centers for transferring manufacturing technology to small and medium-sized firms.

- Developing Standard Reference Materials and Standard Reference Data and calibrating equipment and devices to aid in improving industrial quality control.

- Promoting technology innovation by technically evaluating innovations, inventions, and new technologies.

- Providing technical assistance to private, local, national, and international standards-writing organizations to ensure equity in the marketplace.

Contact the office above for more information on the available services.

* The Journal of Research of the National Bureau of Standards

Superintendent of Documents
Government Printing Office
Washington, DC 20402-9371   202-512-1800

The proceedings of a 1987 symposium, *Accuracy in Trace Analysis-- Accomplishments, Goals, Challenges,* have been reprinted in this special edition of the journal. The 4-day event at NIST covered such topics as the history of trace analysis, robotics in the chemistry lab, measuring vitamins in foods, and the use of microwaves to dissolve samples. The proceedings consist of nearly 140 technical reports.

* Thermal Radiometry

Physics Laboratory
National Institute of Standards and Technology (NIST)
Gaithersburg, MD 20899   301-975-5559

NIST researchers are investigating the use of thermal imaging cameras as a temperature-measuring tool. These devices may prove to be very useful in determining the quality of products and in investigating changes in different processes.

* Thermochemical Tables Available Online

Office of Standard Reference Data
National Institute of Standards and Technology (NIST)
Gaithersburg, MD 20899   301-975-2200

The third edition of the (Joint-Army-Navy-Air Force) *JANAF Thermochemical Tables,* published by NIST, has been computerized to provide scientists and engineers with rapid access to information on the performance of materials at high temperatures. The database is available to subscribers on STN International (Scientific and Technical Network), an on-line private sector retrieval service offered worldwide. The numerical data can be used to make quick performance calculations for chemical reactors such as rocket engines, air pollution control equipment, internal combustion engines, coal gasifiers, and furnaces. The database is designed to list in one table all of the values for a given property of a chemical compound when the values for that compound appear in more than one tabulation. Information can be obtained by chemical name, the formula, or by the *Chemical Abstracts Registry Number.* For information on the new JANAF file through STN, contact the office above.

* Thermomechanical Processing for Metals/ Manufactures

Materials Science and Engineering Laboratory
Division 853
National Institute of Standards and Technology (NIST)
Boulder, CO 80303   303-497-5658

NIST researchers have designed and built a computerized, laboratory scale, hot-deformation apparatus that can simulate the manufacturing processes, such as forging and plate rolling and measure important properties incurred during processing. This approach offers more economy and versatility than the use of pilot scale or production facilities for the development of new alloys or manufacturing schedules.

* Thermophysical Computer Programs

Thermophysics Division
Center for Chemical Engineering

Science and Technology

National Institute of Standards and Technology (NIST)
Gaithersburg, MD 20899   301-975-4020
The Thermophysics Division creates computer programs for the calculation of thermodynamic and transport properties of industrial chemicals and fuels (for improved commercial exchange of fluids and process design).

* Tours of the Facilities
Public Affairs
National Institute of Standards and Technology (NIST)
Gaithersburg, MD 20899   301-975-2758
Free tours of the various facilities at NIST are given on Thursdays at 9:30 a.m. They generally last for two hours, and the public is welcome, but should schedule reservations in advance through Jan Hauber at the office above.

* Trace Gas Measurement Research
Chemical Science and Technology Laboratory
National Institute of Standards and Technology (NIST)
Gaithersburg, MD 20899   301-975-3939
Accurate measurement of gaseous species is of great importance to many industries for applications ranging from quantification of pollutant and toxic gas emissions to the quality control of products. Current NIST research is focusing on new detection systems.

* UV Optics Testbed
Physics Laboratory
National Institute of Standards and Technology (NIST)
Gaithersburg, MD 20899   301-975-6892
The emerging field of high reflectance, normal incidence, soft X-ray/extreme ultraviolet (xuv) optics has a wide range of applications. The ability to produce high-quality images at wavelengths below 40nm has allowed construction of xuv solar telescopes with unprecedented resolution; xuv microscopes able to study living biological samples with sub-micron resolution; and xuv photolithographic systems that will produce the next generation of integrated circuits. NIST is construction a new test facility that will allow for increased resolution and accuracy and will extend measurement capabilities to shorter wavelengths.

* Video Processing
Electronics and Electrical Engineering Laboratory
Metrology Bldg.
National Institute of Standards and Technology (NIST)
Gaithersburg, MD 20899   301-975-4230
Data compression, motion encoding, scan-rate conversion, scientific visualization, image analysis, and other video processing research topics are being explored at NIST using a massively parallel supercomputer, The Princeton Engine, capable of 14 giga instruction per second image processing and simulating video rate signals. Research using this system has focused on advancing the state of the art in high-definition systems.

* Voluntary Laboratory Accreditation
Technology Services
Room A146 TRF
National Institute of Standards and Technology (NIST)
Gaithersburg, MD 20899   301-975-4016
Staff of the NIST National Voluntary Laboratory Accreditation Program evaluate the competencies and technical qualifications of public and private laboratories for conducting specific tests or types of tests in key areas of commerce, health, and safety. Testing provides both as an internal quality check for those certified and as an external identification as a quality laboratory. Contact the staff at NIST to inquire about the types of laboratories certified and certification procedures.

* Weights and Measures Certification
Technology Services
Room A617 Administration Bldg
National Institute of Standards and Technology (NIST)
Gaithersburg, MD 20899   301-975-4004
One of NIST's longest running and most well known programs is assisting the states and local governments in the ensurance of the equity of weights and measures in the market place. The NIST staff produce numerous publications and also maintain an electronic bulletin board to keep people informed of changing developments. Contact this office for more information.

Patents, Trademarks, and Copyrights

Most inventors realize that it's vitally important to protect their idea by copyrighting it and obtaining the necessary patents and copyrights, but did you know that it's also important to look around for loans and other grants to support your business while working on your invention? If you want an idea to become an actual product, you have to invest an awful lot of your time into its research, and not just on a part time basis. Loans and grants programs for inventors help you do just that — for example, Hawaii offers low cost loans to inventors, as do other states around the country. First, let's talk about getting the necessary information concerning trademark and patent procedures.

Patent and Trademark Office

United States patent and trademark laws are administered by the Patent and Trademark Office (PTO). States also have trade secret statutes, which generally state that if you guard your trade secret with a reasonable amount of care, you will protect your rights associated with that secret. The PTO examines patent and trademark applications, grants protection for qualified inventions, and registers trademarks. It also collects, assembles, and disseminates the technological information patent grants. The PTO maintains a collection of more than 5 million United States patents issued to date, several million foreign patents, and 1.2 million trademarks, together with supporting documentation. Here's how to find out what you need to do to patent your idea.

What a Great Idea

To help you get started with patenting your invention, the Patent and Trademark Offices will send you a free booklet upon request called *Summary of How the Patent Process Works*. There are three legal elements involved in the process of invention: the conception of the idea, diligence in working it out, and reducing it to practice — i.e., getting a finished product that actually works. If you have a great idea you think might work, but you need time to develop it further before it is ready to be patented, what should you do?

Protect Your Idea for $6

You can file a Disclosure Statement with the Patent and Trademark Office, and they will keep it in confidence as evidence of the date of conception of the invention or idea.

Disclosure Statement
Commissioner of Patents and Trademarks
Patent and Trademark Office
Washington, DC 20231
Recorded Message   703-557-3158
Disclosure Office   703-308-HELP
Legal Counsel   703-308-HELP

Send an 8 1/2 x 13" drawing, a copy, signed disclosure, SASE, and a check or money order for $6 to file. Upon request, the above office will also send you a free brochure on Disclosure Statements.

This is the best way to keep the idea you are working on completely secret and yet document the date you conceived the idea. You can file the Disclosure Statement at any time after the idea is conceived, but the value of it will depend on how much information you put into it — so put as much detail into this statement as you can.

Another way to document the date of conception is to have someone vouch for you and your idea. Explain your idea to another person who is able to understand it and have them acknowledge what you have said to them in a signed, dated, notarized affidavit. Keep the voucher statement in a safe place in case you should ever need to produce it as proof of conception.

Either of the above two methods produces documentation that can be used as evidence if someone else later claims to have thought of your idea first and patents it before you do. The drawback to the voucher method is that it does not preserve absolute secrecy as does filing a disclosure statement. The person you told may tell someone else, and then you might have a problem.

Telling the World

Another way to document the date of conception is to publish it in a journal. Suppose that while in your basement to see why your old furnace is not working, you trip over your stationary exercise bicycle, which you never use, and hit your head. You also hit upon a way to heat your home by hooking up the furnace to one of the bike wheels and pedalling for 15 minutes. You're not sure if this method will work with any other furnace except your own, but it might. If you publish this or any other idea in a journal, it is protected for a year.

Publication acts as collateral evidence of the date of conception. If you are the first to conceive of an idea, and no one else has previously filed a Disclosure Statement on it or taken a Voucher Affidavit or published it, then for a year no one can patent your idea. Note that during the year you have to patent your invention you may not know whether someone else has documented an earlier conception date. The other catch to this method is that you have only a year to act. The heat is on because after a year **you** are barred from patenting your own invention! This is because the government wants you to use a reasonable amount of diligence in putting the idea to work sooner rather than later.

The Purpose of Documenting the Date of Conception

If someone else should try to patent your idea, filing a Disclosure Statement shows that you thought of it first, although filing this statement does not legally protect your invention. Documentation

Patents, Trademarks, and Copyrights

of the conception date gives you time to patent your invention, and is invaluable if you need to prove when you thought of your idea if a dispute should arise. (Note that filing a Disclosure Statement gives you limited defensive legal protection only if you follow it up with a patent in two years. Unlike a patent, it cannot be used offensively, to stop someone else from patenting the same idea.) When you go to file for a patent, if you and a competitor get into a dispute as to who was the first to invent it, the Patent and Trademark Office (PTO) will hold an Interference Proceeding. If you thought of the idea first, your Disclosure Statement or Voucher Affidavit will go a long way towards establishing that you were the first inventor and should therefore receive the patent for it.

Research Resources That Can Help You Turn Your Idea Into Reality

While diligently working out the details of your invention you can use the extensive resources of over 150,000 scientific and technical journals, articles, and books at the Scientific Document Library at the PTO in Crystal City, VA.

Facilitating public access to the more than 25 million cross-referenced United States patents is the job of PTO's Office of Technology Assessment and Forecast (OTAF), 703-308-0322. It has a master database which covers all United States patents, and searches are available for a fee which is based on the size of the project. The minimum search fee is $150, but no fee is charged if the information you need is already contained in a report they have on hand. This office can run a search for you based on classification, sub-class, country, or company name, but not by work or topic. An OTAF search will not result in an in-depth patent search. (More on that, and how to find classifications in the *Conducting Your Own Patent Search* section below.) OTAF extracts information from its database and makes it available in a variety of formats, including publications, custom patent reports, and statistical reports. The purpose of most of the reports generated by an OTAF search is to reveal patent trends.

Copies of the specifications and drawings of all patents are available from PTO. Design patents and trademark copies are $1.50 each. Plant patents not in color are $10 each, while plant patents in color are $20 each. To make a request, you must have the patent number. For copies, contact:

Commissioner of Patent and Trademarks
U.S. Department of Commerce
U.S. Patent and Trademark Office (PTO)
P.O. Box 9
Washington, DC 20231
Public Information Line   703-308-HELP

Patenting Your Invention

To patent your invention, start by ordering the Patent Booklet called *General Information Concerning Patents*, and Application Form.

Superintendent of Documents
U.S. Government Printing Office
Washington, DC 20402   202-512-1800

The cost is $2 and may be charged to Mastercard, VISA or Choice Card. The booklet must be ordered by its stock number 003-004-00641-2.

The application will ask you for a written description, oath, and drawing where possible. The cost to file for a patent to individuals or small businesses of under 15 employees (defined by SBA standards) is $315. It generally takes 18 months to two years for the PTO to grant a patent, and rights start the date the patent is granted. If you use your invention prior to being granted a patent, you can put "patent pending" on your product. This warns competitors that you have taken the necessary steps, but otherwise affords you no legal protection. Before embarking on the patenting process, you should conduct a patent search to make sure no one else has preceded you.

Conducting Your Own Patent Search

Before investing too much time and money on patenting your idea, you will want to see if anyone has already patented it. The PTO will only conduct searches on a specific inventors' name that you request. The fee is $10 and covers a 10-year time span. You can request this service by calling 703-308-0595. If you wish to hire a professional to do your patent search, consult the local yellow pages or obtain a copy of *Patent Attorneys and Agents Registered to Practice Before the U.S. Patent and Trademark Office*. View this publication at the PTO Search Room, or obtain it from the U.S. Government Printing Office. Even if your search is not as in-depth as that of a patent attorney or a patent agent, you may still find the information that you need. You may conduct your patent search at the Patent and Trademark Office Search Room located at:

Patent and Trademark Office (PTO)
Washington, DC 20231   703-308-0595

You can also conduct your patent search at any one of the 72 Patent Depository Libraries (PDLs) throughout the country. For information about the Patent Depository Library Program and the location of a library near you, call the toll-free number listed below.

Office of Patent Depository Library Programs
U.S. Patent and Trademark Office
2021 Jefferson Davis Hwy., Suite 2004   1-800-435-7735
Arlington, VA 22202   703-308-3924

The mailing address is:
Office of Patent Depository Libraries Office
U.S. Patent and Trademark Office
Suite 2004
Washington, DC 20231

This office distributes the information to the 72 PDLs. The information is kept on CD-Rom discs, which are constantly updated, and you or the library personnel can use them to do a patent search. CD-Rom discs have been combined to incorporate CASSIS (Classification and Search Support Information System). CD-Rom discs do not give you online access to the PTO database. Online access will be available through APS (Automated Patent Systems) within two years. APS is presently available only to patent examiners, public users of the PTO Search Room and to 14 of the 72 Patent Depository Libraries on a pilot program basis. Each PDL with the online APS has its own rules regarding its use. To use the online APS at the PTO Search Room, you must first sign up and take a class at the Search Room. Online access costs $40 per connect hour, and the charge for paper used for printouts is additional.

If you do not live near a PDL, the three CD-Rom discs are available through subscription. You may purchase the Classification disc, which dates back to 1790, for $210; the Bibliography disc, which dates back to 1969, for $210; and the ASIST disc, which contains a roster of patent attorneys, assignees, and other information for $151. You can also conduct your patent search and get a copy of it through commercial database services such as:

Mead Data Central, NEXIS Express, LEXPAT; 1-800-543-6862, 1-800-543-6862, Fax: 513-865-7418. Searches are done free of charge on patent topics. The charge for information found is $30 for a list of abstracts, plus print charges. Copies of patents (which you may decide to order after viewing the listing, or order directly if you already know which patent you want) cost $20. Copies include full text and detailed description of drawings, but no actual drawing because it is pulled from the electronic database.

If complete secrecy or doing your own search is your object, you may also subscribe to LEXPAT through the full library service. The cost is $28 per hour access charge, plus 65 cents per minute connect time. To subscribe call 1-800-843-6476.

Derwent, 1420 Spring Hill Rd., Suite 525, McLean, VA 22102; 1-800-451-3451, 703-790-0400, Fax: 703-790-1426. Patent searches are $360 per hour, plus 80 cents per record and $40 per hour for technical time. Copies of patents are $13-$16 for the first 25 pages and 67 cents for each additional page thereafter.

Rapid Patent, 1921 Jefferson Davis Highway, Suite 1821D, Arlington, VA 22202; 1-800-457-0850, 703-920-5050, Fax: 703-413-0127. Minimum costs for patent searches are: $240 for Mechanical, $290 for Electrical or Chemical. They are done manually. Delivery time is 4 weeks. Copies of patents cost $3.25 for each 25 pages.

CompuServe, 1-800-848-8199. There is a $39.95 one-time fee. Search time is $12.50 per hour or 21 cents per minute. Searches are available for abstracts ($4), full listing ($4), or classification ($4).

If you are going to do your own patent search at your local Patent Depository Library, begin with the *Manual and Index to U.S. Patent Classifications* to identify the subject area where the patent is placed. Then use the CD-Rom discs to locate the patent. CD-Rom discs enable you to do a complete search of all registered patents but do not enable you to view the full patent, with all its specific details. Lastly, view the patent, which will be kept on microfilm, cartridge, or paper. What information there is to view varies by library, depending on what they have been able to purchase. If the library you are using does not have the patent you want, you may be able to obtain it through inter-library loan.

Copies of patents can be ordered from the PTO at 703-308-9726, or more quickly, but for a price, from commercial services such

as Derwent or Rapid Patent. Depending on what each individual PDL has available, copies of patents can be obtained for no fee.

To obtain a certified copy of a patent, call 703-308-9726 (Patent Search Library at the PTO). The fee is $5 and you must have the patent number. For a certified copy of an abstract of titles, the fee is $15. For a certified copy of patent assignments, with a record of ownership from the beginning until present, call 703-308-9726. The cost is $15, and to request specific assignments you must have the reel and frame number.

Trademarks

Registering a trademark for your product or service is the way to protect the recognition quality of the name you are building. The PTO keeps records on more than 1.2 million trademarks and records. Over 500,000 active trademarks are kept on the floor of the library, while "dead" trademarks are kept on microfilm. Books contain every registered trademark ever issued, starting in 1870. You can visit the Patent and Trademark Office to research a trademark. You can then conduct your search manually for no charge or use their Trademark Search System (T-Search) for $40 per hour, plus ten cents per page and $25 per hour for office staff assistance time.

Trademark Search Library
2900 Crystal Dr.
Second Floor, Room 2B30
Arlington, VA 22202   703-308-9800/9805

If you can't do it yourself, you can hire someone to do the search for you. For an agent to do this, consult the local yellow pages under "Trademark Agents/Consultants" or "Trademark Attorneys". You can also locate an agent by calling your local bar association for a list of recommendations.

To conduct your own search at a Patent Depository Library use the CD-Rom disc on trademarks. It is not presently available for purchase. The CD-Rom disc contains trademarks but not images. Images can be found in the *Official Gazette*, which contains most current and pending trademarks. Subscriptions to the *Gazette* for trademarks cost $312 per year. The *Gazette* for patents costs $583 per year. Both are issued every two weeks and can be ordered from the U.S. Government Printing Office. You can also purchase an image file which contains pending and registered trademarks and corresponding serial or registration numbers through Thomson and Thomson by calling 1-800-692-8833. The information contained in it dates back to April 1, 1987 and is updated by approximately 500 images weekly. However, the PDL you use is likely to have an image of the trademark on microfilm or cartridge, and also have copies of the *Official Gazette*. If not, and you have the registration number, you may obtain a copy of the trademark you want for $1.50 from the PTO. Contact:

The Patent and Trademark Office
U.S. Department of Commerce
P.O. Box 9
Washington, DC 20231
Public Information Line   703-557-4636

There are also several commercial services you can use to conduct trademark searches.

Patents, Trademarks, and Copyrights

CompuServe, 1-800-848-8199. Fees are: $39.95 one time charge, plus $12.80 per hour or 21 cents per minute online time, plus $4 per search and $4 for full entry call-up.

Trademark Scan produced by Thomson and Thomson. It can be purchased by calling 1-800-692-8833 (ask for online services), or accessed directly via Dialog. Trademark Scan is updated three times per week, and includes state and federal trademarks, foreign and domestic. To access Trademark Scan you must already have Dialog. The cost is $130 per hour. Call 703-524-8004 or 1-800-334-2564. The fax number for Trademark Producer Scan is 617-786-8273. Users who already own the database should use this number.

Derwent, 1-800-451-3451, is a commercial service that will conduct the search for you. They will access the Trademark Scan database via Dialog. Cost is $60 per mark plus $1 per record. If required, 24-hour turnaround time is available.

Visual image of trademarks are not available on any of the electronic services above.

Online services and database discs for both patents and trademarks are constantly being expanded. For information on an extensive range of existing and projected products, call the PTO Office of Electronic Information at 703-308-0322 and ask for the U.S. Department of Commerce, PTO Office of Information Systems' *Electronic Products Brochure*. For example, there is a Weekly Text File, containing text data of pending and registered trademarks. Information can be called up by using almost any term. It can be purchased from IMSMARQ, 215-834-5089, the Trademark Register through Bell Atlantic Gateway, 1-800-638-6363, and Thomson & Thomson, 1-800-692-8833.

How to Register a Trademark

Get a copy of the booklet, *Basic Facts about Trademarks* from the U.S. Government Printing Office. It is free upon request from the Trademark Search Library by calling 703-308-9800/9805. The mark you intend to use needs to be in use before you apply. The fee to register your trademark is $175. The time to process your registration can take up to 14 months.

The Right Way to Get a Copyright

Copyrights are filed on intellectual property. A copyright protects your right to control the sale, use of distribution, and royalties from a creation in thought, music, films, art, or books. For more information, contact:

Library of Congress
Copyright Office
Washington, DC 20559   202-479-0700
Public Information Office   202-707-3000

If you know which copyright application you require, you can call the Forms Hotline, open 7 days per week, 24 hours per day at 202-707-9100. The fee is $20 for each registration.

The Library of Congress provides information on copyright registration procedures and copyright card catalogs which cover 28 million works that have been registered since 1870. The Copyright Office will research the copyright you need and send you this information by mail. Requests must be made in writing and you must specify exactly what information you require. Contact the Copyright Office, Reference and Bibliography, Library of Congress, 101 Independence Ave., SE, Washington, DC 20559; 202-707-6850, Public Information 707-3000. The fee for the search is $30 per hour. You can get a certificate stating the search was conducted by qualified researchers. There is no fee if you conduct the search yourself, and staff at the Library of Congress will show you how to do it. You may then, if you wish, request a certificate. The Copyright Office will conduct its own search, but your work will probably reduce the time of the search and save you money.

Subscriptions to the following parts of the Library of Congress *Catalogue of Copyright Entries* are available from the Superintendent of Documents, U.S. Government Printing Office, Washington, DC 20402-9325. Each lists material registered since the last issue was published. Order by stock number using Mastercard, VISA, check, or money order. To order, call the Government Printing Office Order Desk at 202-512-1800. Fax for delays in receiving orders: 202-512-2250. For help or complaints call the Superintendent of Documents Office at 202-512-1803 (publications), or 202-512-1806 (subscriptions).

Part 1: Nondramatic Literary Works - this quarterly costs $16 per year. Stock number 730-001-0000-2.

Part 2: Serials and Periodicals - this semiannual costs $5 per year. Stock number 730-002-0000-9.

Part 3: Performing Arts - this quarterly costs $16 per year. Stock number 730-003-0000-5.

Part 4: Motion Pictures and Filmstrips - this semiannual costs $5 per year. Stock number 730-004-0000-1.

Part 5: Visual Arts - this semiannual does not include maps and costs $5 per year. Stock number 730-005-00000-8.

Part 6: Maps - this semiannual costs $4 per year. Stock number 730-006-0000-4.

Part 7: Sound Recordings - this semiannual costs $7.50 per year. Stock number 730-007-0000-1.

Part 8: Renewal - this semiannual costs $5 per year. Stock number 730-008-0000-7.

Agriculture and Farming
Management and Productivity

* See also Careers and Workplace; Research Grants in Every Field Chapter
* See also Selling Overseas: International Trade Chapter
* See also Environment and Nature Chapter
* See also Information from Lawmakers Chapter
* See also Experts Chapter

Most farmers, ranchers, and growers are aware of only a fraction of the resources available from the federal government but consumers, chefs, gardeners, and ordinary folks know even less about the help and information readily accessible from the U.S. Department of Agriculture (USDA). A local telephone call to your USDA extension service will bring instantaneous advice on how to get rid of a wasp's nest or termites. Extension services in local communities offer classes on a wide variety of other topics that range from career opportunities to hydroponic farming. The National Agricultural Library is another mammoth information center with its numerous databases and publications. Youngsters between the ages of 10 to 20 years are eligible for start-up USDA loans to launch businesses ranging from lawn-mowing services to roadside produce stands. Incentives for agriculture cooperatives and new alternative approaches to farming also can be exploited. The government, along with many land grant colleges and universities, can share the latest research findings about soil and water conservation, farmland preservation, crop yields, or genetic engineering. In addition to farming, aquaculture, and forestry information there are answers to questions concerning the quality of meat, poultry, dairy, produce and other food that reaches the supermarket.

Family farmers, agricultural cooperatives, medium size growers, and corporate agribusiness all can benefit from the technical expertise, resources, loan and loan guarantee programs, and other incentives offered by numerous government offices. Efforts to modernize farming in developing countries, notably by the Peace Corps, are included in the International Relations and Defense Chapter.

* African Aquaculture Documents

Aquaculture Information Center
U.S. Department of Agriculture (USDA)   301-504-5558
10301 Baltimore Blvd., Room 304   Fax: 301-504-5472
Beltsville, MD 20705-2351   Internet: aic@nalusda.gov
The second generation of a computerized information project on African aquaculture, called REGIS II had been completed by the NAL, the National Oceanic and Atmospheric Administration (NOAA), and the Food and Agriculture Organizations (FAO) of the United Nations. REGIS II (for REGional Information Systems for African Aquaculture II) is a computer software with easy access to information on African aquaculture. REGIS and REGIS II are simple to use systems that describe, with diagrams, pictures and easy-to-follow text, aquaculture in the African region. The core of information in REGIS II is the full text of a Regional Survey of the Aquaculture Sector in Africa, South of the Sahara. REGIS II is a more powerful version of the original REGIS. A limited supply of REGIS II is available on CD-ROM, free of charge, from the NAL.

* AgNewsFax Service

News Distribution Office
U.S. Department of Agriculture (USDA)   202-720-9045
Washington, DC 20250   Fax: 202-690-3944
You can use a touchtone telephone connected to a fax machine to select and receive immediately on the same machine USDA news releases and other news items; fact sheets on USDA agencies and their programs; and biographical sketches of USDA officials, including agency administrators. Voice prompts guide you through a menu of selections and you may receive up to 10 documents per call. AgNewsFax is available 24 hours a day, 7 days a week.

* AGRICOLA Database

National Agricultural Library (NAL)
Reference Branch, Room 111
U.S. Department of Agriculture (USDA)
10301 Baltimore Blvd.
Beltsville, MD 20782   301-501-5479
The bibliographic database consists of records for literature citation of journal articles, monographs, theses, patents, software, audiovisual materials, and technical reports relating to all aspects of agriculture. It also includes materials not in the NAL collection. Access to AGRICOLA is available on-site, on a cost-recovery basis and online through DIALOG and BRS, and on CD-ROM from several vendors. For more information contact NAL at the above address.

* Agricultural Chemicals

National Agricultural Chemicals Association (NACA)
1155 15th St., NW, Suite 400
Washington, DC 20005   202-296-1585
The National Agricultural Chemicals Association (NACA) consists of companies producing chemical controls for fungi, rodents, pests and weeds. In addition to representing member interests in Washington, DC, NACA also pursues environmental programs. The NACA Alliance for a Clean Rural Environment (ACRE) provides information on the best management practices to help farmers and other users of agricultural chemicals to protect water quality. The ACRE program publishes *Dealer Environment* for agrichemical dealers. The NACA also publishes a pamphlet entitled *Protecting Our Groundwater: A Growers Guide*. Finally, a good source on the NACA is its quarterly newsletter called *Growing Possibilities*. The NACA puts out several other publications, most of which are free. Contact them for a publications list.

* Agricultural Cooperative Service Publications

Agricultural Cooperative Service (ACS)
U.S. Department of Agriculture (USDA)
PO Box 96576
Washington, DC 20090-6576   202-720-2556
The Agricultural Cooperative Service devotes its efforts to preserving and improving the family farm. Family farmers use cooperatives as an extension of their farm businesses to jointly purchase production supplies, process and market products, and perform related services. ACS publications series include:
Agricultural Cooperative Service; Directories; History and Statistics;

Organization: Members, Organizing a Cooperative, Principles and Practices, Structure and Scope;

Agriculture and Farming

Operations: Communications, Education and Training, Finance, Legal and Legislative;

Marketing: Crops - cotton, Food and feed grains, fruits and vegetables, specialty, foreign trade; Livestock - dairy, other; Other marketing;

Purchasing: Animal health, Agrichemicals, Feed, Petroleum, Seed, Other;

Rural Development.

Also inquire about the magazine *Farmers Cooperatives*, which covers all aspects of cooperatives. Annual subscriptions are available through Government Printing Office, 202-512-1800 for $21 annually, domestic. (#701-020-00000-6)

* Agricultural Diseases Database

Emergency Programs Information Center Data Bank
Veterinary Services
Animal and Plant Health Inspection Service (APHIS)
U.S. Department of Agriculture (USDA)
4700 River Rd.
Riverdale, MD 20737   301-734-8687

The Emergency Program Information Center (EPIC) maintains a computerized database with bibliographic information for all literature stored on microfilm by the center. The EPIC Data Bank consists of worldwide literature covering diseases of livestock and poultry exotic to the U.S. Complete services, including bibliographic printouts and copies of cited articles, are primarily for personnel working in Federal and cooperating State animal disease-control and eradication programs. Users outside APHIS are generally only provided citations; however, requests are handled on an individual basis. The center has prepared standard bibliographies on 17 different topics, which are available to the general public. The *PIC Brucellosis file* is included in the AGRICOLA system.

* Agricultural Environmental Engineering

American Society of Agricultural Engineers (ASAE)
2950 Niles Rd.   616-429-0300
St. Joseph, MI 49085   Fax: 616-429-3852
                               Internet: hq@asae.org

The American Society of Agricultural Engineers (ASAE) is the national association for engineers working on problems of importance to agricultural interests including irrigation and other large scale projects with environmental significance. In addition to technical papers and general interest material, the society publishes books in the following substantive areas: power and machinery, forest engineering, energy, Agriculture equipment design, electronics, soil and water, irrigation, wastewater treatment, plant environment, animal housing, food and process engineering, and tractor history. Call or write for a publications list and order form.

* Agricultural Libraries Information Notes

U.S. Department of Agriculture (USDA)
National Agricultural Library (NAL), Room 203
10301 Baltimore Blvd.
Beltsville, MD 20705-2351   301-504-6778

The Agricultural Libraries Information Notes (ALIN) contains information, features and updates on many NAL programs. It also contains a schedule of upcoming activities for those interested in agriculture research. Contact the ALIN editor about getting on the mailing list.

* Agricultural Pests and Insects

Public Awareness, LPAS
Animal and Plant Health Inspection Service (APHIS)
U.S. Department of Agriculture (USDA)
4700 River Road
Riverdale, MD 20737   301-734-8536

The following is a sampling of fact sheets intended for consumers, farmers, scientists, journalists, and others. All publications are free; however, if ordering multiple quantities, an explanation is requested.

Mediterranean Fruit Fly (April 1992). For farmers and the general public, it describes the appearance and life cycle of the fly, and explains how eradication is accomplished by survey, regulatory actions, and control.

Services Provided by APHIS (August 1993). This fact sheet has brief descriptions of the agencies 10 components.

* Agricultural Productivity

Eastern Regional Research Center (ERRC)
U.S. Department of Agriculture (USDA)
600 E. Mermaid Lane
Philadelphia, PA 19118   215-233-6400

Through basic, applied, and developmental research, scientists at nine research centers at the Eastern Regional Research Center (ERRC) are involved with projects to improve productivity of animals and crop plants and reduce losses; develop new and improved products and processing technology; upgrade nutritional value; open new and expand existing domestic and foreign markets; reduce marketing costs; eliminate health-related problems; and minimize energy consumption.

* Agricultural Publications

Office of Public Affairs
Publishing and Visual Communication
U.S. Department of Agriculture (USDA)
Room 542A
Washington, DC 20250   202-720-6623

The U.S. Department of Agriculture (USDA) has literally hundreds of publications available on all aspects of agriculture. Some documents can be purchased through the Government Printing Office (GPO) or the National Technical Information Service (NTIS), while others can be obtained directly from USDA. Publication topics include: agricultural economics, agricultural engineering, conservation, entomology, foresting, home economics, marketing, plant science, rural development, cooperatives, and statistics. Call or write for a free copy of the *List of Available Publications*.

* Agricultural Research Magazine

Superintendent of Documents
U.S. Government Printing Office (GPO)   202-512-1800
Washington, DC 20402   Fax: 202-512-2250

The Agricultural Research Service of the U.S. Department of Agriculture (USDA) publishes a monthly magazine entitled *Agriculture Research*. It contains articles about ongoing research and agricultural programs around the U.S. Subscriptions are available for $28 per year (#701-006-00000-3). It can be ordered from the above address. Information and sample copies can be obtained from ARS at 301-504-8296.

* Agriculture and Food Marketing Revolution

Yearbook Editor, Publications
U.S. Department of Agriculture (USDA)
Room 535-A
Washington, DC 20250   202-720-9434

Each year, the U.S. Department of Agriculture (USDA) publishes a yearbook which explores one theme in depth. The 1988 yearbook, *Marketing U.S. Agriculture*, written by experts from farms, industry, universities, and government, describes the revolution in the food marketing system caused by new technology, social changes, and increased competition for world markets.

* Agriculture Document Delivery Service

National Agriculture Library
U.S. Department of Agriculture (USDA)
Document Delivery Services Branch, 6th floor
10301 Baltimore Blvd., Room 300
Beltsville, MD 20705-2351   301-504-6503

The National Agricultural Library (NAL) supplies agriculture materials not found elsewhere to other libraries. Requests for materials should first be submitted to your local state libraries or university library. Libraries can borrow materials through an inter-library loan system. NAL will photocopy articles for individuals for a fee. Contact the NAL for a fee schedule and for information request requirements.

* Agriculture Electronic Bulletin Board

Public Services Division
National Agricultural Library (NAL)
U.S. Department of Agriculture (USDA)
10301 Baltimore Blvd.
Beltsville, MD 20705-2351   301-504-5113

The Agricultural Library Forum, or ALF, is an electronic bulletin board operated by the NAL. ALF provides a convenient, economical medium for the electronic communication of information about NAL project, products and services. The ALF also provides a forum for the exchange of agricultural information between individuals. It is free of charge, save the cost of the call into the system, and accessible 24 hours a day, 7 days a week. It can be accessed by dialing 301-504-

5496; 301-504-5111; 301-504-5497; or 301-504-6510 from your computer modem. For technical assistance call 301-504-5204. Contact the above office for more information on the ALF system and a free copy of the ALF user guide.

* Agriculture Fact Book, 1994

Superintendent of Documents
U.S. Government Printing Office (GPO)   202-512-1800
Washington, DC 20402   Fax: 202-512-2250

Intended as a handy reference tool, this book offers facts about U.S. agriculture, rural America, food, nutrition, consumer issues, and USDA programs. It contains detailed information about U.S. farm sector, the structure of the USDA's six mission areas rural economic and community development: farm and international trade; food; nutrition; and consumer services; natural resources and environment; marketing and inspection; and science, education and economics. Order #001-000-04616-1, $8.00. A complete listing of publications available is available from the GPO by asking for an agriculture Subject Bibliography or you can call the GPO Fax Watch at 202-512-1716 and request document #162.

* Agriculture Fair Practices

Information Staff
Agricultural Fair Practices Act
Agricultural Marketing Service (AMS)
U.S. Department of Agriculture (USDA)   202-720-8998
Washington, DC 20250   Fax: 202-720-7135

The Agricultural Marketing Service (AMS) administers four major regulatory laws-- the Perishable Agricultural Commodities Act, the Federal Seed Act, the Plant Variety Protection Act, and the Agricultural Fair Practices Act. If a processor has refused to deal with a farmer because the farmer is member of a producers association, the farmer can file a complaint with AMS. The act makes it unlawful for handlers of agricultural commodities, except cotton and tobacco, to coerce, intimidate, or discriminate against producers because they belong to a producers association. Farmers whose rights are violated in this respect can get AMS help in asking the Federal courts to restrain handlers from such unlawful practices. For more information contact this office.

* Agriculture Research Service Programs (ARS)

Information Staff
Beltsville Agricultural Research Center, Room 307A
10301 Baltimore Blvd.
Beltsville, MD 20705   301-504-6264

The Agriculture Research Service (ARS) of the U.S. Department of Agriculture (USDA) conducts research in several areas designed to increase the quality of American crops, livestock, and nutrition. ARS also conducts research designed to improve the competitiveness of U.S. agriculture on the world market. For more information on specific ARS programs, contact the information office listed above.

* Agriculture Trade and Marketing

Agriculture Trade and Marketing Information Center (ATMIC)
National Agricultural Library (NAL)
U.S. Department of Agriculture (USDA)   301-504-5704
10301 Baltimore Blvd.   Fax: 301-504-5472
Beltsville, MD 20705-2351   E-mail: niassanyi@nalusda.gov

The Agriculture Trade and Marketing Information Center (ATMIC) was established in 1987 in response to the concern of policymakers, agricultural experts, farmers, and consumers about the U.S. export decline, implications of world events, and shifting global trends. ATMIC includes information on: agricultural trade and marketing; trade policies; trade barriers; General Agreement on Tariffs and Trade (GATT); trade negotiations; agricultural domestic policy and international trade; transportation of agricultural products; farm exports and farm economy; country marketing profiles; and more. AMTIC also publishes *Vignettes*, a quarterly newsletter focusing on activities, upcoming events, new technologies, resources, and services of interest to the agricultural trade and marketing community.

* Agriculture Yearbooks

Yearbook Editor, Publications
U.S. Department of Agriculture (USDA)
Room 542-A
Washington, DC 20250   202-720-9434

Each year the U.S. Department of Agriculture (USDA) publishes a yearbook that explores one agriculture related topic in depth. Yearbooks have been published since 1894. Between 1894 and 1935 they were simply called *Yearbook of Agriculture*.

Since 1935 each book has had an individual theme. A complete list of book titles is available from the Yearbook office. Books published since 1983 are in print and are available from the Superintendent of Documents (202-512-1800). Available books (with prices) are as follows:

1983 Using Our Natural Resources ($7) 001-000-04387-1
1984 Animal Health - Livestock and Pets ($10) 001-000-04434-6
1985 U.S. Agriculture in a Global Economy ($10) 001-000-04452-4
1986 Research for Tomorrow ($9.50) 001-000-04472-9
1987 Our American Land ($9.50) 001-000-04494-0
1988 Marketing American Agriculture ($9.50) 001-000-04517-2
1989 Farm Management ($9.50) 001-000-04537-7
1990 Americans in Agriculture, Portraits in Diversity ($10)
1991 Agriculture and the Environment ($12) 001-000-04574-1

* Alternative Agricultural Opportunities

Administrators Office
Cooperative State Research and Education Service
U.S. Department of Agriculture (USDA)
Room 305A, Administration Building
Washington, DC 20250   202-720-6283

The U.S. Department of Agriculture (USDA) operates an extension program in 3,165 counties located in all of the 50 states and the U.S. territories. Federal, state, and local governments share in financing and conducting cooperative extension educational programs to help farmers, processors, handlers, farm families, communities, and consumers apply the results of food and agricultural research including Alternative Agricultural Opportunities, which helps farmers use a distinctive approach to alternative crop and livestock enterprises to integrate marketing, management, and production factors into a total business plan.

* Alternative Farming Systems

Alternative Farming Information Center (AFIC)
U.S. Department of Agriculture (USDA)
10301 Baltimore Blvd., Room 304   301-504-6559
Beltsville, MD 20705-2351   Fax: 301-504-5472
                                          Internet: nalafsic@nalusda.gov

This center covers organized farming or gardening that includes low-input, sustainable, or regenerative agriculture. Conservation tillage and other cultivation practices, such as intercropping, crop rotation, and use of green manures, are also covered. The Alternative Farming Information Center (AFIC) has quick bibliographies and other information available free. You can receive a listing of information products that are available. These products are free of charge. Most of the publications on the list are available in either hard copy or electronic format. A few are available only in one or the other. In addition, all electronically available publications are available on the Internet via: National Agricultural Library (NAL's) Gopher: <gopher.nalusda.gov>; Alternative Farming Systems Information Center (AFSIC's) World Wide Web Page: <http://www.inform.umd.edu/EdRes/Topic/AgrEnv/AltFarm>; or NAL's Electronic Bulletin Board System: Agricultural Library Forum (ALF), 301-504-6510. An example of publications available include:

Alternative Crops, 1993, 34 pp, electronic format, QB 93-53
Double Cropping and Interplanting, 1994, 111 pp, hard copy or electronic format, QB 94-51
Farmland Preservation, 1993, 38 pp, hard copy or electronic format, QB 93-57
Green Manures and Cover Crops, 1993, 71 pp, hard copy or electronic format, QB 93-68
Legumes in Crop Rotations, 1994, 121 pp, hard copy or electronic format, QB 94-38
Solar Energy Alternatives for Agriculture, 1993, 64 pp, electronic format, QB 93-33
Sustainable or Alternative Agriculture, 1992, 84, pp, hard copy format, QB 93-03
Wind Energy for Agriculture, 1993, 32 pp, electronic format, QB 93-28

* American Agriculture News Service

Radio News Line
U.S. Department of Agriculture (USDA)
Room 1618
Washington, DC 20250   202-488-8358

This recorded message gives you daily news announcements on a variety of agriculture-related topics.

* Animal Damage Control

Legislative and Public Affairs
Animal and Plant Health Inspection Service (APHIS)

Agriculture and Farming

U.S. Department of Agriculture (USDA)
Room 1147-S — 202-720-2511
Washington, DC 20250 — Fax: 202-720-3982
The Animal Damage Control (ADC) unit helps manage wildlife to minimize potential threats to agriculture and natural resources and to protect threatened and endangered species. ADC cooperates with and provides technical assistance to foreign governments, international organizations, and other Federal, State, local, and private organizations in regard to animal damage and nuisance control.

* Animal Disease Control

Emergency Programs Information Center
Animal-Plant Health Inspection Service
U.S. Department of Agriculture (USDA)
4760 River Road
Riverdale, MD 20737 — 301-734-8687
Veterinary Services (VS) is responsible for protecting the health of U.S. livestock and poultry. VS continually monitors diseases in the U.S. and abroad and investigates suspected incursions of foreign diseases into the U.S. The Information Center has approximately 68,000 articles accessible through the AGRICOLA system. Call for more information and for a list of *Emerpro files* on animal diseases.

* Animal Welfare

Animal Welfare Information Center (AWIC)
U.S. Department of Agriculture (USDA)
10301 Baltimore Blvd. — 301-504-6212
Beltsville, MD 20705-2531 — Fax: 301-504-7125
Internet: awic@nalusda.gov
This center handles matters of animal care and handling, as well as housing and caging, training guides and manuals for animal care personnel, ethical issues involving animals, legislation, and regulation, and testing alternatives for drug toxicology studies. The Center publishes a list containing the titles and order forms for Animal Welfare Information Center (AWIC) bibliographies, reference briefs, fact sheets, series, source guides and other publications electronically and in hard copy. Call or write for a publications list. All publications are free. Publications include:

AWIC Quarterly Newsletter
APHIS Report--Animal Welfare Enforcement
Animal Care and Use Committees (SRB 92-16)
Animal Euthanasia (SRB 93-06)
Animal Models of Disease (QB 95-14)
Animal Welfare Legislation, Regulations, and Guidelines (QB 95-18)
Contacting AWIC (fact sheet)
Licensing and Regulation Under the Animal Welfare Act (APHIS Program Aid 1117)
Environmental Enrichment Information Resources for Nonhuman Primates 1987-1992 (Resource Guide)
Welfare of Experimental Animals (QB 94-04)

* Aquaculture and Fish Farming

Aquaculture Information Center
U.S. Department of Agriculture (USDA)
10301 Baltimore Blvd. — 301-504-5558
Beltsville, MD 20705 — Fax: 301-504-5472
Internet: alc@nalusda.gov
This center covers culture of aquatic plants and animals in freshwater, brackish water, and marine environments. Examples include catfish farming, oyster culture, freshwater prawn culture, and trout farming. Staff can also answer questions about animal parasitology. Patrons can use AquaRef, a system containing aquaculture information on computer. Call or write for a publications list. All publications are free. Publications and bibliographies include:

Aqua Topic Series:
Aquaculture (July 1991)
Fish Waste Utilization (July 1993)
Water Quality in Aquaculture Ponds (June 1992)

Bibliographies and Literature of Agriculture:
BLA #123 Biotechnology of Algae (1992)
BLA #90 The Potentials of Aquaculture (1989)

Additional Resources:
Aquaculture II CD-ROM Packet (1992)
Audiovisuals for Aquaculture (1991)
Directory of Aquaculture Associations (1995)

* Aquaculture Loans

Farmers Home Administration
U.S. Department of Agriculture (USDA)
South Agriculture Building 5420
Washington, DC 20250 — 202-720-1632
The Farmers Home Administration extends credit to aquaculture operators, farmers, ranchers, rural residents, and communities. Loans for aquaculture purposes may generally be used for the husbandry of aquatic organisms under a controlled or selected environment.

* AquaNIC

Agriculture Network Information Center (AquaNIC)
Purdue University
Department of Animal Sciences — 317-494-4862
West Lafayette, IN 47907-1151 — Fax: 317-494-9646
E-mail: meinstei@hub.ansc.purdue.edu
Data: 317-496-1440
AquaNIC is a multi-branched system containing a wide variety of information. Most documents can either be viewed on your computer monitor, downloaded, or a copy sent to your e-mail address. AquaNIC also contains an image directory that holds hundreds of pictures, short videos, and slides in a variety of common image formats. You will also have access to newsletters, calendar of events, news flashes and links to other aquaculture databases on the Internet. Contact this office for more information.

* Bees and Beekeeping

Honeybee Breeding Genetics and Physiology Research Lab
U.S. Department of Agriculture (USDA)
Agriculture Research Service (ARS)
1157 Ben Hur Rd.
Baton Rouge, LA 70820 — 504-767-9280
This Lab does most of its research on protecting bees against pests and disease. Scientists are currently at work trying to protect the beekeeping industry and the public from the advent of the Africanized bees that are due to arrive in mid 1990. Research projects include use of a toxic substance that will attract bees and kill them, a repellent that will keep these aggressive bees from stinging, and ways of protecting commercial queen bee farms from invasion of Africanized bees. The Lab has also recently imported bees from Europe to test them for resistance to certain diseases. The Lab works with the private bee industry and the Agriculture Extension Service to disseminate the results of its work to industry. A free listing of publications is available from this office.

* Biotechnology and Genetic Engineering

Biotechnology Information Center
National Agricultural Library
U.S. Department of Agriculture — 301-504-5340
10301 Baltimore Blvd., 4th Floor — Fax: 301-504-7098
Beltsville, MD 20705-2351 — TDD: 301-504-6856
Internet: biotech@nalusda.gov
Subject areas covered by this center include genetic engineering, plant and animal tissue culture, single cell protein, immobilized enzymes, legislation and regulations, transgenic animals, and detoxification using microbes. The Center's staff will also perform brief, complimentary searches of the AGRICOLA data base on specific topics of your choice, or more exhaustive searches on a cost-recovery basis. Call for a list of free bibliographies and publications. Available free Quick Bibliographies include the following:

QB 95-07 Biotechnology: Forestry and Forest Products, 1992-1995
QB 91-138 Animal Science, 1980-1991
QB 92-25 Breeding and Selecting Crops for Insect Pest Resistance, 1986-1991
QB 94-60 Herbicide Tolerance/Resistance in Plants, 1991-1994
QB 91-38 Single-Cell Protein, 1984-1990

* Biotechnology Information Online

Biotechnology Information Center
National Agricultural Library
U.S. Department of Agriculture
10301 Baltimore Blvd., 4th Floor — 301-504-5340
Beltsville, MD 20705-2351 — Fax: 301-504-7098
TDD: 301-504-6856
The National Biological Impact Assessment Program (NBIAP) is designed to facilitate and assess the safe application of new techniques for genetically modifying

plants, animals and microorganisms to benefit agriculture and the environment. This Information System combines a monthly News Report with direct access to an extensive series of databases. Access to the system is free up to 30 minutes a day. For access dial 703-231-3858 on your computer modem, enter the registration information and choose a password. From then on you can enter the system using a toll free number [800-624-2723]. Contact the Biotechnology Information Center for more information on this service.

* Business Start-Up Loans for 10-20 Year Olds

Youth Project Loans
U.S. Department of Agriculture (USDA)
Farmers Home Administration
Washington, DC 20250   202-720-1632

The U.S. Department of Agriculture (USDA) lends up to $5,000 to youths from 10 to 20 years of age. The loans can be used to support both farm and non-farm ventures, such as small crop farming, livestock farming, roadside stands, and custom work. They are normally made in conjunction with youth groups and require parental consent.

* Chemical and Fertilizer Hotline

Chemical Manufacturers Association
Chemical Referral Center
Chemtreck Information Services
2501 M St. NW
Washington, DC 20037   800-CMA-8200

This toll-free service provides non-emergency referrals to companies that manufacture chemicals and to state and federal agencies for health and safety information and information regarding chemical regulations. It operates 9 a.m. to 6 p.m. eastern time.

* Climate Dial Up Service

Climate Analysis Center/NMC
National Weather Service, W/NMC53
National Oceanic Atmospheric Administration
U.S. Department of Commerce
Washington, DC 20233   202-763-4670

The Climate Dial Up Service is an electronic bulletin board that currently consists of 45 data sets. An example of data sets available are: Monthly and Seasonal Climate Rankings by Areas; Explanation of Degree Day Products; Five Day, Six-to-Ten Day, Seven Day Max and Min, and Monthly and Seasonal Outlooks for Temperature and Precipitation; Weekly and Monthly Heating and Cooling Degree Forecasts; Daily, Weekly and Monthly Summaries of Temperatures and Precipitation Data for More than 6000 Locations Worldwide; and Cumulative Weekly Growing Degree Days For Corn. You can call or write for a free copy of the Climate Dial Up Service Brochure which contains the necessary forms to register and an explanation of fees involved.

* Commodities Market News

Information Staff
Agricultural Marketing Service
U.S. Department of Agriculture (USDA)
Room 3510, South Building
P.O. Box 96456
Washington, DC 20090-6456   202-720-8998

Skilled market reporters gather and document marketing information that is distributed quickly throughout the U.S. via telephone recorders, newspapers, radio, television, and in printed reports. The reports are available for seven commodities: dairy, tobacco, cotton, fruits and vegetables, livestock, grain, and poultry, and they contain information on supply and demand and shipping point reports that cover prices paid by types of sale. Much of the information is gathered and distributed by local field offices via satellite.

* Communicable Diseases Affecting Cattle and Poultry

Animal and Plant Health Inspection Service (APHIS)
Veterinary Services
U.S. Department of Agriculture (USDA)
Washington, DC 20250   202-720-2511

A staff of specialists studies communicable diseases and pests affecting livestock and poultry. They organize and conduct control eradication programs in cooperation with industry and state officials.

* Compost and Improved Soil

Soil Microbial Systems
U.S. Department of Agriculture
Building 318, Room 108 BARC-E
Beltsville, MD 20705   301-504-8163

This office provides technical assistance on the production and use of compost, soil, and microbes. The information from this office is of a highly scientific nature. Your local county extension service can provide more practical information.

* Computer Software

Software Demonstration Center
National Agricultural Library (NAL)
U.S. Department of Agriculture (USDA)
10301 Baltimore Blvd., Room 103
Beltsville, MD 20705-2351   301-504-7114

This collection of software consists of software packages in many areas of agriculture and related subjects, including general-purpose software with applications in the agricultural community. To obtain a current listing of software titles, contact the Software Demonstration Center.

* Consolidated Farm Service Agency (formerly Agricultural Stabilization and Conservation Service)

Information Division
Consolidated Farm Service Agency (CFSA)
P.O. Box 2415
Washington, DC 20013   202-720-7962

The Consolidated Farm Service Agency (CFSA), an agency of the United States Department of Agriculture, administers farm commodity, conservation, environmental protection, and emergency programs. These programs provide for commodity loans and price support payments to farmers; commodity purchases from farmers and processors; acreage reduction; cropland set-aside and other means of production adjustment; conservation cost-sharing; and emergency adjustment. The CFSA has offices in most every state in the country. It also provides an extensive amount of information on commodity support programs available from the USDA and the Commodity Credit Corporation and on Federal Crop Insurance. The most common methods of farm support are price supports, income supports, and supply controls. The following is a list of free fact sheets available from the CFSA on commodity support programs.

Flue-Cured Tobacco, Other Tobaccos, Burley Tobacco, Peanuts, Mohair, Wool, Upland Cotton Program, Extra Long Staple Cotton, Soybeans and Minor Oilseeds, Sugar Beets and Sugarcane, Rye, Rice, Honey, Wheat, Dairy Refund Payment Program, Conservation Reserve Program, Feed Grain Program, Dairy Indemnity Payment Program, Dairy Price Support Program, Wheat Program.

* Crop Acreage Certification

Information Division
Consolidated Farm Service Agency (CFSA)
U.S. Department of Agriculture (USDA)
P.O. Box 2415
Washington, DC 20013   202-720-7962

Farmers certify their crop acreages when they report program crop data, acreage conservation reserve (ACR) and other crop acres. Farmers who are growing barley, corn, grain sorghum, rice, upland cotton, or wheat who wish to be eligible for price support and other program benefits must report crop acreages. Farmers growing crops but not participating in current programs should report acreages to insure the opportunity to fully participate in future programs. For more information on what to certify and procedures for doing so, contact the CFSA.

* Crop and Soil Agronomy

American Society of Agronomy (ASA)
677 South Segoe Rd.
Madison, WI 53711   608-273-8080

The American Society of Agronomy promotes the acquisition and diffusion of knowledge concerning the nature and interrelationship of plants, soils and the environment. Publications: *Agronomy Journal, Crops and Soils, Journal of Environmental Quality, Journal of Natural Resources and Life Science Education, Agronomy News, Crop Science, Soil Science Society of America Journal, Journal of Production Agriculture, Soil Survey Horizons, Agronomy Abstracts*. The Society also publishes numerous books, monographs, and special publications. Call or write for a list of publications as well as the price list for the journals.

Agriculture and Farming

* Crop Insurance Coverage

Manager
Federal Crop Insurance Corporation
U.S. Department of Agriculture (USDA)
2101 L St. NW
Washington, DC 20037   202-254-8224
OR: Your local crop insurance agent

The U.S. Department of Agriculture (USDA) runs a crop insurance program to improve the economic stability of agriculture through a sound system of crop insurance that provides multiple-peril insurance for individual farmers to ensure a basic income against droughts, freezes, insects, and other natural causes of disastrous crop losses. Any owner or operator of farmland who has an insurable interest in a crop in a county where insurance is offered on that crop is eligible unless the land is not classified for insurance purposes.

* Crop Production Losses

Information Division
Consolidated Farm Service Agency (CFSA)
U.S. Department of Agriculture (USDA)
P.O. Box 2415
Washington, DC 20013   202-720-7962

The Consolidated Farm Service Agency (CFSA) administers disaster assistance programs to provide payments to producers sustaining crop production losses in either 1990 or 1991. To be eligible, producers must have less than $2 million gross annual revenue and be in compliance with highly erodible land and wetland conservation provisions of the law. Disaster payments may be made for losses of commercially-grown crops under the categories of participating program crops, nonparticipating program crops, sugar, tobacco, peanuts, soybeans, sunflowers, nonprogram crops and ornamental crops. Contact the CFSA for more information on eligibility and payments.

* Current Awareness Literature Service (CALS)

Information Systems Division
National Agricultural Library (NAL), 5th Floor
U.S. Department of Agriculture (USDA)
10301 Baltimore Blvd.
Beltsville, MD 20705   301-504-6859

The Current Awareness Literature Service is a computer based literature search system designed to keep researchers up to date with current information in their fields. It is available free to USDA personnel. Call for information on developing a profile or for a users guide to the system.

* Dairy Indemnity Payment Program

Consolidated Farm Services Agency (CFSA)
U.S. Department of Agriculture (USDA)
P.O. Box 2415
Washington, DC 20013   202-720-6733

The Dairy Indemnity Payment Program provides indemnity payments to dairy farmers whose milk has been removed from the commercial market because it contained residues of chemicals or toxic substances, including nuclear radiation fallout.

* Educational Programs: Farmers and their Families

Executive Officer
U.S. Department of Agriculture (USDA)
Room 340A, Administration Building
Washington, DC 20250   202-720-4111

The U.S. Department of Agriculture (USDA) operates an extension program in 3,165 counties located in all of the 50 states and the U.S. territories. Federal, state, and local governments share in financing and conducting cooperative extension educational programs to help farmers, processors, handlers, farm families, communities, and consumers apply the results of food and agricultural research. The Extension Service has targeted 9 national initiatives to provide a new focus for educational efforts.

Alternative Agricultural Opportunities: Helps farmers use a distinctive approach to alternative crop and livestock enterprises to integrate marketing, management, and production factors into a total business plan.

Building Human Capital: Helps people develop marketable job skills, make informed career decisions, and expand available opportunities.

Competitiveness and Profitability of American Agriculture: To enhance farmers' competitiveness and profitability, Extension helps farmers improve production, finance, and management skills; develop new technology; adjust profitability to global market changes; and strengthen business and support systems.

Conservation and Management of Natural Resources: Helps people benefit from natural ecosystems without destroying them, sustain a productive natural resource base, market natural resource goods and services, and formulate and implement sound public policies.

Family and Economic Well-Being: Helps families manage finances and make sound financial decisions; confront and deal with such problems as alcohol and drug abuse, teenage pregnancy, and unemployment; and develop strategies for retirement.

Improving Nutrition, Diet, and Health: Extension offers up-to-date information about the relationship of dietary practices to lifestyle factors; the safety, quality, and composition of foods; and consumers' needs and perceptions about the food industry.

Revitalizing Rural America: In cooperation with local governments, Extension programs emphasize how to increase competitiveness and efficiency of rural programs, explore methods to diversify local economies and attract new business, adjust to impact of change, develop ways to finance and deliver services, and train leaders to make sound policy decisions for rural communities.

Water Quality: Work with consumers, producers and local government to learn more about the importance of high-quality ground water and the conservation of water resources. Emphasis is also put on the effects of agricultural chemicals and contaminants on water quality.

Youth at Risk: Extension is helping expand youth outreach resources to meet the needs of youth, develop programs for the most susceptible youth populations, provide leadership and job skills, and increase training of professionals and volunteers to work in communities to prevent and treat problems.

* E-Mail and Internet Access to USDA Copy and Economic Reports

Oya Reiger
Albert R. Mann Library
Cornell University   607-255-2199
Ithaca, NY 14853-4301   E-mail: help@usda.mannlib.cornell.edu

Three agencies of the U.S. Department of Agriculture (USDA), the Economic Research Service (ERS), the National Agricultural Statistics Service (NASS), and the World Agricultural Outlook Board, provide data electronically. Full texts of current statistical and economic analysis reports can be automatically delivered to your electronic mailbox address at no charge. The USDA economics and statistics system on the Internet provides access to more than 140 agricultural data bases and over 70 current reports. Data are distributed free of charge through a Gopher server, Telnet, and anonymous file transfer protocol. Call or write for complete instructions. You can also have this information faxed to you by calling 202-690-3944 from your fax machine and follow the voice prompts to request fact sheet number 3811.

* Emergency Programs

Consolidated Farm Service Agency (CFSA)
Information Division
U.S. Department of Agriculture (USDA)
P.O. Box 2415
Washington, DC 20013   202-720-7962

The Consolidated Farm Service Agency (CFSA) provides assistance to agricultural producers in emergencies caused by natural disasters through: haying and grazing privileges on cropland placed in the Acreage Conservation Reserve and in Conservation Use; the Livestock Feed Program; and the Emergency Conservation Program. Contact the CFSA regarding specific eligibility requirements.

* Emerging Agricultural Technology

Office of Technology Assessment (OTA)
600 Pennsylvania Ave., SE
Washington, DC 20510   202-228-6521

The Office of Technology Assessment (OTA) is studying the emerging agricultural technologies for the 1990s and the structure of the research system that gives rise to these technologies, which include biotechnology, information technology, and low input technology for the food and agricultural sector. Contact Mike Phillips, the project director, for more information.

Be patient. If any phone number is incorrect, call (area code) 555-1212 and request the new listing.

* Erosion Control

Information Division
Consolidated Farm Service Agency (CFSA)
U.S. Department of Agriculture (USDA)
Consolidated Farm Service Agency (CFSA)
P.O. Box 2415
Washington, DC 200131   202-720-3168

The Consolidated Farm Service Agency (CFSA) directs a number of conservation programs to preserve and improve American farmland:

Conservation Reserve Program (CRP): Targets the most fragile farmland by encouraging farmers to stop growing crops on land designated by conservationists as "highly erodible" and plant grass or trees on it instead. The farmer receives rent on the land for a term of ten years. Cost-share programs are also available for permanent planting of grass and trees in these areas.

* ERS AutoFax

Economic Research Service (ERS)
National Agricultural Statistics Service (NASS)
1301 New York Ave. NW   202-219-0510
Washington, DC 20005-4788   Fax: 202-501-6166
                                              AutoFax: 202-219-1107

AutoFax has basic information on current research, farm income, crops, vegetables and specialties, U.S. agricultural trade, and other subjects. Call AutoFax from you fax machine and follow the voice prompts. Request document #0411 for more information and a directory.

* Export of U.S. Farm Products

Foreign Agriculture Service (FAS)
U.S. Department of Agriculture (USDA)
Room 5074-S   202-720-7115
Washington, DC 20570   Fax: 202-720-1727

The Foreign Agriculture Service (FAS) serves as a basic source of information to U.S. agriculture on world crops, policies and markets; administers agricultural import regulations; assists in the export of U.S. farm products; represents U.S. agriculture in foreign trade matters; and administers U.S. Department of Agriculture's (USDA) responsibility for export credit programs and the reporting of export sales. International Cooperative and Development staff coordinates USDA's international training and technical assistance programs; sponsors international research projects and scientific and technical exchanges with agribusinesses; and serves as USDA's liaison with international food and agriculture organizations. Free publications available from this office include:

Desk Reference Guide to U.S. Agricultural Trade (1993)
Farmers Export Arm (1985)
Food and Agriculture Export Directory (1991)
How to Get Information on U.S. Agricultural Trade (1993)
Trade Assistance for U.S. Agriculture Exporters (1989)
U.S. Agricultural Trade Book (1991)
U.S. Export Credit Guarantee Program (1992)
U.S. Export Sales Report

* Farm Credit Administration Freedom of Information Act Requests

Freedom of Information Act Officer
Farm Credit Administration
U.S. Department of Agriculture (USDA)
1510 Farm Credit Drive
McLean, VA 22102   703-883-4000

Contact the office above for Freedom of Information Act requests. Requests for agency records must be made in writing.

* Farm Credit Administration Library

Library
Farm Credit Administration
U.S. Department of Agriculture (USDA)
1501 Farm Credit Drive
McLean, VA 22102   703-883-4296

For information on obtaining reference material through inter-library loan, contact the office above.

* Farm Facility Loan Program

Consolidated Farm Service Agency (CFSA)
U.S. Department of Agriculture (USDA)
P.O. Box 2415
Washington, DC 20013   202-720-6778

The Farm Facility Loan Program helps qualifying farmers obtain on-site storage for their crops. Applications for these loans are accepted by county CFSA offices only during periods announced by the Secretary of Agriculture. Contact the above listed office for more details.

* Farm Labor Housing Loans

Farmers Home Administration
U.S. Department of Agriculture (USDA)
South Agriculture Building 5013
Washington, DC 20250   202-720-5177

The Farmers Home Administration makes loans and grants to finance low-rent housing for domestic farm laborers. Funds may be used to build, buy, improve, or repair farm labor housing and to provide related facilities. Loan funds can also be used to finance some amenities, but cannot be used to refinance debts.

* Farm Management and Improvements

The National Fertilizer and Environmental Center
Tennessee Valley Authority (TVA)
Muscle Shoals Reservation
Muscle Shoals, AL 35660-1010   205-386-2593

The Tennessee Valley Authority (TVA) is involved in a broad range of agricultural services. Thousands of demonstration farms have been created to test agricultural improvements. Current research focuses on farm management and record-keeping, planning and specialization, new crops, weed and pest control, and marketing, as well as continued improvements in fertilizer use and production practices. Current agricultural programs include developing alternative fuels from hardwood trees and farm crops, along with recycling nutrients found in farm and municipal waste.

* Farm Money and Credit Reports

Office of Congressional and Public Affairs
Farm Credit Administration
1501 Farm Credit Drive
McLean, VA 22102-5090   703-883-4056

Information on obtaining publications and documents can be obtained from the office above. Some of the documents it has which are available include news releases issued since January 1, 1972, biographies of Farm Credit Administration (FCA) officials, and speeches by FCA officials. Other publications include:

FCA Handbook - Statutes and Regulations (fee charged)
FCA Examination Manual (Set fee Charged)
FCA Bulletin (Published 10 days after each meeting of the FCA Board)
FCA Report (Published on an as-needed basis)
FCA Annual Report
FCA Biographical Sketches:
A Brief History of the Farm Credit System
Risk Analysis of Farm Credit System: Operations & Outlook
The Farm Credit System: A History of Financial Self Help

* Farm Operating Loans

Farmers Home Administration
U.S. Department of Agriculture (USDA)
South Agriculture Building 5420
Washington, DC 20250   202-720-1632

Operating loans may be used to pay for items needed for farm operations, including livestock, farm and home equipment, feed, seed, fertilizer, fuel, chemicals, and hail and other crop insurance; family living expenses, minor building improvements, purchase of stock in certain cooperative associations, creditor payments; purchase of milk base; and refinancing of debts. Family farmers and ranchers are eligible.

* Farm Ownership Loans

Farmers Home Administration
U.S. Department of Agriculture (USDA)
South Agriculture Building 5420
Washington, DC 20250   202-720-1632

Farm Ownership Loans may be used to buy, improve or enlarge farms. Uses may include construction, improvement, or repair of farm homes and service buildings;

improvement in on-farm water supplies; installation of pollution control or energy conservation measures; refinancing debts; clearing or improving forests; and establishing non-agricultural enterprises to help farmers supplement their income.

* Farm Ownership Loans for Socially Disadvantaged Persons

Farmers Home Administration
U.S. Department of Agriculture (USDA)
South Agriculture Building 5420
Washington, DC 20250   202-720-1632

The Federal Home Administration is authorized by the Agricultural Credit Act of 1987 (P.L. 100-233) to set aside funds for farm ownership loans to eligible members of socially disadvantaged groups who will operate family-size farms. Eligible groups are blacks, American Indians or Alaskan Natives, Hispanics,, and Asians or Pacific Islanders.

* Farm Products Cash Value

National Center for Agricultural Utilization Research
U.S. Department of Agriculture (USDA)
Agriculture Research Service (ARS)
1815 N. University St.
Peoria, IL 61604   309-685-4011

The research goal of this center is to increase the cash value of farm products in domestic and foreign markets through improved quality and safety of food and feed, enhanced use of plant materials as renewable resources, and increased efficiency of crop production.

* Farmer-Owned Lending Institutions

Office of Congressional and Public Affairs
Farm Credit Administration
1501 Farm Credit Drive
McLean, VA 22102-5090   703-883-4056

The Farm Credit System is a network of farmer-owned lending institutions and specialized service organizations. In 1916 Congress created the System to provide American agriculture with a dependable source of credit at competitive rates. Today the System provides more than 25 percent of the total credit used by America's farmers, ranchers, and their cooperatives. The *Farm Credit System Information Guide*, which provides information on the Farm Credit System, including a list of the System's banks, is available free from the office above.

* Farming Cooperatives

Agricultural Cooperative Service
U.S. Department of Agriculture (USDA)
P.O. Box 96576, Room 4207S
Washington, DC 20090-6576   202-720-2556

The U.S. Department of Agriculture (USDA) will assist any group interested in starting or developing agricultural cooperatives, and will also work with them to solve organizational, operational, or management problems. They will also help a cooperative expand export markets.

* Farming Profitability and Competitiveness

Executive Officer
Local Extension Service
U.S. Department of Agriculture (USDA)
Room 340A, Administration Building
Washington, DC 20250   202-720-4111

The U.S. Department of Agriculture (USDA) operates an extension program in 3,165 counties located in all of the 50 states and the U.S. territories. Federal, state, and local governments share in financing and conducting cooperative extension educational programs to help farmers, processors, handlers, farm families, communities, and consumers apply the results of food and agricultural research including Competitiveness and Profitability of American Agriculture: To enhance farmers' competitiveness and profitability, Extension helps farmers improve production, finance, and management skills; develop new technology; adjust profitability to global market changes; and strengthen business and support systems.

* Farmland Conservation Efforts

Information Division
Consolidated Farm Service Agency (CFSA)
U.S. Department of Agriculture (USDA)
P.O. Box 2415
Washington, DC 20013   202-720-3168

The Consolidated Farm Service Agency (CFSA) directs a number of conservation programs to preserve and improve American farmland: Conservation Reserve Program (CRP): Targets the most fragile farmland by encouraging farmers to stop growing crops on land designated by conservationists as "highly erodible" and plant grass or trees on it instead. The farmer receives rent on the land for a term of ten years. Cost-share programs are also available for permanent planting of grass and trees in these areas. Agricultural Conservation Program (ACP): This program is designed to solve soil, water, and related resource problems through costsharing. ACP assistance is available to install soil-saving practices, including terraces, grass, sod waterways, and other measures to control erosion. It also helps reduce sediment, chemicals, and livestock waste that contaminate streams and lakes.

* Farmland Natural Disaster Relief

Office of Government and Public Affairs
U.S. Department of Agriculture (USDA)
Washington, DC 20250   202-720-5237

This free publication provides an overview of the U.S. Department of Agriculture's (USDA) disaster assistance programs. It describes types of assistance available and where to apply for assistance. Local extension agents in each county can approve disaster applications for the following: conservation structures (when located on eligible lands); rehabilitation of farm lands destroyed by disaster; crop payment subsidies for disruption caused by disaster to regular crop schedules; sale of animal feed at below market price in emergency situations; animal grazing on reserve or conservation lands in emergency situations; donation of animal feed to Indian reservations when needed; and donation of grain to migratory wildfowl domains. The federal government will also remove debris from a major disaster from publicly- or privately-owned lands or waters.

* Federal Grain Inspection Service

Public Affairs Office
Federal Grain Inspection Service (FGIS)
Room 1095-S
U.S. Department of Agriculture (USDA)   202-720-5091
Washington, DC 20250   Fax: 202-720-9237

The Federal Grain Inspection Service (FGIS) is responsible for inspecting and weighing grain and related commodities; supervising official, private state grain inspections agencies; and maintaining U.S. grade standards for grain. You may obtain more information from this office or by calling AgNewsFax at 202-690-3944 from your fax machine and request documents 3600 and 3601.

* Fertilizer and Chemical Development

The National Fertilizer and Environmental Center
Tennessee Valley Authority
Muscle Shoals Reservation
Muscle Shoals, AL 35660-1010   205-386-2593

The National Fertilizer Development Center plans and manages research and development programs for new and improved fertilizers and processes for their manufacture; for testing and demonstrating methods of chemical and organic fertilizer use as an aid to soil and water conservation and to the improved use of agricultural and related resources; and for operating and maintaining facilities to serve as a national laboratory for research and development in chemistry and chemical engineering related to fertilizers essential to national defense. The center conducts research to develop improved technology for converting cellulosic materials, including trees, to ethanol and other chemicals. Currently, there is an emphasis to demonstrate ways to minimize pollution problems during the handling and use of fertilizers in order to protect the environment.

* Financial Assistance For Rural Residents and Communities

Farmers Home Administration (FmHA)
U.S. Department of Agriculture
Washington, DC 20250   202-720-4323

The Farmers Home Administration (FmHA) provides financial assistance to rural people and communities that cannot obtain commercial credit at affordable terms. Applicants must be unable to obtain credit from usual commercial sources. Examples of the types of loans available are Emergency Loans, Youth Project Loans, Housing Repair Loans and Grants, and Business and Industry Loan Guarantees.

* Forest Insect and Disease Management

Contact: your State Forester or the state office
of the U.S. Forest Service, usually located
in the state capitol.

To reduce loss and damage to forests and lands by forest insects and diseases, the U.S. Department of Agriculture (USDA) provides technical and financial assistance in prevention, detection, evaluation, and suppression of forest insect and disease outbreaks on state and private lands.

* Forestry Incentives Program

Information Division
Consolidated Farm Service Agency (CFSA)
U.S. Department of Agriculture (USDA)
P.O. Box 2415
Washington, DC 20013   202-720-5783

In the Forestry Incentive Program, the Federal Government shares the cost of planting trees and improving timber stands with private landowners. Contact the Consolidated Farm Service Agency (CFSA) to inquire if your land is eligible and for more information on the program.

* Grain Reserve Program

Consolidated Farm Service Agency (CFSA)
U.S. Department of Agriculture (USDA)
Room 3702, South Building
Washington, DC 20250   202-720-3463

The Grain Reserve Program is authorized for farmer owned wheat, corn, grain, sorghum, oats, and barley. When entry into the Reserve is authorized by the Secretary of Agriculture, producers may enter into a contract extending their 9 month loan an additional 27 months and receive quarterly storage payments. Loans may be repaid at any time. Contact Consolidated Farm Service Agency (CFSA) for more details.

* Great Plains Conservation Work

Soil Conservation Service
U.S. Department of Agriculture (USDA)
Washington, DC 20250   202-205-0027

Land users living in the Great Plains states can seek assistance from the Soil Conservation Service (SCS), which offers technical assistance and cost-sharing funds to farmers, ranchers, and other land users in the Great Plains. Cost-share rates can range up to 80 percent for urgently needed conservation work. Contact SCS or your local Soil Conservation Office.

* Gypsy Moth Control

Printing and Distribution Management Branch
Animal and Plant Health Inspection Service (APHIS)
U.S. Department of Agriculture (USDA)
4700 River Rd.
Riverdale, MD 20737   301-734-7799

The following publication is available free of charge from the Animal and Plant Health Inspection Service (APHIS): *Don't Move the Gypsy Moth* (July 1985). This tells how to make sure outdoor household articles don't spread gypsy moths.

* Horticulture Clearinghouse

Reference Desk
National Agricultural Library
U.S. Department of Agriculture (USDA)
10301 Baltimore Blvd.
Beltsville, MD 20705   301-504-5479

Most questions concerning horticultural or botanical question, economic botany, wild plants of possible use, herbs, bonsai, and floriculture can be answered here. For more information you will be referred to the appropriate information center depending on the nature of your interests.

* Hydroponic Farming

Environmental Research Laboratory
2601 East Airport Dr.   602-741-1990
Tucson, AZ 85706-6985   Fax: 602-573-0852

This lab can provide you with information and expertise on hydroponics, the process of growing crops without soil.

* Insects Identification and Control

Contact your local USDA
Extension Service agent

Technical assistance is available to help you identify and eliminate any problems you may have caused by insects and bugs. You are encouraged to catch one of the insects which are causing the problem and send it in for analysis. Contact your local Extension Service for more information.

* Limited Resource Farm Loans

Farmers Home Administration
U.S. Department of Agriculture (USDA)
South Agriculture Building 5420
Washington, DC 20250   202-720-1632

The Farmers Home Administration makes loans to help low income farmers and ranchers who live on not larger than family farms including small family farms, improve their farming and earn a better living. These loans are made on better terms than ordinary farm loans, and those who cannot pay the regular rate of interest because of low income.

* Livestock and Veterinary Services

Livestock and Poultry Sciences
Room 217, Bldg. 200
Beltsville Agricultural Research Center
Beltsville, MD 20705   301-504-8431

Specialists study many topics, including domestic animal diseases, beef production, dairy production, foreign animal diseases, poultry production and diseases, production of sheep and fur-bearing animals, swine production, and livestock facilities.

* Livestock Rangeland

Rangeland Resources
Bureau of Land Management (BLM)
U.S. Department of the Interior
Washington, DC 20240   202-208-3435

The Bureau of Land Management has administration of 170 million acres of public lands where livestock graze. About 18,800 ranchers and farmers graze livestock on BLM-managed lands. A majority of these permittees have small (less than 100 head) or medium (100 to 500 head) livestock operations.

* Multiple Uses of Crops

Alternative Farming Center
U.S. Department of Agriculture (USDA)
10301 Baltimore Blvd.
Beltsville, MD 20705   301-504-5724

This center covers new crops or new uses for old crops, including forest products and especially crops from which "natural rubber" can be produced.

* National Agricultural Library (NAL) Reference Service

Reference Staff
National Agricultural Library (NAL)
U.S. Department of Agriculture (USDA)
10301 Baltimore Blvd., Room 111
Beltsville, MD 20705-2351   301-504-5204

These services may be requested in person, by phone, or in writing. The Library's subject specialists regularly guide users in search of answers, information or assistance with research. Staff will conduct brief searches on topics of user's choice, conduct exhaustive searches on a cost-recovery basis, furnish bibliographies, guides or fact sheets, or identify current research being conducted by USDA research agencies. Reference services are free up to a point determined by Library management, thereafter fees are charged. Because of limited staff, users are encouraged to consult local libraries first.

* National Agricultural Library Services

National Agricultural Library (NAL)
10301 Baltimore Blvd.
Beltsville, MD 20705-2351   301-504-5755

The National Agricultural Library (NAL) provides comprehensive information services for the food and agricultural sciences through a variety of sources, which include bibliographies, personal reference services, loans, photocopies, and online data files. Services are provided to agricultural colleges, research institutions, government agencies, agricultural associations, industry, individual scientists, and the general public. NAL cooperates with the Library of Congress and the National Library of Medicine to provide access to publications worldwide in the agricultural, chemical, and biological sciences. NAL houses one of the largest collections in the free world on agricultural subjects--2.3 million volumes and 26,000 periodicals--including biology, chemistry, nutrition, forestry, soil sciences, and much more.

* National Agriculture Clearinghouse

National Agricultural Library (NAL)
U.S. Department of Agriculture (USDA)
10301 Baltimore Blvd.
Beltsville, MD 20705-2351   301-504-5755

The National Agricultural Library (NAL) has established 12 specialized information centers to provide enhanced services to its current clientele, as well as to develop new service relationships with the public and private sectors. Aside from agricultural researchers, centers also serve educators, consumers, and the private sector. Each center has a coordinator responsible for planning the center's activities, including reference services, collection development, developing information products, coordinating outreach activities, and establishing distribution networks.

* National Agriculture Statistics

Agricultural Statistics Board
U.S. Department of Agriculture (USDA)
South Agriculture Building, Room 5809
Washington, DC 20250-2351   202-720-7017

The National Agricultural Statistics Service, through its Washington DC headquarters and 45 field offices serving all 50 states, annually publishes hundreds of reports detailing production and prospects for crops, livestock, dairy, and poultry. Other releases outline stocks, prices, labor, weather and similar items concerning farmers, ranchers and those associated with agriculture. Information is gathered from agricultural producers and available to the public. The information is also available electronically through the Departments Computerized Information Delivery (CID) System. When calling, ask for a copy of the *Agricultural Statistics Board Catalogue*, which contains contact names as well as a complete list of reports broken down by topic area. It is available free.

* National Animal Health Monitoring System

Veterinary Services
Animal and Plant Health Inspection Service (APHIS)
U.S. Department of Agriculture (USDA)
4700 River Road
Riverdale, MD 20737   301-734-8687

The National Animal Health Monitoring System (NAHMS) is a cooperative effort to gain health status information about various species of farm animals that will benefit producers, exporters, researchers, practicing veterinarians, and local, state, and federal animal health officials. Information from NAHMS enables producers to improve farm management practices, especially disease control. For more information call or write the office listed above.

* National Association of State Aquaculture Coordinators (NASAC)

Secretary/Treasurer
National Association of State Aquaculture Coordinators (NASAC)
P.O. Box 1163
Richmond, VA 23209   804-371-6094

The National Association of State Aquaculture Coordinators (NASAC) is an affiliate of the National Association of State Departments of Agriculture (NASDA). The Coordinators are responsible for coordinating aquaculture programs at the state or territorial level. The purpose of NASAC is to promote, to encourage, and to assist the development of aquaculture in the United States by enhancing communication among federal, state, and local and tribal government agencies; agricultural research and extension institutions; and trade and marketing organizations. For more information and a Directory of State Aquaculture Coordinators and Contacts contact the office above.

* National Biological Impact Assessment Program (NBIAP) Information Systems

Doug King
National Biological Impact Assessment Program (NBIAP)
Virginia Tech   703-231-3747

120 Engel Hall   Data: 800-624-2723
Blacksburg, VA 24061   Internet: ftp.nbiap.bt.edu

The National Biological Impact Assessment Program (NBIAP) is a United States Department of Agriculture (USDA) program designed to advance agricultural and environmental biotechnology research and promote biosafety by expediting the flow of information. Major NBIAP projects are funded through Information Systems for Biotechnology (ISB), a joint project between Virginia Tech and USDA. ISB maintains extensive textfiles and databases of agbiotech information and produces a monthly News Report, Agbiotech regulations, policy statements and announcements are available, as well as searchable databases of field tests of genetically engineered crops, products approaching commercial release, state biotech regulators and agbiotech companies.

* National Pesticide Telecommunications Network Pesticide Information Hotline (PIN)

National Pesticide Telecommunications Network   800-858-7378
                                                    Fax: 806-743-3094

This service of the U.S. Environmental Protection Agency and Texas Tech University is open 24 hours, 7 days a week. It responds to non-emergency questions about the effects of pesticides, toxicology and symptoms, environmental effects, disposal and cleanup, and safe use of pesticides.

* Non-Farm Enterprise Loans

Farmers Home Administration
U.S. Department of Agriculture (USDA)
South Agriculture Building 6321
Washington, DC 20250-2351   202-720-4323

The Farmers Home Administration makes loans to family farmers and ranchers and gives technical and management assistance for development and operation of non-farm enterprises to supplement farm income. Enterprises for which loans can be made include: repair and service shops, restaurants and grocery stores, camping sites, and riding stables.

* Orchard and Forest Tree Losses

Information Division
Consolidated Farm Service Agency (CFSA)
U.S. Department of Agriculture (USDA)
P.O. Box 2415
Washington, DC 20013   202-720-7962

The CFSA administers disaster assistance programs to provide payments to producers sustaining orchard and forest tree losses in either 1990 or 1991. To be eligible, producers must have less than $2 million gross annual revenue and be in compliance with highly erodible land and wetland conservation provisions of the law. To qualify, owners must own at least one acre of orchard or forest trees, but not more than 500 acres of orchard trees (not more than 1,000 ares in the case of forest trees) and must have owned the trees at the time of the disaster.

* Patent Licensing Opportunities

National Patent Program
Room 401, Building 005
BARC-West
Beltsville, MD 20705   301-504-2518

Government patents resulting from agricultural research discoveries are available for licensing to U.S. companies and citizens. Licenses are offered on a non-exclusive, exclusive, and co-exclusive basis. Non-exclusive licenses are generally granted when no large investment to market a product is expected. Exclusive and co-exclusive licenses are granted when substantial investment is required. Fees for licenses are negotiable. An annual catalog listing all patents available for license plus technical abstracts is available. The necessary regulations and forms are included.

* Patents on Seeds

Plant Variety Protection Office
Commodities Scientific Support Division
Agricultural Marketing Service (AMS)
National Agricultural Library (NAL), Room 500
Beltsville, MD 20705-2351   301-504-2518

Unique seeds, with few exceptions, that are sexually reproduced can be protected by patents, The protection, which extends for 18 years, provides owners with exclusive rights to sell, reproduce, export, and produce the seed.

* Perishable Agricultural Commodities

Information Staff
Agricultural Fair Practices Act
Agricultural Marketing Service (AMS)
U.S. Department of Agriculture (USDA)   202-720-8998
Washington, DC 20250   Fax: 202-720-7135

The Perishable Agricultural Commodities Act (PACA) is designed to encourage fair trading practices in the marketing of fresh and frozen fruits and vegetables. It prohibits unfair and fraudulent practices, and it provides a means of enforcing contracts in interstate or foreign commerce. PACA offices handle complaints involving unfair trading practices, endeavor to bring parties together, and arrange informal settlement of disputes. Representatives regularly furnish advice to growers, shippers, and buyers on their marketing transactions upon request. They also make spot checks from time to time. More information is available from this office.

* Pesticide and Quarantine Programs

Animal and Plant Health Inspection Service (APHIS)
Plant Protection and Quarantine
6505 Belcrest Rd.
Hyattsville, MD 20782   301-436-7799

The U.S. Department of Agriculture (USDA) helps states and growers control or eradicate pests and diseases that cause plant loss. Animal and Plant Health Inspection Service (APHIS) cooperates with state agencies to establish quarantines, pesticide spray programs, or release of sterile insects to reduce pest populations.

* Pesticide Database

National Pesticides Information Retrieval System (NPIRS)
Center for Environmental and Regulatory Systems (CERIS)
U.S. Environmental Protection Agency (EPA)
1231 Cumberland Ave., Suite A   317-494-6614
West Lafayette, IN 47906-1317   Fax: 317-494-9727

The National Pesticide Information Retrieval System (NPIRS), a subscription database of the Center for Environmental and Regulatory Systems (CERIS), provides information on pesticide products which have been registered by the Environmental Protection Agency (EPA). Online databases available on NPIRS include:

Registered pesticide product information - over 23,000 active products and over 59,000 canceled and transferred product registrations. Updated weekly.
Pesticides tolerance indices by chemical or commodity name - lists the allowable residues of pesticides in raw agriculture commodities, processed food, and animal feed. Updated monthly.
Chemical information fact sheet - over 230 registered chemical summaries are available.
Pesticide document management system - over 220,000 citations of studies submitted to EPA in support of pesticide chemical registrations. Updated monthly.
Material safety data sheets (MSD) - over 900 MSDs from 27 chemical manufacturers of pesticides used in the protection of crops, turf, and ornamental plants. Updated quarterly.

* Pesticide Dissipation in Soil

The National Fertilizer and Environmental Center (NFERC)
Tennessee Valley Authority
Muscle Shoals Reservation
Muscle Shoals, AL 35660-1010   205-386-2593

National Fertilizer and Environmental Center (NFERC) researchers are currently evaluating the influence on management practices, such as the use of cover crops and variations in nitrogen application rates, on the absorption and degradation of pesticides in soil. Relative emphasis is placed on the effects on the potential movement of pesticides to groundwater. Laboratory studies have been initiated to examine the effect of cover crop residuals, such as wheat and canola, on adsorption, degradation and movement. For more information, contact principal investigator Sidney S. Harper.

* Pesticides Documents Management System (PDMS)

National Pesticides Information Retrieval System (NPIRS)
Center for Environmental and Regulatory Systems (CERIS)
1231 Cumberland Ave., Suite A   317-494-6614
West Lafayette, IN 47906-1317   Fax: 317-494-9727

The Pesticides Documents Management System (PDMS) is an automated index containing over 220,000 citations of studies or documents, most of which have been submitted to the Environmental Protection Agency (EPA) in support of pesticides registrations. This database had been found useful to pesticides registrants,

consultants, state and federal regulatory officials and others seeking information related to health and safety. The data is updated monthly. The National Pesticides Information Retrieval System (NPIRS) is available by subscription only.

* Pesticides Information Network (PIN)

Office of Pesticide Programs
Environmental Protection Agency (7507C)   703-305-7499
401 M St., SW   Fax: 703-305-6309
Washington, DC 20460   Data: 703-305-5919

The Pesticides Information Network (PIN) provides a contacts directory, pesticide applicator training bibliography, pesticide monitoring inventory, pesticide environmental fate and effects data summaries, and current or suspended pesticides, and restricted use product information. PIN serves as a mechanism for collecting and disseminating pesticide information and provides a source of expertise for pesticide-related activities. There are no access restriction or user fees at this time. PIN is available 24 hours a day, 7 days a week.

* Pesticides Rules and Regulations

Office of Pesticide Programs
Environmental Protection Agency (7506C)
401 M Street, SW   703-305-5805
Washington, DC 20460   Fax: 703-305-5884

The Pesticides Docket provides public access to documentation for each Registration Standard under development when the Agency begins review of data for the Registration Standard or upon publication of a notice setting out the list and sequence of Registration Standards. The docket contains documentation of pre-special and special reviews of pesticides, memoranda, all comments, correspondence, documents, proposals, or other materials concerning a pending pesticide regulatory decision provided to the Agency by a person or party outside of government (other than confidential business information).

* Plant and Entomological Services

Information Staff
Beltsville Agricultural Research Service
U.S. Department of Agriculture
Room 307, Bldg. 307, BARC West
Beltsville, MD 20705   301-504-6875

Specialists study and can provide you with information on biological control of pests, corn and sorghum production, crop mechanization and pest control equipment, crop pollination, bees and honey, insect control, forage crop production, range management, plant genetics and breeding, pesticide use and impacts, plant pathology, weed control, small grains production, sugar crop production, and plant physiology.

* Plant Breeders Protection

Plant Variety Protection Office
U.S. Department of Agriculture
National Agricultural Library (NAL) Building
Agricultural Marketing Service (AMS)
10301 Baltimore Blvd., Room 500
Beltsville, MD 20705-2351   301-504-5518

Federal legislation protects the ownership rights of breeders of plants that reproduce through seeds. The Agricultural Marketing Service will certify whether or not a new variety is entitled to patent protection.

* Plant Genome Data and Information Center

National Agricultural Library (NAL)
U.S. Department of Agriculture (USDA)   301-504-6613
10301 Baltimore Blvd., 4th Floor   Fax: 301-504-7098
Beltsville, MD 20705-2351   Internet: pgenome@nalusda.gov

The Plant Genome Data and Information Center provides a variety of information services and publications on all aspects of plant and animal genome mapping including: nucleotide and protein sequencing; physical and cytogenetic maps; plant breeding efforts based on or using mapping efforts. The Center can furnish you with quick bibliographies or special reference briefs on genome mapping. The information center is also associated with several databases on genetic research. Also ask about *Probe,* the newsletter of the USDA Plant Genome Research Program. Some of the quick bibliographies include:

Artificial Seeds (1993)
DNA Fingerprinting and Plants (1993)
Maize Genome Mapping (1994)

Agriculture and Farming

New Oilseed Crops (1993)
Plant Genome Research Grant Program, First Annual Report (1992)
Probe: The Official Newsletter for the USDA Plant Genome Research Program
  (1991-1993)
Transgenic Tomato (1994)
USDA's Plant Genome Research Program (1991)

* Post-Harvest Processing
Southern Regional Research Center
U.S. Department of Agriculture (USDA)
1100 Robert E. Lee Blvd.
ARS, Box 19687
New Orleans, LA 70179   504-286-4200
Research at this center relates primarily to post-harvest processing, product enhancement, and the safety and use of agricultural commodities produced in the southern U.S.

* Production, Coops, and Marketing Groups
Your local Extension Agent or
Office for the Assistant Secretary
Science and Education Department
U.S. Department of Agriculture (USDA)
Washington, DC 20250   202-720-5923
The USDA will provide educational and technical assistance to any agricultural production or marketing association, group, or cooperative. They provide the latest USDA land grant university research findings, discuss new technology, and share the results of feasibility studies, market analysis reports, and the development of new products and markets.

* Quarterly Report to Congress
Current Information Branch
Agricultural Research Service
U.S. Department of Agriculture, Building 005
Beltsville, MD 20705   301-344-2340
The free *Quarterly Report To Congress* summarizes research findings of projects conducted by USDA. Reports cover livestock, poultry, crops, insect pest control, soil and water resources, human nutrition, post-harvest technology, and commercial uses for commodities.

* Quick Bibliography Series
National Agricultural Library (NAL)
U.S. Department of Agriculture (USDA)
10301 Baltimore Blvd.
Beltsville, MD 20705   301-504-5755
An invaluable resource for the researcher, the *Quick Bibliography* series can provide you with article, book, and conference paper citations and abstracts. Cites are taken from the AGRICOLA system. Contact the NAL information centers to inquire about the availability of *Quick Bibliographies* in your area of interest. They are available free.

* Requirements of the Animal Welfare Act
Animal Welfare Information Center (AWIC)
National Agricultural Library (NAL)
U.S. Department of Agriculture (USDA)   301-504-6212
10301 Baltimore Blvd.   Fax: 301-504-6409
Beltsville, MD 20705-2351   E-mail: awic@nalusda.gov
The Animal Welfare Information Center (AWIC) conducts a quarterly workshop, *Meeting the Information Requirements of the Animal Welfare Act*, which assists researchers in understanding and complying with the Act. The workshop covers legislation, the "alternative concept" in animal research, and the mechanics of developing and executing a literature search on both compact disk and online databases. The workshop also provides hands-on experience in searching online databases relevant to their subject areas.

* Rural Information Center (RIC)
Rural Information Center (RIC)
National Agricultural Library (NAL)   800-633-7701
U.S. Department of Agriculture (USDA)   301-504-5372
10301 Baltimore Blvd., Room 304   Fax: 301-504-5181
Beltsville, MD 20705-2351   E-mail: ric@nalusda.gov

The Rural Information Center (RIC) provides information and referral services to rural citizens working to maintain the vitality of America's rural areas. One of the areas RIC focuses on is the economic competitiveness, management and marketing education, profitability of rural business, including agriculture and natural resource-based enterprises. The Office of Rural Health Policy in the Department of Health and Human Services and the NAL jointly created a rural health information clearinghouse known as the Rural Information Center Health Service (RICHS). RICHS, situated within RIC, is a national clearinghouse for collecting and disseminating information on rural health issues, research findings related to rural health, and innovative approaches to the delivery of rural health care services.

* Seed Quality and Inspection Labs
Federal Seed Lab
U.S. Department of Agriculture (USDA)
Beltsville, MD 20705   301-504-8089
The federal government can test seeds to determine their quality and whether they are free from contamination. They will also prosecute any agent that transfers contaminated or mislabeled seed from state to state. Seeds are examined by or at a state agent's request, and there may be some fee involved.

* Soil and Farmland Protection Programs
Soil Conservation Service (SCS)
U.S. Department of Agriculture (USDA)
P.O. Box 2890
Washington, DC 20013   202-720-9149
Soil surveys are used not only for conservation purposes but also to identify suitable lands for a wide variety of uses, from maintaining crops to urban uses. Information about soil helps prevent major construction mistakes and misuse of land that can be productively put to use. Soil maps identify flood-prone areas and sources of water pollutants. The Soil Conservation Service (SCS) has a tremendous amount of material available on all aspects of soil conservation. The following is a list of some of the publications available from the SCS.

Assistance Available from the SCS - Program Aid 1532
Going Wild with Soil and Water Conservation - Program Aid 1363
Save Soil Systematically - Program Aid 1366
Soil Erosion by Wind - Agriculture Information Bulletin 555
Soil Erosion by Water - Agriculture Information Bulletin 513

* Soil and Water Loans
Farmers Home Administration
U.S. Department of Agriculture (USDA)
South Agriculture Building 5420
Washington, DC 20250   202-720-1632
The Farmers Home Administration makes soil and water loans and provides technical management assistance to owners or operators of farms and ranches for developing, conserving, and making proper use of their land and water resources. Activities eligible for these loans include irrigation, farmstead water, drainage, soil and water conservation, forestry, fish farming, land development, certain pollution abatement or control activities.

* Soil Conservation Technical Expertise
Soil Conservation Service (SCS)
U.S. Department of Agriculture (USDA)
P.O. Box 2890
Washington, DC 20013   202-720-1845
Technical expertise is available in such areas as irrigation, drainage, landscape architecture, construction, sanitary and water quality, and hydrology.

* Soil Conservation Volunteers
The Earth Team
7515 N.E. Ankeny Road
Ankeny, IA 50021   800-THE SOIL
Earth Team volunteers work to improve the soil where they live and represent the local volunteer arms of the Soil Conservation Service (SCS). Call for a free information packet and information on the Earth Team.

* Soil, Water, and Air Sciences
Agriculture Research Service
ARS Information Staff

U.S. Department of Agriculture (USDA)
Room 307-A, Building 005
Beltsville, MD 20705 301-504-6264

Specialists study such topics as environmental quality, erosion and sedimentation, soil fertility and plant nutrition, organic wastes, pesticide degradation, water use efficiency and tillage practices, and weed control. Contact the ARS staff for answers to questions on these and other conservation-related topics.

* State-based Farming Research

Cooperative State Research Service
U.S. Department of Agriculture (USDA)
Washington, DC 20250-2200 202-720-4423

More than half of the publicly funded agricultural research in the U.S. is conducted at State Agricultural Experiment Stations (SAES), located on land-grant universities in each state and territory in the U.S. The SAES serve as an early warning system for problems and opportunities. Such advancements as iodized salt, fluoride toothpaste, and mineral and vitamin additives for food came from these laboratories. Scientists are involved with experiments to reduce food costs for the consumer, reforest our landscape with genetically improved trees free from insects and diseases, produce leaner meat, control pests, prevent acid rain, and fight insect pests. Since the SAES are located at the land-grant universities, the Cooperative Extension Service readily transfers research to the classroom and to citizens.

* Sustainable Agriculture Network (SAN)

Gabriel Hegyes, SAN Coordinator
Alternative Farming System Information Center, Room 304
National Agricultural Library/ARS
U.S. Department of Agriculture (USDA) 301-504-2351
10301 Baltimore Blvd. Fax: 301-504-6409
Beltsville, MD 20705-2351 Internet: gopher.ces.ncsu.edu

The Sustainable Agriculture Network (SAN) is a cooperative effort of university, government, business, and non-profit organizations dedicated to the exchange of scientific and practical information on sustainable agricultural systems. It is a network supporting the exchange of information with a variety of users. The networking takes many forms: print, meetings, as well as electronically. You will have access to SAN databases including SARE/ACE Research Reports, summaries of the projects funded by the USDA/CSRS Sustainable Agriculture Research and Education program; The Directory is a listing of detailed characteristics by individuals and organizations that are willing to share their expertise in sustainable agriculture; Showcase is an annotated bibliography of educational and informational materials; Managing Cover Crops Profitably is a guide for farmers looking for alternatives to chemical fertility and weed control, Discussions Group, members of the group share sources of information and help answer each others; questions (subscribe sanet-mg), and information on more Internet resources (send internet exploring-internet to the address: almanac@esusda.gov). For more information or help accessing SAN, contact the office above.

* Technology Assessment Reports

Office of Technology Assessment (OTA)
Publications Order
U.S. Congress
Washington, DC 20510-8025 202-224-8996

These Office of Technology Assessment (OTA) publications are available through the office above, the Government Printing Office, and the National Technical Information Service. To find out correct ordering information and prices, along with brief summaries of the following studies, contact the OTA office above and request their current publications catalog.

Agriculture and Forestry

Africa Tomorrow: Issues in Technology, Agriculture, and U.S. Foreign Aid (TM-F-31)
Agricultural Postharvest Technology and Marketing Economics Research (TM-F-21)
Assessing Biological Diversity in the United States: Data Considerations (BP-F-39)
Commercial Biotechnology: An International Analysis (BA-218)
Continuing the Commitment: Agricultural Development in the Sahel (F-308)
Enhancing Agriculture in Africa: A Role for Development Assistance (F-356)
Enhancing the Quality of U.S. Grain for International Trade (F-399)
Grain Quality in International Trade: A Comparison of Major U.S. Competitors (F-402)
Grassroots Conservation of Biological Diversity in the United States (BP-F-38)
Grassroots Development: The African Development Foundation (F-378)
Impacts of Applied Genetics: Micro-Organisms, Plants, and Animals (HR-132)
Impacts of Technology on U.S. Cropland and Rangeland Productivity (F-166)

Innovative Biological Technologies for Lesser Developed Countries (BP-F-29)
Pesticide Residues in Food (F-398)
Plants: The Potential for Extracting Protein, Medicines, and Other Useful Chemicals (BP-F-23)
A Review of U.S. Competitiveness in Agriculture Trade (TM-TET-29)
Sustaining Tropical Forest Resources: Reforestation of Degraded Lands (BP-F-18)
Sustaining Tropical Forest Resources: U.S. and International Institutions (BP-F-19)
Technologies To Benefit Agriculture and Wildlife (BP-F-34)
Technologies To Maintain Biological Diversity (F-330)
Technologies To Sustain Tropical Forest Resources (F-214)
Technology and the American Economic Transition (TET-283)
Technology, Public Policy, and the Changing Structure of American Agriculture (F-285)
Technology, Public Policy, and the Changing Structure of American Agriculture: A Special Report for the 1985 Farm Bill (F-272)
Technology, Renewable Resources, and American Crafts (BP-F-27)
Water-Related Technologies for Sustainable Agriculture in U.S. Arid/Semiarid Lands (F-212)
Water-Related Technologies for Sustainable Agriculture in U.S. Arid/Semiarid Lands: Selected Foreign Experience (BP-F-20)
Wetlands: Their Use and Regulation (0-206)
Wood Use: U.S. Competitiveness and Technology (ITE-210) Volume I, (ITE-224) Volume II

* Technology Transfer Information Center (TTIC)

National Agriculture Library (NAL)
U.S. Department of Agriculture (USDA) 301-504-6875
10301 Baltimore Blvd., 4th Floor Fax: 301-504-7098
Beltsville, MD 20705-2351 Internet: ttic@nalusda.gov

The National Agricultural Library (NAL) established the Technology Transfer Information Center (TTIC) in 1989 as a vehicle to get results of research to individuals and organizations. TTIC assists USDA personnel and private sector individuals and firms to locate the technology they need. General literature focuses on such areas as: leadership, innovation, creativity, quality, competitiveness, future trends, and science and technology policy. Literature specific to technology transfer focuses on; Federal and university laboratories; methodologies, processes, and models; intellectual property rights; patents; cooperative research and development agreements; licensing agreements; centers of excellence; incubators; entrepreneurship; and venture capital. The TTIC compile and edit T' Squared, the monthly newsletter of the Technology Transfer Society. Other publications available include:

Generating Solutions to the Hardwood Industry's Technology Based Problems (1991)
Transferring Technologies for the Hardwood Industry: Detection System to Identify Wetwood in Standing Living Trees and in Cut Logs and Boards (1992)
Transferring Technologies for the Hardwood Industry: External and Internal Defect Detection to Optimize Cutting of Hardwood Logs and Lumber (1992)

* Tobacco Inspection

Tobacco Division
U.S. Department of Agriculture (USDA)
Room 520 Annex
AMS, P.O. Box 96456
Washington, DC 20090-6456 202-205-0567

Tobacco sold at auction in designated U.S. markets, along with imported tobacco (except cigar and oriental varieties), are inspected.

* Transportation Services for Agricultural Products

Office of Transportation
U.S. Department of Agriculture (USDA)
P.O. Box 96456
Washington, DC 20250-6456 202-690-1303

This office recognizes that transportation facilities are an integral part of the agribusiness system. Farmers, shippers, farm organizations and local or state agencies who wish to bring about changes in freight service or rates for food products can seek assistance through this office.

* TVA Fertilizer Research and Development

National Fertilizer and Environmental Development Center
Resource Development
Tennessee Valley Authority (TVA)
Muscle Shoals Reservation
Muscle Shoals, AL 35660 205-386-2593

At its National Fertilizer Development Center, the Tennessee Valley Authority

Agriculture and Farming

(TVA) operates the world's leading facility for developing new fertilizer technology. Major objectives of this program have been to reduce energy requirements for fertilizer production and increase the efficiency of fertilizer use. Also, emphasis is on an environmental initiative aimed at avoiding an adverse environmental impact from fertilizer production, distribution, and use. Various activities with agricultural colleges and fertilizer industries take place, including model plant compliance demonstrations and educational audiovisuals.

* USDA Plant Hardiness Zone Map

Superintendent of Documents
U.S. Government Printing Office (GPO)   202-512-1800
Washington, DC 20402   Fax: 202-512-2250

This map consists of a waterproof chart showing ten different zones, each of which represents an area of winter hardiness of the plants of agriculture and natural landscape. It also introduces Zone 11 to represent areas that have average annual minimum temperatures above 40 degrees Fahrenheit (22 degrees Celsius) and that are therefore essentially frost free. The stock number is 001-000-04550-4 and the price is $6.50.

* U.S. Department of Agriculture Economic Agencies Reports

Economic Research Service
U.S. Department of Agriculture (USDA)
1301 New York Avenue, NW
Washington, DC 20005   202-219-0515

The USDA agricultural economics agencies publish a quarterly catalogue entitled *ERS-NASS*. It contains a list of available reports form the Economic Research Service, the National Agricultural Statistics Service, and the World Agricultural Outlook Board. It is available free.

* U.S. Department of Agriculture Resources

Information Office
U.S. Department of Agriculture (USDA)
Office of Public Affairs, Room 507-A
Washington, DC 20250   202-720-2791

The information staff can help you get the facts you need. USDA also publishes a variety of publications. Some of the general, more helpful ones are:

Fact Book of Agriculture. Published annually, this monograph details the mission of the many USDA agencies, and provides a plethora of information about agriculture in the U.S.

How to Get Information from USDA: Lists sources of information in the USDA agencies.

Your United States Department of Agriculture: Provides some history of the USDA and describes how this huge agency serves farms, local communities, as well as the world agricultural communities.

Report of the Secretary of Agriculture: Published annually, this report gives a summary of progress and initiatives for the policy making agencies in USDA--great source of "what's new" at the USDA.

* Water Quality and Natural Resources Education

Executive Officer
Local Extension Service
U.S. Department of Agriculture (USDA)
Room 340A Administration Building
Washington, DC 20250   202-720-7947

The USDA operates an extension program in 3,165 counties located in all of the 50 states and the U.S. territories. Federal, state, and local governments share in financing and conducting cooperative extension educational programs to help farmers, processors, handlers, farm families, communities, and consumers apply the results of food and agricultural research, including Conservation and Management of Natural Resources, which helps people benefit from natural ecosystems without destroying them, sustain a productive natural resource base, market natural resource goods and services, and formulate and implement sound public policies. In the Water Quality program officials work with consumers, producers and local government to teach them more about the importance of high-quality ground water and the conservation of water resources. Emphasis is also put on the effects of agricultural chemicals and contaminants on water quality.

* Water Quality and Preservation

Deputy for Programs
Soil Conservation Service (SCS)
U.S. Department of Agriculture (USDA)
Box 2890
Washington, DC 20013   202-720-4527

The USDA manages a variety of water resource programs to aid landowners and agricultural operators use existing water resources wisely. These programs also promote reclamation and preservation of water sources that have been contaminated or allowed to fall into disrepair. USDA will provide technical and financial assistance for approved projects that meet its criteria.

* Water Quality/Environmental Monitoring

The National Fertilizer and Environmental Center (NFERC)
Agricultural Research Projects
Tennessee Valley Authority (TVA)
Muscle Shoals Reservation
Muscle Shoals, AL 35660-1010   205-386-2593

The National Fertilizer and Environmental Center (NFERC) is currently working to increase awareness of its expertise in environmentally related activities among Congressional staff, administrators of other Federal agencies, such as the Environmental Protection Agency, National Oceanic and Atmospheric Administration, and U.S. Geological Survey (USGS) and many other policy makers. NFERC researchers monitor and comment on legislative proposals and reports.

* Water Quality Information Center (WQIC)

National Agricultural Library (NAL)
U.S. Department of Agriculture (USDA)   301-504-6077
10301 Baltimore Blvd., 4th Floor   Fax: 301-504-7098
Beltsville, MD 20705-2351   E-Mail: wqic@nalusda.gov
                                             Internet: gopher.nalusda.gov
              or http://www.inform.umd.EdRes/Topic/AgrEnv/Water
          Data: 301-504-5496; 301-504-5497; 301-504-5111; 301-504-6510

The Water Quality Information Center (WQIC) was established in 1990 as part of the USDA's coordinated plan responding to the President's initiative on water quality. The primary focus of the Center is on the quality of water resources as they affect or are affected by agricultural production practices. Information from the WQIC is available on the ALF electronic network. Call or write for a publications list. Some of the free bibliographies include:

QB 91-145 Water Quality Implications of Conservation Tillage
QB 91-51 Allocation of Water Resources (1/85-7/90)
QB 94-05 Bioassessment of Water Resources (1/85-12/93)
QB 93-65 Water Quality and Forestry
QB 94-13 Conservation Tillage (1/91-12/93)
QB 94-35 Irrigating Efficiently (1/88-2/94)
QB 93-71 Researching Water Quality (1/89-7/93)
QB 93-03 Sustainable or Alternate Agriculture (1/90-9/92)

* Water Related Resources

Public Affairs Division
Bureau of Reclamation
Department of the Interior
Washington, DC 20240-0001   202-208-4662

The mission of the Bureau of Reclamation is to manage, develop, and protect, water and related resources in an environmentally and economically sound manner in arid and semi-arid lands of the western states. The Reclamation project provides for sustained economic growth, an improved environment, and an enhanced quality of life through the development of a water storage and delivery infrastructure, which provides safe and dependable water supplies and hydroelectric power for agricultural, municipal and industrial users.

* Wood Pests

Your local Forest Service or
Extension Office, or
Forest Insect and Disease Research
U.S. Department of Agriculture (USDA)
P.O. Box 96090
Washington, DC 20090-6090   202-205-1532

The USDA provides technical assistance for insect and diseases to wood, whether it is in use, stored, wood products, or urban trees. All insect and disease suppression projects must meet specific criteria for federal participation.

* Worldwide Access to NAL

Bill Feidt
NAL Library Automation Branch
National Agricultural Library (NAL)
U.S. Department of Agriculture (USDA)   301-504-6813
10301 Baltimore Blvd.   Fax: 301-504-7473
Beltsville, MD 20705-2351   E-mail: wfeidt@nalusda.gov
                                               Internet: gopher.nalusda.gov 70

Immediate electronic access to the resources and services of the National Agricultural
Library (NAL) are now available worldwide through the new NAL Gopher server
and the Internet. Services currently available include access to: NAL Information
Centers; NAL publications and resources; links to agricultural items authored outside
of NAL; and links to 31 other Gopher systems. There are plans to continue adding
new services to the system.

* Young, Beginning, and Small Farmers

Farm Credit Administration (FCA)
1501 Farm Credit Drive
McLean, VA 22102-5090   703-883-4056

Each Federal Land Bank Association, Production Credit Association, Federal Land
Credit Association, and Agricultural Credit Association is required by law, under
policies established by each Farm Credit district board, to prepare a program for
furnishing sound and constructive credit and related services to young beginning, and
small farmers. Specific efforts generally focus on educational efforts and assistance
in the extension of credit. Education programs emphasize the need for sound
recordkeeping and management practices. Credit program assistance usually involves
efforts to coordinate regular loan programs with special assistance from the Federal,
State, and local agencies. For information on specific programs, contact the Farm
Credit Administration.

Food Quality and Distribution

* See also Health and Medicine; Food Facts, Nutrition and Diets Chapter
* See also Consumer Chapter

* Beef and Meat Grading and Certification

Meat Grading and Certification Branch
U.S. Department of Agriculture
Room 2628, P.O. Box 96456
Washington, DC 20090-6456   202-720-1113

All meat is federally inspected on a mandatory basis. All other product grading is voluntary. Grading of meat, poultry, eggs, and dairy products and fresh and processed fruits and vegetables is provided on request for a fee. For further information, contact the appropriate office.

* Child and Adult Care Food Program (CACFP)

Food and Consumer Service
U.S. Department of Agriculture (USDA)
3101 Park Center Drive   703-305-2286
Alexandria, VA 22302   Fax: 703-305-1117

The Child and Adult Care Food Program (CACFP) provides Federal funds and USDA donated foods to nonresidential child care and adult day care facilities to serve nutritious meals and snacks to participants. Federal funds come in the form of reimbursements to participating institutions for meals served under the program. CACFP generally operates in child care centers, outside-school-hours care centers, family day care homes, and certain adult day-care centers. The program spent nearly $1.5 billion in 1995.

* Cotton, Dairy, Produce, Meat Regulations

Information Staff
Agricultural Marketing Service (AMS)
U.S. Department of Agriculture (USDA)
Room 3510, South Building
P.O. Box 96456   202-720-8998
Washington, DC 20090-6456   Fax: 202-720-7135

This office regulates the following segments of the agricultural industry: cotton, dairy products, fruits and vegetables, some livestock, poultry, grains, seeds, and also tobacco.

* Crop Yields and Food Research

Beltsville Agricultural Research Center (BARC)
U.S. Department of Agriculture
10300 Baltimore Ave.
Building 3, Room 223
Beltsville, MD 20705   301-504-6078

The Beltsville Agricultural Research Center (BARC) is among the largest and most diversified agricultural complexes in the world. About 900 scientists and technicians who specialize in a wide variety of research projects, have a long list of accomplishments to their credit. Animal researchers study livestock diseases, animal nutritional needs, and animal genetics and physiology. Plant specialists seek greater crop yields by breeding plants that use light and nutrients more efficiently. Broad research topics include animals, insects, plants, soil, air water, human nutrition, and family resources.

* Dairy Certification

Dairy Grading Branch
Dairy Division
Agricultural Marketing Service (AMS)
U.S. Department of Agriculture (USDA)
Ag Box 0230   202-720-3171
Washington, DC 20250-0230   Fax: 202-720-2643

If you need help in meeting importers' specifications, you can take advantage of a voluntary food quality certification service provided by the Agricultural Marketing Service (AMS). To apply for this service, which is operated on a user-fee basis, you must submit a copy of the contract specifications in advance. AMS staff will review the contract and work with your firm to develop a written specification that can be certified.

* Dairy Products Grading

Dairy Grading Branch
Dairy Division, Room 2750-SAG
U.S. Department of Agriculture
Washington, DC 20250   202-720-3171

All eggs (liquid or frozen) are federally inspected on a mandatory basis. All other product grading is voluntary. Grading of meat, poultry, eggs, and dairy products and fresh and processed fruits and vegetables is provided on request for a fee. For further information, contact the appropriate office.

* Egg Products Inspection

Food Safety and Inspection Service (FSIS)
U.S. Department of Agriculture
Room 1175, South Agriculture
Washington, DC 20250   202-720-7943

Under the Egg Products Inspection Act, the Food Safety and Inspection Service (FSIS) provides continuous mandatory inspection in all plants processing liquid, dried, or frozen egg products. In 1989, the FSIS inspected some 1.6 billion pounds of liquid, frozen, and dried egg products in 83 processing plants. For more technical information, contact the Egg Products Inspection Division, Room 0165S; 202-720-7410.

* Emergency Relief and Excess Food

Commodity Operations Division
U.S. Department of Agriculture
ASCS, Room 5755
South Building
Washington, DC 20250   202-720-4254

The Commodity Credit Corporation buys, stores, and distributes such commodities as dry milk, wheat, rice, and corn, which are acquired through price support programs. The commodities are sent overseas as donations, distributed to domestic food programs, or given to relief agencies in times of emergencies.

* Emergency Food Assistance Program

Public Information Staff
Food and Consumer Service
U.S. Department of Agriculture (USDA)
3101 Park Center Dr.   703-305-2286
Alexandria, VA 22302   Fax: 703-305-1117

The Program gives needy Americans USDA-donated foods for household use. The foods are free, but recipients must meet the program eligibility criteria set by the states. Local agencies, usually food banks, shelters and soup kitchens, are designed by the states to distribute the food.

* Food and Nutrition Information Center

Food and Nutrition Information Center (FNIC)
U.S. Department of Agriculture
10301 Baltimore Blvd., Room 304   301-504-5719
Beltsville, MD 20705-2351   Fax: 301-504-6409

The Food and Nutrition Information Center (FNIC) assists all individuals interested in food and human nutrition. Nutritionists and information specialists help consumers, educators, health professionals, the media, researchers, and others locate information and resources. FNIC provides electronic access to its publications and databases by making them available on floppy disk, through Internet (gopher.nal.usda.gov) and on the ALF bulletin board (301-504-6510/5111) and other information systems. Subjects covered include human nutrition, food service management, nutrition education, food labeling, food safety, and food technology. FNIC supports collaborative efforts to improve access to information. Projects include: a software demonstration center with over 200 software packages available for onsite preview and demonstration; the FDA/USDA Food Labeling Education Information Center that maintains a database of all new food labeling education materials and activities; and a cooperative agreement with the National Food Service Management Institute that employs a food service educator at FNIC to provide assistance to Child Nutrition Program staff. FNIC publishes resource lists of articles and books on popular nutrition topics. Many are also available on disk (supplied by customer), and many are available on the Internet. Topics include:

Food Composition Nutri-Topics
Food and Nutrition Fun for Children
The New Food Label
Vegetarian Nutrition Nutri-Topics
Weight Control and Obesity Nutri-Topics

* Food Distribution Process Studies

Transportation and Marketing Division
Agricultural Marketing Service (AMS)
P.O. Box 96456
U.S. Department of Agriculture
Washington, DC 20090-6456   202-690-1300

Studies are available on a wide variety of markets covering all aspects of the distribution process: wholesaling, packaging, transportation, and more. For a listing of studies available, contact the above office.

* Food Inspection and Official Standards

Food Safety and Inspection Service (FSIS)
U.S. Department of Agriculture
Room 1175, South Building
Washington, DC 20250   202-720-7943

This office inspects all meats, poultry, and egg products shipped interstate and abroad, and ensures that labels on these products are truthful. Food inspection is mandatory for the following animals and birds used for human food: cattle, calves, swine, goats, sheep and lambs, horses, chickens, turkeys, ducks, geese and guineas. FSIS tests product samples for microbial or chemical contaminants.

* Food Irradiation Safety

Food and Nutrition Information Center
U.S. Department of Agriculture
10301 Baltimore Blvd.   301-504-5719
Beltsville, MD 20705   Fax: 301-504-6409

This center covers the use of ionizing radiation to process foods. Print and audio-visual aids are available in food science, nutrition, safety and wholesomeness, labeling, economics, and other subjects.

* Food Market Overviews

Trade Assistance and Promotion Office
Foreign Agricultural Service (FAS)/AGX
U.S. Department of Agriculture (USDA)   202-720-7420
Ag Box 1052   Fax: 202-690-4374
Washington, DC 20250-1052   TDD: 202-690-4837

Information on export markets for U.S. food products is available in *Food Market Overviews* and *Market Focus Reports*.

* Food Nutrition Service Programs

Food and Consumer Service
U.S. Department of Agriculture (USDA)
3101 Park Center Drive   703-305-2286
Alexandria, VA 22302   Fax: 703-305-1117

The USDA Food and Nutrition Service coordinates a variety of programs to get food to those in need. Special Nutrition Programs aim at improving children's nutrition through school breakfast and lunch programs. The Special Supplemental Food Program for Women, Infants, and Children provides specified nutritious food supplements to and nutrition education for pregnant women, nursing women up to 12 months postpartum, non-nursing women up to 6 months postpartum, and children up to 5 years old.

* Food Poisoning or Improper Packaging

Food Safety and Inspection Service
U.S. Department of Agriculture
Washington, DC 20250   800-535-4555

This service takes calls from consumers on cases of meat, egg, or poultry food poisoning or complaints about meat, egg, or poultry spoilage due to improper

packaging or processing. They can also provide you with health-oriented information on safe handling and storage of meats and poultry.

* Food Safety and Supply

Western Regional Research Center
U.S. Department of Agriculture
ARS, 800 Buchanan St.
Albany, CA 94710   510-559-6082

Research here is generally focused on food problems. Scientists try to increase agricultural productivity through preventing loss and ensuring safety of the food supply and improving market quality of agricultural products. They also have a program to find new means to convert agricultural materials to value-added food and nonfood products.

* Food Safety Research

Eastern Regional Research Center (ERRC)
600 East Mermaid Lane
Philadelphia, PA 19118   215-233-6400

The ERRC conducts research to enhance food safety. Their research objectives are: to investigate the chemical and physical parameters that influence the formation of potentially carcinogenic components in foods, particularly cured meats and to develop means for their reduction or elimination; develop methodologies capable of identifying meats and poultry that have been subjected to low dose ionizing radiation; and to investigate the efficacy and safety of ionizing radiation treatments of fresh and processed meats and poultry to improve microbiological safety and shelflife of products while preserving vitamin content. Another ERRC unit carries out microbiological research on eliminating harmful food bacteria.

* Foreign Food Assistance - PL 480

Public Information
Foreign Agricultural Service
U.S. Department of Agriculture
Room 5074, South Building   202-720-7115
Washington, DC 20013   Fax: 202-720-1727

Under the Agriculture Trade Development and Assistance Act of 1954, PL 480, as amended, the Commodity Credit Corporation (CCC) carries out assigned foreign assistance activities, such as the guaranteeing of U.S. agricultural commodities abroad. Major emphasis is also being directed toward meeting the needs of developing nations. The Corporation also encourages U.S. financial institutions to provide financing to developing nations under the Export Credit Guarantee Programs.

* Free Food for Non-Profit Institutions

Food Distribution Program
Food and Consumer Service
U.S. Department of Agriculture (USDA)
3101 Park Center Dr., Room 502   703-305-2286
Alexandria, VA 22302   Fax: 703-305-1117

Thousands of charitable institutions throughout the country rely on foods donated by the U.S. Department of Agriculture (USDA) to help provide meals to needy people. These charitable groups range from churches operating community kitchens for the homeless and destitute, to orphanages and homes for the elderly. Other eligible groups include meals-on-wheels programs, soup kitchens, temporary shelters, correctional institutions offering rehabilitative activities, group homes for the mentally retarded, and hospitals that offer general and long-term care. To be eligible, charitable institutions must be nonprofit and serve meals on a regular basis. They may be either public or nonprofit private institutions that have federal tax-exempt status.

* Fresh Products Quality

Fresh Products Branch
Fruit and Vegetable Division
Agricultural Marketing Service (AMS)
U.S. Department of Agriculture (USDA)
Ag Box 0240   202-720-2093
Washington, DC 20250-0240   Fax: 202-720-0393

If you need help in meeting importers' specifications, you can take advantage of a voluntary food quality certification service provided by the Agricultural Marketing Service (AMS). To apply for this service, which is operated on a user-fee basis, you must submit a copy of the contract specifications in advance. AMS staff will review the contract and work with your firm to develop a written specification that can be certified.

Agriculture and Farming

* Grading Food Products

Agricultural Marketing Service
U.S. Department of Agriculture (USDA)
Room 3510, South Building   202-720-8998
Washington, DC 20250   Fax: 202-720-7135

The U.S. Department of Agriculture (USDA) provides producers, packers, processors, shippers, wholesalers, and consumers with official certification of the quality of food and farm products to aid in establishing a market value for the product. For most commodities a fee is charged to cover the cost of the service, and the service may be conducted during packing or processing or at supply depots. The official grading or inspection certificate is accepted as prima facie evidence in court.

* Grain Inspection

Administrator
Federal Grain Inspection Service
U.S. Department of Agriculture
Room 1099 South Building
Washington, DC 20250   202-720-5091

This office establishes federal standards for grain and performs inspections to ensure compliance. They also regulate the weighing of all grain for export.

* Indian Reservation Food Distribution

Food and Consumer Service (FCS)
U.S. Department of Agriculture
3101 Park Center Drive   703-305-2286
Alexandria, VA 22302   Fax: 703-305-1117

This program provides monthly food packages to Indians living on or near a reservation. While the program is administered federally by the Food and Consumer Service, state agencies are responsible for all aspects of the programs operation.

* Livestock and Meat Standardization

Livestock and Meat Standardization Branch
Livestock and Seed Division
Agricultural Marketing Service (AMS)
U.S. Department of Agriculture (USDA)
Ag Box 0254   202-720-4486
Washington, DC 20250-0254   Fax: 202-690-1988

If you need help in meeting importers' specifications, you can take advantage of a voluntary food quality certification service provided by the Agricultural Marketing Service (AMS). To apply for this service, which is operated on a user-fee basis, you must submit a copy of the contract specifications in advance. AMS staff will review the contract and work with your firm to develop a written specification that can be certified.

* Livestock Health and Safety

Packers and Stockyards Administration
U.S. Department of Agriculture
Room 3403 South Building
Washington, DC 20250   202-720-9528

The agency's overall mission is to assure fair trade practices and competitive markets for livestock, meat, and poultry. Particular attention also is given to protecting consumers and the industry against unfair business practices that can unduly affect meat and poultry distribution and prices. To achieve this mission, the Packers and Stockyards Administration (PS&A) fosters fair and open competition in marketing; guards against deceptive and fraudulent practices; and provides payment protection to those marketing livestock, meat, and poultry. The agency also certifies central filing systems established by states to provide clear title information for farm products.

* Meat and Poultry Inspection

Export Coordination Division
International Programs
Food Safety and Inspection Service (FSIS)
U.S. Department of Agriculture (USDA)
Franklin Court Building, Room 3714
1099 14th St.   202-501-6022
Washington, DC 20250-3700   Fax: 202-501-6929

Meat and poultry products are inspected by the U.S. Department of Agriculture (USDA) Food Safety and Inspection Service to ensure that they are sound, properly labeled, and meet both U.S. standards and the requirements of the importing country.

* Meat, Egg, and Poultry Hotline

Food Safety and Inspection Service
U.S. Department of Agriculture
Washington, DC 20250   800-535-4555

This service takes calls from consumers on cases of meat, egg, or poultry food poisoning or complaints about meat, egg or poultry spoilage due to improper packaging or processing. They can also provide you with health-oriented information on safe handling and storage of meats and poultry. Recorded information is always available on topics such as seasonal foods safety, the preparation and handling of meat and poultry, recalls, labeling and nutrition, and the safe use of cooking equipment.

* Milk Order Marketing Program

Market Information Branch
Dairy Division
Agricultural Marketing Service (AMS)
P.O. Box 96456
Washington, DC 20090-6456   202-720-7461

Federal milk orders define the terms under which handlers of milk in a specified market purchase milk from dairy farmers. They are legal instruments designed to promote orderly market conditions. Orders assist farmers in developing steady, dependable markets and help correct conditions of price instability and needless fluctuations in price. More information is available from the AMS, which can also provide you with the publications: The Federal Milk Marketing Order Program; The Market News; Federal Milk Order Statistics; Questions and Answers On Federal Milk Marketing Orders; and Daily Market News ($30 per year). Recorded phone messages on prices are available as follows:

Chicago . . . . 708-810-9999 ext. 9
Madison, WI 608-224-5088

* Milk Research

Eastern Regional Research Center
600 East Mermaid Lane
Philadelphia, PA 19118   215-233-6400

Biochemical, microbial, and chemical technology research is conducted in critical areas of milk processing and utilization. Results of basic and applied studies are used to develop the science, technology and knowledge needed to improve food quality, processing, and storage.

* Nutrition Education

Public Information Staff
Food and Consumer Service
U.S. Department of Agriculture (USDA)
3101 Park Center Dr.   703-305-2286
Alexandria, VA 22302   Fax: 703-305-1117

The Nutrition Education Training Program is currently the only national school-based nutrition education and training program. It seeks to build good food habits by teaching the fundamentals of nutrition to children, educators, and food service personnel. Some of the things the program supports is development of national nutrition education and training programs for pre-school and school-aged children; development of print and video nutrition education and training materials; analysis and assessment of existing school meal patterns, development of new menus and recipes; training and assistance for local school food service operators; and incentives for schools to comply with the Dietary Guidelines.

* Nutrition Program for the Elderly

Public Information Staff
Food and Consumer Service
U.S. Department of Agriculture (USDA)
3101 Park Center Dr.   703-305-2286
Alexandria, VA 22302   Fax: 703-305-1117

The Nutrition Program for the Elderly (NPE) helps provide elderly persons with nutritionally sound meals through meals-on-wheels programs or in senior citizen centers and similar settings. The NPE is administered by the U.S. Department of Health and Human Services (DHHS), but receives commodity foods and financial support from the U.S. Department of Agriculture (USDA). Under the Older Americans Act of 1965, USDA contributes commodity foods and/or cash to DHHS programs for the elderly. People age 60 or older and their spouses, regardless of age, are eligible for NPE benefits. Indian tribal organizations may select an age below 60 for defining an "older" person for their tribes. There is no income requirement to receive meals under NPE. Each recipient can contribute as much as he or she wishes toward the cost of the meal, but meals are free to those who cannot make any contribution.

* Nutritional Labeling
Product Assessment Division
Food Safety and Inspection Service (FSIS)
U.S. Department of Agriculture (USDA)
Room 329, West End Court Bldg.
1255 22nd St., NW
Washington, DC 20037   202-254-2565

A number of labeling regulations apply across-the-board to all meat and poultry products. These include: appropriate product name; ingredients listed from most to least; net quantity of package contents; name and address of the manufacturer; USDA mark of inspection. The FSIS can provide you with a brochure entitled *Meat and Poultry Products: A Consumer Guide to Content and Labeling Requirements* which details requirements for meat and poultry products labels.

* Packers and Stockyards Program
Packers and Stockyards Administration
U.S. Department of Agriculture (USDA)
Room 3039, South Agriculture
Washington, DC 20250   202-720-7051

The USDA's packers and stockyards specialists work with private producers and trade organizations to investigate complaints and file any complaint on violations of fair and open competition in the marketing of livestock.

* Perishable Agricultural Commodities
PACA Branch
Agricultural Marketing Service
U.S. Department of Agriculture
Room 2095, South Agriculture
Washington, DC 20250   202-720-2272

The USDA's Agricultural Marketing Service (AMS) prohibits unfair trading practices among buyers and sellers of perishable items. The AMS will provide advice on your rights and responsibilities and try to bring disputing parties together for informal settlements.

* Pick Your Own Fruits and Vegetables
Contact your local U.S. Department of Agriculture
Extension Service agent

Many farmers allow consumers to pick produce directly from their fields at substantial savings.

* Poultry Certification
Poultry Grading Branch
Poultry Division
Agricultural Marketing Service (AMS)
U.S. Department of Agriculture (USDA)
Ag Box 0258   202-720-3271
Washington, DC 20250-0258   Fax: 202-720-3165

If you need help in meeting importers' specifications, you can take advantage of a voluntary food quality certification service provided by the Agricultural Marketing Service (AMS). To apply for this service, which is operated on a user-fee basis, you must submit a copy of the contract specifications in advance. AMS staff will review the contract and work with your firm to develop a written specification that can be certified.

* Processed Fruits and Vegetables Certification
Processed Products Branch
Fruit and Vegetable Division
Agricultural Marketing Service (AMS)
U.S. Department of Agriculture
Ag Box 0247   202-720-4693
Washington, DC 20250-0247   Fax: 202-690-1527

If you need help in meeting importers' specifications, you can take advantage of a voluntary food quality certification service provided by the Agricultural Marketing Service (AMS). To apply for this service, which is operated on a user-fee basis, you must submit a copy of the contract specifications in advance. AMS staff will review the contract and work with your firm to develop a written specification that can be certified.

* Protection from Animal Pests and Diseases
Animal and Plant Health Inspection Service
Veterinary Services
U.S. Department of Agriculture
4700 River Rd.
Riverdale, MD 20737   301-734-8687

For control or eradication of livestock/poultry pest or disease, a state government or industry can receive cooperation from the federal government to establish quarantines, vaccination procedures, and destruction of diseased or exposed animals.

* Quality Control Regulations
Marketing Order Administration Branch
U.S. Department of Agriculture
Room 2523, South Agriculture
Washington, DC 20250   202-720-2491

This office administers programs that give growers the authority to work together to develop dependable markets for their products. Methods used include establishing minimum quality standards to keep inferior products from depressing markets for an entire crop, research and promotion projects to improve production, and volume controls to stabilize the short-term rate of commodity shipments.

* Residue Testing of Meat and Poultry
Residue Program
Food Safety and Inspection Service (FSIS)
U.S. Department of Agriculture
Room 305, Annex Bldg.
Washington, DC 20250   202-205-0007

The Food Safety and Inspection Service (FSIS) runs a National Residue Program designed to detect illegal or potentially harmful levels of residues on meat and poultry. Each year the FSIS collects about 1.5 million test results on 450,000 meat and poultry samples from U.S. plants. Call or write for more information on the program.

* Salmonella and Food Safety
Food Safety and Inspection Service (FSIS)
U.S. Department of Agriculture
Room 1180 South Building
Washington, DC 20250   202-690-0351

After 20 years of research, it is still impossible to economically produce "salmonella free" raw meat and poultry. Routine food safety practices can destroy salmonella and other bacteria. The FSIS produces a background information sheet on safe handling of meat and poultry to prevent food borne illness.

* Seed Quality and Inspection Labs
Federal Seed Lab
U.S. Department of Agriculture
Beltsville, MD 20705   301-504-8089

The federal government can test seeds to determine their quality and whether they are free from contamination. They will also prosecute any agent that transfers contaminated or mislabeled seed from state to state. Seeds are examined by or at a state agent's request, and there may be some fee involved.

* Shipping and Storage
Shipper and Exporter Assistance Program
International Transportation Branch
Transportation and Marketing Division
Agricultural Marketing Service (AMS)
U.S. Department of Agriculture (USDA)
Ag Box 0267   202-690-1304
Washington, DC 20250-0267   Fax: 202-690-1340

The Transportation and Marketing Division of the U.S. Department of Agriculture (USDA) Agricultural Marketing Service (AMS) provides publication and guidance to help exporters efficiently use transportation resources and maintain product quality in transit. A series of tip sheets and handbooks are available.

* Summer Food Service Program
Food and Consumer Service
U.S. Department of Agriculture
3101 Park Center Drive   703-305-2286

Alexandria, VA 22302   Fax: 703-305-1117

The Summer Food Service Program funds meals and snacks for children in needy areas when school is not in session. In local areas, the program is operated by local sponsors, which receive reimbursement from USDA. Sponsorship is limited to public or private nonprofit school food authorities; state, local, or municipal county governments; public or private non-profit colleges and universities that are operating the National Youth Sports Program; public or private non-profit residential summer camps; and private non-profit organizations that operate special summer or school vacation programs.

* Technology Assessment Reports

National Technical Information Service
U.S. Department of Commerce   800-553-6847
5285 Port Royal Rd.   703-487-4650
Springfield, VA 22161   Fax: 703-321-8547

These Office of Technology Assessment (OTA) publications are available through the National Technical Information Service (NTIS). To find out correct ordering information and prices, contact NTIS.

Food Information Systems (PB-258171)
Nutrition Research Alternatives (PB-289825)
Open Shelf-Life Dating of Food (PB80-101629)
Organizing and Financing Basic Research To Increase Food Production (PB-273182)
Perspectives on Federal Retail Food Grading (PB-273163)
Pesticide Residues in Food (PB89-136444)

* Transportation and Marketing Division

U.S. Department of Agriculture
Agricultural Marketing Service (AMS)
PO Box 96456
Washington, DC 20090-6456   202-690-1300

On January 1, 1991 USDA's Office of Transportation was incorporated into the Agricultural Marketing Service (AMS) to improve coordination of transportation and marketing policies. The Transportation and Marketing Division (TMD) conducts economic and analyses of domestic and international transportation systems and represents agriculture and rural transportation interests in policy and regulatory forums. TMD also conducts research in cooperation with industry on packaging and refrigeration transport for perishables.

* Volume Food Buyers

Agricultural Marketing Service
U.S. Department of Agriculture (USDA)
Room 3943, South Agriculture

Washington, DC 20250   Poultry Division: 202-720-7693

USDA specialists work with volume food buyers in developing specifications for food commodities using specifications, grades, and standards that have been developed by USDA for this purpose. Graders examine food and certify the food buyers' purchases prior to delivery. Any processor, wholesaler, retailer, hospital, restaurant, governmental agency, educational institution, airline, or other public or private group buying food in large quantities may ask USDA for their inspection services by contacting this office. Fruit/Vegetable division 202-720-6391; Livestock 202-720-2650; general program information 202-720-8998.

* Wholesale Food Distribution

Marketing Facilities Branch
Agricultural Marketing Service (AMS)
U.S. Department of Agriculture (USDA)
Room 2649-S, South Building
Box 96456
Washington, DC 20090-6456   202-720-8317

This office performs general research aimed at getting food on the table more cheaply by working with wholesale food distribution facilities and farmers markets to reduce the price spread between what the farmer gets for his products and what the consumer pays.

* Women, Infants and Children Food Program (WIC)

Food and Consumer Service
U.S. Department of Agriculture
3101 Park Center Drive   703-305-2286
Alexandria, VA 22302   Fax: 703-305-1117

The WIC program provides supplemental foods, plus health care referrals and nutrition education at no cost to low-income pregnant breastfeeding and nonbreastfeeding postpartum women, infants, and young children up to 5 years of age who are found to be at nutritional risk. To be eligible, persons must: meet a state residency requirement; meet an income standard or participate in Aid to Families with Dependent Children Program, the Food Stamp Program, or Medicaid; and be individually determined to be at risk by a health professional.

* World Food Donations

Agency for International Development
Bureau of Food and Humanitarian Assistance
Room 1262 A-NS
320 21st St., NW
Washington, DC 20523-0008   202-647-0220

By working with groups like CARE and the World Food Program, the Food For Peace program helps needy people abroad by sending food and other agricultural commodities.

Trade and Marketing

* See also the International Trade Chapter
* See also the Experts Chapter

* Agricultural Analyses and Forecasts

Economic Research Service and
National Agricultural Statistical Service
U.S. Department of Agriculture
341 Victory Dr.   800-999-6779
Herndon, VA 22070   703-834-0125

Agricultural Statistics Reports estimate production, stocks, inventories, disposition, utilization, and prices of about 40 agricultural commodities and other items such as labor and farm numbers ($20). A catalog of publications is available free of charge.

* Agricultural/Food Trade Policy

Bureau of Economic and Business Affairs
U.S. Department of State
2201 C St., NW, Room 6828
Washington, DC 20520   202-647-7971

This office handles agricultural trade issues and agreements, including the General Agreement on Tariffs and Trade (GATT) negotiations. Besides monitoring such food commodities as coffee, cocoa and jute, this office also is responsible for foreign policy aspects of food aid and shipment, and acts as liaison with the U.S. Department of Agriculture.

* Agricultural Import Quotas

Foreign Agricultural Service
Import Policies and Trade Analysis
U.S. Department of Agriculture
Room 5531 South Building
Washington, DC 20250   202-720-2916

This office regulates the imports of beef, dairy products, and other commodities by administering quotas imposed by the President.

* Agricultural Industry Investigations

Office of Investigations
U.S. International Trade Commission (ITC)
500 E St., SW, Room 615
Washington, DC 20436   202-205-3160

This office coordinates the International Trade Commission's (ITC) investigations involving antidumping, reviews, escape-clause and market disruptions, and determinations of whether imports of agricultural products are interfering with programs of the U.S. Department of Agriculture. For more information regarding these investigations, contact this office.

* Agricultural Marketing Service (AMS)

Public Affairs
U.S. Department of Agriculture (USDA)
Room 3510 South Building
Washington, DC 20250   202-720-8998

The Agricultural Marketing Service (AMS) is the focal point for a variety of marketing programs operated by the USDA. The free publication, *This is the AMS*, provides a good overview of AMS programs.

* Agricultural Trade and Marketing

Agricultural Marketing and Trade Information Center (AMTIC)
U.S. Department of Agriculture
10301 Baltimore Blvd.
Beltsville, MD 20705   301-504-5704

The Agricultural Marketing and Trade Information Center (AMTIC) covers agricultural trade and marketing, trade policies, barriers, trade agreements and negotiations, agricultural domestic policy and international trade, and many other trade-related matters. Staff can also answer questions relating to the economics of

urbanization and urban policies in developing countries. AMTIC publishes *Vignettes*, a quarterly newsletter focusing on upcoming events, new technologies, and resources and services.

* Agriculture Exports Clearinghouse

Information Division
Foreign Agricultural Service
U.S. Department of Agriculture
5074 South Building
Washington, DC 20250   202-720-9330

For supply and demand information of agricultural products in other countries, contact the above office.

* Animal and Pet Import and Export Restrictions

Import--Export Staff Veterinary Services
Animal and Plant Health Inspection Service (APHIS)
U.S. Department of Agriculture (USDA)
Room 1147 South Building
Washington, DC 20250   202-720-2511

The U.S. Department of Agriculture (USDA) will provide certification to exporters or importers of animals and animal products, or pet birds to prevent the introduction of agricultural pests and diseases from foreign countries into the U.S. and to aid exporters meeting foreign importers standards.

* Attache Educational Program (AEP)

Trade Assistance and Planning Office
Foreign Agricultural Service
U.S. Department of Agriculture (USDA)
Ag Box 1052   202-720-7420
Washington, DC 20250-1052   Fax: 202-720-4374

The Attache Educational Program (AEP) enables U.S. agricultural producers and exporters to benefit from the experience of USDA agricultural counselors and trade officers who have recently returned from overseas posting. These officers are available to make presentations, participate in panel discussions and provide one-on-one export counseling. Groups eligible to participate in the AEP include international trade development centers; land grant and historically black colleges and universities; state wide, regional, and national farm organizations; and state departments of agriculture.

* Buyer Alert

AgExport Connection
Foreign Agricultural Service (FAS)/AGX
U.S. Department of Agriculture (USDA)
Ag Box 1052   202-690-3421
Washington, DC 20250-1052   Fax: 202-690-4374

Buyer Alert is a bi-weekly newsletter, distributed by the U.S. Department of Agriculture's (USDA) overseas offices. It can introduce your food, farm and forest products to foreign buyers around the world. *Buyer Alert* helps U.S. exporters reach more than 15,000 importers in nearly 60 countries. Each announcement in the newsletter provides a product description, offer terms, and information about your company. There is a $15 charge for each announcement.

* Commodities Programs

Consolidated Farm Service Agency (CFSA)
U.S. Department of Agriculture
Room 3702, South Agriculture
Washington, DC 20250   202-720-5237

The Consolidated Farm Service Agency (CFSA) administers the Commodity Credit Corporation's (CCC) commodity stabilization programs for wheat, corn, cotton, seed cotton, soybeans, peanuts, rice, tobacco, milk, wool, mohair, barley, oats, sugarbeets, sugarcane, grain sorghum, rye and honey. For most commodities, loans are made directly to producers on the unprocessed commodity through the CFSA's county offices. If market prices rise above loan levels, producers or their agents can pay off their loans and market their commodities. If market prices fail to rise above loan levels, producers or their agents ca forfeit or deliver the commodity to the CCC, thereby discharging their obligations in full.

* Commodity Reports

Reports Officer - Foreign Agricultural Service (FAS)
U.S. Department of Agriculture (USDA)
Room 6078, South Building
Washington, DC 20250-1000   202-720-2115

Commodities reports by USDA officers posted overseas are available to the public at cost. The current subscription program is done by commodity only. Major commodities have weekly reports while other commodities are less frequent. Call FAS for a list of commodity reports, prices, and frequency of publication.

* Dairy Export Incentive Program

Commodity Credit Corporation
Operations Division
U.S. Department of Agriculture (USDA)
Room 4503, South Building
Washington, DC 20250-1000   202-720-2150

The Dairy Export Incentive Program (DEIP) enables U.S. exporters to meet prevailing world prices for targeted dairy products and destinations. Under the program, the USDA pays cash to exporters as bonuses, allowing them to sell certain dairy products in targeting countries at prices below the exporters cost of acquiring them. The program is designed to help U.S. farmers meet subsidized competition and also to demonstrate the quality of U.S. products. Milk powder, butterfat, and Cheddar Cheese are currently eligible for inclusion in DEIP. Contact the FAS for information on qualifications for participating in the program.

* Electronic Access to Trade Leads

U.S. Department of Commerce
STAT-USA
HCHB Room 4885
Washington, DC 20230   202-482-1986

Trade leads are available on a daily basis through the Department of Commerce Economic Bulletin Board (EBB). You can access new trade leads each day or search for previous trade leads by country, product, or date. Free limited access service is available to sample the EBB before subscribing. Connect to the EBB and type GUEST when prompted for user ID. To access the EBB, dial 202-482-3870 for 1200/2400 bps or 202-482-2584 for 9600 bps. You can also access the EBB on the Internet via Telnet at ebb.stat-usa.gov.

* Electronic Export Data Available

Information Division
Foreign Agricultural Service (FAS)
U.S. Department of Agriculture (USDA)
Room 5074, South Building   202-720-7115
Washington, DC 20250   Fax: 202-720-1727

Trade leads are available on a daily basis through the Foreign Agricultural Service (FAS) Home Page. You can access new trade leads each day or search for previous trade leads by country, product, or date. In addition, you can access information on USDA/FAS programs and services, as well as trade statistics and foreign market reports. The Internet address is http://www.usda.gov/fas.

* Expert Export Assistance

Ag Export Connection
Ag Export Services
U.S. Department of Agriculture (USDA)
Washington, DC 20050   202-720-7103

The USDA's Foreign Agricultural Service offers private companies and cooperatives assistance in marketing their products overseas. The Agricultural Information and Marketing Service (AIMS), for example, provides foreign trade opportunities and contacts to U.S. food and agricultural businesses by collecting and publicizing information on foreign buyers and advertising U.S. export availability. The export marketing services offered include Trade Leads, Buyer Alert, Foreign Buyer Lists, and U.S. Supplier Lists. This material is available in print or through various computer information suppliers, for a charge, depending on the information you request.

* Export Certificates

Alcohol Import/Export Branch
Bureau of Alcohol, Tobacco and Firearms
U.S. Department of the Treasury
650 Massachusetts Ave., NW, Room 5400   202-927-8127
Washington, DC 20226   Fax: 202-927-8605

While permission to export is not required for most agricultural products, the Bureau of Alcohol, Tobacco, and Firearms does require export permits for alcoholic beverages.

* Export Credit Guarantees

Export Credit Guarantee Programs
Commodity Credit Corporation
Operations Division
U.S. Department of Agriculture (USDA)
Room 4513, Ag Box 1035
Washington, DC 20250-1035   202-720-3224

This program encourages the development or expansion of overseas markets for U.S. agricultural commodities by providing guarantees on private financing of U.S. exports to foreign buyers purchasing on credit terms. The guarantees ensure that the exporter or banks will be repaid in the event the foreign purchaser breaks their promise to pay for the goods. The USDA programs differ in their length of the credit periods they cover. The Export Credit Guarantee Program (GSM 102) covers loans with credit terms of 90 days to three years. This program issued some $5 billion in guarantees in 1995. The Intermediate Export Credit Guarantee Program (GSM 103) promotes exports on a longer term basis. The CCC considers coverage on sales of any U.S. agricultural commodity that has the potential of expanding U.S. export markets. A U.S. exporter, foreign buyer, or foreign government may submit requests that may result in authorized guarantee coverage.

* Export Enhancement Program

Commodity Credit Corporation Operating Division
Foreign Agricultural Service
U.S. Department of Agriculture (USDA)
Room 4503, South Agriculture   202-720-2150
Washington, DC 20250   Fax: 202-720-0938

The Export Enhancement Program (EEP) helps products produced by U.S. farmers meet competition from subsidizing countries, especially the European Union. Under the program, the U.S. Department of Agriculture pays cash to exporters as bonuses, allowing them to sell U.S. agricultural products in targeted countries at prices below the exporter's costs of acquiring them. Major objectives of the program are to challenge unfair trade practices, to encourage other countries exporting agricultural commodities to undertake serious negotiations on agricultural trade problems, and to expand U.S. agricultural exports.

* Export Opportunities for Small and Minority Businesses

Trade Assistance and Promotion Office
Minority and Small Business Program
Foreign Agricultural Service (FAS)/AGX
U.S. Department of Agriculture (USDA)
Ag Box 1052   202-720-7420
Washington, DC 20250-1052   Fax: 202-720-4374

This office can provide small and minority companies seeking assistance with a broad range of support services and assistance in selling their products overseas.

* Export Opportunities for U.S. Farmer Cooperatives

International Trade Program
Rural Business and Cooperative Development Service (RBCDS)
U.S. Department of Agriculture (USDA)
Ag Box 3252   202-690-1428
Washington, DC 20250-3252   Fax: 202-690-4641

The U.S. Department of Agriculture (USDA) Rural Business and Cooperative Development Service (RBCDS) helps identify export opportunities for U.S. farmer cooperatives and advises cooperatives on strategies for exporting.

* Export Programs

Marketing Operations Staff
Foreign Agricultural Service (FAS)
U.S. Department of Agriculture (USDA)

Ag Box 1042   202-720-5521
Washington, DC 20250-1042   Fax: 202-720-9361

Under its Foreign Markets Development and Market Promotion Programs, the Foreign Agricultural Service (FAS) works with over 70 nonprofit trade associations and state regional trade groups. These program participants initiate and conduct market development activities approved and partially funded by FAS. Projects are designed to: create demand for U.S. agricultural products in foreign markets; introduce U.S. food and agricultural products to potential foreign customers; and show foreign customers how to use U.S. products. FAS also provides some funding to private companies for approved projects to promote branded products through these programs.

* Export Publications

Information Division
Foreign Agricultural Service (FAS)
U.S. Department of Agriculture (USDA)
Room 5074, South Building   202-720-7115
Washington, DC 20250   Fax: 202-720-1727

Foreign Agricultural Service (FAS) brochures, circulars, and fact sheets, available on such topics as FAS agricultural trade offices and attaches abroad, export financing, technical requirements for export products, and *Your Guide to AgExport Services*, are available from this office free of charge. For *Information on U.S. Export Sales*, a weekly report that summarizes sales and exports of selected commodities (52 issues, $175 per year), call 202-720-3273. All other FAS publications are made available through the National Technical Information Service, U.S. Department of Commerce, 5285 Port Royal Rd., Springfield, VA 22161; 800-553-6847, 703-487-4650.

* Farm Export Information Round-the-Clock

Information Division
U.S. Department of Agriculture (USDA)
Room 5074, Foreign Agricultural Service
Washington, DC 20250   202-720-3448

News reports announcing agreements and allocations for farm exports are available by facsimile. Also, 24-hour information is available on export credit guarantee activities and on Export Enhancement Program (EEP) news. The Weekly Roundup of World Production and Trade offers current news items and trade statistics on various commodities, along with a summary of recent developments in world production and trade. To hear recorded messages, call 202-690-1621. To receive information by fax, at 3:30 and 10:30, set your machine to polling and dial 202-720-1728.

* Farm Imports and Exports

ERS/NASS
U.S. Department of Agriculture (USDA)
31 Victory Dr.   800-999-6779
Herndon, VA 22070   703-834-0125

Foreign Agricultural Trade of the United States updates the quantity and value of U.S. farm exports and imports, plus price trends. Subscriptions for one year cost $29.

* Federal Milk Order Programs

U.S. Department of Agriculture (USDA)
Agricultural Marketing Service
Dairy Division
Room 2753, South Building
Washington, DC 20250   202-720-7461

The Federal Milk Order Program sets the prices that producers of milk receive when selling to milk processors. This division collects monthly statistics on prices, numbers of producers, quantities of milk sold, and its final end use. The division also oversees the national dairy promotion and research program, dairy inspection programs, and standards programs with respect to the content of butter and cheese.

* Foreign Buyer and U.S. Supplier Lists

AgExport Connections
Foreign Agricultural Service (FAS)/AGX
U.S. Department of Agriculture (USDA)
Ag Box 1052
Washington, DC 20250-1052   Fax: 202-690-4374
Foreign Buyer Lists: 202-690-3416
U.S. Supplier Lists: 202-690-3421

Foreign Buyer Lists are drawn from a database which contains information on more than 15,000 foreign buyers of food, farm and forest products in nearly 70 countries. The lists provide important details on each firm such as contact person, address,

telephone, fax, and type of product(s) imported. You may order lists by product or by country. U.S. Supplier Lists provide information on about 5,000 U.S. exporters of food, farm and forest products. The lists provide details on each firm such as contact person, address, telephone, fax, annual sales, and products. For further information on these lists, contact the office listed above.

* Import Interference with Agricultural Programs

The Office of Investigations
U.S. International Trade Commission (ITC)
500 E St., SW, Room 615
Washington, DC 20436   202-205-3160

At the direction of the U.S. President, the International Trade Commission (ITC) conducts investigations to determine whether any articles are being or are about to be imported into the U.S. under such conditions and in such quantities as to have a negative effect on the U.S. Department of Agriculture's programs for agricultural commodities or products. If investigation find that import interference exists, the U.S. President may decide to restrict the imports in question by imposing either import fees or quotas.

* Import Requirements

Information on import requirements of foreign countries is available from several U.S. Department of Agriculture (USDA) agencies such as:

Multilateral Trade Policy Affairs Division
Trade Barriers Analysis Group
USDA/FAS/ITP
Ag Box 1022   202-720-6064
Washington, DC 20250-1022   Fax: 202-720-1139
(tariff rates and import quotes)

Food Safety and Technical Services
USDA/FAS
Ag Box 1027   202-720-1301
Washington, DC 20250-1027   Fax: 202-690-0677
(technical requirements for imported foods overseas)

National Center for Import/Export
USDA/APHIS/VS
4700 River Road, Unit 40   301-734-8590
Riverdale, MD 20737-1231   Fax: 301-734-6402
(information on foreign import requirements for livestock)

Export Certification Unit
USDA/APHIS/PPQ
4700 River Rd., Unit 139   301-734-8537
Riverdale, MD 20737-1228   Fax: 301-734-5786
(information on foreign import for fresh vegetables)

Export Coordination Division
International Programs
USDA/FSIS
Franklin Court Bldg., Room 3714
1099 14th St.   202-501-6022
Washington, DC 20250-3700   Fax: 202-501-6929
(foreign imports requirements for meat and poultry)

* International Trade Shows

Trade Show Office
Foreign Agricultural Service (FAS)/AGX
U.S. Department of Agriculture (USDA)
Ag Box 1052   202-690-1182
Washington, DC 20250-1052   Fax: 202-690-4374

The USDA offers a cost-effective service for U.S. firms to explore foreign markets. FAS organizes national pavilions in major international food shows throughout the world. Participation includes individual booths, lounge, advance public relations work, product shipment, and customs clearance for the show. Copies of the current trade show calendar are available.

* Livestock, Meat and Wool Market Reports

Agricultural Marketing Service (AMS)
Livestock and Grain Market News
U.S. Department of Agriculture (USDA)

Be patient. If any phone number is incorrect, call (area code) 555-1212 and request the new listing.

1027

Agriculture and Farming

Room 2623, South Building
P.O. Box 96456
Washington, DC 20090-6456   202-720-8054
The Agricultural Marketing Service (AMS) produces a variety of commodity reports, covering the latest prices and other important information from regional markets around the country. The following reports are available for a fee:

National Carlot Meat Trade Report - Daily
Livestock, Meat and Wool - Weekly
Georgia Livestock - Weekly
California Livestock - Weekly
National Wool Market Review - 33 issues
Grain, Feed and Market News - Weekly
Pacific Northwest Grain Market News - Weekly
Pacific Northwest Feed Market News - Weekly
Hay Market News - Weekly
Rice Market News - Weekly
Bean Market News - Weekly and Annual National
Molasses Market News - Weekly and Annual National
Hops Market News - Monthly
Grain Stocks Report - Weekly
Durum Wheat Reports - Quarterly

Call for current prices. Also request a free copy of *The Market News* Services, which lists numbers in each state for dairy updates and livestock information and grain market information.

* Mandated Dairy Sales Program

Commodity Credit Corporation (CCC)
Operations Division
U.S. Department of Agriculture (USDA)
Room 4503, South Building
Washington, DC 20250-1000   202-720-2150
This program requires that in each of the fiscal years 1990 through 1995 the Commodity Credit Corporation export not less than 150,000 metric tons of CCC owned dairy products. These sales cannot disrupt domestic U.S. markets or world prices and patterns of commercial trade.

* Market News

Agricultural Marketing Service (AMS)
U.S. Department of Agriculture (USDA)
Room 3510, South Agriculture   202-720-8998
Washington, DC 20250   Fax: 202-720-7135
The Federal-State Market News Service, carried out by USDA's Agricultural Marketing Service (AMS) in cooperation with 41 state agencies, U.S. AID, and Agriculture Canada, reports up to the minute information on prices, supply, and demand for most agricultural commodities. The reports cover buying and selling of these commodity groupings: cotton and cottonseed; domestic fruits and vegetables, including truck rates; floral products and specialty crops; livestock, meat, poultry, eggs, grain, hay, feeds and wool; dairy products and tobacco.

* Market Promotion Program (MPP)

Foreign Agricultural Service
Marketing Operations Staff
U.S. Department of Agriculture (USDA)
Room 4932, South Building
Washington, DC 20250   202-720-4327
The Market Promotion Program is designed to increase U.S. exports of farm commodities and value added agricultural commodities. Under the MPP, funds from the Commodity Credit Corporation (some $200 million annually) are used to partially reimburse program participants conducting specific foreign market development projects for eligible products in specified countries. Contact the program for information on products and participants in the program.

* Market Prospects Overseas

Information Division
Foreign Agricultural Service (FAS)
U.S. Department of Agriculture (USDA)
Room 5074 South Building   202-720-7115
Washington, DC 20250   202-720-1727
A series of background publications describing market prospects for U.S. food and farm products in many countries is available from this office.

* Marketing Regulations

Agricultural Marketing Service (AMS)
U.S. Department of Agriculture (USDA)
Room 3071, South Agriculture
Washington, DC 20250   202-720-5115
The Agricultural Marketing Service (AMS) administers and enforces regulatory laws with respect to marketing. Farmers can file complaints under the Agricultural Fair Practices Act if processors refuse to deal with them because they are members of a producer's bargaining or marketing association.

* Plant Import and Export Restrictions

Export Certification Unit
Animal and Plant Health Inspection Service (APHIS)/PPQ
U.S. Department of Agriculture (USDA)
4700 River Rd., Unit 139   301-734-8537
Riverdale, MD 20737-1228   Fax: 301-734-5786
The U.S. Department of Agriculture (USDA) will provide certification to exporters or importers of plants and plant products as well as animals and animal products, or pet birds to prevent the introduction of agricultural pests and diseases from foreign countries into the U.S. and to aid exporters meeting foreign importers standards.

* Publications for Exporters

National Technical Information Service
U.S. Department of Commerce   800-553-6847
5285 Port Royal Rd.   703-487-4650
Springfield, VA 22161   Fax: 703-321-8547
The Foreign Agricultural Service publishes materials to assist U.S. exporters. They include: *AgExporter*, a monthly magazine for agricultural exporters. Articles analyze U.S. agricultural trade, highlighting market opportunities and export promotion activities; *Agricultural Trade Highlights*, a monthly report that gives a timely, thorough review of developments in U.S. agricultural trade.

* Research on Export Markets

Information Center
Economic Research Service (ERS)
U.S. Department of Agriculture (USDA)
1301 New York Ave., NE, Room 110   202-219-0515
Washington, DC 20005-4788   Fax: 202-219-0112
The U.S. Department of Agriculture's (USDA) Economic Research Service (ERS) provides economic and other information on U.S. and foreign agriculture, food, natural resources, rural development and related topics.

* Sunflower and Cottonseed Oil Assistance Programs

Commodity Credit Corporation
Operations Division
U.S. Department of Agriculture (USDA)
Ag Box 1035
Washington, DC 20250-1035   202-720-2150
The Sunflowerseed Oil Assistance Program (SOAP) and the Cottonseed Oil Assistance Program (COAP) are designed to help U.S. exporters meet prevailing world prices for sunflowerseed oil and cottonseed oil in targeted markets. Under the programs, the USDA pays cash to U.S. exporters as bonuses, making up the difference between the higher U.S. cost and lower world market price. Contact the FAS for information on eligibility for participating in the program.

* Tobacco Markets

Agricultural Marketing Service (AMS)
Tobacco Division
Room 502 - Annex Building
P.O. Box 96456
Washington, DC 20090-6456   202-205-0567
The Agricultural Marketing Service Tobacco division issues annual reports on tobacco stocks, and the tobacco market for different grades of tobacco produced. A publications list is also available.

* Trade Assistance

Trade Assistance and Planning Office (TAPO)
Foreign Agricultural Service (FAS)
U.S. Department of Agriculture (USDA)   202-720-7420

Ag Box 1052
Washington, DC 20250-1052

Fax: 202-690-4374
TDD: 202-690-4837

The Trade Assistance and Promotion Office (TAPO) is the first point of contact within USDA's Foreign Agricultural Service (FAS). It serves exporters of U.S. food, farm, and forest products who need foreign market information or information on USDA export programs. This office can provide export counseling and access to foreign market information; provide information and assistance to individuals or firms that are interested in export programs carried out by the FAS and the USDA; help in getting information on export-related programs managed by other federal agencies; and serve as a contact point for minority and small businesses seeking assistance in exporting food, farm, and forest products.

* Trade Leads

Ag Export Connection
Foreign Agricultural Service (FAS)/AGX
U.S. Department of Agriculture (USDA)
Ag Box 1052   202-690-3416
Washington, DC 20250-1052   Fax: 202-690-4374

The USDA issues a weekly publication entitled *Trade Leads*, which lists agricultural products sought by foreign buyers, as well as contact names and phone numbers. Leads are also available by FAX. New trade leads are placed on the machines each Wednesday at 12:00 noon, Eastern time. The same set of leads will be available 24 hours per day. To receive the Trade Leads on your machine, simply dial one of the numbers listed below on your fax machine and then press start. The leads come through like a regular transmission. FAX numbers and the leads they cover are listed below.

Machine 1 - 202-60-2088
Condiments, Candy, Beverages, and Other Specialty Foods.

Machine 2 - 202-690-1753
Grains, Pulses, Grain Products, and Animal Feeds.

Machine 3 - 202-720-5165
Fruits, Vegetables, Nuts (Fresh, Processed, Packaged, or Juices) Meats, Poultry, Seafood, and Dairy Products.

Machine 4 - 202-720-8980
Oils, Oilseeds, and Oilseed products; Live Animals and animal byproducts; Tobacco, Cotton, Seeds for Planting, Nursery Stock, and Cut Flowers; Lumber and Forest Products.

Machine 5 - 202-205-2963
All of the four machines listed above, plus information on up coming Trade Shows, Notice of Foreign Proposals Concerning Standards in Agriculture, and more.

* Wholesale Market Development Program

Wholesale Market Branch
Transportation and Marketing Division
Agricultural Marketing Service (AMS)
U.S. Department of Agriculture (USDA)
P.O. Box 96456
Washington, DC 20090-6456   202-720-8317

The Wholesale Market Development Program conducts research to find new ways to improve the efficiency of American food marketing. An important element of the program is research to develop new wholesale food marketing centers and farmers' markets. Over the years some 75 extensive studies have been conducted in cities throughout the U.S.; about half of these studies have led to the construction of new wholesale food distribution centers and specialized industrial parks for food firms. For more information on this program, contact the AMS. The Branch also has an extensive publications list covering both the Market Development Program as well as commodities and livestock research.

* World Agricultural Databases

Economic Research Service Databases
U.S. Department of Agriculture (USDA)
ERS/NASS
341 Victory Dr.   800-999-6779
Herndon, VA 22070   703-834-0125

The Economic Research Service has developed more than 60 databases dealing in a wide variety of U.S. and world agricultural economics topics. Data products are shipped on DOS-compatible discs or on unlabeled, 9-track 6250 b.p.i. magnetic tapes as appropriate. A complete listing of ERS electronic products and ordering information is available by contacting the above center.

* World Agricultural Outlook Board

Public Affairs Officer
U.S. Department of Agriculture (USDA)
Room 5143, South Building   202-720-5447
Washington, DC 20250   Fax: 202-690-1805

The World Agricultural Outlook Board (WAOB) coordinates USDA's supply and use commodity forecasts and agricultural situation and outlook analyses, publishes the *World Agricultural Supply and Demand Estimates Report*; leads departmental weather, climate and remote sensing activities; assesses weather's impact on agriculture; and coordinates USDA's annual conference. To order WAOB reports, call 800-999-6779.

* World Agricultural Trade Database

Chief, Trade and Marketing Branch
Foreign Agricultural Service
U.S. Department of Agriculture (USDA)
Washington, DC 20250   202-720-1294

The Foreign Agricultural Service (FAS) maintains a database of selected foreign agricultural trade information for the U.S. and 100 nations that conduct agricultural trade. The database contains information from a variety of sources, including United Nations trade tapes from the Food and Agriculture Organization and data from the Bureau of the Census. Examples of retrievable information include long-term U.S. exports by destination; foreign country import and export data; foreign production, supply, and distribution of agricultural products; and other export marketing information. Searches and print-outs are provided on a cost-recovery basis. Staff prefers request by phone so that they can discuss your needs and thereby supply you with appropriate information. To access information on the Internet: http://www.usda.gov/fas or http://www.fao.org/waicent/foaftat/faoftat.htm.

Commodity Divisions:
Tobacco, Cotton and Seeds	202-720-9516
Horticulture and Tropical Products	202-720-6590
Forest Products	202-720-0638
Oilseeds and Products	202-720-7037
Grain and Seed	202-720-6219
Dairy, Livestock, and Poultry	202-720-8031
High Value Products	202-690-0159

Be patient. If any phone number is incorrect, call (area code) 555-1212 and request the new listing.

1029

State Agriculture Information

In most states, agriculture is the leading industry. Farming has become highly specialized, and modern farmers and agribusinesses must stay abreast of a wide range of current data: crop prices, price and production projections, field statistics, test results, and more. The U.S. Department of Agriculture (USDA) publishes the greatest number of reports and surveys in such areas, routinely publishing data on crop conditions, long-term and short-term weather forecasts, research developments, and current and projected market conditions for specific crops at home and abroad. Decisions involving billions of dollars are made each year based on this information.

The U.S. Department of Agriculture (USDA) reports are most often used to track crop and livestock production and prices and to maximize production by ensuring that the best equipment and storage techniques are used for each crop. But the federal government does not hold a monopoly on agricultural information. States also collect and disseminate a great deal of farm data, and obtaining information from a state agency is generally less time-consuming and expensive than going through the USDA offices in Washington, DC.

Market News and Surveys

Individual states contribute to the Market News Service. Major wire services, newspapers, and radio stations use this service to track developments in agriculture. The service is used by virtually all persons involved in the sale or purchase of grain, livestock, poultry, or poultry products, as well as by insurance and investment companies and government agencies.

State agencies often make available employment and income surveys -- publications providing information of farms and the families who operate them, the quality of services provided, income generated from all sources, and analysis of this data. Special state agricultural directories are also a good source of information, providing the name, address, and telephone number of every agricultural producer in a state by commodity. They also include data on production levels, acreage, and farm dollar values for each commodity.

Information on Agribusiness and Growers

In terms of collecting information on agricultural companies, most states maintain a computerized licensing and product registration system and will provide mailing lists for a minimum fee. Included in the databases are names and addresses of agricultural processors, distributors, and manufacturers, as well as all registered products. States maintain records on the number of products and licenses held by each company, and inspection reports for retailers, wholesalers, and packagers are usually available for a fee. In addition, some states require that you file a Freedom of Information Act request to obtain this information.

Marketing or Agricultural Development Programs

State agriculture offices may offer their biggest help in promoting products grown within a state. Each state has a marketing and development program to protect, conserve, and develop state agriculture and natural resources. The objectives of such programs are to develop new and existing markets (including foreign) for state agricultural products and to ensure that state farms and ranches are using the best production techniques available. These offices also:

*   improve agricultural profitability by encouraging the development of value-added products and new, high-value crops.

*   encourage and support research issues which have an impact upon agricultural growth within the state.

*   serve as clearinghouses for trade leads and provide various support services for state farmers and agribusinesses, including grading, inspection, promotion, and market intelligence.

*   assist the agricultural producer, processor, shipper and exporter to expand trade volume and to broaden marketing areas, to reduce distribution and transportation costs, and to gain freer access to foreign markets.

To obtain overseas contracts, companies have their name and product(s) registered in the state export directory free of charge. Foreign investors and importers look to state directories for new ideas and areas in which to expand their business interests.

State departments of agriculture also rent booths at agricultural trade shows both at home and overseas. For example, if you have a small seafood company or are in the pasta and noodle business, renting a booth through the state at the Japan Food Show will go a long way to promote your product and may net you a tax-free trip to the Orient as well.

States also help promote your product overseas and may prove valuable in helping your small businesses expand through foreign franchises. Another example: a popular soft yogurt company was able to franchise in several overseas markets with the help of the Maryland State Agricultural Department.

Statistical Reporting Service (SRS)

The purpose of the Statistical Reporting Service (SRS) is to collect and disseminate current statistics on the nation's agriculture. SRS maintains a network of 45 field offices which service all 50 states through cooperative agreements with state departments of agriculture or state universities. These State Statistical Offices (SSOs) regularly survey thousands of farmers, ranchers, and agribusinesses that voluntarily provide data on a confidential basis.

Statisticians consolidate these reports with field observations, objective yield measurements, and other data to produce state farm and ranch estimates. These data are then forwarded to SRS headquarters in Washington, DC, where they are combined and released as a national profile. In addition, SRS issues about 300 national and 9,000 state farm reports each year. The reports provide broad coverage of agriculture, including 120 crops and 45 livestock items.

Many statistical publications are also available directly from the USDA/NASS Agricultural Statistics Board Publications, Room 5805 South Building, Washington, DC 20250-2000, or call 800-727-9540.

Farm Service Agency

The Farm Service Agency (FSA) helps American agriculture with commodity, credit, export, and risk management programs that improve the economic stability of agriculture and helps farmers adjust to meet demand. These programs help keep enough farmers in business to produce an adequate food supply and to keep consumer prices reasonable.

FSA finances commodity loan programs through the Commodity Credit Corporation (CCC), a government entity for which FSA provides operating personnel. The CCC helps maintain balanced and adequate supplies of farm commodities and helps in their orderly distribution.

FSA administers commodity loan programs for wheat, rice, rye, corn, grain sorghum, barley, oats, soybeans, tobacco, peanuts, cotton, and sugar. FSA programs for crops help stabilize farm income, help create a balance between the supply and demand of these crops, and help farmers at harvest time by providing interim financing.

Under the dairy price support program, CCC buys surplus butter, cheese, and nonfat dry milk from processors at announced prices. These purchases help maintain prices at the legislated support level.

FSA administers the Agricultural Conservation Program (ACP) and the Conservation Reserve Program (CRP), which help preserve and improve America's farmland.

FSA administers the crop insurance program, which provides catastrophic-level coverage that will compensate farmers for crop yield losses of greater than 50 percent at 60 percent of the expected market price. Farmers who participate in other FSA programs must have catastrophic-level insurance.

FSA provides farm loans to those farmers and ranchers who cannot obtain it from conventional lenders due to risk factors. Borrowers can get direct loans, where FSA actually lends the money, or a guaranteed farm loan, where FSA guarantees loans made by eligible lenders. Programs include farm ownership loans, farm operating loans, and a variety of other loans, such as aquaculture loans and both direct and secured loans for socially disadvantaged persons.

FSA offices are located in all 50 states, usually in the state capital. County offices are listed in the telephone directory under "U.S. Department of Agriculture."

State Agricultural Offices

The following is a list of state agricultural departments and the products and services they can provide:

Alabama

Agricultural Statistics Service, M.L. Dantzler, Box 240578, Montgomery, AL 36124-0578; 334-279-3555, Fax: 334-279-3590. Publications: *Alabama Farm Facts* (issued twice monthly): *Agricultural Prices; Crop Production or Forecasts, Intended and Actual Plantings, and Grain Stocks; Fruits, Nuts and Vegetables; Livestock Numbers, Production, Slaughter and Milk; Poultry and Eggs; Broiler Report* (issued each Wednesday); *Crop Weather* (issued each Monday, March-December); *County Data: Cattle, Hogs, Poultry, Corn, Cotton, Hay, Oats, Peanuts, Sorghum Grain, Soybeans, Wheat; Alabama Agricultural Statistics, Fact Sheet on Alabama Agriculture, Alabama Agriculture Perspective.*

Department of Agriculture and Industries, P. O. Box 3336, Montgomery, AL 36109-0336; 334-240-7125. Publications: *Fruit and Vegetable Direct Marketing Directory, Alabama Farmers' Bulletin, Ag Talk, The Alabama Food and Agricultural Export Directory.*

Farm Service Agency Office, P.O. Box 235013, Montgomery, AL 36106; 334-279-3500, Fax: 334-279-3550.

Alaska

State Statistical Service, D.A. Brown, Box 799, Palmer, AK 99645; 907-745-4272, Fax: 907-746-4654. Publications: *Alaska Agricultural Statistics; Alaska Farm Reporter* (monthly); *Crop Weather* (weekly). Combined fee for all three publications is $15 per year.

Department of Natural Resources, Division of Agriculture, P.O. Box 949, Palmer, AK 99645-0949; 907-745-7200, Fax: 907-745-7112. Programs: *Agricultural Revolving Loan Fund, Alaska Grown Program, Alaska Grown Logo Program, Plant Materials Center for Alaskan Grown Plants.* Publications: *Alaska Agricultural Statistics; Alaska Food and Farm Directory.*

Alaska Farm Service Agency, 800 W. Evergreen Ave., Suite 216, Palmer, AK 99645; 907-745-7982, Fax: 907-745-7984.

Arizona

Agricultural Statistics Service, B. L. Boyd, 3003 N. Central Ave., Suite 950, Phoenix, AZ 85012; 602-280-8850, Fax: 602-280-8897. Publications: *Arizona Agricultural Statistics, Crop Release, Livestock Release, Crop and Weather Report, Annual Bulletin.*

Arizona Department of Agriculture, 1688 West Adams, Phoenix, AZ 85007; 602-542-0958, Fax: 602-542-5420. *Annual Report, Agriculture, Arizona Agricultural Statistics.*

Farm Service Agency, 77 E. Thomas Rd., Suite 240, Phoenix, AZ 85012-3118; 602-640-5200, Fax: 602-640-5180.

Arkansas

Agricultural Statistics Service, D. H. Von Steen, Box 3197, Little Rock, AR 72203; 501-324-5145, Fax: 501-324-8160. Publications: *Arkansas Farm Report* (issued twice a month); *Weather and Crop Bulletin; Weekly Broiler* (weekly); *County Estimates; Agricultural Statistics for Arkansas.*

Cooperative Extension Service, University of Arkansas, P.O. Box 391, Little Rock, AR 72203; 501-671-2000, Fax: 501-225-3390. Publication: *Annual Report of Accomplishments.* Publication topics are the following: Agricultural Chemicals, Agricultural Engineering, Agronomy - general, Agronomy - Cotton, Agronomy - Feed Grains, Agronomy - Pastures and Forages, Agronomy - Rice, Agronomy - Soybeans, Clothing and Textiles, Entomology, Farm Management, Fisheries, Food Marketing, Food and Nutrition, Forestry, Horticulture, Livestock and Livestock Products, Marketing, and Plant Pathology.

Farm Service Agency, Federal Building, Room 5416, 700 W. Capitol, Little Rock, AR 72201-3225; 501-378-5220, Fax: 501-324-5895.

Be patient. If any phone number is incorrect, call (area code) 555-1212 and request the new listing.

1031

Agriculture and Farming

California

Agricultural Statistics Service, H. J. Tippett, Box 1258, Sacramento, CA 95806; 916-551-1533, Fax: 916-551-1528. Publications: *California Agriculture; Exports of California Agricultural Products; California Agricultural Export Directory; Summary of County Agricultural Commissioners' Reports; Field Crop Statistics; Prices Received by California Producers for Farm Commodities; Fruit and Nut Acreage, Fruit and Nut Statistics, Grape Crush Report; Grape Acreage Bulletin; Grapes, Raisins, and Wine; Walnuts, Raisins, and Prunes; Vegetable Crops; Livestock Statistics; Eggs, Chickens, and Turkeys; Dairy Industry Statistics, Complete Set of County Agricultural Commissioner Report Data, Commodity by County.*

State of California, Food and Agriculture, 1220 N. St., Sacramento, CA 94271-0001; 916-654-0433, Fax: 916-657-4240. Programs: *Agricultural Export Program (AEP):* first of its kind by a state, AEP provides assistance, service, and support in developing sales in foreign markets. It is a five year matching funds partnership in which the costs of foreign market development are equally shared between the California Department of Food and Agriculture and program cooperators. The program is open to all private companies, marketing boards, and commissions or associations who are producers, processors, or marketers of California agricultural products. The AEP program is developing its own "California specific" trade lead network which will electronically provide information on buyer leads, best market prospects, trade barriers, and export assistance. Publications: *California Department of Food and Agriculture and What it Does for You; California Agriculture: 1990 Statistics; Taste California: 1992 Food and Wine Festivals; Straight From the Farm to You: Farmer to Consumer Direct Marketing; Taste the Californias: California Fresh Produce Guide.*

Farm Service Agency, 1303 J Street, Suite 300, Sacramento, CA 95814-2916; 916-498-5311, Fax: 916-498-5310.

Colorado

Agricultural Statistics Service, C. A. Hudson, Box 150969, Lakewood, CO 80215; 303-236-2300, Fax: 303-236-2299. The Colorado Legislature has eliminated funding for agricultural statistics. Publications: *Agricultural Update* (bi-monthly); *Crop-Weather Report* (weekly, March-November); *Colorado Agricultural Statistics Bulletin* (Annual).

Colorado Department of Agriculture, 700 Kipling St., Suite 4000, Lakewood, CO 80215-1630; 303-239-4100, Fax: 303-239-4125. The Department administers the Colorado Agricultural Development Authority which makes low interest loans to producers.

Farm Service Agency, 655 Parfet Street, Suite E305, Lakewood, CO 80215; 303-236-2866, Fax: 303-236-2879.

Connecticut

For Connecticut agricultural statistics, contact the Marketing Division at the Connecticut Department of Agriculture below.

Connecticut Department of Agriculture, State Office Building, Room 243, 165 Capitol Ave., Hartford, CT 06106; 203-566-4667, Fax: 203-566-6576. Program: Joint Venture Program: $50,000 in matching funds is available to agricultural commodity groups and organizations for promotion of "Connecticut Grown" products. Publications: *Connecticut Grown, Annual Report, Farm Fresh Directory, Connecticut Sugarhouses, Connecticut Wineries, Pick Your Own: Orchards, Vegetables, Christmas Trees, Berries; Connecticut Farmers Markets, Fair List, Connecticut Agricultural Directory, Connecticut Agricultural Statistics.*

Farm Service Agency, 88 Day Hill Road, Windsor, CT 06095; 203-285-8483, Fax: 860-285-8481.

Delaware

Agricultural Statistics Service, 2320 S. Dupont Highway, Dover, DE 19901; 302-739-4811, Fax: 302-697-6287. Publications: *Annual Delaware Agricultural Statistics Report, Delaware Agri-Facts, Delaware Weekly Crop and Weather Report, Delmarva Broiler Chicks.*

Delaware Department of Agriculture, 2320 S. Dupont Highway, Dover, DE 19901; 302-739-4811, Fax: 302-697-6287. Publications: *Delaware Agricultural Statistics, Delaware AGenda, Century Farms, Delaware Land Survey, Report of State Farmland Evaluation Advisory Council, Agricultural Bulletin, Delaware's State Forests, Delaware Agriculture - An Overview, Delaware Farmers Markets Directory, Delaware Food/Agriculture Export Directory, Delaware Produce Buyers Guide, Pesticide Briefs.*

Farm Service Agency, 1201 College Park Dr., Suite 101, Dover, DE 19901; 302-573-6536, Fax: 302-573-6554.

Florida

Agricultural Statistics Services, R. L. Freie, 1222 Woodward St., Orlando, FL 32803; 407-648-6013, Fax: 407-648-6029. Publication: *Florida Agricultural Statistics, Field Crops, Citrus and Tropical Fruits, Vegetables, Celery, Tomatoes, Livestock - Dairy and Poultry, Broilers, Weather and Crop News, Numbers of Workers and Wage Rates, Prices and Cash Receipts, Citrus Acreage and Tree Numbers, Citrus Historic Maturity and Yield, Annual Summaries* for the following crops: Citrus, Vegetables, Livestock, Poultry, Dairy, Field Crops.

Department of Agriculture, Plazaio, The Capitol, Tallahassee, FL 32399-0810; 904-488-3022. Publications: *Annual Report; Agricultural Groups Directory; Dollars and Sense; Flowers, Trees, and Shrubs: Native and Exotic; Native Trees of Florida; Vegetable Gardening; Touring Florida Agriculture; Lemon Log.* Information is also available from the Agricultural Institute of Florida - 904-236-3488.

Farm Service Agency, P.O. Box 141030, Gainesville, FL 36214-1030; 904-372-8549, Fax: 904-372-0599.

Georgia

Agricultural Statistics Service, L. E. Snipes, Stephens Federal Building, Suite 320, Athens, GA 30613; 404-546-2236, Fax: 706-546-2416. Publications: *Georgia Farm Report* includes the following reports: *Crop production, Grain stocks, Vegetable production, Fruit production, Prices received and paid by farmers, Hog inventory, Pig crop, Egg production, Hatchery data, Milk production, Livestock slaughter, Cash receipts, Farm Labor; Weather and Crops; Weekly Hatchery; Georgia Agricultural Facts, Georgia Poultry Facts.*

Department of Agriculture, Capitol Square, 19 Martin Luther King Jr. Drive, Atlanta, GA 30334; 404-656-3645, 800-282-5852, Fax: 404-651-7957. Publications: *Farmers and Consumers Market Bulletin; Annual Report; Agricultural Fact Book.*

Farm Service Agency, P.O. Box 1907, Athens GA 30603-1907; 706-546-2266, Fax: 706-546-2151.

Hawaii

Agricultural Statistics Service, D.A. Martin, State Department of Agriculture Building, 1428 S. King St., Honolulu, HI 96814-2512; 808-973-9588, Fax: 808-541-3495. Publication: *Hawaii Agricultural Statistics; Avocados; Bananas; Coffee; Fruits; Ginger Root; Guavas; Herbs; Macadamia Nuts; Papayas; Pineapples; Sugarcane; Taro; Vegetables; Anthurimes; Floriculture and Nursery Products; Poinsettias; Cattle; Chickens and Eggs; Hogs; Honey; Milk; Crop-Weather Report; Farm Labor; and Prices Paid-Feed.*

Department of Agriculture, P.O. Box 22159, Honolulu, HI 96823-2159; 808-973-9599, Fax: 808-973-9613. Programs: 1) Agricultural Loan Program: credit is available to qualified farmers, partnerships, corporations, and agricultural cooperatives to promote agricultural development in Hawaii. 2) New Farmer Program: provides initial start-up loans to new farmers. 3) Aquaculture Loan Program: provides loans for the development of aquacultural enterprises (independent). Publications: *Annual Report, Hawaii Agricultural and Food Products Export Directory.*

Farm Service Agency, 300 Ala Moana Blvd., Room 5106, P.O. Box 50008, Honolulu, HI 96850; 808-541-2644, Fax: 808-541-2648.

Idaho

Agricultural Statistics Service, R. C. Max, Box 1699, Boise, ID 83701; 208-334-1507, Fax: 208-334-1114. Publication: *Annual Report, Agriculture in Idaho, Potato Reports, Weekly Crop Weather Reports.*

Idaho Department of Agriculture, Marketing and Administration, P.O. Box 790, Boise, ID 83701; 208-332-8530, Fax: 208-334-2170. Program: Rural Rehabilitation Loans: this lending program helps stabilize rural Idaho by providing funds to small family farmers and to youths who want to continue in agricultural pursuits. Publication: *Department of Agriculture Annual Report.*

Farm Service Agency, 3220 Elder Street, Boise, ID 83705; 208-334-1486, Fax: 208-334-1323.

Illinois

Agricultural Statistics Service, J. Clampett, Box 19283, Springfield, IL 62794-9283; 217-492-4295, Fax: 217-492-4291. Publications: *Illinois Farm Report, Illinois Weather and Crop Reports, Annual Summary - Illinois Agricultural Statistics.*

Department of Agriculture, Division of Administrative Services, State Fairgrounds, P.O. Box 19281, Springfield, IL 62794-9281; 217-785-9272, Fax: 217-785-4505.

Be patient. If any phone number is incorrect, call (area code) 555-1212 and request the new listing.

Programs: Illinois Grain Insurance Corporation (IGIC): provides full protection to Illinois farmers who store their grain in country elevators; "T by 2000". This program is a nationwide model aimed at controlling soil erosion of fragile lands by the turn of the century. Publication: *Illinois Agricultural Statistics Annual Summary*.

Farm Service Agency, S. Scates, P.O. Box 19273, Springfield, IL 62794-9723; 217-492-4180, Fax: 217-492-4508.

Indiana

Agricultural Statistics Service, R. W. Gann, 1148 Agricultural Administration Building, Purdue University, Room 223, West Lafayette, IN 47907-1148; 317-494-8371, Fax: 317-494-4315. Publications: *Indiana Agricultural Statistics, Indiana Weekly Crop and Weather Report, Indiana Agriculture Report*.

Indiana Department of Agriculture, Communications, School of Agriculture, Purdue University, 1143 AGAD, West Lafayette, IN 47907-1143; 317-494-8396, Fax: 317-496-1117. Programs: 1) Hoosier Homestead and Hoosier Business Award Programs: farms and businesses that have been a working factor in the same family for at least 100 years receive an award. 2) Treasurer's Farm Program (TFP) provides low interest loans to farmers facing cash flow difficulties. 3) Value Added Grant Program: This program is designed to increase the value of Indiana produced agricultural commodities, thereby increasing the net worth of the state's agriculture. 4) Domestic and International Marketing Program: Works to identify markets within the U.S. and abroad for Indiana Agriculture. Publications: *Indiana Food Processors Directory, Grown in Indiana: You Pick Directory, Agricultural Exports Directory, Indiana Agriculture Book, Indiana Agriculture: A Strategic Plan, Indiana Agricultural Statistics*.

Farm Service Agency, 5981 Lakeside Blvd. Indianapolis, IN 46278-1996; 317-290-3030, Fax: 317-290-3045.

Iowa

Agricultural Statistics Service, D. M. Skow, 210 Walnut St., Room 833, Des Moines, IA 50309; 515-284-4340, Fax: 515-284-4342. Publications: *Iowa Crop Report, Iowa Crops and Weather, Iowa Livestock Report, Agri News*.

Iowa Department of Agriculture, Information Bureau, Wallace Building, E. 9th and Grand Ave., Des Moines, IA 50319; 515-281-5633, Fax: 515-281-6236. Programs: Agricultural Diversification Program: assists farms with an alternative crop and livestock program. Agricultural Development Authority: assists beginning farmers in acquiring agricultural land, property, and agricultural improvements by offering loans at low interest rates. Publications: *Beginning Farmer Loan Program, Iowa Department of Agriculture and Land Stewardship, Recycling: The Right Thing to Do, History of Agriculture in Iowa, Iowa's Apple Orchards, Honey Producers of Iowa, Biennial Report, Agricultural Commodity and Farm Orgainization List for 1991-92*.

Farm Service Agency, 10500 Buena Vista Court, Urbandale, IA 50322; 515-254-1540, Fax: 515-254-1573.

Kansas

Agricultural Statistics Service, T.J. Byram, P.O. Box 3534, Topeka, KS 66601-3534; 913-233-2230, Fax: 913-233-2518. Publications: *Weekly Crop Weather; Crops; Prices; Livestock; Hogs and Pigs; Bluestem Pasture; Grain Marketing and Transportation; Custom Rates; Farm Facts; Wheat Quality; Wheat Varieties; Farm Bankruptcies; Agricultural Land Values*.

State Board of Agriculture, Public Information, 901 Kansas Ave., Topeka, KS 66612-1280; 913-296-3571, Fax: 913-296-8389.

Farm Service Agency, 3600 Anderson Ave. Manhattan, KS 66502-2511; 913-539-3531, Fax: 913-537-9659.

Kentucky

Agricultural Statistics Service, D. D. Williamson, Box 1120, Louisville, KY 40201; 502-582-5293, Fax: 502-582-5114. Publications: *AGRI-NEWS, Crop Weather Reports, Livestock Reports, Dairy Reports, Poultry Reports, Price Reports, Miscellaneous Reports, Crop Weather, County Estimates*.

Department of Agriculture, 7th Floor, 500 Mero St., Frankfort, KY 40601; 502-564-4696, system 800-327-6568, Fax: 502-564-6527. Program: Market News Information: free marketing service to persons across the state who are interested in buying and/or selling farm commodities as well as receiving regional up-to-date farm market prices. Publication: *Kentucky Agricultural Statistics, Produce Directory: Getting What You Pay For; Kentucky Agricultural News, Kentucky Agricultural Facts, Kentucky Agricultural Almanac, Export Directory, Food Products Directory, Christmas Tree Directory, Kentucky Local Agricultural Fairs, Kentucky Livestock, Kentucky Livestock and Grain Report, Gift Guide*.

Farm Service Agency, 771 Corporate Dr., Suite 100, Lexington, KY 40503-5478; 606-224-7601, Fax: 606-224-7691.

Louisiana

Agricultural Statistics Service, A.D. Frank, Box 65038, Baton Rouge, LA 70896-5038; 504-922-1362, Fax: 504-922-0744. Publication: *Statistical Report, Louisiana Farm Reporter, Annual Crop Summary, Weekly Crop-Weather Report, All County Estimates for Cotton, Rice, Soybeans, Wheat, Corn, Sugarcane, Sorghum, and Livestock*.

Department of Agriculture and Forestry, 5825 Florida Blvd., P.O. Box 631, Baton Rouge, LA 70821-0631; 504-922-1234, Fax: 504-922-1253. Program: Farm Youth Loan Program: provides loan and loan guarantees to youths who are involved in an organized school program in agriculture. Publication: *Market Bulletin*.

Farm Service Agency, 3737 Government St. Alexandria, LA 71302-3395; 318-473-7721, Fax: 318-473-7735.

Maine

For specific statistical information on Maine's agricultural products contact the Commissioner's Office of the Department of Agriculture, Food and Rural Resources, 207-287-3871.

Department of Agriculture, Food and Rural Resources, Director of Resource Development, State House Station 28, Augusta, ME 04333; 207-287-3511, Fax: 207-287-7548. Publications: *Maine Agricultural Report, Maine Agricultural Buyers Guide, Producer to Consumer, Peat Task Force Report, How to Organize Agricultural Marketing Cooperatives, Annual Report on the Main Agricultural Fairs, Saving Energy in Rural Maine or Who is Doing What on the Farm, Useable Waste Products for the Farm*.

Farm Service Agency, 444 Stillwater Ave. Suite 1, P.O. Box 406, Bangor, ME 04402-0406; 207-990-9140, Fax: 207-990-9169.

Maryland

Agricultural Statistics Service, M. B. West, 50 Harry S. Truman Parkway, Suite 202, Annapolis, MD 21401; 410-841-5740, Fax: 410-841-5755. Publications: *Maryland Agri-Facts* - which includes the following types of information - crop production, grain stocks, vegetable production, fruit production, prices received and paid by farmers, livestock production and inventories, poultry and egg production, hatchery data, milk production, livestock slaughter, farm income and finance, farm labor, miscellaneous reports; *Maryland Crop Weather; Delmarva Broiler Chicks; Maryland Agricultural Summary*.

Maryland Department of Agriculture, Public Information Office, 50 Harry S. Truman Pkwy., Annapolis, MD 21401; 410-841-5882, Fax: 410-841-5914. Publication: *The Maryland Department of Agriculture Yesterday, Today and Tomorrow; Agricultural Maryland*.

Farm Service Agency, Rivers Center 8335 E. Guillford Rd., Suite 3, Columbia, MD 21406; 410-381-4550, Fax: 410-962-4860.

Massachusetts

For specific agricultural statistics, contact the Department of Food and Agriculture listed below.

Massachusetts Department of Food and Agriculture, Communications Specialist, 100 Cambridge, Boston, MA 02202; 617-727-3018, ext. 170, Fax: 617-727-7235. Programs: Municipal Farmland Identification Program: information on available farmland will be mapped and on record. It provides the communities and farmers with an inventory on the possible crop production of an area and assists in planning decisions. Agricultural Preservation Restriction Program: protects diminishing farmland resources through the purchase of Agricultural Preservation Restrictions, commonly known as development rights.

The Department is currently initiating its own, complimentary data-collection program which will be transformed into a reliable computerized data base. Publications: *Massachusetts Agriculture Annual Report. The Fresh Connection* - newsletter to help local growers find new markets, and to help improve communications between local producers and restaurant chefs, *Farm and Market Report*.

Farm Service Agency, 445 West Street, Amherst, MA 01002-2953; 413-256-0232, Fax: 413-256-6290.

Michigan

Agricultural Statistics Service, D. J. Fedewa, Box 20008, Lansing, MI 48901; 517-377-1831, Fax: 517-377-1829. Publications: *Michigan Agricultural Statistics, Agriculture Across Michigan, Crop Weather, Fruit Survey, Equine Survey*.

Be patient. If any phone number is incorrect, call (area code) 555-1212 and request the new listing.

1033

Department of Agriculture, Press and Public Affairs, P.O. Box 30017, 611 W. Ottawa St., Lansing, MI 48909; 517-373-1104, Fax: 517-335-0628. Program: Agricultural Assistance Network: provides assistance to Michigan farmers and related agribusinesses facing financial hardship as a result of economic crisis. A toll free hotline (1-800-346-FARM) is available to anyone with problems related to loans, human service needs, legal referrals, and financial farm management. Publications: *You Pick Fruit and Vegetable Markets; County Agricultural Economy Directory; Agriculture Business Directory for Exports.*

Farm Service Agency, 3001 Coolidge St., Suite 100, East Lansing, MI 48823-5202; 517-337-6660, Fax: 517-337-6898.

Minnesota

Agricultural Statistics Service, M. Hunst, Box 7068, St. Paul, MN 55107-9983; 612-296-2230, Fax: 612-290-3034. Publications: *Agri-View, Minnesota Weekly Crop-Weather Report, Potato Stocks, Monthly Turkey Report, Minnesota Agricultural Statistics Book.*

Department of Agriculture, Communications Director, J. Renner, 90 West Plato Blvd. Saint Paul, MN 55107-2094; 612-297-1629, Fax: 612-297-5522. Publication: *MDA Update, Stockpot, Nursery News, Pest Report.*

Farm Service Agency, 400 Agribank Bldg. 375 Jackson Street, St. Paul, MN 55101-1852; 612-290-3651, Fax: 612-290-3186.

Mississippi

Agricultural Statistics Service, Thomas L. Gregory, Box 980, Jackson, MS 39205; 601-965-4575, Fax: 601-965-5622. Publication: *Mississippi Agricultural Statistics, Crop Weather Report, Weekly Broiler Report, Ag Report.*

Mississippi Department of Agriculture and Commerce, Public Information Coordinator, P.O. Box 1609, 500 Greymont, Jackson, MS 39215-1609; 601-354-7094, Fax: 601-354-6001. Publication: *Annual Report, Export Trade Directory, Mississippi Market Bulletin.*

Farm Service Agency, P.O. Box 14995 Jackson, MS 39236-4995; 601-965-4300, Fax: 601-965-4184.

Missouri

Agricultural Statistics Service, P.A. Walsh, P.O. Box L, Columbia, MO 65205; 314-876-0950, Fax: 314-876-0973. Publications: *Farm Facts; Crop and Weather Report; Crop and Livestock Report.*

Missouri Department of Agriculture, Public Affairs, P.O. Box 630, 1616 Missouri Blvd., Jefferson City, MO 65102-0630; 314-751-8596, Fax: 314-751-5002. Publication: *Missouri Farm Facts.*

Farm Service Agency, 601 Business Loop, 70 West, Columbia, MO 65203; 314-876-0926, Fax: 314-876-0935.

Montana

Agricultural Statistics Service, P. Stringer, Box 4369, Helena, MT 59604; 406-441-1240, Fax: 406-449-5330. Publication: *Agricultural Statistics Bulletin, Crop Weather Report, Reporter.*

Montana Department of Agriculture, P.O. Box 200201, Helena, MT 59620-0201; 403-444-3144, Fax: 406-444-5409. Agricultural Development, 406-444-2402. Programs: provides financial assistance: makes grants and low interest rate loans available to youth, organizations, and other qualified farmers and ranchers. Publications: *Junior Agricultural Loan Program, Rural Assistance Loan Program, Growth Through Agriculture Loan Program, Hay Hotline.*

Farm Service Agency, P.O. Box 670 Bozeman, MT 59771-0670; 406-587-6872, Fax: 406-587-6887.

Nebraska

Agricultural Statistics Service, W.C. Dobbs, Box 81069, Lincoln, NE 68501; 402-437-5541, Fax: 402-437-5547. Publications: *Nebraska Agricultural Statistics, Crop-Weather, Agri-Facts, Crops and Weather Summary.*

Department of Agriculture, Nebraska Agricultural Development, Public Relations, 301 Centennial Mall South, P.O. Box 94947, Lincoln, NE 68509-4947; 402-471-6860, 800-422-6692, Fax: 402-471-2759. Programs: The Nebraska Department of Agriculture has identified four key areas for development. Livestock - further develop markets for this most important industry; Bulk Commodities - generate trade leads for grain; Value Added - assist companies for international marketing of

Nebraska value added food products; Nontraditional Agriculture - development of new crops for Nebraska agriculture. Publication: *Nebraska Agriculture, Nebraska Agricultural Products Trade Directory, Ag Report, Facts About Nebraska Agriculture, Nebraska Beef.*

Farm Service Agency, P.O. Box 57975 Lincoln, NE 68505-7975; 402-437-5581, Fax: 402-437-5280.

Nevada

Agricultural Statistics Service, C. R. Lies, Box 8880, Reno, NV 89507; 702-784-5584, Fax: 703-784-5766. Publication: *Nevada Agricultural Statistics, Prospective Plantings; Crop Production; Annual Crop Production Summary; Weather, Crops, and Livestock; Farm Income; Livestock Inventory.*

Nevada State Department of Agriculture, Box 11100, Reno, NV 89502; 702-688-1180, Fax: 702-688-1178. Publication: *Nevada and Its Agriculture.*

Farm Service Agency, 1755 East Plumb Lane, Suite 202, Reno, NV 89502; 702-784-5411, Fax: 702-784-5018.

New Hampshire

Agricultural Statistics, Maine, New Hampshire, Vermont, Connecticut, Rhode Island, Massachusetts, A.R. Davis Jr., 22 Bridge St., P.O. Box 1444, Concord, NH 03302-1444; 603-224-9639, Fax: 603-225-1434. Publications: *Ag Review Monthly, Cranberries, Maple, Potato Grade and Size Report, Wild Blueberries, and Crop Weather.*

New Hampshire Department of Agriculture, Markets and Food, P.O. Box 2042, Concord, NH 03302-2042; 603-271-3788, Fax: 603-271-1109. Publication: *Weekly Market Bulletin.*

Farm Service Agency, P.O. Box 1388, Concord, NH 03302-1388; 603-224-7941, Fax: 603-225-1410.

New Jersey

Agricultural Statistics Service, R. J. Battaglia, CN-330 New Warren St., Trenton, NJ 08625; 609-292-6385, Fax: 609-633-2550. Publications: *Farm Facts, Weekly Weather Crop, Annual Vegetable Summary, Fertilizer Report.*

Department of Agriculture, Public Information Office, Health and Agriculture Building, CN-330, Trenton, NJ 08625-0330; 609-292-8896, Fax: 609-292-2978. Programs: administers nine commodity councils dedicated to research, education and agricultural promotion. Agricultural Development Program: through a variety of tours and educational activities, this program informs the non-farming public about New Jersey's agriculture. Publication: *New Jersey Agriculture, Pick Your Own Guide, NJ Certified and Plant Dealers, Roadside Stand Directory, NJ Farm Market Directory.*

Farm Service Agency, Mastoris Professional Plaza, 163 Rte. 130 Building 2, Suite E, Bordentown, NJ 08505; 609-298-3446, Fax: 609-298-8780.

New Mexico

Agricultural Statistics Service, D. G. Gerhardt, Box 1809, Las Cruces, NM 88004; 505-523-8168, Fax: 505-522-7646. Publications: *Weekly Crop Weather, New Mexico Agri-Info:* includes information on Crop Acreages and Production, Livestock Inventory and Production; other publications - *Chile Summary, New Mexico Agricultural Statistics.*

New Mexico Department of Agriculture, Public Relations, NMSU Campus, Box 30005, Dept. 3189, Las Cruces, NM 88003-0005; 505-646-2804, Fax: 505-646-3303. Programs: Rangeland Protection Program: implements brush control programs on lands within the state. ADC Program: assists agricultural producers with the control of prairie dogs and kangaroo rats on rangeland, planted pastures, and field crops. Publications: *Biennial Report, New Mexico Agricultural Export Directory.*

Farm Service Agency, 6200 Jefferson NE, Room 211, Albuquerque, NM 87109; 505-761-4900, Fax: 505-7611-4934.

New York

Agricultural Statistics Service, R.E. Schooley, 1 Winners Circle, Albany, NY 12235; 518-457-5570, Fax: 518-472-4419. Publication: *New York Agricultural Statistics, New York Crop and Livestock Report, Weather and Crops, Fruit, Vegetables, Potatoes, Maple Production, Cash Receipts and Farm Income, Apples in Storage, Cold Storage, Corn, Wheat, Oats, and Hay Acreage and Production by County, Cattle Inventory by County, Milk Production by County, New York Equine Survey.*

New York Department of Agriculture and Markets, Public Affairs, 1 Winners Circle, Albany, NY 12235; 518-457-3136, Fax: 518-485-7782. Program: Institutional

Procurement Assistance Program (l-800-NY-CROPS) assists state institutional facilities in purchasing foods grown, produced,and processed in the state. The program utilizes a computerized database of farmers, institutional buyers, and food wholesalers to provide buyers and sellers with detailed information on sources and marketing opportunities for New York State fresh fruits and vegetables. Publications: *Annual Report, New York Wine Guide, Uncork New York, Export Directory, Local Laws and Agricultural Districts, NYS Community Farmers Market Directory, NYS Guide to Fresh Farm Food, List of Milk Plants and Dealers in NYS, Agricultural Fairs List.*

Farm Service Agency, 441 S. Salina St., Suite 356, 5th Floor, Syracuse, NY 13202; 315-477-6300, Fax: 315-477-6323.

North Carolina

Agricultural Statistics Service, B.M Murphy, Box 27767, Raleigh, NC 27611; 919-856-4394, Fax: 919-856-4139. Publication: *North Carolina Farm Report* - which includes the following reports: Crop Production, Grain Stocks, Vegetable Production, Prices received and paid by farmers, Hog inventory and pig crop, Egg Production, Hatchery data, Milk production, Livestock slaughter, Cash receipts, Farm labor; *Weather and Crops; Broiler Reports, North Carolina Agricultural Statistics; North Carolina Farm Income;* County Estimates of these crops: Corn, Soybeans and Wheat, Tobacco, Peanuts, and Cotton, Sweet potatoes, Cattle and Hogs, Chickens.

North Carolina Department of Agriculture, 2 W. Edenton St., P.O. Box 27647, Raleigh, NC 27611; 919-733-4216, Fax: 919-733-5047. Program: Public Affairs Department features reports on agricultural business violations; Market NewsLine: a new electronic version of market news that transmits instant reports on farm market prices, supply and demand information, and weather. Publications: *Market Summary, Livestock Report, Agricultural Review, Agriculture Information Sourcebook.*

Farm Service Agency, 4407 Bland Rd., Suite 175, Raleigh, NC 27609-6296; 919-790-2957, Fax: 919-790-2954.

North Dakota

Agricultural Statistics Service, R. F. Carver, Box 3166, Fargo, ND 58108-3166; 701-237-5771, Fax: 701-239-5613. Agricultural Statistics.

Department of Agriculture, Public Information, 600 E. Boulevard Ave., 6th Floor, Bismarck, ND 58505-0020; 701-328-2233, Fax: 701-328-4567. Programs: Northern Crops Institute: established to foster cooperation of farm commodity and agri-business organizations. Centennial Farm Award Program: awards given to families who have retained ownership of their farm for 100 years or more. Publication: *North Dakota Biennial Report.*

Farm Service Agency, P.O. Box 3046, Fargo, ND 58108-3046; 701-239-5224, Fax: 701-239-5696.

Ohio

Agricultural Statistics Service, J.E. Ramsey, 200 N. High St., Room 608, Columbus, OH 43215; 614-469-5590, Fax: 614-469-5784. Publication: *Ohio Agricultural Statistics, Ohio Farm Report, Crop-Weather Report, Ohio Farm Income, Timber Prices, Farm Real Estate.*

Ohio Department of Agriculture; Communications Director, 65 South Front St., Room 607, Columbus, OH 43215; 614-752-4505, Fax: 614-466-6124. Programs: Ohio Farm Financial Management Program: offers seminars on Farm Financial Management In Time of Stress; a $500,000 grant is being used to help farmers with new financing techniques using a computer generated program. International Trade Program: designed to foster international trade relationships between foreign buyers and Ohio agribusiness firms via a trade-leads match-making service. The focus of this program is toward small businesses. Publication: *Ohio Food Products Directory.*

Farm Service Agency, 200 North High Street, 540 Federal Building, Columbus, OH 43215-2495; 614-469-6735, Fax: 614-469-2047.

Oklahoma

Agricultural Statistics Section, R. P. Bellinghausen, 2800 N. Lincoln Blvd. Oklahoma City, OK 73105; 405-525-9226, Fax: 405-528-2296. Publication: *Oklahoma Agricultural Statistics; Crop Weather Summary; Farm Statistics.*

State Department of Agriculture, Public Information Coordinator, 2800 North Lincoln Blvd., Oklahoma City, OK 73105-4298; 405-521-3864, Fax: 405-521-4912. Publication: *The Oklahoma Department of Agriculture and You, Poultry Newsletter; Urban Forestry Grant Information; Branch Out in Oklahoma; Certified Greenhouse and Nursery Directory; Hybrid Sorghum; Licensed Commercial and Non Commercial Pesticide Applicators; Firewood Facts; Planting Trees and Shrubs to Improve Wildlife Habitat in Oklahoma.*

Farm Service Agency, 100 USDA, Suite 102, McFarland and Farm Road, Stillwater, OK 74074; 405-742-1177, Fax: 405-742-1130.

Oregon

Agricultural Statistics Service, P.M. Williamson, 1220 S.W. 3rd Avenue, Portland, OR 97204; 503-526-2131, Fax: 503-326-2549. Publication: *Oregon Agriculture and Fisheries Statistics, Crop Weather Report, Agrifacts.*

Department of Agriculture, 635 Capitol St., NE, Salem, OR 97310-0110; 503-986-4559, Fax: 503-986-4747. Publications: *Farming and Ranching in Oregon, Oregon County and State Agricultural Estimates, Commodity Data Sheets* for: grains, hay, field crops, tree fruits and nuts, small fruits and berries, vegetables and truck crops, specialty products, livestock and poultry; the Extension service also publishes a booklet listing an extensive number of publications available.

Also contact Department of Agriculture, Marketing, 121 South West Salmon St., Portland, OR, 97204; 503-229-6734 and the Information Office in Salem; 503-378-3713. Publications: *Department of Agriculture Mission Statement, Export Service Center, Biennial Report, Oregon Agriculture and Fisheries Statistics.*

Farm Service Agency, 7620 SW Mohawk, Tualatin, OR 97062; 503-692-6830, Fax: 503-692-8139.

Pennsylvania

Agricultural Statistics Service, W. C. Evans, 2301 N. Cameron St., Room G-19, Harrisburg, PA 17110; 717-787-3904, Fax: 717-782-4011. Publications: *Statistical Summary, Keystone Digest, Special Dairy Report, Broilers, Annual Manufactured Dairy, Machinery Custom Rates, Weekly Crop and Weather Round-Up.*

Department of Agriculture, 2301 North Cameron St., Harrisburg, PA 17110-9408; 717-787-5085, Fax: 717-772-2780. Publication: *Annual Report.*

Farm Service Agency, One Credit Union Place, Suite 320, Harrisburg, PA 17110-2994; 717-782-4547, Fax: 717-782-4813.

Rhode Island

For specific agricultural statistics in Rhode Island contact the office listed below.

Rhode Island Division of Agriculture and Marketing, 83 Park St., Providence, RI 02903; 401-277-2781, Fax: 401-277-6047. Programs: Purchase of Development Rights: designed to retain agricultural land by purchasing right to develop the land for purposes other than agriculture. Farm, Forest and Open Space: encourages the maintenance of Rhode Island's productive agriculture and forestland. The use value assessment is based on the current use of land rather than the potential development value. Publications: *Weekly Wholesale Reports, Seasonal Crop Reports, Pick-Your-Own* brochures and information, *Farmers Market* brochures and information, *Crop Brochures* featuring Nutritional, Storage, Buying and Cooking information on Rhode Island grown crops. *Rhode Island Agricultural Statistics, Export Directory, Agriculture Facts Book.*

Farm Service Agency, West Bay Office Park, Room 40, 60 Quaker Lane, Warwick, RI 02886; 401-828-8232, Fax: 401-828-5206.

South Carolina

Agricultural Statistics Service, H. J. Power, Box 1911, Columbia, SC 29202; 803-765-5333, Fax: 803-765-5310. Publications: *Weekly Crop Weather; Farm Facts for Field Crops, Fruits and Vegetables; Farm Facts for Livestock and Poultry; Farm Facts for Agriculture Prices; Annual Cash Receipts Bulletin; Vegetable Statistics Bulletin; Fruit Tree Survey Bulletin; Annual Agricultural Statistics Bulletin.*

Department of Agriculture, P.O. Box 11280, Columbia, SC 29211-1280; 803-734-2182, Fax: 803-734-2192. Publications: *Annual Report, individual reports:* Tobacco, Soybean, Cattle, Beef, Pork, Peach, Watermelon, Egg, Peanut and Tomato, Commodity Promotions and Consumer Information, Poultry Grading, Fruit and Vegetables, Ag Study Tours, Small Farms, Fruit and Vegetable Market News, International Trade, Livestock Market News, Consumer Services.

Farm Service Agency, 1927 Thurmond Mall, Suite 100, Columbia, SC 29201-2375; 803-765-5186, Fax: 803-765-5165.

South Dakota

Agricultural Statistics Service, J.C. Ranek, Box 5068, Sioux Falls, SD 57117; 605-330-4235, Fax: 605-330-4379. Publications: *Crop and Livestock Reporter, Crop-Weather Summary, South Dakota Agriculture, South Dakota's Rank in Agriculture.*

Agriculture and Farming

Department of Agriculture, Anderson Building, 445 E. Capitol Ave., Pierre, SD 57501-3185; 605-773-3375, Fax: 605-773-5926. Program: Adult Farm and Ranch Business Management Program: assists farmers and ranchers in developing a farm accounting system. Publications: *Statewide Annual Report, South Dakota Agriculture, South Dakota Exporters Directory, South Dakota Agricultural Statistics, Horizons, Pesticide Program, Guide to Animal Waste Management and Assistance for Livestock Producers, South Dakota Conservation Districts, Gypsy Moth Trapping and Detection Program, Agricultural Marketing Program, Agricultural Enterprise Program, Rural Development Loan Participation, Livestock Loan Programs, Farm Loan Mediation Program, Nursery Inspection Program, Coordinated Soil and Water Conservation Program, Egg Inspection Program, Grassroots Restoration, Register of Big Trees, Protect Your Forest Home From Wildlife, Project Learning Tree, Tree Farming, Chemical Weed Control in Trees, The Capitol Grounds Arboretum Trail, Arbor Day, South Dakota's Forests, Windbreaks.*

Farm Service Agency, 200 Fourth Street SW, Room 208 Huron, SD 57350-2478; 605-352-1160, Fax: 605-352-1195.

Tennessee

Agricultural Statistics Service, G. Danekas, Box 41505, Nashville, TN 37204-1505; 615-781-5300, Fax: 615-781-5303. Publications: *Tennessee Weather and Crops, Tennessee Farm Facts, Agricultural Statistics.*

Department of Agriculture, Ellington Agricultural Center, P.O. Box 40627, Melrose Station, Nashville, TN 37204; 615-360-0117, Fax: 615-360-0333. Program: Overseas Market Program: new-to-export companies receive counseling via state-sponsored educational seminars and individual meetings with marketing personnel. Advice is also available on international financing. Publications: *Tennessee Agriculture* and a selection of marketing publications and directories.

Farm Service Agency, 579 U.S. Courthouse, 801 Broadway, Nashville, TN 37203-3816; 615-736-5555, Fax: 615-736-7801.

Texas

Agricultural Statistics Service, D. S. Findley, Box 70, Austin, TX 78767; 512-482-5581, Fax: 512-482-5956. Publications: *Texas Agricultural Facts, Texas Historic Livestock Statistics, Texas Historic Crops Statistics, Texas County Statistics, Texas Custom Rates Statistics, Texas Citrus Tree Inventory Survey, Weekly Crop-Weather, Monthly Citrus, Monthly Onions, Quarterly Vegetable Acreage, Monthly Cattle on Feed, Weekly Broilers.*

Department of Agriculture, 1700 N. Congress Ave., P.O. Box 12847, Austin, TX 78711; 512-463-7406, Fax: 512-463-7643. Program: International Marketing Program: this network ties into the USDA's computerized trade lead system that spans the world to gather buyer inquiries on a daily basis. Publications: *Texas Agriculture Facts, Gazette, Taste of Texas.*

Farm Service Agency, P.O. Box 2900, College Station, TX 77841-2900; 409-260-9207, Fax: 409-260-9358.

Utah

Agricultural Statistics Service, D. J. Gneiting, Box 25007, Salt Lake City, UT 84125; 801-524-5003, Fax: 801-524-3090. Publications: *Annual Bulletin, Utah Agriculture, Weekly Crop-Weather.*

Department of Agriculture, 350 North Redwood Road, Salt Lake City, UT 84116; 801-533-7104, Fax: 801-538-7126. Programs: 1) Meat and Poultry Inspection Program, 2) Utah Partners for Conservation and Development Program, 3) Insect Treatment Program, 4) Pesticide Collection Program, 5) Geographical Information System (GIS), 6) Utah Sends First Ever Milk to Hong Kong, 7) New Marketing Concept for Utah Alfalfa Hay. Publications: *Market News, Biennial Report.*

Farm Service Agency, 125 S. State St., #4239, Salt Lake City, UT 84138-1189; 801-524-5013, Fax: 801-524-5244.

Vermont

Agricultural Statistics: Vermont is included in the New England State Statistical Office. Contact: New England State Statistical Office, P.O. Box 1444, Concord, NH 03302; 603-224-9639.

Vermont Department of Agriculture, 116 State St., Montpelier, VT 05620-2901; 802-828-2416, Fax: 802-828-2361. Contact: Office of Information for various free directories and brochures including: *Hay Directory and Specialty Foods Directory,* and the following Vermont titles: *Beef, Wool, Game, Cheese, Sugarhouses, Pork, Turkey, Milk, Lamb, Christmas Trees, Maple by Mail.*

Farm Service Agency, 346 Shelburne Street, Burlington, VT 05401-4995; 802-658-2803, Fax: 802-951-6749.

Virginia

Agricultural Statistics Service, R. Bass, Box 1659, Richmond, VA 23213; 804-786-3500, Fax: 804-771-2651. Publications: *Crops and Livestock, Poultry, Milk and Dairy, Prices and Income, Virginia Agricultural Statistics, Tobacco Sales.*

Department of Agriculture and Consumer Service, P.O. Box 1163, Richmond, VA 23209-1163; 804-786-7686, Fax: 804-371-7679. Program: Rural Virginia Development Foundation: researches and evaluates potential venture investment opportunities, established a computerized information exchange system statewide-tel-o-auction, to promote livestock sales. Publications: *Bulletin, Year in Review, Commodity Newsletter.*

Farm Service Agency, 1606 Santa Rosa Rd., Culpeper Bldg., Suite 138, Richmond, VA 23229; 804-287-1500, Fax: 804-287-1723.

Washington

Agricultural Statistics Service, D. A. Hasslen, Box 609, Olympia, WA 98507; 206-586-8919, Fax: 360-902-2091. Publications: *Agri-Facts* which includes the following crop information -*Crop production, Grain Stocks, Vegetables, Fruit, Agricultural Prices, Hogs, Eggs, Milk, Cattle, Cattle on Feed, Farm Labor, Potatoes and Cold Storage; Potato Stocks and Processing; Crop-Weather, Washington Agricultural Statistics Annual.* Publications can also be ordered from Agricultural Statistics Board Publications, U.S. Department of Agriculture, NASS, Room 5829, South Building, Washington, DC 20250-2000.

Department of Agriculture, P.O. Box 42560, Olympia, WA 98504-2560; 360-902-1815, Fax: 360-902-2092. Publications: *Washington State Food and Agricultural Suppliers Directory, Biennial Report, Washington Agricultural Exports Statistical Bulletin, Washington Agricultural Statistics, Washington State Livestock Brand Book, AG-2000 Economic Strategies for Washington Agriculture, The Regulation Handbook for Direct Farm Marketers, Processed Food Marketing in Japan, Business Opportunities Report, Agri-Facts, Crop-Weather Report, Livestock Market News, Fruit and Vegetable Market News, Agriculture Trade Facts, WSDA Pesticide Notes.*

Washington Farm Service Agency, Rock Pointe Tower, Suite 568, W. 316 Boone Ave., Spokane, WA 99201-2350; 509-353-2307, Fax: 509-353-2309.

West Virginia

Agricultural Statistics Service, D. Loos, c/o State Department of Agriculture, 1990 N. Kanawha Blvd East, Charleston, WV 25305; 304-348-2217, Fax: 304-558-0297. Publications: *West Virginia Mountain State Reporter* [includes statistics on major crops and livestock in the state], *West Virginia Crop Weather Bulletin, West Virginia Agricultural Statistics.*

Department of Agriculture, 1900 Kanawha Blvd., East, State Capitol, Charleston, WV 25305; 304-558-3708, Fax: 304-558-2203. Publications: *The Market Bulletin;* The following publications are divided by subject - *Cattle: External Parasite Control, Beef Cattle for Beginners, Herd Health, Identification in West Virginia, Summer Management, Winter Cow Management, Recognizing and Handling Calving Problems, Leptospirosis, an infectious disease of livestock and pets, Abortion in Cattle in West Virginia, Roundworms in Cattle, Breeding Season Management, Dehorning, What You Should Know About Blackleg; Sheep: Quality Lamb Production, Winter Ewe Management, Early Weaning of Lambs; Horses: Housing Recommendations, Broodmare Management, Internal Parasites in Horses, Equine Foot Care, Horses in West Virginia; Goats: Goat Management Guide; Gardening: Growing Strawberries in West Virginia, Gardening for Beginners, Home Vegetable Garden Pest Control, Beginning a Backyard Orchard, West Virginia Home Orchard Spray Schedule, Home Gardening is Fun, Beginning with Grapes - No. 1, Grape Pest Control - No. 2; Bees and Beekeeping: Beekeeping in West Virginia, Transferring Bees from Box Hives into Modern Equipment, The Diagnosis and Treatment of American Foulbrood, Controlling the Wax Moth in Honey Comb, Swarming of Honey Bees; Consumer Guides and Recipes: West Virginia Apples - Consumer Guide and Recipes, A Peach Potpourri, West Virginia Strawberry Recipes, Beef - A Consumer Guide and Recipes, Pork - A Consumer Guide and Recipes, Cooking with Cornmeal, EGG-ceptional Recipes Using Eggs, Egg Facts You Should Know, Turkey Recipes, A Pickle Potpourri, A Roundup of Relishes, 1987 Prizewinning Recipes.*

Farm Service Agency, P.O. Box 1049, Morgantown, WV 26507-1409; 304-291-4351, Fax: 304-291-4097.

Wisconsin

Agricultural Statistics Service, L. Pratt, Box 9160, Madison, WI 53715; 608-264-4848, Fax: 608-264-5271. Publication: *Agricultural Statistics; Dairy Facts;*

Agricultural Land Sales and Rental Rates; Annual Dairy Summary; Custom Rates; Cash Receipts; Farm Costs and Returns; Mink Production; Trout Production. Several publications are available directly from the USDA/NASS Agricultural Statistics Board Publications, Room 5829 South Building, Washington DC 20250-2000. These include: *Wisconsin Farm Reporter; Crop and Weather; Snow and Frost; Vegetables; Manufacturing Grand Milk Prices; Livestock Review; and Poultry.*

Department of Agriculture, 2811 Agriculture Rd., Madison, WI 53704; 608-224-5002, Fax: 608-224-5034. Publications: *Direct Marketing Guide, Take Home Guide.*

Farm Service Agency, 6515 Watts Road, Suite 100, Madison, WI 53719; 608-276-8732, Fax: 608-271-9425.

Wyoming

Agricultural Statistics Service, R.W. Coulter, Box 1148, Cheyenne, WY 82003; 307-772-2181, Fax: 307-772-2398. Publications: *Biweekly Ag Statistics, Winter Wheat Variety, Winter Wheat County Estimates, Barley County Estimates, Hay County Estimates, Sheep and Lamb Loss, Crop Weather Report, Wyoming Agricultural Statistics.*

Department of Agriculture, R. Micheli, 2219 Carey Avenue, Cheyenne, WY 82002; 307-777-6792, Fax: 307-777-6593. Publications: *Understanding the Loan Approval Process, Annual Report, Food Handlers Guide, Wyoming State Fair Preview, Wyoming Agriculture Strategic Plan: 1990-2000, Wyoming Coordinated Resource Management Workbook, Wyoming Farm and Ranch Finance Survey, Wyoming Ag Directory.*

Farm Service Agency, 951 Werner Court, Suite 130, Casper WY 82601; 307-261-5231, Fax: 307-261-5857.

Energy
General Sources

* See also Housing and Real Estate Chapter
* See also Careers and Workplace; Research Grants in Every Field Chapter
* See also Economics, Demographics, and Statistics Chapter
* See also Science and Technology Chapter
* See also Weather and Maps Chapter
* See also Environment and Nature Chapter
* See also Current Events and Homework Chapter
* See also Experts Chapter

As the Persian Gulf War made vividly clear, finding new and more efficient sources and uses of energy is one of the most pressing issues facing the world today. Here you'll find information leads on everything from international energy agreements to how you can better insulate your home to lower your heating bills. Not only can you find out about the newest energy-related legislation or the newest developments in geothermal power, but you'll also find sources on such volatile issues as nuclear reactor safety and offshore oil exploration. Whether you're a business that needs an energy audit or a student doing a report on solar energy, these up-to-date resources will provide you with the answers.

* Advanced Utility Concepts
Advanced Utility Concepts Division, EE-142
U.S. Department of Energy (DOE)
1000 Independence Ave. SW, Room 6H-034
Washington, DC   202-586-0205
This office plans and manages a balanced program for technology research and development to provide the technology base enhancing the use of advanced utility concepts, such as superconductivity, conversion, or transmission options; electrochemistry; battery and storage in electrical utility load leveling; and industrial commercial, and residential applications.

* Agricultural Use of Energy
Director of Information
Economics Management Staff
Economic Research Service
U.S. Department of Agriculture
1301 New York Ave., Room 228
Washington, DC 20005-4788   202-219-0504
The Economic Research Service can provide you with current and historical statistics on energy use, prices, and expenditure in agriculture by fuel source such as gasoline, diesel, liquified petroleum gas, fuel oil, etc. The office can also provide you with information on grain based fuels such as alcohol.

* Albuquerque Operations Office
Public Information Office
U.S. Department of Energy (DOE)
P.O. Box 5400
Albuquerque, NM 87185   505-845-6049
This facility provides field level planning for nuclear weapons research and development. It also provides direction for non weapons projects in the areas of nuclear, solar, wind, and geothermal energy projects as well as waste management and transportation research.

* Alcohol Fuel Plant Permits
Distribution Center
Bureau of Alcohol, Tobacco, and Firearms
U.S. Department of the Treasury
7664-K Fullerton Rd.
Springfield, VA 22150   703-455-7801
The free booklet, *Alcohol Fuel Plants*, #P5000.4, outlines the general provisions of the alcohol fuel plant permit system. Questions and answers are included to clarify certain points in reference to alcohol fuel plant application and operations. If you need further information, contact the Bureau's Regional Office located in your state.

* Alcohol Fuel Production Loans
Office of Alcohol Fuels
Conservation and Renewable Energy EE-80
U.S. Department of Energy (DOE)
1000 Independence Ave., SW, Room 6C-016
Washington, DC 20585   202-586-9220
This office manages departmental programs of Federal assistance for alcohol fuels production. It develops, executes, and administers Federal assistance programs. The market is monitored and the development and utilization of alcohol fuels is encouraged. The office acts as a primary coordinator for alcohol fuels assistance programs with the Department of Agriculture and other Federal agencies, and acts as a liaison with state and local governments.

* American Public Power Association
American Public Power Association
2301 M. St. NW
Washington, DC 20037   202-775-8300
This Association represents municipally owned electric utilities, public utility districts, State and county owned electrical systems and rural cooperatives. It also maintains a 6000 volume library on the electrical power industry as well as compiling statistics and conducting research programs.

* Appliance Labeling
Appliance Division
Conservation and Renewable Energy, EE-431
U.S. Department of Energy (DOE)
1000 Independence Ave., SW, Room 1J018
Washington, DC 20585   202-586-7140
This division carries out the requirements of Public Law 94-163, as amended. Program activities include the development of appliance test procedures, promulgation and implementation of appliance energy conservation standards and technical support and consumer education activities for the Federal Trade Commission appliance labeling program. Energy guide labels, required by law to be on the back of all major appliances, provide information as to energy efficiency and cost of operation of the particular equipment. Contact this office for information on the Appliance Standards Program.

* Appliance Testing and Evaluation
Codes and Standards
Conservation and Renewable Energy EE431
U.S. Department of Energy (DOE)
1000 Independence Ave., SW, Room 1J018
Washington, DC 20585   202-586-9127

The U.S. Department of Energy's (DOE) Building Equipment Division develops or modifies test procedures for measuring energy saving design procedures in major household appliances. The office also develops minimum energy efficiency standards for these appliances. Contact the office for further information.

* Appropriate Technology Assistance Service

Energy Efficiency and Renewable Energy Clearinghouse (EREC)
U.S. Department of Energy (DOE)
P.O. Box 3040   800-363-3732
Merrifield, VA 22116   Fax: 703-893-0400
                                           TDD: 800-273-2952
                                           BBS: 800-273-2955

Energy Efficiency and Renewable Energy Clearinghouse (EREC) provides tailored information and technical and commercialization assistance by toll-free telephone or mail. EREC provides assistance services such as: technical engineering assistance, which can include help with system design, component comparisons, system problem solving, economic analysis, and sources of local help; and commercialization assistance, which includes industry overviews, microeconomic analyses and tailored help to identify and evaluate market trends and locate potential funding sources. In addition to responding to written or phone requests, EREC also responds via a computer bulletin board service.

* Architecture and Engineering

Buildings Systems and Materials Division
Buildings and Community Systems
Conservation and Renewable Energy
U.S. Department of Energy (DOE)
1000 Independence Ave., SW, Room 5E-098
Washington, DC 20585   202-586-9445

The Buildings Systems Division distributes information and runs outreach programs on energy efficient buildings. The work of this Division focuses on how systems, subsystems, and components of buildings function independently and how they interact. This Division also develops and promotes research on construction and operation methods and standards for application to new or existing structures. Contact this office for detailed program information and information on available publications, or contact the National Energy Information Center and the National Technical Information Service for information.

* Atmospheric Fluid Dynamics

Battel Northwest
Richland Operations Office
U.S. Department of Energy
P.O. Box 999
Richland, WA 99352   509-375-2924

This office collects and manages research on atmospheric fluid dynamics as they apply to design, performance, and operation of wind turbines. Recent work includes wind turbine wake research, microscale turbulence analyses for dynamic stress load studies, flow characterization, and micrositing in complex terrain. This laboratory has performed wind energy resource assessments for the U.S. and has also developed an international wind energy resource assessment, Contact this office for more detailed information on its projects.

* Audit and Accounting Files

Division of Public Affairs
Federal Energy Regulatory Commission (FERC)
888 1st St., NE
Washington, DC 20426   202-208-0055

Contact this office for information on examining the accounting files and Federal Energy Regulatory Commission (FERC) audits of gas, electric, and oil companies.

* Automobile Fuel Economy

Motor Vehicle Requirements Division
Office of Market Incentives, Rulemaking
National Highway Traffic Safety Administration (NHTSA)
U.S. Department of Transportation
400 7th Street, SW, Room 5313
Washington, DC 20590   202-366-1740

The National Highway Traffic Safety Administration (NHTSA) issues fuel economy standards and collects information on the technological and economic capabilities of automobile manufacturers to maximize fuel efficiency. Contact this office for information and referrals.

* Basic Energy Sciences Advisory Committee

U.S. Department of Energy (DOE) ER-10
19901 Germantown Rd., Room J-304
Germantown, MD 20874   301-903-5565

This Committee was established in 1986 to provide the Secretary of Energy with advice on elements of the Department's Basic Energy Sciences Program, including advice on long range plans, priorities, and strategies to address more effectively the scientific aspects of basic energy science issues of DOE policies and programs.

* Biofuels

Biofuels Systems Division. EE-331
Conservation and Renewable Energy
U.S. Department of Energy (DOE)
1000 Independence Ave., SW, Room 5F-034
Washington, DC 20585   202-586-8072

Researchers at the U.S.U.S. Department of Energy provide the technology base for the production of cost-competitive liquid and gaseous fuels from biomass resources. During the early stages of biofuels development, DOE provides leadership and sponsors long-term, high-risk research and development (R&D). As technology is developed, industry's level of cooperation and cost sharing increases. Finally, when the technology is sufficiently advanced and the economics are sufficiently defined, industry assumes responsibility for commercialization of the developed technology. Contact this office for the program summary and other information.

* Biomass Energy Directory - 1993

Independent Energy Inc.
620 Central Avenue North
Milaca, MN 56353-1788   612-983-6892

This directory contains listings for hundreds of companies involved in the area of biomass energy. Listings include company name, address, and a description of their activities in the biomass field. The directory sells for $27.50.

* Biomass Feedstock Fuels

Biofuels Systems Division, EE-331
U.S. Department of Energy (DOE)
1000 Independence Ave., SW, Room 5F-034
Washington, DC 20585   202-586-8072

This office directs long-term research and development into increasing supplies of biomass feedstocks. Researchers also develop conversion technologies for producing heat, gas, and liquid fuels from a variety of biomass and municipal waste feedstocks. They also investigate aquatic, herbal, and wood crops with potential for increased biomass yields, as well as related systems. Regional programs focus on technology transfer and matching local feedstocks to conversion technologies.

* Buildings Energy Technology

National Technical Information Service
Department of Commerce   800-553-6847
5285 Port Royal Rd.   703-487-4650
Springfield, VA 22161   Fax: 703-321-8547
                                           TDD: 703-487-4639

This current awareness bulletin abstracts worldwide information on the technology required for economic energy conservation in buildings and communities. The summaries in this publication include information about general buildings, residential buildings, office buildings, schools, municipal and other public buildings, and commercial and industrial buildings. The order number is PB94-900700. The price for a yearly subscription, issued monthly, is $160.

* Bulletins: Ocean Thermal to Wind Power

Science and Technology Division
Reference Section, Library of Congress
10 First Street, SE
Washington, DC 20540-5580   202-707-5580

Informal series of reference guides are issued free from the Science and Technology Division under the general title, *LC Science Tracer Bullet*. These guides are designed to help readers locate published material on subjects about which they have only general knowledge. New titles in the series are announced in the weekly Library of Congress *Information Bulletin* that is distributed to many libraries. Those who have Internet access may download a selection of recent science and technology tracer bullets by telnetting to the Library of Congress gopher, LC Marvel, at Marvel.Loc.gov (Logon ID=Marvel). The following is a list of *Tracer Bullets* currently available:

Be patient. If any phone number is incorrect, call (area code) 555-1212 and request the new listing.

1039

* Center for Science Education

Education Office
National Renewable Energy Laboratory (NREL)
1617 Cole Blvd.
Golden, CO 80401   303-275-3044
                                         Fax: 303-275-3076
                             E-mail: lungl@tcplink,nrel.gov

The National Renewable Energy Laboratory (NREL) and the Department of Energy (DOE) believe it is important to cultivate and inspire a new generation of innovative scientists to discover and invent better ways of using our natural resources. The Education Office is dedicated to supporting the system that produces our future scientists and engineers by strengthening education programs in science, mathematics, and technology. A wide range of education programs reaches students and teachers from kindergarten to graduate studies with special attention to women and other underrepresented populations in the sciences. Contact this office for more information about programs available.

* Community Viability

Office of Community Viability
Energy Division
Department of Housing and Urban Development (HUD)
451 7th St. SW, Room 7244
Washington, DC 20410   202-708-2504

This office serves as the Department of Housing and Urban Development's (HUD) principal coordinator for energy activities and provides advice and staff support on energy matters affecting State and local governments and the general public; provides technical assistance to State and local governments in achieving the energy objectives of programs administered by DOE. This division prepares DOE's 5-Year Energy Plan, administers and participates in demonstrations, feasibility studies, and cooperative efforts with DOE and other agencies in such diverse areas as energy efficiency of buildings, economic/community development, district heating, municipal waste-to-energy systems, energy and the elderly, and sustainable development.

* Computer Control of Power Systems

Power System Control Center-MRBA
Tennessee Valley Authority (TVA)
101 Market St.
Chattanooga, TN 37401   423-751-8678

The Computer Systems Section develops and maintains the software systems that control such functions as economic dispatch, automatic generation control, and logging. Telemetered information from TVA's plants, substations, and from interconnection points with utilities is analyzed and processed to help the load coordinators determine the most economical and reliable method to run the power system. Personnel also are responsible for program development and maintenance of the software for the five area dispatch control centers and a microwave alarm logger.

* Conservation Technology Transfer

State Energy Programs Division, EE-522
Office of Technical Assistance Programs
U.S. Department of Energy (DOE)
1000 Independence Ave., SW, Room 5G-052
Washington, DC 20585   202-586-9187

The Energy Extension Service helps market and transfer energy conservation technology and information to businesses. Contact this office to find more out about the information and technology available. For publications, contact the EREC center at 800-363-3732.

* Consumer Countries

Office of International Energy Policy
Bureau of Economics and Business Affairs
U.S. Department of State
2201 C St., NW, Room 3336
Washington, DC 20520   202-647-2887

This office deals with energy-consuming countries--countries that use more energy than they produce. The primary portfolio is dealing with the International Energy Agency in Paris, which was begun in response to the oil crisis. This office, which coordinates policy regarding energy and energy crises, is broken down into the various energy sources (oil, natural gas, coal, nuclear, solar, wind and electricity) with each looking at the stock and emergency preparedness. They also each follow a handful of countries and track international organizations. Along with the Departments of Energy and Commerce, they try to sell energy when they can.

* Consumers and Energy Issues

Congressional, Intergovernmental and Public Affairs
U.S. Department of Energy (DOE)
1000 Independence Ave., SW, Room 8G-026
Washington, DC 20585   202-586-5373

This office analyzes how U.S. Department of Energy policies affect the public energy consumer. It is a source of referral for specific program information to other offices in the U.S. Department of Energy.

* Consumption Statistics

Energy End-Use Division
Energy Markets and End Use
Energy Information Administration EI-63
U.S. Department of Energy (DOE)
1000 Independence Ave., SW, Room 2F-065
Washington, DC 20585   202-586-1112

The Energy End Use and Integrated Statistics Division designs, develops, tests, maintains, and documents energy consumption surveys and information systems which provide accurate and consistent data on energy end use in the residential, commercial, transportation, and industrial sectors. It provides monthly and annual integrated energy statistics for all sources of energy. This office develops historical and current preliminary estimates of energy supply and disposition balances and energy estimates of energy supply and disposition balances and energy prices and expenditures data and interprets trends and events.

* Cost-Effective Renewable Energy

Office of the Assistant Secretary
Energy Efficiency and Renewable Energy, EE-1
U.S. Department of Energy (DOE)
1000 Independence Ave. SW, Room 6C-016
Washington, DC 20585   202-586-9220

This office formulates and directs programs designed to develop and promote the adoption of cost-effective renewable energy and energy efficiency technologies in conjunction with the states and with partners in the transportation, building, industrial, and utility sectors. It supports research, development, and technology transfer activities.

* Daylight Savings Time

Office of Regulatory Affairs
U.S. Department of Transportation (DOT)
400 7th St. SW, Room 9217
Washington, DC 20590   202-366-4864

This office provides information from the interim (1974) and final (1975) reports to Congress on the operation and effects of daylight saving time experiments in energy use and on other factors.

* Deep Seabed Mining

Karl Jugel
Ocean Minerals and Energy Division
Ocean and Coastal Resource Management
National Oceanic and Atmospheric Administration (NOAA)
U.S. Department of Commerce
1305 East West Hwy.
Silver Spring, MD 20910   301-703-3159 ext. 208

Extensive information is available on deep seabed mining, which includes the annual report to Congress and an updated environmental assessment of National Oceanic and Atmospheric Administration (NOAA) deep seabed mining licensees' exploration plans. This office can provide you with information regarding the research conducted concerning the environmental impact of the mining, as well as information on the regulations and licenses. The 1993 annual reports is particularly good for information.

* Defense Energy Emergencies

Energy Emergency Operations
Emergency Planning Office
U.S. Department of Energy (DOE)
1000 Independence Ave., SW, Room 8F0973
Washington, DC 20585   202-586-3271

This office conducts programs to ensure that the U.S. can meet its defense energy needs and that government and industry can continue their essential functions in a catastrophic emergency. It works to reduce U.S. vulnerability to such emergencies and to help improve energy emergency decision making. Contact the Emergency Operations Center, 202-586-8100 for more information.

* Department of Energy Annual Report

Office of Public Affairs
U.S. Department of Energy (DOE)
1000 Independence Ave., SW, Room 7A145
Washington, DC 20585   202-586-4940

The Division of Budget and Administration prepares the U.S. Department of Energy's annual budget and *Annual Report*. For copies of these and other Department of Energy Publications, contact the office of Public Affairs, a good starting point for any quest for information from the Department of Energy.

* Department of Energy Budget

Office of the Controller
Office of Management and Administration
U.S. Department of Energy (DOE)
1000 Independence Ave., SW, Room 4A105
Washington, DC 20585   202-586-4016

The free publication, *Budget Highlights*, summarizes, in statistics and narrative description, the current budget and programs of the U.S. Department of Energy.

* Department of Energy Bulletin Board System (DOE BBS)

Peter Grahn
Office of Information Technology Services and Operations
U.S. Department of Energy (DOE)   301-903-4613
19901 Germantown Rd.   Technical Problems: 301-903-2500
Germantown, MD 20874   Data: 301-903-1666

The Department of Energy maintains an electronic bulletin board providing information on such topics as policies and procedures and draft directives. Forums can be established for public message areas and discussions of general and/or specific topics. Security features are available to control access to Forums. Teleconferencing is available for users who are online at the same time allowing them to converse with each other. There are file libraries which are collections of files by category that contain material available for downloading. There are no fees involved for the use of this system which operates 24 hours a day 7 days a week.

* Department of Energy Standards

National Technical Information Service
Department of Commerce
5285 Port Royal Rd.   800-553-6847
Springfield, VA 22161   703-487-4650
                                    Fax: 703-321-8547
                                    TDD: 703-487-4639

Department of Energy (DOE) Standards establish uniform engineering and technical requirements for processes, procedures, practices, and methods. Standards may also establish requirements for selection, application, and design criteria of facilities, systems components, and other items. These standards are developed by DOE in cases where adequate non-Government standards or standards from other federal agencies do not exist or are not adequate for the intended application. DOE technical standards also establish acceptable methodologies and acceptance criteria for products and processes to be used in accomplishing the DOE mission. The order number is PB95-974300. It is sold as a yearly subscription and the price will be based on number of issues. A $200 deposit is required.

* Diesel Fuel Recording

Office of Economics
Interstate Commerce Commission
12th St. and Constitution Ave., NW
Washington, DC 20423   202-586-6966

This recording states the average diesel fuel price each week after a survey is taken of fuel stations across the country.

* DOE Energy Education Programs

Office of Energy Research
Office of Science Education, ET-30
U.S. Department of Energy (DOE)
1000 Independence Ave., SW, Room 5B168
Washington, DC 20585   202-586-8949

Education has been an important part of the U.S. Department of Energy's mission since its creation in 1977. While the Department has traditionally concentrated its efforts on education at the University level through graduate fellowships and research appointments, the Department has expanded its approach and now also funds significant programs for precollege education and science literacy. The Office of Science Education was formed within the Office of Energy Research in 1990 to coordinate education programs within the Department. The *Education Programs Catalog* details Dept. of Energy programs at the pre-college, under-graduate, graduate, and general public level. It also contains a list of the National Laboratories run by or affiliated with the Dept. of Energy and the education programs they sponsor.

* DOE Energy Research

Office of Energy Research
U.S. Department of Energy (DOE)
1000 Independence Ave., SW, Room 7B-058
Washington, DC 20585   202-586-5430

The Office of Energy Research gives advice on U.S. Department of Energy research programs, university-based education and training activities, as well as grants and other forms of energy assistance. Office programs support both energy research and technologies that have non-energy related spinoffs. Contact this office for available program information, including the publication, *Programs of the Office of Energy Research*, which provides a summary of office research and education programs.

* DOE Grants

Office of Grants Management, EE-53
U.S. Department of Energy (DOE)
600 Maryland Ave., Suite 220
Washington, DC 20585   202-426-1698

This office manages, through the DOE regional support offices, the Institutional Conservation and Weatherization Assistance Programs. They provide information, technical consultation, and financial assistance for improving energy efficiency processes, systems, and practices in schools, hospitals, residences of the elderly and the low income, and other sectors of high energy dependence. The office also manages the Geothermal Loan Guarantee Program.

* DOE Public Reading Rooms

U.S. Department of Energy (DOE)
Public Reading Room, MA 232.22
1000 Independence Ave., SW, Room GA-138
Washington, DC 20585   800-638-8081

A variety of program documents are available at DOE Public Reading Rooms and Information Offices listed below. A more detailed list is available from this office. Nuclear Regulatory Commission materials are available at the listed NRC Local Public Document rooms. For further information about the Local Public Document Room Program, call the above office.

Albuquerque
Operations Office, National Atomic Museum, P.O. Box 5400, Kirtland Air Force Base, E, Albuquerque, NM 87185-5400; 505-845-4378.

Bartlesville
Institute for Petroleum and Energy Research Library, U.S. Dept. of Energy, 220 N. Virginia Ave., P.O. Box 2128, Bartlesville, OK 74003; 918-337-4371.

Boston
Support Office, U.S. Department of Energy, One Congress St. Suite 1101, Boston, MA 02114-2021; 617-565-9700.

Chicago
University of Illinois, 801 S. Morgan, Chicago, IL 60607; 312-996-2738 .

Idaho
Operations Office, Public Reading Room, 1776 Science Center Drive, P.O. Box 1625, Idaho Falls, ID 83415; 208-526-1144.

Morgantown

Energy Technology Center Library, 3610 Collins Ferry Road, P.O. Box 880, Morgantown, WV 26507-0880; 304-285-4764.

Nevada

Technical Information Resource Center, Public Reading Room, U.S. Department of Energy, P.O. Box 98518, Las Vegas, NV 89193-8518; 702-295-1274.

Oak Ridge

Operations Office, Federal Building, 200 Administration Road, P.O. Box 2001, Oak Ridge, TN 37830; 423-576-1216.

Pittsburgh

Energy Technology Center, U.S. Department of Energy, Cochran Mill Road, Building 95, P.O. Box 10940, Pittsburgh, PA 15236-0940; 412-892-6819.

Richland

Operations Office, U.S. Department of Energy, 100 Sprout Rd., Room 131, P.O. Box 999, Mail Stop H2-53, Richland, WA 99352; 509-376-8583.

Colorado

Rocky Flats Office, Front Range Community College, 3645 West 112 Avenue, Westminster, CO 80030; 303-469-4435.

Livermore

Livermore Public Library, 1000 S. Livermore Ave., Livermore, CA 94550; 510-373-5500.

Savannah River

Operations Office, DOE Public Documents Reading Room, Gregg-Graniteville Library, Second Floor, University of South Carolina-Aiken, 1920 Whiskey Road South, Aiken, SC 29801; 803-725-2919.

* Donation of Energy-Related Laboratory Equipment

University and Industry Programs
Office of Science Education, ET-31
U.S. Department of Energy (DOE)
1000 Independence Ave., SW, Room 5B168   202-586-8947
Washington, DC 20585   Data: 301-258-0953
                          Technical Assistance: 301-975-0103
                                  Internet: fedix.fie.com
                          or www:url:http://ewb.fie.com/

Used energy equipment is donated to nonprofit educational institutions of higher learning for use in appropriate programs. Lists of eligible equipment can be found in the *Energy-Related Laboratory Equipment Guide* and on the Eligible Equipment Grants Access Data System (EEGADS). EEGADS provides an overview of program requirements, information on eligibility, mailing addresses for equipment items at various DOE facilities, terms and conditions of grants awarded under the program, and guidelines for developing a proposal for submission to the program. A User's Guide is available free of charge.

* Economics and Statistics

Economics and Statistics Division
Office of Energy Markets and End Use
Energy Information Administration, EI-81
U.S. Department of Energy (DOE)
1000 Independence Ave., SW, Room 2F-081
Washington, DC 20585   202-586-1441

This office conducts forward-looking analyses of energy demand; generates mid-term and long-term forecasts of energy demand; and develops the demand components of the National Energy Modeling System and other mid and long term models. It produces mid and long term forecasts of macroeconomic and international markets and evaluates policies in these areas. Designs and implements a voluntary reporting system for greenhouse gas emissions and produces reports analyzing the results, according to the requirements of the Energy Policy Act of 1992.

* Electric Power Data

Electric Power Division
Coal, Nuclear, Electric and Alternate Fuels
Energy Information Administration
U.S. Department of Energy (DOE)
1000 Independence Ave., SW
Washington, DC 20585   202-426-1200

This office collects analytical data on electric power supply, including capacity, generation, distribution, fuel use, finances, and rates. It also prepares projections of capacity, generation, fuel use, costs, rates, financial requirements, and distribution of electric power. The effects of policy and regulatory actions on the electric utilities' rates, costs, capacity, generation, distribution, finance, and consumption of input fuels are also studied. Contact this office for more information.

* Electricity - Generation and Transmission

Office of Energy Management
Utility Systems Division, EE-141
U.S. Department of Energy (DOE)
1000 Independence Ave, SW, Room 6H-034
Washington, DC 20585   202-586-2828

This division plans and manages research and development programs that will result in new technologies to improve the generation and transmission of electricity, the reliability of electric networks, and impacts resulting from generating and transmission activities. It also researches new methods and techniques for addressing energy demand and supply options that will enable more efficient delivery and use of energy in community shared systems.

* Electronic Publishing System (EPUB)

National Energy Information Center, EI-231
Energy Information Administration
1000 Independence Ave. SW, Room 1F-048   202-586-8800
Washington, DC 20585   Data: 202-586-2557

The Energy Information Administration maintains the EPUB system to allow the general public to electronically access many of EIA's statistical reports and other selected energy data. The system is a menu-driven, bulletin board type with extensive online help capabilities that can be accessed free of charge 24 hours a day. An EPUB users guide is also available. The following files are accessible on the system: Coal, Nuclear, Electricity; Quarterly Coal Report; Oil and Gas; Winter Fuels Pricing; Winter Fuels Propane; Winter Fuels Distillate; Winter Fuels Report; Oxygenate Data; Weekly Petroleum Status Report; Petroleum Supply Monthly; Petroleum Supply Monthly State stocks; Petroleum Marketing Report; Weekly on-Highway Diesel Prices; Weekly Retail Gasoline Prices; Natural Gas Prices; Energy Forecasts; Monthly Energy Review; EIA Press Releases; EIA Publications Directory; Financial Reporting System; Monthly Petroleum Imports; Upcoming Analyses and Publications; Energy Information Contacts; Monthly Energy Review Features File; Electric Power Monthly; and EIA Products Now on DOE Homepage. EPUB is also available via NTIS Fedworld.

* Energy Analysis

Energy Analysis and Systems Division
Energy Information Administration, EI-53
U.S. Department of Energy (DOE)
1000 Independence Ave. SW
Washington, DC 20585   202-426-1211

This Division develops and maintains statistical information and short term forecasting systems related to coal, nuclear, electric, and alternative fuels. It assesses existing and potential resources and reserves, analyzes historical trends, produces forecasts for the short term, performs quality control, and improves and maintains systems for data collection and analysis.

* Energy and Mineral Resources

Office of Energy
U.S. Geological Survey
National Center, MS 915
Reston, VA 22092   703-648-6470

Investigations of the nature, extent, and origin of the Nation's coal, oil and gas, oil shale, uranium, and geothermal resources are basic to this office's research efforts. Acquired data are placed in computerized databases, such as the National Coal Resources Data System.

* Energy Conference and Symposia

National Technical Information Service
Department of Commerce   800-553-6847
5285 Port Royal Rd.   703-487-4650
Springfield, VA 22161   Fax: 703-321-8547
                                     TDD: 703-487-4639

This bulletin lists conferences, symposia, workshops, congresses and other formal meetings concerned with energy issues. It is divided into two parts: Part 1 lists meetings in chronological order; Part 2 displays the same meetings by subject category. Many full-text papers and proceedings emanating from these conferences later become available as printed publications. The order number is PB95-901500. Sold as a yearly subscription the price will be based on the number of issues. A $180 deposit is required.

* Energy Conservation and Solar Power

Office of Energy Conservation and Energy Management
Tennessee Valley Authority (TVA)
400 W. Summit Hill Dr.
Knoxville, TN 37902   432-632-6000

The Tennessee Valley Authority publishes a number of brochures and information bulletins on energy conservation and on the use of solar energy in your home. The following publications are available free from TVA.

Introduction to Solar Energy
Solar Energy in New Homes
Read Your Electric Meter
Save on Your Electric Bills
Insulate Your Attic
Insulate Your Water Heater
Water Source Heat Pump: How to get home heating and cooling from your own backyard.
The New Variable Speed Heat Pump
Let the Sun Get You in Hot Water
Build-It-Yourself Solar Water Heater
Shading Devices
Seasonal Sun and Home Orientation
Natural Cooling

* Energy Conservation Video

National Audiovisual Center
National Archives and Records Administration
8700 Edgeworth Dr.   800-788-6282
Capitol Heights, MD 20743-3701   301-763-1896

The Media Resource Catalog contains more than 600 programs which are ideal for classrooms, training programs, library collections, and home use.

Energy - The American Experience (29 minutes, color, 1978). With the perspective of over 200 years of history, this program shows the development of different forms of energy under the unique conditions of the American Experience. You see the 60 year changing cycle of energy sources from wood to coal to oil and gas to produce the steam and electrical energy that helped make the U.S. the industrial giant of the world. VHS Video No. TCA06181, $110.00.

* Energy-Efficient and Renewable Energy Technologies

Office of Technical Assistance Programs
U.S. Department of Energy (DOE) EE-54
1000 Independence Ave, SW, Room 5E-036
Washington, DC 20585   202-586-5517

This office develops national and international programs that provide technical assistance to a wide range of energy users and to renewable energy and energy efficiency industries. They coordinate the resources of public and private sector organizations to enhance the role of U.S. energy technologies in the world marketplace and provides technical assistance and information to energy users and the intermediaries, local governments, and trade and professional associations to increase the use of energy-efficient and renewable energy technologies.

* Energy Efficiency and Renewable Energy Network (EREN)

Pam Lowe
National Renewable Energy Laboratory
U.S. Department of Energy (DOE)   303-275-4035
1617 Cole Blvd.   Data: 303-275-INFO
Golden, CO 80401   E-mail: lowep@tcplink.nrel.gov
    Internet URL: http//www.eren.doe.gov
    Technical information: 708-252-3608
or
Energy Efficiency and Renewable Energy Clearinghouse (EREC)
P.O. Box 3408   800-363-3732
Merrifield, VA 22116   Fax: 703-893-0400
    TDD: 800-273-2957

    BBS: 800-273-2955
    E-mail: energyinfo@delphi.com

The Energy Efficiency and Renewable Energy Network (EREN), the sister service of the Energy Efficiency and Renewable Energy Clearinghouse (EREC), gives Internet users a gateway to energy efficiency and renewable energy information from national laboratories and other organizations. Topics available include alternative fuels, energy efficiency topics, wind energy, hydrogen power, and solar energy. EREN provides access to bibliographic information; bulletin boards; databases and information services; documents and data files; links to maps, images, video, sound and text; and discussion groups. Currently EREN has over 60 links to various Internet sites.

* Energy Extension Services

State Energy Programs, EE-522
U.S. Department of Energy (DOE)
1000 Independence Ave. SW, Room 5E-052
Washington, DC 20585   202-586-9187

The Energy Extension Service (EES) provides small-scale energy users, such as individuals, small businesses, and local governments, with personalized information and on-site technical assistance for practical energy conservation, including the uses of renewable energy resources. EES supplies block grants for approved programs. States operate their own EES programs. You can find out what is available in your state by contacting the Energy Director Office. These offices are listed at the end of this section.

* Energy Facts

Superintendent of Documents
Government Printing Office (GPO)
710 N. Capitol St. NW   202-512-1800
Washington, DC 20402   Fax: 202-512-2250

This book provides a reference to a broad range of domestic and international energy data for the general public as well as the technical community. Designed especially for the business person, government worker, or student who needs a quick reference to major facts about energy. Stock #061-003-00829-1, $2.00.

* Energy Information Administration

U.S. Department of Energy (DOE)
1000 Independence Ave., SW, Room 2F-095
Washington, DC 20585   202-586-1094

The Energy Information Administration's *Annual Report* provides a good summary of the Administrations' structure and key informational contacts within the offices. To receive a copy of the report call the National Energy Information Center at 202-586-8800.

* Energy Information Administration (EIA) Homepage

National Energy Information Center, EI-231
Energy Information Administration
Forrestal Bldg., Room 1F-048   202-586-8800
Washington, DC 20585   TDD 202-586-1181
    Internet: http://apollo.osti.gov/html/eia/eiahome.html

The Energy Information Administration (EIA) and the Office of Scientific and Technical Information (OSTI) have established a program that makes selected EIA test products available on the "EIA Homepage," which currently resides on a Mosaic/World Wide Web server at OSTI. The Mosaic technology permits browsing of the hypertext documents by Internet users. EIA New Releases, Short-Term Energy Models, together with the "Energy Data Information Contacts" listing; selected feature articles and press releases; and a natural gas and oil contact information listing are available on the EIA Homepage. EIA will continue to place most upcoming feature articles, press releases, and other items of interest onto this system.

* Energy Information Directory

National Energy Information Center
Energy Information Administration
U.S. Department of Energy (DOE)
1000 Independence Ave., SW, Room E1-231
Washington, DC 20585   202-586-8800

The National Energy Information Center (NEIC) is the central distribution point for most U.S. Department of Energy publications, including the free *Energy Information Administration Publications Directory: A Users Guide*. The *Directory* includes current program information sources; an index of DOE, State, and Federal Agency contacts; a directory of DOE technical information with descriptions of computerized databases and other resources; Congressional Committees and Subcommittees that have jurisdiction over various components of the Civilian Radioactive Waste Management Program; and DOE Public Reading Rooms and Information Offices, and NRC local public document rooms; and listings of selected publications. Also ask for the latest edition of the *Energy Information Directory*, a comprehensive guide to energy information in the Federal government. The NEIC should be an early contact in any energy research project.

* Energy Information Directory of Electronic Products

National Energy Information Center EI-231
Energy Information Administration
1000 Independence Ave., Room 1F-048
Washington, DC 20585   202-586-8800
                                                      TDD: 202-586-1181

The Energy Information Administration Directory of Electronic Products makes available for public use a series of machine-readable data files and computer models. The data files and models are made available to the public on magnetic tapes. In addition, selected data files and models are available on diskette for IBM compatible personal computers. Also available is The Directory of Energy Information Administration Models; it contains descriptions about each model, including the title, acronym, purpose, and more detailed information.

* Energy Inventions and Innovation

Office of National Programs
Inventions and Innovations Division EE-521
U.S. Department of Energy (DOE)
1000 Independence Ave, SW, Room 5E-052
Washington, DC 20585   202-586-1479

Two principal programs of this division, the Energy Related Inventions Program (ERIP) and the Innovative Concepts Program (ICP) help non-Federal entities to identify, evaluate, and provide financial and technical support for inventions and innovations that may have a significant impact on energy production or utilization. ERIP provides assistance for the commercialization of recommended technologies. ICP provides assistance for the development of technologies beyond the concept stage. Contact this office for more information.

* Energy Markets Development/Analysis

Office of Policy, Planning, and Analysis
Office of Electricity, Coal, Nuclear,
 and Renewable Policy
U.S. Department of Energy (DOE)
1000 Independence Ave., SW, Room 7H-075
Washington, DC 20585   202-586-5727

This office analyzes factors that influence energy demand such as economic, technical, environmental, regulatory, and institutional developments. Major areas of concentration include analysis of electrical power, coal, and nuclear resource markets, incentives designed to stimulate production and availability for more efficient use of resources and enhance U.S. energy security.

* Energy Publications Directory, 1977-1994

Energy Information Administration
National Energy Information Center
U.S. Department of Energy (DOE)
1000 Independence Ave.,SW
Washington, DC 20585   202-586-8800

The Energy Information Administration has compiled a massive directory that lists some 895 Energy publications written between 1977 and 1989. The report is indexed by subject, title, and report number. Contact the National Energy Information Center for a copy of the Directory.

* Energy Related Inventions

Program Information
National Institute of Standards and Technology (NIST)
Gaithersburg, MD 20899   301-975-5500

This office provides for the evaluation of ideas and inventions to determine their technical and commercial feasibility, energy conservation or supply value, and practicality; formulates recommendations for Department of Energy (DOE) funding if the technology is promising. Applicants must submit a detailed technical description of the invention and complete the Energy-Related Inventions Evaluation Report Form; the Review process takes from 2 to 8 months. This office works in conjunction with the DOE Energy-Related Inventions Program, 202-586-1479.

* Energy Research Grants

Office of Energy Research
U.S. Department of Energy (DOE)
19901 Germantown Rd.
Germantown, MD 20874   301-903-5544

The Office of Energy Research sponsors research, training, and related activities in the following program areas: Basic Energy Sciences, Field Operations Management, Fusion Energy, Health and Environmental Research, High Energy and Nuclear Physics, Scientific Computing Staff, Superconduction Super Collider, University and Science Education Programs, Program Analysis, and other program areas that are announced in the *Federal Register*. The Office of Energy Research *Grant Application and Guide* lists different research division projects with contact numbers for the programs. It is available free.

* Energy Resource Management and Conservation

Directorate for Energy Policy
Department of Defense
The Pentagon, Room 1D760
Washington, DC 20301-8000   703-697-5981

Reduces energy use through efficiency investments, incentives, and engineering: develops energy use and management policies that achieve environmental goals such as clean air, clean water, solid and hazardous waste minimization; and develops and cosponsors emerging energy technologies for a variety of security, environmental, and economic goals.

* Energy-Saving Equipment in Buildings

Building Equipment Division
Conservation and Renewable Energy EE-422
U.S. Department of Energy (DOE)
1000 Independence Ave., SW, Room 5H-048
Washington, DC 20585   202-586-9130

This Division supplies the private sector with the technological base on which to develop and test high efficiency energy and solar equipment used in operating residential and commercial buildings. This office is also responsible for administration of the Appliance Standards Program. Contact this office for more information.

* Energy Science Research

Accelerator and Fusion Research Division
Lawrence Berkeley Laboratory (LBL)
1 Cyclotron Road
Mail Stop 50-149
Berkeley, CA 94720   510-486-5771

The Lawrence Berkeley Laboratory undertakes a wide ranging research program in Energy Sciences. Research is carried out by four divisions: material sciences, chemical sciences, energy and environment, and earth sciences. LBL pursues basic research and seeks ways of practical application of the basic results. The work of this division of the Laboratory is designed to reflect Energy Department priorities in finding ways to explore and recover energy resources, as well as protecting people and the environment from possible hazards. Contact the above office for further information.

* Environmental Guidance

Office of the Assistant Secretary for Environment,
 Safety and Health
Office of Environmental Policy
U.S. Department of Energy (DOE)
1000 Independence Ave., SW, Room 7A-097
Washington, DC 20585   202-586-6151

This office is responsible for developing written compliance policies, standards, guidance documents, and internal DOE orders which cover the full range of environmental statutes and regulations. The division monitors regulatory and legislative developments, keeps DOE personnel abreast of emerging and changing environmental requirements, coordinates the development of Departmental positions, and serves as the advocate for DOE's position with regard to other agencies rulemaking efforts.

* Environmental Impact Statements

Office of National Environmental Policy Act (NEPA)
Project Assistance
Environment, Safety, and Health

U.S. Department of Energy (DOE)
1000 Independence Ave., SW, Room 3E-080
Washington, DC 20585   202-586-4610

NEPA documents prepared for DOE activities are reviewed and approved through this office to determine whether DOE programs require Environmental Impact Statements. This office also reviews energy-related Environmental Impact Statements from other agencies. Contact this office for more detailed information.

* Environmental Issues and Energy Development

Office of Environmental Analysis, PE-63
Assistant Secretary for Environment, Safety and Health
U.S. Department of Energy (DOE)
1000 Independence Ave., SW, Room 4G-036
Washington, DC 20585   202-586-2061

This office analyzes proposed environmental policies, laws, and regulations to determine their effects on energy development and use. The office also assesses the potential impact on the environment of energy technologies being developed by the Department of Energy, along with the potential impact of national energy strategies at both the national and regional level. Contact the office for more detailed information.

* Environmental Protection, International

Bureau of Oceans and International Environmental and
   Scientific Affairs
U.S. Department of State
2201 C St., NW, Room 4325
Washington, DC 20520   202-647-9266

This office looks at international environmental issues and concerns, such as pollution, acid rain, global climate changes, the ozone, and toxic waste. They monitor bilateral and multilateral agreements, and work with other agencies in trying to develop ways to handle these environmental concerns.

* Environmental Safety and Health Fax System

Environmental Safety and Health, EH-0499
Department of Energy (DOE)
19901 Germantown Rd.
Germantown, MD 20874   301-903-3016
                          Fax: 301-903-6699/6692

Some of the publications available by fax include the Environmental Safety and Health (ES&H) Synergy and the Safety and Health Connection newsletters, Safety and Health Notes, Bulletins, Hazard Alerts, ES&H Updates, DOE News Releases relating to ES&H, and congressional testimony. To use this system you must call from a touch tone phone or a fax machine. Follow the voice prompts to order the publications you want.

* Federal Energy Management

Federal Energy Management Program (FEMP), EE-44
Office of Conservation and Renewable Energy
U.S. Department of Energy (DOE)
1000 Independence Ave., SW, Room 5E-80
Room 5E-080
Washington, DC 20585   202-586-5772

This office plans and manages energy conservation for the Federal Government. Specific objectives include reducing total energy consumption by the Federal Government; increasing efficiencies and reducing costs; altering the fuel mix within the Federal consumption total; enhancing the use of renewable energy fuels; and reducing dependence on imported fuels. The program attempts to set an example for the nation by transferring the Federal energy experience to state and local governments and the private sector. The Federal Energy Management Program (FEMP) Update, published quarterly and the FEMP Annual Report are good sources of information.

* Federal Energy Policy

Commerce Clearing House, Inc.
4025 West Peterson Ave.
Chicago, IL 60646   312-583-8500

The *Federal Energy Guidelines* is a set of loose-leaf publications dealing primarily with DOE programs, certain other Federal energy activities, and general data regarding energy policy are produced from an automated data base. Nongovernment offices can obtain a subscription by contacting the office above. Order # ERG, $1420 yearly.

* Federal Energy Regulatory Commission

Federal Energy Regulatory Commission (FERC)
Division of Public Affairs
888 1st St. NE
Washington, DC 20426   202-208-0004

This office can supply you with information on the work of the Federal Energy Regulatory Commission (FERC). This office can also assist you in obtaining copies of FERC official documents.

* Federal Energy Regulatory Commission Publications

Public Reference Room
Federal Energy Regulatory Commission (FERC)
888 1st St. NE
Room 2A
Washington, DC 20426   202-208-1371

The *Federal Energy Regulatory Commission Publications Directory* provides descriptions, sources, stock numbers, and prices, when applicable, of the latest editions of publications and staff reports issued by the Federal Energy Regulatory Commission or the former Federal Power Commission. Many reports and data files are available on diskette. Contact the office above to obtain a free copy. Orders for FERC publications must be sent in writing.

* Films on Energy Issues

Office of Civilian Radioactive Waste Management (OCRWM)
National Information Center
Department of Energy (DOE)
600 Maryland Ave SW, Suite 760   800-225-6972
Washington, DC 20024   202-488-6720

OCRWM has produced a number of videotapes about the nation's civilian radioactive waste management system. Topics cover all aspects of the OCRWM program, including deep geologic disposal, interim storage, transportation, and the multi-purpose canister concept being developed for storing, transporting, and disposing of commercial spent nuclear fuel. OCRWM videos are available to the public free of charge.

* Financial Statistics and Projections

Economics and Statistics Division
Energy Markets and End Use EI-60
Energy Information Administration
U.S. Department of Energy (DOE)
1000 Independence Ave., SW, Room 2G-089
Washington, DC 20585   202-586-1617

This office compiles economic and financial energy statistics and projections, and periodic assessments of the U.S. energy situation are made. Additionally, it evaluates and interprets current trends and events in the U.S. and international energy situations. For available information and publications, contact this office.

* Forest Biomass Energy

Energy Coordinator
Forest Products and Harvesting Research Staff
U.S. Department of Agriculture, Forest Service
14th & Independence Ave. SW, P.O. Box 96090
Washington, DC 20090-6090   202-205-1565

This office conducts forest biomass energy-related research. The agency coordinates it's research activities with Federal and State agencies, as well as universities. Activities include obtaining, analyzing, and projecting national statistics on woody biomass supply and use, as well as research in silviculture, harvesting, and utilization. The agency also administers national forest lands in a multiple-use approach that includes sales of industrial wood and personal/industrial use of fuel wood.

* Fuel and Vehicle Research and Testing

Vehicle Research and Test Center
Research and Development
National Highway Traffic Safety Administration (NHTSA)
U.S. Department of Transportation
P.O. Box 37
East Liberty, OH 43319   513-666-4511

NHTSA evaluates the effectiveness of Federal Motor Vehicle Safety Standards. This engineering facility performs tests to obtain basic data used to establish standards for safety and fuel safety of motor vehicles. They are also studying the crashworthiness of alternative fuels.

* General Accounting Office Studies

Energy Issue Area Resources
U.S. General Accounting Office (GAO)
441 G. St. NW
Washington, DC 20548   202-512-3841

The GAO's Energy Issue Area conducts in-depth studies of the production, regulation, and consumption of all forms of energy. Aspects of the GAO's work include evaluating the effectiveness of energy security policies and programs, the management of energy research and development programs and nuclear waste disposal programs, the safety of defense and commercial nuclear facilities, and the procedures and controls governing energy programs. Recent reports of interest includes *Bibliography of GAO Documents* January 1986 - December 1989 (GAO/RCED 90-179). To get on the GAO's mailing list or to order this free report, and reports and testimony for 1992 (GAO/RCED-93-131) call 202-512-6000.

* Genetic Research

Life Sciences Program
Lawrence Berkeley Laboratory
One Cyclotron Rd.
Mail Stop Donner
Berkeley, CA 94720   510-486-5771

The Life Sciences Program at the Lawrence Berkeley Laboratory undertakes research into genes and related aspects of genetic structure. It also researches radiobiology, nuclear medicine, biotechnology, and cellular and molecular damage caused by energy-related environmental hazards. Contact this office for more detailed information on its programs.

* Geothermal Energy

Geothermal Technology Division
Conservation and Renewable Energy EE-122
U.S. Department of Energy (DOE)
1000 Independence Ave., SW, Room 5H-065
Washington, DC 20585   202-586-5340

Geothermal energy technology improvements are needed before the more difficult resources--moderate-temperature hydrothermal fluids, geopressured brines, hot dry rock, and magma--can compete economically with conventional power generation technologies. Until these technologies become available for industry use, this resource cannot meet its full potential in the Nation's energy supply mix. This division supports geothermal technology development and transfer through government/ industry cooperation. Research that promises future economic expansion of geothermal development and use is given priority. Contact this office for more information and the program summary.

* Grand Coulee and Other Dams

Public Affairs
Bureau of Reclamation
U.S. Department of the Interior
18th and C Sts., NW
Washington, DC 20240   202-208-4662

Across the West, the Bureau of Reclamation annually supplies over 210,000 billion gallons of water to more than 23 million people for municipal, industrial, and agricultural use. The best known Reclamation projects are the Grand Coulee Dam on the Columbia River and the Hoover Dam on the Colorado River. Project water is delivered to almost 10 million acres of farmland to produce crops valued at $7.5 billion annually. The Bureau's non-polluting hydroelectric powerplants supply electricity to 17 million persons. Reclamation reservoirs also provide millions of visitors with facilities for fishing, swimming, picnicking, and sightseeing.

* Greenhouse Gas Technology Information Exchange (GREENTIE)

Marty Broders
Oak Ridge National Laboratory
P.O. Box 2008
Oak Ridge, TN 37831-6070   423-576-2731

The International Energy Agency and the Organization for Economic Cooperation and Development have jointly organized the Greenhouse Gas Technology Information Exchange (GREENTIE) to improve the transfer of knowledge about the mitigation and abatement of greenhouse gas (GHG) emissions. Opportunities to reduce such emissions exist in industry, commerce, transport, government, and the private home. GREENTIE is maintaining a directory of institutions and expertise in the field of GHG technologies and will use that directory to respond to users' inquiries, identifying suitable sources of information and providing users with a printed report of names and addresses of organizations that can supply the needed technology, information, or technical advice. GREENTIE will not charge for putting users in contact with sources of knowledge, but suppliers of information and services may charge for some of their products. If you have a program that you wish included in the directory, forward it to the U.S. liaison listed above.

* Heat Pump Program

Residential Energy Services Program
Tennessee Valley Authority (TVA)
3N45B Signal Place
1101 Market St. PSC 1F-C
Chattanooga, TN 37402-2801   423-697-4211

TVA and participating local power distributors offer a heat pump program to encourage the installation of energy-efficient heat pumps in existing residential dwellings. The plan includes an on-site inspection to ensure the heat pump is correctly installed. In addition, distributors may offer such incentives as cash payments, electric bill credits, or low-interest loans. Loans may be used for approved weatherization improvements, such as attic and floor insulation and storm windows, installed along with a heat pump. No down payment is required, and customers may take up to 10 years to repay the loans.

* Household Energy Consumption and Expenditures, 1987

Office of Energy Markets and End Use
Energy End Use Division
Energy Information Administration
U.S. Department of Energy (DOE)
1000 Independence Ave., SW, Room 2F-065
Washington, DC 20585   202-586-1122

Household Energy Consumption and Expenditures, 1987 is the second report based on 1987 RECS data. The 1987 RECS, the seventh in a series of national surveys of households and their energy suppliers, provides baseline information on how households in the United States use energy. A randomly selected set of housing units that includes single-family detached homes, townhouses, apartment buildings, condominiums, and mobile homes were selected for the survey. Data from the RECS and a companion survey, the *Residential Transportation Energy Consumption Survey*, are available to the public in published reports such as this one and on public use tapes.

* Housing Energy Characteristics 1987

Office of Energy Markets and End Use
Energy End Use Division
Energy Information Administration
U.S. Department of Energy (DOE)
1000 Independence Ave., SW, Room 2F-065
Washington, DC 20585   202-586-1122

Housing Characteristics 1987 is the first of a series of reports based on data from the 1987 RECS, the seventh in the series of national surveys of households and their energy suppliers. These surveys provide baseline information on how households in the U.S. use energy. Contact this office for more information.

* Hydroelectric Power

Program Analysis Office
Bureau of Reclamation
U.S. Department of the Interior
P.O. Box 25007
Denver CO 80225   303-236-3289

The Bureau of Reclamation is currently operating 49 powerplants at different sites throughout the West. For further information on the impact of hydroelectric power and the Bureau's efforts, contact this office.

* Industrial Energy Bibliography

Office of Scientific and Technical Information
U.S. Department of Energy (DOE)
P.O. Box 62
Oak Ridge, TN 37831   615-423-8104

The *Office of Industrial Technologies Technical Report: A Bibliography* is the first annotated publication containing information on all scientific and technical reports sponsored by the DOE Industrial Energy Conservation Program DOE contractors. Contact this office for information on ordering. The public should first contact NTIS (800-553-6847). Order # DE92-000-497.

* Industrial Energy Conservation

National Technical Information Service
5285 Port Royal Road   800-553-6847
Springfield, VA 22161   703-487-4650

The monthly publication, *Industrial Energy Conservation*, announces the current worldwide information on all aspects of energy conservation in industry, including alternative energy sources; improved materials, equipment, and processes; waste heat recovery; and industrial waste management. This publication contains the abstracts of DOE reports, journal articles, conference papers, patents, theses, and monographs added to the Energy Data Base (EDB) during the past month. Also included is information obtained through acquisition programs or interagency agreements and through the International Energy Agency's Energy Technology Data Exchange or government-to-government agreements. The digests in *IEC* and other citations to information on energy conservation in industry technologies back to 1974 are available for on-line searching and retrieval on EDB. Current information, added daily to EDB, is available to DOE and its contractors through the DOE Integrated Technical Information System. Customized profiles can be developed to provide current information to meet each user's needs. The entire Energy Database is available on commercial on-line retrieval systems. (Order #PB88-933900, $90).

* Industrial Energy Technologies

Office of Industrial Technology
Deputy Assistant Secretary for Conservation
U.S. Department of Energy (DOE)
1000 Independence Ave., SW, Room 6B-052
Washington, DC 20585   202-586-2098

Here researchers develop new energy technologies for improved energy efficiency in the industrial process and greater fuel flexibility. This office can supply you with several basic reports describing what programs are being undertaken. Reports on the results of their studies are available from the National Technical Information Service (NTIS).

* Industrial Programs: Research in Progress

National Technical Information Service
U.S. Department of Commerce
5285 Port Royal Rd.   800-553-6847
Springfield, VA 22161   703-487-4650

The report, *Office of Industrial Programs: Research in Progress* contains summaries for currently active projects supported by the Office of Industrial Programs. The report was prepared from the DOE Research-in-Progress database maintained by the Office of Scientific and Technical Information. Order # DE 90002100, $22.

* Institutional Energy Conservation Grants

Conservation and Renewable Energy Programs, CE-531
Institutional Conservation Program Division
U.S. Department of Energy (DOE)
1000 Independence Ave., SW, Room 5G-063
Washington, DC 20585   202-586-8034

Public and private nonprofit schools and hospitals can get matching, cost-shared grants to make detailed energy analyses and energy-saving capital improvements. The government will contribute 50 percent of the cost of these conservation projects, and in certain hardship cases, they may provide more. Contact this office for more information.

* Integrated Technical Information System

U.S. Department of Energy (DOE)
Office of Scientific and Technical Information (OSTI)
P.O. Box 62
Oak Ridge, TN 37831   423-576-1222

The Integrated Technical Information System (ITIS), developed by the DOE, provides access to DOE databases in the Energy Data Information System; information merging for customized information products; and electronic mail, a communications link among OSTI, DOE, and contractor offices. Library specialists, information managers, and researchers can work from remote terminals to search various databases on ITIS. The following databases are part of the ITIS system.

Energy Science and Technology Database. This database contains citations in associated sciences, medicine ecology and other fields outside the conventional energy areas. The database is updated nightly.

Management Information File (MIF). MIF contains selected data elements from all records entered into the Energy Science and Database since 1974, as well as

Controlled Access File records. MIF records contain enough information for report ordering.

Reports Holding File (RHF). This is a directory of DOE and non-DOE reports processed and held at the Office of Scientific and Technical Information from 1947 to the present.

Research in Progress (RIP). This database contains administrative and technical information on all current and recently completed unclassified research projects performed or funded by the U.S. Department of Energy. Citations are maintained in the database for five years after project completion.

Controlled Access File (CAF). This database contains records of DOE documents and other materials that are not classified but which legal reasons, such as patent or copyright questions, restrict distribution.

Minority Economic Impact (MEI). Found here are bibliographic references to selected books, reports, and journal articles concerned with the impact of energy on minorities.

Nevada Nuclear Waste (NNW). Found here are references to research and site characterization studies for the proposed high-level radioactive waste repository at Yucca Mountain, Nevada. NNW is a subset of the Energy Science and Technology Database.

Energy Science and Technology Software (ESTS). This database contains citations to available software developed in all subject areas relative to programs of the U.S. Department of Energy and the Nuclear Regulatory Commission.

Numeric Database Directory (NDB). This is a directory of machine-readable numeric and factual databases currently available in the field of scientific and technical information. NDB includes descriptions for both federal and private sector databases.

Foreign Research in Progress (FRP). Records of current energy-related research abroad are found here. Information about ongoing foreign research is acquired through exchange agreements with such organizations as the International Energy Agency, International Nuclear Energy Agency, and Energy Technology Data Exchange.

New Technology from DOE (NTD). This database contains brief descriptions of DOE research results having potential for commercialization by U.S. industry. NTD incorporates older materials known as Applications Assessments Records and current Technology Assessment Records submitted by each Office of Research and Technology Applications, as required by the Stevenson-Wydler Technology Innovation Act of 1980.

Contact the office above for more information about on-line access to these databases. The Access fee for this service is $30 per hour plus $.25 per record for downloading/printing.

* Interagency Power Group Briefs

National Technical Information Service
Department of Commerce
5285 Port Royal Rd.   800-553-6847
Springfield, VA 22161   703-487-4650
           Fax: 703-321-8547
           TDD: 703-487-4639

The Government Research and Development Summaries describe the status of all programs in the fields of advanced power research, development and engineering. Members of the Interagency Advanced Power Group (IAPG) are the U.S. Army, Navy, and Air Force, U.S. Department of Energy (DOE) and the National Aeronautics and Space Administration (NASA). Their cooperative effort monitors government-funded research and development producing project briefs. Each project brief contains title; project description; contract number, period, probable completion date and funding; principle investigator name and telephone number; contractor name and address. Directing agency and index terms subscribers who receive any of the project brief packages will also receive the semi-annual IAPG Project Briefs by Field of Interest, and the Annual Completed or Canceled Compilation and Cumulative Annual Project Brief Subject Index which are combined into a single publication.

Chemical projects cover chemical batteries, biochemical devices, simple fuel cell systems, chemical regenerative fuel cell systems, and thermal energy storage. Magnetohydrodynamics covers the magnet hydronamic (MHD) interaction between electromagnetic fields and electrically conducting fields, including fuels, materials, plasma dynamics, and combustion.

Be patient. If any phone number is incorrect, call (area code) 555-1212 and request the new listing.

1047

Electrical projects cover energy conversion to electrical forms (including electrical energy control) by electromechanical, electromagnetic, electrostatic, magnet hydrodynamic, electronic, and solid state devices excluding photovoltaic and photoemissive devices. Specific attention is devoted to magnet hydrodynamics, power conditioning, and superconductivity.

Mechanical projects cover energy conversion to mechanical hydraulic, and pneumatic energy, including working fluids, materials, heat transfer processes, heat transfer and storage equipment, and other components of mechanical conversion systems.

Nuclear projects cover energy conversion from fission, fusion, and radioisotope power sources and other thermal systems that use thermionic systems. These briefs also follow related investigations of plasma dynamics.

Solar projects cover solar radiation collection, storage, and conversion to heat or other energy forms. Photovoltaic and solar thermal devices and related systems are also reported.

Order numbers:

Chemical	PB94-901600FCD
Electrical	PB94-901700FCD
Mechanical	PB94-901800FCD
Nuclear	PB94-901900FCD
Solar	PB94-902000FCD
Magneto-hydrodynamic	PB94-902200FCD
Systems	PB94-910700FCD

Minimum deposit $100 per category, standing order price $5 per brief.

* International Annual Energy Outlook

National Energy Information Center
Energy Information Center
U.S. Department of Energy (DOE)
1000 Independence Ave., SW, Room 1F-048
Washington, DC 20585   202-586-8800

The *Annual Energy Outlook* is a survey of the U.S. and world energy situation. It includes projections of production and prices in the U.S. and overseas. Contact NEIC for information on obtaining a copy of the report.

* International Energy Affairs

International Research and Development Policy
International Technology Cooperation, PO-71
U.S. Department of Energy (DOE)
1000 Independence Ave., SW, Room 1E-218
Washington, DC 20585   202-586-5915

This office coordinates and assists the development of energy research and development cooperation involving the United States and other nations. Contact the office for more detailed information.

* International Energy Data

International and Contingency Information Division
Energy Markets and End Use
Energy Information Administration EI-621
U.S. Department of Energy (DOE)
1000 Independence Ave., SW, Room 2G-060
Washington, DC 20585   202-586-1130

This Branch compiles international energy information, including current international energy market assessments, international energy projections, contingency planning studies, prices, distribution, and other quick response or special purpose analyses. In addition, the Branch reports U.S. energy data to international organizations. Contact office for information on its research reports and publications.

* International Energy Supply

International and Contingency Information Division
Office of Energy Markets and End Use
Energy Information Administration EI-621
U.S. Department of Energy (DOE)
1000 Independence Ave., SW, Room 2G-060
Washington, DC 20585   202-586-1130

This office forecasts international energy supply and demand under various assumptions of international institutional arrangements and other international factors. Contact this office for more detailed program information.

* Lawrence Berkeley Laboratory

Lawrence Berkeley Laboratory
One Cyclotron Rd., Mail Stop 65B
Berkeley, CA 94720   510-486-5771

Lawrence Berkeley Laboratory is a multi-program national laboratory run by the University of California under contract to the U.S. Department of Energy. It undertakes a wide range of unclassified research activities, including Accelerator and Fusion Research, Applied Science, Life Science, Earth Science, Energy Sciences, Engineering, General Sciences, Information and Computing Sciences, Materials and Chemical Sciences, Nuclear Science and Physics. The Laboratory describes its function as being four-fold: research, education, developing and operating national experimental facilities, and fostering productive relations between LBL research programs and private industry. Contact the Public Affairs office for copies of their annual report and catalog of programs. Also ask for a couple sample copies of the *LBL Research Review*, which contains articles on research projects ongoing at the Laboratory.

* Legislation

Division of Public Affairs
Federal Energy Regulatory Commission
888 1st St. NE
Washington, DC 20426   202-208-0870

You can get information on energy-related legislative matters under consideration by Congress, after release by the Committee or Member of Congress involved. For more information current or past legislation, contact this office.

* Legislation on Energy Issues

Governmental Relations
U.S. Department of Energy (DOE)
1000 Independence Ave., SW, Room 8E-070
Washington, DC 20585   202-586-2764

Daily actions by Congress on energy legislation, are tracked through this office, and the staff can provide you with current status of the legislation. The office prepares briefing books and issues papers for U.S. Department of Energy witnesses, and compiles membership lists of Congressional committees concerned with DOE programs. The office also prepares and distributes reports of all daily energy related Congressional activity. Contact this office for more information on current energy legislation.

* Libraries, Energy

The Energy Library
U.S. Department of Energy (DOE)
1000 Independence Ave., SW, Room GA-138
Washington, DC 20585   202-586-9534

This library compiles material on administrative and regulatory matters, non-nuclear research and development and alternative energy sources. The following are the major libraries of the U.S. Department of Energy:

Federal Energy Regulatory Commission Library, 825 N. Capitol Street, NW, Room 8502, Washington, DC 20426; 202-208-2179. Focuses on regulatory matters.

Germantown Branch, U.S. Department of Energy, Germantown Branch, 19901 Germantown Rd., Room GO55, Germantown, MD 20585; 301-903-4301. This library focuses on material on nuclear energy and fossil fuels, energy research, and environmental protection, safety and emergency preparedness.

* Liquid Biomass Fuels in Vehicles

Transportation Technologies
National Alternative Fuels Hotline
U.S. Department of Energy (DOE)
P.O. Box 12316
Arlington, VA 22209   800-423-1363
                              703-528-3500
                              Fax: 703-528-1953

Contact this office for information on the use of liquid biomass fuels in vehicles. The office handles market analysis, market testing, research and development, and commercialization programs involving these fuels. It consolidates information about federal alcohol fuel efforts and education activities designed to increase public awareness and use of alcohol fuels. For further information on available publications, or to be put on the mailing list for the quarterly biofuels update newsletter, contact this office.

* Load Management

Marketing Services
3N45B Signal Pl.
Tennessee Valley Authority (TVA)
1101 Market St.
Chattanooga, TN 37402-2801   423-751-2573

The Tennessee Valley Authority (TVA), in cooperation with power distributors, is trying out a number of ways to flatten out the peaks in consumer power demand, which requires the use of more expensive generating facilities. One of these load management demonstrations involves remote controlled "cycling" of hot water heaters and space-conditioning units in homes. About 120,000 remote switches have been installed for power distributors to investigate larger capacity storage small element water heaters.

* Load Research

Load Research Efforts
Electric Sales Statistics Dept.
Tennessee Valley Authority (TVA)
Power, 1100 Market St.
2N-48A Signal Place
Chattanooga, TN 37402-2801   423-751-7036

Researchers are currently sampling Tennessee Valley Authority (TVA) power customers to determine when and how much electricity they consume. Homes and businesses are monitored to determine hourly load information, which will be gathered for studies of cost of service, rate design, and planning and marketing. Contact this office for more information on power usage statistics in the TVA regions.

* Low Income Energy Assistance

Administration for Children and Families
Office of Community Services
370 L'Enfant Promenade, SW
Washington, DC 20447   202-401-9333

This office administers the Low Income Home Energy Assistance Program (LIHEAP) block grants to the States, Indian tribes, and U.S. territories to assist low-income households with home energy costs through heating and cooling assistance, crisis assistance, and weatherization assistance.

* Maps from TVA

Maps and Surveys Department
Maps Information and Records Unit
1101 Market St., HB 1A
Chattanooga, TN 37401   423-751-6277

The Tennessee Valley Authority can provide you with a variety of maps and land surveys for areas under their jurisdiction. Contact them for a free catalog.

* Marketing Federally Generated Power

Power Marketing Coordination
Office of the Assistant Secretary
Conservation and Renewable Energy
U.S. Department of Energy (DOE)
1000 Independence Ave., SW, Room 8G-061
Washington, DC 20585   202-586-2008

Contact the above office for information on the marketing of power generated at Federal facilities. The Judicial Administrations are listed below:

Alaska Power Administration, Robert J. Cross, Administrator, 2770 Sherwood Avenue, Suite 2B, Juneau, AK 99801-8545; 907-586-7405

Bonneville Power Administration, Randall Hardy, Administrator, P.O. Box 3621, Portland, OR 97208; 503-230-5101

The Bonneville Power Administration serves the Pacific Northwest area including Washington, Oregon, Idaho, and western Montana. It also provides power to California in the summer. In addition to managing a series of hydroelectric and nuclear stations, the Power Administration is also involved in many conservation activities related to Salmon.

Washington, DC Office, Lee Johnson, Assistant Administrator, FORSTL, Room 8G033; 202-586-5640

Southeastern Power Administration, Johnny McAllister, Administrator, Samuel Elbert Building, 2 Public Square, Elberton, GA 30635; 706-213-3805

Headquartered in Elberton, GA, this administration markets surplus power generated at reservoir projects operated in the states of West Virginia, Virginia, North Carolina, South Carolina, Georgia, Florida, Alabama, Mississippi, Tennessee, and Kentucky.

Southwestern Power Administration, JM Shafer, Administrator, P.O. Box 1619, Tulsa, OK 74101; 918-581-7474

This Administration provides power from hydroelectric dams to citizens in Oklahoma, Missouri, Arkansas, Louisiana, Kansas, and Eastern Texas.

Western Area Power Administration, William Clagett, Administrator, 1627 Cole Boulevard, Bldg. 18, Golden, CO 80401; 303-231-1511

* Markets and End Use

Office of Energy Markets and End Use
Energy End Use Division
Energy Information Administration
U.S. Department of Energy (DOE)
1000 Independence Ave., SW, Room 2F-065
Washington, DC 20585   202-586-1122

Here research produces models for short- and medium-term energy demand in end use sectors: residential, industrial, commercial, and transportation. The research includes regional and demographic breakdowns, analyses of market penetration, the impact of conservation, and new technologies. The office can provide you with reports detailing its programs, as well as some subject reports.

* Material Processing

Material Processing Division, EE-234
U.S. Department of Energy (DOE)
1000 Independence Ave. SW, Room 5F-059
Washington, DC 20585   202-586-5377

The Material Processing Division conducts a balanced research and development program for energy intensive industrial processes, such as melting and casting and extracting material from rock and ore. Key industries included steel, aluminum, copper, magnesium. foundry, glass, and cement. The cross-cutting activity of refractory development, as well as research and development on non-metallic materials and process electrolysis, is also part of the program.

* Medical Research

Energy Research, ER-73
Medical Applications and Biophysical Research Division
U.S. Department of Energy (DOE)
19901 Germantown Rd., Room G-159
Germantown, MD 20874-1290   301-903-3153

This office conducts research on advanced radiation and chemical dosimetry techniques. It pursues instrumentation research and development to acquire improved analytical measurement technology. It supports radiological physics research to provide fundamental insights into the interaction of radiation with biological systems. They conduct medical research to develop new radioisotope and radio-pharmaceutical applications for diagnosis and radiation treatment approaches. It supports molecular nuclear medicine research which brings the insights and technology from molecular biology to achieve advanced nuclear medicine methodology.

* Minorities and Energy Programs

National Minority Energy Information Clearinghouse
U.S. Department of Energy (DOE)
1000 Independence Ave., SW, Room 5B-110
Washington, DC 20585   202-586-5876

This Clearinghouse is a centralized repository for information about energy programs and the economic impact of those programs on minorities, minority businesses, and minority educational institutions. The following services are available from the Clearinghouse: research, referrals, information transfer, selective distribution of information, and searches of minority energy information retrieval systems as well as commercial and other Federal databases. The Department of Energy is also forging ahead with programs to encourage more minority participation in the sciences through initiatives such as The Minorities Honors Training and Industrial Assistance Program, the Minority Educational Institution Assistance Program, the Minority Undergraduate Training for Energy-Related Careers Program, and the Minority Math/Science Leadership Development Program and Recognition Program, and the Cooperative Developmental Energy Program. The office also coordinates departmental activities with respect to the Historically Black Colleges and Universities Initiative.

Energy

* National Alternative Fuels Hotline

Transportation Technologies
National Alternative Fuels Hotline   800-423-1363
P.O. Box 12316   703-528-3500
Arlington, VA 22209   Fax: 703-528-1953

The hotline information specialists represent a valuable central source of up-to-the-minuet alternative fuel and vehicle information. Information specialists have strong backgrounds in alternative fuels and they are constantly updating their knowledge through literature monitoring and professional research. Callers include fleet operators, financial analysts, fuel providers, auto manufacturers, university professors and teachers, students, state and federal agencies, inventors and journalists. The hotline operates weekdays from 10am to 6pm.

* National Association of Energy Service Companies

1440 New York Ave, NW
Washington, DC 20005   202-371-7816

Members of this association include individuals and firms providing energy efficiency services or electrical or thermal energy as an unregulated business activity using a range of performance based contacting and financing mechanisms. Its purpose is to provide industry representation at all regulatory levels in the government as well as to inform the public regarding performance contracting and financing of alternative energy and energy conservation programs. Information on activities is available through its quarterly newsletter *NAESCO NEWS*, which is available to members. This office will try to provide you with information requested.

* National Center for Appropriate Technology (NCAT)

P.O. Box 4000
Butte, MT 59702   406-494-4572

The National Center for Appropriate Technology is a non-profit organization whose purpose is to develop and promote practical solutions in the areas of energy, housing, agriculture, and the environment. NCAT helps people choose and implement energy conservation and energy saving renewable technologies. It also works with public utilities and provides information to low-income energy assistance program managers. The NCAT annual report is a good resource of basic information on NCAT. The following is a list of NCAT publications available for a fee.

Conservation in Buildings: A Northwest Perspective, 1985
Window Insulation: How to Sort Through the Options, 1984
Moisture and Home Energy Conservation, 1983
Introducing Supplemental Combustion Air to Gas-Fired Home Appliances, 1983
Using the Earth to Heat and Cool Homes, 1983
NCAT Energy Conservation and Renewable Energy Bibliography, 1992
Directory of State Energy Programs, 1992
Conservation for Window Air Conditioners, 1978
Heat Recovery Ventilation for Housing: Air-to-Air Heat Exchanges, 1984
Energy Efficient Home Construction: Basic Superinsulation Techniques, 1984
Mobile Home Weatherization: A Status Report, 1985
Mobile Home Weatherization: A Guidebook for Installers, 1986
The NCAT/Penelec Mobile Home Weatherization Series, 1990
Community Energy Management: An Introduction to Saving Energy Dollars, 1981
Appropriate Technology Management Information System (ATMIS), 1984
Appropriate Technology at Work, 1983
NCAT's Best: Outstanding Projects Funded by NCAT from 1977 to 1980, 1981
NCAT Technical Publications Catalog, 1992
Solar Greenhouse and Sunspaces: Lessons Learned, 1984
Low-Cost Passive Solar Greenhouses, 1981
Solar Greenhouses: Suggested Reading Lists, 1992
Solar Water Heating: Suggested Reading List 1992
Cold Frame Construction: A Beginners Guide, 1981
The Caterpillar Cold Frame, 1980
Breadbox Solar Water Heaters, 1981
Vertical Solar Air Heaters, 1981
Solar Energy: Suggested Readings, 1992
Drying Wood With the Sun: How to Build a Solar Heated Firewood Dryer, 1983
Homemade Electricity: An Introduction to Small-Scale Wind, Hydro, and
    Photovoltaic Systems, 1984
Photovoltaics: Suggested Readings, 1984
Microhydroelectric Energy: Suggested Readings, 1992
Independent Power Systems: Suggested Readings, 1990
Fuel Alcohol: Answers to Common Questions, 1981
Fuel Alcohol Production: A Selective Survey of Operating Systems, 1981
Making More Fuel Alcohol: An Operator's Guide to Improve Starch Conversion
    and Fermentation, 1981
Alcohol Fuels: Suggested Readings, 1992

* National Energy Information Center

Energy Information Administration (EIA)
U.S. Department of Energy (DOE)
1000 Independence Ave., SW, Room 1F-048
Washington, DC 20585   202-586-8800

The National Energy Information Center can provide you with statistical and analytical data, information, and referral assistance on virtually an energy-related issue. The Center operates the EIA microfilm control center, providing access to data collection surveys and historical documents available to the public. National Energy Information Center (NEIC) Energy Information Administration's data and projections on energy productions, consumption, prices, and supplies, are available by mail or telephone. The NEIC has subject specialists to handle the following areas: Coal, Electrical and Nuclear Power, Natural Gas, Petroleum, Renewable Energy Resources/Conservation, and Data Survey forms.

* National Energy Modeling System (NEMS)

Energy Information Administration, EI-80
Office of Integrated Analysis and Forecasting
U.S. Department of Energy (DOE)
1000 Independence Ave. SW, Room 2F-081
Washington, DC 20585   202-586-2222

This office conducts forward-looking analyses and develops forecasts of alternative energy futures. It develops, applies, and maintains NEMS and other modeling systems needed to analyze and illuminate the complex interactions of the demand, conversion, and supply for all energy sources and their economic and environmental emplaces. They perform analytical studies of integrated energy markets and how they are affected by alternative energy policies and other parameters. It prepares mid- and long-term forecasts of energy markets, penetration of new technologies, and changes in energy, environmental, and macroeconomic policies and international developments. They publish regular reports and special reports as requested. The office coordinates with other EIA offices to maintain data systems needed for inputs to integrated analysis forecasting models and analyses. They also design and implement a voluntary reporting system for greenhouse gas emissions and produces reports analyzing the results according to the requirements of the Energy Policy Act of 1992.

* National Energy Software Center

U.S. Department of Energy (DOE)
Energy Science and Technology Software Center (ESTSC)
P.O. Box 1020   423-576-2606
Oak Ridge, TN 37831-1020   Fax: 423-576-2865
                         Internet: estsc @Adonis.osti.gov
          or Http://Apollo.osti.gov.html/osti/estsc/estsc.html.

Operated under contract for DOE's Office of Scientific and Technical Information, this center is DOE's centralized software management center. Software exchange and information center activities for the U.S. Nuclear Regulatory Commission (NRC) are carried with support from the NRC's Office of Resource Management. ESTSC provides a central computer software information and resource facility in support of DOE and NRC research and development programs. It also serves as a focal point for intra-agency sharing of software and for the transfer and exchange of computer technology to other U.S. and foreign agencies, as well as to the U.S. private sector. Contact the office above for more information.

* National Renewable Energy Laboratory (NREL)

Public Affairs
National Renewable Energy Laboratory (NREL)
1617 Cole Boulevard
Golden, CO 80401   303-275-4090

NREL is the nation's premier national laboratory for research and development in renewable energy and energy efficiency. The Laboratory is a national resource committed to leadership, excellence, and innovation in renewable energy and related technologies. Research activities span several scientific and technical areas and are intended for application in the private sector.

* National Renewable Energy Laboratory (NREL)
Document Distribution

Document Distribution Service
National Renewable Energy Laboratory (NREL)
1617 Cole Blvd. 15/1   303-275-4363
Golden, CO 80401   Fax: 303-275-4053
                         E-mail: evanss@tcplink.nrel.gov

NREL's Document Distribution Service is the central repository for current and some archived documents published by NREL. It is a source for both general interest and technical documents. A free catalog of publications is available.

* National Vehicle and Fuel Emissions Laboratory Library

U.S. Environmental Protection Agency (EPA)
National Vehicle and Fuel Emissions Laboratory Library (NVFEL)
2565 Plymouth Rd.   313-668-4311
Ann Arbor, MI 48105-2498   Fax: 313-668-4368

NVFEL provides information services concentrated on automotive engineering in such areas as air pollution from mobile sources, alternative alcohol fuels, and motor vehicle retrofit devices. The NVFEL collection includes books, subscriptions to journals, abstracts and indexes, bulletins, and newspapers; hard copy documents and technical reports generated by government or private sources; documents on microfiche, including technical reports produced by EPA. The library also has Society of Automotive Engineers papers related to topics in automotive emission, fuel economy, and new automotive technology; Advisory Circulars, Applications for Certification of Light and Heavy Duty Vehicles, Fuel Economy Guides and Rulemaking Analysis. Documents, books, and journals are processed into the EPA Online Library System at 919-549-0720 or via the Internet at epaibm.rtpnc.epa.gov

* New Technology for Department of Energy (NTD)

Polly Blackburn
Integrated Technical Information System
Office of Science and Technical Information
P.O. Box 62
Oak Ridge, TN 37831   423-576-2615

NTD contains brief descriptions of Department of Energy research results that have been potential for commercialization by United States industries. This database is the centralized source on online information on DOE technical innovations and advancements. Each NTD record includes a technology description, patent status, secondary or spinoff applications, literature citations, DOE laboratory and sponsoring information, subject descriptions, and a contact for further information. The NTD is available only to DOE and its contractors.

* News Releases

National Energy Information Center, EI-231
Energy Information Administration (EIA)
Room 1F-048, Forestall Building
Washington, DC 20585   202-586-8800

EIA New Releases is published six times per year and contains information on issues of special interest, periodicals, machine-readable files, and how to order EIA publications. This is a valuable publication for keeping up with the latest publications and developments in EIA.

* NREL Technical Inquiry Service (TIS)

National Renewable Energy Laboratory (NREL)
1617 Cole Blvd.   303-275-4065
Golden, CO 80401   Fax: 303-275-4091
                                      E-mail: rubin@tcplink.nrel.gov

NREL's Technical Inquiry Service informs key audiences, including the scientific, industrial and business communities, about NREL's research and development activities and those of NREL subcontractors. The information is provided in a timely and consistent manner to assist the inquirer in making informed decisions about renewable energy options. TIS also responds to requests for technical information from research organizations, academic institutions, consulting firms, and investment/financial organizations. General renewable energy information requests from consumers (including homeowners and students) should be addressed to the Energy Efficiency and Renewable Energy Clearinghouse (EREC) at 800-363-3732.

* Nuclear Energy Institute

1776 I Street, NW, Suite 400
Washington, DC 20006   202-739-8000

This organization consists of representatives from electrical utilities, manufacturers, industrial firms, research and service organizations, educational institutions, labor groups and government agencies engaged in development and utilization of nuclear energy especially nuclear produced electricity, and other energy matters. It maintains a speakers bureau, compiles statistics and public attitude data. It's library consists of books, articles, periodicals, government documents, and audiovisual material on energy related topics.

* Ocean Energy

Wind Hydro and Oceans Technologies Division
Conservation and Renewable Energy, EE-121
U.S. Department of Energy (DOE)
1000 Independence Ave., SW, Room 5H-047
Washington, DC 20585   202-586-5348

Here researchers develop technologies to harness ocean energy in a cost-effective and environmentally safe manner. Researchers look to develop ocean energy technology to the point where businesses accurately assess whether applications of the technology are viable energy conversion alternatives, or supplements, to systems currently in use. Contact this office for more program information.

* OTA Publications

Superintendent of Documents
Government Printing Office (GPO)
710 N. Capitol St. NW   202-512-1800
Washington, DC 20402   Fax: 202-512-2250

National Technical Information Service (NTIS)   800-553-6847
5285 Port Royal Rd.   703-487-4650
Springfield, VA 22161   Fax: 703-321-8547

The Office of Technology Assessment (OTA) was established by Congress to provide congressional committees with analyses of emerging, difficult, and often highly technical issues. The OTA was abolished in late 1995 but their publications are still available from the Government Printing Office (GPO) and the National Technical Information Service (NTIS). Some of these publications include:

Aging nuclear power plants: managing plant life and decommissioning (1193, 192p)
    GPO# 052-003-01342-8, NTIS# PB94-107588
Energy efficiency: challenges and opportunities for electric utilities (1993, 204p)
    GPO# 052-003-01348-7, NTIS# PB94-107547
Industrial energy efficiency (1993, 152p) GPO# 052-003-01336-3, NTIS#
    PB93-218931
Building energy efficiency (1992, 274p) GPO# 051-003-01280-4, NTIS#
    PB92-169267
Energy efficiency in the Federal Government: government by good example? (1991,
    124p) NTIS# PB91-197905
Energy efficiency technologies for Central and Eastern Europe (1993, 140p) GPO#
    052-003-01321-5, NTIS# PB93-203750
Fueling development: energy technologies for developing countries (1992, 336p)
    GPO# 052-00301279-1, NTIS# PB92-169259
Improving automobile fuel economy: new standards, new approaches (1991, 128p)
    NTIS# PB92-115989
Energy technology choices: shaping our future (1991, 156p) NTIS# PB91-220004
Energy in developing countries (1991, 148p) NTIS# PB91-133694

* Passive Solar Homes: Case Studies

Superintendent of Documents
Government Printing Office (GPO)
710 N. Capitol St. NW   202-512-1800
Washington, DC 20402   Fax: 202-512-2250

This book discusses 13 passive solar houses in Europe and the United States showing the architectural impact of energy conservation and passive/hybrid solar features. Each house is presented as a case study on the design. Stock #061-000-00769-5, $8.50. Other publications available on solar energy include:

Design Context #061-000-00780-6, $9.00
Effects of Solar-Geomagnetically Induces Currents on Electrical Systems in Nuclear Power Stations #052-021-01060-5, $13.00
Public Utilities Supply Solar Energy to Eager Customers #061-000-00827-6, $1.00
Sunspace Basics #061-000-00822-5, $1.00

* Petroleum Overcharge Refunds

Office of Hearings and Appeals, HG-1
U.S. Department of Energy (DOE)
1000 Independence Ave., SW, Room 6G-030
Washington, DC 20585   202-586-5510

Cash refunds are available to any people, business firms, and governments that purchased refined petroleum products in the U.S. between August 1973 and January 1981. This office distributes millions of dollars in oil overcharges collected through the DOE enforcement program between those years. This office can give you further details.

* Petroleum Price Regulation

Economic Regulatory Administration (ERA)
Office of Energy Supply Policy PO-52
Press Office, U.S. Department of Energy (DOE)
1000 Independence Ave., SW, Room 8G-087
Washington, DC 20585   202-586-5667

This office serves as the first public contact point for information on petroleum enforcement actions for crude oil price and allocation regulations prior to January 28, 1981. ERA also regulates natural gas imports and exports; administers programs for the conversion of oil- and gas-fired utilities to alternate fuels; and licenses both exports of electricity from the United State and transmission lines crossing U.S. borders. Contact this office for more information.

* Photovoltaic Materials and Devices

Photovoltaics Division, EE-131
Deputy Assistant Secretary for Renewable Energy
Conservation and Renewable Energy
U.S. Department of Energy (DOE)
1000 Independence Ave., SW, Room 5H-088
Washington, DC 20585   202-586-1721

This office conducts research and development leading toward potentially low-cost, advanced photovoltaic materials and devices which are environmentally sound. Contact this office for more program information.

* Photovoltaics

Office of Solar Energy Conversion, EE-13
Conservation and Renewable Energy
U.S. Department of Energy (DOE)
1000 Independence Ave., SW, Room 5H-072
Washington, DC 20585   202-586-1720

Researchers are currently developing photovoltaic technology--which converts sunlight directly into electricity--for the large-scale generation of economically competitive electric power in the U.S. Eventually photovoltaic energy products will significantly contribute to the mix of renewable energy sources on which the U.S. will depend. Contact this office for its program summary.

* Power Control Centers

Power System Control Center
Tennessee Valley Authority (TVA)
101 Market St. (MRBA)
Chattanooga, TN 37402   423-751-8678

The Tennessee Valley Authority's (TVA) five area dispatch control centers (ADCCs) monitor the 15,000 miles of transmission lines across which power is carried to the distributors of TVA power and large industries in the Valley. The dispatchers at the ADCCs and the load coordinators at the Power System Control Center work together to coordinate the maintenance of the transmission network to ensure the safety of the men working on the lines, and to make sure there are no transmission lines scheduled to be out of service that would cause an interruption in power service.

* Power Information Center

Interagency Advanced Power Group (IAPG)
c/o Horizon Data Corporation
1950 Rolard Clarke Pl., Suite 250
Reston, VA 22091   703-758-0531

The Interagency Advanced Power Group (IAPG) promotes the exchange of information in advanced power fields by 1) maintaining a database of projects sponsored by its member agencies (Army, Navy, Air Force, NASA, and DOE); and 2) arranging semiannual meetings in the following areas of interest: chemical, electrical, magnetohydrodynamics, mechanical, nuclear, solar, and systems research and development. Members of industry and academia who are frequently invited to serve as presenters or participants at these meetings can receive IAPG publications by subscribing to the National Technical Information Service (NTIS). Membership and associated benefits are free to employees of the IAPG member agencies.

* Power System Control

Power System Control Center
Tennessee Valley Authority (TVA)
1101 Market St. (MRBA)
Chattanooga, TN 37402   423-751-8678

The Tennessee Valley Authority (TVA) provides a reliable supply of power at the lowest possible cost to the consumers. This center manages the resources needed to meet the daily load of the TVA power system, the largest in the U.S. Through control of generation, interchange transactions with other utilities, and load management, the staff at the Center ensures that the residents and industrial customers have ample power on hand to meet their needs.

* Press Services

Press Secretary to the Secretary
U.S. Department of Energy (DOE)
Office of Communications
FORSTL, CP-60, Room 8G087
Washington, DC 20585   202-586-5806

The U.S. Department of Energy's (DOE) Press Service produces news releases and answers inquiries from the media of a general nature in all program areas, including nuclear energy and national defense programs within DOE. The office also arranges press conferences and media interviews for the Secretary of Energy and other DOE officials.

* Princeton Plasma Physics Laboratory

Information and Administrative Services
P.O. Box 451
Princeton, NJ 08543   609-243-2755

This lab performs research aimed at the development of magnetic fusion energy as an inexhaustible, safe, and environmentally acceptable means of generating electricity. The laboratory operates two major magnetic fusion devices: the Tokamak Fusion Test Reactor and the Princeton Beta Experiment - Modified. A third device, called Compact Ignition Tokamak is currently under construction. Research at the Princeton lab is also being applied to research in other areas such as X-ray technology and the plasma etchings of electronic circuitry on semiconductor chips.

* Printing and Graphics Division

Energy Technology Visuals Collection (ETVC) HR-842
Department of Energy (DOE)
1000 Independence Ave. SW, Room BH-039
Washington, DC 20585   202-586-9796

The Energy Technology Visuals Collection (ETVC) serves as a central repository for visuals representing the U.S. Department of Energy's (DOE) many research and development activities. The Collection, maintained and operated by the Office of Administrative Services, contains high quality images of over 600 DOE sponsored projects in such areas as fossil fuels, nuclear fission and fusion, biomedical research, solar energy, wind energy, conservation, and environmental activities. Images are available as 8" x 10" prints (color or black and white), and 33mm color slides through the DOE Graphics Branch. Each image requested from the collection is accompanied by a computer-generated data sheet containing caption and background information. An automated cataloging system is used by the ETVC staff to conduct online searches of the database with respect to program, project, technology, and geographic location. ETVC supports DOE personnel; other Federal, State, or local agencies; and the private sector, upon approval, in preparing publications, briefings, and presentations.

* Producing Countries

Office of Energy Producer - Country Affairs
Bureau of Economics and Business Affairs
U.S. Department of State
2201 C St., NW, Room 3329
Washington, DC 20520   202-647-1476

This office handles all foreign affairs concerning energy producing countries. Subjects studies include OPEC, natural gas, uranium, as well as the importing and exporting of oil and gas.

* Propulsion Technology

Office of Advanced Propulsion Systems
Advanced Propulsion Division, EE-322
U.S. Department of Energy (DOE)
1000 Independence Ave, SW, Room 5G-046
Washington, DC 20585   202-586-8012

This office manages the development of a national advanced transportation, propulsion, and demonstration program of advanced engine and vehicular systems development. It emphasized high-risk technology research for advanced propulsion systems such as ceramic gas turbines, adiabatic diesels, low heat rejection designs, as well as research on fuels which could result in lower emissions and improving fuel economy performance.

* Publications

Public Affairs
Division of Public Affairs, PA-1
U.S. Department of Energy (DOE)
1000 Independence Ave., SW, Room 7A-145
Washington, DC 20585   202-586-2050

This office writes and publishes the U.S. Department of Energy's (DOE) newspaper, *DOE This Month* and produces written material describing DOE programs and policies in a variety of formats, including speech texts, talking points, letters to editors, magazine/journal articles, and fact sheets. *DOE This Month* contains articles on recent developments in energy policy as well as new programs and a calendar of upcoming events. Contact this office for more information on the publications available from DOE.

* Regulation

Public Reference Room
Federal Energy Regulatory Commission (FERC)
Office of External Affairs
888 1st St NE, Room 2A
Washington, DC 20426   202-208-1371

The *Annual Report of the Federal Energy Regulatory Commission* details last year's energy regulatory activities of the Federal Energy Regulatory Commission (FERC), as well as giving a summary of the structure and functions of each office within FERC. The report costs $2.75 and requests must be made in writing.

* Regulation Information

Office of Congressional Affairs
Federal Energy Regulatory Commission
U.S. Department of Energy (DOE)
888 1st St. NE
Washington, DC 20585   202-208-0870

This office serves as liaison with Congress, Federal agencies and the public. They coordinate presentation of Commission hearings, briefings, and reviews information pertaining to legislative issues and proposals. In addition, this division responds to inquiries from public industry, interest groups and federal, state and local governments about Commission activities, actions and procedures. The division develops informational and educational materials on energy regulatory subjects and processes and responds to Freedom of Information and Privacy Act requests or other written, and telephone requests for information.

* Regulatory Files

Division of Public Affairs
Federal Energy Regulatory Commission (FERC)
888 1st St. NE
Washington, DC 20426   202-208-2326

Records and files of the Federal Energy Regulatory Commission (FERC) are available for public inspection or copying at FERC's North Capitol Street office. Contact the office of Public Affairs for more detailed information on consulting records. The following is a summary of the available information:

- All filings submitted to the Commission which comprise formal records. This includes applications, petitions and other pleadings requesting FERC action; responses, protests, motions, contracts, briefs, rate schedules, tariffs and related filings; and FERC staff correspondence relating to any proceedings.
- Transcripts of hearings, hearing exhibits, proposed testimony and exhibits filed with the Commission but not yet offered or received in evidence.
- Administrative law judges' actions, orders, and correspondence in connection with FERC proceedings.
- Commission orders, notices, opinions, decisions, letter orders, and approved Commission minutes.
- Agendas and lists of actions taken at Commission meetings, which are open to the public.
- Environmental impact statements prepared by FERC staff pursuant to the National Environmental Policy Act of 1969.
- Agendas, minutes, and draft papers relating to the National Power Survey, Natural Gas Policy Council and other FERC advisory committee meetings, all open to the public.
- Filings and recordings in court proceedings to which the Commission is a party and FERC correspondence with the courts.
- News releases and announcements issued by FERC.
- Subject index of Commission actions.

* Renewable Energy Information Hotline

P.O. Box 3040   800-363-3732
Merrifield, VA 22116   Fax: 703-893-0400
                                        TDD 800-273-2957
                                        BBS 800-273-2955

Energy Efficiency and Renewable Energy Clearinghouse (EREC) answers questions for the general public by toll-free telephone or mail. This center can answer questions on such topics as active/passive solar, solar thermal, photovoltaics, wind, biomass, alcohol fuels, hydroelectric, geothermal, and ocean thermal energy.

* Renewable Energy Publications

National Renewable Energy Laboratory
Technical Inquiry Service
1617 Cole Boulevard
Golden, CO 80401-3393   303-231-1000

You can get any of the following series of documents on the renewable energy programs sponsored by the U.S. Department of Energy at no charge by writing the office above. A list of publications is available and may also be ordered from the National Technical Information Service (NTIS); 703-487-4650.

Solar Building Program Summaries
Wind Energy
Energy Storage and Distribution
Solar Thermal Energy
Biofuels
Geothermal Energy
Photovoltaic Energy
Ocean Energy
Technical and Financial Assistance (for energy conservation)
Energy for Today: Renewable Energy
CORRECT: Committee on Renewable Energy Commerce and Trade

* Renewable Energy Publications

Energy Efficiency and Renewable Energy Clearinghouse (EREC)
P.O. Box 3040   800-363-3732
Merrifield, VA 22116   Fax: 703-893-0400
                                        TDD: 800-273-2957
                                        BBS: 800-273-2955

The following are some of the free energy information publications available through the above Energy Efficiency and Renewable Energy Clearinghouse (EREC) service. Bulk copies are not available. The service asks that each request be limited to 8 publications.

Fact Sheets:
FS 104 Conserving Energy and Heating Your Swimming Pool with Solar Energy.
FS 105 Alternative Heat Sources for Heat Pumps
FS 109 Planning for a Homeowner Installation
FS 110 Converting a Home to Solar Heat
FS 113 Solar Energy Systems Consumer Tips
FS 115 Solar Heat Storage
FS 118 Solar Energy and You (for middle grades)
FS 120 Earth-Sheltered Houses
FS 124 Sunspaces and Solar Greenhouses
FS 135 Wind Energy Systems
FS 141 Energy Efficient Lighting
FS 142 Insulation
FS 150 Municipal Resource Recovery
FS 176 Solar Energy and Your Home: Questions and Answers
FS 178 Low-Cost Passive and Hybrid Solar Retrofits
FS 183 Facts About Ethanol
FS 188 Geothermal Energy
FS 185 Residential Indoor Air Pollution
FS 190 Movable Insulation
FS 203 Caulking and Weatherstripping
FS 204 Hot Water Energy Conservation
FS 207 Buying an Energy Efficient House
FS 208 Moisture Control in Your Home
FS 214 Biofuels as a Source of Energy
FS 216 Improving the Energy Efficiency of Windows
FS 217 Small-Scale Hydropower Systems
FS 218 Learning About Energy Conservation (for elementary grades)
FS 220 Landscaping for Energy-Efficient Homes
FS 222 Energy Efficient Factory Built Homes
FS 224 Home Energy Audits

Energy

* Renewable Energy Technologies

Energy Efficiency and Renewable Energy Clearinghouse (EREC)
P.O. Box 3040
Merrifield, VA 22116   800-363-3732
                                          Fax: 703-893-0400
                                          TDD: 800-273-2957
                                          BBS: 800-273-2955

The Energy Efficiency and Renewable Energy Clearinghouse (EREC) provides information on the full spectrum of renewable energy technologies and energy conservation, including active/passive solar, solar thermal, photovoltaics, wind, biomass, alcohol fuels, hydroelectric, geothermal, and ocean thermal energy. In addition, the Service maintains contact with a nationwide network of public and private organizations that specialize in highly technical or regionally specific information. Information on other programs can also be obtained from EREC.

* Renewable Energy Technologies

Office of Renewable Energy Conversion
Conservation and Renewable Energy, EE-12
U.S. Department of Energy (DOE)
1000 Independence Ave., SW, Room 5H-095
Washington, DC 20585   202-586-8084

This office conducts research and development of biomass energy technology, energy from municipal waste, and geothermal/small hydropower energy technology. They emphasize the development of renewable technology with potential to increase significantly the Nation's supply of fuel, heat, and electricity. Contact the office for program information.

* Research and Technology Development

Program Integration Analysis Division
Office of Energy Research
U.S. Department of Energy (DOE)
19901 Germantown Road
Germantown, MD 20874   301-903-5544

The Office of Energy Research undertakes advanced and fundamental research to support the Energy Department's long-term energy technology development. *Programs of the Office of Energy Research* describes the Office's research activities in sufficient detail to enable researchers to understand current Energy Department research programs. A copy is available free through the office.

* Research Facilities

Office of Energy Research
Office of Field Operations Management
U.S. Department of Energy (DOE)
1000 Independence Ave., SW, Room 3FO477
Washington, DC 20585   202-586-5447

The *Capsule Review of DOE Research and Development and Field Facilities* surveys DOE research facilities, with brief descriptions of the work of the various offices.

* Residential Energy Consumption Database

Office of Energy Markets and End Use
Energy End Use Division

Energy Information Administration
U.S. Department of Energy (DOE)
1000 Independence Ave., SW, Room 2F-065
Washington, DC 20585   202-586-1122

The database, *Technical Documentation, 1984 Residential Energy Consumption Survey and 1985 Residential Transportation Energy Consumption Survey*, contains data concerning energy consumption in the U.S. residential sector. The *RECS* data file contains basic data concerning housing unit characteristics, including weather and weighing variables. The file contains 5,611 sample households from the contiguous U.S. representing 85.8 million weighted households. The 1985 *RTECS* data provide information on how energy is used in households for personal transportation based on the number and type of vehicles per household and, for each vehicle, annual miles traveled, gallons of fuel consumed, type of fuel used, price paid for fuel, and vehicle miles-per-gallon. Contact this office for more information on these databases.

* Rural Utilities Service

Legislative and Public Affairs Staff
U.S. Department of Agriculture (USDA)
14th & Independence Ave. SW
Washington, DC 20250   202-720-1255

The Rural Utilities Service (RUS), a new agency created in late 1994 by the reorganization of the U.S. Department of Agriculture (USDA), seeks to improve the quality of life in rural America via a variety of economic development programs in the electric, telecommunications, water and waste disposal areas. It administers the electric and telephone loan programs previously handled by the Rural Electrification Administration, which was abolished by the reorganization, and the water and waste disposal loan and grant programs, which were previously in the Rural Development Administration. RUS provides financial assistance via direct loans, guarantees of loans made by others, approval of loan security arrangements, which permits agency borrowers emergency water system repairs, technical assistance and replacement and contract technical aid in the water and waste disposal areas.

* Safety Inspections

Office of the Deputy Assistant Secretary for Nuclear and
  Facility Safety, EH-3
U.S. Department of Energy (DOE)
1000 Independence Ave. SW, Room 7A-121
Washington, DC 20585   202-586-2407

This office provides policy and technical assistance to the U.S. Department of Energy (DOE) through the analysis of facility operations, assistance to program managers in implementing nuclear safety assurance programs, and the development of policies and standards. The office reviews accidents and incidents, risk assessments, emergency preparedness plans, and implementation of DOE safety standards including radiological protection. Facilities operating experiences are analyzed for feedback and lessons learned, and vulnerability assessments are conducted of selected high-priority safety issues. Technical experts provide assistance to all facilities to promote and further improve safety.

* Small Business Assistance - Energy

Office of Small and Disadvantaged Business Utilization
U.S. Department of Energy (DOE)
1000 Independence Ave SW, Room 4B080
Washington, DC 20585   202-586-7377

This office is responsible for policy, plans, implementation, and oversight of functions related to programs for small businesses, small disadvantaged businesses, minority and women owned businesses.

* SocioEconomic Research and Analysis Program

National Minority Energy Information Clearinghouse
U.S. Department of Energy (DOE)
1000 Independence Ave., SW, Room 5B-110
Washington, DC 20585   202-586-5876

The Office of Minority programs has begun a major research program to collect information on the energy consumption and expenditure patterns of minorities as compared to other segments of the population. The long range hope is to use the information both to improve the U.S. Department of Energy's (DOE) program sensitivity to minority needs and to expand opportunities for minority owned businesses/entrepreneurs and minority communities. Another goal is to improve the capabilities of the policy sensitive Minority Energy Assessment Model "MEAM" by improving the level of minority representation in the data bank. For more information on this ongoing program, contact the Office of Minority Economic Impact listed above.

* Solar Building Technology

Office of Building Energy Research
Conservation and Renewable Energy, EE-42
U.S. Department of Energy (DOE)
1000 Independence Ave., SW, Room 6A-081
Washington, DC 20585   202-586-1660

Research from this office provides the solar and buildings industries with the technology needed to develop reliable solar systems that can contribute significantly to a building's space heating, hot water, cooling, and lighting requirements at competitive costs. Major research activities are aimed at improving the overall effectiveness of solar water and space heating systems, increasing solar cooling system performance, increasing daylighting system contributions, and increasing overall building energy contributions from individual solar heating, cooling, and daylighting technologies through systems integration. These activities are planned and executed in close cooperation with the solar and building industries to ensure that the results can readily be adopted by the private sector. Contact this office for further information.

* Solar Collector Manufacturing Activity

Superintendent of Documents
Government Printing Office (GPO)
710 N. Capitol St. NW   202-512-1800
Washington, DC 20402   Fax: 202-512-2250

This book presents national and state level data on the U.S. solar thermal collector and photovoltaic cell and module manufacturing industry. It includes detailed information on 1993 U.S. industry total shipments and shipments by market sector, end-use application, and destination. Historical data for comparison are presented for annual shipments of solar thermal collectors for the years 1974 through 1993 and of photovoltaic cells and modules for the years 1982 through 1993. Stock # 061-003-00870-4, $5.50.

* Solar Energy and Wind Information

National Climatic Data Center
National Oceanic and Atmospheric Administration
U.S. Department of Commerce
Federal Building
Asheville, NC 28801   704-271-4800

The National Climatic Data Center has a great deal of information regarding solar energy and wind data. Information includes solar radiation averages, measurements, and sunshine averages, as well as wind statistics. Reference manuals and indexes are also available. Prices vary depending upon the information requested. The Center can provide you with more detailed information regarding the data available.

* Solar Energy Research

National Renewable Energy Laboratory (WREL)
1617 Cole Boulevard
Golden, CO 80401   303-275-4090

The Solar Energy Research Facility (SERF) houses laboratories and offices of scientists involved in photovoltaics, superconductivity, photoconversion, and materials sciences. Research in these and other technologies will ensure that sustainable, clean energy resources will be available. To find out more about SERF contact the Public Affairs Office.

* Solar Thermal Technology

Solar, Thermal, and Biomass Power Technology Division
Conservation and Renewable Energy EE-132
U.S. Department of Energy (DOE)
1000 Independence Ave., SW, Room 5H-088
Washington, DC 20585   202-586-8121

Here researchers are looking to improve the overall performance of solar thermal and biomass systems and provide cost-effective energy options that are strategically secure and environmentally sound. Major research activities include energy collection technology, energy conversion technology, and systems and applications technology for both CR and DR systems. This research is being conducted through research laboratories in close coordination with the solar thermal industry, utility companies, and universities. This research program is also pursuing the development of critical components and subsystems for improved energy collection and conversion devices.

This development follows two basic paths: 1) For CR systems, critical components include stretched membrane heliostats, direct absorption receivers (DARs), and transport subsystems for molten salt heat transfer fluids. These components offer the potential for a significant reduction in system costs; and 2) For DR systems, critical components include stretched membrane dishes, reflux receivers, and Stirling engines. These components will significantly increase system reliability and efficiency, which will reduce costs.

The major thrust of the program is to provide electric power; however, there is an increasing interest in the use of concentrated solar energy for such applications as detoxifying hazardous wastes and developing high-value transportable fuels. These potential uses of highly concentrated solar energy still require additional experiments to prove concept feasibility. The research's goal of economically competitive energy production from solar thermal systems is being cooperatively addressed by both industry and government. Contact this office or the Solar Energy Research Institute for more information and a copy of the program summary.

* State Energy Conservation

Office of Technical and Financial Assistance Conservation
  and Renewable Energy
State Energy Programs, EE-522
U.S. Department of Energy (DOE)
1000 Independence Ave., SW, Room 5E-052
Washington, DC 20585   202-586-9187

To reduce the growth rate of energy demand, States voluntarily participate in a cooperative effort with the U.S. Department of Energy (DOE), which provides technical and cost-shared financial assistance, while the states develop and implement comprehensive plans for achieving specific energy goals. At present, all states, as well as the District of Columbia and U.S. territories, participate in this conservation program. Recent regulatory and legislative changes have given States flexibility to engage in a much broader range of program measures to promote energy efficiency and conservation, thereby enabling them to take advantage of available petroleum violation escrow funds. For more information on this, contact your State office. (Listings are found at the end of this section.)

* Statistics

National Energy Information Center
Energy Information Administration
U.S. Department of Energy (DOE)
1000 Independence Ave., SW, Room E1-231
Washington, DC 20585   202-586-8800

This Center can provide you with National energy statistics and general data services. Contact them for more information on the types available.

* Statistics on Production/Sales

Energy and Chemicals Division
International Trade Commission (ITC)
500 E. St. SW
Washington, DC 20406   202-205-3343

The ITC monitors U.S. production, sales and international trade flows of petroleum, natural gas, and other chemical agents. Contact them for information on acquiring statistics.

* Scientific and Technical Information

Office of Scientific and Technical Information (OSTI)
U.S. Department of Energy (DOE)
P.O. Box 62   423-576-1188
Oak Ridge, TN 37831   Fax: 423-576-2865
                               General Information: 423-576-1569
                                  Technical Reports: 423-576-8401
                                         Data Bases: 423-576-1175

The Office of Scientific and Technical Information (OSTI) provides direction and leadership for the departmentwide Scientific and Technical Information Program, which serves the information needs of DOE and contractor facilities. OSTI collects, processes, and disseminates information resulting from DOE research projects, as well as worldwide information on subjects of interest to DOE researchers; serves as the central processing and distribution point and repository for DOE scientific and technical reports; and develops data bases to provide access to energy literature, DOE research in progress, and DOE-developed software. OSTI also maintains a registry of energy publications produced by DOE for the public. They provide technical guidance, project analysis, and project feasibility assessment to organizations requiring expertise in evaluation project proposals or recommendations. OSTI develops specialized information systems and products in response to the needs of DOE program managers; represents DOE in international technical information exchanges; and provides energy information to the public through the National Technical Information Service and the Government Printing Office.

Energy

* Technology Hotline

Energy Efficiency and Renewable Energy Clearinghouse (EREC)
P.O. Box 3040
Merrifield, VA 22110

800-363-3732
Fax: 703-893-0400
TDD: 800-273-2957
BBS: 800-273-2955

Both businesses and consumers can call this toll-free hotline for information on implementing energy-saving technologies. EREC provides more detailed technical assistance than other programs and helps entrepreneurs develop appropriate technology.

* Tennessee Valley Authority (TVA)

Power Control Center
Tennessee Valley Authority
1101 Market St. (MRBA)
Chattanooga, TN 37401

423-751-8678

The TVA serves an area in the southeast U.S. consisting of 91,000 square miles and over seven million residents in parts of seven states. TVA has a total generating capacity in excess of 32,000 megawatts, made up of 11 operating coal-fired power plants, two licensed nuclear plants, 29 hydro plants, four combustion turbine installations, and the Raccoon Mountain Pumped-Storage Plant. The TVA works toward achieving competitive power rates, a reliable transmission system, research on clean-coal technology, industrial development in the region, improved quality and costs, and excellent fossil and hydro facilities performance.

* TVA Energy Publications

Office of Communications
Governmental and Public Affairs
Tennessee Valley Authority (TVA)
400 W. Summit Hill Dr.
Knoxville, TN 37902

423-632-4402

TVA provides publications on energy for research studies and the general public. They contain general information on the TVA and also specific information on such subjects as dams and steam plants, nuclear power, energy alternatives, and energy conservation, including buying guides for appliances. Though solar energy projects are no longer being carried out at TVA, you can still obtain information on past research. The following is a partial list of publications:

Annual Report
Answers to the Most Frequently Asked Questions About TVA
Financial Statement (of TVA)
History of TVA
Power Quarterly Report
TVA Act (1933 TVA Constitution)
A Student History
Electricity
TVA and Electric Power
TVA and Regional Development

* United States Alternative Fuels Council Research Results

U.S. Department of Energy (DOE)
1000 Independence Ave., SW, Room 7H-021
Washington, DC 20585

202-586-3891

This Council was established in 1990 to provide advice to the Interagency Commission on Alternative Fuels to help in the Commission's efforts to ensure commercial development for alcohol, natural gas, and other potential alternative motor fuels. The council completed their research and no longer exists but you can contact this office for a copy of their results.

* Unleaded Gas and Fuels Assistance

Environmental Protection Agency
Eastern Field Office
401 M St. SW
Washington, DC 20460

202-564-1301

Environmental Protection Agency
Western Field Office
One Denver Place
999 18th St.
Denver, CO 80202-2405

303-969-6474

These enforcement related offices can provide assistance with matters such as emissions tampering questions, spill prevention controls, underground storage tanks, and fuel questions, spill prevention controls, underground storage tanks, and fuel questions such as states that have Oxy programs, cities that have RFG gasoline and high and low sulphur diesel fuel. An 800 number is planned for this service in the near future.

* U.S. House of Representatives: Energy Information

Committee on Energy and Commerce
Majority Staff
2125 Rayburn House Office Building
Washington, DC 20515

202-225-2927

This committee can provide you with a variety of information on energy policy as well as information on legislation currently being considered by the House of Representatives that relates to energy.

* U.S. Senate: Energy Information

Committee on Energy and Natural Resources
Majority Staff
364 Senate Dirksen Office Building
Washington, DC 20510-6150

202-224-4971

This committee can provide you with a variety of information on energy exploration and policy as well as information on current legislation being considered by the Senate relating to energy.

* Waste Operations

Office of Environmental Restoration and Waste Management
Office of Waste Operations
U.S. Department of Energy (DOE)
1000 Independence Ave., SW, Room 6B-170
Washington, DC 20585

202-586-0370

This office is responsible for all DOE facilities, operations, or sites that are used for the storage, treatment, or disposal of radioactive, hazardous waste materials that have been packaged or labelled or used exclusively for long term storage of DOE waste material. Sites and operations managed by the Office of Civilian Radioactive Waste Management are excepted.

* Water Heater Program

Residential Energy Services Program
Tennessee Valley Authority (TVA)
1101 Market St., PSC IF-C
Chattanooga, TN 37402-2801

423-697-4211

The TVA's water heater program is designed to encourage homeowners in the region to install electric water heaters in new and existing homes. The program, available through local power distributors, offers participation incentives, which include cash payments, credits on electric bills, or financing. Water heater distributors may also offer free or reduced-cost water heaters, or make special offers for maintenance or installation. Loans may be used for a heat pump and related items such as electronic air cleaners, programmable thermostats, and extended warranties. No down payment, and the loan may be repaid over a period of up to 10 years.

* Weapons Materials and Planning

Office of Weapons and Surety, DP-21
Weapons Planning Division
U.S. Department of Energy (DOE)
19901 Germantown Road, Room A386
Germantown, MD 20874

301-903-6690

This office is responsible for strategic planning, liaison, and management direction related to the nuclear weapons stockpile, and strategic planning related to nuclear materials. It also manages nuclear weapons planning, acquisition, and retirement. The office also prepares the DOE portion of the annual surety report to the President.

* Weatherization Assistance

Weatherization Assistance Programs Branch, EE-532
U.S. Department of Energy (DOE)
1000 Independence Ave., SW, Room 5G-023
Washington, DC 20585

202-426-1698

To reduce high fuel costs for heating and air conditioning, low-income families, the elderly, and the handicapped can receive assistance to weatherize their homes and apartments. Those in need can have caulking and weatherstripping, heating and cooling system modification, attic insulation, and heating system improvements installed at little or no charge. Contact this office or your state energy office for more detailed information on this assistance.

* Wind Energy Information Contacts

With existing technological resources, a recent study concluded that wind energy could supply 20% of this country's electricity, with advanced technology currently under development, wind energy, in theory, could supply more than the current consumption of electricity of the U.S. Research has been steadily reducing the per kilowatt hour cost of wind generated electricity, making it increasingly economical. The following is a list of contact points for acquiring more information on wind energy development.

U.S. Department of Energy, Washington, DC 20585.
Office of Renewable Energy Conservation, CE-12; 202-586-8084.
Wind/Hydro/Ocean Division, EE-121; 202-586-5348.
National Renewable Energy Laboratory, 1617 Cole Boulevard, Golden, CO 80401-3393; 303-384-6950.
Sandia National Laboratories, P.O. Box 5800, Albuquerque, NM 87185-5800; 505-844-5253.
Albuquerque Operating Office, P.O. Box 5400, Albuquerque, NM 87485-5400; 505-845-5400.

* Wind Energy Test Center

National Renewable Energy Laboratory (NREL)
1617 Cole Boulevard
Golden, CO 80401   303-384-6900/6950

NREL's Wind Energy Test Center is the focal point for wind technology research activities in the U.S. The objective is to establish a technology base in a support industry in confirming the viability of wind energy as an alternative energy source. Basic research in wind turbine dynamics is conducted to understand the random nature of the wind, characterize its complex interaction with the wind turbine, and determine the effects of this interactions on performance, structural loads reliability and lifetime. Research is also scheduled to establish the feasibility of such technological advances as high performance airfoils, variable speed generators, and controls. Cooperative research and test programs with the wind industry will also take place over the next 5 years. NREL can provide you with information on its current activities and publications.

* Wind/Hydro/Ocean Division

Office of Conservation and Renewable Energy
U.S. Department of Energy (DOE)
1000 Independence Ave, SW, Room 5H-047
Washington, DC 20585   202-586-8086

This division is responsible for managing the development, implementation, and evaluation of a national program of technology and development of hydroelectric, wind, and ocean energy.

* State and Territorial Energy Director Offices

Alabama
Science, Technology, and Energy Division, P.O. Box 5690, Montgomery, AL 36103-5690; 205-242-5292, Fax 205-242-0552.

Alaska
Rural Development Division Planning & Development, 520 E. 34th Ave., Anchorage, AK 99503; 907-561-1900 ext. 335, Fax 907-561-4520.

American Samoa
Territorial Energy Office, American Samoan Government, Pago Pago, American Samoa 96799; 011 684-699-1101, Fax 684-699-2835.

Arizona
Dept. of Commerce, 3800 North Central Avenue, Suite 1200, Phoenix, AZ 85012; 602-280-1402, Fax 602-280-1305.

Arkansas
Energy Office, One State Capitol Mall, Suite 4B/215, Little Rock, AR 72201; 501-682-7377, Fax 501-682-7341.

California
Energy Commission, 1516 Ninth Street, MS-31, Sacramento, CA 95814; 916-654-4996, Fax 916-654-4420.

Colorado
Office of Energy Conservation, 1675 Broadway, Suite 1300, Denver, CO 80262-4613; 303-620-4292, Fax 303-620-4288.

Connecticut
Office of Policy and Management, Energy Division, 80 Washington St., Hartford, CT 06106; 203-566-4298, Fax 203-566-1589.

Delaware
Division of Facilities Management, Margaret O'Neill Bldg., P.O. Box 1401, Dover, DE 19903; 302-739-5644, Fax 302-739-6148.

District of Columbia
Energy Office, 613 G Street, NW, Suite 500, Washington, DC 20001; 202-727-1800, Fax 202-727-4700.

Florida
Department of Community Affairs Energy Office, 2740 Centerview Dr., Tallahassee, FL 32399-2100; 904-488-8466, Fax 904-922-5623.

Georgia
Environmental Facilities Authority, Equitable Bldg., Suite 2080, 100 Peachtree St. NW, Atlanta, GA 30303-1901; 404-656-5176, Fax 404-656-7970.

Guam
Energy Office, P.O. Box 2950, Agana, Guam 96910; 671-472-0538.

Hawaii
State Energy Division, Dept. of Planning and Economic Development, 335 Merchant Street, Room 108, Honolulu, HI 96813; 808-587-3812, Fax 808-587-3820.

Idaho
Dept. of Water Resources, Division of Energy Resources, 1301 North Orchard, Boise, ID 83720; 208-327-7866.

Illinois
Office of Energy Conservation and Alternative Energy, 325 West Adams, Room 300, Springfield, IL 62704-1892; 217-785-2800, Fax 217-785-2618.

Indiana
Dept. of Commerce, Division of Energy Policy, One North Capitol, Suite 700, Indianapolis, IN 46204-2248; 317-232-8940, Fax 317-232-8995.

Iowa
Dept. of Natural Resources, Energy Bureau, Wallace State Office Building, Des Moines, IA 50319-0034; 515-281-8681, Fax 515-281-8895.

Kansas
Research and Energy Analysis Division, Kansas Corporation Commission, 1500 S.W. Arrowhead Road, Topeka, KS 66604-4027; 913-271-3100, Fax 913-271-3354.

Kentucky
Division of Energy, Department of Natural Resources, 691 Teton Trail, Frankfort, KY 40601; 502-564-7192, Fax 502-564-7484.

Louisiana
Dept. of Natural Resources, P.O. Box 44156, Baton Rouge, LA 70804-4156; 504-342-2133, Fax 504-342-2707.

Maine
Department of Economics and Community Development, State House Station No. 59, Augusta, ME 04333; 207-624-6802, Fax 207-624-6810.

Maryland
Energy Office, 45 Calvert St., 4th Floor, Annapolis, MD 21401; 410-974-3755, Fax 410-974-2250.

Massachusetts
Division of Energy Resources, Leverett Saltonstall Bldg., 100 Cambridge Street, Room 1500, Boston, MA 02202; 617-727-4732, Fax 617-727-0300.

Michigan
Public Service Commission, Energy Resources Division, P.O. Box 30221, 6545 Mercantile Way, Lansing, MI 48909; 517-334-6270, Fax 517-882-5170.

Minnesota
Energy Information Center, Department of Public Service, Energy Division, 121 7th Place East, Suite 200, St. Paul, MN 55101-2145; 612-296-6025, Fax 612-297-1959.

Be patient. If any phone number is incorrect, call (area code) 555-1212 and request the new listing.

1057

Mississippi
Energy Division, P.O. Box 859, Jackson, MS 39202-3096; 601-359-6600, Fax 601-359-6642.

Missouri
Dept. of Natural Resources, Division of Energy, P.O. Box 176, Jefferson City, MO 65102; 314-751-4000, Fax 314-751-6860.

Montana
Dept. of Natural Resources and Conservation, Energy Division, P.O. Box 202301 Avenue, Helena, MT 59620-2301; 406-444-6754, Fax 406-444-6721.

Nebraska
Energy Office, P.O. Box 95085, State Capitol Building, 9th Floor, Lincoln, NE 68509-5085; 402-471-2867, Fax 402-471-3064.

Nevada
Energy Office, 1050 E. Williams, Suite 401, Carson City, NV 89710; 702-687-4910, Fax 702-687-4914.

New Hampshire
Governor's Energy Office, 57 Regional Dr., Concord, NH 03301-8519; 603-271-2611, Fax 603-271-2615.

New Jersey
Division of Energy Planning and Conservation, State of New Jersey, Board of Public Utility, 2 Gateway Center, Newark, NJ 07102; 201-648-2129, Fax 201-648-7420.

New Mexico
Dept. of Minerals and Natural Resources, Energy Management and Conservation Division, 2400 South Pacheco, Santa Fe, NM 87505; 505-827-5917, Fax 505-827-5912.

New York
State Energy Research and Development Authority, Two Rockefeller Plaza, Albany, NY 12223; 518-473-6251, Fax 518-432-4630.

North Carolina
Dept. of Economic and Community Development, Energy Division, 430 North Salisbury St., Raleigh, NC 27611; 919-733-2230, Fax 919-733-2953.

North Dakota
Office of Intergovernmental Assistance, State Capitol Building, 600 East Boulevard Ave., 14th Floor, Bismarck, ND 58505; 701-224-2094, Fax 701-224-2308.

Ohio
Office of Energy Conservation, Ohio Dept. of Development, 77 South High Street, 26th Floor, Columbus, OH 43215; 614-466-6797, Fax 614-466-1864.

Oklahoma
Dept. of Commerce, Division of Community Affairs and Development, P.O. Box 26980, Oklahoma City, OK 73126-0980; 405-841-5346, Fax 405-841-5199.

Oregon
Dept. of Energy, Conservation Resources Division, 625 Marion Street, NE, Salem, OR 97310-0831; 503-378-4040, Fax 503-373-7806.

Pennsylvania
Energy Office, 116 Pine Street, Harrisburg, PA 17101-1227; 717-783-9981, Fax 717-783-2703.

Puerto Rico
Department of Natural Resources, and Economies, Energy Affairs Administration, P.O. Box 41059-Minillas Station, San Juan PR 00940-2059; 809-721-3960, Fax 809-721-3089.

Rhode Island
Office of Energy Assistance, State House, Room 111, Providence, RI 02903-5872; 401-277-2850, Fax 401-277-5301.

South Carolina
State Energy Office, 1201 Main St., Suite 820, Columbia, SC 29201; 803-737-8030, Fax 803-737-9846.

South Dakota
Governors Office of Energy Policy, 217 West Missouri, Suite 200, Pierre, SD 57501; 605-773-3603, Fax 605-773-4802.

Tennessee
Energy Division, Department of Economic and Community Development, Rachel Jackson Bldg., 320 Sixth Ave., North, 6th Floor, Nashville, TN 37219-5308; 615-741-2994, Fax 615-741-5070.

Texas
Energy Conservation Office, State Insurance Annex Bldg., 221 E 11th St., Austin, TX 78701; 512-463-1931, Fax 512-475-2659.

Utah
Energy Office and Resource Planning, Three Triad Center, Suite 450, Salt Lake City, UT 84180-1204; 801-538-5428, Fax 801-521-0657.

Vermont
Energy Efficiency Division, Department of Public Services, State Office Building, 120 State Street, Montpelier, VT 05620-2601; 802-828-2811, Fax 802-828-2342.

Virgin Islands
Energy Office, Old Customs House, Frederiksted, St. Croix, VI 00840; 809-772-2616, Fax 809-772-0063.

Virginia
Department of Mines, Minerals, and Energy, 202 N. 9th St., 8th Floor, Richmond, VA 23219; 804-692-3219, Fax 804-692-3238.

Washington
State Energy Office, P.O. Box 43165, Olympia, WA 98504-3165; 206-956-2001, Fax 206-956-2217.

West Virginia
Development Office, Energy Efficiency Program, Building 6, Room 553, Capital Complex, Charleston, WV 25305-3011; 304-558-4010, Fax 304-558-3248.

Wisconsin
Energy Bureau, P.O. Box 7868, Madison, WI 53707-7868; 608-266-8234, Fax 608-267-6931.

Wyoming
Division of Economic and Community Development, Barrett Bldg., Cheyenne, WY 82002; 307-777-7284, Fax 307-777-5840.

Northern Mariana Islands
Commonwealth Energy Office, P.O. Box 340, Saipan, CM 96950; 670-322-9229.

Republic of Palau
Ministry, National Resources, Palau Energy Office, P.O. Box 100, Koror, Palau, RP 96940; 011-608-488-2431

Western Caroline Island
State of Yap, Office of Planning and Budget, P.O. Box 471, Kolonia, Yap, WC 96943; 011-691-350-2166.

Be patient. If any phone number is incorrect, call (area code) 555-1212 and request the new listing.

Fossil Fuels: Oil, Coal, and Natural Gas

* Alaska Natural Gas Pipeline

Alaska Natural Gas Pipeline Project
Office of Pipeline Safety, DPS-12
Research and Special Programs Administration, Room 2335
U.S. Department of Transportation
400 7th Street, SW
Washington, DC 20590   202-366-4595

Contact this office for information about the plans, programs, policies, and regulation concerning the Alaska pipeline.

* Alternative Fuel Vehicles

Office of Alternative Fuels, EE-33
U.S. Department of Energy (DOE)
1000 Independence Ave. SW, Room 5G-086
Washington, DC 20585   202-586-9118

This office directs and manages research and demonstration of promising alternative fuel vehicles and production technologies for alternative fuels. The office examines both fuels and engines, and performs the necessary research, testing, information gathering, and data analyses to determine the least costly and most environmentally beneficial combinations. The most effective options for providing personal and freight mobility are identified and promoted.

* Annual Energy Outlook, With Projections to 2010

Superintendent of Documents
Government Printing Office (GPO)
710 N. Capitol St. NW   202-512-1800
Washington, DC 20402   Fax: 202-512-2250

This book includes sections on framing the 1993 energy outlook; energy end use; oil and gas outlook, coal outlook, carbon emissions; and comparison with other forecasts. It also contains appendices and an index. Stock #061-003-00899-5, $15.00

* Atmospheric Fluidized Bed Combustion

Fluidized Bed Combustion Projects
Tennessee Valley Authority
7900 Metropolis Lake Rd.
W. Paducah Shoals, KY 42086   502-443-3626

This office can provide you with up-to-date information on atmospheric fluidized bed combustion, a new technology which burns pulverized coal at a lower temperature than conventional pulverized coal technology in a bed of limestone particles, resulting in lower nitrogen oxide emissions. The by-product is more easily disposed of, and therefore, it is more environmentally desirable. A 160 megawatt atmospheric fluidized bed demonstration plant was recently completed in Paducha, Kentucky, at the Shaunyee Plant. The U.S. Department of Energy's Office of Fossil Fuels also has a contact for this program at 301-903-3991.

* Automotive Fuel Economy Program

Office of Market Incentives
National Highway Traffic Safety Administration (NHTSA)
Department of Transportation (DOT)
400 7th St. SW
Washington, DC 20590   202-366-4936

This publication summarizes the 1993 activities of NHTSA regarding implementation of applicable sections of Title V: "Improving Automotive Fuel Efficiency" of the Motor Vehicle Information and Cost Savings Act of 1972. NHTSA responsibilities in the fuel economy area include: 1) establishing and amending average fuel economy standards for manufacturers of passenger cars and light trucks, as necessary; 2) promulgating regulations concerning procedures, definitions, and reports necessary to support the fuel economy standards; 3) considering petitions for exemption from established fuel economy standards by low volume manufacturers (those producing fewer than 10,000 passenger cars annually worldwide) and establishing alternative standards for them; 4) preparing annual reports to Congress on the fuel economy program; 5) enforcing fuel economy standards and regulations; and 6) responding to petitions concerning domestic production by foreign manufacturers and other matters.

* Basic Energy Fuels Market

Office of Energy, Infrastructure, and Machinery
Energy Division
U.S. Department of Commerce (USDA)
14th & Constitution Ave. NW, Room 4413
Washington, DC 20230   202-482-1466

The primary role of the Office of Energy is to foster and assist the basic energy fuels industries (coal, oil, natural gas, uranium renewable fuels, and electric power generation) and to improve their market competitiveness and participation in international trade.

* Biofuels Data Base

Biofuels Information Center
National Renewable Energy Laboratory (NREL)
1617 Cole Blvd.
Golden, CO 80401   303-275-4347

This is a technical database consisting of abstracted citations of all Department of Energy (DOE) and National Renewable Energy Laboratory (NREL) publications from 1980 to the present that are relevant to the production of transportation fuels from biomass. The data base will soon be available through the Internet.

* Clean Coal Technology

Dr. C. Lowell Miller
Clean Coal Technology
Demonstration Project FE-22/270CC
U.S. Department of Energy
19901 Germantown Rd.
Germantown, MD 20874   301-903-9451

Through the U.S. Department of Energy's (DOE) Clean Coal Technology (CCT) Demonstration Program, the most promising of the advanced coal-based technologies are being moved into the marketplace through demonstration. The demonstration effort is at a large enough scale to generate all data needed by the public sector to judge the commercial potential of the processes being developed. These technologies will reduce or eliminate the economic and environmental impediments that limit the full use of coal, and will work toward resolving the conflict between the increasing use of coal and the growing concern about the environmental impact of such use. Contact the above office for further information, including a copy of their report *Clean Power From Clean Coal*.

* Coal Combustion and Control Systems

Fossil Energy
U.S. Department of Energy
19901 Germantown, Rd.
Germantown, MD 20874   301-903-2795

This office oversees research in atmospheric and pressurized fluidized bed combustion, coal-water mixtures, coal preparation and advanced combustion techniques. The office also develops advanced environmental control technology, including management of solid wastes produced by advanced fossil energy technologies. Contact the office for further program information.

* Coal Education Information

American Coal Foundation
1130 17th St. NW, Suite 220
Washington, DC 20036   202-466-8630

This association provides publications for grades K-12, some of which are available in classroom sets; a film guide, activities and science fair ideas. Also available free of charge is a coal sample kit that contains samples of peat, lignite, bitomous coal and anthracite, along with a brief description of the formation of different types of coal. Also available for purchase or free loan (grades 7-12 and adult groups) is a slide presentation "Understanding the Greenhouse Effect and Global Climate Change." The complete kit numbers 53 slides, a script, teachers guide, brochure, and a one page summary.

* Coal Energy Research

Fluidized Bed Combustion Projects
7900 Metropolis Lake Rd.
W. Paducah, KY 42086   502-443-3626

This office can provide you with information on TVA's two most promising technologies for better use of coal: fluidized bed combustion, and advanced sulfur dioxide control technology to capture sulfur in conventional coal-fired boilers.

* Coal Liquefaction

Pittsburgh Energy Technology Center
P.O. Box 10940
Pittsburgh, PA 15236   412-892-6128

This laboratory conducts research and development in coal liquefaction, alternative fuels, coal slurries, advanced combustion, magnetohydrodynamics, coal preparation, flue gas cleanup, and university coal research. Contact this office for available information on its research.

* Coal Supply and Demand

Coal Branch
Coal, Nuclear, Electric and Alternate Fuels
Energy Information Administration
U.S. Department of Energy
1000 Independence Ave. NW
Washington, DC 20585   202-426-1226

This office monitors all supply and demand aspects of coal, including production, prices, and distribution. It identifies and analyses coal reserves; examines new technologies for deriving energy from coal; and, studies existing and proposed legislation and regulations affecting coal supply and demand. Contact this office for more program information.

* Coal Use Technology Database

Mr. Lloyd Lorenzi, Coordinator
U.S. Department of Energy (DOE)
P.O. Box 10940
Pittsburgh, PA 15236   412-892-6159

The Coal Technology Database supports computer-related studies and information management services in support of the Center's lead program areas. A bibliographic database has been assembled, cataloging nearly 100,000 documents. The database allows for computer-searching of DOE/PETC sponsored research reports, as well as items of historical significance in the field of coal utilization technology. To maximize efficiency, and to avoid unnecessary duplication, the database integrates information from PETC with that from other organizations such as the U.S. Energy Information Administration, the U.S. Geological Survey, State geological surveys, and universities. This cooperation has had the effect of creating an extensive energy information network, in furtherance of the Federal governments's technology transfer mission. Data can be accessed and analyzed in the following coal areas:

Chemical and Physical Properties
Washability
Reserves, Production, and Shipments
Utility Power Plants

* Defense Energy Consumption

Jim Carn
Materiel and Distribution Management Office
Office of the Deputy Undersecretary for Logistics
ODUS (L) MDM
3500 Defense, Pentagon
Washington, DC 20301-3560   703-697-2500

This office can provide you with wholesale petroleum data. For facility energy consumption contact Millard Carr (OASD/EP) at 703-604-6022.

* Electric Plant Cost and Power Production Expenses

Elise Bess
National Energy Information Center, EI-521
Energy Information Administration
Forrestal Building
Washington, DC 20585   202-254-5637

To Order:
National Technical Information Service (NTIS)
U.S. Department of Commerce   800-553-6847
5285 Port Royal Rd.   703-487-4650

Springfield, VA 22161   Fax: 703-321-8547

This database contains information on the historical plant cost of selected hydroelectric, fossil-fueled, steam-electric, gas-turbine, and nuclear steam-electric plants in commercial operation by electric utilities. Also included is the annual cost (exclusive of fixed charges) to electric utilities of producing electric power at these plants. Data are for 100 percent of plant ownership unless otherwise indicated. Data contained include net generating capacity, not generation, net capability, historical plant cost, production expenses, fuel consumption, and fuel costs. Data are taken from the Federal Energy Regulatory Commission (FERC) Form 1 (filed by investor-owned utilities) and the EIA-412 (filed by publicly owned utilities) reports. Data are utility and plant specific. Frequency of update is annual. Time unit of data is yearly. This data is available from NTIS on tape, PB94-501525.

* Energy and Mineral Resources

Office of Energy and Marine Geology
U.S. Geological Survey
Department of Interior (DOI)
National Center, MS 915
Reston, VA 22092   703-648-6470

Investigations of the nature, extent, and origin of the Nation's coal, oil and gas, oil shale, uranium, and geothermal resources are basic to this office's research efforts. Acquired data are placed in computerized databases, such as the National Coal Resources Data System.

* Energy Price Patterns

Energy Markets and Contingency Information Division
Energy Information Administration (EIA), EI-62
U.S. Department of Energy
1000 Independence Ave., SW, Room 2G-060
Washington, DC 20585   202-586-1130

This office performs analyses and short-term forecasting of world oil markets and energy demand patterns and prices. It assesses the factors that influence world energy prices. This office also acts as the center for the collection and analysis of enterprise level data within EIA.

* Export Assistance for Coal and Coal Technologies Industry

National Technical Information Service
U.S. Department of Commerce
5285 Port Royal Rd.   800-553-6847
Springfield, VA 22161   703-487-4650
      Fax: 703-321-8547

The *Guide to Federal Export Assistance Activities Applicable to the U.S. Coal and Coal Technologies Industry* provides coal and coal technology firms with a single reference source for identifying U.S. government agencies, programs, and contacts that might aid in exporting. The *Guide* contains an in-depth discussion of the eight major agencies offering export assistance and identifies pertinent activities performed by other federal agencies that might assist coal and coal technologies exporters. Order # DE 90000949, $48.00.

* Fossil Energy Developments

Office of Communications, FE-5
Fossil Energy, 4G-085
U.S. Department of Energy
1000 Independence Ave. SW, Room 4G-085
Washington, DC 20585   202-586-6503

The Office of Communications coordinates fossil energy communications with external stakeholders, including the general public, business and industry, Congress, and educational institutions. It oversees the preparation and distribution of Fossil Energy pamphlets, fact sheets, audiovisual materials, and educational information. The Office also provides Federal administrative support for the two principal fossil energy advisory committees, the National Petroleum Council and the national Coal Council, and maintains Fossil Energy's correspondence control functions. This information is also available on a dial-in fax service, TechLine 202-586-4300, and on the Internet.

* Fossil Energy Research

Western Research Institute (WRI)
365 N. 9th St.
Laramie, WY 82070   307-721-2011

This fossil energy research center specializes in environmental assessment, extraction process development, and fuels upgrading. Research efforts focus on conversion of oil shale, tar sands, coal, and waste products to useful hydrocarbon products and environmentally acceptable wastes. Contact this Institute for more information on fossil energy.

* Fossil Energy Technology

Fossil Energy, FE-1
Office of the Assistant Secretary
U.S. Department of Energy (DOE)
1000 Independence Ave. SW, Room 4G-084
Washington, DC 20585 202-586-6660

This office oversees the research, development and demonstration of advanced, innovative technologies that can (1) enhance the nation's production and use of natural gas, (2) increase the effectiveness of crude oil exploration and recovery processes, and (3) improve the environmental acceptability and economic performance of energy production from the abundant U.S. coal reserves. They also manage the Strategic Petroleum Reserve, the nation's emergency crude oil stockpile; the production and commercial sale of crude oil, natural gas, and petroleum products from the Naval Petroleum Reserves; and administers certain regulatory functions, including authorizations and permits for natural gas imports and exports, electricity exports, and international power line facilities.

* Fossil Fuel Research Solicitations

National Institute for Petroleum
and Energy Research (NIPER)
P.O. Box 2128
Bartlesville, OK 74005 918-337-4531

The National Institute for Petroleum and Energy Research (NIPER) solicits fossil fuel technology research not only from government agencies, but from the private sector as well. Contact this office for more information.

* Fossil Fuel Technology

Brian Kelch
National Institute for Petroleum
and Energy Research (NIPER)
P.O. Box 2128
Bartlesville, OK 74005 918-337-4556

This office conducts research and development covering all phases of liquid fossil fuel technology. This program includes research on petroleum extraction using enhanced oil recovery methods and improved drilling technology; the extraction of natural gas from Western tight sands; processing and thermodynamic properties of conventional oils, as well as liquid products made from coal, oil shale, and tar sands; recycling of waste lubricating oil; and improving automotive engine emissions. Databases on crude oil analyses, alternative fuels, enhanced oil recovery are maintained, and the public has free access to them. There are over 9000 databases updated on a regular basis. Information is available at no cost in print or online, 918-336-3621.

* Fuel Suppliers and Consumption in the Military

Public Affairs Office
Attn: DFSC-DEB, Lisa Wade
Defense Fuel Supply Center (DFSC)
Defense Logistics Agency
8725 John J. Kingman Rd.
Ft. Belvoir, VA 22060-6222 703-767-9656

This office will supply information on almost anything you will want to know concerning fuel supply in the military. The staff will explain how to contract for the Strategic Petroleum Reserve, and how to request information under the Freedom of Information Act, such as statistics on fuel consumption patterns in the military and copies of current contracts with major suppliers. You may request a free copy of their *Fact Book*, which tells how much was spent on fuel throughout the U.S. Department of Defense, the sources of supply, and how the fuel was allocated. It includes line graphs and pie charts, with a national geographic distribution breakdown. Also ask for a copy of the DFSC's magazine *Fuel Line*.

* Gas Facts, 1992

Department of Statistics
American Gas Association
1515 Wilson Blvd. 703-841-8504
Arlington, VA 22209 Fax: 703-841-8697

This publication contains detailed statistics for 1992 and summary statistics for 1975-

1990 for the gas utility industry which, by definition, consists of the companies engaged in natural gas distribution and transmission. The publication also contains relevant data on the gas producing segment of the industry and key statistics on other energy industries. Sources for this data are Uniform Statistical Report prepared by electric and gas utility companies, various American Gas Association and U.S. government reports.

* Gas Research Institute (GRI)

8600 West Bryn Mawr Avenue
Chicago, IL 60631 312-399-8100

This institute is a non-profit membership organization of the natural gas industry. The Gas Research Institute (GRI) plans, manages, and develops financing for a research and development program designed to advance natural gas supply, transport, storage, and end-use technologies and to conduct related basic research. New products processes and information resulting from GRI's results oriented program provide cost savings and other benefits for the natural gas industry and gas consumers nationwide.

* Intermediate Future Forecasting System (IFFS)

National Energy Information Center, EI-811
Energy Information Administration
Department of Energy (DOE)
Forrestal Building
Washington, DC 20585 202-586-1469
To Order:
National Technical Information Service (NTIS)
U.S. Department of Commerce 800-553-6847
5285 Port Royal Rd. 703-487-4650
Springfield, VA 22161 Fax: 703-321-8547

The Intermediate Future Forecasting System (IFFS) represents United States energy supply, distribution, and consumption by fuel supply and consumption defined for the world crude oil price and a macroeconomic projection of economic growth. A detailed representation of electric utility planning and generation provides the demand for oil, coal, natural gas, hydropower, and nuclear, and the prices of the generated electricity. The model finds an equilibrium price for each fuel by balancing supply and demand to produce and to the year 2010. The data is available on tape from NTIS. Tapes available include PB93-505212 (1993, Low Macro Case), PB-93-505220 (1993, High Macro Case), PB93-505006 (1993, Low World Oil Price), PB93-505014 (1993, High World Oil Price) and PB93-505253 (1993, Reference).

* Morgantown Energy Technology Center

U.S. Department of Energy
Public Affairs Manager
PO Box 880
Morgantown, WV 26507-0880 304-285-4764

The main goal of this center is to work with industry and research organizations to commercialize new ways to find and utilize domestic supplies of coal, oil and natural gas. Research is conducted on site and at many locations throughout the United States.

* Motor Fuel Statistics

Federal Highway Administration
Office of Highway Information Management
U.S. Department of Transportation (DOT)
Washington, DC 20590 202-366-0180

Statistics on highway use of motor fuels, including total use of gasoline; vehicle registration and driver's licenses issued; financing of Federal, State and local highway systems; mileage of roads and streets, including type of pavement; traffic and travel characteristics, including vehicles miles traveled by various types; and characteristics of household base vehicle and person trip making are compiled and published by this office. Most data are by State except for the household based travel data which is a national sample.

* National Councils on Coal and Petroleum

FE-5
1000 Independence Ave. SW, Room 4G-055
Washington, DC 20585 202-586-3867

The National Coal Council (NCC) and the National Petroleum Council (NPC) duties are solely advisory. Their purpose is to provide advice and recommendations on a continuing basis as requested by the Secretary of Energy on general policy matters relating to coal, oil and gas.

* Natural Gas Information

American Gas Association
1515 Wilson Blvd.
Arlington, VA 22209   703-841-8400

This association provides information on sales, finance utilization, research, management, safety, accounting, and all phases of gas transmission and distribution. It also sponsors competitions among primary and secondary students as well as public service and informational advertising. It also compiles a wide range of national and regional statistical, economic, marketing and financial studies as well as developing operating practices and gas rate schedules for virtually all gas companies.

* Naval Petroleum Reserves

Office of Naval Petroleum and Oil Shale Reserves
Fossil Energy, FE-60
U.S. Department of Energy
1000 Independence Ave., SW
Room 3H-076
Washington, DC 20585   202-586-4685

This office oversees the operations of the Naval Petroleum and Oil Shale Reserves, including the protection, conservation, maintenance, and production of Reserves. A Naval petroleum reserve program has existed since before the Second World War. Contact the above office for information or references to further information on the program.

* Office of Natural Gas

Office of Fuels Program
Fossil Energy, FE-50
U.S. Department of Energy
1000 Independence Ave., SW
Room 3H-087
Washington, DC 20585   202-586-9482

Working in conjunction with the State department and other federal agencies, this office performs policy analysis related to the importation and exportation of natural gas. It also works on the major issues involving pipeline systems for natural gas across state and international boundaries.

* Offshore Geologic Resources

Geologic Inquiries
U.S. Geological Survey (USGS)
U.S. Department of the Interior (DOI)
907 National Center
Reston, VA 22092   703-648-4383

Using remotely sensed data, including sidescan sonar and other geophysical surveys, and direct sampling, the U.S. Geological Survey (USGS) studies the geology and assesses the potential mineral and energy resources of the continental margins and the Exclusive Economic Zone of the United States (200 miles from the coastline) and its territories. Also identified are geologic features that must be considered in the selection of sites for offshore drilling platforms and pipelines.

* Offshore Oil and Gas Leasing

Offshore Minerals Management
Mineral Management Service
U.S. Department of the Interior
18th and C Sts., NW, Room 4210
Washington, DC 20240   202-208-3500

This office is responsible for the offshore leasing program, resource evaluation, and classification functions; environmental review of leasing activities; regulation of operations and lease management; and inspection and enforcement activities for all leasable minerals on the Outer Continental Shelf (OCS). In addition, the Service is responsible for the collection of all royalty payments, rentals, bonus payments, fines, penalties, and assessments and for other revenues due the Federal Government and Indian lessors as moneys or royalties-in-kind from the extraction of mineral resources from Federal and Indian lands on-shore and from the leasing and extraction of mineral resources on the OCS.

* Oil and Gas Data

Office of Oil and Gas
Energy Information Administration, EI-40
U.S. Department of Energy
1000 Independence Ave., SW, 2H-058
Washington, DC 20585   202-586-6401

This office designs, develops and maintains oil and gas statistical data and current short-term analytical forecasting information systems. This office also performs data collection, short-term forecasting, and report preparation activities associated with these energy sources.

* Oil and Gas: Economic Issues

International Energy Markets
Office of Policy, Planning, and Analysis, PO-73
U.S. Department of Energy
1000 Independence Ave., SW, 7G-076
Washington, DC 20585   202-586-6832

This office analyzes the international oil and gas markets. Major areas of concentration include economic analyses of the Organization of Petroleum Exporting Countries (OPEC), market responses to changing oil prices, incentives designed to stimulate increased oil production and conservation, and Government policies designed to deregulate oil and gas markets and enhance U.S. energy security.

* Oil and Gas Leasing on Public Lands

Resource Use and Protection
Bureau of Land Management
U.S. Department of the Interior
1849 C St. NW, Room 5627
Washington, DC 20240   202-208-4201

Public lands are available for oil and gas leasing only after they have been evaluated through the Bureau of Land Management. In areas where development of oil and gas resources would conflict with the protection or management of other resources or public land uses, mitigating measures are identified and may appear on leases as either stipulations to uses or as restrictions on surface occupancy. Two types of leases are issued: competitive and noncompetitive.

* Oil and Gas Reserves

Reserves and Natural Gas Division
Energy Information Administration, EI-44
U.S. Department of Energy
1000 Independence Ave., SW
Room BE-054
Washington, DC 20585   202-586-6090

Energy reserves and production are vital to America's energy security for the future. This office maintains statistical and short-term forecasting information systems for domestic oil and gas reserves and production and on the natural gas industry.

* Oil and Gas Royalties

Royalty Management
Mineral Management Service
U.S. Department of the Interior
Kipling at Sixth Ave., Bldg. 85
Box 25165, Mail Stop 3062
Denver, CO 80225   303-231-3230

The Royalty Management Program collects and accounts for bonuses, rentals, and royalties due on the Outer Continental Shelf, federal and Indian mineral leases. It then distributes the money to States, Indians, or other Federal agencies. Owners of federal and Indian leases are required, by regulation and lease terms, to pay an annual lease rental fee and/or monthly royalties on the value of minerals removed or sold from a lease. Mineral revenues from Federal and Indian lands were nearly $4.6 billion in 1990. The publication *Mineral Revenues 1990* details royalties on a state by state basis and also has some interesting figures on oil, gas, and coal production.

* Oil and Gas Technology

Oil and Gas Exploration and Production
Fossil Energy
U.S. Department of Energy (DOE)
1000 Independence Ave. SW, 3E-028
Washington, DC 20585   202-586-5600

This office is responsible for Federal technology programs for recovery of natural gas from hydrocarbon reserves, Eastern gas shales, and Western tight gas sands; for the recovery of methane from coal; and for recovery of other unconventional gas resources. The office is also responsible for the advancement of the science and engineering database for gas extraction technologies. Contact this office for program information. For publication information call 202-586-9534.

* Oil and Natural Gas: Production, Marketing, Legislation

Office of Energy Supply Policy
Policy, Planning and Analysis, PO-52
U.S. Department of Energy
1000 Independence Ave., SW, Room 7H-063
Washington, DC 20585   202-586-5667

This office prepares analyses and advises the Secretary of Energy on government policies affecting the discovery, production, refining, marketing, and consumption of oil and natural gas. This promotes free market policies and regulatory reform, thereby increasing the economic efficiency of oil and natural gas markets, increasing domestic consumer welfare, and reducing the Nation's vulnerability to energy supply disruptions. To accomplish this objective, the staff currently prepares analyses of natural gas legislation, restrictions on Alaskan oil exports, acquisition/drawdown policies for the Strategic Petroleum Reserve, domestic refinery policy, tax reform policy, and the Crude Oil Windfall Profits Tax. Contact this office for information on the availability of these and other reports and program information.

* Oil Recyclers

National Oil Recyclers Association (NORA)
2266 Bellfield Avenue
12429 Cedar Rd., Suite 26
Cleveland, OH 44106-3172   216-791-7316

The National Oil Recyclers Association (NORA) is comprised of primary producers of recycled used oil fuel. Its purpose is to represent the interests of used oil recyclers to the Environmental Protection Agency to ensure regulations on used oil are carried out and to encourage recycling. NORA will send you a free information package upon request.

* Onshore Leasing Program

Energy and Mineral Resources
Bureau of Land Management, BLM 600
Department of Interior
1849 C St. NE, Room 5627
Washington, DC 20240   202-208-4201

This office is responsible for the onshore leasing program, resource evaluation, and classification functions; environmental review of leasing activities; regulation for operations and lease management; and inspection and enforcement activities for all on-shore leasable minerals.

* Outer Continental Shelf Oil and Gas

Operations Management
Minerals Management Service
U.S. Department of the Interior
18th and C Sts., NW, Room 4210
Washington, DC 20240   202-208-3500

Management of the oil and gas operations following leasing agreements with the Mineral Management Service is outlined in the publication, *Managing Oil and Gas Operations on the Outer Continental Shelf*. This booklet describes activities through the drilling and production process to lease relinquishment.

* Petroleum Equipment Industries

Office of Energy, Infrastructure, and Machinery
Energy Division
U.S. Department of Commerce (USDA)
14th & Constitution Ave. NW, Room 4413
Washington, DC 20230   202-482-0680

This office monitors the petroleum equipment industries. It provides industry shipment and trade data and develops trade policy and export promotion programs.

* Petroleum Industry Interest Group

American Petroleum Institute (API)
1220 L St., NW
Washington, DC 20005   202-682-8375

The American Petroleum Institute is the petroleum industry trade association representing major oil companies, independent oil producers and fuel distributors, and service-station owners. It publishes extensive statistics about the industry. Contact this office for a free publications catalog.

* Petroleum Information Systems

Petroleum Marketing Division
Oil and Gas
Energy Information Administration
U.S. Department of Energy
1000 Independence Ave., SW, Room EI-431
Washington, DC 20585   202-586-5986

This office compiles information on crude oil and refined petroleum product prices and the industry market. The office can provide you with regular statistical reports on heating oil, gasoline, and other refined product prices and on sales of fuel oil and kerosene. Contact this office for available information and publications.

* Petroleum Marketing Information

Petroleum Marketing Division
Energy Information Administration, EI-43
U.S. Department of Energy
1000 Independence Ave., SW, Room 2G-051
Washington, DC 20585   202-586-5214

Since 1973 the price of oil has been one of the most important factors influencing economic growth in this country. This office designs, develops, and maintains crude oil and refined petroleum product price and marketing statistical information.

* Petroleum Overcharge Refunds

Office of Hearings and Appeals
U.S. Department of Energy
1000 Independence Ave., SW, Room 6G-087
Washington, DC 20585   202-586-2094

Cash refunds are available to any people, business firms, and governments that purchased refined petroleum products in the U.S. between August 1973 and January 1981. This office distributes millions of dollars in oil overcharges collected through the DOE enforcement program between those years. This office can give you further details.

* Petroleum Research Technology Transfer

Bartlesville Project Office
U.S. Department of Energy
P.O. Box 1398
Bartlesville, OK 74001   918-337-4293
                                        Fax: 918-337-4418

This Center is involved with research and engineering in petroleum and natural gas, including the improvement and demonstration of technologies in exploration, producing, refining, and use. A database on crude oil production and marketed fuel properties is also maintained. Research into automobile fuels is also undertaken. Contact this office for information on the database.

* Petroleum Statistics

Petroleum Supply Division
Oil and Gas
Energy Information Administration, EI-42
U.S. Department of Energy
1000 Independence Ave., SW, Room 2G-020
Washington, DC 20585   202-586-6860

This office compiles statistics and projections for crude oil and refined petroleum products, including their availability, production, imports, processing, transportation, stocks, and distribution. For available information and publications, contact this office.

* Pipeline Safety

Freedom of Information Act Office, DCRI
Office of Pipeline Safety (OPS)
Research and Special Programs Administration
U.S. Department of Transportation
400 7th St., SW
Washington, DC 20590   202-366-9638

OPS establishes and enforces safety standards for the transportation of gas and other hazardous materials by pipeline. A computerized reporting system is maintained to collect and analyze accident and incident data from pipeline operators. Accident reports include the operator's name, the hazardous material involved, description of the accident, and results. For database searches, contact the office listed. There may be a charge. For additional information, call Michelle Silva at 202-366-4578.

Energy

* Public Lands Oil and Gas Leasing

Resource Use and Protection
Bureau of Land Management
U.S. Department of the Interior
1849 C St. NW, Room 5627
Washington, DC 20240   202-208-4201

Public lands are available for oil and gas leasing only after they have been evaluated through the Bureau of Land Management. In areas where development of oil and gas resources would conflict with the protection or management of other resources or public land uses, mitigating measures are identified and may appear on leases as either stipulations to uses or as restrictions on surface occupancy. Two types of leases are issued: competitive and noncompetitive.

* Residential Consumption

Consumer Price Index
Bureau of Labor Statistics (BLS)
U.S. Department of Labor (DOL)
600 E St. NW
Washington, DC 20212   202-606-6985/6982

The Bureau of Labor Statistics (BLS) provides monthly prices for residential consumption of natural gas, electricity, fuel oil, and gasoline. Prices are averaged for 15 U.S. cities and Standard Metropolitan Statistical Areas (SMSA), reflecting different geographic areas and population categories. Price indices for natural gas, fuel oil, gasoline, and other fuels are also available.

* Short-Term Integrated Forecasting System

David Costello
Energy Information Administration, EI-621
National Energy Information Center
U.S. Department of Energy (DOE)
1000 Independence Ave.
Washington, DC 20585   202-586-1468

To Order:
National Technical Information Service (NTIS)
U.S. Department of Commerce (DOC)
5285 Port Royal Rd.   800-553-6847
Springfield, VA 22161   703-487-4650
                                                        Fax: 703-321-8547

Superintendent of Documents
Government Printing Office (GPO)
Washington, DC 20402   202-512-1800
                                                        Fax: 202-512-2250

This database contains forecasts for energy supply, demand, stocks, and prices for each quarter. The petroleum outlook includes detailed projections of domestic crude oil production, motor gasoline, distillate fuel oil, residual fuel oil, other product, and inventories. Other projections include natural gas, coal and electric power. The international petroleum situation is also discussed. This information is available on tape from the National Technical Information Service (NTIS) for $240, order number PB93-505956. Printed material is available from the Government Printing Office (GPO).

* Strategic Petroleum Reserve

New Orleans Project Management Office
Oak Ridge Operations Office
U.S. Department of Energy
900 Commerce Rd. East
New Orleans, LA 70123   504-734-4201

Petroleum Reserves
Fossil Energy
U.S. Department of Energy
1000 Independence Ave., SW, Room 3G-072
Washington, DC 20585   202-586-4410

The Strategic Petroleum Reserve was established to provide a stock of petroleum products to serve as at least a partial cushion in case of another cut off of oil products from overseas. Reports on the reserve and its progress are available from the above offices. The New Orleans office can answer specific questions on project implementation, site locations, construction, technical problems, and related matters, and the Washington office can provide you with information on the project's overall direction.

* Strategic Petroleum Reserve: Quarterly Report

Office of Petroleum Reserves
Assistant Secretary for Fossil Energy
U.S. Department of Energy
1000 Independence Ave., SW, Room 3G-024
Washington, DC 20585   202-586-4410/4625

Strategic Petroleum Reserve: Quarterly Report details the current status of the Strategic Petroleum Reserve project, designed to have a stock on hand of petroleum in case of future supply disruptions. Contact the office of the National Energy Information Center for information on availability.

* Transportation Technology

Office of the Deputy Assistant Secretary
Transportation Technologies, EE-30
U.S. Department of Energy (DOE)
1000 Independence Ave. SW, Room 6B-094
Washington, DC 20585   202-586-8027

Technologies that will improve fuel use efficiency and will result in displacement of petroleum by alternative fuels in transportation are researched. The office evaluates economic, environmental, and energy policies and statutes; current and prospective domestic and international transportation energy demands and utilization; and appropriate application of federal funds. They are responsible for defining and implementing programs that realize the economic and technical potential of advanced transportation technologies, reflect industrial, economic, and financial concerns; and account for the capabilities, decisions, and interests of energy users. The office coordinates national and international programs having a bearing upon the competitive position of U.S. industry.

* Underground Storage Tank Regulations

Office of Underground Storage Tank Docket, 5401
Environmental Protection Agency
4201 M St. SW, Room M-2616   202-260-9720
Washington, DC 20460   Hotline: 800-424-9346
                                                        703-412-9810

The Underground Storage Tank (UST) Docket provides public access to regulatory information supporting the Agency's regulatory action on USTs. As of April 1, 1987, there are seven dockets: (1) UST Notification Form; (2) Technical Standards for USTs Containing Petroleum; (3) Financial Responsibility Requirements for USTs Containing Petroleum; (4) State Program Approval; (5) Report to Congress on Exempt Tanks; (6) Consolidated Rules of Practice Governing the Administrative Assessment of Civil Penalties and Revocation or Suspension of Permits; and (7) Financial Responsibility Requirements for USTs Containing Hazardous Substances.

* World Production and Prices

Energy Plastics Branch
Energy, Chemicals, and Textiles Division
U.S. International Trade Commission (ITC)
500 E St. SW, Room 513
Washington, DC 20436   202-205-3342

Energy related activities of the Commission include the monitoring of production, sales, and international trade of petroleum, natural gas, coke and coal, uranium, and electricity. In addition, the Commission follows developments in biomass and solar and hydropower for energy production, and collects and publishes data on U.S. production and sales of all synthetic organic chemicals, including alternate energy sources, such as alcohols and oxygenages. For information on publications that are available call 202-205-1807.

Nuclear Energy and Waste

* Abnormal Occurrences at Nuclear Facilities

Superintendent of Documents
Government Printing Office (GPO)
Washington, DC 20402   202-512-1800

The Nuclear Regulatory Commission (NRC) prepares a quarterly *Report to Congress on Abnormal Occurrences* which also serves to communicate significant event information to licensees, other government agencies, and the public. This publication reports abnormal occurrences, which are unscheduled incidents or events which the NRL determined significant from the standpoint of public health and safety, involving facilities and activities regulated by the NRL and those regulated by the agreement states. For more information on the content of the reports, contact the Office of Analysis and Evaluation of Operational Data, Nuclear Regulatory Commission, Washington, DC 20555; GPO ordering information, stock # 752-020-00000-1, $6.50 a year, issued quarterly.

* Accidents and Incidents

Division of Operational Events Assessment
Office of Nuclear Reactor Regulation, O-11A1
Nuclear Regulatory Commission (NRC), Room 11 E1
Washington, DC 20055   301-504-1163

This division implements programs and procedures to systematically assess and screen daily reactor events; to provide daily reports; to recommend immediate corrective plant-specific and generic actions; and to coordinate the follow-up to events by assigning and tracking follow-up actions. This Division maintains and administers "on-call officer" roster to assure notification of management for events requiring prompt actions. They also respond to emergencies, and serve as the Incident Assessment Team contact.

* Antitrust Review of Nuclear Industry

Office of the General Counsel
Nuclear Regulatory Commission (NRC)
Room 15B18
Washington, DC 20555-0001   301-415-1740

During the licensing process, the NRC and the Attorney General conduct antitrust reviews of license applications, and an antitrust hearing may be required. Contact this office for more information on past or current antitrust reviews.

* Atomic Energy Films

National Audiovisual Center
National Archives and Records Administration
8700 Edgeworth Dr.   800-788-6282
Capitol Heights, MD 20743-3701   301-763-1896

The Media Resource Catalog contains more than 600 programs which are ideal for classrooms, training programs, library collections, and home use. The following two are about atomic energy.

The Atom Strikes (31 minutes, black & white, 1950) Gives an account of the first experimental atomic bomb blast in New Mexico, aerial views of Hiroshima and Nagasaki bombings, and close-up shots of devastated areas. VHS Video No. TCA13254, $125.00.

Target Nevada (14 minutes, color, 1962) Tells the story of the U.S. Air Force support to the Atomic Energy Commission on continual atomic tests. Covers the delivery of the atom bomb and shows aerial views of nuclear explosions plus the monitoring of blast areas. VHS Video No. TCA08200, $95.00.

* Atomic Safety and Licensing Board Panel

Nuclear Regulatory Commission (NRC)
Room 3E19, T3F23
Washington, DC 20555-0001   301-415-7450

Three-member licensing boards are drawn from this panel. They are made up of lawyers and others with expertise in various technical and environmental fields to conduct public hearings on applications to build and operate nuclear power plants and other matters related to the possession and use of nuclear facilities and materials.

* Audiovisuals, Nuclear Waste

Office of Civilian Radioactive Waste Management (OCRWM)
National Information Center
600 Maryland Ave. SW, Suite 760   800-225-6972
Washington, DC 20024   202-488-6720

OCRWM has produced a number of video tapes about the nation's civilian radioactive waste management system. Topics cover all the OCRWM programs, including deep geologic disposal, interim storage, transportation, and the multi-purpose canister concept being developed for storing, transporting, and disposing of commercial spent nuclear fuel. Videos are available to the public free of charge. Call or write for a brochure describing some of the videos available.

* Bibliographic Retrieval System (BRS)

Elizabeth Yeats
Public Documents Room (PDR)
LL-6
Nuclear Regulatory Commission (NRC)   202-634-3380
2120 L St. NW   Data: 800-270-2787
Washington, DC 20555-0001   202-634-1421

The Bibliographic Retrieval System (BRS) provides online access to the majority of publicly available Nuclear Regulatory Commission (NRC) documents generated by or sent to the NRC and placed in the Public Document Room (PDR) after October 1978 and selected documents for 1967-1978. The database consists of descriptive citations; in 1994, abstracts or full text for selected documents were added. The system was developed to respond to the needs of the public in obtaining agency documents and is tailored to the public. BRS supports search, retrieval, viewing, printing, and ordering of documents. The system can be accessed either on site, using the terminals in the PDR, or off site via a modem. It is available 24 hours a day, 7 days a week. Passwords are required to access BRS, contact the PDR technical librarians for further information 202-634-3273. The librarian can perform searches for the public and generate printouts upon request. The customer is not charged for use of the system but is responsible for cost of off site telecommunications. Information is continuously updated.

* Citizen's Guide to U.S. Nuclear Regulatory Commission

Public Document Room
Nuclear Regulatory Commission (NRC)
2120 L St. NW   800-397-4209
Washington, DC 20037   202-634-3273

The *Citizen's Guide to U.S. Nuclear Regulatory Commission Information* is designed to acquaint the public with the availability of information pertaining to the licensing and regulation of nuclear energy, and of all commercial high-level and low-level radioactive waste and uranium recovery activities in the United States.

* Civilian Reactor Development

Nuclear Energy, NE-40
Office of Facilities
U.S. Department of Energy
19901 Germantown Rd., Room 424
Germantown, MD 20874-1290   301-903-2915

This office manages the design, construction, and operations of the nuclear energy test facilities and Office of Energy Research reactor and supporting facilities, assuring their safe, reliable, and environmentally sound operation and their cost-effective utilization in meeting Department of Energy's missions. It manages the conduct of shutdown activities necessary to place unneeded facilities into an industrial and radiologically safe shutdown condition.

* Construction Permits for Nuclear Facilities

Office of Nuclear Reactor Regulation
Nuclear Regulatory Commission (NRC)
Room 12 D1, O-12 G18
Washington, DC 20555-0001   301-415-1270

Energy

Obtaining an NRC construction permit is the first objective of a utility or other company seeking to operate a nuclear power reactor or other nuclear facility under NRC licensing authority. The process begins with the filing and acceptance of an application, generally comprising many volumes of data, covering both safety and environmental considerations, in accord with NRC requirements and guidance. Contact this office for more information concerning the construction permit process.

* Criminal Incidents

Emergency Programs Center
U.S. Department of Justice
10th St. and Constitution Ave., NW, Room 6101
Washington, DC 20530   202-514-2000

If you would like to know the facts of any case of criminal activity involving nuclear incidents, the files of the Emergency Programs Center is for you. This office of the U.S. Department of Justice coordinates the government's activity in any such case. For instance, if you want the facts on the real-life case of nuclear extortion seen in the movie, *The Falcon and the Snowman*, this is the place to go. Maybe you are interested in writing your own thriller on nuclear espionage; contact the Emergency Programs Center and read accounts of actual incidents to give your writing that tinge of reality. Whatever your interest may be, here's where you'll get the facts.

* Daily Nuclear Documents

Public Document Room (PDR)
Nuclear Regulatory Commission (NRC)
2120 L. Street, NW   800-397-4209
Washington, DC 20037   202-634-3273

The *PDR Daily Accession List* describes agency documents that are made publicly available each weekday. There is ordinarily at least a two-to-three-week delay in the public availability of new documents. The PDR collection includes all publicly available forms of communication generated by NRC or sent to NRC by the companies and institutions it regulates. The Accession Lists are organized by NRC topics, and all documents appropriate to a topic and their file location are listed in one place. A free publication, *How to Use The Public Document Room's Daily Accession List*, is available from the office above, and explains the *Daily Accession List*, the PDR request policy, as well as the classification scheme.

* Decommissioning Nuclear Facilities

Mark Owen, Manager
Remedial Action Program Information Center (RAPIC)
Martin Marietta Energy Systems Inc.
P.O. Box 2003
Building K-1210, MS-7256   423-576-0568
Oak Ridge, TN 37831-7256   Fax: 423-576-6547
                              Internet: rapic@ornl.gov

The *Nuclear Facility Decommissioning and Site Remedial Action* database serves as a comprehensive source of technical information relevant to the DOE Remedial Action Program, under which nuclear facilities are decommissioned and cleaned up. The RAPIC data center scans both foreign and domestic reports, journals, books and theses and currently contains some 8,500 references. Computerized literature searches of RAPIC databases are available upon request at no charge.

* Defense Requirements

Office of Nuclear Weapons Management, DP-22
U.S. Department of Energy (DOE)
19901 Germantown Rd., Room A-301
Germantown, MD 20874   301-903-2402

The planning and execution of the stockpile support and materials policies and programs to assure that national defense requirements are met and developed and managed here. The office is responsible for ensuring the safe and effective operations and maintenance of the Kansas City Plant and for ensuring that production requirements are achieved.

* Development Testing

Office of Development Testing DP-12
U.S. Department of Energy (DOE)
19901 Germantown Rd., Room A-483
Germantown, MD 20874   301-903-3441

This office coordinates, initiates, and implements basic policies for all Defense Programs development and testing activities that are required to support the enduring stockpile and oversees a wide variety of experimental facilities and activities relating to nuclear weapons, including use of the Nevada Test Site.

* Documents on Disk (DOD)

Elizabeth Yeats
Public Documents Room (PDR)
LL-6
Nuclear Regulatory Commission (NRC)
Washington, DC 20555-0001   202-634-3380

This system was developed to provide the public with selected NRC publicly available documents in a very timely manner and in an electronic format that can be loaded (via diskette) into the customer's equipment. Information available includes Commission Meeting Transcripts, Daily Event Reports, selected Federal Register Notices, Plant Status Reports, Preliminary Notification of Occurrences, Secretary Papers, and Staff Requirements Memoranda (SRMs). Information is added as it becomes available. Available only by subscription and the price will vary depending on the amount of information available at the time. The price for one disk is $4.00 but more than one disk might be necessary. For information on obtaining subscriptions contact the Technical Reference Librarian at 202-634-3273.

* Domestic and International Nuclear Issues

Office of Nuclear, Energy, Science and Technology
Office of the Director, NE-1
U.S. Department of Energy (DOE)
1000 Independence Ave. SW, Room 5A-143
Washington, DC 20585   202-586-6450

This office provides technical leadership to address critical domestic and international issues, contribute to energy supply diversity, and advance United States competitiveness and security by providing nuclear products and services that meet the needs of the United States and the world community in a safe environmentally sound, and economical manner, and encourage public involvement in programs and provide information to increase public knowledge.

* Energy Science and Technology Database

Robert W. Rutowski
Office of Scientific and Technical Information System
U.S. Department of Energy (DOE)
P.O. Box 62
Oak Ridge, TN 37831   615-576-9362

The Energy Science and Technology Database is a multidisciplinary database containing bibliographic information for and summaries of all unlimited, unclassified information related to energy and nuclear science and technology from worldwide sources processed at the Department of Energy Office of Scientific and Technical Information. In addition, the database contains over a million citations in subject areas extending beyond energy fields, such as basic scientific studies, computers, environment and pollution, nuclear medicine, and arms control. The data covers all scientific and technical aspects of energy sources (fossil, renewable, and nuclear); energy conservation, consumption, and utilization; energy policy; and the environmental effects of energy production and utilization. The complete DOE database is available through Dialog (File 103) and contains approximately 2.9 million records dating from 1974 to the present.

* Enhanced Participatory Rulemaking Bulletin Board System (EPRBBS)

Christine Daily
Information Resources Management (IRM)
T-9-C24
Nuclear Regulatory Commission (NRC)   Voice: 301-415-6026
Washington, DC 20555-0001   Data: 800-880-6091

This electronic bulletin board system was developed to increase public access to information as part of the Enhanced Participatory Rulemaking process. Background information on the decommissioning rulemaking process are available for download or online viewing. Files containing comments on the rulemaking can be easily uploaded by the caller into a reserved area on the bulletin board, and will be sent to the docket within one business day of receipt. There is no fee from the NRC for the use of this bulletin board.

* Environmental Restoration

Office of the Deputy Assistant Secretary for Environmental Restoration
Environmental Management, EM-40
U.S. Department of Energy (DOE)
1000 Independence Ave. SW, Room 5B-050
Washington, DC 20585   202-586-6331

Programs are managed to ensure that risks to human health and the environment posed by DOE's past operations at its nuclear facilities and sites are eliminated or reduced to prescribed, safe levels. The office assesses and cleans up these sites and facilities contaminated with radioactive, hazardous, and mixed waste.

* Environmental Review of Proposed Nuclear Facilities

Office of Nuclear Reactor Regulation
Nuclear Regulatory Commission (NRC)
Room 12 D1, O-12G18
Washington, DC 20555   301-415-1270

An environmental review begins with an analysis of the consequences to the environment of the construction and operation of the proposed nuclear facility at the proposed site. Upon completion of the analysis, a draft Environmental Statement is published and distributed to all interested parties. Comments are then taken into account in the preparation of a final Environmental Statement. During this same period, the NRC is conducting analysis and preparing a report on the site suitability aspects of the proposed licensing action. Contact this office more information on the review process and reports.

* Exhibits, Nuclear Fission and Fusion

Printing and Graphics Division
Energy Technology Visuals Collection (ETVE), HR-842
Department of Energy (DOE)
1000 Independence Ave. SW, Room BH-039
Washington, DC 20585   202-586-9796

ETVC serves as a central repository for visuals representing DOE's many research and development activities. The Collection, maintained and operated by the Office of Administrative Services, contains high quality images of over 600 DOE sponsored projects in such areas as fossil fuels, nuclear fission and fusion, biomedical research, solar energy, wind energy, conservation, and environmental activities. Images are available as 8" x 10" prints (color or black and white), and 35mm color slides through the DOE Graphics Branch. Each image requested from the collection is accompanied by a computer-generated data sheet containing caption and background information. An automated cataloging system is used by the ETVC staff to conduct online searches of the database with respect to program, project, technology and geographic location. ETVC supports DOE personnel; other federal, state, or local agencies; and the private sector, upon approval, in preparing publications, briefings, and presentations.

* Export and Import Controls

Nuclear Energy and Energy Technology Affairs
Bureau of Oceans and International Environmental
  and Scientific Affairs
U.S. Department of State
2201 C St., NW, Room 7820
Washington, DC 20520   202-647-3978

This office works closely with the Nuclear Regulatory Commission with regard to the licensing requests for nuclear imports and exports. They also study the development and transfer of nuclear technology in foreign countries. This office monitors the Nuclear Non-Proliferation Treaty, making sure that the countries which signed the treaty are following its regulations. They also oversee the export and import of items which are not nuclear, but which could be used for nuclear purposes, such as super computers. The export of these items must follow the guidelines set in the Nuclear Non-Proliferation Treaty.

* Export-Import Licensing

International Programs
Division of Non-proliferation Exports, and Multilateral Relations
Nuclear Regulatory Commission (NRC)
Room 3H1, O-3H5
Washington, DC 20555   301-415-2344

This NRC office formulates and recommends policies concerning nuclear exports and imports, international safeguards, international physical security, nonproliferation matters, and international cooperation and assistance in nuclear safety and radiation protection. NRC is responsible for licensing the import or export of nuclear-related materials and equipment. This export authority extends to production and utilization facilities, to special nuclear and source material, to byproduct materials, and to certain nuclear-related components and other material.

* Freedom of Information Act Requests

Division of Freedom of Information
Nuclear Regulatory Commission (NRC)
Mail Stop T-6D8

Washington, DC 20555-0001   301-415-7169

All Freedom of Information Act Requests should be addressed to the Office listed above.

* Fuel Cycle Plants and Material Safety

Division of Fuel Cycle Safety and Safeguards
Office of Nuclear Material Safety and Safeguards
Nuclear Regulatory Commission (NRC)
Room 8E1, T-8 A33
Washington, DC 20555-0001   301-415-7212

This office analyzes health physics, radiation and nuclear safety, quality, licensing, and follow-up review of all fuel cycle plants. Contact this office for more information on its studies.

* Fuel Cycle Programs

Office of Facilities and Fuel Cycle Programs
Fuel Cycle Programs Division
U.S. Department of Energy
19901 Germantown Rd., F-426
Germantown, MD 20874   301-903-2915

This division manages fuel development and fabrication activities necessary to assure adequate fuel supply for uninterrupted operations by key nuclear test facilities. It also performs equipment development and verification testing to support various fuel cycle options, improve operational efficiency, and reduce future fuel cycle costs.

* Fusion Energy and Basic Science Research

General Sciences
Fusion Energy Research Program
Lawrence Berkeley Laboratory
One Cyclotron Rd.
Bldg. 47-112
Berkeley, CA 94720   510-486-5771

The General Sciences section of the Lawrence Berkeley Laboratory researches the basic nature of matter to provide basic understanding of the elements of the universe, making progress possible in many fields of science. Of particular interest in the work of this division is investigation of the potential development of nuclear fusion energy sources. Contact this office for more information.

* Fusion Technology

Office of Fusion Energy
Energy Research
U.S. Department of Energy
19901 Germantown Rd.
Germantown, MD 20874   301-903-3347

The office works to develop sound physical and engineering technological foundations needed for the design, construction, and operation of complex nuclear fusion experiments and facilities. Contact the office for more detailed program information.

* Generic Communications Electronic Distribution System (GCEDS) Bulletin Board

Andy Kugler
Office of Nuclear Regulatory Research (NRR)
0-8-D22
Nuclear Regulatory Commission   Voice: 301-415-2828
Washington, DC 20555-0001   Data: 800-679-5784

This bulletin board provides electronic distribution of previous and recently released NRC generic communications. GCEDS was developed to 1) identify when an NRC generic communication had been issued; 2) allow faster distribution of generic communications; and 3) allow access to previously issued generic communications. This bulletin board is also available via NTIS FedWorld Gateway #63.

* Guide to Nuclear Regulatory Commission (NRC) Reporting and Recordkeeping Requirements (NUREG-1460)

Mike Collins
Information Resources Management (IRM)
T-6-F33
Nuclear Regulatory Commission (NRC)

Washington, DC 20555-0001   301-415-5876

This system mainly services utilities, State nuclear regulatory agencies, consultants, medical facilities, and business enterprises. It contains a compilation of NRC reporting and recordkeeping requirements that are imposed on licensees and applicants. The information is revised periodically to add new requirements or to remove requirements resulting from NRC rulemakings. NUREG-1460 diskettes are currently provided free of charge to State nuclear regulatory agencies, consultants, medical facilities and business enterprises. This system is planned to become a bulletin board in the near future where it will be available to the public via FedWorld.

* Hazards Ahead: Managing Cleanup, Worker Health and Safety at the Nuclear Weapons Complex

Superintendent of Documents
Government Printing Office
710 N. Capitol St.   202-512-1800
Washington, DC 20402   Fax: 202-512-2250
    TDD: 202-512-2489

This book examines the risks that workers might face in cleaning up contamination at the Nuclear Weapons Complex. It evaluates the effectiveness of the Department of Energy's occupational safety and health programs for cleanup workers. The conclusion, thus far, is that the Department of Energy and its' contractors have devoted little attention to cleanup worker health and safety. (87pp., 1993). Stock #052-003-01316-9, $5.00.

* High-Level Nuclear Waste

High-Level Waste Management Division
Office of Nuclear Material Safety and Safeguards
Nuclear Regulatory Commission (NRC)
Room 7E47, T-7J9
Washington, DC 20555   301-415-7238

This Division develops and manages the Agency's program for the licensing, inspection, and regulation of the U.S. Department of Energy's high-level waste repository program. They also provide the lead for all Agency activities under the Nuclear Waste Policy Act.

* Inertial Fusion

Office of Research and Inertial Fusion, DP-11
U.S. Department of Energy (DOE)
19901 Germantown Rd., Room B-312
Germantown, MD 20874   301-903-5491

This office manages research activities associated with the weapons science and enabling technology base including advanced technologies, inertial fusion, and research and technology development activities such as weapons design and safety research.

* Inspection of Nuclear Reactors

Nuclear Reactor Regulation
Nuclear Regulatory Commission (NRC)
Room 3E1, O-3E4
Washington, DC 20402   301-415-2373

A basic element in Nuclear Regulatory Commission (NRC) reactor regulation is the inspection of licensed reactor facilities to determine the state of reactor safety, to confirm that the operations are in compliance with the provisions of the license, and to ascertain whether other conditions exist which have safety implications serious enough to warrant corrective action. The NRC conducts a program to deal with unsafe or potentially unsafe events or conditions which occur at individual plant sites or other facilities involving licensed operation ("reactive" inspections).

* International Thermonuclear Experimental Reactor

Energy Research, ER-53
International Thermonuclear Experimental Reactor and
  Technology Division
U.S. Department of Energy (DOE)
19901 Germantown Rd., Room G-240
Germantown, MD 20874-1290   301-903-5378

Manages and provides technical director of the U.S. International Thermonuclear Experimental Reactor (ITER) program, as well as managing the U.S. fusion base technology development program for near-term experimental needs. Develops the technologies needed to form, contain, heat, and sustain a reacting fusion plasma, including magnetic, heating, and fueling systems. This division also focuses on elements of fusion devices related to long-term waste issues, safety and environmental considerations, device reliability, tritium production and power extraction.

* Inventory of Power Plants in the United States, 1993

Superintendent of Documents
Government Printing Office
710 N. Capitol St.   202-512-1800
Washington, DC 20402   Fax: 202-512-2250
    TDD: 202-512-2489

This book presents year-end statistics about electric generating units operated by electric utilities in the 50 states and the District of Columbia. It provides a 10-year outlook of future generating unit additions. Organized into: year in review; operable electric generating units; and projected electric generating unit additions. It reflects the statistics of electric generation units as of December 31, 1993. (401 pgs., 1995). Stock #061-003-00888-7, $24.

* Licensee Contractor and Vendor Inspection Status Report

Superintendent of Documents
Government Printing Office
710 N. Capitol St.   202-512-1800
Washington, DC 20402   Fax: 202-512-2250
    TDD: 202-512-2489

Issued quarterly, this presents individual reports on violations of the Nuclear Regulatory Commission standards in nuclear power plant operations, maintenance, or modifications based on inspections performed by NRC personnel. Subscription price is $15 yearly. Stock #752-011-00000-1.

* Licensing Nuclear-Related Operations

Office of Nuclear Reactor Regulation
Nuclear Regulatory Commission (NRC)
Room 12 D1, O-12 G18
Washington, DC 20402   301-415-1270

The Nuclear Regulatory Commission grants licenses for nuclear power operations and other possession and use of nuclear materials, including the transportation and disposal of nuclear materials and wastes. Contact this office for more information on the licensing process.

* Limited Work Authorization

Office of Nuclear Reactor Regulation
Nuclear Regulatory Commission (NRC)
Room 12 D1, O-12 G18
Washington, DC 20555   301-415-1270

The NRC may decide to grant a Limited Work Authorization to an applicant in advance of a final decision on the construction permit, in order to allow certain work to begin at the site. Such a step could save seven months' construction time.

* Local Public Document Rooms

Nuclear Regulatory Commission (NRC)   800-638-8081
Washington, DC 20555   301-492-4344

The Local Public Documents Room (LPDR) in your area can provide you with information on nuclear plants and low level waste disposal facilities in your area. Many of the LPDRs have documents on microfiche for all publicly available documents issued since January 1981.

The following list, organized by state, contains the addresses of LPDR libraries. Under each library is a list of the nuclear facilities whose records are available there. An asterisk along side the listing indicates that the library has a microfiche file containing all NRC publicly available records issued since January 1981. The LPDRS with online access to the NRC Nuclear Documents System: Advanced Design are indicated by the acronym NUDOCS.

Alabama
* Athens Public Library, 405 E. South Street, Athens, AL 35611; 205-232-1233. Browns Ferry Nuclear Power Station; Browns Ferry Low-Level Rad Waste Facility. NUDOCS

* Houston-Love Memorial Library, 212 W. Burdeshaw Street, PO Box 1369, Dothan, AL 36302; 205-793-9767. Joseph M. Farley Nuclear Plant. NUDOCS

* Scottsboro Public Library, 1002 S. Broad St., Scottsboro, AL 35768; 205-574-4335.
Bellefonte Nuclear Plant.

Arizona
* Phoenix Public Library, 1221 N. Central Ave., Phoenix, AZ 85004; 602-495-5052.
Palo Verde Nuclear Station.

Arkansas
* Tomlinson Library, Arkansas Tech University, Russellville, AR 72801; 501-968-0366.
Arkansas Nuclear One. NUDOCS

California
* Humbolt County Library, 421 I Street, Eureka, CA 95501; 707-445-72845
Humbolt Bay Power Plant.

* University of California - Irvine, Main Library, P.O. Box 19557, Irvine, CA 92713; 714-856-7234.
San Onofre Nuclear Station. NUDOCS

* Government Documents Central Library, 828 I, Sacramento, CA 95814; 916-264-2972.
Rancho Seco Nuclear Generating Station. NUDOCS

* California Polytechnic State University, Government Documents and Maps Dept, Robert E. Kennedy Library, San Luis Obispo, CA 93407; 805-756-1364.
Diablo Canyon Power Plant. NUDOCS

Colorado
* Weld Library District, Lincoln Park Branch, 919 7th Street, Greely, CO 80631; 970-350-9210.
Fort St. Vrain Nuclear Generating Station.

Connecticut
* Russell Library, 123 Broad Street, Middletown, CT 06457; 203-347-2520.
Haddam Neck Plant. NUDOCS

* Learning Resources Center, Three Rivers Community Technical College, 574 New London Turnpike, Norwich, CT 06360; 203-885-2346.
Millstone Nuclear Power Station. NUDOCS

Florida
* Technical Services, Coastal Region Library, 8619 W. Crystal Street, Crystal River, FL 33428; 904-795-1706.
Crystal River Nuclear Plant.

* Charles S. Miles Learning Resources Center, Indian River Community College, 3209 Virginia Avenue, Ft. Pierce, FL 34981-5599; 407-462-4757.
St. Lucie Plant. NUDOCS

* Documents Department Library, Florida International University, University Park, Miami, FL 33199; 305-348-3137.
Turkey Point Plant. NUDOCS

Georgia
* Appling County Public Library, 301 City Hall Dr., Baxley, GA 31513; 912-367-8103.
Edwin I. Hatch Nuclear Plant.

* Burke County Library, 412 4th Street, Waynesboro, GA 30830; 706-554-3277.
Alvin W. Vogtle Nuclear Plant.

Illinois
* Byron Public Library District, 109 N. Franklin, P.O. Box 434, Byron, IL 61010; 815-234-5107.
Byron Station.

* Vespasian Warner Public Library District, 310 N. Quincy St., Clinton, IL 61727; 217-935-5174.
Clinton Power Station.

* Dixon Public Library, 221 Hennepin Avenue, Dixon, IL 61021; 815-284-7621.
Quad Cities Station; Sheffield Low-Level Radioactive Waste Disposal Facility.

* Morris Area Public Library District, 604 Liberty St., Morris, IL 60450; 815-942-6880.
Dresden Nuclear Power Station; Morris Operations, General Electric.

* Jacobs Memorial Library, Illinois Valley Community College, Oglesby, IL 61348; 815-224-2720 ext. 397. Lasalle County Station. NUDOCS

* Waukegan Public Library, 128 N. County Street, Waukegan, IL 60085; 708-623-2041.
Zion Nuclear Power Station. NUDOCS

* Government Documents Collection, Wilmington Public Library, 201 South Kankakee Street, Wilmington, IL 60481; 815-476-2834.
Braidwood Station.

Iowa
* Cedar Rapids Public Library, 501 1st Street SE, Cedar Rapids, IA 52401; 319-398-5123.
Duane Arnold Energy Center. NUDOCS

Kansas
* William Allen White Library, Emporia State University, 1200 Commercial Street, Emporia, KS 66801; 316-343-5409.
Wolf Creek Generating Station. NUDOCS

* Washburn University School of Law, Topeka, KS 66621; 913-231-1010 ext. 1785.
Wolf Creek Generating Station. NUDOCS

Kentucky
* Paducah Public Library, 555 Washington St., Paducah, KY 42003; 502-442-2510.
Paducah Gaseous Diffusion Plant.

Louisiana
* Troy H. Middleton Library, Government Documents Department, Louisiana State University, Baton Rouge, LA 70803; 504-388-2570.
River Bend Station. NUDOCS

* Clairborne Parish Library, 901 Edgewood Drive, Homer, LA 71040; 318-927-3845.
Clairborne Enrichment Center.

* Earl K. Long Library, University of New Orleans, Lakefront Drive, New Orleans, LA 70148; 504-286-7275.
Waterford Generating Station. NUDOCS

Maine
* Wiscasset Public Library, High Street, PO Box 367, Wiscasset, ME 04578; 207-882-7161.
Maine Yankee Atomic Power Plant. NUDOCS

Maryland
* Calvert County Public Library, 30 Duke Street, PO Box 405, Prince Frederick, MD 20678; 410-535-0291.
Calvert Cliffs Nuclear Power Plant. NUDOCS

Massachusetts
* Greenfield Community College, Library Learning Resource Center, One College Drive, Greenfield, MA 01301; 413-774-3131.
Yankee Rowe Nuclear Power Station.

* Plymouth Public Library, 132 South Street, Plymouth, MA 02360; 508-830-4250.
Pilgrim Nuclear Power Station. NUDOCS

Michigan
* Hope College, Van Wylen Library, Holland, MI 49423-3698; 616-394-7790.
Pallisades Nuclear Plant.

* Ellis Reference and Information Center, Monroe County Library System, 3700 S. Custer Road, Monroe, MI 48161; 313-241-5277.
Enrico Fermi Atomic Power Plant. NUDOCS

* North Central Michigan College, 1515 Howard Street, Petoskey, MI 49770; 616-348-6615.
Big Rock Point Nuclear Plant. NUDOCS

* Maude Preston Palenske Memorial Library, 500 Market Street, St. Joseph, MI 49085; 616-983-7167.
Donald C. Cook Nuclear Power Plant.

Minnesota
* Minneapolis Public Library, Technology and Science Department, 300 Nicollet Mall, Minneapolis, MN 55401; 612-372-6642.
Monticello Nuclear Generating Plant; Prairie Island Nuclear Station. NUDOCS

Energy

Mississippi
* Judge George W. Armstrong Library, 220 S. Commerce St., Natchez, MS 39120; 601-445-8862.
Grand Gulf Nuclear Station.

Missouri
* Callaway County Public Library, 710 Court Street, Fulton, MO 65251; 314-642-7261.
Callaway Plant.

Nebraska
* Auburn Public Library, 1118 15th Street, PO Box 324, Auburn, NE 68305; 402-274-4023.
Cooper Nuclear Station.

* W Dale Clark Library, Business, Science and Technology Department, 215 S. 15th Street, Omaha, NE 68102; 402-444-4817.
Fort Calhoun Station. NUDOCS

Nevada
* James R. Dickinson Library, University of Nevada at Las Vegas, 4505 Maryland Parkway, Las Vegas, NV 89154; 702-895-1574.
Yucca Mountain Project. NUDOCS

* University of Nevada at Reno, University Library, Government Publications Department, Reno, NV 89557-0044; 702-784-6579.
Yucca Mountain Project. NUDOCS

New Hampshire
* Exeter Public Library, Founders Park, Exeter, NH 03833; 603-772-3101.
Seabrook Nuclear Station. NUDOCS

New Jersey
* Pennsville Public Library, 190 S. Broadway, Pennsville, NJ 08070; 609-678-5473.
Hope Creek Nuclear Station, Shield Alloy Metallurgical Corporation.

* Salem Free Public Library, 112 West Broadway, Salem, NJ 08079; 609-935-0526.
Salem Nuclear Generating Station, Shield Alloy Metallurgical Corporation.

* Ocean County Public Library, 101 Washington Street, Toms River, NJ 08753; 908-349-6200.
Oyster Creek Nuclear Power Plant. NUDOCS

New York
* Buffalo and Erie County Public Library, Science and Technology Department, Lafayette Square, Buffalo, NY 14203; 716-858-7098.
West Valley Demonstration Project.

* Penfield Library, Reference and Documents Department, State University of New York at Oswego, Oswego, NY 13126; 315-341-3566/3564.
James A. Fitzpatrick Nuclear Power Station; Nine Mile Point Nuclear Station. NUDOCS

* Rochester Public Library, Business, Economics and Law Division, 115 South Avenue, Rochester, NY 14604; 716-428-7328.
Robert Emmet Ginna Nuclear Plant. NUDOCS

* Shoreham-Wading River Public Library, Route 25A, Shoreham, NY 11786; 516-929-4488.
Shoreham Nuclear Power Station.

* White Plains Public Library, 100 Martine Avenue, White Plains, NY 10601; 914-422-1477.
Indian Point Station. NUDOCS

North Carolina
* University of North Carolina at Charlotte, J. Murrey Atkins Library, UNCC Station, Charlotte, NC 28223; 704-547-2243.
William B. Mcguire Nuclear Station. NUDOCS

* Cameron Village Regional Library, 1930 Clark Avenue, Raleigh, NC 27605; 919-856-6868.
Shearon Harris Nuclear Power Plant.

* University of North Carolina at Wilmington, William Madison Randall Library, 601 S. College Road, Wilmington, NC 28403; 919-395-3760 (reference desk), 919-395-3277 (documents desk). Brunswick Steam Electric Plant. NUDOCS

Ohio
* Cuyahoga County Public Library, Garfield Heights Branch, 5409 Turney Road, Garfield Heights, OH 44125; 216-475-8178.
Chemerton Corporation.

* Guernsey County District Public Library, 800 Steubenville Ave., Cambridge, OH 43725-2385; 614-432-5946.
Shield Alloy Metallurgical Corporation.

* Perry Public Library, 3753 Main Street, Perry OH 44081; 216-259-3300.
Perry Nuclear Power Plant. NUDOCS

* Portsmouth Public Library, 1220 Gallia St., Portsmouth, OH 45662; 614-354-5688.
Portsmouth Gaseous Diffusion Plant.

* University of Toledo, Government Documents Collection, William Carlson Library, 2801 West Bancroft Avenue, Toledo, OH 43606; 419-537-2171.
Davis-Besse Nuclear Power Station. NUDOCS

Oklahoma
* Stanley Tubbs Memorial Library, 101 E. Cherokee, Sallisaw, OK 74955; 918-775-4481.
Sequoyah Fuels Corporation.

Oregon
* Branford Price Millar Library, Portland State University, 934 SW Harrison, PO Box 1151, Portland, OR 97207; 503-725-4735.
Trojan Nuclear Plant. NUDOCS

Pennsylvania
* BF Jones Memorial Library, 663 Franklin Avenue, Aliquippa, PA 15001; 412-375-7174.
Beaver Valley Power Station. NUDOCS

* Apollo Memorial Library, 219 N. Pennsylvania Avenue, Apollo, PA 15613; 412-478-4214.
B&W Apollo Site; B&W Parks Township Site.

* State Library of Pennsylvania, Law/Government Documents Section, Walnut Street and Commonwealth Avenue, Box 1601, Harrisburg, PA 17105; 717-787-2327.
Three Mile Island Nuclear Station, Peach Bottom Atomic Power Station. NUDOCS

* Pottstown Public Library, 500 High Street, Pottstown, PA 19464; 610-970-6551.
Limerick Generating Station.

* Saxton Community Library, 911 Church Street, Saxton, PA 16678; 814-635-3533.
Saxton Nuclear Experimental Facility.

* Osterhout Free Library, 71 South Franklin Street, Wilkes-Barre, PA 18701; 717-823-0156.
Susquehanna Steam Electric Station.

South Carolina
* Barnwell County Public Library, Hagood Avenue, Barnwell, SC 29812; 803-259-3612.
Barnwell Reprocessing Plant, Barnwell Low-Level Radioactive Waste Disposal Facility.

* Hartsville Memorial Library, Nuclear Information Depository, 147 W. College Ave., Hartsville, SC 29550; 803-332-5115.
H.B. Robinson Plant.

* York County Library, 138 East Black Street, PO Box 10032, Rock Hill, SC 29731; 803-324-3055.
Catawba Nuclear Station.

* Oconee County Library, 501 W. South Broad Street, Wallhalla, SC 29691; 803-638-4133.
Oconee Nuclear Station. NUDOCS

* Fairfield County Library, 300 Washington Street, Winnsboro, SC 29180; 803-635-4971.
Virgil C. Summer Nuclear Station.

Tennessee
* Chattanooga-Hamilton County Library, Business, Science and Technology Department, 1001 Broad Street, Chattanooga, TN 37402; 423-757-5351.

Be patient. If any phone number is incorrect, call (area code) 555-1212 and request the new listing.

Sequoyah Nuclear Plant, Watts Bar Nuclear Plant, Sequoyah Low-Level Radioactive Waste Facility. NUDOCS

Texas
* University of Texas at Arlington, Library-Government Publications/Maps, 702 College, PO Box 19497, Arlington, TX 76019; 817-273-3000 ext. 4968. Comanche Peak Steam Electric Station. NUDOCS

* J.M. Hodges Learning Center, Wharton County Junior College, 911 Boling Highway, Wharton, TX 77488; 409-532-4560. South Texas Project. NUDOCS

Vermont
* Brooks Memorial Library, 224 Main Street, Brattleboro, VT 05301; 802-254-5290. Vermont Yankee Nuclear Power Station. NUDOCS

Virginia
* University of Virginia, Alderman Library, Special Collections Department, Charlottesville, VA 22903-2498. 804-924-3025. North Anna Power Station.

* Swem Library, College of William and Mary, Documents Department, Williamsburg, VA 23185; 804-221-3065. Surry Power Station, Surry Independent Spent Fuel Storage Installation.

Washington
* W.H. Abel Memorial Library, 125 Main Street South, Montesano, WA 98563; 206-249-4211. WPPSS Nuclear Project.

* Richland Public Library, 955 Northgate, Richland, WA 99352; 509-943-7446/7457. WPPSS Nuclear Project, Richland Low-Level Waste Disposal Facility.

Wisconsin
* University of Wisconsin, Cofrin Library, 2420 Nicolet Drive, Green Bay, WI 54311-7001; 414-465-2384/2304. Kewaunee Nuclear Power Plant. NUDOCS

* LaCrosse Public Library, 800 Main Street, LaCrosse, WI 54601; 608-789-7116. Lacross Boiling Water Reactor.

* Joseph Mann Library, 1516 16th Street, Two Rivers, WI 54241; 414-793-5585. Point Beach Nuclear Plant.

* Low-Level Nuclear Waste
Division of Low-Level Waste Management and Decommissioning
Office of Nuclear Material Safety and Safeguards
Nuclear Regulatory Commission (NRC)
Room 7F42, T-7F27
Washington, DC 20555   301-415-7297
This division directs the NCR's program for the licensing, inspection, and regulation to assure safety and quality associated with the management, treatment, and commercial disposal of low-level nuclear waste.

* Material Review and Licensing
Medical, Academic, and Commercial Use Safety Branch
Division of Industrial and Medical Nuclear Safety
Office of Nuclear Material Safety and Safeguards
Nuclear Regulatory Commission (NRC)
Room 8F28, T-8F5
Washington, DC 20555   301-415-7231
This Branch conducts health physics, radiation safety, and other appropriate analyses, licensing, and follow-up review of byproduct, medical, academic, industrial, and other source and special nuclear materials, including the preparation of environmental assessments and impact statements, determination of quality evaluations of sealed sources and devices, and licensing of exempt distribution of consumer products.

* National Codes and Standards
Library
Nuclear Regulatory Commission (NRC)
Washington, DC 20555-0001   301-415-5610
NRC regulations or guides may incorporate or refer to national codes and standards developed by professional societies, such as the American Society of Mechanical

Engineers. NRC has assembled a reference collection consisting of codes and standards in current use. The collection may be consulted by appointment at the NRC Library. Copying is restricted because most codes and standards are copyrighted.

* National Security
Office of the Deputy Assistant Secretary
Military Applications and Stockpile Support, DP-20
U.S. Department of Energy (DOE)
1000 Independence Ave. SW, Room 4B-012
Washington, DC 29585   202-586-4879
This office carries out DOE responsibilities to achieve national security objectives established by the President and assisting in reducing the global nuclear danger by planning for and maintaining a safe, secure, and reliable stockpile of nuclear weapons and associated materials, capabilities technologies in an environmentally sound and cost-effective manner.

* Nuclear Documents System
Information and Records Management Branch
Nuclear Regulatory Commission (NRC)
Washington, DC 20555-0001   301-415-7230
The Nuclear Documents System (NUDOCS) information system stores bibliographic data for more than one million reports, correspondence and other issuances related to the NRC's regulatory, licensing, safety, research, and enforcement programs, including such items as NUREG reports, Regulatory Guides, NRC Regulations, Generic Letters, Inspection Reports, NRC Bulletins, Environmental Reports, and Licensee Events Reports. This service is accessible from anywhere in the United States. Contact this office for information on access.

* Nuclear Documents System, Advanced Design (NUDOCS/AD)
Karen VanDucer
Information Resources Management (IRM)
T-6-C30
Nuclear Regulatory Commission (NRC)
Washington, DC 20555-0001   301-415-7223
NUDOCS/AD provides online identification of documents for retrieval from file centers or microfiche. Items identified in the system represent both public and non-public documents related to licensing, adjudicatory, regulation and inspection activities of the agency. The query system is available from 7:00 AM to 8:00 PM, Monday through Friday. The capacity is provided to download bibliographic information and abstracts or full text for selected documents. The system is used by agency staff and contractors and is available to public users (restricted to those documents that are publicly available) upon written request to the NRC.

* Nuclear Power Plant Performance
Nuclear Energy, Science and Technology
Office of Planning and Analysis
U.S. Department of Energy
19901 Germantown Rd.
Germantown, MD 20874   301-903-3773
This office performs economic analyses to compare the costs of various forms of electrical power generation to nuclear generation, as well as comparing the costs of different nuclear technologies. It also coordinates with the nuclear power industry in developing strategies to address the various impediments to the further development of the nuclear power option. The office maintains a current database on status, performance, and related information on all U.S. nuclear power plants as well as monitoring critical nuclear plant events including emergency situations on a real time basis for the Department of Energy.

* Nuclear Power Publications
Nuclear Energy Institute
1776 I St. NW
Suite 400
Washington, DC 20006-2495   202-739-8000
The Council on Energy Awareness can provide you with a number of publications and videos on nuclear energy. The following publications are available and cost up to $3.50.

Nuclear Energy: What Has It Done For Us Lately? BR0001
Safety in Motion: Transportation of Radioactive Materials BR0002
Nuclear Energy: How Do Nuclear Plants Work? BR0003

Energy

Contact the Council for information on price and availability. Members receive discounts on publications.

* Nuclear Regulatory Commission (NRC)

Office of Public Affairs
Nuclear Regulatory Commission
Washington, DC 20555-0001   301-415-8200

This office serves as a public inquiry point for information on the following:

- Licensing (including decommissioning) of commercial nuclear power plants and other nuclear facilities and the possession and use of nuclear materials for medical, industrial, educational, and research purposes.
- Inspections and investigations designed to assure that licensed activities are conducted in compliance with the agency's regulations and other requirements and enforcement of compliance.
- Search in the areas of safety, safeguards, and environmental assessment and the establishment of regulations, standards, and guidelines governing the use of nuclear facilities and materials.
- Safeguarding nuclear facilities and materials from diversion or sabotage.
- Implementation of agency responsibilities under the Nuclear Waste Policy Act of 1982 (high-level radioactive wastes), the Low-Level Radioactive Waste Policy Act of 1980, and the Uranium Mill Tailings Radiation Control Act of 1978.
- Packaging of radioactive materials for transport.

* Nuclear Regulatory Commission (NRC) Docket Breakdown

Public Document Room
Nuclear Regulatory Commission (NRC)
2120 L Street, NW   800-397-4209
Washington, DC 20555-0001   202-634-3273

Each organization engaged in a nuclear activity licensed and regulated by the Nuclear Regulatory Commission (NRC) is assigned a docket (case) number. Documents exchanged between NRC and the license applicant or licensee are filed together under that number. The docket files are open to the public in the Public Documents Room.

* Nuclear Regulatory Commission (NRC) Information Digest

Division of Budget and Analysis
Office of the Controller
Nuclear Regulatory Commission (NRC)   800-368-5642
Washington, DC 20037   301-415-8200

The *Information Digest* is a great starting source about both the Nuclear Regulatory Commission (NRC) and nuclear power in the U.S. The *Digest* discusses the role of the NRC as a regulatory agency as well as discussing the worldwide commercial nuclear energy sector. Nuclear material safety and waste disposal planning is also discussed. Appendices list a variety of statistics related to nuclear power. Call for your free copy.

* Nuclear Regulatory Commission (NRC) News Releases and Speeches

Public Affairs Office
Nuclear Regulatory Commission (NRC)
Washington, DC 20555-0001   301-415-8200

The NRC Public Affairs Office provides copies of NRC news releases and speeches in response to requests from news media. Members of the media may also be placed on a mailing list to receive copies of all NRC news releases and speeches. The Public Documents Room maintains a complete microform file of NRC and Atomic Energy Commission news releases and speeches. Contact the public affairs office for further information.

* Nuclear Regulatory Commission (NRC) Reports

Superintendent of Documents
Government Printing Office
Washington, DC 20402   202-512-1800

The NRC has several categories of reports available to the public, broken down by specific report code. General Reports, those not case specific, are prepared on a variety of areas related to nuclear power/regulation. Reference reports serve as sources for further information on NRC actions/proceedings. The following reports are available.

Annual Report (NUREG-1145)
Handbook of Acronyms and Initialisms (NUREG-0544)
NRC Organizational Charts (NUREG-0325)
Regulatory and Technical Reports (NUREG-0304)
Report to Congress on Abnormal Occurrences (NUREG-0090)
The List of Documents Made Publicly Available (NUREG-0540)
Staff Practices and Procedures (NUREG-0386)
Nuclear Regulatory Legislation (NUREG-0980)

* Nuclear Regulatory Commission (NRC) Rules and Regulations

Public Document Room
Nuclear Regulatory Commission (NRC)
2121 L St. NW   800-397-4209
Washington, DC 20037   301-634-3273

The NRC issues a loose-leaf publication entitled *U.S. NRC Rules and Regulations*. This four volume set contains all Rules and Regulations, Policy Statements, Memoranda of Understanding, a listing of Regulatory Guides, and brief summaries of selected General Notices issued by the NRC and other agencies that are published in the *Federal Register*. This publication available on a subscription basis from GPO, may be consulted at the Public Document Room and on microfiche at most local public document rooms.

* Nuclear Safety Policy

Office of Nuclear Safety Policy and Standards
Nuclear Safety Policy Division
U.S. Department of Energy
19901 Germantown Rd.
Germantown, MD 20874   301-903-3465

This division manages the development, review, issuance interpretation, and maintenance of the Department's nuclear safety policies. It interfaces with Federal and international agencies professional societies, and advisory committees on nuclear-safety related issues.

* Nuclear Waste Policy Act

Education and Information Division
Office of Civilian Radioactive Waste Management (OCRWM), RW-1
U.S. Department of Energy
1000 Independence Ave., SW, Room 5A-85
Washington, DC 20585   202-586-6842

This legislation established a national policy for safely storing, transporting, and disposing of spent nuclear fuel and high level radioactive waste. This act also established the Office of Civilian Radioactive Waste Management within the U.S. Department of Energy to develop and manage the waste management system. Under this act the U.S. may establish a permanent repository for nuclear waste at Yucca Mountain in Nevada. The act also provides for the construction of a Monitored Retrievable Storage Site (MRS) as a temporary storage place for spent fuel before being transported to permanent sites. The OCRWM can provide you with a background information package on the NWPA and other aspects of nuclear waste transport and storage.

* Office of Civilian Radioactive Waste Management (OCRWM) Homepage

Office of Civilian Radioactive Waste Management (OCRWM)
National Information Center
Department of Energy (DOE)
600 Maryland Ave. SW, Suite 760   800-225-6972
Washington, DC 20024   202-488-6720
                                 Internet: http://www.rw.doe.gov

The Office of Civilian Radioactive Waste Management (OCRWM) Home Page offers instant access 24 hours a day to a range of OCRWM program information and services, including current activities, resource materials, a publications ordering system, and an electronic mailbox for users to submit suggestions about the availability of information on the home page.

* Open and Closed Meetings of the NRC

Office of the Secretary
Nuclear Regulatory Commission (NRC), 16H1
Washington, DC 20555-0001   301-415-1661

The public is welcome to observe all Commission meetings, unless a meeting is closed because it involves one or more of the "exempted" subjects described in NRC Regulations. "Exempted" subjects usually involve classified information, investigations, enforcement actions, internal rules and practices, or personnel matters. Advance notices of Commission meetings are published in the *Federal Register*, posted in the Public Document Room, and mailed to those on a regular list. Contact the Office of the Secretary to be added to the list. Current information on scheduled Commission meetings may be obtained by calling the recorded message number: 301-415-1292. Transcripts are made of Commission meetings. These are available in the Public Document Room for inspection or duplication.

* OpenNet

David Henderson
Office of Scientific and Technical Information
U.S. Department of Energy (DOE)   423-576-3615
P.O. Box 62   Fax: 423-576-2865
Oak Ridge, TN 37831   Internet: http://www.doe.gov

OpenNet provides access to thousands of previously classified documents. The online index will guide users through documents covering topics such as human radiation experiments, nuclear testing, radiation releases, and historical records. The bibliographic database will contain references for all publicly releasable documents declassified by DOE after October 1, 1994. In addition it gives information on more than 265,000 documents from collections at DOE facilities. This database will be continuously updated to include documents as they are released. The system also provides the DOE site location and person to contact to obtain access to the referenced documents.

* Operating Statistics on Nuclear Plants

Licensed Operating Reactors
Superintendent of Documents
Government Printing Office
Washington, DC 20402   202-512-1800

Also referred to as the "Gray Book," *Monthly Operating Units Status Reports* provides data on the operation of nuclear units as timely and accurately as possible. It contains three sections: highlights and statistics for commercial operating units, detailed information on each unit, and an appendix for miscellaneous information such as spent fuel storage capabilities. Order # 752-035-00000-8, $85.00 per year.

* Operations Analysis

Nuclear Operations Analysis Center (NOAC)
Nuclear Regulatory Commission (NRC)
P .O. Box 2009
Oak Ridge National Laboratory
Oak Ridge, TN 37831-8065   615-574-0394

The Nuclear Operations Analysis Center performs analysis tasks, as well as information-gathering activities, for the Nuclear Regulatory Commission. NOAC conducts a number of tasks related to the analysis of nuclear power experience, and develops and manages databases used for these analyses. These databases contain diverse types of information on nuclear power reactors about routine and off-normal operation, including Licensee Event Reports. NOAC publishes "Nuclear Safety", a peer-related technical journal covering significant issues in the field of nuclear safety. Contact this office to obtain a copy.

* Peaceful Uses of Nuclear Technology

Office of Nuclear Technology and Safeguards
Bureau of Oceans and International Environmental
 and Scientific Affairs
U.S. Department of State
2201 C St., NW, Room 7828
Washington, DC 20520   202-647-3310

Concerned with peaceful uses of nuclear power, such as nuclear energy, this office negotiates cooperative agreements with other countries for the safe functioning of nuclear reactors, and also becomes involved where nuclear reactor accidents occur.

* Power Plant Emissions

Radioactive Emissions Standards
Office of Radiation Programs
Environmental Protection Agency (EPA)
401 M St., SW, Room NE108
Washington DC 20460   202-233-9320

The Environmental Protection Agency (EPA), with a number of other federal agencies, protects the public from unnecessary exposure to ionizing radiation. EPA's major responsibilities are to set radioactive emissions standards and exposure limits, assess new technology, and monitor radiation in the environment in four areas: radiation from nuclear accidents, radon emissions, land disposal of radioactive waste, and radiation in groundwater and drinking water. The EPA fulfills these responsibilities by setting emissions standards for nuclear power plants, and for radionuclides in drinking water and in the air. EPA also prescribes work practices to reduce emissions of radon from underground uranium mines, develops radioactive waste disposal standards, and issues guidance to limit occupational exposure.

* Pre-Notification Analysis Support System (PASS)

Judy Holm
Office of Transportation Emergency Management and
 Analytic Services
Office of Environmental Management, EM-26
U.S. Department of Energy (DOE)
1000 Independence Ave. SW
Washington, DC 20585   301-427-1643

For additional information:
Edward Liebow
Battelle Seattle Research Center
400 NE 41st St.
Seattle, WA 98105   206-528-3311
        Internet URL: http://131.167.239.5:8080/es_home/gis/gis/htm

The Pre-Notification Analysis Support System (PASS) consists of locations for all Indian Reservations in the lower 48 states; all Department of Energy facilities that ship or receive radiological materials; and all highway, rail and barge routes over which the materials could be shipped. There are two searchable databases. One database includes names, mailing addresses, and telephone numbers for tribal and state executives for all 50 states. The second database provides information on federal funding distributed to all state and tribal executives by agency and recipient for transportation emergency preparedness assistance dating back to fiscal year 1990.

* Public Participation in Nuclear Licensing

Atomic Safety and Licensing Board Panel
Nuclear Regulatory Commission (NRC)
3E19, T-3F23
Washington, DC 20555-0001   301-415-7450

As part of the licensing process, a mandatory public hearing is carried out by a three-member Atomic Safety and Licensing Board, which then makes an initial decision as to whether a construction permit should be granted. A notice of a public hearing is published in the *Federal Register* and in local newspapers, giving 30 days for members of the public to petition to intervene in the proceeding.

* Radiation in Vicinity of Reactors

Government Printing Office
Superintendent of Documents
Washington, DC 20402   202-512-1800

NRC TLD is a direct radiation monitoring network quarterly publication provides the status and results of the NRC thermoluminescent dosimeter (TLD) direct radiation monitoring. It presents the radiation levels measured in the vicinity of NRC licensed facility sites throughout the country. Stock # 752-014-00000-1, $20 yearly.

* Radioactive Waste Management

National Technical Information Service (NTIS)
5285 Port Royal Rd.
Springfield, VA 22161   703-487-4650

Radioactive Waste Management is a monthly publication that provides digests of current information available on the topics of spent fuel transport and storage, radioactive effluents from nuclear facilities, techniques of processing radioactive waste, remedial actions and environmental aspects of radioactive waste management. Those wishing to receive this publication should request document number PB95-902904, $19.50 single copy price. For a yearly subscription, order #PB95-902900, $195.00.

* Radioactive Waste Management Bulletin

U.S. Department of Energy
Office of Civilian Radioactive Waste Management (OCRWM)
National Information Services Center
600 Maryland Ave., Suite 760   800-225-6972
Washington, DC 20024   202-586-2835

The *OCRWM Bulletin*, a monthly publication, provides information about OCRWM program activities, milestones, events, publications, and documents to assist interested individuals in keeping abreast of the radioactive waste management program.

* Radiological Emergencies

Office of Emergency Response DP-23
U.S. Department of Energy (DOE)
19901 Germantown Rd., Room B-230
Germantown, MD 20874   301-903-3558

This office administers and directs the programs of DOE's emergency response capability to ensure availability and viability to respond to nuclear and radiological emergencies within the United States and abroad. This capability includes seven major radiological emergency response assets/capabilities. It provides overall management and direction for the development and maintenance of Defense Programs Emergency Management System at all Defense Programs facilities.

* Reactor Construction Surveillance

Division Of Reactor Controls and Human Factors
Office of Nuclear Reactor Regulation
Nuclear Regulatory Commission (NRC)
Room 10H1, O-10H5
Washington, DC 20555   301-415-1004

This Division develops and implements a program for assuring quality and reliability of reactor license facilities design, fabrication, construction, testing, and operation.

* Reactor Inventory in the U.S.

Nuclear Energy, Science and Technology
U.S. Department of Energy
19901 Germantown Rd.
Germantown, MD 20874   301-903-4404

Nuclear Reactors Built, Being Built or Planned is a survey of American nuclear reactors in operation, under construction or planned. Contact this office for a copy. This publication is handy reference for information on reactors currently in operation.

* Reactor Programs

Nuclear Energy, Science and Technology
Office of Reactor Programs
U.S. Department of Energy
19901 Germantown Rd.
Germantown, MD 20874   301-903-3218

This office is responsible for the technical direction and management of the advanced liquid metal reactor division and the modular high temperature gas reactor (HTGR) R&D programs. Also included in the responsibilities of this office is the R&D initiative on waste management improvements through actinnide recycle, coordination with the New Production Reactor for common HTGR development tasks, licensing interactions with industry and technology transfer.

* Reactor Safeguards Advisory Committee

Advisory Committee on Reactor Safeguards (ACRS)
Nuclear Regulatory Commission (NRC)
Room 2E7, T-2E26
Washington, DC 20555   301-415-7360

This statutory body of 15 scientists and engineers reviews and makes recommendations to the Commission on all applications to build or operate nuclear power reactors and on related nuclear safety matters. The ACRS provides advice to the Commission on potential hazards of proposed safety standards. The ACRS reviews requests for pre-application site and standard plant approvals, for each application for a construction permit or an operating license for power reactors, and for applications for licenses to construct or operate test reactors.

* Reactor Safety Research

Division of Systems Research Technology
Office of Nuclear Regulatory Research

Nuclear Regulatory Commission (NRC), Room 10E47, T-10G6
Washington, DC 20555   301-415-5741

This Division plans, develops, and directs comprehensive safety research programs for predicting nuclear reactor and plant systems behavior under normal, accident, and severe accident conditions. Responsibilities include evaluating challenges to containments, development of accident source terms, performance and review of probable risk assessments, and accident sequence analysis. Contact this office for more information on the research.

* Reactors and National Security

Office of Security Affairs
U.S. Department of Energy
1000 Independence Ave., SW, Room 4H-093
Washington, DC 20585   202-586-6591

To meet national security requirements, this office acquires and constructs new production reactors, along with developing a strategy to consider their safety, quality, environmental, and performance. Contact this office for further information.

* Reactor Training Center

NRC Technical Training Center
Nuclear Regulatory Commission (NRC)
Osborne Office Center
Chattanooga, TN 37411   423-855-6500

The NRC Technical Training Center (TTC) was established to develop and implement policy and programs for technical training of NCR staff. The TTC provides technical training in broad areas of reactor technology and specialized technical training.

* Reduction, Utilization of Wastes

Office of Waste Reduction Technologies, EE-22
U.S. Department of Energy (DOE)
1000 Independence Ave. SW, Room 5F-035
Washington, DC 20585   202-586-6750

This office develops and maintains a balanced program of research and development on generic technologies enhancing the reduction or utilization of wastes, the application of solar to industrial processes and the delivery of industrial energy with wide application throughout industry and agriculture. The program includes activities in waste heat recovery, improved thermal energy management, cogeneration systems, and waste products utilization and reduction, including municipal solid wastes and waste stream detoxification. The office also performs analyses to identify future technological opportunities and impediments to deployment of proven energy-efficient technologies.

* Regulation Dockets

Superintendent of Documents
Government Printing Office
Washington, DC 20402   202-512-1800

Title List of Documents Made Publicly Available contains descriptions of the information received and generated by the Nuclear Regulatory Commission. The information includes docketed material associated with civilian nuclear power plants and material received and generated by the Commission pertinent to its role as a regulatory agency. "Docketed" refers to the system by which the Commission maintains its regulatory records. A monthly subscription price is available for $67 per year, order #752-025-00000-2.

* Regulation Hotline

Nuclear Regulatory Commission   800-368-5642
Washington, DC 20555-0001   301-415-1292

A telephone recording service has also been established to announce upcoming meetings related to the waste management program of the NRC.

* Regulation Public Documents

Nuclear Regulatory Commission (NRC)
Public Documents Room
2120 L. Street, NW   800-397-4209
Washington, DC 20037   202-634-3273

The Public Document Room maintains over 2 million agency documents in hard copy and microfiche. The majority of these documents relate to the licensing and inspection of nuclear facilities and to the use, transport and disposal of nuclear materials. There is generally about a two week processing delay before documents are available in the PDR. The PDR files are open for public use, and reference librarians assist on-site patrons in their use. The reference staff also respond to telephone and letter requests. The PDR online catalog contains citations to public documents received after October 1978, and the computer searches are free of charge. In addition, the Commission has approximately 100 local Public Document Rooms around the country. Call the office above for information on the locations.

* Regulatory and Technical Reports

Government Printing Office (GPO)
Superintendent of Documents
Washington, DC 20402   202-512-1800

Regulatory and Technical Reports (NUREG 0304) is a quarterly compilation, cumulated annually with the fourth quarter, of regulatory and technical reports and conference proceedings issued by the NRC staff and contractors. GPO ordering information: Order #752-018-00000-6, $8.00.

* Regulatory Bulletins

Public Document Room
Nuclear Regulatory Commission (NRC)   800-397-4209
Washington, DC 20555-0001   202-634-3273

Generic Letters, Bulletins, and *Information Notices* are written NRC notifications sent to groups of licensees that identify specific problems, developments, or other matters of interest of which licensees should be aware or for which the NRC is calling for or recommending specific steps be taken by the licensees. These technical documents are placed in the Public Document Room, and can be automatically sent to interested groups or organizations who are on the mailing list.

* Regulatory Enforcement

Office of Enforcement, O-745
Nuclear Regulatory Commission (NRC)
Washington, DC 20402   301-415-2741

This office develops policies and programs for enforcement of NRC requirements. It manages major enforcement actions and assesses the effectiveness and uniformity of enforcement actions taken by the regional offices. Enforcement powers include notices of violation, fines, and orders for license modification, suspension, or revocation.

* Regulatory Guides

Distribution and Mail Service
Nuclear Regulatory Commission
Washington, DC 20555-0001

Superintendent of Documents
Government Printing Office   202-512-1800
Washington, DC 20402   Fax: 202-512-2250

Nuclear Regulatory Commission (NRC) regulatory guides describe methods acceptable to the NRC staff of implementing specific parts of the Commission's regulations and, in some cases, describe techniques used by the staff in evaluating specific problems or postulated accidents. Guides also may advise applicants regarding information the NRC staff needs in reviewing applications for permits and licenses. Comments on the guides are encouraged. The following guides are currently issued. *Division 1: Power Reactor Guides; Division 2: Research and Test Reactor Guides; Division 3: Fuels and Materials Facilities Guides; Division 4: Environmental and Siting Guides; Division 5: Materials and Plant Protection Guides; Division 6: Product Guides; Division 7: Transportation Guides; Division 8: Occupational Health Guides; Division 9: Antitrust and Financial Review Guides; Division 10: General Guides.* Any member of the public may request a free copy of a specific draft guide when it is announced in the Federal Register, or may be placed on a mailing list to receive future drafts by writing to the distribution and mail services. Active guides may also be consulted at GPO Depository Libraries, at the NRC Public Document Room, and in microfiche at most local public document rooms.

* Regulatory Library

Nuclear Regulatory Commission (NRC)
11545 Rockville Pike
Bethesda, MD 20852   301-415-5610

The Nuclear Regulatory Commission's library is open to the public, and its focus is on nuclear energy. The library does not make loans or allow photocopying of documents, but the public is free to come in and use the facilities on site. It is open M-F from 8:00 to 4:00. Reference staff are available to assist you.

* Regulatory Publications

Superintendent of Documents
Government Printing Office
Washington, DC 20402   202-512-1800

Nuclear Regulatory Commission Issuances is a monthly publication containing opinions, decisions, denials, memorandum, and orders of the Commission, the Atomic Safety and Licensing Appeal Board, the Atomic Safety and Licensing Board, and the Administrative Law Judge. A subscription is available for $54 per year ($3.00 per copy). Semiannual and Quarterly indexes are also available. Order #752-015-00000-7.

* Regulatory Research

Office of Nuclear Regulatory Research
Nuclear Regulatory Commission (NRC)
Room 10F1, T-10F12
Washington, DC 20555-0001   301-415-6802

The Nuclear Regulatory Commission (NRC) is mandated by law to conduct an extensive confirmatory research program in the areas of safety, safeguards, and environmental assessment. In addition, the agency establishes regulations, standards, and guidelines governing the various licensed uses of nuclear facilities and materials.

* Repository for Nuclear Waste

Yucca Mountain Information Office
4101 Meadows Lane
Las Vegas, NV 89107   702-295-1312

The Nuclear Waste Policy Amendments Act of 1987 named Yucca Mountain, Nevada as the only candidate site to be characterized for a repository. Contact this U.S. Department of Energy (DOE) office for further information and for a copy of *DOE's Yucca Mountain Studies,* which explains basic nuclear waste disposal policy in layman's terms and also describes current research being done on the Yucca Mountain site.

* Safeguards

Division of Safeguards and Transportation
Office of Nuclear Material Safety and Safeguards
Nuclear Regulatory Commission (NRC)
Room 8D41, T-8A23
Washington, DC 20555-0001   301-415-7358

This Division develops overall agency safeguards policy and conducts safeguards licensing, inspection, and regulatory functions applicable to nuclear materials, nonreactor facilities, transportation of nuclear materials, and nonreactor inspection activities.

* Safeguards Inspection

Division of Reactor Inspection and Safeguards
Office of Nuclear Reactor Regulation
Nuclear Regulatory Commission (NRC)
Room 12E1, O-12E4
Washington, DC 20555-0001   301-415-7800

This Division performs special reactor inspection, vendor inspections, reactor safeguards licensing, and regulatory effectiveness reviews, and quality assurance reviews for reactors. This Division also performs inspections in response to allegations and reports of defective and substandard components and equipment in nuclear service or being offered for nuclear service.

* Safety Review for Nuclear Plants

Director of Projects
Office of Nuclear Reactor Regulations
Nuclear Regulatory Commission (NRC)
Room 12D9, O-12G18
Washington, DC 20555   301-415-1284

An applicant for a nuclear plant construction permit lays out the proposed nuclear plant design in *Preliminary Safety Analysis Report* (PSAR). The Nuclear Regulatory Commission (NRC) staff examines the applicant's PSAR to determine whether the plant design is safe and consistent with NRC rules and regulations; whether valid methods of calculation were employed and accurately performed; and whether the applicant has conducted its analysis and evaluation in sufficient depth and breadth to support staff approval as to assured adequate levels of safety.

* Savannah River Operations Office

Office of External Affairs
U.S. Department of Energy
PO Box A
Aiken, SC 29802   803-725-2889

As an element of the U.S. Department of Energy (DOE) nuclear weapons complex, the Savannah River Operations Office carries out the following activities: production of special nuclear materials, management of nuclear waste production of naval fuel materials, and the protection and management of environmental resources.

* Speakers, Nuclear Waste

Yucca Mountain Project Office
U.S. Department of Energy
101 Convention Center
Suite P-105
Las Vegas, NV 89109   702-794-7759

Members of the Office of Civilian Radioactive Waste Management (OCRWM) program staff are available to speak to various groups interested in the radioactive waste management program. Qualified speakers can discuss the OCRWM program in general or address specific topics of special interest to a particular organization. To request a speaker from the Speakers' Bureau in the Nevada Project Office, contact the office above.

* Spent Fuel Options

Nuclear Energy Institute
1776 I St., NW, Suite 400
Washington, DC 20006-02495   202-739-8000

The Nuclear Energy Institute can provide you with information on the disposal of spent nuclear fuel as well as facts on other aspects of the nuclear power industry. The Energy Products Research Institute, or EPRI (415-855-2788), a utility operated research institute, may also be able to provide you with technical information concerning ongoing research in this area.

* Standards for Nuclear Safety

Division of Engineering Technology
Office of Nuclear Regulatory Research
Nuclear Regulatory Commission (NRC)
Room 10 E7, T-10 D20
Washington, DC 20555-0001   301-415-3340

This Division plans, develops, and directs comprehensive research programs and standards development for nuclear safety in the design, qualification, construction, inspection, testing, operation, and decommissioning of nuclear power plants. This office maintains liaison and provides technical input to other Federal agencies, the American National Standards Institute, professional societies, and international organizations.

* State Nuclear Programs

State Programs
Office of Governmental and Public Affairs
Nuclear Regulatory Commission (NRC)
Washington, DC 20555-0001   301-415-3340

This office plans and directs the Nuclear Regulatory Commission's (NRC) program of cooperation and liaison with States, local governments, interstate and Indian Tribe organizations. They also develop and direct administrative and contractual programs for coordinating and integrating Federal and State regulatory activities.

* Supply and Demand:
Nuclear and Alternative Fuel

Nuclear and Alternate Fuels Division
Coal, Nuclear, Electric and Alternate Fuels
Energy Information Administration, EI-50
U.S. Department of Energy
1000 Independence Ave. NW, Room 6070
Washington, DC 20585   202-426-1200

The office prepares, analyzes, and projects the availability, production, cost, processing, transportation, and distribution of nuclear and alternate energy sources, including solar, wind, and wood. Contact this office for more information and publications.

* Technical Specifications Plus Bulletin Board System (TS-BBS)

Tom Dunning
Nuclear Regulatory Research
Mail Stop 0-14-D1   301-415-1189
Nuclear Regulatory Commission (NRC)   Data: 800-679-5784
Washington, DC 20555-0001   301-415-1778

This bulletin board provides free online access to Operation Reactor Technical Specifications to support the Nuclear Regulatory Commission's Technical Specifications Improvement Program. Also available on this system are bulletins, circulars, Administrative letters, generic communications, NRC Inspection Manual, Information Notices, and Daily Event Reports. This information is updated daily and dial in capacity is provided 24 hours a day. TS-BBS is also available via NTIS Fedworld Gateway #63 at 703-321-8020.

* Tritium Supply and Recycling

Office of Complex Reconfigurations, DP-25
U.S. Department of Energy (DOE)
1000 Independence Ave. SW, Room 4B-014
Washington, DC 20585   202-586-0838

This office directs the preparation of the Tritium Supply and Recycling Programmatic Environmental Impact Statement. It prepares the recommendations to be included in the Record of Decision (ROD) in which the Secretary of Energy will announce the site and/or technology selected for the future tritium production and recycle facilities. It plans for the implementation of the ROD and prepares the site-specific Environmental Impact Statement regarding tritium production and recycle facilities which will allow DOE to construct a new facility or purchase irradiation services at an existing reactor. The office provides support to the Stockpile Stewardship and Management Programmatic Environmental Impact Statement.

* TVA Nuclear Power Plants

Nuclear Power
Tennessee Valley Authority (TVA)
1101 Market St., LP6A
Chattanooga, TN 37402-2801   423-751-8689

TVA has two licensed nuclear plants with a total of five reactors in operation. Two additional plants, with a total of four reactors, are under construction. The division's responsibilities include demonstrating safe and reliable performance, making sure that operating plants to meet or exceed industry standards of excellence, increasing productivity and reliability of nuclear units to meet or exceed the industry average, and maintaining a competitive human resources program.

* Uranium Enrichment

Nuclear Energy
Office of Uranium Enrichment
U.S. Department of Energy
19901 Germantown Rd.
Germantown, MD 20874   301-903-5922

This office ensures that requirements for uranium enrichment services meet domestic, foreign and U.S. government needs in the most economical, reliable, safe, secure and environmentally acceptable manner.

* Uranium Mine Clean Up

Uranium Mill Tailings Remedial Action Project Office
Albuquerque Operations Office
U.S. Department of Energy
P.O. Box 5400
Albuquerque, NM 87185-5400   505-845-6307

This office performs clean-up activities at 24 inactive uranium mill tailings sites and associated vicinity properties in 11 States and the Navajo Indian Reservation. After clean-up is completed, the sites will be owned by DOE and licensed by the Nuclear Regulatory Commission. You can get further information on U.S. Dept. of Energy nuclear waste management programs from the above office.

* Uranium Mining and the Environment

Grand Junction Projects Office (GJPO)
U.S. Department of Energy
P.O. Box 2567
Grand Junction, CO 81502   303-242-8621

This office assesses the environmental effects of uranium mining and milling operations, and manages uranium leases on lands under DOE control. This office also provides geoscientific support in characterizing sites under consideration as repositories under DOE's Civilian Radioactive Waste Management Program. It also participates in international technical exchanges under several programs administered by the Organization for Economic Cooperation and Development's Nuclear Energy Agency and the International Atomic Energy Agency. Contact this office for further information on DOE nuclear waste management programs.

* Waste Advisory Committee

Advisory Committee on Nuclear Waste
Nuclear Regulatory Commission (NRC)
Room 2E2, T-2E26
Washington, DC 20555-0001   301-415-7360

The Advisory Committee on Nuclear Waste is an independent committee established by the Commission to provide it with advice and recommendations concerning all aspects of nuclear waste management for which the NRC has responsibility. Its primary focus is on waste disposal, but its work also includes other aspects of waste management, such as the handling, processing, transportation, storage, and safeguarding of nuclear wastes, including spent fuel, nuclear wastes mixed with other hazardous substances, and uranium mill tailings.

* Waste Clean Up

Office of Waste Reduction Technology
Nuclear Energy
1000 Independence Ave., SW, Room E435
Washington, DC 20585   202-586-6759

This office provides plans, develops, and executes DOE programs for civilian nuclear waste treatment and low-level waste management. It also works to clean up and decommission both contaminated DOE and legislatively-authorized non-Government facilities and sites. Beneficial uses of nuclear waste byproducts are also studied. Further information on U.S. Department of Energy nuclear waste management programs can be obtained from the above office.

* Waste Management

National Information Center
Office of Civilian Radioactive Waste Management (OCRWM)
U.S. Department of Energy
600 Maryland Ave. SW, Suite 760   800-225-NPWA
Washington, DC 20585   202-488-6720

The *Publications Catalog, Office of Civilian Radioactive Waste Management*, is a detailed summary of office reports and studies on nuclear waste management. This catalog provides citations of selected technical and public information on nuclear waste management. The free brochure, *Managing the Nation's Nuclear Waste*, is also available from this office.

* Waste Management Factsheets

U.S. Department of Energy
Office of Civilian Radioactive Waste Management (OCRWM)
Office of External Relations and Policy
National Information Center
600 Maryland Ave. SW, Suite 760   800-225-6972
Washington, DC 20042   202-488-6720

The Office of Civilian Radioactive Waste Management (OCRWM) has published factsheets that describe the overall OCRWM program, the repository program, the monitored retrievable storage (MRS) system and the transportation program. Call or write for a package.

* Waste Management Information System

Lisa Wachter
Waste Management Information System
U.S. Department of Energy (DOE)
P.O. Box 2003
Mail Stop 7606
Oak Ridge, TN 37831-7606   423-435-2381

The Waste Management Information System (WMIS) is a dynamic system developed as a management and planning tool. The system provides an accurate and complete resource for information pertaining to waste streams and treatment, storage, and disposal facilities throughout the DOE complex. WMIS data exists in two major areas. Treatment, Storage, and Disposal (T/S/D) Capabilities--a compilation of DOE facilities, both existing and planned, for the treatment, storage and disposal of waste. Storage capabilities, capacities, and information on types of acceptable feedstocks are included. Treatment and disposal methodologies are presented with operating parameters and restrictions. The Waste Profiles--data on the various waste streams that have been identified for waste management activities. Data includes generation rates, quantities, characterization, point of contact information, and applicable waste management option. This data is available free of charge by contacting the office listed above.

* Waste Management Publications

U.S. Department of Energy
Office of Civilian Radioactive Waste Management (OCRWM)
Office of External Relations and Policy
National Information Center
600 Maryland Ave. SW, Suite 760   800-225-6972
Washington, DC 20042   202-488-6720

The Office of Civilian Radioactive Waste Management (OCRWM) publications brochure contains descriptions of printed documents on the topic of high-level radioactive waste management that are of interest to Federal, State and local government officials and staff; affected Indian Tribes; advisory groups; special interest groups; the media; information science professionals; and students and the general public.

* Weekly Information Report

Superintendent of Documents
Government Printing Office
710 N. Capitol St.   202-512-1800
Washington, DC 20402   Fax: 202-512-2250
                    TDD: 202-512-2489

Issued weekly, this report from the Nuclear Regulatory Commission Office of the Executive Director for Operations summarizes items of interest and actions taken by the Commission's Offices. Other items of interest include a section on items approved by the Commission, a status report of Freedom of Information Act requests, a list of Request for Proposals issued, contracts awarded and closed out, and a status report from the Three Mile Island Program. Sold as a subscription only for $145.00 Stock #752-005-00000-1.

Weather and Maps
Climate and Forecasts

* *See also Science and Technology; Geology and Earth Science Chapter*
* *See also Current Events and Homework Chapter*

The National Weather Service is a well-known federal institution but the general public probably is unaware of the Landslide Information Center and other government offices which track and analyze climate changes. General information and technical materials on other "Acts of God" such as volcano eruptions and earthquakes are identified in the Science and Technology Chapter. Many agencies are using the most sophisticated methods for cartography from the National Archives to the National Air and Space Administration. By and large the primary distributor of all sorts of maps is the U.S. Geological Survey.

* Acid Rain, Aerosols, and Climate Impact

Environmental Research Laboratory
National Oceanic and Atmospheric Administration
U.S. Department of Commerce
8060 13th St.
Silver Spring, MD 20910   301-427-7684

The Air Resources Laboratory (ARL) performs weather research to understand and predict human influences on the environment, especially those involving atmospheric transport and dispersion of pollutants such as acid rain and ozone. The ARL also monitors and interprets trends in natural and man-made substances, such as CO_425, halocarbons, aerosols, and ozone which can potentially modify the climate. In addition, ARL studies solar radiation for its role in climate change. An annual report is available, which describes in more detail the current research being undertaken.

* Aeronomy Research

Earth's Atmosphere Research
Environmental Research Laboratories
National Oceanic and Atmospheric Administration
U.S. Department of Commerce
325 Broadway
Boulder, CO 80303   303-497-6286

The Aeronomy Laboratory studies the physical and chemical processes of the Earth's atmosphere to advance our capability for monitoring, predicting, and controlling these processes. Recent emphasis is on the greenhouse effect, stratospheric and tropospheric ozone.

* Air Quality and Atmospheric Research

Environmental Sciences Group
Environmental Research Laboratories
National Oceanic and Atmospheric Administration
U.S. Department of Commerce
325 Broadway
Boulder, CO 80303   303-497-6286

The Environmental Sciences Group includes the Climate Research Program (studies of short- and long-term climate change), the Weather Research Program (research to improve short-range weather predictions and warning, especially regarding storm systems and flash floods), the Weather Modification Program (evaluations of data from various states' weather modification programs), and the Program for Regional Observing and Forecasting Services (transfer of technology such as interactive computer workstations to operational agencies like the National Weather Service). Contact the Public Affairs Office for information.

* Atmospheric Sciences Central Library

Central Library
National Oceanic and Atmospheric Administration
U.S. Department of Commerce
6009 Executive Blvd.
Rockville, MD 20852   301-443-8330

The library maintains a collection of books, journals, technical reports, microfiche, and compact discs to support research in the atmospheric sciences, oceanography, geophysics, and related disciplines. The library uses a wide array of products and services to meet its clientele's needs. Computers provide for information retrieval and bibliographic control of materials. Online services include access to hundreds of databases, which are available through systems such as Dialog, BRS, NEXIS, and LEXIS. The library's facilities and collection are available for the general public to use on-site during normal business hours.

* Beaches and Resort Weather Forecasts

Key West, FL	305-296-2011
Myrtle Beach, SC	803-744-3207
Nags Head, NC	919-995-5610
Ocean City, MD	410-289-3223
Orlando, FL	305-851-7510
Rehoboth, DE	302-856-7633
St Petersburg/Tampa, FL	813-645-2506
Virginia Beach, VA	804-853-3013

* Climate Change

Global Change Division
Environmental Protection Agency (EPA)
401 M St., SW
Washington, DC 20460   202-260-8825

This office can provide you with information regarding the effects of global climate change on the U.S. A report to Congress and various articles on the greenhouse effect are available, as well as information on EPA's Sea Level Rise project and the relationship between the changing climate and the coast.

* Climates of the World

National Oceanic and Atmospheric Administration
National Climatic Data Center
Federal Building   704-259-0682
Asheville, NC 28801-2696   704-CLI-MATE

This publication contains: (1) Brief discussions of the principal features of climate of all the continents; (2) Worldwide annual average precipitation (in.), map, and January and July average precipitation (in.) seasonal average maximum/minimum temperatures, and annual extremes of temperature for selected world locations.

* Climatic Information

National Climatic Data Center (NCDC)
National Environmental Satellite, Data and Information Service
U.S. Department of Commerce
Federal Building   704-CLI-MATE
Asheville, NC 28801-2696   704-259-0682

The National Climatic Data Center compiles and distributes global historical climate information. It is the collection center for all United States weather records and the world's largest climate data center. Many millions of weather facts are stored in NCDC's computer banks, available for quick response. Nearly one-third of the inquiries received are from attorneys seeking to establish circumstances surrounding legal events. Simple questions can be answered on the phone; however, those requests which need detailed digging may carry a research charge. Much data is available free or by fee in printed form.

* CLIVUE-CD-ROM

National Climatic Data Center   704-271-4800
Federal Building   Fax: 704-271-4876
Asheville, NC 28801-2733   Internet Access: orders@ncdc.noaa.gov

This CD-ROM was developed in support of a museum exhibit which traveled across the U.S. It contains 1,500-station subset of nearly 8,000 U.S. daily cooperative stations. The user selects a date/area of the U.S. and the CD database is queried for stations within the specified domain having data. Then, the system displays daily maximum/minimum temperatures, precipitation, and snowfall for the site. Graphs showing 7 years, 21 years, and the full period of record are available. The cost is $50.

* Cumulative Climatic Data Summaries

National Climatic Data Center
National Environmental Satellite, Data and Information Service
National Oceanic and Atmospheric Administration
U.S. Department of Commerce
Federal Building
Asheville, NC 28801   704-259-0682

Local Climatological Data is a monthly and annual publication for each of approximately 290 National Weather Service stations. Each issue includes daily and monthly temperatures, dew point temperatures, heating and cooling degree days, weather, precipitation, snowfall, pressure, wind, sunshine, and sky cover. Three-hourly weather observations and hourly precipitation data are also presented for most stations. *Climatological Data* is a monthly and annual publication issued for each state containing much the same information. Contact this office for current prices.

* Cyclones and Other Oceanographic Forecasts

National Oceanographic Data Center
National Oceanic and Atmospheric Administration
Universal Building Room 412
Washington, DC 20235   202-673-5549

The Mariners Weather Log is a unique source of information on marine weather and climate and their effects on operations at sea. Published quarterly by the National Oceanographic Data Center, the *Mariners Weather Log* provides comprehensive coverage of major storms of the North Atlantic and North Pacific, reports and annual summaries on tropical cyclones, information on the National Weather Service's Marine Observation Program, selected shipboard gale and wave observations, and general articles about weather and climate, hazards and safety precautions, and related marine lore. An annual subscription is available for $6 from the Superintendent of Documents, Government Printing Office, Washington, DC 20402; 202-512-1800.

* Environmental Research Publications

Environmental Research Laboratories
National Oceanic and Atmospheric Administration (NOAA)
U.S. Department of Commerce
325 Broadway
Boulder, CO 80303   303-497-6286

As the research arm of the National Oceanic and Atmospheric Administration (NOAA), the Environmental Research Laboratories support the present responsibilities and the development of future services of NOAA. Programs include investigation of ocean processes and their interactions with the atmosphere; studies of the ocean environment as it is affected by waste disposal and development of energy and food resources; atmosphere and ocean research on weather and climate change; and much, much more. *Environmental Research Laboratories Publication Abstracts* lists all scientific and technical papers and reports available in a given year, as well as ordering information. The *Abstracts* are arranged alphabetically by Laboratory, and an author index is included.

* Environmental Satellite Systems

National Environmental Satellite,
 Data And Information Service (NESDIS)
National Oceanic and Atmospheric Administration
U.S. Department of Commerce
Federal Office Bldg. 4
Washington, DC 20233   202-763-4690

The National Environmental Satellite, Data and Information Service manages the nation's civil earth observing satellite systems for meteorology and oceanography. NESDIS operates low-altitude polar-orbiting satellites and high-altitude geostationary satellites which together monitor weather and surface conditions over the entire globe each day, providing advance warning of hurricanes, flash floods, and other severe weather conditions. Its satellites play an increasingly important role in monitoring global climate changes and such related phenomena as changes in ozone distribution over the Earth, plus changes in the marine environment. Contact this office for more information regarding satellite and data topics.

* Federal Emergency Management

Federal Emergency Management Agency (FEMA)
P.O. Box 70274
Washington DC 20024   202-646-3484

The Motion Picture Catalog (FEMA-2) contains a current list of motion pictures of the Federal Emergency Management Agency (FEMA). These films are in 16mm color or black and white. Topics covered include tornadoes, earthquakes, hurricanes, and public safety. Contact FEMA for your free catalog.

* Floods

S. James, Consumer Information Center 2A
P.O. Box 100
Pueblo, CO 81002

In The Event of a Flood explains what to do in a flood, and how to minimize loss of life and property (590Y, $1).

* Floods: Audiovisuals

Public Affairs
National Weather Service
U.S. Department of Commerce
8060 13th. St., Room 1326
Silver Spring, MD 29010   301-427-8090

The National Weather Service has films, videotapes, slide programs, and informational pamphlets dealing with floods. Contact the Public Affairs Office for more information.

* Global Daily Summary (GDS)

National Climatic Data Center   704-271-4800
Federal Building   Fax: 704-271-4876
Asheville, NC 28801-2733   Internet Access: orders@ncdc.noaa.gov

This CD provides access to a 10,000 station set of daily maximum/minimum temperature, daily precipitation, and 3-hourly present weather for the 1977-1991 period of record. The data set includes element flags for suspected erroneous data. A data inventory contains station name, latitude and longitude, elevation, period of record, and the number of observations of available data. The cost is $100.

* Global Tropical and Extratropical Cyclone Climatic Atlas (GTECCA)

National Climatic Data Center   704-271-4800
Federal Building   Fax: 704-271-4876
Asheville, NC 28801-2733   Internet Access: orders@ncdc.noaa.gov

This CD contains all global historic tropical storm track data available for 5 tropical storm basins. Periods of record vary for each basin. Tropical track data includes times, position, storm stage. Narratives for all tropical storms for the 1980-1992 period are included along with basin-wide tropical storm climatological statistics. The cost is $100.

* Global Upper Air Climatic Atlas (GUACA)

National Climatic Data Center   704-271-4800
Federal Building   Fax: 704-271-4876
Asheville, NC 28801-2733   Internet Access: orders@ncdc.noaa.gov

This 2 volume CD set uses 12-year (1980-1991) 2.5 degree gridded upper air climatic summaries derived from the European Centre for Medium Range Weather Forecasts model analyses. It presents upper air statistics for 15 different vertical levels in the Northern/Southern Hemisphere for dry bulb and dewpoint temperature, geopotential height, air density, vector and scaler wind speed. The cost is $200.

* Greenhouse Effect, Ozone and Related Research

Environmental Research Laboratories
National Oceanic and Atmospheric Administration
U.S. Department of Commerce
325 Broadway
Boulder, CO 80303   303-497-6286

Weather and Maps

The Environmental Research Laboratories conducts an integrated program of fundamental research, related technology development, and services to improve understanding and prediction of the geophysical environment comprising the oceans and inland waters, the lower and upper atmosphere, the space environment, and the Earth. Activities at its laboratories address such major areas as stratospheric and tropospheric ozone, the greenhouse effect and atmospheric chemistry, acid rain sources, transport and deposition, ocean role in climate, meteorological phenomena, solar disturbances, and computer modeling of oceanic conditions. Contact this office for more information about the Laboratories.

* Hurricanes and Tropical Weather Research

Environmental Research Laboratories
Atlantic Oceanographic and Meteorological Laboratory (AOML)
National Oceanic and Atmospheric Administration
U.S. Department of Commerce
34301 Rickenbacher Causeway
Miami, FL 33149   305-361-4300

The Atlantic Oceanographic and Meteorological Laboratory performs tropical weather research to improve the description, understanding, and prediction of hurricanes, and to explore methods for modifying them. AOML's oceanographic studies focus on exchanges of energy and matter through the air-sea interface, and hydrothermal processes of mineralization at seafloor spreading centers. An annual report is available which describes the research conducted at AOML, including a listing of the technical reports published by AOML researchers.

* International Station Meteorological Climate Summary (ISMCS) Ver. 2.0 on CD-ROM

National Climatic Data Center   704-271-4800
Federal Building   Fax: 704-271-4876
Asheville, NC 28801-2733   Internet Access: orders@ncdc.noaa.gov

This CD-ROM gives detailed climatological summaries for about 980 locations worldwide. These locations include National Weather Service locations, domestic/overseas Navy/Air Force sites, and selected foreign stations. The cost is $50.

* Lightning Statistics Derived from Storm Data

National Oceanic and Atmospheric Administration
National Climatic Data Center
Federal Building   704-259-0682
Asheville, NC 28801-2696   704-CLI-MATE

Parameters that make up this file are damage categories, fatalities/injuries due to lightning, the location or activity. Contains extreme weather events and related damage information as confirmed by the National Weather Service.

* Mariners Weather Log

National Oceanographic Data Center
National Oceanic and Atmospheric Administration
Universal Building Room 412
Washington, DC 20235   202-673-5549

The Mariners Weather Log is a unique source of information on marine weather and climate and their effects on operations at sea. Published quarterly by the National Oceanographic Data Center, the *Mariners Weather Log* provides comprehensive coverage of major storms of the North Atlantic and North Pacific, reports and annual summaries on tropical cyclones, information on the National Weather Service's Marine Observation Program, selected shipboard gale and wave observations, and general articles about weather and climate, hazards and safety precautions, and related marine lore. An annual subscription is available for $6 from the Superintendent of Documents, Government Printing Office, Washington, DC 20402; 202-512-1800.

* Meteorological National Center

National Meteorological Center
National Weather Service
National Oceanic and Atmospheric Administration
U.S. Department of Commerce
5400 Auth Rd., Room 101
Camp Springs, MD 20033   301-763-8016

At the National Meteorological Center (NMC) in Maryland, more than 100,000 weather observations are incorporated daily into models of the atmosphere to produce weather forecasts from 48 hours to as far as 10 days ahead. Monthly and seasonal predictions of temperature and precipitation over North America also are produced. NMC guidance goes to National Weather Service facilities in every part of the nation where it helps meteorologists and hydrologists prepare local warnings and forecasts.

* Meteorologists Society

American Meteorological Society (AMS)
45 Beacon St.
Boston, MA 02108   617-227-2425

The American Meteorological Society certifies consulting meteorologists and grants a Seal of Approval to television and radio meteorologists. Publications: *Journal of Climate and Applied Meteorology, Journal of Atmospheric Sciences, Journal of Physical Oceanography, Meteorological and Geoastrophysical.*

* Meteorology and Climate Analysis

ASRL-Meteorology
Environmental Protection Agency
Research Triangle Park, NC 27711

This library's major field of interest is the meteorological aspects of air pollution, including model development and application, climatic analysis, and geophysical studies. The library holds a collection of climatic data material consisting of approximately 4,000 climatic data material reports on microfiche, over 400 rolls of film of synoptic data, surface and vorticity charts, and a large body of topographic maps.

* National Climate Information Disc-Vol. 1

National Climatic Data Center   704-271-4800
Federal Building   Fax: 704-271-4876
Asheville, NC 28801-2733   Internet Access: orders@ncdc.noaa.gov

This CD-ROM has monthly sequential temperature, precipitation, and drought data for the 344 climate divisions in the U.S. The data can be viewed in a tabular or graphical format. It also covers the period 1895-1989 and contains 1032 time-series graphs, 4180 maps, and 5400 frames of video animation. The cost is $50.

* National Environmental Data Clearinghouse

NEDRES Office
National Oceanic And Atmospheric Administration
U.S. Department of Commerce
1825 Connecticut Ave., NW, Room 412
Washington, DC 20235   202-673-5548

The National Environmental Data Referral Service (NEDRES) is designed to provide convenient, economical, and efficient access to widely scattered environmental data. NEDRES is a publicly available service which identifies the existence, location, characteristics, and availability conditions of environmental data sets. NEDRES database contains only descriptions, not the actual data. It is a national network of federal, state, and private organizations cooperating to improve access to environmental data. Major subject categories include climatology and meteorology, oceanography, geophysics and geology, geography, hydrology and limnology, terrestrial resources, toxic and regulated substances, and satellite remotely sensed data. NEDRES also produces the following printed catalogs with references to available environmental data on selected topics and regions:

Finding the Environmental Data You Need (free)
NEDRES Memorandum of Agreement (free)
NEDRES Database User Agreement (free)
NEDRES Data Base User Guide ($7.50)
Guideline for the Description of Environmental Data Files for the Nedres Database ($10)
North American Climatic Data Catalog: Part 1 ($10)
North American Climatic Data Catalog: Part 2 ($10)
Satellite Remote Sensing of the Marine Environment: Literature and Data Sources ($10)
Coastal and Estuarine Waters of California, Oregon, and Washington ($10)
Chesapeake Bay and Adjacent Wetlands
Chesapeake Bay Environmental Data Directory (free to federal and state agencies)
Environmental Data Review (free)

For more information on the NEDRES database and the user charges, contact the office listed above.

* National Thunderstorm Frequencies for the Contiguous United States

National Oceanic and Atmospheric Administration
National Climatic Data Center
Federal Building   704-259-0682
Asheville, NC 28801-2696   704-CLI-MATE

This publication presents a narrative description of data utilized and the analysis performed; monthly/annual analyzed charts of the contiguous U.S. depicting the number of thunderstorms; tables of monthly/annual number of thunderstorms for 450 stations; and station listings.

* Northern Hemisphere Extratropical Cyclone Movements

National Oceanic and Atmospheric Administration
National Climatic Data Center
Federal Building   704-259-0682
Asheville, NC 28801-2696   704-CLI-MATE

Copies of these data are available on magnetic tape. Parameters that make up this file are 12-hour (GMT) positions, 10-degree square number, direction of movement, previous 10-degree square number, center movement and speed of movement.

* Ocean and Weather Films

Modern Talking Picture Service
5000 Park Street North
St. Petersburg, FL 33709   800-243-MTPS

The National Oceanic and Atmospheric Administration (NOAA) has produced several films on weather, oceans, and ocean life, which are available for free loan through the Modern Talking Picture Service. These films are most often requested by teachers from elementary schools through universities, as well as members of the general public who are interested in learning about the weather. Some requests have even come from video and commercial film production companies who need shots of lightning and thunder or flash floods for their videos. The titles include:

Down to the Monitor
Estuary
*FAMOUS- Boundary of Creation**
Flood
*Give Me The Tides**
Global Weather Experiment
Hurricane
*Longlines: An Undersea Investigation**
NOAA Corps- The Seventh Service
Sentinels In Space
Sockeye Odyssey
Terrible Tuesday (Tornado Safety)
The Awesome Power
The Great American Fish Story
The Great American Fish Story- The West
The Great American Fish Story- The Northeast
The Great American Fish Story- The South
The Great American Fish Story- The Lakes and Rivers
Trashing the Oceans

For a free descriptive brochure contact: NOAA Public Affairs, U.S. Department of Commerce, Room 6913, Washington DC 20230; 202-377-8090. Films followed by an asterisk are available directly from the National Oceanic and Atmospheric Administration (NOAA).

* Oceanographic Data and Publications

National Oceanic and Atmospheric Administration
U.S. Department of Commerce
1825 Connecticut Ave., NW
Washington, DC 20235   202-673-5549

The National Oceanographic Data Center has a free publications list which includes technical reports and bulletins, as well has a variety of data reports pertaining to oceanographic research.

* Oceanographic Information

National Oceanographic Data Center (NODC)
National Environmental Satellite, Data
 and Information Service
National Oceanic and Atmospheric Administration
U.S. Department of Commerce
1825 Connecticut Ave., NW
Washington, DC 20235   202-673-5549

The National Oceanographic Data Center provides global coverage of oceanographic data and services. The National Oceanographic Data Center's (NODC) databases cover physical and chemical properties of the world's oceans, seas, and estuaries, plus information on selected continental shelf and coastal waters. Researchers using NODC data range from industrial scientists through local, state, and national

government investigators, to university or academic personnel. Information is available in various forms: publications computer plots, computer printouts, magnetic tapes and floppy disks. Simple questions usually can be answered without charge by telephone or mail, but more complicated ones requiring research or computer processing usually carry a fee.

* Online Access and Service Information System (OASIS)

National Climatic Data Center   704-271-4800
Federal Building   Fax: 704-271-4876
Asheville, NC 28801-2733   Internet Access: orders@ncdc.noaa.gov

This has been developed for selected National Climatic Data Center (NCDC) data and metadata files. Once connected to OASIS, users can obtain these files by FTP computer access. Data is placed online as soon as possible after receipt. In addition to data, important metadata is included with the online data. Station histories, data dictionaries, field experiment information, and data inventories are included. Access to the system is via Internet using telnet. Use the address: open192.67.134.72 or open hurricane.ncdc.noaa.gov. The Login is: storm. The Password is: research. The point of contact at the National Climatic Data Center is the Research Customer Service Group: Tom Ross, 704-271-4994, tross@ncdc.noaa.gov or Neal Lott 704-271-4995, nlott@ncdc.noaa.gov.

* Permafrost, Ice Age and Other Publications

Book and Report Sales
Box 25425
Denver, CO 80225   303-236-7476

This is a listing of some of the general interest publications available through the U.S. Geological Survey. They are free unless otherwise indicated.

The Great Ice Age
The Interior of the Earth
Landforms of the United States
Marine Geology: Research Beneath the Sea
Our Changing Continent
Permafrost
Geysers
Glaciers: A Water Resource

* Radiosonde Data of North America 1946-1992

National Climatic Data Center   704-271-4800
Federal Building   Fax: 704-271-4876
Asheville, NC 28801-2733   Internet Access: orders@ncdc.noaa.gov

This CD-ROM contains all available radiosonde data for North America on 4 disks. Periods covered are 1946-1965, 1966-1979, 1980-1989, and 1990-1992. Data includes significant, mandatory, special wind levels for all observation times, and includes geopotential height, temperature, dew point, wind direction, and scaler speed. The cost is $400.

* SAMSON CD Set

National Climatic Data Center   704-271-4800
Federal Building   Fax: 704-271-4876
Asheville, NC 28801-2733   Internet Access: orders@ncdc.noaa.gov

The Solar and Meteorological Surface Observational Network (SAMSON) 3 volume CD set is divided geographically into eastern, central, and western U.S. regions. Contains hourly solar radiation data, plus selected meteorological elements for 1961-1990. It includes both observational/modeled data. Hourly solar elements are: Extraterrestrial horizontal/extraterrestrial direct normal radiation; global, diffuse, and direct normal radiation. Meteorological elements are: Total/opaque sky cover, temperature and dew point, relative humidity, pressure, wind direction/speed visibility, ceiling height, present weather, precipitable water, aerosol optical depth, snow depth, days since last snowfall, and hourly precipitation. The cost is $100 per region or $300 per set.

* Satellite Data

National Climate Center
National Environmental Satellite, Data, and Information Service
National Oceanic and Atmospheric Administration (NOAA)
U.S. Department of Commerce
World Weather Building, Room 100
Washington, DC 20233   301-763-8111

The Satellite Data Services Division (SDSD) of the National Climatic Data Center

Weather and Maps

manages a database of environmental satellite data and information and provides products from this database to requesters. A unique source of data and information, the environmental database contains film imagery and digital data collected by a number of environmental satellites from 1960 to the present. It includes data from the National Oceanic and Atmospheric Administration's (NOAA) operational environmental satellites and selected data from NASA and the U.S. Department of Defense. While much of the data is nominally meteorological, its oceanographic applications have been very extensive, and the data and information has been of interest to agronomists, hydrologists, and geologists. Contact the office listed above for more information on the data and services available.

* Satellites and Other Instruments for Atmosphere, Geodesy, Navigational Study

Office of Legislative Affairs
National Oceanic and Atmospheric Administration
U.S. Department of Commerce
14th St. and Constitution Ave., NW, Room 6228   800-648-6209
Washington, DC 20230   202-842-7460 (DC area)

The National Oceanic and Atmospheric Administration (NOAA) has a free *Product Information Catalog* (PIC) which lists over 600 products related to the atmosphere, oceans, navigation, fisheries, mammals, geodesy, satellites, and other environmental concerns. These products span the range from simple pamphlets to technical reports. Each listing includes price and ordering information. NOAA has designed a system, the NOAA Information Service (NIS) to provide high-speed, automated retrieval of the PIC via an electronic database management system. A NOAA Information Specialist will answer inquiries about NOAA products and services and make in-house referrals to technical representatives. Call 206-526-9403 in Washington State.

* Severe Storms Forecast Center

National Severe Storms Forecast Center (NSSFC)
National Weather Service
National Oceanic and Atmospheric Administration
U.S. Department of Commerce
601 E. 12th St.
Kansas City, MO 64106   816-426-5922

The National Severe Storms Forecast Center is the office responsible for forecasting tornadoes and severe thunderstorms throughout the contiguous United States. In addition to this, NSSFC prepares aviation forecasts and advisories to aircraft in-flight, weather analyses based on interpretation of satellite data, and national weather summaries. The national weather summaries are issued twice daily and are distributed nationally for use by radio, television, newspapers, and other media interests. They are written in narrative form and contain information on significant weather that has occurred in the Nation. An extensive list of technical reports is available from NSSFC, most of which deal with tornado and severe thunderstorm forecasting.

* Solar Energy and Wind Information

National Climatic Data Center
National Oceanic and Atmospheric Administration
U.S. Department of Commerce
Federal Building
Asheville, NC 28801   704-259-0682

The National Climatic Data Center has a great deal of information regarding solar energy and wind data. Information includes solar radiation averages, measurements, and sunshine averages, as well as wind statistics. Reference manuals and indexes are also available. Prices vary depending upon the information requested. The Center can provide you with more detailed information regarding the data available.

* Space Environment Research

Space Environment Laboratory
Environmental Research Laboratories
National Oceanic and Atmospheric Administration
U.S. Department of Commerce
325 Broadway
Boulder, CO 80303   303-497-3313

The Space Environment Laboratory provides real-time space environment monitoring and forecasting services, develops techniques for improving forecasts of solar disturbances and their effect on the near-Earth space environment, and conducts research in solar-terrestrial physics. An annual report is available which goes into more detail about the Laboratory, the research conducted, and lists the technical reports published.

* Storm (Tropical Cyclone) Tracks

National Oceanic and Atmospheric Administration
National Climatic Data Center
Federal Building   704-259-0682
Asheville, NC 28801-2696   704-CLI-MATE

The parameters that make up this 4 magnetic tape file are: time, days the storm lasted, storm identification/position, wind speed, and maximum storm status for each (Tropical Storm, Hurricane, or Subtropical Storm).

* Storms and Natural Disaster Detection

National Ocean Service
National Oceanic and Atmospheric Administration
U.S. Department of Commerce
6001 Executive Blvd.
Rockville, MD 20852   301-443-8487

The Office of Oceanography and Marine Assessments surveys and monitors the oceans, U.S. coastal waters, estuarine waterways, and the Great Lakes to produce data and information products that describe the physical properties of these waters for a wide range of engineering and navigational applications. This office also conducts studies to assess the environmental impact of human activities in U.S. coastal waters. Many of these marine data and information products are essential for protecting life and property from storms and other destructive natural forces. Other marine products, such as predictions of the times and heights of tides and descriptions of tidal currents, are vital for safe navigation.

* Stratospheric Ozone

Global Change Division
Environmental Protection Agency
401 M St., SW, W739
Washington, DC 20460   202-260-7497

This Office can provide you with all the information you need to know regarding the Ozone, including information on ozone-depleting chemicals and ideas for reducing these chemicals. Publications include a *Handbook for Reducing and Eliminating Chlorofluorocarbons In Flexible Polyurethane Foams* and the *Executive Summary of the Ozone Trends Panel*.

* Tornados, Hurricanes and Floods - Free Weather Films

National Weather Service
National Oceanic and Atmospheric Administration
8060 13th St., Room 1326
Silver Spring, MD 20910   301-713-0622

The National Weather Service has several films, videos, and slides available for free loan on such topics as tornados, floods, hurricanes, and winter storms. These films are often used to teach civil defense personnel and storm spotters, and are suitable from grade four through college students. Contact this office for more information and for your free brochure.

* Undersea Research

National Undersea Research Program (NURP)
National Oceanic and Atmospheric Administration (NOAA)
U.S. Department of Commerce
6010 Executive Blvd.
Rockville, MD 20852   301-443-8391

The National Undersea Research Program develops programs and provides support to scientists and engineers for the study of biological, chemical, geological, and physical processes in the world's oceans and lakes. NURP assist researchers in conducting what are considered by NOAA and the marine community to be crucial research programs. In order to execute these programs, NURP provides investigators with a suite of the modern undersea facilities including submersibles, habitats, air and mixed gas SCUBA, and remotely operated vehicles. A major part of the research program is carried out by a network of National Undersea Research Centers. Contact this office for more information on the research conducted or the research centers.

* U.S. Navy Marine Climatic Atlas of the World Ver 1.0

National Climatic Data Center   704-271-4800
Federal Building   Fax: 704-271-4876
Asheville, NC 28801-2733   Internet Access: orders@ncdc.noaa.gov

This CD-ROM includes analysis/display software for climatological averages of atmospheric/oceanographic data. The data are summarized with user-defined 1 and

5 degree grid areas covering the global marine environment. The summaries are produced using predominately ship data collected between 1854-1969. The major elements include air and sea temperature, dewpoint temperature, scaler wind speed, sea-level pressure, wave height, wind/ocean-current roses. The cost is $50.

* Weather Data Archive and Analyses

Selective Guide to Climatic Data Sources
National Climatic Data Center
National Oceanic and Atmospheric Administration
U.S. Department of Commerce
Federal Building
Asheville, NC 28801   704-259-0682

The *Selective Guide to Climatic Data Sources* is designed to assist potential users of climatological information by acquainting them with the various forms in which these data are archived and the products or publications that are prepared from these data. Each listing contains the file name, format, contents, and an abstract. The Data Center also has the ability to prepare other statistical tabulations, climatological analyses, and special studies other than those listed in the *Guide*. Further information on the cost for preparing such specialized products, or the cost for items listed in the *Guide*, may be obtained from the Data Center. A meteorologist is available to assist you in locating appropriate data or answering your questions.

* Weather Duration

National Oceanic and Atmospheric Administration
National Climatic Data Center
Federal Building   704-259-0682
Asheville, NC 28801-2696   704-CLI-MATE

Coverage is for the U.S., Pacific Islands, Virgin Islands, and Puerto Rico. All stations are filed on 1 magnetic tape for 1984; 1 magnetic tape for the current year. Data are sorted by record type, station ID, element type, year/month/day. Weather types included are: thunderstorms, tornado; rain showers; snow pellets, ice crystals; snow showers; sleet; fog, blowing dust and blowing sand; smoke, haze, dust, blowing snow, and ice pellets.

* Weather Films and Publications

National Weather Service
National Oceanic and Atmospheric Administration
U.S. Department of Commerce
8060 13th St., Room 1326
Silver Spring, MD 20910   301-427-8090

A list of films, videotapes, and slides, as well as brochures is available from the National Weather Service. These publications deal with tornados, thunderstorms, floods, and hurricanes. Contact this office for your free list.

* Weather Forecasts

National Weather Service
National Oceanic and Atmospheric Administration
U.S. Department of Commerce
8060 13th St., Room 1326
Silver Spring, MD 20910   301-427-8090

A listing is available of the weather information phone numbers for major cities throughout the U.S., as well as several resort towns. Recordings are available at most National Weather Service offices. For a listing of these phone numbers, see the city's telephone directory under "United States Government, Department of Commerce, National Weather Service" or "Weather." Large capacity weather information recordings are operated by telephone companies at some locations with forecasts supplied by the National Weather Service. For these listings, turn back to the first page of this chapter.

* Weather Forecasts for U.S. Cities

Albany, NY	518-476-1111
Albuquerque, NM	505-821-1111
Atlanta, GA	770-434-6800
Birmingham, AL	205-945-7000
Bismarck, ND	701-223-3700
Boise, ID	208-342-8303
Boston, MA	617-567-4670
Buffalo, NY	716-844-4444
Caribou, ME	207-496-8931
Charleston, WV	304-345-2121

Cheyenne, WY	307-635-9901
Cincinnati, OH	513-241-1010
Cleveland, OH	216-931-1212
Columbia, SC	803-822-1401
Denver, CO	303-337-2500
Des Moines, IA	515-288-1047
Detroit, MI	313-941-7192
Elko, NV	702-738-3018
El Paso, TX	915-562-4040
Eugene, OR	503-484-1200
Fort Worth, TX	214-787-1111
Great Falls, MT	406-453-5469
Indianapolis, IN	317-635-5959
International Falls, MN	218-283-4615
Jackson, MS	601-936-2189
Jacksonville, FL	904-757-3311
Little Rock, AR	501-376-4400
Los Angeles, CA	213-554-1212
Louisville, KY	502-585-1212
Lubbock, TX	806-745-1058
Memphis, TN	901-757-6400
Miami, FL	305-229-4522
Sullivan, WI	414-744-8000
Minneapolis, MN	612-375-0830
New Orleans, LA	504-465-9212
New York City, NY	516-924-0517
Oklahoma City, OK	405-360-5928
Omaha, NE	402-359-9955
Philadelphia, PA	215-936-1212
Phoenix, AZ	602-379-4000
Pittsburgh, PA	412-936-1212
Portland, ME	207-713-0352
Portland, OR	503-236-7575
Raleigh, NC	919-515-8225
Redding, CA	916-221-5613
Reno, NV	702-793-1300
Salt Lake City, UT	801-575-7669
San Antonio, TX	210-737-1400
San Francisco, CA	415-936-1212
Savannah, GA	912-964-1700
Seattle, WA	206-526-6087
Sheridan, WY	307-672-2345
Shreveport, LA	318-635-7575
St. Louis, MO	314-441-8467
Topeka, KS	913-234-2592
Washington, DC	202-936-1212
Wichita, KS	316-942-3102

* Weather Maps

Public Affairs
National Oceanic and Atmospheric Administration
U.S. Department of Commerce
14th St. and Constitution Ave., NW
Room 6013
Washington, DC 20230   202-377-8090

This office has free copies of the weekly series of daily weather maps. The maps include the highest and lowest temperatures chart, and the precipitation areas and amounts chart. Annual subscriptions are available for $60 per year. Contact the Public Affairs Office for more information.

* Weather Reporting Locations

Federal Aviation Administration (FAA)
National Flight Data Center ATM-600
U.S. Dept. of Transportation
800 Independence Ave. SW
Washington, DC 20591   202-267-9272

This database describes all U.S. and select foreign locations that provide the following weather reports: Area Forecasts, Aviation Terminal Forecast, Notice to Airman, Surface Area, Aircraft Report, Transcribed Weather Broadcast, etc. Data includes identifier of reporting facility, state/country, city, latitude/longitude, elevation, weather reporting services provided, collectives, and affected areas. The database available to the public on magnetic tape. Upon written request to the above address, FAA-owned reels will be sent to you to copy and return. The charge for a one-time order is $36. The data is updated as information becomes available.

Weather and Maps

* World Climate Data

National Climatic Data Center
National Oceanic And Atmospheric Administration
U.S. Department of Commerce
Federal Building   704-CLI-MATE
Asheville, NC 28801-2690   704-259-0682

The National Climatic Data Center has a wide variety of world climate data sources, some of which include *Climates of the World, World Weather Records, Monthly Climatic Data for the World, Defense Department Foreign Data*, and *Foreign Data Publications Collection*. They also have several guides and catalogs on world weather. Contact the Center for more information on these and other publications and their current price list.

* World Wide Consolidated Tropical Cyclones

National Oceanic and Atmospheric Administration
National Climatic Data Center
Federal Building   704-259-0682
Asheville, NC 28801-2696   704-CLI-MATE

Parameters that make up this file for each ocean basin are constructed; sequential number of the storm, time, location, highest stage of storm, direction of movement, type of movement/source of data. This magnetic tape contains storm data for 6 separate ocean basins.

Maps and Geography

* Aeronautical Charts

Chart Distribution Branch
National Ocean Service
National Oceanic and Atmospheric Administration (NOAA)
U.S. Department of Commerce
Riverdale, MD 20737   301-436-6990

The National Ocean Service Distribution Branch provides National Oceanic and Atmospheric Administration (NOAA) aeronautical charts and chart-related publication for the U.S. Air Space System. NOAA aeronautical charts depict navigation data and flight regulation information critically important for flight planning, flight navigation, landings and take-offs, and air traffic control. The *Catalog of Aeronautical Charts and Related Publications* contains a brief description of each aeronautical chart and chart-related publication produced by the NOS, as well as aeronautical charts produced by the U.S. Defense Mapping Agency for civilian use. It also includes the price of the chart or publication, other information needed to select and order aeronautical chart products, and a list of NOAA chart sales facilities and authorized commercial chart sales agents.

* Airborne-Geophysical Information

Branch of Geophysics
U.S. Geological Survey (USGS)
MS 964, Box 25046
Denver Federal Center   800-USA-MAPS
Denver, CO 80225   303-236-1343

State index maps and information about available aeromagnetic and aerodiometric maps and profiles can be obtained from this office.

* Alaska AVHRR Companion Disk

U.S. Geological Survey
EROS Data Center   605-594-6151
Sioux Falls, SC 57198   Fax: 605-594-6589

Data on this disk includes Digital Line Graph international boundaries, transportation, and pipeline raster cartographic data. Hydrologic data includes Digital Line Graph streams/water bodies and U.S. Geological Survey (USGS) hydrologic units. Precipitation climate data is also provided. Ecologic data includes major land ecosystems, major physiographics divisions, USGS geology and permafrost, and Dept. of Agriculture soil survey raster images.

* Alaska AVHRR Twice-Monthly Composites

U.S. Geological Survey
EROS Data Center   605-594-6151
Sioux Falls, SC 57198   Fax: 605-594-6589

This series of satellite imagery begins with data collected in 1990 to 1991. Each disk contains 11 composite images for AVHRR Local Area Coverage data for bands 1-5 afternoon-acquired coverage, normalized difference vegetation index images for each composite period, satellite and solar azimuth/relative zenith data for each image pixel, principal roads and the Trans-Alaska Pipeline.

* Antarctic Maps

Distribution Branch
U.S. Geological Survey (USGS), Building 810
Denver Federal Center, Box 25286
Denver, CO 80225   800-USA-MAPS

Antarctic maps are available that show contour intervals of 200 meters and bathymetric information for coastal areas. The 1:250,000 -scale topographic maps are the primary map source for the planning, logistic support, and multidisciplinary investigations of the U.S. Antarctic Research Program. In the 1:500,000 series, the satellite imagery was recorded by NASA's Landsat, including the coastal areas of Wilkes Land and Enderby Land.

* Atlas of Military Installations in U.S.

Directorate for Information Operations and Reports

Washington Headquarters Services
1215 Jefferson Davis Hwy., Suite 1204
Arlington, VA 22202   202-746-0786

The *Atlas/Data Abstract for the United States and Selected Areas* contains a map showing all the military installations and a compendium of U.S. Department of Defense statistics for each state. Write or call for their free catalog list all their publications available through the Government Printing Office, 202-512-1800.

* Automatic Mapping Program

National Technical Information Service
U.S. Department of Commerce
5285 Port Royal Road
Springfield, VA 22151   703-487-4650

The Cartographic Automatic Mapping Program performs many cartographic functions and can be used in conjunction with the World Data Bank II noted below. CAM software, microfiche, and documents are available from the National Technical Information Service.

* Cadastral Survey Publications

Branch of Cadastral Survey Development, SC 678
Bureau of Land Management Service Center
U.S. Department of the Interior
Denver Federal Center, Bldg. 50
P.O. Box 25047
Denver, CO 80225-0047

The following publications on surveying are available from this office:

Surveying Our Public Lands. Informative account of survey history, the growth of the public domain, the rectangular survey system, and the role of the federal cadastral surveyor (Free, #P-25).

Surveys and Surveyors of the Public Domain. To be used in training cadastral surveyors in the application of surveying principles, survey laws and their formation, and a study of the people who performed the surveys ($8, #P-140).

Preparation of Special Instructions. A required quasi-legal document authorizing a cadastral survey or resurvey. The book contains important guidelines for the proper and adequate preparation of this and other related documents ($1.85, #P-171).

Durability of Bearing Trees. Prepared as a guide for cadastral surveyors and others involved in the search for old bearing trees as well as identifying and evaluating various species of trees for marking new bearing trees ($1.40).

Manual of Surveying Instructions, 1973. Describes in detail all aspects of how cadastral surveys are made in conformance to statutory law and its judicial interpretation ($16, Superintendent of Documents, Government Printing Office, 202-512-1800, S/N 024-011-00052-6).

Selected Computations of Astronomical Computations. Discusses the following topics: Motion of the Earth, Solar Time, Sidereal Time, 24-Hour Clock, Time Signals, Azimuth Determination, Polaris, Selected Examples for Azimuth Determination - Sun, Polaris Observation for Azimuth, Equatorial Star Identification Equatorial Star/Hour Angle Observation (Free, #T/N 318).

* Cartographic Archives

Cartographic and Architectural Branch
Special Archives Division
National Archives and Records Administration
8th St. and Pennsylvania Ave., NW
Washington, DC 20408   703-756-6700

The Cartographic and Architectural Branch has over 11 million maps, charts, aerial photographs, architectural drawings, patents, and ship plans, which constitute one of the world's largest accumulations of such documents. The Branch holds architectural and engineering drawings created by civilian and military agencies. All the holdings can be examined in the research room at 841 South Pickett St., Alexandria, VA, from 8:00am to 4:30pm, Monday through Friday. Reproductions can be furnished for a fee.

* Cartographic Research and Experimental Maps

Geographic and Cartographic Research
National Mapping Division
U.S. Geological Survey (USGS)   Reference: 703-648-4302
National Center, MS 521   703-648-4555
Reston, VA 22092   TTY: 703-648-4105

The U.S. Geological Survey acquires, stores, and uses geographic data in studies that combine geographic analyses with new cartographic concepts and techniques. New types of cartographic data and experimental maps result and are used to solve environmental problems and to aid in resource management.

* CCAP: Chesapeake Bay Region (1984-1989) on CD-ROM

National Geophysical Data Center   303-497-6607
325 Broadway, E/GC1, Dept. 961   Fax: 303-497-6513
Boulder, CO 80303-3328 USA   Telex: 592811 NOAA MASC BDR
                                 Internet: info@ngdc.noaa.gov
                                 Voice/TDD: 303-497-6958

The Coastal Change Analysis Project (CCAP), established to study the changes in land cover in coastal areas of the U.S.; shows the Chesapeake Bay region over a 5 year interval. Available for $71.

* Central Cartographer: Defense Mapping Agency

Defense Mapping Agency
Combat Support Center
Attn: Customer Assistance Office   800-826-0342
Washington, DC 20315-0010   301-227-2495

The Defense Mapping Agency makes available at cost a broad range of maps and charts. There are four categories available: aeronautical, topographic, hydrographic, and digital (lists those products available on magnetic tape). Each map costs $2.75 each. Write or call to order copies.

* China Map

Public Affairs Office
Central Intelligence Agency
Washington, DC 20505   703-351-2053

The Central Intelligence Agency Cartographic Automated Mapping Program and World Data Bank have generated a one-page multi-colored map which incorporates the new Pinyin (phonetic alphabet) spelling of names that became effective in 1979. The gazetteer on the reverse side of the map includes both the Pinyin and Wade-Giles rendition of geographic names. This Pinyin Edition (S/N 041-015-00106-0) can be purchased from the Government Printing Office, Washington, DC 20402; 202-512-1800.

* CIA Catalog of Declassified Maps

Public Affairs
Central Intelligence Agency (CIA)
Washington, DC 20505   703-351-2053

The Central Intelligence Agency (CIA) declassifies many of its maps which are available from the National Technical Information Service, 5285 Port Royal Road, Springfield, VA 22161; 703-487-4650. The catalog, titled *CIA Maps and Publications Released to the Public*, is available free from the CIA.

* CIA World and Country Maps

Public Affairs
Central Intelligence Agency
Washington, DC 20505   703-351-2053

Hundreds of maps generated by the Central Intelligence Agency are sold through the National Technical Information Service (NTIS), 5285 Port Royal Rd., Springfield, VA 22161; 703-487-4650. There are country maps as well as maps of continents are available. smaller geographical areas and city maps such as Moscow and Vicinity; Middle East Area Oilfields and Facilities; Israeli Settlement in the Gaza Strip; South Africa: Industrial Activity and Production; Africa Ethnolinguistic Groups.

* Climatic Atlas of the Outer Continental Shelf Waters and Coastal Regional of Alaska; Vol. I--Gulf of Alaska, Vol. II--Bering Sea, Vol. III--Chukchi-Beaufort Sea

National Oceanic and Atmospheric Administration
National Climatic Data Center
Federal Building   704-259-0682
Asheville, NC 28801-2696   704-CLI-MATE

This publication contains narrative information on such hazards as storm surges, superstructure icing, hypothermia, wind chill; extremes data on winds, temperature, and precipitation; planning information on surface currents, bathymetry, sea ice, and aviation weather.

* Climatic Atlas of the United States

National Oceanic and Atmospheric Administration
National Climatic Data Center
Federal Building   704-259-0682
Asheville, NC 28801-2696   704-CLI-MATE

Contains 271 climatic maps and 15 tables for the U.S. showing the national distribution of monthly and annual mean, normal/extreme values of temperature, precipitation, wind, barometric pressure, relative humidity, dewpoint, sunshine, sky-cover, heating-degree days, solar radiation, and evaporation.

* Comet Haley Atlas

Superintendent of Documents
Government Printing Office
Washington, DC 20402   202-512-1800

Census statistics publications are listed in this bibliography. One may send for the Railroad Maps of North America, featuring 5,000 maps and surveys. Weather and political atlases are listed, as well as an atlas to the Comet Haley. Free.

* Conterminous U.S. AVHRR Bi-Weekly Composites

U.S. Geological Survey
EROS Data Center   605-594-6151
Sioux Falls, SC 57198   Fax: 605-594-6589

This series of satellite imagery begins with data collected in 1989. Each disk contains 4 biweekly composite images of AVHRR Local Area Coverage data for bands of 1-5 afternoon-acquired coverage, normalized difference vegetation index images for each composite period, satellite/solar azimuth and relative zenith data for each image pixel, and miscellaneous state, county, climatic/ecological region raster polygons and linework for the entire conterminous United States.

* Conterminous U.S. AVHRR Companion Disk

U.S. Geological Survey
EROS Data Center   605-594-6151
Sioux Falls, SC 57198   Fax: 605-594-6589

Data includes geographic information systems data layers in both raster and DLG3 vector format. Data layers on this disk include: USGS National Geophysical Data Center 30 arc-second digital elevation models, USGS shaded relief/slope data derived from the elevation models, Soil Conservation Service Land Resource Areas, Environmental Protection Agency ecoregions, NOAA climatic regions, and AVHRR biweekly composite and vegetation index for July 15-18, 1991.

* Conterminous U.S. Land Characteristics, 1990

U.S. Geological Survey
EROS Data Center   605-594-6151
Sioux Falls, SC 57198   Fax: 605-594-6589

This disk contains 2 land cover classifications for the lower 48 states in a raster image format. Associated with these classifications are text files containing attributes for the land cover classes. Attributes include vegetation types, vegetation greenness, monthly precipitation, minimum/maximum monthly temperatures, elevation, ecoregion codes, and major land resource areas, among others.

* Digital Cartography

Earth Science Information Center
U.S. Geological Survey (USGS)
507 National Center   800-USA-MAPS
Reston, VA 22092-9998   703-648-6045

U.S. Geodata is the effort of the U.S. Geological Survey to expand its mapping program with digital cartography, involving the collection, storage, processing, analysis, and display of map data with the aid of computers. This includes a collection of planimetric, elevation, and geographic names information. This data may be combined with other data for cartographic applications. Users are able to plot their own maps with appropriate software. Calculations can be performed related to spatial analysis.

* Digital Line Graph (DLG) Data, 1:2,000,000-Scale

U.S. Geological Survey
National Mapping Division
Earth Science Information Center
National Center, MS 507   800-USA-MAPS
Reston, VA 22092   703-648-6045

This CD-ROM contains data for all 50 states, organized in 21 geographic regions. Eight categories are: Political Boundaries, Administrative Boundaries, Streams, Water Bodies, Hysography, Roads/Trails, Railroads, and Cultural Features.

* Digital Orthophoto Demonstration CD-ROM

U.S. Geological Survey
Western Mapping Center
345 Middlefield Rd., MS 531
Menlo Park, CA 94025   415-604-3914

Produced by the U.S. Geological Survey (USGS) National Mapping Division and U.S. Department of Agriculture Soil Conservation Service to demonstrate a new digital cartographic product--the digital orthophoto. These are aerial photographs which have been scan digitized to form raster images, rectified to orthogonal positions, and converted to a UTM projection. These images show promise as datasets for digital mapping systems or geographic information systems.

* Digital Spatial Data and Mapping Software

U.S. Geological Survey (USGS)
Reston-ESIC
507 National Center   800-USA-MAPS
Reston, VA 22092-9998   703-648-6045

The U.S. Geological Survey's Earth Science Information Center (ESIC) now offers inventories of digital spatial data sets and cartographic applications software in two bound listings. These inventories provide up-to-date bibliographic descriptions of data sets and software available from federal, state, and local government agencies and the private sector.

Sources for Digital Spatial Data. Describes more than 500 data sets containing spatially referenced base or thematic categories of data. The data sets are indexed by geographic area of coverage and cross-indexed by type of data.

Sources for Software for Computer Mapping and Related Disciplines. Describes more than 700 subroutines, programs, and systems that can be used in geographic information systems, map and chart plotting and construction, image processing and analysis, surveying, photogrammetry, data modeling and analysis, coordinate conversion, and other applications. Each publication is $22.

* Digital Spatial Data Applications Cooperation

U.S. Geological Survey (USGS)
Reston-ESIC
507 National Center   800-USA-MAPS
Reston, VA 22092   703-648-6045

If your organization is involved in digital spatial data applications, the Earth Science Information Center invites you to contribute information about your holdings. Your data and software may be valuable to other users.

* Digitized Strong-Motion Accelerograms...Earthquakes, 1933-86

U.S. Geological Survey
Branch of Distribution
Open-File Services Section
Box 25425, Federal Center
Denver, CO 80225   303-236-7476

This CD contains uncorrected ground level digital accelerograms recorded at permanent stations in North and Central America. The data were recorded/processed by both government/private agencies. The disk includes 2 database index files containing information from each of the acceleration files, such as station location, earthquake location/magnitude, epicentral distance, and peak acceleration.

* Earth Observation System

Customer User Services
Earth Resources Observation System Data Center (EROS)
U.S. Geological Survey (USGS)
Sioux Falls, SD 57198   605-594-6511

Aerial photographs are available from this center for most geographical regions of the country. Prices range from $6 to $65, depending on whether they are black and white or color photographs. Contact this office for ordering information.

* Earthquake Damage--General Slide Set

National Geophysical Data Center   303-497-6607
325 Broadway, E/GC1, Dept. 961   Fax: 303-497-6513
Boulder, CO 80303-3328 USA   Telex: 592811 NOAA MASC BDR
    Internet: info@ngdc.noaa.gov
    Voice/TDD: 303-497-6958

Illustrates effects caused by 11 earthquakes. Set is designed to give an overview/summary of earthquake effects. Available for $30. Other slide sets are available for $30 each, and are as follows:

Earthquake damage, San Francisco, CA 4/18/06
Earthquake Damage, Mexico City, Mexico, 9/85
Earthquake Damage to Transportation Systems
Earthquake Damage to Schools
Earthquake Damage, Great Alaska Earthquake, 3/64
Earthquake Damage, Southern CA, 1979-1989
Earthquake Damage, the Armenian Soviet Socialist Republic, 12/1988
Earthquake Damage, Loma Prieta, 10/89, Set 1, Loma Prieta Vicinity
Earthquake Damage, Loma Prieta, 10/89, Set, San Francisco and Oakland
Earthquake Damage, Northern Iran, Engineering Aspects, 6/21/90
Environmental Hazards & Mud Volcanoes in Romania
Earthquake Damage, the Cape Mendocino Earthquakes, 4/25-26/92
Earthquake Damage, the Landers and Big Bear Earthquakes, 6/28/92

* Earth-Science Films

Visual Information Services Group
U.S. Geological Survey (USGS)
790 National Center MS 507
Reston, VA 22092   703-648-6045

The Visual Information Services Group provides earth-science movies on a free-loan, short-term (2 or 3 day) basis to educational institutions and professional and scientific societies.

* Geographic Boundaries and International Disputes

Office of the Geographer
Bureau of Intelligence and Research
U.S. Department of State
2201 C St., NW, Room 8742
Washington, DC 20520   202-647-2022

This office distributes several publications which contain a variety of geographical information. Some of them include:

Geographic Notes. Contains brief analyses of current issues relevant to United States foreign policy. These analyses provide a geographical perspective on such foreign policy-related topics such as boundary, sovereignty, and territorial disputes.

International Boundary Studies. This is a series of specific boundary papers.

* Geographic Data and Research

Geographic and Cartographic Research
National Mapping Division
U.S. Geological Survey (USGS)   703-648-4555
National Center, MS 521   Reference: 703-648-4302
Reston, VA 22092   TTY: 703-648-4105

The U.S. Geological Survey acquires, stores, and uses geographic data in studies that combine geographic analyses with new cartographic concepts and techniques. New types of cartographic data and experimental maps result and are used to solve environmental problems and to aid in resource management.

* Geographic Names Information

Branch of Geographic Names
U.S. Geological Survey (USGS)
National Center, MS 523

Reston, VA 22092   703-648-4544

The USGS Branch of Geographic Names maintains a national research, coordinating, and information center to which all problems and inquiries concerning domestic geographic names can be directed. This office compiles name information, manages a names data repository, maintains information files, and publishes materials on domestic geographic names. The USGS, in cooperation with the Board on Geographic Names, maintains the *National Geographic Names Data Base* and compiles *The National Gazetteer of the United States of America* on a state-by-state basis.

* Geological Cartography Exhibits

Exhibits Committee
U.S. Geological Survey (USGS)
790 National Center
Reston, VA 22092   703-648-4357

Exhibits illustrating recent work in cartography, geography, geology, water resources, and other aspects of the USGS research are available to scientific associations for professional meetings and conferences. Contact this office for availability and scheduling information.

* Geological Survey Field Records Collection

Field Records
U.S. Geological Survey (USGS)   Reference: 303-236-1000
MS 914   TTY: 303-236-0998
Box 25046, Federal Center   Photos: 303-236-1010
Denver, CO 80225-0046   303-236-1005

The Field Records collection consists of the original materials produced by the USGS during its field investigations. Holdings include 15,600 notebooks, 2,000 folders, 2,400 map groups, and 60,000 aerial photographs. Upon gaining approval, you may examine these records at the Denver Library or make arrangements for the materials to be sent to a more convenient USGS library.

* Geologic Maps Hotline

Distribution Branch
U.S. Geological Survey (USGS)
Building 810
Denver Federal Center, Box 25286
Denver, CO 80225   800-USA-MAPS

Geologic maps are made by USGS as part of a continuing program of examining geological structure, mineral resources, and products. These maps range in scale from 1:20,000 to 1:2,5000,000, depending on the type of information shown.

Geologic Quadrangle Maps. Show the bedrock, surficial, or engineering geology of selected quadrangles in the United States.
Black-and-White or Multicolor Miscellaneous Field Studies Maps. Are preliminary reports on geologic aspects of mineral and environmental studies.
Mineral Investigations Resource Maps. Feature mineral distribution of metallic and nonmetallic minerals.
Geophysical Investigations Maps. Show the results of surveys to measure geomagnetism, gravity, and radioactivity in selected areas of the country.
State Geologic Maps. Show rock types and named geologic units exposed at the surface, geologic faults, anticlines, and synclines.
Antarctic Geologic Maps. Define rock type and named units of exposed and inferred rocks in ice-free areas.
Oil, Gas, and Coal Investigations Maps.

* Geologic Names Committee

U.S. Geological Survey (USGS)
National Center, MS 902
Reston, VA 22092   703-648-6045

The Geologic Names Committee defines and recommends policy and rules governing stratigraphic nomenclature and classification for the USGS. *Stratigraphic Notes* is published to announce changes in official geologic names usage. Lexicons are compiled that show domestic geologic names usage, and a file is maintained of geologic names reserved future use.

* Geophysics of North America on CD-ROM

National Geophysical Data Center   303-497-6607
325 Broadway, E/GC1, Dept. 961   Fax: 303-497-6513
Boulder, CO 80303-3328 USA   Telex: 592811 NOAA MASC BDR
    Internet: info@ngdc.noaa.gov
    Voice/TDD: 303-497-6958

This land/marine geophysical data includes magnetics, gravity, earthquake seismology, and stress data. A special feature is its color graphics capability. Available for $261.

* Global Ecosystems Data on CD-ROM

National Geophysical Data Center   303-497-6607
325 Broadway, E/GC1, Dept. 961   Fax: 303-497-6513
Boulder, CO 80303-3328 USA   Telex: 592811 NOAA MASC BDR
    Internet: info@ngdc.noaa.gov
    Voice/TDD: 303-497-6958

Selected data on global ecosystems, vegetation, climate topography, soils and other data. Available for $91.

* GLORIA Data--East Coast

U.S. Geological Survey
USGS/NOAA Joint Office for Mapping and Research
National Center, MS 915
Reston, VA 22092-9998   703-648-6525

This disk contains sidescan sonar image data from the 1987 USGS GLORIA surveys of the seafloor of the EEZ off the east coast of the U.S. The pixel data can be shown on a CRT (EGA or VGA) as individual 2-degree geographical areas or selected sub-areas. Software routines allow the user to perform limited process on the data.

* Ground Water, Floods and Other Hydrologic Investigative Maps

Distribution Branch
U.S. Geological Survey (USGS), Building 810
Denver Federal Center, Box 25286
Denver, CO 80225   800-USA-MAPS

Hydrologic investigations atlases are either black and white or multicolor maps showing a wide range of water-resources information, such as depth to ground water, floods, irrigated acreage, producing aquifers, availability of water on Indian lands, surface-water discharge to the oceans, chemical or mineral content of water, surface impoundments, and water temperature.

* Hawaii Volcanism: Impact on the Environment Slide Set

National Geophysical Data Center   303-497-6607
325 Broadway, E/GC1, Dept. 961   Fax: 303-497-6513
Boulder, CO 80303-3328 USA   Telex: 592811 NOAA MASC BDR
    Internet: info@ngdc.noaa.gov
    Voice/TDD: 303-497-6958

Depicts impact of lava flows on communities, vegetation, marine life, roads, and coastlines. Illustrates benefits of volcanism such as geothermal powers, increase in land area of the islands, and opportunities for viewing and studying volcanism in relative safety. Available for $30. Other volcano slide sets are available for $30 and are as follows:

Volcanoes in Eruption, Set I
Volcanic Rocks and Features
Volcanoes in Eruption, Set II
The Eruption of Mount Saint Helens, May 1980
Hawaii Volcanism: Lava Forms
Mount Pinatubo, the June 1991 Eruption
Crater Peak (Mt.Spurr), Alaska Eruptions--1992

* Hydrography and Transportation

U.S. Geological Survey
National Mapping Division
Earth Science Information Center
National Center, MS 507   800-USA-MAPS
Reston, VA 22092   703-648-6045

This CD-ROM contains the 1:100,000 scale hydrography and transportation Digital Line Graph data for the Conterminous United States and Hawaii. Currently available sections include--Northeastern States; Mid-Atlantic States; Southeastern; Florida; Great Lakes States; New Mexico and Arizona; Northwestern States; and Hawaii.

* Is There a Wetland Near You?

National Wetlands Inventory
Fish and Wildlife Service

U.S. Department of Interior
1849 C St., NW
Washington, DC 20240 703-358-2201
The National Wetlands Inventory identifies, plots, and maps all the wetlands in the U.S. These maps are available for sale through the U.S. Geologic Service by calling 800-USA-MAPS.

* Land Use and Land Cover Maps

Distribution Branch
U.S. Geological Survey (USGS), Building 810
Denver Federal Center, Box 25286
Denver, CO 80225 800-USA-MAPS
Land use maps and land cover maps are available for most of the United States. Land use maps refer to human uses of the land (housing and industry) and land cover maps describe the vegetation, water, natural surface, and construction on the land surface. The scale used ranges from 1:100,000 for a few maps in the Western states to 1:250,000 for most other maps.

* Library of Congress Geography and Map Resources

Geography and Map Division
Library of Congress
Washington, DC 20540 202-707-6277
The Library's cartographic collections, which include 4 million maps, nearly 51,000 atlases, 500 globes, and some 8,000 reference books, are the largest and most comprehensive in the world. The collections include atlases published over the last five centuries covering individual continents, countries, states, counties, and cities as well as the world. Official topographic, geologic, soil, mineral, and resource maps and nautical and aeronautical charts are also available for most countries. There are also complete LANDSAT microimage data sets of images produced by several satellites revolving around the Earth. Subscription information on the microfiche data sets is available from EOSAT, 4300 Forbes Blvd., Lanham, MD 20706; 800-344-9933.

* Mapping Research Reference Collection

National Mapping Division Research Reference Collection
U.S. Geological Survey (USGS)
National Center MS 507
Reston, VA 22092 703-648-6045
The National Mapping Division Office of Research maintains a collection of over 3,000 technical reference works in the fields of cartography and geography. The collection also includes the National Mapping Division Historical Archives, containing over 150,000 sheets. Functioning primarily to support research of the National Mapping Division, it is also open for use by other USGS personnel and the public. Items may be borrowed by the public through inter-library loans at local libraries.

* Maps

State affiliate National Cartographic Information Center offices distribute free pamphlets, poster-leaflets, and topographic map indexes. Many State affiliates sell maps of their respective States. The State affiliates also provide ordering assistance for custom cartographic products (including aerial photographic and satellite imagery).

Alabama
Geological Survey of Alabama
P.O. Box O
Tuscaloosa, AL 35486-9780 205-349-2852

Alaska
Geophysical Institute
University of Alaska- Fairbanks
P.O. Box 757320
Fairbanks, AK 99775-7320 907-474-7487

Arizona
Arizona State Land Department
Resource Analysis Division
1616 West Adams
Phoenix, AZ 85007 602-542-4061

Arkansas
Arkansas Geological Commission
3815 West Roosevelt Road
Little Rock, AR 72204 501-663-9714

California
Map and Imagery Laboratory Library
University of California
Santa Barbara, CA 93106 805-961-2779

Connecticut
Natural Resource Center
Department of Environmental Protection
165 Capitol Ave.
Hartford, CT 06106 203-566-2211

Delaware
Delaware Geological Survey
DGS Building
University of Delaware
Newark, DE 19716-7501 302-831-2833

Florida
Florida Resources and Environmental Analysis Center
361 Bellamy Building
Florida State University
Tallahassee, FL 32306-4015 904-644-2883

Georgia
Office of Research and Information
Department of Community Affairs
100 Peachtree St., NW
1200 Equitable Bldg.
Atlanta, GA 30303 404-656-5526

Hawaii
Department of Planning and Economic Development
Kamamalu Building
250 South King St.
Honolulu, HI 96813 808-586-2487

Idaho
Idaho State Historical Library
450 N. Fourth
Boise, ID 83702 208-334-3356

Illinois
University of Illinois at Urbana-Champaign
Map and Geography Library
1408 West Gregory Dr.
Urbana, IL 61801 217-333-0827

Indiana
Agricultural Data Network
214 Entomology Hall, Room 220
Purdue University
West Lafayette, IN 47907-1158 317-494-6305

Iowa
Iowa Geological Survey
109 Trowbridge Hall
Iowa City, IA 52242 319-335-1575

Kansas
Kansas Geological Survey
1930 Constant Avenue
Campus West
The University of Kansas
Lawrence, KS 66046 913-864-3965

Kentucky
Kentucky Geological Survey
228 Mining and Min. Res.
University of Kentucky
Lexington, KY 40506 606-257-5500

Louisiana
Office of Public Works
Department of Transportation and Development
P.O. Box 94245 Capitol Station
Baton Rouge, LA 70804-9245 504-379-1473

Weather and Maps

Maine
Maine Geological Survey
State House Station #22
Augusta, ME 04333 — 207-287-2211

Maryland
Maryland Geological Survey
2300 St. Paul St.
Baltimore, MD 21218 — 410-554-5500

Massachusetts
University of Massachusetts
Cartographic Information Research Services
Blaisdell House
Amherst, MA 01003 — 413-545-0359

Michigan
Division of Land Resource Programs
Michigan Department of Natural Resources
P.O. Box 30048
Lansing, MI 48909-7948 — 517-373-9123

Minnesota
Minnesota State Planning Agency
Land Management Information Center
300 Centennial Office Building
658 Cedar St.
Saint Paul, MN 55155 — 612-296-1201

Mississippi
Geographic Information Systems Division
Mississippi Research and Development Center
3825 Ridgewood Road
Jackson, MS 39211 — 601-982-6606

Missouri
Missouri Department of Natural Resources
Division of Geology and Land Survey
P.O. Box 250
Rolla, MO 65401 — 314-364-1752

Montana
Montana Bureau of Mines and Geology
Montana Tech, Main Hall, Room 200
Butte, Mt 59701 — 406-496-4167

Nebraska
Conservation and Survey Division
University of Nebraska
901 North 17th St.
Lincoln, NE 68508 — 402-472-3471

Nevada
Nevada Bureau of Mines and Geology, MS 178
University of Nevada
Reno, NV 89557 — 702-784-6691

New Hampshire
Documents Department
18 Library Way
University of New Hampshire
Durham, NH 03824 — 603-862-1777

New Jersey
Department of Environmental Protection
New Jersey Geological Survey
29 Artic Parkway
Trenton, NJ 08625 — 609-292-2576

New Mexico
University of New Mexico
Technology Applications Center
2500 Yale SE, Suite 100
Albuquerque, NM 87131 — 505-277-3622

New York
Map Information Unit

New York Department of Transportation
Albany, NY 12232 — 518-457-3555

North Carolina
Geological Survey Section
P.O. Box 27687
Raleigh, NC 27611-7687 — 919-733-2423

North Dakota
North Dakota State Water Commission
State Office Building
900 East Blvd.
Bismarck, ND 58505 — 701-328-2754

Ohio
Ohio Division of Soil and Water Conservation, RELM
Remote Sensing Section- NCIC
Fountain Square, C-2
Columbus, OH 43224 — 614-265-6770

Oklahoma
Oklahoma Geological Survey
100 E. Boyd, Room N131
University of Oklahoma
Norman, Ok 73019 — 405-325-3031

Oregon
Oregon State Library
Public Service
Salem, OR 97310 — 503-378-4277

Pennsylvania
Department of Environmental Resources
Bureau of Topographic and Geologic Survey
P.O. Box 8453
Harrisburg, PA 17105-8453 — 717-787-2169

Rhode Island
Rhode Island Cartographic Information Center
Pell Library
University of Rhode Island
Narragansett, RI 02882 — 401-874-6539

South Carolina
South Carolina Land Resources Conservation Commission
2221 Devine St., Suite 222
Columbia, SC 29205 — 803-734-9100

South Dakota
South Dakota Geological Survey
Science Center
University of South Dakota
Vermillion, SD 57069 — 605-677-5227

Texas
Texas Natural Resources Information System
1700 N. Congress
Austin, TX 78711 — 512-463-8337

Utah
Utah Geological and Mineral Survey
606 Black Hawk Way
Research Park
Salt Lake City, UT 84108-1280 — 801-975-3483

Vermont
University of Vermont
Documents/Map Department
Bailey/Howe Library
Burlington, VT 05405 — 802-656-2503

Virginia
Department of Conservation and Economic Development
Division of Mineral Resources
Box 3667
Charlottesville, VA 22903 — 804-293-5121

Be patient. If any phone number is incorrect, call (area code) 555-1212 and request the new listing.

Washington
Washington State Library
Information Services Division
Olympia, WA 98504 360-753-4027

West Virginia
West Virginia Geological and Economic Survey
West Virginia Cartographic Center
P.O. Box 879
Morgantown, WV 26507-0879 304-594-2331

Wisconsin
State Cartographer's Office
155 Science Hall
550 North Park St.
Madison, WI 53706 608-262-6850

Wyoming
State Engineer
Herschler Building
Cheyenne, WY 82002 307-777-7354

* Maps and Atlases: United States and Foreign
Superintendent of Documents
Government Printing Office
Washington, DC 20402 202-512-1800
Census statistics publications are listed in this bibliography. One may send for the Railroad Maps of North America, featuring 5,000 maps and surveys. Weather and political atlases are listed, as well as an atlas to the Comet Haley. Free.

* Maps of Moon and Planets
Distribution Branch
U.S. Geological Survey (USGS), Building 810
Denver Federal Center, Box 25286
Denver, CO 80225 .... 800-USA-MAPS
The USGS established an astrogeology program on behalf of NASA to support lunar and planetary exploration. Many maps of the Moon, Mars, Venus, and Mercury are available.

* Maps: Technical Information
Geologic Inquiries
U.S. Geological Survey (USGS)
National Center, MS 907
Reston, VA 22092 301-648-6045
To obtain technical information on such geologic topics as earthquakes and volcanoes, energy and mineral resources, the geology of specific areas, and geologic maps, contact this office.

* Meteorological Topographic Maps
ASRL-Meteorology
Environmental Protection Agency
Research Triangle Park, NC 27711
This library's major field of interest is the meteorological aspects of air pollution, including model development and application, climatic analysis, and geophysical studies. The library holds a collection of climatic data material consisting of approximately 4,000 climatic data material reports on microfiche, over 400 rolls of film of synoptic data, surface and vorticity charts, and a large body of topographic maps.

* Mine Companies and Property Ownership Maps
Division of Program Information and Analysis
Surface Mining Reclamation and Enforcement
U.S. Department of the Interior
1951 Constitution Ave., NW
Washington, DC 20240 202-343-5907
Valuable information is available from the mine maps available through the mine map repositories of the Office of Surface Mining Reclamation and Enforcement. Mine and company names, water sources, property ownership of adjoining companies and towns, latitudes and longitudes, coal outcrop seam designations, openings and emergency exits of mines, and gas and power lines are some of the topics covered. This information can be useful to local developers, engineering firms, and energy interests, as well as private citizens.

* Mine Map Repositories
Office of Public Affairs
Surface Mining Reclamation and Enforcement
U.S. Department of the Interior
1951 Constitution Ave., NW
Washington, DC 20240 202-343-4953
The Mine Map Repositories were established in 1970 and are responsible for collecting and archiving mine maps both east and west of the Mississippi River and in Alaska. The brochure, *Mine Map Repositories*, provides information and statistics on the mine map repository facilities of the Office of Surface Mining Reclamation and Enforcement. The five repositories are listed with their addresses and phone numbers. They are located in Pittsburgh, PA, Wilkes-Barre, PA, Denver, CO, Spokane, WA, and Juneau, AK.

* National Atlas Updates
Distribution Branch
U.S. Geological Survey (USGS), Building 810
Denver Federal Center, Box 25286
Denver, CO 80225 .... 800-USA-MAPS
The *National Atlas of the United States* (1970) contains 765 maps and charts on 335 pages. Out of print and no longer for sale, it can still be found in most libraries. However, separate sheets of selected reference maps and thematic maps from the *Atlas* are available from the USGS. Some of the sheets have been updated. Some updated thematic maps include potential natural vegetation (1985), monthly average temperature (1986) monthly minimum temperature (1986), monthly maximum temperature (1986), networks of ecological research (1983), and territorial growth (1986).

* National Gazetteer of the United States of America
Books and Open File Reports
U.S. Geological Survey (USGS)
Box 25425, Federal Center
Denver, CO 80225 303-236-7476
The *National Gazetteer of the United States of America* is a geographic dictionary of place and feature names, published on a state-by-state basis. It includes a glossary of terms and abbreviations, a map of counties in a state, and an alphabetical listing of USGS topographic quadrangle maps of the state, as well as the information contained in the *National Geographic Names Data Base*. Also listed are names of features from other historical sources. Variant names are listed and cross-referenced to their official names. A variant name is any other known name or spelling applied to a feature other than the official name.

* National Mapping Activities
National Mapping Division
U.S. Geological Survey (USGS)
National Center, MS 507 .... 800-USA_MAPS
Reston, VA 22092 703-648-5748
The National Mapping Program of the U.S. Geological Survey compiles, updates, and prints topographic maps as well as thematic maps that combine topographic data with other spatial data, such as geology, hydrology, rainfall, land use, and population. Four regional Mapping Centers, located in Reston, VA, Rolla, MO, Denver, CO, and Menlo Park, CA, are responsible for map production and for coordinating joint mapping activities with other Federal and State agencies. Maps are sold through the Earth Science Information Centers and private dealers.

* National Mapping System
Distribution Branch
U.S. Geological Survey (USGS)
Building 810
Denver Federal Center, Box 25286
Denver, CO 80225 .... 800-USA-MAPS
The USGS National Mapping System is a rich source of numerous types of maps. The brochure, *Catalog of Maps*, describes in detail the different maps available. Contact either the above office for a price list or one of the Earth-Science Information Centers for more information on the maps available.

* National Park Maps
Technical Information Center
National Park Service
Denver Service Center
12795 W. Alameda Parkway

P.O. Box 25287
Denver, CO 80225-0287   303-969-2130

The Technical Information Center has been designated by the National Park Service as the central repository for all National Park Service-generated planning, design, and construction maps, drawings, and reports as well as related cultural, environmental, and other technical documents. Bibliographic data on aerial photography is also maintained. The Center reproduces and delivers copies of the available materials for the Service, other agencies, and the public, both here and abroad. Today, the system has a holding of 100,000 data records, which represent about 500,000 microfilm aperture cards of maps, plans, and drawings; 1,000 records of resource and site aerial photography; and 25,000 planning, design, environmental, cultural resource, and natural resource documents.

* Nautical Charts

Chart Distribution Branch
National Ocean Service
National Oceanic and Atmospheric Administration (NOAA)
U.S. Department of Commerce
Riverdale, MD 20737   301-436-6990

The National Ocean Service produces approximately 1,000 nautical charts for navigation in U.S. estuarine waters and navigable inland waterways, the Great Lakes, and the 2 1/2 million square miles of coastal waters of the United States and its possessions. NOAA *Chart and Map Catalogs* describe nautical charts which are listed in a series of four catalogs, one for each region of the U.S. ocean and coastal waters. NOAA bathymetric maps and special purpose charts are listed in a single catalog. A sixth catalog is a guide to NOAA nautical products and services. The catalogs contain a brief description of each nautical chart, bathymetric map, special purpose chart, and chart-related publication produced by the NOS. They also include the price of the chart of publication, other information needed to select and order nautical charting products, and a list of NOAA chart sales facilities and authorized commercial chart sales agents. Contact this office for your free catalogs.

* Northridge (CA) Earthquake Slide Set, Jan. 17, 1994

National Geophysical Data Center   303-497-6607
325 Broadway, E/GC1, Dept. 961   Fax: 303-497-6513
Boulder, CO 80303-3328 USA   Telex: 592811 NOAA MASC BDR
                                           Internet: info@ngdc.noaa.gov
                                           Voice/TDD: 303-497-6958

Shows the damage from this most expensive earthquake in U.S. history. These sets are available for $30 and are as follows:

Set 1--Community of Northridge: Depicts the damage in the immediate area of this earthquake. Photos showing damage are included.

Set 2--Communities other than Northridge: Depicts damaged structures in Sylmar, Fillmore, Granada Hills, Reseda, Van Nuys, Sherman Oaks, Chatsworth, Santa Monica, and Los Angeles.

The San Fernando Valley Earthquakes: 2/9/71 and 1/17/94: Compares and contrasts these 2 earthquakes that were separated by 10 miles and about 23 years. Disproving the notion that once an earthquake has occurred, an area is safe from future earthquakes.

* Photoimage Maps

Distribution Branch
U.S. Geological Survey (USGS)
Building 810
Denver Federal Center, Box 25286
Denver, CO 80225   800-USA-MAPS

Photoimage maps are published in three types: orthophotomaps, orthoquads, and border maps of US./Mexico and U.S/Canada. Satellite (Landsat) image maps are multi-color photograph-like maps made from data collected by Earth resources satellites. They are available for selected areas in about half of the states, along with such areas as Antarctica, the Bahamas, and Iceland.

* Portraits of the Earth

U.S. Geological Survey (USGS)
Book and Report Sales
Box 25425
Denver, CO 80225   303-236-7476

Geologic Maps: Portraits of the Earth is one of many maps available from the U.S. Geological Survey.

* Railroad Maps of North America

Superintendent of Documents
Government Printing Office
Washington, DC 20402   202-512-1800

Census statistics publications are listed in this bibliography. One may send for the Railroad Maps of North America, featuring 5,000 maps and surveys. Weather and political atlases are listed, as well as an atlas to the Comet Haley. Free.

* Relief Globe Slides

National Geophysical Data Center
NOAA E/GC3 Dept. 874
325 Broadway   303-497-6677
Boulder, CO 80303-3328   Fax: 303-497-6513

Relief Globe Slides is a set of 20 slides containing 14 global view of the Earth in full color shaded relief, showing land and undersea topography. The planet is seen from vantage points over the poles and each major ocean and land mass. Also included are a rectangular Mercator projection view of the whole Earth, as well as displays of crustal plates and their relation to world seismic activity. Other views may be generated on request, either as slides or computer files. The cost is $40.

* Scholarly Sources on Cartography

Smithsonian Institution Press
Dept. 900
Blue Ridge Summit, PA 17214   717-794-2148

Produced by the Woodrow Wilson International Center for Scholars, the *Guides to Scholarly Sources* are designed to be descriptive, evaluative surveys of source materials. The Guide titled *Cartography and Remote Sensing* is divided into two parts. Part I examines area collections - libraries; archives and manuscript depositories; art, film, music, and map collections; and data banks. Part II focuses on pertinent activities of Washington-based organizations, public and private. Given for each are its related functions, materials and products.

* Space Photographs

Customer Services
Earth Resources Observation System Data Center (EROS)
U.S. Geological Survey (USGS)   605-594-6151
Sioux Falls, SD 57198   Fax: 605-594-6589

The Earth Resources Observation System (EROS) Data Center maintains photographs from many of the space missions, including those of the space shuttle, Apollo, and Gemini. Contact the center directly for information concerning specific topics.

* Spitak Earthquake on CD-ROM

National Geophysical Data Center   303-497-6607
325 Broadway, E/GC1, Dept. 961   Fax: 303-497-6513
Boulder, CO 80303-3328 USA   Telex: 592811 NOAA MASC BDR
                                           Internet: info@ngdc.noaa.gov
                                           Voice/TDD: 303-497-6958

Provides seismologists with a complete set of data for the earthquake which occurred in Armenia on 12/7/88. Includes geological/geophysical data collected in years prior to the event. Available for $71.

* State Topographic Maps

Earth Science Information Center
U.S. Geological Survey (USGS)
507 National Center   800-USA-MAPS
Reston, VA 22092   703-648-6045

Two types of directories are now available listing topographic maps for each state. *An Index to Topographic and Other Map Coverage* and its companion, *Catalog of Topographic and Other Published Maps*, contain information on the types of state maps that are available. The *Index* shows you how to locate your general area of interest and then the specific location and name of the area for which you want a map in each state. The *Catalog* lists cities and geographic areas for which maps are available.

* Topographic and Topographic-Bathymetric Maps

Distribution Branch
U.S. Geological Survey (USGS)
Building 810
Denver Federal Center, Box 25286

Denver, CO 80225   800-USA-MAPS

Topographic maps of the U.S. Geological Survey (USGS) use brown contours to show the shape and elevation of the terrain. The maps show and name prominent natural and man-made features. The best known USGS maps are those of the 7.5-minute, 1:24,000-scale quadrangle series. Fifteen-minute maps are also available, particularly for the Hawaiian Islands, but some detail is omitted or generalized. Other topographic maps include the U.S. 1:100,000 scale series, county map series, U.S. 1:250,000-scale series, state map series, National Park series, and shaded-relief maps.

On the topographic-bathymetric maps, contour lines show elevations of the land areas above sea level, and isobaths (depth contours) show the form of the land below the water. Some bathymetric maps also show magnetic and gravity data. The combined map serves the needs of oceanographers, marine geologists, land use planners, physical scientists, conservationists, and others having an interest in management of the coastal zone, the wetlands, and the offshore environment.

* Tsunamis-General Slide Set

National Geophysical Data Center   303-497-6607
325 Broadway, E/GC1, Dept. 961   Fax: 303-497-6513
Boulder, CO 80303-3328 USA   Telex: 592811 NOAA MASC BDR
                                     Internet: info@ngdc.noaa.gov
                                     Voice/TDD: 303-497-6958

Depicts advancing waves, harbor damage, and structural damage from 7 tsunami events which have occurred since 1946 in the Pacific region. Set includes before/after views of Scotch Cap Lighthouse, which was completely washed away by a wave of more than 30 meters. Available for $30. Other tsunamis slide sets available are as follows and available for $30:

The Major Tsunamis of 1992--Nicaragua and Indonesia: Set shows damage from the two tsunami events of 1992. The slides illustrate how a tsunami may affect an area economically and ecologically.

The Hokkaido Nansei-Oki Tsunami, July 12, 1993: Shows the result of one of the largest tsunamis in Japan's history. Views of damage to ships/dwellings/business, and unique views of clocks stopped in time.

* U.S. Geological Survey: New Publications

Branch of Data Systems
U.S. Geological Survey (USGS)
National Center, MS 507   800-USA-MAPS
Reston, VA 22092   703-648-6045

New Publications of the U.S. Geological Survey is a free monthly catalog of new publications released by the U.S. Geological Survey. To be placed on the mailing list, contact the office above.

* U.S. Geological Survey Photographs

Photographic Library, MS 914   Reference: 303-236-1000
U.S. Geological Survey (USGS)   TTY: 303-236-0998
Box 25046, Federal Center   Field Records: 303-236-1005
Denver, CO 80225   Photos: 303-236-1010

The Photographic Library of the U.S. Geological Survey contains a special collection of approximately 250,000 photographs. The Library may be used by the public as well as by personnel of other government agencies. Persons who wish to obtain prints, copy negatives, and duplicate transparencies from the collection are encouraged to visit the library. If this is not possible, the staff will prepare lists of specific photographs in response to requests. Many photographs are selected by searching U.S. Geological Survey publications and are identified by title and number of the publication as well as the number of the page and plate of the figure found. To obtain information on purchasing prints, negatives, or transparencies, contact the library directly.

* Weather Maps

Public Affairs
National Oceanic and Atmospheric Administration
U.S. Department of Commerce
14th St. and Constitution Ave., NW
Room 6013
Washington, DC 20230   202-377-8090

This office has free copies of the weekly series of daily weather maps. The maps include the highest and lowest temperatures chart, and the precipitation areas and amounts chart. Annual subscriptions are available for $60 per year. Contact the Public Affairs Office for more information.

* World Data Bank II

National Technical Information Service
U.S. Department of Commerce
5285 Port Royal Road
Springfield, VA 22151   703-487-4650

The CIA produced a cartographic database which represents natural and man-made features of the world in a digital format. Approximately six million points are contained on five separate geographic area files. All four volumes (PB 87-184-768) on magnetic tape can be purchased from NTIS.

Environment and Nature
General Sources

* See also Careers and Workplace; Research Grants in Every Field Chapter
* See also Vacations and Business Travel Chapter
* See also Health and Medicine Chapter
* See also Energy Chapter
* See also Current Events and Homework Chapter

Ozone depletion, dioxins, chemical dumps, medical waste, and the disappearance of tropical rain forests are just a few of the environmental issues making news headlines daily. These and other topics, including the tug-of-war between conservation and development, are covered in this chapter. Besides the hundreds of Environmental Protection Agency sources, you'll also find several interest and lobby groups which are useful sources on practically any environmental issue, from details about proposed Clean Air Act amendments to municipal garbage incinerators and indoor air quality. Bird watchers and naturalists will find a complete state-by-state listing of the National Wildlife Refuges here, but should also browse through the Vacations and Business Travel Chapter for information on National Parks and other points of interest.

* Aircraft Noise
Noise Abatement Division
Office of Environment and Energy
Federal Aviation Administration (FAA)
U.S. Department of Transportation
800 Independence Ave., SW, Room 900W
Washington, DC 20591   202-267-3553
This Federal Aviation Administration (FAA) division conducts research on reducing noise levels of new aircraft, and retrofitting older aircraft to reduce noise levels.

* Alternative Energy Sources
National Renewable Energy Laboratory
Technical Inquiry Service
1617 Cole Blvd.
Golden, CO 80401   303-275-3000
SERI produces and disseminates technical communication publications, technical articles, awareness publications, videos, and exhibits on energy efficiency and renewable energy with include: solar, photovoltaic, biofuels, wind energy, ocean energy, and energy storage. SERI provides specific technical responses to limited audiences through the Technical Inquiry Service. Contact SERI for more information.

* Arctic and Antarctic Science Stations
Office of Polar Affairs
Bureau of Oceans and International Environmental
  and Scientific Affairs
U.S. Department of State
2201 C St., NW, Room 5805
Washington, DC 20520   202-647-3262
This office is concerned with all issues concerning the Arctic and Antarctic, including the environment and marine life, such as whales and seals. They are also closely involved with the many science stations located on the Antarctic.

* Army Corps of Engineers Publications
U.S. Army Corps of Engineers
Public Affairs
20 Massachusetts Ave., NW
Washington, DC 20314   202-761-0011
The Corps offers free brochures on a wide variety of subjects, including archaeology, camping, environment, erosion control, flood control, flood plain management, history, safety, waste-water treatment and water supply. For a publications list, call or write the above office.

* Asbestos Ombudsman Clearinghouse
Environmental Protection Agency (EPA)
401 M St., SW   800-368-5888
Washington DC 20460   703-557-1938 (in VA)
The assigned mission of the Asbestos Ombudsman Clearinghouse is to provide to the public sector, including individual citizens and community services, information on handling and abatement of asbestos in schools, the workplace, and the home. In addition, interpretation of the asbestos-in-school requirements, and publications are provided to explain recent legislation. More specifically, the Environmental Protection Agency (EPA) Asbestos Ombudsman receives complaints and requests for information and provides assistance with regard to them.

* Asbestos Regulations
Toxic Substances Control Act Information
Environmental Protection Agency (EPA)
401 M St., SW
Washington DC 20460   202-554-1404
This service can provide you with technical information on asbestos, as well information on regulations and publications. They have publications which interpret the regulations, as well as guidance documents on abatement, sampling, respiratory protection, and waste removal.

* Automated Laboratory Library
Central Regional Laboratory (CRL) Library
839 Bestgate Rd.
Annapolis, MD 21401   410-266-9180
This library was established in support of the Regional Laboratory which started in Annapolis in 1964. The subjects in the collection focus on biology, chemistry, ecology, engineering, hazardous waste hydrology, and oceanography. To serve the highly diversified expertise of the laboratory scientists and engineers, material is provided in aquatic biology, analytical chemistry, automated laboratory techniques, industrial wastewater monitoring, toxic and hazardous substances, and mathematical modelling. A special collections covers the Chesapeake Bay.

* Basic Sciences Clearinghouse
Library Services Office
Research Triangle Park, NC 27711   919-541-2777
The Research Triangle Park (RTP) library's collection concentrates on chemical toxicity, all aspects of air pollution as well as the basic sciences, with some coverage of business and economics. Databases maintained here include BRS, CAS On-line, DIALOG, Hazardline, Hazardous Waste Database, and NLM.

* Coast Guard Environmental Protection

Planning Branch, Research and Development Staff
Office of Engineering and Development
U.S. Coast Guard
U.S. Department of Transportation
2100 2nd St., SW, Room 6208
Washington, DC 20593-0001   202-267-1030

Information can be obtained here about research conducted by the Coast Guard in support of its operations and responsibilities. Areas of study include ice operations, ocean dumping, law enforcement, environmental protection, port safety and security, navigation aids, search and rescue procedures, recreational boating, energy, and advanced marine vehicles. For referral to specific personnel working in these areas, contact the Planning Branch.

* Coastal Zone Management

Office of Ocean and Coastal Resource Management
National Ocean Service
National Oceanic and Atmospheric Administration
U.S. Department of Commerce
1305 East West Hwy.
Silver Spring, MD 20910   301-413-0900

To balance the needs for preserving and developing the resources in the U.S. coastal zone, the National Ocean Service (NOS), through its Office of Ocean and Coastal Resource Management, provides the coordination and expertise at the Federal level needed for effective management of these coastal resources. NOS has begun to expand the technical assistance provided to States and territories, emphasizing special area management planning, coastal hazards mitigation, cost-effective coastal management, and the simplification of permit processes for coastal activities.

* Community-College Environmental Curricula Grants

SEEP
Office of Research and Development
Environmental Protection Agency (EPA)
401 M St., SW, Room NE312
Washington DC 20460   202-260-2576

SEEP has agreements with nonprofit organizations to place senior citizens in special positions in Environmental Protection Agency (EPA) programs. The office also awards fellowships to State employees to continue their education concerning the environment. The fellowship applications are given out through the individual states. Contact this office for more information.

* Consumer Publications

Public Information Center
Environmental Protection Agency (EPA)
401 M St., SW, 3404
Washington DC 20460   202-260-7751

The Environmental Protection Agency's (EPA) Public Information Center maintains a wide selection of publications on major environmental topics. The materials distributed by the Center are nontechnical and have been prepared as sources of general environmental information for the public. Technical documents are available through the EPA Library, the National Technical Information Service, or the publishing office within EPA. The *Public Information Center Publications List* is updated monthly and is free.

* Drinking Water Programs

Office of Drinking Water 4601
Environmental Protection Agency (EPA)
401 M St., SW, Room E1011
Washington, DC 20460   202-260-5543

This Environmental Protection Agency (EPA) office develops national programs, technical policies, and regulations for water pollution control and water supply. It also administers part of the Safe Drinking Water Act.

* Ecology Research

National Ecology Center
National Biological Service
4512 McMurray Ave.
Fort Collins, CO 80525   303-226-9100

The center conducts research, develops new tools, and transfers information so that scientists can better understand and manage fish and wildlife resources, habitats, and ecosystems. All endangered marine mammal research is performed here. Workshops

are held in refuge management and habitat model development for those within the Interior Department and scientists in Federal and State agencies and foreign countries. Studies are reported in the Center's *Biological Report* series and through extension education brochures.

* Educational Materials and Programs

Environmental/Energy Education
Land Resources Division
Resource Development
Tennessee Valley Authority (TVA)
Norris, TN 37828   615-632-1640

Much of the Tennessee Valley Authority's (TVA) environmental education effort is accomplished through university-based environmental education centers. The TVA has worked with several universities and colleges across the Valley and seven states to develop environmental education teaching aids and programs for schools, along with workshops for teachers. At the national level, the TVA has been involved in coordinating programs with the Environmental Protection Agency. In addition, TVA offers teacher workshops and interpretive programs for groups at Land Between the Lakes, an experimental area for schools and the public to study total resource management. Contact this office of more information on the TVA's environmental education programs.

* Education Materials from the EPA

Public Information Center
Environmental Protection Agency (EPA)
401 M St., SW, PM-211 B
Washington DC 20460   202-260-7751

Environmental Education Materials For Teachers and Young People is a free annotated list of educational materials on environmental issues. Entries include diverse materials ranging from workbooks and lesson plans to newsletters, films, and computer software intended for young people. Educational materials available from sources other than Environmental Protection Agency (EPA) are listed alphabetically following the name of their sponsoring organization or group. A separate listing of selected EPA publications and other material available from EPA's Public Information Center is included in this pamphlet, as well as a short descriptive list of environmental education resource facilities.

* Energy Conservation - Help Is Just a Phone Call Away

Conservation and Renewable Energy Inquiry and
   Referral Service (CAREIRS)
U.S. Department of Energy
P.O. Box 8900
Silver Spring, MD 20907   800-523-2929

CAREIRS provides fact sheets and bibliographies on the full spectrum of energy efficiency and renewable energy technologies. CAREIRS also maintains a referral network of hundreds of public and private organizations to respond to requests that are regionally or State specific, or highly technical in nature. CAREIRS provides general information on energy efficiency and renewable energy technologies such as: caulking and weatherstripping, efficient windows and lighting systems, recycling, photovoltaics, wind energy, and solar energy.

* Energy Efficiency for You

Public Affairs
U.S. Department of Energy   800-363-3732
Washington, DC 20585   202-586-5575

The U.S. Department of Energy has a wide variety of information available regarding energy efficiency. They have information sheets on automatic and programmable thermostats, solar energy, appliance labeling, fans and ventilation, heat pumps, hot water conservation, insulation, as well as many more. Two booklets that provide a wealth of information as well as some helpful suggestions include: *Tips For Saving Energy In Small Business*, and *Tips For An Energy Efficient Apartment*. All are free.

* Energy Information Clearinghouse

Office of Scientific and Technical Information (OSTI)
U.S. Department of Energy
P.O. Box 62
Oak Ridge, TN 37831   615-576-8401

The Office of Scientific and Technical Information (OSTI) is the program office responsible for managing the U.S. Department of Energy's (DOE) scientific and technical information. OSTI primarily serves the information needs of DOE and its contractors. Information collected and managed by OSTI is also made available

Environment and Nature

through specific databases on superconductivity and new technology and abstract periodicals in specific subject areas such as *Buildings Energy Technology* and *Synthesis Gas Conversion Technology Update*. OSTI also distributes handbooks, brochures, flyers, posters and other information products to the public at no charge.

* Enforcement and Investigations

National Enforcement Investigations Center Library (NEIC)
Building 53, Box 25227
Denver Federal Center
Denver, CO 80225   303-236-5122

This library's collection comprises case files, technical reports, data compilations, and background information used to develop the basis for field studies and enforcement actions; research and development reports on municipal, industrial, and agricultural pollution abatement practices; enforcement conference documents and environmental law materials; technical reference materials covering chemistry, pesticides, toxic substances, air technology, and hazardous wastes. Databases maintained here include BRS, CDS, CIS, Consent Decree System, DIALOG, FINDS, Ground Water On-line, HWDMS, ISI, LEXIS/NEXIS, NLM, PCS, SFFAS, STORET, VV-Text, and Westlaw.

* Enforcement of Environmental Laws

Civil Enforcement
Enforcement and Compliance Monitoring
Environmental Protection Agency (EPA)
401 M St., SW, Room W1035
Washington DC 20460   202-260-4137

When regulated entities fail to comply voluntarily with Environmental Protection Agency (EPA) requirements, the EPA, in partnership with State agencies, can take a number of enforcement actions. These alternatives include compliance promotion; administrative money penalties; negotiated compliance schedules; and ultimately, judicial enforcement involving criminal proceedings in federal court. Contact this office for more information regarding enforcement of environmental laws.

* Environment Library As Close As Your Phone

EPA's National Computer Center
EPA Research Triangle Park Library
Research Triangle Park, NC 27711   919-541-2777

The Environmental Protection Agency (EPA) Online Library System puts a wealth of environmental information at your disposal. Anyone with access to a terminal with a modem can use the system. The holdings of EPA's Network Libraries are accessible using this system. The system can be searched using titles, authors, and keywords. For a User Guide and password information, contact the office listed above.

* Environmental Engineering and Technology

Office of Environmental Engineering and Technology
Office of Research and Development
Environmental Protection Agency (EPA)
401 M St., SW, Room W635E
Washington, DC 20460   202-260-2600

Research in environmental engineering and technology studies pollution from industrial and municipal sources, and analyzes alternative control technologies. Examples of research includes exploring innovative techniques for removing and disposing of pollutants, and developing cost-effective methods of providing safe drinking water.

* Environmental Impact Statements

Special Programs and Analysis Division
Office of Federal Activities
Environmental Protection Agency (EPA)
401 M St., SW, Room 2119
Washington DC 20460   202-260-8799

This office reviews and completes a compliance check on *Environmental Impact Statements* (EISs) to ensure that they meet the criteria required of an EIS. They comment on the impact statement and then publish it in the *Federal Register*. These *Statements* are documents required of Federal agencies by the National Environmental Policy Act for major projects or legislative proposals significantly affecting the environment. A tool for decision making, they describe the positive and negative effects of the undertaking and lists alternative actions. This office can also refer you to a Federal agency responsible for an *Environmental Impact Statement* on a specific topic.

* Environmental Regulations

Superintendent of Documents
Government Printing Office
Washington DC 20402   202-512-1800

Single copies of *Federal Registers* with environmental regulations can be obtained from this office.

* EPA Bibliography

National Technical Information Service (NTIS)
5285 Port Royal Rd.
Springfield, VA 22161   703-487-4650

EPA Publications Bibliography, Quarterly Abstract Bulletin is a quarterly update listing and indexing Environmental Protection Agency (EPA) technical reports and journal articles added to the NTIS collection during the preceding quarter. The fourth issue of each year contains bibliographic citations with abstracts for the preceding quarter and cumulative indexes for the calendar year. Single copies are $25, and a yearly subscription is $90.

* EPA Freedom of Information Requests

Freedom of Information Officer
Environmental Protection Agency (EPA)
401 M St., SW, Room W227
Washington DC 20460   202-260-4048

All Freedom of Information requests should be addressed to the Officer listed above.

* EPA Libraries

EPA Headquarters Library
401 M St., SW
Room 2904 WSM, MC 3404
Washington, DC 20460   202-260-5921

The Environmental Protection Agency (EPA) Headquarters Library provides information services covering a wide range of environmental and related subjects of interest to EPA staff and the general public. Major areas include air and radiation, chemistry, hazardous waste, management, noise abatement, pesticides, resource recovery, solid waste, toxicology, wastewater treatment, water quality, and water supply. Databases maintained here include CAS Online, CIS, DIALOG, Ground Water Online, Hazardous Waste Database, ISI, LEXIS/NEXIS, NLM, and Newsnet. The library's special collection covers hazardous waste.

There are 28 EPA network libraries located in Headquarters, and all regional offices and laboratories to support the EPA offices. The libraries and other information services contain a combined collection of over 128,900 books, 5,088 journals subscriptions, 357,146 hard copy reports, 3,166,500 documents on microfilm and microfiche, 9,000 journal article reprints, and 2,000 maps. A free publication, *Guide to EPA Libraries And Information Services*, lists each of the libraries, as well as their location, collection emphasis, loan policy, and the services they offer. What follows is a list of the EPA's regional libraries:

Region 1 Library
JFK Federal Bldg., Boston, MA 02203; 617-565-3300. The EPA Region I Library's collection still reflects some older New England river basin reports, but has been extensively developed in the areas of air pollution and control, pesticides and toxic substances, groundwater, solid and hazardous waste, health effects, water pollution and control. Databases maintained here include BRS, CAS On-line, CIS, DIALOG, Ground Water On-line, Hazardous Waste Database, and LEXIS/NEXIS. Special collections include the Hazardous Waste collection, Envirofiche since 1980, New England materials: Connecticut, Maine, Massachusetts, New Hampshire, Rhode Island, and Vermont.

Region 2 Library
26 Federal Plaza, New York, NY 10278; 212-264-2881. This library embraces all aspects of EPA's environmental mission. Databases maintained here include DIALOG, Hazardous Waste Database, and ISI. Its general collection covers human resources management.

Region 2 Field Office Library
2890 Woodbridge Ave., Edison, NJ 08837; 908-321-6762. This library includes materials on all EPA programs: air, solid waste, hazardous waste, toxic substances, pesticides, water, and radiation.

Region 3 Library
841 Chestnut St., Philadelphia, PA 19107; 215-597-0580. This Center (IRC) provides information support for a wide range of environmental programs and activities

Be patient. If any phone number is incorrect, call (area code) 555-1212 and request the new listing.

conducted by the Regional office. It also serves as an information resource for the general public. Subject areas include air pollution, pesticides, employee development, radiation, environmental law, toxic substances, hazardous waste, toxicology, management, water pollution, and wetlands. Databases maintained here include CIS, DIALOG, Ground Water On-line, Hazardline, Hazardous Waste Database, and LEXIS/NEXIS. There are also special collections on wetland ecology and hazardous waste and law. In addition, a special effort is made to acquire published information on environmental conditions and trends within the five states and the District of Columbia which comprise Region 3.

Region 4 Library
345 Courtland St., NE, Atlanta, GA 30365-2401; 404-347-4216. The Region 4 Library provides a full range of library and information services, covering subjects from air and water pollution to toxics and hazardous waste with a variety of technical reports, reference books, journals, and online computer services. Databases maintained here include CAS On-line, CIS, DIALOG, Dun & Bradstreet, Hazardous Waste Database, ISI, LEXIS/NEXIS, NLM, NPIRS, and OHS.

Region 5 Library
Library PL-12J, 77 West Jackson Blvd., Room 1670, Chicago, IL 60604; 312-353-2022. The subject areas of this library's collection cover air pollution, air quality, groundwater, hazardous waste, noise, pesticides, recycling and resource recovery, solid waste management, toxic substances, water pollution, water quality, and water supply (drinking water). The emphasis is on the Great Lakes and the six states in the Region: Illinois, Indiana, Michigan, Minnesota, Ohio, and Wisconsin. Databases maintained here include BRS, CIS, DIALOG, Ground Water On-line, Hazardous Waste Database, ISI, LEXIS/NEXIS, NLM, and ORBIT.

Region 6 Library
1445 Ross Ave., Sountain Place, Dallas, TX 75202-2733; 214-665-6424. The EPA Region 6 Library includes materials on all EPA programs: air pollution, radiation, hazardous waste, solid waste, noise, toxic substances, pesticides, and water pollution.

Region 7 Library
726 Minnesota Ave., Kansas City, KS 66101; 913-551-7241. The Region 7 Library provides information on a wide range of environmental subjects of interest to the Regional staff and the general public. Subject areas include agricultural pollution, air pollution, environmental law, hazardous waste, pesticides, radiation, solid waste management, water pollution, water quality, and water supply. Databases maintained here include CIS, Hazardous Waste Database, LEXIS/NEXIS, NLM, and Watstore.

Region 8 Library
999 18th St., Suite 500, Denver, CO 80202-2466; 303-312-6511. The Region 8 Library includes materials on all EPA programs: air, water, hazardous and solid waste, pesticides, toxic substances, noise and radiation, particularly as they relate to the states within the Region. In addition, because the Rocky Mountain area is rich in energy resources, the library collects material relating to energy resource development and its relationship to the environment. And finally, to support other Agency programs, the collection incorporates publications relating to economics, planning, transportation, management and employee development. Databases maintained here include CARL, CIS, DIALOG, Ground Water On-line, and Hazardous Waste Database.

Region 9 Library
215 Fremont St., 6th Floor, San Francisco, CA 94105. The Region 9 Library's major subject areas include air pollution and control, pesticides, environmental health and safety, radiation, hazardous waste, research and development, law, solid waste. Databases maintained include CIS, DIALOG, Hazardline, and Hazardous Waste Database. Special collections here include Environmental Impact Statements, hazardous waste, and speeches given by EPA Senior Staff.

Region 10 Library
1200 Sixth Ave., Seattle, WA 98101; 206-553-1289. The Region 10 Library's holdings include monographs, serials, a basic environmental law collection, EPA reports (both hard copy and microfiche), and local and state government reports. The collection was originally heavily oriented toward water pollution, but has since been developed to encompass all other areas of environmental quality. Databases maintained here include CIS, DIALOG, Ground Water On-line, Hazardous Waste Database, LEXIS/NEXIS, and NLM. Special collections include Environmental Impact Statements and hazardous waste.

* EPA Newsletter
Superintendent of Documents
Government Printing Office
Washington DC 20402   202-512-1800
Published six times a year, the *EPA Journal* presents articles concerning the

environment, state and local actions, and Environmental Protection Agency (EPA) activities. A subscription is available for $8 per year. For more information concerning the EPA Journal contact: Editor, *EPA Journal*, 401 M St, SW, A-107, Washington DC 20460: 202-382-4393.

* Exposure to Toxic Substances
Health and Environment Review Division
Office of Toxic Substances
Environmental Protection Agency (EPA)
401 M St., SW, Room E315B
Washington, DC 20460   202-260-4241
This Environmental Protection Agency (EPA) division studies human and environmental exposure to chemical substances in support of the Office of Toxic Substances (OTS) risk assessment activities. EED provides standards, guidance, and rule development. It reviews available information relevant to chemical exposure to humans and develops guidelines for epidemiological data.

* Free Environment Information
Consumer Information Center
Pueblo, CO 81009
Consumer Information Catalog lists 200 free or low cost publications from a variety of federal agencies. The publications cover environment, health, federal benefits, money management, housing, childcare, employment, small business, education, food and nutrition, consumer protection, and more. The catalog is published quarterly and is free. Write for your free copy.

* Free Technology Newsletter
Center for Environmental Research Information (CERI)
ORD Publications Unit
Environmental Protection Agency (EPA)
Cincinnati, OH 45268   513-569-7369
This free newsletter lists titles and description of printed publications that available from the Center for Environmental Research Information (CERI), including seminar publications, manuals, handbooks, and guides. Also included is a listing of technology transfer seminars and meetings.

* Grants For Your Environmental Research
Research Grants Program
Center for Environmental Research Information
ORD Publications Unit
Environmental Protection Agency (EPA)
26 W. Martin Luther King Jr. Dr.
Cincinnati, OH 45268   513-569-7562
The Environmental Protection Agency (EPA) Research Program Guide provides descriptions of the research programs organized first by media such as air, water, hazardous waste, etc. These categories are further broken down into research foci such as scientific assessment, monitoring and quality assurance, health effects. environmental processes, and engineering technology. Each description is a every broad summary of research being done, where it is occurring, who to contact for more information about the program, and both the approximate total funding for that area and the percentage of total funding which is reserved by EPA for in-house research.

* Greenhouse Effect
Office of Technology Assessment (OTA)
600 Pennsylvania Ave., SE
Washington, DC 20510   202-224-8996
The Office of Technology Assessment (OTA) has studied the major contributors to climate change, ozone depletion, and the greenhouse effect for both the developed and developing world. OTA identifies areas where gains in efficiency, product substitution, conservation, or other options can slow climate change. *Ozone Depletion and the Greenhouse Effect* is the resulting publication.

* Guide to the Environmental Protection Agency
Public Information Center
Environmental Protection Agency (EPA)
401 M St., SW, PM-211B
Washington, DC 20460   202-260-7551
Your Guide to the United States Environmental Protection Agency describes how the EPA is addressing the major environmental problems that confront the U.S. It looks

at the organization, and the laws for which the EPA is responsible, as well as providing a listing of regional offices and research facilities. Contact this office for your free copy.

* Gulf Breeze Environmental Center

Environmental Research Laboratory (ERL) Library
Sabine Island
Gulf Breeze, FL 32561   904-932-9218

The Gulf Breeze Environmental Research Laboratory (GBERL) library provides information services to GBERL employees and the general public. The library's subject areas include aquatic toxicology, microbiology, genetic engineering, pathobiology, marine ecology, and pesticide science. Databases maintained here include DIALOG and Ground Water On-line.

* Health Effects of Chemicals

Health and Environmental Review Division
Office of Toxic Substances
Environmental Protection Agency (EPA)
401 M St., SW, Room E617
Washington, DC 20460   202-260-4241

The Health and Environmental Review Division studies the hazards posed by new chemicals to human health and the environment, and for integrating these studies with exposure information from other EPA divisions.

* Health Risks and the Environment

Research and Development
Environmental Protection Agency (EPA)
401 M St., SW, Room 3100
Washington DC 20460   202-260-5900

This office conducts health assessment research which provides an integrated, scientific basis for evaluating environmental risks and effects stemming from exposure to various substances, and provides data needed to estimate human mortality and illness caused by pollutants.

* Help With Risk Assessment

Office of Toxic Substances
Chemical Library, TS-793
Environmental Protection Agency (EPA)
401 M St., SW
Washington, DC 20460   202-260-3944

Risk Assessment, Management, and Communication: A Guide to Selected Sources is a series of risk management bibliographies. References are gathered from the environmental, medical and scientific literature. Also available is *Communicating Environmental Risks: A Guide to Practical Evaluations* (EPA230-01-91-001), which was designed to help staff evaluate the effectiveness of their risk communication activities.

* Hotlines: EPA State and Local Site-Specific

Region II   800-732-1223
This is a local hotline that provides site-specific regulatory information on Resource Conservation and Recovery Act only in the Region II areas of New York, New Jersey, Puerto Rico, and the Virgin Islands.

Region III   800-438-2474
The EPA Region III Hotline provides general information on Agency programs to the public and makes referrals as needed. It provides this information for all Region III states: Washington, DC, Delaware, Maryland, Pennsylvania, Virginia, and West Virginia.

Region IV   800-241-1754
The EPA Region IV Hotline provides general information on Agency programs to the public and makes referrals as needed. It provides this information for all Region IV states: Alabama, Florida, Georgia, Kentucky, Mississippi, North Carolina, South Carolina, and Tennessee.

Region V   800-621-8431; 800-572-2515 (IL)
The EPA Region V Hotline provides general information on Agency programs to the public and makes referrals as needed. It provides this information for all Region V states: Indiana, Michigan, Illinois, Minnesota, Ohio, and Wisconsin.

Region VII
The Region VII Hotline provides general information on Agency programs to the public and makes referrals a needed. It provides this information for all Region VII states: Iowa, Kansas, Missouri, and Nebraska. Kansas: 800-221-7749; Nebraska, Iowa, and Missouri: 800-223-0425.

Region VII   800-223-0424
The Resource Conservation and Recovery Act Hotline in Region VII provides information on implementation of RCRA in Iowa.

Region VIII   800-525-3022
The Region VIII Hotline provides general information on Agency programs to the public and makes referrals as needed. It provides this information for all Region VIII states: Colorado, Montana, North Dakota, South Dakota, Utah, and Wyoming.

Region IX   800-231-3075
This is a local hotline that provides site-specific regulatory information on Resource Conservation and Recovery Act only in the Region IX areas of Arizona, California, Hawaii, Nevada, Guam, and Samoa.

* How Does The EPA Decide What's Good Or Bad For The Environment?

Environmental Impact
Office of Federal Activities
401 M St., SW
Washington, DC 20460   202-260-5075

An Environmental Impact Statement (EIS) is a document required of federal agencies for major projects or legislative proposals significantly affecting the environment. A tool for decision making, it describes the positive and negative effects of the undertaking and lists alternative actions. The Environmental Protection Agency (EPA) reports all filed environmental impact statements in the *Federal Register* weekly. In addition, EPA's comments on the EIS are also published in the weekly *Federal Register*. For each EIS listed in the Register, a public contact is listed, along with the filing agency name and phone number. Contact the office listed above for referral information on EIS and copies of EPA comments only.

* Indian Affairs Field Offices

Bureau of Indian Affairs
U.S. Department of the Interior
Code 130, Room 4627N
Washington, DC 20240   202-208-3711

For information on American Indian lands, address your correspondence to: Area Director, Bureau of Indian Affairs, followed by the address listed below.

Alaska
P.O. Box 22520, Juneau, AK 99802; 907-586-7177. Serving: Alaska

Arizona
P.O. Box M, Window Rock, AZ 86515; 520-871-5151, ext. 5106. Serving: Navajo Reservations only, Arizona, Utah, and New Mexico
P.O. Box 10, Phoenix, AZ 85001; 602-379-6600. Serving: Arizona, Nevada, Utah, and Idaho

California
Federal Office Building, 2800 Cottage Way, Sacramento, CA 95825; 916-484-4682. Serving: California

Minnesota
Chamber of Commerce Building, 15 South Fifth St., 10th Floor, Minneapolis, MN 55402; 612-349-3631. Serving: Minnesota, Iowa, Michigan and Wisconsin

Montana
316 North 26th St., Billings, MT 59101; 406-247-7943. Serving: Montana and Wyoming

New Mexico
P.O. Box 26567, Albuquerque, NM 87125-6567; 505-766-3170. Serving: Colorado and New Mexico

North Dakota
115 4th Ave., SE, Aberdeen, SD 57401; 605-226-7343. Serving: Nebraska, North Dakota, and South Dakota

Oklahoma
WCD-Office Complex, P.O. Box 368, Anadarko, OK 73005; 405-247-6673. Serving: Kansas and West Oklahoma
Old Federal Building, 5th and Okmulgee St., Muskogee, Oklahoma 74401; 918-687-2296. Serving: East Oklahoma

Oregon
911 North East St., Portland, OR 97232-4182; 503-231-6702. Serving: Oregon, Washington, and Idaho

Virginia
1000 N. Glebe Rd, Arlington, VA 22201; 703-235-3006. Serving: New York, Maine, Louisiana, Florida, North Carolina, Mississippi, Connecticut, and Rhode Island

Eastern Area
1951 Constitution Ave. NW, MS260, Washington, DC 20245; 703-235-2571.

* Innovative/Alternative Environmental Clearinghouse
Innovative/Alternative Projects   304-293-4191
This Clearinghouse provides information on innovative and alternative projects to enable communities and grant applicants to identify and contact other sources with experience in technologies.

* Inspector General's Whistle Blower Hotline
Environmental Protection Agency (EPA)
401 M St., SW
Washington DC 20460   800-424-4000
The Inspector General's Whistle Blower Hotline receives reports of Environmental Protection Agency (EPA) -related waste, fraud, abuse, or mismanagement from public and from EPA and other government employees. All calls are kept confidential. The Hotline operates Monday through Friday, 10:00 a.m. to 3:00 p.m. (EST).

* Insular Islands Assistance
Territorial and International Affairs
U.S. Department of the Interior
18th and C Sts., NW
Washington, DC 20240   202-208-4754
Technical assistance in the areas of social, political, and economic development is given to the Insular Islands by this office. The office is no longer involved in the government of the islands.

* Interior Department Freedom of Information
Freedom of Information Appeals Officer
U.S. Department of the Interior
18th and C Sts., NW, Room 5412
Washington, DC 20240   202-208-5339
Each bureau under the U.S. Department of the Interior has a separate office that handles concerns under the Freedom of Information Act. If you wish to obtain the officer's name within a particular bureau or wish to file with the central office, contact the officer above.

* International Environment Policy
Bureau of Oceans and International Environmental
    and Scientific Affairs
U.S. Department of State
2201 C St., NW, Room 7831
Washington, DC 20520   202-647-1561
International political and economic relationships are increasingly affected by science and technology and by environmental issues. This bureau deals with U.S. foreign policy such specialized fields as nuclear physics, marine science, biotechnology, global climate, acid rain, and wildlife conservation. The bureau also manages bilateral science and technology agreements with ten countries and guides the development and implementation of several hundred other science and technology arrangements.

* International Environmental Conservation
Office of Ecology, Health and Conservation
Bureau of Oceans and International
    Environmental and Scientific Affairs

U.S. Department of State
2201 C St., NW, Room 4325
Washington, DC 20520   202-647-2418
This office handles matters in two basic areas: 1) the conservation of nature and natural resources, such as wildlife, plant issues, and tropical deforestation; 2) international health issues, particularly AIDS. This office also works with other agencies in developing an international approach for the United States in dealing with these problems. Recently, they have been looking at debt leverage in third world countries to set aside land for new parks or to protect habitats.

* International Marine Environmental Efforts
Environmental Coordination Branch
Marine Environmental Response Division
Office of Marine, Safety, Security, and Environmental Protection
U.S. Coast Guard
U.S. Department of Transportation
2100 2nd St., SW, Room 1202
Washington, DC 20593-0001   202-267-0421
Information is available here on the Coast Guard's role in international marine environmental efforts, such as representation in the U.N. International Maritime Consultative Organization. For further information on cooperative environmental efforts, contact the branch listed.

This office also handles all antarctic issues, law of the seas, maritime boundaries, and coordinates international marine science programs. Experts are available to answer questions and provide information.

* International Marine Science and Policy
Office of Marine Science and Polar Affairs
2201 C St., NW, Room 5805
U.S. Department of State
Washington, DC 20520   202-647-3262
This office handles international marine environment concerns, from the protection of whales to cleaning up oil spills, by negotiating bilateral and multilateral agreements.

* Land Use Engineering
Division of Engineering
Bureau of Land Management
U.S. Department of the Interior
1725 I St., NW
Washington, DC 20006   202-452-5125
For technical information concerning environmental engineering of roads, buildings, and recreational structures, contact the above office.

* Law Library
EPA Law Library
401 M St., SW
Room 2902
Washington, DC 20460   202-260-5919
The Environmental Protection Agency (EPA) Law Library provides information services to the Agency's legal and enforcement personnel, and to the ten Regional Counsels. The collection contains approximately 9,000 volumes of legal and law-related material concentrating on Federal law, with special emphasis on administrative and environmental law. Included are statutes, codes, regulations, case reports, digests, citators, and legal reference sources, as well as looseleaf services, newspapers, and 70 current law reviews and periodicals.

* Legislation
Environmental Legislative Library
832 West Tower, 401 M St., SW
Washington, DC 20460   202-260-5425
The Legislative Library primarily supports the Office of Legislative Analysis, but also provides information for other Environmental Protection Agency (EPA) staff on request. The collection consists primarily of federal environmental legislation and related federal information. The library is mainly geared to the current Congress, but there are many older documents in the collection. The library responds to reference requests from EPA staff; supplies copies of Congressional documents when possible; tracks status of current environmental legislation; and compiles current status of pending environmental legislation organized by subject area. Databases maintained include Legi-Slate and the Congressional Quarterly Data Base (CQ)

Environment and Nature

* Minnesota-Based Environmental Lab

Environmental Research Laboratory Library
6201 Congdon Boulevard
Duluth, MN 55804   218-720-5538

This library's major fields of interest are analytical chemistry, fisheries biology, and water pollution. Its general collections cover analytical chemistry and fisheries biology.

* Minority and Disadvantaged Small Business Hotline

Office of Small and Disadvantaged Business Utilization
Environmental Protection Agency (EPA)
401 M St., SW   800-368-5888
Washington DC 20460   202-557-7015 (DC area)

The Small Business Hotline is an EPA-based hotline that gives advice and information to small businesses on complying with Environmental Protection Agency (EPA) regulations. It deals with problems encountered by small-quantity generators of hazardous waste and other small businesses with environmental concerns.

* Monitoring Pollution

Office of Modeling, Monitoring Systems and Quality Assurance
Research and Development
Environmental Protection Agency (EPA)
401 M St., SW, Room 3821
Washington DC 20460   202-260-5776

This office provides data on monitoring systems and quality assurance research which develops standardized methods to measure and monitor pollutants in various media (water, air, soil).

* National Environmental Data Network

National Environmental Data Referral Service
NEDRES Office
National Oceanic And Atmospheric Administration
U.S. Department of Commerce
1825 Connecticut Ave., NW, Room 412
Washington, DC 20235   202-606-4548

The National Environmental Data Referral Service (NEDRES) is designed to provide convenient, economical, and efficient access to widely scattered environmental data. NEDRES is a publicly available service which identifies the existence, location, characteristics, and availability conditions of environmental data sets. NEDRES database contains only descriptions, not the actual data. It is a national network of federal, state, and private organizations cooperating to improve access to environmental data. Major subject categories include climatology and meteorology, oceanography, geophysics and geology, geography, hydrology and limnnology, terrestrial resources, toxic and regulated substances, and satellite remotely sensed data. For more information on the NEDRES database and the user charges, contact the office listed above. NEDRES also produces the following printed catalogs with references to available environmental data on selected topics and regions:

Finding the Environmental Data You Need (free)
NEDRES Memorandum of Agreement (free)
NEDRES Database User Agreement (free)
NEDRES Data Base User Guide ($7.50)
Guideline for the Description of Environmental Data Files for the Nedres Database ($10)
North American Climatic Data Catalog: Part 1 ($10)
North American Climatic Data Catalog: Part 2 ($10)
Satellite Remote Sensing of the Marine Environment: Literature and Data Sources ($10)
Coastal and Estuarine Waters of California, Oregon, and Washington ($10)
Chesapeake Bay and Adjacent Wetlands
Chesapeake Bay Environmental Data Directory (free to federal and state agencies)
Environmental Data Review (free)

* Natural Landmarks Registry

National Registry of Natural Landmarks
National Registry Branch
National Park Service
U.S. Department of the Interior
800 N. Capitol St., NW, Suite 250
Washington, DC 20002   202-343-9536

The Park Service conducts natural region studies to identify areas that are of potential national significance. These areas are then studied in the field by scientists.

Natural areas considered of national significance are cited by the Secretary of the Interior as eligible for recognition as Registered Natural Landmarks. The owner may apply for a certificate and bronze plaque designating the site.

* Natural Resources Library

Natural Resources Library
U.S. Department of the Interior
18th and C Sts., NW
Washington, DC 20240   202-208-5815

Information is provided to the general public on such topics as Native American Indians, mining and minerals issues, land reclamation and management, fish and wildlife, water resources, parks and outdoor recreation, and the preservation of scenic and historic sites. The library is open from 7:45 a.m. to 5:00 p.m., Monday through Friday. Computer searches can also be performed by their reference librarians.

* Need Help Finding the Right Expert?

Technical Assistance Directory
Center for Environmental Research Information
ORD Publications Unit
Environmental Protection Agency (EPA)
Cincinnati, OH 45268   513-569-7369

The *Technical Assistance Directory* is a free publication which lists programs, areas of expertise, and primary contacts in each of the major research and development areas within the Environmental Protection Agency (EPA). This information is provided to improve communication and technology transfer, and would be useful for the environmental community, other federal agencies, and individuals who need to locate specific programs within ORD.

* One-Stop Shopping for Environmental Data

Gerald Barton
NOAA/NODC
1825 Connecticut Ave., NW
Washington, DC 20235   202-606-4548

The *NOAA Earth System Data Directory* helps pull together all the National Oceanic and Atmospheric Administration (NOAA) data files that are scattered throughout the U.S. This is an online computer guide to environmental data. This office can also provide you with a free monthly newsletter, *Earth System Monitor*, which is a guide to NOAA's Data and Information Services.

* Oregon-Based Environmental Lab

Environmental Research Laboratory Library
200 SW 35th St.
Corvallis, OR 97333   541-254-4600

The Corvallis Environmental Research Laboratory (CERL) Library was established in 1966 with an emphasis on marine, estuarine, and fresh water quality, air and terrestrial research. At present the laboratory has three branches: Toxics and Pesticides, Hazardous Materials, and Water, and the Air. Research concerns acid precipitation and its effects on the ecosystem, wildlife toxicology, genetic engineering, wetlands, and hazardous waste. Databases maintained here include CIS, DIALOG, and NLM. General collections of the library include acid rain, air pollution-ecology, biology, estuarine research, genetic engineering, wetlands, wildlife toxicology. The library's special collection covers acid rain.

* Outer Continental Shelf Management

Offshore Minerals Management
Mineral Management Service
U.S. Department of the Interior
18th and C Sts., NW
Washington, DC 20240   202-208-3530

Management of the oil and gas operations following leasing agreements with the Mineral Management Service is outlined in the publication, *Managing Oil and Gas Operations on the Outer Continental Shelf*. This booklet describes activities through the drilling and production process to lease relinquishment.

* Outside Help for the EPA

Science Advisory Board (SAB), A-101
Environmental Protection Agency (EPA)
401 M St., SW, Room 1145 West Tower
Washington, DC 20460   202-260-4126

The Science Advisory Board (SAB) was established by Congress to provide independent scientific and engineering advice to the Administrator of the Environmental Protection Agency (EPA) on the technical basis for EPA regulations. The SAB deals with risk assessment (hazard identification, dose-response assessment, exposure assessment, and risk characterization) and only that portion of risk management that deals strictly with the technical issues associated with various control options. The SAB produces approximately 25 scientific reports a year in addition to a monthly newsletter called *Happenings*, and the *Annual Report of the Staff Director*.

* Park Service Technical Information

Technical Information Center
National Park Service
Denver Service Center
12795 W. Alameda Parkway
P.O. Box 25287
Denver, CO 80225-0287   303-969-2130

The Technical Information Center has been designated by the National Park Service as the central repository for all National Park Service-generated planning, design, and construction maps, drawings, and reports as well as related cultural, environmental, and other technical documents. Bibliographic data on aerial photography is also maintained. The Center reproduces and delivers copies of the available materials for the Service, other agencies, and the public, both here and abroad. Today, the system has a holding of 100,000 data records, which represent about 500,000 microfilm aperture cards of maps, plans, and drawings; 1,000 records of resource and site aerial photography; and 25,000 planning, design, environmental, cultural resource, and natural resource documents.

* Pipeline Safety

Office of Pipeline Safety (OPS)
Research and Special Programs Administration
U.S. Department of Transportation
400 7th Street, SW
Washington, DC 20590   202-366-4572

The Office of Pipeline Safety (OPS) establishes and enforces safety standards for the transportation of gas and other hazardous materials by pipeline. A computerized reporting system is maintained to collect and analyze accident and incident data from pipeline operators. Accident reports include the operator's name, the hazardous material involved, description of the accident, and results. For database searches, contact the office listed. There may be a charge.

* President's Council on Environmental Quality

Council on Environmental Quality
722 Jackson Place, NW
Washington, DC 20503   202-395-5750

This office was established by the National Environmental Policy Act of 1969 to formulate and recommend national policies to promote the improvement of the quality of the environment. There are three members on the Council appointed by the President by and with the consent of the Senate. The Council's major responsibilities are to provide opinion and policy advice to the President on environmental matters, to act with White House advisors and other agencies to develop international environmental policy, to interact as a liaison with representatives of foreign governments and international organizations about global environmental issues, to assist in coordinating federal environmental programs that involve more than one agency, to act in the review process for proposed legislation on environmental quality, and to prepare the annual *Environmental Quality Report* on environmental activities of all levels of government and of private entities.

* Prevent Pollution Near You

Pollution Prevention Clearinghouse
Pollution Prevention Office
Environmental Protection Agency (EPA)
401 M St., SW
Washington, DC 20460   202-260-3810

Through the Pollution Prevention Information Clearinghouse (PPIC), the Environmental Protection Agency's (EPA) Pollution Prevention Office provides information on government and industry pollution prevention programs, grant and project funding opportunities, upcoming events, conferences, and seminars and contains the Electronic Information Exchange System (EIES). The EIES is a computerized information network that anyone can access, either through a PC with appropriate communication software or through the RCRA/Superfund Hotline (800-424-9346). The EIES lists documents available, provides a directory of experts and calendar of events, and enables you to leave your question on the bulletin board and the appropriate person will respond. The hotline provides a telephone service to answer or refer any pollution prevention questions, access information in the PPIC, provide instruction on accessing the EIES databases, and assist in document searches and ordering.

* Public Access to EPA Actions

Environmental Protection Agency (EPA)
401 M St., SW
Washington DC 20460   202-260-5926

The Public Information Reference Unit provides public access to regulatory information supporting the Environmental Protection Agency's (EPA) actions administered under the Clean Air Act and the Clean Water Act. Records are submitted to this office by the programs within EPA or the regions for public inspection and photocopying. This office also has information supporting other EPA regulations issued under the following statutes: Resource Conservation and Recovery Act, Safe Drinking Water Act, Noise Control Act, and the Marine Protection, Research and Sanctuaries Act.

* Quality Assurance

Office of Modeling, Monitoring Systems
   and Quality Assurance
Research and Development
Environmental Protection Agency (EPA)
401 M St., SW, Room 3702
Washington DC 20460   202-260-5767

This office provides data on monitoring systems and quality assurance research which develops standardized methods to measure and monitor pollutants.

* Radon and Radiation Control

Office of Radiation Programs
Environmental Protection Agency (EPA)
401 M St., SW, Room NE108
Washington DC 20460   202-260-7400

The Environmental Protection Agency (EPA), with a number of other federal agencies, protects the public from unnecessary exposure to ionizing radiation. EPA's major responsibilities are to set radioactive emissions standards and exposure limits, assess new technology, and monitor radiation in the environment in four areas: radiation from nuclear accidents, radon emissions, land disposal of radioactive waste, and radiation in groundwater and drinking water. The EPA fulfills these responsibilities by setting emissions standards for nuclear power plants, and for radionuclides in drinking water and in the air. EPA also prescribes work practices to reduce emissions of radon from underground uranium mines, develops radioactive waste disposal standards, and issues guidance to limit occupational exposure.

* Radon: Citizen's Guide

Public Information Center
Environmental Protection Agency (EPA)
401 M St., SW, MC 3404
Washington DC 20460   202-260-7751

A Citizen's Guide to Radon helps readers understand the radon problem and decide if they need to take action to reduce radon levels in their homes. It explains what radon is, how it is detected, and what the results mean. Contact this office for your free copy.

* Radon Indoors

Radon Division
Office of Radiation Programs
Environmental Protection Agency (EPA)
401 M St., SW, Room NE200
Washington DC 20460   202-260-9622

The Environmental Protection Agency's (EPA) indoor radon program assists states in identifying areas with high indoor radon levels, researches, demonstrates, and evaluates techniques to reduce radon levels, and establishes standard methods for measuring radon levels. Contact this office for more information on radon standards.

* Reclamation Bibliography

Superintendent of Documents
Government Printing Office
Washington, DC 20402   202-512-1800

Publications on priorities within the Bureau are listed, including the safety of dams and a water measurement manual used in irrigation and municipal water facilities.

Environment and Nature

* Regulatory Information References

Environmental Protection Agency (EPA)
401 M St., SW
Washington DC 20460   202-260-5926

PIRU provides public access to regulatory information supporting the Agency's actions administered under (1) the Clean Air Act (primarily the State Implementation Plans), and (2) the Clean Water Act (primarily the Effluent Limitation Guidelines). Records are submitted to PIRU (indexed) by the programs within Environmental Protection Agency (EPA) or the Regions for public inspection and photocopying. PIRU also has information supporting other EPA regulations issued under the following statutes: Resource Conservation and Recovery Act (RCRA), Safe Drinking Water Act, Noise Control Act, and The Marine Protection, Research and Sanctuaries Act.

* Research Center

Andrew W. Briedenbach Environmental
Research Center Library
26 W. Martin Luther King
Cincinnati, OH 45268   513-569-7703

The major subjects in this library's collection are bacteriology, biology, biotechnology, chemistry, engineering, hazardous wastes, hydrobiology, microbiology, solid waste management, toxicology, water pollution, and water quality. Databases maintained here include BRS, CAS On-line, CIS, DIALOG, Dun & Bradstreet, Hazardous Waste Database, LEXIS/NEXIS, NLM, Toxline, and Toxnet. General collections include bacteriology, biology, biotechnology, microbiology, physics, solid waste management. This library's special collections cover the environment, Canada, legal issues, hazardous waste, and solid waste.

* Research Labs

Environmental Research Laboratories
National Oceanic and Atmospheric Administration
U.S. Department of Commerce
325 Broadway
Boulder, CO 80303   303-497-6286

The Environmental Research Laboratories conducts an integrated program of fundamental research, related technology development, and services to improve understanding and prediction of the geophysical environment comprising the oceans and inland waters, the lower and upper atmosphere, the space environment, and the Earth. Activities at its laboratories address such major areas as stratospheric and tropospheric ozone, the greenhouse effect and atmospheric chemistry, acid rain sources, transport and deposition, ocean role in climate, meteorological phenomena, solar disturbances, and computer modeling of oceanic conditions. . *Environmental Research Laboratories Programs and Plans* is a free publication which contains highlights of Laboratory accomplishments and abbreviated summaries of immediate objectives. More comprehensive and detailed descriptions of activities, results, and plans may be found in the laboratories' annual reports.

* Research and Technology Transfer

Center for Environmental Research Information (CERI)
Environmental Protection Agency (EPA)
401 M St., SW
Washington DC 20460   513-569-7562

The Office of Research and Development (ORD) has centralized most of its information distribution and technology transfer activities in the Center for Environmental Research Information (CERI) listed above. CERI also serves as a central point of distribution for ORD research results and reports.

* Resident Environmental Education

Environmental/Energy Education
Land Between The Lakes
Resource and Development
Tennessee Valley Authority
Golden Pond, KY 42211   502-924-1309

The Youth Station and Brandon Spring at Land Between The Lakes operates the residential education program to promote better environmental understanding, aesthetic appreciation, and man's place in nature. These dorm-style activity areas are open year-round and accommodate kindergarten through college-level groups. Groups are welcome to carry out their own programs, or the staff can help in developing them. Activities include canoeing, pond studies, and nature walks. With Murray (Kentucky) State University Center for Environmental Education, the staff provides additional workshops for area teachers and in-service students.

* Resource Conservation and Recovery Act Docket

Environmental Protection Agency (EPA)
1235 Jefferson Davis Hwy.
Crystal City, VA   703-603-9230

This Docket provides public access to regulatory information supporting the Agency's actions under the Resource Conservation and Recovery Act (RCRA). Records support *Federal Register* notices, Delisting Petitions, and other Office of Solid Waste (OSW) publications. RCRA Docket publishes a semiannual catalog of frequently requested documents. The RCRA Docket staff performs two primary functions: maintaining the docket and responding to information requests. The activities which are required for each function include maintaining the RCRA Docket, tracking regulations, organizing and storing information, and distributing and ordering documents.

* Resource Conservation and Recovery Hotline

CERCLA/RCRA Hotline
Environmental Protection Agency (EPA)
401 M St., SW   800-424-9346
Washington DC 20460   703-920-9810

This hotline answers questions concerning the Resource Conservation and Recovery Act, Superfund, and hazardous waste regulations. Requests for certain documents from the *Federal Register* and public laws are also handled in addition to referral to appropriate contacts. See also RCRA/CERCLA Hotline and Superfund Hotline.

* Right to Know Information Center (PIC)

Environmental Protection Agency (EPA)
401 M St., SW
Washington DC 20460   202-260-2080

The Public Information Center answers inquiries from the public about Environmental Protection Agency (EPA), its programs, and activities and offers a variety of general, non-technical information materials.

* Safe Drinking Water Hotline

Environmental Protection Agency (EPA)
401 M St., SW
Washington DC 20460   800-426-4791

The Safe Drinking Water Hotline responds to questions concerning the Safe Drinking Water Act, Water Standards, Regulations, and the Underground Injection Program. It will also provide selected publications relevant to these issues. It operates Monday through Friday, 8:30 a.m. to 4:30 p.m. (EST).

* Sea-Grant Colleges

Office of Oceanic Research Programs
National Oceanic and Atmospheric Administration
U.S. Department of Commerce
1335 East-West Hwy.
Silver Spring, MD 20910   800-631-2114

The National Sea Grant College Program is a national network of over 300 colleges, universities, research institutions, and consortia working in partnership with industry and the federal government to support Great Lakes and marine research, education, and extension services. This program provides support for institutions engaged in comprehensive marine research, education, and advisory service programs, supports individual projects in marine research and development, and sponsors education of ocean scientists and engineers, marine technicians, and other specialists at selected colleges and universities.

* Small Business EPA-Help Hotline

Environmental Protection Agency (EPA)
401 M Street SW   800-368-5888
Washington, DC 20460   202-557-1938

The Small Business Hotline is an EPA-based hotline that gives advice and information to small businesses on complying with Environmental Protection Agency (EPA) regulations. It deals with problems encountered by small-quantity generators of hazardous waste and other small businesses with environmental concerns.

* Space Environment and Solar-Terrestrial Physics

Space Environment Laboratory
Environmental Research Laboratories
National Oceanic and Atmospheric Administration

U.S. Department of Commerce
325 Broadway
Boulder, CO 80303   303-497-3313

The Space Environment Laboratory provides real-time space environment monitoring and forecasting services, develops techniques for improving forecasts of solar disturbances and their effect on the near-Earth space environment, and conducts research in solar-terrestrial physics. An annual report is available which goes into more detail about the Laboratory, the research conducted, and lists the technical reports published.

* State Environmental Libraries

The following is a list of State Environmental Libraries which is part of an Environmental Protection Agency (EPA) initiative to support information sharing between EPA and the States. The collections vary from State to State, each having their own area of emphasis. These libraries are good local starting places.

Alabama
Alabama Public Library Service
6030 Monticello Dr.
Montgomery, AL 37130   334-277-7330

Alaska
Alaska Department of Environmental Conservation Library
P.O. Box O
3032 Vintage Park Blvd.
Juneau, AK 99811-1800   907-465-2692

Arizona
Attorney General
Civil Division Research Room
1275 W. Washington
Phoenix, AZ 85007   602-542-1410

Arizona Department of Environmental Quality Library
2005 N. Central Ave.
Phoenix, AZ 85004   602-257-6959

Arizona Department of Water Resources Library
15 South 15th Ave.
Phoenix, AZ 85007   602-417-2400

Arkansas
Arkansas Department of Pollution Control and Ecology
Records Section
8001 National Dr.
Little Rock, AR 72209   501-682-0744

California
State Water Resources Control Board Law Library
901 P St.
Sacramento, CA 95801   916-323-0220

California Air Resources Board Library
2020 L St.
Sacramento, CA 95812   916-323-8376

Toxic Substances Control Division
Technical Reference Library
714/744 P St., P.O. Box 806
Sacramento, CA 95812-0806   916-324-5898

California State Resources Agency Library
1416 Ninth St., Room 117
Sacramento, CA 95814   916-654-0640

Delaware
Superfund Branch Library
Department of Natural Resources and Environmental Control
Superfund Branch
715 Grantham Lane
New Castle, DE 19720   302-323-4540

Florida
Environmental Library of Sarasota County
7112 Curtiss Ave.
Sarasota, FL 34231   813-316-1242

Florida Department of Environmental Regulation Information Center
2600 Blair Stone Rd.
Tallahassee, FL 32301   904-488-0890

State of Florida
Department of Natural Resources
903 W. Tennessee St.
Tallahassee, FL 32304-7795   904-488-9380

Georgia
Fernbank Science Center Library
156 Heaton Park Dr., NE
Atlanta, GA 30307   404-378-4311

Hawaii
Hawaii State Library
634 Pensacola St.
Honolulu, HI 96813   808-586-3500

Illinois
Illinois Hazardous Waste Research and Information Center Library
One East Hazelwood Dr.
Champaign, IL 61820   217-333-8957

Illinois Environmental Protection Agency Library
2200 Churchill Rd.
Springfield, IL 62794-9276   217-782-9691

Indiana
Indiana Department of Environmental Management Law Library
100 N. Senate Ave.
Indianapolis, IN 46206   317-232-8603

Iowa
Technical Library
Iowa Department of Natural Resources
Henry A. Wallace Building
Des Moines, IA 50319   515-281-5145

Kansas
Kansas Department of Health and Environment Library
Forbesfield Bldg. 740
Topeka, KS 66620   913-296-1500

Kentucky
Environmental Protection Information Center
14 Reilly Rd.
Frankfort, KY 40601   502-564-2150

Louisiana
Air Quality Information Resources Center
Air Quality Division
Department of Environmental Protection
625 North Fourth St., 8th Floor
Baton Rouge, LA 70804   504-342-1241

Ground Water Protection Library
Ground Water Protection Division
Department of Environmental Protection
P.O. Box 44274
Baton Rouge, LA 70804   504-342-1234

Waste Minimization Library
P.O. Box 44066
Baton Rouge, LA 70804   504-765-0511

Water Resources Library
Water Resources Division
Department of Environmental Protection
P.O. Box 44274
Baton Rouge, LA 70804   504-765-0634

Maine
Department of Environmental Protection and
 Department of Conservation Library
State House, Station #17
Augusta, ME 04333   207-287-7688

Environment and Nature

Maryland
Maryland State Department of the Environment
Toxics Information Center
2500 Broening Highway
Baltimore, MD 21224   410-631-3818

Massachusetts
Massachusetts Water Resources Authority Library
100 First Ave.
Boston, MA 02129   617-242-6000

State Library of Massachusetts
State House, Room 341
Boston, MA 02133   617-727-2590

Michigan
Michigan Department of Natural Resources
Surface Water Quality Division
P.O. Box 30273
Lansing, MI 48909-7773   517-373-6794

Minnesota
Minnesota Department of Natural Resources
DNR Library
500 Lafayette Rd., Box 21
St. Paul, MN 55155   612-296-1305

Minnesota Pollution Control Agency
520 Lafayette Rd. North
St. Paul, MN 55155   612-296-7719

Montana
Department of Natural Resources and Conservation
 Research Center
1520 East Sixth Ave.
Helena, MT 59620   406-444-6700

New Hampshire
New Hampshire Department of Environmental Services
6 Hazen Dr.
Concord, NH 03301   603-271-2975

New Jersey
New Jersey Department of Environmental Protection
Information Resource Center
432 East State St, CN409
Trenton, NJ 08625   609-984-2249

North Carolina
Environmental Resources Library
North Carolina Department of Environment, Health, and Natural Resources
P.O. Box 27687
512 N. Salisbury St.
Raleigh, NC 27611   919-733-4984

North Dakota
North Dakota State Department of Health and Consolidated Laboratories
P.O. Box 5520
Bismarck, ND 58506-5520   701-328-5150

Ohio
Ohio Environmental Protection Agency Library
1800 Watermark Dr.
Columbus, OH 43266   614-644-3024

Oklahoma
Oklahoma Department of Libraries
U.S. Documents Division
200 Northeast 18th St.
Oklahoma City, OK 73105   405-521-2502

Puerto Rico
Centro de Informacion
Environmental Quality Board
Biblioteca
Apartado 11488
Santurce, Puerto Rico 00910   809-767-7712

South Carolina
South Carolina Department of Health and Environmental
Control Library
Mill Building
2600 Bull St.
Columbia, SC 29201   803-737-3945

Texas
Texas Air Control Board Library
6330 Highway 290 East
Austin, TX 78723   512-451-5711

Texas Water Commission Library
1700 North Congress
P.O. Box 13087
Austin, TX 78711-3087   512-239-0020

Virginia
Bureau of Toxic Substances Library
Virginia Department of Health
1500 E. Main St., Room 124
Richmond, VA 23218   804-786-1763

Virginia State Water Control Board Library
2111 North Hamilton St.
P.O. Box 11143
Richmond, VA 23230   804-367-6340

Washington
Department of Ecology Library
P.O. Box 47600
Olympia, WA 98504   360-407-6150

Wisconsin
Department of Natural Resources
P.O. Box 7921
Madison, WI 53707   608-266-8933

Alternate State Environmental Contacts
The following states do not have an environmental library, but are willing to provide environmental information upon request at the address and phone number listed below their state name.

Colorado
Colorado Department of Health
4210 East 11th Ave.
Denver, CO 80220   303-866-5901

Colorado Joint Review Process
Department of Natural Resources
1313 Sherman St., Room 719
Denver, CO 80203   303-866-3311

Connecticut
Department of Environmental Protection
122 Washington St.
Hartford, CT 06106   860-424-3000

Idaho
Idaho Department of Health and Welfare
Division of Environment
450 West State St, Fifth Floor
Boise, ID 83720   208-334-5839

Mississippi
Mississippi Department of Natural Resources
Southport Center
2380 Highway 880 West
P.O. Box 20305
Jackson, MS 39289   601-961-5000

Missouri
Missouri Department of Environmental Quality
Jefferson State Office Building
Jefferson City, MO 65102   314-751-3443

Nebraska
Nebraska Department of Environmental Quality
301 Centennial Mall South, Fourth Floor
P.O. Box 94877
Lincoln, NE 68509   402-471-4223

Nevada
Nevada Department of Conservation and Natural Resources
201 South Fall St.
Carson City, NV 89710   702-687-4670

New York
New York Department of Environmental Conservation
50 Wolf Rd.
Albany, NY 12233   518-457-5400

Rhode Island
Rhode Island Department of Environmental Management
9 Hayes St.
Providence, RI 02908   401-277-2771

North Dakota
Department of Water and Natural Resources
523 East Capitol St.
Pierre, SD 57501   605-773-3151

Tennessee
Bureau of Environment
Tennessee Department of Environment
150 9th Ave.
Nashville, TN 32247   615-532-0200

Utah
Division of Environmental Health
Utah Department of Health
288 North 1460 West
Salt Lake City, UT 84116   801-538-4400

Vermont
Vermont Environmental Board
58 East State St., Drawer 20
Montpelier, VT 05620-3201   802-828-3309

West Virginia
State of West Virginia
Department of Natural Resources
Charleston, WV 25305   304-558-3315

Wyoming
Department of Environmental Quality
122 West 25th St.
Cheyenne, WY 82002   307-777-7938

* Tennessee Valley Authority Environmental Policy

Environmental Quality Staff
Tennessee Valley Authority (TVA)
Summer Place Building
Knoxville, TN 37902-6604   615-632-6578

Environmental protection and enhancement are a natural part of all Tennessee Valley Authority (TVA) programs that affect the water, air, and land. This office provides centralized environmental guidance and direction to the entire agency, and is TVA's point of contact with Federal and State environmental regulators. To ensure meaningful citizen involvement in TVA's environmental activities and decisions, this office conducts periodic meetings with members of the environmental community to discuss matters of mutual interest. The public is also kept informed through advertised public meetings and the news media.

* Terminology and Acronyms

Public Information Center
Environmental Protection Agency (EPA)
401 M St., SW, PM 3404
Washington DC 20460   202-260-7751

The free *Glossary of Environmental Terms and Acronym List* is designed to provide you with an explanation of the more commonly used environmental terms appearing in the Environmental Protection Agency (EPA) publications, news releases, and other Agency documents. The terms and definitions in this publication were selected to give the user a general sense of what a term or phrase means in relatively non-technical language. Contact this office for your free copy.

* Territorial and International Affairs

Territorial and International Affairs
U.S. Department of the Interior
1849 C St., NW
Washington, DC 20240   202-208-4822

International affairs within the U.S. Department of the Interior are handled by this office. If more than one Bureau is involved in an international effort, this office acts as the coordinator and liaison between the Department and the foreign constituent. The Department of the Interior has administrative responsibility for coordinating Federal policy in the territories of American Samoa, Guam, the Virgin Islands and the Trust Territory of the Pacific Islands, as well as oversight of all federal programs and funds in the freely associated states of the Republic of the Marshall Islands and the Federated States of Micronesia.

* Testing at the EPA

EPA Test Methods
Region 1 Library
Environmental Protection Agency (EPA)
JFK Federal Building
Boston, MA 02203   617-565-3298

Test methods are approved procedures for measuring the presence and concentration of physical and chemical pollutants, evaluating properties, such as toxic properties, of chemical substances, or measuring the effects of substances under various conditions. *Index to EPA Test Methods* consists of the following three sections: Numeric List by method number, Alphabetical List by chemical substance or method name, and Source List by document number. This is an attempt to coordinate, in one publication, an index to sources of EPA test methods and sampling procedures for laboratory analysis.

* Training Clearinghouse

EPA Institute
Environmental Protection Agency (EPA)
401 M St., SW
Washington DC 20460   202-260-3297

The national clearinghouse for all Agency training activities, from environmental science to enforcement to personal and professional development. The Institute focuses on in-house training, but serves as the Agency's training "broker" with other Federal agencies, State, and local governments, associations, and environmental organizations. Contact this Institute for more information on specific training programs.

* Transit Environments

Environment Division
Policy and International Affairs
Office of the Secretary of Transportation
U.S. Department of Transportation
400 7th Street, SW, Room 9217
Washington, DC 20590   202-366-4366

This is the U.S. Department of Transportation (DOT) contact point for environmental issues. Staff can provide you with information and referrals on such subjects as highway beautification, transportation architecture, bicycle paths, historic preservation activities, environmental impact statements, and disabled access.

* TVA Natural Resources Protection

Resource Development
Tennessee Valley Authority (TVA)
400 W. Summit Hill Dr.
Knoxville, TN 37921   615-632-6367

The Tennessee Valley Authority's (TVA) work with natural resources involves the whole range of environmental concerns. Today, with 20 million acres of forests in the Valley, TVA is working to adapt computer-age management to this valuable resource. TVA lakes and their 11,000 miles of shoreline provide an extensive resource for waterfowl protection, game management, and fisheries research. Industrial development and increased population intensify the necessity of protecting the natural environment. Research and testing continue to seek better ways to protect air and water; to dispose of and make use of wastes; to plan for the wise use and

Environment and Nature

management of land; and to protect and preserve water tables and mineral resources, along with free-flowing streams, plants, and animal life.

* Undersea Research

National Undersea Research Program (NURP)
National Oceanic and Atmospheric Administration (NOAA)
U.S. Department of Commerce
6010 Executive Blvd.
Rockville, MD 20852   301-413-0900

The National Undersea Research Program (NURP) develops programs and provides support to scientists and engineers for the study of biological, chemical, geological, and physical processes in the world's oceans and lakes. NURP assist researchers in conducting what are considered by National Oceanic and Atmospheric Administration (NOAA) and the marine community to be crucial research programs. In order to execute these programs, NURP provides investigators with a suite of the modern undersea facilities including submersibles, habitats, air and mixed gas SCUBA, and remotely operated vehicles. A major part of the research program is carried out by a network of National Undersea Research Centers. Contact this office for more information on the research conducted or the research centers.

* Up-To-The-Minute Research

Center for Environmental Research Information
Environmental Protection Agency (EPA)
ORD Publications Unit
Cincinnati, OH 45268   513-569-7369

The *ORD Publication Announcement* lists titles of printed publications from the Office of Research and Development (ORD). These lists provide interested parties with access to the broad range of currently available documents produced by ORD. Contact this office for your free copy.

* Want to Commercialize the Latest Technology?

Office of Technology Transfer and Regulatory Support
Larry Fradkin
Office of Research and Development
Environmental Protection Agency (EPA)
26 W. Martin Luther King Dr.
Cincinnati, OH 45268   513-569-7960

The Federal Technology Transfer Act makes possible cooperative research and development agreements (CRDAs) between federal laboratories, industry, and academic institutions. CRDAs set forth the terms of government/industry collaboration to develop and commercialize new technologies. Information about the FTTA and the associated CRDAs can be obtained from this office. They also have a one-page flier on the opportunities for Cooperative R&D with the EPA: The Federal Technology Transfer Act.

* Water Quality Criteria

Standards and Applied Science Division
Office of Water Regulations and Standards
Environmental Protection Agency (EPA)
401 M St., SW, Room E829
Washington, DC 20460   202-260-7301

The Clean Water Act requires each state to set water quality standards for every dignifican body of surface water within its borders. To set these standards, states specify the uses of each body of water (such as drinking water, recreation, commercial fishing), and restrict pollution to levels that permit those uses. The EPA assists the states in setting these standards and monitors them to make sure they meet the minimum required.

* What's the Latest at the EPA

EPA Publications
Information Management and Services Division, PM-211D
Environmental Protection Agency (EPA)
401 M St., SW
Washington, DC 20460   202-260-7751

The *EPA Publications Bibliography* contains bibliographic citations with abstracts for reports generated by Environmental Protection Agency (EPA). It lists and indexes EPA technical reports and journal articles submitted to National Technical Information Service (NTIS). This Bibliography is available for sale: National Technical Information Service (NTIS), Springfield, VA 22161; 703-487-4650, 800-553-NTIS.

* Woodsy Owl and Children's Materials

U.S. Department of Agriculture
Forest Service, P.O. Box 96090
Washington, DC 20090-6090   202-205-1785

To increase children's awareness of our delicate environment, the Forest Service's Woodsy Owl campaign has a variety of free materials available, including coloring sheets, detective sheets, song sheets, patches, *Woodsy Owl on Camping* (brochure), and stickers.

Water and Air Quality

* Acid Rain and Aquatic Species Chart

Superintendent of Documents
Government Printing Office
Washington, DC 20402   202-512-1800

The wall chart, *Acid Rain: The Effect on Aquatic Species*, illustrates the survival of selected aquatic species in an acidic environment. Information is given on acid rain, its causes, and the effect on aquatic life. Measures 17 by 22 inches (S/N 024-010-00675-7, $3.25).

* Acid Rain Headquarters

National Acid Precipitation Assessment
    Program (NAPAP)
1110 Vermont Ave., NW
Suite 810
Washington, DC 20005   202-296-1002

The National Acid Precipitation Assessment Program (NAPAP) was established because of concern that acid rain might contribute to adverse effects on aquatic systems, forests, agricultural crops, construction materials and cultural resources, atmospheric visibility, and human health. NAPAP coordinates federally funded research and assessment activities concerning acid rain, and investigates the causes and effects of acid rain, as well as analyzing alternative strategies to control or mitigate those effects. NAPAP compiled the most comprehensive and quality-assured database ever assembled for an environmental issue. Major activities of NAPAP will include interagency research, monitoring and assessment to determine whether acid rain impacts are reduced as a result of the mandated emissions reductions, and to assess the value of the improvements. A free quarterly newsletter is available which contains articles and information concerning acid rain, as well as listing recent NAPAP publications. Several important publications are available from: Superintendent of Documents, Government Printing Office, Washington, DC 20402; 202-512-1800.

* *National Acid Precipitation Assessment Program 1990: Integrated Assessment Report*

* *1989 Annual Report of the National Acid Precipitation Assessment Program to the President and Congress, June 1990* (available from NAPA)

* *Background on Acidic Deposition and the National Acid Precipitation Assessment Program, September 5, 1990* (available from NAPA)

* *Acidic Deposition: State of Science and Technology* (6,200 pages long; a separate 250-page Summary Document is also available)

VOLUME 1 Emissions, Atmospheric Processes and Deposition

Report 1	Emissions Involved in Acidic Deposition Processes
Report 2	Atmospheric Processes Research and Process Model Development
Report 3	Regional Acid Deposition Modeling
Report 4	The Regional Acid Deposition Model and Engineering Model
Report 5	Evaluation of Regional Acidic Deposition Models
Report 6	Deposition Monitoring: Methods and Results
Report 7	Air Quality Measurements and Characterizations for Terrestrial Effects Research
Report 8	Relationships Between Atmospheric Emissions and Deposition/Air Quality

VOLUME 2 Aquatic Processes and Effects

Report 9	Current Status of Surface Water Acid-Base Chemistry
Report 10	Watershed and Lake Processes Affecting Surface Water Acid-Base Chemistry
Report 11	Historical Changes in Surface Water Acid-Base Chemistry in Response to Acidic Deposition
Report 12	Episodic Acidification of Surface Waters Due to Acidic Deposition
Report 13	Biological Effects of Changes in Surface Water Acid-Base Chemistry
Report 14	Methods for Projecting Future Changes in Surface Water Acid-Base Chemistry
Report 15	Liming Acidic Surface Waters

VOLUME 3 Terrestrial, Materials, Health and Visibility Effects

Report 16	Changes in Forest Health and Productivity in the United States and Canada
Report 17	Development and Use of Tree and Forest Response Models
Report 18	Response of Vegetation to Atmospheric Deposition and Air Pollution
Report 19	Effects of Acidic Deposition on Materials
Report 20	Processes of Deposition t Structures
Report 21	Distribution of Materials Potentially at Risk from Acidic Deposition
Report 22	Direct Health Effects of Air Pollutants Associated with Acidic Precursor Emissions
Report 23	Indirect Health Effects Associated with Acidic Deposition
Report 24	Visibility: Existing and Historical Conditions- Causes and Effects

VOLUME IV Control Technologies, Future Emissions, and Effects Valuation

Report 25	Technologies and Other Measures for Controlling Emissions: Performance, Costs and Applicability
Report 26	Methods for Modeling Future Emissions and Control Costs
Report 27	Methods for Valuing Acidic Deposition and Air Pollution Effects

* Acid Rain Program

Atmospheric Deposition Analysis
Water Resources Division
U.S. Geological Survey
National Center, MS 416
Reston, VA 22092   703-648-6876

The U.S. Geological Survey, in cooperation with other federal agencies and many state agencies, is participating in a coordinated nationwide program to monitor the chemical composition of precipitation and selected streams and lakes that are now or may be affected by acid rain. Selected watersheds are also being studied to gain a better understanding of the hydrologic and geochemical processes that determine whether or not acid rain will ultimately affect the quality of water coming from the watershed.

* Air and the TVA

Atmospheric Science Department
Tennessee Valley Authority (TVA)
P.O. Box 1010
Muscle Shoals, AL 35662   205-386-2342

The Department assesses trends in regional air quality, identifies air quality problems in the Valley, and provides technical assistance to air regulatory agencies and industry in correcting air quality problems. Information documents are produced to inform the public of regional air quality (both indoor and outdoor) problems and issues.

* Air Pollutants, Asbestos and Consumer Safety Hotline

Consumer Product Safety Commission (CPSC) Hotline
5401 Westbard Avenue
Bethesda, MD 20207   800-638-2772

The Consumer Product Safety Commission (CPSC) hotline provides information on consumer safety and guidelines on exposure to formaldehyde, asbestos, and air pollutants. They offer copies of studies and other related documents.

* Air Pollution and State Motor Vehicle Inspections

Records and Motor Vehicle Services Division (NTS-43)
National Highway Traffic Safety Administration (NHTSA)
U.S. Department of Transportation
400 7th Street, SW
Washington, DC 20590   202-727-6680

The National Highway Traffic Safety Administration's (NHTSA) Motor Vehicle Inspection Program is aimed at providing car owners with preventative information on what repairs are needed to achieve greater safety, lower pollution, and better mileage. The annual *Study of the State Motor Vehicle Inspection Program* is available from this office.

Environment and Nature

* Air Pollution Emissions Hotline

Control Technology Center Hotline   919-541-0800

The Control Technology Center (CTC) Hotline is the component of Environmental Protection Agency's (EPA) Air Toxics Strategy. The Hotline provides information to State and local pollution control agencies on sources of emissions of air toxics. It operates Monday through Friday, 8:00 a.m. to 4:30 p.m. (EST). It also offers a wide range of engineering assistance and technical guidance. A quarterly newsletter containing relevant articles and a list of CTC publications is available.

* Air Quality and Climate Change

Atmospheric Sciences Department
Tennessee Valley Authority (TVA)
Resource Development
Chemical Engineering Bldg.
Muscle Shoals, AL 35660   205-386-2556

The Tennessee Valley Authority (TVA) is working on a large scale air pollution control program. A current report, *How Clean Is Our Air?*, evaluates the levels of traditional air pollutants, as well as discussing emerging air quality issues, which include regional oxident pollution, acidic deposition, indoor air quality, toxic air pollutants, and climate change. A full-scale report will focus on various specific regional programs that address these issues. One example, the Middle Tennessee Ozone Study, is investigating the levels and sources of ozone in the greater Nashville metropolitan area as a cooperative effort between the TVA and the Tennessee Division of Air Pollution Control. Contact this office for more information on the study and the regional air quality control programs.

* Air Quality Planning and Standards

Office of Air Quality Planning and Standards
Environmental Protection Agency
Research Triangle Park, NC 27711   919-541-5618

This office develops national standards for air quality, emission standards for new stationary and mobile sources, and emission standards for hazardous pollutants. Contact this office for information on specific standards.

* Air Quality Standards Library

Office of Air Quality Planning
and Standards (OAQPS) Library
826 Mutual Plaza, MD-16
Research Triangle Park, NC 27711   919-541-5618

This library focuses on air pollution and control technology, including material on costs, chemical technology, minerals, and statistics. The reference collection emphasizes chemistry and engineering.

* Air Resources Laboratory (ARL)

Environmental Research Laboratory
National Oceanic and Atmospheric Administration
U.S. Department of Commerce
1315 East West Hwy.
Silver Spring, MD 20910   301-713-2458

The Air Resources Laboratory (ARL) performs weather research to understand and predict human influences on the environment, especially those involving atmospheric transport and dispersion of pollutants such as acid rain and ozone to distances up to thousands of kilometers. The ARL also monitors and interprets trends in natural and man-made substances, such as CO425, halocarbons, aerosols, and ozone which can potentially modify the climate. In addition, ARL studies solar radiation for its role in climate change. An annual report is available, which describes in more detail the current research being undertaken at ARL.

* Air Risk Hotline

Pollutant Assessment Branch, MD-13
Environmental Protection Agency
Research Triangle Park, NC 27711   919-541-0888

The primary purpose of the Air Risk Hotline is to provide an initial quick response based upon available health and exposure data and the expertise of Environmental Protection Agency (EPA) and its contractors. They can answer any question from companies, industry, or other EPA offices regarding indoor or outdoor air and can direct your call to the appropriate expert. The Clearinghouse collects, classifies, and disseminates air toxics information submitted by state and local air agencies. The database contains two categories of information: air pollution control agency data and citations/abstracts.

* Air Toxics Information Clearinghouse

National Air Toxics Information Clearinghouse
Environmental Protection Agency, MD-13
Research Triangle Park, NC 27711   919-541-0850

The National Air Toxics Information Clearinghouse (NATICH) assists states in developing air toxics programs and setting emission levels. The Clearinghouse has a bimonthly newsletter, special reports, and a computerized database.

* Aquaculture Information

Aquaculture Information Center
National Agricultural Library Building
Beltsville, MD 20705   301-504-5704

This Information Center can answer questions regarding the culture of aquatic plants and animals in freshwater, brackish, and marine environments. They can also handle requests on eel culture, alligator farming, Spirulina farming, and aqatic snail culture (no fisheries industry information). They have access to a database, bibliographic information, and other publications.

* Aquatic Plants

Aquatic Biology Department
Resource Development
River Basin Operations, Water Resources
Tennessee Valley Authority (TVA)
Muscle Shoals, AL 35660   205-386-2278

Tennessee Valley Authority's (TVA) two major weapons for controlling the spread of pesky aquatic plants, such as Eurasian watermilfoil, spiny-leaf naiad, and hydrilla in its reservoirs, is the winter and summer draw downs and the selective spraying of herbicides. Reservoir levels may be lowered several feet in the late summer to dry out and kill the roots of these plants embedded in shallow areas of the reservoirs; while at other times, lake levels may be held higher than normal to prevent sunshine from penetrating to the bottom and thus prevent germination and growth of new colonies. Selective use of approved herbicides in high priority use areas, such as swimming beaches, developed shoreline, and marinas, is another effective control method. Several experimental control strategies also are being tested on TVA lakes. One of the most promising is a cooperative effort between TVA and the U.S. Army Corps of Engineers. TVA proposes to conduct large scale demonstrations on Guntersville reservoir on the use of Grass Carp, hydrilla fly, a fungus to control watermilfoil, and other methods being currently tested on a smaller scale by the Corps Waterways Experiment Station.

* Aquatic Toxicology and Water Quality Research

Environmental Research Laboratory Library
College Station Rd.
Athens, GA 30605   706-546-3302

The Athens Environmental Research Laboratory (ERL) Library provides information services covering a wide range of environmental and management subjects. Subject areas include aquatic toxicology, microbiology, biology, pesticides, chemistry, water pollution, engineering, and water quality. Databases maintained here include CIS, DIALOG, and Ground Water On-line.

* Bibliography: Water Pollution and Resources

Superintendent of Documents
Government Printing Office
Washington, DC 20402   202-512-1800

Water conservation and management books are featured. The *National Water Summary* books on hydrologic events and the subscription service, *Soil and Water Conservation News*, are among the selections. Free.

* Boulder Canyon and Other Water Projects

Office of Public Affairs
Bureau of Reclamation
U.S. Department of the Interior
P.O. Box 25007
Denver Federal Center
Denver, CO 80225   303-236-7000

Contact the office above for their recent publications listing. Topics available include the following: annual reports and project data from the Bureau, Boulder Canyon Project reports, design standards, engineering manuals, research reports, technical records, and design and construction records, and other reports on subjects such as canals, dams, economic planning, environment, geology and rock mechanics, hydrology, and safety.

* Chesapeake Bay Regional Library

Central Regional Laboratory (CRL) Library
839 Bestgate Rd.
Annapolis, MD 21401   410-266-9180

This library was established in support of the Regional Laboratory which started in Annapolis in 1964. The subjects in the collection focus on biology, chemistry, ecology, engineering, hazardous waste hydrology, and oceanography. To serve the highly diversified expertise of the laboratory scientists and engineers, material is provided in aquatic biology, analytical chemistry, automated laboratory techniques, industrial wastewater monitoring, toxic and hazardous substances, and mathematical modelling. A special collections covers the Chesapeake Bay.

* Clean Air Act

Air Docket
Environmental Protection Agency
401 M St., SW, Room M 1500
Washington DC 20460   202-260-7548

The Air Docket provides public access to regulatory information which supports the Agency's actions administered under the Clean Air Act. The docket consists of files containing a series of file folders for each category of documents. Most of the records are on microfilm. Contact this office for more information.

* Clean Lakes Clearinghouse

Environmental Protection Agency
401 M St., SW
Washington, DC 20460   800-726-5253

The main purpose of the Clean Lakes clearinghouse is to collect, organize, and disseminate information on lake restoration, protection, and management to researchers, Environmental Protection Agency (EPA) personnel, lake managers, and state and local governments. A computerized database provides abstracts and citations to journal articles, technical reports, and conference papers. The Clearinghouse also responds to inquiries and provides printed bibliographies on lake topics. There is a Clean Lakes Clearinghouse Information Packet available free of charge. The Clearinghouse operated by the Terrene Institute for the EPA offers several EPA publications on lake topics including posters, fact sheets, Nonpoint Source publications, and the following:

Handbooks

Handle with Care: Your Guide to Preventing Water Pollution ($9.95)
Organizing Lake Users: A Practical Guide ($10)
Urban Runoff and Stormwater Management Handbook ($4.50)
Your ABC Guide to the Environment ($12.95)
Lake Maintenance Handbook (TBA)
Decisionmaker's Stormwater Handbook (TBA)
Pesticide Publications (TBA)

The regional offices of the Clean Lakes program are as follows:

Region 1
Water Management Division
U.S. EPA-Region 1
JFK Federal Building
Boston, MA 02203   617-565-3515
(CT, ME, MA, NH, RI, VT)

Region II
U.S. EPA-Region II
Room 805
290 Broadway
New York, NY 10007   212-637-3000
(NJ, NY, PR, VI)

Region III
U.S. EPA-Region III
841 Chestnut St.
Philadelphia, PA 19107   215-597-9800
(DE, DC, MD, PA, VA, WV)

Region IV
U.S EPA-Region IV
345 Courtland St., NE
Atlanta, GA 30365   404-347-2126
(AL, FL, GA, KY, MS, NC, SC, TN)

Region V
U. S. EPA-Region V
230 S. Dearborn St.
Chicago, IL 60604   312-886-0209
(IL, IN, MN, OH, WI)

Region VI
U.S. EPA-Region VI
1445 Ross Ave.
Dallas, TX 75202   214-665-6444
(AR, LA, NM, OK, TX)

Region VII
U.S. EPA-Region VII
Water Management Div.
726 Minnesota Ave.
Kansas City, KS 66101   913-551-7500
(IA, KS, MO, NE)

Region VIII
U.S. EPA-Region VIII
Suite 5000, 999 18th St.
Denver, CO 80202   303-312-6268
(CO, MT, ND, SD, UT, WY)

Region IX
U.S. EPA-Region IX
75 Hawthorn St.
San Francisco, CA 94105   415-744-2018
(AS, AZ, CA, GU, HI, MP, NV, TT)

Region X
U.S. EPA-Region X
1200 Sixth Ave.
Seattle, WA 98101   206-553-1200
(AK, ID, OR, WA)

* Dam Safety

Engineering and Research
Bureau of Reclamation
U.S. Department of the Interior
P.O. Box 25007
Denver, CO 80225   303-236-6988

Safety of dams will continue to be a Bureau of Reclamation priority. The Department revises safety ratings annually, based on the latest technical information available for each dam operated by the Bureau.

* Dams and Steam Plants

Governmental and Public Affairs
Community Relations
Tennessee Valley Authority (TVA)
400 W. Summit Hill Dr.
Knoxville, TN 37902   615-632-2101

Washington Representative
Tennessee Valley Authority (TVA)
412 1st St, Room 300
Washington, DC 20444   202-479-4412

The Tennessee Valley Authority (TVA) has constructed a system of dams and reservoirs to promote navigation on the Tennessee River and its tributaries, and to control destructive flood waters in the Tennessee and Mississippi drainage basins, and to also produce electric power. Citizens are welcome to tour and visit the dams and steam plants.

* Deep Seabed Mining

Ocean Minerals and Energy Division
National Ocean Service
National Oceanic and Atmospheric Administration
U.S. Department of Commerce
1305 East West Hwy.
Washington, DC 20235   301-713-3066

Extensive information is available on deep seabed mining, which includes the annual report to Congress and an updated environmental assessment of National Oceanic and

Be patient. If any phone number is incorrect, call (area code) 555-1212 and request the new listing.

1109

Environment and Nature

Atmospheric Administration (NOAA) deep seabed mining licensees' exploration plans. This office can provide you with information regarding the research conducted concerning the environmental impact of the mining, as well as information on the regulations and licenses.

* Drinking Water Rules and Regulations

Environmental Protection Agency
401 M Street SW
Washington, DC 20460   202-260-3027

The Drinking Water Docket currently contains information on the following regulatory phases: (1) Volatile Organic Chemical (VOC) (Phase I); (2) Fluoride (Phase IIA); (3) Synthetic Organic Chemicals (SOC) (Phase II); (4) Surface Water Treatment Rule (SWTR); and (5) Radionuclides (Phase III). Others will be developed as new Maximum Contaminant Level Goals (MCLG) and Maximum Contaminant Levels (MCL) are proposed. These materials include appropriate *Federal Register* notices, letters, public hearing transcripts, National Drinking Water Advisory Council materials, public comments, technical support documents, and other materials.

* Drought Information

Tom Ross
Hydrologic Information Unit
Water Resources Division
U.S. Geologic Survey
419 National Center
Reston, VA 22092   703-648-6814

The Hydrologic Information Unit has up-to-date information on the drought conditions. They have over 500 collection sites from which they draw their data. They also have some limited historical information on droughts.

* Effluent Guidelines

Office of Science and Technology
Environmental Protection Agency
401 M St., SW
Washington DC 20460   202-260-7120

The Clean Water Act was designed to control the discharge of pollution into U.S. waters. Any industry that pumps waste water into U.S. waters must have a permit. The Environmental Protection Agency (EPA) develops effluent guidelines which set pollution limits for specific industries.

* Emissions Clearinghouse

Emission Factor Clearinghouse, MD-14
Environmental Protection Agency
Research Triangle Park, NC 27711   919-541-5477

The Clearinghouse is a means of exchanging information on air pollution control matters. It addresses the criteria pollutants and toxic substances from stationary and area sources, as well as mobile sources. Emission Factor Clearinghouse Newsletter is issued quarterly, and contains information on recent publications, inquiries about EPA emission inventory policy, newly developed emission factors, and requests for assistance in dealing with general or specific air pollution emissions. The Clearinghouse does have a database.

* Emissions Hotline

Control Technology Center Hotline   919-541-0800

The Control Technology Center Hotline is the component of Environmental Protection Agency's (EPA) Air Toxics Strategy. The Hotline provides information to State and local pollution control agencies on sources of emissions of air toxics. It operates Monday through Friday, 8:00 a.m. to 4:30 p.m. (EST).

* English and Spanish Publications

Book and Report Sales
Box 25425
Denver, CO 80225   303-202-4200

This is a listing of some of the general interest publications available through the U.S. Geological Survey. They are free unless otherwise indicated.

Glaciers: A Water Resource
Ground Water
Ground Water and the Rural Homeowner
Rain: A Water Resource (Also available in Spanish)
River Basins of the United States

Save Water....Save Money
Water in the Urban Environment: Erosion and Sediment
The Water of the World
Water Use in the United States
What Is Water? (Also available in Spanish)
Why Is the Ocean Salty? (Also available in Spanish)

* Global Change

Atmospheric Pollution Prevention Division
Environmental Protection Agency
401 M St., SW
Washington, DC 20460   202-233-9190

This office works on curbing the use of greenhouse gases, such as Carbon dioxide and methane gas. They also work to protect the ozone layer through writing the national regulations for the Clean Air Act. They can provide you with information regarding global change.

* Great Lakes Research

Great Lakes Environmental Research Laboratory
Environmental Research Laboratories
National Oceanic and Atmospheric Administration (NOAA)
2205 Commonwealth Blvd.
Ann Arbor, MI 48105   313-741-2235

The Great Lakes Environmental Research Laboratory (GLERL) conducts research in support of resource management and environmental services in coastal and estuarine water, with special emphasis on the Great Lakes. The scientific programs are organized into six coordinated research programs considered critical to the NOAA mission and Great Lakes problems, and include: non-indigenous species, coordinated ecosystem research, climate variability and global change, pollutant effects, and marine hazards and water management. Contact this office for more information.

* Greenhouse Effects and the Ozone

Climate Monitoring and Diagnostics Laboratory
Environmental Research Laboratories
National Oceanic and Atmospheric Administration
Boulder, CO 80303-3328   303-497-6966

Much of the Laboratory's advanced research focuses on three contemporary issues: greenhouse gas climate warming, stratospheric ozone depletion, and El Nino-Southern Oscillation effects on larger space-scale weather and climate. Levels are increasing for the gases that cause changes in the atmosphere, such as choloroflourocarbons. New, less damaging, but not damage free species are being introduced (ex. hydroflourocarbons), and this lab is responsible for long-term monitoring of these species.

* Greenhouse Effect - What Is It and What Are We Doing About It?

Committee on Earth and Environmental Sciences
c/o U.S. Geological Survey
107 National Center
Reston, VA 22092   703-648-4450

The Global Change Research Program was developed by a U.S. Federal interagency group, the Working Group on Global Change of the Committee on Earth and Environmental Sciences (CEES). An unprecedented partnership has evolved not only among the agencies of the U.S. government with global and regional environmental science responsibilities, but also with the scientific community. The agencies involved included the U.S. Departments of Interior, Energy, Commerce, and Agriculture, as well as the EPA, NASA, and NSF. The CEES formulated a comprehensive plan for the U.S. Global Change Research Program in *Our Changing Planet: The FY 1990 Research Plan*. This Plan reviewed the Earth system changes that have occurred in the past, the forces that are at work today, and the strengths and weaknesses in current environmental monitoring, understanding of fundamental processes, and predictive capabilities. *Our Changing Planet: The FY 1991 Research Plan* focused on establishing the research required to provide the scientific information needed as input to current environmental policy issues, e.g., stratospheric ozone depletion and climate change, including greenhouse warming. This publication outlines the research proposed, policy issues, current knowledge, the problems being faced, and possible solutions. The agency research projects that make up the Program are summarized in the Appendix. The FY 1992 Report continues this theme outlining the research being conducted by each agency. This Office can assist you in locating the researcher responsible for conducting a specific experiment for further information.

* Groundwater and Contaminants

Robert S. Kerr Environmental Research
Laboratory Library
P.O. Box 1198
Ada, OK 74820   405-332-8800

The Robert S. Kerr Environmental Research Laboratory (RSKERL) is the Agency's center of expertise for investigation of the soil and subsurface environment. Important areas of research at RSKERL include the study of the chemical and microbial contamination of groundwater and the mathematical and computer modeling of both the movement of groundwater and the influence of various contaminants in this area of the environment. Sources of pollution, as well as migration and degradation of pollutants, are all topics of concern at RSKERL. Databases maintained here include Ground Water On-line.

* Groundwater Management

Resource Management
Bureau of Reclamation
U.S. Department of the Interior
P.O. Box 25007
Denver CO 80225   303-312-6624

A priority of the Bureau of Reclamation is groundwater management. The Bureau continues to work with state, regional, and local entities in support of the theory that the responsibility for groundwater management, allocation, and protection rests with the states. Several programs are focused on coordinating the use of surface water and groundwater, desalinization and improvement of water quality, control of high water tables through drainage, and technical assistance to other governmental agencies.

* Help Close to Home for Your Indoor Air Issues

Indoor Air Division (ANR-445-W)
Office of Air and Radiation
Environmental Protection Agency
401 M St., SW
Washington, DC 20460   703-308-8470

The Directory of State Indoor Air Contacts is a guide to locating individuals who can provide information and assistance on indoor air quality problems. It brings together information on more than 17 issues, from asbestos to wood preservatives, for the range of agencies involved in addressing those issues, from health agencies to energy departments. In most states, as well as at the federal level, indoor air quality issues are dealt with by a variety of agencies with the authority or expertise to focus on a particular problem or set of problems. This free directory is intended to make it easier to find the right contact.

* Home Water Treatment

R. Woods
Consumer Information Center-2A
P.O. Box 100
Pueblo, CO 81002

Buying a Home Water Treatment Unit is a pamphlet which discusses various units on the market and how to protect yourself from deceptive sales practices (429Y, $1.50).

* How Much Water Do We Have?

WATSTORE Program
Water Resources Division
U.S. Geological Survey
National Center
Reston, VA 22092   703-648-5656

Water-data stations at selected locations throughout the U.S. are used by the Geological Survey to obtain records on stream discharge (flow) and stage (height), reservoir and lake stage and storage, ground water levels, well and spring discharge, and the quality of surface and ground water. These data provide a continuing record of the quantity and quality of the nation's surface- and ground-water resources. All data collected are stored in WATSTORE (National Water Data Storage and Retrieval System), and can be retrieved in machine-readable form or as computer printed tables or graphs, statistical analyses, and digital plots.

* How Much Water Do You Use?

National Water-Use Information Program
Branch of Water-Use Information
U.S. Geological Survey
Reston, VA 22092   703-648-5670

This program provides for the comprehensive and systematic collection of data on water use throughout the U.S. Cooperating states collect the water-use data and aggregate these data by county and hydrologic unit. The point data are stored in a state level data base; the aggregated data are compiled by the Geological Survey for incorporation into the computerized National Water-use Data System.

* Hydroelectric Power

Resource Management
Bureau of Reclamation
U.S. Department of the Interior
P.O. Box 25007
Denver CO 80225   303-236-1058

The Bureau of Reclamation is currently operating 49 powerplants at different sites throughout the West. This office has design and technical and other publications on hydroelectric power. They can answer questions and refer you to other experts in the field. For further information on the impact of hydroelectric power and the Bureau's efforts, contact this office.

* Hydrographic Research

Commission Personnel Division
NOAA Corps
National Oceanic and Atmospheric Administration (NOAA)
U.S. Department of Commerce
11400 Rockville Pike
Rockville, MD 20852   301-460-4768

The NOAA Corps is the uniformed service of the U.S. Department of Commerce responsible for operating and managing National Oceanic and Atmospheric Administration's (NOAA) fleet of hydrographic, oceanographic, and fisheries-research ships and for supporting NOAA scientific programs. Engineering, computer science, mathematics, and science baccalaureate or higher degree graduates are sought for positions in the Corps.

* Is Your Drinking Water Safe?

Public Information Center (PIC)
Environmental Protection Agency
401 M St., SW, PM 3404
Washington, DC 20460   202-260-7751

The Public Information Center (PIC) can provide you with free general publications on the safety of your drinking water, including: *Is Your Drinking Water Safe?* - This brochure explains the Safe Drinking Water Act, drinking water standards, what the numbers mean, and your state resources.

* Lake Protection and Restoration

Clean Lakes Program
Office of Water Regulations and Standards
Environmental Protection Agency
401 M St., SW
Washington DC 20460   202-260-7105

The Environmental Protection Agency's (EPA) Clean Lakes Program provides technical and financial assistance to States for programs dealing with lake restoration and protection.

* Lead and Your Drinking Water

Public Information Center
Environmental Protection Agency
401 M St., SW, PM 3404
Washington DC 20460   202-260-7751

The free brochure, *Lead and Your Drinking Water*, explains the dangers of lead in your drinking water, how it gets there, and steps you can take to remove the lead.

* Local Air Pollution Control Hotline

Best Available Control Technology
Lowest Achievable Emission Rate Clearinghouse
Environmental Protection Agency
Research Triangle Park, NC 27711   919-541-2736

This Clearinghouse was established to enable state and local air pollution control agencies to exchange information on Reasonably Available Control Technology, BACT/LAER determinations for new or modified sources, and to facilitate more consistent emission levels.

Environment and Nature

* Marine, Coastal, Estuarine Water Quality

Environmental Research Laboratory Library
South Ferry Rd.
Narragansett, RI 02882   401-782-3025

The Environmental Research Laboratory Narragansett (ERLN), with its field station in Newport, Oregon, is the Environmental Protection Agency's (EPA) center for marine, coastal, and estuarine water quality research. General collections cover aquatic toxicology, biological oceanography, biomedical science, coastal research, fisheries biology, marine biology, marine ecology, marine organisms. The special collections cover: ○ Estuarine and marine disposal and discharge of complex wastes, dredged materials, and other wastes; ○ Water use designation and quality criteria for estuarine and marine water and sediment; ○ Environmental assessment of ocean discharge.

* Marine Environment and Ocean Dumping

Wetlands, Oceans, and Watersheds
Environmental Protection Agency
401 M St., SW
Washington DC 20460   202-260-7102

This office carries out the duties covered under the Marine Protection, Research and Sanctuaries Act, which is designed to protect the marine environment from the harmful effects of ocean dumping. The Act establishes a permit program to ensure that ocean dumping does not cause degradation of the marine environment. Contact this office for more information on ocean dumping regulation.

* Mosquito Control

Aquatic Biology Department
River Basin Operations
Water Resources
122OSA
Tennessee Valley Authority (TVA)
Muscle Shoals, AL 35660   205-386-3430

This office investigates complaints regarding the mosquito population around the Tennessee Valley Authority (TVA) waters and lands. They will use an adulticide and a larvaicide if needed. This office has done research regarding the killing of mosquitoes. They also run an inspection program May through October. If you have a mosquito problem outside the TVA jurisdiction, contact your local health department. You may be part of a mosquito control abatement district. The health department may also have information regarding mosquitoes.

* Motor Vehicle Emissions

Motor Vehicle Emissions Laboratory Library
2565 Plymouth Rd.
Ann Arbor, MI 48105   313-668-4311

This library provides information services concentrated on automotive engineering to Environmental Protection Agency (EPA) staff and the general public. Subject areas include air pollution from mobile sources, alternative alcohol fuels, and motor vehicle retrofit devices.

* Motor Vehicle Emissions

Motor Vehicle Anti-Tampering Program
Office of Mobile Sources
EN-397F
401 M St., SW
Washington, DC 20460   202-260-2640

The Motor Vehicle Anti-Tampering Program is administered by the Office of Mobile Sources. The program provides the public (especially gas station and garage owners, and the oil and gas industry) with information pertaining to enforcement of tampering regulations in the form of pamphlets and public documents as well as information over the phone. They inspect gas stations and garages regarding compliance with tampering regulations and coordinate state and local inspection programs. Staff can answer questions concerning regulation, gasoline additives and emissions standards. They also can respond to catalytic converter warranty inquiries.

* Municipal, Recreation, Industrial Water Supply

U.S. Department of Agriculture (USDA)
Deputy for Programs, SCS
Box 2890
Washington, DC 20013   202-720-4527

The U.S. Department of Agriculture (USDA) manages a variety of water resource programs to aid landowners and agricultural operators use existing water resources

wisely. These programs also promote reclamation and preservation of water sources that have been contaminated or allowed to fall into disrepair and to monitor recreation, municipal, and industrial water supply.

* National Ocean Service

National Oceanic and Atmospheric Administration
U.S. Department of Commerce
6001 Executive Blvd.
Rockville, MD 20852   301-413-0900

The Office of Ocean Resources, Conservation and Assessments surveys and monitors the oceans, U.S. coastal waters, estuarine waterways, and the Great Lakes to produce data and information products that describe the physical properties of these waters for a wide range of engineering and navigational applications. This office also conducts studies to assess the environmental impact of human activities in U.S. coastal waters. Many of these marine data and information products are essential for protecting life and property from storms and other destructive natural forces. Other marine products, such as predictions of the times and heights of tides and descriptions of tidal currents, are vital for safe navigation.

* National Water Conditions Monthly Update

Hydrologic Information Unit
Water Resources Division
U.S. Geological Survey
419 National Center
Reston, VA 22092   703-648-6817

National Water Conditions is a monthly summary of hydrologic conditions in the United States and southern Canada. Subscriptions are free upon application.

* Ocean and Coastal Pollution

National Ocean Service
National Oceanic and Atmospheric Administration
U.S. Department of Commerce
6001 Executive Blvd.
Rockville, MD 20852   301-413-0900

This office surveys and monitors the oceans, U.S. coastal waters and the Great Lakes to produce data and information products that are critically important for offshore oil and gas exploration, dredging operations, coastal and offshore construction, seafloor mining, waste disposal management, and for protecting the marine environment from the adverse effects of ocean and coastal pollution.

* Ocean Dumping Surveillance and Marine Technology

Library, Coast Guard Research and Development Center
U.S. Coast Guard
U.S. Department of Transportation
Avery Point
Groton, CT 06340-6096   203-441-2648

Marine research is conducted here in areas such as ice technology, navigation instrumentation technology, ocean dumping surveillance, pollution, search and rescue techniques, and marine fire and safety technology. This library is a good starting point for obtaining specific information about what research is done by the Center and for referrals to appropriate experts.

* Oceanographic Corps Jobs

Commission Personnel Division
NOAA Corps
National Oceanic and Atmospheric Administration (NOAA)
U.S. Department of Commerce
11400 Rockville Pike
Rockville, MD 20852   301-443-8648

The NOAA Corps is the uniformed service of the U.S. Department of Commerce responsible for operating and managing National Oceanic and Atmospheric Administration's (NOAA) fleet of hydrographic, oceanographic, and fisheries-research ships and for supporting NOAA scientific programs. Engineering, computer science, mathematics, and science baccalaureate or higher degree graduates are sought for positions in the Corps.

* Ocean Pollution Information Network

Ocean Pollution Data and
 Information Network/CCRO
National Oceanographic Data Center

     Be patient. If any phone number is incorrect, call (area code) 555-1212 and request the new listing.

National Oceanic and Atmospheric Administration
1825 Connecticut Ave., NW
Washington, DC 20235   202-606-4539
The Ocean Pollution Data and Information Network (OPDIN) facilitates user access to ocean pollution data and information generated by 11 participating Federal departments and agencies. OPDIN provides a wide range of products and services to researchers, managers, and others who need data and information about ocean pollution. OPDIN is managed by the Central Coordination and Referral Office (CCRO). The CCRO maintains a directory of Federal ocean pollution data and information systems and services, lists of ocean pollution scientists and managers and their fields of expertise, and annually-updated catalogs of Federal marine pollution research, development, and monitoring projects. The CCRO also provides information and advice about ocean pollution data management and processing, as well as copies of catalogs, directories, technical reports, data inventories, and data products.

* Oil and Chemical Spills Hotline

National Response Center (NRC)
Office of Marine Safety, Security, and Environmental Protection
U.S. Coast Guard
U.S. Department of Transportation
2100 2nd St., SW, Room 2611 800-424-8802
Washington, DC 20593   202-267-2188
The National Response Center (NRC) is the initial point of contact for reporting oil, chemical, radiological, and biological incidents. This is an emergency hotline. NRC's National Strike Force assists federal coordinators on the scene in responding to pollution accidents. For further details, or to report information, contact the Center toll-free.

* Ozone Database

Office of Air and Radiation
Environmental Protection Agency
401 M St., SW
Washington, DC 20460   202-260-7400
OZONET is an electronic database that supplies information regarding substitutes and alternative processes to ozone-depleting solvents. In addition, it includes contacts, regulatory information, relevant articles, an electronic bulletin board, and other services.

* Ozone Production

Aeronomy Laboratory
Environmental Research Laboratory
National Oceanic and Atmospheric Administration
Boulder, CO 80303   303-497-5785
Extensive research is being conducted concerning regional and global ozone production, as well as studying the ozone in the Antarctic. Research is also being conducted on hydrocloroflourocarbons which are becoming the substitutes for the ozone-destroying CFCs. This laboratory can direct you to the appropriate researcher for your area of interest, and can provide you with relevant articles and reports.

* Pacific Research

Pacific Marine Environmental Laboratory
Environmental Research Laboratories
National Oceanic and Atmospheric Administration
7600 Sand Point Way NE
Bin No. C15700
Seattle, WA 98115   206-526-6810
The Pacific Marine Environmental Laboratory carries out interdisciplinary scientific investigations in oceanography, marine meteorology, and related subjects. Current programs focus on climate, marine observation and prediction, marine resources, and marine environmental assessment. Contact this office for further information.

* Pollution Response Operations

Pollution Response Branch
Marine Environmental Response Division
Office of Marine Safety, Security,
 and Environmental Protection
U.S. Coast Guard
U.S. Department of Transportation
2100 2nd St., SW, Room 2100 202-267-0518
Washington, DC 20593-0001 202-267-2611

This office responds to requests for marine environmental protection information from Congress and other federal agencies, state agencies, schools, industries, and the general public. Data is available on laws relating to the protection of the marine environment, incidents involving releases of oil or other hazardous substances, and federally funded spill response operations.

* Project Skywater: Cloud Seeding

Cloud Seeding - Project Skywater
Water Augmentation Group, Code D-3720
Research and Laboratory Services Division
Bureau of Reclamation
U.S. Department of the Interior
P.O. Box 25007
Denver, CO 80225-0007   303-236-4346
Project Skywater is a weather modification project which attempts to change natural phenomena such as clouds, rain, snow, hail, lightning, thunderstorms, tornadoes, fog, and hurricanes so they are more beneficial or less destructive. Foreign assistance programs are also underway with Morocco, and Thailand.

* Radon Hotline

National Radon Hotline
Box 16622
Alexandria, VA 22302   800-767-7236
This is a 24 hour toll-free hotline where a message records your name and address and a brochure on radon is sent via first class mail. The brochure gives some basic information concerning radon, as well as information on a radon detection kit available from the National Safety Council.

* Radon Removal

Public Information Center PM 3404
Environmental Protection Agency
401 M St., SW
Washington, DC 20460   202-260-7751
The Environmental Protection Agency (EPA) has published the following free publications regarding radon and its removal;

A Citizen's Guide to Radon: What It Is And What To Do About It- designed to help readers understand the radon problem and decide if they need to take action to reduce radon levels in their homes.

Removal Of Radon From Household Water- the EPA is studying ways to reduce radon in houses; including methods to remove the gas from water to prevent its release in houses when the water is used. While the work has not yet answered all the questions about household water treatment systems, they are publishing what information they have that may be of immediate use to homeowners.

Radon Reduction in New Construction- This is designed to provide radon information for those involved in new construction and to introduce methods that can be used during construction to minimizer radon entry and facilitate its removal after construction is complete.

Radon Reduction Methods: A Homeowner's Guide- This is designed for homeowners who have already tested their houses for radon and decided that they need to take some action, as well as those who are still uncertain. The information provided should be helpful for homeowners who have the skills and equipment needed for "do-it-yourself" radon reduction work, as well as for homeowners who decide to hire contractors to perform the needed work.

* Regional Hydrologists

Water Resources Division
U.S. Geological Survey
409 National Center
Reston, VA 22092   703-648-5215
The U.S. Geological Survey has the following hydrologist field offices:

Northeastern Region
Regional Hydrologist, U.S. Geological Survey, 433 National Center, Reston, VA 22092; 703-648-5817. Serving: CT, DE, IL, IN, ME, MD, MA, MI, MN, NH, NJ, NY, OH, PA, RI, VT, VA, DC, WV, WI

Southeastern Region
Regional Hydrologist, U.S. Geological Survey, Spalding Woods Office Park, Suite

160, 3850 Holcomb Bridge Rd., Norcross, GA 30092; 404-409-7700. Serving: AL, AR, FL, GA, KY, LA, MS, NC, PR, SC, TN, Virgin Islands

Central Region
Regional Hydrologist, U.S. Geological Survey, Mail Stop 406, Box 25046, Denver Federal Center, Lakewood, CO 80225; 303-236-5920. Serving: CO, IA, KS, MO, MT, NE, NM, ND, OK, SD, TX, UT, WY

Western Region
Regional Hydrologist, U.S. Geological Survey, 345 Middlefield Rd., Mail Stop 470, Menlo Park, CA 94025. Serving: AK, AR, CA, Guam, HI, ID, NV, OR, WA

* Rural Non-Source Water Pollution

U.S. Department of Agriculture (USDA)
Deputy for Programs
Soil Conservation Service (SCS)
Box 2890
Washington, DC 20013   202-720-4527

The U.S. Department of Agriculture (USDA) manages a variety of water resource programs to aid landowners and agricultural operators use existing water resources wisely. The Rural Clean Water Program to reduce non-source water pollution is one of its programs, which aims to prevent or reduce the amount of sediment, chemicals, livestock wastes, and other agricultural pollutants from entering streams and lakes.

* Safe Drinking Water Hotline

Environmental Protection Agency
401 M Street SW
Washington, DC 20460   800-426-4791

The Safe Drinking Water Hotline responds to questions concerning the Safe Drinking Water Act, Water Standards, Regulations, and the Underground Injection Program. It will also provide selected publications relevant to these issues. It operates Monday through Friday, 8:30 a.m. to 4:30 p.m. (EST).

* Sea-Grant Colleges

Office of Oceanic Research Programs
National Oceanic and Atmospheric Administration
U.S. Department of Commerce
1335 East-West Hwy.
Silver Spring, MD 20910   301-713-2448

The National Sea Grant College Program is a national network of over 300 colleges, universities, research institutions, and consortia working in partnership with industry and the federal government to support Great Lakes and marine research, education, and extension services. This program provides support for institutions engaged in comprehensive marine research, education, and advisory service programs, supports individual projects in marine research and development, and sponsors education of ocean scientists and engineers, marine technicians, and other specialists at selected colleges and universities.

* State Drinking Water Programs

State Programs Division
Office of Drinking Water
Environmental Protection Agency
401 M St., SW, Room E1101
Washington DC 20460   202-260-5526

This office oversees the drinking water regulations that are part of the Clean Water Act at the regional and State level. They make sure a State's standards meet at least the minimum requirements of the law, and they are also responsible for their enforcement.

* State Radon Contacts

Your State Radon Office can answer all your questions regarding radon, including providing informational brochures and referrals for testing and removal of radon gas.

Alabama
Radiological Health Branch
Alabama Department of Public Health
State Office Building
Montgomery, AL 36130   334-261-5313

Alaska
Alaska Department of Health and Social Services

P.O. Box 110613
Juneau, AK 99811   907-465-3019

Arizona
Arizona Radiation Regulatory Agency
4814 South 40th St.
Phoenix, AZ 85040   602-255-4845

Arkansas
Division of Radiation Control and Emergency Management
Arkansas Department of Health
4815 W. Markham St.
Little Rock, AR 72205   501-661-2301

California
Indoor Quality Program
California Department of Health Services
2151 Berkeley Way
Berkeley, CA 94704   415-540-2134

Colorado
Radiation Control Division
Colorado Department of Health
4300 Cherry Creek Dr., South
Denver, CO 80220-1530   303-460-4768

Connecticut
Connecticut Department of Public Health
Toxic Hazards Section EEOH
150 Washington St.
Hartford, CT 06106   203-566-8167

Delaware
Division of Public Health
Delaware Bureau of Environmental Health
P.O. Box 637
Dover, DE 19903   302-739-4731

District of Columbia
DC Department of Consumer and Regulatory Affairs
614 H St., NW, Room 1016
Washington, DC 20001   202-727-7728

Florida
Florida Office of Radiation Control
Building 18, Sunland Center
P.O. Box 15490
Orlando, FL 32858   305-297-2095

Georgia
Georgia Department of Natural Resources
Environmental Protection Division
7 Martin Luther King Dr., Room 139
Atlanta, GA 30334   404-656-6905

Hawaii
Environmental Protection and Health Services Division
Hawaii Department of Health
591 Ala Moana Blvd.
Honolulu, HI 96813   808-586-4304

Idaho
Radiation Control Section
Idaho Department of Health and Welfare
Statehouse Mall
Boise, ID 83720   208-334-5879

Illinois
Illinois Department of Nuclear Safety
Office of Environmental Safety
1035 Outer Park Dr.
Springfield, IL 62704   800-225-1245 (in State)

Indiana
Division of Industrial Hygiene and Radiological Health
Indiana State Board of Health
1330 W. Michigan St.

P.O. Box 1964
Indianapolis, IN 46206   317-633-0153

Iowa
Bureau of Environmental Health
Iowa Department of Public Health
Lucas State Office Building
Des Moines, IA 50319   515-281-7781

Kansas
Kansas Department of Health and Environment
Forbes Field, Building 740
Topeka, KS 66620   913-296-1535

Kentucky
Radiation Control Branch
Cabinet of Human Resources
275 East Main St.
Frankfort, KY 40621   502-564-3700

Louisiana
Louisiana Radiation Protection Division
P.O. Box 14690
Baton Rouge, LA 70898   504-765-0141

Maine
Division of Health Engineering
Maine Department of Human Services
10 State House Station
Augusta, ME 04333   207-287-5338

Maryland
Radiation Control
Department of the Environment
7th Floor Mailroom
201 W. Preston St.   410-333-3130
Baltimore, MD 21201   800-872-3666

Massachusetts
Radiation Control Program
Massachusetts Department of Public Health
23 Service Center   413-586-7525
North Hampton, MA 01060   617-983-6874 (Boston)

Michigan
Michigan Department of Public Health
Division of Radiological Health
3423 N. Martin Luther King Jr. Blvd.
P.O. Box 30195
Lansing, MI 48909   517-335-8190

Minnesota
Section of Radiation Control
P.O. Box 9441
717 SE Delaware St.
Minnesota Department of Health   612-623-5350
Minneapolis, MN 55440   800-652-9747

Mississippi
Division of Radiological Health
Mississippi Department of Health
P.O. Box 1700
Jackson, MS 39215   601-354-6657

Missouri
Bureau of Radiological Health
Missouri Department of Health
1730 E. Elm, P.O. Box 570
Jefferson City, MO 65102   314-751-6083

Montana
Occupational Health Bureau
Montana Department of Health and
  Environmental Sciences
836 Front St.
Helena, MT 59620   406-444-3671

Nebraska
Division of Radiological Health
Nebraska Department of Health
301 Centennial Mall South
P.O. Box 95007
Lincoln, NE 68509   402-471-2168

Nevada
Radiological Health Section
Health Division
Nevada Department of Human Resources
400 W. King St., Room 102
Carson City, NV 89710   702-687-5394

New Hampshire
New Hampshire Radiological Health Program
Health and Welfare Building
6 Hazen Dr.
Concord, NH 03301   603-271-4588

New Jersey
New Jersey Department of Environmental Protection
380 Scotch Rd. CN-411   609-530-4000
Trenton, NJ 08625   800-648-0394

New Mexico
Surveillance Monitoring Section
New Mexico Radiation Protection Bureau
P.O. Box 968
Santa Fe, NM 87504   505-827-2957

New York
Bureau of Environmental Radiation Protection
New York State Health Department
Empire State Plaza, Corning Tower   518-473-3613
Albany, NY 12237   800-458-1158

North Carolina
Radiation Protection Section
North Carolina Department of Human Resources
3825 Barrett Dr.
Raleigh, NC 27609   919-571-4141

North Dakota
Division of Environmental Engineering
North Dakota State Department of Health and Consolidated Laboratories
Missouri Office Building
1200 Missouri Ave., Room 304
Bismarck, ND 58502   701-328-2348

Ohio
Bureau of Radiation Protection
Ohio Department of Health
246 N. High St.   614-644-2727
Columbus, OH 43212   800-523-4439

Oklahoma
Radiation and Special Hazards Service
Oklahoma State Department of Health
1000 North 10th
Oklahoma City, OK 73117-2199   405-271-6868

Oregon
Oregon State Health Department
800 North East Oregon 21
Portland, OR 97232   503-731-4014

Pennsylvania
Bureau of Radiation Protection
Pennsylvania Department of Environmental Resources
P.O. Box 2063
Harrisburg, PA 17120   717-787-2480

Puerto Rico
Puerto Rico Radiological Health Division
GPO Call Box 70184
Rio Piedras, PR 00936   809-767-3563

Be patient. If any phone number is incorrect, call (area code) 555-1212 and request the new listing.   **1115**

Environment and Nature

Rhode Island
Division of Occupational Health and Radiological Control
Rhode Island Department of Health
3 Capitol Hill, Room 206
Providence, RI 02908 — 401-277-2438

South Carolina
Bureau of Radiological Health
South Carolina Department of Health and Environmental Control
2600 Bull St.
Columbia, SC 29201 — 803-737-7400

South Dakota
Office of Air Quality and Solid Waste
South Dakota Department of Water and Natural Resources
Joe Foss Building
523 E. Capital
Pierre, SD 57501 — 605-773-3153

Tennessee
Division of Air Pollution Control
9th Floor, NCNX
401 CHurch St.
Nashville, TN 37243-1531 — 615-532-0554

Texas
Bureau of Radiation Control
Texas Department of Health
1100 West 49th St.
Austin, TX 78756 — 512-834-6688

Utah
Bureau of Radiation Control
Utah State Department of Environmental Quality
168 North 1950 West
P.O. Box 84114-4850
Salt Lake City, UT 84116 — 801-538-6734

Vermont
Division of Occupation and Radiological Health
Vermont Department of Health
Administration Building
108 Cherry St.
P.O. Box 70
Burlington, VT 05402 — 802-865-7730

Virginia
Bureau of Radiological Health
Department of Health
1500 E. Main St., Room 217 — 804-786-5932
Richmond, VA 23219 — 800-468-0138

Washington
Environmental Protection Section
Washington Office of Radiation Protection
Thurston AirDustrial Center
Building 5
Olympia, WA 98504-7827 — 360-753-5962

West Virginia
Industrial Hygiene Division
West Virginia Department of Health
151 11th Ave.
South Charleston, WV 25303 — 304-348-3526

Wisconsin
Division of Health
Section of Radiation Protection
Wisconsin Department of Health and Social Services
1414 E. Washington Ave., Room 96
Madison, WI 53703 — 608-267-4782

Wyoming
Wyoming Department of Health and Social Services
Hathway Building
4th Floor
Cheyenne, WY 82002 — 307-777-7956

* Toxic Substances in Water

Toxic Substances Hydrology Program (TSHP)
Water Resources Division
U.S. Geological Survey
National Center
Reston, VA 22092 — 703-648-6862

The Toxic Substances Hydrology Program (TSHP) is an interdisciplinary program designed to provide the hydrologic information necessary both to improve waste-disposal practices and also to help mitigate existing and future surface and groundwater contamination problems. This program focuses on the occurrence, movement, and fate of toxic substances in the hydrologic system by 1) studying major types of contaminants of ground and surface waters, and 2) developing new methods and protocols to assess the extent of contamination.

* Unleaded Gas and Fuels Hotline

Environmental Protection Agency
Region I
JFK Federal Bldg.
Boston, MA 02203 — 800-821-1237

The Unleaded Fuel Tank Hotline is an enforcement-related line that takes calls about tampering with vehicles, pumps, and other problems related to unleaded fuels. It provides this service for Region I states: Connecticut, Massachusetts, New Hampshire, Rhode Island, Vermont.

* Want to Know More About Acid Rain?

Acid Rain Division
Environmental Protection Agency
401 M St., SW
Washington, DC 20460 — 202-233-9150

Acid rain affects both the health of humans and our environment and is an issue with which the Environmental Protection Agency (EPA) is actively involved. EPA can provide information on research, regulation, and other issues associated with acid rain. EPA publishes *Acid Rain: A Student's First Sourcebook* designed for grades 4-8 and their teachers, which describes the effects of acid rain, solutions, experiments, and activities. This office also has EPA Journal articles on acid rain, background information, and updates on EPA's activities. The EPA is part of the National Acid Precipitation Assessment Program, and is conducting the National Surface Water Survey designed to provide information on the status of lakes and streams believed to be susceptible to change as a result of acid rain. Contact this office for more information.

* Wastewater Information

Wastewater Treatment and Information Exchange
Bulletin Board System
P.O. Box 6064
Morgantown, WV 26506 — 304-293-4191

This Bulletin Board allows for the exchange of information on wastewater related material through its main board and its specialized conferences. They also publish a *User's Guide*.

* Wastewater Treatment Clearinghouse

Small Flows Clearinghouse
613 N. Spruce St.
Morgantown, WV 26506-6064 — 800-624-8301

The National Small Flows Clearinghouse provides information on wastewater treatment technologies for small communities, and participates in a national training effort to assist states in implementing small flows technology at the community level. Two free newsletters are produced by the Clearinghouse. *Small Flows* provides technical information and is geared toward the engineering and regulatory communities, and *Pipeline* presents information about various wastewater topics for community officials. The Clearinghouse has a computer bulletin board, databases, provides telephone consultation and referral service, maintains a large inventory of instructional products (books, brochures, and videotapes) and instructional materials. Workshops, seminars, and presentations are also sponsored. This clearinghouse was mandated by the Clean Water Act Amendments of 1977.

* Water Clearinghouse

Water Resources Scientific Information Center (WRSIC)
Water Resources Division
U.S. Geological Survey
National Center

Reston, VA 22092   703-648-6821

The Water Resources Scientific Information Center (WRSIC) was established to increase the availability and knowledge of water-related scientific and technical information. WRSIC abstracts water-resource publications from throughout the world and makes this information available to the water-resources community and the public through publications and computerized bibliographic information services.

* Water Conservation

U.S. Department of Agriculture (USDA)
Deputy for Programs
Soil Conservation Service (SCS)
Box 2890
Washington, DC 20013   202-720-4527

The U.S. Department of Agriculture (USDA) manages a variety of water resource programs to aid landowners and agricultural operators use existing water resources including Resource Conservation and Development which encourages state and local governments and non-profit organizations to develop programs to accelerate water conservation and development.

* Water Contamination by Metals

Environmental Technology Division
Bureau of Mines
U.S. Department of the Interior
118 7th St., NW, MS 6205
Washington, DC 20241   202-501-9630

Researchers at the Bureau of Mines are working on low-cost ways to deal with the problem of acid drainage at abandoned mines. They are developing computer programs to predict potential drainage at new mines and to develop ways to treat the water after it's been contaminated. The Bureau's environmental research also addresses the problem of solid waste disposal and soil and water contaminated by metals. Technologies are developed that will reduce or remove the threats that these wastes pose.

* Water Data Exchange (NAWDEX)

National Water Data Exchange
Water Resources Division
U.S. Geological Survey
National Center, MS 421
Reston, VA 22092   703-648-5677

The National Water Data Exchange is a confederation of Federal and non-Federal water-oriented organizations working together to improve access to available water data. Information on sites for which water data is available, the types of data available, and the organizations that store the data is available from NAWDEX.

* Water Online and Other Databases

Environmental Research Laboratory Library
College Station Rd.
Athens, GA 30613   706-542-0621

The Athens Environmental Research Laboratory (ERL) Library provides information services covering a wide range of environmental and management subjects. Subject areas include aquatic toxicology, microbiology, biology, pesticides, chemistry, water pollution, engineering, and water quality. Databases maintained here include CIS, DIALOG, and Ground Water On-line.

* Water Pollution

Nonpoint Source Information Exchange
Office of Water Assessment and Watershed Protection Division
401 M St., SW
Environmental Protection Agency
Washington, DC 20460   202-260-7085

The Nonpoint Source Information Exchange provides response to inquiries regarding the management of nonpoint sources of water pollution and the Environmental Protection Agency's (EPA) control program under Section 319 of the Clean Water Act. Publications include *Nonpoint Sources NEWS-NOTES* and a *Technical Bulletin*.

* Water Pollution and Hydrobiology Clearinghouse

Andrew W. Briedenbach Environmental
Research Center Library
26 W. Martin Luther King
Cincinnati, OH 45268   513-569-7703

The major subjects in this library's collection are bacteriology, biology, biotechnology, chemistry, engineering, hazardous wastes, hydrobiology, microbiology, solid waste management, toxicology, water pollution, and water quality. Databases maintained here include BRS, CAS On-line, CIS, DIALOG, Dun & Bradstreet, Hazardous Waste Database, LEXIS/NEXIS, NLM, Toxline, and Toxnet. General collections include bacteriology, biology, biotechnology, microbiology, physics, and solid waste management. This library's special collections cover the environment, Canada, legal issues, hazardous waste, and solid waste.

* Water Quality Assessment

Office of Water Quality
Water Resources Division
U.S. Geological Survey
National Center, MS 412
Reston, VA 22092   703-648-6884

The National Water Quality Assessment Program is designed to address a wide range of water-quality issues that include chemical contamination, acidification, eutrophication, salinity, sedimentation, and sanitary quality. The program strives to provide nationally consistent descriptions of current water-quality conditions and to define long-term trends in water quality.

* Water Quality Information Center

National Agriculture Library Building
Beltsville, MD 20705   301-504-6875

This Information Center can answer questions regarding the quality of freshwater and coastal water resources, point and nonpoint source pollution of both surface and ground water, the quality of drinking water, wetlands issues, and much more,. They have access to a database, bibliographies, and other publications. Contact the Center for more information.

* Water Quality Networks

Office of Water Quality
Water Resources Division
U.S. Geological Survey
National Center, MS 412
Reston, VA 22092   703-648-6884

The National Water-Quality Networks Program describes and appraises the Nation's water resources. The largest of these networks is the National Stream Quality Accounting Network (NASQAN), which consists of more than 400 sampling sites used to measure a comprehensive list of physical and chemical characteristics on a quarterly or bimonthly schedule to fulfill information needs of national and regional water resources planners and managers. Other networks within the program include the Radiochemical Surveillance Network, the Tritium Network, and the Hydrologic Bench-Mark Network. This last network monitors the natural streamflow and water quality of small river basins that are known to be relatively little affected by man's activities.

* Water Research Grants

Office of External Research
Water Resources Division
U.S. Geological Survey
National Center, MS 409
Reston, VA 22092   703-648-6807

The Water Research Grants Program is a national program of grants to support technology development and research in major water resource problem areas. State Water Resources Research and Technology Institutes, qualified educational institutions, private foundations, private firms, individuals, and agencies of local or state governments are eligible to receive grants on a dollar-for-dollar matching basis for research concerning any aspect of a water-resource related problem deemed to be in the national interest.

* Water Resources Activities

Hydrologic Information Unit
Water Resources Division
U.S. Geological Survey
419 National Center
Reston, VA 22092   703-648-6817

The current hydrology program in each state is outlined in pamphlets entitled *Water-Resources Activities of the Geological Survey in (State)*. Pamphlets are available through the regional hydrologists offices listed elsewhere in this book.

Environment and Nature

* Water Resources Clearinghouse

Water Resources Scientific Information Center (WRSIC)
U.S. Geological Survey
421 National Center
Reston, VA 22092   703-648-6821

The Water Resources Scientific Information Center (WRSIC) was established as a national center to increase the availability and knowledge of water-related scientific and technical information. To accomplish this purpose, WRSIC abstracts water resources publications from throughout the world and makes this bibliographic information available to the water resources community and the public through publications and computerized bibliographic information services.

* Water Resources Division District Offices

The Water Resources Division District Offices are NAWDEX Assistance Centers that provide the public with information on WATSTORE and answer questions on the water resources of their specific regions. Each State publishes an Annual Report on Water Resources Data, and can provide you with information on surface-water resources, water supply and use, ground water quality, and groundwater resources. They also publish current water-resources activities in your State, which includes a publication list and other hydrologic information.

Alabama
Water Resources Division District Office
U.S. Geological Survey
520 19th Ave.
Tuscaloosa, AL 35401   205-752-8104

Alaska
Water Resources Division District Office
U.S. Geological Survey
4230 University Dr., Suite 201
Anchorage, AK 99508-4664   907-786-7100

Arizona
Water Resources Division District Office
U.S. Geological Survey
375 South Usoid 5719
Tucson, AZ 85719   520-670-0661

Arkansas
Water Resources Division District Office
U.S. Geological Survey
401 Hardin Rd.
Little Rock, AR 72211   501-228-3600

California
Water Resources Division District Office
U.S. Geological Survey
Federal Building
Room W-2233
2800 Cottage Way
Sacramento, CA 95825   916-979-2605

Colorado
Water Resources Division District Office
U.S. Geological Survey
Box 25046, Federal Center
Mail Stop 415
Denver, CO 80225   303-236-4882

Connecticut
Connecticut Office Water Resources Division
U.S. Geological Survey
525 Ribicoff Federal Building
450 Main St.
Hartford, CT 06103   203-240-3060

Delaware
Delaware Office
Water Resources Division
U.S. Geological Survey
1201 Federal Building
300 South New Street
Dover, DE 19904   302-734-2506

Florida
Water Resources Division District Office
U.S. Geological Survey
227 North Bronough St., Suite 3015
Tallahassee, FL 32301   904-681-7620

Georgia
Water Resources Division District Office
U.S. Geological Survey, Suite B
3039 Amwiller Rd., Suite 130   770-903-9100
Atlanta, GA 30360   404-986-6860

Hawaii
Water Resources Division District Office
U.S. Geological Survey
677 Ala Moana Blvd., Room 415
Honolulu, HI 96850   808-522-8290

Idaho
Water Resources Division District Office
U.S. Geological Survey
230 Collins Rd..
Boise, ID 83702   208-387-1300

Illinois
Water Resources Division District Office
U.S. Geological Survey
Champaign County Bank Plaza
102 East Main, Fourth Floor
Urbana, IL 61801   217-344-0037

Indiana
Water Resources Division District Office
U.s. Geological Survey
5957 Lakeside Blvd.
Indianapolis, IN 46278   317-290-3333

Iowa
Water Resources Division District Office
U.s. Geological Survey
P.O. Box 1230
269 Federal Building
400 South Clinton St.
Iowa City, IA 52244   319-337-4191

Kansas
Water Resources Division District Office
U.S. Geological Survey
4821 Quiail Crest Place
Lawrence, KS 66049-3839   913-842-9909

Kentucky
Water Resources Division District Office
U.S. Geological Survey
2301 Bradley Ave.
Louisville, KY 40217   502-635-8000

Louisiana
Water Resources Division District Office
U.s. Geological Survey
3535 South Sherwood Forest, Suite 120
Baton Rouge, LA 70816   504-389-0281

Maine
Maine Office
Water Resources Division
U.S. Geological Survey
26 Ganneston Dr.
Augusta, ME 04330   207-622-8201

Maryland
Water Resources Division District Office
U.S. Geological Survey
208 Carroll Building
8600 LaSalle Rd.
Towson, MD 21286   410-512-4800

Massachusetts
Water Resources Division District Office
U.S. Geological Survey
150 Causeway St., Suite 1309
Boston, MA 02114
617-565-6860

Michigan
Water Resources Division District Office
U.S. Geological Survey
6520 Mercantile Way, Suite 5
Lansing, MI 48910
517-887-8903

Minnesota
Water Resources Division district office
U.S. Geological Survey
702 Post Office Building
St. Paul, MN 55101
612-229-2600

Mississippi
Water Resources Division District Office
U.S. Geological Survey
308 S. Airport Rd.
Pearl Mississippi
Jackson, MS 39208
601-965-4600

Missouri
Water Resources Division District Office
U.S. Geological Survey
Mail Stop 200
1400 Independence Rd.
Rolla, MO 65401
314-341-0824

Montana
Water Resources Division District Office
U.S. Geological Survey
301 South Park Ave.
428 Federal Building
Drawer 10076
Helena, MT 59626
406-449-5363

Nebraska
Water Resources Division District Office
U.S. Geological Survey
406 Federal Building
100 Centennial Mall, North
Lincoln, NE 68508
402-437-5082

Nevada
Nevada Office Water Resources Division
U.S. Geological Survey
224 Federal Building
705 North Plaza St.
Carson City, NV 89701
702-882-1388

New Hampshire
New Hampshire Office
Water Resources Division
U.S. Geological Survey
525 Clinton St., RFD 2
Bow, NH 03301
603-225-4681

New Jersey
Water Resources Division District Office
U.S. Geological Survey
Mountain View Office Park, Suite 206
810 Bear Tavern Rd.
West Trenton, NJ 08628
609-771-3900

New Mexico
Water Resources Division District Office
U.S. Geological Survey
720 Western Bank Building
505 Marquette, Northwest
Albuquerque, NM 87102
505-262-5300

New York
Water Resources Division District Office
U.S. Geological Survey
P.O. Box 1669
343 U.S. Post Office and Courthouse Building
Albany, NY 12201
518-434-5300

North Carolina
Water Resources Division District Office
U.S. Geological Survey
P.O. Box 2857
300 Fayetteville Street Mall
436 Century Postal Station
Raleigh, NC 27602
919-856-4510

North Dakota
Water Resources Division District Office
U.S. Geological Survey
821 East Interstate Ave.
Bismarck, ND 58501
701-250-4601

Ohio
Water Resources Division District Office
U.S. Geological Survey
975 West Third Ave.
Columbus, OH 43212
614-469-5553

Oklahoma
Water Resources Division District Office
U.S. Geological Survey
202 North West 66
Building 7
Oklahoma City, OK 73116
405-843-7570

Oregon
Water Resources Division District Office
U.S. Geological Survey
16015 South E. Cherry Blossom Dr.
Portland, OR 97216-3159
503-251-3200

Pennsylvania
Water Resources Division District Office
U.S. Geological Survey
840 Marriot St.
Lemoyne, PA 17143-1586
717-730-6900

Puerto Rico
Water Resources Division District Office
U.S. Geological Survey
GPO Box 4424
GSA Center, Building 652
Highway 28, Pueblo Viejo
San Juan, PR 00936
809-783-4660

Rhode Island
Rhode Island Office
Water Resources Division
U.S. Geological Survey
Pastore Federal Building and U.S. Post Office
Room 237
Providence, RI 02903
401-528-5135

South Carolina
Water Resource Division District Office
U.S. Geological Survey
Suite 658
1835 Assembly St.
Columbia, SC 29201
803-750-6100

South Dakota
Water Resources Division District Office
U.S. Geological Survey
317 Federal Building
200 Fourth St., SW
Huron, SD 57350
605-353-7176

Tennessee
Water Resources Division District Office
U.S. Geological Survey

Be patient. If any phone number is incorrect, call (area code) 555-1212 and request the new listing.

1119

A-10 Broadway, Suite 500
Nashville, TN 37203   615-736-5424

Texas
Water Resources Division District Office
U.S. Geological Survey
649 Federal Building
300 East Eighth St.
Austin, TX 78701   512-832-5791

Utah
Water Resources Division District Office
U.s. Geological Survey
Room 1016
Administration Building
1745 West 1700 South
Salt Lake City, UT 84104   801-524-5663

Vermont
See listing for Massachusetts

Virginia
Virginia Office
Water Resources Division
U.W. Geological Survey
3600 West Broad St., Room 606
Richmond, VA 23230   804-278-4750

Washington
Water Resources Division District Office
U.S. Geological Survey
1201 Pacific Ave., Suite 600
Tacoma, WA 98402   206-593-6510

West Virginia
Water Resources Division District Office
U.S. Geological Survey
603 Morris St.
Charleston, WV 25301   304-347-5130

Wisconsin
Water Resources Division District Office
U.S. Geological Survey
6417 Normandy Lane
Madison, WI 53719   608-274-3535

Wyoming
Water Resources Division District Office
U. S. Geological Survey
2617 E. Lincoln Way, Suite B
Cheyenne, WY 82001-5662   307-778-2931

* Water Resources Information
Hydrologic Information Unit (HIU)
Water Resources Division
U.S. Geological Survey
National Center, MS 419
Reston, VA 22092   703-648-6817

Contact this office for requests for general information on water resources of an area or the Nation and on activities of the Water Resources Division. The Hydrologic Information Unit (HIU) answers general questions on hydrology, water resources, hydrologic mapping, publications, activities, projects, and services of the Water Resources Division, making referrals to appropriate field and Headquarters offices when necessary. HIU also maintains limited stocks of Geological Survey general-interest publications. This publication series consists of short presentations in the form of leaflets, booklets, essay reprints, brochures, and water fact sheets.

* Water Resources Library
Departmental Library
Bureau of Reclamation
U.S. Department of the Interior
P.O. Box 25007, D7923I
Denver Federal Center
Denver, CO 80225-0007   303-236-6963

This library within the Bureau of Reclamation holds a wealth of information on the Bureau's water conservation activities. Library materials may be used only at the library or may be checked out through the inter-library loan system at your local library. Key topics include hydrology engineering, groundwater management, dam safety, soil mechanics, and business related issues.

* Water Resources: National Survey
National Water Summary Branch
Water Resources Division
U.S. Geological Survey
National Center, MS 407
Reston, VA 22092   703-648-6851

The National Water Summary Program brings together information about the availability, quantity, quality, and use of water resources and organizes it in ways to show the Nation's water resources condition to national, state, and local officials and to the general public. *National Water Summary Reports* are published annually.

* Watershed Protection
U.S. Department of Agriculture (USDA)
Deputy for Programs, SCS
Box 2890
Washington, DC 20013   202-720-4527

The U.S. Department of Agriculture (USDA) manages a variety of water resource programs to aid landowners and agricultural operators use existing water resources wisely including Watershed Protection Projects which provides flood management prevention; watershed protection; and agricultural water management.

* Water Supply, Flood Plain Management
U.S. Army Corps of Engineers
Public Affairs
20 Massachusetts Ave., NW
Washington, DC 20314   202-272-0011

The Corps offers free brochures on a wide variety of subjects, including archaeology, camping, environment, erosion control, flood control, flood plain management, history, safety, waste-water treatment and water supply. For a publications list, call or write the above office.

* Water Supply Situation
Resource Management
Bureau of Reclamation
U.S. Department of the Interior
P.O. Box 25007
Denver Federal Center
Denver, CO 80225   303-236-3289

The Bureau assists water users and development agencies in reviewing state and federal water laws in an ongoing effort to conserve the Nation's water supply.

* Western Reservoirs and Water Projects Photographs and Videos
Visual Communication Services
Bureau of Reclamation
U.S. Department of the Interior
P.O. Box 25007, Denver Federal Center
Denver, CO 80225   303-236-7000

Photographs depicting Bureau of Reclamation activities may be borrowed from this office. Videocassettes, slide shows, black and white photos, and color slides are available, showing water and power activities, such as recreation, irrigation, agriculture, research, and reservoirs, within the Western region. The following videos are available for free loan:

A Bursting Bubble - Cavitation
A New Horizon
Adventure in Glen Canyon
Build-up On The Bighorn
California Flooding
Central Arizona Project-Lifeline to the Future
Central Utah Project
Challenge at Glen Canyon
Coachella Canal Relining
The Colorado
The Columbia A Fountain of Life

Design and Construction of Safe Dams
From Snowfall to Sandstone
Giant on the Bighorn
Great Web of Water
Hoover Dam
Hoover Dam Construction
Hoover Dam 50th Anniversary
How Water Won the West
Hydropower
Hydropower - a Twentieth Century Force
Lake Powell - Jewel of the Colorado
Living Waters of the Colorado
Miracle of Water
Mountain Skywater
New Technologies and New Solutions
Operation Glen Canyon
Powering One Corner of the World
Rio Grande-Ribbon of Life
Take Pride in America
Take Pride in America - A Legacy of Caring
Taming of Black Canyon
Teton - Decision and Disaster
To Build A Dream - The Story of Hoover Dam
Water In The West - Tomorrow's Challenge

* Western Water Quality and Supply

Engineering and Research
Bureau of Reclamation
U.S. Department of the Interior
P.O. Box 25007
Denver, CO 80225   303-236-6988

The Bureau of Reclamation provides programs and leadership to improve water quality, to eliminate environmental pollution and protect Western water supplies from other threats of pollution. Other related programs include fish and wildlife enhancement, reduction of salinity and other pollutants in streams and reservoirs, agricultural drainage control, and protection against contamination of underground and surface water sources.

* Wetlands Protection

Office of Wetlands Protection
Environmental Protection Agency (EPA)
401 M St., SW
Washington DC 20460   202-260-7791

This office implements Environmental Protection Agency (EPA) statutory responsibilities in the Clean Water Act as they relate to the filling of wetlands and other aquatic resources. Designed to raise the importance of wetlands, this office works with other governmental bodies to encourage wetlands protection.

* Wild and Scenic Rivers

Land and Renewable Resources
Bureau of Land Management (BLM)
U.S. Department of the Interior
18th and C Sts., NW
Washington, DC 20240   202-208-4896

The Bureau of Land Management (BLM) manages about 2,200 miles of the Wild and Scenic River System, primarily in the western United States. These areas are located in the directory, *Recreation Guide to BLM Public Lands*, available from the Office of Public Affairs, Bureau of Land Management, U.S. Department of the Interior, Washington, DC 20240.

* Undersea Research

National Undersea Research Program (NURP)
National Oceanic and Atmospheric Administration (NOAA)
U.S. Department of Commerce
6010 Executive Blvd.
Rockville, MD 20852   301-413-0900

The National Undersea Research Program (NURP) develops programs and provides support to scientists and engineers for the study of biological, chemical, geological, and physical processes in the world's oceans and lakes. NURP assist researchers in conducting what are considered by NOAA and the marine community to be crucial research programs. In order to execute these programs, NURP provides investigators with a suite of the modern undersea facilities including submersibles, habitats, air and mixed gas SCUBA, and remotely operated vehicles. A major part of the research program is carried out by a network of National Undersea Research Centers. Contact this office for more information on the research conducted or the research centers.

Forests and Land Conservation

* *See also Business and Industry Chapter*
* *See also Vacations and Business Travel Chapter*

* Abandoned Mine Land Reclamation

Office of Surface Mining Reclamation and Enforcement
U.S. Department of the Interior
1951 Constitution Ave., NW
Washington, DC 20240   202-208-2553

The surface mining law requires that operators pay a reclamation fee for each ton of coal produced. These fees are deposited with the U.S. Treasury in a fund called the Abandoned Mine Reclamation Fund and are used to reclaim sites that were mined and left unreclaimed before the surface mining law was enacted in 1977. Fifty percent of the fees collected in a state that has approved reclamation and regulatory programs is returned to that state for use in its reclamation program. The other fifty percent is the Federal share. This portion is used by the Office of Surface Mining Reclamation and Enforcement to address public health and safety emergencies caused by past mining practices, and to fund high-priority reclamation projects in non-program states. To obtain your state contact for the abandoned mine land reclamation program, contact the office above.

* A Forest in Your Community?

Urban and Community Forestry
Forest Service, U.S. Department of Agriculture
14th and Independence Ave., SW
Washington, DC 20250   202-205-1694

The Urban and Community Forestry program promotes and improves the economic, environmental, and social well-being of communities through the planting and management of trees, shrubs, and other vegetation. These efforts enhance the city environment, make important contributions to soil, water, and air quality, and help conserve energy and reduce atmospheric carbon dioxide. Contact this office for more information.

* Agents and Rangers for Public Lands

Office of Public Information
Bureau of Land Management (BLM)
U.S. Department of the Interior
18th and C Sts., NW
Washington, DC 20240-0001   202-208-3435

As a caretaker of more than 300 million acres, the Bureau of Land Management (BLM) manages and protects these lands and the resources associated with them. BLM has highly trained Special Agents and uniformed rangers to enforce applicable Federal laws on public lands. Special agents are responsible for conducting criminal investigations and making arrests. Rangers primarily patrol the public lands where they prevent law violations and assist stranded visitors. Contact the office above for the pamphlet *Protecting Public Land Resources* for a listing of Field Offices to contact for employment.

* Bureau of Land Management State Offices

Bureau of Land Management (BLM)
U.S. Department of the Interior
Washington, DC 20240   202-452-5125

Specific information about opportunities to enjoy the benefits of the public lands and resources can best be obtained from the state office responsible for the areas of interest:

Alaska
Bureau of Land Management, 701 C St., P.O.Box 13, Anchorage, AK 99513; 907-271-5555

Arizona
Bureau of Land Management, 3707 N 7th St., Phoenix, AZ 85014; 602-893-6701

California
Bureau of Land Management, Federal Building, Room E-2841, 2800 Cottage Way, Sacramento, CA 95825; 916-978-4746

Colorado
Bureau of Land Management, 2850 Youngfield St., Lakewood, CO 80215; 303-239-3600. Also serves Kansas

Eastern States
Bureau of Land Management, 7450 Boston Blvd., Springfield, VA 22153; 703-440-1700. Serves states bordering and east of the Mississippi River.

Idaho
Bureau of Land Management, 3380 Americana Terr., Boise, ID 83706; 208-384-3000.

Montana
Bureau of Land Management, 222 N 32nd Street, P.O. Box 36800, Billings, MT 59107; 406-255-2913. Also serves North Dakota and South Dakota.

Nevada
Bureau of Land Management, 300 Booth St., P.O. Box 12000, Reno, NV 89520; 702-785-6400.

New Mexico
Bureau of Land Management, South Federal Pl., P.O. Box 1449, Santa Fe, NM 87501; 505-988-6316. Also serves Oklahoma and Texas.

Oregon
Bureau of Land Management, 825 NE Multnomah St., P.O. Box 2965, Portland, OR 97208; 503-231-6274. Also serves Washington.

Utah
Bureau of Land Management, 324 South State Street, Suite 301, Salt Lake City, UT 84111-2303; 801-539-4021.

Wyoming
Bureau of Land Management, 5353 Yellowstone Rd., P.O. Box 82009, Cheyenne, WY 82001; 307-775-6256. Also serves Nebraska.

* Bureau of Reclamation Regional Offices

Bureau of Mines
U.S. Department of Interior
1951 Constitution Avenue, NW
Washington, DC 20240   202-501-9649

Here are the regional offices which enforce strip mining and reclamation laws:

Lower Colorado Region
Box 427, Nevada Hwy. and Park St., Boulder City, NV 89005; 702-293-8420

Mid-Pacific Region
2800 Cottage Way, Sacramento, CA 95825; 916-978-4919

Pacific Northwest Region
1150 North Curtis Rd., Boise, ID 83706-1234; 208-378-5020

Upper Colorado Region
Box 11568, 125 S. State St., Salt Lake City, UT 84147; 801-524-5403

Great Plains Region
Box 36900, 316 N. 26th St., Billings, MT 59107; 406-247-7610

* Cadastral Survey

Branch of Cadastral Survey Development
Bureau of Land Management (BLM)
U.S. Department of the Interior
1849 C St., NW
Washington, DC 20240   202-452-5125

The Office of Cadastral Surveys is responsible for the creation, restoration, marking, and defining of the boundaries of public lands. Under the cadastral system, the public domain is plotted into a grid of squares, each approximately 6 miles to the side, called "townships." In recent years, modern technology has replaced the traditional "chain" measuring tape with electronic instruments. Microwave, light wave, laser beam, photogrammetry, and gyroscopic orientations are among the scientific mediums integrated in the cadastral surveyor's array of working tools.

* Christmas Trees - Free
Division of Forestry, Bureau of Land Management (BLM)
U.S. Department of the Interior
Washington, DC 20240　　202-452-7755
The Bureau of Land Management (BLM) officials issue permits to cut Christmas trees for a nominal fee on Bureau of Land Management-administered lands in the 11 Western states and Alaska. Free-use permits are available from the Bureau to non-profit organizations for timber and trees to be used exclusively by that organization. This excludes the resale of any free timber or trees by those organizations.

* Cooperative Forest Fire Control
Fire Protection Staff
U.S. Department of Agriculture
Forest Service, P.O. Box 96090
Washington, DC 20090-6090　　202-205-1508
State and Federal governments cooperate to protect non-federal timberland, potential timberland, certain non-forested watershed lands, and other rural lands from serious fire damage. For information, contact a regional forester or area Forest Service director or the above office.

* Cooperative Forest Insect and Disease Management
Contact: your State Forester or the state office of the
U.S. Forest Service, usually located in the state capitol.
To reduce loss and damage to forests and lands by forest insects and diseases, the U.S. Department of Agriculture (USDA) provides technical and financial assistance in prevention, detection, evaluation, and suppression of forest insect and disease outbreaks on state and private lands.

* Erosion Control
Information Division
U.S. Department of Agriculture
Agricultural State Conservation Service (ASCS)
P.O. Box 205
Kansas City, MO 64141　　202-720-5237
The Agricultural State Conservation Service (ASCS) directs a number of conservation programs to preserve and improve American farmland. One of these is the Conservation Reserve Program (CRP), which targets the most fragile farmland by encouraging farmers to stop growing crops on land designated by conservationists as "highly erodible" and plant grass or trees on it instead. The farmer receives rent on the land for a term of ten years. Cost-share programs are also available for permanent planting of grass and trees in these areas.

* Federal Lands Energy Leasing
Offshore Minerals Management
Mineral Management Service
U.S. Department of the Interior
18th and C Sts., NW
Washington, DC 20240　　202-208-6906
The Mineral Management Service leases the rights to explore and develop oil and gas on Federal lands of the continental shelf. The "shelf" is made up of the submerged offshore areas lying seaward of the territorial sea to a depth of 200 meters (656 feet) and beyond that area to that depth which allows for mineral exploration. The brochure, *Leasing Energy Resources on the Outer Continental Shelf*, explains the leasing procedure and gives a history of the program.

* Fire and Land Management
Fire and Aviation Management
Bureau of Land Management (BLM)
U.S. Department of the Interior
1849 C St., NW, #5627
Washington, DC 20240　　202-208-5099

The Bureau of Land Management's (BLM) fire management program is divided into two areas: wildfire suppression and prescribed fire. Wildfire suppression includes all aspects of preparing for, detecting, and fighting wildland fire, and for rehabilitation of severely burned areas. Fire is also used under prescribed conditions to help achieve land management objectives. An average of 700 prescribed (intentionally set and controlled) fires are conducted each year by BLM to make room for new forage for livestock and wildlife. They are also used to prepare a site for seeding or the planting of seedlings.

* Fire Safety Bibliography
Superintendent of Documents
Government Printing Office
Washington, DC 20402　　202-512-1800
Fire safety publications are listed, including improving the fire safety of cigarettes and the effect of cigarettes on the ignition of furnishings. Free.

* Forest and Park Films
Office of Public Affairs
National Park Service
U.S. Department of the Interior
P.O. Box 37127
Washington DC 20013　　202-208-7394
The National Park Service has an extensive list of films available for rent or sale. The films cover a variety of topics including parks, history, great Americans, and travel. Often they are used for all grade levels, as well as various civic organizations and clubs, such as Civil War Round Tables. Contact the Park Service for a listing of their films and ordering information. The Harpers Ferry Historical Association serves as a distributing agency for the Park Service and can be reached at: Harpers Ferry Historical Association Inc., P.O. Box 197, High St., Harpers Ferry, WV 25425; 304-535-6881.

* Forest Fire Reports
Aviation and Fire Management
U.S. Department of Agriculture
Current Forest Fire Situation
Washington, DC 20013　　202-205-1486
This office can provide you with information on forest fires anywhere in the U.S. They maintain all statistics for forest fires. During the fire season (June-Sept.), a special fire hotline is established to answer questions on current fires. For that number, contact Public Affairs, 202-205-0957.

* Forest Management and Education Worldwide
Natural Resources Sector
Office of Training and Programming Support
Peace Corps
1990 K St., NW
Washington, DC 20526　　202-606-3100
Working in 38 countries, forestry specialists design and execute forest management plans designed to help combat the overcutting, droughts, and deserts that are beginning to threaten many tropical forests around the world. They also help establish nurseries, curricula in environmental education, and skills in tropical fruit cultivation.

* Forest Products Utilization
Cooperative Forestry
Forest Service
U.S. Department of Agriculture
P.O. Box 96090
Washington, DC 20090-6090　　202-205-1661
Technical assistance is available to wood processors and harvesters of wood products in cooperation with private consultants and state agencies. Assistance can range from improving efficiency to marketing assistance.

* Forest Ranger Recruitment
Forest Service
U.S. Department of Agriculture
Recruitment
P.O. Box 2417
Washington, DC 20013　　703-235-2730
Contact this office for information on a career as a forest ranger.

Environment and Nature

* Forest Research and Technical Expertise

Deputy for Research
Forest Service
U.S. Department of Agriculture
Box 90690
Washington, DC 20090-6090   202-205-1507

Basic research is conducted by a large staff on such topics as forest insects and diseases, forest fire and atmosphere sciences, forest resource economics, biodiversity, global climate change, watershed and aquatic habitat, range and wildlife ecology, wood chemistry and fiber products, and structural and forest system engineering.

* Forest Service Films

Office of Public Affairs
Forest Service
U.S. Department of Agriculture
P.O. Box 96090
Washington DC 20090   202-205-1438

The Forest Service maintains regional film libraries across the country. The films cover a wide range of topics, such as acid rain and management of national forests, and many of the newer ones cover region-specific issues. The films are appropriate for elementary school children through college, as well as foresters. Most of the films from the Forest Service are available for free loan. Contact the film library nearest you for a free catalog and ordering information.

Region I
Film Library
U.S.D.A.
University of Montana
Missoula, Montana 59812   406-243-5976

Region II
J&A Film Service
P.O. Box 20034
Denver CO 80220   303-321-3030

Region III
Public Service Audience Planners
5341 Derry Ave., Suite PNQ
Aqaura Hills, CA 91301   818-865-1233

Region IV
Utah State Library
USU
Audiovisual Service, UMC-31
Logan, UT 84322   801-797-2633

Region V
California- same as Region III

Region X
Alaska Department of Education
Attn: State Libraries
P.O. Box 110571
Juneau, AK 99811   907-465-2910

* Forest Service Regional Offices

Public Affairs
14th and Independence Ave., SW
Washington, DC 20250   202-205-1760

The Forest Service has an annual report which outlines the activities of each of its programs. Contact the office listed above for your free copy. The following is a list of Forest Service Regional Offices:

Forest Service, USDA
Northern Region (R-1)
Federal Building
P.O. Box 7669
Missoula, MT 59807   406-329-3511

Forest Service, USDA
Rocky Mountain Region (R-2)
P.O. Box 25127
Lakewood, CO 80225-0127   303-275-5735

Forest Service, USDA
Southwestern Region (R-3)
Federal Building
517 Gold Ave., SW
Albuquerque, NM 87102   505-842-3293

Forest Service, USDA
Intermountain Region (R-4)
Federal Building
324 25th St.
Ogden, UT 84401   801-625-5352

Forest Service, USDA
Pacific Southwest Region (R-5)
630 Sansome St.
San Francisco, CA 94111   415-705-2870

Forest Service, USDA
Pacific Northwest Region (R-6)
333 SW First St.
P.O. Box 3623
Portland, OR 97208   503-326-2971

Forest Service, USDA
Southern Region (R-8)
1720 Peachtree Rd., NW
Atlanta, GA 30367   404-347-2384

Forest Service, USDA
Western Region (R-9)
310 West Wisconsin Ave.
Room 500
Milwaukee, WI 53203   414-297-3693

Forest Service, USDA
Alaska Region (R-10)
P.O. Box 21628
Juneau, AK 99802   907-586-8863

* Forests and Land Management

Forestry Division
Bureau of Land Management (BLM)
U.S. Department of the Interior
1620 L St., NW
Washington, DC 20240   202-452-1755

The Bureau of Land Management administers 90 million acres of forested lands, most of which are in Alaska. In the lower 48 states, some 26 million acres are managed, including 21 million acres of woodlands and 5 million acres of commercial forest lands.

* Forests Near TVA Reservoirs

River Basin Operations
Land Resources
Natural Resources Management
Forest Resource Development
Tennessee Valley Authority (TVA)
Norris, TN 37828   615-632-1631

The Forest Resource Development staff maintains forests around the Tennessee Valley Authority's (TVA) reservoirs to prevent development and thereby protect the water from siltation. The forests are kept in good health to allow for hunting--within the bounds of state regulations--and recreational parks. The Service also creates jobs and encourages economic development by assisting industry in utilizing forest resources. The staff also works with state agencies in reforestation efforts and fire control programs.

* Free Books and Posters on Forests

Forest Service Publications
Forest Service
U.S. Department of Agriculture
Washington, DC 20090   202-205-1760

The Forest Service publishes the following fact sheets, booklets and posters, which they offer free to the public. Contact the Office listed above for a current publications list. Titles include:

Making Paper from Trees
How a Tree Grows (poster)
Why Leaves Change (Color)
What the Forest Service Does
How a Tree Grows (Booklet)
Forestry Fact Sheet
How Fire Ruins Timber
Conservation Fact Sheet
Suggestions for Intergrating Forestry in the Modern Curriculum
Wilderness Sanitation
What we get from Trees (poster, Color and B&W)
Career Profiles
Investigating Your Community Environment
You Can Be a Forest Service Volunteer
Investigating Your Environment (Packet)
State Trees and Arbor Day
Is the Water Safe
Plant A Tree for a Special Occasion
The National Resource and Environmental Education Program of the Forest Service
Room to Roam
Timeless Heritage
A Guide to Your National Forests (map)
Managing the Range

* Free Land Films and Videos

Division of Public Affairs
Bureau of Land Management (BLM)
U.S. Department of the Interior
Washington DC 20240   202-452-5125

The Bureau of Land Management (BLM) has produced three films, three videos, and a slide show dealing with areas covered by BLM. Titles include:

Promise of the Land (film)- explains multiple use management on public lands.

Dapples, Bays, Pintos and Grays (film)- presents wild horse and burro adopt a horse program.

Antiquities (film)- details issue of looting and vandalism of our cultural resources.

Measuring America: The Cadastral Story (slide show)- explains cadastral surveying.

BLM Backcountry Byways (video)- looks at recreational opportunities provided by BLM's backcountry byways program.

Fish and Wildlife 2000 (video)- explains managing wildlife and fisheries habitat on public lands.

Automating the Past (video)- details effort at automating old land records.

These films are often requested by educational institutions (elementary and junior high), as well as civic organizations interested in the outdoors or finding out how their tax dollars are being spent. Even the Boy Scouts have borrowed films for evening entertainment. Contact this office for more information on the films and videos available for free loan.

* Gold Prospecting

Publications Department
Bureau of Mines
U.S. Department of the Interior
18th and C Sts., NW, Room 2647
Washington, DC 20240   202-501-9649

The publications department of the Bureau of Mines distributes the free booklet, *How To Mine and Prospect for Gold.*

* Great Plains Conservation Work

Soil Conservation Service
U.S. Department of Agriculture
P.O. Box 2890
Washington, DC 20013   202-720-4525

Land users living in the Great Plains states can seek assistance from the Soil Conservation Service (SCS), which offers technical assistance and cost-sharing funds to farmers, ranchers, and other land users in the Great Plains. Cost-share rates can

range up to 80 percent for urgently needed conservation work. Contact SCS or your local Soil Conservation Office.

* Help With Forest Pests

Forest Pest Management
Forest Service
U.S. Department of Agriculture
14th and Independence Ave., SW
Washington, DC 20250   202-205-1600

Forest Pest Management provides protection from insects and diseases on all Federal and non-Federal lands. Pest management projects also helped protect recreation areas, wildlife habitats, and watersheds. The Forest Service aerial and ground surveys detected and evaluated vegetation damage or pest populations on 134 million acres of National Forest System lands and 44 million acres of other Federal lands. For information on pest outbreak prevention and suppression contact the office listed above.

* Indian Land Trust

Office of Trust
Bureau of Indian Affairs
U.S. Department of the Interior
18th and C Sts., NW
Washington, DC 20240   202-208-5831

This office manages some 53 million acres of land held in trust by the United States for Indians. Tribes are helped in protecting their lands and in developing their forest, water, mineral, and energy resources.

* Land Management Library

Bureau of Land Management (BLM) Library
R5150A
U.S. Department of the Interior
Denver Federal Center
P.O. Box 25047
Denver, CO 80225   303-236-6649

A vast collection of information on issues concerning land management is available to the public through this library. The reference staff and an automated card catalog system aid researchers in exploring the following topics: cadastral engineering; forest resources management; land reserve studies; legislation and public land laws; range management; watershed management; mineral, oil, and gas leasing; oil shale; and conservation and use of public lands.

* Land Use and Land Cover Maps

Distribution Branch
U.S. Geological Survey
Building 810
Denver Federal Center, Box 25286
Denver, CO 80225   800-USA-MAPS

Land use maps and land cover maps are available for most of the United States. Land use maps refer to human uses of the land (housing and industry) and land cover maps describe the vegetation, water, natural surface, and construction on the land surface. The scale used ranges from 1:100,000 for a few maps in the Western states to 1:250,000 for most other maps.

* Livestock Rangeland

Rangeland Resources
Bureau of Land Management (BLM)
U.S. Department of the Interior
1725 I St., NW
Washington, DC 20006   202-452-7773

The Bureau of Land Management has administration of 170 million acres of public lands where livestock graze. About 18,800 ranchers and farmers graze livestock on BLM-managed lands. A majority of these permittees have small (less than 100 head) or medium (100 to 500 head) livestock operations.

* Minerals Management Service Field Offices

Bureau of Mines
U.S. Department of Interior
1951 Constitution Avenue, NW
Washington, DC 20240   202-208-3983

U.S. Department of Interior has the following regional offices:

Environment and Nature

Atlantic Region
381 Elden St., Suite 1109, Herndon, VA 22070-4817; 703-787-1113

Alaska
949 E. 36th Ave., Suite 604, Anchorage, AK 99508-4302; 907-271-6070

Gulf of Mexico
1201 Elmwood Park Blvd., New Orleans, LA 70123-2394; 504-736-2595

Pacific Region
1340 W. 6th St., Los Angeles, CA 90017; 213-894-2050

Central Region
6th Ave. and Kipling St., Bldg. 85, Lakewood, CO 80225; 303-231-3162

* Mining Claims on Federal Lands
Energy and Mineral Resources
Bureau of Land Management (BLM)
U.S. Department of the Interior
18th and C Sts., NW
Washington, DC 20240   202-208-4201

The brochure, *Staking a Mining Claim on Federal Lands*, describes the procedure you will follow to stake a mining claim on public lands. Claims are granted to individuals for particular pieces of land, valuable for specific mineral deposits. Questions concerning the definition of a mining claim and the technicalities of recording and maintaining mining claims are also covered.

* National Firefighting Coordination
Fire and Aviation Management
Bureau of Land Management (BLM)
U.S. Department of the Interior
1725 I St., NW
Washington, DC 20006   202-208-5099

The goal of the Boise Interagency Fire Center is to provide the nationwide coordination of fire support activities among Federal and state firefighting agencies. The Fire Center is also called upon to help during many types of natural disasters when local, state, and regional resources are exhausted.

* National Park OffShore Oil Leases Revenues
Land Resources Division
National Park Service
U.S. Department of the Interior
800 N. Capitol St., NW
Washington, DC 20002   202-343-4828

The National Park System is able to purchase land for its use with the revenues received from offshore oil leases. Revenues from these leases also are credited to the Land and Water Conservation Fund and the Historic Preservation Fund for efforts in these areas.

* National Park Service Regional Offices
National Park Service
U.S. Department of the Interior
1100 L St., NW
Washington, DC 20005   202-208-7394

Here are the contact points for the field offices of the National Park Service.

Alaska
2525 Gambell St., Room 107, Anchorage, AK 99503; 907-271-2737

Mid-Atlantic
143 South Third St., Philadelphia, PA 19106; 215-597-3679. Serving: PA, VA, WV, DE, MD

Midwest
1709 Jackson St., Omaha, NE 68102; 402-221-3448. Serving: NE, MO, KS, IA, IL, IN, WI, MI, MN, OH

National Capital
1100 Ohio Dr., SW, Washington, DC 20242; 202-619-7222

North-Atlantic
15 State St., Boston, MA 02109-3572; 617-223-5200. Serving: NY, NJ, CT, RI, MA, NH, VT, ME

Pacific Northwest
2001 6th Avenue, Seattle, WA 98104; 206-220-4000. Serving: WA, OR, ID

Rocky Mountains
12795 W. Alameda Pkwy., P.O. Box 25287, Denver, CO 80225; 303-969-2000. Serving: MT, ND, SD, WY, UT, CO

Southeast
75 Spring St., Atlanta, GA 30303; 404-331-5187. Serving: MS, TN, AL, GA, FL, SC, NC, KY, Virgin Is., PR

Southwest
P.O. Box 728, Santa FE, NM 87504-0728; 505-988-6375. Serving: NM, TX, LA, OK, AR

Western
600 Harrison, Suite 600, P.O. Box 36063, San Francisco, CA 94107; 415-556-0560. Serving: CA, AZ, NV, HI, Guam, Northern Marianas Is., Am Samoa, Micronesia, Marshall Is., Palau.

* Native American Indians Land Rights
Office of Public Affairs
Bureau of Indian Affairs
U.S. Department of the Interior
18th and C Sts., NW
Washington, DC 20240   202-208-7315

The free booklet, *American Indians Today: Answers to Your Questions, 1988*, contains useful information on the Native American Indians and their relationship to the Bureau of Indian Affairs. Programs within the Bureau, including education, health services, and housing are briefly outlined and contain recent statistics. Many questions are answered within the booklet, including the rights of the Indians to own land and have their own governments. A map locates the Indian lands and communities, showing Federal and State Indian Reservations and other Indian groups. An excellent bibliography, prepared by the Smithsonian Institution, is included.

* Need Some Help Managing Your Forest?
Forest Resource Management
Forest Service
U.S. Department of Agriculture
14th and Independence Ave., SW
Washington, DC 20090-6090   202-205-1374

The Forest Resource Management program cooperates with State forestry agencies to provide technical assistance to non-industrial private landowners for managing their forest lands. During 1990, this program helped landowners manage 3.5 million acres by assistance through multi-resource management plans.

* Offshore Information
Office of Offshore Information and Publication
Minerals Management Service
381 Elden St., MS 642
Herndon, VA 22070   703-787-1000

The Minerals Management Service manages more than a billion offshore acres and collects billions of dollars in mineral revenues annually. One of its two primary missions is to run the federal government's program for managing mineral resources on the Outer Continental Shelf (OCS). The Offshore Information Office can provide you with any information regarding the OCS, including publications on leasing and managing energy resources, brochures on oil-spill prevention, as well as scientific and technical publications of the Offshore Minerals Management Program.

* Outdoor Recreation
Land Between The Lakes (LBL)
Tennessee Valley Authority (TVA)
100 Van Morgan Dr.
Golden Pond, KY 42211   502-924-5602

The Land Between the Lakes (LBL) is a 40-mile long, wooded peninsula bordered on three sides by the water of Kentucky Lake and Lake Barkley. LBL is a national outdoor recreation and environmental education area managed by the Tennessee Valley Authority (TVA). In LBL you can enjoy camping, hiking, fishing, bicycling, sightseeing, and other traditional outdoor activities. Four State resort parks are nearby which have lodging and restaurant facilities. For more information including maps, an LBL calendar of events, and other information, contact the address listed above.

* Pacific Yew - Anticancer Drug

Jim Sanders, Forest Service
U.S. Department of Agriculture
14th and Independence Ave., SW
Washington, DC 20250   202-205-1772

Taxol, a chemical extracted from the Pacific Yew, is an extremely effective anticancer drug. Patients with ovarian cancer have shown a 40 percent response rate to taxol treatment even when they had previously shown no response to other drugs. Breast cancer patients are predicted to show a 50-percent response. Taxol is expected to become a major cancer-treating chemical. This will require a large and steady supply of the raw material- Pacific yew bark. Attempts to produce taxol synthetically have not been successful. The National Cancer Institute and the Forest Service are working together on short and long-range approaches to the taxol supply from Pacific yew bark. To provide long-term bark supply, the Institute and the Forest Service are collecting bark and branchlet samples to send to the Institute for taxol-content determination and to the National Forest Genetic Tectrophoresis Laboratory for test of genetic variation. Mr. Sanders has a wealth of information on taxol, including the range, amount collect, and current research. He can also refer you to the proper researchers for more technical information.

* Parks Pass

National Park Service
U.S. Department of the Interior
P.O. Box 37127
Washington, DC 20013   202-208-7394

Some federal parks, refuges and facilities can be entered and used free of charge. Other areas and facilities require payment of entrance fees, user fees, special recreation permit fees, or some combination. There are five Congressionally authorized entrance passes. The annual Golden Eagle passport and the two lifetime passes, the Golden Age Passport and Golden Access Passport, can be used at all federally operated outdoor recreation areas which charge entrance fees. The Federal Duck Stamp serves as an annual entrance fee permit to national wildlife refuges, and Park Pass is an annual entrance permit to a specific park. Contact the office listed above for more information.

* Public Lands National Parks

Division of Interpretation
National Park Service
U.S. Department of the Interior
1800 N. Capitol St., NW, Suite 56
Washington, DC 20002   202-523-5270

The National Park Service assists its facilities in planning and carrying out their exhibits and visitor programs. Their future plans include more involvement in environmental education programs to be offered at the Park Service sites.

* Public Lands Oil and Gas Leasing

Energy and Mineral Resources Division
Bureau of Land Management (BLM)
U.S. Department of the Interior
18th and C Sts., NW
Washington, DC 20240   202-208-4201

Public lands are available for oil and gas leasing only after they have been evaluated through the Bureau of Land Management. In areas where development of oil and gas resources would conflict with the protection or management of other resources or public land uses, mitigating measures are identified and may appear on leases as either stipulations to uses or as restrictions on surface occupancy. Two types of leases are issued: competitive and noncompetitive.

* Public Lands Photos

Forestry, Range, Realty
Office of Public Affairs
Bureau of Land Management (BLM)
U.S. Department of the Interior
18th and C Sts., NW
Washington, DC 20240   202-208-5717

Thousands of black and white photographs and color slides are available, including forestry, realty, minerals, and range subjects.

* Public Lands Recreation

Office of Public Affairs
Bureau of Land Management (BLM)

U.S. Department of the Interior
18th and C Sts., NW
Washington, DC 20240   202-452-7155

In recognition of the importance of outdoor recreation to Americans, *Recreation 2000 Executive Summary* sets forth the commitment of the Bureau of Land Management to the management of outdoor recreation resources in public lands. The plan highlights the areas in which the Bureau intends to concentrate future efforts, such as visitor information, resource protection, land ownerships, partnerships, volunteers, tourism programs, facilities, and permits, fees, and concessions.

* Public Land Renewable Resources Management

Land and Renewable Resources
Bureau of Land Management (BLM)
U.S. Department of the Interior
18th and C Sts., NW
Washington, DC 20240   202-208-4896

The Bureau of Land Management issues leases, rights-of-way, and use permits for a wide variety of public lands including parks; power transmission and distribution lines; petroleum products collection and transmission systems.

* Public Lands Revenue: Grazing, Timber Sales, Mining

Management Services
Bureau of Land Management (BLM)
U.S. Department of the Interior
18th and C Sts., NW
Washington, DC 20240   202-208-4864

This office collects and disburses revenues and receipts generated from public lands. The Bureau of Land Management is a primary generator of revenues in the Federal government, with more than $800 million collected annually from a variety of sources, including timber sales, sale of public lands, grazing leases, right-of-way leases, permits, and mineral receipts.

* Public Land Statistics

Superintendent of Documents
Government Printing Office
Washington, DC 20402   202-512-1800

The publication, *Public Land Statistics*, contains valuable information regarding the land administered by the Bureau of Land Management. Tables include the following topics: land disposition and use, range management, resource conservation and development, forest management, wildlife habitat management, wild horse and burro management, cultural resource management, outdoor recreation, areas of critical environmental concern, energy and mineral resources, public land surveys, fire protection, and finance.

* Publications On National Parks

Office of Public Affairs
National Park Service
U.S. Department of the Interior
Washington, DC 20240   202-208-4747

The Office of Public Affairs can provide you with a list of publications available from the National Park Service. They publish the *National Park Handbooks*, which are compact introductions to the great natural and historic places administered by the Park Service. They are published to promote understanding and enjoyment of the parks. Each is intended to be informative reading and a useful guide before, during, and after a park visit. They also publish the following general publications:

The National Parks: Camping Guide 1991
The National Parks: Index 1989
The National Parks: Lesser-Know Areas
The National Parks: Shaping the System
The National Park System Map and Guide, 1990 edition
Welcome to Washington, 1990 edition
The White House

* Rural Community Fire Protection

Fire and Aviation Management Staff
Forest Service, U.S. Department of Agriculture
14th and Independence Ave., SW
Washington, DC 20250   202-205-1483

The Farmers Home Administration funds Rural Community Fire Protection, and the Forest Service administers the program in cooperation with State foresters. The

Environment and Nature

program contributes matching funds to strengthen volunteer fire departments in communities of less than 10,000 people. The funds provide for organizing, training, and equipping rural fire departments.

* Smokey Bear and Fire Prevention

Smokey Bear Headquarters
U.S. Forest Service
14th and Independence Ave., NW
Washington, DC 20250   202-205-1483

To make children aware of the campaign to fight forest fires, the Forest Service makes a variety of materials available to children, including posters, signs, patches, bookmarks, bumper stickers, and comic books.

* Soil and Farmland Protection Programs

Soil Conservation Service (SCS)
U.S. Department of Agriculture
P.O. Box 2890
Washington, DC 20013   202-720-4543

Soil surveys are used not only for conservation purposes but also to identify suitable lands for a wide variety of uses, from maintaining crops to urban uses. Information about soil helps prevent major construction mistakes and misuse of land that can be productively put to use. Soil maps identify flood-prone areas and sources of water pollutants.

* Soil Conservation Technical Expertise

Soil Conservation Service (SCS)
U.S. Department of Agriculture
P.O. Box 2890
Washington, DC 20013   202-720-4543

Technical expertise is available in such areas as irrigation, drainage, landscape architecture, construction, sanitary and water quality, and hydrology.

* State Soil-Saving Conservation

Information Division
U.S. Department of Agriculture
ASCS, P.O. Box 205
Kansas City, MO 64141   816-926-6502

The Agricultural State Conservation Service (ASCS) directs a number of conservation programs to preserve and improve American farmland. One of these is the Agricultural Conservation Program (ACP): This program is designed to solve soil, water, and related resource problems through costsharing. ACP assistance is available to install soil-saving practices, including terraces, grass, sod waterways, and other measures to control erosion. It also helps reduce sediment, chemicals, and livestock waste that contaminate streams and lakes.

* Soil, Water, and Air Sciences

ARS Information Staff
U.S. Department of Agriculture
Room 307-A, Building 005
Beltsville, MD 20705   301-344-2340

Specialists study such topics as environmental quality, erosion and sedimentation, soil fertility and plant nutrition, organic wastes, pesticide degradation, water use efficiency and tillage practices, and weed control. Contact the ARS staff for answers to questions on these and other conservation-related topics.

* Strip Mining and Reclamation

Office of Public Affairs
Office of Surface Mining Reclamation and Enforcement
U.S. Department of Interior
1951 Constitution Avenue, NW
Washington, DC 20240   202-208-2553

This office works to protect people and the environment from the side-effects of coal mining, while continuing to regulate coal mining. Lands that were affected by past coal mining operations must be repaired if left unreclaimed or abandoned. Technical assistance is provided to states so that they can perform their responsibilities under the surface mining law. State personnel are trained in the technical aspects of surface mining, such as soil compaction, revegetation, and groundwater hydrology, so that they can better enforce regulations. An *Annual Report* is available.

* Strip Mining Enforcement Offices Nationwide

Office of Surface Mining Reclamation and Enforcement
U.S. Department of Interior (DOI)
1951 Constitution Avenue, NW
Washington, DC 20240   202-208-2553

The following are field offices of the Department of the Interior's (DOI) Surface Mining and Reclamation Office:

Albuquerque
505 Marqueppe NW, Suite 100, Albuquerque, NM 87102; 505-248-5070

Alton
Alton Federal Bldg., 501 Belle St., Alton, IL 62002; 618-463-6460

Appalachia
1300 New Circle Rd., NE, Suite 100, Lexington, KY 40505; 606-233-2792

Ashland
Federal Bldg., Room 120, 1430 Greenup Ave., Ashland, KY 41101; 606-325-4735

Beckley
323 Harper Park Dr., Beckley, WV 25801; 304-255-5265

Birmingham
280 W. Valley, Room 302, Homewood, AL 35209; 205-731-0890

Big Stone Gap
1941 Neely Rd., Suite 201, Big Stone Gap, VA 24219; 703-523-4303

Casper
Federal Bldg., 100 East B St., Room 2128, Casper, WY 82601-1918; 307-261-5776

Columbus
4480 Refugee Rd., Columbus, OH 43232; 614-866-0578

Chattanooga
900 Georgia Ave., Room 30, Chattanooga, TN 37402; 615-752-5175

Charleston
603 Morris St., Charleston, WV 25301; 304-347-7158

Denver
Bldg. 20, Room B2015, P.O. Box 25065, Denver CO 80225; 303-236-0331

Eastern
Ten Parkway Center, Pittsburgh, PA 15220; 412-937-2828

Harrisburg
Harrisburg Transportation Ctr., Third Fl., Suite 3C, 4th and Market Sts., Harrisburg, PA 17101; 717-782-4036

Hazard
516 Village Lane, Hazard, KY 41701; 606-439-5843

Indianapolis
Minton-Capehart Federal Bldg., 575 N. Penn St., Room 301, Indianapolis, IN 46204; 371-226-6700

Johnstown
Penn Traffic Bldg., Room 20, 319 Washington St., Johnston, PA 15901; 814-533-4223

Knoxville
530 Gay St., Suite 500, Knoxville, TN 37902; 615-673-4504

Lexington
2675 Regency Rd., Suite 28, Lexington, KY 40504; 606-233-2494

London
P.O. Box 1048, London, KY 40741; 606-878-6440

Lebanon
Two Acre Task Force: P.O. Box 487, Lebanon, VA 24266; 703-889-4032

Madisonville
100 YMCA Dr., Madisonville, KY 42431; 502-825-4500

Morgantown
P.O. Box 886, Morgantown, WV 26507; 304-291-4004

Norris
P.O. Box 295, Norris, TN 37828; 615-632-1699

Olympia
Columbia Commons, 3773 C Martini Way East, Suite 104, Olympia, WA 98506; 360-753-9538

Pikesville
Division of Audit Management, First National Bank, Room 608B, 334 Main St., Pikesville, KY 41505; 606-432-4123

Prestonburgh
P.O. Box 306, 2664 West Mountain Parkway, West Prestonburg, KY 41618; 606-432-8145

Springfield
600 East Monroe St., Room 20, Springfield IL 62701; 217-492-4495

Tulsa
5100 East Skelley Dr., Suite 470, Tulsa, OK 74135; 918-581-6430

Wilkes-Barre
20 N. Penn. Ave., Suite 3323, Wilkes-Barre, PA 18701; 717-826-6333

Western Region
1999 S. Broadway, Suite 3320, Denver, CO 80202; 303-236-3546

* Timber and Woodland Analysis

River Basin Operations
Natural Resources Management
Land Resources, Forestry Resource Development
Tennessee Valley Authority
Norris, TN 37828   615-632-1631

This Land Resources group has developed a number of user-friendly, reliable, PC software programs, which allow the public, the timber industry, and consultants to analyze timber supply, inventory, and finances by providing growth and yield information. Inventory processing helps foresters to determine maximum financial returns by calculating, for example, the optimal time to schedule harvesting. To stay abreast of all new technologies, this resource group also conducts safety seminars, field days, and hardware demonstrations, and to stay abreast of all new technology.

* Tree Growing and Lumber Bibliography

Superintendent of Documents
Government Printing Office
Washington, DC 20402   202-512-1800

Tree publications are listed, including those of interest to tree growers and the lumber industry. Also featured is a guide to Christmas Tree diseases and books listing the tropical timbers of the world. Free.

* Utilize Your Forest Wisely

Forest Products Utilization
Forest Service
U.S. Department of Agriculture
14th and Independence Ave., SW
Washington, DC 20250   202-205-1394

Utilization, marketing, and technology transfer activities are important aspects of the outreach delivery provided by Cooperative Forestry staff. Key accomplishments include the monthly technology transfer newsletter *Utilization and Marketing Review* which provides current information on research and technology transfer to assist scientists and nonindustrial private landowners. Also available includes the *Technology Opportunities* packet, which contains concepts, emerging technologies, recent developments, and state-of-the-art knowledge from the Forest Products Laboratory and experiment stations. The Integrated Mill Production and Recovery Options for Value and Efficiency (IMPROVE) System package will increase sawmill, veneer mill, or plywood plant output by improving manufacturing efficiency. Other technology transfer activities include central tire inflation, wood protection using diffusible preservatives, and hardwood use for structural application.

* Wetlands and Land Conservation

Information Division
U.S. Department of Agriculture
ASCS, P.O. Box 205
Kansas City, MO 64141   202-720-5237

The Agricultural State Conservation Service (ASCS) directs a number of conservation programs which plant trees, improve timberstands, prevent loss of wetlands for migratory waterfowl, and control water pollution.

* Wildland Fire Database

FIREBASE Operations
U.S. Department of Agriculture Forest Service
Boise Interagency Fire Center
3905 Vista Ave.
Boise, ID 83705   208-387-5512

FIREBASE is a collection of bibliographic citations and abstracts of wildland fire-related information. The database is international in scope and topic include wildland fire detection; prevention and suppression; fire management analysis; planning and training; and fire statistics, indexes, and hazards.

* Youth Conservation Corps Regional Offices

Washington Office
Youth Program Officer
National Park Service
U.S. Department of the Interior
Room 4415, P.O. Box 37127
1100 L St., NW
Washington, DC 20013-7127   202-343-5514

Youngsters interested to gain experience in environmental protection can contact the nearest field office of the National Park Service listed below to inquire about summer job opportunities:

Alaska
2525 Gambell St., Room 107, Anchorage, AK 99503; 907-261-2690

Mid-Atlantic
Second and Chestnut Sts., Philadelphia, PA 19106; 215-597-2284. Serving: PA, VA, WV, DE, MD

Midwest
1709 Jackson St., Omaha, NE 68102; 402-221-3431. Serving: NE, MO, KS, IA, IL, IN, WI, MI, MN, OH

National Capital
1100 Ohio Dr., SW, Washington, DC 20242; 202-619-7222

North-Atlantic
15 State St., Boston, MA 02109-3572; 617-223-5200. Serving: NY, NJ, CT, RI, MA, NH, VT, ME

Pacific Northwest
83 South King St., Suite 212, Seattle, WA 98104; 206-220-4000. Serving: WA, OR, ID

Rocky Mountains
12795 W. Alameda Pkwy, P.O. Box 25287, Denver, CO 80225; 303-969-2875. Serving: MT, ND, SD, WY, UT, CO

Southeast
75 Spring St., Atlanta, GA 30303; 404-331-5185. Serving: MS, TN, AL, GA, FL, SC, NC, KY, Virgin Is., PR

Southwest
P.O. Box 728, Santa FE, NM 87504-0728; 505-988-6100. Serving: NM, TX, LA, OK, AR

Western
450 Golden Gate Ave., P.O. Box 36063, San Francisco, CA 94102; 415-556-0560. Serving: CA, AZ, NV, HI, Guam, Northern Marianas Is., Am Samoa, Micronesia, Marshall Is., Palau.

Environment and Nature

Fish and Wildlife

* See also Vacations and Business Travel Chapter

* Acid Rain and Aquatic Species Chart
Superintendent of Documents
Government Printing Office
Washington, DC 20402   202-512-1800

The wall chart, *Acid Rain: The Effect on Aquatic Species*, illustrates the survival of selected aquatic species in an acidic environment. Information is given on acid rain, its causes, and the effect on aquatic life. Measures 17 by 22 inches (S/N 024-010-00675-7 $3.25).

* Alaska Fish and Wildlife Research
Alaska Fish and Wildlife Research Center
U.S. Fish and Wildlife Service
1011 E. Tudor Rd.
Anchorage, AK 99503   907-786-3512

The Alaska Fish and Wildlife Research Center in Anchorage, in association with its field stations in Kodiak and Fairbanks, is responsible for planning and conducting research on fish, wildlife, and their habitats in Alaska. Areas of research include: the status and trends of marine mammal populations; the distribution, abundance, and population trends of coastal and marine birds; waterfowl population dynamics; productivity and stock of anadromous fish; advanced technology and its use in studying arctic and subarctic fish and wildlife; and identifying and resolving conflicts between wildlife and the utilization of Alaska's natural resources.

* Arctic and Antarctic Science Stations
Office of Polar Affairs
Bureau of Oceans and International Environmental and Scientific Affairs
U.S. Department of State
2201 C St., NW, Room 5801
Washington, DC 20520   202-647-3262

This office is concerned with all issues concerning the Arctic and Antarctic, including the environment and marine life, such as whales and seals. They are also closely involved with the many science stations located on the Antarctic.

* Bald Eagles and Peregrine Falcons
U.S. Department of the Army
Chemical Research Development and Engineering Center
Aberdeen Proving Ground, MD 21010-5423   301-671-4912

While the Center's primary mission is concerned with research on chemical defensive material, the Center has become very involved in wildlife conservation programs because of its location on the Chesapeake Bay. The Center is especially experienced in a Bald Eagle program and a Peregrine Falcon program. Fact sheets on these and other wildlife issues may be obtained by writing or calling the above office.

* Banded Waterfowl Recovery
Office of Migratory Bird Research
Pawtuxent Wildlife Research Center
U.S. Fish and Wildlife Service
Laurel, MD 20708   301-497-5500

If you happen to capture, find, or shoot a banded bird is obtained, you should remove the band, flatten and tape it securely to a piece of heavy paper or cardboard, and mail it to the address above. Include the following information: 1) Names and address of person sending the band: 2) All numbers and letters on the band (in case the band is lost from the envelope); 3) Date the band was obtained; 4) Place where band was found (mileage and direction from the nearest town, including County and State); 5) How the band was obtained (on a bird shot, found dead, etc.). Mark the envelope *Hand Cancel.*

* Bird Strikes
Airport Safety Data Group
Office of Airport Standards
Federal Aviation Administration

U.S. Department of Transportation
800 Independence Ave., SW, Room 615
Washington, DC 20591   202-267-8792

Birds being accidentally sucked into jet engines is a serious aviation hazard. Contact this office for information on where bird strikes occur.

* Birds Bibliography
Superintendent of Documents
Government Printing Office
Washington, DC 20402   202-512-1800

This listing includes booklets on the Atlantic Barrier Islands and their plant and animals life, the Chesapeake Bay's bird population, and field guide to fifty birds to observe in your own town. The Duck Stamp Collection subscription service is also outlined. Free.

* Birds, Buffalo, and Other Publications
U.S. Fish and Wildlife Service
4401 N. Fairfax Dr.
Arlington, VA 22203   703-358-1711

For a free listing of general interest publications from the Fish and Wildlife Service, contact the office above. General interest publications are available free of charge, but when ordering more than five publications, the need must be justified. Titles include the following:

American Bald Eagle
America's Sea Turtles
Attracting and Feeding Birds
Chesapeake Bay
Conservation Notes on American Buffalo
Ducks at a Distance
Duck Stamp Story
Endangered Species
Facts about Federal Wildlife Laws
Lead Poisoning in Waterfowl
People and Wildlife-Public Involvement in Fish and Wildlife Administration
Waterfowl Regulations

Also available is a *Wildlife Biologue Series* of various species of wildlife, including endangered species. The series includes a one page life history of the species. They are free of charge when ordering under five copies. Contact the above office for a listing.

* Buffalo and Cattle Refuges
Division of Refuges
U.S. Fish and Wildlife Service
4401 N. Fairfax Dr.
Arlington, VA 22203   703-358-1744

Buffalo and Texas longhorn cattle, as well as deer and elk, can be enjoyed at wildlife refuges maintained by the U.S. Department of the Interior. Wichita Mountains in Oklahoma and Fort Niobrara in Nebraska preserve these animals in their natural habitat. The government periodically auctions these animals to the public at these locations. For more information, contact the refuge managers directly: Fort Niobrara National Wildlife Refuge, Hidden Timber Route, HC 14, Box 67, Valentine, NE 69201; 402-376-3789. Witchita Mountains Wildlife Refuge, Rt. 1, Box 448, Indiahoma, OK 73552; 405-429-3222. You can see Buffalo also at the National Bison Range in Moiese, Montana. For more information on this refuge, contact National Bison Range, Moiese, MT 59824; 406-644-2211.

* Captive Breeding of Endangered Species
Patuxent Wildlife Research Center
U.S. Fish and Wildlife Service
Laurel, MD 20708   301-497-5500

The Endangered Species Branch at Patuxent conducts research on several endangered species in their native habitats throughout the United States and its territories. Current studies focus on such species as the Puerto Rican parrot, California condor, Hawaiian forest birds, Kirtland's warbler, and eastern timber wolf. Along with studying the endangered species, the scientists breed them in captivity for release to bolster wild populations. Key endangered species, as well as closely related surrogate species, are maintained for captive propagation research. The physiological, behavioral, and veterinary characteristics of these species are evaluated to gain a better understanding of possible biological problems as well as to assist with management of the species in the wild.

* Conservation Law Enforcement Training

Law Enforcement Division
U.S. Fish and Wildlife Service
4401 N. Fairfax Dr.
Arlington, VA 22203   703-358-1949

Through this division, state conservation officers are trained in the area of criminal law as it applies to the enforcement of wildlife protection.

* Duck and Geese Population

North American Waterfowl Management Plan
U.S. Fish and Wildlife Service
Federal Building
Fort Snelling
Twin Cities, MN 55111   612-290-3131

The United States and Canada have joined forces to reverse the decline in certain populations of ducks and geese. This plan has inspired cooperation between Federal, Provincial, and State governments, as well as private conservation agencies in the two countries. Joint ventures, formed among public and private corporations, are developing economic incentives to change land use practices, striking agreements with private landowners, and improving water management.

* Duck Stamps

Federal Duck Stamp Office
U.S. Fish and Wildlife Service
1849 C Street, NW
Suite 2058
Washington, DC 20240   202-208-4355

The Federal Duck Stamp program has become one of the most successful conservation programs ever initiated. To date, over 350 million duck stamp dollars have gone to preserve over 4 million acres of wetland refuges for North American waterfowl. A sheet of duck stamps from 1987-1988, Redheads, can be purchased for $10, as well as the 1988-1989 Snow Goose stamps. The 1989-1990 Lesser Scaup stamps are available for $12.50, and the 1990-1992 Black-bellied Whispering Ducks for $12.50. To order your Duck Stamps, contact U.S. Postal Service, Philatelics Sales Division, Washington, DC 20265-9997.

Subscriptions to the Duck Stamp Collection are available at $12 each from the Superintendent of Documents. The collection includes a data sheet on each duck stamp issued since the first one in 1934. Each sheet includes a photograph of the stamp and original art, short biography of the artist, names of the designers and engravers, inscription, first date of sale, and number of stamps sold. The subscription service provides the entire collection to date plus one update per year for an indeterminate period of time.

* Duck Stamp Design Competition

Federal Duck Stamp Office
U.S. Fish and Wildlife Service
4401 N. Fairfax Drive
Arlington, VA 22203   202-208-5508

Each year, a Duck Stamp Design Competition is held, with the winning design chosen by a panel of waterfowl and art experts. Any artist can enter the contest by submitting a 7 X 10 inch waterfowl design and paying an entry fee. The winner receives a pane of stamps bearing his or her design. Winning artists also sell prints of their prize entries which are eagerly sought by collectors.

* Ecosystems and Wildlife Habitat Models

National Ecology Center
U.S. Fish and Wildlife Service
4512 McMurray Ave.
Fort Collins, CO 80525-2899   303-226-9100

The center conducts research, develops new tools, and transfers information so that

scientists can better understand and manage fish and wildlife resources, habitats, and ecosystems. All endangered marine mammal research is performed here. Workshops are held in refuge management and habitat model development for those within the Interior Department and scientists in Federal and State agencies and foreign countries. Studies are reported in the Center's *Biological Report* series and through extension education brochures.

* Endangered Species

S. James
Consumer Information Center 2A
P. O. Box 100
Pueblo, CO 81002

Endangered Species is a publication which explains government efforts to protect and restore species in danger of extinction and what you can do to help (587Y, $1).

* Endangered Wildlife and Plants

Office of Endangered Species
U.S. Fish and Wildlife Service
4401 N. Fairfax Dr.
Arlington, VA 22203   703-358-2171

The Fish and Wildlife Service follows a formal procedure in determining which species should be placed on the *U.S. List of Endangered and Threatened Wildlife and Plants*. The proposed ruling is published in the *Federal Register*, and after a suitable period for public comment and possible revision, it is published as a final rule. To obtain a listing of the endangered and threatened wildlife and plants and other information on this topic, contact the office above.

* Exotic and Warm Water Fish Husbandry

National Fisheries Research Center
U.S. Fish and Wildlife Service Biological Center
7920 NW 71 St.
Gainesville, FL 32553   904-378-8181

Exotic and warm water fish of the southeastern United States and the Gulf Coast are studied at the National Fisheries Research Center in Gainesville, Florida, and at its field station in Marion, Alabama. Research of fish husbandry of southeastern fishes is also conducted. Aquatic weed control as it relates to the survival of these fishes is also a priority.

* Fish and Marine Life Bibliography

Superintendent of Documents
Government Printing Office
Washington, DC 20402   202-512-1800

Fisheries and fish research publications are featured in this bibliography, along with marine fish posters of the California, Great Lakes, and Gulf and South Atlantic waters. Free.

* Fish and Wildlife Cooperative Research

Cooperative Fish and Wildlife National Biologic Center
Research Units Center
U.S. Fish and Wildlife Service
4401 N. Fairfax Dr.
Arlington, VA 22203   703-358-1709

Cooperative fish and wildlife research field stations are located at various universities throughout the country. Research finds answers to a broad spectrum of fish and wildlife management questions, from habitat requirements of individual species to the effects of development projects on populations of fish and wildlife. Graduate education is provided to resource managers at the M.S. and Ph.D. levels and in-service training and continuing education is given to employees of conservation agencies. Technical assistance is made available to fish and wildlife resource managers and to the public. For a complete listing of field stations, contact the office above.

* Fish and Wildlife Films and Videos

Office of Public Affairs
Fish and Wildlife Service (FWS)
U.S. Department of Interior
Washington DC 20240   202-208-5611

The Fish and Wildlife Service has many films and videos available for free loan and are distributed through their regional offices. Some of the topic areas covered include current research and environmental issues, as well as fish and wildlife. The Offices also distribute some non-FWS videos which cover similar topics. Some of the titles available include:

America's Wetland
Wildlife, Wetlands and You- The Duck Stamp Story
Chain of Life- The Aleutian Islands
So Little Time
Where The Fish Will Be
Patuxent Wildlife Research Center
The Role of Research
A Great White Bird
Birds of the Indian Monsoon
In Celebration of America's Wildlife

These films are used in elementary schools through college, and are often part of environmental group meetings. Contact your regional office for a free catalog, or contact the Office of Public Affairs for information regarding the Office nearest you.

* Fish and Wildlife Photographs

Audio Visuals
U.S. Fish and Wildlife Service
18th and C Sts., NW
Washington, DC 20240   202-208-5611

The Audio Visual Department of the U.S. Fish and Wildlife Service has an extensive collection of both black and white pictures and color slides of fish and wildlife. There is no charge for their lending service, which extends 30 or 90 days. If the photographs or slides are used in publications, the photographer and the U.S. Fish and Wildlife Service must be given credit.

* Fish and Wildlife Technical Publications

Office of Information Transfer
U.S. Fish and Wildlife Service
317 W. Prospect
Fort Collins, CO 80522   970-484-2836

Many technical publications are produced by the U.S. Fish and Wildlife Service. Copies of publications are available to selected individuals or organizations concerned with environmental issues.

Resource Publication
Fish and Wildlife Leaflet
Investigations in Fish Control
Fish Disease Leaflet
North American Fauna
Fish and Wildlife Research
Fish and Wildlife Technical Report
Biological Report

Fisheries Review and *Wildlife Review* are also available on a subscription basis from the Superintendent of Documents, Government Printing Office, 202-512-1800. *Fisheries Review* is $16/year and *Wildlife Review* is $22/year.

* Fish and Wildlife Year 2000

Office of Public Affairs
Bureau of Land Management
U.S. Department of the Interior
18th and C Sts., NW
Washington, DC 20240   202-452-5125

The full-color brochure, *Fish and Wildlife 2000: A Plan for the Future*, describes the future management plan of the public lands and their resources. These resources include recreation, range, forest, minerals, watershed, fish and wildlife, wilderness and natural, scenic, scientific, educational, and cultural values. A strategic plan is outlined, including the management of wildlife habitats, fisheries habitats, threatened and endangered species, and human resources.

* Fish Disease and Chemical Cures

National Fisheries Research Center
U.S. Fish and Wildlife Service
P.O. Box 818
LaCrosse, WI 54602-0818   608-783-6451

The National Fisheries Research Center at LaCrosse, Wisconsin, has been designated by the Fish and Wildlife Service to negotiate registration for fishery chemicals with regulatory agencies. Pesticides are registered with the U.S. Environmental Protection

Agency, and therapeutants for controlling fish diseases are registered with the U.S. Food and Drug Administration. Once a fishery chemical is registered by the Federal government, states will generally allow the use of that chemical for fish culture and management.

* Fisheries Contaminant Research

National Fisheries Contaminant Research Center
U.S. Fish and Wildlife Service
Rt. 2, 4200 New Haven Rd.
Columbia, MO 65201   314-875-5399

All fisheries contaminant research under the U.S. Fish and Wildlife Service, except for the Great Lakes area, is conducted at the National Fisheries Contaminant Research Center and its eight field stations. The Center is actively studying the effects of pesticides and other contaminants on aquatic ecosystems. Research equipment is designed to study the long-term effects of contaminants on growth, life stages, and biochemistry of fishes and other aquatic forms under realistic pollution conditions. The Center has capabilities to conduct special studies of national concern with striped bass, Atlantic and Pacific salmon, grayling, and Arctic char. Scientists and special groups are welcome at the Center, and special arrangements can be made for visiting scientists to conduct cooperative research with laboratory investigators.

* Fish Hatcheries Scientific Advice

Office of Information Transfer
U.S. Fish and Wildlife Service
1025 Pennock Pl., Suite 212
Fort Collins, CO 80524   970-226-9100

This office distributes technical information to scientists, refuge managers, and fish hatchery managers within and outside of the U.S. Fish and Wildlife Service. At office meetings scientists present research findings and provide technical advice to others. In turn, they have a rare opportunity to meet the users of their findings face to face. Information is also transferred through synthesis documents, which bring together information from a variety of sources on a particular topic of interest. Each package is then distributed to a specific audience, such as refuge managers or fish hatchery managers. Contact the office above to be placed on the mailing list for periodic announcements of new publications.

* Fish Health Research

National Fisheries Center
U.S. Fish and Wildlife Service
Box 700
Kearneysville, WV 25430   304-725-8461 x5333

The National Fisheries Center and its five field stations are world-renowned as a focal point for fish health research and fisheries development. Studies include nutrition, genetics, diseases, management technology, and technical services. The facility contains a training academy of fish husbandry.

* For The Latest Ecology Research. . .

National Ecology Research Center
4512 McMurry Ave.
Fort Collins, CO 80525   303-226-9100

There is a continuing need for information that can help resolve the myriad of natural resource issues facing endangered species, nongame and declining species, and on a larger scale, terrestrial, riverine, and wetlands systems. The National Ecology Research Center strives to fill these needs. The Centers develop new technologies, conduct research on threatened and endangered animals, and give attention to nongame and declining species. The following is a list of field research stations, including some of the research which they conduct.

San Simeon, CA- movements, reproductive biology, and foraging ecology of sea otters; distribution and and seasonal abundance of birds and reptiles in riparian areas near Piedras Blancas.

Santa Cruz, CA- interaction of sea otters with their nearshore food resources.

Gainesville, FL- long-term life history and population studies of manatees, reptiles, and amphibians.

Albuquerque, NM- ecology, distribution, and status of reptiles and amphibians in the arid southwest.

Washington, DC- curation of the North American collection of amphibians, eptiles, birds, and mammals at the U.S. National Museum of Natural History; status of amphibians in the eastern United States.

Auburn, AL- aquatic research and instream flow assessments for fishes, mussels, and insects.

* Grain Surpluses for Wildlife

Commodities Operations
U.S. Department of Agriculture
ASCS, Room 2415
Washington, DC 20013   202-720-3217

Upon request of the U.S. Department of the Interior, bulk grain is available in emergency situations to feed wildlife and birds as long as grain surpluses exist.

* Great Lakes Fish Spawning and Survival

National Fisheries Research Center
U.S. Fish and Wildlife Service
1451 Green Rd.
Ann Arbor, MI 48105   313-994-3331

The primary objective of the National Fisheries Research Center in Ann Arbor and its eight biological stations and research vessels is to develop the knowledge and technical basis for assessing, protecting, enhancing, and rehabilitating the valuable resources and habitats of the Great Lakes. Laboratory experiments provide information on how natural and man-induced changes in the lakes may affect important fish populations. Particular emphasis is placed upon the spawning requirements, survival of early life stages, and forage requirements of important species such as lake trout.

* Marine Environmental Pollution Response

Pollution Response Branch
Marine Environmental Response Division
Office of Marine Safety, Security and Environmental Protection·
U.S. Coast Guard
U.S. Department of Transportation
2100 2nd St., SW, Room 2104
Washington, DC 20593-0001   202-267-2611

This office responds to requests for marine environmental protection information from Congress and other federal agencies, state agencies, schools, industries, and the general public. Data is available on laws relating to the protection of the marine environment, incidents involving releases of oil or other hazardous substances, and federally funded spill response operations.

* Marine Life Posters

Superintendent of Documents
Government Printing Office
Washington, DC 20402   202-512-1800

The following is a list of Marine Life Posters available from the National Marine Fisheries Service through the Government Printing Office. The posters are printed on washable non-glare plasticized paper, and cost $5.50 each.

Marine Fishes of the California Current and Adjacent Waters
Marine Fishes of the Gulf and South Atlantic
Fishes of the Great Lakes
Mollusks and Crustaceans of the Coastal U.S.

* Marine Mammals Rescue and Protection

Office of Protected Resources
National Marine Fisheries Service
National Oceanic and Atmospheric Administration
U.S. Department of Commerce
1335 East-West Hwy.
Silver Spring, MD 20910   301-713-2322

The Marine Mammal Protection Act commits the United States to long-term management and research programs to conserve and protect these animals. Marine mammals may be taken for scientific research, public display, and incidentally to commercial fishing. The National Marine Fisheries Service grants or denies requests for exemptions, issues permits, carries out research and management programs, enforces the Act, participates in international programs, and issues rules and regulations to carry out its mission to conserve and protect marine mammals. An annual report is available for the Office of Protected Resources, which gives detailed information regarding the activities of the Office. This office can also provide you with copies of the Act, and the publication *Proceedings of the Workshop to Review and Evaluate Whale Watching Programs and Management Needs.*

* Migratory Bird Research

Migratory Birds Research Branch
Patuxent Wildlife Research Center
U.S. Fish and Wildlife Service
Laurel, MD 20708   301-497-5623

Research at Patuxent on migratory game birds includes methods of assessing the status of various species, discovering reasons for declines in particular bird populations, and investigating relationships between bird populations and environmental variables to determine ecologically sound resource management techniques. Non-game migratory bird research at Patuxent studies particular habitat requirements for breeding, migration, and wintering.

* National Fisheries Library

U.S. Fish and Wildlife Service
P.O. Box 818
LaCrosse, WI 54602-0818   608-783-6451

The Center's library has the world's most complete collection of publications on fishery chemicals, their use, and their effects on the environment. Computer hook-ups provide access to over 200 databases.

* National Wildlife Refuges Visitor's Guide

Office of Public Affairs
U.S. Fish and Wildlife Service
18th and C Sts., NW
Washington, DC 20240   703-358-1711

National Wildlife Refuges: A Visitor's Guide is a listing of all of the National Wildlife Refuges that provide visitor opportunities; not all of the refuges in the system are included. A map locating each of these refuges is featured, along with public facilities, including visitor's centers, foot trails, auto tours, bicycling, boating, environmental study areas, hunting, fishing, camping, picnicking, swimming, and food and lodging. For a state-by-state listing of these refuges, see the listing below under "Wildlife Refuges National System."

* Nuisance Fish Control

National Fisheries Research Center
U.S. Fish and Wildlife Service
P.O. Box 818
LaCrosse, WI 54602-0818   608-783-6451

The National Fisheries Research Center at La Crosse, along with its field station at Hammond Bay, Michigan, have played an important role in the development and registration of toxicants that are useful for controlling populations of the dreaded sea lamprey, a predator of Great Lakes fishes. Intensive research and control efforts have greatly reduced the sea lamprey population through the use of larval lampricides. The Center is also responsible for all research under the U.S. Fish and Wildlife Service to control nuisance fish.

* Ocean and Coastal Pollution

Ocean Resources, Conservation, and Assessments
National Ocean Service
National Oceanic and Atmospheric Administration
U.S. Department of Commerce
6001 Executive Blvd.
Rockville, MD 20852   301-413-0900

This office surveys and monitors the oceans, U.S. coastal waters and the Great Lakes to produce data and information products that are critically important for offshore oil and gas exploration, dredging operations, coastal and offshore construction, seafloor mining, waste disposal management, and for protecting the marine environment from the adverse effects of ocean and coastal pollution.

* Parrots, Gray Whale and 2,700 Videos and Films

National Audiovisual Center
8700 Edgeworth Dr.
Capitol Heights, MD 20743-3701   800-788-6282

The National Audiovisual Center contains more than 2,700 titles of videocassettes, films and slide/sound programs. Among them are some wonderful presentations produced by the National Park Service and the U.S. Fish and Wildlife Service. Materials may be rented or purchased. Contact the Audiovisual Center for specific information. Some titles include:

Environment and Nature

Everglades: Seeking a Balance
Gulf Island Beaches, Bays, Sands, and Bayous
California Gray Whale
Environmental Awareness
Giant Sequoia
One Man's Alaska
Sanctuary: The Great Smoky Mountains
Crater Lake
Yellowstone
Washington, DC: Fancy Free
Glacier Bay
Bighorn Canyon Experience
Cape Cod
What is a Mountain?
Living Waters of the Big Cypress
National Parks: Our Treasured Lands
Mt. McKinley
America's Wetlands
Parrots of Luquillo
Where the Fish Will Be
Patuxent Wildlife Research Center
Minnesota Valley National Wildlife Refuge

* Patuxent Wildlife Center Film

National Audiovisual Center
8700 Edgeworth Dr.
Capitol Heights, MD 20743-3701   800-788-6282

This film informs the viewers about the wildlife research activities at the Patuxent Wildlife Research Center in Laurel, Maryland. It describes the wildlife research on endangered species, environmental contaminants, migratory waterfowl, and urban wildlife carried on at the center and at field stations around the world. This 20 minute film is available on 16mm film, and on Beta and VHS videocassettes. The film can be rented for $40 or purchased for $210. The videocassettes can be purchased for $95 each.

* Restoring America's Wildlife

Superintendent of Documents
Government Printing Office
Washington, DC 20402   202-512-1800

Illustrated with photographs and paintings by nationally known artists, *Restoring America's Wildlife 1937-1987* describes the impact of modern wildlife management on nearly a score of popular species and describes the many economic and recreational opportunities created by the Pittman-Robertson Federal Aid in Wildlife Restoration Act. 1986 (S/N 024-010-00671-4, $20).

* River and Water Films

Visual Communication Services
Bureau of Reclamation
P.O. Box 25007
D-1500
Denver, CO 80225   303-236-6973

The Bureau of Reclamation provides water for farms, towns, and industries, and is responsible for the generation of hydroelectric power, river regulation and flood control, outdoor recreation opportunities, and the enhancement and protection of fish and wildlife habitats. There are films available for free loan on a variety of the Bureau's projects. The titles include:

Central Arizona Project- Lifeline to the Future
California Flooding
Cofferdam Failure
How Water Won the West
Rio Grande- Ribbon of Life
To Build A Dream- The Story of Hoover Dam
Take Pride in America
Hoover Dam 50th Anniversary
Guam, USA
Commonwealth of the Northern Mariana Islands
Managing the Floods of '86- California's Ordeal
A Page In Time
The Colorado
Central Utah Project
Challenge At Glen Canyon Dam
Colorado River Operations

From Snowfall to Sandstone
Hydropower
Hydropower "A 20th Century Force"
Horizons
Waterpower 87 Wrap Up
For Want of Water
Taming of Black Canyon
The Spillways of Glen Canyon Dam
1983 The Record Water Year
Yuma Desalting Plant

These films are most often requested by elementary and junior high school teachers, or by people who have visited the dams while on vacation and would like to learn more about them. Contact the Bureau for more information regarding these videos.

* Salmon and Other Pacific Fish

National Fisheries Research Center
U.S. Fish and Wildlife Service
Building 204, Naval Station Puget Sound
Seattle, WA 98115-5007   206-526-6282

Fishery research problems of the Pacific Coast, except for those of Alaska, are solved at the National Fisheries Research Center in Seattle, Washington, and at its field stations in Cook, Washington, Nordland, Washington, and Reno, Nevada. Projects involving the study of Pacific salmon, trout, and steelhead provide valuable information to the economy of the Pacific Northwest and to the recreational fishing of this area. The Center has two main research groups: fish health and environment, and fish ecology. Willard Field Station near Cook, Washington, studies fish living in the Columbia River Basin and the effects of many hydropower projects in the area. The Marrowstone Field Station in Nordland, Washington, is the U.S. Fish and Wildlife Service's only marine laboratory where salmon and steelhead are studied as they leave their native streams and enter the oceans. The third field station in Reno, Nevada, works with threatened and endangered species native to the area.

* Saltwater Fish and Shellfish Stocks

Public Affairs
National Marine Fisheries Service
National Oceanic and Atmospheric Administration
U.S. Department of Commerce
1335 East-West Hwy.
Silver Spring, MD 20910   301-713-2370

The National Marine Fisheries Service (NMFS) manages the country's stocks of saltwater fish and shellfish for both commercial and recreational interests. NMFS administers and enforces the Magnuson Fishery Conservation and Management Act to assure that fishing stays within sound biological limits, and that U.S. commercial and recreational fishermen have the opportunity to harvest all the available fish within these limits. Several hundred Fisheries Service scientists conduct research relating to these management responsibilities in science and research centers in 15 states and the District of Columbia. Many of these laboratories have evolved a major field of interest, and have special knowledge of the fish in their geographical area that leads to predictions of abundance, economic forecasts, and direct assistance to sport fishermen and commercial fishing businesses.

* Toxic Chemicals in Fish

Office of Ocean Resources Conservation and Assessment (ORCA)
National Ocean Service
National Oceanic and Atmospheric Administration
6001 Executive Blvd.
Rockville, MD 20852   301-713-2989

The Office of Ocean Resources Conservation and Assessment (ORCA) monitors the concentrations of toxic chemicals and trace elements in bottom-feeding fish, shellfish, and sediments at almost 300 coastal and estuarine locations in the US. The program's objective is to determine the status and long-term trends of toxic contamination. Samples are analyzed to determine levels of DDTs, PCBs, PAHs, and toxic trace elements (e.g. mercury and lead).

* U.S. Fish and Wildlife Regional Offices

U.S. Fish and Wildlife Service
Washington, DC 20240   202-208-5634

Here are the field offices of the Interior Department's Fish and Wildlife Service.

Region 1
911 NE 11th Street, Portland, OR 97232; 503-231-6121

Region 2
Box 1306, Albuquerque, NM 87103; 505-248-6282

Region 3
Federal Building, Fort Snelling, MN 55111; 612-725-3563

Region 4
Richard B. Russell Federal Building, 75 Spring St., SW, Atlanta, GA 30303; 404-679-7319

Region 5
300 Westgate Center Dr., Hadley, MA 02158; 413-253-8200

Region 6
Box 25486, Denver Federal Center, Denver, CO 80225; 303-236-7920

Region 7
1011 E. Tudor Rd., Anchorage, AK 99503; 907-786-3542

Region 8
1849 C St., NW, Washington, DC 20240; 202-208-6394

* Vertebrate Research

Biological Survey/National Ecology Center
U.S. Fish and Wildlife Service
U.S. Department of the Interior
Museum of Natural History Building
10th and Constitution Ave., NW
Washington, DC 20560   202-357-1930

This laboratory performs systematic and ecological studies of vertebrates and their communities, particularly in their relationship to land use practices. Studies also include work with endangered species. Qualified researchers may inquire about possible study through the laboratory.

* Volunteers: Fish and Wildlife Service

U.S. Fish and Wildlife Service
Washington, DCC 20240   202-208-5634

Would you like to spend some time banding birds at a national wildlife refuge, feeding fish at a national fish hatchery, or doing research in a laboratory? Then consider volunteering with the U.S. Fish and Wildlife Service. There are no age requirements; however, anyone under 18 must have written parental approval. Young people under 16 years of age are encouraged to volunteer as part of a supervised group, such as a Boy Scout troop, Girl Scout troop, or 4H Club. Contact one of the U.S. Fish and Wildlife regional offices for possible volunteer programs in your area.

* Waterfowl and Migratory Birds

Northern Prairie Science Center
U.S. Fish and Wildlife Service
8711 37th St., SE
Jamestown, ND 58401   701-252-5363

This research center gathers information to improve the management of migratory birds, particularly waterfowl west of the Mississippi River. Results of their studies are applied to National Wildlife Refuges and other Federal, State, and private lands. Field and experimental studies are conducted from the headquarters near Jamestown, North Dakota, and through field stations at Woodworth, North Dakota; Davis, California; and La Crosse, Wisconsin. Studies are also conducted on the ecology of the prairie pothole and upper Mississippi River areas.

* Waterfowl Hunting Regulations

Office of Migratory Bird Management
U.S. Fish and Wildlife Service
4401 N. Fairfax Dr.
Arlington, VA 22203   703-358-1714

Aerial surveys of waterfowl breeding populations and habitats, post-hunting surveys, and the banding program provide useful biological data for developing annual waterfowl hunting regulations. Before the rules are set, the current waterfowl picture is presented to the public through news releases, publication of proposed regulations in the *Federal Register*, and a series of late July and early August public meetings where survey data and Fall flight forecasts are reviewed. The decisions of each state are then published in the *Federal Register*.

* Wetlands and Wintering Waterfowl

National Wetlands Research Center
U.S. Fish and Wildlife Service
1010 Gause Blvd.
Slidell, LA 70458   504-646-7564

This center focuses on research and development studies of issues related to the protection, restoration, and management of wetlands, with an emphasis on wintering waterfowl. The Center gathers data on plant and animal ecology in both managed and natural wetland systems. Most current information is published in the *Biological Report* series. Field stations are located in Baton Rouge, LA, Corpus Christi, TX, and Vicksburg, MS.

* Wetlands Information

Public Information Center
Environmental Protection Agency (EPA)
401 M St., SW, MS 3404
Washington, DC 20460   202-260-7751

The U.S. is losing one of its most valuable and perhaps irreplaceable resources - the wetlands. Today less than half of the U.S.'s original wetlands remain. The Environmental Protection Agency (EPA) has an Environmental Backgrounder which provides information on the wetlands, as well as laws, sanctions, and EPA and State actions. Further information is available.

* Wetlands Protection

Office of Wetlands Protection
Environmental Protection Agency (EPA)
401 M St., SW
Washington DC 20460   202-260-7791

This office implements Environmental Protection Agency (EPA) statutory responsibilities in the Clean Water Act as they relate to the filling of wetlands and other aquatic resources. Designed to raise the importance of wetlands, this office works with other governmental bodies to encourage wetlands protection.

* Wetlands Protection Hotline

Geo/Resource Consultants, Inc.
1555 Wilson Blvd. Suite 500
Arlington, VA 22209   800-832-7828

The Environmental Protection Agency's Wetlands Protection Hotline is responsive to public interest, questions and requests for information about the values and functions of wetlands, and options for their protection. The Hotline acts as the central point of contact for the Wetlands Protection Division of the Office of Wetlands, Oceans, and Watersheds to provide a wide range of oral and written information on wetlands protection efforts involving EPA and other public and private programs. *Wetlands Protection: A Local Government Handbook* is available which reviews federal and state laws and programs that promote wetlands preservation. In addition, the Hotline uses an extensive contact list to provide referrals to callers when necessary. The Hotline also provides information on the availability of wetlands related documents and accepts requests for certain wetlands publications.

* Wetlands Video

National Association of Conservation Districts
P.O. Box 855
League City, TX 77574   800-825-5547

The U.S. Department of Agriculture and Interior, as well as private corporations cooperatively produces a 23-minute videotape which includes interviews with five farmers who believe there is a place for wetlands on their farms. Also included are brief overviews of wetlands losses, restoration methods, and sources of help in wetlands conservation and restoration. The video is available for $10.

* Whale Watching

Office of Protected Resources
National Marine Fisheries Service
National Oceanic and Atmospheric Administration
U.S. Department of Commerce
1335 East-West Hwy.
Silver Spring, MD 20910   301-713-2322

The Marine Mammal Protection Act commits the United States to long-term management and research programs to conserve and protect these animals. The National Marine Fisheries Service grants or denies requests for exemptions, issues permits, carries out research and management programs, enforces the Act, participates in international programs, and issues rules and regulations to carry out its mission to conserve and protect marine mammals. An annual report is available for the Office of Protected Resources, which gives detailed information regarding the activities of the Office. This office can also provide you with copies of the Act, and two publications: *First Aid For Stranded Marine Mammals*, and *Proceedings of the Workshop to Review and Evaluate Whale Watching Programs and Management Needs.*

* Wild Burros and Horses for Adoption

Office of Public Information
Bureau of Land Management (BLM)
U.S. Department of the Interior
18th and C Sts., NW
Washington, DC 20240-0001   202-452-5125

Wild burros and horses that roam on public lands are put up for adoption after a short time to decrease their numbers. If you are interested in adopting one of these animals, you should contact a local BLM adoption center, and there is a fee of $125 per horse and $75 per burro. You must also transport the animals home and provide for their future upkeep. The booklet, *So You'd Like to Adopt A Wild Horse Or Burro?*, answers many of the questions you might have when handling this responsibility. Contact the office above for the adoption centers near you.

* Wildlife Contaminant Research

Environmental Contaminants Research Branch
Patuxent Wildlife Research Center
U.S. Fish and Wildlife Service
Laurel, MD 20708   301-497-5704

Research on environmental contaminants is one of the major efforts at the Patuxent Wildlife Research Center. Field research is conducted at contaminated sites and demonstrates the relation between the presence of contaminants in the environment or tissues of a wildlife species and the degree of risk to the species. Controlled laboratory studies measure effects of mixtures of chemical contaminants on growth, survival, reproduction, metabolism, behavior, and well-being.

* Wildlife Disease Control

National Wildlife Health Research Center
U.S. Fish and Wildlife Service
6006 Schroeder Rd.
Madison, WI 53711   608-271-4640

This center offers services and conducts activities to prevent and control wildlife diseases. Workshops and seminars are sponsored at the Center and other locations throughout the country. The information produced through research findings and field observations is issued in the form of original articles in scientific journals, *Service Research Information Bulletins*, brochures, and special communications projects. A video presentation on lead poisoning in migratory birds was recently produced that is now widely used by the conservation community.

* Wildlife Habitats on Public Lands

Wildlife and Fisheries Division
Bureau of Land Management (BLM)
U.S. Department of the Interior
1725 I St., NW
Washington, DC 20006   202-208-5171

Wildlife habitats for more than 3,000 species are managed on public lands by the Bureau of Land Management. Included in this count are 140 threatened or endangered plant and animal species. The Bureau also protects and manages the key riparian areas along 85,000 miles of streams. BLM manages habitats for one out of every five big game animals in the United States, including caribou, brown and grizzly bears, desert bighorn sheep, moose, mule deer, and antelope.

* Wildlife Import Restrictions

Publications Unit
U.S. Fish and Wildlife Service
4401 N Fairfax Dr.
Arlington, VA 22203   703-358-1711

Before travelling overseas, learn what items cannot be imported. Write for a copy of *Facts About Federal Wildlife Laws* and a list of protected species at the above address.

* Wildlife Refuge National System

Refuges and Wildlife
U.S. Fish and Wildlife Service
18th and C Sts., NW
Washington, DC 20240   703-358-1744

The National Wildlife Refuge System is a network of United States lands and waters managed specifically for the enhancement of wildlife. Refuges are vitally important for they provide food, water, shelter, and space for approximately 60 endangered species and hundreds of species of birds, mammals, reptiles, amphibians, fish, and plants. Over 440 refuges, encompassing over 90 million acres in 49 states and five trust territories, now comprise the system. An estimated 30 million people visit these lands annually:

Alabama

Bon Secour, P.O. Box 1650, Gulf Shores, AL 36542; 334-968-8623. Choctaw, Box 808, 2704 Westside College Ave., Jackson, AL 36545; 334-246-3583. Eufaula, Rte. 2, Box 97-B, Eufaula, AL 36027; 334-687-4065. Wheeler (Blowing Wind Cave, Fern Cave, Watercress Darter), Rte. 4, Box 250, Decatur, AL 35603; 334-353-7243.

Alaska

Alaska Maritime (Alaska Peninsula Unit, Bering Sea Unit, Chukchi Sea Unit, Gulf of Alaska Unit), 2355 Richman Dr., Homer, AK 99603; 907-235-6546. Aleutian Islands Unit, Box 5251, Naval Air Station Adak, FBO Seattle, WA 98791; 907-592-2406. Alaska Peninsula (Becharof), P.O. Box 277, King Salmon, AK 99613; 907-246-3339. Arctic, Box 20, 101-12th Ave., Fairbanks, AK 99701; 907-456-0250. Innoko, Box 69, McGrath, AK 99627; 907-524-3251. Izembek, Box 127, Cold Bay, AK 99571; 907-532-2445. Kanuti, Box 11, 101-12th Ave., Fairbanks, AK 99701; 907-456-0329. Kenai, 2139 Ski Hill Road, Soldotna, AK 99669-2139; 907-262-7021. Kodiak, 1390 Buskin River Rd., Kodiak, AK 99615; 907-487-2600. Koyukuk, P.O. Box 287, Galena, AK 99741; 907-656-1231. Nowitna, P.O. Box 287, Galena, AK 99741; 907-656-1231. Selawik, P.O. Box 270, Kotzebue, AK 99572; 907-442-3799. Tetlin, P.O. Box 155, Tok, AK 99780; 907-883-5312. Togiak, P.O. Box 270, Dillingham, AK 99576; 907-842-1063. Yukon Delta, P.O. Box 346, Bethel, AK 99559; 907-543-3151. Yukon Flats, Box 14, 101-12th Ave., Fairbanks, AK 99701; 907-456-0440.

Arizona

Buenos Aires, P.O. Box 109, Sasabe, AZ 85633; 502-823-4251. Cabeza Prieta, 1611 N. Second Ave., Ajo, AZ 85321; 502-387-6483. Cibola, P.O. Box AP, Blythe, CA 92226; 502-857-3253. Havasu, P.O. Box 3009, Needles, CA 92363; 619-326-3853. Imperial, P.O. Box 72217, Martinez Lake, AZ 85365; 502-783-3371. Kofa, P.O. Box 6290, 356 W. 1st, Yuma, AZ 85366-6290; 502-783-7861. San Bernardino, Rural Rte. 1. Box 228R, Douglas, AZ 85607; 502-364-2104.

Arkansas

Felsenthal (Overflow), P.O. Box 1157, Crossett, AR 71635; 501-364-3167. Holla Bend (Logan Caves), Box 1043, 115 S. Denver St., Russellville, AR 72801; 501-968-2800. N.E. Arkansas Refuges, P.O. Box 279, Turrell, AR 72384; 501-343-2595. Big Lake, P.O. Box 67, Manila, AR 72442; 501-564-2429. Cache River, P.O. Box 279, Turrell, AR 72384; 501-343-2595. Wapanocca, P.O. Box 279, Turrell, AR 72384; 501-343-2595. White River, Box 308, 321 W. 7th St., De Witt, AR 72042; 501-946-1468.

California

Cibola, P.O. Box AP, Blythe, CA 92226; 520-857-3253. Havasu, P.O. Box 3009, Needles, CA 92363; 619-326-3853. Imperial, P.O. Box 72217, Martinez Lake, AZ 85365; 520-783-3371. Kern (Bitter Creek, Blue Ridge, Hopper Mountain, Pixley, Seal Beach), P.O. Box 670, Delano, CA 93216-0219; 805-725-2767, 805-725-5284. Klamath Basin Refuges (Bear Valley (OR), Clear Lake, Klamath Forest (OR), Lower Klamath (OR & CA), Tule Lake, Upper Klamath (OR)), Rte. 1, Box 74, Tule Lake, CA 96134; 916-667-2231. Modoc, P.O. Box 1610, Alturas, CA 96101; 916-233-3572. Sacramento (Butte Sink WMA, Delevan, Willow Creek-Lurline WMA), Rte. 1, Box 311, Willows, CA 95988; 916-934-2801. 906 W. Sinclair Rd., Calipatria, CA 92233; 619-348-5278, 619-348-5310. Tijuana Slough (Coachella Valley, Sweetwater Marsh), P.O. Box 335, Imperial Beach, CA 92032; 619-575-1290. San Francisco Bay (Antioch Dunes, Castle Rock, Ellicott Slough, Farallon, Humboldt Bay, Salinas Lagoon, San Pablo Bay), P.O. Box 524, Newark, CA 94560; 510-792-0222. San Luis (East Grasslands WMA, Grasslands WMA, Kesterson, Merced, San Joaquin River), P.O. Box 2176, Los Banos, CA 93635; 209-826-3508.

Colorado

Alamosa/Monte Vista, P.O. Box 1148, Alamosa, CO 81101; 303-589-4021. Arapaho (Bamforth (WY), Hutton Lake (WY), Pathfinder (WY)), P.O. Box 457, Walden, CO 80480; 303-723-8202. Browns Park, 1318 Hwy. 318, Maybell, CO 81640; 303-365-3613.

Connecticut
Salt Meadow, P.O. Box 307, Charlestown, RI 02813; 401-364-9124. Stewart B. McKinney, U.S. Federal Bldg., Room 210, 915 Lafayette Blvd., Bridgeport, CT 06604; 203-579-5617.

Delaware
2591 Waithall Neck Rd., Smyrna, DE 19977; 302-653-9345. Prime Hook, Rte. 3, Box 195, Milton, DE 19968; 302-684-8419.

Florida
Arthur R. Marshall Loxahatchee (Hobe Sound), 10216 Lee Rd., Boynton Beach, FL 33437; 407-732-3684. Chassahowitzka (Crystal River, Egmont Key, Passage Key, Pinellas), 7798 S. Suncoast Blvd., Homosassa, FL 32646; 941-353-8442. Florida Panther (Ten Thousand Lakes), 3860 Tailgate Blvd., Suite 30, Naples, FL 33942; 813-472-1100. J.N. "Ding" Darling (Caloosahatchee, Island Bay, Matlacha Pass, Pine Island), One Wildlife Dr., Sanibel, FL 33957; 813-472-1100. Lake Woodruff, P.O. Box 488, DeLeon Springs, FL 32130; 904-985-4673. Lower Suwannee (Cedar Keys), 16450 NW 31st Place, Chiefland, FL 32626; 904-493-0238. Merritt Island (Pelican Island, St. Johns), P.O. Box 6504, Titusville, FL 32780; 305-867-0667. National Key Deer (Crocodile Lake, Great White Heron, Key West), P.O. Box 510, Big Pine Key, FL 33043; 305-872-2239. St. Marks, P.O. Box 68, St. Marks, FL 32355; 904-925-6121. St. Vincent, P.O. Box 447, Apalachicola, FL 32329; 904-653-8808.

Georgia
Eufaula, Rte. 2, Box 97-B, Eufaula, AL 36027; 334-687-4065. Okefenokee (Banks Lake), Rte. 2, Box 3330, Folkston, GA 31537; 912-496-7366. Piedmont, Rte. 1, Box 670, Round Oak, GA 31038; 912-986-5441. Savannah Coastal Refuges (Blackbeard Island, Harris Neck, Pinckney Island (SC), Savannah, Tybee, Wassaw, Wolf Island), 1000 Business Center Rd., Savannah, GA 31405; 912-652-4415.

Hawaii
Hawaiian and Pacific Islands Complex, P.O. Box 50167, 300 Ala Moana Blvd., Honolulu, HI 96850; 808-541-1201. Hakalau Forest, 154 Waianuenue Ave., Federal Bldg., Room 219, Hilo, HI 96720; 808-933-6915. Kilauea Point, P.O. Box 87, Kilauea, Kauai, HI 96754; 808-828-1413. Remote Island Refuges (Baker Island, Hawaiian Islands, Howland Island, Jarvis Island, Johnston Atoll, Rose Atoll), P.O. Box 50167, 300 Ala Moana Blvd., Honolulu, HI 96850; 808-541-1201. Wetlands Refuges (Hanalei, Huleia, James C. Campbell, Kakahaia, Pearl Harbor), P.O. Box 50167, 300 Ala Moana Blvd., Honolulu, HI 96850; 808-541-1201.

Idaho
Deer Flat, 13751 Upper Embankment Rd., Nampa, ID 83686; 208-467-9278. Kootenai, HCR 60, Box 283, Bonners Ferry, ID 83805; 208-267-3888. Southeast Idaho Refuge Complex (Oxford Slough WPA), 1246 Yellowstone Ave., A-4, Pocatello, ID 83201-4372; 208-237-6615. Bear Lake, 370 Webster, Box 9, Montpelier, ID 83254; 208-847-1757. Camas, 2150 E. 2350 N., Hamer, ID 83245; 208-662-5423. Grays Lake, 74 Grays Lake Rd., Wayan, ID 83285; 208-574-2755. Minidoka, Rte. 4, P.O. Box 290, Rupert, ID 83350; 208-436-3589.

Illinois
Chautauqua (Meredosia), 19031 CR2105N, Havana, IL 62644; 309-535-2290. Crab Orchard, P.O. Box J, Carterville, IL 62918; 618-997-3344. Mark Twain, 1704 N. 24th St., Great River Plaza, Quincy, IL 62301; 217-224-8580. Annada District, P.O. Box 107, Annada, MO 63330; 314-847-2333. Brussels District, P.O. Box 142, Brussels, IL 62013; 618-883-2524. Wapello District, 10728 County Rd., x61, Wapello, IA 52653; 319-523-6982. Upper Mississippi River National Wildlife and Fish Refuge, 51 East 4th St., Winona, MN 55987; 507-452-4232. Savanna District, Post Office Bldg., Savanna, IL 61074; 815-273-2732. Cypress Creek, Route 1, Box 53D, Ullin, IL 62992; 618-634-2231.

Indiana
Muscatatuck, 12985 E. Highway 50, Seymour, IN 47274; 812-522-4352. Patoka, 2630 E. State Rd., Winslow, IN 47598; 812-789-2724.

Iowa
DeSoto, Rte. 1, Box 114, Missouri Valley, IA 51555; 712-642-4121. Union Slough, 1710 360th St., Titonka, IA 50480; 515-928-2523. Upper Mississippi River National Wildlife and Fish Refuge, 51 East 4th St., Winona, MN 55987; 507-452-4232. McGregor District, P.O. Box 460, McGregor, IA 52157; 319-873-3423. Walnut Creek, P.O. Box 399, Prairie City, IA 50228; 515-994-2415.

Kansas
Flint Hills, P.O. Box 128, Hartford, KS 66854; 316-392-5553. Kirwin, Rte. 1, Box 103, Kirwin, KS 67644; 913-543-6673. Quivira, Rte. 3, Box 48A, Stafford, KS 67578; 316-486-2393.

Louisiana
Bogue Chitto (Breton, Delta), 1010 Gause Blvd., Bldg. 936, Slidwell, LA 70458; 504-646-7555. Cameron Prairie, Rte. 1, Box 643, Bell City, LA 70630; 318-598-2216. Catahoula, P.O. Drawer Z, Rhinehart, LA 71363-0201; 318-992-5261. D'Arbonne (Upper Ouachita), P.O. Box 3065, Monroe, LA 71201; 318-325-1735. Lacassine (Shells Keys), 209 Nature Rd., Lake Arthur, LA 70549; 318-774-5923. Lake Ophelia, P.O. Box 256, Marksville, LA 71351; 318-253-4238. Sabine, Hwy. 27, 3000 Main St., Hackberry, LA 70645; 318-762-3816. Tensas River, Rte. 2, Box 295, Tallulah, LA 71282; 318-574-2664. Louisiana WMD, P.O. Box 1601, Monroe, LA 71210; 318-325-1735.

Maine
Moosehorn (Cross Island, Carlton Pond WPA, Franklin Island, Seal Island, Sunkhaze Meadows), P.O. Box 1077, Calais, ME 04619; 207-454-3521. Petit Manan, P.O. Box 279, Milbridge, ME 04658; 207-546-2124. Pond Island, Northern Blvd., Plum Island, Newburyport, MA 01950; 508-465-5753. Rachel Carson, Rte. 2, Box 751, Wells, ME 04090; 207-646-9226. Sunkhaze Meadows, USDA Bldg., Room 221, Orono, ME 04469; 207-827-6138.

Maryland
Blackwater (Martin, Susquehanna), 2145 Key Wallace Dr., Cambridge, MD 21613; 410-228-2692. Chincoteague, Box 62, Chincoteague, VA 23336; 804-336-6122. Eastern Neck, 1730 Eastern Neck Rd., Rock Hall, MD 21661; 410-639-7056. Patuxent, Rte. 197, Laurel, MD 20708; 410-497-5605.

Massachusetts
Great Meadows (John Hay (NH), Massasoit, Monomoy, Nantucket, Oxbow, Wapack (NH)), Weir Hill Rd., Sudbury, MA 01776; 508-443-4661. Parker River (Pond Island (ME), Thacher Island), Northern Blvd., Plum Island, Newburyport, MA 01950; 508-465-5753. Rachel Carson, 321 Port Rd., Wells, ME 04090; 207-646-9226.

Michigan
Seney (Harbor Island, Huron), Seney, MI 49883; 906-586-9851. Shiawassee (Michigan Islands, Wyandotte), 6975 Mower Rd., Rte. 1, Saginaw, MI 48601; 517-777-5930.

Minnesota
Agassiz, Middle River, MN 56737; 218-449-4115. Big Stone, 25 NW 2nd St., Ortonville, MN 56278; 612-839-3700. Minnesota Valley, 3815 E. 80th St., Bloomington, MN 55425; 612-854-5900. Minnesota Wetlands Complex, Rte. 1, Box 76, Fergus Falls, MN 56537; 218-739-2291. Morris WMD, Rte. 1, Box 877, Mill Dam Rd., Morris, MN 56267; 612-589-1001. Detroit Lakes WMD, Rte. 3, Box 47D, Detroit Lakes, MN 56501; 218-847-4431. Fergus Falls WMD, Rte. 1, Box 76, Fergus Falls, MN 56537; 218-739-2291. Litchfield WMD, 971 E. Frontage Rd., Litchfield, MN 55355; 612-693-2849. Rice Lake (Mille Lacs, Sandstone), Rte. 2, Box 67, McGregor, MN 55760; 218-768-2402. Sherburne, Rte. 2, Zimmerman, MN 55398; 612-389-3323. Tamarac, Rural Rte., Rochert, MN 56578; 218-847-2641. Upper Mississippi River Complex, 555 Lester Ave., Onalosua, WI, 54650; 608-783-8405. Upper Mississippi River National Wildlife and Fish Refuge (IA, IL, MN, WI), 51 East 4th St., Winona, MN 55987; 507-452-4232. Winona District, 51 East 4th St., Winona, MN 55987; 507-452-4232.

Mississippi
Mississippi Sandhill Crane, 7200 Coane Ln., Gautier, MS 39553; 601-497-6322. Noxubee, Rte. 1, Box 142, Brooksville, MS 39739; 601-323-5548. Yazoo (Hillside, Mathews Brake, Morgan Brake, Panther Swamp), Rte. 1, Box 286, Hillandale, MS 38748; 601-839-2638. Mississippi WMD, P.O. Box 1070, Grenada, MS 38901; 601-226-8286. St. Catherine Creek, P.O. Box 1639, Natchez, MS 39122; 601-442-6696.

Missouri
Mingo, Rte. 1, Box 103, Puxico, MO 63960; 314-222-3589. Squaw Creek, P.O. Box 101, Mound City, MO 64470; 816-442-3187. Swan Lake, P.O. Box 68, Sumner, MO 64681; 816-856-3323.

Montana
Benton Lake, 922 Boot Great Lake, Black Eagle, MT 59404; 406-727-7400. Bowdoin (Black Coulee, Creedman Coulee, Hewitt Lake, Lake Thibadeau), P.O. Box J, Malta, MT 59538; 406-654-2863. Charles M. Russell (Hailstone, Halfbreed Lake, Lake Mason, Nichols Coulee, UL Bend, War Horse), P.O. Box 110, Lewistown, MT 59457; 406-538-8706. Fort Peck Wildlife Station, P.O. Box 166, Fort Peck, MT 59223; 406-526-3464. Jordan Wildlife Station, P.O. Box 63, Jordan, MT 59337; 406-557-6145. Sand Creek Wildlife Station, P.O. Box 89, Roy, MT 59471; 406-464-5181. Lee Metcalf, P.O. Box 257, Stevensville, MT 59870; 406-777-5552. Medicine Lake (Lamesteer), 233 North Shore Rd., Medicine Lake, MT 59247; 406-789-2305. National Bison Range (Nine-Pipe, Pablo), Moiese, MT 59824; 406-644-2211.

Environment and Nature

Northwest Montana WMD (Swan River), 780 Creston Hatchery Rd., Kalispell, MT 59901; 406-758-6868. Red Rock Lakes, Monida Star Rte., Box 15, Lima, MT 59739; 406-276-3347.

Nebraska
Crescent Lake (North Platte), HC 68, Box 21, Ellsworth, NE 69340; 308-762-4893. DeSoto, Rte. 1, Box 114, Missouri Valley, IA 51555; 712-642-4121. Fort Niobrara/Valentine, Hidden Timber Route, HC 14, Box 67, Valentine, NE 69201; 402-376-3789. Valentine, Hidden Timber Route, HC 14, Box 67, Valentine, NE 69201; 402-376-3789. Rainwater Basin WMD, P.O. Box 1686, Kearney, NE 68847; 308-236-5015.

Nevada
Desert National Wildlife Range (Amargosa Pupfish Station), 1500 North Decatur Blvd., Las Vegas, NV 89108; 702-646-3401. Ash Meadows, P.O. Box 2660, Pahrump, NV 89041; 702-372-5435. Pahranagat, Box 510, Alamo, NV 89001; 702-725-3417. Ruby Lake, Ruby Valley, NV 89833; 702-779-2237. Sheldon, P.O. Box 111, Lakeview, OR 97630; 503-947-3315. Stillwater (Anaho Island, Fallon), P.O. Box 1236, Fallon, NV 89407-1236; 702-423-5128.

New Hampshire
John Hay, Weir Hill Rd., Sudbury, MA 01776; 508-443-4661. Wapack, Weir Hill Rd., Sudbury, MA 01776; 508-443-4661.

New Jersey
Edwin B. Forsythe (Brigantine Division), Great Creek Rd., Box 72, Oceanville, NJ 08231; 609-652-1665. Barnegat Division, P.O. Box 544, 70 Collinstown Rd., Barnegat, NJ 08005; 609-698-1387. Great Swamp, Pleasant Plains Rd., RD 1, Box 152, Basking Ridge, NJ 07920; 201-425-1222. Killcohook, Suite 104, Scott Plaza 2, Philadelphia, PA 19113; 610-521-0662. Supawna Meadows, RD 3, Box 540, Salem, NJ 08079; 609-935-1487.

New Mexico
Bitter Lake, P.O. Box 7, Roswell, NM 88201; 505-622-6755. Bosque del Apache, P.O. Box 1246, Socorro, NM 87801; 505-835-1828. San Andres, P.O. Box 756, Las Cruces, NM 88004; 505-382-5047. Sevilleta, General Delivery, San Acacia, NM 87831; 505-864-4021. Grulla, P.O. Box 179, Umbarger, TX 79091; 806-499-3382. Las Vegas, Rte. 1, Box 399, Las Vegas, NM 87701; 505-425-3581. Maxwell, P.O. Box 276, Maxwell, NM 87728; 505-375-2331.

New York
Iroquois, P.O. Box 1101, Casey Rd., Alabama, NY 14003; 716-948-9154. Montezuma, 3395 Rte. 5/20 East, Seneca Falls, NY 13148; 315-568-5987. Wertheim (Amagansett, Conscience Point, Elizabeth A. Morton, Lido Beach, Oyster Bay, Seatuck, Target Rock), P.O. Box 21, Shirley, NY 11967; 516-286-0485. Seatuck, P.O. Box 21, Shirley, NY 11967; 516-581-1538.

North Carolina
Alligator River (Currituck), P.O. Box 1969, Manteo, NC 27954; 919-473-1131. Pea Island, 919-987-2394. Great Dismal Swamp, 3100 Desert Rd., P.O. Box 349, Suffolk, VA 23434; 804-986-3705. Mackay Island, P.O. Box 39, Knotts Island, NC 27950; 919-429-3100. Mattamuskett (Cedar Island, Pungo, Swanquarter), Rte. 1, Box N-2, Swanquarter, NC 27885; 919-926-4021. Roanoke River, 102 Dundee St., Box 430, Windsor, NC 27983; 919-794-5326.

North Dakota
Arrowwood (Chase Lake, Slade), 7745 11th St., SE, Pingree, ND 58476; 701-285-3341. Long Lake, 1200 353rd St., SE, Moffit, ND 58560; 701-387-4397. Valley City WMD, 11515 River Rd., Valley City, ND 58072; 701-845-3466. Audubon, Rural Rte. 1, Coleharbor, ND 58531; 701-442-5474. Lake Ilo, Dunn Center, ND 58626; 701-548-8110. Des Lacs (Lake Zahl), P.O. Box 578, Kenmare, ND 58746; 701-385-4046. Crosby WMD, P.O. Box 148, Crosby, ND 58730; 701-965-6488. Lostwood, Rural Rte. 2, Box 98, Kenmare, ND 58746; 701-848-2722. Devils Lake WMD (Lake Alice, Sullys Hill National Game Preserve), P.O. Box 908, Devils Lake, ND 58301; 701-662-8611. J. Clark Salyer, Box 66, Upham, ND 58789; 701-768-2548. Kulm WMD, P.O. Box E, Kulm, ND 58456; 701-647-2866. Tewaukon, 9754 134 1/2 Ave., SE, Cayuga, ND 58013; 701-724-3598. Upper Souris, Rural Rte. 1, Box 163, Foxholm, ND 58738; 701-468-5467.

Ohio
Ottawa (Cedar Point, West Sister Island), 14000 W. State Rte. 2, Oak Harbor, OH 43449; 419-898-0014.

Oklahoma
Little River (Little Sandy), P.O. Box 340, Broken Bow, OK 74728; 405-584-6211. Salt Plains, Rte. 1, Box 76, Jet, OK 73749; 405-626-4794. Sequoyah (Oklahoma Bat Caves), Rte. 1, Box 18A, Vian, OK 74962; 918-773-5251. Tishomingo, Rte. 1, Box

151, Tishomingo, OK 73460; 405-371-2402. Washita (Optima), Rte. 1, Box 68, Butler, OK 73625; 405-664-2205. Wichita Mountains Wildlife Refuge, Rte. 1, Box 448, Indiahoma, OK 73552; 405-429-3221.

Oregon
Klamath Forest and Upper Klamath, Rte. 1, Box 74, Tule Lake, CA 96134; 916-667-2231. Lewis and Clark, HC 01, Box 910, Ilwaco, WA 98624-9707; 360-484-3482. Malheur, HC 72, Box 245, Princeton, OR 97721; 503-493-2612. Sheldon/Hart Mountain Complex, P.O. Box 111, 18 S. G St., Lakeview, OR 97630; 503-947-3315. Sheldon, 18 S. G St., Lakeview, OR 97630; 503-947-3315. Hart Mountain, P.O. Box 111, Room 308, U.S. Post Office Bldg., Lakeview, OR 97630; 503-947-3315. Umatilla (Cold Springs, McKay Creek), P.O. Box 700, Umatilla, OR 97882; 503-922-3232. McNary, P.O. Box 544, Burbank, WA 99323; 509-547-4942. Toppenish, 21 Pumphouse Rd., Toppenish, WA 98948; 509-865-2405. Western Oregon Refuge Complex, 26208 Finley Refuge Rd., Corvallis, OR 97333; 503-757-7236. Ankeny, 2301 Wintel Rd., Jefferson, OR 97352; 503-327-2444. Baskett Slough, 10995 Hwy. 22, Dallas, OR 97338; 503-623-2749. William L. Finley (Bandon Marsh, Cape Meares, Oregon Islands, Three Arch Rocks), 26208 Finley Refuge Rd., Corvallis, OR 97333; 503-757-7236.

Pennsylvania
Erie, RD 1, Wood Duck Ln., Guys Mills, PA 16327; 814-789-3585. Tinicum National Environmental Center (Killcohook (NJ)), Suite 104, Scott Plaza 2, Philadelphia, PA 19113; 610-521-0662. Supawna Meadows (NJ), RD 3, Box 540, Salem, NJ 08079; 609-935-1487.

Puerto Rico
Caribbean Islands (Buck Island (Virgin Islands), Cabo Rojo, Culebra, Desecheo, Green Cay (Virgin Islands), Sandy Point (Virgin Islands)), Box 510, Carr. 301, KM 5.1, Boqueron, PR 00622; 809-851-7258.

Rhode Island
Ninigret (Block Island, Pettaquamscutt Cove, Sachuest Point, Salt Meadow (CT), Trustom Pond), P.O. Box 307, Charlestown, RI 02813; 401-364-9124. Stewart B. McKinney, U.S. Federal Bldg., Room 210, 915 Lafayette Blvd., Bridgeport, CT 06604; 203-579-5617.

South Carolina
Cape Romain, 5801 Highway 17 N., Awendaw, SC 29429; 803-928-3368. Carolina Sandhills, Rte. 2, Box 330, McBee, SC 29101; 803-335-8401. Pee Dee, P.O. Box 780, Wadesboro, NC 28170; 704-694-4424. Pinckney Island, 1000 Business Center Rd., Savannah, GA 31405; 912-944-4415. Santee, Rte. 2, Box 370, Summerton, SC 29148; 803-478-2217. Ace Basin, P.O. Box 848, Hollywood, SC 29449; 803-889-3084.

South Dakota
Lacreek, HC 5, Box 114, Martin, SD 57551; 605-685-6508. Lake Andes (Karl E. Mundt), Rural Rte. 1, Box 77, Lake Andes, SD 57356; 605-487-7603. Madison WMD, P.O. Box 48, Madison, SD 57042; 605-256-2974. Sand Lake (Pocasse), Rural Rte. 1, Box 25, Columbia, SD 57433; 605-885-6320. Waubay, Rural Rte. 1, Box 379, Waubay, SD 57273; 605-947-4521.

Tennessee
Cross Creeks, Rte. 1, Box 556, Dover, TN 37058; 615-232-7477. Hatchie (Chickasaw, Lower Hatchie), 4172 Highway 76 S., Brownsville, TN 38012; 901-772-0501. Reelfoot (Lake Isom), 4343 Highway 157, Union City, TN 38261; 901-538-2481. Tennessee, P.O. Box 849, Paris, TN 38242; 901-642-2091.

Texas
Anahuac (Moody), P.O. Box 278, Anahuac, TX 77514; 409-267-3337. McFaddin/Texas Point, P.O. Box 609, Sabine Pass, TX 77655; 409-971-2909. Aransas (Matagorda), P.O. Box 100, Austwell, TX 77950; 512-286-3559. Attwater Prairie Chicken, P.O. Box 119, Eagle Lake, TX 77434; 409-234-5940. Brazoria (Big Boggy), 1212 N. Velasco, Suite 200, Angleton, TX 77516-1088; 409-849-7771. San Bernard, 1212 N. Velasco, Suite 200, Angleton, TX 77516-1088; 409-849-7771. Buffalo Lake (Grulla (NM)), P.O. Box 179, Umbarger, TX 79091; 806-499-3382. Muleshoe, P.O. Box 549, Muleshoe, TX 79347; 806-946-3341. Hagerman, Rte. 3, Box 123, Sherman, TX 75090-9564; 214-786-2826. Laguna Atascosa, P.O. Box 450, Rio Hondo, TX 78583; 210-748-3607. Lower Rio Grande Valley/Santa Ana Complex, 320 N. Main, Room A-225, McAllen, TX 78501; 210-630-4636.

Utah
Fish Springs, P.O. Box 568, Dugway, UT 84022; 801-831-5353. Ouray (Bear River Migratory Bird Refuge), 866 S. Main, Bingham City, UT 84302; 801-723-5887.

Vermont
Missisquoi, P.O. Box 163, Swanton, VT 05488; 802-868-4781.

Be patient. If any phone number is incorrect, call (area code) 555-1212 and request the new listing.

Virginia

Back Bay (Plum Tree Island), 4005 Sandpiper Rd., P.O. Box 6286, Virginia Beach, VA 23456; 804-721-2412. Chincoteague (Wallops Island), Box 62, Chincoteague, VA 23336; 804-336-6122. Eastern Shore of Virginia (Cedar Island, Fisherman Island), 5003 Hallett Circle, Cape Charles, VA 23310; 804-331-2760. Great Dismal Swamp (Nansemond), 3100 Desert Rd., P.O. Box 349, Suffolk, VA 23434; 804-986-3705. Mason Neck (Featherstone, Marumsco), 14416 Jefferson Davis Hwy., Suite 20A, Woodbridge, VA 22191; 703-690-1297. Presquile, P.O. Box 620, Hopewell, VA 23860; 804-458-7541.

Washington

Columbia (Saddle Mountain), 735 E. Main St., P.O. Drawer F, Othello, WA 99344; 509-488-2668. McNary, P.O. Box 308, Burbank, WA 99323; 509-547-4942. Nisqually (San Juan Islands), 100 Brown Farm Rd., Olympia, WA 98506; 360-753-9467. Coastal Refuges Office (Dungeness, Protection Island, Washington Islands), P.O. Box 698, Sequim, WA 98382; 360-457-8451. Ridgefield (Pierce Ranch, Steigerwald Lake), 301 N. Third St., P.O. Box 457, Ridgefield, WA 98642; 360-887-4106. Toppenish, Rte. 1, Box 1300, Toppenish, WA 98948; 509-865-2405. Turnbull, S. 26010 Smith Rd., Cheney, WA 99004; 509-235-4723. Umatilla, P.O. Box 700, Umatilla, OR 97882; 503-922-3232. Willapa (Lewis and Clark (OR)), HC 01, Box 910, Ilwaco, WA 98624-9707; 360-484-3482. Julia Butler Hansen (Formerly Columbian White-tailed Deer), P.O. Box 566, Cathlamet, WA 98612; 360-795-3915. Conboy Lake, P.O. Box 5, Glenwood, WA 98619; 509-364-3410.

Wisconsin

Horicon (Fox River, Gravel Island, Green Bay), W. 4279 Headquarters Rd., Mayville, WI 53050; 414-387-2658; Necedah, Star Rte. West, Box 386, Necedah, WI 54646; 608-565-2551. Upper Mississippi River Complex, 555 Lester Ave., Onalasua, WI 54650; 608-783-8405. Trempealeau, W 28488 Refugee Rd., Trempealeau, WI 54661; 608-539-2311. Upper Mississippi River National Wildlife and Fish Refuge, 51 East 4th St., Winona, MN 55987; 507-452-4232. La Crosse District, P.O. Bldg., Box 415, La Crosse, WI 54601-0415; 608-783-8405.

Wyoming

Bamforth, P.O. Box 457, Walden, CO 80480; 303-723-8202. Hutton Lake, P.O. Box 457, Walden, CO 80480; 303-723-8202. National Elk Refuge, P.O. Box C, Jackson, WY 83001; 307-733-9212. Pathfinder, P.O. Box 457, Walden, CO 80480; 303-723-8202. Seedskadee, P.O. Box 100, Green River, WY 82935; 307-875-2187.

* Wildlife Refuge Regional Offices

Region 1
911 NE 11th Ave., Portland, OR 97232; 503-231-6118, 503-231-6214.

Region 2
P.O. Box 1306, Albuquerque, NM 87103; 505-248-6282, 505-248-6802.

Region 3
Federal Bldg., Fort Snelling, Twin Cities, MN 55111; 612-725-3563, 612-725-3507.

Region 4
Richard B. Russell Federal Bldg., 75 Spring St., SW, Atlanta, GA 30303; 404-679-7152.

Region 5
300 Westgate Center Dr., Hadley, MA 01035; 413-253-8200, 617-965-9222.

Region 6
Box 25486, Denver Federal Center, Denver, CO 80225; 303-236-7920, 303-236-8145.

Region 7
1011 E. Tudor Rd., Anchorage, AK 99503; 907-786-3542, 907-786-3545.

* Youth Conservation Corps

United States Youth Conservation Corps
U.S. Fish and Wildlife Service
National Park Service
Washington, DC 20240   202-343-5514

The Youth Conservation Corps is a summer employment program for young men and women, ages 15 through 18, who work, learn, and earn wages accomplishing needed conservation work on public lands. The program is also administered by the Forest Service of the U.S. Department of Agriculture. Projects include constructing trails, building campground facilities, planting trees, collecting litter, clearing streams, improving wildlife habitats, and office work. Limited positions are available.

Hazardous and Solid Waste

* See also Health and Medicine; Chemicals, Toxics, and Other Health Hazards Chapter

* 45,000 Pesticide Products Inventory

Office of Pesticide Programs
Environmental Protection Agency (EPA)
401 M St., SW
Washington DC 20460   703-305-7090

The Environmental Protection Agency (EPA) administers two Congressionally mandated statutes to control the more than 45,000 pesticide products registered for use in the United States. The EPA monitors the distribution and use of these pesticides, issuing civil or criminal penalties for violations. EPA also sets tolerances or maximum legal limits for pesticide residues on food commodities and feed grains to prevent consumer exposure to unsafe pesticide levels.

* Animal Poison Control Hotline

National Animal Poison Control Center   217-333-3611

The National Animal Poison Control Center, at The University of Illinois, provides 24-hour consultation in diagnosis and treatment of suspected or actual animal poisonings or chemical contaminations. Its emergency response team will rapidly investigate such incidents in North America, and perform laboratory analysis of feeds, animal specimens, and environmental materials for toxicants and chemical contaminants.

* Arctic Environmental Assessment

Office of Ocean Resources Conservation and Assessment (ORCA)
National Ocean Service
National Oceanic and Atmospheric Administration
6001 Executive Blvd.
Rockville, MD 20852   301-443-8487

The Office of Ocean Resources Conservation and Assessment (ORCA) manages a large scientific program of environmental assessments on the effects of oil and gas development on Alaska's outer continental shelf. General areas of investigation include description of Alaskan coastal and marine environments and ecosystems, development of pollutant transport models, and evaluation of the potential effects of petroleum development on coastal and marine resources.

* Asbestos in Your Home

R. Woods, Consumer Information Center-2A
P.O. Box 100
Pueblo, CO 81002

Asbestos in the Home discusses what asbestos is and the dangers it presents; how to tell if it's in your home and what to do about it (124Y, $1.50).

* Chemical Hazards Guide

Publications Dissemination
National Institute for Occupational Safety and Health
4676 Columbia Parkway
Cincinnati, Ohio 45226   513-533-8287

A Pocket Guide To Chemical Hazards is intended as a source of general industrial hygiene information for workers, employers, and occupational health professionals. It presents key information and data in abbreviated tabular for 398 chemicals or substance groupings that are found in the work environment and that have existing Occupational Safety and Health Administration regulations. The information includes chemical structures or formulas, identification codes, synonyms, exposure limits, chemical and physical properties, incompatibilities and reactivities, measurement methods, respirator selections, signs and symptoms of exposure, and procedures for emergency treatment. This Guide is free.

* Chemical Hazards Management Bibliography

Superintendent of Documents
Government Printing Office
Washington, DC 20402   202-512-1800

Hazardous and toxic waste management are topics within this bibliography. A pocket guide to chemical hazards and a septic systems and ground-water protection guide are featured. Free.

* Chemical Health and Safety Hotline

Chemical Referral Center   800-CMA-8200
                                                  202-887-1315 (in DC)

This toll-free service provides non-emergency referrals to companies that manufacture chemicals and to state and federal agencies for health and safety information and information regarding chemical regulations. It operates 9 a.m. to 6 p.m. eastern time. Residents in Arkansas can call 202-887-1315 collect.

* Chemical Risk Management

Chemical Control Division
Office of Toxic Substances
Environmental Protection Agency (EPA)
401 M St., SW, Room E513
Washington DC 20460   202-260-3749

This office performs the risk management functions for the Office of Toxic Substances. They manage the new chemical and biotechnology programs.

* Chemicals' Impact on Eagles and Falcons

U.S. Department of the Army
Chemical Research Development and Engineering Center
Aberdeen Proving Ground, MD 21010-5423   301-671-4345

While the Center's primary mission is concerned with research on chemical defensive material, the Center has become very involved in wildlife conservation programs because of its location on the Chesapeake Bay. The Center is especially experienced in a Bald Eagle program and a Peregrine Falcon program. Fact sheets on these and other wildlife issues may be obtained by writing or calling the above office.

* Chemicals in Your Community

Public Information Center
Environmental Protection Agency (EPA)
401 M St., SW, MS 3404
Washington, DC 20460   202-260-7751

Congress passes a law designed to help America's communities deal safely wand effectively with the many hazardous substances that are used throughout our society. The law is called the Emergency Planning and Community Right-to-Know Act; and this booklet has been written to help you understand and take advantage of your rights and opportunities under this far-reaching law. The first part of the guide describes how the law works; what its provisions were intended to accomplish; and how all members of the community can play an active part in making sure the law is carried out. The second part discusses specific groups and organizations affected by the law; describes what they can do or are required to do to make it work; and tells how they can benefit from it.

* Concerned About Pesticides?

Public Information Center
Environmental Protection Agency (EPA)
401 M St., SW, MS 3404
Washington, DC 20460   202-260-7751

The Environmental Protection Agency (EPA) has several publications which provide the consumer with information concerning pesticides. Some of the publications include:

Citizen's Guide to Pesticides- An informative brochure describing how to choose and use pesticides, how to pick a pest control company, and what to do in the event of a problem.

Regulating Pesticides- This brochure explains EPA's registration process and how they classify pesticides.

* Damage Assessment

Office of Ocean Resources Conservation and Assessment (ORCA)
National Ocean Service
National Oceanic and Atmospheric Administration
6001 Executive Blvd.
Rockville, MD 20852   301-713-2989

The Office of Ocean Resources Conservation and Assessment (ORCA) conducts comprehensive assessments of damages to National Oceanic and Atmospheric Administration (NOAA) trust resources from discharges of oil or releases of hazardous substances. ORCA works with the Environmental Protection Agency (EPA) to address natural resource concerns at these sites through its cleanup efforts. ORCA conducts damage assessments to enable NOAA to file claims against the potentially responsible parties. ORCA is currently working to assess damages resulting from the Exxon Valdez oil spill in Alaska.

* Dioxin Hotlines

The following hotlines provide callers with information on dioxin and related concerns for contaminated areas in New York, New Jersey, and Missouri:

New Jersey 800-346-5009
New York 800-722-1223
Missouri 800-892-5009

* Do You Want to Learn More About Hazardous Substances?

Public Information Center
Environmental Protection Agency (EPA)
401 M St., SW, MS 3404
Washington, DC 20460   202-260-2080

Hazardous Substances In Our Environment: A Citizen's Guide to Understanding Health Risks and Reducing Exposure is a guidebook which can help answer questions you may have about health risks from hazardous substances after reading statements in newspapers, book and government reports. The term hazardous substances can apply to any man-made or naturally occurring chemical or mineral substance found in air, water, soil, or food that can cause any type of human illness. Part 1 describes different hazardous substances and how they get into your environment, and Part 2 describes government actions, community activities and personal actions you can take. Also included is a list of publications and resources for further information.

* Emergency Plans for Acutely Toxic Chemicals

Emergency Planning and Community Right to Know   800-535-0202
                                                    202-260-3810

This Environmental Protection Agency (EPA) hotline provides communities with help in preparing for accidental releases of toxic chemicals by providing documents and other publications necessary. Communities can call to obtain interim guidelines regarding *Acutely Toxic Chemicals*. These guidelines cover organizing a community, developing a chemical contingency plan, and gathering site-specific information. The hotline also provides a list of more than 400 acutely toxic chemicals. They can also direct you to sources for obtaining information about chemicals stored in your community.

* Environmental Hazards in Your Home

R. Woods
Consumer Information Center-2A
P.O. Box 100
Pueblo, CO 81002

Homebuyer's Guide to Environmental Hazards explains the dangers of radon, asbestos, lead, hazardous waste, contaminated ground water, and formaldehydes. This publication explains the risks, what to do, and where to get help (432Y, $1.50).

* Fishery Chemicals Research

National Fisheries Research Center
U.S. Fish and Wildlife Service
P.O. Box 818
LaCrosse, WI 54602-0818   608-783-6451

The National Fisheries Research Center at LaCrosse, Wisconsin, has been designated by the Fish and Wildlife Service to negotiate registration for fishery chemicals with

regulatory agencies. Pesticides are registered with the National Research Agency, and therapeutants for controlling fish diseases are registered with the U.S. Food and Drug Administration. Once a fishery chemical is registered by the Federal government, states will generally allow the use of that chemical for fish culture and management.

* Geologic Hazards and Hazardous Waste

Geologic Inquiries
U.S. Geological Survey
911 National Center
Reston, VA 22092   703-648-4380

This division evaluates environmental hazards which are associated with earthquakes, volcanoes, floods, droughts, toxic materials, landslides, subsidence, and other ground failures. Methods of hazards prediction are developed through the study of the Earth's internal structure. Engineering problems are identified and solved, including problems in the selection of sites for power stations, highways, bridges, dams, and hazardous waste disposal.

* Guide to Hazardous Waste Publications

Headquarters Library
Environmental Protection Agency (EPA)
401 M St., SW, MS 3404
Washington, DC 20460   202-260-5934

The Hazardous Waste Superfund Collection is housed in 17 libraries in the Environmental Protection Agency (EPA) Library Network. This publication explains the various document types comprising the Hazardous Waste Superfund collection, including sources of documents, contacts, public access, and information pertaining to the availability of documents. This is published annually.

* Hazardous Materials Technical Hotline

Hazardous Materials Technical Center   800-638-8958
                                              301-468-8858

This center provides various services related to hazardous materials, including a clearinghouse technical inquiry line, a newsletter for the U.S. Department of Defense about hazardous materials, maintenance of a collection of publications on hazardous management, and abstracting and publishing of literature related to hazardous materials. The services provided are free only to the U.S. Department of Defense; others must pay a fee to use them.

* Hazardous Material Transportation Accidents

Information Systems Division (DHM-63)
Office of Hazardous Materials Transportation
Research and Special Programs Administration
U.S. Department of Transportation
400 7th Street, SW, Room 8112
Washington, DC 20590   202-366-4555

This division collects and analyzes accident data from transporters of hazardous materials by highway, rail, air, and water and from container manufacturers. Information stored in the database includes the hazardous material involved, transporter name and mode, packaging used, cause of accident, and results. Contact the above office for searches. There may be a charge.

* Hazardous Materials Transportation Hotline

U.S. Department of Transportation Department Hotline
400 7th Street, SW, Room 8112
Washington, DC 20590   202-366-1111

This U.S. Department of Transportation Hotline provides informational assistance pertaining to federal regulations for transportation of hazardous materials. This includes those regulations contained in CFR-49.

* Hazardous Waste Bibliography and Technology Transfer

Office of Solid Waste and Emergency Response
Environmental Protection Agency (EPA)
401 M St., SW
Washington DC 20460   202-260-4761

This bibliography, prepared by the Technology Transfer Task Force, lists and abstracts the most important technical materials that should be readily available to all Federal and State hazardous waste staffs and their contractors. It assigns each document a level of importance as primary reference documents for Federal and State headquarters, regional, and field staffs. Contact this office to obtain a copy.

Environment and Nature

* Hazardous Waste Hotline

RCRA/Superfund Hotline
Environmental Protection Agency (EPA)
401 M St., SW   800-424-9346
Washington DC 20460   703-920-9810

Under the Resource Recovery and Conservation Act, the Environmental Protection Agency (EPA) is responsible for identifying general and specific categories of hazardous wastes, developing standards, and enforcing compliance with those standards. Hazardous wastes regulated under RCRA include toxic substances, caustics, pesticides, and other flammable, corrosive, or explosive materials. EPA establishes criteria for classifying land disposal facilities according to their environmental acceptability and publishes a national inventory of unacceptable facilities. Contact this hotline for more information on hazardous wastes and the regulations associated with them. A free catalog is available.

* Hazardous Waste Ombudsman Hotline

Hazardous Waste Ombudsman Program
Environmental Protection Agency (EPA)
401 M St., SW
Washington DC 20460   202-260-9361

The Environmental Protection Agency (EPA) has established this office to handle complaints from the public and regulated community, and to assist them in resolving problems concerning any program or requirement under the hazardous waste law. The Hazardous Waste Ombudsman Program assists citizens and the regulated community who have had problems voicing a complaint or getting a problem resolved about hazardous waste issues. It serves as a last resort to the RCRA/CERCLA Hotline.

Region 1 617-573-5758
Region 2 212-264-2980
Region 3 215-597-9636
Region 4 404-347-7109
Region 5 312-886-0981
Region 6 214-655-6760
Region 7 913-551-7680
Region 8 303-293-1603
Region 9 415-744-2074
Region 10 206-553-4280

* Help With Chemical Assessment Problems

Office of Toxic Substances
Environmental Protection Agency (EPA)
401 M St., SW
Washington, DC 20460   202-260-3442

The Chemical Assessment Desk is an outreach service to other Environmental Protection Agency (EPA) Offices. The Desk offers technical consultation and information on chemical risk-related issues under the Office of Toxic Substances (OTS) Existing Chemicals Program. The Desk also provides estimates of chemical toxicity and environmental fate based on structure-activity relationships in the absence of experimental data, assists in identifying related risk assessment activities, and provides comments on technical aspects of OTS evaluations and risk assessments. For State and local agencies, the Chemical Assessment Desk operates through Regional coordinators as follows:

Region 1
Boston 617-565-3704

Region 2
New York 201-637-3000

Region 3
Philadelphia 215-597-7904

Region 4
Atlanta 404-347-4216

Region 5
Chicago 312-886-6006

Region 6
Dallas 214-665-6444

Region 7
Kansas City 913-551-7000

Region 8
Denver 303-312-6415

Region 9
San Francisco 415-974-7280

Region 10
Seattle 206-442-1072

* Help with Solid Waste Issues

RCRA Information Center
Environmental Protection Agency (EPA)
401 M St., SW
Washington, DC 20460   800-424-9346

Is your community facing or edging toward a solid waste crisis? Do you understand all the available solid waste management options and how to integrate them to your community's advantage? To help local solid waste managers address these questions, the Environmental Protection Agency (EPA) has compiled and published the *Decision-Maker's Guide to Solid Waste Management*. This free publication will help you devise and implement a solid waste management system that benefits your community economically and environmentally.

* Lead-Based Paint

R. Woods, Consumer Information Center
P.O. Box 100
Pueblo, CO 81002

What You Should Know About Lead-Based Paint in Your Home explains how lead poisoning is hazardous to you and your family's health. Learn how to detect lead in paint, what to do to reduce exposure, and safety guidelines for removing lead-based paint (435Y, $1.50).

* National Response Center Hotline

Coast Guard Hotline   800-424-8802
      202-267-2675

This U.S. Department of Transportation National Response Center can be used to report spills of oil and other hazardous materials where required. It can also be used to report incidents in transportation where hazardous materials are responsible for death, serious injury, property damage in excess of $50,000 or continuing danger to life and property.

* New Pesticide Registration

Registration Division
Office of Pesticide Programs
Pesticides and Toxic Substances
Environmental Protection Agency (EPA)
401 M St., SW
Washington DC 20460   703-305-5447

The Environmental Protection Agency (EPA) registers (licenses) thousands of pesticide products for use in and around homes. No pesticide may legally be sold in the U.S. unless its label bears an EPA registration number. The Federal Insecticide, Fungicide and Rodenticide Act (FIFRA), which governs the registration of pesticides, prohibits the use of any pesticide products in a manner that is inconsistent with product labeling. Contact this office for more information.

* Northeast Industrial Waste Clearinghouse

Northeast Industrial Waste Exchange   315-422-6572

The Northeast Industrial Waste Exchange provides information on waste exchange in the Northeast but with access to other areas. This exchange joins those who generate waste with those who desire waste.

* Nuclear Waste Hydrology

Nuclear Waste Program
Water Resources Division
U.S. Geological Survey
National Center, MS 410
Reston, VA 22092   703-648-5719

Hydrologic and geologic research and field studies are conducted to develop better understanding of radionuclide transport in ground-water systems. The program also supports Interior's role in the national high-level nuclear waste repository program, providing information on the management of low-level nuclear waste.

* Ocean Dumping

Office of Marine and Estuarine Protection
Environmental Protection Agency (EPA)
401 M St., SW
Washington DC 20460   202-260-1952

This office carries out the duties covered under the Marine Protection, Research and Sanctuaries Act, which is designed to protect the marine environment from the harmful effects of ocean dumping. The Act establishes a permit program to ensure that ocean dumping does not cause degradation of the marine environment. Contact this office for more information on ocean dumping regulation.

* Oil and Chemical Spills Hotline

National Response Center (NRC)
Marine Environmental Response Division
Office of Marine Safety, Security, and
    Environmental Protection
U.S. Coast Guard
U.S. Department of Transportation
2100 2nd St., SW, Room 2611   800-424-8802
Washington, DC 20593   202-267-2188

The National Response Center (NRC) receives reports of oil and hazardous substance spills, investigates incidents, initiates civil penalty actions, monitors cleanups, and coordinates federally funded spill response operations. NRC's National Strike Force assists federal coordinators on the scene in responding to pollution accidents. For further details, or to report information, contact the Center toll-free.

* Oil Spills and Hazardous Waste Response Hotline

Coast Guard Hotline
U.S. Coast Guard
U.S. Department of Transportation
2100 2nd St., SW, Room 2611   800-424-8802
Washington, DC 20593   202-426-2675

This U.S. Department of Transportation National Response Center can be used to report spills of oil and other hazardous materials where required. It can also be used to report incidents in transportation where hazardous materials are responsible for death, serious injury, property damage in excess of $50,000 or continuing danger to life and property.

* PCBs and Asbestos Hotline

Toxic Substances Control Act Hotline
Environmental Protection Agency (EPA)
401 M St., SW
Washington DC 20460   202-554-1404

The Toxic Assistance Office at the Environmental Protection Agency (EPA) will answer questions and offer general and technical assistance on the Toxic Substances Control Act (TSCA). Staff will help to obtain guidance on TSCA regulations, including guidance on PCBs and asbestos issues. Publications are also available through the hotline.

* Pesticide Information Hotline

National Pesticide Telecommunications Network   800-858-7378
    806-743-3091 (TX)

This service of the U.S. Environmental Protection Agency and Texas Tech University is open 24 hours, 7 days a week. It responds to non-emergency questions about the effects of pesticides, toxicology and symptoms, environmental effects, disposal and cleanup, and safe use of pesticides.

* Pesticide Problems

Frank Davido
Pesticide Incident Response Officer
Field Operations Division (H-7506C)
Office of Pesticide Programs
Environmental Protection Agency (EPA)
401 M St., SW
Washington, DC 20460   703-305-0576

The Environmental Protection Agency (EPA) is interested in receiving information on any adverse effects associated with pesticide exposure. You should provide as complete information as possible, including any official investigation report of the incident and medical records concerning adverse health effects. Medical records will be held in confidence.

* Pesticides and Toxic Substances Library

Office of Toxic Substances Library
401 M St., SW
Washington, DC 20460   202-260-3944

Part of the Office of Pesticides and Toxic Substances, the Office of Toxic Substances (OTS) Library houses collections relevant to toxic substances. The library also maintains some pesticides publications. Hours of operation are Monday through Friday, 8:00 a.m. to 4:30 p.m. Databases maintained here include DIALOG, NLM, STN, and CIS.

* Pesticides Database

Pesticides Information Retrieval System
CERIS
1231 Cumberland Avenue, Suite A
N. Lafayette, IN 47906   317-494-7309

This computer database provides public access to current information on over 36,000 pesticide products. The system development has been jointly funded by the U.S. Department of Agriculture (USDA) and the Environmental Protection Agency (EPA) and is managed by Purdue University.

* Pesticides Rules and Regulations

Environmental Protection Agency (EPA)
401 M Street SW
Washington, DC 20460   703-305-5805

The Pesticides Docket provides public access to documentation for each Registration Standard under development when the Agency begins review of data for the Registration Standard or upon publication of a notice setting out the list and sequence of Registration Standards. The docket contains documentation of pre-special and special reviews of pesticides, memoranda, all comments, correspondence, documents, proposals, or other materials concerning a pending pesticide regulatory decision provided to the Agency by a person or party outside of government (other than confidential business information).

* Pipeline Safety

Office of Pipeline Safety (OPS)
Research and Special Programs Administration
U.S. Department of Transportation
400 7th Street, SW
Washington, DC 20590   202-366-4572

The Office of Pipeline Safety (OPS) establishes and enforces safety standards for the transportation of gas and other hazardous materials by pipeline. A computerized reporting system is maintained to collect and analyze accident and incident data from pipeline operators. Accident reports include the operator's name, the hazardous material involved, description of the accident, and results. For database searches, contact the office listed. There may be a charge.

* Poison Control Centers

24 hours a day, 7 days a week

These centers answer specific questions about situations involving poisons. While most calls received involve questions regarding children, a significant number of calls involve adults exposed to some form of toxic substance. These Centers provide medical treatment guidance and can answer general questions about air toxics, including paint fumes and pesticides. Regional poison control centers service many areas throughout the United States.

Alabama Poison Center
205-345-0600
800-462-0800 (AL only)

Arizona Poison Control System
602-626-7899
602-626-6016 (Tucson)
602-253-3334 (Phoenix)
800-362-0101 (AZ only)

Central Ohio Poison Center
614-722-2636
614-228-1323
800-682-7625

Blodgett Regional Poison Center
800-632-2727 (616 area code only)

Cardinal Glennon Children's Hospital Regional Poison Center
314-772-8300
314-772-5200
800-392-9111 (MO only)

Maryland Poison Center
410-528-7606
410-528-7701
800-492-2414 (MD only)

Sharlope Poison Control Center
919-684-8111
800-848-6946 (NC only)

Georgia Poison Control Center
404-616-9000
800-282-5846 (GA only)

Hennepin Regional Poison Center (Minnesota)
612-347-3144
612-347-3141
612-347-6219 (TTY)

Intermountain Regional Poison Control Center
801-581-7504
801-581-2151
800-456-7707 (UT only)

Kentucky Regional Poison Center of Kosair Children's Hospital
502-589-8222
800-722-5725 (KY only) (TDD)

Long Island Regional Poison Control Center
516-542-2323

Los Angeles County Medical Association Regional Poison Control Center
213-222-3212
800-777-6476

Louisiana Regional Poison Control Center
318-675-6364
800-256-9822 (LA only)

Massachusetts Poison Control System
617-355-6607
617-232-2120
800-682-9211 (MD only)

Michigan Poison Control Center
313-745-5329
313-745-5711
800-764-7661 (313 area code only)
800-572-1655 (remainder of MI)

Mid-Plains Poison Center
402-390-5434
402-390-5555
800-955-9119 (NE only)

New Jersey Poison Information and Education System
201-926-7443
201-923-0764
800-764-7661 (NJ only)

New Mexico Poison and Drug Information Center
505-277-4261
505-843-2551
800-432-6866 (NM only)

New York City Poison Control Center
212-764-7667
212-340-4494

North Central Texas Poison Center
214-590-5000
800-764-7661 (TX only)

Oregon Poison Control and Drug Information Center
503-415-5799
503-494-8968 (Portland, OR)
800-452-7165

Pittsburgh Poison Center
412-692-5600
412-681-6669

Rocky Mountain Poison Center
303-893-3784
303-629-1123
800-332-3073 (CO only)
800-525-5042 (MT only)
800-442-2702 (WY only)

San Diego Regional Poison Center
619-543-6000
800-876-4766

San Francisco Gay Area Regional Poison Control Center
800-523-2222

Southwest Ohio Regional Poison Control System
513-558-5111
800-872-5111

Tampa Bay Regional Control System
813-251-6911
813-253-4444
800-282-3171

Texas State Poison Center
409-772-3332 (Houston)
713-654-1701 (Austin)
800-764-7661 (TX only)

UCDMC Regional Poison Control Center
916-734-3692
800-342-9293

West Virginia Poison Center
304-347-1212
304-348-4211
800-642-3625 (WV only)

Washington DC
202-625-3333

* Pollution Prevention and the Environment
Public Information Center
Environmental Protection Agency (EPA)
401 M St., SW, MS 3404
Washington, DC 20460   202-260-7751

The Environmental Protection Agency's (EPA) Public Information Center supplies non-technical publications about the environment and related issues, including information on household hazards, family recycling tips, and book suggestions for all ages. All of these are free and provide a wealth of helpful information.

Books for Young People on Environmental Issues
Earth Trek...Explore Your Environment
The President's Environmental Youth Awards
1991 Gas Mileage Guide: EPA Fuel Economy Estimates
Be An Environmentally Alert Consumer
Citizen's Guide to Pesticides
Citizen's Guide to Radon: What It Is and What To Do About It
Environmental Enforcement: A Citizen's Guide
A Family Guide to Pollution Prevention
Glossary of Environmental Terms and Acronym List
The Inside Story: A Guide to Indoor Air Quality
Meeting the Environmental Challenge
Protecting Our Ground Water
Superfund: Looking Back, Looking Ahead
Termiticides: Consumer Information

* Radioactive and Radon Exposure

Office of Radiation Programs
Environmental Protection Agency (EPA)
401 M St., SW, Room NE108
Washington DC 20460   202-260-9600

The Environmental Protection Agency (EPA), with a number of other federal agencies, protects the public from unnecessary exposure to ionizing radiation. EPA's major responsibilities are to set radioactive emissions standards and exposure limits, assess new technology, and monitor radiation in the environment in four areas: radiation from nuclear accidents, radon emissions, land disposal of radioactive waste, and radiation in groundwater and drinking water. The Environmental Protection Agency fulfills these responsibilities by setting emissions standards for nuclear power plants, and for radionuclides in drinking water and in the air. The Environmental Protection Agency also prescribes work practices to reduce emissions of radon from underground uranium mines, develops radioactive waste disposal standards, and issues guidance to limit occupational exposure.

* Recycling Help for Teachers

RCRA Docket Information Center
Office of Solid Waste
Environmental Protection Agency (EPA)
401 M St., SW   800-424-9346
Washington, DC 20460   202-260-2080

Let's Reduce and Recycle: Curriculum for Solid Waste Awareness provides lesson plans for grades K-12, and is a curriculum guide that emerged as part of a public education campaign to promote recycling awareness. Activities, skits, bibliographies, and other resources are included. This is a free publication.

* Recycling Information

Public Information Center
Environmental Protection Agency (EPA)
401 M St., SW, MS 3404
Washington DC 20460   202-260-7751

Recycling publications are available that provide information about successful recycling programs initiated by state and local agencies. They describe private recycling efforts and joint recycling ventures of government and businesses.

* Resource Conservation and Recovery Act (RCRA)

Environmental Protection Agency (EPA)
401 M St., SW
Washington, DC 20460   703-603-9230

The Resource Conservation and Recovery Act (RCRA) Docket provides public access to regulatory information supporting the Environmental Protection Agency's (EPA) actions under the Resource Conservation and Recovery Act. Records support *Federal Register* notices, *Delisting Petitions*, and other Office of Solid Waste publications. RCRA Docket publishes a semiannual catalog of frequently requested documents titled, *A Catalog of Hazardous and Solid Waste Publications*. Contact this office for more information on these and other RCRA documents.

* Resource Recovery Emergency Response Hotline

Resource Conservation and Recovery Act (RCRA)
On-Scene Coordinators Hotline   214-767-2666

The Resource Conservation and Recovery Act On-Scene Coordinators Hotline in Region VI responds 24 hours a day to questions and to reports of chemical spills and other emergencies for all Region VI states: Arkansas, Louisiana, New Mexico, Oklahoma, and Texas.

* Restricted Pesticides

Office of Pesticides and Toxic Substances
Environmental Protection Agency (EPA)
Washington, DC 20460   703-305-5805

This office has a publication titled *Suspended, Cancelled and Restricted Pesticides* which is a summary and clarification of actions taken by the Environmental Protection Agency (EPA) for pesticides that the Agency has suspended, cancelled, or otherwise restricted because of concern for potentially adverse effects. This listing identifies the current status and references the legal history of each pesticide, as well as the criteria of concern for which the chemical was reviewed by the Agency (EPA/EN-342).

* Save the Whales

Office of Ocean Affairs
U.S. Department of State, Room 5805
Washington, DC 20520   202-647-3262

This office can provide you with up to the minute information on the protection of whales. They put together the U.S. whaling policy, attend meetings of the international whaling commission, and follow the mandates of the Marine Mammal Protection Act. This office can direct you to other organizations and associations concerned with the protection of whales.

* Solid Waste Information Clearinghouse and Hotline

Solid Waste Information Clearinghouse
P.O. Box 7219
8750 Georgia Ave., Suite 140
Silver Spring, MD 20910   800-67-SWICH

The Solid Waste Information Clearinghouse and Hotline (SWICH) was developed to help increase the availability of information in the field of solid waste management, and is comprised of a library system and an electronic bulletin board (EBB). The library includes journals, reports, studies, proceedings, periodicals, case studies, curricula, films and videotapes all focusing on solid waste issues. Topic covered include source reduction, recycling, composting, planning, education and training, public participation, legislation and regulation, waste combustion, collection, transfer, disposal, landfill gas, and special wastes. The EBB provides updated information on solid waste issues including: meeting and conference information, message inquiries, case studies, new technologies, new publications, expert contact information, and much more. A quarterly newsletter is also published.

* Solid Waste Management Clearinghouse

Andrew W. Briedenbach Environmental
Research Center Library
26 W. Martin Luther King
Cincinnati, OH 45268   513-569-7703

The major subjects in this library's collection are bacteriology, biology, biotechnology, chemistry, engineering, hazardous wastes, hydrobiology, microbiology, solid waste management, toxicology, water pollution, and water quality. Databases maintained here include BRS, CAS On-line, CIS, DIALOG, Dun & Bradstreet, Hazardous Waste Database, LEXIS/NEXIS, NLM, Toxline, and Toxnet. General collections include bacteriology, biology, biotechnology, microbiology, physics, solid waste management. This library's special collections cover the environment, Canada, legal issues, hazardous waste, and solid waste.

* State Pesticide Agencies

State Pesticide Agencies regulate the use of pesticides and license people who purchase restricted use permits and for people who use it for their business, such as farmers. Typically, people must pass a test, carry a certain amount of insurance, and attend recertification classes in order to get a license. This office can answer question regarding pesticide use, and can explain the label on your pesticide container. If you hired someone to treat your home or yard, and you had damage as a result of that treatment, you should contact this office. They are charged with seeing that pesticides are used properly, and will investigate your complaint.

REGION 1
Connecticut
Director
Department of Environmental Protection
Hazardous Materials
Waste Management Bureau
State Office Building
79 Elm Street
Hartford, CT 06106   203-424-3369

Maine
Director, Board of Pesticide Control
Dept. of Agriculture
State House- Station 28
Augusta, ME 04333   207-287-2731

Massachusetts
Chief, Pesticides Bureau
Dept. of Food and Agriculture
100 Cambridge St., 21st Floor
Boston, MA 02202   617-727-2863

Environment and Nature

New Hampshire
Director
Division of Pesticides Control
Department of Agriculture
P.O. Box 2042
Concord, NH 03302   603-271-3550

Rhode Island
Chief, Division of Agriculture and Marketing
Dept. of Environmental Management
22 Hayes St.
Providence, RI 02908   401-277-2781

Vermont
Director, Plant Industry Division
Dept. of Agriculture
116 State St., Drawer 20
Montpelier, VT 05620   802-828-2431

REGION 2
New Jersey
Chief, Bureau of Pesticide Control
NJ Dept. of Environmental Protection
380 Scoutch Rd.
West Trenton, NJ 08625   609-530-4123

New York
Director
Bureau of Pesticides
Department of Environmental Conservation
Room 404, 50 Wolf Rd.
Albany, NY 12233-0001   518-457-7482

Puerto Rico
Director
Analysis and Registration of Agricultural Materials
Division of Laboratory
Puerto Rico Dept. of Agriculture
P.O. Box 10163
Santurce, PR 00908   809-796-1715

Virgin Islands
Director
Pesticide Programs
Division of Natural Resources Management
Dept. of Conservation and Cultural Affairs
14 F Bldg.
111 Watergut Homes
Christiansted, St. Croix
U.S. Virgin Islands 00820   809-773-0565

REGION 3
Delaware
Delaware Dept. of Agriculture
2320 S. DuPont Highway
Dover, DE 199901   302-739-4811

District of Columbia
Pesticide Section
Dept. of Consumer and Regulatory Affairs
District of Columbia
2100 Martin Luther King Dr., SE
Washington, DC 20020   202-645-6080

Maryland
Chief
Pesticide Applicators Law Section
Maryland Dept. Of Agriculture
50 Harry S. Truman Parkway
Annapolis, MD 21401   410-841-5710

Pennsylvania
Chief
Agronomic Services
Bureau of Plant Industry

PA Dept. Of Agriculture
32301 N. Cameron St.
Harrisburg, PA 17110   717-787-4843

Virginia
Supervisor
Office of Pesticide Services
VA Dept. of Agriculture and Consumer Service
P.O. Box 1163
Richmond, VA 23218   804-786-3798

West Virginia
Plant Industries Division
W VA Dept. of Agriculture
State Capitol Bldg.
1900 Kanawha Blvd. E.
Charleston, WV 25305   304-558-2212

REGION 4
Alabama
Director
Agricultural Chemistry/Plant Industry Division
Alabama Dept. of Agriculture and Industries
P.O. Box 336
Montgomery, AL 36109   334-240-7239

Florida
Pesticide Registration Section
Bureau of Pesticides
Division of Inspection
Dept. of Agriculture and consumer Services
25 Conner Blvd., MD-2
Tallahassee, FL 32399   904-487-2130

Georgia
Agricultural Manager
Entomology and Pesticides Division
Dept. of Agriculture
19 Martin Luther King Jr. Drive, SW
Atlanta, GA 30334   404-656-4958

Kentucky
Director
Division of Pesticides
Kentucky Dept. of Agriculture
100 Fair Oaks Lane, 5th Floor
Frankfort, KY 40601   502-564-7274

Mississippi
Division of Plant Industry
Dept. of Agriculture and Commerce
P.O. Box 5207
Mississippi State, MS 99762   601-325-3390

North Carolina
Administrator
Pesticides
Food and Drug Pesticide Section
Dept. of Agriculture
P.O. Box 27647
Raleigh, NC 27611   919-733-3556

South Carolina
Head
Pesticide
Dept. of Pesticide Regulation/Pest Control
256 Poole Agriculture Center
Clemson University
Clemson, SC 29634   803-656-3171

Tennessee
Director
Plant Industries Division
Dept. of Agriculture
P.O. Box 40627, Melrose Station
Nashville, TN 37204   615-360-0130

REGION 5

Illinois
Chief
Bureau of Plant and Apiary Protection
Dept. of Agriculture
State Fair Ground
P.O. Box 19281
Springfield, IL 62794   217-785-2427

Indiana
Administrator, Pesticide
Office of the State Chemist
Dept. of Biochemistry
Purdue University
West Lafayette, IN 47907   317-494-1492

Michigan
Pesticide and Plant Pest Management Division
Dept. of Agriculture
Ottawa Building
N. Tower, 4th Floor
611 W. Ottawa St.
P.O. Box 30017
Lansing, MI 48909   517-373-1087

Minnesota
Director, Division of Agronomy Services
Dept. of Agriculture
90 West Plato Blvd.
St. Paul, MN 55107   612-296-1161

Ohio
Specialist in Charge of Pesticide Regulation
Division of Plant Industry
Dept. of Agriculture
8995 East Main St.
Reynoldsburg, OH 43068   614-866-6361

Wisconsin
Director
Groundwater and Regulatory Service Section
Dept. of Agriculture
Trade and Consumer Protection
2211 Agriculture Dr.
P.O. Box 8911
Madison, WI 53708   608-266-9459

REGION 6

Arkansas
Director
Division of Feed, Fertilizer and Pesticides
Arkansas State Plant Board
#1 Natural Resources Dr.
Little Rock, AR 72205   501-225-1598

Louisiana
Office of Agricultural and Environmental Sciences
Louisiana Dept. of Agriculture
P.O. Box 3596
Baton Rouge, LA 760821   504-925-3763

New Mexico
Director
Division of Agricultural and Environmental Services
N.M. State Dept. of Agriculture
P.O. Box 3005-3AQ1
N.M. State University
Las Cruces, NM 88003   505-646-2133

Oklahoma
Chief
Pest Management Section
Plant Industry Division
Oklahoma State Dept. of Agriculture
2800 N. Lincoln Blvd.
Oklahoma City, OK 73105   405-521-3864

Texas
Director
Division of Agricultural and Environmental Sciences
Texas Dept. of Agriculture
P.O. Box 12847
Austin, TX 78711   512-463-7534

REGION 7

Iowa
Supervisor, Pesticide Control Bureau Section
Iowa Dept. of Agriculture
Henry A. Wallace Building
E. 9th St. and Grand Ave.
Des Moines, IA 50319   515-281-8591

Kansas
Director, Plant Health Division
Kansas State Board of Agriculture
109 SW 9th St.
Topeka, KS 66612   913-296-2263

Missouri
Supervisor, Bureau of Pesticide Control
Dept. of Agriculture
P.O. Box 630
Jefferson City, MO 65102   314-751-2462

Nebraska
Director
Bureau of Plant Industry
Nebraska Dept. of Agriculture
301 Centennial Mall South
Lincoln, NE 68509   402-471-2341

REGION 8

Colorado
Supervisor, Pesticide Section
Division of Plant Industry
Colorado Dept of Agriculture
700 Kipling St., Suite 4000
Lakewood, CO 80215   303-239-4140

Montana
Administrator, Agricultural Science Division
Montana Dept. of Agriculture
P.O. Box 200201
303 N. Roberts
Helena, MT 59620   406-444-2944

North Dakota
Director
Pesticide/Noxious Weed Division
N.D. Dept. of Agriculture
600 East Boulevard, 6th Floor
Bismarck, ND 58505   701-328-4756

South Dakota
Director
Division of Regulatory Services
S.D. Dept. of Agriculture
Anderson Bldg.
445 East Capitol
Pierre, SC 57501   605-773-3724

Utah
Director, Division of Plant Industries
Utah Dept. of Agriculture
350 North Redwood Rd.
Salt Lake City, UT 84116   801-538-7123

Wyoming
Manager, Pesticide Division
Wyoming Dept. of Agriculture
2219 Carey Ave.
Cheyenne, WY 82002   307-777-6590

Be patient. If any phone number is incorrect, call (area code) 555-1212 and request the new listing.

1147

Environment and Nature

REGION 9

Arizona
Director
Agricultural Chemical and Environmental Services Division
AZ Commission of Agriculture and Horticulture
1688 West Adams, Suite 103
Phoenix, AZ 85007 — 602-542-4373

California
Associate Deputy Director
Division of Pest Management
Environmental Protection and Worker Safety
California Dept. of Food and Agriculture
1220 N. St.
Sacramento, CA 95814 — 916-322-6315

Hawaii
Director, Division of Plant Industry
Hawaii Dept. of Agriculture
P.O. Box 22159
Honolulu, HI 96822 — 808-973-9530

Nevada
Director, Division of Plant Industry
Nevada Dept. of Agriculture
350 Capitol Hill Ave.
P.O. Box 11100
Reno, NV 89502 — 702-688-1180

Guam
Director
Air and Land Program Division
Guam Environmental Protection Agency
P.O. Box 2999
Agana, GU 96910

American Samoa
Director, Dept. of Agriculture
P.O. Box 366
Pago Pago, American Samoa 96799

Trust Territory of the Pacific Islands
Executive Officer, Trust Territory
Environmental Protection Board
Office of the High Commissioner
Trust Territory of the Pacific Islands
Saipan, Mariana Islands 96950

Commonwealth of the Northern Mariana Islands
Environmental Engineer
Division of Environmental Quality
Commonwealth of the Northern Mariana Island
Dr. Torres Hospital
Saipan Mariana Island 96950

REGION 10

Idaho
Chief
Bureau of Pesticides
Idaho Dept. of Agriculture
P.O. Box 790
Boise, ID 83701 — 208-334-3243

Oregon
Assistant Chief
Plant Division
Oregon Dept. of Agriculture
635 Capitol St., NE
Salem, OR 97301

Washington
Chief
Chemicals Branch
Washington Dept. of Agriculture
P.O. Box 42560
Olympia, WA 98504 — 360-902-1800

Alaska
Director Division of Environmental Health
Alaska Dept. of Environmental Conservation
P.O. Box "O"
Juneau, AK 99811 — 907-465-2609

* Superfund Cleanup Bulletin Board

Clean-Up Information Bulletin Board System (CLU-IN)
OSWER Electronic Bulletin Board, OS-110W
Environmental Protection Agency (EPA)
401 M St., SW — 301-589-8368
Washington, DC 20460 — 301-589-8366

The CLU-IN Bulletin Board offers a number of services including online messages and bulletins; computer files, programs, and databases, and Special Interest Group conference areas. The system targets those involved in hazardous waste remediation and corrective action activities, and is intended to provide an efficient mechanism for the exchange of technological information. CLU-IN is open to the public although access to several Special Interest Group areas are restricted to use by select EPA employees.

* Superfund Compensation and Liability Regulations

Environmental Protection Agency (EPA)
401 M Street SW
Washington, DC 20460 — 202-260-3046

The Superfund Docket provides public access to information supporting all regulatory decisions issued under the Comprehensive Environmental Response, Compensation, Liability Act of 1980 (CERCLA) as amended. This includes records of proceeding under the Emergency Planning and Community Right to Know Act of 1986, Title III of the Superfund Amendments and Reauthorization Act (SARA) of 1986. The Docket also includes CERCLA guidance documents and information supporting rulemaking under authority of Section 3012 of the Resource Conservation and Recovery Act.

* Superfund Hotline

Environmental Protection Agency (EPA)
401 M St., SW — 800-424-9346
Washington DC 20460 — 703-920-9810 (DC area)

This hotline answers questions concerning the Resource Conservation and Recovery Act, Superfund, and hazardous waste regulations. Requests for certain documents from the *Federal Register* and public laws are also handled in addition to referral to appropriate contacts. The hotline operates 8:30 a.m. to 7:30 p.m. (EST). A free catalogue of publications is available.

* Superfund National Priorities List Regional Docket Contacts

Nancy Smith, HSS-CAN-7
US EPA, Region 1
J.F. Kennedy Federal Bldg.
Boston, MA 02203 — 617-573-9697

Ben Conetta
US EPA, Region 2
26 Federal Plaza, Room 13-1000
New York, NY 10278 — 212-637-3152

Kurt Schenk, 3HW13
US EPA, Region 3
841 Chestnut St.
Philadelphia, PA 19107 — 215-597-6633

Deborah Vaugyn-Wright
US EPA, Region 4
345 Courtland St., NE
Atlanta, GA 30365 — 404-347-5065

Jeanne Griffin, 5HSM-TUB7
US EPA, Region 5
230 South Dearborn St.
Chicago, IL 60604 — 312-886-3007

Bill Taylor, 6H-MA
US EPA, Region 6

1445 Ross Ave.
Dallas, TX 75202   214-665-6701

Karla Ashberry
US EPA, Region 7-Library
726 Minnesota Ave.
Kansas City, KS 66101   913-551-7595

Gregory Oberley, 8HWM-SM
US EPA, Region 8
999 18th St., Suite 500
Denver, CO 80202   303-312-6931

US EPA, Region 9
1235 Mission St.
San Francisco, CA 94103   415-744-2347

David Bennett, HW-093
US EPA, Region 10
1200 Sixth Ave.
Seattle, WA 98101   206-553-2103

* Toxicology Databases and Clearinghouse

Andrew W. Briedenbach Environmental
   Research Center Library
26 W. Martin Luther King Dr.
Cincinnati, OH 45268   513-569-7703

The major subjects in this library's collection are bacteriology, biology, biotechnology, chemistry, engineering, hazardous wastes, hydrobiology, microbiology, solid waste management, toxicology, water pollution, and water quality. Databases maintained here include BRS, CAS On-line, CIS, DIALOG, Dun & Bradstreet, Hazardous Waste Database, LEXIS/NEXIS, NLM, Toxline, and Toxnet. General collections include bacteriology, biology, biotechnology, microbiology, physics, solid waste management. This library's special collections cover the environment, Canada, legal issues, hazardous waste, and solid waste.

* Toxic Substances Control Act Hotline

Environmental Protection Agency (EPA)
401 M Street SW
Washington, DC 20460   202-554-1404

The Toxic Assistance Office at Environmental Protection Agency (EPA) will answer questions and offer general and technical assistance on the Toxic Substances Control Act (TSCA). Staff will help you obtain guidance on TSCA regulations including guidance on PCBs and asbestos issues.

* Toxic Substances Non-Confidential Information

Office of Toxic Substances
Non-Confidential Information Center
401 M St., SW
Northeast Mall, Room B002
Washington, DC 20460   202-260-3944

This office's library covers chemical literature in areas of biotechnology, health, chemical industry and process technology, international chemical control, ecology, and pesticides.

* Toxic Substances Rules and Regulations

Office of Toxic Substances
Environmental Protection Agency (EPA)
401 M Street SW
Washington, DC 20460   202-260-3587

The Office of Toxic Substances (OTS) Public Information Office houses the official copies of all OTS administrative records supporting regulatory decisions promulgated under the Toxic Substances Control Act (TSCA). The Public Information Office also maintains original materials submitted by industry in compliance with TSCA regulations. The contents of the dockets vary according to the proposed regulation and the particular Section of the Act which is being promulgated. However, generally all dockets contain the following types of supporting documentation: *Federal Register* notices; various health, environmental, and exposure assessment documents; published references; communications; and test data.

* Transportation of Hazardous Materials

Office of Hazardous Materials Transportation
Research and Special Programs Administration
U.S. Department of Transportation
400 7th Street, SW
Washington, DC 20590-0001   202-366-2301

This office can provide you with information on the transportation of hazardous materials by highway, rail air, and water. Data is collected directly from industry and also via compliance inspections by field staff. The quarterly *Hazardous Material Newsletter* is available free from the office above.

* Underground Storage Tank Docket

Environmental Protection Agency (EPA)
401 M Street SW
Washington, DC 20460   703-603-9231

The Underground Storage Tank (UST) Docket provides public access to regulatory information supporting the Agency's regulatory action on USTs. As of April 1, 1987, there are seven dockets: (1) UST Notification Form; (2) Technical Standards for USTs Containing Petroleum; (3) Financial Responsibility Requirements for USTs Containing Petroleum; (4) State Program Approval; (5) Report to Congress on Exempt Tanks; (6) Consolidated Rules of Practice Governing the Administrative Assessment of Civil Penalties and Revocation or Suspension of Permits; (7) Financial Responsibility Requirements for USTs Containing Hazardous Substances; and (8) Category insurance of and administrated hearings for corrective action orders for UST.

* Underground Storage Tanks

Office of Underground Storage Tanks
Solid Waste and Emergency Response
Environmental Protection Agency (EPA)
401 M St., SW, Room 2107
Washington, DC 20460   703-603-9231

Storage tanks for volatile liquids have been buried underground to reduce the risk of fire and explosion, but leaking tanks are a major source of groundwater contamination and a great risk to human health and the environment. The Environmental Protection Agency (EPA) has issued regulations addressing leak detection, corrective action requirements, standards for new tanks, and other tank management practices. This Office can provide you with details concerning leaking tanks, as well as information regarding the cleanup required.

* Waste Reduction and Minimization Hotline

Waste Minimization Hotline, Region III
Environmental Protection Agency (EPA)
841 Chestnut St.   800-826-5320
Philadelphia, PA 19107   800-334-2467 (PA)

The Waste Minimization Hotline provides technical assistance and education on waste minimization. It provides this information for all Region III states: Washington, DC, Delaware, Maryland, Pennsylvania, Virginia, and West Virginia.

* What Helps with Oil Spills and Other Problems?

Office of Ocean Resources Conservation
   and Assessment (ORCA)
National Ocean Service
National Oceanic and Atmospheric Administration
6001 Executive Blvd.
Rockville, MD 20852   301-713-2989

As the Scientific Support Coordinator to the Coast Guard, The Office of Ocean Resources Conservation and Assessment (ORCA) provides critical information on spill trajectory projections, chemical hazard analyses, and assessment of marine and estuarine sensitivity to spills. ORCA's Hazardous Materials (HAZMAT) Response Program responds to about 100 oil spills a year. The program provides similar support to the EPA's Superfund Program during emergency responses at, and for the cleanup of, abandoned hazardous waste sites in coastal areas. The program has implemented the CAMEO (Computer-Aided Management of Emergency Operations) program designed to help emergency planners and first responders safely handle chemical accidents. CAMEO currently is being used by over 3,000 fire departments.

Freedom of Information Act
Government Records and Privacy

A Citizen's Guide on Using the Freedom of Information Act and
the Privacy Act of 1974 to Request Government Records

Introduction

A popular Government without popular information or the means of acquiring it, is but a Prologue to a Farce or a Tragedy or perhaps both. Knowledge will forever govern ignorance, and a people who mean to be their Governors, must arm themselves with the power knowledge gives. — James Madison

The Freedom of Information Act (FOIA) established a presumption that records in the possession of agencies and departments of the Executive Branch of the United States government are accessible to the people. This was not always the approach to federal information disclosure policy. Before enactment of the Freedom of Information Act in 1966, the burden was on the individual to establish a right to examine these government records. There were no statutory guidelines or procedures to help a person seeking information. There were no judicial remedies for those denied access.

With the passage of the FOIA, the burden of proof shifted from the individual to the government. Those seeking information are no longer required to show a need for information. Instead, the "need to know" standard has been replaced by a "right to know" doctrine. The government now has to justify the need for secrecy.

The FOIA sets standards for determining which records must be made available for public inspection and which records can be withheld from disclosure. The law also provides administrative and judicial remedies for those denied access to records. Above all, the statute requires federal agencies to provide the fullest possible disclosure of information to the public.

The Privacy Act of 1974 is a companion to the FOIA, and serves to regulate federal government agency recordkeeping and disclosure practices. The Act allows most individuals to seek access to federal agency records about themselves. The Act requires that personal information in agency files be accurate, complete, relevant, and timely. The Act allows the subject of a record to challenge the accuracy of the information. The Act requires that agencies obtain information directly from the subject of the record and that information gathered for one purpose not be used for another purpose. As with the FOIA, the Privacy Act provides civil remedies for individuals whose rights have been violated.

Another important feature of the Privacy Act is the requirement that each federal agency publish a description of each system of records maintained by the agency that contains personal information. This prevents agencies from keeping secret records.

The Privacy Act also restricts the disclosure of personally identifiable information by federal agencies. Together with the FOIA, the Privacy Act permits disclosure of most personal files to the individual who is the subject of the files. The two laws restrict disclosure of personal information to others when disclosure would violate privacy interests.

While both the FOIA and the Privacy Act encourage the disclosure of agency records, both laws also recognize the legitimate need to restrict disclosure of some information. For example, agencies may withhold information classified in the interest of national defense or foreign policy, trade secrets, and criminal investigatory files. Other specifically defined categories of confidential information may also be withheld.

The essential feature of both laws is that they make federal agencies accountable for information disclosure policies and practices. While neither law grants an absolute right to examine government documents, both laws provide a right to request records and to receive a response to the request. If a requested record cannot be released, the requester is entitled to a reason for the denial. The requester has a right to appeal the denial and, if necessary, to challenge it in court.

These procedural rights granted by the FOIA and the Privacy Act make the laws valuable and workable. The disclosure of government information cannot be controlled by arbitrary or unreviewable actions.

Which Act to Use

The access provisions of the FOIA and the Privacy Act overlap in part. The two laws have different procedures and different exemptions. As a result, sometimes information exempt under one law will be disclosable under the other.

In order to take maximum advantage of the laws, an individual seeking information about himself or herself should normally cite both laws. Requests by an individual for information that does not relate solely to himself or herself should be made under the FOIA.

Congress intended that the two laws be considered together in the processing of requests for information. Many government agencies will automatically handle requests from individuals in a way that will maximize the amount of information that is disclosable. However, a requester should still make a request in a manner that is most advantageous and that fully protects all available legal rights. A requester who has any doubts about which law to use should always cite both the FOIA and the Privacy Act when seeking documents from the federal government.

The Scope of the Freedom of Information Act

The federal Freedom of Information Act applies to documents held by agencies in the executive branch of the federal Government. The executive branch includes cabinet departments, military departments, government corporations, government controlled corporations, independent regulatory agencies, and other establishments of the executive branch.

The FOIA does not apply to elected officials of the federal government, including the President, Vice President, Senators, and Congressmen, or the federal judiciary. The FOIA also does not apply to private companies; persons who received federal contracts or grants; tax-exempt organizations; or state or local governments.

All states and some localities have passed laws like the FOIA that allow people to request access to records. In addition, there are other federal and state laws that may permit access to documents held by organizations not covered by the FOIA.

What Records Can Be Requested Under FOIA?

The FOIA requires agencies to publish or make available some types of information. This includes: (1) Description of agency organization and office addresses; (2) statements of the general course and method of agency operation; (3) rules of procedure and descriptions of forms; (4) substantive rules of general applicability and general policy statements; (5) final opinions made in the adjudication of cases; and (6) administrative staff manuals that affect the public. This information must either be published or made available for inspection and copying without the formality of an FOIA request.

All other "agency records" may be requested under the FOIA. However, the FOIA does not define "agency record." Material that is in the possession, custody, or control of an agency is usually considered to be an agency record under the FOIA. Personal notes of agency employees may not be agency records. A record that is not an "agency record" will not be available under the FOIA.

The form in which a record is maintained by an agency does not affect its availability. A request may seek a printed or typed document, tape recording, map, computer printout, computer tape, or a similar item.

Of course, not all records that can be requested must be disclosed. Information that is exempt from disclosure is described below in the section entitled "Reasons Access May Be Denied Under the FOIA."

The FOIA carefully provides that a requester may ask for records rather than information. This means that an agency is only required to look for an existing record or document in response to an FOIA request. An agency is not obliged to create a new record to comply with a request. An agency is not required to collect information it does not have. Nor must an agency do research or analyze data for a requester.

Requesters may ask for existing records. Requests may have to be carefully written in order to obtain the information that is desired. Sometimes, agencies will help a requester identify the specific document that contains the information being sought. Other times, a requester may need to be creative when writing an FOIA request in order to identify an existing document or set of documents containing the desired information.

There is a second general limitation on FOIA request. The law requires that each request must reasonably describe the records being sought. This means that a request must be specific enough to permit a professional employee of the agency who is familiar with the subject matter to locate the record in a reasonable period of time.

Because different agencies organize and index records in different ways, one agency may consider a request to be reasonably descriptive while another agency may reject a similar request as too vague. For example, the Federal Bureau of Investigation has a central index for its primary record system. As a result, the FBI is able to search for records about a specific person. However, agencies that do not maintain a central name index may be unable to conduct the same type of search. These agencies may reject a similar request because the request does not describe records that can be identified.

Requesters should make their requests as specific as possible. If a particular document is required, it should be identified as precisely as possible, preferably by date and title. However, a request does not have to be that specific. A requester who cannot identify a specific record should clearly explain his or her needs. A requester should make sure, however, that the request is broad enough to cover the information that is needed.

For example, assume that a requester wants to obtain a list of toxic sites near his home. A request to the Environmental Protection Agency for all records on toxic waste would cover many more records than are needed. The fees for such a request might be very high, and it is possible that the request might be rejected as too vague.

A request for all toxic waste sites within three miles of a particular address is very specific. But is unlikely that EPA would have an existing record containing data organized in that fashion. As a result, the request might be denied because there is no existing record containing the information.

The requester might do better to ask for a list of toxic waste sites in his city, county, or state. It is more likely that existing records might contain this information. The requester might also want to tell the agency in the request letter exactly what information is desired. The additional explanation will help the agency to find a record that meets the request.

Many people include their telephone number in their requests. Sometimes questions about the scope of a request can be resolved quickly when the agency employee and the requester talk. This is an efficient way to resolve questions that arise during the processing of FOIA requests.

It is to everyone's advantage if requests are as precise and as narrow as possible. The requester benefits because the request can be processed faster and cheaper. The agency benefits because it can do a better job of responding to the request. The agency will

Freedom of Information Act

also be able to use its scarce resources to respond to more requests. The FOIA works best when both the requester and the agency act cooperatively.

Making an FOIA Request

The first step in making a request under the FOIA is to identify the agency that has the records. An FOIA request must be addressed to a specific agency. There is no central government records office that services FOIA requests.

Often, a requester knows beforehand which agency has the desired records. If not, a requester can consult a government directory such as the *United States Government Manual*. This manual has a complete list of all the federal agencies, a description of agency functions, and the address of each agency. A requester who is uncertain about which agency has the records that are needed can make FOIA requests at more than one agency.

All agencies normally require that FOIA requests be in writing. Letters requesting records under the FOIA can be short and simple. No one needs a lawyer to make an FOIA request. The Appendix to this section contains a sample request letter.

The request letter should be addressed to an agency's FOIA officer or to the head of the agency. The envelope containing the written request should be marked "Freedom of Information Act Request" in the bottom left-hand corner.

There are three basic elements to an FOIA request letter. First, the letter should state that the request is being made under the Freedom of Information Act. Second, the request should identify the records that are being sought as specifically as possible. Third, the name and address of the requester must be included.

In addition, under the 1986 amendments to the FOIA, the fees chargeable vary with the status or purpose of the requester. As a result, requesters may have to provide additional information to permit the agency to determine the appropriate fees. Different fees can be charged to commercial users, representatives of the news media, educational and non-commercial scientific institutions, and individuals. The next section explains the new fee structure in more detail.

There are several optional items that are often included in an FOIA request. The first is the telephone number of the requester. This permits an agency employee processing a request to talk to the requester if necessary.

A second optional item is a limitation on the fees that the requester is willing to pay. It is common for requesters to ask to be contacted if the charges will exceed a fixed amount. This allows a requester to modify or withdraw a request if the cost is too high.

A third optional item sometimes included in an FOIA request is a request for waiver or reduction of fees. The 1986 amendments waived or reduced the rules for fee waivers. Fees must be waived or reduced if disclosure of the information is in the public interest because it is likely to contribute significantly to public understanding of the operations or activities of the government and is not primarily in the commercial interest of the request. Decisions about granting fee waivers are separate from and

different from decisions about the amount of fees that can be charged to requesters.

Requesters should keep a copy of their request letter and related correspondence until the request has been fully resolved.

Fees and Fee Waivers

FOIA requesters may have to pay fees covering some or all of the costs of processing their request. As amended in 1986, the law establishes three types of charges that may be imposed on requesters. The 1986 law makes the process of determining the applicable fees more complicated. However, the new rules reduce or eliminate entirely the cost for small, non-commercial requests.

First, fees can be imposed to recover the costs of copying documents. All agencies have a fixed price for making copies using copying machines. Requesters are usually charged the actual cost of copying computer tapes, photographs, or other nonstandard documents.

Second, fees can also be imposed to recover the costs of searching for documents. This includes the time spent looking for material responsive to a request. Requesters can minimize search charges by making clear, narrow requests for identifiable documents whenever possible.

Third, fees can be charged to recover review costs. Review is the process of examining documents to determine whether any portion is exempt from disclosure. Before the effective date of the 1986 amendments, no review charges were imposed on any requester. Effective April 25, 1987, review charges may be imposed on commercial requesters only. Review charges only include costs incurred during the initial examination of a document. An agency may not charge for any costs incurred in resolving issues of law or policy that may arise while processing a request.

Different fees apply to different categories of requesters. There are three basic groups of FOIA requesters. The first includes representatives of the news media, and educational or noncommercial scientific institutions whose purpose is scholarly or scientific research. Requesters in this category who are not seeking records for commercial use can only be billed for reasonable standard document duplication charges. A request for information from a representative of the news media is not considered to be for commercial use if the request is in support of a news gathering or dissemination function.

The second group includes FOIA requesters seeking records for commercial use. Commercial use is not defined in the law, but generally includes profit making activities. Commercial users pay reasonable standard charges for document duplication, search, and review.

The third group of FOIA requesters includes everyone not included in either of the first two groups. People seeking information for their own use, public interest groups, and non-profit organizations are examples of requesters who fall into the third group. Charges for these requests are limited to reasonable standard charges for document duplication and search. No review charges may be imposed. The 1986 amendments did not change the fees charged to these requesters.

Be patient. If any phone number is incorrect, call (area code) 555-1212 and request the new listing.

Small requests are free to requesters in the first and third groups. This includes all requesters except commercial users. There is no charge for the first two hours of search time and the first 100 pages of documents. Noncommercial requesters who limit their requests to a small number of easily found records will not pay any fees.

In addition, the law also prevents agencies from charging fees if the cost of collecting the fee would exceed the amount collected. This limitation applies to all requests, including those seeking documents for commercial use. Thus, if the allowable charges for any FOIA request are small, no fees are imposed.

Each agency sets charges for duplication, search, and review based on its own costs. The amount of these charges is included in the agency FOIA regulations. Each agency also sets its own threshold for minimum charges.

The 1986 FOIA amendments changed the law on fee waivers. The new rules require that fees must be waived or reduced if disclosure of the information is in the public interest because it is likely to contribute significantly to public understanding of the operations or activities of the government and is not primarily in the commercial interest of the requester.

The new rules for fees and fee waivers have created some confusion. Determinations about fees are separate and apart from determinations about eligibility for fee waivers. For example, a news reporter may only be charged duplication fees and may ask that the duplication fees be waived. There is no need for a reporter to ask for a waiver of search and review costs because search and review costs are not charged to reporters.

Only after a requester has been categorized to determine applicable fees does the issue of a fee waiver arise. A requester who seeks a fee waiver should include a separate request in the original request letter. The requester should describe how disclosure will contribute to the public understanding of the operations or activities of the government. The sample request letter in the Appendix includes optional language asking for a fee waiver.

Any requester may ask for a fee waiver. Some will find it easier to qualify than others. A news reporter who is charged only duplication costs may still ask that the charges be waived because of the public benefits that will result from disclosure. Representatives of the news media and public interest groups are very likely to qualify for a waiver of fees. Commercial users will find it more difficult to qualify.

The eligibility of other requesters will vary. A key element in qualifying for a fee waiver is the relationship of the information to public understanding of the operations or activities of government. Another important factor is the ability of the requester to convey that information to other interested members of the public. A requester is not eligible for a fee waiver solely because of indigence.

Requirements for Agency Responses

Each agency is required to determine within ten days (excluding Saturdays, Sundays, and legal holidays) after the receipt of a request whether to comply with the request. The actual disclosure of documents is required to follow promptly thereafter. If a request for records is denied in whole or in part, the agency must tell the requester the reasons for the denial. The agency must also tell the requester that there is a right to appeal any adverse determination to the head of the agency.

The FOIA permits agencies to extend the time limits up to ten days in unusual circumstances. These circumstances include the need to collect records from remote locations, review large numbers of records, and consult with other agencies. Agencies are supposed to notify the requester whenever an extension is invoked.

The statutory time limits for responses are not always met. Agencies sometimes receive an unexpectedly large number of FOIA requests at one time and are unable to meet the deadlines. Some agencies assign inadequate resources to FOIA offices. The Congress does not condone the failure of any agency to meet the law's limits. However, as a practical matter, there is little that a requester can do about it. The courts have been reluctant to provide relief solely because the FOIA's time limits have not been met.

The best advice to requesters is to be patient. The law allows a requester to consider a request to be denied if it has not been decided within the time limits. This permits the requester to file an administrative appeal. However, this is not always the best course of action. The filing of an administrative or judicial appeal does not normally result in any faster processing of the request.

Agencies generally process requests in the order in which they were received. Some agencies will expedite the processing of urgent requests. Anyone with a pressing need for records should consult with the agency FOIA officer about how to ask for expedited treatment of requests.

Reasons Access May Be Denied Under the FOIA

An agency may refuse to disclose an agency record that falls within any of the FOIA's nine statutory exemptions. The exemptions protect against the disclosure of information that would harm national defense or foreign policy, privacy of individuals, proprietary interests of business, functioning of government, and other important interests.

A record that does not qualify as an "agency record" may be denied because only agency records are available under the FOIA. Personal notes of agency employees may be denied on this basis.

An agency may withhold exempt information, but it is not always required to do so. For example, an agency may disclose an exempt internal memorandum because no harm would result from its disclosure. However, an agency is not likely to agree to disclose an exempt document that is classified or that contains a trade secret.

When a record contains some information that qualifies as exempt, the entire record is not necessarily exempt. Instead, the FOIA specifically provides that any reasonably segregable portions of a record must be provided to a requester after the deletion of the portions that are exempt. This is a very important

Freedom of Information Act

requirement because it prevents an agency from withholding an entire document simply because one line or one page is exempt.

Exemption 1: Classified Documents

The first FOIA exemption permits the withholding of properly classified documents. Information may be classified to protect it in the interest of national defense or foreign policy. Information that has been classified as "Confidential," "Secret," or "Top Secret" under the procedures of the Executive Order on Security Classification can qualify under the first exemption.

The rules for classification are established by the President and not the FOIA or other law. The FOIA provides that, if a document has been properly classified under the President's rules, the document can be withheld from disclosure.

Classified documents may be requested under the FOIA. An agency can review the document to determine if it still requires protection. In addition, the Executive Order on Security Classification establishes a special procedure for requesting the declassification of documents. If a requested document is declassified, it can be released in response to an FOIA request. However, a document that was formerly classified may still be exempt under other FOIA exemptions.

Exemption 2: Internal Personnel Rules and Practices

The second FOIA exemption covers matters that are related solely to an agency's internal personnel rules and practices. As interpreted by the courts, there are two separate classes of documents that are generally held to fall within exemption two.

First, information relating to personnel rules or internal agency practices is exempt if it is a trivial administrative matter of no genuine public interest. A rule governing lunch hours for agency employees is an example.

Second, internal administrative manuals can be exempt if disclosure would risk circumvention of law or agency regulations. In order to fall into this category, the material will normally have to regulate internal agency conduct rather than public behavior.

Exemption 3: Information Exempt Under Other Laws

The third exemption incorporates into the FOIA other laws that restrict the availability of information. To qualify under exemption three, a statute must require that matters be withheld from the public in such a manner as to leave no discretion to the agency. Alternatively, the statute must establish particular criteria for withholding or refer to particular types of matters to be withheld.

One example of a qualifying statute is the provision of the Tax Code prohibiting the public disclosure of tax returns and tax law designating identifiable census data as confidential. Whether a particular statute qualifies under Exemption 3 can be a difficult legal determination.

Exemption 4: Confidential Business Information

The fourth exemption protects from public disclosure two types of information: trade secrets and confidential business information. A trade secret is a commercially valuable plan, formula, process, or device. This is a narrow category of information. An example of a trade secret is the recipe for a commercial food product.

The second type of protected data is commercial or financial information obtained from a person and privileged or confidential. The courts have held that data qualifies for withholding if disclosure by the government would be likely to harm the competitive position of the person who submitted the information. Detailed information on a company's marketing plans, profits, or costs can qualify as confidential business information. Information may also be withheld if disclosure would be likely to impair the government's ability to obtain similar information in the future.

Only information obtained from a person other than a government agency qualifies under the fourth exemption. A person is an individual, a partnership, or a corporation. Information that an agency created on its own cannot normally be withheld under Exemption 4.

Although there is no formal requirement under the FOIA, many agencies will notify a submitter of business information that disclosure of the information is being considered. The submitter can file suit to block disclosure under the FOIA. Such lawsuits are generally referred to as "reverse" FOIA lawsuits because the FOIA is being used in an attempt to prevent rather than to require disclosure of information. A reverse FOIA lawsuit may be filed when a submitter of documents and the government disagree whether the information is confidential.

Exemption 5: Internal Government Communications

The FOIA's Exemption 5 applies to internal government documents. One example is a letter from one government department to another about a joint decision that has not yet been made. Another example is a memorandum from an agency employee to his supervisor describing options for conducting the agency's business.

The purpose of the exemption is to safeguard the deliberative policymaking processes of government. The exemption encourages frank discussions of policy matters between agency officials by allowing supporting documents to be withheld from public disclosure. The exemption also protects against premature disclosure of policies before final adoption.

While the policy behind the fifth exemption is well accepted, the application of the exemption is complicated. Exemption 5 may be the most difficult FOIA exemption to understand and apply. For example, the exemption protects the policymaking process, but it does not protect purely factual information related to the policy process. Factual information must be disclosed unless it is inextricably intertwined with protected information about an agency decision.

Protection for the decision making process is appropriate only for the period while decisions are being made. Thus, the Exemption 5 has been held to distinguish between documents that are pre-decisional and therefore may be protected, and those which are post-decisional and therefore not subject to protection. Once a policy is adopted, the public has a greater interest in knowing the basis for the decision.

Be patient. If any phone number is incorrect, call (area code) 555-1212 and request the new listing.

The exemption also incorporates some of the privileges that apply in litigation involving the government. For example, papers prepared by the government's lawyers are exempt in the same way that papers prepared by private lawyers for clients are not available through discovery in civil litigation.

Exemption 6: Personal Privacy

Exemption 6 covers personnel, medical, and similar files the disclosure of which would constitute a clearly unwarranted invasion of personal privacy. This exemption protects the privacy interests of individuals by allowing an agency to withhold from disclosure intimate personal data kept in government files. Only individuals have privacy interests. Corporations and other legal persons have no privacy rights under the sixth exemption.

The exemption requires agencies to strike a balance between an individual's privacy interests and the public's right to know. However, since only a clearly unwarranted invasion of privacy is a basis for withholding, there is a perceptible tilt in favor of disclosure in the exemption. Nevertheless, the sixth exemption makes it hard to obtain information about another individual without the consent of the individual.

The Privacy Act of 1974 also regulates the disclosure of personal information about individuals. The FOIA and the Privacy Act overlap in part, but there is no inconsistency. Individuals seeking records about themselves should cite both laws when making a request. This ensures that the maximum amount of disclosable information will be released. Records that can be denied to an individual under the Privacy Act are not necessarily exempt under the FOIA.

Exemption 7: Law Enforcement

Exemption 7 allows agencies to withhold law enforcement records in order to protect the law enforcement process from interference. The exemption was amended slightly in 1986, but it still retains six specific subexemptions.

Exemption (7)(A) allows the withholding of law enforcement records that could reasonably be expected to interfere with enforcement proceedings. This exemption protects active law enforcement investigations from interference through premature disclosure.

Exemption (7)(B) allows the withholding of information that would deprive a person of the right to a fair trial or an impartial adjudication. This exemption is rarely used.

Exemption (7)(C) recognizes that individuals have a privacy interest in information maintained in law enforcement files. If the disclosure of information could reasonably be expected to constitute an unwarranted invasion of personal privacy, the information is exempt from disclosure. The standards for privacy protection in Exemption 6 and Exemption (7)(C) differ slightly. Exemption (7)(C) refers only to unwarranted invasions of personal privacy rather than to clearly unwarranted invasions.

Exemption (7)(D) protects the identity of confidential sources. Information that could reasonably be expected to reveal the identity of a confidential source is exempt. A confidential source can include a state, local, or foreign agency or authority, or a private institution that furnished information on a confidential basis. In addition, the exemption protects information furnished by a confidential source if the data was compiled by a criminal law enforcement authority during a criminal investigation or by an agency conducting a lawful national security intelligence investigation.

Exemption (7)(E) protects from disclosure information that would reveal techniques and procedures for law enforcement investigations or prosecutions or that would disclose guidelines for law enforcement investigations or prosecutions if disclosure of the information could reasonably be expected to risk circumvention of the law.

Exemption (7)(F) protects law enforcement information that could reasonably be expected to endanger the life or physical safety of any individual.

Exemption 8: Financial Institutions

Exemption 8 protects information that is contained in or related to examination, operating, or condition reports prepared by or for a bank supervisory agency such as the Federal Deposit Insurance Corporation, or the Federal Reserve, or similar agencies.

Exemption 9: Geological Information

Exemption 9 covers geological and geophysical information, data, and maps about wells. This exemption is rarely used.

FOIA Exclusions

The 1986 amendments to the FOIA gave limited authority to agencies to respond to a request without confirming the existence of the requested records. Ordinarily, any proper request must receive an answer stating whether there is any responsive information, even if the requested information is exempt from disclosure.

In some narrow circumstances, acknowledgement of the existence of a record can produce consequences similar to those resulting from disclosure of the record itself. In order to avoid this type of problem, the 1986 amendments established three "record exclusions." However, these exclusions do not broaden the ability of agencies to withhold documents.

The exclusions allow agencies to treat certain exempt records as if the records were not subject to the FOIA. Agencies are not required to confirm the existence of three specific categories of records. If those records are requested, agencies may state that there are no disclosable records responsive to the request. However, these exclusions give agencies no authority to withhold additional categories of information from the public.

The first exclusion is triggered when a request seeks information that is exempt because disclosure could reasonably be expected to interfere with a current law enforcement investigation. There are specific prerequisites for the application of this exclusion. First, the investigation in question must involve a possible violation of criminal law. Second, there must be a reason to believe that the subject of the investigation is not already aware that the investigation is underway. Third, disclosure of the existence of the records — as distinguished from contents of the records — could reasonably be expected to interfere with enforcement proceedings.

When all three of these conditions are present, an agency may respond to an FOIA request for investigatory records as if the records are not subject to the requirements of the FOIA. In other words, the agency's response does not have to reveal that it is conducting an investigation.

The second exclusion applies to informant records maintained by a criminal law enforcement agency under the informant's name or personal identifier. The agency is not required to confirm the existence of these records unless the informant's status has been officially confirmed. This exclusion helps agencies to protect the identity of confidential informants. Information that might identify informants has always been exempt under the FOIA.

The third exclusion applies only to records maintained by the Federal Bureau of Investigation which pertain to foreign intelligence, counterintelligence, or international terrorism. When the existence of those type of records is classified, the FBI may treat the records as not subject to the requirements of FOIA.

This exclusion does not apply to all classified records on the specific subjects. It only applies when the records are classified and when the existence of the records is also classified. Since the underlying records must be classified before the exclusion is relevant, agencies have no new substantive withholding authority.

In enacting these exclusions, congressional sponsors stated that it was their intent that agencies must inform FOIA requesters that these exclusions are available for agency use. Requesters who believe that records were improperly withheld because of the exclusions can seek judicial review.

Administrative Appeal Procedures

Whenever an FOIA request is denied, the agency must inform the requester of the reasons for the denial and the requester's right to appeal the denial to the head of the agency. A requester may appeal the denial of a request for a document or for fee waiver. A requester may contest the type or amount of fees that were charged. A requester may appeal any other adverse determination including a rejection of a request for failure to describe adequately the documents being requested. A requester can also appeal because the agency failed to conduct an adequate search for the documents that were requested.

A person whose request was granted in part and denied in part may appeal the partial denial. If an agency has agreed to disclose some but not all of the requested documents, the filing of an appeal does not affect the release of the documents that are disclosable. There is no risk to the requester in filing an appeal.

The appeal to the head of an agency is a simple administrative appeal. A lawyer can be helpful, but no one must have a lawyer to file an appeal. Anyone who can write a letter can file an appeal. Appeals to the head of the agency often result in the disclosure of some records that have been withheld. A requester who is not convinced that the agency's initial decision is correct should appeal. There is no charge for filing an appeal.

An appeal is filed by sending a letter to the head of the agency. The letter must identify the FOIA request that is being appealed. The envelope containing the letter of appeal should be marked in the lower left hand corner with the words "Freedom of Information Act Appeal."

Many agencies assign a number to all FOIA requests that are received. The number should be included in the appeal letter, along with the name and address of the requester. It is a common practice to include a copy of the agency's initial decision letter as part of the appeal, but this it not required. It can also be helpful for the requester to include a telephone number in the appeal letter to insure a faster response.

An appeal will normally include the requester's arguments supporting disclosure of the documents. A requester may include any facts or any arguments supporting the case for reversing the initial decision. However, an appeal letter does not have to contain any arguments at all. It is sufficient to state that the agency's initial decision is being appealed. The Appendix to this section includes a sample appeal letter.

The FOIA does not set a time limit for filing an administrative appeal of an FOIA denial. However, it is good practice to file an appeal promptly. Some agency regulations establish a time limit for filing an administrative appeal. A requester whose appeal is rejected by an agency because it is too late may refile the original FOIA request and start the process again.

A requester who delays filing an appeal runs the risk that the documents could be destroyed. However, as long as an agency is considering a request or an appeal, the agency must preserve the documents.

An agency is required to make a decision on an appeal within twenty days (excluding Saturdays, Sundays, and federal holidays). It is possible for an agency to extend the time limits by an additional ten days. Once the time period has elapsed, a requester may consider a that the appeal has been denied and may proceed with a judicial appeal. However, unless there is an urgent need for records, this is not always the best course of action. The courts are not sympathetic to appeals based solely on an agency's failure to comply with the FOIA's time limits.

Filing a Judicial Appeal

When an administrative appeal is denied, a requester has the right to appeal the denial in court. An FOIA appeal can be filed in the United States District Court in the district where the requester lives. The requester can also file suit in the district where the documents are located or in the District of Columbia. When a requester goes to court, the burden of justifying the withholding of documents is on the government. This is a distinct advantage for the requester.

Requesters are sometimes successful when they go to court, but the results vary considerably. Some requesters who file judicial appeals find that an agency will disclose some documents previously withheld rather than fight about disclosure in court. This does not always happen, and there is no guarantee that the filing of a judicial appeal will result in any additional disclosure.

Most requesters require the assistance of an attorney to file a judicial appeal. A person who files a lawsuit and substantially prevails may be awarded reasonable attorney fees and litigation costs reasonably incurred. Some requesters may be able to handle their own appeal without an attorney. Since this is not a litigation guide, details of the judicial appeal process have not been included. Anyone considering filing an appeal can begin by reviewing the provisions of the FOIA on judicial review.

The Privacy Act of 1974

The Privacy Act of 1974 provides safeguards against an invasion of privacy through the misuse of records by federal agencies. In general, the Act allows citizens to learn how records are collected, maintained, used, and disseminated by the federal government. The Act also permits individuals to gain access to most personal information maintained by federal agencies and to seek amendment of any incorrect or incomplete information.

The Privacy Act applies to personal information maintained by agencies in the executive branch of the federal government. The executive branch includes cabinet departments, military departments, government corporations, government controlled corporations, independent regulatory agencies, and other establishments in the executive branch. Agencies subject to the Freedom of Information Act (FOIA) are also subject to the Privacy Act. The Privacy Act does not generally apply to records maintained by state and local governments or private companies or organizations.

The Privacy Act grants rights only to United States citizens and to aliens lawfully admitted for permanent residence. As a result, foreign nationals cannot use the Act's provisions. However, foreigners may use the FOIA to request records about themselves.

The only records subject to the Privacy Act are records about individuals that are maintained in a system of records. The idea of a "system of records" is unique to the Privacy Act and requires explanation.

The Act defines a "record" to include most personal information maintained by an agency about an individual. A record contains information about education, financial transactions, medical history, criminal history, or employment history. A system of records is a group of records from which information is actually retrieved by name, social security number, or other identifying symbol assigned to an individual.

Some personal information is not kept in a system of records. This information is not subject to the provisions of the Privacy Act, although access may be requested under the FOIA. Most personal information in government files is subject to the Privacy Act.

The Privacy Act also establishes general records management requirements for federal agencies. In summary, there are five basic requirements that are more relevant to individuals.

First, agencies must establish procedures allowing individuals to see and copy records about themselves. An individual may also seek to amend any information that is not accurate, relevant, timely, or complete. The rights to inspect and to correct records

are the most important provisions of the Privacy Act. This section explains in more detail how an individual can exercise these rights.

Second, agencies must publish notices describing all systems of records. The notices include a complete description of personal-data recordkeeping policies, practices, and systems. This requirement prevents the maintenance of secret record systems.

Third, agencies must make reasonable efforts to maintain accurate, relevant, timely, and complete records about individuals. Agencies are prohibited from maintaining information about how individuals exercise rights guaranteed by the First Amendment to the U.S. Constitution unless maintenance of the information is specifically authorized by statute or relates to authorized law enforcement activity.

Fourth, the Act establishes rules governing the use and disclosure of personal information. The Act specifies that information collected for one purpose may not be used for another purpose without notice to or the consent of the subject of the record. The Act also requires that agencies keep a record of some disclosures of personal information.

Fifth, the Act provides legal remedies that permit individuals to seek enforcement of rights under the Act. In addition, there are criminal penalties that apply to federal employees who fail to comply with the Act's provisions.

Locating Records

There is no central index of federal government records. An individual who wants to inspect records about himself or herself must first identify which agency has the records. Often, this will not be difficult. For example, an individual who was employed by the federal government knows that the employing agency or the Office of Personnel Management maintains personnel files.

Similarly, an individual who receives veterans' benefits will normally find the related records at the Veterans Administration or at the Defense Department. Tax records are maintained by the Internal Revenue Service, social security records by the Social Security Administration, passport records by the State Department, etc.

For those who are uncertain about which agency has the records that are needed, there are several sources of information. First, an individual can ask an agency that might maintain the records. If that agency does not have the records, it may be able to identify the proper agency.

Second, a government directory such as the *United States Government Manual* contains a complete list of all federal agencies, a description of agency functions, and the address of the agency and its field offices. An agency responsible for operating a program normally maintains the records related to that program.

Third, a Federal Information Center can help to identify government agencies, their functions, and their records. These centers, which are operated by the General Services Administration, serve as clearinghouses for information about the federal government. There are several dozen Federal Information Centers throughout the country.

Be patient. If any phone number is incorrect, call (area code) 555-1212 and request the new listing.

1157

Fourth, the Office of Federal Register publishes an annual compilation of system of records notices for all agencies. These notices contain a complete description of each record system maintained by each agency. The compilation — which is published in five large volumes — is the most complete reference for information about federal agency personal information practices. The information that appears in the compilation is also published occasionally in the *Federal Register*.

The compilation — formally called Privacy Act Issuance — may be difficult to find. Copies will be available in some federal depository libraries and possibly in other libraries as well. Although the compilation is the best single source of detailed information about personal records maintained by the federal agencies, it is not necessary to consult the compilation before making a Privacy Act request.

A requester is not required to identify the specific system of records that contains the information being sought. It is sufficient to identify the agency that has the records. Using information provided by the requester, the agency will determine which system of records has the files that have been requested.

Those who request records under the Privacy Act can help the agency by identifying the type of records being sought. Large agencies maintain dozens or even hundreds of different record systems. A request is processed faster if the requester tells the agency that he or she was employed by the agency, was the recipient of benefits under an agency program, or had other specific contacts with the agency.

Making a Privacy Act Request for Access

The fastest way to make a Privacy Act request is to identify the specific system of records. The request can be addressed to the system manager. Few people do this. Instead, most people address their requests to the head of the agency that has the records or the agency's Privacy Act Officer. The envelope containing the written request should be marked "Privacy Act Request" in the bottom left-hand corner.

There are three basic elements to a request for records under the Privacy Act. First, the letter should state that the request is being made under the Privacy Act. Second, the letter should include the name, address, and signature of the requester. Third, the request should describe as specifically as possible the records that are wanted. The Appendix to this section includes a sample Privacy Act request letter. It is a common practice for an individual seeking records about himself or herself to make the request both under the Privacy Act of 1974 and the Freedom of Information Act. See the discussion in the front of this section concerning which act to use.

A requester can describe the records by identifying a specific system of records, by describing his or her contacts with an agency, or by simply asking for all records about himself or herself. The broader and less specific a request is, the longer it may take for an agency to respond.

It is a good practice for a requester to describe the type of records that he or she expects to find. For example, an individual seeking a copy of his service record in the Army should state he was in the Army and include the approximate dates of service. This will help the Defense Department narrow its search to record systems that are likely to contain the information being sought. An individual seeking records from the Federal Bureau of Investigation may ask that files in specific field offices be searched in addition to the FBI's central office files. The FBI dose not routinely search field office records without a specific request.

Agencies generally require requesters to provide some proof of identity before records will be disclosed. Agencies may have different requirements. Some agencies will accept a signature; others may require a notarized signature. If an individual goes to the agency to inspect records, standard personal identification may be acceptable. More stringent requirements may apply if the records being sought are especially sensitive.

Agencies will inform requesters of special identification requirements. Requesters who need records quickly should first consult regulations or talk to the agency's Privacy Act Officer to find out how to provide adequate identification.

An individual who visits an agency office to inspect a Privacy Act record may wish to bring along a friend or relative to review the record. When a requester brings another person, the agency may ask the requester to sign a written statement authorizing discussion of the record in the presence of that person.

It is a crime to knowingly and willfully request or obtain records under the Privacy Act under false pretenses. A request for access under the Privacy Act can be made only by the subject of the record. An individual cannot make a request under the Privacy Act for a record about another person. The only exception is for a parent or legal guardian who can request records for a minor or a person who has been declared incompetent.

Fees

Under the Privacy Act, fees can be charged only for the cost of conveying records. No fees may be charged for the time it takes to search for the records or the time it takes to review the records to determine if any exemptions apply. This is a major difference from the FOIA. Under the FOIA, fees can sometimes be charged to recover search costs and review costs. The different fee structure in the two laws is one reason many requesters seeking records about themselves cite both laws. This minimizes allowable fees.

Many agencies will not charge fees for making copies of files under the Privacy Act, especially when the files are small. If paying the copying charges is a problem, the requester should explain in the request letter. An agency can waive fees under the Privacy Act.

Requirements for Agency Responses

Unlike FOIA, there is no fixed time when an agency must respond to a request for access to records under the Privacy Act. It is good practice for an agency to acknowledge receipt of a Privacy Act request within ten days and to provide the requested records within thirty days.

At many agencies, FOIA and Privacy Act requests are processed by the same personnel. When then is a backlog of requests, it takes longer to receive a response. As a practical matter, there is little that a requester can do when an agency response is delayed.

Agencies generally process requests in the order in which they were received. Some agencies will expedite the processing of urgent requests. Anyone with a pressing need for records should consult the agency Privacy Act Officer about how to ask for expedited treatment of requests.

Reasons Access May Be Denied Under the Privacy Act

Not all records about an individual must be disclosed under the Privacy Act. Some records may be withheld to protect important government interests such as national security or law enforcement.

The Privacy Act exemptions are different from the exemptions of the FOIA. Under the FOIA, any record may be withheld from disclosure if it contains exempt information when a request is received. The decision to apply an FOIA exemption is made only after a request has been made. In contrast, Privacy Act exemptions apply not only to records but to systems of records. Before an agency can apply a Privacy Act exemption, the agency must first issue a regulation stating that there may be exempt records in that system of records. Thus, there is a procedural prerequisite for the application of the Privacy Act exemptions.

Without reviewing agency regulations, it is hard to tell whether particular Privacy Act records are exempt from disclosure. However, it is a safe assumption that any system of records that qualifies for an exemption has been exempted by the agency.

Since most record systems are not exempt, the exemptions are not relevant to most requests. Also, agencies do not automatically rely upon the Privacy Act exemptions unless there is a specific reason to do so. Thus, some records that are exempt may be disclosed upon request.

Because Privacy Act exemptions are complex and used infrequently, most requesters need not worry about them. The exemptions are discussed here for those interested in the law's details and for reference when an agency withholds records. Anyone interested in more information about the Privacy Act's exemptions can begin by reading the relevant sections of the Act.

The Privacy Act's exemptions differ from those of the FOIA in another important way. The FOIA is essentially a disclosure law. Information exempt under the FOIA is exempt from disclosure only. That is not true under the Privacy Act. It imposes many separate requirements on personal records. No system of records is exempt from all Privacy Act requirements.

For example, no system of records is ever exempt from the requirement that a description of the system be published. No system of records can be exempted from the limitations on disclosure of the records outside the agency. No system is exempt from the requirement to maintain an accounting for disclosures. No system is exempt from the restriction against the maintenance of unauthorized information on the exercise of First Amendment rights. All systems are subject to the requirement that reasonable efforts be taken to assure that records disclosed outside the agency be accurate, complete, timely, and relevant. Agencies must maintain proper administrative controls and security for all systems. Finally, The Privacy Act's criminal penalties remain fully applicable to each system of records.

1. General Exemptions

There are two general exemptions under the Privacy Act. The first applies to all records maintained by the Central Intelligence Agency. The second general exemption applies to selected records maintained by an agency or component whose principal function is any activity pertaining to criminal law enforcement. Records of these criminal law enforcement agencies can be exempt under the Privacy Act if the records consists of (A) information compiled to identify individual criminal offenders and which consist only of identifying that and notations of arrests, the nature and disposition of criminal charges, sentencing, confinement, release, and parole or probation status: (B) criminal investigatory records associated with an identifiable individual; or (C) reports identifiable to a particular individual compiled at any stage from arrest through release from supervision.

Systems of records subject to these general exemptions may be exempted from many of the Privacy Act's requirements. Exemption from the Act's access and correction provisions is the most important. Individuals have no right under the Privacy Act to ask for a copy of records that are generally exempt or to seek correction of erroneous records.

In practice, these exemptions are not as expansive as they sound. Most agencies that have exempt records will accept and process Privacy Act requests. The records will be reviewed on a case-by-case basis. Agencies will often disclose any information that does not require protection. Agencies also tend to follow a similar policy for requests for correction.

Individuals interested in obtaining records from the Central Intelligence Agency or from law enforcement agencies should not be discouraged from making requests for access. Even if the Privacy Act access exemption is applied, portions of the records may still be disclosable under the FOIA. This is a primary reason individuals should cite both the Privacy Act and the FOIA when requesting records.

The general exemption from access does not prevent requesters from filing a lawsuit under the Privacy Act when access is denied. The right to sue under the FOIA is not changed because of a Privacy Act exemption.

2. Specific Exemptions

There are seven specific Privacy Act exemptions that can be applied to many systems of records. Records subject to these exemptions are not exempt from as many of the Act's requirements as are the records subject to the general exemptions. However, records exempt under the specific exemptions are exempt from the Privacy Act's access and correction provisions. Nevertheless, since the access and correction exemptions are not always applied when available, those seeking records should not be discouraged from making a request. Also, the FOIA can be used to seek access to records exempt under the Privacy Act.

Freedom of Information Act

The first specific exemption covers record systems containing information that is properly classified. Classified information is also exempt from disclosure under the FOIA. Information that has been classified in the interest of national defense or foreign policy will normally be unavailable under either the FOIA or the Privacy Act.

The second specific exemption applies to systems of records containing investigatory material compiled for law enforcement purposes other than material covered by the general law enforcement exemption. The specific law enforcement exemption is limited when — as a result of the maintenance of the records — an individual is denied any right, privilege, or benefit to which he or she would be entitled by federal law or for which he or she would otherwise be entitled. In such a case, disclosure is required except where disclosure would reveal the identity of a confidential source who furnished information to the government under an express promise that the identity of the source would be held in confidence. If the information was collected from a confidential source before the effective date of the Privacy Act (September 27, 1975), an implied promise of confidentiality is sufficient to permit withholding of the identity of the source.

The third specific exemption applies to systems of records maintained in connection with providing protective services to the President of the United States or other individuals who receive protection from the Secret Service.

The fourth specific exemption applies to systems of records required by statute to be maintained and used solely as statistical records.

The fifth specific exemption covers investigatory material compiled solely to determine suitability, eligibility, or qualifications for federal civilian employment, military service, federal contracts, or access to classified information. However, this exemption applies only to the extent that disclosure of information would reveal the identity of a confidential source who provided the information under a promise of confidentiality.

The sixth specific exemption applies to systems of records that contain testing or examination of material used solely to determine individual qualifications for appointment or promotion in federal service, but only when disclosure would compromise the objectivity or fairness of the testing or examination process. Effectively, this exemption permits withholding of questions used in employment tests.

The seven specific exemption covers evaluation material used to determine potential for promotion in the armed services. The material is only exempt to the extent that disclosure would reveal the identity of a confidential source who provided the information under a promise of confidentiality.

3. Medical Records

Medical records maintained by federal agencies — for example, records at Veterans Administration hospitals — are not formally exempt from the Privacy Act's access provisions. However, the Privacy Act authorizes a special procedure for medical records that operates, at least in part, like an exemption.

Agencies may deny individuals direct access to medical records, including psychological records, if the agency deems it necessary. An agency normally reviews medical records requested by an individual. If the agency determines that direct disclosure is unwise, it can arrange for disclosure to a physician selected by the individual or possibly to another person chosen by the individual.

4. Litigation Records

The Privacy Act's access provisions include a general limitation on access to litigation records. The Act does not require an agency to disclose to an individual any information compiled in reasonable anticipation of a civil action or proceeding. This limitation operates like an exemption, although there is no requirement that the exemption be applied to a system of records before it can be used.

Administrative Appeal Procedures for Denial of Access

Unlike the FOIA, the Privacy Act does not provide for an administrative appeal of the denial of access. However, many agencies have established procedures that will allow Privacy Act requesters to appeal a denial of access without going to court. An administrative appeal is often allowed under the Privacy Act, even though it is not required, because many individuals cite both the FOIA and Privacy Act when making a request. The FOIA provides specifically for an administrative appeal, and agencies are required to consider an appeal under the FOIA.

When a Privacy Act request for access is denied, agencies usually inform the requester of any appeal rights that are available. If no information on appeal rights is included in the denial letter, the requester should ask the Privacy Act Officer. Unless an agency has established an alternative procedure, it is possible that an appeal filed directly with the head of the agency will be considered by the agency.

When a request for access is denied under the Privacy Act, the agency explains the reason for the denial. The explanation must name the system of records and explain which exemption is applicable to the system. An appeal may be made on the basis that the record is not exempt, that the system of records has not been properly exempted, or that the record is exempt but no harm to an important interest will result if the record is disclosed.

There are three basic elements to a Privacy Act appeal letter. First, the letter should state that the appeal is being made under the Privacy Act of 1974. If the FOIA was cited when the request for access was made, the letter should state that the appeal is also being made under the FOIA. This is important because the FOIA grants requesters statutory appeal rights.

Second, a Privacy Act appeal letter should identify the denial that is being appealed and the records that were withheld. The appeal letter should also explain why the denial of access is improper or unnecessary.

Third, the appeal should include the requester's name and address. It is good practice for a requester to also include a telephone number when making an appeal. The Appendix at the end of this section includes a sample letter of appeal.

Be patient. If any phone number is incorrect, call (area code) 555-1212 and request the new listing.

Amending Records Under the Privacy Act

The Privacy Act grants an important right in addition to the ability to inspect records. The Act permits an individual to request a correction of a record that is not accurate, relevant, timely, or complete. This remedy allows an individual to correct errors and to prevent those errors from being disseminated by the agency or used unfairly against the individual.

The right to seek a correction extends only to records subject to the Privacy Act. Also, an individual can only correct errors contained in a record that pertains to himself or herself. Records disclosed under the FOIA cannot be amended through the Privacy Act unless the records are also subject to the Privacy Act. Records about unrelated events or about other people cannot be amended unless the records are in a Privacy Act file maintained under the name of the individual who is seeking to make the correction.

A request to amend a record should be in writing. Agency regulations explain the procedures in greater detail, but the process is not complicated. A letter requesting an amendment of a record will normally be addressed to the Privacy Act Officer of the agency or to the agency official responsible for the maintenance of the record system containing the erroneous information. The envelope containing the request should be marked "Privacy Act Amendment Request" on the lower left corner.

There are five basic elements to a request for amending a Privacy Act record.

First, the letter should state that it is a request to amend a record under the Privacy Act of 1974.

Second, the request should identify the specific record and the specific information in the record for which an amendment is being sought.

Third, the request should state why the information is not accurate, relevant, timely, or complete. Supporting evidence may be included with the request.

Fourth, the request should state what new or additional information, if any, should be included in place of the erroneous information. Evidence of the validity of the new or additional information should be included. If the information in the file is wrong and needs to be removed rather than supplemented or corrected, the request should make this clear.

Fifth, the request should include the name and address of the requester. It is a good idea for the requester to include a telephone number. The Appendix includes a sample letter requesting amendment of a Privacy Act record.

Appeals and Requirements for Agency Responses

An agency that receives a request for amendment under the Privacy Act must acknowledge receipt of the request within ten days (not including Saturdays, Sundays, and legal holidays). The agency must promptly rule on the request. The agency may make the amendment requested. If so, the agency must notify any person or agency to which the record had previously been disclosed of the correction.

If the agency refuses to make the change requested, the agency must inform the requester of: (1) the agency's refusal to amend the record; (2) the reason for refusing to amend the request; and (3) the procedures for requesting a review of the denial. The agency must provide the name and business address of the official responsible for conducting the review.

An agency must decide an appeal of a denial of a request for amendment within thirty days (excluding Saturdays, Sundays, and legal holidays), unless the time period is extended by the agency for good cause. If the appeal is granted, the record will be corrected.

If the appeal is denied, the agency must inform the requester of the right to judicial review. In addition, a requester whose appeal has been denied also has the right to place in the agency file a concise statement of disagreement with the information that was the subject of the request for amendment.

When a statement of disagreement has been filed and an agency is disclosing the disputed information, the agency must mark the information and provide copies of the statement of disagreement. The agency may also include a concise statement of its reasons for not making the requested amendments. The agency must also give a copy of the statement of disagreement to any person or agency to whom the record had previously been disclosed.

Finding a Judicial Appeal

The Privacy Act provides a civil remedy whenever an agency denies access to a record or refuses to amend a record. An individual may sue an agency if the agency fails to maintain records with accuracy, relevance, timeliness, and completeness as is necessary to assure fairness in any agency determination and the agency makes a determination that is adverse to the individual. An individual may also sue an agency if the agency fails to comply with any other Privacy Act provision in a manner that has an adverse effect on the individual.

The Privacy Act protects a wide range of rights about personal records maintained by federal agencies. The most important are the right to inspect records and the right to seek correction of records. Other rights have also been mentioned here, and still others can be found in the text of the Act. Most of these rights can become the subject of litigation.

An individual may file a lawsuit against an agency in the federal district court in which the individual lives, in which the records are situated, or in the District of Columbia. A lawsuit must be filed within two years from which the basis for the lawsuit arose.

Most individuals require the assistance of an attorney to file a judicial appeal. An individual who files a lawsuit and substantially prevails may be awarded reasonable attorney fees and litigation costs reasonably incurred. Some requesters may be able to handle their own appeal without an attorney. Since this is not a litigation guide, details about the judicial appeal process have not been included. Anyone considering filing an appeal can begin by reviewing the provisions of the Privacy Act on civil remedies.

Freedom of Information Act

Appendix: Sample Request and Appeal Letters

A. Freedom of Information Act Request Letter

Agency Head [or Freedom of Information Act Officer]
Name of Agency
Address of Agency
City, State, Zip Code
Re: Freedom of Information Act Request.

Dear_____:

This is a request under the Freedom of Information Act.

I request that a copy of the following documents [or documents containing the following information] be provided to me: [identify the documents or information as specifically as possible].

In order to help determine my status to assess fees, you should know that I am (insert a suitable description of the requester and the purpose of the request).

[Sample requester descriptions:

a representative of the news media affiliated with the newspaper (magazine, television station, etc.) and this request is made as part of news gathering and not for a commercial use.

affiliated with an educational or noncommercial scientific institution and this request is made for a scholarly or scientific purpose.

an individual seeking information for personal use and not for a commercial use.

affiliated with a private corporation and am seeking information for use in the company business.]

[Optional] I am willing to pay fees for this request up to a maximum of $XXX. If you estimate that the fees will exceed this limit, please inform me first.

[Optional] I request a waiver of all fees of this request. Disclosure of the requested information to me is in the public interest because it is likely to contribute significantly to public understanding of the operations or activities of the government and is not primarily in my commercial interest. [Include a specific explanation.]

Thank you for your consideration of this request.

Sincerely,
Name
Address
City, State, Zip Code
Telephone number [Optional]

B. Freedom of Information Act Appeal Letter

Agency Head or Appeal Officer
Name of Agency
Address of Agency
City, State, Zip Code
Re: Freedom of Information Act Appeal

Dear_____:

This is an appeal under the Freedom of Information Act.

On (date), I requested documents under the Freedom of Information Act. My request was assigned the following identification number: XXXXX. On (date), I received a response to my request in a letter signed by (name of official). I appeal the denial of my request.

[Optional] The documents that were withheld must be disclosed under the FOIA because * * *.

[Optional] I appeal the decision to deny my request for a waiver of fees. I believe that I am entitled to a waiver of fees. Disclosure of the documents I requested is in the public interest because the information is likely to contribute significantly to public understanding of the operations or activities of government and is not primarily in my commercial interests. (Provide details)

[Optional] I appeal the decision to require me to pay review costs for this request. I am not seeking the documents for a commercial use. (Provide details)

[Optional] I appeal the decision to require me to pay search charges for this request. I am a reporter seeking information as part of news gathering and not for commercial use.

Thank you for your consideration of this appeal.

Sincerely,

Name
Address
City, State, Zip Code
Telephone number [Optional]

C. Privacy Act Request for Access Letter

Privacy at Officer [or System of Records Manager]
Name of Agency
City, State, Zip Code
Re: Privacy Act Request for Access.

Dear_____:

This is a request under the Privacy Act of 1974.

I request a copy of any records [or specifically named records] about me maintained at your agency.

[Optional] To help you to locate my records, I have had the following contacts with your agency: [mention job applications, periods of employment, loans or agency programs applied for, etc.).

[Optional] Please consider that this request is also made under the Freedom of Information Act. Please provide any additional information that may be available under the FOIA.

[Optional] I am wiling to pay fees for this request up to a maximum of $ XXX. If you estimate that the fees will exceed this limit, please inform me first.

[Optional] Enclosed is [a notarized signature or other identifying document] that will verify my identity.

Thank you for your consideration of this request.

Sincerely,

Name
Address
City, State, Zip Code
Telephone number [Optional]

D. Privacy Act Denial of Access Letter

Agency Head or Appeal Officer
Name of Agency
City, State, Zip Code
Re: Appeal of Denial of Privacy Act Access Request.

Dear____:

This is an appeal under the Privacy Act of the denial of my request for access to records.

On (date), I requested access to records under the Privacy Act of 1974. My request was assigned the following identification number: XXXXX. On (date), I received a response to my request in a letter signed by (name of official). I appeal the denial of my request.

[Optional] The records that were withheld should be disclosed to me because * * *.

[Optional] Please consider that this appeal is also made under the Freedom of Information Act. Please provide any additional information that may be available under the FOIA.

Thank you for your consideration of this appeal.

Sincerely,

Name
Address
City, State, Zip Code
Telephone number [Optional]

E. Privacy Act Request to Amend Records

Privacy Act Officer [or System of Records Manager]
Name of Agency
City, State, Zip Code
Re: Privacy Act Request to Amend Records

Dear____:

This is a request under the Privacy Act to amend records about myself maintained by your agency.

I believe that the following information is not correct: [Describe the incorrect information as specifically as possible].

The information is not (accurate) (relevant) (timely) (complete) because * * *.

[Optional] Enclosed are copies of documents that show that the information is incorrect.

I request that the information be [deleted] [changed to read:]

Thank you for your consideration of this request.

Sincerely,

Name
Address
City, State, Zip Code
Telephone number [Optional]

F. Privacy Act Appeal of Refusal to Amend Records

Agency Head or Appeal Officer
Name of Agency
City, State, Zip Code
Re: Privacy Act Request to Amend Records

Dear____:

This is an appeal made under the Privacy Act of the refusal of your agency to amend records as I requested.

On (date), I was informed by (name of official) that my request was rejected. I appeal the rejection of my request.

The rejection of my request for amendment was wrong because * * *.

[Optional] I enclose additional evidence that shows that the records are incorrect and that the amendment I requested is appropriate.

Thank you for your consideration of this appeal.

Sincerely,

Name
Address
City, State, Zip Code
Telephone number [Optional]

Federal FOIA Offices

The Office of Information and Privacy (OIP) is the principal contact point within the executive branch for advice and policy guidance on matters pertaining to the administration of the Freedom on Information Act (FOIA). Through OIP's FOIA Counselor Service, experienced FOIA attorneys are available to respond to FOIA-related inquiries at the U.S. Department of Justice, Office of Information and Privacy, 10th and Constitution Ave., NW, Room 7238, Washington, DC 20530, 202-514-4251.

The following list contains the principal FOIA legal and administrative contacts at all federal agencies that deal regularly with FOIA matters. In some instances (e.g., the U.S. Department of Defense), all major agency components are listed individually under the agency. In other instances (e.g., the Food and Drug Administration), major agency components are listed separately. In still other instances (e.g., the U.S. Department of Labor), no components are listed, as it is the agency's preference that all FOIA contacts be made through its main FOIA office.

All telephone numbers are FTS numbers unless a local area code is shown. Where both the legal and the administrative contacts (marked "L" and "A," respectively) are at the same address, the common address follows the name of the administrative contact. OIP should be notified whenever there is a change in a legal or administrative contact or any change in title, telephone number, or address.

Administrative Conference of the United States
Gary J. Edles (202-254-7020) (L)
General Counsel
2120 L St., NW, Suite 500
Washington, DC 20037

Agency for International Development
Willette L. Smith (703-516-1849) (A)
FOIA Coordinator
Room 1101, SA-16
Washington, DC 20523-1608

Agriculture Department
Milton E. Sloane (202-720-8164) (A)
FOIA/PA Coordinator
Room 536A, Admin. Bldg.
Washington, DC 20250-1300

Kenneth E. Cohen (202-720-5565) (L)
Room 2321, South Bldg.
Washington, DC 20250-1400

Arms Control and Disarmament Agency
Frederick Smith, Jr. (202-647-3596) (L)
Office of the General Counsel
320 21st St., NW, Room 5635
Washington, DC 20451

Central Intelligence Agency
John H. Wright (703-351-2770) (A)
Information and Privacy Coordinator
Paula A. Sweeney (703-874-3118) (L)
Washington, DC 20505

Commerce Department
Brenda Dolan (202-482-4115) (A)
FOIA/PA Officer
Gordon B. Fields (202-482-5384) (L)
Chief, General Law Division
14th St. and Constitution Ave., NW
Washington, DC 20230

Commission on Civil Rights
Emma Monroig (202-376-8351) (L)
Solicitor

624 9th St., NW, Room 632
Washington, DC 20425

Commodity Futures Trading Commission
Edward W. Colbert (202-254-3382) (A)
Assistant Sec'y to the Commission
Glynn L. Mays (202-254-9880) (L)
Senior Assistant General Counsel
2033 K St., NW
Washington, DC 20581

Comptroller of the Currency
Frank Vance, Jr. (202-874-4700) (A)
Disclosure Officer
Lester Scail (202-874-4460) (L)
Administrative and Internal Law Division
Washington, DC 20219

Consumer Product Safety Commission
Todd A. Stevenson (301-504-0785) (A)
FOI Officer and Deputy Secretary
Alan C. Shakin (301-504-0980) (L)
Assistant General Counsel
Washington, DC 20207

Corporation for National and Community Service
Kenneth Priebe (202-606-5000) (A)
FOIA/PA Officer
1201 New York Ave., NW, Room 6103F
Washington, DC 20525

Customs Service, U.S.
Gwen Contee (202-482-6970) (A)
Paralegal Specialist, ORR
Kathryn C. Peterson (202-482-6970) (L)
Chief, Disclosure Law Branch, ORR
Washington, DC 20229

Defense Department
Charlie Y. Talbott (703-697-1180) (A)
OATSD (PA), Room 2C757
Stewart F. Aly (703-695-6804) (L)
OGC/LC, Room 3C962
The Pentagon
Washington, DC 20301

Air Force
Anne P. Rollins (703-697-3492) (A)
SAF/AAIQ
Room 4A1088E Pentagon
Washington, DC 20330-1610

Army
Rose Marie Christensen (703-607-3377) (A)
SAID-IDP-F/P
1725 Jefferson Davis Hwy., Suite 201
Arlington, VA 22202-4102

Defense Contract Audit Agency
Dave Henshall (703-274-4400) (A)
Information and Privacy Adviser
Cameron Station (CMR)
Alexandria, VA 22304-6178

Defense Finance and Accounting Service
Jean Marie Ward (703-607-2821) (A)
1931 Jefferson Davis Hwy, Room 416
Arlington, VA 22240

Defense Information Systems Agency
Robin M. Berger (703-607-6515) (A)
Code R/GC, 701 S. Courthouse Rd.
Arlington, VA 22204-2199

Defense Intelligence Agency
Robert P. Richardson (202-373-8361) (A)
Chief, FOIA Staff, Code PSP/FOIA
Washington, DC 20340-5100

Defense Logistics Agency
Barry Christensen (703-617-7583) (A)
DASC-RP, Cameron Station
Alexandria, VA 22304-6100

Defense Mapping Agency
Helen Sharetts-Sullivan (703-285-9315) (A)
8613 Lee Hwy. (A-7)
Fairfax, VA 22031-2137

Defense Nuclear Agency
Nell M. Hayes (703-325-7095) (A)
Public Affairs Office
6801 Telegraph Rd., Room 113
Alexandria, VA 22310-3398

Marine Corps
B.L. Thompson (703-614-3685) (A)
HQMC (ARAD)
2 Navy Annex
Washington, DC 20380-1775

National Reconnaissance Office
Mary Jo Kingsley (703-892-0147) (A)
External Relations
1040 Defense Pentagon
Washington, DC 20301-1040

National Security Agency
Gerald Stroudt (301-688-6527) (A)
Chief, FOIA/PA Branch
Office of Information Policy, N5131
Ft. George G. Meade, MD 20755-6000

Navy
Doria M. Lama (703-614-2817) (A)
CNO (N09B30)
Room 5E521
200 Navy Pentagon
Washington, DC 20350-2000

Office of the Inspector General
Nadine K. Dulacki (703-604-9775) (A)
FOIA/PA Office

400 Army Navy Dr., Room 405
Arlington, VA 22202-2884

Defense Nuclear Facilities Safety Board
Carole C. Morgan (202-208-6433) (A)
FOIA Officer
Office of Reference and Document Management
William Shields (202-208-6387) (L)
Office of the General Counsel
625 Indiana Ave., NW, Suite 700
Washington, DC 20004

Education Department
Maria Teresa Cueva (202-708-4753) (A)
FOIA Specialist
ROB3, Room 5624
Robert Wexler (202-401-6700) (L)
Office of the General Counsel
Room 4433
600 Independence Ave., SW
Washington, DC 20202

Energy Department
GayLa D. Sessoms (202-586-5955) (A)
Director, FOIA-PA Division, HR-78
Ralph D. Goldenberg (202-586-8665) (L)
Assistant General Counsel, GC-80
1000 Independence Ave., SW
Washington, DC 20585

Environmental Protection Agency
Jeralene G. Green (202-260-4048) (A)
FOIA Officer (A-1105)
Marlyne Lipfert (202-260-5472) (L)
Office of General Counsel (2379)
401 M St., SW
Washington, DC 20460

Equal Employment Opportunity Commission
Thomas Schlageter (202-663-4669) (L)
Assistant Legal Counsel
Office of Legal Counsel
1801 L St., NW
Room 6034
Washington, DC 20507

Executive Office of the President, Office of Administration
Carol Ehrlich (202-395-6963) (A)
Acting FOIA Officer
Nelson Cunningham (202-395-2273) (L)
General Counsel
479 Old Executive Office Bldg.
Washington, DC 20503

Export-Import Bank
Stephen G. Glazer (202-563-3431) (L)
Deputy General Counsel
811 Vermont Ave., NW, Room 957
Washington, DC 20571

Farm Credit Administration
Mark McBeth (703-883-4345) (A)
FOI Officer
Jane M. Virga (703-883-4071) (L)
1501 Farm Credit Dr.
McLean, VA 22102-5090

Federal Aviation Administration
Valerie G. Collins (202-267-3108) (A)
FOIA Program Director, APA-200
LeAnne Faulkner (202-376-6406) (L)
Manager, General Law Branch, AGC-110
800 Independence Ave., SW
Washington, DC 20591

Freedom of Information Act

Federal Communications Commission
Kathy Conley (202-418-0210) (A)
Records Management Branch, Room 234
Lawrence S. Schaffner (202-418-1720) (L)
Assistant General Counsel, Room 616
1919 M St., NW
Washington, DC 20554

Federal Deposit Insurance Corporation
Dianne M. Salva (202-898-3819) (A)
Senior Attorney, Room F-405
Thomas A. Schulz (202-736-0520) (L)
Assistant General Counsel, Room H-5018
550 17th St., NW
Washington, DC 20429

Federal Election Commission
Ron Harns (202-219-4155) (A)
FOIA Officer
Vincent J. Convery, Jr. (202-219-3690) (L)
Office of General Counsel
999 E St., NW
Washington, DC 20463

Federal Emergency Management Agency
Sandra B. Jackson (202-646-3840) (A)
FOI/PA Specialist, Room 840
Office of the General Counsel
Spence W. Perry (202-646-4105) (L)
Deputy General Counsel, Room 840
500 C St., SW
Washington, DC 20472

Federal Energy Regulatory Commission
Rebecca F. Schaffer (202-208-1088) (A)
Office of External Affairs, Room 9200
Denise M. O'Brien, (202-208-0457) (L)
Office of the General Counsel, Room 8002
825 N. Capitol St., NE
Washington, DC 20426

Federal Labor Relations Authority
Michael D. Nossaman (202-482-6602) (A)
Assistant General Counsel
David M. Smith (202-482-6695) (L)
Solicitor
607 14th St., NW
Washington, DC 20424

Federal Maritime Commission
Joseph C. Polking (202-523-5725) (A)
Secretary of the Commission
800 N. Capitol St., NW
Room 1046
Washington, DC 20573

Federal Mediation and Conciliation Service
Eileen Hoffman (202-606-5444) (L)
General Counsel
2100 K St., NW
Washington, DC 20427

Federal Mine Safety and Health Review Commission
Richard Baker (202-653-5625) (L)
Executive Director
1730 K St., NW
Room 6030
Washington, DC 20006

Federal Reserve Board
Elaine M. Boutilier (202-452-2418) (L)
Legal Division
20th and C Sts., NW
Room B1051B
Washington, DC 20551

Federal Trade Commission
Sandra Bolden (202-326-2406) (A)
FOIA/PA Officer
William Golden (202-326-2494) (L)
Office of the General Counsel
Sixth St. and Pennsylvania Ave., NW
Washington, DC 20580

Food and Drug Administration
Gerald H. Deighton (301-443-6310) (A)
Director, FOI Staff
5600 Fishers Lane, (HFI-30)
Rockville, MD 20857

Foreign Claims Settlement Commission
Judith H. Lock (202-616-6986) (A)
Administrative Officer
600 E St., NW
Room 6002
Washington, DC 20579

General Accounting Office
Nola Casieri (202-512-2960) (A)
Office of Policy
James M. Lager (202-512-8170) (L)
Assistant General Counsel
441 G St., NW
Washington, DC 20548

General Services Administration
Mary Cunningham (202-501-1659) (A)
Information Management Division
Helen C. Maus (202-501-1460) (L)
18th and F Sts., NW
Washington, DC 20405

Health and Human Services Department
Rosario Cirrincione (202-690-7453) (A)
Director, FOIA/Privacy Division
Room 645F, HHH Bldg.
Richard Friedman (202-619-0162) (L)
Office of the General Counsel
Room 5362, Cohen Bldg.
Washington, DC 20201

Health Care Finance Administration
Arthur Weatherbee (410-966-5352) (A)
Director, FOIA Office
6325 Security Blvd.
Room 100, Prof. Bldg.
Baltimore, MD 21207

Housing and Urban Development Department
Yvette Magruder (202-708-3054)
Departmental FOIA Officer, Room 10139
Jeffrey Rock (202-708-0622) (L)
Attorney Advisor, Room 10246
451 7th St., SW
Washington, DC 20410

Interior Department
Alexandra Mallus (202-208-5342) (A)
Departmental FOIA Officer (PMO-5412)
Robert Moll (202-208-5216) (L)
Assistant Solicitor (MS-6531)
1849 C St., NW
Washington, DC 20240

Internal Revenue Service
John R. Nelson (202-622-6250) (A)
Chief, FOIA Branch
Office of Disclosure
Peter V. Filpi (202-622-4560) (L)
Assistant Chief Counsel
1111 Constitution Ave., NW
Washington, DC 20224

Be patient. If any phone number is incorrect, call (area code) 555-1212 and request the new listing.

International Trade Commission
Donna R. Koehnke (202-205-2000) (A)
Secretary to the Commission
500 E St., SW
Washington, DC 20436

Interstate Commerce Commission
John Atkisson (202-927-6317) (A)
FOIA/PA Officer, Room 4136
Henri F. Rush (202-927-7312) (L)
General Counsel, Room 5211
12th and Constitution Ave., NW
Washington, DC 20423

Justice Department
Patricia Harris (202-514-1938) (A)
FOIA/PA Section, Room B-324
Justice Management Division
Washington, DC 20530

Richard L. Huff (202-514-FOIA) (L)
Daniel J. Metcalfe
Co-Directors, Room 7238
Office of Information and Privacy
Washington, DC 20530

Antitrust Division
Ann Lea Harding (202-514-2692) (A)
Acting FOIA/PA Officer, Room 3250
Washington, DC 20530

Bureau of Prisons
Renee Barley (202-514-6655) (A)
FOIA Administrator, Room 738 (HOLC)
Washington, DC 20534

Civil Division
James M. Kovakas (202-514-2319) (A)
FOIA/PA Office, Room 808, 901 E St.
Elizabeth A. Pugh (202-514-3178) (L)
Assistant Branch Director
Federal Programs Branch, Room 1062, 901 E St.
Leonard Schaitman (202-514-3441) (L)
Assistant Director
Appellate Staff, Room 3614
Washington, DC 20530

Civil Rights Division
Nelson D. Hermilla (202-514-4209) (A)
Chief, FOI/PA Branch, Room 8000 NYAV
Washington, DC 20530

Criminal Division
Marshall Williams (202-616-0307) (A)
Chief, FOIA Unit, Room 1075, 1001 G St.
Washington, DC 20530

Drug Enforcement Administration
Thomas H. Wingate (202-307-7596) (A)
Chief, FOI Section, Room W-6268 LP-2
Washington, DC 20537

Environment and Natural Resources Division
Brett Grosko (202-514-4362) (A)
Paralegal Specialist, Room 2129
Washington, DC 20530

Executive Office for U.S. Attorneys
Bonnie L. Gray (202-616-6757) (A)
Attorney-in-Charge, Room 7100 BICN
Washington, DC 20530

Federal Bureau of Investigation
J. Kevin O'Brien (202-324-5520) (A)
Chief, FOI/PA Section
Room 6296 JEH
Washington, DC 20535

Immigration and Naturalization Service
Magda S. Ortiz (202-514-1722) (A)
FOIA/PA Branch, Room 5240 CAB
Washington, DC 20536

INTERPOL
Yvonne A. Holley (202-616-9000) (A)
FOIA/PA Specialist, Suite 600 BICN
Washington, DC 20530

Marshals Service
Florastine P. Graham (202-307-9054) (A)
FOI/PA Officer
600 Army Navy Drive
Arlington, VA 22202-4210

Office of the Inspector General
Deborah M. Briscoe (202-616-0646) (A)
Paralegal Specialist, Room 4261
Washington, DC 20530

Parole Commission
Pamela Posch (202-492-5959) (A)
Paralegal Specialist
5550 Friendship Blvd., Room 420
Chevy Chase, MD 20815

Tax Division
Pamela J. Martin (3202-307-0462) (A)
FOIA Unit, Room 6823 JCB
Washington, DC 20530

Labor Department
Miriam McD. Miller (202-219-8188) (L)
Office of the Solicitor, Room N-2428
200 Constitution Ave., NW
Washington, DC 20210

Legal Services Corporation
JoAnn Gretch (202-336-8813) (L)
FOIA Administrator
750 1st St., NE
Washington, DC 20002-4250

Library of Congress
Copyright Office
William C. Froelich (202-707-8394) (A)
Senior Attorney-Advisor
Marilyn Kretsinger (202-707-8380) (L)
1st St. and Independence Ave., SE
Washington, DC 20540

Merit Systems Protection Board
Michael H. Hoxie (202-653-7200) (A)
FOIA/PA Officer
Lew Fischer (202-653-7171) (L)
General Counsel
1120 Vermont Ave., NW
Washington, DC 20419

National Aeronautics and Space Administration
Patricia M. Riep-Dice (202-358-1764) (A)
FOIA Officer (Code PSN)
Pamela Werner (202-358-2085) (L)
Senior Attorney (Code GG)
300 E St., SW
Washington, DC 20546

National Archives and Records Administration
Mary Ronan (202-501-5461) (A)
FOIA Officer
Christopher M. Runkel (202-501-5535) (L)
Acting General Counsel
7th St. and Pennsylvania Ave., NW
Washington, DC 20408

Be patient. If any phone number is incorrect, call (area code) 555-1212 and request the new listing.

1167

National Credit Union Administration

Patricia A. Slye (703-518-6540) (A)
Office of the General Counsel
1775 Duke St.
Alexandria, VA 22314

National Endowment for the Arts

Melody Wayland (202-682-5418) (A)
FOIA Officer, Room 517
Karen Christensen (202-682-5418) (L)
General Counsel, Room 517
1100 Pennsylvania Ave., NW
Washington, DC 20506

National Endowment for the Humanities

Michael S. Shapiro (202-606-8322) (L)
General Counsel, Room 530
1100 Pennsylvania Ave., NW
Washington, DC 20506

National Labor Relations Board

John J. Toner (202-273-1944) (A)
Associate Executive Secretary, Room 11600
John W. Hornbeck (202-273-3847) (L)
Office of Legal Research, Room 10612
1099 14th St., NW
Washington, DC 20570

National Mediation Board

Ronald M. Etters (202-523-5944) (L)
General Counsel
1301 K St., NW, Suite 250
Washington, DC 20572

National Oceanic and Atmospheric Administration

Maria C. Krug (301-413-0610) (A)
FOIA/PA Officer
Room 714, WSC-5
Rockville, MD 20852-3809

National Railroad Passenger Corporation (AMTRAK)

Medaris W. Oliveri (202-906-2728) (A)
FOIA Officer
Law Department
William F. Erkelenz (202-906-3975) (L)
General Solicitor
60 Massachusetts Ave., NE
Washington, DC 20002

National Science Foundation

M.E. Schoolmaster (202-306-1070) (A)
FOIA Officer
Office of Legislative and Public Affairs, Room 1245
D. Matthew Powell (703-306-1060) (L)
Assistant General Counsel, Room 1265
4201 Wilson Blvd.
Arlington, VA 22230

National Security Council

David Van Tassel (202-456-9201) (A)
Director, Access Management
392 Old Executive Office Bldg.
Washington, DC 20506

National Transportation Safety Board

Michael Levins (202-382-6700) (A)
Director, Office of Administration
Jane F. Mackall (202-382-1952) (L)
Office of General Counsel
490 L'Enfant Plaza East, SW
Washington, DC 20594

Nuclear Regulatory Commission

Russell A. Powell (301-415-7169) (A)
Chief, FOIA/LPDR

Mary Pat Siemien (301-415-1565) (L)
Office of the General Counsel
Washington, DC 20555

Occupational Safety and Health Review Commission

Linda A. Whitsett (202-606-5398) (A)
FOIA Officer
Office of Public Information
Earl R. Ohman, Jr. (202-606-5410) (L)
General Counsel
1120 20th St., NW, 9th Floor
Washington, DC 20036-3419

Office of Government Ethics

William Gressman (202-523-5757) (L)
Associate General Counsel
1201 New York Ave., NW, Suite 500
Washington, DC 20005-3917

Office of Management and Budget

Darrell A. Johnson (202-395-5715) (A)*
Deputy Assistant Director for Administration
9206 New Executive Office Bldg.
Steven D. Aitken (202-395-4728) (L)
Assistant General Counsel
464 Old Executive Office Bldg.
Washington, DC 20503

* For policy guidance on FOIA fee matters, contact the Office of Management and Budget's (OMB) Virginia Huth at 202-395-3785. Privacy Act Officers may call OMB's Maya Bernstein at 202-395-3785 for Privacy Act policy guidance.

Office of Personnel Management

Leslie Crawford (703-908-8565) (A)
Office of Information Technology
Room CHP-500
Stephanie Peters (202-606-1920) (L)
Office of the General Counsel
Room TRB-7353
1900 E St., NW
Washington, DC 20415

Office of Science and Technology Policy

Barbara Ferguson (202-456-6001) (A)
Administrative Officer
431 Old Executive Office Bldg.
Washington, DC 20500

Office of Special Counsel

Cathleen M. Sadio (202-653-6005) (L)
General Attorney
1730 M St., NW, Suite 300
Washington, DC 20036-4505

Office of Thrift Supervision

Kathy Semone (202-906-5900) (A)
Director, Information Services
Public Affairs Office
1700 G St., NW
Washington, DC 20552

Office of U.S. Trade Representative

Sybia Harrison (202-395-3432) (A)
FOIA Officer
Office of the General Counsel
600 17th St., NW
Washington, DC 20506

Office of the Vice President

Kumiki Gibson (202-456-7022) (L)
Counselor to the Vice President
Old Executive Office Bldg.
Washington, DC 20501

Panama Canal Commission
Barbara A. Fuller (202-634-6441) (A)
Assistant to the Secretary for Commission Affairs
1825 I St., NW, Suite 1050
Washington, DC 20006-5402

Peace Corps
Tom Peirce (202-606-3261) (A)
FOIA Analyst
Thomas Tighe (202-606-3114) (L)
Associate General Counsel
1990 K St., NW
Washington, DC 20526

Pension Benefit Guaranty Corporation
E. William Fitzgerald (202-326-4040) (A)
Disclosure Officer, Room 240
Philip R. Hertz (202-326-4004) (L)
Associate General Counsel, 3rd Floor
1200 K St., NW
Washington, DC 20005

Postal Service
Donna M. Peak (202-268-2924) (A)
Acting Records Officer
Fred Eggleston (202-268-2962) (L)
Chief Counsel, Ethics and Information Law
475 L'Enfant Plaza West, SW
Washington, DC 20260

Railroad Retirement Board
Stephen Bartholow (312-751-4935) (L)
Deputy General Counsel
Office of the General Counsel
844 Rush St.
Chicago, IL 60611

Securities and Exchange Commission
Hannah R. Hall (202-942-4320) (A)
FOIA Officer
John H. Heinz (202-942-0871) (L)
450 5th St., NW
Washington, DC 20549

Selective Service System
Henry N. Williams (703-235-2050) (L)
General Counsel
1515 Wilson Blvd.
Arlington, VA 22209-2425

Small Business Administration
Beverly K. Linden (202-401-8203) (A)
Chief, Office of FOI/PA
Christopher Holleman (202-205-6645) (L)
Office of General Counsel
409 3rd St., SW
Washington, DC 20416

Social Security Administration
Vince Sanudo (410-965-2737) (A)
FOIA Officer, Room 4-C-5, Annex
Robert Crowe (410-965-3155) (L)
Office of General Counsel
Room 612, Altmeyer Bldg.

6401 Security Blvd.
Baltimore, MD 21235

State Department
Frank M. Machak (202-647-7740) (A)
FOIA Coordinator, Room 1239
John W. Kropf (202-647-5154) (L)
Attorney-Adviser, Room 5425
2201 C St., NW
Washington, DC 20520

Tennessee Valley Authority
Mark R. Winter (615-751-2523) (A)
FOIA Officer
1101 Market St.
Chattanooga, TN 37402

Maureen H. Dunn (615-632-4131) (L)
400 West Summit Hill Dr.
Knoxville, TN 37902

Transportation Department
Dorothy A. Chambers (202-366-4542) (A)
Chief, FOIA Division (C-12)
Robert I. Ross (202-366-9154) (L)
Office of General Counsel (C-10)
400 7th St., SW
Washington, DC 20590

Treasury Department
Alana Johnson (202-622-0930) (A)
Disclosure Officer, Room 1054
David L. Dougherty (202-622-0450) (L)
Office of General Counsel, Room 1410
1500 Pennsylvania Ave., NW
Washington, DC 20220

United States Information Agency
Lola L. Secora (202-619-5499) (A)
FOIA/PA Officer
Lorie J. Nierenberg (202-619-6084) (L)
Assistant General Counsel
301 4th St., SW
Washington, DC 20547

United States Secret Service
James P. O'Neill (202-435-5838) (A)
FOIA/PA Officer
Liaison Division, Room 720
1800 G St., NW
Washington, DC 20223

Veterans Affairs Department
Donald L. Nielson (202-535-8272) (A)
Director, Information Mgt. Service (045A4)
Mark McDonough (202-273-6382) (L)
Office of General Counsel (024K4)
810 Vermont Ave., NW
Washington, DC 20420

The White House
Office of the Counsel to the President
The White House (202-456-7903)
1600 Pennsylvania Ave., NW
Washington, DC 20500

Be patient. If any phone number is incorrect, call (area code) 555-1212 and request the new listing.

1169

State FOIA Offices

How to Use State Open Records Laws: Freedom of Information

Just as the Freedom of Information Act, enacted by Congress in 1966, gave individuals the right to request and receive information held by the federal government, all states have laws giving the public access to their government records. Many of these laws, often called the Open Record laws, are modeled after the federal act.

The state statutes have some similarities. What is covered under the act, for example, invariably includes all books, maps, photographs and other documents made or received by any government agency in transaction with public business. And just as the federal act has exemptions to the rules, so do the state laws. While most of them exempt personnel, medical and other personal files, as well as criminal intelligence information and "trade secrets," there are less common ones. For example, in South Dakota, commercial fertilizer reports are exempt. In Florida, information provided to an agency for the purpose of ride-sharing arrangements is exempt, and in New Hampshire, meat inspection records are closed.

Companies can get a wide range of information from the state's Open Records laws. Here are a few examples of how these laws have been successfully used at the state level:

Bookstore Gets School Reading List
In Maryland, a bookstore used the state Open Records Law to obtain the required reading list for various courses at the state university in order to stock those books for the coming school year.

Plumber Opens Up Contracting Info
A plumbing company in New York that was the unsuccessful bidder for a project was granted access through the Open Records Law to the successful bid proposal as well as the agency's findings.

Environmental Group Obtains Damaging Drinking Water Study
In New York, an environmental group was able to get reports, analyses, and records concerning soil borings regarding a drinking water treatment plant prepared by a consulting firm for the City of Niagara Falls.

Hospital Gets Billing Practices of Competitors
In Illinois, a hospital in the same market as another hospital was able to get information on its competitive billing practices concerning ambulance service.

Advertiser Gets State's Mailing List
Through the Open Records Law in Mississippi, a company wishing to expand its advertising list was able to get a list of all the state residents who had a driver's license.

The way laws are administered varies. Some states have time limits for agencies to respond to requests -- usually between three and ten working days; others do not. Some states have administrative review processes available to individuals who have been denied their request. In other states a person's only recourse is to go court. Some laws state whether or not the motive of the requester is relevant in allowing access to records; some provide sanctions for violations of the statutes, others do not.

In addition, several states publish pamphlets explaining their law and how to file a request for records. New York, for example, has a Committee on Open Government composed of members from the government and the public. It furnishes advice to agencies, the public and the news media and annually reports its recommendations and observations to the governor and the legislature. Unlike the federal act, which has been amended only a few times, state acts are often changed on a frequent basis.

Information on a state's FOIA can usually be obtained from the office of attorney general. Listed below are their addresses, telephone numbers, and some information about the laws and their exemptions. The common exemptions -- personal records, criminal investigation files, library and academic files -- are not listed for each state. Some of the exemptions that are listed are exempted by other state laws.

States may charge fees to cover the cost of searches and/or the cost of copying records.

State Freedom of Information Offices

Alabama
Office of Attorney General, Alabama State House, 11 South Union Street, Montgomery, AL 36130; 334-242-7300. Exemptions include income tax returns, records of child care facilities, certain conservation and natural resource information.

Alaska
Office of Attorney General, Department of Law, P.O. Box 110300, State Capitol, Juneau, AK 99811; 907-465-3600. Exemptions because of other state laws include: geological and other information submitted for persons applying to lease or buy land, reports, logs and surveys held by the Department of Natural Resources relating to oil wells for which a permit to drill was issued by the department, information contained in audit reports or tax returns. There is a ten working day time limit for responding to requests.

Arizona
Office of Attorney General, 1275 W. Washington, Phoenix, AZ 85007; 602-542-4266. Exemptions include consumer fraud reports, racketeering investigations, minutes of executive sessions of public bodies.

Arkansas
Office of Attorney General, 200 Tower Bldg., 323 Carter St., Little Rock, AR 72201; 501-682-2007. Exemptions include state income tax records, grand jury minutes. Records specifically declared open include motor vehicle citations and blood alcohol tests, payroll records of covered bodies and juvenile court records. Records must be made available within three working days at the time of the request.

California
Office of Attorney General, Department of Justice, 1300 I St., Sacramento, CA 95814; 916-324-5437. Exemptions include requests for bilingual election materials,

Be patient. If any phone number is incorrect, call (area code) 555-1212 and request the new listing.

records of regulation of financial institutions, records of utility systems development or market or crop reports, and real estate appraisals. Agencies have 10 working days to comply with request. If denied access, an individual may request a review with the Information Practices Coordinator.

Colorado

Office of Attorney General, 1525 Sherman Street, Third Floor, Denver, CO 80203; 303-866-3611. Access may be denied for information pertaining to licensing, specific details of state research projects, real estate appraisals by the state before any purchase. Records must be turned over within three working days after a request is made.

Connecticut

Freedom of Information Commission, 1820 Trinity St., Hartford, CT 06106; 203-566-5682. Exemptions include real estate appraisals, collective bargaining, anti-trust investigations, states sales and use tax. Any person denied the records requested may appeal to the Freedom of Information Commission.

Delaware

Office of the Attorney General, 820 North French Street, Eighth Floor, Wilmington, DE, 19801; 302-577-3047. Exemptions include labor negotiations, anonymous contributors to charity, and records of permits for concealed weapons.

District of Columbia

Office of Corporate Counsel, District Building, 441 4th St., NW, Washington, DC; 202-727-6248. Exemptions include information related to civil anti-trust investigations, fire loss information furnished by insurer to fire marshal. Records declared open include names, salaries, title and dates of employment of all employees or officers of the mayor and an agency.

Florida

Office of Attorney General, The Capitol, Tallahassee, FL 32399-1050; 904-487-1963. Exemptions include home addresses, phone numbers and photos of law enforcement personnel. Records held legally open include autopsy reports, inspection records of nursing homes compiled by the Department of Health, appraisal reports of land acquisitions made by a city, vote sheets, final orders and other documents of the Public Service Commission.

Georgia

Office of Attorney General, Department of Law, 40 Capital Square, SW, Atlanta, GA 30334-1300; 404-656-3300. Exemptions include tax returns, medical peer review group records. Records declared to be confidential by court decision or attorney general's opinions include: salary information of county employees contained only in personnel files and not included as part of another public record.

Hawaii

Department of Attorney General, Hawaii State Capitol, 425 Queen St., Honolulu, HI 96813; 808-586-1500. Exemptions through other state laws include applications for licenses to manufacture or sell motor vehicles, fire investigation records of county fire chiefs may be withheld. There is no time limit for responding to requests.

Idaho

Office of Attorney General, P.O. Box 83720, Boise, ID 83720-0010; 208-334-2400. Exemptions include papers filed with the judicial council or masters appointed by the supreme court concerning removal, discipline or retirement of judges or justices.

Illinois

Office of Attorney General, State of Illinois, 500 S. Second St., Springfield, IL 62706; 217-782-1090. Exemptions include taxpayer information, research data, proposals and bids for contracts, grants and agreements, architects' and engineers' plans.

Indiana

Office of Attorney General, 219 State House, Indianapolis, IN 46204; 317-232-6201. Exemptions include information concerning research conducted under the auspices of institutions of higher learning. Information that may be withheld includes negotiations in progress with industrial, research, or commercial prospects.

Iowa

Office of Attorney General, Department of Justice, Hoover Building, Des Moines, IA, 50319; 515-281-5164. Exemptions include: appraisal information for possible public land purchase, Iowa Development Commission information on industrial prospects in negotiations, and financial statements submitted to the state Commerce Commission. Records that have been legally open include the Book of Accounts required to be kept by county auditors, and jury lists.

Kansas

Office of Attorney General, Kansas Judicial Center, 301 SW 10th Ave., Topeka, KS 66612-1597; 913-296-2215. Exemptions include appraisals of property, software programs, well samples, logs and surveys, census and research records, and records of utility customers.

Kentucky

Office of Attorney General, Capitol Building, P.O. Box 2000, Frankfort, KY 40602; 502-564-7600. Exemptions include details of possible real estate acquisitions, prospective locations of unannounced business. Records legally open include coroner's reports, tax records in the custody of the property valuation administrator, records of disciplinary actions of the state board of medical licensure. A public body must respond in three working days to a request.

Louisiana

Office of Attorney General, Department of Justice, P.O. Box 94005, Baton Rouge, LA 70804; 504-342-7013. Exemptions include tax return information, financial institution records, confidential mineral reports, records in control of supervisor of public funds. Records held open under the law includes: budget requests of a city parish, records of associations of public officials. An agency has three days to respond to a request.

Maine

Office of Attorney General, State House Station - Six, Augusta, ME 04333; 207-626-8800. Exemptions include materials prepared exclusively for labor negotiations, information on hazardous waste. Records legally opened include private appraisal reports obtained by the Bureau of Parks and Recreation in connection with proposed land acquisitions. A public official has 10 days to respond to a request.

Maryland

Office of Attorney General, 200 St. Paul Place, Baltimore, MD 21202; 410-576-6300. Records that may be withheld include details of state research projects, real estate appraisals made for state. Records that must be withheld include confidential financial, geological, data, professional licensing records of individuals. Response to a request must not exceed 30 days.

Massachusetts

Office of Attorney General, One Ashburton Place, Boston, MA 02108; 617-727-2200. Exemptions include real estate appraisals, name and address of any person contained in an application to carry firearms.

Michigan

Department of Attorney General, 525 W. Ottawa St., Lansing, MI 48913; 517-373-1110. Exemptions include public bids, real estate appraisals, archaeological site information, records of any campaign committee. A public body has five working days to respond to a request.

Minnesota

Office of Attorney General, 102 Capitol Building, St. Paul, MN 55155; 612-296-6196. Exemptions include property complaint data, real estate appraisals, social recreation data, energy and financial data, public safety data.

Mississippi

Office of Attorney General, P.O. Box 220, Jackson, MS 39205; 601-359-3680. Exemptions include individual tax records, certain appraisal records, archaeological records, commercial and financial records.

Missouri

Office of Attorney General, Supreme Court Building, P.O. Box 899, Jefferson City, MO 65102; 314-751-3321. Exemptions include records of state militia, records of national guard, records of labor negotiations.

Montana

Office of Attorney General, Justice Building, 215 N. Sanders, P.O. Box 201401, Helena, MT 59620; 406-444-2026. Exemptions include unfair trade practices investigations, artificial insemination information, certain vehicle accident reports, reports of financial institutions to the Department of Commerce, and tax records. There is no time limit for responding to a request.

Nebraska

Office of Attorney General, 2115 State Capitol Building, Lincoln, NE 68509; 402-471-2682. Exemptions include appraisal and negotiation records concerning purchase or sale of property, sales and use tax records, and income tax records.

Freedom of Information Act

Nevada

Office of Attorney General, Heroes Memorial Building, Capitol Complex, Carson City, NV 89710; 702-687-4170. Exemptions include certain vital statistics, certain divorce records, certain prison commission records.

New Hampshire

Office of Attorney General, State Capitol Annex, 33 Capitol St., Concord, NH 03301-6397; 603-271-3658. Exemptions include certain bank records, Cancer Commission records, certain records of Human Rights Commission, records of malpractice claims, certain tax information. Records legally open include city real estate records, salary information of school boards.

New Jersey

Office of Attorney General, Richard Highes Complex Center, CN-081, Trenton, NJ 08620; 609-984-1548. Exemptions include cancer incidence reports, certain records of Casino Control Commission, Health Department Research Studies, audits of life insurance companies.

New Mexico

Office of Attorney General, P.O. Box 1508, Santa Fe, NM 87504-1508; 505-827-6000. Exemptions include certain historical or educational materials, certain vital statistics.

New York

Department of State, Committee On Open Government, 162 Washington Ave., Albany NY 12231; 518-474-2518. Exemptions include records that if disclosed would impair contract awards and collective bargaining. An agency must respond to a request within five business days of receipt of request.

North Carolina

Attorney General's Office, Department of Justice, P.O. Box 629, Raleigh, NC 27602-0629; 919-733-3377. Exemptions include certain bank records, commercial feed information, communicable disease records, national guard records, and tax records.

North Dakota

Office of the Attorney General, State Capitol, 600 East Blvd., Bismarck, ND 58505; 701-328-2210. Exemptions include air pollution records, health department studies, medical review records, legislative investigation records, veterans' records. Records legally open include medical coroner's records, school district records, State Highway Department records, Water Conservation Commission records, state engineer records, and records of charitable records on file with the secretary of state.

Ohio

Office of Attorney General, State Office Tower, 30 E. Broad St., Columbus, OH 43215; 614-466-4320. Exemptions include victim impact statements, tax information, statistics concerning veterans' exposure to caustic agents. Records legally open include city jail logs, employee address and payroll records of township trustees, complaints filed with the Division of Real Estate.

Oklahoma

Office of Attorney General, State of Oklahoma, 2300 N. Lincoln, Suite 112, State Capitol, Oklahoma City, OK 73105; 405-521-3921. Exemptions include income tax returns filed with the Oklahoma Tax Commission, certain bank records, income tax records, motor vehicle accident reports.

Oregon

Department of Justice, Justice Building, 1162 Court St., NE, Salem, OR 97310; 503-378-4400. Exemptions include records received or compiled by the superintendent of banks, mortality studies, motor vehicle accident reports, bank examinations, corporate tax information, personal property tax returns.

Pennsylvania

Office of Attorney General, Strawberry Square, 16th Floor, Harrisburg, PA 17120; 717-787-3391. Exemptions include records of the state ethics commission, records of the Judicial Inquiry and Review Board, records of the PA Crime Commission. Records legally open include salaries and employment addresses of Commonwealth employees.

Rhode Island

Department of Attorney General, 72 Pine St., Providence, RI 02903; 401-274-4400. Exemptions include charitable contributions requesting anonymity, collective bargaining, all tax returns, real estate appraisals and engineering feasibility estimates.

South Carolina

Office of Attorney General, Rembert C. Dennis Building, P.O. Box 11549, Columbia, SC 29211; 803-734-3970. Exemptions include income tax returns, certain records of the Board of Financial Institutions, Board of Dentistry records, contagious disease records, certain information given to the Securities Commission, State Development Board records. Each public body has 15 days to respond to a written request.

South Dakota

Office of Attorney General, 500 E. Capitol, State Capitol Building, Pierre, SD 57501; 605-773-3215. Exemptions include commercial fertilizer reports, taxpayer information, hospital inspection information, savings and loan association records.

Tennessee

Office of Attorney General, 500 Charlotte Ave., Nashville, TN 37243-0486; 615-741-6474. Exemptions include appraisal of real and personal property, bank examinations, records of the Medical Review Committee, tax records.

Texas

Office of Attorney General, Supreme Court Building, P.O. Box 12548, Austin, TX 78711-2548; 512-463-2100. Exemptions include real and personal property appraisals and purchase price, agency reports concerning the supervision of financial institutions, geological information concerning wells, personal property tax records, sales use tax records.

Utah

Office of Attorney General, 236 State Capitol, Salt Lake City, UT 84114; 801-538-1015. Exemptions include income tax returns, certain Insurance Commission records, certain Liquor Control Commission records, motor vehicle accident reports, sales tax returns, savings and loan association records.

Vermont

Office of Attorney General, 109 State St., Montpelier, VT 05609; 802-828-3171. Exemptions include tax return records, real estate appraisals, contract negotiation records. A right to appeal a request denial to the agency head exists.

Virginia

Office of Attorney General, 900 E. Main St., Richmond, VA 23219; 804-786-2071.

Washington

Public Disclosure Commission, 403 Evergreen Plaza, Mail Stop F-42, P.O. Box 40100, Olympia, WA 98504-0100; 360-753-6200. Exemptions include taxpayer information, real estate appraisals, research data, information identifying archaeological sites, bank exams, salary and fringe information survey.

West Virginia

Office of Attorney General, 1900 Kanawha Blvd., East, Building 1, E26, Charleston, WV 25305; 304-558-2021. Exemptions include motor vehicle accident reports, labor dispute records, tax returns, bar disciplinary records.

Wisconsin

Department of Justice, 123 W. Washington Ave., P.O. Box 7857, Madison, WI 53707-7857; 608-266-1221. Exemptions include air pollution control records, savings bank exams, public utility accident reports.

Wyoming

Office of Attorney General, 123 Capitol Building, Cheyenne, WY 82002; 307-777-7841. Exemptions may include details of research projects, real estate appraisals. Other statutory exemptions include motor vehicle accident reports, hospital inspection records, use tax records.

Information from Lawmakers
Tracking Federal Legislation

The U.S. Congress is accustomed to answering questions and sharing information with the public. Here is how you can quickly learn about any bill or resolution pending before the House of Representatives or Senate:

Free Legislation Database

This Bill Status Office can tell you the latest action on any federal legislation within seconds. Every bill and resolution for the current session as well as all House and Senate legislation dating back to 1975 are contained in LEGIS, a computerized database. When you call, it is best to give a key word or phrase (i.e., product liability, hazardous waste) which will help the congressional aides search LEGIS. This office can provide such detailed information as:

Have any bills been introduced covering a given topic?
Who is the sponsor of the bill?
How many co-sponsors are there?
When was it introduced?
Which committees have the bills been referred to?
Have any hearings been held?
Has there been any floor action?
Has a similar bill been introduced in the other chamber?
Has there been any action on the other side of the Hill?
Have the House and Senate agreed to a compromise bill?
Has the bill been sent to the White House?
Has the President signed or vetoed the bill?
What is the PL (public law) number?

Telephone assistance is free, and printouts from LEGIS are available for $.20 per page with a $5 minimum, but must be picked up at the Bill Status Office. However, by making arrangements with your Representative's or Senator's office, you can avoid this nominal charge and also have the printout mailed to your home or office. Contact: LEGIS, Office of Legislative Information, Ford Building, 3rd and D Streets, SW, Room 696, Washington, DC 20515; 202-225-1772.

Bill Sponsor's Legislative Assistant

The aide to the Senator or Representative who is the sponsor of a particular bill is the best person to contact next. The Bill Status Office can tell you the sponsor, and the Capitol Hill Switchboard at 202-224-3121 can transfer you to the appropriate office; then ask to speak to the person in charge of the particular bill. Usually, this congressional aide will offer to send you a copy of the bill, a press announcement, and other background information. Don't lose this opportunity to get your first of many predictions about the likelihood of the bill becoming law.

Committee Staff

Committees and subcommittees are the real work centers of the Congress. After you touch base with the Bill Status Office

(LEGIS), it is wise to double-check that information with the House or Senate committees which have jurisdiction over the legislation you are tracking. The Capitol Hill Switchboard at 202-224-3121 can connect you with any committee. Once you reach the committee staffer who handles the bill in question, you are now in a position of obtaining the following information:

Are hearings expected to be held?
Has the subcommittee or committee chair promised a vote on the measure?
What is the timetable for committee "markup" and consideration of amendments?
What is the Administration's position on the legislation?
Has the committee filed its report on the bill?
Is there any action on a similar proposal on the other side of the Hill?

You can get free copies of House bills, resolutions, and House committee reports by sending a self-addressed mailing label to the House Document Room, 2nd and D Sts., SW, Room B18, Washington, DC 20515; 202-225-3456. Similarly, you can direct your requests for Senate documents to the Senate Document Room, Senate Hart Bldg., Room B-04, Washington, DC 20510; 202-224-7860. Public laws, often called slip laws, can be obtained from either the House or Senate Document Rooms, but call the Bill Status Office to get the public law number. You can get printed copies of hearings by contacting the committee which conducted the inquiry, but expect several months lag time before it becomes available.

If the legislation you are concerned about is scheduled for action on the floor of the House or Senate, you can monitor its activity by the hour by listening to the following recorded messages:

House of Representatives Cloakroom
Democrat 202-225-7400
Republican 202-225-7430

Senate Cloakroom
Democrat 202-224-8541
Republican 202-224-8601

Play Constituent

Your Representative's or Senator's office also can help with your questions about specific bills, particularly when you have difficulty getting through to committee or subcommittee staffers. Remember that Members of Congress are eager to serve their constituents, especially for simple requests such as sending you

Information from Lawmakers

copies of bills or new public laws. The Capitol Hill Switchboard Operator at 202-224-3121 can connect you with the Washington office of your Representative and Senators.

Additional Tools for Monitoring Federal Legislation

There are sophisticated variations of the free LEGIS database described above. One reason for the growth of commercial databases is that direct online access to LEGIS is limited to Members of Congress and their staff. The following databanks cover every bill or resolution pending before the current session:

* Electronic Legislative Search System
This online system tracks all current federal legislation (as well as all 50 states) and also provides introductory bill summaries and legislative histories. Contact: Commerce Clearinghouse, 4025 W. Peterson Avenue, Chicago, IL 60646, 312-583-8500.

* Legi-Slate
This computerized system provides information based primarily on the *Congressional Record*, the official edited transcript of the House and Senate floor proceedings. This database also contains committee schedules, all recorded votes and analyses voting patterns. Contact: Legi-Slate, 777 N.Capitol St., NE, Suite 900, Washington, DC 20002; 202-898-2300.

* Washington Alert Service
This database covers all bills introduced in the U.S. Congress and includes information on committee schedules, release of committee reports and other documents, all recorded votes as well as full text of the publication, *CQ Weekly Report*. Contact: Congressional Quarterly, 1414 22nd Street, NW, Washington, DC 20037; 202-887-8500.

There are plenty of specialized trade publications designed to help lobbyists stay apprised of developments on the Hill. Online access is available to some of these newsletters, for instance, the Bureau of National Affairs' *Daily Tax Advance* and *Daily Congressional and Presidential Calendar* (BNA OnLine, 1227 25th St., NW, Room 3-268, Washington, DC 20037; 800-728-7964 or 202-728-7962). Another example is Budgetrack, a database produced by the editors of *Aviation Week and Space Technology*, which monitors the budget for the U.S. Defense Department and NASA from presidential submission to final congressional action (Budgetrack is available online from Data Resources, Inc., 1750 K St., NW, Washington DC 20006).

The American Enterprise Institute, the Brookings Institution, and other Washington-based think tanks generate position papers on specific legislative initiatives and often will share their information with the public. Other useful outside sources which can shed light on activities on the Hill are both small, specialized trade associations and large ones, for example, the National Paint and Coating Association and the U.S. Chamber of Commerce. How successful you are at getting these organizations to help you depends in large measure on how good you are on the telephone.

Congressional Experts

An estimated 4,000 legislative assistants and committee aides fall into the category of "professional staff." Because these congressional aides often draft bills and amendments and play a critical role in the negotiations with special interest groups, they are valuable sources of information, but some are much more open and candid than others. When dealing with these experts, remember they are at the beck and call of an elected official. It doesn't hurt to appeal to their egos and offer to call them when they aren't quite so busy.

Investigations and Special Reports

There are approximately 20 congressional committees and subcommittees which do not have legislative authority but serve as watchdogs with responsibility for reviewing existing laws. Some examples include the Senate Permanent Subcommittee on Investigations, House Select Committee on Aging, the Joint Economic Committee, and the House Science and Technology Subcommittee on Investigations and Oversight. These congressional panels conduct full-scale hearings on a wide range of subjects. A complete listing of these committees appears in the U.S. Congress Committees section. Some hearings conducted by the House Energy and Commerce Subcommittee on Oversight and Investigations during the 104th Congress include the following examples:

"Need for Cancer Patient Access to Unproved Treatment"
"Department of Energy's Expenditures and Use of Travel Fund"
"Allegations of FDA Abuse of Funds"

Many of these committees will put you on their mailing lists to receive notices of upcoming hearings as well as their *Committee Calendar*, which lists all of the hearings held during the previous year.

Congressional Caucuses

Approximately 100 non-legislative caucuses formed by Members of Congress serve as in-house think tanks. Some of these coalitions, such as the Congressional Clearinghouse on the Future, provide information to the public. The House Steel Caucus, the Senate Coal Caucus, the Congressional Port Caucus, and others work to get their particular legislative initiatives through the Congress. The staff directors of these organizations can be good sources because these congressional aides have access to all government studies and also have close contact with industry and special interests that the caucus is going to bat for.

Many of these "informal groups" dissolve after work on its legislative priorities is completed, so you should expect that these organizations come and go. A list of these organizations appear next in U.S. Congress Committees section. Note that the Capitol Hill Switchboard at 202-224-3121 or your Member of Congress can help you find out if a particular special interest caucus exists. A list of the current caucuses appears in the U.S. Congress Committee section.

Federal Agencies Legislative Affairs Offices

Every federal department and agency has an office which makes the Administration's case for the President's proposed budget or legislation. These offices within the executive branch usually are termed the "Offices of Legislative Affairs," which concentrate on particular bills. This is in contrast to an agency's own Office of Congressional Relations, which tends to respond to requests made by lawmakers or their staff. The office of legislative affairs also makes available written testimony by agency officials who appeared as witnesses at congressional hearings.

Arms of Congress

In addition to the 47 House and Senate committees, the following four organizations produce volumes of information and reports to aid lawmakers. These studies and recommendations by these arms of Congress are available to the public.

* Congressional Budget Office
House Office Building Annex 2
2nd and D Streets SW
Washington, DC 20515   202-226-2800
Scorekeeping reports, special studies and other economic assessments are all available free to the public.

* Congressional Research Service (CRS)
Library of Congress
See also the Current Events and Homework Chapter for a comprehensive listing of all CRS studies which cover practically every current event topic. (You must arrange to get copies of any CRS publications through your Member of Congress.)

* General Accounting Office
Office of Public Affairs Room 7049
441 G Street NW
Washington, DC 20548   202-512-4800
Reports and audit information about every government program.

U.S. Congress Committees

There is virtually *no* subject that is ignored by some office of the legislative branch of the federal government. Why? The voters back home raise all sorts of concerns with their elected officials. Every special interest group lobbies for this or that. And, each year the President proposes a federal budget which affects every taxpayer. Since Congress controls the government's purse strings, lawmakers ultimately decide the fate of practically every issue facing the country.

Every subject, from aquaculture to zinc, is monitored by some congressional employee. Many committees have authority over all these subjects. Over 100 House and Senate committees and subcommittees oversee the defense; the U.S. Department of Housing and Urban Development is subject to the jurisdiction of over 84 committees; and 54 House panels and 21 Senate panels have responsibility for some aspect of the "War on Drugs." Using the seven phone call rule, you will find someone who can be a useful information source. It may be an aide who works directly for a Senator or Congressman, a subcommittee staffer who serves either the Democratic or Republican Members of that subcommittee, an employee at one of the special interest congressional organizations such as the Senate Wine Caucus, or a specialist at the Congressional Research Service or another think tanks of the legislative branch.

The staff at the committees, subcommittees, special interest caucuses, and other congressional organizations listed here can all share their expertise over the phone, refer you to other specialists, and send publications to you free of charge. Congress tends to be particularly responsive to information requests because almost every legislator wants your vote.

Telephone Connection with Lawmakers and Staff

Although there is no central office for the U.S. Congress, the central switchboard operators at 202-224-3121 can connect you with every Washington office of every Senator, every member of the House of Representatives, every committee, and most of the in-house congressional caucuses. To contact members of the Senate staff call or write the Senate Locator, U.S. Senate, Washington, DC 20510; 202-224-3207, or the House Finance office, U.S. Capitol, Washington, DC 20515; 202-225-6514. You needn't bother with room numbers and office buildings when writing to various offices. Simply address correspondence to any Senator or Senate office, followed by U.S. Capitol, Washington, DC 20510; and for any Member of the House or House committee, write the U.S. Capitol, Washington, DC 20515.

Senate Legislative Committees

The work of drafting and considering legislation is done largely by 16 "standing" or permanent committees. They evaluate proposed federal laws authored by individual Senators, the executive branch, and outside organizations and experts. Each bill and resolution is usually referred to the appropriate committee or committees, which may report a bill out in its original form, favorably or unfavorably recommend amendments, or allow the proposed legislation to die in committee without action. Committees are divided into subcommittees which conduct hearings, consider and amend legislation, and may either approve or reject the bills. On behalf of the Senate, these committees, with rare exception, determine what reaches the floor. In the process they modify--sometimes extensively--proposals referred to them.

In addition, committees serve as congressional watchdogs of the executive branch. They oversee the organization and operations of the executive branch agencies and are responsible for knowing how efficiently and effectively the agencies perform their duties and whether and how they are carrying out the intent of the laws enacted by Congress. Under the Senate's "advise and consent" responsibility, these committees decide whether or not to confirm the President's nominees to the executive and judicial branches.

These legislative committees produce reams of studies, committee reports, published hearings, and the committee staff are specialists in the areas which fall within the committee's jurisdiction. Both the majority committee staff, currently the Republicans who control the Senate, and the minority staff, the Democratic committee staff, operate independently of one another and both can provide different viewpoints on issues, predictions about the fate of particular bills, and suggest people to contact both in the executive branch and organizations lobbying for or against pending legislation.

* Senate Committee on Agriculture, Nutrition and Forestry

Suite SR-328A Russell Senate Office Building
Washington, DC 20510   202-224-2035
Topics covered: agriculture; forestry and forest reserves; farm credit; school nutrition; and food stamp programs. For subcommittees, call the main number.

Subcommittees:
Production and Price Competitiveness
Marketing, Inspection and Product Promotion
Forestry, Conservation, and Rural Revitalization
Research, Nutrition, and General Legislation

* Senate Committee on Appropriations

Suite S-128 Capitol
Washington, DC 20510   202-224-3471

Topics covered: appropriations of revenues for executive agencies and Federal programs.

Subcommittees:

Agriculture and Related Agencies	202-224-5270
Commerce, Justice, State, and Judiciary	202-224-7236
Defense	202-224-7255
District of Columbia	202-224-2731
Energy and Water Development	202-224-7234
Foreign Operations	202-224-7251
Interior and Related Agencies	202-224-7233
Labor, Health and Human Services, Education, and Related Agencies	202-224-7230
Legislative Branch	202-224-7246
Military Construction	202-224-7271
Transportation and Related Agencies	202-224-7281
Treasury, Postal Service, and General Government	202-224-7337
VA, HUD and Independent Agencies	202-224-7234

* Senate Committee on the Armed Services

Suite SR-228 Russell Senate Office Building
Washington, DC 20510   202-224-3871

Topics covered: military and defense matters.

Subcommittees:

Acquisition and Technology	202-224-3871
Air Land Forces	202-224-3871
Personnel	202-224-3871
Readiness	202-224-3871
Seapower	202-224-3871
Strategic Forces	202-224-3871

* Senate Committee on Banking, Housing, and Urban Affairs

Suite SD-534 Dirksen Senate Office Building
Washington, DC 20510   202-224-7391

Topics covered: banks and other financial institutions; public and private housing; Federal monetary policy; urban development; mass transit; and certain foreign trade matters. For subcommittees, call main number.

Subcommittees:

Financial Institutions and Regulatory Relief	
International Finance	
Securities	
Housing Opportunity and Community Development	202-224-9205
HUD Oversight and Structure	

* Senate Committee on the Budget

SD-621 Dirksen Senate Office Building
Washington, DC 20510   202-224-0642

Topics covered: coordination of appropriations and revenues in Federal budget. This committee has no subcommittees.

* Senate Committee on Commerce, Science, and Transportation

Suite SD-508 Dirksen Senate Office Building
Washington, DC 20510   202-224-5115

Topics covered: regulation of interstate transportation, including railroads, buses, trucks, ships, pipelines, and civil aviation; Coast Guard; Merchant Marine; science and technology research policy; communications; non-military aeronautical and space sciences; coastal zone management; and oceans policy.

Subcommittees:

Aviation	202-224-4852
Communications	202-224-5184
Consumer	202-224-5183
Science, Technology, and Space	202-224-8172
Surface Transportation and Merchant Marine	202-224-4852
National Ocean Policy Study	202-224-8172

* Senate Committee on Energy and Natural Resources

Suite SD-304 Dirksen Senate Office Building
Washington, DC 20510   202-224-4971

Topics covered: regulation, conservation, and research and development of all forms of energy; mining; national parks; wilderness areas and historical sites; and territorial possessions of the U.S.

Subcommittees:

Energy Production and Regulation	202-224-5754
Energy Research and Development	202-224-6621
Forests and Public Land Management	202-224-2752
Oversight and Investigations	202-224-6441
Parks, Historic Preservation, and Recreation	202-224-2852

* Senate Committee on Environment and Public Works

Suite SD-410 Dirksen Senate Office Building
Washington, DC 20510   202-224-6176

Topics covered: environmental protection; water resources and flood control; public works and buildings; highways; and noise pollution. For subcommittees, call the main number.

Subcommittees:

Clean Air and Wetlands
Private Property and Nuclear Safety
Superfund
Transportation and Infrastructure
Drinking Water, Fisheries,, and Wildlife

* Senate Committee on Finance

Suite SD-219 Dirksen Senate Office Building
Washington, DC 20510   202-224-4515

Topics covered: taxes; tariffs; import quotas; old-age and survivors insurance; Medicare; unemployment insurance; general revenue sharing. For subcommittees, call the main number.

Subcommittees:

Long-Term Growth, Debt, and Deficit Reduction
Medicaid and Health Care for Low-Income Families
Social Security and Family Policy
International Trade
Medicare and Long Term Care and Health Insurance
Taxation and IRS Oversight

* Senate Committee on Foreign Relations

Suite SD-450 Dirksen Senate Office Building
Washington, DC 20510   202-224-4651

Topics covered: foreign policy; treaties; diplomatic affairs; United Nations.

Subcommittees:

African Affairs	202-224-4774
East Asian and Pacific Affairs	202-224-6441
European Affairs	202-224-4814
International Economic Policy, Export and Trade Promotion	202-224-4944
International Operations	202-224-5344
Near Eastern and South Asian Affairs	202-224-5941
Western Hemisphere and Peace Corps Affairs	202-224-3643

* Senate Committee on Governmental Affairs

Suite SD-340 Dirksen Senate Office Building
Washington, DC 20510   202-224-4751

Topics covered: budget and accounting matters; organization and reorganization of executive branch; intergovernmental relations; municipal affairs of the District of Columbia; civil service; postal service; and the census.

Subcommittees:

Post Office and Civil Service	202-224-2254

Information from Lawmakers

Oversight of Government Management, District of Columbia . . . 202-224-3682
Permanent Subcommittee on Investigations 202-224-3721

* Senate Committee on the Judiciary

Suite SD-224
Dirksen Senate Office Building
Washington, DC 20510   202-224-5225

Topics covered: Federal courts and judges; civil rights and civil liberties; constitutional amendments; interstate compacts; legislative apportionment; antitrust and monopoly; and immigration and naturalization.

Subcommittees:

Antitrust, Business Rights and Competition 202-224-9494
Constitution, Federalism, and Property Rights 202-224-8081
Administrative Oversight and Courts 202-224-6736
Immigration 202-224-6098
Terrorism, Technology and Government Information 202-224-6791
Youth Violence 202-224-7572

* Senate Committee on Labor and Human Resources

Suite SD-428 Dirksen Senate Office Building
Washington, DC 20510   202-224-5375

Topics covered: education, labor, health, and public welfare.

Subcommittees:

Aging 202-224-0136
Children and Families 202-224-5800
Education, Arts, and Humanities 202-224-2962
Disabilities Policies 202-224-7139
Office on Labor and Employment 202-224-6770
Office on Health Policy 202-224-3191

* Senate Committee on Rules and Administration

Suite SR-305 Russell Senate Office Building
Washington, DC 20510   202-224-6352

Topics covered: rules of the Senate; Senate employees; management of the Senate; Federal elections; Presidential succession; the Smithsonian Institution; the Library of Congress. The Committee has no subcommittees.

* Senate Committee on Small Business

Suite SR-428A Russell Senate Office Building   202-224-5175
Washington, DC 20510   Fax: 202-224-4885

Topics covered: measures relating to small businesses generally, and to the Small Business Administration. The committee has no subcommittees.

* Senate Committee on Veterans' Affairs

Suite SR-412 Russell Senate Office Building
Washington, DC 20510   202-224-9126

Topics covered: veterans' affairs, including pensions, medical care, life insurance, education, and rehabilitation. This Committee has no subcommittees.

Senate Think Tanks and Committees

Congressional studies and policy options are byproducts of these Senate committees. Usually established for a limited period of time, these committees ordinarily deal with more specific issues and problems than do the legislative committees. The political party organizations are permanent committees, but others are usually established for a specific period of time or until the project for which they have been created has been completed. Most select committees may investigate, study, and make recommendations, but they have no authority to make legislation. The Select and Special Committees of the Senate are as follows:

Special Committee on Aging
Room SD G-31 Dirksen Senate Office Building; Washington, DC 20510-6400; 202-224-5364.

Select Committee on Ethics
Room SH-220 Hart Senate Office Building; Washington, DC 20510-6425; 202-224-2981.

Select Committee on Indian Affairs
Room SH-838 Hart Senate Office Building; Washington, DC 20510-6450; 202-224-2251; Fax: 224-2309.

Select Committee on Intelligence
Room SH-211 Hart Senate Office Building; Washington, DC 20510-6475; 202-224-1700.

Special Committee to Investigate Whitewater
Room SD-534, Dirksen Senate Office Building, Washington, DC 20510; 202-224-7391.

House of Representatives Legislative Committees

The work of drafting and considering legislation is done largely by 19 committees. The jurisdictions of the House committees are similar to the 16 Senate committees; however, the House subcommittees usually play a much more important role than their Senate counterparts. The committees and subcommittees, with rare exception, determine what legislation will be considered by the entire House. In the process they modify--sometimes extensively--proposals referred to them. The committees, like the Senate committees, serve as congressional watchdogs of the executive branch. They oversee the organization and operations of the executive branch agencies--for knowing how efficiently and effectively the agencies perform their duties, and for knowing whether and how they are carrying out the intent of the laws enacted by Congress. These legislative committees are tremendous generators of information on all the issues over which they have jurisdiction, and both the committee and subcommittee staff are accessible and useful contacts.

* Committee on House Oversight

1309 Longworth House Office Building
Washington, DC 20515   202-225-2061

Topics covered: House administration and management; Federal election legislation; Library of Congress; and the Smithsonian Institution. This committee has no subcommittees.

* Committee on Science

2320 Rayburn House Office Building   202-225-8772
Washington, DC 20515   Fax: 202-225-8280

Topics covered: astronautical research and development; energy research and development; space; and scientific research and development.

Subcommittees:

Basic Research 202-225-9662
Energy and Environment 202-225-9662
Space and Aeronautics 202-225-7878
Technology 202-225-8848

* House Committee on Agriculture

1301 Longworth House Office Building
Washington, DC 20515   202-225-2171

Topics covered: agriculture and forestry measures, including farm credit, crop insurance, soil conservation, rural electrification, domestic marketing, and nutrition. All subcommittees may be reached through the main committee number.

Subcommittees:
Department Operations, Nutrition and Foreign Agriculture
Resource Conservation, Research, and Forestry
Livestock, Dairy, and Poultry
General Farm Commodity
Risk Management, Specialty Crop

* House Committee on Appropriations
H-218 Capitol Building
Washington, DC 20515   202-225-2771
Topics covered: appropriation of revenue for executive agencies and Federal programs and activities.

Subcommittees:
Agriculture, Rural Development, Food and Drug Administration
  and Related Agencies 202-225-2638
Commerce, Justice, State, The Judiciary, and
  Related Agencies 202-225-3351
District of Columbia 202-225-5338
Energy and Water Development 202-225-3421
Foreign Operations, Export Financing, and Related Programs ... 202-225-2041
Interior 202-225-3081
Labor, Health and Human Services, Education, and
  Related Agencies 202-225-3508
Legislative 202-225-5338
Military Construction 202-225-3047
National Security 202-225-2847
Transportation 202-225-2141
Treasury, Postal Service, and General Government 202-225-5834
VA, HUD, and Independent Agencies 202-225-3241

* House Committee on Banking, Finance, and Urban Affairs
2129 Rayburn House Office Building
Washington, DC 20515   202-225-7502
Topics covered: banking and currency legislation; international financial organizations; public and private housing.

Subcommittees:
Capital Markets, Securities and
  Government-Sponsored Enterprises 202-226-0469
Domestic and International Monetary Policy 202-226-0473
Financial Institutions and Consumer Credit 202-225-2258
General Oversight and Investigations 202-226-3280
Housing and Community Opportunity 202-225-6634

* House Committee on the Budget
309 Cannon House Office
Washington, DC 20515   202-226-7270
Topics covered: coordination of spending and revenues in federal budget. This committee has no special task forces or subcommittees.

* House Committee on Economic and Educational Opportunity
2181 Rayburn House Office Building
Washington, DC 20515   202-225-4527
Topics covered: education and labor legislation, including vocational rehabilitation, minimum wage legislation, and school lunch programs. All subcommittees may be reached through the main committee number.

Subcommittees:
Employer-Employee Relations
Workforce Protections
Early Childhood, Youth and Families
Oversight and Investigations
Postsecondary Education, Training and Life Long Learning

* House Energy and Commerce Committee
2125 Rayburn House Office Building
Washington, DC 20515   202-225-2927

Topics covered: National energy policy generally, including energy pricing, transmission, and conservation; interstate commerce; communications; securities and exchanges; health care; biomedical research; railroads and railroad labor; and consumer affairs and protection. All subcommittees may be reached through the main committee number.

Subcommittees:
Commerce, Trade, and Hazardous Materials
Energy and Power
Health and the Environment
Oversight and Investigations
Telecommunications and Finance

* House Committee on Government Reform and Oversight
2157 Rayburn House Office Building
Washington, DC 20515   202-225-5074
Topics covered: Executive branch reorganization, intergovernmental relations, and revenue sharing.

Subcommittees:
Civil Service 202-225-6427
District of Columbia 202-225-6751
Government Management, Information, and Technology 202-225-5147
Human Resources and Intergovernmental Relations 202-225-2548
National Economic Growth, Natural Resources,
  and Regulatory Affairs 202-225-4407
National Security, International Affairs, and Criminal Justice ... 202-225-2577
Postal Service 202-225-3741

* House Committee on International Relations
2170 Rayburn House Office Building
Washington, DC 20515   202-225-5021
Topics covered: foreign relations; international trade and economic policy; Food For Peace; international commodity agreements.

Subcommittees:
Africa 202-226-7812
Asia and the Pacific 202-226-7825
International Economic Policy and Trade 202-225-3345
International Operations and Human Rights 202-225-5748
Western Hemisphere 202-226-7820

* House Committee on Public Works, Transportation and Infrastructure
2165 Rayburn House Office Building
Washington, DC 20515   202-225-9446
Topics covered: public buildings and roads; bridges and dams; flood control; rivers and harbors; watershed development; mass transit; surface transportation excluding railroads; and civil aviation.

Subcommittees:
Aviation 202-226-3220
Coast Guard/Maritime Transportation 202-226-3552
Public Buildings and Economic Development 202-225-3014
Railroads 202-226-0727
Surface 202-225-6715
Water 202-225-4360

* House Committee on Resources
1324 Longworth House Office Building
Washington, DC 20515   202-225-2761
Topics covered: public lands; national parks and military cemeteries; irrigation; reclamation; U.S. territories and possessions; Indian affair; and regulation of domestic nuclear energy industry.

Subcommittees:
Energy and Mineral Resources 202-225-9297
Fisheries, Wildlife, and Oceans 202-226-0200
National Parks, Forests, and Lands 202-226-7736
Native American and Insular Affairs 202-226-7393
Water and Power Resources 202-225-8331

Information from Lawmakers

* House Committee on Rules

H-312 Capitol Building
Washington, DC 20515   202-225-9191

Topics covered: resolutions governing the disposition of business on the House floor; rules of the House (except for the House Code of Official Conduct); and waivers relating to legislative deadlines imposed by the Congressional Budget Act.

Subcommittees:

Rules of the House	202-225-8925
The Legislative Process	202-225-1547

* House Committee on Small Business

2361 Rayburn House Office Building
Washington, DC 20515   202-225-5821

Topics covered: measures related to small business generally, and to the Small Business Administration.

Subcommittees:

Government Programs	202-225-8944
Regulation and Paperwork	202-225-7797
Procurement, Exports, and Business Opportunities	202-225-9638
Tax and Finance	202-225-7673

* House Committee on Standards of Official Conduct

HT-2, Capitol Building
Washington, DC 20515   202-225-7103

Topics covered: enforcement of Code of Official Conduct. The Committee has no subcommittees.

* House Committee on Veterans' Affairs

335 Cannon House Office Building
Washington, DC 20515   202-225-3527

Topics covered: veterans' affairs, including pensions, medical care, life insurance, education, and rehabilitation.

Subcommittees:

Hospitals and Health Care	202-225-9154
Compensation, Pension, and Memorial Affairs	202-225-3569
Education, Training, Employment, and Housing	202-225-9166

* House Committee on Ways and Means

1102 Longworth House Office Building
Washington, DC 20515   202-225-3625

Topics covered: taxation, social security, tariffs, and health care programs financed through payroll taxes.

Subcommittees:

Health	202-225-3943
Human Resources	202-225-1025
Oversight	202-225-7601
Social Security	202-225-9263
Trade	202-225-6649

* Judiciary Committee of the House

2138 Rayburn House Office Building
Washington, DC 20515   202-225-3951

Topics covered: Federal courts; constitutional amendments; immigration and naturalization; Presidential succession; antitrust and monopolies; impeachment resolutions; and patents, trademarks, and copyrights.

Subcommittees:

Commercial and Administrative Law	202-225-2825
Constitution	202-226-7680
Courts and Intellectual Property	202-225-5741
Crime	202-225-3926
Immigration and Claims	202-225-5727

* National Security Committee

2120 Rayburn House Office Building
Washington, DC 20515   202-225-4151

Topics covered: defense matters, including procurement practices, weapons systems, manpower, military intelligence, naval petroleum reserves, and military applications of nuclear energy.

Subcommittees:
Investigations
Military Installations and Facilities
Military Personnel
Military Procurement
Military Readiness
Military Research and Development
Special Oversight Panel on Morale, Welfare, and Recreation
Special Oversight Panel on the Merchant Marines

House Investigative Committees and Think Tanks

Many of these House committees conduct hearings and issue reports and recommendations. The Committee on Intelligence, which oversees the Central Intelligence Agency (CIA) and other national security operations, has both investigative and legislative authority. Several of these select committees, such as the Committee on Aging and the Committee on Children, Youth, and Family, will most likely continue their work well into the 1990s. The various political party organizations, such as the Democratic Study Group, issue numerous policy papers on such broad issues as health care, education, and defense. Don't overlook these committees; the staff experts are very knowledgeable.

Permanent Select Committee on Intelligence
Room H-405, The Capitol Building, Washington, DC 20515; 202-225-4121. Subcommittees may be reached through the main committee number.

Subcommittees
Human Intelligence, Analysis, and Counter Intelligence
Technical and Tactical Intelligence

Democratic Congressional Campaign Committee
430 South Capitol St., SE, Washington, DC 20003; 202-863-1500.

Democratic Steering and Policy Committee
Room H-226, The Capitol Building, Washington, DC 20515; 202-225-8550.

Democratic Study Group
Room 1422, Longworth House Office Building, Washington, DC 20515; 202-225-5858.

National Republican Congressional Committee
320 First St., SE, Washington, DC 20003; 202-479-7000.

Republican Policy Committee
2471 Rayburn House Office Building, Washington, DC 20515; 202-225-6168.

Minority WHIP Committee
H107 Capitol Building, Washington, DC 20515; 202-225-0197.

Joint Committees of the U.S. Congress

Congress uses joint committees for study and administrative purposes. Usually joint committees study broad and complex areas of interest to the entire Congress. They are usually permanent bodies composed of an equal number of House and Senate members. Members of these committees are appointed under the provisions of the measure establishing them.

Joint Committee on the Library of Congress
Room SH-711, House Annex I, Washington, DC 20510; 202-224-3753.

Joint Committee on Printing
Room SH-818, U.S. Hart Senate Office Building, Washington, DC 20510-6650; 202-224-5241; Fax: 224-1176. Arm of the Committee: Congressional Record Index Office; U.S. Government Printing Office, Room C-738, North Capitol and H Sts., Washington, DC 20401; 202-512-0275.

Joint Committee on Taxation
SD-204 Dirksen Office Building, Washington, DC 20510; 202-224-5569.

Joint Economic Committee
Room SD-G01 Dirksen Senate Office Building, Washington, DC 20510; 202-224-5171.
Subcommittees: International Economic Policy Technology and National Security Economics; Economic Growth, Trade, and Taxes; Fiscal and Monetary Policy; Economic Goals and Intergovernmental Policy; Economic Resources and Competitiveness; and Investment, Jobs, and Prices; Education and Health.

Congressional Budget Office
2nd and D Streets, SW, Washington, DC 20515; 202-226-2621. This nonpartisan think tank works closely with the House and Senate Budget Committees and helps lawmakers analyze both the fiscal and budgetary consequences of legislation and the interaction between the federal budget and the nation's economy. CBO maintains current tabs of spending actions, prepares cost estimates for bills, provides funding alternatives for bills, reports annual projections for new budget activities, and issues advisory reports that estimate whether the projected deficit exceeds that allowed by law.

Special Interest Congressional Organizations

Congressional Member Organizations (CMOs) —commonly known as informal groups, caucuses, coalitions, or ad hoc task forces--are voluntary associations of Members of Congress created to play a role in the policy process. Unlike the formal leadership and party organizations, these groups operate without direct recognition in the chamber rules or line item appropriations. At least 114 congressional member organizations are currently operating. Listed below are some of the groups which Senators and Congressmen have formed to exercise a stronger voice about certain regional, ethnic, industrial, or other concerns related to their state or congressional district. Some caucuses have a primary mission to disseminate information, while others serve as an informal in-house lobby on various policies. Listed are groups which may be of particular interest to the public as all caucuses produce reports, monitor legislation, and can serve as useful resources. Included is the chairperson of each group.

Albanian Issues Caucus
Elito L. Engel, Room 1433, Longworth House Office Building, Washington, DC 20515; 202-225-2464

An Artistic Discovery
George Gekas, Room 2410 Rayburn House Office Building, Washington, DC 20515; 202-225-4315

Auto Parts Task Force
Sander Levin, Room 2230, Rayburn House Office Building, Washington, DC 20515; 202-225-4961

Bipartisan Regulatory Reform Caucus
Thomas Bliley, Room 2241 Rayburn House Office Building, Washington, DC 20515; 202-225-2815

Children, Youth and Family Caucus
Barbara Rose Collins, Room 401 Cannon House Office Building, Washington, DC 20515; 202-225-2261

CMO on Terrorism and Unconventional Warfare
Jim Saxton, Room 339 Cannon House Office Building, Washington, DC 20515; 202-225-4765

Congressional Automotive Caucus
Dale Kildee, Room 2187 Rayburn House Office Building, Washington, DC 20515; 202-225-3611

Congressional Aviation and Space Caucus
Herbert Bateman, Room 2350 Rayburn House Office Building, Washington, DC 20515; 202-225-4261

Congressional Bearing Caucus
Nancy L. Johnson, Room 343 Cannon House Office Building, Washington, DC 20515; 202-225-4476

Congressional Black Caucus
Donald Payne, Room 2244 Rayburn House Office Building, Washington, DC 20515; 202-225-3436

Congressional Caucus for Women's Issues
Nita Lowey, Room 2421 Rayburn House Office Building, Washington, DC 20515; 202-225-6506

Congressional Caucus on Armenian Issues
Frank Pallone, Room 420 Cannon House Office Building, Washington, DC 20515; 202-225-4671

Congressional Caucus on India and Indian-Americans
Frank Pallone, Room 420 Cannon House Office Building, Washington, DC 20515; 202-225-4671

Congressional Coalition on Population and Development
Connie Morella, Room 106 Cannon House Office Building, Washington, DC 20515; 202-225-5341

Congressional Coastal Caucus
Frank Pallone, Room 420 Cannon House Office Building, Washington, DC 20515; 202-225-4671

Congressional Empowerment Caucus
Curt Weldon, Room 2452 Rayburn House Office Building, Washington, DC 20515; 202-225-2011

Congressional Family Caucus
Tom Coburn, Room 511 Cannon House Office Building, Washington, DC 20515; 202-225-2701

Congressional Fire Services Caucus
Sherwood Boehlert, Room 2246 Rayburn House Office Building, Washington, DC 20515; 202-225-3665

Congressional Hispanic Caucus
Ed Pastor, Room 223 Cannon House Office Building, Washington, DC 20515; 202-225-4065

Congressional Human Rights Caucus
John Edward Porter, Room 2373 Rayburn House Office Building, Washington, DC 20515; 202-225-4835

Congressional Law Enforcement Caucus
Jim Lightfoot, Room 2161 Rayburn House Office Building, Washington, DC 20525; 202-225-3806

Congressional Missile Defense Caucus
Curt Weldon, Room 2452 Rayburn House Office Building, Washington, DC 20515; 202-225-2011

Congressional Narcotics Abuse and Control Caucus
Charles Rangel, Room 2354 Rayburn House Office Building, Washington, DC 20215; 202-225-4365

Congressional Oil and Gas Educational Forum
Jim McCrery, Room 225 Cannon House Office Building, Washington, DC 20515; 202-225-2777

Congressional Shipbuilding Caucus
Jim Longley, Room 226 Cannon House Office Building, Washington, DC 20515; 202-225-6116

Be patient. If any phone number is incorrect, call (area code) 555-1212 and request the new listing.

1181

Information from Lawmakers

Congressional Steel Caucus
Ralph Regula, Room 2309 Rayburn House Office Building, Washington, DC 20515; 202-225-3876

Congressional Sunbelt Caucus
Thad Cochran, SR-326 Russell Building, Washington, DC 20510; 202-224-5054

Congressional U.S. Former Soviet Union Energy Caucus
Curt Weldon, Room 2452 Rayburn House Office Building, Washington, DC 20515; 202-225-2011

Conservative Opportunity Society
Thomas Ewing, Room 1317 Longworth House Office Building, Washington, DC 20515; 202-225-2371

Constitutional Caucus
J.D. Hayworth, Room 1023 Longworth House Office Building, Washington, DC 20515; 202-225-2190

Constitutional Liberty Caucus
Jack Metcalf, Room 507 Cannon House Office Building, Washington, DC 20515; 202-225-2605

Democratic Study Group
David Skaggs, Room 1124 Longworth House Office Building, Washington, DC 20515; 202-225-2161

Environmental and Energy Study Conference
Jan Meyers, Room 2303 Rayburn House Office Building, Washington, DC 20515; 202-225-2865

Forestry 2000 Task Force
Sonny Callahan, Room 2418 Rayburn House Office Building, Washington, DC 20515; 202-225-4931

House Army Caucus
John McHugh, Room 416 Cannon House Office Building, Washington, DC 20515; 202-225-4611

House Gaming Caucus
John B. Ensign, Room 414 Cannon House Office Building, Washington, DC 20515; 202-225-5965

House Medical Technology Caucus
Jim Ramstad, Room 103 Cannon House Office Building, Washington, DC 20515; 202-225-2871

House Pro-Life Caucus
Christopher Smith, Room 2370 Rayburn House Office Building, Washington, DC 20515; 202-225-3765

House Renewable Energy Caucus
Dan Schaefer, Room 2353 Rayburn House Office Building, Washington, DC 20515; 202-225-7882

Interstate 69 Mid-Continent Highway Caucus
John Hostettler, Room 1404 Longworth house Office Building, Washington, DC 20515; 202-225-4636

Jobs and Fair Trade Caucus
Duncan Hunter, Room 2265 Rayburn House Office Building, Washington, DC 20515; 202-225-5672

Manufacturing Task Force
Bob Franks, Room 429 Cannon House Office Building, Washington, DC 20515; 202-225-5361

National Security Caucus
Duncan Hunter, Room 2265 Rayburn House Office Building, Washington, DC 20515; 202-225-5672

New York Congressional Delegation
Charles Rangel, Room 2354 Rayburn House Office Building, Washington, DC 20515; 202-225-4365

Northeast-Midwest Congressional Coalition
Bob Franks, Room 429 Cannon House Office Building, Washington, DC 20515; 202-225-5361

Older Americans Caucus
Ron Wyden, Room 1111 Longworth House Office Building, Washington, DC 20515; 202-225-4811

Peace Accord Monitoring Group
Eliot Engel, Room 1433 Longworth House Office Building, Washington, DC 20515; 202-225-2464

Progressive Caucus
Bernard Sanders, Room 213 Cannon House Office Building, Washington, DC 20515; 202-225-4115

Small Business Survival Caucus
Bill Zellif, Room 1210 Longworth House Office Building, Washington, DC 20515; 202-225-5456

Western Caucus
James Hansen, Room 2466 Rayburn House Office Building, Washington, DC 20515; 202-225-0453

Be patient. If any phone number is incorrect, call (area code) 555-1212 and request the new listing.

Legislative Branch Sources

In addition to the powerful information sources of congressional committees and think tanks, the offices of your U.S. Senators and Representatives can be very helpful. In this section you'll also find out where to find financial information on federal campaign finance, television coverage of Congress, congressional salaries, and even how to get a flag that was raised over the U.S. Capitol.

* Bicentennial Celebration and Free Publications

Legislative Resource Center
House of Representatives
B-18 Cannon Building
Washington, DC 20515-6701   202-225-1153

The Office of the Historian acts as a clearinghouse for historical information on the House of Representatives, for the members, the public, and the press. Books and other reference information. The following publications are available free of charge from the Office:

A Guide to Research Collections of Former Members of the U.S. House of Representatives 1789-1987
Women in Congress
Origins of the U.S. House of Representatives: A Documentary Record

* Bills and Laws: Document Rooms

House Document Room
U.S. House of Representatives
2nd and D Sts.,SW, B-18   202-225-3456
Washington, DC 20515-6622   Fax: 202-226-4362

Senate Document Room
Senate Hart Office Bldg., Room B-04   202-224-7860
Washington, DC 20510-7106   Fax: 202-228-2815

Free copies of all bills introduced in the House and Senate are available. Legislation approved by committees and also passed by the full House and/or Senate along with committee reports are available free of charge. To request a bill, you must send a self-addressed mailing label and include the bill number or report number. No more than six requests may be presented at a time. Requests for Senate documents may be made to either of your Senators, and your Representative can get copies of House bills and reports. The Document Rooms maintain current files of legislation including public laws (slip laws). Periodically public laws on a variety of subject areas are compiled and are available for $160 per session from the Government Printing Office.

* Biographical Directory of the U.S. Congress 1774-1989

Superintendent of Documents
Government Printing Office
Washington, DC 20402   202-512-1800

The Biographical Directory of the U.S. Congress 1774-1989, contains authoritative biographies of the more than 11,000 men and women who have served in the U.S. Congress from 1789 to 1989, and in the Continental Congress between 1774 and 1789. Many features include a listing of all chairmen of standing committees, all major formal leadership positions, bibliographic citations, and major revisions of political party affiliations reflecting the latest scholarship. You'll also find complete rosters of State congressional delegations for the First through 100th Congresses. This bicentennial edition is the most comprehensive *Biographical Directory of the United States Congress* ever issued. The latest edition published at the beginning of the 101st Congress is available through the Government Printing Office for $82.

* Calendar of the House of Representatives and History of Legislation

Superintendent of Documents
Government Printing Office
Washington, DC 20402   202-512-1800

House Document Room
U.S. House of Representatives
2nd and D Sts., SW, B-18   202-225-3456
Washington, DC 20515-6622   Fax: 202-226-4362

This calendar contains a list of bills in conference, a list of bills through conference, the *Union Calendar*, the *House Calendar*, a history of actions on each bill of the current session, a subject index of active legislation, and more. It is a weekly (when Congress is in session) publication available on subscription for $247 a year. Free copies can be picked up at the House Document Room.

* Campaign Finance Information

Press Office
Federal Election Commission (FEC)
999 E Street, NW
Washington, DC 20463   202-219-4155

Staff of the Press Office are the Federal Election Commission's (FEC) official media spokespersons. In addition to publicizing FEC actions and releasing statistics on campaign finance, they respond to all questions from representatives of the print and broadcast media.

* Campaign Finance Records

Public Records Office
Federal Election Commission (FEC)
999 E Street, NW
Washington, DC 20463   202-219-4140

Commission disclosure of campaign finance activity is based on the reports submitted by political committees. These reports, available from the Public Records Office within 48 hours of receipt as required by law, focus on the flow of money in and out of campaigns and the sources of campaign support.

* Congress and the Nation

Clerk of the House
House of Representatives
The Capitol
Washington, DC 20515   202-225-7000

Congress and the Nation is a summary of material in the *Congressional Quarterly Almanac*. *Volume I* covers the years 1945-1964; thereafter, it is published every four years.

* Congressional Directory

Superintendent of Documents
Government Printing Office
Washington, DC 20402   202-512-1800

The *Congressional Directory* has been the official handbook for the Congress since 1821 and is also widely used by Federal agency officials and the general public. Its contents include lists of addresses, rooms, and phone numbers of Members, biographical sketches of Members, Capitol officers and officials, committees, departments, and information on diplomatic offices and statistics. It also includes lists of members of the press admitted to the House and Senate galleries. The *1989-1990 Official Congressional Directory of the 101st Congress* is available for $15 in paperback, $20 in hardback, and $25 for a hardback copy with a thumb index.

* Congressional Documents, Reports, and Hearings

Law Library
Library of Congress   202-707-5079
Washington, DC 20540   202-707-5065

All Senate and House documents, reports, hearings since 1970, and all bills back to the First Congress are available. Material can be obtained on microfilm.

Information from Lawmakers

* Congressional Leaders and Presiding Officers

Chief of Staff for Vice President
Old Executive Office Bldg, Room 276
Washington, DC 20501 — 202-456-6605

Speaker's Office
Room H-204, The Capitol
Washington, DC 20510 — 202-225-0600

Senate Minority Leader
Room S-221, The Capitol
Washington, DC 20510 — 202-224-5556

Senate Majority Leader
141 Hart Building
Washington, DC 20510 — 202-224-3135

The Vice President of the United States is the Presiding Officer of the Senate, and in his absence the duties are taken over by a President pro tempore, elected by that body, or someone designated by him. The Presiding Officer of the House of Representatives, the Speaker, is elected by the House; he may designate any Member of the House to act in his absence. The Senate Majority Leader is elected at the beginning of each new Congress by a majority vote of the Senators in the political party which controls the Senate. In cooperation with their party organizations, leaders are responsible for the design and achievement of a legislative program involving legislation, expediting noncontroversial measures, and keeping Members informed regarding proposed action on pending business. The Majority Leader serves as an ex officio member of this party's policy making and organizational bodies and is aided by an assistant floor leader (whip) and a party secretary.

* Congressional Record: House and Senate Floor Debate

Superintendent of Documents
Government Printing Office
Washington, DC 20402 — 202-512-1800

Proceedings of Congress are published in the *Congressional Record*, which is issued when Congress is in session. Publication of the *Record* began in March of 1873; it was the first record of debate officially reported, printed, and published directly by the Federal Government. The *Daily Digest of the Congressional Record*, printed in the back of each issue of the *Record*, summarizes the proceedings of that day in each House, and before each of their committees and subcommittees, respectively. The *Digest* also presents the legislative program for each day and, at the end of the week, gives the program for the following week. The subscription price is $225 per year. For information on the Senate portion of the *Congressional Record*, call 202-224-2658; for the House portion, call 202-224-5848; for information on committee activities, call Senate 202-224-2120; House 202-225-4470.

* Congressional Record Index

House Documents Room
U.S. House of Representatives
2nd and D Sts. SW, B-18
Washington, DC 20515-6622 — 202-225-3456

About once every two weeks, the *Congressional Record Index* is distributed listing *Congressional Record* matters by subject, member, bill number, bill title and every other sort of cross-reference combination. For instance, you can look up a member's name and find everything he or she introduced, made remarks on, submitted, reported, and gave a speech about. You can also look up a subject and find all related articles, editorials, bills, letters, tables, and press releases included during the previous two weeks in the *Congressional Record*.

* Congressional Telephone Directories

The Superintendent of Documents
Government Printing Office
Washington, DC 20402 — 202-512-1800

Telephone directories for the U.S. Senate and the House of Representatives are available for sale. Abbreviated pamphlets providing Members and committees telephone numbers and addresses are available from the Secretary of the Senate and the Clerk of the House.

* Daily Congressional Schedule

Published weekdays in the *Washington Post* newspaper, the *Today in Congress* column gives a daily rundown on times and subjects of all House and Senate committee hearings and meetings and indicates which are open to the public.

* Election Assistance

Federal Election Commission (FEC)
Information Services
999 E Street, NW
Washington, DC 20463 — 202-219-3420

In an effort to promote voluntary compliance with the law, this office provides technical assistance to candidates and committees and others involved in elections. Staff will research and answer questions on the Federal Election Campaign Act and FEC regulations, procedures, and advisory opinions; direct workshops on the law; and publish a wide range of materials.

* Federal Campaign Finance Law Complaints

Federal Election Commission (FEC)
999 E Street, NW
Washington, DC 20463 — 202-219-3690

If you believe a violation of the Federal campaign finance law has taken place, you may file a complaint with the Federal Election Commission. Send the Commission a letter explaining why you believe the law may have been violated, describe the specific facts and circumstances, and name the individuals or organizations responsible. The letter must be sworn to, signed, and notarized. Complaints of alleged violations receive case numbers and are called MURs, Matters Under Review.

* Federal Election Commission Publications

Federal Election Commission (FEC)
Information Services
999 E Street, NW — 202-219-3420
Washington, DC 20463 — 800-424-9530

The following publications are available free of charge from the Federal Election Commission (FEC):

Federal Election Campaign Laws. A complete compilation of Federal election campaign laws.
FEC Regulations. FEC regulations appear in Title 11 of the Code of Federal Regulations, including subject indexes.
FEC Record. This monthly newsletter is the primary source of information on FEC activity, covering reporting, advisory opinions, litigation, legislation, statistics, regulations compliance, and more.
FEC Annual Report.
Supporting Federal Candidates: A Guide for Citizens. For the general public, this booklet discusses how citizens can support Federal candidates through contributions, volunteer work, and independent expenditures.
The First 10 Years. Graphs and text describe the FEC's work during its first decade, including a brief history of campaign finance legislation and an overview of FEC operations.
Campaign Guides. Four separate guides explain how the law affects candidates, parties, corporations/unions, and nonconnected PACs. Election law requirements are explained and illustrated with examples of completed FEC forms.
The FEC and the Federal Campaign Finance Law. Gives a brief overview of the major provisions of the Federal Election Campaign Act and the FEC's role in administering it.
Public Funding of Presidential Elections. For the general public, this brochure gives a brief history of Presidential public funding and describes how the process works.
Using FEC Campaign Finance Information. Explains how to gather information about the financial activity of Federal political committees. It describes FEC's computer indexes and ways to use them.

* Federal Elections Clearinghouse

Federal Election Commission (FEC)
999 E Street, NW
Washington, DC 20463 — 202-219-3670

The Election Clearinghouse assists election officials and the general public by responding to inquiries concerning the electoral process, publishing research, and conducting workshops on all matters related to Federal election administration.

* Federal Elections Library

Federal Election Commission (FEC) Library
999 E Street, NW, Room 801
Washington, DC 20463 — 202-219-3312

The FEC Library's collection includes basic legal research tools and materials dealing with political campaign finance, corporate and labor political activity, and campaign finance reform. The Library staff prepares indexes to Advisory Opinions and Matters Under Review (MURs), as well as a *Campaign Finance and Federal Election Law Bibliography*, which are available for purchase from the FEC's Public Records Office.

* Financial Disclosure Database on Federal Candidates

Federal Election Commission (FEC)
Data Systems Development Division
999 E Street, NW
Washington, DC 20463   202-219-3730

The Federal Election Commission (FEC) maintains a computer database of information from all reports filed by political committees, individuals, and other entities since 1972. The data is sorted into indexes which permit a detailed analysis of campaign finance activity and, additionally, provide a tool for monitoring contribution limitations. The data can be searched by specific candidate or contributor. By contacting this office, individuals can have searches done on twenty names or less free of charge. For searches of more than 20 names, cost varies depending on computer time needed.

* General Accounting Office Bibliographic Database

General Accounting Office (GAO)/IHSF
P.O. Box 6015
Gaithersburg, MD 20877   202-512-4400

The General Accounting Office (GAO) maintains a database which provides bibliographic information on GAO documents and reports. The studies cover a vast array of subjects, as the agency must produce a report on any topic Congress assigns. Reports have ranged from financial audits of government agencies to policy studies of health-related programs. Searches are generally conducted by subject area and specific time period. Searches and printouts are available free of charge by calling 202-512-6000. GAO will also mail you up to five copies of any report listed, without charge. Each copy requested beyond that is $2. Contact the office above for information regarding the contents of the reports.

* General Accounting Office Congressional Staff Assignments

Congressional Relations
General Accounting Office (GAO)
441 G St., NW, Room 7125
Washington, DC 20548   202-512-4400

Each year the General Accounting Office (GAO) assigns between 75 to 125 staff members directly to Congressional committees to help carry out their responsibilities or to assist them in using the results of GAO studies. In addition, GAO provides staff assistance to committees having jurisdiction over revenues, appropriations, and expenditures, and often to other committees as well. The agency does not, however, assign staff to individual members of Congress.

* History of the Senate

Senate Historical Office
Secretary of the Senate
The Capitol, Room SH 201
Washington, DC 20510   202-224-6900

The Senate Historical Office collects and disseminates information on Senate history and Senate members, including photographs, unpublished documents, and oral history. A free newsletter, *Senate History*, is available, as well as a series of addresses to the Senate on subjects related to its history and traditions, including a list of citations with dates, subjects, and page numbers.

* House Committees Roster

Clerk of the House
House of Representatives
The Capitol
Washington, DC 20515   202-225-7000

This listing contains all official and unofficial House committees. The members of each committee are included.

* House Leadership and Ceremonial Posts

Office of the House Democratic Leader
Room H-214, The Capitol
Washington, DC 20515   202-225-0100

Office of the House Majority Leader
Room H-329, The Capitol
Washington, DC 20515   202-225-0600

The leadership of the House of Representatives is elected at the beginning of each Congress. Under the tradition of the two party system in the United States, the leader of the party with the largest number of Members becomes the Majority Leader. The Minority Leader is invariably the Member nominated by the minority party for the Senate.

Sergeant at Arms of the House
Room H-124, The Capitol
Washington, DC 20515   202-225-2456

This office enforces the rules of the house and maintains decorum during sessions of the House. The Sergeant at Arms also is in charge of the Mace, the symbol of legislative power and authority. Maintaining the general security of the House buildings and the Capitol is his major responsibility. Another major responsibility is management of the House bank which disburses Members' salaries and travel expenses.

Clerk of the House
Room H-154, The Capitol
Washington, DC 20515   202-225-7000

The Clerk is the chief legislative, administrative, and budgetary officer of the U.S. House of Representatives. The Clerk is responsible for directing legislative activities of the House, such as keeping the Journal, taking all votes, certifying passage of bills, and processing all legislation. The Clerk also prepares the budget for the House, disburses funds, serves as the contracting officer of the House, and issues a report available to the public on salaries and expenses. In addition, the Clerk is the purchaser and provider of all furnishings, office equipment, and office supplies.

Chaplain of the House
Room HB-25, The Capitol
Washington, DC 20515   202-225-2509

The Chaplain is responsible for the opening prayer at each session of the House, and occasionally invites other clergy to serve as guest chaplains. The Chaplain's Office also coordinates use of the Prayer Room and makes arrangements for pastoral services for Members and staff.

* House of Representatives Research and Library

U.S. House of Representatives and Committees Library
Cannon House Office Bldg., Room B 18
Washington, DC 20515   202-225-0462

This library is the official depository of House documents, reports, bills, and more. Its primary function is to serve House members and their staffs. It is open to the public, but no photocopying is permitted.

* House Telephone Directory

The Committee on House Oversight
1339 Longworth House Office Building
Washington, DC 20515   202-225-2061

The *House Telephone Directory* is produced yearly by the Committee on House Administration. It provides a listing for representatives, a listing for House committees, an alphabetical staff listing, a listing of staffs by representatives, a listing of staffs by committee, listings for senators and Senate committees, a listing for executive branch leaders, a listing for government agencies, and more. It is available for $17 from the Superintendent of Documents, Government Printing Office, 202-512-1800.

* How Our Laws Are Made

Superintendent of Documents
Government Printing Office   202-512-1800
Washington, DC 20402   Fax: 202-512-2250

The booklet, *How Our Laws Are Made*, is prepared by the House of Representatives and provides a plain language explanation of how a legislative idea travels the complex passageways of the federal lawmaking process to become a statute. It is available for $2.50 from the Superintendent of Documents.

* Legislative Archives

National Archives and Records Administration
7th St. and Pennsylvania Ave., NW, Room 8E
Washington, DC 20408   202-501-5350

The Legislative Archives Center is responsible for the appraisal, preservation,

Information from Lawmakers

arrangement, description, reference service, and outreach activities associated with all records of the U.S. Senate, House of Representatives, congressional committees, and agencies. The Center includes the Legislative Reference Branch, which provides reference services to Congress and the public pertaining to congressional records, and the Legislative Projects Branch, which has just completed writing two guides to the congressional records.

* Legislative Branch Audit Site

Audit Oversight and Liaison
Accounting and Information Division
General Accounting Office
441 G St., NW, Room 6123
Washington, DC 20548   202-512-9489

This office assists Congress by doing 15 regular annual financial audits of such units as the House Recording Studio and the Senate Restaurant. On a less formal basis, the staff also offers advice and assistance on administrative matters. For free copies (up to five) of Audit Site reports, contact: Information Handling and Support Facilities, General Accounting Office, P.O. Box 6015, Gaithersburg, MD 20877; 202-512-6000.

* Legislative Histories and Research

Law Library
Library of Congress, LM240
Washington, DC 20540   202-707-5065

The Law Library compiles legislative histories which include versions of new public statutes from the time of introduction, through congressional hearings, House and Senate floor debate, vote tallies, and votes.

* Live TV Coverage of House and Senate Chambers

Cable Satellite Public Affairs Network (C-SPAN)
400 North Capitol St., NW, Suite 650
Washington, DC 20001   202-737-3220

C-SPAN is a basic cable service specializing for more than a decade in the coverage of Congress. It shows lawmaking in the raw on Capitol Hill. Created to provide live gavel-to-gavel coverage of the U.S. House of Representatives C-SPAN II began in 1986 to cablecast the live sessions off the U.S. Senate, in their entirety. In addition, C-SPAN offers a front row seat to other public events from the nation's capitol and across the country. Events are aired without commentary or analysis. Each morning at 8 and each evening at 6:30, the network presents "Viewer Call-in" where viewer's questions about major news events are discussed. To receive C-SPAN call your local cable company.

* New Federal Laws

Office of the Federal Register
National Archives and Records Administration
800 N. Capitol St. NW, Room 700
Washington, DC 20408   202-523-5230

This office receives all laws enacted by Congress for publication in the *Federal Register* and can provide information regarding these laws. They also publish *United States Statutes at Large*, a compilation of laws enacted during a particular year.

* New Laws: Free Copies of These Statutes

House Documents Room
U.S. House of Representatives
2nd and D Sts. SW, B-18
Washington, DC 20515-6622   202-226-3456

The 104th Congress has passed only 106 laws to date. For a complete listing of the new laws passed by the 104th Congress, contact the House Documents Room and ask for a House Calendar which will list the new laws and their bill numbers.

* Online Access to FEC Financial Database

Federal Election Commission (FEC)
Press Office
999 E Street, NW   800-424-9530
Washington, DC 20463   202-219-3730

The Federal Election Commission (FEC) offers an online computer information system designed for owners of personal computers. The system furnishes campaign finance information in formatted computer indexes and in raw data form. For a specific candidate or committee, the system provides the following information for election cycles beginning in 1985: total receipts and expenditures; total cash on hand; and total debts owed. Contact this office for more information on accessing this information.

* Photographs of Every Member of Congress

The Superintendent of Documents
Government Printing Office
Washington, DC 20402   202-512-1800

The *Congressional Pictorial Directory* contains photographs of the President, Vice President, members of the Senate and House, Officers of the Senate and House, Officials of the Capitol, and a list of the Senate delegations and an alphabetical list of senators and representatives. The paperback edition is $5.50, and the hardback copy is $16.

* Presidential Political Appointments: The "Plum" Book

Senate Government Affairs Committee
Dirksen Office Building, Room SD 353
Washington, DC 20510

Superintendent of Documents
Government Printing Office
Washington, DC 20402   202-512-1800

U.S. Policy and Supporting Positions, more commonly known as the *Plum Book*, lists some 3,000 political appointment jobs and describes the type of appointment, tenure, grade, and salary. It is available for sale at the Superintendent of Documents, Government Printing Office for $13 per copy.

* Public Laws Tape Recording

Office of the Federal Register
National Archives and Records Administration
800 N. Capitol St. NW, Room 700
Washington, DC 20408   202-523-6641

This recording lists the most recent laws which have come to the office for publication in the *Federal Register*.

* Published Congressional Hearings

Documents Clerk
Relevant House Committee   202-225-3456
Relevant Senate Committee   202-224-7860

Superintendent of Documents
Government Printing Office
Washington, DC 20402   202-512-1800

House and Senate committees and subcommittees conduct hundreds of informational and investigative hearings practically every week of the year. All of these congressional hearings are published and often available free of charge from the documents clerk of the committee or subcommittee which held the hearings. Many of the hearings also are sold by the Superintendent of Documents, Government Printing Office.

* Radio Coverage of Committee Hearings and International Events

C-SPAN Audio Networks
400 North Capitol St., NW, Suite 650
Washington, DC 20001   202-737-3220

The C-SPAN Audio Networks were created to provide audio coverage of congressional committee hearings and other public affairs events. They are intended to supplement the round-the-clock floor coverage of the House and Senate provided by the C-SPAN and C-SPAN II cable television networks. In addition, the Audio Networks air international public affairs events through retransmissions of foreign English-language shortwave radio programming. C-SPAN Audio I combines the Washington, DC, and international programming. Future audio programming will provide historical perspective through programming of public events from the past, drawn from the National Archives and other Sources. C-SPAN Audio 2 provides 24-hour retransmissions of the BBC World Service.

* Raise a Flag Over the Capitol

c/o The Capitol
Washington, DC 20515   202-224-3121

You can arrange to purchase flags that have been flown over the Capitol by getting in touch with your U.S. Senator or Representative. A certificate signed by the Architect of the Capitol accompanies each flag. Flags are available for purchase in sizes of 3'x5' or 5'x8' in fabrics of cotton and nylon.

* Salaries and Expenses of House of Representatives

Members and Employees
House Document Room
U.S. House of Representatives
2nd and D Sts. SW, B-18
Washington, DC 20515-6622   202-225-3456

The *Report of the Clerk of the House* includes the salaries of House members' staffs, committee staffs, and House officers and employees. This quarterly report includes a listing of House expenditures.

* Salaries and Expenses of U.S. Senators and Their Staff

Senate Document Room
Room B-04 Senate Hart Office Building
Washington, DC 20510   202-224-7860

The biannual *Report of the Secretary of the* Senate lists expenditures and details the salaries of senators' staff, members, committee staff members, and officers and employees of the Senate.

* Senate Committees Roster

Office of the Secretary of the Senate
The Capitol, Room S-208
Washington, DC 20510   202-224-2115

A listing is available of official Senate committees. These include the members of each committee. Also available is the *A Class List of Senators*, which gives the names of all Senators, their states, their party affiliations, and the year they are up for reelection.

* Senate Leadership or Ceremonial Posts

Office of Republican Leader
Room S-230, The Capitol
Washington, DC 20510   202-224-3135

The Minority Leader is elected at the beginning of each new Congress by the Senators in the political party which does not have a working majority in the Senate. This leader works closely with its party organizations and currently with the White House in terms of getting the President's legislative program enacted.

Secretary of the Senate
Room S-208, The Capitol
Washington, DC 20510   202-224-2115

The Secretary is the custodian of the seal of the Senate, and handles the payroll for the Senators, officers, committee staff, and employees, and issues a report disclosing such salaries and expenses. The Secretary's executive duties include certification of extracts from the Journal of the Senate; the attestation of bills and joint, concurrent, and Senate resolutions; in impeachment trials, issuance, under the authority of the Presiding Officer, of all orders, mandates, writs, and precepts, authorized by the Senate; and certification of the President of the United States of the advice and consent of the Senate to ratification of treaties and the names of persons confirmed or rejected upon the nomination of the President.

Sergeant at Arms of the Senate
Room S-321, The Capitol   202-224-2341
Washington, DC 20510   Fax: 224-7690

The Senate elects the Sergeant at Arms who serves as its Executive Officer. As law enforcement officer, the Sergeant of Arms has statutory power to make arrests; to locate absentee Senators for a quorum; and to enforce Senate rules and regulations. As Protocol Officer, he is responsible for many aspects of ceremonial functions, including the Presidential inauguration; funeral arrangements of Senators who die in office; escorting the President when he addresses a Joint Session of Congress or attends any function in the Senate; and escorting heads of state when they visit the Senate.

Chaplain of the Senate
Room SH-204A, Hart Senate Office Bldg.
Washington, DC 20510   202-224-2510

The Chaplain of the Senate serves as pastor to the Senators and their families. He opens the sessions of the Senate each day with a prayer. His office is a resource center for information concerning the Bible, various religious denominations, and the subject of religion in general.

* Senate Research and Library

Senate Library
The Capitol, Suite S-332
Washington, DC 20510   202-224-7106

The Senate Library is the official depository of senate documents. Its primary function is service to Senate members and their staffs. To use the library a researcher must have a letter of introduction from a Senator.

* State Access to Financial Disclosure Database

Federal Election Commission (FEC)
Public Records Office   202-219-4140
999 E Street, NW   Web Site: www.fec.gov
Washington, DC 20463   FTP: ftp.fec.gov

Under the State Access Program, individuals and organizations in 30 states now have immediate online access to several standard Federal Election Commission (FEC) computer indexes which provide descriptive information on all registered political committees, the total receipts and disbursements of committees, and a listing of all PAC contributions to federal candidates. Participating states with operational terminals within their State Election Offices include: Arizona, Colorado, Connecticut, Georgia, Illinois, Iowa, Massachusetts, Michigan, New Jersey, New Mexico, Ohio, Tennessee, Vermont, Washington, and Wisconsin.

* State Election Finance Records

Federal Election Commission (FEC)
Public Records Office
999 E Street, NW   800-424-9530
Washington, DC 20463   202-219-4140

Researchers can obtain campaign finance reports from the records office in each state. Contact this Federal Election Commission (FEC) office to order a list of the names, addresses, and phone numbers of national and state disclosure offices.

* Treaties and Nominations

Senate Document Room
Hart Building, Room B-04
Washington, DC 20510   202-224-7860

For information on and copies of treaties submitted to the Senate for ratification, contact the Senate Document Room or your Senators.

* World's Largest Law Library

Law Library
Library of Congress
Washington, DC 20540   202-707-5065

As the world's largest and most comprehensive library of foreign, international, and comparative law, the Law Library provides information for all known legal systems including common law, civil law, Roman law, canon law, Chinese law, Jewish and Islamic law, and ancient and medieval law. Specialists with knowledge of more than fifty languages provide reference and research service in all known legal systems. U.S. legislative documents housed here include the *Congressional Record* (and its predecessors), the serial set, a nearly complete set of bills and resolutions, current documents, committee prints, reports, hearings, etc. and a complete set of U.S. Supreme Court records and briefs and collections of U.S. Court of Appeals records and briefs. The law library has only two divisions:

Western Law Division
United States, Australia, Canada, Great Britain, India, New Zealand, Pakistan, certain other countries of the British Commonwealth and their dependent territories, Eire, Spain and Portugal, Latin America, Puerto Rico, the Philippines, and Spanish-and Portuguese-language states of Africa: 202-707-5077.

Eastern Law Division
Nations of Europe and their possessions, except Spain and Portugal, nations of East and Southeast Asia including China, Indonesia, Japan, Korea, Thailand, and former British and French possessions in the area, Middle Eastern countries, including the Arab states, Turkey, Iran, and Afghanistan, and all African countries except Spanish-and Portuguese-language states and possessions: 202-707-5085.

Tracking State Legislation

* See also Information Starting Places; State Information Starting Places Chapter
* See also Current Events and Homework Chapter

Bill Status Information

Most state legislatures maintain an office responsible for providing bill status information to the public. In Ohio, for example, a bank of telephone reference experts answer questions about current or past legislation on any given subject. The researchers rely on their own files and also have access to a computerized database updated by the Senate Clerk's office. Usually these offices can search their databases or indexes in several ways, by keyword or phrase, by specific subject, or by state senator or representative.

About half of the legislatures can send you this information in the form of a computer printout free of charge. In those states which do not operate a central bill status office, it is necessary to contact the Clerk of the House for information on bills pending before the House and similarly a call to the Secretary or Clerk of the Senate for updates on legislation pending before that body. Many legislatures have toll-free numbers which can be accessed only if you are calling from inside the state. Most of the State House hotlines operate just during the regular session of the legislature and, as you might expect, some of the "800" numbers change from one session to the next.

Your initial call to the bill status office will lead you to the appropriate committees, and if no action has been taken on a particular bill, this legislative information office can provide you with the sponsor of the legislation whom you can call directly for more details.

Copies of Bills and Other Legislative Documents

In most states, the legislative information office can send you copies of bills. Indiana is the only state that charges $.10 per page if the bill is more than 10 pages long. All states print the bills at the time of introduction. Over half reprint the amended legislation after committee action, and about two-thirds of all chambers print the legislation after the floor vote. Unlike the U.S. Congress, legislative documentation is skimpy when it comes to committee hearings as well as floor debate. Only about a third of all legislative bodies tape all committee sessions. You can make arrangements with the Clerk's office to listen to the tapes, and some states, like the Minnesota House, sell audio tapes of committee meetings and floor debates for $12.50 per copy. For copies, call 612-296-3398.

Advanced Strategy for Monitoring One or All 50 State Legislatures

Coverage of a state legislature can be substantially enhanced in many ways; some are inexpensive and others can be costly:

* Clipping Service:
Newspapers, especially those published in the state capital, can prove to be a cost effective way of staying informed provided the issues of concern are controversial or significant enough to capture the attention of the local media.

* Local Chamber of Commerce:
This organization may offer information about certain issues it is following on behalf of the business community.

* Stringers:
Often expensive, but there may be no substitute for hiring someone who is in frequent contact with legislators and is a familiar face in the document rooms and statehouse corridors.

* Governor's Legislative Liaison Office:
On major legislative initiatives and politically "hot" issues, try telephoning this office.

* National Conference of State Legislators (NCSL):
Although this organization serves legislators, the staff will respond to requests from the public. The Conference maintains a list of reports and studies by investigative committees in all 50 states. Access to its in-house database may be possible in the future. This national organization of state legislators and legislative staff aims to improve the quality and effectiveness of state legislators, to ensure states a strong, cohesive voice in the federal decision-making process and to foster interstate communication and cooperation. Contact either of the two offices at 1560 Broadway, Suite 700, Denver, CO 80202; 303-830-2200; or 444 North Capitol St., NW, Suite 515, Washington, DC 20001; 202-624-5400.

* Council of State Governments/State Information Center:
This arm of the Council of State Governments publishes several useful directories, including *The Book of States*, *State Administration Officials Classified By Function*, and *State Legislative Leadership Committees and Staff*. Its database may soon be available to the public. Contact: State Information Center, Council of State Governments, P.O. Box 11910, Iron Works Pike, Lexington, KY 40578; 606-244-8000.

* Commerce Clearing House (CCH):
CCH offers the "State Legislative Reporting Service" as well as the Electronic Legislative Search System. The Reporting Service allows you to select only those legislatures you are interested in, whereas the online search system tracks all current legislation in all 50 states. Contact: CCH, 4025 West Peterson Avenue, Chicago, IL 60646; 312-583-8500.

* Information for Public Affairs:
This private firm offers online access to its database containing the status of legislation pending before the current session of all

50 state legislatures. Contact: IPA, 2101 K St., Sacramento, CA 95816; 916-444-0840.

* Other Private Legislative Reporting Services:
Legi-Tech Corporation and other firms specialize in tracking one or two statehouses. About half of the legislatures are covered by such information brokers.

Reports and Resources Available from State Legislatures

A trend among state legislatures is the creation of special investigative committees which have responsibility for oversight and often the power to subpoena. These watchdogs usually have permanent full-time staff and produce reports throughout the year. Frequent contact with these committees is necessary to stay informed about their activities.

Here is a sampling of reports issued by the Virginia Joint Legislative Audits and Review Committee:

> *Outpatient Care in Virginia*
> *Medical Assistance Programs in Virginia: An Overview*
> *Homes for Adults in Virginia*
> *Social Services (including day care) in Virginia*
> *Vehicle Cost Responsibility in Virginia*
> *Highway Construction, Maintenance, and Transit Needs*
> *The Occupational and Professional Regulatory System*
> *Consolidation of Office Space in Northern Virginia*
> *Special Report: Use of State-Owned Aircraft*
> *Towns in Virginia*
> *Virginia's Correctional System: Population Forecasting*

Even those legislatures that compress their work into 60 or 90 day sessions are active year-round. Information about hearings, meetings, and reports produced throughout the Interim can be provided by each state house legislative information office.

State Legislatures: Bill Status Information Offices

You will find more than 50 information offices listed here because some state houses do not have one centralized legislature reference office.

Alabama
Senate Bill Status, 11 S.Union, Room 716, New State House, Montgomery, AL 36130-4600; 334-242-7826. This office can respond to questions about all Senate bills and refer you to the appropriate committee, document room, etc.

House Bill Status, 11 S.Union, Room 512, New State House, Montgomery, AL 36130-4600; 334-242-7627. This office can provide information on all bills pending before the House of Representatives and can refer you to the appropriate committees, document rooms, etc.

Alaska
Legislative Information, 130 Seward St., Suite 313, Juneau, AK 99801-2197; 907-465-4648. This office can provide information on the status of House and Senate bills. It can do subject searches by accessing a database but at this time Legislative Information cannot provide computer printouts. Copies of bills will be sent out by this office.

Arizona
Information Desk, House of Representatives, State House, 1700 West Washington Street, Phoenix, AZ 85007; 602-542-4221. This Information Desk is the best starting point to learn the status of all bills pending before the House of Representatives. This office will refer you to the appropriate committees, document room, etc.

Senate Information Desk, State House, 1700 West Washington Street, Phoenix, AZ 85007; 602-542-3559. This Information Desk maintains current information on all bills pending before the Arizona Senate. This office will refer you to the appropriate committees, document rooms, etc.

Arkansas
Office of Legislative Counsel, State Capitol Building, Room 315, Little Rock, AR 72201; 501-682-1937. This office can provide status information on all legislation pending before the House of Representatives and the Senate. It also has scheduling information and can you refer you to the appropriate committees, document rooms, etc.

California
Office of the Chief Clerk, State Assembly, State Capitol, Room 3196, Sacramento, CA 95814; 916-445-3614. This office can respond to questions regarding legislation pending before the State Assembly and Assembly committees. This office can refer you to the appropriate offices in the State Capitol such as the document rooms.

Secretary of the Senate, State Capitol, Room 3044, Sacramento, CA 95814; 916-445-4251. This office can provide information about bills pending before the Senate and the Senate committees. The Secretary of the Senate also will refer you to appropriate offices in the State Capitol such as where to obtain copies of Senate bills.

Colorado
Legislative Information Center, 200 E. 14th St., Room 022, Denver, CO 80203; 303-866-3055. This office can provide information on the status of both House and Senate bills. The Legislative Information Center also can send you copies of bills as well as mail out status sheets which target on bills pertaining to a specific subject.

Connecticut
Bill Information Room, Law and Legislative Reference Dept., State Library, 231 Capitol Avenue, Hartford, CT 06106; 203-566-5736. This office can provide information about both House and Senate bills and send you copies of bills. Besides doing a key word or subject search, this office can mail you a printout of all legislation pertaining to one topic.

Delaware
Division of Research, Legislative Counsel, Legislative Hall, Dover, DE 19901; 302-739-4114; 800-282-8545. This office can provide status information on both House and Senate bills and send you copies of bills. It can access a legislative computerized database and do searches for free. The toll-free number operates year-round.

Florida
Legislative Information Division, 111 W. Madison St., Room 704, Tallahassee, FL 32399-1400; 904-488-4371; 800-342-1827. This office can provide status information on all House and Senate bills. It can send you single copies of up to 10 bills and mail out printouts of all House and Senate bills pertaining to a specific subject.

Georgia
Clerk of the House, 309 State Capitol, Atlanta, GA 30334; 404-656-5015. This office can provide up-to-date information on all House bills and send you copies of House bills. The Clerk of the House also will search its database to tell you all legislation that has been introduced on a specific topic.

Secretary of the Senate, State Capitol, Room 353, Atlanta, GA 30334; 404-656-5040; 800-282-5803. This office can respond to questions about all bills pending before the Georgia Senate. The Secretary of the Senate can send you copies of Senate bills and search its database for legislation pertaining to a specific subject.

Hawaii
Clerk of the House, State Capitol of Hawaii, Honolulu, HI 96813; 808-586-6400. This office can respond to questions about bills pending before the House and refer you to the appropriate offices in the State Capitol such as the document room.

Information from Lawmakers

Clerk of the Senate, State Capitol of Hawaii, Honolulu, HI 96813; 808-586-6720. This office can provide status information on all legislation pending before the Hawaii Senate. It can refer you to the appropriate offices in the State Capitol such as the document room.

Idaho

Legislative Services Research and Information, 700 W. Jefferson, Lower Level East, P.O. Box 83720, Boise, ID 83720-0054; 208-334-2475. This office can give you information on the status of all House and Senate bills. It also can send you copies of bills as well as a printout of all legislation pertaining to a specific topic.

Illinois

Clerk of the House, State Capitol Building, Room 424, Springfield, IL 62706; 217-782-6010; 800-252-6300. This office can respond to questions about both House and Senate bills, and provide you with copies of bills. The Clerk's office can send you printouts, for example, a list of all bills sponsored by one legislator.

Indiana

Legislative Information, Legislative Services Agency, 302 State House, Indianapolis, IN 46204; 317-232-9856. The agency can give you bill status information and do searches by bill number, subject or legislator. Legislative Information can send you copies of bills but charge $.15 per page.

Iowa

Legislative Information Office, State Capitol, Room 16, Des Moines, IA 50319; 515-281-5129. This office can provide information on all House and Senate bills and send you copies of bills. It can access a computerized database and mail you a printout of all legislation pertaining to a specific subject.

Kansas

Legislative Reference, State Library, State Capitol Third Floor, 343-N, Topeka, KS 66612; 913-296-2149; 800-432-3924. This office can tell you the status of all current House and Senate legislation as well as provide bill histories. Legislative Reference can send you copies of bills and voting records.

Kentucky

Bill Status, State Capitol Annex, Room T-3, Frankfort, KY 40601; 502-564-8100; 800-776-9158. This office can provide information on House and Senate bills pending before the legislature. It can also send you copies of bills.

Louisiana

Legislative Research Library, House of Representatives, P.O. Box 94012, Baton Rouge, LA 70804-9012; Senate Docket 504-342-2365; House Docket 504-342-6458. During the session, call the toll-free PULS Line, 800-256-3793 (if out-of-state, 504-342-2456) for bill status information and to have them send you copies of House and Senate bills. When the legislature is not in session, contact the Legislative Research Library, 504-342-4914.

Maine

Legislative Information Office, State House Station 100, Room 314, Augusta, ME 04333; 207-287-1692. This office can respond to questions about House and Senate bills and do key word or subject searches of its database.

Maryland

Legislative Information Desk, Dept. of Legislative Reference, 90 State Circle, Annapolis, MD 21401; 410-841-3886; 800-492-7122. This office can provide status information on all House and Senate bills and send you copies of bills. It also can provide you with a printout of all bills which pertain to a specific subject area.

Massachusetts

Citizen Information Service, 1 Ashburton Place, 16th Floor, Boston, MA 02108; 617-727-7030. This office can provide bill status information and supply copies of bills but you must know the bill number. To obtain bill numbers and other information contact the Clerk of the House which is listed below.

Clerk of the House, House of Representatives, State House, Boston, MA 02133; 617-722-2356. This office can respond to questions about House and Senate bills and will refer you to the document room and other appropriate offices within the State House.

Michigan

Clerk of the House, State Capitol, Lansing, MI 48909; 517-373-0135. This office can provide information on the status of House bills and can do searches of its database to identify legislation which pertains to a specific subject. It will refer you to the House document room for copies of bills.

Secretary of the Senate, P.O. Box 30036, Lansing, MI 48909-7536; 517-373-2400. This office can provide Senate bill status information and also can send you copies of bills.

Minnesota

House Index Office, State Capitol Building, Room 211, St Paul, MN 55155; 612-296-6646. This office can tell you the status of all House bills but will refer you to the Chief Clerk's office (612-296-2314) for copies of all House bills. It can search its database to identify all bills that pertain to a specific subject.

Senate Index Office, State Capitol Building, Room 231, St Paul, MN 55155, 612-296-2887. This office can provide bill status information on all Senate legislation and will refer you to the Secretary of the Senate if you want to obtain copies of bills. It can search its database and identify all bills pertaining to a specific subject.

Mississippi

House Docket Room, PO Box 1018, New Capitol Room 305, Jackson, MS 39215; 601-359-3358. This office can tell you the status of all House bills and send you copies of proposed laws pending before the House.

Senate Docket Room, PO Box 1018, New Capitol Room 308, Jackson, MS 39215; 601-359-3229. This office can respond to questions about bills pending before the Mississippi Senate and send you copies of Senate bills.

Missouri

House Information Bill Status, State Capitol, Room 307B, Jefferson City, MO 65101; 314-751-3659. This office can provide information on bills pending before the House and will refer you to the appropriate offices within the State Capitol such as the document room.

Senate Research, State Capitol Room B-9, Jefferson City, MO 65101; 314-751-4666. This office can respond to questions about bills pending before the Senate and will refer you to the appropriate offices such as the document room.

Montana

Legislative Counsel, State Capitol, Room 138, Helena, MT 59620; 406-444-3064, 800-333-3408. The in-state toll-free number may change in subsequent sessions of the Montana legislature. The Legislative Counsel office can respond to inquiries year-round and send you copies of bills.

Nebraska

Hotline, Office of the Clerk, State Capitol, Room 2018, Lincoln, NE 68509; 402-471-2709; 800-742-7456. This office operates an in-state hotline during the session that can provide information on all bills pending before this unicameral legislature. The Clerk can respond to questions year-round.

Nevada

Chief Clerk of the Assembly, Legislative Building, 401 S. Carson St., Carson City, NV 89710; 702-687-5739. This office can provide information about the status of bills pending before the Assembly. The Chief Clerk will refer you to the appropriate offices in the State Capitol such as the documents room or the Clerk of the Senate.

New Hampshire

State Library Reference and Information Services, 20 Park Street, Concord, NH 03301; 603-271-2239. This office can respond to questions about House and Senate bills pending before the legislature. It can send you copies of bills and search its database for bills pertaining to specific subject areas.

Be patient. If any phone number is incorrect, call (area code) 555-1212 and request the new listing.

New Jersey

Office of Legislative, Services - Bill Room, Executive Statehouse, Room #6, Statehouse CN 068, Trenton, NJ 08625; 609-292-6395; 800-792-8630. This office can provide information about House and Senate legislation and send you copies of bills. It will refer you to other offices within the State House if necessary.

New Mexico

Legislative Counsel, State Capitol, Room 311, Santa Fe, NM 87503; 505-986-4600. This office can provide bill status information on House and Senate legislation. It will refer you to the appropriate offices within the State Capitol such as the document room.

New York

Public Information Office, Room 202 LOB 2nd Floor Empire State Plaza, Albany, NY 12248; 518-455-4218. This office can provide information on the status of House and Senate bills and send you copies of bills. It may refer you to your local library if you want a search done to identify all bills which pertain to a specific subject.

North Carolina

State Legislative Building, Legislative Library, Raleigh, NC 27601; 919-733-7779. This office can provide information about House and Senate bills and will refer you to the appropriate offices within the State Capitol such as where to obtain copies of bills.

North Dakota

Legislative Counsel Library, State Capital, 2nd Floor, Bismarck, ND 58505; 701-328-2916. This office can provide information about House and Senate bills year-round and will refer you to appropriate offices in the State Capitol. The legislature maintains an in-state toll-free number during the biannual session.

Ohio

Legislative Information, State House, Columbus, OH 43266-0604; 614-466-8842; 800-282-0253. This office can provide information on the status of House and Senate legislation and do subject searches. This telephone bank of researchers will route your requests (i.e., copies of bills). In-state toll-free access is available throughout the year.

Oklahoma

Chief Clerk, House of Representatives, State Capitol Bldg., Oklahoma City, OK 73105; 405-521-2711, 800-522-8502. This office can respond to questions about bills pending before the House and Senate. It will refer you to the appropriate offices within the State Capitol.

Oregon

Legislative Library, State Capitol S-347, Salem, OR 97310; 503-378-8871, 800-332-2313. This office can provide information on House and Senate bills year-round. During the biannual session the legislature offers an in-state toll-free number for bill information.

Pennsylvania

Legislative Reference Bureau, History Room, Main Capitol Building, Room 648, Harrisburg, PA 17120-0033; 717-787-2342. This office can provide information on House and Senate bills be consulting its card index and computerized database. It will refer you to the appropriate offices, for example, where to obtain copies of bills.

Rhode Island

Legislative Information Line, State House, Room #2, Providence, RI 02903; 401-751-8833; 800-547-8880. This office can provide you with information on the status of House and Senate bills and send you copies of bills. It will refer you to the appropriate legislators or committees.

South Carolina

Legislative Information Systems, Room 112, Blatt Building, 1105 Pendleton St., Columbia, SC 29201; 803-734-2923, 800-922-1539. This office can respond to inquiries about House and Senate bills and will refer you to the appropriate offices such as where to obtain copies of bills. It can do subject searches but is unable to send out a printout.

South Dakota

Public Information Clerk, Legislative Research Counsel, State Capitol Building, 500 East Capitol, Pierre, SD 57501; 605-773-4498, 605-773-4296. They can provide information on the status of House and Senate bills. They can access a computerized database and do a search to identify legislation which pertains to a specific subject.

Tennessee

Office of Legislative Services, Room G-20, War Memorial Bldg, Nashville, TN 37243; 615-741-3511. This office can provide information on House and Senate bills and will send you copies of bills. It can identify all legislation pending on specific subjects.

Texas

Legislative Reference Library, PO Box 12488, Capitol Station, Austin, TX 78711; 512) 463-1252. This office can provide information on the status of all House and Senate bills. It can search its database to identify all legislation which pertains to a specific subject. It will refer you to the appropriate offices such as the document room. The in-state toll-free access number changes yearly.

Utah

Legislative Research and General Counsel, 436 State Capitol, Salt Lake City, UT 84114; 801-538-1032. This office can respond to questions about House and Senate bills. It will refer you to the appropriate offices within the State Capitol.

Vermont

Vermont Legislative Counsel, 115 State St., Montpelier, VT 05633-5301; 808-828-2231. This office responds to House and Senate Bill Status questions. They will refer you to the appropriate offices.

Virginia

Legislative Information, House of Delegates, P.O. Box 406, Richmond, VA 23218; 804-786-6530. This office can provide information on House and Senate bills and can send you copies of bills. It can consult a printed index which is updated daily to identify bills which pertain to a specific subject.

Washington

House Workroom, Legislative Building, Third Floor Capitol Campus, P.O. Box 40600, Olympia, WA 98504-0600; 360-786-7780; 800-562-6000. This office can provide information on the status of bills pending before the House. It can also provide copies of bills. The toll-free number (out of state should call 360-786-7763) is in operation only during the session.

Senate Workroom, Legislative Building AS32, Third Floor Capitol Campus, P.O. Box 40482, Olympia, WA 98504-0482; 360-786-7592; 800-562-6000. This office can provide information on bills pending before the Senate and can supply you with copies of bills. An in-state toll-free number (out of state call 360-786-7763) provides both House and Senate bill information but only during the session.

West Virginia

Clerk of the House, House of Delegates, 1900 Kanawha Blvd. E, Bldg.1, Room M212, Charleston, WV 25305-0470; 304-340-3200. This office can respond to questions about legislation pending before the House of Delegates and House committees. It will refer you to the appropriate offices in the State Capitol such as where to obtain legislative documents.

Clerk of the Senate, 1900 Kanawha Blvd. E, Bldg., Room M-211, Charleston, WV 25305-0470; 304-357-7800. This office can provide information on the status of bills pending before the Senate. It will refer you to the appropriate offices in the State Capitol.

Wisconsin

Legislative Reference Bureau, 100 N. Hamilton St., POB 2037, Madison, WI 53701-2037; 608-266-0341; 800-362-9472. The legislature operates a Legislative Hotline

Be patient. If any phone number is incorrect, call (area code) 555-1212 and request the new listing.

Information from Lawmakers

during the session (if calling from inside Madison, dial 608-266-9960). The Legislative Reference Bureau can respond to questions year-round will refer you to the document room, etc.

Wyoming

Legislative Service Office, State Capitol Building, Room 213, Cheyenne, WY 82002; 307-777-7881, 800-342-9570 within Wyoming. When the Wyoming legislature is not in session it is necessary to contact this office. During the session, bill status questions are best directed to the two offices noted below.

Senate Information Clerk, State Capitol Building, Cheyenne, WY 82002; 307-777-6185. This office can respond to questions about the status of bills pending before the Senate. It will refer you to the Bill Room to obtain copies of bills.

House Information Clerk, Bill Status, State Capitol Building, Cheyenne, WY 82002; 307-777-6185; 800-342-9570 (in state only). This office can provide current information on legislation pending before the House. It will refer you to the proper offices in the State Capitol, for instance, the Bill Room.

Be patient. If any phone number is incorrect, call (area code) 555-1212 and request the new listing.

Books and Libraries
Library of Congress

The Library of Congress is the world's largest library, but there are more than dusty old books stored here. The more than 20 million books in 470 languages that it holds represent less than a fourth of the holdings of the Library. There are 3,000,000 books in the science and technology field. There are also massive collections of manuscripts, maps, music, prints and photographs, and film. In 1800 the Library was founded simply to help Congress make the laws. But now the Library is much more. For instance, more than a million handicapped readers borrow materials in braille and recorded forms each year. And the Library also registers copyright for books, music, films, computer programs, and other works. In celebration of the arts, the Library holds concerts by the Juilliard String Quartet, poetry readings, folk music and dance performances, and showings of classic films. More than 900 specialists provide extensive research and analysis for Congress, much of which is available to you through your Congressman's office. The Library is a major world center for scholarly research with specialists in its 22 reading rooms and in other areas ready to provide information on just about any subject you can name. And much of this information is available to you from exhaustive databases both in printed form and on magnetic tape.

New!! Visit the Library of Congress via the Internet. Find out about the Library's history. View exhibits of the Library of Congress and read about upcoming events. You can visit reading rooms. Access electronic publications and conference proceedings. View items from digitized historical collections (American Memory). LC Online Systems includes a POW/MIA database as well as others. So, don't hesitate to grab a board and surf through history. Internet address: http://www.loc.gov (to reach the LC Home Page).

* Books Published Since 1454
Enhanced Catalog Division
LA 2004, Library of Congress
Washington, DC 20540   202-707-5965
The *National Union Catalog* lists the world's books published since 1454 and held in approximately 1,100 North American libraries and other union catalogs that record the location of books in Slavic, Hebraic, Japanese, and Chinese languages (if Romanized). The catalog is produced on microfiche, and is in many libraries.

* Center for the Book: Reading Project
Center for the Book
Library of Congress
Washington, DC 20540   202-707-5221
A partnership between the federal government and private industry, the Center for the Book works closely with other organizations to explore important issues dealing with books and educational communities. The Center encourages reading and research about books and reading and serves as a catalyst by bringing together authors, publishers, librarians, booksellers, educators, scholars, and readers to discuss common concerns. Four primary concerns are: television and the printed word, reading development, international role of the book, and publishing. The center is funded by tax-deductible contributions.

* Central Intelligence Agency Declassified Reports
Photoduplication Service
Library of Congress
Washington, DC 20540   202-707-5650
The Library of Congress distributes CIA reports that have been released to the public. These reports detail foreign government structures, trade news, economic conditions, and industrial development. Orders must be prepaid or charged to a standing account at the Library of Congress. For $13, the Photoduplication Service can also provide you with a list of CIA reports available. Reports can be purchased on microfilm for $30 per reel if you write to: CIA, Office of Public and Agency Information, Washington, DC, 20205; the list of CIA Reports is free.

* Children's Literature Center
Children's Literature Center
National Programs
Library of Congress

Washington, DC 20540   202-707-5535
The Center prepares lists and scholarly bibliographies and provides other reference services for individuals who serve children, including scholars, writers, teachers, librarians, and illustrators. The center also has many publishers' catalogs that list titles to be published in the upcoming year, a wide range of periodicals about children's literature, and lists from rare and used book sellers. *Books for Children*, a guide to reference sources for children's literature published annually for $1 per issue, is available from the Superintendent of Documents, Government Printing Office, Washington, DC 20402; 202-512-1800. Guides available:
#6-1989-S/N 030-00100-133-4
#7-1990- S/N 030-001-00135-1
#8-1991- S/N 030-001-00138-5

* Computer-Generated Bibliographies
Customer Services Section
Cataloging Distribution Service
Library of Congress
Washington, DC 20541   202-707-6100
Readers who cannot do their own research in the Library of Congress can request a search of its catalog databases on a fee basis. Through this service, a bibliographic listing referred to as Select Marc; Retrospective Conversion Service, can provide you with their complete manual on readable magnetic tape.

* Congressional Documents, Reports, and Hearings
Law Library
Library of Congress
Washington, DC 20540   202-707-5079
All Senate and House documents, reports, hearings since 1970, and all bills back to the First Congress are available. Material can be obtained on microfilm.

* Congressional Research Service (CRS) Reports
Contact your Member of Congress   202-224-3121
Refer to Current Events Reports and Homework Chapter
for complete listing of these reports and issue briefs.
The Congressional Research Service at the Library of Congress prepares hundreds of non-partisan background *Reports* each year on current issues, large and small, domestic and foreign, social and political. CRS also publishes hundreds of major *Issue Briefs* each year designed to keep members of Congress informed on timely

issues. Written in simple and direct language, these briefs provide background information and are updated daily. Free printed copies can be obtained from your Congressman's office. *Audio Briefs* are audio cassette programs produced on topics of Congressional interest, including specially produced programs on issues before Congress featuring CRS experts and nationally recognized experts. CRS products are listed in the *Guide to CRS Products*, published quarterly, and in monthly cumulative supplements entitled *Update to the Guide to CRS Products*. Copies are available from your Congressman.

* Copernicus to Star Wars

Science and Technology Division
Library of Congress
Washington, DC 20540 . 202-707-5639

The Science and Technology collection contains more than 3 million scientific and technical books and pamphlets and 3 million technical reports, including those issued by the U.S. Department of Energy, NASA, the U.S. Department of Defense, and other government agencies. The collections, which are particularly strong in aeronautical materials, contain first editions of Copernicus and Newton and the personal papers of the Wright Brothers and Alexander Graham Bell. Computer terminals provide principal access to the collections. Special scientific finding aids, such as abstracting and indexing journals, are part of the division's reference collection. This Division also prepares an informal series of reference guides called *Tracer Bullets*, which are available free upon request. More extensive bibliographies are published from time to time.

* Copyright Examining Practices

Copyright Office
Certifications and Documents
Library of Congress
Washington, DC 20559 202-707-6800

The *Compendium II of Copyright Office Practices* is intended as a general guide for those with special interest in copyright examining practices which concern the registration of applications for copyright under the 1976 Copyright Act. It is available for $62 from the Government Printing Office, Washington, DC 20402; 202-512-1800.

* Copyright Office

Copyright Office
Library of Congress
Washington, DC 20559 202-707-3000

The Library of Congress Copyright Office grants exclusive rights to reproduce or prepare derivative works on the copyrighted work in copies or on phonorecords and to distribute them to the public by sale, rental, lease, or loan. Copyrightable works include books, periodicals, and other literary works; musical compositions, song lyrics, dramas, and dramatico-musical compositions; pantomimes and choreographic works; pictorial, graphic, and sculptural works; motion pictures and other audiovisual works; and sound recordings. The Library provides information on copyright registration procedures and copyright card catalogs covering more than 16 million works that have been registered since 1870.

* Copyright Record

Copyright Catalog Office
Library of Congress, Room 549
Washington, DC 20559 202-707-5063

Information on copyrights from 1978 to the present is available online through terminals located in the Copyright Office, and records on all copyrights back to the 1800s are kept in the Copyright Card Catalog.

* Copyright Research Service

Copyright Office
Reference and Bibliographic Section
Library of Congress
Washington, DC 20559 202-707-6850

For a fee of $20 per hour, the Copyright Office will research the copyright you need and send you the information by mail. Requests must be in writing, and you must specify exact details you require.

* Domestic and Foreign Periodicals Division

Serial and Government Publication Division
Library of Congress, LM 133
Washington, DC 20540 202-707-5647

The Library of Congress has an extensive collection of both domestic and foreign periodicals, government serials, microfilms, and newspapers.

* Folklife Center

American Folklife Center
Library of Congress
Washington, DC 20540-8100 202-707-5510

This Center collects and maintains archives, conducts scholarly research, and coordinates the development of field projects, performances, exhibitions, festivals, workshops, publications, and audiovisual programs on American folklife. *Folk Life Center News* is a free quarterly newsletter on folklife activities and programs. The Center maintains and administers an extensive collection of folk music, folk culture, ethnomusicology, and grass-roots oral history--both American and international--in published and unpublished forms. The Archive houses more than 30,000 hours of folk-related recordings, manuscripts, and raw materials. The Archive Reading Room contains more than 4,000 books and periodicals, plus unpublished theses, and dissertations, field notes, and many textual and some musical transcriptions and recordings. A free listing of the Archive's publications is available.

* Free LOC Catalog Cards

Cataloging Distribution Service
Library of Congress
Washington, DC 20541 202-707-6100

Individuals or organizations wishing to establish libraries may receive Library of Congress catalog cards free by establishing an account with the above office.

* Geography and Maps Division

Geography and Map Division
Library of Congress
Washington, DC 20540 202-707-6277

The Library's cartographic collections, which include 4 million maps, nearly 51,000 atlases, 500 globes, and some 8,000 reference books, are the largest and most comprehensive in the world. The collections include atlases published over the last five centuries covering individual continents, countries, states, counties, and cities as well as the world. Official topographic, geologic, soil, mineral, and resource maps and nautical and aeronautical charts are also available for most countries. There are also complete LANDSAT microimage data sets of images produced by several satellites revolving around the Earth. Subscription information on the microfiche data sets is available from EOSAT, 4300 Forbes Blvd., Lanham, MD 20706; 800-344-9933.

* High School and Intercollegiate Debate Topics

Your Member of Congress 202-224-3121

A series of free reports are prepared by the Congressional Research Service of the Library of Congress that contain pertinent excerpts, bibliographic references, and other materials related to debate topics for that year. For high school debate teams, the topics are selected by the National University Extension Service Association, and for college, the topics are selected by the American Speech Association.

* Historical Sound Recordings Division

Motion Picture, Broadcasting,
and Recorded Sound Division
Room 338
Library of Congress
Washington, DC 20540 202-707-5840

The sound recording collection reflects the entire spectrum of history of sound from wax cylinders to quadraphonic discs and includes such diverse media as wire recordings, aluminum discs, zinc discs, acetate-covered glass discs, rubber compound discs, and translucent plastic discs. The division has also recently made all of its materials recorded prior to 1909 available on 8-inch compressed audio discs for individual users in the Recorded Sound Reading Room using a micro computer. Included are the Berliner collection, from the company which invented and introduced disc recording, radio news commentaries from 1944 to 1946, eyewitness descriptions of marine combat and House of Representatives debates. For purchase by researchers, the Division's laboratory is prepared to make taped copies of recordings in good physical condition, when not restricted by copyright, performance rights, or provisions of gift or transfer. The requester is responsible for any necessary search--by mail or in person--of Copyright Office records to determine the copyright status of specific recordings. The Division also offers copies of some of its holdings for sale in disc form. These include a number of LP records of folk music, poetry, and other literature.

* Humanities Library

National Endowment for the Humanities (NEH)
1100 Pennsylvania Ave., NW
Room 217
Washington, DC 20506   202-606-8244

This library focuses on the needs and interests of the National Endowment for the Humanities (NEH) and has materials on a variety of humanities-related subjects. Individuals may use this library by appointment only.

* Information On Demand

National Reference Service
Library of Congress, LJ 144
Washington, DC 20540   202-707-5522

If you need information that is contained in the material in the Library of Congress collections, the reference staff will find it for you and relay it over the phone. If the information you require is too extensive, however, the reference staff will refer you to private researchers who work on a fee basis.

* Last Resort Interlibrary Loan

Loan Division
Library of Congress
Washington, DC 20540   202-707-5444

The Loan Division will loan materials to other libraries when they have exhausted other means of locating the material. If you are having trouble finding material, first contact your local library.

* Law Library on All Legal Systems

Law Library
Library of Congress
Washington, DC 20540   202-707-5079

As the world's largest and most comprehensive library of foreign, international, and comparative law, the Law Library provides information for all known legal systems including common law, civil law, Roman law, canon law, Chinese law, Jewish and Islamic law, and ancient and medieval law. Specialists with knowledge of more than fifty languages provide reference and research service in all known legal systems. U.S. legislative documents housed here include the *Congressional Record* (and its predecessors), the serial set, a nearly complete set of bills and resolutions, current documents, committee prints, reports, hearings, etc. plus a complete set of U.S. Supreme Court records and briefs and collections of U.S. Court of Appeals records and briefs. The law library has only two divisions:

Western Law Division
United States, Australia, Canada, Great Britain, India, New Zealand, Pakistan, certain other countries of the British Commonwealth and their dependent territories, Eire, Spain and Portugal, Latin America, Puerto Rico, the Philippines, and Spanish- and Portuguese-language states of Africa: 202-707-5077.

Eastern Law Division
Nations of Europe and their possessions, except Spain and Portugal, nations of East and Southeast Asia including China, Indonesia, japan, Korea, Thailand, and former British and French possessions in the area, Middle Eastern countries, including the Arab states, Turkey, Iran, and Afghanistan, and all African countries except Spanish- and Portuguese-language states and possessions: 202-707-5085.

* Legislative Histories and Research

Law Library
Library of Congress, LM240
Washington, DC 20540   202-707-5065

The Law Library compiles legislative histories which include versions of new public statutes from the time of introduction, through congressional hearings, House and Senate floor debate, vote tallies, and votes.

* Library of Congress Color Slides

Photoduplication Service
Library of Congress
Washington, DC 20540   202-707-5640

Color slides of the Library's buildings and items from its collections are available starting at $15 per slide.

* Library of Congress Free Catalog

Office Systems Services
Library of Congress (LC)
Washington, DC 20540   202-707-5590

The free annual catalog, *Publications in Print*, offers a comprehensive listing of the materials published by or in cooperation with the Library of Congress. Publications may be in print, recorded, or video formats. As new Library of Congress publications are issued, they are announced in the weekly *Library of Congress Information Bulletin*, and in the *Monthly Catalog of United States Government Publications* available from the Superintendent of Documents, Government Printing Office, Washington, DC 20402; 202-512-1800.

* Library of Congress Tours

Visitor Services Office
Library of Congress
Washington, DC 20540   202-707-5458

The Visitor Services Office shows a film tour, (Monday to Friday starting at 8:30 a.m. until 9:00 p.m., and Saturday and Sunday starting at 8:30 a.m. until 5:30 p.m.) of the Library every half hour. Actual tours of the Library are conducted at 11:00 a.m., and 2:00 p.m., weekdays. The tours highlight the art and architecture of the Thomas Jefferson Building, and provide an overview of the Library activities. Tour reservations for groups over 10 must be made in advance.

* Library Services for Blind and Physically

Handicapped Readers Reference Section
National Library Service for the Blind and
    Physically Handicapped
Library of Congress
Washington, DC 20542   202-707-9275
OR: Your local library

The National Library Service (NLS) maintains a large collection of books, magazines, journals, and music materials in braille, large type, and recorded formats for individuals who cannot read or use standard printed materials because of temporary or permanent visual loss or physical limitations. Reading materials and necessary playback equipment for books on record and cassette are distributed through a national network of cooperating libraries. Books in the collection are selected on the basis of their appeal to a wide range of interests. Bestsellers, biographies, fiction, and how-to books are in great demand.

* Madison Gift Shop

Madison Gift Shop
Library of Congress
Washington, DC 20541

Two of the most popular books in the gift shop are the *Handbook of the New Library of Congress* ($7.95(and *Jefferson's Legacy: A Brief History of the Library of Congress* ($9.50). The books are filled with the Library's history, architecture, exhibits, and holdings. Mail orders are excepted with an additional fee for shipping and handling.

* Main Reading Room

Main Reading Room
National Reference Service
Library of Congress
Room LJ 100
Washington, DC 20540   202-707-5522

Located on the first floor of the Thomas Jefferson Building, the main reading room contains material on American history, economics, fiction, language and literature, political science, government documents, and sociology. A reference collection for these materials is also housed there. These reading rooms are not equipped to answer reference questions over the telephone, but will provide information on their collections, hours of operation, and the like.

Social Science	202-707-5522
Microform	202-707-5522
Local History and Genealogy	202-707-5522
Newspapers and Current Periodicals	202-707-5690
Science	202-707-5639
Law Library	202-707-5079
Performing Arts Library at the Kennedy Center	202-707-6245

Be patient. If any phone number is incorrect, call (area code) 555-1212 and request the new listing.

1195

Books and Libraries

Motion Picture, Broadcasting, and Recorded Sound 202-707-8572
Archive of Folk Culture 202-707-5510
Prints and Photographs 202-707-6394
Manuscripts 202-707-5387
Music 202-707-5507
Rare Book and Special Collections 202-707-5434
Geography and Map 202-707-6277
Hispanic 202-707-5397
European 202-707-4515
Asian 202-707-5423
African and Middle Eastern Division 202-707-5528

* Manuscripts Division

Manuscript Division
Special Collections, LM 102
Library of Congress
Washington, DC 20540-4780   202-707-5387

More than 40 million pieces of manuscript material are housed in the Manuscript Division, including the letters, diaries, speech drafts (including the copy of the Gettysburg Address), scrapbooks, telegrams, and so forth of influential people. For instance, the Library owns the papers of 23 of the presidents from George Washington to Calvin Coolidge, as well as materials of Clara Barton, Sigmund Freud, and Benjamin Franklin. The Manuscript is open to persons engaged in serious research who present proper identification. Hours of operation are 8:30 a.m. to 5:00 p.m., Monday through Saturday (except national holidays).

* Motion Picture and Broadcasting Division

Motion Picture, Broadcasting, and Recorded
  Sound Division, LM 336
Library of Congress
Washington, DC 20540   202-287-5840

The Library of Congress's film and television collections contain more than 100,000 titles, and more than 1,000 titles are added each month through copyright deposit, purchase, gift, or exchange. Items selected from copyright deposits include feature films and short works of all sorts, fiction and documentary, exemplifying the range of current film and video production. The collections also include some 90,000 stills. The film and television collections are maintained for research purposes. Limited viewing and listening facilities for individual users are provided in the reading rooms.

* Music Arts Reading Room

Music Arts Reading Room
Room LM113
Library of Congress
Washington, DC 20540   202-707-5507

The Performing Arts Reading Room houses the Library of Congress's non-book collections in the performing arts area: music, dance, sound recordings, motion pictures, and television. The collection includes more than 4,000,000 pieces of music and manuscripts, some 300,000 books and pamphlets, and about 350,000 sound recordings reflecting the development of music in Western civilization from earliest times to the present. Reference services are available. Adjacent to the reading room is the Recorded Sound Reference Center, Room LM 115, 202-707-7833, for users primarily interested in sound recordings and radio materials. Listening facilities are available in the reading room, but their use is limited of those doing research of a specific nature leading to publication or production. Musicians who wish to play music drawn from the Library's collection may use the piano available in an adjacent sound proof room.

* Newspapers and Periodicals From Around the World

Library of Congress
Washington, DC 20540   202-707-5690

Hundreds of different newspapers and periodicals from all fifty states and countries around the world are available on microfilm for $35 for domestic and $40 for foreign publications. Subscriptions are available or single issues can be ordered. Orders must be prepaid or charged to a standing account at the Library of Congress.

* Performing Arts

Performing Arts
John F. Kennedy Center for Performing Arts

2700 F St., NW   Library: 202-416-8780
Washington, DC 20566   Exec ofc: 202-416-8000

The Performing Arts Library is a joint project of the Library of Congress and the Kennedy Center, and offers information and reference assistance on dance, theater, opera, music, film and broadcasting.

* Preservation: Newspapers to Motion Pictures

National Preservation Program Office
Library of Congress, LMG 21
Washington, DC 20540   202-707-1840

The Preservation Office is involved in a constant race against time to preserve its millions of items from disintegration. Newspapers are immediately microfilmed, motion pictures are rushed to refrigerated vaults, manuscripts are put in fumigating vaults, and maps are encased in polyester envelopes. But the main problem for preservationists is acid and its affect on paper. Recently the Library's chemists developed a technique whereby wood pulp books are placed in huge vacuum tanks which are flooded with diethyl zinc gas, thus deacidifying them for another hundred years. Research continues on longstanding preservation problems. A series of leaflets on various preservation and conservation topics is available from the office.

* Prints and Photographs Division

Prints and Photographs Division
Library of Congress, LM 337
Washington, DC 20540-4840   202-707-6394

More than 10 million items in the Library of Congress (LC) chronicle American life and society from its earliest days to the present through its prints and photographs. Items include architectural plans, posters, cartoons, drawings, and advertising labels. Reference librarians will assist those doing their own research, and they can furnish names of freelance picture researchers for individuals who cannot get to the Library of Congress themselves.

* Private Library Space for Researchers

Research Facilities Section
General Reading Rooms
Library of Congress
Washington, DC 20540   202-707-5211

For increased convenience, full-time scholars and researchers may apply for study desks in semi-private areas within the Library of Congress.

* Publishers' ISBN Catalog Numbers

Cataloging-in-Publication
Library of Congress
Washington, DC 20540   202-707-6372

Through a program in cooperation with American publishers to print cataloging information in current books, Library of Congress card catalog numbers are assigned by the Cataloging-in-Publication Office prior to publication.

* Rare Books Division

Rare Book and Special Collections Division
Library of Congress
LJ 256
Washington, DC 20540   202-707-5434

The Rare Books Division contains about 300,000 volumes and 200,000 pamphlets, broadsides, theater playbills, title pages, manuscripts, posters, and photographs. The collection includes documents of the first fourteen congresses of the United States, the personal libraries of Thomas Jefferson and Harry Houdini, incunabula; miniature books and dime novels, and the Russian Imperial collection. The division has its own central card catalog plus special card files that describe individual collections or special aspects of books from many collections.

* Reproduce Library of Congress Materials

Photoduplication Service
Library of Congress, G1011
Washington, DC 20540   202-707-5640

Photostats, microfilms, and other photocopies of manuscripts, prints, photographs, maps, and book materials not subject to copyright and other restrictions are available for a fee. In general, there is, however, a four-to-six-week turnaround time for this service. Order forms for photo reproduction and price schedules for this and other copying services are available.

* Science and Technology Resources

National Reference Services
Library of Congress
Washington, DC 20540   202-707-5522

The *Science, Technology, and Social Science Database* is a computerized directory of more than 14,000 organizations or individuals who will provide information to the general public on topics primarily in science, technology, and the social sciences. Citations generally contain the name of the organization or person, mailing address, telephone number, areas of interest, special collections, publications, and special services.

* Science Information Tracer Bullets

Science and Technology Division
National Reference Services
Library of Congress (LC)
Washington, DC 20540   202-707-5522

The *LC Science Tracer Bullet* is an informal series of literature guides designed to help a reader begin to locate published materials on a subject about which he or she has only a general knowledge. Among its major features are a weighted list of subject headings to be used in searching a card, book, or computer catalog; lists of basic texts, bibliographies, state-of-the-art reports, conference proceedings, or government publications; a list of abstracting and indexing services useful in finding journal articles and technical reports; and the names and addresses of organizations to contact for additional information. Because these compilations are intended to put a reader "on target," they are called *Tracer Bullets*. New titles in the series are announced in the *Library of Congress Information Bulletin* that is distributed to many libraries. Each Bullet is available, without charge, from the Science Reference Section of the Science and Technology Division at the address given above.

TB No.Title

81-3	Alcoholism
81-5	Wind Power
81-6	Pets and Pet Care
81-9	Cable Television (Cable TV)
81-10	Manned Space Flight
81-11	Mariculture
81-13	Wood As Fuel
81-14	Volcanoes
81-15	History of American Agriculture
81-17	Epilepsy
82-1	Food Additives
82-2	Gardening
82-3	Earth Sheltered Buildings
82-4	Extraterrestrial Life
82-5	Jet Engines and Jet Aircraft
82-6	Biological Control of Insects
82-9	Sickle Cell Anemia
83-1	Biofeedback
83-2	Powder Metallurgy
83-3	Hazardous Wastes (Non-nuclear)
83-4	Science Policy
83-5	Plant Exploration and Introduction
83-6	Mental Retardation
83-7	Quarks
83-9	Geothermal Energy
83-10	High Technology
84-1	Aquaculture
84-2	Edible Wild Plants
84-3	Japanese Science and Technology
84-4	Sharks
84-5	Scientific and Technical Libraries: Administration and Management
84-7	Biotechnology
85-1	Herbs and Herb Gardening
85-2	Landscape Gardening
85-3	Endangered Species (Animals)
85-4	Computer Security
85-6	Acupuncture
85-7	CAD/CAM (Computer Aided Design/Computer Aided Manufacture)
85-8	Anorexia Nervosa/Bulimia
85-10	Rose Culture
86-1	Artificial Intelligence
86-2	Mars (Planet)
86-3	Jojoba and Other Oilseed Plants
86-4	Composite Materials
86-5	Electromagnetic Fields--Physiological and Health Effects
86-6	Diabetes Mellitus
86-8	Indoor Air Pollution
86-11	Acid Rain
87-1	Asbestos
87-2	Alzheimer's Disease
87-3	Cellular Radio
87-4	The History of Technology
87-5	Science and Technology in China
87-6	Stress: Physiological and Psychological Aspects
87-7	Osteoporosis
87-8	The Future: Science and Technology Enter the 21st Century
87-9	Microcomputers
87-10	Tribology
87-11	Inventions and Inventors
87-12	Optical Disc Technology
88-1	Algae
88-2	Fiber Optics
88-3	Biographical Sources in the Sciences
88-5	Soil Erosion
88-6	Noise Pollution
89-1	Science Policy--Foreign and International
89-2	Japanese Technology
89-3	Space Science Projects
89-4	Municipal Solid Waste Management
89-5	Human Diet and Nutrition
89-6	Endangered Species (Plants)
89-7	Allergy and Asthma
89-8	Earthquakes and Earthquake Engineering
89-9	Blacks in Science and Related Disciplines
89-10	Halocarbons and the Stratospheric Ozone Layer
90-1	Soviet Union and Eastern Europe: State of the Environment
90-2	Environmental Science Projects
90-3	High Speed Rail Transportation
90-4	Poisonous Plants
90-5	The Crisis in Science Education
90-6	Women in the Sciences
90-7	Freshwater Ecology
90-8	Astronomy and Astrophysics
90-9	Chemical and Biological Warfare
90-10	The Brain: An Overview
91-1	Unidentified Flying Objects
91-2	Civil Engineering: Public Works/Infrastructure
91-3	Dyslexia
91-4	Bioethics
91-5	Desalination
91-6	Career Opportunities in the Sciences
91-7	Breast Cancer
91-8	Medicinal Plants
91-9	Acquired Immunodeficiency Syndrome (AIDS)
91-10	Dolphins
91-11	Chemical Exposure: Toxicology, Safety, and Risk Assessment
91-12	Science Fair Projects

* Selling to the Library of Congress

Procurement and Supply Division
Library of Congress
1701 Brightseat Rd.
Landover, MD 20785   202-707-0419

Those interested in doing business with the Library of Congress must request the pamphlet, *How and What We Purchase* from the above office in writing.

* Social Science Resource Center

National Reference Services
Library of Congress
Washington, DC 20540   202-707-5522

The *Science, Technology, and Social Science Database* is a computerized directory of more than 14,000 organizations or individuals who will provide information to the general public on topics primarily in science, technology, and the social sciences. Citations generally contain the name of the organization or person, mailing address, telephone number, areas of interest, special collections, publications, and special services.

Books and Libraries

* Sound Recordings of Poetry and Other Literature

Motion Picture, Broadcasting,
and Recorded Sound Division
Library of Congress
Washington, DC 20540   202-707-5840

The Library of Congress offers copies of some of its poetry and literature holdings for sale in disc form. Contact this office for information on what's available, along with prices.

* Surplus Books Giveaway

Exchange and Gift Division
Library of Congress
Washington, DC 20540   202-707-9511

Tens of thousands of surplus books in a wide variety of subjects are available to government agencies, private citizens, and non-profit organizations. The books come from a wide variety of sources including extras from the Copyright Division, books that are not acquired by not selected for the Library's collections, and from private gifts. Government agencies can select from the books available first at no charge. The general public (referred to as book dealers by the Library) can select from books next. They must bid on books by the lot, and the minimum bid is $25. Everything left over is available to non-profit organizations free of charge.

* Telephone Reference Service

Library of Congress
Washington, DC 20540   202-707-5522

This service provides information to callers about the collections within the Library of Congress and how they can be used. In planning your research, remember that the Library of Congress is the library of last resort--all other inter-library loan avenues must be exhausted before you may borrow a book from the Library of Congress. Always begin your research with your local library.

Federal Libraries

* African Art

Smithsonian Institution
950 Independence Ave., SW
Washington, DC 20560 202-357-4875

The Library maintains a collection of 15,000 books and 280 periodical titles on traditional and contemporary arts of Africa, including sculptural and decorative arts, ethnography, anthropology, craft, architecture, archeology, history, oral tradition and folklore, and African retentions in the New World. The Library is open to the public by appointment.

* Agriculture, U.S. Department of

National Agricultural Library (NAL)
10301 Baltimore Blvd.
Beltsville, MD 20705 301-504-5755

The National Agricultural Library (NAL) provides comprehensive information services for the food and agricultural sciences through a variety of sources, which include bibliographies, personal reference services, loans, photocopies, and online data files. Services are provided to agricultural colleges, research institutions, government agencies, agricultural associations, industry, individual scientists, and the general public. NAL cooperates with the Library of Congress and the National Library of Medicine to provide access to publications worldwide in the agricultural, chemical, and biological sciences. NAL houses one of the largest collections in the free world on agricultural subjects--1.6 million volumes--including biology, chemistry, nutrition, forestry, soil sciences, and much more.

* Air Force, U.S. Department of the

Resource Library
SAF/PAR
Washington, DC 20330-1000 703-697-4100

This library is not open to the public but they do accept mail requests. They have general information about the air force, as well as biographies. Mail requests to the address listed above.

* Air Force, U.S. Department of the

History Library
USAF/CHO, Building 5681
Bolling Air Force Base
Washington, DC 20330 202-767-0412

The library is open to the public from 10am to 3pm. Collection includes history of Air Force, history of aircraft, and biographies dating back to WWI. Call for appointment.

* Air Force, U.S. Department of the

Historical Resource Center
AFHRA/R3Q
Maxwell A.F.B., AL 36112-6678 334-953-5342

Open 9am to 4pm. This is a repository of all Air Force historical documents. It contains 550,000 documents and 60 million pages of information.

* American History Branch

National Museum of American History
Smithsonian Institute
Room 5016
14th and Constitution Ave., NW
Washington, DC 20560 202-357-2414

The Library houses a collection of 165,000 volumes of book and bound journals on engineering, transportation, military history, science, applied science, decorative arts, and domestic and community life in addition to American history and the history of science and technology. They have special collections of trade literature and materials about world fairs. The Library is open to the public by appointment, 10am to 5pm, Monday-Friday.

* Architect of the Capitol

U.S. Capitol Bldg.
Curators Office
House Terrace Level, #3
Washington, DC 20515 202-225-1222

This small reference library is open by appointment only. It is open 9am-4:30pm, Monday through Friday, and one must secure a visitor's pass to enter.

* Arms Control and Disarmament Agency (ACDA), U.S.

320 21st St., NW, Room 5840
Washington, DC 20451 202-647-5969

As a complement to the much larger State Department Library, the ACDA Library maintains a current collection of books, periodicals, documents, and reference materials relevant to arms control and disarmament issues. The library also includes an information retrieval system and inter-library loan services. Individuals wishing to use the library must call and make an appointment.

* Arts and Museum Management Library

National Endowment for the Arts (NEA)
1100 Pennsylvania Ave., NW
Washington, DC 20506 202-682-5485

This library focuses on the needs and interests of the National Endowment for the Arts (NEA) and has materials on the arts and arts management. Individuals may use this library by appointment only.

* Binational Libraries and Cultural Centers Worldwide

Library Programs Division
Bureau of Educational and Cultural Affairs
U.S. Information Agency (USIA)
301 Fourth St., SW, Room 314
Washington, DC 20547 202-619-4597

The U.S. Information Agency (USIA) maintains or supports 156 libraries and reading rooms in 95 countries, as well as library programs at 111 binational centers in 24 countries. Collections focus on fostering foreign understanding of U.S. people, history, and culture. A bi-weekly bibliography, listing 80-100 titles on international relations and developments in the U.S., is one of many library services provided for the overseas posts, including reference and research assistance.

* Commerce, U.S. Department of

1400 and Constitution Ave. NW, Room 7046
Washington, DC 20230 202-482-5511

This collection includes business directories, periodicals, and newspapers.

* Comptroller of Currency, Office of the

U.S. Department of the Treasury
250 E. St., SW
Washington, DC 20219 202-874-4720

Open by appointment on Tuesdays and Thursdays.

* Congressional Budget Office

2nd and D Sts., SW, Room 472
Washington, DC 20515 202-226-2635

Open 9am to 5:30pm, Monday through Friday to federal employees only, this library contains information on economics and studies on the budget process. Appointment preferred.

* Consumer Product Safety Commission (CPSC)

5401 Westbard Ave., NW, Room 546
Washington, DC 20207 301-504-0044

Books and Libraries

The Consumer Product Safety Commission (CPSC) library's collection includes reference materials on engineering, economics, and health sciences, which CPSC staff and other researchers may use for background on product safety issues. The library does not include CPSC documents and publications. Open to the public 8:30am to 5pm, Monday to Friday.

* Court of Appeals for the Federal Circuit and U.S. Claims Court, U.S.

Library
717 Madison Place, NW
Washington, DC 20439   202-633-5871
This joint library is accessible only to members of the Bar and those involved in cases within the courts.

* Customs Services, U.S.

U.S. Department of Treasury
1301 Constitution Ave., NW
Washington, DC 20229   202-927-1350
This library is open by appointment only to researchers.

* Defense, U.S. Department of

Pentagon Library
Room 1A518, Pentagon
Washington, DC 20310   703-697-4301
This library is open to Department of Defense employees, 9am to 4pm, Monday-Friday. Inquiries will be directed to another appropriate library.

* Doris and Henry Dreyfuss Study Center

Cooper-Hewitt Museum
Smithsonian Institution's National Museum of Design
2 East 91st St.
New York, NY 10128   212-860-6887
The Study Center and Library serve as a resource for scholars, researchers, designers, and students for the study of design. This library contains fifty thousand volumes, with specialized holdings in decorative arts, textiles, and needlework, wallcoverings, architecture, pattern and ornament, landscape design, industrial design, interior design, theater design, and graphic design. Researchers are asked to call or write in advance. Photographs may be ordered through the museum's Photographic Services Department.

* Education, U.S. Department of
Reference Facility

555 New Jersey Ave., NW, MS-1139
Washington, DC 20208   202-219-1692
Collection focuses on education and related social sciences information.

* Energy, U.S. Department of

1000 Independence Ave., SW, Room GA138
Washington, DC 20585   202-586-9534
This energy library is available to U.S. Department of Energy employees, government employees from other agencies, members of the armed forces if in uniform, and for those escorted by a U.S. Department of Energy employee.

* Environmental Protection Agency

401 M St., SW, Room 2904
Mail Code 3404   Reference Desk 202-260-5921
Washington, DC 20460   Main Desk 202-260-5922
The library's collection focuses on environmental issues.

* Federal Aviation Administration

800 Independence Ave., SW, Room 930
Washington, DC 20591   202-267-3115
Open to the public 9am to 4pm. Collection focuses on commercial and general aviation. Historical aviation information is located at Smithsonian's Air and Space Museum.

* Federal Communications Commission (FCC)

1919 M St., NW, Suite 639
Washington, DC 20554   202-418-0451
The Federal Communications Commission (FCC) Library is a collection of various types of legal and technical information. The legal collection includes federal and statutory case histories, indexes, reference works, treatises, and looseleaf services. The technical collection covers telecommunications and related subjects. The library also includes a special collection of cross-indexed legislative histories dating back to the early beginnings of communications law, along with a special collection of trade journals, and law and literature reviews. It is open to the public 1pm to 4pm, Monday-Friday.

* Federal Deposit Insurance Corporation (FDIC)

550 17th St., NW, Room 4060
Washington, DC 20429   202-898-3631
The FDIC library collection focuses on banking law, with emphasis on bank regulation and supervision, state codes, deposit insurance, international banking, bankruptcy, and consumer affairs. The library is open to the public Tuesdays through Thursdays, 8:30am to 5:15pm. Call at least one day in advance to make an appointment to visit.

* Federal Emergency Management Agency

500 C St., SW, Room 123
Washington, DC 20472   202-646-3768/3769
The library's collection focuses on emergency management topics. Open to the public 8am to 4:30pm.

* Federal Reserve Board Research

Room BC241
20th St. and Constitution Ave., NW
Washington, DC 20551   202-452-3333
The Federal Reserve System research library contains material on banking, finance, economics, and other areas related to the Federal Reserve System. The library is open to the public on Thursdays from 9-5. Appointment required. Call one day in advance.

* Federal Reserve System Banking Law

Room B1066
20th St. and Constitution Ave., NW
Washington, DC 20551   202-452-3284
For information on specific banking laws, contact the Federal Reserve System Banking Law Library. It is open 9am to 5pm, Monday-Friday by appointment only.

* Federal Trade Commission (FTC)

6th and Pennsylvania Ave., NW
Room 630
Washington, DC 20580   202-326-2395
Contact the Federal Trade Commission's (FTC) library to use the 120,000 volumes on legal, economic, and business subjects, 1,500 periodicals, interlibrary loans, and photocopy facilities. It is open to the public 8:30am - 5pm, Monday-Friday. A picture I.D. required.

* General Accounting Office

441 G St., NW, Room 7016
Washington, DC 20548   202-512-5180
This library provides information of General Accounting Office (GAO) interest and has access to databases, government documents, dissertations, research in progress, and organizations. *Library Focus*, published monthly, lists the latest books acquired. It is open to the public 8am to 4:45pm, Monday-Friday, picture I.D. required.

* General Accounting Office Law Library

441 G St., NW, Room 7056
Washington, DC 20548   202-512-2585
This library's references include the Legislative History Collection, which documents the creation of public documents and bills. The collection can be read in the library on weekdays between 8am and 4:45pm. A picture ID is required.

* General Services Administration
18th and F Sts., NW, Room 1033
Washington, DC 20405 202-501-2789
The collection includes the Federal Acquisition Institute library. It is open to the public 8am to 4:30pm, Monday-Friday for research only. Book check out is not available.

* Health and Human Services, U.S. Department of
Information Center
P.O. Box 1133 301-565-4167 in MD
Washington, DC 20013 800-336-4797
This center should be the initial phone call because it can direct you to more specialized clearinghouses as well as health organizations and foundations. The Information Center, through its resource files and database (DIRLINE), responds to questions regarding health concerns and can send publications, bibliographies, and other material. A library focusing on health topics is open to the public, 9am-5pm, Monday-Friday, advance notice is preferred. The National Health Information Center Library is located at 1010 Wayne Dr., Silver Springs, MD 20091. The Center also produces many different directories, and resource guides, which are available for a minimal cost. A publications catalog is free of charge.

* House of Representatives Research and Library
Cannon House Office Bldg., Room B-18
Washington, DC 20515 202-225-0462
This library is the official depository of House documents, reports, bills, and more. Its primary function is to serve House members and their staffs. It is open to the public, but no photocopying is permitted. The hours are 9am to 5:30pm Monday through Friday.

* Housing and Urban Development (HUD), U.S. Department of
Library
451 7th St., SW, Room 8141
Washington, DC 20410 202-708-2370
This library contains a wealth of information on financing, home building, mortgages, and other HUD related topics. Also included are archival documents of old housing agencies. Hours are 8:45am - 5:15pm, Monday through Friday. The Program Information Center at the Library is a source of information on HUD programs. The number is 202-755-6420.

* Information Agency (USIA), U.S.
Programs Division
Bureau of Educational and Cultural Affairs
301 Fourth St., SW, Room 314
Washington, DC 20547 202-619-4597
The U.S. Information Agency (USIA) maintains or supports 156 libraries and reading rooms in 95 countries, as well as library programs at 111 binational centers in 24 countries. Collections focus on fostering foreign understanding of U.S. people, history, and culture. A bi-weekly bibliography, listing 80-100 titles on international relations and developments in the U.S., is one of many library services provided for the overseas posts, including reference and research assistance.

* Information Agency (USIA), U.S.
301 Fourth St., SW, Room 135
Washington, DC 20547 202-619-5947
The Washington library of the U.S. Information Agency (USIA) houses a varied collection, including a Russian language section. Access is restricted: permission to use the library can be obtained through the Office of Congressional and Public Liaison, address above, Room 602, Congressional 202-619-6828, Public 202-619-4355.

* Interior, U.S. Department of the
Natural Resources Library
18th and C Sts., NW
Washington, DC 20240 202-208-5815
Information is provided on such topics as Native American Indians, mining and minerals, land reclamation and management, fish and wildlife, water resources, parks and outdoor recreation, and the preservation of scenic and historic sites. The library is open from 7:45am - 5pm, Monday through Friday.

* Interior, U.S. Department of the
U.S. Geological Survey Library
National Center, MS 950, 4th Floor
Reston, VA 22092 703-648-4302
This library contains valuable publications on subjects related to the Geological Survey; however geology, including ground water and water resources, is the primary topic. The hours are 7:30am -4:15pm, Monday through Friday.

* International Development Cooperation Agency, U.S.
1601 N. Kent St., Room 105
Rosslyn, VA

Agency for International Development (AID)
Development Information Center (Mailing Address)
Room 105 SA18
Washington, DC 20523-1801 703-875-4818
The reference desk is open between 10am and 4pm, Monday-Friday. They maintain a database listing all of Agency for International Development (AID) materials. It includes 150 journals of country development, strategy statements.

* International Trade Commission (ITC), U.S.
International Trade Library
Office of Data Systems
500 E St., SW, Room 300
Washington, DC 20436 202-205-2630
As one of the most extensive libraries on international trade in the United States, the International Trade Commission's (ITC) main library maintains a 100,000-volumes and subscribes to about 2,400 periodicals. Publications on international trade and U.S. tariff commercial policy are housed along with many business and technical journals. An audiovisual room enables visitors to listen to audio tapes and to view video tapes relating to international trade. A rare-book room is also maintained, and the library staff has begun to establish special collection areas for use with ongoing ITC projects. The library is open to the public from 9am to 5pm.

* International Trade Commission (ITC) Law Library
500 E St., SW, Room 614
Washington, DC 20436 202-205-3287
The Law Library, a resource of the ITC's Office of the General Counsel, contains more than 10,000 volumes, participates in an exchange program with other libraries, and maintains a comprehensive file on documents on legislation affecting U.S. trade. It is open to the public for research.

* John F. Kennedy Center for the Performing Arts
Performing Arts Library
2700 F St., NW
Washington, DC 20566 202-416-8000
The Performing Arts Library is a joint project of the Library of Congress and the Kennedy Center, and offers information and reference assistance on dance, theater, opera, music, film, and broadcasting. It is open Tuesday through Saturday.

* Justice, U.S. Department of
U.S. Parole Commission
Public Reading Room
U.S. Department of Justice
5550 Friendship Blvd.
1 N. Park Bldg.
Chevy Chase, MD 20015 301-492-5990

Federal Bureau of Investigation
Public Reading Room
U.S. Department of Justice
9th St. and Pennsylvania Ave., NW
Washington, DC 20535 202-324-3477
Open by appointment only.

* Labor, U.S. Department of
200 Constitution Ave., NW, Room N2439
Washington, DC 20210 202-219-6992
Collection includes information on trade unions, labor movements, women issues, and legal and regulatory topics related to labor.

Books and Libraries

* Land Management Library, Bureau of

U.S. Department of the Interior
SC 653
Denver Federal Center
6th Ave. and Kippling
P.O. Box 25047
Denver, CO 80225   303-236-6649

A vast collection of information on issues concerning land management is available to the public through this library. The following topics are included: cadastral engineering; forest resources management; land reserve studies; legislation and public land laws; range management; watershed management; mineral, oil and gas leasing; oil shale; and conservation and use of public lands. Open 8am - 4:30pm.

* Library of Congress

Washington, DC 20540   202-707-5000 General information
                                   202-707-6372 catalog number

The Library of Congress is the world's largest library, but there are more than dusty old books stored here. The more than 20 million books in 470 languages that it holds represent less than a fourth of the holdings of the Library. There are also massive collections of manuscripts, maps, music, prints and photographs, and film. In 1800 the Library was founded simply to help Congress make the laws. But now the Library is much more. For instance, more than a million handicapped readers borrow materials in braille and recorded forms each year. And the Library also registers copyright for books, music, films, computer programs, and other works. In celebration of the arts, the Library holds concerts by the Juilliard String Quartet, poetry readings, folk music and dance performances, and showings of classic films. More than 900 specialists provide extensive research and analysis for Congress, much of which is available to you through your Congressman's office. The Library is a major world center for scholarly research with specialists in its 22 reading rooms and in other areas ready to provide information on just about any subject you can name. And much of this information is available to you from exhaustive databases both in printed form and on magnetic tape.

* Library of Congress International Law Library

Washington, DC 20540   202-707-5080

As the world's largest and most comprehensive library of foreign, international, and comparative law, the Law Library provides information for all known legal systems including common law, civil law, Roman law, canon law, Chinese law, Jewish and Islamic law, and ancient and medieval law. Specialists with knowledge of more than fifty languages provide reference and research service in all known legal systems. U.S. legislative documents housed here include the *Congressional Record* (and its predecessors), the serial set, a nearly complete set of bills and resolutions, current documents, committee prints, reports, hearings, etc. plus a complete set of U.S. Supreme Court records and briefs and collections of U.S. Court of Appeals records and briefs. The law library has only two divisions:

Western Law Division

United States, Australia, Canada, Great Britain, India, New Zealand, Pakistan, certain other countries of the British Commonwealth and their dependent territories, Eire, Spain and Portugal, Latin America, Puerto Rico, the Philippines, and Spanish- and Portuguese-language states of Africa: 202-707-5077.

Eastern Law Division

Nations of Europe and their possessions, except Spain and Portugal, nations of East and Southeast Asia including China, Indonesia, japan, Korea, Thailand, and former British and French possessions in the area, Middle Eastern countries, including the Arab states, Turkey, Iran, and Afghanistan, and all African countries except Spanish- and Portuguese-language states and possessions: 202-707-5085.

* Library of Congress Law Library

Legislative Histories and Research
LM 240
Washington, DC 20540   202-707-5080

This section of the library provides information on legislative history.

* Library of Congress: Services for Readers with Vision Impairment and Handicaps

Library Services for Blind and Physically Handicapped
Readers Reference Section
National Library Service for the Blind and Physically Handicapped

Washington, DC 20540   202-707-9287
or: Your local library

The National Library Service (NLS) maintains a large collection of books, magazines, journals, and music materials in braille, large type, and recorded formats for individuals who cannot read or use standard printed materials because of temporary or permanent visual loss or physical limitations. Reading materials and necessary playback equipment for books on record and cassette are distributed through a national network of cooperating libraries. Books in the collection are selected on the basis of their appeal to a wide range of interests. Bestsellers, biographies, fiction, and how-to books are in great demand.

* Merit Systems Protection

1120 Vermont Ave., NW, Room 828
Washington, DC 20419   202-653-7133

The Library's collection specializes in legal aspects of personnel issues. A reference librarian on staff can direct you to appropriate resources. The library is open to the public, but you should call for an appointment.

* Minerals Management Service

Resource Center
Congressional Liaison Office
U.S. Department of the Interior
18th and C Sts., NW
Room 4241
Washington, DC 20240   202-208-3502

This small reference center contains documents including offshore minerals management statistics from the Service. Hours are 8am - 4pm, Monday through Friday. Please call ahead for an appointment.

* National Aeronautics and Space Administration

300 E. St., SW
Washington, DC 20546   202-358-0168

The library focuses on aeronautics and space information. It is open to the public from 7:30am to 5pm, Monday through Friday.

* National Air and Space Museum Branch

National Air and Space Museum
7th and Independence Ave., SW
Room 3100
Washington, DC 20590   202-357-3133

This library houses more than 30,000 books, 4,700 periodical titles, 6,000,000 technical reports, and is enriched by a documentary archival collection which includes 900,000 photographs, drawings, and other documents. The scope of the collection covers history of aviation and space, flight technology, aerospace industry, biography, lighter-than-air technology and history, rocketry, earth and planetary sciences, and astronomy. The Library is open to the public by appointment, 10am to 4pm, Monday-Friday.

* National Credit Union Administration (NCUA)

1775 Duke St.
Alexandria, VA 22314   703-518-6540

The NCUA Law Library is open to the public. A part-time librarian is on duty to offer assistance. You must call for an appointment.

* National Endowment for the Arts (NEA)

1100 Pennsylvania Ave., NW
Washington, DC 20506   202-682-5485

This library focuses on the needs and interests of the National Endowment for the Arts (NEA) and has materials on the arts and arts management. Individuals may use this library by appointment only.

* National Endowment for the Humanities (NEH)

1100 Pennsylvania Ave., NW
Room 216
Washington, DC 20506   202-606-8244

This library focuses on the needs and interests of the National Endowment for the Humanities (NEH) and has materials on a variety of humanities--related subjects. Individuals may use this library by appointment only, 8am - 5pm, Monday-Friday.

* National Energy Information Center

Public Reading Room
U.S. Department of Energy
1000 Independence Ave., SW, Room 1F048
Washington, DC 20585   202-586-8800

This reading room contains research materials pertaining to the energy industry. Hours are 8am - 5pm, Monday through Friday. A picture ID is required.

* National Gallery of Art

Constitution and 6th St., NW
Washington, DC 20565   202-842-6511

The Gallery's library has over 150,000 volumes with a specialty in Renaissance and Baroque art. The collection covers the period from Post-Byzantine to the present, focusing on the history and criticism of art. The stacks themselves are closed; however, the library is open to the public, but you should call for the hours to make an appointment.

* National Labor Relations Board

1099 14th St., NW
Washington, DC 20570   202-273-3720

The Board's library collection focuses on labor law and labor relations. The library is open to the public and no appointment is necessary.

* National Mediation Board Reading Room

1425 K Street, NW
Washington, DC 20570   202-523-5996

Mediation files are available for inspection by appointment.

* National Science Foundation

4201 Wilson Blvd.
Arlington, VA 22230   703-306-0658

The library is open to the public between 9am and 5pm, Monday-Friday. Specialty is science policy, technological innovation, research and development management, science and engineering education.

* National Technical Institute for the Deaf (NTID)

NTIC Resource Center
One Lomb Memorial Dr.
Rochester, NY 14623   716-475-6823

* National Zoological Park Branch

Education/Administration Building
3000 Connecticut Ave., NW
Washington, DC 20008   202-673-4771

This library houses a collection of 3,500 books and 350 periodical titles on animal behavior, animal nutrition, capture and care of animals in captivity, conservation and endangered species, horticulture, pathology, veterinary medicine, and zoology. The library is open to the public by appointment.

* Natural History Branch Library

Smithsonian Institute
10th and Constitution Ave., NW, Room 51
Washington, DC 20560   202-357-4696

This library houses 330,000 books and bound journals and receives 1,963 journal subscriptions. The library consists of a main location and several subject-based locations. Topics covered include biology, geology, paleontology, ecology, anthropology, botany, entomology, and mineral sciences. Call to make an appointment or for information on the location of the subject-based libraries.

* Navy, U.S. Department of the Navy Library

9th and M Sts.
Building 44
Washington Navy Yard
Washington, DC 20374-5060   202-433-4132

Open 9am to 4pm, Monday, Tuesday, Thursday, and Friday. The library contains historical information dating back to the 18th century. They have historical documents and abstracts. They loan books through the interlibrary loan system.

* Nuclear Regulatory Commission

Two White Flint North Bldg.
11555 Rockville Pike
Rockville, MD 20852   301-415-5610

The library is open to the public from 8am to 4pm.

* Occupational Safety and Health Review Commission

One Lafayette Centre
1120 20th St., NW
Washington, DC 20036   202-606-5410

The collection focuses on federal laws. It is open to the public from 8:30am to 4:45pm.

* Office of Personnel Management

1900 E Street, NW, Room 4516
Washington, DC 20415   202-606-1381

The library is open to the public between 8:30am to 4:30pm by appointment only. The specialty of the library is personnel management

* Peace Corps

1900 K Street, NW
Room 5353
Washington, DC 20526   202-606-3307

The library is open to the public between 8:30am to 4:30pm. The specialty of the library is the countries the Peace Corps serves and Peace Corps services, volunteerism, and languages.

* Postal Service, U.S.

475 L'Enfant Plaza, SW
Room 11800
Washington, DC 20260-1641   202-268-2904

Along with a working collection of materials in law, the social sciences, and technology, the Postal Library contains a unique collection of postal materials, legislative files from the 71st Congress to date, reports, pamphlets, clippings, photographs, general postal histories, periodicals of the national postal employee organizations, Universal Postal Union studies, and Postal laws and regulations handbooks and manuals. The library is open to the public weekdays from 9am to 4pm. Reading Rooms are located on the 11th Floor North.

* Presidential Libraries

National Archives and Records Administration
8th St. and Pennsylvania Ave., NW
Room 104
Washington, DC 20408   202-501-5700

Through the Presidential Libraries, which are located on sites selected by the presidents and built with private funds, the National Archives preserves and makes available for use the Presidential records and personal papers that document the actions of a particular president's administration. In addition to providing reference services on Presidential documents, each library prepares documentary and descriptive publications and operates a museum to exhibit documents, historic objects, and other memorabilia of interest to the public. Each library provides research grants to scholars and graduate students for the encouragement of research in Presidential libraries' holdings and of publication or works based on such research. Public programs of the libraries include conferences, lectures, films, tours, commemorative events, and seminars. For further information, contact the President library of your choice.

Herbert Hoover Library, West Branch, IA 52358; 319-643-5301
Franklin D. Roosevelt Library, Hyde Park, NY 12358; 914-229-8114
Harry S. Truman Library, Independence, MO 64050; 816-833-1400
Dwight D. Eisenhower Library, Abilene, KS, 67410; 913-263-4751
John F. Kennedy Library, Boston, MA 02125; 617-929-4545
Lyndon B. Johnson Library, Austin, TX 78705; 512-916-5137
Gerald R. Ford Library, Ann Arbor, MI 48109; 313-741-2218
Gerald R. Ford Museum, Grand Rapids, MI 49504; 616-451-9263
Nixon Presidential Materials Staff, College Park, MD 20740; 301-713-6950
Jimmy Carter Library, Atlanta, GA 30307; 404-331-3942
Ronald Reagan Library, Simi Valley, CA, 93065; 805-522-8444
George Bush Materials Project, College Station, TX 77840; 409-260-9554

Be patient. If any phone number is incorrect, call (area code) 555-1212 and request the new listing.

1203

Books and Libraries

* Reclamation, Bureau of

Water Resources Library
U.S. Department of the Interior
P.O. Box 25007, D79231
Denver Federal Center
6th and Kippling
Denver, CO 80225-000   303-236-6963

The key topics covered at this library include hydrology engineering, groundwater management, dam safety, soil mechanics, and business related issues. Materials can be checked out only through the inter-library loan system.

* Securities and Exchange Commission (SEC)

450 5th St., NW
Washington, DC 20549   202-942-7090

The Securities and Exchange Commission (SEC) Library contains resource material on Federal Securities Laws, accounting, economics, and other general financial information. It also houses all SEC published materials. The library is open to the public from 9am to 5:30pm, Monday through Friday.

* Senate Research and Library

The Capitol, Suite S-332
Washington, DC 20510   202-224-7106

The Senate Library is the official depository of senate documents. Its primary function is service to Senate members and their staffs. To use the library a researcher must have a letter of introduction from a Senator.

* Small Business Administration

409 3rd St., SW   202-205-7033 Main Library
Washington, DC 20416   202-205-6849 Law Library

To review reference material pertaining to small business, contact the SBA's library. The library is open to the public for reference use only.

* Smithsonian Astrophysical Observatory (SAO)

Smithsonian Institute
Perkin Building
Center for Astrophysics
60 Garden St.
Cambridge, MA 02138   617-495-7289

The collection of 50,000 books and 600 current journal titles are owned jointly by SAO and Harvard College Observatory. Subjects covered include all aspects of astronomy and astrophysics, related fields of physics, mathematics, engineering, and computer science. The library is open to the public by appointment.

* Smithsonian Institution Libraries

10th St. and Constitution Ave., NW
Washington, DC 20560   202-357-2139

The libraries of the Smithsonian Institution include approximately 950,000 volumes, with strengths in natural history, museology, history of science, and the humanities. Inquiries on special subjects or special collections should be addressed to the appropriate branch library or to the Central Reference and Loan.

* Smithsonian Museum Support Center

Smithsonian Institution
4210 Silver Hill Rd.   301-238-3666
Suitland, MD 20746   Fax: 301-238-3667

This library provides information about conservational of materials and museum objects, conservation science, which includes archaeometry, the study of museum environments, and the analysis of materials by such means as x-ray, diffraction, and gas chromatography. This library is open to the public by appointment.

* State, U.S. Department of

2201 C St., NW, Room 3239
Washington, DC 20520   202-647-1099
Mailing address:
U.S. Dept. of State
A/OIS/LR, Room 3239
Washington, DC 20520-2442

The library, whose collection specializes in the area of foreign affairs, is open to the public only if the information you are looking for cannot be found elsewhere in the Washington area. You must, however, call for an appointment.

* Supreme Court of the United States

Library
1 First St., NE
Washington, DC 20543   202-479-3037

Supreme Court records and briefs are available to the public for reproduction. However, only government attorneys and members of the Bar are permitted to use the general collection.

* Tennessee Valley Authority (TVA)

Tennessee Valley Authority (TVA)
Corporate Library
400 W. Summit Hill Dr., WT 2F
Knoxville, TN 37902   423-632-3464

The Tennessee Valley Authority (TVA) library facilities are open to the public, 8am to 4:45pm, Monday-Friday, while its specialty libraries cater to various organizations within TVA. Cataloged books, current technical journals, and reports relating to ongoing research in each division are available.

* Transportation, U.S. Department of

400 7th St., SW
Room 2200
Washington, DC 20590   202-366-0746

Collection covers all modes of transportation except aviation. The library is open 9am to 4pm with limited staff.

* Treasury, U.S. Department of

1500 Pennsylvania Ave., NW, Room 5310
Washington, DC 20220   202-622-0045

By appointment only. The collection includes law, economics, and finance information.

* U.S. Trade Representative, Office of the

Public Documents Room
Executive Office of the President
600 17th St., NW, Room 101
Washington, DC 20506   202-395-6186

You must schedule an appointment to visit this documents area, open 10 to 12am and 1 to 4 pm, Monday through Friday.

* Veterans Affairs, U.S. Department of

Central Office Library
810 Vermont Ave., NW
Washington, DC 20420   202-565-4612

Library resources include circulation collections of books, journals, and audiovisuals. Open to the public, 9am to 5pm, Monday-Friday.

Government Printing Office

The U.S. Government Printing Office (GPO) along with the National Technical Information Service (NTIS) are Uncle Sam's primary publishers. The Superintendent of Documents at GPO is the official sales agent for many government publications. Approximately 21,000 titles are for sale in a wide variety of subject areas, including business and industry, children and families, careers, and energy. There are how-to guides, government manuals, and in-depth studies on nearly every subject imaginable. GPO publishes many different types of listings of their publications, from the popular *U.S. Government Books*, which lists selected popular recent releases, to the exhaustive *Publications Reference File*, which lists *all* GPO titles. GPO also provides access to their publications through a nationwide system of 1400 libraries and through 24 bookstores located across the country. Online connection through DIALOG is also possible.

* 320 Subject Bibliographies

Subject Bibliography Index
Superintendent of Documents
Government Printing Office (GPO)   202-512-1800
Washington, DC 20402   Fax: 202-512-2250

More than 320 subject bibliographies listing books, periodicals, and subscriptions published by government agencies are available free from the Government Printing Office. Topics range from accidents to zoning, and touch on most facets of human life. A complete listing of these subject bibliographies, called the *Subject Bibliography Index*, is available free upon request.

* Bestsellers from Uncle Sam

U.S. Government Books
Free Catalog
P.O. Box 37000
Washington, DC 20013-7000

The Government Printing Office has a catalog of new and popular books sold by the government about agriculture, energy, children, space, health, history, business, vacations, and much more. Find out what government books are all about by ordering this free catalog.

* Bookstores Around the Country

Superintendent of Documents
Government Printing Office (GPO)
Office of Marketing, Stop: SM
Washington, DC 20402   202-512-2420

The Government Printing Office (GPO) operates 24 bookstores that display and sell the most popular of the more than 21,000 titles for sale by the government. If the bookstore does not stock the book you are looking for, they will order it and have it sent to you. Bookstores accept VISA, MasterCard, and Superintendent of Documents deposit account orders. All stores are open Monday through Friday, except Kansas City which is open 7 days a week. The following is a listing of the bookstores:

Alabama
U.S. Government Bookstore, O'Neill Building, 2021 Third Ave., North, Birmingham, AL 35203; 205-731-1056, Fax: 205-731-3444

California
U.S. Government Bookstore, ARCO Plaza, C-Level, 505 South Flower St., Los Angeles, CA 90071; 213-239-0844, Fax: 213-239-0848
U.S. Government Bookstore, Marathon Plaza, Room 141-S, 303 2nd St., San Francisco, CA 94107; 415-512-2770, Fax: 415-512-2270

Colorado
U.S. Government Bookstore, Room 117, Federal Building, 1961 Stout St., Denver, CO 80294; 303-844-3964, Fax: 303-844-4000
U.S. Government Bookstore, Norwest Bank Building, 201 West 8th St., Pueblo, CO 81003; 719-544-3142, Fax: 719-544-0719

District of Columbia
U.S. Government Bookstore, U.S. Government Printing Office, 710 N. Capitol St., NW, Washington, DC 20401; 202-512-0132, Fax: 202-512-1355

U.S. Government Bookstore, 1510 H St. NW, Washington, DC 20005; 202-653-5075, Fax: 202-376-5055

Florida
U.S. Government Bookstore, 100 West Bay St., Suite 100, Jacksonville, FL 32202; 904-353-0569, Fax: 904-353-1290

Georgia
U.S. Government Bookstore, First Union Plaza, 999 Peachtree St. NE, Suite 120, Atlanta, GA 30300-3064; 404-347-1900, Fax: 404-347-1897

Illinois
U.S. Government Bookstore, One Congress Center, 401 South State St., Suite 124, Chicago, IL 60605; (312) 353-5133, Fax: 312-353-1590

Maryland
U.S. Government Bookstore, U.S. Government Printing Office, Warehouse Sales Outlet, 8660 Cherry Lane, Laurel, MD 20707; 301-953-7974; 301-792-0262, Fax: 301-498-8999

Massachusetts
U.S. Government Bookstore, Thomas P. O'Neill Building, 10 Causeway St., Room 169, Boston, MA 02222; 617-720-4180, Fax: 617-720-5753

Michigan
U.S. Government Bookstore, Suite 160, Federal Building, 477 Michigan Ave., Detroit, MI 48226; 313-226-7816, Fax: 313-226-4698

Missouri
U.S. Government Bookstore, 120 Bannister Mall, 5600 E. Bannister Rd., Kansas City, MO 64137; 816-765-2256, Fax: 816-767-8233

New York
U.S. Government Bookstore, Room 110, 26 Federal Plaza, New York, NY 10278; 212-264-3825, Fax: 212-264-9318

Ohio
U.S. Government Bookstore, Room 1653, Federal Building, 1240 E. 9th St., Cleveland, OH 44199; 216-522-4922, Fax: 216-522-4714
U.S. Government Bookstore, Room 207, Federal Building, 200 N. High St., Columbus, OH 43215; 614-469-6956, Fax: 614-469-5374

Oregon
U.S. Government Bookstore, 1305 SW First Ave., Portland, OR 97201-5801; 503-221-6217, Fax: 503-225-0663

Pennsylvania
U.S. Government Bookstore, Robert Morris Building, 100 N. 17th St., Philadelphia, PA 19103; 215-636-1900, Fax: 215-636-1903
U.S. Government Bookstore, Room 118, Federal Building, 1000 Liberty Ave., Pittsburgh, PA 15222; 412-644-2721, Fax: 412-644-4547

Texas
U.S. Government Bookstore, Room 1C50, Federal Building, 1100 Commerce St., Dallas, TX 75242; 214-767-0076, Fax: 214-767-9239

U.S. Government Bookstore, Texas Crude Building, 801 Travis St., Suite 120, Houston, TX 77002; 713-228-1187, Fax: 713-228-1180

Washington
U.S. Government Bookstore, Room 194, Federal Building, 915 Second Ave., Seattle, WA 98174; 206-553-4270, Fax: 206-553-6717

Wisconsin
U.S. Government Bookstore, Room 150, Rouse Federal Building, 310 W. Wisconsin Ave., Milwaukee, WI 53202; 414-297-1304, Fax: 414-297-1300

* Catalog of Federal Domestic Assistance
Superintendent of Documents
Government Printing Office (GPO)   202-512-1800
Washington, DC 20402   Fax: 202-512-2250

The *Catalog of Federal Domestic Assistance* is government-wide summary of financial and non-financial Federal programs, projects, services, and activities that provide assistance or benefits to the American public administered by departments and establishments of the Federal government. It describes the type of assistance available and the eligibility requirements for the particular assistance being sought, with guidance on how to apply. Also intended to improve coordination and communication between the federal government and state and local governments. Annual subscriptions, which consist of a basic manual and supplementary material for an indeterminate period, are $60.

* Congressional Record and Calendars
Superintendent of Documents
Congressional Information Specialist, Stop: SSOI
Government Printing Office (GPO)   202-512-1800
Washington, DC 20402   Fax: 202-512-2250

The Government Printing Office (GPO) publishes major Congressional publications, including the *Congressional Record*, House and Senate *Calendars*, all bills and laws, and related information. All of this information is available by subscription.

* Data Tapes of Government Publications
Superintendent of Documents
Government Printing Office (GPO)
941 N. Capitol St.   202-512-1800
Washington, DC 20402   Fax: 202-512-2250

Government publications produced in electronic format are now available in magnetic tape form. Tapes may be purchased on an individual tape basis or by subscription. Individual publications on tape include the *Budget of the United States*, the *Congressional Directory*, and the *Government Manual*. Some of the subscriptions available are the *Congressional Record*, *Federal Register*, and *Daily Bills*.

* Deposit Accounts for Government Publications
U.S. Government Printing Office (GPO)
Receipts and Processing Branch
Stop: SSOR
Washington, DC 20402   202-512-0822

Deposit accounts are a convenient way to order materials from the Government Printing Office (GPO). A minimum of $50 is required to open the account, and monthly statements are issued. Telephone orders are accepted for any account containing sufficient funds, and order forms are provided for mail orders.

* Discounts on Government Books
Superintendent of Documents
Director, Documents Sales Service
Government Printing Office (GPO)   202-512-1800
Washington, DC 20402   Fax: 202-512-2250

Designated bookdealers and educational institution bookstores receive a 25 percent discount on publications and subscriptions whether single copies or in bulk. Any customers ordering 100 or more copies of a publication to be delivered to the same address may also receive the discount.

* Federal Depository Libraries
Superintendent of Documents
Library Marketer
Stop: SM
Washington, DC 20402   202-512-2420

A national system of nearly 1400 public, academic, and law libraries maintains collections of most government publications. The libraries are located in nearly every state. Their staffs will help you with research questions and can provide information on price and order numbers if you wish to purchase copies. If your library does not have the publication you need, they will borrow it for you. To determine which library serves you, contact your public library or the above.

* Federal Register
Superintendent of Documents
Government Printing Office (GPO)   202-512-1800
Washington, DC 20402   Fax: 202-512-2250

The *Federal Register*, with daily issues Monday through Friday, except on a legal holidays, announces to the public regulations and legal notices issued by Federal agencies. These include Presidential proclamations and Executive orders and Federal agency documents having general applicability and legal effect, documents required to be published by Act of Congress and other Federal agency documents of public interest. Subscribers to this service will automatically receive copies of the *Federal Register Index* and the *Code of Federal Regulations*, and *LSA List of CFR Sections Affected*, at no additional cost. Subscriptions are $544 per year; or $272.50 for six months; or $8 for single copies.

* Government Periodicals and Subscription Services
Superintendent of Documents
Government Printing Office (GPO)   202-512-1800
Washington, DC 20402   Fax: 202-512-2250

Better known as PL 36, *Government Periodicals and Subscription Services* lists all materials available on a subscription basis complete with ordering information and order forms. Single copies of this publication are available.

* Government Publications: Complete Listing
Superintendent of Documents
Government Printing Office (GPO)   202-512-1800
Washington, DC 20402   Fax: 202-512-2250

A complete master file of Government Printing Office (GPO) publications, entitled *Sales Publications Reference File* (PRF), is available by subscription on microfiche for $125, and magnetic tape $850, from GPO. It is also available to subscribers of the DIALOG Information Retrieval System. Users of the system can perform on-line searches of GPO's sales inventory to determine if the publication is for sale, if the item is in stock, and its stock number and current price. DIALOG users can order documents via DIALORDER, a feature of DIALOG, Information Service, Inc., 3460 Hillview Ave., Palo Alto, CA 94304.

* Government Publications Ordering Information
Superintendent of Documents
Government Printing Office (GPO)   202-512-1800
Washington, DC 20402   Fax: 202-512-2250

Orders for government books, pamphlets, posters, and periodicals can be placed by calling the above telephone number between 7:30 a.m. and 4:00 p.m., eastern time. This number may also be used to obtain catalogs of publications plus information on prices, stock numbers, and availability of sales publications. Orders may be charged to MasterCard, VISA, or prepaid Superintendent of Documents deposit accounts.

* How to Do Business With the Government Printing Office
Government Printing Office (GPO)
General Procurement Division, Stop: MMG
Washington, DC 20401   202-512-0916

If you are interested in doing business with the Government Printing Office (GPO), contact the above office to be put on a bidder list and to receive the 129 Commodities Newsletter and brochure, *How to do Business With the GPO*.

* Information on Government Printing Office Publications
Superintendent of Documents
Research and Analysis Section
Stop: SSOP   202-512-1800
Washington, DC 20402   Fax: 202-512-2250

Call or write at the above address for general information on materials available from the Government Printing Office (GPO) or for bibliographies, catalogs, or current brochures. For more extensive information on government published information, contact the nearest Federal Depository Library, which maintains copies of all GPO-published materials. To find the library nearest you, contact your local library.

* International Orders

Superintendent of Documents
Government Printing Office (GPO)   202-512-1800
Washington, DC 20402   Fax: 202-512-2250

Orders for delivery outside the U.S. are subject to a 25% surcharge to provide for the special handling required by international mailing regulations. Orders are mailed surface mail unless airmail is requested (at an additional cost). Payment must accompany every order in U.S. dollars and be in the form of a check drawn on a bank located in the U.S. or Canada, a UNESCO coupon, or an International Postal Money Order made payable to the Superintendent of Documents.

* Mailing Lists

Superintendent of Documents
Government Printing Office (GPO)
Mail List User Program, Stop: SM   202-512-1800
Washington, DC 20402   Fax: 202-512-2250

Individuals interested in direct mail promotions to subscribers of government periodicals can obtain paid subscriber lists for approximately 70 different government periodicals from the Government Printing Office. The lists are available on a one-time use basis only.

* New Government Titles

Superintendent of Documents
Government Printing Office (GPO)   202-512-1800
Washington, DC 20402-9325   Fax: 202-512-2250

The *New Books* catalog is a sampling of new releases from the Government Printing Office (GPO). It is organized by subject area such as agriculture, education, computers, and transportation. These bimonthly listings are available free on a subscription basis. Contact the above address or your nearest U.S. Government bookstore.

* Printing Contracts from Government Printing Office

Government Printing Office (GPO)
Bid Section
Stop: PPSB
Washington, DC 20401   202-512-0526

The Government Printing Office (GPO) awards approximately 46,000 printing contracts to commercial printers each year. To get in on the action, ask for the GPO bidders's information packet, which contains everything necessary to get started.

* Priority Publication Announcements

Government Printing Office (GPO)
Office of Marketing, Stop: SM   202-512-1800
Washington, DC 20401   Fax: 202-512-2250

If you are interested in staying up to date in a certain subject, you can request that notification be sent to you when the government publishes something new in your area of interest. The Government Printing Office (GPO) maintains lists of materials--called *Priority Announcements*--for nearly 100 subject areas, free from GPO.

* Selling Ink to Government Printing Office

Government Printing Office (GPO)
Ralph Miller
Stop: QC
Washington, DC 20401   202-512-0785

If you are a commercial contractor interested in selling ink to the Government Printing Office (GPO), write or call for the brochure, *How to Sell Ink to GPO*, which is designed to provide the necessary information.

* Selling Paper to Government Printing Office

Government Printing Office (GPO)
Paper Procurement Section
Stop: MMPP
Washington, DC 20401   202-512-2022

Information is available on procedures for selling paper to GPO.

* Standing Orders: Government Publications

Standing Order Specialist
Publication Order Branch
Stop SSOP
Government Printing Office (GPO)
Washington, DC 20402-9322   202-512-2315

For your convenience, the Government Printing Office (GPO) has instituted a standing order service for many recurring publications. This allows you to place an order once and automatically receive all subsequent editions or issuances in the same series. For complete information and the necessary authorization form, contact the above office.

* Tours of Government Printing Office

Government Printing Office (GPO)
Office of Public Affairs
Stop: PA
Washington, DC 20401   202-512-1995

For a tour of the world's largest printing plant, contact the above office. Tours given by appointment only on Tuesday, Wednesday, Thursday, beginning at 9:00 AM. Maximum of 20 per tour group, more than one group may be taken at a time.

Government Databases and Internet Access
Federal Government Databases and Bulletin Boards

Much of the data found in the thousands of federal databases are not available anywhere else, which makes them unique and invaluable sources of information for research on almost any topic. And because the government agencies do not make an effort to solicit public access, in many instances the existence of government databases is known to only a few specialists. In those cases where commercial vendors are selling government data, you will discover that you can get the data directly from the federal or state agency for much less money. Searches and printouts of many of these databases can be arranged, and often a tape or diskette of a file can be purchased. There are literally tens of thousands of databases generated by federal agencies. Here is just a sampling of what is available. If you are looking for databases other than those listed below, refer to the Information Starting Places Chapter or review Information USA's reference books, the *Federal Data Base Finder* and the *State Data and Database Finder*.

* Acid Rain (SN 92017)

David Westenbarger
Economic Research Service
U.S. Department of Agriculture (USDA)
1301 New York Ave., NW
Washington, DC 20005-4788 — 202-219-0429
Ordering information — 800-999-6779

This database contains Spring (April-June) and summer (July-September) estimates of nitrate and sulfate wet dispositions in kilograms per hectare by state and county by year for the Northeastern and Middle Atlantic regions. This data is available on one 3.5" disk for $25.

* Adoption Databases

National Adoption Information Clearinghouse
11426 Rockville Pike
Suite 410 — 301-231-6512
Rockville, MD 20852-3007 — Fax: 301-984-8527

This clearinghouse maintains the nation's most comprehensive library of adoption materials, offering a broad array of data on the subject. Resources/services related to child treatment focused on special needs adoptions, including children who have been abused or neglected by their birth parents. The cost depends on the information requested.

* Advance Monthly Retail Sales (CB)

Customer Services
Bureau of the Census
U.S. Department of Commerce — 301-457-4100
Washington, DC 20223 — Fax: 301-457-4714

This file presents, in the form of a press release, advance monthly estimates of retail store sales by kind-of business groups. The report includes seasonally adjusted estimates and percentage changes for major kind-of-business groups based on a subsample of the Census Bureau's monthly retail trade survey respondents. It shows advance estimates for the current month, preliminary and final estimates of the 2 preceding months, and final estimates for the same 2 months a year ago. The estimates are both unadjusted and adjusted for seasonal variations and trading-day differences. Also included are additional preliminary and final monthly sales estimates for the previous months for firms with 11 or more retail stores. This data is also available online through CENDATA. For information about CENDATA content and online services, contact CompuServe or Dialog Information Services. The cost depends on the information requested.

* Aerial Photography Summary Record System on CD-ROM

National Mapping Division
U.S. Geological Survey
U.S. Department of the Interior
12201 Sunrise Valley Dr.
National Center, MS 501
Reston, VA 22092 — 800-USA-MAPS

This system describes aerial photography projects that meet specified criteria over a given geographic area of the United States. There are two databases in the system: the Aerial Photography Summary Record System (APSRS) database and the contributor's database. The Aerial Photography Summary Record System database includes the following fields: agency, latitude and longitude, state/county, date of coverage, project code, scale, focal length, film type, sensor class, percentage of cloud cover/quadrangle covered, and remarks. It describes aerial photography projects that meet specified criteria for 7.5 minute quadrangle areas of the United States. The CD-ROM contains more than 2.5 million records referencing the holdings of more than 600 contributors from federal, state, and local government agencies, universities, and private industry. The contributor's database contains the name, address, and phone number of a contributor. The CD-ROM contains licensed software for searching, sorting, displaying, printing, and exporting the data. This CD-ROM is available for $57 each.

* Agricultural Library Forum (ALF)

National Agricultural Library (NAL)
U.S. Department of Agriculture (USDA)
10301 Baltimore Blvd. — 301-504-5204
Beltsville, MD 20705 — Data: 301-504-5496
— Data: 301-504-5497
— Data: 301-504-6510
— Data: 301-504-5111

The Agricultural Library Forum (ALF) provides a convenient, low-cost tool for electronically accessing information about National Agricultural Library (NAL) products and services and for exchanging agricultural information and resources. ALF supports three types of communications: NAL bulletins, messaging and conferencing between users, and file transfers. It is available 24 hours/day; 7 days/week.

* AGRICultural Online Access Database (AGRICOLA)

Technical Services Division
National Agricultural Library (NAL)
U.S. Department of Agriculture (USDA)
10301 Baltimore Blvd.
Beltsville, MD 20705 — 301-504-5479
To order:
National Technical Information Service (NTIS)
U.S. Department of Commerce
5285 Port Royal Rd. — 703-487-4650
Springfield, VA 22161 — Fax: 703-321-8547

AGRICOLA is a bibliographic database consisting of records for literature citations of journal articles, monographs, thesis, patents, software, audiovisual materials and technical reports relating to all aspects of agriculture. It is one of the largest collections of agricultural literature in the world with over 2 million volumes. AGRICOLA has been available in magnetic tape form since 1970. It currently has over 3.1 million records. AGRICOLA has many access points, searching approaches include: personal and corporate authors, subject category codes, date of journal issues, journal titles or journal title abbreviations, languages of text, source codes, subject heading, and indexing terms. Online access is offered by the following commercial vendors: Dialog, CDP Technologies. Magnetic tapes for both the current and retrospective files may be purchased from National Technical Information Service (NTIS). The cost is available upon request.

* Airman Certificate Data

Airman Certification Branch, AVN-460
Federal Aviation Administration (FAA)
U.S. Department of Transportation (DOT)
P.O. Box 25082
Oklahoma City, OK 73125   405-954-3261

The information in this file deals with the operation and performance of certificated airmen — pilots, other flight crew members, instructors, mechanics, parachute riggers, control tower operators, and dispatchers. It includes accident involvement, violations, and written and practical examination results. Principal reports are: Airman Directory (hard copy and machine-readable certification information), Federal Aviation Administration (FAA) Statistical Handbook of Aviation, U.S. Civil Airmen Statistics, and listings of designated examiners (hard copy). To obtain copies of the data tape at no cost, send a written request to the office listed above.

* Alcohol News Databases

National Clearinghouse for Alcohol and Drug Information
U.S. Department of Health and Human Services
P.O. Box 2345   301-468-2600
Rockville, MD 20847   800-729-6686

This clearinghouse offers 2 databases: the Daily News Summaries Database; the Prevention Materials Database. These databases are designed for anyone who is interested in changing the environment surrounding youth alcohol use/problems. The Daily News Summaries Database consists of summaries of new stories relevant to alcohol policy. The Industry Materials Database, draws on the Marine Institute's collection of materials by/for, and about the alcoholic beverage industry. For those interested in environmental strategies for prevention, this database provides hard to find citations and abstracts containing data on new products, marketing campaigns, sponsorships, policy changes, other developments in the alcohol environment. This database contains over 3,000 records. The cost is $12 per disk for information from the Prevention Materials database, and $20 per disk from the Daily News Summaries Database.

* Alcohol Storage and Production Facilities

Gerald LaRusso
Information Systems Division
Bureau of Alcohol, Tobacco and Firearms (ATF)
U.S. Department of the Treasury
650 Massachusetts Ave., NW, Room 6001
Washington, DC 20226   202-927-7870

This file covers alcohol storage and production facilities in the United States and Puerto Rico. Information on the type of facility and product handled are contained in the record. There are ten data fields showing capacities in hundreds of gallons for the following: (a) daily maximum production for 100-159 proof alcohol; (b) daily maximum production for 160-189 proof alcohol; (c) daily maximum production for 190-194 proof alcohol; (d) daily maximum production for 195-200 proof alcohol; (e) average amount stored for 100-159 proof alcohol; (f) average amount stored for 160-189 proof alcohol; (g) average amount stored for 190-194 proof alcohol; (h) average amount stored for 195-200 proof alcohol; (i) maximum storage capacity for the facility; and (j) total number of storage units (includes drum/barrels and tanks). This file was last updated in 1981 and contains 248 records. The database is no longer updated by FEMA, but it is maintained by the Bureau of Alcohol, Tobacco, and Firearms (ATF) where the file is updated annually. A written request is required to obtain information from ATF. There may be a processing fee depending on the size of the file and the size of the request.

* Animal Welfare Licensee System (AWA)

Regulatory Enforcement and Animal Care (REAC)
Animal and Plant Health Inspection Service (APHIS)
U.S. Department of Agriculture (USDA)
4700 River Rd.
Riverdale, MD 20737   301-734-7833

The system allows the Animal and Plant Health Inspection Service to keep track of licensed and dealers and exhibiters as well as registered animal carriers, intermediate handlers and research facilities. The system contains the registration or license numbers and the addresses of businesses that deal with warm blooded animals. Searches of some over 6,000 records are possible by registration and license numbers and by the geographic location of the business. Printouts and tapes are available on a cost recovery basis.

* Approved Prescription Drugs

Gerald Deighton
Freedom of Information Staff HFI-35
U.S. Food and Drug Administration
U.S. Department of Health and Human Services
5600 Fishers Lane
Rockville, MD 20857   301-443-6310
Database Administration Branch   301-443-6770

The Food and Drug Administration maintains a database of approved prescription drugs. The following data is retrievable for each drug: trade and generic name, manufacturer, and date of Food and Drug Administration approval. Started in 1964 and updated daily, the database contains several thousand records. For more information on the contents of this system, contact the Food and Drug Administration, Database Administration Branch. All requests for searches must be directed in writing to the Freedom of Information staff listed above. Information is provided on a cost recovery basis.

* Art Theft FBI Database

Federal Bureau of Investigation (FBI)
U.S. Department of Justice
9th St. and Pennsylvania Ave., NW
Washington, DC 20535   202-324-4192

The *National Stolen Art File* is a database which lists all currently missing works of art reported as stolen from either public or private collections in the United States. Information from this database is not available to the public.

* Attorney Roster File (PB81-133167XDD)

Office of Public Affairs
U.S. Patent and Trademark Office
U.S. Department of Commerce
2011 Crystal Dr.
Arlington, VA 22202   703-305-8341
To order:
National Technical Information Service (NTIS)
U.S. Department of Commerce
5285 Port Royal Rd.   703-487-4650
Springfield, VA 22161   Fax: 703-321-8547

The Attorney Roster File consists of records of those attorneys and/or agents who are registered to practice before the U.S. Patent and Trademark Office, who also wish to have their names and addresses published in the yearly publication of *Attorneys and Agents Registered to Practice before the U.S. Patent and Trademark Office*. The Attorney Roster Master File is in a 5 position numeric control number order. The records are arranged on the master file in this order for update purposes. The Master File is updated on a quarterly schedule. The updates consist of record changes, deletions of records, and addition of records. From the Attorney Roster Master File an extract tape for National Technical Information Service (NTIS) is generated. This tape contains all names and preferred publication addresses requested by each attorney/agent, and is sorted in zip code sequence (major) and alphabetical last name, first name sequence (minor). The block size is 3080; record size is 308 and blocking factor is 10. The internal label identification value is ATYR44550540TS1M. Source tape is in ASCII character set. Character set restricts preparation to 9 track, one-half inch tape only. Identify recording mode by specifying density only. The price is $360.

* Bird Banding Database

John Tautin
Bird Banding Laboratory
National Biological Service
U.S. Department of the Interior
Laurel, MD 20708   301-497-5790

This database contains information about game and non-game birds banded and/or recovered since the Banding Program began in 1921. Records exist on all birds banded in North America as well as their recovery from all over the world. The database is international in scope, as birds have been recovered by participants in countries such as Russia, Brazil and India. The database is used to produce quarterly reports to the person who bands the bird and certificates of appreciation to band reporters. It is also used for extensive data analysis of migratory bird populations. The database contains 2.6 million banding records. Searches and printouts are available. Depending upon the nature of your request, you may or may not be charged a fee. There is no determined fee schedule.

* Black Population in the United States: March 1992

Customer Services
Bureau of the Census
U.S. Department of Commerce   301-457-4100

Washington, DC 20223   Fax: 301-457-4714

This file provides statistics on the demographic, social, and economic status of the Black population. The data covers population growth, educational attainment, family composition, employment, income, earnings, and poverty status. This data is available online through CENDATA. The cost depends on the information requested.

* Cardiac Pacemaker Registry (CPR)

Gerald Deighton
Freedom of Information Staff HFI-35
U.S. Food and Drug Administration
U.S. Department of Health and Human Services
5600 Fishers Lane
Rockville, MD 20857   301-443-6310

This registry contains data on all pacemakers and leads paid for under Medicare since April of 1985. Some information cannot be released. Searches are done on a cost recovery basis, and requests must be submitted in writing.

* Census of Fatal Occupational Injuries

William Eisenberg, Data Manager
Office of Safety, Health, and Working Conditions
Bureau of Labor Statistics (BLS)
U.S. Department of Labor (DOL)
2 Massachusetts Ave., NE
Washington, DC 20212   202-606-6304

This program provides information on all fatal work injuries by state during a given year. The source of data includes death certificates, state worker compensation reports, state coroner reports and other documents. Information is updated yearly and only information for the current year is available. This data is available free of charge in printed form only from the Office of Publications at the address above.

* Characteristics of Teachers

Customer Services
Bureau of the Census
U.S. Department of Commerce   301-457-4100
Washington, DC 20233   Fax: 301-457-4714

This tabulation, originally prepared for the National Center for Education Statistics, provides selected characteristics of teachers for the United States, regions, divisions, and states. The selected characteristics include: age, sex, race, Spanish origin, family and household type, aggregate earnings, aggregate family income, and various categories of income type. Data for the United States regions, and divisions are on 1 tape reel at 6250 bpi; data for states also are on 1 reel at 6250 bpi. The cost depends on the information requested.

* Child Abuse and Neglect CD-ROM

National Clearinghouse on Child Abuse and Neglect Information
U.S. Department of Health and Human Services
P.O. Box 1182   703-385-7565
Washington, DC 20013-1182   Fax: 703-785-3206

This database is targeted to researchers, policymakers, and administrators from many disciplines who are working to prevent and treat child abuse and neglect. Subscriptions are available to qualifying organizations worldwide: libraries, universities, social and health care providers, law firms, policymakers, public agencies, professional associations, etc.. Any qualified professional or institution can obtain this CD-ROM free, provided you write to the above address on your organization's letterhead, stating your professional interest in the database and how you will actively promote the disc within your organization. The cost depends on information requested.

* Climate Assessment Bulletin Board (CABB)

George Fulwood
National Meteorological Center W353
National Oceanographic and Atmospheric Administration (NOAA)
5200 Auth Rd., Room 805
Washington, DC 20233   301-763-8071

The system is designed for easy public access and provides users with information about short-term climate conditions in the United States and throughout the world. Anyone with a compatible terminal (most home computers are) and telephone linkup can obtain a password and dial directly into the system. Users can then select from a menu of 50 datafiles summarizing meteorological data on a weekly, monthly and seasonal basis. Examples of data include: temperature, precipitation, weather indexes, heating and cooling days, energy conditions, and assessment of climate on crops. The

system contains global surface data collected from 6,000 stations worldwide. Data is contributed from 8,000 stations worldwide. The system is updated continually. For the price of a phone call, anyone with compatible equipment can use the system. Contact Mr. Fulwood's office at the National Oceanographic and Atmospheric Administration (NOAA) to find out if your terminal and telephone linkup are compatible. His office will give you an eight-letter password and the telephone number you can use to enter the system. The users fee ranges from $48-$600.

* Clivue CD-ROM

National Climatic Data Center (NCDC)
National Environmental Satellite Data and
    Information Service (NESDIS)
National Oceanic and Atmospheric Administration (NOAA)
U.S. Department of Commerce
Federal Building   704-271-4800/4871
Asheville, NC 28801-4876   Fax: 704-271-4876

The CD-ROM contains a 1,500-station subset of the National Climatic Data Center's (NCDC) nearly 8,000 United States daily cooperative stations. The user selects a date and area of the United States and the CD-ROM database is queried for stations within the specified domain having data. Then, the system displays daily maximum and minimum temperatures, precipitation, and snowfall for the site. Graphs showing 7 years, 21 years, and the full period of record (varies by station) for the station(s) are available. Visual displays allow users to view trends, variability, and extremes. This is a joint NCDC and Franklin Institute product. The cost is $50.

* Commercial Bank Mortgages Survey

David Cristy
Office of Information Policies and Systems (IPS)
U.S. Department of Housing and Urban Development (HUD)
451 7th Street, SW, Room 4176
Washington, DC 20410   202-708-2374

This system is used by the Office of Financial Management, Housing, to survey originations, purchase, sales, repayments, and holdings of mortgage loans by commercial banks. The commercial bank survey, when combined with similar surveys for savings and loan associations, mortgage companies and life insurance companies, provides the only comprehensive source of data on developments in the national market. Databases maintained are current month plus previous month's master and history. The Housing Systems Division is responsible for this system. The information in this database may be subject to Privacy Act restrictions. If information is released, there may be a processing fee. All requests must be made in writing.

* Comprehensive Airmen Information System

Airmen Certification Branch, AVN-460
Federal Aviation Administration (FAA)
U.S. Department of Transportation (DOT)
P.O. Box 25082
Oklahoma City, OK 73125   405-954-3205

This system was first developed in 1993 and is updated continually. Data includes information on personal, medical, and certification status of individuals associated with civil aviation operations including pilots, mechanics, and flight crews. Limited information is available in printed form at no cost.

* Consular Arrest System

Overseas Citizen Office
U.S. Department of State
Bureau of Consular Affairs
2201 C St., NW
CA/EX Room 4820A
Washington, DC 20520   202-647-5225
To order:
Initial Processing Unit
Information and Privacy Act Office
U.S. Department of State
2201 C St., NW, Room 1512
Washington, DC 20520-1512   202-647-6070

This database maintains current information on Americans in prison in foreign countries in order to respond to requests for this information from the Congress, other federal government agencies, and the public. The file contains up to 71 data elements covering personal identity data, arrest information, judicial status of the case, and reports on the personal welfare of the prisoner. There are approximately 21,000 active and inactive cases in the datafile. Requests for information contained in the database must be made through the Freedom of Information Act office. The cost for obtaining the information is charged according to a fee schedule of: professional time at $12 per hour, clerical time at $7 per hour, and reproduction of documents at $.10 per page.

* Credit Data on Individual Debtors System

Ilga Pakalns
Office of the Secretary (O/SECY)
U.S. Department of Labor (DOL)
Room N-4309, Frances Perkins Building
200 Constitution Ave., NW
Washington, DC 20210   202-219-8362

The purpose of this system is to assemble in one system information on individuals who are indebted to the Department of Labor for the purpose of determining collectibility of debts and taking appropriate actions to collect or otherwise resolve the debts. The categories of records in this system include commercial credit reports, correspondence to and from the debtor, information or records relating to the debtor's current whereabouts, assets, liabilities, income and expenses, debtor's personal financial statements, and other information such as social security number, address, nature, amount and history of the debt, and other records and reports relating to the implementation of the Debt Collection Act of 1982, including any investigative reports or administrative review matters. The system is updated as information becomes available.

* Credit Information in Export-Import Bank

Robert Camp
Export-Import Bank of the United States
811 Vermont Ave, NW, Room 1050
Washington, DC 20571   202-566-4690

This database contains a wide variety of information regarding the services the Export-Import Bank provides. Users can access information in a variety of ways, including providing data on their dealings with a particular exporter, identifying exporters in a particular state, and listing the total amounts authorized to a particular foreign entity. The system is updated daily. Simple requests can be handled over the phone. More detailed requests may require a Freedom of Information Act (FOIA) letter. The price will vary depending on the amount of information requested.

* Database for Pilot Study of Nutrient Content of School Lunches (PB84-196906XDD)

Office of Analysis and Evaluation
Food and Nutrition Information Center
National Agricultural Library (NAL) Building
Room 304
U.S. Department of Agriculture (USDA)
Beltsville, MD 20705   301-504-5719
To order:
National Technical Information Service (NTIS)
U.S. Department of Commerce
5285 Port Royal Rd.   703-487-4650
Springfield, VA 22161   Fax: 703-321-8547

This file is the base file for computation of the nutrient content of school lunches. The 1,044 foods are those most frequently used in school lunch service nationwide. The data set was developed in conjunction with software for a USDA Food and Nutrition Service (FNS) pilot test. The entire system is being field tested and all aspects are subject to extensive revision. The software, documentation, manuals, and data set in its final form will only be made available when testing is completed, and if approved by FNS.

* Database Search Service

Federal Communications Commission (FCC)
1919 M St., NW
Washington, DC 20554   202-418-0200
To order:
International Transcription Service (ITS)
2100 M St., NW, Suite 140
Washington, DC 20037   202-857-3800

All public information on Federal Communications Commission (FCC) databases, including information on broadcasting, citizen radio service, microwave applications, common carriers, and financial and operating expenses are available on letter sized paper from an FCC duplicating contractor, International Transcription Service (ITS). The cost for this service is $15 per hour for research and retrieval time and $.07 per page.

* Detailed Occupation by Industry and Other Characteristics

Customer Services
Bureau of the Census
U.S. Department of Commerce   301-457-4100
Washington, DC 20233   Fax: 301-457-4714

This special tabulation consists of three tabulations with data for employed persons for the Nation and states. In addition, the second tabulation (occupation by industry) has data for standard metropolitan statistical areas (SMSAs). The data is available on 2 tape reels at 6250 bpi; United States and states, 1 reel; SMSAs, 1 reel. The cost depends on the information requested.

* Dietary Risk Evaluation System (DRES)

Jim Kariya
Environmental Protection Agency (EPA)
401 M St., SW
Washington, DC 20460   703-305-6028

The system estimates exposure to pesticides in the diet by combining information concerning residues on raw agricultural commodities with information on consumption of those commodities. It then compares the estimated exposure level to a toxicologically relevant dose. It is used in the Office of Pesticide Planning's (OPP) decision making process for granting or revoking pesticide tolerance. The data is updated at least quarterly. Limited information is available at no cost.

* Directory of Federal Contractors and Cognizant Audit Offices

Lorraine Byars (CMO)
Defense Contract Audit Agency (DCAA)
U.S. Department of Defense (DOD)
Cameron Station
Alexandria, VA 22304-6178   703-274-5821

This directory identifies the company names, addresses, and telephone numbers of approximately 30,000 contractors which perform work for the Department of Defense and other government agencies for which Defense Contract Audit Agency (DCAA) conducts audits. The database and related software is contained on two 3.5" disks, and requires approximately 10 million bytes. Also provided, materials available to the public in hard copy form for nominal fee by contacting the above address are as follows: *DCAA Contract Audit Manual* (DCAAM 7640.1); *Index of DCAA Numbered Publications* (DCAAI 5025.2); *Index of DCAA Memorandums for Regional Directors (MRDs)* (DCAAI 5025.13); and *Directory of DCAA offices* (DCAAP 5100.1). The Headquarters, DCAA is scheduled to be relocated to Fort Belvoir, VA in 1995. The new address and telephone number are not available at this time.

* Directory of Federal Laboratories and Technology Resources (FATD) Database (PB94-500568XDD)

National Center for Health Statistics
Public Health Service
U.S. Department of Health and Human Services
6525 Belcrest Rd.
Hyattsville, MD 20782   301-436-8500
To order:
National Technical Information Service (NTIS)
U.S. Department of Commerce
5285 Port Royal Rd.   703-487-4650
Springfield, VA 22161   Fax: 703-321-8547

The Directory of Federal Laboratories and Technology Resources database contains descriptions of over 1,000 federal research and engineering laboratories and other facilities that are available for use by the private sector. Entries are divided into 31 subject categories and provide information on the nature and extent of the resources available (e.g. expertise, information, equipment, facilities, special services). Each entry includes name, address, and contact person. The database is updated every 2 years. Access can be gained through CDP Technologies. The cost is $2000.

* Driver License Administration Requirements and Fees

Mary Teets, Highway Statistics Division
Federal Highway Administration (FHWA)
U.S. Department of Transportation (DOT)
400 7th St., SW
Washington, DC 20590   202-366-9211

This data covers the administrative requirements and qualifications necessary to

Government Databases and Internet Access

obtain drivers' licenses in the 50 states, the District of Columbia, and Canada. This system contains narrative summary and 10 detailed tables showing data by state, including requirements for regular licenses and classified licenses; training; examination and renewal; license reciprocity; fees; and suspension, revocation, and reinstatement provisions. Data is updated biennially. Contact the office listed above for price.

* Duck Breeding Ground Survey Database

Graham Smith
Office of Migratory Bird Management
U.S. Fish and Wildlife Service
U.S. Department of the Interior
Laurel, MD 20708   301-497-5860

This survey estimates the size of breeding waterfowl populations in the north-central United States and Canada. The data exists from 1955 to present. This annual survey is conducted May through June. It is the most extensive and long term survey in the world in terms of wildlife species. Information from this survey is most reliable for the most abundant and widely distributed species such as the mallard; it is less so for species of low abundance or for those species whose nesting range is partly outside the survey area. Information is public, and questions will be answered for members of the general public. Search requests are accepted through state agencies and University Land Grant Programs. The cost depends on the information requested.

* Earthquake Database

National Geophysical Data Center (NGDC)
National Environmental Satellite Data and
    Information Service (NESDIS)
National Oceanic and Atmospheric Administration (NOAA)
U.S. Department of Commerce
325 Broadway   301-497-6826
Boulder, CO 80303   Fax: 303-497-6513
                                         Voice/TDD: 303-497-6958
                                 Internet: info@mail.ngdc.noaa.gov

This file contains information from 2100 B.C. to the present. Retrievals can be made using various criteria, such as geographic area, magnitude, time period, maximum intensity. Other databases include the Significant Earthquakes and Earthquake Intensity databases. Call for price information.

* Economic Bulletin Board (EBB)

STAT-USA
Economics and Statistics Administration
Room H4885   202-482-1986
Washington, DC 20230   Fax: 202-482-2164
                                           Access TDD: 202-482-1526
                                     E-mail: rwendling@doc.gov
                              Internet/Telnet: ebb.stat-usa.gov

The Economic Bulletin Board (EBB) is managed by STAT-USA and is the world's leading source of government sponsored business administration. On the Economic Bulletin Board you get late-breaking business developments minutes after they happen, and in-depth analyses of markets, products, and economic trends. More than 5,000 files are available 24 hours a day, 7 days a week. Some of the most popular files include: Business Cycle Indicators, Daily Trade Opportunities (TOPs), Consumer Price Index, Nose and T-Bill Auction Results, and much more. A free limited-access service is available to those who would like to get acquainted with Electronic Bulletin Board before subscribing. Call the Electronic Bulletin Board and type GUEST when prompted for a User ID. An annual subscription to the Electronic Bulletin Board is $45. Connect time charges also apply, but users receive $20 worth of free connect time with their paid subscription.

* Economic Research Service (ERS) Electronic Data Products CD-ROM (SN 93050)

Jim Horsfield
Economic Research Service
U.S. Department of Agriculture (USDA)
1301 New York Ave., NW
Washington, DC 20005-4788   202-219-0698
Ordering Information   800-999-6779

This file combines files from 118 Economic Research Service (ERS) electronic data products (current and revised versions) on a standard CD-ROM disc. Included on the disc are over 6,500 Lotus 1-2-3 worksheet files, ASCII text files describing each data product, and easy to use software to locate and download files for use with your favorite analytical package. This data is available on one CD-ROM disc for $150.

* Electronic Publishing System (EPUB)

National Energy Information Center, EI-231
Energy Information Administration (EIA)
U.S. Department of Energy (DOE)
Forrestal Building, Room 1F-048   202-586-8800
Washington, DC 20585   Data: 202-586-2557
TDD for deaf or hearing impaired   202-586-1181
Technical Assistance   202-586-8959
                                          Internet: fedworld.gov

The Energy Information Administration (EIA) maintains the Electronic Publishing System (EPUB). The general public are allowed to access many of EIA's reports and some selected energy data. The EPUB is a bulletin-board-type that can be accessed free of charge for 24 hours a day. Users can download reports to their printer, or download reports to their Personal Computer or to a diskette. Samples of files accessible are as follows: *Weekly Coal Production Report (WCPR):* Statistics on United States production of bituminous coal, lignite, production of Pennsylvania anthracite. *Winter Fuels Natural Gas (WFRG):* Statistics on natural gas in underground storage for the 5 most recent months. Data is on base and working gas in storage. *Short-Term Energy Outlook (STEO):* Quarterly forecast for the next 4 quarters of the United States energy supply/demand summary; forecast assumptions; energy prices; domestic supply/disposition of petroleum in low/mid/high world oil price scenarios. *Financial Reporting System:* Contains tables from EIA's Performance Profiles of Major Energy Producers on operating statistics, profit ratios, cash flows, income taxes, development/production expenses, etc. Personal computer users must provide the following in order to access the Electronic Publishing System (EPUB): Baud Rate: 300-2400 bps; Data Bits: 8; Stop Bits: 1; No Parity; Duplex: Full; Terminal Type: (e.g. ANSI, ANSI-BBS, VT100). For more information, obtain the *EPUB User's Guide*, available from the National Energy Information Center. This system can also be accessed on the Internet through Fedworld, Gateway number 16.

* Federal Domestic Assistance Programs (FDAP)

Jerry Varner
Federal Domestic Assistance Catalog Staff (WKU)
General Services Administration (GSA)
Reporters Building
300 7th St., SW
Room 101
Washington, DC 20407   202-708-5126

The Federal Domestic Assistance Programs (FDAP) is a computerized question-answer system designed to provide rapid access to federal domestic assistance program information. Information provided is determined by user input, including type of applicant, type of assistance, and specific categories of interest. Output includes a list of program numbers and titles, the full text of selected programs, or sections of text. A keyword search function has been added. States have designated access points where FDAP searches may be requested. To connect to the system, you must first register with the General Services Administration. There is a subscription fee of $50.

* Federal Procurement Data Center (FPDC)

Brenda Johnson
Federal Procurement Data Center
General Services Administration (GSA)
Reporters Bldg.
300 7th St., SW
Washington, DC 20407   202-401-1529

The Federal Procurement Data Center (FPDC) stores information about federal procurement actions, from 1979 to present, that totaled $25,000 or more. The system will eventually contain 45 data elements, including: purchasing or contracting office; date of award; principal place of performance; dollars obligated; principal product or service; business and labor requirements; type of procurement action; methods of contracting; socioeconomic data; name and address of contractor; and foreign trade data. The database was started in 1979 and contains two million records. Approximately 400,000 contract actions are added yearly. Searches and printouts are available on a cost recovery basis. Requests should be made in writing. If a search on a contractor is requested, the Contractor Establishment Code (CEC) number will be helpful.

* Federal Reserve Economic Data (FRED) Bulletin Board

Research and Public Information
The Federal Reserve Bank of St. Louis
P.O. Box 442   314-444-8562 ext. 8807
St. Louis, MO 63166   Data: 314-621-1824

The Federal Reserve Economic Data (FRED) provides current United States and international economic and financial data, including daily United States interest rates, historical data on money and business indicators, and regional economic data for Arkansas, Illinois, Indiana, Kentucky, Mississippi, Missouri and Tennessee. Weekly United States monetary data is updated on FRED Thursday by 5:30 PM Central time. The Master File (file directory 15) contains a listing of all FRED files that are available for viewing or downloading and new user information. Once connected the system will instruct you on how to register and enter your password. FRED is a free service that is available 24 hours a day, 7 days a week, limited to 1 hour of log on time a day.

* Federal Tax Forms on CD-ROM

Linda Wallace
Internal Revenue Service (IRS)
U.S. Department of the Treasury
1111 Constitution Ave., NW
Washington, DC 20224   202-927-4288
To order:
Superintendent of Documents
U.S. Government Printing Office
P.O. Box 371954   202-512-1800
Pittsburgh, PA 15250-7954   Fax: 202-512-2250
                                         BBS: 202-512-1387

The 1994 CD-ROM includes Internal Revenue Service Taxpayer Information Publication (TIPS) and approximately 3000 pages of topic-oriented tax information. This will be released on a three-issue subscription basis with cumulative CD-ROMs released in December, January, and February to provide access to earlier-approved forms in December, with the later-approved items being added in the subsequent releases. The search and display software has been upgraded and will make it easier to locate information across all products on the CD-ROM. Users will be able to electronically search, view-on-screen, or print out any of the items contained on the CD-ROM. The CD-ROM is available for sale through the Government Printing Office. You may also order through the Government Printing Office's Federal Bulletin Board System (BBS). The cost for the three issue subscription is $69, and the stock number is 648-094-00004-3. New CD-ROMs will be issued annually.

* Financial Disclosure Database on Federal Candidates

Direct Access Program
Federal Election Commission (FEC)
999 E St., NW   800-424-9530
Washington, DC 20463   202-219-3730

The Financial Disclosure database has both financial and reference information on every candidate for federal office since 1977 and on contributing Political Action Committees and political parties. The system can be searched by specific candidate or contributor, and retrievable data includes exact dollar amounts and contact information. The database was started in 1977 and contains nearly 3.5 million records. It is updated daily. Searches and printouts amounting to 20 records or less are available free of charge. A nominal fee is charged for each additional record.

* Fish and Wildlife Reference Service (FWRS) Database

U.S. Fish and Wildlife Service
U.S. Department of the Interior   301-492-6402
5430 Governor Ln., Suite 110   800-582-3421
Bethesda, MD 20814-2142   Fax: 301-569-4059

The Fish and Wildlife Reference Service (FWRS) operates a bibliographic database containing indexed fish and wildlife-related documents from the following sources: the Federal Aid in Fish and Wildlife Restoration Program; the Adronomous Fish Conservation Program; the Endangered Species Grants program; and work done at the Cooperative Fishery and Wildlife Agencies. Documents are selected for their research value to biologists in more than one state. Indexed materials include reports, published papers, technical publications, theses, and special materials such as endangered species recovery plans. Subject coverage includes birds, botany, fish management, hunting and fishing, water resources, pesticides, land use, habitat management and many other topics. The database has 25,000 records, some dating back to 1915, and is updated quarterly. Bibliographic searches and documents can be obtained from FWRS. Employees of state and federal Natural Resource agencies are considered to be FWS "cooperators". Free literature searches are performed for "cooperators" and they are not charged for photocopying and microfiche services unless the cost exceeds $10. All others are termed "clients" and are charged a flat fee of $30 for a new literature search, 10 cents per page for copies of documents on file and 50 cents per fiche for copies of reports. The FWRS database will be available on the Internet by mid-1995.

* Food Spending in American Households, 1980-88 (SN 90005 B)

David Smallwood
Economic Research Service
U.S. Department of Agriculture (USDA)
1301 New York Ave., NW
Washington, DC 20005-4788   202-219-1265
Ordering information   800-999-6779

This database contains detailed data from 1980-1992 on household food expenditures by major food groups and by household demographic characteristics. It includes data on food price trends and percent of households purchasing selected food items in a week. The prices range from $35-$55.

* Foreign Geographic Names

Geographic Names Branch (GNB)
Hydro-Graphic Topal-Graphic Center
Defense Mapping Agency
U.S. Department of Defense (DOD)
Washington, DC 20315   301-227-3880

This database manages information about all standardized foreign geographic names approved by the Geographic Names Branch (GNB). The system is searchable by foreign country and its subdivisions such as listing of a particular country's rivers, populated places, or valleys. Retrievable data include proper name and spelling, longitude/latitude, and type of feature (i.e., city, mountain, administrative area, etc). In the near future, records will exist on all foreign countries. Searches and printouts are expected to be available on a cost recovery basis.

* Foreign Hourly Compensation Costs

Patricia Capdevielle
Bureau of Labor Statistics (BLS)
U.S. Department of Labor (DOL)
2 Massachusetts Ave., NE
Washington, DC 20212   202-606-5654

This database contains annual levels of hourly compensation costs for production workers in all manufacturing and 30 component industries for the United States and 30 foreign countries or areas from 1975. Data is adjusted for comparability and presented both in national currency and in United States dollars. This data is available on one disk for $55.

* Foreign Importer Listings Database

Agricultural Information Marketing Service
Foreign Agriculture Service
U.S. Department of Agriculture (USDA)
Room 4951, South Building
14th St. and Independence Ave., SW
Washington, DC 20250   202-720-7103

This system includes names, addresses and telex numbers of firms currently dealing in food and agricultural products in specific countries and of companies which have requested United States products during the past three years. Listings are available for: 1) all foreign countries for a single product or 2) all importers of all agricultural products in a single country. There is a nominal fee for each listing.

* Foreign Living Costs--Allowances and Differentials Program

Erle Curtis, Office of Allowances
U.S. Department of State
3005 Massachusetts Ave., NW, Room 205
Washington, DC 20520   703-875-7949
To order:
Superintendent of Documents
Government Printing Office (GPO)
Washington, DC 20402   202-512-1800

This system, updated every 2 to 4 weeks, measures cost of living, cost of permanent housing, cost of temporary lodging, and cost of dependents education in foreign areas where United States government employees are assigned. Based on analysis of costs, appropriate rates of allowances and travel per diem are established to reimburse employees for extraordinary costs of living. Basic reports contain 700 prices for 200 different items. About 700 foreign locations are rated. Information available to the public through the Government Printing Office includes: *U.S. Department of State Indexes of Living Costs Abroad, Quarterly Allowances, Hardship Differentials, Standardized Regulations (Government Civilians, Foreign Areas)* stock number 744-

Be patient. If any phone number is incorrect, call (area code) 555-1212 and request the new listing.

1213

Government Databases and Internet Access

011-0000-1, $5.50 for a quarterly subscription; and *Maximum Per Diem Allowances for Foreign Areas* stock number 744-008-00000-0, $24 for a monthly subscription.

* Foreign-Owned Agricultural Land Datafile (SN 87015)

Peter DeBraal, Economic Research Service
U.S. Department of Agriculture (USDA)
1301 New York Ave., NW
Washington, DC 20005-4788
Ordering Information   202-219-1011
    800-999-6779

This data is from 13,000 reports filed under the Alien Foreign Investment Disclosure Act of 1978. It includes foreign-owned agricultural land by states and counties as on 12/31/93. The data is available on two 3.5" disks for $35.

* Geographic Names Information System (GNIS)

Roger Payne, Manager
Geographic Names Information System (GNIS)
U.S. Geological Survey
U.S. Department of the Interior
12201 Sunrise Valley Dr.
National Center, MS 523   703-648-5920
Reston, VA 22092   800-USA-MAPS
Questions   703-648-4544

The Geographic Names Information System (GNIS) is an automated data system developed by the U.S. Geological Survey to standardize and disseminate information on geographic names. Primary information is provided for all know places, features, and areas in the United States identified by a proper name. The system is composed of 3 databases: National Geographic Names Database (NGN), U.S. Geological Survey Topographic Map Names Database, and Generic Database. The Generic Database defines the terms used by U.S. Geological Survey for 63 broad categories of feature types found in the National Geographic Names (NGN) Database (i.e., "stream" is used for rivers, creeks, brooks, etc.). It also contains annotated bibliographic listings of sources used to create the NGN Database. The National Geographic Names (NGN) and U.S. Geological Survey (USGS) Topographic Map Names Database are described in separate entries in this section. Printouts and searches from the Geographic Names Information System (GNIS) are available on a cost recovery basis. This information is available in almost very type of format, including diskette for personal computers. It will soon be available on the Internet.

* Glacier Photo Index

Pat Hoffman
World Data Center A: Glaciology
Cooperative Institute for Research in Environmental Science
Campus Box 449
University of Colorado
Boulder, CO 80309   303-492-5171

The Glacier Photo Index is an inventory of glacier photographs taken since the mid-1960s by the U.S. Geological Survey. The database contains aerial photographs from the Pacific Northwest of the United States (including Alaska) and parts of Canada. Retrievable information includes photograph name, date, location and geological features. Information can be retrieved by 20 different categories. The database contains approximately 120,000 records and is updated yearly. Searches and printouts are available on a cost recovery basis.

* Greenhouse and Nursery Statistics, 1960-88 (SN 90024 A-B)

Doyle Johnson, Economic Research Service
U.S. Department of Agriculture (USDA)
1301 New York Ave., NW
Washington, DC 20005-4788
Ordering information   202-219-0296
    800-999-6779

This is a comprehensive database covering production, supply, consumption, prices, and sales of floricultural and environmental horticultural products. It includes United States and state data as well as world trade data. A version of this database is included on the Economic Research Service (ERS) CD-ROM, #93050. Prices for this information range from $35-$85.

* Investment Adviser Directory, August 1977 - November 1991, and December 8, 1995

Margaret Adams, Archives Specialist
Reference Services (NSXA)

Center for Electronic Records
National Archives and Records Administration   301-713-6645
8601 Adelphi Rd.   Fax: 301-713-6911
College Park, MD 20740-6001   Internet: cer@nara.gov

This electronic data set is comprised of 2 files. These computer-readable datafiles and documentation are in the custody of the National Archives and Records Administration, Center for Electronic Records. Copies of electronic records are available either on 9-track magnetic tape or on 2480-class tape cartridge. Reproductions of electronic records are on a cost recovery basis and cost is dependent on output media and technical specifications (encoding, labeling, and blocksize). Contact the Center for Electronic Records for further information about the content of the records, a price quotation, and ordering instructions. A complete list of files can be ordered from the National Archives and Records Administration. It is available online through the use of a File Transfer Protocol (FTP) and on the National Archives Gopher Server.

* "Labor News" Electronic Bulletin Board

Office of Public Affairs
U.S. Department of Labor (DOL)   202-219-8831
200 Constitution Ave., NW   Data: 202-219-4784
Washington, DC 20210   Fax: 202-219-9600

Labor News is a free electronic bulletin Board providing a variety of labor related information and is available to anyone with a computer, a modem, and communications software. Information is updated daily and includes new releases, selected publications, public labor oriented forums and connection to major Occupational Safety and Health Administration (OSHA) databases. To register directly, load the following parameters into your computer: BAUD Speed: 300, 1200, 2400, 9600, 14,400, Parity: none, Data bits: 8, Stop bit: 1. After you have made a connection to Labor News, follow the registration prompts. Users must pay any toll for long distance calls. This bulletin board operates 24 hours a day, 7 days a week.

* Lists of Airline Employees Protected Under the Rehire Program

Tony Massey
Bureau of Labor Management Relations and Cooperative Programs
U.S. Department of Labor (DOL)
Room N-5402, Frances Perkins Building
200 Constitution Ave., NW
Washington, DC 20210   202-219-6231

The lists will assist covered air carriers in verifying job applicants' protected status. The categories of records in this system include lists that contain employees' names, social security numbers (if available), occupational specialties and reporting covered carrier. These records are retrieved alphabetically by covered carrier and name of employee. The records are updated as information becomes available. All information from this system requires a written Freedom of Information Act request.

* Manufacturing Plants and Chemical Registry

National Institute of Occupational Safety and Health
Division of Surveillance Hazard Evaluation
4676 Columbia Parkway
Cincinnati, OH 45226   513-841-4491

The National Institute of Occupational Safety and Health (NIOSH) maintains two databases, the National Occupational Hazard Survey Databases I and II, which contain surveys of 5,000 manufacturing plants each. NIOSH administers a questionnaire, investigates health and safety programs, and conducts an inventory of chemicals. Through the databases, NIOSH can identify potential exposure agents, describe health and safety programs, and by chemical can develop estimates of number of people exposed. There is no charge for information.

* Marine Minerals CD-ROM

National Geophysical Data Center (NGDC)
National Environmental Satellite Data and
    Information Service (NESDIS)
National Oceanic and Atmospheric Administration (NOAA)
U.S. Department of Commerce   301-497-6826
325 Broadway   Fax: 303-497-6513
Boulder, CO 80303   Voice/TDD: 303-497-6958
    Internet: info@mail.ngdc.noaa.gov

This CD-ROM contains the results of a nine year cooperative between the National Geophysical Data Center (NGDC), National Oceanic and Atmospheric Administration's (NOAA) National Ocean Service, and the Minerals Management Service, to compile a comprehensive computerized bibliography and geochemical database on offshore hard mineral resources. Both personal computer (PC) and Macintosh software are included. The cost is $57.

* Medical and Dental Laboratories

Data Liaison, Bureau of the Census
U.S. Department of Commerce
Suitland Federal Center, Room 1021-3   301-763-2360
Washington, DC 20233   Fax: 301-763-4469

This file covers establishments primarily engaged in providing professional analytic or diagnostic services to the medical profession, to the patient on prescription by a physician, and establishments primarily engaged in making dentures and artificial teeth for the dental profession. The cost depends on the information requested.

* Medical Device Reporting System (MDR)

Gerald Deighton
Freedom of Information Staff HFI-35
U.S. Food and Drug Administration
U.S. Department of Health and Human Services
5600 Fishers Lane
Rockville, MD 20857   301-443-6310

The system collects reports of deaths, injuries, and malfunctions related to the use of medical devices. The database is updated daily and covers 1984 to present. For more information contact the National Center for Health Statistics at 301-436-8500. Searches are done on a cost recovery basis, and requests must be submitted in writing.

* Military Family Clearinghouse (MFC)

Military Family Clearinghouse (MFC)
U.S. Department of Defense (DOD)   703-696-5806
4015 Wilson Boulevard, Suite 903   800-336-4592
Arlington, VA 22203-5190   Fax: 703-696-6344

The Military Family Clearinghouse (MFC) was established to support the professional community that helps families cope with the unique challenges of military life. Specific information related to child abuse and neglect is available, as well as information on aspects of military life that are stressful for parents, such as family separations, reunions, occupational hazards, and the current downsizing of the Armed Forces.

* Military Hospitals in the United States

Joint Data Systems Support Center (JDSSC)
Deputy Assistant Secretary of Defense (Information Management)
U.S. Department of Defense
Pentagon, Room 3E172
Washington, DC 20310-3040   703-692-2788

This file provides information on military hospitals in the United States. Due to the nature of security classification of this data, a more detailed description is available only to those with the proper security clearance and a need-to-know. The cost depends on the information requested.

* National Agricultural Library (NAL) Databases

Alvetta Pindell
Reference Section, Room 100
National Agricultural Library (NAL)
U.S. Department of Agriculture (USDA)
10301 Baltimore Blvd.
Beltsville, MD 20705   301-504-5204

The National Agricultural Library (NAL) is a national and international resource for the collection and dissemination of information on all aspects of agriculture. United States state and local agencies including state experiment stations and extension services, United States individuals including college and university students and faculty can receive services up to the threshold level without charge. Threshold level service is defined as one hour of staff time of $25 in computer usage costs. Services beyond the threshold level are provided for a fee. Computer time costs vary according to the database(s) searched, time spent on-line, and the number of references printed. Charges are for telecommunications linkages, direct online costs and for the offline prints, if any.

* National Atlas

National Mapping Division
U.S. Geological Survey

U.S. Department of the Interior
12201 Sunrise Valley Dr.
National Center, MS 523
Reston, VA 22092   800-USA-MAPS

This system is utilized with the geographic names information system (GNIS) of the U.S. Geological Survey; consists of variable length records containing data recorded in the index to the National Atlas of the United States; this information refers to well-known places, physical features and administrative areas such as national parks; information consists of text, numeric data and codes; topics covered are name, feature, class, geographic coordinates, population, state, county and key reference to a map in national atlas. The cost depends on the information requested.

* National Earthquake Information Center (NEIC)

National Earthquake Information Center
U.S. Geological Survey
U.S. Department of the Interior
Denver Federal Center
Box 25046, Mail Stop 967   303-273-8500
Denver, CO 80225   Data: 800-358-2663

This center compiles, computes and distributes digital and analog data on earthquakes that have occurred around the world. The database contains information on the time, location, depth, magnitude and other characteristics of each earthquake. The National Earthquake Information Center (NEIC) receives information by real-time direct transmission from monitoring stations, telecommunications from monitoring centers, by airmail delivery from stations outside the United States and by direct computer link. In 1985, NEIC assumed responsibility for filming and distributing microfiche copies of Worldwide Seismic Station Network (WWSSN) seismograms. Data is also published in the Preliminary Determination of Epicenter (PDE) monthly listing and through Quick Epicenter Determinations (QED). Quick Epicenter Determinations are now available to individuals and groups having access to a 300 baud modem. Call the above number for an information packet for computer access.

* National Endowment for the Arts (NEA) Grants Management System

Andrea F. Fowler, Information Management Division
National Endowment for the Arts
National Foundation on the Arts and the Humanities
1100 Pennsylvania Ave., NW, Room 815
Washington, DC 20506   202-682-5757

One of the principal ways in which the National Endowment for the Arts fulfills its mission to encourage and support American arts and artists is through the awarding of grants to individuals and organizations. The Arts Endowment receives between 15,000-16,000 applications for grant awards annually, and awards between 4,000-5,000 grants per year. To facilitate the management and control of application and grant information received and processed at the Arts Endowment, an automated computer system was developed for the agency. The Grants Management System is an in-office, online system which allows agency users to invoke various functions (e.g., maintenance, searching and reporting functions) interactively through menus. The system operates in a WANG VS environment. The Grants Management System contains pertinent information about applicants/grantees and the projects which are recommended for award. A written request is generally required to obtain information from the Grants Management System. Information is available on a cost-reimbursable basis.

* National Snow and Ice Data Center

World Data Center-A for Glaciology (Snow and Ice)
University of Colorado   303-492-1834/5171
Boulder, CO 80309   Fax: 303-492-2468
    Telex: 7401426 WDCA UC
    Telemail: (NSIDC/OMNET) MAIL/USA
    (Attn: Data Request Services)
    Internet: nsidc@kryos.colorado.edu
    Vax Mail: KRYOS::NSIDC

World Data Center (WDC)-A for Glaciology (Snow and Ice) in Boulder, Colorado, is one of three international data centers serving the discipline. Co-located with WDC is the National Snow and Ice Data Center (NSIDC) established by the National Oceanic and Atmospheric Administration (NOAA) in 1982. This center functions as a national information and referral center for the snow and ice community. Many of the data sets held are common to both the WDC and NSIDC although some are only available within the latter organization framework. WDC/NSIDC archives digital data on numerous areas of snow and ice research. The majority of data sets are of snow cover and sea ice, but there are also data relating to glacial geophysics, Great Lakes ice-related environmental studies, and satellite microwave research.

Government Databases and Internet Access

* Nursing Demand Model: Combined Report

Public Health Services
U.S. Department of Health and Human Services
National Center for Health Statistics
6525 Belcrest Rd.
Hyattsville, MD 20782   301-436-8500
To order:
National Technical Information Service (NTIS)
U.S. Department of Commerce
5285 Port Royal Rd.   703-487-4650
Springfield, VA 22161   Fax: 703-321-8547

This combined report contains a complete set of documentation covering all aspects of the development of the Nursing Demand Model. The model analytically describes the demand the number of full time equivalent nurses employers would actually hire given market condition for the major sectors of the health care system in the states of the United States. The 3 major components of nursing are treated by the model: Registered Nurse, Licensed Practical and Vocational Nurses and Nursing Personnel. The software is available on 5.25" diskettes (order number PB94-501616) or 3.5" diskettes (order number PB94-504370) for $140.

* Nutrient Data Bank Bulletin Board

David B. Haytowitz
Nutrient Data Laboratory
Agricultural Research Service
U.S. Department of Agriculture   301-734-8491
4700 River Rd., Unit 89   Data: 301-734-5078
Riverdale, MD 20737   E-mail: info-12@info.umd.edu
             Internet: telnet info.umd.edu

The Nutrient Data Bank Bulletin Board is sponsored by the Nutrient Data Laboratory (NDL) of the U.S. Department of Agriculture (USDA), Agricultural Research Service. It is operated as a public service to provide information about current NDL publications and computer files on the nutrient composition of foods. Announcements about Nutrient Data Bank Conferences and other relevant topics ar also included. The information is presented in the form of bulletins that can be viewed directly or captured on a disk for review at your convenience. In addition, datafiles are available to download for use on computers using MS-DOS or PC-DOS. These include data from *Agriculture Handbook No. 8, Composition of Foods, Home and Garden Bulletin No. 72, Nutritive Value of Foods; Home Economics Research Report No. 48, Sugar Content of Selected Foods*, sections of *Home Economics Research Report No. 50, Nutrient Content of the United States Food Supply*, National Nutrient Database for Child Nutrition Programs (NNDCNP), and computer files from USDA's Nutrient Database for Food Consumption Surveys and the Dietary Analysis Program for microcomputers. The computer is online 24 hours a day, 7 days a week, with a few hours a month set aside for performing maintenance work on the computer and files. There is no charge for this service.

* Patent Attorney Roster File

Office of Products Development/OIPD
U.S. Patent and Trademark Office
U.S. Department of Commerce
Crystal Plaza 2, Room 9D30   703-308-0555
Washington, DC 20231   Fax: 703-308-0493

The file contains records for attorneys and/or agents who are registered to practice before the Patent and Trademark Office (PTO) who also wish to have their names and addresses published in the yearly publication which lists them. It contains names and addresses in the last name, first name sequence. It contains approximately 12,500 records per file. The file is updated as requested and is available from the PTO office above for $100 on cartridge, $110 on 9 track tape, and $95 on diskette. Write for agreement and technical specifications.

* Patent Full Text File

Office of Products Development/OIPD
U.S. Patent and Trademark Office
U.S. Department of Commerce
Crystal Plaza 2, Room 9D30   703-308-0555
Washington, DC 20231   Fax: 703-308-0493

The file, updated weekly, contains the full text of each patent exclusive of the drawings. Some of the fields in each patent record include: filing date; serial number; patent number; patent title; issue date; inventor's name; assignee; tables; and claims. It contains approximately 1,000,000 patents with 75,000 added each year (1,600 per issue). The time period covered is January 1975 to present. Patent Full Text is available on cartridge for $5295 or on 9 track tape for $7710 per year from the Patent and Trademark office above. Write for agreement and technical specifications.

The database is also available for online commercial searching on Mead Data Central's LEXPAT System.

* Pension and Welfare Benefits Administration (PWBA) Public Disclosure System

Office of Technical Assistance and Inquires
Pension and Welfare Benefits Administration (PWBA)
U.S. Department of Labor (DOL)
200 Constitution Ave., NW
Washington, DC 20210   202-219-8776

Pension and Welfare Benefits Administration completed development of its Public Disclosure System automation project which links mainframe files to a Local Area Network (LAN) based delivery system. This system used Automated-Tape-To-Print (ATP) technology that was partially adapted from an existing IRS graphics system. This has resulted in the elimination of 650,000 microfiche in Pension and Welfare Benefits Administration's public disclosure program for Form 5500C and 5500R filings for 1990 and subsequent years. Information about these forms and other documents such as Annual Reports, the Employee Retirement Income Security Act (ERISA), Master Trust Reports, Advisory Opinion Letters, and Apprenticeship and Other Training Plans Notices can be viewed in person at the Public Disclosure Room, Room N-5507, or requests can be taken over the phone or by mail.

* Pesticide Product Information System (PPIS)

Jim Beech, Office of Pesticide Programs
Environmental Protection Agency (EPA)
401 M St., SW
Washington, DC 20460   202-305-5439

The Pesticide Product Information System contains information concerning all pesticide products registered in the United States. It includes registrant name and address, chemical ingredients, toxicity category, brand name, etc. The system is updated when necessary. Limited information is available in printed form.

* Poison Control Inquiry Database (1962-80) (PB80-202534XDD)

Office of Public Affairs
U.S. Department of Health and Human Services
200 Independence Ave., SW
Washington, DC 20201
General Information   202-619-0257
To order:
National Technical Information Service (NTIS)
U.S. Department of Commerce
5285 Port Royal Rd.   703-487-4650
Springfield, VA 22161   Fax: 703-321-8547

This database is a computerized listing of the 5 x 8 Poison Control Product Cards which the Division of Poison Control makes available to the poison control centers. Each product is identified by a numeric code and a product category. It also includes information concerning symptoms that can be expected from a poisoning caused by each product and suggested acceptable treatments. The price for this data is $240.

* Procurement Automated Source System (PASS)

Your local SBA Office
or
Glen Harwood
Procurement Automated Source System
Small Business Administration (SBA)
409 Third St., SW   800-827-5722
Washington, DC 20416   202-205-6469

Updated daily, the Procurement Automated Source System (PASS) is a centralized inventory and referral system of small businesses interested in being prime contractors for federal agencies or subcontractor for companies. More than 39,000 minority owned, 53,000 female owned and over 60,000 veteran owned businesses nationwide are listed in the fields of research and development, manufacturing, construction and services. PASS uses a keyword system which identifies the capabilities of the company. The system can be searched for firms by geographic location, type of ownership, labor surplus area, zip code, minority type and over 3,000 keywords. PASS, started in October 1978, currently holds reports about 220,000 firms and increases by 200 firms monthly. There are 300 direct access users. Anyone seeking to purchase a product or service from a small business can contact Small Business Administration (SBA) to have a search run. Firms wanting to be listed (no charge) should contact the SBA regional PASS specialist. Federal agencies and prime contractors have online direct access to PASS, and can receive searches and printouts free of charge.

* Public Libraries Universe 1973/1977/1981/1988/ 1989/1990

Jack Dusatko
Office of Educational Research and Improvement
Public Information Division
Education Information Branch
U.S. Department of Education
555 New Jersey Ave., NW   202-219-1522
Washington, DC 20208-5641   800-424-1616

This file covers data collected from 8,968 libraries and includes each one's name, location, population of area served, number of service outlets, full-time equivalent staff, income, operational expenditures, capital outlay, library collection, public service hours per year, library services per year, and interlibrary loans. This data is available on tape for $175.

* Snow Survey Centralized Forecasting System (CFS)

James Marron, Water and Climate Center
Natural Resources Conservation Service
U.S. Department of Agriculture (USDA)
101 SW Main St., Suite 1700
Portland, OR 97204-3225   503-414-3047

The Centralized Forecasting System (CFS) is an automated information system related to water supply forecasting such as streamflow, precipitation, snow depth and snow water equivalent, and reservoir data. This data is available for the current water year (September 30 through October 1) and for historical water years. Numerous routines and interactive programs for manipulating water supply data are included in utility programs within CFS. CFS also provides access to hydro-meteorologic data and interpretative products for a wide variety of governmental agencies and the general public. The system can be accessed by most computers, and it is menu driven for ease of use. This data resides in an automated database consisting of monthly data for 1,700 snow courses, 600 stream gauges, 300 reservoirs, and 1,200 precipitation stations as well as daily data from 550 SNOTEL sites and 18,000 climatological stations. The cost depends on the information requested.

* State Data Center Bulletin Board

State and Regional Program Staff
Data User Services Division
Bureau of the Census
U.S. Department of Commerce   301-457-1305
Washington, DC 20233   Data: 301-457-2310

This free electronic bulletin board system is open to the public with some restrictions. Depending on need, other organizations may qualify. The 24-hour system can be used to request answers to technical questions, place orders for computer tapes and books, locate training opportunities and seminars related to demographic data, copy free public domain software, read Census Bureau press releases, and obtain statistical information. Available census data includes: county population estimates for the entire country; statistical profiles for each state; and ranking files for each states, in 40 to 50 statistical categories. The cost depends on the information requested.

* Substance Abuse Information Database (SAID) Diskette

Office of the Assistant Secretary for Policy (OSAP)
U.S. Department of Labor (DOL)
200 Constitution Ave., NW
Washington, DC 20210   800-808-0965

This is a free software program from the Department of Labor (DOL). The program is designed to provide employers with information for establishing employee drug abuse awareness programs and employee counseling. The Substance Abuse Information Database also includes guidelines for employers in dealing with drug-addicted employees. The Office of the Assistant Secretary for Policy does plan on establishing a Substance Abuse Information Database Bulletin Board Service in the future.

* Sudden Infant Death Syndrome

National Sudden Infant Death Syndrome Resource Center (NSRC)
U.S. Department of Health and Human Services
8201 Greensboro Dr., Suite 600   703-821-8955 x249 or x474
McLean, VA 22102-3843   Fax: 703-821-2098

This Center responds to inquiries and provides information about Sudden Infant Death Syndrome/Sudden Infant Death Syndromes-related topics. The National Sudden Infant Death Syndrome Resource Center is an affiliation of the National Center for Education in Maternal and Child Health. Primary subject areas are: infant mortality; apnea; apnea monitoring; death investigation; and bereavement. On matters of child abuse and neglect, the Center provides information about: infant death investigations; autopsies and autopsy protocols; the distinction between Sudden Infant Death Syndrome and child abuse fatalities. The cost depends on information requested.

* Tides - Hourly Heights

Tidal Datums Section (N/OMA123)
National Ocean Service
U.S. Department of Commerce
1305 East West Hwy.
Silver Spring, MD 20910   301-713-2877

Tidal hourly heights are the records of the height of the water level (in feet) for each hour of each day at tide observation stations. All heights are referenced to a datum. All tide data is processed in monthly increments and added to the station datafile. Users of this data include: federal, state, and local agencies, waterborne commerce, port authorities, marinas, coastal industries, engineering, surveying, construction firms, law firms, academia and foreign governments. The records for stations in the National Tide Observation Network (NTON) are available on hard copy and on tape with costs determined by format and amount of information ordered.

* Tomato Statistics (SN 92010)

Gary Lucier, Economic Research Service
U.S. Department of Agriculture (USDA)
1301 New York Ave., NW
Washington, DC 20005-4788   202-219-0117
Ordering information   800-999-6779

This file contains United States and state data, 1960-90, on tomato acreage, yield, production, and value; monthly prices and price indexes; monthly shipments and arrivals; price spreads; and United States trade in fresh tomatoes and tomato products. Also included are tomato acreage and production in major producing countries and cost of production estimates for major United States production areas. This data is available on two 3.5" disks for $35.

* Trademark New Pending Application File

Office of Products Development/OIPD
U.S. Patent and Trademark Office
U.S. Department of Commerce
Crystal Plaza 2, Room 9D30   703-308-0555
Washington, DC 20231   Fax: 703-308-0493

The file contains the following information on each trademark application: serial number, filing date, word mark, mark drawing code, date published for opposition, owner name and address, and other data. It contains approximately 1,200 Trademark Applications per update. The time period covered is January 19, 1988 to present. The file is available for $6,030 per year, with weekly updates, from the Patent and Trademark office above. Write for agreement and technical specifications. Thomson & Thomson offers commercial searching through Dialog, Inc.

* Training Technology Resource Center (TTRC)

Employment and Training Administration
U.S. Department of Labor (DOL)   202-219-5600
200 Constitution Ave., NW   800-488-0901
Washington, DC 20210   Data: 800-767-0806
     Data, DC area: 202-219-5941
     Fax: 202-219-4858

This is an online database with limited public access during a 5 year test program beginning in 1992. Training Technology Resource Center is a central repository of information on best practices and emerging training technology and serves as a mechanism for dissemination of such information to employers and employer representatives nationwide. The Training Technology Resource Center also provides computer assisted demonstrations for governmental policy markers, educators, trainers, and representatives, from the business community.

* Union Address Data Tape

Bernard Peterson, Office of Assessments
Mine and Safety Health Administration
U.S. Department of Labor (DOL)
4015 Wilson Blvd.
Arlington, VA 22203-1984   703-235-1484

Gene Coffey, Office of Assessments
U.S. Department of Labor (DOL)
P.O. Box 25367
Denver Federal Center
Denver, CO 80225-0367   303-231-5432

This tape was developed to provide union address data in automated form for interested parties. The tape contains mine identification (ID), union ID, union name, local number, representative's name and an address. Selection options are: coal mines only; metal/nonmetal mines only; both coal and metal/nonmetal mines; all mines except abandoned mines; and all mines including abandoned mines. The estimated cost is $50. A written Freedom of Information Act request is required. This office is currently in transition. At this time, the data can be obtained from the Virginia Office of Assessments. In the future, data may be obtained from the Denver Office of Assessments.

* U.S. Department of Housing and Urban Development (HUD) Business Partners Bulletin Board System

Linda Cantrell, Policy Systems
Computer Division

U.S. Department of Housing and Urban Development (HUD)
451 7th St., SW
Washington, DC 20410   202-708-0766

This system provides current information to U.S. Department of Housing and Urban Development's (HUD) business partners and contractors pertaining to a wide range of issues pertaining to the housing field. Information available includes information on HUD programs, results of HUD programs, notices, and an electronic mail feature that allows users of this system to communicate with each other. At this time, this system is not available to the public. To gain access, you must register with the office listed above to receive the necessary access code.

* Veterans Wheelchair Games

Larry Long (141D7)
U.S. Department of Veteran Affairs
810 Vermont Ave., NW
Washington, DC 20420   202-535-7279

The purpose of this system is to provide support for the annual Veterans Wheelchair Games by registering and keeping records of participants and results. Data includes names of participants, types of games and results. The cost depends on the information requested.

Government on the Internet

The fastest growing segment of the government is information and data on the Internet. Basic economics will insure that this cyber-goldmine will continue to grow. Both state and federal governments have more incentive to place their information on the Internet than they do in making it available in any other form. Our democracy requires them to make its information available to the public, but with the current mode of government cutbacks, agencies have discovered that the cheapest way to do this is on the Internet. It is bound to become one of the cheapest and easiest ways to obtain government information. So if you are not wired yet, you may want to look into it. It's getting easier and easier every day.

* Administration on Aging

Website: gopher://WWW.AoA.dhhs.gov:80/hGET%20/aoa.html
E-mail: comments@ban-gate.aoa.dhhs.gov

As the population ages, more and more information and assistance is available for those over age 60. At this site, you can read about the Administration on Aging's (AoA) overall mission and use the Eldercare Locator or the National Aging Information Center links to get detailed information on senior services and other aging issues and concerns.

* Advanced Research Projects Agency

Website: http://www.arpa.mil/
E-mail: webmaster@arpa.mil

The Advanced Research Projects Agency (ARPA) helps maintain United States technological superiority and guards against unforeseen technological advances by potential adversaries. This site also contains a Small Business Support Center, which describes all kinds of ARPA projects and opportunities for small businesses. For example, you can find out about the Small Business Innovation Research Program, which can help a small business find federally funded research and development money! (If you have any questions, e-mail sbir@arpa.mil).

* Agency for Toxic Substances and Disease Registry

Website: http://atsdr1.atsdr.cdc.gov:8080/atsdrhome.html
E-mail: lmp1@atsoaa1.em.cdc.gov

This agency was designed to provide information on preventing exposure to hazardous substances from waste sites, unplanned releases, and other pollution sources. Download information on the Agency for Toxic Substances and Disease Registry (ATSDR) and gain quick access to hundreds of online documents on hazardous substances, or explore the topic in more detail on other WWW sites.

* AirForceLINK

Website: http://www.dtic.dla.mil:80/airforcelink/

Are you interested in seeing some Air Force lithographs or Airman Art? How about hearing a radio program or watching a TV clip about the Air Force without having to leave your computer? Or maybe you are interested in reading biographies of famous Air Force leaders, or brushing up on your major weapons systems knowledge. Whatever your preference, you'll find it on the AirForceLINK. There is also a news section here, so you might want to check in often.

* American Charities Home Page

Website: http://www.charities.org/
E-mail: nancym@charities.org

This site is valuable for its extensive list of charities, including those addressing human rights, health and education.

* American Job Bank

Website: http://www.AJB.dri.us/

For people who are currently unemployed, or are looking for a different career path, this is a perfect site. It provides three options – you can either search the nationwide American Job Bank, jump directly to your state's employment web site, or look at employer maintained job listings.

* Amtrak

Website: http://www.amtrak.com/

Take your next vacation by train and use this site to plan your trip. Amtrak can help with affordable travel packages that will save you the hassle - and risk - of driving. This site includes detailed descriptions of Amtrak's routes in all parts of the country, as well as vacation package offers and information on how to make reservations. You can also check out the travel hints section or "Amtrak's Great American Vacations" - a section dedicated to vacation routes by rail.

* Arms Control and Disarmament Agency

Website: http://www.acda.gov/organ.htm

Discover how the government pursues arms control and nuclear disarmament in the post Cold-War era. Read publications such as a report on the Conference on Security and Cooperation in Europe. Also, read up on disarmament fellowship grants, the people who run the Arms Control and Disarmament Agency (ACDA), or browse through the alphabet soup section for a glossary of common arms-control acronyms.

* ArmyLINK – The U.S. Army Home Page

Website: http://www.army.mil/

At the time of this research, there were 280 Army or Army related home pages that one could access from ArmyLink. Who knows how many there will be in the future? One thing for sure – there is enough information here to answer even the most intricate questions. (Check at ftp://ftp.army.mil/ftp-anon/PUB/ to see just how much information is available – from technological manuals to a list of retirees).

* ArtsEdge – John F. Kennedy Center for the Performing Arts

Website: http://artsedge.kennedy-center.org/

For those who are interested in new art, this page is worth a visit. Several collections of online art have been assembled here, mostly made by students. Also there are job listings, a guest forum, and a research center on art topics.

* Asia/Pacific Home Page

Website: http://www.ita.doc.gov/region/asia/pacific
E-mail: keim@USITA.gov

This site provides detailed information on export opportunities, trade conditions and business climates for all of the countries in Asia and the Pacific except Japan. (For information on Japan, visit the *Japan Export Information Center Home Page* at www.ita.doc.gov/regional/geo_region/japan). This site includes a hotlink to an FAQ section about doing business in the region, as well as *Hot Issues* and *Trade Events* corners.

Business and trade information is available for many countries, including Hong Kong, China, Singapore, and Thailand. This is a great starting point if you want information about business in Asia and the Pacific!

* Bonneville Power Administration

Website: http://www.bpa.gov/
E-mail: krkane@bpa.gov

This administration markets the power of 29 federal dams in the Pacific Northwest, and that's a lot of power. It also has built one of the largest and most reliable systems in the country for transmitting electricity. Download maps and publications

Be patient. If any phone number is incorrect, call (area code) 555-1212 and request the new listing.

1219

on such diverse topics as electromagnetic field research, energy conservation, and wildlife conservation in energy development areas. The Bonneville Power Administration (BPA) also offers and opportunity for teachers to download and order information online (such as curricula and classroom posters). Click on the technical solution section and discover how BPA uses such advanced tools as Computer-Aided Design Drafting to build and run its massive energy projects.

* BosniaLINK

Website: http://www.dtic.dla.mil/bosnia/

BosniaLINK provides the latest news about the NATO peacekeeping mission in Bosnia, including maps and charts of the operation, read the latest news releases, speeches and testimony, and transcripts of the briefings. You can even take a look at some photographs directly from the Bosnian hot zones, and send your support directly to the troops.

* Bureau of Land Management

Website: http://info.er.usgs.gov/doi/bureau-land-management.html
E-mail: webmaster@blm.gov

The Bureau of Land Management administers what remains of the nation's vast public land holdings. Even though these have fallen from over 1.8 billion acres to 272 million acres - this is a great place to learn more about the agency and what it offers. Use the online Website directory or visit the FAQ section for information on farming, conservation and other opportunities. Remember, 272 million acres is still a lot of land - and breathing room.

* Centers for Disease Control Home Page

Website: http://www.cdc.gov/

The Centers for Disease Control (CDC) is the national agency charged with monitoring the nation's health, and this site is dedicated entirely to disease and health risk prevention. Here you'll find information on the illnesses and diseases they watch, whether it's the flu or food poisoning. A separate page is dedicated to scientific data, surveillance, and health statistics. Funding, training, and employment opportunities also are available.

* Central Intelligence Agency

Website: http://www.odci.gov/cia/

Available from the Central Intelligence Agency (CIA) are several exciting and informative publications and Q&A sections. You can take a virtual tour of the CIA headquarters, read about the CIA vision, mission, and values, and discover what information is made available to the public. Several texts are available in an electronic format online, including:

The World Factbook 1995
1995 Factbook on Intelligence
CIA Maps and Publications Released to the Public
DCI and DDCIs of Central Intelligence
Chiefs of State and Cabinet Members of Foreign Governments
Intelligence Literature: Suggested Reading List

* Commodity Futures Trading Commission

Website: http://www.cftc.gov/cftc

Available from this page is general background information about the Commodity Futures Trading Commission (CFTC), several financial publications and reports (the titles and content change often), press releases, speeches, and job vacancies listing.

* Consumer Product Safety Commission

Site: gopher://cpsc.gov/

Among other material, publications are available on the following topics:

Children's Furniture
Children's Safety
Toy Safety
Recreational Safety
Fire and Burn Prevention
Industry and Businesses
Carbon Monoxide
Power Equipment
Child Drowning Prevention
Household Products
Art Materials

Electrical Safety
Indoor Air Quality
Poison Prevention

* Copyright Office

Site: gopher://marvel.loc.gov/11/copyright

From this gopher site, you can download documents on copyright basics, copyright registration, international copyright, works not protected by copyright, and other useful information regarding copyright laws and procedures.

* Counter-Terrorism Rewards Program

Website: http://www.clark.net/pub/heroes
E-mail: bsmith@heroes.net

Information is available on three rewards programs: counter-terrorism, counter-narcotics, and passport and visa. The U.S. government is offering up to $4 million dollars for information preventing acts of international terrorism against United States persons or property, or leading to the arrest or conviction of terrorist criminals responsible for such acts. Find out what you can do to prevent terrorism and narcotics export.

* DefenseLINK

Website: http://www.dtic.dla.mil/defenselink/

This is the where to find out almost anything about the people who bravely defend our country. Through the main page of DefenseLINK - you can link to the Office of the Secretary of Defense, the Joint Chiefs of Staff, the Army, Navy, Air Force, and Marine Corps, the Coast Guard, the U.S. Army Reserve, the National Guard, the Combatant Commands, and other components of the U. S. Armed Forces. This site also contains the latest news and a fact file that contains information on ammunition, missiles, rockets and torpedoes, shelters, tanks, vehicles, weapons systems, and other military paraphernalia. It also includes the latest official news releases and an FAQ section, and other publications, including speeches on defense issues and a Guide to Defense Organization and Functions.

* Earthquake Information from the U.S. Geological Survey

Website: http://quake.wr.usgs.gov/
E-mail: michael@andreas.wr.usgs.gov

Would you like some information on a recent earthquake, anywhere around the world? Visit this site, and you'll get a whole lot more. When was the last earthquake? Get seismographic plots and news on active faultlines. Besides immediate earthquake data, this site also offers descriptions of studies performed around San Francisco Bay and in Southern California, where seismologists predict the Big One could occur within the next 20 years. You can also try "seismosurfing" – a link that takes you to an outstanding index of other earthquake resources on the Internet.

* Empowerment Zones and Enterprise Communities Internet Home Page

Website: http://www.ezec.gov/

This agency was designated by the President to help poor communities empower themselves to achieve economic progress. Find out how the government is helping people help themselves.

* Environmental Protection Agency

Website: http://www.epa.gov
E-mail: support@unixmail.ripnc.epa.gov

Care about the environment? Want some tips on how to help preserve it? Here you can find out how. This site claims to have the largest repository of Agency publications with more than 5,500 available titles. There are too many publications here to describe, but chances are if it has to do with the environment, the Environmental Protection Agency (EPA) has it. Some of the more popular titles are:

Dos and Don'ts Around the Home.
The Consumer's Handbook For Reducing Solid Waste
Citizen's Guide to Pest Control and Pesticide Safety
Protect Your Family From Lead In Your Home
What you can do to reduce air pollution
Your automobile and the environment.
You and Clean Water
Volunteer to monitor our water resources

You can also check out the EPA programs and initiatives, contract and grant opportunities, rules and regulations, citizen information, and free software!

* Environmental Research Laboratories

Website: http://www.erl.noaa.gov/
E-mail: britt@erl.noaa.gov

This site is kept by the Office of Oceanic and Atmospheric Research in Silver Spring, MD, and focuses on fundamental research, technology development, and services to improve understanding of the Earth and its oceans and inland water, the lower and upper atmosphere, and the space environment. Some of the more interesting information on this site is the overview of the Environmental Research Laboratory's (ERL) mission, and links to such environmental research laboratories as those studying the atmosphere and space environments. There is also an extensive list of links that will interest environmentalists of any age.

* Executive Direction and Management Offices of the Department of Justice

Office of the Attorney General
(http://gopher.usdoj.gov/offices/oag.html). Read a short biography of the current Attorney General or browse the offices' job descriptions' and its mission statement.

Office of the Deputy Attorney General
(http://gopher.usdoj.gov/offices/dag.html). Job responsibilities and a brief biography of the Deputy Attorney General are available.

Office of the Associate Attorney General
(http://gopher.usdoj.gov/offices/asag.html). Read about the current Associate Attorney General and the office's responsibilities.

Office of the Solicitor General
(http://gopher.usdoj.gov/offices/osg.html). Find out about the person charged with deciding what cases the Government should ask the Supreme Court to review, and what the government's position should be.

Office of Legislative Affairs
(http://gopher.usdoj.gov/offices/ola.html). A short job description of the person in charge of the Office of Legislative Affairs (OLA) and agency functions.

Justice Management Division
(http://gopher.usdoj.gov/offices/jmd.html). Explore the agency in charge of programs such as budget and financial management, personnel management and training, equal opportunity programs, automatic data processing and telecommunications, security, records management, procurement, real property and materiel management, and for all other matters pertaining to organization, management and administration.

Office of Professional Responsibility
(http://gopher.usdoj.gov/offices/opr.html). A brief notice about the office and its functions within the U.S. Justice Department.

Office of the Inspector General
(http://gopher.usdoj.gov/offices/oig.html). The Inspector General is responsible for providing leadership and assisting management in promoting economy, efficiency, and effectiveness within the Department. Find out how.

* Export Import Bank

Website: http://www.exim.gov/
E-mail: WebAdmin@exim.gov

Would you like to find out how to finance selling a product overseas? The opportunity is here. Also, read the latest press releases, summaries of board meetings, or subscribe to the online newsletter.

* Federal Aviation Administration

Website: http://web.fie.com/web/fed/faa/
E-mail: dot-m@fedix.fie.com

Before you take your next flight, you might want to explore the Federal Aviation Administration (FAA) site and its powerful search engine. Information includes:

- A Quarterly Newsletter for Educators;
- Legal Information about FAA;
- Regional, State, and Employment Programs;
- Education Programs (includes grant information!);

If you need more information after visiting this site, here are two more:

- For all kinds of technical questions about airplanes, visit the **FAA Technical Center Home Page** at http://www.tc.faa.gov/
- FAA Library Site: ftp://fwux.fedworld.gov/pub/faa/faa.htm
  This FTP site has an archive of various manuals, knowledge tests, and information files regarding the airplane industry. Check in often, the list is updated daily!

* Federal Bureau of Investigation Home Page

Website: http://www.fbi.gov/

Did you know that the Federal Bureau of Investigation (FBI) employs 10,158 special agents and 13,711 support personnel? Even if you did, there are lots of other interesting facts to be found at the FBI home page. Here's what's available:

FBI Fact Sheet
Location of FBI Field Offices
FBI Frequently Asked Questions File
A listing of high-profile FBI investigations
A counterintelligence and counterterrorism corner
Information on FBI Headquarters tour!
Yearly crime statistics
FBI Community Relations Program

* Federal Bureau of Prisons

Website: http://ww.usdoj.gov/bop/bop.html

Do you know the average age of a prison inmate? How the percentage of life sentences? The average cost of inmate confinement? If you'd like to find out, visit this page. Also read the general overview of the Bureau of Prisons (BOP) and the latest corrections research. An interesting section to visit is *Facilities* – a brief overview of the U.S. penal institutions.

* Federal Deposit Insurance Company

Website: http://www.fdic.gov/

This site contains a mission statement that broadly outlines its (Federal Deposit Insurance Corporation) current tasks. A link is available to the Federal Deposit Insurance Corporation (FDIC) Corporate Library which publishes a number of guides to information about the FDIC and the banking industry. Some of the titles that are here: *Bank Rating and Analysis Services, Important Banking Legislation, S&L Crisis: A Chrono-Bibliography*. You can also download a wealth of data on FDIC-insured institutions, information on banking from FDIC's Division of Research and Statistics, a Survey of Real Estate Trends that asks market observers from all federal bank and thrift regulatory agencies about developments during the prior three months in their real estate markets), and other info of interest to consumers.

* Federal Emergency Management Agency

Website: http://www.fema.gov/

The Federal Emergency Management Agency (FEMA) was created to help victims of natural disasters and other crisis situations. This page contains information on how they do it, and their plans for the future. This site includes tips on preparing for natural disasters, and what to do following hurricanes, earthquakes, or floods. There is also a library where you can download publications on topics such as filing a flood insurance claim and managing emergencies for businesses. The photo file contains images from the Oklahoma City bombing, the Northridge earthquake, and several floods and hurricanes. A good search engine is available for anyone doing research on natural disasters.

* Federal Energy Regulatory Commission

Website: http://www.fedworld.gov/ferc/ferc.html

This commission regulates the way natural gas, oil, and electricity is delivered through interstate commerce. Also find out about the agency's connection to hydroelectric and environmental matters.

* Federal Information Exchange Home Page

Website: http://www.fie.com/

A premium research center for governmental and education purposes alike. Several indexes are available: Fedix for Federal Job Opportunities, Molis for Minority Colleges and Universities, ERA (Electronic Research Administration, which joins several government agencies), and RAMS (Research of Education Resources).

Government Databases and Internet Access

* Federal Judicial Center Home Page

Website: http://www.fjc.gov
Publications available here include:

Reference Manual on Scientific Evidence
Guideline Sentencing: An Outline of Appellate Case Law on Selected Issues
Guideline Sentencing Update
District Court Response to Amended Fed. R. Civ. P. 26.
Voluntary Arbitration in Eight Federal District Courts
Court-Annexed Arbitration in Ten District Courts
The Consequences of Mandatory Minimum Prison Terms: A Summary of Recent Findings
Studying the Role of Gender in the Federal Courts: A Research Guide
Electronic Media Coverage of Federal Civil Proceedings: An Evaluation:
The Bail Reform Act of 1984
Stalking the Increase in the Rate of Federal Civil Appeals
Manual for Complex Litigation

* Federal Trade Commission

Website: http://www.ftc.gov/
Has online fraud touched your life yet? To make sure it never does, visit this FTC site and browse through *Consumer Alert! Online Scams.* Or check out other consumer information on telemarketing, telecommunications, and FCC licenses, or browse its FAQ and News sections.

* FinanceNet

Website: http://www.financenet.gov/
One of the most popular sites on the 'Net, FinanceNet has a lot to offer. You can check out the library, join a mailing list, or participate in a discussion forum if you want to research a specific question. This site also lists major government asset sales - check here if something is going on in your area. A huge job opportunities section is available for those who are interested.

* Food and Drug Administration Home Page

Website: http://www.fda.gov/
If you are wondering about drug interactions, dietary supplements or whether melatonin spells Fountain of Youth in a pill, start here. Extensive information is available on the following topics:

Animal Drugs
Biologics
Cosmetics
Human Drugs
Foods
Toxicology
Medical Devices and Radiological Health
Inspection and Imports

* General Services Administration

Website: http://www.gsa.gov/
This site contains valuable advice and information from the General Services Administration (GSA). Here you can find information about almost everything, from cars and employment to food and nutrition. You can also find out about federal travel and property pages that GSA manages, as well as how to do business with GSA.

* General Services Administration, Cultural and Environmental Affairs

Website: http://www.gsa.gov/pbs/pt/pts/cultural.html
E-mail: webmaster@gsa.gov
This division maintains three programs: Art-in-Architecture, Fine Arts Collection, and Historic Federal Buildings. Information is available on all of them. Search the data by state, by artist, or any other keyword. Very convenient!

* Government Information Sharing Project

Website: http://govinfo.kerr.orst.edu/
This is an excellent starting point for anyone doing research on demographics, economics, or public education. The site offers searchable databases on subjects like population estimates by age, sex, and race. Regional economic information also is available for years 1969-1993, and you can explore the U.S. Imports/Exports History from 1990-1994.

* Government Printing Office

Website: http://www.access.gpo.gov/
Information is what the Internet is all about, and that's exactly what the Government Printing Office (GPO) promises to deliver. Clients can get immediate access to several online databases (like the Federal Register and the Unified Agenda, the Federal Depository Libraries) and even request information directly from the GPO. For those who are willing to pay a cheap price for some data and facts, there's an *Information for Sale* section available, as well.

* GulfLink

Website: http://www.dtic.dla.mil/gulflink/
This site is dedicated entirely to Persian Gulf Veteran Illnesses. A features and news section is also available. Here is a list of some of the documents available at this site:

Clinical Evaluation Program for Gulf War Veterans
Comprehensive Clinical Evaluation Program (CCEP) for Gulf War Veterans, August 1995
Defense Science Board Task Force Report: Persian Gulf War Health Effects, June 1994
Federal Activities Related to the Health of Persian Gulf Veterans: Dept. of Veterans Affairs, March 1995
Unexplained Illnesses Among Desert Storm Veterans

* Health Care Financing Administration

Website: http://www.hcfa.gov/
This site includes reports on the Medicare and Medicaid programs. You can download publications like the Medicare Handbook or the Guide for Health Insurance for People with Medicare. Also, check up on the latest research, news, press releases, speeches, and testimony by Health Care Financing Administration (HCFA) officials.

* Inspector General's Network

Website: http://www.sbaonline.sba.gov/ignet/ig.html
E-mail: jedye@fred.net
Read the reports issued by the U.S. Government Agencies, check the hotline numbers to report fraud, waste and abuse, and check out job opportunities, training information, as well the *Journal of Public Inquiry*, a publication of the Federal Inspectors General.

* International Data Center

Website: http://www.cdidc.org:65120/
E-mail: Tae Kan@cdidc.org

* Internal Revenue Service (IRS)

Website: http://www.irs.ustreas.gov/prod/cover.html
OK, here is a surprise: the Internal Revenue Service (IRS) has created a web page that's well-designed, relevant and informative. There's lots of information available: for one, there's a detailed section on TeleFile, a system that lets you file taxes right over the telephone. Then there is a forms and publications sections. There you can find such exciting titles as *Publ 15 Circular E, Employer's Tax Guide* and *1194 Publ 378 Fuel Tax Credits and Refunds*, as well as 104 other files. You can also retrieve over 550 tax forms, such as Form W-3PR and Form CT-1. The IRS News Stand is also interesting to visit: a wide variety of newsletters and helpers are available for download.

* Joint Chiefs of Staff

Website: http://www.dtic.dla.mil/defenselink/jcs/index.html
E-mail: jberger@dtic.mil
This is the site for information on the men and women who direct our troops. Read job descriptions for the Chairman and Vice Chairman of the Joint Chiefs of Staff, the most powerful of our warriors. Also read about the U.S. Army Chief of Staff, Chief of Naval Operations, Commandant of the Marine Corps, and the Chief of the U.S. Air Force Staff. You can also learn the history of the Joint Chiefs of Staff, and read an overview of our national security structure.

* Legal and Policy Offices

Website: http://gopher.usdoj.gov/offices/offices.html
Provides easy access to the following offices:

Community Relations Service
Office of Justice Programs
Executive Office for U.S. Attorneys
Executive Office for U.S. Trustees
Office of Intelligence Policy and Review
Office of Legal Counsel
Office of Policy Development
Immigration and Naturalization Service
Office of Information and Privacy
Foreign Claims Settlement Commission of the United States
Office of Public Affairs
Executive Office for Immigration Review

* Library of Congress

Website: http://www.loc.gov/
While there may not be as much on the Library of Congress web page as there is in the Library itself, this site still covers a lot of ground. Access is available to:

General Information and Publications (including the *Civilization* magazine), employment information, and a virtual tour;

Federal Legislation (including access to THOMAS and LOCIS, information systems);

Foreign and International Governments information;

Research and Collections Services (including digital collections and reference collections).

* Litigation Organizations of the U.S. Department of Justice

Website: http://gopher.usdoj.gov/divisions/divisions.html
This site provides instant and simple access to the Civil Rights, Antitrust, Civil, Criminal, Environment and Natural Resources, and Tax divisions of the U.S. Department of Justice. Also includes a link to the United States Attorneys' home page.

Civil Rights Division

(http://gopher.usdoj.gov/crt/crt-home.html). Read the latest speeches concerning civil rights issues; view descriptions of cases that impacted American civil rights movement, and browse through the information of several acts, such as Americans With Disabilities Act.

Civil Division

(http://gopher.usdoj.gov/civil/civil.html). Read an overview of the civil division, as well as the online brochure that describes the role and stricture of the division.

Antitrust Division

(http://gopher.usdoj.gov/atr/atr.htm). The home site of the agency that's responsible for the promotion and protection of the competitive process in the American economy. Browse the antitrust guidelines, international agreements, speeches by senior officials of the Antitrust Division, congressional testimony, press releases, and antitrust cases and appellate briefs.

Criminal Division

(http://gopher.usdoj.gov/criminal/criminal-home.html). Read a brief description of the criminal division's function within the U.S. Department of Justice.

Tax Division

(http://gopher.usdoj.gov/tax/tax.html). Find out what the tax division does and who to contact for further information.

* Minority Information Service

Website: http://web.fie.com/fedix/aid.html
Available here is a description of funding opportunities for programs that deal with minorities, such as Stay-In-School Program and Cooperative Education. Links are also available to other minorities-related sites on the Internet.

* NASA Office of Aeronautics: Human Factors

Website: http://olias.arc.nasa.gov
E-mail: shafto@eos.arc.nasa.gov
Ever wonder who works for NASA? Well, you don't have to wonder anymore: it's all here. The NASA Human Factors site includes:

- *FMS Bluecoat Digest*, an Internet mailing list and online monthly magazine dealing with the design and use of modern flight deck automation;
- Aviation acronyms and abbreviations and the Pilot/Controller Glossary; An online publications page with the latest from NASA;
- A list of Human Factors department personnel;
- Interesting studies and research;
- A list of the latest hard-copy publications as well as some related sites on the Net.

* NASA'S Shuttle Web

http://shuttle.nasa.gov/
khumpri@gp.301.jsc.nasa.gov
This site contains all sorts of exciting information about NASA's shuttle projects, including pictures, sounds, and movies of different phases of the latest shuttle mission. Take a tour of launch and landing facilities, get detailed information about each mission, check out images direct from NASA Television, learn background information about the shuttle and its crew, and even follow the countdown on the launch clock. This is a great site for kids.

* National AIDS Clearinghouse Web Server

Website: http://cdcnac.aspensys.com:86/
At this site you can download numerous documents dealing with various aspects of AIDS and HIV infection, or use the Internet order form to receive information in the mail. Find out what's new in AIDS research and prevention. Visit other 'Net services by using the provided links, or find the right contact on AIDS-related information through an online phone directory.

* National Archives and Records Administration

Website: http://www.nara.gov/
E-mail: webmaster@nara.gov
If you don't want to travel to Washington, D.C. to look up important old records and other documents, there might be a National Archives and Records Administration (NARA) office in your city. Check here for locations and hours. Also visit the Online Exhibit Hall to view such documents as The Charters of Freedom, The Emancipation Proclamation, even poster art from WWII. A Digital Classroom provides information and resources for teachers, and information on various professional services - such as records management, grants, and archival management - is also available at this site.

* National Coordination Office for High Performance Computing and Communications

Website: http://www.hpcc.gov/index.html
Find out how the government is helping the U.S. computer and communications technology remain the best in the 21st century. Several agency reports and newsletters, such as *High Performance Computing and Communications: Foundation for America's Information Future* are available online. Links are available to grants and awards section, as well as the White House technology information page.

* National Endowment for the Humanities

Website: http://www.neh.fed.us/
E-mail: alifson@neh.fed.us
This site contains information on several National Endowment for the Humanities (NEH) programs, including grants for students and teachers. A section is also available for current NEH grantees. You can also find out about deadline changes, recent awards, and current news at NEH.

* National Institute for Literacy Home Page

Website: http://novel.nifl.gov/
Find out what's going on with the U.S. government's struggle against illiteracy. You can join one of the several forums available on the topic, read about the current events and information, or browse the *Internet Directory of Literacy and Adult Education Resources*.

Be patient. If any phone number is incorrect, call (area code) 555-1212 and request the new listing.

1223

Government Databases and Internet Access

* National Institutes of Health

Website: http://www.nih.gov/home.html

E-mail: nihinfo@od3ltm1.od.nih.gov

The National Institutes of Health (NIH) web page is one of the best starting points for anyone looking for medical resources – be it the latest research on AIDS or bone marrow transplants, or simply whether a cold medicine works. Information is available on grants from NIH to the research labs around the country who are doing all the work. This site also provides links to NIH's individual agencies, most of which have their own web pages. This includes the National Cancer Institute, the National Eye Institute, the National Heart, Lung, and Blood Institute, the National Institute of Drug Abuse, the National Institute of Mental Health, the National Library of Medicine, and lots more. Be sure to check out the *Library and Literature Resources* section at this site for the latest research in the health and medical journals.

* National Park Service

Website: http://www.nps.gov/nps

This site provides more information about wide open spaces. At publication, the service's page was still being built, but it looks like a winner for nature lovers and anyone planning a vacation. Check in soon!

* National Performance Review

Website: http://www.npr.gov

A project by Vice-President Al Gore, the National Performance Review presents recent reports and highlights of the nation's progress. Reports on such diverse topics as law enforcement, business, and veterans issues are available. There's also a huge library section, which includes the latest executive orders and presidential memos. The site's news room contains speeches, statements, and announcements made by both the President and the Vice-President.

* National Science Foundation

Website: http://www.nsf.gov

E-mail: Webmaster@nsf.gov

This site provides information about the latest in technology, science, and engineering. You can read the latest science and technology news or explore grant opportunities.

* National Security Agency

Website: http://www.nsa.gov:8080/

While this page is still under development, there is one extremely interesting section here: The National Cryptologic Museum. Online exhibits are available on the KGB, The Black Chamber, and "Enigma". You can also read the National Security Agency's (NSA) Mission Statement, find out what the NSA is all about, and explore the Director's Page.

* NavyOnLine Home Page

Website: http://www.ncts.navy.mil/

E-mail: navyonline@ncts.navy.mil

Would you like to know the next time the Blue Angels are planning a flyover? Or how to send mail to sailors participating in the Bosnia operations? Explore any of the other 2,214 items publicly available through the Navy Public Affairs Library at this site. All you have to do is point your WWW browser to the URL listed above.

* Nuclear Regulatory Commission

Website: http://www.nrc.gov/

E-mail: clhl@nrc.gov

There are currently 109 commercial nuclear power plants licensed to operate in 32 states. Read about the reactors, nuclear material, radioactive waste disposal, and the latest news and information concerning the Nuclear Regulatory Commission (NRC). Find out how the nuclear industry works and how safe it actually is.

* Office of Justice Programs

Website: http://gopher.usdoj.gov/ojp/ojp-home.html

You can read the overview of the Office of Justice Programs, the main function of which is to make the Nation's justice system more efficient and effective in preventing and controlling crime. The four bureaus administrated by the Office of Justice are:

Bureau of Justice Assistance

(http://gopher.usdoj.gov/ojp/bja.html). This bureau is responsible for providing financial and technical assistance to State and local units of government to control drug abuse, drug trafficking, and violent crime. Find out more about it at this site.

Bureau of Justice Statistics

(http://gopher.usdoj.gov/ojp/bjs.html). This bureau deals strictly with cold numbers of crime. Discover who is provided with the statistics that the bureau assembles and how you may contact them to be put on a mailing list, or receive some publications.

National Institute of Justice

(http://gopher.usdoj.gov/ojp/nij.html). This is the primary research and development agency for the U.S. Department of Justice. Find out what its mission is and how it goes about carrying it out.

Office of Juvenile Justice and Delinquency Prevention

(http://gopher.usdoj.gov/ojp/ojjdp.html).

* Office of Nonproliferation and National Security

Website: http://www.nn.doe.gov/nn/

Find out how the government is trying to eliminate the spread of nuclear weapons, including reports such as *Reducing the Nuclear Danger: Inventory of U.S. Department of Energy Nonproliferation and Nuclear Threat Reduction Initiatives.* Examine the department's organizational charts, testimony to Congress, and unclassified publications. This page was under construction at the time of this review, but it promises a wealth of information for anyone concerned about nuclear arms.

* Oil Spill Public Information Center

Website: http://www.alaska.net:80/~ospic/

E-mail: ospic@calvino.alaska.net

This is a page dedicated to the Exxon Valdez Oil Spill that took place in Alaska in 1989. You can check out the magnitude of this catastrophe by exploring the map of the spill, looking at scenes of the oil spill, and reading the Natural Resource Damage Assessment and Restoration Project Final Reports.

* Peace Corps

Website: http://www.clark.net/pub/peace/PeaceCorps.html

So would you like to do something radically different? Change the world for the better? The Peace Corps provides the perfect opportunity, and their home page is the perfect example of how useful the Internet can really be. Information is available about:

Where the Peace Corps is recruiting and where it needs volunteers;
The countries where the Peace Corps is active;
Minimum requirements for volunteering and how to volunteer;
What you'll actually do once you get to the country;
Publications and technical information;

* Pentagon

Website: http://www.dtic.dla.mil/defenselink/pubs/pentagon/index.html

"Each day, Pentagon employees have 4,200 clocks to watch, drink from 691 water fountains, and consume 4,500 cups of coffee, 1,700 pints of milk and 6,800 soft drinks ... and use 284 rest rooms." This is among the many interesting facts that you'll find on the Pentagon home site. You can also download the following publications:

Airman: The Flagship U.S. Air Force Magazine
Army Weapon Systems Handbook
Cooperative Threat Reduction Handbook
Defense Issues: Important Speeches
DoD Directives and Instructions
DoD Forms and Reports
DoD Manpower Statistics
DoD Procurement Statistics
Guide to DoD Organization and Functions
Pentagon Informational Brochure
United States Security Strategy for Europe and NATO
Soldiers: The Official U.S. Army Magazine

Be patient. If any phone number is incorrect, call (area code) 555-1212 and request the new listing.

* Public Health Service

Website: http://phs.os.dhhs.gov/phs/phs.html
E-mail: asmith2@oash.ssw.dhhs.gov

Here you can find information from the agencies and programs charged with researching the nation's health and new drug research - including the Food And Drug Administration and the National Institutes of Health. You can read the latest Public Health Service (PHS) news releases and access an extensive database of health-related WWW sites.

* Securities and Exchange Commission

Website: http://www.sec.gov/

This page is designed to provide basic information about the Securities and Exchange Commission (SEC) and its mission. You'll find sections on SEC rulemaking and policy, a public statements file, as well as *What Every Investor Should Know* – a guide to safe investing.

* Small Business Advancement National Center

Website: http://161.31.2.174/index.html
E-mail: chrisb@cc1.uca.edu

The Small Business Advancement National Center (SBANC) helps small businesses, entrepreneurs, educators, economic development officers, and small business counselors. Information is available here on many programs for small businesses, including Small Business Advancement Training, training and internships for high school students, and lots more. SBANC even offers some software packages designed specifically for the small business owner! Publications are available the following topics:

Family Business
International Business
Legal
Miscellaneous
Industry Profiles
Government
Business Marketing
Business Planning
Small Business Demographics
Small Business Institute
Information / Computers
Small Business Development
Finance
Education
Tax / Accounting

* Smithsonian Institution Home Page

Website: http://www.si.edu/

This is the 150th Anniversary of the Smithsonian, and it's a great place to visit in cyberspace. You can take a virtual tour of the museum, subscribe to the Smithsonian news group, and even do some virtual shopping at its museum shopping mall. This site also has information on the latest exhibitions at the Smithsonian's museums and galleries and the National Zoo.

* Social Security Online

Website: http://www.ssa.gov/SSA_Home.html

All you ever wanted to know about Social Security programs is here. You can download information about retirement, survivors benefits, disability pay, as well as other programs. Various forms are available online, as are a number of helpful publications. Those who are interested can download the Social Security Benefit Estimate Program and calculate their own retirement benefits. Teachers might be interested in a special kit to help them educate students about the agency and its services.

* Supreme Court

Website: http://www.law.cornell.edu/supct/supct.table.html

This site contains all the Supreme Court rulings from 1990 to 1995. Also here are some selected pre-1990's decisions (including school prayer, copyright, and Roe v. Wade decisions). Also, you can sign up on a mailing list to keep current with the 1996 Supreme Court activities.

* Tax Analysts Home Page

Website: http://www.tax.org/

A service mostly for tax professionals, Tax Analysts nevertheless has some useful information for any taxpayer. The most interesting section is "Tax Notes NewsWire", a section with the most up-to-date tax happenings. You can subscribe to several moderated newsgroups, including one dedicated entirely to banks and other financial institutions. This site also has a customer service section and a catalog of tax products - even a suggestion box.

* The White House

Website: http://www.whitehouse.gov/
E-mail: feedback@www.whitehouse.gov

"I hope you find this a useful way to find answers to your questions, a better way to let me know what you think, and a powerful way to find information you can use — whether you are in Nome, Alaska or right down Pennsylvania Avenue," says the President in welcoming visitors to the first ever White House Internet site. From this site, you can visit with the First Family, check who's new in the President's cabinet, get information on White House tours, and catch up on the latest news from the President's and the Vice-President's offices. And if you have some important message to pass on to the President, you can do that here, too!

* U.S. Agency For International Development

Website: http://www.info.usaid.gov/

The U.S. Agency For International Development (USAID) describes itself as "an independent federal government agency that conducts foreign assistance and humanitarian help to advance the political and economic interests of the United States." This site has information on how USAID helps developing nations achieve economic growth and improve health care services through its relief efforts. USAID's other missions include promoting democracy and protecting the global environment.

* U.S. Department of Agriculture (USDA) Home Page

Website: http://www.usda.gov/
E-mail: vpowell@usda.gov

The U.S. Department of Agriculture's home page is jam-packed with information and links. Included on the site are the USDA Program Missions, descriptions of USDA's subdivisions and their programs, USDA's News and Current Information, and even the history of USDA. Some of the other resources available from the USDA on the Internet are:

USDA Agricultural Marketing Services Home Page
(http://www.usda.gov/ams/titlepag.htm).
This site explains USDA's Agricultural Marketing Service's (AMS) mission, including descriptions of the services offered by each AMS division, a section on AMS and consumers, and a list of available publications.

Foreign Agricultural Service
(http://www.usda.gov:8000/fas/index.html)
The Foreign Agricultural Service (FAS) is responsible for representing the interests of American farmers overseas. You'll find information about FAS' long-term and short-terms goals, as well as national agricultural trade strategies. and a listing and explanation of available FAS programs, services, resources, and publications.

FCS Library
(ftp://fwux.fedworld.gov/pub/fcs/fcs.htm). Why buy an expensive book on nutrition when you can get the information free from the government? Based on government research, this library includes reports and publications on diet and nutrition, including federal guidelines. You can even find out what the President's diet plan will be next year!

State Rural Development Councils
(http://www.rurdev.usda.gov/nrdp/nrdpsrdc.html). Lists contact people in all the states. Check this out if you have any questions about agricultural developments in your state.

* U.S. Department of Commerce Information Services via World Wide Web

Website: http://www.doc.gov/
E-mail: stat-usa@doc.gov

This web site provides the mission statement and general facts about the Department of Commerce. This page also features links to other sites administered by the Department of Commerce, including:

Census Bureau Home Page
(http://www.census.gov/). In addition to current census figures, this site covers a broad range of other topics, including the economy, genealogy, population and housing studies, a range of current market statistics and much more!

Be patient. If any phone number is incorrect, call (area code) 555-1212 and request the new listing.

1225

Government Databases and Internet Access

Bureau of Economic Analysis Home Page
(http://www.bea.doc.gov/). Information about Bureau of Economic Analysis (BEA) and its many publications is available here, as are several information and data files about BEA's economic programs.

Bureau of Export Administration
(http://www.doc.gov/resources/BX-info.html). Provides information about the Bureau and its goals.

Economic Development Administration
(http://www.doc.gov/resources/EDA_info.html). This site includes interesting facts about the Economic Development Administration (EDA) and several of its programs, such as the Economic Conversion Information Exchange, and the latest news and announcements about economic conditions in the country.

International Trade Administration Home Page
(http://www.ita.doc.gov/). The International Trade Administration (ITA) has only one mission: to help U. S. companies sell products and services abroad while helping to sustain and create new jobs for United States workers. It includes information on emerging markets, a Hot Issues and Announcements corner, ITA's Customer Service Standards statement, as well as links to other related sites.

National Institute of Standards and Technology WWW - Home Page
(http://www.nist.gov/). This site is dedicated to the latest advanced technology and innovation. Information on the Baldridge Award for quality, National Institute of Standards and Technology (NIST) research, and industry programs is available, as are the latest progress reports from the NIST and an electronic newsletter on institute developments.

National Oceanic and Atmospheric Administration
(http://www.noaa.gov/noaa-image-home.html). If you care about the environment, this is the page to visit. It covers such topics as global warming, protected species, weather warnings and forecasts, coastal ecosystems, and more. From here you can also visit other National Oceanic and Atmospheric Administration (NOAA) agencies, such as the National Ocean Service, National Weather Service, Office of Global Programs, Office of Ocean and Earth Sciences, and others.

U.S. Patent and Trademark Office
(http://www.uspto.gov/). From here, you can search the U. S. Patent Office's Bibliographic Data Base, the AIDS Patent Data Base, find out about the pending public hearings on new patents, as well as receive free advice on how to obtain a patent for your latest great.

U.S. Travel and Tourism Administration
(http://www.doc.gov/resources/csd/csustta.html). This site provides information about U.S. Travel and Tourism Administration's (USTTA) mission, activities and services, publications, and contact information. A great place to get the latest information about vacation spots without having to buy a travel guide.

Economics and Statistics Administration
(http://www.doc.gov/resources/ESA_info.html). This site offers links to STAT-USA, The Bureau of the Census, and the Bureau of Economic Analysis, all subdivisions of the Economics and Statistics Administration (ESA). Also available is ESA's mission statement and information on other sources of economic data.

Information Infrastructure Task Force
(http://iitf.doc.gov/). If you wonder what "information infrastructure" means, visit this site, it's the group that maps the information highway.

Climate Prediction Center
(http://nic.fb4.noaa.gov/). Everything you ever wanted to know about the world's hot (or cold) zones.

National Telecommunications and Information Administration
(http://www.ntia.doc.gov/). The second half of the twentieth is rightfully called the Information Age. Find out what's new in telecommunications and information technology at this site, as well as international and domestic policy addressing the information boom.

* U.S. Department of Education
Website: http://www.ed.gov
The U.S. Department of Education has a lot to offer teachers, students and parents - and anyone else concerned about the quality of education in our country. Here is just some of the information available on the Internet:

News from the Department of Education. The latest educational news, including announcements of new funding opportunities, press releases, transcripts of speeches and testimony made by the Secretary of Education, etc.

Guides, including *A Teacher's Guide to the Department of Education, A Researcher's Guide to the Department of Education,* and a whole list of publications designed to address parents' concerns about their children's education. Examples include:

> *Helping Your Child Learn Math*
> *Helping Your Child Learn to Read*
> *Helping Your Child Learn History*
> *Helping Your Child Get Ready for School*
> *Help Your Child Improve in Test Taking*
> *Help Your Child Learn to Write Well*
> *Helping Your Child Use the Library*
> *Helping Your Child Learn Geography*
> *Helping Your Child Learn Science*
> *Helping Your Child Learn Responsible Behavior*
> *Helping Your Child With Homework*
> *Helping Your Child Succeed in School*

Information for those interested in applying for an educational grant or a contract;

A list of programs supported by the Department;

A complete, indexed list of publications is available online from the Department of Education (there's tons of them!)

* U.S. Department of Health And Human Services
Website: http://www.os.dhhs.gov/
E-mail: thompson@os.dhhs.gov
All consumers need reliable information. What better source is there than the government, and what better medium than the Internet? From this site, you can download information on:

Foodborne illnesses, food labeling, nutrition and seafood;

Consumer guidelines on AIDS, cancer, pain control, back problems, mammograms, flu, foot care, hearing, and other illnesses and diseases;

Emerging infectious disease information;

Health information for seniors;

The Citizens Guide to Prevention Resources (for assistance in finding help for those with drug and alcohol problems);

Traveler's health page, for information on what vaccines you need if you are planning a visit to a foreign country or what to take to prevent jetlag or sea sickness in getting there;

Medicare and Medicaid programs;

Where to write for "vital" records, such as certificates of birth, death, marriage, or divorce;

GrantsNet, a project intended to provide the public with electronic grant information;

Transcripts of various health-related research and data;

Gopher site for Agency of Aging (gopher.os.dhhs.gov/11/dhhs/aoa/aoa).

* U.S. Department of Housing and Urban Development
Website: http://www.hud.gov/
E-mail: webmaster@hud.gov
This site is worth seeing if only its design. There's an 800 Number phone directory for assistance on a variety of housing issues, such as community improvement and fair housing rules. There's a *Community Connections* section where communities can find information about a full range of U.S. Department of Housing and Urban Development (HUD) programs that communities can use to spur growth and create new opportunities. Also, there's *Step-Up* – information about jobs for low-income citizens. For people who are looking to buy a new house or fix up the one they already own, there are guides and publications available.

* U.S. Department of the Interior

Website: http://info.er.usgs.gov/doi/doi.html
E-mail: cnethawa@ridgisd.er.usgs.gov

On this site, you can find information regarding some of our most precious national treasures – including endangered species - and the fish and other wildlife that call this country home (also check out the *U. S. Fish and Wildlife Service* at http://www.fws.gov/). The U.S. Department of the Interior also offers training, employment, and volunteer opportunities for students and others interested in preserving nature. It's worth a look!

* U.S. Department of Justice Home Page

Website: http://www.usdoj.gov/
E-mail: web@usdoj.gov

Would you like detailed information about the UNABomber? Or an online visit with Attorney General Janet Reno? How about reading President Clinton's latest speech on affirmative action? It's all here, as well as:

Americans with Disabilities Act Information;

PAVNET – Partnership Against Violence, a "virtual library of information about violence and youth-at-risk, representing data from seven different federal agencies".

The U.S. Department of Justice gopher server.

* U.S. Department of Labor

Website: http://www.dol.gov/
E-mail: webmaster@dol.gov (only technical issues)

This site provides information about the U.S. Department of Labor (including an organizational chart, a mission statement, history, and annual report for the Department). Also available are the complete texts of the Department's press releases and congressional testimony. Other information includes labor-related data, grant and contract opportunities, as well as statutory and regulatory information for DOL's agencies.

* U.S. Department of State

Website: http://dosfan.lib.uic.edu/index.html
E-mail: alfred@uic.edu

Information is available on a wide range of topics – from Secretary Christopher Warren's latest press-conference, to travel warnings directly from the U.S. Department of State (DOS), to an International Affairs column. Available, also, is a listing for contacts and phone numbers of the DOS at home as well as abroad. The site also offers an opportunity to take a photographic tour of the U.S. Department of State headquarters in Washington, D.C.

* U.S. Department of Transportation

Website: http://www.dot.gov/
E-mail: webmaster@www.dot.gov

This web site is still under construction at this time.

* U.S. Department of the Treasury

Website: http://www.ustreas.gov/
E-mail: dale.servetrick@treas.sprint.com

Do you own a small business? Are you thinking about buying one? If so, this page is of interest for you. Information is available on:

Small Business Specialists in Each Bureau
Forecast of Contract Opportunities - Fiscal Year 1996
Small Business Subcontracting Opportunities Directory
Contractor Profile Database
Electronic Payment by Treasury - Vendor Express Program
What Treasury Buys
Small, Minority and Women-Owned Business Conferences

Also here is information on auctions of seized property, savings bonds, financial statistics at the University of California, San Diego, and treasury bureaus and services.

* U.S. Department of Veterans Affairs Home Page

Website: http://www.va.gov/

This page is dedicated to issues that pertain to war veterans and has lots of stuff for them to check out. There is a section which explains the VA benefits to which every veteran is entitled. Also available is a benefits manual (which can be downloaded), and a list of facilities where the vets can go for help. This page is updated often, and offers extensive coverage of veteran-related news, speeches, and press releases.

* U.S. Fire Administration

Website: http://www.fema.gov/netc/usfa1.shtml

Sections are available on:

USFA Organization
Public education
Fire data
National Fire Academy
Publications
National Fallen Firefighters Memorial
National Emergency Training Center
Learning Resource Center
Research and technology
Frequently asked questions
What's new at USFA

* U.S. Global Change Research Information Office

Website: http://www.gcrio.org/
E-mail: chood@gcrio.org

This page is designed to provide the viewer with access to global change and environmental data from around the world. You can download electronic documents on the global environment, as well as connect to other Internet servers dealing with the same issues. Information is available on a variety of issues from a variety of sources, so check it out!

* U.S. House of Representatives Home Page

Website: http://www.house.gov/

Have you ever wondered about the legislative process and how those bills and resolutions are handled? You can find out. There's also a contact list for Members and committees affiliated with the House. For those who are interested (or are forced into) legal research, the following documents are available:

The U.S. Code
Constitution
Constitutional amendments
Declaration of Independence
Annapolis Convention
Articles of Confederation
Bill of Rights
Budget
Code of Federal Regulations
Congressional Record
Court decisions and rules
Declaration of Independence
Equal Rights Amendment
Federal Register
Federalist Papers
General Accounting Office (GAO) Reports
General Services Administration (GSA) publications
Hearings
House Documents
Jefferson, Works of Thomas
Legislation
Paine, Works of Thomas
Presidential documents
Reports of the House and Senate
Rules of the House and Senate
Statutes
Lots, lots more, including international law, legal profession directories, and treaties.

* U.S. Information Agency

Website: http://www.usia.gov/
E-mail: inquiry@usia.gov

The U.S. Information Agency (USIA) explains and supports American foreign policy and promotes U.S. national interest through a wide range of overseas information programs. How? For starters, it maintains more than 211 posts in 147 countries where it is known as USIS, or the U.S. Information Service. The other sections posted on this site include:

Be patient. If any phone number is incorrect, call (area code) 555-1212 and request the new listing.

1227

Government Databases and Internet Access

Mission
People
Budget
Exchange Activities
Broadcasting
Information Programs
US-NIS Exchanges
East European Initiatives
Research and Media Reaction
History
Authority (Law)

* U.S. Postal Service

Website: http://www.usps.gov/

In addition to delivering mail, the U.S. Postal Service (USPS) is now delivering in cyberspace! Several "mailboxes" are available: one for today's features, one for your business, and one that's F.Y.I. You can even check on the postal rates from your house to anywhere in the USA (and beyond).

* U.S. Secret Service

Website: http://www.ustreas.gov/treasury/bureaus/usss/usss.html

Read the Secret Service mission statement or visit with the agency's director.

* U.S. Senate

Website: http://www.senate.gov/
E-mail: webmaster@scc.senate.gov

Available here is a directory of senators (including the e-mail addresses, if applicable). Also available is information about the Senate Committee System, a glossary of Senate terms, and a virtual tour of the U.S. Capitol. (If you don't have access to the World Wide Web, try the Senate gopher at gopher.senate.gov).

* U.S. Sentencing Commission

Website: http://www.ussc.gov/
E-mail: webmaster@ussc.gov

Break the law, go to jail - or not. Read at this site about how the government establishes sentencing policies and practices for federal courts.

* Voice of America

Site: gopher://gopher.voa.gov/

In many isolated parts of the world, Voice of America (VOA) *is* America. This site describes in great detail how the VOA operates. Information is available on its broadcast programs into China, Cuba, and other parts of the world where television and radio are controlled and censored by the current government. You can also check out the Worldnet television schedules and contact Voice of America by E-mail (a list of public addresses also is available).

* Volcano Observatories on the 'Net:

The Alaska Volcano Observatory
(http://www.avo.alaska.edu/). Get up-to-the minute news about volcano activity in Alaska and the North Pacific regions, the outlying domestic areas that are part of the Ring of Fire - the most active volcanic area on earth. Download maps, location figures, summary tables and text, databases, and satellite images. According to this site, there are over 40 volcanoes that the observatory is following.

Hawaiian Volcano Observatory "Volcano Watch"
(http://www.soest.hawaii.edu/hvo/). While Volcano Watch is primarily for citizens of Hawaii, it should interest anyone concerned with volcanic activity. A two-year archive of the observatory's newsletter also is available here.

* Women's Bureau

Website: http://www.dol.gov/dol/wb

Read information about the Women's Bureau, its media releases, and a list of programs and activities. You can also download online publications relating to women's labor, such as *20 Facts About Women's Labor*. You can also admire some of Women's Bureau/posters, available online!

Be patient. If any phone number is incorrect, call (area code) 555-1212 and request the new listing.

Federal Legislators on the Internet

The following is a listing of Federal Congressional E-Mail Addresses and Web Sites. This information was compiled from the Senate and House Gophers, CAPWEB, David Morgan (http://www.geopages.com/CapitolHill/1007/), and contributions from individual citizens.

You can get an updated version from the University of Michigan Library Gopher: Path: Social Sciences/ Government/U.S. Government: Legislative Branch/E-Mail Addresses. It is also available through the Documents Center's web site: http://www.lib.umich.edu/ libhome/Documents.center/ federal.html and the ULIBRARY Gopher's web interface: gopher://una.hh.lib.umich.edu:70/00/socsci/poliscilaw/uslegi/conemail.

Web sites appear after the complete list of Senate and House E-Mail addresses. These are official web sites only. If you are looking for political campaign and political party web sites, they are available through CAPWEB's Political Page (http://policy.net/capweb/political.html) or David Morgan's Congress home page (http://www.geopages.com/Capitol Hill/1007/.

United States Senate

Each listing includes the state, party affiliation, senator's name, and senator's e-mail address.

ST	PT	Name	E-Mail Address
AK	R	Stevens, Ted	Senator_Stevens@stevens.senate.gov
AK	R	Murkowski, Frank	email@murkowski.senate.gov
AL	R	Shelby, Richard	senator@shelby.senate.gov
AR	D	Bumpers, Dale	senator@bumpers.senate.gov
AZ	R	Kyl, Jon	info@kyl.senate.gov
AZ	R	McCain, John	Senator_McCain@mccain.senate.gov
CA	D	Boxer, Barbara	senator@boxer.senate.gov
CA	D	Feinstein, Dianne	senator@feinstein.senate.gov
CO	R	Brown, Hank	senator_brown@brown.senate.gov
CO	R	Campbell, Ben N.	data@nighthorse.falcontech.com
CT	D	Dodd, Christopher	sen_dodd@dodd.senate.gov
CT	D	Lieberman, Joseph	senator_lieberman@lieberman.senate.gov
DE	D	Biden, Joe	senator@biden.senate.gov
FL	D	Graham, Bob	bob_graham@graham.senate.gov
FL	R	Mack, Connie	senator_mack@jec.senate.gov
GA	R	Coverdell, Paul	senator_coverdell@coverdell.senate.gov
IA	D	Harkin, Tom	tom_harkin@harkin.senate.gov
IA	R	Grassley, Charles	chuck_grassley@grassley.senate.gov
ID	R	Craig, Larry	larry_craig@craig.senate.gov
ID	R	Kempthorne, Dirk	dirk_kempthorne@kempthorne.senate.gov
IL	D	Simon, Paul	senator@simon.senate.gov
IL	D	Moseley-Braun, Carol	senator@moseley-braun.senate.gov
IN	R	Lugar, Richard	lugar@iquest.net
KY	D	Ford, Wendell	wendell_ford@ford.senate.gov
KY	R	McConnell, Mitch	senator@mcconnell.senate.gov
LA	D	Breaux, John	senator@breaux.senate.gov
LA	D	Johnston, J.Bennett	senator@johnston.senate.gov
MA	D	Kennedy, Ted	senator@kennedy.senate.gov
MA	D	Kerry, John	john_kerry@kerry.senate.gov
MD	D	Mikulski, Barbara	senator@mikulski.senate.gov
MD	D	Sarbanes, Paul	senator@sarbanes.senate.gov
ME	R	Cohen, William	billcohen@cohen.senate.gov
MI	D	Levin, Carl	senator@levin.senate.gov
MI	R	Abraham, Spencer	michigan@abraham.senate.gov
MN	R	Grams, Rod	mail_grams@grams.senate.gov
MN	D	Wellstone, Paul	senator@wellstone.senate.gov
MO	R	Ashcroft, John	john_ashcroft@ashcroft.senate.gov
MS	R	Cochran, Thad	senator@cochran.senate.gov
MT	D	Baucus, Max	max@baucus.senate.gov
MT	R	Burns, Conrad	conrad_burns@burns.senate.gov
NC	R	Faircloth, Lauch	senator@faircloth.senate.gov
NC	R	Helms, Jesse	jesse_helms@helms.senate.gov
ND	D	Conrad, Kent	senator@conrad.senate.gov
ND	D	Dorgan, Byron	senator@dorgan.senate.gov
NE	D	Kerrey, Bob	bob@kerrey.senate.gov
NH	R	Gregg, Judd	mailbox@gregg.senate.gov
NH	R	Smith, Bob	opinion@smith.senate.gov
NJ	D	Bradley, Bill	senator@bradley.senate.gov
NM	D	Bingaman, Jeff	Senator_Bingaman@bingaman.senate.gov
NM	R	Domenici, Pete	senator_domenici@domenici.senate.gov
NV	D	Reid, Harry	senator_reid@reid.senate.gov
NY	R	D'Amato, Alfonse	senator_al@damato.senate.gov
NY	D	Moynihan, Daniel P.	senator@dpm.senate.gov
OH	R	Dewine, Michael	senator_dewine@dewine.senate.gov
OH	D	Glenn, John	caroline@cua3.csuohio.edu
OK	R	Nickles, Don	senator@nickles.senate.gov
OR	D	Wyden, Ron	wyden@teleport.com
PA	R	Santorum, Rick	senator@santorum.senate.gov
PA	R	Specter, Arlen	senator_specter@specter.senate.gov
RI	R	Chafee, John	senator_chafee@chafee.senate.gov

Be patient. If any phone number is incorrect, call (area code) 555-1212 and request the new listing.

1229

SC	R	Thurmond, Strom	senator@thurmond.senate.gov
SC	D	Hollings, Ernest	senator@hollings.senate.gov
SD	D	Daschle, Thomas	tom_daschle@daschle.senate.gov
SD	R	Pressler, Larry	larry_pressler@pressler.senate.gov
TN	R	Thompson, Fred	senator_thompson@thompson.senate.gov
TN	R	Frist, Bill	senator_frist@frist.senate.gov
TX	R	Gramm, Phil	info@gramm96.org
TX	R	Hutchison, Kay	senator@hutchison.senate.gov
UT	R	Bennett, Robert	senator@bennett.senate.gov
UT	R	Hatch, Orrin	senator_hatch@hatch.senate.gov
VA	D	Robb, Charles	senator_robb@robb.senate.gov
VA	D	Robb, Charles	vascr@CapAccess.org
VA	R	Warner, John	senator@warner.senate.gov
VT	D	Leahy, Patrick	senator_leahy@leahy.senate.gov
VT	R	Jeffords, Jim	vermont@jeffords.senate.gov
WA	D	Murray, Patty	senator_murray@murray.senate.gov
WA	R	Gorton, Slade	Senator_Gorton@gorton.senate.gov
WI	D	Feingold, Russell	russell_feingold@feingold.senate.gov
WI	D	Kohl, Herbert	senator_kohl@kohl.senate.gov
WV	D	Rockefeller, Jay	senator@rockefeller.senate.gov
WY	R	Simpson, Alan	senator@simpson.senate.gov

Senate Committee on Small Business . . . . . . committee@small-bus.senate.gov

Senate Special Committee on Aging . . . . mailbox@aging.senate.gov

Senate Republican Policy Committee . . . . webmaster@rpc.senate.gov

United States House of Representatives

Each listing includes the state, district number, party affiliation, representative's name, and representative's e-mail address.

ST	DS	PT	Name	E-Mail Address
AL	2	R	Everett, Terry	everett@hr.house.gov
AL	5	D	Cramer, Bud	budmail@hr.house.gov
AL	6	R	Bachus, Spencer	sbachus@hr.house.gov
AR	3	R	Hutchinson, Tim	timhutch@hr.house.gov
AR	4	R	Dickey, Jay	jdickey@hr.house.gov
AZ	2	D	Pastor, Ed	edpastor@hr.house.gov
AZ	5	R	Kolbe, Jim	jimkolbe@hr.house.gov
AZ	6	R	Hayworth, J.D.	hayworth@hr.house.gov
CA	1	R	Riggs, Frank	repriggs@hr.house.gov
CA	3	D	Fazio, Vic	dcaucus@hr.house.gov
CA	6	D	Woolsey, Lynn	woolsey@hr.house.gov
CA	7	D	Miller, George	gmiller@hr.house.gov
CA	8	D	Pelosi, Nancy	sfnancy@hr.house.gov
CA	10	R	Baker, Bill	bbaker@hr.house.gov
CA	12	D	Lantos, Tom	talk2tom@hr.house.gov
CA	13	D	Stark, Pete	petemail@hr.house.gov
CA	14	D	Eshoo, Anna	annagram@hr.house.gov
CA	15	R	Campbell, Tom	campbell@hr.house.gov
CA	16	D	Lofgren, Zoe	zoegram@lofgren.house.gov
CA	17	D	Farr, Sam	samfarr@hr.house.gov
CA	19	R	Radanovich, George	george@hr.house.gov
CA	22	R	Seastrand, Andrea	andrea22@hr.house.gov
CA	25	R	McKeon, Howard	tellbuck@hr.house.gov
CA	36	D	Harman, Jane	jharman@hr.house.gov
CA	42	D	Brown, George E.	talk2geb@hr.house.gov
CA	47	R	Cox, Christopher	chriscox@hr.house.gov
CA	48	R	Packard, Ron	rpackard@hr.house.gov
CA	49	R	Bilbray, Brian	bilbray@hr.house.gov

ST	DS	PT	Name	E-Mail Address
CO	2	D	Skaggs, David	skaggs@hr.house.gov
CO	6	R	Schaefer, Dan	schaefer@hr.house.gov
CT	2	D	Gejdenson, Sam	bozrah@hr.house.gov
CT	4	R	Shays, Christopher	cshays@hr.house.gov
DE	AL	R	Castle, Michael	delaware@hr.house.gov
FL	5	D	Thurman, Karen	kthurman@hr.house.gov
FL	6	R	Stearns, Cliff	cstearns@hr.house.gov
FL	9	R	Bilirakis, Michael	truerep@hr.house.gov
FL	12	R	Canady, Charles	canady@hr.house.gov
FL	15	R	Weldon, Dave	fla15@hr.house.gov
FL	20	D	Deutsch, Peter	pdeutsch@hr.house.gov
FL	23	D	Hastings, Alcee	hastings@hr.house.gov
GA	3	R	Collins, Mac	rep3mac@hr.house.gov
GA	4	R	Linder, John	jlinder@hr.house.gov
GA	6	R	Gingrich, Newton	georgia6@hr.house.gov
GA	8	R	Chambliss, Saxby	saxby@hr.house.gov
GA	10	R	Norwood, Charlies	ga10@hr.house.gov
GU	AL	D	Underwood, Robert	guamtodc@hr.house.gov
IA	2	R	Nussle, James	nussleia@hr.house.gov
ID	1	R	Chenoweth, Helen	askhelen@hr.house.gov
IL	1	D	Rush, Bobby	brush@hr.house.gov
IL	4	D	Gutierrez, Luis	luisg@hr.house.gov
IL	12	D	Costello, Jerry	jfcil12@hr.house.gov
IL	13	R	Fawell, Harris	hfawell@hr.house.gov
IL	14	R	Hastert, Dennis	dhastert@hr.house.gov
IL	20	D	Durbin, Richard	durbin@hr.house.gov
IN	2	R	McIntosh, David	mcintosh@hr.house.gov
IN	3	D	Roemer, Tim	troemer@hr.house.gov
IN	4	R	Souder, Mark	souder@hr.house.gov
IN	8	R	Hostettler, John	johnhost@hr.house.gov
IN	9	D	Hamilton, Lee	hamilton@hr.house.gov
KS	1	R	Roberts, Pat	emailpat@hr.house.gov
KS	2	R	Brownback, Sam	brownbak@hr.house.gov
KS	4	R	Tiahrt, Todd	tiahrt@hr.house.gov
KY	1	R	Whitfield, Ed	edky01@hr.house.gov
KY	3	D	Ward, Mike	mikemail@hr.house.gov
KY	4	R	Bunning, Jim	bunning4@hr.house.gov
LA	5	R	McCrery, Jim	mccrery@hr.house.gov
MA	5	D	Meehan, Martin	mtmeehan@hr.house.gov
MA	6	R	Torkildsen, Peter	torkma06@hr.house.gov
MA	9	D	Moakley, Joe	jmoakley@hr.house.gov
MD	2	R	Ehrlich, Robert	rallen@lattanze.loyola.edu
				ehrlich@hr.house.gov
MD	3	D	Cardin, Ben	cardin@hr.house.gov
MD	4	D	Wynn, Albert	alwynn@hr.house.gov
ME	2	D	Baldacci, John	baldacci@hr.house.gov
MI	1	D	Stupak, Bart	stupak@hr.house.gov
MI	2	R	Hoekstra, Peter	tellhoek@hr.house.gov
MI	2	R	Hoekstra, Peter	usavoice@hr.house.gov
MI	3	R	Ehlers, Vernon	congehlr@hr.house.gov
MI	4	R	Camp, Dave	davecamp@hr.house.gov
MI	7	R	Smith, Nick	repsmith@hr.house.gov
MI	8	R	Chrysler, Dick	chrysler@hr.house.gov
MI	13	D	Rivers, Lynn	lrivers@hr.house.gov
MI	14	D	Conyers, John	jconyers@hr.house.gov
MN	1	R	Gutknect, Gil	gil@hr.house.gov
MN	2	D	Minge, David	dminge@hr.house.gov
MN	3	R	Ramstad, Jim	mn03@hr.house.gov
MN	4	D	Vento, Bruce	vento@hr.house.gov
MN	5	D	Sabo, Martin	msabo@hr.house.gov

MN	6	D	Luther, Bill	tellbill@hr.house.gov
MN	7	D	Peterson, Collin	tocollin@hr.house.gov
MN	8	D	Oberstar, James	oberstar@hr.house.gov
MO	2	R	Talent, James	talentmo@hr.house.gov
MO	3	D	Gephardt, Richard	gephardt@hr.house.gov
MO	8	R	Emerson, Bill	bemerson@hr.house.gov
MS	2	D	Thompson, Bennie	ms2nd@hr.house.gov
NC	2	R	Funderburk, David	funnc02@hr.house.gov
NC	4	R	Heineman, Frederick	thechief@hr.house.gov
NC	5	R	Burr, Richard	mail2nc5@hr.house.gov
NC	7	D	Rose, Charlie	crose@hr.house.gov
NC	9	R	Myrick, Sue	myrick@hr.house.gov
NC	10	R	Ballenger, Cass	cassmail@hr.house.gov
NC	11	R	Taylor, Charles	chtaylor@hr.house.gov
NC	12	D	Watt, Mel	melmail@hr.house.gov
ND	AL	D	Pomeroy, Earl	epomeroy@hr.house.gov
NE	2	R	Christensen, Jon	talk2jon@hr.house.gov
NH	1	R	Zeliff, Bill	zeliff@hr.house.gov
NH	2	R	Bass, Charlie	cbass@hr.house.gov
NJ	1	D	Andrews, Robert	randrews@hr.house.gov
NJ	7	R	Franks, Bob	franksnj@hr.house.gov
NJ	11	R	Frelinghuysen, Rodney	njeleven@hr.house.gov
NJ	12	R	Zimmer, Dick	dzimmer@hr.house.gov
NM	3	D	Richardson, Bill	billnm03@hr.house.gov
NV	1	R	Ensign, John	ensign@hr.house.gov
NY	1	R	Forbes, Michael	mpforbes@hr.house.gov
NY	2	R	Lazio, Rick	lazio@hr.house.gov
NY	3	R	King, Peter	peteking@hr.house.gov
NY	7	D	Manton, Thomas	tmanton@hr.house.gov
NY	8	D	Nadler, Jerrold	nadler@hr.house.gov
NY	13	R	Molinari, Susan	molinari@hr.house.gov
NY	15	D	Rangel, Charles	rangel@hr.house.gov
NY	16	D	Serrano, Jose	jserrano@hr.house.gov
NY	17	D	Engel, Eliot	engeline@hr.house.gov
NY	18	D	Lowey, Nita	nitamail@hr.house.gov
NY	19	R	Kelly, Sue	dearsue@hr.house.gov
NY	21	D	McNulty, Michael	mmcnulty@hr.house.gov
NY	23	R	Boehlert, Sherwood	boehlert@hr.house.gov
NY	26	D	Hinchey, Maurice	hinchey@hr.house.gov
NY	27	R	Paxon, Bill	bpaxon@hr.house.gov
OH	2	R	Portman, Rob	portmail@hr.house.gov
OH	4	R	Oxley, Michael	oxley@hr.house.gov
OH	10	R	Hoke, Martin	hokemail@hr.house.gov
OH	13	D	Brown, Sherrod	sherrod@hr.house.gov
OH	15	R	Pryce, Deborah	pryce15@hr.house.gov
OH	17	D	Traficant, James	telljim@hr.house.gov
OK	5	R	Istook, Jr. Ernest	istook@hr.house.gov
OR	1	D	Furse, Elizabeth	furseor1@hr.house.gov
OR	4	D	DeFazio, Pete	pdefazio@hr.house.gov
OR	5	R	Bunn, Jim	askbunn@hr.house.gov
PA	7	R	Weldon, Curt	curtpa7@hr.house.gov
PA	11	D	Kanjorski, Paul	kanjo@hr.house.gov
PA	12	D	Murtha, John	murtha@hr.house.gov
PA	13	R	Fox, Jon	jonfox@hr.house.gov
PA	15	D	McHale, Paul	mchale@hr.house.gov
PA	16	R	Walker, Robert	pa16@hr.house.gov
SC	1	R	Sanford, Mark	sanford@hr.house.gov
SC	5	D	Spratt, John	jspratt@hr.house.gov
SC	6	D	Clyburn, James	jclyburn@hr.house.gov
TN	5	D	Clement, Bob	clement@hr.house.gov
TN	9	D	Ford, Harold	hford@hr.house.gov

TX	1	D	Chapman, Jim	jchapman@hr.house.gov
TX	2	D	Wilson, Charles	cwilson@hr.house.gov
TX	3	R	Johnson, Sam	samtx03@hr.house.gov
TX	6	R	Barton, Joe	barton06@hr.house.gov
TX	10	D	Doggett, Lloyd	doggett@hr.house.gov
TX	24	D	Frost, Martin	frost@hr.house.gov
TX	25	D	Bentsen, Ken	bentsen@hr.house.gov
TX	29	D	Green, Gene	ggreen@hr.house.gov
UT	2	R	Waldholtz, Enid	enidutah@hr.house.gov
UT	3	D	Orton, Bill	ortonut3@hr.house.gov
VA	2	D	Pickett, Owen	opickett@hr.house.gov
VA	6	R	Goodlatte, Bob	talk2bob@hr.house.gov
VA	8	D	Moran, Jim	repmoran@hr.house.gov
VA	9	D	Boucher, Rick	ninthnet@hr.house.gov
VA	11	R	Davis, Tom	tomdavis@hr.house.gov
VT	AL	I	Sanders, Bernie	bsanders@igc.apc.org
WA	1	R	White, Rick	repwhite@hr.house.gov
WA	3	R	Smith, Linda	asklinda@hr.house.gov
WA	8	R	Dunn, Jennifer	dunnwa08@hr.house.gov
WA	9	R	Tate, Randy	rtate@hr.house.gov
WI	1	R	Neumann, Mark	mneumann@hr.house.gov
WI	2	R	Klug, Scott	badger02@hr.house.gov
WI	4	D	Kleczka, Gerald	jerry4wi@hr.house.gov
WI	5	D	Barrett, Tom	telltom@hr.house.gov
WI	6	R	Petri, Tom	tompetri@hr.house.gov
WI	8	R	Roth, Toby	roth08@hr.house.gov
WI	9	R	Sensenbrenner, James	sensen09@hr.house.gov
WV	2	D	Wise, Robert	bobwise@hr.house.gov
WV	3	D	Rahall, Nick	nrahall@hr.house.gov

House Committee on Commerce . . . . commerce@hr.house.gov

House Committee on Economic and Educational Opportunities
    Subcommittee on Employer-Employee Relations . slabmgnt@hr.house.gov

House Committee on Resources . . . . resource@hr.house.gov

House Committee on Science . . . . science@hr.house.gov

House Commitee on Science (minority) . . . . scidems@hr.house.gov

House Committee on Small Business . . . . smbizcom@hr.house.gov

House Republican Policy Committee . . . . repubpol@hr.house.gov

Congressional Web Sites

* United States Senate Web Sites

Generic web pages are available for all Senators by name or state at the Senate web site (http://www.senate.gov). Each listing below includes the state, party affiliation, senator's name, and web site address.

ST	PT	Name	Web Site
AK	R	Murkowski, Frank	http://www.senate.gov/~murkowski/
			http://www.state.ak.us/local/akpages/CONGRESS/aksenfm.htm
AK	R	Stevens, Ted	http://www.senate.gov/~stevens/
			http://www.state.ak.us/local/akpages/CONGRESS/aksents.htm
AZ	R	Kyl, Jon	http://aspin.asu.edu/~pctp/kyl/kyl.html
AZ	R	McCain, John	http://aspin.asu.edu/~pctp/mccain/mccain.html
CA	D	Boxer, Barbara	http://www.senate.gov/~boxer/
CA	D	Feinstein, Dianne	http://www.senate.gov/~feinstein/
CO	R	Campbell, Ben Nighthorse	http://www.falcontech.com/nighthorse/
CT	D	Dodd, Christopher	http://www.uconn.edu/dodd/dodd.html
CT	D	Lieberman, Joseph	http://www.senate.gov/~lieberman/

Be patient. If any phone number is incorrect, call (area code) 555-1212 and request the new listing.

1231

Government Databases and Internet Access

DE D Biden, Joe . . . . http://www.senate.gov/~biden/

FL D Graham, Bob . . . . http://www.senate.gov/~graham/
FL R Mack, Connie . . . . http://www.senate.gov/~mack/

IA D Harkin, Tom . . . . http://www.senate.gov/~harkin/

ID R Craig, Larry . . . . http://www.senate.gov/~craig/
ID R Kempthorne, Dirk . . . . http://www.senate.gov/~kempthorne/

IL D Simon, Paul . . . . http://www.senate.gov/~simon/

KY D Ford, Wendell . . . . http://www.senate.gov/~ford/

LA D Breaux, John . . . . http://www.senate.gov/~breaux/
LA D Johnston, Bennett . . . . http://www.senate.gov/~johnston/

MA D Kennedy, Ted
            http://www.ai.mit.edu/projects/iiip/Kennedy/homepage.html
            http://www.senate.gov/~kennedy/
MA D Kerry, John . . . . http://www.senate.gov/~kerry/

MD D Mikulski, Barbara . . . . http://www.senate.gov/~mikulski/
MD D Sarbanes, Paul . . . . http://www.senate.gov/~sarbanes/

ME R Cohen, William . . . . http://www.senate.gov/~cohen/

MI D Levin, Carl . . . . http://www.senate.gov/~levin/

MN R Grams, Rod . . . . http://www.senate.gov/~grams/
MN D Wellstone, Paul . . . . http://www.senate.gov/~wellstone/

MO R Ashcroft, John . . . . http://www.senate.gov/~ashcroft/

MT D Baucus, Max . . . . http://www.senate.gov/~baucus/

ND D Conrad, Kent . . . . http://www.senate.gov/~conrad/
ND D Dorgan, Byron http://www.bps.k12.nd.us/Dorgan/Dorgan.html

NE D Kerrey, Bob . . . . http://www.senate.gov/~kerrey/

NH R Smith, Robert . . . . http://www.senate.gov/~smith/

NJ D Bradley, Bill . . . . http://www.senate.gov/~bradley/

NM D Bingaman, Jeff . . . . http://www.senate.gov/~bingaman/

NV D Reid, Harry . . . . http://www.senate.gov/~reid/

NY D Moynihan, Daniel Patrick . . . . . http://www.senate.gov/~moynihan/

OH D Glenn, John . . . . http://little.nhlink.net/john-glenn/
OH R DeWine, Michael . . . . http://www.senate.gov/~dewine/

OK R Nickles, Don . . . . http://www.senate.gov/~nickles/

OR D Wyden, Ron . . . . http://www.house.gov/wyden/welcome.html

PA R Santorum, Rick . . . . http://www.senate.gov/~santorum/

SC D Hollings, Ernest . . . . http://www.senate.gov/~hollings/
SD D Daschle, Thomas . . . . http://www.senate.gov/~daschle/

TN R Frist, Bill . . . . http://www.senate.gov/~frist/
            http://www.surgery.mc.vanderbilt.edu/frist/frist.html

TX R Hutchison, Kay Bailey . . . . http://www.senate.gov/~hutchison/

UT R Bennett, Robert . . . . http://www.senate.gov/~bennett/
UT R Hatch, Orrin . . . . http://www.senate.gov/~hatch/

VA D Robb, Charles . . . . http://www.senate.gov/~robb/
VA R Warner, John . . . . http://www.senate.gov/~warner/

VT D Leahy, Patrick . . . . http://www.senate.gov/~leahy/
VT R Jeffords, Jim . . . . http://www.senate.gov/~jeffords/

WA D Murray, Patty . . . . http://www.senate.gov/~murray/

WI D Feingold, Russell . . . . http://www.senate.gov/~feingold/
WI D Kohl, Herbert . . . . http://www.senate.gov/~kohl/

WV D Rockefeller, Jay . . . . http://www.senate.gov/~rockefeller/

WY R Simpson, Alan . . . . http://www.senate.gov/~simpson/

Senate . . . . http://www.senate.gov

Senate Committee on Energy and Natural
    Resources . . . . http://www.senate.gov/~energy/

Senate Committee on Small Business . . . . http://www.senate.gov/~sbc/

Senate Committee on Veterans Affairs . . . . http://www.senate.gov/~svac/

Senate Democratic Policy Committee . . . . http://www.senate.gov/~dpc/

Senate Republican Conference . . . . http://www.senate.gov/~src/

Senate Republican Policy Committee . . . . http://www.senate.gov/~rpc/

Senate Office of the Legal
    Counsel . . . . . ftp://ftp.senate.gov/committee/legal/general/lchome.html

Senate Special Committee on Aging . . . . http://www.senate.gov/~aging/

* United States House of Representatives

Generic web sites are also available for House members under http://www.house.gov/
mbr_dir/membr_dir.html. Each listing below includes state, district number, party
affiliation, representative's name, and web site address.

ST DS PT Name . . . . Web Site

AK AL R Young, Don
            http://www.state.ak.us/local/akpages/CONGRESS/akcondy.htm

AL 1 R Callahan, Sonny . http://www.house.gov/callahan/welcome.html
AL 3 D Browder, Glen . . . http://www.house.gov/browder/welcome.html
AL 5 D Cramer, Bud . . . . http://www.house.gov/cramer/welcome.html

AZ 1 R Salmon, Matt . . http://aspin.asu.edu/~pctp/salmon/salmon.html
AZ 2 D Pastor, Ed . . . . http://aspin.asu.edu/~pctp/pastor/pastor.html
            http://www.house.gov/pastor/welcome.html
AZ 3 R Stump, Bob . . . . . http://aspin.asu.edu/~pctp/stump/stump.html
AZ 4 R Shadegg, John . http://aspin.asu.edu/~pctp/shadegg/shadegg.html
AZ 5 R Kolbe, Jim . . . . http://www.house.gov/kolbe/welcome.html
            http://www.arizona.edu/kolbe/kolbe.html
AZ 6 R Hayworth, John D.
            . . . . http://aspin.asu.edu/~pctp/hayworth/hayworth.html

CA 3 D Fazio, Vic . . . . http://www.house.gov/fazio/welcome.html
CA 7 D Miller, George
            . . . . http://www.house.gov/georgemiller/welcome.html
CA 8 R Pelosi, Nancy . . . . http://www.house.gov/pelosi/welcome.html
CA 9 D Dellums, Ron . . . http://www.house.gov/dellums/welcome.html
CA 12 D Lantos, Tom . . . . http://www.house.gov/lantos/welcome.html
CA 14 D Eshoo, Anna . . . . http://www-eshoo.house.gov
CA 15 R Campbell, Tom . . . . http://www.campbell.org/
CA 16 D Lofgren, Zoe . . . . http://www.house.gov/lofgren/welcome.html
CA 17 D Farr, Sam . . . . http://www.house.gov/farr/welcome.html
CA 19 R Radanovich, George
            . . . . http://www.house.gov/radanovich/welcome.html
CA 40 R Lewis, Jerry . . . . http://www.house.gov/jerrylewis/
CA 41 R Kim, Jay . . . . . . http://www.house.gov/kim/welcome.html
CA 46 R Dornan, Robert
            . . . . http://www.umr.edu/~sears/primary/dornan.html
CA 47 R Cox, Christopher . . . . http://www.house.gov/cox/
CA 48 R Packard, Ron . . . . http://www.house.gov/packard/welcome.html
CA 49 R Bilbray, Brian . . . http://www.house.gov/bilbray/welcome.html

CT 2 D Gejdenson, Samuel
            . . . . http://www.house.gov/gejdenson/welcome.html

CT 4 R Shays, Christopher . http://www.house.gov/shays/welcome.html

DE AL R Castle, Michael .... http://www.house.gov/castle/welcome.html

FL 4 R Fowler, Tillie .... http://www.house.gov/fowler/welcome.html
FL 5 D Thurman, Karen . http://www.house.gov/thurman/welcome.html
FL 6 R Stearns, Cliff .... http://www.house.gov/stearns/welcome.html
FL 9 R Bilirakis, Michael http://www.house.gov/bilirakis/welcome.html
FL 23 D Hastings, Alcee
.... http://www.house.gov/alceehastings/welcome.html

GA 1 R Kingston, Jack .... http://www.gasou.edu/first_district
GA 8 R Chambliss, Saxby
.... http://www.house.gov/chambliss/welcome.html

GU AL D Underwood, Robert
.... http://www.house.gov/underwood/welcome.html

IA 1 R Leach, Jim ...... http://www.house.gov/leach/welcome.html

IL 1 D Rush, Bobby ..... http://www.house.gov/rush/welcome.html
IL 15 R Ewing, Thomas ... http://www.house.gov/ewing/welcome.html
IL 20 D Durbin, Richard .. http://www.house.gov/durbin/welcome.html

IN 3 D Roemer, Tim .... http://www.house.gov/roemer/welcome.html
IN 4 R Souder, Mark .... http://www.house.gov/souder/welcome.html
IN 8 R Hostettler, John .... johnhost@hr.house.gov
http://www.house.gov/hostettler/welcome.html
IN 9 D Hamilton, Lee .. http://www.house.gov/hamilton/welcome.html

KS 2 R Brownback, Sam
.... http://www.house.gov/brownback/welcome.html
KS 4 R Tiahrt, Todd ..... http://www.house.gov/tiahrt/welcome.html

LA 5 R McCrery, Jim ... http://www.house.gov/mccrery/welcome.html

MA 4 D Frank, Barney .... http://www.house.gov/frank/welcome.html
MA 9 D Moakley, Joe ... http://www.house.gov/moakley/welcome.html

MD 2 R Ehrlich, Robert
..... http://lattanze.loyola.edu:80/research/Ehrlich/index.html
MD 3 D Cardin, Benjamin .. http://www.house.gov/cardin/welcome.html
MD 4 D Wynn, Albert ..... http://www.house.gov/wynn/welcome.html
+MD 7 D Mfume, Kweisi ... http://www.house.gov/mfume/welcome.html

MI 2 R Hoekstra, Peter .. http://www.house.gov/hoekstra/welcome.html
MI 3 R Ehlers, Vern .... http://www.house.gov/ehlers/welcome.html
MI 7 R Smith, Nick ... http://www.house.gov/nicksmith/welcome.html
MI 8 R Chrysler, Dick .. http://www.house.gov/chrysler/welcome.html
MI 14 D Conyers, John ... http://www.house.gov/conyers/welcome.html

MN 4 D Vento, Bruce .... http://www.house.gov/vento/welcome.html
MN 5 D Sabo, Martin ..... http://www.house.gov/sabo/welcome.html
MN 6 D Luther, Bill .... http://www.house.gov/luther/welcome.html
MN 7 D Peterson, Collin
.... http://www.house.gov/collinpeterson/welcome.html
MN 8 D Oberstar, James . http://www.house.gov/oberstar/welcome.html

MO 2 R Talent, James .... http://www.house.gov/talent/welcome.html
MO 8 R Emerson, Bill ... http://www.house.gov/emerson/welcome.html

MS 2 D Thompson, Bennie
.... http://www.house.gov/thompson/welcome.html

NC 5 R Burr, Richard ...... http://www.house.gov/burr/welcome.html

NE 2 R Christensen, Jon
.... http://www.house.gov/christensen/welcome.html

NH 1 R Zeliff, William .... http://www.house.gov/zeliff/welcome.html

NJ 7 R Franks, Bob .. http://www.house.gov/bobfranks/welcome.html
NJ 13 D Menendez, Bob http://www.house.gov/menendez/welcome.html

NY 1 R Forbes, Michael ... http://www.house.gov/forbes/welcome.html
NY 2 R Lazio, Rick .... http://www.house.gov/lazio/welcome.html
NY 8 D Nadler, Jerrold .... http://www.house.gov/nadler/welcome.html

NY 16 D Serrano, Jose .... http://www.house.gov/serrano/welcome.html
NY 21 D McNulty, Michael http://www.house.gov/mcnulty/welcome.html
NY 23 R Boehlert, Sherwood
.... http://www.house.gov/boehlert/welcome.html

OH 2 R Portman, Rob ... http://www.house.gov/portman/welcome.html
OH 4 R Oxley, Michael .... http://www.house.gov/oxley/welcome.html
OH 7 R Hobson, David ... http://www.house.gov/hobson/welcome.html
OH 10 R Hoke, Martin ..... http://www.house.gov/hoke/welcome.html

OK 1 R Largent, Steve .... http://www.house.gov/largent/welcome.html

OR 4 D DeFazio, Pete http://darkwing.uoregon.edu/~pdefazio/index.html

PA 12 D Murtha, John .... http://www.house.gov/murtha/welcome.html
PA 15 D McHale, Paul .... http://www.house.gov/mchale/welcome.html
PA 16 R Walker, Robert ... http://www.house.gov/walker/welcome.html

RI 1 D Kennedy, Patrick
.... http://www.house.gov/patrickkennedy/welcome.html

SC 5 D Spratt, John ..... http://www.house.gov/spratt/welcome.html

TN 3 R Wamp, Zach .... http://www.house.gov/wamp/welcome.html
TN 4 R Hilleary, Van ... http://www.house.gov/hilleary/welcome.html
TN 5 D Clement, Bob ... http://www.house.gov/clement/welcome.html
TN 9 D Ford, Harold ...... http://www.house.gov/ford/welcome.html

TX 3 R Johnson, Same
.... http://www.house.gov/samjohnson/welcome.html
TX 6 R Barton, Joe .... http://www.house.gov/barton/welcome.html
TX 21 R Smith, Lamar . http://www.house.gov/lamarsmith/welcome.html
TX 22 R Delay, Tom .... http://www.house.gov/delay/welcome.html
TX 25 D Bentsen, Ken ... http://www.house.gov/bentsen/welcome.html
TX 26 R Armey, Dick ..... http://www.house.gov/armey/welcome.html
TX 29 D Green, Gene ...... http://www.house.gov/green/welcome.html

VA 1 R Bateman, Herbert . http://www.house.gov/bateman/welcome.html
VA 9 R Boucher, Rick ... http://www.house.gov/boucher/welcome.html

WA 1 R White, Rick .... http://www.house.gov/white/welcome.html
WA 3 R Smith, Linda .. http://www.house.gov/lindasmith/welcome.html
WA 9 R Tate, Randy .... http://home.worldweb.net/tate

WI 1 R Neumann, Mark http://www.house.gov/neumann/welcome.html
WI 3 R Gunderson, Steve
.... http://www.house.gov/gunderson/welcome.html
WI 5 D Barrett, Tom ..... http://www.house.gov/barrett/welcome.html
WI 8 R Roth, Toby .... http://www.house.gov/roth/welcome.html
WI 9 R Sensenbrenner, James
.... http://www.house.gov/sensenbrenner/welcome.html

WV 2 D Wise, Bob .... http://www.house.gov/wise/welcome.html
+Resigned 2-18-96; web site still active

House Web Site .... http://www.house.gov/

House Banking/Subcommittee on Domestic and Intl Monetary
http://www.house.gov/castle/banking/welcome.html

House Economics and Educational Opportunity
http://www.house.gov/eeo/welcome.html

House Government Reform and Oversight
http://www.house.gov/reform/welcome.html

House Judiciary .... http://www.house.gov/judiciary/welcome.html

House Resources .... http://www.house.gov/resources/welcome.html

House Science .... http://www.house.gov/science/welcome.html

House Science (Democrats)
http://www.house.gov/science_democrats/welcome.html

House Standards of Official Conduct
http://www.house.gov/ethics/ethics_memos.html

Government Databases and Internet Access

House Transportation . . . . . . http://www.house.gov/transportation/welcome.html

House Democratic Caucus . . . http://www.house.gov/demcaucus/welcome.html

House Democratic Leadership . . . . http://www.house.gov/democrats/

House Leadership . . . . http://www.house.gov/orgs_pub_hse_ldr_www.html

House Majority Whip . . . . . http://www.house.gov/majoritywhip/welcome.html

House Republican Conference . . . . . http://www.house.gov/gop/conference.html

House Republican Policy Committee:
        http://www.house.gov/republican-policy/policyhome.htm

* Joint Committee Web Sites

Joint Committee on Printing . . . . http/www.access.gpo.gov/demo/jcp.html

Joint Economic Committee http://www.town.hall.org:80/places/jec
        http://www.senate.gov/~jec/
        http://www.house.gov/jec/welcome.html
(House Republicans on JEC)

Congressional Black Caucus . . . . http://drum.ncsc.org/~carter/CBC.html

State Governments on the Internet

Alabama

AlaWeb Home Page (State of Alabama)
Website: http://alaweb.asc.edu

Find out what's new in Alabama. Read information about the state government, the state capitol, tours, education programs, media, and more. You can even look at a detailed map of the state, browse the state's business directory, or get in touch with state officials through E-mail.

Alaska

State of Alaska's Home Page
Website: http://www.state.ak.us/

Connect to Alaska state department sites, including the Department of Labor, Department of Public Safety, even the University of Alaska. At this site, you can also explore the FAQ section, find out what's new in the state, and read the Top 10 List!

Arizona

State of Arizona Services via World Wide Web
Website: http://www.state.az.us/

Connect to the executive, legislative, and judicial branches of Arizona government, including its congressional delegation. Other interesting sites also are available.

Arkansas

Government Relations of Arkansas
Website: http://www.uark.edu/~govinfo

Click on the directory of state legislators, the legislative and judicial branches, or visit the executive offices to find out how to contact them and visit their web sites.

California

California Home Page
Website: http://www.ca.gov/
E-mail: webmaster@teale.ca.gov

Explore the Golden State: read about it's history, economy, culture, and natural resources - or simply find out the best places to take a vacation in California. There is also a section on doing business in California, as well as information on living, learning, and working there. Read the welcome message from the Governor and connect to other state agencies on the Net.

Colorado

State of Colorado Home Page
Website: http://www.state.co.us/

Thinking about taking a vacation in the Rockies? There's no better place to get the information you need than at this site. Explore Colorado government sites, learn about the different communities around the state, or find out about educational opportunities. If you are interested in doing business in Colorado, there is a lot of excellent information here, too.

Connecticut

State of Connecticut Home Page
Website: http://www.ctstateu.edu/state.html

Read about Connecticut's recreational features, including environmental and natural resources. Also, this site includes information on economic, educational, health and social services, government and law, transportation, and even state libraries. It is an excellent source for both residents and visitors.

Delaware

State of Delaware
Website: http://www.state.de.us/

Visit the Peach State and find out what's new. A huge fact file is available for people who are interested in the state's past, present, and future. Those who want to visit should first stop by the tourist section. Residents might be interested in investigating the economic development section, and students can find out about higher education opportunities in the state.

Florida

Florida Department of State
Website: http://www.dos.state.fl.us/

The most comprehensive directory of government Internet sites in the Sunshine State is right here. You might also want to read 'elections online' -- a progressive site of comprehensive information about state and federal elections. You can also browse through Florida Facts and History or connect to the DOS Divisions for more information.

Georgia

Georgia Online
Website: http://www.state.ga.us/

While it takes a long time to load, the Georgia state home page offers a wealth of information in return. From here you can explore the Governor's web page, county, city, and region web servers, Department of Human Resources web pages, the Georgia Senate and House of Representatives, the Georgia Statewide Academic and Medical System, the Department of Archives and History, and much more. You can even review the state's weather, sports (think Olympics!), and a number of other interesting Web servers.

Hawaii

Hawaii Tourism Office
Website: http://www.hawaii.gov/tourism

Hawaii has miles of beaches, volcanoes and flowers galore. Who wouldn't want to visit? Take the smart approach to planning your trip at this site. The library has the latest research reports on the islands, or stop by the Hawaii Visitors Bureau for useful tourism information.

Idaho

State of Idaho Home Page
Website: http://www.state.id.us/

Business information is available on a calendar of events, cities, counties, and education. A government agency directory search is available for congressional delegation, executive branch, judicial branch, legislative department, phone list, and state government agencies. Internet Information Sources include organizations and special interest groups, recreation and tourism, and weather.

Illinois

State of Illinois
Website: http://www.state.il.us/

Connect to the state agencies, educational institutions, libraries and museums in Illinois. Also get legislative information, some data and advice about tourism, or simply search the site for any specific information you are looking for. You can even visit the State Police.

Indiana

Access Indiana Web Index
Website: http://www.state.in.us/index/index.html

This is a comprehensive index of most government Internet resources in Indiana. Links are available to a number of sites, including the state archives. Career placement, education, county government, crime, elections, employment, and business information is available, as is a state history. This site is updated every week.

Iowa

State of Iowa Home Page
Website: http://www.state.ia.us/

Visit Iowa. Get information on doing business, going to school, or simply taking a vacation in the state. This site also offers extensive information job opportunities, government resources, and 'Iowa Links' -- a database of non-governmental Internet resources in Iowa and elsewhere. Please sign the guest book on your way out.

Kansas

Information Network of Kansas Home Page
Website: http://www.ink.org/

Here is information on state government, education, banking, insurance, and business and commerce issues, as well as other facets of life in Kansas. Other interesting sections include a Children's Network — with links to other neat sites for kids -- and the Libraries site, with links to Kansas state libraries. Those who are interested can subscribe to the Information Network of Kansas (INK) and get free technical support and communications software.

Be patient. If any phone number is incorrect, call (area code) 555-1212 and request the new listing.

1235

Government Databases and Internet Access

Kentucky

Commonwealth of Kentucky Web Server
Website: http://www.state.ky.us/

Take a virtual tour of Kentucky, link to other Kentucky web servers, and try your luck at finding information that you need at the Commonwealth server.

Louisiana

Info Louisiana
Website: http://www.state.la.us/

Louisiana will send you a detailed state map and visitors' guide for absolutely nothing. Take advantage of this deal. This site also offers extensive information on Louisiana legislature, education, and state department sites, even job listings!

Maine

Maine State Government WWW Home Page
Website: http://www.state.me.us/

This site offers information on various state and quasi-state agencies, Maine's cities and towns, or the state's weather, its Yellow Pages -- even the Maine State Lottery! You can also find links to other states' web servers, as well as links to federal government and U.S. Congress sites.

Maryland

State of Maryland Home Page
Website: http://www.maryland.umd.edu/

Think crabs. Think Orioles. Would you like to find out what events are planned in Maryland this month? Check the *Calendar of Events*. Don't have time to visit the state? Take a virtual tour of museums and historic places, or simply take a peak at Maryland towns and cities at this site. If you want to do business in the state, or want to check out library resources or education opportunities, there is also information here.

Massachusetts

Commonwealth of Massachusetts – MAGNet
Website: http://www.state.ma.us/

This well-organized site is both quick and efficient. *Massachusetts Government* is an hierarchical map of the Commonwealth, showing branches of government, Constitutional office,s and the departments under them. The reference shelf will help you find online publications from the state. Internet Connections lists other useful Internet resources, if you can't find the information you need here.

Minnesota

State of Minnesota
Website: http://www.state.mn.us/

Look through the Minnesota Accommodations, Events, and Arts and Sport Calendar Interactive Database at this site. Also available are links to state government offices, *All About Minnesota*, several state directories, and *Tools of Democracy*, a site on Minnesota's democratic heritage.

Mississippi

State of Mississippi
Website: http://www.state.ms.us/

This page offers quite a few links in a very succinct format. Just point and click, and you can visit every state government department that has a home page. Most are of interest mainly to residents, but the education and library pages can be useful for anyone.

Missouri

Missouri State Government Home Page
Website: http://www.state.mo.us/

Visit the Missouri Executive Branch and Executive Department sites. Links are also available to the Legislative and Judicial branches. You can also browse the Missouri State Telephone Directory and review any recent job openings. Those who are interested can look through Show-Me Missouri Cyberspace Tradeshow, which features a wealth of information on Missouri communities, products, and industrial properties.

Montana

Montana Online
Website: http://www.mt.gov/

Everything you wanted to know about traveling in Montana is right at your fingertips: you can download information on camping and lodging, events and attractions, recreation and adventure, and other travelers' services. Online information and data is also available on government, education, employment, and weather conditions in the state.

Michigan

Michigan State and Local Government on the Web
Website: http://www.lib.umich.edu/libhome/Documents.center/mich.html

This is one of the most comprehensive state directories on the Internet. From here you can connect to state and local government sites. Obtain census data, read about politics, statistics, and weather, find out some details about Michigan's budget, or browse through local laws. Too much information is available to list.

Nebraska

Nebraska Online Home Page
Website: http://www.nol.org/

This site has links to the following Nebraska networks: Bank Net, Legal Net, Insurance Net, Library Net, State Net, Community Net, Internet Services, and Customer Utilities.

New Hampshire

WEBSTER: The New Hampshire State Government Online Information Center
Website: http://www.state.nh.us/

There are several ways to find information about New Hampshire at this site. You can use the New Hampshire State Government Locator to view a hierarchical listing of all the branches of the government, or click on *State Information* to look for state information sorted by subject. The State Tourist Information section provides some important information for visitors and vacationers. Local Government Internet Resources and Internet Resources provide links to other relevant sites, and there is a page for anyone interested in education in New Hampshire.

New Jersey

State of New Jersey
Website: http://www.state.nj.us/

Visitors to this site can quickly and easily find information on business, consumer affairs, colleges and universities, employment opportunities, weather, and even lottery results in New Jersey. Residents might be especially interested in the links to the judicial, legislative, and executive branches of the government.

New Mexico

State of New Mexico Services via World Wide Web
Website: http://www.state.nm.us/

This web server carries important information on tourism, the state's labor market, its libraries and museums, training opportunities, and educational opportunities in New Mexico. You can also download the state's legislative session and legislative calendars for 1996, and contact the Office of the Governor, elected officials in Washington, and state legislators. A list of state agency phone numbers is also available.

North Carolina

State of North Carolina
Website: http://www.sips.state.nc.us/

Links are available to all state government sites in North Carolina. Connect to the Department of Agriculture, Department of Travel and Tourism, Department of Cultural Resources, State Library, Department of Labor, State Board of Elections, and more. The education information services include the NC community college system, UNC, and K-12 schools. Links are available to other government resources in case you don't find the information you need.

North Dakota

State of North Dakota
Website: http://www.state.nd.us/

Connect to the North Dakota state government, K12 schools, and business sites. Those who are interested in regional information can access the sensitive North Dakota Map for information servers in specific areas.

Ohio

State of Ohio Front Page
Website: http://www.ohio.gov/

Links are available to the executive branch of the Ohio government and other state agencies, including the agriculture, development, and education councils. You can also connect to the judicial and legislative branches. Information is available about employment, transportation, public utilities, libraries, and other topics of interest.

Oklahoma

Oklahoma Home Page
Website: http://www.oklaosf.state.ok.us/

Learn about current events in Oklahoma or contact various government web servers in Oklahoma. Resources include the Oklahoma State Senate, House of Representatives, Secretary of State, Tax Commission, and state agencies. Potential

Be patient. If any phone number is incorrect, call (area code) 555-1212 and request the new listing.

visitors might be interested in the State Arts Council, Oklahoma Tourism and Recreation, or the Oklahoma Horse Racing Commission. Useful information is also available on transportation, public safety, science and technology, and even the state's weather.

Oregon

Oregon On-Line
Website: http://www.state.or.us/

This site is divided into four sections: Government, Community, Business, and Education resources. The government section includes links to various departments, such as Oregon State Archives, Oregon Department of Fish and Wildlife, Department of Human Resources, Secretary of State, Arts Commission, Justice Services Division, even the Oregon Lottery. You can also connect to web sites of all elected officials, and search for their E-mail addresses. The Communities section includes links to almost every local Internet resource available, while the Commerce and Education sections offer valuable information to those who are looking to do business or study in Oregon.

Pennsylvania

Commonwealth of Pennsylvania
Website: http://www.state.pa.us/

This site should interest both locals and anyone considering traveling to Pennsylvania for any reason. Links are available to various government servers, including both state and local resources. The visitor's guide should, once it has been completed, contain important information for travelers. Information is also available on economic development, education, and technological progress in the state.

Rhode Island

Rhode Island
Website: http://www.ids.net./ri/ri.htm

Find the information you need about the Ocean State's government, as well as its business, entertainment, tourism, weather, education, local media, education, and recreation opportunities. You can even review the club scene.

South Carolina

State of South Carolina Public Information Center
Website: http://www.state.sc.us/

This site has information available on the history of the Palmetto State, as well as links to government, education, and commerce and tourism resources. You can also connect to other state web servers and federal sites.

South Dakota

State of South Dakota
Website: http://www.state.sd.us/

This site offers you a chance to learn about South Dakota and contact the various web servers in the state. Read about the state's signs and symbols, download the Department of Tourism's 1996 Calendar of Events, sign the on-line guest book, and even put yourself on a South Dakota mailing list. Job and labor information also is available, as are the offices of all state officials and departments.

Tennessee

Tennessee's WWW Home Page
Website: http://www.state.tn.us/

Visit the Volunteer State, and gain easy access to the following information sources: Department of Employment Security, Tennessee Supreme Court, Department of Education, Department of Financial Institutions, Office for Information Resources / Telecommunications, State of Tennessee Information Systems Plan, and Secretary of State. You can also download the official 1995 vacation guide to Tennessee, or get the latest weather update. Please keep in mind that the server was under construction at the time of this review.

Texas

State of Texas WWW Server
Website: http://www.texas.gov/

Information is available for visitor and tourist, job seekers, people looking to do business in Texas and anyone interested in playing the state lottery. Links are also available to government sources, including councils of government servers and county and city information listings. Other sites of interest listed here include Texas-ONE, with services for businesses, and interactive maps of Texas.

Utah

State of Utah WWW Home Page
Website: http://www.state.ut.us/

Information available at this site includes: Proposed Department of Workforce Services, Upcoming State Conferences, SmartUTAH, Governor's State-of-the-State Address, 1996 Utah Legislative Bills and Legislative Information, Ski Utah - The Greatest Snow on Earth Ski Conditions, Utah Job Listings, Digital Signatures Information, and Utah's Complete Alphabetical Agency Listing. You can also link to other sites for information on the state legislature, courts, elections, state agencies, public and higher education, cities and towns, and counties.

Vermont

State of Vermont Home Page
Website: http://www.cit.state.vt.us/

Here you'll find links to various government departments and agencies, including Vermont's Department of Agriculture, Food and Markets, Department of Education, Department of Libraries gopher, Department of Public Services, Department of Travel and Tourism, and others. Also connect to Vermont education resources to find links to colleges, universities, and K12 schools. Resources for travelers include *Vermont Life* Magazine, and a Vermont calendar of events.

Virginia

Virginia
Website: http://www.state.va.us/

This site has information for residents and tourists alike. Visitor's Guide lets you explore Virginia's events and festivals, its history, natural areas, recreational activities, restaurants, and more. Government links will connect you to both state and local government, including legislative information, information technology resources, state government Internet addresses – plus federal offices. Links are also available to educational and community sites.

Washington

Olympus – A Washington State Public Information Server
Website: http://olympus.dis.wa.gov/

Here is where to discover information on doing business with and in Washington state. You can also link to *Home Page Washington*, the state government server. Home Page Washington (http://www.wa.gov/) offers links to Washington State Legislature and Courts, the Governor's office, and a state government index. Information is also available on business and commerce, education, employment, environment and natural resources, health and social services, recreation, technology, tourism, and transportation in Washington. You can even read a short document on Washington's history.

West Virginia

West Virginia Travel and Recreation
Website: http://wvweb.com/www/travel_recreation/Tourism_Home_Page2.html

Get information on family resorts, mountain biking, lodging, skiing, special events, and state parks in West Virginia. Here you'll also find information on local weather and special events in the state.

Wisconsin

State of Wisconsin Web Page
Website: http://badger.state.wi.us/

Here you'll find links to Wisconsin state agencies, departments and its legislature, as well as city, county and local government web sites. There is a special site dedicated to tourism, and anyone interested in the state's history will find it all here. This site was under construction, so check it for more information!

Wyoming

Wyoming
Website: http://www.state.wy.us/state/welcome.html

Anyone interested in Wyoming should check here. Information is available on business and industry, tourism, online services, state government, and educational opportunities. You can visit the Governor's virtual office, sign the virtual guest book, and even take a virtual tour of the state! Tourists will this a great place to visit before they pack their bags.

Be patient. If any phone number is incorrect, call (area code) 555-1212 and request the new listing.

1237

More Info-Power Hits

Every chapter is filled with all sorts of free publications, posters, and gift ideas. Some special souvenirs and freebies are grouped here along with an assortment of other odds and ends ranging from pet advice to beekeeping.

* 50th Wedding Anniversary Card Signed by the President

Presidential Correspondence
White House
1600 Pennsylvania Ave., NW
Washington, DC 20500   202-456-1111

50th wedding anniversary cards and 80th birthday cards signed by the President are available to the public. The requests must be written and should be received at least one month before the event. Photographs are also available through a written request. Contact the office above, 9 a.m.-5 p.m.

* 80th Birthday Card Signed by the President

Presidential Correspondence
White House
1600 Pennsylvania Ave., NW
Washington, DC 20500   202-456-1111

Birthday cards signed by the President are available to the public. The requests must be written and should be received at least one month before the event. Photographs are also available through a written request. Contact the office above, 9 a.m.-5 p.m.

* Aerial Photographs

Customer User Services
Earth Resources Observation System Data Center (EROS)
U.S. Geological Survey
Sioux Falls, SD 57198   605-594-6511

Aerial photographs are available from this center for most geographical regions of the country. Prices range from $6 to $65, depending on whether they are black and white or color photographs. Contact this office for ordering information.

* American Flags

U.S. Flag Office
Room HT-16
Washington, DC 20515   202-224-3121

You can arrange to purchase flags that have been flown over the Capitol by getting in touch with your U.S. Senator or Representative. A certificate signed by the Architect of the Capitol accompanies each flag. Flags are available for purchase in sizes of 3 x 5 or 5 x 8 in fabrics of cotton and nylon.

* Animal Poison Control Hotline

National Animal Poison Control Center
        900-680-0000 $2.95 per minute or
        800-548-2423 $30 per case, charge on a major credit card

The National Animal Poison Control Center, at The University of Illinois, provides 24-hour consultation in diagnosis and treatment of suspected or actual animal poisonings or chemical contaminations. Its emergency response team will rapidly investigate such incidents in North America, and perform laboratory analysis of feeds, animal specimens, and environmental materials for toxicants and chemical contaminants.

* Bees and Beekeeping

Honeybee Breeding Genetics
and Physiology Research Lab
U.S. Department of Agriculture
ARS, 1157 Ben Hur Rd.
Baton Rouge, LA 70820   504-767-9280

Scientists are currently at work trying to protect the beekeeping industry and the public from the advent of the Africanized bees that are due to arrive in mid 1990.

Research projects include use of a toxic substance that will attract bees and kill them, a repellent that will keep these aggressive bees from stinging, and ways of protecting commercial queen bee farms from invasion of Africanized bees.

* Bugs and Other Household Pests

Biological Assessment
U.S. Department of Agriculture
4700 River Rd., Unit 133
Riverdale, MD 20737   301-734-8896
OR local County Cooperative Extension Service

Free technical advice is available to aid in controlling cockroaches and other critters. To identify an insect, the local county cooperative extension service often will ask you to send a representative sample in order to suggest the best way to rid your home of this menace.

* Cheese Making

Dairy Laboratory
U.S. Department of Agriculture, AR-NER
Eastern Regional Center
600 East Mermaid Lane
Wyndmoor, PA 19038   215-233-6400

The Dairy Lab has accumulated information on the process of making cheese at home and can share their expertise with you.

* Christmas Trees

Wildlife, Fisheries, Rangeland, Forestry Group
Bureau of Land Management (BLM)
U.S. Department of the Interior
1849 C St., NW
Washington, DC 20240   202-451-7770

The BLM officials issue permits to cut Christmas trees for a nominal fee on Bureau of Land Management-administered lands in the 11 Western states and Alaska. Free-use permits are available from the Bureau to non-profit organizations for timber and trees to be used exclusively by that organization. This excludes the resale of any free timber or trees by those organizations.

* Comet Halley Atlas

Superintendent of Documents
Government Printing Office
Washington, DC 20402   202-512-1800

Census statistics publications are listed in this bibliography. One may send for the Railroad Maps of North America, featuring 5,000 maps and surveys. Weather and political atlases are listed, as well as an atlas to the Comet Halley. Free.

* Dial the Exact Time: The Master Clock

Atomic Clock, Naval Observatory
3450 Massachusetts Ave.   202-653-1507 (TIME)
Washington, DC 20392-5100   202-653-1800

The Observatory's Master Clock is the source for all standard time in the United States. For the correct time, call the number above, or dial 1-900-410-TIME if you are outside of the DC area.

* First Lady's Daily Schedule

Office of the First Lady
Old Executive Office Bldg., Room 100
Washington, DC 20500   202-456-2960

For more information write or call to the office above.

* Free County Educational Programs

Executive Officer
State Research Education and Cooperative Extension Service
U.S. Department of Agriculture (USDA)
Room 335, Administration Building
Washington, DC 20250   202-720-3377

The U.S. Department of Agriculture (USDA) operates an extension program in 3,165 counties located in all of the 50 states and the U.S. territories. Federal, state, and local governments share in financing and conducting cooperative extension educational programs to help farmers, processors, handlers, farm families, communities, and consumers apply the results of food and agricultural research. The Extension Service helps people develop marketable job skills, make informed career decisions, and expand available opportunities. It offers guidance to families such as ways to manage finances and make sound financial decisions; confront and deal with such problems as alcohol and drug abuse, teenage pregnancy, and unemployment; and develop strategies for retirement. The extension offers up-to-date information about the relationship of dietary practices to lifestyle factors. Another major area is revitalizing rural America: programs emphasize how to increase competitiveness and efficiency of rural programs, explore methods to diversify local economies and attract new business, adjust to impact of change, develop ways to finance and deliver services, and train leaders to make sound policy decisions for rural communities. It works with consumers, producers and local government to learn more about the importance of high-quality ground water and the conservation of water resources. Emphasis is also put on the effects of agricultural chemicals and contaminants on water quality. The extension is helping expand youth outreach resources to meet the needs of youth, develop programs for the most susceptible youth populations, provide leadership and job skills, and increase training of professionals and volunteers to work in communities to prevent and treat problems.

* Free Firewood

Contact your nearest forest ranger \

Where supply exceeds demand, free firewood is available from public lands. Just contact your nearest forest ranger.

* Free Manure

College Park Holsteins
University of Maryland Dairy Barns
College Park, MD 20742   301-405-1298

Many Extension Service offices offer free manure for gardeners. In the Washington, DC, area, manure is available by the barrel or truckload at the above address.

* Geologic Publications: Caves to Volcanoes

U.S. Geological Survey
Branch of Publications
Box 25286
Denver, CO 80225   303-202-4700

This is a listing of some of the general interest publications available through the U.S. Geological Survey. They are free unless otherwise indicated.

The Antarctic and its Geology
Eruptions of Hawaiian Volcanoes: Past, Present and Future ($4)
Eruptions of Mount St. Helens: Past, Present, and Future ($2.75)
Geologic History of Cape Cod, Massachusetts
Geology of Caves
The Great Ice Age
The Interior of the Earth
Landforms of the United States
Marine Geology: Research Beneath the Sea
Our Changing Continent
Permafrost
The San Andreas Fault
Volcanoes
Geysers
Gold
Natural Steam for Power
Glaciers: A Water Resource
Elevations and Distances in the United States
Geologic Maps: Portraits of the Earth
Building Stones of Our Nation's Capital
Steps to the Moon
Tree Rings: Timekeepers of the Past
The Naming (and Misnaming) of America

* Greeting Cards and Gift Items

Madison Gift Shop
Library of Congress
Washington, DC 20540   202-707-0204

Many gift items, including greeting cards, notepaper, bookplates, posters, recordings, T-shirts, are available from the gift shop, which is open 9 a.m. to 5 p.m., Monday through Saturday.

* Medals of the United States Mint

Customer Service Center
U.S. Mint
U.S. Department of the Treasury
10001 Aerospace Rd.
Lanham, MD 20706   202-283-2646

You can purchase many different types of medals that honor famous people from the U.S. Mint. Medals of all of the U.S. Presidents are available in 3" and 1 5/16" sizes. The Secretaries of the Treasury are featured in a 3" medal series, as well as the Directors of the Mint. Various medals has been issued that commemorate veterans, and famous army and navy heroes. Others include aviation heroes, leaders and statesmen, those who contributed to the arts and culture, doctors, and Chief Justices of the Supreme Court. Checks or Visa and MasterCard payments are accepted.

* Moon and Planets Maps

Distribution Branch
U.S. Geological Survey (USGS)
Building 810
Denver Federal Center
Box 25046
Denver, CO 80225-0046   800-USA-MAPS

The USGS established an astrogeology program on behalf of NASA to support lunar and planetary exploration. Many maps of the Moon, Mars, Venus, and Mercury are available.

* National Atlas Updates

Distribution Branch
U.S. Geological Survey (USGS)
Building 810
Denver Federal Center, Box 25046
Denver, CO 80225-0046   800-USA-MAPS

The *National Atlas of the United States* (1970) contains 765 maps and charts on 335 pages. Out of print and no longer for sale, it can still be found in most libraries. However, separate sheets of selected reference maps and thematic maps from the *Atlas* are available from the USGS. Some of the sheets have been updated. Some updated thematic maps include potential natural vegetation (1985), monthly average temperature (1986) monthly minimum temperature (1986), monthly maximum temperature (1986), networks of ecological research (1983), and territorial growth (1986).

* Nation's Capitol: History, Books, Tapes

U.S. Capitol Historical Society
200 Maryland Ave., NE
Washington, DC 20002   202-543-8919

A non-profit educational organization chartered by Congress, this historical society puts out many publications, including *We the People* and *Washington Past and Present*. The society also sells VHS video cassette tapes, such as *City Out of Wilderness*, which tells the story of Washington, DC, and the Capitol. It sells for $35, which including postage, or $30 in the Capitol. *Place of Resounding Deeds*, a thirty minute video tour of the Capitol, sells for $29.95 with postage, or $25 in the Capitol. The society has a sales desk in the rotunda with miscellaneous items such as postcards and various books for the public. Symposiums are held annually and are published for the public. Speakers from the Society are available provided advance notice is given.

* Pet Food and Medications

Center for Veterinary Medicine
Division of Animal Feeds
Food and Drug Administration (FDA)
7500 Standish Place, Room 431, HFV 220
Rockville, MD 20855   301-594-1623

The Food and Drug Administration is responsible for ensuring that animal drugs, devices, and medicated feeds are safe and effective and that food from treated animals is safe to eat. They also make sure the animal and pet foods are safe and properly labeled. Flyers and memos are available for the general public and professionals regarding veterinary medicine. The *FDA Veterinarian*, a bimonthly publication, outlines the latest developments in the field of veterinary medicine, and is available for $5 per year from Superintendent of Documents, Government Printing Office, Washington, DC 20402, 202-512-1800.

* Pet Problems and Sickness

Executive Officer
U.S. Department of Agriculture
SEA, Room 33A
Administration Building
Washington, DC 20250   202-720-3377
OR local County Cooperative Extension Service

Free technical advice is available to aid in diagnosing sick pets. Your local county cooperative extension service often will analyze your pet's stool and offer guidance over the telephone.

* Pets and Animal Health

Public Information, LPAS
Animal and Plant Health Inspection Service (APHIS)
U.S. Department of Agriculture
4700 River Rd.
Riverdale, MD 20737   301-734-5386

Pets--They Need Proper Care to Travel by Air is one of the publications available free. Many other fact sheets are published by the Animal and Plant Health Inspection Service (APHIS) such as housing and caging, training guides and manuals for animal care personnel.

* Presidential Homes and Washington Buildings

Bureau of Engraving and Printing
U.S. Department of the Treasury
14th and C Sts., SW, Room 522A
Washington, DC 20228   202-874-3714/3715

Vignettes of famous Washington buildings and presidential homes are available in the 6" x 8" size for $4. The Great Seal of the U.S. and the Department of Treasury Seal, lithographed in color, are also available.

* Presidential Portraits

Bureau of Engraving and Printing
U.S. Department of the Treasury
14th and C Sts., SW, Room 522A
Washington, DC 20228   202-874-3714/3715

Small presidential portraits (6" x 8") and larger presidential portraits (9" x 12") are available from the Bureau of Engraving and Printing for $4 and $4.50, respectively. Prices are slightly less at the facility store. There are also 6" x 8" portraits of the Chief Justices of the Supreme Court, available for $4.

* President's Schedule

Office of Presidential Scheduling
The White House
Old Executive Office Bldg., Room 185 1/2
Washington, DC 20500   202-456-7560

Contact this office for information on the President's daily schedule, or call 202-456-2343 to hear a recorded message.

* Public Debt Donations

Office of the Commissioner
Bureau of the Public Debt
U.S. Department of the Treasury
999 E St., NW, Room 553
Washington, DC 20239   202-219-3300

Since the U.S. Government maintains a public debt of more than $1.9 trillion dollars, and is currently paying $176 billion in interest to pay off this debt, they are asking for donations from the general public to pay off the debt. The Treasury has an account into which money received as gifts is deposited. The money is used to pay at maturity, or to redeem or buy before maturity, an obligation of the Government included in the public debt. Donations can be sent to: Bureau of the Public Debt, Department G, Washington, DC 20239-0601.

* Rock Collecting

U.S. Geological Survey
Branch of Publications, Box 25286
Denver, CO 80225   303-202-4700

Collecting Rocks is a free booklet available from the USGS for those youngsters and adults interested in pursuing this hobby and learning more about geology.

* Sick Plants

Executive Officer
U.S. Department of Agriculture
SEA, Room 33A Administration Building
Washington, DC 20250   202-720-3377
OR local County Cooperative Extension Service

Free technical advice is available to aid in diagnosing and curing diseases of indoor and outdoor plants by contacting your local county cooperative extension service.

* Space Photographs

Customer Services
Earth Resources Observation System Data Center (EROS)
U.S. Geological Survey
Sioux Falls, SD 57198   605-594-6511

The EROS Data Center maintains photographs from many of the space missions, including those of the space shuttle, Apollo, and Gemini. Contact the center directly for information concerning specific topics.

* Stamp Collecting

Philatelic Sales Division
P.O. Box 449995
Kansas City, MO 64144-9995   816-455-0970

Anyone interested in philately, the collecting and study of stamps, can receive a free booklet called *Introduction to Stamp Collecting*.

* Tell the President!

The President of the United States
White House
1600 Pennsylvania Avenue, NW
Washington, DC 20500   202-456-7639

White House operators will take messages for the president. You can also write to the Commander-in-Chief and share your views about current issues.

* Wild Burros and Horses for Adoption

Office of Public Information
Bureau of Land Management
U.S. Department of the Interior
18th and C Sts., NW
Washington, DC 20240-0001   202-452-5125

Wild burros and horses that roam on public lands are put up for adoption after a short time to decrease their numbers. If you are interested in adopting one of these animals, you should contact a local BLM adoption center, and there is a fee of $125 per horse and $75 per burro. You must also transport the animals home and provide for their future upkeep. The booklet, *So You'd Like to Adopt A Wild Horse Or Burro?*, answers many of the questions you might have when handling this responsibility. Contact the office above for the adoption centers near you.

* Wine: Home Production

National Agriculture Library
U.S. Department of Agriculture
Beltsville, MD 20705   301-504-5248

The U.S. Department of Agriculture has accumulated documentation and can share information to assist you in making wine at home.

* Woodsy Owl: Toys for Tots

U.S. Department of Agriculture
Forest Service, P.O. Box 96090
Washington, DC 20090-6090   202-205-1785

To increase children's awareness of our delicate environment, the Forest Service's Woodsy Owl campaign has a variety of materials available, including coloring sheets, detective sheets, song sheets, patches, and stickers.

The Government Works for Kids, Too

The government offers a bonanza of information and services specifically designed for kids, and those who love kids. When we first started to do research into what was offered, it was a bit like opening Pandora's box. We discovered an unexpected bounty of material. To our surprise, there are publications, programs, slides, games, and even computer software available for personal and classroom use. So, whether you are a student, parent, teacher or scout leader, why not take advantage of the wealth. Here are a few ideas to get you started.

Term Papers with Pizazz

When I was in school, the first mention of a term paper caused me to nod off in my seat. I knew that, like it or not, I would be spending the next month copying out-of-date facts from a dusty encyclopedia. Fortunately, this no longer has to be the case. Kids today can take advantage of publications that are available from the government with up-to-the-minute facts and figures.

Say your elementary age child wants to do a term paper on a particular animal, bird or reptile that interests him. The U.S. Fish and Wildlife Service has dozens of easy-to-read brochures and publications on anything from armadillos to weasels. There are also publications devoted just to endangered species such as the Brown Pelican or Spotted Owl.

If a history paper is assigned, why have your child read second-hand accounts when first-hand reports are available? The National Archives puts out a publication, *A More Perfect Union: The Creation of the U.S. Constitution* that contains facsimiles of the featured documents and transcriptions of what the founding fathers wrote. If he is more interested in recent events, the U.S. Government Printing Office has a transcript of the Apollo 11 post-flight press conference with the astronauts' actual descriptions of what it was like to travel into space.

Decorating in a Flash

Why not decorate your child's bedroom with a colorful poster or map? The Smithsonian offers portraits of such historical figures as Frederick Douglass or Sitting Bull for a nominal fee. Or, start teaching your child about geology at home. The U.S. Geological Survey has a number of geologic maps available for purchase.

If your classroom needs a little sprucing up, the Environmental Protection Agency offers the colorful poster, *Ride the Wave of the Future: Recycle Today!* for all grade levels. It is a great teaching aid to help promote recycling activities in the classroom. Are your kids space happy? The National Aeronautics and Space Administration produces posters for educators, students, and the general public through the U.S. Government Printing Office. Posters range from a near life-sized picture of an astronaut to a poster detailing the size and make-up of the planets.

Teacher Opportunities

Teachers who are interested in attending workshops have a wide selection of government sponsored programs from which to choose. For example, the NASA Education Workshop for Elementary School Teachers (NEWEST) gives outstanding elementary teachers a chance to personally experience the U.S. aerospace program. Or, if your interests lie closer to home, the National Museum of Natural History offers workshops for elementary and middle school teachers on topics ranging from dinosaurs to ocean reefs.

The earth sciences is just one topic that is covered in teacher workshops held each summer by Aerospace Education Services Program (AESP) specialists at NASA field centers, elementary and secondary schools, and on college campuses. Workshops cover astronomy, life in space, principles of rocketry and remote sensing and include hands-on activities to help teachers incorporate what they learn into classroom programs and activities.

Classroom Tools for the 90's

NASA also offers a large selection of computer software education materials that are available for the classroom. The Hubble Space Telescope, Space Shuttle Commander and Astronomy diskettes are available for use on Apple Computers. The U.S. Public Information Agency also puts out a guide, *Environmental Education Materials for Teachers and Young People (Grades K-12)* which includes computer software designed to teach students how to keep our environment clean.

Teachers can use films to teach schoolchildren about the importance of aeronautics through a program sponsored through the National Air and Space Museum. Or, introduce them to the visual arts. The National Gallery of Art now loans films free of charge to educational institutions, community groups and individuals.

The examples above are just a sampling of what is available. The following chapter includes a long list of classroom resources plus enough information, products and services to keep kids busy from kindergarten through graduation.

4-H

California Energy Extension Service
1400 Tenth St., Room 209
Sacramento, CA 95814   916-323-4388
The *4-H Home Conservation Guide* is a collection of 12 hands-on projects which teach home energy conservation skills for a 4-H group.

ACID RAIN

Public Information Center
U.S. Environmental Protection Agency
401 M Street, SW, MS 3404
Washington, DC 20460   202-260-2080

The Government Works for Kids, Too

The EPA frequently receives requests for information on acid rain from school systems, teachers, and individuals. In response to these requests, EPA has developed the study guide *Acid Rain: The Student's First Sourcebook*. The purpose of the guide, which is for students in grades 4-8, is to help students better understand the science, citizen actions, and research issues that are part of the acid rain problem. *EPA's Acid Rain Program: Charting a New Course in Environmental Protection* and the *Environmental Backgrounder: Acid Rain* are two additional publications which provide information on the acid rain issue.

> Office of Environmental Education
> Pennsylvania Department of Education
> 333 Market St.
> Harrisburg, PA 17126   717-783-6994

Acid rain is one of the many topics covered in Paul E. Beals' activity book *The Newspaper: A Tool for Teaching Environmental Awareness*. It also covers topics such as forest preservation, waste disposal, and recycling. This activity book contains newspaper articles and uses them to teach about environmental awareness.

AFRICAN-AMERICAN ART

> Office of Educational Program
> National Museum of American Art
> Smithsonian Institution
> Washington, DC 20560   202-357-3095

African-American Art: 20th Century Selections is a brochure appropriate for teachers of grades 5-12 which discusses various African-American artists.

> Division of Education, Room B1026
> National Museum of American History
> Smithsonian Institution
> Washington, DC 20560

Field to Factory: Afro-American Migration, 1915-1940 is an educational kit which teaches about the migration of Afro-American from 1915-1940. It is appropriate for grades upper-elementary and up and is available at a cost.

> Education Office
> Federal Aviation Administration
> U.S. Department of Transportation (DOT)
> DOT Building
> Room PL100
> 800 Independence Ave., SW
> Washington, DC 20591   202-267-3383

The *August Martin Activities Book* is a great tool to help teach your child about the world's first black airline pilot. This office will refer you to your local regional office to request the book.

AGRICULTURE

> Ag in the Classroom
> Room 317-A Administration Building
> U.S. Department of Agriculture
> Washington, DC 20350

The mission of the U.S. Department of Agriculture's Ag in the Classroom program is to help students in grades K-12 acquire the knowledge needed to become agriculturally literate. The objective of Ag in the Classroom is to encourage educators to teach more about our food and fiber system and the role of agriculture in our economy and society. The program is primarily carried out in each state by a group composed of educators, government officials, and representatives from agricultural organizations and agribusinesses. Materials available for the program include the following appropriate for elementary-school educators:

Resource Guide to Educational Materials About Agriculture: A Project of Ag in the Classroom. This guide provides a listing of materials relating to agriculture that are available from private and public sources. The listings are divided into four sections: Printed Materials; Audio-Visuals and Audio-Visual Kits; Resource Guides or Catalogs; and miscellaneous items such as posters, wall charts, and computer software. Materials included are primarily about agriculture and related issues. Those concerned with nutrition, food preparation (recipes), promotional information, or buying advice on food and fiber are not included.

Library Guide to Books About Agriculture describes books with factual information about agriculture as well as fiction with an agricultural theme.

Ag in the Classroom Folders are attractive pocket folders which can be used for conferences, teacher training workshops, etc.

Ag in the Classroom Brochures are red, white, and blue and are eye-catching and informative. Distribute them at fairs, teacher conferences, or other outreach activities.

Glossary of Farm Terms, a "mini-dictionary" of farm terms, was originally prepared by Bank of America NT&SA in 1983 and has been revised and reprinted by USDA with permission of Bank of America.

Ag in the Classroom Notes is a bimonthly newsletter about Ag in the Classroom activities around the country.

Ag in the Classroom Fact Sheet is a one-page summary of Ag in the Classroom: its purpose, the basic concepts, how it works, and the role of the U.S. Department of Agriculture.

State Updates tell about Ag in the Classroom organizations and activities in each state and lists the State Contacts.

Model State Action Plan helps states organize task forces to implement Ag in the Classroom programs.

Ag in the Classroom Exhibit in red, white, and blue -- table-top or free-standing -- can be borrowed for fairs, conferences, and conventions.

Video Tapes that can be borrowed and copied.
1986 Ag in the Classroom shows how Ag in the Classroom works and offers a glimpse of enthusiastic teachers and students involved in Ag in the Classroom around the country. (16 minutes.)

America's Most Crucial Industry helps viewers of all ages understand agriculture's vital role in the American economy. This tape can also be purchased for $12 from: Video Transfer, 4709-B Arundel Avenue, Rockville, MD 20852. (14 minutes.)

AIDS

> S. James
> Consumer Information Center - Y
> P.O. Box 100
> Pueblo, CO 81002

AIDS and the Education of Our Children: A Guide for Parents and Teachers addresses issues and questions you may face when talking with children about AIDS. It also lists sources for more information. 34 pp. (1988 ed.) 550X.

AIR POLLUTION

> Resource Center
> Public Education and Risk Communication Division
> Environmental and Occupational Health Sciences Institute
> 45 Knightsbridge Road
> Piscataway, NJ 08854   908-932-0110

Children in grades 4-6 can also learn about air pollution through the following two videos. *Keeping the Lid on Air Pollution* is a 20 min. video about Terry who has a homework assignment which is to write about two pollution controls. He ends up inside the school library computer and learns about different types of air pollutants (focusing on ozone) and air pollution controls. *The Inside Story on Air Pollution* is a 19 min. video about Danny, Terry's friend, and his sister who go into the computer to investigate the sources and health effects of indoor air pollution in the home. They also learn how to reduce and prevent indoor air pollution problems. Contact the office above for cost and ordering information:

> Resource Center
> Public Education and Risk Communication Division
> Environmental and Occupational Health Sciences Institute
> 681 Frelinghuysen Rd.
> Piscataway, NJ 08854   908-445-0110

Fifth grade educators can use the lesson plan *Exploring Air Pollution* to teach their students about air pollution. This lesson plan helps students learn about major sources of air pollutants (including indoor air pollution) and their major health impacts. The concepts of occupational safety and health are introduced. They also learn about methods for reducing air pollution and about the role of government agencies and regulations in protecting worker and community health.

ALCOHOL AND DRUG ABUSE PREVENTION

> National Clearinghouse for Alcohol and Drug Information
> P.O. Box 2345
> Rockville, MD 20852   301-468-2600

Elementary School Children and Alcohol Education includes audiovisuals, programs descriptions, professional and organizational resources to assist educators and parents of young childcare. It is available free from the office above. (# MS315)

> Drug Video Program
> Office of Public Affairs
> U.S. Department of Education
> 400 Maryland Ave., SW
> Washington, DC 20202

Drug prevention videos are available from the U.S. Department of Education for parents and educators. Originally designed for schools these video programs are now available for home use. Each program is closed captioned and comes with its own Parent's or Teacher's Guide to help you discuss each program's message and the serious problem of drug abuse with your child. Programs for elementary children include:

The Drug Avenger. ($35, 73 minutes, 16-page Parent's Guide, 1988, VHS Order No. DGA17535). Three children from the future travel back to the 20th Century to take on the life-threatening problem of drug abuse in 10 animated programs.

Fast Forward Future. ($30, 61 minutes, 23-page Teacher's Guide, 1988., VHS Order No. DGA 17532). Actor Richard Kiley as "Mentor" shows three elementary students the future with the Fast Forward machine. The students see the effects of using drugs and staying drug free.

Straight Up. ($40, 90 minutes, 2-page Teacher's Guide, 1988, VHS Order No. DGA17529). Academy award winning actor Lou Gosset, Jr., as Cosmo takes a boy named Ben, played by Chad Allen of NBC's "Our House", on a journey in the "fate" elevator. Ben's travels teach him valuable lessons about why drugs are harmful and how to refuse them.

> Demand Reduction Section
> Drug Enforcement Administration
> U.S. Department of Justice
> Washington, DC 20537   202-307-7936

Healthy Bodies Don't Need Drugs! Learning and Activity Book is a fifteen-page publication designed to educate children about the need to take care of their bodies and to say "No!" to drugs.

> National Crime Prevention Council
> 1700 K Street, NW, 2nd Floor
> Washington, DC 20006   202-466-6272

Help teach your children to say "No!" through the use of the following McGruff materials. They are available from the National Crime Prevention Council. Materials include:

Elementary School Materials Package. This package contains materials that can be photocopied for students and parents. It was sent to 51,000 elementary schools, and limited quantities are still available from the National Crime Prevention Council. Free.

If You Want to Fit In, Be Drug Free: Welcome to McGruff's Drug-Free Park. This colored poster shows McGruff with children playing basketball, baseball, riding bicycles, and reading - all alcohol- and other drug-free activities. $2.50.

Licensed Products Package. The National Crime Prevention Council has many specialty items available to teach elementary youth about prevention. This package includes information on a talking robot, a puppet package, stickers, calendars, and many other items. Free.

McGruff's Drug Abuse Prevention Kit. This kit includes different games, puzzles, a video, and recorded songs for children. Two items are for parents, and they give tips for teaching children how to say no. Materials come as reproducible masters. $30.

McGruff's Drug Abuse Prevention Kit: The No Show. The video is part of McGruff's Drug Abuse Prevention Kit. All parts of the Kit including the video, are reproducible for nonprofit educational purposes. Animation is used throughout 25 percent of the video. The video kids create a rock video about refusing drugs. $12.

To Be What You Want To Be: Be Drug Free. This poster has people from many professions with the slogan "To be what you want to be, be drug free". It has room for the child to draw himself into the picture. $2.50.

> National Clearinghouse for Alcohol and Drug Information
> P.O. Box 2345   800-729-6686
> Rockville, MD 20852   301-468-2600

The National Clearinghouse for Alcohol and Drug Information (NCADI) is an excellent source of information for alcohol and drug abuse prevention. In 1987 it was established as the central point within the Federal Government for current print and audiovisual materials about alcohol and other drugs. NCADI answers more than 18,000 telephone and mail inquiries each month and distributes some 18 million printed items a year, which include the following posters and publications appropriate for elementary school children:

Ayundando a sus alumnos a decirle que no (Helping Your Students Say "No") Teacher's Guide (1990). In English and Spanish, explains the effects of alcohol on the body, why children start to drink, how teachers can help their students say "No" to alcohol and deal with the first signs of drinking, and where teachers can go for more information. 13 pp. PH284.

Buzzy's Rebound: Fat Albert and the Cosby Kids (1990). In comic book format, depicts the story of Buzzy, a young basketball player and friend of the Cosby Kids, who gets into trouble with alcohol and is helped by his coach, and a school counselor. 18 pp. PH232.

The Fact Is ... You Can Prevent Alcohol and Other Drug Problems Among Elementary School Children (1988). Includes videotapes, program descriptions, and professional and organizational resources to assist educators and parents of young children. 17 pp. MS349.

Growing Up Drug Free: A Parent's Guide to Prevention (1989). This handbook outlines what children at four key stages of development should know about drugs and suggests family activities to reinforce children's motivation to avoid alcohol and other drugs. 52 pp. PHD533.

The Herschel Walker Poster (1989). Herschel Walker, football star, salutes the drug-free youth of America in a 22 in. by 27 in. color poster. Reference is made to NCADI as a source for more information. AVD45.

Learning to Live Drug Free: A Curriculum Model for Prevention (1990). Provides a flexible framework for classroom-based prevention efforts for kindergarten through grade 12. Presents the states of child development as they relate to drug prevention, facts about drugs, suggested lesson plans, tips on working with parents and the community, and a resource section for further information. Teachers can learn how to integrate prevention messages into their classroom presentations. BKD51.

Little League Drug Education Program (1991). This video has two parts: Part 1, Friend to Friend, Featuring Orel Hershiser, is directed toward today's Little Leaguer. The film tells the story of a Little League player who is tempted by drugs. Part 2, Big League Advice: Helping Your Little Leaguers Say No, is for parents and coaches of Little League players. The film depicts a discussion among Little League parents and baseball Hall-of-Famers 'Hank' Aaron and Jim Palmer. These great ball players offer frank and important advice to parents on how to talk to young people about drugs and alcohol. 30 minutes. VHS29.

Live the Dream, Say No to Alcohol and Drug Abuse (1989). Poster features Dr. Martin Luther King, Jr. Appropriate for all ages, 15 1/2 in. by 22 in. AV165.

McGruff's Surprise Party (1989). A comic book that helps children understand the importance of saying "No" to alcohol and other drugs, as told by McGruff, the crime dog. Also teaches children techniques for resisting peer pressure. For ages 8 to 10. 14 pp. PH271.

McGruff: Say 'No' to Crack and Other Drugs (1989). Bright red and white poster featuring McGruff, the Crime Dog. McGruff tells kids that crack is poison and a very dangerous drug. Tells them to say a big "no" and walk away. Also provides the NIDA hotline number (800-662-HELP) and a cocaine hotline number (800-COCAINE). 64 in. by 88 in. AVD14.

Parent Training is Prevention (1991). Contains information to help communities identify and carry out programs on parenting. Details roles parents play in rearing children who are free of alcohol and other drug problems, highlights ethnic and cultural considerations, and gives characteristics of effective prevention programs. 184 pp. BK 184.

Pointers for Parents Card (1989). Provides easy steps parents can take to help prevent their child from using alcohol or other drugs. Excellent handout for special events such as fairs, workshop, or conferences. 3 1/2 in. by 8 1/2 in. card. PH260.

Prevention Resource Guide: Elementary Youth (1991). This Resource Guide includes materials specifically developed for youth that may be used in an elementary school setting, as well as relevant information on parenting. It is designed for teachers, administrators, and program leaders who come in contact with elementary youth. 23 pp. MS421.

The Government Works for Kids, Too

Quick List: 10 Steps to Help Your Child Say "No" (1990). Also available in Spanish. Identifies ten things that parents can do to help their children stay away from alcohol and other drugs, from talking with your child to being a good role model. Three-panel fold out mini-poster. PH230.

Snappy Answers Card for Kids (1989). Suggests responses young people can use to say "No" if offered alcohol or other drugs. Excellent handout for special events such as fairs, workshops, or school events. 3 1/2" by 8 1/2" card. PH 261.

> National Clearinghouse for Alcohol and Drug Information
> P.O. Box 2345
> Rockville, MD 20852   800-729-6686

Use the *Be Smart Game* board game to help teach your children to say "No!" to drugs. It is printed on a heavy sheet of paper, allows two-four players, and requires dice and a coin for each player. Going around the board, players have opportunities to say "No!" to drugs and to discover alternate activities.

ALLIGATORS

> U.S. Fish and Wildlife Service
> U.S. Department of the Interior
> 4401 N. Fairfax Drive, Mail Stop 130
> Arlington, VA 22203   703-358-1711

Use the publication, *American Alligator*, to help teach your children about one type of endangered species. Contact the office above to receive a publication on this and other endangered species.

AMERICAN INDIANS

> Attn: Public Inquiries Office
> Bureau of Indian Affairs
> Mail Stop 2620 (MIB)
> U.S. Department of Interior
> Washington, DC 20240   202-208-3711

The U.S. Department of Interior's Bureau of Indian Affairs is a wonderful source of information for those who want to teach their children about American Indians. Use the booklet *American Indians Today: Answers to Your Questions* to help answer some of the common questions your children may have about Indians. Teach your children about famous Indians through the use of *Famous Indians: A Collection of Short Biographies*. From Pocahontas to Sitting Bull, this publication describes the history and lives of twenty famous American Indians. Help your children locate the Indian reservation nearest them through *Indian Land Areas*. This map of the United States displays federal Indian reservations, along with state reservations.

> Office of Education, Room 212
> Mail Stop 158
> National Museum of Natural History
> Washington, DC 20560   202-357-2747

Use the slide set *Native Peoples of North America* to enhance curricula for school children. It is available for a three-week loan free of charge from The National Museum of Natural History.

> Office of Public Information
> Department of Anthropology
> National Museum of Natural History
> Smithsonian Institution
> Washington, DC 20560   202-357-1592

The Department of Anthropology of the National Museum of Natural History has a wonderful selection of bibliographies and leaflets on American Indians, including *Native American Resources*, a bibliography of reading material for elementary school children. Use this and the following publications to enlighten your children about the American Indian culture:

American Indian Basketry. Bibliography
American Indian Food. Bibliography
American Indian Languages. Leaflet.
Arts and Crafts of the American Indians of the Southwest. Bibliography.
Arts and Crafts of the Northwest Coast Indians and Eskimos. Bibliography.
Arts and Crafts of the Plains Indians. Bibliography.
Genealogical Research. Leaflet.
Native American Games, Dances, and Crafts. Bibliography.
Native American Resources. Bibliography.
Native Americans. Bibliography.
North American Indian Art. Bibliography.
North American Indian Healing and Medicine. Bibliography.
North American Indian Mythology. Bibliography.

North American Indian Ritual and Religion. Bibliography.
North American Indian Silverwork. Bibliography.
North American Indian Women. Bibliography.
North American Symbolism and Design. Bibliography.
Origin of the American Indians. Leaflet.
Southwest Indian Pottery. Bibliography.
Southwest Indian Textiles and Weaving. Bibliography.

> Office of Public Information
> Department of Anthropology
> National Museum of Natural History
> Smithsonian Institution
> Washington, DC 20560   202-357-1592

Educators can use the *North American Indians* teacher's resource packet to find out how to obtain different teaching materials. Available at no charge.

> Photographic Services
> American History Building, Room CB-054
> Smithsonian Institution
> Washington, DC 20560   202-357-1933

The *Sitting Bull* poster provides an excellent visual tool for those who want to educate their children about American Indians. Cost is $3.

> Office of Education, Room 212
> Mail Stop 158
> National Museum of Natural History
> Washington, DC 20560   202-357-2747

The National Museum of Natural History has several different programs and activities held throughout the school year for visiting preschool and elementary school children. For Indian enthusiasts there is the *Indian Walkaround*, a teacher-directed walk-through of the Indian and Eskimo halls. Volunteers staff small display stations throughout the exhibit, offer objects to touch, and tell about the people who made them. There also is *Indians and Eskimos*. Sitting in front of museum exhibits and using Indian children's toys, students learn what grandparents of Indian children did in the past, what parents do today, and what Indian children might do when they grow up. Lesson includes Eskimo, Woodland, Plains, Northwest Coast, and Southwest peoples. For grades 1 and up there also are museum lesson tours. With *Indians and Eskimos* students discover the wide diversity of the indigenous cultures past and present in North America. On the tour they explore the relationships between environment and culture by focusing on the basic human need for food, shelter, clothing, and tools. Teachers are urged to request pre-visit materials that will help them before and during the visit. Call the office above to obtain the dates of these programs and activities.

ANCIENT CULTURES

> Office of Education, Room 212
> Mail Stop 158
> National Museum of Natural History
> Washington, DC 20560   202-357-2747

A slide set on *Ancient Cultures: 10,000 B.C. - 600 A.D.* is available for a three-week loan free of charge from the National Museum of Natural History.

ANIMALS

> Office of Public Affairs
> National Institute of Mental Health
> 5600 Fishers Lane, Room 7C02
> Rockville, MD 20857   301-443-4513

Let's Visit a Research Laboratory: Introduction and Lesson Plans (for schoolchildren in grades 2-5) helps answer the many questions children may have about research laboratories. The supplemental poster that is included provides teachers with helpful illustrations for classroom discussion and activities.

> Office of Education, Room 212
> Mail Stop 158
> National Museum of Natural History
> Washington, DC 20560   202-357-2747

The National Museum of Natural History is an excellent place to teach your students about different types of animals. Several programs and activities on animals are held throughout the school year for visiting preschool and elementary school children. Activities for preschool and kindergarten children include:

Animals - students see real examples of the different kinds of animals that make up the Animal Kingdom - birds, mammals, fish, amphibians, and reptiles - and learn to tell them apart by using external characteristics.

Discover Dinosaurs - students receive a short introduction to "what is a fossil?" by means of a puppet show, investigate dinosaur skeletons and dioramas in the Dinosaur Hall, and participate in hands-on activities relating to dinosaur exhibits.

Museum lesson tours for grades 1 and up include *Animals, Endangered Species and Extinction,* and *Prehistoric Life.* Teachers are urged to request pre-visit materials that will help them before and during the visit.

> Office of Education, Room 212
> Mail Stop 158
> National Museum of Natural History
> Washington, DC 20560   202-357-2747

The National Museum of Natural History offers two workshops for teachers (of elementary and middle school students) interested in preparing a visit for their classes to the museum. *Dinosaurs* is a walk through the Dinosaur Hall to help teachers and aides design a visit for their classes, followed by an informal lecture on major dinosaur groups represented in the exhibit hall. *Climate and Endangered Species* is a workshop designed to help teachers and aides design a visit or prepare for a guided tour. The identification of all endangered and extinct modern animals on exhibit is followed by an informal talk about why certain groups of animals are more vulnerable than others. For specific dates and more information contact the office above.

> U.S. Fish and Wildlife Service
> U.S. Department of the Interior
> 4401 N. Fairfax Drive
> Mail Stop 130
> Arlington, VA 22203   703-358-1711

Would you or your child like to learn about endangered species such as the grizzly bear, spotted owl or gray wolf? Why not decorate your classroom or child's bedroom with some of the 30 portraits of fish they have available? The U.S. Fish and Wildlife Service has dozens of easy-reading brochures and publications which can provide information for school reports, 4-H club assignments, or Boy Scout projects. Some of the publications include the following:

American Bald Eagle
Conservation Note 5 - Bird Banding: The Hows and Whys
Conservation Note 6 - Snakes (In Press)
Conservation Note 8 - Migration of Birds (In Press)
Conservation Note 11 - Pronghorn Antelope
Ducks Get Sick, Too
Endangered Species
Endangered and Threatened Wildlife and Plants
Estuaries: Cradles of Life
In Celebration of America's Wildlife - Teacher's Guide to Learning
Know Before You Go
National Wildlife Refuges - A Visitor's Guide
Waterfowl for the Future

Available also are publications on endangered species:
General Information
American Alligator
Red Wolf
Gray Wolf
California Condor
Black-Footed Ferret
Grizzly Bear
Whooping Crane
Bald Eagle
Polar Bear
Spotted Owl

Other publications include those on:
Beaver
Giant Panda
Dolphins
Key Deer
Pronghorn Antelope
Sandhill Crane
Coyote
Bobcat
Rocky Mountain Goat
Muskrat
Black Bear
Cougar
Opossum
Armadillo

Trumpeter Swan
American Elk
Pacific Salmon
Caribou
Trout
Racoon
Prairie Dog
Great Horned Owl
Snowy Owl
Ring-necked Pheasant
Life in a Fox Den
American Buffalo

Posters available include:
Raptors - Hunters On the Wing!
Steel Shot - Are You Using the Right Load?
The Difference Between Endangered and Extinct is Forever
Wetlands - We need 'em...- Wildlife needs 'em too.

> Natural Heritage Division
> Illinois Department of Conservation
> 524 S. 2nd St.
> Springfield, IL 62706

Nature Discovery II: Wild Mammals of Illinois is a publication for students and teachers and is available to teachers in Illinois. It includes various activities on different mammals and even has a "Guide to Mammal Signs". The publication is written for children in grades 4-8.

> Public Information Center
> U.S. Environmental Protection Agency
> 401 M Street, SW, MS 3404
> Washington, DC 20460   202-260-2080

Use the coloring book *Save Our Species: Endangered Species Coloring Book* to introduce your children to 21 endangered and threatened plants and animals found in the United States. As they color the pages, they will journey to oceans, swamps, deserts, and islands and bring to life a variety of plants and animals.

> Center for Veterinary Medicine
> Food and Drug Administration
> Public Health Service
> U.S. Department of Health and Human Services
> 5600 Fishers Lane
> Rockville, MD 20857   301-295-8755

Prepare your child how to care for a pet before it arrives. The Center for Veterinary Medicine has several fact sheets which parents can use to teach their children how to care for pets properly.

ANTELOPES

> U.S. Fish and Wildlife Service
> U.S. Department of the Interior
> 4401 N. Fairfax Drive
> Mail Stop 130
> Arlington, VA 22203   703-358-1711

The U.S. Fish and Wildlife Service has publications on various kinds of animals including the Pronghorn Antelope.

ARCHAEOLOGY

> Office of Education, Room 212
> Mail Stop 158
> National Museum of Natural History
> Washington, DC 20560   202-357-2747

Use the slide set *An Introduction to Archaeology* to learn more about archaeology. It is available for a three-week loan free of charge from the National Museum of Natural History.

ARCHITECTURE

> Architect of the Capitol
> Washington, DC 20515   202-225-1200

The United States Capitol contains a wealth of architectural history. Publications are provided from the office above which can be used to teach schoolchildren about the history of the U.S. Capitol so that they may attain a greater appreciation of U.S. history and architecture. The publications include the following:

Architects of the Capitol
Flags Over the East and West Central Fronts of the United States Capitol
Cornstalk or Corncob Columns and Capitals
*History of the Old Subway Transportation System Connecting the Capitol and
    the Russell Office Building*
Minton Title in the U.S. Capitol
Statuary Hall: Old Hall of the House
Statue of Freedom
The Architecture of the Unites States Capitol
The Canopy in the Rotunda of the U.S. Capitol
The United States Capitol
The United States Capitol: A Brief Architectural History
Those Who Have Lain in State in the Rotunda

National Graphic Center
205 West Jefferson Street
Falls Church, VA 22046   703-533-8700

Learn about the U.S. Capitol's architecture through photographs and slides from the
Collection of the Architect of the Capitol.

ART

Office of Educational Program
National Museum of American Art
Smithsonian Institution
Washington, DC 20560   202-357-3095

Afro-American Art: 20th Century Selections is a brochure appropriate for grades 5-12
which discusses various African-American artists.

Office of Elementary and Secondary Education
Arts and Industries Building
Room 1163
Smithsonian Institution
Washington, DC 20560   202-357-3049

The Smithsonian Institution's Office of Elementary and Secondary Education has an
excellent guide to educational materials from the Smithsonian Institution, the
National Gallery of Art, and the John F. Kennedy Center for the Performing Arts.
The *Resource Guide For Teachers* is available from the office above.

National Gallery of Art
Publications Mail Order Department
2000B South Club Drive
Landover, MD 20785   301-322-5900

Enlighten your students or children with reproductions from the National Gallery of
Art. The National Gallery of Art lists hundreds of different portraits and paintings
available in postcards, plaques, double mats, 11x14" format, or large unframed
reproductions. Included also is information on ordering slides.

Department of Extension Programs
National Gallery of Art
Washington, DC 20565

The National Gallery of Art is continually exploring ways to develop awareness in
the visual arts and make its collections accessible to everyone, no matter how far
away from the Gallery they may live. They now have an Extension Program which
loans slide programs, films, and videocassettes free of charge to educational
institutions, community groups, and to individuals throughout the U.S. Write to the
office above for more information on how you may bring the National Gallery of Art
to your students.

Office of Educational Program
National Museum of American Art
Smithsonian Institution
Washington, DC 20560   202-357-3095

Use the kit of African-American Art and Public Sculpture to teach children in grades
5-12 about African-American art.

Office of Elementary and Secondary Education
Smithsonian Institution
Washington, DC 20560   202-357-2404

Art to Zoo is a publication dedicated to promoting the use of community resources
among students and teachers nationally. It brings news from the Smithsonian
Institution to teachers of grades three through eight. Its purpose is to help teachers
use museums, parks, libraries, zoos, and many other resources within their
community to open up learning opportunities for their students. Contact the above
address if you want your school to be placed, free of charge, on the *Art to Zoo*
mailing list.

AUSTRALIA

Education Department
Kennedy Center
Washington, DC 20566   202-416-8800

Teach your students about Australia's performing arts (music, drama, dance) through
the use of the booklet *An Australian Experience*. For students in grades 1-8. $1 copy;
$2 shipping and handling.

AVIATION

Education Office
Federal Aviation Administration
U.S. Department of Transportation
400 7th Street, SW
Washington, DC 20590   202-366-7500

Help teach your children about the history of aviation and the role it plays in today's
society through the publications available from the Federal Aviation Administration's
Education Office. These publications are designed to provide instructional materials
consisting of accurate, timely information to enrich and enhance general study
programs with concepts relating to aviation. The following publications are
distributed free of charge:

Aviation and Space Curriculum Guide K-3. The purpose of this guide is to provide
an array of aviation and space activities which may be used by teachers to enrich
locally-designed programs.

Aviation Science Activities for Elementary Grades. Pamphlet containing science
demonstrations pertaining to physical properties of air. Experiments use simple
equipment.

Demonstration Aids for Aviation Education. Set of science teaching strategies for
independent or classroom work.

How We Made the First Flight. In Orville Wright's own words, a description of his
and Wilbur's first flights.

Nuestro Primer Vuelo. Spanish version of How We Made the First Flight.

Teacher's Guide for Aviation Education for Grades 2-6. Study unit lessons of
science, health, social studies, communications arts, and career education.

August Martin Activities Book. Learning activities based on a biography of the
world's first black airline pilot.

A Trip to the Airport. Contains English-Spanish bilingual materials. Bilingual text
plus supplemental teaching materials.

A Flying Start. Tells the basic story of flying and getting a private pilot license.

AWARDS PROGRAMS

EPA Region 1
(Connecticut, Massachusetts, Maine, New Hampshire, Rhode Island,
Vermont)
JFK Federal Building
Boston, MA 02203   617-565-3398

EPA Region 2
(New Jersey, New York, Puerto Rico, Virgin Islands)
290 Broadway
New York, NY 10007-1866   212-637-5000

EPA Region 3:
(Delaware, Maryland, Pennsylvania, Virginia, West Virginia, District of
Columbia)
841 Chestnut Street
Philadelphia, PA 19107   215-597-9814

EPA Region 4:
(Alabama, Florida, Georgia, Kentucky, Mississippi, North Carolina, South
Carolina, Tennessee)
345 Courtland Street NE
Atlanta, GA 30365   404-347-3004

EPA Region 5:
(Illinois, Indiana, Michigan, Minnesota, Ohio, Wisconsin)

77 W. Jackson Blvd.
Chicago, IL 60604
312-353-2072

EPA Region 6:
(Arkansas, Louisiana, New Mexico, Oklahoma, Texas)
1445 Ross Avenue
Dallas, TX 75202-2733
214-665-6444

EPA Region 7:
(Iowa, Kansas, Missouri, Nebraska)
726 Minnesota Avenue
Kansas City, KS 66101
913-551-7003

EPA Region 8:
(Colorado, Montana, North Dakota, South Dakota, Utah, Wyoming)
One Denver Place
999 18th Street
Denver, CO 80202-2405
303-293-1647

EPA Region 9:
(Arizona, California, Hawaii, Nevada, American Samoa, Guam, Trust Territories of the Pacific)
75 Hawthorne Street
San Francisco, CA 94105
415-744-1020

EPA Region 10:
(Alaska, Idaho, Oregon, Washington)
1200 Sixth Avenue
Seattle, WA 98101
800-424-4EPA
206-553-1200

Help get some recognition for your child's interest in saving the environment by sponsoring him or her in the President's Environmental Youth Awards Program. The program encourages individuals, school classes, schools, summer camps, public interest groups, and youth organizations to promote local environmental awareness and to channel this awareness into positive community involvement. To be eligible, a young person, or group of young persons, must have completed an environmental project while in grades kindergarten through twelve, and the project must be sponsored by at least one adult representative of their school, camp, youth group, or public interest group. For additional information, contact your regional office listed below:

Martin Luther King Jr. Federal Holiday Commission
451 7th St., SW, Suite 5182
Washington, DC 20410

The Martin Luther King Jr. Federal Holiday Commission has an awards program for those individuals and organizations that are in keeping with Dr. King's standards of service to others. For more information obtain the *National and International Martin Luther King Jr. Heritage Action Project Guidelines* publication from the office above.

President's Council on Physical Fitness and Sports
701 Pennsylvania Ave., NW, Suite 205
Washington, DC 20005
202-272-3421

American youth have participated in the Presidential Physical Fitness Award Program or the "President's Challenge" since 1966. The program includes all young people from ages six through 17, including those students with special needs. In addition, two awards have been added to go with the prestigious Presidential Physical Fitness Award for outstanding achievement. The National Physical Fitness Award was introduced in 1987 and is for those who reach a basic yet challenging level of fitness. A new award called the Participant Physical Fitness Award, introduced in the Fall of 1991, is for those who attempt the President's Challenge but don't qualify for a Presidential or National Award. The booklet *Get Fit! A Handbook for Youth Ages 6-17* will help children become as physically fit as they can be.

Take Pride in America
P.O. Box 1339
Jessup, MD 20794

A national awards program exists with the Take Pride in America campaign. Take Pride in America is a public awareness campaign specifically designed to restore respect for the Nation's public lands and to promote voluntary stewardship of America's vast and valuable resources.

BADGERS

U.S. Fish and Wildlife Service
U.S. Department of the Interior
4401 N. Fairfax Drive, Mail Stop 130
Arlington, VA 22203
703-358-1711

Upper elementary school children can use the publication *Badger* to learn more about this interesting animal.

BATS

U.S. Fish and Wildlife Service
U.S. Department of the Interior
4401 N. Fairfax Drive, Mail Stop 130
Arlington, VA 22203
703-358-1711

Bats and Their Conservation can serve as a supplement when teaching about this unusual animal.

Department of Vertebrate Zoology
Room 369, National Museum of Natural History
Smithsonian Institution
Washington, DC 20560

The Smithsonian Institution has available the pamphlet *Bats* which can help answer questions children may have on bats. For students in grades 1-9. Free.

BEARS

U.S. Fish and Wildlife Service
U.S. Department of the Interior
4401 N. Fairfax Drive, Mail Stop 130
Arlington, VA 22203
703-358-1711

Would you like to teach your child about bears? You can do so through the publication *Grizzly Bear*, available from the office above.

BEAVERS

U.S. Fish and Wildlife Service
U.S. Department of the Interior
4401 N. Fairfax Drive, Mail Stop 130
Arlington, VA 22203
703-358-1711

Learn about beavers through the U.S. Fish and Wildlife Service's publication *Beaver*.

BILINGUALISM

Center for Applied Linguistics
118 22nd Street NW
Washington, DC 20037-0037
202-429-9551

The Educational Resources Information Center (ERIC) is a nationwide information network designed to provide users with ready access to education literature. The ERIC System, managed by the U.S. Department of Education, Office of Educational Research and Improvement, consists of 16 Clearinghouses, four Adjunct Clearinghouses, and 4 support components. One of the Clearinghouses, *Languages and Linguistics*, specializes in languages and language sciences; all aspects of second language instruction and learning in all commonly and uncommonly taught languages, including English as a second language; bilingualism and bilingual education; cultural education in the context of second language learning; intercultural communication; study abroad and international education exchange; all areas of linguistics, including theoretical and applied linguistics, sociolinguistics, and psychololinguistics.

BILL OF RIGHTS

Education Branch (NEEE)
National Archives and Records Administration
Washington, DC 20408
202-501-5525

Teach upper elementary and secondary students about the Bill of Rights through the use of the National Archives teaching aid, *Bill of Rights*. Published by the National Archives and SIRS, Inc., it contains about 50 reproductions of documents - charts, photographs, letters, drawings, and posters - and a detailed teacher's guide. The materials deal with certain key issues of the period, with governmental and political responses to these issues, and with public attitudes. Cost is $40 each. To order, send a purchase order to: SIRS, Inc., P.O. Box 2348, Boca Raton, FL 33427-2348: or call toll free: 800-232-SIRS (except AK and FL call collect 407-994-0079). To find out what grade level it is appropriate for and for information on other teaching aids contact the office above.

BIRDFEEDERS

U.S. Fish and Wildlife Service
U.S. Department of the Interior
4401 N. Fairfax Drive, Mail Stop 130
Arlington, VA 22203
703-358-1711

The Government Works for Kids, Too

Would you like to build your child a birdfeeder? Use the U.S. Fish and Wildlife Service's publication, *Homes for Birds* to learn how to do so.

BIRDS

U.S. Fish and Wildlife Service
U.S. Department of the Interior
4401 N. Fairfax Drive
Mail Stop 130
Arlington, VA 22203   703-358-1711

The U.S. Fish and Wildlife Service is a wonderful resource of information on different kinds of birds, from ducks to pelicans. Listed below are some of the publications they have available:

Conservation Note 1- Birds
Conservation Note 4 - America's Upland Game Birds
Conservation Note 8 - Migration of Birds (In Press)
Diving Ducks
Ducks Get Sick, Too
California Condor
Whooping Crane
Bald Eagle
Spotted Owl
Trumpeter Swan
Great Horned Owl
Snowy Owl
Ring-necked Pheasant

BOARD GAMES

National Clearinghouse for Alcohol and Drug Information
P.O. Box 2345
Rockville, MD 20852   800-729-6686

Have fun saying "No!" to drugs when playing the *Be Smart Game*, a board game printed on a heavy sheet of paper. It requires dice and a coin for each player and allows two-four players. Going around the board, players have opportunities to say "No!" to drugs and to discover alternate activities.

Energy Center
Sonoma State University
1801 East Cotati Ave.
Rohnert Park, CA 94928   707-664-2577

Learn about California history and geography from an energy perspective with the board game *California Challenge: An Educational Tour of California* (appropriate for children in grades 4-5.) The cost is $20 for a full game which includes instructions, map, cards, 4 game pieces and 1 die.

BOBCATS

U.S. Fish and Wildlife Service
U.S. Department of the Interior
4401 N. Fairfax Drive
Mail Stop 130
Arlington, VA 22203   703-358-1711

Teach your children about bobcats after reading the publication *Bobcat*.

BUFFALO

U.S. Fish and Wildlife Service
U.S. Department of the Interior
4401 N. Fairfax Drive
Mail Stop 130
Arlington, VA 22203   703-358-1711

Use the publication *American Buffalo* to enlighten your children about this interesting animal.

CALIFORNIA

Energy Center
Sonoma State University
1801 East Cotati Ave.
Rohnert Park, CA 94928   707-664-2577

Learn about California history and geography from an energy perspective with the board game *California Challenge: An Educational Tour of California* (appropriate for children in grades 4-5.) The cost is $20 for a full game which includes instructions, map, cards, 4 game pieces and 1 die.

California Air Resources Board
Public Information Office
P.O. Box 2815
Sacramento, CA 95812   916-322-2990

The California Air Resources Board has materials available for Californians. Single copies are available free to non-Californians as well.

CARBON MONOXIDE

Public Information Center
U.S. Environmental Protection Agency
401 M Street, SW, MS 3404
Washington, DC 20460   202-260-2080

Use the publication *Environmental Backgrounder: Ozone and Carbon Monoxide* to supplement science curricula when teaching about the pollutants carbon monoxide and ozone.

CARIBBEAN FESTIVALS

Office of Education, Room 212
Mail Stop 158
National Museum of Natural History
Washington, DC 20560   202-357-2747

Use the instructional kit *Caribbean Festival Arts* to teach your school children about the festivals of the Caribbean (based on the 1989 exhibition Caribbean Festival Arts).

CARIBOU

U.S. Fish and Wildlife Service
U.S. Department of the Interior
4401 N. Fairfax Drive, Mail Stop 130
Arlington, VA 22203   703-358-1711

Would you like to teach your kids about caribou? The U.S. Fish and Wildlife Service can help you by sending you the publication *Caribou*.

CD-ROMS

Education Services Department
MRC 305
National Air and Space Museum
Mail Response Room
Washington, DC 20560   202-786-2109

If you are an educator and are interested in teaching your kids aerospace-related information through the use of CD-roms, you may want to visit the Education Resource Center (ERC) of the National Air and Space Museum (NASM). Additional information on the ERC and other NASM educational programs may be obtained by writing to the address above.

CHESAPEAKE BAY

U.S. Fish and Wildlife Service
U.S. Department of the Interior
4401 N. Fairfax Drive
Mail Stop 130
Arlington, VA 22203   703-358-1711

For Chesapeake Bay enthusiasts who would like to enlighten their children about this area of water, let the U.S. Fish and Wildlife Service send you the publications *Chesapeake Bay - Its Beauty and Bounty* and *Chesapeake Bay Restoration*.

Smithsonian Environmental Research Center
P.O. Box 28
Edgewater, MD 21037   301-798-4424

Are you planning on taking your students on a field trip to the Chesapeake Bay? Then get the loose-leaf manual *Estuarine Dock Activities Guidebook*. Includes information on crabs, oyster bars, weather and tides. For students in grades 4-6. $9.50.

Public Information Center
U.S. Environmental Protection Agency
401 M Street, SW, MS 3404
Washington, DC 20460   202-260-2080

Use the coloring book *Chessie: A Chesapeake Bay Story*, to help teach kids the importance of keeping the Chesapeake Bay clean. Learn about Chessie, popularized cousin of Nessie (Scotland's Loch Ness monster), a sea monster who people have reported seeing for at least half a century. Through hearing the tale of Chessie children will learn how and why we all need to keep the Chesapeake Bay clean.

CHICAGO RIVER

Public Information Office
Metropolitan Water Reclamation District of Greater Chicago
100 East Erie
Chicago, IL 60611   312-751-6633
Learn how the city of Chicago helps keep the Chicago River and Lake Michigan clean. *Color It Blue* is a coloring book which offers children a creative way of learning about sewage treatment.

CIVIL WAR

Education Branch (NEEE)
National Archives and Records Administration
Washington, DC 20408   202-501-6172
Teach your upper elementary and secondary students about the Civil War through the use of the teaching unit, *The Civil War: Soldiers and Civilians*. Published by the National Archives and SIRS, Inc., the unit contains about 50 reproductions of documents - charts, photographs, letters, drawings, and posters -and a detailed teacher's guide. The materials deal with certain key issues of the period, with governmental and political responses to these issues, and with public attitudes. The cost is $40. To order, send a purchase order to: SIRS, Inc., P.O. Box 2348, Boca Raton, FL 33427-2348: or call toll free: 800-3327-0513 (except AK and FL call collect 407-994-0079). To find out for what grade level it is appropriate, and for information on other teaching aids, contact the office above.

CLOUDS

Superintendent of Documents
Dept. 33
Washington, DC 20402   202-512-1800
Use the *Cloud Code Chart* to help teach children about cloud formations. This chart illustrates and describes the 36 cloud formations according to the international system of classification. 1972. Rep. 1988. 31 x 19 ins. Shipped folded. (S/N 003-018-00050-4, $2.25).

COAL

Office of Fossil Energy Communications
1000 Independence Ave., SW
Room 4G-085
Washington, DC 20585   202-586-6503
Teach kids where coal comes from and the importance of it. *Dinosaurs and Power Plants* is a 16-page brochure designed for students that relates the story of mining and drilling for coal, gas, and oil, the environmental concerns involved, and modes of transportation. *Clean Coal Technology* is also available.

Office of Fossil Energy, Room 4G 085
U.S. Department of Energy
1000 Independence Ave., SW
Washington, DC 20585   202-586-6503
Call the office above to receive *The Clean Coal Path* poster. It traces the route of several new advances in the clean use of coal, America's most abundant fossil energy resource. During the 1990s, many of these improvements will be used for the first time in power plants to generate new supplies of electricity without polluting the nation's air.

COAST GUARD, U.S.

Public Affairs
U.S. Coast Guard
U.S. Department of Transportation
2100 Second Street, SW
Washington, DC 20593-0001   .   202-267-1587
Our Day with the Coast Guard provides a fun way for children to learn about the U.S. Coast Guard. By providing information in a coloring book format, kids can learn what it's like to be in the Coast Guard. The coloring book includes activities such as a maze and connect-the-dots.

COLLEGES

Higher Education Clearinghouse
The George Washington University
One Dupont Circle, NW, Suite 630
Washington, DC 20036-1183   202-296-2597
The Educational Resources Information Center (ERIC) is a nationwide information network designed to provide users with ready access to education literature. The

ERIC System, managed by the U.S. Department of Education, Office of Educational Research and Improvement, consists of 16 Clearinghouses, four Adjunct Clearinghouses, and 4 support components. One of the Clearinghouses, *Higher Education* contains information on topics relating to college and university conditions, problems, programs, and students; curricular and instructional programs; and institutional research at the college or university level.

COLORADO

U.S. Geological Survey
P.O. Box 25425
Denver, CO 80225
Mountains and Plains: Denver's Geologic Setting is an excellent source of information about the nature and structure of the rocks that underlie Denver, Colorado, and part of the adjacent Front Range. Provides a road log to explain the natural features of the area. Students can use this publication to supplement special reports and science projects.

COLORING BOOKS

Department of Air Pollution Control
Commonwealth of Virginia
P.O. Box 10089
Richmond, VA 23240   804-694-1366
Get your kids interested in the need for clean air through the coloring book *Airy Canary Learns to Fly*. It is about a bird who is having difficulty learning to fly because of the presence of Nasty Nitrogen Dioxide, Otto Ozone the Air Pollutant, and Sully Sulfur Dioxide. Children in the lower elementary grades will enjoy coloring this 16-page book, while learning about pollutants and the need for healthy air.

Beth Lester
P.O. Box 10089
Richmond, VA 23240   804-786-7913
Available from the office above are the coloring books *Color Your Environment* and *Air Bear*. Single copies are free; check for prices on quantity orders.

Public Information Center
U.S. Environmental Protection Agency
401 M Street, SW, MS 3404
Washington, DC 20460   202-260-2080
For at least half a century people have reported seeing a "sea monster" in the Chesapeake Bay. Affectionately known as "Chessie," popularized cousin of Nessie (Scotland's Loch Ness monster), the creature is reported to be gentle and good natured. In the coloring book *Chessie: A Chesapeake Bay Story*, Chessie discusses how and why we need to keep the Chesapeake Bay clean.

Public Information Office
Metropolitan Water Reclamation District of Greater Chicago
100 East Erie
Chicago, IL 60611   312-751-6633
Learn how the city of Chicago helps keep the Chicago River and Lake Michigan clean. *Color It Blue* is a coloring book which offers children a creative way of learning about sewage treatment.

Public Information Center
U.S. Environmental Protection Agency
401 M Street, SW, MS 3404
Washington, DC 20460   202-260-2080
Save Our Species: Endangered Species Coloring Book will introduce children to 21 endangered and threatened plants and animals found in the United States. As they color the pages, they will journey to oceans, swamps, deserts, and islands and bring to life a variety of plants and animals.

Public Information Center
U.S. Environmental Protection Agency
401 M Street, SW, MS 3404
Washington, DC 20460   202-260-2080
Children will enjoy learning about the need for recycling while reading and coloring the publication, *There Lived a Wicked Dragon*. Written by Martha Finan for the federal solid waste management programs, it provides a creative way to learn about an important issue.

Office of Public Affairs
U.S. Environmental Protection Agency
77 West Jackson
Chicago, IL 60604   312-886-7935

The Government Works for Kids, Too

Teach your kids how to take care of the earth through the coloring book *The Happy Earth Day Coloring and Activities Book*.

Bureau of Mines
U.S. Department of the Interior
Cochrans Mill Road
P.O. Box 18070
Pittsburgh, PA 15236   412-892-4338

Contact the office above to receive a copy of the poster "The Rock, Coal". Children will enjoy learning the importance of keeping the environment clean.

Public Affairs
U.S. Coast Guard
U.S. Department of Transportation
2100 Second Street, SW
Washington, DC 20593-0001   202-267-1587

Our Day with the Coast Guard provides a fun way for children to learn about the U.S. Coast Guard. By providing information in a coloring book format, kids can learn what it's like to be in the Coast Guard. The coloring book includes activities such as a maze and connect-the-dots.

COMET, HALLEY'S

NASA CORE
Lorain County Joint Vocational School
15181 Route 58 South
Oberlin, OH 44074   216-774-1051

NASA CORE makes available to educators an educational aid on Halley's Comet. Appropriate for grades 4 -12 are the slides *The Return of Halley's Comet* which examine an event heralded by man since the beginning of time.

COMIC BOOKS

Smithsonian Institution Traveling Exhibition Service
1100 Jefferson Dr., SW
Room 3146
Washington, DC 20560

As a teacher did you ever want to use comics in the classroom? M. Thomas Inge's publication *Comics in the Classroom* can help you to do so. It is a teacher's guide and contains suggestions for both the elementary and secondary levels. $1.

National Clearinghouse for Alcohol and Drug Information
P.O. Box 2345   800-729-6686
Rockville, MD 20852   301-468-2600

In 1987, the National Clearinghouse for Alcohol and Drug Information was established as the central point within the Federal Government for materials about alcohol and other drugs. A few of the publications available are in comic book format, so kids can enjoy reading them while learning about important issues. The following two comic books are appropriate for elementary kids:

McGruff's Surprise Party (1989). A comic book that helps children understand the importance of saying "No" to alcohol and other drugs, as told by McGruff, the crime dog. Also teaches children techniques for resisting peer pressure. For ages 8 to 10. 14 pp. PH271.

Forest Service
U.S. Department of Agriculture
14th and Independence, SW
P.O. Box 96090
Washington, DC 20090-6090   202-205-1510

Fire prevention can also be taught through the use of comic books. The comic book *The True Story of Smokey Bear* is one of many fire prevention materials available from the office above.

Food and Drug Administration
Consumer Communications HFE-88
Rockville, MD 20857

Dennis the Menace Takes a Poke at Poison is a comic book that teaches children to "always ask first" before they taste. Write to the office above for a free copy.

Office of Public Information
Texas Water Development Board
P.O. Box 13231
Austin, TX 78711-3231   512-463-8422

Comic books appropriate for environmental education programs may be found in the *Environmental Education Books*, which lists water and environmental education

programs and/or materials suitable for use in public schools. In addition to comic books, materials listed include classroom curriculum, and pamphlets.

COMMUNITY RESOURCES

Office of Elementary and Secondary Education
Smithsonian Institution
Washington, DC 20560   202-357-2404

Art to Zoo is a publication dedicated to promoting the use of community resources among students and teachers nationally. It brings news from the Smithsonian Institution to teachers of grades three through eight. Its purpose is to help teachers use museums, parks, libraries, zoos, and many other resources within their community to open up learning opportunities for their students. Write to the address above if you want your school to be placed, free of charge, on the *Art to Zoo* mailing list.

COMPUTER GRAPHICS

Education Division
NASA Headquarters
Washington, DC 20546

NASA Spacelink is a collection of NASA information and educational materials stored on a computer at the Marshall Space Flight Center in Huntsville, Alabama. The system may be accessed over regular telephone lines. Classroom materials include computer graphics in addition to a variety of information useful in the classroom.

COMPUTER SOFTWARE

NASA CORE
Lorain County Joint Vocational School
15181 Route 58 South
Oberlin, OH 44074   216-774-1051

The NASA Central Operation of Resources for Educators (CORE) serves as the national distribution center for NASA produced education materials. Computer Software (on 5 1/4" diskettes for use on Apple Computers) includes the following:

Astronomy. Programs provide a variety of calculation functions including rising and setting times, planet locations, eclipse dates, calendar conversions and astrophotography data. Educational programs include the "Griffith Observatory Museum Disk" which contains an astronomy term hangman game, a space exploration and astronomy quiz, and a program about the user's birth dates on the planets. Produced by public domain sources. Grade 4 - 6.

Hubble Space Telescope Educational Software Project. Four Apple II disks with reproducible information sheets and reference materials: *Windows to the Universe* chronicles the history of astronomical observations from the unaided eye through the Hubble Space Telescope; *Telescopes* explains the science of optics and the design and characteristics of telescopes; *Introduction to the Hubble Space Telescope* explains the design and operation of the Hubble Space Telescope; *Images From Space* describes the process through which light is captured by the Hubble space Telescope and converted into images on Earth; *Activities Disk* contains a collection of classroom activities and illustrations relating to telescopes; *Glossary* contains an Appleworks data base of more than 300 astronomy terms. Also includes two Macintosh Applications Software (requires Pagemaker program 3.02 version or higher): *Hubble Space Telescope Model* contains the pattern and instructions for making a detailed model of NASA's Hubble Space Telescope: *Telescope Primer* outline of the basic principles behind the design and operation of telescopes. Includes many diagrams that can be enlarged and used for making transparencies. Grade 5 - 8.

Space Shuttle Mission Facts Data Base. A data base that provides information on the first 30 space shuttle missions including: mission number, orbiter, date, commander and pilot. To use this data base you must have the Apple works program. Produced by Oklahoma State University. Grade K - Adult.

Space Shuttle Commander. Side A introduces students to Newton's laws of motion by asking them to imagine that they are the commander of the space shuttle. Takes a nonmathematical approach to this topic and concentrates on concept formation. Side B contains four question banks to use for practice or evaluation. Copyrighted by and reproduced with permission from Lloyd P. Reiber. Grade 4 - 8.

Education Division, MRC 305
National Air and Space Museum
Washington, DC 20560   202-786-2109

The Education Resource Center (ERC) of the National Air and Space Museum (NASM) is open to teachers of all levels and disciplines and offers teachers access to educational materials pertaining to aviation, space, and the Museum's collections. Aerospace-related public domain computer software is available for use with Apple II series and IBM PC computers and is available for duplication when you visit the ERC, as well as through the mail. In both cases, teachers must provide blank diskettes. (Contact the ERC for a current catalog and mail-in procedures.) A growing collection of IBM PC and Apple II series commercial software on aerospace topics is also available on a preview-only basis for visiting teachers.

Ag in the Classroom
Room 317-A, Administration Building
U.S. Department of Agriculture
Washington, DC 20350

Ag in the Classroom is a U.S. Department of Agriculture program designed to help students in grades K-12 acquire the knowledge needed to become agriculturally literate. The program is primarily carried out in each state by a group composed of educators, government officials, and representatives from agricultural organizations and agribusinesses. Computer software and other educational materials are available. Contact the office above for a copy of the *Resource Guide to Educational Materials About Agriculture: A Project of Ag in the Classroom* which lists where to obtain these materials.

Public Information Center
U.S. Environmental Protection Agency
401 M Street, SW, MS 3404
Washington, DC 20460   202-260-2080

Environmental Education Materials for Teachers and Young People (Grades K-12) is an excellent source of resources for educators interested in teaching their students how to keep our environment clean. Computer software is just one of the many types of materials available. Contact the office above to obtain a copy.

CONDORS

U.S. Fish and Wildlife Service
U.S. Department of the Interior
4401 N. Fairfax Drive, Mail Stop 130
Arlington, VA 22203   703-358-1711

Learn about the intriguing bird, the condor, so you can teach your children about it. Call the U.S. Fish and Wildlife Service for the following publication, the *California Condor*.

CONSTELLATIONS

R. Woods, Consumer Information Center - Y
P.O. Box 100
Pueblo, CO 81002

Stars in Your Eyes: A Guide to the Northern Skies contains helpful hints on how to find the seven best known constellations and an explanation on how they were named. 23 pp. (1988. DOD) 155X. $1.50. Write to the office above to receive a copy.

CONSTITUTION, U.S.

Education Branch (NEEE)
National Archives and Records Administration
Washington, DC 20408   202-501-6172

Interested in teaching your upper elementary students about the U.S. Constitution? Contact the Education Branch of the National Archives for the publication *A More Perfect Union: The Creation of the U.S. Constitution* (#200105, ISBN 0-922333-24-X). This particular booklet includes a historical introduction, transcriptions, and facsimiles of the featured documents, and can be ordered from the address above. (8 1/2 x 11, approx. 25 pages each, illustrations, 1986. Softcover only, $2.50 each.) Also available is the teaching unit *The Constitution: Evolution of a Government*. Published by the National Archives and SIRS, Inc., this unit contains about 50 reproductions of documents - charts, photographs, letters, drawings, and posters - and a detailed teacher's guide. The materials deal with certain key issues of the period, with governmental and political responses to these issues, and with public attitudes. The unit's cost is $40. To order, send a purchase order to: SIRS, Inc., P.O. Box 2348, Boca Raton, FL 33427-2348: or call toll free: 800-3327-0513 (except AK and FL call collect 407-994-0079). For information on other educational materials available contact the address above.

COUGARS

U.S. Fish and Wildlife Service
U.S. Department of the Interior
4401 N. Fairfax Drive, Mail Stop 130

Arlington, VA 22203   703-358-1711

Call the U.S. Fish and Wildlife Service to obtain their publication *Cougar* so you can learn more about this fascinating animal.

COUNSELING

Counseling and Personnel Services Clearinghouse
University of Michigan
School of Education, Room 2108
610 East University Street
Ann Arbor, MI 48109-1259   313-764-7563

The Counseling and Personnel Services Clearinghouse of the Educational Resources Information Center (ERIC) prepares and supervises counselors at all educational levels. It is a resource for counselors seeking information on the theoretical development of counseling and guidance; personnel procedures such as testing and interviewing and the analysis and dissemination of the resultant information; group and case work; nature of pupil, student, and adult characteristics; personnel workers and their relation to career planning; family consultations; and student orientation activities.

CRATERS

Venus Names, Magellan Project Office
Mail Stop 230-310
Jet Propulsion Laboratory
4800 Oak Grove Drive
Pasadena, CA 91109   818-354-4321

Get your students interested in the craters on Venus by having them help choose an official name for them! Scientists of the Magellan Project, in association with the U.S. Geological Survey, are inviting the public to propose names of notable women for the many impact craters and large volcanic vents being discovered on Venus by the Magellan spacecraft's imaging radar. Names sent to the Magellan Project offices at NASA's Jet Propulsion Laboratory will be compiled for the Working Group of Planetary Systems Nomenclature, a committee of the International Astronomical Union (IAU). The IAU gives final approval to names for bodies in the solar system. Because the IAU meets only every 3 years and its last meeting was in July, 1991, names newly proposed for Venusian features will not be considered until the following meeting in 1994. But names proposed this year, if accepted as provisional by the nomenclature committee, may be used on published maps and in articles, pending final approval by the IAU. For more information, including the criteria for the names submitted, write to the office above.

CREATIVE THINKING

Project XL
U.S. Patent and Trademark Office
Washington, DC 20231   703-305-8341

PROJECT XL has been initiated by the U.S. Patent and Trademark Office as a national partnership designed to encourage proliferation of such programs and to develop new programs and materials which will promote critical and creative thinking and problem-solving skills for all children in our nation's schools. Through critical and creative thinking and problem-solving, ideas become reality as children create inventive solutions, illustrate their ideas, and make models of their inventions. The *Inventive Thinking Curriculum Project* provides children with opportunities to develop and practice higher order thinking skills. Call the office above to obtain a copy of this teacher's guide and *The Inventive Thinking Resource Directory*, a directory designed to assist the classroom teacher or school administrator who is interested in helping students become better thinkers, problem-solvers, and decision makers. Also available is *Black Innovators in Technology: Inspiring a New Generation*.

CUBA

Education Branch (NEEE)
National Archives and Records Administration
Washington, DC 20408   202-501-6172

Available for educators of upper elementary through secondary schools is *The Cuban Missile Crisis: Kennedy's Address to the Nation* (#200113, ISBN 0-911333-59-2, $2.50.), a teaching aid available from the National Archives. It contains a historical introduction and transcriptions and facsimiles of the featured documents.

CULTURE

Office of Education, Room 212
Mail Stop 158
National Museum of Natural History

Washington, DC 20560   202-357-2747

The National Museum of Natural History has a workshop for elementary and middle school teachers on understanding culture. *Understanding Culture: Introducing Culture Into Your Classroom and/or Curricula*. The workshop provides an understanding of culture and how it works, a perspective on world cultures and the concepts of multiculturalism and Eurocentrism. Included are suggestions for resources, learning activities, and strategies for integrating an understanding of culture into social studies, geography, history, biology, language arts, art, sociology, and anthropology. Workshop involves using museum exhibits for teaching.

CURRICULUM, ELEMENTARY SCHOOLS

Superintendent of Documents
Dept. 33
Washington, DC 20402   202-512-1800

James Madison Elementary School: A Curriculum for American Students presents a model elementary school curriculum for kindergarten through the eighth grade. It includes suggestions for teaching English, social studies (history, geography, and civic), mathematics, science, foreign languages, fine arts, physical education, and health. It also includes profiles of seven actual schools which have demonstrated curricular excellence. 1988. 61 pp. (S/N 065-000-00350-3, $2.50).

DATA BASES

NASA CORE
Lorain County Joint Vocational School
15181 Route 58 South
Oberlin, OH 44074   216-774-1051

Teach your students interesting facts about the Space Shuttle missions. Use the *Space Shuttle Mission Facts Data Base* to obtain information on the first 30 space shuttle missions including mission number, orbiter, date, commander and pilot. To use this data base you must have the Apple works program. Appropriate for kids in grades K-12. Produced by Oklahoma State University.

Educational Resources Information Center (ERIC)
Office of Educational Research and Improvement (OERI)
U.S. Department of Education
555 New Jersey Ave., NW
Washington, DC 20208-5720   202-219-2289

The Educational Resources Information Center (ERIC) is a nationwide information network designed to provide users with ready access to education literature. Established in 1966 to make educational research and practice available from a single source, ERIC collects, analyzes, and distributes information from local, state, federal, and international agencies, as well as private sources. At the heart of ERIC is the largest education database in the world - containing more than 735,000 bibliographic records of documents and journal articles; approximately 2,600 records are added monthly. Papers, conference proceedings, literature reviews, and curricula materials, along with articles from nearly 800 education-related journals, are indexed and abstracted for entry into the ERIC database.

DEER

U.S. Fish and Wildlife Service
U.S. Department of the Interior
4401 N. Fairfax Drive
Mail Stop 130
Arlington, VA 22203   703-358-1711

Call the U.S. Fish and Wildlife Service to obtain its publication called *Key Deer*.

DEERE, JOHN

Department of Public Programs
Room MBB66
National Museum of American History
Smithsonian Institution
Washington, DC 20560   202-357-4184

Would your students or children like a poster of a 1924 John Deere Model D farm tractor? Cost is $8.

DINOSAURS

Office of Education, Room 212
Mail Stop 158
National Museum of Natural History
Washington, DC 20560   202-357-2747

The National Museum of Natural History periodically conducts workshops for elementary and middle school teachers. One of the workshops is *Dinosaurs* which includes a walk through the Dinosaur Hall to help teachers and aides design a visit for their classes, followed by an informal lecture on major dinosaur groups represented in the exhibit hall.

Office of Education, Room 212
Mail Stop 158
National Museum of Natural History
Washington, DC 20560   202-357-2747

Available from the National Museum of Natural History is the slide set *Dinosaurs and Other Giants*. It is available for a three-week loan free of charge. Use it to enhance curricula for school children.

Office of Education, Room 212
Mail Stop 158
National Museum of Natural History
Washington, DC 20560   202-357-2747

Discover Dinosaurs is a program for preschool and kindergarten children offered by the National Museum of Natural History. In this program students receive a short introduction to "What is a fossil?" by means of a puppet show, investigate dinosaur skeletons and dioramas in the Dinosaur Hall, and participate in hands-on activities relating to dinosaur exhibits.

DOGS

Center for Veterinary Medicine
Food and Drug Administration
Public Health Service
U.S. Department of Health and Human Services
7500 Standish Pl.
Rockville, MD 20855   301-594-1740

Dogs are one of the many pets children like to have. There are many factors, however, involved in the care and feeding of a household pet. The office above has several fact sheets which parents can use to teach their children how to care for pets properly.

Office of Public Affairs
National Institute of Mental Health
Public Health Service
U.S. Department of Health and Human Services
5600 Fishers Lane, Room 13C05
Rockville, MD 20857   301-443-4513

Dogs are also one of the many types of animals used for medical research. By learning how scientists perform medical research in laboratories, children can better understand how and why doctors are able to help people to get well. *Let's Visit a Research Laboratory: Introduction and Lesson Plans* (for schoolchildren in grades 2-5) helps answers the many questions children may have about research laboratories. The supplemental poster that is included provides teachers with helpful illustrations for classroom discussion and activities.

U.S. Fish and Wildlife Service
U.S. Department of the Interior
4401 N. Fairfax Drive
Mail Stop 130
Arlington, VA 22203   703-358-1711

Learn about the prairie dog through the publication *Prairie Dog*.

DOLPHINS

U.S. Fish and Wildlife Service
U.S. Department of the Interior
4401 N. Fairfax Drive
Mail Stop 130
Arlington, VA 22203   703-358-1711

Would you like to learn more about the gentle and intriguing mammal, the dolphin? Contact the U.S. Fish and Wildlife Service for the publication *Dolphins*.

DOUGLASS, FREDERICK

Smithsonian Institution Traveling Exhibition Service
1100 Jefferson Drive, SW
Room 3146
Washington, DC 20560

Help teach your children about Frederick Douglass through the poster *The Frederick Douglass Years: 1817-1895*. It includes biographies of abolitionists and black leaders, and a bibliography. Cost is $1.

DRAMA

Education Department
Kennedy Center
Washington, DC 20566   202-416-8800

Introduce theater to children in grades K-6 with help from the booklet *Imaginations at Work: Kids Invent Theatre*. $2.50 copy; $2 shipping and handling.

DRUG AND ALCOHOL ABUSE PREVENTION

National Clearinghouse for Alcohol and Drug Information
P.O. Box 2345
Rockville, MD 20852   800-729-6686

Drug prevention videos are available from the U.S. Department of Education for parents and educators. Originally designed for schools these video programs are now available for home use. Each program is closed captioned and comes with its own Parent's or Teacher's Guide to help you discuss each program's message and the serious problem of drug abuse with your child. Programs for elementary children include:

The Drug Avenger. ($8.50, 73 minutes, 16-page Parent's Guide, 1988, VHS Order No. DGA17535). Three children from the future travel back to the 20th Century to take on the life-threatening problem of drug abuse in 10 animated programs.

Fast Forward Future. ($8.50, 61 minutes, 23-page Teacher's Guide, 1988., VHS Order No. DGA 17532). Actor Richard Kiley as "Mentor" shows three elementary students the future with the Fast Forward machine. The students see the effects of using drugs and staying drug free.

Straight Up. ($8.50, 90 minutes, 2-page Teacher's Guide, 1988, VHS Order No. DGA17529). Academy award winning actor Lou Gosset, Jr., as Cosmo takes a boy named Ben, played by Chad Allen of NBC's "Our House", on a journey in the "fate" elevator. Ben's travels teach him valuable lessons about why drugs are harmful and how to refuse them.

Demand Reduction Section
Drug Enforcement Administration
U.S. Department of Justice
Washington, DC 20537   202-307-7936

Healthy Bodies Don't Need Drugs! Learning and Activity Book is a fifteen-page publication designed to educate children about the need to take care of their bodies and to say "No!" to drugs.

National Crime Prevention Council
1700 K Street, NW, 2nd Floor
Washington, DC 20006   202-466-6272

Help teach your children to say "No!" through the use of the following McGruff materials. They are available from the National Crime Prevention Council. Materials include:

Elementary School Materials Package. This package contains materials that can be photocopied for students and parents. It was sent to 51,000 elementary schools, and limited quantities are still available from the National Crime Prevention Council. Free.

If You Want to Fit In, Be Drug Free: Welcome to McGruff's Drug-Free Park. This colored poster shows McGruff with children playing basketball, baseball, riding bicycles, and reading - all alcohol- and other drug-free activities. $2.50.

Licensed Products Package. The National Crime Prevention Council has many specialty items available to teach elementary youth about prevention. This package includes information on a talking robot, a puppet package, stickers, calendars, and many other items. Free.

McGruff's Drug Abuse Prevention Kit. This kit includes different games, puzzles, a video, and recorded songs for children. Two items are for parents, and they give tips for teaching children how to say no. Materials come as reproducible masters. $30.

McGruff's Drug Abuse Prevention Kit: The No Show. The video is part of McGruff's Drug Abuse Prevention Kit. All parts of the Kit including the video, are reproducible for nonprofit educational purposes. Animation is used throughout 25 percent of the video. The video kids create a rock video about refusing drugs. $12.

To Be What You Want To Be: Be Drug Free. This poster has people from many professions with the slogan to be what you want to be, be drug free. It has room for the child to draw himself into the picture. $2.50.

National Clearinghouse for Alcohol and
 Drug Information
P.O. Box 2345   800-729-6686
Rockville, MD 20852   301-468-2600

The National Clearinghouse for Alcohol and Drug Information is an excellent source of information for alcohol and drug abuse prevention. In 1987 it was established as the central point within the Federal Government for current print and audiovisual materials about alcohol and other drugs. NCADI answers more than 18,000 telephone and mail inquiries each month and distributes some 18 million printed items a year, which include the following posters and publications appropriate for elementary school children:

Ayudando a sus alumnos a decirle que no (Helping Your Students Say "No") Teacher's Guide (1990). In English and Spanish, explains the effects of alcohol on the body, why children start to drink, how teachers can help their students say "No" to alcohol and deal with the first signs of drinking, and where teachers can go for more information. 13 pp. PH284.

Buzzy's Rebound: Fat Albert and the Cosby Kids (1990). In comic book format, depicts the story of Buzzy, a young basketball player and friend of the Cosby Kids, who gets into trouble with alcohol and is helped by his coach, and a school counselor. 18 pp. PH232.

Elementary School Children and Alcohol Education includes audiovisuals, programs descriptions, professional and organizational resources to assist educators and parents of young childcare. It is available free from the office below. MS315.

The Fact Is ... You Can Prevent Alcohol and Other Drug Problems Among Elementary School Children (1988). Includes videotapes, program descriptions, and professional and organizational resources to assist educators and parents of young children. 17 pp. MS349.

Growing Up Drug Free: A Parent's Guide to Prevention (1989). This handbook outlines what children at four key stages of development should know about drugs and suggests family activities to reinforce children's motivation to avoid alcohol and other drugs. 52 pp. PHD533.

The Herschel Walker Poster (1989). Herschel Walker, football star, salutes the drug-free youth of America in a 22 in. by 27 in. color poster. Reference is made to NCADI as a source for more information. AVD45.

Learning to Live Drug Free: A Curriculum Model for Prevention (1990). Provides a flexible framework for classroom-based prevention efforts for kindergarten through grade 12. Presents the states of child development as they relate to drug prevention, facts about drugs, suggested lesson plans, tips on working with parents and the community, and a resource section for further information. Teachers can learn how to integrate prevention messages into their classroom presentations. BKD51.

Little League Drug Education Program (1991). This video has two parts: Part 1, Friend to Friend, Featuring Orel Hershiser, is directed toward today's Little Leaguer. The film tells the story of a Little League player who is tempted by drugs. Part 2, Big League Advice: Helping Your Little Leaguers Say No, is for parents and coaches of Little League players. The film depicts a discussion among Little League parents and baseball Hall-of-Famers 'Hank' Aaron and Jim Palmer. These great ball players offer frank and important advice to parents on how to talk to young people about drugs and alcohol. 30 minutes. VHS29.

Live the Dream, Say No to Alcohol and Drug Abuse (1989). Poster features Dr. Martin Luther King, Jr. Appropriate for all ages, 15 1/2 in. by 22 in. AV165.

McGruff's Surprise Party (1989). A comic book that helps children understand the importance of saying "No" to alcohol and other drugs, as told by McGruff, the crime dog. Also teaches children techniques for resisting peer pressure. For ages 8 to 10. 14 pp. PH271.

McGruff: Say 'No' to Crack and Other Drugs (1989). Bright red and white poster featuring McGruff, the Crime Dog. McGruff tells kids that crack is poison and a very dangerous drug. Tells them to say a big "no" and walk away. Also provides the NIDA hotline number (800-662-HELP) and a cocaine hotline number (800-COCAINE). 64 in. by 88 in. AVD14.

Parent Training is Prevention (1991). Contains information to help communities identify and carry out programs on parenting. Details roles parents play in rearing children who are free of alcohol and other drug problems, highlights ethnic and cultural considerations, and gives characteristics of effective prevention programs. 184 pp. BK 184.

The Government Works for Kids, Too

Pointers for Parents Card (1989). Provides easy steps parents can take to help prevent their child from using alcohol or other drugs. Excellent handout for special events such as fairs, workshop, or conferences. 3 1/2 in. by 8 1/2 in. card. PH260.

Prevention Resource Guide: Elementary Youth (1991). This Resource Guide includes materials specifically developed for youth that may be used in an elementary school setting, as well as relevant information on parenting. It is designed for teachers, administrators, and program leaders who come in contact with elementary youth. 23 pp. MS421.

Quick List: 10 Steps to Help Your Child Say "No" (1990). Also available in Spanish. Identifies ten things that parents can do to help their children stay away from alcohol and other drugs, from talking with your child to being a good role model. Three-panel fold out mini-poster. PH230.

Snappy Answers Card for Kids (1989). Suggests responses that young people can use to say "No" if offered alcohol or other drugs. Excellent handout for special events such as fairs, workshops, or school events. 3 1/2 in. by 8 1/2 in. card. PH 261.

Drug Enforcement Administration
U.S. Department of Justice
Washington, DC 20537   202-307-7977

The *Soozie and Katy* workbook was created to acquaint children with the purpose of medicine, its appropriate use, the legal distribution of drugs, and the dangers which can accompany misuse. Appropriate for home and classroom discussion, it begins with the idea that each child is responsible for the care of his body and should protect it. Teaching the child the doctor-pharmacist-parent sequence of drug distribution will help the child accept the administration of medicine without fear, and it will also begin to explore the idea that there are illegal channels of drug distribution.

National Clearinghouse for Alcohol and Drug Information
P.O. Box 2345
Rockville, MD 20852   800-729-6686

Use the *Be Smart Game* board game to help teach your children to say "No!" to drugs. It is printed on a heavy sheet of paper, allows two-four players, and requires dice and a coin for each player. Going around the board, players have opportunities to say "No!" to drugs and to discover alternate activities.

R. Woods
Consumer Information Center
Pueblo, CO 81008

Growing Up Drug Free (#551X) is an educational booklet intended for parents, available at no charge. To order, send a written request (including the stock number) to the above address.

DUCKS

U.S. Fish and Wildlife Service
U.S. Department of the Interior
4401 N. Fairfax Drive
Mail Stop 130
Arlington, VA 22203   703-358-1711

The U.S. Fish and Wildlife Service has several publications available on ducks including *Diving Ducks*, and *Ducks Get Sick, Too*. Teach your students about these adorable birds!

EAGLES

U.S. Fish and Wildlife Service
U.S. Department of the Interior
4401 N. Fairfax Drive
Mail Stop 130
Arlington, VA 22203   703-358-1711

Use the U.S. Fish and Wildlife Service's publications to teach your students about our national symbol, the bald eagle. Call to receive *Bald Eagle*.

EARTH SCIENCES

Elementary and Secondary Programs Branch
Educational Affairs Division
Mail Code XEE
NASA Headquarters
Washington, DC 20546

The earth sciences is just one topic that is covered in teacher workshops held each summer by Aerospace Education Services Program (AESP) specialists at NASA field centers, elementary and secondary schools, and on college campuses. Workshops also cover astronomy, aeronautics, life in space, principles of rocketry, and remote sensing. A typical workshop includes how-to and hands-on activities to help teachers incorporate what they learn into classroom activities and programs to supplement existing curricula.

Missouri Department of Natural Resources
Division of Geology and Land Survey
P.O. Box 250
Rolla, MO 65401

Earthquakes in Missouri contains information not only about earthquakes in Missouri but also general information on understanding earthquakes, measuring earthquakes, and the hazards of earthquakes. This publication can serve as an educational aid for upper-elementary school children learning about earthquakes.

Geologic Inquiries Group
U.S. Geological Survey
907 National Center
Reston, VA 22092   703-648-4383

The office above answers questions on topics such as the geology of specific areas, geologic maps and mapping, earthquakes, and energy and mineral resources. Educators and students can contact the office if they have any questions relating to these topics.

Geologic Inquiries Group
U.S. Geological Survey
907 National Center
Reston, VA 22092   703-648-4383

The *Selected Packet of Geologic Teaching Aids* is prepared for elementary school teachers (and high school teachers) of general science, geography, social studies, environmental education and other earth science-related subjects. It contains leaflets, booklets, reference lists, and an activity sheet ("Make Your Own Paper Model of a Volcano"). To receive a packet, send a request on school letterhead indicating the subject that is taught and the grade level to the office listed above.

Earth Science Information Center
U.S. Department of the Interior
1849 C Street, NW, Room 2650
Washington, DC 20240   202-208-4047

Contact the office above for information on the U.S. Geological Survey's map products and earth science publications. They may help answer questions you have.

U.S. Geological Survey
P.O. Box 25425
Denver, CO 80225

The following publications are an excellent source of information for both upper elementary students and educators. Students can use them to supplement special reports and science projects and teachers can use them to enhance their curricula. To obtain single copies write to the office above.

"The Big Five" - Some Facts and Figures on our Nation's Largest Rivers. Presents statistics for maximum, minimum, and mean flows for the Nation's largest rivers -- the Mississippi, St. Lawrence, Columbia, Ohio, and the Missouri.

A Brief History of the U.S. Geological Survey. Describes the bureau's growth, activities, and achievements from its founding in 1879 to its centennial in 1979.

Collecting Rocks. Describes the origin of major rock types and how rocks can provide clues to the Earth's history. Includes suggestions for starting a rock collection, identifying specimens, and housing such a collection.

Earthquakes. Explains the nature and causes of earthquakes. Describes the techniques used to detect, record, measure, and predict seismic disturbances. Provides historical data on several world-famous earthquakes that have occurred since 1755.

The Exclusive Economic Zone: An Exciting New Frontier. Describes the geologic processes that form the ocean floors. Discusses the importance of the mineral potential of the Exclusive Economic Zone, which provides the Nation with nearly 3 billion acres of new frontier for study and exploration.

Geologic Maps: Portraits of the Earth. Explains the nature of geologic maps, how they are made, and the ways they may be used to determine relationships of rocks on and beneath the Earth's Surface. Shows examples of maps.

Geologic Time. Explains relative and radiometric time scales and how geologists measure the age of the Earth. Illustrates the scientific processes that are used to interpret the Earth's geologic history.

Be patient. If any phone number is incorrect, call (area code) 555-1212 and request the new listing.

Gold. Discusses the nature of gold, its origins, and the geologic environments in which it is commonly found. Provides information about the uses of gold and a brief historical account of production in the U.S.

Glaciers: A Water Resource. Discusses the relationship between glacial ice and the amount of water on land surfaces. Describes the types of glaciers, their origins, and the natural processes that regulate the melting of ice.

Ground Water: An Undervalued Resource. Describes the need for using ground water, the role of ground water in the economy, and an analysis of regional aquifer systems. Discusses the ways in which ground water and surface water interact.

Ground Water and the Rural Homeowner. Presents a short description of ground water, some of the problems associated with ground water, and some suggestions for help with problems.

Ground Water Contamination--No "Quick Fix" in Sight. Explains how ground water is contaminated by septic tanks or cesspools, municipal lagoons, sewers, landfills, or tailings piles, and the need for further research in contamination prevention.

How Much Water in a 12-ounce Can? A Perspective on Water-Use Information. Provides information on how water was a free resource but now is considered an expensive commodity. Demonstrates how the ever-increasing use of water by industry and in the home is depleting existing supplies.

The Hydrologic Cycle. Explains the natural process by which water is circulated from the seas to the atmosphere, to the land, and back to the seas in a continuous cycle.

The Interior of the Earth. Explains the structure and nature of the Earth's crust, mantle, and core. Describes the procedures used to obtain this information through studies of seismic wave patterns.

John Wesley Powell's Exploration of the Colorado River. Describes Powell's daring voyage in 1869 through the canyons of the Colorado River, starting at Green River Station, Wyoming, and ending at the junction of the Colorado and Virgin Rivers in Arizona.

Landforms of the United States. Discusses the sculpturing of landforms and the effects of wind, water, and chemical processes. Lists major physiographic divisions of the U.S. and describes their characteristic features.

Mountains and Plains: Denver's Geologic Setting. Describes the nature and structure of the rocks that underlie Denver, Colorado, and part of the adjacent Front Range. Provides a road log to explain the natural features of the area.

The Naming (and Misnaming) of America. Describes how some localities came to be names, the derivation of these geographic names, and why the U.S. Board on Geographic Names was established.

Natural Steam for Power. Describes the investigation of geothermal steam as a potential source of energy for power needs worldwide. Discusses the nature and behavior of steam formed underground.

Our Changing Continent. Discusses the evidence and techniques scientists use to reconstruct the history of the changing land surface of the North American continent.

Permafrost. Defines permafrost and summarizes its geographic distribution. Explains how construction activities alter local permafrost conditions and discusses how best to counteract unfavorable changes.

Prospecting for Gold in the United States. Describes various kinds of gold deposits and their locations. Offers a brief review of the problems faced by present-day prospectors and lists available maps and services.

Rain: A Water Resource. Provides information on the annual precipitation in areas of the United States, with specific data on several major cities. Explains how to express rainfall as quantities of water. Also available in Spanish.

River Basins of the United States: A Series. Lists basic facts including historical notes, flow characteristics, and physical statistics on selected river basins.

Safety and Survival in an Earthquake. Describes the hazards posed by earthquakes and offers instructions for individual action before, during, and after a tremor to minimize loss of life and damage to property. Also available in Spanish.

The San Andreas Fault. Describes the nature, behavior, and earthquake history of this major fault system that extends from northern California to the Gulf of California.

Tree Rings: Timekeepers of the Past. Explains how past environmental conditions have been recorded in tree rings and how scientists interpret this information.

Volcanic Hazards at Mount Shasta, California. Describes the kinds of volcanic activity that have occurred in the past, shows areas that could be affected in the future, and suggests ways of reducing the risks.

Volcanoes. Describes the principal types of volcanoes, different types of eruptions, associated volcanic phenomena, their geologic settings, and how volcanoes are monitored. Explains how volcanic activity endangers and helps mankind.

Water Dowsing. Provides a brief history of water dowsing. Explains how hydrologists of the USGS and other agencies use scientific methods to locate ground water.

Water in the Urban Environment: Erosion and Sediment. Explores the dual role that water plays as both as resource and a hazard. Discusses possible actions that minimize erosion and sedimentation.

The Water of the World. Discusses the amount of water contained in the world's atmosphere, on the surface, and underground. Describes the world's water balance.

Water Use in the United States, 1980. Summarizes the use of the Nation's water supply for domestic, industrial, rural, and irrigation purposes.

What is Water?. Describes the basic chemical properties of water and its diverse physical characteristics. Briefly explains the formation of water on Earth. Also available in Spanish.

Why is the Ocean Salty? Discusses the origin of the oceans and the sources of their salinity. Also available in Spanish.

EARTHQUAKES

Geologic Inquiries Group
U.S. Geological Survey
907 National Center
Reston, VA 22092   703-648-4383

Would you like to teach your students or children about earthquakes, but you have some questions about them yourself? Call the Geologic Inquiries Group of the U.S. Geological Survey. This office answers questions not only on topics such as earthquakes, but also questions on energy and mineral resources, the geology of specific areas, and geologic maps and mapping.

Missouri Department of Natural Resources
Division of Geology and Land Survey
P.O. Box 250
Rolla, MO 65401

Earthquakes in Missouri contains information not only about earthquakes in Missouri but also general information on understanding earthquakes, measuring earthquakes, and the hazards of earthquakes. This publication can serve as an educational aid for upper-elementary school children learning about earthquakes.

U.S. Geological Survey
P.O. Box 25425
Denver, CO 80225

The following publications are an excellent source of information on earthquakes for both upper elementary students and educators. Students can use them to supplement special reports and science projects and teachers can use them to enhance their curricula. To obtain single copies write to the office above.

Earthquakes. Explains the nature and causes of earthquakes. Describes the techniques used to detect, record, measure, and predict seismic disturbances. Provides historical data on several world-famous earthquakes that have occurred since 1755.

Safety and Survival in an Earthquake. Describes the hazards posed by earthquakes and offers instructions for individual action before, during, and after a tremor to minimize loss of life and damage to property. Also available in Spanish.

The San Andreas Fault. Describes the nature, behavior, and earthquake history of this major fault system that extends from northern California to the Gulf of California.

ECOLOGY

U.S. Fish and Wildlife Service
U.S. Department of the Interior

4401 N. Fairfax Drive
Mail Stop 130
Arlington, VA 22203   703-358-1711
Learn more about ecology through the U.S. Fish and Wildlife Service's publication *Ecology*.

EISENHOWER, DWIGHT D.

Education Branch (NEEE)
National Archives and Records Administration
Washington, DC 20408   202-501-6172
Atoms for Peace: Dwight D. Eisenhower's Address to the United Nations (#200016, ISBN 0-911333-76-2) is booklet offered to teachers of upper elementary through secondary school students. It includes a historical introduction and transcriptions and facsimiles of the featured documents. Cost is $2.50.

ELECTRICITY

National Energy Information Center (NEIC)
Energy Information Administration, EI-231
1000 Independence Ave., SW, Room 1F-048
Washington, DC 20585   202-586-8800
Do you have a question about electricity? Contact the National Energy Information Center which is the information dissemination service for DOE's Energy Information Administration (EIA). It is responsible for the collection, analysis, and distribution of energy statistics and provides 20 information sheets free. In addition to electricity, these one-page capsules cover such energy topics as petroleum, natural gas, coal, and renewable energy. Also available is *Energy Facts*, a pocket-size statistical reference providing brief facts on a variety of domestic and international energy data.

ELKS

U.S. Fish and Wildlife Service
U.S. Department of the Interior
4401 N. Fairfax Drive
Mail Stop 130
Arlington, VA 22203   703-358-1711
The publication *American Elk* may provide new information on this intriguing animal.

ELLINGTON, DUKE

Department of Public Programs
Room BB53
National Museum of American History
Smithsonian Institution
Washington, DC 20560   202-357-4187
Use the poster *Duke Ellington* to educate your students about this extraordinary person.

EMANCIPATION PROCLAMATION

Education Branch (NEEE)
National Archives and Records Administration
Washington, DC 20408   202-501-6172
The Education Branch of the National Archives offers teachers of upper elementary through secondary school students publications and teaching units to aid in the teaching of historical documents and eras. *The Emancipation Proclamation* (#200103, ISBN 0-911333-40-1) is one of these teaching aids. This booklet includes a historical introduction and transcriptions and facsimiles of the featured documents. Cost is $2.50.

ENDANGERED SPECIES

U.S. Fish and Wildlife Service
U.S. Department of the Interior
4401 N. Fairfax Drive
Mail Stop 130
Arlington, VA 22203   703-358-1711
Would you like to teach your students about endangered species? The Fish and Wildlife has some excellent publications to help you. Call them to receive *Endangered Species*, and *Pesticide Use and Endangered Species*.

Office of Education, Room 212
Mail Stop 158
National Museum of Natural History
Washington, DC 20560   202-357-2747
The National Museum of Natural History conducts a visiting program, include one on endangered species. The museum has on display over 100 mounted specimens of animals that are endangered. With *Endangered Species and Extinction* students learn about changes on our planet and discover how those changes affect life on Earth. Choose either a "Modern" (living endangered species and immediate reasons for their problems - recommended for K-3) or "Fossil and Modern" (global climate changes as documented in fossil and modern scientific record - recommended for Grade 3 and up) focus.

Office of Education, Room 212
Mail Stop 158
National Museum of Natural History
Washington, DC 20560   202-357-2747
The National Museum of Natural History also conducts workshops for teachers, including *Climate and Endangered Species*. This workshop is designed to help teachers and aides design a visit or prepare for a guided tour. The identification of all endangered and extinct modern animals on exhibit is followed by an informal talk about why certain groups of animals are more vulnerable than others.

ENERGY EDUCATION (CONSERVATION AND AWARENESS)

Energy Center
Sonoma State University
1801 East Cotati Ave.
Rohnert Park, CA 94928   707-664-2577
The teaching activity/game *California Challenge: An Educational Tour of California* highlights California history and geography from an energy perspective, and is appropriate for children in grades 4-5. The cost is $20 for a full game which includes instructions, map, cards, 4 game pieces and 1 die.

Energy Efficiency and Renewable Energy Clearinghouse
P.O. Box 3048
Merrifield, VA 22116   800-363-3732
The office above has information sheets that educators can use to supplement their curricula. They include the following:

Biofuels as a Source of Energy
Geothermal Energy
Hot Water Energy Conservation
Learning About Energy Conservation
Learning About Renewable Energy
Ocean Energy
Recycling Waste to Save Energy
Renewable Energy: An Overview
Renewable Energy Reading List for Young Adults
Solar Energy and You
Sunspaces
Wood Fuel

Office of Fossil Energy, Room 4G 085
U.S. Department of Energy
1000 Independence Ave., SW
Washington, DC 20585   202-586-6503
Call the office above to receive *The Clean Coal Path* poster. It traces the route of several new advances in the clean use of coal, America's most abundant fossil energy resource. During the 1990s, many of these improvements will be used for the first time in power plants to generate new supplies of electricity without polluting the nation's air.

Bureau of Mines
U.S. Department of the Interior
Cochrans Mill Road
P.O. Box 18070
Pittsburgh, PA 15236   412-892-4338
Children in the upper elementary grades will enjoy the *Coal Products Tree* illustration and learning all the products that are available from coal. While all the common products are listed, some surprisingly uncommon ones are listed as well, including baking powder, perfumes, and food preservatives.

Energy Efficiency and Renewable Energy Clearinghouse
P.O. Box 3048
Merrifield, VA 22116   800-363-3732
Conservation Activities for the Classroom lists activities that other teachers have used to promote awareness of energy conservation and renewable energy in the classroom.

Office of Fossil Energy Communications
1000 Independence Ave., SW, Room 4G-085
Washington, DC 20585   202-586-6503

Teach kids where coal comes from and the importance of it. *Dinosaurs and Power Plants* is a 16-page brochure designed for students that relates the story of mining and drilling for coal, gas, and oil, the environmental concerns involved, and modes of transportation. *Clean Coal Technology* is also available.

Energy Center
Sonoma State University
1801 East Cotati Ave.
Rohnert Park, CA 94928   707-664-2577

Conserve and Renew: Energy Activities is a collection in interdisciplinary energy activities for children in grades 4-6 to be used either as a unit on energy, or as individual activities to complement existing curricula. While the main focus is on conservation and renewables, recycling and ethics are also included. Cost is $10.

Energy Efficiency and Renewable Energy Clearinghouse
P.O. Box 3048
Merrifield, VA 22116   800-363-3732

Educators can use the publication *Learning About Energy Conservation* to teach their students the meaning of renewable and nonrenewable energy and ways in which one can conserve energy. Call the office above for a copy of this ten page publication.

National Energy Information Center
Energy Information Administration
Forrestal Building
1000 Independence Ave., SW, Room 1F-048
Washington, DC 20585   202-586-8800

Energy Education Resources is the result of a study undertaken by the National Energy Information Center (NEIC), a service of the Energy Information Administration (EIA), to provide its customers with a list of generally available free or low-cost energy-related educational materials for primary and secondary students and educators. The list is updated once a year.

Energy Efficiency and Renewable Energy Clearinghouse
P.O. Box 3048
Merrifield, VA 22116   800-363-3732

What is Your Energy I.Q.? is a two page publication students can use to test their energy I.Q. Questions asked include: What is energy from the sun called? Why do we need to conserve our nonrewable forms of energy? and What changes sunlight into electricity?

National Energy Information Center, EI-231
Energy Information Administration
Forrestal Building
Washington, DC 20585   202-586-8800

Contact the office above for a copy of *Energy Information Sheets*, available free of charge. Information ranging from crude oil production to coal consumption to nuclear power generation is provided. The information can be used by teachers and upper elementary students to supplement curricula and reports.

California Energy Extension Service
1400 Tenth St., Room 209
Sacramento, CA 95814   916-323-4388

The Energy Tech-Knowledgy Program promotes energy awareness to children in grades kindergarten through junior high. Grade-level specific materials are available to teachers and are designed to make it easy for them to include energy conservation education as part of their regular classroom instruction. Contact the office above for more information.

Office of Plans and Evaluations
Office of Nuclear Energy
U.S. Department of Energy
1000 Independence Ave., SW
Washington, DC 20585   202-586-9720

Would you like to teach your students about nuclear energy? The office above has several publications available, some of which are listed below, to more fully understand this valuable source of energy and the role it plays. Teachers can supplement their science curricula with the use of these publications:

Answers to Questions
Approaches to Nuclear Safety
Atoms to Electricity
The First Reactor
High-Level Nuclear Waste: A Safe, Permanent Solution
The History of Nuclear Energy

How Nuclear Energy Plants Work
Light Water Breeder Reactor
Low-Level Nuclear Waste: Safe, Permanent Disposal
Nuclear Energy: Benefit for All Americans
Nuclear Energy Economics
Nuclear Energy Plant Safety
The Nuclear Fuel Cycle
Nuclear Power in Space
Nuclear Powerplant Safety: Design and Planning
Nuclear Powerplant Safety: Operations
Nuclear Powerplant Safety: Source Terms
Radiation in Perspective
Radiosotopes: Today's Applications
Understanding Radiation

Bureau of Mines
U.S. Department of the Interior
Cochrans Mill Road
P.O. Box 18070
Pittsburgh, PA 15236   412-892-4338

The Petroleum Tree illustration shows all the dozens of products that are obtainable from crude oil. This illustration serves as an excellent learning tool for students in the upper elementary grades.

Energy Efficiency and Renewable Energy Clearinghouse
P.O. Box 3048
Merrifield, VA 22116   800-363-3732

People are trying to find new ways to heat their homes, factories, offices, and schools without using so much expensive oil and gas. *Solar Energy and You* helps teach children about solar energy and solar heat. Call the office above for this four page publication.

U.S. Geological Survey
P.O. Box 25425
Denver, CO 80225

Natural Steam for Power describes the investigation of geothermal steam as a potential source of energy for power needs worldwide. Discusses the nature and behavior of steam formed underground.

Governor's Office of Planning and Research
1400 Tenth St., Room 209
Sacramento, CA 95814   916-322-2316

This Service is a U.S. Department of Energy funded program which provides information and training on renewable energy and energy efficiency to schools, small businesses and Indian tribes. It provides materials for the teacher, including lesson plans and class activities for grades kindergarten through twelve. An available publication, *Animated Bibliography, A Sample of Energy Education Curriculum Materials: K-12*, lists available materials and where to obtain them. All are free of charge.

Florida Energy Office
2704 Centerview Dr.
Tallahassee, FL 32399-2100   904-488-2475

This office focuses on solar energy and conservation. *Solar and Energy Conservation Projects for Students* was produced by the Florida Solar Energy Center and is available from the office above to elementary school teachers. Another publication, *Energy Research Projects Guide*, will assist students in their selection of an energy topic for science fair projects. Also available is the *Florida Middle School Energy Education Project*. All are free of charge.

Nebraska Energy Office
1200 N St., Suite 110
P.O. Box 95085
Lincoln, NE 68509   402-471-2867

The office above provides energy-related curriculum materials, including instructional materials (films), video tapes, curriculum guides, slides, and resource books and materials, and are available to Nebraska educators only.

ENVIRONMENTAL AWARENESS

Public Information Center
U.S. Environmental Protection Agency (EPA)
401 M Street, SW, MS 3404
Washington, DC 20460   202-260-2080

Acid rain affects both the health of humans and our environment and is an issue with which the EPA is actively involved. EPA frequently receives requests for information on acid rain from school systems, teachers, and individuals. In response to these

The Government Works for Kids, Too

requests, EPA has developed the study guide *Acid Rain: The Student's First Sourcebook*. The purpose of the guide, which is for students in grades 4-8, is to help students better understand the science, citizen actions, and research issues that are part of the acid rain problem. *EPA's Acid Rain Program: Charting a New Course in Environmental Protection* and the *Environmental Backgrounder: Acid Rain* are two additional publications which provide information on the acid rain issue.

Department of Air Pollution Control
Commonwealth of Virginia
P.O. Box 10009
Richmond, VA 23240   804-698-4000

Airy Canary Learns to Fly is a coloring book about Airy Canary, a bird who is having difficulty learning to fly because of the presence of Nasty Nitrogen Dioxide, Otto Ozone the Air Pollutant, and Sully Sulfur Dioxide. Children in the lower elementary grades will enjoy coloring this 16-page book, while learning about pollutants and the need for clean air.

Office of Environmental Education
Pennsylvania Department of Education
333 Market St.
Harrisburg, PA 17126   717-783-6994

The Baily Twins' Outdoor Adventures is an illustrated publication with stories, games, and activities, designed to teach upper elementary schoolchildren about the environment.

Illinois Environmental Protection Agency
Office of Public Information
2200 Churchill Road
P.O. Box 19276
Springfield, Illinois 62794-9276   217-782-5562

Books for Young People on Environmental Issues is a selection of books from 1970 to present prepared by Gretl Cox of EPA's Headquarters Library. It is arranged in two sections. The first section is for children from kindergarten through the sixth grade with books grouped by grade level. The second section is for students in grades seven through twelve; books are listed by subject area.

Bureau of Mines
U.S. Department of the Interior
Cochrans Mill Road
P.O. Box 18070
Pittsburgh, PA 15236   412-892-4338

Children in grades K-5 will enjoy watching the video *Call Me Can* (18:20 mins.). Can is a lively aluminum beverage can who calls out one day in a grocery store to a young boy named Dan. Can has new and exciting stories to tell Dan about recycling, and sings a song about how wonderful it is to be made of aluminum, because he can be recycled over and over. There is no charge for borrowing this video. It is available in 3/4" U-Matic and 1/2" VHS formats only.

Public Information Center
U.S. Environmental Protection Agency
401 M Street, SW, MS 3404
Washington, DC 20460   202-260-2080

For at least half a century people have reported seeing a "sea monster" in the Chesapeake Bay. Affectionately known as "Chessie," popularized cousin of Nessie (Scotland's Loch Ness monster), the creature is reported to be gentle and good natured. In the coloring book *Chessie: A Chesapeake Bay Story*, Chessie discusses how and why we need to keep the Chesapeake Bay clean.

Public Information Office
Metropolitan Water Reclamation District of Greater Chicago
100 East Erie
Chicago, IL 60611   312-751-6633

Learn how the city of Chicago helps keep the Chicago River and Lake Michigan clean. *Color It Blue* is a coloring book which offers children a creative way of learning about sewage treatment.

Texas Water Development Board
Office of Public Information
P.O. Box 13231
Austin, TX 78711-3231   512-936-0830

Do You Know How to Keep Our Water Clean? is a publication written for children which addresses the need for a clean environment. It discusses the "story on water" and recycling. It is a twenty page publication which ends with a crossword puzzle.

Office of Coastal Zone Management
National Oceanic and Atmospheric Administration
3300 Whitehaven St., NW

Washington, DC 20235

Coastal Awareness: A Resource Guide for Teachers in Elementary Science was developed for elementary school teachers who would like to instill in children and young adults an appreciation of the ecologic value of the coast. (Resource Guides for junior high and high school teachers are also available). The purpose of this guide is not to present a definitive work on coastal ecology, but to entice teachers to explore ecological aspects of coastal awareness. A more complete understanding of the coast requires study of the interactions of ecology with economics, humanities, and government. An understanding of coastal ecological processes will aid students as they participate in future decision making.

National Oceanic and Atmospheric Administration
U.S. Department of Commerce
14th and Constitution Ave., NW
Washington, DC 20230   202-482-6090

The need to protect our nation's coasts is becoming increasingly important. Use the following films (which are appropriate for elementary-age children) to educate your students about coastal awareness. They may be obtained without charge by writing to the office above. A catalogue is also available listing other films and ordering information.

NOAA - A Year of Anniversaries
The National Weather Service Modernization
NOAA Serves
CAMEO (Computer-Aided Management of Emergency Operations)
The SARSAT/COSPAS Story

Public Information Center
U.S. Environmental Protection Agency
401 M Street, SW, MS 3404
Washington, DC 20460   202-260-2080

Environmental Education Materials for Teachers and Young People (Grades K-12) is an excellent source of resources for educators. Entries are diverse with materials described ranging from workbooks to curriculum plans, to posters and pamphlets, to newsletters, films, and computer software. The publication's citations have been organized into two major sections according to the private and public sector organizations that have developed and produced environmental education materials for teachers, other educators, and students. A third section describes opportunities for educators to participate in workshops and to use other resources that can enable them to better cover environmental topics in their work with young people.

Public Information Center
U.S. Environmental Protection Agency
401 M Street, St., MS 3404
Washington, DC 20460   202-260-2080

Children will enjoy learning about the need for recycling while reading and coloring the publication, *There Lived a Wicked Dragon*. Written by Martha Finan for the federal solid waste management programs, it provides a creative way to learn about an important issue.

Public Information Center
U.S. Environmental Protection Agency
401 M Street, SW, MS 3404
Washington, DC 20460   202-260-2080

The *Glossary of Environmental Terms and Acronyms List* can help educators and students clarify the meaning of environmental terms. It is designed to give the user an explanation of the more commonly used environmental terms appearing in EPA publications, news releases, and other Agency documents available to the general public.

Public Information Office
Metropolitan Water Reclamation District of Greater Chicago
100 East Erie
Chicago, IL 60611   312-751-6633

Earth Trek....Explore Your Environment is an activity book designed to educate elementary schoolchildren about our need to protect our water, air, and land. The booklet's layout allows its pages to be duplicated so that each student can have a copy for use in class.

Public Information Center
U.S. Environmental Protection Agency
401 M Street, SW, MS 3404
Washington, DC 20460   202-260-2080

General Motors has produced a video entitled *I Need the Earth and the Earth Needs Me*. Initially distributed by the Environmental Protection Agency to 4th graders, it is available from the Public Information Center to children of all ages. Children will enjoy watching this video while learning the importance of keeping our air, water, and soil clean.

Public Information Center
U.S. Environmental Protection Agency (EPA)
401 M Street, SW, MS 3404
Washington, DC 20460   202-260-2080

Earthnotes is published in February, May, August and November by the Environmental Protection Agency. It is the intent of EPA to provide an open forum for the exchange of teaching aids, comments, and brief essays concerning environmental education in the elementary grades.

Education Specialist: SSI
Ohio Department of Natural Resources
Division of Litter Prevention and Recycling
1889 Fountain Square Ct. - F-2
Columbus, OH 43224   614-265-6333

Super Saver Investigators is an interdisciplinary environmental studies activity guide book about solid waste, recycling, and natural resources for grades kindergarten through 8th and was developed by the Ohio Department of Natural Resources in cooperation with the Ohio Department of Education and Ohio teachers actively involved in environmental studies education. *Super Saver Investigators* contains over 65 hands-on learning activities for grades K-8. The activities are related to science and social studies lessons normally taught by elementary teachers. The activities include skill-building handouts in language arts, math, reading comprehension, creative writing, art and design. It is made available to schools and teachers in Ohio at no cost, through workshops or inservice training. For out-of-state requests there is a charge. Call or write for availability and price information.

EPA Region 1:
(Connecticut, Massachusetts, Maine, New Hampshire, Rhode Island, Vermont)
JFK Federal Building
Boston, MA 02203   617-565-3400

EPA Region 2:
(New Jersey, New York, Puerto Rico, Virgin Islands)
290 Broadway
New York, NY 10007   212-637-5000

EPA Region 3:
(Delaware, Maryland, Pennsylvania, Virginia, West Virginia, District of Columbia)
841 Chestnut Street
Philadelphia, PA 19107   215-597-9370

EPA Region 4:
(Alabama, Florida, Georgia, Kentucky, Mississippi, North Carolina, South Carolina, Tennessee)
345 Courtland Street NE
Atlanta, GA 30365   404-347-3004

EPA Region 5:
(Illinois, Indiana, Michigan, Minnesota, Ohio, Wisconsin)
230 South Dearborn Street
Chicago, IL 60604   312-353-2000

EPA Region 6:
(Arkansas, Louisiana, New Mexico, Oklahoma, Texas)
1445 Ross Avenue
Dallas, TX 75202-2733   214-655-6444

EPA Region 7:
(Iowa, Kansas, Missouri, Nebraska)
726 Minnesota Avenue
Kansas City, KS 66101   913-551-7000

EPA Region 8:
(Colorado, Montana, North Dakota, South Dakota, Utah, Wyoming)
One Denver Place
999 18th Street
Denver, CO 80202-2405   303-312-6312

EPA Region 9:
(Arizona, California, Hawaii, Nevada, American Samoa, Guam, Trust Territories of the Pacific)
75 Hawthorne Street
San Francisco, CA 94105   415-744-1305

EPA Region 10:
(Alaska, Idaho, Oregon, Washington)
1200 Sixth Avenue   800-424-4EPA
Seattle, WA 98101   206-553-1200

Young people in all fifty states are invited to participate in the President's Environmental Youth Awards program, which offers them, individually and collectively, an opportunity to become an environmental force within their community. The program encourages individuals, school classes, schools, summer camps, public interest groups, and youth organizations to promote local environmental awareness and to channel this awareness into positive community involvement. To be eligible, a young person, or group of young persons, must have completed an environmental project while in grades kindergarten through twelve, and the project must be sponsored by at least one adult representative of their school, camp, youth group, or public interest group. For additional information on this awards program, contact your regional office (see listings above).

Office of Public Affairs
U.S. Environmental Protection Agency
77 West Jackson Blvd., PI-195
Chicago, IL 60604   312-886-2395

Children of all ages will enjoy coloring *The Happy Earth Day Coloring and Activities Book* while learning how to take care of the earth. For a free copy, contact the office above.

Resource Center
Public Education and Risk Communication Division
Environmental and Occupational Health Sciences Institute
681 Frelinghuysen Rd.
Piscataway, NJ 08855   908-445-0110

"Healthy Environment - Healthy Me" is a interdisciplinary, supplementary environmental and occupational health curriculum. As an "environmental health promotion" curriculum, it is designed to provide young people with the knowledge and understanding for creating a safe and healthful environment at home, in their future workplaces and in their communities. The primary audience is schoolchildren in kindergarten through sixth grade. Lesson plans and videos are available.

Videos
(VHS 1/2" $85 each, 3/4" $99 each, previews $25 - previews are available for 2 weeks, the fee may be applied to the purchase price).

Alexandria's Clean-Up Fix-Up Parade (15 min., grades K-2)
Alexandria decides to get the community involved in a litter pick-up campaign after seeing the harm that litter caused a swan family in the park.

Alu-Man the Can (15 min., grades K-3)
This video teaches children about recycling through the adventures of Alu-Man the Can, Nettie Newspaper, Benjamin J. Bottle III, and Mr. "G" the garbage can.

Safety Sense (14 min., grades K-3)
Jason and Alice are safety detectives as they explore the possible health hazards of using and storing hazardous products incorrectly.

Sam's Safety Star Award (15 min., grades 1-3)
Sam, the TV camera, learns that risks are part of everyday activities like crossing the road, driving a bicycle, swimming and riding in a car. He learns to look and think before he acts.

Down the Drain (22 min., grades 3-5)
As Chris begins to pour some Polish-All down the drain, the sink comes alive. The animated sink explains why certain products can pollute the water supply. Chris learns the proper way to dispose of hazardous waste.

Keeping the Lid on Air Pollution (20 min., grades 4-6)
Terry has a homework assignment to write about two pollution controls. He ends up inside the school library computer and learns about different types of air pollutants (focusing on ozone) and air pollution controls.

The Inside Story on Air Pollution (19 min., grades 4-6)
Danny, Terry's friend, and his sister go into the computer to investigate the sources and health effects of indoor air pollution in the home. They also learn how to reduce and prevent indoor air pollution problems.

What to Do With All Our Garbage? (20 min., grades 4-6)
Kate, Jenny, and Greg explore the garbage crisis and possible solutions. Source reduction, recycling, sanitary landfills and incineration are discussed. The focus is on what consumers can do to reduce the amount of garbage we generate.

The Government Works for Kids, Too

Lessons
($29 each)

My Environment and Me (Kindergarten)
Children learn why clean water, air and soil are important for people to stay healthy. They also learn about taking responsibility for keeping the environment clean by doing an "environmental clean-up."

Recycling: A Community Pollution Solution (First Grade)
Children explore the health consequences of living in a polluted environment and specifically the problems of garbage disposal and solid waste management. Children learn about recycling aluminum, glass and newspaper - one positive community solution to the garbage problem.

Using My Safety Sense (Second Grade)
Children learn to identify and safely handle hazardous household products by recognizing warning words on labels, demonstrating proper storage of products, and practicing handling emergencies with confidence.

Creating a Safer Environment (Third Grade)
As "Safety Detectives" children search out safe situations and hazardous situations in their school and at home. Using problem solving skills they identify a safety problem involving a threat to their health, suggest positive solutions, carry out one solution, and analyze the results. They also learn to discriminate between risks caused by individual behavior and risks caused by the actions or non-actions of those responsible for maintaining a safe environment.

Exploring Water Pollution Issues (Fourth grade)
Students discuss water pollution and the steps individuals and groups can take to protect water quality. The hydrologic cycle, water conservation, waste-water treatment and correct disposal methods of hazardous household wastes are covered. Children research water pollution issues and develop a newspaper to communicate the information they have learned.

Exploring Air Pollution Issues (Fifth Grade)
Students learn about major sources of air pollutants (including indoor air pollution) and their major health impacts. The concepts of occupational safety and health are introduced. They also learn about methods for reducing air pollution and about the role of government agencies and regulations in protecting worker and community health.

Garbage, Garbage, Garbage (Sixth Grade)
Students examine technical topics in solid waste management, specifically: source reduction, recycling, sanitary landfills, incineration, hazardous waste, and household hazardous waste.

Water Watch, Division of Water
Department for Environmental Protection
Frankfort Office Park
14 Reilly Road
Frankfort, KY 40601   502-564-3410
Contact the office above to obtain a copy of *A Field Guide to Kentucky Lakes and Wetlands*. This booklet offers an illustrated guide and discussion for field observation along and within Kentucky's lakes and wetlands. It can be used by educators and upper elementary schoolchildren.

Water Watch
Division of Water
Department for Environmental Protection
Frankfort Office Park
14 Reilly Road
Frankfort, KY 40601   502-564-3410
A Field Guide to Kentucky Rivers and Streams was developed for Water Watch, a public participation program that encourages citizens to adopt a stream, lake or wetland, and then gain hands on experience in protecting and enhancing their adopted water resource. To learn about Kentucky's rivers and streams, contact the office above.

Water Watch
Division of Water
Department for Environmental Protection
Frankfort Office Park
14 Reilly Road
Frankfort, KY 40601   502-564-3410
For information on wild rivers in Kentucky, contact the office above to obtain the brochure, *Kentucky Wild Rivers*. Learn about the Kentucky wild river system and the uses of the rivers.

Office of Environmental Education
Pennsylvania Department of Education
333 Market St.
Harrisburg, PA 17126   717-783-6994
Land and Soil is a publication comprised of several activities for schoolchildren, and is designed to promote environmental awareness.

Office of Environmental Education
Pennsylvania Department of Education
333 Market St.
Harrisburg, PA 17126   717-783-6994
Paul E. Beals' publication *The Newspaper: A Tool for Teaching Environmental Awareness* is an activity book for children in grades K-12. It covers such topics as acid rain, forest preservation, waste disposal, and recycling. This activity book contains newspaper articles and uses them to teach about environmental awareness.

Forest Service
U.S. Department of Agriculture
14th and Independence, SW
P.O. Box 96090
Washington, DC 20090-6090   202-205-0957
Suggestions for Incorporating Forestry into the School Curriculum (FS-62) is a brochure intended to provide a variety of suggestions for incorporating the study of forestry and other environmental topics within existing school curricula. By incorporating environmental studies into existing programs, the teacher is able not only to add a new dimension to the material but also to further the understanding of the environment as an integral part of all other studies.

Forest Service
U.S. Department of Agriculture
14th and Independence, SW
P.O. Box 96090
Washington, DC 20090-6090   202-205-0957
The publication *Why Leaves Change Color* (FS-12) can be used by adults and upper elementary schoolchildren to learn why leaves change their color. It also contains instructions on how to copy leaves with crayons and how to make leaf prints with a stamp pad.

Bureau of Mines
U.S. Department of the Interior
Cochrans Mill Road
P.O. Box 18070
Pittsburgh, PA 15236   412-892-4338
Contact the office above to receive a copy of the coloring book *Take Pride in America with Mark Trail*. Children will enjoy coloring in the pictures while learning the importance of keeping the environment clean.

Public Information Center
U.S. Environmental Protection Agency
401 M Street, SW, MS 3404
Washington, DC 20460   202-260-2080
Learn about the pollutants ozone and carbon monoxide in the *Environmental Backgrounder: Ozone and Carbon Monoxide*. This six-page publication provides important information on these two major public health concerns and can be used by educators to supplement science curricula.

Office of Environmental Education
Pennsylvania Department of Education
333 Market St.
Harrisburg, PA 17126   717-783-6994
Available from the office above is *The Friendly Forest Fun Book*, an activity book designed to help elementary teachers enhance students' awareness and knowledge about Pennsylvania's forest lands, the resources the forest provides to both wildlife and the consumer, and the enjoyment that can be obtained from the proper use of our forests.

Office of Environmental Education
Pennsylvania Department of Education
333 Market St.
Harrisburg, PA 17126   717-783-6994
I'm a Blue Ribbon Recycler! is an activity book that teaches children in grades K-6 about the various aspects of recycling. This includes teaching about trash, environmental shopping, and composting. The activity book concludes by awarding the user a blue ribbon. Its fun activities, which include coloring and connecting-the-dots, encourage children to learn about recycling in a creative manner.

Forest Service
U.S. Department of Agriculture
14th and Independence, SW
P.O. Box 96090
Washington, DC 20090-6090   202-205-0957

To learn more about recycling and the Forest Service's involvement in it, contact the office above for a copy of *Expanding Recycling Horizons*.

Public Information Center
U.S. Environmental Protection Agency
401 M Street, SW, MS 3404
Washington, DC 20460   202-260-2080
or
Resource Conservation and Recovery Act
Hotline   800-424-9346

The following materials are available from either office above.

Recycle Today! Educational Materials for Grades K-12 (EPA/530-SW-90-025). Presents the goals and objectives of EPA's School Recycling Program, and describes this handbook as well as the following materials.

Let's Reduce and Recycle: Curriculum for Solid Waste Awareness (EPA/530-SW-90-005). Presents lessons and activities to teach students in grades K-12 about solid waste generation and management. Each unit presents a series of related lessons with vocabulary words, discussion questions, and projects. Practical teaching aids, such as handouts, worksheets, clip art, and a short skit are also included, along with a bibliography of additional sources of information.

Adventures of the Garbage Gremlin: Recycle and Combat a Life of Grime (EPA/530-SW-90-024). Introduces students in grades 4-7 to the benefits of book approach. Students are lead on an adventure in which their peers foil the "Garbage Gremlin" and learn about recycling.

Ride the Wave of the Future: Recycle Today! (EPA/530-SW-90-010). Promotes recycling through a colorful poster designed to appeal to all grade levels. Can be displayed in conjunction with recycling activities or used to help foster recycling.

School Recycling Programs: A Handbook for Educators (EPA/530-SW-90-023). Describes a number of school recycling program options, along with step-by-step instructions on how to set one up. It focuses on implementing actual recycling projects as a way of teaching the importance and benefits of recycling.

Energy Efficiency and Renewable Energy Clearinghouse
P.O. Box 3048
Merrifield, VA 22116   800-363-3732

Available from this office is *Recycling: What You Can Do*. This two page publication discusses the reasons to recycle and what materials can be recycled.

Public Information Center
U.S. Environmental Protection Agency
401 M Street, SW, MS 3404
Washington, DC 20460   202-260-2080

The poster *Beneficial Use of Sewer Sludge: Land Application* discusses the various uses of sewer sludge. It shows how sewer sludge is a valuable resource that can be used to improve plant growth and soil quality.

Soil Conservation Service
U.S. Department of Agriculture
P.O. Box 2890
Washington, DC 20013   202-720-5157

Publications are available from the office above to help teach elementary school children about soil conservation. One educational publication includes the program aid, *Teaching Soil and Water Conservation: A Classroom and Field Guide*.

Forest Service
U.S. Department of Agriculture
14th and Independence, SW
P.O. Box 96090
Washington, DC 20090-6090   202-205-0957

Trees offer many benefits to the environment and play a vital role in reducing water and wind erosion, keeping rivers and streams clean, and counteracting the greenhouse effect. To learn more about trees and how they help the environment, contact the office above to receive a copy of *Trees are the Answer....to America's Growing Environmental Concerns*. Also available is *What We Get From Trees* which lists the various products, ranging from chewing gum to mop handles, which come from trees.

Forest Service
U.S. Department of Agriculture
14th and Independence, SW
P.O. Box 96090
Washington, DC 20090-6090   202-205-0957

The poster *How a Tree Grows* (FS-8) teaches about photosynthesis, enzymes, and the various parts of a tree. Its colorful illustrations make it a useful teaching aid. The eight-page publication *How a Tree Grows* supplements the poster and provides more information on how a tree grows.

Texas Water Development Board
Office of Public Information
P.O. Box 13231
Austin, TX 78711-3231   512-239-0012

Land Use and the Water Cycle is a black and white poster which illustrates the water cycle and different uses of land. It can be used by educators as a teaching aid or by students as a component to a report.

Texas Water Development Board
Office of Public Information
P.O. Box 13231
Austin, TX 78711-3231   512-239-0012

The Texas Water Education Network Directory is a collection of water education materials suitable for use in public schools.

Texas Water Development Board
Office of Public Information
P.O. Box 13231
Austin, TX 78711-3231   512-239-0012

Water Education Teams, or WETs, are groups of young people who work together to understand and preserve the water resources in their local environment. The WET Project in intended as a supplemental or extracurricular activity for schoolchildren, or a special project for youth organizations. WETs select and survey a local surface water body, which may be a creek, lake, stream, reservoir or river. Then, through water testing, local observation and problem solving, WETs work to identify existing or potential sources of pollution. The students conclude by preparing community awareness projects to share what they have learned. Contact the office above to receive a copy of the *WET Project Instruction Handbook* which contains WET student activities, teacher resources and references, and sections on the basics of water quality. There also is a section of indoor/outdoor activities for areas without access to a body of water.

Texas Water Development Board
Office of Public Information
P.O. Box 13231
Austin, TX 78711-3231   512-239-0012

Do You Know How to Keep Water Clean? is a four page publication on water conservation written for children and describes the various ways in which water conservation can be achieved.

Public Information Center (MS 3404)
U.S. Environmental Protection Agency
401 M Street, SW, MS 3404
Washington, DC 20460

America's Wetlands: Our Vital Link Between Land and Water provides information on the types of wetlands, wetland values, status and trends of wetlands, and wetlands protection. Both educators and students can benefit from the information provided.

Forest Service
U.S. Department of Agriculture
14th and Independence, SW
P.O. Box 96090
Washington, DC 20090-6090   202-205-1389

Give a hoot! Don't pollute! *Woodsy Owl's 1991-92 Campaign Catalog* is filled with dozens of items children can use (such as bike stickers, bookmarks, name tags, balloons, pens, pencils, lunch bags) that have the Woodsy Owl logo on them. Contact the office above for a catalog or the National Association of State Foresters/Woodsy Owl Campaign at 803-737-8800.

Public Information Office
California Air Resources Board
P.O. Box 2815
Sacramento, CA 95812   916-322-2990

Contact the office above to receive materials aimed to Californians. Single copies available free to non-Californians as well.

Legislation and Public Affairs
California Integrated Waste Management Board
1020 9th Street, Suite 300
Sacramento, CA 95814   916-255-2473

Contact the office above for information on the Solid Waste Environmental Education Program (SWEEP). It includes two lesson plans, *The Wizards of Waste* (grades 2-4) and *The Trash Monster* (grades 5-7). Each 10-lesson plan includes a teacher's guide, a filmstrip and cassette tape, pre- and post-lesson tests, picture cards, home information leaflets, and pupil booklets. Also includes self-contained, interdisciplinary units designed to teach students resource conservation skills they can apply in their daily lives. Free list including price information is available upon request.

Public Information
Florida Department of Environmental Protection
3900 Commonwealth Blvd.
Tallahassee, FL 32399-2400   904-488-9334

Call the office above for information on receiving *Your Environment (Grades 3-8)*, a 21-page booklet about Florida's environment for students. It includes puzzles, games, suggestions on how you can help the environment, and contacts for further information.

Division of Natural Heritage
Illinois Department of Natural Resources
Lincoln Town Plaza
524 South Second Street
Springfield, IL 62701   217-785-8774

This office makes available to Illinois teachers the curriculum guide *Nature Discovery 2 - Wild Mammals of Illinois* (grades K-8).

Environmental Education Consultant
Iowa State Department of Education
Grimes State Office Building
Des Moines, Iowa 50319   515-281-3146

Available is a bibliography of books relating to children's literature that presents a listing of selected publications and describes a learning cycle approach to using literature. The story makes students aware of an environmental concept and provides an application phase, whereby students can apply their knowledge through hands on experiences. Also available is the *Iowa Developed Energy Activity Sampler K-12 (IDEAS)*, a 1989 edition of energy education materials. The packets (K-2 and 3-5 and 6-12) offer multidisciplinary teaching and learning possibilities. Each activity is presented within a learning cycle consisting of a framework of an awareness stage, conceptual development stage and application stage. Materials are provided free to Iowa educators. Educators outside Iowa can request more information including cost from the address above.

Department for Environmental Protection
Kentucky Natural Resources and
Environmental Protection Cabinet
Frankfort Office Park
14 Reilly Road
Frankfort, KY 40601   502-564-3410

Free pamphlets available include *Kentucky Wild Rivers* and *10 Ways You Can Help Keep Kentucky Water Resources Clean. A Field Guide to Kentucky Rivers and Streams* and *A Field Guide to Kentucky Lakes and Wetlands* are available to teachers. Also available is information on the *Water Watch Program*, a program conducted by the Division of Water with services designed to encourage and support citizen participation in the wise management of community water resources, including streams, lakes, wetlands and groundwater. Any individual, group, family, organization, school or business can become an official "Kentucky Water Watcher".

Donna Spreitzer
California Local Government Commission
909 12th St., #205
Sacramento, CA 95814   916-448-1198

Available from this office is *Toxic is My Home? You Bet!*, for grades K-3, 4-6, 7-8, and 9-12 (available in Spanish only). Developed by Golden Empire Health Planning Center as a one-week course of instruction, this school curriculum identifies: toxics in the home environment; methods for reducing exposure to household toxics; unsafe circumstances involving toxic products; and safer alternatives to using such products. Step by step teaching instructions, masters for worksheets, teacher answer guides, and evaluation methods are all included.

Director
Bureau of Environmental Education
New York State Department of Environmental Conservation
50 Wolf Road, Room 504

Albany, NY 12233-4500

Pamphlets describing various materials are available to New York State teachers.

David Landis
Division of Litter and Prevention Recycling
Ohio Department of Natural Resources
Fountain Square, Bldg. F-2
Columbus, OH 43224   614-265-6444

Available from the office above is *Super Saver Investigators* (grades K-8), an interdisciplinary environmental studies activity guidebook about solid waste, recycling, and natural resources. It contains over 65 hands-on learning experiences related to science and social studies lessons normally taught by elementary teachers. Includes skill-building handouts in language arts, math, reading comprehension, creative writing, art and design. Illustrations enhance student interest. Test is secured in a 3-ring binder. For cost and ordering information write to above addressee.

San Francisco Recycling Program
1145 Marnet, Suite 401
San Francisco, CA 94102   415-554-3400

Available from this office is *Fourth R* (grades K-5), a curriculum on recycling, reuse, and waste reduction. Send $10 payable to City and County of San Francisco. Resource fact sheets and general recycling information are available free upon request.

Renee Carlson
Office of Public Information
Texas Natural Resources Commission
P.O. Box 13087
Capitol Station
Austin, TX 78711-3087   512-239-1000

The W.E.T. (Water Education Team) Program (grades 4-6) is intended to supplement the regular elementary curriculum or for use as a special project by youth organizations. However, many of the activities are appropriate for K-12 classes. Water Education Teams work together to understand and preserve the water resources in their local environment. Through water quality activities, student teams study pollution problems, understand the importance of water and realize the need to preserve water supplies. Adopt-a-Creek activities enable students to survey a local body of water, test its waters and help resolve its problems. Indoor/outdoor activities provide hands on experiments for students in areas where no surface water is available.

Office of Public Information
Texas Natural Resources Commission
P.O. Box 13087
Austin, TX 78711-3087   512-239-1000

The annual publication, *Texas Water Education Network Directory*, lists water and environmental education programs and/or materials suitable for use in public schools. A contact is provided for each resource listed. The materials listed include classroom curriculum, comic books, pamphlets, dramas, speakers bureaus, workshops, seminars, and field trip opportunities.

University of California Extension Media Center
2000 Center St., 4th Floor
Berkeley, CA 94704   510-642-0460

A free catalog listing environmental films and videos for young people is available upon request.

Jan Lingenfelter
Washington State Department of Ecology
4350 150th Ave., NE
Redmond, WA 98052-5301   206-867-7043

Available from the office above is *A-Way With Waste*, 3rd Edition, 1990 (grades K-12), a waste management and recycling curriculum and school program. The goal of the program is to reduce waste and increase recycling at home, at school and in the community. It includes a 602 page interdisciplinary guide of 117 activities. Three sections cover concepts in Solid Waste Management, Hazardous Waste, and Waste and Water. Articles, research reports, glossary, bibliography, fact sheets and resources are also included. This book is free to Washington State teachers who take a workshop. Write or call for prices to purchase curriculum.

Environmental Protection Agency
Public Information Center MS 3404
401 M St., SW
Washington, DC 20460

All materials listed below are free. Note: materials listed are available as of Winter 1991. Selection of materials changes periodically.

I Need the Earth and the Earth Needs Me (grade 4). A curriculum for fourth graders. Package includes a videocassette and companion teacher's guide. General Motors provided the packages to all fourth grade teachers in spring 1990. Suggest checking school's library before requesting a package. Request must be on school letterhead.

Earth Trek...Explore Your Environment (grades 3,4,5). Illustrated booklet describes measures to protect water, air, and land, safe uses of toxic substances and pesticides, and federal environmental laws. Booklet's layout allows its contents, including student activities, to be duplicated.

Books for Young People on Environmental Issues (grades K-12). A selected bibliography of published books on environmental issues, which are generally available at local public libraries.

President's Environmental Youth Awards (grades K-12). Information on carrying out environmental projects that may earn regional and national awards for students. Brochure includes application.

Educators Earth Day Sourcebook (grades K-6 and 7-12). Booklets on how to incorporate Earth Day into the classroom every day.

Don't Bug Me (grades K-3). A pamphlet illustrating the safe use of pesticides. Includes pictures and captions.

Acid Rain: A Student's First Source Book (Teachers and students grades 4-8). Content explains what acid rain is, its impact on people, on natural and man-made materials, and resources. Tell what can and is being done to combat it. Book suggests classroom and individual activities and describes experiments students can perform. Glossary and bibliography complete the content.

Once There Lived a Wicked Dragon (grades K-4). A story/coloring book about the need to protect the environment, and what the world would be like if we didn't.

Limited quantities of the following are available for residents in the six-state Region 5 area (Illinois, Indiana, Michigan, Minnesota, Ohio, Wisconsin).

The Happy Earth Day (grades K-3). Coloring and activities book that informs children on simple ways to preserve and conserve.

Film Brochure. Lists films available to educational and organized group audiences free of charge.

50 Ways to Make Your World a Better Place (grades K-12). Poster lists common sense ideas to help protect and improve your home and community environment.

Welcome to the Wetlands (grades K-12). Coloring poster explains how wetlands help us and what is a threat to wetlands. Included is information on animals, birds, fish and plants that thrive in wetlands.

> U.S. EPA Region 5
> Office of Public Affairs
> 77 West Jackson Blvd., PI-195
> Chicago, IL 60604   312-353-2000

The following materials are available to New York and Pennsylvania residents in addition to Region 5 residents.

The Great Lakes in My World (grades K-8). Environmental Education curriculum that focuses on the Great Lakes.

Great Minds, Great Lakes Curriculum Sampler (grades K-12). This is a companion piece to both *The Great Lakes in My World* and *The Great Lakes Environmental Atlas*.

> Information Services
> Great Lakes Regional Office
> International Joint Commission
> P.O. Box 32869
> Detroit, MI 48232-2869   313-226-2170

More than 600 educators were surveyed to produce the publication *Directory of Great Lakes Education Materials*, a free-for-the-requesting directory that contains information on pamphlets, technical reports, booklets, videotapes, curriculum based and classroom-based materials for classes concentrating on Great Lakes studies.

ESKIMOS

> Office of Education
> Room 212, Mail Stop 158

> National Museum of Natural History
> Washington, DC 20560   202-357-2747

Indians and Eskimos is one of the several programs and activities held throughout the school year for visiting preschool and elementary school children by the National Museum of Natural History. With this particular program students (sitting in front of museum exhibits and using Indian children's toys) learn what grandparents of Indian children did in the past, what parents do today, and what Indian children might do when they grow up. Lesson includes Eskimo, Woodland, Plains, Northwest Coast, and Southwest peoples. Teachers are urged to request pre-visit materials that will help them before and during the visit.

> Indian Arts and Crafts Board
> Mail Stop 4004 (MIB)
> U.S. Department of Interior
> Washington, DC 20240   202-208-3773

Would you like to give your child some crafts made by Eskimos? An easy way to do this is to obtain the publication *Indian, Eskimo, Aleut Owned and Operated Arts and Crafts Businesses: Source Directory*. It serves as an essential resource for students, parents, and teachers who wish to obtain authentic Indian arts and crafts.

ESTUARIES

> U.S. Fish and Wildlife Service
> U.S. Department of the Interior
> 4401 N. Fairfax Drive
> Mail Stop 130
> Arlington, VA 22203   703-358-1711

Estuaries: Cradles of Life provides information on estuaries so you can teach your students about them.

> Smithsonian Environmental Research Center
> P.O. Box 28
> Edgewater, MD 21037   410-798-4424

Are you planning on taking your students on a field trip to the Chesapeake Bay? Then get the loose-leaf manual *Estuarine Dock Activities Guidebook*. Includes information on crabs, oyster bars, weather and tides. For students in grades 4-6. $9.50.

> National Audiovisual Center
> 8700 Edgeworth Dr.
> Capitol Heights, MD 20743   800-788-6282

Estuary is a 28-minute film which shows the threats to estuarine resources and stresses the importance of estuaries. It is appropriate for elementary-age children and may be obtained without charge by writing to the office above.

FERRETS

> U.S. Fish and Wildlife Service
> U.S. Department of the Interior
> 4401 N. Fairfax Drive
> Mail Stop 130
> Arlington, VA 22203   703-358-1711

The U.S. Fish and Wildlife Service's publication *Black-Footed Ferret* will introduce you and your upper-elementary child to this interesting and unusual animal.

FILMS

> Education Division, MRC 305
> Education Resource Center
> National Air and Space Museum
> Washington, DC 20560   202-786-2109

Use films to teach your schoolchildren about the importance of aeronautics. The Education Resource Center (ERC) of the National Air and Space Museum (NASM) has a large collection of filmstrips available for preview. The Center offers teachers access to educational materials pertaining to aviation, space, and the Museum's collections, and is open to teachers of all levels and disciplines. NASM-produced filmstrips may be obtained from the National Audiovisual Center, 8700 Edgewood Drive, Capitol Heights, MD 20743, 301-763-1896. For information on other material available from the Center, contact the office above.

> Department of Extension Programs
> National Gallery of Art
> Washington, DC 20565

The National Gallery of Art is continually exploring ways to develop awareness in the visual arts and make its collections accessible to everyone, no matter how far away from the Gallery they may live. Films are now available for loan free of charge

The Government Works for Kids, Too

to educational institutions, community groups, and to individuals throughout the U.S. Write to the office above for more information on how you may bring the National Gallery of Art to your students.

National Oceanic and Atmospheric Administration
U.S. Department of Commerce
14th and Constitution Ave., NW
Washington, DC 20230 202-482-6090

The National Oceanic and Atmospheric Administration makes available films appropriate for elementary-age children. They may be obtained without charge by writing to the office above. A catalogue is available listing other films and ordering information.

NOAA - A Year of Anniversaries
The National Weather Service Modernization
NOAA Serves
CAMOE (Computer-Aided Management of Emergency Operations)
The SARSAT/COSPAS Story

Institute of Agriculture and Natural
Resources Nebraska
Cooperative Extension Service
University of Nebraska - Lincoln
Department of Entomology
210 Plant Industry Bldg.
Lincoln, NE 68583-0816 402-472-2123

Environmental films concerning the use of nonchemical control of pests and low uses of pesticides are available from the office above. A pamphlet which describes videotapes and a field scout manual can also be purchased.

University of California Extension Media Center
2000 Center St., 4th Floor
Berkeley, CA 94704 510-642-0460

Environmental films for young people can also be obtained from the address above. For a free catalog, contact this office.

U.S. EPA Region 5
Office of Public Affairs
77 West Jackson Blvd., PI-195
Chicago, IL 60604 312-353-2000

Available from the U.S. Environmental Protection Agency (for residents in the six-state Region 5 area -- Illinois, Indiana, Michigan, Minnesota, Ohio, Wisconsin) is the publication *Film Brochure*, which lists films available to educational and organized group audiences free of charge.

Warning and Forecast Branch, W/OM11
National Weather Service
National Oceanic and Atmospheric Administration
SSMCII
1325 East West Highway, Room 14370
Silver Spring, MD 20910

Weather warning and forecast films can be used by educators to teach school children about safety during natural disasters. The following 16 mm films are available:

Minneapolis Tornado of July 1986 (Copyrighted)
Terrible Tuesday
Day of the Killer Tornadoes
Tornado at Pleasant Hill
Tornado: A Spotter's Guide (Copyrighted)
Tornado: On the Spot Training (silent and with soundtrack)
Neosho
The Awesome Power
Flash Flood
Flood
A Lady Named Camille
Hurricane Decision
Hurricane
Survival in the Cold
An Ill Wind
Rising Waters
Watch Along the Watershed
Earthwatch
NOAA, A Global View
Galaxy
Before It Hits Home
Hurricane: Before the Storm

Hurricane Aetna: Date with Disaster
Cities Don't Die
Winter Storm

NASA CORE
Lorain County Joint Vocational School
15181 Route 58 South
Oberlin, OH 44074 216-774-1051

Propulsion: Space Shuttle is one film available from the National Aeronautics and Space Administration's (NASA) Central Operation of Resources for Educators (CORE). This particular film, appropriate for children in grades 4-12, highlights the NASA Space Transportation System, its functions, and possible uses for the future.

FINE ARTS

California Energy Extension Service
1400 Tenth St., Room 209
Sacramento, CA 95814 916-323-4388

Learning about the fine arts should be an essential part of a child's education, as should learning about energy awareness. Classroom activities integrating the two can be found in the publication *100 Ways to Celebrate NEED*. This guide promotes energy awareness and links lessons to not only the fine arts, but also to science, social studies, history, economics, and the language arts. It contains 100 activities for children in grades K-12, along with a glossary and teacher background information.

FIRE PREVENTION

United States Fire Administration
National Academy
Federal Emergency Management Agency
16825 S. Seton Avenue
Emmitsburg, MD 21727 301-447-1122

The U.S. Fire Administration has developed a public education program called "Curious Kids Set Fires" to help reduce fire deaths by education and counseling the child setter. Contact the office above to receive a kit, which includes: handouts for the school classroom, lesson plans and poster for teachers, camera-ready print public service announcements, a press release announcing your local program, a sample letter for the local paper, a resource guide with additional materials you may want to get, and descriptions of pre-adolescent fire prevention and counseling programs from other communities.

Attn: Sesame Street Fire Safety
Federal Emergency Management Agency
P.O. Box 70274
Washington, DC 20024

The Sesame Street Fire Safety Project was developed by the Community Education Services division of the Children's Television Workshop (CTW). The first edition of the *Sesame Street Fire Safety Resource Book* is still available in English and Spanish versions. The second edition of the *Sesame Street Fire Safety Book* contains the original Muppet skits and activities that inspired thousands to teach young children fire safety. Each book is accompanied by an audio cassette that contains five songs. Also included is a five page color brochure highlighting the Sesame Street research study on mass media fire education for young children. To order your free copy, write to the office above.

Forest Service
U.S. Department of Agriculture
14th and Independence, SW
P.O. Box 96090
Washington, DC 20090-6090 202-205-0957

Contact the office above to receive Smokey Bear fire prevention materials, including *The True Story of Smokey Bear* comic book.

FEMA Warehouse
P.O. Box 70274
Washington, DC 20024 202-646-3484

Contact the office above for the following publications:

Arson Resource Directory
Public Fire Education Resource Directory
Public Fire Education Today: Fire Service Programs From Across America
Juvenile Firesetter Handbook: Dealing with Children Ages 7-14
Interviewing and Counseling Juvenile Firesetters: The Child Under Seven Years of Age
Adolescent Firesetter Handbook: Ages 14-18

Be patient. If any phone number is incorrect, call (area code) 555-1212 and request the new listing.

Bureau of Fire Prevention
Chicago Fire Department
444 North Dearborn St.
Chicago, IL 60610   312-744-4762

Contact the office above for information on "Mike, Tom, and Matches", a fire prevention slide presentation on burn prevention and the dangers on match play suitable for children in grades three to six. Cost: $12 (slides with script), $15 (slides, script and tape).

Program Coordinator
Juvenile Firesetters Program
300 N. 4th St.
Columbus, OH 43215   614-222-7641

This fire prevention program includes a psychological assessment through interviews based on USFA/FEMA Agency guidelines as well as an extensive fire education program. The coordinator follows up on the firesetter periodically for two years. The Consumer Product Safety Division's "Little Birdie Told Me" is used with younger children. Many National Fire Protection Association programs are used to educate older children. A 13-unit training manual is currently being produced which discusses past programs as well as existing programs, the difference between juvenile firesetting and juvenile arson, arson laws, and fire safety education. The Columbus Fire Department has also formed the Strategic Action for Fire Education Committee (SAFE) in cooperation with the city council. SAFE has developed a preschool fire safety education curriculum based on Sesame Street characters.

Executive Director
Fall River Firefighters' Museum Program
1345 Olden St.
Box 2888
Fall River, MA 02720   508-674-1810

This program is a good example of networking in the community to provide the services necessary for a comprehensive program. By working with state mental health agencies and the court system the Museum is able to offer services such as psychological counseling that the organization couldn't afford to contract with privately. All materials used are original. These include slide presentations, video presentations and flannel board activities. Letters to parents incorporating preschool safety lessons in Cambodian and Portuguese have also been developed. The program works with firesetters of all ages.

Fire Investigator
Juvenile Firesetter Program
Mesa Fire Department
13 W. 1st St.
Mesa, AZ 85201   602-644-2622

The Mesa fire prevention program emphasizes working with the family. For example, after the first meeting the family is asked to plan a home drill together. Children who graduate from the program are named "Junior Fire Marshals representing Mesa" and are given fire marshal badges to underscore the importance of fire safe behavior. Educational materials used include pamphlets on E.D.I.T.H. (Exit Drills in the Home), and a slide show developed by the Mesa Fire Department. They have developed a slide show on responsible and irresponsible uses of fire; one directed to juvenile boys, and one directed to juvenile girls.

Fire Commissioner
Juvenile Firesetters Intervention Program
Bureau of Investigation
250 Livingston Street
Brooklyn, NY 11201   718-694-2109

The fire investigators in this program have police powers to ensure that children and their families attend education and/or counseling sessions. The program provides a good example of networking as well as data collection and storage. E.D.I.T.H. pamphlets are used as well as "Stop, Drop, and Roll" educational materials. Materials include: a picture book illustrating safe/unsafe uses of fire; a comprehensive annual report; a school survey which indicates that many more children play with fires than most people suspect; and some literature developed in Spanish.

Juvenile Firesetter Program Coordinator
55 Southwest Ash
Portland, OR 97204   503-823-3806

In this program the entire family is involved in counseling and fire safety education. Educational techniques used include the following film/TV spots: "Donald Duck's Fire Survival Plan" (Walt Disney Educational Media Company), "Matches" (Coronet MTI Film and Video), and "Smush the Fire Out" (Coronet MTI Film and Video). Literature produced includes "Beyond Burned Fingers" - a one-half hour video on firesetting and Portland's program, TV PSA on their Juvenile Firesetter program which urges parents to call in with questions, and the Oregon Juvenile Firesetter Resource Directory - a statewide resource manual.

Fire Related Youth (FRY) Coordinator
150 Plymouth Avenue South
Public Safety Building, Room 300
Rochester, NY 14614   716-428-7036

This fire prevention program is a very well known program in which the fire investigators have police powers to ensure participation. Fire Related Youth (FRY) also works closely with the University of Rochester which offers a variety of excellent resources including psychological counseling and data analysis. Materials include: a study revealing that play is extremely widespread among school-age children; a curriculum for primary schools which incorporates fire safety education into general education; and two annual reports which include valuable information on the setting problem and setting up and maintaining a program.

Public Educator
Fireplay Intervention Program
110 E. 11th St.
St. Paul, MN 55101   612-228-6203

This program teaches curiosity setters about the dangers of fire. Educational materials used include *Matches, Lighters, Crackers are not Toys* by Dorothy Schad (part of the *Safety Town* series) for preschoolers to seven-year olds. For children ages 7 to 10 they offer *If You Could See Me Now* with pictures of burn victims, available from the Tulsa, Oklahoma, Fire Department. They had printed flyers describing the program put into grocery bags. St. Paul is currently developing a pamphlet describing the program. They have also developed a computer program designed to store information on all setters.

Fire Chief
San Francisco Fire Department
260 Golden Gate Ave.
San Francisco, CA 94102   415-558-3300

The San Francisco program has evolved over many years. From 1971-1979 it was a counseling program. From 1979-1986 it used the "Firehawks" fighter buddy system which provided adult companions for child firesetters. Since 1987, the U.S. Fire Administration / Federal Emergency Management Agency intervention and education guidelines have been followed. Educational techniques used include the National Fire Protection Association's "Learn Not to Burn" materials. The program's philosophy is positive - scare tactics such as pictures of burn victims are not used.

Juvenile Firesetters Prevention
Task Force
3600 Tremont Road
Upper Arlington, OH 43221   614-457-5080

The task force provides a variety of services including: a general public awareness campaign; family interview/screening sessions to determine the cause of firesetting; family intervention sessions to assist families with local mental health referrals when necessary; and maintaining communications with local juvenile justice and protective services. Educational techniques used include Project Burn Prevention education materials. Daniel Strohl's program has developed a puppet show for younger children. For the older child, demonstrations on such topics as flammable vapors have been created. A manual describing Upper Arlington's program and interviewing techniques has also been developed.

FLOODS

Warning and Forecast Branch, W/OM11
National Weather Service
National Oceanic and Atmospheric Administration
SSMCII
1325 East West Highway, Room 14370
Silver Spring, MD 20910

Educators can use the following audiovisuals to teach school children about safety during flash floods.

16 mm Films:
The Awesome Power
Flash Flood
Flood

Videotape:
The Awesome Power

Slides:
Flash Floods: Myths or Realities
Flash Flood Preparedness

The Government Works for Kids, Too

FLORIDA

Communications Office
Department of Environmental Education
3900 Commonwealth Blvd.
Mail Station 30
Tallahassee, FL 32399   904-488-9334

Call the office above for information on receiving *Your Environment (Grades 3-8)*, a 21-page booklet about Florida's environment for students. It includes puzzles, games, suggestion on how you can help the environment, and contacts for further information.

FORESTS

Office of Environmental Education
Pennsylvania Department of Education
333 Market St.
Harrisburg, PA 17126   717-783-6994

Available from the office above is *The Friendly Forest Fun Book*, an activity book designed to help elementary teachers enhance students' awareness and knowledge about Pennsylvania's forest lands, the resources the forest provides to both wildlife and the consumer, and the enjoyment that can be obtained from the proper use of our forests.

Forest Service
U.S. Department of Agriculture
14th and Independence, SW
P.O. Box 96090
Washington, DC 20090-6090   202-205-0957

Suggestions for Incorporating Forestry into the School Curriculum (FS-62) is a brochure intended to provide a variety of suggestions for incorporating the study of forestry and other environmental topics within existing school curricula. By incorporating environmental studies into existing programs, the teacher is able not only to add a new dimension to the material but also to further the understanding of the environment as an integral part of all other studies.

Office of Education, Room 212
Mail Stop 158
National Museum of Natural History
Washington, DC 20560   202-357-2747

Old-Growth Forests: Moist, Massive, and Magnificent is an instructional kit available from the National Museum of Natural History. Slides, videos, teacher's guides to classroom activities and discussions, and a wall poster provide teachers and group leaders with a range of tools for investigating the ecology of old-growth forests, their benefits, and the controversy over our use of them. It is designed for grades 6-8 but easily adapted for younger and older students. Material may be used effectively without a museum visit. Kit may be borrowed for one week. The Museum also offers a visiting program and a teacher workshop on this topic; call the office above to receive more information.

FOXES

U.S. Fish and Wildlife Service
U.S. Department of the Interior
4401 N. Fairfax Drive, Mail Stop 130
Arlington, VA 22203   703-358-1711

Reading *Life in a Fox Den* is one way to learn about how foxes live. Use this publication to educate your children about the lives of foxes.

GAS, NATURAL

National Energy Information Center (NEIC)
Energy Information Administration, EI-231
U.S. Department of Energy
1000 Independence Ave., SW, Room 1F-048
Washington, DC 20585   202-586-8800

Would you like to learn more about natural gas? Information on natural gas can be obtained from The National Energy Information Center (NEIC) of the U.S. Department of Energy. The NEIC provides one-page information sheets not only on natural gas but also on petroleum, coal, electricity, and renewable energy.

Office of Fossil Energy Communications
1000 Independence Ave., SW
Room 4G-085
Washington, DC 20585   202-586-6503

Public education-related information on natural gas and other sources of energy are available from the office above. *Dinosaurs and Power Plants*, a 16-page brochure

designed for students that relates the story of mining and drilling for coal, gas, and oil, is available free.

GEMINI MISSIONS

NASA CORE
Lorain County Joint Vocational School
15181 Route 58 South
Oberlin, OH 44074   216-774-1051

Gemini Science is a video, appropriate for students in grades 4 and up, in which scientists explain life science experiments developed for the Gemini missions. It includes a brief synopsis of the missions.

GEOGRAPHY

R. Woods
Consumer Information Center
Pueblo, CO 81008

Get your child interested in an important, but often neglected, aspect of education - geography. *Helping Your Child Learn Geography* ($.50, #454X) provides tips to both parents and educators.

U.S. Geological Survey
P.O. Box 25425
Denver, CO 80225

A great way to get your students interested in geography is to teach them how localities got their names. Use the publication *The Naming (and Misnaming) of America* to learn how some localities came to be named, the derivation of these geographic names, and why the U.S. Board on Geographic Names was established.

GEOLOGY

Geologic Inquiries Group
U.S. Geological Survey
907 National Center
Reston, VA 22092   703-648-4383

This office answers questions on topics such as earthquakes, energy and mineral resources, the geology of specific areas, and geologic maps and mapping. Educators and students can contact the office if they have any questions relating to the topics above.

Geologic Inquiries Group
U.S. Geological Survey
907 National Center
Reston, VA 22092   703-648-4383

The *Selected Packet of Geologic Teaching Aids* is prepared for elementary school teachers (and high school teachers) of general science, geography, social studies, environmental education and other earth science-related subjects. It contains leaflets, booklets, reference lists, and an activity sheet ("Make Your Own Paper Model of a Volcano"). To receive a packet, send a request on school letterhead indicating the subject that is taught and the grade level to the office listed above.

GLACIERS

U.S. Geological Survey
P.O. Box 25425
Denver, CO 80225

Glaciers: A Water Resource discusses the relationship between glacial ice and the amount of water on land surfaces. Describes the types of glaciers, their origins, and the natural processes that regulate the melting of ice. Upper elementary teachers can use it to help teach their students about glaciers.

GOATS

U.S. Fish and Wildlife Service
U.S. Department of the Interior
4401 N. Fairfax Drive, Mail Stop 130
Arlington, VA 22203   703-358-1711

Rocky Mountain Goat will introduce your students to this interesting animal.

GREAT LAKES

U.S. EPA Region 5
Office of Public Affairs
77 West Jackson Blvd, PI-195
Chicago, IL 60604   312-353-2000

If you live in Illinois, Indiana, Michigan, Minnesota, Ohio or Wisconsin, you can obtain the publication *The Great Lakes in My World* (grades K-8), an environmental education curriculum that focuses on the Great Lakes. *Great Minds, Great Lakes Curriculum Sampler* (grades K-12), a companion piece to both *The Great Lakes in My World* and *The Great Lakes Environmental Atlas*, is also available to residents from the states noted above, in addition to New York and Pennsylvania.

GROUND WATER
U.S. Geological Survey
P.O. Box 25425
Denver, CO 80225

Do you want your students to do a report on ground water? Have them obtain the following publications for information:

Ground Water: An Undervalued Resource. Describes the need for using ground water, the role of ground water in the economy, and an analysis of regional aquifer systems. Discusses the ways in which ground water and surface water interact.

Ground Water and the Rural Homeowner. Presents a short description of ground water, some of the problems associated with ground water, and some suggestions for help with problems.

Ground Water Contamination--No "Quick Fix" in Sight. Explains how ground water is contaminated by septic tanks or cesspools, municipal lagoons, sewers, landfills, or tailings piles, and the need for further research in contamination prevention.

GUTHRIE, WOODY
Smithsonian/Folkways Recordings
416 Hungerford Dr., Suite 320
Rockville, MD. 20850

Introduce your child to Woody Guthrie's children's songs, available for purchase from Smithsonian/Folkways Recordings. Administered by the Smithsonian Institution's Office of Folklife Programs, Folkways Records is one of the ways the Office supports cultural conservation and continuity, integrity, and equity for traditional artists and cultures. Children's recordings are one of the many categories of recordings available. Children's songs by Pete Seeger and Ella Jenkins can also be purchased, along with dozens of recordings by lesser-known yet still very talented artists.

HALLEY'S COMET
NASA CORE
Lorain County Joint Vocational School
15181 Route 58 South
Oberlin, OH 44074   216-774-1051

The Return of Halley's Comet examines an event heralded by man since the beginning of time, Halley's Comet and its place in the Universe. Available as slides for grades 4-12.

Teaching Resource Center
Jet Propulsion Laboratory
4800 Oak Grove Dr., Mail Stop CS-530
Pasadena, CA 91109   818-354-6916

Halley's Comet is a slide set available to teachers for $6. It consists of twenty 35 mm slides held in a plastic vue-file sleeve which will fit into a three ring binder. It can be an excellent educational aid for classroom use.

HANDICAPPED CHILDREN
Council for Exceptional Children
1920 Association Drive
Reston, VA 22091-1589   703-620-3660

Education literature on handicapped children is available from the Education Resources Information Center (ERIC), a nationwide information network designed to provide users with ready access to education literature. Information on all aspects of the education and development of disabled and gifted children, including identification, assessment, intervention, and enrichment, both in special settings and within the mainstream, is available.

HEAT, SOLAR
Energy Efficiency and Renewable Energy Clearinghouse
P.O. Box 3048
Merrifield, VA 22116   800-363-3732

People are trying to find new ways to heat their homes, factories, offices, and schools without using so much expensive oil and gas. *Solar Energy and You* helps teach children about solar energy and solar heat.

HUBBLE SPACE TELESCOPE
NASA CORE
Lorain County Joint Vocational School
15181 Route 58 South
Oberlin, OH 44074   216-774-1051

Are you looking for some computer software that can help teach your kids about the Hubble Space Telescope? *Hubble Space Telescope Educational Software Project* includes four Apple II disks with reproducible information sheets and reference materials. *Windows to the Universe* chronicles the history of astronomical observations from the unaided eye through the Hubble Space Telescope. *Telescopes* explains the science of optics and the design and characteristics of telescopes. *Introduction to the Hubble Space Telescope* explains the design and operation of the Hubble Space Telescope. *Images From Space* describes the process through which light is captured by the Hubble Space Telescope and converted into images on Earth. *Activities Disk* contains a collection of classroom activities and illustrations relating to telescopes. *Glossary* contains an Appleworks data base of more than 300 astronomy terms. Also includes two Macintosh Applications Software (requires Pagemaker program 3.02 version or higher); *Hubble Space Telescope Model* contains the pattern and instructions for making a detailed model of NASA's Hubble Space Telescope; and *Telescope Primer* which is an outline of the basic principles behind the design and operation of telescopes. Includes many diagrams that can be enlarged and used for making transparencies. For children in grades 5-8.

HURRICANES
Warning and Forecast Branch, W/OM11
National Weather Service
National Oceanic and Atmospheric Administration
SSMCII
1325 East West Highway, Room 14370
Silver Spring, MD 20910

The office above has the following audiovisuals available which can be used by educators to teach school children about safety during natural disasters.

16 mm Films:
A Lady Named Camille
Hurricane Decision
Hurricane

Videotapes:
Hurricane
Before the Hurricane Strikes
Everyday Weather Project: Hurricanes

Slides:
Hurricane Hugo
Hurricane Eloise
Hurricane Preparedness
Hurricane Alicia
Hurricane Frederick

ILLINOIS
Natural Heritage Division
Illinois Department of Conservation
524 S. 2nd St.
Springfield, IL 62706

Nature Discovery II: Wild Mammals of Illinois is a publication for students and teachers and is available to teachers in Illinois. It includes various activities on different mammals and even has a "Guide to Mammal Signs". The publication is written for children in grades 4-8.

INDIA
Office of Education, Room 212
Mail Stop 158
National Museum of Natural History
Washington, DC 20560   202-357-2747

The Living Arts of India is an instructional kit available on loan for a three-week period. Based on the Aditi exhibition (1985), this truly comprehensive kit is contained in a large, brass-bound Indian dowry box. Designed for elementary and secondary students, the kit includes a library of books, pamphlets and catalogs, two dozen objects, a 45-minute videotape, four audio tapes, a two-volume teacher's manual plus four supplemental manuals on children's games, theater activities, Indian fairs and festivals, and Mughul art and history.

INDIANS, AMERICAN

Attn: Public Inquiries Office
Bureau of Indian Affairs
Mail Stop 1340
U.S. Department of Interior
Washington, DC 20240   202-208-3711

The U.S. Department of Interior's Bureau of Indian Affairs often receives inquiries from students who have questions about American Indians. Publications are available to help answer questions. They serve as a wonderful source of information for students and teachers. The publications available include:

Famous Indians: A Collection of Short Biographies. From Pocahontas to Sitting Bull, this publication describes the history and lives of twenty famous American Indians. All were leaders in a great struggle to preserve treasured lands and lifeways. With their tribesmen, they are inseparably linked to our country's history from its earliest beginnings through generations of growth.

Indian Land Areas. This map of the United States displays federal Indian reservations, along with state reservations. It serves as an essential teaching aid for schoolchildren who are learning about Indian reservations.

Office of Education, Room 212
Mail Stop 158
National Museum of Natural History
Washington, DC 20560   202-357-2747

The National Museum of Natural History has programs and activities held throughout the school year for visiting preschool and elementary school children. Programs on American Indians include:

Indian Walkaround: (For preschool and kindergarten children.) The Indian Walkaround is a teacher-directed walk-through of the Indian and Eskimo halls. Volunteers staff small display stations throughout the exhibit, offer objects to touch, and tell about the people who made them. Students find out about different kinds of Indians and Eskimos, examine authentic Native American artifacts, and participate in hands-on activities.

Indians and Eskimos: (For preschool and kindergarten children.) Sitting in front of museum exhibits and using Indian children's toys, students learn what grandparents of Indian children did in the past, what parents do today, and what Indian children might do when they grow up. Lesson includes Eskimo, Woodland, Plains, Northwest Coast, and Southwest peoples.

Indians and Eskimos: (For grades 1 and up.) Students discover the wide diversity of the indigenous cultures past and present in North America. On the tour they explore the relationships between environment and culture by focusing on the basic human need for food, shelter, clothing, and tools. Students also examine authentic Indian and Eskimo artifacts, both contemporary and old, to complete the learning experience.

JENKINS, ELLA

Smithsonian/Folkways Recordings
416 Hungerford Dr., Suite 320
Rockville, MD. 20850

Administered by the Smithsonian Institution's Office of Folklife Programs, Folkways Records is one of the ways the Office supports cultural conservation and continuity, integrity, and equity for traditional artists and cultures. Ella Jenkins is one of those artists whose recordings are available for purchase. Children's songs by Pete Seeger and Woody Guthrie can also be purchased, along with dozens of recordings by lesser-known yet still very talented artists.

JUPITER

Teaching Resource Center
Jet Propulsion Laboratory
4800 Oak Grove Dr.
Mail Stop CS-530
Pasadena, CA 91109   818-354-6916

The Teacher Resource Center of the Jet Propulsion Laboratory makes available educational aids for classroom use, including the slide/cassette program *Jupiter: Voyagers 1 & 2* ($11) and the video *Jupiter, Saturn, Uranus and Neptune* ($25).

KENNEDY CENTER FOR THE PERFORMING ARTS

Office of Elementary and Secondary Education
Arts and Industries Building
Room 1163, MRC-402
Smithsonian Institution
Washington, DC 20560   202-357-3049

The John F. Kennedy Center for the Performing Arts is one of several resources which provides educational materials for teachers. The *Resource Guide for Teachers* contains educational materials available from the Kennedy Center, in addition to the National Gallery of Art and the Smithsonian Institution. The materials include bibliographies, posters, slide sets, films teacher's manuals, videocassettes, and curriculum units.

KENNEDY SPACE CENTER

Teaching Resource Center
Jet Propulsion Laboratory
4800 Oak Grove Dr.
Mail Stop CS-530
Pasadena, CA 91109   818-354-6916

Kennedy Space Center Tour is a video which will delight curious minds. Cost is $25.

KENNEDY, JOHN F.

Education Branch (NEEE)
National Archives and Records Administration
Washington, DC 20408   202-501-6172

Use two documents available from the Education Branch of the National Archives and Records Administration to help teach your students about John F. Kennedy's presidential speeches. *Kennedy's Inaugural Address of 1961* (#200110, ISBN 0-911333- 53-3) and *The Cuban Missile Crisis: Kennedy's Address to the Nation* (#200113, ISBN 0-911333-59-2) are part of a series of booklets which focus on some of the great documents that have shaped the course of U.S. history. Each booklet includes a historical introduction, transcriptions and facsimiles of the featured documents. 8 1/2 x 11, approx. 25 pages each, illustrations, 1986. Softcover only, $2.50 each.

KENTUCKY

Department for Environmental Protection
Frankfort Office Park
14 Reilly Road
Frankfort, KY 40601   502-564-3410

Free pamphlets available include *Kentucky Wild Rivers* and *10 Ways You Can Help Keep Kentucky Water Resources Clean. A Field Guide to Kentucky Rivers and Streams* and *A Field Guide to Kentucky Lakes and Wetlands* are available to teachers. Also available is information on the *Water Watch Program*, a program conducted by the Division of Water with services designed to encourage and support citizen participation in the wise management of community water resources, including streams, lakes, wetlands and groundwater. Any individual, group, family, organization, school or business can become an official "Kentucky Water Watcher".

KING, JR.; MARTIN LUTHER

Martin Luther King Jr. Federal Holiday Commission
451 7th St., SW, Suite 5182
Washington, DC 20410

Are you looking for educational materials to help teach your students about Martin Luther King, Jr.? Look no further than the Martin Luther King, Jr., Federal Holiday Commission. Available items include pledge cards, posters, teaching materials, and selected speeches. Use this resource to heighten your students knowledge of Dr. King.

National Clearinghouse for Alcohol and Drug Information
P.O. Box 2345   800-729-6686
Rockville, MD 20847   301-468-2600

Use the poster *Live the Dream, Say No to Alcohol and Drug Abuse* (1989) to help teach your kids about Martin Luther King, Jr., and the need to say no to alcohol and drugs. Appropriate for all ages, 15 1/2 in. by 22 in. AV165.

LANGUAGES

Center for Applied Linguistics
118 22nd Street NW
Washington, DC 20037-0037   202-429-9551

The Educational Resources Information Center (ERIC) is a nationwide information network designed to provide users with ready access to education literature. The ERIC System, managed by the U.S. Department of Education, Office of Educational Research and Improvement, consists of 16 clearinghouses, four adjunct clearinghouses, and four support components. One of those clearinghouses contains information on languages and language sciences. It includes information on all aspects of second language instruction and learning in all commonly and uncommonly taught languages, including English as a second language; bilingualism and bilingual education; cultural education in the context of second language learning; intercultural communication; study abroad and international education exchange; all areas of linguistics, including theoretical and applied linguistics, sociolinguistics, and psychololinguistics.

LEAVES

Forest Service
U.S. Department of Agriculture
14th and Independence, SW
P.O. Box 96090
Washington, DC 20090-6090 202-205-0957

The publication *Why Leaves Change Color* (#FS-12) can be used by adults and upper elementary schoolchildren to learn about this natural process. It also contains instructions on how to copy leaves with crayons and how to make leaf prints with a stamp pad.

LITTLE LEAGUE

National Clearinghouse for Alcohol and Drug Information
P.O. Box 2345 800-729-6686
Rockville, MD 20852 301-468-2600

The video *Little League Drug Education Program* (1991) combines a child's interest in Little League with a parent's desire to teach him how to say no to drugs and alcohol. This video has two parts: Part 1, "Friend to Friend", featuring Orel Hershiser, is directed toward today's Little Leaguer. The film tells the story of a Little League player who is tempted by drugs. Part 2, "Big League Advice: Helping Your Little Leaguers Say No", is for parents and coaches of Little League players. The film depicts a discussion among Little League parents and baseball Hall-of-Famers 'Hank' Aaron and Jim Palmer. These great ball players offer frank and important advice to parents on how to talk to young people about drugs and alcohol. 30 minutes. VHS29.

LOUISIANA PURCHASE

Education Branch (NEEE)
National Archives and Records Administration
Washington, DC 20408 202-501-6172

The Louisiana Purchase (ISBN 0-911333-54-1) is part of the Milestone Document series available from the National Archives and Records Administration. This ongoing series of booklets focuses on some of the great documents that have shaped the course of U.S. history. The booklet includes a historical introduction and transcriptions and facsimiles of the featured documents. 8 1/2 x 11, approx, 25 pages, illustrations, 1986. Softcover only, $3.50 each.

MAPS

Geologic Inquiries Group
U.S. Geological Survey
907 National Center
Reston, VA 22092 703-648-4383

The geology of specific areas can be taught through the use of maps. The Geologic Inquiries Group has various kinds of geologic maps available for you to purchase.

MARS

Teaching Resource Center
Jet Propulsion Laboratory
4800 Oak Grove Dr.
Mail Stop CS-530
Pasadena, CA 91109 818-354-6916

The Teaching Resource Center of the Jet Propulsion Laboratory has selected video programs on space and planetary subjects available, including a few about the planet Mars. They also have available the video *Mars and Mercury* ($25).

NASA CORE
Lorain County Joint Vocational School
15181 Route 58 South
Oberlin, OH 44074 216-774-1051

Mars and Life on Mars is a video that depicts a mission to Mars involving three vehicles launched from Earth, six months of interplanetary travel, and the establishment of a base on the martian soil. For students in grades 4-8.

MATH

California Energy Extension Service
1400 Tenth St., Room 209
Sacramento, CA 95814 916-323-4388

Energy Math is a set of materials which will assist in integrating the primary math and physical science curricula with respect to the energy theme. Teacher-led activities, learning center activities, and self-correcting worksheets for individual completion are all included.

The Ohio State University
1928 Kenny Rd.
Columbus, OH 43210 614-292-6717

Science, Mathematics, and Environmental Education (SE) is one of the many clearinghouses that are a part of the Educational Resources Information Center (ERIC), a nationwide information network designed to provide users with ready access to education literature. This particular clearinghouse provides information on science, mathematics, and environmental education at all levels, and within these three broad subject areas, the following topics; development of curriculum and instructional materials; teachers and teacher education; learning theory/outcomes (including the impact of parameters such as interest level, intelligence, values, and concept development upon learning in these fields); educational programs; engineering; research and evaluative studies; medical applications; and computer applications.

R. Woods
Consumer Information Center
Pueblo, CO 81008

Help Your Child Learn Math ($0.50, #452X) is one of the many publications for parents available from the Consumer Information Center. Make check or money order payable for Superintendent of Documents. For a copy, send your check or money order to the address above.

MEDICAL RESEARCH

National Institute of Mental Health
U.S. Department of Health and Human Services
5600 Fishers Lane, Room 7C02
Rockville, MD 20857 301-443-4513

By learning how scientists perform medical research in laboratories, children can better understand how and why doctors are able to help people to get well. *Let's Visit a Research Laboratory: Introduction and Lesson Plans* (for schoolchildren in grades 2-5) helps answer the many questions children may have about research laboratories. The supplemental poster that is included provides teachers with helpful illustrations for classroom discussion and activities.

MERCURY FLIGHTS

NASA CORE
Lorain County Joint Vocational School
15181 Route 58 South
Oberlin, OH 44074 216-774-1051

Project Mercury: An Early Step is a video appropriate for students in grades four and up that summarizes the project Mercury flights of the 60's. It shows the designing and building of the spacecraft, the training of the seven original astronauts, the MR-2 launch with the chimp HAM, and highlights of Alan Shepard's first flight, as well as the flights of other Mercury astronauts.

MERCURY (PLANET)

Teaching Resource Center
Jet Propulsion Laboratory
4800 Oak Grove Dr.
Mail Stop CS-530
Pasadena, CA 91109 818-354-6916

Show your students the video *Mars and Mercury* and watch their interest grow as they learn about these planets. Cost is $25.

METRIC SYSTEM

Superintendent of Documents
Government Printing Office

Washington, DC 20402   202-512-1800

The National Institute of Standards and Technology (formerly the National Bureau of Standards) of the U.S. Department of Commerce has produced a 29"x45" poster called *The Modernized Metric System*. Available from the Superintendent of Documents, Government Printing Office (special publication 304), it is an excellent visual tool educators can use to teach their students about the metric system.

MIGRATION

Division of Publications
Room B1026
National Museum of American History
Smithsonian Institution
Washington, DC 20560   202-357-4573

Appropriate for upper elementary through twelfth grade students is the educational outreach kit, *Field to Factory: Afro-American Migration, 1915-1940*. It includes a teacher's manual, slides, and poster, in addition to other educational tools.

MINERALS

Bureau of Mines
U.S. Department of the Interior
Cochrans Mill Road
P.O. Box 18070
Pittsburgh, PA 15236   412-892-4338

Minerals in 1991 contains information on 34 minerals identified as highly important to the economy or defense of the United States. Students in the upper elementary grades can use this brochure to learn about various minerals, including copper, gold, silver, and tin.

Bureau of Mines
U.S. Department of the Interior
Cochrans Mill Road
P.O. Box 18070
Pittsburgh, PA 15236   412-892-4338

To learn about your state's mineral activities, contact the office above for a copy of *Minerals in the 50 States*. This publication contains historical information and is an excellent resource for schoolchildren who need to write reports on the history of their state.

Geologic Inquiries Group
U.S. Geological Survey
907 National Center
Reston, VA 22092   703-648-4383

Do you have a question on mineral resources? Contact the Geologic Inquiries Group. This office answers questions not only on mineral resources, but also questions on earthquakes, energy resources, the geology of specific areas, and geologic maps and mapping.

Office of Education
Room 212
Mail Stop 158
National Museum of Natural History
Washington, DC 20560   202-357-2747

The National Museum of Natural History has a visiting program for grades one and up called *Rocks and Minerals*. In it students are introduced to rocks and the major rock-forming minerals by examining exhibited specimens in the Earth and Mineral exhibition halls and by participating in a hands-on classroom activity. Students distinguish between rocks and minerals; identify seven common minerals using the physical properties of luster, color, hardness, and streak; classify seven rock specimens according to their origin (igneous, sedimentary, or metamorphic); and explore the relationship between texture and mineral composition of rocks and the processes that form them.

Office of Education
Room 212
Mail Stop 158
National Museum of Natural History
Washington, DC 20560   202-357-2747

The National Museum of Natural History also has workshops for teachers, including one called *Rocks and Minerals*. Here teachers can work with a geologist in developing ways to introduce students to rocks and minerals. Time is spent in the Earth and Mineral exhibition halls, as well as in a classroom. Activities are designed to provide experience in distinguishing between a rock and a mineral, describing minerals by their physical properties, and using rock texture to classify rocks according to their origin.

MISSOURI

Missouri Department of Natural Resources
Division of Geology and Land Survey
P.O. Box 250
Rolla, MO 65401

Students who wish to learn interesting facts about Missouri should obtain the publication *Earthquakes in Missouri*. It contains information not only about earthquakes in Missouri but also general information on understanding earthquakes, measuring earthquakes, and the hazards of earthquakes. This publication can serve as an educational aid for upper-elementary school children.

MONEY

Bureau of Engraving and Printing
U.S. Department of the Treasury
14th and C St., SW
Washington, DC 20228   202-874-3019

Did you know that 95% of the notes printed each year are used to replace notes already in circulation? That 48% of the notes printed are $1 notes? These facts and others can be obtained from the Bureau of Engraving and Printing. Parents and teachers can use the information to provide a greater appreciation of U.S. currency. Children can use it to supplement school reports. Some of the information sheets available include:

Bibliography of Numismatic Books and Periodicals
Changes in $1 From July 1929
Difference Between United States Notes and Federal Reserve Notes
Engravers and Engraving
Expanded Use of the Motto "In God We Trust" in United States Currency
Fun Facts About Dollars
The Great Seal of the United States
Use of the National Motto "In God We Trust" on United States Currency
The Story of Money

Bureau of Engraving and Printing
U.S. Department of the Treasury
14th and C St., SW
Washington, DC 20228   202-874-3019

The Bureau of Engraving and Printing is pleased to offer uncut currency for sale to the general public. Imagine a child's surprise and curiosity when they see uncut currency! Contact the office above for more information. Prices are:

One ($1) Notes	Visitors Center	Mail Order
4-subject	$ 7.50	$10.25
16-subject	$21.50	$28.00
32-subject	$40.50	$47.00

Two ($2) Notes	Visitors Center	Mail Order
4-subject	$12.00	$14.75
16-subject	$38.50	$45.00

MOON

NASA CORE
Lorain County Joint Vocational School
15181 Route 58 South
Oberlin, OH 44074   216-774-1051

NASA CORE makes available to educators educational slides and videos, including the following three educational aids. *Moon Landing - Apollo 11* is a set of slides that tells the story of the most famous spaceflight in history, man's first moon landing. Appropriate for students in grades 4-12. *Return To The Moon Videoconference Kit* is a video of the taping of an interactive teleconference on January 26, 1990. Students joined Apollo astronaut Michael Collins and NASA guest educator Dr. Lynn Bondurant on a "Return to the Moon", participating in a series of unique problem-solving and hands on activities. Accompanying curriculum material includes an activity booklet, slides and a moon map (for grades 5-8). *The Time of Apollo* is a video tribute to the historical accomplishments of the Apollo missions (for grades 4-adult).

Teaching Resource Center
Jet Propulsion Laboratory
4800 Oak Grove Dr.
Mail Stop CS-530   800-345-6707
Pasadena, CA 91109   818-354-6916

The video *Apollo Moon Landings* ($25) is available from the Teacher Resource Center of the Jet Propulsion Laboratory.

MOTOR RACING

Photographic Services
American History Building
Room CB-054, Smithsonian Institution
Washington, DC 20560
202-357-1933

American Motor Racing: Richard Petty Car is a wonderful color poster available for all car enthusiasts. $10.

MOTORCYCLES

Department of Publications
Room MBB66
National Museum of American History
Smithsonian Institution
Washington, DC 20560
202-357-1487

Get your child the color poster *American Motorcycles, 1900-1940*. $8.

MUSIC

Smithsonian/Folkways Recordings
416 Hungerford Dr., Suite 320
Rockville, MD. 20850

Administered by the Smithsonian Institution's Office of Folklife Programs, Folkways Records is one of the ways the Office supports cultural conservation and continuity, integrity, and equity for traditional artists and cultures. Children's recordings are one of the many categories of recordings available. Children's songs by Pete Seeger, Ella Jenkins, and Woody Guthrie can be purchased, along with dozens of recordings by lesser-known yet still very talented artists. They include *Latin American Folk Songs Sung in Spanish by Chago Rodrigo*, *Singing Streets: The Childhood Memories of Ireland and Scotland*, *Children's Songs from Spain*, and *French Folk Songs for Children*. Write to the office above to obtain *The Whole Folkways Catalogue* which contains these and other recordings.

MUSKRATS

U.S. Fish and Wildlife Service
U.S. Department of the Interior
4401 N. Fairfax Drive, Mail Stop 130
Arlington, VA 22203
703-358-1711

Interested in learning more about the muskrat? Obtain the publication *Muskrat* from the U.S. Fish and Wildlife Service.

NATIONAL AERONAUTICS AND SPACE ADMINISTRATION

Superintendent of Documents
Government Printing Office
Washington, DC 20402
202-512-1800

The National Aeronautics and Space Administration produces educational publications for educators, students, and the general public. All are offered for sale by the Superintendent of Documents, Government Printing Office. Prices may change.

NASA CORE
Lorain County Joint Vocational School
15181 Route 58 South
Oberlin, OH 44074
216-774-1051

The NASA Central Operation of Resources for Educators (CORE), established in cooperation with Lorain County Joint Vocational School, serves as the national distribution center for NASA produced education materials. For a minimal charge the NASA CORE will provide a valuable service to educators unable to visit one of the NASA Teacher Resource Centers (TRC), by making NASA educational audiovisual materials available through its mail order service. Also available are different memorabilia items which can be used by teachers as awards for students. They include a NASA logo patch, pencils, hats, T-shirts, mugs, and astronaut ice cream.

Elementary and Secondary Programs Branch
Educational Affairs Division
Mail Code XEE
NASA Headquarters
Washington, DC 20546

The Aerospace Education Services Program (AESP), previously known as Spacemobile, is the Educational Affairs Division's premier outreach program. AESP specialists, all former teachers themselves, reach millions of students each year. They cross the country from September to June each year, assisting schools so students and teachers can see first-hand what NASA is all about. Visits are scheduled by field center, and because each field center performs a specific service for NASA, each center's program is a little different from the others. All emphasize current NASA programs, such as the Space Shuttle and the Freedom Space Station. Because of this program's popularity, a visit should be requested well in advance. Although field centers make every effort to accommodate the date a school requests, there is currently about a 2-year waiting list.

Education Division
NASA Headquarters
Washington, DC 20546

NASA Spacelink is a collection of NASA information and educational materials stored on a computer at the Marshall Space Flight Center in Huntsville, Alabama. The system may be accessed over regular telephone lines. It is designed to communicate with a wide variety of computers and modems, especially those most commonly found in classrooms and home. NASA Spacelink is free, but you'll owe your phone company for long distance calls. It includes a listing of all the major NASA educational programs. Subjects include the Aerospace Education Services Project, Urban Community Enrichment Program, Summer High School Apprenticeship Research Program, Space Science Student Involvement Project, Teacher Workshops, Educators Mailing List, Telelectures, Teacher Resource Centers, and Science Fair support. Classroom materials include a variety of information useful in the classroom, including space science lesson plans and activities (all grade levels and many subjects), astronomy information, film/video list, computer programs, career information, computer graphics, and a source list for pictures, posters, and other educational materials.

Elementary and Secondary Programs Branch
Educational Affairs Division
Mail Code XEE
NASA Headquarters
Washington, DC 20546

Aerospace Education Services Program (AESP) specialists conduct workshops for teachers each summer at NASA field centers, elementary and secondary schools, and on college campuses. Workshops cover astronomy, aeronautics, life in space, principles of rocketry, earth sciences, and remote sensing. A typical workshop includes how-to and hands-on activities to help teachers incorporate what they learn into classroom activities and programs to supplement existing curricula.

NATIONAL AIR AND SPACE MUSEUM

Education Division, MRC 305
National Air and Space Museum
Washington, DC 20560
202-786-2109

The Education Resource Center (ERC) of the National Air and Space Museum (NASM) is open to teachers of all levels and disciplines. The ERC offers teachers access to educational materials pertaining to aviation, space, and the Museum's collections. These materials are produced by NASM, the National Aeronautics and Space Administration (NASA), and other government agencies, and private organizations. Additional information on the ERC and other NASM educational programs may be obtained by writing to the address above. Educational materials include the following:

Curriculum Packages: Complete units on specific topics are available on request for grades K-12. Write and tell them the subjects and grades you teach, and they will be happy to send you the appropriate packages. Requests must be made by teachers on school letterhead.

Lesson Plans: Hundreds of classroom activities on aerospace-related topics, arranged according to subject and grade levels, are available for duplication when you visit the ERC. This service is not available through the mail.

Public Domain Software: Aerospace-related public domain computer software for use with Apple II series and IBM PC computers is available for duplication when you visit the ERC, as well as through the mail. In both cases, teachers must provide blank diskettes. Contact the ERC for a current catalog and mail-in procedures.

Commercial Software: A growing collection of IBM PC and Apple II series commercial software on aerospace topics is available on a preview-only basis for visiting teachers.

Videodiscs and CD-Roms: Visit the ERC to preview our growing collection of these new audiovisual formats.

Filmstrips: The ERC's large collection of filmstrips is available for preview. NASM-produced filmstrips may be obtained from the National Audiovisual Center, 8700 Edgewood Drive, Capitol Heights, MD 20743, 301-763-1896.

Be patient. If any phone number is incorrect, call (area code) 555-1212 and request the new listing.

1271

The Government Works for Kids, Too

Videos: Hundreds of videos can be previewed at the ERC. Videos must be rented or purchased from their respective suppliers.

Slide Sets: A variety of slide sets are available for preview in the ERC. The NASM-produced "Milestones of Flight" set is available through NASA CORE.

Other Resources: A variety of resources such as science kits, posters, brochures, and catalogs are available as reference materials.

"Skylines" Newsletter: The Education Division publishes a newsletter for teachers. Please write and ask to be placed on our mailing list.

ERC Workshops: Half-day workshops, to aid educators in utilizing the ERC, are scheduled on request. Participants receive assistance in compiling educational units to meet specific needs.

Other Workshops: Throughout the year, the Education Division offers aerospace-related teacher workshops that are announced in the Skylines newsletter. Contact the Education Division for more information.

Tours and Group Reservations: Free docent-led tours of the Museum are offered year-round for school groups, on a variety of subjects and grade levels. Reservations must be made by mail at least three weeks in advance but no earlier than eight weeks in advance of visit. School group reservation for the Einstein Planetarium and Langley Theater are also available. Request a current tour brochure and reservation form from the Tour Scheduling Office, MRC 305, National Air and Space Museum, Washington, DC 20560.

NATIONAL ARCHIVES

Education Branch (NEEE)
National Archives and Records Administration
Washington, DC 20408   202-501-6172

The National Archives preserves and makes available to the public the permanently valuable records of the U.S. Government. It offers teachers from the upper elementary grades through the secondary levels a workshop called *Primarily Teaching* that introduces them to the holdings and organization of the National Archives. *Primarily Teaching* emphasizes secondary strategies, but educators at all levels adapt them to their particular needs. Participants will learn how to do research in historical records; to create classroom material from records; and to present documents in ways that sharpen students' skills and enthusiasm for history, social studies, and the humanities.

Education Branch (NEEE)
National Archives and Records Administration
Washington, DC 20408   202-501-6172

The Education Branch of the National Archives offers teachers of upper elementary through secondary school students publications and teaching units to aid in the teaching of historical documents and eras. They include "Milestone Documents", an ongoing series of booklets which focus on some of the great documents that have shaped the course of U.S. history. (Each booklet includes a historical introduction and transcriptions and facsimiles of the featured documents.) Also available is "Teaching With Documents", an invaluable aid to teachers who wish to enliven their curriculum through the use of primary sources. This collection of articles began as a feature series appearing in Social Education, the journal of the National Council for the Social Studies. Each essay highlights on National Archives document and provides practical suggestions for using the documents in several classroom settings.

NATIONAL GALLERY OF ART

Office of Elementary and Secondary Education
Arts and Industries Building
Room 1163, Smithsonian Institution
Washington, DC 20560   202-357-3049

The *Resource Guide for Teachers* contains educational materials available not only from the National Gallery of Art, but the John F. Kennedy Center for the Performing Arts and the Smithsonian Institution as well. The materials include bibliographies, posters, slide sets, films teacher's manuals, videocassettes, and curriculum units. Below are some materials listed in the *Resource Guide*.

NATIONAL MUSEUM OF NATURAL HISTORY

Office of Education, Room 212
Mail Stop 158
National Museum of Natural History
Washington, DC 20560   202-357-2747

The National Museum of Natural History offers visiting programs for school children and workshops for teachers. *Old Growth Forests*, *Animals*, and *Dinosaurs* are a few of the programs for kids, and *Endangered Species and Extinction*, *Rocks and Minerals*, and *Oceans* are a few of the workshops for teachers. For information on these and other services available, including slide sets, contact the office above.

NEPTUNE

NASA CORE
Lorain County Joint Vocational School
15181 Route 58
Oberlin, OH 44074   216-774-1051

Voyager Encounters Neptune is a set of color photographs taken when Voyager encountered Neptune in August of 1989. It includes pictures of the Great Dark Spot, Neptune's rings and Triton. Appropriate for children in grades 4-12.

Teaching Resource Center
Jet Propulsion Laboratory
4800 Oak Grove Dr.
Mail Stop CS-530
Pasadena, CA 91109   818-354-6916

A video is available entitled *Jupiter, Saturn, Uranus and Neptune* ($25).

NORTH AMERICAN CONTINENT

U.S. Geological Survey
P.O. Box 25425
Denver, CO 80225

Our Changing Continent is a publication that discusses the evidence and techniques scientists use to reconstruct the history of the changing land surface of the North American continent.

NUCLEAR ENERGY

Office of Plans and Evaluations
Office of Nuclear Energy
U.S. Department of Energy
1000 Independence Ave., SW
Washington, DC 20585   202-586-6450

Since 1982, nuclear energy has been second only to coal as an energy source for the production of electricity in the United States, surpassing oil, natural gas, and hydroelectric power. The office above has several publications available, some of which are listed below, to more fully understand this valuable source of energy and the role it plays. Teachers can supplement their science curricula with the use of these publications:

Answers to Questions
Approaches to Nuclear Safety
Atoms to Electricity
The First Reactor
High-Level Nuclear Waste: A Safe, Permanent Solution
The History of Nuclear Energy
How Nuclear Energy Plants Work
Light Water Breeder Reactor
Low-Level Nuclear Waste: Safe, Permanent Disposal
Nuclear Energy: Benefit for All Americans
Nuclear Energy Economics
Nuclear Energy Plant Safety
The Nuclear Fuel Cycle
Nuclear Power in Space
Nuclear Powerplant Safety: Design and Planning
Nuclear Powerplant Safety: Operations
Nuclear Powerplant Safety: Source Terms
Radiation in Perspective
Radiosotopes: Today's Applications
Understanding Radiation

National Energy Information Center, EI-231
Energy Information Administration
Forrestal Building
Washington, DC 20585   202-586-8800

Information on nuclear power generation is available from the National Energy Information Center. The NEIC offers free of charge *Energy Information Sheets*, which contain information on topics ranging from crude oil production to coal consumption to nuclear power generation.

OCEANS

U.S. Geological Survey
P.O. Box 25425
Denver, CO 80225

The U.S. Geological Survey has two publications available on oceans. *Why is the Ocean Salty?* discusses the origin of the oceans and the sources of their salinity (also available in Spanish) and *The Exclusive Economic Zone: An Exciting New Frontier* describes the geologic processes that form the ocean floors.

Office of Education, Room 212
Mail Stop 158
National Museum of Natural History
Washington, DC 20560   202-357-2747

The National Museum of Natural History has several workshops for teachers including one on oceans. In this workshop teachers become familiar with ancient and modern reefs and how ocean populations have changed over time. They also learn the ecology of and strategies for competing in a water environment and survey briefly the problems in today's ocean environments.

OIL

National Energy Information Center, EI-231
Energy Information Administration
Forrestal Building
Washington, DC 20585   202-586-8800

Crude oil production is one of the many topics covered in the National Energy Information Center's *Energy Information Sheets.* Information ranging from the above to coal consumption to nuclear power generation is provided. The information can be used by teachers and upper elementary students to supplement curricula and reports.

Office of Fossil Energy Communications
1000 Independence Ave., SW, Room 4G-085
Washington, DC 20585   202-586-6503

The office above provides technical and public education-related information on oil, coal, and natural gas technologies, and the Nation's petroleum reserves. It offers *Dinosaurs and Power Plants*, a 16-page brochure designed for students that relates the story of mining and drilling for coal, gas, and oil; environmental concerns; and modes of transportation.

OPOSSUM

U.S. Fish and Wildlife Service
U.S. Department of the Interior
4401 N. Fairfax Drive, Mail Stop 130
Arlington, VA 22203   703-358-1711

Do you know much about this marsupial? Find out more by reading the publication *Opossum*.

OWLS

U.S. Fish and Wildlife Service
U.S. Department of the Interior
4401 N. Fairfax Drive
Mail Stop 130
Arlington, VA 22203   703-358-1711

Is your child fascinated with owls? Obtain the publication *Spotted Owl* and *Great Horned Owl* so she can learn more about them.

OZONE

Public Information Center
U.S. Environmental Protection Agency
401 M Street, SW, MS 3404
Washington, DC 20460   202-260-2080

Learn about the pollutants ozone and carbon monoxide in the *Environmental Backgrounder: Ozone and Carbon Monoxide*. This six-page publication provides important information on these two major public health concerns and can be used by educators to supplement science curricula.

PALEOANTHROPOLOGY

Office of Education, Room 212
Mail Stop 158
National Museum of Natural History
Washington, DC 20560   202-357-2747

What Does It Mean to Be Human? Human Origins is one of several visiting programs offered by the National Museum of Natural History. Here students in grades one and up can learn about the family history of humankind. Students investigate human's place in nature, identify characteristics of our genus and species, and trace the biological and cultural evolution of humankind to the end of the last Ice Age. By examining real skeletal materials, replicas of fossils, and ancient stone tools, students get a feel for the real stones, bones and methods of paleoanthropology.

PANAMA CANAL

Panama Canal Commission
1825 I Street, NW, Suite 1050
Washington, DC 20006   202-634-6441

Would you like to teach your students or children about the Panama Canal? Call the office above to receive a copy of the publications, *Panama Canal: The Vital Link for World Trade* and *The Panama Canal: Pictorial Map*. Both of these publications provide interesting facts and information about the Panama Canal.

PANDAS

U.S. Fish and Wildlife Service
U.S. Department of the Interior
4401 N. Fairfax Drive
Mail Stop 130
Arlington, VA 22203   703-358-1711

Pandas are such an interesting animal. Help your child learn more about them by reading the publication *Giant Panda*.

PEDESTRIAN SAFETY

National Highway Traffic Safety Administration
U.S. Department of Transportation
400 Seventh St., SW
Washington, DC 20590   202-366-0910

Contact the office above to receive publications on pedestrian safety. Appropriate for elementary children are *Safe Street Crossing for Kids: A Planning Guide* and *Safe Street Crossing for Kids: A Program that Works*.

PEN PALS

U.S. Postal Service Olympic Pen Pal Club
P.O. Box 9419
Gaithersburg, MD 20898-9419

Children six years and older who enjoy writing may be interested in joining Stamper, the U.S. Postal Service Olympic Pen Pal Club. For $5.95 a child receives a pen pal's name and address along with a Stamper sign, a Stamper calendar, an extra-thick note pad, a big world map, a Stamper activity book, an official membership card and button, a Stamper frame, and Stamper stationery. Write to the address above for more information.

PENNSYLVANIA

Office of Environmental Education
Pennsylvania Department of Education
333 Market St.
Harrisburg, PA 17126   717-783-6994

Available from the office above is *The Friendly Forest Fun Book*, an activity book designed to help elementary teachers enhance students' awareness and knowledge about Pennsylvania's forest lands, the resources the forest provides to both wildlife and the consumer, and the enjoyment that can be obtained from the proper use of our forests.

PESTICIDES

Public Information Center
401 M St., SW, MS 3404
Washington, DC 20460

Don't Bug Me, for grades K-3, is a pamphlet illustrating the safe use of pesticides and includes pictures and captions.

PESTS

Cooperative Extension Service
University of Nebraska - Lincoln
Department of Entomology

210 Plant Industry Bldg.
Lincoln, NE 68583-0816   402-472-2123

Educational materials on the topic of integrated pest management of crops are available from the Institute of Agriculture and Natural Resources at the University of Nebraska. A free catalog which lists environmental films and videotapes for young people's viewing is also available.

PETROLEUM

National Energy Information Center (NEIC)
Energy Information Administration, EI-231
U.S. Department of Energy
1000 Independence Ave., SW, Room 1F-048
Washington, DC 20585   202-586-8800

Petroleum is one of several types of energy used today. The National Energy Information Center (NEIC) provides information on petroleum and other energy sources, such as natural gas, coal, electricity and renewable energy. Students can use the information provided on the one-page information sheets for science reports.

PETS

Center for Veterinary Medicine
Food and Drug Administration
Public Health Service
U.S. Department of Health and Human Services
7500 Standish Place
Rockville, MD 20855   301-594-1755

There are many factors involved in the care and feeding of a household pet. The office above has several fact sheets which parents can use to teach their children how to care for pets properly.

PETTY, RICHARD

Photographic Services
American History Building
Room CB-054
Smithsonian Institution
Washington, DC 20560   202-357-1933

The color poster *American Motor Racing: Richard Petty Car* is available for $10.

PHEASANTS

U.S. Fish and Wildlife Service
U.S. Department of the Interior
4401 N. Fairfax Drive
Mail Stop 130
Arlington, VA 22203   703-358-1711

Teach your students about pheasants after reading the *Ring-necked Pheasant* publication.

PHYSICAL FITNESS

Physical Fitness Award Program
President's Council on Physical Fitness and Sports
701 Pennsylvania Ave., NW, Suite 250
Washington, DC 20004   202-272-3421

American youth have participated in the Presidential Physical Fitness Award Program or the "President's Challenge" since 1966. The program includes all young people from ages six through 17, including those students with special needs. In addition, two awards have been added to go with the prestigious Presidential Physical Fitness Award for outstanding achievement. The National Physical Fitness Award was introduced in 1987 and is for those who reach a basic yet challenging level of fitness. A new award called the Participant Physical Fitness Award, introduced in the Fall of 1991, is for those who attempt the President's Challenge but don't qualify for a Presidential or National Award. The booklet *Get Fit! A Handbook for Youth Ages 6-17* will help children become as physically fit as they can be.

PLANETS

R. Woods
Consumer Information Center - Y
P.O. Box 100
Pueblo, CO 81002

Full-color photos and descriptions of the planets in the solar system can be found in the publication *A Look at the Planets*. Includes data on space explorations. 8 pp. (1985. NASA) 150X. $1. Write to the above address.

Superintendent of Documents
Government Printing Office
Washington, DC 20402   202-512-1800

Information Summaries: Our Planets At a Glance is a 16-page publication that serves as an excellent source of concise information on the planets. Use it as a supplement to science curricula.

Superintendent of Documents
Government Printing Office
Washington, DC 20402   202-512-1800

The publication *Comparing the Planets* introduces comparative planetology by presenting information gathered from National Aeronautics and Space Administration (NASA) space missions. In addition to showing the size of planets and their distance from the Sun, it describes planets in terms of composition, density, atmosphere, and geology. Printed in color. 32x56 inches. 1979. Stock No. 033-000-00744-2. $3.50.

POCAHONTAS

Attn: Public Inquiries Office
Bureau of Indian Affairs
Mail Stop 2620 (MIB)
U.S. Department of Interior
Washington, DC 20240   202-208-3711

The publication *Famous Indians: A Collection of Short Biographies* describes the history and lives, from Pocahontas to Sitting Bull, of twenty famous American Indians. All were leaders in a great struggle to preserve treasured lands and lifeways. With their tribesmen, they are inseparably linked to our country's history from its earliest beginnings through generations of growth. This publication is a wonderful source of information for students and teachers.

POISON

Food and Drug Administration
Consumer Communications HFE-88
Rockville, MD 20857

Most products are made to look attractive so people will buy them -- even products that can be poisonous. But things made attractive for consumers are also attractive to children. Many poisonings that occur involve children who are too young and innocent to "know better." *Dennis the Menace Takes a Poke at Poison* is a comic book that teaches children to "always ask first" before they taste. Write to the office above for a free copy.

POSTERS

Department of Public Programs
Room BB53, National Museum of American History
Smithsonian Institution
Washington, DC 20560   202-357-4187

The color poster *A More Perfect Union* is an excellent educational aid to use when teaching students about the Japanese American internment that occurred during World War II. $8.

Photographic Services
American History Building
Room CB-054
Smithsonian Institution
Washington, DC 20560   202-357-1933

The color poster *American Motor Racing: Richard Petty Car* is available for $10.

Department of Public Programs
Room CC53
National Museum of American History
Smithsonian Institution
Washington, DC 20560   202-357-4187

Get your child the color poster *American Motorcycles, 1900-1940*. $8.

Department of Public Programs
Room CC53
National Museum of American History
Smithsonian Institution
Washington, DC 20560   202-357-4187

For Duke Ellington enthusiasts, this office has the poster *Duke Ellington*, available for $6.

Smithsonian Institution Traveling Exhibition Service
1100 Jefferson Drive, SW

Room 3146
Washington, DC 20560
Use the poster *The Frederick Douglass Years: 1817-1895* to help teach your children about Frederick Douglass. The poster includes biographies of abolitionists and black leaders, and a bibliography. Cost is $1.

Photographic Services
American History Building
Room CB-054
Smithsonian Institution
Washington, DC 20560   202-357-1933
Sitting Bull is a poster available for $3 from the Smithsonian Institution.

National Crime Prevention Council
1700 K Street, NW, 2nd Floor
Washington, DC 20006   202-466-6272
For drug prevention educators there is the poster *To Be What You Want To Be: Be Drug Free*. This poster has people from many professions with the slogan "To be what you want to be, be drug free." The poster has room for the child to draw himself into the picture. $2.50.

National Clearinghouse for Alcohol and Drug Information
P.O. Box 2345   800-729-6686
Rockville, MD 20847   301-468-2600
The following poster is available from the National Clearinghouse for Alcohol and Drug Information and are appropriate for elementary school children:

Live the Dream, Say No to Alcohol and Drug Abuse (1989). Poster features Dr. Martin Luther King, Jr. Appropriate for all ages, 15 1/2 in. by 22 in. AV165.

Superintendent of Documents
Dept. 33
Washington, DC 20402   202-512-1800
The American Soldier, Set No. 2 is a set of 10 color posters reproducing paintings of American servicemen and women over the 100-year period from 1863 to 1963. (Includes an explanatory booklet). Use these posters to help teach your children about American history. All posters are 9 x 13 inches and are printed on fine white paper suitable for framing. (S/N 008-020-00227-5, $6, 1989, shipped flat).

Office of Fossil Energy, Room 4G 085
U.S. Department of Energy
1000 Independence Ave., SW
Washington, DC 20585   202-586-6503
Call the office above to receive *The Clean Coal Path* poster. It traces the route of several new advances in the clean use of coal, America's most abundant fossil energy resource. During the 1990's, many of these improvements will be used for the first time in power plants to generate new supplies of electricity without polluting the nation's air.

U.S. Fish and Wildlife Service
U.S. Department of the Interior
4401 N. Fairfax Drive
Mail Stop 130
Arlington, VA 22203   703-358-1711
The U.S. Fish and Wildlife Service has several posters available to be used by educators, 4-H clubs, or Boy Scout organizations. They include:

Raptors - Hunters On the Wing!
Steel Shot - Are You Using the Right Load?
The Difference Between Endangered and Extinct is Forever
Wetlands - We need 'em...- Wildlife needs 'em too.

Forest Service
U.S. Department of Agriculture
14th and Independence, SW
P.O. Box 96090
Washington, DC 20090-6090   202-205-0957
The poster *How a Tree Grows* (FS-8) teaches about photosynthesis, enzymes, and the various parts of a tree. Its colorful illustrations make it a very useful teaching aid. The eight-page publication *How a Tree Grows* supplements the poster and provides more information on how a tree grows.

Forest Service
U.S. Department of Agriculture
14th and Independence, SW
P.O. Box 96090
Washington, DC 20090-6090   202-205-0957

Available from this office is the poster *What We Get From Trees* (FS-68). It lists the various products, ranging from chewing gum to mop handles, which come from trees.

United States Fire Administration
National Academy
Federal Emergency Management Agency
16825 S. Seton Avenue
Emmitsburg, MD 21727   301-447-6771
A poster is one of many educational aids included in the U.S. Fire Administration public education kit called "Curious Kids Set Fires." The program was developed to help reduce fire deaths by educating and counseling the child setter. Contact the office above to receive the kit, which also includes handouts for the school classroom, lesson plans for teachers, camera-ready print public service announcements, a press release announcing your local program, a sample letter for the local paper, a resource guide with additional materials you may want to get, and descriptions of pre-adolescent fire prevention and counseling programs from other communities.

Superintendent of Documents
Government Printing Office
Washington, DC 20402   202-512-1800
The National Aeronautics and Space Administration (NASA) produces posters for educators, students, and the general public. All are offered for sale by the Superintendent of Documents, Government Printing Office. Prices may change. Contact your regional GPO outlet or call the office above. The posters include:

Space Shuttle. Shows the external configuration, and internal design and construction of the Space Shuttle. Printed in color. 30x42 inches. Folded. 1978. Stock No. 033-000-00743-4. $3.50.

Comparing the Planets. Introduces comparative planetology by presenting information gathered from NASA space missions. In addition to showing the size of planets and their distance from the Sun, it describes planets in terms of composition, density, atmosphere, and geology. Printed in color. 32x56 inches. 1979. Stock No. 033-000-00744-2. $3.50.

Spacelab Wallsheet. Spacelab and Space Shuttle orbiter during a hypothetical mission. Inserts show life cycle of Spacelab from assembly to launch, different Spacelab configurations, and parts of the vehicle. Printed in color. 43x44 inches. 1983. Stock No. 033-000-00903-8. $3.75.

Space Suit Wallsheet. Near-life-sized poster of Bruce McCandless on his first spacewalk using the manned maneuvering unit. The space suit is labeled showing its various components. Printed in color. 36x56 inches. 1990. Stock No. 033-000-01067-2. $5.50.

International Cometary Explorer Wallsheet. Depicts comet and International Cometary Explorer (ICE) spacecraft, and lists mission details. Printed in color. 37x41 inches. 1985. Stock No. 033-000-00958-5. $4.

Superintendent of Documents
Government Printing Office
Washington, DC 20402   202-512-1800
The National Institute of Standards and Technology (formerly the National Bureau of Standards) of the U.S. Department of Commerce has produced a 29"x45" poster called *The Modernized Metric System*. Available from the Superintendent of Documents (special publication 304), it is an excellent visual tool educators can use to teach their students about the metric system.

Education Division
NASA Headquarters
Washington, DC 20546
Are you looking for more posters available from NASA? NASA Spacelink is a collection of NASA information and educational materials stored on a computer at the Marshall Space Flight Center in Huntsville, Alabama. It includes a listing of all the major NASA educational programs. Classroom materials include a variety of information useful in the classroom (in addition to posters) including space science lesson plans and activities (all grade levels and many subjects), astronomy information, film/video list, computer programs, career information, computer graphics, and a source list for pictures, and other educational materials.

Bureau of Mines
U.S. Department of the Interior
Cochrans Mill Road
P.O. Box 18070
Pittsburgh, PA 15236   412-892-4431

The Government Works for Kids, Too

The Petroleum Tree illustration shows all the dozens of products that are obtainable from crude oil. This illustration serves as an excellent learning tool for students in the upper elementary grades.

Texas Water Development Board
Office of Public Information
P.O. Box 13231
Austin, TX 78711-3231   512-936-0833

Land Use and the Water Cycle is a black and white poster which illustrates the water cycle and different uses of land. It can be used by educators as a teaching aid or by students as a component to a report.

Government Printing Office (GPO)
Superintendent of Documents
Washington, DC 20402-9325   202-512-1800

National Park Service posters and charts are colorful commemorative pieces by well-know artists. They can be used to brighten any classroom. Prices vary from $3.75 to $7 a copy. They include the following:

The Alpine Northwest
The Atlantic Barrier Islands
The Canyon Country
The Desert
Edgar Allan Poe
Everglades
George Washington Carver
Glacier Bay
Greater Yellowstone: Panorama
Hawaii Volcanoes
North Cascades Panorama
The Rocky Mountains
The Sierra Range
Statue of Liberty
Yosemite Panorama

Educational Programs Branch
Room 105
National Oceanic and Atmospheric Administration (NOAA)
11400 Rockville Pike
Rockville, MD 20852   301-443-8031

Natural Hazard Watch and Warning with Safety Rules for: Tornadoes, Hurricanes, Floods, Flash Floods, Thunderstorms/Lightning, Winter Storms is a mini-poster that provides easy-to-read information on what to do when there is a natural hazard.

U.S. EPA Region 5
Office of Public Affairs
77 West Jackson Blvd., PI-195
Chicago, IL 60604   312-353-2000

Welcome to the Wetlands is a coloring poster (for grades k-12) that explains how wetlands help us and what is a threat to wetlands. Included is information on animals, birds, fish and plants that thrive in wetlands. Limited quantities are available for residents in the six-state Region 5 area (Illinois, Indiana, Michigan, Minnesota, Ohio, Wisconsin).

POWELL, JOHN WESLEY

U.S. Geological Survey
P.O. Box 25425
Denver, CO 80225

Do you want to teach your students about John Wesley Powell? Obtain the publication *John Wesley Powell's Exploration of the Colorado River*. It describes Powell's daring voyage in 1869 through the canyons of the Colorado River, starting at Green River Station, Wyoming, and ending at the junction of the Colorado and Virgin Rivers in Arizona.

PRESIDENTS

Bureau of Engraving and Printing
U.S. Department of the Treasury
14th and C St., SW
Room 602-11A
Washington, DC 20228   202-874-2778

Presidential portraits and portraits of the Chief Justices can be purchased from the office above. Teachers can hang these portraits in a classroom or students can use them if they need to present a report on a president. Also available are vignettes of federal government buildings.

RAIN (See also Acid Rain)

U.S. Geological Survey
P.O. Box 25425
Denver, CO 80225

Rain: A Water Resource provides information on the annual precipitation in areas of the United States, with specific data on several major cities. Explains how to express rainfall as quantities of water. Also available in Spanish.

READING

Indiana University
Smith Research Center, Suite 150
2805 East 10th Street
Bloomington, IN 47408-2698   812-855-5847

The Educational Resources Information Center (ERIC) is a nationwide information network designed to provide users with ready access to education literature. It has sixteen clearinghouses, including one which makes available literature on reading and communication skills. The Reading and Communication Skills clearinghouse also has information on educational research and instruction development in reading, writing, speaking, and listening; identification, diagnosis, and remediation of reading problem; speech communication (including forensics), mass communication, interpersonal and small group interaction, interpretation, rhetorical and communication theory, speech sciences, and the theater.

R. Woods
Consumer Information Center
Pueblo, CO 81008

The following booklets and pamphlets on reading may be ordered from the Consumer Information Center. Make check or money order payable to Superintendent of Documents. Send your request to the address above and give the item numbers of the publications you want. Prices include postage and handling.

Help Your Child Become a Good Reader, $.50, 449X
Helping Your Child Use the Library, $.50, 455X
Becoming a Nation of Readers: What Parents Can Do, $.50, 447X

Reading is Fundamental
600 Maryland Ave., SW
Suite 600
Washington, DC 20024   202-287-3220

Reading is Fundamental has several publications available at a small charge, including:

Building a Family Library
Children Who Can Read, But Don't....
Children's Bookshelf: A Parent's Guide to Choosing Good Books
Choosing Good Books for Your Children
Encouraging Soon-to-Be Readers
Family Storytelling
Helping Your Children Become Readers/Como Ayudar a Que Sus Ninos Sean Buenos Lectores
Magazines and Family Reading
Reading Aloud to Your Children
Reading is Fun!
Reading is Fun! Tips for Parents of Children Age Birth to 8 Years
The RIF Guide to Encouraging Young Readers
Summertime Reading
TV and Reading
Upbeat and Offbeat Activities to Encourage Reading
When We Were Young: Favorite Books of RIF Kids, RIF Volunteers and Readers of Renown

RECYCLING

Public Information Center
U.S. Environmental Protection Agency
401 M Street, SW, MS 3404
Washington, DC 20460   202-260-2080

Help children learn about the need for recycling while reading and coloring the publication, *There Lived a Wicked Dragon*. Written by Martha Finan for the Federal solid waste management programs, it provides a creative way to learn about an important issue.

Education Specialist: SSI
Ohio Department of Natural Resources
Division of Litter Prevention and Recycling

1889 Fountain Square Ct. - F-2
Columbus, OH 43224   614-265-6333

Are you looking for some activities your students can do to help teach them about recycling? *Super Saver Investigators* is an interdisciplinary environmental studies activity guide book about recycling (in addition to solid waste and natural resources) for grades kindergarten through 8th and was developed by the Ohio Department of Natural Resources in cooperation with the Ohio Department of Education and Ohio teachers actively involved in environmental studies education. *Super Saver Investigators* contains over 65 hands-on learning activities for grades K-8. The activities are related to science and social studies lessons normally taught by elementary teachers. The activities include skill-building handouts in language arts, math, reading comprehension, creative writing, art and design. It is made available to schools and teachers in Ohio at no cost, through workshops or inservice training. For out-of-state requests there is a charge.

Resource Center
Public Education and Risk Communication Division
Environmental and Occupational Health Sciences Institute
681 Frelinghuysen Rd.
Piscataway, NJ 08854   908-445-0110

"Healthy Environment - Healthy Me" is a interdisciplinary, supplementary environmental and occupational health curriculum. As an "environmental health promotion" curriculum, it is designed to provide young people with the knowledge and understanding for creating a safe and healthful environment at home, in their future workplaces and in their communities. The primary audience is schoolchildren in kindergarten through sixth grade. Both lesson plans and videos are available. Those that help teach about the importance of recycling include:

Videos
(VHS 1/2" $85 each, 3/4" $99 each, previews $25 - previews are available for 2 weeks, the fee may be applied to the purchase price).
Alu-Man the Can (15 min., grades K-3)
This video teaches children about recycling through the adventures of Alu-Man the Can, Nettie Newspaper, Benjamin J. Bottle III, and Mr. "G" the garbage can.

What to Do With All Our Garbage? (20 min., grades 4-6)
In this video Kate, Jenny, and Greg explore the garbage crisis and possible solutions. Source reduction, recycling, sanitary landfills and incineration are discussed. The focus is on what we as consumers can do to reduce the amount of garbage we generate.

Lessons
($29 each)
Recycling: A Community Pollution Solution (First Grade)
Children explore the health consequences of living in a polluted environment and specifically the problems of garbage disposal and solid waste management. Children learn about recycling aluminum, glass and newspaper - one positive community solution to the garbage problem.

Garbage, Garbage, Garbage (Sixth Grade)
Students examine technical topics in solid waste management, specifically: source reduction, recycling, sanitary landfills, incineration, hazardous waste, and household hazardous waste.

Forest Service
U.S. Department of Agriculture
14th and Independence, SW
P.O. Box 96090
Washington, DC 20090-6090   202-205-0957

To learn more about recycling and the Forest Service's involvement in it, call the office above for a copy of *Expanding Recycling Horizons*.

Public Information Center
U.S. Environmental Protection Agency
401 M Street, SW, MS 3404
Washington, DC 20460   202-260-2080
or
Resource Conservation and Recovery Act
Hotline   800-424-9346

The following recycling materials are available from either office listed below.

Recycle Today! Educational Materials for Grades K-12 (EPA/530-SW-90-025). Presents the goals and objectives of EPA's School Recycling Program, and describes this handbook as well as the following materials.

Let's Reduce and Recycle: Curriculum for Solid Waste Awareness (EPA/530-SW-90-005). Presents lessons and activities to teach students in grades K-12 about solid

waste generation and management. Each unit presents a series of related lessons with vocabulary words, discussion questions, and projects. Practical teaching aids, such as handouts, worksheets, clip art, and a short skit are also included, along with a bibliography of additional sources of information.

Adventures of the Garbage Gremlin: Recycle and Combat a Life of Grime (EPA/530-SW-90-024). Introduces students in grades 4-7 to the benefits of book approach. Students are lead on an adventure in which their peers foil the "Garbage Gremlin" and learn about recycling.

Ride the Wave of the Future: Recycle Today! (EPA/530-SW-90-010). Promotes recycling through a colorful poster designed to appeal to all grade levels. Can be displayed in conjunction with recycling activities or used to help foster recycling.

School Recycling Programs: A Handbook for Educators (EPA/530-SW-90-023). Describes a number of school recycling program options, along with step-by-step instructions on how to set one up. It focuses on implementing actual recycling projects as a way of teaching the importance and benefits of recycling.

Energy Efficiency and Renewable Energy Clearinghouse
P.O. Box 3048
Merrifield, VA 22116   800-363-3732

Available from this office is *Recycling: What You Can Do*. This two page publication discusses the reasons to recycle and what materials can be recycled.

Office of Environmental Education
Pennsylvania Department of Education
333 Market St.
Harrisburg, PA 17126   717-783-6994

Recycling is one of several topics covered in Paul E. Beals' publication *The Newspaper: A Tool for Teaching Environmental Awareness*, an activity book for children in grades K-12. It also covers such topics as acid rain, forest preservation, and waste disposal. This activity book contains newspaper articles and uses them to teach about environmental awareness.

Energy Efficiency and Renewable Energy Clearinghouse
P.O. Box 3048
Merrifield, VA 22116   800-363-3732

Recycling Waste to Save Energy is an information sheet available to educators.

Energy Center
Sonoma State University
1801 East Cotati Ave.
Rohnert Park, CA 94928   707-664-2577

Conserve and Renew: Energy Activities is a collection in interdisciplinary energy activities for children in grades 4-6 to be used either as a unit on energy, or as individual activities to complement existing curricula. While the main focus is on conservation and renewables, recycling and ethics are also included. Cost is $10.

Jan Lingenfelter
Washington State Department of Ecology
4350 150th Ave., NE
Redmond, WA 98052-5301   206-867-7043

Available from the office above is *A-Way With Waste*, 3rd Edition, 1990 (grades K-12), a waste management and recycling curriculum and school program. The goal of the program is to reduce waste and increase recycling at home, at school and in the community. It includes a 602 page interdisciplinary guide of 117 activities. Three sections cover concepts in Solid Waste Management, Hazardous Waste, and Waste and Water. Articles, research reports, glossary, bibliography, fact sheets and resources are also included. This book is free to Washington State teachers who take a workshop. Write or call for prices to purchase curriculum.

RIVERS

U.S. Geological Survey
P.O. Box 25425
Denver, CO 80225

The U.S. Geological Survey makes available dozens of publications, two of which are about rivers. Students can use them to supplement special reports and science projects and teachers can use them to enhance their curricula. The publications are:

"The Big Five" - Some Facts and Figures on our Nation's Largest Rivers. Presents statistics for maximum, minimum, and mean flows for the Nation's largest rivers -- the Mississippi, St. Lawrence, Columbia, Ohio, and the Missouri.

River Basins of the United States: A Series. Lists basic facts including historical notes, flow characteristics, and physical statistics on selected river basins.

Be patient. If any phone number is incorrect, call (area code) 555-1212 and request the new listing.

1277

Water Watch
Division of Water
Department for Environmental Protection
Frankfort Office Park
14 Reilly Road
Frankfort, KY 40601   502-564-3410

A Field Guide to Kentucky Rivers and Streams was developed for Water Watch, a public participation program that encourages citizens to adopt a stream, lake or wetland, and then gain hands on experience in protecting and enhancing their adopted water resource.

ROCKETS

NASA Education Division
NASA Headquarters
Washington, DC 20546

Rockets: A Teaching Guide for an Elementary Science Unit on Rocketry is a teaching guide which emphasizes hands-on involvement. Background information about the history of rockets and basic science explaining why rockets work can be found within the publication. The unit also includes basic concepts of rocket control and descriptions of different kinds of rockets.

Elementary and Secondary Programs Branch
Educational Affairs Division
Mail Code XEE
NASA Headquarters
Washington, DC 20546

The principles of rocketry is one of many topics covered in the Aerospace Education Services Program (AESP) workshops held each summer for teachers at NASA field centers, elementary and secondary schools, and on college campuses. Workshops also cover astronomy, aeronautics, life in space, earth sciences, and remote sensing. A typical workshop includes how-to and hands-on activities to help teachers incorporate what they learn into classroom activities and programs to supplement existing curricula. Contact the office above for more detailed information.

ROCKS

U.S. Geological Survey
P.O. Box 25425
Denver, CO 80225

Is your child a rock collector? Then get the publication *Collecting Rocks*. It describes the origin of major rock types and how rocks can provide clues to the Earth's history, and includes suggestions for starting a rock collection, identifying specimens, and housing such a collection.

Office of Education, Room 212
Mail Stop 158
National Museum of Natural History
Washington, DC 20560   202-357-2747

The National Museum of Natural History has several different programs and activities held throughout the school year for visiting preschool and elementary school children, including a visiting program on rocks and minerals. In this program, students are introduced to rocks and the major rock-forming minerals by examining exhibited specimens in the Earth and Mineral exhibition halls and by participating in a hands-on classroom activity. Students distinguish between rocks and minerals; identify seven common minerals using the physical properties of luster, color, hardness, and streak; classify seven rock specimens according to their origin (igneous, sedimentary, or metamorphic); and explore the relationship between texture and mineral composition of rocks and the processes that form them.

Office of Education, Room 212
Mail Stop 158
National Museum of Natural History
Washington, DC 20560   202-357-2747

The National Museum of Natural History also conducts workshops for teachers. In the workshop *Rocks and Minerals*, teachers work with a geologist in developing ways to introduce students to rocks and minerals. Time is spent in the Earth and Mineral exhibition halls, as well as in a classroom. Activities are designed to provide experience in distinguishing between a rock and a mineral, describing minerals by their physical properties, and using rock texture to classify rocks according to their origin.

ROOSEVELT, FRANKLIN D.

Education Branch (NEEE)
National Archives and Records Administration

Washington, DC 20408   202-501-6172

The Education Branch of the National Archives offers teachers of upper elementary through secondary school students publications and teaching units to aid in the teaching of historical documents and eras. They include the following two addresses given by Franklin D. Roosevelt, which are part of the "Milestone Documents" series. Each booklet includes a historical introduction and transcriptions and facsimiles of the featured documents. (8 1/2 x 11, approx. 25 pages each, illustrations, 1986, softcover only, $2.50 each). The publications are:

Franklin D. Roosevelt's Inaugural Address of 1933 (#200112, ISBN 0-911333-69-X)

On War Against Japan: Franklin D. Roosevelt's "Day of Infamy" Address of 1941 (#200114, ISBN 0-911333-70-3)

SALMON

U.S. Fish and Wildlife Service
U.S. Department of the Interior
4401 N. Fairfax Drive
Mail Stop 130
Arlington, VA 22203   703-358-1711

The publication *Pacific Salmon* may provide you and your child with insights into this fascinating fish.

SATELLITES

NASA CORE
Lorain County Joint Vocational School
15181 Route 58 South
Oberlin, OH 44074   216-774-1051

Portrait of Earth: The Story of Satellites is a videocassette that explains what satellites are and how they perform their daily tasks in orbit around our planet. Captioned at the 2nd, 3rd, and 4th grade levels.

SATURN

Superintendent of Documents
Government Printing Office
Washington, DC 20402   202-512-1800

The Voyager Flights to Jupiter and Saturn is a nontechnical guide describing the Voyager flights from the Jupiter and Saturn flybys. Illustrated. 62 pages. 1982. Stock No. 033-000-00854-6. $5.50.

NASA CORE
Lorain County Joint Vocational School
15181 Route 58 South
Oberlin, OH 44074   216-774-1051

Voyagers 2 Encounter Saturn is a set of slides that illustrates Voyager's most significant discoveries about Saturn, including incredible rings, erupting volcanoes and cyclonic storms. Appropriate for grades 4-12.

Teaching Resource Center
Jet Propulsion Laboratory
4800 Oak Grove Dr.
Mail Stop CS-530
Pasadena, CA 91109   818-354-6916

Saturn: Voyager 1 and *Saturn: Voyager 2* are two separate sets of color slides with cassette narration. ($11 each. Each 40 slide/cassette program listed below contains 40 color slides and an audio cassette narration with audible beep tones).

SCHOOL ACHIEVERS

Superintendent of Documents
Dept. 33
Washington, DC 20402   202-512-1800

How to Help Your Children Achieve in School explains how to help your children improve their study skills, both at home and in school. Tips on maintaining interest and attention are given, and techniques for effective notetaking, studying, remembering, and taking tests are explained. 1983. 28 pp. (S/N 065-000-00176-4, $3.75).

SCHOOL IMPROVEMENT

Superintendent of Documents
Dept. 33
Washington, DC 20402   202-512-1800

Call the office above to obtain *Experiences in School Improvement: Story of 16 American Districts*. It discusses the experiences and recommendations of selected high school principals and superintendents. Some of the recommendations include: redesigning schools to create more productive working and learning environments; changing the structure of the teaching career; developing a system to evaluate administrators effectively and accurately; allowing schools to make more of their own decisions, then holding them accountable for results; and much more. 1988. 91 pp. (S/N 065-000-00343-1, $4.50).

SCIENCE

The Ohio State University
1929 Kenny Rd.
Columbus, OH 43210   614-292-6717

The Science, Mathematics, and Environmental Education Clearinghouse is part of the Educational Resources Information Center (ERIC), a nationwide information network designed to provide users with ready access to education literature. This particular clearinghouse provides information on science, mathematics, and environmental education at all levels, and within these three broad subject areas, the following topics; development of curriculum and instructional materials; teachers and teacher education; learning theory/outcomes (including the impact of parameters such as interest level, intelligence, values, and concept development upon learning in these fields); educational programs; engineering; research and evaluative studies; medical applications; and computer applications.

R. Woods
Consumer Information Center
Pueblo, CO 81008

Helping Your Child Learn Science (#611X) is a free publication for parents available from the Consumer Information Center. To order write to the address above.

Department 900
Smithsonian Institution Press
Blue Ridge Summit, PA 17294   717-794-2148

Are you looking for science projects for your students? Then get the publication *Smithsonian Surprises: An Educational Activity Book* by Sara Toney. Appropriate for students in grades K-12. $7.95; $2.25 postage and handling first book, $1 each additional book.

SEEGER, PETE

Smithsonian/Folkways Recordings
944 L'Enfant Plaza, SW, Suite 2600
Washington, DC 20560   202-287-3262

Pete Seeger is one of several artists whose recordings are available for purchase from Folkways Records, which is administered by the Smithsonian Institution's Office of Folklife Programs. Children's songs by Ella Jenkins and Woody Guthrie can also be purchased, along with dozens of recordings by lesser-known yet still very talented artists.

SESAME STREET

Attn: SSFS
FEMA
P.O. Box 70274
Washington, DC 20024

The Sesame Street Fire Safety Project was developed by the Community Education Services division of the Children's Television Workshop (CTW). The first edition of the *Sesame Street Fire Safety Resource Book* is still available in English and Spanish versions. The second edition of the *Sesame Street Fire Safety Book* contains the original Muppet skits and activities that inspired thousands to teach young children fire safety. Each book is accompanied by an audio cassette that contains five songs. Also included is a five page color brochure highlighting the Sesame Street research study on mass media fire education for young children. To order your free copy, write to the office above.

SHARKS

Office of Education, Room 212
Mail Stop 158
National Museum of Natural History
Washington, DC 20560   202-357-2747

Shark Tub is an instructional kit produced by the National Museum of Natural History as a classroom enhancement for the temporary exhibit *Sharks! Fact and Fantasy* (1990), and can be used to supplement any science curriculum. Dive gear tub (3x2x2 ft.) contains small shark specimens, dried shark jaws, shark leather, shark

vertebrae, an egg case, a fossil tooth, and other hands-on materials. Curriculum and reference materials are included. Reserve kit by calling 202-357-2811. Teachers must pick up and return tub at the museum, Monday through Saturday, 10:30 to 4, or Sunday, 12-5. If shipping is necessary, shipping fee is required in advance. It is available on loan for a three-week period and may be requested by writing to the office above.

SITTING BULL

Photographic Services
American History Building, Room CB-054
Smithsonian Institution
Washington, DC 20560   202-357-1933

The poster, *Sitting Bull*, is available for $3 for educators and parents who would like to expose their students and children to famous American Indians.

Attn: Public Inquiries Office
Bureau of Indian Affairs
Mail Stop 2620 (MIB)
U.S. Department of Interior
Washington, DC 20240   202-208-3711

From Pocahontas to Sitting Bull, the publication, *Famous Indians: A Collection of Short Biographies*, describes the history and lives of twenty famous American Indians. All were leaders in a great struggle to preserve treasured lands and lifeways. With their tribesmen, they are inseparably linked to our country's history from its earliest beginnings through generations of growth.

SKYLAB

NASA CORE
Lorain County Joint Vocational School
15181 Route 58 South
Oberlin, OH 44074   216-774-1051

The videocassette, "Our Laboratories in Space," examines some of the scientific and medical experiments that were completed on Skylab, the Apollo-SOYUZ Test Project and future experiments to be conducted on the space shuttle. The slides *3 Flights of Skylab* recounts man's first attempt to establish a permanent laboratory in space. Both are appropriate for grades 4 and up.

SLIDES

Education Resource Center
Education Division, MRC 305
National Air and Space Museum
Washington, DC 20560   202-786-2109

The National Air and Space Museum offers to teachers of all levels and disciplines educational materials, including slides, pertaining to aviation, space, and the Museum's collections.

Office of Education, Room 212
Mail Stop 158
National Museum of Natural History
Washington, DC 20560   202-357-2747

Slide sets are available for a three-week loan free of charge from the National Museum of Natural History. The slides sets are:

Ancient Cultures: 10,000 B.C. - 600 A.D.
Dinosaurs and Other Giants
Glaciers: Geological Evidence
An Introduction to Archaeology
Introduction to the Natural History Museum
Native Peoples of North American

NASA CORE
Lorain County Joint Vocational School
15181 Route 58 South
Oberlin, OH 44074   216-774-1051

The NASA Central Operation of Resources for Educators (CORE), established in cooperation with Lorain County Joint Vocational School, serves as the national distribution center for NASA produced education materials. For a minimal charge the NASA CORE will provide a valuable service to educators unable to visit one of the NASA Teacher Resource Centers (TRC), by making NASA educational audiovisual materials available through its mail order service. Slides available include:

Human Space Flight: Living in Space. Explanation of how astronauts live and work in the Space Shuttle environment. Grades 4 -12.

The Government Works for Kids, Too

Propulsion: Space Shuttle. Highlights the NASA Space Transportation System, its functions, and possible uses for the future. Grades 4 - 12.

America in Space: The First 25 Years. Details America's long string of successful space accomplishments, culminating in the Apollo 11 moon landing, the Voyager Missions, and the Space Shuttle program. Grades 4 -12.

Moon Landing - Apollo 11. Tells the story of the most famous spaceflight in history, man's first moon landing. Grades 4 - 12.

The Story of the Flight of Apollo-SOYUZ. Highlights the first meeting between America and Russia in space. Three astronauts and two cosmonauts rendezvoused in orbit, docked and entered each other's craft.

Voyagers Encounter Jupiter. Focuses on the flights of Voyagers I and II as one of the most successful and revealing unmanned spaceflights in history. Grades 4 - 12.

Voyagers 2 Encounter Saturn. Illustrates Voyager's most significant discoveries about Saturn, including incredible rings, erupting volcanoes and cyclonic storms. Grades 4 - 12.

Best of the Space Shuttle 1977-1984. Examines shuttle highlights from the first dramatic shuttle flights to the on-going array of spectacular space walks and experiments. Grades 4 - 12.

The Story of Our Universe. This information-packed program explores the Universe and all of its other worldly phenomena. Grades 4 - 12.

The Return of Halley's Comet. Examines an event heralded by man since the beginning of time, Halley's Comet, and discusses its place in the Universe. Grades 4 - 12.

3 Flights of Skylab. Recounts man's first attempt to establish a permanent laboratory in space. Grades 4 - 12.

Transformations of Flight. A series of slides which present the numbers 1-10 being transformed into ten different air and spacecraft in the history of flight. These slides successfully compliment the videotape also found in this catalog. Produced by the Smithsonian Institution. Grades K - 3.

Voyager Encounters Neptune. Color photographs taken when Voyager encountered Neptune in August of 1989. Includes pictures of the Great Dark Spot, Neptune's rings and Triton. Grades 4 - 12.

Department of Extension Programs
National Gallery of Art
Washington, DC 20565

The National Gallery of Art is continually exploring ways to develop awareness in the visual arts and make its collections accessible to everyone, no matter how far away from the Gallery they may live. They now have an Extension Program which loans not only slide programs, but films and videocassettes to educational institutions, community groups, and to individuals throughout the U.S. free of charge. Write to the office above for more information on how you may bring the National Gallery of Art to your students.

Nebraska Energy Office
9th Floor
State Capitol
P.O. Box 95085
Lincoln, NE 68509   402-471-2867

Energy-related slides and other instructional materials, (including video tapes, curriculum guides, and resource books and materials) are available to Nebraska educators only from the office above.

Warning and Forecast Branch, W/OM11
National Weather Service
National Oceanic and Atmospheric Administration
SSMCII
1325 East West Highway, Room 14370
Silver Spring, MD 20910

The following slides can be used by educators to teach school children about safety during natural disasters. They include:

Tornado Slides:
A Slide Series Supplement to "Tornado: A Spotter's Guide"
Tornado Preparedness
Tornado Safety in Residence

The Safest Place in Schools
A Look at the Tornado and other Local Storms

Thunderstorm Slides:
Advanced Meteorologist/Spotter Training Slide Series
When Lightning Strikes

Flash Flood/Flood Slides:
Flash Floods: Myths or Realities
Flash Flood Preparedness

Hurricane Slides:
Hurricane Hugo
Hurricane Eloise
Hurricane Preparedness
Hurricane Alicia
Hurricane Frederick

Winter Storm Slides:
Winter Storms, The Deceptive Killers

Finley Holiday Films
12607 E. Philadelphia St.
Wittier, CA 90601   800-345-6707

Below are selected color slide packages on space and planetary subjects which can be excellent educational aids for classroom use. These slides were produced by the Jet Propulsion Laboratory. To receive an order form contact the office above.

Color Slides with Cassette Narration
($11 each. Each 40 slide/cassette program listed below contains 40 color slides and an audio cassette narration with audible beep tones. Each set comes in its own plastic storage box.)
Our Universe
Apollo 11: The First Moon Landing
Apollo 17: The Final Mission
Viking Lands on Mars
Jupiter: Voyagers 1 & 2
Mt. St. Helens Erupts
Saturn: Voyager 1
Saturn: Voyager 2
History of the Universe: Space Art by Don Dixon
America in Space
Best of the Space Shuttle 1977-1984

Slide Sets
($6 each. Each 20-slide set consists of twenty 35 mm slides held in a plastic vue-file sleeve which will fit into a three ring binder. Many sets have a fact sheet included which lists the title of the slides and may have a brief description or topic.)
Voyager Missions, Computer Graphics
Manned Space Flight: Mercury, Gemini, Apollo, Apollo-Soyuz, Skylab
Space Shuttle Mission STS-1
Earth: Views from Moon and Space Shuttle
Galtech/JPL Facilities
JPL Recent Projects 1973-1983
JPL Historical Missions: Jato, Explorer, Ranger, Surveyor, Mariner
Voyager Missions to Jupiter
Vikings Missions to Mars
Mariner 9 Mission to Mars, Black and White
Voyager Mission to Saturn
IRAS, Set 1, Infrared Astronomical Satellite
Halley's Comet
Voyager Mission to Uranus
IRAS, Set 2, Infrared Astronomical Satellite
Future Missions, Set 2
Voyager Mission to Neptune
Magellan Mission to Venus
Neptune Computer Graphics, Set 2

SMITHSONIAN INSTITUTION
Office of Elementary and Secondary Education
Arts and Industries Building
Room 1163
Smithsonian Institution
Washington, DC 20560   202-357-3049

The easiest way to find out what educational materials the Smithsonian Institution has available is to obtain the publication *Resource Guide for Teachers*. The materials include bibliographies, posters, slide sets, films, teacher's manuals, videocassettes, and curriculum units. The publication also includes materials available from the National Gallery of Art and the John F. Kennedy Center for the Performing Arts.

SMOKEY BEAR

Forest Service
U.S. Department of Agriculture
14th and Independence, SW
P.O. Box 96090
Washington, DC 20090-6090   202-205-0957

Get in touch with the office above to receive Smokey Bear fire prevention materials, including *The True Story of Smokey Bear* comic book.

SNAKES

U.S. Fish and Wildlife Service
U.S. Department of the Interior
4401 N. Fairfax Drive
Mail Stop 130
Arlington, VA 22203   703-358-1711

The U.S. Fish and Wildlife Service has publications on snakes including *Conservation Note 6 - Snakes* and *Snakes*.

SOCIAL STUDIES

Indiana University
Social Studies Development Center
2805 East 10th Street, Suite 120
Bloomington, IN 47408-2698   812-855-3838

The Educational Resources Information Center (ERIC) is a nationwide information network designed to provide users with ready access to education literature, including literature on social studies. The Social Studies/Social Science Education (SO) Clearinghouse contains literature on all levels of social studies and social science education; the contributions of history, geography, and other social science disciplines; applications of theory and research to social science education; education as a social science; comparative education (K-12); content and curriculum materials on social topics such as law-related education ethnic studies, bias and discrimination, aging, and women's equity. Music and art education are also covered.

SOLAR ENERGY

Florida's Governor's Energy Office
2740 Centerview Dr.
Tallahassee, FL 32399   904-488-2475

Solar and Energy Conservation Projects for Students was produced by the Florida Solar Energy Center and is available from the office above to elementary school teachers. Another publication, *Energy Research Projects Guide,* will assist students in their selection of an energy topic for science fair projects. Also available is the *Florida Middle School Energy Education Project.* All are free of charge.

Energy Efficiency and Renewable Energy Clearinghouse
P.O. Box 3048
Merrifield, VA 22116   800-363-3732

People are trying to find new ways to heat their homes, factories, offices, and schools without using so much expensive oil and gas. *Solar Energy and You* helps teach children about solar energy and solar heat. Call the office above for this four page publication.

SOLAR SYSTEM

NASA CORE
Lorain County Joint Vocational School
15181 Route 58 South
Oberlin, OH 44074   216-774-1051

The NASA Central Operation of Resources for Educators (CORE) serves as the national distribution center for NASA produced education materials, including the video *Our Solar System.* This video teaches the names, orbital positions, and characteristics of each planet using the phrase "my very educated mother just served us nine pizza pies". The program is animated, set to music, and appropriate for early elementary grades. Grade 2 - 6.

SOLDIERS

Superintendent of Documents
Dept. 33

Washington, DC 20402   202-512-1800

The American Soldier, Set No. 2 is a set of 10 color posters reproducing paintings of American servicemen and women over the 100-year period from 1863 to 1963. (Includes an explanatory booklet). Use these posters to help teach your children about American history. All posters are 9 x 13 inches and printed on fine white paper suitable for framing. (S/N 008-020-00227-5, $6, 1989, shipped flat).

SPACE EXPLORATION

Superintendent of Documents
Government Printing Office
Washington, DC 20402   202-512-1800

The National Aeronautics and Space Administration produces educational publications for educators, students, and the general public. All are offered for sale by the Superintendent of Documents, Government Printing Office. Prices may change.

NASA CORE
Lorain County Joint Vocational School
15181 Route 58 South
Oberlin, OH 44074   216-774-1051

The NASA Central Operation of Resources for Educators (CORE), established in cooperation with Lorain County Joint Vocational School, serves as the national distribution center for NASA produced education materials. For a minimal charge the NASA CORE will provide a valuable service to educators unable to visit one of the NASA Teacher Resource Centers (TRC), by making NASA educational audiovisual materials available through its mail order service. Also available are different memorabilia items which can be used by teachers as awards for students. They include a NASA logo patch, pencils, hats, T-shirts, mugs, and astronaut ice cream.

Elementary and Secondary Programs Branch
Educational Affairs Division
Mail Code XEE
NASA Headquarters
Washington, DC 20546

The Aerospace Education Services Program (AESP), previously known as Spacemobile, is the Educational Affairs Division's premier outreach program. AESP specialists, all former teachers themselves, reach millions of students each year. They cross the country from September to June each year, assisting schools so students and teachers can see first-hand what NASA is all about. Visits are scheduled by field center, and because each field center performs a specific service for NASA, each center's program is a little different from the others. All emphasize current NASA programs, such as the Space Shuttle and the Freedom Space Station. Because of this program's popularity, a visit should be requested well in advance. Although field centers make every effort to accommodate the date a school requests, there is currently about a 2-year waiting list.

Education Division
NASA Headquarters
Washington, DC 20546

NASA Spacelink is a collection of NASA information and educational materials stored on a computer at the Marshall Space Flight Center in Huntsville, Alabama. The system may be accessed over regular telephone lines. It is designed to communicate with a wide variety of computers and modems, especially those most commonly found in classrooms and home. NASA Spacelink is free, but you'll owe your phone company for long distance calls. It includes a listing of all the major NASA educational programs. Subjects include the Aerospace Education Services Project, Urban Community Enrichment Program, Summer High School Apprenticeship Research Program, Space Science Student Involvement Project, Teacher Workshops, Educators Mailing List, Telelectures, Teacher Resource Centers, and Science Fair support. Classroom materials include a variety of information useful in the classroom, including space science lesson plans and activities (all grade levels and many subjects), astronomy information, film/video list, computer programs, career information, computer graphics, and a source list for pictures, posters, and other educational materials.

Elementary and Secondary Programs Branch
Educational Affairs Division
Mail Code XEE
NASA Headquarters
Washington, DC 20546

Aerospace Education Services Program (AESP) specialists conduct workshops for teachers each summer at NASA field centers, elementary and secondary schools, and on college campuses. Workshops cover astronomy, aeronautics, life in space, principles of rocketry, earth sciences, and remote sensing. A typical workshop includes how-to and hands-on activities to help teachers incorporate what they learn into classroom activities and programs to supplement existing curricula.

The Government Works for Kids, Too

Education Division, MRC 305
National Air and Space Museum
Washington, DC 20560   202-786-2109

The Education Resource Center (ERC) of the National Air and Space Museum (NASM) is open to teachers of all levels and disciplines. The ERC offers teachers access to educational materials pertaining to aviation, space, and the Museum's collections. These materials are produced by NASM, the National Aeronautics and Space Administration (NASA), and other government agencies, and private organizations. Additional information on the ERC and other NASM educational programs may be obtained by writing to the address above. Educational materials include the following:

Curriculum Packages: Complete units on specific topics are available on request for grades K-12. Write and tell them the subjects and grades you teach, and they will be happy to send you the appropriate packages. Requests must be made by teachers on school letterhead.

Lesson Plans: Hundreds of classroom activities on aerospace-related topics, arranged according to subject and grade levels, are available for duplication when you visit the ERC. This service is not available through the mail.

Public Domain Software: Aerospace-related public domain computer software for use with Apple II series and IBM PC computers is available for duplication when you visit the ERC, as well as through the mail. In both cases, teachers must provide blank diskettes. Contact the ERC for a current catalog and mail-in procedures.

Commercial Software: A growing collection of IBM PC and Apple II series commercial software on aerospace topics is available on a preview-only basis for visiting teachers.

Videodiscs and CD-Roms: Visit the ERC to preview our growing collection of these new audiovisual formats.

Filmstrips: The ERC's large collection of filmstrips is available for preview. NASM-produced filmstrips may be obtained from the National Audiovisual Center, 8700 Edgewood Drive, Capitol Heights, MD 20743, 301-763-1896.

Videos: Hundreds of videos can be previewed at the ERC. Videos must be rented or purchased from their respective suppliers.

Slide Sets: A variety of slide sets are available for preview in the ERC. The NASM-produced "Milestones of Flight" set is available through NASA CORE.

Other Resources: A variety of resources such as science kits, posters, brochures, and catalogs are available as reference materials.

"Skylines" Newsletter: The Education Division publishes a newsletter for teachers. Please write and ask to be placed on our mailing list.

ERC Workshops: Half-day workshops, to aid educators in utilizing the ERC, are scheduled on request. Participants receive assistance in compiling educational units to meet specific needs.

Other Workshops: Throughout the year, the Education Division offers aerospace-related teacher workshops that are announced in the Skylines newsletter. Contact the Education Division for more information.

Tours and Group Reservations: Free docent-led tours of the Museum are offered year-round for school groups, on a variety of subjects and grade levels. Reservations must be made by mail at least three weeks in advance but no earlier than eight weeks in advance of visit. School group reservation for the Einstein Planetarium and Langley Theater are also available. Request a current tour brochure and reservation form from the Tour Scheduling Office, MRC 305, National Air and Space Museum, Washington, DC 20560.

Superintendent of Documents
Government Printing Office
Washington, DC 20402   202-512-1800

In June 1984 President Reagan announced a new NASA education program, "Operation Liftoff". This program is designed to encourage pupils in the nation's elementary schools to take a greater interest in mathematics and science. NASA responded to this announcement with a plan to reach students in their formative years in the elementary grades. Operation Liftoff complements the widely acclaimed educational programs NASA now offers at the secondary and university levels. *Living in Space - Operation Liftoff Elementary Space Program: A Resource Guide With Activities for Elementary School Teachers*, one of Operation Liftoff's publications, is available for sale from the office above.

Finley Holiday Films
12607 E. Philadelphia St.
Wittier, CA 90601   800-345-6707

Below are selected video programs and color slide packages on space and planetary subjects which can be excellent educational aids for classroom use. These were produced by the Jet Propulsion Laboratory. To receive an order form contact the office above.

Videos
($25 each. Available in VHS and Beta formats, PAL VHS format for use in Europe and Australia only where indicated by a "*".)
1st Flight of Space Shuttle STS-1 (30 min.)
Universe (30 min.)
Apollo Moon Landings (56 min.)
History of Flight (56 min.)
Mars and Mercury (the planets) (52 min.)
Mercury and Gemini Spacecraft Missions (56 min.)
Eruption of Mt. St. Helens (30 min.)
America in Space: 1st 25 Years (50 min.)
Shuttle Flights STS-1 thru STS-8 (60 min.)
Jupiter, Saturn, Uranus and Neptune (30 min.)
The Dream is Alive, IMAX (40 min.)
Kennedy Space Center Tour (42 min.)
We Remember: Shuttle Pioneers '81-'87 (60 min.)
Voyager Missions Animation Only (30 min.)

Color Slides with Cassette Narration
($11 each. Each 40 slide/cassette program listed below contains 40 color slides and an audio cassette narration with audible beep tones. Each set comes in its own plastic storage box.)
Our Universe
Apollo 11: The First Moon Landing
Apollo 17: The Final Mission
Viking Lands on Mars
Jupiter: Voyagers 1 & 2
Mt. St. Helens Erupts
Saturn: Voyager 1
Saturn: Voyager 2
History of the Universe: Space Art by Don Dixon
America in Space
Best of the Space Shuttle 1977-1984

Slide Sets
($6 each. Each 20-slide set consists of twenty 35mm slides held in a plastic vue-file sleeve which fits into a three ring binder. Many sets include a fact sheet which lists the title of the slides and may have a brief description or topic.)
Voyager Missions, Computer Graphics
Manned Space Flight: Mercury, Gemini, Apollo, Apollo-Soyuz, Skylab
Space Shuttle Mission STS-1
Earth: Views from Moon and Space Shuttle
Galtech/JPL Facilities
JPL Recent Projects 1973-1983
JPL Historical Missions: Jato, Explorer, Ranger, Surveyor, Mariner
Voyager Missions to Jupiter
Vikings Missions to Mars
Mariner 9 Mission to Mars, Black and White
Voyager Mission to Saturn
IRAS, Set 1, Infrared Astronomical Satellite
Halley's Comet
Voyager Mission to Uranus
IRAS, Set 2, Infrared Astronomical Satellite
Future Missions, Set 2
Voyager Mission to Neptune
Magellan Mission to Venus
Neptune Computer Graphics, Set 2

SPACE SHUTTLE
NASA CORE
Lorain County Joint Vocational School
15181 Route 58 South
Oberlin, OH 44074   216-774-1051

For a minimal charge the NASA Central Operation of Resources for Educators (CORE) CORE will provide a valuable service to educators unable to visit one of the NASA Teacher Resource Centers (TRC), by making NASA educational audiovisual materials available through its mail order service. Audiovisual materials which contain information on the Space Shuttle and are appropriate for certain elementary grades include the following:

Videocassettes:

Opening New Frontiers: The Orbital Flight Tests of the Space Transportation System. Covers the first four test missions of the Space Shuttle Columbia, STS flights, 1,2,3, and 4. Also includes events leading up to the first launch, President Reagan's speech after the fourth landing, and highlights of the Orbital Flight Test Program. Grade 4 - 10.

Milestones of Flight. This program was produced by the National Air and Space Museum and is based on the museum's "Milestones of Flight" Gallery. It traces the history of flight from Langley's first attempts to the Space Shuttle. Uses live footage from many history making events. Grade 4 - 10.

Shuttle: A Remarkable Flying Machine. Features the first historic flight of the Space Shuttle Columbia. Highlights include the liftoff on April 12, 1981, the onboard activities of Young and Crippen and a spectacular landing on Rogers Dry Lake bed in California. Grade 4 - adult.

We Deliver: Summary of Shuttle Flights 5,6,7 & 8. Covers the first four operational missions of the Space Transportation System, STS flight 5,6,7 & 8. Stresses the operational common denominator of these missions - satellite deployment. Also includes significant secondary achievements such as the first female astronaut, first black astronaut, first night launch and landing, and some of the more important onboard experiments. Grade 4 - adult.

To Dream...To Learn. The first segment of this program documents two Ohio schools who outfitted school buses as Space Shuttles. The school bus "ground shuttles" were sent on "missions" during which students learned a great deal about space travel. The second half of this program shows shuttle astronauts demonstrating toys during space shuttle mission 51-D. Students were asked to speculate as to how the toys would react in the weightless environment of space. Grade 4 - adult.

NASA Images: Episode 1. Several films about the U.S.'s efforts to land a man on the moon are presented. Subjects discussed include: guidance, navigation, footage from the first manned moon landing and research aircraft which led to the Space Shuttle development. Grade 4 - 12.

Slides:

Human Space Flight: Living in Space. Explanation of how astronauts live and work in the Space Shuttle environment. Grade 4 -12.

America in Space: The First 25 Years. Details America's long string of successful space accomplishments, culminating in the Apollo 11 moon landing, the Voyager Missions, and the Space Shuttle program. Grade 4 -12.

Best of the Space Shuttle 1977-1984. Examines shuttle highlights from the first dramatic shuttle flights to the on-going array of spectacular space walks and experiments. Grade 4 - 12.

Filmstrip Program:

Propulsion: Space Shuttle. Highlights the NASA Space Transportation System, its functions, and possible uses for the future. Grade 4 - 12.

Computer Software (5 1/4" diskettes for use on Apple Computers):
Space Shuttle Mission Facts Data Base. A data base that provides information on the first 30 space shuttle missions including: mission number, orbiter, date, commander and pilot. To use this data base you must have the Apple works program. Produced by Oklahoma State University. Grade K - Adult.

Space Shuttle Commander. Side A introduces students to Newton's laws of motion by asking them to imagine that they are the commander of the space shuttle. Takes a nonmathematical approach to this topic and concentrates on concept formation. Side B contains four question banks to use for practice or evaluation. Copyrighted by and reproduced with permission from Lloyd P. Reiber. Grade 4 - 8.

Superintendent of Documents
Government Printing Office
Washington, DC 20402   202-512-1800
Are you looking for more information on the Space Shuttle? The National Aeronautics and Space Administration produces educational publications for educators, students, and the general public, including those listed below on the Space Shuttle. All are offered for sale by the Superintendent of Documents, Government Printing Office (GPO). Prices may change. Contact your regional GPO outlet or call the office above. Materials appropriate for the elementary grades include the following:

Aboard the Space Shuttle (publication). Describes what it would be like to travel into space on a typical Space Shuttle mission, including clothing, food, what the various compartments look like, etc. Illustrated in color. 32 pages. 1980. Stock No. 033-00-00806-6. $2.75.

Teaching Resource Center
Jet Propulsion Laboratory
4800 Oak Grove Dr.
Mail Stop CS-530
Pasadena, CA 91109   818-354-6916
For slides:
Finley Holiday Films
12607 E. Philadelphia St.
Wittier, CA 90601   800-345-6707
Below are selected video programs and color slide packages on the Space Shuttle. To receive an order form contact the office above.

Videos
($25 each. Available in VHS and Beta formats, PAL VHS format for use in Europe and Australia only where indicated by a "*".)
1st Flight of Space Shuttle STS-1 (30 min.)
Shuttle Flights STS-1 thru STS-8 (60 min.)
We Remember: Shuttle Pioneers '81-'87 (60 min.)

Color Slides with Cassette Narration
($11 each. Each 40 slide/cassette program listed below contains 40 color slides and an audio cassette narration with audible beep tones. Each set comes in its own plastic storage box.)
Best of the Space Shuttle 1977-1984

Slide Sets
($6 each. Each 20-slide set consists of twenty 35 mm slides held in a plastic vue-file sleeve which will fit into a three ring binder. Many sets have a fact sheet included which lists the title of the slides and may have a brief description or topic.)
Space Shuttle Mission STS-1
Earth: Views from Moon and Space Shuttle

SPEAKING
Indiana University
Smith Research Center, Suite 150
2805 East 10th Street
Bloomington, IN 47408-2698   812-855-5847
The Reading and Communication Skills (CS) Clearinghouse is part of the Educational Resources Information Center (ERIC), a nationwide information network designed to provide users with ready access to education literature. Literature is available on reading, english, and communication skills (verbal and nonverbal), preschool through college; educational research and instruction development in reading, writing, speaking, and listening; identification, diagnosis, and remediation of reading problem; speech communication (including forensics), mass communication, interpersonal and small group interaction, interpretation, rhetorical and communication theory, speech sciences, and the theater. Preparation of instructional staff and related personnel in these areas. All aspects of reading behavior with emphasis on physiology, psychology, sociology, and teaching; instructional materials, curricula, tests/measurement, and methodology at all levels of reading; the role of libraries and other agencies in fostering and guiding reading; and diagnostics and remedial reading services in schools and clinical settings.

STAMPS CLUBS
U.S. Postal Service
Ben Franklin Stamp Club Program (BFSC)
Washington, DC 20260-6755
In 1974 the U.S. Postal Service established the Benjamin Franklin Stamp Club Program to create an awareness of stamps and to demonstrate their educational and entertaining benefits to students in the fourth through seventh grades. Stamp collecting is an enjoyable experience that teaches important skills applicable to every day life (for example, organization, appreciation of valuable objects, the value of money and how to manage money). Teachers or administrators interested in starting clubs can call their local postmaster or, for more information on the BFSC Program, write to the office above.

STARS
R. Woods
Consumer Information Center - Y
P.O. Box 100
Pueblo, CO 81002
Stars in Your Eyes: A Guide to the Northern Skies contains helpful hints on how to

find the seven best known constellations and an explanation on how they were named. 23 pp. (1988. DOD) 155X. $1.50. Write to the office above to receive a copy.

STEAM

U.S. Geological Survey
P.O. Box 25425
Denver, CO 80225

The publication *Natural Steam for Power* describes the investigation of geothermal steam as a potential source of energy for power needs worldwide. It also discusses the nature and behavior of steam formed underground.

STREAMS

Water Watch
Division of Water
Department for Environmental Protection
Frankfort Office Park
14 Reilly Road
Frankfort, KY 40601   502-564-3410

A Field Guide to Kentucky Rivers and Streams was developed for Water Watch, a public participation program that encourages citizens to adopt a stream, lake or wetland, and then gain hands on experience in protecting and enhancing their adopted water resource. *Kentucky Wild Rivers* is also available from the office above.

TEACHER WORKSHOPS

Education Resource Center
Education Division, MRC 305
National Air and Space Museum
Washington, DC 20560   202-786-2109

The Education Resource Center (ERC) of the National Air and Space Museum (NASM) is open to teachers of all levels and disciplines. The ERC offers teachers access to educational materials pertaining to aviation, space, and the Museum's collections. They offer half-day workshops, to aid educators in utilizing the ERC, and are scheduled on request. Participants receive assistance in compiling educational units to meet specific needs.

Office of Education, Room 212
Mail Stop 158
National Museum of Natural History
Washington, DC 20560   202-357-2747

The National Museum of Natural History Workshops for Teachers offers the following workshops for elementary and middle school teachers. Contact the office above for specific dates.

Old Growth Forests: Learn about the ecology of old growth forests from a Forest Service ranger. Review materials available for pre- and post-visit activities, including the instructional kit. Join the ranger to explore the temporary exhibit about old growth forests.

Indian Walkaround: The workshop reviews Walkaround logistics, presents background information on Native Americans, and ideas for classroom activities. This year's topic is "Native American Traditional Clothing, Then and Now." Logistical information includes teachers' and parents' roles, storage of coats and lunches, the Walkaround route, and what to expect.

Dinosaurs: A walk through the Dinosaur Hall to help teachers and aides design a visit for their classes, followed by an informal lecture on major dinosaur groups represented in the exhibit hall.

Climate and Endangered Species: A workshop designed to help teachers and aides design a visit or prepare for a guided tour. The identification of all endangered and extinct modern animals on exhibit is followed by an informal talk about why certain groups of animals are more vulnerable than others.

Seeds of Change: Become acquainted with the ideas, issues, and information embodied in the concept of the Columbian Exchange and in the exhibit *Seeds of Change*. Gather suggestions on using the exhibition with social studies, geography, and history classes and projects. Workshop includes activities in the exhibit and in the classroom.

Rocks and Minerals: Work with a geologist in developing ways to introduce students to rocks and minerals. Time is spent in the Earth and Mineral exhibition halls, as well as in a classroom. Activities are designed to provide experience in: 1)

distinguishing between a rock and a mineral, 2) describing minerals by their physical properties, and 3) using rock texture to classify rocks according to their origin.

Oceans: Become familiar with ancient and modern reefs and how ocean populations have changed over time. Learn the ecology of and strategies for competing in a water environment. Survey briefly the problems in today's ocean environments.

Understanding Culture: Introducing Culture Into Your Classroom and/or Curricula: Culture is a major concept in social studies, language and literature, history, art, philosophy - and in life. The workshop provides an understanding of culture and how it works, a perspective on world cultures and the concepts of multiculturalism and Eurocentrism. Included are suggestions for resources, learning activities, and strategies for integrating an understanding of culture into social studies, geography, history, biology, language arts, art, sociology, and anthropology. Workshop involves using museum exhibits for teaching.

National Science Teachers Association
Space, Science, and Technology Programs
1742 Connecticut Ave., NW
Washington, DC 20009   202-328-5800

The NASA Education Workshop for Elementary School Teachers (NEWEST) gives outstanding elementary teachers a chance to personally experience the U.S. aerospace program. As a NEWEST participant, you will spend two weeks during the summer at one of NASA's research centers learning about the latest in space and aeronautics activities. You will work with NASA experts and elementary curriculum specialists to fit the wealth of materials you will receive into your classroom teaching.

Elementary and Secondary Programs Branch
Educational Affairs Division
Mail Code XEE
NASA Headquarters
Washington, DC 20546

Aerospace Education Services Program (AESP) specialists conduct workshops for teachers each summer at NASA field centers, elementary and secondary schools, and on college campuses. Workshops cover astronomy, aeronautics, life in space, principles of rocketry, earth sciences, and remote sensing. A typical workshop includes how-to and hands-on activities to help teachers incorporate what they learn into classroom activities and programs to supplement existing curricula.

Education Branch (NEEE)
National Archives and Records Administration
Washington, DC 20408   202-501-6172

The National Archives preserves and makes available to the public the permanently valuable records of the U.S. Government. It offers teachers from the upper elementary grades through the secondary levels a workshop called *Primarily Teaching* that introduces them to the holdings and organization of the National Archives. *Primarily Teaching* emphasizes secondary strategies, but educators at all levels adapt them to their particular needs. Participants will learn how to do research in historical records; to create classroom material from records; and to present documents in ways that sharpen students' skills and enthusiasm for history, social studies, and the humanities.

Texas Parks and Wildlife Department
Ilo Hiller, Project WILD Coordinator
4200 Smith School Rd.
Austin, TX 78744

Project Wild is an award-winning environmental and conservation education program of instructional workshops and supplementary materials for teachers of kindergarten through high school age youth which prepares students to be responsible decision makers. The *Project Wild* materials are distributed free of charge to teachers and youth group leaders who attend one of the Texas Parks and Wildlife sponsored six-hour instructional workshops. The *Project Wild* guides cannot be purchased or obtained in any other manner.

TEACHING

American Association of Colleges for Teacher Education
One Dupont Circle NW, Suite 610
Washington, DC 20036-1186   202-293-2450

The Educational Resources Information Center (ERIC) is a nationwide information network designed to provide users with ready access to education literature. ERIC collects, analyzes, and distributes information from local, state, federal, and international agencies, as well as private sources. It consists of 16 clearinghouses including the Teacher Education Clearinghouse. The clearinghouse contains information on school personnel at all levels; teacher selection and training, preservice and inservice preparation, and retirement; the theory, philosophy, and practice of teaching; curricula and general education not specifically covered by other Clearinghouses; and all aspects of physical, health, and recreation education.

TELESCOPE, HUBBLE SPACE

NASA CORE
Lorain County Joint Vocational School
15181 Route 58 South
Oberlin, OH 44074   216-774-1051

Computer software is available on the Hubble Space Telescope. The *Hubble Space Telescope Educational Software Project* consists of four Apple II disks with reproducible information sheets and reference materials: *Windows to the Universe* chronicles the history of astronomical observations from the unaided eye through the Hubble Space Telescope; *Telescopes* explains the science of optics and the design and characteristics of telescopes; *Introduction to the Hubble Space Telescope* explains the design and operation of the Hubble Space Telescope; *Images From Space* describes the process through which light is captured by the Hubble Space Telescope and converted into images on Earth; *Activities Disk* contains a collection of classroom activities and illustrations relating to telescopes; *Glossary* contains an Appleworks data base of more than 300 astronomy terms. Also includes two Macintosh Applications Software (requires Pagemaker program 3.02 version or higher): *Hubble Space Telescope Model* contains the pattern and instructions for making a detailed model of NASA's Hubble Space Telescope: *Telescope Primer* outline of the basic principles behind the design and operation of telescopes. Includes many diagrams that can be enlarged and used for making transparencies. Grade 5-8.

THUNDERSTORMS

Warning and Forecast Branch, W/OM11
National Weather Service
National Oceanic and Atmospheric Administration
SSMCII
1325 East West Highway, Room 14370
Silver Spring, MD 20910   301-713-0622

The office above has the following audiovisuals available which can be used by educators to teach school children about safety during natural disasters:

Thunderstorm Videotape:
Everyday Weather Project: Thunderstorms

Thunderstorm Slides:
Advanced Meteorologist/Spotter Training Slide Series
When Lightning Strikes

TIME, GEOLOGIC

U.S. Geological Survey
P.O. Box 25425
Denver, CO 80225

The publication *Geologic Time* explains relative and radiometric time scales and how geologists measure the age of the Earth. It also illustrates the scientific processes that are used to interpret the Earth's geologic history.

TORNADO

Warning and Forecast Branch, W/OM11
National Weather Service
National Oceanic and Atmospheric Administration
SSMCII
1325 East West Highway, Room 14370
Silver Spring, MD 20910   301-713-0622

The office above has the following audiovisuals available which can be used by educators to teach school children about safety during natural disasters.

Tornado 16 mm Films:
Minneapolis Tornado of July 1986 (Copyrighted)
Terrible Tuesday
Day of the Killer Tornadoes
Tornado at Pleasant Hill
Tornado: A Spotter's Guide (Copyrighted)
Tornado: On the Spot Training (silent and with soundtrack)
Neosho

Tornado Videotapes:
Minneapolis Tornado of July 1986 (Copyrighted)
Terrible Tuesday
Day of the Killer Tornadoes
Tornado: A Spotter's Guide (Copyrighted)
Tornado: On the Spot Training (silent and with soundtrack)
Tornado Near Ellis, Kansas
Neosho

Tornado Slides:
A Slide Series Supplement to "Tornado: A Spotter's Guide"
Tornado Preparedness
Tornado Safety in Residence
The Safest Place in Schools
A Look at the Tornado and other Local Storms

TOXICS

Local Government Commission
909 12th St., #205
Sacramento, CA 95814   916-448-1198

Available from this office is *Toxic is My Home? You Bet!*, for grades K-3, 4-6, 7-8, and 9-12 (available in Spanish only). Developed by Golden Empire Health Planning Center as a one-week course of instruction, this school curriculum identifies: toxics in the home environment; methods for reducing exposure to household toxics; unsafe circumstances involving toxic products; and safer alternatives to using such products. Step by step teaching instructions, masters for worksheets, teacher answer guides, and evaluation methods are all included.

TREES

U.S. Geological Survey
P.O. Box 25425
Denver, CO 80225

Tree Rings: Timekeepers of the Past explains how past environmental conditions have been recorded in tree rings and how scientists interpret this information.

Forest Service
U.S. Department of Agriculture
14th and Independence, SW
P.O. Box 96090
Washington, DC 20090-6090   202-205-0957

Trees offer many benefits to the environment and play a vital role in reducing water and wind erosion, keeping rivers and streams clean, and counteracting the greenhouse effect. To learn more about trees and how they help the environment, contact the office above to receive a copy of *Trees are the Answer....to America's Growing Environmental Concerns*.

Forest Service
U.S. Department of Agriculture
14th and Independence, SW
P.O. Box 96090
Washington, DC 20090-6090   202-205-0957

The publication *Why Leaves Change Color* (FS-12) can be used by adults and upper elementary schoolchildren to learn why leaves change their color. It also contains instructions on how to copy leaves with crayons and how to make leaf prints with a stamp pad.

Forest Service
U.S. Department of Agriculture
14th and Independence, SW
P.O. Box 96090
Washington, DC 20090-6090   202-205-0957

The poster *How a Tree Grows* (FS-8) teaches about photosynthesis, enzymes, and the various parts of a tree. Its colorful illustrations make it a very useful teaching aid. The eight-page publication *How a Tree Grows* supplements the poster and provides more information on how a tree grows.

Forest Service
U.S. Department of Agriculture
14th and Independence, SW
P.O. Box 96090
Washington, DC 20090-6090   202-205-0957

Available from this office is the poster *What We Get From Trees* (FS-68). It lists the various products, ranging from chewing gum to mop handles, which come from trees.

TRUMAN

Education Branch (NEEE)
National Archives and Records Administration
Washington, DC 20408   202-501-6172

The Truman Years: 1945-1953 is a teaching unit available from the Education Branch of the National Archives. It is published by the National Archives and SIRS, Inc., and is designed to help students of U.S. history, government, and economics

The Government Works for Kids, Too

understand the process by which history is written and to develop analytical skills. It contains about 50 reproductions of documents - charts, photographs, letters, drawings, and posters - and a detailed teacher's guide. The materials deal with certain key issues of the period, with governmental and political responses to these issues, and with public attitudes.

U.S. CAPITOL

Architect of the Capitol
Washington, DC 20515   202-225-1200

Photographs and slides of the U.S. Capitol from the Collection of the Architect of the Capitol are available from the National Graphic Center, 205 West Jefferson Street, Falls Church, VA 22046 (703-533-8700). Teachers can use them to supplement a history lesson.

U.S. COAST GUARD

Public Affairs
U.S. Coast Guard
U.S. Department of Transportation
Washington, DC 20593-0001   202-267-1587

Our Day with the Coast Guard provides a fun way for children to learn about the U.S. Coast Guard. By providing information in a coloring book format, kids can learn what it's like to be in the Coast Guard. The coloring book includes activities such as a maze and connect-the-dots.

U.S. FISH AND WILDLIFE SERVICE

U.S. Fish and Wildlife Service
U.S. Department of the Interior
4401 N. Fairfax Drive, Mail Stop 130
Arlington, VA 22203   703-358-1711

Would you or your child like to learn more about America's sea turtles, diving ducks, or the golden eagle? Or what about endangered species such as the grizzly bear, spotted owl or gray wolf? Or why not decorate your classroom or child's bedroom with some of the 30 portraits of fish they have available? The U.S. Fish and Wildlife Service has dozens of easy-reading brochures and publications which can provide information for school reports, 4-H club assignments, or Boy Scout projects.

UNIVERSE

Teaching Resource Center
Jet Propulsion Laboratory
4800 Oak Grove Dr.
Mail Stop CS-530
Pasadena, CA 91109   818-354-6916

Two educational aids are available from the office above. The video *Universe* (30 min.) is available for $25 and the set of color slides with cassette narration *Our Universe* is available for $11.

UNIVERSITIES

The George Washington University
One Dupont Circle, NW, Suite 630
Washington, DC 20036-1183   202-296-2597

The Higher Education Clearinghouse has education literature on topics relating to college and university conditions, problems, programs, and students; curricular and instructional programs, and institutional research at the college or university level; federal program, professional education (medicine, law, etc.), professional continuing education, collegiate computer-assisted learning and management, graduate education, university extension programs, teaching-learning, legal issues and legislation, planning, governance, finance, evaluation, inter-institutional arrangements, management of institutions of higher education, and business or industry educational programs leading to a degree.

URANUS

Teaching Resource Center
Jet Propulsion Laboratory
4800 Oak Grove Dr.
Mail Stop CS-530
Pasadena, CA 91109   818-354-6916

Are you looking for materials to teach your children about Uranus. Contact the office above for *Jupiter, Saturn, Uranus and Neptune* (30 min.), a video for $25, and the slide set *Voyager Mission to Uranus*, $6.

NASA CORE
Lorain County Joint Vocational School
15181 Route 58 South
Oberlin, OH 44074   216-774-1051

Voyager, The Grand Tour is a computer animated video that highlights the significant features discovered by Voyagers 1 and 2 as these spacecraft traveled past the outer planets of Jupiter, Saturn, Uranus and Neptune. Copyrighted and reproduced with permission from Martin Marietta. For educational use only. Grade 4 - 12.

VENUS

Finley Holiday Films
12607 E. Philadelphia St.
Wittier, CA 90601   800-345-6707

The slide set *Magellan Mission to Venus* is available for $6 from the office above.

VIDEOS

NASA CORE
Lorain County Joint Vocational School
15181 Route 58 South
Oberln, OH 44074   216-774-1051

Aerospace-related videos are available from the NASA CORE of the National Air and Space Museum (NASM). NASA CORE offers teachers access to educational materials pertaining to aviation, space, and the Museum's collections. These materials are produced by NASM, the National Aeronautics and Space Administration (NASA), and other government agencies, and private organizations.

Ag in the Classroom
Room 317-A Administration Building
U.S. Department of Agriculture
Washington, DC 20350

Ag in the Classroom produces videos to help students in grades K-12 acquire the knowledge needed to become agriculturally literate. The objective of Ag in the Classroom is to encourage educators to teach more about our food and fiber system and the role of agriculture in our economy and society. The program is primarily carried out in each state by a group composed of educators, government officials, and representatives from agricultural organizations and agribusinesses. Materials available for the program include the following videos for elementary-school educators. The videos are:

1986 Ag in the Classroom shows how Ag in the Classroom works and offers a glimpse of enthusiastic teachers and students involved in Ag in the Classroom around the country. (16 minutes.)

America's Most Crucial Industry helps viewers of all ages understand agriculture's vital role in the American economy. This tape can also be purchased for $12 from: Video Transfer, 4709-B Arundel Avenue, Rockville, MD 20852. (14 minutes.)

Department of Extension Programs
National Gallery of Art
Washington, DC 20565

The National Gallery of Art is continually exploring ways to develop awareness in the visual arts and make its collections accessible to everyone, no matter how far away from the Gallery they may live. They now have an Extension Program which loans not only videocassettes, but also slide programs and films, free of charge to educational institutions, community groups, and to individuals throughout the U.S. Write to the office above for more information on how you may bring the National Gallery of Art to your students.

NASA CORE
Lorain County Joint Vocational School
15181 Route 58 South
Oberlin, OH 44074   216-774-1051

The NASA Central Operation of Resources for Educators (CORE), established in cooperation with Lorain County Joint Vocational School, serves as the national distribution center for NASA produced education materials. For a minimal charge the NASA CORE will provide a valuable service to educators unable to visit one of the NASA Teacher Resource Centers (TRC), by making NASA educational audiovisual materials available through its mail order service. Videocassettes appropriate for certain elementary grades include the following:

A Man's Reach Should Exceed His Grasp. Presents the story of flight and man's reach for new freedom through aviation and the exploration of space. From the Wright Brother's flight at Kitty Hawk to the landing on the moon and future

Be patient. If any phone number is incorrect, call (area code) 555-1212 and request the new listing.

missions to the planets, the tape depicts the fulfillment of the ancient dream of flight. Grade 4 - 9.

Opening New Frontiers: The Orbital Flight Tests of the Space Transportation System. Covers the first four test missions of the Space Shuttle Columbia, STS flights, 1,2,3, and 4. Also includes events leading up to the first launch, President Reagan's speech after the fourth landing, and highlights of the Orbital Flight Test Program. Grade 4 - 10.

Milestones of Flight. This program was produced by the National Air and Space Museum and is based on the museum's "Milestones of Flight" Gallery. It traces the history of flight from Langley's first attempts to the Space Shuttle. Uses live footage from many history making events. Grade 4 - 10.

Transformations of Flight. An animated video that presents ten important air and spacecraft in the history of flight. Includes a lesson guide. Produced by the Smithsonian Institution. Grade K - 3.

Portrait of Earth: The Story of Satellites. The film explains what satellites are and how they perform their daily tasks in orbit around our planet. Captioned at the 2nd, 3rd, and 4th grade levels.

Space Station: The Next Logical Step. Chronicles space milestones preceding the proposed Space Station. Focuses on man's desire to spend more time working and living in space and illustrates a possible Space Station design. Grade 4 - 6.

The Time of Apollo. In the year 1961, the President of the U.S. stated, "This nation should commit itself to achieving the goal, before this decade is out, of landing a man on the Moon and returning him safely to Earth." This program is a tribute to the historical accomplishments of the Apollo missions. Grade 4 -adult.

Shuttle: A Remarkable Flying Machine. Features the first historic flight of the Space Shuttle Columbia. Highlights include the liftoff on April 12, 1981, the onboard activities of Young and Crippen and a spectacular landing on Rogers Dry Lake bed in California. Grade 4 - adult.

We Deliver: Summary of Shuttle Flights 5,6,7 & 8. Covers the first four operational missions of the Space Transportation System, STS flight 5,6,7 & 8. Stresses the operational common denominator of these missions - satellite deployment. Also includes significant secondary achievements such as the first female astronaut, first black astronaut, first night launch and landing, and some of the more important onboard experiments. Grade 4 - adult.

The Dream Is Alive. Narrated by Walter Cronkite, *The Dream Is Alive* gives you a window seat on the shuttle. Share the astronaut's experiences of working, eating and sleeping in zero gravity....look back at our magnificent Earth and witness an exciting satellite repair. Copyrighted by the Smithsonian Institution/Lockheed Corporation. Grade 4 - adult.

To Dream...To Learn. The first segment of this program documents two Ohio schools who outfitted school buses as Space Shuttles. The school bus "ground shuttles" were sent on "missions" during which students learned a great deal about space travel. The second half of this program shows shuttle astronauts demonstrating toys during space shuttle mission 51-D. Students were asked to speculate as to how the toys would react in the weightless environment of space. Grade 4 - adult.

Our Solar System. Teaches the names, orbital positions, and characteristics of each planet using the phrase "my very educated mother just served us nine pizza pies". The program is animated, set to music, and appropriate for early elementary grades. Grade 2 - 6.

Voyager, The Grand Tour. A computer animated video that highlights the significant features discovered by Voyagers 1 and 2 as these spacecraft traveled past the outer planets of Jupiter, Saturn, Uranus and Neptune. Copyrighted and reproduced with permission from Martin Marietta. For educational use only. Grade 4 - 12.

Mars, The Next Step. Depicts a mission to Mars involving three vehicles launched from Earth, six months of interplanetary travel, and the establishment of a base on the martian soil. Grade 4 - 8.

Return To The Moon Videoconference Kit. Taping of an interactive teleconference on January 26, 1990. Students joined Apollo astronaut Michael Collins and NASA guest educator Dr. Lynn Bondurant on a "Return to the Moon", participating in a series of unique problem-solving and hands on activities. Accompanying curriculum material includes: and activity booklet, slides and a moon map. Grade 5 - 8.

Zero-G and Space Suits. Describes the space suit worn by Apollo astronauts. The three major parts of the suit are described. Weightlessness is also examined and

explained with animation, and Newton's three laws of motion are presented. Astronauts are shown in zero-gravity and in an extravehicular activity. Grade 4 - adult.

Project Mercury: An Early Step. Summarizes the project Mercury flights of the 60's. Shows the designing and building of the spacecraft, the training of the seven original astronauts, the MR-2 launch with the chimp HAM, and highlights of Alan Shepard's first flight, as well as the flights of other Mercury astronauts. Grade 4 - adult.

Gemini Science. Scientists explain life science experiments developed for the Gemini missions. Includes a brief synopsis of the missions. Grade 4 - adult.

Our Laboratories in Space. Examines some of the scientific and medical experiments that were completed on Skylab, the Apollo-SOYUZ Test Project and future experiments to be conducted on the space shuttle. Grade 4- adult.

NASA Images: Episode 1. Several films about the U.S.'s efforts to land a man on the moon are presented. Subjects discussed include: guidance, navigation, footage from the first manned moon landing and research aircraft which led to the Space Shuttle development. Grade 4 - 12.

NASA Images: Episode 2. Historic film documenting NASA highlights from 1967 and a 1968 Apollo flight are shown. 1967 highlights include the first unmanned test flight of the Saturn V moon rocket as well as footage showing satellite launches. A second documentary film, "The Flight of Apollo 7" shows the first manned Earth-orbital Apollo mission. Grade 4 - 12.

NASA Images: Episode 3. Three motion picture segments are presented including clips from a 1977 animated film "Space Spider Robot". The Space Spider project, now inactive, was designed to "weave" large structures in space. A historic 1967 film shows step-by-step animation of manned moonflights which were to follow in future years. Finally, a 1979 film shows how jet engines were tested for noise levels. Grade 4 - 12.

NASA Images: Episode 4. Fascinating footage from two 1974 films about weightlessness about Skylab, NASA's first "Space Station". Why weightlessness occurs in spacecraft in low Earth orbit, Newton's laws, and how fluids act in microgravity are described by scientist-pilot Dr. Owen Garriott who was on the crew of the second manned skylab mission. Grade 4 - 12.

> Drug Video Program
> Office of Public Affairs
> U.S. Department of Education
> 400 Maryland Ave., SW
> Washington, DC 20202

Originally designed for schools, these programs are now available for home use. Each program is closed captioned and comes with its own parent's or teacher's guide to help you discuss each program's message and the serious problem of drug abuse with your child. Contact the office above for ordering information. Programs for elementary children include:

The Drug Avenger. ($35, 73 minutes, 16-page Parent's Guide, 1988, VHS Order No. DGA17535). Three children from the future travel back to the 20th Century to take on the life-threatening problem of drug abuse in 10 animated programs.

Fast Forward Future. ($30, 61 minutes, 23-page Teacher's Guide, 1988., VHS Order No. DGA 17532). Actor Richard Kiley as "Mentor" shows three elementary students the future with the Fast Forward machine. The students see the effects of using drugs and staying drug free.

Straight Up. ($40, 90 minutes, 2-page Teacher's Guide, 1988, VHS Order No. DGA17529). Academy award winning actor Lou Gosset, Jr., as Cosmo takes a boy named Ben, played by Chad Allen of NBC's "Our House", on a journey in the "fate" elevator. Ben's travels teach him valuable lessons about why drugs are harmful and how to refuse them.

> State Capitol
> Nebraska Energy Office
> 9th Floor
> P.O. Box 95085
> Lincoln, NE 68509   402-471-2867

Energy-related video tapes in addition to curriculum guides, slides, and resource books and materials, are available to Nebraska educators only.

> Resource Center
> Public Education and Risk Communication Division
> Environmental and Occupational Health Sciences Institute
> 681 Frelinghuysen Rd.
> Piscataway, NJ 08855   908-445-0110

Be patient. If any phone number is incorrect, call (area code) 555-1212 and request the new listing.

1287

The Government Works for Kids, Too

"Healthy Environment - Healthy Me" is a interdisciplinary, supplementary environmental and occupational health curriculum. As an "environmental health promotion" curriculum, it is designed to provide young people with the knowledge and understanding for creating a safe and healthful environment at home, in their future workplaces and in their communities. The primary audience is schoolchildren in kindergarten through sixth grade. Videos include:

Alexandria's Clean-Up Fix-Up Parade (15 min., grades K-2)
Alexandria decides to get the community involved in a litter pick-up campaign after seeing the harm that litter caused a swan family in the park.

Alu-Man the Can (15 min., grades K-3)
This video teaches children about recycling through the adventures of Alu-Man the Can, Nettie Newspaper, Benjamin J. Bottle III, and Mr. "G" the garbage can.

Safety Sense (14 min., grades K-3)
Jason and Alice are safety detectives as they explore the possible health hazards of using and storing hazardous products incorrectly.

Sam's Safety Star Award (15 min., grades 1-3)
Sam, the TV camera, learns that risks are part of everyday activities like crossing the road, driving a bicycle, swimming and riding in a car. He learns to look and think before he acts.

Down the Drain (22 min., grades 3-5)
As Chris begins to pour some Polish-All down the drain, the sink comes alive. The animated sink explains why certain products can pollute the water supply. Chris learns the proper way to dispose of hazardous waste.

Keeping the Lid on Air Pollution (20 min., grades 4-6)
Terry has a homework assignment to write about two pollution controls. He ends up inside the school library computer and learns about different types of air pollutants (focusing on ozone) and air pollution controls.

The Inside Story on Air Pollution (19 min., grades 4-6)
Danny, Terry's friend, and his sister go into the computer to investigate the sources and health effects of indoor air pollution in the home. They also learn how to reduce and prevent indoor air pollution problems.

What to Do With All Our Garbage? (20 min., grades 4-6)
Kate, Jenny, and Greg explore the garbage crisis and possible solutions. Source reduction, recycling, sanitary landfills and incineration are discussed. The focus is on what we as consumers can do to reduce the amount of garbage we generate.

> University of California Extension Media Center
> 2176 Shattuck Ave.
> Berkeley, CA 94704   415-642-0460

A free catalog listing environmental films and videos for young people is available upon request from the office above.

> Information Services
> Great Lakes Regional Office
> P.O. Box 32869
> Detroit, MI 48232-2869   313-226-2170

Video tapes relating to Great Lake Studies are listed in the *Directory of Great Lakes Education Materials*. More than 600 educators were surveyed to produce the publication, a free-for-the-requesting directory that contains information on video tapes, pamphlets, technical reports, booklets, curriculum based and classroom-based materials for classes concentrating on Great Lakes studies.

> Warning and Forecast Branch, W/OM11
> National Weather Service
> National Oceanic and Atmospheric Administration
> SSMCII, 1325 East West Highway, Room 14370
> Silver Spring, MD 20910   301-713-0622

The office above has the following warning and forecast videotapes available which can be used by educators to teach school children about safety during natural disasters. They include:

Tornado Videotapes:
Minneapolis Tornado of July 1986 (Copyrighted)
Terrible Tuesday
Day of the Killer Tornadoes
Tornado: A Spotter's Guide (Copyrighted)
Tornado: On the Spot Training (silent and with soundtrack)
Tornado Near Ellis, Kansas
Neosho

Thunderstorm Videotapes:
Everyday Weather Project: Thunderstorms

Hurricane Videotapes
Hurricane
Before the Hurricane Strikes
Everyday Weather Project: Hurricanes

> Cooperative Extension Service
> University of Nebraska - Lincoln
> Institute of Agriculture and Natural
>   Resources Nebraska
> Department of Entomology
> 210 Plant Industry Bldg.
> Lincoln, NE 68583-0816   402-472-2123

The Institute promotes the use of nonchemical control of pests and low uses of pesticides. The Institute has a free brochure which describes educational materials on the topic of integrated pest management of crops. A pamphlet which describes videotapes and a field scout manual can also be purchased from the address above. A free catalog which lists environmental films and videotapes for young people's viewing is available. Programs are available on a rental basis.

> Teaching Resource Center
> Jet Propulsion Laboratory
> 4800 Oak Grove Dr.
> Mail Stop CS-530
> Pasadena, CA 91109   818-354-6916

Below are selected video programs on space and planetary subjects which can be excellent educational aids for classroom use. To receive an order form contact the office above. The videos include:

1st Flight of Space Shuttle STS-1 (30 min.)
Universe (30 min.)
Apollo Moon Landings (56 min.)
History of Flight (56 min.)
Mars and Mercury (the planets) (52 min.)
Mercury and Gemini Spacecraft Missions (56 min.)
Eruption of Mt. St. Helens (30 min.)
America in Space: 1st 25 Years (50 min.)
Shuttle Flights STS-1 thru STS-8 (60 min.)
Jupiter, Saturn, Uranus and Neptune (30 min.)
The Dream is Alive, IMAX (40 min.)
Kennedy Space Center Tour (42 min.)
We Remember: Shuttle Pioneers '81-'87 (60 min.)
Voyager Missions Animation Only (30 min.)

VOLCANOES

> Geologic Inquiries Group
> U.S. Geological Survey
> 907 National Center
> Reston, VA 22092   703-648-4383

The *Selected Packet of Geologic Teaching Aids* is prepared for elementary school teachers (and high school teachers) of general science, geography, social studies, environmental education and other earth science-related subjects. It contains leaflets, booklets, reference lists, and an activity sheet entitled "Make Your Own Paper Model of a Volcano". To receive a packet, send a request on school letterhead indicating the subject that is taught and the grade level to the office listed below.

WASHINGTON, GEORGE

> National Archives Teaching Aids
> Education Branch (NEEE)
> National Archives and Records Administration
> Washington, DC 20408   202-501-6172

Washington's Inaugural Address of 1789 (#200101, ISBN 0-911333-39-8) is available as a teaching unit from the National Archives Teaching Aids Education Branch (NEEE). This booklet includes a historical introduction and transcriptions and facsimiles of the featured documents. 8 1/2 x 11, approx. 25 pages each, illustrations, 1986. Softcover only, $2.50 each.

WASTE DISPOSAL

> Office of Environmental Education
> Pennsylvania Department of Education
> 333 Market St.

Harrisburg, PA 17126   717-783-6994

Paul E. Beals' publication *The Newspaper: A Tool for Teaching Environmental Awareness* is an activity book for children in grades K-12. It covers such topics as acid rain, forest preservation, waste disposal, and recycling. This activity book contains newspaper articles and uses them to teach about environmental awareness.

WATER

U.S. Geological Survey
P.O. Box 25425
Denver, CO 80225

The following publications are an excellent source of information for both upper elementary students and educators. Students can use them to supplement special reports and science projects and teachers can use them to enhance their curricula. To obtain single copies write to the office above.

Ground Water: An Undervalued Resource. Describes the need for using ground water, the role of ground water in the economy, and an analysis of regional aquifer systems. Discusses the ways in which ground water and surface water interact.

Ground Water and the Rural Homeowner. Presents a short description of ground water, some of the problems associated with ground water, and some suggestions for help with problems.

Ground Water Contamination--No "Quick Fix" in Sight. Explains how ground water is contaminated by septic tanks or cesspools, municipal lagoons, sewers, landfills, or tailings piles, and the need for further research in contamination prevention.

How Much Water in a 12-ounce Can? A Perspective on Water-Use Information. Provides information on how water was a free resource but now is considered an expensive commodity. Demonstrates how the ever-increasing use of water by industry and in the home is depleting existing supplies.

The Hydrologic Cycle. Explains the natural process by which water is circulated from the seas to the atmosphere, to the land, and back to the seas in a continuous cycle.

Water Dowsing. Provides a brief history of water dowsing. Explain how hydrologists of the USGS and other agencies use scientific methods to locate ground water.

Water in the Urban Environment: Erosion and Sediment. Explores the dual role that water plays as both as resource and a hazard. Discusses possible actions that minimize erosion and sedimentation.

The Water of the World. Discusses the amount of water contained in the world's atmosphere, on the surface, and underground. Describes the world's water balance.

Water Use in the United States, 1980. Summarizes the use of the Nation's water supply for domestic, industrial, rural, and irrigation purposes.

What is Water?. Describes the basic chemical properties of water and its diverse physical characteristics. Briefly explains the formation of water on Earth. Also available in Spanish.

Why is the Ocean Salty? Discusses the origin of the oceans and the sources of their salinity. Also available in Spanish.

Texas Water Development Board
Office of Public Information
P.O. Box 13087
Austin, TX 78711-3087   512-239-0028

Do You Know How to Keep Our Water Clean is a publication written for children which addresses the need for a clean environment. It discusses the "story on water" and recycling. It is a twenty page publication which ends with a crossword puzzle.

Texas Water Development Board
Office of Public Information
P.O. Box 13087
Austin, TX 78711-3087   512-239-0028

Land Use and the Water Cycle is a black and white poster which illustrates the water cycle and different uses of land. It can be used by educators as a teaching aid or by students as a component to a report.

Texas Water Development Board
Office of Public Information
P.O. Box 13087
Austin, TX 78711-3087   512-239-0028

The Texas Water Education Network Directory is a collection of water education materials suitable for use in public schools.

Texas Water Development Board
Office of Public Information
P.O. Box 13087
Austin, TX 78711-3087   512-239-0028

Water Education Teams, or WETs, are groups of young people who work together to understand and preserve the water resources in their local environment. The WET Project is intended as a supplemental or extracurricular activity for schoolchildren, or a special project for youth organizations. WETs select and survey a local surface water body, which may be a creek, lake, stream, reservoir or river. Then, through water testing, local observation and problem solving, WETs work to identify existing or potential sources of pollution. The students conclude by preparing community awareness projects to share what they have learned. Contact the office above to receive a copy of the *WET Project Instruction Handbook* which contains WET student activities, teacher resources and references, and sections on the basics of water quality. There also is a section of indoor/outdoor activities for areas without access to a body of water.

Texas Water Development Board
Office of Public Information
P.O. Box 13087
Austin, TX 78711-3087   512-239-0028

Invasion of the Water Hogs is a four page publication on water conservation written for children and describes the various ways in which water conservation can be achieved.

Public Information Center
U.S. Environmental Protection Agency
401 M Street, SW, MS 3404
Washington, DC 20460   202-260-2080

America's Wetlands: Our Vital Link Between Land and Water provides information on the types of wetlands, wetland values, status and trends of wetlands, and wetlands protection. Both educators and students can benefit from the information provided.

Kentucky Natural Resources and Environmental Protection Cabinet
Department for Environmental Protection
Frankfort Office Park
18 Reilly Road
Frankfort, KY 40601   502-564-3410

Free pamphlets available include *Kentucky Wild Rivers* and *10 Ways You Can Help Keep Kentucky Water Resources Clean. A Field Guide to Kentucky Rivers and Streams* and *A Field Guide to Kentucky Lakes and Wetlands* are available to teachers. Also available is information on the *Water Watch Program*, a program conducted by the Division of Water with services designed to encourage and support citizen participation in the wise management of community water resources, including streams, lakes, wetlands and groundwater. Any individual, group, family, organization, school or business can become and official "Kentucky Water Watcher".

WEATHER

Superintendent of Documents
Dept. 33
Washington, DC 20402   202-512-1800

Use the *Cloud Code Chart* to help teach children about cloud formations. This chart illustrates and describes the 36 cloud formations according to the international system of classification. 1972. Rep. 1988. 31 x 19 ins. Shipped folded. (S/N 003-018-00050-4, $2.25).

Warning and Forecast Branch, W/OM11
National Weather Service
National Oceanic and Atmospheric Administration
SSMCII
1325 East West Highway, Room 14370
Silver Spring, MD 20910   301-713-0622

The office above has the following audiovisuals available which can be used by educators to teach school children about safety during natural disasters:

Tornado 16 mm Films

Minneapolis Tornado of July 1986 (Copyrighted)
Terrible Tuesday
Day of the Killer Tornadoes
Tornado at Pleasant Hill
Tornado: A Spotter's Guide (Copyrighted)
Tornado: On the Spot Training (silent and with soundtrack)
Neosho

The Government Works for Kids, Too

Tornado Videotapes
Minneapolis Tornado of July 1986 (Copyrighted)
Terrible Tuesday
Day of the Killer Tornadoes
Tornado: A Spotter's Guide (Copyrighted)
Tornado: On the Spot Training (silent and with soundtrack)
Tornado Near Ellis, Kansas
Neosho

Tornado Slides
A Slide Series Supplement to "Tornado: A Spotter's Guide"
Tornado Preparedness
Tornado Safety in Residence
The Safest Place in Schools
A Look at the Tornado and other Local Storms

Thunderstorm Videotapes
Everyday Weather Project: Thunderstorms

Thunderstorm Slides
Advanced Meteorologist/Spotter Training Slide Series
When Lightning Strikes

Flash Flood 16 mm Films
The Awesome Power
Flash Flood
Flood

Flash Flood Videotapes
The Awesome Power

Flash Flood/Flood Slides
Flash Floods: Myths or Realities
Flash Flood Preparedness

Hurricane 16 mm Films
A Lady Named Camille
Hurricane Decision
Hurricane

Hurricane Videotapes
Hurricane
Before the Hurricane Strikes
Everyday Weather Project: Hurricanes

Hurricane Slides
Hurricane Hugo
Hurricane Eloise
Hurricane Preparedness
Hurricane Alicia
Hurricane Frederick

Tsunami Video
1983 Sea of Japan Tsunami

Winter Storm 16 mm film
Survival in the Cold

Winter Storm Videotapes
Survival in the Cold

Winter Storm Slides
Winter Storms, The Deceptive Killers

Additional 16 mm Films
An Ill Wind
Rising Waters
Watch Along the Watershed
Earthwatch
NOAA, A Global View
Galaxy
Before It Hits Home
Hurricane: Before the Storm
Hurricane Aetna: Date with Disaster
Cities Don't Die
Winter Storm

Educational Programs Branch
National Oceanic and Atmospheric Administration (NOAA)
1305 East West Hwy
Silver Spring, MD 20910   301-713-1170
The office above provides educational materials to educators and the public. They can tailor requests for appropriate grade levels and curricula. Some of their weather publications include the following (which are appropriate for grades 3-6):

The Amateur Weather Forecaster. Learn the importance of keeping a weather log, some of the most common weather instruments, and some reliable weather forecasting statements.

Watch Out....Storms Ahead! Owlie Skywarn's Weather Book. Includes weather warnings, tornado facts, flash flood and winter storm instructions.

Natural Hazard Watch and Warning with Safety Rules for: Tornadoes, Hurricanes, Floods, Flash Floods, Thunderstorms/Lightning, Winter Storms. This mini-poster provides easy-to-read information on what to do when there is a natural hazard.

WETLANDS

Public Information Center
U.S. Environmental Protection Agency
401 M Street, SW, MS 3404
Washington, DC 20460
America's Wetlands: Our Vital Link Between Land and Water provides information on the types of wetlands, wetland values, status and trends of wetlands, and wetlands protection. Both educators and students can benefit from the information provided.

Water Watch
Division of Water
Department for Environmental Protection
Frankfort Office Park
14 Reilly Road
Frankfort, KY 40601   502-564-3410
Contact the office above to obtain a copy of *A Field Guide to Kentucky Lakes and Wetlands.* This booklet offers an illustrated guide and discussion for field observation along and within Kentucky's lakes and wetlands. It can be used by educators and upper elementary schoolchildren.

U.S. EPA Region 5
Office of Public Affairs
77 West Jackson Blvd., PI-195
Chicago, IL 60604   312-353-2000
Welcome to the Wetlands (grades K-12) is a coloring poster that explains how wetlands help us and what is a threat to wetlands. Included is information on animals, birds, fish and plants that thrive in wetlands. Limited quantities of the following are available for residents in the six-state Region 5 area (Illinois, Indiana, Michigan, Minnesota, Ohio, Wisconsin).

WHOOPING CRANES

U.S. Fish and Wildlife Service
U.S. Department of the Interior
4401 N. Fairfax Drive
Mail Stop 130
Arlington, VA 22203   703-358-1711
The publication *Whooping Crane* will teaching you more about this interesting bird.

WILDLIFE CONSERVATION

Texas Parks and Wildlife Department
Ilo Hiller, Project WILD Coordinator
4200 Smith School Rd.
Austin, TX 78744
Project Wild is an award-winning environmental and conservation education program of instructional workshops and supplementary materials for teachers of kindergarten through high school age youth which prepares students to be responsible decision makers. The *Project Wild* materials are distributed free of charge to teachers and youth group leaders who attend one of the Texas Parks and Wildlife sponsored six-hour instructional workshops. The *Project Wild* guides cannot be purchased or obtained in any other manner.

Public Information Center
U.S. Environmental Protection Agency
401 M Street, SW, MS 3404

Be patient. If any phone number is incorrect, call (area code) 555-1212 and request the new listing.

Washington, DC 20460   202-260-2080

Save Our Species: Endangered Species Coloring Book will introduce children to 21 endangered and threatened plants and animals found in the United States. As they color the pages, they will journey to oceans, swamps, deserts, and islands and bring to life a variety of plants and animals.

U.S. Fish and Wildlife Service
U.S. Department of the Interior
4401 N. Fairfax Drive
Mail Stop 130
Arlington, VA 22203   703-358-1711

Would you or your child like to learn more about America's sea turtles, diving ducks, or the golden eagle? Or what about endangered species such as the grizzly bear, spotted owl or gray wolf? Or why not decorate your classroom or child's bedroom with some of the 30 portraits of fish they have available? The U.S. Fish and Wildlife Service has dozens of easy-reading brochures and publications which can provide information for school reports, 4-H club assignments, or Boy Scout projects.

WOLVES

U.S. Fish and Wildlife Service
U.S. Department of the Interior
4401 N. Fairfax Drive
Mail Stop 130
Arlington, VA 22203   703-358-1711

Two publications are available from the U.S. Fish and Wildlife Service for those interested in wolves, *Red Wolf* and *Gray Wolf* publications.

WOODSY OWL

Forest Service
U.S. Department of Agriculture
14th and Independence, SW
P.O. Box 96090
Washington, DC 20090-6090   202-205-0957

Give a hoot! Don't pollute! *Woodsy Owl's 1991-92 Campaign Catalog* is filled with dozens of items children can use (such as bike stickers, bookmarks, name tags, balloons, pens, pencils, lunch bags) that have the Woodsy Owl logo on them. Contact the office above for a catalog or the National Association of State Foresters/Woodsy Owl Campaign at 803-737-8800.

WRIGHT BROTHERS

NASA CORE
Lorain County Joint Vocational School
15181 Route 58 South
Oberlin, OH 44074   216-774-1051

The videocassette *A Man's Reach Should Exceed His Grasp* presents the story of flight and man's reach for new freedom through aviation and the exploration of space. From the Wright Brother's flight at Kitty Hawk to the landing on the moon and future missions to the planets, the tape depicts the fulfillment of the ancient dream of flight. Grade 4 - 9.

Education Office
Federal Aviation Administration
U.S. Department of Transportation
400 7th Street, SW
Washington, DC 20590   301-322-4961

Use the publication *How We Made the First Flight* to teach your children about the Wright brothers experiences. Written in Orville Wright's own words, it is a description of his and Wilbur's first flights.

WRITING

Indiana University
Smith Research Center, Suite 150
2805 East 10th Street
Bloomington, IN 47408-2698   812-855-5847

Education literature on writing can be obtained from one of the Educational Resources Information Center (ERIC) clearinghouses called Reading and Communication Skills. Literature is available on reading, english, and communication skills (verbal and nonverbal), preschool through college; educational research and instruction development in reading, writing, speaking, and listening; identification, diagnosis, and remediation of reading problem; speech communication (including forensics), mass communication, interpersonal and small group interaction, interpretation, rhetorical and communication theory, speech sciences, and the theater.

Current Events and Homework

Whether you are struggling with a school term paper or are eager to impress your boss by obtaining the latest statistics and analysis on practically any subject, help is right at hand. Few people, even those of us living in Washington, DC, are aware of all the studies generated around the clock by a division of the Library of Congress. Approximately 500 PhDs working at the Congressional Research Service (CRS) grind out these reports on almost any topic imaginable and these studies are constantly made available to all 525 members of Congress.

Your U.S. Representative and Senators have immediate access to over 10,000 reports on current events through a computerized online network. And a phone call or letter to one of your legislators is all it takes for you to tap into this rich information resource. To get copies of these reports, you must go through the office of your U.S. Representative or Senator. There is no charge for these concise reports which are unquestionably the "best information value" because the material is prepared by other experts in federal government agencies as well as from the private sector. Researchers, students of all ages, marketing reps, entrepreneurs, and ordinary citizens should take advantage of this information gold mine.

The Reason Why These Reports Are Constantly Updated

If a congressional committee plans an investigation, for example, on the home health care situation, the CRS specialists will complete a background study and their findings will be available to anyone in the public domain. If a lawmaker is concerned about the situation in Poland, these experts will prepare a complete analysis of the situation and when warranted, will update it daily as events change. If a Congressman is going to address an industry group on a subject like "Captive Off-Shore Insurance Companies", most likely his staff is going to rely on the information generated by CRS. They can tap into this database and find a 10 to 30-page report written by an expert who spends much of his or her career doing nothing but studying this subject.

CRS Reports Are Easy to Understand ... They're Written for Congressmen

Although these studies are prepared by PhDs, you don't have to worry about understanding them. These reports summarize historical context as well as fast breaking developments and are presented in layman's language. Also, the CRS adheres to its non-partisan mission to serve all members of Congress. One rationale for getting CRS studies is to see what material legislators and their staff are using as background information, whether it be for speeches or policy decisions. In addition to covering most business or student subject areas, these reports are an easy way to stay current on complex world events and issues of peripheral concern.

How to Get a Report

Getting your hands on a half a dozen reports can be easy. Just remember you cannot get studies directly from CRS but only by contacting a Member's Washington or district office. It is important to have the proper title or publication number of the CRS report that you are requesting. If you don't receive copies in a week or two, a follow-up phone call may be necessary. Keep in mind that helping constituents in this way is a welcome task for an elected official, especially when a legislator's reelection is close at hand. If you find one office uncooperative, try another. Remember we each have two Senators and one Representative. You can contact all legislators in Washington, DC by calling the Capitol Hill Switchboard at 202-224-3121.

Sample Entry

It is next to impossible to get the *CRS Index to Reports and Issues Briefs* which is why we've reproduced it here. In addition to reports, this list includes Issue Briefs, which are summaries of CRS reports. At the end of the chapter you will find two other CRS products, Info Packs, and Audio Briefs.

To make sure you understand the way these reports are listed, we have dissected one entry here.

* Polygraph Testing: Employee and Employer Rights: Issue Brief, Gail McCallion IB87126

Polygraph Testing: Employee and Employer Rights = Title
Issue Brief = Issue Brief (rather than a full length CRS report)
Gail McCallion = Congressional Research Service Author
IB87126 = Report Number

Although these reports are available through your U.S. Representative or Senator, you may be able to contact the author of the report directly at: Congressional Research Service, Library of Congress, Washington, DC 20540, 202-707-5700. Also, after reading the reports or issue briefs, you may want to follow up and check with the CRS specialist to track down any of his or her articles which have been published in trade publications. Since the Congressional Research Service is only in the habit of responding to requests from Congress, it is especially important to treat CRS experts with respect.

These thousand or so reports are grouped under several hundred subject categories. It may require browsing through this chapter to find the category heading of interest. You'll notice that certain categories are cross-references, for example, under "Labor--Earnings and Benefits" you'll be instructed to "see Labor--Policies and Legislation." If you are unable to find a particular category or have no luck locating a report on a given subject, ask your Member of Congress to send you the most recent CRS list of reports for that particular issue. Of course, new reports are added to the CRS immense portfolio every day to reflect developments both at home and abroad.

Current Events and Homework

Abortion
* Abortion: Info Pack IP001A
* Abortion Law Development: A Brief Overview, Karen J. Lewis 95-724 A
* Abortion: Legislative Response; Issue Brief, Karen J. Lewis and Thomas P. Carr IB95095
* Abortion Procedures, Irene Stith-Coleman 95-1101 SPR
* Abortion Services and Military Medical Facilities, David D. Burrelli 95-387 F
* RICO and Political Protest: The Implications of NOW v. Scheidler, Kenneth R. Thomas 94-108 A

Acid Rain
* see Air Pollution -- Law and Legislation

* Adarand Constructors, Inc. v. Pena
* The Supreme Court Decision in Adarand Constructors Inc. v. Pena: Federal Contracting and Disadvantaged Business Enterprises, Charles V. Dale 95-137 A

Adolescent Childbearing
* see Children

Adult Day Care
* see Aged

Adult Education Act
* Adult Education Act: Reauthorization Factsheet, Paul M. Irwin and Richard N. Apling 94-882 EPW
* Adult Education Program Trends, Paul M. Irwin 94-951 EPW

Aeronautics
* see Transportation -- Aviation

AFDC
* see Welfare -- Children

Affirmative Action
* see Minorities

Afghanistan
* see also South Asia
* Afghanistan: Current Issues & U.S. Policy Interests, Kenneth Katzman 95-533 F

Africa
* see Africa (Sub-Saharan), Middle East and North Africa

Africa (Sub-Saharan)
* Africa: U.S. Foreign Assistance Issues; Issue Brief, Raymond W. Copson IB95052
* Angola: A Chronology of War and Endeavors Toward Peace, Patrice Curtis 94-843 F
* Angola: U.S. Interests; Issue Brief, Patrice K. Curtis IB95045
* Burundi Crisis, Theodros Dagne 95-458 F
* Cote D'Ivoire (Ivory Coast): Briefing Paper, Raymond W. Copson 94-859 F
* Ghana: Briefing Paper, Raymond W. Copson 94-830 F
* Kenya: Briefing Paper, Raymond W. Copson 95-775 F
* Mozambique: Post Election Prospects, Raymond W. Copson, 94-984 ENR
* Nigeria: Briefing Paper, Raymond W. Copson 94-715 F
* Organization of African Unity: Briefing Paper, Brenda Branaman 94-824 F
* Rwandan Crisis: A Chronology, August 1994-June 1995, Theodros Dagne 95-773 F
* Rwanda's Humanitarian Situation and the U.S. Response, Lois McHugh 94-617 F
* Somalia: Current Developments, Drawdowns, and Implications, Alfred B. Prados 94-817 F
* Somalia: Update, Objectives and Options; Videoprogram, Raymond Copson VT93-1363
* South Africa Aid: U.S. Assistance Package for FY 1994-1996, Larry Nowels 94-851 F

* South Africa: Politics, Economic Development, U.S. Assistance, Brenda Branaman 95-414 F
* South Africa: The Current Situation; Info Pack, IP340S
* South African Humanitarian Needs, Brenda M. Branaman 93-1005 F
* South African Transition: Scenario, Major Actors, Current Problems, Issues for U.S. Policy, Raymond Copson 93-947 F
* South Africa's Elections and Prospects for the Future; Videoprogram, Raymond Copson VT94-1329
* South Africa's Elections: Economic Problems and Prospects; Videoprogram, Raymond Copson VT94-1379
* South Africa's Elections: Politics and Prospects for the Future: Audio Brief AB50298

Aged
* see also Health Policy, Pensions, Social Security
* Adult Day Care: A Fact Sheet, Carol O'Shaughnessy 94-757 EPW
* Aged: A Profile; Info Pack IP003A
* Evolution of Section 202: Housing for the Elderly, Susan M. Vanhorenbeck 93-645 E
* Home Equity Conversion: An Overview, Bruce Foote 95-274 E
* Housing for Older Persons Act of 1995: H.R. 660, Susan M. Vanhorenbeck 95-443 E
* Older Americans Act Amendments of 1992, Carol O'Shaughnessy 93-329 EPW
* Older Americans Act: Brief History of Legislation and Funding, Carol O'Shaughnessy and Molly Forman 93-400 EPW
* Older Americans Act FY 1995 Budget: Fact Sheet, Carol O'Shaughnessy and Molly Forman 94-607 EPW
* Older Americans Act FY 1996 Budget: Fact Sheet, Carol O'Shaughnessy and Molly R. Forman 95-916 EPW
* Older Americans Act Nutrition Program: Fact Sheet, Carol O'Shaughnessy 95-379 EPW
* Older Americans Act: 104th Congress Issues, Carol O'Shaughnessy 95-32 EPW
* Senior Community Service Employment Program: Background, FY 1996 Budget Request and 104th Congress Legislation, Carol O'Shaughnessy 95-244 EPW
* White House Conference on Aging: Fact Sheet, Carol O'Shaughnessy 94-574 EPW

Aged -- Health
* Brain Disorders in the Elderly, Irene Stith-Coleman 95-748 SPR
* Case Management Standards in State Community-Based Long-Term Care Programs for Older Persons With Disabilities, Carol O'Shaughnessy 94-96 EPW
* Health Benefits for Retirees: Employer-Based Plans, Beth C. Fuchs 93-428 EPW
* Health: Long-Term Care; Info Pack IP402H
* Long-Term Care for Elderly: Issue Brief, Richard J. Price IB95039
* Medicaid: Eligibility for the Aged, Disabled, and Blind, Richard J. Price 94-297 EPW
* Medicaid: Long-Term Care and the Elderly, Richard J. Price 93-302 EPW
* Tax Incentives for Elderly Home Care, Louis Alan Talley 93-805 E

Agricultural Exports
* see Agriculture -- Foreign Trade

Agriculture
* see also Emergency Management, Hazardous Substances
* Agricultural Issues: Info Pack, IP295A
* Agricultural Provisions of the House Reconciliation, Geoffrey S. Becker and Jasper Womach 95-1056 ENR
* Agricultural Provisions of the Senate Reconciliation Bill, Geoffrey S. Becker and Jasper Womach 95-1055 ENR
* Agriculture and the Environment: Audio Brief, John Blodgett, etc. AB50303
* Agriculture and the FY 1996 Budget: Issue Brief, Ralph M. Chite IB95031
* Bovine Somatotropin (BST or BGH): Questions and Answers on a New Dairy Technology, Ralph M. Chite 93-1041 ENR
* Comparing Levels of Farm Support Across Selected Commodities, Jasper Womach and Geoffrey Becker 95-840 ENR
* Federal Marketing Orders for Fruits, Vegetables, and Specialty Crops, Geoffrey S. Becker 95-326 ENR

* Research and Education Funding in the U.S. Department of Agriculture, Christine M. Matthews 95-525 SPR
* USDA: Background on the Department and Reorganization Issues, Geoffrey S. Becker, 92-613 ENR
* USDA Reorganization Legislation in the 103rd Congress: A Section-by-Section Description, Geoffrey S. Becker 94-798 ENR

Agriculture -- Foreign Trade
* Agricultural Export Programs, Food Aid and the Farm Bill, Charles C. Hanrahan and Remy Jurenas 95-391 S
* Agriculture in the North American Free Trade Agreement, Charles C. Hanrahan 92-958 S
* Agriculture in the Uruguay Round: An Assessment, Charles C. Hanrahan 94-582 S
* Export Enhancement Program: Background and Current Issues, Lenore Sek 95-388 ENR
* NAFTA and Sugar, Remy Jurenas 93-986 ENR
* U.S. Agricultural Trade: Trends, Composition, Direction, and Policy, Charles E. Hanrahan, etc. 95-809 S
* U.S.-Canadian Agricultural Trade Disputes, Carl Ek and Charles E. Hanrahan 94-270 F

Agriculture -- Policies and Legislation
* Agricultural Credit: 1995 Farm Bill Issues; Issue Brief, Ralph M. Chite IB95096
* Agricultural Research and Extension: Current Issues, Jean M. Rawson 93-83 ENR
* Agriculture and Clean Water: Provisions of S. 2093, Claudia Copeland 94-476 ENR
* An Assessment of the Agricultural Impacts of H.R. 2199, A. Barry Carr 94-229 ENR
* Conservation Compliance: Policy Issues for the 1995 Farm Bill, Jeffrey Zinn 95-6 ENR
* Conservation Cost-Share Programs for Agriculture: An Introduction, Jeffrey A. Zinn 95-339 ENR
* Conservation Reserve Program: Policy Issues for the 1995 Farm Bill, Jeffrey Zinn 95-8 ENR
* Conservation Titles in the 1995 Farm Bill: A Comparison, Jeffrey Zinn 95-1106 ENR
* The Economics of Agricultural Policy, A. Barry Carr, 92-198 ENR
* Farm Commodity Deficiency Payments: Where and to Whom?, Paul W. Barkley 94-434 ENR
* Farm Commodity Legislation: Chronology 1933-93, Geoffrey S. Becker, 94-576 ENR
* Farm Commodity Programs: Feed Grains, Carl W. Ed 93-402 ENR
* Farm Commodity Programs: Financing and Costs, Geoffrey S. Becker and Ralph M. Chite, 94-575 ENR
* Farm Commodity Programs: Peanuts, Remy Jurenas, 95-318 ENR
* Farm Commodity Programs: Sugar, Remy Jurenas 95-317 ENR
* Farm Commodity Programs: Surplus Management, Geoffrey S. Becker 94-583 ENR
* Farm Commodity Programs: The Dairy Price Support Program, Ralph M. Chite 94-690 ENR
* Farm Commodity Programs: Wheat, Carl W. Ek 93-881 ENR
* Farm Disaster Payments: Recent History and Specialty Crop Issues, Ralph M. Chite 94-283 ENR
* Farm Price Support Operations: Wheat, Feed Grains, Cotton, Rice, and Soybeans, Geoffrey S. Becker and Jasper Womach 95-531 ENR
* Farm Program Target Prices, Geoffrey S. Becker 95-874 ENR
* Farm Programs: A Comparison of Selected Budget Reconciliation Legislation; Issue Brief, Geoffrey S. Becker IB95116
* Farmer Mac: The Legislative Development of the Agricultural Secondary Market, Ralph M. Chite 95-1045 ENR
* The Federal Crop Insurance Reform Act of 1994, Ralph M. Chite 94-836 ENR
* Federal Farm Promotion ("Check-Off") Programs, Geoffrey S. Becker 95-353 ENR
* Food and Farm Support under USDA's Section 32 Fund, Geoffrey S. Becker 94-655 ENR
* Foods and Biotechnology: FDA's Regulatory Policy; Proceedings of a Seminar, July 22, 1992, Irene Stith-Coleman, 93-712 SPR
* Fruit and Vegetable Issues in the 104th Congress, Brenda Branaman 95-1061 ENR
* Grazing Fees: A Primer, Betsy A. Cody, 95-1 ENR
* Increasing Cigarette Excise Taxes: Implications for Tobacco Farming, Jasper Womach 94-344 ENR
* An Introduction to Farm Commodity Programs, Geoffrey S. Becker, 94-577 ENR
* Legal Issues Related to Livestock Watering in Federal Grazing Districts, Pamela Baldwin 94-688 A
* Milk Marketing Orders: Background and Current Policy Issues, Ralph M. Chite 95-267 ENR

* The Perishable Agricultural Commodities Act, Geoffrey S. Becker 95-285 ENR
* Previewing the 1995 Farm Bill Debate, Jasper Womach 94-709 ENR
* Reduced Farm Commodity Support: Economic Assessments; Videoprogram, Jasper Womach VT95-1343
* Selected CRS Reports Available on Food and Agricultural Topics, Environment and Natural Resources Policy Division, Food and Drug Section 94-880 ENR
* Senator Lugar's Farm Bill Questions: Responses From Academia, Environment and Natural Resources Policy Division 95-1094 ENR
* Soil and Water Conservation Policy Issues for the 1995 Farm Bill; Issue brief, Jeffrey A. Zinn IB95027
* Sustainable Agriculture, Jean M. Rawson 95-1062 ENR
* Tobacco Price Support: An Overview of the Program, Jasper Womach 95-129 ENR
* U.S. Tobacco Production: Prospects for the Future, Jasper Womach 94-672 ENR
* Wetlands and Agriculture: Policy Issues in the 1995 Farm Bill, Jeffrey Zinn 95-7 ENR
* What Exactly is a Farm Bill?, Jasper Womach, etc. 95-199 ENR
* 1995 Farm Bill Issues, Jean Yavis Jones 95-219 ENR
* The 1995 Farm Bill: Dairy; Issue Brief, Ralph M. Chite IB95103
* The 1995 Farm Bill: Food and Agricultural Policy: A Checklist of CRS Products, Ted L. Burch 94-883 L
* The 1995 Farm Bill: Overview; Issue Brief, Jean M. Rawson IB95058
* The 1995 Bill: Sugar; Issue Brief, Remy Jurenas IB95117
* The 1995 Farm Bill Targeting Program Benefits; Issue Brief IB95102
* 1995 Farm Bill: The Economic Setting; Audio Brief, Jasper Womach AB50308
* 1995 Farm Bill: The Economic Setting; Videoprogram, Jasper Womach VT94-1355
* 1995 Farm Bill: The Policy Setting; Audio Brief, Charles S. Hanrahan AB50309
* 1995 Farm Bill: The Policy Setting; Videoprogram, Geoffrey Becker VT95-1301
* The 1995 Farm Bill: Wheat, Feed Grains, Cotton, Rice, and Oilseeds; Issue Brief, Geoffrey S. Becker and Jasper Womach IB95082

Aid to Families with Dependent Children
* see Welfare -- Children

AIDS
* see Medicine -- AIDS

Air Pollution
* see also Clean Air Act, Emergency Management
* California Air Quality FIP - A Fact Sheet, Susan L. Mayer 95-491 ENR
* Heavy Duty Diesel Engines and Their Fuel: Can They Survive Clean Air Regulations?, David E. Gushee, 95-961 ENR
* Implementation of the Reformulated Gasoline Program, Susan L. Mayer 95-850 ENR

Air Pollution -- Law and Legislation
* Air Pollution--Clean Air Act: Info Pack IP008A
* Air Quality: Impacts of Trip Reduction Programs on States and Affected Employers, Maura K. Flechtner, 93-745 ENR
* Air Quality Implementing the Clean Air Act Amendments of 1990; Issue Brief, Susan Mayer IB91022
* Alternative Fuels and Reformulated Gasoline: Issue Brief, David Bushee, IB91008
* Clean Air Act Issues in the 104th Congress: Issue Brief, Susan L. Mayer IB95034
* EPA's Implementation of the Clean Air Act Amendments of 1990: The First Two Years, Susan L. Mayer 93-268 ENR
* Ethanol and Clean Air: The "Reg-Neg" Controversy and Subsequent Events, Migdon Segal, 93-614 SPR
* Implementing Acid Rain Legislation: Issue Brief, Larry Parker, IB91035
* Implementing the Clean Air Act Amendments of 1990: Where are We Now?, Susan L. Mayer 95-234 ENR

Air Pollution -- Ozone
* CFC Phase-Out: Future Problem for Air Conditioning Equipment?, David Gushee 93-382 S Bills in the
* Climate Change: Three Policy Perspectives, Larry Parker and John Blodgett 94-816 ENR
* Global Climate Change: Issue Brief, John Justus and Wayne Morrissey IB89005
* Global Climate Change: Policy Issues; Videoprogram VT91-857
* Greenhouse Effect and Ozone Depletion; Info Pack, IP405G
* Montreal Protocol Negotiations: Should the HCFC Phaseout Schedule be Accelerated in 1995?, David Gushee 94-788 S
* The Stratospheric Ozone Layer: Regulatory Issues; Issue Brief, David Gushee IB89021

Airline Industry
* see Transportation -- Aviation

Be patient. If any phone number is incorrect, call (area code) 555-1212 and request the new listing.

1295

Current Events and Homework

Albania
* Romania, Bulgaria, Albania: Recent Developments; Issue Brief, Sergiu Verona, IB92064

Alcoholism
* see Drug Abuse

Algeria
* see also Middle East and North Africa
* Algeria in Crisis: Situation Update, Carol Migdalovitz 94-241 F

Alternative Energy Sources
* see Energy -- Alternative Sources

American Dream Restoration Act
* The American Dream Restoration Act: Tax Provisions, Gregg A. Eisenwein 95-395 E

Americans With Disabilities Act
* AIDS Discrimination: The Federal Response, Mark Eddy 94-818 GOV
* The Americans With Disabilities Act: An Overview of Major Provisions, Nancy Lee Jones 92-306 A
* The Americans With Disabilities Act: Equal Employment Opportunity Commission Proposed Regulations on Equal Employment Opportunity for Individuals With Disabilities, Nancy Lee Jones 92-83 A
* Americans With Disabilities Act: Final Rules and Information Sources, James W. Watson, 92-311 A
* The Americans With Disabilities (ADA): Implementation Issues, Nancy Lee Jones 93-815 A
* Americans With Disabilities Act (ADA) Requirements Concerning the Provision of Interpreters by Doctors, Nancy L. Jones 94-345 A
* The Americans With Disabilities Act: Info Pack IP443A

Amtrak
* see also Transportation
* Selected Labor Protections Regarding Transit, Amtrak, and Freight Railroads: Issue Brief, Stephen Thompson IB95097

Angola
* Angola: A Chronology of War and Endeavors Toward Peace, Patrice Curtis 94-843 F
* Angola: U.S. Interests; Issue Brief, Patrice Curtis IB95045

Animals
* Brief Summaries of Federal Animal Protection Statutes, Henry Cohen 94-731 A
* The Convention on International Trade in Endangered Species: Its Past and Future, M. Lynne Corne 94-675 ENR
* The Endangered Species Act and Private Property: A Legal Primer, Robert Meltz 93-346 A
* Endangered Species: Continuing Controversy; Issue Brief, M. Lynn Corn IB95003
* Endangered Species: Info Pack IP192E
* Habitat Modification and the Endangered Species Act: The Sweet Home Decision, Pamela Baldwin 95-778 A
* The Listing of a Species: Legal Definitions and Biological Realities, M. Lynn Corn and Joshua P. Nowlis 92-944 ENR
* Marine Mammal Protection Act Amendments of 1994, Eugene H. Buck 94-751 ENR
* The Northern Right Whale, M. Lynne Corn 95-493 ENR
* Reintroduction of Wolves, Jennifer A. Heck 92-524 ENR
* The Steel Jaw Leghold Trap: Issues and Concerns, M. Lynne Corn 93-356 ENR
* Wildlife Restoration Projects Fund, Louis Alan Talley 95-1097 E

Antarctica
* Antarctica: Environmental Protection, Research and Conservation of Resources, James E. Mielke and Marjorie Ann Browne 95-476 SPR

Antitrust
* see Business

Appropriations
* see Budgets -- Process

Arctic National Wildlife Refuge
* Arctic Oil, Arctic Refuge; Videoprogram, M. Lynne Corn VT91-1489

Armenia
* see also U.S.S.R.
* Armenia-Azerbaijan Conflict: Issue Brief, Carol Migdalovitz, IB92109
* Armenia: Basic Facts, Carol Migdalovitz 95-245F

Arms Control
* see Defense Policy -- Nonproliferation

Arms Control and Disarmament Agency
* Arms Control and Disarmament Agency: Background and Current Issues, Steven A. Hildreth 95-692 F

Arms Sales and Transfers
* see Foreign Aid

Arts
* see Humanities

Asia
* see Central Asia, East Asia, South Asia

Asia Pacific Economic Cooperation (Organization)
* APEC-Asia Pacific Economic Cooperation: Free Trade and Other Issues, Dick Nanto 93-926 E
* Asia-Pacific Economic Cooperation (APEC) and the Indonesia "Summit" in 1994, Dick Nanto 94-242 E

Astronautics
* see Space Activities

Asylum
* see Immigration

Atomic Energy
* see Energy -- Nuclear

Atomic Weapons
* see Weapons Systems-- Nuclear Weapons

Australia
* see Oceania

Authorization
* see Budgets -- Process

Autism
* see Disabled

Azerbaijan
* see also Central Asia
* Armenia-Azerbaijan Conflict: Issue Brief, Carol Migdalovitz, IB92109
* Azerbaijan: Basic Facts, Keith Berner 95-337 F

Balanced Budgets
* see Budgets -- Deficits

Balkans
* see Bosnia-Hercegovina, Croatia, Macedonia (Skopje), Slovenia

Baltic States
* see also Europe, Individual Countries
* The Baltic Republics: U.S. Policy Concerns; Issue Brief, Vita Bite IB90075

Bangladesh
* see also South Asia
* Bangladesh: Background and U.S. Policy Interests, Barbara L. LePoer 94-684 F

Banking
* see Finance -- Banks, International Finance -- Banks

Bankruptcy
* see Business

Be patient. If any phone number is incorrect, call (area code) 555-1212 and request the new listing.

Base Closings

* see Defense Policies -- Bases

Bayh-Dole Act

* see Patent and Trademarks Act

Belarus

* see also Europe
* Belarus: Basic Facts, Steven Woehrel 95-776 F

Biotechnology

* see Medicine -- Drugs, Technology

Birth Control

* see Abortion, Medicine

Blacks

* see Minorities -- Blacks

Block Grants

* see State and Local Government

Board of Governors of the Federal Reserve System (U.S.)

* see also Finance
* Audits of the Federal Reserve System: Past, Present and Proposed, Pauline Smale 94-784 E
* Board of Governors of the Federal Reserve System: History, Membership, and Current Issues, Pauline H. Smale, 95-292 E
* Changing the Monetary Policy Goals under the Full Employment Act, Thomas Woodward 95-168 E
* Depository Institution Regulatory Agencies: Restructuring Proposals, F. Jean Well, 93-315 E
* Federal Reserve Accountability and Independence: Recent Legislation and Oversight, F. Jean Wells 95-12 A
* Federal Reserve Independence, William Jackson, 93-557 E
* Federal Reserve Interest Rate, Bank Interest Rate, and Bank Profitability Relationships in the Recent Financial Cycle, William Jackson 94-587 E
* Federal Interest Rate Changes, 1994-1995, G. Thomas Woodward 95-781 E
* Federal Reserve Interest Rate Increases, 1994-1995, G. Thomas Woodward 95-241 E
* Federal Reserve System; Info Pack IP105F
* Redefining the Federal Reserve's Monetary Policy Mandate, G. Thomas Woodward 95-394 E

Bolivia

* see also Latin America
* Bolivia: Briefing Paper, Nina M. Serafino 95-680 F

Bosnia-Hercegovina

* see also Europe -- Conflicts
* The Balkans--U.S. and International Policy Options: Summary of a CRS Seminar, Julie Kim, 93-696 F
* Bosnia & Macedonia: U.S. Military Operations; Issue Brief, Steven Bowman, IB93056
* Bosnia-Former Yugoslavia: Civil War in the Balkans; Info Pack IP466B
* Bosnia-Former Yugoslavia: Ongoing Conflict and U.S. Policy: Issue Brief, Steven J. Woehrel IB91089
* Bosnia-Hercegovina and Former Yugoslavia: Policy Issues and Options, Steven Woehrel 95-777 F
* Bosnia-Hercegovina Conflict and the 103rd Congress: Policy Debates and Summary of Major Legislation, Julie Kim and Dianne Rennack 94-1008 F
* Bosnia-Hercegovina Conflict: Chronology of Events in the Former Yugoslavia, June 1, 1993-May 31, 1994, Julie Kim and Steve Woehrel 94-522 F
* Bosnia-Hercegovina Federation: One Year of Muslim-Croat Cooperation, Julie Kim 95-496 F
* Bosnia: U.S. Objectives, Military Options, Serbian Responses, Mark M. Lowenthal, 93-408 S
* Bosnian Brierpatch: Military Options, Mid-1995, John M. Collins 95-732 S
* NATO Beyond Bosnia, Stanley R. Sloan 94-977 S
* War Crimes in the Former Yugoslavia: Selected References, Valentin Leskovsek 94-762 L

Bracero Program

* Immigration: The Labor Market Effects of Temporary Alien Farm Worker Program, Linda Levine 95-712 E

Brady Handgun Violence Prevention Act

* The Brady Handgun Control Act: Constitutional Issues, Dorothy Schrader 94-885 S
* Brady Handgun Violence Prevention Act, Harry L. Hogan and Keith Bea 94-14 GOV

Branch Davidians (Cult)

* Branch Davidian Siege at Ranch Apocalypse Near Waco, Texas: A Chronology, Suzanne Cavanagh 95-582 GOV

Breast Cancer

* see Women

Breast Implants

* see Women

Btu Tax

* see Taxation -- Consumption Taxes

Budget and Government Spending

* see Budgets, Defense Economics, Economic Policy, State and Local Government, Taxation

Budget Deficits

* see Budgets -- Deficits

Budget Process

* see Budgets -- Process

Budgets

* Budgets and Economic Policy: Which Direction in 1993; Videoprogram, William Cox and Donald Kiefer VT93-1307
* Budget for Fiscal Year 1995: An Overview; Info Pack IP483B
* The Budget for Fiscal Year 1995: Issue Brief, Philip Winters IB94012
* Budget for Fiscal Year 1996: Info Pack, IP502B
* The Budget for Fiscal Year 1996: Issue Brief, Phillip Winters IB95056
* The Economic and Budget Outlook; Videoprogram, Gail Makinen and Philip Winters VT95-1311
* The Federal Budget: Components and Trends (FY 1992); Videoprogram, VT93-1301
* Federal Budget Issues: A Checklist of CRS Products 95-552 L
* The Federal Money Trail: Data Sources on Federal Aid, Grants, Loans, Procurement in States and Local Areas, James R. Riehl 95-637 C
* The Grace Commission, Gary Galemore 93-741 GOV
* The Relative Size of the Public Sector in Selected Nations: Fact Sheet, Gregg A. Esenwein 95-801 E
* The U.S. Fiscal Position: A Comparison With Selected Industrial Nations, Gregg A. Esenwein 94-558 E

Budgets -- Deficits

* The "A to Z Spending Reduction Plan": A Brief Summary and Assessment, Edward Davis 94-454 GOV
* A Balanced Budget Constitutional Amendment: Background and Congressional Options, James V. Saturno 95-48 GOV
* A Balanced Budget Constitutional Amendment: Economic Issues, William A. Cox, etc. 94-76 S
* Balanced Budget Constitutional Amendment; Videoprogram, William Cox, etc. VT94-1311
* Balanced Budget Issues: Info Pack IP463B
* A Balanced Federal Budget: Major Statutory Provisions, Robert Keith and Edward Davis 95-69 GOV
* The Debt Limit, Issue Brief IB93054
* Debt Management: An Overview of Concepts and Policy Options, James Bickley 94-569 E
* The Debt, the Deficit, and the Means of Financing, Philip D. Winters 94-1004 E
* Deficit Reduction and Federal Debt: Background and Statistics; Info Pack IP488D
* The Deficit Reduction Fund, Philip D. Winters 94-292 E
* Economic Principles for Deficit Reduction: Audio Brief, William Cox, etc. AB50318
* The Macroeconomic Effects of Deficit Reduction, Brian W. Cashell 95-66 E
* Major Deficit Reduction Measurements Enacted in Recent Years, David Koitz and

Current Events and Homework

Michele Harlan 94-719 EPW
* Measuring the Federal Budget Deficit, Brian W. Cashell 94-637 E
* Public Debt Reduction Fund, Louis Allan Talley 94-482 E
* Reducing the Deficit: Economic Principles, Bill Cox, etc. VT95-1324
* Value-Added Tax as a New Revenue Source: Issue Brief, James M. Bickley IB91078
* Will Deficit Reduction Stimulate the Economy?, Thomas Woodward 93-802 E

Budgets -- Process
* Annual Appropriations Measures and Rescission Measures Considered in 1995: Issue Brief, Sandy Streeter IB950404
* Appropriations Procedures in Congress, Stanley Bach 94-1009 S
* The Authorization/Appropriation Process; Videoprogram, Walter Kravitz VT91-875
* Budget Enforcement Procedures: Application to Social Security Revenues and Spending, Edward Davis and Robert Keith, 95-255 GOV
* Budget for FY 1996: Congressional Budget Resolutions, Philip Winters 95-744 E
* Budget Process Changes Adopted in August 1993, Edward Davis and Robert Keith 93-778 GOV
* Budget Process Changes in the House-Passed Reconciliation Act of 1993, Robert Keith and Edward Davis 93-583 GOV
* Budget Process Changes Made in the Rules of the House in January 1995 (H. Res.), Robert Keith 95-432 GOV
* Budget Process Changes Made in the 102nd-103rd Congresses (1991-1994), Robert Keith and Edward Davis 95-457 GOV
* Budget Process: Info Pack IP012B
* Continuing Appropriation Acts: Summary Data for Fiscal Years 1977-1995, Edward Davis and Robert Keith 95-78 GOV
* Continuing Resolutions and Funding Gaps: Fiscal Years 1981-1995, Robert Keith and Edward Davis 95-77 GOV
* Dynamic Revenue Estimating, Jane Gravelle, 94-1000 S
* Economic Forecasts and the Budget, Brian W. Cashell 95-222 E
* Fiscal Responsibility; Videoprogram, Louis Fisher and Bob Keith VT95-1302
* The House Appropriations Process, 1789-1993, Louis Fisher 93-729 S
* Impoundment Reform Proposals; Issue Brief, Virginia McMurtry IB89148
* Item Veto: Bibliography-in-Brief, Tangela G. Roe 95-393 L
* Legislative Line Item Veto Bills: Comparing S. 4 and S. 14 (as Reported), Louis Fisher, etc. 95-273 S
* Line Item Veto: Info Pack IP287L
* Manual on the Federal Budget Process, Allen Schick, etc. 91-902 GOV
* Measuring Budgetary Change, Philip Winters 94-568 E
* Omnibus Budget Reconciliation Legislation: The Timing of Legislative Action, Robert Keith, etc. 94-955 GOV
* Point of Order in the Congressional Budget Process, Edward Davis 94-874 GOV
* The President's Budget: Dates of Submission of the Mid-Session Review (FY 1980-1995), Robert Keith 95-349 GOV
* Proposed and Actual Budget Totals for the Fiscal Years 1980 Through 1994, Philip D. Winters 95-67 E
* Proposed Changes in the Discretionary Spending Limits and the Pay-as-You-Go Process, Edward Davis and Robert Keith 95-436 GOV
* The Senate's "Byrd Rule" Against Extraneous Matter in Reconciliation Measures, Robert Keith and Edward Davis 95-362 GOV
* The Senate's Byrd Rule Against Extraneous matter in Reconciliation Measures: A Fact Sheet, Robert Keith and Edward Davis 95-707 GOV

Budgets -- Programs
* Access to Student Loans and the Senate Proposal for Restructuring under H.R. 2264, Dennis Zimmerman and Barbara Miles 93-660 E
* Administration FY 1995 Budget Proposals for Assisted Housing, Grace Milgram 94-131 E
* Agriculture and the FY 1996 Budget: Issue Brief, Ralph M. Chite IB95031
* Amtrak and the 104th Congress: Issue Brief, Stephen J. Thompson IB95081
* Appropriations for FY 1996: Agriculture, Ralph M. Chite 95-624 ENR
* Appropriations for FY 1996: Defense, Stephen Daggett, 95-622 F
* Appropriations for FY 1996: Departments of Commerce, Justice and State, the Judiciary, and Related Agencies, Edward Knight 95-632 E
* Appropriations for FY 1996: District of Colombia, Suzanne Cavanagh and Nonna A. Noto 95-628 GOV
* Appropriations for FY 1996: Energy and Water, Carl E. Behrens and Marc Humphries, 95-625 ENR
* Appropriations for FY 1996: Foreign Operations, Larry Nowels 95-623 ENR
Appropriations for FY 1996: Interior, Alfred Greenwood 95-629 ENR
* Appropriations for FY 1996: Labor, Health and Human Services, and Education, Paul M. Irwin 95-633 EPW
* Appropriations for FY 1996: Legislative Branch, Paul Dwyer 95-626 GOV
* Appropriations for FY 1996: Military Construction, George H. Siehl 95-621 F
* Appropriations for FY 1996: Overview, Michael Anderson 95-620 C

* Appropriations for FY 1996: Transportation, John W. Fischer 95-627 E
* Appropriations for FY 1996: Treasury, Postal Service, Executive Office of the President, and General Government, Sylvia Morrison 95-630 E
* Appropriations for FY 1996: VA, HUD, and Independent Agencies, Susan Vanhorenbeck 95-631 E
* Appropriations for Selected Health Programs, FY 1980-FY 1993, Edward R. Klebe 93-125 EPW
* Appropriations Measures and Amounts: Summary Tables, Sandy Streeter and Matthew Ginsburg 95-920 GOV
* Authority to Tap Trust Funds and Establish Payment Priorities If the Debt Limit is Not Increased, Thomas Nicola and Morton Rosenberg 95-1109 A
* Budget for FY 1996: Fact Sheet on the House and Senate Budget Committees' Resolutions, Philip D. Winters 95-585 E
* Budget Reconciliation FY 1996: CRS Products and Resources, Janet Kline 95-967 EPW
* Child Nutrition: Program Information, Data, and Analysis, Jean Yavis Jones 93-165 EPW
* Continuing Appropriations Acts: Brief Overview of Recent Practices, Edward Davis 95-992 GOV
* Continuing Resolutions and Funding Gaps: Selected Data for Fiscal Years 1977-1995, Robert Keith and Edward Davis 95-995 GOV
* Corporation for National and Community Service Programs: A Summary, Dale H. Robinson 95-278 EPW
* Debt Limit Increases, 1980-1995, Philip D. Winters 95-825 E
* The Deficit Reduction Lock-Box Act of 1995 (H.R. 1162): Fact Sheet, Robert Keith 95-951 GOV
* Department of Education Funding FY 1995 and FY 1996, Paul M. Irwin 95-331 EPW
* The Department of Energy's FY 1996 Budget: Issue Brief, Marc Humphries IB95043
* Economic Development Administration: Reinventing or Elimination; Issue Brief IB95100
* The Economic Effects of a Large Federal Debt, Brian W. Cashell 95-996 E
* Energy Efficiency: A New National Outlook? Issue Brief IB95085
* Entitlement Caps, Jim Cornelius 95-719 EPW
* Entitlements and Other Mandatory Spending, Kenneth Cahill and Michele Harlan 94-348 EPW
* Entitlements and the Budget; Videoprogram, Richard Rimkunas and David Koitz VT95-1313
* Environmental Protection Agency: FY 1995 Budget; Issue Brief, Martin R. Lee IB94013
* Environmental Protection Agency: FY 1996 Budget; Issue Brief, Martin R. Lee IB95048
* Federal Budget Chronology: Fiscal Year 1996, J. Michael Anderson 95-584 C
* Federal Budget Issues: A Checklist of CRS Products, 95-552 L
* Federal Employees and the FY 1995 Budget; Issue Brief, James P. McGrath IB94031
* Federal Employees and the FY 1996 Budget: Issue Brief, James P. McGrath IB95033
* Federal Land Sales: Possible Revenues, Ross Gorte 95-345 ENR
* Federal Programs that Could Financially Benefit Business Enterprises, Edward Knight and Vivian Catherine Jones 95-535 E
* Food and Farm Support under USDA's Section 32 Fund, Geoffrey S. Becker 94-655 ENR
* Foreign Aid Budget and Policy Issues for the 104th Congress: Issue Brief, Larry Nowels IB950202
* Foreign Food Assistance: PL 480 Budget Facts, Susan P. Epstein 94-204 F
* Foreign Policy Budget: A Checklist of CRS Products, Sherry B. Shapiro 95-551 L
* Foreign Policy Rescissions and Supplemental Appropriations for FY 1995, Larry Knowels IB95041
* The FY 1995 HUD Budget: Disposition of Multifamily Properties, Bruce B. Foote 94-250 E
* Housing Appropriations for FY 1995: Proposed Rescissions; Issue Brief, Bruce E. Foote IB95079
* HUD Appropriations for FY 1995: Proposed Rescissions, Bruce Foote 95-354 E
* The HUD Budget for FY 1995: Housing for Special Needs Persons, Susan Vanhorenbeck 94-130 E
* Immigration and Naturalization Service Funding and the Administration's FY 1996 Immigration Initiative, William J. Krouse 95-478 EPW
* Intelligence Spending: Should Total Amounts Be Made Public?, Elizabeth Bazan, etc. 94-261 E
* Investment of the Social Security Trust Funds: A Fact Sheet, Geoffrey Kollmann 93-886 EPW
* The Largest Entitlement Programs, Kenneth Cahill 93-410 EPW
* Legislative Branch Budget Authority, FY 1968-FY 1995, Paul Dwyer, etc. 95-762 GOV

* Legislative Line Item Veto Bills in the 104th Congress: Comparing H.R. 2 (As Passed by the House) and S. 4 (As Passed by the Senate), Louis Fisher 95-273 S
* Magnuson Fishery Conservation and Management Act Reauthorization: Issue Brief, Eugene Buck IB95036
* Mandatory Spending in President Clinton's FY 1996 Budget Proposal: A Fact Sheet, Dawn Nuschler and Richard Rimkunas IB95036
* Medicaid Reform and FY 1996 Budget: Issue Brief, Melvina Ford IB95099
* Medicaid: 1995 Budget, Melvina Ford 94-210 EPW
* Medicaid and the Budget Process: A Fact Sheet, James R. Storey 95-694 EPW
* Migrant Education: Fact Sheet on FY 1996 Budget Proposals, Bob Lyke 95-280 EPW
* The National Aeronautics and Space Administration: An Overview With FY 1995 and FY 1996 Budget Summaries, David P. Radzanowski and Stephen J. Garber 95-336 SPR
* National Aeronautics and Space Administration's (NASA) Fiscal Year 1995 Budget Request, David P. Radzanowski 94-280 SPR
* Older Americans Act FY 1995 Budget: Fact Sheet, Molly Forman, etc. 94-607 EPW
* Older Americans Act: 104th Congress Issues, Carol O'Shaughnessy 95-32 EPW
* President Clinton's Federal "Investment" Proposals; Videoprogram, William Cox, etc. VT94-1332
* Proposed Changes in the Discretionary Spending Limits and the Pay-As-You-Go Process, Edward Davis and Robert Keith 95-436 GOV
* Recent Federal Outlays (FY 1990-1994) by Department and Agency and Function, Philip Winters 95-132 E
* Research and Development Funding: Fiscal Year 1996; Issue Brief, Michael E. Davey IB95037
* The Rural Electrification Administration: Background and Current Issues, Carl Ek and Amy Abel 91-614 ENR
* SBA's Disaster Loan Program: Consolidated Loss Rate and Subsidy Cost Rate, James Bickley 94-800 E
* Social Security: Its Removal from the Budget and Procedures for Considering Changes to the Program, David Koitz 95-206 EPW
* Social Welfare Mandatory and Discretionary Spending in the Fiscal Year 1996 Budget: A Fact Sheet, Dawn Nuschler 95-303 EPW
* Social Welfare Spending in Fiscal Year 1994: A Fact Sheet, Dawn Nuschler 94-864 EPW
* Social Welfare Spending in President Clinton's 1994 Budget Proposal, Gene Falk, etc. 93-397 EPW
* Social Welfare Spending in the Fiscal Year 1996 Budget: A Fact Sheet, Dawn Nuschler and Richard Rimkunas 95-251 EPW
* Social Welfare Spending in the FY 1995 Recession/Supplemental Appropriations Bill Conference Agreement: A Fact Sheet, Dawn Nuschler 95-619 EPW
* Social Welfare Spending in the FY 1995 Rescission/Supplemental Package: A Fact Sheet, Dawn Nuschler 95-619 EPW
* Social Welfare Spending in the FY 1995 Rescission/Supplemental Package: A Fact Sheet, Dawn Nuschler 95-330 EPW
* Social Welfare Spending in the FY 1996 Budget Resolution Conference Agreement, Dawn Nuschler and Richard Rimkunas 95-814 EPW
* Social Welfare Spending in the Senate's FY 1995 Rescission/Supplemental Appropriations Bill: A Fact Sheet, Dawn Nuschler 95-456 EPW
* Social Welfare Spending Targets in the House Budget Resolution , Dawn Nuschler, etc. 95-586 EPW
* Social Welfare Spending Targets in the Senate Budget Resolution, Dawn Nuschler and Richard Rimkunas 95-587 EPW
* Transportation Trust Funds: The Off-Budget Debate; Issue Brief, John F. Fischer IB95038
* Vetoes of Legislative Branch Appropriations, Gary L. Galemore 95-847 GOV
* Violent Crime Control Act of 1994: Crime Prevention Funding With FY 1995 Appropriations, David Teasley 94-878 GOV
* 1995 Budget Perspectives: Federal Spending for Social Welfare Programs, Gene Falk, etc. 94-216 EPW

Bulgaria
* see also Europe
* Romania, Bulgaria, Albania: Recent Developments; Issue Brief, Sergiu Verona, IB92064

Burma
* see also East Asia
* Burma: Briefing Paper, Larry Niksch 94-725 F

Burundi
* see also Africa (Sub-Saharan)
* Burundi Crisis, Theodros Dagne 95-458 F

Business
* A Bankruptcy Primer: Liquidation and Reorganization Under the U.S. Bankruptcy Code, Robin Jewler 95-302 A
* Brownfields Program: Cleaning Up Urban Industrial Sites, Mark Reisch 95-454 ENR
* Business: Doing Business With the Federal Government; Info Pack IP305B
* Comparison of Some Antitrust Provisions, Janice E. Rubin 94-212 A
* Corporate Executive Pay: Capping the Tax Deduction, Gerald Mayer 95-653 E
* Discriminatory Pricing and the Robinson Patman Act: An Overview; Some Exceptions, Janice E. Rubin 94-726 A
* Employee Stock Ownership Plans: Background and Policy Issues, Gerald Mayer 94-421 E
* Federal Government Corporations in Perspective, Ronald C. Moe 95-703 GOV
* Federal Regulation: Issue in Balancing Costs and Benefits: A Checklist of CRS Products, Felix Chin 95-141 L
* Federal Regulatory Reform: An Overview; Issue Brief, Roger Garcia IB95035
* General Overview of the United States Antitrust Law, Janice Rubin 95-116 A
* Japan-U.S. 1995 Automotive Dispute: Impact of 100 Percent Tariffs on Automobile Dealers by State, Penelope Fay Heavener 95-718 C
* The Largest Corporations in the United States: Information and Addresses from the Forbes 500, Felicia G. Kolp 95-716 C
* Manufacturing, Technology, and Competitiveness: Issue Brief, Wendy Schacht IB92025
* Minority and Women Owned Business Programs of the Federal Government, Mark Eddy 95-757 GOV
* Privatization: Meanings, Rationale, and Limits, Ronald C. Moe 95-522 GOV
* Steel Imports from Russia and Their Implications for Steel Markets, David J. Cantor 95-554 E
* The Supreme Court Decision in Adarand Constructors Inc. v. Pena: Federal Contracting and Disadvantaged Business Enterprises, Charles V. Dale 95-137 A
* Taxation of Mail Order Sales: A Fact Sheet, Arnold Solomon 95-655 C
* United States Regulations: Finding Regulatory Material, Mark Gurevitz 90-590 A

Business -- Small Business
* Defense Economic Conversion: Adjustment Assistance for Small Business, Bruce K. Mulock 93-423 E
* Federal Taxation of Small Business: A Brief Summary, David Brumbaugh 94-328 E
* Health Care Reform: An Employer Mandate and Small Business, Gerald Mayer 94-888 EPW
* H.R. 1215 and the Expensing Allowance for Smaller Businesses, Gerald Mayer 95-528 E
* Impact of the Omnibus Budget Reconciliation Act of 1993 on Small Businesses, Gerald Mayer 94-44 E
* The National Employee Savings Trust (NEST) Proposal, Ray Schmitt 95-803 EPW
* SBA's Disaster Loan Program: Consolidated Loss Rate and Subsidy Cost rate, James M. Bickley 94-800 E
* Secondary Market for Small Business Loans, Mark Jickling 93-758 E
* Small Business Administration: A Fact Sheet, Bruce K. Mulock 95-652 E
* Small Business and Job Creation, Bruce K. Mulock 95-284 E
* Small Business and the Stock Market, Mark Jickling, 94-366 E
* Small Business Assistance Programs; Sources of Information; Info Pack IP422S
* Small Business: Definitions and Demographics, Bruce K. Mulock 94-327 E
* Small Business: Definitions and Demographics: An issue Overview, Bruce K. Mulock 94-420 E
* Small Business Tax Subsidy Proposals, Jane G. Gravelle 93-316 S

Business, Industry and Consumer Affairs
* see Business, Consumers, Finance, Technology, Telecommunication

Byrne Programs
* see Criminal Justice

Cable Television
* see Telecommunication -- Television

Cambodia
* see also South Asia
* Cambodia: Peace Agreement, Elections and Beyond; Issue Brief, Robert G. Sutter IB93048

Campaign Funds
* see Congress -- Apportionment and Elections, Elections -- Finance

Canada
* Canada: Briefing Paper, Carl Ek 94-640 F

Be patient. If any phone number is incorrect, call (area code) 555-1212 and request the new listing.

1299

Current Events and Homework

* The Canadian Health Care System in 1993, Joan Sokolovsky 93-910 EPW
* Capital Gains and Securities Transactions Taxation in Canada: Fact Sheet, Gregg A. Esenwein and Philip D. Winters 94-832 E
* Immigration and Naturalization Laws: A Nine Country Comparison, Ruth Ellen Wasem, etc. 93-755 EPW
* The Quebec Sovereignty Question, Carl Ek and Stephen F. Clarke 94-886 F
* U.S.-Canadian Agricultural Trade Disputes, Carl Ek and Charles Hanrahan 94-270 F

Cancer
* see Medicine, Women

Capital Gains Tax
* see Taxation -- Capital Gains

Capital Punishment
* see Criminal Justice -- Capital Punishment

Caribbean Area
* see also Latin America
* Caribbean Basin Countries: Implications of a North American Free Trade Agreement, Lenore M. Sek and Mark P. Sullivan 93-551 E
* Caribbean-U.S. Relations: Issues for Congress; Issue Brief, Mark P. Sullivan, IB92047

Carl D. Perkins Vocational and Applied Technology Education Act
* Carl D. Perkins Vocational and Applied Technology Education Act: Reauthorization Overview, Paul M. Irwin and Richard N. Apling 94-427 EPW
* Vocational Education and Special Populations, Richard N. Apling and Sylvie Moulan 94-940 EPW
* Vocational Education Program Trends, Richard N. Apling 95-11 EPW

Census of Population and Housing
* see also Government Information
* House Apportionment Following the 2000 Census: Preliminary Projections, David C. Huckabee 95-104 GOV

Central America
* see Latin America

Central Asia
* see also East Asia, Europe, Russia, South Asia
* Armenia-Azerbaijan Conflict: Issue Brief, Carol Migdalovitz IB92109
* Armenia: Basic Facts, Carol Migdalovitz 95-245 F
* Azerbaijan: Basic Facts, Jim Nichol 95-337 F
* Central Asia's New States: Political Developments and Implications for U.S.; Issue Brief, Jim Nichol IB93108
* Georgia (Republic): Basic Facts, Jim Nichol 94-608 F
* Kazakhstan: Basic Facts, Jim Nichol 95-497 F
* Kyrgyzstan: Basic Facts, Jim Nichol 95-613 F
* Tajikistan: Basic Facts, Kenneth Katzman 94-697 F
* Transcaucasus Newly Independent States: Political Development and Implications: Jim Nichol IB95024
* Turkmenistan: Basic Facts, Jim Nichol 95-609 F
* Uzbekistan: Basic Facts, Jim Nichol 95-520 F

Chechnya
* Beyond Chechnya: Some Options for Russia & the West, John P. Hardt 95-338 S
* Chechnya Confrontation, Jim Nichol 95-79 F
* Russian Conflict in Chechnya and Implications for the United States, Stuart D. Goldman and Jim Nichol 95-207 F

Chemical Warfare
* see Weapons Systems

Chemicals
* see Hazardous Substances

Child Abuse
* see Children

Child Care
* see Children

Child Nutrition
* see Food

Child Support
* see Children

Child Welfare
* see Welfare -- Children

Children
* see also Disabled, Families
* Adolescent Childbearing: Fact Sheet on Trends and Consequences, Ruth Ellen Wasem, 94-983 EPW
* Adoption: Federal Programs and Issues, Dale H. Robinson 91-131 EPW
* Adoption: Parental Rights and Children's Interests, Gina Marie Stevens 94-618 A
* The Child Abuse and Family Violence Acts, as Amended in FY 1992, Dale H. Robinson 93-272 EPW
* Child Abuse: Info Pack IP019 C
* Child Care: A Comparison of House and Senate Legislation, Karen Spar 95-696 EPW
* Child Care in the 104th Congress: An Issue Summary, Karen Spar IB95009
* Child Day Care Centers: A List of Resources for Starting and Operating a Child Day Care Center, Marjorie Washington 04-432 C
* Child Day Care: Info Pack IP306C
* Child Immunization Provisions in the Omnibus Budget Reconciliation Act of 1993, P.L. 103-66, Melvina Ford 93-781 EPW
* Child Labor and Public Policy: Legislative and Administrative Issues; Issue Brief, William G. Whittaker IB94057
* Child Nutrition: Issues in the 104th Congress; Issue Brief, Jean Yavis Jeans IB95047
* Child Nutrition: Program Information, Data, and Analysis, Jean Yavis Jones 93-165 EPW
* Child Pornography: Constitutional Principles and Federal Statutes, Henry Cohen 95-406 A
* Child Support: Changes Enacted or Proposed in the 103rd Congress, Gina M. Stevens, etc. 95-142 A
* The Child Support Enforcement Program: A Fact Sheet, Carmen D. Solomon 93-4 EPW
* The Child Support Enforcement Program: Policy and Practice, Carmen D. Solomon 89-659 EPW
* Child Support Enforcement: Welfare Reform in the 104th Congress, Carmen D. Solomon 95-401 EPW
* Child Welfare, Child Abuse, and Related Issues in the 104th Congress; Issue Brief, Karen Spar, etc. IB95029
* Child Welfare Programs: A Fact Sheet, Karen Spar 94-950 EPW
* Children's Rights: United Nations Convention on the Rights of the Child; Info Pack IP493C
* Children's Social Service Issues in the 104th Congress, Dale Robinson 95-97 EPW
* Convention on the Rights of the Child: A Fact Sheet, Vita Bite 95-304 F
* Federal Child Care Programs: Background and FY 1995 Budget Information, Anne C. Stewart 94-172 EPW
* Federal Programs for Children and Their Families, Dale Robinson 93-59 EPW
* Federal Programs for Children and Their Families: An Overview, Dale Robinson 93-221 EPW
* "Kinship" Foster Care: An Emerging Federal Issue, Karen Spar 93-856 EPW
* The Knox "Clothed Children" Child Pornography Case and the Congressional response, Henry Cohen 94-753 A
* Legislation on Protection of Pupil or Family Rights in Federally Assisted Programs, Wayne Riddle and Richard N. Apling 95-76 EPW
* Medicaid: Maternal and Child Health, Melvina Ford 93-700 EPW
* Orphanages: A New Issue in Welfare Reform, Karen Spar 94-986 EPW
* Sudden Infant Death Syndrome (SIDS): Risk Factors and Federal Research Funding Levels, Edith Cooper 95-315 SPR
* Television Violence: A Survey of Selected Social Science Research Linking Violent Program Viewing Program Viewing With Aggression in Children and Society, Edith Cooper, 95-593 SPR
* Television Violence: Info Pack IP476T
* Violence on Television: What Can Technology Do?, Science Policy Research Division 93-710 SPR
* Welfare Reform: Adolescent Pregnancy Issues, Ruth Allen Wasem 94-591 EPW
* Welfare Reform and Child Support; Videoprogram, Vee Burke, etc. VT93-1324
* Welfare, Work and Child Support: Effects on Single Parent Families, Thomas Gabe 93-504 EPW
* Youth Development: Legislative Issues Fact Sheet, Ruth Ellen Wasem, 95-994 EPW

Be patient. If any phone number is incorrect, call (area code) 555-1212 and request the new listing.

Chile
* Chile: Briefing Paper, Mark P. Sullivan 94-813 F
* Chile-United States Free Trade Agreement?, Raymond J. Ahearn and Nina M. Serafino, 92-423 F
* Chilean Trade and Economic Reform: Implications for NAFTA Accession, J.F. Hornbeck 95-751 E

China
* see also East Asia, Hong Kong, Taiwan
* China After Deng Xiaoping -- Implications for the United States, Robert G. Sutter 95-465 S
* China as a Security Concern in Asia: Perceptions, Assessment and U.S. Options, Robert G. Sutter and Shirley Kan 95-46 S
* China in Transition: Changing Conditions and Implications for U.S. Interests, Robert G. Sutter, etc, 93-1061 S
* China's Changing Conditions: Issue Brief, Robert G. Sutter IB93114

China -- Foreign Relations
* China in World Affairs--U.S. Policy Choices, Robert G. Sutter, 95-265 S
* China Policy: Managing U.S.-PRC-Taiwan Relations After President Lee's Visit to the U.S., Robert Sutter 95-727 S
* China-U.S. Relations in a Post-Cold War World: Info Pack IP460C
* China-U.S. Relations: Issue Brief, Robert G. Sutter and Kerry Dumbaugh IB94002
* China's Sinister View of U.S. Policy: Origins, Implications and Options, Robert Sutter 95-750 S
* Chinese Missile and Nuclear Proliferation: Issues for Congress; Issue Brief, Shirley A. Kan and Robert Shuey IB92056
* Chinese Nuclear Weapons and Arms Control Policies: Implications and Options for the United States, Robert G. Sutter 94-422 S
* The Hong Kong Crisis of 1993-Origins, Competing Priorities, and Outcomes., Robert G. Sutter 93-455 S

China -- Trade
* China and the General Agreement on Tariffs and Trade, George D. Holliday 94-723 E
* China: Current U.S. Sanctions, Kerry Dumbaugh 94-92 F
* The China-U.S. Trade Agreement on Intellectual Property Rights: Implications for China-U.S. Trade Relations, Wayne M. Morrison 95-463 E
* China-U.S. Trade Issues: Issue Brief, Wayne Morrison IB91121
* China U.S. Trade, MFN Status, and Economic Relations: Info Pack IP489C
* China's MFN Status: Implications of the 1994 Decision, Kerry Dumbaugh 94-531 F
* Granting Most-Favored-Nation Status to China as a Market Economy Country, Vladimir N. Pregelj 94-514 E
* Most-Favored Nation Status of the People's Republic of China: Issue Brief, Vladimir N. Pregelj IB92094
* U.S. Commercial Relations With Japan and China; Videoprogram, Dick Nanto VT94-1309

Church-State Issues
* see Religion

Citizen Militias
* see Criminal Justice

Civil Liberties
* see also Civil Rights
* AIDS Discrimination: The Federal Response, Maek Eddy 94-818 GOV
* The Communications Decency Act of 1995, Henry Cohen 95-510 A
* The Constitutional and Statutory Rights to Health Care, Kathleen Swendiman 94-64 A
* Freedom of Speech and Press: Exceptions to the First Amendment, Henry Cohen 94-654 A
* Homosexual Rights: Bibliography-in-Brief, 1993-1994, Jean M. Bowers 94-742 L
* Homosexuals and U.S. Military Personnel Policy, David Burrelli 93-52 F
* Legislation on Protection of Pupil or Family Rights in Federally Assisted Programs, Wayne Riddle and Richard N. Appling 95-76 EPW
* Obscenity: Constitutional Principles and Federal Statutes, Henry Cohen 95-804 A
* The Religious Freedom Restoration Act, David M. Ackerman 94-15 A
* RICO and Political Protest: The Implication of NOW v. Scheidler, Kenneth R. Thomas 94-108 A
* Supreme Court: Church and State Cases, 1994-95 Term; Issue Brief, David M. Ackerman IB95015
* Supreme Court Decisions Interpreting Section 504 of the Rehabilitation Act of 1973, Nancy Lee Jones 95-70 A

* The Voting Rights Act of 1995, as Amended: Its History and Current Issues, Garrine P. Laney 95-896 GOV
* Wiretapping & Electronic Surveillance: The Electronic Communications Privacy Act and Related Matters, Charles Doyle 92-959 A

Civil Liberties and Rights -- Privacy
* see Civil Liberties, Civil Rights, Minorities, Women

Civil Rico
* see Criminal Justice

Civil Rights
* see also Aged, Civil Liberties, Criminal Justice, Disabled, Minorities, Religion, Women
* Affirmative Action and Equal Employment Opportunity: Info Pack IP424A
* Affirmative Action Employment, Andorra Bruno 95-165 GOV
* The Americans With Disabilities Act (ADA): Implementation Issues, Nancy Lee Jones 93-815 A
* The American with Disabilities Act: Info Pack IP443A
* The Civil Rights Act of 1991: A Legal History and Analysis, Charles V. Dale 92-85 A
* Civil Rights Protection in the United States: Brief Summaries of Constitutional Amendments, Federal Law and Executive Orders, Leslie Gladstone 93-148 GOV
* Sexual Harassment in the Workplace: Selected References, 1991-1993, Jean M. Bowers 94-121 L

Civil Rights Acts
* see Civil Rights

Civil Service
* see Pensions -- Government

Civil Service Retirement System
* see Pensions -- Government

Clean Air Act
* see also Air Pollution
* Air Pollution--Clean Air Act: Info Pack IP008A
* Air Quality: Impacts of Trip Reduction Programs on States and Affected Employers, Maura K. Flechtner, 93-745 ENR
* Air Quality: State Plans and Sanctions, Susan L. Mayer 93-1062 ENR
* Alternative Fuels and Reformulated Gasoline; Issue Brief, David Gushee IB91008
* CFC Phaseout: Future Problem for Air Conditioning Equipment?, David E. Gushee, 93-382 S
* Clean Air Act Issues for the 104th Congress: Issue Brief, Susan L. Mayer IB95034
* Environmental Protection Legislation in the 103rd Congress: Issue Brief, Environment and Natural Resources Policy Division, IB93007
* EPA's Implementation of the Clean Air Act Amendments of 1990: The First Two Years, Susan L. Mayer, 93-268 ENR
* Ethanol and Clean Air: The "Reg-Neg" Controversy and Subsequent Events, Migdon Segal, 93-614 SPR
* Implementing Acid Rain Legislation: Issue Brief, Larry Parker IB91035
* Implementing the Clean Air Act Amendments of 1990: Where Are We Now?, Susan Mayer 95-234 ENR

Clean Water Act
* see also Water Pollution
* Clean Water Act Legislation: Summary of S. 1114, Claudia Copeland, 93-626 ENR
* Clean Water Act Reauthorization; Issue Brief, Claudia Copeland IB93013
* Clean Water Act Section 401: Background and Current issues, Claudia Copeland 95-2 ENR
* Clean Water Issues in the 104th Congress, Claudia Copeland 94-825 ENR
* Clean Water Legislation in the 103rd Congress: A Legislative Rollercoaster, Claudia Copeland 94-750 ENR
* Clean Water Summary of H.R. 961, as Passed, Claudia Copeland 95-427 ENR
* Environmental Protection Legislation in the 103rd Congress; Issue Brief, Environment and Natural Resources Policy Division, IB93007
* Implications of Linking Clean Water Spending to the Rate of Inflation, Claudia Copeland 95-216 ENR
* PUD No. 1 of Jefferson County v. Washington Department of Ecology: An Expansive Interpretation of State Authority under the Clean Water Act, Ellen M. Lazarus 94-601 A
* Rural Water Supply and Sewer Systems: Background Information, Claudia Copeland 94-838 ENR
* Stormwater Permits: Status of EPA's Regulatory Program, Claudia Copeland, 94-811 ENR

Be patient. If any phone number is incorrect, call (area code) 555-1212 and request the new listing.

1301

Current Events and Homework

* Toxic Pollutants and the Clean Water Air Act: Current Issues, Claudia Copeland 93-849 ENR
* Wastewater Treatment: Overview and Background, Claudia Copeland 94-822 ENR
* Water Quality: Implementing the Clean Water Act; Issue Brief, Claudia Copeland, IB89102
* Wetlands Protection: Issues in the 104th Congress:, Issue Brief, Jeffrey A. Zinn, etc., IB95028
* Wetlands Legislation: Comparison of Two Bills, Claudia Copeland 95-796 ENR

Climate Change (Global Climate Change)
* see Air Pollution -- Ozone

Clipper Chip
* see also Technology
* The Clipper Chip Encryption, Stephen Gould 94-298 SPR

Colombia
* see also Latin America
* Colombia: Briefing Paper, Nina Serafino 95-588 F

Columbus Day
* Speech Material; Columbus Day; Info Pack IP380C

Commemorations
* see also General Interest
* Commemorative Legislation, Stephen W. Stathis 93-407 GOV
* Flag Desecration and Flag Misuse Laws in the United States, Vastine D. Platte 95-182 A
* Flag Protection: A Brief History and Summary of Recent Supreme Court Decisions and Proposed Constitutional Amendment, 95-709 A
* Speech Material: Abraham Lincoln's and George Washington's Birthdays; Info Pack IP373A
* Speech Material: Columbus Day; Info Pack IP380C
* Speech Material: Fourth of July; Info Pack IP377F
* Speech Material: Graduation; Info Pack IP379S
* Speech Material: Labor Day; Info Pack IP374L
* Speech Material: Martin Luther King, Jr.'s Birthday; Info Pack IP372M
* Speech Material: Memorial Day; Info Pack IP376M
* Speech Material: Thanksgiving Day; Info Pack IP381T
* Speech Material: Veterans Day; Info Pack IP378V

Commodities
* see Agriculture -- Policies and Legislation

Commodity Credit Corporation
Farm Commodity Programs: Financing and Costs, Geoffrey S. Becker, etc. 94-575 ENR
* Farm Commodity Programs: Surplus Management, Geoffrey S. Becker 94-583 ENR
* An Introduction to Farm Commodity Programs, Geoffrey S. Becker, 94-577 ENR

Common Sense Legal Reforms Act
* Common Sense Legal Reforms Act of 1995: Title I--Civil Justice Reform (Attorneys' Fees, Products Liability, Etc.), Henry Cohen 95-27 A
* Legal Reforms Passed by the House: Issue Brief, Henry Cohen, etc. IB95030
* Proposed Reform of Private Securities Litigation: Title II of the Common Sense Legal Reforms Act, Michael V. Seitzinger 95-68 A

Communications
* see also Telecommunication
* Commemorative Postage Stamps: History, Selection Criteria, and Revenue Raising Potential, Bernevia M. McCalip 94-376 E
* English as the Official Language of the United States: An Overview, Steven R. Aleman, etc. 95-1054 EPW
* Federal Appropriations to the U.S. Postal Service: A More Stringent Policy Toward Reduced-Rate Mail, Bernevia McCalip IB95083
* Freedom of Speech and Press: Exceptions to the First Amendment, Henry Cohen 94-654 A
* Legal Analysis of Proposals to Make English the Official Language of the United States Government, Charles V. Dale, etc. 95-1043 A
* Mail Service in the United States: Exploring Options for Improvement, Bernard A. Gelb 95-1105 E
* Multiple Broadcast Ownership Restrictions, Kevin M. Greely 95-852 A

* Postal Rate Increases: The Process and Their Impact on Mail Volume, Bernevia McCalip 94-889 E
* Postal Service's Mail Monopoly: Is It Time for a Change? Issue Brief, Bernevia McCalip IB95083
* Public Broadcasting: Issues in the 104th Congress; Issue Brief, Bernevia McCalip IB95063
* Public Speaking and Speech Writing: Selected References, Jean M. Bowers 94-860 L

Communications Decency Act
* The Communications Decency Act of 1995, Henry Cohen 95-510 A
* The Communications Decency Act of 1995, as Passed by the Senate, Henry Cohen 95-783 A

Communist Countries
* see China, Cuba

Community Development Banking
* see Finance -- Banks

Community Development Block Grant Program (U.S.)
* Community Development Block Grants: An Overview, Eugene Boyd 95-440 GOV

Community Development Block Grants
* see Urban Affairs

Community Reinvestment Act
* The Community Reinvestment Act and the President's Initiative for Reform, Jean Wells 94-520 E
* The Community Reinvestment Act and the President's Initiative for Reform: An Issue Review, F. Jean Wells 94-557 E

Community Services Block Grant
* Community Services Block Grants and Related Programs, Karen Spar 92-779 EPW

Competitiveness
* see Trade

Comprehensive Terrorism Prevention Act
* Comprehensive Terrorism Prevention Act of 1995, S. 735, as Introduced: A Summary, Charles Doyle 95-580 S

Computers
* see Technology -- Computers

Congress
* see also Apportionment and Elections, Budget Process, Executive Relations, Foreign Relations, Legislative Procedure and Operations, Members, Offices, Oversight
* Architect of the Capitol: Appointment, Duties, and Operations, Mildred L. Amer 95-343 GOV
* Casework in a Congressional Office, John S. Pontius 95-1111 GOV
* Census Adjustment: Impact on Reapportionment and Redistricting, David C. Huckabee 94-649 GOV
* Characteristics of Congress, Videoprogram, Walter Kravitz VT91-876
* Commissions and Boards to Which House Party Leaders Appoint Representatives and Private Citizens, Faye M. Bullock 95-836 GOV
* Comparison of Current House Gift Rule to Gift Limitation Proposals, Jack Maskell 95-1104 A
* Congress: An Overview, Walter J. Oleszek, 92-59 S
* Congress in the Public Eye: Media and Public Opinion; Videoprogram, Steven Roberts, etc. VT91-949
* Congress: Info Pack, IP022C
* Congress: Issues for the 104th Congress; Info Pack, Congressional Reference Division, IP497C
* Congressional Gift and Lobbying Regulation: Current Law and Legal Issues for Reform, Jack H. Maskall 95-832 A
* Congressional Pensions: Illustrative Effects of Proposed Reductions, Carolyn Merck 95-686 EPW
* The Congressional Research Service, Evelyn Howard 94-691 PGM
* The Congressional Scene: Selected Publications Covering the Congress, Pamela M. Dragovich 94-958 C
* Gift Prohibition Legislation in the House in the 104th Congress: A Comparison of Major Provisions, Richard Sachs 95-911 GOV
* House and Senate Campaign Receipts and Sources of Funds: 1980-1994, Joseph E. Cantor 95-1087 GOV

* How to Obtain Copies of Videotapes of Proceedings of Congress and Network and Cable Television Broadcasts, Michele M. Springer 95-728 C
* Legislative Branch Budget Authority, FY 1968-FY 1995, Paul Dwyer ETC. 95-762 GOV
* Legislative Branch Employment, 1960-1995, Paul Dwyer, etc. 95-1113 GOV
* Legislative Ethics in Democratic Countries: Comparative Analysis of Standards, Stephen F. Clarke etc. 94-325 A
* Members of the U.S. Congress Who Have Served Thirty Years or More, Mildred Amer 93-840 GOV
* Members Roundtable: What We Ought To Know About Our National Legislature; Videoprogram, Wyche Fowler, etc VT91-867
* Salaries and Allowances: The Congress, Paul E. Dwyer 95-831 GOV
* Salaries of Members of Congress: An Overview, Paul E. Dwyer 95-898 GOV
* Salaries of Members of Congress, 1789-1995, Paul E. Dwyer 95-459 GOV
* Staff Depositions in Congressional Investigations, Jay R. Shamansky 95-949 A
* Time and History on the Hill, David McCullough VT91-909
* Toward and Informed Legislator: The Development of the Congressional Research Service; Videoprogram, Charles Mathias, Jr., etc. VT91-950
* U.S. Government: Info Pack IP162U
* Washington and the U.S. Capitol Building: Info Pack IP132W
* Women in the United States Congress, Mildred L. Amer 95-905 GOV
* The 104th Congress: Key Issues and Early Agenda, Congressional Research Service 94-966 D

Congress -- Apportionment and Elections

* Campaign Activities by Congressional Staff: Audio Brief AB50118
* Campaign Activities by Congressional Staff: Videoprogram, Jack Maskell VT91-916
* Campaign Finance Bills Passed by House and Senate in the 103rd Congress: Comparative Highlights, Joseph E. Cantor 94-97 GOV
* Campaign Finance Reform: Full Text Comparison of H.R. # and S.3 (103rd Congress) and Current Law, Joseph E. Cantor etc. 94-98 GOV
* Census Adjustment: Impact on Reapportionment and Redistricting, David C. Huckabee 94-649 GOV
* Congressional and State Reapportionment and Redistricting: A Legal Analysis, Thomas M. Durbin, etc. 95-793 A
* Congressional Districts: Objectively Evaluating Shapes, David Huckabee 94-449 GOV
* Congressional Districts: Sources of Maps and Demographic Information, Judith Frazier 93-681 C
* Congressional Redistricting: Federal Law Controls a State Process, David Huckabee 93-1060 GOV
* Districts of the 103rd Congress: Hispanic Population-Data and Rankings, David C. Huckabee, 94-9 GOV
* House Apportionment Following the 2000 Census: Preliminary Projections, David C. Huckabee 95-104 GOV
* House of Representatives: Setting the Size at 435, David Huckabee 95-791 GOV
* An Overview of Miller V. Johnson--Georgia's Majority-Minority Congressional Redistricting Plan, Thomas M. Durbin 95-770 A
* Procedure for House Contested Election Cases, Thomas Durbin, etc. 95-61 A
* Reelection Rates of House Incumbents: 1790-1994, David C. Huckabee 95-361 GOV
* Re-Election Rates of Senate Incumbents: 1790-1994, David C. Huckabee 95-415 GOV
* Removal of Members of Congress from Office, Jack Maskell 94-745 A
* Special Elections and Membership Changes in the 103rd Congress: Second Session, Thomas H. Neale, 95-737 GOV
* Term Limits; Info Pack IP439T
* Term Limits for Federal and State Legislators, Sula P. Richardson, 94-287 GOV
* Term Limits for Members of Congress, Sula P. Richardson 94-915 GOV
* Term Limits for Members of Congress: Background and Contemporary Issues; Issue Brief, Sula P. Richardson IB95021
* The Unconstitutionality of State Congressional Term Limits: An Overview of U.S. Terms Limits, Inc. v. Thornton, Thomas M. Durbin 95-646 A

Congress -- Budget Process

* see Budgets -- Process

Congress -- Executive Relations

* see also Congress--Foreign Relations, Congress--Oversight
* GATT and Other Trade Agreements: Congressional Action by Statute or by Treaty? Louis Fisher 94-890 S
* Separate But Equal: Two Hundred Years of Legislative-Executive-Judicial Relations; Videoprogram, Louis Fisher, etc. VT91-955
* The Supreme Court Appointment Process: Audio Brief, Denis Steven Rutkus, AB50276

* Why Certain Trade Agreements Are Approved as Congressional-Executive Agreements Rather Than as Treaties, Jeanne J. Grimmett 94-766 A

Congress -- Foreign Relations

* see also Presidents
* Foreign Policy Roles of the President and Congress, Ellen C. Collier, 93-20 F
* Presidential Emergency Powers: The War Powers Act of 1933, David M. Ackerman 95-753 A
* Protection of Classified Information by Congress: Practices and Proposals for Change, Frederick M. Kaiser 95-252 GOV
* War Powers and U.N. Military Actions: A Brief Background of the Legislative Framework, Ellen C. Collier 93-1058 F
* War Power Resolution: A Brief Summary of Pro and Con Agreements, Ellen C. Collier 93-984 F
* War Powers Resolution: Info Pack, IP131 W
* War Powers Resolution: Presidential Compliance; Issue Brief, Ellen C. Collier, IB81050
* The War Powers Resolution: The Controversial Act's Search for a Successful Litigation Posture, Raymond J. Celada and David M. Ackerman 93-1065 A
* The War Powers Resolution: Twenty Years of Experience, Ellen C. Collier 94-42 F
* War Power Restrictions: Selected Excerpts from Legislation Enacted in the 103rd Congress, Ellen C. Collier 95-49 F

Congress -- Legislative Procedure and Operations

* The Amending Process in the House of Representatives, Stanley Bach, 91-605 RCO
* The Amending Process in the Senate, Stanley Bach 93-113 S
* Amending the U.S. Constitution: By Congress or by Constitutional Convention, Thomas M. Durbin, 95-589 A
* Bills Introduced and Laws Enacted: Selected Legislative Statistics 1947-1994, Rozanne M. Barry 95-233 C
* A Brief Overview of Floor Procedure in the House of Representatives, Stanley Bach, 89-59 S
* Budget Process Changes Made in the Rules of the House in January 1995 (H. Res. 6), Robert Keith 95-432 GOV
* Caucuses and Legislative Service Organizations of the 103rd Congress, 2nd Session: An Informational Directory, Sula P. Richardson 94-707 GOV
* Commemorative Legislation, Stephen W. Stathis, 93-407 GOV
* Committee of the Whole: An Introduction, Ilona Nickels 85-943 GOV
* The Committee System in the U.S. Congress, Carol Hardy Vincent 95-591 GOV
* Committee System: Rules Changes in the House, 104th Congress, Judy Schneider 95-187 GOV
* Committee of the United States House of Representatives, Carol Hardy Vincent 95-608 GOV
* Committee of the United States Senate, Carol Hardy Vincent 95-473 GOV
* Conference Committee and Related Procedures: An Introduction, Stanley Bach 91-576 GOV
* The Congressional Record: A User's Guide; Videoprogram, Ilona Nickels, VT92-879
* The Congressional Record; Content, History and Issues, Mildred L. Amer, 93-60 GOV
* Congressional Reform: Info Pack IP462C
* Congressional Reform: Rules, Campaign Finance, and Lobbying; Videoprogram, Ilona Nickels VT94-1318
* Congressional Reform: 103rd Congress, Issue Brief, Frederick H. Pauls and Judy Schneider, IB93084
* The Congressional Research Service, Evelyn Howard, 93-635 PGM
* Congressional Roll Call and Other Recorded Votes: Statistical Summary of 1st Through 103rd Congresses (1789-1994), John Pontius 95-247 GOV
* CRS One-Day Legislative Institute: A Checklist of CRS Products, Tangela G. Roe 95-176 L
* Guiding a Bill Through the Legislative Process, Ilona B. Nickels 94-322 GOV
* House Committee Reports: Required Contents, Judy Schneider 95-282 GOV
* House Committee Rules in the 103rd Congress: Comparison of Selected Provisions, Brad Vander Linden 93-994 GOV
* House of Representatives Procedures and Operations: A Checklist of CRS Products, George Walser 95-16L
* How to Follow Current Federal Legislation and Regulations, Carol D. Davis 95-314 C
* Impeachment: An Overview of Constitutional Provisions, Procedures, and Practice Elizabeth B. Bazan 95-243 A
* The Joint Committee on Printing: A Brief Overview, Harold C. Relyea 95-425 GOV
* Joint Committee on the Library: Duties and Responsibilities, Paul S. Runquist 95-721 GOV

Be patient. If any phone number is incorrect, call (area code) 555-1212 and request the new listing.

1303

* Legislative Activity in Committee: The Impact of Senate Rule, Stanley Bach 95-9S
* Legislative Procedure: An Introduction; Info Pack, IP247L
* Legislative Procedure: An Introductory Guide to Sources, Pamela M. Dragovich 94-629 C
* Legislative Procedures and the Legislative Agenda in the House of Representatives, Stanley Bach 94-975 S
* Legislative Procedures of the U.S. Congress; Videoprogram, Walter Oleszek VT91-915
* The Legislative Process on the House Floor: An Introduction, Stanley Bach 95-563 S
* The Legislative Process on the Senate Floor: An Introduction, Stanley Bach 91-520 GOV
* Legislative Reorganization Act of 1946: Summary of Provisions, Frederick H. Pauls 91-593 RCO
* Minority Rights and Senate Procedures, Stanley Bach 94-978 S
* A New "Corrections Calendar" for the House, Walter J. Oleszek 95-722 S
* Parliamentary Reference Sources: An Introductory Guide, Ilona Nickels, 95-700 GOV
* The President Pro Tempore of the Senate: History and Authority of the Office, Richard C. Sachs 95-181 GOV
* The Proposed Legislative Reorganization Act of 1994: Issue Brief, Walter J. Oleszek IB94039
* Quorums in House Floor Proceedings: An Introduction, Stanley Bach 94-895 S
* Resolving Legislative Differences in Congress: Conference Committees and Amendments Between the Houses, Stanley Bach, 91-538 RCO
* Senate Legislative Floor Procedures: Videoprogram, Stanley Bach VT91-920
* Senate Procedure and Operations: A Checklist of CRS Products, George Walser 95-17 L
* Senate Rules and Practices on Committee, Subcommittee, and Chairmanship Assignment Limitations, as of October 31, 1994, Judy Schneider 94-849 GOV
* The Senate's "Byrd Rule" Against Extraneous Matter in Reconciliation Measures, Robert Keith, 95-707 GOV
* Special Rules in the House of Representatives, Stanley Bach 91-730 S
* Super-Majority Voting Requirements for Tax Increases: A Constitutional Analysis Jay R. Shampansky 95-299 A
* Suspension of the Rules in the House of Representatives, Stanley Bach 92-185 GOV
* Trade Agreements: Renewing the Negotiating and Fast Track Implementing Authority; Issue Brief, Vladimir N. Pregelj IB95089

Congress -- Members
* Black Members of the United States Congress, 1789-1993, Mildred L. Amer 93-671 GOV
* Brief Comparison of Retirement Eligibility and Benefits for Members of Congress and Executive Branch Personnel, Carolyn L. Merck 93-721 EPW
* Brief Facts About Congressional Pensions, Carolyn L. MercK 94-740 EPW
* Congressional Pensions: Illustrative Effects of Proposed Reductions, Carolyn L. Merck 95-686 EPW
* Former Speakers of the House: Office Allowances, Franking Privilege, and Staff Assistance, Paul Dwyer 95-386 GOV
* Legal and Congressional Ethics Standards of Relevance to Those Who Lobby Congress, Jack Maskell, 91-163 A
* Length of Service for Representatives and Senators: 1st-103rd Congresses, David C. Huckabee 95-426 GOV
* Lists of Members of Congress and Their Committee Assignments: A Guide to Sources, 92-530 C
* Membership of the 104th Congress: A Profile, Mildred L. Amer, 95-205 GOV
* Organizations That Rate Members of Congress on Their Voting Records, Kathy Doddridge 95-26 C
* Post Employment, "Revolving Door", Restrictions for Legislative Branch Members and Employees, Jack Maskell 95-52 A
* Retirement for Members of Congress, Carolyn L. Merck 94-969 EPW
* Salaries of Members of Congress, 1789-1995, Paul E. Dwyer 95-459 GOV
* Selected Privileges and Courtesies Extended to Former Members of the House of Representatives, Mildred Amer 94-861 GOV
* Selected Privileges and Courtesies Extended to Former Senators, Mildred Amer 95-501 A
* The Senate Chaplaincy, Charles H. Whittier 86-916 GOV
* Territorial Delegates to the U.S. Congress: A Brief History, Andorra Bruno, 93-616 GOV
* Voting Records of Members of Congress: A Self-Help Guide to Their Compilation, Jennifer Manning 94-992 C

Congress -- Offices
* Basic Reference Sources for Use by Congressional Offices: An Annotated Selected of Publications and Services, Rita Jimenez, 95-57 C

* Casework in a Congressional Office, John S. Pontius etc, 94-904 C
* Congress' Exemption from Selected Major Legislation: A Legal Analysis, Jay R. Shampansky etc, 92-294 A
* Congressional Accountability Act of 1995 95-557 A
* Congressional Casework: Approaches and Considerations; Audio Brief, Congressional Research Service, AB50254
* Congressional Casework: Approaches and Considerations; Videoprogram, Congressional Research Service, VT92-1344
* Congressional Staff Guide to Finding Information in CRS Reading Rooms/Reference Centers, Merete F. Gerli, 95-121 C
* Congressional Member Office Operations, Fredrick H. Pauls and John S. Pontius 92-882 S
* Congressional Office Operations: A Checklist of CRS Products, George Walser 95-93 L
* Congressional Office Operations and Staffing: Selected References, Fred H. Pauls 92-63 S
* Congressional Office Operations: Info Pack IP151C
* Congressional Staff: An Analysis of Their Roles, Functions, and Impacts, Paul S. Rundquist, etc. 92-90 S
* Fair Employment Practices in Congress: Authorizing Legislation and House/Senate Comparison Leslie Gladstone 94-996 GOV
* Family and Medical Leave Act: Provisions Applicable to Congressional Offices, Leslie W. Gladstone, 93-454 GOV
* Legislative History: A Guide for Constituents, Mark Gurevitz 89-596 A
* Legislative Research: A Guide to Conducting Legislative Research in a Congressional Office; Info Pack, IP321L
* Legislative Research in Congressional Offices: A Primer, Clay H. Welborn 95-657 GOV
* Managing Projects and Grand Work: Videoprogram, Congressional Research Service VT94-1346
* Preparing Legislative Histories; Videoprogram, David Siddall VT91-910

Congress -- Oversight
* see also Congress--Executive Relations
* Congressional Oversight: Audio Brief, Walter Oleszak, etc. AB50319
* Congressional Oversight: Videoprogram, Walter Oleszek, etc. VT95-1326
* Effective Oversight: Planning for the Future; Videoprogram, Richard Bolling, etc. VT91-917
* Executive Perspectives on Oversight; Videoprogram, Eileen Siddman, etc. VT91-952
* Former Members View Oversight; Videoprogram, Gilbert Gude, etc. VT91-954
* Inspectors General: Resources for Oversight; Videoprogram, Thomas Novotny, etc. VT91-956
* Investigative Oversight: An Introduction to the Law, Practice and Procedure of Congressional Inquiry, Morton Rosenberg 95-464 A
* A Member's Reflections on Oversight; Videoprogram, John Moss VT91-913
* Outside Perspectives on Oversight; Turning the Tables on Congress; Videoprogram, Tom Novotny, VT91-877
* Oversight and Congressional Policymaking; Videoprogram, John Dingell VT91-912
* Oversight Authority and Major Procedures; Videoprogram, Mark Nadel, etc. VT91-951
* Oversight in Action: A Variety of Experiences; Videoprogram, Morton Rosenberg, etc. VT91-953
* Powers and Constraints of Oversight; Videoprogram, Antonin Scalia, etc. VT91-911
* The Role of Media in Oversight; Videoprogram, Henry Hubbard, etc. VT91-914

Congress and Foreign Policy
* see Congress -- Foreign Relations

Congressional Accountability Act
* Congressional Accountability Act of 1995, American Law Division 95-557 A

Congressional Budget Process
* see Budgets -- Process

Congressional Districts
* see Congress-Apportionment and Elections

Congressional Elections
* see Congress-Apportionment and Elections

Congressional Ethics
* see Congress -- Members

Congressional Oversight
* see Congress -- Oversight

Congressional Pay
* see Congress -- Members

Congressional-Presidential Relations
* see Congress -- Executive Relations, Congress -- Foreign Relations, War Powers Resolution

Congressional Record
* The Congressional Record: A User's Guide; Videoprogram, Ilona Nickels, VT92-879

Congressional Research Service
* The Congressional Research Service, Evelyn Howard 94-691 PGM
* Toward an Informed Legislator: The Development of the Congressional Research Service; Videoprogram, Charles Mathias, Jr., Mary Rose Oakar, Richard Bolling, Daniel Boorstin, and Gilbert Gude VT91-950

Conservation of Wildlife
* see Animals

Constitution (U.S.)
* Amending the U.S. Constitution: By Congress or by Constitutional Convention, Thomas M. Durbin, 95-589 A
* Balanced-Budget Constitutional Amendment; Videoprogram, William Cox, etc. VT94-1311
* Constitution of the United States: Bibliography-in-Brief, Tangela G. Roe 95-37 L
* The Constitution of the United States, Including the Bill of Rights, and the Declaration of Independence: A Guide to Obtaining Copies, Pamela G. Dragovich 95-442 C
* Constitution of the United States: Including the Bill of Rights: Info Pack, IP339C
* Impeachment: An Overview of Constitutional Provisions, Procedure and Practice, Elizabeth B. Bazan 95-243 A
* Ratification of Amendments to the U.S. Constitution, David Huckabee 95-316 GOV

Consumer Price Index
* see Economic Policy

Consumer Protection
* see Consumers

Consumers
* Consumer Attitude Indexes: What Are They and What Do They Mean?, Gail Makinen 95-407 E
* Consumer Credit Issues: Info Pack IP498C
* Fifty-State Surveys on Selected Products Liability Issues, Henry Cohen and La Vonne Mangan 95-300 A
* Legal Reform Bill Pending in the Senate; Issue Brief, Henry Cohen 95-597 A
* Products Liability: A Legal Overview: Archived Issue Brief, Henry Cohen IB77021

Consumption Taxes
* see Taxation--Consumption Taxes

Contract with America
* Adoption Tax Credit Proposal, Louis Allan Talley 94-957 E
* Budget Process Changes Made in the Rules of the House in January 1995, Robert Keith 95-432 GOV
* Child Care in the 104th Congress, Dale Robinson 95-97 EPW
* Committee System: Rules Changes in the House, 104th Congress, Judy Schneider 95-187 GOV
* Common Sense Legal Reforms Act of 1995: Title I Civil Justice Reform (Attorney's Fees, Products, Liability, Etc.), Henry Cohen 95-27 A
* The Contract with America Tax Relief Act: An overview of the House Bill, David L. Brumbaugh 95-735 E
* The Contract With America Tax Relief Act (H.R. 1215), David L. Brumbaugh 95-813 E
* Contract With America Tax Relief Act of 1995: Revenue and Distributional Effects, Greg A. Esenwein 95-498 E
* Crime Issues; Videoprogram, Charles Doyle, etc. VT95-1307
* Crime Prevention: A Brief Overview, Suzanne Cavanagh, etc. VT95-140 GOV
* Distributional Effects of Tax Provisions in the Contract With America as Reported by the Ways and Means Committee, Jane G. Gravelle 95-455 S

* Entitlements and the Budget; Videoprogram Richard Rimkunas, etc. VT95-1313
* Environmental Protection: From 103rd to the 104th Congress, by Environment and Natural Resources Policy Division, Martin R. Lee 95-58 ENR
* Environmental Protection Legislation in the 104th Congress: Issue Brief, Martin R. Lee IB95004
* Environmental Reauthorization and Regulatory Reform: Recent Developments, John Blodgett 95-3 ENR
* The Estate Tax Exemption and the House Republican Contract, Salvatore Lazzari 95-167 E
* Executive Branch Reorganization: Issue Brief, Harold C. Relyea IB93026
* Fair Employment Practices in Congress: Authorizing Legislation and House/Senate Comparison, Leslie Gladstone 94-996 GOV
* The Family Tax Credit, Gregg A. Esenwein 95-507 E
* Fiscal Responsibility; Videoprogram, Louis Fisher and Bob Keith VT95-1302
* H.R. 1215 and the Expensing Allowance for Smaller Businesses, Gary Guenther 95-528 E
* Immigration and Federal Assistance: Issues and Legislation; Issue Brief, Joyce C. Vialet and Larry M. Eig IB94037
* Indexing Capital Gains for Inflation: Complexity and Related Issues, Harry G. Gourevitch 95-437 S
* Individual Retirement Account Issues and Savings Accounts Proposals: Issue Brief, James R. Storey IB89085
* Individual Retirement Accounts (IRAs) and Related Proposals, Jane G. Gravelle 95-420 S
* Item Veto and Expanded Impoundment Proposals; Issue Brief, Virginia McMurtry IB89148
* Key Foreign and Defense Policy Issues in the 104th Congress, Ellen C. Collier 95-28 F
* Legal Reforms Passed by the House: Issue Brief, Henry Cohen and Michael Seitzinger IB95030
* Legislation on Protection of Pupil or Family Rights in Federally Assisted Programs, Wayne Riddle and Richard N. Apling 95-76 EPW
* Legislative Line Item Veto Bills: Comparing S. 4 and S. 14 (as Reported), Louis Fisher and Virginia A. McMurtry 95-273 S
* Line Item Veto: Info Pack IP287L
* Mandates and the Congress, Sandra Osbourn 95-62 GOV
* Mandates Relief for State and Local Government Bill of 1994: A Summary of Provisions, Sandra S. Osbourn 95-55 GOV
* The Neutral Cost Recovery System and the House Republican Contract, David L. Brumbaugh, etc. 95-161 E Contract,
* Older Americans Act: 104th Congress Issues, Carl O'Shaughnessy 95-32 EPW
* Paperwork Reduction and Information Resources Management, Stephanie Smith 95-453 GOV
* Property Rights: Comparison of H. R. 9 as Passed and S. 605 as Introduced, Robert Meltz 95-509 A
* The Property Rights Issue; Videoprogram, Robert Meltz and Jeffrey A. Zinn VT95-1323
* Proposed Reform of Private Securities Litigation: Title II of the Common Sense Legal Reforms Act, Michael V. Seitzingeer 95-68 A
* Risk and Cost-Benefit Provisions in House and Senate Bills, Linda-Jo Schierow 95-576 ENR
* Social Security: Repeal of 1993 Provision that Increased Taxation of Benefits; Issue Brief, Geoffrey C. Kollman IB94056
* Transportation Trust Funds: The Off-Budget Debate; Issue Brief, John C. Fischer IB95038
* Unfunded Mandate Reform Act: A Brief Summary, Sandra S. Osbourn 95-246 GOV
* U.S. Geological Survey: Its Mission and Its Future, James E. Mielke 95-145 SPR
* Welfare: Durational Residency Requirements, Gina Marie Stevens 95-357 A
* Welfare Proposal in the Contract With America, Vee Burke 94-989 EPW
* Welfare Reform: Background and Key Issues, James R. Storey 95-72 EPW
* Welfare Reform: How the House-Passed Bill Would Change Family Cash Welfare, Vee Burke 95-495EPW
* Welfare Reform; Videoprogram, Vee Burke, etc. VT95-1306
* Wetland Issues in the 104th Congress: Issue Brief, Jeffrey A. Zinn, etc. IB95028
* The 104th Congress: Key Issues and Early Agenda, Congressional Research Service 94-966 D

Controlled Substances Act
* Federal Sanctions Imposed for Violations of the Controlled Substances Act and Related Statutes: Recent Developments, Charles Doyle 94-768 S

Convention on Biological Diversity
* Biological Diversity: Issues Related to the Convention on Biodiversity, Susan R. Fletcher 95-598 ENR
* Biological Diversity Treaty: Fact Sheet, Susan Fletcher 95-596 ENR

Current Events and Homework

Conventional Weapons
* see Weapon Systems -- Weapon Facts

Copyright Act
* see Intellectual Property

Copyright Term Extension Act
* Proposed U.S. Copyright Term Extension, Dorothy Schrader 95-799 S

Corporation for National and Community Service
* Corporation for National and Community Service Programs: A Summary, Dale H. Robinson 95-278 EPW

Corporation Taxes
* see Taxation -- Business Taxes

Corporations
* see Business Taxation -- Business Taxes

Credit
* see Finance -- Banks

Credit Unions
* see Finance -- Banks

Crime Control
* see Criminal Justice

Crimes and Offenses
* see Criminal Justice

Criminal Justice
* Anti-Crime Funding in the Fiscal 1995 Commerce, Justice, State Appropriations Act (H.R. 4603): A Summary, David Teasley 94-679 GOV
* Anti-Crime Initiatives: Community Policing and Citizen Involvement: Selected References, 1992-1994, Tangela G. Roe 94-381 L
* Anti-Crime Initiatives: Issues, Approaches, and Federal Involvement; Selected References, 1992-1994 94-384 L
* Anti-Crime Initiatives: Sentencing, Prisons, and Prisoners; Selected References, 1992-1994 Tangela G. Roe 94-380 L
* Anti-Crime Initiatives: Youth and Violence: Selected References, 1992-1994 Tangela G. Roe 94-382 L
* The Brady Handgun Control Act: Constitutional Issues, Dorothy Schrader 94-885 S
* Branch Davidian Siege at Ranch Apocalypse New Waco, Texas: A Chronology by Suzanne Cavanagh and David Teasley 95-582 GOV
* Child Pornography: Constitutional Principles and Federal Statutes, Henry Cohen 95-406 A
* Citizen Militias: Selected References, 1994-1995, Tangela Roe 95-567 L
* Community Anti-Crime Weed and Seed Program: Recent Developments, Suzanne Cavanagh and David Teasley 94-827 GOV
* Community Policing: An Overview, David Teasley 94-350 GOV
* Comprehensive Terrorism Prevention Act of 1995, S. 735, as Introduced: A Summary, Charles Doyle 95-580 S
* Crime Control Act of 1994: Selected Highlights of H.R. 3355 as Passed, Charles Doyle, etc. 94-682 S
* Crime Control: Asset Forfeiture Funds and Equitable Sharing of Forfeited Assets, Andorra Bruno 95-980 GOV
* Crime Control Assistance Through the Byrne Programs, Keith Bea 95-81 GOV
* Crime Control Comparison of House and Senate Legislation of the 103rd Congress, 2nd Session, Charles Doyle, etc. 94-358 S
* Crime Control: Federal Initiatives; Info Pack IP310C
* Crime Control: Summary of Financial Assistance Available to State and Local Governments, Keith Bea 95-258 GOV
* Crime Control: Summary of the Violent Crime Control and law Enforcement Act of 1994, Charles Doyle 94-910 S
* Crime Control: The Federal Response; Issue Brief, Suzanne Cavanagh IB90078
* Crime, Drug and Gun Control; Videoprogram, Elizabeth Bazan etc. VT94-1312
* Crime Issues: A Checklist of CRS Products, Tangela G. Roe 95-160 L
* Crime Issues; Videoprogram, Charles Doyle etc. VT95-1307
* Crime Prevention: A Brief Overview, Suzanne Cavanagh and David Teasley 95-140 GOV
* Explosives and Taggants: Congressional Consideration, Keith Bea 95-640 GOV
* The Fair Labor Standards Act: Minimum Wage Protection for Prison Inmate Workers and for Non-Prison Labor, William G. Whittaker 93-895 E

* Hate Crime: An Overview, Suzanne Cavanagh etc. 93-157 GOV
* Hate Crime: Recent Developments, Suzanne Cavanagh etc. 94-855 GOV
* Hate Violence in the United States: Background and Current Dimensions, William W. Ellis 95-616 S
* Juvenile Justice and Delinquency Prevention: Background and Current Issues, Suzanne Cavanagh etc. 92-633 GOV
* Juvenile Justice and Delinquency Prevention Reauthorization Act of 1992: Summary of Major Provisions, Suzanne Cavanagh etc. 92-821 GOV
* The Knox "Clothed Children" Child Pornography Case and the Congressional Response, Henry Cohen 94-753 A
* Law Enforcement Assistance Block Grant Proposals, 104th Congress, Keith Bea 95-731 GOV
* Law Enforcement Availability Pay, Barbara L. Schwemle 95-189 GOV
* The Legal System and Controversy: Women, Gays, Minorities, the Poor, the Aged, and the Disabled: Selected References, 1990-1993, Tangela G. Roe 93-748 L
* Lorton: D.C. Correctional Facilities, JoAnne O'Bryant 95-689 GOV
* The National Guard, State Defense Forces, and the Militias: Official and Unofficial Status, Robert L. Goldich 95-574 F
* Obscenity: Constitutional Principles and Federal Statutes, Henry Cohen 95-804 A
* The Oklahoma City Bombing Investigation: A Chronology, David Teasley and Suzanne Cavanagh 95-902 GOV
* Oklahoma City Bombing: Underlying Federal Response Authorities, Raphael Perl etc. 95-538 GOV
* "Operation Garden Plot"--Military Response to Civil Disturbances: Fact Sheet, Edward F. Bruner 95-1014 F
* Pornography in the United States: A Brief Overview, Leslie W. Gladstone 95-759 GOV
* The Posse Comitatus Act & Related Matters: The Use of the Military to Executive Civilian Law, charles Doyle 95-964 S
* President Clinton's Terrorism Proposal Omnibus Counterterrorism Act of 1995, H.R. 896/S. 390 as Introduced: A Summary Charles Doyle 95-558 S
* Prison Boot Camps: Selected References, 1988-1995, Jean M. Bowers 94-308 L
* Prisons: Policy Options for Congress; Issue Brief Keith Bea IB92061
* Randy Weaver Case at Rugby Ridge, Idaho: A Chronology, David Teasley, etc. 95-581 GOV
* RICO: A Brief Sketch, Charles Doyle 93-750 A
* RICO and Political Protest: The Implications of NOW v. Scheidler, Kenneth R. Thomas 94-108 A
* Social Security: Withholding Benefits from Prisoners and Others Who Are Institutionalized for Criminal Acts, David Koitz 94-494 EPW
* Television Violence: A Survey of Selected Social Security Research Linking Violent Program Viewing With Aggression in Children and Society, Edith Fairman 95-593 SPR
* Television Violence: An Overview, Edith Fairman 95-144 SPR
* Television Violence: Bibliography of Selected Research Reports, Edith Sutterlin 95-466 L
* Television Violence: Info Pack, IP476T
* Terrorism: Background and Issues for Congress; Issue Brief, Elizabeth Bazan and Larry Eig IB95086
* Terrorism: Comparison of Senate Omnibus Bills of the 104th Congress, Charles Doyle 95-600 S
* Unauthorized Militia: A Brief Sketch of State and Federal Laws Proscribing or Regulating Paramilitary Activities, Charles Doyle 95-683 S
* U.S. Bureau of Alcohol, Tobacco, and Firearms, Suzanne Cavanagh etc, 93-451 GOV
* Violence Against Women: An Overview, Suzanne Cavanagh etc. 94-142 GOV
* Violence in Schools: An Overview, Liane E. White etc. 94-141 EPW
* Violence on Television: What Can Technology Do?, by Science Policy Research Division, Technology and Information Policy Section, 93-710 SPR
* Violent and Abusive Behavior: A Public Health Approach, Edith Fairman Cooper, 93-73 SPR
* Violent Crime: An Overview Suzanne Cavanagh etc. 94-625 GOV
* Violent Crime Control Act of 1994: Crime Prevention Funding With FY 1995 Appropriations, David Teasly 94-878 GOV
* Violent Crime Control and Enforcement Act: Selected Comparative Highlights of the House (H.R. 4092/H.R.3355), Charles Doyle etc. 94-372 S
* When the Young Violate Federal Criminal Law: Federal Juvenile Frequency Act & Related Matters, Charles Doyle 93-320 A
* White-Collar Crime: A Conceptual and Statistical Overview, Suzanne Cavanagh and David Teasley 94-75 GOV
* Youth Gangs: An Overview, Suzanne Cavanagh and David Teasley 92-491 GOV
* Youth Gangs: Recent Developments, Suzanne Cavanagh 94-934 GOV

Criminal Justice--Capital Punishment
* Capital Punishment: A Brief Overview, Suzanne Cavanagh and David Teasley 95-505 GOV
* Capital Punishment: Bibliography-in-Brief, 1992-1994, Tangela G. Roe 95-45 L

* Capital Punishment: Info Pack IP015C
* Crime Control Act of 1994: Capital Punishment Provisions Summarized, Charles Doyle 94-721 S
* The Death Penalty Before the Supreme Court: Capital Punishment 1987-1994, Dorothy Schrader 94-553 A
* Federal Habeas Corpus: Background and Issues, Charles Doyle 95-320 S
* Present Federal Death Penalty Statutes, Elizabeth B. Bazan 95-321 A
* Racial Justice and Capital Punishment: The Racially Discriminatory Capital Sentencing Provisions of the House Passed crime Bill (H.R. 4092/H.R. 3355), Charles Doyle 94-386 S

Criminal Justice -- Gun Control
* The Assault Weapons Ban: Review of Federal Laws Controlling Possession of Certain Firearms, Dorothy Schrader 95-108 S
* "Assault Weapons": Military-Style Semiautomatic Firearms Facts and Issues, Keith Bea, 92-434 GOV
* Brady Handgun Control Act: Constitutional Issues, Dorothy Schrader 94-885 S
* Brady Handgun Violence Prevention Act, Harry Hogan, 94-14 GOV
* Does United States v. Lopez Affect the Gun-Free Schools Provisions of the Improving America's Schools Act of 1994?, Elizabeth B. Bazan 95-647 A
* Federal Gun Control Laws: The Second Amendment and Other Constitutional Issues, Dorothy Schrader 95-220 S
* Firearms Possession by Convicted Felons: State Law Imposing and Abrogating Restrictions, P. L. Morgan 95-325 A
* Gun Control: Bibliography-in-Brief, 1992-1994, Tangela G. Roe 94-837 L
* Gun Control: Info Pack, IP051G
* Gun Control: Issue Brief, Keith Bea IB94007

Criminal Justice -- Sentences
* Federal Sanctions Imposed for Violations of the Controlled Substances Act and Related Statutes: Recent Developments, Charles Doyle 94-768 S
* How the Federal Sentencing Guidelines Work, Charles Doyle 94-323 S
* Mandatory Minimum Sentencing for Federal Crimes: Overview and Analysis, Suzanne Cavanagh and David Teasley 93-539 GOV
* "Three Strikes" Provisions: Mandatory Life Sentences for Violent Offenders, Suzanne Cavanagh etc. 94-143 GOV
* "Three Strikes" Provisions: Recent Federal Development, Suzanne Cavanagh 94-876 GOV
* Truth in Sentencing: Summary of Implicated State Laws, Charles Doyle 93-310 S

Critical Technologies
* see Technology

Croatia
see also Europe
* Croatia: Armed Conflict Resumed, New U.N. Mandate, Prospects for Peace or War, Julie Kim 95-643 F

Crop Insurance
* see Agriculture -- Policies and Legislation

Cuba
* Cuba: Issues for Congress; Issue Brief, Mark P. Sullivan IB94005
* Cuba: U.S. Economic Sanctions, Dianne E. Rennack and Mark P. Sullivan 95-248 F
* Cuba-U.S. Relations: A Chronology of Key Events, Steve McCollum and Mark P. Sullivan 95-618 F
* Cuba-U.S. Relations: Should the United States Reexamine Its Policy?, Mark P. Sullivan 94-759 F
* Cuban Adjustment Act of 1966, Larry M. Eig, 93-253 A
* Cuban Migration: Legal Basics, Larry M. Eig 94-692 A
* Cuban Migration to the U.S.: Trends and Issues, Ruth Ellen Wasem, 95-659 EPW
* Guantanamo Bay Naval Base, Cuba: Background and Current Issues, Ronald O'Rourke and Mark P. Sullivan 94-701 F
* Radio and Television Broadcasting to Cuba: Background and Current Issues, Susan B. Epstein and Mark P. Sullivan 94-636 F

Cyprus
* see also Europe
* Cyprus: Status of U.N. Negotiations; Issue Brief, Ellen B. Laipson IB89140
* Greece and Turkey: Current Foreign Aid Issues: Issue Brief, Carol Migdalovitz, IB86065

Czech Republic
* see Europe

* The Czech Republic and Slovakia; Implications of the Split, Francis T. Miko, 93-66 F
* Poland, Czech Republic, Slovakia, and Hungary: Recent Developments; Issue Brief, Julie Kim etc., IB92051

Czechoslovakia
* see Czech Republic, Slovakia

Dairy Industry
* see Agriculture -- policies and Legislation

Davis-Bacon Act
* see also Labor -- Policies and Legislation
* The Davis-Bacon Act: Action During the 104th Congress; Issue Brief, William G. Whittaker IB94058
* The Davis-Bacon Act: Institutional Evolution and Public Policy, William Whittaker 94-408 E
* The Davis Bacon Act: Institutional Evolution and Public Policy, William G. Whittaker 94-460 E
* Davis-Bacon Coverage: Facilities Built for Lease to the Federal Government, William G. Whittaker 94-431 E
* Davis-Bacon: The Act and the Literature, William G. Whittaker 94-908 E

Day Care
* see Children

Daylight Savings Time
* see Science Policy

Death Penalty
* see Criminal Justice -- Capital Punishment

Debt (International)
* see International Finance -- Foreign Loans

Defense
* see Defense Economics, Defense Policy, Weapons Systems

Defense Budgets
* see Defense Economics -- Defense Budgets

Defense Contracts
* see Defense Economics

Defense Conversion
* see Defense Economics

Defense Economics
* see also Defense Policy, Weapons Systems
* Costs of Major U.S. Wars and Recent U.S. Military Operations, Stephen Daggett 94-995 F
* Defense Conversion: Info Pack, IP474D
* Defense Economic Adjustment and Conversion After the Cold War: Selected, Annotated References, 1990-1994, Edward Knight and Robert S. Kirk 94-317 E
* Defense Economic Adjustments, Military Base Closures, and Other Defense Conversion Issues: A Checklist of CRS Products, Valentin Leskovsek 95-155 L
* Defense Economic Conversion: Adjustment Assistance for Small Business, Bruce K. Mulock, 93-423 E
* Defense Funding for FY 1995: Congressional Action on Supplemental Appropriations and Offsetting Rescissions, Stephen Daggett 95-1112 F
* Defense Industry in Transition: Issues and Options for Congress; Issue Brief, Gary J. Pagliano, IB92122
* Federal Role in Defense Economic Adjustment and Conversion, 94-538 E
* Federal Role in Defense Economic Adjustment and Conversion: An Overview, Edward Knight 94-665 E
* Lockheed and Martin Marietta Merger: Potential Concerns for Congress, 94-765 F

Defense Economics--Defense Budgets
* A Comparison of Clinton Administration and Bush Administration Long-Term Defense Budget Plans for FY 1994-99, Stephen Daggett 95-20 F
* Defense Authorization and Appropriations for FY 1996: Major Weapons and Other Defense Programs; Issue Brief IB95087
* Defense Budget: Alternative Measures of Costs of Military Commitments Abroad,

Be patient. If any phone number is incorrect, call (area code) 555-1212 and request the new listing.

1307

Current Events and Homework

Stephen Daggett 95-726 F

* Defense Budget Cuts and the Economy; Issue Brief, Economics Division IB90012
* Defense Budget for FY 1990: Congressional Action; Archived Issue Brief, Stephen Daggett IB89054
* Defense Budget for FY 1995: Data Summary, Keith Berner etc. 94-128 F
* Defense Budget for FY 1996: Data Summary, Paul J. Graney 95-295 F
* Defense Budget for FY 1996: Major Issues and Congressional Action: Issue Brief, Stephen Daggett IB95049
* Defense Budget: How Much for Defense in the Post-Cold War World; Videoprogram, Robert Goldich etc., VT93-1308
* A Defense Budget Primer, Keith Berner etc., 93-317 F
* Defense Funding for FY 1995: Congressional Action on Supplemental Appropriations; Issue Brief, Stephen Daggett IB95042
* Defense Policy and Budget Issues: A Checklist of CRS Products, Valentin Leskovsek 95-684 L
* Defense Policy and Budget Issues; Videoprogram, Stephen Daggett etc. VT95-1315
* Defense Spending: Does the Size of the Budget Fit the Size of the Force?, Stephen Daggett 94-199 F
* Defense Spending: Effects of the Declining Dollar on the Department of Defense Budget, Kathleen Hicks 95-663 F
* Defense Spending: Info Pack, Congressional Reference Division IP434D
* Military Contingency Operations: Search for a New Funding Mechanism, Nina Serafino 95-636 F
* Military Spending by Foreign Nations: Data from Selected Public Forces, Stephen Daggett 95-472 F
* The U.S. Military in International Peacekeeping : The Funding Mechanism, Nina Serafino 94-95 F

Defense Industry
* see Defense Economics

Defense Policy
* Clinton Foreign and Defense Policy Issues for the Congress; Videoprogram, John Collins etc. VT94-1310
* Comprehensive Terrorism Prevention Act of 1995, S. 735, as Introduced: A Summary, Charles Doyle 95-580 S
* Current National Emergency Issues: A Brief Overview, Harold Relyea 94-596 GOV
* Defense Burdensharing: Is Japan's Host Nation Support a Model for Other Allies?, Stephen Daggett 94-515 F
* Defense Department Bottom-Up Review: Results and Issues, Edward F. Bruner 93-839 F
* Defense Modeling and Simulation, Richard M. Nunno 95-592 SPR
* Defense Policy and Budget Issues: A Checklist of CRS Products, Valentin Leskovsek 95-684 L
* Defense Policy and Budget Issues, Videoprogram, Stephen Daggett, etc. VT95-1315
* Defense Policy and Budget Issues: A Checklist of CRS Products, Valentin Leskovsek 95-684 L
* Defense Policy: Threats, Force Structure, and Budget Issues; Issue Brief, Robert L. Goldich and Stephen Daggett IB90013
* Defense R&D Primer, Richard Nunno 95-173 SPR
* Defense Reinvestment and the Technology Reinvestment Project: Issue Brief, John Moteff IB93078
* The Defense Science and Technology Strategy, Kurt F. McPherson and Richard M. Nunno 95-185 SPR
* Department of Deafness Readiness Preservation Authority, Louis Fisher 95-447 S
* Department of Energy Abolition? Implications for the Nuclear Weapons Program, Jonathan Medalia 95-1020 F
* DOD Support for University Based Research, Michael E. Davey 94-1001 SPR
* DOD's Advanced Concepts and Technology Demonstrations, John D. Moteff 95-283 SPR
* DOD's Dual-Use Strategy, John Moteff 95-322 SPR
* DOD's Federally Funded Research and Development Centers, Michael Davey 95-489 SPR
* DOD's Independent Research and Development Program: Changes and Issues, Michael E. Davey and Dahlia Stein 93-1051 SPR
* Four U.S. "Air Forces:" Overlap Alternatives, Allen Howey 93-823 F
* Global Burdensharing in the Post-Cold War World, Stanley R. Sloan 93-892 S
* HIV/AIDS and Military Manpower Policy: Issue Brief, David F. Burrelli IB95114
* Instances of Use of United States Armed Forces Abroad, 1798-1993, Ellen Collier 93-890 F
* Intelligence Implications of the Military Technical Revolution, Richard A. Best Jr. 95-560 F
* Key Foreign and Defense Policy Issues in the 104th Congress, Ellen C. Collier 95-28 F

* Military Child Care Provisions: Background and Legislation, David F. Burrelli and Kristin Archick 95-985 F
* Military Command, Control, and Communications: Basic Facts and Selected Issues of C3, Edward F. Bruner 94-487 F
* Military Deployments to the Persian Gulf Region, Steven Bowman 94-790 F
* Military Intervention: A Checklist of Key Considerations, John Collins 95-788 S
* Military Operations Other Than War: Implications for the U.S. Air Force, Sanford S. Terry 94-286 F
* Military Preparedness: Principles Compared With U.S. Practices, John M. Collins 94-48 S
* Military Retirement and Personnel Management: Should Active Duty Military Careers Be Lengthened?, Robert Goldich 95-1118 F
* Military Roles and Missions: A Framework for Review, John M. Collins 95-517 S
* Military Space Program: Issues for 104th Congress, Marcia S. Smith 95-95 SPR
* The National Defense Stockpile : A Historical Perspective, Alfred R. Greenwood 95-5 ENR
* The National Defense Stockpile: The FY 1996 Annual Materials Plan, Alfred R. Greenwood 95-577 ENR
* National Emergency Powers, Harold Relyea 93-985 GOV
* The National Guard, State Defense Forces, and the Militias: Official and Unofficial Status, Robert L. Goldich 95-574 F
* Naval Force-Structure Planning: Breaking Old Habits of Thought, Ronald O'Rourke 93-332 F
* The Naval Petroleum Reserves: Proposed Sale and Issues, Robert Bamberger 95-293 ENR
* Nuclear Weapons Proliferation: The Role of Security Assurances in Nonproliferation Policy, Amy F. Woolf and Ross Kaplan 95-984 F
* The Open Skies Treaty, Amy Woolf 95-10098 F
* Peacekeeping: The Debate Over U.S. Policy; Videoprogram, Stanley Sloane etc. VT95-1310
* Persian Gulf Region: U.S. Post-War Security Interests, Alfred Prados 93-586 F
* Persian Gulf Security Issues; Videoprogram, Alfred Prados etc. VT93-1306
* POW's and MIA's: Status and Accounting Issues; Issue Brief, Robert L. Goldich IB92101
* Prepositioned Weapons, Equipment, and Supplies: Overviews and Evaluations, John M. Collins 95-1073 S
* Roles and Functions of U.S. Combat, John M. Collins 93-72 S
* Roles and Missions Commission: Legislative Proposals, Edward F. Bruner and Brian A. Tallerico 95-1031 F
* Special Operations Forces: An Assessment, 1986-1993, John M. Collins 93-697 S
* State Income Taxation of Military Personnel and United States Citizens Residing Outside of the United States, John Luckey 95-895 A
* Terrorism and U.S. Foreign Policy Options; Issue Brief, Raphael Perl IB95086
* Terrorism: Comparison of Senate Omnibus Bills of the 104th Congress, Charles Doyle 95-600 S
* Terrorism: Info Pack IP299T
* Terrorism the Future, and U.S. Foreign Policy: Issue Brief, Raphael L. Perl IB95112
* The United States and the Use of Force in the Post-Cold War World: Toward Self-Deterrence?, Stanley R. Sloan 94-581 S
* The U.S.-Euratom Nuclear Cooperation Agreement, Zachary S. Davis 95-359 ENR
* U.S. Military Dispositions: Fact Sheet, Edward F. Bruner 95-829 F
* U.S. Military Operations, 1965-1994 (Not Including Vietnam): Data on Casualties, Decorations, and Personnel Involved, Robert L. Goldich and John C. Schaefer 94-529 F
* U.S. National Security: Current and Future Threats and U.S. Policies; Selected References, Sherry B. Shapiro 95-1000 L
* The Use of Force: Key Contemporary Documents, Stephen Daggett and Nina Serafino 94-805 F
* War Powers Resolution: Presidential Compliance; Issue Brief Richard F. Grimmett IB81050
* The War Powers Resolution: Twenty Years of Experience, Ellen C. Collier 94-42 F
* War Powers Restrictions: Selected Excerpts from Legislation Enacted in the 103rd Congress, Ellen C. Collier 95-49 F

Defense Policy--Alliances
* Combined Joint Task Forces (CJTF) and New Missions for NATO, Stanley R. Sloan 94-249 F
* NATO Enlargement and Russia: From Cold War to Cold Peace, Stanley R. Sloan and Steve Woerhrel 95-594 S
* NATO: Fact Sheet, Karen E. Donfried 92-919 F
* The NATO Strategy Review: Negotiating the Future of the North Atlantic Alliance, Stanley R. Sloan 91-379 RCO
* The NATO Summit: Transatlantic Relations at a Crossroads, Stanley R. Sloan 93-939 S

Be patient. If any phone number is incorrect, call (area code) 555-1212 and request the new listing.

* NATO's Future: Info Pack IP425N
* Partnership for Peace, Paul E. Gallis 94-351 F
* South Korea: U.S. Defense Obligations, Larry A. Niksch 94-300 F

Defense Policy--Bases

* Base Closures: The Issue of Reviewability by the Courts, Andrew Mayer 93-960 F
* Guantanamo Bay Naval Base, Cuba: Background and Current Issues, Ronald O'Rourke and Mark P. Sullivan 94-701 F
* Military Base Closures: Issues for the 104th Congress; Issue Brief, Andrew C. Mayer and David E. Lockwood IB92113
* Military Base Closures: Status of Major Designated Sites, George H. Siehl 95-263 F

Defense Policy--Nonproliferation

* The ABM Treaty and Theater Missile Defense: Proposed Changes and Potential Implications, 94-374 F
* Arms Control and Disarmament: A Catalog of Recent Activities, Amy F. Woolf etc. 95-134 F
* Arms Control and Disarmament Agency: Background and Current Issues, Steven A. Hildreth 95-692 F
* Ballistic and Cruise Missile Forces of Foreign Countries, Robert Shuey 95-688 F
* Ballistic Missile Dismantlement: Process Implications, Thomas Lester 95-747 F
* Ballistic Missiles Defenses: Info Pack IP496B
* Chinese Missile and Nuclear Proliferation: Issues for Congress; Issue Brief, Shirley A. Kan and Robert Shuey IB92056
* Nonproliferation Export Controls in Eastern Europe and the Former Soviet Union, Theodore Galdi 94-850 F
* Nonproliferation Regimes: Policies to Control the Spread of Nuclear, Chemical and Biological Weapons and Missiles, Zachary S. Davis etc. 93-237 ENR
* North Korea: U.S. Policy and Negotiations to Halt Its Nuclear Weapons Program; an Annotated Chronology and Analysis, Richard P. Cronin 94-905 F
* North Korean Nuclear Controversy: Defining Treaties, Agreements, and Terms, Larry Niksch and Zachary Davis 94-752 F
* North Korea's Nuclear Weapons Program; Issue Brief, Amy F. Woolf IB91141
* Nuclear Arms Control and Nuclear Threat Reduction: Issues and Agenda; Issue Brief, Amy F. Woolf IB94054
* Nuclear Arms Control at the Washington Summit: Early Deactivation of Ballistic Missiles, Amy Woolf 94-782 F
* Nuclear Arms Control Implementation : Next Steps for START I and Beyond, Amy F. Woolf 95-305 F
* Nuclear Dilemmas: Nonproliferation Comprehensive Test Ban, and Stockpile Stewardship, Jonathan E. Medalia 94-1007 F
* The Nuclear Nonproliferation Treaty Extension: A Fact Sheet, Zachary S. Davis 95-289 ENR
* Nuclear Nonproliferation Policy Issues in the 102nd Congress: Issue Brief, Warren Donnelly and Zachary S. Davis IB91023
* Nuclear Nonproliferation Strategies for South Asia, Zachary S. Davis 94-385 ENR
* Nuclear Weapons in the Former Soviet Union: Location, Command and Control: Issue Brief, Amy F. Woolf and Theodore Galdi IB91144
* Nuclear Weapons Materials: Dismantlement and Disposal in the States of the Former Soviet Union; Issue Brief, Warren H. Donnelly and Zachary Davis IB91129
* Proliferation Control Regimes: Background and Status, Theodore W. Galdi etc. 95-547 F
* The Proliferation of Nuclear and Chemical Weapons; Videoprogram, Theodore W. Galdi Etc. VT94-1330
* South Asia: Background and Recent Developments in U.S. Nuclear Nonproliferation Efforts, Barbara Leitch 95-215 F
* The START and START II Arms Control Treaties: Background and Issues, Amy F. Woolf 93-617 F
* START II: Central Limits and Force Structure Implications, Amy F. Woolf 93-35 F
* Strategic Arms Reduction Treaty (START I & II): Verification and Compliance Issues; Issue Brief, Amy Woolf IB91139
* Theater Ballistic Missile Defense Policy, Missions and Programs: Current Status, Steven Hildreth 93-585 F
* Theater Missile Defense: Indigenous Programs and Interest Among U.S. Friends and Allies, Steven A. Hildreth 94-379 F
* Theater Missile Defense: Issues for 104th Congress; Issue Brief, Steven Hildreth IB95012
* U.S. Counterproliferation Doctrine: Issues for Congress, Zachary S. Davis etc. 94-734 ENR

Defense Policy--Personnel

* Abortion Services and Military Medical Facilities, David Burelli 95-387 F
* Army Reserve Component Reforms and the Bottom-Up Review: Issues for Congress, Robert L. Goldich 94-8 F
* COLAs for Military Retirees: Summary of Congressional and Executive Branch Action Since 1982, Robert L. Goldich 94-7 F
* Homosexuals and U.S. Military Personnel Policy, David Burrelli 93-52 F
* Illnesses Related to the Persian Gulf Experience, Samuel Merrill 92-886 SPR
* Medal of Honor, History and Issues, David Burrelli 95-519 F
* Military and Civilian Pay: Is There a Gap?, David Burrelli 95-492 F
* Military Benefits for Former Spouses: Legislation and Policy Issues, David Burrelli 94-778 F
* Military Manpower and Compensation: FY 1996 Legislative Issues; Issue Brief, Robert L. Goldich IB95044
* Military Medical Care Services: Questions and Answers; Issue Brief, Richard A. Best IB93103
* Military Medicine and National Health Care Reform, Richard A. Best 94-570 F
* Military Retiree Health Care: Base Closures and Realignments, David Burrelli and Elizabeth A. Dunstan 95-435 F
* Military Retirement and Veterans' Compensation: Concurrent Receipt Issues, Robert L. Goldich and Carolyn L. Merck 95-469 F
* The Military Survivor Benefit Plan: A Description of Its Provisions, David Burrelli 94-779 F
* Women in the Armed Forces: Issue Brief, David Burrelli IB92008

Defense Procurement

* see Defense Economics -- Procurement

Defense Spending

* see Defense Economics

Deficit Reduction

* see Budgets -- Deficits

Deforestation

* see Natural Resources -- Forests

Deposit Insurance

* see Finance -- Banks

Derivatives

* see Finance, International Finance

Desegregation of Schools

* see Elementary and Secondary, Education

Developing Countries

* AIDS in the Developing World: The International Response, Lois McHugh 93-1016 F
* GATT: The Uruguay Round Agreement and Developing Countries, Susan Epstein 95-260 F
* International Financial Institutions and Environment: Multilateral Development Banks and the Global Environment Facility, Susan Fletcher and Betsy A. Cody 94-173 ENR
* Population and Development: The 1994 Cairo Conference, Curt Tarnoff 94-533 F

Developmental Disabilities

* see Disabled

Dietary Supplement Health and Education Act

* Dietary Supplement Health and Education Act of 1994: P.L. 103-417, Donna V. Porter 94-965 SPR
* Dietary Supplements: Brief Chronology of Recent Events, Donna Porter 94-981 SPR

Dietary Supplements

* see Food -- Labeling and Safety

Disability Insurance

* see Social Security -- Benefits

Disabled

* see also Americans with Disabilities Act and Rehabilitation Act
* Accessibility for Persons With Disabilities in Federally Funded Buildings, Mary F. Smith 92-541 EPW
* The Americans With Disabilities Act (ADA): An Overview of Major Provisions, Nancy Lee Jones 92-306 A

Current Events and Homework

* The American With Disabilities Act (ADA): Implementation Issues, Nancy Lee Jones 93-815 A
* Americans With Disabilities Act (ADA) Requirements Concerning the Provision of Interpreters by Doctors, Nancy Lee Jones 95-345 A
* American With Disabilities Act (ADA) Requirements Concerning the Provision of Interpreters by Doctors, Nancy L. Jones 92-83 A
* Americans With Disabilities Act: Final Rules and Information Sources, James W. Watson 92-311 A
* The Americans With Disabilities Act: Info Pack IP443A
* Autism: Background Information and Federal Research Funding Levels, Edith Fairman Cooper 95-451 SPR
* Business Tax Provisions of Benefit to the Handicapped, Louis Alan Talley 93-783 E
* Changes in Home Care Use by Disabled Elderly Persons: 1982-1989, Korbin Liu and Kenneth Manton 94-398 EPW
* Developmental Disabilities Programs: Background, FY 1994 Reauthorization, and Funding, Carol O'Shaughnessy and Mary F. Smith 94-66 EPW
* Developmental Disabilities Programs: FY 1996 Funding Proposals, Carol O'Shaughnessy and Melissa W. Zimmerman 95-1011 EPW
* Disabled and Blind Child Recipients of Supplemental Security Income (SSI): Background and Concerns, Carmen D. Solomon 93-897 EPW
* Federal Tax Code Provisions of Interest to the Disabled and Handicapped, Louis Alan Talley 95-916 E
* The Individuals With Disabilities Education Act: Congressional Intent, Nancy Lee Jones 95-669 A
* The Individuals With Disabilities Education Act (IDEA): Legal Issues Surrounding the Least Restrictive Environment, Nancy L. Jones 95-286 A
* Individuals With Disabilities Education Act: Reauthorization Overview, Steven R. Aleman 94-156 EPW
* Individuals With Disabilities Education Act: Summary of Current Programs, Steven R. Aleman 95-675 EPW
* Medicaid: Eligibility for the Aged, Disabled, and Blind, Richard J. Price 94-297 EPW
* Medicaid Services for Persons With Developmental Disabilities, Mary F. Smith 93-742 EPW
* Rehabilitation Act of 1973: Brief Background and Funding History, Carol O'Shaughnessy and Mary Smith 94-509 EPW
* Rehabilitation Act: 104th Congress Legislation, Carol O'Shaughnessy 95-802 EPW
* Rental Housing for the Disabled, Susan M. Vanhorenbeck 94-177 E
* Social Security Disability Issues: Fact Sheet, David Koitz 94-402 EPW
* Special Education: Issues in the State Grant Program of the Individuals With Disabilities Education Act, Steven R. Aleman 95-438 EPW
* Status of the Disability Programs of the Social Security Administration, 1994, David Koitz, etc. 94-477 EPW
* Supreme Court Decisions Interpreting Section 504 of the Rehabilitation Act of 1973, Nancy Lee Jones 95-70 A
* Violence in Schools and the Individuals With Disabilities Education Act, Nancy Lee Jones 95-107 A
* Vocational Education and Special Programs Populations, Richard N. Apling and Sylvie Moulin 94-940 EPW
* Vocational Rehabilitation Act and Related Programs for Persons With Disabilities: Brief Description and FY 1995 Budget Request, Carol O'Shaughnessy and Mary Smith 94-224 EPW

Disarmament
* see Defense Policy -- Nonproliferation

Disasters
* see Emergency Management

Discrimination
* see Civil Liberties, Civil Rights, Minorities, Women

Discrimination in Employment
* see Minorities

Diseases
* see Medicine

District of Columbia
* Appropriations for FY 1996: District of Colombia, Suzanne Cavanagh and Nonna A. Noto 95-628 GOV
* DC Statehood: The Historical Context and Recent Congressional Actions, Garrine P. Laney 94-492 GOV
* District of Colombia Financial Responsibility and Management Assistance Act of 1995; Issue Brief Nonna A. Noto, etc. IB95069

* District of Columbia Public Schools: Status of Federal Legislation Affecting Them, Wayne Riddle 95-1030 EPW
* District of Colombia: Relationship to the Federal Government; Issue Brief, Suzanne Cavanagh and David Teasley IB95074
* The District of Colombia's Relationship to the Federal Government: A Brief Overview, Suzanne Cavanagh and David Teasley 95-247 GOV
* Inexpensive Hotels and Housing in Washington, DC, Bette A. Alberts 95-544 PGM
* Lorton: D.C. Correctional Facilities, JoAnne O'Bryant 95-689 GOV
* Washington, DC and the U.S. Capitol Building: Info Pack, IB132W

Doe v. Bolton
* see Abortion

Domestic Terrorism
* see Criminal Justice

Domestic Volunteer Service Act
* Domestic Volunteer Service Act Programs, Dale Robinson 94-982 EPW

Dropouts
* see Elementary and Secondary Education

Drug Abuse
* The Alcohol, Drug Abuse, and Mental Health Administration (ADAMHA) Reorganization Act of 1992, Edward R. Klebe etc., 93-597 EPW
* Asset Forfeiture and the War on Drugs: Selected References, Jean M. Bowers 95-869 L
* Drug Abuse and Control: Info Pack, IP030D
* Cocaine Sentencing: Federal Sentencing Guideline Proposals, Charles Doyle 95-1032 S
* Drug Abuse Statistics--The National Household Survey: Background and Policy Concerns, David Teasley, 92-610 GOV
* Drug Control Budget: An Overview, David Teasley 95-943 GOV
* Fetal Alcohol Syndrome and Fetal Alcohol Effects: Background Information and Congressional Concern, Edith Fairman 95-935 SPR
* Health Care Fact Sheet: Drug Abuse Resistance Education (DARE), Celinda Franco and Edward Klebe 95-740 EPW
* Health Care Fact Sheet: Illicit Drug Use in the U.S., Edward R. Klebe etc., 93-300 EPW
* Mental Illness and Substance Abuse Disorders: Background Information Related to Health Care Reform, Edith Fairman Cooper 94-544 SPR
* Mortality and Economic Costs Attributable to Smoking and Alcohol Abuse, C. Stephen Redhead, 93-426 SPR
* The Safe and Drug-Free Schools and Communities Act, Celinda Franco 95-372 EPW

Drug Abuse -- International Narcotics Control
* Drug Control: International Policy and Options: Issue Brief, Raphael F. Perl, IB88093
* Drug Supply Control: 104th Congress; Issue Brief, David Teasley IB95025
* International Drug Control: Recent Developments and Issues for Congress, Raphael F. Perl 93-923 F
* NAFTA: Implications for Illicit Drug Supply in the United States, Raphael F. Perl 93-972 F
* Narcotics and Dangerous Drug Control: Landmark U.S. Enactments and Treaty Ratifications, Harry Hogan 94-614 GOV
* U.S. International Drug Control Programs: Agencies and Budgets, Jonathan E. Sanford, 93-500 F

Drug Abuse -- Policies and Legislation
* Anti-Crime Initiatives: Drug Control: Selected References, 1992-1994, Tangela G. Roe 94-383 L
* Community Anti-Crime Weed and Seed Program: Recent Developments, Suzanne Cavanagh and David Teasley 94-827 GOV
* Crime Control: Comparison of House and Senate Legislation of the 103rd Congress, 2nd Session, Charles Doyle, etc. 94-358 S
* Crime, Drug and Gun Control; Videoprogram, Elizabeth Bazan, etc. VT94-1312
* Drug Abuse: Treatment, Prevention and Education: Selected References, Jean M. Bowers 94-994 L
* Federal Sanction Imposed for Violations of the Controlled Substances Act and Related Statutes: Recent Developments, Charles L. Doyle 94-768 S
* Medicaid Services for Substance Abuse Treatment, Edward R. Klebe 93-764 EPW
* Medicare Coverage for Mental Illness and Substance Abuse, Edward R. Klebe 94-331 EPW
* Substance Abusers: New Rules for Disability Benefits from Supplemental Security

Be patient. If any phone number is incorrect, call (area code) 555-1212 and request the new listing.

Income and Social Security Disability Insurance, Carmen D. Solomon 95-291 EPW
* Supplemental Security Income (SSI) Drug Addicts and Alcoholics: Welfare Reform in the 104th Congress, Carmen D. Solomon 95-433 EPW

Drug Abuse Control
* see Drug Abuse

Drugs
* see Medicine -- Drugs

Earned Income Tax Credit
* see Taxation -- Personal Income Tax

Earth Summit
* see Environmental Protection

East Asia
* Asia Pacific Economic Cooperation (APEC) and the Indonesia "Summit' in 1994, Dick K. Nanto 94-242 E
* Asian Trade, Foreign Policy, and Security Issues; Audio Brief, Dick Nanto, etc. AB50312
* Capital Gains and Securities Transactions Taxation in Japan: Fact Sheet, Gregg Esenwein and Philip D. Winters 94-891 E
* Chemical Agent Attack in Tokyo, Steven R. Bowman 95-411 F
* China's Changing Conditions: Issue Brief, Robert G. Sutter IB93114
* Chinese Migration to the United States: Trends and Issues, Ruth Ellen Wasem 93-727 EPW
* Chinese Nuclear Weapons and Arms Control Policies: Implications and Options in the United States, Robert G. Sutter 94-422 S
* Defense Burdensharing: Is Japan's Host Nation Support a Model for Other Allies?, Stephen Daggett 94-515 F
* Japan's Budget: Role in Economic Policymaking, James K. Jackson 94-278 E
* Japan's Looming Bank Crisis: A Half Trillion Dollars in Non-Performing Loans?, Dick K. Nanto 94-667 E
* Oil in Vietnam: A Review of Foreign and Domestic Activities, Dario Scuka 93-416 E
* Political Change in Japan and the United States; Videoprogram, Richard Cronin VT93-1365
* Regional Security Consultative Organizations in East Asia and Their Implications for the United States, Larry Niksch 94-79 F
* South Korea: U.S. Defense Obligations, Larry A. Niksch 94-300 F

East Asia -- Foreign Relations
* China as a Security Concern in Asia: Perceptions, Assessment, and U.S. Options, Robert G. Sutter and Shirley Kan 95-46 S
* China in World Affairs--U.S. Policy Choices, Robert G. Sutter 95-265 S
* China Policy: Managing U.S.-PRC-Taiwan Relations After President Lee's Visit to the U.S., Robert Sutter 95-727 S
* China-U.S. Relations in a Post-Cold War World: Info Pack IP460C
* China-U.S. Relations: Issue Brief, Robert G. Sutter and Kerry Dumbaugh IB94002
* China's Sinister View of U.S. Policy: Origins, Implications, and Options, Robert Sutter 95-750 S
* East Asia: Challenges for U.S. Policy Makers; Videoprogram, Ray Ahearn, etc. VT92-181
* East Asia: The New Triangular Relationship, Implications for U.S. Influence, and Options for U.S. Policy, Robert G. Sutter 94-463 S
* The Hong Kong Crisis of 1993--Origins, Competing Priorities, and Outcomes, Robert G. Sutter 93-455 S
* Hong Kong's Transition to Chinese Rule: Issues, U.S. Interests, U.S. Options, Robert G. Sutter 95-743 S
* Indonesia: Recent Developments and U.S. Policy; Summary of a CRS Seminar, Larry Niksch 94-390 F
* Japan-U.S. Relations: Issues for Congress in the 1990's; Issue Brief, Robert G. Sutter IB94008
* Korea: Procedural and Jurisdictional Questions Regarding Possible Normalization of Relations With North Korea, Congressional Research Service 94-933 S
* Korea: U.S. South Korean Issues in the 1990s; Issue Brief, Robert G. Sutter IB94038
* Korean Crisis, 1994 Military Geography, Military Balance, Military Options, John M. Collins 94-311 S
* Korean Peninsula Tensions: North Korea and Nuclear Weapons; Info Pack IP484K
* North Korea: Military Relations With the Middle East, Rinn-Sup Shinn and Kenneth Katzman 94-754 F
* North Korea: U.S. Policy and Negotiations to Halt Its Nuclear Weapons Program; an Annotated Chronology and Analysis, Richard P. Cronin 94-905 F
* North Korean Nuclear Controversy: Defining Treaties, Agreements, and Terms,

Larry Niksch and Zachary Davis 94-752 F
* North Korea's nuclear Weapon Program: U.S. Policy Options, Richard Cronin, etc. 94-470 F
* Singapore: Background and U.S. Policy Issues, Barbara Leitch LePoer 95-658 F
* South Korea Under Kim Young Sam: Trends, Nuclear and Other Issues, Rinn-Sup Shinn and Robert G. Sutter 94-599 F
* Taiwan: Recent Developments and U.S. Policy Choices; Issue Brief, Robert Sutter IB94006
* U.S.-Indonesian Relations, Larry Niksch 94-233 F
* Vietnam in Transition and Vietnamese Relations With the United States, Robert G. Sutter 95-254 S
* Vietnam: Procedural and Jurisdictional Questions Regarding Possible Normalization of U.S. Diplomatic and Economic Relations, Robert G. Sutter, etc. 94-633 S
* Vietnam-U.S. Relations: The Debate Over Normalization; Issue Brief, Robert G. Sutter IB93081

East Asia -- Politics and Government
* Burma: Briefing Paper, Larry Niksch 94-725 F
* Cambodia: Peace Agreement, Elections, and Beyond; Issue Brief, Robert G. Sutter IB93048
* China After Deng Xiaoping--Implications for the United States, Robert G. Sutter 95-465 S
* China in Transition: Changing Conditions and Implications for U.S. Interests, Robert G. Sutter, etc. 93-1061 S
* Hong Kong's political Transition: Implications for U.S. Interests; Issue Brief, Robert G. Sutter IB94051
* Indonesia: Briefing Paper, Larry Niksch 94-706 F
* Japan's New Era of Coalition Governance: Implications for U.S. Interests, Richard P. Cronin 95-390 F
* Japan's Ongoing Political Instability: Implications for U.S. Interests, Richard P. Cronin 94-550 F
* Japan's Uncertain Political Transition; Issue Brief, Rinn-Sup Shinn IB94045
* Laos: Briefing Paper, Larry Niksch 95-798 F
* Mongolia: Briefing Paper, Larry Niksch 95-667 F
* North Korea After Kim Il Sung, Rinn S. Shinn 94578 F
* North Korea After Kim Il Sung: A CRS Roundtable: Audio Brief, Robert Sutter AB50305
* North Korea After Kim Il Sung: A CRS Roundtable; Videoprogram, Robert Sutter VT94-1348
* Philippines: Briefing Paper, Larry Niksch 95-565 F
* Thailand: Briefing Paper, Raymond J. Ahearn 94-796 F

East Asia -- Trade
* APEC--Asia Pacific Economic Cooperation: Free Trade and Other Issues, Dick Nanto 93-926 E
* APEC, EAEC, and Free Trade in the Asia Pacific, Dick Nanto 94-914 E
* China and the Agreement on Tariffs and Trade, George D. Holliday 94-723 E
* China: Current U.S. Sanctions, Kerry Dumbaugh 94-92 F
* The China-U.S. Trade Agreement on Intellectual Property Rights: Implications for China-U.S. Trade Relations, Wayne M. Morrison 95-463 E
* China's MFN Status: Implications of the 1994 Decision, Kerry Dumbaugh 94-531 F
* Deregulation as Market Opening in Japan, Dick K. Nanto 95-224 E
* Dispute Settlement under the WTO and Trade Problems With Japan, Dick Nanto 95-42 E
* Financial Services Trade With Japan, Dick Nanto 95-418 E
* Granting Most-Favored-Nation Status to China as a Market Economy Country, Vladimir N. Pregelj 94-514 E
* The Japan-U.S. Automobile and Parts Trade Dispute, Dick Nanto, etc. 95-725 E
* Japan-U.S. Automotive Framework Talks: Issue Brief, Gwenell L. Bass IB94055
* Japan-U.S. Trade Agreements, 1980-1993, William H. Cooper 94-481 E
* Japan-U.S. Trade and Economic Relations: Info Pack IP201J
* Japan-U.S. Trade Negotiations under the Framework: Status and Alternative Approaches, William H. Cooper 94-620 E
* Japan-U.S. Trade Negotiations: Will the Deadlock Be Broken?, Raymond Ahearn 94-724 F
* Japan-U.S. 1995 Automotive Dispute: Impact of 100 Percent Tariffs on Automobile Dealers by State, Penelope Fay Heavner 94-764 F
* Japanese and U.S. Involvement in Asia and the Pacific: Comparative Data and Analysis, Richard P. Cronin 94-764 F
* Japanese Investment in Asia; Videoprogram, Dick Nanto VT95-1341
* Japan's Keiretsu: Industrial Groups as Trade Barriers, Dick Nanto VT95-1341
* Japan's Response to U.S. Trade Barriers, Dick Nanto 94-82 E
* Japan's Response to U.S. Trade Pressures: End of an Era?, Raymond Ahearn 95-714 F
* A "Managed Trade" Policy Toward Japan? Wayne M. Morrison, etc. 94-524 E

Be patient. If any phone number is incorrect, call (area code) 555-1212 and request the new listing.

1311

Current Events and Homework

* Most-Favored Nation Status of the People's Republic of China: Issue Brief IB92094
* Regional Free Trade Partners and U.S. Interests: What's Next? Raymond J. Ahearn 95-392 F
* South Korea's Economy and Trade, Dick K. Nanto 94-624 E
* U.S. Commercial Relations With Japan and China; Videoprogram, Dick Nanto VT94-1309
* U.S. Economic Trade, and Financial Relations With Asia: A Statistical Overview, James Jackson, etc. 94-590 E
* U.S. Japan Trade Confrontation: Economic Perspective and Policy Options, Craig Elwell and Alfred Reifman 94-526 E
* U.S. Japan Trade: Framework Talks and Other Issues: Issue Brief, William H. Cooper IB95019

East-West Trade
* see Trade

Eastern Europe
* see Europe

Economic Conditions
* see Economic Policy

Economic Policy
* see also Budgets, Finance
* Budget and Economic Policy: Which Direction in 1993; Videoprogram William Cox and Donald Keifer VT93-1307
* Changing the Monetary Policy Goals under the Full Employment Act, G. Thomas Woodward 95-168 E
* Competitiveness: Economic Issue or Illusion?, Craig Elwell 94-424 E
* The Composite Index of Leading Economic Indicators, Brian Cashell 94-869 E
* Consumer Attitude Indexes: What Are They and What do They Mean?, Gail Makinen 95-407 E
* Consumer Price Index: Background and Current Issues; Info Pack IP505C
* The Consumer Price Index: A Brief Overview, Brian W. Cashell 93-637 E
* The Consumer Price Index: Background and Recent Controversies, Barry Molefsky 94-217 E
* The Consumer Price Index: Is It Biased?, Brian W. Cashell 95-654 E
* Current Economic Conditions and Selected Forecasts: Issue Brief, Gail Makinen IB89044
* The Economic and Budget Outlook; Videoprogram, Gail Makinen and Philip Winters VT95-1311
* Economic Comparisons of Mexico, Canada, and the United States: Implications for the NAFTA, Arlene Wilson 93-669 E
* Economic Development in the United States: Theory, Problems, and Federal Policy Response, J.F. Hornbeck 93-1022 E
* Economic Development in the United States: Theory, Problems, and Federal Policy Responses; an Issue Overview, J.F. Hornbeck 94-651 E
* Economic Forecasts and the Budget, Brian W. Cashell 95-222 E
* Gross National Product or Gross Domestic Product: What Difference Does It Make?, Brian W. Cashell 93-570 E
* Inflation and the Real Minimum Wage: Factsheet, Brian W. Cashell 94-899 E
* Inflation: Its Current Status; Issue Brief, Gail Makinen IB90129
* Monetary Policy: Current Policy and Conditions; Issue Brief, Gail E. Makinen IB1110
* A New Measure of Real GDP, Brian W. Cashell 95-892 E
* President Clinton's Federal "Investment" Proposals; Videoprogram, William Cox, etc. VT94-1332
* Quarterly Economic Outlook; Videoprogram, Gail Makinen VT95-1342
* Redefining the Federal Reserve's Monetary Policy Mandate, G. Thomas Woodward 95-394 E
* Saving in the United States: Why Is It Important and How Has It Changed?, Brian W. Cashell and Gail Makinen 94-54 E
* The "Sovereignty" Proposal: An Appraisal, Gail E. Makinen and Thomas Woodward 94-789 E
* The U.S. Fiscal Position: A Comparison With Selected Industrial Nations, Gregg Esenwein 94-558 E
* The Weaker Dollar and Its Effects on the U.S. Economy, Gail Makinen 95-715 E
* Will Deficit Reduction Stimulate the Economy? G. Thomas Woodward 93-802 E

Economic Statistics
* see Economic Policy

Ecuador
* see Latin America

Educate America Act
* Goals 200: Educate America Act--Citations to U.S. Code, Mary Ann Wolfe 94-342 A
* Goals 2000: Overview and Analysis, James B. Stedman 94-490 EPW
* A New Federal Role in Elementary and Secondary Education; Videoprogram, Wayne Riddle, etc. VT94-1316

Education
* see Education Policy, Elementary and Secondary Education, Higher Education, Job Training

Education Funding
* see Higher Education -- Student Aid

Education of Handicapped Children
* see Disabled

Educational Policy
* see also Elementary and Secondary Education, Higher Education
* Department of Education Funding, FY 1995 and FY 1996, Paul Irwin 95-331 EPW
* Educational Department: Debate Over Its Cabinet Level Status, Wayne Riddle, etc. 95-693 EPW
* Education Department: Proposals to Change Its Status, Wayne Riddle, etc. 95-754 EPW
* Education: Funding Issues; Info Pack IP199E
* Education Issues in the 104th Congress: A Checklist of CRS Products, M. Alexandra Salinas 95-111 L
* Education: Issues of Quality and Reform; Info Pack IP256E
* Federal Education Funding: A 1995 Perspective, Paul M. Irwin 95-217 EPW
* Federal Program for Children and Their Families, Dale Robinson 93-59 EPW

Educational Reform
* see Elementary and Secondary Education

EEC Countries
* see Europe

Egypt
* see also Middle East and North Africa
* Egypt-U.S. Relations: Issue Brief, Clyde R. Mark IB93087

El Salvador
* see also Latin America
* El Salvador and U.S. Aid: Congressional Action in 1992, K. Larry Storrs 93-310 F
* El Salvador and U.S. Aid: Congressional Action in 1993 and 1994, K. Larry Storrs 95-327 F
* El Salvador under Calderon Sol: U.S. Foreign Assistance Decisions; Issue Brief, K. Larry Storrs IB94048

Elderly
* see Aged

Election Law
* see Congress -- Apportionment and Elections, Elections

Elections
* see also Congress--Apportionment and Elections, Politics and Elections--Election Law, Presidents (U.S.)
* Asian American Electoral Participation and Representation, Kevin Coleman 94-893 GOV
* Black Electoral Participation and Representation , Kevin Coleman and Daryl Harris 93-1063 GOV
* Campaign Finance Legislation in the 104th Congress, Joseph E. Cantor 95-559 GOV
* Campaign Management: Selected References, Jean M. Bowers 94-730 L
* Congressional Districts: Sources of Maps and Demographic Information, Judy Frazier 93-681 C
* Congressional Primaries in 1996, Kevin Coleman 95-1015
* Congressional Redistricting: Federal Law Controls a State Process, David Huckabee 93-1060 GOV
* Elections for House, Senate, and President, 1900-1994: Nationwide Vote Totals and Seats Won, David Huckabee 95-978 GOV
* The Election Process in the United States, Kevin Coleman, etc. 95-800 GOV

Be patient. If any phone number is incorrect, call (area code) 555-1212 and request the new listing.

* Electoral Structure and Representative Government: Selected References, Tangela G. Roe 95-1108 L
* First Amendment Issues and Major Supreme Court Decisions Relating to Campaign Finance Laws, Thomas M. Durbin 92-48 A
* The National Voter Registration Act of 1993, "Motor-Voter.", Royce Crocker 94-276 GOV
* National Voter Registration: Issue Brief, Royce Crocker IB95073
* Political Activities: Regulations to Implement the Hatch Act Reform Amendments of 1993, Barbara M. Schwemle 94-275 GOV
* Political Activities 103rd Congress; Amendments to the Hatch Act, Barbara Schwemle 93-235 GOV
* The Presidential Primaries and Caucuses in 1996: A Calendar, Kevin Coleman 95-701 GOV
* Presidential Primaries and Caucuses in 1996: A Preliminary Calendar, Kevin Coleman 95-701 GOV
* Racial and Ethnic Electoral Districting: A Checklist of CRS products, 94-897 L
* Term Limits for Federal and State Legislators, Sula P. Richardson 94-287 GOV
* Term Limits for Members of Congress: Background and Contemporary Issues; Issue Brief, Sula P. Richardson IB95021
* Term Limits: Info Pack IP439T
* Voter Registration and Turnout: 1948-1992, Royce Crocker 94-22 GOV
* Voter Registration and Turnout, 1994, Royce Crocker 95-237 GOV
* Voter Registration by State and Party Affiliation, Judith B. Frazier 95-677 C
* Voter Registration and Turnout: 1994 Royce Crocker 95-237 GOV
* The Voting Rights Act of 1965: A Legal Overview, L. Paige Whitaker 91-736 A

Elections--Finance
* Campaign Finance Bills Passed by House and Senate in the 103rd Congress: Comparative Highlights, Joseph E. Cantor 94-97 GOV
* Campaign Finance: Info Pack IPO14C
* Campaign Finance Legislation in the 103rd Congress, Joseph E. Cantor 94-972 GOV
* Campaign Finance Legislation in the 104th Congress, Joseph E. Cantor 95-559 GOV
* Campaign Finance Reform: Full Text Comparison of H.R. 3 and S. 3 (103rd Congress) and Current Law, Joseph E. Cantor and L. Paige Whitaker 94-98 GOV
* Campaign Finance: Selected References, Jean M. Bowers 95-481 L
* Campaign Financing in Federal Elections: A Guide to the Law and Its Operation, Joseph E. Cantor 93-932 GOV
* Campaign Financing: Issue Brief, Joseph E. Cantor IB87020
* Congressional Reform: Rules, Campaign Finance, and Lobbying; Videoprogram, Joe Cantor, etc. VT94-1318
* Political Action Committees (PACs): Sources for Lists of PACs, Judith Frazier 92-538 C
* Political Action Committees: Selected References, Jean M. Bowers 95-482 L
* Soft Money in Campaign Finance Reform: Issue Brief, Thomas M. Durbin and M. Ann Wolfe IB93079

Electrification
* see Energy

Electronic Communications Privacy Act
* Wiretapping & Electronic Surveillance: The Electronic Communications Privacy Act and Related Matters, Charles Doyle 92-959 A

Elementary and Secondary Education
* Adult Education Act: Reauthorization Factsheet, Paul Irwin and Richard N. Apling 94-882 EPW
* Bilingual and Immigrant Education: Status in the 104th Congress, Steven R. Aleman 95-999 EPW
* Carl D. Perkins Vocational and Applied Technology Education Act: Reauthorization Overview, Richard N. Appling and Paul M. Irwin 94-427 EPW
* Does United States v. Lopez Affect the Gun-Free Schools Provisions of the Improving America's Schools Act of 1994?, Elizabeth B. Bazan 95-647 A
* Education Finance Incentive Grant Under ESEA Title I, Liane White 95-963 EPW
* Education Issues of Quality and Reform; Info Pack IP256E
* Education of the Gifted and Talented: Background and Funding, Susan Boren 95-945 EPW
* Elementary and Secondary Education Act: Reauthorization Summary, Steven Aleman 94-828 EPW
* Family Educational Rights and Privacy Act: P.L. 103-382 Amendments, Richard N. Apling 94-980 EPW
* Federal Support of School Choice: Background and Options, Wayne Riddle and James Stedman 95-344 EPW
* Goals 2000: Educate America Act--Citations to U.S. Code, Mary Ann Wolfe 94-342 A

* Goals 2000: Educate America Act Implementation Status and Issues, James B. Stedman, etc. 95-502 EPW
* Goals 2000: Overview and Analysis, James B. Stedman 94-490 EPW
* Head Start Fact Sheet, Anne C. Stewart 94-103 EPW
* Head Start in the 104th Congress, Dale H. Robinson 95-431 EPW
* High School Dropouts: An Overview, Robert F. Lyke 94-747 EPW
* Improving America's School Act: An Overview of P.L. 103-382, James B. Stedman 94-872 EPW
* The Individuals With Disabilities Education Act (IDEA): Legal Issues Surrounding the Least Restrictive Environment, Nancy L. Jones 95-286 A
* Individuals With Disabilities Education Act: Reauthorization Overview, Steven R. Aleman 94-156 EPW
* Individuals With Disabilities Education Act: Reauthorization Overview, Steven R. Aleman 95-675 EPW
* Information Technologies in Elementary and Secondary Education: Background and Federal Policy Issues; Issue Brief, James B. Stedman IB93071
* Legislative Prayer and School Prayer: The Constitutional Difference, David M. Ackerman 94-821 A
* Migrant Education: Fact on FY 1996 Budget Proposals, Bob Lyke 95-280 EPW
* National Curriculum Content Standards, James B. Stedman 94-963 EPW
* A New Federal Role in Elementary and Secondary Education; Videoprogram, Wayne Riddle, etc. VT94-1316
* Prayer and Religion in the Public Schools: What Is, and Is Not, Permitted, David Ackerman 93-680 A
* Prayer in the Public Schools: Legislative Status and Background; Issue Brief, David Ackerman and James Sayler IB95080
* Private Management of Public Schools: Status and Issues, Liane White 95-461 EPW
* The Right of Undocumented Alien Children to Basic Education: An Overview of Plyer v. Doe, Larry M. Eig 94-804 A
* School Desegregation Update: Summary and Analysis of the Supreme Court's Opinion in Missouri v. Jenkins, Kevin B. Greely 95-767 A
* School Facilities Infrastructure: Background and Funding, Susan Boren 95-1090 EPW
* School Prayer: Info Pack IP494 S
* School Prayer: The Congressional Response, 1962-1994, David Ackerman 94-829 A
* Science, Engineering, and Mathematics Education: Issue Brief, Christine M. Matthews IB92026
* Special Education: Issues in the State Grant Program of the Individuals With Disabilities Act, Steven R. Aleman 95-438 EPW
* Violence in Schools: An Overview, Liane E. White 94-141 EPW
* Violence in Schools and the Individuals With Disabilities Education Act, Nancy Lee Jones 95-107 A
* Women's Educational Equity Act: An Overview, Laura L. Monagle 94-857 EPW

Elementary and Secondary Education Act
* Elementary and Secondary Education Act: Reauthorization Summary, Steven R. Aleman 94-828 EPW
* Improving America's Schools Act: An Overview of P.L. 103-382, James B. Stedman 94-872 EPW
* Migrant Education: Fact Sheet on FY 1996 Budget Proposals, Bob Lyke 95-280 EPW
* A New Federal Role in Elementary and Secondary Education; Videoprogram, Wayne Riddle, etc. VT94-1316

Emergency Management
* A Descriptive Analysis of Federal Relief, Insurance, and Loss Reduction Programs for Natural Hazards, Malcolm Simmons, etc. 94-195 ENR
* Disaster Management: Issue Brief, Keith Bea IB93094
* Disaster Policy Options: Federal Aid or Insurance; Issue Brief, Rawle O'King IB95120
* Disaster Relief Program Summaries, Keith Bea 95-1048 GOV
* Farm Disaster Payments: Recent History and Specialty Crop Issues, Ralphe M. Chite 94-283 ENR
* The Federal Crop Insurance Reform Act of 1994, Ralph M. Chite 94-836 ENR
* FEMA and Disaster Relief, JoAnne Bryant 95-378 GOV
* U.S. Natural Disasters: State Exposures and Private Insurance Coverage, Rawle O. King 94-991 E

Employee Retirement Income Security Act
* Health Benefit Plans: ERISA and the States, Joan Sokolovsky, 93-747 EPW
* Pension Issues; Info Pack IP428P
* Private Pension Facts and Issues, Ray Schmitt, 93-448 EPW
* Private Pension Plan Standards: A Summary of ERISA, Ray Schmitt 94-506 EPW

Current Events and Homework

Employment
* see Labor--Employment and Unemployment

Employment Discrimination
* see Minorities

Endangered Species Act
* The Convention on International Trade in Endangered Species: Its Past and Future, Lynne Corn 94-675 ENR
* The Endangered Species Act and Private Property: A Legal Primer, Robert Meltz, 93-346 A
* Endangered Species: Continuing Controversy; Issue Brief, M. Lynne Corn, IB95003
* Endangered Species: Info Pack IP192E
* The Listing of a Species: Legal Definitions and Biological Realities, M. Lynne Corn, 92-944 ENR
* Reintroduction of Wolves, Jennifer A. Heck 92-524 ENR

Energy
* Department of Energy Laboratories: Capabilities and Missions, William C. Boesman 93-752 SPR
* Department of Energy Programs: History, Status, Options, Carl L. Behrens, etc. 95-908 ENR
* The Department of Energy's FY 1996 Budget: Issue Brief, Marc Humphries, etc. IB95043
* Domestic Natural Gas: Past, Present, and Future, Joseph P. Riva 94-504 SPR
* Energy Efficiency: A New National Outlook? Issue Brief, Fred J. Sissine IB95085
* Energy Policy: Info Pack IP447E
* Energy Tax Provisions in the Energy Policy Act of 1992, Salvatore Lazzari 94-525 E
* Fossil Energy Research and Development: Whither Coal? Issue Brief, Larry Parker IB94020
* The Low-Income Home Energy Assistance: A Fact Sheet, Jennifer A. Reisner and Joe Richardson 94-211 EPW
* Minerals Management Service Functions: Devolve to the States? Marc Humphries 95-785 ENR
* The Naval Petroleum Reserves: Proposed Sale and Issues, Robert L. Bamberger 95-293 ENR
* Outer Continental Shelf Leasing for Oil and Gas Development: Issue Brief, Lawrence C. Kumins IB95115
* Power Marketing Administrations: A Time for Change?, Larry Parker 95-356 ENR
* Power Marketing Administrations: Reassessing the Federal Role; Issue Brief, Larry Parker IB95093
* The Presidential Domestic Natural Gas and Oil Initiative, Joseph Riva 94-677 SPR
* Privatizing the United States Enrichment Corporation: Issue Brief IB95111
* Public Utilities Holding Company Act of 1935: Legislative History, Background and Recent Amendments, Ellen Lazarus 93-266 A
* Residential Energy Costs and LIHEAP, Bernard A. Gelb 95-350 E
* Rural Electric and Telephone Programs: Background and Issues, Carl Ek and Amy Abel 95-266 F
* The Rural Electrification Administration: Background and Current Issues, Carl Ek and Amy Abel 91-614 ENR
* Tennessee Valley Authority's Power Program--A Fact Sheet, Amy Abel and Mark Holt 95-249 ENR
* West Coast Oil Exports, Lawrence C. Kumins 95-214 ENR
* World Oil Production After Year 2000: Business as Usual or Crises?, Joseph P. Riva 95-925 SPR

Energy--Alternative Sources
* Alcohol Fuel Tax Incentives and EPAs Renewable Oxygenate Requirement, Salvatore Lazzari 94-785 E
* Alternative Fuels and Reformulated Gasoline: Issue Brief, David Gushee IB91008
* Alternative Transportation Fuels: Oil Import and Btu Tax Issues; David E. Gushee IB93009
* Ethanol and Clean Air: The "Reg-Neg" Controversy and Subsequent Events, Migdon Segal 93-614 SPR
* Ethanol and Reformulated Gasoline: The Renewable Oxygenate Standard, Susan Mayer 94-613 ENR
* Hydrogen: Technology and Policy, Daniel Morgan and Fred Sissine 95-540 SPR
* Impact of Highway Fuel Taxes on Alternative Fuel Vehicle Economics, David E. Gushee 94-247 ENR
* Renewable Energy: A New National Outlook; Issue Brief, Fred Sissine IB93063
* Tax Incentives for Alcohol Fuels, Salvatore Lazzari 95-261 E

Energy--Nuclear
* The Future of the Nuclear Weapons Laboratories. Part II: Civilian Issues, Jonathan E. Medalia 93-901 F

* High Level Nuclear Waste Disposal--A Fact Sheet, mark Holt 93-958 ENR
* Human Radiation Experiments and Radiation Safety: Selected References, 1981-1994, Bonnie f. Mangan 94-626 L
* Magnetic Fusion Energy--A Fact Sheet, Richard E. Rowberg 94-1003 S
* Magnetic Fusion Energy: Issue Brief, Richard E. Rowberg IB91039
* Nuclear Energy Policy: Issue Brief, Marc Holt and Warren Donnelly IB88090
* Nuclear Energy: Safety and Waste Issues; Info Pack IP074N
* Pakistan's Nuclear Activities: Legislation Related to the Cutoff of U.S. Aid, Richard Cronin, etc. 93-1036 F
* The Tokamak Physics Experiment: Description and Issues--An Update, Richard Rowberg 94-990 S
* Waste Isolation Pilot Plant--A Fact Sheet, Mark Holt 93-997 ENR

Energy--Petroleum
* The Arctic National Wildlife Refuge: Issue Brief, M. Lynne Corn, etc. IB95071
* Arctic Oil, Arctic Refuge; Videoprogram, M. Lynne Corn VT91-1489
* Automobile Fuel Economy Standards: Another Cup of CAFE? Issue Brief, Robert Bamburger IB90122
* Domestic Oil: Past, Present, and Future, Joseph P. Riva, Jr. 94-263 SPR
* Domestic U.S. Crude Oil: A Declining Asset, Joseph P. Riva, Jr. 95-479 SPR
* Iranian Military Buildup: What Sort of Threat to Persian Gulf Oil Supply?, Lawrence C. Kumins and Kenneth Katzman 95-572 ENR

Energy Policy
* see Energy

Enterprise Zones
* see Urban Affairs

Entitlement Programs
* see Welfare Entitlements

Environmental Health
* see Air Pollution, Environmental Protection, Water Pollution

Environmental Protection
* see also Air Pollution, Hazardous Substances, Solid Wastes, Water Pollution
* Acoustic Thermometry of Ocean Climate: Marine Mammal Issues, Eugene Buck 95-603 ENR
* Agriculture and the Environment: Audio Brief, John Blodgett, etc. AB50303
* Antarctica: Environmental Protection, Research and Conservation of Resources, James Mielke and Marjorie Ann Browne 95-476 SPR
* Border Environment Cooperation Commission and North American Development Bank: Background and Issues, Mary Tiemann and J.F. Hornbeck 95-184 ENR
* Brownfields Program: Cleaning Up Urban Industrial Sites, Mark Reisch 95-454 ENR
* Dioxin: Reassessing the Risk, Linda-Jo Schierow 95-1059 ENR
* A Directory of Some Interest Groups and Governmental Organizations Concerned With National Environmental Policies, Linda-Jo Schierow 93-831 ENR
* DOE Environmental Technology Development - A Fact Sheet, Mark Holt 94-230 ENR
* EPA, Risk Assessment, and Congress, John E. Blodgett 94-109 ENR
* International Financial Institutions and Environment: Multilateral Development Banks and the Global Environmental Facility, Susan R. Fletcher and Betsy A. Cody 94-173 ENR
* Market-Based Environmental Management: Issues in Implementation, Environment and Natural Resources Policy Division 94-213 ENR
* Risk and Cost-Benefit Provisions in House and Senate Bills, Linda-Jo Schierow 95-576 ENR
* Risk Assessment; Info Pack IP503R
* The Role of Risk Analysis and Risk Management in Environmental Protection: Issue Brief, Linda-Jo Schierow IB94036
* Sources of Information on the Environment, Kori Calvert 95-649
* Superfund Fact Book, Environmental and Natural Resources Policy Division 94-464 ENR

Environmental Protection--Policy
* Congress and International Environmental Policy, Susan R. Fletcher 93-695 ENR
* Environmental Policy and the Economy: Conflicts and Concordances, John Blodgett 95-147 ENR
* Environmental Protection Agency: FY 1995 Budget; Issue Brief, Martin R. Lee IB94013
* Environmental Protection Agency: FY 1996; Issue Brief Martin R. Lee IB95048
* Environmental Protection and the Unfunded Mandates Debate, Environment and Natural Resources Policy Division 94-739 ENR

Be patient. If any phone number is incorrect, call (area code) 555-1212 and request the new listing.

* Environmental Protection: From 103rd to the 104th Congress, Environment and Natural Resources Policy Division 95-58 ENR
* Environmental Protection Issues for the 104th Congress: A Checklist of CRS Products, Ted L. Burch 95-100 L
* Environmental Protection Laws and Treaties: Reference Guide, Environment and Natural Resources Policy Division 91-136 ENR
* Environmental Protection Legislation in the 103rd Congress: Issue Brief, Environment and Natural Resources Policy Division IB93007
* Environmental Protection Legislation in the 104th Congress, Issue Brief, Martin R. Lee IB95004
* Environmental Reauthorizations and Regulatory Reform: Recent Developments, John Blodgett 95-3 ENR
* Excise Tax Financing of Federal Trust Funds, Nonna A. Noto and Louis Alan Talley 93-6 E
* GATT, Trade Liberalization, and the Environment: An Economic Analysis, Arlene Wilson 94-291 E
* Lead-Based Paint Poisoning Prevention: Federal Mandates for Local Government-- A Fact Sheet, Linda Jo Schierow 93-91 ENR
* North American Free Trade Agreement: Environment Provisions and Issues, Mary Tiemann 93-760 ENR
* Summaries of Environmental Laws Administered by the Environmental Protection Agency, Martin R. Lee, etc. 95-59 ENR
* Trade and Environment: GATT and NAFTA, Susan Fletcher and Mary Tiemann 94-165 ENR
* Voluntary Program to Reduce pollution, James E. McCarthy 95-817 ENR

Equal Employment Opportunity
* see Minorities

ERISA
* see Employee Retirement Income Security Act Pensions

Estonia
* see also Europe
* The Baltic Republics: U.S. Policy Concerns; Issue Brief, Vita Bite IB90075

Ethanol
* see Energy--Alternative Sources

Ethics in Government
* see Congress--Members, Politics and Government

Ethics in Government Act
* Overview of the Independent Counsel Provisions of the Ethics in Government Act, Jack Maskell 94-732 A

Ethiopia
* Ethiopia: An Overview of the Transition Period, Ted Dagne 95-851 F

Ethnic Groups
* see Minorities

Europe
* see also Conflicts, Defense, Integration, Politics and Government, and Trade
* Capital Gains and Securities Transactions Taxation in Germany: Fact Sheet, Gregg A. Esenwein and Phillip D. Winters 95-51 E
* Capital Gains and Securities Transactions Taxation in the United Kingdom: Fact Sheet, Gregg A. Esenwein 94-920 E
* East Central European Economic Trends: Issue Brief, John Hardt and Phillip Kaiser IB93074
* Economic Issues for Summits in Moscow and Kiev, John Hardt and Phillip Kaiser 95-516 S
* Expenditure Tax Proposals in Other Countries; Sweden, Harry G. Gourevitch 95-550 S
* German Foreign Policy and U.S. Interests: Current Issues, Karen Donfried 95-564 F
* Greece and Turkey Current Foreign Aid Issues: Issue Brief, Carol Migdalovitz IB86065
* Immigration and Naturalization Laws: A Nine Country Comparison, Ruth Ellen Wasem, etc. 93-755 E
* Ireland and Northern Ireland: U.S. Aid, Investment, and Trade, Karen Donfried 94-997 F
* The Petroleum Status of Hungary, Joseph P. Riva 95-114 ENR
* Retroactive Tax Laws in Western Europe, Edith Palmer, etc. LL93-8

Europe--Conflicts
* The Balkans--U.S. and International Policy Options: Summary of CRS Seminar, Julie Kim 93-696 F
* Bosnia & Macedonia: U.S. Military Operations; Issue Brief, Steven Bowman IB93056
* Bosnia-Former Yugoslavia: Civil War in the Balkans; Info Pack IP466B
* Bosnia-Former Yugoslavia: Ongoing Conflict and U.S. Policy: Issue Brief, Steven J. Woehrel IB91089
* Bosnia-Hercegovina and Former Yugoslavia: Policy Issues and Options, Steven Woehrel 95-777 F
* Bosnia-Hercegovina Conflict and the 103rd Congress: Policy Debates and Summary of Major Legislation, Julie Kim and Dianne E. Rennack 94-1008 F
* Bosnia-Hercegovina Conflict: Chronology of Events in the Former Yugoslavia, June 1, 1993-May 31, 1994, Julie Kim and Steven Woehrel 94-522 F
* Bosnia-Hercegovina Federation: One Year of Muslim-Croat Cooperation, Julie Kim 95-496 F
* Bosnia-Hercegovina: Summary of the Debate on a Unilateral Lifting of the Arms Embargo, Steven Woehrel 95-477 F
* Bosnia-Hercegovina: Support from Islamic Countries, Kenneth Katzman, etc. 93-596 F
* Bosnia-Hercegovina's Partition and U.S. Policy, Steven Woehrel 93-904 F
* Bosnia: U.S. Objectives, Military Options, Serbian Responses, Mark Lowenthal 93-408 S
* Bosnian Brierpatch: Military Options, Mid-1995, John M. Collins 95-732 S
* Croatia: Armed Conflict Resumed, New U.N. Mandate, Prospects for Peace or War, Julie Kim 95-643 F
* Cyprus: Status of U.N. Negotiations; Issue Brief, Carol Migdalovitz IB89140
* Macedonia-Albanian Ethic Tensions: Chronology of the Confrontation in Tetovo, Julie Kim 95-381 F
* Northern Ireland and the Peace Process: The Joint Declaration of December 1993 Revisited, Karen Donfried 95-515 F
* Northern Ireland: IRA Cease-Fire, Karen Donfried 94-693 F
* Northern Ireland: The Peace Process; Videoprogram, Karen Donfried VT95-1340
* War Crimes in the Former Yugoslavia: Selected References, Valentin Leskovsek 94-762 L

Europe--Defense
* European Proposals for a New Atlantic Community, Stanley R. Sloan 95-374 S
* European Security: Bosnia, Russia, and NATO's Future; Audio Brief, Paul Gallis, etc. AB50310
* European Security: Bosnia, Russia, and NATO's Future; Videoprogram, Paul Gallis, etc. VT95-1303
* European Security Conference: The Balladur Plan, Paul E. Gallis 94-335 F
* NATO Beyond Bosnia, Stanley R. Sloan 94-977 S
* NATO: Congress Addresses Expansion of Alliance; Issue Brief Paul E. Gallis IB95076
* NATO: Enlargement in Central Europe, Paul E. Gallis 94-879 F
* NATO Enlargement: Partnership for Peace Members--On the Road to Alliance Membership? Paul E. Gallis 95-468 F
* NATO Enlargement and Russia: From Cold War to Cold Peace, Stanley R. Sloan and Steve Woehrel 95-594 S
* The NATO Strategy Review: Negotiating the Future of the North Atlantic Alliance, Stanley R. Sloan 91-379 RCO
* The NATO Summit: Transatlantic Relations at a Crossroads, Stanley R. Sloan 93-939 S
* NATO's Future: Info Pack IP425N
* Partnership for Peace, Paul E. Gallis 94-351 F
* Ukraine: Nuclear Weapons and U.S. Interests, Steven Woehrel 94-253 F
* The U.S.-Euratom Nuclear Cooperation Agreement, Zachary Davis 95-359 ENR
* U.S. Policy Toward Russia and NATO, Stanley R. Sloan 94-871 S
* The Western European Union, Paul F. Gallis 95-758 F

Europe--Integration
* European Monetary Union by the Year 2000?, Arlene Wilson 94-777E
* European Union: Economic Integration; Info Pack IP408E
* The New Europe: 1992 and Beyond; Videoprogram, Steven Woehrel, etc. VT92-665
* Nordic EU Membership: Issues for Congress, Carl Ek 95-385 F

Europe--Politics and Government
* The Baltic Republics: U.S. Policy Concerns; Issue Brief, Vita Bite IB90075
* Belarus: Basic Facts, Steven Woehrel 95-776 F
* Britain: Current Issues and Relations With the United States, Paul Gallis 94-967 F
* The Czech Republic and Slovakia; Implications of the Split, Frances T. Miko 93-66 F

Be patient. If any phone number is incorrect, call (area code) 555-1212 and request the new listing.

1315

* Economic Crisis in Ukraine: Dangers and Opportunities, John P. Hardt 94-668 S
* Finland: Briefing Paper, Carl Ek 95-635 F
* German-American Relations in the New Europe: Issue Brief, Karen Donfried IB91018
* Germany: Electoral Trends and Implications for the United States, Karen Donfried 95-240 F
* Italy: Parliamentary Elections; a Changing of the Guard?, Paul E. Gallis 94-259 F
* Macedonia: Basic Facts, Julie Kim 95-771 F
* Moldova Republic: Basic Facts, Steven Woehrel 95-403 F
* Norway: Briefing Paper, Carl Ek 95-708 F
* Poland, Czech Republic, Slovakia, and Hungary: Recent Developments; Issue Brief, Julie Kim and Frances Miko IB92051
* Romania, Bulgaria, Albania: Recent Developments; Issue Brief , Julie Kim and Carl Ek IB92064
* Roundtable on Northern Ireland; Videoprogram, Karen Donfried VT93-1364
* Slovenia: Basic Facts, Julie Kim 95-786 F
* Ukraine: Issue Brief, Steven Woehrel IB92072
* Ukraine's Uncertain Future and U.S. Policy, Steven Woehrel 94-738 F
* United Kingdom: Briefing Paper, Karen Donfried 94-758 F

Europe--Trade
* EC Trade With the United States and the Rest of the World: A Statistical Overview, Glennon J. Harrison 93-685 E
* The European Union: The World's Largest Trading Bloc., Glennon J. Harrison and Vivian Jones 95-43 E
* European Union-U.S. Trade Relations, Glennon J. Harrison 95-342 E
* NAFTA and the EC as Trading Blocs: A Distinction With a Difference, Glennon J. Harrison 93-864 E
* Regional Free Trade Partners and U.S. Interests: What's Next?, Raymond J. Ahearn 95-392 F
* U.S. Access to the EC Market: Opportunities, Concerns, and policy Challenges, Raymond A. Ahearn 92-514 F
* U.S.-European Union Trade and Investment, Glennon J. Harrison 95-34 E

European Community
* see Europe--Integration
* EC Trade with the United States and the Rest of the World: A Statistical Overview, Glennon J. Harrison, 93-685 E
* European Union: Economic Integration; Info Pack IP408E
* NAFTA and the EC as Trading Blocs: A Distinction With A Difference, Glennon J. Harrison 93-864 E
* U.S. Access to the EC Market: Opportunities, Concerns, and Policy Changes, Raymond J. Ahearn 92-514 F

Exchange Rates
* see International Finance

Excise Taxes
* see Taxation-Consumption Taxes

Executive Departments
* Alternative Dispute Resolution: Selected References, Jean M. Bowers 95-660 L
* Awards of Attorneys' Fees by Federal Courts and Federal Agencies, Henry Cohen 94-970 A
* Cost-Benefit Analysis: Issues in its Use in Regulation, John L. Moore 95-760 ENR
* DOE Environmental Technology Department--A Fact Sheet, Mark Holt 94-230 ENR
* Economic Development Administration: A Fact Sheet, Bruce K. Mulock 95-617 E
* Ecosystem Management: Federal Agency Activities, M. Lynn Corn, etc. 94-339 ENR
* Executive Perspectives on Oversight: Videoprogram, Eileen Siddman, Charles Bingman, etc. VT91-952
* Federal Government Corporations in Perspective, Ronald C. Moe 95-703 GOV
* Federal Regulatory Reform: An Overview; Issue Brief, Roger Garcia IB95035
* Food and Drug Administration: Selected Funding Data, Donna U. Vogt, 94-1002 SPR
* Government Management Reform Act of 1994: An Overview, Jennifer Suttle 95-942 GOV
* Government Performance and Results Act, P.L. 103-62; Interim Status Report; Revised, Genevieve J. Knezo 95-713 SPR
* Hotlines, Bulletin Boards, and Other Useful Government Telephone Numbers: Info Pack IP106H
* Inspectors General: Resources for Oversight; Videoprogram, Thomas Novotny, etc. VT91-956

* Major Federal Land Management Agencies: Management of Our Nation's Lands and Resources, Betsy A. Cody 95-599 ENR
* The National Biological Service, M. Lynne Corn 95-746 ENR
* Outcomes Research, Clinical Practice Guidelines, and the Agency for Health Care Policy and Research, Bernice Reyes-Akinbileje 94-488 SPR
* An Overview of NASA, Stephen J. Garber and David P. Radzanowski 95-101 SPR
* Presidential Appointments to Full-Time Positions in Executive Departments During the 103rd Congress, Rogelio Garcia 94-453 GOV
* Presidential Appointments to Full-Time Positions in Independent and Other Agencies, 103rd Congress, Rogelio Garcia 94-473 GOV
* Presidential Appointments to Full-Time Positions on Regulatory and Other Collegial Boards and Commissions, 103rd Congress, Rogelio Garcia 94-628 GOV
* The President's Cabinet, Ronald C. Moe 93-271 GOV
* Proposals to Eliminate the U.S. Department of Commerce: An Issue Overview, Edward Knight 95-834 E
* Recent Federal Outlays (FY 1990-1994) by Department and Agency and by Function, Philip Winters 95-132 E
* Separate But Equal: Two Hundred Years of Legislative-Executive-Judicial Relations; Videoprogram, Louis Fisher, etc. VT91-955
* Statutory Office of Inspector General, Frederick M. Kaiser 94-153 GOV
* Tennessee Valley Authority's Power Program--A Fact Sheet, Amy Abel and Mark Holt 95-249 ENR
* United States Regulations: Finding Regulatory Material, Mark Gurevitz 90-590 A
* U.S. Bureau of Alcohol, Tobacco, and Firearms, Suzanne Cavanagh and David Teasley 93-451 GOV
* U.S. Government: Info Pack IP162U
* Women Appointed to Full-Time Civilian Positions by President Clinton in 1993, Rogelio Garcia 94-272 GOV

Executive Departments--Reorganization
* The Alcohol, Drug Abuse, and Mental Health Administration (ADAMHA) Reorganization Act of 1992, Edward R. Klebe and Karen M. Judge 93-597 EPW
* Department of Energy Programs: History, Status, Options, Carl L. Behrens, etc. 95-508 ENR
* The Department of Energy's FY 1996 Budget: Issue Brief, Marc Humphries IB95043
* A Department of Science and Technology: A Recurring Theme, William C. Boesman 95-235 SPR
* Economic Development Administration: Reinventing or Elimination; Issue Brief, Bruce Mulock IB95100
* Education Department: Debate over Its Cabinet-Level Status, Wayne Riddle, etc. 95-693 EPW
* EPA Risk Assessment, and Congress, John E. Blodgett 94-109 ENR
* Executive Branch Reorganization: Issue Brief, Harold C. Relyea IB93026
* Food and Drug Administration: Selected Funding and Policy Issues, Donna Vogt 95-422 SPR
* The Grace Commission, Gary L. Galemore 93-741 GOV
* HUD's 1996 Budget and Reinvention Proposals, Morton J. Schussheim 95-462 S
* Implementation of National Performance Review Recommendations: General Government, Harold C. Relyea 93-936 GOV
* The National Performance Review, Harold C. Relyea 93-862 GOV
* National Performance Review: A New Look at the Federal Bureaucracy; Info Pack IP478N
* A New HUD? The Administration Proposal, Susan Vanhorenbeck 95-452 E
* Public Health Service: Program Consolidations; Issue brief, Edward Klebe IB95098
* Railroad Retirement Board: Background and Analysis of Issues Raised by Proposals to End Federal Administration, Dennis Snook 93-949 EPW
* Railroad Retirement Board: National Performance Review II, Dennis Snook 93-928 EPW
* Reforming Government: The Grace Commission and the National Performance Review, Harold Relyea and Gary L. Galemore 93-933 GOV
* Reinventing Government and the 103rd Congress: A Brief Overview, Harold Reylea 93-859 GOV
* Reinventing Government: The First Year, Harold C. Reylea 95-209 GOV
* Reinventing HUD: The Missions and Management of the Department of Housing and Urban Development, Morton Schussheim 94-854 S
* Social Security as an Independent Agency: A Fact Sheet, David Koitz 94-262 EPW
* U.S. Geological Survey: Its Mission and Its Future, James Mielke 95-145 SPR
* USDA: Background on the Department and Reorganization Issues, Geoffrey Becker 92-613 ENR
* USDA Reorganization Legislation in the 103rd Congress: A Section-by-Section Description, Geoffrey S. Becker 94-798 ENR

Executive Organization
* see Executive Departments

Export Administration Act
* Export Administration Act of 1994: Side-by-Side, Glennon J. Harrison 94-266 E

Export Enhancement Program
* Export Enhancement Program: Background and Current Issues, Lenore Sek 95-388 ENR

Export-Import Bank of the United States
* The Export-Import Bank: Background and Current Policy Issues, James K. Jackson 95-341 E

Exports
* see Agriculture--Foreign Trade, Foreign Trade--Imports and Exports

Fair Housing Act
* The Fair Housing Act: A Legal Overview, Henry Cohen 95-710 A

Fair Labor Standards Act
* see also Policies and Legislation
* The Fair Labor Standards Act: An Overview of Issues Before the 104th Congress: Issue Brief, William G. Whittaker IB95008
* The Fair Labor Standards Act: Changes Made by the 101st Congress and Their Implications, William G. Whittaker, 92-50 E
* The Fair Labor Standards Act: Minimum Wage Protection for Prison Inmate Workers and for non-Prison Labor, William G. Whittaker 93-895

Families
* see also Children
* Adoption: Parental Rights and Children's Interests, Gina Marie Stevens 94-618 A
* Adoption Tax Credit Proposal, Louis Alan Talley 94-957 E
* Adoption Tax Credit Proposal of Family Reinforcement -- H.R. 1215; Issue Brief, Louis Alan Talley IB95066
* The Child Abuse and Family Violence Act, as Amended in FY 1992, Dale H. Robinson 93-272 EPW
* Domestic Violence: Data, Federal Programs, and Selected Issues, Dale Robinson 95-865 EPW
* Family and Medical Leave, Leslie W. Gladstone 94-388 GOV
* Family and Medical Leave Act: Provisions Applicable to Congressional Offices, Leslie W. Gladstone 93-454 GOV
* Family and Medical Leave Legislation; Issue Brief, Leslie W. Gladstone IB86132
* Family Law: Authority of Congress to Legislate on Domestic Relations Questions, Lou Fields, etc. 89-152 A
* Family Leave: Info Pack, IP237F
* The Family Preservation and Support Program: Background and Description, Karen Spar 93-967 EPW
* The Family Tax Credit, Greg A. Esenwein 95-507 E
* Family Violence: Background Issues, and the State and Federal Response, Dale H. Robinson 92-356 EPW
* Federal Programs for Children and Their Families, Dale Robinson 93-59 EPW
* Federal Programs for Children and Their Families: An Overview, by Education and Public Welfare Division, Dale Robinson 93-221 EPW
* Federal Requirements for AFDC Programs: Comparison of 1935 and 1995 Law, Vee Burke HV 84 C
* Medicaid: Maternal and Child Health, Melvina For, 93-700 EPW
* Mother-Only Families: Trends and Issues, Carmen D. Solomon, 93-582 EPW
* Sick Leave for Federal Employees: Amendments to Law, Barbara Schwemle 95-22 GOV
* USIA Au Pair Program, Susan B. Epstein and Elizabeth A. Dunstan 95-256 F

Family Educational Rights and Privacy Act
* Family Educational Rights and Privacy Act: P.L. 103-382 Amendments, Richard N. Apling 94-980 EPW

Family Leave
* see Families

Family Planning
* see Medicine

Family Preservation and Support Program
* The Family Preservation and Support Program: Background and Description, Karen Spar 93-967 EPW

Family Violence
* see Children, Families

Far East
* see East Asia

FDIC
* see Federal Deposit Insurance Corporation, Finance--Banks

Federal Aid to Education
* see Education Policy, Elementary and Secondary Education, Higher Education

Federal Aid to Housing
* see Housing

Federal Budget
* see Budgets

Federal Crop Insurance Reform Act
* The Federal Crop Insurance Reform Act of 1994, Ralph M. Chite 94-836 ENR

Federal Deposit Insurance Corporation
* see also Finance--Banks
* Commercial Banks, Thrifts, and Credit Unions: The Federal Regulatory Structure, F. Jean Wells 93-773 E
* Depository Institution Regulatory Agencies: Restructuring Proposals, F. Jean Wells, 93-315 E
* FDIC and RTC: Recent Obstacles in Savings and Loan Litigation, L. Marlon Fields and M. Maureen Murphy 94-670 A
* Federal Deposit Insurance Premium Changes, William Jackson and Barbara Miles 95-441 E

Federal Employees
* see Government Employees

Federal Employees' Retirement System
* see Government Employees -- Pay and Benefits, Pensions --Government

Federal Helium Program
* The Federal Helium Program: The Reaction Over Inert Gas, James E. Mielke 95-197 SPR

Federal Juvenile Delinquency Act
* When the Young Violate Federal Criminal Law: Federal Juvenile Delinquency Act and Related Matters, Charles Doyle 95-774 S

Federal Pay
* see Government Employees -- Pay and Benefits

Federal Reserve System
* see Board of Governors of the Federal Reserve System (U.S.), Finance

Federal Tort Claims Act
* Federal Tort Claims Act: Current Legislative and Judicial Issues, Henry Cohen 95-717 A

Federal Transit Act
* Selected Labor Protection Regarding Transit, Amtrak, and Freight Railroads: Issue Brief IB95097

FERS
* see Pensions--Government

Finance
* Audits of the Federal Reserve System: Past, Present and Proposed., Pauline Smale 94-784 E
* Bank Mergers and Competition, F. Jean Wells 95-1046 E
* Banking and Finance Issues: A Checklist of CRS Products, Felix Chin 95-113 L
* Banking and Insurance Interaction in the Financial Institutions Regulatory Relief Act of 1995: The Baker Amendment and Controller's Moratorium, William Jackson 95-972 E
* Banks and Thrifts and FY 1996 Budget Reconciliation, F. Jean Wells and Barbara Miles 95-1012 E
* Banks and Thrifts: Securities & Insurance Powers, M. Maureen Murphy 95-936 A
* Board of Governors of the Federal Reserve System: History, Membership, and Current Issues, Pauline H. Smale 95-292 E

Be patient. If any phone number is incorrect, call (area code) 555-1212 and request the new listing.

1317

Current Events and Homework

* Changing the Monetary Policy Goals Under the Full Employment Act, Thomas Woodward 95-168 E
* Derivatives: Issue Brief, Mark D. Jickling IB95011
* Commercial Banks and Savings Associations: Alike or Distinct?, William Jackson 95-977 E
* Community Reinvestment Act Compliance Issues, William Jackson 95-842 E
* Comparison of Securities Litigation Reform Bills Passed by the House and the Senate, Michael V. Seitzinger 95-822 A
* Contract Abrogation in the Context of Savings & Loan Agreements Involving Regulatory Goodwill: Windstar v. United States-F.sd-(Fed. Cir. 1995), Maureen M. Murphy 95-958 A
* Corporate-Owned Life Insurance: Tax Issues, Jack Taylor 95-990 E
* Electronic Banking: Legal Underpinnings, Maureen Murphy 95-1080 A
* Electronic Money: Technology and Retail Payment, F. Jean Wells 95-828 E
* Electronic Money: Technology and Retail Payment Mechanisms; an Issue Overview 95-878 E
* Federal Disaster Insurance for Homeowners: Policy Issues in the 104th Congress, Rawle O. King 95-1023 E
* Federal Reserve Accountability and Independence: Recent Legislation and Oversight, Jean Wells 95-12 E
* Federal Reserve Independence, William Jackson 93-557 E
* Federal Reserve Interest Changes, 1994-1995, G. Thomas Woodward 95-781 E
* Federal Reserve Interest Rate Increases, 1994-1995, G. Thomas Woodward 95-241 E
* Federal Reserve System: Info Pack IP105E
* Financial Derivatives: Definitional and Uncertainty, Kevin F. Winch 95-568 E
* Financial Services Industry Policy Issues: Diversification and Regulation; Issue Brief, F. Jean Wells IB95065
* Gold: Frequently Asked Questions About U.S. Government Holdings, Carolyn V. Torsell 93-1048 C
* Hedge Funds, Mark Jickling 94-511 E
* Insurance Solvency Regulations: Is There A Federal Role?, Rawle King 94-936 E
* Legal Reforms Passed by the House: Issue Brief, Henry Cohen and Michael Seitzinger IB95030
* Monetary Policy: Current Policy and Conditions; Issue Brief, Gail E. Makinen IB91110
* Redefining the Federal Reserve's Monetary Policy Mandate, G. Thomas Woodward 95-394 E
* The Savings Association Insurance Fund Undercapitalization and Legislative Options: An Update, Barbara L. Miles 95-1084 E
* Securities Litigation Reform Bills: Comparison of H.R. 1058 as Passed by the House, and S. 240, as Marked Up, Michael V. Seitzinger 95-830 A
* Securities Market Deregulation Proposals in the 104th Congress: Issue Brief, Kevin F. Winch IB95109
* Securities Transaction Settlement: Key Transitional Issues Related to T+3, Gary Shorter 95-899 E
* Shareholder Litigation Reform: Have Frivolous Securities Suits Exploded?, An Issue Overview, Gary W. Shorter 95-695 E
* Smart Cards: Fact Sheet, Pauline Smale 95-965 E
* Taxation of Life Insurance Companies: Policy Holder Dividends and Section 809, Jack Taylor 95-678 E
* The Thrift Charter: Should It Be Eliminated?, F. Jean Wells 95-931 E
* U.S. Natural Disasters: State Exposures and Private Insurance Coverage, Rawle O. King 94-991 E

Finance--Banks
* Bank Insurance Activities: An Economic Analysis, William Jackson 94-68 E
* Bank Insurance Powers, M. Maureen Murphy 94-24 A
* Bank Regulatory Agency Consolidation Proposals: A Structural Analysis; An Issue Overview, F. Jean Wells and William Jackson 94-256 E
* Bank Sales of Insurance: Recent Litigation, M. Maureen Murphy 95-446 A
* Banking and Finance Issues: A Checklist of CRS Products, Felix Chin 95-113 L
* Banking and Finance Issues: Recent Congressional Activities and a Preview for 1995, F. Jean Wells, etc. 94-998 E
* Banking and Finance Issues: Recent Congressional Activities and a Preview for 1995; an Issue Overview, Jean Wells, etc. 94-1010 E
* Banking Issues: An Overview; Info Pack IP429B
* Banks' Sale of Mutual Funds: Legislative and Regulatory Issues; An Overview, Gary W. Shorter 95-102 E
* Banks' Sale of Mutual Funds: Regulatory and Legislative Issues, Gary W. Shorter 94-875 E
* Commercial Banks, Thrifts, and Credit Unions: The Federal Regulatory Structure, F. Jean Wells and Pauline H. Smale 93-773 E
* Community Development Banking and Financial Institutions: The Administration's Proposal; an Issue Overview, F. Jean Wells and William Jackson 93-698 E
* Community Development Financial Services: Alternative Legislative Approaches, F. Jean Wells and William Jackson 93-483 E

* Community Development Lenders: Policy Options and the Track Record, F. Jean Wells and William Jackson 93-483 E
* Community Development Revolving Loan Program for Credit Unions, Pauline Smale 94-819 E
* The Community Reinvestment Act After FIRREA, M. Maureen Murphy 91-754 A
* The Community Reinvestment Act and the President's Initiative for Reform, F. Jean Wells 94-520 E
* The Community Reinvestment Act and the President's Initiative for Reform: An Issue Review 94-557 E
* Depository Institution Regulatory Agencies: Restructuring Proposals, F. Jean Wells 93-315 E
* Depository Institution Regulatory Agencies: Restructuring Proposals; an Issue Overview , F. Jean Wells 93-818 E
* Fair Trade in Financial (Banking and Securities) and the General Agreement on Trade In Services, William Jackson 95-270 E
* Fair Trade in Financial Services: Legislation and the GATT, William Jackson 94-279 E
* FDIC and RTC: Recent Obstacles in Savings and Loan Litigation, L. Marlon Fields and M. Maureen Murphy 94-670 A
* Federal Deposit Insurance Premium Changes, William Jackson and Barbara Miles 95-441 E
* Federal Reserve Interest Rate, Bank Interest Rate, and Bank Profitability Relationships in the Recent Financial Cycle, William Jackson 94-587 E
* Financial Diversification, Bank Subsidiaries, and Holding Companies, William Jackson and F. Jean Wells 95-348 E
* Financial Institutions, Community Development, and Fair Lending: Federal Initiatives, F. Jean Wells and William Jackson 94-727 E
* Financial Institutions, Markets, and Regulators: A Structural Analysis, Jean Wells and William Jackson 95-297 E
* Financial Institutions, Markets, and Regulators: A Structural Analysis; an Issue Overview, Jean Wells and William Jackson 95-405 E
* Financial Regulation: An Overview, Jean Wells and William Jackson 95-397 E
* Financial Services Industry Legislative Issues: A Glossary of Terms, Jean Wells, etc. 95-569 E
* Foreign Investment in American Banking: Competitiveness, Legislation, and Regulation William Jackson 94-705 E
* Glass-Steagall Act Reform, William Jackson 95-467 E
* Nationwide (Interstate) Banking: An Update, William Jackson 95-749 E
* Resolution Trust Corporation Completion Act, M. Maureen Murphy 94-74 A
* The Reigle Community Development and Regulatory Improvement Act of 1994, Titles I and II: Community Development, Consumer Protection, Small Capital Formation, Maureen Murphy 94-700 A
* The Reigle Community Development and Regulatory Improvement Act of 1994, Titles III-VI: Paperwork Reduction, Regulatory Improvement, Money Laundering, Maureen Murphy 94-696 A
* The Reigle-Neal interstate Banking and Branching Efficiency Act of 1994, Maureen Murphy 94-744 A
* Salomon Brothers' Violations: Explanation, Consequences, and Options for Reform: Issue Brief, James M. Bickley and Mark Jickling IB91134
* Savings and Loan Cleanup Cost: Fact Sheet, Barbara Miles 95-133 E
* The Savings Association Insurance Fund: Undercapitalization and Legislative Options, Barbara L. Miles 94-896 A
* Universal Banking (Deposits and Diversified Industries in One Company?): An Issue Overview, William Jackson 95-734 E
* Whitewater/Madison Guaranty S7L Affairs: Info Pack IP487W

Finance -- Securities
* Chaos Theory in Financial Markets: Overview and Annotated bibliography, Kevin Winch and Pamela Hairston 95-228 E
* Merging the CFTC and the SEC?, Mark Jickling 95-698 E
* Proposed Reform of Private Securities Litigation: Title II of the Common Sense Legal Reforms Act, Michael V. Seitzinger 95-68 A
* Securities Litigation Legislation in the Senate: Issue Brief, Michael V. Seitzinger IB95070
* Securities Litigation Reform: A Comparison of Legislative Proposals, Mark Jickling 95-281 E
* Securities Litigation Reform Bills: Comparison of H.R. 1058, as Passed by the House, and S. 240 and S. 67, as Introduced, Michael V. Seitzinger 95-642 A
* Securities Litigation Reform: Have Frivolous Shareholder Suits Exploded?, Gary W. Shorter 95-656 E
* Shareholder Litigation Reform: Have Frivolous Securities Suits Exploded?, Gary W. Shorter 95-695 E

Financial Aid to Students
* see Higher Education -- Student Aid

Financial And Fiscal Affairs
* see Budgets, Economic Policy, Finance, International Finance, Money and Banking

Financial Institutions
* see Finance -- Banks, International Finance -- Banks

Financial Institutions Reform, Recovery and Enforcement Act
* The Community Reinvestment Act After FIRREA, M. Maureen Murphy 91-754 A

Finland
* see also Europe
* Finland: Briefing Paper, Carl Ek 95-635 F

FIRREA
* see Financial Institutions Reform, Recovery, and Enforcement Act

Fiscal Policy
* see Budgets

Fisheries
* see Marine Resources--Fisheries

Flags
* see History (U.S.)

Food
* Child Nutrition: Issues in the 104th Congress; Issue Brief, Jean Yavis Jones IB95047
* Child Nutrition: Program Information, Data, and Analysis, Jean Yavis Jones 93-165 EPW
* Child Nutrition Programs: Facts and Issues, Jean Davis Jones and Joe Richardson 95-230 ENR
* The Delaney Clause Effects on Pesticide Policy, Donna U. Vogt 95-514 SPR
* Domestic Food Assistance: 1995 Program Facts and Proposals, Jean Yavis Jones 95-73 ENR
* Domestic Food Programs: Reconciliation and Welfare Reform Proposals, Jean Yavis Jones 95-1096 ENR
* The Emergency Food Assistance Program: TEFAP Facts and Issues, Jean Yavis Jomnes 94-695 ENR
* Food Additive Regulations: A Chronology, Donna U. Vogt 95-857 ENR
* Food and Drug Administration: Selected Funding Policy Issues, Donna Vogt 95-422 SPR
* Food and Drug Administration: Selected Funding Data, Donna U. Vogt 94-1002 SPR
* Food Assistance Block Grants in the Personal Responsibility Act, Joe Richardson 95-196 EPW
* Food Assistance Programs: Nutrition Standards, Donna V. Porter 95-733 SPR
* Food Stamp Reform: A Brief Summary, Joe Richardson 95-366 EPW
* Food Stamps: Background and Funding, Joe Richardson 94-85 EPW
* How the Food Stamp Program Works: 13th Edition, Joe Richardson 92-935 EPW
* The "Hunger" Issue and Federal Food Assistance, Jean Yavis 93-414 EPW
* National School Lunch Facts and Issues, Jean Yavis Jones 95-475 ENR
* Older Americans Act Nutrition Program: Fact Sheet, Carol O'Shaughnessy 95-379 EPW
* Selected CRS Reports Available on Food and Agricultural Topics, Environmental and Natural Resources Policy Division 94-880 ENR
* Special Supplemental Nutrition Program for Women, Infants, and Children (WIC): A Fact Sheet, Melvina Ford 94-361 EPW
* Special Supplemental Nutrition Program for Women, Infants, and Children (WIC): Funding Issues, Joe Richardson 95-335 EPW

Food -- Labeling and Safety
* The Delaney Clause: The Dilemma of Regulating Health Risk for Pesticide Residues, Donna U. Vogt, 92-800 SPR
* The Delaney Dilemma: Regulating Pesticide Residues in Foods--Seminar Proceedings, March 16, 1993, Donna U. Vogt, 93-510 SPR
* Dietary Supplement Health and Education Act of 1994: P.L. 103-417, Donna V. Porter 94-965 SPR
* Dietary Supplements: Brief Chronology of Recent Events, Donna V. Porter, 94-918 SPR
* Dietary Supplements: Use and Regulation, Donna V. Porter, 94-208 SPR
* FDA's Enforcement Authorities for Foods: Are They Adequate?, Donna U. Vogt 94-441 SPR

* Food Safety: Congressional Options for Revising the Pesticide Residue System, Donna U. Vogt 94-760 SPR
* Food Safety Issues in the 104th Congress: Issue Brief, Donna U. Vogt IB95061
* Foodborne Illness: Recent Outbreaks of Escherichia Coli 0157:H7, Donna U. Vogt 94-99 SPR
* Foodborne Illness: What Does the Data Tell Us?, Donna U. Vogt 94-917 SPR
* Foods and Biotechnology: FDA's Regulatory Policy; Proceedings of a Seminar, July 22, 1992, Irene Stith-Coleman, 93-712 SPR
* Meat and Poultry Inspection: Background and Current Issues, Geoffrey S. Becker, 93-574 ENR
* Seafood Inspection Issues, Geoffrey Becker, 95-290 ENR

Food, Agriculture, Conservation, and Trade Act
* Agricultural Research and Extension: Current Issues, Jean M. Rawson, 93-83 ENR
* Farm Commodity Legislation: Chronology, 1933-93, Geoffrey S. Becker 94-576 ENR
* Farm Disaster Payments: Recent History and Specialty Crop Issues, Ralph Chite 94-283 ENR

Food Labeling
* see Food--Labeling and Safety

Food Relief Programs
* see Foreign Aid

Food Safety
* see Food--Labeling and Safety

Food Stamp Plan
* see Food

Foreign Aid
* see also Defense Policy, Trade
* Africa: U.S. Foreign Assistance Issues; Issue Brief, Raymond W. Copson IB95052
* AIDS in the Developing World: The International Response, Lois McHugh 93-1016 F
* Bosnia & Macedonia: U.S. Military Operations; Issue Brief, Steven Bowman IB93056
* Central America and U.S. Foreign Assistance: Issues for Congress; Issue Brief, Mark P. Sullivan IB84075
* Child Survival: Renewed Focus in U.S. Foreign Aid, Lois McHugh 95-868 F
* Conventional Arms Transfers in the Post-Cold War Era, Richard F. Grimmett, 93-852 F
* Conventional Arms Transfers to Developing Nations, 1987-1994, Richard F. Grimmett 95-862 F
* Conventional Arms Transfers: President Clinton's Policy Directive, Richard F. Grimmett 95-639 F
* Defense and Foreign Aid Budget Analysis and the Use of Constant Dollars, Alice C. Maroni, etc. 86-154 F
* DOD Assistance to Foreign Humanitarian and Disaster Relief: The Current Congressional Controversy, Nina Serafino 95-976 F
* El Salvador and U.S. Aid: Congressional Action in 1992, K. Larry Storrs 93-310 F
* Foreign Aid: Answers to Basic Questions, Curt Tarnoff 92-309 F
* Foreign Aid Budget and Policy Issues for the 104th Congress: Issue Brief, Larry Q. Nowels IB95020
* Foreign Aid: Info Pack IP044F
* Foreign Aid Reform Legislation: Background, Contents and Issues, Larry Q. Nowles 94-23 F
* Foreign Aid: Review of Major Studies From 1980-1995, Larry Q. Nowels 95-946 F
* Foreign Assistance: An Overview of U.S. Aid Agencies and Programs, Jonathan E. Sanford and Pamela D. Richardson 96-506 F
* Foreign Assistance and Commercial Interests: The Aid for Trade Debate, Curt Tarnoff etc. 93-528 F
* Foreign Food Assistance: P.L. 480 Budget Facts, Susan B. Epstein 94-204 F
* Foreign Policy Budget: A Checklist of CRS Products, Sherry Shapiro 95-551 L
* Foreign Policy Rescissions and Supplemental Appropriations for FY 1995; Larry Q. Nowels IB95041
* Greece and Turkey: Current Foreign Aid Issues: Issue Brief, Carol Migdalovitz IB86065
* International Disaster Assistance: Cost to the United States of Six Recent Crises, Lois McHugh 95-835 F
* International Population and Family Planning Programs: Issues for Congress; Issue Brief, Shirley Kan IB85187
* Israel: U.S. Foreign Assistance; Issue Brief, Clyde Mark IB85066

Be patient. If any phone number is incorrect, call (area code) 555-1212 and request the new listing.

1319

* Fair Trade in Financial Services: Legislation and the GATT, William Jackson 94-279 E
* The GATT Accord: Implications for U.S. Foreign Policy , Richard P. Cronin and Paul E. Gallis 94-186 F
* The GATT and Other Trade Agreements: Congressional Action by Statute or by Treaty?, Louis Fisher 94-890 S
* GATT and Regional Free Trade Agreements, George D. Holliday 93-989 E
* GATT and the Pharmaceutical Industry: Prospective Effects of the Uruguay Round on the Industry, Sylvia Morrison 94-831 E
* The GATT and the WTO: An Overview, Arlene Wilson 95-424 E
* GATT (General Agreement on Tariffs and Trade): Background Information, Penelope Fay Heavner 94-238 C
* GATT: General Agreement on Tariffs and Trade; Info Pack IP481G
* GATT: The Uruguay Round Agreement and Developing Countries, Susan P. Epstein 95-260 F
* GATT, Trade Liberalization, and the Environment: An Economic Analysis, Arlene Wilson 94-291 E
* How Will the Uruguay Round of GATT Affect the U.S. Computer Industry?, Sylvia Morrison 94-840 E
* Intellectual Property Rights and the Uruguay Round of Multilateral Trade Talks: Economic Affects, Lenore Sek 94-722 E
* Pension Provisions Enacted With the General Agreement on Tariffs and Trade, Ray Schmitt 95-212 EPW
* A Reappraisal of the Economic Effects of the 1994 GATT Agreement, Alfred Reifman and Craig Elwell 94-659 S
* Telecommunications Services: Provisions in the Uruguay Round and in NAFTA, Angeles Villarreal 94-653 E
* Trade and Environment: GATT and NAFTA, Susan Fletcher and Mary Tiemann 94-165 ENR
* Trade, Competitiveness, and International Economic Policy: A Bibliography of CRS Products, Robert Howe 93-611 L
* Trade Policy in the 104th Congress, George D. holliday 95-485 E
* The Uruguay Round: A Review of Major Issues by Congressional Research Service, Lenore Sek 94-294 E
* Uruguay Round of Trade Negotiations: A Checklist of CRS Products, Robert Howe 95-370 L
* The Uruguay Round of Trade Negotiations; Videoprogram, Lenore Sek VT94-1301
* Uruguay Round: Reform of the Safeguard Provisions of GATT, George holliday 95-275 E
* Why Certain Trade Agreements Are Approved as Congressional-Executive Agreements Rather than as Treaties, Jeanne J. Grimmett 94-766 A
* World Trade Organization: Institutional Issues and Dispute Settlement, Jeanne J. Grimmett 94-627 A

General Interest

* see History (U.S.) and References Sources
* Additions to the Major Issues File: Issue Brief IB95001
* Addresses for Presidential Libraries and Selected Historic Sites, Vanessa Cieslak 95-25 C
* Basic References Sources for Congressional Offices: An Annotated Selection of Publications and Services, Maureen Bearden 95-57 C
* Black History Month: Info Pack IP344B
* The Congressional Scene: Selected Publications Covering the Congress, Pamela M. Dragovich 94-958 C
* The Congressional Staff Guide to Finding Information in CRS Reading Rooms and Reference Centers, Merete F. Gerli 95-121 C
* The Constitution of the United States, Including the Bill of Rights and the Declaration of Independence: A Guide to Obtaining Copies, Pamela M. Dragovich 95-442 C
* Fax-on-Demand Services Available from Federal Government Agencies, Glenda Richardson 95-434 C
* The Federal Money Trail: Data Sources on Federal Aid, Grants, Loans, and Procurement in States and Local Areas, James R. Riehl 95-637 C
* Foreign Companies in the United States: A Guide to Lists and Directories, Vanessa Cieslak 94-737 C
* Fund Raising Techniques for Groups: Selected References, 1988-1993, Robert S. Kirk 93-825 L
* Grants and Foundation Support: Selected Sources of Information on Government and Private Funding 95-1036 C
* Hispanic Heritage Month: Info Pack IP427H
* Hotlines, Bulletin Boards, and Other Useful Government Telephone Numbers: Info Pack IP106H
How to Find Information About a Subject: A Guide to Reference Materials in Local Libraries, Merete Gerli 90-155 C
* How to Find Information in a Library, Suzy Platt 94-483 C
* How to Follow Current Federal Legislation and Regulations, Carol D. Davis 95-314 C

* How to Obtain Copies of Videotapes of Proceedings of Congress and Network and Cable Television Broadcasts, Michelle M. Springer 95-728 C
* Inexpensive Hotels and Housing in Washington, D.C., Bette Alberts 95-544 PGM
* The Largest Corporations in the United States: Information and Addresses from the Forbes 500, Felicia G. Kolp 95-716 C
* Legislative History: A Guide for Constituents, Mark Guretiz 89-596 A
* Legislative Procedure: An Introductory Guide to Sources, Pamela B. Dragovich 94-629 C
* Legislative Research in Congressional Offices: A Primer, Clay H. Welborn 95-657 GOV
* Lists of Members of Congress and Their Committee Assignments: A Guide to Sources, Jon R. Simon 92-530 C
* Lobbyists and Interest Groups: A List of Information Sources, Jon R. Simon 94-669 C
* Native American Heritage: Info Pack IP454N
* Organizations that Rate Members of Congress on Their Voting Records, Kathy Doddridge 95-26 C
* Political Action Committees (PACs): Sources for Lists of PACs, Judith B. Frazier 92-538 C
* Public Speaking and Speechwriting: Selected References, Jean Bowers 94-860 L
* Sources of Information on the Environment, Kori Calvert 95-649 C
* SCORPIO Reference Manual, Congressional Research Service 95-941 AU
* SCORPIO Self-Teaching Workbook, Theodore Moore and Tarria Burwell 91-908 AU
* Speech Material: Abraham Lincoln's and George Washington's Birthday's; Info Pack IP373A
* Speech Material: Columbus Day; Info Pack IP380C
* Speech Material: Fourth of July; Info Pack Info Pack IP377F
* Speech Material: Graduation; Info Pack IP379S
* Speech Material: Labor Day; Info Pack IP374L
* Speech Material: Martin Luther King, Jr.'s Birthday; Info Pack IP372M
* Speech Material: Memorial Day; Info Pack IP376M
* Speech Material: Thanksgiving Day; Info Pack IP381T
* Speech Material: Veterans Day; Info Pack IP378V
* Speechwriting and Delivery: Info Pack IP139S
* United States Law: Finding Statutory Material, Thomas B. Ripy etc., 90-110 A
* Voting Records of Members of Congress: A Self-Help Guide to Their Compilation, Jennifer Manning 94-992 C
* Where to Get Publications from the Executive and Independent Agencies: A Directory of Sources for Official Documents, Janet Hayes etc., 95-54 C

General Interest -- Grants

* Fund Raising Techniques for Groups: Selected References, 1988-1993, Robert S. Kirk 93-825 L
* Grant Proposal Development, Rhoda Newman 90-430 C
* Grants and Foundation Support: Info Pack IP050G
* Grants and Foundation Support: Selected Sources of Information on Government and Private Funding, Rita Tehan and Rhoda Newman 92-498 C
* Managing Projects and Grant Work: Videoprogram, CRS VT94-1346

General Mining Law

* Hardrock Mining, the 1872 Law, and the U.S. Economy, Bernard A. Gelb 94-540 E
* Mining Law Reform: The Impact of a Royalty, Marc Humphries 94-438 ENR
* Reforming the General Mining Law of 1872: A Comparison of S. 775 and H.R. 322, Marc Humphries 93-632 ENR
* The 1872 Mining Law: Time for Reform?, Issue Brief, Marc Humphries IB89130

Geological Survey (U.S.)

* U.S. Geological Survey: Its Mission and Its Future, James E. Mielke 95-145 SPR

Georgia Republic

* see also Central Asia
* Georgia (Republic): Basic Facts, Jim Nichol 94-608 F

Germany

* see Eastern Europe
* Capital Gains and Securities Transactions Taxation in Germany: Fact Sheet, Gregg A. Esenwein and Philip D. Winters 95-51 E
* German Foreign Policy and U.S. Interests: Current Issues, Karen Donfried 95-564 F
* Germany: Electoral Trends and Implications for the United States, Karen Donfried 95-240 F

Ghana

* see also Africa (Sub-Saharan)
* Ghana: Briefing Paper, Raymond W. Copson 94-830 F

Be patient. If any phone number is incorrect, call (area code) 555-1212 and request the new listing.

1321

Current Events and Homework

Glass-Steagall Act
* see also Finance
* Banking Issues: An Overview; Info Pack IP429B
* Glass-Steagall Act Reform, William Jackson 95-467 E

Global Climatic Changes
* see Air Pollution--Ozone

Global Positioning System
* GPS Satellite Navigation and Positioning and the DOD's Navstar Global Positioning System, David A. Turner and Marcia S. Smith 94-171 SPR

Goals 2000
* Goals 2000: Educate America Act-Citations to U.S. Code, Mary Ann Wolfe 94-342 A
* Goals 2000: Overview and Analysis, James B. Stedman 94-490 EPW
* A New Federal Role in Elementary and Secondary Education; Videoprogram, Wayne Riddle, etc. VT94-1316

Gore, Al
* The National Performance Review, Harold C. Relyea 93-862 GOV
* National Performance Review: A New Look at the Federal Bureaucracy; Info Pack IP478N
* Reinventing Government and the 103rd Congress: A Brief Overview, Harold C. Relyea 93-859 GOV

Government Contracts
* see Public Contracts

Government Employees
* Age at Retirement for Federal: A Fact Sheet, Carolyn L. Merck 94-826 EPW
* Architect of the Capitol: Appointment, Duties, and Operations, Mildred L. Amer and Paul S. Rundquist 95-343 GOV
* Career Guidance and Federal Job Information: Info Pack IP016C
* Federal Employees and the FY 1996 Budget: Issue Brief, James P. McGrath IB95033
* Federal Jobs: New Application Procedures, Barbara L. Schwemle 95-82 GOV
* Federal Pay: Fiscal Year 1996 Salary Adjustments, Barbara Schwemle 95-997 GOV
* Federal Structure and Fire Fighters: Amendments to the Pay System, Barbara Schwemle 95-959 GOV
* Hatch Act Amendments: Political Activity and the Civil Service; Issue Brief Barbara L. Schwemle IB87153
* Internships and Fellowships: Congressional, Federal, and Other Work Experience Opportunities, Barbara Hillson 95-887 C
* National Performance Review: A New Look at the Federal Bureaucracy; Info Pack IP478N
* Performance Management and the Federal Government, Barbara Schwemle 95-1068 GOV
* Political Activities: Regulations to Implement the Hatch Act Reform Amendments of 1993, Barbara L. Schwemle 94-275 GOV
* Political Activities: 103rd Congress; Amendments to the Hatch Act, Barbara L. Schwemle 93-235 GOV
* Ramspeck Act: Proposed Repeal of the Legislative and Judicial Provision, Barbara Scwemle 95-819 GOV
* Restrictions on Lobbying Congress with Federal Funds, Jack Maskell 95-382 A
* Shutdown of the Federal Government: Effects on the Federal Workforce, James P. McGrath 95-906 GOV
* Summer Job Opportunities in the Federal Government, Rita Jiminez 94-467 C
* Whistleblower Protections for Federal Employees, L. Paige Whitaker 90-41 A

Government Employees -- Pay and Benefits
* Brief Comparison of Retirement Eligibility and Benefits for Members of Congress and Executive Branch Personnel, Carolyn L. Merck 93-721 EPW
* Cost-of-Living Adjustment for Federal Civil Service Annuities, Carolyn L. Merck 94-834 EPW
* Early Retirement, Buy-Outs, and Separation Benefits for Federal Employees, Carolyn L. Merck 94-295 EPW
* Federal Civil Service Early Retirement and Separation Benefits: A Fact Sheet, Carolyn L. Merck 93-326 EPW
* Federal Civil Service Retirement:Comparing the Generosity of Federal and Private-Sector Retirement Systems, Education and Public Welfare Division 95-687 EPW
* Federal Civil Service Retirement Systems in FY 1994: Participation, Benefits, and Costs, Carolyn L. Merck 94-289 EPW
* Federal Employees and the FY 1995 Budget: Issue Brief, James P. McGrath,

IB94031
* Federal Employees Pay Comparability Act: Locality-Based Pay, Barbara L. Schwemle 94-53 GOV
* Federal Pay: Fiscal Year 1995 Increases to the General Schedule, Barbara Schwemle 94-1011 GOV
* Federal Retirement: Proposals for Change, Carolyn L. Merck 95-449 EPW
* Federal Retirement Systems: Background and Design Concepts, Carolyn L. Merck 94-929 EPW
* Federal Retirement: The Administration's FY 1996 Budget Proposals, Carolyn L. Merck 95-383 EPW
* Financing the Federal Civil Service Retirement Programs, Carolyn L. Merck 94-973 EPW
* Health Care Reform: The Federal Employees Health Benefits Program, Celinda Franco 94-392 EPW
* Law Enforcement Availability Pay, Barbara L. Scwemle 95-189 GOV
* Retirement for Federal Employees: A Fact Sheet, Carolyn L. Merck 93-97 EPW
* Salaries of Federal Officials, Sharon Gressle 95-226 GOV
* Salary of the U.S. President Compared With That of Other High-Level Government Officials, Sharon S. Gressle 95-203 GOV
* Sick Leave for Federal Employees: Amendments to Law, Barbara L. Schwemle 95-22 GOV
* Survivor Benefits for Families of Federal Civil Service Workers and Retirees, Carolyn L. Merck 95-18 EPW
* 1994 Federal Pay Situation Report, James P. McGrath 93-944 GOV

Government Information
* Access to Government Information in the United States, Harold C. Relyea 91-697 GOV
* The Administration and Operation of the Freedom of Information Act: An Overview, 1966-1991, Harold c. Relyea 93-977 GOV
* Census Adjustment: Impact on Reapportionment and Redistricting, David C. Huckabee 94-649 GOV
* The Federal Statistical System Under Review, Jennifer D. Williams 95-885 GOV
* Freedom of Information Act/Privacy Act: A Guide to Their Use; Info Pack, IP047F
* Government Publications--How, What, When, Where, and Why: Info Pack, IP264G
* The Joint Committee on Printing: A Brief Overview, Harold C. Relyea 95-425 GOV
* Paperwork Reduction and Information Resources Management, Stephanie Smith 95-453 GOV
* Population and Development: The 1994 Cairo Conference, Curt Tarnoff 94-533 F
* United States Regulations: Finding Regulatory Material, Mark Gurevitz 90-590 A
* Where to Get Publications from the Executive and Independent Agencies: A Directory of Sources for Official Documents, Janet Hays etc. 95-54 C

Government Performance and Results Act
* Government Performance and Results Act, P.L. 103-62: Interim Status Report; Revised, Genevieve J. Knezo 95-713 SPR

Government Procurement
* see Public Contracts

Government Regulation
* see Business, Executive Departments, Finance

Government Spending
* see Budgets

Grants
* see General -- Interests

Great Britain
* see Europe
* Britain: Current Issues and Relations With the United States, Paul E. Gallis 94-967 F
* Capital Gains and Securities Transactions Taxation in the United Kingdom: Fact Sheet Gregg Esenwein 94-920 E
* Expenditure Tax Proposals in Other Countries, Harry G. Gourevitch 95-662 S
* United Kingdom: Briefing Paper, Karen Donfried 94-758 F

Greece
* see also Europe
* Greece and Turkey: Current Foreign Aid Issues; Issue Brief, Carol Migdalovitz IB86065

Greenhouse Effect
* see Air Pollution--Ozone

Guatemala
* see also Latin America
* Guatemala and Allegations of Improper CIA, State and Defense Department Activities, K. Larry Storr 95-690 F
* Guatemala: Background and Relations With the United States Since 1985, K. Larry Storrs 95-610 F
* Guatemala's Human Rights Record, 1985-1995, and Prominent Recent Human Rights Cases, K. Larry Storr 95-611 F

Gun Control
* see Criminal Justice -- Gun Control

Gun Free Schools Act
* Does United States v. Lopez Affect the Gun-Free Schools Provisions of the Improving America's School Act of 1994?, Elizabeth B. Bazan 95-647 A

Guyana
* see also Latin America
* Guyana: Briefing Paper, Mark P. Sullivan and Stephen Hirsch 95-606 F

Haiti
* see also Latin America
* Haiti After President Aristide's Return: Concerns of the 104th Congress; Issue Brief, Patrick Curtis IB95090
* Haiti and Asylum Seekers: A Chronology of Major Events, Ruth Ellen Wasem and Maureen Taft-Morales 94-378 EPW
* Haiti: Background to the Overthrow of President Aristide, Maureen Taft-Morales 93-931 F
* Haiti: Chronology of Its Troubled Path Toward Democracy, Steven R. Bowman, Etc. 94-852 F
* Haiti: Efforts to Restore President Aristide, 1991-1994, Maureen Taft-Morales 95-602 F
* Haiti: Info Pack IP47911
* Haiti: Operation Uphold Democracy Facts and Figures, Steven R. Bowman 94-735 F
* Haitian Migration: Statistical and Chronological Fact Sheet, Ruth Ellen Wasem 94-170 EPW
* Haiti's Economic Recovery Program and U.S. Aid: A Fact Sheet, Larry Nowels 95-90 F
* Haiti's Political Crisis: U.S. Policy Options, Maureen Taft-Morales and Steven R. Bowman 94-567 F
U.S. Aid to Haiti: Policy and Perils; Videoprogram, Maureen Taft-Morales VT95-1380
* The U.S. Occupation of Haiti, 1915-1934, Richard A. Best 94-459 F

Halifax Economic Summit
* The Halifax "Emergency Financing Mechanism:" Expanding the General Arrangements to Borrow, Patricia A. Wertman 95-768 E

Handicapped
* see Disabled

Hatch Act
* see also Government Employees
* Hatch Act Amendments: Political Activity and the Civil Service: Archived Issue Brief, Barbara Schwemle IB87153
* Political Activities: Regulations to Implement the Hatch Act Reform Amendments of 1993, Barbara L. Schwemle 94-275 GOV

Hate Crimes
* see Criminal Justice

Hazardous Substances
* see also Solid Wastes
* The Delaney Clause: The Dilemma of Regulating Health Risk for Pesticide Residues, Donna U. Vogt 92-800 SPR
* The Delaney Dilemma: Regulating Pesticide Residues in Foods--Seminar Proceedings, Donna U. Vogt 93-510 SPR
* Hazardous Waste Management and the Superfund Program: Info Pack IP094H
* Pesticide Policy Issues: Issue Brief, Linda-Jo Schierow IB95016
* Toxic Pollutants and the Clean Water Act: Current Issues, Claudia Copeland 93-849 ENR

Hazardous Wastes
* see Solid Wastes, Superfund

Head Start Program
* see Elementary and Secondary Education

Health Care Costs
* see Health Policy -- Finance

Health Care Reform
* see Health Policy -- Reform

Health Facilities
* see Medicine -- Facilities/Personnel

Health Insurance
* see Health Policy -- Insurance

Health Policy
* see also Medicine
* The Canadian Health Care System in 1993, Joan Sokolovsky 93-910 EPW
* Changes in Home Care Use by Disabled Elderly Persons: 1982-1989, Korbin Liu and Kenneth Manton 94-398 EPW
* Child Immunization Provisions in the Omnibus Budget Reconciliation Act of 1993, P.L. 103-66, Melvina Ford 93-781 EPW
* Coal Industry Retiree Health Benefit Reachback Relief: House Budget Reconciliation Bill Provisions, Nonna A. Noto 95-1064 E
* Federal Employees Health Benefits Program, Ray Schmitt 94-615 EPW
* Health Care Fact Sheet: Maternal and Child Health Block Grant, Edward R. Klebe 94-867 EPW
* Health Care Fraud and Abuse, Jennifer O'Sullivan and Melissa Thompson 95-720 EPW
* Health Care Reform in the 104th Congress: A Checklist of CRS Products, Alexandra Salinas 95-172 L
* Health Insurance: Reforming the Private Market, Beth Fuchs, etc. 95-877 EPW
* Health Services for American Indians and Alaska Natives, Edward R. Klebe and Karen M. Judge 93-975 EPW
* Rural Health Care Initiatives in Current Law, Celinda Franco 95-329 EPW

Health Policy -- Finance
* Appropriations for Selected Health Programs, FY 1980-FY 1993, Edward R. Klebe 93-125 EPW
* Health Care Costs: Bibliography-in-Brief, 1990-1993, M. Alexandra Salinas 93-874 L
* Health Care Fact Sheet: An International Comparison of Spending Ambulatory Care, Impatient Services, and Pharmaceutical Supplies, Richard Rimkunas 94-43 EPW
* Health Care Fact Sheet: Increase in Health Care Prices, Richard Rimkunas, etc. 95-175 EPW
* Health Care Fact Sheet: International Health Spending, Richard Rimkunas 93-987 EPW
* Health Care Fact Sheet: 1993 National Health Spending, Richard Rice and Richard Rimkunas 94-952 EPW
* Health Care Spending and Medical Care Prices: Info Pack IP223H
* Long-Term Care for the Elderly: Issue Brief, Richard J. Price IB95039
* Tax Incentives for Elderly Home Care, Louis Allan Talley 93-805 E

Health Policy -- Insurance
* Health Benefits: Employer Costs and Employee Coverage, Linda Levine 94-545 E
* Health Benefits for Retirees: Employer-Based Plans, Beth C. Fuchs 93-428 EPW
* Health Care: Federal Tax Subsidies for Health Insurance, Gerald Mayer 95-601 E
* Health Insurance Continuation Coverage Under COBRA: Issue Brief, Beth C. Fuchs IB87182
* Health Insurance Cost and Coverage: Tax System Approaches; Issue Brief, Mark Merlis and Beth C. Fuchs IB95026
* Health Insurance: Employer Mandated Benefits Under COBRA; Info Pack IP389H
* Universal Health Insurance and Uninsured People: Effects on Use and Cost, Stephen M. Long and Susan Marquis 94-689 EPW

Health Policy -- Medicaid
* Medicaid: ABCs of Current Law, Melvina Ford 95-918 EPW
* Medicaid: A Fact Sheet, Melvina Ford and Mark Merlis 95-38 EPW
* Medicaid: An Overview, Mark Merlis IP468M
* Medicaid: An Overview; Info Pack IP468M

Current Events and Homework

* Medicaid: Audio Brief, Mark Merlis and Melvina Ford AB50316
* Medicaid: Eligibility for Families, Children, and Pregnant Women, Jennifer O'Sullivan 93-240 EPW
* Medicaid: Eligibility for the Aged, Disabled and Blind, Richard J. Price 94-297 EPW
* Medicaid: Long-Term Care and the Elderly, Richard J. Price 93-302 EPW
* Medicaid: Maternal and Child Health, Melvina Ford 93-700 EPW
* Medicaid: Program and Demonstration Waivers, Mark Merlis 95-109 EPW
* Medicaid Program Description and Recent Trends, Mark Merlis 95-863 EPW
* The Medicaid Program; Videoprogram, Mark Merlis and Melvina Ford VT95-1322
* Medicaid Reform and FY 1996 Budget: Issue Brief, Melvina Ford IB95099
* Medicaid Services for Persons With Developmental Disabilities, Mary F. Smith 93-742 EPW
* Medicaid Services for Substance Abuse treatment, Edward R. Klebe 93-764 EPW
* Medicaid Services for the Mentally Ill, Edward R. Klebe 93-761 EPW
* Medicaid: Spousal Impoverishment Protection, Richard Price 95-1053 EPW
* Medicaid: 1995 Budget, Melvin Ford 94-210 EPW

Health Policy -- Medicare

* Health Care Fact Sheet: Original Medicare Cost Estimates, Jennifer O'Sullivan and Bud Graves 93-834 EPW
* Medicare, Jennifer O'Sullivan and Richard Price 95-44 EPW
* Medicare: A Checklist of CRS Products, M. Alexandra Salinas 95-87 L
* Medicare: An Overview; Info Pack IP467M
* Medicare and the Budget Process: A Fact Sheet, James Storey 95-694 EPW
* Medicare Coverage for Mental Illness and Substance Abuse, Edward R. Klebe 93-331 EPW
* Medicare: Description of Hospital Reimbursement of Inpatient Hospital Care under the Prospective Payment System, Celinda M. Franco 93-230 EPW
* Medicare: Financing the Part A Hospital Insurance Program, Jennifer O'Sullivan 95-650 EPW
* Medicare Home Health Benefit, Richard Price 95-1009 EPW
* Medicare Income-Related Financing: Options and Analysis, Beth C. Fuchs 95-752 EPW
* Medicare: Issue Brief, Jennifer O'Sullivan and Richard Price IB95054
* Medicare: Payments to Physicians, Jennifer O'Sullivan 95-21 EPW
* Medicare Reform: Automatic Spending Cuts to Meet Budget Targets, James R. Storey 95-1038 EPW
* Medicare Reforms: Changes in Projected Spending Under H.R. 2425, Madeline Smith 95-1065 EPW
* Medicare Reimbursement Policies, Celinda Franco, etc. 95-765 EPW
* Medicare Secondary Payer Program, Jennifer O'Sullivan 94-573 EPW
* Medicare SELECT, Jennifer O'Sullivan 94-962 EPW
* Medicare Taxes, Taxes, and Government Contributions for 1995, David Koitz 94-21 EPW
* Medicare: The Restructuring Debate; Issue brief, Beth Fuchs, etc. IB95108
* Qualified Medicare Beneficiary Program, Jennifer O'Sullivan 95-854 EPW
* Rescissions to FY 1995 Health Budget of the Department of Health and human Services, Celinda Franco 95-334 EPW
* Social Security and Medicare Taxes and Premiums: A Fact Sheet, David Koitz 94-28 EPW

Health Policy -- Reform

* Biotechnology, Breakthrough Drugs, and Health Care Reform: Lessons from the NIH-University-Industry Relationship, Wendy H. Schacht 94-375 SPR
* Cigarette Taxes to Fund Health Care Reform: An Economic Analysis, Jane G. Gravelle and Dennis Zimmerman 94-214 E
* Comparison of Some Antitrust Provisions, Janice E. Rubin 94-212 A
* Constitutional and Statutory Rights to Health Care, Kathleen S. Swendiman 94-64 A
* The Financial Outlook for Social Security and Medicare, David Koitz and Geoffrey Kollman 95-543 ENR
* Health Benefit Plans: ERISA and the States, Joan Sokolovsky 93-747 EPW
* Health Care Fact Sheet: Health Care Reform in the 104th Congress, Beth C. Fuchs 95-138 EPW
* Health Care Reform: An Employer Mandate and Small Business, Gerald Mayer 94-888 EPW
* Health Care Reform and Investment in New Drug Development, Gary Guenther 95-179 E
* Health Care Reform and National Information Infrastructure, Stephen B. Gould 94-770 SPR
* Health Care Reform: Audio Brief, Beth Fuchs AB50315
* Health Care Reform: Cost Containment; Videoprogram, Mark Merlis VT93-1371
* Health Care Reform in the 104th Congress: A Checklist of CRS Products, M. Alexandra Salinas 95-172 L
* Health Care Reform in the 104th Congress; Info Pack IP421H

* Health Care Reform: Legislation in the 103rd Congress, Mark Merlis 94-717 EPW
* Health Care Reform: Prevention and Medical Research; Videoprogram, Pamela Smith, etc. VT94-1314
* Health Care Reform: The Clinton Plan; Videoprogram, Congressional Research Service, VT93-1362
* Health Care Reform: The Federal Employees Health Benefits Program, Celinda Franco 94-392 EPW
* Health Care Reform, Videoprogram, Beth Fuchs and Mark Merlis VT95-1316
* Health Care Reform: Where Do We Go From Here?, Videoprogram Beth Fuchs and Mark Merlis VT94-1378
* Health Care Reform: Where Does Medical Research Fit In?, Pamela W. Smith 94-870 SPR
* Medical Savings Accounts, Bob Lyke 94-597 EPW
* Mental Illness and Substance Abuse Disorders: Background Information Related to Health Care Reform, Edith Fairman Cooper 94-544 SPR
* Military Medicine and National Health Care Reform, Richard A. Best 94-570 F
* Outcomes Research, Clinical Practice Guidelines, and the Agency for Health Care Policy and Research, Bernice Reyes-Akinbileje 94-488 SPR
* Paying for Health Care Reform: The Role of Cost Savings, Nonna A. Noto 94-666 E
* The President's Health Care Reform Plan and Drug Development in the Biotechnology Industry, Gary Guenther 94-346 E
* Summary Comparison of Selected Health Care Reform Bills, Education and Public Welfare Division 94-185 EPW
* Tax Aspects of Health Care Reform: The Tax Treatment of Health Care Providers, Harry G. Gourevitch 94-369 S

Health Security Act

* see also Health Policy -- Reform
* Health Care Reform: The Federal Employees Health Benefits Program, Celinda Franco 94-392 EPW
* Summary Comparison of Selected Health Care Reform Bills, Education and Public Welfare Division 94-185 EPW

Higher Education

* Appropriations Directed by Congress to Specific Colleges and Universities, for Research and Development and Research-Related Facilities, FY 1992, Genevieve J. Knezo 93-684 SPR
* Indirect Costs at Academic Institutions: Background and Controversy; Issue Brief, Genevieve J. Knezo IB91095
* Indirect Costs for R&D at Higher Education Institutions: Annotated Chronology of Major Federal Policies, Genevieve J. Knezo 94-646 SPR
* Institutional Eligibility: The Higher Education Amendments of 1992, Margot Schenet 93-861 EPW
* Speech Material: Graduation; Info Pack IP379S

Higher Education -- Student Aid

* Access to Student Loans and the Senate Proposal for Restructuring Under H.R. 2264, Dennis Zimmerman, etc. 93-660 E
* The Federal Direct Student Loan Program, Margot Schenet 95-110 EPW
* The Federal Family Education Loan Programs, Margot A. Schenet 94-810 EPW
* Federal Family Education Loans: Reduced Costs, Direct Lending, and National Income, Barbara Miles etc. 93-247 E
* The Federal Pell Grant Program, Margot A. Schenet 94-532 EPW
* Federal Taxation of Student Aid, Bob Lyke 94-749 EPW
* Financial Aid for Native American Post-Secondary Students, Rita Jimenez 93-172 C
* Financial Aid for Students; Info Pack, IP042F
* Guaranteed Student Loans vs. Direct Lending: Where Are the Savings? An Issue Overview, Barbara L. Miles etc. 93-552 E
* Minority Scholarships and Title VI of the Civil Rights Act of 1964: A Legal Analysis, Kevin B. Greely 92-245 A
* National Service: Info Pack IP475N
* Recent Changes in Federal Student Aid, Margot A. Schenet 94-10 EPW
* The Student Loan Marketing Association: Charter Rescission, Barbara Miles 95-590 E
* Student Loans: The Clinton Administration's Direct Loan Proposal; Issue Brief, Charlotte J. Fraas IB93075
* Tuition Tax Deduction: Issue Raised by the President's Proposal, Bob Lyke 95-186 EPW

Higher Education Act

* see also Education Policy, Higher Education
* Institutional Eligibility: The Higher Education Amendments of 1992, Margot A. Schenet 93-861 EPW

Be patient. If any phone number is incorrect, call (area code) 555-1212 and request the new listing.

Highways
* see Transportation

Hispanic Americans
* see Minorities

History (U.S.)
* see also General Interest
* Black History and Culture: Bibliography-in-Brief, Tangela G. Roe 95-136 L
* Black Members of the United States Congress: 1789-1993, Mildred L. Amer 93-671 GOV
* Constitution of the United States: Bibliography-in-Brief, Tangela G. Roe 95-37 L
* Constitution of the United States Including the Bill of Rights: Info Pack IP339C
* Constitution of the United States: Its History, Development and Amending Process; Info Pack, IP339C
* Flag Desecration and Flag Misuse Law in the United States, Vastine Davis Platte 95-182 A
* Flag Etiquette: Info Pack IP365 F
* Flag Protection: A Brief History and Summary of Recent Supreme Court Decisions and Proposed Constitutional Amendment, John Luckey 95-709 A
* Hispanic Heritage Month: Info Pack IP427H
* Hispanic Tradition and Achievement in the United States, Garrine P. Laney 93-906 GOV
* The House Appropriations Process, 1789-1993, Louis Fisher 93-729 S
* Inauguration of the President: Info Pack, IP316I
* Medal of Honor: History and Issues, David F. Burrelli 95-519 F
* The President Pro Tempore of the Senate: History and Authority of the Office, Richard C. Sachs 95-181 GOV
* The President's Cabinet, Ronald C. Moe 93-271 GOV
* The Presidency of the United States: An Introductory Bibliography to Their Writings, James Sayler 93-1043 GOV
* Speech Material: Abraham Lincoln's and George Washington's Birthdays; Info Pack, IP373A
* Speech Material: Columbus Day; Info Pack, IP380C
* Speech Material: Fourth of July; Info Pack, IP377F
* Speech Material: Martin Luther King's Birthday; Info Pack, IP372M
* Speech Material: Thanksgiving Day; Info Pack, IP381T
* Time and History on the Hill, David McCullough VT91-909

Holidays
* see General Interest -- Speechwriting

Homeless
* see Welfare

Homosexual Rights
* see Civil Liberties

Hong Kong
* see also East Asia
* The Hong Kong Crisis of 1993--Origins, Competing Priorities, and Outcomes, Robert Sutter 93-455 S
* Hong Kong's Political Transition: Implications for U.S. Interests; Issue Brief, Robert Sutter and James Casey IB94051
* Hong Kong's Transition to Chinese Rule: Issues, U.S. Interests, U.S. Options, Robert

Hospitals
* see Medicine -- Facilities/Personnel

House of Representatives
* see Congress

Housing
* For Homeless see Welfare
* Administration FY 1995 Budget Proposals for Assisted Housing, Grace Milgram 94-131 E
* Budget Resolutions: The Effect on Housing Programs, Bruce E. Foote 95-672 E
* Discrimination in Mortgage Lending: What Do We Know?, Barbara L. Miles 94-708 E
* Economic Principles for Deficit Reduction: Audio Brief, William Cox, etc. AB50318
* Evolution of Section 202: Housing for the Elderly, Susan M Vanhorenbeck, 93-645 E
* The Fair Housing Act: A Legal Overview, Henry Cohen 95-710 A

* The Family Self-Sufficiency Program Susan Vanhorenbeck 94-541 E
* Fannie Mae and Freddie Mac, Barbara Miles 95-373 E
* The Federal Home Loan Banks: An Issue Overview, Barbara Miles 95-1017 E
* The Federal Housing Administration: Refund of Mortgage Insurance Premiums, Bruce E. Foote 95-474 E
* The Federal National Mortgage Association: "Fannie Mae" and Its Impact 2000 Program 94-795 C
* The FY 1995 HUD Budget: Disposition of Multifamily Properties, Bruce E. Foote 94-250 E
* Help for First-Time Buyers, Richard Bourdon 94-437 E
* Home Equity Conversion: An Overview, Bruce E. Foote 95-274 E
* The HOME Program in the 103rd Congress: A Brief Introduction, Eugene Boyd 94-694 GOV
* The Housing Community Development Act of 1992: Highlights and Analysis, Economics Division 93-377 S
* Housing Community Development: Issues Facing the 103rd Congress, Morton Schussheim 94-209 S
* Housing and Real Estate Tax Provisions in the Omnibus Budget Reconciliation Act of 1993, E. Richard Bourdon 93-887 E
* Housing Appropriations for FY 1995: Proposed Rescissions; Issue Brief Bruce E. Foote IB95079
* Housing for Older Persons Act of 1995: H.R. 660, Susan Vanhorenbeck 95-443 E
* Housing Legislation: Budget-Saving Provisions in the FY 1996 Reconciliation Proposals, Bruce E. Foote 95-1019 E
* Housing Policy and Implications for Current Programs: Info Pack IP417H
* Housing Programs of VA and FHA: A Comparison 93-545 E
* H.R. 1691, the Homesteading and Neighborhood Restoration Act of 1995, Bruce E. Foote 95-1072 E
* HUD Appropriations for FY 1995: Proposed Rescissions, Bruce E. Foote 95-354 E
* The HUD Budget for FY 1995: Housing for Special Needs Persons, Susan Vanhorenbeck 94-130 E
* HUD Housing Assistance Programs: Their Current Status, Grace Milgram 94-304 E
* HUD Programs That Provide and Support Homeownership Opportunities, Pearl Thomas 95-810 E
* HUD's Shelter Programs for the Homeless, Susan Vanhorenbeck 93-246 E
* Lead-Based Paint Poisoning Prevention: Federal Mandates for Local Governments - A Fact Sheet, Linda Jo Schierow 93-91 ENR
* The Low Income Housing Tax Credit: Should the Program Be Ended After 1997?, Richard Bourdon 95-1058 E
* A New HUD? The Administration Proposal, Susan Vanhorenbeck 95-452 E
* The Real Estate Settlement Procedures Act: Is it Working?, Richard Bourdon 94-841 E
* The Real Estate Settlement Procedures Act: The Four Issues, Bruce Foote 95-1085 E
* Reinventing HUD: The Missions and Management of the Department of Housing and Urban Development, Morton J. Schussheim 94-854 S
* Rental Housing for the Disabled., Susan M. Vanhorenbeck 94-177 E
* Rollover of Gain on the Sale of a Principle Residence, Louis Alan Talley 95-1018 E
* Trends in Funding and Numbers of Households in HUD Assisted Housing, Fiscal Years 1975-1994, Grace Milgram 94-579 E

Housing Assistance
* see Housing

Housing for the Aged
* see Aged

Housing Subsidies
* see Housing

Human Rights
* see International Affairs

Humanities
* For Information on Grants, see General Interest -- Grants
* Arts and Humanities: Funding and Reauthorization in the 104th Congress, Susan Boren 95-190 EPW
* How to Find Information in a Library, Suzy Platt 94-483 C
* Library Services and Construction Act: Reauthorization Issues, Wayne Riddle IB95002
* National Foundation on the Arts and the Humanities Act of 1965: Reauthorization Fact Sheet, Susan Boren and Ruth Ann Stewart 93-417 EPW
* Rap and Rock Music Lyrics: Bibliography-in-Brief, Tangela G. Roe 94-251 L

Be patient. If any phone number is incorrect, call (area code) 555-1212 and request the new listing.

1325

Current Events and Homework

Hungary
* see also Europe
* The Petroleum Status of Hungary, Joseph P. Riva 95-114 ENR
* Poland, Czech Republic, Slovakia, and Hungary: Recent Developments: Issue Brief, Julie Kim etc. IB92051

Illegal Aliens
* see Immigration

Immigration
* California's Proposition 187: A Brief Overview, Larry M. Eig 95-39 A
* Chinese Migration to the United States: Trends and Issues, Ruth Ellen Wasem 93-727 EPW
* Haiti and Asylum Seekers: A Chronology of Major Events, Ruth Ellen Wasem and Maureen Taft Morales 94-378 EPW
* Haitian Migration: Statistical and Chronological Fact Sheet, Ruth Ellen Wasem 94-170 EPW
* Illegal Aliens: Bibliography-in-Brief, Karen Alderson 95-859 L
* Illegal Immigration: Facts and Issues, Joyce Vialet 95-29 EPW
* Immigration: A Checklist of CRS Products, Karen L. Alderson 95-128 L
* Immigration Economic Aspects; Bibliography-in-Brief, Karen Alderson 95-858 L
* Immigration Fact Sheet: The "H-2A" Temporary Agricultural Worker Program, Joyce C. Violet 95-1069 EPW
* Immigration Fundamentals, Joyce Vialet 95-56 EPW
* Immigration: Illustrating the Asylum Process, Ruth Ellen Wasem etc. 93-865 EPW
* Immigration Legislation in the 104th Congress, Joyce Vialet 95-881 EPW
* Immigration: Numerical Limits on Permanent Admissions, Joyce C. Vialet and Molly R. Forman 94-146 EPW
* Immigration: Recent Estimates of the U. S. Illegal Alien Population, Jennifer D. Williams 95-523 GOV
* Immigration Reform: Bibliography-in-Brief 95-860 L
* Immigration: The Economic Impact; Info Pack IP4911
* Immigration: The Effects on Native-Born Workers, Linda Levine 95-408 E
* Immigration: The Effects on Native-Born Workers; an Issue Overview, Linda Levine 95-439 E
* Immigration: The Labor Market Effects of Temporary Alien Farm Worker Program, Linda Levine 95-712 E
* Immigration: What Is PRUCOL?, Joyce Vialet 94-710 EPW
* Immigration's Contribution to the Size of the U.S. Population, Ruth Ellen Wasem 94-116 EPW
* Law on Refugees in Selected Countries, Law Library of Congress, Mya Saw Shin LL95-1
* Native and Naturalized Citizens and Non-Citizens: An Analysis of Poverty Status, Welfare Benefits, and Other Factors, Michael J. O'Grady 95-276 EPW
* Naturalization of Immigrants: Facts and Issues, Ruth Ellen Wasem 95-279 EPW
* A North American Free Trade Agreement and Immigration, Joyce C. Vialet 93-62 EPW
* U.S. Citizenship of Persons Born in the United States to Alien Parents, Margaret Mikyung 94-664 A
* Vietnam Repatriation Debate, Lois McHugh 95-891 F
* Welfare: Legal Immigrant Eligibility for Benefits Under the House and Senate-Passed H.R. $, Joyce Vialet 95-1037 EPW

Immigration -- Law and Legislation
* Alien Eligibility for Federal Assistance, Joyce C. Vialet and Larry M. Eig 94-73 EPW
* Alien Eligibility Requirements for Major Federal Assistance Programs, Larry M. Eig and Joyce C. Vialet 93-1046 A
* Asylum Facts and Issues, Ruth Ellen Wasem 94-314 EPW
* Basic Questions on U.S. Citizenship and Naturalization, Larry M.Eig 92-246 A
* A Brief History of U.S. Immigration Policy, Joyce Vialet 91-141 EPW
* California's Proposition 187: A Brief Overview, Larry M. Eig 95-39 A
* Cuban Adjustment Act of 1966, Larry M. Eig 93-253 A
* Cuban and Haitian Asylum Seekers: Recent Trends, Ruth Ellen Wasem 94-410 EPW
* Cuban Migration: Legal Basics, Larry M. Eig 94-692 A
* Cuban Migration to the U.S.: Trends and Policy Issues, Ruth Ellen Wasem 95-659 EPW
* Immigration and Asylum Policies of Selected Countries, by Foreign Affairs and National Defense Division 94-307 F
* Immigration and Federal Assistance: Issues and Legislation; Issue Brief, Joyce C. Vialet and Larry M. Eig IB94037
* Immigration and Naturalization Service Funding and the Administration's FY 1996 Immigration Initiative, William J. Krouse 95-478 EPW
* Immigration and Refugee Policy; Videoprogram, Joyce Vialet and Ruth Wasem VT94-1328

* Immigration Issues: Info Pack IP164I
* Immigration; Proposition 187; Info Pack IP495I
* Naturalization of Immigrants: Policy, Trends, and Issues, Ruth Ellen Wasem 95-298 EPW
* Refugee Assistance in the Foreign Aid Bill: Problems and Prospects; Issue Brief, Lois McHugh IB89150
* Refugees in U.S. Foreign Policy, Lois McHugh 95-23 F
* The Right of Undocumented Alien Children to Basic Education: An Overview of Plyer v. Doe, Larry M. Eig 94-804 A

Imports
* see Trade--Imports and Exports

Impoundment of Funds
* see Budgets -- Process

Improving America's Schools Act
* Family Educational Rights and Privacy Act: P.L. 103-382 Amendments, Richard N. Apling 94-980 EPW
* Improving America's School Act: An Overview of P.L. 103-382, James B. Stedman 94-872 EPW

Income
* see Economic Policy

Income Tax
* see Taxation

Indexing (Economic Policy)
* see Budgets, Pensions, Social Security, Taxation, Welfare

India
* see also South Asia
* India-U.S. Relations; Issue Brief, Barbara Le Poer IB93097
* The Kashmir Dispute: Historical Background to the Current Struggle, Richard P. Cronin, etc. 91-563 F

Indian Gaming Regulatory Act
* The Indian Gaming Regulatory Act Amendments Act of 1994, S. 2230, (103rd Cong. 2nd Sess.): A Brief Analysis M. Maureen Murphy 94-674 A
* Indian Gaming Regulatory Act: Judicial and Administrative Interpretations, M. Maureen Murphy 93-793 A

Indians
* see Minorities -- Native Americans

Individual Retirement Accounts
* see Pensions

Individuals With Disabilities Education Act
* The Individuals With Disabilities Education Act: Congressional Intent, Nancy Lee Jones 95-669 A
* The Individuals With Disabilities Education Act (IDEA): Legal Issues Surrounding the Least Restrictive Environment, Nancy L. Jones 95-286 A
* Individuals With Disabilities Education Act: Reauthorization Overview, Steven R. Aleman 94-156 EPW
* Individuals With Disabilities Education Act: Summary of Current Programs, Steven R. Aleman 95-675 EPW
* Special Education: Issues in the State Grant Program of Individuals With Disabilities Education Act, Steven R. Aleman 95-438 EPW
* Violence in Schools and the Individuals With Disabilities Education Act, Nancy Lee Jones 95-107 A

Indonesia
* see also South Asia
* Indonesia: Briefing Paper, Larry Niksch 94-706 F
* Indonesia: Recent Developments and U.S. Policy; Summary of CRS Seminar, Larry Niksch 94-390 F
* U.S.-Indonesian Relations, Larry Niksch 94-233 F

Industrial Competitiveness
* see Trade

Be patient. If any phone number is incorrect, call (area code) 555-1212 and request the new listing.

Industrial Technology
* see Technology

Industry
* see Business, Technology, Telecommunication, Trade

Inflation
* see Economic Policy

Information
* see Communications, Government Information, Telecommunication

Information and Privacy
* see Civil Liberties

Information Superhighway
* see Telecommunication -- Superhighway

Infrastructure
* see also Public Contracts, Solid Wastes, Transportation, Urban Affairs, Water Resources
* Transportation Infrastructure: Conditions, Needs, and Financing, J.F. Hornbeck 93-676 E
* Transportation Infrastructure: Economic Issues and Public Policy Alternatives, J.F. Hornbeck 93-107 E

Inspector General Act
* Statutory Offices of Inspector General, Frederick M. Kaiser 94-153 GOV

Inspectors General
* see Executive Departments

Insurance
* see Finance, Health Policy -- Insurance

Intellectual Property
* The Bayh-Dole Act: Patent Policy and the Commercialization of Technology, Wendy Schacht 94-501 SPR
* The China-U.S. Trade Agreement on Intellectual Property Rights: Implications for China-U.S. Trade Relations, Wayne M. Morrison 95-463 E
* Copyright and Fair Use After Acuff-Rose and Texaco, Dorothy Schrader 95-888 S
* Copyright Restoration for Public Domain Works, Dorothy Schrader 94-645 A
* Criminal Copyright Infringement: Proposal to Impose Criminal Liability on Nonprofit Infringers and Felony Liability for Transmissions, Dorothy Schrader 95-1035 S
* Enforcement of Intellectual Property Rights Under the GATT 1994 TRIPS Agreements, Dorothy Schrader 94-228 A
* Enforcement of Intellectual Property Rights Under the NAFTA, Dorothy Schrader 94-72 A
* Intellectual Property Provisions of the GATT 1994: "The TRIPS Agreement", Dorothy Schrader 94-302 A
* Intellectual Property Provisions of the NAFTA, Dorothy Schrader 94-59 A
* Intellectual Property Rights and the Uruguay Round of Multilateral Trade Talks: Economic Effects, Lenore Sek 94-722 E
* Performance Rights in Digital Transmissions of Sound Recordings, Douglas Weimer 95-924 A
* Proposed U.S. Copyright Term Extension, Dorothy Schrader 95-799 S
* Television Satellite Carrier License Extension: Retransmission of Network and "Superstation" Video Programming to Home Satellite Dishes, Dorothy Schrader 94-680 A
* U.S. Trade Laws and Intellectual Property Rights, Glennon Harrison 95-355 E

Intelligence Activities
* Intelligence Implications of the Military Technical Revolution, Richard A. Best 95-560 F
* Intelligence Issues and the 104th Congress: Issue Brief, Richard A. Best IB95018
* Intelligence Issues in the 1990s, Richard A. Best 93-176 F
* Intelligence Spending: Should Total Amounts Be Made Public?, Elizabeth B. Bazan and Richard A. Best 94-261 F
* "National Security" as a Concept: Does It Need to Be "Redefined"?, Mark M. Lowenthal 93-12 S
* The National Security Council: An Organizational Assessment, Richard A. Best, etc. 93-517 F

* Peacekeeping: Intelligence Requirements, Richard A. Best 94-394 F
* Protection of Classified Information By Congress, Practices and Proposals for Change, Frederick M. Kaiser 95-252 GOV
* Security Classification Policy and Procedure--Executive Order 12958: The Clinton Administration Directive, Harold C. Relyea 95-711 GOV

Intergovernmental Fiscal Relations
* see State and Local Government

International Labor Organization
* International Labor Organization: A Fact Sheet, Losi McHugh 95-766 F

International Affairs
* Biological Diversity: Issues Related to the Convention on Biodiversity, Susan R. Fletcher 95-598 ENR
* Biological Diversity Treaty: Fact Sheet, Susan R. Fletcher 95-596 ENR
* Convention on the Rights of the Child: A Fact Sheet, Vita Bite 95-304 F
* Coups D'etat Worldwide, Attempted and Accomplished January 1991-December 1993, Karen Donfried 94-333 F
* Cyprus: Status of U.N. Negotiations; Issue Brief Carol Migdalovitz IB89140
* The Global Information Infrastructure (GII) and the G-& Meeting in Brussels: Issues for Congress, Glenn J. McLoughlin and Marcia S. Smith 95-532 SPR
* Human Rights Treaties: A Summary of Provisions and Status in the U.S. Ratification Process, Vita Bite 95-191 F
* Human Rights Treaties: Racial Discrimination, Women's Rights and Children's Rights--Some Issues for U.S. Ratification, Vita Bite 93-654 F
* International Broadcasting: Consolidation of U.S. Radio Services, Kennon H. Nakamura and Susan B. Epstein 94-29 F
* International Labor Organization: A Fact Sheet, Lois McHugh 95-766 F
* Iraqi Compliance With Cease-Fire Agreements: Issue Brief, Kenneth Katzman IB92117
* Israeli-Palestinian Agreement, Carol Migdalovitz 93-797 F
* The Law of the Sea Convention and U.S. Policy Issue Brief, Marjorie Ann Browne IB950101
* Law of the Sea Convention: Status of the Convention and Agreement, Marjorie Ann Browne 95-612 F
* The Middle East Peace Talks: Issue Brief, Carol Migdalovitz IB91137
* Palestinians and Middle East Peace: Issues for the United States: Issue Brief, Clyde Mark IB93052
* Population and Development: The 1994 Cairo Conference, Curt Tarnoff 94-533 F
* Regional Security Consultative Organizations in East Asia and Their Implications for the United States, Larry Niksch 94-79 F
* U.N. Development Program: A Fact Sheet, Lois McHugh 95-578 F
* U.N. Fourth World Conference on Women, Vita Bite and Lois McHugh 95-607 F
* U.N. Regular Budget Funding: Issues for Congress, Vita Bite 95-645 F
* U.N. System Funding: Congressional Issues; Issue Brief Vita Bite IB86116
* United Nations Convention on the Law of the Sea: Living Resources Provisions, Eugene H. Buck 95-4 ENR
* United Nations Industrial Development Organization: A Fact Sheet, Lois McHugh 95-736 F
* United Nations Regular Budget Contributions: Members Compared, 1989-1994, Marjorie Ann Browne 95-571 F
* United Nations: Selected References, 1990-1993, Ursula Roosmaa and Sherry Shapiro 94-77 L
* The United States and International Human Rights Treaties: A Summary of Provisions and Status in the Ratification Process, Vita Bite 92-991 F
* War Crimes in the Former Yugoslavia: Selected References, Valentin Leskovsek 94-762 L
* World Health Organization: A Fact Sheet, Lois McHugh 95-166 F

International Affairs -- Peacekeeping
* Military Contingency Operations: Search for a New Funding Mechanism, Nina M. Serafino 95-636 F
* Multinational Peacekeeping Operations: Proposals to Enhance Congressional Oversight; Issue Brief Richard F. Grimmett IB95006
* Peace Keeping: PDD-25 and Issues for Congress: Info Pack IP492P
* Peacekeeping and Conflict Management Activities: A Discussion of Terminology, Stanley R. Sloan 93-1017 S
* Peacekeeping and U.S. Foreign Policy: Implementing PDD-25; Issue Brief, Nina M. Serafino IB94043
* Peacekeeping in Future U.S. Foreign Policy, Mark M. Lowenthal 94-260 S
* Peacekeeping: Issues for the Congress; Videoprogram, Marjorie Ann Browne, etc. VT94-1343
* Peacekeeping: Issues of U.S. Military Involvement; Issue Brief, Nina Serafino 95-787 E

Be patient. If any phone number is incorrect, call (area code) 555-1212 and request the new listing.

1327

Current Events and Homework

* United Nations Peacekeeping: Issues for Congress; Issue Brief, Marjorie Ann Browne IB90103
* United Nations Peacekeeping Operations: Country Participation, Marjorie Ann Browne 95-556 F
* United Nations Peacekeeping Operations, Marjorie Ann Browne 95-555 F
* United Nations Peacekeeping Operations: Force Commanders/Chief Military Observers for Current Operations, Marjorie Ann Browne 95-524 F
* United Nations Peacekeeping Operations, 1988-1993: Background Information, Marjorie Ann Browne 94-193 F
* U.S. Forces and Multinational Commands: PDD-25 and Precedents, Edward F. Bruner 94-887 F
* The U.S. Military in International Peacekeeping: The Funding Mechanism, Nina M. Serafino 94-95 F
* U.S. Participation in U.N. Military Actions: Is Advance Congressional Approval Needed?, Louis Fisher 95-480 S
* The Use of Force: Key Contemporary Documents, Stephen Daggett and Nina Serafino 94-805 F

International Banking
* see International Finance--Banks

International Competitiveness
* see Trade

International Debt
* see International Finance--Foreign Loans

International Economic Relations
* see Foreign Aid, International Finance, Trade

International Finance
* Derivative Financial Markets, Kevin F. Winch, etc. 93-943 E
* Derivative Financial Markets: An Issue Overview, Mark Jickling and Kevin F. Winch 93-983 E
* Dollar Depreciation in Early 1995, Arlene Wilson 95-741 E
* The Dollar: Why It Is Weak and Why Worry?, William A. Cox 94-537 S
* The Exchange-Rate System: Return to Bretton Woods?, Alfred Reifman, 94-956 S
* The Exchange Stabilization Fund, Arlene Wilson 95-262 E
* The Global Information Infrastructure (GII) and the G-7 Meeting in Brussels: Issues for Congress, Glenn J. McLoughlin 95-532 SPR
* NAFTA and the Peso-Dollar Exchange Rate, Arlene Wilson 94-496 E
* Strengthening the International Monetary System: Lessons of the Mexican Crisis, Alfred Reifman 95-595 S
* The Weaker Dollar and Its Effects on the U.S. Economy, Gail Makinen 95-715 E
* The Yen/Dollar Exchange Rate, James K. Jackson 94-644 E

International Finance -- Banks
* Banking and Finance in the North American Free Trade Agreement, William Jackson 93-560 E
* Financial Services Trade With Japan, Dick K. Nanto, 95-418 E
* Foreign Investment in American Banking: Competitiveness, Legislation, and Regulation, William Jackson 94-705 E
* International Monetary Fund and World Bank: Info Pack IP245I
* Multilateral Development Banks: Issues for Congress; Issue Brief, Jonathan E. Sanford IB87218
* Multilateral Development Banks: U.S. Contributions FY 1984-95, Jonathan E. Sanford 94-571 F
* Would a Currency Board Have Prevented Mexico's Financial Crisis?, Gail Makinen 95-271 E
* Caribbean Basin Countries: Implications of a North American Free Trade Agreement, Lenore M. Sek and Mark P. Sullivan 93-551 E
* Foreign Companies in the United states: A Guide to Lists and Directories, Vanessa Cieslak 94-737 C
* Foreign Direct Investment in the United States: Issue Brief, James K. Jackson IB93011
* Japanese Investment in Asia; Videoprogram, Dick Nanto VT95-1341
* Mexico's Changing Policy Toward Foreign Investment and NAFTA Implications: An Issue Overview, M. Angeles Villarreal 93-782 E
* Mexico's Changing Policy Toward Foreign Investment and NAFTA Implications, M. Angeles Villarreal 93-668 E
* Oil and Natural Gas in the Russian Federation, Joseph P. Riva 93-732 SPR
* Oil in Vietnam: A Review of Foreign and Domestic Activities, Dairo Scuka 93-416 E
* The Overseas Private Investment Corporation: Background and Current Policy Issues, James K. Jackson and Wayne M. Morrison 95-644 E

* Trade, Competitiveness, and International Economic Policy: A Bibliography of CRS Products, Robert Howe 93-611 L
* U.S. Access to the EC Market: Opportunities, Concerns, and Policy Changes, Raymond J. Ahearn 92-514 F
* U.S. Direct Investment Abroad, James K. Jackson 95-204 E
* U.S. Direct Investment in Mexico, James K. Jackson 93-522 E
* U.S. Economic, Trade, and Financial Relations With Asia: A Statistical Overview, James K. Jackson and Wayne M. Morrison 94-590 E

International Finance -- Foreign Loans
* Debt Owed to the United States by Foreign Countries: Recent Rescheduling and Forgiveness, Jonathan E. Sanford 93-1010 F
* The Halifax "Emergency Financing Mechanism:", Expanding the General Agreements to Borrow, Patricia A. Wertman 95-768 E
* International Financial Institutions and Environment: Multilateral Development Banks and the Global Environment Facility, Susan R. Fletcher and Betsy A. Cody 94-173 ENR
* Japan's Looming Bank Crisis: A Half Trillion Dollars in Non-Performing Loans?, Dick Nanto 94-667 E
* The Mexican Economic Crisis: U.S. Jobs, Illegal Immigrants, and Systemic Risk, Glennon J. Harrison 95-225 E
* Mexican Financial Crises, 1982 and 1995: Similarities and Differences, Patricia A. Wertman 95-239 E
* The Mexican Peso Devaluation and Swap Arrangements, Arlene Wilson 95-169 E
* Mexico and Proposed U.S. Loan Guarantees: Background and Issues, Glennon J. Harrison and J.F. Hornbeck 95-183 E
* Mexico's Financial Crisis and U.S. Support Efforts, K. Larry Storrs 95-211 F
* Mexico's 1995 Economic Program and the IMF, Patricia A. Wertman 95-428 E
* Russian Economic Reform and the IMF: Mission Possible?, Issue Brief Patricia A. Wertman IB95055
* U.S. Government Foreign Loans and Loan Guarantees: A Brief Overview, Patricia A. Wertman 95-195 E
* U.S. Government Foreign Loans and Loan Guarantees: Managing Subsidies, Patricia A. Wertman 95-151 E

International Law
* see International Affairs

International Monetary Fund
* see also International Finance-Banks
* International Monetary Fund and World Bank: Info Pack, IP245I
* Mexico's 1995 Economic Program and the IMF, Patricia A. Wertman 95-428 E
* Russian Economic Reform and the IMF: Mission Possible? Issue Brief, IB95055
* Strengthening the International Monetary System: Lessons of the Mexican Crisis, Alfred Reifman 95-595 S

International Relations
* see International Affairs

International Trade
* see Trade

Internet
* see Telecommunication--Superhighway

Iran
* see also Middle East and North Africa
* Iran and Iraq: U.S. National Security Problems Since the Gulf War — A Chronology, Kenneth Katzman 94-561 F
* Iran: Current Development and U.S. Policy; Issue Brief, Kenneth Katzman IB93033
* Iran: The People's Mojahedin Organization of Iran, Kenneth Katzman 94-683 F
* Iran: U.S. Containment Policy, Kenneth Katzman 94-652 F
* Turkey's Military Offensive in Northern Iraq, Carol Migdalovitz 95-487 F

Iraq
* see also Middle East and North Africa
* Iran and Iraq: U.S. National Security Problems Since the Gulf War — A Chronology July 1993-July 1994, Kenneth Katzman 94-561 F
* Iraq: Current Sanctions, Long Term Threat, and U.S. Policy Options, Kenneth Katzman 94-465 F
* Iraqi Compliance With Cease-Fire Agreement: Issue Brief, Kenneth Katzman IB92117

IRAs
* see Pensions

Ireland
* see also Europe
* Ireland and Northern Ireland: U.S. Aid, Investment, and Trade Karen Donfried 94-997 F

Israel
* see also Middle East and North Africa
* Israel: U.S. Foreign Assistance Facts; Issue Brief, Clyde Mark IB85066
* Israeli-United States Relations: Issue Brief, Clyde R. Mark IB82008
* Israel's Request for U.S. Loan Guarantees: Issue Brief, Larry Q. Nowels and Clyde Mark IB91103
* Jordanian-Israeli Peace Treaty, Alfred B. Prados 94-842 F
* Middle East Peace Prospects: Info Pack IP397M

Italy
* see also Europe
* Italy: Parliamentary Elections; a Changing of the Guard?, Paul E. Gallis 94-259 F

Item Veto
* see Budgets--Process

Ivory Coast
* see also Africa (Sub-Saharan)
* Cote D'Ivoire (Ivory Coast): Briefing Paper, Raymond W. Copson 94-859 F

Jamaica
* see also Latin America
* Jamaica: Briefing Paper, Mark Sullivan and Stacey Williams 95-60 F

Japan
* see also East Asia
* Capital Gains and Securities Transactions Taxation in Japan: Fact Sheet, Gregg A. Esenwein and Philip D. Winters 94-891 E
* Chemical Agent Attack in Tokyo, Steven R. Bowman 95-411 F
* Defense Burdensharing: Is Japan's Host Nation Support a Model for Other Allies?, Stephen Daggett 94-515 F
* Immigration and Naturalization Laws: A Nine Country Comparison, Ruth Ellen Wasem and Kersi Shroff 93-755 EPW
* Japan-U.S. Relations: Issues for Congress in the 1990's; Issue Brief Robert G. Sutter IB94008
* Japan's Budget: Role in Economic Policymaking, James K. Jackson 94-278 E
* Japan's Looming Bank Crisis: A Half a Trillion Dollars in Non-Performing Loans?, Dick K. Nanto 94-667 E
* Japan's New Era of Coalition Governance: Implications for U.S. Interests and Policy, Richard P. Cronin 94-550 F
* Japan's Uncertain Political Transition; Issue Brief, Rinn-Sup Shinn IB94045
* Political Change in Japan and the United States: Videoprogram, Richard Cronin VT93-1365

Japan -- Foreign Trade
* Deregulation as Market Opening in Japan, Dick K. Nanto 95-224E
* Dispute Settlement Under WTO and Trade Problems With Japan, Dick K. Nanto 95-42 E
* Financial Services Trade With Japan, Dick K. Nanto 95-418 E
* The Japan-U.S. Automobile and Parts Trade Dispute, Dick K. Nanto, etc. 95-725 E
* Japan-U.S. Automotive Framework Talks: Issue Brief, Gwenell L. Bass IB94055
* Japan-U.S. Trade Agreements 1980-1993, William H. Cooper 94-481 E
* Japan-U.S. Trade and Economic Relations: Info Pack IP201J
* Japan-U.S. Trade Negotiations Under the Framework: Status and Alternative Approaches, William H. Cooper 94-620 E
* Japan-U.S. Trade Negotiations: Will the Deadlock Be Broken?, Raymond J. Ahearn 94-724 F
* Japan-U.S. 1995 Automotive Dispute: Impact of 100 Percent Tariffs on Automobile Dealers by State, Penelope Fay Heavner 95-718 C
* Japanese and U.S. Economic Involvement in Asia and the Pacific: Comparative Data and Analysis, Richard P. Cronin 94-764 F
* Japanese Investment in Asia; Videoprogram, Dick Nanto VT95-1341
* Japan's Keiretsu: Industrial Groups as Trade Barriers, Dick C. Nanto 94-82 E
* Japan's Response to U.S. Trade Pressures: End of an Era?, Raymond J. Ahearn 95-714 F
* A "Managed Trade" Policy Toward Japan?, Wayne M. Morrison, etc. 94-524 E
* U.S. Commercial Relations With Japan and China: Videoprogram, Dick Nanto VT94-1309

* U.S.-Japan Trade Confrontation: Economic Perspective and Policy Options, Craig Elwell and Alfred Reifman 94-526 E
* U.S.-Japan Trade: Framework Talks and Other Issues: Issue Brief, William H. Cooper IB95019

Jefferson County v. Washington Dept. of Ecology
* PUD No. 1 of Jefferson County v. Washington Department of Ecology: An Expansive Interpretation of State Authority under the Clean Water Act, Ellen M. Lazarus 94-601 A

Jerusalem
* Jerusalem, Clyde R. Mark 94-755 F

Job Creation and Wage Enhancement Act
* Job Creation and Wage Enhancement Act: Tax Provisions; Issue Brief, David L. Brumbaugh and Gregg A. Esenwein IB95059

Job Opportunities and Basic Skills Program
* see also Job Training
* Job Opportunities and Basic (JOBs) Program: Basic Facts, Vee Burke 94-282 EPW
* The Job Opportunities and Basic Skills (JOBS) Program: Recent Funding Statistics and Trends, Gene Falk 95-755 EPW

Job Training
* Adjustment Assistance for Workers Dislocated by the North American Free Trade Agreement, Ann M. Lordeman and James R. Storey 94-52 EPW
* Adult Education Program Trends, Paul M. Irwin 94-951 EPW
* Creating a Federal Employment and Training System: An Overview, Richard N. Apling and Ann Lordeman 94-144 EPW
* Employer Education Assistance: Overview of Tax Status, Bob Lyke 94-761 EPW
* Job Opportunities and Basic (JOBs) Program: Basic Facts, Vee Burke 94-282 EPW
* The Job Opportunities and Basic Skills (JOBs) Program: Recent Funding Statistics and Trends, Gene Falk 95-755 EPW
* The Job Training Partnership Act: A Compendium of Programs, Molly R. Forman and Ann M. Lordeman 94-862 EPW
Jobs for Welfare Recipients, Linda Levine 94-457 E
* Jobs for Welfare Recipients An Issue Overview, Linda Levine 94-461 E
* Jobs: Job Training and the Labor Market; Info Pack IP246J
* School-to-Work Transition: Issues and Legislation in the 2nd Session of the 103rd Congress, Richard N. Apling 94-216 EPW
* Targeted Jobs Tax Credit: Youth Apprentices as an Eligible Group, Linda Levine 93-562 E
* Tax Incentives to Train or Retrain the Work Force, Nonna A. Noto and Louis Alan Talley 93-739 E
* Trade Adjustment Assistance: A Fact Sheet, James R. Storey 94-478 EPW
* Trade Adjustment Assistance: The Program for Workers, James R. Storey 94-801 EPW
* Training for Dislocated Workers under the Job Training Partnership Act, Ann Lordeman 92-901 EPW
* Vocational Education and Special Populations, Richard N. Apling and Sylvie Moulin 94-940 EPW
* Vocational Education: Major Provisions of the 1990 Amendments (P.L. 101-392), Paul M. Irwin and Richard N. Apling 91-675 EPW
* Vocational Education Program Trends, Richard N. Apling 95-11 EPW
* Work Programs for Welfare Recipients: A Look at Past Efforts, Karen Spar 95-761 EPW

Job Training Partnership Act
* Job Training Partnership Act: A Compendium of Programs, Molly R. Forman and Ann M. Lordeman 94-862 EPW
* Jobs: Job Training and the Labor Market; Info Pack IP246J
* Training for Dislocated Workers Under the Job Training Partnership Act, Ann Lordeman 92-901 EPW

Jordan
* see also Middle East and North Africa
* Jordan: U.S. Relations and Bilateral Issues; Issue Brief, Alfred Prados IB93085
* Jordanian-Israeli Peace Treaty, Alfred B. Prados 94-842 F

Judiciary
* see Law

Juvenile Delinquency
* see Criminal Justice

Kashmir

* see also South Asia
* The Kashmir Dispute: Historical Background to the Current Struggle, Richard P. Cronin and Barbara Leitch LePoer 91-563 F

Kazakhstan

* see also Central Asia
* Kazakhstan: Basic Facts, Jim Nichol 95-497 F

Kenya

* see also Africa (Sub-Saharan)
* Kenya: Briefing Paper, Raymond W. Copson 95-775 F

Kim, Young Sam

* South Korea Under Kim Young Sam: Trends, Nuclear and Other issues, Rinn-Sup Shinn and Robert G. Sutter 94-599 F

King, Martin Luther

* Martin Luther King, Jr.'s Birthday: Bibliography-in-Brief, Jean Bowers 93-43 L
* Speech Material: Martin Luther King's Birthday; Info Pack, IP372M

Korea

* see also North Korea, South Korea

Koresh, David

* Branch Davidian Siege at Ranch Apocalypse Near Waco Texas: A Chronology, Suzanne Cavanagh and David Teasley 95-582 GOV

Kyrgyzstan

* see also Central Asia
* Kyrgyzstan: Basic Facts, Jim Nichol 95-613 F

Labor

* Does Trade Reduce Wages of U.S. Workers?, Craig Elwell 94-288 E
* Education Matters: Earnings by the Highest Year of Schooling Completed, linda Levine 95-1081 E
* Employee Compensation: A Fact Sheet, Linda Levine 95-756 E
* Employee Stock Ownership Plans: Background and Policy Issues, Gerald Mayer 94-421 E
* Immigration: The Labor Market Effects of Temporary Alien Farm Worker Program, Linda Levine 95-712 E
* International Labor Organization: A Fact Sheet, Lois McHugh 95-766 F
* Labor-Management Corporation : A Glossary of Terms, 94-516 C
* The Male-Female Wage Gap: A Fact Sheet, Linda Levine 95-661 E
* The Minimum Wage: An Overview of Issues Before the 104th Congress; Issue Brief, William G. Whittaker IB95091
* Real Wage Trends: An Overview, Gail McCallion 95-537 E
* Real Wage Trends: An Overview; An Issue Overview, Gail McCallion 95-664 E
* Resume Writing: The Basics, Rita Jimenez 93-587 C
* Selected Labor Protections Regarding Transit, Amtrak, and Freight Railroads: Issue Brief, Stephen Thompson IB95097
* Sexual Orientation Discrimination in Employment: Legislation and Issues in the 104th Congress, Mark Eddy 94-592 GOV
* Social Security: Coverage of Household Workers; A Fact Sheet, Geoffrey Kollmann 94-114 EPW
* Speech Material: Labor Day; Info Pack IP374L
* Strike Replacements: Developments in the 104th Congress, Gail McCallion 95-651 E
* Union Membership by State, Gail McCallion 94-907 E
* Union Membership Decline: Competing Theories and Economic Implications, Gail McCallion 93-759 E
* Workforce Diversity in the 1990s: Bibliography-in-Brief, 1990-1994, Robert Howe 94-63 L

Labor -- Employment and Unemployment

* Career Guidance and Federal Job Information: Info Pack IP016C
* Displaced Workers in the Current Legislative Context, Linda Levine 95-932 E
* Effects of Trade on U.S. Jobs and Wages, James K. Jackson 94-69 E
* Employment Abroad; Info Pack IP065E
* Employment-at-Will: A Legal Overview, Robin Jeweler 94-605 A
* Employment Trends: A Fact Sheet, Linda Levine 95-763 E
* Equal Employment Opportunity and Affirmative Action: Bibliography-in-Brief, 1993-1995, Tangela G. Roe 95-371 L
* Hispanics in the Labor Force: A Brief Statistical Portrait, Gail McCallion 94-563 E

* How the Unemployment Compensation System Works, James R. Storey 94-11 EPW
* Immigration: The Effects on Native-Born Workers, Linda Levine 95-408 E
* Immigration: The Effects on Native-Born Workers; an Issue Overview, Linda Levine 95-439 E
* Jobs: Job Training and the Labor Market; Info Pack IP246J
* NAFTA and Jobs: An Overview, Alfred Reifman 92-955 S
* NAFTA: U.S. Employment and Wage Effects, Mary Jane Bolle 93-447 E
* NAFTA: U.S. Jobs and Industry Trade Trends After One Year, Mary Jane Bolle 95-605 E
* Plant Closings, Mass Layoffs and Worker Dislocations: Data Issues, Mary Jane Bolle 93-355 E
* Railroad Retirement and Unemployment Benefits: A Summary of Benefits, Financing, and History Dennis W. Snook 95-47 EPW
* Railroad Retirement and Unemployment Benefits: History, Provisions of Financing, Dennis W. Snook 92-765 EPW
* Railroad Unemployment Benefits: Proposed Changes, Dennis W. Snook 95-117 EPW
* Right-to-Work Laws, Gail McCallion 95-805 E
* Small Business and Job Creation, Bruce K. Mulock 95-284 E
* Trade Adjustment Assistance: A Fact Sheet, James R. Storey 94-478 EPW
* Unemployment Benefits: Legislative Issues in the 104th Congress, James R. Storey 95-742 EPW
* Unemployment Compensation in the Group of Seven Nations: An International Comparison, James R. Storey 95-867 EPW
* Union Membership Statistics, Gail McCallion 95-989 E
* Union Membership Trends: A Fact Sheet, Gail McCallion 95-915 E
* Worker Rights Provisions in Fast-Track for Chile: Pros and Cons, Mary Jane Bolle 95-826 E

Labor -- Policies and Legislation

* Affirmative Action Revisited: Legal Overview and Prospectus, Charles V. Dale and Kevin B. Greely 95-223 A
* Child Labor and Public Policy: Legislative and Administrative Issues; Issue Brief, William G. Whittaker IB94057
* The Davis-Bacon Act: Action During the 104th Congress; Issue Brief, William G. Whittaker IB94058
* The Davis-Bacon Act: Institutional Evolution and Public Policy, William G. Whittaker 94-408 E
* The Davis Bacon Act: Institutional Evolution and Public Policy; an Issue Overview, William G. Whittaker 94-460 E
* Davis-Bacon Coverage: Facilities Built for Lease to the Federal Government, William G. Whittaker 94-431 E
* Davis-Bacon: The Act and the Literature, William G. Whittaker 94-908 E
* The Fair Labors Standards Act: An Overview of Issues Before the 104th Congress; Issue Brief, William G. Whittaker IB95008
* The Fair Labor Standards Act: Changes Made by the 101st Congress and Their Implications, William G. Whittaker 92-50 E
* The Fair Labor Standards Act: Consideration During the 102nd Congress; Issue Brief, William G. Whittaker IB91020
* Fair Labor Standards Act: Minimum Wage Protection for Prison Inmate Workers and for Non-Prison Labor, William G. Whittaker 93-895 E
* The Federal Minimum Wage and Select Bibliography, William G. Whittaker 95-202 E
* Inflation and the Real Minimum Wage: Fact Sheet, Brian W. Cashell 94-899 E
* Labor Controversies: Suspension of Davis Bacon; Open-Shop Bidding Requirements; And, "Beck" Rights, Gail McCallion, etc. 93-458 E
* Labor Issues in the 104th Congress: The First Session, by Congressional Research Service, 95-98 E
* OSHA Reform Bills in the 103rd Congress: Comparison With Current Law, Mary Jane Bolle 94-523 E
* OSHA Reform in the 104th Congress: Issue Brief, Edward Rappaport IB95092
* Proposed OSHA Reform in the 103rd Congress: Costs and Benefits, Mary Jane Bolle 94-671 E
* Regulatory Reform: Implications for OSHA, Mary Jane Bolle 95-213 E
* Regulatory Reform: Implications for OSHA: An Issue Overview, Mary Jane Bolle 95-250 E
* Strike Replacement: Issue Brief, Gail McCallion IB93021
* Strike Replacements: Major Legislation Since the 100th Congress 94-353 C
* Targeted Jobs Tax Credit: Prospects in the 104th Congress; Issue Brief, Linda Levine IB95005
* Targeted Jobs Tax Credit: Youth Apprentices as an Eligible Group, Linda Levine 93-562 E
* Trade Adjustment Assistance: The Program for Workers, James R. Storey 94-801 EPW
* Trade Agreements and the International Labor Standards of the ILO, Lois McHugh 94-535 F
* Workers' Compensation, Joe Richardson 91-396 EPW

Be patient. If any phone number is incorrect, call (area code) 555-1212 and request the new listing.

1331

* Common Sense Legal Reforms Act of 1995: Title I-Civil Justice Reform (Attorneys' Fees Products Liability, Etc.), Henry Cohen 95-27 A
* Congressional and State Reapportionment and Redistricting: A Legal Analysis, Thomas B. Durbin and L. Paige Whitaker 95-793 A
* The Constitutionality of Federal Tort Reform, Henry Cohen 95-797 A
* Court Rulings During 1994 on Constitutional Taking Claims Against the United States, Robert Meltz 95-790 A
* Exclusionary Rule: Brief Overview of the Federal Fourth Amendment Rule and Related Matters, Charles Doyle 95-384 S
* Federal Tort Claims Act: Current Legislative and Judicial Issues, Henry Cohen 95-717 A
* Fifty-State Surveys on Selected Products Liability Issues, Henry Cohen and La Vonne Mangan 95-300 A
* "Good Behavior" Tenure of Some Federal Judges, P.L. Morgan 95-450 A
* The Judicial Compensation Clause of the United States Constitution, P.L. Morgan 95-879 A
* Legal Reform Bills Pending in the State; Issue Brief, Henry Cohen IB95068
* Legal Reforms Passed by the House: Issue Brief, Henry Cohen and Michael Seitzinger IB95030
* The Legal Services Corporation, Henry Cohen 95-470 A
* Legal Services Corporation: Basic Facts and Current Status, Karen Spar 95-178 EPW
* The Legal System and Controversy: Women, Gays, Minorities, the Poor, the Aged, and the Disabled: Selected References, 19990-1993, Tangela G. Roe 93-748 L
* Overview of the Independent Counsel Provisions of the Ethics in Government Act, Jack Maskell 94-732 A
* Preparing Legislative Histories; Videoprogram, David Siddall VT91-910
* Product Liability Bills Passed By the House and the Senate: Side-by-Side Analysis, Henry Cohen 95-597 A
* Professional Qualifications for Appointment to the Federal Judiciary, P.L. Morgan 95-404 A
* Property Rights: Comparison of H.R. 9 a Passed and S. 605 as Introduced, Robert Meltz 95-509 A
* Property Rights: Info Pack IP504P
* The Property Rights Issue, Robert Meltz 95-200 A
* The Property Rights Issue: Audio Brief, Robert Meltz and Jeffrey A. Zinn VT95-1323
* Property Rights Legislation in the 103rd Congress, Robert Meltz 94-588 A
* Separate But Equal: Two Hundred Years of Legislative-Executive-Judicial Relations; Videoprogram, Louis Fisher, etc. VT91-955
* Supreme Court Appointment Process, Denis Steven Rutkus 94-355 GOV
* The Supreme Court Appointment Process: Audio Brief, Denis Steven Rutkus AB50276
* Supreme Court Opinions: October 1994 Term, George Costello 95-808 A
* United States Law: Finding Statutory Material, Thomas B. Ripy, etc. 90-110 A
* U.S. Government: Info Pack IP162U

Law, Crime, and Justice
* see Criminal Justice, Drug Abuse, Intelligence Activities, Law

Law Enforcement Availability Pay Act
* Law Enforcement Availability Pay, Barbara L. Schwemle 95-189 GOV

Lebanon
* see also Middle East and North Africa
* Hizballah: A Radical Militia in Lebanon, Kenneth Katzman 93-905 F
* Lebanon: The Current Crisis, Issue Brief, Clyde R. Mark IB89118

Legal Services Corporation
* The Legal Services Corporation, Henry Cohen 95-470 A

Legislative Procedure
* see Congress-Legislative Procedure and Operations

Libraries
* see Humanities

Library of Congress
* Joint Committee on the Library: Duties and Responsibilities, Paul S. Rundquist 95-721 GOV

Library Services and Construction Act
* Library Services and Construction Act: Reauthorization Issues, Wayne Riddle IB95002

Libya
* see also Middle East and North Africa
* Libya: Issue Brief, Clyde E. Mark IB93109

Lincoln, Abraham
* Speech Material: Abraham Lincoln's and George Washington's Birthdays; Info Pack, IP373A

Line Item Veto
* see Budgets -- Process

Lithuania
* see also Europe
* The Baltic Republics: U.S. Policy Concerns, Issue Brief, Vita Bite IB90075

Lobbying
* see Politics and Government

Local Finance
* see State and Local Government

Long-Term Care
* see Aged -- Health

Low Income Energy Assistance
* see Energy

Lumber Trade
* see Natural Resources -- Forests

Macedonia (Skopje)
* see also Europe
* Bosnia & Macedonia: U.S. Military Operations; Issue Brief, Steven Bowman IB93056
* Macedonia: Basic Facts, Julie Kim 95-771 F
* Macedonia-Albanian Ethnic Tensions: Chronology of the Confrontation in Tetovo, Julie Kim 95-381 F

Magnuson Fishery Conservation and Management Act
* Magnuson Fishery Conservation and Management Act Reauthorization: Issue Brief, Eugene H. Buck IB95036
* Social Aspects of Federal Fishery Management, Eugene H. Buck 95-553 ENR

Mandates
* see State and Local Government

Manpower Training Programs
* see Job Training

Marine Mammal Protection Act
* see also Marine Resources -- Fisheries
* Acoustic Thermometry of Ocean Climate: Marine Mammal Issues, Eugene H. Buck 95-603 ENR
* Marine Mammal Protection Act Amendments of 1994, Eugene H. Buck 94-751 ENR

Marine Resources
* see also Infrastructure
* Acoustic Thermometry of Ocean Climate: Marine Mammal Issues, Eugene H. Buck 95-603 ENR
* Deep Seabed Mining: U.S. Interests and the U.N. Convention on the Law of the Sea, James E. Mielke 95-471 SPR
* Federal Agency Programs in Living Aquatic Resources and Aquatic Habitat Protection, Eugene Buck 95-937 ENR
* Individual Transferable Quotas in Fishery Management, Eugene Buck 95-849 ENR
* The Law of the Sea Convention and U.S. Policy: Issue Brief, Marjorie Ann Browne IB95010
* Living Aquatic Resource Laws and Treaties: Reference Guide, Eugene Buck 95-174 ENR
* Marine Ecosystem Management, Eugene H. Buck 93-679 ENR
* Oceans and Coastal Resources: A Briefing Book, Alfred R. Greenwood 95-313 ENR
* United Nations Convention on the Law of the Sea: Living Resources Provisions, Eugene H. Buck 95-4 ENR

* Wetlands Issues in the 104th Congress: Issue Brief, Jeffrey Zinn and Claudia Copeland IB95028
* Wetlands Issues: Info Pack IP423W
* Wetlands Legislation: Comparison of Two Bills, Claudia Copeland 95-796 ENR

Marine Resources -- Fisheries

* Aquaculture and the Federal Role, Eugene H. Buck and Geoffrey S. Becker 93-798 ENR
* Atlantic Bluefin Tuna: International Management of a Shared Resource, Eugene H. Buck 95-367 ENR
Magnuson Fishery Conservation and Management Act Reauthorization: Issue Brief, Eugene Buck IB95036
* The Magnuson Fishery Conservation and Management Act: Reauthorization Issues, Eugene Buck 93-88 ENR
* Marine Mammal Protection Act Amendments of 1994, Eugene H. Buck 94-751 ENR
* The Northern Right Whale, Lynne Corn 95-493 ENR
* Overcapitalization in the U.S. Commercial Fishing Industry, Eugene H. Buck 95-296 ENR
* Seafood Inspection Issues, Geoffrey S. Becker 95-290 ENR
* Social Aspects of Federal Fishery Management, Eugene H. Buck 95-553 ENR
* Summaries of Major Laws Implemented by the National Marine Fisheries Service, Eugene H. Buck 95-460 ENR

Meat
* see Food -- Labeling and Safety

Medicaid
* see Health Policy -- Medicaid

Medical Care Reform
* see Health Policy -- Reform

Medical Economics
* see Health Policy -- Finance

Medical Personnel
* see Medicine -- Facilities/Personnel

Medical Records
* see Medicine

Medicare
* see Health Policy -- Medicare

Medicine
* see also Health Policy
* Alzheimer's Disease: Federal Research Funding and Programs, C. Stephen Redhead 95-14 SPR
* Appropriations for Selected Health Programs FY 1981-1995, Celinda Franco, etc. 95-987 EPW
* Cancer Research: Selected Federal Spending and Morbidity and Mortality Statistics, Judith A. Johnson 95-268 SPR
* Diabetes, Donna U. Vogt 95-146 SPR
* Drug Regulation: Historical Overview and Current Reform, Blanchard Randall 95-962 SPR
* Emerging Infectious Diseases: A Selected Bibliography, Karen L. Alderson 95-545 L
* Environmental Tobacco Smoke and Lung Cancer Risk, Stephen Redhead 95-1115 SPR
* FDA's Medical Device Review Process, Bernice Reyes-Akinileje 95-779 SPR
* Foodborne Illness: What Do the Data Tell Us?, Donna U. Vogt 94-917 SPR
* Health Care Fact Sheet: Health Centers Programs, Melvina Ford and Edward Klebe 94-865 EPW
* Health Care Fact Sheet: Indian Health Service, Edward L. Klebe 94-866 EPW
* Health Care Reform: Prevention and Medical Research; Videoprogram, Pamela Smith, etc. VT94-1314
* Health Care Reform: Where Does Medical Research Fit In?, Pamela W. Smith 94-870 SPR
* Homeless Mentally Ill Persons: Problems and Programs, Karen M. Judge and Edward R. Klebe 93-728 EPW
* Hospital Length-of-Stay for Obstetrical Care, Sharon Kearney 95-1114 EPW
* Human Embryo Research, Irene Stith-Coleman 95-910 SPR
* Human Fetal Tissue Transplantation Research, Irene Stith-Coleman 95-886 SPR

* Human Radiation Experiments and Radiation Safety: Selected References, 1981-1994, Bonnie F. Mangan 94-626 L
* Infectious Diseases: Emerging and Reemerging Threats to Public Health in the United States, Judith A. Johnson 95-534 SPR
* International Population and Family Planning Programs: Issues for Congress; Issue Brief, Shirley Kan and Curt Tarnoff IB85187
* Medicaid Services for Mentally Ill, Edward R. Klebe 93-761 EPW
* Medical Use of Marijuana: Policy and Regulatory Issues, Blanchard Randall 93-308 SPR
* Medicare Coverage for Mental Illness and Substance Abuse, Edward R. Klebe 94-331 EPW
* Mental Illness and Substance Abuse Disorders: Background Information Related to Health Care Reform, Edith Fairman Cooper 94-544 SPR
* Mortality and Economic Costs Attributable to Smoking and Alcohol Abuse, C. Stephen Redhead 93-426 SPR
* National Health Service Corps, Celinda M. Franco 95-323 EPW
* The National Institutes of Health: An Overview, Pamela W. Smith 95-96 SPR
* Organ Transplantation and Bone Marrow Transplantation: Background and Federal Role, Pamela W. Smith and Irene Stith-Coleman 95-811 SPR
* Outcomes Research, Clinical Practice Guidelines, and the Agency for Health Care Policy and Research, Bernice Reyes-Akinbileje 94-488 SPR
* Protection of Human Subjects in Research, Irene Stith-Coleman 94-179 SPR
* Public Health Service: Program Consolidations; Issue Brief, Edward Klebe IB95098
* Smoking: Federal Actions; Info Pack IP486S
* Sudden Infant Death Syndrome (SIDS): Risk Factors and Federal Research Funding Levels, Edith Fairman Cooper 95-315 SPR
* The Surgeon General of the United States, Mark V. Wright 94-663 C
* The Title X Family Planning Program, Melvina Ford 95-665 EPW
* World Health Organization: A Fact Sheet, Lois McHugh 95-166 F

Medicine -- AIDS
* AIDS: Acquired Immune Deficiency Syndrome; Info Pack IP261A
* AIDS and Other Diseases: Selected Federal Spending and Mortality Statistics, Judith A. Johnson 95-363 SPR
* AIDS Discrimination: The Federal Response, Mark Eddy 94-818 GOV
* AIDS: Federal Funding for Research and Prevention, FY 81-FY 96, Judith A. Johnson 95-352 SPR
* AIDS in the Developing World: The International Response, Lois McHugh 93-1016 F
* Ryan White Comprehensive AIDS Resources Emergency (CARE) Act of 1990, Bud Graves 94-252 EPW

Medicine -- Drugs
* Biotechnology, Breakthrough Drugs, and Health Care Reform: Lessons from the NIH-University-Industry Relationship, Wendy Schacht 94-375 SPR
* Federal Support for Pharmacology and Medical Device-Related Research and Development, Bernice Reyes-Akinbileje 93-452 SPR
* Food and Drug Administration: Selected Funding and Policy Issues, Donna U. Vogt 95-422 SPR
* GATT and the Pharmaceutical Industry: Prospective Effects of the Uruguay Round on the Industry, Sylvia Morrison 94-831 E
* Health Care Reform and Investment in New Drug Development, Gary Guenther 95-179 E
* Prescription Drug Prices: The Effects of Generics, Formularies, and Other Market Changes, Sylvia Morrison 93-740 E
* The President's Health Care Reform Plan and Drug Development in the Biotechnology Industry, Gary Guenther 94-346 E

Medicine -- Facilities/Personnel
* Case Management Standards in State Community-Based Long-Term Care Programs for Older Persons With Disabilities, Carol O'Shaughnessy and Richard Price 94-96 EPW
* Clinical Laboratory Improvement Amendments of 1988, Jennifer O'Sullivan 94-898 EPW
* Health Care: Physician Self-Referrals, Jennifer O'Sullivan 95-19 EPW
* The Hill-Burton Program, Celinda Franco and Edward R. Klebe 94-88 EPW
* Medical Malpractice: Issue Brief, Jennifer O'Sullivan IB92086
* Medicare: Payments to Physicians, Jennifer O'Sullivan 95-21 EPW
* Military Medical Care Services: Questions and Answers; Issue Brief, Richard A. Best IB93103
* Tax Aspects of Health Care Reform: The Tax Treatment of Health Care Providers, Harry G. Gourevitch 94-369 S

Members of Congress
* see Congress--Members

Be patient. If any phone number is incorrect, call (area code) 555-1212 and request the new listing.

1333

Current Events and Homework

Mental Illness
* see Medicine

Mentally Retarded
* see Disabled

Mexican Peso Crisis
* see Mexico

Mexico
* Doing Business With Mexico: Sources of Information, Penelope Fay Heavner 94-543 C
* The Exchange Stabilization Fund, Arlene Wilson 95-262 E
* Mexican Challenges in 1994: Uprising in Chiapas Assassinations, Elections, and Devaluation, K. Larry Storrs 95-527 F
* The Mexican Economic Crisis: U.S. Jobs, Illegal Immigrants, and Systematic Risk, Glennon J. Harrison 95-225 E
* The Mexican Economy Under the Salinas Administration: The Macroeconomic Foundations, Patricia A. Wertman 93-1049 E
* The Mexican Financial Crises, 1982 and 1995: Similarities and Differences, Patricia A. Wertman 95-239 E
* The Mexican Peso and Devaluation and Swap Arrangements, Arlene Wilson 95-169 E
* Mexico and Proposed U.S. Loan Guarantees: Background and Issues, Glennon J. Harrison and J.F. Hornbeck 95-183 E
* Mexico: Chronology of Major Events, January 1993 to April 1995, K. Larry Storrs 95-504 F
* Mexico: Problems and Prospects; Info Pack IP358M
* Mexico and Zedillo: Implications for U.S. Mexico Relations; A Checklist of CRS Products, Sherry B. Shapiro 95-423 L
* Mexico-U.S. Relations: Issues for the 104th Congress; Issue Brief, K. Larry Storrs, etc. IB95078
* Mexico's Changing Policy Toward Foreign Investment: NAFTA Implications:An Issue Overview, M. Angeles Villarreal 93-668 E
* Mexico's Financial Crisis and U.S. Support Efforts, K. Larry Storrs 95-211 F
* Mexico's 1995 Economic Program and the IMF, Patricia A. Wertman 95-428 E
* Strengthening the International Monetary System: Lessons of the Mexican Crisis, Alfred Reifman 95-595 S
* United States-Mexico Economic Relations: Has NAFTA Made A Difference, J.F. Hornbeck 95-398 E
* U.S. Direct Investment in Mexico, James K. Jackson 93-522 E
* Would a Currency Board Have Prevented Mexico's Financial Crisis? 95-271 E

MIAs
* see Defense Policy

Middle East and North Africa
* Hamas and Palestinian Islamic Jihad: Recent Developments, Sources of Support, and Implications for U.S. Policy, Clyde Mark and Kenneth Katzman 94-993 F
* Hamas: The Organization, Goals and Tactics of a Militant Palestinian Organization, James P. Wootten 93-511 F
* Hizballah: A Radical Militia in Lebanon, Kenneth Katzman 93-905 F
* Saudi Arabia: Commercial Disputes With U.S. Firms, Alfred B. Prados 95-666 F

Middle East and North Africa -- Defense
* Iran and Iraq: U.S. National Security Problems Since the Gulf War--A Chronology July 1993-July 1994, Kenneth Katzman 94-561 F
* Iranian Military Buildup: What Sort of Threat to Persian Gulf Oil Supply?, Lawrence C. Kumins and Kenneth Katzman 95-572 ENR
* Iraqi Compliance With Cease-Fire Agreements: Issue Brief, Kenneth Katzman IB92117
* Middle East Arms Supply: Recent Control Initiatives; Issue Brief, Alfred B. Prados IB91113
* Military Deployments to the Persian Gulf Region, Steven R. Bowman 94-790 F
* Persian Gulf Region: U.S. Post-War Security Interests, Alfred Prados 93-586 F
* Turkey's Military Offensive in Northern Iraq, Carol Migdalovitz 95-487 F

Middle East and North Africa -- Foreign Aid
* Greece and Turkey: Current Foreign Aid Issues: Issue Brief, Carol Migdalovitz IB86065
* Israel: U.S. Foreign Assistance; Issue Brief, Clyde Mark IB85066
* Israel's Request for U.S. Loan Guarantees: Issue Brief, Larry Nowels and Clyde Mark IB91103
* Middle East and North Africa: U.S. Aid FY 1993, 1994, 1995, Clyde Mark 94-274 F

* North Korea: Military Relations With the Middle East, Rinn-Sup Shinn and Kenneth Katzman 94-754 F
* West Bank/Gaza Strip: U.S. Foreign Assistance, Clyde Mark 93-689 F

Middle East and North Africa -- Foreign Policy
* Egypt-United States Relations: Issue Brief, Clyde Mark IB93087
* Iran: U.S. Containment Policy, kenneth Katzman 94-652 F
* Iran: U.S. Trade Regulation and Legislation, Kenneth Katzman and Lawrence Kumins 95-419 F
* Iraq: Current Sanctions, Long Term Threat, and U.S. Policy Options, Kenneth Katzman 94-465 F
* Israeli-United States Relations: Issue Brief, Clyde Mark IB82008
* Jordan: U.S. Relations and Bilateral Issues; Issue Brief, Alfred B. Prados IB93085
* Saudi Arabia: Post War Issues and U.S. Relations; Issue Brief, Alfred B. Prados IB93113
* Syrian-U.S. Relations: Issue Brief, Alfred Prados IB92075
* Turkey: Ally in a Troubled Region, Carol Migdalovitz 93-835 F
* Turkey: Political and Economic Change and Implications for the United States, Carol Migdalovitz 94-741 F

Middle East and North Africa -- Peace
* The Golan Heights, Clyde Mark 95-308 F
* Israeli-Palestinian Agreement, Carol Migdalovitz 93-797 F
* Jordan-Israel Peace Treaty: Implementation Dates, Clyde Mark 94-877 F
* Jordanian-Israeli Peace Treaty, Alfred B. Prados 94-842 F
* Middle East Peace and Security Issues: Audio Brief, Alfred Prados, etc. AB50311
* Middle East Peace and Security Issues; Videoprogram, Alfred Prados, etc. VT95-1304
* Middle East Peace Breakthrough: A CRS Roundtable; Videoprogram, Congressional Research Service VT93-1360
* Middle East Peace Prospects: Info Pack IP397M
* The Middle East Peace Talks: Issue Brief, Carol Migdalovitz IB91137
* Palestinians and Middle East Peace: Issues for United States; Issue Brief, Clyde Mark IB92052
* Syrian Positions on Peace With Israel: Official Statements Since September 1993, Alfred Prados 95-324 F

Middle East and North Africa -- Politics and Government
* Algeria in Crisis: Situation Update, Carol Migdalovitz 94-241 F
* Iran: The People's Mojahedin Organization of Iran, Kenneth Katzman 94-683 F
* Jerusalem, Clyde Mark 94-755 F
* Lebanon: The Current Crisis; Issue Brief, Clyde Mark IB89118
* Libya: Issue Brief, Clyde Mark IB93109
* Morocco: Situation Update, Carol Migdalovitz 95-410 F
* Turkey's Kurdish Imbroglio and U.S. Policy, Carol Migdalovitz 94-267 F
* United Arab Emirates: Background and U.S. Relations, Alfred Prados and Ross Kaplan 95-730 F

* Migrant Education
* see Elementary and Secondary Education

* Migration
* see Immigration

Military Assistance
* see Foreign Aid

Military Bases
* see Defense Policy -- Bases

Military Pensions
* see Pensions -- Government

Military Personnel
* see Defense Policy -- Personnel

Military Retirement
* see Defense Policy -- Personnel

Miller v. Johnson
* An Overview of Miller v. Johnson--Georgia's Majority-Minority Congressional Redistricting Plan, Thomas M. Durbin 95-770 A

Minimum Wage
* see Labor -- Policies and Legislation

Minorities

* Affirmative Action and Equal Employment Opportunity: Info Pack IP424A
* Affirmative Action in Employment, Andorra Bruno 95-165 GOV
* Affirmative Action in the 104th Congress: Selected Legislation; Issue Brief, Andorra Bruno IB95094
* Affirmative Action Revisited: Legal Overview and Prospectus, Charles V. Dale and Kevin B. Greely 95-223 A
* Asian American Electoral Participation and Representation, Kevin Coleman 94-893 GOV
* The Civil Rights Act of 1991: A Legal History and Analysis, Charles V. Dale 92-85 A
* Civil Rights Protection in the United States: Brief Summaries of Constitutional Amendments, Federal Laws, and Executive Orders, Leslie Gladstone 93-148 GOV
* Discrimination in Mortgage Lending: What Do We Know?, Barbara L. Miles 94-708 E
* Districts of the 103rd Congress: Hispanic Population-Data and Rankings, David C. Huckabee 94-9 GOV
* Fair Employment Practices in Congress: Authorizing Legislation and House/Senate Comparison, Leslie Gladstone 94-996 GOV
* Hate Crime: Recent Developments, Suzanne Cavanagh and David teasley 94-855 GOV
* Hate Crime: An Overview, Suzanne Cavanaugh and David Teasley 93-157 GOV
* Hate Violence in the United States: Background and Current Dimensions, William W. Ellis 95-616 S
* Hispanic Heritage Month: Info Pack IP427H
* Hispanic Tradition and Achievement in the United States, Garrine P. Laney 93-906 GOV
* Hispanics in the Labor Force: A Brief Statistical Portrait, Gail McCallion 94-563 E
* The Legal System and Controversy: Women, Gays, Minorities, the Poor, the Aged, and the Disabled: Selected References, 1990-1993, Tangela G. Roe 93-748 L
* Minority and Women-Owned Business Programs of the Federal Government, Mark Eddy 95-757 GOV
* Racial Justice and Capital Punishment: The Racially Discriminatory Capital Sentencing Provisions of the House Passed Crime Bill (H.R. 4092/H.R. 3355), Charles Doyle 94-386 S
* The Supreme Court Decision in Adarand Constructors Inc. v. Pena: Federal Contracting and Disadvantaged Business Enterprises, Charles V. Dale 95-137 A
* The Voting Rights Act of 1965: A Legal Overview, L. Paige Whitaker 91-736
* Workforce Diversity in the 1990s: Bibliography-in-Brief, 1988-1991, Robert Howe 94-63 L

Minorities -- Black

* Black Americans: A Checklist of CRS Products, Tangela Roe 95-512 L
* Black Electoral Participation and Representation, Kevin Coleman and Daryl Harris 93-1063 GOV
* Black History and Culture: Bibliography-in-Brief, Tangela G. Roe 95-136 L
* Black History Month: Info Pack IP344B
* Black Members of the United States Congress: 1789-1993, Mildred L. Amer 93-671 GOV
* An Overview of Miller v. Johnson--Georgia's Majority-Minority Congressional Redistricting Plan, Thomas M. Durbin 95-770 A
* Rap and Rock Music Lyrics: Bibliography-in-Brief, Tangela G. Roe 94-251 L
* Speech Material: Martin Luther King, Jr.'s Birthday, Info Pack IP372M

Minorities--Native Americans

* Federal Indian Law: Sources of General Information, Dana Ely 94-820 A
* Financial Aid for Native American Post-Secondary Students, Rita Jimenez 93-172 C
* Health Care Fact Sheet: Indian Health Service, Edward R. Klebe 94-866 EPW
* Health Services for American Indians and Alaska Natives, Edward Klebe and Karen M. Judge 93-975 EPW
* Indian Gaming: A Short Glossary of Some Financial Terms Used in Gaming, Roger Walke 93-555 GOV
* The Indian Gaming Regulatory Act of 1994, S. 2230, (103rd Cong, 2nd Sess.): A Brief Analysis, M. Maureen Murphy 94-674 A
* Indian Gaming Regulatory Act: Judicial and Administrative Interpretations, M. Maureen MURPHY 93-793 a
* Native American Heritage: Bibliography-in-Brief, Tangela G. Roe 94-815 L
* Native American Heritage: Info Pack IP454N

Missiles

* see Weapons Systems -- Nuclear Weapons

Missing in Action

* see Defense Policy

Moldova

* see also Europe
* Moldova Republic: Basic Facts, Sergiu Verona 92-182 F

Monetary Policy

* see Finance

Mongolia

* see also East Asia
* Mongolia: Briefing Paper, Rinn Sup Shinn 95-667 F

Morocco

* see also Middle East and North Africa
Morocco: Situation Update, Carol Migdalovitz 95-410 F

Most Favored Nation Trade Policies

* see Trade -- Policy

Motor Voter Laws

* see Elections

Mozambique

* see also (Sub-Saharan)
* Mozambique: Post Election Prospects, Patrice Curtis 94-984

Multilateral Development Banks

* see International Finance -- Banks

Multinational Corporations

* see International Corporations

NAFTA

* see North American Free Trade Agreement

Narcotics

* see Drug Abuse

National and Community Service Trust Act

* Domestic Volunteer Service Act Programs, Dale Robinson 94-982 EPW
* The National and Community Service Trust Act of 1993: Description and Related Programs, Dale H. Robinson 95-746 ENR

National Debt

* see Budgets -- Deficits

National Defense

* see Defense Policy

National Endowments

* see Humanities

National Foundation on the Arts and the Humanities Act

* National Foundation on the Arts and the Humanities Act of 1965: Reauthorization Fact Sheet, Susan Bowen and Ruth Ann Stewart 93-417 EPW

National Hispanic Heritage Month

* Hispanic Heritage Month: Info Pack IP427H

National Information Infrastructure

* see also Technology -- Computers
* Health Care Reform and National Information Infrastructure, Stephen B. Gould 94-770 SPR
* The National Information Infrastructure: The Federal Role; Issue Brief, Stephen B. Gould and Glenn J. McLoughlin IB95051

National Institutes of Health (U.S.)

* Biotechnology, Breakthrough Drugs, and Health Care Reform: Lessons from the NIH-University-Industry Relationship, Wendy H. Schacht 94-375 SPR
* Health Care Reform: Where Does Medical Research Fit In?, Pamela W. Smith 94-870 SPR
* The National Institutes of Health: An Overview, Pamela W. Smith 95-96 SPR

National Organization for Women v. Scheidler

* RICO and Political Protest: The Implications of NOW v. Scheidler, Kenneth Thomas 94-108 A

Be patient. If any phone number is incorrect, call (area code) 555-1212 and request the new listing.

1335

National Performance Review (U.S.)

* Implementation of National Performance Review Recommendations: General Government, Harold C. Relyea 93-936 GOV
* Minerals Management Service Functions: Devolve to the States?, Marc Humphries 95-785 ENR
* The National Performance Review, Harold C. Relyea 93-862 GOV
* National Performance Review: A New Look at the Federal Bureaucracy; Info Pack IP478N
* Railroad Retirement Board: Summary of Issues Posed the National Performance Review's Proposal to End the Board's Function, Dennis W. Snook 93-928 EPW
* Reforming Government: The Grace Commission and the National Performance Review, Harold C. Relyea and Gary L. Galemore 93-933 GOV
* Reinventing Government and the 103rd Congress: A Brief Overview, Harold C. Relyea 93-859 GOV
* Reinventing Government: The First Year, Harold C. Relyea 95-209 GOV

National Security Council (U.S.)

* The National Security Council: An Organizational Assessment, Richard A. Best and Mark M. Lowenthal 93-517 F

National Service

* see Social Services

National Voter Registration Act

* The National Voter Registration Act of 1993, "Motor-Voter"., Royce Crocker 94-276 GOV
* National Voter Registration Act of 1993 ("Motor Voter"): Comparison of H.R. 2 (103rd Cong.) as Passed by the House and the Senate, L. Paige Whitaker 93-351 A
* National Voter Registration: Issue, Royce Crocker IB95073

Native Americans

* see Minorities -- Native Americans

NATO

* see North Atlantic Treaty Organization

Natural Disasters

* see Emergency Management

Natural Gas

* see Energy

Natural Resources

* see also Energy, Marine Resources, Public Lands, Water Resources
* The Arctic National Wildlife Refuge: Issue Brief, M. Lynne Corn and Lawrence C. Kummins IB95071
* Arctic Oil, Arctic Refuge; Videoprogram, M. Lynne Corn, VT91-1489
* Biological Diversity: Issues Related to the Convention on Biodiversity, Susan Fletcher 95-598 ENR
* Biological Diversity Treaty: Fact Sheet, Susan R. Fletcher 95-596 ENR
* Conservation Compliance: Policy Issues for the 1995 Farm Bill, Jeffrey Zinn 95-6 ENR
* Ecosystem Management: Federal Agency Activities, M. Lynne Corn, etc. 94-339 ENR
* Ecosystem Management Tools and Techniques: Proceedings of a CRS Workshop, Wayne A. Morrissey 95-430 SPR
* Ecosystems, Biomes, and Watersheds: Definition and Use, M. Lynne Corn 93-655 ENR
* The Federal Helium Program: The Reaction Over an Inert Gas, James E. Mielke 95-197 SPR
* Federal Sales of Natural Resources: Allocation and Pricing Systems, Ross W. Gorte 93-1035 ENR
* The Forest Service and Bureau of Land Management: History and Analysis of Merger Proposals, Ross Gore and Betsy Cody 95-1117 ENR
* The Forest Service Budget: Trust Funds and Special Accounts, Ross Gorte 95-604 ENR
* Forest Service Timber Sale Practices and Procedures: Analysis of Alternative Systems, Ross W. Gorte 95-1077 ENR
* Hardrock Mining, the 1872 Law, and the U.S. Economy, Bernard A. Gelb 94-540 E
* International Forest Agreements: Current Status, Susan Fletcher 95-960 ENR
* An Introduction to Major Natural Resource Issues in the 104th Congress 95-92 ENR
* Land and Water Conservation Fund: Current Funding, Ross Gorte 95-970 ENR

* The Major Federal Land Management Agencies: Management of Our Nation's Lands and Resources, Environment and Natural Resources Policy Division, 95-599 ENR
* Minerals Management Service Functions: Devolve to the States?, Marc Humphries 95-785 ENR
* Mining Law Reform: The Impact of a Royalty, Marc Humphries 94-438 ENR
* The National Biological Service, M. Lynne Corn 95-746 ENR
* The National Defense Stockpile: The FY 1996 Annual Materials Plan, Alfred R.Greenwood 95-577 ENR
* Natural Resource "Subsidy" Issues, Issue Brief, Ross W. Gorte, Environmental and Natural Resources Division IB95022
* Reforming the General Mining Law of 1872: A Comparison of S. 775 and H.R. 322, Marc Humphries 93-632 ENR
* The Rural Abandoned Mine Program--A Fact Sheet, Duane A. Thompson 95-706 ENR
* U.S. Geological Survey: Its Mission and Its Future, James E. Mielke 95-145 SPR
* The 1872 Mining Law: Time to Reform?; Issue Brief, Marc Humphries IB89130

Natural Resources -- Forests

* Below-Cost Timber Sales, Ross W. Gorte 95-15 ENR
* Clearcutting in the National Forests, Adela Backiel and Ross W. Gorte 92-707 ENR
* Deforestation: An Overview of Global Programs and Agreements, Julie Lyke and Susan R. Fletcher 92-764 ENR
* Forest Fires and Forest Health, Ross W. Gorte 95-511 Enr
* Forest Health, Ross W. Gorte 95-548 ENR
* Lumber Prices, Ross W. Gorte 94-122 ENR
* Mahoganies: International Protection?, M. Lynne Corn 94-802 ENR
* Restricting Softwood Log Exports: Policy and Legal Implications, Kenneth R. Thomas and Ross W. Gorte 93-738 ENR
* Salvage Timber Sales and Forest Health, Ross W. gorte 95-364 ENR

Negotiated Rates Act

* The Truckline Undercharge Problem and the Negotiated Rates act, K.R. DeJarnette 94-776 E

Nicaragua

* see also Latin America
* Nicaragua: Background and U.S. Policy Concerns, K. Larry Storrs and Maureen Taft-Morales 94-440 F

Nigeria

* see also Africa (Sub-Saharan)
* Nigeria: Briefing Paper, Raymond W. Copson 94-715 F

Nominations

* see Executive Departments

Nonproliferation

* see Defense Policy--Nonproliferation

North American Free Trade Agreement

* see also Canada, Latin America -- Foreign Trade, Mexico
* Adjustment Assistance for Workers Dislocated by the North American Free Trade Agreement, Ann M. Lordeman and James R. Storey 94-52 EPW
* Agriculture in the North American Free Trade Agreement, Charles E. Hanrahan 92-958 S
* Banking and Finance in the North American Free Trade Agreement, William Jackson 93-560 E
* Border Environment Cooperation Commission and North American Development Bank: Background and Issues, Mary Tiemann and J.F. Hornbeck 95-184 ENR
* Caribbean Basin Countries: Implications of a North American Free Trade Agreement, Lenore M. Sek, etc. 93-551 E
* Caribbean Basin Interim Trade Program ("CBI Parity"): Fact Sheet, Vladimir N. Pregelj 95-236 E
* Caribbean Basin Interim Trade Program: Issue Brief, Vladimir N. Pregelj IB95050
* Chilean Trade and Economic Reform: Implications for NAFTA Accession, J.F. Hornbeck 95-751 E
* Doing Business With Mexico: Sources of Information, Penelope Fay Heavner 94-543 C
* Economic Comparisons of Mexico, Canada, and the United States: Implications for the NAFTA, Arlene Wilson 93-669 E
* Enforcement of Intellectual Property Rights Under the NAFTA, Dorothy Schrader 94-72 A
* Intellectual Property Provisions of the NAFTA, Dorothy Schrader 94-59 A

* Mexican-U.S.-Canadian Automotive Trade Issues, Gwenell L. Bass and M. Angeles Villarreal 93-961 E

* Mexico's Changing policy Toward Foreign Investment and Implications: An Issue Overview, M. Angeles Villarreal 93-782 E

* Mexico's Changing Policy Toward Foreign Investment: NAFTA Implications, M. Angeles Villarreal 93-668 E

* NAFTA: A Broad Economic Perspective, Arlene Wilson 93-974 E

* NAFTA and Jobs: An Overview, Alfred Reifman 92-955 S

* NAFTA and Sugar, Remy Jurenas, 93-986 ENR

* NAFTA and the EC as Trading Blocs: A Distinction With a Difference, Glennon Harrison 93-864 E

* NAFTA and the Peso-Dollar Exchange Rate, Arlene Wilson 94-496 E

* NAFTA Decisions and U.S. -Mexico Relations, K. Larry Storrs 93-991 F

* NAFTA: Implications for Illicit Drug Supply to the United States, Raphael F. Perl 93-972 F

* NAFTA: The North American Free Trade Agreement; Info Pack IP445N

* NAFTA: U.S. Employment and Wage Effects, Mary Jane Bolle 93-447 E

* NAFTA: U.S. Jobs and Industry Trade Trends After One Year; an Issue Overview, Mary Jane Bolle 95-648 E

* NAFTA: U.S. Jobs and Industry Trade Trends After One Year, Mary Jane Bolle 95-605 E

* A North American Free Trade Agreement and Immigration, Joyce C. Vialet 93-62 EPW

* North American Free Trade Agreement: Bibliography-in-Brief, Robert Howe 94-960 L

* North American Free Trade Agreement: Environmental Provisions and Issues, Mary Tiemann 93-760 ENR

* Telecommunications Services: Provisions in the Uruguay Round and in NAFTA, M. Angeles Villarreal 94-653 E

* Trade and Environment: GATT and NAFTA, Susan R. Fletcher and Mary Tiemann 94-165 ENR

* Trade and the Americas: Issue Brief, Raymond J. Ahearn IB95017

* Trade, Competitiveness, and International Economic Policy: A Bibliography of CRS Products, Robert Howe 93-611 L

* Trade Policy in the 104th Congress, George D. Holliday 95-485 E

* United States-Mexico Economic Relations: Has NAFTA Made a Difference, J.F. Hornbeck 95-398 E

* U.S.-Canadian Agricultural Trade Disputes, Carl Ek and Charles E. Hanrahan 94-270 F

* U.S. Direct Investment in Mexico, James K. Jackson 93-522 E

* Why Certain Trade Agreements Are Approved as Congressional-Executive Agreements Rather Than as Treaties, Jeanne J. Grimmett 94-766 A

North Atlantic Treaty Organization

* Combined Joint Task Forces (CJTF) and New Missions for NATO, Stanley R. Sloan 94-249 F

* NATO: Congress Addresses Expansion of Alliance; Issue Brief, Paul E. Gallis IB95076

* NATO Enlargement and Russia: From Cold War to Cold Peace, Stanley R. Sloan and Steve Woehrel 95-594 S

* NATO Enlargement in Central Europe, Paul E. Gallis 94-879 F

* NATO Enlargement: Partnership for Peace Members-On the Road for Alliance Membership?, Foreign Affairs and National Defense Division, Paul E. Gallis 95-468 F

* NATO: Fact Sheet, Karen E. Donfried 92-919 F

* The NATO Strategy Review: Negotiating the Future of the North Atlantic Alliance, Stanley R. Sloan, 91-379 RCO

* The NATO Summit: Transatlantic Relations at a Crossroads, Stanley R. Sloan 93-939 S

* NATO's Future: Info Pack IP425N

* Partnership for Peace, Paul E. Gallis 94-351 F

* U.S. Policy Toward Russia and NATO, Stanley R. Sloan 94-871 S

North Korea

* Korea: Procedural and Jurisdictional Questions Regarding Possible Normalization of Relations With North Korea, Congressional Research Service 94-933 S

* Korean Crisis, 1994 Military Geography, Military Balance, Military Options, John M. Collins 94-311 S

* Korean Peninsula Tensions: North Korea and Nuclear Weapons; Info Pack IP484K

* North Korea After Kim Il Sung, Rinn S. Shinn 94-578 F

* North Korea After Kim Il Sung: A CRS Roundtable: Audio Brief, Robert Sutter AB50305

* North Korea After Kim Il Sung: A CRS Roundtable; Videoprogram, Robert Sutter VT94-1348

* North Korea: Military Relations With the Middle East, Rinn-Sup Shinn and Kenneth Katzman 94-754 F

* North Korea: U.S. Policy and Negotiations to Halt Its Nuclear Weapons Program; an Annotated Chronology and Analysis, Richard P. Cronin 94-905 F

* North Korean Nuclear Controversy: Defining Treaties, Agreements, and Terms, Larry Niksch and Zachary Davis 94-752 F

* North Korea's Nuclear Weapons Program; Issue Brief, Larry Niksch IB91141

* North Korea's nuclear Weapons Program: U.S. Policy Options, Richard Cronin, etc. 94-470 F

North Vietnam

* see Vietnam

Northern Ireland

* see also Europe

* Northern Ireland and the Peace Process: The Joint Declaration of December 1993 Revisited, Karen Donfried 95-515 F

* Northern Ireland: IRA Cease-Fire, Karen Donfried IB94025

* Northern Ireland: The Peace Process; Videoprogram, Karen Donfried VT95-1340

* Roundtable on Northern Ireland; Videoprogram, Karen Donfried VT93-1364

Nuclear Energy

* see Energy -- Nuclear

Nuclear Waste

* see Solid Wastes

Nuclear Weapons

* see Weapons -- Nuclear Weapons

Nutrition

* see Food

Occupational Health and Safety

* see Labor -- Policies and Legislation

Occupational Training

* see Job Training

Oceania

* APEC--Asia Pacific Economic Cooperation: Free Trade and Other Issues, Dick K. Nanto 93-926 E

* APEC, EAEC, and Free Trade in the Asia Pacific, Dick K. Nanto 94-914 E

* Asian-Pacific Economic Cooperation (APEC) and the Indonesia "Summit" in 1994, Dick K. Nanto 94-242 E

* Australia, New Zealand, and the Pacific Islands: Issues for the Policy in the 1990s, Robert G. Sutter 94-930 S

* Australia, New Zealand, and the Pacific Islands: Issues for U.S. Policy in the 1990s, Robert G. Sutter 95-794 S

* Palau: Briefing Paper, Robert G. Sutter 95-40 S

* Papua New Guinea: Briefing Paper, Rinn Sup Shinn 95-702 F

* U.S. Economic, Trade, and Financial Relations With Asia: A Statistical Overview, James K. Jackson and Wayne M. Morrison 94-590 E

Oil

* see Energy -- Petroleum

Oil Import Tax

* see Taxation -- Consumption

Oklahoma City Bombing

* see Criminal Justice

Old Age

* see Aged

Older Americans Act

* see also Aged

* Older Americans Act Amendments of 1992, Carol O'Shaughnessy 93-329 EPW

* Older Americans Act: Brief History of Legislation and Funding, Carol O'Shaughnessy, etc. 93-400 EPW

* Older Americans Act FY 1995 Budget: Fact Sheet, Carol O'Shaughnessy and Molly Forman 94-607 EPW

Be patient. If any phone number is incorrect, call (area code) 555-1212 and request the new listing.

1337

* Older Americans Act Nutrition Program, Carol O'Shaughnessy, 95-379 EPW
* Older Americans Act: 104th Congress Issues, Carol O'Shaughnessy 95-32 EPW
* Senior Community Service Employment Program: Background, FY 1996 Budget Request and 104th Congress legislation, Carol O'Shaughnessy 95-244 EPW

Omnibus Budget Reconciliation Act
* Budget Process Changes in the House-Passed Reconciliation Act of 1993, Robert Keith and Edward Davis 93-583 GOV
* Capital Gains Revisions, Arnold Solomon 94-357 C
* Child Immunization Provisions in the Omnibus Budget Reconciliation Act of 1993, P.L. 103-66, Melvina Ford 93-781 EPW
* Housing and Real Estate Tax Provisions in the Omnibus Budget Reconciliation Act of 1993, Richard Bourdon 93-887 E
* Impact of Omnibus Budget Reconciliation Act of 1993 on Small Businesses, Gerald Mayer 94-44 E
* Marriage Tax Penalties After the Omnibus Budget Reconciliation Act of 1993, Gregg A. Esenwein 93-1000 E
* Transportation Fuel Taxes After the 1993 Budget Act: How Much? For What? And for How Long?, Bernard A. Gelb 93-888 E

Omnibus Counterterrorism Act
* President Clinton's Terrorism Proposal Omnibus Counterterrorism Act of 1995, H.R. 896/S. 390 as Introduced: A Summary, Charles Doyle 95-558 S

Opec Countries
* see Middle East and North Africa

Orphanages
* see Children

OSHA
* see Labor -- Policies and Legislation

Oversight
* see Congress -- Oversight

Ozone
* see Air Pollution -- Ozone

Pacific Area
* see Oceania

PACs
* see Elections -- Finance

Pakistan
* see also South Asia
* The Kashmir Dispute: Historical Background to the Current Struggle, Richard P. Cronin, etc., 91-563 F
* Pakistan Aid Cutoff: U.S. Nonproliferation and Foreign Policy Consideration; Issue Brief, Richard P. Cronin, IB90149
* Pakistan-U.S. Relations: Issue Brief, Barbara LePoer IB94041
* Pakistan's Nuclear Activities: Legislation Related to the Cutoff of U.S. Aid, Richard P. Cronin and Barbara Leitch LePoer 93-1036 F

Palau
* Palau: Briefing Paper, Robert G. Sutter 95-40 S

Palestine
* Middle East Peace Prospects: Info Pack IP397M

Palestinian Conflict
* see Middle East and North Africa

Panama
* see also Latin America
* Panama-U.S. Relations: Continuing Policy Concerns; Issue Brief, Mark P. Sullivan IB92088

Paperwork Reduction Act
* Paperwork Reduction and Information Resources Management Stephanie Smith 95-453 GOV

Papua New Guinea
* see also Oceania
* Papua New Guinea: Briefing Paper, Rinn Sup Shinn 95-702 F

Patent and Trademarks Act
* The Bayh-Dole Act: Patent Policy and the Commercialization of Technology, Wendy H. Schacht 94-501 SPR

PDD-25
* see Foreign Policy

Peacekeeping
* see International Affairs -- Peacekeeping

Pension Benefit Guarantee Corporation
* see also Pensions
* Pension Benefit Guaranty Corporation: A Fact Sheet, Ray Schmitt 95-118 EPW
* Pension Benefit Guaranty Corporation: Proposals to Shore Up the Single-Employer Program; Issue Brief, Ray Schmitt IB92106
* Pension Issues: Challenges to Retirement Income Security, Ray Schmitt 93-613 EPW
* Pension Provisions Enacted With the General Agreement on Tariffs and Trade, Ray Schmitt 95-212 EPW

Pensions
* see also Social Security
* Effect on Pension Integration on Retirement Benefits, Ray Schmitt, etc. 94-974 EPW
* Health Benefit Plans: ERISA and the States, Joan Sokolovsky 93-747 EPW
* Individual Retirement Account Issues and Savings Accounts Proposals: Issue Brief, James R. Storey IB89085
* Individual Retirement Accounts: Fact Sheet, James R. Storey 94-83 EPW
* Individual Retirement Accounts (IRAs) and Related Proposals, Jane G. Gravelle 95-420 S
* The National Employee Savings Trust (NEST) Proposal, Ray Schmitt 95-803 EPW
* Pension Benefit Guarantee Corporation: A Fact Sheet, Ray Schmitt, 95-212 EPW
* Pension Issues: Challenges to Retirement Income Security, Ray Schmitt 93-613 EPW
* Pension Issues: Info Pack IP428P
* Pension Portability Clearinghouse, Ray Schmitt 95-445 EPW
* Pension Provisions Enacted With the General Agreement on Tariffs and Trade, Ray Schmitt 95-212 EPW
* Private Pension Facts and Issues, Ray Schmitt 94-555 EPW
* Private Pension Plan Standards: A Summary of ERISA, Ray Schmitt 94-506 A
* Proposal to Tax Pension Plans, Ray Schmitt 95-400 EPW
* Railroad Retirement and Unemployment Benefits: A Summary of Benefits, Financing, and History, Dennis W. Snook 95-47 EPW
* Railroad Retirement and Unemployment Benefits: History, Provisions, and Financing, Dennis W. Snook 92-765 EPW
* Railroad Retirement Board: Background and Analysis of Issues Raised by Proposals to End Federal Administration, Dennis W. Snook 93-949 EPW
* Railroad Retirement Board: Summary of Issues Posed by the National Performance Review's Proposal to End the Board's Function, Dennis W. Snook 93-928 EPW
* Rules Governing Salary Reduction Retirement Plans, James R. Storey, 94-65 EPW
* Section 401 (K) Retirement Plans: A Fact Sheet, James R. Storey 95-180 EPW
* Trends in Private Pension Plans: Is There Cause for Concern?, Ray Schmitt and Gene Falk 94-373 EPW

Pension -- Government
* Age at Retirement for Federal Employees: A Fact Sheet, Carolyn L. Merck 94-826 EPW
* Benefits and Pay Increases in Selected Federal Programs, 1969-1995, Carolyn L. Merck 94-971 EPW
* Brief Comparison of Retirement Eligibility and Benefits for Members of Congress and Executive Branch Personnel, Carolyn L. Merck 93-721 EPW
* Brief Facts About Congressional Pensions, Carolyn L. Merck 94-740 EPW
* COLAs for Military Retirees: Summary of Congressional and Executive Branch Action Since 1982, Robert L. Goldich 94-7 F
* Cost-of-Living Adjustments for Federal Civil Service Annuities, Carolyn L. Merck 94-834 EPW
* Early Retirement, Buy-Outs, and Separation Benefits for Federal Employees, Carolyn L. Merck 94-295 EPW
* Federal Civil Service Early Retirement and Separation Benefits: A Fact Sheet, Carolyn L. Merck 93-326 EPW
* Federal Civil Service Retirement: Comparing the Generosity of Federal and

Private-Sector Retirement Systems, by Education and Public Welfare Division, Income Maintenance Section 95-687 EPW
* Federal Civil Service Retirement Systems in FY 1994: Participation, Benefits and Costs, Carolyn L. Merck 94-289 EPW
* Federal Retirement: Proposals for Change, Carolyn L. Merck 95-449 EPW
* Federal Retirement Systems: Background and Design Concepts Carolyn Merck 95-383 EPW
* Financing the Federal Civil Service Retirement Programs, Carolyn L. Merck 94-973 EPW
* Military Benefits for Former Spouses: Legislation and Policy Issues, David Burrelli 94-778 F
* Military Retirement: Major Legislative Issues; Issue Brief, Robert Goldich IB85159
* The Military Survivor Benefit Plan: A Description of the Provisions, David F. Burrelli 94-779 F
* Payment Schedule for Military and Civil Service Retiree Cost-of-Living Adjustments, FY 1994-19999: A Fact Sheet, Carolyn L. Merck 94-462 EPW
* Retirement for Federal Employees: A Fact Sheet, Carolyn L. Merck 93-97 EPW
* Retirement for Members of Congress, Carolyn L. Merck 94-969 EPW
* Survivor Benefits for Families of Federal Civil Service Workers Retirees, Carolyn L. Merck 95-18 EPW
* Veterans' Pensions: Fact Sheet, Dennis W. Snook 95-269 EPW

People's Republic of China
* see China

Persian Gulf
* see Middle East and North Africa

Personal Responsibility Act
* Child Nutrition Programs: Facts and Issues, Jean Javis Joans and Joe Richardson 95-230 ENR
* Child Support Enforcement: Welfare Reform in the 104th Congress, Carmen D. Solomon 95-401 EPW
* Family Cash Welfare: Comparison of House-Passed and Senate Finance Committee Versions of H. R. 4, Vee Burke 95-691 EPW
* Food Assistance Block Grants in the Personal Responsibility Act, Joe Richardson 95-196 EPW
* Older Americans Act: 104th Congress issues, Carol O'Shaughnessy 95-32 EPW
* Supplemental Security Income (SSI) Children: Welfare Reform in the 104th Congress, Carmen D. Solomon 95-402 EPW
* Supplemental Security Income (SSI): Comparison of House Passed and Senate Finance Versions of H.R. $, Carmen D. Solomon 95-704 EPW
* Supplemental Security Income (SSI) Drug Addicts and Alcoholics: Welfare Reform in the 104th Congress, Carmen D. Solomon 95-433 EPW
* Welfare Proposal in the Contract With America, Vee Burke 94-989 EPW
* Welfare Reform: How the House-Passed Bill Would Change Family Cash Welfare, Vee Burke 95-495 EPW
* Welfare Reform: Implications of H.R. 4 for Child Welfare Services, Karen Spar 95-566 EPW
* Welfare Reform: The Family Cap, Carmen D. Solomon 95-503 EPW
* Welfare Reform: The House-Passed Bill (H.R. $), Vee Burke, etc. 95-375 EPW

Peru
* see also Latin America
* Peru: Briefing Paper, Nina Serafino 94-797 F

Peso Crisis
* see Mexico

Pesticides
* see Hazardous Substances

Petroleum
* see Energy -- Petroleum

Pharmaceutical Industry
* see Medicine -- Drugs

Philippines
* see also East Asia
* Philippines: Briefing Paper, Larry Niksch 95-565 F

Poland
* see also Europe
* Poland, Czech Republic, Slovakia, and Hungary: Recent Developments; Issue Brief, Julie Kim and Francis Miko IB92051

Police
* see Criminal Justice

Political Action Committees
* see Elections -- Finance

Political Ethics
* see Congress -- Members, Politics and Government

Politics
* see Politics and Government

Politics and Government
* American National Government: An Overview, Frederick M. Kaiser 94-600 GOV
* Interest Groups and Lobbying: Selected References, 1991-1994, Jean M. Bowers 94-527 L
* Legal and Congressional Ethics Standards of Relevance to Those Who Lobby Congress, Jack Maskell 91-163 A
* Legislative Ethics in Democratic Countries: Comparative Analysis of Financial Standards, Stephen F. Clarke 94-325 A
* The Lobbying Disclosure Act of 1993, S. 349, as Amended and Passed by the Senate: An Overview, Richard C. Sachs 93-493 GOV
* Lobbying Disclosure Bills in the 103rd Congress: S. 349 and H.R. 823 Compared, Richard C. Sachs 94-119 GOV
* Lobbying: Info Pack IP066L
* Lobbyists and Interest Groups: A List Information Sources, Barbara Hillson 94-669 C
* Overview of the Independent Counsel Provisions of the Ethics in Government Act, Jack Maskell 94-732 A
* Political Action Committees: Selected References, Jean M. bowers 95-482 L
* Post Employment, "Revolving Door," Restrictions for Legislative Branch Members and Employees, Jack Maskell 95-52 A
* Regulating Interest Groups and Lobbyists: Issues in the 104th Congress; Issue Brief Richard C. Sachs IB95014
* Restrictions on Lobbying Congress With Federal Funds, Jack Maskell 95-382 A

Poor
* see Welfare

Population
* see Government Information

Poverty
* see Welfare

Power Resources
* see Energy

POWs
* see Defense Policy

Prayer in the Public Schools
* see Elementary and Secondary Education

Prescription Drugs
* see Medicine -- Drugs

Presidential Appointments
* see Executive Departments

Presidential-Congressional Relations
* see Congress--Executive Relations, Congress--Foreign Relations, Presidents, War Powers Resolution

Presidents (U.S.)
* Addresses for Presidential Libraries and Selected Historic Sites, Vanessa Cieslak 95-25 C
* Executive Office of the President Funding Levels Requested and Enacted Fiscal 1979-Fiscal 1996, Sharon Gressle 95-880 GOV
* Federal Presidential Libraries, Harold C. Relyea 95-389 GOV
* Former Presidents: Federal Pension and Retirement Benefits Summary of Provisions, Stephanie Smith 95-723 GOV
* Former Presidents: Federal Pension and Retirement Benefits: Summary of Provisions, Stephanie Smith 95-723 GOV

Be patient. If any phone number is incorrect, call (area code) 555-1212 and request the new listing.

1339

Current Events and Homework

* Pardoning Power of the President, P.L. Morgan 95-1049 A
* Presidential and Vice Presidential Succession, Thomas H. Neale 95-561 GOV
* Presidential Primaries and Caucuses in 1996: A Preliminary Calendar, Kevin Coleman 95-701 GOV
* Presidents of the United States: An Introductory Bibliography to Their Writings, James Sayler 93-1043 GOV
* Salary of the President of the United States Compared With That of Other High-Level Government Officials, Sharon Gressle 95-203 GOV
* Whitewater/Madison Guaranty S&L Affairs: Info Pack IP487W

Presidents -- Duties/Powers

* Current National Emergency Issues: A Brief Overview, Harold C. Relyea 94-596 GOV
* Executive Orders and Proclamations, John Contrubis 95-772 A
* Foreign Policy Roles of the President and Congress, Ellen C. Collier 93-20 F
* Item Veto and Expanded Impoundment Proposals; Issue Brief, Virginia A. McMurtry IB89148
* Item Veto: Bibliography-in-Brief, Tangela G. Roe 95-393 L
* Legislative Line Item Veto Bills: Comparing S. 4 and S. 14 (as Reported), Louis Fisher and Virginia A. McMurtry 95-273 S
* Line Item Veto: Info Pack IP287L
* National Emergency Powers, Harold C. Relyea 93-985 GOV
* Presidential Directives, Harold C. Relyea 95-139 GOV
* Presidential Emergency Powers: The War Powers Act of 1933, David M. Ackerman 95-753 A
* War Powers and U.N. Military Actions: A Brief Background of the Legislative Framework, Ellen C. Collier 93-1058 F
* War Powers Resolution: Info Pack IP131W
* War Powers Resolution: Presidential Compliance; Issue Brief, Richard F. Grimmett IB81050

President's Private Sector Survey on Cost Control (U.S.)

* The Grace Commission, Gary l. Galemore 93-741 GOV
* Reforming Government: The Grace Commission and the National Performance Review, Harold C. Relyea and Gary L. Galemore 93-933 GOV

Press
* see Communications

Price Discrimination
* see Business

Prisons
* see Criminal Justice

Procurement
* see Defense Economics -- Budgets, Public Contracts

Products Liability
* see Consumers

Proliferation
* see Defense Policy -- Nonproliferation

Property Insurance
* see Finance

Property Rights
* see Law

Public Broadcasting
* see Telecommunication

Public Contracts
* see also Defense Economics
* Business: Doing Business With the Federal Government: Info Pack IP305B
* The Buy American Act, John R. Luckey 94-554A
* Civilian Procurement Reform Efforts, Stephanie Smith 94-225 GOV
* Competition in Federal Public Contracting, Michael V. Seitzinger 93-334 A
* The Davis-Bacon Act: Action During the 104th Congress; Issue Brief, William G. Whittaker IB94058
* The Davis-Bacon Act: Institutional Evolution and Public Policy, William G. Whittaker 94-408 E
* The Davis-Bacon Act: Institutional Evolution and Public Policy; an Issue

Overview, William G. Whittaker 94-460 E
* Davis-Bacon Coverage: Facilities Built for Lease to the Federal Government, William G. Whittaker 94-431 E
* Davis-Bacon: The Act and the Literature, William G. Whittaker 94-908 E
Federal Procurement: A Brief Overview, Stephanie Smith 95-208 GOV
* Government Procurement and U.S. Trade Policy, William H. Cooper 95-369 E
* The Supreme Court Decision in Adarand Constructors Inc. v. Pena: Federal Contracting and Disadvantaged Business Enterprises, Charles V. Dale 95-137 A

Public Debt Reduction Fund
* Public Debt Reduction Fund, Louis Alan Talley 94-482 E

Public Finance
* see Budgets

Public Health
* Health Policy, Medicine

Public Lands
* see also Natural Resources
* Bureau of Land Management Authorization, Betsy A. Cody and Pamela Baldwin 95-429 ENR
* Changes in Federal Rangeland Management: Current Proposals, Betsy A. Cody 95-816 ENR
* Court Rulings During 1993 on Constitutional Taking Claims Against the United States, Robert Meltz 94-728 A
* Court Rulings During 1994 on Constitutional Taking Claims Against the United States, Robert Meltz 95-790 A
* Ecosystems, Biomes, and Watersheds: Definition and Use, M. Lynne Corn 93-655 ENR
* Federal Land and Resource Management: A Primer, Ross W. Gorte, etc. 93-787 ENR
* Federal Land Sales: Possible Land Revenues, Ross Gorte 95-345 ENR
* Federal Sales of Natural Resources: Allocation and Pricing Systems, Ross W. Gorte 93-1035 ENR
* Grazing Fees: A Primer, Betsy A. Cody 95-1 ENR
* The Major Federal Land Management Agencies: Management of Our Nation's Lands and Resources, Betsy A. Cody, etc. 95-599 ENR
* Management Planning for Forest Service and Bureau of Land Management Lands: A Report of a CRS Workshop, Pamela Baldwin 95-1070 A
* PILT (Payments in Lieu of Taxes): Somewhat Simplified, M. Lynne Corn 95-259 ENR
* Property Rights: Info Pack IP504P
* The Property Rights Issue; Videoprogram, Robert Meltz and Jeffrey A. Zinn VT95-1323
* When the United States Takes Property: Legal Principles, Robert Meltz 91-339 A
* Wilderness Overview and Statistics, Ross W. Gorte, 94-976 ENR

Public Speaking
* see General Interest -- Speechwriting

Public Utility Holding Company Act
* The Public Utility Holding Company Act of 1935: Legislative History, Background and Recent Amendments, Ellen Lazarus 93-266 A

Public Welfare
* see Welfare

Public Works
* see Infrastructure, Public Contracts, Transportation

Puerto Rico
* Puerto Rico: Political Status Options: Issue Brief, Garrine P. Laney IB89065
* Statehood for Puerto Rico: The Effect on Social Welfare Programs, Carolyn L. Merck, 91-47 EPW

Qatar
* see Middle East and North Africa

Racketeer Influenced and Corrupt Organizations Act
* see Criminal Justice

Radioactive Wastes
* see Solid Wastes

Be patient. If any phone number is incorrect, call (area code) 555-1212 and request the new listing.

Ranch Apocalypse (Waco, Texas)
* Branch Davidian Siege at Ranch Apocalypse Near Waco, Texas: A Chronology, Suzanne Cavanagh and David Teasley 95-582 GOV

RCRA
* see Resource Conservation and Recovery Act

Real Estate Settlement Procedures Act
* The Real Estate Settlement Procedures Act: Is It Working?, Richard Bourdon 94-841 E

Recreation
* Natural Resources

Recycling
* see Solid Wastes

Reemployment Act
* Trade Adjustment Assistance: A Fact Sheet, James R. Storey 94-478 EPW

Refugees
* see Immigration

Regional Development
* see Infrastructure, Rural Affairs, Urban Affairs

Regulatory Reform
* see Business, Executive Departments, Finance

Rehabilitation Act
* see also Disabled
* Rehabilitation Act of 1973: Brief Background and Funding History, Carol O'Shaughnessy and Mary F. Smith 94-509 EPW
* Supreme Court Decisions Interpreting Section 504 of the Rehabilitation Act of 1973, Nancy Jones 95-70 A

Reinventing Government
* see Executive Departments -- Reorganization, National Performance Review (U.S.)

Religion
* Branch Davidian Siege at Ranch Apocalypse Near Waco, Texas: A Chronology, Suzanne Cavanagh and David Teasley 95-582 GOV
* Developments in the Law of Church and State Since 1980, David Ackerman 95-866 A
* Hamas: The Organization, Goals, and Tactics of a Militant Palestinian Organization, James P. Wootten 93-511 F
* Legislative Prayer and School Prayer: The Constitutional Difference, David M. Ackerman 94-821 A
* Prayer and Religion in the Public Schools: What Is, and Is Not, Permitted, David M. Ackerman 93-680 A
* Prayer in the Public Schools: Legislation Status and Background; Issue Brief, David M. Ackerman and James Sayler IB95080
* The Religious Freedom Restoration Act, David M. Ackerman 94-15 A
* School Prayer: The Congressional Response, 1962-1994, David M. Ackerman 94-829 A
* Supreme Court: Church and State Cases, 1994-95 Term; Issue Brief, David M. Ackerman IB95015

Religious Freedom Restoration Act
* The Religious Freedom Restoration Act, David M. Ackerman 94-15 A

Renewable Energy
* see Energy -- Alternative Sources

Rescissions
* see Budgets

Research and Development
* see Science Policy -- Research

Resolution Trust Corporation
* FDIC and RTC: Recent Obstacles in Savings and Loan Litigation, L. Marlon Fields, and M. Maureen Murphy 94-670 A

* Resolution Trust Corporation Completion Act, M. Maureen Murphy 94-74 A
* Savings and Loan Cleanup Cost: Fact Sheet, Barbara Miles 95-133 E

Resource Conservation and Recovery Act
* see also Solid Wastes
* Environmental Protection Legislation in the 103rd Congress; Issue Brief, Environmental and Natural Resources Policy Div. IB93007
* Recycled Content Legislation: Audio Brief, James McCarthy AB50241
* Solid Waste Issues: Issue Brief, James E. McCarthy IB95023

Retirement
* see Defense Policy -- Personnel, Government Employees -- Pay and Benefits, Pensions, Social Security

Retirement Equity Act
* Women's Pension Equity: A Summary of the Retirement Equity Act of 1984, Ray Schmitt 84-217 EPW

RICO
* see Criminal Justice

Riegle Community Development and Regulatory Improvement Act
* The Riegle Community Development and Regulatory Improvement Act of 1994, Titles I and II: Community Development Consumer Protection, Small Capital Formation, M. Maureen Murphy 94-700 A
* The Riegle Community Development and Regulatory Improvement Act of 1994, Titles III and IV: Paperwork Reduction, Regulatory Improvement, Money Laundering, M. Maureen Murphy 94-696 A

Riegle-Neal Interstate Banking and Branching Efficiency Act
* The Riegle-Neal Interstate Banking and Branching Efficiency Act of 1994, M. Maureen Murphy 94-744 A

Right of Asylum
* see Immigration

Robinson-Patman Act
* Discriminatory Pricing and the Robinson-Patman Act: An Overview: Some Exceptions, Janice E. Rubin 94-726 A

Rock Music Lyrics
* see Arts and Humanities

Roe v. Wade
* see Abortion

Romania
* see also Europe
* Romania, Bulgaria, Albania: Recent Developments; Issue Brief, Sergiu Verona IB92064

Rural Abandoned Mine Program
* The Rural Abandoned Mine Program--A Fact Sheet, Duane M. Thompson 95-706 ENR

Rural Affairs
* Economic Development Administration: A Fact Sheet, Bruce K. Mulock 95-617 E
* Health Care Fact Sheet: Access to Health Care in Rural Areas, Celinda M. Franco and Karen M. Judge 93-673 EPW
* Rural Development: An Overview, Sandra Osbourn 95-956 GOV
* Rural Electric and Telephone Programs: Background and Issues, Carl Ek and Amy Abel 95-266 F
* The Rural Electrification Administration: Background and Current Issues, Carl Ek and Amy Abel 91-614 ENR
* Rural Health Care Initiatives in Current Law, Celinda Franco 95-329 EPW
* Rural Water Supply and Sewer Systems: Background Information, Claudia Copeland 94-838 ENR

Rural Areas and Policy
* see Rural Affairs

Be patient. If any phone number is incorrect, call (area code) 555-1212 and request the new listing.

1341

Current Events and Homework

Rural Electrification
* see Energy

Russia
* see also Central Asia, Europe
* Crime in Russia: Situation Update, Jim Nichol 95-486 F
* Economic Issues for Summits in Moscow and Kiev, John P. Hardt and Phillip Kaiser 95-516 S
* Moscow Summit, May 10, 1995: Outcome & Implications, Jim Nichol 95-676 F
* NASA's Space Station Program: A New Focus--Foreign Policy, Marcia S. Smith 94-70 SPR
* NATO Enlargement and Russia: From Cold War to Cold Peace, Stanley R. Sloan and Steve Woehrel 95-594 S
* Nonproliferation Export Controls in Eastern Europe and the Former Soviet Union, Theodor Galdi 94-850 F
* Nuclear Weapons in the Former Soviet Union: Location, Command and Control; Issue Brief, Amy F. Woolf and Theodor W. Galdi IB91144
* Oil and Natural Gas in the Russian Federation, Joseph P. Riva, Jr. 93-732 SPR
* Russia and U.S. Foreign Policy: Parameters of the Current Debate, Mark M. Lowenthal 94-491 S
* Russian and Other Former Soviet Union Armed Forces: Issue Brief, Edward F. Bruner IB92014
* Russian Economic Reform and the IMF: Mission Impossible? issue Brief, Patricia A. Wertman IB95055
* Russian Foreign Trade: Prospects and Implications for the United States, William H. Cooper 94-988 E
* Russian Nuclear Reactor and Conventional Arms Transfers to Iran, Stuart D. Goldman, etc. 95-641 F
* Russian Officer Resettlement Program, Steven J. Woehrel 95-287 F
* The Space Station Program: Progress and Challenges, Marcia S. Smith 95-674 SPR
* Steel Imports From Russia and Their Implications for Steel Markets, David J. Cantor 95-554 E
* United States-Russian Economic Partnership: Benefits and Risks, John P. Hardt 94-892 S
* U.S. Policy Toward Russia and NATO, Stanley R. Sloan 94-871 S

Russia -- Foreign Aid
* Conditions on U.S. Foreign Assistance to Russia, Curt Tarnoff 95-769 F
* The Former Soviet Union and U.S. Foreign Aid:Implementing the Assistance Program, Curt Tarnoff 95-170 F
* The Former Soviet Union and U.S. Foreign Assistance: Issue Brief, Curt Tarnoff IB95077
* The Former Soviet Union: Assistance From the International Financial Institutions, Jonathan E. Sanford 95-218 F

Russia -- Politics and Government
* Beyond Chechnya: Some Options for Russia and the West, John P. Hardt 95-338 S
* Chechnya Confrontation, Jim Nichol 95-79 F
* Crime in Russia: Context and Implications for U.S. Interests, Jim Nichol 94-718 F
* Russia and the Commonwealth of Independent States: Info Pack IP233R
* Russia and the NIS; Videoprogram, Stuart Goldman VT94-1308
* Russia: Economic Conditions and Prospects for Reform, William H. Cooper 94-406 E
* Russia: Issue Brief, Stuart D. Goldman and Steven J. Woehrel IB92089
* Russian Conflict in Chechnya and Implications for the United States, Stuart D. Goldman and Jim Nichol 95-207 F
* Russia's Emerging Foreign and Defense Policy, Stuart D. Goldman 94-493 F
* Russia's New Parliament, Stuart D. Goldman 94-844 F
* Russia's Political Shutdown: A CRS Panel Discussion; Videoprogram, Congressional Research Service VT93-1361
* U.S.-Russian Washington Summit September 27-28, 1994: Outcome and Implications for U.S. Interests, Jim Nichol 94-787 F

Rwanda
* see also Africa (Sub-Saharan)
* Rwandan Crisis: A Chronology, August 1994-June 1995, Theodros Dagne 95-773 F
* Rwanda's Humanitarian Situation and the U.S. Response, Lois McHugh 94-617 F

Ryan White Comprehensive AIDS Resources Emergency (CARE) Act
* Ryan White Comprehensive AIDS Resources Emergency (CARE) Act of 1990, Bud Graves 94-252 EPW

Safe Drinking Water Act
* Rural Water Supply and Sewer Systems: Background Information, Claudia Copeland 94-838 ENR
* Safe Drinking Water Act Amendments of 1994: Summary of S. 2019, as Passed, Mary Tiemann 94-606 ENR
* Safe Drinking Water Act Reauthorization Issues, Mary Tiemann 95-780 ENR

Safe Schools
* see Elementary and Secondary Education

Sanctions
* see Trade -- Policy

Satellites
* see Space Activities

Saudi Arabia
* see also Middle East and North Africa
* Saudi Arabia: Commercial Disputes With U.S. Firms, Alfred B. Prados 95-666 F
* Saudi Arabia: Post-War Issues and U.S. Relations; Issue Brief, Alfred B. Prados IB93113

Savings
* see Economic Policy

Savings and Loan Institutions
* see Finance -- Banks

Savings Association Insurance Fund
* The Savings Association Insurance Fund: Undercapitalization and Legislative Options, Barbara L. Miles 94-896 E

School Choice
* see Elementary and Secondary Education

School Desegregation
* see Elementary and Secondary Education

School Dropouts
* see Elementary and Secondary Education

School Lunch Program
* see Food

School Prayer
* see Elementary and Secondary Education

Schools
* see Education Policy, Elementary and Secondary Education, Higher Education, Job Training

Science and Technology
* see Intellectual Property, Medicine, Science Policy, Space Activities, Technology, Telecommunication

Science Policy
* Daylight Saving Time, Heidi G. Yacker 91-386 C
* A Department of Science and Technology: A Recurring Theme, William C. Boesman 95-235 SPR
* The Difference Between DOD Programs That Develop Dual-Use Technologies and DOD's Dual-Use Technology Development Programs--A Fact Sheet, John D. Moteff 95-738 SPR
* International Science and Technology: Issues for U.S. Policy Makers, Glenn J. McLoughlin 94-733 SPR
* Major Science and Technology Programs: Megaprojects and Presidential Initiatives, Trends Through FY 1995, Genevieve J. Knezo 95-31 SPR
* Risk Assessment: Info Pack IP503R
* Science and Technology Issues 104th Congress, First Session, Science Policy Research Division 95-84 SPR
* Science, Engineering, and Mathematics Education: Issue Brief, Christine M. Matthews IB92026

Science Policy -- Research
* Appropriations Directed by Congress to Specific Colleges and Universities, for

Research and Development and Research-Related Facilities, FY 1992, Genevieve J. Knezo and Richard E. Rowberg 93-684 SPR

* Big Science and Technology Projects: Analysis of 30 Selected U.S. Government Projects, William C. Boesman 94-687 SPR

* Child Day Care Centers: A List of Resources for Starting and Operating a Child Day Care Center,Marjorie Washington 94-432 C

* Cooperative R&D: Federal Efforts to Promote Industrial Competitiveness: Issue Brief, Wendy H. Schacht IB89056

* Cooperative Research and Development Agreements, Wendy H. Schacht 95-150 SPR

* Defense R&D Primer, Richard M. Nunno 95-173 SPR

* The Defense Science and Technology Strategy, Kurt F. McPherson and Richard M. Nunno 95-185 SPR

* Department of Energy Laboratories: A New Partnership With Industry?, Wendy H. Schacht 93-844 SPR

* DOD Support for University Based Research, Michael E. Davey 94-1001 SPR

* DOD's Federally Funded Research and Development Centers, Michael E. Davey 95-489 SPR

* DOD's Independent Research and Development Program: Changes and Issues, Michael E. Davey and Dahlia Stein 93-1051 SPR

* The DOE Multiprogram Nuclear Weapons Laboratories, William C. Boesman 94-916 SPR

* Federal R&D Policies and Priorities: A Checklist of CRS Products, Bonnie F. Mangan 95-123 L

* The Future of the Nuclear Weapons Laboratories. Part II: Civilian Issues, Jonathan E. Medalia 93-901 F

* High-Energy Physics Research: Description and Issues, Richard Rowberg and Daniel Morgan 95-210 S

* Indirect Costs at Academic Institutions: Background and Controversy; Issue Brief, Genevieve J. Knezo IB91095

* Indirect Costs for R&D at Higher Education Institutions: Annotated Chronology of Major Federal Policies, Genevieve J. Knezo 94-646 SPR

* Is DOD the Place to Fund Dual-Use Technology?, John D. Moteff 93-496 SPR

* Major Science and Technology Programs: Megaprojects and Presidential Initiatives, Trends Through FY 1996, Requested, Genevieve J. Knezo 95-490 SPR

* R&D Partnerships: Government-Industry Collaboration, Wendy H. Schacht 95-499 SPR

* Research and Development Funding: Fiscal Year 1996; Issue Brief, Michael E. Davey IB95037

* Research and Development: Priority Setting and Consolidation in Science Budgeting; Issue Brief, Genevieve J. Knezo IB94009

* Research and Education Funding in the U.S. Department of Agriculture, Christine M. Matthews 95-525 SPR

* The Research and Experimentation Tax Credit: Issue Brief, Gary Guenther IB92039

* Science Megaprojects: A Status Report on Policy Options for Priority-Setting and International Cooperation, Genevieve J. Knezo 95-764 SPR

Securities Industry
* see Finance -- Securities

SEMATECH
* see also Technology
* SEMATECH: issues and Options; Issue Brief, Glenn J. McLoughlin IB93024

Senate
* see Congress

Senior Community Service Employment Program
* Senior Community Service Employment Program: Background, FY 1996 Budget Request and 104th Congress Legislation, Carol O'Shaughnessy 95-244 EPW

Sentencing
* see Criminal Justice -- Sentences

Sex Discrimination
* see Women

Sexual Harassment
* see Women

Singapore
* Singapore: Background and U.S. Policy Issues, Barbara LePoer 95-658 F

Slovakia
* see also Europe

* The Czech Republic and Slovakia: Implications of the Split, Frances T. Miko 93-66 F

* Poland, Czech Republic, Slovakia, and Hungary: Recent Developments; Issue Brief, Julie Kim and Francis Miko IB92051

Slovenia
* see also Europe
* Slovenia: Basic Facts, Julie Kim 95-786 F

Small Business
* see Business -- Small Business

Social Security
* Social Security: An Introduction; IP153S
* Social Security as an Independent Agency: A Fact Sheet, David Koitz 94-262 EPW
* Social Security: Brief Facts and Statistics, David Koitz 94-27 EPW
* Social Security Issues; Videoprogram, Geoffrey Kollman VT94-1319
* The Social Security Number: Chronology of Federal Developments Affecting Its Use, Kathleen S. Swendiman, 91-825 A
* Social Security: The Relationship of Taxes and Benefits for Past, Present, and Future Retirees, Geoffrey Kollman 95-149 EPW

Social Security -- Benefits
* Determination of Taxable Social Security Benefits Under New Law: A Fact Sheet, Geoffrey Kollmann 93-336 EPW
* Effects on Pension Integration on Retirement Benefits, Ray Schmitt, etc. 94-974 EPW
* Means Testing Social Security Benefits: An Issue Summary, Geoffrey Kollmann 94-791 EPW
* Social Security Benefits Are Not Paid for the Month of Death: A Fact Sheet, David Koitz 94-402 EPW
* Social Security: Coverage of Household Workers; A Fact Sheet, Geoffrey Kollmann 94-114 EPW
* Social Security Disability Issues: Fact Sheet, Geoffrey Kollmann 94-402 EPW
* The Social Security Earnings Test: A Fact Sheet, Geoffrey Kollmann 94-20 EPW
* The Social Security " Notch": Info Pack IP266S
* Social Security Notch Issue: A Summary, David Koitz 95-188 EPW
* Social Security: Proposed Modifications to the Earnings Test; Issue Brief, Geoffrey Kollmann IB89114
* Social Security: Repeal of 1993 Provision That Increased Taxation of Benefits; Issue Brief, Geoffrey Kollmann IB94056
* Social Security: The Cost-of-Living Adjustment in January 1995, David Koitz and Geoffrey Kollmann 94-803 EPW
* Social Security: The Purpose of the Government Pension Offset Provisions and Examples of How It Works, David Koitz 92-375 EPW
* Social Security: Withholding Benefits From Prisoners and Others Who Are Institutionalized for Criminal Acts, David Koitz 94-494 EPW
* Social Security's Government Pension Offset: A Fact Sheet, Carolyn Merck and Geoffrey Kollman 91-854 EPW
* Status of the Disability Programs of the Social Security Administration, 1994, David Koitz, etc. 94-477 EPW
* Substance Abusers: New Rules for Disability Benefits From Supplemental Security Income and Social Security Disability Insurance, Carmen D. Solomon 95-291 EPW
* Summary of Major Changes in the Social Security Cash Benefits Program: 1935-1994, Geoffrey Kollmann. 94-36 EPW
* Supplemental Security Income (SSI): Changes Made by the 104th Congress, Carmen D. Solomon, 95-433 EPW
* The Windfall Benefit Provision: A Fact Sheet, Geoffrey Kollmann 94-125 EPW

Social Security -- Finance
* Budget Enforcement Procedures: Application to Social Security Revenues and Spending, Edward Davis and Robert Keith 95-255 GOV
* The Financial Outlook for Social Security and Medicare, David Koitz, 95-543 EPW
* How Long Does It Take New Retirees to Recover the Value of Their Social Security Taxes? Geoffrey Kollmann, 94-5 EPW
* Investment of the Social Security Trust Funds: A Fact Sheet, Geoffrey Kollmann 93-886 EPW
* Social Security and Medicare Taxes and Premiums: A Fact Sheet, David Koitz 94-28 EPW
* Social Security Financing and Taxation: Recent Issues; Info Pack, IP435S
* Social Security: Its Removal From the Budget and New Procedures for Considering Changes to the Program, David Koitz, 93-23 EPW
* Social Security Taxes: Where Do Surplus Taxes Go and How Are They Used?, David Koitz 94-593 EPW
* Social Security's Treatment Under the Federal Budget: A Summary, David Koitz 95-206 EPW

Be patient. If any phone number is incorrect, call (area code) 555-1212 and request the new listing.

1343

Current Events and Homework

Social Services
* see Aged, Children, Disabled, Educational Policy, Families, Food, Health Policy, Housing, Job Training, Veterans, Welfare
* AmeriCorps National Service Programs: Info Pack IP475A
* Children's Social Service Issues in the 104th Congress, Dale Robinson 95-97 EPW
* Corporation for National and Community Service Programs: A Summary, Dale H. Robinson 95-278 EPW
* Domestic Volunteer Service Act Programs, Dale Robinson 94-25 EPW
* Linking Human Services: Waivers to Block Grants, Ruth Ellen Wasem 94-987 EPW
* The National and Community Service Trust Act of 1993: Description and Related Programs, 94-25 EPW
* Restructuring Human Services: From Waivers to Block Grants: A Checklist of CRS Products, Edith Sutterlin 95-201 L
* Social Services Block Grants: A Fact Sheet (Title XX of the Social Security Act), Karen Spar 94-953 EPW

Solid Wastes
* see also Superfund
* Brownfields Program: Cleaning Up Urban Industrial Sites, Mark Reisch 95-454 ENR
* Civilian Nuclear Waste Disposal: Issue Brief, Mark Holt IB92059
* Flow Control of Solid Wastes: Issues and Options, James E. McCarthy 94-265 ENR
* Hazardous Waste and the Superfund Program: Info Pack IP094H
* High-Level Nuclear Waste Disposal--A Fact Sheet, Mark Holt 93-958 ENR
* Interstate Shipment of Municipal Solid Waste, James E. McCarthy, etc., 93-743 ENR
* Interstate Shipment of Municipal Solid Waste: 1995 Update, James E. McCarthy 95-570 ENR
* Nuclear Weapons Production Complex: Environmental Compliance and Waste; Issue Brief, Mark Holt IB90074
* Recycled Content Legislation: Audio Brief, James McCarthy AB50241
* Recycling, Info Pack IP437R
* Solid Waste Issues: Issue Brief, James E. McCarthy, IB95023
* Solid Waste Legislation in the 104th Congress: A Comparison, James E. McCarthy 95-682 ENR
* Solid Waste Management: Info Pack IP396S
* Superfund Fact Book, Environmental and Natural Resources Policy Division 94-464 ENR
* Superfund Reauthorization Issues in the 104th Congress: Issue Brief, Mark Reisch IB95013
* Superfund Reform Act of 1994: A Summary of the Bill Reported to the House, Mark Reisch 94-720 ENR
* Taxes to Finance Superfund, Salvatore Lazzari 94-519 E
* Waste Isolation Pilot Plant--A Fact Sheet, Mark Holt 93-997 ENR

Somalia
* see also Africa (Sub-Saharan)
* Somalia: Current Developments, Drawdowns, and Implications, Alfred B. Prados 94-817 F
* Somalia: Update, Objectives and Options; Videoprogram, Raymond Copson VT93-1363

South Africa
* see also Africa (Sub-Saharan)
* South Africa Aid: U.S. Assistance Package for FY 1994-1996, Larry Nowels 94-851 F
* South Africa: Politics, Economic Development, U.S. Assistance, Brenda Branaman 95-414 F
* South Africa: The Current Situation, Info Pack IP340S
* South African Humanitarian Needs, Brenda M. Branaman 93-1005 F
* South African Transition: Scenario, Major Actors, Current Problems, Issues for U.S. Policy, Raymond W. Copson 93-947 F
* South Africa's Elections and Prospects for the Future; Videoprogram, Raymond Copson VT94-1329
* South Africa's Elections: Politics and Prospects for the Future: Audio Brief AB50298

South America
* see Latin America

South Asia
* see also Central Asia, East Asia
* Afghanistan: Current Issues and U.S. Policy Concerns, Kenneth Katzman 95-533 F

* Bangladesh: Background and U.S. Policy Interests, Barbara L. LePoer 94-684 F
* India-U.S. Relations: Issue Brief, Barbara LePoer IB93097
* The Kashmir Dispute: Historical Background to the Current Struggle, Richard P. Cronin and Barbara LePoer 91-563 F
* Nuclear Nonproliferation Strategies for South Asia, Zachary S. Davis 94-385 ENR
* Pakistan-U.S. Relations: Issue Brief, Barbara LePoer IB94041
* Pakistan's Nuclear Activities: Legislation Related to the Cutoff of U.S. Aid, Richard P. Cronin and Barbara LePoer 93-1036 F
* South Asia: Background and Recent Developments in U.S. Nuclear Nonproliferation Efforts, Barbara Leitch LePoer 95-215 F
* South Asia: U.S. Interests and Policy Issues, Richard P. Cronin and Barbara LePoer 93-243 F

South Korea
* see also North Korea
* Korea-U.S.-South Korean Issues in the 1990's; Issue Brief, Robert G. Sutter IB94038
* Korean Peninsula Tensions: North Korea and Nuclear Weapons; Info Pack IP484K
* South Korea Under Kim Young Sam: Trends, Nuclear and Other Issues, Rinn Sup Shinn and Robert G. Sutter 94-599 F
* South Korea: U.S. Defense Obligations, Larry Niksch 94-300 F
* South Korea's Economy and Trade, Dick K. Nanto 94-624 E

South Vietnam
* see Vietnam

Soviet Nuclear Capacity
* see Russia

Soviet Union (Former)
* see Central Asia, Europe, Russia

Space Activities
* GPS: Satellite Navigation and Positioning and the DOD's Navstar Global Positioning System, David A. Turner and Marcia S. Smith 94-171 SPR
* Military Space Program: Issues for the 104th Congress, Marcia S. Smith 95-95 SPR
* NASA's Space Station Program: A New Focus--Foreign Policy, Marcia S. Smith 94-70 SPR
* The National Aeronautics and Space Administration: An Overview With FY 1995 and FY 1996 Budget Summaries, David P. Radzanowski and Stephen J. Garber 95-336 SPE
* National Aeronautics and Space Administration's (NASA) Fiscal Year 1995 Budget Request, David P. Radzanowski 94-280 SPR
* An Overview of NASA, Stephen G. Garber and David P. Radzanowski 95-101 SPR
* Public and Commercial Land Remote Sensing from Space: Landsat &, Lewis and Clark, and Private Systems, David P. Radzanowski 95-346 SPR
* Reusable Launch Vehicle (RLV) Technology , David P. Radzanowski and Stephen J. Garber 95-311 SPR
* Space Activities of the United States, CIS, and Other Launching Countries/Organizations: 1957-1994, Marcia Smith 95-873 SPR
* Space Launch Vehicles: Government Requirements and Commercial Competition; Issue Brief, Marcia S. Smith and David P. Radzanowski IB93062
* The Space Station Program: Progress and Challenges, Marcia S. Smith 95-674 SPR
* Space Stations: Issue Brief, Marcia S. Smith IB93017
* U.S. Space Programs: Issue Brief, Marcia S. Smith IB93011

Space Policy
* see Space Activities

Space Station
* see Space Activities

Spanish Americans (U.S.)
* see Minorities

Speechwriting
* see General Interest --Speechwriting

Sports
* Baseball, Economics, and Public Policy: Issue Brief, William A. Cox and Dennis Zimmerman IB94052
* The Baseball Strike and Federal Policy: An Economic Analysis, William A. Cox and Dennis Zimmerman 95-152 E

Be patient. If any phone number is incorrect, call (area code) 555-1212 and request the new listing.

Spotted Owl
* see Animals

State and Local Government
* Air Quality: Impacts of Trip Reduction Programs on States and Affected Employers, Maura K. Flechtner 93-745 ENR
* Alternative Dispute Resolution: Selected References, Jean M. Bowers 95-660 L
* American Federalism, 1776 to 1995: Significant Events, Eugene Boyd 95-518 GOV
* Block Grants: An Overview, Eugene Boyd and Sandra Osbourn 95-264 GOV
* Citizen Initiative Proposals Appearing on State Ballots, 1976-1992, Lisa Oakley and Thomas P. Neale 95-288 GOV
* Community Development Block Grant Programs: Bibliography-in-Brief, Jean M. Bowers 95-562 L
Community Development Block Grants: An Overview, Eugene Boyd 95-440 GOV
* Community Development Programs; Videoprogram, Eugene Boyd and Morton Schussheim VT95-1328
* Community Services Block Grants and Related Programs, Karen Spar 92-779 EPW
* Congressional and State Reapportionment and Redistricting: A Legal Analysis, Thomas M. Durbin and L. Paige Whitaker 95-793 A
* Crime Control: Summary of Financial Assistance Available to State and Local Governments, Keith Bea 95-258 GOV
* D.C. Statehood: The Historical Context and Recent Congressional Actions, Garrine P. Laney 94-492 GOV
* Environmental Protection and the Unfunded Mandates Debate , Environment and Natural Resource Policy Division, Martin R. Lee 94-739 ENR
* Financial Control Boards Cities in Distress, Nonna A. Noto and Lillian Rymarowicz 95-328 E
* Flow Control of Solid Wastes: Issues and Options, James McCarthy 94-265 ENR
* Food Assistance Block Grants in the Personal Responsibility Act, Joe Richardson 95-196 EPW
* Investment Losses in Orange County, CA: Is There a Federal Policy Role?, Dennis Zimmerman and Mark Jickling 95-193 E
* Law Enforcement Assistance Block Grant Proposals, 104th Congress, Keith Bea 95-731 GOV
* Legislative Prayer and School Prayer: The Constitutional Difference, David M. Ackerman 94-821 A
* Linking Human Services: Waivers to Block Grants, Ruth Ellen Wasem 94-987 EPW
* Mandates and the Congress, Sandra Osbourn 95-62 GOV
* Mandates Relief for State and Local Government Bill of 1994: A Summary of Provisions, Sandra S. Osbourn 95-55 GOV
* Municipal Reorganization: Chapter 9 of the U.S. Bankruptcy Code, Robin Jewler 95-177 A
* PILT (Payments in Lieu of Taxes): Somewhat Simplified, M. Lynne Corn 95-259 ENR
* Small-Issue Industrial Development Bonds, Dennis Zimmerman 94-771 E
* Social Services Block Grants: A Fact Sheet (Title XX of the Social Security Act), Karen Spar 94-953 EPW
* The " Sovereignty" Proposal: An Appraisal, Gail E. Makinen and G. Thomas Woodward 94-789 E
* State Tax Structures: Tax Bases, Dennis Zimmerman 94-713 E
* Taxation of Mail Order Sales: A Fact Sheet, Arnold Solomon 95-655 C
* Term Limits for Federal and State Legislators, Sula P. Richardson 94-287 GOV
* Unfunded Mandate Reform Act: A Brief Summary, Sandra Osbourn 95-246 GOV
* Unfunded Mandates: Info Pack IP500U
* Washington D.C. and the U.S. Capitol Building: Info Pack IP132W
* Welfare Reform: Financing Welfare Through Block Grants, Gene Falk 95-685 EPW
* Welfare Reforms Proposed by State Commissions, Louisa J. Hierholzer and Carmen D. Solomon 93-969 EPW

State Taxation
* see State and Local Government

Steel Industry
* see Business

Strategic Arms Reduction Talks
* see Defense Policy -- Nonproliferation

Strategic Arms Reduction Treaty
* see also Defense Policy -- Nonproliferation
* The START and START II Arms Control Treaties: Background and Issues, Amy F. Woolf 93-617 F
* START II: Central limits and Force Structure Implications, Amy Woolf 93-35 F
* Strategic Arms Reduction Treaty (START I and II): Verification and Compliance Issues; Issue Brief, Amy F. Woolf IB91139

Stratospheric Ozone Layer
* see Air Pollution -- Ozone

Student Aid
* see Higher Education -- Student Aid

Student Loans
* see Higher Education -- Student Aid

Superfund
* see also Solid Wastes
* Brownfields Program: Cleaning Up Urban Industrial Sites, Mark Reisch 95-454 ENR
* Environmental Protection Agency: FY 1996 Budget; Issue Brief, Martin R. Lee IB95048
* Environmental Protection Legislation in the 103rd Congress; Issue Brief, Environmental and Natural Resources Policy Division. Environmental Protection Section IB93007
* Hazardous Waste Management and the Superfund Program: Info Pack, IP094H
* Indoor Air Pollution: Issue Brief, Mira Courpas, Christopher H. Dodge and Fred J. Sissine. IB88092
* Summaries of Environmental Laws Administered by the Environmental Protection Agency, Martin R. Lee 95-59 ENR
* Superfund Fact Book, Environment and Natural Resources Policy Division, Mark Reisch 94-464 ENR
* Superfund Reauthorization Issues in the 104th Congress: Issue Brief, Mark Reisch IB95013
* Superfund Reform Act of 1994: A Summary of the Bill Reported to the House, Mark Reisch 94-720 ENR
* Taxes to Financial Superfund, Salvatore Lazzari 94-519 E

Supplemental Security Income Program
* see Welfare

Support of Dependents
* see Children

Supreme Court
* see Law

Sweden
* see also Europe
* Expenditure Tax Proposals in Other Countries; Sweden, Harry G. Gourevitch 95-550 S

Syria
* see also Middle East and North Africa
* Syrian Positions on Peace With Israel: Official Statements Since September 1993, Alfred B. Prados 95-324 F
* Syrian-U.S. Relations: Issue Brief, Alfred Prados IB92075

Taggants
* see Criminal Justice

Taiwan
* see also East Asia
* China Policy: Managing U.S.-PRC-Taiwan Relations After President Lee's Visit to the U.S., Robert Sutter 95-727 S
* Taiwan: Recent Developments and U.S. Policy Choices; Issue Brief, Robert G. Sutter IB94006

Tajikistan
* see also Central Asia
* Tajikistan: Basic Facts, Liam Wasley, 94-697 F

Taking Decisions
* see Law

Taxation
* see also Business Taxes, Capital Gains Tax, Consumption Taxes, Personal Income Tax

* Alcohol Fuels Tax Incentives and EPAs Renewable Oxygenate Requirement, Salvatore Lazzari 94-785 E
* The Bipartisan Commission on Entitlement and Tax Reform, David Koitz 94-806 EPW
* Contract With America Tax Relief Act of 1995: Revenue and Distribution Effects, Gregg A. Esenwein 95-498 E
* Distributional Effects of Tax Provisions in the Contract with America as Reported by the Ways and Means Committee, Jane G. Gravelle 95-455 S
* Expenditure Tax Proposals in Other Countries; Britain Harry G. Gourevitch 95-662 S
* Expenditure Tax Proposals in Other Countries; Sweden, Harry G. Gourevitch 95-550 S
* Expiring Tax Provisions: Issue Brief, David L. Brumbaugh and Sylvia Morrison IB95064
* Job Creation and Wage Enhancement Act: Tax Provisions; Issue Brief, Gregg A. Esenwein, etc. IB95059
* The Level of Taxes in the United States, 1940-Present: Fact Sheet, David L. Brumbaugh 95-812 E
* Major Tax Issues in the 104th Congress: A Summary; Issue brief, David L. Brumbaugh IB95053
* The Neutral Cost Recovery System and the House Republican Contract, David L. Brumbaugh and Jane G. Gravelle 95-161 E
* The Omnibus Budget Reconciliation Act of 1993: An Overview of the Tax Provisions, Gregg A. Esenwein and David L. Brumbaugh 93-810 E
* The Research and Experimentation Tax Credit: Issue Brief, Gary Guenther IB92039
* Retroactive Tax Laws in Western Europe, Law Library of Congress, Edith Palmer LL93-8
* The Size and Distribution of the Federal Tax Burden, Gregg A. Esenwein 94-530 E
* Super-Majority Voting Requirements for Tax increases: A Constitutional Analysis, Jay R. Shampansky 95-299 A
* Tax-Gap: Concept and Relationship Enforcement, James M. Bickley 94-41 E
* Tax Policy: A Checklist of CRS Products, Felix Chin 95-546 L
* Tax Policy: Savings and Investment Incentives; Videoprogram, David Brumbaugh and Jane Gravelle VT95-1305
* Tax Proposals at the Outset of the 104th Congress: An Outline, Gregg Esenwein and David Brumbaugh 95-74 E
* Tax Proposals in the President's FY 1996 Budget: Issue Brief, Salvatore Lazzari IB95072
* Tax Proposals--104th Congress: Info Pack IP501T
* Taxes in 1993: The Clinton and Congressional Agendas; Videoprogram, Donald Kiefer, etc. VT93-1312
* U.S. Federal Taxes in Puerto Rico, David L. Brumbaugh 94-428 E

Taxation -- Business Taxes

* Business Tax Provisions of Benefit to the Handicapped, Louis Alan Talley 93-783 E
* Comparison of 501 (C) (3) and 501 (C) (4) Organization, Marie B. Morris 95-421 A
* Corporate Executive Pay: Capping the Tax Deduction, Gerald Mayer 95-653 E
* Federal Excise Tax on Beer, Louis Alan Talley 94-900 E
* Federal Taxation of Small Business: A Brief Summary, David L. Brumbaugh 94-328 E
* The Home Office Deduction: An Unresolved Issue, Sylvia Morrison and Marie B. Morris 95-368 E
* How to Set Up a Tax-Exempt Organization, Marie B. Morris 94-227 A
* H.R. 1215 and the Expensing Allowance for Smaller Businesses, Gary Guenther 95-528 E
* Impact of the Omnibus Budget Reconciliation Act of 1993 on Small Businesses, Gerald Mayer 94-44 E
* The Possessions Tax Credit: Economic Analysis of the 1993 Revisions, David L. Brumbaugh 94-650 E
* Small Business Tax Subsidy Proposals, Jane G. Gravelle 93-316 S
* The Targeted Jobs Tax Credit: Prospects in the 104th Congress; Issue Brief, Linda Levine IB95005
* Targeted Jobs Tax Credit: Youth Apprentices as an Eligible Group, Linda Levine 93-562 E
* Tax Aspects of Health Care Reform: The Tax Treatment of Health Care Providers, Harry G. Gourevitch 94-369 S
* Tax Incentives to Train or Retrain the Work Force, Nonna A. Noto, etc., 93-739 E
* The Tax Treatment of Exempt Organizations: Intermediate Sanctions, Harry G. Gourevitch 94-901 S
* Taxation of Life Insurance Companies: Policyholder Dividends and Section 809, Jack Taylor 95-678 E
* Taxation of S Corporations, Partnerships, and Proprietorships in FY 1994 Budget

Reconciliation Bills, Gerald Mayer 93-644 E
* Taxes to Finance Superfund, Salvatore Lazzari 94-519 E
* Transfer Pricing and Taxes: Background and Issues, David L. Brumbaugh 94-823 E

Taxation -- Capital Gains

* Capital Gains and Securities Transactions Taxation in Canada: Fact Sheet, Gregg A. Esenwein and Philip D. Winters 94-832 E
* Capital Gains and Securities Transactions Taxation in Germany: Fact Sheet, Gregg A. Esenwein and Philip D. Winters 95-51 E
* Capital Gains and Securities Transactions Taxation in Japan: Fact Sheet, Gregg A. Esenwein and Philip D. Winters 94-891 E
* Capital Gains and Securities Transactions Taxation in the United Kingdom: Fact Sheet, Gregg Esenwein 94-920 E
* Capital Gains Revisions, Arnold Solomon 94-357 C
* Capital Gains Tax Issues and Proposals: An Overview, Jane G. Gravelle, 95-64 S
* Indexing Capital Gains for Inflation: Complexity and Related Issues, Harry G. Gourevitch 95-437 S

Taxation -- Consumption Taxes

* Alternative Transportation Fuels: Oil Import and Btu Tax Issues; Issue Brief, David E. Gushee IB93009
* Cigarette Taxes to Fund Health Care Reform: An Economic Analysis, Jane G. Gravelle and Dennis Zimmerman 94-214 E
* Energy Tax Provisions in the Energy Policy Act of 1992, Salvatore Lazzari 94-525 E
* Excise Tax Financing of Federal Trust Funds, Nonna A. Noto and Louis Alan Talley 93-6 E
* Excise Tax Rates for Alcohol, Tobacco, and Gasoline Adjusted for Inflation, Louis Alan Talley and Brian W. Cashell 94-466 E
* Federal Excise Taxes on Gasoline and the Highway Trust Fund: A Short History, Louis Alan Talley 94-354 E
* Federal Excise Taxes on Tobacco Products: A Summary of Present Law and a Legislative History, Thomas B. Ripy and Mildred C. Washington 94-47 A
* Flat Rate Consumption Taxes: Fact Sheet, Gregg A. Esenwein and James M. Bickley 95-549 E
* History and Economics of U.S. Excise Taxation of Luxury Goods, Louis Alan Talley, Jack Taylor and Dennis Zimmerman, 94-714 E
* Impact of Highway Fuel Taxes on Alternative Fuel Vehicle Economics, David E. Gushee 94-247 ENR
* Increasing Cigarette Excise Taxes: Implications for Tobacco Farming, Jasper Womach 94-344 ENR
* The Prospective Tax Increase on Commercial Jet Fuel, Salvatore Lazzari 95-396 E
* Tax Incentives for Alcohol Fuels, Salvatore Lazzari 95-261 E
* A Tax on Consumed Income, Gregg Esenwein 93-57 E
* Transportation Fuel Taxes After the 1993 Budget Act: How Much? For What? And for How Long?, Bernard A. Gelb 93-888 E
* Value-Added Tax as a New Revenue Source: Issue Brief, James M. Bickley IB91078
* Value-Added Tax: Concepts, Policy Issues, and OECD Experiences, James M. Bickley, 94-41 E
* A Value-Added Tax Contrasted With a National Sales Tax: Issue Brief, James M. Bickley. IB92069
* Value-Added Tax: Revenue Estimates for FY 95, James M. Bickley 93-687 E

Taxation -- Personal Income Tax

* Adoption Tax Credit Proposal, Louis Alan Talley 94-957 E
* Adoption Tax Credit Proposal of Family Reinforcement--H.R. 1215; Issue Brief, Louis Alan Talley IB95066
* The American Dream Restoration Act: Tax Provisions, Gregg A. Esenwein 95-395 E
* Conflicting Equity Goals of the Federal Income Tax Marriage Neutrality, Progressivity, and Equal Taxation of Couples With Equal Incomes Gregg A. Esenwein 93-630 E
* The Constitutionality of Retroactive Tax Increases: United States v. Carlton, Harry G. Gourevitch 94-508 S
* The Contract With America Tax Relief Act: An Overview of the House Bill, David Brumbaugh 95-735 E
* The Contract With America Tax Relief Act (H.R. 1215), David Brumbaugh 95-813 E
* Determination of Taxable Social Security Benefits under New Law: A Fact Sheet, Geoffrey Kollmann 93-336 EPW
* The Distribution of the Federal Tax Burden: Fact Sheet, Gregg A. Esenwein 95-807 E
* The Earned Income Tax Credit; a Fact Sheet, James R. Storey 94-396 EPW

* The Earned Income Tax Credit: A Growing Form of Aid to Children, James R. Storey, 95-542 EPW
* The Earned Income Tax Credit: Benefit Amounts, James R. Storey 94-399 EPW
* The Earned Income Tax Credit (EITC) Current Law and the Clinton Proposal: Characteristics of Eligible Families, Thomas Gabe, 93-546 EPW
* Employer Education Assistance: Overview of Tax Status, Bob Lyke 94-761 EPW
* The Estate Tax Exemption and the House Republican Contract, Salvatore Lazzari 95-167 E
* The Family Tax Credit, Gregg A. Esenwein 95-507 E
* Federal Estate, Gift, and Generation-Skipping Taxes: A Legislative History and Description of Current Law, John R. Luckey. 95-416 A
* Federal Taxation of Student Aid, Bob Lyke, 94-749 EPW
* Federal Taxes and the Territories: An Overview, David L. Brumbaugh 94-498 E
* Flat Tax Proposals: An Overview; Issue brief, James M. Bickley IB95060
* Frequently Asked Questions Concerning the Federal Income Tax, John R. Luckey, 92-303 A
* Health Care: Federal Tax Subsidies for Health Insurance, Gerald Mayer 95-601 E
* Health Insurance Cost and Coverage: Tax System Approaches; Issue Brief, Mark Merlis and Beth C. Fuchs IB95026
* A History of Federal Estate, Gift, and Generation-Skipping Taxes, John R. Luckey 95-444 A
* Housing and Real Estate Tax Provisions in the Omnibus Budget Reconciliation Act of 1993, E. Richard Bourdon 93-887 E
* Individual Income Tax Rates; 1995, Gregg A. Esenwein. 94-780 E
* Marriage Tax Penalties After the Omnibus Budget Reconciliation Act of 1993, Gregg A. Esenwein 93-475 E
* The Neutral Taxation of Capital Gains Income Under the Individual Income Tax, Gregg A. Esenwein 94-395 E
* An Overview of Current Flat Rate Tax Proposals, James M. Bickley and Gregg Esenwein 95-221 E
* Pension Issues: Info Pack, IP428P
* Proposal to Tax Pension Plans, Ray Schmitt 95-400 EPW
* Public Debt Reduction Fund, Louis Alan Talley 94-482 E
* Some Economic Issues Associated With the Current Tax Cut Debate, Gregg Esenwein 95-194 E
* Special Tax Rules for Members of Congress, Robert B. Burdette 95-501 A
* Tax Incentives for the Elderly Home Care, Louis Alan Talley 93-805 E
* Tax Policy: Family Tax Issues; Videoprogram, Greg Esenwein, etc. VT95-1314
* Tax Provisions Affecting Senior Citizens, Louis Alan Talley and Jack Taylor 95-513 E
* Taxpayer Rights in Dealing With the IRS About Income Taxes, Marie B. Morris 93-77 A
* Tuition Tax Deduction: Issue Raised by the President's Proposal, Bob Lyke 95-186 EPW

Technology and Civilization

* The Bayh-Dole Act: Patent Policy and the Commercialization of Technology 94-501 SPR
* Big Science and Technology Projects: Analysis of 30 Selected U.S. Government Projects, William C. Boesman 94-687 SPR
* Biotechnology, Breakthrough Drugs, and Health Care Reform: Lessons from the NIH-University-Industry Relationship, Wendy H. Schacht 94-365 SPR
* The Clipper Chip Encryption System, Stephen Gould 94-298 SPR
* Critical Technologies: Legislative and Executive Branch Activities, Genevieve J. Knezo. 93-734 SPR
* Defense Modeling and Simulation, Richard M. Nunno 95-592 SPR
* Defense Reinvestment and the Technology Reinvestment Project: Issue Brief, John D. Moteff IB93078
* The Defense Science and Technology Strategy, Kurt McPherson and Richard Nunno 95-185 SPR
* Department of Energy Laboratories: A New Partnership With Industry?, Wendy Schacht 93-844 SPR
* Department of Energy Laboratories: Capabilities and Missions, William C. Boesman 93-752 SPR
* The Difference Between DOD Programs That Develop Dual-Use Technologies and DOD's Dual Use Technology Development Programs--A Fact Sheet, John D. Moteff 95-738 SPR
* DOD's Advanced Concept and Technology Demonstrations, John D. Moteff 95-283 SPR
* DOD's Dual-Use Strategy, John D. Moteff 95-322 SPR
* DOD's Technology Reinvestment Project (TRP): Friend or Foe? John D. Moteff 95-86 SPR
* Fax-on-Demand Services Available From Federal Government Agencies, Glenda Richardson 95-434 C
* The Federal Role in Technology Development, Wendy H. Schacht 95-50 SPR
* Flat Panel Display (FPD) Technology: An Introduction to the Issues, Richard M. Nunno and Glenn J. McLoughlin 95-10 SPR

* Industrial Competitiveness and Technological Advancement: Debate Over Government Policy; Issue Brief, Wendy H. Schacht, IB91132
* Information Technologies in Elementary and Secondary Education: Background and Federal Policy Issues; Issue Brief, James B. Stedman IB93071
* International Science and Technology: Issues for U.S. Policymakers, Glenn J. McLoughlin 94-733 SPR
* Is DOD the Place to Fund Dual-Use Technology?, John D. Moteff. 93-496 SPR
* Major Science and Technology Programs: Megaprojects and Presidential Initiatives, Trends Through FY 1995, Genevieve J. Knezo, Science Policy Research Division 95-31 SPR
* Major Science and Technology Programs: Megaprojects and Presidential Initiatives, Trends Through FY 1996 Requested, Genevieve J. Knezo 95-490 SPR
* Manufacturing, Technology, and Competitiveness: Issue Brief, Wendy H. Schacht. IB92025
* R7D Partnerships: Government-Industry Collaboration, Wendy H. Schacht 95-499 SPR
* The Research and Experimentation Tax Credit: Issue Brief IB92039
* Science and Technology Issues, 104th Congress, First Session, Science Policy Research Division 95-84 SPR
* SEMATECH: Issues and Options; Issue Brief, Glenn J. McLoughlin IB93024
* Technology Policy Initiatives in the Clinton-Gore Administration, Glenn McLoughlin and Wendy Schacht 93-357 SPR
* Technology Transfer: Utilization of Federally Funded Research and Development; Issue Brief, Wendy Schacht IB85031

Technology -- Computers

* The Computer Industry, GATT, and the Uruguay Round, Sylvia Morrison 94-949 E
* Flat Panel Display Technology: What is the Federal Role?, Glenn J. McLoughlin and Richard M. Nunno 95-417 SPR
* Health Care Reform and National Information Infrastructure, Stephen B. Gould 94-770 SPR
* The High Performance Computing and Communications (HPCC) Program: An Introduction, Glenn J. McLoughlin 95-272 SPR
* How Will the Uruguay Round of GATT Affect the U.S. Computer Industry?, Sylvia Morrison 94-840 E
* The Information Superhighway: An Annotated Glossary, James Riehl 94-468 C
* Information Superhighway and Telecommunications Regulation: A Checklist of CRS Products, Bonnie F. Mangan 95-124 L
* Information Superhighway and the Internet: Info Pack IP4901
* The Information Superhighway: Status and Congressional Issues, Marcia S. Smith and Glenn J. McLoughlin 95-53 SPR
* The Information Superhighway: Status and Issues, Marcia S. Smith 94-954 SPR
* SCORPIO Self-Teaching Workbook, Theodore Moore and Tarria Burwell 91-908 AU

Technology Reinvestment Project (U.S.)

* DOD's Technology Reinvestment Project (TRP): Friend or Foe?, John D. Moteff 95-86 SPR

Technology Transfer

* see Technology

Teenage Pregnancy

* see Children

Telecommunication

* see Superhighway, Telephone Television
* Auctions of PCS Radiofrequency Spectrum Licenses: Issue Brief, Richard M. Nunno 94-444 SPR
* Bell Operating Company Entrance into the Alarm Industry, Angele A. Gilroy 95-806 E
* The Communications Decency Act of 1995, as Passed by the Senate, Henry Cohen 95-783
* Fax-on-Demand Services Available from Federal Government Agencies, Glenda Richardson 95-434 C
* How to Obtain Copies of Videotapes of Video Proceedings of Congress and Network and Cable Television Broadcasts, Michele M. Springer 95-728 C
* International Broadcasting: Consolidation of U.S. Radio Services, Kennon M. Nakamura and Susan B. Epstein 94-29 F
* Law of the Sea Convention: Status of the Convention and Agreement, Marjorie Ann Browne 95-612 F
* The Rural Electrification Administration: Background and Current Issues, Carl Ek and Amy Abel 91-614 ENR
* Telecommunications: Pioneer's Preference and Broad Band PCS, Angele A. Gilroy 94-873 E

Be patient. If any phone number is incorrect, call (area code) 555-1212 and request the new listing.

1347

Current Events and Homework

* Telecommunications Regulatory Reform: A Brief Overview, Angele A. Gilroy 95-80 E
* Telecommunications Regulatory Reform: Issue Brief, Angele A. Gilroy IB95067
* Telecommunications Services: Provisions in the Uruguay Round and in Nafta, M. Angeles Villarreal 94-653 E
* U.S. Telecommunications Infrastructure: Projected Future Evolution, Stephen Gould 93-161 SPR
* The Viacom Transaction and Beyond: The Federal Communications Commission Tax Certificate program, Angele A. Gilroy 95-319 SPR
* Wiretapping and Electronic Surveillance: The Electronic Communications Privacy Act and Related Matters, Charles Doyle 92-959 A

Telecommunication -- Superhighway

* Health Care Reform and the National Information Infrastructure, Stephen B. Gould 94-770 SPR
* The Information Superhighway: An Annotated Glossary, James Riehl 94-468 C
* Information Superhighway and Telecommunications Regulation: A Checklist of CRS Products, Bonnie F. Mangan 95-124 L
* Information Superhighway and the Internet: Info Pack IP4901
* The Information Superhighway: Status and Congressional Issues, Marcia Smith and Glenn J. McLoughlin 95-53 SPR
* The Information Superhighway: Status and Issues, Marcia S. Smith 94-954 SPR
* The National Information Infrastructure: The Federal Role; Issue Brief, Stephen B. gould and Glenn J. McLoughlin IB95051
* Welcome to Cyberia: An Internet Guide, Rita Tehan 94-471 C

Telecommunication -- Telephone Industry

* The American Telephone and Telegraph Company Divestiture: Background, Provisions, and Restructuring, Angela A. Gilroy, 94-510 E
* Bell Operating Company Entrance into the Alarm Industry, Angele G. Gilroy 94-451 E
* The Communications Decency Act of 1995, Henry Cohen 95-510 A
* Telephone/Cable Crossownership: A Time for Reassessment?, Angele A. Gilroy 93-658 E
* Telephone/Cable Crossownership: A Time for Reassessment? An Issue Overview, Angele A. Gilroy 93-674 E
* Telephone Companies-And Six Other Contributors to Competition in Local Telephone Service, David B. Hack. 93-234 SPR
* Telephone Industry Issues: Info Pack, IP257T

Telecommunication -- Television

* Cable Television Industry: The Top 25 Cable Multiple System Operators, James Riehl 95-99 C
* Cable TV: Info Pack, IP104C
* Television Satellite Carrier License Extension: Retransmission of Network and "Superstation" Video Programming to Home Satellite Dishes, Dorothy Schrader 94-680 A
* Television Violence: A Survey of Selected Social Science Research Linking Violent Program Viewing With Aggression in Children and Society , Edith Fairman Cooper 95-593 SPR
* Television Violence: An Overview, Edith Fairman Cooper 95-144 SPR
* Television Violence: Bibliography of Selected Research Reports, Edith Sutterlin 95-466 L
* Television Violence: Info Pack IP476T
* Violence on Television: What Can Technology Do?, Science Policy Research Division, Technology and Information Policy Section 93-710 SPR

Telephone Industry

* see Telecommunication -- Telephone

Television

* see Telecommunication --Television

Tennessee Valley Authority

* Tennessee Valley Authority's Power Program-A Fact Sheet, Amy Abel and Mark Holt 95-249 ENR

Term Limits

* see Congress -- Apportionment and Elections

Territories

* Federal Taxes and the Territories: An Overview, David L. Brumbaugh 94-498 E
* The Possessions Tax Credit: Economic Analysis of the 1993 Revisions, David L. Brumbaugh 94-650 E
* Puerto Rico: Political Status Options; Issue Brief, Garrine P. Laney IB89065

* Statehood for Puerto Rico: The Effect on Social Welfare Programs, Carolyn Merck, 91-47 EPW
* U.S. Federal Taxes in Puerto Rico, David L. Brumbaugh 94-428 E

Terrorism

* see Defense Policy

Thailand

* see also East Asia
* Thailand: Briefing Paper, Raymond J. Ahearn 94-796 F

Third World

* see Developing Countries

Timber Industry

* see Natural Resources -- Forests

Tobacco Industry

* see Agriculture -- Policies and Legislation

Toxic Substances

* see Hazardous Substances

Trade

* see also Agriculture -- Foreign Trade, Foreign Aid
* APEC--Asia Pacific Economic Cooperation: Free Trade, and Other Issues, Dick K. Nanto 93-926 E
* APEC, EAEC, and Free Trade in the Asia Pacific, Dick K. Nanto 94-914 E
* Asia-Pacific Economic Cooperation (APEC) and the Indonesia "Summit" in 1994, Dick K. Nanto 94-242 E
* Competitiveness: Economic Issue or Illusion?, Craig Elwell 94-424 E
* Cooperative R7D: Federal Efforts to Promote Industrial Competitiveness; Issue Brief, Wendy Schacht IB89056
* Does Trade Reduce Wages of U.S. Workers?, Craig Elwell 94-288 E
* Effects of Trade on U.S. Jobs and Wages, James Jackson 94-69 E
* European Union: Economic Integration; Info Pack IP408E
* The European Union: The World's Largest Trading Bloc, Glennon Harrison and Vivian Jones 95-43 E
* European Union-U.S. Trade Relations, Glennon J. Harrison 95-342 E
* Foreign Assistance and Commercial Interests: The Aid for Trade Debate, Curt Tarnoff and Larry Q. Nowels 93-578 F
* Japanese Investment in Asia; Videoprogram, Dick Nanto VT95-1341
* Russian Foreign Trade: Prospects and Implications for the United States, William H. Cooper 94-988 E
* Saudi Arabia: Commercial Disputes With U.S. Firms, Alfred Prados 95-666 F
* Trade, Competitiveness, and International Economic Policy: A Bibliography of CRS Products, Robert Howe 93-611 L
* U.S.-European Union Trade and Investment, Glennon J. Harrison 95-34 E
* U.S. International Trade: Data and Forecasts; Issue Brief, Dick K. Nanto IB94053
* U.S. Trade Performance: Recent Trends and Prospects, Craig Elwell 95-131 E

Trade -- Agreements

* Adjustment Assistance for Workers Dislocated by the North American Free Trade Agreement, Ann Lordeman and James R. Storey 94-52 EPW
* Agriculture in the North American Free Trade Agreement, Charles E. Hanrahan 92-582 S
* Agriculture in the Uruguay Round: An Overview, 94-582 S
* Antidumping and the Uruguay Round: An Overview, Arlene Wilson 95-192 E
* Banking and Finance in the North American Free Trade Agreement, William Jackson 93-560 E
* Caribbean Basin Countries: Implications of a North American Free Trade Agreement, 93-551 E
* Caribbean Basin Interim Trade Program ("CBI Parity"): Fact Sheet, Vladimir N. Pregelj 95-236 E
* Caribbean Basin Interim Trade Program: Issue Brief, IB95050
* Chile-United States Free Trade Agreement?, Raymond J. Ahearn and Nina M. Serafino 92-423 F
* Chilean Trade and Economic Reform: Implications for NAFTA Accession, J. F. Hornbeck 95-751 E
* China and the General Agreement on Tariffs and Trade, George D. Holliday 94-723 E
* The China-U.S. Trade Agreement on Intellectual Property Rights: Implications for China-U.S. Trade Relations, Wayne M. Morrison 95-463 E
* The Computer Industry, GATT and the Uruguay Round, Sylvia Morrison 94-949 E

* The Convention on International Trade in Endangered Species: Its Past and Future, M. Lynn Corn 94-675 ENR
* Dispute Settlement Under Free Trade Agreements and the GATT, Jeanne Grimmett 93-82 A
* Dispute Settlement under the WTO and Trade problems With Japan, Dick K. Nanto 95-42 E
* Economic Comparisons of Mexico, Canada, and the United States: Implications for the NAFTA, Arlene Wilson 93-669 E
* Enforcement of Intellectual Property Rights Under the GATT 1994 TRIPS Agreements, Dorothy Schrader 94-228 A
* Enforcement of Intellectual Property Rights Under the NAFTA, Dorothy Schrader 94-72 A
* Fair Trade in Financial Services: Legislation and the GATT, William Jackson 94-279 E
* Financial Services Trade With Japan, Dick K. Nanto 95-418 E
* The GATT Accord: Implications for U.S. Foreign Policy, Richard Cronin and Paul E. Gallis 94-186 F
* GATT and Other Trade Agreements: Congressional Action by Statute or by Treat?, Louis Fisher 94-890 S
* GATT and Regional Free Trade Agreements, George D. Holliday 93-989 E
* GATT and the Pharmaceutical Industry: Prospective Effects of the Uruguay Round on the Industry, Sylvia Morrison 94-831 E
* The GATT and the WTO: An Overview, Arlene Wilson 95-424 E
* GATT (General Agreement on Tariffs and Trade): Background Information, Penelope Fay Heavner 94-238 C
* GATT: General Agreement on Tariffs and Trade; Info Pack IP481G
* GATT: The Uruguay Round Agreement and Developing Countries, Susan B. Epstein 95-260 F
* GATT, Trade Liberalization, and the Environment: An Economic Analysis, Arlene Wilson 94-291 E
* How Will the Uruguay Round of GATT Affect the U.S. Computer Industry?, Sylvia Morrison 94-840 E
* Intellectual Property Provisions of the GATT of 1994: "The TRIPS Agreement", Dorothy Schrader 94-302 A
* Intellectual Property Provisions of the NAFTA, Dorothy Schrader 94-59 A
* Intellectual Property Rights and the Uruguay Round of Multilateral Trade Talks: Economic Effects, Lenore Sek 94-722 E
* Japan-U.S. Trade Agreements, 1980-1993, William H. Cooper 94-481 E
* Japan-U.S. Trade Negotiations: Will the Deadlock be Broken?, Raymond J. Ahearn 94-724 F
* Mexican-U.S.-Canadian Automotive Trade Issues, Gwenell L. Bass and M. Angeles Villarreal 93-961 E
* Mexico's Changing Policy Toward Foreign Investment and NAFTA Implications: An Issue Overview, M. Angeles Villarreal 93-782 E
* Mexico's Changing Policy Toward Foreign Investment: NAFTA Implications: An Issue Overview, M. Angeles Villarreal 93-668 E
* NAFTA: A Broad Economic Perspective, Arlene Wilson 93-974 E
* NAFTA and Jobs: An Overview, Alfred Reifman 92-955 S
* NAFTA and Sugar, Remy Jurenas 93-986 ENR
* NAFTA and the EC as Trading Blocs: A Distinction with a Difference, Glennon J. Harrison 93-864 E
* NAFTA and the Peso-Dollar Exchange Rare, Arlene Wilson 94-496 E
* NAFTA Decisions and U.S.-Mexico Relations, K. Larry Storrs 93-991 F
* NAFTA: Implications for Illicit Drug Supply to the United States, Raphael F. Perl 93-972 F
* NAFTA: The North American Free Trade Agreement; Info Pack IP445N
* NAFTA: U.S. Employment and Wage Effects, Mary jane Bolle 93-447 E
* NAFTA: U.S. Job Industry Trade Trends After One Year ; An Issue Overview, Mary Jane Bolle 95-648 E
* NAFTA: U.S. Jobs and Industry Trade Trends After One Year, Mary Jane Bolle 95-605 E
* A North American Free Trade Agreement and Immigration, Joyce C. Vialet 93-62 EPW
* North American Free Trade Agreement: Bibliography-in-Brief, Robert Howe 94-960 L
* North American Free Trade Agreement: Environmental Provisions and Issues, Mary Tiemann 93-760 ENR
* Pension Provisions Enacted With the General Agreement on Tariffs and Trade, Ray Schmitt 95-212 EPW
* A Reappraisal of the Economic Effects of the 1994 GATT Agreement, Alfred Reifman and Craig Elwell 94-659 S
* Telecommunications Services: Provisions and the Uruguay Round and in NAFTA, M. Angeles Villarreal 94-653 E
* Trade Agreements and the International Labor Standards of the ILO, Lois McHugh 94-535 F
* Trade and Environments: Renewing the Negotiating and Fast Track Implementing Authority; Issue Brief, Vladimir N. Pregelj IB95089

* Trade and Environment: GATT and NAFTA, Susan R. Fletcher and Mary Tiemann 94-165 ENR
* Trade and the Americas: Issue Brief, Raymond J. Ahearn IB95017
* Trade Prospects in the Western Hemisphere, Raymond J. Ahearn 94-660 F
* United States-Mexico Economic Relations: Has NAFTA made a Difference, J.F. Hornbeck 95-398 E
* The Uruguay Round: A Review of Major Issues, Congressional Research Service, Lenore Sek 94-294 E
* Uruguay Round of Trade Negotiations: A Checklist of CRS Products, Robert Howe 95-370 L
* The Uruguay Round of Trade Negotiations; Videoprogram, Lenore Sek VT94-1301
* Uruguay Round: Reform of the Safeguard Provisions of GATT, George Holliday 95-275 E
* U.S.-Canadian Agricultural Trade Disputes, Carl Ek and Charles E. Hanrahan 94-270 F
* U.S. Interests in Western Hemisphere Free Trade, Raymond J. Ahearn and Alfred Reifman 93-8988 F
* U.S. Trade Laws and Intellectual Property Rights, Glennon J. Harrison 95-355 E
* Why Certain Trade Agreements Are Approved as Congressional- Executive Agreements Rather Than as Treaties, Jeanne J. Grimmett 94-766 A
* World Trade Organization: Institutional Issues and Dispute Settlement, Jeanne J. Grimmett 94-627 A

Trade -- Imports/Exports

* see also Agriculture -- Trade
* Asian Trade, Foreign Policy, and Security Issues; Videoprogram, Dick K. Nanto, etc. VT95-1312
* China-U.S. Trade Issues: Issue Brief, Wayne Morrison IB91121
* China-U.S. Trade, MFN Status, and Economic Relations: Info Pack IP489C
* Deregulation as Market Opening in Japan, Dick k. Nanto 95-224 E
* Doing Business With Mexico: Sources of Information, Penelope Fay Heavener 94-543 C
* EC Trade With United States and the Rest of the World: A Statistical Overview, Glennon J. Harrison 93-685 E
* The Economics of Export Controls, Glennon J. Harrison 95-575 E
* The Economics of Export Promotion, Wayne M. Morrison 93-354 E
* Export Administration Act of 1994: Side-by-Side, Glennon J. Harrison 94-266 E
* Export Controls: Background and Issues, Glennon J. Harrison 94-30 E
* Export Controls in the 103rd Congress: New Issues, New Policies?, Glennon J. Harrison 94-277 E
* Export Enhancement Program: Background and Current Issues, Lenore Sek 95-388 ENR
* The Export-Import Bank: Background and Current Policy Issues, James K. Jackson 95-341 E
* Exporting: Major Federal Programs and Basic Information Sources, Carolyn C. Smith 94-499 C
* Generalized System of Preferences, George D. Holliday 95-679 E
* The Japan-U.S. Automobile and Parts Trade Dispute, Dick Nanto, etc. 95-725 E
* Japan-U.S. Automotive Framework Talks: Issue Brief, Gwenell L. Bass IB94055
* Japan-U.S. Trade and Economic Relations: Info Pack IP201J
* Japan-U.S. 1995 Automotive Dispute: Impact of 100 Percent Tariffs on Automotive Dealers by State, Penelope Fay Heavner 95-718 C
* Japan's Response to U.S. Trade pressures: End of an Era?, Raymond J. Ahearn 95-714 F
* Mahoganies: International Protection?, M. Lynne Corn 94-802 ENR
* Nonproliferation Export Controls in Eastern Europe and the Former Soviet Union, Theodore Galdi 94-850 F
* An Overview of NASA's Mission to Planet Earth, David P. Radzanowski and Stephen J. Garber 95-312 SPR
* Restricting Softwood Log Exports: Policy and Legal Implications, Kenneth R. Thomas and Ross W. Gorte 93-738 ENR
* Section 301: Its Operation and Prospects for Future Use by the United States, Wayne M. Morrison 95-360 E
* Steel Imports from Russia and Their Implications for Steel Markets, David J. Cantor 95-554 E
* Tied Aid Credits: Background and Current Policy Issues, James Jackson 94-412 E
* Trade Adjustment Assistance: A Fact Sheet, James R. Storey 94-478 EPW
* United States Exports by State: A Guide for the U.S. Congress, Dario Scuka 94-472 E
* U.S. Access to the EC Market: Opportunities, Concerns, and Policy Challenges, Raymond J. Ahearn 92-514 F
* U.S. Agricultural Trade: Trends, Composition, Direction, and Policy, Charles E. Hanrahan, etc. 95-809 S
* U.S. Commercial Relations With Japan and China; Videoprogram, Dick Nanto VT94-1309
* U.S. Japan Trade: Framework Talks and Other Issues: Issue Brief, William H. Cooper IB95019

Be patient. If any phone number is incorrect, call (area code) 555-1212 and request the new listing.

1349

Current Events and Homework

Trade -- Policy

* APEC, EAEC, and Free Trade in the Asia Pacific, Dick K. Nanto 94-914 E
* China: Current U.S. Sanctions, Kerry Dumbaugh 94-92 F
* China's MFN Status: Implications of the 1994 Decision, Kerry Dumbaugh 94-531 F
* Fair Trade in Financial Services (Banking and Securities) and the General Agreement on Trade in Services, William Jackson 05-260 E
* Government Procurement and U.S. Trade Policy, William H. Cooper 95-369 E
* Granting Most-Favored-Nation Status to China as a Market Economy Country, Vladimir N. Pregelj 94-514 E
* Iran: U.S. Trade Regulation and Legislation, Kenneth Katzman and Lawrence Kumins 95-419 F
* Japan-U.S. Trade Negotiations Under the Framework: Status and Alternative Approaches, William H. Cooper 94-620 E
* Japan's Keiretsu: Industrial Groups as Trade Barriers, Dick K. Nanto 94-82 E
* A "Managed Trade" Policy Toward Japan?, Wayne Morrison, etc. 94-524 E
* Most-Favored-Nation Policy of the United States; Issue Brief, Vladimir N. Pregelj IB93107
* Most-Favored-Nation Status of the People's Republic of China: Issue Brief, Vladimir N. Pregelj IB92094
* Regional Free Trade Partners and U.S.Interests: What's Next?, Raymond Ahearn 95-392 F
* The Trade and Development Agency, Susan B. Epstein 93-717 F
* Trade Issues: A Checklist of CRS Products, Robert Howe 95-127 L
* Trade Issues in the 104th Congress: Bibliography-in-Brief, Robert Howe 95-483 L
* Trade Issues: Info Pack IP263T
* Trade Policy in an Economic Perspective, Craig K. Elwell 95-529 E
* Trade Policy in the 104th Congress, George D. Holliday 95-4485 E
* U.S.-Japan Trade Confrontation: Economic Perspective and Policy Options, Craig Elwell and Alfred Reifman 94-526 E

Trade Negotiations
* see Trade -- Agreements

Transportation

* Air Quality: Impacts of Trip Reduction Programs on States and Affected Employers, Maura K. Flechtner 93-745 ENR
* Amtrak and the 104th Congress: Issue Brief, Stephen J. Thompson IB95801
* Automobile Fuel Economy Standards: Another Cup of CAFE?, Issue Brief, IB90122
* Federal Excise Taxes on Gasoline and the Highway Trust Fund: A Short History, Louis Alan Talley 94-354 E
* Federal Programs That Could Financially Benefit Business Enterprises, Edward Knight and Vivian C. Jones 95-535 E
* Highway Demonstration Projects: Background and Economic Policy Issues, J.F. Hornbeck 94-572 E
* Intelligent Transportation Systems Program: Benefits, Costs, and Concerns, Paul F. Rothberg 95-347 SPR
* The Interstate Commerce Commission and the 104th Congress: S. 440 and Other Legislation, Migdon Segal, etc. 95-795 SPR
* The National Highway System: Background and Status, William A. Lipford 94-257 E
* Rail Market Dominance: Is ICC Regulation Still Needed?, Stephen Thompson 94-775 E
* Railroad Retirement and Unemployment Benefits: A Summary of Benefits, Financing, and History, Dennis W. Snook 95-47 EPW
* Railroad Unemployment Benefits: Proposed Changes, Dennis W. Snook 95-117 EPW
* Selected Labor Protections Regarding Transit, Amtrak, and Freight Railroads: Issue Brief, Stephen Thompson IB95097
* Transit Funding Under the Highway Flexibility Option: A Summary, William A. Lipford 95-536 E
* Transportation Fuel Taxes After the 1993 Budget Act: How Much? For What? And for How Long?, Bernard A. Gelb 93-888 E
* Transportation Infrastructure: Economic Issues and Public Policy Alternatives, J.F. Hornbeck 93-676 E
* Transportation Infrastructure: Economic Issues and Public Policy Alternatives, J.F. Hornbeck 93-107 E
* Transportation Program Finances and Selected Policy Issues, Stephen J. Thompson 94-506 E
* Transportation Trust Funds: The Off-Budget Debate; Issue brief, John F. Fischer IB95038
* The Truckline Undercharge Problem and the Negotiated Rates Act, K.R. DeJarnette 94-776 E

Transportation -- Aviation
* The Airport Improvement Program: Background, and Some Options for using Federal Finance Resources More Effectively, Stephen J. Thompson 94-67 E
* The Commercial Jet Aircraft Industry: An Issues Overview, John W. Fischer 94-781 E
* Commuter and Large Air Carriers: Is It Time for One Level of Safety?, Glen Moore 95-351 SPR
* The Prospective Tax Increase on Commercial Jet Fuel, Salvatore Lazzari 95-396 E
* Reorganization of the Federal Aviation Administration: Safety and Efficiency Issues, John W. Fischer 94-371 E
* Wind Tunnels: Proposal for a New National Wind Tunnel Complex, David P. Radzanowski and John J. Sloan 95-103 SPR

Treaties
* see International Affairs

Treaty on the Non-Proliferation of Nuclear Weapons
* The Nuclear Non-Proliferation Treaty Extension: A Fact Sheet, Zachary S. Davis 95-289 ENR

Trucking
* see Transportation

Tunisia
* see Middle East and North Africa

Turkey
* see also Central Asia, Europe
* Greece and Turkey: Current Foreign Aid Issues: Issue Brief, Carol Migdalovitz. IB86065
* Turkey: Ally in a Troubled Region, Carol Migdalovitz IB86065
* Turkey: Political and Economic Change and Implications for the United States, Carol Migdalovitz 94-741 F
* Turkey's Kurdish Imbroglio and U.S. Policy, Carol Migdalovitz 94-267 F
* Turkey's Military Offensive in Northern Iraq, Carol Migdalovitz 95-487 F

Turkmenistan
* see also Central Asia
* Turkmenistan Republic: Basic Facts, Jim Nichol, 95-609 F

Ukraine
* see also Europe
* Economic Crisis in Ukraine: Dangers and Opportunities, John P. Hardt 94-668 S
* Economic Issues for Summits in Moscow and Kiev, John P. Hardt and Phillip Kaiser 95-516 S
* Ukraine: Issue Brief, Stevan Woehrel IB92072
* Ukraine Nuclear Weapons and U.S. Interests, Stephen Woehrel 94-253 F
* Ukraine's Uncertain Future and U.S. Policy, Stephen Woehrel 94-738 F

Undocumented Aliens
* see Immigration

Unemployment
* see Labor -- Employment and Unemployment

Unemployment Compensation
* see Labor -- Employment and Unemployment

Unfunded Mandate Reform Act
* Unfunded Mandate Reform Act: A Brief Summary, Sandra Osbourn 95-246 GOV

Unfunded Mandates
* see State and Local Government

United Arab Emirates
* see also Middle East and North Africa
* United Arab Emirates: Background and U.S. Relations, Alfred P. Prados and Ross Kaplan 95-730 F

United Nations
* Cyprus: Status of U.N. Negotiations; Issue Brief, Carol Migdalovitz IB89140
* U.N. Regular Budget Funding: Issues for Congress, Vita Bite 95-645 F
* U.N. System Funding: Congressional Issues; Issue Brief, Vita Bite. IB86116

* United Nations Peacekeeping: Historical Overview and Current Issues, Marjorie Ann Browne, 90-96 F
* United Nations Peacekeeping: Issues for Congress; Issue Brief, Marjorie Ann Browne, IB90103
* United Nations Peacekeeping Operations, 1988-1993: Background Information, Marjorie Ann Browne, 94-193 F
* United Nations Regular Budget Contributions: Members Compared, 1989-1994, Marjorie Ann Browne 95-571 F
* United Nations: Selected References, 1990-1993, Ursula Roosmaa and Sherry Shapiro 94-77 L

United Nations Conference on Environment and Development (1992: Rio de Janeiro, Brazil)
* Congress and International Environmental Policy, Susan R. Fletcher. 93-695 ENR
* Deforestation: An Overview of Global Programs and Agreements, Julie Lyke and Susan R. Fletcher, 92-764 ENR
* Oceans and Coastal Resources: A Briefing Book, Alfred R. Greenwood 95-313 ENR

United Nations Conference on the Law of the Sea
* Deep Seabed Mining: U.S. Interests and the U.N. Convention on the Law of the Sea, James E. Mielke 95-471 SPR

United States Postal Service
* see Communications

United States v. Knox
* The Knox "Clothed Children" Child Pornography Case and the Congressional Response, Henry Cohen 94-753 A

United States v. Lopez
* Does United States v. Lopez Affect the Gun-Free Schools Provisions of the Improving America's Schools Act of 1994?, Elizabeth B. Bazan 95-647 A

United States Sentencing Commission
* Federal Sentencing Guidelines, Suzanne Cavanagh, 91-499 GOV
* United States Sentencing Commission: Preliminary Analysis, Charles Doyle. 89-308 A

Uranium
* see Nuclear Energy

Urban Affairs
* Community Development Banking and Financial Institutions: The Administration's Proposal; an Issue Overview, F. Jean Wells and William Jackson 93-698 E
* Community Development Block Grant Programs: Bibliography-in-Brief, Jean M. Bowers 95-562 L
* Community Development Block Grants: An Overview, Eugene Boyd 95-440 GOV
* Community Development Financial Services: Alternative Legislative Approaches, F. Jean Wells and William Jackson 93-1024 E
* Community Development Programs; Videoprogram, Eugene Boyd and Morton Schussheim VT95-1328
* Community Development Revolving Loan Program for Credit Unions, Pauline Smale 94-819 E
* Community Reinvestment Act and Regulatory Relief, F. Jean Wells 95-521 E
* Economic Development Administration: A Fact Sheet, Bruce K. Mulock 95-617 E
* Empowerment Zones/Enterprise Communities Program: Background and Analysis of Economic Issues, Bruce K. Mulock 95-494 E
* Housing and Community Development: Issues Facing the 103rd Congress, Morton Schussheim 94-209 S

Urban and Regional Development
* see Infrastructure, Public Lands, Rural Affairs, Urban Affairs

Uruguay Round
* see General Agreement on Tariffs and Trade

U.S. Agency for Health Care Policy and Research
* Outcomes Research, Clinical Practice Guidelines, and the Agency for Health Care Policy and Research, Bernice Reyes-Akinbileje 94-488 SPR

U.S. Air Force
* see Defense Policy

U.S. Alcohol, Drug Abuse, and Mental Health Administration
* The Alcohol, Drug Abuse, and Mental Health Administration (ADAMHA) Reorganization Act of 1992, Edward R. Klebe, etc. 93-597 EPW

U.S. Architect of the Capitol
* Architect of the Capitol: Appointment, Duties, and Operations, Mildred L. Amer and Paul S. Rundquist 95-343 GOV

U.S. Army
* see Defense Policy

U.S. Attorney General's Commission on Pornography
* Pornography in the United States: A Brief Overview, Leslie W. Gladstone 95-759 GOV

U.S. Bureau of Alcohol, Tobacco, and Firearms
* Branch Davidian Siege at Ranch Apocalypse Near Waco, Texas: A Chronology, Suzanne Cavanagh and David Teasley 95-582 GOV
* U.S. Bureau of Alcohol, Tobacco, and Firearms, Suzanne Cavanagh 93-451 GOV

U.S. Bureau of Land Management
* Bureau of Land Management Authorization, Betsy A. Cody and Pamela Baldwin 95-429 ENR

U.S. Bureau of the Census
* see Government Information

U.S. Central Intelligence Agency
* see Intelligence Activities

U.S. Congress, House, Committee on Appropriations
* The House Appropriations, Process, 1789-1993, Louis Fisher 93-729 S

U.S. Congress, Joint Committee on Printing
* The Joint Committee on Printing: A Brief Overview, Harold C. Relyea 95-425 GOV

U.S. Congress, Joint Committee on the Library
* Joint Committee on the Library: Duties and Responsibilities, Paul S. Rundquist 95-721 GOV

U.S. Congress, Joint Committee on the Organization of Congress
* The Proposed Legislative Reorganization Act of 1994: Issue Brief, Walter J. Oleszek IB94039

U.S. Congress, Senate, Office of the President Pro Tempore
* The President Pro Tempore of the Senate: History and Authority of the Office, Richard C. Sachs 95-181 GOV

U.S. Dept. of Agriculture
* see Agriculture

U.S. Dept. of Defense
* see Defense Policy

U.S. Dept. of Education
* see Education Policy, Elementary and Secondary Education, Higher Education

U.S. Dept. of Energy
* see Energy

U.S. Dept. of Housing and Urban Development
* see Housing

U.S. Dept. of Justice
* see Civil Liberties and Rights, Law

U.S. Environmental Protection Agency
* see Environmental Protection

Be patient. If any phone number is incorrect, call (area code) 555-1212 and request the new listing.

1351

Current Events and Homework

U.S. Federal Aviation Administration
* see Transportation

U.S. Federal Bureau of Investigation
* Branch Davidian Siege at Ranch Apocalypse Near Waco, Texas: A Chronology, Suzanne Cavanagh and David Teasley 95-582 GOV

U.S. Federal Communications Commission
* Auctions of PCS Radiofrequencies, Richard M. Nunno 94-444 SPR

U.S. Federal Election Commission
* see Elections

U.S. Federal Emergency Management Agency
* see Emergency Management

U.S. Federal Housing Administration
* see Housing

U.S. Food and Drug Administration
* see Food, Medicine

U.S Forest Service
* see Natural Resources

U.S. General Services Administration
* Civilian Procurement Reform Efforts, Stephanie Smith 94-225 GOV

U.S. Immigration and Naturalization Service
* see Immigration

U.S. Immigration Border Patrol
* The Border Patrol: Facts and Issues, William J. Krouse 94-648 EPW

U.S. Indian Health Service
* Health Services for American Indians and Alaska Natives, Edward R. Klebe and Karen M. Judge 93-975 EPW

U.S. National Aeronautics and Space Administration
* see Space Activities

U.S. National Institute for Standards and Technology
* Flat Panel Display (FPD) Technology: An Introduction to the Issues, Richard M. Nunno and Glenn J. Mcloughlin 95-10 SPR

U.S. National Marine Fisheries Service
* Summaries of Major Laws Implemented by the National Marine Fisheries Service, Eugene H. Buck 95-460 ENR

U.S. National Park Service
* see Public Lands

U.S. Nuclear Regulatory Commission
* see Energy -- Nuclear

U.S. Occupational Safety and Health Administration
* see Labor

U.S. Postal Service
* see Communications

U.S. Public Health Service
* see also Health Policy, Medicine
* Public Health Service: Program Consolidations; Issue Brief Edward Klebe IB95098
* The Surgeon General of the United States, Mary V. Wright 94-663 C

U.S. Social Security Administration
* see Social Security

U.S. Supreme Court
* see Law

U.S. Trade and Development Agency
* The Trade and Development Agency, Susan B. Epstein 93-717 F

U.S. Veterans Administration
* see Veterans

U.S. as a Debtor Nation
* see Foreign Aid, International Finance

U.S. Government
* see Executive Departments

U.S. Navy
* see Defense Policy

U.S. Railroad Retirement Board
* see Pensions

U.S. Term Limits, Inc. v. Thornton
* The Unconstitutionality of State Congressional Term Limits: An Overview of U.S. Terms Limits, Inc. v. Thornton (Sup. Ct. Doc. No. 93-1456), Thomas M. Durbin 95-646 A

User Fees
* see Budgets

Uzbekistan
* see Central Asia
* Uzbek Republic: Basic Facts, Jim Nichol, 95-520 F

Value-Added Tax
* see Taxation--Consumption Taxes

Venezuela
* see also Latin America
* Venezuela: Political and Economic Situation and U.S.-Venezuelan Relations, Mark P. Sullivan 94-362 F

Veterans
* Housing Programs of VA and FHA: A Comparison, Bruce E. Foote. 93-545 E
* Illnesses Related to the Persian Gulf Experience, Samuel Merrill. 92-886 SPR
* Major Veterans' Legislation in the 103rd Congress, Anne C. Stewart, etc. 94-609 EPW
* Military Retirement and Veterans' Compensation: Concurrent Receipt Issues, Robert L. Goldich and Carolyn L. Merck 95-469 F
* Speech Material: Veterans Day; Info Pack. IP378V
* Veterans' Educational Assistance Programs, Mary F. Smith and William J. Krouse 94-221 EPW
* Veterans' Health Care Program: A Fact Sheet, Anne C. Stewart. 94-611 EPW
* Veterans' Pensions: Fact Sheet, Dennis W. Snook 95-269 EPW

Veterans Day
* Speech Material: Veterans Day; Info Pack. IP378V

Vietnam
* Oil in Vietnam: A Review of Foreign and Domestic Activities, Dario Scuka. 93-416 E
* Vietnam in Transition and Vietnamese Relations With the United States, Robert G. Sutter 95-254 S
* Vietnam: Procedural and Jurisdictional Questions Regarding Possible Normalization of U.S. Diplomatic and Economic Relations, Alan K. Yu, etc., 94-633 S
* Vietnam-U.S. Relations: The Debate Over Normalization; Issue Brief, Robert G. Sutter. IB93081

Violence
* see Criminal Justice

Violence on Television
* see Telecommunication -- Television

Violent Crime Control and Law Enforcement Act
* Anti-Crime Funding in the Fiscal 1995 Commerce, Justice, State Appropriations Act (H.R. 4603): A Summary, David Teasley 94-679 GOV

Be patient. If any phone number is incorrect, call (area code) 555-1212 and request the new listing.

* The Assault Weapons Ban: Review of Federal Laws Controlling Possession of Certain Firearms, Dorothy Schrader 95-108 S
* Crime Control Act of 1994: Capital Punishment Provisions Summarized., Charles Doyle 94-721 S
* Crime Control Act of 1994: Selected Highlights of H.R. 3355 as Passed, Charles Doyle 94-682 S
* Crime Control: Comparison of House and Senate Legislation of the 103rd Congress, 2nd Session, Charles Doyle, etc. 94-358 S
* Crime Control: Summary of Financial Assistance Available to State and Local Governments, Keith Bea 95-258 GOV
* Crime Control: Summary of the Violent Crime Control and Law Enforcement Act of 1994, Charles Doyle 94-910 S
* Crime Issues; Videoprogram, Charles Doyle, etc. VT95-1307
* Crime Prevention: A Brief Overview, Suzanne Cavanagh and David Teasley 95-140 GOV
* Hate Crime: Recent Developments, Susan Cavanagh and David Teasley 94-855 GOV
* Present Federal Death Penalty Statues, Elizabeth B. Bazan 95-321 A
* "Three Strikes" Provisions: Recent Federal Developments, Suzanne Cavanagh 94-876 GOV
* Truth in Sentencing: Summary of Implicated State Laws, Charles Doyle 95-310 S
* Violent Crime Control Act of 1994: Crime Prevention Funding With FY 1995 Appropriations, David Teasley 94-878 GOV
* Violent Crime Control Enforcement Act: Selected Comparative Highlights of the House (H.R. 4092/H.R. 3355) and Senate Bills (S. 1607/H.R.3355), Charles Doyle 94-372 S
* Youth Gangs: Recent Developments, Suzanne Cavanagh 94-934 GOV

Vocational Education
* see Job Training

Vocational Rehabilitation Act
* Vocational Rehabilitation Act and Related Programs for Persons With Disabilities: Brief Description and FY 1995 Budget Request, Carol O'Shaughnessy and Mary Smith 94-224 EPW

Volunteers and Volunteer Program
* see Social Services

Voting
* see Elections

Voting Rights Act
* Congressional and State Reapportionment and Redistricting: A Legal Analysis, Thomas M. Durbin and L. Paige Whitaker 95-793 A
* Congressional Redistricting: Federal Law Controls a State Process, David C. Huckabee 93-1060 GOV
* The Voting Rights Act of 1965 as Amended., Paul Downing. 84-203 GOV
* The Voting Rights Act of 1965: A Legal Overview, L. Paige Whitaker, 91-736 A

War and Peace
* see Defense Policy, Foreign Policy, International Affairs, War Powers Resolution

War Powers Act
* Presidential Emergency Powers: The War Powers Act of 1933, David M. Ackerman 95-753 A

War Powers Resolution
* War Powers and U.N. Military Actions: A Brief Background of the Legislative Framework, Ellen C. Collier 93-1058 F
* War Powers Resolution: A Brief Summary of Pro and Con Arguments, Ellen C. Colier 93-984 F
* War Powers Resolution: Info Pack, IP131W
* War Powers Resolution: The Controversial Act's Search for a Successful Litigation Posture, Raymond J. Celada and David M. Ackerman 93-1065 A
* The War Powers Resolution: Twenty Years Experience, Ellen C. Collier 94-42 F
* War Powers Restrictions: Selected Excerpts from Legislation Enacted in the 103rd Congress, Ellen C. Collier 95-49 F

Washington, DC
* see District of Columbia

Washington, George
* Speech Material: Abraham Lincoln's and George Washington's Birthdays; Info Pack, IP373A

Waste Isolation Pilot Plant
* Waste Isolation Pilot Plant--A Fact Sheet, Mark Holt 93-997 ENR

Waste Management
* see Solid Wastes

Water Pollution
* see also Clean Water Act
* Agriculture and Clean Water: Provisions of S. 20093, Claudia Copeland 94-476 ENR
* An Assessment of the Agricultural Impacts of H.R. 2199, Barry Carr 94-229 ENR
* Clean Water Act Legislation: Summary of S. 1114, Claudia Copeland. 93-626 ENR
* Clean Water Act Reauthorization: Issue Brief, Claudia Copeland, IB93013
* Clean Water Act Section 401: Background and Current Issues, Claudia Copeland 95-2 ENR
* Clean Water Issues in the 104th Congress, Claudia Copeland 94-446 ENR
* Clean Water Legislation in the 103rd Congress: A Legislative Rollercoaster, Claudia Copeland 94-750 ENR
* Clean Water: Summary of H.R. 961, as Passed, Claudia Copeland 95-427 ENR
* Implications of Linking Clean Water Spending to the Rate of Inflation, Claudia Copeland 95-216 ENR
* PUD No. 1 of Jefferson v. Washington Department of Ecology: An Expansive Interpretation of State Authority Under the Clean Water Act, Ellen M. Lazarus 94-601 A
* Rural Water Supply and Sewer Systems: Background Information, Claudia Copeland 94-838 ENR
* Safe Drinking Water Act Amendments of 1994: Summary of S. 2019, as Passed, Mary Tiemann 94-606 ENR
* Safe Drinking Water Act: Implementing the 1986 Amendments; Issue Brief, Mary E. Tiemann. IB91041
* Safe Drinking Water Act Reauthorization Issues, Mary Tiemann 95-780 ENR
* Stormwater Permits: Status of EPA's Regulatory Program, Claudia Copeland. 94-811 ENR
* Toxic Pollutants and the Clean Water Act: Current Issues, Claudia Copeland 93-849 ENR
* Wastewater Treatment: Overview and Background, Claudia Copeland 94-822 ENR
* Water Quality: Implementing the Clean Water Act; Archived Issue Brief, Claudia Copeland IB89102
* Water Quality Issues: Info Pack IP369W
* Wetlands Legislation: Comparison of Two Bills, Claudia Copeland 95-796 ENR

Water Pollution Prevention and Control Act
* Agriculture and Clean Water Provisions of S. 2093, Claudia Copeland 94-476 ENR

Water Resources
* see also Emergency Management, Water Pollution
* Ecosystems, Biomes, and Watersheds: Definition and Use, M. Lynne Corn 93-655 ENR
* Legal Issues Related to Livestock Watering in Federal Grazing Districts, Pamela Baldwin 94-688 A
* Rural Water Supply and Sewer Systems: Background Information, Claudia Copeland 94-838 ENR
* Safe Drinking Water Act: Implementing the 1986 Amendments; Issue Brief, Mary E. Tiemann, IB91041
* Safe Drinking Water Act Reauthorization Issues, Mary Tiemann 95-780 ENR
* Water Quality Issues: Info Pack. IP369W
* Wetlands and Agriculture: Policy Issues in the 1995 Farm Bill, Jeffrey Zinn 95-7 ENR
* Wetlands Legislation: Comparison of Two Bills, Claudia Copeland 95-796 ENR

Weapons
* see Weapons Systems

Weapons Facts
* see Weapons Systems -- Weapons Facts

Weapons Systems
* Chemical Weapons Convention of 1993: Ratification and Implementation Issues, Steven R. Bowman 94-246 F
* Chemical Weapons: Issues for Congress; Issue Brief, Steven Bowman IB94029
* DOE and Its Weapons Laboratories: A Summary, William Boesman 94-999 SPR
* Nuclear, Biological, and Chemical Weapons Proliferation: Potential Military Countermeasures, John M. Collins, etc. 94-528 S
* The Proliferation of Nuclear and Chemical Weapons; Videoprogram, Theodor Galdi, etc. VT94-1330

Be patient. If any phone number is incorrect, call (area code) 555-1212 and request the new listing.

1353

Current Events and Homework

Weapons Systems -- Nuclear Weapons
* Ballistic and Cruise Missile Forces of Foreign Countries, Robert Shuey 95-688 F
* Ballistic Missile Defenses: Info Pack IP496B
* Chinese Nuclear Weapons and Arms Control Policies: Implications for the United States, Robert G. Sutter. 94-422 S
* The DOE Multiprogram Nuclear Weapons Laboratories, William C. Boesman 94-916 SPR
* Missile Defense: Proposals, Programs, and Treaty Constraints, Robert D. Shuey and Steven A. Hildreth 95-24 F
* North Korea's Nuclear Weapons Program: U.S. Policy Options, Richard Cronin 94-470 F
* Nuclear Weapons Production Complex: Environmental Compliance and Waste; Issue Brief, Mark Holt, IB90074
* Nuclear Weapons Stockpile Stewardship: The Role of Livermore and Los Alamos National Laboratories, Jonathan E. Medalia 94-418 F
* Nuclear Weapons Testing and Negotiation of a Comprehensive Test Ban Treaty: Issue Brief, Jonathan Medalia IB92099
* Theater Ballistic Missile Defense Policy, Missions and Programs: Current Status, Steven A. Hildreth. 93-585 F
* Theater Missile Defense: Issues for the 104th Congress; Issue Brief, Steven A. Hildreth IB95012
* Weapons of Mass Destruction: The Impact of Proliferation on U.S. Military Posture, John M. Collins 95-673 S

Weapons Systems -- Weapons Facts
* Antitank Guided Missile: U.S. Army's Non-Portable Medium System; Issue Brief, Edward F. Bruner, IB91130
* Bomber Non-Nuclear Roles: Background to the Heavy Bomber Debate, Theodor W. Galdi 95-699 F
* The C-17 Cargo Plane Production Status Issue Brief, James P. Wooten, IB93041
* F/A - 18E/F Aircraft Program: Issue Brief, Bert H. Cooper IB92035
* F-16 Aircraft Issues: Debate Over Continued Procurement, Bert Cooper 94-642 F
* F-22 Aircraft Program: Issue Brief, Bert H. Cooper. IB87111
* Navy Attack Submarine Programs: Issues for Congress; Issue Brief, Ronald O'Rourke IB91098
* Navy DDG-51 Destroyer Procurement Rate: Issues and Options for Congress, Ronald O'Rourke 94-343 F
* Navy New Attack Submarine (NSSN) Program: Is It Affordable?, Ronald O'Rourke 94-643 F
* Tactical Aircraft Modernization: Issues for Congress; Issue Brief, Bert H. Cooper IB92115
* V-22 Osprey Tilt-Rotor Aircraft (Weapons Facts): Issue Brief, Bert H. Cooper IB86103

Welfare
* Alien Eligibility for Federal Assistance, Joyce C. Vialet and Larry M. Eig 94-73 EPW
* Alien Eligibility Requirements for Major Federal Assistance Programs, Larry M. Eig and Joyce C. Vialet 93-1046 A
* Benefits for Persons with Limited Income: FY 1975-1992, Vee Burke 93-877 EPW
* Cash and Noncash Benefits for Persons with Limited Income: Eligibility Rules, Recipient and Expenditure Data, FY 1990-92, Vee Burke 93-832 EPW
* Homeless Assistance: Funding and Legislation in the 104th Congress, Dale Robinson 95-697 EPW
* Homeless Assistance: Programs and Funding Issues, Ruth Ellen Wasem and Dale H. Robinson 94-3 EPW
* Homeless in America: Info Pack IP314H
* Homeless Mentally Ill Persons: Problems and Programs, Karen Judge and Edward R. Klebe 93-728 EPW
* HUD's Shelter Programs for the Homeless, Susan Vanhorenbeck 95-130 E
* Immigration: What Is PRUCOL?, Joyce Vialet 94-710 EPW
* Jobs for Welfare Recipients, Linda Levine 94-457 E
* Jobs for Welfare Recipients: An Issue Overview, Linda Levine 94-461 E
* The Low-Income Home Energy Assistance Program, Joe Richardson and Louisa Hierholzer 94-881 EPW
* Native and Naturalized Citizens and Non-Citizens: An Analysis of Poverty Status, Welfare Benefits, and Other Factors, Michael J. O'Grady 95-276 EPW
* Recent Statistics on Poverty in the United States, Thomas Gabe 94-863 EPW
* Recipiency of Federal and State Government Benefits Among Families in 1993, Dawn Nuschler and Gene Falk 94-711 EPW
* Redefining Poverty in the United States: National Academy of Science Panel Recommendations, Thomas B. Gabe 95-539 EPW
* Residential Energy Costs and LIHEAP, Bernard A. Gelb 95-350 E
* State Welfare Initiatives, Jennifer A. Neisner 94-183 EPW
* Supplemental Security Income (SSI): A Fact Sheet, Carmen D. Solomon 94-486 EPW

* Trends in Poverty in the U.S. (1959 to 1993): A Fact Sheet, Thomas Gabe 94-853 EPW
* Welfare: Durational Residency Requirements, Gina Marie Stevens 95-357 A
* Welfare-to-Work Programs: Lessons Learned, Vee Burke 94-37 EPW
* Welfare (Dis)incentives in the Welfare System, Thomas Gabe and Gene Falk 95-105 EPW

Welfare -- Children
* AFDC Recipients and Employer Wage Subsidies, Linda Levine 94-839 E
* AFDC Recipients and Employer Wage Subsidies: An Overview, Linda Levine 94-858 E
* AFDC Reform: Why Again?, Vee Burke 95-63 EPW
* Aid to Families With Dependent Children (AFDC): A Fact Sheet, Carmen D. Solomon 94-340 EPW
* Aid to Families With Dependent Children (AFDC): Need Standards, Payment Standards, and Maximum Benefits, Carmen D. Solomon and Jennifer A. Neisner 95-229 EPW
* Child Nutrition Programs: Facts and Issues, Jean Javis Jones and Joe Richardson 95-230 ENR
* Child Support Assurance: United States Initiatives and Experience in Other Countries, Carmen D. Solomon and Louisa Hierholzer 93-167 EPW
* The Child Support Enforcement Program: Policy and Practice, Carmen D. Solomon 89-659 EPW
* Child Welfare, Child Abuse, and Related Issues in the 104th Congress; Issue Brief, Karen Spar and Dale H. Robinson IB95029
* Child Welfare Programs: A Fact Sheet, Karen Spar 94-950 EPW
* Children Welfare: State Services and Federal Programs, Karen Spar 92-455 EPW
* Children's Social Service Issues in the 104th Congress, Dale Robinson 95-97 EPW
* Disabled and Blind Child Recipients of Supplemental Security Income (SSI): Background and Concerns, Carmen D. Solomon 93-897 EPW
* The Earned Income Tax Credit: A Growing Form of Aid to Low-Income Workers, James R. Storey 94-396 EPW
* The Earned Income Tax Credit: A Growing Form of Aid to Low-Income Workers, James R. Storey 95-542 EPW
* The Earned Income Tax Credit: Benefit Amounts, James R. Storey 94-399 EPW
* The Earned Income Tax Credit (EITC) Current Law and the Clinton Proposal: Characteristics of Eligible Families, Thomas Gabe 93-546 EPW
* Family Cash Welfare: Comparison of House-Passed and Senate Finance Committee Versions of H.R. 4, Vee Burke 95-691 EPW
* The Family Preservation and Support Program: Background and Description, Karen Spar 93-967 EPW
* The Family Support Act of 1988: How it Changes the Aid to Families With Dependent Children (AFDC) and Child Support Enforcement Programs, Carmen D. Solomon 88-702 EPW
* Federal Programs for Children and Their Families, Dale Robinson 93-59 EPW
* Federal Programs for Children and Their Families: An Overview, Education and Public Welfare Division, Dale Robinson 93-221 EPW
* Financial Institutions, Community Development, and Fair Lending: Federal Initiatives, F. Jean Wells and William Jackson 94-727 E
* Job Opportunities and Basic (JOBs) Program: Basic Facts, Vee Burke 94-282 EPW
* Poverty and Welfare Among Urban Children: A Fact Sheet, Vee Burke 94-118 EPW
* Supplemental Security Income (SSI) Children: Welfare Reform in the 104th Congress, Carmen D. Solomon 95-402 EPW
* Welfare: A Review of Studies About Time Spent on Welfare, Gene Falk 94-539 EPW
* Welfare Reform and Child Support; Videoprogram, Vee Burke, etc. VT93-1324
* Welfare Reform: FY 1994 Expenditures for Aid to Families With Dependent Children, Gene Falk 95-358 EPW
* Welfare Reform: Implications of H.R. 4 for Child Welfare Services, Karen Spar 95-566 EPW
* Welfare Reform: The Family Cap, Carmen D. Solomon 95-504 EPW

Welfare -- Entitlements
* The Bipartisan Commission on Entitlement and Tax Reform, David Koitz 94-806 EPW
* Entitlement Caps, Jim Cornelius 95-719 EPW
* Entitlement Spending: A Fact Sheet, Richard Rimkunas 94-94 EPW
* Entitlement Spending: Info Pack IP477E
* Entitlements and Other Mandatory Spending, Kenneth R. Cahill and Michele Harlan 94-348 EPW
* Entitlements and the Budget, Videoprogram, Richard Rimkunas and David Koitz VT95-1313
* Entitlements: Brief Descriptions of the Largest Programs, Kenneth Cahill 94-115 EPW

Be patient. If any phone number is incorrect, call (area code) 555-1212 and request the new listing.

* The Largest Entitlement Programs, Kenneth Cahill 93-410 EPW
* Mandatory Spending in President Clinton's FY 1996 Budget Proposal: A Fact Sheet, Dawn Nuschler and Richard Rimkunas 95-277 EPW
* Social Welfare Mandatory and Discretionary Spending in the Fiscal Year 1996 Budget: A Fact Sheet, Dawn Nuschler 95-303 EPW
* Social Welfare Spending in Fiscal Year 1994: A Fact Sheet, Dawn Nuschler 94-864 EPW
* Social Welfare Spending in President Clinton's 1994 Budget Proposal, Gene Falk, etc. 93-397 EPW
* Social Welfare Spending in the Fiscal Year 1996 Budget: A Fact Sheet, Dawn Nuschler, etc. 95-251 EPW
* Social Welfare Spending in the FY 1995 Rescission/Supplemental Appropriations Bill Conference Agreement: A Fact Sheet, Dawn Nuschler 95-619 EPW
* Social Welfare Spending in the FY 1995 Rescission/Supplemental Package: A Fact Sheet, Dawn Nuschler 95-330 EPW
* Social Welfare Spending in the FY 1996 Budget Resolution Conference Agreement, Dawn Nuschler and Richard Rimkunas 95-814 EPW
* Social Welfare Spending in the Senate's FY 1995 Rescissions/Supplemental Appropriations Bill: A Fact Sheet, Dawn Nuschler 95-456 EPW
* Social Welfare Spending Targets in the House Budget Resolution, Dawn Nuschler, etc. 95-586 EPW
* Social Welfare Spending Targets in the Senate Budget Resolution, Dawn Nuschler, etc. 95-587 EPW
* 1995 Budget Perspectives: Federal Spending for Social Welfare Programs, Gene Falk, etc. 94-215 EPW

Welfare -- Reform
* Child Support Enforcement: Welfare Reform in the 104th Congress, Carmen D. Solomon 95-401 EPW
* Clinton Welfare Reform Proposal: Issue Summary, Vee Burke 94-84 EPW
* Federal Budget Chronology Fiscal Year 1996, Carmen D. Solomon and Vee Burke 94-584 EPW
* How States Are Reforming Welfare Through Waivers; Videoprogram, Jennifer Neisner VT95-1327
* Restructuring Human Services: From Waivers to Block Grants; a Checklist of CRS Products, Edith Sutterlin 95-201 L
* Supplemental Security Income (SSI): Comparison of House-Passed and Senate Finance Versions of H.R. 4, Carmen D. Solomon 95-704 EPW
* Supplemental Security Income (SSI) Drug Addicts and Alcoholics: Welfare Reform in the 104th Congress, Carmen D. Solomon 95-433 EPW
* Welfare Proposal in the Contract With America, Vee Burke 94-989 EPW
* Welfare Reform: A Comparison of H.R. 3500 and S. 1795 With Current Policy, Carmen D. Solomon 94-176 EPW
* Welfare Reform: Background and Key Issues, James R. Storey 95-72 EPW
* Welfare Reform: Financing Welfare Through Block Grants, Gene Falk 95-685 EPW
* Welfare Reform: How the House-Passed Bill Would Change Family Cash Welfare, Vee Burke 95-495 EPW
* Welfare Reform: Implications for Federal/State Financing Arrangements, Carmen Solomon, etc. 95-231 EPW
* Welfare Reform: Implications for Work and Welfare, the Role of Work Incentives and Work Requirement, Thomas Gabe and Gene Falk 95-198 EPW
* Welfare Reform: Info Pack IP098W
* Welfare Reform: Issue Brief, Vee Burke IB93034
* Welfare Reform Proposals: Brief Descriptions, Vee Burke 94-638 EPW
* Welfare Reform: The House Passed Bill (H.R. 4), Vee Burke, etc. 95-375 EPW
* Welfare Reform; Videoprogram, Vee Burke, etc. VT95-1306
* Welfare Reforms Proposed by State Commissions, Louisa J. Hierholzer and Carmen D. Solomon 93-969 EPW
* Work Programs for Welfare Recipients: A Look at Past Efforts, Karen Spar 95-761 EPW

West Bank
* see also Middle East and North Africa
* Middle East Peace Prospects: Info Pack IP397M

Western Europe
* see Europe

Wetlands
* see Marine Resources

Whistleblowers
* see Government Employees

White House Conference on Aging
* White House Conference on Aging: Fact Sheet, Carol O'Shaughnessy 94-574 EPW

WIC Program
* see Food

Wilderness Areas
* see Public Lands

Wildlife
* see Animals

Women
* see also Civil Liberties, Civil Rights, Pensions
* Breast Cancer, Judith A. Johnson 94-236 SPR
* Equal Employment Opportunity and Affirmative Action: Bibliography-in-Brief, 1993-1995, Tangela G. Roe 95-371 L
* The Male-Female Wage Gap: A Fact Sheet, Linda Levine 95-661 E
* Minority and Women-Owned Business Programs of the Federal Government, Mark Eddy 95-757 GOV
* Selected Women's Health Conditions: Federal Spending and Prevalence, Science Policy Research Division 93-670 SPR
* Sexual Harassment: A History of Federal Law, Charles V. Dale 93-495 A
* Sexual Harassment in the Workplace: Selected References, 1991-1993, Jean M. Bowers 94-121 L
* U.N. Fourth World Conference on Women, Vita Bite and Lois McHugh 95-607 F
* Violence Against Women: An Overview, Suzanne Cavanagh, etc. 94-142 GOV
* Women Appointed to Full-Time Civilian Positions by President Clinton in 1993, Rogelio Garcia 94-272 GOV
* Women in Armed Forces: Issue Brief, David Burelli IB92008
* Women's Educational Equity Act: An Overview, Laura L. Monagle 94-857 EPW
* Women's Health Research, Judith A. Johnson and Irene-Stith-Coleman 94-495 SPR

Women's Educational Equity Act
* Women's Educational Equity Act: An Overview, Laura L. Monagle 94-857 EPW

Women's Health Issues
* see Women

Workers' Compensation
* see Labor -- Policies and Legislation

World Bank
* Deforestation: An Overview of Global Programs and Agreements, Julie Lyke, etc. 92-764 ENR
* International Financial Institutions and Environment: Multilateral Development Banks and the Global Environment Facility, Susan R. Fletcher and Betsy A. Cody 94-173 ENR
* International Monetary Fund and World Bank: Info Pack IP245I
* Multilateral Development Banks: Issues for the 101st Congress; Archived Issue Brief, Jonathan E. Sanford, IB87218

World Health Organization
* World Health Organization: A Fact Sheet, Lois McHugh, 95-166 F

World Trade Organization
* see also Trade
* Dispute Settlement Under the WTO and Trade Problems With Japan, Dick K. Nanto 95-42 E

Yellowstone National Park
* Reintroduction of Wolves, Jennifer A. Heck 92-524 ENR

Yemen
* see Middle East and North Africa

Youth Employment
* see Labor

Yugoslavia (Former)
* see Bosnia-Hercegovina

Be patient. If any phone number is incorrect, call (area code) 555-1212 and request the new listing.

1355

Current Events and Homework

Audio Brief List

Agriculture and the Environment: Audio Brief, AB50303
Asia Trade, Foreign Policy, and Security Issues: Audio Brief, AB50312
Brazil-U.S. Relations: Audio Brief, AB50324
1995 Farm Bill: The Economic Setting; Audio Brief, AB50308
1995 Farm Bill: The Policy Setting: Audio Brief, AB50309
Campaign Activities by Congressional Staff: Audio Brief, AB50118
Congressional Casework: Approaches and Considerations; Audio Brief, AB50254
Congressional Oversight: Audio Brief, AB50319
Economic Principles for Deficit Reduction: Audio Brief, AB50318
Health Care Reform: Audio Brief, AB50315
Japanese Investment in Asia: Audio Brief, AB50322
Latin America: Key Issues in U.S. Policy; Audio Brief, AB50314
Medicaid Program: Audio Brief, AB50316
Middle East Peace and Security Issues: Audio Brief, AB50311
Monitoring Foreign Elections: Audio Brief, AB50300
North Korea After Kim Il Sung: Audio Brief, AB50305
Property Rights Issue: Audio Brief, AB50317
Recycled Content Legislation: Audio Brief, AB50241
South Africa's Elections: Economic Problems and Prospects; Audio Brief AB50298
The Supreme Court Appointment Process: Audio Brief, AB50276
U.S. Policy Towards Iraq: Audio Brief, AB50323

Info Pack Listing

Abortion: Info Pack, IP001A
Affirmative Action: Info Pack, IP424A
Aged: Info Pack, IP003A
Agriculture: The 1995 Farm Bill; Info Pack, IP295A
AIDS: Acquired Immune Deficiency Syndrome; Info Pack, IP261A
Air Pollution-Clean Air Act: Info Pack, IP008A
The Americans With Disabilities Act: Info Pack, IP443A
Americorps National Service Programs: Info Pack, IP475N
Balanced Budget Issues: Info Pack, IP463B
Ballistic Missile Defenses: Info Pack, IP496B
Banking in the United States: An Overview, Info Pack, IB429B
Black History Month: Info Pack, IP344B
Bosnia-Former Yugoslavia: Civil War in the Balkans: Info Pack, IP466B
Budget for Fiscal Year 1995: An Overview: Info Pack, IP483B
Budget for FY 1996: Info Pack, IP502B
Budget Process: Info Pack, IP012B
Business: Doing Business With the Federal Government; Info Pack, IP305B
Cable TV: Info Pack, IP104C
Campaign Finance: Info Pack, IP014C
Capital Punishment: Info Pack, IP015C
Career Guidance and Federal Job Information: Info Pack, IP016C
Child Abuse; Info Pack, IP019C
Child Day Care: Info Pack, IP306C
Children's Rights: United Nations Convention on the Rights of the Child, IP493C
China-U.S. Relations in a Post-Cold War World, IP460C
China-U.S. Trade, MFN Status, and Economic Relations, IP489C
Congress: Info Pack, IP022C
Congress: Issues for the 104th Congress; Info Pack, IP497C
Congressional Office Operations: Info Pack, IP151C
Congressional Reform, IP462C
Constitution of the United States: Its History, Development, and Amending Process; Info Pack, IP339C
Crime Control: Federal Initiatives; Info Pack IP310C
Defense Conversion, IP474D
Defense Spending: Info Pack, IP434D
Deficit Reduction Issues: Info Pack, IP488D
Drug Abuse in America: Info Pack, IP303D
Drug Abuse: Treatment, Prevention and Education: Info Pack, IP400D
Drug Control: Existing Federal Laws and Pending Legislation, Info Pack IP030D
Education: Funding Issues: Info Pack, IP199E
Education: Issues of Quality and Reform; Info Pack IP256E
El Salvador: Info Pack, IP121E
Endangered Species: Info Pack, IP192E
Energy Policy: Info Pack, IP447E
Entitlement Spending, IP477E
European Community: The Economic Integration Info Pack, IP408E
Family Leave, IP237F
Federal Reserve System: Info Pack, IP105F
Financial Aid for Students; Info Pack, IP042F

The Flag: Info Pack, IP365F
Flag Etiquette: Info Pack IP365F
Foreign Aid: Info Pack, IP044F
Foreign Policy: Info Pack, IP297F
GATT: General Agreement on Tariffs and Trade IP481G
Government Publications--How, What, When, Where, and Why: Info Pack, IP264G
Grants and Foundation Support: Info Pack, IP050G
Greenhouse Effect and Ozone Depletion: Info Pack, IP405G
Gun Control: Info Pack, IP051G
Haiti: Info Pack, IP479H
Hazardous Waste and the Superfund Program; Info Pack, IP094H
Health Care Reform: Overview of Major Proposals: Info Pack, IP421H
Health Care Costs: Info Pack, IP223H
Health Insurance: Employer Benefits Required under COBRA: Info Pack, IP389H
Health: Long-Term Care: Info Pack, IP402H
Homeless in America: Info Pack, IP314H
Hotlines and Other Useful Government Telephone Numbers: Info Pack, IP106H
Housing Policy and Implications for Current Programs; Info Pack, IP417H
How to Follow Current Federal Legislation and Regulations: Info Pack, IP122H
Immigration and Refugee Policy: Info Pack, IP164I
Immigration: the Economic Impact: Info Pack, IP491I
Immigration: Proposition 187: Info Pack, IP495I
Information Superhighway and the Internet: Info Pack, IP490I
International Monetary Fund and World Bank: Info Pack, IP245I
Internships and Fellowships: Info Pack, IP063I
Japan-U.S. Trade and Economic Relations: Info Pack, IP201J
Jobs: The Employment Situation and Job Training Programs: Info Pack, IP246J
Korean Peninsula Tensions: North Korea and Nuclear Weapons: Info Pack, IP484K
Legislative Procedure: An Introduction; Info Pack, IP247L
Legislative Research: A Guide to Conducting Legislative Research in a Congressional Office; Info Pack, IP321L
Line Item Veto: Info Pack, IP287L
Lobbying: Info Pack, IP066L
Medicaid: An Overview: Info Pack, IP066L
Medicare: An Overview: Info pack, IP467M
Medicare Payments to Hospitals and Physicians: Info Pack, IP317M
Mexico: Problems and Prospects: Info Pack, IP358M
Middle East Peace Prospects: Info Pack, IP397M
NAFTA: The North American Free Trade Agreement: Info Pack, IP445N
National Performance Review: Info Pack, IP478N
Native American Heritage,: Info Pack IP425N
NATO: Conventional Arms Control and Related Political Issues: Info Pack, IP425N
Nuclear Energy: Safety and Waste Issues; Info Pack, IP074N
Peacekeeping: PDD-25 and Issues for Congress: Info Pack IP492P
Pension Issues; Info Pack IP428P
Political Action Committees (PACs): Info Pack, IP196P
Property Rights Issues: Info Pack, IP504P
Recycling: Info Pack, IP437R
Retirement Systems for Federal Employees: Info Pack, IP205R
Risk Assessment: Info Pack, IP503R
Russia and the Commonwealth of Independent States: Info Pack, IP233R
School Prayer: Info Pack, IP494S
Small Business Assistance Programs Sources of Information: Info Pack, IP422S
Smoking Federal Actions: Info Pack, IP486S
Social Security: Current Issues, Benefits and Financing: Info Pack, IP153S
Social Security Financing and Taxation: Recent Issues; Info Pack, IP435S
Social Security: National Committee to Preserve Social Security and Medicare; Info Pack, IP345S
The Social Security "Notch": Info Pack, IP266S
Solid Waste Management: Info Pack, IP396S
South Africa: The Current Situation: Info Pack, IP340S
Speech Material: Abraham Lincoln's and George Washington's Birthdays; Info Pack, IP373A
Speech Material: Captive Nations Week: Info Pack, IP375C
Speech Material; Columbus Day; Info Pack IP380C
Speech Material: Fourth of July; Info Pack, IP377F
Speech Material: Graduation; Info Pack, IB379G
Speech Material: Labor Day; Info Pack, IP374L
Speech Material: Martin Luther King's Birthday; Info Pack, IP372M
Speech Material: Thanksgiving Day; Info Pack, IP381T
Speech Material: Veterans Day; Info Pack, IP378V
Speechwriting and Delivery: Info Pack, IP139S
Tax Proposals: 104th Congress: Info Pack, IP501T
Telephone Industry Issues: Info Pack, IP257T
Television Violence: Info Pack, IP439T
Term Limits; Info Pack IP439T
Terrorism: Info Pack, IP299T

Trade Issues and Trade Deficits: Background, Statistics, and Proposed Legislation:
Info Pack, IP263T
U.S. Government: Info Pack, IP162U
War Powers Resolution: Info Pack, IP131W

Washington, DC and the U.S. Capitol Building: Info Pack, IP132W
Water Resources: Quality and Quantity: Info Pack, IP369W
Welfare and Poverty: Info Pack, IP098W
Wetlands Issues: Info Pack, IP423W

Be patient. If any phone number is incorrect, call (area code) 555-1212 and request the new listing.

1357

11,500 Free Experts
Acronyms

You may have heard of the "seven-phone call rule" for tracking down an expert who will help you for free. Well, now you can throw that phrase out the window. With this handy list of 11,500 government experts you are likely to find the right subject specialist in only ONE phone call.

Do you have a new idea to revolutionize the crayon market? Shetty Sundar at the U.S. International Trade Commission has spent her career analyzing this market. Want to know how many women-owned businesses there are in the United States? Contact Elaine Emanuel at the Bureau of Census and she will give you the official data. You'll find 60 bureaucrats listed in this chapter who are experts in computers and the computer industry. You will also find experts on sewing machines, eggs, fish nets, and robots. Remember each of these professionals has devoted his or her life work to studying a specific area and will share their knowledge without charging a penny **just as long as you treat them right.** (Refer to the *Information is Power* chapter for guidance on how to deal with bureaucrats.)

The abbreviations for the federal agency which precede an expert's telephone number are spelled out below. If you have trouble with a telephone number, after all, numbers change all the time, simply contact the agency directly.

AAAI =	American Academy of Allergy and Immunology, 611 East Wells Street, Milwaukee, WI 53202, 800-822-2762
AAF =	Aplastic Anemia Foundation of America, P.O. Box 22689, Baltimore, MD 21201, 800-747-2820
AAFP =	American Academy of Family Physicians, 8880 Ward Pkwy., Kansas City, MO 64114, 800-274-2237
AAKP =	American Association of Kidney Patients, 100 S. Ashley Dr., Suite 280, Tampa, FL 33602, 800-749-2257
AAPS =	Association of American Physicians and Surgeons, 1601 North Tucson Boulevard, Suite 9, Tucson, AZ 85716, 800-635-1196
AARP =	American Association of Retired Parents, 601 E Street, NW, Washington, DC 20049, 800-424-2277
ABLEDATA =	ABLEDATA, 8455 Colesville Road, Suite 935, Silver Spring, MD 20910, 800-227-0126
ABTA =	American Brain Tumor Association, 2720 River Road, Suite 146, Des Plaines, IL 60018, 800-886-2282
ACA =	American Council on Alcoholism, 5024 Campbell Boulevard, Suite H, Baltimore, MD 21236, 800-527-5344
ACB =	American Council of the Blind (ACB), 1155 15th Street, Suite 720, NW, Washington, DC 20005, 800-424-8666
ACCESS =	The Access Group, 1776 Peachtree Road, NW, Atlanta, GA 30309, 800-821-8580
ACED =	Advocacy Center for the Elderly and Disabled, 210 O'Keefe Avenue, Suite 700, New Orleans, LA 70112, 800-960-7705
ACLM =	American College of Legal Medicine, 611 East Wells St., Milwaukee, WI 53202, 800-433-9137
ACP =	American College of Physicians, Independence Mall West, Sixth Street at Race, Philadelphia, PA 19106, 800-523-1546
ACS =	American Cancer Society, 1599 Clifton Road, NE, Atlanta, GA 30329, 800-227-2345
ACTIS =	AIDS Clinical Trials Information Service, P.O. Box 6421, Rockville, MD 20849, 800-874-2572
ACYF =	Administration for Children and Youth and Families, HHS, 901 D St., SW, Washington, DC 20447, 202-401-9200
ADEAR =	Alzheimer's Disease Education and Referral (ADEAR) Center, P.O. Box 8250, Silver Spring, MD 20907, 800-438-4380
ADH =	Alcohol and Drug Helpline, 4578 Highland Drive, Salt Lake City, UT 84117, 800-821-4357
AERO =	Aeronational (Air ambulance transport), P.O. Box 538, Washington, PA 15301, 800-245-9987
AF =	Arthritis Foundation, 1314 Spring Street NW, Atlanta, GA 30309, 800-283-7800
AFB =	American Foundation for the Blind, 15 West 16th Street, New York, NY 10011, 800-232-5463
AGING =	Delaware Division of Aging, Department of Health and Social Services, 1901 North Dupont Highway, New Castle, DE 19720, 800-223-9074
AGRI =	National Agriculture Statistics Service, U.S. Dept. of Agriculture, 14th and Independence Ave., SW, Washington, DC 20250, 202-219-0610
AGSG =	Alliance of Genetic Support Groups, 35 Wisconsin Circle, Suite 440, Chevy Chase, MD 20815, 800-336-4363
AHA =	American Heart Association, 415 North Charles Street, P.O. Box 17025, Baltimore, MD 21203, 800-242-8721
AHASC =	American Heart Association Stroke Connection, 7272 Greenville Avenue, Dallas, TX 75231, 800-553-6321
AHCPR =	Agency for Health Care Policy and Research, HHS, 2101 East Jefferson St., Ste. 501, Rockville, MD 20852, 301-594-1364
AHCPR =	AHCPR Clearinghouse, P.O. Box 8547, Silver Spring, MD 20907, 301-594-1364
AID =	Agency for International Development, 2201 C Street NW, Washington, DC 20523, 202-647-9620
AID ATLANTA =	AID Atlanta, 1438 West Peachtree Street, NW, Atlanta, GA 30309, 800-551-2728
AIDS =	AIDS Action Committee of Massachusetts, 131 Clarendon Street, Boston, MA 02116, 800-669-0696
AIPM =	American Institute for Preventive Medicine, 30445 Northwestern Highway, Suite 350, Farmingham Hills, MI 48334, 800-345-2476
Air AA =	Air Ambulance America, 5804 Sunset Drive, Miami, FL 33156, 800-262-8526
AKF =	American Kidney Fund, 6110 Executive Blvd, Suite 1010, Rockville, MD 20852, 800-638-8299
ALM =	ALM International (American Leprosy Missions), One ALM Way, Greenville, SC 29601, 800-537-7679
Al-Anon =	Alateen Family Group Hotline, P.O. Box 862, Midtown Station, New York, NY 10018-0862, 800-344-2666
ALS =	American Lupus Society, 3914 Del Arno Blvd., Suite 922, Torrance, CA 90503, 800-331-1802
ALSA =	Amyotrophic Lateral Sclerosis Association, 21021 Ventura Boulevard, Suite 321, Woodland Hills, CA 91364, 800-782-4747
Alz. Assc. =	Alzheimer's Association, 919 N. Michigan Ave., Suite 1000, Chicago, IL 60611, 800-272-3900

AMC =	AMC Cancer Information and Counseling Line, 1600 Pierce Street, Denver, CO 80214, 800-525-3777
AMHCA =	American Mental Health Counselors Association, 5999 Stevenson Avenue, Alexandria, VA 22304, 800-326-2642
AOA =	Administration on Aging, HHS, 330 Independence Avenue, Washington, DC 20201, 202-619-0556
APA =	American Paralysis Association, 500 Morris Avenue, Springfield, NJ 07081, 800-225-0292
APDA =	American Parkinson's Disease Association, 60 Bay Street, Suite 401, Staten Island, NY 10301, 800-223-2732
ARE =	Alcohol Rehab for the Elderly , P.O. Box 267, Hopedale, IL 61747, 800-354-7089
Arthritis =	Arthritis Consulting Service, 4620 North State Road 7, Suite 206, Ft. Lauderdale, FL 33319, 800-327-3027
ASDS =	American Society for Dermatologic Surgery, 930 Meachum, Schaumburg, IL 60173, 800-441-2737
ASH =	Assistant Secretary for Health, U.S. Department of Health and Human Services, 200 Independence Avenue, SW, Room 719-H, Hubert Humphrey Bldg., Washington, DC 20201, 202-401-9215
ASHA =	American Social Health Association, P.O. Box 13827, Research Triangle Park, NC 27709, 800-227-8922
ASLHA =	American Speech-Language-Hearing Association Consumer Hotline, 10801 Rockville Pike, Kensington, MD 20852, 800-638-8255
ASA =	Ankylosing Spondylitis Association, 511 North La Cienga, Suite 216, Los Angeles, CA 90048, 800-777-8189
ASPO =	American Society for Psychoprophylaxis in Obstetrics (ASPO/Lamaze), 1200 19th Street, Suite 300, NW, Washington, DC 20036, 800-368-4404
ASPRS =	American Society of Plastic and Reconstructive Surgeons, 444 East Algonquin Road, Arlington Heights, IL 60005, 800-635-0635
AST =	Association of Surgical Technologists, 7108 S. Alton Way, Englewood, CO, 80112, 800-637-7433
ASTHMA =	Asthma and Allergy Foundation of America, 1125 15th Street, Suite 502, NW, Washington, DC 20005, 800-727-8462
ATRIAL-FIB =	Atrial Fibrillation (AF) Hotline, 625 N. Michigan Ave., Chicago, IL 60611, 800-423-1925
ATS =	American Trauma Society, 8903 Presidential Parkway, Suite 512, Upper Marlboro, MD 20772, 800-556-7890
ATSDR =	Agency for Toxic Substances and Disease Registry, HHS, 1600 Clifton Rd., NE, Mail Stop 828, Atlanta, GA 30333, 404-639-0727
BACK PAIN =	Back Pain Hotline, 3801 West 15th Street, Plano, TX 75075, 800-247-2225
BATTEN =	Batten Disease Support and Research Association, 2600 Parsons Ave., Columbus, OH 43207, 800-448-4570
BCC =	Blind Children's Center, 4120 Marathon St., P.O. Box 29159, Los Angeles, CA 90029, 800-222-3566
BE HEALTHY =	Be Healthy Inc., 51 Saltrock Road, Baltic, CT 06330, 800-433-5523
BEHCETS =	American Behcet's Association Inc.,P.O. Box 54963, Minneapolis, MN 55454, 800-723-4238
BEIB =	Biomedical Engineering and Instrumentation Branch, NIH, 9000 Rockville Pike, Bldg. 13, Bethesda, MD 20892, 301-496-1131
BHCDA =	Bureau of Health Care Delivery and Assistance, HHS, 5600 Fishers Lane, Room 7-05, Rockville, MD 20857, 301-443-3376
BJSCONTA =	U.S. Department of Justice, 10th and Constitution Avenue, NW, Washington, DC 20530, 202-514-2000
BMS =	American Board of Medical Specialists, 47 Perimeter Center East, Suite 500, Atlanta, GA 30346, 800-776-2378
BRAILLE =	Braille Institute, 741 North Vermont Avenue, Los Angeles, CA 90029, 800-272-4533
BVA =	Blinded Veterans Association, 477 H Street, NW, Washington DC 20001, 800-669-7079
CAF =	Cooley's Anemia Foundation, 29-09 26th Avenue, Flushing, NY 11354, 800-221-3571
CAN =	National Resource Center on Child Abuse and Neglect, 63 Inverness Drive East, Englewood, CO 80112, 800-227-5242
CC =	Clinical Center, NIH, 9000 Rockville Pike, Bldg. 10, Bethesda, MD 20892, 301-496-4251
CCA =	Children's Craniofacial Association, 10210 North Central Expressway, Suite 230, Dallas, TX 75231, 800-535-3643
CCCF =	Candlelighters Childhood Cancer Foundation, 7910 Woodmont Avenue, Suite 400, Bethesda, MD 20814, 800-366-2223
CCFA =	Crohn's and Colitis Foundation of America, 386 Park Avenue South, 17th Floor, New York, NY 10016-8804, 800-932-2423
CDC =	Centers for Disease Control, HHS, Room 2067, Bldg. 1, Atlanta, GA 30333, 404-639-3286
CDCC =	CDC National AIDS Clearinghouse, P.O. Box 6003, Rockville, MD 20849, 800-458-5231
CENSUS =	Data Users Service Division, Customer Service, Bureau of Census, U.S. Department of Commerce, Washington, DC 20233, 301-457-4100
CFF =	Cystic Fibrosis Foundation, 6931 Arlington Road, Bethesda, MD 20814, 800-344-4823
CFIDS =	Chronic Fatigue and Immune Dysfunction Syndrome Association (CFIDS), P.O. Box 220398, Charlotte, NC 28222, 800-442-3437
CH =	Child Help USA, 6463 Independence Avenue, Woodland Hills, CA 91367, 800-422-4453
CHI =	Children's Hospice International, 700 Princess Street, Alexandria, VA 22314, 800-242-4453
CHILD =	Child Find of America, P.O. Box 277, New Paltz, NY 12561, 800-426-5678
CHILDWATCH =	Childwatch, P.O. Box 1368, Jackson, MI 49204, 800-222-1464
Chiro Assc =	American Chiropractic Association, 1701 Clarendon Blvd., Arlington, VA 22209, 800-327-1129
CIRC =	Chemical Information Referral Center, 2501 M St., NW, Washington, DC 20037, 800-262-8200
CLMA =	Contact Lens Manufacturers Association, 421 King St., Suite 224, Alexandria, VA 22314, 800-343-5367
CLSF =	Cornelia de Lange Syndrome Foundation, 60 Dyer Ave., Collinsville, CT 06022, 800-223-8355
CNTYCOM =	Country Desk Officers, International Trade Administration, U.S. Department of Commerce, Washington, DC 20230, 202-482-3809
CNTYMINE =	Bureau of Mines, U.S. Department of Interior, 810 7th St., NW, Washington, DC 20241, 202-501-9649
CNTY STATE =	United States Department of State, 2201 C St., NW, Washington, DC 20520, 202-647-6407
COCAINE =	Cocaine Anonymous, 3740 Overland Avenue, Suite G, Los Angeles, CA 90034, 800-347-8998
COMMERCE =	Industry Experts, Public Affairs, International Trade Administration, U.S. Department of Commerce, Washington, DC 20230, 202-482-3809
CPF =	Cleft Palate Foundation, 1218 Grandview Avenue, Pittsburgh, PA 15211, 800-242-5338
CPSC =	Consumer Product Safety Commission, 4330 East West Highway, Bethesda, MD 20814, 800-638-2772
CR =	Child Research, 155 Plan Way, Warwick, RI 02886, 800-556-7918
CRNL =	American Institute for Cancer Research Nutrition Line, 1759 R. Street NW, Washington, DC 20009, 800-843-8114
CUSTOMS =	U.S. Customs Service, Department of the Treasury, Customs Information Exchange, U.S. Customhouse, Code 20437, 6 World Trade Center, New York, NY 10048, 212-466-3956
DAS =	Division of Administrative Services, NIH, Building 1, 9000 Rockville Pike, Bethesda, MD 20892, 301-496-5787
DC =	District of Columbia

11,500 Free Experts

DCRT =	Division of Computer Research and Technology, NIH, 9000 Rockville Pike, Bethesda, MD 20892, 301-496-2122
DEO =	Division of Equal Opportunity, NIH, 9000 Rockville Pike, Bldg. 31, Bethesda, MD 20892, 301-496-6301
DF =	Devereux Foundation, 19 South Waterloo Road, Devon, PA 19333, 800-345-1292
Diabetes =	American Diabetes Association, 1660 Duke Street, Alexandria, VA 22314, 800-232-3472
DIET =	Nutrition Information Service, Univ. of Alabama at Birmingham, Webb Bldg., Room 447, UAB Station, Birmingham, AL 35294, 800-231-3438
DMCH =	Division of Maternal and Child Health, HHS, 5600 Fishers Lane, Rockville, MD 20857, 301-443-2250
DN =	Division of Nursing, HHS, 5600 Fishers Lane, Rockville, MD 20857, 202-401-9215
DOT =	Department of Transportation, 400 7th Street, SW, Washington, DC 20590, 202-366-4570
DPCS =	Division of Primary Care Services, HHS, 5600 Fishers Lane, Rockville, MD 20857, 301-443-2403
DPM =	Division of Personnel Management, NIH, 9000 Rockville Pike, Bldg. 1, Bethesda, MD 20892, 301-496-2400
DRF =	Deafness Research Foundation, Nine E. 38th St., 7th Fl., New York, NY 10016, 800-535-3323
DRG =	Division of Research Grants, NIH, 9000 Rockville Pike, Bldg. 31, Bethesda, MD 20892, 301-594-7248
DRR =	Division of Research Resources, NIH, 9000 Rockville Pike, Bldg. 31, Bethesda, MD 20892, 301-594-2000
DRS =	Division of Research Services, NIH, 9000 Rockville Pike, Bldg. 12, Room 4007, Bethesda, MD 20892, 301-496-4131
ECONOMICS =	Bureau of Economic Analysis, U.S. Department of Commerce, Washington, DC 20230, 202-606-9900
EFA =	Epilepsy Foundation of America, 4351 Garden City Dr., Suite 406, Landover, MD 20785, 800-332-1000
ELDERCARE =	Eldercare Locator, 1112 16th Street, Suite 100, NW, Washington, DC 20036, 800-677-1116
ELDERCARE I =	Sound Options, Inc., (Eldercare issues), 917 Pacific Avenue, Suite 608, Tacoma, WA 98402, 800-628-7649
Emb. Afghan. =	Afghanistan, Republic of, 2341 Wyoming Avenue, NW, Washington, DC 20008, 202-234-3770
Emb. Albania =	Albania, Republic of, 1511 K Street, NW, Suite 1010, Washington, DC 20005, 202-223-4942
Emb. Algeria =	Algeria, Democratic & Popular Republic of, 2118 Kalorama Road, NW, Washington, DC 20008, 202-265-2800
Emb. Angola =	Angola, Republic of, 1899 L Street, NW, Suite 400, Washington, DC 20036, 202-785-1156
Emb. Antigua =	Antigua and Barbuda, Suite 4M, 3400 International Dr., NW, Washington, DC 20008, 202-362-5211
Emb. Arg. =	Argentine Republic, 1600 New Hampshire Avenue, NW, Washington, DC 20009, 202-939-6400
Emb. Armenia =	Armenia, Republic of, 1660 L Street, NW, Suite 210, Washington, DC 20036, 202-628-5766
Emb. Austral.=	Australia, 1601 Massachusetts Avenue, NW, Washington, DC 20036, 202-797-3000
Emb. Austria =	Austria, 3524 International Court, NW, Washington, DC 20008, 202-895-6700
Emb. Azerbaijan =	Azerbaijan, Republic of, 927 15th Street, Suite 700, Washington, DC 20005, 202-842-0001
Emb. Bahamas =	Bahamas, Commonwealth of The, 2220 Massachusetts Avenue, NW, Washington, DC 20008, 202-319-2660
Emb. Bahrain =	Bahrain, State of, 3502 International Drive, NW, Washington, DC 20008, 202-342-0741
Emb. Bangladesh =	Bangladesh, People's Republic of, 2201 Wisconsin Ave., NW, Washington, DC 20007, 202-342-8372
Emb. Barbados =	Barbados, 2144 Wyoming Avenue, NW, Washington, DC 20008, 202-939-9200
Emb. Belarus =	Belarus, Republic of, Suite 1619, New Hampshire Ave., NW, Washington, DC 20009, 202-986-1604
Emb. Belgium =	Belgium, 3330 Garfield Street, NW, Washington, DC 20008, 202-333-6900
Emb. Belize =	Belize, 2535 Massachusetts Avenue, NW, Washington, DC 20008, 202-332-9636
Emb. Benin =	Benin, Republic of, 2737 Cathedral Avenue, NW, Washington, DC 20008, 202-232-6656
Emb. Bolivia =	Bolivia, 3014 Massachusetts Avenue, NW, Washington, DC 20008, 202-483-4410
Emb. Bosnia =	Bosnia and Herzegovina, 1707 L Street, Suite 760, NW, Washington, DC 20036, 202-833-3612
Emb. Botswana =	Botswana, Republic of, 3400 International Drive, Suite 7M, NW, Washington, DC 20008, 202-244-4990
Emb. Brazil =	Brazil, 3006 Massachusetts Avenue, NW, Washington, DC 20008, 202-745-2700
Emb. Brunei =	Brunei, State of Brunei Darussalam, 2600 Virginia Avenue, Suite 300, NW, Washington, DC 20037, 202-342-0159
Emb. Bulgaria =	Bulgaria, Republic of, 1621 22nd Street, NW, Washington, DC 20008, 202-387-7969
Emb. Burkina Faso =	Burkina Faso, 2340 Massachusetts Avenue, NW, Washington, DC 20008, 202-332-5577
Emb. Burundi =	Burundi, Republic of, 2233 Wisconsin Ave., Suite 212, NW, Washington, DC 20007, 202-342-2574
Emb. Cameroon =	Cameroon, Republic of, 2349 Massachusetts Ave., NW, Washington, DC 20008, 202-265-8790
Emb. Canada =	Canada, 501 Pennsylvania Avenue, NW, Washington, DC 20001, 202-682-1740
Emb. Cape Verde =	Cape Verde, Republic of, 3415 Massachusetts Ave., NW, Washington, DC 20007, 202-965-6820
Emb. CAR =	Central African Republic, 1618 22nd Street, NW, Washington, DC 20008, 202-483-7800
Emb. Chad =	Chad, Republic of, 2002 R Street, NW, Washington, DC 20009, 202-462-4009
Emb. Chile =	Chile, 1732 Massachusetts Avenue, NW, Washington, DC 20036, 202-785-1746
Emb. China =	China, People's Republic of, 2300 Connecticut Ave., NW, Washington, DC 20008, 202-328-2500
Emb. Colombia =	Colombia, 2118 Leroy Place, NW, Washington, DC 20008, 202-387-8338
Emb. Comoros =	Comoros, Federal and Islamic Republic of the, 336 E 45th, 2nd Floor, New York City, NY 10017, 212-
Emb. Congo =	Congo, Republic of, 4891 Colorado Avenue, NW, Washington, DC 20011, 202-726-0825
Emb. Costa Rica =	Costa Rica, 2114 South Street, NW Washington, DC 20008, 202-234-2945
Emb. Cote d' Ivore =	Cote d'Ivoire, Republic of 2424 Massachusetts Ave., NW, Washington, DC 20008, 202-797-0300
Emb. Croatia =	Croatia, Republic of, 2343 Massachusetts Ave., NW, Washington, DC 20008, 202-588-5899
Emb. Cyprus =	Cyprus, Republic of, 2211 R St., NW, Washington, DC 20008, 202-462-5772
Emb. Czech Rep. =	Czech Republic, 3900 Spring of Freedom Street, NW, Washington, DC 20008, 202-363-6315
Emb. Denmark =	Denmark, 3200 Whitehaven Street, NW, Washington, DC 20008, 202-234-4300
Emb. Djibouti =	Djibouti, Republic of, 1156 15th Street, Suite, 515, NW, Washington, DC 20005, 202-331-0270
Emb. Dom. Rep. =	Dominican Republic, 1715 22nd Street, NW, Washington DC 20008, 202-332-6280
Emb. Ecuador =	Ecuador, 2535 15th Street, NW, Washington, DC 20009, 202-234-7200

Be patient. If any phone number is incorrect, call (area code) 555-1212 and request the new listing.

Emb. Egypt =	Egypt, Arab Republic of, 3521 International Court, NW, Washington, DC 20008, 202-895-5400
Emb. El Salvador =	El Salvador, 2308 California Street, NW, Washington, DC 20008, 202-265-9671
Emb. Equat. Guinea =	Equatorial Guinea (temporary), 57 Magnolia Avenue, Mt. Vernon, NY 10553, 914-738-9584
Emb. Eriteria =	Eriteria, State of, 910 17th Street, Suite 400, NW, Washington, DC 20006, 202-429-1991
Emb. Estonia =	Estonia, 1030 15th Street, Suite 1000, NW, Washington, DC 20005, 202-789-0320
Emb. Ethiopia =	Ethiopia, 2134 Kalorama Road, NW, Washington, DC 20008, 202-234-2281
Emb. Fiji =	Fiji, Republic of, 2233 Wisconsin Ave., Suite 240, NW, Washington, DC 20007, 202-337-8320
Emb. Finland =	Finland, 3301 Massachusetts Avenue, NW, Washington, DC 20008, 202-298-5800
Emb. France =	France, 4101 Reservoir Road, NW, Washington, DC 20007, 202-944-6000
Emb. Gabon. =	Gabonese Republic, 2233 Wisconsin Ave., Suite 200, NW, Washington, DC 20007, 202-797-1000
Emb. Gambia =	Gambia, 1155 - 15th Street, Suite 1000, NW, Washington, DC 20005, 202-785-1399
Emb. Georgia =	Georgia, Republic of (temporary), 1511 K St., Suite 424, NW, Washington, DC 20005, 202-393-6060
Emb. Germany =	Germany, Federal Republic of, 4645 Reservoir Rd., NW, Washington, DC 20007, 202-298-4000
Emb. Ghana =	Ghana, 3512 International Drive, NW, Washington, DC 20008, 202-686-4520
Emb. Greece =	Greece, 2221 Massachusetts Avenue, NW, Washington, DC 20008, 202-939-5800
Emb. Grenada =	Grenada, 1701 New Hampshire Avenue, NW, Washington, DC 20009, 202-265-2561
Emb. Guatem. =	Guatemala, 2220 R Street, NW, Washington, DC 20008, 202-745-4952
Emb. Guinea =	Guinea, Republic of, 2112 Leroy Place, NW, Washington, DC 20008, 202-483-9420
Emb. Guin.-Biss. =	Guinea-Bissau, Republic of, 918 16th Street, NW, Washington, DC 20006, 202-872-4222
Emb. Guyana =	Guyana, 2490 Tracy Place, NW, Washington, DC 20008, 202-265-6900
Emb. Haiti =	Haiti, Republic of, 2311 Massachusetts Avenue, NW, Washington, DC 20008, 202-332-4090
Emb. Holy See =	Holy See, The Apostolic Nunciature, 3339 Massachusetts Avenue, NW, Washington, DC 20008, 202-333-7121
Emb. Hond. =	Honduras, 3007 Tilden Street, NW, Washington, DC 20008, 202-966-7702
Emb. Hungary =	Hungary, Republic of, 3910 Shoemaker Street, NW, Washington, DC 20008, 202-362-6730
Emb. Iceland =	Iceland, 2022 Connecticut Avenue, NW, Washington, DC 20008, 202-265-6653
Emb. India =	India, 2107 Massachusetts Avenue, NW, Washington, DC 20008, 202-939-7000
Emb. Indon. =	Indonesia, Republic of, 2020 Massachusetts Ave., NW, Washington, DC 20036, 202-775-5200
Emb. Iranian =	Iranian Interests Section, 2209 Wisconsin Avenue, NW, Washington, DC 20007, 202-965-4990
Emb. Ireland =	Ireland, 2234 Massachusetts Avenue, NW, Washington, DC 20008, 202-462-3939
Emb. Israel =	Israel, 3514 International Drive, NW, Washington, DC 20008, 202-364-5500
Emb. Italy =	Italy, 1601 Fuller Street, NW, Washington, DC 20009, 202-328-5500
Emb. Jamaica =	Jamaica, 1520 New Hampshire Avenue, NW, Washington, DC 20036, 202-452-0660
Emb. Japan =	Japan, 2520 Massachusetts Avenue, NW, Washington, DC 20008, 202-939-6700
Emb. Jordan =	Jordan, Hashemite Kingdom of, 3504 International Dr., NW, Washington, DC 20008, 202-966-2664
Emb. Kazakh. =	Kazakhstan, Republic of, 3421 Massachusetts Ave., NW, Washington, DC 20008, 202-333-4504
Emb. Kenya =	Kenya, Republic of, 2249 R Street, NW, Washington, DC 20008, 202-387-6101
Emb. Korea =	Korea, 2450 Massachusetts Avenue, NW, Washington, DC 20008, 202-524-9273
Emb. Krgyzs. =	Kyrgyzstan, Kyrgz Republic, 1511 K St., Suite 706, NW Washington, DC 20005, 202-347-3732
Emb. Laos =	Laos, Lao People's Democratic Republic, 222 S St., NW, Washington, DC 20008, 202-332-6416
Emb. Latvia =	Latvia, 4325 17th Street, NW, Washington, DC 20011, 202-726-8213
Emb. Lebanon =	Lebanon, 2560 28th Street, NW, Washington, DC 20008, 202-939-6300
Emb. Lesotho =	Lesotho, Kingdom of, 2511 Massachusetts Avenue, NW, Washington, DC 20008, 202-797-5533
Emb. Liberia =	Liberia, Republic of, 5201 16th Street, NW, Washington, DC 20011, 202-723-0437
Emb. Lithuania =	Lithuania, Republic of, 2622 16th Street, NW, Washington, DC 20009, 202-234-5860
Emb. Luxemb. =	Luxembourg, 2200 Massachusetts Avenue, NW, Washington, DC 20008, 202-265-4171
Emb. Madagas. =	Madagascar, Democratic Republic of, 2374 Massachusetts Avenue, NW, Washington, DC 20008, 202-265-5525
Emb. Malawai =	Malawi, 2408 Massachusetts Avenue, NW, Washington, DC 20008, 202-797-1007
Emb. Malaysia =	Malaysia, 2401 Massachusetts Avenue, NW, Washington, DC 20008, 202-328-2700
Emb. Mali =	Mali, Republic of, 2130 R Street, NW, Washington, DC 20008, 202-332-2249
Emb. Malta =	Malta, 2017 Connecticut Avenue, NW, Washington, DC 20008, 202-462-3611
Emb. Marsh. Isl. =	Marshall Islands, Republic of, 2433 Massachusetts Avenue, NW, Washington, DC 20008, 202-234-5414
Emb. Maurit. =	Mauritania, Islamic Republic of, 2129 Leroy Place, NW, Washington, DC 20008, 202-232-5700
Emb. Mauritius =	Mauritius, 4301 Connecticut Avenue, Suite 441, NW, Washington, DC 20008, 202-244-1491
Emb. Mexico =	Mexico, 1911 Pennsylvania Avenue, Suite 441, NW, Washington, DC 20006, 202-728-1600
Emb. Micronesia =	Micronesia, Federated States of, 1725 N Street, NW, Washington, DC 20036, 202-223-4383
Emb. Moldova =	Moldova, Republic of, 1511 K Street, Suite 329, NW, Washington, DC 20005, 202-783-3012
Emb. Mongolia =	Mongolia, 2833 M Street, NW, Washington, DC 20007, 202-333-7117
Emb. Morocco =	Morocco, Kingdom of, 1601 21st Street, NW, Washington, DC 20009, 202-462-7979
Emb. Mozam. =	Mozambique, Republic of, 1990 M St., Suite 570, NW, Washington, DC 20036, 202-293-7146
Emb. Myanmar =	Myanmar, Union of, 2300 S Street, NW, Washington, DC 20008, 202-332-9044
Emb. Nambia =	Nambia, Republic of, 1605 New Hampshire Avenue, NW, Washington, DC 20009, 202-986-0540
Emb. Nepal =	Nepal, 2131 Leroy Place, NW, Washington, DC 20008, 202-667-4550
Emb. Nether. =	Netherlands, 4200 Wisconsin Ave., NW, Washington, DC 20016, 202-244-5300

11,500 Free Experts

Emb. New Zea. =	New Zealand, 37 Observatory Circle, NW, Washington, DC 20008, 202-328-4800
Emb. Nicar. =	Nicaragua, 1627 New Hampshire Avenue, NW, Washington, DC 20009, 202-939-6570
Emb. Niger =	Niger, Republic of, 2204 R Street, NW, Washington, DC 20008, 202-483-4224
Emb. Nigeria =	Nigeria, Federal Republic of, 1333 16th Street, NW, Washington, DC 20036, 202-986-8400
Emb. Norway =	Norway, 2720 34th Street, NW, Washington, DC 20008, 202-333-6000
Emb. Oman =	Oman, Sultanate of, 2535 Belmont Road, NW, Washington, DC 20008, 202-387-1980
Emb. Pakistan =	Pakistan, 2315 Massachusetts Avenue, NW, Washington, DC 20008, 202-939-6200
Emb. Panama =	Panama, Republic of, 2862 McGill Terrace, NW, Washington, DC 20008, 202-483-1407
Emb. Papua N. G. =	Papua New Guinea, 1615 New Hampshire Avenue, NW, Washington, DC 20008, 202-745-3680
Emb. Paraguay =	Paraguay, 2400 Massachusetts Avenue, NW, Washington, DC 20008, 202-483-6960
Emb. Peru =	Peru, 1700 Massachusetts Avenue, NW, Washington, DC 20036, 202-833-9860
Emb. Phillip. =	Philippines, 1600 Massachusetts Avenue, NW, Washington, DC 20036, 202-467-9300
Emb. Poland =	Poland, Republic of, 2640 16th Street, NW, Washington, DC 20009, 202-234-3800
Emb. Portugal =	Portugal, 2125 Kalorama Road, NW, Washington, DC 20008, 202-328-8610
Emb. Qatar =	Qatar, State of, 600 New Hampshire Ave., Suite 1180, NW, Washington, DC 20037, 202-338-0111
Emb. Romania =	Romania, 1607 23rd Street, NW, Washington, DC 20008, 202-332-4846
Emb. Russia =	Russia, Federation, 2650 Wisconsin Avenue, NW, Washington, DC 20007, 202-298-5700
Emb. Rwanda =	Rwanda, Republic of, 1714 New Hampshire Ave., NW, Washington, DC 20009, 202-232-2882
Emb. St. Kitts =	Saint Kitts and Nevis, 2100 M Street, Suite 608, NW, Washington, DC 20037, 202-833-3550
Emb. St. Lucia =	Saint Lucia, 2100 M Street, Suite 309, NW, Washington, DC 20037, 202-463-7378
Emb. St. Vincent =	Saint Vincent and the Grenadines, 1717 Massachusetts Avenue, Suite 102, NW, Washington, DC 20036, 202-462-7806
Emb. Saudi Arabia =	Saudi Arabia, 601 New Hampshire Avenue, NW, Washington, DC 20037, 202-342-3800
Emb. Senegal =	Senegal, Republic of, 2112 Wyoming Avenue, NW, Washington, DC 20008, 202-234-0540
Emb. Seych. =	Seychelles, Republic of, 820 Second Ave., Suite 900F, New York City, NY 10017, 212-687-9766
Emb. Sierre Leo. =	Sierre Leone, 1701 19th Street, NW, Washington, DC 20009, 202-939-9261
Emb. Singap. =	Singapore, Republic of, 3501 International Place, NW, Washington, DC 20009, 202-537-3100
Emb. Slovak. =	Slovakia, Republic of, 2201 Wisconsin Avenue, Suite 380, NW, Washington, DC 20007, 202-965-5161
Emb. Sloven. =	Slovenia, Republic of, 1525 New Hampshire Ave., NW, Washington, DC 20036, 202-667-5363
Emb. S. Africa =	South Africa, 3051 Massachusetts Avenue, NW, Washington, DC 20008, 202-232-4400
Emb. Spain =	Spain, 2375 Pennsylvania Avenue, NW, Washington, DC 20037, 202-452-0100
Emb. Sri Lanka =	Sri Lanka, Democratic Socialist Rep. of, 2148 Wyoming Avenue, NW, Washington, DC 20008, 202-483-4825
Emb. Sudan =	Sudan, Republic of, 2210 Massachusetts Avenue, NW Washington, DC 20008, 202-338-8565
Emb. Suriname =	Suriname, Republic of, 4301 Connecticut Avenue, Suite 108, NW, Washington, DC 20008, 202-244-7488
Emb. Swazi. =	Swaziland, Kingdom of, 3400 International Drive, NW, Washington, DC 20008, 202-362-6683
Emb. Sweden =	Sweden, 1501 M Street, NW, Washington, DC 20005, 202-467-2600
Emb. Switz. =	Switzerland, 2900 Cathedral Avenue, NW, Washington, DC 20008, 202-745-7900
Emb. Syria =	Syrian Arab Republic, 2215 Wyoming Avenue, NW, Washington, DC 20008, 202-232-6313
Emb. Tanzan. =	Tanzania, United Arab Republic of, 2139 R Street, NW, Washington, DC 20008, 202-939-6125
Emb. Thailand =	Thailand, 2300 Kalorama Road, NW, Washington, DC 20007, 202-939-6125
Emb. Togo =	Togo, Republic of, 202-483-7200 Massachusetts Avenue, NW, Washington, DC 20008, 202-234-4212
Emb. Trinida =	Trinidad and Tobago, Republic of, 1708 Massachusetts Avenue, NW, Washington, DC 20036, 202-467-6490
Emb. Tunisia =	Tunisia, 1515 Massachusetts Avenue, NW, Washington, DC 20005, 202-862-1850
Emb. Turkey =	Turkey, Republic of, 1714 Massachusetts Avenue, NW, Washington, DC 20036, 202-659-8200
Emb. Turkmen. =	Turkmenstein, Republic of, 1511 K St., Suite 412, NW, Washington, DC 20005, 202-737-8400
Emb. Uganda =	Uganda, Republic of, 5909 16th Street, NW, Washington, DC 20011, 202-726-7100
Emb. Ukraine =	Ukraine, 3350 M Street, NW, Washington, DC 20007, 202-333-0606
Emb. U. Arab =	United Arab Emirates, 3000 K Street, Suite 600, NW, Washington, DC 20007, 202-336-6500
Emb. U.K. =	United Kingdom and Northern Ireland, 3100 Massachusetts Avenue, NW, Washington, DC 20008, 202-462-1340
Emb. Uruguay =	Uruguay, 1918 F Street, NW, Washington, DC 20006, 202-331-1313
Emb. Uzbek. =	Uzbekistan, Republic of, 1511 K Street, Suite 600, NW, Washington, DC 20007, 202-638-4266
Emb. Venezuela =	Venezuela, Republic of, 1099 30th Street, NW, Washington, DC 20007, 202-342-2214
Emb. W. Samoa =	Western Samoa, 820 Second Avenue, Suite 800, New York City, NY 10017, 212-599-6196
Emb. Yemen =	Yemen, Republic of, 2600 Virginia Ave., Suite 705, NW, Washington, DC 20037, 202-965-4760
Emb. Yugo. =	Yugoslavia, 2410 California Street, NW, Washington, DC 20008, 202-462-6566
Emb. Zaire =	Zaire, Republic of, 1800 New Hampshire Avenue, NW, Washington, DC 20009, 202-234-7690
Emb. Zambia =	Zambia, Republic of, 2419 Massachusetts Avenue, NW, Washington, DC 20008, 202-265-9717
Emb. Zimbabwe =	Zimbabwe, Republic of, 1608 New Hampshire Ave., NW, Washington, DC 20009, 202-332-7100
ENDO =	Endometriosis Association, P.O. Box 92187, Milwaukee, WI 53202, 800-992-3636
EPA =	Environmental Protection Agency, 401 M St., Washington, DC 20460
EPILEPSY =	Bowman Gray School of Medicine, Epilepsy Information Service, Medical Center Boulevard, Winston-Salem, NC 27157, 800-642-0500
EX-IM Bank =	Export - Import Bank, 811 Vermont Avenue, NW, Washington, DC 20571, 202-565-3200
FAA =	Federal Aviation Administration, 800 Independence Avenue, SW, Washington, DC 20591, 202-565-3202
FACE =	American Academy of Facial Plastic and Reconstructive Surgery, 1101 Vermont Avenue, Suite 304, NW, Washington, DC 20005, 800-332-3223

Be patient. If any phone number is incorrect, call (area code) 555-1212 and request the new listing.

FAES = Foundation for Advanced Education in the Sciences, Inc., NIH, One Cloister Ct., Bldg. 60, Suite 230, Bethesda, MD 20814-1460, 301-496-7976

FCC = Federal Communications Commission, 1919 M St., NW, Room 734, Washington, DC 20554-0001, 202-418-0200

FCCS = Foundation Center Customer Service, 79 Fifth Ave. at 16th St., New York, NY 10003, 800-424-9836

FDA = Food and Drug Administration, HHS, 5600 Fishers Lane, Room 1505 Parklawn Bldg., Rockville, MD 20857, 301-443-1130

FFAR = French Foundation for Alzheimer's Research, 11620 Wilshire Boulevard, Suite 820, Los Angeles, CA 90025, 800-477-2243

FHWA = Federal Highway Administration, 400 7th Street, SW, Washington, DC 20590, 202-366-0660

FIC = Fogarty International Center, NIH, 9000 Rockville Pike, Bldg. 38, Bethesda, MD 20892, 202-496-2075

FRA = Federal Railroad Administration, 400 7th Street, SW, Washington, DC 20590, 202-366-0881

FRAGILE X = National Fragile X Foundation, 1441 York Street, Suite 215, Denver, CO 80206, 800-688-8765

FRS = Federal Reserve System, Twentieth Street and Constitution Avenue, NW, Washington, DC 20551, 202-452-3618

FS = Forest Service, U.S. Department of Agriculture, Auditors Building, 201 14th Street, S.W., Washington, DC 20250, 202-720-3760

FWS = Fish and Wildlife Service, Department of the Interior, 1849 C Street, N.W., Washington, DC 20240, 202-208-5634

FTC = Federal Trade Commission, 6th St. and Pennsylvania Avenue, NW, Washington, DC 20580, 202-326-2180

GAO = Government Accounting Office, 441 G Street, NW, Washington, DC 20548, 202-512-3000

GAUCHER = National Gaucher Foundation, 11140 Rockville Pike, Suite 350, Rockville, MD 20852, 800-925-8885

GLADNEY = Edna Gladney Center, 2300 Hemhill, Fort Worth, TX 76110, 800-452-3639

GRIEF = Grief Recovery Helpline, 8306 Wilshire Blvd., Suite 21A, Beverly Hills, CA 90211, 800-445-4808

GSPT = Good Samaritan Project Teen, 3030 Walnut Street, Kansas City, MO 64108, 800-234-8336

GUIDE DOG = Guide Dog Foundation for the Blind, 371 E. Jericho Turnpike, Smithtown, NY 11787, 800-548-4337

HAA = Histiocytosis Association of America, 609 New York Road, Glassboro, NJ 08028, 800-548-2758

HANDI = Hemophilia and AIDS/HIV Network for the Dissemination of Information (HANDI), 110 Greene St., Suite 406, New York, NY 10012, 800-424-2634

HCFA = Health Care Financing Administration, HHS, 200 Independence Ave., SW, Room 435-H, Hubert Humphrey Bldg., Washington, DC 20201, 202-966-3206

HDSA = Huntington's Disease Society of America, 140 West 22nd Street, Sixth Floor, New York, NY 10011, 800-345-4372

HEARING = Hearing Helpline, P.O. Box 1840, Washington, DC 20013, 800-424-8576

HEAT = Higher Education and Adult Training for People With Handicaps Resource Center, One Dupont Circle, Suite 800, Washington, DC 20036, 800-544-3284

HEARTSPRING = Heartspring, 2400 Jardine Drive, Wichita, KS 67219, 800-835-1043

HEI = Hospice Education institute, Five Essex Square, Suite 3-B, Essex, CT 06426-0713, 800-331-1620

HEPATITIS = American Liver Foundation Hepatitis Hotline, 1425 Pompton Avenue, Cedar Grove, NJ 07009, 800-223-0179

HERO = Health Education Resource Organization (HERO), 101 West Read Street, Suite 825, Baltimore, MD 21201, 800-638-6252

HGF = Human Growth Foundation, 7777 Leesburg Pike, Suite 202S, Falls Church, VA 22043, 800-451-6434

HH = Better Hearing Institute Hearing Helpline, 5021-B Backlick Rd., Annandale, VA 22003, 800-327-9355

HHS = Regional Directors, U.S. Department of Health and Human Services (HHS), Room 638-E, Hubert Humphrey Bldg., 200 Independence Avenue, SW, Washington, DC 20201, 202-619-0257

HHSREG = Regional Directors, U.S. Department of Health and Human Services (HHS), Room 638-E, Hubert Humphrey Bldg., 200 Independence Avenue, SW, Washington, DC 20201, 202-619-0257

HIAA = Health Insurance Association of America, 1025 Connecticut Avenue, NW, Washington, DC 20036, 800-635-1271

HILL-BURTON = Hill-Burton Free Hospital Care Hotline, Rockville, MD 20857, 800-638-0742

HIP = Help for Incontinent People, P.O. Box 544, Union, SC 23979, 800-252-3337

HIS = Heart Information Service, Texas Heart Institute, P.O. Box 20345, Houston, TX 77225, 800-292-2221

HOMELESS Y = Covenant House, Homeless youth), 346 West 17th Street, New York, NY 10011, 800-999-9999

HOSPICE = National Hospice Organization, 1901 N. Moore St., Suite 901, Arlington, VA 22209, 800-658-8898

HRSA = Health Resources and Services Administration, HHS, 5600 Fisher Lane, Room 1443, Parklawn Bldg., Rockville, MD 20857, 301-443-3376

HS = International Hearing Society, 20361 Middlebelt Road, Livonia, MI 48152, 800-521-5247

ID-ALERT = Medic Alert Foundation International, 2323 Colorado, Turlock, CA 95381, 800-432-5378

IDF = Immune Deficiency Foundation, 3565 Ellicott Mills Drive, Unit B-2, Ellicott City, MD 21044, 800-296-4433

IHS = Indian Health Service, HHS, Room 6-35, Parklawn Bldg., Rockville, MD 20857, 301-443-3593

IG = Inspector General, Office of, HHS, 330 Independence Avenue, SW, Room 5259, HHS Cohen Bldg., Washington, DC 20201, 800-368-5779

JAN = Job Accommodation Network, West Virginia University, 918 Chestnut Ridge Road, P.O. Box 6080, Morgantown, WV 26506, 800-526-7234

JDF = Juvenile Diabetes Foundation, 432 Park Avenue South, 16th Floor, New York, NY 10016, 800-223-1138

JUST SAY NO = Just Say No International, 2101 Webster Street, Suite 1300, Oakland, CA 94612, 800-258-2766

KCF = Kevin Collins Foundation for Missing Children, Box 590473, San Francisco, CA 94159, 800-272-0012

KIDSRIGHTS = Kidsrights, 10100 Park Cedar Drive, Charlotte, NC 28210, 800-892-5437

La LECHE = La Leche League International, P.O. Box 1209, Franklin Park, IL 60131, 800-525-3243

LABOR = Bureau of Labor Statistics, U.S. Department of Labor, 2 Massachusetts Avenue, NW, Washington, DC 20212, 202-606-5886

LIGHTHOUSE = National Center for Vision and Aging, The Lighthouse, 111 E. 59th St., New York, NY 10022, 800-334-5497

LPA = Little People of America, P.O. Box 9897, Washington, DC 20016, 800-243-9273

LSA = Leukemia Society of America, 600 Third Ave., 4th Floor, New York, NY 10016, 800-955-4572

LUNG LINE = National Jewish Center for Immunology and Respiratory Medicine, Lung Line, 1400 Jackson Street, Denver, CO 80206, 800-222-5864

LUPUS = Lupus Foundation of America, 4 Research Pl., Suite 180, Rockville, MD 20850, 800-558-0121

LYME = Lyme Disease Foundation, One Financial Plaza, Hartford, CT 06103, 800-886-5963

MAA = Medical Awareness Association, 3421 M St. NW, Suite 303, Washington, DC 20007, 800-899-0005

Be patient. If any phone number is incorrect, call (area code) 555-1212 and request the new listing.

1363

MADD =	Mother Against Drunk Driving, 511 East John Carpenter Freeway, Suite 700, Irving, TX 75062, 800-438-6233
MAPB =	Medical Arts and Photography Branch, 9000 Rockville Pike, Bldg. 10, Bethesda, MD 20892, 301-496-5787
MARROW =	National Marrow Donor Program, 3433 Broadway Street, NE, Suite 400, Minneapolis, MN 55413, 800-627-7692
MD =	Maryland
MED-ETHX =	National Reference Center for Bioethics Literature, Georgetown University, Washington, DC 20057, 800-633-3849
MEDICARE =	MEDICARE Issues Hotline, 200 Independence Ave., SW, Washington, DC 20201, 800-638-6833
METRO-HELP =	National Runaway Switchboard, 3080 North Lincoln, Chicago, IL 60657, 800-621-4000
MGF =	Myasthenia Gravis Foundation, 222 S. Riverside Plaza, Suite 1540, Chicago, IL 60606, 800-541-5454
MHRC =	Office of Minority Health Resource Center, P.O. Box 37337, Washington, DC 20013, 800-444-6472
MINES =	Division of Mineral Commodities, U.S. Department of Interior, 810 7th St., NW, Washington, DC 20241, 202-501-9649
MNEF =	Meniere's Network of the Ear Foundation at Baptist Hospital, 2000 Church Street, Box 111, Nashville, TN 37236, 800-545-4327
NABS =	National Alliance of Blind Students, 1155 15th Street, Suite 720, NW, Washington, DC 20005, 800-424-8666
NAC =	National Adoption Center, 1500 Walnut St., Suite 701, Philadelphia, PA 19102, 800-862-3678
NACH =	National Association for the Craniofacially Handicapped, P.O. Box 11082, Chattanooga, TN 37401, 800-332-2373
NAEYC =	National Association for the Education of Young Children, 1509 16th Street, NW, Washington, DC 20036, 800-424-2460
NAF =	National Abortion Federation, 1436 U St., Suite 103, NW, Washington, DC 20009, 800-772-9100
NARHA =	North American Riding for the Handicapped (NARHA), P.O. Box 33150, Denver, CO 80233, 800-369-7433
NAL =	National Agricultural Library, Beltsville, MD 20705, 301-504-5755
NAPARE =	National Center for Perinatal Addiction, Research and Education, 200 North Michigan Avenue, Suite 300, Chicago, IL 60601
NAPVI =	National Association for Parents of the Visually Impaired, P.O. Box 317, Watertown, MA 02272, 800-562-6265
NAPWA =	National Association of People with AIDS (NAPWA), P.O. Box 18345, Washington, DC 20036, 800-673-8538
NARIC =	National Rehabilitation Information Center, 8455 Colesville Road, Suite 935, Silver Spring, MD 20910, 800-346-2742
NARS =	National Association of Radiation Survivors, P.O. Box 278, Live Oak, CA 95953, 800-798-5102
NASA =	National Aeronautics and Space Administration, Washington, DC 20546, 202-358-0000
NCA =	National Council on Aging, 409 Third Street, SW, Washington, DC 20024, 800-424-9046
NCADDH =	National Council on Alcoholism and Drug Dependence Hopeline, 12 West 21st Street, Suite 700, New York, NY 10010, 800-622-2255
NCAH =	National Child Abuse Hotline, Box 630, Hollywood, CA 90028, 800-422-4453
NCCAF =	National Council on Child Abuse and Family Violence, 1155 Connecticut Avenue, Suite 300, NW, Washington, DC 20036, 800-222-2000
NCDB =	National Center for Drugs and Biologics, NIH, 9000 Rockville Pike, Bldg. 29, Bethesda, MD 20892, 301-496-5787
NCFS =	National Clearinghouse on Family Support and Children's Mental Health, Portland State University, P.O. Box 751, Portland, OR 97202, 800-628-1696
NCH =	National Cocaine Hotline, P.O. Box 100, Summit, NJ 07902, 800-262-2463
NCHS =	National Center for Health Statistics, HHS, 6525 Belcrest Rd., Hyattsville, MD 20782, 301-436-7019
NCI =	National Cancer Institute, NIH, 9000 Rockville Pike, Bldg. 31, Bethesda, MD 20892, 301-496-5583
NCJRS =	National Criminal Justice Reference Service, P.O. Box 6000, Rockville, MD 20850, 800-851-3420
NCMEC =	National Center for Missing and Exploited Children, 2101 Wilson Boulevard, Suite 550, Arlington, VA 22201, 800-843-5678
NCNR =	National Center for Nursing Research, NIH, 9000 Rockville Pike, Bldg. 31, Bethesda, MD 20892, 301-496-0207
NCPG =	National Council on Problem Gambling, 445 West 59th Street, Room 1521, New York, NY 10019, 800-522-4700
NCS =	National Center for Stuttering, 200 East 33rd Street, New York, NY 10016, 800-221-2483
NCYD =	National Center for Youth with Disabilities (NCYD), University of Minnesota, 420 Delaware Street, SE, Minneapolis, MN 55455, 800-333-6293
NDC =	National Dairy Council, 10255 West Higgins, #900, Rosemont, IL 60018, 800-426-8271
NDSC =	National Down Syndrome Congress, 1605 Chantilly Dr., Suite 250, Atlanta, GA 30324, 800-232-6372
NDSS =	National Down Syndrome Society, 666 Broadway, New York, NY 10012, 800-221-4602
NDVH =	National Domestic Violence Hotline, P.O. Box 463100, Mt. Clemens, MI 48043, 800-333-7233
NEA =	National Endowment for the Arts, 1100 Pennsylvania Avenue, N.W., Washington DC 20506, 202-682-5400
NECH =	New England Center for Headache, 778 Long Ridge Road, Stamford, CT 06902, 800-245-0088
NECP =	National Eye Care Project, P.O. Box 9688, San Francisco, CA 94101, 800-222-3937
NEH =	National Endowment for the Humanities, 1100 Pennsylvania Avenue, N.W., Washington, DC 20506, 202-606-8438
NEI =	National Eye Institute, NIH, 9000 Rockville Pike, Bldg. 31, Bethesda, MD 20892, 301-496-5248
NEIC =	National Energy Information Center, Energy Information Administration, Department of Energy, E1-231, Forrestal Bldg., Washington, DC 20585, 202-586-8800
NERF =	National Eye Research Foundation, 910 Skokie Blvd., #207A, Northbrook, IL 60062, 800-621-2258
NESS =	National Easter Seal Society, 70 East Lake Street, Chicago, IL 60601, 800-221-6827
NFDI =	National Foundation for Depressive Illness, P.O. Box 2257, New York, NY 10116, 800-248-4344
NFPA =	National Fire Protection Association, Batterymarch Park, Quincy, MA 02269, 800-344-3555
NHAS =	National Hearing Aid Society, 20361 Middlebelt Road, Livonia, MI 48152, 800-521-5247
NHF =	National Headache Foundation, 5252 North Western Avenue, Chicago, Il 60625, 800-843-2256
NHIC =	National Health Information Center, P.O. Box 1133, Washington, DC 20013, 800-336-4797
NHIF =	National Head Injury Foundation, 1176 Massachusetts Avenue, Suite 100, NW, Washington, DC 20036, 800-444-6443
NHLBI =	National Heart, Lung,and Blood Institute, NIH, 9000 Rockville Pike, Bldg. 31, Bethesda, MD 20892, 301-496-4236
NHTSA =	National Highway Traffic Safety Administration, 400 7th Street, SW, Washington, DC 20590, 202-366-2540
NIA =	National Institute on Aging, NIH, 9000 Rockville Pike, Bldg. 31, Bethesda, MD 20892, 800-222-2225
NIAID =	National Institute of Allergy and Infectious Diseases, NIH, 9000 Rockville Pike, Bldg. 31, Bethesda, MD 20892, 301-496-5717

Be patient. If any phone number is incorrect, call (area code) 555-1212 and request the new listing.

NIAMS =	National Institute of Arthritis and Musculoskeletal and Skin Diseases, 9000 Rockville Pike, Bldg. 31, Bethesda, MD 20892, 301-496-8188
NICCYH =	National Information Center for Children and Youth with Handicaps, P.O. Box 1492, Washington, DC 20013, 800-695-0285
NICHD =	National Institute of Child Health and Human Development, NIH, 9000 Rockville Pike, Bldg. 31, Bethesda, MD 20892, 301-496-5133
NIDA =	National Institute on Drug Abuse, HHS, 5600 Fishers Lane, Rockville, MD 20857, 301-443-6245
NIDDK =	National Institute of Diabetes and Digestive and Kidney Diseases, NIH, 9000 Rockville Pike, Bldg. 31, Bethesda, MD 20892, 301-496-3583
NIDR =	National Institute of Dental Research, NIH, 9000 Rockville Pike, Bldg. 31, Bethesda, MD 20892, 301-496-4261
NIEHS =	National Institute of Environmental Health Sciences, NIH, Research Triangle Park, NC 27709, 919-541-3345
NIGMS =	National Institute of General Medical Sciences, NIH, 5333 Westbard Avenue, Room 926, Bethesda, MD 20892, 301-496-7301
NIH =	National Institutes for Health, 9000 Rockville Pike, Bldg 1, Room 126, Bethesda, MD 20892, 301-496-5787
NIMH =	National Institute of Mental Health, NIH, 5600 Fishers Lane, Rockville, MD 20857, 301-443-4513
NINDS =	National Institute of Neurological Disorders and Stroke, 9000 Rockville Pike, Bldg. 31, Bethesda, MD 20892, 301-496-5751
NIRE =	National Institute for Rehabilitation Engineering, P.O. Box T, Hewitt, NJ 07421, 800-736-2216
NIST =	National Institute of Standards and Technology, Gaithersburg, MD 20899, 301-975-3058
NKF =	National Kidney Foundation, 30 East 33rd, New York, NY 10016, 800-622-9010
NLM =	National Library of Medicine, 8600 Rockville Pike, Bethesda, MD 20894, 301-496-6095
NLN =	National Lymphedema Network, 2211 Post St., Suite 404, San Francisco, CA 94115, 800-541-3259
NMSS =	National Multiple Sclerosis Society (NMSS), 733 Third Avenue, Sixth Floor, New York, NY 10017, 800-344-4867
NNF =	National Neurofibromatosis Foundation (NNF), 120 Wall St., New York, NY 10005, 800-323-7938
NOAH =	National Organization for Albinism and Hypopigmentation, 1530 Locust St., #29, Philadelphia, PA 19102, 800-473-2310
NOD =	National Organization on Disability (NOD), 910 16th Street, NW, Suite 600, Washington, DC 20006, 800-248-2253
NORD =	National Organization for Rare Disorders, P.O. Box 8923, New Fairfield, CT 06812, 800-999-6673
NPF =	National Parkinson Foundation, 1501 NW Ninth Ave., Miami, FL 33136, 800-327-4545
NPTN =	National Pesticide Telecommunications Network, Texas Tech University, Thompson Hall, Room S129, Lubbock, TX 79430, 800-858-7378
NRC =	United States Nuclear Regulatory Commission, 11555 Rockville Pike, Rockville, MD 30852, 301-415-8200
NRCHMI =	National Resource Center on Homelessness and Mental Illness, 262 Delaware Avenue, Delmar, NY 12054, 800-444-7415
NRPF =	National Retinitis Pigmentosa Foundation, 1401 Mount Royal Avenue, Fourth Floor, Baltimore, MD 21217, 800-683-5555
NRSF =	National Reye's Syndrome Foundation, Inc., P.O. Box 829, Bryan, OH 43506, 800-233-7393
NSC =	National Safety Council, 1121 Spring Lake Drive, Itasca, Il 60613, 800-621-7619
NSCIA =	National Spinal Cord Injury Association, 545 Concord Ave., Cambridge, MA 02138, 800-962-9629
NSWS =	Coast Guard Hotline, 2100 Second Street, SW, Washington, DC 20593, 800-368-5647
NSSOP =	National Second Surgical Opinion Program, Health Care Financing Administration, 200 Independence Avenue, SW, Washington, DC 20201, 800-638-6833
NTSA =	National Tuberous Sclerosis Association, 8000 Corporate Drive, Suite 120, Landover, MD 20785, 800-225-6872
NTSB =	National Transportation Safety Board, 490 L'Enfant Plaza, SW, Washington DC 20594, 202-382-6735
OA =	American Osteopathic Association, 142 East Ontario Street, Chicago, IL 60611, 800-621-1773
OB =	Office of Biologics, NIH, 9000 Rockville Pike, Bldg. 29, Bethesda, MD 20892, 301-594-2000
OCA =	Office of Consumer Affairs, HHS, 1620 L St., NW, Ste. 700, Washington, DC 20036, 202-395-7904
OC =	Office of Communications, NIH, 9000 Rockville Pike, Bldg. 1, Bethesda, MD 20892, 301-496-4461
OCR =	Office for Civil Rights, HHS, 300 Independence Avenue, SW, Room 5044, HHS Cohen Bldg., Washington, DC 20201, 202-619-0671
OD =	Office of the Director, NIH, 9000 Rockville Pike, Bldg. 1, Bethesda, MD 20892, 301-496-2960
ODRD =	National Information Center for Orphan Drugs and Rare Diseases, P.O. Box 1133, Washington, DC 20013, 800-456-3505
ODS =	Orton Dyslexia Society, Chester Building, Suite 382, 8600 La Salle Road, Baltimore, MD 21286, 800-222-3123
OERT =	Office of Extramural Research and Training, NIH, P.O. Box 12233, Research Triangle Park, NC 27709, 919-541-7723
OHDS =	Office of Human Development Services, HHS, 200 Independence Avenue, SW, Washington DC 20201, 202-395-7904
OHS =	Occupational Hearing Service, Dial A Hearing Screen Test, P.O. Box 1880, Media, PA 19063, 800-222-3277
OPIC =	Overseas Private Investment Corporation, 1100 New York Avenue, NW, Washington, DC 20527, 202-336-8710
OPM =	Office of Personnel Management, 1900 E Street, NW, Washington, DC 20415, 202-606-1800
OPRR =	Office for Protection from Research Risks, NIH, 9000 Rockville Pike, Bldg. 31, Bethesda, MD 20892, 301-496-1357
ORGAN =	Living Bank (Organ Donation), P.O. Box 6725, Houston, TX 77265, 800-528-2971
ORS =	Office of Research Services, NIH, 9000 Rockville Pike, Bldg. 1, Bethesda, MD 20892, 301-496-2215
PBA =	Prevention Blindness America, 500 E. Remington Rd., Schaumburg, IL 60173, 800-331-2020
PCMS =	Primary Care Management Systems, 224 East Clara Street, Port Hueneme, CA 93041, 800-444-9999
PDF =	Parkinson's Disease Foundation, Columbia-Presbyterian Medical Center, 650 West 168th Street, New York, NY 10032, 800-457-6676
PEC =	Peace Corps, 1990 K St., NW, Washington, DC 20526, 202-606-3862
PF =	National Psoriasis Foundation, 6600 SouthWest 92nd Avenue, Suite 300, Portland, OR 97223, 800-248-0886
PHS =	Public Health Service, HHS, Office of Communication, 200 Independence Avenue, SW, Washington, DC 20201, 202-690-7694
PMS =	People's Medical Society, 462 Walnut Street, Allentown, PA 18102, 800-624-8773
PPFA =	Planned Parenthood Federation of America, 810 Seventh Ave., New York, NY 10019, 800-230-7526
PKD-CURE =	Polycystic Kidney Disease Research Foundation, 922 Walnut Street, Suite 411, Kansas City, MO 64106, 800-753-2873
PRN =	USP Practitioners Reporting Network, 12601 Twinbrook Pkwy., Rockville, MD 20852, 800-487-7776
PROJECT =	Project Inform, 1965 Market Street, Suite 220, San Francisco, CA 94103, 800-822-7422
PTO =	Patent and Trademark Office, Crystal Mall 1, 1911 Jefferson Davis Highway, Arlington, VA 22202, 703-308-3924
RICHS =	Rural Information Center Health Service, 10301 Baltimore Avenue, Room 304, Beltsville, MD 20705, 800-633-7701

Be patient. If any phone number is incorrect, call (area code) 555-1212 and request the new listing.

11,500 Free Experts

R&P Found. =	R P Foundation Fighting Blindness, 1401 Mount Royal Avenue, Fourth Floor, Baltimore, MD 21217, 800-683-5555
Runaway =	Runaway Hotline, P.O. Box 12428, Austin, TX 78711, 800-231-6946
Safe Sitter =	Safe Sitter, 1500 North Ritter Avenue, Indianapolis, IN 46219, 800-255-4089
SAMHSA =	Substance Abuse and Mental Health Service Administration, 5600 Fishers Lane, Rockville, MD 20857, 301-443-8956
SBA =	Small Business Administration, 409 Third Street, SW, Washington, DC 20416, 202-205-6766
SBAA =	Spina Bifida Association of America, 45900 MacArthur Boulevard, Suite 250, Washington, DC 20007, 800-621-3141
SCIH =	Spinal Cord Injury Hotline, 2201 Argonne Drive, Baltimore, MD 21218, 800-526-3456
SEC =	United States Securities and Exchange Commission, 450 5th Street, NW, Washington, DC 20549, 202-942-4040
Self-Help =	Self-Help Network of Kansas, Wichita State University, 1845 Fairmont, Campus Box 34, Wichita, KS 67260, 800-445-0116
SF =	Simon Foundation, 3621 Thayer Street, Evanstown, IL 60201, 800-237-4666
SFARF =	Sarcoidosis Family Aid and Research Foundation, P.O. Box 22868, Newark, NJ 07101, 800-223-6429
Shriners =	Shrine Hospital Referral Line, 2900 Rocky Point Drive, Tampa, FL 33607, 800-237-5055
Sickle Cell =	Sickle Cell Disease Association of America, Inc., 3345 Wilshire Boulevard, Suite 1106, Los Angeles, CA 90010, 800-421-8453
SIDS =	Sudden Infant Death Syndrome Alliance, 10500 Little Patuxent Parkway, Suite 420, Colombia, MD 21044, 800-221-7437
SS =	Sjogren's Syndrome Association, 3201 West Evans Drive, Phoenix, AZ 85023, 800-395-6772
SSA =	Social Security Administration, 6401 Security Blvd., Room 932, Altmeyer Bldg., Baltimore, MD 21235, 410-965-8904
SSAREG =	Public Information Contacts, Social Security Administration, 6401 Security Blvd., Room 932, Altmeyer Bldg., Baltimore, MD 21235, 410-965-8904
STROKE =	National Stroke Association, 8480 East Orchard Road, Suite 1000, Englewood, CO 80111, 800-787-6537
SWF =	Sturge-Weber Foundation, P.O. Box 460931, Aurora, CO 80046, 800-627-5482
TOUGHLOVE =	TOUGHLOVE, P.O. Box 1069, Doylestown, PA 18901, 800-333-1069
TRADREP =	Office of the U.S. Trade Representative, 600 17th St., NW, Washington, DC 20506, 202-482-5820
Treasury =	Department of the Treasury, 1500 Pennsylvania Avenue, NW, Washington, DC 20220, 202-622-1610
TRIPOD =	Tripod Grapevine, 2901 North Keystone Street, Burbank, CA 91504, 800-352-8888
TSA =	Tourette Syndrome Association (TSA), 42-40 Bell Boulevard, Bayside, NY 11361, 800-237-0717
UCPA =	United Cerebral Palsy Association, Inc., 1522 K Street, NW, Suite 1112, Washington, DC 20005, 800-872-5827
ULF =	United Leukodystrophy Foundation, 2304 Highland Drive, Sycamore, IL 60178, 800-728-5483
UMD =	University of Maryland, University of Maryland-College Park, College Park, MD 20742, 301-405-1000
UNOS =	United Network for Organ Sharing (UNOS), P.O. Box 13770, Richmond, VA 23225, 800-243-6667
UOA =	United Ostomy Association, 36 Executive Park, Suite 120, Irvine, CA 92714, 800-826-0826
USA-KIDS =	Missing Children Help Center, 410 Ware Blvd., Suite 400, Tampa, FL 33619, 800-872-5437
USF =	United Sclerodema Foundation, P.O. Box 399, Watsonville, CA 95077, 800-722-4673
USITC =	Office of Industries, U.S. International Trade Commission, 500 E. St., SW, Washington, DC 20436, 202-205-3334
USCG =	United States Coast Guard, 2100 2nd Street, SW, Washington, DC 20593, 202-267-1587
USIA =	United States Information Agency, 301 4th Street, SW, Washington, DC 20547, 202-619-4355
UVA =	University of Virginia, Office of Television News, Booker House, PO Box 9018, Charlottesville, VA 22906-9018, 804-924-0311
VA =	Virginia
VIC =	Visitor Information Center, NIH, 9000 Rockville Pike, Bldg.10, Bethesda, MD 20892, 301-496-6308
VNAA =	Visiting Nurses Association of America, 3801 East Florida Avenue, Suite 900, Denver, CO 80210, 800-426-2547
VRP =	Veterinary Resources Program, NIH, 9000 Rockville Pike, Bldg. 14, Bethesda, MD 20892, 301-496-4000
VVAOV =	Vietnam Veterans Agent Orange Victims, P.O. Box 2465, Darien, CT 06820, 800-521-0198
Wisconsin =	Wisconsin Clearinghouse (Drug and alcohol prevention educational materials and publications), University of Wisconsin, P.O. Box 1468, Madison, WI 53701, 800-322-1468
World Bank =	World Bank, 1818 H Street, NW, Washington DC 20433, 202-477-1234
WSF =	Women's Sports Foundation Information and Referral Service, Eisenhower Park, East Meadow, NY 11554, 800-227-3988
YMCA =	YMCA of the USA, 101 North Wacker, Chicago, IL 60606, 800-872-9622
Y-Me =	Y-Me National Breast Cancer Organization, 212 West Van Buren, Fourth Floor, Homewood, IL 60607, 800-221-2141

Be patient. If any phone number is incorrect, call (area code) 555-1212 and request the new listing.

Experts

A

Abaca....Cook, Lee USITC 202-205-3471

Abetalipoproteinemia....Staff NHLBI 301-496-4236

Abortion (Research Relating to)....Staff NICHD 301-496-5133

Abortion (Research Relating to)....Staff CDC 404-639-3286

Abortion (Research Relating to)....Staff NCHS 301-436-8500

Abortion/Surveillance Data....Sims, Anne CDC 404-639-3286

Abortion....Staff National Abortion Federation 800-772-9100

Above Ground Storage Tanks....Staff EPA 202-260-1130

Abrasion (Corneal)....Staff NEI 301-496-5248

Abrasive Products....Presbury, Graylin COMMERCE 202-482-5158

Abrasive....DeSapio, Vincent USITC 202-205-3435

Abrasives, Natural....Austin, Gordon MINES 202-501-9388

Abrasives, Manmade....Austin, Gordon MINES 202-501-9388

Abrasives....Bell, Mark L. PTO 703-308-3823

ABS resins....Misurelli, Denby USITC 202-205-3362

Absences from Work, Empl/Unempl Statistics....Staff LABOR 202-606-6378

Abuse of Processing-Non-Hearing (audio)....Staff FCC 202-418-2780

Abuse of Process-Non-Hearing....Staff FCC 202-418-1600

Abuse Liability....Staff NIDA 301-496-5248

Abuse Liability....Mona Brown NIDA 301-443-6245

Access....Staff FCC 202-418-1595

Accessories....Weiss, Martin CUSTOMS 212-466-5881

Accident Statistics....Staff CDC 404-329-3286

Accident Statistics....Staff NCHS 301-496-8500

Accident Prevention and the Elderly....Staff NIA 301-496-1752

Accounting Services....Bedore, James USITC 202-205-3424

Accounting Issues....Staff FCC 202-418-0800

Accounting and Related Issues....Lee, Ronald CENSUS 301-763-5435

Accounting....Chittum, J. Marc COMMERCE 202-482-0345

Accreditation (Health Professions)....Staff HRSA/BHPr 301-443-3376

Accreditation (Nurse Training)....Staff HRSA/BHPr 301-443-5786

Acetal resins....Misurelli, Denby USITC 202-205-3362

Acetates....Michels, David USITC 202-205-3352

Acetic acid....Michels, David USITC 202-205-3352

Acetone....Michels, David USITC 202-205-3352

Acetoricinoleic acid ester....Johnson, Larry USITC 202-205-3351

Achondroplasia....Staff NICHD 301-496-5133

Achondroplasia....Staff NIAMS 301-496-8188

Acid, oleic....Randall, Rob USITC 202-205-3366

Acid, stearic....Randall, Rob USITC 202-205-3366

Acid Rain....Jordy, George NEIC 301-903-2971

Acid Rain....Staff EPA 202-233-9150

Acidosis....Staff NICHD 301-496-5133

Acids, inorganic....Trainor, Cynthia USITC 202-205-3354

Acne (Cystic)....Staff NIAMS 301-496-8188

Acne....Staff NIAMS 301-496-8188

Acoustic Neuroma....Staff NIDCD 301-296-7243

Acoustic Neuroma....Staff NINDS 301-496-5751

Acoustics....Gellner, Michael L. PTO 703-308-1436

Acquired Immune Deficiency Syndrome (AIDS)....Staff PHS 800-342-2437

Acquired Immune Deficiency Syndrome (AIDS)....Staff NCI 301-496-5583

Acquired Immune Deficiency Syndrome (AIDS)....Staff NIAID 301-496-5717

Acquisitions, Land....Staff FWS 202-358-2200

Acquisitions....Staff FCC 202-418-0930

Acromegaly....Staff NIDDK 301-496-3583

Acrylates....Michels, David USITC 202-205-3352

Acrylic resins....Misurelli, Denby USITC 202-205-3362

Acrylonitrile....Michels, David USITC 202-205-3352

ACTH, Excessive Secretion....Staff NHLBI 301-496-4236

Actinide Chemistry....Marianelli, Robert NEIC 301-903-5808

Activated carbon....Randall, Bob USITC 202-205-3366

Acupuncture (Animal Studies)....NIDA 301-443-6245

Acupuncture....Staff NINDS 301-496-5751

Acute Leukemia....Staff NCI 301-496-5583

Acute Hemorrhagic Conjunctivitis....Staff NEI 301-496-5248

Acute Puncture (Animal Studies)....Staff NIDA 301-443-6245

Acyclic plasticizers....Johnson, Larry USITC 202-205-3351

ADA for Economic Development....Sclater, Jeanne SBA 202-205-6552

Adaption to Clinical Illness....NINR 301-496-0207

Adding Machines....Baker, Scott USITC 202-205-3386

Addison's Disease....Staff NIDDK 301-496-3583

Addressing machines....Baker, Scott USITC 202-205-3386

Adenoma of the Thyroid....Staff NIDDK 301-496-3583

Adherence to Therapeutic Regimens....Staff NINR 301-496-0207

Adhesive Bonding....Simmons, David A. PTO 703-308-1972

Adhesives/Sealants....Prat, Raimundo COMMERCE 202-482-0128

Adhesives....Jonnard, Aimison USITC 202-205-3350

Adipic acid esters....Johnson, Larry USITC 202-205-3351

Adjudication....Gaskins, Carla Justice Stat 202-508-8546

Adjudication....Langan, Patrick Justice Stat 202-616-3490

Administration, Director, Office of....Burke, Sally NLM 301-496-6491

Administrative Law Judges....Parker, Lewis, F. FTC 202-326-3632

Administrative Law Judges....Jones, Shirley J. FTC 202-326-3634

Administrative Law Judges....Timony, James P. FTC 202-326-3635

Administrative Law Judges....Cabell, Henry B. FTC 202-326-3642

Administrative Law Judges....Harriger, Patricia A. FTC 202-326-3626

Administrative Systems Training....Staff OD/DPM 301-496-6211

Administrative Procedure Act....Staff FCC 202-418-1720

Admission (Health Professions Schools)....Staff BHPr 301-443-3376

Admission Procedures (Patient)....Staff CC 301-496-4891

Admissions (Patient)....Staff CC 301-496-3315

Adolescence....Staff NIMH 301-443-4513

Adolescence....Staff NICHD 301-496-5133

Adolescent Drug Use....Brown, Mona NIDA 301-443-6245

Adolescent Pregnancy....Staff NICHD 301-496-5133

Adolescent Pregnancy....Sheeran, Patrick NICHD 301-594-4004

Adoption....Kharfen, Michael ACF 202-401-9215

Adoption....Staff National Adoption Center (NAC) 800-862-3678

Adrenal Gland....Staff NIDDK 301-496-3583

Adrenal Insufficiency....Staff NICHD 301-496-5133

Adrenoleukodystrophy....Staff NINDS 301-496-5751

Adrenomyeloneuropathy....Staff NINDS 301-496-5751

Adult Education....Staff FAES 301-496-7976

Advanced Industrial Concepts....Gunn, Marvin NEIC 202-586-2826

Advanced Solid Rocket Motor....Staff NASA 205-544-5041

Advanced Studies....Staff FIC 301-496-2516

Advanced Technology....Uriano, G.A. NIST 301-975-5187

Advanced Training (Registered Nurse)....Staff BHPr 301-443-5786

Advanced TV-General Engineering....Staff FCC 202-418-2190

Advanced TV-Legal....Staff FCC 202-418-2130

Advertising services....Evans, Katherine USITC 202-205-3407

Advertising Questions....Staff FCC 202-418-1430

Advertising....Frederick, Eliot COMMERCE 202-482-1134

Advertising....Zanot, Eric J. UMD 301-405-2429

Advisory Committees....Staff OD 301-496-2123

Adynamia....Staff NINDS 301-496-5751

Aerodynamic Research....Staff NASA 804-864-6123

Aeroelasticity Research....Staff NASA 804-864-6123

Aeronautics Research....Staff NASA 804-864-6123

Aeronautics....Jordan, Charles PTO 703-308-0918

Aeronautics....Koehler, Keith NASA 804-824-1579

Aeronautics....Rachul, Lori NASA 216-433-8806

Aeronautics....Whitehead, Robert NASA 202-358-2693

Aerospace, Aircraft and Parts Industry Group....Roycroft, John C. SEC 202-942-1960

Aerospace Financing Issues....Jackson, Jeff COMMERCE 202-482-6234

Aerospace Industry Analysis....McDonald, Eric COMMERCE 202-482-1237

Aerospace Industry Data....McDonald, Eric COMMERCE 202-482-1237

Aerospace Market Promo.....Largay, Tony COMMERCE 202-482-6236

Aerospace Information and Analysis....McDonald, Eric COMMERCE 202-482-1237

Aerospace Market Development....Largay, Tony COMMERCE 202-482-6236

Aerospace Policy and Analysis....Bender, Juliet COMMERCE 202-482-1233

Aerospace Technology....Ellis, Linda NASA 216-433-2900

Aerospace Trade Policy Issues....Bender, Juliet COMMERCE 202-482-1233

Aerospace Trade Promo....Bender, Juliet COMMERCE 202-482-1233

Aerospace - Marketing Support....Pederson, Heather COMMERCE 202-482-1228

Aerospace - Space Programs....Farner, Peter COMMERCE 202-482-2232

Aerospace - Space Marketing Support....Pederson, Heather COMMERCE 202-482-6239

Affiliate Transactions....Staff FCC 202-418-0850

Affiliates, Domestic....Nardolilli, Pamela FRS 202-452-3289

Affiliates, Foreign....Clubb, Christopher FRS 202-452-3778

Afghanistan/Minerals....Kuo, Chin Cnty Mines 202-501-9693

Afghanistan (Kabul)....Staff Cnty State 202-647-9552

Afghanistan.....Mohabbat, Yar Mohammad Cnty Embassy 202-234-3770

Afghanistan.....Azizian, Abdul Aziz Cnty Embassy 202-234-3770

Afghanistan....Gilman, Timothy Cnty Commerce 202-482-2954

Afghanistan....Hutchings, Dayna Cnty Export-Import Bank 202-565-3737

Afghanistan....Sayeh, Antoinette M. Cnty World Bank 202-473-4719

Afghanistan....VanRenterghem, Cynthia Cnty Treasury 202-622-0343

Afghanistan....Winchester, Rebecca Cnty USIA 202-619-6528

Africa....Jones, Walter OPIC 202-336-8654

AG Indexes with options....Fichert, David CFT 312-353-3181

Agammaglobulinemia....Staff NIAID 301-496-5717

Agar agar....Jonnard, Aimison USITC 202-205-3350

Age and Sex (U.S.)....Staff CENSUS 301-457-2397

Age Search (Access to Personal Census Records)....Staff CENSUS 301-457-1167

Age-Related Muscular Degeneration....Staff NEI 301-496-5248

Ageism....Staff NIA 800-222-2225

Agenesis of the Corpus Callosum....Staff NINDS 301-496-5751

Agent Orange....Sims, Anne CDC 404-639-3286

Agent Orange victims....Staff Vietnam Veterans Agent Orange Victims 800-521-0198

Ageusia....Staff NIDCD 301-496-7243

Agglomerating machinery....Greene, William USITC 202-205-3405

Aging-Related Maculopathy....Staff NEI 301-496-5248

Aging, Administration on....Benson, William AOA 202-619-0556

Aging and vision....Staff The Lighthouse 800-334-5497

Aging (Mental Health)....Staff NIMH 301-443-4513

Aging, National Institute on....Torres-Gil, Fernando AOA 301-401-4634

Aging....Sprott, Richard L. FAES 301-496-4996

Aging....Staff NIA 301-496-1752

Aging....Staff National Council on the Aging (NCA) 800-424-9046

Agnogenic Myeloid Metaplasia....Staff NHLBI 301-496-4236

Agreements--Collective Bargaining/Public File....Cimini, Michael LABOR 202-606-6275

Agribusiness, Major Proj.....Bell, Richard COMMERCE 202-482-2460

Agricultural Affairs/trade matters....Early, Suzanne US Trade Rep 202-395-6127

Agricultural Chemicals....Maxey, Francis P. COMMERCE 202-482-0128

Agricultural Credit....Walraven, Nicholas 202-452-2655

Agricultural Finances - Cash Receipts....Williams, Roberts Agri 202-219-0804

Agricultural Finances - Cash Receipts....Dixon, Connie Agri 202-219-0805

Agricultural Finances - Costs and Returns....Dismukes, Robert Agri 202-219-0840

Agricultural Finances - Costs and Returns....Morehart, Mitch Agri 202-219-0801

Agricultural Finances - Credit and Financial Markets....Ryan, Jim Agri 202-219-0798

Agricultural Finances - Credit and Financial Markets....Sullivan, Pat Agri 202-219-0719

Agricultural Finances - Credit and Financial Markets-World....Baxter, Tim Agri 202-219-0708

Agricultural Finances - Credit and Financial Markets....Stam, Jerry Agri 202-219-0892

Agricultural Finances - Farm Real Estate Taxes....DeBraal, Peter Agri 202-219-1011

Agricultural Finances - Farm, Annual....Strickland, Roger Agri 202-219-0807

Agricultural Finances - Farm Household....Bentley, Susan 202-219-0931

Agricultural Finances - Future Markets....Heifner, Richard Agri 202-219-0868

Agricultural Finances - Futures Markets - Crops....Plato, Gerry Agri 202-501-6763

Agricultural Finances - Income - Farm Forecast....McElroy, Bob Agri 202-219-0802

Agricultural Finances - Prices, Parity and Indexes-Received....Vanderberry, Herb Agri 202-720-5446

Agricultural Finances - Prices, Parity and Indexes - Paid....Kleweno, Doug Agri 202-720-4214

Agricultural Finances - Prices, Parity and Indexes....Milton, Bob Agri 202-720-3570

Agricultural Finances - Production Costs - Livestock....Shapouri, H. Agri 202-219-1491

Agricultural Finances - Production Costs - Sweeteners....Clauson, Annette Agri 202-219-0890

Agricultural Finances - Production Costs - Sweeteners....Buzzanell, Peter Agri 202-219-0888

Agricultural Finances - Production Costs....Kleweno, Doug Agri 202-720-4214

Agricultural Finances - Production Costs - Crops....Dismukes, Robert Agri 202-219-0840

Agricultural Finances - Production Costs - Dairy....Matthews, Ken Agri 202-219-0710

Agricultural Finances - Subsidies....Mabbs-Zeno, Carl Agri 202-219-0631

Agricultural Finances - Subsidies....Nelson, Fred Agri 202-219-0695

Agricultural Finances - Taxes....Durst, Ron Agri 202-219-0897

Agricultural Finances - Wages and Labor:...Oliveira, Victor Agri 202-219-0033

Agricultural Finances....Hacklander, Duane Agri 202-219-0798

Agricultural Finances....Morehart, Mitch Agri 202-219-0801

Agricultural Lands....Staff FWS 703-358-1744

Agricultural Machinery....Fravel, Dennis USITC 202-205-3404

Agricultural Machinery....Weining, Mary COMMERCE 202-482-4708

Agricultural Subsidies....Johnson, Jim Agri 202-219-0001

Agricultural Trade and Marketing Information Center....Lassanyi, Mary NAL 301-504-5509

Agriculture, Crop Statistics....Hutton, Linda CENSUS 301-763-8569

Agriculture, Data Requirements and Outreach....Wilson, Ewen CENSUS 301-763-8555

Agriculture, Farm Economics....Liefer, James A. CENSUS 301-763-8514

Agriculture, General Information....Staff CENSUS 800-523-3215

Agriculture, Guam....Hoover, Kent CENSUS 301-763-8564

Agriculture Issues....Harman, John W. GAO 202-512-5138

Agriculture, Livestock Statistics....Hutton, Linda CENSUS 301-763-8569

Agriculture, No. Marianas....Hoover, Kent CENSUS 301-763-8564

Agriculture, Puerto Rico....Hoover, Kent CENSUS 301-763-8564

Agriculture, State - Virginia, Richmond....Bass, R. Agri 804-786-3500

Agriculture, State - West Virginia, Charleston....Loos, Dave Agri 304-558-2217

Agriculture, State - Alabama, Montgomery....Kleweno, Dave Agri 334-279-3555

Agriculture, State - Alaska, Palmer....Brown, D.A. Agri 907-745-4272

Agriculture, State - Arizona, Phoenix....Sherman, W. M. Agri 602-288-8850

Agriculture, State - Arkansas, Little Rock....Klugh, B.F. Agri 501-324-5145

Agriculture, State - California, Sacramento....Tippett, H.J. Agri 916-498-5161

Agriculture, State - Colorado, Lakewood....Hudson, C.A. Agri 303-236-2300

Agriculture, State - Delaware, Dover....Feurer, T.W. Agri 302-736-4811

Agriculture, State - Florida, Orlando....Freie, R.L. Agri 407-648-6013

Agriculture, State - Georgia, Athens....Snipes, L.E. Agri 404-546-2236

Agriculture, State - Hawaii, Honolulu....Martin, D.A. Agri 808-973-2907

Agriculture, State - Idaho, Boise....Gerhardt, D.G. Agri 208-334-1507

Agriculture, State - Illinois, Springfield....Clampet, J.L. Agri 217-492-4295

Agriculture, State - Indiana, West Lafayette....Gann, R.W. Agri 317-494-8371

Agriculture, State - Iowa, Des Moines....Sands, J. Agri 515-284-4340

Agriculture, State - Kansas, Topeka....Bryam, T.J. Agri 913-233-2230

Agriculture, State - Kentucky, Louisville....Williamson, D. D. Agri 502-582-5293

Agriculture, State - Louisiana, Baton Rouge....Frank, A.D. Agri 504-922-1362

Agriculture, State - Maryland, Annapolis....West, M.B. Agri 410-841-5740

Agriculture, State - Michigan, Lansing....Fedewa, D.J. Agri 517-377-1831

Agriculture, State - Minnesota, St. Paul....Hunts, M. Agri 612-296-2230

Agriculture, State - Mississippi, Jackson....Gregory, T. Agri 601-965-4575

Agriculture, State - Missouri, Columbia....Walsh, P.A. Agri 314-876-0950

Agriculture, State - Montana, Helena....Stringer, M. Agri 406-449-5303

Agriculture, State - Nebraska, Lincoln....Dobbs, B. Agri 402-437-5541

Agriculture, State - Nevada, Reno....Owens, M. J. Agri 702-784-5584

Agriculture, State - New Jersey, Trenton....Battaglia, R.J. Agri 609-292-6385

Agriculture, State - New Mexico, Las Cruces....Gore, C.E. Agri 505-522-6023

Agriculture, State - New England - Concord, NH....Davis, A.R. Agri 603-224-9639

Agriculture, State - New York, Albany....Schooley, R.E. Agri 518-457-5570

Agriculture, State - North Carolina, Raleigh....Murphy, R.M. Agri 919-856-4394

Agriculture, State - North Dakota, Fargo....Beard, L. W. Agri 701-239-5306

Agriculture, State - Ohio, Columbus....Ramey, J.E. Agri 614-469-5590

Agriculture, State - Oklahoma, Oklahoma City....Beloyed, B. Agri 405-525-9226

Agriculture, State - Oregon, Portland....Rowley, H. K. Agri 503-326-2131

Agriculture, State - Pennsylvania, Harrisburg....Evans, W.C. Agri 717-787-3904

Agriculture, State - South Carolina, Columbia....Graham, R. Agri 803-765-5333

Agriculture, State - South Dakota, Sioux Falls....Ranek, J.C. Agri 605-330-4235

Agriculture, State - Tennessee, Nashville....Danekas, G. Agri 615-781-5300

Agriculture, State - Texas, Austin....Findley, D. S. Agri 512-482-5581

Agriculture, State - Utah, Salt Lake City....Gneiting, D.J. Agri 801-524-5003

Agriculture, State - Washington, Tumwater....Hasslen, D.A. Agri 360-902-1940

Agriculture, State - Wisconsin, Madison....Pratt, L.H. Agri 608-224-4848

Agriculture, State - Wyoming, Cheyenne....Coulter, R.W. Agri 307-772-2181

Agriculture/trade matters....Kaska, Edward US Trade Rep 202-395-3320

Agriculture, Virgin Islands....Hoover, Kent CENSUS 301-763-8564

Agriculture....Rosine, John FRS 202-452-2971

Agroforestry....Huke, Susan FS 202-235-9461

Aid to Families with Dependent Children (AFDC)....Kharfen, Michael ACF 202-401-9215

AID ATLANTA....Staff Georgia Dept. of Health 800-551-2728

AIDS (Acquired Immune Deficiency Syndrome)....Arthur, Lawrence PHS 202-690-5471

AIDS and IV drug abuse....Brown, Mona NIDA 301-443-6245

AIDS Clinical Trials....Staff ACTIS 800-874-2572

AIDS Dementia....Staff NINDS 301-496-5751

AIDS Drugs....Staff Project Inform 800-334-7422

AIDS Education at Work....Staff AIDS Action Committee of Massachusetts 800-669-0696

AIDS/HIV....Waller, Robert CDC 404-639-2928

AIDS, Neurological Symptoms or Effects of....Staff NINDS 301-496-5751

AIDS, Neurological Symptoms or Effects of....Staff NIDCD 301-496-7243

AIDS, Pediatric....Staff NICHD 301-496-5133

AIDS, Research Facilities....Staff NCRR 301-594-7938

AIDS...Staff Good Samaritan Project Teen (GSPT) 800-234-8336

AIDS....Staff NAPWA 800-673-8538

AIDS....Staff NCI 301-496-5583

AIDS....Staff NIAID 301-496-5717

AIDS....Staff PHS Hotline 800-342-2437

Air and Radiation....Staff EPA 202-260-7400

Air and Energy Policy Division....Staff EPA 202-260-5490

Air Compressors, Gas....McDonald, Edward COMMERCE 202-482-2107

Air Conditioners....Francke, Eric CUSTOMS 212-466-5669

Air conditioners....Mata, Ruben USITC 202-205-3403

Air Conditioning Equipment....Bell, Richard COMMERCE 202-482-3509

Air Division....Staff EPA 202-260-7606

Air Enforcement Division....Staff EPA 202-564-2260

Air Environmental Laws....Wallo, Andrew NEIC 202-586-4996

Air Gas Compressors, Trade Promo.....Heimowitz, Leonard COMMERCE 202-482-0558

Air/Ground Communication....Johnson, Nathaniel FAA 202-287-7027

Air Pollution Training....Staff EPA 919-541-2401

Air Pollution Control Equipment....Jonkers, Loretta COMMERCE 202-482-0564

Air Pollution and Respiratory Health....Etzel, Ruth CDC 404-488-7320

Air Quality (Outdoor Cities)....Staff EPA 202-260-1023

Air Quality Planning and Standards....Staff EPA 202-541-5615

Air Quality Management Division....Staff EPA 202-541-0886

Air Risc Hotline....Staff EPA 919-541-0888

Air Taxi....Hakala, Katherine M FAA 202-267-8086

Air Traffic Control Equipment (Market Support)....Smerkanich, Audrey COMMERCE 202-482-6235

Air Traffic Rules....Matthews, Reginald FAA 202-267-8783

Air Traffic....Pollard, William FAA 202-267-3666

Air transportation services....Lahey, Kathleen USITC 202-205-3409

Air Transportation Services....Lahey, Kathleen USITC 202-205-3409

Airborne Science and Applications....Staff NASA 415-604-3934

Aircraft Accident Investigation....Rawson, John D FAA 202-267-8190

Aircraft and Aircraft Engines, Trade Promo.....Smerkanich, Audrey COMMERCE 202-482-6235

Aircraft and Aircraft Engines, Market Support....Pederson, Heather COMMERCE 202-482-6239

Aircraft Auxiliary Equipment, Market Support....Pederson, Heather COMMERCE 202-482-1228

Aircraft Certification Service....McSweeney, Thomas E FAA 202-267-8235

Aircraft Engines, Trade Promo.....Smerkanich, Audrey COMMERCE 202-482-6235

Aircraft Fuel Economy Research....Rachul, Lori NASA 216-433-8806

Aircraft Noise Abatement Research....Rachul, Lori NASA 216-433-8806

Aircraft Operating Problems Research....Koehler, Keith NASA 804-824-1579

Aircraft Parts, Trade Promo/Aux Equipment....Smerkanich, Audrey COMMERCE 202-482-6235

Aircraft Parts, Market Support....Smerkanich, Audrey COMMERCE 202-482-6235

Aircraft Propulsion....Rachul, Lori NASA 216-433-8806

Aircraft Radio Licenses-Technical Questions....Staff FCC 202-418-0680

Aircraft Radio Licenses-General Questions....Staff FCC 800-322-1117

Aircraft Reliability Research....Rachul, Lori Ann NASA 216-433-8806

Aircraft Testing....Staff NASA 804-864-3314

Aircraft....Dicerbo, Mario CUSTOMS 212-466-5672

Aircraft....Andersen, Peder USITC 202-205-3409

Airlines....Alford, Eugene COMMERCE 202-482-5071

Airport Equipment, Trade Promo....Smerkanich, Audrey COMMERCE 202-482-6235

Airport Equipment, Market Support....Smerkanich, Audrey COMMERCE 202-482-6235

Airports, Ports, Harbors, Major Projects....Smith, Jay COMMERCE 202-482-4642

Airport Safety....Mudd, Leonard E FAA 202-267-3053

Airway Facilities Training Program....Kruger, Mike FAA 202-366-7400

Airway facilities....Archilla, Joaquin FAA 202-267-8181

Al-Anon....Staff Alateen Family Group Hotline 800-344-2666

Alarms, burglar and fire....Scott, Baker USITC 202-205-3386

Alaska Joint Board....Staff FCC 202-418-0830

Albania....Altheim, Stephen Cnty Treasury 202-622-0125

Albania....Amick, Jack Peace Corps 202-606-3548

Albania....Corwin, Elizabeth Cnty USIA 202-619-5055

Albania....Dawson, Kathleen Cnty Treasury 202-622-5815

Albania....Dilja, Lubin Cnty Embassy 202-223-4942

Albania....Keller, Jeremy Cnty Commerce 202-482-4915

Albania....LeMaster, Cheryl Peace Corps 202-606-3547

Albania....Staff Cnty State 202-647-3747

Albania....Stillwell, Carol Cnty TDA 703-875-4357

Albania....Varallyay, Julius G. Cnty World Bank 202-473-7210

Albania....Waxman-Lenz, Roberta Cnty Export-Import Bank 202-565-3742

Albania....Xheph, Mustafa Cnty Embassy 202-223-4942

Albania\Minerals....Steblez, Walter Cnty Mines 202-501-9672

Albinism (Eyes)....Staff NEI 301-496-5248

Albinism....Staff National Organization for Albinism and Hypopigmentation (NOAH) 800-473-2310

Albright's Syndrome....Staff NIDDK 301-496-3583

Albright's Syndrome....Staff NICHD 301-496-5133

Albright's Syndrome....Staff NIAMS 301-496-8188

Albums (autograph, photograph)....Twarok, Chris USITC 202-205-3314

Alcohol Abuse and Alcoholism, National Institute on....Miller, Diane NIAAA 301-443-3860

Alcohol and Aging....Staff NIAAA 301-443-3860

Alcohol and Cancer....Staff NCI 301-496-5583

Alcohol and Cancer....Staff NIAAA 301-443-3860

Alcohol and Aging....Staff NCADI 301-468-2600

Alcohol and Aging....Staff NIA 301-496-1752

Alcohol, elderly....Alcohol Rehab for the Elderly (ARE) 800-354-7089

Alcohol Fuels....Costello, Raymond NEIC 202-586-8072

Alcohol Fuels....Russell, John NEIC 202-536-8053

Alcohol Fuels....Staff NEIC 202-586-9920

Alcohol, oleyl....Randall, Rob USITC 202-205-3366

Alcohol....Alcohol and Drug Helpline 800-821-4357

Alcohol....Staff NAPARE 800-638-2229

Alcohol....Staff NCADI 301-468-2600

Alcohol....Staff NIAAA 301-443-3860

Alcohol....Staff Office of Alcohol and Drug Programs 800-932-0912

Alcoholic Beverages....Kenney, Cornelius COMMERCE 202-482-2428

Alcoholic beverage labeling....Staff ATF 202-927-7777

Alcoholic beverage permits....Staff ATF 202-927-8100

Alcoholism prevention....Staff Wisconsin Clearinghouse 800-322-1468

Alcoholism....Staff NIAAA 301-443-3860

Alcoholism....Staff NCADI 301-468-2600

Alcoholism....Staff American Council on Alcoholism (ACA) 800-527-5344

Alcoholism....Staff National Council on Alcoholism and Drug Dependence Hopeline (NCADDH) 800-622-2255

Alcohols, polyhydric, fatty acids....Land, Eric USITC 202-205-3349

Alcohols....Michels, David USITC 202-205-3352

Aldehydes....Brady, Thomas CUSTOMS 212-466-5747

Aldehydes....Michels, David USITC 202-205-3352

Aldosteronism....Staff NHLBI 301-496-4236

Alexander's Syndrome....Staff NINDS 301-496-5751

Algeria/Minerals....Michalski, Bernadette Cnty Mines 202-501-9699

Algeria (Algiers)....Staff Cnty State 202-647-4680

Algeria....Belkadi, Mouloud Cnty Embassy 202-265-2800

Algeria....Bencherif, Hadji Osmane Cnty Embassy 202-265-2800

Algeria....Clement, Claude/Cerone, Chris Cnty Commerce 202-482-1860

Algeria....Early, Evelyn Cnty USIA 202-619-6528

Algeria....El Baroudy, Samia Cnty World Bank 202-473-2370

Algeria....Imam, Fahmila Cnty Export-Import Bank 202-565-3738

Algeria....Mandel, Pamela Cnty AID 202-663-2617

Algeria....VanRenterghem, Cynthia Cnty Treasury 202-622-0343

Alien Restricted Permits....Staff FCC 202-418-2780

Aliferis, Peter V. GAO 202-512-4707

Alkali metals....Connant, Kenneth USITC 202-205-3346

Alkaloids....Nesbitt, Elizabeth USITC 202-205-3355

Alkaptonuria....Staff NHLBI 301-496-4236

Alkylating Agents....Staff NCI 301-496-5583

Allergic Rhinitis....Staff NIAID 301-496-5717

Allergic Diseases....Kaliner, Michael A. FAES 301-496-9314

Be patient. If any phone number is incorrect, call (area code) 555-1212 and request the new listing.

1369

11,500 Free Experts

Allergies (Eyes)....Staff NEI 301-496-5248

Allergies....Staff NIAID 301-496-5717

Allergies....Staff American Academy of Allergy and Immunology (FACE) 800-822-2762

Allergy and Infectious Diseases, National Inst. of....Randall, Patricia NIH 301-496-5717

Allergy....Staff Asthma and Allergy Foundation of America (ASTHMA) 800-727-8462

Allied Health Professions....Staff HRSA/BHPr 301-443-3376

Allocations FM....Staff FCC 202-418-2180

Almaty....Eighmy, Thomas Cnty AID 202-647-6920

Almonds....Burket, Stephen USITC 202-205-3318

Alopecia....Staff NIAMS 301-496-8188

Alpaca....Shelton, Linda USITC 202-205-3457

Alpers Syndrome....Staff NINDS 301-496-5751

Alpha-1-antitrypsin Deficiency (liver)....Staff NIDDK 301-654-3810

Alpha-1-antitrypsin Deficiency (lung)....Staff NHLBI 301-496-4236

Alternate energy....Foreso, Cynthia USITC 202-205-3348

Alternate Fuels Statistics....Geidl, John NEIC 202-254-5570

Alternate Long Distance Service Providers....Staff FCC 202-418-1544

Alternate Dispute Resolution....Staff FCC 202-418-0960

Alternative Farming Systems Information Center....Gates, Jane NAL 301-504-5724

Alternative Fuels Data Center....Eberhardt, James NEIC 202-586-9837

Alternative Fuels....Ferrell, John NEIC 202-586-8072

Alternative Medicine....Staff OD 301-402-2466

Alternative Motor Fuels....Bower, Marc NEIC 202-586-3891

Altitude....Staff NHLBI 301-496-4236

Alumina....Conant, Kenneth USITC 202-205-3346

Aluminum compounds....Greenblatt, Jack USITC 202-205-3353

Aluminum Extrud. Alum Rolling....Cammarota, David COMMERCE 202-482-5157

Aluminum Forgings, Electro....Cammarota, David COMMERCE 202-482-5157

Aluminum Sheet, Plate/Foil....Cammarota, David COMMERCE 202-482-5157

Aluminum....McNay, Deborah USITC 202-205-3425

Aluminum....Plunkert, Patricia MINES 202-501-9419

Alumni (NIH)....Staff FAES 301-530-0567

Alveolar Bone (Regeneration/Resorption)....Staff NIDR 301-496-4261

Alveolar Microlithiasis....Staff NHLBI 301-496-4236

Alveolar Proteinosis....Staff NHLBI 301-496-4236

Alzheimer's Disease....Staff NINDS 301-496-5751

Alzheimer's Disease....Staff NIDCD 301-496-7243

Alzheimer's Disease....Staff NIA 301-496-1752

Alzheimer's Disease....Staff NIMH 301-443-4513

Alzheimer's Disease....Staff Alzheimer's Association 800-272-3900

Alzheimer's Disease....Staff ADEAR 800-438-4380

Alzheimer's Research....Staff French Foundation for Alzheimer's Research (FFAR) 800-477-2243

AM Antennas, Directional....Staff FCC 202-418-2660

AM Stereo....Staff FCC 301-725-1585

AM Technical Standards Applications....Staff FCC 202-418-2660

Amateur (Ham) Radio-Antenna Ordinance Preemption....Staff FCC 202-418-0680

Amateur (Ham) Radio-Application forms....Staff FCC 800-322-1117

Amateur (Ham) Radio-Compliance....Staff 202-418-0680

Amateur (Ham) Radio-Engineering....Staff FCC 202-418-0680

Amateur (Ham) Radio-Exam Availability....Staff FCC 202-418-0680

Amateur (Ham) Radio-Forfeitures....Staff FCC 202-418-0680

Amateur (Ham) Radio-General....Staff FCC 800-322-1117

Amateur (Ham) Radio-Interference to TV/Phone etc....Staff FCC 202-418-1170

Amateur (Ham) Radio-Operating Questions....Staff FCC 202-418-0680

Amateur (Ham) Radio-Reciprocal Licenses....Staff FCC 800-322-1117

Amateur (Ham) Radio-Revocations....Staff FCC 202-418-0680

Amateur (Ham) Radio-Status....Staff 800-322-1117

Amateur (Ham) Radio-Status Licenses....Staff FCC 800-322-1117

Amateur (Ham) Radio-Technical....Staff FCC 202-418-0680

Amaurotic Idiocy....Staff NINDS 301-496-5751

Ambergris....Land, Eric USITC 202-205-3349

Ambiguous Genitalia....Staff NICHD 301-496-5133

Amblyopia....Staff NEI 301-496-5248

Ambulance and Rescue Squads....Staff FCC 717-337-1212

Ambulance....Staff Air Ambulance of America (Air AA) 800-262-8526

Ambulance....Staff Aeronational (Air ambulance transport) 800-245-9987

Ambulatory Patient Centers....Staff CC 301-496-3141

Amebiasis....Staff NIAID 301-496-5717

American Disability Act (ADA)....Staff FCC 202-418-0190

American fisheries products....Corey, Roger USITC 202-205-3327

American Nurses' Association....Staff NIH 816-474-5720

American Sign Language....Staff NIDCD 301-496-7243

Amides, fatty acids of (surface-active agents)....Land, Eric USITC 202-205-3349

Amides....Michels, David USITC 202-205-3352

Amines, fatty acids of (surface-active agents)....Land, Eric USITC 202-205-3349

Amines....Michels, David USITC 202-205-3352

Amino acids....Michels, David USITC 202-205-3352

Amino Acid Disorders....Staff NICHD 301-496-5133

Amino nitrogen....Hollrah, Glen H. PTO 703-308-4552

Ammonia....Trainor, Cynthia USITC 202-205-3354

Ammonium nitrate, fertilizer....Trainor, Cynthia USITC 202-205-3354

Ammonium nitrate, fuel-sensitized....Johnson, Larry USITC 202-205-3351

Ammonium nitrate, non-explosive or non-fertilizer....Greenblatt, Jack USITC 202-205-3353

Ammonium phosphate....Greenblatt, Jack USITC 202-205-3353

Ammonium sulfate....Greenblatt, Jack USITC 202-205-3353

Ammunition....Jordan, Charles PTO 703-308-0918

Ammunition....Luther, Dennis USITC 202-205-3498

Amniocentesis....Staff NICHD 301-496-5133

Amphetamines....Staff NIDA 301-443-6245

Amplifiers....Puffert, Douglas USITC 202-205-3402

Amplifiers....Sherman, Thomas USITC 202-205-3389

Amusement games....Millin, Vincent PTO 703-308-1065

Amusement devices....Love, John PTO 703-308-0873

Amyloid Polyneuropathy....Staff NINDS 301-496-5751

Amyloidosis (cardiac)....Staff NHLBI 301-496-4236

Amyloidosis....Staff NIDDK 301-654-4415

Amyloidosis....Staff NEI 301-496-5248

Amyloidosis....Staff NIAMS 301-496-8188

Amyotonia Congenita....Staff NINDS 301-496-5751

Amyotrophic Lateral Sclerosis....Staff NIDCD 301-496-7243

Amyotrophic Lateral Sclerosis....Staff NINDS 301-496-5751

Amyotrophic Lateral Sclerosis....Staff ALS 800-782-4747

Anabolic Steroids....Staff NIDA 301-443-6245

Analgesic-Associated Nephropathy....Staff NIDDK 301-654-4415

Analgesics....Nesbitt, Elizabeth USITC 202-205-3355

Analog computational computers....Envall, Roy PTO 703-305-9706

Analysis and Data, Producer Price Indexes....Howell, Craig LABOR 202-606-7704

Analysis....Clark, Stephen FRS 202-452-3752

Analytical Chemistry....Staff NIGMS 301-496-7301

Analytical chemistry....Housel, James PTO 703-308-4027

Analytical Instruments....Nealon, Marquarite COMMERCE 202-482-3411

Analytical Instrument (Trade Promo)....Manzolino, Frank COMMERCE 202-482-2991

Anaphylaxis....Staff NIAID 301-496-5717·

Anaplasia....Staff NCI 301-496-5583

Andalusite....DeSapio, Vincent USITC 202-205-3435

Andean Affairs....Lenzy, Karen US Trade Rep 202-395-5190

Andorra....Staff Cnty State 202-647-1412

Anemia (Hemolytic and Aplastic)....Staff NHLBI 301-496-4236

Anemia (Hemolytic and Aplastic)....Staff NCI 301-496-5583

Anemia....Staff NIDDK 301-496-3583

Anencephaly....Staff NINDS 301-496-5751

Anesthesiology (Dental)....Staff NIDR 301-496-4261

Anesthesiology....Staff NIGMS 301-496-7301

Aneurysm (Brain or Spinal)....Staff NINDS 301-496-5751

Aneurysm....Staff NHLBI 301-496-4236

Angelman's Disease....Staff NINDS 301-496-5751

Angina Pectoris....Staff NHLBI 301-496-4236

Angioedema....Staff NIAID 301-496-5717

Angiography....Staff NHLBI 301-496-4236

Angioplasty....Staff NHLBI 301-496-4236

Angles, shapes, and sections (steel)....Kaplan, Stephanie USITC 202-205-3436

Angola (Luanda)....Staff Cnty State 202-647-8434

Angola/Minerals....Mobbs, Philip Cnty Mines 202-501-9674

Angola....Daniels, Gussie Cnty AID 202-647-4328

Angola....Holm-Olsen, Finn Cnty Commerce 202-482-4228

Angola....Kotze, Joan Cnty Treasury 202-622-0333

Angola....Maybury-Lewis, Anthony Cnty Export-Import Bank 202-565-3739

Angola....Patel, Praful C. Cnty World Bank 202-473-4250

Angola....Patricio, Jose Goncalves Martins Cnty Embassy 202-785-1156

Angola....Schwartz, Larry Cnty USIA 202-619-6904

Angola....Silva, Jose Maria Cnty Embassy 202-785-1156

Angora....Shelton, Linda USITC 202-205-3457

Anguilla....Brooks, Michelle Cnty Commerce 202-482-2527

Anguilla....Wilkins, Michele Cnty Export-Import Bank 202-565-3743

Aniline Dyes (and Cancer)....Staff NCI 301-496-5583

Animal Bedding....Staff OD/DL 301-496-1160

Animal (Caging, Housing, Watering)....Staff NCRR 301-594-7933
Animal Colonies and Models (Special)....Staff DRR 301-594-7933
Animal Feeds....Conte, Ralph CUSTOMS 212-466-5759
Animal feeds....Pierre-Benoist, John USITC 202-205-3320
Animal Food....Staff OD/DL 301-496-1160
Animal Genetics....Staff NCRR 301-496-5255
Animal Health....Staff NCRR 301-496-4463
Animal husbandry....Love, John PTO 703-308-0873
Animal husbandry....Mancene, Gene PTO 703-308-2696
Animal Husbandry....Staff NCRR 301-496-2527
Animal Models for Aging Research....Staff NIA 301-496-1752
Animal Nutrition....Staff NCRR 301-496-4481
Animal oil, fats, greases....Reeder, John USITC 202-205-3319
Animal Research (Intramural)....Staff OD/DC 301-496-8740
Animal Research (Intramural)....Staff NCRR 301-594-7938
Animal Research....Staff OD/DC 301-496-8740
Animal Research....Staff NCRR 301-594-7938
Animal Resources Program....Staff NCRR 301-594-7938
Animal Sanitation....Staff OD/ORS 301-496-2960
Animal Welfare Information Center....Larson, Jean NAL 301-504-5215
Animal Welfare Policy....Staff OPRR 301-496-7163
Animal Welfare....Staff NIDA 301-443-6245
Animal Welfare....Staff NCRR 301-594-7938
Animal Welfare....Staff OD/DC 301-496-8740
Animals: Guide for the Care and Use of Lab Animals....Staff NCRR
    301-594-7938
Aniridia....Staff NEI 301-496-5248
Ankylosing Spondylitis....Staff Ankylosing Spondylitis Association (ASA)
    800-777-8189
Ankylosing Spondylitis....Staff NIAMS 301-496-8188
Anorexia Nervosa....Staff NIMH 301-496-4513
Anorexia Nervosa....Staff NICHD 301-496-5133
Anosmia....Staff NIDCD 301-496-7243
Anosmia....Staff NINDS 301-496-5751
Anoxia....Staff NHLBI 301-496-4236
ANSI Committee 63....Staff FCC 301-725-1585
Antarctica/Minerals....Doan, David Cnty Mines 202-501-9678
Antenatal Diagnosis....Staff NICHD 301-496-5133
Antenna measurements....Repjar, Andrew G. NIST 303-497-5703
Antenna Structures and Towers....Staff FCC 800-322-1117
Antenna Survey....Staff FCC 800-322-1117
Antenna....Kitzmiller, John USITC 202-205-3387
Antennas....Hajec, Donald PTO 703-308-4075
Anthracite....Foreso, Cynthia USITC 202-205-3348
Anthrax....Staff NIAID 301-496-5717
Anti-inflammatory agents....Nesbitt, Elizabeth USITC 202-205-3355
Anti-infective agents....Nesbitt, Elizabeth USITC 202-205-3355
Antialphatrypsin....Staff NIDDK 301-496-3583
Antibiotics....Staff NIAID 301-496-5717
Anticoagulant Drugs....Staff NHLBI 301-496-4236
Anticonvulsants....Nesbitt, Elizabeth USITC 202-205-3355
Antidiuretic Hormone....Staff NHLBI 301-496-4236
Antidiuretic Hormone....Staff NIDDK 301-496-3583
Antigens....Nucker, Christine M PTO 703-308-4028
Antigua/Barbuda....Brooks, Michelle Cnty Commerce 202-482-2527
Antigua and Barbuda (St. John's)....Staff Cnty State 202-647-2621
Antigua/Minerals....Torres, Ivette Cnty Mines 202-501-9670
Antigua....Lewis, Patrick Albert Cnty Embassy 202-362-5211
Antigua....Marcus, Anthony Cnty Treasury 202-622-1218
Antigua....Nallari, Raj R. Cnty World Bank 202-473-8697
Antigua....Prosper, Debbie Cnty Embassy 202-362-5211
Antigua....Wilkins, Michele Cnty Export-Import Bank 202-565-3743
Antihistamines....Nesbitt, Elizabeth USITC 202-205-3355
Antimetabolites....Staff NCI 301-496-5583
Antimony compounds....Greenblatt, Jack USITC 202-205-3353
Antimony....Carlin, James Jr., MINES 202-501-9426
Antimony....Lundy, David USITC 202-205-3439
Antipyretics....Nesbitt, Elizabeth USITC 202-205-3355
Antiques....Mushinske, Larry CUSTOMS 212-466-5739
Antiques....Spalding, Josephine USITC 202-205-3498
Antisocial Behavior....Staff NIMH 301-496-4513
Antithrombin III Deficiency....Staff NHLBI 301-496-4236
Antitrust Laws....Nardolilli, Pamela FRS 202-452-3289
Antiviral drug products....Boring, Daniel L. FAES 301-594-5029
Antiviral Substances....Staff NIAID 301-496-5717
Anxiety Disorders....Staff NIMH 301-496-4513
Aorta....Staff NHLBI 301-496-4236

Aortic Valve....Staff NHLBI 301-496-4236
Aortic Insufficiency/Stenosis....Staff NHLBI 301-496-4236
Aortitis....Staff NHLBI 301-496-4236
Apes and Monkeys (Medical Research)....Staff NCRR 301-594-7938
Aphakia....Staff NEI 301-496-5248
Aphasia (due to Stroke)....Staff NINDS 301-496-5751
Aphasia....Staff NIDCD 301-496-7243
Aphasia....Staff NINDS 301-496-5751
Aphthous Stomatitis-Recurrent....Staff NIDR 301-496-4261
Aplastic Anemia....Staff Aplastic Anemia Foundation of America (AAF)
    800-747-2820
Aplastic Anemia....Staff NHLBI 301-496-4236
Apparatus, Filtering/Purifying....Francke, Eric CUSTOMS 212-466-5669
Apparel and Textiles Industry Group....Owings, Christopher SEC 202-942-1900
Apparel, Body Supporting....Burtnik, Brian CUSTOMS 212-466-5880
Apparel, Food and Raw Materials, Intl. Price Ind....Frumkin, Rob LABOR
    202-606-7106
Apparel, Knit Wearing: Men's....Ryan, Mary CUSTOMS 212-466-5877
Apparel, Knit Wearing: Boys'....Ryan, Mary CUSTOMS 212-466-5877
Apparel, Leather....Weiss, Martin CUSTOMS 212-466-5881
Apparel, Miscellaneous....DeGaetano, Angela CUSTOMS 212-466-5540
Apparel, Plastic Wearing....Weiss, Martin CUSTOMS 212-466-5881
Apparel, Women's Woven Wearing....Schiazzano, Patricia CUSTOMS
    212-466-5866
Apparel, Woven Wearing: Men's....Shea, Gerard CUSTOMS 212-466-5878
Apparel, Woven Wearing: Boys'....Shea, Gerard CUSTOMS 212-466-5878
Apparel....Dulka, William COMMERCE 202-482-4058
Appeals....Staff FCC 202-418-1740
Appliances, Small....Smyth, James CUSTOMS 212-466-2084
Appliances....Duvall, Steven SEC 202-942-1950
Application Status-All Private Radio....Staff FCC 800-322-1117
Application Status-AM....Staff FCC 202-418-2670
Application Status-FM....Staff FCC 202-418-2730
Application Status-TV....Staff FCC 202-418-1630
Applications Fraud-Cellular....Staff FCC 202-418-1320
Applications Fraud-Private Radio....Staff FCC 202-418-0620
Appraisals, Land....Staff FWS 703-358-1713
Apraxia (speech)....Staff NIDCD 301-496-7243
Apraxia....Staff NIDCD 301-496-7243
Apraxia....Staff NINDS 301-496-5751
Aquaculture Information Center....McVey, Eileen NAL 301-504-5558
Aquaculture....Harvey, Dave Agri 202-219-0085
Aquaculture....Little, Robert Agri 202-720-6147
Aquaculture....Moore, Joel Agri 202-720-3244
Aquaculture....Staff FWS 703-358-1715
Aquatic Species Management....Staff FWS 703-358-1710
Aquatic Resource Education....Staff FWS 703-358-2156
Arachnoid Cyst....Staff NINDS 301-496-5751
Arachnoiditis....Staff NINDS 301-496-5751
Aran Duchenne Spinal Muscular Dystrophy....Staff NINDS 301-496-5751
Arboretum, National Library....Fernandez, Katya NAL 202-245-4538
ARC (AIDS-Related Complex)....Staff NIAID 301-496-5717
ARC Injection....Staff Project Inform 800-334-7422
Arch Glazing Petition....Giles, Ken CPSC 301-504-0580
Archaeology Research....Staff NEH 202-606-8210
Archaeology....Staff FWS 703-358-1786
Architecture Services....Polly, Laura USITC 202-205-3408
Architecture, Urban Planning....Beatley, Timothy UVA 904-924-6459
Architecture....Bowler, Alyssa PTO 703-305-9702
Architecture....Harris, William M. UVA 804-924-6450
Area Measurement....Hirschfeld, Don CENSUS 301-457-1099
Argentina (Buenos Aires)....Staff Cnty State 202-647-2401
Argentina/Minerals....Velasco, Pablo Cnty Mines 202-501-9677
Argentina....Granillo Ocampo, Raul Enrique Cnty Embassy 202-939-6400
Argentina....Hagerstrom, Mark V. Cnty World Bank 202-473-9208
Argentina....Jaureguiberry, Nora L. Cnty Embassy 202-939-6400
Argentina....Leeb, Howard Cnty USIA 202-619-5867
Argentina....Mye, Randolph Cnty Commerce 202-482-1548
Argentina....Neil, Jeff Cnty Treasury 202-622-1268
Argentina....Prevot, Babette Cnty AID 202-647-4359
Argentina....Wilkins, Michele Cnty Export-Import Bank 202-565-3743
Argon....Conant, Kenneth USITC 202-205-3346
Armenia....Carlen, James Cnty Treasury 202-622-0122
Armenia....Kreslins, Dagnija Cnty AID 202-736-4317
Armenia....Levine, Richard Cnty MINES 202-501-9682
Armenia....Nanagulian, Rouben Robert Cnty Embassy 202-628-5766
Armenia....O'Keefe, Monica Cnty USIA 202-619-5057

Be patient. If any phone number is incorrect, call (area code) 555-1212 and request the new listing.

1371

Armenia....Ruhl, Onno Cnty World Bank 202-458-9119
Armenia....Shugarian, Rouben Robert Cnty Embassy 202-628-5766
Armenia....Staff Cnty State 202-647-8671
Armenia....Stillwell, Carol Cnty TDA 703-875-4357
Armenia....Viksnins, Helen Peace Corps 202-606-5517
Armenia....Waxmen-Lenz, Roberta Cnty Export-Import Bank 202-565-3742
Armenia....Wootton, Nicholas Peace Corps 202-606-5519
Arms....Luther, Dennis USITC 202-205-3497
Arnold-Chiari Malformations....Staff NINDS 301-496-5751
Arrhythmias....Staff NHLBI 301-496-4236
Arsenic compounds....Greenblatt, Jack USITC 202-205-3353
Arsenic....Conant, Kenneth USITC 202-205-3346
Arsenic....Loebenstein, Roger MINES 202-501-9416
Art, works of....Spalding, Josephine USITC 202-205-3498
Art Services....Staff NCRR 301-496-2868
Arteriosclerosis (Cerebral)....Staff NINDS 301-496-5751
Arteriosclerosis....Staff NHLBI 301-496-4236
Arteriovenous Malformations (Cerebral and Spinal)....Staff NINDS 301-496-5751
Arteritis (eyes)....Staff NEI 301-496-5248
Arthritis and Musculoskeletal and Skin Dis., Nat'l Ins....Raab, Connie NIH
    301-496-8118
Arthritis Information Clearinghouse....Staff NIAMS 301-495-4484
Arthritis....Staff Arthritis Foundation (AF) 800-283-7800
Arthritis....Staff Arthritis Consulting Services 800-327-3027
Arthritis....Staff NIAMS 301-496-8188
Arthritis....Staff NIA 301-496-1752
Arthrogryposis Multiplex Congenita....Staff NIAMS 301-496-8188
Arthrogryposis Multiplex Congenita....Staff NIAMS 301-496-8188
Arthroscopy....Staff NIAMS 301-496-8188
Article carriers....Recia, Henry PTO 703-308-1382
Article dispensing....Olszewski, Robert PTO 703-308-2588
Article handling....Huppert, Michael PTO 703-308-1107
Artificial Blood Vessels....Staff NHLBI 301-496-4236
Artificial flowers of man-made fibers....Cook, Lee USITC 202-205-3471
Artificial flowers....Spalding, Josephine USITC 202-205-3498
Artificial Heart Valves....Staff NHLBI 301-496-4236
Artificial Heart....Staff NHLBI 301-496-4236
Artificial Insemination....Staff NICHD 301-496-5133
Artificial Intelligence Research....Staff NASA 713-483-5111
Artificial Intelligence....Montgomery, Shelagh COMMERCE 202-482-0571
Artificial Intelligence....Staff NLM 301-496-9300
Artificial Joints....Staff NIAMS 301-496-8188
Artificial Lung....Staff NHLBI 301-496-4236
Artificial mixtures of fatty substances....Randall, Rob USITC 202-205-3366
Artificial Pancreas....Staff NIDDK 301-496-3583
Artificial Skin....Staff NIGMS 301-496-7301
Aruba/Minerals....Rabchevsky, George Cnty Mines 202-501-9680
Aruba....Brooks, Michelle Cnty Commerce 202-482-2527
Aruba....Marcus, Anthony Cnty Treasury 202-622-1218
Aruba....Wilkins, Michele Cnty Export-Import Bank 202-565-3743
Asbestos Action Program (Technical Questions)....Staff EPA 202-260-3904
Asbestos and Cancer....Staff NCI 301-496-5583
Asbestos and the Workplace....Sims, Anne CDC 404-639-3286
Asbestos/Cement Products....Pitcher, Charles COMMERCE 202-482-0132
Asbestos Clearinghouse....Staff EPA 800-368-5888
Asbestos Ombudsman Clearinghouse/Hotline....Staff EPA 800-368-5888
Asbestos Ombudsman and Small Business Clearinghouse....Staff EPA
    703-305-5938
Asbestos Publications....Staff EPA 202-554-1404
Asbestos....Virta, Robert MINES 202-501-9384
Asbestos....White, Linda USITC 202-205-3427
Asbestosis....Staff NHLBI 301-496-4236
Asbestosis....Staff CDC/NIOSH 404-639-3286
ASEAN....Paine, George Cnty Commerce 202-482-3877
Ashgabat....Eighmy, Thomas Cnty AID 202-647-6920
Asia/trade matters....Lund, Christina US Trade Rep 202-395-6813
Asia/trade matters....Cassidy, Robert US Trade Rep 202-395-3430
Asia/trade matters....Byrons, Wendy C. US Trade Rep 202-395-3900
Asia....Greenberg, Richard OPIC 202-336-8616
Asparagus....McCarty, Timothy USITC 202-205-3324
Aspartame, Neurological Effects of....Staff NINDS 301-496-5751
Asperger's Syndrome....Staff NINDS 301-496-5751
Aspergillosis....Staff NIAID 301-496-5717
Asphalt, Natural....Solomon, Cheryl C. MINES 202-501-9393
Asphalt....White, Linda USITC 202-205-3427
Asphyxia....Staff NINDS 301-496-5751
Aspirin Allergy....Staff NIAID 301-496-5717

Aspirin-Myocardial Infarction Study (AMIS)....Staff NHLBI 301-496-4236
Assembly Equipment....Abrahams, Edward COMMERCE 202-482-0312
Assessment and Management of Side Effects of Disease Treatments....Staff NINR
    301-496-0207
Assessment and Management of Symptoms NINR 301-496-0207
Assistant Commissioner, Compensation Levels and Trnd....MacDonald, Kathleen
    M. LABOR 202-606-6302
Assistant Commissioner, Consumer Prices and Price Index....Greenlef, Joan
    LABOR 202-606-6952
Assistant Commissioner, Empl/Unempl. Stats, Curr. Empl. An....Bregger, John E.
    LABOR 202-606-6388
Assistant Commissioner, Empl/Unempl. Stats, Fed/State....Vacant LABOR
    202-606-6500
Assistant Commissioner, Industry Prices and Pr. Index....Vacant LABOR
    202-606-7700
Assistant Commissioner, Intl. Price Indexes....Reut, Katrina LABOR
    202-606-7100
Assistant Commissioner, Safety, Health and Work. Cond....Eisenberg, William M.
    LABOR 202-606-6304
Assisted Circulation....Staff NHLBI 301-496-4236
Assistive Devices....Staff NIDCD 301-496-7243
Associate Commissioner, Compensation and Work. Cond....Vacant LABOR
    202-606-6300
Associate Commissioner, Empl/Unempl Stats....Plewes, Thomas J. LABOR
    202-606-6400
Associate Commissioner, Employment Projections....Kutscher, Ronald LABOR
    202-606-5700
Associate Commissioner, Prices and Living Cond.....Dalton, Kenneth LABOR
    202-606-6960
Associate Commissioner, Productivity and Technology.....Dean, Edwin R. LABOR
    202-606-5600
Asthma....Staff Asthma and Allergy Foundation of America 800-727-8462
Asthma....Staff NIAID 301-496-5717
Asthma....Staff NHLBI 301-496-4236
Astigmatism....Staff NEI 301-496-5248
Astronaut appearances....Clary, Tawna NASA 202-358-1718
Astronaut Training....Staff NASA 713-483-5111
Astronomy Research....Gundy, Cheryl NASA 301-338-4707
Astronomy....Chevalier, Roger A. UVA 804-924-7494
Astrophysical Research....Katz, Jessie NASA 301-286-5566
Asymmetric Septal Hypertrophy (ASH)....Staff NHLBI 301-496-4236
Ataxia Telangiectasia....Staff NINDS 301-496-5751
Ataxia Telangiectasia....Staff NCI 301-496-5583
Ataxia....Staff NINDS 301-496-5751
Atelectasis....Staff NHLBI 301-496-4236
Atherosclerosis (Effect on Vision)....Staff NEI 301-496-5248
Atherosclerosis (Cerebral)....Staff NINDS 301-496-5751
Atherosclerosis....Staff NHLBI 301-496-4236
Athetosis....Staff NINDS 301-496-5751
Athlete's Foot....Staff NIAID 301-496-5717
Athlete's Heart....Staff NHLBI 301-496-4236
Athletic equipment....Witherspoon, Ricardo USITC 202-205-3496
Atmospheric Science Research....Staff NASA 804-864-6122
Atmospheric and Indoor Air Programs....Staff EPA 202-233-9140
Atomic Physics....Wiese, W.L. NIST 301-975-3200
Atomic Safety and Licensing Board....Cotter, Paul NRC 301-415-7450
Atomic Vapor Laser Isotope Separation Plant....Lowe, Owen W. NEIC
    301-903-5161
Atopic Dermatitis....Staff NIAMS 301-496-8188
Atopic Dermatitis....Staff NIAID 301-496-5717
Atrial Fibrillation....Staff AF Hotline 800-423-1925
Atrial Fibrillation....Staff NHLBI 301-496-4236
Atrophy....Staff NINDS 301-496-5751
Attention Deficit Disorder....Staff NINDS 301-496-5751
Attention Deficit Disorder....Staff NICHD 301-496-5133
Attention Deficit Disorder....Staff NIMH 301-443-4513
Attribution of Ownership of Mass Media Licenses....Staff FCC 202-418-1630
Auction Hotline....Staff FCC 202-418-1400
Auctions....Staff FCC 202-418-1400
Audio components....Puffert, Douglas USITC 202-205-3402
Audio systems....Kuntz, Curt PTO 703-305-4708
Audio Visual Services....Siegmund, John COMMERCE 202-482-4781
Audiology (Clinical Center patients)....Staff CC 301-496-5368
Audiovisual Material (For Health Prof. Education)....Staff NLM 301-496-6095
Audiovisual Materials (Nursing)....Staff HRSA/BHPr 301-443-5786
Auditory System....Staff NIDCD 301-496-7243

Audits....Staff FCC 202-418-0820

Augmentative Devices....Staff NIDCD 301-496-7243

Aural Rehabilitation....Staff NIDCD 301-496-7243

Australia (Canberra)....Staff Cnty State 202-647-9691

Australia....Bouck, Gary (Bus.)/Golike, William (Policy) Cnty Commerce 202-482-2471

Australia....Coyne, Bruce J. Cnty Embassy 202-797-3000

Australia....Demeter, Katalin Cnty World Bank 202-458-4661

Australia....Imam, Fahmila Cnty Export-Import Bank 202-565-3738

Australia....Jabbs, Theodore Cnty USIA 202-619-5836

Australia....Lyday, Travis Cnty Mines 202-501-9695

Australia....Russell, Donald Eric Cnty Embassy 202-797-3000

Australia....Vacant Cnty Treasury 202-622-0166

Austria (Vienna)....Staff Cnty State 202-647-1484

Austria/Minerals....Plachy, Josef Cnty Mines 202-501-9673

Austria....Combs, Philip Cnty Commerce 202-482-2920

Austria....Gosnell, Peter Cnty Export-Import Bank 202-565-3733

Austria....Lemaistre, Alice Cnty USIA 202-619-6184

Austria....Mackour, Oscar Cnty Treasury 202-622-0145

Austria....Stift, Desiree Cnty Embassy 202-895-6700

Austria....Tuerk, Helmet Cnty Embassy 202-895-6700

Autism....Staff NICHD 301-443-5133

Autism....Staff NIMH 301-443-4513

Autism....Staff NINDS 301-496-5751

Auto Industry Affairs Parts/Suppliers....Reck, Robert O. COMMERCE 202-482-1418

Auto Industry Affairs....Keitz, Stuart COMMERCE 202-482-0554

Auto Parts/Suppliers (Trade Promotions)....White, John C. COMMERCE 202-482-0671

Autoimmune Disease....Staff NIAID 301-496-5717

Autoimmune Disease....Staff NIAMS 301-496-8188

Automated Clearinghouse....Young, Florence FRS 202-452-3955

Automatic Teller Machine Theft....Kaplan, Carol Justice Stat 202-307-0759

Automation (Laboratory Apparatus and Processes)....Staff NCRR/BEIB 301-496-4426

Automobile - Catalytic Converters....Staff EPA 202-233-9090

Automobile Emissions- Recalls....Staff EPA 202-233-9260

Automobile Emissions....Staff EPA 202-260-7647

Automobile - Imports....Staff EPA 202-233-9660

Automobile Loans....Luckett, Charles FRS 202-452-2925

Automobile Parts....Topolansky, Adam USITC 202-205-3394

Automobile Warranty Information....Staff EPA 202-233-9100

Automobiles....Desoucey, Robert CUSTOMS 212-466-5667

Automobiles....Hagey, Michael USITC 202-205-3392

Automotive and other Vehicles Industry Group....Daly, James M. SEC 202-942-1800

Autonomic drugs....Nesbitt, Elizabeth USITC 202-205-3355

Auxiliary Antennas/Transmitters-AM....Staff FCC 202-418-2660

Auxiliary Antennas/Transmitters-FM....Staff FCC 202-418-2740

Auxiliary Antennas/Transmitters-TV FCC 202-418-1630

Availability of Nursing Resources-Quality Patient Care....Staff NINR 301-496-0207

Avascular Necrosis....Staff NIAMS 301-496-8188

Average Retail Food Prices--Monthly, CPI....Cook, William LABOR 202-606-6988

Average Retail Prices and Indexes of Fuels and Utilities.....Adkins, Robert LABOR 202-606-6985

Average Retail Prices and Indexes, Motor Fuels Only....Chelena, Joseph LABOR 202-606-6982

Aversives....Giles, Ken CPSC 301-504-0580

Aviation and Helicopter Services....Alford, Eugene COMMERCE 202-482-5071

Aviation, International....Gretch, Paul DOT 202-366-2423

Aviation Licenses....Staff FCC 717-337-1212

Aviation Medicine....Jordon, Jon L FAA 202-267-3535

Aviation Safety Analysis....Bermingham, Barry DOT 202-366-4466

Aviation Safety Information....Edwards, Carolyn FAA 202-366-5995

Aviation Safety....Huettner, Charles FAA 202-267-9613

Aviation safety....Loeb, Bernie NTSB 202-382-6610

Avionics Marketing....Pederson, Heather COMMERCE 202-482-2835

Avionics Testing....Deason, Billie A. NASA 713-483-5111

Azerbaijan....Adoteye, Philip C. Cnty World Bank 202-473-5509

Azerbaijan....Carlen, James Cnty Treasury 202-622-0122

Azerbaijan....Kreslins, Dagnija Cnty AID 202-736-4317

Azerbaijan....Kurbanov, Fakhratdin Cnty Embassy 202-842-0001

Azerbaijan....Levine, Richard Cnty MINES 202-501-9682

Azerbaijan....O'Keefe, Monica Cnty USIA 202-619-5057

Azerbaijan....Pashayev, Hafiz Mir Jalal Cnty Embassy 202-842-0001

Azerbaijan....Staff Cnty State 202-647-8671

Azerbaijan....Waxmen-Lenz Cnty Export-Import Bank 202-565-3742

Azides....Johnson, Larry USITC 202-205-3351

Azo chemistry....Lee, Mary PTO 703-308-4546

B

B-19 Infection (Human Parvovirus)....Staff NICHD 301-496-5133

Baby Bottle Tooth Decay....Staff NIDR 301-496-4261

Baby carriages, strollers, and parts....Abrahamson, Dana USITC 202-205-3430

Baby Walkers....Tyrrell, Elaine CPSC 301-504-0580

Baccalaureate Nursing Schools....Staff HRSA/BHPr 301-443-6333

Back Pain....Staff Back Pain Hotline 800-247-2225

Back Problems....Staff NIAMS 301-496-8188

Back Problems....Staff NINDS 301-496-5751

Bacterial Endocarditis....Staff NHLBI 301-496-4236

Bacterial Meningitis....Staff NIAID 301-496-5717

Bacterial Meningitis....Staff NIDCD 301-496-7243

Bacteriologic Media....Staff OD/ORS 301-496-6017

Bacteriology....Staff NIAID 301-496-5717

Bags or sacks....Cook, Lee USITC 202-205-3471

Bags....Gorman, Kevin CUSTOMS 212-466-5893

Bahamas (Nassau)....Staff Cnty State 202-647-2621

Bahamas/Minerals....Rabchevsky, George Cnty Mines 202-501-9670

Bahamas....Carey, Sheila Gweneth Cnty Embassy 202-319-2660

Bahamas....Donaldson, Timothy Baswell Cnty Embassy 202-319-2660

Bahamas....Head, Alfred Cnty USIA 202-619-6835

Bahamas....Hume, Susan Cnty World Bank 202-473-2407

Bahamas....Marcus, Anthony Cnty Treasury 202-622-1218

Bahamas....Siegelman, Mark Cnty Commerce 202-482-5880

Bahamas....Wilkins, Michele Cnty Export-Import Bank 202-565-3743

Bahrain (Manama)....Staff Cnty State 202-647-6572

Bahrain/Minerals....Michalski, Bernadette Cnty Mines 202-501-9699

Bahrain....Abdulkader, Mohammed Ibrahim Cnty Embassy 202-342-0741

Bahrain....Abdulla, Muhammad Abdul Ghaffer Cnty Embassy 202-342-0741

Bahrain....Clement, Claude Cnty Commerce 202-482-5545

Bahrain....Farah, Ahmed Cnty World Bank 202-473-2649

Bahrain....Maybury-Lewis Anthony Cnty Export-Import Bank 202-565-3739

Bahrain....Mercer, Dorothy Cnty Treasury 202-622-0184

Bahrain...Vacant Cnty USIA 202-619-6528

Bail (Federal)....Kaplan, Carol Justice Stat 202-307-0759

Bakery Products....Janis, William V. COMMERCE 202-482-2250

Balance of Payments, Chief....Bach, Christopher L., ECONOMIC 202-606-9545

Balance (Normal and Disordered)....Staff NIDCD 301-496-7243

Balkin States....Staff Cnty Commerce 202-482-2645

Ball Bearings....Reise, Richard COMMERCE 202-482-3489

Balls, sports and play....Witherspoon, Ricardo USITC 202-205-3496

Baltic Republics....Altheim, Stephen Cnty Treasury 202-622-0125

Baltic States....Staff Cnty State 202-647-3187

Baltics....Visknins, Helen Peace Corps 202-606-5517

Baltimore Longitudinal Study of Aging....Staff NIA 410-558-8139

Baltimore Longitudinal Study of Aging....Staff NIA 301-496-1752

Bamboo....Hoffmeier, Bill USITC 202-205-3321

Bandages, impregnated w/ medicinals....Randall, Rob USITC 202-205-3366

Banding, Bird....Staff FWS 703-358-0205

Bangladesh/Minerals....Kuo, Chin Cnty Mines 202-501-9693

Bangladesh (Dhaka)....Staff Cnty State 202-647-9552

Bangladesh....Frederick, David Cnty AID 202-647-5863

Bangladesh....Hutchings, Dayna Cnty Export-Import Bank 202-565-3737

Bangladesh....Kabir, Humayun Cnty Staff Embassy 202-342-8372

Bangladesh....Lowenstein, Linda Cnty World Bank 202-458-0428

Bangladesh....McCoy, Ethel Cnty Treasury 202-622-0336

Bangladesh....Simmons, John Cnty Commerce 202-482-2954

Bangladesh....Swaleheen, Mushfiq Us Cnty Embassy 202-342-8372

Bangladesh....Winchester, Rebecca Cnty USIA 202-619-6528

Bank Acquisitions....Simon, David FRS 202-452-3611

Bank credit Cards....Hurt, Adrienne FRS 202-452-2412

Bank for International Settlements....Siegman, Charles FRS 202-452-3308

Bank Rates on Business loans....English, William FRS 202-736-5645

Banking, International....Frankel, Allen FRS 202-452-3578

Banking services....Melly, Chrisopher USITC 202-205-3461

Banking services.... USITC 202-205-3436

Banking....Shuman, John COMMERCE 202-482-3050

Bankruptcy Reorganizations....Berman, Michael A. SEC 202-942-0810

Banks Industry Group....Tow, A. Richard SEC 202-942-1760

Banks....Staff SEC 202-942-7040

Be patient. If any phone number is incorrect, call (area code) 555-1212 and request the new listing.

1373

Barbados/Minerals....Rabchevsky, George Cnty Mines 202-501-9670
Barbados....Blackman, Courtney N. Cnty Embassy 202-939-9200
Barbados....Brooks, Michelle Cnty Commerce 202-482-2527
Barbados....Clarke, Roy Cnty Embassy 202-939-9200
Barbados....Head, Alfred Cnty USIA 202-619-6835
Barbados....Marcus, Anthony Cnty Treasury 202-622-1218
Barbados....Scoseria, Carmen C. Cnty World Bank 202-473-8677
Barbados....Staff Cnty State 202-647-2130
Barbados....Wilkins, Michele Cnty Export-Import Bank 202-565-3743
Barbasco....Wanser, Stephen USITC 202-205-3363
Barbiturates....Nesbitt, Elizabeth USITC 202-205-3355
Barbiturates....Staff NIDA 301-443-6245
Barbuda/Minerals....Torres, Ivette Cnty Mines 202-501-9680
Barbuda....Lewis, Patrick Albert Cnty Embassy 202-362-5211
Barbuda....Marcus, Anthony Cnty Treasury 202-622-1218
Barbuda....Nallari, Raj R. Cnty World Bank 202-473-4250
Barbuda....Prosper, Debbie Cnty Embassy 202-362-5211
Barge Freight Index....Schambach, Duane CFT 312-353-9022
Barite....Johnson, Larry USITC 202-205-3351
Barite....Searls, James, P. MINES 202-501-9407
Barium carbonate....Johnson, Larry USITC 202-205-3351
Barium compounds....Greenblatt, Jack USITC 202-205-3353
Barium pigments....Johnson, Larry USITC 202-205-3351
Barium sulfate...Johnson, Larry USITC 202-205-3351
Barium....Lundy, David USITC 202-205-3439
Barlow's Syndrome (Mitral Valve Prolapse)....Staff NHLBI 301-496-4236
Barrettes....Burns, Gail USITC 202-205-2501
Bars (steel)....Kaplan, Stephanie USITC 202-205-3436
Bartter's Syndrome....Staff NHLBI 301-496-4236
Basal Cell....Staff NCI 301-496-5583
Basic Energy Sciences....Staff NEIC 301-903-3081
Basic Paper and Board Mfg....Branley, Gary COMMERCE 202-482-0375
Basic Research....Staff NIGMS 301-496-7301
Basketwork, wickerwork, related products....Hoffmeier, Bill USITC 202-205-3321
Bathing caps....Jones, Jackie USITC 202-205-3466
Bathing caps....Hamey, Amy USITC 202-205-3465
Bathroom facilities....Recia, Henry PTO 703-308-1382
Batten Disease....Staff Battan Disease Support and Research Association 800-448-4570
Batten's Disease....Staff NINDS 301-496-5751
Battered Spouses....Staff NIMH 301-443-4513
Battered Spouses....Staff Hot-Line 301-654-1881
Batteries, Storage....Larrabee, David COMMERCE 202-482-0607
Batteries....Curran, David CUSTOMS 212-466-4680
Batteries....Eaton, Russell NEIC 202-586-0205
Batteries....Polly, Laura USITC 202-205-3408
Battery manufacturing....Hearn, Brian E. 703-308-2552
Battery-Driven Vehicles....Alpaugh, Richard NEIC 202-586-1477
Bauxite, Alumina, Prim Alum....Cammarota, David COMMERCE 202-482-5157
Bauxite calcined....White, Linda USITC 202-205-3427
Bauxite for metal....McNay, Deborah USITC 202-205-3425
Bauxite....Sehnke, Errol D. MINES 202-501-9421
Bay rum or bay water....Land, Eric USITC 202-205-3349
BCG (Bacillus Calmette-Guerin)....Staff NCI 301-496-5583
Beads, articles of....Witherspoon, Ricardo USITC 202-205-3489
Beads....Witherspoon, Ricardo USITC 202-205-3489
Beans, ex oilseed....McCarty, Timothy USITC 202-205-3324
Bearings, ball and roller....Polly, Laura USITC 202-205-3408
Bearings....Riedl, Karl CUSTOMS 212-466-5493
Bechet's Disease (eyes)....Staff NEI 301-496-5248
Becker's Muscular Dystrophy....Staff NINDS 301-496-5751
Bed Wetting....Staff NICHD 301-443-5133
Bed Wetting....Staff NIDDK 301-654-4415
Bedding....Hansen, John CUSTOMS 212-466-5854
Bedding....Sweet, Mary Elizabeth USITC 202-205-3455
Beds....Cuomo, Peter PTO 703-308-0827
Beef....Ludwick, David USITC 202-205-3329
Beepers-Common Carrier....Staff FCC 202-418-1330
Beepers-Private Carrier Paging and Microwave....Staff FCC 202-418-0620
Beer....Harney, Amy USITC 202-205-3465
Behavioral and Social Sciences....Staff NICHD 301-496-6832
Behavioral and Social Sciences....Staff NIMH 301-443-4513
Behavioral Pharmacology....Staff NIDA 301-443-6245
Behavioral Therapy....Staff NIDA 301-443-6245
Behcet's Disease (Neurological Effects of)....Staff NINDS 301-496-5751
Behcet's Disease (Systemic)....Staff NIDR 301-496-4261
Behcet's Disease (Systemic)....Staff NIAMS 301-496-8188

Behcet's....Staff American Behcet's Association Inc. 800-723-4238
Belarus....Carlen, James Cnty Treasury 202-622-0122
Belarus....Garg, Prabhat Cnty World Bank 202-473-2171
Belarus....Gontcharenok, Vladimir Cnty Embassy 202-986-1604
Belarus....Levine, Richard Cnty MINES 301-501-9682
Belarus....Martynov, Serguei Nikolaevich Cnty Embassy 202-986-1604
Belarus....McCleod, Evelyn Cnty AID 202-736-7646
Belarus....O'Keefe, Monica Cnty USIA 202-619-5057
Belarus....Staff Cnty State 202-647-6764
Belarus....Waxman-Lenz, Roberta Cnty Export-Import Bank 202-565-3742
Belgium (Brussels)....Staff Cnty State 202-647-6592
Belgium/Minerals....Zajac, William Cnty Mines 202-501-9671
Belgium....Adam, Andre Cnty Embassy 202-333-6900
Belgium....Bensimon, Simon Cnty Commerce 202-482-5041
Belgium....Gosnell, Peter Cnty Export-Import Bank 202-565-3733
Belgium....Holloway, Barbara Cnty Treasury 202-622-0098
Belgium....Kulla, Morgan Cnty USIA 202-619-6853
Belgium....Lepage, Christian Cnty Embassy 202-333-6900
Belize/Minerals....Velasco, Pablo Cnty Mines 202-501-9677
Belize (Belize City)....Staff Cnty State 202-647-3381
Belize....Brooks, Michelle Cnty Commerce 202-482-2527
Belize....Cambell, Edward Cnty AID 202-647-4105
Belize....Erlandson, Barbara Peace Corps 202-606-3624
Belize....Haylock, Claude Bromwell Cnty Embassy 202-332-9636
Belize....John Herrman Cnty TDA 703-875-4357
Belize....Lindo, Dean R. Cnty Embassy 202-332-9636
Belize....Neil, Jeff Cnty Treasury 202-622-1268
Belize....Opstein, Sally Cnty USIA 202-619-5864
Belize....Scoseria, Carmen C. Cnty World Bank 202-473-8677
Belize....Wilkins, Michele Cnty Export-Import Bank 202-565-3743
Bell's Palsy....Staff NINDS 301-496-5751
Belting and Hose....Prat, Raimundo COMMERCE 202-482-0128
Belting, industrial....Cook, Lee USITC 202-205-3471
Belting of rubber or plastics (for machinery)....Misurelli, Denby USITC 202-205-3362
Belts, apparel: Leather....Jones, Jackie USITC 202-205-3466
Belts, apparel: Other mens and boys....Sweet, Mary Elizabeth USITC 202-205-3455
Belts, apparel: Other womens and girls....Sweet, Mary Elizabeth USITC 202-205-3455
Bemiconductor Prod. Equipment....Andrews, Michael COMMERCE 202-482-2795
Benign Prostatic Hyperplasia....Staff NIDDK 301-654-4415
Benign Congenital Hypotonia....Staff NINDS 301-496-5751
Benign Mucosal Pemphigoid....Staff NIAMS 301-496-8188
Benin (Cotonou)....Staff Cnty State 202-647-1540
Benin/Minerals....Mobbs, Philip Cnty Mines 202-501-9679
Benin....Baily, Jess Cnty USIA 202-619-5900
Benin....Barber, Ed Cnty Treasury 202-622-1730
Benin....Bezek, Jill Cnty TDA 703-875-4357
Benin....Brown, Arthur Peace Corps 202-606-3237
Benin....Guidi, Kouassi Cnty Embassy 202-232-6656
Benin....Henke, Debra Cnty Commerce 202-482-5149
Benin....Maybury-Lewis Anthony Cnty Export-Import Bank 202-565-3739
Benin....Moreno-Herrero, Bianca Cnty World Bank 202-473-9178
Benin....Swift, Gail Peace Corps 202-606-3136
Benin....Tonoukouin, Lucien Edgar Cnty Embassy 202-232-6656
Bensenoid intermediates, miscellaneous....Matusik, Ed USITC 202-205-3356
Bentonite....DeSapio, Vincent USITC 202-205-3435
Benzene....Raftery, Jim USITC 202-205-3365
Benzenoid plastics....Misurelli, Denby USITC 202-205-3362
Benzenoid varnishes....Johnson, Larry USITC 202-205-3351
Benzenoid paints....Johnson, Larry USITC 202-205-3351
Benzenoid plasticizers....Johnson, Larry USITC 202-205-3351
Benzo(a)pyrene....Staff NCI 301-496-5583
Benzodiazepines....Staff NIDA 301-443-6245
Benzoic acid....Matusik, Ed USITC 202-205-3356
Berger's Disease....Staff NIDDK 301-654-4415
Beriberi (Nutritional)....Staff NIDDK 301-496-3583
Beriberi (Neurological)....Staff NINDS 301-496-5751
Bermuda/Minerals....Rabchevsky, George Cnty Mines 202-501-9670
Bermuda (Hamilton)....Staff Cnty State 202-647-8027
Bermuda....Brooks, Michelle Cnty Commerce 202-482-2527
Bernard-Soulier Syndrome....Staff NIDDK 301-496-3583
Beryllium compounds....Greenblatt, Jack USITC 202-205-3353
Beryllium....Kramer, Deborah A. MINES 202-501-9394
Beryllium....Lundy, David USITC 202-205-3439
Beryllium....Males, Barbara COMMERCE 202-482-0606

Best's Disease....Staff NEI 301-496-5248
Beta-thalassemia (Cooley's Anemia)....Staff NHLBI 301-496-4236
Betatron....Staff NCI 301-496-5583
Beverages, Alcoholic....Harney, Amy USITC 202-205-3465
Beverages, Alcoholic....Maria, John CUSTOMS 212-466-5730
Beverages Industry Group....Roycroft, John C. SEC 202-942-1960
Beverages, Non-alcoholic....Dennis, Alfred USITC 202-205-3316
Beverages....Kenney, Cornelius COMMERCE 202-482-2428
Bhutan/Minerals....Wu, John Cnty Mines 202-501-9697
Bhutan....Gilman, Timothy Cnty Commerce 202-482-2954
Bhutan....Gradisher, Thomas Cnty USIA 202-619-5529
Bhutan....Hutchings, Dayna Cnty Export-Import Bank 202-565-3737
Bhutan....McCoy, Ethel Cnty Treasury 202-622-0336
Bhutan....Nicholaws, Peter Cnty World Bank 202-458-0420
Bhutan....Staff Cnty State 202-647-2141
Bicycles and parts....Seastrum, Carl USITC 202-205-3493
Bicycles....Desoucey, Robert CUSTOMS 212-466-5667
Bicycles....Tyrrell, Elaine CPSC 301-504-0580
Bicycles....Vanderwolf, John COMMERCE 202-482-0348
Bilateral Agreements....Staff FIC 301-496-5903
Biliary Cirrhosis....Staff NIDDK 301-496-3583
Bilirubinemia....Staff NICHD 301-496-5133
Billed Party Preference....Staff FCC 202-418-1594
Billfolds....Seastrum, Carl USITC 202-205-3493
Billiard cloth....Cook, Lee USITC 202-205-3471
Billing and Collections....Staff FCC 202-418-1995
Binge Eating....Staff NIMH 301-496-443-4513
Binocular Vision....Staff NEI 301-496-5248
Binswanger's Disease....Staff NINDS 301-496-5751
Bio-related Chemistry....Staff NIGMS 301-496-7301
Bio-related Chemistry....Staff NIGMS 301-496-7301
Biochemical genetics....Gottesman, Susan FAES 301-496-3524
Biochemistry Instrumentation....Staff NCRR 301-594-7938
Biochemistry....Litchen, Michael J. FAES 301-496-3393
Biodegradable Plastics....Staff EPA 202-260-5649
Bioethics Literature....Staff National Center for Bioethics Literature 800-633-3849
Bioethics of Clinical Decisionmaking....Staff NINR 301-496-0207
Bioethics....Bonkovsky, Frederick O. FAES 301-496-2429
Biofeedback....Staff NHLBI 301-496-4236
Biofeedback....Staff NIMH 301-443-4513
Biofuels....Morrer, Richard NEIC 202-586-9315
Biogasoline....Moorer, Richard NEIC 202-586-9315
Biohazard Control....Staff OD/ORS 301-496-2960
Biohazard Identification....Staff OD/ORS 301-496-2960
Biohazards (Cancer Research)....Staff NCI 301-496-5583
Biological Community Profiles....Staff FWS 703-358-1715
Biological Information Services....Goshorn, Jeanne C. NLM 301-496-1131
Biological Models and Materials Resources Program....Staff NCRR 301-594-7906
Biology....Block, Gene D. UVA 804-924-3606
Biomedical Communications....Staff NLM 301-496-6308
Biomedical Computer Centers....Staff NCRR 301-496-5411
Biomedical Engineering....Staff NIGMS 301-496-7301
Biomedical Engineering....Staff NCRR/BEIB 301-496-4741
Biomedical Information Services....Spann, Melvin L. NLM 301-496-1131
Biomedical Research Training and Fellowships....Staff NIGMS 301-496-7301
Biomedical Research Training and Fellowships....Staff DRG 301-594-7248
Biomedical Research Technology Program....Staff NCRR 301-593-7934
Biomedical Research Support Program....Staff NCRR 301-594-7947
Biomedical Research Technology Programs....Staff NCRR 301-594-7934
Biometrics....Huque, Mohammad FAES 301-443-4594
Bioorganic Chemistry....Kirk, Kenneth L. FAES 301-496-2619
Biophysics....Staff NIGMS 301-496-7301
Biopsy....Staff NCI 301-496-5583
Biotechnology Information Center....Dobert, Raymond NAL 301-504-5947
Biotechnology Information....Staff NLM 301-496-2475
Biotechnology, Trade Promo....Kimmel, Edward COMMERCE 202-482-3640
Biotechnology....Arakaki, Emily COMMERCE 202-482-0128
Biotechnology....Levin, Morris FAES 301-405-1056
Biotechnology....Moore, Mike PTO 703-308-4474
Biotechnology....Powell, L.J. NIST 301-975-2627
Bipolar Disorder....Staff NIMH 301-443-4513
Bird meat....Newman, Douglas USITC 202-205-3328
Birth Defects and Genetic Diseases....Erickson, David J. CDC 404-488-7160
Birth Defects and Developmental Disabilities....Adams, M. J. CDC 404-488-7150
Birth Defects (Developmental)....Staff NICHD 301-496-5133
Birth Defects (Neurological)....Staff NINDS 301-496-5751
Birth Defects....Staff Cornelia de Lange Syndrome Foundation (CLSF) 800-223-8355

Birth Place....Hansen, Kristin CENSUS 301-457-2454
Birth Weight....Staff NICHD 301-496-5133
Birth....Staff NICHD 301-496-5133
Bishkek....Eighmy, Thomas Cnty AID 202-647-6920
Bismuth compounds....Greenblatt, Jack USITC 202-205-3353
Bismuth....Brown, Robert Jr. MINES 202-501-9577
Bismuth....Lundy, David USITC 202-205-3439
Bituminous coal....Foreso, Cynthia USITC 202-205-3348
Black Lung Disease....Gambino, Phil SSA 410-965-8904
Black Lung Disease....Sims, Anne CDC 404-639-3286
Black Holes....Staff NASA 410-338-4514
Black powder....Johnson, Larry USITC 202-205-3351
Blankets....Sweet, Mary Elizabeth USITC 202-205-3455
Blasting caps....Johnson, Larry USITC 202-205-3351
Blastomycosis....Staff NIAID 301-496-5717
Bleaching machines....Greene, William USITC 202-205-3405
Blepharitis....Staff NEI 301-496-5248
Blepharospasm....Staff NINDS 301-496-5751
Blepharospasm....Staff NEI 301-496-5248
Blind (Rehabilitation and Research)....Staff NEI 301-496-5248
Blind students....Staff National Alliance of Blind Students (NABS) 800-424-8666
Blind....ACB 800-424-8666
Blind....Staff American Foundation for the Blind (AFB) 800-232-5463
Blindness....Staff R P Foundation Fighting Blindness 800-683-5555
Blindness....Staff Blind Children's Center (BCC) 800-222-3566
Blindness....Staff Prevent Blindness America (PBA) 800-331-2020
Blindness....Staff Blinded Veterans Association (BVA) 800-669-7079
Bloch-Sulzberger Syndrome (Neurological Effects)....Staff NINDS 301-496-5751
Blood Brain Barrier....Staff NINDS 301-496-5751
Blood Cells....Staff NHLBI 301-496-4236
Blood Coagulation....Staff NHLBI 301-496-4236
Blood Diseases....Staff NHLBI 301-496-4236
Blood Donations....Staff CC 301-496-1048
Blood Fractions....Staff NHLBI 301-496-4236
Blood Groups....Staff NHLBI 301-496-4236
Blood Plasma....Staff NHLBI 301-496-4236
Blood Plasma....Staff FDA/NCDB/OB 301-496-4396
Blood Pressure....Staff NHLBI 301-496-4236
Blood Resources (National)....Staff NHLBI 301-496-4236
Blood Substitutes....Staff NHLBI 301-496-4236
Blood Vessels....Staff NHLBI 301-496-4236
Blouses....Sweet, Mary Elizabeth USITC 202-205-3455
Blowers and Fans....Jonkers, Loretta COMMERCE 202-482-0564
Blowers....Riedl, Karl CUSTOMS 212-466-5493
Boat Building, Major Proj.....Vanderwolf, John COMMERCE 202-482-0348
Boat Radios....Staff FCC 202-418-0680
Boats, Craft....Vanderwolf, John COMMERCE 202-482-0348
Boats, Pleasure....Vanderwolf, John COMMERCE 202-482-0348
Boats, Pleasure....Lahey, Kathleen USITC 202-205-3409
Boats....Wholey, Patrick CUSTOMS 212-466-5668
Body Weight....Staff NIDDK 301-496-3583
Body-supporting garments, includes corset/brassieres....Sundar, Shetty USITC 202-205-3486
Boilers....Francke, Reic CUSTOMS 212-466-5669
Boilers....Fravel, Dennis USITC 202-205-3404
Bolivia (La Paz)....Staff Cnty State 202-647-3076
Bolivia/Minerals....Velasco, Pablo Cnty Mines 202-501-9677
Bolivia....Anne McKinney Cnty TDA 703-875-4357
Bolivia....Clapham, Lizzie Cnty Peace Corps 202-606-3499
Bolivia....Davis, Janice Peace Corps 202-606-3198
Bolivia....Epstein, Sharon Cnty AID 202-647-4358
Bolivia....Hunt, Rebecca Cnty Commerce 202-482-2521
Bolivia....Iwase, Noriko Cnty World Bank 202-473-0137
Bolivia....Jarvis, Catherine Cnty USIA 202-619-5867
Bolivia....Lopez, Miguel Antonio Cnty Embassy 202-483-4410
Bolivia....Neil, Jeff Cnty Treasury 202-622-1268
Bolivia....R. Petricevic, Andres Cnty Embassy 202-483-4410
Bolivia....Wilkins, Michele Cnty Export-Import Bank 202-565-3743
Bolivian Hemorrhagic Fever....Staff NIAID 301-496-5717
Bolting cloth....Cook, Lee USITC 202-205-3471
Bolts....Brandon, James USITC 202-205-3433
Bonds, Technical Information....Decorleto, Donna FRS 202-452-3956
Bone, articles of....Spalding, Josephine USITC 202-205-3498
Bone black....Johnson, Larry USITC 202-205-3351
Bone char....Randall, Rob USITC 202-205-3366
Bone Disorders....Staff NIAMS 301-496-8188
Bone Marrow Transplantation....Staff NIAID 301-496-5717

Be patient. If any phone number is incorrect, call (area code) 555-1212 and request the new listing.

1375

Bone Marrow Transplantation....Staff NHLBI 301-496-4236
Bone Marrow Transplantation....Staff NCI 301-496-5583
Bone Marrow Failure....Staff NHLBI 301-496-4236
Bone Marrow....Staff National Marrow Donor Program (MARROW) 800-654-1247
Book Store (Clinical Center)....Staff FAES 301-496-5274
Bookbinding machinery....Lusi, Susan USITC 202-205-3400
Books (Export Promo)....Kimmel, Edward COMMERCE 202-482-3640
Books-Information-NIH Library....Staff NCRR 301-496-2184
Books-Information-NIH Library....Staff NLM 301-496-6095
Books....Abramowitz, Carl CUSTOMS 212-466-5733
Books....Lofquist, William S. COMMERCE 202-482-0379
Books....Twarok, Chris USITC 202-205-3314
Borax....Greenblatt, Jack USITC 202-205-3353
Borderline Personality Disorder....Staff NIMH 301-443-4513
Boric acid....Trainor, Cynthia USITC 202-205-3354
Boron compounds....Greenblatt, Jack USITC 202-205-3353
Boron....Greenblatt, Jack USITC 202-205-3353
Boron....Lyday, Phyllis A. MINES 202-501-9405
Bosnia....Alkalaj, Sven Cnty Embassy 202-833-3612
Bosnia....Dzirlo, Sakir Cnty Embassy 202-833-3612
Bosnia....Staff Cnty State 202-736-7677
Bosnia....Steblez, Walter Cnty MINES 202-501-9672
Bosnia-Herce....Waxman-Lenz Roberta Cnty Export-Import Bank 202-565-3742
Bosnia-Herzegovina....Fraile-Ordonez, Maria Cnty World Bank 202-473-4838
Bosnia-Herzegovina....Altheim, Stephen Cnty Treasury 202-622-0125
Bosnia-Herzegovina....Corwin, Elizabeth Cnty USIA 202-619-5055
Botswana/Minerals....Antonides, Lloyd Cnty Mines 202-501-9686
Botswana (Gaborone)....Staff Cnty State 202-647-8433
Botswana....Bowler, Gina Peace Corps 202-606-3644
Botswana....Fox, Russell Peace Corps 202-606-3645
Botswana....Holm-Olsen, Finn Cnty Commerce 202-482-4228
Botswana....Lane, Bernard Cnty AID 202-647-4228
Botswana....Maybury-Lewis Anthony Cnty Export-Import Bank 202-565-3739
Botswana....Moorad, Mustaq Ahmed Cnty Embassy 202-244-4990
Botswana....Patel, Praful C. Cnty World Bank 202-473-4250
Botswana....Rauch, Margie Cnty Treasury 202-622-0251
Botswana....Schwartz, Larry Cnty USIA 202-619-6904
Botswana....Sebele, Botseletse Kingsley Cnty Embassy 202-244-4990
Botswana....Younge, Nathan Cnty TDA 703-875-4357
Bottles, pails and dishes, of rubber of plastics....Raftery, Jim USITC 202-205-3365
Botulism....Staff NIAID 301-496-5717
Boundaries of Legal Areas, State Boundary Certifica....Sobel, Joel CENSUS 301-457-1099
Boundaries of Legal Areas, Boundary Changes....Goodman, Nancy CENSUS 301-457-1099
Bowel Diseases, Inflammatory....Staff NIDDK 301-496-5583
Bowen's Disease....Staff NCI 301-496-5583
Brachial Plexus Injuries....Staff NINDS 301-496-5751
Bradycardia....Staff NHLBI 301-496-4236
Braids, other....Shelton, Linda USITC 202-205-3457
Braille....Staff Braille Institute 800-272-4553
Brain Banks....Staff NINDS 301-496-5751
Brain Injury....Staff NINDS 301-496-5751
Brain Tumor....Staff American Brain Tumor Association (ABTA) 800-886-2282
Brain Tumor....Staff NIDCD 301-496-7243
Brain Tumor....Staff NINDS 301-496-5751
Brain Tumor....Staff NCI 301-496-5583
Brain....Staff NIMH 301-443-4513
Brain....Staff NINDS 301-496-5751
Brake systems....Oberleitner, Robert PTO 703-308-3569
Brakes....Oberleitner, Robert PTO 703-308-3569
Brass....Lundy, David USITC 202-205-3439
Brazil (Brasilia)....Staff Cnty State 202-647-9407
Brazil/Minerals....Gurmendi, Alfredo Cnty Mines 202-501-9681
Brazil....de Araujo, Fredrico Cesar Cnty Embassy 202-745-2700
Brazil....Farris, Larry Cnty Commerce 202-482-3871
Brazil....Flecha De Lima, Paulo-Tarso Cnty Embassy 202-202-745-2700
Brazil....Korff, Michael Cnty USIA 202-619-6835
Brazil....Marcus, Anthony Cnty Treasury 202-622-1218
Brazil....Maybury-Lewis Anthony Cnty Export-Import Bank 202-565-3739
Brazil....Parel, Chris Cnty World Bank 202-473-3918
Brazil....Prevot, Babette Cnty AID 202-647-4359
Bread and other baked goods....Schneider, Greg USITC 202-205-3326
Breast Cancer....Staff Y-Me National Breast Cancer Association 800-221-2141
Breast Cancer....Staff NCI 301-496-5583

Breast Implants....Staff FDA 800-532-4440
Breast Milk....Staff NICHD 301-496-5133
Breeder reactor....Greenblatt, Jack USITC 202-205-3353
Brick, ceramic....White, Linda USITC 202-205-3427
British Indian Ocean Territories (BIOT)....Staff Cnty State 202-647-8913
British Pound with options....Lang, Dawn M. CFT 312-353-9018
Broadcast News....Barkin, Steve UMD 301-405-2412
Broadcast services (Radio, Television)....Staff OD/OC 301-496-5895
Broadcasting Satellites....Staff FCC 202-418-1610
Broadcasting services....Huthoefer, Lori USITC 202-205-3303
Broiler with options....Fichert, David CFT 312-353-3181
Bromine....Conant, Kenneth USITC 202-205-3346
Bromine....Lyday, Phyllis A. MINES 202-501-9405
Bronchiectasis....Staff NHLBI 301-496-4236
Bronchitis (Chronic)....Staff NHLBI 301-496-4236
Brooms....Burns, Gail USITC 202-205-2501
Brucellosis....Staff NIAID 301-496-5717
Brunei/Minerals....Wu, John Cnty Mines 202-501-9697
Brunei (Bandar Seri Begawan)....Staff Cnty State 202-647-3276
Brunei....Abdul Latif, Hali Jaya bin Cnty Embassy 202-342-0159
Brunei....Cung, Raphael Cnty Commerce 202-482-3877
Brunei....Gilroy, Meg Cnty USIA 202-619-5836
Brunei....Imam, Fahmila Cnty Export-Import Bank 202-565-3738
Brunei....Shelton, Alison Cnty Treasury 202-622-0354
Brunei....Sukaimi, Janeh Cnty Embassy 202-342-0159
Brushes....Brownchweig, Gilbert CUSTOMS 212-466-5744
Brushes....Burns, Gail USITC 202-205-2501
Bruxism....Staff NIDR 301-496-4261
Bubonic Plague....Staff NIAID 301-496-5717
Buckets....Staff CPSC 301-504-0580
Buckles....Brandon, James USITC 202-205-3433
Budget Issues....Psner, Paul L. GAO 202-512-9573
Budget Issues....Irving, Paul L. GAO 202-512-9573
Buerger's Disease (Thromboangiitis Obliterans)....Staff NHLBI 301-496-4236
Builders Hardware....Williams, Franklin COMMERCE 202-482-0132
Builders' Wares....Burtnik, Brian CUSTOMS 212-466-5880
Building boards....Hoffmeier, Bill USITC 202-205-3321
Building components (wood)....Hoffmeier, Bill USITC 202-205-3321
Building Environment....Hill, James E. NIST 301-975-5851
Building Materials and Construction....Pitcher, Charles B. COMMERCE 202-482-0132
Building Materials, Trade Policy....Pitcher, Charles COMMERCE 202-482-0132
Building materials....Frohnsdorff, Geoffrey J. NIST 301-975-6706
Building Materials....Frohnsdorff, G.J. NIST 301-975-6706
Buildings, Energy Efficient....Kapus, Theodore NEIC 202-586-9123
Bulbar Palsy....Staff NINDS 301-496-5751
Bulbs (lamps)....Cutchin, John USITC 202-205-3396
Bulgaria (Sofia)....Staff Cnty State 202-647-0310
Bulgaria/Minerals....Steblez, Walter Cnty Mines 202-501-9672
Bulgaria....Amick, Jack Peace Corps 202-606-3548
Bulgaria....Amick, Jack Peace Corps 202-606-3548
Bulgaria....Botoucharova, Snejana Damianova Cnty Embassy 202-387-7969
Bulgaria....Gallagher, Tricia Cnty Treasury 202-622-0117
Bulgaria....Keller, Jeremy Cnty Commerce 202-482-4915
Bulgaria....Kraske, Huda Cnty World Bank 202-473-3564
Bulgaria....LeMasters, Cheryl Peace Corps 202-606-3547
Bulgaria....Petkov, Latchezar Cnty Embassy 202-387-7969
Bulgaria....Stillwell, Carol Cnty TDA 703-875-4357
Bulgaria....Waxman-Lenz, Roberta Cnty Export-Import Bank 202-565-4742
Bulimia....Staff NICHD 301-496-5133
Bulimia....Staff NIMH 301-443-4513
Bulletin Boards....Staff FCC 202-418-0940
Bulletin Board....Staff CENSUS 301-457-2310
Bullous Pemphigoid....Staff NIAMS 301-496-8188
Bunker "C" fuel oil....Foreso, Cynthia USITC 202-205-3348
Buprenorphine....Staff NIDA 301-443-6245
Bureau of Competition - Accounting....Broberg, Evelyn S. FTC 202-326-2569
Bureau of Competition - Accounting....Painter, David T. FTC 202-326-2574
Bureau of Competition - Accounting....Rowe, Ronald Baylor FTC 202-326-2610
Bureau of Competition - Accounting....Steffen, Boris J. FTC 202-326-2573
Bureau of Competition - Administration....Baumgartner, Phillip A. FTC 202-326-2546
Bureau of Competition - Administration....Foster, Patricia A. FTC 202-326-2852
Bureau of Competition - Administration....Kennedy, Chandra FTC 202-326-2547
Bureau of Competition - Administration....Kereszturi, Joyce A. FTC 202-326-2541
Bureau of Competition - Administration....McGraw, Jeanne M. FTC 202-326-2565
Bureau of Competition - Administration....Onley, Essie FTC 202-326-2544

Bureau of Competition - Administration....Shelton, Joyce A. FTC 202-326-2856

Bureau of Competition - Administration....Salters, Willie FTC 202-326-2561

Bureau of Competition - Compliance.....Clayborne, Delores M. FTC 202-326-2152

Bureau of Competition - Compliance....Baruch, Roberta S. FTC 202-326-2861

Bureau of Competition - Compliance....Davidson, Kenneth FTC 202-326-2863

Bureau of Competition - Compliance....Ducore, Daniel P. FTC 202-326-2526

Bureau of Competition - Compliance....Eckhaus, Joseph FTC 202-326-2665

Bureau of Competition - Compliance....Gill, Pamela A. FTC 202-326-2765

Bureau of Competition - Compliance....Lawler, Stewart FTC 202-326-3181

Bureau of Competition - Compliance....Libby, Kenneth A. FTC 202-326-2694

Bureau of Competition - Compliance....Ortiz, Rafael A. FTC 202-326-2672

Bureau of Competition - Compliance....Patel, Chirag FTC 202-326-2824

Bureau of Competition - Compliance....Piotrowski, Elizabeth A. FTC 202-326-2623

Bureau of Competition - Compliance....Rohlck, Eric C. FTC 202-326-2681

Bureau of Competition - Compliance....Schenoff, Anne K. FTC 202-326-2031

Bureau of Competition - Compliance....Scott, Pauline FTC 202-326-2670

Bureau of Competition - Compliance....Seymour, Jane R. FTC 202-326-2678

Bureau of Competition - Compliance....Strong, Arthur FTC 202-326-3478

Bureau of Competition - Compliance....Von Nirschel, David FTC 202-326-3213

Bureau of Competition - Compliance....Williams, Tonya FTC 202-326-2054

Bureau of Competition - Compliance....Youngwood, Gordon FTC 202-326-2808

Bureau of Competition - Gen. Lit. (Assoc and Business).....Lomax, Joan C. FTC 202-326-2901

Bureau of Competition - Gen. Lit. (Assoc and Business)....Catt, Malcolm L. FTC 202-326-2911

Bureau of Competition - Gen. Lit. (Assoc and Business)....Cox, Kent FTC 202-326-2058

Bureau of Competition - Gen. Lit. (Assoc and Business)....Boynton, Evelyn B. FTC 202-326-2737

Bureau of Competition - Gen. Lit. (Assoc and Business).....Veney, Wanda M. FTC 202-326-2895

Bureau of Competition - Gen. Lit. (Assoc and Business)....McCartney, P. Abbott FTC 202-326-2695

Bureau of Competition - Gen. Lit. (Assoc and Business)....Oppenheim, Martha H. FTC 202-326-2941

Bureau of Competition - Gen. Lit. (Assoc and Business)....Hoagland, John R. FTC 202-326-2893

Bureau of Competition - Gen. Lit. (Assoc and Business)....Draluck, Jonathan FTC 202-326-2564

Bureau of Competition - Gen. Lit. (Assoc and Business)....McNeely, Michael FTC 202-326-2904

Bureau of Competition - Gen. Lit. (Assoc and Business).....Marks, Randall FTC 202-326-2571

Bureau of Competition - Gen. Lit. (Assoc and Business)....Zimmerman, Seth B. FTC 202-326-2914

Bureau of Competition - Gen. Lit. (Assoc.and Business)....Harcketts, J. Dennis FTC 202-326-2783

Bureau of Competition - Gen. Lit. (Energy and Food)....Skubel, Marmichael O. FTC 202-326-2611

Bureau of Competition - Gen. Lit. (Energy and Food)....Wilensky, Steven FTC 202-326-2650

Bureau of Competition - Gen. Lit. (Energy and Food)....Washington, Norris FTC 202-326-2606

Bureau of Competition - Gen. Lit. (Energy and Food)....Frumin, Jill M. FTC 202-326-2758

Bureau of Competition - Gen. Lit. (Energy and Food)....Jones, Robert FTC 202-326-2740

Bureau of Competition - Gen. Lit. (Energy and Food)....Krulla, Rhett R. FTC 202-326-2608

Bureau of Competition - Gen. Lit. (Energy and Food)....Henning, Renee S. FTC 202-326-2621

Bureau of Competition - Gen. Lit. (Energy and Food)....Hershey, Micheline FTC 202-326-2191

Bureau of Competition - Gen. Lit. (Energy and Food)....Schneider, Marc FTC 202-326-2062

Bureau of Competition - Gen. Lit. (Energy and Food)....Dodson, Beverly A. FTC 202-326-2939

Bureau of Competition - Gen. Lit. (Energy and Food)....Licker, Naomi FTC 202-326-2851

Bureau of Competition - Gen. Lit. (Energy and Food)....Fishkin, James FTC 202-326-2663

Bureau of Competition - Gen. Lit. (Energy and Food)....Petrizzi, Maribeth FTC 202-326-2615

Bureau of Competition - Gen. Lit. (Energy and Food)....Salemi, Constance M. FTC 202-326-2643

Bureau of Competition - Gen. Lit. (Energy and Food)....Lipson, Frank FTC 202-326-2617

Bureau of Competition - Gen. Lit. (Energy and Food)....Nolan, Arthur J. FTC 202-326-2770

Bureau of Competition - Gen. Lit. (Energy and Food)....Tovsky, Robert S. FTC 202-326-2634

Bureau of Competition - Gen. Lit. (Energy and Food)....Silver, Daniel FTC 202-326-3102

Bureau of Competition - Gen. Lit. (Energy and Food)....McDonald, Carol E. FTC 202-326-2616

Bureau of Competition - Gen. Lit. (Energy and Food)....Shapiro, Barbara K. FTC 202-326-2633

Bureau of Competition - Gen. Lit. (Energy and Food)....Villavicencio, Alice M. FTC 202-326-3155

Bureau of Competition - Gen. Lit. (Energy and Food)....Richman, Peter FTC 202-326-2563

Bureau of Competition - Gen. Lit. (Energy and Food)....Proctor, Barbara FTC 202-326-2630

Bureau of Competition - Gen. Lit. (Energy and Food)....Liedquist-Scott, Philo FTC 202-326-2631

Bureau of Competition - Gen. Lit. (Energy and Food)....Schildkraut, Marc G. FTC 202-326-2622

Bureau of Competition - Gen. Lit. (Energy and Food)....Lawrence, Jo Ann FTC 202-326-2642

Bureau of Competition - Gen. Lit. (Energy and Food)....Joseph, Anthony Low FTC 202-326-2910

Bureau of Competition - Gen. Lit. (Energy and Food)....Johnson, Dennis F. FTC 202-326-2712

Bureau of Competition - Gen. Lit. (Health Care)....Hilder, Elizabeth FTC 202-326-2545

Bureau of Competition - Gen. Lit. (Health Care)....Jones, Patricia Y. FTC 202-326-2942

Bureau of Competition - Gen. Lit. (Health Care)....Narrow, David M. FTC 202-326-2744

Bureau of Competition - Gen. Lit. (Health Care)....Greene, Stephanie FTC 203-326-2925

Bureau of Competition - Gen. Lit. (Health Care)....Moreland, Judith A. FTC 202-326-2776

Bureau of Competition - Gen. Lit. (Health Care)....White, Christine FTC 202-326-3707

Bureau of Competition - Gen. Lit. (Health Care)....Maxwell, Sally L. FTC 202-326-2674

Bureau of Competition - Gen. Lit. (Health Care)....Brazille, Lorraine FTC 202-326-2059

Bureau of Competition - Gen. Lit. (Health Care)....Schwartz, Allison FTC 202-326-2926

Bureau of Competition - Gen. Lit. (Health Care)....Osnowitz, Steve FTC 202-326-2746

Bureau of Competition - Gen. Lit. (Health Care)....Pender, David FTC 202-326-2549

Bureau of Competition - Gen. Lit. (Health Care)....Allen, Patricia FTC 202-326-3176

Bureau of Competition - Gen. Lit. (Health Care)....Bissegger, Michael R. FTC 202-326-2154

Bureau of Competition - Gen. Lit. (Health Care)....Voss, Oscar M. FTC 202-326-2750

Bureau of Competition - Gen. Lit. (Health Care)....Blumenreich, Linda FTC 202-326-2751

Bureau of Competition - Gen. Lit. (Health Care)....Tucker, Deborah FTC 202-326-2766

Bureau of Competition - Gen. Lit. (Health Care)....Bellack, George R. FTC 202-326-2763

Bureau of Competition - Gen. Lit. (Health Care)....Davis, Rendell A., Jr. FTC 202-326-2894

Bureau of Competition - Gen. Lit. (Health Care)....Connelly-Draper, Molly FTC 202-326-2760

Bureau of Competition - Gen. Lit. (Health Care)....Langley, Stephanie FTC 202-326-2944

Bureau of Competition - Gen. Lit. (Health Care)....Gibbs, Garry FTC 202-326-2767

Bureau of Competition - Gen. Lit. (Health Care)....Friedman, Alan J. FTC 202-326-2742

Bureau of Competition - Gen. Lit. (Health Care)....Horoschak, Mark J. FTC 202-326-3688

Bureau of Competition - Gen. Lit. (Health Care)....Schorr, Gary FTC 202-326-3063

Bureau of Competition - Gen. Lit. (Health Care)....Brownman, Joseph S. FTC 202-326-2605

Be patient. If any phone number is incorrect, call (area code) 555-1212 and request the new listing.

1377

Bureau of Competition - Gen. Lit. (Health Care)....Bruno, Marian FTC 202-326-2846

Bureau of Competition - Gen. Lit. (Health Care)....Clark-Coleman, Sheila FTC 202-326-2759

Bureau of Competition - Gen. Lit. (Health Care)....Meier, Markus FTC 202-326-2781

Bureau of Competition - Gen. Lit. (Mergers)....Scribner, John E. FTC 202-326-3271

Bureau of Competition - Gen. Lit. (Mergers)....Weber, John C. FTC 202-326-2829

Bureau of Competition - Gen. Lit. (Mergers)....Woodard, Carolyn FTC 202-326-2706

Bureau of Competition - Gen. Lit. (Non-Mergers)....Waldeck, Cecelia FTC 202-326-3669

Bureau of Competition - Gen. Lit. (Non-Mergers)....Mills, Karen FTC 202-326-2052

Bureau of Competition - Gen. Lit. (Non-Mergers)....Sockwell, Stephen W., Jr. FTC 202-326-2950

Bureau of Competition - Gen. Lit. (Non-Mergers)....Seesel, John H. FTC 202-326-2702

Bureau of Competition - Gen. Lit. (Non-Mergers)....Hahm, Kevin K. FTC 202-326-2306

Bureau of Competition - Gen. Lit. (Non-Mergers)....Stevens, Peer L. FTC 202-326-3154

Bureau of Competition - Gen. Lit. (Non-Mergers)....Hackley, Jacqueline FTC 202-326-2729

Bureau of Competition - Gen. Lit. (Non-Mergers)....Abrahamsen, Dana FTC 202-326-2906

Bureau of Competition - Gen. Lit. (Non-Mergers)....Spriggs, Valicia A. FTC 202-326-2839

Bureau of Competition - Gen. Lit. (Non-Mergers)....Kinzelman, Gregory FTC 202-326-2073

Bureau of Competition - Gen. Lit. (Non-Mergers)....Antalics, Michael FTC 202-326-2821

Bureau of Competition - Gen. Lit. (Non-Mergers)....Bloom, Morris A. FTC 202-326-2707

Bureau of Competition - Gen. Lit. (Non-Mergers)....Nolan, Paul FTC 202-326-2770

Bureau of Competition - Gen. Lit. (Non-Mergers)....Costilo, L. Barry FTC 202-326-2024

Bureau of Competition - Gen. Lit. (Non-Mergers)....Inglefield, David L. FTC 202-326-2637

Bureau of Competition - Gen. Lit. (Non-Mergers)....Menna, Mark FTC 202-326-2722

Bureau of Competition - Gen. Lit. (Non-Mergers)....Cook, Robert FTC 202-326-2771

Bureau of Competition - Gen. Lit. (Non-Mergers)....Riddell, Stephen FTC 202-326-2721

Bureau of Competition - Gen. Lit. (Non-Mergers)....Gray, Jessica FTC 202-326-3342

Bureau of Competition - Gen. Lit. (Non-Mergers)....Johnson, Joyce FTC 202-326-2576

Bureau of Competition - Gen. Lit. (Non-Mergers)....Parker, Patrice FTC 202-326-2837

Bureau of Competition - Gen. Lit. (Non-Mergers)....Nagata, Ernest A. FTC 202-326-2714

Bureau of Competition - Gen. Lit. (Non-Mergers)....Cunningham, Linda FTC 202-326-2638

Bureau of Competition - Gen. Lit. (Non-Mergers)....Moscatelli, Catharine FTC 202-326-2749

Bureau of Competition - Gen. Lit. (Non-Mergers)....Dagen, Richard FTC 202-326-2628

Bureau of Competition - Gen. Lit. (Non-Mergers)....Easterling, Wallace W. FTC 202-326-2936

Bureau of Competition - Gen. Lit. (Non-Mergers)....Lanning, William FTC 202-326-3361

Bureau of Competition - Gen. Lit. (Non-Mergers)....Cole, Judith A. FTC 202-326-2693

Bureau of Competition - Gen. Lit. (Non-Mergers)....Doyle, Robert W., Jr. FTC 202-326-2819

Bureau of Competition - Gen. Lit. (Non-Mergers)....Dugan, John, F. FTC 202-326-2715

Bureau of Competition - Gen. Lit. (Non-Mergers)....Barnes, Rosenna FTC 202-326-2796

Bureau of Competition - Gen. Lit. (Non-Mergers)....McDuffie, Lourine FTC 202-326-2735

Bureau of Competition - General Litigation (Mergers)....Levy, Richard A. FTC 202-326-2814

Bureau of Competition - General Litigation (Mergers)....Brooks, Sylvia M. FTC 202-326-2682

Bureau of Competition - General Litigation (Non-Mergers)....Forster, Mary C. FTC 202-326-2212

Bureau of Competition - General Litigation....Malester, Ann B. FTC 202-326-2682

Bureau of Competition - General Litigation....Elmore, Ernest FTC 202-326-3109

Bureau of Competition - General Litigation....Miller, Anne E. FTC 202-326-2806

Bureau of Competition - General Litigation....Feldman, Dawn FTC 202-326-2064

Bureau of Competition - General Litigation....Jex, Elizabeth FTC 202-326-3273

Bureau of Competition - General Litigation....Berg, Karen E. FTC 202-326-2960

Bureau of Competition - General Litigation....Bernstein, Steven K. FTC 202-326-2423

Bureau of Competition - General Litigation....Moskowitz, Lenore H. FTC 202-326-2779

Bureau of Competition - General Litigation....Mendel, Jacqueline FTC 202-326-2603

Bureau of Competition - General Litigation....Stephenson, Patricia FTC 202-326-2877

Bureau of Competition - General Litigation....Triggs, Casey FTC 202-326-2804

Bureau of Competition - General Litigation....Tahyar, Benjamin FTC 202-326-2889

Bureau of Competition - General Litigation.....Blunt, Deborah M. FTC 202-326-2145

Bureau of Competition - General Litigation....Wilkinson, Laura FTC 202-326-2830

Bureau of Competition - General Litigation....Pettee, Susan P. FTC 202-326-2826

Bureau of Competition - General Litigation....Holden, James FTC 202-326-2963

Bureau of Competition - General Litigation....Pickett, Robert FTC 202-326-2682

Bureau of Competition - General Litigation....Moiseyev, Michael FTC 202-326-3106

Bureau of Competition - General Litigation....Higgins, Claudia R. FTC 202-326-2682

Bureau of Competition - General Litigation....Heydenreich, Melissa FTC 202-326-2543

Bureau of Competition - International Antitrust....Parisi, John J. FTC 202-326-2133

Bureau of Competition - International Antitrust....Karlsson, Paul FTC 202-326-2566

Bureau of Competition - International Antitrust....Feuillan, Jacques C. FTC 202-326-2379

Bureau of Competition - International Antitrust....Schimpff, Kirsten M. FTC 202-326-2731

Bureau of Competition - Mergers....Berman, Jacqueline FTC 202-326-3769

Bureau of Competition - Mergers....Bush, Michele B. FTC 202-326-2619

Bureau of Competition - Mergers....Faulk, Linda M. FTC 202-326-2822

Bureau of Competition - Mergers....Foreman, Elaine FTC 202-326-2531

Bureau of Competition - Mergers....Koberstein, Nicholas R. FTC 202-326-2743

Bureau of Competition - Mergers....Mahan, Carrie FTC 202-326-3680

Bureau of Competition - Mergers....Perez, Christina FTC 202-326-2048

Bureau of Competition - Mergers....Piercy, Carey FTC 202-326-2962

Bureau of Competition - Mergers....Taylor, Pamela FTC 202-326-2237

Bureau of Competition - Mergers....Waldman, Craig A. FTC 202-326-2602

Bureau of Competition - Mergers...Martin, Lisa FTC 202-326-2888

Bureau of Competition - Office of the Director....Clark, Barbara A. FTC 202-326-2562

Bureau of Competition - Office of the Director....Greenbaum, Joan S. FTC 202-326-2629

Bureau of Competition - Office of the Director....Green, Geoffrey FTC 202-326-2641

Bureau of Competition - Office of the Director...Egan, James C., Jr. FTC 202-326-2886

Bureau of Competition - Office of the Director....Arquit, Kevin J. FTC 202-326-2556

Bureau of Competition - Office of the Director....White, Roxanne FTC 202-326-4954

Bureau of Competition - Office of the Director....Winslow, Walter T., Jr. FTC 202-326-2560

Bureau of Competition - Office of the Director....Steptoe, Mary Lou FTC 202-326-2584

Bureau of Competition - Office of the Director....Taylor, Mildred E. FTC 202-326-2553

Bureau of Competition - Office of the Director....Whitener, Mark D. FTC 202-326-2845

Bureau of Competition - Office of the Director....Baer, William J. FTC 202-326-2952

Bureau of Competition - Office of the Director....Rowe, Ronald A. FTC 202-326-2610

Bureau of Competition - Policy and Evaluation....Morse, Howard FTC 202-326-2949

Bureau of Competition - Policy and Evaluation....Mongoven, James F. FTC 202-326-2879

Bureau of Competition - Policy and Evaluation....Cariaga, Frances P. FTC 202-326-2882

Bureau of Competition - Policy and Evaluation....Doying, William A.E. FTC 202-326-2582

Bureau of Competition - Policy and Evaluation....Averitt, Neil W. FTC 202-326-2885

Bureau of Competition - Policy and Evaluation....Hadley, Benjamin FTC 202-326-2598

Bureau of Competition - Premerger Notification.....Moss, Betty W. FTC 202-326-3650

Bureau of Competition - Premerger Notification....Ovuka, Nancy M. FTC 202-326-2609

Bureau of Competition - Premerger Notification....Epps, Melea R.C. FTC 202-326-2705

Bureau of Competition - Premerger Notification....Cohen, Victor FTC 202-326-2849

Bureau of Competition - Premerger Notification....Hancock, Thomas F. FTC 202-326-2946

Bureau of Competition - Premerger Notification....Kaplan, Jeffrey FTC 202-326-2943

Bureau of Competition - Premerger Notification....Horton, Renee A. FTC 202-326-2842

Bureau of Competition - Premerger Notification....Choslovsky, Jonathan FTC 202-326-2639

Bureau of Competition - Premerger Notification....Rubenstein, Hy David FTC 202-326-2887

Bureau of Competition - Premerger Notification....Smith, Richard B. FTC 202-326-2850

Bureau of Competition - Premerger Notification....Sipple, John M., Jr. FTC 202-326-2862

Bureau of Competition - Premerger Notification....Sharpe, Patrick FTC 202-326-2848

Bureau of Competition - Premerger Notification....Schechter, William I. FTC 202-326-3119

Bureau of Competition - Premerger Notification....Peay, Sandra M. FTC 202-326-2844

Bureau of Competition....Krauss, Joseph FTC 202-326-2713

Bureau of Consumer Affairs - Advertising Practices....Bloom, Jeffrey I. FTC 202-326-3327

Bureau of Economics - Antitrust....Ferguson, James M. FTC 202-326-3386

Bureau of Economics - Antitrust....Saltzman, Harold E. FTC 202-326-3459

Bureau of Economics - Antitrust....Wu, Lawrence FTC 202-326-2229

Bureau of Economics, Director's Office....Wise, Michael O. FTC 202-326-3344

Bureau of Economics - Office of the Director....Painter, Susan FTC 202-326-3370

Bureau of Economics - Policy Analysis....Person, Brenda W. FTC 202-326-2554

Burkina Faso....Foster, Whitney P. Cnty World Bank 202-473-4653

Burkina Faso....Maybury-Lewis Anthony Cnty Export-Import Bank 202-565-3739

Burkina Faso....Baily, Jess Cnty USIA 202-619-5900

Burkina Faso....Kotze, Joan Cnty Treasury 202-622-0333

Burkina Faso....Ouedraogo, Gaetan R. Cnty Embassy 202-332-5577

Burkina Faso....Ouedraogo, Oulemayne Cnty Embassy 202-332-5377

Burkina Faso (Ouagadougou)....Staff Cnty State 202-647-2791

Burkina Faso....Michelini, Philip Cnty Commerce 202-482-4388

Burkina Faso/Minerals....Mobbs, Philip Cnty Mines 202-501-9679

Burkina....Saulters, Willie Cnty AID 202-647-6039

Burkitt's Lymphoma....Staff NCI 301-496-5583

Burma/Minerals....Wu, John Cnty Mines 202-501-9697

Burma (Myanmor)....Dwight, Lawrence Cnty Treasury 202-622-0356

Burma (Myanmar)....Paine, George Cnty Commerce 202-482-3877

Burma (Rangoon)....Staff Cnty State 202-647-7108

Burma....Camp, Bea Cnty USIA 202-619-5837

Burma....Ntahomvukiye, Severin Cnty Embassy 202-342-2574

Burma....Respess, Rebecca Cnty TDA 703-875-4357

Burn care for children....Staff Shriners Hospital Referral Line 800-237-5055

Burn Research....Staff NIGMS 301-496-7301

Burning Mouth Syndrome....Staff 301-496-4261

Bursitis....Staff NIAMS 301-496-8188

Burundi (Bujumbura)....Staff Cnty State 202-647-3139

Burundi/Minerals....Antonides, Lloyd Cnty Mines 202-501-9686

Burundi....Barber, Ed Cnty Treasury 202-622-1730

Burundi....Goode, Sachiko Peace Corps 202-606-3695

Burundi....Henning, Herman Cnty USIA 202-619-5926

Burundi....Irabahinyuje-Sakubu, Beatrice Cnty Embassy 202-3422574

Burundi....Lloyd, Linda Cnty AID 202-647-9809

Burundi....Maybury-Lewis Anthony Cnty Export-Import Bank 202-565-3739

Burundi....Michelini, Philip Cnty Commerce 202-482-4388

Burundi....Wilhelm, Vera A. Cnty World Bank 202-473-4366

Buses....Hagey, Michael USITC 202-205-3392

Business Administration....Allen, Brandt R. UVA 804-924-4842

Business Cycle Indicators....Statistical Indicators Staff ECONOMIC 202-606-5366

Business Data Centers....Staff CENSUS 301-457-1305

Business Establishment List, Empl/Unempl. Stats....Searson, Michael LABOR 202-606-6469

Business Forms....Bratland, Rose Marie COMMERCE 202-492-0380

Business/Industry Data Centers....Staff CENSUS 301-457-2580

Business Initiatives....Harrison, Monika SBA 202-205-6665

Business Investment...Funk, Charles CENSUS 301-763-2542

Business Licenses....Staff FCC 717-337-1212

Business Opportunities, Small and Disadvantaged Utilization....Staff HUD 202-708-1428

Business Opportunities....Staff FCC 202-416-0934

Business Outlook, Chief....Vacant ECONOMIC 202-606-5365

Business Radio....Staff FCC 717-337-1212

Business Statistics, Business Owners' Characterist....McCutcheon, Donna CENSUS 301-457-2568

Business Statistics, County Business Patterns....Hanczaryk, Paul CENSUS 301-457-2580

Business Statistics, Minority Businesses....McCutcheon, Donna CENSUS 301-457-2568

Businesses, Disadvantaged....Smith, Gloria NEIC 202-586-7377

Businesses, Minority-Owned....Smith, Gloria NEIC 202-586-7377

Businesses, Women-Owned....Smith, Gloria NEIC 202-586-7377

Butadiene....Raftery, Jim USITC 202-205-3365

Butane....Land, Eric USITC 202-205-3349

Butter....Ludwick, David USITC 202-205-3329

Buttons....Shildneck, Ann USITC 202-205-3499

Butyl alcohol....Michels, David USITC 202-205-3352

Butyl benzyl phthalate....Johnson, Larry USITC 202-205-3351

Butyl oleate....Johnson, Larry USITC 202-205-3351

Butyl rubber....Misurelli, Denby USITC 202-205-3362

Butyl stearate....Johnson, Larry USITC 202-205-3351

Butylene....Raftery, Jim USITC 202-205-3365

Bypass Surgery....Staff NHLBI 301-496-4236

Byssinosis (Brown Lung Disease)....Staff NHLBI 301-496-4236

C

C.A.R.....Maybury-Lewis, Anthony Cnty Export-Import Bank 202-565-3739

Cable-Aeronautical Radio....Staff FCC 202-416-0903

Cable Broadcasting....Siegmund, John COMMERCE 202-482-4781

Cable Equipment Capability....Staff FCC 202-416-0903

Cable Forms....Staff FCC 202-416-0919

Cable-Franchising Authority....Staff FCC 202-416-0940

Cable-General Inquiries Western U.S.....Staff FCC 202-416-0953

Cable-General Inquiries Southern U.S.....Staff FCC 202-416-0860

Cable-General Inquiries Central U.S.....Staff FCC 202-416-0876

Cable-General Inquiries Northeastern U.S.....Staff FCC 202-416-0859

Cable Leakage Index....Staff FCC 202-416-0903

Cable-Signal Leakage....Staff FCC 202-416-0903

Cable-Small Systems Hotline....Staff FCC 202-416-0818

Cable Special Relief Petitions....Staff FCC 202-416-0903

Cable System Files....Staff FCC 202-416-0921

Cable-Technical Standards....Staff FCC 202-416-0903

Cable Television Franchising....Staff FCC 202-416-0940

CAD/CAM/CAE Software....Swann, Vera A. COMMERCE 202-482-0396

Cadastral Surveys....Staff FWS 703-358-1713

Cadmium....Kuck, Peter MINES 202-501-9436

Cadmium....Lundy, David USITC 202-205-3439

Caffeine and its compounds....Nesbitt, Elizabeth USITC 202-205-3355

Calcium carbonate....Johnson, Larry USITC 202-205-3351

Calcium carbonate....Tepordei, Valentin V. MINES 202-501-9392

Calcium compounds....Greenblatt, Jack USITC 202-205-3353

Calcium pigments....Johnson, Larry USITC 202-205-3351

Calcium sulfate....Johnson, Larry USITC 202-205-3351

Calcium....Greenblatt, Jack USITC 202-205-3353

Calcium....Miller, Michael MINES 202-501-9409

Calculators....Baker, Scott USITC 202-205-3386

Calculus....Staff NIDR 301-496-4261

Calendaring machines....Lusi, Susan USITC 202-205-3400

Calendar of Events....Staff OD/OC 301-496-2266

California MTC (Manufacturing Technology Center)....Chernesky, John J. NIST 310-353-3060

Call Signs Allocation....Staff FCC 202-418-1680

Call Signs - Availability Only....Staff FCC 202-418-0270

Call Signs Block Allocation....Staff FCC 202-653-8126

Call Signs - Radio....Staff FCC 202-418-1680

Call Signs - TV....Staff FCC 202-418-1680

Calligraphy....Staff FWS 202-208-4111

Calling Card....Staff FCC 202-418-1530

Cambodia/Minerals....Lyday, Travis Cnty Mines 202-501-9695

Cambodia....Camp, Bea Cnty USIA 202-619-5837

Cambodia....Imam, Fahmila Cnty Export-Import Bank 202-565-3738

Cambodia....Pho, Hong-Phong B. Cnty Commerce 202-482-3877

Cambodia....Respess, Rebecca Cnty TDA 703-875-4357

Cambodia....Sanaka, Yoshio Cnty World Bank 202-458-0628

Cambodia....Schneider, Todd Cnty Treasury 202-622-0335

Cambodia....Staff Cnty State 202-647-3133

Cameos....Witherspoon, Ricardo USITC 202-205-3489

Cameras....Kiefer, Barbara CUSTOMS 212-466-5685

Cameroon (Yaounde)....Staff Cnty State 202-647-1707

Cameroon/Minerals....Dolley, Thomas Cnty Mines 202-501-9690

Cameroon....Barber, Ed Cnty Treasury 202-622-1730

Cameroon....Bezek, Jill Cnty TDA 703-875-4357

Cameroon....Henke, Debra Cnty Commerce 204-482-5149

Cameroon....Henning, Herman Cnty USIA 202-619-5926

Cameroon....Jordon, Kim Peace Corps 202-606-3097

Cameroon....Khouzam, Magda Cnty World Bank 202-473-4701

Cameroon....Maybury-Lewis Anthony Cnty Export-Import Bank 202-565-3739

Cameroon....Mendouga, Jerome Cnty Embassy 202-265-8790

Cameroon....Ndzengue, Pierre Cnty Embassy 202-265-8790

Cameroon....Trouba, Larry Peace Corps 202-606-3998

Cameroon....Vandergriff, Teresa Cnty AID 202-647-9207

Camphor....Randall, Rob USITC 202-205-3366

Canada (Ottawa)....Staff Cnty State 202-647-2170

Canada/Minerals....Heydari, Michael Cnty Mines 202-501-9688

Canada/trade matters....Burckey, Claude US Trade Rep 202-395-3412

Canada....Chretien, Raymond A.J. Cnty Embassy 202-682-1740

Canada....Don, Jonathan Cnty Commerce 202-482-3101

Canada....Gosnell, Peter Cnty Export-Import Bank 202-565-3733

Canada....Kulla, Morgan Cnty USIA 202-619-6853

Canada....Pascoe, Pat Cnty Treasury 202-622-0093

Canada....Wright, Robert Cnty Embassy 202-265-8790

Canadian Dollar with options....Bice, David CFT 312-353-7880

Canavan's Disease....Staff NINDS 301-496-5751

Cancer and Aging....Staff NIA 301-496-1752

Cancer and Aging....Staff NCI 301-496-5583

Cancer Control Program....Staff NCI 301-496-5583

Cancer Information Service....Staff NCI 800-422-6237

Cancer Institute, National....Nealon, Eleanor NIH 301-496-6631

Cancer Institute, National....Newman, Patricia NIH 301-496-6641

Cancer Prevention....Sunnarborg, Katharyn CDC 404-488-5080

Cancer (Reproductive Tract)....Staff NICHD 301-496-5133

Cancer (Reproductive Tract)....Staff NCI 301-496-5583

Cancer Research....Staff NCI 301-496-5583

Cancer....Staff ACS 800-227-2345

Cancer....Staff AMC Cancer Information and Counseling Line 800-525-3777

Cancer....Staff CIC 800-4-CANCER

Candida....Staff NIDR 301-496-4261

Candida....Staff NIAID 301-496-5717

Candidiasis....Staff NIAID 301-496-5717

Candidiasis....Staff NIDR 301-496-4261

Candles....Brownchweig, Gilbert CUSTOMS 212-466-5744

Candles....Randall, Rob USITC 202-205-3366

Candy....Maria, John CUSTOMS 212-466-5730

Canes....Spalding, Josephine USITC 202-205-3498

Canker Sores....Staff NIDR 301-496-4261

Canned Goods....Williams, Janis COMMERCE 202-482-2250

Canoes....Lahey, Kathleen USITC 202-205-3409

Capacitors....Malison, Andrew USITC 202-205-3391

Capacitors....Reynolds, Bruce A. PTO 703-308-3305

Capacitors....Vacant CUSTOMS 212-466-5673

Cape Verde....Radisic, Gradimir Cnty World Bank 202-473-7539

Cape Verde....Hutchings, Dayna Cnty Export-Import Bank 202-565-3737

Cape Verde....Baily, Jess Cnty USIA 202-619-5900

Cape Verde....Vandergriff, Teresa Cnty AID 202-647-9207

Cape Verde....Barber, Ed Cnty Treasury 202-622-1730

Cape Verde....Younge, Nathan Cnty TDA 703-875-4357

Cape Verde....Santon, Corentino, Virgilio Cnty Embassy 202-965-6820

Cape Verde....Barbosa, Jose Eduardo Cnty Embassy 202-965-6820

Cape Verde....Michelini, Philip Cnty Commerce 202-482-4388

Cape Verde....Mitchell, Willis Peace Corps 202-606-3708

Cape Verde (Praia)....Staff Cnty State 202-647-1596

Cape Verde Islands/Minerals....Mobbs, Philip Cnty Mines 202-501-9679

Capital Flows, International....Stekler, Lois FRS 202-452-3716

Capital Measurement, Productivity Research....Harper, Michael LABOR 202-606-5603

Capital Punishment....Greenfeld, Lawrence Justice Stat 202-616-3281

Capitation Grants for Health Professions Schools....Staff HRSA/BHPr 301-443-6880

Capitation Grants for Nurse Training....Staff HRSA/BHPr 301-443-5786

Caprolactam monomer....Matusik, Ed USITC 202-205-3356

Caps....Hamey, Amy USITC 202-205-3465

Caps....Jones, Jackie USITC 202-205-3466

Captioning....Staff NIDCD 301-496-7243

Carbohydrate products....Robinson, Douglas PTO 703-308-2897

Carbohydrates....Breneman, Bruce PTO 703-308-3324

Carbon activated....Randall, Bob USITC 202-205-3366

Carbon and graphite electrodes....Cutchin, John USITC 202-205-3396

Carbon black....Johnson, Larry USITC 202-205-3351

Carbon Black....Prat, Raimundo COMMERCE 202-482-0128

Carbon dioxide....Conant, Kenneth USITC 202-205-3346

Carbon disulfide....Conant, Kenneth USITC 202-205-3346

Carbon Products....Brownchweig, Gilbert CUSTOMS 212-466-5744

Carbon tetrachloride....Michels, David USITC 202-205-3352

Carbon....Johnson, Larry USITC 202-205-3351

Carboxylic acids....Michels, David USITC 202-205-3352

Carboxymethyl cellulose salts (surface active)....Land, Eric USITC 202-205-3349

Carcalon (Krebiozen)....Staff NCI 301-496-5583

Carcinogen Assessment....Staff EPA 202-260-3814

Carcinogen....Staff NCI 301-496-5583

Carcinogenesis....Donovan, Paul J. FAES 301-846-1245

Carcinoma....Staff NCI 301-496-5583

Card cases....Seastrum, Carl USITC 202-205-3493

Cardiac Arrest....Staff NHLBI 301-496-4236

Cardiac Disease....Staff NHLBI 301-496-4236

Cardiac Pacemakers....Staff NHLBI 301-496-4236

Cardiomegaly....Staff NHLBI 301-496-4236

Cardiomyopathy (Hypertrophic, Dilated)....Staff NHLBI 301-496-4236

Cardiomyoplasty....Staff NHLBI 301-496-4236

Cardiopulmonary Resuscitation (CPR)....Staff NHLBI 301-496-4236

Cardiovascular Disease....Staff NHLBI 301-496-4236

Cardiovascular drugs....Nesbitt, Elizabeth USITC 202-205-3355

Cardioversion....Staff NHLBI 301-496-4236

Carditis....Staff NHLBI 301-496-4236

Career Criminals....Langan, Patrick Justice Stat 202-616-3490

Career Criminals....Greenfeld, Lawrence Justice Stat 202-616-3281

Careers in Nursing....Staff DRR 301-443-5786

Caregiving and Older People....Staff NIA 301-496-1752

Caribbean Basin....Dowling, Jay Cnty Commerce 202-482-1648

Caribbean Development Bank....Nallari, Raj R. 202-473-8697

Caribbean Primate Research Center....Staff NCRR 301-594-7933

Caribbean....Allgeir, Peter US Trade Rep 202-395-6135

Caries....Staff NIDR 301-496-4261

Carotid Artery Disease....Staff NHLBI 301-496-4236

Carpal Tunnel Syndrome....Staff NIAMS 301-496-8188

Carpal Tunnel Syndrome....Staff NINDS 301-496-5751

Carpets....Sweet, Mary Elizabeth USITC 202-205-3455

Carrier Identification Codes....Staff FCC 202-0940

Carrier Common Line Charge...Staff FCC 202-418-1595

Carrots....McCarty, Timothy USITC 202-205-3324

Carrying Cases....Gorman, Kevin CUSTOMS 212-466-5893

Cartography....Staff FWS 703-358-1713

Case....Swann, Vera COMMERCE 202-482-0396

Casein....Randall, Rob USITC 202-205-3366

Cash registers....Baker, Scott USITC 202-205-3386

Castile soap....Land, Eric USITC 202-205-3349

Casting machines....Greene, William USITC 202-205-3405

Castleman's Disease....Staff NHLBI 301-496-4236

Cat Cry Syndrome (Cri Du Chat)....Staff NICHD 301-496-5133

Cat Scratch Fever....Staff NIAID 301-496-5717

Catalytic compositions....Beck, Shrive PTO 703-308-3808

Catalytic Converters....Staff EPA 202-233-9020

Cataplexy....Staff NINDS 301-496-5751

Cataract....Staff NEI 301-496-5248
Catheterization (Cardiac or Heart)....Staff NHLBI 301-496-4236
Cathode-Ray tubes....Kitzmiller, John USITC 202-205-3387
Cattle (Feeder) with options....Fichert, David CFT 312-353-3181
Cattle with options....Fichert, David CFT 312-353-3181
Caulking compounds....Johnson, Larry USITC 202-205-3351
Caulks....Johnson, Larry USITC 202-205-3351
Caustic potash....Conant, Kenneth USITC 202-205-3346
Caustic soda....Conant, Kenneth USITC 202-205-3346
Caymans....Brooks, Michelle Cnty Commerce 202-482-2527
CB Radio-General Licensing....Staff FCC 800-322-1117
CB Radio Service....Staff FCC 202-418-0680
CB Radio-Technical Questions....Staff FCC 202-418-0680
CD Players....Dicerbo, Mario CUSTOMS 212-466-5672
CD-ROM....Staff CENSUS 301-457-1234
CDC Information Center....Kennedy, Joan U. CDC 404-639-1601
CDC Information Center (Database)....Staff CDC 404-639-1718
CEA (Carcinoembryonic Antigen)....Staff NCI 301-496-5583
Cedar leaf....Land, Eric USITC 202-205-3349
Celiac Disease....Staff NIDDK 301-496-3583
Celiac Disease....Staff NIAID 301-496-5717
Cell Aging....Staff NIA 301-496-1752
Cell Bank....Staff NIGMS 301-496-7301
Cell Biology....Staff NIGMS 301-496-7301
Cellular Function....Staff NIGMS 301-496-7301
Cellular General....Staff FCC 202-418-1310
Cellular Immunology....Finerty, John FAES 301-496-7815
Cellular Mobile Radio....Staff FCC 202-418-1310
Cellular Structure....Staff NIGMS 301-496-7301
Cellular Telephone Fraud....Staff FCC 804-441-6472
Cellular Unserved Areas....Staff FCC 202-418-1320
Cellular Unserved Areas....Staff FCC 202-418-1320
CellularVision....Staff FCC 202-418-0871
Cement compositions....Bell, mark L. PTO 703-308-3823
Cement, hydraulic....White, Linda USITC 202-205-3427
Cement Plants, Major Proj.....Brandes, Jay COMMERCE 202-482-3352
Cement....Clifton, James R. NIST 301-975-6707
Cement....Pitcher, Charles COMMERCE 202-482-0132
Cement....Solomon, Cheryl C. MINES 202-501-9393
Cements, dental....Randall, Rob USITC 202-205-3366
Cements of rubber, vinyl, etc.....Jonnard, Aimison USITC 202-205-3350
CENDATA....Staff CENSUS 301-457-1214
Census and You (Monthly Newsletter)....Tillman, Neil CENSUS 301-457-1221
Census and You (Monthly Newsletter)....Morton, Jackson CENSUS 301-457-1221
Census Awareness (Regional Offices)....Staff CENSUS 301-457-2032
Census Catalog....McCall, John CENSUS 301-457-1221
Census Customer Service Fax Number....Staff CENSUS 301-457-4714
Census Geographic Concepts....Staff CENSUS 301-457-1099
Census History....Solomon, Les CENSUS 301-457-1167
Census of Retail Trade, Virgin Islands....Hoover, Kent CENSUS 301-763-8564
Census of Retail Trade, Puerto Rico....Hoover, Kent CENSUS 301-763-8564
Census of Retail Trade, Guam....Hoover, Kent CENSUS 301-763-8564
Census of Selected Service Industries, Virgin Isl....Hoover, Kent CENSUS 301-763-8564
Census of Selected Service Industries, Puerto Rico....Hoover, Kent CENSUS 301-763-8564
Census of Selected Service Industries, Guam....Hoover, Kent CENSUS 301-763-8564
Census of Wholesale Trade, Virgin Islands....Hoover, Kent CENSUS 301-763-8564
Census of Wholesale Trade, Guam....Hoover, Kent CENSUS 301-763-8564
Census of Wholesale Trade, Puerto Rico....Hoover, Kent CENSUS 301-763-8564
Census Personnel Locator....Staff CENSUS 301-457-4608
CENTAM....Staff Cnty State 202-647-3381
Centenarians....Staff NIA 301-496-1752
Center for Hazardous Materials Hotline....Staff EPA 800-334-2467
Centers for Disease Control....Staff CDC 404-329-3291
Centers of Population....Hirschfeld, Don CENSUS 301-457-1099
Central African Republic....Michelini, Philip Cnty Commerce 202-482-4388
Central African Republic (Bangui)....Staff Cnty State 202-647-1707
Central African Republic....Cohen, Ellen Cnty World Bank 202-473-4463
Central African Republic....Gaba, N'dinga Cnty Embassy 202-483-7800
Central African Republic/Minerals....Dolley, Thomas Cnty Mines 202-501-9690
Central African Republic....Henning, Herman Cnty USIA 202-619-5926
Central African Republic....Koba, Henry Cnty Embassy 202-483-7800
Central African Republic....Palghat, Kathy Cnty Treasury 202-622-0332
Central African Republic....Bezek, Jill Cnty TDA 703-875-4357

Central Auditory Processing Disorders....Staff NIDCD 301-496-7243
Central Core Disease....Staff NINDS 301-496-5751
Central Europe/trade matters....Novelli, Catherine US Trade Rep 202-395-4620
Central Europe....Brereton, Barbara OPIC 202-336-8617
Central Storeroom....Staff OD/DL 301-496-9156
Centrifuges....Greene, William USITC 202-205-3400
Ceramic construction articles....White, Linda USITC 202-205-3427
Ceramic Gas Turbines....Sebestyen, Thomas NEIC 202-586-8012
Ceramic sanitary fixtures....Fulcher, Nancy USITC 202-205-3434
Ceramic table, kitchen articles....McNay, Deborah USITC 202-205-3425
Ceramics (Advanced)....Shea, Moira COMMERCE 202-482-0128
Ceramics Machinery....Shaw, Eugene COMMERCE 202-482-3494
Ceramics....Freiman, Stephen W. NIST 301-975-6119
Ceramics....Freiman, S.W. NIST 301-975-6119
Ceramics....Kalkines, George CUSTOMS 212-466-5794
Cereal breakfast foods....Schneider, Greg USITC 202-205-3326
Cereal grains....Pierre-Benoist, John USITC 202-205-3320
Cerebellar Arteriovenous Malformations....Staff NINDS 301-496-5751
Cerebellar Arteriosclerosis....Staff NINDS 301-496-5751
Cerebellar Ataxia....Staff NINDS 301-496-5751
Cerebellar Lesions....Staff NINDS 301-496-5751
Cerebral Death....Staff NINDS 301-496-5751
Cerebral Degeneration....Staff NINDS 301-496-5751
Cerebral Palsy....Staff NIDCD 301-496-7243
Cerebral Palsy....Staff United Cerebral Palsy Associations, Inc. (UCPA) 800-872-5827
Cerebral Palsy....Staff NINDS 301-496-5751
Cerebrotendious Xanthomatosis....Staff NINDS 301-496-5751
Cerebrovascular Disease....Staff NINDS 301-496-5751
Cerium compounds....Greenblatt, Jack USITC 202-205-3353
Cerium....DeSapio, Vincent USITC 202-205-3435
Ceroid Lipofuscinosis....Staff NINDS 301-496-5751
Certificates of Deposit....Reid, Brian FRS 202-452-3589
Certifications-Equipment Authorization....Staff FCC 301-725-1585
Cervical Disorders (Non-Malignancy)....NICHD 301-496-5133
Cervical Spine Disorders....Staff NIAMS 301-496-8188
Cesium compounds....Greenblatt, Jack USITC 202-205-3353
Cesium....Reese, Robert G., Jr. MINES 202-501-9413
Chad (N'Djamena)....Staff Cnty State 202-647-1707
Chad/Minerals....Dolley, Thomas Cnty Mines 202-501-9690
Chad....Cisse, Amadou B. Cnty World Bank 202-473-3345
Chad....Favitsou-Boulandi, Lemaye Cnty Embassy 202-462-4009
Chad....Henning, Herman Cnty USIA 202-619-5926
Chad....Kotze, Joan Cnty Treasury 202-622-0333
Chad....Mahamat-Saleh, Ahmat Cnty Embassy 202-462-4009
Chad....Michelini, Philip Cnty Commerce 202-482-4388
Chad....Saulters, Willie Cnty AID 202-647-6039
Chad....Trouba, Larry Peace Corps 202-606-3998
Chad....Waxman-Lenz, Roberta Cnty Export-Import Bank 202-565-3742
Chad....Younge, Nathan Cnty TDA 703-875-4357
Chagas' Disease....Staff NIAID 301-496-5717
Chain, of base metal....Kaplan, Stephanie USITC 202-205-3436
Chairman's Office.....Hamill, James C., Jr. FTC 202-326-2107
Chairs....Spalding, Josephine USITC 202-205-3498
Chalazion....Staff NEI 301-496-5248
Chalk (pigment grade)....Johnson, Larry USITC 202-205-3351
Chalks....Seastrum, Carl USITC 202-205-3493
Channel black....Johnson, Larry USITC 202-205-3351
Chaparral Tea....Staff NCI 301-496-5583
Chaplains (Hospital)....Staff CC 301-496-3407
Character Qualifications....Staff FCC 202-428-1600
Characteristics of Injuries and Illnesses, Comp. Wk....Biddle, Elyce LABOR 202-606-6170
Charcoal Broiling of Meat....Staff NCI 301-496-5583
Charcot-Marie-Tooth Disease....Staff NINDS 301-496-5751
Charge Syndrome....Staff NICHD 301-496-5133
Check controlled....Huppert, Michael PTO 703-308-1107
Check-writing machines....Scott, Baker USITC 202-205-3386
Chediak-Higashi Syndrome....Staff NIAID 301-496-5717
Cheese....Ludwick, David USITC 202-205-3329
Chelation Therapy (For Arterios., Hemosiderosis)....Staff NHLBI 301-496-4236
Chemical and Petroleum Branch....Staff EPA 919-541-5673
Chemical and Physical Hazards....Kapolka, Robert J. CDC 404-639-3147
Chemical compositions....Lieberman, Paul PTO 703-308-2523
Chemical Elements....Brady, Thomas CUSTOMS 212-466-4769
Chemical Elements....Conant, Kenneth USITC 202-205-3346
Chemical Emergency Preparedness and Prevention....Staff EPA 202-260-8600

Be patient. If any phone number is incorrect, call (area code) 555-1212 and request the new listing.

1381

Chemical gas purification processes....Lewis, Michael M. PTO 703-308-2535

Chemical Hazards....Staff OD/ORS 301-496-2960

Chemical Information Services....Hazard, George F. NLM 301-496-1131

Chemical Kinetics....Lias, S. NIST 301-975-2562

Chemical Measurement Techniques....Patrinus, Aristides NEIC 301-903-3251

Chemical pathology....Copeland, Edmund FAES 301-594-7154

Chemical Plants, Major Proj.....Haraguchi, Wally COMMERCE 202-482-4877

Chemical Reactors....Warden, Robert PTO 703-308-2920

Chemical safety....Staff CPSC 301-504-0580

Chemical Sciences....Marianelli, Robert NEIC 301-903-5808

Chemical Spills National Response Center....Staff EPA 202-426-2675

Chemical Spills....Staff FWS 202-208-2148

Chemicals and Allied Products....Kelly, Michael COMMERCE 202-482-0128

Chemicals Industry Group....Tow, A. Richard SEC 202-942-1760

Chemicals (Technical and Non-Technical Questions)....Staff EPA 202-260-3850

Chemicals....Elkins, John Customs 202-482-7020

Chemicals....Shaw, Eugene COMMERCE 202-482-3494

Chemistry of hydrocarbons....Beck, Shrive PTO 703-308-3808

Chemotherapy (Cancer)....Staff NCI 301-496-5583

Chemotherapy (Effect on Teeth)....Staff NIDR 301-496-4261

Chesapeake Bay Program....Staff EPA 410-267-0061

Chicken pox....Staff NIAID 301-496-5717

Chief Economist, BEA....Triplett, Jack E. ECONOMIC 202-606-9603

Child abnormalities....Staff Human Growth Foundation (HGF) 800-451-6434

Child Abuse and Neglect....Kharfen, Michael ACF 202-401-9215

Child abuse....Staff National Child Abuse Hotline (NCAH) 800-422-4453

Child Abuse....Staff National Resource Center on Child Abuse and Neglect (CAN) 800-227-5242

Child Abuse....Staff OHDS/ACYF 301-205-8646

Child Abuse...Staff National Council on Child Abuse and Family Violence (NCCAF) 800-222-2000

Child Care Information (Preschool)....Staff NIH 301-496-5144

Child Care, Population....Bachu, Amara CENSUS 301-457-2416

Child Care, Population....O'Connell, Martin CENSUS 301-457-2416

Child Development....Staff OHDS/ACYF 301-775-7782

Child Exploitation....Burgasser, George C. Justice 202-514-5780

Child Find....Staff Child Find of America 800-I-AM-LOST

Child Help....Staff Child Help USA (CH) 800-422-4453

Child Neglect....Staff National Resource Center on Child Abuse and Neglect (CAN) 800-227-5242

Child Rearing....Staff NIMH 301-443-4513

Child safety....Staff CPSC 301-504-0580

Child....Staff Child Reach (CR) 800-556-7918

Childbirth....Staff NICHD 301-496-5133

Childbirth....Staff HRSA/BHCDA/DMCH 301-443-2170

Childhood Malignancies....Staff NCI 301-496-5583

Childhood Mental Illness....Staff NIMH 301-443-4515

Childhood Progressive Dementia....Staff NINDS 301-496-5751

Children with disabilities born to Vietnam Veterans....Staff Access Group 800-821-8580

Children (Gifted)....Staff NIMH 301-443-4515

Children's Attitudes Towards Aging....Staff NIA 301-496-1752

Children's Inn (NIH)....Staff 301-496-5672

Children's Mental Health....Staff Family Support and Children's Mental Health 800-628-1696

Children's TV Enforcement....Staff FCC 202-418-1630

Children's TV Renewal....Staff FCC 202-418-1630

Childwatch....Staff National Child Safety Council 800-222-1464

Chile/Minerals....Velasco, Pablo Cnty Mines 202-501-9677

Chile....Augusto, Suzana Campos Cnty World Bank 202-473-9096

Chile....Biehl, John Cnty Embassy 202-785-1746

Chile....Clapham, Lizzie Peace Corps 202-606-3499

Chile....Davis, Janice Peace Corps 202-606-3198

Chile....Geiser, Barbara Cnty Treasury 202-622-1271

Chile....John Herrman Cnty TDA 703-875-4357

Chile....Leeb, Howard Cnty USIA 202-619-5867

Chile....Montes, Joaquin Cnty Embassy 202-785-1746

Chile....Prevot, Babette Cnty AID 202-647-4359

Chile....Staff Cnty State 202-647-2407

Chile....Turner, Randy Cnty Commerce 202-482-1703

Chile....Wilkins, Michele Cnty Export-Import Bank 202-565-3743

Chilean Affairs....Early, Jane US Trade Rep 202-395-5190

Chimpanzee Breeding and Research Program....Staff NCRR 301-594-7938

China Affairs....Stites, Richard Cnty USIA 202-619-5839

China/Minerals....Tse, Pui-Kwan Cnty Mines 202-501-9696

China, People's Republic of (Beijing)....Staff Cnty State 202-647-6300

China (policy analyst)....Siegal, Byron US Trade Rep 202-395-5070

China (policy planning)....Weisel, Barbara US Trade Rep 202-395-5070

China/trade matters....Lee, Sands US Trade Rep 202-395-3900

China/trade matters....Lehr, Deborah US Trade Rep 202-395-5050

China/trade matters....Cantilina, Amy US Trade Rep 202-395-5050

China....Daoyu, Li Cnty Embassy 202-328-2500

China....Dong, Buming Cnty Embassy 202-328-2501

China....Dwight, Lawrence Cnty Treasury 202-622-0356

China....Frye, Lisa Peace Corps 202-606-0956

China....Huston, Christy Peace Corps 202-606-0970

China....Hutchings, Dayna Cnty Export-Import Bank 202-565-3737

China....Respess, Rebecca Cnty TDA 703-875-4357

China....Rix, David C. Cnty World Bank 202-458-5517

China....Tsui, Tom C. Cnty World Bank 202-458-0432

Chinaware articles....McNay, Deborah USITC 202-205-3425

Chinaware....Bratland, Rosemarie COMMERCE 202-482-0380

Chinaware....Kalkines, George CUSTOMS 212-466-5794

Chiropractic Association....Staff ACA 800-327-1129

Chlamydial Infections....Staff NIAID 301-496-5717

Chlorides, nonmetallic....Conant, Kenneth USITC 202-205-3346

Chlorine....Conant, Kenneth USITC 202-205-3346

Chlorofluorocarbons....Michels, David USITC 202-205-3352

Chlorofluorocarbons (CFC)....Staff EPA 202-233-9410

Chloroform....Michels, David USITC 202-205-3352

Chocolate....Gallagher, Joan USITC 202-205-3317

Chocolate....Maria, John CUSTOMS 212-466-5730

Cholera....Staff NIAID 301-496-5717

Cholesteatoma....Staff NIDCD 301-496-7243

Cholesterol....Staff NHLBI/IC 301-251-1222

Chondromalacia....Staff NIAMS 301-496-8188

Chondrosarcoma....Staff NCI 301-496-5583

Chordoma....Staff NCI 301-496-5583

Choriocarcinoma....Staff NCI 301-496-5583

Chorionic Villus Sampling (CVS)....Staff 301-496-5133

Choroiditis....Staff NEI 301-496-5248

Christmas Island/Minerals....Lyday, Travis Cnty Mines 202-501-9695

Christmas Decorations....Rauch, Theodore CUSTOMS 212-466-5892

Chrome pigments....Johnson, Larry USITC 202-205-3351

Chromium compounds....Greenblatt, Jack USITC 202-205-3353

Chromium....Papp, John F. MINES 202-501-9438

Chromium....Presbury, Graylin COMMERCE 202-482-5158

Chromium....Yost, Charles USITC 202-205-3432

Chronic Bronchitis....Staff NHLBI 301-496-4236

Chronic Disease Prevention....Byers, Tim CDC 404-488-5099

Chronic Disease Nutrition....Byers, Tim E. CDC 404-488-5099

Chronic EBV....Staff NIAID 301-496-5717

Chronic Fatigue Syndrome....Staff NIAID 301-496-5717

Chronic Fatigue Syndrome....Staff CFIDS 800-442-3437

Chronic Fatigue Syndrome....Staff NINDS 301-496-5751

Chronic Fatigue Syndrome....Staff NIMH 301-443-4513

Chronic Granulomatous Disease....Staff NIAID 301-496-5717

Chronic Hepatitis with Rheumatic Disease.....Staff NIAMS 301-496-8188

Chronic Infections....Staff NIAID 301-496-5717

Chronic Myelogenous Leukemia....Staff NCI 301-496-5583

Chronic Obstructive Lung Disease (COPD)....Staff NHLBI 301-496-4236

Chronic Obstructive Lung Disease (COPD)....Staff NCNR 301-496-0526

Churg-Strauss Syndrome....Staff NIAID 301-496-5717

Cicatricial Pemphigoid....Staff NEI 301-496-5248

Cigarette Lighters....Maruggi, Al CPSC 301-504-0580

Cigarette Safety....Kaplan, Kathy CPSC 301-504-0580

Cigarettes, Research....Staff NCI 301-496-5583

Cigars and cigarettes....Harney, Amy USITC 202-205-3465

Cigars and cigarettes holders....Burns, Gail USITC 202-205-2501

Cigars and cigarettes lighters....Burns, Gail USITC 202-205-2501

Cinchona bark alkaloids and their salts....Nesbitt, Elizabeth USITC 202-205-3355

Cincinnati - Regional Office....Moore, William GAO 513-684-7125

Cinnamon oil (essential oil)....Land, Eric USITC 202-205-3349

Circulation/Circulatory System....Staff NHLBI 301-496-4236

Circumcision....Staff NICHD 301-496-5133

Cirrhosis....Staff NIDDK 301-496-3583

Cirrhosis....Staff NIAAA 301-443-3860

Citizens' Agreements....Staff FCC 202-418-1430

Citizenship....Staff CENSUS 301-457-2403

Citral....Land, Eric USITC 202-205-3349

Citrates....Michels, David USITC 202-205-3352

Citric acid....Michels, David USITC 202-205-3352

Citrus fruits....Dennis, Alfred USITC 202-205-3316

Civet....Land, Eric USITC 202-205-3349

Civil Aircraft Agreement....Bender, Juliet COMMERCE 202-482-4222
Civil Aviation Security....Flynn, Cathal FAA 202-267-9863
Civil Aviation Security Operations....Osmus, Lynne FAA 202-267-8537
Civil Aviation....Alford, Eugene COMMERCE 202-482-5071
Civil Cases (Federal)....Kaplan, Carol Justice Stat 202-307-0759
Civil Engineering....Demetsky, Michael J. UVA 804-924-6362
Civil Money Penalties....Holtz, Judy IG 202-619-1142
Clackerballs....Tyrell, Elaine CPSC 301-504-0850
Class A Power Increase Applications....FCC 202-418-2720
Classification System, Standard Industrial, Em/Un....Bennott, William LABOR 202-606-6474
Classification....Hartman, Frank CENSUS 301-763-7182
Classified electrical applications....Tarcza, Thomas C. PTO 703-308-1689
Classified mechanical applications....Jordan, Charles PTO 703-308-0918
Claudication....Staff NHLBI 301-496-4236
Clays....DeSapio, Vincent USITC 202-205-3435
Clays....Virta, Robert MINES 202-501-9384
Clean Lakes Program....Staff EPA 202-260-5904
Clean LAN/Waste Lan Hotline....Staff EPA 703-908-2066
Cleaners, under 10 lbs each....Randall, Rob USITC 202-205-3366
Cleaning apparatus....Recia, Henry PTO 703-308-1382
Cleaning machinery....Jackson, Georgia USITC 202-205-3399
Cleaning machines (textile)....Greene, William USITC 202-205-3405
Cleaning....Bedore, James USITC 202-205-3424
Cleaning....Goldberg, Gerald PTO 703-308-5443
Cleanwater Act....Staff EPA 202-260-5700
Clearances (News Releases)....Staff OD/OC 301-496-2535
Clearing Houses, Automated....Young, Florence FRS 202-452-3955
Clearinghouse for Census Data Services....Staff CENSUS 301-457-1305
Cleft Lip....Staff NIDR 301-496-4261
Cleft Palate....Staff Cleft Palate Foundation (CPF) 800-242-5338
Cleft Palate....Staff NIDR 301-496-4261
Climate Change Division....Staff EPA 202-260-8825
Clinical Center (Reception and Information Desk)....Staff CC 301-496-3141
Clinical Electives for Medical Students at Clinical Center....Staff CC 301-496-2427
Clinical Information System (CLINFO)....Staff NCRR 301-594-7945
Clinical Medicine (Animals)....Staff NCRR 301-496-1076
Clinical Pathology....Staff CC 301-496-5668
Clinical Research Applications of Computer Technology.....Staff NCRR 301-594-7938
Clinical Research Centers....Staff NCRR 301-594-7945
Clinical Research....Staff CC 301-496-4891
Clocks....Luther, Dennis USITC 202-205-3497
Clocks....Schwartz, Stanley CUSTOMS 212-466-5895
Closure fasteners....Cuomo, Peter PTO 703-308-0827
Closures, stoppers, seals, lids, caps, rubber or plastic....Trainor, Cynthia USITC 202-205-3354
Clotting Disorders....Staff NHLBI 301-496-4236
Clove oil (essential oil)....Land, Eric USITC 202-205-3349
CMV Retinitis....Staff NEI 301-496-5248
CO/Fuel Gas Detectors....Staff Reuben CPSC 301-504-0580
Coal and Minerals....Staff FWS 703-358-2183
Coal and Electricity....Como, Anthony NEIC 202-586-5935
Coal Exports....Rasmussen, Joghn COMMERCE 202-482-1466
Coal Exports....Yancik, Joseph J. COMMERCE 202-482-1466
Coal Related Securities....Chavez, Carlos SEC 202-942-2970
Coal Statistics....Geidl, John NEIC 202-254-5570
Coal-tar pitch....Foreso, Cynthia USITC 202-205-3348
Coal tar, crude....Foreso, Cynthia USITC 202-205-3424
Coal Technology Export Program....Swink, Denise NEIC 202-586-0559
Coal, Technology....Vacant NEIC 202-586-1650
Coal Workers' Pneumoconiosis (Black Lung Disease)....Staff NHLBI 301-496-4236
Coal....Biggerstaff, Margie NEIC 202-586-3867
Coal....Foreso, Cynthia USITC 202-205-3348
Coal....Karsteter, Dorothy NEIC 202-586-4216
Coarctation of the Aorta....Staff NHLBI 301-496-4236
Coast Station Licenses....Staff FCC 717-337-1212
Coast Station Rules and Hearings....Staff FCC 202-632-7175
Coastal Anadromous Fish....Staff FWS 703-358-1718
Coastal Barrier Coordination....Staff FWS 703-358-2183
Coastal Barrier Research....Staff FWS 703-358-1710
Coated fabric apparel....Jones, Jackie USITC 202-205-3466
Coated Garments: Boys'....Raftery, William CUSTOMS 212-466-5851
Coated Garments: Women's....Raftery, William CUSTOMS 212-466-5851
Coated Garments: Men's....Raftery, William CUSTOMS 212-466-5851

Coating compositions....Bell, Mark L. PTO 703-308-3823
Coating elements....Hafer, Robert PTO 703-308-2674
Coating machines....Greene, William USITC 202-205-3405
Coats, Women's Knit....Crowley, Michael CUSTOMS 212-466-5852
Coats' Disease....Staff NEI 301-496-5248
Cobalt compounds....Greenblatt, Jack USITC 202-205-3353
Cobalt....Lundy, David USITC 202-205-3439
Cobalt....Presbury, Graylin COMMERCE 202-482-5158
Cobalt....Shedd, Kim B. MINES 202-501-9420
Cobalt....Staff NCI 301-496-5583
Cocaine....Staff Cocaine Anonymous 800-347-8998
Cocaine....Staff National Cocaine Hotline (NCH) 800-262-2463
Cocaine....Staff NIDA 301-443-6245
Cochlear Implant....Staff NIDCD 301-496-7243
Cockayne's Syndrome....Staff NIA 301-496-1752
Cocks and valves....Mata, Ruben USITC 202-205-3403
Cocoa....Gallagher, Joan USITC 202-205-3317
Coffee and Tea....Gray, Fred Agri 202-219-0888
Coffee....Maria, John CUSTOMS 212-466-5730
Coffee....Schneider, Greg USITC 202-205-3326
Cogan's Syndrome....Staff NEI 301-496-5248
Cogeneration Energy Systems....Walter, Donald NEIC 202-586-2090
Cognition....Staff NICHD 301-496-5133
Cognition....Staff NIMH 301-443-4513
Coin Distribution....Epps, James FRS 202-452-2222
Coin handling....Huppert, Michael PTO 703-308-1107
Coin purses....Seastrum, Carl USITC 202-205-3493
Coinage....Epps, James FRS 202-452-2222
Coke for fuel....Foreso, Cynthia USITC 202-205-3348
Coke, calcined (non-fuel)....White, Linda USITC 202-205-3427
Cold Storage....Lange, John Agri 202-720-0585
Coley's Mixed Toxins....Staff NCI 301-496-5583
Colitis....Staff Crohn's and Colitis Foundation of America 800-932-2423
Colitis....Staff NIDDK 301-496-3583
Collagen Disease....Staff NIAMS 301-496-8188
Collagen Disease....Staff NHLBI 301-496-4236
Collagen/Collagenase....Staff NIDR 301-496-4261
Collapsed Lung....Staff NHLBI 301-496-4236
Collective Bargaining Agreements Analysis....Cimini, Michael LABOR 202-606-6275
Collective Bargaining Settlements, Major, Comp/Wk....Devine, Janice M. LABOR 202-606-6276
Collective Bargaining--Public File, Agreements....Cimini, Michael LABOR 202-606-6275
Colombia (Bogota)....Staff Cnty State 202-647-3023
Colombia/Minerals....Rabchevsky, George Cnty Mines 202-501-9670
Colombia....Jarvis, Catherine Cnty USIA 202-619-5867
Colombia....Lleras, Carlos Cnty Embassy 202-387-8338
Colombia....Parkinson, Katherine Cnty Treasury 202-622-5292
Colombia....Pizano Salazar, Diego Cnty Embassy 202-387-8338
Colombia....Schneider, John Cnty AID 202-647-4365
Colombia....Wallentin, Eduardo Cnty World Bank 202-473-5600
Colombia....Wilkins, Michele Cnty Export-Import Bank 202-565-3743
Color Blindness (Deficiency)....Staff NEI 301-496-5248
Colorectal Neoplasms....Staff NCI 301-496-5583
Coloring Matter....Joseph, Stephanie CUSTOMS 212-466-5768
Colostomy....Staff NIDDK 301-654-3810
Columbia....Moore, Paul Cnty Commerce 202-482-1659
Columbium....Cunningham, Larry D. MINES 202-501-9443
Columbium....Lundy, David USITC 202-205-3439
Columbium....Presbury, Graylinn, C. COMMERCE 202-482-5158
Coma....Staff NINDS 301-496-5751
Combs....Brownchweig, Gilbert CUSTOMS 212-466-5744
Combs....Burns, Gail USITC 202-205-2501
Commerce....DeMong, Richard F. UVA 804-924-3227
Commercial Aircraft (Trade Policy)....Bender, Juliet COMMERCE 202-482-4222
Commercial Development of Space....Norwood, Robert NASA 202-358-2320
Commercial/Indus Refrig....Bell, Richard COMMERCIAL 202-482-5126
Commercial Lighting Fixtures....Bodson, John COMMERCE 202-482-0681
Commercial Operator Licenses....Staff FCC 202-418-0680
Commercial Operators....Staff FCC 202-418-0680
Commercial Printing....Lofquist, William COMMERCE 202-482-0379
Commercial Printing....Lofquist, William COMMERCE 202-482-0379
Commercial Radio Operator Licensing....Staff FCC 202-418-0680
Commercial Radio apps.- Gen. Radiotelephone operator....Staff FCC 202-418-0680
Commercial Radio apps.- Global Maritime FCC 202-418-0680

Commercial Radio apps.- Radar Endorsement....Staff FCC 202-418-0680

Commercial Radio apps.- Radio Telegraph licenses....Staff FCC 202-418-0680

Commercial Radio apps.- Restricted Permit....FCC 202-418-0680

Commercial Rulings....Durant, John Customs 202-482-6990

Commercial Space Ventures....Norwood, Robert NASA 202-358-2320

Commissioned Officer Information....Staff OD/DPM 301-496-4212

Commissioner, Special Assistant to Office of....Barkume, Anthony J. LABOR 202-606-7808

Commissioner, Special Assistant to Office of....Parks, William LABOR 202-606-7807

Commissioner's Office - Azcuenaga, Mary L.....Buek, Alexandra P. FTC 202-326-2145

Commissioner's Office - Azcuenaga, Mary L.....Heim, Joan L. FTC 202-326-2145

Commissioner's Office - Azcuenaga, Mary L.....Parrish, Pearl D. FTC 202-326-2145

Commissioner's Office - Azcuenaga, Mary L.....Jeter, LaJuan J. FTC 202-326-2145

Commissioner's Office - Azcuenaga, Mary L.....Bokat, Karen G. FTC 202-326-2912

Commissioner's Office - Azcuenaga, Mary L.....Warden, John B. FTC 202-326-2145

Commissioner's Office - Chairman's Office....Anderson, Rita D. FTC 202-326-2109

Commissioner's Office....Yao, Dennis A. FTC 202-326-2171

Commissioner's Office....Simmons, Gwendolynn FTC 202-326-2172

Commissioner's Office....Steiger, Janet D. FTC 202-326-3400

Commissioner's Office, Mary Azcuenaga....Pahl, Thomas B. FTC 202-326-2145

Commissioner's Office....Engle, Mary Koelbel FTC 202-326-3161

Commissioner's Office - Office of the Chairman....Rosenfeld, Dana FTC 202-326-2113

Commissioner's Office - Office of the Chairman....Bond, Ronald S. FTC 202-326-3424

Commissioner's Office - Owen, Deborah K.....Eisenstat, Philip FTC 202-326-2157

Commissioner's Office - Pitofsky, Robert....Etchison, Glenda L. FTC 202-326-3401

Commissioner's Office....Pitofsky, Robert FTC 202-326-2100

Commissioner's Office....Starek, Roscoe B., III FTC 202-326-2150

Commissioner's Office - Starek, Roscoe B., III....Armendariz, Rebecca FTC 202-326-2124

Commissioner's Office - Starek, Roscoe B., III....Cook, Barbara A. FTC 202-326-2150

Commissioner's Office - Starek, Roscoe B., III....Davis, Megan Wagner FTC 202-326-2127

Commissioner's Office - Starek, Roscoe B., III....Norris, Catherine FTC 202-326-2123

Commissioner's Office - Steiger, Janet D.....Anderson, Emily FTC 202-326-2109

Commissioner's Office - Steiger, Janet D.....Armstrong, Katherine FTC 202-326-3250

Commissioner's Office - Steiger, Janet D.....Miles, Elizabeth D. FTC 202-326-2108

Commissioner's Office - Steiger, Janet D.....Conn, David FTC 202-326-2114

Commissioner's Office - Steiger, Janet D.....Cohen, William E. FTC 202-326-2110

Commissioner's Office - Steiger, Janet D.....Crist, Sandy FTC 202-326-2105

Commissioner's Office - Steiger, Janet D.....Vedova, Holly K. FTC 202-326-3237

Commissioner's Office - Steiger, Janet D.....White, Robert S. FTC 202-326-2102

Commissioner's Office - Varney, Christine....Labuda, Laurie FTC 202-326-3315

Commissioner's Office - Yao, Dennis A.....Thompson, Patricia V. FTC 202-326-2169

Commissioner's Office - Yao, Dennis A.....Harris, LaVerne H. FTC 202-326-2170

Commissioner's Office - Yao, Dennis A.....Vecchi, Christa Van Anh FTC 202-326-3166

Commissioner's Office - Yao, Dennis A.....Corley, Derry L. FTC 202-326-2168

Commissioner's Office - Yao, Dennis A.....Murphy, R. Dennis FTC 202-326-3524

Commissioner's Office - Yao, Dennis A.....Dahdouh, Thomas FTC 202-326-2263

Commissioner's Office - Yao, Dennis A.....DeSanti, Susan S. FTC 202-326-2167

Commodity and Programs and Policies - Crops....Evans, Sam Agri 202-219-0840

Commodity Flow Survey....Fowler, John CENSUS 301-457-2108

Common Cold....Staff NIAID 301-496-5717

Commonwealth of Independent States....Levine, Richard Cnty Mines 202-501-9685

Commonwealth of Independent States....Staff Peace Corps 202-606-3973

Commonwealth of Independent States....Staff Cnty State 202-647-9559

Commonwealth of Independent States....Staff Peace Corps 202-606-3973

Communicable and Infectious Diseases....Staff NIAID 401-496-5717

Communicable and Infectious Diseases....Staff CDC 404-639-3534

Communication Human (Disorders)....Staff NIMH 401-443-4513

Communication Human (Disorders)....Staff NINDS 401-496-5751

Communication Human (Disorders)....Staff NIDCD 401-496-7243

Communication Human (Normal)....Staff NIDCD 301-496-7243

Communications Industry Group....Owings, Christopher SEC 202-942-1900

Communications Office....Lachance, Janice R. OPM 202-606-1800

Communications....Combs, William SBA 202-205-6606

Communications....Stillman, Rona B. GAO 202-512-6412

Communications....Stillman, Rona B. GAO 202-512-6412

Community Affairs....Loney, Glenn FRS 202-452-3585

Community Corrections and Detention....Clark, John R. Justice Stat 202-514-8585

Community Development....England-Joseph, Judy GAO 202-512-7631

Community Energy Systems....Gunn, Marvin E. NEIC 202-586-2826

Community Health Centers....Staff HRSA 301-443-3376

Community of License Changes AM....Staff FCC 202-418-2660

Community of License Changes FM....Staff FCC 202-418-2180

Community of License Changes TV....Staff FCC 202-418-2180

Community Planning and Development....Staff HUD 202-708-0270

Community Reinvestment Act....Soboeiro, John FRS 202-452-3838

Community Services Program....Kharfen, Michael ACF 202-401-9215

Commuter Aircraft....Hakala, Katherine M FAA 202-267-8086

Commuting, Population....Boertein, Celia CENSUS 301-457-2454

Commuting....Salopek, Phil CENSUS 301-457-2454

Comoros (Moroni)....Staff Cnty State 202-647-6473

Comoros/Minerals....Antonides, Lloyd Cnty Mines 202-501-9674

Comoros....Barber, Ed Cnty Treasury 202-622-1730

Comoros....Bezek, Jill Cnty TDA 703-875-4357

Comoros....Eap, Pisei Phlong Cnty World Bank 202-473-4364

Comoros....Imam, Fahmila Cnty Export-Import Bank 202-565-3738

Comoros....Larsen, Mark Cnty USIA 202-619-4894

Comoros....Schmitz, Virginia Peace Corps 202-606-3334

Comoros....Walkins, Chandra Cnty Commerce 202-482-4564

Comparative Renewals AM/FM Stations....Staff FCC 202-418-2780

Comparative Renewals TV Stations....Staff FCC 202-418-1630

Comparative Medicine Program....Staff NCRR 301-594-7933

Compensation Administration....Mikowicz, Jerome OPM 202-606-2858

Compensation and Working Conditions, Asst. Commis.....Vacant LABOR 202-606-6300

Compensation and Working Conditions, Employee Ben.....Staff LABOR 202-606-6222

Compensation and Working Conditions, Employer Costs....Rogers, Brenda LABOR 202-606-6206

Compensation and Working Conditions, Industry injuries and illness....Staff LABOR 202-606-6180

Compensation and Working Conditions, Recorded Message....24-hour hotline LABOR 202-606-7828

Compensation and Working Conditions, Supp. Data....Biddle, Elyce LABOR 202-606-6170

Compensation and Working Conditions, Supp. Data....Biddle, Elyce LABOR 202-606-6170

Compensation and Working Conditions, Work Injury Report Surveys....Jackson, Ethel LABOR 202-606-6167

Compensation Levels and Trends, Asst. Commis.....MacDonald, Kathleen M. LABOR 202-606-6302

Competitive Bidding....Staff FCC 202-418-2030

Competitiveness Issues....Mendelowitz, Allan I. 202-512-5889

Complaints by Investors....Staff SEC 202-942-7040

Complaints Telephone (consumer)....Staff FCC 202-632-7553

Composites, Advanced....Manion, James COMMERCE 202-482-5157

Composting (Yardwaste and Municipal Solid Waste)....Staff EPA 703-308-7258

Compulsory Treatment (Drug Abuse)....Staff NIDA 301-443-6245

Computational Molecular Biology....Staff DRCT 301-496-1141

Computational Aerodynamics....Farrar, Diane NASA 415-604-3934

Computer and Communication Systems, Director of....Bennett, Harry D. NLM 301-496-1351

Computer and DP Services....Inoussa, Mary COMMERCE 202-482-5820

Computer and DP Services....Atkins, Robert G. COMMERCE 202-482-4781

Computer applications....Teska, Kevin PTO 703-305-9704

Computer Consulting....Adkins, Robert COMMERCE 202-482-4781

Computer control systems....Envall, Roy PTO 703-305-9706

Computer Crime....Kaplan, Carol Justice Stat 202-307-0759

Computer/data processing services....Bringe, Julie USITC 202-205-3390

Computer, Midrange....Woods, Clay COMMERCE 202-482-3013

Computer, Personal....Miles, Timothy O. COMMERCIAL 202-482-2990

Computer, Personal....Woods, R. Clay COMMERCE 202-482-3013

Computer, Portable....Hoffman, Heidi M. COMMERCE 202-482-0569

Computer Professional Services....Atkins, Robert COMMERCE 202-482-4781

Computer, Super....Streete, Jonathan P. COMMERCE 202-482-0480

Computer Systems and Services, Chief....Doyle, James P. ECONOMIC 202-606-9909

Computer systems...Harvey, Jack PTO 703-305-9704

Computerized Search Services....Staff NIH 301-496-6095

Computerized Search Services....Staff NCRR/NIH Library 301-496-1156

Computers and Business Equipment, Office of....Inoussa, Mary COMMERCE 202-482-5820

Computers in Medical Research....Staff DCRT 301-496-6203

Computers in Medical Research....Staff NCRR 301-594-7934

Computers Industry Group...Duvall, Steven C. SEC 202-942-1900

Computers, Midrange....Hoffman, Heidi M. COMMERCE 202-482-2053

Computers, Trade Promo.....Fogg, Judy A. COMMERCE 202-482-4936

Computers, Workstations....Sirceter, Jonathan COMMERCE 202-482-0480

Computers....Stillman, Rona B. GAO 202-512-6412

Concrete and products....White, Linda USITC 202-205-3427

Concrete....Clifton, James R. NIST 301-975-6707

Condensate, lease....Foreso, Cynthia USITC 202-205-3348

Conductors....Cutchin, John USITC 202-205-3396

Conductors....Picard, Leo PTO 703-308-0538

Conduit....Cutchin, John USITC 202-205-3396

Conduits....Curran, David CUSTOMS 212-466-5680

Conduits....Recia, Henry PTO 703-308-1382

Condyloma....Staff NIAID 301-496-5717

Confectionery Products....Kenney, Cornelius COMMERCE 202-482-2428

Confectionery....Gallagher, Joan USITC 202-205-3317

Confidentiality and Privacy Issues....Gates, Jerry CENSUS 301-457-2516

Confidentiality of Data....Kaplan, Carol Justice Stat 202-307-0759

Congenital Abnormalities....Staff NEI 301-496-5248

Congenital Abnormalities....Staff NINDS 301-496-5751

Congenital Abnormalities....Staff NICHD 301-496-5133

Congenital Adrenal Hyperplasia....Staff NIDDK 301-496-3583

Congenital Adrenal Hyperplasia....Staff NICHD 301-496-5133

Congenital Heart Disease....Staff NHLBI 301-496-4236

Congenital Infections....Staff NIAID 301-496-5717

Congestive Heart Failure....Staff NHLBI 301-496-4236

Congo (Brazzaville)....Staff Cnty State 202-647-3139

Congo/Minerals....Dolley, Thomas Cnty Mines 202-501-9690

Congo....Boussoukou-Boumba, Pierre Damien Cnty Embassy 202-726-0825

Congo....Henke, Debra Cnty Commerce 202-482-5149

Congo....Henning, Herman Cnty USIA 202-619-5926

Congo....Maybury-Lewis, Anthony Cnty Export-Import Bank 202-565-3739

Congo....Palghat, Kathy Cnty Treasury 202-622-0332

Congo....Sachika, Goode Peace Corps 202-606-3695

Congo....Wilson, Michael Cnty World Bank 202-473-4714

Congo....Younge, Nathan Cnty TDA 703-875-4357

Congressional Affairs....Staff CENSUS 301-457-2171

Congressional Districts, Boundaries....Ramirez, Lourdes CENSUS 301-457-1099

Congressional Districts, Address Locations....Staff CENSUS 301-457-1050

Congressional Districts, Component Areas....Ramirez, Lourdes CENSUS 301-457-1099

Congressional Inquiries....Staff SEC 202-942-0014

Congressional Relations Office....Hall, Dorian J. FTC 202-326-2195

Congressional Relations....Kando, Carol A. FTC 202-326-3152

Conjunctivitis....Staff NEI 301-496-5248

Connective Tissue Diseases....Staff NIAMS 301-496-8188

Consensus Development Conferences....Staff OD/OMAR 301-496-1143

Conservation....Staff NEIC 202-586-8800

Constipation and Aging....Staff NIA 301-496-1752

Constipation....Staff NIDDK 301-654-3810

Construction and Forestry, PPI, Prices/Lv. Cond....Davies, Wanda LABOR 202-606-7713

Construction, Domestic....MacAuley, Patrick COMMERCE 202-482-0132

Construction, Machinery....Heimowitz, L. COMMERCE 202-482-0558

Construction Machinery....Heimowitz, L. COMMERCE 202-482-0558

Construction paper....Rhodes, Richard USITC 202-205-3322

Construction Permit Extensions AM....Staff FCC 202-418-2670

Construction Permit Extensions FM....Staff FCC 202-418-2710

Construction Permit Extensions TV....Staff FCC 202-418-1630

Construction services....Polly, Laura USITC 202-205-3408

Construction Statistics, Census/Industry Surveys....Kristoff, James CENSUS 301-457-2813

Construction Statistics, Constr Authorzd by Bldg Permit....Hoyle, Linda CENSUS 301-457-4641

Construction Statistics, New Residential, Charact....Berman, Steve CENSUS 301-457-4666

Construction Statistics, New Residential, Sales....Berman, Steve CENSUS 301-457-4666

Construction Statistics, New Residential, House Complet....Fondelier, David CENSUS 301-457-4703

Construction Statistics, New Residential, In Select MSA....Jacobson, Dale CENSUS 301-457-4666

Construction Statistics, New Residential, Housing Start....Fondelier, David CENSUS 301-457-4703

Construction Statistics, Residential Alterations....Huesman, Joe CENSUS 301-457-1605

Construction Statistics, Residential Repairs....Huesman, Joe CENSUS 301-457-1605

Construction Statistics, Value New Constr Put in Place....Roff, Joe CENSUS 301-457-1605

Consulting services....DeSapio, Vincent USITC 202-205-3435

Consumer Affairs, Energy Affairs....Gauldin, Michael NEIC 202-586-5373

Consumer Affairs (all press inquiries)....Freidlander, Bernice OCA 202-395-7904

Consumer Affairs Compliance....Loney, Glenn FRS 202-452-3585

Consumer Assistance....Staff FCC 202-418-0190

Consumer Complaints about Financial Institutions....Whitehead, Myrna L FRS 202-452-3693

Consumer Expenditure Survey....Dopkowski, Ron CENSUS 301-457-3914

Consumer Expenditure Survey, Prices, Data Tapes....Passero, William LABOR 202-606-6900

Consumer Expenditure Survey, Prices and Liv. Cond....Jacobs, Eva LABOR 202-606-6900

Consumer Expenditure Survey, Surv. Data and Tapes....Passero, William LABOR 202-606-6900

Consumer Expenditure Survey, Surv. Oper., Pr/Lv.....Dietz, Richard LABOR 202-606-6872

Consumer Goods....Bodansky, Harry COMMERCE 202-482-5783

Consumer Price Indexes, Avg. Ret. Pr., Fuels and Util.....Adkins, Robert LABOR 202-606-6985

Consumer Price Indexes, Avg. Retail Food Pr--Mo.....Cook, William LABOR 202-606-6988

Consumer Price Indexes, Pr/Lv. Con, Data Diskettes....Gibson, Sharon LABOR 202-606-6968

Consumer Price Indexes, Prices and Living Cond.....Jackman, Patrick LABOR 202-606-6952

Consumer Price Indexes, Prices and Living Cond.....Jackman, Patrick LABOR 202-606-6952

Consumer Price Indexes, Prices and Living Conditions....Staff LABOR 202-606-7000

Consumer Price Indexes, Recorded CPI Detail....24-Hour Hotline LABOR 202-606-7828

Consumer Prices and Price Indexes, Asst. Comm....Greenlef, Joan LABOR 202-606-6952

Consumer Protection Bureau - Advertising Practices....Jones, Deitra FTC 202-326-3151

Consumer Protection Bureau - Advertising Practices....Ostheimer, Michael FTC 202-326-2699

Consumer Protection Bureau - Advertising Practices....Renant, Danielle FTC 202-326-3247

Consumer Protection Bureau - Advertising Practices....Kolish, Elaine D. FTC 202-326-3042

Consumer Protection Bureau - Advertising Practices....Johnson, Barbara J. FTC 202-326-3149

Consumer Protection Bureau - Advertising Practices....Hoppock, Theodore H. FTC 202-326-3087

Consumer Protection Bureau - Advertising Practices....Momin, Karim C. FTC 202-326-2418

Consumer Protection Bureau - Advertising Practices....Fremont, Laura FTC 202-326-2649

Consumer Protection Bureau - Advertising Practices....Greisman, Lois C. FTC 202-326-3404

Consumer Protection Bureau - Advertising Practices....Guelzow, Lynn F. FTC 202-326-2386

Consumer Protection Bureau - Advertising Practices....Kopchik, Lisa B. FTC 202-326-3139

Consumer Protection Bureau - Advertising Practices....Pulley, Samichie K. FTC 202-326-3147

Consumer Protection Bureau - Advertising Practices....Warder, Nancy S. FTC 202-326-3048

Consumer Protection Bureau - Advertising Practices....Rusk, Michelle K. FTC 202-326-3148

Consumer Protection Bureau - Advertising Practices....Rosso, Rosemary FTC 202-326-2174

Consumer Protection Bureau - Advertising Practices....Skidmore, Patricia A. FTC 202-326-3050

Consumer Protection Bureau - Advertising Practices....Bank, Kevin M. FTC
202-326-2675

Consumer Protection Bureau - Advertising Practices....Murray, Joanna C. FTC
202-326-3256

Consumer Protection Bureau - Advertising Practices....Levin, Toby M. FTC
202-326-3156

Consumer Protection Bureau - Advertising Practices....Maher, Anne FTC
202-326-2987

Consumer Protection Bureau - Advertising Practices....Mazis, Michael B. FTC
202-326-2613

Consumer Protection Bureau - Advertising Practices....Fink, Duane E. FTC
202-326-3145

Consumer Protection Bureau - Advertising Practices....Fair, Lesley A. FTC
202-326-3081

Consumer Protection Bureau - Advertising Practices....Ashford, LaToya C. FTC
202-326-3467

Consumer Protection Bureau - Advertising Practices....Cohn, Susan FTC
202-326-3053

Consumer Protection Bureau - Advertising Practices....Johnson, Barbara J. FTC
202-326-3149

Consumer Protection Bureau - Advertising Practices....Priesman, Phillip FTC
202-326-2484

Consumer Protection Bureau - Advertising Practices....Evans, Janet M. FTC
202-326-2125

Consumer Protection Bureau - Advertising Practices....Watts, Marianne R. FTC
202-326-3074

Consumer Protection Bureau - Advertising Practices....Thomas, Sheri FTC
202-326-3398

Consumer Protection Bureau - Advertising Practices....Wilkenfeld, Judith D. FTC
202-326-3150

Consumer Protection Bureau - Advertising Practices....Peeler, C. Lee FTC
202-326-3090

Consumer Protection Bureau - Advertising Practices....Winston, Joel FTC
202-326-3153

Consumer Protection Bureau - Advertising Practices....Knight, Sydney FTC
202-326-2162

Consumer Protection Bureau - Advertising Practices....Dahl, Brian A. FTC
202-326-3182

Consumer Protection Bureau - Advertising Practices....Davidson, Michael FTC
202-326-2454

Consumer Protection Bureau - Advertising Practices....Forbes, Georgianna A. FTC
202-326-3183

Consumer Protection Bureau - Advertising Practices....Del Borello, Michael FTC
202-326-3051

Consumer Protection Bureau - Advertising Practices....Colbert, Lynne J. FTC
202-326-3571

Consumer Protection Bureau - Advertising Practices....Cleland, Richard FTC
202-326-3088

Consumer Protection Bureau - Advertising Practices....Dershowitz, Michael FTC
202-326-3158

Consumer Protection Bureau - Advertising Practices....Axelroad, Benjamin FTC
202-326-3008

Consumer Protection Bureau - Consumer and Bus. Educ.....Vawter, Irene FTC
202-326-3268

Consumer Protection Bureau - Consumer and Bus. Educ....Holz, Dawne FTC
202-326-3087

Consumer Protection Bureau - Consumer and Bus. Educ.....Shanoff, Carolyn FTC
202-326-3270

Consumer Protection Bureau - Consumer and Bus. Educ.....Tressler, Colleen P.
FTC 202-326-2368

Consumer Protection Bureau - Credit Practices....Cohen, Stephen FTC
202-326-3222

Consumer Protection Bureau - Credit Practices....Brinckerhoff, Clarke FTC
202-326-3208

Consumer Protection Bureau - Credit Practices....Credle, Lillie R. FTC
202-326-2975

Consumer Protection Bureau - Credit Practices....Lamb, Cynthia S. FTC
202-326-3001

Consumer Protection Bureau - Credit Practices....Wilmore, Sandra FTC
202-326-3169

Consumer Protection Bureau - Credit Practices....Sellers, Evelyn FTC
202-326-3226

Consumer Protection Bureau - Credit Practices....Morris, Lucy Eggersten FTC
202-326-3295

Consumer Protection Bureau - Credit Practices....Silverman, Steven D. FTC
202-326-2460

Consumer Protection Bureau - Credit Practices....Hansberry, Grace A. FTC
202-326-3236

Consumer Protection Bureau - Credit Practices....Nixon, Judith M. FTC
202-326-3173

Consumer Protection Bureau - Credit Practices....Isaac, Ronald G. FTC
202-326-3231

Consumer Protection Bureau - Credit Practices....Acuff, Victoria R. FTC
202-326-2773

Consumer Protection Bureau - Credit Practices....Kane, Thomas E. FTC
202-326-2304

Consumer Protection Bureau - Credit Practices....Reynolds, Carole L. FTC
202-326-3230

Consumer Protection Bureau - Credit Practices....Keller, Christopher W. FTC
202-326-3159

Consumer Protection Bureau - Credit Practices....D'Entremont, Donald FTC
202-326-2736

Consumer Protection Bureau - Credit Practices....Chang, Nina FTC 202-326-2708

Consumer Protection Bureau - Credit Practices....Cohen, Stephen L. FTC
202-326-3222

Consumer Protection Bureau - Credit Practices....Taylor, Brenda A. FTC
202-326-3125

Consumer Protection Bureau - Credit Practices....Medine, David FTC
202-326-3224

Consumer Protection Bureau - Credit Practices....Twohig, Peggy FTC
202-326-3210

Consumer Protection Bureau - Credit Practices....Yates, Valerie FTC
202-326-3494

Consumer Protection Bureau - Credit Practices....Carroll, Millicent FTC
202-326-2696

Consumer Protection Bureau - Credit Practices....Childs, Beverly R. FTC
202-326-3174

Consumer Protection Bureau - Credit Practices....Baheri, Leila M. FTC
202-326-5610

Consumer Protection Bureau - Credit Practices....Brown, Connie FTC
202-326-3212

Consumer Protection Bureau - Credit Practices....Taylor, Carletta D. FTC
202-326-3225

Consumer Protection Bureau - Credit Practices....Barrios, Jarrett FTC
202-326-3183

Consumer Protection Bureau - Credit Practices....Wahl, Hughes E. FTC
202-326-2999

Consumer Protection Bureau - Education....Jones, Michael J. FTC 202-326-2421

Consumer Protection Bureau - Enforcement....Boyle, Terrence J. FTC
202-326-3016

Consumer Protection Bureau - Enforcement....Brewer, Joel N. FTC 202-326-2967

Consumer Protection Bureau - Enforcement....Cowen, Jonathan FTC
202-326-2533

Consumer Protection Bureau - Enforcement....Dingfelder, Justin FTC
202-326-3017

Consumer Protection Bureau - Enforcement....Dublin, Brenda J. FTC
202-326-2976

Consumer Protection Bureau - Enforcement....Easton, Robert E. FTC
202-326-3029

Consumer Protection Bureau - Enforcement....Ecklund, Stephen C. FTC
202-326-2841

Consumer Protection Bureau - Enforcement....Feinstein, Jeffrey E. FTC
202-326-2372

Consumer Protection Bureau - Enforcement....Frankle, Janice Podoll FTC
202-326-3022

Consumer Protection Bureau - Enforcement....Frisby, Robert FTC 202-326-2098

Consumer Protection Bureau - Enforcement....Graybill, Dean C. FTC
202-326-3284

Consumer Protection Bureau - Enforcement....Kelly, Deborah H. FTC
202-326-3003

Consumer Protection Bureau - Enforcement....Koman, Joseph J., Jr. FTC
202-326-3014

Consumer Protection Bureau - Enforcement....Lewis, Ronald D. FTC
202-326-2985

Consumer Protection Bureau - Enforcement....Martin, Vada L. FTC 202-326-3002

Consumer Protection Bureau - Enforcement....Massie, Thomas D. FTC
202-326-2982

Consumer Protection Bureau - Enforcement....McMurtrey, Nathan FTC
202-326-2308

Consumer Protection Bureau - Enforcement....Metrinko, Peter FTC 202-326-2104

Consumer Protection Bureau - Enforcement....Mickum, George B. FTC
202-326-3132

Consumer Protection Bureau - Enforcement....Mills, James G. FTC 202-326-3035

Consumer Protection Bureau - Enforcement....Pate, Jeffrey FTC 202-326-2305

Consumer Protection Bureau - Enforcement....Phillips, Joyce D. FTC
202-326-3041

Consumer Protection Bureau - Enforcement....Purcell, Adam FTC 202-326-2038

Consumer Protection Bureau - Enforcement....Rodriguez, Edwin FTC 202-326-3147

Consumer Protection Bureau - Enforcement....Sacks, Ruth S. FTC 202-326-3033

Consumer Protection Bureau - Enforcement....Sciacca, Michael FTC 202-326-2305

Consumer Protection Bureau - Enforcement....Tatum, Barbara FTC 202-326-2978

Consumer Protection Bureau - Enforcement....Thomas, Beverly J. FTC 202-326-2938

Consumer Protection Bureau - Enforcement....Toufexis, Rose FTC 202-326-3011

Consumer Protection Bureau - Enforcement....Vecellio, Constance M. FTC 202-326-2966

Consumer Protection Bureau - Enforcement....Welther, Michael S. FTC 202-326-2038

Consumer Protection Bureau - Enforcement....Wilenzick, Marc B. FTC 202-326-2442

Consumer Protection Bureau - Enforcement....Wright, Janet FTC 202-326-2980

Consumer Protection Bureau - Marketing Practices....D'Mara, Jeffries FTC 202-326-2264

Consumer Protection Bureau - Marketing Practices....Stone, Christopher FTC 202-326-3138

Consumer Protection Bureau - Marketing Practices....Ireland, Robert S. FTC 202-326-3114

Consumer Protection Bureau - Marketing Practices....Shetty, Vaishali FTC 202-326-2149

Consumer Protection Bureau - Marketing Practices....Jennings, Carol FTC 202-326-3010

Consumer Protection Bureau - Marketing Practices....Hile, Allen FTC 202-326-3122

Consumer Protection Bureau - Marketing Practices....Harrington, Eileen FTC 202-326-3127

Consumer Protection Bureau - Marketing Practices....Kresses, Mamie FTC 202-326-2070

Consumer Protection Bureau - Marketing Practices....Hodapp, Lawrence FTC 202-326-3105

Consumer Protection Bureau - Marketing Practices....Singer, John Andrew FTC 202-326-3234

Consumer Protection Bureau - Marketing Practices....Tregillus, Craig FTC 202-326-2970

Consumer Protection Bureau - Marketing Practices....Torok, David FTC 202-326-3075

Consumer Protection Bureau - Marketing Practices....Quaresima, Richard A. FTC 202-326-3130

Consumer Protection Bureau - Marketing Practices....Reznek, Sarah FTC 202-326-2213

Consumer Protection Bureau - Marketing Practices....Pitofsky, Sally Forman FTC 202-326-3318

Consumer Protection Bureau - Marketing Practices....Shikiar, Robert FTC 202-326-3009

Consumer Protection Bureau - Marketing Practices....Luehr, Paul H. FTC 202-326-2236

Consumer Protection Bureau - Marketing Practices....Guerard, Collot FTC 202-326-3338

Consumer Protection Bureau - Marketing Practices....Haynes, William L. FTC 202-326-3107

Consumer Protection Bureau - Marketing Practices....Howard, Patricia S. FTC 202-326-2321

Consumer Protection Bureau - Marketing Practices....Howard, Myra FTC 202-326-2047

Consumer Protection Bureau - Marketing Practices....Grant, Elizabeth FTC 202-326-3299

Consumer Protection Bureau - Marketing Practices....Feinstein, Mary S. FTC 202-326-3064

Consumer Protection Bureau - Marketing Practices....Schwanke, Marianne K. FTC 202-326-3165

Consumer Protection Bureau - Marketing Practices....Banks, Nicole O. FTC 202-326-2264

Consumer Protection Bureau - Marketing Practices....Danielson, Carole I. FTC 202-326-3115

Consumer Protection Bureau - Marketing Practices....Modell, Shira D. FTC 202-326-3116

Consumer Protection Bureau - Marketing Practices....Rowan, Thomas P. FTC 202-326-3129

Consumer Protection Bureau - Marketing Practices....Toporoff, Steven FTC 202-326-3135

Consumer Protection Bureau - Marketing Practices....Morris, Beverly M. FTC 202-326-3260

Consumer Protection Bureau - Marketing Practices....Salsburg, Daniel FTC 202-326-3032

Consumer Protection Bureau - Marketing Practices....Kupchyk, Areta L. FTC 202-326-2014

Consumer Protection Bureau - Marketing Practices....Johnson, Delores M. FTC 220-326-3124

Consumer Protection Bureau - Marketing Practices....Norton, Lawrence FTC 202-326-3126

Consumer Protection Bureau - Marketing Practices....Vera, Martha W. FTC 202-326-3096

Consumer Protection Bureau - Marketing Practices....Hudging, Iona FTC 202-326-2927

Consumer Protection Bureau - Marketing Practices....Cook, John M. FTC 202-326-2056

Consumer Protection Bureau - Marketing Practices....Cohn, Thomas A. FTC 202-326-3532

Consumer Protection Bureau - Marketing Practices....Howerton, Kent C. FTC 202-326-3013

Consumer Protection Bureau - Office of Director....Hutchins, Clovia FTC 202-326-3215

Consumer Protection Bureau - Office of Director....Grossman, Beth M. FTC 202-326-3019

Consumer Protection Bureau - Office of Director....Maronick, Thomas J. FTC 202-326-2291

Consumer Protection Bureau - Office of Director....Jung, Louise R. FTC 202-326-2989

Consumer Protection Bureau - Office of Director....Broder, Betsy FTC 202-326-2968

Consumer Protection Bureau - Office of Director....Chung, Jock K. FTC 202-326-2984

Consumer Protection Bureau - Office of Director....Parnes, Lydia B. FTC 202-326-2676

Consumer Protection Bureau - Office of Director....Legal, Sharon V. FTC 202-326-3240

Consumer Protection Bureau - Office of Director....Bernstein, Jodie FTC 202-326-3430

Consumer Protection Bureau - Office of Director....Morris, Lee Willis FTC 202-326-3312

Consumer Protection Bureau - Office of Director....Enright, Maureen FTC 202-326-3160

Consumer Protection Bureau - Office of Director....Brown, Gloria FTC 202-326-3047

Consumer Protection Bureau - Operations....Bow, Kimberley D. FTC 202-326-3252

Consumer Protection Bureau - Operations....Branch, Nicole FTC 202-326-2086

Consumer Protection Bureau - Operations....Burruss, James S., Jr. FTC 202-326-3261

Consumer Protection Bureau - Operations....Clark, Randal S. FTC 202-326-3685

Consumer Protection Bureau - Operations....Cossette, Darlene M. FTC 202-326-3255

Consumer Protection Bureau - Operations....Mandak, Dondra M. FTC 202-326-3246

Consumer Protection Bureau - Operations....Miller, Sylvia FTC 202-326-3258

Consumer Protection Bureau - Operations....Moten, Verletta FTC 202-326-6252

Consumer Protection Bureau - Operations....Peterson, Mark D. FTC 202-326-3731

Consumer Protection Bureau - Operations....Solomon, Tsione FTC 202-326-3251

Consumer Protection Bureau - Operations....Tharrington, Nicole L. FTC 202-326-2416

Consumer Protection Bureau - Operations....Tufts, Tamar FTC 202-326-2411

Consumer Protection Bureau - Service Industry....Sheer, Alain FTC 202-326-3321

Consumer Protection Bureau - Service Industry....Breslaueer, Alan D. FTC 202-326-2430

Consumer Protection Bureau - Service Industry....Osinbajo, Deborah A. FTC 202-326-3316

Consumer Protection Bureau - Service Industry....Gordimer, Douglas FTC 202-326-3003

Consumer Protection Bureau - Service Industry....Hippsley, Heather FTC 202-326-3285

Consumer Protection Bureau - Service Industry....Katz, Michael A. FTC 202-326-3123

Consumer Protection Bureau - Service Industry....Friedman, Robert D. FTC 202-326-3297

Consumer Protection Bureau - Service Industry....Owens, Denise FTC 202-326-3277

Consumer Protection Bureau - Service Industry....Bowie, Darren FTC 202-326-2018

Consumer Protection Bureau - Service Industry....Jones, Elaine FTC 202-326-3622

Be patient. If any phone number is incorrect, call (area code) 555-1212 and request the new listing.

1387

Consumer Protection Bureau - Service Industry....Spiegel, David R. FTC 202-326-3281

Consumer Protection Bureau - Service Industry....Stevenson, Hugh FTC 202-326-3511

Consumer Protection Bureau - Service Industry Practices....Bash, Eric FTC 202-326-2892

Consumer Protection Bureau - Service Industry....Spiro, Daniel A. FTC 202-326-3288

Consumer Protection Bureau - Service Industry....Lamberton, Peter W. FTC 202-326-3274

Consumer Protection Bureau - Service Industry....Mooradian, Jeffrey FTC 202-326-3086

Consumer Protection Bureau - Service Industry....Aliza, Ben FTC 202-326-2905

Consumer Protection Bureau - Service Industry....Toone, Cassandra L. FTC 202-326-3276

Consumer Protection Bureau - Service Industry....Kinscheck, Renate FTC 202-326-3283

Consumer Protection Bureau - Service Industry Pract....Crowley, John A. FTC 202-326-3280

Consumer Protection Bureau - Service Industry....Rothchild, John FTC 202-326-3307

Consumer Protection Bureau - Service Industry....Wagner, Connie FTC 202-326-3309

Consumer Protection Bureau - Service Industry....Dolan, James Reilly FTC 202-326-3292

Consumer Protection Bureau - Service Industry....Chambers, Sylvia J. FTC 202-326-3286

Consumer Protection Bureau - Service Industry....Williams, Gwendolyn C. FTC 202-326-3311

Consumer Protection Bureau - Service Industry Practices.....Daynard, Matthew FTC 202-326-3291

Consumer Protection Bureau - Service Industry....Abdullah, Raouf FTC 202-326-3024

Consumer Protection Bureau - Service Industry....Gurwitz, Stephen FTC 202-326-3272

Consumer Protection Bureau - Service Industry....Kelly, Richard F. FTC 202-326-3304

Consumer Protection Bureau - Service Industry Prac....Michaels, Jason J. FTC 202-326-2239

Consumer Protection Bureau - Service Industry....Jones-Thompson, Gwendolyn L. FTC 202-326-3305

Consumer Protection Bureau - Service Industry Prac....Mills, Sondra FTC 202-326-2673

Consumer Protection Bureau - Service Industry....Fields, Mary C. FTC 202-326-3098

Consumer Protection Bureau - Service Industry....Lesemann, Dana FTC 202-326-3146

Consumer Protection Bureau - Service Industry....Gross, Walter, III FTC 202-326-3319

Consumer Protection Bureau - Service Industry....Fix, David FTC 202-326-3298

Consumer Protection Bureau - Service Industry Practices....Chua, Michele FTC 202-326-3248

Consumer Protection Bureau....Jackson, Howard R. FTC 202-326-3170

Consumer Protection Bureau....Brody, Jay D. FTC 202-326-2419

Consumer Protection Bureau....Bertrand, Jenna R. FTC 202-326-2823

Consumer Protection Bureau....Lefevre, John F. FTC 202-326-3209

Consumer Protection Bureau....Blickman, Neil J. FTC 202-326-3038

Consumer Protection Bureau....Bonanno, Peter FTC 202-326-2495

Consumer Protection, Business Education....Jansen, Bonnie FTC 202-326-2988

Contact Lens....Staff Contact Lens Manufacturers Association (CLMA) 800-343-5367

Contact Lenses....Staff NEI 301-496-5248

Containers Industry Group....Duvall, Steven SEC 202-942-1950

Containers, of base metal....Fulcher, Nancy USITC 202-205-3434

Containers (of wood)....Hoffmeier, Bill USITC 202-205-3321

Containment Systems....Barrett, Richard J. NRC 301-415-3627

Contaminants, Environmental....Staff FWS 703-358-2148

Contest Giveaway....Staff FCC 202-418-1430

Continental Shelf, Outer....Staff FWS 202-358-2183

Continuous Ambulatory Peritoneal Dialysis (CAPD)....Staff NIDDK 301-654-4415

Contraception....Staff NICHD 301-496-5133

Contraceptives....Cruzan, Susan FDA 301-443-3285

Contraceptives....Staff NICHD 301-496-5133

Contract Policy....Staff OD/OA 301-496-6014

Contractors, Building Materials and Related Services....Duvall, Steven SEC 202-942-1950

Control levers....Cuomo, Peter PTO 703-308-0827

Conventional Fossil Fuel Power (Major Projects)....Dollison, Robert COMMERCE 202-482-2733

Conventions, Exhibits....Dickinson, Joanne CENSUS 301-457-1191

Converted Paper Prod....Stanley, Gary COMMERCE 202-482-0375

Converters....Greene, William USITC 202-205-3405

Conveyors....Olszewski, Robert PTO 703-308-2588

Cook Islands....Respess, Rebecca Cnty TDA 703-875-4357

Cook Islands....Berghage, Jeff Peace Corps 202-606-1098

Cook Islands....Staff Cnty State 202-647-3546

Cooley's Anemia....Staff Cooley's Anemia Foundation (CAF) 800-221-3571

Cooley's Anemia....Staff NHLBI 301-496-4236

Cooperative Forestry....Liu, Karen FS 202-205-1378

Copper Wire Mills....Mains, Barbara COMMERCE 202-482-0606

Copper compounds....Greenblatt, Jack USITC 202-205-3353

Copper/Brass Mills....Mains, Barbara COMMERCE 202-482-0606

Copper....Edelstein, Daniel MINES 202-501-9415

Copper....Lundy, David USITC 202-205-3439

Copra and coconut oil....Reeder, John USITC 202-205-3319

Cor Pulmonale....Staff NHLBI 301-496-4236

Cordage machines....Greene, William USITC 202-205-3405

Cordage....Konzet, Jeffrey CUSTOMS 212-466-5885

Cordless Telephone....Staff FCC 202-653-6288

Cork and cork products....Hoffmeier, Bill USITC 202-205-3321

Corn with options....Amato, David CFT 312-353-9025

Corn, field....Reeder, John USITC 202-205-3319

Corneal Disorders....Staff NEI 301-496-5248

Corneal Transplantation....Staff NEI 301-496-5248

Cornelia deLange Syndrome....Staff NICHD 301-496-5133

Coronary Artery Surgery Study (CASS)....Staff NHLBI 301-496-4236

Coronary Angioplasty....Staff NHLBI 301-496-4236

Coronary Artery Disease....Staff NHLBI 301-496-4236

Coronary Bypass....Staff NHLBI 301-496-4236

Coronary Disease....Staff NHLBI 301-496-4236

Corporate Filings....Staff SEC 202-942-8090

Corporate Financial Audits....Gramling, Robert W. GAO 202-512-9406

Corrections - Community....Baunach, Phyllis Jo Justice Stat 202-307-0361

Corrections - General....Baunach, Phyllis Jo Justice Stat 202-307-0361

Corrections - General....Beck, Allen Justice Stat 202-616-3277

Corrections - General....Greenfeld, Lawrence Justice Stat 202-616-3281

Corrections - General....Innes, Christopher Justice Stat 202-724-3121

Corrections - General....Kane, Patrick R. Justice Stat 202-307-3226

Corrections - General....Kline, Susan Justice Stat 202-724-3118

Corrections - General....Stephan, James Justice Stat 202-616-3289

Corrections....Beck, Allen Justice Stat 202-616-3277

Corrections....Innes, Christopher Justice Stat 202-724-3121

Corrections....Staff Justice Stat 202-307-3106

Corrections....Greenfeld, Lawrence Justice Stat 202-616-3281

Corrections....Baunach, Phyllis Jo Justice Stat 202-307-0361

Corrosion Inhibition....Warden, Robert PTO 703-308-2920

Corrosion....Ricker, Richard E. NIST 301-975-6023

Corundum-Emery....Austin, Gordon MINES 202-501-9388

Cosmetic and Toiletry Preparations....Joseph, Stephanie CUSTOMS 212-466-5768

Cosmetic Allergy....Staff FDA 202-205-4231

Cosmetic creams....Land, Eric USITC 202-205-3349

Cosmetics (Export Promo)....Kimmel, Ed COMMERCE 202-482-3460

Cosmetics, perfumery, toilet preparations....Land, Eric USITC 202-205-3349

Cosmetics....Bailey, John E. FDA 202-205-4530

Cost Allocation Models....Staff FCC 202-418-0810

Cost of Capital Audits....Staff FCC 202-418-0850

Cost of Crime - General....Rand, Michael Justice Stat 202-616-3494

Cost of Crime - General....Lindgren, Sue Justice Stat 202-307-0760

Cost of Crime - To Government....Lindgren, Sue Justice Stat 202-307-0760

Cost of Crime - To Victims....Klaus, Patsy Justice Stat 202-307-0776

Cost-of-Living Abroad, Productivity and Technology....Capdevielle, Patricia LABOR 202-606-5654

Costa Rica....Stanton, Dan Peace Corps 202-606-3620

Costa Rica...Wilkins, Michele Cnty Export-Import Bank 202-565-3743

Costa Rica....Opstein, Sally Cnty USIA 202-619-5864

Costa Rica....Vandenbos, James Cnty AID 202-647-9541

Costa Rica....Bayly, Rachel Cnty Treasury 202-622-1266

Costa Rica....Quintanilla, Rosalinda Cnty World Bank 202-473-7673

Costa Rica....Picado, Sonia Cnty Embassy 202-234-2945

Costa Rica....Silva, Carlos Cnty Embassy 202-234-2945

Costa Rica....Davis, Janice Peace Corps 202-606-3198

Costa Rica....Siegelman, Mark Cnty Commerce 202-482-5680

Costa Rica (San Jose)....Staff Cnty State 202-647-3518

Costa Rica/Minerals....Rabchevsky, George Cnty Mines 202-501-9670

Costochondritis....Staff NIAMS 301-496-8188

Costume Jewelry, Trade Promo....Beckham, R. COMMERCE 202-482-5478

Cote d'Ivoire....Maybury-Lewis Anthony Cnty Export-Import Bank 202-565-3739

Cote d'Ivoire....Palghat, Kathy Cnty Treasury 202-622-0332

Cote D'Ivoire....van Trotsenburg, Axel Cnty World Bank 202-473-6794

Cote d'Ivoire....Koumoue, Koffi Moise Cnty Embassy 202-797-0300

Cote d'Ivoire....Bezek, Jill Cnty TDA 703-875-4357

Cote d'Ivoire....Akeo, Severin Mathias Cnty Embassy 202-797-0300

Cote d'Ivoire....Peprah-Mensah, Felicia Peace Corps 202-606-3186

Cote d'Ivoire (Abidjan)....Staff Cnty State 202-647-1540

Cote d'Ivoire (Ivory Coast)....Dolley, Thomas Cnty Mines 202-501-9690

Cotton Seed Oil....Janis, William V. COMMERCE 202-482-2250

Cotton - World....Whitton, Carolyn Agri 202-219-0826

Cotton....Latham, Roger Agri 202-720-5944

Cotton....Meyer, Leslie Agri 202-219-0840

Cotton....Skinner, Robert Agri 202-219-0840

Cotton....Sweet, Mary Elizabeth USITC 202-205-3455

Cottonseed and cottonseed oil....Reeder, John USITC 202-205-3319

Council of Europe....Staff Cnty State 202-647-1708

Counseling (Drug Abuse)....Staff NIDA 301-443-6245

Counterfeit Notes...Cameron, Jon FRS 202-452-2220

Country Exposure Reports....Adams, Sarah FRS 202-452-2634

County Business Patterns....Hanczaryk, Paul CENSUS 301-457-2580

County and City Data Books....Cevis, Wanda CENSUS 301-457-1166

Courier Services....Elliot, Fred COMMERCE 202-482-1134

Court Appeals....Gaskins, Carla Justice Stat 202-508-8546

Court Appeals....Langan, Patrick Justice Stat 202-616-3490

Court Appeals....Lindgren, Sue Justice Stat 202-307-0760

Court Case Processing Time....Gaskins, Carla Justice Stat 202-508-8546

Court Case Processing Time - Federal....Kaplan, Carol Justice Stat 202-307-0759

Court Caseload....Gaskins, Carla Justice Stat 202-508-8546

Court Caseload....Langan, Patrick Justice Stat 202-616-3490

Court Organization....Gaskins, Carla Justice Stat 202-508-8546

Court Organization....Langan, Patrick Justice Stat 202-616-3490

Courts....Gaskins, Carla Justice Stat 202-508-8546

Courts....Langan, Patrick Justice Stat 202-616-3490

Coxsackie Virus (Hand-Food and Mouth Disease)....Staff NIAID 301-496-5717

Coxsackie Virus (Hand-Foot and Mouth Disease)....Staff NICHD 301-496-5133

Cranes....Greene, William USITC 202-205-3405

Craniofacial, children....Staff Children's Craniofacial Association 800-535-3643

Craniofacial Malformations....Staff NIDR 301-496-4261

Craniofacially handicapped....Staff National Association for the Craniofacially Handicapped 800-332-2373

Crayons....Seastrum, Carl USITC 202-205-3493

Creams, cosmetic....Land, Eric USITC 202-205-3349

Cretinism....Staff NIDDK 301-496-3583

Creutzfeldt-Jakob Disease....Staff NINDS 301-496-5751

Cri Du Chat (Cat Cry Syndrome)....Staff NICHD 301-496-5133

Crib Death (SIDS)....Staff NICHD 301-496-5133

Crib Toys....Tyrrell, Elaine CPSC 301-504-0580

Crigler-Najar Syndrome....Staff NIDDK 301-654-3810

Crime and the Elderly....Staff NIA 301-496-1752

Crime and the Elderly....Staff NIA 301-496-1752

Crime and Drug Abuse....Staff NIDA 301-443-6245

Crime Incidence, Rates, and Trends....Chaiken, Jan Justice Stat 202-307-0765

Crime Incidence, Rates, and Trends....Klaus, Patsy Justice Stat 202-307-0776

Crime Incidence, Rates, and Trends....Rand, Michael Justice Stat 202-616-3494

Crime Incidence, Rates, and Trends....Taylor, Bruce Justice Stat 202-616-3498

Crime, Location of....Kinderman, Charles Justice Stat 202-616-3489

Crime Measurement Methods....Taylor, Bruce Justice Stat 202-616-3498

Crime Measurement Methods....Rand, Michael Justice Stat 202-616-3494

Crime Measurement Methods....Kinderman, Charles Justice Stat 202-616-3489

Crime, organized....Singer, Laura S. SEC 202-942-4542

Crime, organized....Zelinsky, Yuri SEC 202-942-4846

Crime, Population...Hoff, Gail CENSUS 301-457-3925

Crime Prevention Measures....Staff Justice Stat 202-466-6272

Crime Seasonality....DeBarry, Marshall Justice Stat 202-616-3489

Crime Severity....Klaus, Patsy Justice Stat 202-307-0776

Crime Types: Federal, Bank Robbery, Computer....Scalia, John Justice Stat 202-616-3276

Crime Types: Homicide....White, Paul Justice Stat 202-307-0771

Crime Types: Homicide....Zawitz, Marianne Justice Stat 202-616-3499

Crime Types: Rape, Robbery, Assault, Theft....Klaus, Patsy Justice Stat 202-307-0776

Crime Types: Rape, Robbery, Assault, Theft....Harlow, Caroline Justice Stat 202-307-0757

Crime Types: Rape, Robbery, Assault, Theft....Rand, Michael Justice Stat 202-616-3494

Criminal Defendants - Federal....Kaplan, Carol Justice Stat 202-307-0759

Criminal Defendants....Gaskins, Carla Justice Stat 202-508-8546

Criminal Defendants....Langan, Patrick Justice Stat 202-616-3490

Criminal History Data Quality....Kaplan, Carol Justice Stat 202-307-0759

Criminal Justice Agencies....Lindgren, Sue Justice Stat 202-307-0760

Criminal Justice Expenditure and Employment....Lindgren, Sue Justice Stat 202-307-0760

Criminal Justice....Staff NCJRS 800-851-3420

Crisis Intervention....Staff Primary Care Management Systems (PCMS) 800-444-9999

Critical Care Medicine Department....Staff CC 301-496-9565

Croatia....Altheim, Stephen Cnty Treasury 202-622-0125

Croatia....Corwin, Elizabeth Cnty USIA 202-619-5055

Croatia....Cosic, Kresimir Cnty Embassy 202-588-5899

Croatia....Elwan Ann E. Cnty World Bank 202-473-2435

Croatia....Sarcevic, Peter A. Cnty Embassy 202-588-5899

Croatia....Staff Cnty State 202-736-7361

Croatia....Waxman-Lenz, Roberta Cnty Export-Import Bank 202-565-3742

Croatia...Rabchevsky, George Cnty MINES 202-501-9670

Crohn's disease....Staff Crohn's and Colitis Foundation of America 800-932-2423

Crohn's Disease....Staff NIAID 301-496-5717

Crohn's Disease....Staff NIDDK 301-654-3810

Crop Protection....Staff FWS 703-358-2043

Cross Interest Policy....Staff FCC 202-418-2130

Cross Ownership TV/Cable....Staff FCC 202-416-0856

Cross-Eye....Staff NEI 301-496-5248

Crude cresylic acid....Foreso, Cynthia USITC 202-205-3348

Crude Oil....Linville, Bill NEIC 918-337-4375

Crude Oil....Heath, Charles NEIC 202-586-6860

Crude petroleum....Foreso, Cynthia USITC 202-205-3348

Crushing machines....Greene, William USITC 202-205-3405

Cryofibrinogenemia....Staff NHLBI 301-496-4236

Cryoglobulinemia....Staff NHLBI 301-496-4236

Cryolite....White, Linda USITC 202-205-3427

Cryosurgery (Eyes)....Staff NEI 301-496-5248

Cryosurgery....Staff NCI 301-496-5583

Cryptococcosis....Staff NIAID 301-496-5717

Cryptosporidiosis....Staff NIAID 301-496-5717

Cuba (Havana)....Staff Cnty State 202-647-9272

Cuba/Minerals....Rabchevsky, George Cnty Mines 202-501-9681

Cuba....Marcus, Anthony Cnty Treasury 202-622-1218

Cuba....Shumake, Josie Cnty USIA 202-619-5864

Cuba....Siegelman, Mark Cnty Commerce 202-482-5680

Cuba....Wilkins, Michele Cnty Export-Import Bank 202-565-3743

Cucumbers....McCarty, Timothy USITC 202-205-3324

Cued Speech.....Staff NIDCD 301-496-7243

Culm....Foreso, Cynthia USITC 202-205-3348

Cupric oxide....Conant, Kenneth USITC 202-205-3346

Cuprous oxide....Conant, Kenneth USITC 202-205-3346

Current Analysis of U.S. Export and Import Price Ind....Vachris, Michelle LABOR 202-606-7155

Current Business Analysis....Fox, Douglas R. ECONOMIC 202-606-9683

Current Business Statistics....Statistical Series Staff ECONOMIC 202-606-9607

Current-Carrying Wiring Devices....Whitley, Richard A. COMMERCE 202-482-0682

Current Employment Analysis, Assist. Comm. Empl/Unempl....Bregger, John E. LABOR 202-606-6388

Current Wage Developments, Comp. and Working Cond....Cimini, Michael LABOR 202-606-6275

Curtains....Sweet, Mary Elizabeth USITC 202-205-3455

Cushing's Syndrome....Staff NICHD 301-496-5133

Cushing's Syndrome....Staff NIDDK 301-496-3583

Cushing's Syndrome....Staff NINDS 301-496-5751

Cushing's Syndrome....Staff NHLBI 301-496-4236

Cushions....Spalding, Josephine USITC 202-205-3498

Customer Service....Staff CENSUS 301-457-4100

Cut flowers....Burket, Stephen USITC 202-205-3318

Cut Flowers....Conte, Ralph CUSTOMS 212-466-5759

Cutis Laxa....Staff NHLBI 301-496-4236

Cutlery....Bello, Felix USITC 202-205-3120

Cutlery....Bratland, Rosemarie COMMERCE 202-482-0380

Cutlery....Preston, Jacques CUSTOMS 212-466-5488

Cutting machines textile....Greene, William USITC 202-205-3405

Cyclic Idiopathic Edema....Staff NHLBI 301-496-4236

Cyclitis....Staff NEI 301-496-5248

Be patient. If any phone number is incorrect, call (area code) 555-1212 and request the new listing.

1389

Cyprus (Nicosia)....Staff Cnty State 202-647-6113
Cyprus/Minerals....Mobbs, Philip Cnty Mines 202-501-9679
Cyprus....Corro, Ann Cnty Commerce 202-482-3945
Cyprus....Hutchings, Dayna Cnty Export-Import Bank 202-565-3737
Cyprus....Jacovides, Andrew Cnty Embassy 202-462-5772
Cyprus....Mehra, Suman Cnty World Bank 202-473-2247
Cyprus....Miltiadou, Miltos Cnty Embassy 202-462-5772
Cyprus....Santoro, Eugene Cnty USIA 202-619-6582
Cyprus....VanRenterghem, Cynthia Cnty Treasury 202-622-0343
Cystic Fibrosis....Staff Cystic Fibrosis Foundation (CFF) 800-344-4823
Cystic Fibrosis (Pancreas)....Staff NIDDK 301-496-3583
Cystic Acne....Staff NIAMS 301-496-8188
Cystinosis....Staff NICHD 301-496-5133
Cystinuria....Staff NIDDK 301-654-4415
Cystitis....Staff NIDDK 301-654-4415
Cytology....Staff NCI 301-496-5583
Cytomegalic Inclusion Disease....Staff NIDCD 301-496-7243
Cytomegalic Inclusion Disease....Staff NINDS 301-496-5751
Cytomegalovirus (Congenital)....Staff NHLBI 301-496-4236
Cytomegalovirus (Congenital)....Staff NEI 301-496-5248
Cytomegalovirus (Congenital)....Staff NICHD 301-496-5133
Cytomegalovirus (Congenital)....Staff NIAID 301-496-5717
Czech Republic....Waxman-Lenz, Roberta Cnty Export-Import Bank 202-565-3742
Czech Republic....Gallagher, Tricia Cnty Treasury 202-622-0117
Czech Republic....Hewer, Ulrich Albert Cnty World Bank 202-473-2279
Czech Republic....Bazala, Razvigor Cnty USIA 202-619-5055
Czech Republic....Ann Lien Cnty TDA 703-875-4357
Czech Republic....Lockwood, Jennifer Peace Corps 202-606-3607
Czech Republic....Schiel, Russell Peace Corps 202-606-3606
Czech Republic....Mowrey, Mark Cnty Commerce 202-482-4915
Czech....Vancura, Petr Cnty Embassy 202-363-6316
Czech....Zantovsky, Michael Cnty Embassy 202-363-6315
Czechoslovakia/Minerals....Steblez, Walter Cnty Mines 202-501-9672
Czechoslovakia (Prague)....Staff Cnty State 202-647-1457

D

D-Mark with options....Bice, David CFT 312-353-7880
D'Jibouti....Watkins, Chandra Cnty Commerce 202-482-4564
Dairy Products - Milk, Ice Cream, etc.....Buckner, Dan Agri 202-720-4448
Dairy Products - Milk, Ice Cream, etc.....Miller, Jim Agri 202-219-0770
Dairy Products - Milk, Ice Cream, etc.....Short, Sara Agri 202-219-0769
Dairy products....Ludwick, David USITC 202-205-3329
Dairy Products....Janis, William V. COMMERCE 202-482-2250
Dairy....Staff National Dairy Council (NDC) 800-426-8271
Dam Safety....Staff FWS 703-358-1719
Dance....Moyeda, Cynthia NEA 202-682-5435
Dance....Sonntag, Doug NEA 202-682-5000
Dandy-Walker Syndrome....Staff NINDS 301-496-5751
Dangerous drugs....Van Vliet, Theresa Justice 202-514-0917
Darier's Disease....Staff NIAMS 301-496-8188
Data Acquisition Systems....Brown, Dwayne NASA 202-358-1726
Data and Tapes, Consumer Expend. Survey, Prices....Passero, William LABOR 202-606-6900
Database management systems....Black, Thomas PTO 703-305-9707
Database Management....Staff DCRT 301-496-6256
Database Services....Inoussa, Mary COMMERCE 202-482-5820
Databases (Bibliograpic Information)....Staff NLM 301-496-6095
Data Diskettes, Employment Projections....Bowman, Charles LABOR 202-606-5702
Data Diskettes and Tapes, State and Area Labor Force....Marcus, Jessie LABOR 202-606-6392
Data Diskettes, Consumer Price Indexes, Pr/Lv. Con....Gibson, Sharon LABOR 202-606-6968
Data Diskettes and Tapes, Empl. and Wages, Empl/Unempl....Buso, Michael LABOR 202-606-6499
Data Diskettes, Prices and Living Conditions....Rosenberg, Elliott LABOR 202-606-7728
Data processing machines....Bringe, Julie USITC 202-205-3390
Data processing services....Xavier, Neil USITC 202-205-3450
Data processing services....Atkins, Robert G. COMMERCE 202-482-4781
Data Tapes, Industry-Occup. Matrix, Empl. Proj.....Turner, Delores LABOR 202-606-5730
Data Tapes, Productivity and Technology....Kriebel, Bertram LABOR 202-606-5606
Day Care....Kharfen, Michael ACF 202-401-9215

Daytime Broadcasting....Staff FCC 202-418-2660
Deafness, National Institute of....Allen, Marin NIH 301-496-7243
Deafness....Staff Deafness Research Foundation (DRF) 800-535-3323
Deafness....Staff NIDCD 301-496-7243
Death and Dying....Staff NIA 301-443-1752
Death and Dying....Staff NIMH 301-443-4515
Decalcomanias (decals)....Twarok, Chris USITC 202-205-3314
Decennial Census, 1990 Counts f/Current Boundaries....Miller, Joel CENSUS 301-457-1099
Decennial Census, Content and Tabula, Program Design....Berman, Patricia CENSUS 301-457-3960
Decennial Census, Content, General....Berman, Patrica A. CENSUS 301-457-3960
Decennial Census, Content, General....Paez, Al CENSUS 301-457-3995
Decennial Census, Count Information....Staff CENSUS 301-457-2933
Decennial Census, Count Information....Staff CENSUS 301-457-2131
Decennial Census, Count Questions, 1990 Census....Kobilarcik, Ed CENSUS 301-457-3994
Decennial Census, Demographic Analysis....Robinson, Gregg CENSUS 301-457-2103
Decennial Census, Housing Data, Special Tabuls. of....Bonnette, Robert CENSUS 301-763-8553
Decennial Census, Litigation....Gregg, Valerie CENSUS 301-457-4102
Decennial Census, Population Data, Special Tab. of....Cowan, Rosemarie CENSUS 301-457-2408
Decennial Census, Post-Enumeration Surveys....Hogan, Howard CENSUS 301-457-2665
Decennial Census, Publications, General....Hemming, Robert CENSUS 301-457-4130
Decennial Census, Publications, General....Hemming, Robert CENSUS 301-457-4130
Decennial Census, Reapportionment....Turner, Marshall CENSUS 301-457-4039
Decennial Census, Redistricting....Turner, Marshall CENSUS 301-457-4039
Decennial Census, Sampling Methods....Woltman, Henry CENSUS 301-457-4199
Decennial Census, Tabulations, General....Porter, Gloria CENSUS 301-457-4019
Decennial Census, Tabulations, General....Stark, Billie CENSUS 301-457-4158
Decennial Census, User-Defined Area Program....Quasney, Adrienne CENSUS 301-457-3819
Decennial Management....Miskusa, Susan CENSUS 301-457-2933
Decennial Planning Division....LaMacchia, Robert CENSUS 301-457-1022
Decibel Information....Staff NIDCD 301-496-7243
Decontamination (Radioactive Spills)....Staff OD/ORS 301-496-2254
Decontamination....Staff OD/ORS 301-496-2960
Decubitus Ulcers....Staff NIAMS 301-496-8188
Decubitus Ulcers....Staff NIA 301-496-1752
Deep Vein Thrombosis....Staff NHLBI 301-496-4236
Deep Space Communications Complex....Wood, Alan S. NASA 818-354-5011
Defense Audit....Connor, David M. GAO 202-512-9095
Defense Energy Programs....Reis, Victor NEIC 202-586-2177
Degenerative Joint Disease....Staff NIAMS 301-496-8188
Degenerative Basal Ganglia Disease....Staff NINDS 301-496-5751
Deglutition....Staff NIDR 301-496-4261
Dejerine-Sottas Disease....Staff NINDS 301-496-5751
Delayed Puberty....Staff NICHD 301-496-5133
Delivery devices....Olszewski, Robert PTO 703-308-2588
Delivery of Nursing Care....Staff NINR 301-496-0207
Dementia....Staff NIMH 301-443-4513
Dementia....Staff NINDS 301-496-5751
Dementia....Staff NIA 301-496-1752
Demographic Programs, Statistical Research....Waite, Preston CENSUS 301-457-4287
Demographic Studies, Center for....Wetzel, James R. CENSUS 301-457-4076
Demography of Aging....Staff NIA 301-496-1752
Demography....Staff NICHD 301-496-5133
Demyelinating Diseases....Staff NINDS 301-496-5751
Dengue....Staff NIAID 301-496-5717
Denmark/Minerals....Zajac, William Cnty Mines 202-501-9671
Denmark (Copenhagen)....Staff Cnty State 202-647-5669
Denmark....Dyvig, Peter Cnty Embassy 202-234-4300
Denmark....Gosnell, Peter Cnty Export-Import Bank 202-565-3733
Denmark....Holloway, Barbara Cnty Treasury 202-622-0098
Denmark....Hoppe, Christian Cnty Embassy 202-234-4300
Denmark....Kendall, Maryanne Cnty Commerce 202-482-3254
Denmark....Rankin-Galloway, Honore Cnty USIA 202-619-5283
Dental Amalgams....Staff NIDR 301-496-4261
Dental Assistants (Education)....Staff HRSA/BHPr 301-443-1173
Dental Care Programs (Aged, Handicapped, Prepaid)....Staff HRSA 301-443-6853
Dental cements....Randall, Rob USITC 202-205-3366

Dental Diseases/Disorders....Staff NIDR 301-496-4261
Dental Implants....Staff NIDR 301-496-4261
Dental materials....Tesk, John A. NIST 301-975-6799
Dental Research, National Institute of....Jacquet, Brent NIH 301-496-6705
Dental Restorative Materials....Staff NIDR 301-496-4261
Dental Sealants....Staff NIDR 301-496-4261
Dental X-rays....Staff NIDR 301-496-4261
Dentistry....Mancene, Gene PTO 703-308-2696
Dentobacterial Plaque Infection....Staff NIDR 301-496-4261
Dentures....Staff NIDR 301-496-4261
Depression and Aging....Staff NIMH 301-443-4513
Depression and Aging....Staff NIA 301-496-1752
Depression....Staff National Foundation for Depressive Illness (NFDI) 800-248-4344
Depression....Staff NIMH 301-443-4513
Depth Perception....Staff NEI 301-496-5248
Deputy Director BEA....Landefeld, Steven ECONOMIC 202-606-9602
Deputy Commissioner, Office of....Barron, William G. LABOR 202-606-7802
Dermatitis Herpetiformis....Staff NIAMS 301-496-8188
Dermatological agents....Nesbitt, Elizabeth USITC 202-205-3355
Dermatology....Staff American Society for Dermatologic Surgery (ASDS) 800-441-2737
Dermatology....Staff NIAMS 301-496-8188
Dermatology....Staff NCI 301-496-5583
Dermatomyositis....Staff NIAMS 301-496-8188
Dermatomyositis....Staff NINDS 301-496-5751
Dermographism....Staff NIAID 301-496-5717
DES (Diethylstilbestrol)....Staff NCI 301-496-5583
DES (Diethylstilbestrol)....Staff NICHD 301-496-5133
DES (Diethylstilbestrol)....Staff FDA 301-443-3170
Desalination/Water Reuse....Wheeler, Frederica COMMERCE 202-482-3509
Design Services....Staff NCRR 301-496-5566
Designer Drugs....Staff NIDA 301-443-6245
Detergents....Joseph, Stephanie CUSTOMS 212-466-5768
Detergents....Land, Eric USITC 202-205-3349
Developmental Disabilities and Birth Defects....Adams, M.J., Jr. CDC 404-488-7150
Developmental Disabilities....Kharfen, Michael ACF 202-401-9215
Developmental Disorders....Staff NIDCD 301-496-7243
Developmental Disorders....Staff NINDS 301-496-5751
Developmental Disorders....Staff NICHD 301-496-5133
Developmental Endocrinology....Chrousos, George P. FAES 301-496-5800
Developmental Endocrinology....Chrousos, George FAES 301-496-4686
Developmentally Disabled....Staff Devereux Foundation 800-345-1292
Devic's Syndrome....Staff NINDS 301-496-5751
Dextrine....Randall, Rob USITC 202-205-3366
Di(2-ethylhexyl) adipate....Johnson, Larry USITC 202-205-3351
Di(2-ethylhexyl) phthalate....Johnson, Larry USITC 202-205-3351
Diabetes and Aging (Type 1 and Type 2)....Staff NIA 301-654-3327
Diabetes and Aging (Type 1 and Type 2)....Staff NIDDK 301-654-3327
Diabetes (And Arteriosclerosis)....Staff NHLBI 301-496-4236
Diabetes and Gum Disease....Staff NIDR 301-496-4261
Diabetes and Pregnancy....Staff NICHD 301-496-5133
Diabetes Clearinghouse....Staff NIDDK 301-654-3327
Diabetes, Digestive and Kidney Disorders, Nat'l Inst....Singer, Betsy NIH 301-496-3583
Diabetes Insipidus....Staff NIDDK 301-654-3327
Diabetes (Juvenile)....Staff NIDDK 301-654-3327
Diabetes Mellitus....Staff NIDDK 301-654-3327
Diabetes with Insulin Allergy or Resistance....Staff NIAID 301-496-5717
Diabetes with Insulin Allergy or Resistance....Staff NIDDK 301-654-3327
Diabetes....Staff American Diabetes Association 800-232-3472
Diabetes....Staff Juvenile Diabetes Foundation 800-223-1138
Diabetes....Taylor, Simeon FAES 301-496-2596
Diabetic Eye Disease....Staff NIDDK 301-654-3327
Diabetic Eye Disease....Staff NEI 301-496-5248
Diabetic Neuropathy....Staff NINDS 301-496-5751
Diabetic Neuropathy....Staff NIDDK 301-654-3327
Diabetic Retinopathy....Staff NEI 301-496-5248
Diabetic Retinopathy....Staff NIDDK 301-654-3327
Diagnostic Laboratories for Animal Disease....Staff NCRR 301-594-7933
Diagnostic Radiology....Staff CC 301-496-7700
Dial-a-Porn Complaints....Staff FCC 202-632-7553
Dialysis, Kidney....Staff NIDDK 301-654-4415
Diamond, Industrial....Prebury, Graylin COMMERCE 202-482-5158
Diamond....Austin, Gordon MINES 202-501-9388
Diamond-Blackfan Syndrome....Staff NHLBI 301-496-4236

Diamonds....DeSapio, Vincent USITC 202-205-3435
Diarrheal Illnesses....Staff NIAID 301-496-5717
Diarrheal Illnesses....Staff NIDDK 301-654-3810
Diathermy Approval....Staff FCC 301-725-1585
Diatomite....Taylor, Harold MINES 202-501-9754
Diatomite....White, Linda USITC 202-205-3427
Dictation machines....Puffert, Douglas USITC 202-205-3402
Diego Garcia....Staff Cnty State 202-647-6453
Dietary Restriction....Staff NIA 301-496-1752
Diethylstilbestrol (DES)....Staff NCI 301-496-5583
Diethylstilbestrol (DES)....Staff FDA 301-443-3170
Diethylstilbestrol (DES)....Staff NICHD 301-496-5133
Diffuse Sclerosis....Staff NINDS 301-496-5751
Digestive Diseases Clearinghouse....Staff NIDDK 301-654-3810
Digestive Diseases....Staff NIDDK 301-654-3810
Digital communications....Olms, Douglas W. PTO 703-305-4703
Digital communications....Chin, Stephen PTO 703-305-4714
Digital computers....Envall, Roy PTO 703-305-9706
Digital data error correction....Envall, Roy PTO 703-305-9706
Digital Device Measurements....Staff FCC 301-725-1585
Dijbouti....Larsen, Mark Cnty USIA 202-619-4894
Dijbouti....McKoy, Ethel Cnty Treasury 202-622-0336
Dilsobutylene....Raftery, Jim USITC 202-205-3365
Dilsodecyl phthalate....Johnson, Larry USITC 202-205-3351
Dinnerware of ceramic....McNay, Deborah USITC 202-205-3425
Dioctyl phthalates....Johnson, Larry USITC 202-205-3351
Diphtheria....Staff NIAID 301-496-5717
Diploma Schools of Nursing....Staff HRSA/BHPr 301-443-5786
Direct Mail....Elliot, Fred COMMERCE 202-482-1134
Director, Office of the....Lindberg, Donald A. NLM 301-496-6221
Director, BEA....Carson, Carol S. ECONOMIC 202-606-9600
Director's Office - Information Services....Brill, Kendra J. FTC 202-326-2607
Director's Office....Rich, Jessica FTC 202-326-2148
Disabilities....Staff NOD 800-248-2253
Disability Benefits, Social Security....Gambino, Phil SSA 410-965-8904
Disabled....Staff ABLEDATA 800-227-0126
Disabled....Staff Advocacy Center for the Elderly and Disabled (ACED) 800-960-7705
Disaster Assistance....Kulik, Bernard SBA 202-205-6734
Disc Drives, Diskettes....Valverde, Daniel COMMERCE 202-482-0573
Discoid Lupus Erythematosus....Staff NIAMS 301-496-8188
Discouraged Workers, Empl./Unempl. Stats....Hamel, Harvey LABOR 202-606-6378
Discouraged Workers, Employment Statistics....Hamel, Harvey LABOR 202-606-6378
Disease Information Hotline.... CDC 404-332-4555
Disease Prevention....Staff NINR 301-496-0207
Disequilibrium....Staff NIDCD 301-496-7243
Disinfection....Staff OD/ORS 301-496-2960
Displaced Workers, Empl/Unempl Statistics....Gardner, Jennifer LABOR 202-606-6378
Disposal (Animal Waste, Dead Animal, Infect. Materials)....Staff OD/ORS 301-496-2960
Distillate fuel oil....Foreso, Cynthia USITC 202-205-3348
Distilled Water....Staff OD/ORS 301-496-2960
Distribution services....Luther, Dennis USITC 202-205-3497
Diuretics....Staff NHLBI 301-496-4236
Diurnaldystonia....Staff NINDS 301-496-5751
Diverticulitis....Staff NIDDK 301-654-3810
Diverticulosis....Staff NIDDK 301-654-3810
Divorce Statistics....Staff CDC 301-436-8500
Dizziness....Staff NIDCD 301-496-7243
Dizziness....Staff NINDS 301-496-5751
Djibouti, Republic of (Djibouti)....Staff Cnty State 202-647-5684
Djibouti/Minerals....Antonides, Lloyd Cnty Mines 202-501-9686
Djibouti....Bouraleh, Issa Daher Cnty Embassy 202-331-0270
Djibouti....Hutchings, Dayna Cnty Export-Import Bank 202-565-3737
Djibouti....Morin, Denyse E. Cnty World Bank 202-473-9732
Djibouti....Olhaye, Roble Cnty Embassy 202-331-0270
DMSO (Dimethylsulfoxide)....Staff NCI 301-496-5583
DMSO (Dimethylsulfoxide)....Staff FDA/NCDB 301-443-1016
DNA Chemistry....Reeder, Dennis NIST 301-975-3128
DNA....Staff NIGMS 301-496-7301
DNA....Staff OD/OSPL 301-496-9838
Docket Information....Staff FCC 202-418-1740
Docket Information Court of Appeals....Staff FCC 202-418-1770
Docket Information FCC Adjudicatory Proceedings....Staff FCC 202-418-1780

Be patient. If any phone number is incorrect, call (area code) 555-1212 and request the new listing.

1391

Docket Information Supreme Court....Staff FCC 202-418-1770
Doll carriages, stroller, and parts....Abrahamson, Dana USITC 202-205-3430
Dolls....Abrahamson, Dana USITC 202-205-3430
Dolls....Hodgen, Donald COMMERCE 202-482-3346
Dolls....Wong, Alice CUSTOMS 212-466-5538
Dolomite, dead burned....DeSapio, Vincent USITC 202-205-3435
Domestic Oil Reserves Statistics....Petersen, Jimmie NEIC 202-586-6401
Domestic Violence....Staff Michigan Coalition Against Domestic Violence 800-333-7233
Domestic Violence....Langan, Patrick Justice Stat 202-616-3490
Domestic Violence....Rand, Michael Justice Stat 202-616-3494
Domestic Violence....Klaus, Patsy Justice Stat 202-307-0776
Dominica (Roseau)....Staff Cnty State 202-647-2130
Dominica/Minerals....Rabchevsky, George Cnty Mines 202-501-9670
Dominica....Brooks, Michelle Cnty Commerce 202-482-2527
Dominica....Marcus, Anthony Cnty Treasury 202-622-1218
Dominica....Nallari, Raj R. Cnty World Bank 202-473-8697
Dominica....Watty, Edward I. Cnty Embassy 202-334-6781
Dominica....Wilkins, Michele Cnty Export-Import Bank 202-565-3743
Dominican Republic....Wilkins, Michele Cnty Export-Import Bank 202-565-3743
Dominican Republic...Parkinson, Katherine Cnty Treasury 202-622-5292
Dominican Republic....Quehl, Scott Cnty World Bank 202-473-8652
Dominican Republic....Head, Alfred Cnty USIA 202-619-6835
Dominican Republic.. Cnty TDA 703-875-4357
Dominican Republic....Ariza, Jose Del Carmen Cnty Embassy 202-332-6280
Dominican Republic....Suro, Dario Cnty Embassy 202-332-6280
Dominican Republic....Soto, Rodrigo Cnty Commerce 202-482-5680
Dominican Republic....Almaguer, Antoinette Peace Corps 202-606-3322
Dominican Republic....Menyhart, Krista Peace Corps 202-606-3323
Dominican Republic (Santo Domingo)....Staff Cnty State 202-647-2620
Dominican Republic/Minerals....Rabchevsky, George Cnty Mines 202-501-9670
Down Syndrome....Staff National Down Syndrome Society (NDSS) 800-221-4602
Down Syndrome....Staff National Down Syndrome Congress (NDSC) 800-232-6372
Down Syndrome....Staff NICHD 301-496-5133
Down apparel....Jones, Jackie USITC 202-205-3466
Draperies....Sweet, Mary Elizabeth USITC 202-205-3455
Drawing instruments....Roth, Jordon USITC 202-205-3467
Dresses....Crowley, Michael CUSTOMS 212-466-5852
Dresses....Sweet, Mary Elizabeth USITC 202-205-3455
Dressing machines (textile)....Greene, William USITC 202-205-3405
Drilling Mus/Soft Compounds....Vacant COMMERCE 202-482-0564
Drink-preparing machines....Jackson, Georgia USITC 202-205-3399
Drinking Water Branch....Staff EPA 202-260-5526
Drinking Water Standards....Staff EPA 202-260-7575
Drinking and Cancer....Staff NCI 301-496-5583
Drug Abuse, in Workplace....Brown, Mona NIDA 301-443-6245
Drug Abuse, National Institute on....Brown, Mona NIDA 301-443-6245
Drug Abuse, Prenatal....Brown, Mona NIDA 301-443-6245
Drug Abuse Treatment....Hurley, Joan NIDA 301-443-6549
Drug Abuse Treatment....Staff NIDA 301-443-6549
Drug Allergy....Staff NIAID 301-496-5717
Drug Enforcement Administration....Staff DEA 202-307-1000
Drug Hemolytic Anemia....Staff NIDDK 301-496-3583
Drug prevention....Staff Wisconsin Clearinghouse 800-322-1468
Drug Purpura....Staff NIDDK 301-496-3583
Drug Research Survey....Staff NIDA 301-443-6245
Drug Resistance....Staff NIAID 301-496-5717
Drug Test Guidelines....Brown, Mona NIDA 301-443-6245
Drugs and Aging....Staff NIA 301-496-1752
Drugs and Drug Labeling: AIDS Drugs....Williams, Bradford FDA 301-443-3285
Drugs and Drug Labeling....Lecos, Chris FDA 202-205-4144
Drugs and Drug Labeling: Generic....Sporn, Douglas FDA 301-594-0340
Drugs and Drug Labeling: Orphan Drugs....Cruzan, Susan FDA 301-443-3285
Drugs and Drug Labeling: Over-the Counter....Weintraub, Michael FDA 301-594-1924
Drugs and Drug Labeling: Prescription Drugs, Biologic....Fazzari, Frank FDA 301-594-2073
Drugs and Drug Labeling: Women's Issues (Drugs)....Staff FDA 301-443-3285
Drugs and Prisoners....Stephan, James Justice Stat 202-616-3289
Drugs and Prisoners....Baunach, Phyllis Jo Justice Stat 202-307-0361
Drugs (Cancer)....Staff NCI 301-496-5583
Drugs (Cardiac)....Staff NHLBI 301-496-4236
Drugs (Eyes)....Staff NEI 301-496-5248
Drugs - General....Lindgren, Sue Justice Stat 202-307-0760
Drugs Industry Group....Daly, James M. SEC 202-942-1800
Drugs, natural....Nesbitt, Elizabeth USITC 202-205-3355

Drugs, synthetic....Nesbitt, Elizabeth USITC 202-205-3355
Drugs (Use and Abuse)....Staff NIDA 301-443-6245
Drugs....Alcohol and Drug Helpline 800-821-4357
Drugs....Hurt, William COMMERCE 202-482-0128
Drugs....Staff NAPARE 800-638-2229
Drugs....Staff National Council on Alcoholism and Drug Dependence Hopeline (NCADDH) 800-622-2255
Drugs....Staff HUD Drug Information and Strategy Clearinghouse 800-955-2232
Drugs....Staff Office of Drug and Alcohol Programs 800-932-0912
Drunk driving....Staff MADD 800-438-6233
Drunk Driving....Zawitz, Marianne Justice Stat 202-616-3499
Dry Edible Beans....Budge, Arvin Agri 202-720-4285
Dry Edible Beans....Plummer, Charles Agri 202-219-0009
Dry Edible Beans....Lucier, Gary Agri 202-219-0884
Dry Eyes....Staff NEI 301-496-5248
Dry-cleaning machines....Jackson, Georgia USITC 202-205-3399
Drying machines....Jackson, Georgia USITC 202-205-3399
Duchenne Muscular Dystrophy....Staff NINDS 301-496-5751
Duchenne Muscular Dystrophy....Staff NIAMS 301-496-8188
Duck Stamps....Staff FWS 202-208-4354
Dumping Toxic Waste....Staff EPA 202-260-1024
Dumping vehicles....Huppert, Michael PTO 703-308-1107
Dupuytren's Contracture....Staff NIAMS 301-496-8188
Dupuytren's Contracture....Staff NINDS 301-496-5751
Durable Consumer Goods....Ellis, Kevin M. COMMERCE 202-482-1176
Dushanabe....Eighmy, Thomas Cnty AID 202-647-6920
Dust Inhalation Diseases (Pneumonoconioses)....Staff FDA 301-443-3170
Dust Inhalation Diseases (Pneumonoconioses)....Staff NHLBI 301-496-4236
Dust Inhalation Diseases (Pneumonoconioses)....Staff CDCW/NIOSH 404-639-3286
Dwarfism....Staff Little People of America (LPA) 800-243-9273
Dwarfism....Staff NICHD 301-496-5133
Dyeing machines....Greene, William USITC 202-205-3405
Dyeing....Lieberman, Paul PTO 703-308-2552
Dyes....Wanser, Stephen USITC 202-205-3363
Dynamite....Johnson, Larry USITC 202-205-3351
Dysarthia....Staff NIDCD 301-496-7243
Dysarthria....Staff NINDS 301-496-5751
Dysautonomia....Staff NINDS 301-496-5751
Dysentery....Staff NIAID 301-496-5717
Dysfluency....Staff NIDCD 301-496-7243
Dysgeusia....Staff NIDCD 301-496-7243
Dysgraphia....Staff NINDS 301-496-5751
Dyskinesia....Staff NINDS 301-496-5751
Dyslexia....Staff Orton Dyslexia Society (ODS) 800-222-3123
Dyslexia....Staff NIMH 301-443-4513
Dyslexia....Staff NINDS 301-496-5751
Dyslexia....Staff NICHD 301-496-5133
Dyslexia....Staff NIDCD 301-496-7243
Dysmenorrhea....Staff NICHD 301-496-5133
Dysphagia....Staff NIDCD 301-496-7243
Dyspnea....Staff NHLBI 301-496-4236
Dyspraxia (Speech)....Staff NIDCD 301-496-7243
Dyspraxia....Staff NINDS 301-496-5751
Dystonia Musculorum Deformans (Torsion Dystonia)....Staff NINDS 301-496-5751
Dystonia....Staff NINDS 301-496-5751
Dystonia....Staff NIDCD 301-496-7243

E

E. Caribbean....Brooks, Michelle Cnty Commerce 202-482-4464
E.Q. Guinea....Maybury-Lewis, Anthony Cnty Export-Import Bank 202-565-3739
Ear Infection....Staff NIDCD 301-496-7243
Ear Wax....Staff NIDCD 301-496-7243
Earnings, Employment and Earnings Publication....Green, Gloria LABOR 202-606-6376
Earnings, Foreign Countries, Productivity and Tech.....Capdevielle, Patricia LABOR 202-606-5654
Earnings, Population Survey....Mellor, Earl LABOR 202-606-6378
Earnings Publication....Green, Gloria LABOR 202-606-6376
Earnings, Real--News Release, Empl/Unempl. Stats....Hiles, David LABOR 202-606-6547
Ears....Staff Meniere's Network of the Ear Foundation 800-545-4327
Earth-moving machines....Polly, Laura USITC 202-205-3408
Earth Observing System (EOS)....Staff NASA 301-286-5566

Earthenware, articles of....McNay, Deborah USITC 202-205-3425
Earthenware....Bratland, Rosemarie COMMERCE 202-482-0380
Earthenware....Kalkines, George CUSTOMS 212-466-5794
Earthquake Engineering....Lew, H.S. NIST 301-975-6061
East Caribbean....Almaguer, Antoinette Peace Corps 202-606-3322
Easter Seal....Staff National Easter Seal Society 800-221-6827
Eastern Caribbean....Feingold, David Cnty AID 202-647-4106
Eastern Europe....Brereton, Barbara OPIC 202-336-8617
Eastern Europe/trade matters....Underwood, Jennifer US Trade Rep 202-395-4620
Eastern European Health Scientist Exchange Program....Staff FIC 301-496-4784
Eating Disorders....Staff NIMH 301-443-4513
Eaton-Lambert Myasthenic Syndrome....Staff NINDS 301-496-5751
ECG....Staff NHLBI 301-496-4236
Echocardiography....Staff NHLBI 301-496-4236
Eclampsia/Preeclampsia....Staff NICHD 301-496-5133
Ecological Effects Branch....Staff EPA 202-305-7347
Econometrics, Ass't to Director....Hirsch, Albert A. ECONOMIC 202-606-9627
Economic Accounts, Associate Director for National....Parker, Robert P. ECONOMIC 202-606-9607
Economic Census Products....Zeisset, Paul CENSUS 301-457-4116
Economic Development....Forbes, Patricia SBA 202-205-6657
Economic Growth/Empl Proj, Associate Commissioner....Kutscher, Ronald LABOR 202-606-5700
Economic Growth/Empl Proj, Data Diskettes....Bowman, Charles LABOR 202-606-5702
Economic Growth/Empl Proj, Economic Growth Proj....Saunders, Norman LABOR 202-606-5723
Economic Growth/Empl Proj, Ind-Occpl Empl Matrix....Turner, Delores LABOR 202-606-5730
Economic Growth/Empl Proj, Labor Force Projection....Fullerton, Howard LABOR 202-606-5711
Economic Growth/Empl Proj, Occupational Projections....Rosenthal, Neal LABOR 202-606-5701
Economic Growth/Empl Proj, Occupational Outlook Hand....Pilot, Michael LABOR 202-606-5703
Economic Growth/Empl Proj, Occupational Outlook Quarterly....Staff LABOR 202-606-5707
Economic Impact Studies....Atkinson, William J. SEC 202-942-8020
Economic Programs, Statistical Research....Monsour, Nash J. CENSUS 301-457-4978
Economic Projections, Employment Projections....Saunders, Norman LABOR 202-606-5723
Economics Bureau - Antitrust....Brogan, Robert D. FTC 202-326-3508
Economics Bureau - Antitrust....Callison, Elizabeth FTC 202-326-3521
Economics Bureau - Antitrust....Coate, Malcolm FTC 202-326-3351
Economics Bureau - Antitrust....Creswell, Jay S., Jr. FTC 202-326-3519
Economics Bureau - Antitrust....Dobson, Douglas C. FTC 202-326-3465
Economics Bureau - Antitrust....Fisher, Alan A. FTC 202-326-3516
Economics Bureau - Antitrust....Gessler, Kevin O. FTC 202-326-2306
Economics Bureau - Antitrust....Gessler, Geary A. FTC 202-326-3463
Economics Bureau - Antitrust....Gladieux, Jennifer FTC 202-326-3507
Economics Bureau - Antitrust....Glasner, David FTC 202-326-3345
Economics Bureau - Antitrust....Griffith, Carolyn FTC 202-326-3450
Economics Bureau - Antitrust....Gulyn, Peter FTC 202-326-2194
Economics Bureau - Antitrust....Harmon, Bernadette D. FTC 202-326-3449
Economics Bureau - Antitrust....Hoskin, Daniel FTC 202-326-3372
Economics Bureau - Antitrust....Howell, John M. FTC 202-326-3456
Economics Bureau - Antitrust....Iosso, Thomas FTC 202-326-2720
Economics Bureau - Antitrust....Iosso, Ilona FTC 202-326-3355
Economics Bureau - Antitrust....John, Tammy FTC 202-326-3462
Economics Bureau - Antitrust....Layher, William N. FTC 202-326-3515
Economics Bureau - Antitrust....Levinson, Robert FTC 202-326-3517
Economics Bureau - Antitrust....Levinson, Robert FTC 202-326-3517
Economics Bureau - Antitrust....Levy, Roy FTC 202-326-3353
Economics Bureau - Antitrust....Ludwick, Richard FTC 202-326-2246
Economics Bureau - Antitrust....Martin, Fred FTC 202-326-3514
Economics Bureau - Antitrust....Nelson, Steven R. FTC 202-326-3523
Economics Bureau - Antitrust....Patterson, Margaret A. FTC 202-326-3472
Economics Bureau - Antitrust....Pegram, William M. FTC 202-326-3336
Economics Bureau - Antitrust....Pidano, Charles FTC 202-326-3454
Economics Bureau - Antitrust....Rodriguez, Armando FTC 202-326-3616
Economics Bureau - Antitrust....Sacher, Seth B. FTC 202-326-2606
Economics Bureau - Antitrust....Silvia, Louis FTC 202-326-3471
Economics Bureau - Antitrust....Simpson, John D. FTC 202-326-3451
Economics Bureau - Antitrust....Tatem, Lewis FTC 202-326-3373
Economics Bureau - Antitrust....Wadbrook, Clare FTC 202-326-3420
Economics Bureau - Antitrust....Wagner, Curtis FTC 202-326-3348

Economics Bureau - Antitrust....Williams, Mark FTC 202-326-3374
Economics Bureau - Antitrust....Zichterman, Elizabeth C. FTC 202-326-3410
Economics Bureau - Consumer Protection....Braman, Susan FTC 202-326-3163
Economics Bureau - Consumer Protection....Lean, David F. FTC 202-326-3480
Economics Bureau - Consumer Protection....Mulholland, Joseph FTC 202-326-3378
Economics Bureau - Consumer Protection....Boorstein, Randi M. FTC 202-326-3482
Economics Bureau - Consumer Protection....Daniel, Lisa M. FTC 202-326-3394
Economics Bureau - Consumer Protection....Silversin, Louis FTC 202-326-3385
Economics Bureau - Consumer Protection....Hertzendorf, Mark FTC 202-326-2768
Economics Bureau - Consumer Protection....VanderNat, Peter FTC 202-326-3518
Economics Bureau - Consumer Protection....Wells, Pamela L. FTC 202-326-3371
Economics Bureau - Consumer Protection....Lacko, James FTC 202-326-3387
Economics Bureau - Consumer Protection....Cox, Carolyn FTC 202-326-3434
Economics Bureau - Consumer Protection....Small, Helen W. FTC 202-326-3375
Economics Bureau - Consumer Protection....Anderson, Keith B. FTC 202-326-3428
Economics Bureau - Consumer Protection....Pappalardo, Janis K. FTC 202-326-3380
Economics Bureau - Consumer Protection....Butters, Gerald R. FTC 220-326-3393
Economics Bureau - Consumer Protection....Porter, Russell FTC 202-326-3460
Economics Bureau - Economic Policy Analysis....Ippolito, Pauline M. FTC 202-326-3477
Economics Bureau - Economic Policy Analysis....Stansel, James C. FTC 202-326-3481
Economics Bureau - Economic Policy Analysis....Reiffen, David FTC 202-326-2027
Economics Bureau - Economic Policy Analysis....Kelly, Kenneth H. FTC 202-326-3358
Economics Bureau - Economic Policy Analysis....Daniel, Tim FTC 202-326-3520
Economics Bureau - Economic Policy Analysis....Barnes, Davina G. FTC 202-326-3346
Economics Bureau - Economic Policy....Koopmans, Reinout M. FTC 202-326-3497
Economics Bureau - Economic Policy Analysis....Breen, Denis A. FTC 202-326-3447
Economics Bureau - Economic Policy Analysis....Kim, Andrew FTC 202-326-3363
Economics Bureau - Economic Policy Analysis....Hilke, John C. FTC 202-326-3483
Economics Bureau - Economic Policy Analysis....Yangh, Jun Cheol FTC 202-326-2057
Economics Bureau - Economic Policy Analysis....Kiely, Eileen FTC 202-326-3382
Economics Bureau - Economic Policy Analysis....Morkre, Morris E. FTC 202-326-3365
Economics Bureau - Economic Policy Analysis....Vita, Mike FTC 202-326-3493
Economics Bureau - Economic Policy Analysis....Wellford, Charissa FTC 202-326-3020
Economics Bureau - Economic Policy Analysis....Grawe, Oliver FTC 202-326-3445
Economics Bureau - Economics Policy Analysis....Yi, Seong Gu FTC 202-326-3368
Economics Bureau - European Assistance....Kneuper, Robert FTC 202-326-3469
Economics Bureau - General Counsel Brashears, Nicole K. FTC 202-326-2455
Economics Bureau - Office of the Director....Johnson, Janice C. FTC 202-326-3332
Economics Bureau - Office of the Director....Brown, Mary FTC 202-326-3429
Economics Bureau - Office of the Director....Carpenter, Lynn J. FTC 202-326-3390
Economics Bureau - Office of the Director....Harris, Kyle FTC 202-326-3399
Economics Bureau - Office of the Director....Altrogge, Phyllis D. FTC 202-326-3464
Economics Bureau - Office of the Director....Baker, Jonathon FTC 202-326-2930
Economics Bureau - Office of the Director....Deyak, Timothy FTC 202-326-3379
Economics Bureau - Office of the Director....Samuels, Carolyn FTC 202-326-3412
Economics Bureau - Office of the Director....Meadows, Chrystal E. FTC 202-326-3489
Economics Bureau - Office of the Director....Richards, Karin F. FTC 202-326-2601
Economics Bureau - Office of the Director....Rosano, William V. FTC 202-326-3422
Economics Bureau - Office of the Director....Farber, Leslie FTC 202-326-3510
Economics Bureau - Office of the Director....Roberts, Gary FTC 202-326-2937
Economics Bureau - Office of the Director....Pautler, Paul A. FTC 202-326-3357

Be patient. If any phone number is incorrect, call (area code) 555-1212 and request the new listing.

1393

11,500 Free Experts

Economics Bureau - Office of the Director....Williams, Cheryl G. FTC 202-326-3418

Economics Bureau - Office of the Director....Treakle, Coletta A. FTC 202-326-3481

Economics Bureau - Policy....Breen, Denis A. FTC 202-326-3447

Economics Bureau....Schumann, Lawrence FTC 202-326-3359

Economics Bureau....Ward, Michael R. FTC 202-326-2096

Economics....Elzinga, Kenneth G. UVA 804-924-6752

Economizers....Fravel, Dennis USITC 202-205-3404

Ectodermal Dysplasias....Staff NIAMS 301-496-8188

Ectodermal Dysplasias....Staff NIDR 301-496-4261

Ectopic Hormones....Staff NIDDK 301-496-3583

Ectopic Pregnancy....Staff NICHD 301-496-5133

Ecuador (Quito)....Staff Cnty State 202-647-3338

Ecuador/Minerals....Velasco, Pablo Cnty Mines 202-501-9677

Ecuador....Bayly, Rachel Cnty Treasury 202-622-1266

Ecuador....Clapham, Lizzie Corps 202-606-3499

Ecuador....Davis, Janice Peace Corps 202-606-3198

Ecuador....Epstein, Sharon Cnty AID 202-647-4358

Ecuador....Hentschel, Jesko S. Cnty World Bank 202-458-1936

Ecuador....Jarvis, Catherine Cnty USIA 202-619-5867

Ecuador....John Herrman Cnty TDA 703-875-4357

Ecuador....Moore, Paul Cnty Commerce 202-482-1659

Ecuador....Salvador, Gonzalo Cnty Embassy 202-234-7200

Ecuador....Teran-Teran, Edgar Cnty Embassy 202-234-7200

Ecuador...Wilkins, Michele Cnty Export-Import Bank 202-565-3743

Eczema....Staff NIAID 301-496-5717

Eczema....Staff NIAMS 301-496-8188

Edema....Staff NHLBI 301-496-4236

Edible gelatin....Jonnard, Aimison USITC 202-205-3350

Edible preparations....Schneider, Greg USITC 202-205-3326

Education and Curriculum Support Projects....Jackson, Dorothy CENSUS 301-457-1210

Education, Environmental....Staff FWS 703-358-1786

Education Facilities, Major Proj.....White, Barbara COMMERCE 202-482-4160

Education (Nursing)....Staff HRSA/BHPr/DN 301-443-5786

Education Programs....Stephens, Richard NEIC 202-586-2366

Education Services....Evans, Katherine USITC 202-205-3407

Education....Bunker, Linda K. UVA 804-924-0740

Education....Gibbs, Anette UVA 804-924-3880

Education....Morra, Linda G. GAO 202-512-7014

Education....Rhile, Howard G. GAO 202-512-6418

Education....Staff National Association for the Education of Young Children (NAEYC) 800-424-2460

Educational Attainment, Empl/Unempl. Stats....Staff LABOR 202-606-6378

Educational Attainment, Employment Statistics....Staff LABOR 202-606-6378

Educational devices....Mancene, Gene PTO 703-308-2696

Educational Programs....Frank Owens NASA 202-358-1110

Educational Programs....Richardson, Deborah NAL 301-504-5779

Educational/Training....Chandorsekara,A. COMMERCE 202-482-1318

Eggs....Newman, Douglas USITC 202-205-1318

Egypt, Arab Republic of (Cairo)....Staff Cnty State 202-647-1228

Egypt/Minerals....Dolley, Thomas Cnty Mines 202-501-9690

Egypt....El Sayed, Ahmed Maher Cnty Embassy 202-244-4319

Egypt....Hoppenbrouwer, Laurens M. Cnty World Bank 202-473-2716

Egypt....Hutchings, Dayna Cnty Export-Import Bank 202-565-3737

Egypt....McKoy, Ethel Cnty Treasury 202-622-0336

Egypt....Ramzy, Ezzeldin Cnty Embassy 202-244-5131

Egypt....Sams, Thomas/Wright, Corey Cnty Commerce 202-482-1860

Egypt....Squire, Margo Cnty USIA 202-619-5529

Egypt....Vacant Cnty AID 202-663-2610

Ehlers-Danlos Syndrome....Staff NIAMS 301-496-8188

Eisenmenger's Syndrome....Staff NHLBI 301-496-4236

EKG....Staff NHLBI 301-496-4236

El Salvador....Wilkins, Michele Cnty Export-Import Bank 202-565-3743

El Salvador....Parkinson, Katherine Cnty Treasury 202-622-5292

El Salvador....Barrett, Kathleen Cnty AID 202-647-9535

El Salvador....Opstein, Sally Cnty USIA 202-619-5864

El Salvador....Fluckiger, Stefan Cnty World Bank 202-473-0093

El Salvador....Anne McKinney Cnty TDA 703-875-4357

El Salvador....Sol, Ana Cristina Cnty Embassy 202-265-9671

El Salvador....Soler, Ana Vilma Cnty Embassy 202-265-9672

El Salvador/Minerals....Velasco, Pablo Cnty Mines 202-501-9677

El Salvador (San Salvador)....Staff Cnty State 202-647-3681

El Salvador....Lee, Helen Cnty Commerce 202-482-2528

Elastic fabrics....Shelton, Linda USITC 202-205-3457

Elastomers....Misurelli, Denby USITC 202-205-3362

Eldercare....Staff Eldercare Locator 800-677-1116

Eldercare....Staff Sound Options, Inc. 800-628-7649

Elderly, alcohol....Alcohol Rehab for the Elderly 800-354-7089

Elderly (Drug Abuse)....Staff NIDA 301-443-6245

Elderly Victims....Klaus, Patsy Justice Stat 202-307-0776

Elderly....Staff Advocacy Center for the Elderly and Disabled (ACED) 800-960-7705

Elec/Power Gen/Transmission and Dist Eqt (Trade Pro)....Kostalas, Anthony COMMERCE 202-482-2390

Electric and Hybrid Propulsion Systems....Barber, Kenneth NEIC 202-586-2198

Electric and Nuclear Power....Welch, Thomas NEIC 202-586-8800

Electric and Nuclear Power....Jeffers, William NEIC 202-586-8800

Electric charge systems....Pellinen, David PTO 703-308-0538

Electric Energy Statistics....Hutzler, Mary NEIC 202-586-2222

Electric heating....Reynolds, Bruce A. PTO 703-308-3305

Electric Industrial Apparatus Nec....Bodson, John COMMERCE 202-482-0681

Electric Machinery and Trans., Producer Price Index....Yatsko, Ralph LABOR 202-606-7745

Electric-Magnetic Field Technical Questions....Staff EPA 202-260-9640

Electric Networks....Brewer, Robert H. NEIC 202-586-2828

Electric photocopying....Grimely, Arthur PTO 703-308-1373

Electric resistance heating devices....Reynolds, Bruce A. PTO 703-308-3305

Electric sound and visual signalling apparatus....Baker, Scott USITC 202-205-3386

Electric Vehicles....Barber, Kenneth NEIC 202-586-2198

Electric welding....Reynolds, Bruce A. PTO 703-308-3305

Electrical Articles....Curan, David CUSTOMS 212-466-4680

Electrical Engineering....Papantoni-Kazakos, Panayota UVA 804-924-6102

Electrical housings for mounting assemblies....Picard, Leo PTO 703-308-0538

Electrical Industry....Daly, James M. SEC 202-942-1800

Electrical measuring....Weider, Kenneth PTO 703-305-4707

Electrical music tone generation....Shoop, William M. PTO 703-308-3103

Electrical Power Plants, Major Proj.....Dollison, Robert COMMERCE 202-482-2733

Electrical safety....Staff CPSC 301-504-0580

Electrical Structures....Curan, David CUSTOMS 212-466-4680

Electrical switches and arc suppression....Pellinen, David PTO 703-308-0538

Electrical systems and devices, protection....Pellinen, David PTO 703-308-0538

Electrical testing....Chilcot, Richard PTO 703-305-4716

Electrical testing....Weider, Kenneth PTO 703-305-4707

Electrical Vol Standards....Staff CPSC 301-504-0580

Electricity Transmission....Brewer, Robert NEIC 202-586-2828

Electricity Transmission, Health Effects of....Brewer, Robert NEIC 202-586-2828

Electricity....Petersons, Oskars NISt 301-975-2400

Electricity....Sugg, William COMMERCE 202-482-1466

Electrocardiogram....Staff NHLBI 301-496-4236

Electrochemical processes....Niebling, John F. PTO 703-308-3325

Electrochemical products....Niebling, John F. PTO 703-308-3325

Electroheological fluids....Lieberman, Paul PTO 703-308-2552

Electromagnetic control systems....Pellinen, David PTO 703-308-0538

Electromagnetic fields....Newell, Allen C. NIST 303-497-3131

Electromagnets....Picard, Leo PTO 703-308-0538

Electromechanical appliances....Jackson, Georgia USITC 202-205-3399

Electron Physics....Clark, C.W. NIST 301-975-3709

Electron Microscopy....Staff DRS/BEIB 301-496-2599

Electron Microscopy....Staff NIDR 301-496-4261

Electron Microscopy....Staff NCRR 301-496-5545

Electronic Components/Prod and Test Eqt, Trade Promo.....Ruffin, Marlene COMMERCE 202-482-0570

Electronic Database Services....Inoussa, Mary COMMERCE 202-482-5820

Electronic Equipment Marketing....Staff FCC 202-418-1170

Electronic Fund Transfer Crime....Kaplan, Carol Justice Stat 202-307-0759

Electronic Industry....Daly, James M. SEC 202-942-1800

Electronic, (Legislation)....Donnelly, Margaret COMMERCE 202-482-5466

Electronic Prod. and Test.....Ruffin, Marlene COMMERCE 202-482-0570

Electronic Prod. and Test (Export Promo)....Ruffin, Marlene COMMERCE 202-482-0570

Electronic technology....Puffert, Douglas USITC 202-205-3402

Electronic tubes....Malison, Andrew USITC 202-205-3391

ElectroOptical Instruments, Trade Promo.....Manzolillo, Franc COMMERCE 202-482-2991

Electrophotography....McCarnish, Marion PTO 703-308-3961

Electrothermic appliances....Jackson, Georgia USITC 202-205-3399

Elementary and Secondary Education Programs....Staff NEH 202-606-8377

Elements, chemical....Conant, Kenneth USITC 202-205-3346

Elephantiasis....Staff NIAID 301-496-5717

Elevators, Moving Stairways....Weining, Mary COMMERCE 202-482-4708

Elevators....Greene, William USITC 202-205-3405

Elevators....Olszewski, Robert PTO 703-308-2588

Eligibility Criteria (Grants)....Staff DRG 301-594-7248

Embolism....Staff NHLBI 301-496-4236

Embroidery machines....Greene, William USITC 202-205-3405

Emergency Broadcast System....Staff FCC 202-418-1220

Emergency Medical Services....Staff FCC 717-337-1212

Emergency Plan. and Community Right-to-Know Hotline....Staff EPA
800-535-0202

Emergency Response....Brockman, Kenneth E. NRC 301-415-7482

Emigration....Fernandez, Edward CENSUS 301-457-2103

Emission Standards....Staff EPA 919-541-5571

Emissions Standards Division....Staff EPA 919-541-5571

Emotionally Handicapped....Staff Devereux Foundation 800-345-1292

Emphysema....Staff NHLBI 301-496-4236

Empl/Unempl Stats, (ES202), Empl/Wgs Ind....Bush, Joseph LABOR
202-606-6492

Empl/Unempl Stats, Assistant Commis.....Plewes, Thomas J. LABOR
202-606-6400

Empl/Unempl Stats, Benchmarks....Getz, Patricia LABOR 202-606-6521

Empl/Unempl Stats, Business Establishment List....Searson, Michael LABOR
202-606-6469

Empl/Unempl Stats, Curr. Empl. An, Assistant Commis.....Bregger, John E.
LABOR 202-606-6388

Empl/Unempl Stats, National Data, Data Diskettes....Staff LABOR 202-606-6551

Empl/Unempl Stats, Occl Empl/Unempl, Occpl Empl Sv....Johnson, Lawrence
LABOR 202-606-6517

Empl/Unempl Stats, State Data, Demographic Charact....Biederman, Edna LABOR
202-606-6392

Empl/Unempl Stats, Std Occupational Classification....McElroy, Michael LABOR
202-606-6516

Empl/Unempl Stats, Std Industrial Classification....Bennott, William LABOR
202-606-6474

Empl/Unempl Stats, Unempl Ins Stats, Establ Record....Cimini, Michael LABOR
202-606-6275

Empl/Unempl Stats, Unempl Ins Stats, Claimant Data....Terwilliger, Yvonne
LABOR 202-606-6392

Empl.and Wages, Empl/Unempl, Data Diskettes and Tapes....Buso, Michael
LABOR 202-606-6499

Employee Assistance Programs (Drug- Related)....Staff NIDA 301-443-6245

Employee Benefit Survey, General Info., Comp./Wk. Con....Staff LABOR
202-606-6222

Employee Benefit Survey, Health and Life Insur.....Blostin, Allan LABOR
202-606-6240

Employee Benefit Survey, Retirement and Capital Acc....Houff, James LABOR
202-606-6238

Employee Benefits, Compensation and Working Condition....Staff LABOR
202-606-6199

Employee Relations....Marks, Marjorie OPM 202-606-2920

Employer Costs for Employee Comp, Comp and Working....Rogers, Brenda
LABOR 202-606-6199

Employment Analysis, Current, Assist. Comm. Empl/Unempl....Bregger, John E.
LABOR 202-606-6388

Employment and Earnings Period. Empl/Unempl. Stats....Green, Gloria LABOR
202-606-6376

Employment and Unempl. Stats. Earnings, Pop. Survey....Mellor, Earl LABOR
202-606-6378

Employment and Unempl. Stats. Longitud. Data/Gr.Flow....Horvath, Francis
LABOR 202-606-6345

Employment and Unempl. Stats., Mass Layoff Stats.....Siegel, Lewis LABOR
202-606-6404

Employment and Unempl. Stats., Minimum Wage Data....Haugen, Steve LABOR
202-606-6378

Employment and Unempl. Stats., Multiple Jobholders....Stinson, John LABOR
202-606-6373

Employment and Unempl. Stats., Older Workers....Rones, Philip LABOR
202-606-6378

Employment and Unempl. Stats., Part-time Workers....Nardone, Thomas LABOR
202-606-6378

Employment and Unempl. Stats. States Est. Surv. Data....Podgornik, Guy LABOR
202-606-6534

Employment and Unempl. Stats., States Est. Surv.....Shipp, Kenneth LABOR
202-606-6519

Employment and Unempl. Stats, Working Poor....Herz, Diane LABOR
202-606-6378

Employment and Unempl. Stats, Flexitime and Shift....Mellor, Earl LABOR
202-606-6378

Employment and Unempl. Stats, Labor Force Data Disk....Marcus, Jessie LABOR
202-606-6392

Employment and Unempl. Stats, Est. Surv.....Seifert, Mary Lee LABOR
202-606-6552

Employment, Area Data....Shipp, Kenneth LABOR 202-606-6519

Employment Cost Index, Comp. and Working Cond.....Shelly, Wayne LABOR
202-606-6206

Employment Information....Whitford, Richard OPM 202-606-2605

Employment Projections, Assistant Commis.....Kutscher, Ronald LABOR
202-606-5700

Employment Projections, Data Diskettes....Bowman, Charles LABOR
202-606-5702

Employment Projections, Economic Growth....Saunders, Norman LABOR
202-606-5723

Employment Projections, Productivity and Technology....Franklin, James LABOR
202-606-5709

Employment Projections, Productivity and Technology....Fullerton, Howard
LABOR 202-606-5711

Employment Requirements Tables, Productivity and Tech....Franklin, James
LABOR 202-606-5709

Employment Statistics....Palumbo, Thomas CENSUS 301-763-8574

Employment Stats, Area Data, Employment....Shipp, Kenneth LABOR
202-606-6519

Employment Stats, Area Data, Demog Charact....Biederman, Edna LABOR
202-606-6392

Employment Stats, Curr Empl Anal., Assist. Commis.....Bregger, John E. LABOR
202-606-6388

Employment Stats, Discouraged Workers....Hamel, Harvey LABOR 202-606-6378

Employment Stats, Displaced Workers....Horvath, Francis LABOR 202-606-6345

Employment Stats, Dropouts....Cohany, Sharon LABOR 202-606-6378

Employment Stats, Earn Stats, Qrtly Empl and Wage....Bush, Joseph LABOR
202-606-6492

Employment Stats, Earnings Publication....Green, Gloria LABOR 202-606-6376

Employment Stats, Educational Attainment....Staff LABOR 202-606-6376

Employment Stats, Employment Publication....Green, Gloria LABOR
202-606-6376

Employment Stats, Family Charactr of Labor Force....Hayghe, Howard LABOR
202-606-6378

Employment Stats, Ind Earn Stats, Mthly Payr Surv....Seifert, Mary Lee LABOR
202-606-6552

Employment Stats, Ind Empl Stats, Mthly Payr Surv....Seifert, Mary Lee LABOR
202-606-6552

Employment/Unempl Stats, Associate Commissioner....Plewes, Thomas J. LABOR
202-606-6400

Employment/Unempl Stats, Machine Readable Data....Green, Gloria LABOR
202-606-6376

Employment/Unempl Stats, Minorities....Cattan, Peter LABOR 202-606-6378

Employment/Unempl Stats, Older Workers....Rones, Philip LABOR 202-606-6378

Employment/Unempl Stats, Permanent Plant Closings....Siegel, Lewis LABOR
202-606-6404

Employment/Unempl Stats, Permanent Mass Layoffs....Siegel, Lewis LABOR
202-606-6404

Employment/Unempl Stats, Real Earnings, News Release....Hiles, David LABOR
202-606-6547

Employment/Unempl Stats, State Data, Employment....Shipp, Kenneth LABOR
202-606-6519

Employment/Unempl Stats, Students....Cohany, Sharon LABOR 202-606-6378

Employment/Unempl Statistics, Trends....Staff LABOR 202-606-6378

Employment/Unempl Stats, Veterans....Cohany, Sharon LABOR 202-606-6378

Employment/Unempl Stats, Women....Hayghe, Howard LABOR 202-606-6378

Employment/Unempl Stats, Work-life Estimates....Horvath, Francis LABOR
202-606-6345

Employment....Morra, Linda G. GAO 202-512-7014

Employment....Palumbo, Thomas CENSUS 301-763-8574

Enamel....Staff NIDR 301-496-4261

Enamels....Johnson, Larry USITC 202-205-3351

Encephalitides....Staff NINDS 301-496-5751

Encephalitis Lethargica....Staff NINDS 301-496-5751

Encephalitis....Staff NIAID 301-496-5717

Encephalitis....Staff NINDS 301-496-5751

Encephalomyelitis....Staff NINDS 301-496-5751

Encopresis....Staff NIDDK 301-654-3810

Encopresis....Staff NICHD 301-496-5133

End Stage Renal Disease....Staff NIDDK 301-496-3583

Endangered Species Bulletins, Tech.....Staff FWS 703-358-2166

Endangered Species....Staff FWS 703-358-1710

Endangered Species Listing....Staff FWS 703-358-2171

Be patient. If any phone number is incorrect, call (area code) 555-1212 and request the new listing.

1395

Endangered Species Permits....Staff FWS 703-358-2104
Endangered Species Recovery Plans....Staff FWS 703-358-2171
Endocarditis....Staff NHLBI 301-496-4236
Endocardium....Staff NHLBI 301-496-4236
Endocrine Gland....Staff NICHD 301-496-5133
Endocrinologic Muscle Disease....Staff NINDS 301-496-5751
Endocrinology of Aging....Staff NIA 301-496-1752
Endocrinology (Sexual Development)....Staff NICHD 301-496-5133
Endocrinology....Staff NIDDK 301-496-3583
Endodontics....Staff NIDR 301-496-4261
Endometriosis....Staff Endometriosis Association (ENDO) 800-992-3636
Endometriosis....Staff NICHD 301-496-5133
Energy and Environ. Sys.....Greer, Damon COMMERCE 202-482-5456
Energy Assist. Block Grant/For Low Income Families....Kharfen, Michael ACF 202-401-9215
Energy Assist. Block Grant/For Low Income Families....Staff ACF 202-401-9215
Energy Biosciences Research....Rabson, Robert NEIC 301-903-2873
Energy, Commodities....Oddenino, Charles L. COMMERCE 202-482-1466
Energy, Commodities....Yancik, Joseph J. COMMERCE 202-482-1466
Energy Conservation Programs....Staff FWS 703-358-1719
Energy Conservation....Freedman, Karen NEIC 202-586-8800
Energy Conservation....Staff J. NEIC 800-523-2929
Energy Demand Policy....Staff NEIC 202-586-4444
Energy Efficient Buildings....Oliver, Robert NEIC 202-586-9127
Energy Efficient Buildings....Kapus, Theodore NEIC 202-586-9123
Energy Industry Group....Owings, Christopher SEC 202-942-1900
Energy Information Statistics....Bishop, Yvonne NEIC 202-254-5419
Energy Information Statistical Standards....Bishop, Yvonne NEIC 202-254-5419
Energy, International....Melick, William FRS 202-452-2296
Energy Inventions....Staff NEIC 202-586-1479
Energy Issues....Rezendes, Victor S. GAO 202-512-3841
Energy Management Education....Stephens, Richard NEIC 202-586-8949
Energy Markets Short-Term Forecasting....Staff NEIC 202-586-1441
Energy Pollutant Research....Krey, Philip W. NEIC 212-620-3616
Energy, Producer Price Index....Caswell, Maria LABOR 202-606-7722
Energy-Related Business Assistance....Everett, George NEIC 800-428-2525
Energy-Related Inventions and Innovations....Staff NEIC 202-586-1479
Energy-Related Inventions Program (ERIP)....Staff NEIC 202-586-1479
Energy-Related Inventions Program....Lewett, P. NIST 301-975-5504
Energy, Renewable....Davis, Michael J. NEIC 202-586-9220
Energy, Renewable....Ervin, Christine COMMERCE 202-482-0556
Energy, Solar....Burch, Gary NEIC 202-586-8121
Energy statistics....Miller, Renee NEIC 202-254-5507
Energy Supply Policy....Coburn, Leonard NEIC 202-586-5667
Energy Technical Assistance....Bowes, Ronald NEIC 202-586-5517
Energy....Tsao, Che Sheung FRS 202-452-3898
Enforcement Operations....Hess, Frederick Justice 202-514-3684
Enforcement....Walton, Steve Customs 202-927-1600
Engine Design....Sebestyen, Thomas NEIC 202-586-8012
Engineering (Biomedical)....Staff DCRT 301-496-1111
Engineering (Biomedical)....Staff NIGMS 301-496-7301
Engineering (Biomedical)....Staff NCRR 301-496-4426
Engineering/Construction Services, Trade Promo.....Mc Auley COMMERCE 202-482-0132
Engineering resins....Misurelli, Denby USITC 202-205-3362
Engineering services....Polly, Laura USITC 202-205-3408
Engines....Anderson, Peder USITC 202-205-3388
Engines...Vacant CUSTOMS 212-466-5673
Enteritis...Staff NIDDK 301-654-3810
Enterprise Statistics....Salyers, Eddie CENSUS 301-763-7234
Enterprise Statistics....Staff CENSUS 301-763-7234
Entertainment Industries....Siegmund, John COMMERCE 202-482-4701
Entertainment services....R-Archila, Laura USITC 202-205-3488
Environment, Safety and Health Concerns....Gilbertson, Mark NEIC 202-586-5042
Environment services....Bedore, James USITC 202-205-3424
Environmental Affairs....Bond, Michael OPIC 202-336-8613
Environmental Carcinogens....Staff NCI 301-496-5583
Environmental Contaminants....Staff FWS 703-358-2148
Environmental Control....Staff OD/ORS 301-496-3537
Environmental control....Vacant PTO 703-308-0101
Environmental Coordination....Staff FWS 703-358-2183
Environmental Crimes....Sarachan, Ronald Justice 202-272-9875
Environmental Economics, Chief....Rutledge, Gary L. ECONOMIC 202-606-5350
Environmental Education....Staff FWS 703-358-1786
Environmental Education....Staff EPA 202-260-4965
Environmental Enforcement....Cruden, John C. Justice 202-514-1604
Environmental Hazards and Health Effects....Ngi, Eric CDC 404-488-7350

Environmental Health Sciences, Nat'l Institute of....Lee, Christopher A. NIH 919-541-3819
Environmental Health, National Center for....Jackson, Richard J. CDC 404-488-7000
Environmental Health....Staff NIEHS 919-541-3345
Environmental Issues - General Information Hotline....Staff EPA 800-759-4372
Environmental Mutagenesis....Staff NIEHS 919-541-3345
Environmental Pollution...Staff NIDCD 301-496-7243
Environmental Protection Issues....Guerro, Peter F. GAO 202-512-6111
Environmental Requirements for Laboratory Animals....Staff OD 301-496-1357
Environmental Review....Newberry, Scott F. NRC 301-415-1183
Environmental Safety....Staff OD/ORS 301-496-3537
Environmental Sciences....Allen, Ralph O. UVA 804-982-4922
Environmental Standards and Requirements....Staff FCC 202-418-1700
Environmental Statistics and Information....Staff EPA 202-260-2680
Environmental Teratology....Staff NIEHS 919-541-3345
Environmental Toxicology....Zeeman, Maurice G. FAES 202-260-1237
Environmental Trade Promo.....Mack, Midred COMMERCE 202-482-0516
Enzymes....Nesbitt, Elizabeth USITC 202-205-3355
Eosinophilic Granuloma of the Lung....Staff NHLBI 301-496-4236
Eosinophilic Syndrome....Staff NIAID 301-496-5717
EPA Action Line....Staff EPA 800-223-0425
EPA Journal....Staff EPA 202-260-6643
EPA Recycling Program....Staff EPA 202-260-4928
Epidemic Aid/Disease Outbreaks.....Sims, Anne CDC 404-639-3286
Epidemiology of Aging....Staff NIA 301-496-1752
Epidemiology/Biostatistics....Hirsch, Robert FAES 202-994-7778
Epidemiology....Anello, Charles FAES 301-443-4227
Epidemiology....Diehl, Scott R. FAES 301-295-1671
Epidemiology....Friedman, Lawrence M. FAES 301-496-2533
Epidemiology....Stewart, John CDC 404-639-3629
Epidermodysplasis Verruciformis....Staff NIAMS 301-496-8188
Epidermolysis Bullosa....Staff NIAMS 301-496-8188
Epiglottitis...Staff NIAID 301-496-5717
Epikeratophakia....Staff NEI 301-496-5248
Epilepsy....Chandler, Jerry L. FAES 301-496-1846
Epilepsy....Epilepsy Foundation of America (EFA) 800-332-1000
Epilepsy....Staff Epilepsy Information Service 800-642-0500
Epilepsy....Staff NINDS 301-496-5751
Epistaxis (Nosebleed)....Staff NHLBI 301-496-4236
Epoxides....Michels, David USITC 202-205-3352
Epoxidized ester....Johnson, Larry USITC 202-205-3351
Epoxidized linseed oils....Johnson, Larry USITC 202-205-3351
Epoxidized soya oils....Johnson, Larry USITC 202-205-3351
Epoxy polymers....Bleutge, John PTO 703-308-2363
Epoxy resins....Misurelli, Denby USITC 202-205-3362
Epstein-Barr Syndrome....Staff NIAID 301-496-5717
Epstein-Barr Virus....Staff NIAID 301-496-5717
Equal Employment Opportunity Compliance....Patrick, Erline SBA 202-205-6750
Equal Employment Opportunity....Staff OD/DEO 301-496-6301
Equatorial Guinea....Barber, Ed Cnty Treasury 202-622-1730
Equatorial Guinea....Wilson, Michael J. Cnty World Bank 202-473-4714
Equatorial Guinea....Henning, Herman Cnty USIA 202-619-5926
Equatorial Guinea....Biyogo Nsue, Teodoro Cnty Embassy 919-738-9584
Equatorial Guinea (Malabo)....Staff Cnty State 202-647-1707
Equatorial Guinea....Jefferson, Deborah Peace Corps 202-606-3709
Equatorial Guinea....Mitchell, Willis Peace Corps 202-606-3708
Equatorial Guinea....Michellini, Philip Cnty Commerce 202-482-4388
Equatorial Guinea/Minerals....Dolley, Thomas Cnty Mines 202-501-9690
Equipment Authorization Certification....Staff FCC 301-725-1585
Equipment leasing....Bedore, James USITC 202-205-3424
Equipment Measurement Authorization....Staff FCC 301-725-1585
ERIP (Energy-Related Inventions Program)....Staff NEIC 202-586-1479
Eritica....McKoy, Ethel Cnty Treasury 202-622-0336
Eritrea....Antonides, Lloyd Cnty MINES 202-501-9686
Eritrea....Berhe, Arefaine Cnty Embassy 202-429-1991
Eritrea....Ggani, Ejaz Cnty World Bank 202-473-4819
Eritrea....Hutchings, Dayna Cnty Export-Import Bank 202-565-3737
Eritrea....Kahsai, Amdemicael Cnty Embassy 202-429-1991
Eritrea....Staff Cnty State 202-647-6485
Eritrea....Thorman, Peter Cnty AID 202-647-7986
Erythema Elevatum Diutinum....Staff NIAMS 301-496-8188
Erythema Multiforme....Staff NIAID 301-496-5717
Erythema Nodosum....Staff NIAID 301-496-5717
Erythroblastosis Fetalis....Staff NICHD 301-496-5133
Erythrocytes (Red Blood Cells)....Staff FDA/NCDB 301-496-3556
Erythrocytes (Red Blood Cells)....Staff NHLBI 301-496-4236

Erythromelalgia....Staff NHLBI 301-496-4236

Erythropoietin....Staff NHLBI 301-496-4236

Esophageal Disorders....Staff NIDDK 301-654-3810

Esophagus, Carcinoma....Staff NCI 301-496-5583

Esotropia....Staff NEI 301-496-5248

Essential oils....Land, Eric USITC 202-205-3349

Essential Hypertension....Staff NHLBI 301-496-4236

Establishment Survey, Data Disk.....Podgornik, Guy LABOR 202-606-6534

Establishment Survey, Emp/Unemp....Shipp, Kenneth LABOR 202-606-6519

Establishment Survey, National, Empl/Unempl.....Seifert, Mary Lee LABOR 202-606-6552

Establishment Survey, Natl., Indus. Classif. Empl/Unempl....Getz, Patricia LABOR 202-606-6521

Establishment Survey, States and Areas, Data Diskette....Podgornik, Guy LABOR 202-606-6534

Establishment Survey, States and Areas, Empl/Unemp....Shipp, Kenneth LABOR 202-606-6519

Esters, fatty-acid, of polyhydric alcohols....Land, Eric USITC 202-205-3349

Esters....Lee, May PTO 703-308-4546

Estimates and Incidence/Industry Injuries and Illness....Staff LABOR 202-606-6180

Estonia....Altheim, Stephen Cnty Treasury 202-622-0125

Estonia....Ann Lien Cnty TDA 703-875-4357

Estonia....Ilves, Toomes Hendrik Cnty Embassy 202-789-0320

Estonia....Jovanovic, Djordje Cnty World Bank 202-473-4070

Estonia....Kross, Eerik-Niiles Cnty Embassy 202-789-0320

Estonia....Levine, Richard Cnty Mines 202-501-9682

Estonia....Robinson, Susan Cnty USIA 202-619-6853

Estonia....Staff Cnty State 202-647-3187

Estonia....Viksnins, Helen Peace Corps 202-606-5517

Estonia....Waxman-Lenz, Roberta Cnty Export-Import Bank 202-565-3742

Estonia....Wootton, Nicholas Peace Corps 202-606-5519

Estrogen Therapy....Staff NIA 301-496-1752

Estrogen Replacement Therapy....Staff NIA 301-496-1752

Estrogen Replacement Therapy....Staff NIAMS 301-496-8188

Estrogen Replacement Therapy....Staff NICHD 301-496-5133

Estrogen Replacement Therapy....Staff NCI 301-496-5583

Estrogen Replacement Therapy....Staff FDA 301-443-3170

Ethane....Land, Eric USITC 202-205-3349

Ethanol....Brady, Thomas CUSTOMS 212-466-5747

Ethanolamines....Michels, David USITC 202-205-3352

Ethers, fatty-acid, of polyhydric alcohols....Land, Eric USITC 202-205-3349

Ethers....Brady, Thomas CUSTOMS 212-466-4769

Ethers....Michels, David USITC 202-205-5747

Ethics....NCHGR 301-402-0911

Ethiopia/Minerals....Antonides, Lloyd Cnty Mines 202-501-9686

Ethiopia (Addis Ababa)....Staff Cnty State 202-647-6485

Ethiopia....Adugna, Fisseha Cnty Embassy 202-234-2282

Ethiopia....Gebhart, George E. Cnty World Bank 202-473-7502

Ethiopia....Gebre-Christos, Berhane Cnty Embassy 202-234-2281

Ethiopia....Hutchings, Dayna Cnty Export-Import Bank 202-565-3737

Ethiopia....Larsen, Mark Cnty USIA 202-619-4894

Ethiopia....McKoy, Ethel Cnty Treasury 202-622-0336

Ethiopia....Pryor, Jeanne Cnty AID 202-647-7988

Ethiopia....Watkins, Chandra Cnty Commerce 202-482-4564

Ethyl alcohol (ethanol) for nonbeverage use....Michels, David USITC 202-205-3352

Ethylene dibromide....Michels, David USITC 202-205-3352

Ethylene glycol....Michels, David USITC 202-205-3352

Ethylene oxide....Michels, David USITC 202-205-3352

Ethylene-propylene rubber....Misurelli, Denby USITC 202-205-3362

Ethylene....Raftery, Jim USITC 202-205-3365

Eurasia/trade matters....Novelli, Catherine US Trade Rep 202-395-4620

Eurodollars with options....SIA Manasses CFT 312-353-9027

Europe/trade matters....Marcich, Chris US Trade Rep 202-395-4620

Europe/trade matters....Kaska, Edward US Trade Rep 202-395-3320

European Affairs/trade matters....Mowrey, Mark US Trade Rep 202-395-4620

European Assistance....Moore, Erroll FTC 202-326-2071

European Communities....Staff Cnty State 202-647-1708

European Community....Ludolph, Charles Cnty Commerce 202-482-5276

European Economic Community (EEC)....Staff Cnty State 202-647-1708

European Economic Community....Staff Cnty State 202-647-1708

European Free Trade Association (EFTA)...Staff Cnty 202-647-2395

European Services....Kaska, Edward US Trade Rep 202-395-3320

European Space Agency....Staff Cnty State 202-647-2395

European Union....Currie, James Cnty Embassy 202-862-9500

European Union....Van AGT, Andreas Cnty Embassy 202-862-9500

Evaluation and Incident Investigation....Rubin, Stuart D. NRC 301-415-7480

Ewing's Sarcoma....Staff NCI 301-496-5583

Ex Parte Rules....Staff FCC 202-418-1740

Ex Parte Rules....Staff FCC 202-418-1720

Excimer Laser (Eye)....Staff NEI 301-496-5248

Executive Director's Office....Wiggs, Barbara B. FTC 202-326-2196

Executive Director's Office....Lustic, Barbara FTC 202-326-2088

Executive Director's Office.....Blumenthal, Don M. FTC 202-326-2255

Executive Director's Office....Woods, James M. FTC 202-326-2232

Executive Director's Office....Hunter, Nancy L. FTC 202-326-2202

Executive Director's Office....Holland, Peggy FTC 202-326-3426

Executive Director's Office....Giffin, James M. FTC 202-326-2209

Executive Director's Office....Zytnick, Joseph FTC 202-326-2224

Executive Director's Office....Walton, Robert, III FTC 202-326-2205

Executive Director's Office....Straight, Rosemarie FTC 202-326-2207

Executive Director's Office - Starek, Roscoe B. III....Yi, Seoung Gu FTC 202-326-2127

Executive Director's Office....Miller, Sula FTC 202-326-2199

Executive Director's Office....Kelsey, Teresa J. FTC 202-326-2196

Executive Director's Office....Pham, Tuan FTC 202-326-2241

Executive Director's Office....Proctor, Alan FTC 202-326-2204

Executive Director's Office - Automated Systems....Mills, Mark C. FTC 202-326-3214

Exec. Director's Office - Automated Systems....Momeni, Ali FTC 202-326-2232

Exec. Director's Office - Automated Systems....Morris, Derrick FTC 202-326-2116

Exec. Director's Office - Automated Systems....Johnson, Loretta FTC 202-326-3624

Exec. Director's Office - Automated Systems....Barnes, Doug FTC 202-326-2269

Exec. Director's Office - Automated Systems....Feldmann, Lester A. FTC 202-326-2216

Exec. Director's Office - Automated Systems....Frank, F. Michael FTC 202-326-2217

Exec. Director's Office - Automated Systems....Lewis, Matthew FTC 202-326-2791

Exec. Director's Office - Automated Systems....Johnson, Gracie E. FTC 202-326-2211

Exec. Director's Office - Automated Systems....Pulliam, Denise M. FTC 202-326-2508

Exec. Director's Office - Automated Systems....Chambers, Michael D. FTC 202-326-2379

Exec. Director's Office - Automated Systems....DeVaughn, Willetta FTC 202-326-2233

Exec. Director's Office - Automated Systems....Condor, Karen FTC 202-326-3402

Exec. Director's Office - Automated Systems....Chmielewski, Richard FTC 202-326-2402

Exec. Director's Office - Automated Systems....Greynolds, Mark C. FTC 202-326-2290

Exec. Director's Office - Automated Systems....Lynch, Dennis FTC 202-326-2840

Exec. Director's Office - Automated Systems....Krupinski, Robert FTC 202-326-2231

Exec. Director's Office - Automated Systems....Edwards, Kathleen N. FTC 202-326-2240

Exec. Director's Office - Automated Systems....Anthony, Edward M. FTC 202-326-3527

Exec. Director's Office - Automated Systems....Dawson, Curtis FTC 202-326-2036

Exec. Director's Office - Automated Systems....Hales, Gregory E. FTC 202-326-2795

Exec. Director's Office - Automated Systems....Williams, Ken FTC 202-326-2082

Exec. Director's Office - Automated Systems....Massey, Karla FTC 202-326-3570

Exec. Director's Office - Automated Systems....St. Claire, Susan L. FTC 202-326-2227

Exec. Director's Office - Automated Systems....Pascoe, George FTC 202-326-3405

Exec. Director's Office - Automated Systems....Rougeau, Brian FTC 202-326-2952

Exec. Director's Office - Automated Systems....Lou, Linda FTC 202-326-2994

Exec. Director's Office - Automated Systems....Luhrs, Rick FTC 202-326-2404

Exec. Director's Office - Automated Systems....Lucas, Lionel FTC 202-326-2166

Exec. Director's Office - Automated Systems....Snyder, I. Michael FTC 202-326-2298

Exec. Director's Office - Automated Systems....Llewellyn, David W. FTC 202-326-3639

Exec. Director's Office - Automated Systems....Vermillion, Bonnie FTC 202-326-2226

Exec. Director's Office - Automated Systems....Overholt, Roberta FTC 202-326-2228

Be patient. If any phone number is incorrect, call (area code) 555-1212 and request the new listing.

1397

Exec. Director's Office - Automated Systems....Pitt, Julia K. FTC 202-326-2445

Exec. Director's Office - Automated Systems....Enger, Craig C. FTC 202-326-2898

Exec. Director's Office - Automated Systems....Enger, Erik L. FTC 202-326-2238

Exec. Director's Office - Automated Systems....Robertson, Diana FTC 202-326-2230

Executive Director's Office - Automated Systems....Smith, Jeff M. FTC 202-326-2529

Executive Director's Office - Automated Systems....Sheriff, Jennifer L. FTC 202-326-2913

Executive Director's Office - Automated Systems....Nguyen, Minh FTC 202-326-2604

Executive Director's Office - Budget and Finance....Hendershot, Alec R. FTC 202-326-3334

Executive Director's Office - Budget and Finance....Thorpe, Wilhelmina FTC 202-326-2219

Executive Director's Office - Budget and Finance....Fielding, Parcellena FTC 202-326-2312

Executive Director's Office - Budget and Finance....Smith, Virginia FTC 202-326-2784

Executive Director's Office - Budget and Finance....Delacruz, Margaret A. FTC 202-326-2322

Executive Director's Office - Budget and Finance....Thompson, Carl M. FTC 202-326-2337

Executive Director's Office - Budget and Finance....Simms, Anthony FTC 202-326-2325

Executive Director's Office - Budget and Finance....Haynes, Donna M. FTC 202-326-2327

Executive Director's Office - Budget and Finance....Arnold, Richard D., II FTC 202-326-2314

Executive Director's Office - Budget and Finance....Rodriguez, Lenore FTC 202-326-2190

Executive Director's Office - Budget and Finance....Farmer, Melissa S. FTC 202-326-2251

Executive Director's Office - Budget and Finance....Savell, Toby Sunshine FTC 202-326-2422

Executive Director's Office - Budget and Finance....Feggins, Payne D. FTC 202-326-2315

Executive Director's Office - Budget and Finance....Hailes, Gail E. FTC 202-326-2318

Executive Director's Office - Budget and Finance....Spriggs, Shari FTC 202-326-2339

Executive Director's Office - Budget and Finance....Hodge, Denise D. FTC 202-326-2324

Executive Director's Office - Budget and Finance....Reinertson, Diane L. FTC 202-326-2051

Executive Director's Office - Budget and Finance....Murphy, Jon FTC 202-326-2328

Executive Director's Office - Budget and Finance....Woodson, Louise V. FTC 202-326-3301

Executive Director's Office - Budget and Finance....Lancaster, Dorothy M. FTC 202-326-2488

Executive Director's Office - Budget and Finance....McLaughlin, Narvarius W. FTC 202-326-2329

Executive Director's Office - Information Management....Baella, Thomas FTC 202-326-2384

Executive Director's Office - Information Management....De La Cruz, Dexter FTC 202-326-2432

Executive Director's Office - Information Management....Jennings, Bruce FTC 202-326-2383

Executive Director's Office - Information Management....Knott, Margie FTC 202-326-2833

Executive Director's Office - Information Management....Ottie, Denise B. FTC 202-326-2381

Executive Director's Office - Information Mangement....Brown, Gregory FTC 202-326-3697

Executive Director's Office - Information Services....Adams, Bonita FTC 202-326-2528

Executive Director's Office - Information Services....Ajibawo, Abiola S. FTC 202-326-2530

Executive Director's Office - Information Services....Bacon, Geraldine G. FTC 202-326-2380

Executive Director's Office - Information Services....Baella, Thomas G. FTC 202-326-2031

Executive Director's Office - Information Services....Barber, Lisa FTC 202-326-2947

Executive Director's Office - Information Services....Barsant, Adolph FTC 202-326-2250

Executive Director's Office - Information Services....Blades, Donna L. FTC 202-326-3005

Executive Director's Office - Information Services....Bolden, Sandra B. FTC 202-326-2406

Executive Director's Office - Information Services....Booker, Lance FTC 202-326-2523

Executive Director's Office - Information Services....Borlase, Michele FTC 202-326-2302

Executive Director's Office - Information Services....Carter-Johnson, Jean FTC 202-326-2405

Executive Director's Office - Information Services....Chambers, Dewayne W. FTC 202-326-3036

Executive Director's Office - Information Services....Conrad, Jean FTC 202-326-2378

Executive Director's Office - Information Services....Cunningham, Jack FTC 202-326-2387

Executive Director's Office - Information Services....Curtin, Frank FTC 202-326-2280

Executive Director's Office - Information Services....Douglass, Franklin S. FTC 202-326-2376

Executive Director's Office - Information Services....Eperson, Patricia C. FTC 202-326-2420

Executive Director's Office - Information Services....Golden, Keith G. FTC 202-326-2410

Executive Director's Office - Information Services....Hammonds, Estelle FTC 202-326-2388

Executive Director's Office - Information Services....Harewood, Stanley M. FTC 202-326-3028

Executive Director's Office - Information Services....Hermingstyne, Dawn A. FTC 202-326-2878

Executive Director's Office - Information Services....Hutchins, Barry FTC 202-326-2373

Executive Director's Office - Information Services....Hynes, Barbara A. FTC 202-326-2389

Executive Director's Office - Information Services....Johnson, Dana FTC 202-326-2431

Executive Director's Office - Information Services....Johnson, Phyllis A. FTC 202-326-2507

Executive Director's Office - Information Services....Kennedy, Patty FTC 202-326-2013

Executive Director's Office - Information Services....Kuykendall, Eunice, Jerusha E. FTC 202-326-2413

Executive Director's Office - Information Services....Leonard, Lynne C. FTC 202-326-3684

Executive Director's Office - Information Services....Long, Marcus D. FTC 202-326-2660

Executive Director's Office - Information Services....Maisel, Theodore A. FTC 202-326-2415

Executive Director's Office - Information Services....Moore, Joyce M. FTC 202-326-3018

Executive Director's Office - Information Services....Moynahan, Eileen FTC 202-326-2449

Executive Director's Office - Information Services....Pierce, Marilyn S. FTC 202-855-1000

Executive Director's Office - Information Services....Reese, Genevieve E. FTC 202-326-2409

Executive Director's Office - Information Services....Titzer, Kristine L. FTC 202-326-2407

Executive Director's Office - Information Services....Tucker, Francenia FTC 202-326-3037

Executive Director's Office - Information Services....Woodson, Margaret B. FTC 202-326-2417

Executive Director's Office - Library....Sullivan, R. Elaine FTC 202-326-2385

Executive Director's Office - Personnel....Allen, Gelinda A. FTC 202-326-2876

Executive Director's Office - Personnel....Axelrod, Harold FTC 202-326-2790

Executive Director's Office - Personnel....Berry, Chrishania R. FTC 202-326-2363

Executive Director's Office - Personnel....Carter, Carole A. FTC 202-326-2550

Executive Director's Office - Personnel....Caton, Kathleen FTC 202-326-2342

Executive Director's Office - Personnel....Cooper, Erica FTC 202-326-2021

Executive Director's Office - Personnel....Crayton, Erika L. FTC 202-326-2022

Executive Director's Office - Personnel....Davis, Elliot FTC 202-326-2022

Executive Director's Office - Personnel....Harris, Barbara A. FTC 202-326-2428

Executive Director's Office - Personnel....Holmes, Ann FTC 202-326-2345

Executive Director's Office - Personnel....Kotecki, Naldyne FTC 202-326-2427

Executive Director's Office - Personnel....La Veille, Monica FTC 202-326-2361

Executive Director's Office - Personnel....McCoy, Catherine M. FTC 202-326-2358

Executive Director's Office - Personnel....Miller-Duncan, Glenda FTC 202-326-2367

Executive Director's Office - Personnel....Schwarz, Mae FTC 202-326-2341

Executive Director's Office - Personnel....Skipper, Brenda FTC 202-326-2365

Executive Director's Office - Personnel....Smith, Del FTC 202-326-2357

Executive Director's Office - Personnel....Smith, Jhana FTC 202-326-2384

Executive Director's Office - Personnel....Steinberg, Sharon FTC 202-326-2364

Executive Director's Office - Personnel....Yates, Diedra M. FTC 202-326-2354

Executive Director's Office - Procurement and Gen. Services.....Moore, David L. FTC 202-326-2277

Executive Director's Office - Procurement and Gen. Services.....Hutcherson, Willie S. FTC 202-326-2297

Executive Director's Office - Procurement and Gen. Services.....Vogt, Eric FTC 202-326-2259

Executive Director's Office - Procurement and Gen. Services....Greulich, Sherron FTC 202-326-2271

Executive Director's Office - Procurement and Gen. Services.....Moore, Francenia K. FTC 202-326-2872

Executive Director's Office - Procurement and Gen. Services.....Justice, Julius FTC 202-326-2275

Executive Director's Office - Procurement and Gen. Services.....Hymon, James F. FTC 202-326-3736

Executive Director's Office - Procurement and Gen. Services....Lorette, Barbara D. FTC 202-326-2260

Executive Director's Office - Procurement and Gen. Services....Clayborne, Charles FTC 202-326-2272

Executive Director's Office - Procurement and Gen. Services....Elliott, George T. FTC 202-326-2278

Executive Director's Office - Procurement and Gen. Services.....Wheeler, Bruce FTC 202-326-2270

Executive Director's Office - Procurement and Gen. Services.....Wells, Ernest L. FTC 202-326-2248

Executive Director's Office - Procurement and Gen. Services....Enos, Mary Ann FTC 202-326-2266

Executive Director's Office - Procurement and Gen. Services.....Goines, Russell E. FTC 202-326-2267

Executive Director's Office - Procurement and Gen. Services....Vasser, Robert M. FTC 202-326-2245

Executive Director's Office - Procurement and Gen. Services....Brewer, Ronald L. FTC 202-326-2243

Executive Director's Office - Procurement and Gen. Services....Walker, William FTC 202-326-2343

Executive Director's Office - Procurement and Gen. Services....Dickerson, William F. FTC 202-326-3735

Executive Director's Office - Procurement and Gen. Services....Woods, Donna K. FTC 202-326-2296

Executive Director's Office - Procurement and Gen. Services....Armstead, Gloria FTC 202-326-2262

Executive Director's Office - Procurement and Gen. Services....Bolden, Skipp D. FTC 202-326-2273

Executive Director's Bureau - Procurement and Gen. Services....Rice, Melvin L. FTC 202-326-2297

Executive Director's Office - Procurement and Gen Services....Royster, Lawrence D., Sr. FTC 202-326-2251

Executive Director's Office - Procurement and Gen. Services....Wilson, Ricardo M. FTC 202-326-2261

Executive Director's Office - Procurement and Gen. Services....Hayes, Ronald FTC 202-326-3734

Executive Director's Office - Procurement and Gen. Services....Green, Theresa Y. FTC 202-326-2243

Executive Director's Office - Procurement and Gen. Services.....Simpson, Flossie I. FTC 202-326-2297

Executive Director's Office - Procurement and Gen. Services.....Sefchick, Jean FTC 202-326-2258

Executive Director's Office - Procurement and Gen. Services....Gillette, Brian K. FTC 202-326-2253

Executive Director's Office - Procurement and Gen. Services.....Meritt, Claude O., Jr. FTC 202-326-2286

Exercise Physiology....Staff NIAMS 301-496-8188

Exercise and Aging....Staff NIA 301-496-1752

Exercise and the Heart....Staff NHLBI 301-496-4236

Exercising devices....Apley, Richard PTO 703-308-0305

Exercising devices...Love, John PTO 703-308-0873

Exhibits, Conventions....Dickinson, Joanne CENSUS 301-457-1191

Exhibits and Publications (Printing)....Beckwith, Frances NLM 301-496-6308

Exotic Fish....Staff FWS 703-358-1718

Exotic Species....Staff FWS 703-358-1718

Exotropia....Staff NEI 301-496-5248

Expanded Interconnection....Staff FCC 202-418-1576

Expanded Band AM....Staff FCC 202-418-2670

Experimental Aerodynamics....Staff NASA 415-604-5000

Experimental Aerodynamics....Mewhinney, Michael NASA 415-604-3937

Experimental Allergic Encephalomyelitis (EAE)....Staff NINDS 301-496-5751

Experimental Immunology....O'Shea, John FAES 301-496-6026

Explosive devices...Jordan, Charles PTO 703-308-0918

Explosives...Johnson, Larry USITC 202-205-3351

Explosives....Kramer, Deborah MINES 202-501-9394

Explosives....Maxey, Francis P. COMMERCE 202-482-0128

Explosives....Preston, Jacques CUSTOMS 212-466-5488

Export and Import Price Indexes, Curr. Anal.....Vachris, Michelle LABOR 202-606-7155

Export Trading Company Affairs....Muller, George COMMERCE 202-482-5131

Exposure Assessment Group....Staff EPA 202-260-8909

Extramural Associates Program....Staff OD/OERT 301-496-9728

Extrapyramidal Disorders....Staff NINDS 301-496-5751

Eye Banks....Staff NEI 301-496-5248

Eye Care....Staff NEI 301-496-5248

Eye Diseases....Staff NEI 301-496-5248

Eye Exercises....Staff NEI 301-496-5248

Eye Health Education Program....Staff NEI 301-496-5248

Eye Institute, National....Stein, Judith NIH 301-496-5248

Eye (Radiation and Ultra Violet Effect)....Staff FDA/NCDRH 301-594-2205

Eye (Statistics)....Staff NCHS 301-436-8500

Eye Strain....Staff NEI 301-496-5248

Eye....Staff National Eye Care Project (NECP) 800-222-3937

Eye....Staff National Eye Research Foundation (NERF) 800-621-2258

Eyeglasses....Johnson, Christopher USITC 202-205-3488

Eyeglasses....Staff NEI 301-496-5248

F

FAA Clearance EMI Problems....Staff FCC 202-418-2780

Fabric folding machines....Greene, William USITC 202-205-3405

Fabricated Metal Construction Materials....Williams, Franklin COMMERCE 202-482-0132

Fabrics: billiard cloth....Cook, Lee USITC 202-205-3471

Fabrics: bolting cloth....Cook, Lee USITC 202-205-3471

Fabrics, Coated or Laminated....Barth, George CUSTOMS 212-466-5884

Fabrics: coated....Cook, Lee USITC 202-205-3471

Fabrics: elastic....Shelton, Linda USITC 202-205-3457

Fabrics: embroidered....Konzet, Jeffrey CUSTOMS 212-466-5885

Fabrics: embroidered....Shelton, Linda USITC 202-205-3457

Fabrics: impression....Shelton, Linda USITC 202-205-3457

Fabrics, knit....Konzet, Jeffrey CUSTOMS 212-466-5885

Fabrics: knit....Shelton, Linda USITC 202-205-3457

Fabrics: narrow....Shelton, Linda USITC 202-205-3457

Fabrics, nonwoven....Barth, George CUSTOMS 212-466-5884

Fabrics: nonwoven....Sussman, Donald USITC 202-205-3470

Fabrics: oil cloths....Cook, Lee USITC 202-205-3471

Fabrics: tapestry, woven....Shelton, Linda USITC 202-205-3457

Fabrics, Technical....Barth, George CUSTOMS 212-466-5884

Fabrics: tire....Cook, Lee USITC 202-205-3471

Fabrics: tracing cloth....Cook, Lee USITC 202-205-3471

Fabrics: Tufted....Shelton, Linda USITC 202-205-3457

Fabrics, Woven....Tytelman, Alan CUSTOMS 212-466-5896

Fabrics, woven: cotton....Shelton, Linda USITC 202-205-3457

Fabrics, woven: glass....McNay, Deborah USITC 202-205-3425

Fabrics: woven: jute....Cook, Lee USITC 202-205-3471

Fabrics, woven: manmade fibers....Shelton, Linda USITC 202-205-3457

Fabrics, woven: pile....Shelton, Linda USITC 202-205-3457

Fabrics, woven: silk....Shelton, Linda USITC 202-205-3457

Fabrics: woven, wool....Shelton, Linda USITC 202-205-3457

Fabry's Disease....Staff NICHD 301-496-5133

Fabry's Disease....Staff NINDS 301-496-5751

Fabry's Disease....Staff NHLBI 301-496-4236

Facial Surgery....Staff American Academy of Facial Plastic and Reconstructive Surgery (FACE) 800-332-3223

Facial Neuralgia (Tic Douloureux)....Staff NINDS 301-496-5751

Facilities Management....Bass, Robert C. FTC 202-326-2265

Facilities Management....Lampkins, Gladys M. FTC 202-326-2307

Facilities Management....Alston, Jerome FTC 202-326-2301

Facilities Management....Morris, Patrick A. FTC 202-326-2309

Facilities Management....Singleton, Frieda FTC 202-326-2580

Be patient. If any phone number is incorrect, call (area code) 555-1212 and request the new listing.

1399

Facilities Management....Morris, J. Wayne FTC 202-326-2310
Facsimile (FAX)--Wire....Staff FCC 202-326-2625
Facsimile....Coles, Edward L. PTO 703-305-4712
Factory Automation Systems....Bloom, Howard NIST 301-975-3508
FAES (Foundation for Adv. Educa. in the Sciences)....Staff FAES 301-496-7976
Fainting (Syncope)....Staff NHLBI 301-496-4236
Fair Credit Billing Act....Hurt, Adrienne FRS 202-452-2412
Fair Credit Reporting Act....Gell, Jane FRS 202-452-3667
Fair Housing Act....Loney, Glenn FRS 202-452-3585
Fair Housing and Equal Opportunity....Staff HUD 202-708-3735
Fairness Doctrine Enforcement....Staff FCC 202-418-1440
Falconry....Staff FWS 703-358-1821
Falls and Frailty....Staff NIA 301-496-1752
Familial Ataxia Telangiectasia....Staff NCI 301-496-5583
Familial Ataxia Telangiectasia....Staff NINDS 301-496-5751
Familial Dysautonomia (Riley-Day Syndrome)....Staff NINDS 301-496-5751
Familial Hypercholesterolemia....Staff NHLBI 301-496-4236
Familial Hypertension....Staff NHLBI 301-496-4236
Familial Mediterranean Fever....Staff NIAMS 301-496-8188
Familial Periodic Paralysis....Staff NINDS 301-496-5751
Familial Spastic Paraparesis....Staff NINDS 301-496-5751
Families....Staff CENSUS 301-457-2394
Family and Aging....Staff NIA 301-496-1752
Family Characteristics of Labor Force....Hayghe, Howard LABOR 202-606-6378
Family Issues....Lewis, Terry ACYF 202-205-8102
Family Medicine Training....Staff HRSA/BHPr 301-443-1467
Family Nursing Practitioner....Staff HRSA/BHPr 301-443-6333
Family Physicians....Staff American Academy of Family Physicians (AAFP) 800-274-2237
Family Planning (Research)....Staff NICHD 301-496-5133
Family Planning....Staff ASH 301-594-4008
Family Planning....Staff NCNR 301-496-0526
Family Size....Staff NICHD 301-496-5133
Family support....Staff Family Support and Mental Health 800-628-1696
Family Violence....Staff National Council on Child Abuse and Family Violence (NCCAF) 800-222-2000
Family....Staff Family Care Givers Alliance (FCGA) 800-445-8106
Fanconi's Anemia....Staff NHLBI 301-496-4236
Fans....Mata, Ruben USITC 202-205-3403
Farm Bill....Staff FWS 703-358-2043
Farm Machinery....Weining, Mary COMMERCE 202-482-4708
Farm Population....Dahmann, Don CENSUS 301-457-2413
Farmlands....Staff FWS 703-358-2043
Farms and Land - Farm Numbers....Ledbury, Dan Agri 202-720-1790
Farms and Land - Farm Output and Productivity....Douvelis, George Agri 202-219-0840
Farms and Land - Farm Real Estate....Beach, Doug Agri 202-219-0443
Farms and Land - Foreign Land Ownership....DeBraal, Peter Agri 202-219-1011
Farms and Land - Land Ownership and Tenure....Wunderlich, Gene Agri 202-219-0427
Farms and Land - Land Use....Daugherty, Arthur Agri 202-219-0424
Farms and Land - World....Urban, Francis Agri 202-219-0717
Farsightedness....Staff NEI 301-496-5248
Fasteners (Industrial)....Reise, Richard COMMERCE 202-482-3489
Fasteners (Nails, Screws, Etc.)....Fitzgerald, John CUSTOMS 212-466-5492
Fasteners....Cuomo, Peter PTO 703-308-0827
Fats and Oils....Janis, William V. COMMERCE 202-482-2250
Fats and vegetable oils and their products....Reeder, John USITC 202-205-3319
Fatty acid amides....Land, Eric USITC 202-205-3349
Fatty acid esters of polyhydric alcohols....Land, Eric USITC 202-205-3349
Fatty acid quaternary ammonium salts (surface act)....Land, Eric USITC 202-205-3349
Fatty acids....Randall, Rob USITC 202-205-3366
Fatty alcohols of animal or vegetable origin....Randall, Rob USITC 202-205-3366
Fatty and Aromatic Substances....Joseph, Stephanie CUSTOMS 212-466-5768
Fatty ethers of animal or vegetable origin....Randall, Rob USITC 202-205-3366
Fatty substances derived from animal, marine, veg....Randall, Rob USITC 202-205-3366
Fear of Crime....Rand, Michael Justice Stat 202-616-3494
Fear of Crime....Lindgren, Sue Justice Stat 202-307-0760
Fear of Crime....Klaus, Patsy Justice Stat 202-307-0776
Feather products....Spalding, Josephine USITC 202-205-3498
Feathers....Steller, Rose USITC 202-205-3323
Febrile Convulsions....Staff NINDS 301-496-5751
Febrile Seizures....Staff NICHD 301-496-5133
Federal Energy Regulatory Commission....Schaffer, Rebecca NEIC 202-208-0004
Federal Information Center....Staff 800-347-1997

Federal Justice....Kaplan, Carol Justice Stat 202-307-0759
Federal Reserve Bulletin....Dykes, S Ellen FRS 202-452-3952
Federal Reserve Regulatory Service....Lahm, Diana FRS 202-452-3547
Federal Reserve System Publications....Kyles, Linda FRS 202-452-3244
Federal Tax Deposits....Bermudez, Michael FRS 202-452-3954
Feed Grains - Corn, Sorghum, Barley, Oats - World....Morgan, nancy Agri 202-501-8511
Feed Grains - Corn, Sorghum, Barley, Oats....Riley, Peter Agri 202-501-8512
Feed Grains - Corn, Sorghum, Barley, Oats....Van Lahr, Charles Agri 202-720-7369
Feed Grains - Corn, Sorghum, Barley, Oats....Dowdy, William Agri 202-720-3843
Feeds, animal....Pierre-Benoist, John USITC 202-205-3320
Fees General....Staff FCC 202-418-0192
Fees Private Radio...Staff FCC 800-322-1117
Fees Regulatory....Staff FCC 202-418-0192
Feldspar....Potter, Michael J. MINES 202-501-9387
Feldspar....White, Linda USITC 202-205-3427
Fellowships and Training in Laboratory Animal Medicine and Science....Staff NCRR 301-594-7933
Fellowships for Research Training in Nursing....Staff NINR 301-496-0207
Fellowships for Research Training in Toxicology....Staff NIEHS 919-755-4022
Female Offenders - Federal....Kaplan, Carol Justice Stat 202-307-0759
Female Offenders....Conley, Joyce Justice Stat 202-633-2214
Female Victims....Klaus, Patsy Justice Stat 202-307-0776
Fencing, Metal....MacAuley, Patrick COMMERCE 202-482-0132
Ferments....Nesbitt, Elizabeth USITC 202-205-3355
Ferricyanide blue....Johnson, Larry USITC 202-205-3351
Ferrites....Cutchin, John USITC 202-205-3396
Ferroalloys Products....Presbury Greylin COMMERCE 202-482-5158
Ferroalloys....Houck, Gerald MINES 202-501-9439
Ferroalloys....Yost, Charles USITC 202-205-3432
Ferrocerium....Johnson, Larry USITC 202-205-3351
Ferrocyanide blue....Johnson, Larry USITC 202-205-3351
Ferrous Scrap....Bell, Charles COMMERCE 202-482-0608
Fertility/Births....Bachu, Amara CENSUS 301-457-2416
Fertility/Births....O'Connell, Martin CENSUS 301-457-2416
Fertility Drugs....Staff NICHD 301-496-5133
Fertility....Staff NICHD 301-496-5133
Fertilizers....Brownchweig, Gilbert CUSTOMS 212-466-5744
Fertilizers....Maxey, Francis P. COMMERCE 202-482-0128
Fertilizers....Trainor, Cynthia USITC 202-205-3354
Fetal Alcohol Syndrome....Staff NIAAA 301-443-3860
Fetal Alcohol Syndrome....Staff NICHD 301-496-5133
Fetal Alcohol Syndrome Prevention....Hymbaugh, Karen CDC 404-488-7370
Fetal Development (Drug Effects)....Staff NIDA 301-443-6245
Fetal Monitoring....Staff NICHD 301-496-5133
Fetus....Staff NICHD 301-496-5133
Fever Blisters....Staff NIDR 301-496-4261
Fever....Staff NIAID 301-496-5717
Fiber Optic Devices....Bovernick, Rodney PTO 703-305-3594
Fibers....Konzet, Jeffrey CUSTOMS 212-466-5885
Fibers: abaca....Cook, Lee USITC 202-205-3471
Fibers: alpaca....Steller, Rose USITC 202-205-3323
Fibers: angora....Steller, Rose USITC 202-205-3323
Fibers: camel hair....Steller, Rose USITC 202-205-3323
Fibers: cashmere....Steller, Rose USITC 202-205-3323
Fibers: cotton....Sweet, Mary Elizabeth USITC 202-205-3455
Fibers: flax....Cook, Lee USITC 202-205-3471
Fibers: jute....Cook, Lee USITC 202-205-3471
Fibers: manmade....Shelton, Linda USITC 202-205-3457
Fibers: silk....Shelton, Linda USITC 202-205-3457
Fibers: sisal and henequen....Cook, Lee USITC 202-205-3471
Fibers: wool....Steller, Rose USITC 202-205-3323
Fibrillation....Staff NHLBI 301-496-4236
Fibrin....Randall, Rob USITC 202-205-3366
Fibrinolysis....Staff NHLBI 301-496-4236
Fibroid Tumors....Staff NICHD 301-496-5133
Fibromuscular Dysplasia....Staff NHLBI 301-496-4236
Fibromuscular Hyperplasia....Staff NIAMS 301-496-8188
Fibromyalgia....Staff NIAMS 301-496-8188
Fibrositis....Staff NIAMS 301-496-8188
Fibrotic Lung Diseases....Staff NHLBI 301-496-4236
Fibrous Dysplasia....Staff NINDS 301-496-5751
Fibrous Dysplasia....Staff NIAMS 301-496-8188
Field Enforcement Actions...Staff FCC 202-418-1170
Fifth Disease....Staff NIAID 301-496-5717
Fiji/Minerals....Lyday, Travis Cnty Mines 202-501-9695

Fiji (Suva)....Staff Cnty State 202-647-3546
Fiji....Berghage, Jeff Peace Corps 202-606-1098
Fiji....Davies, Irene Cnty World Bank 202-458-2481
Fiji....Harmnam, Judy Cnty Embassy 202-337-8320
Fiji....Imam, Fahmila Cnty Export-Import Bank 202-565-3738
Fiji....Jabbs, Theodore Cnty USIA 202-619-5836
Fiji....Nacuva, Pita Kewa Cnty Embassy 202-337-8320
Fiji....Respess, Rebecca Cnty TDA 703-875-4357
Fiji....Shelton, Alison Cnty Treasury 202-622-0354
Filariasis....Staff NIAID 301-496-5717
Filberts....Burket, Stephen USITC 202-205-3318
File management systems....Black, Thomas PTO 703-305-9707
Filling apparatus....Recia, Henry PTO 703-308-1382
Film (photographic)....Baker, Scott USITC 202-205-3386
Film, plastics....Misurelli, Denby USITC 202-205-3362
Film....Brownchweig, Gilbert CUSTOMS 212-466-5744
Films, Wildlife Video....Staff FWS 202-205-5611
Filters/Purifying Equipment....Wheeler, Fredrica COMMERCE 202-482-3509
Finance and Management Ind.....Candilis, Wray O. COMMERCE 202-482-0339
Finance....Goerl, Vincette L. 202-927-0600
Financial Assistance....Cox, John R. SBA 202-205-6490
Financial Industry Group....Roycroft, John C. SEC 202-942-1960
Financial Interest....Staff FCC 202-418-2130
Financial Management Policies....Hill, John W. GAO 202-512-8549
Financial Management....Hill, John W. GAO 202-512-8549
Financial services....Melly, Christopher USITC 202-205-3461
Financial Syndication....Staff FCC 202-418-2130
Finders Preference...Staff FCC 800-322-1117
Fine/industrial arts....Zarfus, Lou PTO 703-305-3260
Fine arts....Shooman, Ted PTO 703-305-3170
Finland (Helsinki)....Staff Cnty State 202-647-5669
Finland/Minerals....Plachy, Jozef Cnty Mines 202-501-9673
Finland....Gosnell, Peter Cnty Export-Import Bank 202-565-3733
Finland....Holloway, Barbara Cnty Treasury 202-622-0098
Finland....Kendall, Maryanne Cnty Commerce 202-482-3254
Finland....Polho, Aapo Cnty Embassy 202-298-5800
Finland....Rankin-Galloway, Honore Cnty USIA 202-619-5283
Finland....Valtasaari, Jukka Cnty Embassy 202-298-5800
Fire extinguishers....Mitchell, David PTO 703-308-0361
Fire Management....Staff FWS 202-208-2595
Fire protection....Cowart, Everett CDC 404-639-3148
Fire protection....Staff National Fire Protection Association (NFPA) 800-344-3555
Fire Research Laboratory....Wright, R.N. NIST 301-975-5900
Fire Safety Engineering....Fowell, A. NIST 301-975-6863
Fire safety....Staff CPSC 301-504-0580
Fire Science....Gann, R.G. NIST 301-6866
Fire....Staff FCC 717-337-1212
Firearm licenses....Staff ATF 404-679-5040
Far East....Staff GAO 808-541-1250
Firearms importing....Staff ATF 202-927-8320
Firearms....Jordan, Charles PTO 703-308-0918
Firearms....Luther, Dennis USITC 202-205-3497
Firearms....Preston, Jacques CUSTOMS 212-466-5488
Firewood....Hoffmeier, Bill USITC 202-205-3321
Fireworks....Johnson, Larry USITC 202-205-3351
Fireworks....Staff CPSC 301-504-0580
First aid kits....Randall, Rob USITC 202-205-3366
Fish and Wildlife Service....Staff EPA 202-208-5634
Fish and Wildlife Law Enforcement....Staff FWS 703-358-1949
Fish and Wildlife Reference Service....Staff FWS 703-358-2156
Fish and Wildlife News....Staff FWS 202-208-5634
Fish Broodstock Program....Staff FWS 703-358-1715
Fish Conservation and Management Act....Staff 703-358-1715
Fish Control Chemicals....Staff FWS 703-358-1715
Fish Culture Information....Staff FWS 703-358-1715
Fish Disease Diagnosis/Control....Staff FWS 703-358-1715
Fish Diseases/Research....Staff FWS 703-358-1715
Fish, Exotic....Staff FWS 703-358-1718
Fish Habitat Research....Lennartz, Michael R. FS 202-205-1524
Fish Hatcheries....Staff FWS 703-358-1715
Fish Health Centers....Staff FWS 703-358-1715
Fish Husbandry....Staff FWS 703-358-1715
Fish Law Enforcement....Staff FWS 703-358-1949
Fish nets and netting....Cook, Lee USITC 202-205-3471
Fish nets and nettings....Barth, George CUSTOMS 212-466-5884
Fish oils....Reeder, John USITC 202-205-3319
Fish Propagation....Staff FWS 703-358-1715

Fish Stocks....Staff FWS 703-358-1715
Fish....Conte, Ralph CUSTOMS 212-466-5759
Fish....Corey, Roger USITC 202-205-3327
Fisheries, Major Proj.....Bell, Richard COMMERCE 202-482-2460
Fishery Information Systems....Staff FWS 703-558-1861
Fishing on Refuges....Staff FWS 703-358-2043
Fishing tackle....Witherspoon, Ricardo USITC 202-205-3489
Flags....Cook, Lee USITC 202-205-3471
Flares....Johnson, Larry USITC 202-205-3351
Flashlights....Cutchin, John USITC 202-205-3396
Flat glass and products....Lukes, James USITC 202-205-3426
Flat goods....Seastrum, Carl USITC 202-205-3493
Flat goods....Gorman, Kevin CUSTOMS 212-466-5893
Flat panel displays....Malison, Andrew USITC 202-205-3391
Flaxseed and linseed oil....Reeder, John USITC 202-205-3319
Flight Control Research....Witherspoon, John NASA 804-864-6170
Flight Research Programs....Lovato, Nancy NASA 805-258-3448
Flight Services....Whatley, David FAA 202-267-9090
Flight simulating machines....Andersen, Peder USITC 202-205-3388
Flight Simulation Research....Hutchison, Jane NASA 415-604-4968
Flight Standards....Accardi, Thomas C FAA 202-267-8237
Floaters....Staff NEI 301-496-5248
Floating structures....Lahey, Kathleen USITC 202-205-3409
Floor coverings, textile....Sweet, Mary Elizabeth USITC 202-205-3465
Floor Coverings....Hansen, John CUSTOMS 212-466-5854
Flooring (wood)....Hoffmeier, Bill USITC 202-205-3321
Floppy Baby (Nemaline Myopathy)....Staff NINDS 301-496-5751
Floral waters....Land, Eric USITC 202-205-3349
Floriculture....Johnson, Doyle Agri 202-501-7949
Floriculture....Rogers, Latham Agri 202-720-5944
Flour (grain)....Pierre-Benoist, John USITC 202-205-3320
Flour....Vacant COMMERCE 202-482-2428
Flower and foliage: artificial, other....Spalding, Josephine USITC 202-205-3498
Flower and foliage: preserved, other....Spalding, Josephine USITC 202-205-3498
Flowers, Artificial....Rauch, Theodore CUSTOMS 212-466-5892
Flowers....Janis, William V. COMMERCE 202-482-2250
Flu and Older People....Staff NIA 301-496-1752
Flu...Staff NIAID 301-496-5717
Fluid conveying....Mitchell, David PTO 703-308-0361
Fluid Power....McDonald, Edward COMMERCE 202-482-0680
Fluorescein Angiography....Staff NEI 301-496-5248
Fluoridation....Reeves, Thomas CDC 404-639-8377
Fluoridation....Staff CDC 404-639-8377
Fluoridation....Staff NIDR 301-496-4261
Fluoride Research....Staff NIDR 301-496-4261
Fluorine....Conant, Kenneth USITC 202-205-3346
Fluorocarbons....Michels, David USITC 202-205-3352
Fluorosis....Staff NIDR 301-496-4261
Fluorspar....DeSapio, Vincent USITC 202-205-3435
Fluorspar....Miller, Michael MINES 202-501-9409
Fluxes....Michaels, David USITC 202-205-3352
FM Antennas, Directional....Staff FCC 202-418-2740
FM Application Status....Staff FCC 202-418-2730
FM Blanketing Interference...Staff FCC 202-418-2740
FM Boosters Legal....Staff FCC 202-418-1690
FM Boosters Technical....Staff FCC 202-418-1690
FM Technical Standards....Staff FCC 202-418-2740
FM Translators Legal/Policy....Staff FCC 202-418-1690
FM Translators Technical....Staff FCC 202-418-1690
Foams....Kight, John PTO 703-308-2453
Fogarty Scholars....Staff FIC 301-496-4161
Fogarty Publications....Staff FIC 301-496-2075
Foil, metal: aluminum....Yost, Charles USITC 202-205-3432
Foil, metal: other....Lundy, David USITC 202-205-3439
Folk Arts....Sheehy, Daniel NEA 202-682-5449
Food Additives/Dyes....Corwin, Emil FDA 202-205-4144
Food Additives....Staff FDA 301-205-4144
Food and Nutrition Information Center....Facinoli, Sandy NAL 301-504-5414
Food and Chemicals, Prices/Lv. Cond....Hippen, Roger LABOR 202-606-7715
Food, Apparel, and Raw Materials, Intl. Price Ind.....Frumkin, Rob LABOR 202-606-7106
Food - Food Assistance and Nutrition....Smallwood, Dave Agri 202-219-1265
Food - Food Assistance ....Smallwood, Dave Agri 202-219-1265
Food - Food Away From Home....Price, Charlene Agri 202-501-6765
Food - Food Consumption....Putnam, Judy Agri 202-501-7413
Food - Food Demand and Expenditures....Blaylock, James Agri 202-219-0900
Food - Food Demand and Expenditures....Haidacher, Richard Agri 202-219-0868

Be patient. If any phone number is incorrect, call (area code) 555-1212 and request the new listing.

1401

Food - Food Demand and Expenditures (World)....Stallings, Dave Agri 202-219-0708

Food - Food Manufacturing and Retailing....Handy, Charles Agri 202-219-0859

Food - Food Manufacturing....Gallo, Tony Agri 202-219-1260

Food - Food Policy (World)....Westcott, Paul Agri 202-219-0840

Food - Food Policy - World....Lynch, Loretta Agri 202-219-0689

Food - Food Policy....Kuhn, Betsey Agri 202-219-0409

Food - Food Policy....Smallwood, Dave Agri 202-219-1265

Food - Food Safety and Quality....Roberts, Tanya Agri 202-219-0857

Food - Food Safety and Quality....Unnevehr, Laurian Agri 202-219-0400

Food - Food Wholesaling....Epps, Walter Agri 202-219-0866

Food Grains - Rice....Kerestes, Daniel Agri 202-720-9526

Food Grains - Wheat....Allen, Ed Agri 202-219-0831

Food Grains - Wheat....Siegenthaler, Vaughn Agri 202-720-8068

Food Industry Group....Daly, James M. SEC 202-942-1800

Food Issues....Harman, John W. GAO 202-512-5138

Food Labeling....Corwin, Emil FDA 202-205-4144

Food - Marketing Margins and Statistics....Haidacher, Richard Agri 202-219-0870

Food - Marketing Margins and Statistics....Dunham, Denis Agri 202-219-0870

Food - Marketing Margins and Statistics....Elitzak, Howard Agri 202-219-1254

Food - Marketing Margins and Statistics....Handy, Charles Agri 202-219-0866

Food - preparing machines....Jackson, Georgia USITC 202-205-3399

Food - Price Spreads (Meat)....Duewer, Larry Agri 202-219-0712

Food Prices and Consumer Index....Clauson, Annette Agri 202-501-6552

Food Prices and Consumer Price Index....Elitzak, Howard Agri 202-219-1254

Food Prices Retail, Consumer Expenditure Survey....Cook, William LABOR 202-606-6988

Food Products Machinery....Shaw, Gene COMMERCE 202-482-3494

Food, Raw Materials, and Apparel, Intl. Price Ind....Frumkin, Rob LABOR 202-606-7106

Food Retailing....Kaufman, Phil Agri 202-219-0728

Food Retailing....Kenney, Cornelius COMMERCE 202-482-2428

Food safety....Karstadt, Myra FAES 202-332-9110

Food....Elkins, John Customs 202-482-7020

Foot Disorders....Staff NIAMS 301-496-8188

Footwear with Uppers of Rubber, Plastic or Leather....Foley, Richard CUSTOMS 212-466-5890

Footwear....Byron, James E. COMMERCE 202-482-4034

Footwear....Shildneck, Ann USITC 202-205-3499

Forbearance (Nondominant)....Staff FCC 202-418-1573

Forecasting Prison Populations....Staff Justice Stat 202-307-7703

Foreign Banks with U.S. Branches....O'Day, Kathleen FRS 202-452-3786

Foreign Born Population....Staff CENSUS 301-457-2403

Foreign Countries--Hourly Compensation Costs....Capdevielle, Patricia LABOR 202-606-5654

Foreign Countries, Labor Force and Unemployment....Sorrentino, Constance LABOR 202-606-5654

Foreign Countries--Prices, Prod. and Tech.....Godbout, Todd LABOR 202-606-5654

Foreign Countries--Productivity, Unit Labor Costs....Neef, Arthur LABOR 202-606-5654

Foreign Exchange Markets....Smith, Ralph W FRS 202-452-3712

Foreign Exchange Rates....Decker, Patrick J FRS 202-452-3314

Foreign Governments....Duvall, Steven SEC 202-942-1950

Foreign Language Education....Staff NEH 202-606-8373

Foreign Margin Stock List....Wolffrum, Margaret A FRS 202-452-2781

Foreign Medical Students....Shaffer, Sylvia HRSA 301-443-3376

Foreign Missions....Picard, James Customs 202-646-5056

Foreign Official Reserves....Smith, Ralph FRS 202-452-3712

Foreign Patents....Dell'Orto, Kathleen PTO 703-308-3278

Foreign Program Distribution....Staff FCC 202-418-2780

Foreign Radio Ownership....Staff FCC 202-418-2780

Foreign Scientists Assistance....Staff FIC 301-472-6166

Foreign Securities Margin Requirements....Holz, Scott FRS 202-452-2781

Foreign Service....Klang, Gordon OPM 202-606-0961

Foreign Trade Data Services....Staff CENSUS 301-457-3041

Foreign Trade Data Services....Higbee, Reba CENSUS 301-457-3041

Foreign Trade, Shippers Export Declaration....Blyweiss, Hal CENSUS 301-457-1086

Foreign Trade, U.S.....Morisse, Kathryn A FRS 202-452-3773

Foreign trade zones....Burns, Gail USITC 202-205-2501

Foreign Trust Activities....Vinnedge, Donald R FRS 202-452-2717

Foreign TV Ownership....Staff FCC 202-418-1630

Forest Diseases....Smith Richard S. FS 202-205-1532

Forest Fire Sciences....Donoghue, Linda R. FS 202-205-1561

Forest Insects....Powell, Janine FS 202-205-1532

Forest Products, Domestic Construction....Kristensen, Chris COMMERCE 202-482-0384

Forest Products, Trade Policy....Stanley, Gary COMMERCE 202-482-0375

Forest Products....Stanley, Gary COMMERCE 202-482-0375

Forest Products....Vacant FS 202-205-1565

Forest Protection....Staff FWS 703-358-2043

Forest Radio Service....Staff FCC 717-337-1212

Forest Recreation and Urban Forestry....Ewert, Alan FS 202-205-1092

Forestry and Construction, Prices and Living Cond....Davies, Wanda LABOR 202-606-7714

Forestry and Construction, Prices and Living Cond.....Davies, Wanda LABOR 202-606-7714

Forestry Atmospheric Deposition Research....Dunn, Paul H. FS 202-205-1524

Forestry Ecosystem Research....Ruark, Gregory FS 202-205-1524

Forestry, Global Change Research....Niebla, Elvia E. FS 202-205-1561

Forestry, Land Reclamation....Duscher, Karl FS 202-205-1244

Forestry, Lands and Resource Information....Holmes, Chris FS 202-205-1006

Forestry, Mineral Materials....Marshall, Steve FS 202-205-1246

Forestry, Oil and Gas Analysis....Holm, Melody FS 303-236-9376

Forestry, Pesticide Use....Staff FS 202-205-1600

Forestry, Soils Program....Avers, Peter FS 202-205-0977

Forestry, Solid Leasable Minerals....Kurcaba FS 202-205-1239

Forestry, Water Rights Program....Glasser, Steve FS 202-205-1475

Forestry, Water Rights....Glasser, Steve FS 202-205-1475

Forestry Wetlands Research....Ryan, Douglas FS 202-205-1524

Forfeiture....Zawitz, Marianne Justice Stat 202-616-3499

Forged-steel grinding balls....Polly, Laura USITC 202-205-3408

Forgings Semifinished Steel....Bell, Charles COMMERCE 202-482-0608

Fork-lift trucks....Polly, Laura USITC 202-205-3408

Formaldehyde....Michels, David USITC 202-205-3352

Fossil Energy....Siegal, Linda NEIC 202-586-6660

Fossil Fuel Power Generation, Major Proj.....Dollison, Robert COMMERCE 202-482-2733

Foster Care....Kharfen, Michael ACF 202-401-9215

Foundation....Staff Foundation Center Customer Service (FCCS) 800-424-9836

Foundry Equipment....Kemper, Alexis COMMERCE 202-482-5956

Foundry Industry....Bell, Charles COMMERCE 202-482-0608

Foundry products....Bello, Felix USITC 202-205-3120

Fracture Healing....Staff NIAMS 301-496-8188

Fragile X Syndrome....Staff National Fragile X Foundation 800-688-8765

Fragile X Syndrome....Staff NICHD 301-496-5133

France/Minerals....Newman, Harold R. Cnty Mines 202-501-9669

France (Paris)....Staff Cnty State 202-647-1412

France....Andreani, Jacques Cnty Embassy 202-944-6000

France....Gosnell, Peter Cnty Export-Import Bank 202-565-3733

France....Mikalis, Elana Cnty Commerce 202-482-6008

France....Seifkin, David Cnty USIA 202-619-6582

France....Vacant Cnty Treasury 202-622-0166

France....Villemur, Patrick Cnty Embassy 202-944-6000

Franchising services....Melly, Christopher USITC 202-205-3461

Fraud Hotline, HUD....Staff HUD 800-347-3735

Fraud, Scientific....Staff OASH/ORI 301-443-3400

Fraud, Waste and Abuse-Investigations, Audits....Holtz, Judy IG 202-619-1149

Fraud....Herera, Maria Customs 202-927-1510

Free Trade Area of the Americas (FTAA)....Lenzy, Karen US Trade Rep 202-395-5190

Freedom of Information Act General....Staff FCC 202-418-0210

Freedom of Information, Office of....Leathers, Laura CDC 404-639-2388

Freedom of Information Office....Christian, Darlene PHS 301-443-5252

Freedom of Information....Staff OD/DC 301-496-5633

French Guinea/Minerals....Gurmendi, Alfredo Cnty Mines 202-501-9681

French Antilles....Staff Cnty State 202-647-2620

French Polynesia....Staff Cnty State 202-647-3546

Freon (chlorofluorocarbons)....Michels, David USITC 202-205-3352

Friedreich's Ataxia....Staff NINDS 301-496-5751

Friends of the Clinical Center....Staff FOCC/CC 301-402-0193

Frohlich's Syndrome (Adiposogenital Dystrophy)....Staff NICHD 301-496-5133

Frohlich's Syndrome (Adiposogenital Dystrophy)....Staff NIDDK 301-496-3583

Frohlich's Syndrome (Adiposogenital Dystrophy)....Staff NINDS 301-496-5751

Frozen Fruits, Vegetables and Specialties....William, Janis V. COMMERCE 202-482-2250

Fructose....Randall, Rob USITC 202-205-3366

Fruit, edible, ex citrus....Frankel, Lee USITC 202-205-3315

Fruits and Vegetables....Hopardt, Stanley CUSTOMS 212-466-5760

Fruits and Tree Nuts....Bertelsen, Diane Agri 202-219-0884

Fruits and Tree Nuts....Hintzman, Kevin Agri 202-720-5412

Fruits and Tree Nuts....Shields, Dennis Agri 202-219-0884

Fruits and Tree Nuts - Tree Nuts....Johnson, Doyle Agri 202-219-0884

Fuchs' Dystrophy....Staff NEI 301-496-5248

Fuel Cycle Safety and Safeguards....Burnett, Robert F. NRC 301-415-7212

Fuel, jet....Foreso, Cynthia USITC 202-205-3348

Fuel oil, bunker "C"....Foreso, Cynthia USITC 202-205-3348

Fuel oil, navy special....Foreso, Cynthia USITC 202-205-3348

Fuel oil (nos. 1, 2, 3, 4, 5, 6)....Foreso, Cynthia USITC 202-205-3348

Fuels and Chemical Analysis....Staff EPA 313-668-4557

Fuels and Utilities Index, Monthly....Adkins, Robert LABOR 202-606-6985

Fuels and Utilities Retail Prices, Consumer Price Index....Adkins, Robert LABOR 202-606-6985

Fulminates....Johnson, Larry USITC 202-205-3351

Fumes (Hazardous)....Staff OD/ORS 301-496-2960

Functional fluids....Lieberman, Paul PTO 703-308-2552

Fund Raising...Staff FCC 202-418-1720

Fungal Infections....Staff NIAID 301-496-5717

Fungal Diseases (Eyes)....Staff NEI 301-496-5248

Funnel Chest (Pectus Excavatum)....Staff NHLBI 301-496-4236

Fur and furlike apparel....Hamey, Amy USITC 202-205-3465

Fur and furlike apparel....Jones, Jackie USITC 202-205-3466

Fur Goods....Byron, James E. COMMERCE 202-482-4034

Furfural....Michels, David USITC 202-205-3352

Furnace black....Johnson, Larry USITC 202-205-3351

Furnaces....Francke, Reic CUSTOMS 212-466-5669

Furnaces....Mata, Ruben USITC 202-205-3403

Furnaces....Staff CPSC 301-504-0580

Furnishings....Hansen, John CUSTOMS 212-466-5854

Furniture....Hodgen, Donald COMMERCE 202-482-3346

Furniture....Mushinske, Larry CUSTOMS 212-466-5739

Furniture....Spalding, Josephine USITC 202-205-3498

Furskins....Steller, Rose USITC 202-205-3323

Fuse/Burn....Giles, Ken CPSC 301-504-0580

Fused Alumina, (Abrasive)....Austin, Gordon MINES 202-501-9388

Fuses: Blasting...Johnson, Larry USITC 202-205-3351

Fuses: electrical....Malison, Andrew USITC 202-205-3391

Fusion Energy....Greenblatt, Jack USITC 202-205-3353

Fusion Energy....Davies, Anne NEIC 301-903-4941

Fusion Plasma....Crandall, David NEIC 301-903-4596

Futures Trading....Homer, Laura FRS 202-452-2781

Fuzzy Logic....Montgomery, Sheila COMMERCE 202-482-0397

G

G. Bissaue....Fossum, Linnea Peace Corps 202-606-3708

G6PD Deficiency....Staff NHLBI 301-496-4236

Gabon (Libreville)....Staff Cnty State 202-647-3139

Gabon/Minerals....Mobbs, Philip Cnty Mines 202-501-9679

Gabon....Boundoukou-Latha, Paul Cnty Embassy 202-797-1000

Gabon....Henke, Debra Cnty Commerce 202-482-5149

Gabon....Henning, Herman Cnty USIA 202-619-5926

Gabon....Jefferson, Deborah Peace Corps 202-606-3709

Gabon....Maybury-Lewis Anthony Cnty Export-Import Bank 202-565-3739

Gabon....Mitchell, Willis Peace Corps 202-606-3708

Gabon....Nguembi, Fidele Moussavou Cnty Embassy 202-797-1000

Gabon....Palghat, Kathy Cnty Treasury 202-622-0332

Gabon....Wilson, Michael J. Cnty World Bank 202-473-4714

Gabon....Younge, Nathan Cnty TDA 703-875-4357

Galactorrhea....Staff NIDDK 301-496-3583

Galactosemia....Staff NICHD 301-496-5133

Galactosemia....Staff NINDS 301-496-5751

Galactosemia....Staff NIDDK 301-496-3583

Galileo Flight Project....Wilson, James NASA 818-354-5011

Gallbladder....Staff NIDDK 301-654-3810

Gallium....Kramer, Deborah A. MINES 202-501-9394

Gallium....Lundy, David USITC 202-205-3439

Gallstones....Staff NIDDK 301-654-3810

Gambia, The (Banjul)....Staff Cnty State 202-647-4567

Gambia/Minerals....Dolley, Thomas Cnty Mines 202-501-9690

Gambia....Baily, Jess Cnty USIA 202-619-5900

Gambia....Barber, Ed Cnty Treasury 202-622-1730

Gambia....Bezek, Jill Cnty TDA 703-875-4357

Gambia....Bowler, Gina Peace Corps 202-606-3644

Gambia....Brown, Edward K. Cnty World Bank 202-473-4834

Gambia....Dibba, Aminatta Cnty Embassy 202-785-1399

Gambia....Fox, Russell Peace Corps 202-606-3644

Gambia....Hutchins, Dayna Cnty Export-Import Bank 202-565-3737

Gambia....Michelin, Philip Cnty Commerce 202-482-4388

Gambia....Niec, Rebecca Cnty AID 202-647-9206

Gambia....Tunkara, Kemo Cnty Embassy 202-785-1379

Gambling problem....Staff National Council on Problem Gambling (NCPG) 800-522-4700

Game animals....Steller, Rose USITC 202-205-3323

Games and Childrens' Vehicles....Hodgen, Donald COMMERCE 202-482-3346

Games....Abrahamson, Dana USITC 202-205-3430

Games....McKenna, Thomas CUSTOMS 212-466-5475

Gaming Enforcement....Staff FCC 202-418-1430

Gamma Ray Observatory....Shannon, Ernie NASA 301-286-6256

Gamma Ray Observatory....Staff NASA 301-286-8102

Garage Door Openers--Licenses....Staff FCC 717-337-1212

Garage Door Operators....Staff CPSC 301-504-0580

Garnet....Austin, Gordon MINES 202-501-9388

Garters and suspenders....Sweet, Mary Elizabeth USITC 202-205-3455

Gas generators....Fravel, Dennis USITC 202-205-3404

Gas Industry Group....Daly, James M. SEC 202-942-1800

Gas oil....Foreso, Cynthia USITC 202-205-3348

Gas-operated metalworking appliances....Fravel, Dennis USITC 202-205-3404

Gas Reserves Statistics....Lique, Diane NEIC 202-586-6090

Gas Vol Standards....Staff CPSC 301-504-0580

Gaseous Diffusion Plants (GDP)....Alexander, James NEIC 615-576-0885

Gases, Greenhouse....Patrinus, Aristides NEIC 301-903-5348

Gaskets/Gasketing Materials....Reiss, Richard COMMERCE 202-482-3489

Gasoline, Retail Prices....Chelena, Joseph LABOR 202-606-6982

Gasoline....Foreso, Cynthia USITC 202-205-3348

Gastric Hypersecretion....Staff NIDDK 301-654-3810

Gastrinoma....Staff NIDDK 301-654-3810

Gastritis....Staff NIDDK 301-654-3810

Gastrointestinal Disorders....Staff NIDDK 301-654-3810

Gastrointestinal Tract Diseases....Staff NIDDK 301-654-3810

GATT....Hasha, Gene Agri 202-219-0818

Gaucher's Disease....Staff National Gaucher Foundation 800-925-8885

Gaucher's Disease....Staff NINDS 301-496-5751

Gauze, impregnated with medicinals....Randall, Rob USITC 202-205-3366

Gaza....Roberts, Nigel Cnty World Bank 202-473-2241

GBF/DIME System....Staff CENSUS 301-457-1305

Gears....Riedl, Karl CUSTOMS 212-466-5493

Gelatin, articles of....Spalding, Josephine USITC 202-205-3498

Gelatin, edible....Jonnard, Aimison USITC 202-205-3350

Gelatin, inedible....Jonnard, Aimison USITC 202-205-3350

Gelatin, photographic....Jonnard, Aimison USITC 202-205-3350

Gelatin....Brownchweig, Gilbert CUSTOMS 212-466-5744

Gem Stones....Austin, Gordon MINES 202-501-9388

Gems....DeSapio, Vincent USITC 202-205-3435

Gemstones, imitation....Witherspoon, Ricardo USITC 202-205-3489

Gen. Indus. Mach. Nec, Exc 35691....Shaw, Eugene COMMERCE 202-482-2204

GenBank (Genetic Sequence Data Bank)....Staff NLM 301-496-2475

Gene Mapping....Staff NCHGR 301-402-0911

Gene Therapy...Staff NHLBI 301-496-4236

Gene Therapy....Staff NCI 301-496-5583

Gene Therapy....Staff OD/OSPL 301-496-9838

General Agreement on Trade and Tariffs (GATT)....Klein, Cecelia US Trade Rep 202-395-3063

General Aviation Aircraft (Market Support)....Green, Ron COMMERCE 202-482-4228

General Clinical Research Centers Program....Staff NCRR 301-594-7945

General Counsel.....Plyler, Joyce FTC 202-326-2155

General Counsel....Vidas, Sandra M. FTC 202-326-2456

General Counsel's Office....Ballard, Sonia D. FTC 202-326-2669

General Forms...Staff FCC 202-418-0210

General Information - Environmental Issues Hotline....Staff EPA 800-759-4372

General Information....Staff CENSUS 301-457-4100

General Information....Staff FCC 202-418-0190

General Litigation (Assoc. and Business Practices)....Abrahamsen, Dana FTC 202-326-2906

General Litigation (Assoc. and Business Practices)....Alexander, Janice FTC 202-326-2891

General Litigation (Health Care)....Allen, Patricia A. FTC 202-326-3176

General Litigation....Lord, Terry Justice 202-514-1026

General, Medical Sciences, National Institute of....Dieffenbach, Ann NIH 301-496-7301

General Mobile Radio Service General....Staff FCC 800-322-1117

General Mobile Radio Service Technical....Staff FCC 202-418-0680

General Mobile Licenses....Staff FCC 717-337-1212

General Mobile Radio Service....Staff FCC 717-337-1212

Generator Sets/Turbines (Major Proj)....Dollison, Robert COMMERCE 202-482-2733

Be patient. If any phone number is incorrect, call (area code) 555-1212 and request the new listing.

1403

Generators....Cutchin, John USITC 202-205-3396
Genetic counseling....Biesecker, Barbara B. FAES 301-496-3979
Genetic Pancrea. Involv. not due to Cystic Fibrosis....Staff NIDDK 301-496-3583
Genetics, Animal Monitoring....Staff NCRR 301-496-9188
Genetics, Developmental....Adhya, Sankar L. FAES 301-496-2495
Genetics of Aging....Staff NIA 301-496-1752
Genetics....Bale, Sherri J. FAES 301-402-2679
Genetics....Francomano, Clair FAES 301-402-8255
Genetics....Staff Alliance of Genetic Support Groups (AGSG) 800-336-4363
Genetics....Staff NIGMS 301-496-7301
Genetics....Staff NIDCD 301-496-7243
Genetics....Staff NIDR 301-496-4261
Genetics....Staff NINDS 301-496-5751
Genetics....Staff NICHD 301-496-5133
Genital Warts....Staff NIAID 301-496-5717
Genital Herpes....Staff NIAID 301-496-5717
Genome....Staff NCHGR 301-402-0911
Geology....Goodell, Grant UVA 804-4-0559
Geometrical instruments....Goldberg, Gerald PTO 703-308-5443
Geophysical Phenomena Research....Staff NASA 415-604-3937
Geophysical Research....Shannon, Ernie 301-286-6256
Georgia....Carlen, James Cnty Treasury 202-622-0122
Georgia....Djaparidze, Tedo Cnty Embassy 202-393-5959
Georgia....Hall, Christopher L. Cnty World Bank 202-473-4418
Georgia....Kreslins, Dagnija Cnty AID 202-736-4317
Georgia....Levine, Richard Cnty Mines 202-501-9682
Georgia....Makharadze, Gueorgui Cnty Embassy 202-393-5959
Georgia....Skipper, Thomas Cnty USIA 202-619-5057
Georgia....Staff Cnty State 202-647-8671
Georgia....Waxmen-Lenz, Roberta Cnty Export-Import Bank 202-565-3742
Geoscience Research....Coleman, James NEIC 301-903-5822
Geothermal Energy....Jelacic, Al 202-586-5340
Geothermal Loan Guarantee Program....Staff NEIC 202-586-1539
Geriatric Medicine....Staff NIA 301-496-1752
Geriatric Psychiatry....Staff NIA 301-496-1752
Geriatric Psychiatry....Staff NIMH 301-443-4515
Geriatrics....Dutta, Chhanda FAES 301-496-1033
Geriatrics....Staff NIA 301-496-1752
German Measles (Rubella)....Staff NIAID 301-496-5717
Germanium oxides....Conant, Kenneth USITC 202-205-3346
Germanium....Lundy, David USITC 202-205-3439
Germanium....Schnecke, Errol MINES 202-501-9421
Germany, East/Minerals....Zajac, William Cnty Mines 202-501-9671
Germany....Chrobog, Juergen Cnty Embassy 202-298-4000
Germany....Fisher, Brenda Cnty Commerce 202-482-2435
Germany....Gosnell, Peter Cnty Export-Import Bank 202-565-3733
Germany....Kloepfer, Joan Cnty Commerce 202-482-2841
Germany....Larsen, John Commerce 202-482-2434
Germany....Lemaistre, Alice Cnty USIA 202-619-6184
Germany....Mackour, Oscar Cnty Treasury 202-622-0145
Germany....Matussek, Thomas Cnty Embassy 202-298-4000
Germany....Staff Cnty State 202-647-2005
Germfree Rodents....Staff NCRR 301-496-5255
Gerontology....Staff NIA 301-496-1752
Gerson Method....Staff NCI 301-496-5583
Gerstmann's Syndrome....Staff NICHD 301-496-5133
Gestation....Staff NICHD 301-496-5133
Ghana (Accra)....Staff Cnty State 202-647-1596
Ghana/Minerals....van Oss, Hendrik Cnty Mines 202-501-9687
Ghana....Brown, Arthur Peace Corps 202-606-3137
Ghana....Effah-Apenteng, Nana Cnty Embassy 202-686-4520
Ghana....Henke, Debra Cnty Commerce 202-482-5149
Ghana....Maybury-Lewis Anthony Cnty Export-Import Bank 202-565-3739
Ghana....Najm, Fauzia Cnty World Bank 202-473-4981
Ghana....O'Neal, Adrienne Cnty USIA 202-619-6904
Ghana....Palghat, Kathy Cnty Treasury 202-622-0332
Ghana....Spio-Garbrah, Ekwow Cnty Embassy 202-686-4520
Ghana....Swift, Gail Peace Corps 202-606-3136
Ghana....Wilburn, Adolph Cnty AID 202-647-9339
Ghana....Younge, Nathan Cnty TDA 703-875-4357
Giant Cell Arteritis....Staff NEI 301-496-5248
Giardiasis....Staff NIAID 301-496-5717
Gibraltar....Staff Cnty State 202-647-8027
Giftware (Export Promo)....Beckham, Reginald COMMERCE 202-482-5478
Gigantism....Staff NIDDK 301-496-3583
Gilbert's Syndrome....Staff NIDDK 301-496-3583
Gilles de la Tourette's Disease....Staff NINDS 301-496-5751

Gingivitis....Staff NIDR 301-496-4261
Glace fruit and vegetable substances....Frankel, Lee USITC 202-205-3315
Glands....Staff NIDDK 301-496-3583
Glass articles, nspf....Lukes, James USITC 202-205-3426
Glass containers....Lukes, James USITC 202-205-3426
Glass fiber....Lukes, James USITC 202-205-3426
Glass, Flat....Williams, Franklin COMMERCE 202-482-0132
Glass (flat)....Lukes, James USITC 202-205-3426
Glass yarn....Lukes, James USITC 202-205-3426
Glass....Bunin, Jacob CUSTOMS 212-566-5796
Glassblowing....Staff NCRR/BEIP 301-496-5195
Glassware (Issue and Washing)....Staff OD/ORS 301-496-4595
Glassware....Bratland, Rosemarie COMMERCE 202-482-0380
Glassware....McNay, Deborah USITC 202-205-3425
Glassworking machines....Fravel, Dennis USITC 202-205-3404
Glaucoma....Staff NEI 301-496-5248
Glazing compounds....Johnson, Larry USITC 202-205-3351
Gliomas....Staff NINDS 301-496-5751
Global Change Division....Staff EPA 202-233-9190
Global Change (service issues)....Wright, Janet NAL 202-720-3434
Global Changes (technical issues)....Rand, Roberta NAL 301-504-6684
Global Climate Change....Galas, David J. NEIC 301-903-3251
Global Commodity Outlook....Whitton, Carolyn Agri 202-219-0825
Globoid Cell Leukodystrophy....Staff NINDS 301-496-5751
Glomerulonephritis....Staff NIDDK 301-654-4415
Gloves (Work)....Byron, James E. COMMERCE 202-482-4034
Gloves....Burtnik, Brian CUSTOMS 212-466-5880
Gloves....Jones, Jackie USITC 202-205-3466
Glucose Intolerance....Staff NIDDK 301-654-3327
Glue, articles of....Spalding, Josephine USITC 202-205-3498
Glue, of animal or vegetable origin....Jonnard, Aimison USITC 202-205-3350
Glue size....Jonnard, Aimison USITC 202-205-3350
Glue....Brownchweig, Gilbert CUSTOMS 212-466-5744
Gluten Intolerance....Staff NIDDK 301-654-3810
Glycerine....Michels, David USITC 202-205-3352
Glycogen Storage Disease....Staff NICHD 301-496-5133
Glycogen Storage Disease....Staff NIDDK 301-496-3583
Glycols....Michels, David USITC 202-205-3352
Glycoside products....Robinson, Douglas PTO 703-308-2897
Goats....Steller, Rose USITC 202-205-3323
Goiter....Staff NIDDK 301-496-3583
Gold compounds....Greenblatt, Jack USITC 202-205-3353
Gold with options....Rosenfeld, David CFT 312-353-9026
Gold....Lucus, John M. MINES 202-501-9417
Gold....McNay, Deborah USITC 202-205-3425
Golf equipment....Witherspoon, Ricardo USITC 202-205-3496
Gonads....Staff NICHD 301-496-5133
Gonorrhea....Staff NIAID 301-496-5717
Goodpasture's Syndrome....Staff NIDDK 301-496-3583
Goodpasture's Syndrome....Staff NHLBI 301-496-4236
Gout....Staff NIAMS 301-496-8188
Government and Foreign Affairs....Cooper, Alice H. UVA 804-924-4660
Government and Foreign Affairs....Abraham, Henry J. UVA 804-924-3958
Government and Foreign Affairs....Jordan, David C. UVA 804-924-3298
Government Business Operations Issues....Gadsby, J. William GAO 202-512-8387
Government Contracting....Dumaresq, Thomas SBA 202-205-6460
Government-Press Relations, Broadcast Journalism....Holman, Ben UMD 301-405-2420
Government-Press relations....Hiebert, Ray E. UMD 301-405-2419
Government, Productivity in, Prod. and Tech.....Forte, Darlene J. LABOR 202-606-5621
Government....Galbraith, Karl D. ECONOMIC 202-606-9778
Governments, Criminal Justice Statistics....Stevens, Alan CENSUS 301-457-1550
Governments, Employment....Wulf, Henry CENSUS 301-457-1486
Governments, Federal Expenditure Data....McArthur, Robert CENSUS 301-457-1565
Governments, Finance....Wulf, Henry CENSUS 301-457-1486
Governments, Governmental Organization....Kellerman, David CENSUS 301-457-1586
Governments, Operations Support and Analysis....Fanning, William CENSUS 301-457-1515
Governments, Taxation....Wulf, Henry CENSUS 301-457-1486
Graduate Courses....Staff FAES 301-496-7976
Grain Dust Project....Cheney, Sheldon NAL 301-504-4204
Grain Mill Products....Janis, William V. COMMERCE 202-482-2250
Grain products, milled....Reeder, John USITC 202-205-3319
Grain....Conte, Ralph CUSTOMS 212-466-5759

Grains....Pierre-Benoist, John USITC 202-205-3320

Granite....White, Linda USITC 202-205-3427

Grant Application Kits....Staff DRG 301-594-7248

Grants and Awards (General)....Staff DRG 301-594-7248

Grants and Awards (Statistics)....Staff 301-594-7248

Grants Associates Program....Staff OD/OERT 301-496-1736

Grants (Medical Libraries)....Staff NLM 301-496-4221

Granulocytopenia....Staff NIDDK 301-496-3583

Granulomatous Diseases....Staff NIAID 301-496-5717

Grape Cure....Staff NCI 301-496-5583

Grapefruit oil (essential oil)....Land, Eric USITC 202-205-3349

Graphite....Taylor, Harold A. MINES 202-501-9754

Graphite....White, Linda USITC 202-205-3427

Grasslands....Staff FWS 703-358-2043

Grateful Med (Software for Information Retrieval)....Staff NLM 301-496-6308

Grave's Disease (Eye Complications)....Staff NEI 301-496-5248

Grave's Disease (General Information)....Staff NIDDK 301-496-3583

Grease, lubricating....Foreso, Cynthia USITC 202-205-3348

Great Lakes Fisheries....Staff FWS 703-358-1718

Great Lakes MTC (Manufacturing Technology Center)....Sutherland, George H. NIST 216-432-5300

Greece (Athens)....Staff Cnty State 202-647-6113

Greece/Minerals....Zajac, William Cnty Mines 202-501-9671

Greece....Corro, Ann Cnty Commerce 202-482-3945

Greece....Holloway, Barbara Cnty Treasury 202-622-0098

Greece....Hutchings, Dayna Cnty Export-Import Bank 202-565-3737

Greece....Kokossis, Constantin Cnty Embassy 202-939-5800

Greece....Santoro, Eugene Cnty USIA 202-619-6582

Greece....Tsilas, Loucas Cnty Embassy 202-939-5800

Greenhouse Gases....Patrinus, Aristides NEIC 301-903-3251

Greenland/Minerals....Zajac, William Cnty Mines 202-501-9672

Greenland....Staff Cnty State 202-647-5669

Greensand....Searls, James P. MINES 202-501-9407

Greeting Cards....Bratland, Rose Marie COMMERCE 202-482-0380

Grenada (St. George's)....Staff Cnty State 202-647-2621

Grenada....Brooks, Michelle Cnty Commerce 202-482-2527

Grenada....Marcus, Anthony Cnty Treasury 202-622-1218

Grenada....Modeste, Denneth Cnty Embassy 202-265-2561

Grenada....Nallari, Raj R. Cnty World Bank 202-473-8697

Grenada....Rabchevsky, George Cnty Mines 202-501-9670

Grenada....Wilkins, Michele Cnty Export-Import Bank 202-565-3743

Grenadines....Layne, Kingsley Cnty Embassy 202-462-7806

Grenadines....Marcus, Anthony Cnty Treasury 202-622-1218

Grenadines....Nallari, Raj R. Cnty World Bank 202-473-8697

Grenadines....Norris, Cecily A. Cnty Embassy 202-462-7846

Grief....Staff Grief Recovery Hotline 800-445-4808

Grinding machines....Greene, William USITC 202-205-3405

Ground fish....Corey, Roger USITC 202-205-3327

Ground Water and Drinking Water....Staff EPA 202-250-5543

Ground Water Exploration and Development....Wheeler, Frederica COMMERCE 202-482-3509

Ground Water Protection....Staff EPA 202-260-7077

Group Quarters, Population....Smith, Denise CENSUS 301-457-2378

Growth and Development....Staff NICHD 301-496-5133

Growth Hormone Deficiency....Staff NIDDK 301-496-3583

Growth Hormone Deficiency....Staff NICHD 301-496-5133

Guadeloupe (Basse-Terre)....Staff Cnty State 202-647-2620

Guadeloupe/Minerals....Rabchevsky, George Cnty Mines 202-501-9670

Guadeloupe....Brooks, Michelle Cnty Commerce 202-482-2527

Guatemala (Guatemala City)....Staff Cnty State 202-647-1145

Guatemala/Minerals....Velasco, Pablo Cnty Mines 202-501-9677

Guatemala....Anne McKinney Cnty TDA 703-875-4357

Guatemala....Bayly, Rachel Cnty Treasury 202-622-1266

Guatemala....Berz, Cristina N. Cnty World Bank 202-473-3901

Guatemala....Erlandson, Barbara Peace Corps 202-606-3624

Guatemala....Lee, Helen Cnty Commerce 202-482-2527

Guatemala....Mulet, Edmond Cnty embassy 202-745-4952

Guatemala....Opstein, Sally Cnty USIA 202-619-5864

Guatemala....Toriello, Magdalena Cnty Embassy 202-745-4953

Guatemala....Vandenbos, James Cnty AID 202-647-9541

Guatemala....Wilkins, Michele Cnty Export-Import Bank 202-565-3743

Guest Researchers (Foreign)....Staff FIC 301-496-6166

Guide dog....Staff Guide Dog Foundation for the Blind 800-548-4337

Guide for the Care and Use of Laboratory Animals....Staff NCI 301-496-5545

Guide to Grants and Contracts....Staff OD 301-496-1789

Guides....Young, Gary CENSUS 301-457-1221

Guillain-Barre Syndrome (Polyneuritis)....Staff NINDS 301-496-5751

Guinea Bissau....Barber, Ed Cnty Treasury 202-622-1730

Guinea Bissau....Cabral, Alfredo Lopes Cnty Embassy 202-872-4222

Guinea Bissau....Younge, Nathan Cnty TDA 703-875-4357

Guinea Bissau...Garcia, Ligia Maria Cnty Embassy 202-265-6901

Guinea Bissau (Bissau)....Staff Cnty State 202-647-4567

Guinea Bissau...Michelin, Philip Cnty Commerce 202-482-4388

Guinea Bissau....Baily, Jess Cnty USIA 202-619-5900

Guinea Bissau....Edwards, Jennifer R. Cnty World Bank 202-473-4875

Guinea Bissau....Waxman-Lenz, Roberta Cnty Export-Import Bank 202-565-3742

Guinea Bissau....Wickman, Cam Cnty AID 202-647-6335

Guinea Bissau/Minerals....Dolley, Thomas Cnty Mines 202-501-9690

Guinea (Conakry)....Staff Cnty State 202-647-3407

Guinea/Minerals....Izon, David Cnty Mines 202-501-9674

Guinea....Ansoumane, Camara Cnty Embassy 202-483-9420

Guinea....Baily, Jess Cnty USIA 202-619-5900

Guinea....Barber, Ed Cnty Treasury 202-622-1730

Guinea....Bezek, Jill Cnty TDA 703-875-4357

Guinea....Esposito, Dina Cnty AID 202-647-7887

Guinea....Martinez, Carmen Cnty World Bank 202-473-4734

Guinea....Michelin, Philip Cnty Commerce 202-482-4388

Guinea....Trouba, Larry Peace Corps 202-606-3695

Guinea....Waxman-Lenz, Roberta Cnty Export-Import Bank 202-565-3742

Guinea...Barry, Elhadj Boubacar Cnty Embassy 202-483-9420

Gulf Corporation Council....Staff Cnty State 202-647-6562

Gum Disease....Staff NIDR 301-496-4261

Gums and resins....Reeder, John USITC 202-205-3319

Gun cotton....Johnson, Larry USITC 202-205-3351

Gun tracing....Staff ATF 304-274-4100

Gunpowder....Johnson, Larry USITC 202-205-3351

Guns and Ammunition....Vanderwolf, John COMMERCE 202-482-0348

Gut, articles of....Spalding, Josephine USITC 202-205-3498

Gut; catgut, whip gut, oriental gut, and wormgut....Ludwick, David USITC 202-205-3329

Guyana (Georgetown)....Staff Cnty State 202-647-2621

Guyana/Minerals....Doan, David Cnty Mines 202-501-9678

Guyana....Boonma, Sawai Cnty World Bank 202-473-3058

Guyana....Brooks, Michelle Cnty Commerce 202-482-2527

Guyana....Feingold, David Cnty AID 202-647-4106

Guyana....Ishmael, Mohammed Ali Odeen Cnty Embassy 202-265-6900

Guyana....John Herrman Cnty TDA 703-875-4357

Guyana....Korff, Michael Cnty USIA 202-619-6835

Guyana....Marcus, Anthony Cnty Treasury 202-622-1218

Guyana....Wilkins, Michele Cnty Export-Import Bank 202-565-3743

Gynecological Research....Nelson, Lawrence FAES 301-496-4686

Gynecology....Staff NICHD 301-496-5133

Gynecomastia....Staff NICHD 301-496-5133

Gynecomastia....Staff NIDDK 301-496-3583

Gypsum board....Hoffmeier, Bill USITC 202-205-3321

Gypsum....Austin, Gordon MINES 202-501-9388

Gypsum....White, Linda USITC 202-205-3427

Gyrate Atrophy....Staff NEI 301-496-5248

H

Habeas Corpus....Kaplan, Carol Justice Stat 202-307-0759

Habitat Management....Staff FWS 703-358-1718

Habitat Models....Staff FWS 703-358-1710

Habitat Resources Research....Staff FWS 703-358-1710

Hafnium....Gambogi, Joseph MINES 202-501-9390

Hafnium....Lundy, David USITC 202-205-3439

Hailey's Disease....Staff NIDDK 301-496-3583

Hair, articles of.... USITC 202-205-3498

Hair curlers, nonelectric....Burns, Gail USITC 202-205-3501

Hair loss....Staff NIAMS 301-496-8188

Hair ornaments....Brownchweig, Gilbert CUSTOMS 212-466-5744

Hair ornaments....Burns, Gail USITC 202-205-2501

Hair Spray....Staff FDA 301-245-1061

Hair Testing (Drug Abuse)....Staff NIDA 301-443-6245

Hair....Steller, Rose USITC 202-205-3323

Haiti/Minerals....Rabchevsky, George Cnty Mines 202-501-9678

Haiti (Port-au-Prince)....Staff Cnty State 202-736-4707

Haiti....Almaguer, Antoinette Peace Corps 202-606-3322

Haiti....Casimir, Jean Cnty Embassy 202-332-4090

Haiti....Fluckiger, Stefan Cnty World Bank 202-473-0093

Haiti....Geiser, Barbara Cnty Treasury 202-622-1271

Haiti....Head, Alfred Cnty USIA 202-619-6835

Be patient. If any phone number is incorrect, call (area code) 555-1212 and request the new listing.

1405

Haiti....Joseph, Louis Harold Cnty Embassy 202-332-4092

Haiti....Siegelman, Mark Cnty Commerce 204-482-5680

Haiti....Wilkins, Michele Cnty Export-Import Bank 202-565-3743

Halides, nonmetallic....Conant, Kenneth USITC 202-205-3346

Hallervorden-Spatz Disease....Staff NINDS 301-496-5751

Hallucinogens....Staff NIDA 301-443-6245

Halogenated hydrocarbons....Michels, David USITC 202-205-3352

Halogens....Conant, Kenneth USITC 202-205-3346

Hand/Edge Tools Ex Mach TI/Saws....Abrahams, Edward COMMERCE 202-482-0312

Hand, Foot, and Mouth Disease....Staff NIAID 301-496-5717

Hand Saws, Saw Blades....Abrahams, Edward COMMERCE 202-482-0312

Hand tools: household....Brandon, James USITC 202-205-3433

Hand tools with self-contained motor....Cutchin, John USITC 202-205-3396

Hand tools: other....Brandon, James USITC 202-205-3433

Hand Tools....Birnbaum, Melvyn CUSTOMS 212-466-5487

Hand-Schueller-Christian Syndrome....Staff NHLBI 301-496-4236

Handbags....Byron, James E. COMMERCE 202-482-4034

Handbags....Gorman, Kevin CUSTOMS 212-466-5893

Handbags....Seastrum, Carl USITC 202-205-3493

Handbook, Occupational Outlook, Empl. Projections....Pilot, Michael LABOR 202-606-5703

Handicapped Discrimination....Haynes, Marcella OCR 202-619-0671

Handicapped (severely)....Staff National Institute for Rehabilitation Engineering (NIRE) 800-736-2216

Handicapped....Staff ABLEDATA 800-227-0126

Handicapped....Staff NARHA 800-369-7433

Handicapped....Staff National Information Center for Children and Youth with Handicaps (NICCYH) 800-695-0285

Handkerchiefs....Hamey, Amy USITC 202-205-3465

Handkerchiefs....Jones, Jackie USITC 202-205-3466

Handwork yarns: cotton....Warlick, William USITC 202-205-3459

Handwork yarns: manmade fibers....Warlick, William USITC 202-205-3459

Handwork yarns: wool....Shelton, Linda USITC 202-205-3457

Hansen's Disease....Staff NIAID 301-496-5717

Happy Puppet Syndrome....Staff NINDS 301-496-5751

Harada's Disease....Staff NEI 301-496-5248

Harassing Telephone Calls....Staff FCC 202-632-7553

Hard Surfaced Floor Coverings....McCauley, Patrick COMMERCE 202-482-0132

Hard-to-Reach Populations....Staff NIDA 301-443-6245

Hardboard....Hoffmeier, Bill USITC 202-205-3321

Hardening of the Arteries....Staff NHLBI 301-496-4236

Hashimoto's Disease....Staff NIDDK 301-496-3583

Hashimoto's Disease....Staff NHLBI 301-496-4236

Hats....Hamey, Amy USITC 202-205-3465

Hats....Jones, Jackie USITC 202-205-3466

Hay Fever....Staff NIAID 301-496-5717

Hay....Baker, Allen Agri 202-219-0839

Hay....Tice, Thomas Agri 202-219-0840

Hazard Screening....Giles, Ken CPSC 301-504-0580

Hazardous Chemical Spills....Staff FWS 703-358-2148

Hazardous materials....Chipkevich, Bob NTSB 202-382-6585

Hazardous Materials....Eldridge, K USCG 202-267-1577

Hazardous Site Evaluation....Staff EPA 202-603-8850

Hazardous Substances Information Office....Siegel, Sidney NLM 301-496-5022

Hazardous Substances Information....Staff NLM 301-496-1131

Hazardous substances....DeBerry, Elizabeth FAES 301-496-5022

Hazardous Waste Cleanups....Staff EPA 703-603-8710

Hazardous Waste Disposal Unit....Staff EPA 202-307-8833

Hazardous Waste Disposal....Lytle, Jill NEIC 202-586-0370

Hazardous Waste Enforcement - General....Staff EPA 703-412-9810

Hazardous Waste Ombudsman Hotline....Staff EPA 800-262-7937

Hazardous Waste Publications....Staff EPA 703-603-8710

Hazardous Waste Spills - Emergency Response....Staff EPA 202-260-9361

Hazardous Waste - Superfund....Staff EPA 703-412-9810

Hazardous Waste Transporting Generating or Permits....Staff EPA 202-233-9160

Hazardous Wastes....Staff 404-639-0615

Head Injuries....Staff National Head Injury Foundation 800-444-6443

Head Injury....Staff NINDS 301-496-5751

Head Injury....Staff NIDCD 301-496-7243

Head Lice (Pediculosis)....Staff NIAID 301-496-5717

Head Start...Kharfen, Michael ACF 202-401-9215

Headache....Staff NINDS 301-496-5751

Headaches....Staff New England Center for Headache (NECH) 800-245-0088

Headaches....Staff National Headache Foundation (NHF) 800-843-2256

Headwear....Hamey, Amy USITC 202-205-3465

Headwear....Jones, Jackie USITC 202-205-3466

Headwear....Weiss, Martin CUSTOMS 212-466-5881

Health and Environmental Research....Patterson, Elsie NEIC 301-903-2987

Health and Life Insurance, Comp. and Working Condition....Blostin, Allan LABOR 202-606-6240

Health and medical services....Johnson, Christopher USITC 202-205-3488

Health care industry advancements....Staff Medical Awareness Association (MAA) 800-899-0005

Health Care - Nurse....Brooke, Joan FTC 202-326-2120

Health Care Policy and Research, Agency for....Gaus, Clifton R. AHCPR 301-594-6662

Health Care Policy and Research, Agency for....Gaus, Clifton R. AHCPR 301-594-6662

Health Care Resources....Shaffer, Sylvia HRSA 301-443-3376

Health Care Technology....Holohan, Thomas AHCPR 301-594-4023

Health Care....Staff Agency for Health Care Policy and Research Clearinghouse....Staff (AHCPR) 800-358-9295

Health Effects Division....Staff EPA 202-305-7351

Health Effects of Electricity Transmission....Brewer, Robert NEIC 202-586-2828

Health Expenditures (U.S. Totals)....Hardy, Robert HCFA 202-966-3206

Health Financing Issues....Ratner, Jonathan GAO 202-512-7107

Health Information Programs Development, Dir. of....Siegel, Elliot R. NLM 301-496-8834

Health Maintenance Organizations (HMOs)....Hardy, Robert HCFA 202-966-3206

Health Manpower Education....Staff HRSA/BHPr 301-827-3365

Health Policy, Office of....Staff EPA 202-260-5900

Health Professionals....Staff HRSA/BHPr 301-827-3365

Health Professions and Health Profession Loans....Staff HRSA 301-827-3365

Health Promotion and Disease Prevention....Stoiber, Susanne ASH 202-205-0152

Health Promotion and Disease Prevention....Sims, Anne CDC 404-639-3286

Health Promotion....Staff NINR 301-496-0207

Health Services Research Information....Cahn, Marjorie NLM 301-496-0176

Health Statistics, National Center for....Sandra, Smith NCHS/CDC 301-436-7551

Health Surveys....Mangold, Robert CENSUS 301-457-3879

Health....Francis, Simon COMMERCE 202-482-2697

Health....Staff National Health Information Center (NHIC) 800-336-4797

Health....Staff American Social Health Association (ASHA) 800-227-8922

Health....Staff HHS Hotline 800-368-5779

Healthy Start....McCann, Thurma HRSA 301-443-0543

Hearing Aid....Staff International Hearing Society (HS) 800-521-5247

Hearing impaired....Staff Tripod Grapevine 800-352-8888

Hearing impaired....Staff Hearing Helpline 800-424-8576

Hearing Loss and Aging....Staff NIA 301-496-1752

Hearing Loss and Aging....Staff NINDS 301-496-5751

Hearing Loss and Aging....Staff CC 301-496-5368

Hearing....Staff Occupational Hearing Service (OHS) 800-222-3277

Hearing....Staff Hearing Helpline 800-327-9355

Hearing....Staff American Speech-Language-Hearing Association Consumer Helpline (ASLHA) 800-638-8255

Hearing....Staff National Hearing Aid Society (NHAS) 800-521-5247

Hearing....Staff NINDS 301-496-5751

Hearing....Staff NIDCD 301-496-7243

Heart Attacks....Staff NHLBI 301-496-4236

Heart Block....Staff NHLBI 301-496-4236

Heart Disease....Staff NHLBI 301-496-4236

Heart-Lung Machines....Staff NHLBI 301-496-4236

Heart, Lung and Blood Inst.....Bellicha, Terry NIH 301-496-4236

Heart Murmurs....Staff NHLBI 301-496-4236

Heart Pacemaker....Staff NHLBI 301-496-4236

Heart Transplantation....Staff NHLBI 301-496-4236

Heart Valves....Staff NHLBI 301-496-4236

Heart....Staff American Heart Association (AHA) 800-242-8721

Heart....Staff Heart Information Service (HIS) 800-292-2221

Heat-insulating articles....DeSapio, Vincent USITC 202-205-3435

Heat process equipment....Lusi, Susan USITC 202-205-2334

Heat-Resistant Materials....Staff NASA 804-864-6120

Heat Stroke and Aging....Staff NIA 301-496-1752

Heat Tapes....Staff CPSC 301-504-0580

Heat Treating Equipment....Kemper, Alexis COMMERCE 202-482-5956

Heating Equipment Ex. Furnaces....Bodson, John COMMERCE 202-482-3509

Heavy Metals (Cadmium, Zinc, Mercury)....Staff NIEHS 919-541-3345

Helicopter Services....Johnson, C. William COMMERCE 202-482-5012

Helicopters, Market Support....Smarkanich, Audrey COMMERCE 202-482-2835

Helicopters (Trade Promo)....Vacant COMMERCE 202-482-1228

Helicopters....Green, Ron COMMERCE 202-482-4222

Heliotropin....Land, Eric USITC 202-205-3349

Helium, Division of Helium Field Operations....Leachman, William D. MINES 806-376-2604

Helium....Conant, Kenneth USITC 202-205-3346
Helpline (Workplace, Drug-Related)...Staff NIDA 301-443-6245
Hemangiomas....Staff NHLBI 301-496-4236
Hematology....Finlayson, John FAES 301-496-5544
Hemiplegia....Staff NINDS 301-496-5751
Hemochromatosis....Staff NHLBI 301-496-4236
Hemodialysis....Staff NIDDK 301-654-4415
Hemoglobin Genetics....Staff NIDDK 301-496-3583
Hemoglobinopathies....Staff NIDDK 301-496-3583
Hemolytic Anemia....Staff NHLBI 301-496-4236
Hemolytic Anemia....Staff NIDDK 301-496-3583
Hemolytic Disease (Newborn)....Staff NICHD 301-496-5133
Hemolytic Disease (Newborn)....Staff NHLBI 301-496-4236
Hemophilia and AIDS....Staff HANDI 800-424-2634
Hemophilia....Staff NHLBI 301-496-4236
Hemophilus Influenzae....Staff NIAID 301-496-5717
Hemorrhagic Diseases....Staff NHLBI 301-496-4236
Hemorrhagic Diseases....Staff NIDDK 301-496-3583
Hemorrhoids....Staff NIDDK 301-654-3810
Hemorrhoids....Staff NHLBI 301-496-4236
Hemosiderosis....Staff NHLBI 301-496-4236
Henoch-Schonlein Purpura....Staff NIAID 301-496-5717
Henoch-Schonlein Purpura....Staff NICHD 301-496-5133
Hepatitis (Treatment of Acute or Chronic)....Staff NIAID 301-496-5717
Hepatitis (Treatment of Acute or Chronic)....Staff NIDDK 301-654-3810
Hepatitis....Margolis, Harold CDC 404-639-2339
Hepatitis....Staff American Liver Foundation Hepatitis Hotline 800-223-0179
Hepatitis....Staff NIAID 301-496-5717
Hepatitis....Staff NIDDK 301-496-3583
Herbicide-Fungicides....Staff EPA 202-305-6250
Herbicides....Hollrah, Glen H. PTO 703-308-4552
Heredity and Cancer....Staff NCI 301-496-5583
Hereditary Angioedema....Staff NIAID 301-496-5717
Hereditary Cerebellar Ataxia....Staff NINDS 301-496-5751
Hereditary Emphysema....Staff NHLBI 301-496-4236
Hereditary Hemorrhagic Telangiectasia....Staff 301-496-4236
Hereditary Movement Disorders....Staff NINDS 301-496-5751
Hereditary Nervous System Tumors....Staff NINDS 301-496-5751
Hereditary Spastic Paraplegia....Staff NINDS 301-496-5751
Hereditary Spherocytosis....Staff NHLBI 301-496-4236
Heritable Disorders of Connective Tissue....Staff NIAMS 301-496-8188
Heritable Disorders of Connective Tissue....Staff NHLBI 301-496-4236
Hernias (Abdominal, Bladder)....Staff NIDDK 301-654-3810
Herniated Disc....Staff NIAMS 301-496-8188
Heroin....Staff NIDA 301-443-4265
Herpes (Nervous System Involvement)....Staff NINDS 301-496-5751
Herpes Simplex (Eye Effects)....Staff NEI 301-496-5248
Herpes Simplex Virus (Oral Lesions)....Staff NIDR 301-496-4261
Herpes Simplex Virus (Type II)....Staff NIAID 301-496-5717
Herpes Zoster (Shingles)....Staff NINDS 301-496-5751
Herpes Zoster-Varicella Infections....Staff NIAID 301-496-5717
Herzegovina....Alkalaj, Sven Cnty Embassy 202-833-3612
Herzegovina....Dzirlo, Sakir Cnty Embassy 202-833-3613
Herzegovina....Steblez, Walter cnty MINES 202-501-9672
Heterocyclic Compounds....Brady, Thomas CUSTOMS 212-466-5747
Hiatal Hernia....Staff NIDDK 301-496-3583
Hiccups....Staff NHLBI 301-496-4236
Hide cuttings....Trainor, Cynthia USITC 202-205-3354
Hides....Steller, Rose USITC 202-205-3323
High Alpha Technology....Staff NASA 805-866-8569
High Blood Pressure....Staff NIA 301-496-1752
High Blood Pressure....Staff NHLBI 301-496-4236
High-Density Lipoproteins (HDL)....Staff NHLBI 301-496-4236
High Energy Fuel Research....Rachul, Lori NASA 216-443-8806
High School Program for Minorities....Staff NCRR 301-594-7947
High School Senior Survey....Staff NIDA 301-443-4265
High Tech Trade, U.S. Competitiveness....Hatter, Victoria L. COMMERCE 202-482-3895
High Voltage Electron Microscopy....Staff NCRR 301-594-7934
High Voltage Electron Microscopy....Staff NCRR 301-594-7934
High Voltage Transmission Lines....Klunder, Kurt NEIC 202-586-2826
Highway Advisory Radio....Staff FCC 202-418-0620
Highway Institute, National....Shrieves, George M FHWA 703-285-2770
Highway safety....Bennett, Clark FHWA 202-366-1153
Highway safety....Osterman, Joseph NTSB 202-382-6854
Highway Statistics....Walsh, William NHTSA 202-366-1503
Hill-Burton Health Facilities....Shaffer, Sylvia HRSA 301-443-3376

Hip Replacement....Staff NIAMS 301-496-8188
Hirsutism....Staff NIAMS 301-496-8188
Hispanic and Other Ethnic Population Statistics....Staff CENSUS 301-457-4100
Histiocytosis....Staff Histiocytosis Association of America (HAA) 800-548-2758
Histiocytosis....Staff NHLBI 301-496-4236
Histiocytosis....Staff NCI 301-496-5583
Histoplasmosis (Eye)....Staff NEI 301-496-5248
Histoplasmosis....Staff NIAID 301-496-5717
Historical Medical Prints and Photographs....Staff NLM 301-496-5961
Historical Prints and Photographs....Keister, Lucinda NLM 301-496-5961
Historical statistics....Staff CENSUS 301-457-1166
Historical Statistics....Staff CENSUS 301-457-1166
History of Medicine....Teigen, Philip NLM 301-496-5405
History of Medicine....Staff NLM 301-496-5405
History of NIH....Staff OD/OC 301-496-6610
History....Braun, Herbert UVA 701-924-6397
HIV/AIDS....Jaffe, Harold W. CDC 404-639-2000
HIV immunoassays....Nucker, Christine M PTO 703-308-4028
HIV Infection....Staff NCI 301-496-5583
HIV Infection....Staff NIAID 301-496-5717
HIV Injection....Staff Project Inform 800-334-7422
HIV: Oral Complications....Staff NIDR 301-496-4261
Hives....Staff NIAID 301-496-5717
Hoarseness....Staff NIDCD 301-496-7243
Hoaxes-Broadcast....Staff FCC 202-418-1430
Hodgkin's Disease....Staff NCI 301-496-5583
Hogs (live) with options....Prentice, Jon CFT 312-353-8647
Hogs....Newman, Douglas USITC 202-205-3328
Hoists/Overhead Cranes....Wiening, Mary COMMERCE 202-482-4708
Holy See....Cacciavillan, Most Reverend Agostino Cnty Embassy 202-333-7121
Home and Community Based Care (Medicaid)....Hardy, Robert HCFA 202-966-3206
Home Care, Nursing Home Care, Hospital Care....Staff NCNR 301-496-0526
Home furnishings....Sweet, Mary Elizabeth USITC 202-205-3455
Home Health Care....Hardy, Robert HCFA 202-966-3206
Home Mortgage Disclosure....Wood, John C FRS 202-452-2412
Home safety....Staff CPSC 301-504-0580
Homeless Population....Taeuber, Cynthia CENSUS 301-457-2378
Homeless youth....Staff Covenant House 800-999-9999
Homeless....Kharfen, Michael ACF 202-401-9215
Homeless....Staff HUD 202-708-1480
Homeless....Staff NIDA 301-443-4265
Homelessness....Staff National Resource Center on Homelessness and Mental Illness 800-444-7415
Homocystinuria....Staff NHLBI 301-496-4236
Homocystinuria....Staff NICHD 301-496-5133
Honduras/Minerals....Rabchevsky, George Cnty Mines 202-501-9670
Honduras (Tegucigalpa)....Staff Cnty State 202-647-4980
Honduras....Anne McKinney Cnty TDA 703-875-4357
Honduras....Baier, Kraig Cnty AID 202-647-9555
Honduras....Bowyer, Nicolette Cnty World Bank 202-473-8724
Honduras....Flores Bermudez, Roberto Cnty Embassy 202-966-7702
Honduras....Lee, Helen Cnty Commerce 202-482-2528
Honduras....Lostumbo, Julie Peace Corps 202-606-3620
Honduras....Murray, Mandy Peace Corps 202-606-3321
Honduras....Opstein, Sally Cnty USIA 202-619-5864
Honduras....Parkinson, Katherine Cnty Treasury 202-622-5292
Honduras....Rodezno-Fuentes, Salvador Cnty Embassy 202-966-2604
Honduras....Wilkins, Michele Cnty Export-Import Bank 202-565-3743
Honey - Prices....Schuchardt, Rick Agri 220-720-7737
Honey - Prod.....Kruchten, Tom Agri 202-690-4870
Honey....Hoff, Fred Agri 202-219-0883
Hong Kong/Minerals....Tse, Pui-Kwan Cnty Mines 202-501-9696
Hong Kong/trade matters....Cantilina, Amy US Trade Rep 202-395-5050
Hong Kong....Hutchings, Dayna Cnty Export-Import Bank 202-565-3737
Hong Kong....Dwight, Lawrence Cnty Treasury 202-622-0356
Hong Kong....Bakar, Sheila Cnty Commerce 202-482-3932
Hong Kong....Staff Cnty State 202-647-6300
Hoof, articles of....Spalding, Josephine USITC 202-205-3498
Hoofs, crude....Ludwick, David USITC 202-205-3329
Hooks and eyes....Brandon, James USITC 202-205-3433
Hormone Distribution....Staff NIDDK 301-496-3583
Hormones and Cancer....Staff NCI 301-496-5583
Hormones (Sex)....Staff NICHD 301-496-5133
Hormones....Nesbitt, Elizabeth USITC 202-205-3355
Hormones....Staff NIDDK 301-496-3583
Horn, crude....Ludwick, David USITC 202-205-3329

Horn, articles of....Spalding, Josephine USITC 202-205-3498

Horology....Shoop, William M. PTO 703-308-3103

Horse Racing Programming and Advertising....Staff FCC 202-418-0200

Horses....Steller, Rose USITC 202-205-3323

Horticultural machinery....Fravel, Dennis USITC 202-205-3404

Hose and Belting....Prat, Raimundo COMMERCE 202-482-0128

Hose, industrial....Cook, Lee USITC 202-205-3471

Hose, of rubber or plastics....Misurelli, Denby USITC 202-205-3362

Hoses....Mazzola, Joan CUSTOMS 212-466-5880

Hosiery....Linkins, Linda USITC 202-205-3469

Hospice Care....Staff NIA 301-496-1752

Hospice Care....Staff NCI 301-496-5583

Hospice....Hardy, Robert HCFA 202-966-3206

Hospice....Staff National Hospice Organization 800-658-8898

Hospice....Staff Children's Hospice International (CHI) 800-242-4453

Hospice....Staff Hospice Education Institute 800-331-1620

Hospital Administrators....Staff HRSA/BHPr 301-443-2134

Hospital-Based Schools of Nursing....Staff HRSA/BHPr 301-443-2134

Hospital Care Statistics....Pokras, Robert CDC 301-436-7125

Hospital care....Staff Hill-Burton Free Hospital Care Hotline 800-638-0742

Hospital Infections....Staff NIAID 301-496-5717

Hotel and Restaurant Eq., Export Promo.....Kimmel, Edward K. COMMERCE 202-482-3640

Hotels and Motels....Sousane, J. Richard COMMERCE 202-482-4582

Hotline (Fraud and Abuse)....Holtz, Judy IG 202-619-1142

Hourly Compensation Costs, Foreign Countries....Capdevielle, Patricia LABOR 202-606-5654

Household Appliances....Harris, John M. COMMERCE 202-482-1178

Household Articles, Metal....Smyth, James CUSTOMS 212-466-2084

Household Articles Plastic....Rauch, Theodore CUSTOMS 212-466-5892

Household Estimates for States and Counties....Staff CENSUS 301-457-2465

Household Furniture....Hodgen, Donald COMMERCE 202-482-3346

Household Hazardous Waste....Staff EPA 202-260-5649

Household Wealth....Eller, T.J. CENSUS 301-763-8578

Households Touched by Crime....Rand, Michael Justice Stat 202-616-3494

Housewares....Beckham, Reginald COMMERCE 202-482-5478

Housing, American Housing Survey....Montfort, Edward CENSUS 301-763-8551

Housing and Real Estate Industry....Parratt, Shelley SEC 202-942-1840

Housing and Urban Development. Major Proj.....White, Barbara COMMERCE 202-482-4160

Housing, Components of Inventory Change Survey....Williams, Barbara CENSUS 301-763-8551

Housing Construction....Cosslett, Patrick COMMERCE 202-482-5125

Housing, Decennial Census....Bonnette, Robert CENSUS 301-763-8553

Housing, Income Statistics....Staff CENSUS 301-763-8576

Housing, Indian....Staff HUD 202-708-0950

Housing, Information....Bonnette, Robert CENSUS 301-763-8553

Housing Issues....England-Joseph, Judy GAO 202-512-7631

Housing, Market Absorption....Smoler, Anne CENSUS 301-763-8165

Housing, Multifamily....Staff HUD 202-708-2495

Housing, New York City Housing and Vacancy Survey....Fronczek, Peter CENSUS 301-763-8165

Housing, Public....Staff HUD 202-708-0950

Housing, Single Family....Staff HUD 202-708-3175

Housing, Vacancy Data....Collis, Robert CENSUS 301-763-8165

Housing....Staff HUD 800-245-2691

Howard Hughes Medical Institute....Staff 301-215-8500

Hubble Space Telescope (HST)....Katz, Jesse NASA 301-286-5566

Hubble Space Telescope....Villard, Ray NASA 301-338-4514

HUD Fraud Hotline....Staff HUD 800-347-3735

Human Development....Staff NICHD 301-443-5133

Human Genetic Mutant Cell Repository....Staff NIGMS 301-496-7301

Human Papilloma Virus (HPV)....Staff NCI 301-496-5583

Human Papilloma Virus (HPV)....Staff NIAID 301-496-5717

Humane Transport of Fish and Wildlife....Staff FWS 703-358-2095

Hungary (Budapest)....Staff Cnty State 202-647-3238

Hungary/Minerals....Steblez, Walter Cnty Mines 202-501-9671

Hungary....Ann Lien Cnty TDA 703-875-4357

Hungary....Banklaki, Gyorgy Cnty Embassy 202-362-6730

Hungary....Bazala, Razvigor Cnty USIA 202-619-5055

Hungary....Hewer, Ulrich Albert Cnty World Bank 202-473-2279

Hungary....Horvath, Gabor Cnty Embassy 202-362-6730

Hungary....Jackson, Juhan Cnty Treasury 202-622-0766

Hungary....Lockwood, Jennifer Peace Corps 202-606-3607

Hungary....Scheil, Russell Peace Corps 202-606-3606

Hungary....Touhey, Brian Cnty Commerce 202-482-4915

Hungary....Waxman-Lenz, Roberta Cnty Export-Import Bank 202-565-3742

Hunt's Disease....Staff NINDS 301-496-5751

Hunter Education Programs....Staff FWS 703-358-2156

Hunter's Syndrome....Staff NIDDK 301-496-3583

Hunting and Fishing Survey, National....Staff FWS 703-358-2156

Hunting, Refuges....Staff FWS 703-358-2043

Huntington's Disease....Staff Huntington's Disease Society of America (HDSA) 800-345-4372

Huntington's Disease....Staff NINDS 301-496-5751

Hurler's Syndrome....Staff NIDDK 301-496-3583

Hurler's Syndrome....Staff NICHD 301-496-5133

Hyaline Membrane Disease....Staff NICHD 301-496-5133

Hyaline Membrane Disease....Staff NHLBI 301-496-4236

Hybrid....Envall, Roy PTO 703-305-9706

Hydranencephaly....Staff NINDS 301-496-5751

Hydraulics....Riedl, Karl CUSTOMS 212-466-5493

Hydrazine....Conant, Kenneth USITC 202-205-3346

Hydro Power Plants, Major Proj.....Dollison, Robert COMMERCE 202-482-2733

Hydrocarbon Geoscience Research....Hochoheiser, Bill NEIC 202-586-5614

Hydrocarbons....Brady, Thomas CUSTOMS 212-466-5747

Hydrocarbons....Raftery, Jim USITC 202-205-3365

Hydrocephalus....Staff NICHD 301-496-5133

Hydrocephalus....Staff NINDS 301-496-5751

Hydrochloric acid....Trainor, Cynthia USITC 202-205-3354

Hydroelectric Energy....Loose, Ronald NEIC 202-586-5348

Hydroelectric Power Projects....Staff FWS 703-358-2183

Hydroelectric Power....Loose, Ronald NEIC 202-586-5348

Hydrofluoric acid....Trainor, Cynthia USITC 202-205-3354

Hydrogen....Conant, Kenneth USITC 202-205-3346

Hydroxides, inorganic....Conant, Kenneth USITC 202-205-3346

Hygienists (Education)....Staff HRSA/BHPr 301-443-6837

Hyperactivity....Staff NINDS 301-496-5751

Hyperactivity....Staff NIMH 301-443-4513

Hyperactivity....Staff NICHD 301-496-5133

Hyperacusis....Staff NIDCD 301-496-7243

Hyperbaric Chamber - UMD Shock Trauma Center....Staff 410-328-8869

Hyperbaric Oxygenation....Staff NHLBI 301-496-4236

Hyperbilirubinemia....Staff NIDDK 301-496-3583

Hyperbilirubinemia....Staff NICHD 301-496-5133

Hypercalcemia....Staff NIDDK 301-496-3583

Hypercalciuria....Staff NIDDK 301-496-3583

Hypercholesterolemia....Staff NHLBI 301-496-4236

Hyperglycemia....Staff NIDDK 301-496-3583

Hyperkeratosis....Staff NIAMS 301-496-8188

Hyperlipidemia....Staff NHLBI 301-496-4236

Hyperlipoproteinemia....Staff NHLBI 301-496-5343

Hyperparathyroidism....Staff NIDDK 301-496-3583

Hyperpyrexia (heat stroke/heat exhaustion)....Staff NIA 301-496-1752

Hypersensitivity Pneumonitis....Staff NIAID 301-496-5717

Hypersonic Engines....Staff NASA 804-864-3305

Hypersonic Aircraft....James, Donald G. NASA 415-604-3935

Hypertension....Staff NCNR 301-496-0526

Hypertension....Staff NHLBI 301-496-4236

Hyperthermia (heat stroke/heat exhaustion)....Staff NIA 301-496-1752

Hyperthermia....Staff NCI 301-496-5583

Hyperthyroidism....Staff NIDDK 301-496-3583

Hypertriglyceridemia....Staff NHLBI 301-496-4236

Hypertrophic Cardiomyopathy....Staff NHLBI 301-496-4236

Hyperuricemia....Staff NIDDK 301-496-3583

Hyperventilation....Staff NHLBI 301-496-4236

Hypnotics....Nesbitt, Elizabeth USITC 202-205-3355

Hypobetalipoproteinemia....Staff NHLBI 301-496-4236

Hypocomplementemic Glomerulonephritis....Staff NIAID 301-496-5717

Hypogammaglobulinemia....Staff NHLBI 301-496-4236

Hypogeusia Hereditary Deafness....Staff NIDCD 301-496-7243

Hypoglycemia....Staff NIDDK 301-496-3583

Hypoglycemia....Staff NHLBI 301-496-4236

Hypogonadism....Staff NICHD 301-496-5133

Hypogonadism....Staff NIDDK 301-496-3583

Hypokalemia....Staff NHLBI 301-496-4236

Hypokalemic Periodic Paralysis....Staff NINDS 301-496-5751

Hypolipoproteinemia....Staff NIDDK 301-496-3583

Hypoparathyroidism....Staff NIDDK 301-496-3583

Hypopigmentation....Staff National Organization for Albinism and Hypopigmentation 800-473-2310

Hypopituitarism....Staff NIDDK 301-496-3583

Hypoplastic Anemia....Staff NHLBI 301-496-4236

Hyposmia....Staff NIDCD 301-496-7243

Hypospadias....Staff NICHD 301-496-5133
Hypotension....Staff NHLBI 301-496-4236
Hypothalamus....Staff NICHD 301-496-5133
Hypothalamus....Staff NIDDK 301-496-3583
Hypothermia (Accidental)....Staff NIA 301-496-1752
Hypothyroidism, Goitrous....Staff NIA 301-496-3583
Hypotonia....Staff NINDS 301-496-5751
Hypoventilation....Staff NHLBI 301-496-4236
Hypoxia....Staff NHLBI 301-496-4236
Hypsarrhythmia....Staff NINDS 301-496-5751

I

Ice (Methamphetamine)....Staff NIDA 301-443-4265
Iceland Disease....Staff NINDS 301-496-5751
Iceland/Minerals....Plachy, Jozef Cnty Mines 202-501-9673
Iceland (Reykjavik)....Staff Cnty State 202-647-5669
Iceland....Benediktsson, Elinor Cnty Embassy 202-265-6653
Iceland....Gosnell, Peter Cnty Export-Import Bank 202-565-3733
Iceland....Holloway, Barbara Cnty Treasury 202-622-0098
Iceland....Jonsdottir Ward, Margaret Cnty Embassy 202-265-6654
Iceland....Kendall, Maryanne Cnty Commerce 202-482-3254
Iceland....Rankin-Galloway, Honore Cnty USIA 202-619-5283
Ichthyosis....Staff NIAMS 301-496-8188
Idiopathic Autonomic Insufficiency....Staff NHLBI 301-496-4236
Idiopathic Hypertrophic Subaortic Stenosis (IHSS)....Staff NHLBI 301-496-4236
Idiopathic Infantile Arterial Calcification....Staff NHLBI 301-496-4236
Idiopathic Inflammatory Myopathy....Staff NINDS 301-496-5751
Idiopathic Osteoporosis....Staff NIAMS 301-496-8188
Idiopathic Pulmonary Fibrosis....Staff NHLBI 301-496-4236
Idiopathic Thrombocytopenic Purpura (ITP)....Staff NHLBI 301-496-4236
Idiopathic Thrombocytopenic Purpura (ITP)....Staff NIDDK 301-496-3583
IGE....Staff NIAID 301-496-5717
IGE....Staff NIAID 301-496-5717
Ignition equipment....Topolansky, Adam USITC 202-205-3394
Ileitis....Staff NIDDK 301-654-3810
Image analysis....Moore, David K. PTO 703-305-4706
Image Processing....Staff DCRT 301-496-2250
Image Processing....Staff DCRT 301-496-7963
Imaging (Brain)....Staff NINDS 301-496-5751
Imaging....Staff NCRR 301-594-7934
Imaging....Staff NCRR 301-496-4741
Immigration (Legal/Undocumented)....Frenandez, Edward CENSUS 301-457-2103
Immigration....Staff ACF 202-401-9215
Immune Deficiency....Immune Deficiency Foundation....Staff (IDF) 800-296-4433
Immune Deficiency Diseases....Staff NIAID 301-496-5717
Immunization, Disease....Orenstein, Walter A. CDC 404-639-8200
Immunization....Sims, Anne CDC 404-639-3286
Immunizations (Foreign Travel)....Staff CDC 404-639-3286
Immunoassays and other binding assays....Scheiner, Toni PTO 703-308-3983
Immunogens....Nucker, Christine M PTO 703-308-4028
Immunology (Cancer)....Staff NCI 301-496-5583
Immunology....Staff American Academy of Allergy and Immunology (AAAI) 800-822-2762
Immunology....Staff Lung Line 800-222-5864
Immunology....Staff NIAID 301-496-5717
Immunotherapy (Cancer)....Staff NCI 301-496-5583
Impaired Health Professionals....Staff NIDA 301-443-6245
Implantable Defibrillator....Staff NHLBI 301-496-4236
Implants, Lens....Staff NEI 301-496-5248
Impotence....Staff NIDDK 301-654-4415
Impotence....Staff NIMH 301-443-4515
In vivo diagnostics....Hollrah, Glen H. PTO 703-308-4552
In Vitro Fertilization....Staff NICHD 301-496-5133
Inactive Waste Site Cleanup....Duffy, Leo P. NEIC 202-586-7710
Inactive Waste Site Management....Duffy, Leo P. NEIC 202-586-7710
Inappropriate Antidiuretic Hormone Syndrome....Staff NHLBI 301-496-4236
Inborn Errors of Metabolism....Staff NHLBI 301-496-4236
Inborn Errors of Metabolism....Staff NICHD 301-496-5133
Inborn Errors of Metabolism....Staff NINDS 301-496-5751
Inborn Errors of Metabolism....Staff NICHD 301-496-5133
Inborn Heart Defects....Staff NHLBI 301-496-4236
Incapacitation....Greenfeld, Lawrence Justice Stat 202-616-3281
Incapacitation....Langan, Patrick Justice Stat 202-616-3490
Incident Response....Congel, Frank NRC 301-415-7476
Incidental Radiation Devices....Staff FCC 202-653-6288

Incinerators....Staff EPA 703-308-8434
Income Security Issues....Ross, Jane GAO 202-512-7215
Incontinence....Staff Simon Foundation 800-237-4666
Incontinence....Staff NIDDK 301-654-4415
Incontinence....Staff NIA 301-496-1752
Incontinent people....Staff Help for Incontinent People 800-252-3337
Incontinentia Pigmenti....Staff NINDS 301-496-5751
Independent States/trade matters....Underwood, Jennifer US Trade Rep 202-395-4620
Index Medicus....Staff NLM 301-496-6308
Indexes of Fuels and Utilities, Monthly....Adkins, Robert LABOR 202-606-6985
India/Minerals....Lyday, Travis Cnty Mines 202-501-9695
India (New Delhi)....Staff Cnty State 202-647-2141
India/trade matters....Ruzicka, Rick US Trade Rep 202-395-6813
India....Gradisher, Thomas Cnty USIA 202-619-5529
India....Hardy, Nancy Cnty AID 202-647-6967
India....Hutchings, Dayna Cnty Export-Import Bank 202-565-3737
India....Nickel, William C. Cnty World Bank 202-458-0336
India....Quinn, Lois Cnty Treasury 202-622-0092
India....Ray, Siddhartha Cnty Embassy 202-939-7000
India....Sibal, Kanwal Cnty Embassy 202-939-7000
India....Simmons, John/Crown, John/Gilman, Tim Cnty Commerce 202-482-2954
Indian Fisheries Resources/Treaties....Staff FWS 703-358-1718
Indian Health....Kendrick, Tony IHS 301-44-3593
Indian Health....Trujillo, Michael IHS 301-443-1083
Indian Housing....Staff HUD 202-708-0950
Indian Hunting, Migratory Birds....Staff FWS 703-358-1714
Indian Resources....Meshorer, Hank Justice 202-272-4111
Indian Wildlife Assistance....Staff FWS 703-358-1718
Indians - Administration for Native Americans....Kharfen, Michael ACF 202-401-9215
Indigent Defense....Gaskins, Carla Justice Stat 202-508-8546
Indium....Brown, Robert Jr. MINES 202-501-9577
Indium....Lundy, David USITC 202-205-3439
Indo-China....Vermillion, James Cnty AID 202-647-4528
Indonesia (Jakarta)....Staff Cnty State 202-647-3276
Indonesia/Minerals....Kuo, Chin Cnty Mines 202-501-9693
Indonesia....Freeman, Kay Cnty AID 202-647-4507
Indonesia....Garrity, Moique P. Cnty World Bank 202-473-4952
Indonesia....Gilroy, Meg Cnty USIA 202-619-5836
Indonesia....Goddin, Karen Cnty Commerce 202-482-3877
Indonesia....Imam, Fahmila Cnty Export-Import Bank 202-565-3738
Indonesia....Rahman, Talaat Cnty TDA 703-875-4357
Indonesia....Shelton, Alison Cnty Treasury 202-622-0354
Indonesia....Siregar, Arifin Mohamad Cnty Embassy 202-775-5200
Indonesia....Sukarna, Muchamad Cnty Embassy 202-775-5200
Indoor Air Division, National Program....Staff EPA 202-233-9030
Indoor Air Division....Staff EPA 202-233-9030
Indoor Air Quality....Persily, Andrew K. NIST 301-975-6418
Induced Movement Disorders....Staff NINDS 301-496-5751
Industrial arts....Word, A. Hugo PTO 703-305-3171
Industrial ceramics....DeSapio, Vincent USITC 202-205-3435
Industrial Chemicals and Cancer....Staff NCI 301-496-5583
Industrial Chemicals (Effects on Human Health)....Staff NIEHS 919-541-3345
Industrial Chemicals....Hurt, William A. COMMERCE 202-482-0128
Industrial Classification, Est. Surv, Natl. Emp/Unemp....Getz, Patricia LABOR 202-606-6521
Industrial diamonds....DeSapio, Vincent USITC 202-205-3435
Industrial Drives/Gears....Reiss, Richard COMMERCE 202-482-3489
Industrial electric furnaces....Reynolds, Bruce A. PTO 703-308-3305
Industrial/fine arts....Douglas, Alan PTO 703-305-3255
Industrial gases....Conant, Kenneth USITC 202-205-3346
Industrial gases....Hurt, William COMMERCE 202-482-0128
Industrial hygiene....Gaunce, Jean A. CDC 404-639-3415
Industrial hygiene....Staff OD/ORS 301-496-2960
Industrial licenses....Staff FCC 717-337-1212
Industrial Minerals, Assistant Branch Chief....Morse, D. MINES 202-501-9402
Industrial Minerals, Assistant Branch Chief....Mozian, Z. MINES 202-501-9396
Industrial Minerals, Chief, Branch of....Barsotti, Aldo F. MINES 202-501-9399
Industrial Organic Chemicals....Hurt, William COMMERCE 202-482-0128
Industrial Prices and Price Indexes, Asst. Commis.....Staff LABOR 202-606-7700
Industrial Process Controls....Bodson, John COMMERCE 202-482-0681
Industrial Process Controls....Nealon, Marguerite COMMERCE 202-482-0411
Industrial Productivity....Swink, Denis NEIC 202-586-9232
Industrial Solid (Non Hazardous) Waste....Staff EPA 202-260-4807
Industrial Structure....Davis, Lester A. COMMERCE 202-482-4924
Industrial Technology Transfer....Sisson, Kurt NEIC 202-586-6750

Be patient. If any phone number is incorrect, call (area code) 555-1212 and request the new listing.

1409

Industrial Trucks....Wiening, Mary COMMERCE 202-482-4608

Industry and Commodity Classification....Kristoff, James CENSUS 301-457-2813

Industry Data Centers....Rowe, John CENSUS 301-457-1305

Industry - Occupational Employment Matrix....Turner, Delores LABOR 202-606-5730

Industry Projections and Economic Growth, Empl. Pro....Bowman, Charles LABOR 202-606-5702

Industry/trade matters....Phillips, Don 202-395-5656

Industry Wage Surveys, Comp. and Work. Conditions....Staff LABOR 202-606-6245

Inedible gelatin....Jonnard, Aimison USITC 202-205-3350

Inertial Confinement Fusion....Davies, Nelia NEIC 301-903-4941

Infant Formula....Corwin, Emil FDA 202-205-4144

Infant Mortality/"Health Start"....Smith, Sandra CDC 301-436-7135

Infant Mortality/"Healthy Start"....Shaffer, Sylvia HRSA 301-443-3376

Infant Mortality....Staff NCHS 301-436-8500

Infant Mortality....Staff CDC 404-488-5141

Infant Mortality....Staff NICHD 301-496-5133

Infant Nutrition....Staff NICHD 301-496-5133

Infant placement....Staff Edna Gladney Center 800-452-3639

Infant Suffocation....Tyrrell, Elaine CPSC 301-504-0580

Infantile Muscular Atrophy....Staff NIAMS 301-496-5751

Infantile Muscular Atrophy....Staff NINDS 301-496-5751

Infantile Spinal Muscular Atrophy....Staff NINDS 301-496-5751

Infants (Care)....Staff HRSA 301-443-6600

Infants' accessories or apparel....Sweet, Mary Elizabeth USITC 202-205-3455

Infections....Staff NIAID 301-496-5717

Infectious Arthritis....Staff NIAMS 301-496-8188

Infectious Eye Disease....Staff NEI 301-496-5248

Infectious Materials (Disposal)....Staff OD/ORS 301-496-2960

Infectious Mononucleosis....Staff NIAID 301-496-5717

Infectious Wastes....Staff EPA 202-260-8551

Infertility....Staff NICHD 301-496-5133

Inflammatory Bowel Disease....Staff NIAID 301-496-5717

Inflammatory Bowel Disease....Staff NIDDK 301-496-3583

Inflatable Articles....McKenna, Thomas CUSTOMS 212-466-5475

Influenza....Sims, Anne CDC 404-639-3286

Influenza....Staff NIAID 301-496-5717

Infomercials....Staff FCC 202-418-1430

Information Centers Branch....Frank, Robyn NAL 301-504-5414

Information Industries....Inoussa, Mary C. COMMERCE 202-482-5820

Information Programs....Pindell, Alvetta NAL 301-504-5204

Information Retrieval Services....Staff NLM 301-496-6095

Information Retrieval Services....Staff NCRR/NIH Library 301-496-1156

Information Services, Chief,....DiCesare, Constance LABOR 202-606-5887

Information services....Huthoefer, Lori USITC 202-205-3303

Information Specialists, Publ. and Special Studies....Staff LABOR 202-606-7828

Infraction Reports--International....Staff FCC 202-653-8138

Infrared Astronomy....Hutchison, Jane NASA 415-604-4968

Ingot molds....Greene, William USITC 202-205-3405

Inhalants....Staff NIDA 301-443-6245

Inherited Blood Abnormalities....Staff NHLBI 301-496-4236

Inherited Blood Abnormalities....Staff NIDDK 301-496-3583

Inherited Metabolic Disorders....Staff NIDDK 301-496-3583

Inherited Neurologic Abnormalities....Staff NINDS 301-496-5751

Injunctions....Staff FCC 202-632-7112

Injuries (Eye)....Staff NEI 301-496-5248

Injury Prevention and Control....Rosenberg, Mark L. CDC 404-488-4690

Ink powders....Johnson, Larry USITC 202-205-3351

Ink....Brownchweig, Gilbert CUSTOMS 212-466-5744

Inks....Johnson, Larry USITC 202-205-3351

Inland Fish and Reservoirs....Staff FWS 703-358-1710

Innovation....Levinson, Terry NEIC 202-586-1479

Inorganic acids....Trainor, Cynthia USITC 202-205-3354

Inorganic Chemicals....Hurt, William COMMERCE 202-482-0128

Inorganic compounds and mixtures....Greenblatt, Jack USITC 202-205-3353

Inorganic compounds and mixtures....DiMaria, Joseph CUSTOMS 212-466-4769

Inorganic compounds....Lewis, Michael M. PTO 703-308-2535

Inorganic hydroxides....Conant, Kenneth USITC 202-205-3346

Inorganic oxides....Conant, Kenneth USITC 202-205-3346

Inorganic pigments....Kostallas, Anthony COMMERCE 202-482-0128

Inorganic silicon compounds....Chaudhuri, Olik PTO 703-308-2546

Insanity Defense....Baunach, Phyllis Jo Justice Stat 202-307-0361

Insect-Borne Infections....Staff NIAID 301-496-5717

Insect Stings Allergy....Staff NIAID 301-496-5717

Insecticide-Rodenticides....Staff EPA 703-305-5200

Insects, Forest....Lyon, Robert FS 202-205-1532

Insomnia....Staff NIMH 301-443-4513

Inspector General Whistle Blower Hotline....Staff EPA 800-424-4000

Institutional Conservation Methods....Volk, Robert NEIC 202-586-8034

Instrument Development....Staff DRS/BEIB 301-496-4741

Instrument Development....Staff NCRR 301-496-4741

Instrument Research....Staff NCRR 301-594-7934

Instruments: controlling....Moller, Ruben USITC 202-205-3495

Instruments: dental....Johnson, Christopher USITC 202-205-3488

Instruments, drafting....Losche, Robert CUSTOMS 212-466-5670

Instruments: drawing....Roth, Jordon USITC 202-205-3467

Instruments Industry Group....Owings, Christopher SEC 202-942-1900

Instruments: mathematical calculating....Roth, Jordon USITC 202-205-3467

Instruments, measuring and Controlling....Riedl, Karl CUSTOMS 212-466-5493

Instruments, measuring or checking....Moller, Ruben USITC 202-205-3495

Instruments: medical....Johnson, Christopher USITC 202-205-3488

Instruments: musical....Witherspoon, Ricardo USITC 202-205-3489

Instruments, navigational....Losche, Robert CUSTOMS 212-466-5670

Instruments: navigational....Roth, Jordon USITC 202-205-3467

Instruments: surgical....Johnson, Christopher USITC 202-205-3488

Instruments: surveying....Roth, Jordon USITC 202-205-3467

Instruments: testing....Moller, Ruben USITC 202-205-3495

Insulation....MacAuley, Patrick COMMERCE 202-482-0132

Insulators, ceramic....Cutchin, John USITC 202-205-3396

Insulators....Picard, Leo PTO 703-308-0538

Insulinomas....Staff NIDDK 301-496-3583

Insurance Claimants (Unempl). Empl/Unempl.Stats.....Terwilliger, Yvonne LABOR 202-606-6392

Insurance Industry Group....Duvall, Steven SEC 202-942-1950

Insurance Programs....Flynn, William OPM 202-606-0600

Insurance....Bedore, James USITC 202-205-3424

Insurance....Health Insurance Association of America....Staff 800-635-1271

Insurance....McAdam, Bruce COMMERCE 202-482-0348

Integrity (Scientific)....Staff OASH/ORI 301-443-3400

Intellectual Development....Staff NICHD 301-496-5133

Intellectual Property Rights, Services....Siegmund, John E. COMMERCE 202-482-4781

Inter-Government Affairs....Staff FCC 202-418-1900

Interconnection....Staff FCC 202-418-1576

Interest Bearing Notes....Montecalvo, Alyssa FRS 202-452-3471

Interest Rate, Foreign....Decker, Patrick FRS 202-452-3314

Interest Rate, Domestic....Culbreth, Leonard FRS 202-452-2853

Interest on Deposits....Ireland, Oliver FRS 202-452-3625

Interest on Federal Reserve Notes....Evans, Gregory L FRS 202-453-3945

Interest on Savings Account....Reid, Brian FRS 202-452-3589

Interference-General....Staff FCC 202-418-0190

Interferon....Staff NCI 301-496-5583

Interferon....Staff NIAID 301-496-5717

Interindustry Economics, (Acting Chief)....Maley, Leo C. ECONOMIC 202-606-9634

Intermittent Claudification....Staff NHLBI 301-496-4236

International Activities, Fish and Wildlife....Staff FWS 703-358-1754

International Activities....Glickman, Marianne NEA 202-682-5422

International Activities....Staff FIC 301-496-1415

International Affairs, NASA....Rahn, Debra NASA 202-358-1639

International Affairs....Browning, Douglas M. Customs 202-927-0400

International Affairs....Kelley, Joseph E. GAO 202-512-4128

International Affairs....Proctor, George W. Justice 202-514-0000

International, Analysis-US Transact's w/Unaffil Foreigners....DiLullo, Anthony J. ECONOMIC 202-606-9558

International, Analysis of US Transact-Unaffiliated Foreigner....Whichard, Obie G. ECONOMIC 202-606-9890

International, Annual Surveys-US Transact's w/Unaffil Foreigners....Emond, Christopher J. ECONOMIC 202-606-9826

International Audit Organization....Kelley, Joseph GAO 202-512-4128

International Aviation....Bauerlein, Joan W FAA 202-267-3213

International Aviation....Gretch, Paul DOT 202-366-2423

International, Benchmark Survey-US Transact's w/Unaffil For.....Kozlow, Ralph ECONOMIC 202-606-9853

International, Capital Expend. of Major-Owned Foreign Affil.....Fahim-Nadir, Mahnaz ECONOMIC 202-606-9828

International Conferences....Staff FIC 301-496-2516

International Coordination and Liason....Staff FIC 301-496-4784

International Crime Data....Kalish, Carol Justice Stat 202-307-0235

International Economics, Associate Director....Pollack, Gerald A. ECONOMIC 202-606-9602

International Economics, Balance of Payments....Bach, Christopher L. ECONOMIC 202-606-9545

International Economics, Current Account Estimates....Bach, Christopher ECONOMIC 202-606-9545

International Economics, Current Account Analysis....DiLullo, Anthony J. ECONOMIC 202-606-9558

International Economics, Special Analysis....Lawson, Ann ECONOMIC 202-606-9462

International Energy Analysis....Pumphrey, David NEIC 202-586-6832

International Fellowship Programs....Staff FIC 301-496-1653

International Finance....Mendelowitz, Allan I. GAO 202-512-5889

International, For. Dir US Invest. - New Investment Surv.....Cherry, Joseph ECONOMIC 202-606-9817

International, For. Dir US Invest. New Investment Surv Anal....Fahim-Nadir, Mahnaz ECONOMIC 202-606-9828

International, Foreign Dir. US Invest, Benchmark and Annual Anal....Mataloni, Raymond D. ECONOMIC 202-606-9867

International, Foreign Dir. US Invest, Benchmark and Annual Surv....Galler, David H. ECONOMIC 202-606-9835

International, Foreign Military Sales....Atherton, Daniel ECONOMIC 202-606-9593

International Forestry....Sirmon, Jeff M. FS 202-205-1650

International, Government Transactions....Bach, Christopher ECONOMIC 202-606-9545

International Health Activities....Vogel, Linda ASH 301-443-1774

International Health....Davis, Joe H. CDC 404-639-2101

International Information Center....Sutton, Cynthia FRS 202-452-3411

International Investment, Chief....Barker, Betty L. ECONOMIC 202-606-9805

International Liaison....Kenney, James B FAA 202-267-3719

International Major Projects....Thibault, Robert COMMERCE 202-482-5225

International, Merchandise Trade....Murad, Howard ECONOMIC 202-606-9572

International, Multinat'l Corps, Analysis of Activities....Mataloni, Raymond J. ECONOMIC 202-606-9867

International Operations....Staff COMMERCE 202-482-0300

International Patent Documentation....Auton, Gary PTO 703-305-5122

International Policy....Staff FCC 202-418-1460

International Price Indexes, Assist. Commiss.....Reut, Katrina LABOR 202-606-7100

International Price Indexes, Food, Raw Matls, Appl....Frumkin, Rob LABOR 202-606-7106

International Price Indexes, Machinery....Costello, Brian LABOR 202-606-7107

International Price Indexes, Revision, Pr/Lv.Cond.....Reut, Katrina LABOR 202-606-7100

International, Private Capital Transactions....Scholl, Russell B. ECONOMIC 202-606-9579

International Programs, Director....Vacant NLM 301-496-6481

International Programs....Cutrell,John FHA 202-366-0111

International, Quarterly and Annual Balance of Payments Data....Fouch, Gregory G. ECONOMIC 202-606-5577

International, Quarterly and Annual Balance of Payments Anal....Fouch, Gregory G. ECONOMIC 202-606-5577

International Research and Awards....Staff FIC 301-496-1653

International Research....Staff NEH 202-606-8204

International Statistics, Africa....Rowe, Patricia CENSUS 301-457-1358

International Statistics, Asia....Rowe, Patricia CENSUS 301-457-1358

International Statistics, China, People's Republic....Harbaugh, Christina CENSUS 301-457-1360

International Statistics, Europe....Stanecki, Karen CENSUS 301-457-1406

International Statistics, International Data Base....Johnson, Peter CENSUS 301-457-1403

International Statistics, Latin America....Rowe, Patricia CENSUS 301-457-1358

International Statistics, North America....Rowe, Patricia CENSUS 301-457-1358

International Statistics, Oceania....Rowe, Patricia CENSUS 301-457-1358

International Statistics of Common Carriers....Staff FCC 202-418-0940

International Statistics, Soviet Union....Stanecki, Karen CENSUS 301-457-1406

International Statistics, Women in Development....Rowe, Patricia CENSUS 301-457-1358

International Studies Program....Staff FIC 301-496-2516

International Thermonuclear Experimental Reactor....James, Thomas R. NEIC 301-903-5378

International Trade Compliance....Seidel, Stuart P. Customs 202-482-6920

International Trade....Fisher, Irene SBA 202-205-6720

International Trade....Mendelowitz, Allan I GAO 202-512-5889

International Transportation and Trade....Levine, Arnold DOT 202-366-4368

International Transportation....Watts, Patricia ECONOMIC 202-606-9589

International Travel....Bolyard, Joan E. ECONOMIC 202-606-9550

International, US Direct Investment Abroad, Analysis....Zeile, William ECONOMIC 202-606-9893

International, US Direct Invest. Abroad, Payments Data Bal.....New, Mark W. ECONOMIC 202-606-9875

International, US Direct Invest. Abroad, Benchmark and Annual Sur....Walker, Patricia G. ECONOMIC 202-606-9889

International Visitor Program....Salisbury, Diane DOD 703-614-6543

International Visitors Program....Vandrovec, Gene CENSUS 301-457-2816

International Visitors Program....Pane Pinto, Nina CENSUS 301-457-2816

International..Staff FCC 202-418-0680

Internet information....Staff CENSUS 301-457-1242

Interplanetary Space Probes....Brown, Dwayne C. NASA 202-358-1726

Interstate Land Sales Registration....Staff HUD 202-708-0502

Interstitial Cystitis....Staff NIDDK 301-654-4415

Interstitial Lung Diseases....Staff NHLBI 301-496-4236

Interstitial Nephritis....Staff NIDDK 301-654-4415

Intestinal Malabsorption Syndrome....Staff NIDDK 301-654-3810

Intracranial Aneurysm....Staff NINDS 301-496-5751

Intraocular Lenses....Staff NEI 301-496-5248

Intrauterine Growth Retardation....Staff NICHD 301-496-5133

Introduced Species, Fish and Wildlife....Staff FWS 703-358-1718

Inventions, Energy-Related....Staff NEIC 202-586-1479

Investigations....Staff FCC 202-418-1170

Investigative Programs....DeVaughn, Stephen Customs 202-9271500

Investment in Plant and Equipment....Hansen, Kenneth CENSUS 301-457-4755

Investment Management....Muir, S. Cassin COMMERCE 202-482-0346

Investment....Stillman, Robert SBA 202-205-6510

Iodine....Conant, Kenneth USITC 202-205-3346

Iodine....Lyday, Phillis A. MINES 202-501-9405

Ionizing Radiation....Coursey, B.M. NIST 301-975-5584

Ionosphere....Staff FCC 202-653-8166

Iran/Minerals....Heydari, Michael Cnty Mines 202-501-9688

Iran....Austin, Ken Cnty Treasury 202-622-0174

Iran....Fitzgerald-Wilks, Kate/Thanos, Paul Cnty Commerce 202-482-1860

Iran....Hutchings, Dayna Cnty Export-Import Bank 202-565-3737

Iran....Staff Cnty State 202-647-6111

Iran....Vaurs, Rene Cnty World Bank 202-473-5034

Iran....Winchester, Rebecca Cnty USIA 202-619-6528

Iraq (Baghdad)....Staff Cnty State 202-647-5692

Iraq/Minerals....Antonides, Lloyd Cnty Mines 202-501-9686

Iraq....Austin, Kim Cnty Treasury 202-622-0174

Iraq....Hutchings, Dayna Cnty Export-Import Bank 202-565-3737

Iraq....Macgregor, John Cnty World Bank 202-473-7311

Iraq....Sams, Thomas/Wright, Corey Cnty Commerce 202-482-1860

Iraq....Vacant Cnty USIA 202-619-6528

Iraqi....Al-Tai, A.M. Cnty Embassy 202-483-7500

Iraqi....Hamed, Fadhel H. Cnty Embassy 202-483-7500

Ireland (Dublin)....Staff Cnty State 202-647-6585

Ireland/Minerals....Newman, Harold R. Cnty Mines 202-501-9669

Ireland....Collins, Michael Cnty Embassy 202-462-3939

Ireland....Fitzpatrick, Boyce Cnty Commerce 202-482-2177

Ireland....Gallagher, Dermot A. Cnty Embassy 202-462-3939

Ireland....Gosnell, Peter Cnty Export- Import Bank 202-565-3733

Ireland....Kulla, Morgan Cnty USIA 202-619-6853

Ireland....Mackour, Oscar Cnty Treasury 202-622-0145

Iridocyclitis....Staff NEI 301-496-5248

Iritis....Staff NEI 301-496-5248

Iron and Steel....Houck, Gerald MINES 202-501-9439

Iron and Steel Scrap....Houck, Gerald MINES 202-501-9439

Iron and Steel Slag....Solomon, Cheryl S. MINES 202-501-9393

Iron blues....Johnson, Larry USITC 202-205-3351

Iron compounds....Greenblatt, Jack USITC 202-205-3353

Iron Deficiency Anemia....Staff NIDDK 301-496-3583

Iron Deficiency Anemia....Staff NHLBI 301-496-4236

Iron ore....Kirk, William S. MINES 202-501-9430

Iron ore....MacKnight, Peg USITC 202-205-3431

Iron oxide pigments....Potter, Michael MINES 202-501-9387

Irrigation, Major Proj.....Weining, Mary COMMERCE 202-482-4608

Irritable Bowel Syndrome....Staff NIDDK 301-654-3810

Isador....Staff NCI 301-496-5583

Ischemia....Staff NHLBI 301-496-4236

Ischemic Heart Disease....Staff NHLBI 301-496-4236

Isinglass....Jonnard, Aimison USITC 202-205-3350

Islet Cell Hyperplasia....Staff NIDDK 301-496-3583

Islet Cell Transplants....Staff NIDDK 301-496-3583

Isobutane....Raftery, Jim USITC 202-205-3365

Isobutylene....Raftery, Jim USITC 202-205-3365

Isocyanates....Kight, John PTO 703-308-2453

Isoprene....Raftery, Jim USITC 202-205-3365

Isopropyl myristate....Johnson, Larry USITC 202-205-3351

Isotope Production....Erb, Donald NEIC 301-903-5338

Be patient. If any phone number is incorrect, call (area code) 555-1212 and request the new listing.

1411

Isotopes....Staff NCI 301-496-5583
Israel/Minerals....Izon, David Cnty Mines 202-501-9674
Israel (Tel Aviv)....Staff Cnty State 202-647-3672
Israel....Gur, Shlomo Cnty Embassy 202-364-5500
Israel....Hughes, Elizabeth Cnty Treasury 202-622-0183
Israel....Hutchings, Dayna Cnty Export-Import Bank 202-565-3737
Israel....Rabinovich, Itamar Cnty Embassy 202-364-5500
Israel....Slatterry, John Cnty AID 202-663-2613
Israel....Thanos, Paul Cnty Commerce 202-482-1860
Israel....Winton, Donna Cnty USIA 202-619-6528
Italy/Minerals....Newman, Harold Cnty Mines 202-501-9669
Italy (Rome)....Staff Cnty State 202-647-3746
Italy....Biancheri, Boris Cnty Embassy 202-328-5500
Italy....Fagiolo, Boris Cnty Embassy 202-328-5500
Italy....Fitzpatrick, Boyce Cnty Commerce 202-482-2177
Italy....Gosnell, Peter Cnty Export-Import Bank 202-565-3733
Italy....Holloway, Barbara Cnty Treasury 202-622-0098
Italy....Santoro, Eugene Cnty USIA 202-619-6582
ITFS Legal Policy....Staff FCC 202-418-1610
ITFS Technical Application....Staff FCC 202-418-1610
IVDS Application Status....Staff FCC 800-322-1117
IVDS Auction Information....Staff FCC 202-418-0660
IVDS Auction Winners....Staff FCC 202-418-0660
Ivory, articles of....Spalding, Josephine USITC 202-205-3498
Ivory Coast/Minerals....van Oss, Hendrik Cnty Mines 202-501-9687
Ivory Coast....Michelini, Philip Cnty Commerce 202-482-4388
Ivory Coast....Wickman, Cam Cnty AID 202-647-6335
Ivory Coast....Baily, Jess Cnty USIA 202-619-5900
Ivory Coast....Palghat, Kathy Cnty Treasury 202-622-0332
Ivory, tusks....Ludwick, David USITC 202-205-3329

J

Jackets: mens and boys....Sweet, Mary Elizabeth USITC 202-205-3455
Jackets: womens and girls....Sweet, Mary Elizabeth USITC 202-205-3455
Jails, Inmates, and Crowding....DeWitt, Charles Justice Stat 202-307-2942
Jails, Inmates, and Crowding....Greenfeld, Lawrence Justice Stat 202-616-3281
Jails, Inmates, and Crowding....Stephan, James Justice Stat 202-616-7273
Jails, Inmates, and Crowding....Baunach, Phyllis Jo Justice Stat 202-307-0361
Jakob-Creutzfeldt Disease....Staff NINDS 301-496-5751
Jamaica (Kingston)....Staff Cnty State 202-647-2620
Jamaica/Minerals....Rabchevsky, George Cnty Mines 202-501-9670
Jamaica....Almaguer, Antoinette Peace Corps 202-606-3322
Jamaica....Anne McKinney Cnty TDA 703-875-4357
Jamaica....Bayly, Rachel Cnty Treasury 202-622-1266
Jamaica....Bernal, Richard Leighton Cnty Embassy 202-452-0660
Jamaica....Bryan, Basil Keith Cnty Embassy 202-452-0660
Jamaica....Cambell, Edward Cnty AID 202-647-4105
Jamaica....Head, Alfred Cnty USIA 202-619-6835
Jamaica....Nallari, Raj Cnty World Bank 202-473-8697
Jamaica....Siegelman, Mark Cnty Commerce 202-482-5680
Jamaica....Wilkins, Michele Cnty Export-Import Bank 202-565-3743
Jams and Jellies....William, Janis COMMERCE 202-482-2250
Jams, jellies, and marmalades....Frankel, Lee USITC 202-205-3315
Jansky-Bielschowsky Disease....Staff NINDS 301-496-5751
Japan/Minerals....Wu, John Cnty Mines 202-501-9697
Japan (policy analyst)....Siegal, Byron US Trade Rep 202-395-5070
Japan (policy planning)....Weisel, Barbara US Trade Rep 202-395-5070
Japan/trade matters....Burns, David US Trade Rep 202-395-5050
Japan/trade matters....Sands, Lee US Trade Rep 202-395-3900
Japan/trade matters....Wolff, Derek US Trade Rep 202-395-3900
Japan (Tokyo)....Staff Cnty State 202-647-3152
Japan....Gosnell, Peter Cnty Export-Import Bank 202-565-3733
Japan....Hashimoto, Hiroshi Cnty Embassy 202-939-6700
Japan....Kuriyama, Takakazu Cnty Embassy 202-939-6700
Japan....Leslie, E./Kennedy, E./Christian, A. Cnty Commerce 202-482-2425
Japan....Loevinger, David G. Cnty Treasury 202-622-0159
Japan....Spector, Brooks Cnty USIA 202-619-5838
Japan....Wolff, Derek US Trade Rep 202-395-5070
Japanese Yen with options....Bice, David CFT 312-353-7880
Jerusalem....Winton, Donna Cnty USIA 202-619-6528
Jet fuel....Foreso, Cynthia USITC 202-205-3348
Jewelry, Export Promo.....Beckham, Reginald COMMERCE 202-482-5478
Jewelry....Harris, John M. COMMERCE 202-482-1178
Jewelry....Schwartz, Stanley CUSTOMS 212-466-5895
Jewelry....Witherspoon, Ricardo USITC 202-205-3489

Job Vacancy Stats, Employment Statistics....Butani, Shail LABOR 202-606-6400
Joint Replacement....Staff NIAMS 301-496-8188
Jordan (Amman)....Staff Cnty State 202-647-1022
Jordan/Minerals....Dolley, Thomas Cnty Mines 202-501-9690
Jordan....Hughes, Elizabeth Cnty Treasury 202-622-0174
Jordan....Hutchings, Dayna Cnty Export-Import Bank 202-565-3737
Jordan....Macgregor, John Cnty World Bank 202-473-7311
Jordan....Mufti, Faris Sh. Cnty Embassy 202-966-2664
Jordan....Slatterry, John Cnty AID 202-663-2613
Jordan....Tarawneh, Fayez A. Cnty Embassy 202-966-2664
Jordan....Winton, Donna Cnty USIA 202-619-6528
Jordan....Wright, Corey/Samms, Thomas Cnty Commerce 202-482-1860
Joseph's Disease....Staff NINDS 301-496-5751
Joubert Syndrome....Staff NINDS 301--496-5751
Journal, EPA....Staff EPA 202-260-6643
Journal Information....Staff NCRR/NIH Library 301-496-2184
Journal Information....Staff NLM 301-496-6095
Journalism research methods....Newhagan, John D. UMD 301-405-2417
Judges....Gaskins, Carla Justice Stat 202-508-8550
Judges....Langan, Patrick Justice Stat 202-616-3490
Judiciary....Gaskins, Carla Justice Stat 202-508-8550
Judiciary....Langan, Patrick Justice Stat 202-616-3490
Juices, fruit....Dennis, Alfred USITC 202-205-3316
Juices, vegetable....Dennis, Alfred USITC 202-205-3316
Juices....Maria, John CUSTOMS 212-466-5730
Jurisdictional Separations...Staff FCC 202-418-0830
Just Say No....Staff Just Say No International 800-258-2766
Justice Issues....Rabkin, Norman J. GAO 202-512-8777
Juvenile Corrections....Baunach, Phyllis Jo Justice Stat 202-307-0361
Juvenile Corrections....Kline, Susan Justice Stat 202-724-3118
Juvenile Delinquency....Staff NIMH 301-443-4513
Juvenile Diabetes....Staff NIDDK 301-654-3327
Juvenile Mascular Degeneration....Staff NEI 301-496-5248
Juvenile Rheumatoid Arthritis....Staff NIAMS 301-496-8188
Juvenile Spin. Musc. Atrophy (Kug.-Wel. Disease)....Staff NINDS 301-496-5751
Juveniles - General....Lindgren, Sue Justice Stat 202-307-0760
Juxtaglomerular Hyperplasia (Bartter's Syndrome)....Staff NHLBI 301-496-4236

K

Kanner's Syndrome....Staff NINDS 301-496-5751
Kaolin....DeSapio, Vincent USITC 202-205-3435
Kaposi's Sarcoma....Staff NCI 301-496-5583
Kawasaki Disease....Staff CDC 401-639-3286
Kawasaki Disease....Staff NIAID 301-496-5717
Kawasaki Disease....Staff NHLBI 301-496-4236
Kazakhstan....Eighmy, Thomas Cnty AID 202-647-6920
Kazakhstan....Essenbaev, Mara T. Cnty Embassy 202-333-4507
Kazakhstan....Konishi, Motoo Cnty World Bank 202-458-0507
Kazakhstan....Levine, Richard Cnty Mines 202-501-9682
Kazakhstan....Resnick, Bonnie Cnty Treasury 202-622-0108
Kazakhstan....Rossate, Julie Peace Corps 202-606-3040
Kazakhstan....Shamson, Tanya Cnty TDA 703-875-4357
Kazakhstan....Skipper, Thomas Cnty USIA 202-619-5057
Kazakhstan....Souleimenov, Touleoutai Cnty Embassy 202-333-4504
Kazakhstan....Staff Cnty State 202-647-6869
Kazakhstan....Waxman-Lenz, Roberta Cnty Export-Import Bank 202-565-3742
Kearns-Sayre Syndrome....Staff NINDS 301-496-5751
Keloid....Staff NIAMS 301-496-8188
Kenya/Minerals....Izon, David Cnty Mines 202-501-9692
Kenya (Nairobi)....Staff Cnty State 202-647-6479
Kenya....Bezek, Jill Cnty TDA 703-875-4357
Kenya....Kipkorir, Benjamin Edgar Cnty Embassy 202-387-6101
Kenya....Kotze, Joan Cnty Treasury 202-622-0333
Kenya....Larsen, Mark Cnty USIA 202-619-4894
Kenya....Magnus, Charles Cnty World Bank 202-473-4154
Kenya....Maybury-Lewis, Anthony Cnty Export-Import Bank 202-565-3739
Kenya....Muriithi, Geoffrey K. Cnty Embassy 202-387-6101
Kenya....Schmitz, Virginia Peace Corps 202-606-3334
Kenya....Terry, Carlton Cnty AID 202-647-5584
Kenya....Watkins, Chandra Cnty Commerce 202-482-4564
Keratitis....Staff NEI 301-496-5248
Keratoconus....Staff NEI 301-496-5248
Keratomileusis...Staff NEI 301-496-5248
Keratoplasty....Staff NEI 301-496-5248
Keratosis....Staff NIAMS 301-496-8188

Kerosene....Foreso, Cynthia USITC 202-205-3348

Ketones....Michels, David USITC 202-205-3352

Key cases....Seastrum, Carl USITC 202-205-3493

Keyboards....Peng, John PTO 703-305-4945

Kidney Dialysis....Hardy, Robert HCFA 220-690-6145

Kidney Disease....Staff Polycystic Kidney Disease Research Foundation (PKD Cure) 800-753-2873

Kidney Fund....Staff American Kidney Fund (AKF) 800-638-8299

Kidney Patients....Staff AAKP Patients 800-749-2257

Kidney Stones....Staff NIDDK 301-654-4415

Kidney, Urology Clearinghouse....Staff NIDDK 301-468-6345

Kidney....Staff National Kidney Foundation (NKF) 800-622-9010

Kidney....Staff NIDDK 301-654-4415

Kidsrights....Staff Kidsrights 800-892-5437

Kienback's Disease....Staff NIAMS 301-496-8188

Kiribati (Gilbert Islands)/Minerals....Lyday, Travis Cnty Mines 202-501-9695

Kiribati (Tarawa)....Staff Cnty State 202-647-3546

Kiribati....Rahman, Talaat Cnty TDA 703-875-4357

Kiribati....Davies, Irene Cnty World Bank 202-458-2481

Kiribati....Imam, Fahmila Cnty Export-Import Bank 202-565-3738

Kiribati....Shelton, Alison Cnty Treasury 202-622-0354

Kitchen Cabinets....Wise, Barbara COMMERCE 202-482-0375

Kleine-Levin Syndrome....Staff NINDS 301-496-5751

Klinefelter's Syndrome....Staff NICHD 301-496-5133

Knee Replacement....Staff NIAMS 301-496-8188

Knitting machines....Greene, William USITC 202-205-3405

Knotted Netting....Konzet, Jeffrey CUSTOMS 212-466-5885

Koch Antitoxins....Staff NCI 301-496-5583

Korea, North and South....Staff Cnty State 202-647-7717

Korea, North/Minerals....Kuo, Chin Cnty Mines 202-501-9693

Korea, South/Minerals....Kuo, Chin Cnty Mines 202-501-9693

Korea....Ban, Ki Moon Cnty Embassy 202-524-9273

Korea....Donius, Jeffrey/Duvall, Dan Cnty Commerce 202-482-4390

Korea....Park, Kun Woo Cnty Embassy 202-524-9273

Korea....Schneider, Todd Cnty Treasury 202-622-0335

Korea....Shetty, Sundhir Cnty World Bank 202-458-1939

Korea....Spector, Brooks Cnty USIA 202-619-5838

Korea-North....Imam, Fahmila Cnty Export-Import Bank 202-565-3738

Korea-South....Imam, Fahmila Cnty Export-Import Bank 202-565-3738

Krabbe's Disease....Staff NINDS 301-496-5751

Krebiezen (Carcalon)....Staff NCI 301-496-5583

Krgyz Republic....Eighmy, Thomas Cnty AID 202-647-6920

Kryrgyzstan....Skipper, Thomas Cnty USIA 202-619-5057

Kugelberg-Welander Disease (Juv. Spi. Mus. Atoph.)....Staff NINDS 301-496-5751

Kuru....Staff NINDS 301-496-5751

Kuwait (Kuwait)....Staff Cnty State 202-647-6562

Kuwait/Minerals....Michalski, Bernadette Cnty Mines 202-501-9699

Kuwait....Al-Sabah, Mohammed Sabah Al-Salim Cnty Embassy 202-966-0702

Kuwait....Al-Saif, Salah Hamdan Cnty Embassy 202-966-0702

Kuwait....Austin, Ken Cnty Treasury 202-622-0174

Kuwait....Farah, Ahmed Cnty World Bank 202-473-2649

Kuwait....Vacant Cnty USIA 202-619-6528

Kuwait....Wright, Corey/Sams, Thomas Cnty Commerce 202-482-1680

Kuwait....Maybury-Lewis, Anthony Cnty Export-Import Bank 202-565-3739

Kyanite-Mullite....Potter, Michael J. MINES 202-501-9387

Kyanite....DeSapio, Vincent USITC 202-205-3435

Kyphosis....Staff NIAMS 301-496-8188

Kyrghyzstan....Koff, Allison S. Cnty TDA 703-875-4357

Kyrghyzstan....Rossate, Julie Peace Coprs 202-606-3040

Kyrgyz Republic....Cooke, Nancy J. Cnty World Bank 202-473-8727

Kyrgyzstan....Chukin, Almas Cnty Embassy 202-347-3732

Kyrgyzstan....Levine, Richard Cnty Mines 202-501-9682

Kyrgyzstan....Omuraliev, Jumgalbek O. Cnty Embassy 202-347-3732

Kyrgyzstan....Resnick, Bonnie Cnty Treasury 202-622-0108

Kyrgyzstan....Staff Cnty State 202-647-6859

Kyrgyzstan....Waxman-Lenz, Roberta Cnty Export-Import Bank 202-565-3742

L

La Leche....Staff La Leche League International 800-525-3243

Labels....Cook, Lee USITC 202-205-3471

Labor Composition, Multifactor Productivity, Hrs.....Rosenblum, Larry LABOR 202-606-5606

Labor Force and Unemployment, Foreign Countries....Sorrentino, Constance LABOR 202-606-5654

Labor Force Data, Data Disk and Tapes....Marcus, Jessie LABOR 202-606-6392

Labor Force Data, machine-readable data, Empl/Un....Green, Gloria LABOR 202-606-6376

Labor Force Projections....Fullerton, Howard LABOR 202-606-5711

Labor Force, State and Area Tapes and Diskettes....Marcus, Jessie LABOR 202-606-6392

Labor Management Relations....Foley, Phyllis G. OPM 202-606-2930

Laboratory Animals....Staff NCRR 301-496-2527

Laboratory Animals....Staff NCRR 301-496-5545

Laboratory devices....Aziz, Kaiser J. FAES 301-594-3084

Laboratory Glassware....Staff OD/ORS 301-496-4595

Laboratory Instruments, Trade Promo.....Manzalillo, Frank COMMERCE 202-482-2991

Laboratory Instruments....Nealon, Marguerite COMMERCE 202-482-3411

Labyrinthine Hydrops....Staff NIDCD 301-496-7243

Labyrinthitis....Staff NINDS 301-496-5924

Labyrinthitis....Staff NIDCD 301-496-7243

Lace....Cook, Lee USITC 202-205-3455

Lace....Konzet, Jeffrey CUSTOMS 212-466-5885

Lacemaking machines....Greene, William USITC 202-205-3405

Lacings....Cook, Lee USITC 202-205-3455

Lacquers....Johnson, Larry USITC 202-205-3351

Lacrimal Glands....Staff NEI 301-496-5248

Lactation....Staff NICHD 301-496-5133

Lactose Intolerance....Staff NIDDK 301-654-3810

Lactose....Randall, Rob USITC 202-205-3366

Laetrile....Staff NCI 301-496-5583

Lakes....Wanser, Stephen USITC 202-205-3363

Lamb....Steller, Rose USITC 202-205-3323

Laminar Flow Rooms....Staff OD/ORS 301-496-2960

LAMM (Heroin Treatment)....Staff NIDA 301-443-6245

Lamp black....Johnson, Larry USITC 202-205-3351

Lamps (bulbs)....Cutchin, John USITC 202-205-3396

Lamps....Kalkines, George CUSTOMS 212-466-5794

Land Acquisition....Kollins, William J. Justice 202-272-6776

Land and Space Based Remote Sensing Instruments....Staff NASA 804-864-6170

Land and Water Conservation Fund....Staff FWS 703-358-1713

Land Disposal....Staff EPA 202-260-4687

Land Disposition, Fish and Wildlife....Staff FWS 703-358-1713

Land Fields....Staff EPA 202-260-4687

Land Mobile Frequent Assignment Techniques....Staff FCC 717-337-1411

Land Mobile Radio Service (Private)-Legal....Staff FCC 202-418-0620

Land Mobile Service (Private)-General....Staff FCC 800-322-1117

Land Resource Usage and Analysis....Staff FWS 703-358-1706

Land Transportation....Staff FCC 717-337-1212

Land vehicles....Focarino, Margaret PTO 703-308-0885

Langerhans-Cell Granulomatosis....Staff NHLBI 301-496-4236

Language and journalism....McAdams, Katherine C. UMD 301-405-2423

Language Development....Staff NINDS 301-496-5924

Language Development....Staff NIDCD 301-496-7243

Language Development....Staff NICHD 301-496-5133

Language....Staff American Speech-Language-Hearing Association Consumer Helpline 800-638-8255

Language....Staff CENSUS 301-457-2464

Language....Staff NINDS 301-496-5924

Language....Staff NIDCD 301-496-7243

Laos/Minerals....Lydays, Travis Cnty Mines 202-501-9694

Laos (Vientiane)....Staff Cnty State 202-647-3133

Laos....Camp, Bea Cnty USIA 202-619-5837

Laos....Imam, Fahmila Cnty Export-Import Bank 202-565-3738

Laos....Pho, Hong-Phong B. Cnty Commerce 202-482-3875

Laos....Phommachanh, Hiem Cnty Embassy 202-332-6416

Laos....Respess, Rebecca Cnty TDA 703-875-4357

Laos....Schneider, Todd Cnty Treasury 202-622-0335

Laos....Soukhathivong, Seng Cnty Embassy 202-332-6417

Laryngeal Nodules....Staff NIDCD 301-496-7243

Laryngectomy....Staff NIDCD 301-496-7243

Laryngitis....Staff NIDCD 301-496-7243

Laser Angioplasty....Staff NHLBI 301-496-4236

Laser (Cancer Surgery)....Staff NCI 301-496-5583

Laser Energy Conversion Techniques....Staff NASA 804-864-6122

Laser (Tatoo Removal/Dermatology)....Staff 301-496-8188

Laser Treatment (Eyes)....Staff NEI 301-496-5248

Lasers, Trade Promo....Manzolilo, Frank COMMERCE 202-482-2991

Lasers....Bovernick, Rodney PTO 703-305-3594

Lassa Fever....Staff NIAID 301-496-5717

Latin America....Greenberg, Richard OPIC 202-336-8616

Latin America/trade matters....Frechette, Myles US Trade Rep 202-395-6135
Latvia....Altheim, Stephen Cnty Treasury 202-622-0125
Latvia....Ann Lien Cnty TDA 703-875-4357
Latvia....Jovanovic, Djordje Cnty World Bank 202-473-4070
Latvia....Kalnins, Ojars Erikas Cnty Embassy 202-726-8213
Latvia....Levine, Richard Cnty Mines 202-501-9682
Latvia....Robinson, Susan Cnty USIA 202-619-6853
Latvia....Staff Cnty State 202-647-3187
Latvia....Upmacis, Ints Cnty Embassy 202-726-8214
Latvia....Viksnins, Helen Peace Corps 202-606-5517
Latvia....Waxman-Lenz, Roberta Cnty Export-Import Bank 202-565-3742
Latvia....Wooton, Nicholas Peace Corps 202-606-5519
Launch Vehicles....Brown, Dwayne C. NASA 202-453-8956
Laundry machines....Jackson, Georgia USITC 202-205-3399
Laurence-Moon-Bardet-Biedl Syndrome....Staff NINDS 301-496-5751
Law Enforcement....Saunders, Norman T USCG 202-267-0977
Law Enforcement....Harris, Daniel C. GAO 202-512-8720
Law Enforcement, Prosecution and Courts - State....Manson, Donald Justice Stat
    202-616-3491
Lawn and Garden Equipment....Hodgen, Donald COMMERCE 202-482-3348
Layoff Statistics, Empl/ Unempl. Stats.....Siegel, Lewis LABOR 202-606-6404
Lead Based Paints....Staff CDC 404-639-3286
Lead compounds....Greenblatt, Jack USITC 202-205-3353
Lead Encephalopathy....Staff NINDS 301-496-5751
Lead for pencils....Seastrum, Carl USITC 202-205-3493
Lead pigments....Johnson, Larry USITC 202-205-3351
Lead Poisoning Anemia....Staff NHLBI 301-496-4236
Lead Poisoning Prevention....Giles, Ken CPSC 301-504-0580
Lead Poisoning Prevention....Forney, David B. CDC 404-488-7330
Lead Poisoning....Grigg, Bill PHS 202-690-6867
Lead Poisoning....Staff NIEHS 919-541-3345
Lead Poisoning....Staff CDC 404-639-3286
Lead Products....Larrabee, David COMMERCE 202-482-0607
Lead....Smith, Gerald MINES 202-501-9431
Lead....White, Linda USITC 202-205-3427
Learning Center for Interactive Technology....Staff NLM 301-496-6280
Learning Disabilities....Staff NIDCD 301-496-7243
Learning Disabilities....Staff NIMH 301-443-4513
Learning Disabilities....Staff NINDS 301-496-5751
Learning Disabilities....Staff NICHD 301-496-5133
Lease condensate....Foreso, Cynthia USITC 202-205-3348
Leasing Equipment and Vehicles....Uzella, Elinore COMMERCE 202-482-4654
Leather apparel....Hamey, Amy USITC 202-205-3465
Leather apparel....Jones, Jackie USITC 202-205-3466
Leather footwear parts....Shildneck, Ann USITC 202-205-3499
Leather, Producer Price Index....Paik, Soon LABOR 202-606-7714
Leather Products....Byron, James E. COMMERCE 202-482-4034
Leather Tanning....Byron, James E. COMMERCE 202-482-4034
Leather....Steller, Rose USITC 202-205-3323
Lebanon (Beirut)....Staff Cnty State 202-647-6148
Lebanon/Minerals....Michalski, Bernadette Cnty Mines 202-501-9699
Lebanon....Hoppenbrouwer, Laurens M. Cnty World Bank 202-473-2716
Lebanon....Maalouf, Massoud Cnty Embassy 202-939-6300
Lebanon....Slatterry, John Cnty AID 202-663-2613
Lebanon....Tabbarah, Riad Cnty Embassy 202-939-6300
Lebanon....VanRenterghem, Cynthia Cnty Treasury 202-622-0343
Lebanon....Winton, Donna Cnty USIA 202-619-6528
Lebanon...Wright, Corey/Sams, Thomas Cnty Commerce 202-482-1860
Lebanon...Hutchings, Dayna Cnty Export-Import Bank 202-565-3737
Leber's Disease....Staff NEI 301-496-5248
Left Ventricular Assist Device (LVAD)....Staff NHLBI 301-496-4236
Legal Medicine....Staff American College of Legal Medicine 800-433-9137
Legal Services....Huthoefer, Lori USITC 202-205-3303
Legal Services....Chittum, J. Marc. COMMERCE 202-482-0345
Legg-Perthes Disease....Staff NIAMS 301-496-8188
Legionella Pneumophila....Staff CDC 404-639-3286
Legionella Pneumophila....Staff NIAID 301-496-5717
Legionnaire's Disease....Staff CDC 404-639-3286
Legionnaire's Disease....Staff NIAID 301-496-5717
Legislation....Gregg, Valerie CENSUS 301-457-4102
Legislation....Jones, Thomas CENSUS 301-457-2512
Legislative Affairs....Staff FCC 202-418-1900
Legislative Information....Staff OD/DLA 301-496-3471
Legislative Reviews....Clark, David L. GAO 202-512-9489
Legislative Reviews....Cark, David L. GAO 202-512-9489
Leigh's Disease (Subacute Necrotizing Encephal.)....Staff NINDS 301-496-5751
Leishmaniasis....Staff NIAID 301-496-5717

Leisure (resorts) Industry Group....Roycroft, John C. SEC 202-942-1960
Lemon oil (essential oil)....Land, Eric USITC 202-205-3349
Lennox-Gastaut Syndrome....Staff NINDS 301-496-5751
Lens Implants....Staff NEI 301-496-5248
Lens....Staff NEI 301-496-5248
Lenses....Johnson, Christopher USITC 202-205-3488
Leprosy....Staff ALM International 800-537-7679
Leprosy....Staff NIAID 301-496-5717
Lesch-Nyhan Disease....Staff NIMH 301-443-4513
Lesch-Nyhan Disease....Staff NIDDK 301-496-3583
Lesch-Nyhan Disease....Staff NINDS 301-496-5751
Lesotho/Minerals....Mobbs, Philip Cnty Mines 202-501-9679
Lesotho (Maseru)....Staff Cnty State 202-647-8434
Lesotho....Barber, Ed Cnty Treasury 202-622-1730
Lesotho....Bulane, Eunice M. Cnty Embassy 202-797-5533
Lesotho....Holm-Olsen, Finn Cnty Commerce 202-482-4228
Lesotho....Jones, Donald Peace Corps 202-606-3246
Lesotho....Khabele, Moliehi Cnty Embassy 202-797-5534
Lesotho....Kohlman, Mark Peace Corps 202-606-3247
Lesotho....Lane, Bernard Cnty AID 202-647-4228
Lesotho....Maybury-Lewis, Anthony Cnty Export-Import Bank 202-565-3739
Lesotho....Patel, Praful C. Cnty World Bank 202-473-4250
Lesotho....Schwartz, Larry Cnty USIA 202-619-6904
Lesotho....Younge, Nathan Cnty TDA 703-875-4357
Letterer-Siwe Syndrome....Staff NHLBI 301-496-4236
Leukemia....Staff Leukemia Society of America (LSA) 800-955-4572
Leukemia....Staff NCI 301-496-5583
Leukoaraiosis....Staff NINDS 301-496-5751
Leukodystrophy....Staff United Leukodystrophy Foundation (ULF) 800-728-5483
Leukodystrophy....Staff NINDS 301-496-5751
Leukoencephalopathy....Staff NINDS 301-496-5751
Leukoplakia....Staff NIDR 301-496-4261
Levulose....Randall, Rob USITC 202-205-3366
Liberia/Minerals....Izon, David Cnty Mines 202-501-9674
Liberia (Monrovia)....Staff Cnty State 202-647-1658
Liberia....Blackett, Konah K. Cnty Embassy 202-723-0437
Liberia....Maybury-Lewis, Anthony Cnty Export-Import Bank 202-565-3739
Liberia....Michelini, Philip/Cerone, Chris Cnty Commerce 202-482-4388
Liberia....Morlu, John S. Cnty Embassy 202-723-0437
Liberia....O'Neal, Adrienne Cnty USIA 202-619-6904
Liberia....Palghat, Kathy Cnty Treasury 202-622-0332
Liberia....Wright, Minnie Cnty AID 202-647-8288
Liberia...Tallroth, Nils Borje Cnty World Bank 202-473-4876
Librarians Office....Staff NCRR/NIH 301-496-2447
Library (DCRT)....Staff DCRT 301-496-1658
Library (National Library of Medicine)....Staff NLM 301-496-6095
Library (NIH)....Staff NCRR/NIH 301-496-1156
Library Services....Staff NCRR/NIH Library 301-496-2447
Library Tours....Staff NCRR/NIH Library 301-496-1156
Library - Toxic Substances....Staff EPA 202-260-3944
Library....Staff CENSUS 301-763-5042
Libya/Minerals....Dolley, Thomas Cnty Mines 202-501-9690
Libya (Tripoli)....Staff Cnty State 202-647-4674
Libya....Clement, Claude Cnty Commerce 202-482-5545
Libya....Early, Evelyn Cnty USIA 202-619-6528
Libya....El Baroudy, Samia Cnty World Bank 202-473-2370
Libya....Hutchings, Dayna Cnty Export-Import Bank 202-565-3737
Libya....VanRenterghem, Cynthia Cnty Treasury 202-622-0343
Lice....Staff NIAID 301-496-5717
License Renewal....Newberry, Scott F. NRC 301-415-1183
Licenses-Cellular....Staff FCC 202-418-1320
Licenses (Common Carrier Mobile Services)....Staff FCC 202-418-1330
Licenses, Federal Permits....Staff FWS 703-358-2183
Lichen Planus....Staff NIAMS 301-496-8188
Lichen Planus....Staff NIDR 301-496-4261
Liechtenstein....Gosnell, Peter Cnty Export-Import Bank 202-565-3733
Liechtenstein....Staff Cnty State 202-647-1484
Life Cycle....Staff NIA 301-496-1752
Life Expectancy....Staff NIA 301-496-1752
Life Extension....Staff NIA 301-496-1752
Life Insurance and Health, Comp. and Working Cond.....Blostin, Allan LABOR
    202-606-6240
Life on Other Planets....Staff NASA 415-604-3934
Life Review....Staff NIA 301-496-1752
Life Sciences Research....Staff NASA 713-438-5111
Lifeline....Staff FCC 202-418-0940
Light oil....Foreso, Cynthia USITC 202-205-3348

M

Machine Tool Accessories....Abrahams, Edward COMMERCE 202-482-0312

Machinery, Agricultural....Wholey, Patrick CUSTOMS 212-466-5668

Machinery, Excavating....Wholey, Patrick CUSTOMS 212-466-5668

Machinery, Heavy Industrial....Horowitz, Alan CUSTOMS 212-466-5494

Machinery Industry Group....Duvall, Steven SEC 202-942-1950

Machinery, International Price Indexes, Prices and Liv. Cond....Costello, Brian LABOR 202-606-7107

Machinery, International Price Indexes....Costello, Brian LABOR 202-606-7107

Machinery, Office and Textile....Brodbeck, Arthur CUSTOMS 212-466-5490

Machinery, Prices and Living Conditions....Alterman, William LABOR 202-606-7108

Machinery, Printing....Francke, Eric CUSTOMS 212-466-5669

Machinery....Amernick, Marvin Customs 202-482-7030

Machines: agricultural or horticultural....Fravel, Dennis USITC 202-205-3404

Machines and machinery: adding....Baker, Scott USITC 202-205-3386

Machines and machinery: addressing....Baker, Scott USITC 202-205-3386

Machines and machinery: agglomerating....Greene, William USITC 202-205-3405

Machines and machinery: agricultural or horticultural....Fravel, Dennis USITC 202-205-3404

Machines: bookbinding....Lusi, Susan USITC 202-205-2334

Machines: calculators....Baker, Scott USITC 202-205-3386

Machines: cash registers....Baker, Scott USITC 202-205-3386

Machines: casting machines....Greene, William USITC 202-205-3405

Machines: checkwriting....Baker, Scott USITC 202-205-3386

Machines: cleaning (heat process equipment)....Lusi, Susan USITC 202-205-2334

Machines: cleaning (textiles)....Greene, William USITC 202-205-3405

Machines: coating....Greene, William USITC 202-205-3405

Machines: converters....Greene, William USITC 202-205-3405

Machines: cordage....Greene, William USITC 202-205-3405

Machines: crushing....Greene, William USITC 202-205-3405

Machines: cutting....Greene, William USITC 202-205-3405

Machines: data processing....Bringe, Julie USITC 202-205-3390

Machines: dressing....Greene, William USITC 202-205-3405

Machines: drink preparing....Jackson, Georgia USITC 202-205-3399

Machines: dry cleaning....Jackson, Georgia USITC 202-205-3399

Machines: drying....Jackson, Georgia USITC 202-205-3399

Machines: dyeing....Greene, William USITC 202-205-3405

Machines: earth moving....Polly, Laura USITC 202-205-3408

Machines: embroidery....Greene, William USITC 202-205-3405

Machines: fabric folding....Greene, William USITC 202-205-3405

Machines: farm....Fravel, Dennis USITC 202-205-3404

Machines: flight simulators....Anderson, Peder USITC 202-205-3388

Machines: food preparing....Jackson, Georgia USITC 202-205-3399

Machines: horticultural....Fravel, Dennis USITC 202-205-3404

Machines: mining....Polly, Laura USITC 202-205-3408

Machines: office copying....Baker, Scott USITC 202-205-3386

Machines: packaging....Jackson, Georgia USITC 202-205-3399

Machines: paper....Lusi, Susan USITC 202-205-2334

Machines: paperboard....Lusi, Susan USITC 202-205-2334

Machines: postage franking....Baker, Scott USITC 202-205-3386

Machines: printing....Greene, William USITC 202-205-3405

Machines: pulp....Lusi, Susan USITC 202-205-2334

Machines: reeling....Greene, William USITC 202-205-3405

Machines: rolling (metal)....Fravel, Dennis USITC 202-205-3404

Machines: rolling nes....Lusi, Susan USITC 202-205-2334

Machines: rolling (textile)....Greene, William USITC 202-205-3405

Machines: rolling (textile)....Greene, William USITC 202-205-3405

Machines: screening....Greene, William USITC 202-205-3405

Machines: sealing....Jackson, Georgia USITC 202-205-3399

Machines: sewing....Greene, William USITC 202-205-3405

Machines: shoe....Fravel, Dennis USITC 202-205-3404

Machines: sorting....Greene, William USITC 202-205-3405

Machines, spraying: agricultural/horticultural....Fravel, Dennis USITC 202-205-3404

Machines, spraying: other....Lusi, Susan USITC 202-205-2334

Machines: stone processing....Greene, William USITC 202-205-3405

Machines: stoneworking....Fravel, Dennis USITC 202-205-3404

Machines, textile: bleaching....Greene, William USITC 202-205-3405

Machines, textile: calendaring and rolling....Greene, William USITC 202-205-3405

Machines, textile: cleaning....Greene, William USITC 202-205-3405

Machines, textile: coating....Greene, William USITC 202-205-3405

Machines, textile: drying....Greene, William USITC 202-205-3405

Machines, textile: dyeing....Greene, William USITC 202-205-3405

Machines, textile: embroidery....Greene, William USITC 202-205-3405

Machines, textile: knitting....Greene, William USITC 202-205-3405

Machines, textile: lacemaking....Greene, William USITC 202-205-3405

Machines, textile: printing....Greene, William USITC 202-205-3405

Machines, textile: spinning....Greene, William USITC 202-205-3405

Machines, textile: tobacco....Jackson, Georgia USITC 202-205-3399

Machines, textile: tools, machine....Fravel, Dennis USITC 202-205-3404

Machines, textile: vending....Jackson, Georgia USITC 202-205-3399

Machines, textile: washing....Greene, William USITC 202-205-3405

Machines, textile: weaving....Greene, William USITC 202-205-3405

Machines, textile: weighing....Lusi, Susan USITC 202-205-2334

Macroglobulinemia and Myeloma....Staff NCI 301-496-5583

Macromolecular biology....Chalberg, Mark FAES 496-0938

Macular Degeneration....Staff NEI 301-496-5248

Madagascar/Minerals....Dolley, Thomas Cnty Mines 202-501-9690

Madagascar, Republic of (Antananarivo)....Staff Cnty State 202-647-5684

Madagascar....Bezek, Jill Cnty TDA 703-875-4357

Madagascar....Cashion, Gerald Cnty AID 202-647-6154

Madagascar....Hubert, Elaine A. Cnty World Bank 202-473-5507

Madagascar....Imam, Fahmila Cnty Export-Import Bank 202-565-3738

Madagascar....Kotze, Joan Cnty Treasury 202-622-0333

Madagascar....Larsen, Mark Cnty USIA 202-619-4894

Madagascar....Rafidinarivo, Jocelyn Victor Cnty Embassy 202-265-5525

Madagascar....Rajaonarivelo, Pierrot Cnty Embassy 202-265-5525

Madagascar....Schmitz, Virginia Peace Corps 202-606-3334

Madagascar....Watkins, Chandra Cnty Commerce 202-482-4564

Magazines....Bratland, Rose Marie COMMERCE 202-482-0380

Magentic Resonance Imaging....Staff NCI 301-496-5583

Magnesite: crude....White, Linda USITC 202-205-3427

Magnesite: dead burned....DeSapio, Vincent USITC 202-205-3435

Magnesium and Mg Comps....Kramer, Deborah A. MINES 202-501-9394

Magnesium compounds....Greenblatt, Jack USITC 202-205-3353

Magnesium....Cammarota, David COMMERCE 202-482-5157

Magnesium....DeSapio, Vincent USITC 202-205-3435

Magnetic Confinement....Willis, John NEIC 301-903-4095

Magnetic devices....Cutchin, John USITC 202-205-3396

Magnetic Fusion....Finn, Thomas G. NEIC 202-586-5444

Magnetic Materials....Bennett, Lawrence H. NIST 301-975-5966

Magnetic Resonance Imaging....Staff NHLBI 301-496-4236

Magnetic Resonance Imaging....Staff NINDS 301-496-5751

Magnetic Switches....Picard, Leo PTO 703-308-0538

Magnetics....Fickett, Fred NIST 303-497-3785

Mailing services....Xavier, Neil USITC 202-205-3450

Main Studi Rule....Staff FCC 202-418-1430

Mainframes....Iverson, Sean COMMERCE 202-482-1987

Maintenance services....Bedore, James USITC 202-205-3424

Major Industries, Technological Trends in....Riche, Richard LABOR 202-606-5626

Major Market Index with options....Fedinets, Robert P. CFT 312-353-9016

Major Projects....Thiebeault, Robert COMMERCE 202-482-5225

Malabsorptive Diseases....Staff NIDDK 301-654-3810

Malaria....Campbell, Carlos C. CDC 404-488-4046

Malaria....Staff NIAID 301-496-5717

Malawi....Kumbatira, MacKienzie M. Cnty Embassy 202-797-1007

Malawi....Younge, Nathan Cnty TDA 703-875-4357

Malawi (Lilongwe)....Staff Cnty State 202-647-6473

Malawi/Minerals....Mobbs, Philip Cnty Mines 202-501-9679

Malawi....Chokani, Willie Cnty Embassy 202-797-1007

Malawi....Elliot, William Cnty AID 202-647-0011

Malawi....Holm-Olsen, Finn Cnty Commerce 202-482-4228

Malawi....Imam, Fahmila Cnty Export-Import Bank 202-565-3738

Malawi....Jewett, Woody Peace Corps 202-606-3635

Malawi....Kotze, Joan Cnty Treasury 202-622-0333

Malawi....Patel, Praful C. Cnty World Bank 202-473-4250

Malawi....Schwartz, Larry Cnty USIA 202-619-6904

Malaysia (Kuala Lumpur)....Staff Cnty State 202-647-3276

Malaysia/Minerals....Wu, John Cnty Mines 202-501-9697

Malaysia....Abdul Majid, Dato Mohamed Cnty Embassy 202-328-2700

Malaysia....Cung, Raphael Cnty Commerce 202-482-3877

Malaysia....Dwor-Frecaut, Dominique Cnty World Bank 202-473-2970

Malaysia....Gilroy, Meg Cnty USIA 202-619-5836

Malaysia....Imam, Fahmila Cnty Export-Import Bank 202-565-3738

Malaysia....Jamalluddin, Zainal Abidin Cnty Embassy 202-328-2700

Malaysia....VanRenterghem, Cynthia Cnty Treasury 202-622-0343

Maldive Islands....Gradisher, Thomas Cnty USIA 202-619-5529

Maldives....Benbrahim, Abderraouf Cnty World Bank 202-458-2637

Maldives....Imam, Fahmila Cnty Export-Import Bank 202-565-3738

Maldives....McKoy, Ethel Cnty Treasury 202-622-0336

Maldives....Simmons, John Cnty Commerce 202-482-2954

Maldives....Staff Cnty State 202-647-2351

Mali/Minerals....van Oss, Hendrik Cnty Mines 202-501-9687
Mali Republic (Bamako)....Staff Cnty State 202-647-2791
Mali....Baily, Jess Cnty USIA 202-619-5900
Mali....Bezek, Jill Cnty TDA 703-875-4357
Mali....Cisse, Siragatou Ibrahim Cnty Embassy 202-332-2249
Mali....Darkins, William Cnty AID 202-647-5990
Mali....Kone, Yassoungo Cnty Embassy 202-332-2249
Mali....Kwakwa, Victoria Cnty World Bank 202-473-4658
Mali....Michelini, Philip Cnty Commerce 202-482-4388
Mali....Palghat, Kathy Cnty Treasury 202-622-0332
Mali....Posner, Mara Peace Corps 202-606-3004
Mali....Waxman-Lenz, Roberta Cnty Export-Import Bank 202-565-3742
Malignancy....Staff NCI 301-496-5583
Malnutrition....Staff NIDDK 301-496-3583
Malnutrition....Staff NICHD 301-496-5133
Malocclusion....Staff NIDR 301-496-4261
Malpractice (Medical)....Staff HRSA 301-443-3376
Malta/Minerals....Plachy, Josef Cnty Mines 202-501-9673
Malta (Valletta)....Staff Cnty State 202-647-3746
Malta....Borg Oliver De Puget, Albert Cnty Embassy 202-462-3611
Malta....Emmett, Annemarie Peace Corps 202-606-3196
Malta....Gosnell, Peter Cnty Export-Import Bank 202-565-3733
Malta....Grima Baldacchino, Vanessa Cnty Embassy 202-462-3612
Malta....Jill Bezek Cnty TDA 703-875-4357
Malta....McLaughlin, Robert Cnty Commerce 202-482-3748
Malta....Santoro, Eugene Cnty USIA 202-619-6582
Malta....Schildwachter, Christy Peace Corps 202-606-3196
Malta....VanRenterghem, Cynthia Cnty Treasury 202-622-0343
Malta....Vaurs, Rene Cnty World Bank 202-473-5034
Malts....Pierre-Benoist, John USITC 202-205-3320
Mammals, Marine....Staff FWS 703-358-1718
Mammography....Staff NCI 301-496-5583
Management consulting....Chittum, J. Marc COMMERCE 202-482-0345
Management consulting services....DeSapio, Vincent USITC 202-205-3435
Manganese compounds....Greenblatt, Jack USITC 202-205-3334
Manganese....Fulcher, Nancy USITC 202-205-3434
Manganese....Jones, Thomas S. MINES 202-501-9428
Manganese....Presbury, Graylin COMMERCE 202-482-5158
Mania....Staff NIMH 301-443-4513
Manifold Business Forms....Bratland, Rose Marie COMMERCE 202-482-0380
Manmade fiber....Dulka, William COMMERCE 202-482-4058
Manmade fibers....Freund, Kimberlie USITC 202-205-3456
Manmade fibers....Shelton, Linda USITC 202-205-3457
Manmade fibers....Warlick, William USITC 202-205-3459
Manned Flight....Phelps, Patti NASA 407-867-4444
Mantles....Vacant USITC 202-205-3343
Manufacturers, Nondurables....Zampogna, Michael CENSUS 301-457-4810
Manufacturers Operations Division....Staff EPA 202-233-9240
Manufacturers, Prod Data, Nondurables, Census/Annual Svy....Zampogna, Michael CENSUS 301-457-4810
Manufacturers, Prod Data, Durables, Census/Annl Svy....Hansen, Kenneth CENSUS 301-457-4755
Manufacturers, Prod Data, Nondurables, Cur Indrl Rp....Flood, Thomas CENSUS 301-457-2589
Manufacturers, Special Topics, Concentration....Hait, Andy CENSUS 301-457-4769
Manufacturers, Special Topics, Inventories....Menth, Kathy CENSUS 301-457-4832
Manufacturers, Special Topics, Monthly Shipments....Menth, Kathy CENSUS 301-457-4832
Manufacturers, Special Topics, Orders....Menth, Kathy CENSUS 301-457-4832
Manufacturers, Special Topics, Pollution Abatement....Champion, Elinor CENSUS 301-457-4701
Manufacturers, Special Topics, Research/Develop Capa....Champion, Elinor CENSUS 301-457-4701
Manufacturing, Durables (Census/Annual Survey)....Hansen, Kenneth CENSUS 301-457-4755
Manufacturing Extension Partnership (MEP)....Nanzetta, Phil NIST 301-975-5020
Manufacturing Industry Group....Parratt, Shelley SEC 202-942-1840
Manufacturing Technology Centers....Carr, K NIST 301-975-4676
Maple Syrup Urine Disease....Staff NIDDK 301-496-3583
Maps, 1980 Census Map Orders....Baxter, Leila CENSUS 812-288-3192
Maps, 1990 Census....Staff CENSUS 301-457-4100
Maps, Cartographic Operations....Staff CENSUS 301-457-4100
Maps, Computer Mapping....Broome, Fred CENSUS 301-457-1056
Marble, breccia, and onyx....White, Linda USITC 202-205-3427
MARC (Minority Access to Research Careers)....Staff NIGMS 301-496-7301

Marfan's Syndrome....Staff NHLBI 301-496-4236
Marfan's Syndrome....Staff NEI 301-496-5248
Marfan's Syndrome....Staff NIAMS 301-496-8188
Margarine....Janis, William V. COMMERCE 202-482-2250
Marijuana (Effect on Glaucoma)....Staff NEI 301-496-5248
Marijuana (In Urine)....Staff NIDA 301-443-6245
Marine Inspections Investigations....Staff FCC 202-418-1170
Marine Insurance....Johnson, C. William COMMERCE 202-482-5012
Marine Investigation....Gibson, Larry USCG 202-267-1430
Marine Mammal Research....Staff FWS 703-358-1718
Marine Mammals....Staff FWS 703-358-1718
Marine Pollution Control....Staff EPA 202-260-8448
Marine Radio Exemptions....Staff FCC 202-418-0680
Marine Radio....Staff FCC 202-418-0680
Marine Recreational Equipment, Export Promo.....Beckham, Reginald COMMERCE 202-482-5478
Marine Resources....Kilbourne, James C. Justice 202-272-4421
Marine Safety Evaluation....Sheek, Steve USCG 202-267-1417
Marine Safety Center....Walsh, Thomas USCG 202-366-3877
Marine safety....Murtagh, Marjorie NTSB 202-382-6860
Marine Services....Staff FCC 717-337-1212
Marital Characteristics of Labor Force....Hayghe, Howard LABOR 202-606-6378
Marital Status....Saluter, Arlene CENSUS 301-457-2465
Maritime Services....Lahey, Kathleen USITC 202-205-3409
Maritime Shipping....Johnson, C. William COMMERCE 202-482-5012
Marker (Cancer)....Staff NCI 301-496-5583
Marketing Promo., Basic Ind.....Trafton, Donald R. COMMERCE 202-482-2493
Marketing Rules....Staff FCC 301-725-1585
Marketing....Gethers, Sandra Customs 202-482-6980
Marketing....Morin, Bernard A. UVA 804-924-3477
Marriage Statistics....Heuser, Robert CDC 301-436-8954
Mars Exploration....Ulrich, Peter B. NASA 202-358-0315
Marsh Land....Staff FWS 703-358-2043
Marshall Islands....Imam, Fahmila Cnty Export-Import Bank 202-565-3738
Marshall Islands....Shelton, Alison Cnty Treasury 202-622-0354
Marshall Islands....Davies, Irene Cnty World Bank 202-458-2481
Marshall Islands....Rahman, Talaat Cnty TDA 703-875-4357
Marshall Islands....Jefferson, Mary Peace Corps 202-606-1038
Marshall Islands, De Brum, Banny Cnty Embassy 202-234-5414
Marshall Islands....Kendall, Wilfred I Cnty Embassy 202-234-5414
Marshall Islands (Majuro)....Staff Cnty State 202-647-0108
Martinique/Minerals....Rabchevsky, George Cnty Mines 202-501-9670
Martinique (Fort-de-France)....Staff Cnty State 202-647-2620
Martinique....Brooks, Michelle Cnty Commerce 202-482-2527
Mary Woodard Lasker Center for Health, Education and Research....Staff 301-951-6700
Mass Layoff Statistics, Empl/Unempl. Stats.....Siegel, Lewis LABOR 202-606-6404
Mass Layoff Statistics, Employment/Unemployment....Siegel, Lewis LABOR 202-606-6404
Mass Layoffs, Employment Statistics....Siegel, Lewis LABOR 202-606-6404
Mass media and society....Stepp, Jr., Carl UMD 301-405-2428
Mass Spectrometers....Staff NCRR 301-594-7934
Mastectomy....Staff NCI 301-496-5583
Mastication....Staff NIDR 301-496-4261
Mastocytosis....Staff NIAID 301-496-5717
Matches....Johnson, Larry USITC 202-205-3351
Materials, Advanced....DeSapio, Vincent COMMERCE 202-482-3435
Materials Reliability....McHenry, H.I. NIST 303-497-3268
Maternal and Child Health....Vacant HRSA 301-443-3376
Maternal and Child Nutrition....Wong, Faye L. CDC 404-488-5099
Maternal Drug Use....Staff NIDA 301-443-6245
Maternity home....Staff Edna Gladney Center 800-452-3639
Mathematical Modeling....Staff DCRT 301-496-1121
Mattresses....Spalding, Josephine USITC 202-205-3498
Mauritania/Minerals....Michalski, Bernadette Cnty Mines 202-501-9699
Mauritania (Nouakchott)....Staff Cnty State 202-647-3407
Mauritania....Carrere, Noel Cnty World Bank 202-473-7213
Mauritania....Early, Evelyn Cnty USIA 202-619-6528
Mauritania....Hanson, Julie Peace Corps 202-606-3004
Mauritania....Iyahi, Ismail Ould Cnty Embassy 202-232-5700
Mauritania....McKoy, Ethel Cnty Treasury 202-622-0336
Mauritania....Posner, Mara Cnty Commerce 202-482-4388
Mauritania....Saulters, Willie Cnty AID 202-647-6039
Mauritania....Waxman-Lenz, Roberta Cnty Export-Import Bank 202-565-3742
Mauritania....Younge, Nathan Cnty TDA 703-875-4357
Mauritania....Diaw, Amadou Cnty Embassy 202-232-5700

Be patient. If any phone number is incorrect, call (area code) 555-1212 and request the new listing.

1417

Mauritius (Port Louis)....Staff Cnty State 202-647-6473
Mauritius/Minerals....Antonides, Lloyd Cnty Mines 202-501-9686
Mauritius....Akpa, Emmanuel Cnty World Bank 202-473-4367
Mauritius....Barber, Ed Cnty Treasury 202-622-0336
Mauritius....Dhalladoo, Israhyananda Cnty Embassy 202-244-1492
Mauritius....Imam, Fahmila Cnty Export-Import Bank 202-565-3738
Mauritius....Larsen, Mark Cnty USIA 202-619-4894
Mauritius....Neewoor, Anund Priyay Cnty Embassy 202-244-1491
Mauritius....Watkins, Chandra Cnty Commerce 202-482-4564
MBS resins....Misurelli, Denby USITC 202-205-3362
McArdle's Disease....Staff NICHD 301-496-5133
McArdle's Disease....Staff NIDDK 301-496-3583
McArdle's Disease....Staff NINDS 301-496-5751
Measles Encephalitis....Staff NINDS 301-496-5751
Measles Immunization....Staff CDC 404-639-8225
Measles....Staff NIAID 301-496-5717
Meat and Dairy Products....Conte, Ralph CUSTOMS 212-466-5759
Meat, inedible....Ludwick, David USITC 202-205-3329
Meat Products....William, Janis COMMERCE 202-482-2250
Meat....Staff Hotline Agriculture 800-535-4555
Mechanical and Aerospace Engineering....Jacobson, Ira D. UVA 804-924-6217
Mechanical Power Transmission Eqmt. Nec.....Reise, Richard COMMERCE 202-482-3489
Mechanical registers....Gellner, Michael L. PTO 703-308-1436
Mechanical safety....Staff CPSC 301-504-0580
Meconium Aspiration Syndrome....Staff NICHD 301-496-5133
Media Arts....O'Doherty, Brian NEA 202-682-5452
Media (Bacteriologic)....Staff OD/ORS 301-496-6017
Media Inquiries....Staff FCC 202-418-0500
Medic Alert....Staff Medic Alert Foundation 800-432-5378
Medicaid....Hardy, Robert HCFA 202-966-3206
Medicaid....Scanlon, William GAO 202-512-4561
Medical apparatus....Johnson, Christopher USITC 202-205-3488
Medical Care for Aged....Staff NIA 301-496-1752
Medical Devices....Cruzan, Susan FDA 301-443-3285
Medical Facilities, Major Proj.....Haraguchi, Wallace COMMERCE 202-482-4877
Medical Fraud/Quackery....Adams, Betsy FDA 301-443-4177
Medical Informatics....Staff NLM 301-496-9300
Medical Information System (MIS)....Staff CC 301-496-7946
Medical Instruments, Trade Promo.....Keen, George B. COMMERCE 202-482-2010
Medical Instruments....Fuchs, Michael COMMERCE 202-482-0550
Medical Instruments....Preston, Jacques CUSTOMS 212-466-5488
Medical materials....Tesk, John A. NIST 301-975-6799
Medical Nuclear Safety....Cool, Donald NRC 301-415-7197
Medical Photography....Staff NCRR/MAPB 301-496-5995
Medical School Grants....Staff HRSA 301-443-1433
Medical Scientist Training Program....Staff NIGMS 301-496-7301
Medical Specialists....Staff American Board of Medical Specialists (BMS) 800-776-2378
Medical Staff Fellowship Training Program....Staff CC 301-496-2427
Medical Statistics....Flegal, Katherine CDC 301-436-7075
Medical Subject Headings....Schuyler, Peri L. NLM 301-496-1495
Medical Waste....Staff EPA 202-260-8551
Medical Waste....Staff EPA 202-260-8551
Medically Underserved Areas....Vacant HRSA 301-443-3376
Medicare....Hickman, Peter HCFA 202-690-5950
Medicare....Staff HCFA 800-638-6833
Medicine for the Public (Lect., Videos, Booklets)....Staff CC 301-496-2563
Medicine, Legal....Staff American College of Legal Medicine 800-433-9137
Medicine, National Library of....Lindberg, David 301-496-6221
Mediterranean Fever....Staff NIAMS 301-496-8188
Mediterranean Fever....Staff NIAID 301-496-5717
Mediterranean/trade matters....Marcich, Chris US Trade Rep 202-395-4620
Mediterranean/trade matters....Richards, Timothy US Trade Rep 202-395-3320
Mediterranean/trade matters....Jones, Chris US Trade Rep 202-395-3320
Mediterranean/trade matters....Marcich, Christopher US Trade Rep 202-395-4620
Medlars/Medline....Staff NLM 301-496-6193
Meige's Syndrome (Facial Dystonia)....Staff NIDCD 301-496-7243
Meige's Syndrome (Facial Dystonia)....Staff NINDS 301-496-5751
Melamine resins....Misurelli, Denby USITC 202-205-3362
Melamine....Michels, David USITC 202-205-3352
Melanoma....Staff NEI 301-496-5248
Melanoma....Staff NCI 301-496-5583
MELAS....Staff NINDS 301-496-5751
Melkerson's Syndrome....Staff NINDS 301-496-5751
Memory Loss....Staff NIA 301-496-1752

Memory....Staff NIMH 301-443-4513
Memory....Staff NINDS 301-496-5751
Meniere's Disease....Staff NINDS 301-496-5751
Meniere's Disease....Staff NIDCD 301-496-7243
Meningitis....Perkins, Bradley CDC 404-639-2215
Meningitis....Staff NIAID 301-496-5717
Meningitis....Staff NINDS 301-496-5751
Meningocele....Staff NICHD 301-496-5133
Meningocele....Staff NINDS 301-496-5751
Meningococcal Meningitis....Staff NIAID 301-496-5717
Menkes' Disease....Staff NINDS 301-496-5751
Menopause....Staff NIA 301-496-1752
Menstruation....Staff NICHD 301-496-5133
Mental Health and Aging....Staff NIA 301-496-1752
Mental Health and Aging....Staff NIMH 301-443-4513
Mental health....Baron, David A. FAES 301-496-4588
Mental Health....Staff American Mental Health Counselors Association (AMHCA) 800-326-2642
Mental Health....Staff National Mental Health Association Information Center (NMHAI) 800-969-6642
Mental Illness....Staff National Resource Center on Homelessness and Mental Illness (NRCHMI) 800-444-7415
Mental Retardation (PCMR)....Kharfen, Michael ACF 202-401-9215
Mental Retardation....Staff NICHD 301-496-5133
Mentally handicapped....Staff Devereux Foundation (DF) 800-345-1292
Menthol....Land, Eric USITC 202-205-3349
Mercury compounds....Greenblatt, Jack USITC 202-205-3353
Mercury, Fluorspar....Manion, James J. COMMERCE 202-482-5157
Mercury in Fish....Staff EPA 202-208-5634
Mercury Poisoning....Staff NINDS 301-496-5751
Mercury....Conant, Kenneth USITC 202-205-3346
Mercury....Jasinski, Stephen MINES 202-501-9418
Mergers and Acquisitions....Staff FCC 202-632-4887
Metabolic Disorders....Staff NIDDK 301-496-3583
Metabolic (Nervous System)....Staff NINDS 301-496-5751
Metabolism (Inborn Errors)....Staff NINDS 301-496-5751
Metabolism (Inborn Errors)....Staff NICHD 301-496-5133
Metachromatic Leukodystrophy....Staff NINDS 301-496-5751
Metal Articles....Birnbaum, Melvyn CUSTOMS 212-466-5487
Metal Building Products....Williams, Franklin COMMERCE 202-482-0132
Metal Cookware....Harris, John COMMERCE 202-482-0380
Metal Cutting Machine Tools....Bratland, Rosemarie COMMERCE 202-482-0380
Metal Cutting Tools Fr Mach Tools....Vacant COMMERCE
Metal Foils....Fitzgerald, John CUSTOMS 212-466-5492
Metal Forming Machine Tools....Pilaroscia, Megan COMMERCE 202-482-0609
Metal Metabolism....Staff NIDDK 301-496-3583
Metal Powders....Malos, Barbara COMMERCE 202-482-0606
Metal Producers Industry Group...Parratt, Shelley SEC 202-942-1840
Metal rolling mills....Fravel, Dennis USITC 202-205-3404
Metal working machines....Fravel, Dennis USITC 202-205-3404
Metallurgy-alloys....Sillbaugh, Jan H PTO 703-308-3829
Metallurgy Research....Thomas, Iran NEIC 301-903-3426
Metallurgy....Pugh, E.N. NIST 301-975-5960
Metallurgy....Pugh, E. Neville NIST 301-975-5960
Metals and Mining Industry Group....Tow, A. Richard SEC 202-942-1760
Metals, Assistant Branch Chief....Butterman, W. MINES 202-501-9425
Metals, Assistant Branch Chief....Sibley, S.F. MINES 202-501-9344
Metals, Chief, Branch of....Makar, Harry MINES 202-501-9432
Metals, Prices and Living Conditions....Kazanowski, Edward LABOR 202-606-7735
Metals, Secondary....Cammarota, David COMMERCE 202-482-5157
Metals....Amernick, Marvin Customs 202-482-7030
Metals....Fitzgerald, John CUSTOMS 212-466-5492
Metalworking Equipment Nec.....McGibbon, Patrick COMMERCE 202-482-0314
Metalworking....Pilarosca, Megan COMMERCE 202-482-0609
Metastases....Staff NCI 301-496-5583
Metastic Tumors (Central Nervous System)....Staff NINDS 301-496-5751
Meteorological instruments....Roth, Jordon USITC 202-205-3467
Meteorological Research....Staff John NASA 301-286-1584
Methacrylates....Michels, David USITC 202-205-3352
Methadone....Staff NIDA 301-443-6245
Methamphetamine and Heavy Metal Contamination....Staff NIDA 301-443-6245
Methane....Land, Eric USITC 202-205-3349
Methane....Moorer, Richard NEIC 202-586-9315
Methanol....Joseph, Stephanie CUSTOMS 212-466-5768
Methodology, Prices and Living Conditions....Rosenberg, Elliott LABOR 202-606-7728

Methyl alcohol (methanol)....Michels, David USITC 202-205-3352

Methyl ethyl ketone....Michels, David USITC 202-205-3352

Methyl oleate....Johnson, Larry USITC 202-205-3351

Methylene Chloride....Giles, Ken CPSC 301-504-0580

Metropolitan Areas (MSAs), Population....Fitzsimmons, James CENSUS 301-457-2422

Metropolitan Areas....Fitzsimmons, James CENSUS 301-457-2422

Mexican Affairs....Melle, John US Trade Rep 202-395-3412

Mexican Affairs....Amirthanayagam, Aruna US Trade Rep 202-395-3412

Mexico (Mexico, D.F.)....Staff Cnty State 202-647-9894

Mexico/Minerals....Heydari, Michael Cnty Mines 202-501-9688

Mexico/trade matters....Roh, Charles US Trade Rep 202-395-5663

Mexico....De Lara-Rangel, Salvador Cnty Embassy 202-728-1600

Mexico....Herzog, Jesus Silva Cnty Embassy 202-728-1600

Mexico....Hill, Derek Cnty Treasury 202-622-1269

Mexico....Prevot, Babette Cnty AID 202-647-4359

Mexico....Ricks, Shawn Cnty Commerce 202-482-0300

Mexico....Shumake, Josie Cnty USIA 202-619-5864

Mexico....Swannack-Nunn, Susan Cnty World Bank 202-458-2472

Mexico....Wilkins, Michele Cnty Export-Import Bank 202-565-3743

Mica....Hedrick, James MINES 202-501-9412

Mica....Presbury, Graylin COMMERCE 202-482-5158

Mica....White, Linda USITC 202-205-3427

Mice (Genetic Resource)....Staff NCRR 301-496-5255

Microanalysis Science....Velapoldi, RA NIST 301-975-3917

Microbiological Monitoring....Staff OD/ORS 301-496-2960

Microbiology....Garges, Susan FAES 301-496-1019

Microcephaly....Staff NINDS 301-496-5751

Microcephaly....Staff NICHD 301-496-5133

Micronesia....Imam, Fahmila Cnty Export-Import Bank 202-565-3738

Micronesia....Lukan, James Leo Cnty Embassy 202-223-4383

Micronesia....Marehalau, Jesse B. Cnty Embassy 202-223-4383

Micronesia....Shelton, Alison Cnty Treasury 202-622-0354

Micronesia....Staff Cnty State 202-647-0108

Microorganisms Control....Staff OD/ORS 301-496-2960

Microphones....Puffert, Douglas USITC 202-205-3402

Microscopes....Johnson, Christopher USITC 202-205-3488

Microtrach....Staff NHLBI 301-496-4236

Microtropia....Staff NEI 301-496-5248

Microvascular Angina....Staff NHLBI 301-496-4236

Microvascular Surgery....Staff NINDS 301-496-5751

Mid-America MTC (Manufacturing Technology Center)....Clay, Paul E. NIST 913-649-4333

Middle East/trade matters....Jones, Chris US Trade Rep 202-395-3320

Middle East....Jones, Walter OPIC 202-336-8654

Middle Ear Infections....Staff NINDS 301-496-5751

Middle Ear Infections....Staff NIDCD 301-496-7243

Midwest MTC (Manufacturing Technology Center)....Taback, Michael NIST 313-769-4377

Migraine (Headache)....Staff NINDS 301-496-5751

Migrant Health....Shaffer, Sylvia HRSA 301-443-3376

Migration, Current Statistics....Hansen, Kristin CENSUS 301-457-2454

Migratory Bird Research....Staff FWS 703-358-1713

Mild Retardation Prevention.... CDC 404-488-7370

Military Lands, Wildlife....Staff FWS 703-358-1718

Military Operations....Gebicke, Mark E. GAO 202-512-5140

Milk Intolerance....Staff NIDDK 301-654-3810

Milk....Ludwick, David USITC 202-205-3329

Millinery ornaments....Spalding, Josephine USITC 202-205-3498

Millwork....Williams, Franklin COMMERCE 202-482-0132

Minamata Disease (Mercury Poisoning)....Staff NINDS 301-496-5751

Mineral Based Cons. Materials, Asphalt....Pitcher, Charles B. COMMERCE 202-482-0132

Mineral Based Const. Mats., Clay....Pitcher, Charles B. COMMERCE 202-482-0132

Mineral Based Const. Mats., Concrete....Pitcher, Charles B. COMMERCE 202-482-0132

Mineral Based Cons. Mats., Gypsum....Pitcher, Charles B. COMMERCE 202-482-0132

Mineral Based Cons. Mats., Stone....Pitcher, Charles B. COMMERCE 202-482-0132

Mineral Industries....Horning, Patricia CENSUS 301-457-4680

Mineral Metabolism....Staff NIDDK 301-496-3583

Mineral oil....Foreso, Cynthia USITC 202-205-3348

Mineral salts....Randall, Rob USITC 202-205-3366

Mineral substances, miscellaneous....Lundy, David USITC 202-205-3439

Mineral wool....White, Linda USITC 202-205-3427

Minerals (and Vitamins)....Staff NHLBI 301-496-4236

Minerals in the World Economy/Minerals....Kimbell, Charles Cnty Mines 202-501-9659

Minerals, Non-Metallic....Bunin, Jacob CUSTOMS 212-566-5796

Minimal Brain Dysfunction....Staff NINDS 301-496-5751

Minimal Brain Dysfunction....Staff NIMH 301-443-4513

Minimum Wage Data, Empl/Unempl. Stats.....Haugen, Steve LABOR 202-606-6378

Minimum Wage Data, Employment/Unemployment....Haugen, Steve LABOR 202-606-6378

Mining Industry Group....Tow, A. Richard SEC 202-942-1760

Mining Machinery, Trade Promo....Zanetakos, George COMMERCE 202-482-0552

Mining Machinery....McDonald, Edward COMMERCE 202-482-0680

Mining machines....Polly, Laura USITC 202-205-3408

Mining....Polly, Laura USITC 202-205-3408

Mining....Staff FCC 717-337-1212

Mink....Kruchten, Tom Agri 202-690-4870

Minorities (Drug Data)....Staff NIDA 301-443-6245

Minorities, Empl./ Unempl. Stats.....Cattan, Peter LABOR 202-606-6378

Minority Access to Research Careers (MARC)....Staff NIGMS 301-496-7301

Minority Aging....Staff NIA 301-496-1752

Minority Biomedical Research Support (MBRS)....Staff NIGMS 301-496-7301

Minority Health....Simpson, Clay E. ASH 301-443-5084

Minority Health....Staff Minority Health Resource Center 800-444-6472

Minority High School Student Research Apprentices....Staff NCRR 301-594-7947

Minority Institutions Program....Staff NCRR 301-594-7944

Minority Owned Businesses....Strang, Valerie CENSUS 301-763-5726

Minority Ownership Policies....FCC 202-418-2130

Mirror Fusion Systems....Brewer, Robert NEIC 202-586-2828

Misarticulation....Staff NIDCD 301-496-7243

Miscellaneous animal products....Ludwick, David USITC 202-205-3329

Miscellaneous articles of pulp and paper....Rhodes, Richard USITC 202-205-3322

Miscellaneous benzenoid intermediates....Matusik, Ed USITC 202-205-3356

Miscellaneous fish products....Corey, Roger USITC 202-205-3327

Miscellaneous products....Spalding, Josephine USITC 202-205-3498

Miscellaneous Reimbursable....Godoy, Francisco FTC 202-326-3757

Miscellaneous Textile and Related Articles....Gualario, Vito CUSTOMS 212-466-5886

Miscellaneous vegetable products....Pierre-Benoist, John USITC 202-205-3320

Miscellaneous wood products....Hoffmeier, Bill USITC 202-205-3321

Misconduct (Scientific)....Staff OASH/ORI 301-443-3400

Missing Children....Staff Kevin Collins Foundation for Missing Children 800-272-0012

Missing Children....Staff Missing Children Help Center 800-875-5437

Mitochondrial Myopathies....Staff NINDS 301-496-5751

Mitral Valve....Staff NHLBI 301-496-4236

Mixed Connective Tissue Disease....Staff NIAMS 301-496-8188

Mixtures (artificial) of fatty substances....Randall, Rob USITC 202-205-3366

Mixtures of inorganic compounds....Greenblatt, Jack USITC 202-205-3353

Mixtures of organic compounds....Michels, David USITC 202-205-3352

Mobile Homes....Cosslett, Patrick COMMERCE 202-482-5125

Mobius Syndrome...Staff NINDS 301-496-5751

Moccasins....Shildneck, Ann USITC 202-205-3499

Model Airplanes....Staff FCC 717-337-1212

Model Rocket Motors....Staff CPSC 301-504-0580

Models (Animal)....Staff NCRR 301-594-7933

Models (Mathematical)....Staff NCRR 301-496-5771

Models (Non-Mammalian)....Staff NCRR 301-594-7906

Models (Radio Controlled)-Cars....Staff FCC 202-418-0680

Models (Radio Controlled)-Planes....Staff FCC 202-418-0680

Models....Abrahamson, Dana USITC 202-205-3430

Modular High Temperature Reactors....Rosen, Sol NEIC 301-903-1642

Molasses....Vacant USITC 202-205-3454

Molders' boxes, forms, and patterns....Greene, William USITC 202-205-3405

Molding....Francke, Eric CUSTOMS 212-466-5669

Molding....Woo, Jay PTO 703-308-3793

Moldings, wooden....Hoffmeier, Bill USITC 202-205-3321

Moldova....Leanca, Iurie Cnty Embassy 202-783-3012

Moldova....Levine, Richard Cnty Mines 202-501-9682

Moldova....McCleod, Evelyn Cnty AID 202-736-7646

Moldova....Rebecca Respess Cnty TDA 703-875-4357

Moldova....Ruhl, Omno Cnty World Bank 202-458-9119

Moldova....Skipper, Thomas Cnty USIA 202-619-5057

Moldova....Staff Cnty State 202-647-8671

Moldova....Tau, Nicolae Cnty Embassy 202-783-3012

Moldova...Carlen, James Cnty Treasury 202-622-0122

Be patient. If any phone number is incorrect, call (area code) 555-1212 and request the new listing.

1419

Moldova...Waxman-Lenz, Roberta Cnty Export-Import Bank 202-565-3742
Molecular Beam Epitaxy....Comas, James NIST 301-975-2061
Molecular Biology....Davies, David R. FAES 301-496-4295
Molecular Biology....Staff NIGMS 301-496-7301
Molecular Biology....Staff NIDA 301-443-6245
Molecular Cardiology....Adelstein, Robert S. FAES 301-496-1865
Molecular Genetics....Staff NIGMS 301-496-7301
Molecular Pharmacology....Kohn, Kurt W. FAES 301-496-5941
Molecular Physics....Suenram, R. NIST 301-975-2377
Molybdenum compounds....Greenblatt, Jack USITC 202-205-3932
Molybdenum....Blossom, John MINES 202-501-9435
Molybdenum...DeSapio, Vincent USITC 202-205-3435
Molybdenum....Presbury, Graylin COMMERCE 202-482-5158
Monaco....Staff Cnty State 202-647-2633
Money Laundering.....Greenberg, Theodore S. Justice 202-514-1758
Mongolia/Minerals....Wu, John Cnty Mines 202-501-9697
Mongolia/trade matters....Cantilina, Amy US Trade Rep 202-395-5050
Mongolia...Dawagiv, Luvsandorj Cnty Embassy 202-333-7117
Mongolia....Frye, Lisa Peace Corps 202-606-0970
Mongolia....Hahm, Hongjoo J. Cnty World Bank 202-458-2346
Mongolia....Howell, Charles Cnty AID 202-647-4515
Mongolia....Huston, Christine Peace Corps 202-606-0970
Mongolia....Hutchings, Dayna Cnty Export-Import Bank 202-565-3737
Mongolia....Narankuu, Khalzhuu Cnty Embassy 202-333-7117
Mongolia....Respess, Rebecca Cnty TDA 703-875-4357
Mongolia....Schneider, Todd Cnty Treasury 202-622-0335
Mongolia....Staff Cnty State 202-647-6300
Mongolia....Vacant Cnty Commerce 202-482-2462
Mongolism (Down Syndrome)....Staff NICHD 301-496-5133
Monitoring Station Protection....Staff FCC 202-418-1210
Monoclonal Gammopathy....Staff NHLBI 301-496-4236
Monofilaments, manmade....Shelton, Linda USITC 202-205-3457
Mononucleosis....Staff NIAID 301-496-5717
Monorails....Wiening, Mary COMMERCE 202-482-4708
Monosodium glutamate....Land, Eric USITC 202-205-3349
Monserrat/Minerals....Rabchevsky, George Cnty Mines 202-501-9670
Monthly Labor Review, Exec. Ed., Public and Spec Stud....Fisher, Robert W. LABOR 202-606-5903
Monthly Product Announcement....Kilbride, Mary CENSUS 301-457-1221
Montserrat....Brooks, Michelle Cnty Commerce 202-482-2527
Moon Exploration....Keegan, Sarah NASA 703-271-5591
Morocco/Minerals....Dolley, Thomas Cnty Mines 202-501-9690
Morocco (Rabat)....Staff Cnty State 202-647-4675
Morocco....Benaissa, Mohamed Cnty Embassy 202-462-7979
Morocco....Clement, Claude/Cerone, Chris Cnty Commerce 202-482-2527
Morocco....Early, Evelyn Cnty USIA 202-619-6528
Morocco....Emmett, Annemarie Peace Corps 202-606-3196
Morocco....Imam, Fahmila Cnty Export-Import Bank 202-565-3738
Morocco....Mandel, Pamela Cnty AID 202-663-2617
Morocco....Schildwachter, Christy Peace Corps 202-606-3196
Morocco....Schneider, Todd Cnty Treasury 202-622-0335
Morocco....Stillwell, Carol Cnty TDA 703-875-4357
Morocco....Tourougui, Abdelhamid Cnty Embassy 202-462-7982
Morocco....Vaurs, Rene Cnty World Bank 202-473-5034
Mortality Rates (Cancer)....Staff NCI 301-496-5583
Mortality Statistics....Rosenbery, Harry CDC 301-436-8884
Mortgage Backed Securities....Lang, Dawn M. CFT 312-353-9018
Mortgages Industry Group....Roycroft, John C. SEC 202-942-1960
Motion pictures....Gellner, Michael L. PTO 703-308-1436
Motion pictures....R-Archila, Laura USITC 202-205-3411
Motion pictures....Seigmund, John COMMERCE 202-482-4781
Motion Sickness....Staff NIDCD 301-496-7243
Motor Carrier Standards....Scapellato, James E FHWA 202-366-1790
Motor Carrier....Staff FCC 717-337-1212
Motor Carriers....Rea, Samuel W P FHWA 202-366-1724
Motor control systems....Shoop, William M. PTO 703-308-3103
Motor Fuels, Only, Avg. Ret. Prices and Indexes....Chelena, Joseph LABOR 202-606-6982
Motor Neuron Disease....Staff NINDS 301-496-5751
Motor oil....Foreso, Cynthia USITC 202-205-3348
Motor transportation services....Lahey, Kathleen USITC 202-205-3409
Motor vehicle bodies....Mitchell, David PTO 703-308-0361
Motor vehicle wheels....Mitchell, David PTO 703-308-0361
Motor vehicles: armored vehicles....Polly, Laura USITC 202-205-3408
Motor vehicles auto ind. Affairs....Warner, Albert COMMERCE 202-482-0669
Motor vehicles: buses....Hagey, Michael USITC 202-205-3392
Motor vehicles: fork-lift/self-propelled trucks....Hagey, Michael USITC 202-205-3392

Motor vehicles: passenger autos....Hagey, Michael USITC 202-205-3392
Motor vehicles: snowmobiles....Polly, Laura USITC 202-205-3408
Motor vehicles: tractors, extruck tractors....Fravel, Dennis USITC 202-205-3404
Motor vehicles: trucks (includes truck tractors)....Hagey, Michael USITC 202-205-3392
Motor vehicles....Focarino, Margaret PTO 703-308-0885
Motor vehicles....Kashnikow, Andres PTO 703-308-1137
Motor Vehicles....Warner, Albert T. COMMERCE 202-482-0669
Motorcycles....Desoucey, Robert CUSTOMS 212-466-5667
Motorcycles....Topolansky, Adam USITC 202-205-3394
Motorcycles....Vanderwolf, John COMMERCE 202-482-0348
Motors: electric....Bodson, John COMMERCE 202-482-0681
Motors: electric....Cutchin, John USITC 202-205-3396
Motors: non-electric....Andersen, Peder USITC 202-205-3388
Motors....Smyth, James CUSTOMS 212-466-2084
Movement Disorders....Staff NINDS 301-496-5751
Moya-Moya Disease....Staff NINDS 301-496-5751
Mozambique (Maputo)....Staff Cnty State 202-647-8433
Mozambique/Minerals....van Oss, Hendrik Cnty Mines 202-501-9687
Mozambique....Cossa, Berta Celestino Cnty Embassy 202-293-7146
Mozambique....Holm-Olsen, Finn Cnty Commerce 202-482-4228
Mozambique....Imam, Fahmila Cnty Export-Import Bank 202-565-3738
Mozambique....Mendelson, Deborah Cnty AID 202-647-2965
Mozambique....Patricio, Hipolito Periera Zozimo 202-293-7146
Mozambique....Pomerantz, Phyllis R. Cnty World Bank 202-473-7170
Mozambique....Rauch, Margie Cnty Treasury 202-622-0251
Mozambique....Schwartz, Larry Cnty USIA 202-619-6904
MPTP (New Heroin)....Staff NIDA 301-443-6245
Mucolipidoses....Staff NINDS 301-496-5751
Mucopolysacchardios....Staff NINDS 301-496-5751
Mucopolysacchardios....Staff NIDDK 301-496-3583
Mucopolysaccharidosis....Staff NIAMS 301-496-8188
Mufflers (apparel)....Hamey, Amy USITC 202-205-3465
Mufflers (apparel)....Jones, Jackie USITC 202-205-3466
Multi-Infarct Dementia....Staff NIA 301-496-1752
Multi-Infarct Dementia....Staff NINDS 301-496-5751
Multifactor Productivity, Labor Composition, Hrs.....Rosenblum, Larry LABOR 202-606-5606
Multifamily Housing....Staff HUD 202-708-2495
Multilateral trade negotiations....Lavoral, Warren US Trade Rep 202-395-3324
Multiple Basal Cell Carcinoma....Staff NCI 301-496-5583
Multiple Myeloma....Staff NCI 301-496-5583
Multiple Ownership Rules Radio....Staff FCC 202-418-2780
Multiple Ownership Rules TV....Staff FCC 202-418-1630
Multiple Personality Disorder...Staff NIMH 301-443-4513
Multiple Risk Factor Intervention Trial....Staff NHLBI 301-496-4236
Multiple Sclerosis....Staff NINDS 301-496-5751
Multiple Sclerosis....Staff NMSS 800-344-4867
Multiple Sclerosis....Staff NIDCD 301-496-7243
Multiple Warts....Staff NCI 301-496-5583
Multiplex communications....Olms, Douglas W. PTO 703-305-4703
Multiply-handicapped children....Staff Heartspring 800-835-1043
Mumps....Staff NIAID 301-496-5717
Munchausen's Syndrome...Staff NIMH 301-443-4513
Muni Bonds with options....SIA Manasses CFT 312-35-39027
Municipal Solid Waste Management....Staff EPA 703-308-7258
Municipal Solid Waste Management - Combustion....Staff EPA 703-308-8254
Municipal Waste....Sisson, Kurt D. NEIC 202-586-6750
Murmurs (Heart)....Staff NHLBI 301-496-4236
Muscle Disorders....Staff NINDS 301-496-5751
Muscle Disorders....Staff NIAMS 301-496-8188
Muscle Wasting....Staff NIAMS 301-496-8188
Muscle Wasting....Staff NINDS 301-496-5751
Muscular Atrophy....Staff NINDS 301-496-5751
Muscular Atrophy....Staff NIAMS 301-496-8188
Muscular Dystrophy....Staff NINDS 301-496-5751
Muscular Fatigue....Staff NINDS 301-496-5751
Musculoskeletal Fitness....Staff NIAMS 301-496-8188
Museums and Historic Orgns. Projects....Staff NEH 202-606-8284
Museum of Medical Research....Staff OD/OC 301-496-6610
Mushrooms....McCarty, Timothy USITC 202-205-3324
Music....Gellner, Michael L. PTO 703-308-1436
Music....Handy, D. Antoinette NEA 202-682-5445
Music....Siegmund, John COMMERCE 202-482-4781
Musical instruments, accessories....Witherspoon, Ricardo USITC 202-205-3489
Musical instruments, parts....Witherspoon, Ricardo USITC 202-205-3489
Musical Instruments....Kalkines, George CUSTOMS 212-466-5794

Musical Instruments....Harris, John COMMERCE 202-482-1178
Musk, grained or in pods....Land, Eric USITC 202-205-3349
Mutual Funds....Muir, S. Cassin COMMERCE 202-482-0349
Mutual Recognition Agreements....Staff FCC 301-725-1585
Myanmar....Brideau-Hall, Rebecca Cnty World Bank 202-458-0517
Myanmar....Imam, Fahmila Cnty Export-Import Bank 202-565-3738
Myanmar....Sein, Paw Lwin Cnty Embassy 202-332-9045
Myanmar....U Thaung, Daw May Kyi Sein Cnty Embassy 202-332-9044
Myasthenia Gravis....Staff Myasthenia Gravis (MGF) 800-541-5454
Myasthenia Gravis....Staff NINDS 301-496-5751
Mycobacterial Infections....Staff NIAID 301-496-5717
Mycoplasma....Staff NIAID 301-496-5717
Mycosis Fungoides....Staff NCI 301-496-5583
Mycotoxins....Staff NIEHS 919-541-3345
Myelodysplastic Syndromes....Staff NCI 301-496-5583
Myelodysplastic Syndromes....Staff NHLBI 301-496-4236
Myelofibrosis....Staff NHLBI 301-496-4236
Myelofibrosis....Staff NCI 301-496-5583
Myeloma....Staff NCI 301-496-5583
Myeloproliferative Disorders....Staff NHLBI 301-496-4236
Myocardial Infarction....Staff NHLBI 301-496-4236
Myocardium....Staff NHLBI 301-496-4236
Myoclonus....Staff NINDS 301-496-5751
Myofascial Pain Syndrome....Staff NIAMS 301-496-8188
Myopia....Staff NEI 301-496-5248
Myositis Ossificans....Staff NIAMS 301-496-8188
Myositis....Staff NIAMS 301-496-8188
Myositis....Staff NINDS 301-496-5751
Myotonia Atrophica....Staff NINDS 301-496-5751
Myotonia Atrophica....Staff NIAMS 301-496-8188
Myotonia Congenita....Staff NINDS 301-496-5751
Myotonia Congenita....Staff NIAMS 301-496-8188
Myotonia Congenita....Staff NICHD 301-496-5133
Myotonia Dystrophica....Staff NINDS 301-496-5751
Myotonia....Staff NIAMS 301-496-8188
Myths on Aging....Staff NIA 301-496-1752

N

NAFTA....Reba, Maria Customs 202-927-1488
Nails....Yost, Charles USITC 202-205-3442
Naltrexone....Staff NIDA 301-443-6245
Namibia/Minerals....Heydari, Michael Cnty Mines 202-501-9688
Namibia....Bezek, Jill Cnty TDA 703-875-4357
Namibia....Daniels, Gussie Cnty AID 202-647-4328
Namibia....Holm-Olsen, Finn Cnty Commerce 202-482-4228
Namibia....Isaack, Japhet Cnty Embassy 202-986-0540
Namibia....Jones, Donald Peace Corps 202-606-3246
Namibia....Kohlman, Mark Peace Corps 202-606-3247
Namibia....Kolomoh, Tuliameni Cnty Embassy 202-986-0540
Namibia....Maybury-Lewis, Anthony Cnty Export-Import Bank 202-565-3739
Namibia....Patel, Praful C. Cnty World Bank 202-473-4250
Namibia....Rauch, Margie Cnty Treasury 202-622-0251
Namibia....Schwartz, Larry Cnty USIA 202-619-6904
Namibia....Staff Cnty State 202-647-9429
Naphtha....Foreso, Cynthia USITC 202-205-3348
Naphthalene (refined)....Matusik, Ed USITC 202-205-3356
Napkins, cloth....Sweet, Mary Elizabeth USITC 202-205-3455
Narcolepsy....Staff NINDS 301-496-5751
Narcotics....Van Vliet, Theresa Justice 202-514-0917
Narrow fabrics....Shelton, Linda USITC 202-205-3457
NASA Engineering....Rachul, Lori NASA 216-433-8806
NASA Innovation....Paules, Granville NASA 202-358-0706
NASA Mission Safety....Brown, Dwayne C. NASA 202-358-1726
NASA Science and Engineering Labs....Staff NASA 205-544-9492
NASA Scientific Balloon Program....Koehler, Keith NASA 804-824-1579
NASA Sounding Rocket Program....Koehler, Keigh NASA 804-824-1579
NASA Tethered Satellite....Staff NASA 205-544-9492
Natality, Marriage and Divorce Statistics....Heuser, Robert CDC 301-436-8954
Natality Statistics....Heuser, Robert CDC 301-436-8954
National Air Data Branch....Staff EPA 919-541-5582
National Air Toxic Information Clearinghouse....Staff EPA 919-541-0850
National, Business Cycle Indicators....Webb, Michael ECONOMIC 202-606-5590
National Cancer Program....Staff NCI 301-496-5583
National, Capital Consumption....Shelby, Herman ECONOMIC 202-606-9721
National, Capital Expenditures....Moylan, Carol ECONOMIC 202-606-9711

National, Capital Stock....Musgrave, John C. ECONOMIC 202-606-9721
National Center for Biotechnology Information....Staff NLM 301-496-2475
National Cholesterol Education Program....Staff NHLBI 301-496-0554
National, Composite Indexes....Robinson, Charles S. ECONOMIC 202-606-4500
National, Computer Price Index....Sadee, Nadia ECONOMIC 202-606-9736
National, Construction....Lane, Lance ECONOMIC 202-606-9726
National, Corporate Profits and Taxes....Petrick, Kenneth A. ECONOMIC 202-606-9738
National Crime Survey - Data Tapes....Taylor, Bruce Justice Stat 202-616-3498
National Crime Survey - Data Tapes....Rand, Michael Justice Stat 202-616-3494
National Crime Survey - Data Tapes....DeBerry, Marshall Justice Stat 202-307-0775
National Crime Survey - General....DeBerry, Marshall Justice Stat 202-307-0775
National Crime Survey - General....Dodge, Richard Justice Stat 202-616-3485
National Crime Survey - General....Harlow, Caroline Justice Stat 202-307-0757
National Crime Survey - General....Klaus, Patsy Justice Stat 202-307-0776
National Crime Survey - General....Rand, Michael Justice Stat 202-616-3494
National Crime Survey - General....Taylor, Bruce Justice Stat 202-616-3498
National Crime Survey - Redesign....Dodge, Richard Justice Stat 202-616-3485
National Crime Survey - Redesign....Taylor, Bruce Justice Stat 202-616-3498
National Crime Survey - Supplements....Kindermann, Charles Justice Stat 202-616-3489
National Crime Survey....DeBarry, Marshall Justice Stat 202-307-0775
National Crime Survey....Rand, Michael Justice Stat 202-616-3494
National Crime Survey....Taylor, Bruce Justice Stat 202-616-3498
National, Cyclically-Adjusted Budget....Michael Webb ECONOMIC 202-606-5590
National, Depreciation....Shelby, Herman ECONOMIC 202-606-9721
National, Disposable Personal Income....Lally, Paul ECONOMIC 202-606-9743
National, Dividends....Petrick, Kenneth A. ECONOMIC 202-606-9738
National, Employee Benefit Plans....Lally, Paul ECONOMIC 202-606-9743
National, Employee Compensation....Lally, Paul ECONOMIC 202-606-9743
National Environmental Policy Act....Staff FCC 202-418-1700
National Environmental Policy Act (NEPA)....Rudy, Gregory NEIC 202-586-2177
National, Environmental Studies....Rugledge, Gary L. ECONOMIC 202-606-5350
National Establishment Survey, Empl/Unempl....Seifert, Mary Lee LABOR 202-606-6552
National Establishment Survey, Indust. Classif. E/Un....Getz, Patricia LABOR 202-606-6521
National Exchange Carrier Association Policy....Staff FCC 202-418-0940
National Eye Health Education Program (NEHEP)....Staff NEI 301-496-5248
National, Farm Output, Product, and Income....Smith, George ECONOMIC 202-606-9746
National, Federal Govt., Contributions and Transfers....Tsehaye, Benyam ECONOMIC 202-606-5591
National, Federal Govt Defense Purchases of Goods and Services....Galbraith, Karl D. ECONOMIC 202-606-9793
National, Federal Govt Nondefense Purchases-Goods and Services....Labella, Ramen ECONOMIC 202-606-5593
National, Federal Govt., Receipts and Expenditures....Dobbs, David T. ECONOMIC 202-606-9776
National Fish Hatchery System....Staff FWS 703-358-1715
National Forest System....Reynolds, Gary FS 202-205-1523
National, GNP by Industry....Yuskavage, Robert ECONOMIC 202-606-5307
National, GNP, Computer Tapes, Disks and Printouts....Barnes, Phyllistine ECONOMIC 202-606-9700
National, GNP, Current Estimates....Mannering, Virginia H. ECONOMIC 202-606-9732
National, Gross Private Domestic Investment....Moylan, Carol ECONOMIC 202-606-9711
National Health Issues....Nadel, Mark V. GAO 202-512-7119
National Health Service Corps....Shaffer, Sylvia HRSA 201-443-3376
National High Blood Pressure Education Program....Staff NHLBI 301-496-0554
National Household Survey....Staff NIDA 301-443-6245
National Hunting and Fishing Survey....Staff FWS 703-358-2156
National Income and Wealth, Auto Output....McCully, Clint ECONOMIC 202-606-9735
National Income and Wealth, Chief....Donahoe, Gerald F. ECONOMIC 202-606-9715
National Information Center....Hannan, Maureen FRS 202-452-3618
National Information Infrastructure....Staff FCC 202-418-0940
National, Input-Output Annual Tables....Horowitz, Karen ECONOMIC 202-606-5587
National, Input-Output, Benchmark Tables....Planting, Mark A. ECONOMIC 202-606-5586
National, Input-Output Tables, Computer Tapes, Disks and Print....Clark, Vanessa ECONOMIC 202-606-5307
National, Input-Output Tables, Goods-Producing Industry....Bonds, Belinda ECONOMIC 202-606-5586

Be patient. If any phone number is incorrect, call (area code) 555-1212 and request the new listing.

1421

National, Input-Output Tables, Services Producing Industry....Lawson, Ann ECONOMIC 202-606-5586
National Institute of Corrections....Thigpen, Morris L. Justice 202-307-3106
National, Interest Income and Payments....Schuster, Mary Kate ECONOMIC 202-606-9740
National, Inventories....Wasshausen, David B. ECONOMIC 202-606-9752
National, Inventory/Sales Ratios....Wasshausen, David B. ECONOMIC 202-606-9752
National, Methodology....Beckman, Barry A. ECONOMIC 202-606-9662
National, National Income....Taub, Leon ECONOMIC 202-606-9722
National, Net Exports....Krincek, Corrine ECONOMIC 202-606-9729
National Oral Health Information Clearinghouse: A Resource for Special Care Patients....Staff NIDR 301-402-7364
National, Output Measures....Ehemann, Christian ECONOMIC 202-606-9717
National Partnership Clearinghouse....Staff OPM 202-606-2940
National, Personal Consumption Expenditures, Autos....Johnson, Everette P. ECONOMIC 202-606-9725
National, Personal Consumption Expenditures, Other Goods....Key, Greg ECONOMIC 202-606-9727
National, Personal Consumption Expenditures, Prices....McCully, Clint ECONOMIC 202-606-9735
National, Personal Consumption Expenditures, Services....Myung, Han ECONOMIC 202-606-9719
National, Personal Consumption Expenditures....McCully, Cling ECONOMIC 202-606-9735
National, Personal Income....Lally, Paul ECONOMIC 202-606-9743
National Pesticides Survey....Staff EPA 202-260-7570
National Pesticides Telecommunications Network....Staff EPA 800-858-7378
National, Plant and Equipment Expenditures....Crawford, Jeffrey W. ECONOMIC 202-606-9713
National Pollutant Discharge Elimination System....Staff EPA 703-821-4823
National, Pollution Abatement and Control Spending....Rutledge, Gary L. ECONOMIC 202-606-5350
National Pregnancy and Health Survey....Staff NIDA 301-443-6245
National, Price Measures (Fixed-Weighted)....Hook, Mimi W. ECONOMIC 202-606-9723
National, Producers' Durable Equipment....Crawford, Jeffrey W. ECONOMIC 202-606-9713
National Projections, States and Metro. Areas....Sullivan, David ECONOMIC 202-606-5594
National, Proprietors' Income, Nonfarm....Abney, Willie J. ECONOMIC 202-606-9701
National Radon Hotline....Staff EPA 800-767-7236
National, Rental Income....McBride, Denise ECONOMIC 202-606-9733
National Research Service Awards....Staff DRG 301-594-7248
National, Residential Construction....Lane, Lance ECONOMIC 202-606-9726
National, Savings....Donahoe, Gerald F. ECONOMIC 202-606-9715
National Security Analysis....Davis, Richard A. GAO 202-512-3504
National Services Information Centers.... CENSUS 301-763-1384
National, State and Local Govt, Purchases of Goods and Services.....Peters, Donald L. ECONOMIC 202-606-5594
National, State and Local Govt., Receipts and Expend.....Sullivan, David F. ECONOMIC 202-606-5594
National, Statistical Series....Young, Mary D. ECONOMIC 202-606-9677
National, Structures....Lane, Lance ECONOMIC 202-606-9726
National, UN and OCED System of National Accounts....Seskin, Eugene ECONOMIC 202-606-9744
National, Wages and Salaries....Schlitzer, Tracey D. ECONOMIC 202-606-9763
National, Wealth Estimates....Herman, Shelby ECONOMIC 202-606-9721
Native American Affairs....Stamps, Quanah SBA 202-205-6552
NATO (North Atlantic Treaty Organization)....Staff Cnty State 202-736-7299
Natural gas liquids (NGL)....Land, Eric USITC 202-205-3349
Natural Gas....Altman, Paula NEIC 202-586-8800
Natural Gas....Cogan, Jonathan NEIC 202-586-8800
Natural Gas....Gillett, Tom COMMERCE 202-482-1466
Natural gas....Land, Eric USITC 202-205-3349
Natural Gas....Tomaszewski, Clifford NEIC 202-586-9482
Natural pearls....Witherspoon, Ricardo USITC 202-205-3489
Natural resins....Kight, John PTO 703-308-2453
Natural resources and Related Equipment....Daly, James M. SEC 202-942-1800
Natural Resources...Duffus, James GAO 202-512-7756
Natural rubber....Misurelli, Denby USITC 202-205-3362
Natural, Synthetic Rubber....Raymundo, PRAT COMMERCE 202-482-0128
Nauru/Minerals....Lyday, Travis Cnty Mines 202-501-9695
Nauru....Imam, Fahmila Cnty Export-Import Bank 202-565-3738
Nauru....Staff Cnty State 202-647-3546
Nauru...Shelton, Alison Cnty Treasury 202-622-0251

Naval Reactor Propulsion....Staff NEIC 412-476-7200
Navigation, Air or Water....Staff FCC 202-632-7175
Navigation Safety....Staff Coast Guard Hotline 800-368-5647
Navigational instruments....Jordon, Roth USITC 202-205-3467
Navy special fuel oil....Foreso, Cynthia USITC 202-205-3348
Nearsightedness....Staff NEI 301-496-5248
Neckties....Sweet, Mary Elizabeth USITC 202-205-3455
Nemaline Myopathy (Floppy Baby)....Staff NINDS 301-496-5751
Neonatal Adaptation....Staff NICHD 301-496-5133
Neonatal Asphyxia....Staff NINDS 301-496-5751
Neonatal Respiratory Distress Syndrome...Staff NHLBI 301-496-4236
Neoplasms (Trophoblastic)....Staff NCI 301-496-5583
Nepal (Kathmandu)....Staff Cnty State 202-647-1450
Nepal/Minerals....Wu, John Cnty Mines 202-501-9697
Nepal....Dhungana, Basudev Prasad Cnty Embassy 202-667-4550
Nepal....Gilman, Timothy Cnty Commerce 202-482-2954
Nepal....Hutchings, Dayna Cnty Export-Import Bank 202-565-3737
Nepal....Paudel, Yug Nath S. Cnty Embassy 202-667-4550
Nepal....Phillips, Scott Peace Corps 202-606-1053
Nepal....Prennushi, Giovanna Cnty World Bank 202-473-2641
Nepal....Respess, Rebecca Cnty TDA 703-875-4357
Nepal....VanRenterghem, Cynthia Cnty Treasury 202-622-0343
Nepal....Winchester, Rebecca Cnty USIA 202-619-6528
Nepheline Syenite....Potter, Michael J. MINES 202-501-9387
Nephritis....Staff NIDDK 301-654-4415
Nephrocalcinosis....Staff NIDDK 301-654-4415
Nephrolithiasis....Staff NIDDK 301-654-4415
Nephrotic Syndrome....Staff NIDDK 301-654-4415
Nerve Damage....Staff NINDS 301-496-5751
Netherlands Antille....Wilkins, Michele Cnty Export-Import Bank 202-565-3743
Netherlands Antilles....Brooks, Michelle Cnty Commerce 202-482-2527
Netherlands Antilles (Curacao)....Staff Cnty State 202-647-2620
Netherlands Antilles/Minerals....Rabchevsky, George Cnty Mines 202-501-9670
Netherlands/Minerals....Zajac, William Cnty Mines 202-501-9671
Netherlands (The Hague)....Staff Cnty State 202-647-6557
Netherlands....Bensimon, Simon Cnty Commerce 202-482-5401
Netherlands....Gosnell, Peter Cnty Export-Import Bank 202-565-3733
Netherlands....Hamer, Alphons C.M. Cnty Embassy 202-244-5300
Netherlands....Holloway, Barbara Cnty Treasury 202-622-0098
Netherlands....Jacobovits De Szeged, Adriaann Pieter Roetert Cnty Embassy 202-244-5300
Netherlands....Kulla, Morgan Cnty USIA 202-619-6853
Nettings: fish....Cook, Lee USITC 202-205-3471
Nettings: other....Sweet, Mary Elizabeth USITC 202-205-3455
Neural Prostheses...Staff NINDS 301-496-5751
Neural Stimulation....Staff NINDS 301-496-5751
Neural Stimulation....Staff NIDCD 301-496-7243
Neural Tube Defects....Staff NICHD 301-496-5133
Neural Tube Defects....Staff NINDS 301-496-5751
Neuralgia....Staff NINDS 301-496-5751
Neuritis (Peripheral Neuropathy)....Staff NINDS 301-496-5751
Neuro-Ophthalmology....Staff NEI 301-496-5248
Neuroaxonal Dystrophy....Staff NINDS 301-496-5751
Neurobiology (Drug-Related)....Staff NIDA 301-443-6245
Neuroblastoma....Staff NEI 301-496-5248
Neurochemistry....Quarles, Richard FAES 301-496-6647
Neuroendocrinology....Bondy, Caroline FAES 301-496-6664
Neurofibromatosis (von Recklinghausen's)....Staff NINDS 301-496-5751
Neurofibromatosis (von Recklinghausen's)....Staff NIDCD 301-496-7243
Neurofibromatosis....Staff NNF 800-323-7938
Neurogenic Arthropathy....Staff NINDS 301-496-5751
Neurogenic Disability (Mouth and Pharynx)....Staff NIDR 301-496-4261
Neurologic Disease....Staff NINDS 301-496-5751
Neurological Disorders and Stroke, Nat'l Inst. of....Emr, Marian NIH 301-496-5924
Neurology....Grafman, Jordan FAES 301-496-0220
Neuromuscular Disease....Staff NINDS 301-496-5751
Neuromyelitis (Devic Syndrome)....Staff NINDS 301-496-5751
Neuromyopathies....Staff NINDS 301-496-5751
Neuromyositis....Staff NINDS 301-496-5751
Neuronal Ceroid Lupofuscinoses....Staff NINDS 301-496-5751
Neuropathies....Staff NINDS 301-496-5751
Neuropharmacology....Staff NINDS 301-496-5751
Neuroscience....Staff NINDS 301-496-5751
Neuroscience....Staff NIMH 301-443-4513
Neurosclerosis....Staff NINDS 301-496-5751
Neurosyphilis....Staff NINDS 301-496-5751

Neurotoxicity....Staff NINDS 301-496-5751
Neurotoxicity....Staff NIDA 301-443-6245
Nevis....Irish, John P. Cnty Embassy 202-686-2636
New Caledonia/Minerals....Lyday, Travis Cnty Mines 202-501-9695
New Caledonia....Staff Cnty State 202-647-3546
New Drug Synthesis and Chemistry of Drugs....Staff NIDA 301-443-6245
New Releases....Staff OD/OC 301-496-2535
New Zealand/Minerals....Lyday, Travis Cnty Mines 202-501-9695
New Zealand (Wellington)....Staff Cnty State 202-647-9691
New Zealand....Bouck, Gary (Bus.)/Golike, William (Policy) Cnty Commerce 202-482-3647
New Zealand....Cooper, Fiona Ruth Cnty Embassy 202-328-4800
New Zealand....Imam, Fahmila Cnty Export-Import Bank 202-565-3738
New Zealand....Jabbs, Theodore Cnty USIA 202-619-5836
New Zealand....Mackour, Oscar Cnty Treasury 202-622-0145
New Zealand....Wood, L. John Cnty Embassy 202-328-4800
Newborn....Staff NICHD 301-496-5133
News Gathering and Publishing....Staff FCC 717-337-1212
Newspaper management....Kenney, Alisa V. UMD 301-405-2427
Newspapers....Bratland, Rose Marie COMMERCE 202-482-0380
Newsprint....Twarok, Chris USITC 202-205-3314
NFA Firearms....Staff ATF 202-927-8340
Nicaragua (Managua)....Staff Cnty State 202-647-2205
Nicaragua/Minerals....Rabchevsky, George Cnty Mines 202-501-9670
Nicaragua....Bowyer, Nicolette L. Cnty World Bank 202-473-8724
Nicaragua....Dowling, Jay Cnty Commerce 202-482-1648
Nicaragua....Eckerson, David Cnty AID 202-647-9551
Nicaragua....Erlandson, Barbara Peace Corps 202-606-3624
Nicaragua....John Herrman Cnty TDA 703-875-4357
Nicaragua....Marcus, Anthony Cnty Treasury 202-622-1218
Nicaragua....Mayorga-Cortes, Roberto Genaro Cnty Embassy 202-939-6570
Nicaragua....Opstein, Sally Cnty USIA 202-619-5864
Nicaragua....Wilkins, Michele Cnty Export-Import Bank 202-565-3743
Nicaragua....Wong-Valle, Jorge Cnty Embassy 202-939-6570
Nickel compounds....Greenblatt, Jack USITC 202-205-3353
Nickel Products....Presbury, Graylin COMMERCE 202-482-0575
Nickel....Kuck, Peter H. MINES 202-501-9436
Nickel....Lundy, David USITC 202-205-3439
Nicotine...Staff NIDA 301-443-6245
Niemann-Pick Disease....Staff NINDS 301-496-5751
Niemann-Pick Disease....Staff NEI 301-496-5248
Niger/Minerals....Izon, David Cnty Mines 202-501-9674
Niger (Niamey)....Staff Cnty State 202-647-2791
Niger....Baily, Jess Cnty USIA 202-619-5900
Niger....Cisse, Amadou Cnty World Bank 202-473-4652
Niger....Michelini, Philip Cnty Commerce 202-482-4388
Niger....Palghat, Kathy Cnty Treasury 202-622-0332
Niger....Posner, Mara Peace Corps 202-606-3004
Niger....Sangare, Moussa Cnty Embassy 202-483-4227
Niger....Seydou, Adamou Cnty Embassy 202-483-4224
Niger....Waxman-Lenz, Roberta Cnty Export-Import Bank 202-565-3742
Niger....Werlin, Louise Cnty AID 202-647-8125
Niger....Younge, Nathan Cnty TDA 703-875-4357
Nigeria (Abuja)....Staff Cnty State 202-647-1597
Nigeria/Minerals....Izon, David Cnty Mines 202-501-9674
Nigeria....Bezek, Jill Cnty TDA 703-875-4357
Nigeria....Bowler, Gina Peace Corps 202-606-3644
Nigeria....Denton, Hazel Cnty World Bank 202-473-4895
Nigeria....Fox, Russell Peace Corps 202-606-3645
Nigeria....Henke, Degra Cnty Commerce 202-482-5149
Nigeria....Kazaure, Zubair Mahmud Cnty Embassy 202-986-8400
Nigeria....Maybury-Lewis, Anthony Cnty Export-Import Bank 202-565-3739
Nigeria....O'Neal, Adrienne Cnty USIA 202-619-6904
Nigeria....Onah, Adoga Cnty Embassy 202-986-8400
Nigeria....Palghat, Kathy Cnty Treasury 202-622-0332
Nigeria....Woodruff, Neil Cnty AID 202-647-6321
Night Blindness....Staff NEI 301-496-5248
Nightwear....DeGaetano, Angela CUSTOMS 212-466-5540
Nikkei with options....Fedinets, Robert P. CFT 312-353-9016
Nitric acid....Trainor, Cynthia USITC 202-205-3354
Nitriles....Lee, Mary PTO 703-308-4546
Nitrites....Michels, David USITC 202-205-3352
Nitrites....Staff NIDA 301-443-6245
Nitrogen Compounds....Joseph, Stephanie CUSTOMS 212-466-5768
Nitrogen....Cantrell, Raymond MINES 202-501-9411
Nitrogen....Conant, Kenneth USITC 202-205-3346
Nitrogenous fertilizers....Trainor, Cynthia USITC 202-205-3354

Nitrosamines....Staff NCI 301-496-5583
Niue....Berhage, Jeff Peace Corps 202-606-1098
Niue....Rahman, Talaat Cnty TDA 703-875-4357
Nobel Prize....Staff NIGMS 301-496-7301
Noise Information....Staff EPA 202-260-4996
Noise....Staff NIDCD 301-496-7243
Noise....Staff NINDS 301-496-5751
Non-alcoholic Beverages....Manogue, Robert COMMERCE 202-482-2428
Non-bank Acquisitions....Greene, D Christopher FRS 202-452-2263
Non-benzenoid resins....Misurelli, Denby USITC 202-205-3362
Non-cash Collections....DeCorleto, Donna FRS 202-452-3956
Non-commercial Educational Stations-FM Apps....Staff FCC 202-418-2710
Non-current Carrying Wiring Devices....Bodson, John COMMERCE 202-482-0681
Non-durable Goods....Simon, Leslie B. COMMERCE 202-482-0341
Non-electric Machinery, Prices and Living Cond.....Dickerson, Bryandt LABOR 202-606-7744
Non-electric motors and engines....Andersen, Peder USITC 202-205-3388
Non-energy Related Inventions Program....Lewett, G.P. NIST 301-975-5504
Non-enumerated products....Spalding, Josephine USITC 202-205-3498
Non-Farm Proprietors' Income and Employment....Levine, Bruce ECONOMIC 202-606-9260
Non-ferrous Foundries....Bell, Charles COMMERCE 202-482-0608
Non-ferrous Metals....Cammorota, David COMMERCE 202-482-5157
Non-Game Wildlife....Staff FWS 703-358-1718
Non-Hodgkins Malignant Lymphoma....Staff NCI 301-496-5583
Non-infectious Chemical Agents (Eff. on Human Hea.)....Staff NIEHS 919-541-3345
Non-metallic article shaping....Silbaugh, Jan H PTO 703-308-3829
Non-metallic elements....Lewis, Michael M. PTO 703-308-2535
Non-metallic Minerals Nec....Manion, James J. COMMERCE 202-482-0575
Non-residential Constr (Domestic)....MacAuley, Patrick COMMERCE 202-482-0132
Non-Toxic Shot....Staff FWS 703-358-1714
North America Affairs....Weiss, David US Trade Rep 202-395-3412
North American Numbering Plan....Staff FCC 202-418-0940
Northeast MTC (Manufacturing Technology Center)....Tebbano, Mark NIST 518-283-1010
Norwalk Agent....Staff NIAID 301-496-5717
Norway/Minerals....Plachy, Josef Cnty Mines 202-501-9673
Norway (Oslo)....Staff Cnty State 202-647-5669
Norway....Devlin, James Cnty Commerce 202-482-4414
Norway....Gosnell, Peter Cnty Export-Import Bank 202-565-3743
Norway....Klepsvik, Karsten Cnty Embassy 202-333-6000
Norway....Mackour, Oscar Cnty Treasury 202-622-0145
Norway....Rankin-Galloway, Honore Cnty USIA 202-619-5283
Norway....Vibe, Kjeld Cnty Embassy 202-333-6000
Nosebleed (Epistaxis)....Staff NHLBI 301-496-4236
Notes, Counterfeit....Cameron, Jon FRS 202-452-2220
Notes, Technical Information....Decorleto, Donna FRS 202-452-3956
Notes, Treasury....DeCorleto, Donna FRS 202-452-3956
Nuclear Energy Institute....Davis, Edward NEIC 202-484-2660
Nuclear Energy Statistics....Geidl, John NEIC 202-254-5570
Nuclear Energy....Greenblatt, Jack USITC 202-205-3353
Nuclear Enforcement....Lieberman, James NRC 301-415-2741
Nuclear Facility Safety....Pearson, Orin NEIC 202-586-2407
Nuclear Fusion....Davies, Anne NEIC 301-903-4941
Nuclear (Heart Pacemaker)....Staff NHLBI 301-496-4236
Nuclear Magnetic Resonance Spectrometers....Staff NCRR 301-594-7934
Nuclear Magnetic Resonance....Becker, Edwin D. FAES 301-496-1024
Nuclear Material Safety and Safeguards....Paperiello, Carl J. NRC 301-415-7800
Nuclear Medicine Department....Staff CC 301-496-6455
Nuclear Physics....Hendrick, David NEIC 301-903-3613
Nuclear Power Plants....Werner, Thomas NEIC 301-903-3773
Nuclear Power Plants, Major Proj.....Dollison, Robert COMMERCE 202-482-2733
Nuclear Power Projects....Staff FWS 703-358-2183
Nuclear Reactor Regulation....Russell, William T. NRC 301-415-1270
Nuclear Reactors....Duraiswamy, Sam NRC 301-415-7364
Nuclear Safety Issues....Black, Richard NEIC 301-903-0102
Nuclear Safety Regulations....Rollow, Thomas NEIC 202-586-2407
Nuclear Waste....Major, Richard K. NRC 301-415-7366
Nuclear Weapons Stockpiles....Ford, John NEIC 301-903-3782
Number Research, Price and Index, Pr/Lv. Cond....Zieschang, Kimberly LABOR 202-606-6573
Numerical Controls Fr. Mach. Tools....Pilaroscia, Megan COMMERCE 202-482-0609
Numerical controls....Malison, Andrew USITC 202-205-3391

Be patient. If any phone number is incorrect, call (area code) 555-1212 and request the new listing.

1423

Nursery Trade Catalogs....Ho, Judith NAL 301-504-5876
Nurses....Staff Visiting Nurse Association of America (VNAA) 800-426-2547
Nursing Department....Staff CC 301-496-5661
Nursing Homes and Care....Staff HRSA 301-443-3376
Nursing Homes....Hardy, Robert HCFA 202-966-3206
Nursing Homes....Staff NIA 301-496-1752
Nursing Interventions....Staff NINR 301-496-0207
Nursing Research, National Center for....Pollin, Geraldine NIH 301-496-0207
Nursing Research, National Center for....McBride, Esther NIH 301-496-0207
Nursing Systems....Staff NCNR 301-496-0526
Nutrition and Aging....Staff NIA 301-496-1752
Nutrition and Cancer....Staff NCI 301-496-5583
Nutrition, Cancer Research....Staff American Institute for Cancer Research
Nutrition Hotline 800-843-8114
Nutrition, Maternal and Child....Wong, Faye L. CDC 404-488-5099
Nutrition Research Coordination....Staff OD 301-496-9281
Nutrition...Hubbard, Van S. FAES 301-594-7573
Nutrition....Meyers, Linda ASH 202-205-9007
Nutrition....Staff Nutrition Information Service (DIET) 800-231-3438
Nutrition....Staff NICHD 301-496-5133
Nutrition....Staff HRSA/DMCH 301-443-4026
Nutrition....Staff NIDDK 301-496-3583
Nutrition....Stoiber, Suzanne ASH 202-205-0152
Nutrition....Trowbridge, Frederick L. CDC 404-488-5090
Nutritional Statistics....Kuczmarski, Robert CDC 301-436-7072
Nuts, Bolts, Washers....Reise, Richard COMMERCE 202-482-3489
Nuts, Edible....Burket, Stephen USITC 202-205-3318
Nuts, Edible....Janis, William V. COMMERCE 202-482-2250
Nuts....Conte, Ralph CUSTOMS 212-466-5759
Nystagmus....Staff NEI 301-496-5248

O

Oakum....Cook, Lee USITC 202-205-3471
Oats with options....Gore, Philip CFT 312-886-3044
Obesity in Children....Staff NHLBI 301-496-4236
Obesity in Children....Staff NICHD 301-496-5133
Obesity....Staff NIDDK 301-496-3583
Obesity....Staff NHLBI 301-496-4236
Obesity....Staff NIMH 301-496-4513
Obscene Broadcasts....Staff FCC 202-418-1430
Obscenity....Burgasser, George C. Justice 202-514-5780
Obsessive-Compulsive Disorder...Staff NIMH 301-443-4513
Occupation Statistics....Priebe, John/Masumura, Wilfred CENSUS 301-763-8574
Occupational Data/Current Survey, Empl/Unempl.St.....Staff LABOR
    202-606-6378
Occupational Diseases....Staff CDC/NIOSH 404-639-3286
Occupational Lung Disease....Staff NHLBI 301-496-4236
Occupational Medicine....Gebus, George NEIC 301-903-7385
Occupational Mobility, Occup. Data, Empl/Unempl. Data...Rones, Philip LABOR
    202-606-6378
Occupational Outlook Handbook, Employment Proj.....Pilot, Michael LABOR
    202-606-5703
Occupational Outlook Quarterly, Empl. Proj.....Fountain, Melvin LABOR
    202-606-5707
Occupational Projections....Rosenthal, Neal LABOR 202-606-5701
Occupational Safety and Health, National Institute for....Sims, Anne CDC
    404-639-3286
Occupational Safety and Health....Poster, Diane CDC 404-639-3061
Occupational Safety....Gibbs, Roy NEIC 301-903-4343
Ocean Biological Experiments....Koehler, Keith NASA 802-824-1579
Ocean Energy....Loose, Ronald NEIC 202-586-5348
Ocean Physics Research....Koehler, Keith NASA 804-824-1579
Ocean Shipping....Johnson, William C. COMMERCE 202-482-5012
Ocean Thermal Energy....Loose, Ronald NEIC 202-586-5348
Oceania/trade matters....Stillman, Betsy US Trade Rep 202-395-6813
Oceans and Coastal Protection Division....Staff EPA 202-260-1952
Oceans and Watersheds....Staff EPA 202-260-7166
Ocular Hypertension....Staff NEI 301-496-5248
Oculocraniosomatic Neuromuscular Disease....Staff NINDS 301-496-5751
Odor....Staff NIDCD 301-496-7243
Odor....Staff NINDS 301-496-5751
Odoriferous Compounds....Joseph, Stephanie CUSTOMS 212-466-5768
Odoriferous or aromatic substances....Land, Eric USITC 202-205-3349
Offal....Ludwick, David USITC 202-205-3329
Offender-based Transaction Statistics....Manson, Donald Justice Stat 202-616-3491

Offender-based Transaction Statistics....Langan, Patrick Justice Stat 202-616-3490
Offenders - Federal....Kaplan, Carol Justice Stat 202-307-0759
Offenders, Female....Baunach, Phyllis Jo Justice Stat 202-307-0361
Offenders, Female - Federal....Kaplan, Carol Justice Stat 202-307-0759
Offenders....Baunach, Phyllis Jo Justice Stat 202-307-0361
Offenders....Beck, Allen Justice Stat 202-616-3277
Offenders....Greenfeld, Lawrence Justice Stat 202-616-3281
Offenders....Stephan, James Justice Stat 202-616-7273
Office copying machines....Baker, Scott USITC 202-205-3386
Office Equipment Industry Group....Duvall, Steven SEC 202-942-1950
Office machines....Baker, Scott USITC 202-205-3386
Office of Congressional Relations....Leslie, Louise M. FTC 202-326-2195
Office of Congressional Relations....Prendergast, William B. FTC 202-326-2195
Office of Congressional Relations....Hall, Dorian J. FTC 202-326-2186
Office of Consumer and Competition Advocacy....Laney, Veronica FTC
    202-326-2249
Office of Inspector General-Audits....Staff FCC 202-418-0470
Office of Inspector General-Complaints....Staff FCC 202-418-0470
Office of Inspector General-Investigations....Staff FCC 202-418-0470
Office of Inspector General....Staff FCC 202-418-0470
Office of Inspector General....Trzeciak, Adam R. FTC 202-326-2435
Office of Inspector General....Treitsch, Dennis R. FTC 202-326-2581
Office of Inspector General....Zirkel, Frederick J. FTC 202-326-2800
Office of Inspector General....Williams, Joyce E. FTC 202-326-2313
Office of Public Affairs....Mack, Brenda A. FTC 202-326-2182
Office of Public Affairs....Leslie, John T. FTC 202-326-2178
Office of Public Affairs....Shaipro, Howard FTC 202-326-2176
Office of Public Affairs....Farrell, Claudia FTC 202-326-2181
Office of Public Affairs....Elder, Donald FTC 202-326-2181
Office of the Commissioner....Azcuenaga, Mary L. FTC 202-326-2145
Office of the Executive Director....Milton, Kathleen FTC 202-326-3253
Office of the General Counsel....Rittner, Kathleen FTC 202-326-2498
Office of the General Counsel....Rowan, Michael FTC 202-326-2489
Office of the General Counsel....Coleman, Jill E. FTC 202-326-2414
Office of the General Counsel....Kane, Maryanne S. FTC 202-326-2450
Office of the General Counsel....Levine, Joanne L. FTC 202-326-2474
Office of the General Counsel....Freedman, Bruce G. FTC 202-326-2464
Office of the General Counsel....DeLuca, Nancy F. FCC 202-326-2460
Office of the General Counsel....Etheridge, Monica M. FTC 202-326-2666
Office of the General Counsel....Dooley, Frederick E. FTC 202-326-2443
Office of the General Counsel....DuPree, Scott E. FTC 202-326-2479
Office of the General Counsel....Fields, Kwasi A. FTC 202-326-2452
Office of the General Counsel....DeMille-Wagman, Lawrence FTC 202-326-2448
Office of the General Counsel....Winerman, Marc L. FTC 202-326-2451
Office of the General Counsel....Wagman, Lawrence FTC 202-326-2448
Office of the General Counsel....Goosby, Consuella M. FTC 202-326-2486
Office of the General Counsel....Greenfield, Gary M. FTC 202-326-2753
Office of the General Counsel....Cummins, Jerold D. FTC 202-326-2471
Office of the General Counsel....Golden, William P. FTC 202-326-2494
Office of the General Counsel....Murphy, John T. FTC 202-326-2457
Office of the General Counsel....Crockett, Elaine FTC 202-326-2453
Office of the General Counsel....Isenstadt, Ernest J. FTC 202-326-2473
Office of the General Counsel....Spears, James M. FTC 202-326-2480
Office of the General Counsel....Worthy, Betty J. FTC 202-326-2459
Office of the General Counsel....White, Christian S. FTC 202-326-2476
Office of the General Counsel....Hurwitz, James D. FTC 202-326-2847
Office of the General Counsel....Dawson, Rachel Miller FTC 202-326-2463
Office of the General Counsel....Kaye, Ira S. FTC 202-326-2426
Office of the General Counsel....Neal, Valary FTC 202-326-2066
Office of the General Counsel....Orlans, Melvin H. FTC 202-326-2475
Office of the General Counsel....Shaffer, Jay C. FTC 202-326-2557
Office of the General Counsel....Pressley, Doris P. FTC 202-326-2916
Office of the General Counsel....Lewis, Tina M. FTC 202-326-2465
Office of the General Counsel....Polydor, Cheryl L. FTC 202-326-2279
Office of the General Counsel....Melman, Leslie R. FTC 202-326-2478
Office of the General Counsel....Shonka, David C. FTC 202-326-2436
Office of the General Counsel....Miller, Rachel Dawson FTC 202-326-2463
Office of the General Counsel....Tang, Alexander FTC 202-326-2447
Office of the Secretary.....Felder, Clayrine K. FTC 202-326-2153
Office of the Secretary....Ashe, Maurice FTC 202-326-2516
Office of the Secretary....Berman, Benjamin I. FTC 202-326-2513
Office of the Secretary....Bradley, Tasha FTC 202-326-3347
Office of the Secretary....Carson, Diane B. FTC 202-326-2515
Office of the Secretary....Clark, Donald S. FTC 202-326-2514
Office of the Secretary....Donohue, Richard C. FTC 202-326-3112
Office of the Secretary....Dowdle, Walter D. FTC 202-326-2505
Office of the Secretary....Foster, Elizabeth M. FTC 202-326-2187

Office of the Secretary....Liebman, Marvin FTC 202-326-2069
Office of the Secretary....Lofty, Bernita V. FTC 202-326-3117
Office of the Secretary....Pierce, Diane E. FTC 202-326-2519
Office of the Secretary....Plummer, C. Landis FTC 202-326-2520
Office of the Secretary....Reynolds, Ronald H. FTC 202-326-2521
Office of the Secretary....Stephen, David FTC 202-326-2512
Office of the Secretary....Tanner, Trina A. FTC 202-326-2517
Office of the Secretary....Thielen, John J. FTC 202-326-2506
Office of the Secretary....Tinker, Wallace FTC 202-326-2192
Office of the Secretary....Williams, Linda A. FTC 202-326-2515
Office of the Secretary....Wood, Dolores A. FTC 202-326-2518
Offshore Radio Telecommunications Service....Staff FCC 202-653-5560
Oil and Gas Development and Refining, Maj. Proj.....Miles, Max COMMERCE 202-482-0679
Oil and Gas (Fuels Only)....Gillett, Tom COMMERCE 202-482-1466
Oil and Gas Leasing on Fish and Wildlife Refuges....Staff FWS 703-358-2183
Oil and Gas Statistics....Peterson, Jimmie NEIC 202-586-6401
Oil and Hazardous Material Spills....Staff EPA 202-267-2675
Oil and Hazardous Material Spills Response Hotline....Staff EPA 800-424-8802
Oil Field Machinery, Trade Promo.....Miles, Max COMMERCE 202-482-0679
Oil Field Machinery....Vacant COMMERCE 202-482-0680
Oil Industry Group....Daly, James M. SEC 202-942-1800
Oil, lubricating....Foreso, Cynthia USITC 202-205-3348
Oil Pollution....Staff EPA 703-603-8707
Oil Shale, Major Proj.....Bell, Richard COMMERCE 202-482-2460
Oil Shale Reserves Management....Furiga, Richard NEIC 202-586-4410
Oil Spills - Emergency Response Division....Staff EPA 800-424-8802
Oil Spills....Staff FWS 703-358-2148
Oil, Used....Staff EPA 703-603-8707
Oilcloth....Cook, Lee USITC 202-205-3471
Oils, Animal and Vegetable....Maria, John CUSTOMS 212-466-5730
Oils, essential....Land, Eric USITC 202-205-3349
Oilseeds - Soybeans, Sunflowers....Sanford, Scott 202-501-8550
Oilseeds - Soybeans, Sunflowers....Ash, Mark Agri 202-219-0838
Oilseeds - Soybeans, Sunflowers - World....Castaneda, Jaime Agri 202-219-0826
Oilseeds - Soybeans, Sunflowers....Kerestes, Dan Agri 202-270-9526
Oilseeds....Reeder, John USITC 202-205-3319
Older Drivers....Staff NIA 301-496-1752
Older Women....Staff NIA 301-496-1752
Older Workers, Empl/Unempl. Stats.....Rones, Philip LABOR 202-606-6378
Oleic acid ester....Johnson, Larry USITC 202-205-3351
Oleic acid....Randall, Rob USITC 202-205-3366
Oleyl alcohols....Randall, Rob USITC 202-205-3366
Olivopontocerebellar Atrophy....Staff NINDS 301-496-5751
Oman/Minerals....Michalski, Bernadette Cnty Mines 202-501-9699
Oman (Muscat)....Staff Cnty State 202-647-6571
Oman....Al-Dhahab, Abdulla Moh'd Aqueel Cnty Embassy 202-387-1980
Oman....Al-Rawas, Ghazi Said Cnty Embassy 202-387-1981
Oman....Konigshofer, Friedrich Cnty World Bank 202-473-2988
Oman....Mabury-Lewis, Anthony Cnty 202-565-3739
Oman....Mercer, Dorothy Cnty Treasury 202-622-0184
Oman....Thanos, Paul Cnty Commerce 202-482-1860
Oman....Vacant Cnty USIA 202-619-6528
Oman....Vacant Cnty AID 202-663-2620
On Site Contractor Employees....Saunders, Paristina FTC 202-326-2243
On Site Contractor Employees....Hallman, Kevin J. FTC 202-326-2243
On Site Contractor Employees....Lathern, Ronald C. FTC 202-326-2290
On Site Contractor Employees....Gardner, Kevin P. FTC 202-326-2243
On Site Contractor Employees....Cassagnol, Pascale FTC 202-326-2088
On Site Contractor Employees....Baxter, Robert L., II FTC 202-326-2243
Onchocerciasis....Staff NEI 301-496-5248
Onchocerciasis....Staff NIAID 301-496-5717
Oncology....Staff NCI 301-496-5583
One-Way Paging and Signaling....Staff FCC 202-653-8157
Online Information Retrieval Services....Staff NCRR/NIH Library 301-496-1156
Online Information Retrieval Services....Staff NLM 301-496-6095
Open Network Architecture....Staff FCC 202-418-1571
Ophthalmia Neonatorum....Staff NEI 301-496-5248
Ophthalmic Congenital and Genetic Disease....Staff NEI 301-496-5248
Ophthalmic....Johnson, Christopher USITC 202-205-3488
Ophthalmology Research....Staff NEI 301-496-5248
Oppenheim's Disease (Amyotonia Congenita)....Staff NINDS 301-496-5751
Optic Atrophy....Staff NEI 301-496-5248
Optic Neuritis....Staff NEI 301-496-5248
Optic....Tarcza, Thomas C. PTO 703-308-1689
Optical communication....Chilcot, Richard PTO 703-305-4716
Optical elements....Johnson, Christopher USITC 202-205-3488

Optical Equipment....Kiefer, Barbara CUSTOMS 212-466-5685
Optical goods....Johnson, Christopher USITC 202-205-3488
Optical measuring....Chilcot, Richard PTO 703-305-4716
Optical Physics....Clark, C.W. NIST 301-975-3709
Optical testing....Chilcot, Richard PTO 703-305-4716
Optics....Gellner, Michael L. PTO 703-308-1436
Optometry Research....Staff NEI 301-496-5248
Oral Cancer....Staff NCI 301-496-5583
Oral Cancer....Staff NIDR 301-496-4261
Oral Contraceptives....Staff NICHD 301-496-5133
Oral Health....Marianos, Donald W. CDC 404-488-4452
Oral Surgery-Intravenous Sedation....Staff NIDR 301-496-4261
Orange oil (essential oil)....Land, Eric USITC 202-205-3349
Ordering Info (Computer Software, Publications)....Customer Services Staff CENSUS 301-457-4100
Ores....Fitzgerald, John CUSTOMS 212-466-5492
Organ Donation....Staff UNOS 800-243-6667
Organ donation....Staff Living Bank 800-528-2971
Organ Donations (Eyes)....Staff NEI 301-496-5248
Organ Transplants....Braslow, Judy HRSA 301-443-7577
Organ Transplants/Medicare, Medicaid Funding....Hardy, Robert HCFA 202-966-3206
Organic acids....Michels, David USITC 202-205-3352
Organic Analytical Research....May, Willie E. NIST 301-975-3108
Organic Brain Syndrome...Staff NINDS 301-496-5751
Organic Brain Syndrome....Staff NINDS 301-496-5751
Organic Chemicals....Kelly, Michael COMMERCE 202-482-0128
Organization for Economic Cooperation and Develop.....Staff Cnty State 202-647-2469
Organized Crime....Coffey, Paul E. Justice 202-514-3594
Organo-metallic compounds....Michels, David USITC 202-205-3352
Organo-Sulfur Compounds....Winters, William CUSTOMS 212-466-5747
Original Telephone and Telephone Plant Cost....Staff FCC 202-632-3772
Orotic Aciduria....Staff NIDDK 301-654-4415
Orphan drugs....Staff National Information Center for Orphan Drugs and rare Diseases 800-456-3505
Orphan Drugs....Haffner, Marlene FDA 301-443-4903
Orphan Drugs....Staff FDA 301-443-4903
Orphan Drugs....Staff NINDS 301-496-5751
Orphan Drugs....Staff OD 301-402-4336
Orthodontics....Staff NIDR 301-496-4261
Orthognathic Surgery....Staff NIDR 301-496-4261
Orthokeratology....Staff NEI 301-496-5248
Orthopedic care for children...Staff Shriners Hospital Referral Line 800-237-5055
Orthopedic Disorders....Staff NIAMS 301-496-8188
Orthopedic Implants....Staff NIAMS 301-496-8188
Orthopedics instruments....Apley, Richard PTO 703-308-0305
Orthostatic Hypotension....Staff NINDS 301-496-5751
Orthostatic Hypotension....Staff NHLBI 301-496-4236
Orthotics....Staff NIAMS 301-496-8188
Osgood-Schlatter Disease...Staff NIAMS 301-496-8188
Osler-Weber-Rendu Syndrome....Staff NHLBI 301-496-4236
Ossein....Jonnard, Aimison USITC 202-205-3350
Osteitis Deformans....Staff NIAMS 301-496-8188
Osteoarthritis with Age....Staff NIA 301-496-1752
Osteoarthritis....Staff NIA 301-496-1752
Osteoarthritis....Staff NIAMS 301-496-8188
Osteochondrosis....Staff NIAMS 301-496-8188
Osteogenesis Imperfecta....Staff NICHD 301-496-5133
Osteogenesis Imperfecta....Staff NIAMS 301-496-8188
Osteogenesis....Staff NIAMS 301-496-8188
Osteogenic Sarcoma....Staff NCI 301-496-5583
Osteomalacia....Staff NIAMS 301-496-8188
Osteomyelitis....Staff NIAMS 301-496-8188
Osteonecrosis....Staff NIAMS 301-496-8188
Osteopathic Medicine....Staff American Osteopathic Association (OA) 800-621-1773
Osteoporosis with Age....Staff NIAMS 301-496-8188
Osteoporosis....Staff NICHD 301-496-5133
Osteoporosis....Staff NIAMS 301-496-8188
Osteosclerosis (Osteopetrosis)....Staff NICHD 301-496-5133
Osteosclerosis (Osteopetrosis)....Staff NIAMS 301-496-8188
Ostomy....Staff United Ostomy Association (UOA) 800-826-0826
Ostomy....Staff NIDDK 301-654-3810
OTC (over-the-counter margin stock list)....Wolffrum, Margaret FRS 202-452-2781
Otitis Media....Staff NIDCD 301-496-7243

Be patient. If any phone number is incorrect, call (area code) 555-1212 and request the new listing.

1425

Otitis Media....Staff NIAID 301-496-5717
Otitis Media....Staff NICHD 301-496-5133
Otosclerosis....Staff NIDCD 301-496-7243
Otosclerosis....Staff NINDS 301-496-5751
Ototoxic Drugs....Staff NIDCD 301-496-7243
Outdoor Air - Cities....Staff EPA 202-260-5575
Outdoor Lightning Fixtures....Bodson, John COMMERCE 202-482-0681
Outdoor Power (Export Promo)....Hodgen, Donald COMMERCE 202-482-3346
Outer Continental Shelf....Staff FWS 703-358-2183
Ovarian Cancer....Staff NCI 301-496-5583
Ovens....Mata, Ruben USITC 202-205-3403
Oviduct....Staff NICHD 301-496-5133
Ovulation....Staff NICHD 301-496-5133
Ovum....Staff NICHD 301-496-5133
Oxalosis and Hyperoxaluria....Staff NIDDK 301-654-3810
Oxides, inorganic....Conant, Kenneth USITC 202-205-3346
Oxygen....Conant, Kenneth USITC 202-205-3346
Oxygenators (Artificial Lungs)....Staff NHLBI 301-496-4236
Ozone - Stratospheric....Staff EPA 919-541-5526

P

Pacemaker (Cardiac/Heart)....Staff NHLBI 301-496-4236
Pacemakers....Cruzan, Susan FDA 301-443-3285
Pacific Islands (General)....Staff Cnty State 202-647-3546
Pacific Islands....Bouck, Gary (Bus.)/Golike, William (Policy) Cnty Commerce 202-482-2471
Pacific Nations....Jabbs, Theodore Cnty USIA 202-619-5836
Pacific/trade matters....Lake, Charles US Trade Rep 202-395-3900
Pacific/trade matters....Cassidy, Robert US Trade Rep 202-395-3430
Pacific/trade matters....Lund, Christina US Trade Rep 202-395-6813
Packages....Goldberg, Gerald PTO 703-308-5443
Packaging Machinery....Shaw, Gene COMMERCE 202-482-3494
Packaging machines....Jackson, Georgia USITC 202-205-3399
Paget's Disease of Bone (Osteitis Deformans)....Staff NIAMS 301-496-8188
Paget's Disease of the Skin....Staff NCI 301-496-5583
Paging--One Way....Staff FCC 717-337-1212
Pain and the Elderly....Staff NIA 301-496-1752
Pain (Cancer Related)....Staff NCI 301-496-5583
Pain (Oral-Facial)....Staff NIDR 301-496-4261
Pain (Pharmacology)....Staff NIDA 301-443-6245
Pain....Staff NINDS 301-496-5751
Pain....Staff NIDR 301-496-1752
Paint rollers....Burns, Gail USITC 202-205-2501
Paint sets, artist's....Johnson, Larry USITC 202-205-3351
Paint....Brownchweig, Gilbert CUSTOMS 212-466-5744
Paintings....Mushinske, Larry CUSTOMS 212-466-5739
Paints/Coatings....Prat, Raimundo COMMERCE 202-482-0128
Paints....Johnson, Larry USITC 202-205-3351
Pajamas....Sweet, Mary Elizabeth USITC 202-205-3455
Pakistan (Islamabad)....Staff Cnty State 202-647-9823
Pakistan/Minerals....Kuo, Chin Cnty Mines 202-501-9693
Pakistan....Fardoust, Shahrokh Cnty World Bank 202-473-3049
Pakistan....Ghazanfar, Agha Cnty Embassy 202-939-6200
Pakistan....Gilman, Timothy Cnty Commerce 202-482-2954
Pakistan....Hutchings, Dayna Cnty Export-Import Bank 202-565-3737
Pakistan....Kiranbay, Carol Cnty AID 202-647-6967
Pakistan....Lodhi, Maleeha Cnty Embassy 202-939-6200
Pakistan....Ordonez, Miguel Peace Corps 202-606-3118
Pakistan....VanRenerghem, Cynthia Cnty Treasury 202-622-0343
Pakistan....Winchester, Rebecca Cnty USIA 202-619-6528
Palau (Koror)....Staff Cnty State 202-647-0108
Palau....Imam, Fahmila Cnty Export-Import Bank 202-565-3738
Palau....Lyday, Travis Cnty Mines 202-501-9695
Palestine....Hughes, Elizabeth Cnty Treasury 202-622-0174
Palm oil....Reeder, John USITC 202-205-3319
Palmitic acid esters....Johnson, Larry USITC 202-205-3351
Palpitation....Staff NHLBI 301-496-4236
Palsy, Cerebral....Staff NINDS 301-496-5751
Palsy, Progressive Supranuclear....Staff NINDS 301-496-5751
Panama/Minerals....Rabchevsky, George Cnty Mines 202-501-9670
Panama (Panama City)....Staff Cnty State 202-647-4986
Panama....Anne McKinney Cnty TDA 703-875-4357
Panama....Arias, Ricardo Alberto Cnty Embassy 202-483-1407
Panama....Berz, Cristina Cnty World Bank 202-473-3901
Panama....Geiser, Barbara Cnty Treasury 202-622-1271

Panama....Lee, Helen Cnty Commerce 202-482-2528
Panama....Lostumbo, Julie Peace Corps 202-606-3620
Panama....Murray, Mandy Peace Corps 202-606-3321
Panama....Shumake, Josie Cnty USIA 202-619-5864
Panama....Suescam Alfaro, Alfredo Cnty Embassy 202-483-1407
Panama....Wilkins, Michele Cnty Export-Import Bank 202-565-3743
Pancreatic Diseases....Staff NIDDK 301-654-3810
Panencephalitis....Staff NINDS 301-496-5751
Panic Disorder....Staff NIMH 301-443-4513
Pantyhose....Shetty, Sundar USITC 202-205-3486
Pantyhose....DeGaetano, Angela CUSTOMS 212-466-5540
Pap Smear....Staff NCI 301-496-5583
Paper and Board Packaging....Stanley, Gary COMMERCE 202-482-0375
Paper and Paper Products....Abromowitz, Carl CUSTOMS 212-466-5733
Paper Industries Machinery....Abrahams, Edward COMMERCE 202-482-0312
Paper Industry Group....Owings, Christopher SEC 202-942-1900
Paper machines....Lusi, Susan USITC 202-205-2334
Paper, products of....Twarok, Chris USITC 202-205-3314
Paper....Rhodes, Richard USITC 202-205-3322
Paper....Stanley, Gary COMMERCE 202-482-0375
Paperboard machines....Lusi, Susan USITC 202-205-2334
Paperboard, products of....Twarok, Chris USITC 202-205-3314
Paperboard....Rhodes, Richard USITC 202-205-3322
Papermakers' felts....Cook, Lee USITC 202-205-3471
Papermaking materials....Rhodes, Richard USITC 202-205-3322
Papillomavirus and Cancer....Staff NCI 301-496-5583
Papillomavirus....Staff NIAID 301-496-5717
Papua New Guinea....Imam, Fahmila Cnty Export-Import Bank 202-565-3738
Papua New Guinea....Jabbs, Theodore Cnty USIA 202-619-5836
Papua New Guinea....Schneider, Todd Cnty Treasury 202-622-0335
Papua New Guinea....Hamidian-Rad, Pirouz Cnty World Bank 202-473-4879
Papua New Guinea....Respess, Rebecca Cnty TDA 703-875-4357
Papua New Guinea....Ekivaki-Seruvatu, Alofa Cnty Embassy 202-745-3680
Papua New Guinea....Watangia, Kepas Isimel Cnty Embassy 202-745-3680
Papua New Guinea....Nagle, Douglas Peace Corps 202-606-3290
Papua New Guinea....Schell, Russell Peace Corps 202-606-3231
Papua New Guinea....Lee, Allison Peace Corps 202-606-0983
Papua New Guinea/Minerals....Lyday, Travis Cnty Mines 202-501-9695
Papua New Guinea (Port Moresby)....Staff Cnty State 202-647-3546
Parachutes....Andersen, Peder USITC 202-205-3388
Paraguay (Asuncion)....Staff Cnty State 202-647-2296
Paraguay/Minerals....Gurmendi, Alfredo Cnty Mines 202-501-9681
Paraguay....Anne McKinney Cnty TDA 703-875-4357
Paraguay....Augusto, Suzana C. Cnty World Bank 202-473-9096
Paraguay....Erlandson, Barbara Peace Corps 202-606-3499
Paraguay....Geiser, Barbara Cnty Treasury 202-622-1271
Paraguay....Gonzalez, Federico A. Cnty Embassy 202-483-6961
Paraguay....Leeb, Howard Cnty USIA 202-619-5867
Paraguay....Mye, Randolph Cnty Commerce 202-482-1548
Paraguay....Prevot, Babette Cnty AID 202-647-4359
Paraguay....Prieto, Jorge G. Cnty Embassy 202-483-6960
Paraguay....Ross, Rebecca Peace Corps 202-606-3575
Paraguay....Wilkins, Michele Cnty Export-Import Bank 202-565-3743
Paralysis Agitans....Staff NINDS 301-496-5751
Paralysis, Periodic....Staff NINDS 301-496-5751
Paralysis....Staff American Paralysis Association (APA) 800-225-0292
Paramedical Training....Staff HRSA/BHPr 301-443-5794
Paramyotonia Congenita....Staff NINDS 301-496-5751
Paranoia....Staff NIMH 301-443-4513
Paraosmia....Staff NIDCD 301-496-7243
Paraplegia....Staff NINDS 301-496-5751
Parasitic Disease....Staff NIAID 301-496-5717
Parasitic Diseases....Staff CDC 404-488-7760
Parasitology....Staff NIAID 301-496-5717
Parathyroid Disorders....Staff NIDDK 301-496-3583
Parenthood....Staff Planned Parenthood Federation of America (PPFA) 800-230-7526
Parenting....Staff Positive Pregnancy and Parenting Fitness 800-433-5523
Parents of Visually Impaired....Staff National Association for Parents of the Visually Impaired (NAPVI) 800-562-6265
Paris Air Show....Staff COMMERCE 202-482-2835
Parkinson's Disease....Staff American Parkinson's Disease Association (APDA) 800-223-2732
Parkinson's Disease....Staff 800-457-6676
Parkinson's Disease....Staff National Parkinson Foundation (NPF) 800-327-4545
Parkinson's Disease....Staff NINDS 301-496-5751
Parkinson's Disease....Staff NIDCD 301-496-7243

Parkinsonism-Dementia....Staff NINDS 301-496-5751

Parole and Parolees....Greenfeld, Lawrence Justice Stat 202-616-3281

Parole and Parolees....Huggins, M. Wayne Justice Stat 202-307-3106

Paroxysmal Atrial Tachycardia (PAT)....Staff NHLBI 301-496-4236

Paroxysmal Nocturnal Hemoglobinuria....Staff NIAID 301-496-5717

Paroxysmal Nocturnal Hemoglobinuria....Staff NHLBI 301-496-4236

Pars Planitis....Staff NEI 301-496-5248

Part-time Workers, Employment/Employment....Nardone, Thomas LABOR 202-606-6378

Particle Beams....Wood, Robert NEIC 301-903-5535

Particle board....Hoffmeier, Bill USITC 202-205-3321

Party favors....Abrahamson, Dana USITC 202-205-3430

Parvovirus Infections....Staff NIAID 301-496-5717

Passenger autos, trucks, and buses....Hagey, Michael USITC 202-205-3392

Pasta....Manogue, Robert COMMERCE 202-482-2428

Patents, Fish and Wildlife....Staff FWS 703-358-1938

Pathogen-Free Mice and Rats....Staff NCRR 301-496-5255

Pathology....Elin, Ronald J. FAES 301-496-5668

Patient Activities Department....Staff CC 301-496-2276

Patient Dumping....Holtz, Judy IG 202-619-1142

Patient Emergency Fund...Staff CC 301-496-2381

Patient Referrals...Staff CC 301-496-4891

Paving Materials, Asphalt....McCauley, Patrick COMMERCE 202-482-0132

Paving Materials, Concrete....Pitcher, Charles COMMERCE 202-482-0132

Pay Telephone Compensation....Staff FCC 202-418-0960

PC-MATLAB....Staff DCRT 301-496-1122

PC-MLAB....Staff DCRT 301-402-1942

PC-MLAB...Staff DCRT 301-496-1122

PCBs (Polychlorinated Biphenyl) Chem. Regulations....Staff EPA 202-260-3933

PCP...Staff NIDA 301-443-6245

PCS-Auctions Hotline....Staff FCC 202-418-1400

Peanuts - World....McCormick, Ian Agri 202-219-0840

Peanuts....Burket, Stephen USITC 202-205-3318

Peanuts....Ropel, Stephen Agri 202-720-8843

Peanuts....Sanford, Scott Agri 202-219-0835

Pearl essence....Johnson, Larry USITC 202-205-3351

Pearls....Witherspoon, Ricardo USITC 202-205-3489

Peat moss....Trainor, Cynthia USITC 202-205-3354

Peat....Cantrell, Raymond MINES 202-501-9411

Pectin....Janis, William V. COMMERCE 202-482-2250

Pectin....Jonnard, Aimison USITC 202-205-3350

Pectus Excavatum (Funnel Chest)....Staff NHLBI 301-496-4236

Pedodontics....Staff NIDR 301-496-4261

Peer Review Organizations (PROs)....Hardy, Robert HCFA 202-966-3206

Peer Review Orgs./Sanctions....Holtz, Judy IG 202-619-1142

Peer Review Process (Grants)....Staff DRG 301-594-7248

Pelizaeous-Merzbacher Disease....Staff NINDS 301-496-5751

Pelvic Inflammatory Disease....Staff NIAID 301-496-5717

Pemphigoid (Ocular)....Staff NEI 301-496-5248

Pemphigoid....Staff NIAMS 301-496-8188

Pemphigus Vulgaris....Staff NIAMS 301-496-8188

Pencils/Pens, etc....Vanderwolff, John COMMERCE 202-482-0348

Pencils....Seastrum, Carl USITC 202-205-3493

Pencils....Smyth, James CUSTOMS 212-466-2084

Penicillin....Nesbitt, Elizabeth USITC 202-205-3355

Pens....Smyth, James CUSTOMS 212-466-2084

People/China....McCall, Laura Cnty Commerce 202-482-3583

People/China....McQueen, Cheryl Cnty Commerce 202-482-3932

People with handicaps....People with Handicaps Resource Center 800-544-3284

People....Staff People's Medical Society 800-624-8773

Peptic Ulcers....Staff NIDDK 301-654-3810

Perchloroethylene....Michels, David USITC 202-205-3352

Percutaneous Transluminal Coronary Angioplasty...Staff NHLBI 301-496-4236

Perfumery, cosmetics, and toilet preps....Land, Eric USITC 202-205-3349

Periarteritis Nodosa....Staff NIAID 301-496-5717

Periarteritis Nodosa....Staff NHLBI 301-496-4236

Pericardial Tamponade....Staff NHLBI 301-496-4236

Pericarditis....Staff NHLBI 301-496-4236

Pericardium....Staff NHLBI 301-496-4236

Perilymph Fistula...Staff NIDCD 301-496-7243

Perinatal Biology....Staff NICHD 301-496-5133

Periodic Paralysis....Staff NINDS 301-496-5751

Periodicals Reading Room....Krug, Patricia NAL 301-504-5204

Periodicals....Bratland, Rose Marie COMMERCE 202-482-0380

Periodontal Diseases....Staff NIDR 301-496-4261

Peripheral Nerve Tumor....Staff NINDS 301-496-5751

Peripheral Neuropathy (Neuritis)....Staff NINDS 301-496-5751

Peripheral Vascular Disease....Staff NHLBI 301-496-4236

Perlite....Bolen, Wallace P. MINES 202-501-9389

Permit Information, Fish and Wildlife....Staff FWS 703-358-2104

Pernicious Anemia....Staff NIDDK 301-496-3583

Peroneal Muscular Atrophy....Staff NINDS 301-496-5751

Peroxides and Acetals....Brady, Thomas CUSTOMS 212-466-5747

Peroxides, inorganic....Conant, Kenneth USITC 202-205-3346

Personal leather goods....Seastrum, Carl USITC 202-205-3493

Personality....Staff NIMH 301-443-4513

Persons with disabilities....Staff Job Accommodation Network 800-526-7234

Pertussis....Staff NIAID 301-496-5717

Peru (Lima)....Staff Cnty State 202-647-3360

Peru/Minerals....Gurmendi, Alfredo Cnty Mines 202-501-9681

Peru....Entwistle, Janet K. Cnty World Bank 202-473-0130

Peru....Hunt, Rebecca Cnty Commerce 202-482-2521

Peru....Jarvis, Catherine Cnty USIA 202-619-5867

Peru....Luna, Ricardo V. Cnty Embassy 202-833-9860

Peru....Parkinson, Katherine Cnty Treasury 202-622-5292

Peru...Quesada, Luis Cnty Embassy 202-833-9869

Peru....Schneider, John Cnty AID 202-647-4365

Peru....Wilkins, Michele Cnty Export-Import Bank 202-565-3743

Pesticide Hotline....Staff EPA 806-743-3095

Pesticide Information....Staff EPA 202-305-5919

Pesticide Monitoring Programs, National....Staff FWS 703-358-2148

Pesticide Monitoring....Staff FWS 703-358-2148

Pesticides and Toxic Substances....Staff EPA 202-235-5300

Pesticides and Toxic Enforcement....Staff EPA 202-260-4544

Pesticides Information Center....Staff EPA 202-305-5919

Pesticides....Hollrah, Glen H. PTO 703-308-4552

Pesticides....Reilly, Cornelius CUSTOMS 212-466-5770

Pesticides....Staff National Pesticide Telecommunications Network 800-858-7378

Pesticides....Staff NIEHS 919-541-3345

Pesticides....Wanser, Stephen USITC 202-205-3363

Pet animals (live)....Steller, Rose USITC 202-205-3323

Pet Food....Manogue, Robert COMMERCE 202-482-2428

Pet Products (Export Promo)....Kimmel, Edward K. COMMERCE 202-482-3640

Petrochemicals Plants, Major Proj.....Max, Miles COMMERCE 202-482-0679

Petrochemicals, Cyclic Crudes....Kelly, Michael COMMERCE 202-482-0128

Petrochemicals....Kelly, Michael COMMERCE 202-482-0128

Petroleum, Crude and Refined Products....Gillett, Tom COMMERCE 202-482-1466

Petroleum (Ground Level)....Staff EPA 919-541-5526

Petroleum Offshore Drilling....Staff FCC 717-337-1212

Petroleum Products Markets....Cook, John NEIC 202-586-5214

Petroleum Statistics....Heath, Charles NEIC 202-586-6860

Petroleum....Brady, Thomas CUSTOMS 212-466-5747

Petroleum....Christian, Trisha NEIC 202-586-8800

Petroleum....Foreso, Cynthia USITC 202-205-3348

Petroleum....Withrow, Leola NEIC 202-586-8800

Peyronie's Disease....Staff NIDDK 301-654-4415

Phacoemulsification....Staff NEI 301-496-5248

Pharmaceuticals....Reilly, Cornelius CUSTOMS 212-466-5770

Pharmaceuticals....Hurt, William COMMERCE 202-482-0128

Pharmacology Information System (PROPHET)....Staff NCRR 301-594-7934

Pharmacology Research Associate Training Program....Staff NIGMS 301-496-7301

Pharmacology/Toxicology....Staff NIGMS 301-496-7301

Pharmacology/Toxicology....Staff NIEHS 919-541-3345

Pharynx....Staff NIDR 301-496-4261

Phenois....Kight, John PTO 703-308-2453

Phenol....Matusik, Ed USITC 202-205-3356

Phenolic resins....Misurelli, Denby USITC 202-205-3362

Phenylketonuria (PKU)....Staff NICHD 301-496-5133

Pheochromocytema....Staff NHLBI 301-496-4236

Philippines (Manila)....Staff Cnty State 202-647-1221

Philippines/Minerals....Lyday, Travis Cnty Mines 202-501-9695

Philippines....Basilio, Antonio I. Cnty Embassy 202-467-9300

Philippines....Camp, Bea Cnty USIA 202-619-5837

Philippines....Imam, Fahmila Cnty Export-Import Bank 202-565-3738

Philippines....Khan, Shamina Cnty World Bank 202-458-2895

Philippines....Paine, George Cnty Commerce 202-482-3875

Philippines....Philip, Scott Peace Corps 202-606-1053

Philippines....Quinn, Lois Cnty Treasury 202-622-8014

Philippines....Rabe, Raul Ch. Cnty Embassy 202-467-9300

Philippines....Rahman, Talaat Cnty TDA 703-875-4357

Phlebitis....Staff NHLBI 301-496-4236

Phlebothrombosis....Staff NHLBI 301-496-4236

Be patient. If any phone number is incorrect, call (area code) 555-1212 and request the new listing.

1427

Phobias....Staff NIMH 301-496-4513

Phonograph and parts....Puffert, Douglas USITC 202-205-3402

Phonograph records....Puffert, Douglas USITC 202-205-3402

Phonographic equipment....Puffert, Douglas USITC 202-205-3402

Phonographs....Puffert, Douglas USITC 202-205-3402

Phosphate Rock....Cantrell, Raymond MINES 202-501-9411

Phosphatic fertilizers....Trainor, Cynthia USITC 202-205-3354

Phosphoric acid esters....Johnson, Larry USITC 202-205-3351

Phosphoric acid....Trainor, Cynthia USITC 202-205-3354

Phosphorous esters....Lee, Mary PTO 703-308-4546

Phosphorus compounds....Conant, Kenneth USITC 202-205-3346

Phosphorus....Trainor, Cynthia USITC 202-205-3354

Photocells....Malison, Andrew USITC 202-205-3391

Photocoagulation....Staff NEI 301-496-5248

Photocopy Services....Staff NIH Library/DRS 301-496-2983

Photocopying apparatus....Baker, Scott USITC 202-205-3386

Photocopying....Gellner, Michael L. PTO 703-308-1436

Photographic chemicals....Wanser, Stephen USITC 202-205-3363

Photographic Equipment and Supplies....Watson, Joyce COMMERCE 202-482-0574

Photographic film: scrap....Baker, Scott USITC 202-205-3386

Photographic film: waste....Baker, Scott USITC 202-205-3386

Photographic gelatin....Jonnard, Aimison USITC 202-205-3350

Photographic supplies....Baker, Scott USITC 202-205-3386

Photographs (Historical)....Staff NLM 301-496-5961

Photographs....Twarok, Chris USITC 202-205-3314

Photography....Gellner, Michael L. PTO 703-308-1436

Photography....Staff NCRRR 301-496-5995

Photovoltaics....Rannels, James E. NEIC 202-586-1720

PHS Commissioned Corps....Griss, William ASH 202-690-6867

Phthalic acid esters....Johnson, Larry USITC 202-205-3351

Phthalic anhydride....Matusik, Ed USITC 202-205-3356

Physical Environment. Agents (Effect on Hum. Hea.)....Staff NIEHS 919-541-3345

Physical Fitness and Sports, President's Council on....Perlmutter, Sandy ASH 202-272-3421

Physical Mapping....Staff NCHGR 301-402-0911

Physician's Assistant....Staff HRSA/BHPr 301-443-5794

Physicians....Staff Association of American Physicians and Surgeons (AAPS) 800-635-1196

Physicians...Staff American College of Physicians (ACP) 800-523-1546

Physics....McCarthy, James UVA 701-924-6783

Physiology....Staff NIGMS 301-496-7301

Pi-Mesons (Cancer Treatment)....Staff NCI 301-496-5583

Pi-Mesons (Cancer Treatment)....Staff NCI 301-496-5583

Pick's Disease....Staff NIA 301-496-1752

Pick's Disease....Staff NINDS 301-496-5751

Pickwickian Syndrome....Staff NHLBI 301-496-4236

Pig iron....MacKnight, Peg USITC 202-205-3431

Pigmented Villonodular Synovitis....Staff NIAMS 301-496-8188

Pigments, inorganic....Johnson, Larry USITC 202-205-3351

Pigments, organic....Wanser, Stephen USITC 202-205-3363

Pigments....Bell, Mark L. PTO 703-308-3823

Pigments....Brownchweig, Gilbert CUSTOMS 212-466-5744

Pillow blocks....Fravel, Dennis USITC 202-205-3404

Pillowcases....Sweet, Mary Elizabeth USITC 202-205-3455

Pillows....Spalding, Josephine USITC 202-205-3498

Pinball machines....Abrahamson, Dana USITC 202-205-3430

Pinene....Michels, David USITC 202-205-3352

Pink Eye....Staff NEI 301-496-5248

PinWorms....Staff NIAID 301-496-5717

Pipe, of rubber or plastics....Misurelli, Denby USITC 202-205-3362

Pipeline safety....Jackson, Larry NTSB 202-382-0670

Pipelines (Major Promo)....Miles, Max COMMERCE 202-482-0679

Pipes, tobacco....Burns, Gail USITC 202-205-2501

Pitch from wood....Randall, Rob USITC 202-205-3366

Pituitary Tumors....Staff NICHD 301-496-5133

Pituitary Tumors....Staff NIDDK 301-496-3583

Pituitary Tumors....Staff NINDS 301-496-5751

Pityriasis Rubra Pilaris....Staff NIAMS 301-496-8188

Pityriasis....Staff NIAMS 301-496-8188

PKU (Phenylketonuria)....Staff NICHD 301-496-5133

PL-480 Program....Staff FIC 301-496-1653

Placenta....Staff NICHD 301-496-5133

Plant Closings Statistics....Siegel, Lewis LABOR 202-606-6404

Plant Genome Information Center....McCarthy, Susan NAL 301-504-6613

Plants, live....Burket, Stephen USITC 202-205-3318

Plants....Conte, Ralph CUSTOMS 212-466-5759

Plaque (Dental)....Staff NIDR 301-496-4261

Plasma Cell Cancer....Staff NCI 301-496-5583

Plaster products....White, Linda USITC 202-205-3427

Plastic Construction Products, Most....Williams, Franklin COMMERCE 202-482-0132

Plastic Materials....Raimundo, Prat COMMERCE 202-482-0128

Plastic processes....Silbaugh, Jan H PTO 703-308-3829

Plastic Products Machinery....Robinson, Raymond COMMERCE 202-482-0610

Plastic Products....Prat, Raimundo COMMERCE 202-482-0128

Plastic Sheet....Mazzola, Joan CUSTOMS 212-466-5880

Plastic Surgeons....Staff American Society of Plastic and Reconstructive Surgeons 800-635-0635

Plastic wood....Johnson, Larry USITC 202-205-3351

Plasticizers....Johnson, Larry USITC 202-205-3351

Plastics, Biodegradable....Staff EPA 703-308-7259

Plastics products....Raftery, Jim USITC 202-205-3365

Plastics....Misurelli, Denby USITC 202-205-3362

Platelet Abnormalities....Staff NIDDK 301-496-3583

Platelet Requests....Staff CC 301-496-3608

Platelet Requests....Staff NCI 301-496-5583

Platelet Requests....Staff NHLBI 301-496-4236

Plateletpheresis Center....Staff CC 301-496-4321

Platinum compounds....Greenblatt, Jack USITC 202-205-3353

Platinum Group Metals....Trease, Robert Jr. MINES 202-501-9413

Platinum group metals....McNay, Deborah USITC 202-205-3425

Platinum....Rosenfeld, David CFT 312-353-9026

Pleasure boats....Lahey, Kathleen USITC 202-205-3409

Pleurisy....Staff NHLBI 301-496-4236

Plumbing Fixtures and Fittings....Shaw, Robert COMMERCE 202-482-0132

Plumbing Fixtures....Pitcher, Charles COMMERCE 202-482-0132

Plutonium....Greenblatt, Jack USITC 202-205-3353

Plywood/Panel Products....McNamara, Kathy COMMERCE 202-482-0375

Plywood....Hoffmeier, Bill USITC 202-205-3321

PMS (Premenstrual Syndrome)....Staff NIMH 301-443-4515

PMS (Premenstrual Syndrome)....Staff NICHD 301-496-5133

Pneumococcal Infections....Staff NIAID 301-496-5717

Pneumoconioses (Dust Inhalation Disease)....Staff NHLBI 301-496-4236

Pneumocystis Carinii....Staff NIAID 301-496-5717

Pneumonia and Older People....Staff NIA 301-496-1752

Pneumonia....Staff NIAID 301-496-5717

Pneumothorax....Staff NHLBI 301-496-4236

Point-of-Use Water Treatment....Vacant COMMERCE 202-482-3509

Point-to-Point Microwave Common Carrier....Staff FCC 202-634-1706

Poison Control Ctrs.....Staff VA 202-625-3333

Poison Control Ctrs.....Staff MD 800-492-2414

Poison Control Ctrs.....Staff DC 202-625-3333

Poison Control Ctrs.....Staff MD 410-528-7701

Poison Ivy....Staff NIAID 301-496-5717

Poland/Minerals....Steblez, Walter Cnty Mines 202-501-9671

Poland (Warsaw)....Staff Cnty State 202-647-4139

Poland....Ann Lien Cnty TDA 703-875-4357

Poland....Azemien, Susan Cnty Treasury 202-622-2887

Poland....Horvai, Andras Cnty World Bank 202-473-3046

Poland....Jaroszynski, Andrzej Cnty Embassy 202-234-3801

Poland....Kozminski, Jerzy Cnty Embassy 202-234-3800

Poland....Lockwood, Jennifer Peace Corps 202-606-3607

Poland....Robinson, Susan Cnty USIA 202-619-6853

Poland....Schiel, Russell Peace Corps 202-606-3606

Poland....Waxman-Lenz, Roberta Cnty Export-Import Bank 202-565-3742

Poland....Zuck, Audrey Cnty Commerce 202-482-4915

Pole Attachments....Staff FCC 202-634-1861

Police Statistics....Manson, Donald Justice Stat 202-616-3491

Police Statistics....White, Paul Justice Stat 202-307-0771

Polioencephalitis (Cerebral Poliomyelitis)....Staff NINDS 301-496-5751

Poliomyelitis....Staff NIAID 301-496-5717

Polishes under 10 lbs each....Randall, Rob USITC 202-205-3366

Political campaign agendas in US and Britain....Gurevitch, Michael UMD 301-405-2418

Pollen Allergy....Staff NIAID 301-496-5717

Pollution (Air, Waste, Water)....Staff EPA 202-260-7606

Pollution Abatement Reporting....Staff FWS 703-358-1719

Pollution Control Equipment....Jonkers, Loretta COMMERCE 202-482-0564

Pollution Funds Center....Sheehan, Daniel USCG 703-235-4720

Pollution Prevention Division....Staff EPA 202-260-3557

Pollution Prevention Policy....Staff EPA 202-260-8621

Polyarteritis....Staff NHLBI 301-496-4236

Polycarbonate resins....Misurelli, Denby USITC 202-205-3362
Polychondritis....Staff NIAMS 301-496-8188
Polycystic Kidney Disease....Staff NIDDK 301-654-4415
Polycystic Ovary Syndrome....Staff NICHD 301-496-5133
Polycythemia (Vera)....Staff NHLBI 301-496-4236
Polycythemia (Vera)....Staff NCI 301-496-5583
Polyester resins....Misurelli, Denby USITC 202-205-3362
Polyesters....Kight, John PTO 703-308-2453
Polyethylene terephthalate (PET) resins....Misurelli, Denby USITC 202-205-3362
Polyethylene....Misurelli, Denby USITC 202-205-3362
Polyhydric alcohols, fatty acids of, animal/veg....Land, Eric USITC 202-205-3349
Polyhydric alcohols of polysaccharides and rare....Randall, Rob USITC 202-205-3366
Polyhydric alcohol....Michels, David USITC 202-205-3352
Polyisoprene rubber....Misurelli, Denby USITC 202-205-3362
Polymers....Misurelli, Denby USITC 202-205-3362
Polymers....Smith, L.E. NIST 301-975-6762
Polymyalgia Rheumatica....Staff NIAMS 301-496-8188
Polymyositis....Staff NINDS 301-496-5751
Polymyositis....Staff NIAMS 301-496-8188
Polyneuritis (Guillain-Barre Syndrome)....Staff NINDS 301-496-5751
Polyostotic Fibrous Dysplasia (Albright's Syndr.)....Staff NIAMS 301-496-8188
Polypropylene....Misurelli, Denby USITC 202-205-3362
Polyps and Cancer....Staff NCI 301-496-5583
Polyps, Colon....Staff NIDDK 301-496-3583
Polyps, Colon....Staff NCI 301-496-5583
Polysaccharides....Randall, Rob USITC 202-205-3366
Polysiloxanes....Bleutge, John PTO 703-308-2363
Polystyrene resins....Misurelli, Denby USITC 202-205-3362
Polysulfides....Bleutge, John PTO 703-308-2363
Polyurethane resins....Misurelli, Denby USITC 202-205-3362
Polyvinyl alcohol resins....Misurelli, Denby USITC 202-205-3362
Polyvinyl chloride....Misurelli, Denby USITC 202-205-3362
Pompe's Disease....Staff NIDDK 301-496-3583
Pompe's Disease....Staff NINDS 301-496-5751
Poor, Working, Employment/Unemployment Statistics....Herz, Diane LABOR 202-606-6378
Population, Age and Sex (States, Counties)....Staff CENSUS 301-457-2422
Population, Aging....Kinsella, Kevin CENSUS 301-457-1371
Population, Apportionment....Staff CENSUS 301-457-2381
Population, Citizenship....Staff CENSUS 301-457-2403
Population, Commuting....Boertein, Celia CENSUS 301-457-2454
Population, Consumer Expenditure Survey....Hoff, Gail CENSUS 301-457-3925
Population, Crime....Hoff, Gail CENSUS 301-457-3925
Population, Disability....McNeil, Jack CENSUS 301-763-8300
Population Dynamics and Problems....Staff NICHD 301-496-5133
Population Ecology, Fish and Wildlife....Staff FWS 703-358-1710
Population, Education....Staff CENSUS 301-457-2464
Population, Estimates....Staff CENSUS 301-457-2422
Population, General Information....Staff CENSUS 301-457-2422
Population, Group Quarters....Smith, Denise CENSUS 301-457-2378
Population Health Studies....Goldsmith, Robert NEIC 301-903-5926
Population, Homeless....Clark, Annette CENSUS 301-457-2378
Population Information....Staff CENSUS 301-457-2422
Population, Language....Staff CENSUS 301-457-2464
Population, Longitudinal Surveys....Higgins, Sarah CENSUS 301-457-3801
Population, National Estimates....Staff CENSUS 301-457-2422
Population, National Surveys....Staff CENSUS 301-457-2422
Population, Outlying Areas....Levin, Michael CENSUS 301-457-2327
Population, Place of Birth....Hansen, Kristin CENSUS 301-457-2454
Population, School District Data....Ingold, Jane CENSUS 301-457-2408
Population, State and Outlying Areas Estimates....Staff CENSUS 301-457-2422
Population, State Projections....Staff CENSUS 301-457-2422
Population Survey (Current), Earnings, Empl/Unempl.....Mellor, Earl LABOR 202-606-6378
Porcelain Electrical Supplies, Part....Whitley, Richard A. COMMERCE 202-482-2213
Pork bellies with options....Prentice, Jon CFT 312-353-8647
Pork....Newman, Douglas USITC 202-205-3328
Porphuria....Staff NHLBI 301-496-4236
Porphyria....Staff NIAMS 301-496-8188
Porphyria....Staff NIDDK 301-654-3810
Port Safety....Sabol, Albert USCG 202-267-0489
Port Security....Sabol, Albert USCG 202-267-0489
Portugal (Lisbon)....Staff Cnty State 202-647-1412
Portugal/Minerals....Newman, Harold R. Cnty Mines 202-501-9669
Portugal....Double, Mary Beth Cnty Commerce 202-482-4508

Portugal....Feliz-Alves, Rui Cnty Embassy 202-328-8610
Portugal....Gosnell, Peter Cnty Export-Import Bank 202-565-3733
Portugal....Guimaraes, Fernando Andresen Cnty Embassy 202-328-8610
Portugal....Holloway, Barbara Cnty Treasury 202-622-0098
Portugal....Seifkin, David Cnty USIA 202-619-6582
Portugal....Szaszkiewicz, Barbara Cnty World Bank 202-473-4374
Position Emission Tomography....Wood, Robert NEIC 301-903-5355
Positional Vertigo....Staff NIDCD 301-496-7243
Positron Emission Tomography....Staff NINDS 301-496-5751
Postage-franking machines....Baker, Scott USITC 202-205-3386
Postal Services....Staff OD/DAS (Mailroom) 301-496-5651
Postdoctoral Fellowships....Staff DRG 301-594-7248
Postdoctoral Fellowships....Staff OD/OERT 301-496-1963
Postherpetic Neuralgia....Staff NINDS 301-496-5751
Postnatal Care....Staff NICHD 301-496-5133
Postpartum Depression....Staff NIMH 301-443-4513
Postpolio Muscular Atrophy....Staff NINDS 301-496-5751
Postpolio Syndrome....Staff NINDS 301-496-5751
Postural Hypotension....Staff NHLBI 301-496-4236
Potash....Searls, James P. MINES 202-501-9407
Potash....Trainor, Cynthia USITC 202-205-3354
Potassic fertilizers....Trainor, Cynthia USITC 202-205-3354
Potassium and sodium salts from coconut and other oils....Land, Eric USITC 202-205-3349
Potassium chloride....Trainor, Cynthia USITC 202-205-3354
Potassium compounds....Greenblatt, Jack USITC 202-205-3353
Potassium (Content of Foods)....Staff NHLBI 301-496-4236
Potatoes....Budge, Arvin Agri 202-720-4285
Potatoes....Lucier, Gary Agri 202-219-0117
Potatoes....McCarty, Timothy USITC 202-205-3324
Potatoes....Plummer, Charles Agri 202-219-0009
Pottery....Bratland, Rosemarie COMMERCE 202-482-0380
Pottery....McNay, Deborah USITC 202-205-3425
Poultry - Broilers, Turkeys, Eggs....Milton, Madison Agri 202-219-1192
Poultry - Broilers, Turkeys, Eggs....Christensen, Lee Agri 202-219-0714
Poultry - Broilers, Turkeys, Eggs - World....Witucki, Larry Agri 202-219-0766
Poultry - Broilers, Turkeys and Eggs....Little, Robert Agri 202-720-6147
Poultry - Broilers, Turkeys, Eggs....Krutchen, Tom Agri 202-690-4870
Poultry - Broilers, Turkeys and Eggs....Moore, Joel Agri 202-720-3244
Poultry Products....Hodgen, Donald A. COMMERCE 202-482-3346
Poultry....Newman, Douglas USITC 202-205-3328
Poultry....Staff Hotline Agriculture 800-535-4555
Poverty Statistics, Current Surveys....Staff CENSUS 301-763-8578
Powder, smokeless....Johnson, Larry USITC 202-205-3351
Powered-Lift Technology....Waller, Peter NASA 415-604-3938
Prader-Willi Syndrome....Staff NICHD 301-496-5133
Precious Metal Jewelry....Harris, John M. COMMERCE 202-482-1178
Precious stones....DeSapio, Vincent USITC 202-205-3435
Precocious Puberty....Staff NICHD 301-496-5133
Predator Control, Fish and Wildlife....Staff FWS 703-358-1718
Preemption of State Laws....Staff FCC 202-418-1720
Prefabricated Buildings, Metal....Williams, Franklin COMMERCE 202-482-0132
Prefabricated Buildings, Wood....Cosslett, Patrick COMMERCE 202-482-0132
Pregnancy and Infant Health....Atrash, Hani K. CDC 404-488-5147
Pregnancy....Staff NAPARE 800-638-2229
Pregnancy....Staff Positive Pregnancy and Parenting Fitness 800-433-5523
Pregnancy....Staff NICHD 301-496-5133
Pregnancy....Staff NCNR 301-496-0526
Prematurity....Staff NICHD 301-496-5133
Prenatal Care....Staff NICHD 301-496-5133
Prenatal Nutrition....Staff NICHD 301-496-5133
Prepared Meats....Manogue, Robert COMMERCE 202-482-2428
Presbycusis/Hearing and Aging....Staff NIA 301-496-1752
Presbycusis/Hearing and Aging....Staff NINDS 301-496-5751
Presbycusis/Hearing and Aging....Staff NIDCD 301-496-7243
Presbycusis....Staff NIDCD 301-496-7243
Presbycusis....Staff NINDS 301-496-5751
Presbyopia....Staff NEI 301-496-5248
Prescription Drug Abuse...Staff NIDA 301-443-6245
Presenile Dementia....Staff NINDS 301-496-5751
Presenile Dementia....Staff NIMH 301-443-4513
Presenile Dementia....Staff NIA 301-496-1752
Preservation and Access Program....Pindell, Alvetta NAL 301-504-5204
Press Information....Staff CENSUS 301-457-2974
Pretrial Release and Crime - Federal....Kaplan, Carol Justice Stat 202-307-0759
Prevention Research (Drug Abuse)...Staff NIDA 301-443-6245
Preventive Health Block Grant....Sims, Anne CDC 404-639-3286

Be patient. If any phone number is incorrect, call (area code) 555-1212 and request the new listing.

1429

Preventive Medicine....Staff American Institute for Preventive Medicine (AIPM) 800-345-2476

Price Caps....Staff FCC 202-418-1520

Price and Index Number Research, Prices/Lv. Cond....Zieschang, Kimberly LABOR 202-606-6573

Price Indexes (Consumer) Prices and Liv. Cond.....Jackman, Patrick LABOR 202-606-6952

Price Indexes, International, Assist. Commiss.....Reut, Katrina LABOR 202-606-7100

Prices, Foreign Countries, Prod. and Technol.....Godbout, Todd LABOR 202-606-5654

Prices/Living Conds, Assist. Commis.....Dalton, Kenneth LABOR 202-606-6960

Prices/Living Conds, Assist. Commis, Consumer Price Index....Greenlef, Joan LABOR 202-606-6950

Prices/Living Conds, Assist. Commis, Consumer Prices....Greenlef, Joan LABOR 202-606-6950

Prices/Living Conds, Associate Commissioner....Dalton, Kenneth LABOR 202-606-6960

Prices/Living Conds, Consumer Expenditure Survey Data....Passero, William LABOR 202-606-6900

Prices/Living Conds, Consumer Expenditure Survey Operations....Dietz, Richard LABOR 202-606-6872

Prices/Living Conds, Consumer Expenditure Survey Tapes....Passero, William LABOR 202-606-6900

Prices/Living Conds, Consumer Expenditure Survey....Jacobs, Eva LABOR 202-606-6900

Prices/Living Conds, Consumer Expenditure Survey....Jacobs, Eva LABOR 202-606-6900

Prices/Living Conds, Consumer Price Indexes....Jackman, Patrick LABOR 202-606-6952

Prices/Living Conds, Consumer Price Indexes....Staff LABOR 202-606-7000

Prices/Living Conds, CPI, Data Diskettes....Gibson, Sharon LABOR 202-606-6968

Prices/Living Conds, CPI Recorded Detail....24-Hour Hotline LABOR 202-606-7828

Prices/Living Conds, Data Diskettes....Rosenberg, Elliott LABOR 202-606-7728

Prices/Living Conds, Data Diskettes....Rosenberg, Elliott LABOR 202-606-7728

Prices/Living Conds, Dept. Store Inventory....Gibson, Sharon LABOR 202-606-6968

Prices/Living Conds, Electric machinery and Transpor....Yatsko, Ralph LABOR 202-606-7747

Prices/Living Conds, Estd Retail Food Price, Mthly....Cook, William LABOR 202-606-6988

Prices/Living Conds, Food, Raw Matls, Apprl....Frumkin, Rob LABOR 202-606-7106

Prices/Living Conds, Forestry and Construction....Davies, Wanda LABOR 202-606-7714

Prices/Living Conds, Index Number Research Studies....Zieschang, Kimberly LABOR 202-606-6573

Prices/Living Conds, Indexes, Fuels, Mthly....Adkins, Robert LABOR 202-606-6985

Prices/Living Conds, Indexes, Utils, Mthly....Adkins, Robert LABOR 202-606-6985

Prices/Living Conds, Intl Price Indexes....Reut, Katrina LABOR 202-606-7100

Prices/Living Conds, Intl. Pr., Machinery....Costello, Brian LABOR 202-606-7107

Prices/Living Conds, Intl. Prices, Revision....Reut, Katrina LABOR 202-606-7100

Prices/Living Conds, Leather....Paik, Soon LABOR 202-606-7714

Prices/Living Conds, Machinery....Alterman, William LABOR 202-606-7108

Prices/Living Conds, Metals....Kazanowski, Edward LABOR 202-606-7735

Prices/Living Conds, Non-electric mach.....Dickerson, Bryandt LABOR 202-606-7744

Prices/Living Conds, Non-electric Machinery....Dickerson, Bryandt LABOR 202-606-7744

Prices/Living Conds, PPI, Forestry....Davies, Wanda LABOR 202-606-7714

Prices/Living Conds, PPI, Current Analysis....Howell, Craig LABOR 202-606-7705

Prices/Living Conds, Price Research Studies....Zieschang, Kimberly LABOR 202-606-6753

Prices/Living Conds, Producer Price Indexes....Tibbetts, Thomas LABOR 202-606-7700

Prices/Living Conds, Recorded CPI Summary....24-Hour quickline LABOR 202-606-6994

Prices/Living Cond., Recorded PPI Detail....24-hour hotline LABOR 202-606-7828

Prices/Living Conds, Retail Prices, Fuels, Mthly....Adkins, Robert LABOR 202-606-6985

Prices/Living Conds, Retail Prices, Gasoline....Chelena, Joseph LABOR 202-606-6982

Prices/Living Conds, Retail Prices, Utils, Mthly....Adkins, Robert LABOR 202-606-6985

Prices/Living Conds, Services....Gerduk, Irwin LABOR 202-606-7748

Prices/Living Conds, Statistical Methods....Hedges, Brian LABOR 202-606-6897

Prices/Living Conds, Textiles....Paik, Soon LABOR 202-606-7714

Prices/Living Conds, Transportation Equipment....Yatsko, Ralph LABOR 202-606-7747

Primary Biliary Cirrhosis....Staff NIDDK 301-654-3810

Primary Lateral Sclerosis....Staff NINDS 301-496-5751

Primary Ovarian Failure....Staff NICHD 301-496-5133

Primary Plastics....Reilly, Cornelius CUSTOMS 212-466-5770

Primate Research Centers Program....Staff NCRR 301-496-5175

Primate Research....Staff NCRR 301-594-7938

Prime mover dynamo plants....Pellinen, David PTO 703-308-0538

Prime Time Access Rule...Staff FCC 202-418-2130

Principe....Blackwell, Gloria Peace Corps 202-606-3998

Principe....Edwards, Jennifer R. Cnty World Bank 202-473-4875

Principe....Swezey, Virginia Peace Corps 202-606-3998

Printed circuit boards....Malison, Andrew USITC 202-205-3391

Printed matter....Twarok, Chris USITC 202-205-3314

Printed Matter....Abramowitz, Carl CUSTOMS 212-466-5733

Printing devices....Burr, Edgar PTO 703-308-0979

Printing and Publishing....Lofquist, William COMMERCE 202-482-0379

Printing ink....Johnson, Larry USITC 202-205-3351

Printing machines (textiles)....Greene, William USITC 202-205-3405

Printing machines....Lusi, Susan USITC 202-205-2334

Printing Trades Machines/Equipment....Robinson, Raymond COMMERCE 202-482-0610

Printing Trade Services....Lofquist, William COMMERCE 202-482-0379

Prisoner Surveys, National Prisoner Statistics....Hoff, Gail CENSUS 301-457-3925

Prisons, Prisoners, and Crowding....Greenfeld, Lawrence Justice Stat 202-616-3281

Prisons, Prisoners, and Crowding....Stephan, James Justice Stat 202-616-7273

Prisons, Prisoners, and Crowding....Huggins, Wayne M. Justice Stat 202-307-3106

Prisons, Prisoners, and Crowding....Baunach, Phyllis Jo Justice Stat 202-307-0361

Prisons, Prisoners, and Crowding....Beck, Allen Justice Stat 202-616-3277

Prisons, Prisoners, and Crowding....Innes, Christopher Justice Stat 202-724-3121

Privacy and Security of Data....Kaplan, Carol Justice Stat 202-307-0759

Private Carriers Communications....Staff FCC 717-337-1212

Private Coast Stations....Staff FCC 202-418-0680

Private Operational Fixed Services....Staff FCC 717-337-1212

Private Security....Zawitz, Marianne Justice Stat 202-616-3499

Privatization of Corrections....Lindgren, Sue Justice Stat 202-307-0760

Prize Giveaway....Staff FCC 202-418-1430

Probation and Probationers....Greenfeld, Lawrence Justice Stat 202-616-3281

Procaine....Staff NIA 301-496-1752

Process Control Instruments, Trade Promo.....Manzolilo, Frank COMMERCE 202-482-2991

Process Control Instruments....Nealon, Margaret COMMERCE 202-482-3411

Process Measurements....Rosasco, GJ NIST 301-975-2609

Procurement Services....Staff OD/ORS 301-496-3181

Producer Price Indexes, Analysis and Data....Howell, Craig LABOR 202-606-7704

Producer Price Indexes, Analysis and Data....Howell, Craig LABOR 202-606-7704

Producer Price Indexes, Electric Machinery and Trans....Yatsko, Ralph LABOR 202-606-7747

Producer Price Indexes, Forestry and Construction....Davies, Wanda LABOR 202-606-7713

Producer Price Indexes, Metals....Kazanowski, Edward LABOR 202-606-7735

Producer Price Indexes Prices/Living Cond.....Tibbetts, Thomas LABOR 202-606-7700

Producer Price Indexes, Textiles and Leather....Paik, Soon LABOR 202-606-7714

Product defects....Staff USP Practitioners Reporting Network 800-487-7776

Product manufacturing....Envall, Roy PTO 703-305-9706

Product safety....Staff CPSC 301-504-0580

Product safety....Staff CPSC 800-638-2772

Productivity and Technology, Assist. Commis.....Dean, Edwin R. LABOR 202-606-5600

Productivity and Technology, Associate Commissioner....Dean, Edwin R. LABOR 202-606-5600

Productivity and Technology, Compensation, For. Countries....Capdevielle, Patricia LABOR 202-606-5654

Productivity and Technology, Cost-of-Living Abroad....Capdevielle, Patricia LABOR 202-606-5654

Productivity and Technology, Data Diskettes....Fulco, Lawrence J. LABOR 202-606-5604

Productivity and Technology, Data Tapes....Kriebel, Bertram LABOR 202-606-5606

Productivity and Technology, Data Tapes....Kriebel, Bertram LABOR 202-606-5606

Productivity and Technology, Earnings, Foreign Countries....Capdevielle, Patricia LABOR 202-606-5654

Productivity and Technology, Employment Projections....Franklin, James LABOR 202-606-5709

Productivity and Technology, Employment Requirement Tbls....Franklin, James LABOR 202-606-5709

Productivity and Technology, For Countries, Other Econ In....Neef, Arthur LABOR 202-606-5654

Productivity and Technology, Foreign Countries, Labor For....Sorrentino, Constance LABOR 202-606-5654

Productivity and Technology, Foreign Countries, Productivity....Neef, Arthur LABOR 202-606-5654

Productivity and Technology, Foreign Countries, Unemployment....Sorrentino, Constance LABOR 202-606-5654

Productivity and Technology, Productivity and Costs-News Release....Fulco, Lawrence J. LABOR 202-606-5604

Productivity and Technology, Productivity in Government....Forte, Darlene J. LABOR 202-606-5621

Productivity and Technology, Productivity Research....Harper, Michael LABOR 202-606-5603

Productivity and Technology, Productivity Trends Federal Govt....Ardolini, Charles W. LABOR 202-606-5618

Productivity and Technology, Tech Trends, Major Ind....Riche, Richard LABOR 202-606-5626

Productivity in Government, Productivity and Tech.....Forte, Darlene J. LABOR 202-606-5621

Productivity, Multifactor, Labor Composition, Hrs.....Rosenblum, Larry LABOR 202-606-5606

Productivity Research, Capital Measurement, Pr/Tch....Harper, Michael LABOR 202-606-5603

Productivity Trends in Selected Industries....Ardolini, Charles W. LABOR 202-606-5618

Productivity Trends in Selected Ind. and Fed. Gov't....Ardolini, Charles W. LABOR 202-606-5618

Productivity, Unit Labor Costs, Foreign Countries....Neef, Arthur LABOR 202-606-5654

Professional Services....Staff OPM 202-606-4400

Professional services....Xavier, Neil USITC 202-205-3450

Progeria....Staff NIA 301-496-1752

Progestins and Progesterone....Staff NICHD 301-496-5133

Progestins and Progesterone....Staff HRSA/DMCH 301-443-4026

Progressive Cerebral Degeneration....Staff NINDS 301-496-5751

Progressive Dementia in Children....Staff NINDS 301-496-5751

Progressive Infantile Spinal Muscular Atrophy....Staff NINDS 301-496-5751

Progressive Leukodystrophy....Staff NINDS 301-496-5751

Progressive Multifocal Leukoencephalopathy....Staff NINDS 301-496-5751

Progressive Muscular Atrophy....Staff NINDS 301-496-5751

Progressive Supranuclear Palsy....Staff NINDS 301-496-5751

Progressive Systemic Sclerosis....Staff NINDS 301-496-5751

Progressive Systemic Sclerosis....Staff NIAMS 301-496-8188

Project LASER Volunteer Programs....Widenhofer, Karen NASA 205-544-3234

Project LASER Discovery Lab....Armstrong, Pat NASA 205-544-1798

Projections, Labor Force, Employment Projections....Fullerton, Howard LABOR 202-606-5711

Projections, Occupational, Empl. Proj.....Rosenthal, Neal LABOR 202-606-5701

Projectors (photographic)....Baker, Scott USITC 202-205-3386

Propagation Research, Fish and Wildlife....Staff FWS 703-358-1710

Propane....Land, Eric USITC 202-205-3349

Property Utilization....Staff OD/OL 301-496-4247

Propulsion Systems....Brogan, John NEIC 202-586-1477

Propylene glycol....Michels, David USITC 202-205-3352

Propylene oxide....Michels, David USITC 202-205-3352

Propylene....Raftery, Jim USITC 202-205-3365

Prosecution....Gaskins, Carla Justice Stat 202-508-8550

Prosecution....Langan, Patrick Justice Stat 202-616-3490

Prostaglandins....Staff NICHD 301-496-5133

Prostaglandins....Staff NHLBI 301-496-4236

Prostate Enlargement....Staff NIDDK 301-654-4415

Prostate/Hyperplasia of the Prostate....Staff NIDDK 301-654-4415

Prostate/Hyperplasia of the Prostate....Staff NIA 301-496-1752

Prostatitis....Staff NIDDK 301-654-4415

Prosthesis (Hearing)....Staff NIDCD 301-496-7243

Prostheses (Heart and Blood Vessel)....Staff NHLBI 301-496-4236

Prostheses (Orthotics)....Staff NIAMS 301-496-8188

Prosthetic devices....Green, Randall PTO 703-308-2912

Prosthetic devices....Staff NINDS 301-496-5751

Prosthodontics....Staff NIDR 301-496-4261

Protection of Human Subjects...Staff OD/OPRR 301-496-7005

Protein Abnormalities with Neurologic Disease....Staff NINDS 301-496-5751

Protein C and S....Staff NHLBI 301-496-4236

Protein Engineering....Staff DCRT 301-496-1100

Prurigo Nodularis....Staff NIAMS 301-496-8188

Pseudogout....Staff NIAMS 301-496-8188

Pseudohypoparathyroidism....Staff NIDDK 301-496-3583

Pseudomonas Infections....Staff NIAID 301-496-5717

Pseudosenility....Staff NIA 301-496-1752

Pseudotumor Cerebri....Staff NINDS 301-496-5751

Pseudotumor Cerebri....Staff NEI 301-496-5248

Pseudoxanthoma Elasticum....Staff NHLBI 301-496-4236

Psittacosis....Staff NIAID 301-496-5717

Psoriasis....Staff National Psoriasis Foundation (PF) 800-248-0886

Psoriasis....Staff NIAMS 301-496-8188

Psoriatic Arthritis....Staff NIAMS 301-496-8188

Psychology....Allen, Joseph P. UVA 804-982-4727

Psychology....McCarty, Richard UVA 804-924-4730

Psychoneuroimmunomodulation....Staff NINDS 301-496-5751

Psychopathology....Staff NIDA 301-443-6245

Psychopharmacology....Staff NIMH 301-443-4513

Psychoprophylaxis....Staff American Society for Psychoprophylaxis in Obstetrics 800-368-4404

Psychotherapeutic agents....Nesbitt, Elizabeth USITC 202-205-3355

Psychotherapy/Counseling....Staff NIDA 301-443-6245

Psychotic Episodes....Staff NIMH 301-443-4513

Pterygium....Staff NEI 301-496-5248

Ptosis....Staff NEI 301-496-5248

Public Affairs, Office of....Sims, Anne CDC 404-639-3286

Public Affairs Office....Murfy, Alexander FTC 202-326-2180

Public Affairs....Corlett, Cleve E. GAO 202-512-4800

Public Affairs....Hayden, Elizabeth A. NRC 301-415-8200

Public Coast Stations....Staff FCC 202-418-0680

Public Defense....Gaskins, Carla Justice Stat 202-508-8550

Public File Requirements AM/FM/TV....Staff FCC 202-418-1430

Public Health and Safety....Ziemer, Paul NEIC 202-586-6151

Public Health Issues....Nadel, Mark V. GAO 202-512-7119

Public Health System....Nicola, Ray CDC 404-639-1904

Public Health....Fintor, Lou FAES 301-496-5410

Public Housing....Staff HUD 202-708-0950

Public Information, Director, Office of....Mehnert, Robert NLM 301-496-6308

Public Information, Fish and Wildlife Service....Staff FWS 202-208-5634

Public Information Office - Atlanta....Mull, Daryl SSAREG 404-331-0612

Public Information Office - Boston....Czarnowski, Kurt SSAREG 617-565-2881

Public Information Office - Chicago....Mahler, Mary SSAREG 312-353-7092

Public Information Office, Chief....Mohn, Ingrid A. ECONOMIC 202-606-9900

Public Information Office - Dallas....O'Neil, Dee SSAREG 214-767-4191

Public Information Office - Denver....Taylor, Peter SSAREG 303-844-4441

Public Information Office - Kansas City....Nolker, Bud SSAREG 816-426-6191

Public Information Office - New York....Clark, John SSAREG 212-264-2500

Public Information Office - Philadelphia....Edward, Dana SSAREG 215-597-3747

Public Information Office - San Francisco....Walker, Leslie SSAREG 415-744-4664

Public Information Office - Seattle....Farrell, Dan SSAREG 206-615-2660

Public Information Office....Kendrick, Tony IHS 301-443-3593

Public Information Office....Velez, Larry OCR 202-619-1587

Public Information Office....Grigg, Bill ASH 202-690-6867

Public Information Office....Holtz, Judy IG 202-619-1142

Public Information Office....Gambino, Phil SSA 410-965-8904

Public Information Office....Kharfen, Michael ACF 202-401-9215

Public Information Office....Helsing, James SAMHSA 301-443-8956

Public Information Center....Staff EPA 202-260-2080

Public Information Office....Murry, Kevin AHCPR 594-1364

Public Information Office....Hardy, Robert HCFA 301-966-3206

Public Information Office....Shaffer, Sylvia HRSA 202-443-3376

Public Information Office....O'Hara, James FDA 301-443-1130

Public Information....Maulsby, Richard PTO 703-305-8341

Public inquiries....Moye, Melba D. NTSB 202-382-6787

Public inquiries....Staff DOD 703-697-5737

Public Opinion About Crime....Zawitz, Marianne Justice Stat 202-616-3499

Public Opinion About Crime....Lindgren, Sue Justice Stat 202-307-0760

Public relations, magazine journalism....Grunig, Larissa A. UMD 301-405-2431

Public relations theory and techniques....Zerbinos, Eugenia UMD 301-405-2430

Public relations....Grunig, James E. UMD 301-405-2416

Public relations....Vacant USITC 202-205-3410

Public Services Division....Lacroix, Eve-Marie NLM 301-496-5501
Public Surveys, Fish and Wildlife Service....Staff FWS 703-358-1730
Public Transportation Systems....Vacant FTA 202-366-4995
Public Use, Fish and Wildlife Hatcheries....Staff FWS 703-358-1715
Public Use, Fish and Wildlife Refuges....Staff FWS 703-358-1786
Public-Use Microdata Samples....Campbell, Carmen CENSUS 301-457-1139
Publication Clearance...Staff OD/OC 301-496-4143
Publication Grants....Staff NLM 301-496-6131
Publications and Special Studies, Assoc. Com....Klein, Deborah P. LABOR
    202-606-5900
Publications Information, Public. and Spec. Studies....Staff LABOR 202-606-7828
Publications (Inquiries) and NLM Photos/Slides....Beckwith, Frances NLM
    301-496-6308
Publications Office, Recorded Current....24-Hour Hotline LABOR 202-606-7828
Publications Office, Press Officer....Hoyle, Kathryn LABOR 202-606-5902
Publications Office, TDD (Telecom. Device for Deaf)....TDD LABOR
    202-606-5897
Publications....Colby, Lloyd SEC 202-942-4040
Publishing Industry Group....Roycroft, John C. SEC 202-942-1960
Publishing....Lofquist, William COMMERCE 202-482-0379
Puerto Rico....Siegelman, Mark Cnty Commerce 202-482-5680
Pulleys....Fravel, Dennis USITC 202-205-3404
Pulmonary Alveolar Proteinosis....Staff NHLBI 301-496-4236
Pulmonary Angiomyomatosis....Staff NHLBI 301-496-4236
Pulmonary Diseases (Infectious/Allergenic)....Staff NIAID 301-496-5717
Pulmonary Diseases (Non-Inf., Non-All., Non-Tum.)....Staff NHLBI
    301-496-4236
Pulmonary Diseases (Tumorous/Cancerous)....Staff NCI 301-496-5583
Pulmonary Edema....Staff NHLBI 301-496-4236
Pulmonary Embolism....Staff NHLBI 301-496-4236
Pulmonary Emphysema....Staff NHLBI 301-496-4236
Pulmonary Fibrosis....Staff NHLBI 301-496-4236
Pulmonic Stenosis....Staff NHLBI 301-496-4236
Pulp, articles of....Rhodes, Richard USITC 202-205-3322
Pulp machines....Lusi, Susan USITC 202-205-2334
Pulp Mills, Major Proj.....Miles, Max COMMERCE 202-482-0679
Pulpmills....Stanley, Gary COMMERCE 202-482-0375
Pulpwood....Hoffmeier, Bill USITC 202-205-3321
Pumice....Bolen, Wallace P. MINES 202-501-9389
Pumice....White, Linda USITC 202-205-3427
Pumps, air and vacuum....Mata, Ruben USITC 202-205-3403
Pumps, liquid....Mata, Ruben USITC 202-205-3403
Pumps, Pumping Eqmt....Vacant COMMERCE 202-482-0680
Pumps, Valves, Comp (Trade Promo.)....Zanetakos, George COMMERCE
    202-482-0552
Pumps....Riedl, Karl CUSTOMS 212-466-5493
Pure Red Cell Aplasia....Staff NHLBI 301-496-4236
Purpara....Staff NHLBI 301-496-4236
Purpura....Staff NIDDK 301-654-4415
Purpura....Staff NIAMS 301-496-8188
Putty....Johnson, Larry USITC 202-205-3351
Puzzles....Abrahamson, Dana USITC 202-205-3430
Pyelonephritis....Staff NIDDK 301-654-4415
Pyorrhea....Staff NIDR 301-496-4261
Pyrethrum....Wanser, Stephen USITC 202-205-3363
Pyridine....Foreso, Cynthia USITC 202-205-3348

Q

Qatar (Doha)....Staff Cnty State 202-647-6572
Qatar/Minerals....Izon, David Cnty Mines 202-501-9674
Qatar....Al-Khari, Ali Saad Cnty Embassy 202-338-0111
Qatar....Al-Thani, Sheikh Abdulrahman bin Saud Cnty Embassy 202-338-0111
Qatar....Konigshofer, Friedrich Cnty World Bank 202-473-2988
Qatar....Mercer, Dorothy Cnty Treasury 202-622-0184
Qatar....Thanos, Paul Cnty Commerce 202-482-1870
Qatar....Vacant Cnty USIA 202-619-6528
Quadriplegia....Staff NINDS 301-496-5751
Quality Control--Common Carrier....Staff FCC 202-418-1500
Quantum Physics....Leone, S.R. NIST 303-497-6807
Quanum Metrology....Deslaattes, R.D. NIST 301-975-4841
Quarantine, Disease....Perez, Tony D. Charles R. CDC 404-639-8107
Quarterly Financial Report....Lee, Ronald CENSUS 301-763-5435
Quarterly, Occupational Outlook, Empl. Proj.....Rosenthal, Neal LABOR
    202-606-5701
Quartz Crystal....Austin, Gordon MINES 202-501-9388

Quartzite....White, Linda USITC 202-205-3427
Quasars....Staff NASA 205-544-0034
Quatar....Mabury-Lewis Anthony Cnty Export-Import Bank 202-565-3739
Quaternary ammonium salts, fatty acids....Land, Eric USITC 202-205-3349
Quebracho....Wanser, Stephen USITC 202-205-3363
Quill, articles of....Spalding, Josephine USITC 202-205-3498
Quilts....Sweet, Mary Elizabeth USITC 202-205-3455

R

Rabies....Staff NIAID 301-496-5717
Race Statistics....Staff CENSUS 301-457-2453
Racing shells....Hagey, Michael USITC 202-205-3392
Racketeering....Coffey, Paul E. Justice 202-514-3594
Radar apparatus....Kitzmiller, John USITC 202-205-3387
Radial Keratotomy....Staff NEI 301-496-5248
Radiant energy systems....Dzierzynski, Paul PTO 703-308-4822
Radiation, Effect on Eyes....Staff NEI 301-496-5248
Radiation, Effect on Teeth....Staff NIDR 301-496-4261
Radiation Environmental Laws....Wallo, Andrew NEIC 202-586-4996
Radiation, Nervous System....Staff NINDS 301-496-5751
Radiation, Nonionizing....Staff OD/ORS 301-496-2960
Radiation, Nonionizing....Staff NIEHS 919-541-3345
Radiation Programs, Office of....Staff EPA 202-233-9320
Radiation Protection....Staff D. CDC 404-639-3147
Radiation Questions....Staff EPA 202-233-9280
Radiation Safety Badges....Staff OD/ORS 301-496-2254
Radiation Safety Officer....Staff NIH 301-496-2254
Radiation Safety (Radio. Spills, Lab. Surveys)....Staff OD/ORS 301-496-5774
Radiation Safety....Cruzan, Susan FDA 301-443-3285
Radiation Safety....Staff FDA 301-594-4752
Radiation Studies Division....Staff EPA 202-233-9340
Radiation Studies....Smith, James M. CDC 404-488-7040
Radiation survivors....Staff National Association of Radiation Survivors
    800-798-5102
Radiation....Staff NCI 301-496-5583
Radio and TV Broadcast Eqpmt....Siegmund, John COMMERCE 202-482-4781
Radio apparatus and parts....Kitzmiller, John USITC 202-205-3387
Radio Control Radio Service....Staff FCC 202-418-0680
Radio Industry....Owings, Christopher SEC 202-942-1900
Radio navigational apparatus....Kitzmiller, John USITC 202-205-3387
Radio Noise....Staff FCC 301-725-1585
Radio Ownership Regulations (Broadcast)....Staff FCC 202-418-2780
Radio receivers....Kitzmiller, John USITC 202-205-3387
Radio....Tarcza, Thomas C. PTO 703-308-1689
Radioactive Materials (Shipping and Receiving)....Staff OD/ORS 301-496-2254
Radioactive Waste Disposal....Lytle, Jill NEIC 202-586-0370
Radioactive Waste Disposal at NIH (Solid and Liquid)....Staff OD/ORS
    301-496-2254
Radiolocation--Industrial....Staff FCC 717-337-1212
Radiometric Physics....Parr, A.C. NIST 301-975-3739
Radionuclide Techniques in CV Diagnosis....Staff NHLBI 301-496-4236
Radios....Dicerbo, Mario CUSTOMS 212-466-5672
Radioscope Power Systems....Lane, Robert NEIC 301-903-4362
Radiotelephone Equipment....Staff FCC 301-725-1585
Radiotherapy (Cancer)....Staff NCI 301-496-5583
Radium....Staff NCI 301-496-5583
Radon Division....Staff EPA 202-233-9370
Radon Information....Staff EPA 202-233-9370
Radon Publications....Staff EPA 202-260-9370
Rags....Cook, Lee USITC 202-205-3471
Rail, locomotives....Lahey, Kathleen USITC 202-205-3409
Railroad Development....McQueen, James T FRA 202-366-9660
Railroad Equipment....Wholey, Patrick CUSTOMS 212-466-5668
Railroad Safety Analysis....Leeds, John G FRA 202-366-9186
Railroad Safety....Fine, Bruce FRA 202-366-0895
Railroad safety....Lauby, Robert NTSB 202-382-6845
Railroad Services....Wolfe, Claudia COMMERCE 202-482-5086
Railroads Industry Group....Parratt, Shelley SEC 202-942-1840
Railroads (Major Proj)....Smith, Jay L COMMERCE 202-482-4642
Railroads....Staff FCC 717-337-1212
Railway equipment....Oberleitner, Robert PTO 703-308-2569
Railway rolling stock....Lahey, Kathleen USITC 202-205-3409
Railway switches....Huppert, Michael PTO 703-308-1107
Railways, spring devices....Oberleitner, Robert PTO 703-308-3569
Railway track....Huppert, Michael PTO 703-308-1107

Rain Forests....Martin, R. Michael FS 703-235-1676
Rainwear....Shetty, Sundar USITC 202-205-3457
Ramsey Hunt Syndrome....Staff NINDS 301-496-5751
Ramsey Hunt Syndrome....Staff NIDCD 301-496-7243
Range Research...Lennartz, Michael R. FS 202-205-1524
Rape....Baldwin, Elaine NIMH 301-443-4536
Rare diseases....Staff National Organization for Rare Disorders 800-999-6673
Rare diseases....Staff National Information Center for Orphan Drugs and Rare Diseases 800-456-3505
Rare Diseases....Staff OD 301-496-1454
Rare Disorders (Neurological)....Staff NINDS 301-496-5751
Rare-earth metals....Conant, Kenneth USITC 202-205-3346
Rare-earth compounds....Greenblatt, Jack USITC 202-205-3353
Rare Earths....Hedrick, James B. MINES 202-501-9412
Rare saccharides....Randall, Rob USITC 202-205-3366
Rattan....Hoffmeier, Bill USITC 202-205-3321
Raw Materials, Food, and Apparel, Intl. Price Ind.....Frumkin, Rob LABOR 202-606-7106
Raynaud's Disease....Staff NHLBI 301-496-4236
Raynaud's Syndrome....Staff NIAMS 301-496-8188
RCRA/Superfund (OUST Hotline)....Staff EPA 800-424-9346
RCRA Information Hotline....Staff EPA 415-744-2074
Reactor Analysis....Rosenthal, Jack E. NRC 301-415-7488
Reactor Controls....Boger, Bruce NRC 301-415-1004
Reactor Radiation....Rowe, J.M. NIST 301-975-6210
Reactor Radiation....Rowe, Michael J. NIST 301-975-6210
Reading Development....Staff NICHD 301-496-5133
Reading Development....Staff NIDCD 301-496-7243
Reading Development....Staff NINDS 301-496-5751
Reading Disorders....Staff NINDS 301-496-5751
Reading Disorders....Staff NIDCD 301-496-7243
Reading Disorders....Staff NICHD 301-496-5133
Reading Disorders....Staff Dept. of Education 202-245-8707
Real Earnings--News Release, Empl/Unempl. Stats....Hiles, David LABOR 202-606-6547
Real Estate and Housing Industry....Parratt, Shelley SEC 202-942-1840
Reasonable Access....Staff FCC 202-418-1440
Recalls (Automobile Emissions)....Staff EPA 202-233-9240
Recalls (drugs)....Adams, Betsy FDA 301-443-3285
Recalls (food)....Corwin, Emil FDA 202-205-4144
Receptacles....Sewell, Paul T PTO 703-308-2126
Recidivism....Beck, Allen Justice Stat 202-616-3277
Recidivism....Greenfeld, Lawrence Justice Stat 202-616-3281
Recidivism....Shipley, Bernard Justice Stat 202-307-7703
Recombinant DNA Activity....Staff OD 301-496-9838
Recombinant DNA....Staff NIAID 301-496-5717
Recombinant DNA....Staff NIGMS 301-496-7301
Reconstituted crude petroleum....Foreso, Cynthia USITC 202-205-3348
Reconstructive Surgeons....Staff American Society of Plastic and Reconstructive Surgeons 800-635-0635
Reconstructive Surgery....Staff American Academy of Facial Plastic and Reconstructive Surgery 800-332-3223
Record Retention Requirement...Staff FCC 202-418-0210
Recorded CPI Detail, Prices and Living Cond.....24-Hour Hotline LABOR 202-606-7828
Recorded Messages, Compensation and Working Condition....24-hour hotline LABOR 202-606-7828
Records Imaging Processing System....Staff FCC 202-418-0293
Records, tapes and recording media....Puffert, Douglas USITC 202-205-3402
Recovery Plans, Endangered Species....Staff FWS 703-358-2183
Recreation, Fish and Wildlife Recreation....Staff FWS 703-358-1715
Recreation, Refuges....Staff FWS 703-358-1786
Recreational Equipment, Export Promo.....Beckham, Reginald COMMERCE 202-482-5478
Rectifiers....Vacant CUSTOMS 212-466-5673
Recurrent Fever....Staff NIAID 301-496-5717
Recurrent Pyogenic Infections....Staff NIAID 301-496-5717
Recycling (General Issues)....Staff EPA 202-260-6261
Recycling Program (EPA)....Staff EPA 703-308-8300
Red Blood Cells (Erythrocytes)....Staff NHLBI 301-496-4236
Red Blood Cells (Erythrocytes)....Staff FDA/NCDB 301-496-3556
Reeling machines....Greene, William USITC 202-205-3405
Refarming of Shared Spectrum....Staff FCC 202-418-0620
Reference and Users Service....Kulp, Leslie NAL 301-504-6875
Reference Center....Staff FCC 202-418-0270
Reference Desk....Staff NAL 301-504-5479
Reference Services....Staff NCRR/NIH Library 301-496-2184

Reference Services...Staff NLM 301-496-6095
Reflex Sympathetic Dystrophy Syndrome....Staff NIAMS 301-496-8188
Reflux Nephropathy....Staff NIDDK 301-496-3583
Refractive Errors....Staff NEI 301-496-5248
Refractories....DeSapio, Vincent USITC 202-205-3435
Refractory Anemia....Staff NHLBI 301-496-4236
Refractory glass....Bell, Mark L. PTO 703-308-3823
Refractory Products....Duggan, Brian COMMERCE 202-482-0610
Refrigerants....Lieberman, Paul PTO 703-308-2552
Refrigeration equipment....Mata, Ruben USITC 202-205-3403
Refrigeration....Francke, Eric CUSTOMS 212-466-5669
Refrigeration....Radebaugh, Ray NIST 303-497-3710
Refsum's Disease....Staff NINDS 301-496-5751
Refugee Resettlement....Kharfen, Michael ACF 202-401-9215
Regeneration (CNS)...Staff NINDS 301-496-5751
Regional Affairs, Western Hemisphere....Eppler, Dale US Trade Rep 202-395-5190
Regional, BEA Economic Areas....Trott, Jr., Edward A. ECONOMIC 202-606-9231
Regional Director - Atlanta....Ford-Roegner, Patricia HHSREG 404-331-2442
Regional Director - Boston....Johnston, Philip HHSREG 617-565-1500
Regional Director - Chicago....Weiss, Elaine HHSREG 312-353-5160
Regional Director - Dallas....Montoya, Patricia HHSREG 214-767-3301
Regional Director - Denver....Carey, Margaret HHSREG 303-844-3372
Regional Director - Kansas City....Steele, Kathleen HHSREG 816-426-2821
Regional Director - New York....Greene, Alison HHSREG 212-264-4600
Regional Director - Philadelphia....Yeakel, Lynn H. HHSREG 215-596-6492
Regional Director - San Francisco....Phelon, Ronald W. FTC 415-744-7920
Regional Director - San Francisco....Grantland, Johnson HHSREG 415-556-6746
Regional Director - Seattle....McBride, Patricia HHSREG 206-615-2010
Regional, Disposable Personal Income....Brown, Robert ECONOMIC 202-606-9246
Regional, Dividends, Interest and Rental Income....Jolley, Charles A. ECONOMIC 202-606-9257
Regional Economic Analysis, Chief....Kort, John R. ECONOMIC 202-606-9221
Regional Economic Measurement, Chief....Knox, Hugh ECONOMIC 202-606-9605
Regional, Economic Situation, Current....Friedenberg, Howard L. ECONOMIC 202-606-9216
Regional Economics, Associate Director....Knox, Hugh W. ECONOMIC 202-606-9605
Regional Economics, Associate Director....Knox, Hugh W. ECONOMIC 202-606-9605
Regional Enteritis....Staff NIDDK 301-654-3810
Regional, Farm Proprietors' Income and Employment....Zavrel, James M. ECONOMIC 202-606-9290
Regional, Gross State Product Estimates....Staff ECONOMIC 202-606-4500
Regional Medical Libraries....Staff NLM 301-496-4777
Regional, Methodology....Bailey, Wallace K. ECONOMIC 202-606-9254
Regional Office -....Cooper, Joanne FTC 202-326-2257
Regional Office - ....Dowdy, Lemuel W. FTC 202-326-2981
Regional Office - ....Wallace, Cheryl J. FTC 202-326-3712
Regional Office - Atlanta....Alphin, Katherine B. FTC 404-347-7520
Regional Office - Atlanta....Bolen, Ida FTC 404-347-7046
Regional Office - Atlanta....Brennan, Virginia FTC 404-347-7540
Regional Office - Atlanta....Carlone, Ralph GAO 404-679-1800
Regional Office - Atlanta....Couillou, Chris M. FTC 404-347-7517
Regional Office - Atlanta....Davis, Paul K. FTC 404-347-7524
Regional Office - Atlanta....Foster, Andrea FTC 404-347-7516
Regional Office - Atlanta....House, Nicole L. FTC 404-347-7541
Regional Office - Atlanta....Kirtz, Harold E. FTC 404-347-7522
Regional Office - Atlanta....Laitsch, Ronald E. FTC 404-347-7535
Regional Office - Atlanta....Liebes, Cinday A. FTC 404-347-7514
Regional Office - Atlanta....Ozburn, Chris Edmonds FTC 404-347-7515
Regional Office - Atlanta....Powell, Saundra FTC 404-347-4836
Regional Office - Atlanta....Rohrer, James T. FTC 404-347-7534
Regional Office - Atlanta....Schanker, Barbara S. FTC 404-347-7518
Regional Office - Atlanta....Staff CENSUS 404-730-3833
Regional Office - Atlanta....Taylor, Mark FTC 404-347-7512
Regional Office - Atlanta....Walton, Doris P. FTC 404-347-7532
Regional Office - Atlanta....Whittaker, Ingrid FTC 404-347-7536
Regional Office - Atlanta....Williams, Addie L. FTC 404-347-7510
Regional Office - Boston....Arleo, Jonathon FTC 617-424-5960
Regional Office - Boston....Barry, Daniel FTC 617-424-5960
Regional Office - Boston....Block, Paul G. FTC 617-424-5960
Regional Office - Boston....Bolton, Barbara E. FTC 617-424-5960
Regional Office - Boston....Caverly, Andrew FTC 617-424-5960

Be patient. If any phone number is incorrect, call (area code) 555-1212 and request the new listing.

1433

Regional Office - Boston....Cooper, Gary S. FTC 617-424-5960
Regional Office - Boston....Dugan, John T. FTC 617-424-5960
Regional Office - Boston....Gray, Jessica D. FTC 617-424-5960
Regional Office - Boston....Greenberg, Sara FTC 617-424-5960
Regional Office - Boston....Haley, Mary G. FTC 617-424-5960
Regional Office - Boston....Harrington, Diane J. FTC 617-424-5960
Regional Office - Boston....Hughes, Thomas M. FTC 617-424-5960
Regional Office - Boston....Keniry, David I., Jr. FTC 617-424-5960
Regional Office - Boston....Morse, Phoebe D. FTC 617-424-5960
Regional Office - Boston....Ols, John M. GAO 617-565-7555
Regional Office - Boston....Robertson, Terry L. FTC 617-424-5960
Regional Office - Boston....Staff CENSUS 617-424-0510
Regional Office - Boston....Wood, Kristie FTC 617-424-5960
Regional Office - Boston....Wood, Pamela J. FTC 617-424-5960
Regional Office - Charlotte....Staff CENSUS 704-371-6142
Regional Office - Chicago....Baker, Steven C. FTC 312-353-8156
Regional Office - Chicago....Damtoft, Russel W. FTC 312-353-3771
Regional Office - Chicago....Daniels, Janice A. FTC 312-353-7178
Regional Office - Chicago....DiGiulio, Barbara A. FTC 312-353-7178
Regional Office - Chicago....Dodge, Karen D. FTC 312-353-4448
Regional Office - Chicago....Franczyk, Nicholas J. FTC 312-353-7957
Regional Office - Chicago....Fuller, Catherine R. FTC 312-353-5576
Regional Office - Chicago....Genda, Christine M. FTC 312-353-5261
Regional Office - Chicago....Hallerud, John C. FTC 312-353-5575
Regional Office - Chicago....Hughes, Timothy T. FTC 312-353-4431
Regional Office - Chicago....Krause, Alan E. FTC 312-353-4441
Regional Office - Chicago....Luke, John H. GAO 312-220-7600
Regional Office - Chicago....McGrew, Theresa M. FTC 312-353-5532
Regional Office - Chicago....Miller, Michael T. FTC 312-353-5260
Regional Office - Chicago....Olson, Mary E. FTC 312-353-4427
Regional Office - Chicago....Russell, Thomas J. FTC 312-353-4523
Regional Office - Chicago....Smith, Michele FTC 312-353-5045
Regional Office - Chicago....Staff CENSUS 708-562-1740
Regional Office - Chicago....Tortorice, Mary E. FTC 312-353-4435
Regional Office - Chicago....Williams, Vassoria L. FTC 312-353-4426
Regional Office - Chicago....Wronka, Kathleen F. FTC 312-353-4442
Regional Office - Cleveland....Amdur, Ilene FTC 216-522-4210
Regional Office - Cleveland....Balster, Steven W. FTC 216-574-2425
Regional Office - Cleveland....Broyles, Phillip FTC 216-522-4217
Regional Office - Cleveland....Doubrava, Brenda W. FTC 216-574-2426
Regional Office - Cleveland....Greene, Willie L. FTC 216-574-2427
Regional Office - Cleveland....Griffiths, Stephanie M. FTC 216-574-2428
Regional Office - Cleveland....Hessoun, Bonnie T. FTC 216-574-2429
Regional Office - Cleveland....Lerner, Louis L. FTC 312-353-5528
Regional Office - Cleveland....Mendenhall, John M. FTC 216-574-2432
Regional Office - Cleveland....Milgrom, Michael FTC 216-574-2433
Regional Office - Cleveland....Pirrone, Jaclyn S. FTC 216-574-2434
Regional Office - Cleveland....Plottner, David V. FTC 216-574-2435
Regional Office - Cleveland....Powell, Catherine F. FTC 216-574-2436
Regional Office - Cleveland....Rose, Michael B. FTC 216-574-2437
Regional Office - Cleveland....Sternlicht, Melissa FTC 216-522-4210
Regional Office - Cleveland....Stewart, Douglas FTC 216-574-2429
Regional Office - Cleveland....Vantusko, Mary Jo. FTC 216-522-4208
Regional Office - Cleveland....Williams, Brinley H. FTC 216-574-2439
Regional Office - Cleveland....Zeman, Gerald C. FTC 216-522-2440
Regional Office - Dallas....Arthur, Susan E. FTC 214-767-5517
Regional Office - Dallas....Black, Michael R. FTC 202-326-3457
Regional Office - Dallas....Blackman, Claire R. FTC 214-767-5503
Regional Office - Dallas....Donsky, Robin L. FTC 214-767-5503
Regional Office - Dallas....Elliott, James E. FTC 214-767-5509
Regional Office - Dallas....Garcia, Ernestina FTC 214-767-5503
Regional Office - Dallas....Golder, James R. FTC 214-767-5508
Regional Office - Dallas....Gosha-Nelson, Jannette FTC 214-767-5503
Regional Office - Dallas....Griggs, W. David FTC 214-767-5510
Regional Office - Dallas....Hickman, Joseph L. FTC 214-767-5503
Regional Office - Dallas....Kennedy, Gary D. FTC 214-767-5512
Regional Office - Dallas....Lenamond, Leslee A. FTC 214-767-5503
Regional Office - Dallas....Malmberg, Kristin L. FTC 214-767-5513
Regional Office - Dallas....McCowan, Curtistene S. FTC 214-767-5503
Regional Office - Dallas....Morgan, Maridel S. FTC 214-767-5503
Regional Office - Dallas....Peterson, Robert A. GAO 214-777-5700
Regional Office - Dallas....Shepherd, Judith L. FTC 214-767-5510
Regional Office - Dallas....Spears, Debby H. FTC 214-767-5503
Regional Office - Dallas....Staff CENSUS 214-767-7105
Regional Office - Dallas....Weart, Steven E. FTC 214-767-5516
Regional Office - Denver....Brew, Thomas J. GAO 303-572-7317
Regional Office - Denver....Carter, Thomas B. FTC 214-767-5518

Regional Office - Denver....Charter, Janice FTC 303-844-2868
Regional Office - Denver....Cole, Pamela M. FTC 303-844-2255
Regional Office - Denver....Cramer, Norman FTC 303-844-2275
Regional Office - Denver....Dahnke, Jeffrey FTC 303-844-2254
Regional Office - Denver....Farrand, Kelli A. FTC 303-844-2276
Regional Office - Denver....Gomez, Cynthia FTC 303-844-3082
Regional Office - Denver....Huff, Jan FTC 303-844-3590
Regional Office - Denver....Keese, Deborah C. FTC 303-844-2276
Regional Office - Denver....Kessler, Jonathan FTC 303-844-2276
Regional Office - Denver....Kraus, Loretta FTC 303-844-2273
Regional Office - Denver....Naylor, Sharon L. FTC 303-844-3576
Regional Office - Denver....Nickerson, Eric FTC 303-844-3584
Regional Office - Denver....Palmquist, Elizabeth FTC 303-844-2274
Regional Office - Denver....Staff CENSUS 303-969-7750
Regional Office - Denver....Wild, Claude C., III FTC 303-844-3571
Regional Office - Detroit....Staff CENSUS 313-259-1875
Regional Office - Kansas City....Staff CENSUS 913-551-6711
Regional Office - Kansas City....Watts, James R. GAO 913-384-7418
Regional Office - Los Angeles...Farias, Eliana R. FTC 310-235-7890
Regional Office - Los Angeles...Stock, Linda M. FTC 310-235-7896
Regional Office - Los Angeles...Harris, Robbie R. FTC 310-235-7890
Regional Office - Los Angles....Staff CENSUS 818-904-6339
Regional Office - Los Angeles...Willis, Elizabeth M. FTC 310-575-7971
Regional Office - Los Angeles...Willins, Paul K. FTC 310-235-7968
Regional Office - Los Angeles...Ell, Victor GAO 213-346-8045
Regional Office - Los Angeles...Syta, Thomas J. FTC 310-235-7879
Regional Office - Los Angeles...Staples, Greg FTC 310-235-7990
Regional Office - Los Angeles...Jacobs, John D. FTC 310-235-6602
Regional Office - Los Angeles...Smart, Bret S. FTC 310-235-7975
Regional Office - Los Angeles...Roark, Paul R. FTC 310-235-7870
Regional Office - Los Angeles...Frauens, Sue L. FTC 310-235-6140
Regional Office - Los Angeles...Guler, Ann M. FTC 310-235-7966
Regional Office - Los Angeles...Sekovich, Dale S. FTC 310-235-7572
Regional Office - Los Angeles...Donaldson, Nancy D. FTC 310-235-7890
Regional Office - Los Angeles...Deitch, Russell S. FTC 310-235-7965
Regional Office - Los Angeles...French, Kathy S. FTC 310-575-6138
Regional Office - Los Angeles...Dawson, Darlene FTC 310-235-7974
Regional Office - Los Angeles...McKown, Raymond E. FTC 310-235-7962
Regional Office - New York....Bloom, Michael J. FTC 212-264-1201
Regional Office - New York....D'Amato, Donald G. FTC 212-264-1223
Regional Office - New York....Au, Alice FTC 212-264-1210
Regional Office - New York....Loughnan, Alan FTC 212-264-1232
Regional Office - New York....Oteri, Patricia FTC 212-264-9804
Regional Office - New York....Goldsmith, Harriet S. FTC 212-264-1208
Regional Office - New York....McLean, Rhonda J. FTC 212-264-1211
Regional Office - New York....Roth, Marc S. FTC 212-264-8855
Regional Office - New York....Fischman, Ethel B. FTC 212-264-4688
Regional Office - New York....Waldman, Ronald FTC 212-264-1242
Regional Office - New York....Lopez, Digna FTC 212-264-0716
Regional Office - New York....Lipkowitz, Eugene FTC 212-264-1230
Regional Office - New York....Eichen, Robin E. FTC 212-264-1250
Regional Office - New York....Staff CENSUS 212-264-4730
Regional Office - New York....Paynter, Carole FTC 212-264-1225
Regional Office - New York....DiFilippi, Anna GAO 212-264-0962
Regional Office - New York....Chandrika, Kapadia FTC 212-264-1205
Regional Office - Norfolk....Stevens, Joe B. GAO 804-552-8112
Regional Office - San Francisco....Badger, Linda K. FTC 415-744-7920
Regional Office - San Francisco....Aguilar, Lisa FTC 415-744-7920
Regional Office - San Francisco....Harris, Lisa A. FTC 415-744-7920
Regional Office - San Francisco....Newmann, David M. FTC 415-744-7920
Regional Office - San Francisco....Phelon, Ronald FTC 415-744-7920
Regional Office - San Francisco....Weigand, John FTC 415-744-7920
Regional Office - San Francisco....Steinitz, Sidney FTC 202-326-3282
Regional Office - San Francisco....Kauffman, Craig D. FTC 415-744-7920
Regional Office - San Francisco....Gold, Matthew FTC 415-744-7920
Regional Office - San Francisco....Sodergren, Harold G. FTC 415-744-7920
Regional Office - San Francisco....O'Brien, Kerry FTC 415-744-7920
Regional Office - San Francisco....McCormick, Thomas P. GAO 415-904-2200
Regional Office - San Francisco....Kundig, Sylvia J. FTC 415-744-7920
Regional Office - San Francisco....Klurfeld, Jeffrey A. FTC 415-744-7920
Regional Office - San Francisco....Stone, Ralph E. FTC 415-744-7920
Regional Office - San Francisco....Wright, Gerald E. FTC 415-744-7920
Regional Office - San Francisco....Steiner, Jerome M., Jr. FTC 415-744-7920
Regional Office - San Francisco....Wodinsky, Erika R. FTC 415-744-7920
Regional Office - Seattle....Benfield, Mary T. FTC 206-220-6350
Regional Office - Seattle....Brook, Randall H. FTC 206-220-6350
Regional Office - Seattle....Decker, Kathryn FTC 206-220-6350

Be patient. If any phone number is incorrect, call (area code) 555-1212 and request the new listing.

Regional Office - Seattle....Durham, Eleanor FTC 206-220-6350
Regional Office - Seattle....Fournier, Dean A. FTC 206-220-6350
Regional Office - Seattle....France, Laureen FTC 206-220-6350
Regional Office - Seattle....Harwood, Charles A. FTC 206-220-6350
Regional Office - Seattle....Hensley, Patricia A. FTC 206-220-6350
Regional Office - Seattle....Kirkwood, John B. FTC 206-220-6350
Regional Office - Seattle....Lipinsky, Joseph FTC 206-220-6350
Regional Office - Seattle....Meissner, James K. GAO 206-287-4810
Regional Office - Seattle....Nielsen, Kathryn C. FTC 206-220-6350
Regional Office - Seattle....Samter, Nadine S. FTC 206-220-6350
Regional Office - Seattle....Schroeder, Robert J. FTC 206-220-6350
Regional Office - Seattle....Schuller, Stella A. FTC 206-220-6350
Regional Office - Seattle....Silveira, Robert FTC 206-220-6350
Regional Office - Seattle....Staff CENSUS 206-728-5314
Regional Office - Seattle....Stansell, Maxine FTC 206-220-6350
Regional Office - Seattle....Thorleifson, Tracy S. FTC 206-220-6350
Regional Office - Seattle....Woods, K. Shane FTC 206-220-6350
Regional Office - Seattle....Zerbe, Richard O. FTC 206-220-6350
Regional Office - Seattle....Zweibel, George J. FTC 206-220-6350
Regional, Personal Income and Employment, Counties....Hazan, Linnea ECONOMIC 202-606-9254
Regional, Personal Income and Employment, Metro Area....Hazan, Linnea ECONOMIC 202-606-9254
Regional, Personal Income and Employment, States....Hazan, Linnea ECONOMIC 202-606-9254
Regional, Projections-States and Metropolitan Areas....Pigler, Carmen C. ECONOMIC 202-606-9227
Regional, Requests for Pers. Income and Employment Data....Information System Staff ECONOMIC 202-606-5360
Regional, Shift-Share Analysis....Kort, John R. ECONOMIC 202-606-9221
Regional, State Ecometric Modeling....Lienesch, C. Thomas ECONOMIC 202-606-9223
Regional, State Quarterly Personal Income....Whiston, Isabelle B. ECONOMIC 202-606-4500
Regional, Transfer Payments....Brown, Robert ECONOMIC 202-606-4500
Regional, Wage and Salary Income and Employment....Carnevale, Sharon ECONOMIC 202-606-9247
Registers....Hajec, Donald PTO 703-308-4075
Regulators....Topolansky, Adam USITC 202-205-3394
Regulatory and International Safeguards....Sherr, Theodore S. NRC 301-415-7218
Regulatory Flexibility Act....Staff FCC 202-418-1720
Rehabilitation Medicine Department....Staff CC 301-496-4733
Rehabilitation....Staff National Rehabilitation Information Center 800-346-2742
Rehabilitation....Staff NIA 301-496-1752
Reiter's Syndrome....Staff NIAMS 301-496-8188
Relays....Curran, David CUSTOMS 212-466-5680
Reliability and Risk Assessment....Baranowsky NRC 301-415-7493
Religious Studies....Childress, James F. UVA 701-924-3741
Remission....Staff NCI 301-496-5583
Remote Control Rules....Staff FCC 202-2190
Remote Sensing Techniques....Sullivan, Nancy NASA 601-688-3341
Remote Sensor Systems....Koehler, Keith NASA 804-824-1579
Renal Artery Stenosis....Staff NHLBI 301-496-4236
Renal Disorders in Children....Staff NIDDK 301-654-4415
Renal Glycosuria....Staff NIDDK 301-654-4415
Renal Hypertension....Staff NIDDK 301-654-4415
Renal Tubular Acidosis....Staff NIDDK 301-654-4415
Renal Vascular Disease....Staff NIDDK 301-654-4415
Renewable Energy Conversion....Staff NEIC 800-528-2929
Renewable Energy Equipment....Garden, Les COMMERCE 202-482-0556
Renewable Energy Resources....King, Marion NEIC 202-586-8800
Renewable Energy Resources....Freedman, Karen NEIC 202-586-8800
Renewable Energy....Davis, Michael J. NEIC 202-586-9220
Renewals Radio....Staff FCC 202-418-2780
Renewals TV....Staff FCC 202-418-1630
Renovascular Hypertension....Staff NHLBI 301-654-4415
Rental (Scientific)....Staff DRS 301-496-4131
Reporting Crime to Police....Harlow, Caroline Justice Stat 202-307-0757
Reproductive Disorders....Staff NICHD 301-496-5133
Rescue Squads....Staff FCC 717-337-1212
Research Aircraft....Brown, Dwayne C. NASA 202-358-1726
Research and Development....Price, James B. COMMERCE 202-482-4781
Research Career Development....Staff DRG 301-594-7248
Research (ethical issues)....Staff OD/OERT 301-496-7005
Research Grants....Staff DRG 301-594-7248
Research Industry Group....Owings, Christopher SEC 202-942-1900
Research Training....Staff DRG 301-594-7248

Research Training....Staff NIGMS 301-496-7301
Residence Adjustment....Zabronsky, Daniel ECONOMIC 202-606-4500
Residential Lighting Fixtures....Bodson, John COMMERCE 202-482-0681
Residual fuel oil....Foreso, Cynthia USITC 202-205-3348
Resistors....Josephs, Irwin CUSTOMS 212-466-5673
Resistors....Malison, Andrew USITC 202-205-3391
Resistors...Reynolds, Bruce A. PTO 703-308-3305
Resorts Industry Group....Roycroft, John C. SEC 202-942-1960
Resorts (leisure)....Roycroft, James M. SEC 202-942-1960
Resource Conservation and Reclamation Act (RCRA)....Traceski, Thomas NEIC 202-586-2481
Resources for Research....Staff NCRR 301-594-7938
RESPA (real estate settlement procedures act)....Goodman, Sheilah FRS 202-452-3667
Respiratory devices....Burr, Edgar PTO 703-308-0979
Respiratory Diseases (Infectious/Allergenic)....Staff NIAID 301-496-5717
Respiratory Diseases (Non-In., Non-All., Non-Tum.)....Staff NHLBI 301-496-4236
Respiratory Diseases (Tumorous/Cancerous)....Staff NCI 301-496-5583
Respiratory Diseases....Anderson, Larry CDC 404-639-3596
Respiratory Distress Syndrome...Staff NHLBI 301-496-4236
Respiratory medicine....Staff Lung Line 800-222-5864
Respiratory Syncytial Virus....Staff NIAID 301-496-5717
Restless Leg Syndrome....Staff NINDS 301-496-5751
Retail Trade, Advance Monthly Sales....Piencykoski, Ronald CENSUS 301-457-2713
Retail Trade, Annual Sales....Piencykoski, Ronald CENSUS 301-457-2713
Retail Trade, Census....Staff CENSUS 301-457-2687
Retail Trade, Monthly Trade Report....True, Irving CENSUS 301-457-2706
Retail Trade, Monthly Inventories....Piencykoski, Ronald CENSUS 301-457-2713
Retail Trade....Burroughs, Helen COMMERCE 202-482-1542
Retailing Industry Group....Tow, A. Richard SEC 202-942-1960
Retinal Degeneration....Staff NEI 301-496-5248
Retinal Detachment....Staff NEI 301-496-5248
Retinal Diseases....Dudley, Peter A. FAES 301-496-5884
Retinal Diseases....Staff NEI 301-496-5248
Retinal Vascular Disease....Staff NEI 301-496-5248
Retinitis Pigmentosa....Staff National Retinitis Pigmentosa Foundation (NRPF) 800-683-5555
Retinitis Pigmentosa....Staff NEI 301-496-5248
Retinoblastoma....Staff NEI 301-496-5248
Retinopathies....Staff NEI 301-496-5248
Retired persons....Staff AARP 800-424-2277
Retirement and Capital Acc, Employee Benefit Survey....Houff, James LABOR 202-606-6238
Retirement Programs....Titus, Frank D. OPM 202-606-0300
Retirement....Staff NIA 301-496-1752
Rett's Syndrome....Staff NINDS 301-496-5751
Reunion/Minerals....Antonides, Lloyd Cnty Mines 202-501-9686
Reunion....Staff Cnty State 202-647-2453
Reye's Syndrome....Staff National Reye's Syndrome Foundation, Inc. (NRSF) 800-233-7393
Reye's Syndrome....Staff NINDS 301-496-5751
Rh Factor....Staff NHLBI 301-496-4236
Rhabdomyosarcoma and Undifferentiated Sarcomas....Staff NCI 301-496-5583
Rhenium....Blossom, John W. MINES 202-501-9435
Rhenium....Lundy, David USITC 202-205-3439
Rheumatic Fever....Staff NIAID 301-496-5717
Rheumatic Heart....Staff NHLBI 301-496-4236
Rheumatoid Arthritis....Staff NIAMS 301-496-8188
Rhinitis....Staff NIAID 301-496-5717
Rhodium compounds....Greenblatt, Jack USITC 202-205-3353
Ribbons: inked....Cook, Lee USITC 202-205-3471
Ribbons: other....Shelton, Linda USITC 202-205-3457
Ribbons: typewriter....Shelton, Linda USITC 202-205-3457
Rice Milling....Manogue, Robert COMMERCE 202-482-2428
Rice with options....Sepsey, Judy CFT 312-353-9025
Rice...Reeder, John USITC 202-205-3319
Ricinoleic acid esters....Johnson, Larry USITC 202-205-3351
Rickets, Vitamin-D Resistant....Staff NIDDK 301-496-3583
Rickettsial Diseases....Staff NIAID 301-496-5717
Riding crops....Spalding, Josephine USITC 202-205-3498
Riding Mowers....Staff CPSC 301-504-0580
Rifles....Luther, Dennis USITC 202-205-3497
Right-of-Way....Orski, Barbara K FHWA 202-366-0342
Riley-Day Syndrome....Staff NINDS 301-496-5751
Ringworm....Staff NIAID 301-496-5717

Be patient. If any phone number is incorrect, call (area code) 555-1212 and request the new listing.

1435

River Blindness....Staff NIAID 301-496-5717
River Blindness....Staff NEI 301-496-5248
Roads, Railroads, Mass Trans (Major Proj)....Smith, Jay L. COMMERCE 202-482-4642
Robot Metrology....Goodwin, Kenneth R. NIST 301-975-3421
Robotics Research....Staff NASA 713-483-8693
Robots....Pilaroscia, Megan COMMERCE 202-482-0609
Rocky Mountain Spotted Fever....Staff NIAID 301-496-5717
Rods, plastics....Misurelli, Denby USITC 202-205-3362
Roller Bearings....Reise, Richard COMMERCE 202-482-3489
Rolling machines, except metal....Lusi, Susan USITC 202-205-2334
Rolling Mill Machinery....Green, William COMMERCE 202-482-3405
Rollings mills, metal....Fravel, Dennis USITC 202-205-3401
Romania (Bucharest)....Staff Cnty State 202-647-4272
Romania/Minerals....Steblez, Walter Cnty Mines 202-501-9672
Romania....Amick, Jack Peace Corps 202-606-3548
Romania....Anne McKinney Cnty TDA 703-875-4357
Romania...Bazala, Razvigor Cnty USIA 202-619-5055
Romania...Botez, Mihail Horia Cnty Embassy 202-332-4846
Romania....Green, Pam Cnty Commerce 202-482-4915
Romania...Jackson, Juhan Cnty Treasury 202-622-0766
Romania....LeMaster, Cheryl Peace Corps 202-606-3547
Romania...Mateescu, Radu Cnty Embassy 202-332-4848
Romania....Szaszkiewicz, Barbara Cnty World Bank 202-473-4374
Romania....Waxman-Lenz, Roberta Cnty Export-Import Bank 202-565-3742
Roofing, Asphalt....Franklin, William COMMERCE 202-482-0132
Root Caries....Staff NIDR 301-496-4261
Rope....Cook, Lee USITC 202-205-3471
Rosemary oil (essential oil)....Land, Eric USITC 202-205-3349
Rotary Ablation....Staff NHLBI 301-496-4236
Rotavirus....Staff NIAID 301-496-5717
Rouges....Land, Eric USITC 202-205-3349
Rubber and Plastic Articles....Mazzola, Joan CUSTOMS 212-466-5880
Rubber, natural....Misurelli, Denby USITC 202-205-3362
Rubber Products....Prat, Raimundo COMMERCE 202-482-0128
Rubber Sheet....Mazzola, Joan CUSTOMS 212-466-5880
Rubber, Synthetic and Natural....Joseph, Stephanie CUSTOMS 212-466-5768
Rubber, synthetic....Misurelli, Denby USITC 202-205-3362
Rubber....Prat, Raimundo COMMERCE 202-482-0128
Rubbers....Kight, John PTO 703-308-2453
Rubella....Staff NIAID 301-496-5717
Rubeola....Staff NIAID 301-496-5717
Rubidium....Reese, Jr., Robert MINES 202-501-9413
Rugs....Hansen, John CUSTOMS 212-466-5854
Rugs....Sweet, Mary Elizabeth USITC 202-205-3455
Rule Questions....Staff FCC 202-418-0680
Runaway Youth/Homeless....Kharfen, Michael ACF 202-401-9215
Runaways....Staff Runaway Hotline 800-231-6946
Runaways....Staff National Runaway Switchboard (NRS) 800-621-4000
Rural Aged....Staff NIA 301-496-1752
Rural Development - Agric. and Community Linkages....Schluter, Gerald Agri 202-219-0785
Rural Development - Business and Industry....Bernat, Andrew Agri 202-219-0539
Rural Development - Community Development....Sears, David Agri 202-219-0546
Rural Development - Credit and Financial Markets....Sullivan, Pat Agri 202-219-0721
Rural Development - Employment....Parker, Tim Agri 202-219-0541
Rural Development - Employment....Swaim, Paul Agri 202-219-0553
Rural Development - Local Government Finance....Reeder, Richard Agri 202-219-0551
Rural Development - Policy....Reeder, Richard Agri 202-219-0551
Rural Development....McGranahan, David Agri 202-219-0533
Rural Development....Long, Dick Agri 202-219-0530
Rural Health....Human, Jeffrey HRSA 301-443-0835
Rural Health....Staff Rural Information Health Service 800-633-7701
Rural Information Center....John, Patricia NAL 301-504-5372
Rural Residence....Staff CENSUS 301-457-1200
Russia....Cavanagh, Stacy Peace Corps 202-606-3974
Russia....Fabrizio, Lynn Cnty Commerce 202-482-0988
Russia....Koff, Allison S. Cnty TDA 703-875-4357
Russia....Levine, Richard Cnty Mines 202-501-9682
Russia....Luhmann, Eric OPIC 202-336-8621
Russia....MacManus, Joseph USIA 202-619-5057
Russia....McGrew, Wes Cnty Treasury 202-622-2876
Russia....Moore, Anne Peace Corps 202-606-3973
Russia....Olive, Marsha M. Cnty World Bank 202-473-7331
Russia....Staff Cnty State 202-647-9806

Russia....Vorontsov, Yuli M. Cnty Embassy 202-298-5700
Russia....Waxman-Lenz, Roberta Cnty Export-Import Bank 202-565-3742
Russia....Westin, Richard Cnty World Bank 202-473-8261
Russia....Whittle, Dennis B. Cnty World Bank 202-473-8518
Russia...Baldwin, Pamela Cnty AID 202-736-4627
Russian Wheat Aphids Project....Olson, Wayne NAL 301-504-5204
Rwanda (Kigali)....Staff Cnty State 202-647-3139
Rwanda/Minerals....Antonides, Lloyd Cnty Mines 202-501-9686
Rwanda....Barber, Ed Cnty Treasury 202-622-1730
Rwanda....English, Linda K. Cnty World Bank 202-473-5049
Rwanda....Henning, Herman Cnty USIA 202-619-5926
Rwanda....Lloyd, Linda Cnty AID 202-647-9809
Rwanda....Maybury-Lewis, Anthony Cnty Export-Import Bank 202-565-3739
Rwanda....Michelini, Philip Cnty Commerce 202-482-4388
Rwanda....Mutaboba, Joseph W. Cnty Embassy 202-232-2882

S

S-Franc with options....Bice, David CFT 312-35-37880
S&P 500 Index with options....Fedinets, Robert P. CFT 312-353-9016
S&P MidCap400 Index with options....Fedinets, Robert P. CFT 312-353-9016
Saccharin....Land, Eric USITC 202-205-3349
Saddlery and Harness Products....Byron, James COMMERCE 202-482-4034
Safe Drinking Water Hotline....Staff EPA 800-426-4791
Safes....Cuomo, Peter PTO 703-308-0827
Safety Equipment, Trade Promo.....Umstead, Dwight COMMERCE 202-482-2410
Safety Glasses...Staff OD/ORS 301-496-2960
Safety, Health and Work. Cond, Asst. Commiss.....Eisenberg, William M. LABOR 202-606-6304
Safety, Navigation....Staff Coast Guard Hotline 800-368-5647
Safety Program...Staff OD/ORS 301-496-1357
Safety recommendations....Sweedler, Barry M. NTSB 202-382-6810
Safety....Schulman, Lawrence FTA 202-366-4052
Safety....Staff National Safety Council 800-621-7619
Salicin....Randall, Rob USITC 202-205-3366
Saliva....Staff NIDR 301-496-4261
Salivary System Diseases....Staff NIDR 301-496-4261
Salmonella Infections....Staff NIAID 301-496-5717
Salmonellosis and Turtles....Staff CDC 404-639-3286
Salt....Greenblatt, Jack USITC 202-205-3353
Salt....Kostick, Dennis S. MINES 202-501-9410
Salts, inorganic....Greenblatt, Jack USITC 202-205-3353
Salts, organic....Michels, David USITC 202-205-3352
Sampling Methods, Current Programs....Waite, Preston J. CENSUS 301-457-4287
San Marino....Gosriell, Peter Cnty Export-Import Bank 202-565-3733
San Marino....Staff Cnty State 202-647-2453
SAN resins....Misurelli, Denby USITC 202-205-3362
Sanction of Health Providers....Holtz, Judy IG 202-619-1142
Sand and Gravel, Construction....Bolen, Wallace MINES 202-501-9389
Sand and Gravel, Industrial....Bole, Wallace MINES 202-501-9389
Sand....White, Linda USITC 202-205-3427
Sandals....Shildneck, Ann USITC 202-205-3499
Sanitation....Staff OD/ORS 301-496-2960
Santavuori Disease....Staff NINDS 301-496-5751
Sao Tome....Maybury-Lewis, Anthony Cnty Export-Import Bank 202-565-3739
Sao Tome....Edwards, Jennifer R. Cnty World Bank 202-473-4875
Sao Tome....Henning, Herman Cnty USIA 202-619-5926
Sao Tome....Younge, Nathan Cnty TDA 703-875-4357
Sao Tome....Jefferson, Deborah Peace Corps 202-606-3709
Sao Tome....Willis, Mitchell Peace Corps 202-606-3708
Sao Tome and Principe....Barber, Ed Cnty Treasury 202-622-1730
Sao Tome and Principe....Michelini, Philip Cnty Commerce 202-482-4388
Sao Tome and Principe....Staff Cnty State 202-647-3139
Sao Tome and Principe/Minerals....Dolley, Thomas Cnty Mines 202-501-9690
Saphenous Vein Bypass Grafts....Staff NHLBI 301-496-4236
Saran....Misurelli, Denby USITC 202-205-3362
Sarcoidosis....Sarcoidosis Family Aid and Research Foundation (SFARF) 800-223-6429
Sarcoidosis....Staff NIAID 301-496-5717
Sarcoidosis....Staff NHLBI 301-496-4236
Sarcoidosis....Staff NEI 301-496-5248
Sarcoma of Bone and Soft Tissue....Staff NCI 301-496-5583
Sarcoma....Staff NCI 301-496-5583
Sardines....Corey, Roger USITC 202-205-3327
Satellite Communications....Rachul, Lori NASA 216-433-8806
Satellite Design....Staff NASA 301-286-5566

Satellite Spread Spectrum....Staff FCC 301-725-1585
Satellite Testing....Staff NASA 301-286-1584
Satellite Tracking....Staff NASA 301-286-1584
Satellites, Communications....Cooper, Patricia COMMERCE 202-482-4466
Satin white....Johnson, Larry USITC 202-205-3351
Saudi Arabia....Maybury-Lewis, Anthony Cnty Export-Import Bank 202-565-3739
Saudi Arabia....Vacant Cnty USIA 202-619-6528
Saudi Arabia....Curry, David Cnty Treasury 202-622-2140
Saudi Arabia....Ahmad, Mirza Qamar Cnty World Bank 202-473-2652
Saudi Arabia....Kattan, Ahmed A. Cnty Embassy 202-342-3800
Saudi Arabia....Bin Sultan, His Royal Highness Prince Bandar Cnty Embassy 202-342-3800
Saudi Arabia....Cerone, Christopher/Clement, Claude Cnty Commerce 202-482-1860
Saudi Arabia/Minerals....Michalski, Bernadette Cnty Mines 202-501-9699
Saudi Arabia (Riyadh)....Staff Cnty State 202-647-7550
Sausages....Ludwick, David USITC 202-205-3329
Saving and Loans Industry Group....Tow, A. Richard SEC 202-942-1760
Scabies....Staff NIAID 301-496-5717
Scales....Lusi, Susan USITC 202-205-2334
Scandium....Hedrick, James B. MINES 202-501-9412
Scars....Staff NIAMS 301-496-8188
Scarves....Hamey, Amy USITC 202-205-3465
Scarves....Jones, Jackie USITC 202-205-3466
Schilder's Disease....Staff NINDS 301-496-5751
Schistosomiasis....Staff NIAID 301-496-5717
Schizophrenia....Staff NIMH 301-443-4513
Scholars-in-Residence....Staff FIC 301-496-4161
School District Data....Ingold, Jane CENSUS 301-457-2408
Schwanoma....Staff NCI 301-496-5583
Sciatica....Staff NINDS 301-496-5751
Sciatica....Staff NIAMS 301-496-8188
Science and Technology Research Programs....Staff NEH 202-606-8210
Science Issues....Rezendes, Victor S. GAO 202-512-3841
Scientific Computing Resource Center....Staff DCRT 301-402-3488
Scientific Information Center....Rosicky, Henry PTO 703-308-0808
Scientific Instruments, Trade Promo.....Manzolilo, Frank COMMERCE 202-482-2991
Scientific Literature....Brown, Maxine PTO 703-308-4473
Scientific Measurement/Control Equipment....Nealon, Marguerite COMMERCE 202-482-3411
Scientific Visualization....Fowler, Howland NIST 301-975-2703
Scleroderma....Staff United Scleroderma Foundation (USF) 800-722-4673
Scleroderma....Staff NIAMS 301-496-8188
Scleroderma....Staff NHLBI 301-496-4236
Sclerosis, Multiple....Staff NINDS 301-496-5751
Sclerosis....Staff NINDS 301-496-5751
Sclerotherapy....Staff NHLBI 301-496-4236
Scoliosis....Staff NIAMS 301-496-8188
SCOR (Specialized Centers of Research)....Staff NHLBI 301-496-4236
Scrap cordage....Cook, Lee USITC 202-205-3471
Screening machines....Greene, William USITC 202-205-3405
Screw Machine Products....Reise, Richard COMMERCE 202-482-3489
Screws, Washers....Reise, Richard COMMERCE 202-482-3489
Screws....Brandon, James USITC 202-205-3433
Sculptures....Mushinske, Larry CUSTOMS 212-466-5739
Seabirds....Staff FWS 703-358-1821
Sealing machinery....Lusi, Susan USITC 202-205-2334
Seasonal Adjustment Methodology, Empl/Unempl. Stats....McIntire, Robert LABOR 202-606-6345
Seat belts....Cook, Lee USITC 202-205-3471
Sebacic acid esters....Johnson, Larry USITC 202-205-3351
Securities industries....Melly, Christopher USITC 202-205-3461
Security and Commodity Brokers....Muir, S. Cassin COMMERCE 202-482-0349
Security Interests in a License....Staff FCC 202-418-2130
Sedatives (Hypnotics)....Staff NIDA 301-443-6245
Sedatives....Nesbitt, Elizabeth USITC 202-205-3355
Seed Trade Catalogs....Ho, Judith NAL 301-504-5876
Seeds, field and garden....Pierre-Benoist, John USITC 202-205-3320
Seeds, oil-bearing....Reeder, John USITC 202-205-3319
Seeds, spice....Schneider, Greg USITC 202-205-3326
Seeds....Conte, Ralph CUSTOMS 212-466-5759
Segawa's Dystonia....Staff NINDS 301-496-5751
Selenium compounds....Greenblatt, Jack USITC 202-205-3353
Selenium....Conant, Kenneth USITC 202-205-3346
Selenium....Jasinski, Stephen MINES 202-501-9418
Self-Help....Staff Self-Help Network of Kansas 800-445-0116

Self-Help....Staff TOUGHLOVE 800-333-1069
Self Protection, Justifiable Use of Force....Zawitz, Marianne Justice Stat 202-616-3499
Semiconductor device manufacturing....Hearn, Brian E. PTO 703-308-2552
Semiconductor devices....James, Andrew PTO 703-308-4894
Semiconductor stock materials....Hearn, Brian E. PTO 703-308-2552
Semiconductors....Josephs, Irwin CUSTOMS 212-466-5673
Semiconductors....Malison, Andrew USITC 202-205-3391
Semiconductors....Roark, Robin COMMERCE 202-482-3090
Senegal (Dakar)....Staff Cnty State 202-647-2865
Senegal/Minerals....Dolley, Thomas Cnty Mines 202-501-9690
Senegal....Baily, Jess Cnty USIA 202-619-5900
Senegal....Bezek, Jill Cnty TDA 703-875-4357
Senegal....Boccara, Bruno Cnty World Bank 202-473-4689
Senegal....Gueye, Silcarneyni Cnty Embassy 202-234-0541
Senegal....Hutchings, Dayna Cnty Export-Import Bank 202-565-3737
Senegal....Michelini, Philip Cnty Commerce 202-482-4388
Senegal....Owens, Susan Peace Corps 202-606-3185
Senegal....Palghat, Kathy Cnty Treasury 202-622-0332
Senegal....Seck, Mamadou Mansour Cnty Embassy 202-234-0540
Senegal....Woodruff, Neil Cnty AID 202-647-6321
Senile Dementia....Staff NIMH 301-443-4513
Senile Dementia....Staff NINDS 301-496-5751
Senile Dementia....Staff NIA 301-496-1752
Senile Macular Degeneration....Staff NEI 301-496-5248
Sensorimotor Research....Zoltick, Brad J. FAES 301-496-9375
Sensorineural Hearing Loss...Staff NIDCD 301-496-7243
Sentencing - Federal....Kaplan, Carol Justice Stat 202-307-0759
Sentencing....Baunach, Phyllis Jo Justice Stat 202-307-0361
Sentencing....Gaskins, Carla Justice Stat 202-508-8546
Sentencing....Kane, Patrick R. Justice Stat 202-307-3226
Septal Defects....Staff NHLBI 301-496-4236
Serbia....Jackson, Juhan Cnty Treasury 202-622-0766
Serbia....Staff Cnty State 202-647-2452
Serbia....Steblez, Walter Cnty Mines 202-501-9672
Serbia....Waxman-Lenz, Roberta Cnty Export-Import Bank 202-565-3742
Serbia-Montenegro....Corwin, Elizabeth Cnty USIA 202-619-5055
Service Industries, Census....Moody, Jack CENSUS 301-457-2689
Service Industries, Communication....Zabelsky, Thomas CENSUS 301-457-2766
Service Industries, Current Selected Service Report....Zabelsky, Thomas CENSUS 301-457-2766
Service Industries, Finance....Marcus, Sidney CENSUS 301-457-2790
Service Industries, Insurance....Marcus, Sidney CENSUS 301-457-2790
Service Industries, Real Estate....Marcus, Sidney CENSUS 301-457-2790
Service Industries, Transportation....Shoemaker, Dennis CENSUS 301-457-2786
Service Industries, Utilities....Shoemaker, Dennis CENSUS 301-457-2786
Service Industries....Parratt, Shelley SEC 202-942-1840
Service Industry Practices....Alcock, Jane FTC 404-347-7537
Service Industry Practices....Abdullah, Raouf M. FTC 202-326-3024
Service Industry Practices....Aliza, Ben FTC 202-326-2905
Services, Data Base....Cleveland, Douglas COMMERCE 202-482-3314
Services, Prices/Lv. Cond....Gerduk, Irwin LABOR 202-606-7748
Services, Telecom....Edwards, Daniel COMMERCE 202-482-4466
Services, Telecom....Elliot, Fred COMMERCE 202-482-1134
Services/trade matters....Broadman, Harry US Trade Rep 202-395-3606
Severe Accident Branch....Barrett, Richard J. NRC 301-415-3627
Sewage Sludge - Beneficial Use/Technology Transfer....Staff EPA 202-260-8488
Sewage Treatment - Industrial Pretreatment Program....Staff EPA 202-260-8488
Sewing and knitting needles....MacKnight, Peg USITC 202-205-3431
Sewing machine needles....Greene, William USITC 202-205-3405
Sewing machines....Greene, William USITC 202-205-3405
Sewing Notions....Rauch, Theodore CUSTOMS 212-466-5892
Sewing thread: cotton....Warlick, William USITC 202-205-3459
Sewing thread: manmade fibers....Warlick, William USITC 202-205-3459
Sewing thread: silk....Shelton, Linda USITC 202-205-3457
Sewing thread: wool....Shelton, Linda USITC 202-205-3457
Sex and Aging....Staff NIA 301-496-1752
Sex Change....Staff NICHD 301-496-5133
Sex Determination....Staff NICHD 301-496-5133
Sex Hormones....Staff NICHD 301-496-5133
Sexual Development....Staff NICHD 301-496-5133
Sexually Transmitted Diseases....Staff NIAID 301-496-5717
Sexually Transmitted Diseases and HIV Prevention....Morse, Stephen CDC 404-639-3222
Seychelles (Victoria)....Staff Cnty State 202-647-6473
Seychelles/Minerals....Antonides, Lloyd Cnty Mines 202-501-9686
Seychelles....Akpa, Emmanuel Cnty World Bank 202-473-4367

Seychelles....Imam, Fahmila Cnty Export-Import Bank 202-565-3738
Seychelles....Larsen, Mark Cnty USIA 202-619-4894
Seychelles....Marengo, Marc M. Cnty Embassy 212-687-9766
Seychelles....Schmitz, Virginia Peace Corps 202-606-3334
Seychelles....Shelton, Alison Cnty Treasury 202-622-0354
Seychelles....Watkins, Chandra Cnty Commerce 202-482-4564
Seychelles....Younge, Nathan Cnty TDA 703-875-4357
Sezary Syndrome....Staff NIAMS 301-496-8188
Shale oil....Foreso, Cynthia USITC 202-205-3348
Shared Energy Cooperatives....Gunn, Marvin Jr. NEIC 202-586-2826
Shared Instrumentation Grant....Staff NCRR 301-594-7947
Shawls....Jones, Jackie USITC 202-205-3466
Sheep....Steller, Rose USITC 202-205-3323
Sheet feeding....Olszewski, Robert PTO 703-308-2588
Sheet, plastics....Misurelli, Denby USITC 202-205-3362
Sheets, bed....Sweet, Mary Elizabeth USITC 202-205-3455
Shell, articles of....Spalding, Josphine USITC 202-205-3498
Shellac and other lacs....Reeder, John USITC 202-205-3319
Shellac, varnish....Johnson, Larry USITC 201-205-3351
Shellfish....Conte, Ralph CUSTOMS 212-466-5759
Shellfish....Newman, Douglas USITC 202-205-3328
Shells, crude....Steller, Rose USITC 202-205-3323
Shingles and older people....Staff NIA 301-496-1752
Shingles and shakes (wood)....Hoffmeier, Bill USITC 202-205-3321
Shingles, asphalt....Rhodes, Richard USITC 202-205-3322
Shingles (Herpes Zoster)....Staff NINDS 301-496-5751
Shingles, Wood....Wise, Barbara COMMERCE 202-482-0375
Ship Earth Stations....Staff FCC 202-632-7175
Ship Inspections....Staff FCC 202-632-7014
Ship Licensing....Staff FCC 717-337-1212
Ship Rules/Exemptions....Staff FCC 202-632-7175
Ships....Jordan, Charles PTO 703-308-0918
Shirts....Holoyda, Olha USITC 202-205-3467
Shock (Cardiogenic)....Staff NHLBI 301-496-4236
Shock (Hemorrhagic)....Staff NHLBI 301-496-4236
Shock Trauma Center....Staff UMD 301-528-6294
Shoe machinery....Fravel, Dennis USITC 202-205-3404
Shoe making....Sewell, Paul T PTO 703-308-2126
Shoe parts....Shildneck, Ann USITC 202-205-3499
Shoes....Sewell, Paul T PTO 703-308-2126
Shoes....Shildneck, Ann USITC 202-205-3499
Short Range Aids to Navigation....Kline, William USCG 202-267-0980
Short Stature....Staff NICHD 301-496-5133
Short-Term Forecasts of Energy Markets....Kilgore, Calvin NEIC 202-586-1617
Shorts....DeGaetano, Angela CUSTOMS 212-466-5540
Shorts: mens and boys....Sweet, Mary Elizabeth USITC 202-205-3455
Shorts: womens and girls....Sweet, Mary Elizabeth USITC 202-205-3455
Shotguns....Robinson, Hazel USITC 202-205-3496
Shrimp....Newman, Douglas USITC 202-205-3328
Shy-Drager Syndrome....Staff NINDS 301-496-5751
Shy-Drager Syndrome....Staff NIMH 301-443-4513
Shy-Drager Syndrome....Staff NHLBI 301-496-4236
Sickle Cell Disease....Staff Sickle Cell Disease Association of America, Inc. 800-421-8453
Sickle Cell Anemia....Staff NHLBI 301-496-4236
Sideroblastic Anemia....Staff NHLBI 301-496-4236
Siding (wood)....Hoffmeier, Bill USITC 202-205-3321
SIDS....Staff SIDS Alliance 800-221-7437
Sierra Leone (Freetown)....Staff Cnty State 202-647-4567
Sierra Leone/Minerals....Michalski, Bernadette Cnty Mines 202-501-9699
Sierra Leone....Waxman-Lenz, Roberta Cnty Export-Import Bank 202-565-3742
Sierra Leone....Palghat, Kathy Cnty Treasury 202-622-0332
Sierra Leone....Tallroth, Nils Borje Cnty World Bank 202-473-4876
Sierra Leone....O'Neal, Adrienne Cnty USIA 202-619-6904
Sierra Leone....Kargbo, Thomas Kahota Cnty Embassy 202-939-9261
Sierra Leone....Herring, Debra Peace Corps 202-606-3644
Sierra Leone....Michelini, Philip Cnty Commerce 202-482-4388
Sierra Leone....McCormick, Michael L. Peace Corps 202-606-3644
Sierre Leone....Williams, Gustavus Cnty Embassy 202-939-9261
Sight Substitution Systems....Staff NEI 301-496-5248
Signal Processing/Analysis....Staff DCRT 301-496-6561
Signal Processing/Analysis....Staff DCRT 301-496-2959
Silent Ischemia....Staff NHLBI 301-496-4236
Silica....White, Linda USITC 202-205-3427
Silicon Carbide Abrasive....Austin, Gordon MINES 202-501-9388
Silicon Characterization....Ehrstein, James R. NIST 301-975-2060
Silicon....Conant, Kenneth USITC 202-205-3346

Silicon....Cunningham, Larry D. MINES 202-501-9443
Silicone resins....Misurelli, Denby USITC 202-205-3362
Silicones....Michels, David USITC 202-205-3352
Silk....Freund, Kimberlie USITC 202-205-3456
Silk....Shelton, Linda USITC 202-205-3457
Silk....Warlick, William USITC 202-205-3459
Sillimanite....DeSapio, Vincent USITC 202-205-3435
Silver compounds....Greenblatt, Jack USITC 202-205-3353
Silver with options....Rosenfeld, David CFT 312-353-9026
Silver....McNay, Deborah USITC 202-205-3425
Silver....Reese, Jr., Robert G. MINES 202-501-9413
Silverware....Harris, John COMMERCE 202-482-1178
Singapore/Minerals....Tse, Pui-Kwan Cnty Mines 202-501-9696
Singapore (Singapore)....Staff Cnty State 202-647-3278
Singapore....Cung, Raphael Cnty Commerce 202-482-3877
Singapore....Gilroy, Meg Cnty USIA 202-619-5836
Singapore....Imam, Fahmila Cnty Export-Import Bank 202-565-3738
Singapore....Selverajah, A. Cnty Embassy 202-537-3100
Singapore....Shelton, Alison Cnty Treasury 202-622-0354
Single Family Housing....Staff HUD 202-708-3175
Sinusitis....Staff NIAID 301-496-5717
Sirups....Vacant USITC 202-205-3454
Sitters....Staff Safe Sitters 800-255-4089
Sjogren's Syndrome....Staff Sjogren's Syndrome Association (SS) 800-395-6772
Sjogren's Syndrome....Staff NEI 301-496-5248
Sjogren's Syndrome....Staff NINDS 301-496-5751
Sjogren's Syndrome....Staff NIDR 301-496-4261
Sjogren's Syndrome....Staff NIAMS 301-496-8188
Sjogren's Syndrome....Staff NIAID 301-496-5717
Ski equipment....Witherspoon, Richardo USITC 202-205-3489
Skin and Aging....Staff NIAMS 301-496-8188
Skin and Aging....Staff NIA 301-496-1752
Skin and Sunlight....Staff NIAMS 301-496-8188
Skin and Sunlight....Staff NCI 301-496-5583
Skin Cancer....Staff NCI 301-496-5583
Skin Diseases....Staff NIAMS 301-496-8188
Skins (animal)....Steller, Rose USITC 202-205-3323
Skirts, Knit and Woven....DeGaetano, Angela CUSTOMS 212-466-5540
Skirts....Sweet, Mary Elizabeth USITC 202-205-3455
Slack....Foreso, Cynthia USITC 202-205-3348
Slacks, mens and boys....Sweet, Mary Elizabeth USITC 202-205-3455
Slacks, womens and girls....Sweet, Mary Elizabeth USITC 202-205-3455
Slate....White, Linda USITC 202-205-3427
Slavic Republic....Schiel, Russell Peace Corps 202-606-3606
Slavic Republic....Lockwood, Jennifer Peace Corps 202-606-3607
Sleep and Aging....Staff NIA 301-496-1752
Sleep and Aging....Staff NIMH 301-443-4513
Sleep Apnea....Staff NHLBI 301-496-4236
Sleep Disorders....Staff NIMH 301-443-4513
Sleep Disorders....Staff NINDS 301-496-5751
Sleep Disturbances....Staff NIMH 301-443-4513
Sleepwear....Staff CPSC 301-504-0580
Slide fasteners....Shildneck, Ann USITC 202-205-3499
Slippers....Shildneck, Ann USITC 202-205-3499
Slovak Republic....Altheim, Stephen Cnty Treasury 202-622-0125
Slovak Republic....Hewer, Ulrich A. Cnty World Bank 202-473-2279
Slovak Republic....Ann Lien Cnty TDA 703-875-4357
Slovakia....Bazala, Razvigor Cnty USIA 202-619-5855
Slovakia....Burian, Peter Cnty Embassy 202-965-5161
Slovakia....Housh, Tony Cnty Treasury 202-622-7456
Slovakia....Lichardus, Branislav Cnty Embassy 202-965-5161
Slovakia....Staff Cnty State 202-647-3191
Slovakia....Steblez, Walter Cnty Mines 202-501-9672
Slovakia....Waxman-Lenz, Roberta Cnty Export-Import Bank 202-565-3742
Slovenia....Corwin, Elizabeth Cnty USIA 202-619-5055
Slovenia....Elwan, Ann E. Cnty World Bank 202-473-2435
Slovenia....Gallagher, Tricia Cnty Treasury 202-622-0117
Slovenia....Petric, Ernest Cnty Embassy 202-667-5363
Slovenia....Staff cnty State 202-736-7152
Slovenia....Steblez, Walter Cnty Mines 202-501-9672
Slovenia....Waxman-Lenz, Roberta Cnty Export-Import Bank 202-565-3742
Slovenia....Zore, Gregor S. Cnty Embassy 202-667-5363
Slow Viruses....Staff NINDS 301-496-5751
Small and Woman-Owned Business Opportunities....Staff HUD 202-708-1428
Small Business Innovation Research....Staff OD/OER 301-496-1968
Small Business Trade Policy....Lino Prosak, Sylvia COMMERCE 202-482-4792
Small Cell Carcinoma....Staff NCI 301-496-5583

Small Telcos....Staff FCC 202-418-1530

Smallpox....Staff NIAID 301-496-5717

Smell (Disorders)....Staff NINDS 301-496-5751

Smell (Disorders)....Staff NIDCD 301-496-7243

Smoke and Toxic Gas Prediction.....Mulholland, George W. NIST 301-975-6695

Smoke Detectors....Giles, Ken CPSC 301-504-0580

Smokeless powder....Johnson, Larry USITC 202-205-3351

Smokeless Tobacco (Oral Complications)....Staff NCI 301-496-5583

Smokeless Tobacco (Oral Complications)....Staff NIDR 301-496-4251

Smokers' articles....Conte, Ralph CUSTOMS 212-466-5759

Smokers' articles....Burns, Gail USITC 202-205-3501

Smoking and Health....Eriksen, Michael P. CDC 404-488-5701

Smoking and Health....Hensley, Timothy CDC 404-488-5705

Smoking and Health....Staff NIDA 301-443-5583

Smoking and Health, Public Information....McKenna, Jeffrey P. CDC 404-488-5705

Smoking and Heart Disease....Staff NHLBI 301-496-4236

Smoking (Cancer related)....Staff NCI 301-496-5583

SMR-Business Opportunities....Staff FCC 202-418-0620

SMR-Enforcement: Channel....Staff FCC 800-322-1117

SMR-Interpretations....Staff FCC 202-418-0620

Smuggling Investigations....Cockrell, Robert Customs 202-927-1530

Snackfood....Manogue, Robert COMMERCE 202-482-2428

Snap fasteners....Shildneck, Anna USITC 202-205-3499

Soap, castile....Land, Eric USITC 202-205-3349

Soap, surface-active agents, synthetic detergent....Land, Eric USITC 202-205-3349

Soap, toilet....Land, Eric USITC 202-205-3349

Soaps, Detergents, Cleansers....Hurt, William COMMERCE 202-482-0128

Soaps....Joseph, Stephanie CUSTOMS 212-466-5768

Soapstone....White, Linda USITC 202-205-3427

Social and Behavioral Research on Aging....Staff NIA 301-496-1752

Social and Behavioral Sciences....Staff NICHD 301-496-6832

Social and Behavioral Sciences....Staff NIMH 301-443-4513

Social Security...Staff SSA 800-772-1213

Social Services Block Grant.... ACF 202-401-9215

Social Work Department....Staff CC 301-496-2381

Sociology of Journalism....Levy, Mark R. UMD 301-405-2389

Sociology....Caplow, Theodore UVA 703-924-6397

Soda ash....Conant, Kenneth USITC 202-205-3346

Sodium and potassium salts of oils, greases, fat....Land, Eric USITC 202-205-3349

Sodium Ash....Kostick, Dennis S. MINES 202-501-9410

Sodium benzoate....Matusik, Ed USITC 202-205-3356

Sodium bicarbonate....Conant, Kenneth USITC 202-205-3346

Sodium carbonate....Conant, Kenneth USITC 202-205-3346

Sodium compounds....Greenblatt, Jack USITC 202-205-3353

Sodium hydroxide....Conant, Kenneth USITC 202-205-3346

Sodium Sulfate....Kostick, Dennis S. MINES 202-501-9410

Sodium....Conant, Kenneth USITC 202-205-3346

Sodium....Lecos, Chris FDA 202-205-4144

Soft Drink....Manogue, Robert COMMERCE 202-482-2428

Software, Export Promo....Fogg, Judy COMMERCE 202-482-4936

Software services....Warlick, William USITC 202-205-3459

Software....Hijikata, Heidi C. COMMERCE 202-482-0569

Software....Smolenskni, Mary COMMERCE 202-482-0551

Solar Burns (Eye Effects)....Staff NEI 301-496-5248

Solar Cells/Photovoltaic Devices/Small Hydro....Garden, Les COMMERCE 202-482-0556

Solar Energy Conversion....Kelly, Margurite NEIS 303-275-4099

Solar Energy Conversion....Annan, Robert H. NEIC 202-586-1720

Solar energy....Foreso, Cynthia USITC 202-205-3348

Solar Equipment, Geoth....Garden, Les COMMERCE 202-482-0556

Solar Equipment Ocean/Biomass....Garden, Les COMMERCE 202-482-0556

Solar Phenomena Research....Staff NASA 415-604-3937

Solar System Exploration....Farrar, Diane NASA 415-604-3934

Solar Thermal and Biomass Power....Burch, Gary NEIC 202-586-8121

Solid Waste Disposal (Radioactive)....Staff OD/ORS 301-496-2254

Solid Waste Disposal....Staff OD/ORS 301-496-3537

Solid Waste Information Clearinghouse Hotline....Staff EPA 800-677-9424

Solid Waste Management (Municipal)....Staff EPA 202-260-5856

Solid Waste Office of....Staff EPA 202-260-4627

Solomon Islands (Honiara)....Staff Cnty State 202-647-3546

Solomon Islands/Minerals....Lyday, Travis Cnty Mines 202-501-9695

Solomon Islands....Imam, Fahmila Cnty Export-Import Bank 202-565-3738

Solomon Islands....Davies, Irene Cnty World Bank 202-458-2481

Solomon Islands....Shelton, Alison Cnty Treasury 202-622-0354

Solomon Islands....Rahman, Talaat Cnty TDA 703-875-4357

Solomon Islands....Schell, Russell Peace Corps 202-606-3231

Solomon Islands....Morona, Catherine Peace Corps 202-606-0982

Solomon Islands....Lee, Allison Peace Corps 202-606-0983

Somalia/Minerals....Antonides, Lloyd Cnty Mines 202-501-9686

Somalia (Mogadishu)....Staff Cnty State 202-647-6453

Somalia....Ghani, Ejaz Syed Cnty World Bank 202-473-4819

Somalia....Gold, Ricki Cnty AID 202-647-7977

Somalia....Hutchings, Dayna Cnty Export-Import Bank 202-565-3737

Somalia....Larsen, Mark Cnty USIA 202-619-4894

Somalia....McKoy, Ethel Cnty Treasury 202-622-0336

Somalia....Watkins, Chandra Cnty Commerce 202-482-4564

Somatization Disorder...Staff NIMH 301-443-4513

Sorbitol....Randall, Rob USITC 202-205-3366

Sorting machines....Greene, William USITC 202-205-3405

Sound signaling apparatus....Baker, Scott USITC 202-205-3386

Sounding Rocket Program....Koehler, Keith NASA 804-824-1579

Sounding Rockets....Brown, Dwayne C. NASA 202-358-1726

South Africa/Minerals....van Oss, Henrik Cnty Mines 202-501-9687

South Africa, Republic of (Pretoria)....Staff Cnty State 202-647-8252

South Africa....Barrington, Belinda Cnty AID 202-647-4229

South Africa....Kilan, Andre Cnty Embassy 202-232-4400

South Africa....Mabury-Lewis, Anthony Cnty Export-Import Bank 202-565-3739

South Africa....Patel, Praful C. Cnty World Bank 202-473-4250

South Africa....Rauch, Margie Cnty Treasury 202-622-0251

South Africa....Schwartz, Larry Cnty USIA 202-619-6904

South Africa....Solomon, Emily Cnty Commerce 202-482-5148

South Africa....Sonn, Franklin Cnty Embassy 202-232-3400

South Asia/trade matters....Stillman, Betsy US Trade Rep 202-395-6813

South Asia/trade matters....Ruzicka, Rick US Trade Rep 202-395-6813

South Pacific Commission....Staff Cnty State 202-647-3546

Southeast Asia/trade matters....Damond, Joseph US Trade Rep 202-395-6813

Southeast MTC (Manufacturing Technology Center)....Bishop, Jim NIST 803-252-6976

Southern Cone Affairs....Murphy, Sean US Trade Rep 202-395-3324

Southern Cone Market....Chopra, Karen US Trade Rep 202-395-5190

Soy Products....Manogue, John COMMERCE 202-482-3428

Soybean Meal with options....Schambach, Duane CFT 312-353-9000

Soybean oil with options....Schambach, Duane CFT 312-353-9000

Soybeans and soybean oil....Reeder, John USITC 202-205-3319

Soybeans with options....Schambach, Duane CFT 312-353-9000

Space Communications....Brown, Dwayne C. NASA 202-358-1726

Space Derived Technology....Dunbar, Brian NASA 202-358-1547

Space Exploration....Keegan, Sarah NASA 202-358-1902

Space Flight Systems....Rachul, Lori NASA 216-433-8806

Space Flight....Campion, Edward S. NASA 202-358-1780

Space Flight....Cast, Jim NASA 202-358-1779

Space Industry Machinery, Nec....Farner, Kim COMMERCE 202-482-2232

Space Policy Development....Farner, Kim COMMERCE 202-482-2232

Space Propulsion....Rachel, Lori NASA 216-433-8806

Space Remote Sensing Commercialization....Sullivan, Nancy NASA 601-688-3341

Space Science and Applications....Braukus, Michael NASA 202-358-1979

Space Science and Applications....Cleggett-Haleim, Paula NASA 202-358-0883

Space Shuttle Engine Testing....Sullivan, Nancy NASA 601-688-3341

Space Shuttle Program....Staff NASA 713-483-5111

Space Shuttle Propulsion Testing....Sullivan, Nancy NASA 601-688-3341

Space Shuttle Research....Staff NASA 804-864-6122

Space Shuttle....Malone, June NASA 205-544-7061

Space Shuttle....James, Donald G. NASA 415-604-3935

Space Station Freedom....Rachul, Lori NASA 216-433-8806

Space Station Freedom....Simmons, Mike NASA 205-544-6537

Space technology....Norwood, Robert NASA 202-358-2320

Space Technology....Staff NASA 205-544-6538

Space Vehicle Testing....Buckingham, Bruce NASA 407-867-2468

Space Vehicle Testing....Buckingham, Bruce NASA 407-867-2468

Space Vehicle Testing....Buckingham, Bruce NASA 407-867-2468

Spacecraft....Anderson, Peder USITC 202-205-3388

Spacelab Missions Operations....Staff NASA 205-544-9492

Spacelab....Hess, Mark NASA 202-358-1778

Spain (Madrid)....Staff Cnty State 202-647-1412

Spain/Minerals....Newman, Harold R. Cnty Mines 202-501-9669

Spain....de Ojeda, Jaime Cnty Embassy 202-452-0100

Spain....Double, Mary Beth Cnty Commerce 202-482-4508

Spain....Gosnell, Peter Cnty Export-Import Bank 202-565-3733

Spain....Holloway, Barbara Cnty Treasury 202-622-0098

Spain....Rodriguez, Dario Polo Cnty Embassy 202-728-2340

Spain....Seifkin, David Cnty USIA 202-619-6582

Spanish, Italian and Portuguese languages....Opere, Fernando UVA 804-924-7159

Spasmodic Dysphonia....Staff NINDS 301-496-5924
Spasmodic Dysphonia....Staff NIDCD 301-496-7243
Spasmodic Torticollis....Staff NINDS 301-496-5751
Spasms (Arteries)....Staff NHLBI 301-496-4236
Spastic Hemiplegia....Staff NINDS 301-496-5751
Spastic Paraplegia....Staff NINDS 301-496-5751
Spastic Quadriplegia....Staff NINDS 301-496-5751
Spasticity....Staff NINDS 301-496-5751
Special classification provisions....Roth, Jordon USITC 202-205-3467
Special Collections Program....Pindell, Alvetta NAL 301-504-5204
Special Events...Staff CC 301-496-3475
Special Foreign Currency Program....Staff FIC 301-496-1653
Special Industry Machinery, Nec....Shaw, Eugene COMMERCE 202-482-3494
Special Investigations....Rosenbaum, Eli M. Justice 202-616-2492
Special Population Censuses....Csellar, Elaine CENSUS 301-457-1429
Special Topics - Agricultural History....Bowers, Douglas Agri 202-219-0787
Special Topics - Alternative Crops....Glaser, Lewrene Agri 202-219-0091
Special Topics - Biotechnology (Dairy)....Caswell, Margaret Agri 202-219-0417
Special Topics - Biotechnology....Reilly, John Agri 202-219-0450
Special Topics - Commodity Programs and Policies-Honey....Hoff, Fred Agri 202-219-0883
Special Topics - Commodity Programs and Policies-Sugar....Buzanelli, Peter Agri 202-219-0888
Special Topics - Commodity Programs and Policies-Tobacco....Grise, Verner Agri 202-219-0890
Special Topics - Commodity Programs and Policies....Harwood, Joy Agri 202-219-0840
Special Topics - Economic Linkages to Agriculture....Edmondson, William Agri 202-219-0785
Special Topics - Energy....Gill, Mohinder Agri 202-219-0464
Special Topics - Farm Labor Market....Whitener, Leslie Agri 202-219-0932
Special Topics - Farm Labor Laws....Runyan, Jack Agri 202-219-0932
Special Topics - Farm Machinery....Vesterby, Marlow Agri 202-219-0422
Special Topics - Farm Structure....Whitener, Leslie Agri 202-219-0932
Special Topics - Fertilizer....Rives, Sam Agri 202-720-2324
Special Topics - Fertilizer....Taylor, Harold Agri 202-219-0464
Special Topics - Geographic information Systems....Heimlich, Ralph Agri 202-219-0431
Special Topics - Macroeconomic Conditions (World)....Baxter, Tim Agri 202-219-0706
Special Topics - Macroeconomic Conditions....Denbaly, Mark Agri 202-219-0779
Special Topics - Natural Resource Policy (World)....Urban, Francis Agri 202-219-0717
Special Topics - Natural Resource Policy....Ribaudo, Marc Agri 202-219-0444
Special Topics - Natural Resource Policy....Osborn, Tim Agri 202-219-0401
Special Topics - Pesticides....Bull, Len Agri 202-501-8288
Special Topics - Pesticides....Love, John Agri 202-219-0388
Special Topics - Pesticides....Padgitt, Merritt Agri 202-219-0433
Special Topics - Pesticides....Rives, Sam Agri 202-720-2324
Special Topics - Pesticides....Vandeman, Ann Agri 202-219-0089
Special Topics - Population - World....Urban, Francis Agri 202-219-0705
Special Topics - Population....Beale, Calvin Agri 202-219-0482
Special Topics - Population....Swanson, Linda Agri 202-219-0557
Special Topics - Seeds....Gill, Mohinder Agri 202-219-0464
Special Topics - Soil Conservation....Magleby, Richard Agri 202-219-0436
Special Topics - Soil Conservation....Osborn, Tim Agri 202-219-1030
Special Topics - Sustainable Agriculture....Vandeman, Ann Agri 202-219-0433
Special Topics - Sustainable Agriculture....Baumes, Harry Agri 202-219-1019
Special Topics - Trade....Anderson, Margot Agri 202-219-0449
Special Topics - Trade....Krissoff, Barry Agri 202-219-0681
Special Topics - Transportation....Hutchinson, T.Q. Agri 202-219-0840
Special Topics - Water and Irrigation....Moore, Michael Agri 202-219-0411
Special Topics - Water and Irrigation....Gollehon, Noel Agri 202-219-0413
Special Topics - Water Quality....Rives, Sam Agri 202-720-2324
Special Topics - Water Quality....Ribaudo, Marc Agri 202-501-8387
Special Topics - Water Quality....Crutchfield, Steve Agri 202-219-0444
Special Topics - Weather....Preston, Greg Agri 202-219-7621
Special Topics - Weather....Ripley, Brad Agri 202-720-1444
Species Profiles, Fish and Wildlife....Staff FWS 703-358-1710
Specific Language Impairment (SLI)....Staff NIDCD 301-496-7243
Spectacles....Johnson, Christopher USITC 202-205-3488
Speech and Language Disorders....Staff NIDCD 301-496-7243
Speech and Language Disorders....Staff NICHD 301-496-5133
Speech and Language Disorders....Staff NINDS 301-496-5924
Speech....Staff American Speech-Language-Hearing Association Consumer Helpline (ASLHA) 800-638-8255
Speech....Staff NIDCD 301-496-7243

Speech....Staff NIDR 301-496-4261
Speed changers....Fravel, Dennis USITC 202-205-3404
Speed Changers....Reise, Richard COMMERCE 202-482-3489
SPF (Specific Pathogen Free) Animal Breeding Research Program....Staff NCRR 301-594-7933
Sphingolipidoses Mucopolysaccharidoses and Stor. Dis.....Staff NINDS 301-496-5751
Sphingolipidoses....Staff NINDS 301-496-5751
Spices....Conte, Ralph CUSTOMS 212-466-5759
Spices....Schneider, Greg USITC 202-205-3326
Spielmeyer-Sjogren's Disease....Staff NINDS 301-496-5751
Spina Bifida....Staff Spina Bifida Association of America (SBAA) 800-621-3141
Spina Bifida....Staff NIDCD 301-496-7243
Spina Bifida....Staff NINDS 301-496-5751
Spina Bifida....Staff NICHD 301-496-5133
Spinal Arachnoiditis....Staff NINDS 301-496-5751
Spinal Cord Injuries....Staff Hotline 800-526-3456
Spinal Cord Injuries....Staff National Spinal Cord Injury Association (NSCIA) 800-962-9629
Spinal Cord Injury....Staff NINDS 301-496-5751
Spinal Cord Lesions....Staff NINDS 301-496-5751
Spinal Cord Tumors....Staff NINDS 301-496-5751
Spinal Muscular Atrophy....Staff NINDS 301-496-5751
Spinning machines....Greene, William USITC 202-205-3405
Spinocerebellar Degeneration....Staff NINDS 301-496-5751
Split Channel Operations....Staff FCC 202-653-5560
Spondyloarthropathies....Staff NIAMS 301-496-8188
Spondylolisthesis....Staff NIAMS 301-496-8188
Sponge, articles of....Spalding, Josephine USITC 202-205-3498
Sponges, marine....Ludwick, David USITC 202-205-3329
Spongy Degeneration...Staff NINDS 301-496-5751
Sporting Goods and Athletic....Vanderwolf, John COMMERCE 202-482-0348
Sporting Goods, Export Promo.....Beckham, Reginald COMMERCE 202-482-5478
Sporting goods....Millin, Vincent PTO 703-308-1065
Sporting goods....Love, John PTO 703-308-0873
Sporting goods....Witherspoon, Ricardo USITC 202-205-3489
Sporting Goods....McKenna, Thomas CUSTOMS 212-466-5475
Sports Medicine....Staff NIAMS 301-496-8188
Spraying devices....Kashnikow, Andres PTO 703-308-1137
Spraying machinery: other....Lusi, Susan USITC 202-205-2334
Spraying machinery: agricultural/horticultural....Fravel, Dennis USITC 202-205-3404
Squamous Cell....Staff NCI 301-496-5583
Sri Lanka (Colombo)....Staff Cnty State 202-647-2351
Sri Lanka/Minerals....Kuo, Chin Cnty Mines 202-501-9693
Sri Lanka....Imam, Fahmila Cnty Export-Import Bank 202-565-3738
Sri Lanka....Benbrahim, Abderraouf Cnty World Bank 202-458-2637
Sri Lanka....McKoy, Ethel Cnty Treasury 202-622-0336
Sri Lanka....Gradisher, Thomas Cnty USIA 202-619-5529
Sri Lanka....Rahman, Talaat Cnty TDA 703-875-4357
Sri Lanka....Dhanapala, Janantha Cudah Cnty Embassy 202-338-8565
Sri Lanka....Dharmawardhane, Asoka G. Cnty Embassy 202-483-4026
Sri Lanka....Simmons, John Cnty Commerce 202-482-2954
Sri Lanka....Phillips, Scott Peace Corps 202-606-1053
St. Bartholomey....Brooks, Michelle Cnty Commerce 202-482-2527
St. Kitts and Nevis....Edwards, Erstein Mallet Cnty Embassy 202-686-2636
St. Kitts and Nevis....Rabchevsky, George Cnty Mines 202-501-9670
St. Kitts and Nevis....Marcus, Anthony Cnty Treasury 202-622-1218
St. Kitts/Nevis....Wilkins, Michele Cnty Export-Import Bank 202-565-3743
St. Kitts-Nevis....Brooks, Michelle Cnty Commerce 202-482-2527
St. Kitts/Nevis....Nallari, Raj R. Cnty World Bank 202-473-8697
St. Kitts....Irish, John P. Cnty Embassy 202-686-2636
St. Lucia....Brooks, Michelle Cnty Commerce 202-482-2527
St. Lucia....Edmunds, Joseph Edsel Cnty Embassy 202-364-6792
St. Lucia....John Herrman Cnty TDA 703-875-4357
St. Lucia....Mallet, Juliet Elaine Cnty Embassy 202-364-6793
St. Lucia....Marcus, Anthony Cnty Treasury 202-622-1218
St. Lucia....Nallari, Raj R. Cnty World Bank 202-473-8697
St. Lucia....Rabchevsky, George Cnty Mines 202-501-9670
St. Lucia....Wilkins, Michele Cnty Export-Import Bank 202-565-3743
St. Martin....Brooks, Michelle Cnty Commerce 202-482-2527
St. Vincent Grenadines....Brooks, Michelle Cnty Commerce 202-482-2527
St. Vincent Grenadines....Rabchevsky, George Cnty Mines 202-501-9670
St. Vincent....Layne, Kingsley Cnty Embassy 202-462-7806
St. Vincent....Marcus, Anthony Cnty Treasury 202-622-1218
St. Vincent....Nallari, Raj R. Cnty World Bank 202-473-8697

Be patient. If any phone number is incorrect, call (area code) 555-1212 and request the new listing.

St. Vincent....Norris, Cecily A. Cnty Embassy 202-462-7846

St. Vincent....Wilkins, Michele Cnty Export-Import Bank 202-565-3743

St. Vitus Dance (Sydenham Chorea)....Staff NINDS 301-496-5751

Stained Teeth (Tetracycline)....Staff NIDR 301-496-4261

Stains....Johnson, Larry USITC 202-205-3351

Standard Industrial Classification, Empl/Unempl....Bennott, William LABOR 202-606-6474

Standard Occupational Classification, Empl/Unempl....McElroy, Michael LABOR 202-606-6516

Staphylococcal Infections....Staff NIAID 301-496-5717

Staple fibers, manmade....Sweet, Mary Elizabeth USITC 202-205-3455

Starches, chemically treated....Randall, Rob USITC 202-205-3366

Starches....Pierre-Benoist, John USITC 202-205-3320

Stargardt's Disease....Staff NEI 301-496-5248

State and Area Labor Force Data, Data Disk and Tapes....Marcus, Jessie LABOR 202-606-6392

State and Area Labor Force Data, Demog. Char. E/Un....Biederman, Edna LABOR 202-606-6392

State and Metropolitan Area Data Books....Cevis, Wanda CENSUS 301-457-1166

State and Outlying Area Estimates....Staff CENSUS 301-457-1099

State Data Center Program....Jones, Tim CENSUS 301-457-1305

State Drug Abuse Services (Standards and Requirements)....Staff NIDA 301-443-6245

State Energy Programs....Demetrops, James NEIC 202-586-9187

State Projections....Staff CENSUS 301-457-2422

State Rates/Infrastructure....Staff FCC 202-418-0940

States and Areas Establishment Survey, Data Disk.....Podgornik, Guy LABOR 202-606-6534

States and Areas Establishment Survey, Empl/Unempl....Shipp, Kenneth LABOR 202-606-6519

Static molds....Woo, Jay PTO 703-308-3793

Statistical Abstract....King, Glenn CENSUS 301-457-1171

Statistical Areas....Staff CENSUS 301-763-3827

Statistical Briefs....Bernstein, Robert CENSUS 301-457-1221

Statistical Consulting...Staff DCRT 301-496-6037

Statistical Engineering....Lundegard, Robert J. NIST 301-975-2840

Statistical Methods, Prices and Living Cond.....Hedges, Brian LABOR 202-606-6897

Statistical Research for Demographic Programs....Hoy, Easley CENSUS 301-457-4978

Statistical Research for Economic Programs....Hoy, Easley CENSUS 301-457-4978

Statistical Surveys, National Fish and Wildlife....Staff FWS 703-358-1730

Statistician, Chief....Young, Allan H. ECONOMIC 202-606-9607

Statistics (Blindness and Visual Disorders)....Staff NEI 301-496-5248

Statistics (Health)....Staff CDC 404-639-3286

Statistics (Health)....Staff NCHS 301-496-8500

Statistics....Dillingham, Steven Justice Stat 202-307-0765

Staurolite....Austin, Gordon MINES 202-501-9388

Stearic acid....Randall, Rob USITC 202-205-3366

Stearic acid esters....Randall, Rob USITC 202-205-3366

Steatite....White, Linda USITC 202-205-3427

Steel: angles, shapes, and sections....Kaplan, Stephanie USITC 202-205-3436

Steel: bars....Kaplan, Stephanie USITC 202-205-3436

Steel, Basic Shapes and Forms....Ilardi, Paula CUSTOMS 212-466-5476

Steel Industry Products....Bell, Charles COMMERCE 202-482-0608

Steel: Ingots, blooms, and billets....MacKnight, Peg USITC 202-205-3431

Steel: pipe and tube and fittings....Bello, Felix USITC 202-205-3120

Steel: Pipes....Bello, Felix USITC 202-205-3120

Steel: plate....MacKnight, Peg USITC 202-205-3431

Steel: rails....Yost, Charles USITC 202-205-3432

Steel: sheet....MacKnight, Peg USITC 202-205-3431

Steel: strip....MacKnight, Peg USITC 202-205-3431

Steel: tubes....Bello, Felix Karen USITC 202-205-3120

Steel: waste and scrap....Kaplan, Stephanie USITC 202-205-3436

Steel: wire rods....Yost, Charles USITC 202-205-3442

Steel: wire....Yost, Charles USITC 202-205-3442

Steele-Richardson Disease....Staff NINDS 301-496-5751

Stents...Staff NHLBI 301-496-4236

Stereo apparatus....Puffert, Douglas USITC 202-205-3402

Sterilization....Staff NICHD 301-496-5133

Sterilization....Warden, Robert PTO 703-308-2920

Steroid Contraceptives....Staff NICHD 301-496-5133

Steroid Hormones....Stoney, Simons S. FAES 301-496-6797

Steroid Hypertension....Staff NHLBI 301-496-4236

Steroids....Staff NIDA 301-443-6245

Stevens-Johnson Syndrome....Staff NIAID 301-496-5717

Stiff Man Syndrome....Staff NINDS 301-496-5751

Still's Disease....Staff NIAMS 301-496-8188

Stimulants....Staff NIDA 301-443-6245

Stomach Cancer....Staff NCI 301-496-5583

Stone and products....White, Linda USITC 202-205-3427

Stone, Crushed....Tepordei, Valentin V. MINES 202-501-9392

Stone, Dimension....Taylor, Harold A. MINES 202-501-9754

Stone House...Staff FIC 301-496-1213

Stone-processing machines....Greene, William USITC 202-205-3405

Stone....Bunin, Jacob CUSTOMS 212-566-5796

Stoneware articles....McNay, Deborah USITC 202-205-3425

Stoneworking machines....Fravel, Dennis USITC 202-205-3404

Storage Batteries....Larrabee, David COMMERCE 202-482-0607

Storm Water....Staff EPA 703-821-4823

Storm Water Hotline....Staff EPA 703-821-4823

Stoves/Woodburning....Staff EPA 919-541-2733

Strabismus....Staff NEI 301-496-5248

Stranger-to-Stranger Crime....Rand, Michael Justice Stat 202-616-3494

Streptococcal Infections....Staff NIAID 301-496-5717

Streptokinase....Staff NHLBI 301-496-4236

Stress and Aging....Staff NIA 301-496-1752

Stress (EKG)....Staff NHLBI 301-496-4236

Stress....Staff NIMH 301-496-4513

Striatonigral Degeneration....Staff NINDS 301-496-5751

Stroke (Hypertension)....Staff NHLBI 301-496-4236

Stroke....Staff American Heart Association Stroke Connection (AHASC) 800-553-6321

Stroke....Staff National Stroke Association (Stroke) 800-787-6537

Stroke....Staff NINDS 301-496-5751

Stroke....Staff NIDCD 301-496-7243

Strontium compounds....Greenblatt, Jack USITC 202-205-3353

Strontium pigments....Johnson, Larry USITC 202-205-3351

Strontium....Lundy, David USITC 202-205-3439

Strontium....Ober, Joyce A. MINES 202-501-9406

Structures of base metals....Kaplan, Stephanie USITC 202-205-3436

Structures....Lew, H.S. NIST 301-975-6061

Student Conservation Programs, Fish and Wildlife....Staff FWS 703-358-1786

Students, Youth, and Dropouts, Empl/Unempl. Stats.....Cohany, Sharon LABOR 202-606-6378

Studio Transmitter Links, Common Carrier....Staff FCC 202-418-1500

Studio Transmitter Links, Mass Media....Staff FCC 202-418-2600

Sturge Weber Syndrome....Staff Sturge Weber Foundation (SWF) 800-627-5482

Sturge-Weber Syndrome....Staff NINDS 301-496-5751

Stuttering....Staff National Center for Stuttering (NCS) 800-221-2483

Stuttering....Staff NIDCD 301-496-7243

Stuttering....Staff NINDS 301-496-5751

Sty....Staff NEI 301-496-5248

Styrene (monomer)....Matusik, Ed USITC 202-205-3356

Styrene resins....Misurelli, Denby USITC 202-205-3362

Subacute Necrotizing Encephalomyelopathy (Leighs')....Staff NINDS 301-496-5751

Subacute Sclerosing Panencephalitis....Staff NINDS 301-496-5751

Subarachnoid Cyst...Staff NINDS 301-496-5751

Subarachnoid Hemorrhage....Staff NINDS 301-496-5751

Subscriber line Charge....Staff FCC 202-418-1595

Subseabed Disposal Research....Warnick, Walter NEIC 301-903-3122

Substance Abuse....Staff Primary Care Management Systems (PCMS) 800-444-9999

Substance Abuse Prevention, Office of....Setal, Mel 301-443-9936

Sudan (Khartoum)....Staff Cnty State 202-647-6475

Sudan/Minerals....Antonides, Lloyd Cnty Mines 202-501-9686

Sudan....Abdalla, Elsadig Bakheit Cnty Embassy 202-338-8570

Sudan....Ghani, Ejaz Syed Cnty World Bank 202-473-4819

Sudan....Hill, Megan Cnty AID 202-647-8100

Sudan....Hutchings, Dayna Cnty Export Import Bank 202-565-3737

Sudan....Squire, Margo Cnty USIA 202-619-5529

Sudan....Suliman, Ahmed Cnty Embassy 202-338-8565

Sudan....VanRenterghem, Cynthia Cnty Treasury 202-622-0343

Sudan....Watkins, Chandra Cnty Commerce 202-482-4564

Sudanophilic Leukodystrophy....Staff NINDS 301-496-5751

Sudden Cardiac Death....Staff NHLBI 301-496-4236

Sudden Infant Death Syndrome....Staff NICHD 301-496-5133

Sugar and Sweeteners....Lord, Ronald Agri 202-219-0888

Sugar and Sweeteners....Buzzanell, Peter Agri 202-219-0886

Sugar and Sweeteners....Preston, Greg Agri 202-720-7621

Sugar....Maria, John CUSTOMS 212-466-5730

Sugar....Vacant USITC 202-205-3454

Suicide...Baldwin, Elaine NIDA 301-443-4536
Suicide....Staff NIMH 301-443-4513
Suit-Jackets....Crowley, Michael CUSTOMS 212-466-5852
Suits....Crowley, Michael CUSTOMS 212-466-5852
Suits: men's and boys'....Sweet, mary Elizabeth USITC 202-205-3455
Suits: women's and girls'....Sweet, Mary Elizabeth USITC 202-205-3455
Sulfides, nonmetallic....Conant, Kenneth USITC 202-205-3346
Sulfiting Agents....Lecos, Chris FDA 202-205-1144
Sulfur dioxide....Conant, Kenneth USITC 202-205-3346
Sulfur....Ober, Joyce MINES 202-501-9406
Sulfur....Trainor, Cynthia USITC 202-205-3354
Sulfuric acid....Trainor, Cynthia USITC 202-205-3354
Sulfuryl chloride....Conant, Kenneth USITC 202-205-3346
Summer Research Fellowship Program....Staff CC 301-496-2427
Sunlight and Skin Cancer....Staff NCI 301-496-5583
Sunshine....Staff FCC 202-418-1720
Supercomputers....Iverson, Sean COMMERCE 202-482-1987
Superconducting Super Collider Project....Hall, James NEIC 214-708-2521
Superconductivity....Eaton, Russell NEIC 202-586-0205
Superconductors....Lieberman, Paul PTO 703-308-2552
Superconductors....Chiarado, Roger COMMERCE 202-482-0402
Supercritical fluid extraction....Chesler, Stephen N. NIST 301-975-3102
Superfund Hazardous Waste....Staff EPA 800-231-3075
Superfund....Sims, Anne CDC 404-639-3286
Superfund....Staff EPA 202-260-7703
Superphosphates....Trainor, Cynthia USITC 202-205-3354
Supersonic (Mach 1-5) Engine Testing....Staff NASA 804-864-6125
Supervisory Training....Staff OD/DPM 301-496-6211
Supplemental Security Income (SSI)....Gambino, Phil SSA 410-965-8904
Supplies (Central Storeroom)....Staff OD/DAS 301-496-3273
Surety Guarantees....Kleeschulte, Dorothy D. SBA 202-205-6540
Surface Active Agents....Joseph, Stephanie CUSTOMS 212-466-5768
Surface-active agents....Land, Eric USITC 202-205-3349
Surgeon General....Manley, Audrey PHS 202-690-6467
Surgeons....Staff Association of American Physicians and Surgeons (AAPS) 800-635-1196
Surgery (Cancer)....Staff NCI 301-496-5583
Surgery, diagnostics....Howell, Kyle PTO 703-308-3256
Surgery, medicators....Rosenbaum, Fred PTO 703-308-2991
Surgery (Oral)....Staff NIDR 301-496-4261
Surgery, treatment....Howell, Kyle PTO 703-308-3256
Surgical apparatus....Johnson, Christopher USITC 202-205-3488
Surgical instruments (endoscopes)....Apley, Richard PTO 703-308-0305
Surgical instruments....Hafer, Robert PTO 703-308-2674
Surgical instruments....Mancene, Gene PTO 703-308-2696
Surgical instruments....Pellegrino, Stephen PTO 703-308-0871
Surgical Opinion, second....Staff National Second Surgical Opinion Program 800-638-6833
Surgical Treatment of Heart Disease....Staff NHLBI 301-496-4236
Suriname/Minerals....Gurmendi, Alfredo Cnty Mines 202-501-9681
Suriname (Paramaribo)....Staff Cnty State 202-647-2620
Suriname....Brooks, Michelle Cnty Commerce 202-482-2527
Suriname....Hume, Susan Cnty World Bank 202-473-2407
Suriname....John Herrman Cnty TDA 703-875-4357
Suriname....Korff, Michael Cnty USIA 202-619-6835
Suriname....Neil, Jeff Cnty Treasury 202-622-1268
Suriname....Udenhout, Willem E. Cnty Embassy 202-244-7489
Suriname....van Dillenburg, Georgine Cnty Embassy 202-244-7490
Suriname....Wilkins, Michele Cnty Export-Import Bank 202-565-3743
Survey Data and Tapes, Consumer Expend. Surv.....Passero, William LABOR 202-606-6900
Survey of Consumer Finances....Fries, Gerhard FRS 202-452-2578
Survey of Income and Program Participation (SIPP)....Eargle, Judy CENSUS 301-763-8375
Survey Operations, Consumer Expend. Survey. Pr/Lv....Dietz, Richard LABOR 202-606-6872
Surveys, Migratory Birds....Staff FWS 703-358-1714
Surveys, National Fish and Wildlife....Staff FWS 703-358-2156
Surveys, Waterfowl Harvest....Staff FWS 703-358-6300
Surveys, Waterfowls Population....Staff FWS 703-358-1838
Sutures, surgical....Randall, Rob USITC 202-205-3366
Swallowing Disorders....Staff NIDCD 301-496-7243
Swallowing Disorders...Staff NIDR 301-496-4261
Swaziland (Mbabane)....Staff Cnty State 202-647-8434
Swaziland/Minerals....van Oss, Hendrik Cnty Mines 202-501-9687
Swaziland....Barber, Ed Cnty Treasury 202-622-1730
Swaziland....Bezek, Jill Cnty TDA 703-875-4357

Swaziland....Burns, Paul Peace Corps 202-606-3634
Swaziland....Holm-Olsen, Finn Cnty Commerce 202-482-4228
Swaziland....Jewett, Woody Peace Corps 202-606-3635
Swaziland....Kanya, Mary M. Cnty Embassy 202-362-6683
Swaziland....Lane, Bernard Cnty AID 202-647-4228
Swaziland....Maybury-Lewis, Anthony Cnty Export-Import Bank 202-565-3739
Swaziland....Nhlabatsi, Lindiwe Audrey Cnty Embassy 202-362-6685
Swaziland...Patel, Praful C. Cnty World Bank 202-473-4250
Swaziland....Schwartz, Larry Cnty USIA 202-619-6904
Sweat Gland Disorders....Staff NIAMS 301-496-8188
Sweaters....Crowley, Michael CUSTOMS 212-466-5852
Sweaters....Sweet, Mary Elizabeth USITC 202-205-3455
Sweatshirts....Crowley, Michael CUSTOMS 212-466-5852
Sweatshirts....Sweet, Mary Elizabeth USITC 202-205-3455
Sweden/Minerals....Plachy, Josef Cnty Mines 202-501-9673
Sweden (Stockholm)....Staff Cnty State 202-647-5669
Sweden....Devlin, James Cnty Commerce 202-482-4414
Sweden....Ekman, Andreas Eric Cnty Embassy 202-462-2600
Sweden....Gosnell, Peter Cnty Export-Import Bank 202-565-3733
Sweden....Mackour, Oscar Cnty Treasury 202-622-0145
Sweden....Rankin-Galloway, Honore Cnty USIA 202-619-5283
Sweden....Sihver Liljegren, Carl Henrik Cnty Embassy 202-467-2600
Swimwear, Adult....Shea, Gerard CUSTOMS 212-466-5878
Swimwear, Childrens'....Kirschner, Bruce CUSTOMS 212-566-5865
Swimwear: womens and girls....Sweet, Mary Elizabeth USITC 202-205-3455
Swimwear....Hamey, Amy USITC 202-205-3465
Swimwear....Jones, Jackie USITC 202-205-3466
Swine Flu....Staff NIAID 301-496-5717
Switches, Electric....Malison, Andrew USITC 202-205-3391
Switches, telephone....Hylton, Lori USITC 202-205-3450
Switches....Recia, Henry PTO 703-308-1382
Switchgear and Switchboard Apparatus....Bodson, John COMMERCE 202-482-0681
Switzerland (Bern)....Staff Cnty State 202-647-1484
Switzerland/Minerals....Plachy, Josef Cnty Mines 202-501-9673
Switzerland....Combs, Philip/Wright, Corey Cnty Commerce 202-482-2920
Switzerland....Gosnell, Peter Cnty Expert-Import Bank 202-565-3733
Switzerland...Jagmetti, Carlo Cnty Embassy 202-745-7900
Switzerland....Joseph, Jean-Claude Cnty Embassy 202-745-7900
Switzerland....Lemaistre, Alice Cnty USIA 202-619-6184
Switzerland....Mackour, Oscar Cnty Treasury 202-622-0145
Sydenham's Chorea....Staff NINDS 301-496-5751
Synchrotron Resources...Staff NCRR 301-594-7934
Syncope (Fainting)....Staff NHLBI 301-496-4236
Syndrome X....Staff NHLBI 301-496-4236
Synfuel Plants....Frye, Keith NEIC 301-903-2098
Synovitis....Staff NIAMS 301-496-8188
Synthesis Gas....Der, Victor NEIC 301-903-2700
Synthetic detergents....Land, Eric USITC 202-205-3349
Synthetic iron oxides and hydroxides....Johnson, Larry USITC 202-205-3351
Synthetic natural gas (SNG)....Land, Eric USITC 202-205-3349
Synthetic rubber....Misurelli, Denby USITC 202-205-3362
Syphilis....Staff NIAID 301-496-5717
Syria/Minerals....Michalski, Bernadette Cnty Mines 202-501-9699
Syria....Al-Moualem, Walid Cnty Embassy 202-232-6313
Syria....Austin, Ken Cnty Treasury 202-622-0174
Syria....Hutchings, Dayna Cnty Export-Import Bank 202-565-3737
Syria....Mukherjee, Mohua Cnty World Bank 202-473-3022
Syria....Sarra, Suleiman Cnty Embassy 202-232-6313
Syria....Winton, Donna Cnty USIA 202-619-6528
Syria....Wright, Corey/Sams, Thomas Cnty Commerce 202-482-5506
Syrian Arab Republic (Damascus)....Staff Cnty State 202-647-1131
Syringomyelia....Staff NINDS 301-496-5751
System Integration....Atkins, Robert COMMERCE 202-482-4781
Systemic Lupus Erythematosus....Staff NIAMS 301-496-8188
Systolic Hypertension in the Elderly (SHEP)....Staff NIA 301-496-1752
Systolic Hypertension in the Elderly (SHEP)....Staff NHLBI 301-496-4236

T

T-Bills, Technical Information....Decorleto, Donna FRS 202-452-3956
T-Bills with options....SIA Manasses CFT 312-353-9027
T-Bonds with options....Redheffer, Nancy L. CFT 312-353-9015
T-Cell Deficiency....Staff NIAID 301-496-5717
T-Notes (2,5, 6-10) with options....Redheffer, Nancy L. CFT 312-353-9015
T-Notes/Bonds (Zeros) with options....Redheffer, Nancy L. CFT 312-353-9015

T-Shirts, Knit....DeGaetano, Angela CUSTOMS 212-466-5540

T-Shirts....Sweet, Mary Elizabeth USITC 202-205-3455

Tablecloths....Sweet, Mary Elizabeth USITC 202-205-3455

Tachycardia....Staff NHLBI 301-496-4236

Tactile Devices....Staff NIDCD 301-496-7243

Taiwan Coordination....Staff Cnty State 202-647-7711

Taiwan/Minerals....Tse, Pui-Kwan Cnty Mines 202-501-9696

Taiwan....Aschneider, Todd Cnty Treasury 202-622-0335

Taiwan....Davis, Ian/Chu, Robert/Duvall, Dan Cnty Commerce 202-482-4390

Taiwan....Hutchings, Dayna Cnty Export-Import Bank 202-565-3737

Tajikistan....Ghasimi, Mohammad R. Cnty World Bank 202-473-6858

Tajikistan....Levine, Richard Cnty Mines 202-501-9682

Tajikistan....Resnick, Bonnie Cnty Treasury 202-622-0108

Tajikistan....Skipper, Thomas Cnty USIA 202-619-5057

Tajikistan....Staff Cnty State 202-647-6757

Tajikistan....Waxman-Lenz, Roberta Cnty Export-Import Bank 202-565-3742

Tajikistan....Eighmy, Thomas Cnty AID 202-647-6920

Takayasu's Arteritis....Staff NIAID 301-496-5717

Take Pride in America Program, Fish and Wildlife....Staff FWS 703-358-2156

Talc....Virta, Robert MINES 202-501-9384

Talc....White, Linda USITC 202-205-3427

Tall oil....Randall, Rob USITC 202-205-3366

Tangier Disease....Staff NINDS 301-496-5751

Tangier Disease....Staff NHLBI 301-496-4236

Tanning products and agents....Wanser, Stephen USITC 202-205-3363

Tantalum....Cunningham, Larry D. MINES 202-501-9443

Tantalum....Lundy, David USITC 202-205-3439

Tantalum....Presbury, Graylin COMMERCE 202-482-5158

Tanzania (Dar es Salaam)....Staff Cnty State 202-647-6473

Tanzania/Minerals....Izon, David Cnty Mines 202-501-9692

Tanzania....Burns, Paul Peace Corps 202-606-3634

Tanzania....Holm-Olsen, Finn Cnty Commerce 202-482-4228

Tanzania....Imam, Fahmila Cnty Export-Import Bank 202-565-3738

Tanzania....Jewett, Woody Peace Corps 202-606-3635

Tanzania....Kotze, Joan Cnty Treasury 202-622-0333

Tanzania....Larsen, Mark Cnty USIA 202-619-4894

Tanzania....Mwendwa, John Mathew Cnty Embassy 202-939-6125

Tanzania....Nyirabu, Charles Musama Cnty Embassy 202-939-6125

Tanzania....Pulaski, Stephan Cnty AID 202-647-5588

Tanzania....Shaw, William Cnty World Bank 202-473-0138

Tanzania....Younge, Nathan Cnty TDA 703-875-4357

Tape Players....Dicerbo, Mario CUSTOMS 212-466-5672

Tape players....Puffert, Douglas USITC 202-205-3402

Tape recorders and players, audio....Puffert, Douglas USITC 202-205-3402

Tape recordings....Puffert, Douglas USITC 202-205-3402

Tapestries....Hansen, John CUSTOMS 212-466-5854

Tapestries....Sweet, Mary Elizabeth USITC 202-205-3455

Taps....Mata, Ruben USITC 202-205-3403

Tar Sands....Der, Victor NEIC 301-903-2700

Tar sands oil....Foreso, Cynthia USITC 202-205-3348

Tardive Dyskinesia....Staff NINDS 301-496-5751

Tardive Dyskinesia....Staff NIMH 301-443-4513

Tarsal Tunnel Syndrome....Staff NINDS 301-496-5751

Tashkent....Eighmy, Thomas Cnty AID 202-647-6920

Taste and Smell Dysfunction....Staff NIDCD 301-496-7243

Taste and Smell Dysfunction....Staff NINDS 301-496-5751

Taste....Staff NIDCD 301-496-7243

Tax Policy....Stathis, Jennie S. GAO 202-512-5407

Tay-Sach's Disease....Staff NINDS 301-496-5751

Tea....Janis, William V. COMMERCE 202-482-2250

Tea....Maria, John CUSTOMS 212-466-5730

Tea....Schneider, Greg USITC 202-205-3326

Technical Assistance....Schulman, Lawrence FTA 202-366-4052

Technical Information Center....Rosicky, Henry PTO 703-308-0808

Technological Developments and Nursing Care....Staff NINR 301-496-0207

Technologists....Staff Association of Surgical Technologists 800-637-7433

Technology Assessment OD/OMAR 301-496-1143

Technology Centers, Fish....Staff FWS 703-358-1714

Technology Demonstration Center....Richardson, Deborah NAL 301-504-5779

Technology Services....Heydemann, P.L.M. NIST 301-975-4500

Technology Transfer Information Center....Hayes, Kathleen NAL 301-504-6875

Technology Transfer...Staff OD/OIA 301-496-7057

Technology Trends In Major Industries....Riche, Richard LABOR 202-606-5626

Technology....Shane, Richard SBA 202-205-6450

Teenage Pregnancy....Eddinger, Lucy ASH 202-690-8335

Teeth....Staff NIDR 301-496-4261

Telangiectasis (Rendu-Osler-Weber Dis., Syndrome)....Staff NHLBI 301-496-4236

Telecommunications, Cellular....Gossack, Linda COMMERCE 202-482-4466

Telecommunications, CPE....Pham, Phuangm COMMERCE 202-482-0399

Telecommunication Devices for the Deaf....Staff FCC 202-639-6999

Telecommunications, Fiber Optics....Mocenigo, Anthony COMMERCE 202-482-2953

Telecommunications for Deaf, Public and Spec. Studies....TDD LABOR 202-219-7090

Telecommunications, Major Projects....Paddock, Rick COMMERCE 202-482-5235

Telecommunications, Network Equipment....Henry, John COMMERCE 202-482-1193

Telecommunications, Network Equipment....Henry, John COMMERCE 202-482-1193

Telecommunications, Radio....Gossack, Linda COMMERCE 202-482-4466

Telecommunications, Satellites....Cooper, Patricia COMMERCE 202-482-4466

Telecommunications, Services....Elliot, Fred COMMERCE 202-482-1134

Telecommunications Services....Shefrin, Ivan COMMERCE 202-482-4661

Telecommunications, Trade Promo.....Vacant COMMERCE 202-482-2952

Telecommunications, TV Broadcast Equip.....Rettig, Thersa E. COMMERCE 202-482-4466

Telecommunications....Eisenzopf, Reinhard PTO 703-305-4711

Telecommunications....Edwards, Daniel COMMERCE 202-482-4466

Telegraph and telephone apparatus....Hylton, Lori USITC 202-205-3450

Telegraph Industry Group....Owings, Christopher SEC 202-942-1900

Telegraphy....Chin, Stephen PTO 703-305-4714

Telephone Equipment Interconnection....Staff FCC 202-418-0200

Telephone Lines....Staff FCC 202-418-0200

Telephone services....Hylton, Lori USITC 202-205-3450

Telephone Telegraph Rates....Staff FCC 202-418-0200

Telephones, Wireless....Dicerbo, Mario CUSTOMS 212-466-5672

Telephones....Vacant CUSTOMS 212-466-5673

Telephony....Dwyer, James L. PTO 703-305-4701

Telephony....Kuntz, Curt PTO 703-305-4708

Telescopes....Johnson, Christopher USITC 202-205-3488

Teletext Services....Elliot, Fred COMMERCE 202-482-1134

Television Advertising Intercity Relays....Staff FCC 202-418-1430

Television Advertising....Staff FCC 202-418-0200

Television camera....Razavi, Michael PTO 703-305-4713

Television equipment....Kitzmiller, John USITC 202-205-3387

Television Industry Group....Owings, Christopher SEC 202-942-1900

Television Political Broadcasting Fairness....Staff FCC 202-418-1440

Television Programming....Staff FCC 202-418-1430

Television Religious Petition....Staff FCC 202-418-0200

Television Translators....Staff FCC 202-418-1650

Television....Groody, James J. PTO 703-305-4702

Television....Chin, Tommy PTO 703-305-4715

Televisions....Dicerbo, Mario CUSTOMS 212-466-5672

TELEX, International and Domestic....Staff FCC 202-632-7265

Tellurium compounds....Greenblatt, Jack USITC 202-205-3353

Tellurium....Jasinski, Stephen MINES 202-501-9418

Temporal Arteritis....Staff NHLBI 301-496-4236

Temporal Arteritis (Eyes)....Staff NEI 301-496-5248

Temporal Arteritis (Neurological Aspects of)....Staff NINDS 301-496-5751

Temporomandibular Joint Disorders....Staff NIDR 301-496-4261

Tender Offers Proxy Contests....Staff FCC 202-418-1630

Tendonitis....Staff NIAMS 301-496-8188

Tennis equipment....Witherspoon, Richardo USITC 202-205-3489

Tents and tarpaulins....Cook, Lee USITC 202-205-3471

Territorial Exclusivity....Staff FCC 202-418-2120

Terrorism....Reynolds, James S. Justice 202-514-0849

Test Procedures-Equipment....Staff FCC 301-725-1585

Test Site Descriptions....Staff FCC 202-418-1430

Test Tube Babies....Staff NICHD 301-496-5133

Testicular Cancer....Staff NCI 301-496-5583

Tetanus....Staff NIAID 301-496-5717

Tethered Cord...NINDS 301-496-5751

Tetraethyl lead....Michels, David USITC 202-205-3352

Tetralogy of Fallot....Staff NHLBI 301-496-4236

Tetramer of proplyene....Raftery, Jim USITC 202-205-3365

Tetramethyl lead....Michels, David USITC 202-205-3352

Tetrapropylene....Raftery, Jim USITC 202-205-3365

Textile calendaring and rolling machines....Greene, William USITC 202-205-3405

Textile finishing agents....Land, Eric USITC 202-205-3349

Textile Machinery....Mangor, Jon COMMERCE 202-482-2732

Textile machines....Greene, William USITC 202-205-3405

Textile washing, bleaching, dyeing, machines....Greene, William USITC 202-205-3405

Textiles and Apparel Industry Group....Owings, Christopher SEC 202-942-1900

Be patient. If any phone number is incorrect, call (area code) 555-1212 and request the new listing.

1443

Textiles and Leather, Prices and Living Conditions....Paik, Soon LABOR 202-606-7714

Textiles, Trade Promo....Mangor, Jon COMMERCE 202-482-2732

Textiles....Dulka, William A. COMMERCE 202-482-4058

Textiles....Goldberg, Gerald PTO 703-308-5443

Textiles....Hubbard, Volenick Customs 202-482-7050

Thailand (Bangkok)....Staff Cnty State 202-647-7108

Thailand/Minerals....Lyday, Travis Cnty Mines 202-501-9695

Thailand....Camp, Bea Cnty USIA 202-619-5837

Thailand....Chompoopet, Wilaiwan Cnty Embassy 202-944-3600

Thailand....Dwor-Frecaut, Dominique Cnty World Bank 202-473-2970

Thailand....Frye, Lisa Peace Corps 202-606-0970

Thailand....Hower, Mark Peace Corps 202-606-5517

Thailand....Huston, Christine Peace Corps 202-606-0970

Thailand....Imam, Fahmila Cnty Export-Import Bank 202-565-3738

Thailand....Kelly, Jean Cnty Commerce 202-482-3877

Thailand....Respess, Rebecca Cnty TDA 703-875-4357

Thailand....VanRenterghem, Cynthia Cnty Treasury 202-622-0343

Thailand...Xuto, Manaspas Cnty Embassy 202-944-3600

Thalassemia....Staff NIDDK 301-496-3583

Thalassemia....Staff NHLBI 301-496-4236

Thallium compounds....Greenblatt, Jack USITC 202-205-3353

Thallium....Sehnke, Errol Mines 202-501-9421

Theater....McCord, Karyl NEA 202-682-5425

Theories of Aging....Staff NIA 301-496-1752

Therapeutic Compositions....Robinson, Douglas PTO 703-308-2897

Therapy devices....Apley, Richard PTO 703-308-0305

Thermal Switches....Picard, Leo PTO 703-308-0538

Thermodynamics....Lias, S. NIST 301-975-2562

Thermophysics....Kayser, R.F. NIST 301-975-2483

Thoracic-Outlet Syndrome....Staff NINDS 301-496-5751

Thoratic-Outlet Syndrome....Staff NHLBI 301-496-4236

Thorium compounds....Greenblatt, Jack USITC 202-205-3353

Thorium....DeSapio, Vincent USITC 202-205-3435

Thorium....Hedrick, James B. MINES 202-501-9412

Thread: cotton....Warlick, William USITC 202-205-3459

Thread: manmade fibers....Warlick, William USITC 202-205-3459

Thread: silk....Shelton, Linda USITC 202-205-3467

Threatened Species Permits, Fish and Wildlife....Staff FWS 703-358-2104

Thrift Acquisitions....Koonjy, Diane FRS 202-452-3274

Thrift Acquisitions....Wassom, Molly FRS 202-452-2305

Throat Disorders...Staff NIDCD 301-496-7243

Thrombasthenia....Staff NIDDK 301-496-3583

Thrombocythemia....Staff NHLBI 301-496-4236

Thrombocytopenia....Staff NHLBI 301-496-4236

Thrombocytopenia....Staff NIDDK 301-496-3583

Thromboembolism....Staff NHLBI 301-496-4236

Thrombolysis....Staff NHLBI 301-496-4236

Thrombophlebitis....Staff NHLBI 301-496-4236

Thrombosis....Staff NHLBI 301-496-4236

Thyroid (Adenoma of)....Staff NIDDK 301-496-3583

Thyroiditis....Staff NIDDK 301-496-3583

Thyroma....Staff NCI 301-496-5583

Thyrotoxic Myopathy...Staff NINDS 301-496-5751

Thyroxine-iodine....Staff NIDDK 301-496-3583

Tic Douloureux (Trigeminal Neuralgia)....Staff NINDS 301-496-5751

Ticks....Staff NIAID 301-496-5717

TIGER, Applications....Carbaugh, Larry CENSUS 301-457-1305

TIGER, Future Plans....Staff CENSUS 301-457-1100

Tiger, Products....Carbaugh, Larry CENSUS 301-457-1242

TIGER System Products....Staff CENSUS 301-457-4100

Tights....DeGaetano, Angela CUSTOMS 212-466-5540

Tiles, ceramic....McNay, Deborah USITC 202-205-3425

Timber Management...Hesse, David FS 202-205-0893

Timber Management, Fish and Wildlife....Staff FWS 703-358-2043

Time and Frequency....Sullivan, D.B. NIST 303-497-3772

Time Served in Prison - Federal....Kaplan, Carol Justice Stat 202-307-0759

Time Served in Prison....Greenfeld, Lawrence Justice Stat 202-616-3281

Time Served in Prison....Innes, Christopher Justice Stat 202-724-3121

Time Served in Prison....Beck, Allen Justice Stat 202-616-3277

Time switches....Luther, Dennis USITC 202-205-3497

Timing apparatus....Luther, Dennis USITC 202-205-3497

Tin compounds....Greenblatt, Jack USITC 202-205-3353

Tin Products....Presbury, Graylin COMMERCE 202-482-5158

Tin....Carlin, Jr., James F. MINES 202-501-9426

Tin....DeSapio, Vincent USITC 202-205-3435

Tinnitus....Staff NINDS 301-496-5751

Tinnitus....Staff NIDCD 301-496-7243

Tires and tubes, of rubber of plastics....Raftery, Jim USITC 202-205-3365

Tires....Prat, Raimundo COMMERCE 202-482-0128

Tires....Rauch, Theodore CUSTOMS 212-466-5892

Tissue Culture Cells (Freezing and Storage)....Staff OD/ORS 301-496-2960

Tissue Culture Media....Staff OD/ORS 301-496-6017

Tissue Plasminogen Activator (TPA)....Staff NHLBI 301-496-4236

Tissue Typing....Staff NHLBI 301-496-4236

Tissue Typing....Staff NIAID 301-496-5717

Titanium compounds....Greenblatt, Jack USITC 202-205-3353

Titanium dioxide....Johnson, Larry USITC 202-205-3351

Titanium pigments....Johnson, Larry USITC 202-205-3351

Titanium....DeSapio, Vincent USITC 202-205-3435

Titanium....Gambogi, Joseph MINES 202-501-9390

Tobacco and tobacco products....Harney, Amy USITC 202-205-3465

Tobacco machines....Jackson, Georgia USITC 202-205-3399

Tobacco pipes....Burns, Gail USITC 202-205-3501

Tobacco products....Love, John PTO 703-308-0873

Tobacco Products....Kenney, Cornelius COMMERCE 202-482-2428

Tobacco....Capehart, Tom Agri 202-219-0822

Tobacco....Conte, Ralph CUSTOMS 212-466-5759

Tobacco....Grise, Verner Agri 202-219-0890

Tobacco....Millin, Vincent PTO 703-308-1065

Tobacco....Preston, Greg Agri 202-720-7621

Tobago....Korff, Michael Cnty USIA 202-619-6835

Tobago....Lewin, Michael Cnty World Bank 202-473-8684

Tobago....Marcus, Anthony Cnty Treasury 202-622-1218

Tobago....Massiah, Joan Cnty Embassy 202-467-6490

Tobago....McKnight, Corinne Arvelle Cnty Embassy 202-467-6490

Togo (Lome)....Staff Cnty State 202-647-1540

Togo/Minerals....Izon, David Cnty Mines 202-501-9674

Togo....Baily, Jess Cnty USIA 202-619-5900

Togo....Barber, Ed Cnty Treasury 202-622-1730

Togo....Bezek, Jill Cnty TDA 703-875-4357

Togo....Dailly, Jean-Paul Cnty World Bank 202-473-4743

Togo....Henke, Debra Cnty Commerce 202-482-3317

Togo....Maybury-Lewis, Anthony Cnty Export-Import Bank 202-565-3739

Togo....Sanchez, Patricia Peace Corps 202-606-3237

Togo....Wickman, Cam Cnty AID 202-647-6335

Toilet preps, cosmetics, and perfumery....Land, Eric USITC 202-205-3349

Toilet soaps....Land, Eric USITC 202-205-3349

Toiletries....Mancene, Gene PTO 703-308-2696

Toll Fraud Complaints....Staff FCC 202-418-0960

Toluene....Raftery, Tim USITC 202-205-3365

Tomatoes....McCarty, Timothy USITC 202-205-3324

Toners....Wanser, Stephen USITC 202-205-3363

Tonga/Minerals....Lyday, Travis Cnty Mines 202-501-9695

Tonga (Nuku'alofa)....Staff Cnty State 202-647-3546

Tonga....Berghage, Jeff Peace Corps 202-606-1098

Tonga....Davies, Irene Cnty World Bank 202-458-2481

Tonga....Imam, Fahmila Cnty Export-Import Bank 202-565-3738

Tonga....Respess, Rebecca Cnty TDA 703-875-4357

Tongue....Staff NIDR 301-496-4261

Tongue....Staff NIDCD 301-496-7243

Tools/Dies/Jigs/Fixtures....Pilaroscia, Megan COMMERCE 202-482-0609

Tools, Machine....Losche, Robert CUSTOMS 212-466-5670

Topical drug products....Chkravarty, Alaka G. FAES 301-443-4595

Topographic Map (USGS) Indexes, Fish and Wildlife....Staff FWS 703-358-1713

Topped crude petroleum....Foreso, Cynthia USITC 202-205-3348

Torsion Dystonia (Dystonia Musculorum Deformans)....Staff NINDS 301-496-5751

Torticollis (Wryneck)....Staff NINDS 301-496-5751

Toto....Olson, Susan Peace Corps 202-606-3136

Tourette Syndrome....Staff TSA 800-237-0717

Tourette Syndrome....Staff NINDS 301-496-5751

Tourette Syndrome....Staff NIMH 301-443-4513

Tourette Syndrome....Staff NIDCD 301-496-7243

Tourism (Major Proj)....White, Barbara COMMERCE 202-482-4160

Tourism services....Ludolph, Josephine COMMERCE 202-482-3575

Tourism services....Sloane, Leonard USITC 202-205-3311

Tours (Campus)....Staff OD/VIC 301-496-1776

Tours....Staff CC 301-496-3475

Tours....Staff NLM 301-496-6308

Tow, manmade....Sweet, Mary Elizabeth USITC 202-205-3455

Towels....Hansen, John CUSTOMS 212-466-5854

Towels....Sweet, Mary Elizabeth USITC 202-205-3455

Towers--Painting and Lighting of....Staff FCC 202-632-7521

Toxic Shock Syndrome....Staff NICHD 301-496-5133
Toxic Shock Syndrome....Staff NIAID 301-496-5717
Toxic Shock Syndrome....Staff CDC 401-639-3286
Toxic Substances and Disease Registry, Agency for....Greenwell, Mike ATSDR 404-639-0727
Toxic Substances Library....Staff EPA 202-260-3944
Toxicology Branch....Staff EPA 703-305-6121
Toxicology/Pharmacology....Staff NIEHS 919-541-3345
Toxicology/Pharmacology....Staff NIGMS 301-496-7707
Toxicology Program, National....Stopinski, Helen NIEHS/NIH 919-541-3991
Toxicology Programs/Special. Information Services....Staff NLM 301-496-1131
Toxicology Programs/Specialized Information Services...Staff NLM 301-496-1131
Toxicology....Davis, Barbara D. FAES 703-603-8823
Toxicology....DeRosa, Christopher CDC 404-639-6300
Toxics Branch....Staff EPA 703-235-5320
TOXNET....Staff NLM 301-496-1131
Toxocariasis....Staff NEI 301-496-5248
Toxoplasmosis....Staff NEI 301-496-5248
Toxoplasmosis....Staff NIAID 301-496-5717
Toys and Games (Export Promo)....Beckham, Reginald COMMERCE 202-482-5478
Toys for pets, christmas deco, figurines, etc....Raftery, Jim USITC 202-205-3365
Toys....Abrahamson, Dana USITC 202-205-3430
Toys....Hodgen, Donald COMMERCE 202-482-3346
Toys....Wong, Alice CUSTOMS 212-466-5538
Toys....Hafer, Robert PTO 703-308-2674
Trace Gas Measurement Techniques....Guenther, Franklin R. NIST 301-975-3939
Trace Metals (and CVD)....Staff NHLBI 301-496-4236
Trachoma....Staff NEI 301-496-5248
Track Suits....Crowley, Michael CUSTOMS 212-466-5852
Tractors (except truck tractors)...Fravel, Dennis USITC 202-205-3404
Tractors....Wholey, Patrick CUSTOMS 212-466-5668
Trade Related Employment....Teske, Gary R.A. COMMERCE 202-482-2056
Trademark Search Library....Staff PTO 703-308-9800
Traffic Safety Programs....Brownlee, Michael NHTSA 202-366-1755
Traffic Safety....Zawitz, Marianne Justice Stat 202-616-3499
Trailers and other vehicles not self-propelled....Polly, Laura USITC 202-205-3408
Training (Biological Safety and Control)....Staff OD/ORS 301-496-2960
Training Courses....Staff CENSUS 301-457-1210
Training....Rhile, Howard G. GAO 202-512-6418
Training....Staff OD/DPM 301-496-6211
Transceivers....Kitzmiller, John USITC 202-205-3387
Transformation (Cell)....Staff NCI 301-496-5583
Transformers....Bodson, John COMMERCE 202-482-0681
Transformers....Cutchin, John USITC 202-205-3396
Transformers....Josephs, Irwin CUSTOMS 212-466-5673
Transfusional Hemosiderosis....Staff NHLBI 301-496-4236
Transient Ischemic Attacks....Staff NHLBI 301-496-4236
Transient Ischemic Attacks....Staff NINDS 301-496-5751
Transplantation (Cornea)....Staff NEI 301-496-5248
Transplantation Immunology....Staff NIAID 301-496-5717
Transplants (He, Valv, Lung, Blo, Vess, Vei, Ar)....Staff NHLBI 301-496-4236
Transplants (Liver, Pancreas, Kidney)....Staff NIDDK 301-496-3583
Transplants (Organ Procurement)....Staff HRSA 301-443-7577
Transport....Staff FCC 202-418-1590
Transportation Equipment, Producer Price Index....Yatsko, Ralph LABOR 202-606-7747
Transportation Issues....Mead, Kenneth M. GAO 202-512-3766
Transportation Services....Johnson, William COMMERCE 202-482-5012
Transportation, Truck Inventory and Use....Bostic, William CENSUS 301-457-2797
Transportation....Staff OD/Motor Pool 301-496-3426
Transposition of the Great Vessels....Staff NHLBI 301-496-4236
Transsexuality....Staff NICHD 301-496-5133
Transverse Myelitis....Staff NINDS 301-496-5751
Trapping, Hatcheries....Staff FWS 703-358-1715
Trapping, Refuges....Staff FWS 703-358-2043
Trauma Research (Cent. Ner. Sys., Head, Spin. Cr.)....Staff NINDS 301-496-5751
Trauma Research....Staff NIDCD 301-496-7243
Trauma Research....Staff NIGMS 301-496-7301
Trauma....Staff American Trauma Society 800-556-7890
Travel and Tourism....Ludolp, Josephine COMMERCE 202-482-3575
Travel goods....Seastrum, Carl USITC 202-205-3493
Travel Surveys....Cannon, John CENSUS 301-457-3877
Treaties, Indian Fisheries....Staff FWS 703-358-1718
Treatment Improvement, Office for....Hurley, Joan NIDA 301-443-6549

Tremors....Staff NINDS 301-496-5751
Tremors....Staff NIDCD 301-496-7243
Trench Mouth....Staff NIDR 301-496-4261
Trichinosis....Staff NIAID 301-496-5717
Trichloroethylene....Michels, David USITC 202-205-3352
Trichomoniasis....Staff NIAID 301-496-5717
Trichotillomania....Staff NIMH 301-443-4513
Trichotillomania....Staff NINDS 301-496-5751
Tricks....Abrahamson, Dana USITC 202-205-3430
Tricuspid Atresia....Staff NHLBI 301-496-4236
Tricuspid Valve....Staff NHLBI 301-496-4236
Tricycles....Abrahamson, Dana USITC 202-205-3430
Trigeminal Neuralgia (Tic Douloureux)....Staff NINDS 301-496-5751
Triglycerides....Staff NHLBI 301-496-4236
Trimellitic acid esters....Johnson, Larry USITC 202-205-3351
Trinidad and Tobago/Minerals....Torres, Ivette Cnty Mines 202-501-9680
Trinidad and Tobago (Port-of-Spain)....Staff Cnty State 202-647-2621
Trinidad and Tobago....Brooks, Michelle Cnty Commerce 202-482-2527
Trinidad....Korff, Michael Cnty USIA 202-619-6835
Trinidad....Lewin, Michael Cnty World Bank 202-473-8684
Trinidad....Marcus, Anthony Cnty Treasury 202-622-1218
Trinidad....Massiah, Joan Cnty Embassy 202-467-6490
Trinidad....McKnight, Corinne Arvelle Cnty Embassy 202-467-6490
Trinidad....Wilkins, Michele Cnty Export-Import Bank 202-565-3743
Trinitrotoluene....Johnson, Larry USITC 202-205-3351
Tripoli....Austin, Gordon MINES 202-501-9388
Tropical Diseases....Staff NIAID 301-496-5717
Tropical Forestry....Martin, Michael R. FS 703-235-9461
Tropical Spastic Paraparesis....Staff NINDS 301-496-5751
Trousers....DeGaetano, Angela CUSTOMS 212-466-5540
Trousers: mens and boys....Sweet, Mary Elizabeth USITC 202-205-3455
Trousers: women's and girls'....Sweet, Mary Elizabeth USITC 202-205-3455
Truck tractors....Hagey, Michael USITC 202-205-3392
Trucking Services....Wolfe, Claudia COMMERCE 202-482-5086
Trucks....Hagey, Michael USITC 202-205-3392
Truncus Arteriosus....Staff NHLBI 301-496-4236
Truth in Leasing....Poindexter, Obrea FRS 202-452-2412
Truth in Lending....Williams, Manley FRS 202-452-3667
Trypanosomiasis....Staff NIAID 301-496-5717
Trypsinogen Deficiency....Staff NIDDK 301-496-3583
TSH, Excessive Secretion....Staff NIDDK 301-496-3583
TTY - Population Information....Staff CENSUS 301-763-5020
Tuberculosis....Jereb, John CDC 404-639-8123
Tuberculosis....Staff NIAID 301-496-5717
Tuberculosis....Staff CDC 404-639-1819
Tuberous Sclerosis....Staff National Tuberous Sclerosis Association 800-225-6872
Tuberous Sclerosis....Staff NINDS 301-496-5751
Tubes for pneumatic tires....Raftery, Jim USITC 202-205-3365
Tubes....Josephs, Irwin CUSTOMS 212-466-5673
Tubing, of rubber or plastics....Misurelli, Denby USITC 202-205-3362
Tularemia....Staff NIAID 301-496-5717
Tumor, Brain....Staff American Brain Tumor Association 800-886-2282
Tumor Immunology....Staff NCI 301-496-5583
Tumor....Staff NCI 301-496-5583
Tumors (Eye)....Staff NEI 301-496-5248
Tumors with Endocrine Function....Staff NIDDK 301-496-3583
Tuna....Corey, Roger USITC 202-205-3327
Tungsten compounds....Greenblatt, Jack USITC 202-205-3353
Tungsten....Amey, Earle B. MINES 202-501-9427
Tungsten....Lundy, David USITC 202-205-3439
Tunisia/Minerals....Dolley, Thomas Cnty Mines 202-501-9690
Tunisia (Tunis)....Staff Cnty State 202-647-3614
Tunisia....DiMeo, Pam Peace Corps 202-606-3196
Tunisia....Early, Evelyn Cnty USIA 202-619-6528
Tunisia....El Baroudy, Samia Cnty World Bank 202-4473-2370
Tunisia....Emmett, Anne Marie Peace Corps 202-606-3196
Tunisia....Ennifar, Azouz Cnty Embassy 202-862-1850
Tunisia....Imam, Fahmila Cnty Export-Import Bank 202-565-3738
Tunisia....Mandel, Pamela Cnty AID 202-663-2617
Tunisia....Romdhani, Oussama Cnty Embassy 202-862-1850
Tunisia....Schneider, Todd Cnty Treasury 202-622-0335
Tunisia....Stillwell, Carol Cnty TDA 703-875-4357
Tunisia....Wright, Corey/Sams, Thomas Cnty Commerce 202-482-1860
Turkey (Ankara)....Staff Cnty State 202-647-6114
Turkey/Minerals....van Oss, Hendrik Cnty Mines 202-501-9687
Turkey....Ayas, Esref Cnty Embassy 202-659-8200
Turkey....Corro, Ann Cnty Commerce 202-482-3945

Be patient. If any phone number is incorrect, call (area code) 555-1212 and request the new listing.

1445

Turkey....Hutchings, Dayna Cnty Export-Import Bank 202-565-3737
Turkey....Kandemir, Nuzhet Cnty Embassy 202-659-8200
Turkey....Lee, Nancy Cnty Treasury 202-622-2916
Turkey....Mehra, Suman Cnty World Bank 202-473-2247
Turkey....Santoro, Eugene Cnty USIA 202-619-6582
Turkmenistan....Annaberdiev, Tchamazar Cnty Embassy 202-737-4800
Turkmenistan....Eighmy, Thomas Cnty AID 202-647-6920
Turkmenistan....Leijonhufvud, Christina E. Cnty World Bank 202-473-8146
Turkmenistan....Resnick, Bonnie Cnty Treasury 202-622-0108
Turkmenistan....Rossate, Julie Peace Corps 202-606-3040
Turkmenistan....Shamson, Tanya Cnty TDA 703-875-4357
Turkmenistan....Staff Cnty State 202-647-6757
Turkmenistan....Ugur, Halil Cnty Embassy 202-737-4800
Turkmenistan....Waxman-Lenz, Roberta Cnty Export-Import Bank 202-565-3742
Turkmenistan....Skipper, Thomas Cnty USIA 202-619-5057
Turks/Caicos....Wilkins, Michele Cnty Export-Import Bank 202-565-3743
Turks and Caicos Islands....Siegelman, Mark Cnty Commerce 202-482-5680
Turner Syndrome....Staff NICHD 301-496-5133
Turntables....Puffert, Douglas USITC 202-205-3402
Turpentine....Randall, Rob USITC 202-205-3336
Turtles (Salmonellosis)....Staff CDC 404-639-3286
Tuvalu (Funafuti)....Staff Cnty State 202-647-3546
Tuvalu....Berghage, Jeff Peace Corps 202-606-1098
Tuvalu...Rahman, Talaat Cnty TDA 703-875-4357
Tuvalu....Shelton, Alison Cnty Treasury 202-622-0354
TV Answer....Staff FCC 202-418-0620
TV Broadcasting....Siegmund, John COMMERCE 202-482-4781
TV Channel Interference....Staff FCC 202-418-2190
TV Communications Eqmt....Gossack, Linda COMMERCE 202-482-4466
TV Receiver-Noise Figures....Staff FCC 301-725-1585
TV Satellite Stations-General Policy....Staff 202-418-2130
TV Satellite Stations-Specific TV Station....Staff FCC 202-418-1630
TV Technical Standards....Staff FCC 202-418-1630
TV Violence....Baldwin, Elaine 301-443-4536
Twine....Cook, Lee USITC 202-205-3471
Typewriters....Baker, Scott USITC 202-205-3386
Typewriting devices....Burr, Edgar PTO 703-308-0979
Typhoid Fever....Staff NIAID 301-496-5717

U

Uganda (Kampala)....Staff Cnty State 202-647-6479
Uganda/Minerals....Izon, David Cnty Mines 202-501-9692
Uganda....Downs, Peter Cnty AID 202-647-5583
Uganda....Goode, Sachiko Peace Corps 202-606-3695
Uganda....Katenta-Apuli, Stephen Cnty Embassy 202-726-7100
Uganda....Kotze, Joan Cnty treasury 202-622-0354
Uganda....Larsen, Mark Cnty USIA 202-619-4894
Uganda....Lucyk, Chris Cnty Commerce 202-482-1104
Uganda....Masutti, Maria L. Cnty World Bank 202-473-4751
Uganda....Maybury-Lewis, Anthony Cnty Export-Import Bank 202-565-3739
Uganda....Ssenyomo, Ahmed Cnty Embassy 202-726-7101
Uganda....Young, Nathan Cnty TDA 703-875-4357
Ukraine....Ann Lien Cnty TDA 703-875-4357
Ukraine....Balkind, Jeffrey Cnty World Bank 202-458-9116
Ukraine....Bloemkamp, Sandra Cnty World Bank 202-458-9109
Ukraine....Carlen, James Cnty Treasury 202-622-0122
Ukraine....Marchuk, Vadym E. Cnty Embassy 202-333-0606
Ukraine....McCleod, Evelyn Cnty AID 202-736-7646
Ukraine....O'Keefe, Monica Cnty USIA 202-619-5057
Ukraine....Shcherbak, Yuriy Mikolayevych Cnty Embassy 202-333-0606
Ukraine....Staff Cnty State 202-647-8671
Ukraine....Viksnins, Helen Peace Corps 202-606-5517
Ukraine....Waxman-Lenz, Roberta Cnty 202-565-3742
Ukraine....Wooton, Nicholas Peace Corps 202-606-5519
Ulcerative Colitis....Staff NIDDK 301-496-3583
Ulcerative Lesions (Oral)....Staff NIDR 301-496-4261
Ulcers (Fingers, Toes, Arms, Legs)....Staff NHLBI 301-496-4236
Ulcers (Oral) NIDR 301-496-4261
Ulcers (Skin) NIAMS 301-496-8188
Ulcers (Stomach)....Staff NIDDK 301-654-3810
Ultrasonics Equipment....Staff FCC 202-653-8247
Umbrellas....Spalding, Josephine USITC 202-205-3498
Underground Nuclear Testing....Williams, Irvin NEIC 301-903-5341
Underwear....Burtnik, Brian CUSTOMS 212-466-5880
Underwear....Sweet, Mary Elizabeth USITC 202-205-3455

Unemployment and Labor Force, Foreign Countries....Sorrentino, Constance LABOR 202-606-5654
Unemployment Statistics....Palumbo, Thomas CENSUS 301-763-8574
Unfinished oils....Foreso, Cynthia USITC 202-205-3348
Uniform Crime Reports - Redesign Implementation....White, Paul Justice Stat 202-307-0771
Uniform Crime Reports - Redesign Implementation....Manson, Donald Justice Stat 202-616-3491
Unions, Employee Associations, Membership, Comp/Wk....Cimini, Michael LABOR 202-606-6275
Unit Labor Costs, Productivity....Neef, Arthur LABOR 202-606-5654
United Arab Emirates (Abu Dhabi)....Staff Cnty State 202-647-6558
United Arab Emirates/Minerals....Izon, David Cnty Mines 202-501-9674
United Arab Emirates....Al-Shaali, Mohammad bin Hussein Cnty Embassy 202-338-6500
United Arab Emirates....Al-Romaithi, Mohammed Cnty Embassy 202-338-6500
United Arab Emirates....Austin, Ken Cnty Treasury 202-622-0174
United Arab Emirates....Vacant Cnty USIA 202-619-6528
United Arab Emirates....Clement, Claude Cnty Commerce 202-482-5545
United Kingdom (London)....Staff Cnty State 202-647-6587
United Kingdom of Great Britain and Northern Ireland....Renwick, Sir Robin Cnty Embassy
United Kingdom/Minerals....Newman, Harold R. Cnty Mines 202-501-9669
United Kingdom....Gosnell, Peter Cnty Export-Import Bank 202-565-3733
United Kingdom....Kulla, Morgan Cnty USIA 202-619-6853
United Kingdom....Mackour, Oscar Cnty Treasury 202-622-0145
United Kingdom....McLaughlin, Robert Cnty Commerce 202-482-3748
United Kingdom....Phillips, Patricia Cnty Embassy 202-462-1340
Universal joints....Topolansky, Adam USITC 202-205-3394
Universal Service Fund....Staff FCC 202-418-0850
Universal Service....Staff FCC 202-418-1594
Unresectable Chrondosarcoma or Osteogenic Sarcoma....Staff NCI 301-496-5583
Upholstery fabrics....Sweet, Mary Elizabeth USITC 202-205-3455
Upper Atmosphere Research Satellite....Loughlin, John NASA 301-286-5565
Upper Atmosphere Research Satellite....Staff NASA 301-286-2806
Upper Midwest MTC (Manufacturing Technology Center)....Pounds, Jan NIST 612-338-7722
Uranium Enrichment....Haberman, Norton NEIC 301-903-4321
Uranium compounds....Greenblatt, Jack USITC 202-205-3353
Uranium oxide....Greenblatt, Jack USITC 202-205-3353
Uranium (statistics only) Hilliard, Henry Cnty MINES 202-501-9429
Uranium....DeSapio, Vincent USITC 202-205-3435
Uranium....Sugg, William COMMERCE 202-482-1466
Urban and Community Forestry Programs....Hatfield, Laura-Ziegler FS 202-205-0823
Urban Residence....Staff CENSUS 301-457-2381
Urban/Rural Residence....Staff CENSUS 301-457-2381
Urea resins....Misurelli, Denby USITC 202-205-3362
Urea....Trainor, Cynthia USITC 202-205-3354
Uremia....Staff NIDDK 301-654-4415
Uric Acid Kidney Stones....Staff NIDDK 301-654-4415
Urinary Incontinence....Staff NIA 301-496-1752
Urinary Tract Diseases....Staff NIDDK 301-654-4415
Urinary Tract Infections....Staff NIDDK 301-654-4415
Urinary Tract Tumors....Staff NIDDK 301-496-5583
Urine Volume....Staff NIDDK 301-654-4415
Urokinase....Staff NHLBI 301-496-4236
Urolithiasis....Staff NIDDK 301-654-4415
Urticaria....Staff NIAID 301-496-5717
Uruguay/Minerals....Gurmendi, Alfredo Cnty Mines 202-501-9681
Uruguay (Montevideo)....Staff Cnty State 202-647-2296
Uruguay....Hagerstrom, Mark V. Cnty World Bank 202-473-9208
Uruguay....John Herrman Cnty TDA 703-875-4357
Uruguay....Leeb, Howard Cnty USIA 202-619-5867
Uruguay....Macgillycuddy, Eduardo Cnty Embassy 202-331-1313
Uruguay....Moerzinger, Alvaro Cnty Embassy 202-331-1316
Uruguay....Neil, Jeff Cnty Treasury 202-622-1268
Uruguay....Prevot, Babette Cnty AID 202-647-4359
Uruguay....Ross, Rebecca Peace Corps 202-606-3575
Uruguay....Turner, Roger Cnty Commerce 202-482-1495
Uruguay....Vacant Peace Corps 202-606-3376
Uruguay....Wilkins, Michele Cnty Import Bank 202-565-3743
US Trade and Foreign Agriculture - Africa and Mideast....Kurtzig, Mike Agri 202-219-0636
US Trade and Foreign Agriculture - Asia - East....Dycke, John Agri 202-219-0610
US Trade and Foreign Agriculture - Asia - South....Vocke, Gary Agri 202-219-0610

US Trade and Foreign Agriculture - Canada....Stout, Jim Agric 202-219-0610
US Trade and Foreign Agriculture - China....Cooke, Frederick Agri 202-219-0610
US Trade and Foreign Agriculture - Developing Economies....Mathia, Gene Agri 202-219-0680
US Trade and Foreign Agriculture - Eastern Europe....Koopman, Robert Agri 202-219-0621
US Trade and Foreign Agriculture - Eastern Europe....Cochrane, Nancy Agri 202-219-0650
US Trade and Foreign Agriculture - Exports and Imports....Greene, Joel Agri 202-219-0816
US Trade and Foreign Agriculture - Exports....Ackerman, Karen Agri 202-219-0243
US Trade and Foreign Agriculture - Food Aid....Missiaen, Margaret Agri 202-219-0652
US Trade and Foreign Agriculture - Food Aid Programs....Suarez, Nydia Agri 202-219-0821
US Trade and Foreign Agriculture - Former Soviet Union....Foster, Christian Agri 202-219-0624
US Trade and Foreign Agriculture - Latin America....Link, John Agri 202-219-0689
US Trade and Foreign Agriculture - Pacific Rim....Coyle, William Agri 202-219-0610
US Trade and Foreign Agriculture - Programs....Ackerman, Karen Agri 202-219-0821
US Trade and Foreign Agriculture - Trade and Finance....Roningen, Vern Agri 202-219-0683
US Trade and Foreign Agriculture - Trade and Finance....Haley, Steve Agri 202-219-0666
US Trade and Foreign Agriculture - Western Europe....Normile, MaryAnn Agri 202-219-0774
US Trade and Foreign Agriculture....Baxter, Tim Agri 202-219-0708
US Trade and Foreign Agriculture....Stallings, David Agri 202-219-0688
Usher's Syndrome....Staff NIDCD 301-496-7243
Usher's Syndrome....Staff NEI 301-496-5248
USSR (Moscow)....Staff Cnty State 202-647-8671
Uterus....Staff NICHD 301-496-5133
Utility, Retail Prices....Adkins, Robert LABOR 202-606-6985
Uveitis....Staff NEI 301-496-5248
Uzbekistan....Butayarov, Turdiqui Cnty Embassy 202-638-4267
Uzbekistan....Eighmy, Thomas Cnty AID 202-647-6920
Uzbekistan....Koff, Allison S. Cnty TDA 703-875-4357
Uzbekistan....Rajagopalan, V.N. Cnty World Bank 202-473-2958
Uzbekistan....Resnick, Bonnie Cnty Treasury 202-622-0108
Uzbekistan....Rossate, Julie Peace Corps 202-606-3040
Uzbekistan....Skipper, Thomas Cnty USIA 202-619-5057
Uzbekistan....Staff Cnty State 202-647-6765
Uzbekistan....Teshabaev, Fatikah Cnty Embassy 202-638-4266

V

Vacancies, NIH Recording....Staff NIH 301-496-2403
Vaccine Licensing....Staff FDA 301-443-8995
Vaccinés....Nesbitt, Elizabeth USITC 202-205-3355
Vaccines....Nucker, Christine M PTO 703-308-4028
Vaccines....Staff FDA/NCDB/OB 301-594-2090
Vaccines....Staff NIAID 301-496-5717
Vacuum cleaners....Jackson, Georgia USITC 202-205-3399
Vaginitis....Staff NIAID 301-496-5717
Valves and cocks....Mata, Ruben USITC 202-205-3403
Valves (Heart)....Staff NHLBI 301-496-4236
Valves, Pipefittings Ex Brass....Reise, Richard COMMERCE 202-482-3489
Valves....Riedl, Karl CUSTOMS 212-466-5493
Valvular Heart Disease....Staff NHLBI 301-496-4236
Valvuloplasty....Staff NHLBI 301-496-4236
Vanadium compounds....Greenblatt, Jack USITC 202-205-3353
Vanadium....Hilliard, Henry E. MINES 202-501-9429
Vanadium....Lundy, David USITC 202-205-3439
Vanatu (Port Vila)....Staff Cnty State 202-647-3546
Vanillin....Land, Eric USITC 202-205-3349
Vanuatu/Minerals....Lyday, Travis Cnty Mines 202-501-9695
Vanuatu....Davies, Irene Cnty World Bank 202-458-2481
Vanuatu....Imam, Fahmila Cnty Export-Import Bank 202-565-3738
Vanuatu....Lee, Allison Peace Corps 202-606-0983
Vanuatu....Marona, Catherine Peace Corps 202-606-0983
Vanuatu....Respess, Rebecca Cnty TDA 703-875-4357
Vanuatu....Schell, Russell Peace Corps 202-606-3231

Vanuatu....Shelton, Alison Cnty Treasury 202-622-0354
Varicella, Congenital....Staff NINDS 301-496-5751
Varicose Ulcers...Staff NHLBI 301-496-4236
Varicose Veins....Staff NHLBI 301-496-4236
Varnish....Brownchweig, Gilbert CUSTOMS 212-466-5744
Varnishes....Johnson, Larry USITC 202-205-3351
Vascular Collapse....Staff NHLBI 301-496-4236
Vasculitis...Staff NIAID 301-496-5717
Vasculitis....Staff NINDS 301-496-5751
Vasculitis....Staff NHLBI 301-496-4236
Vasectomy....Staff NICHD 301-496-5133
Vatican....Staff Cnty State 202-647-3746
VCRs....Dicerbo, Mario CUSTOMS 212-466-5672
VD (Control and Treatment)....Staff CDC 800-227-8922
VD....Staff NIAID 301-496-5717
Vector-Borne Infectious Diseases....Gubler, Duane J. CDC 303-221-6428
Vegetable fibers (except cotton)....Cook, Lee USITC 202-205-3471
Vegetable glue....Jonnard, Aimison USITC 202-205-3350
Vegetables - Fresh....Brewster, Jim Agri 202-720-7688
Vegetables - Proc.....Budge, Arvin Agri 202-720-4285
Vegetables....Hamm, Shannon Agri 202-219-0886
Vegetables....Hintzman, Kevin Agri 202-720-5412
Vegetables....Love, John Agri 202-219-0388
Vegetables....Lucier, Gary Agri 202-219-0884
Vegetables....Manogue, Robert COMMERCE 202-482-3428
Vegetables....McCarty, Timothy USITC 202-205-3324
Vehicle Crash Avoidance Research....Leasure, William NHTSA 202-366-5662
Vehicle performance....Clark, John NTSB 202-382-6634
Vehicle Propulsion Systems....Allsup, Jerry NEIC 202-586-9118
Vehicle Research....Monk, Michael NHTSA 513-666-4511
Vehicle Safety Compliance....Hellmuth, Robert NHTSA 202-366-2832
Vehicle Testing....Monk, Michael NHTSA 513-666-4511
Vehicles, Special Purpose....Desoucey, Robert CUSTOMS 212-466-5667
Veiling....Sweet, Mary Elizabeth USITC 202-205-3455
Vending machines....Jackson, Georgia USITC 202-205-3399
Venereal Disease (Control and Treatment)....Staff CDC 404-639-3286
Venereal Disease....Staff NIAID 301-496-5717
Venezuela (Caracas)....Staff Cnty State 202-647-3023
Venezuela/Minerals....Torres, Ivette Cnty Mines 202-501-9680
Venezuela....Bayly, Rachel Cnty Treasury 202-622-1266
Venezuela....Echeverria, Pedro Luis Cnty Embassy 202-342-2214
Venezuela....Hatfield, Ziegler Cnty Commerce 202-482-4303
Venezuela....Head, Alfred Cnty USIA 202-619-6835
Venezuela....Maybury-Lewis, Anthony Cnty Export-Import Bank 202-565-3739
Venezuela....Prevot, Babette Cnty AID 202-647-4359
Venezuela....Velez, Francisco Jose cnty Embassy 202-342-2214
Venezuela....Zermeno, Mayra R. Cnty World Bank 202-473-0141
Venous Insufficiency...Staff NHLBI 301-496-4236
Venous Thrombosis....Staff NHLBI 301-496-4236
Ventilation....Staff OD/ORS 301-496-2960
Ventricular Septal Defect...Staff NHLBI 301-496-4236
Vermiculite....Potter, Michael J. MINES 202-501-9387
Vertical Blanking Interval TV....Staff FCC 202-418-2190
Vertigo....Staff NIDCD 301-496-7243
Vertigo....Staff NINDS 301-496-5751
Vestibular Neuronitis....Staff NIDCD 301-496-7243
Vestibular System....Staff NIDCD 301-496-7243
Vests, mens'....Jones, Jackie USITC 202-205-3466
Veterans Affairs....Bechet, Leon J. SBA 202-205-6773
Veterans, Employment Statistics....Cohany, Sharon LABOR 202-606-6378
Veterans Status....Jones, Selwyn CENSUS 301-763-8574
Veterans Status....Palumbo, Thomas CENSUS 301-763-8574
Veterinary instruments....Johnson, Christopher USITC 202-205-3488
Veterinary Medicine....Snider, Sharon FDA 301-443-3285
Vibrotactile Aids....Staff NIDCD 301-496-7243
Victim and Witness Assistance Programs....Kaplan, Carol Justice Stat 202-307-0759
Victim and Witness Assistance Programs....Zawitz, Marianne Justice Stat 202-616-3499
Victims of Crime....Taylor, Bruce Justice Stat 202-616-3498
Victims of Crime....Klaus, Patsy Justice Stat 202-307-0776
Victims of Crime....Meister, Brenda G. Justice Stat 202-307-5983
Victims of Crime....Rand, Michael Justice Stat 202-616-3494
Video Data Service Interactive....Staff FCC 202-418-0680
Video Dialtone....Staff FCC 202-418-1580
Video games....Abrahamson, Dana USITC 202-205-3430
Video Marketplace....Staff FCC 202-418-1580

Be patient. If any phone number is incorrect, call (area code) 555-1212 and request the new listing.

1447

Video processing....Field, Bruce F. NIST 301-975-4230
Video Services....Elliot, Fred COMMERCE 202-482-1134
Video Transmission--Common Carrier....Staff FCC 202-418-1500
Videotape Productions....Staff NCRR 301-496-4700
Videotex Services....Elliot, Fred COMMERCE 202-482-1134
Vietnam/Minerals....Lyday, Travis Cnty Mines 202-501-9695
Vietnam....Camp, Bea Cnty USIA 202-619-5837
Vietnam....Ha, Huy Thong Cnty Embassy 202-861-0737
Vietnam....Haldane, Donna Cnty World Bank 202-458-0456
Vietnam....Imam, Fahmila Cnty Export-Import Bank 202-565-3738
Vietnam....Le, Bang Van Cnty Embassy 202-861-0737
Vietnam....Pho, Hong-Phong B. Cnty Commerce 202-482-3877
Vietnam....Rahman, Talaat Cnty TDA 703-875-4357
Vietnam....Schneider, Todd Cnty Treasury 202-622-0335
Vietnam....Staff Cnty State 202-647-3132
Vincent's Infection....Staff NIDR 301-496-4261
Vinyl chloride monomer....Michels, David USITC 202-205-3352
Vinyl resins or plastics....Misurelli, Denby USITC 202-205-3362
Violations, Fish and Wildlife Laws....Staff FWS 703-358-1949
Violent Crime....Reynolds, James S. Justice 202-514-0849
Viral products....Klinman, Dennis FAES 301-496-8492
Virgin Islands (US)....Soto, Rodrigo Cnty Commerce 202-482-5680
Virgin Islands (UK)....Brooks, Michelle Cnty Commerce 202-482-4464
Virology....Staff NIAID 301-496-5717
Virus (Cancer Related)....Staff NCI 301-496-5583
Virus Tumor Biology....Brady, John FAES 301-496-0988
Vision and aging....Staff The Lighthouse 800-334-5497
Vision and Aging....Staff NIA 301-496-1752
Vision and Aging....Staff NEI 301-496-5248
Vision Care (Statistics)....Staff NCHS 301-436-8500
Visitor Centers, Hatcheries....Staff FWS 703-358-1715
Visual Arts....Staff NEA 202-682-5448
Visual communications....Carter, H. UMD 301-405-2408
Visual displays....Oberley, Alvin E. PTO 703-305-4709
Visual signaling apparatus....Baker, Scott USITC 202-205-3386
Vital Statistics, Division of....Curtin, Lester CDC 301-436-8951
Vital Statistics, Family Growth Survey....Staff CDC 301-436-8500
Vitamin E (and Cardiovascular Disease)....Staff NHLBI 301-496-4236
Vitamin Supplements and Aging....Staff NIA 301-496-1752
Vitamins C,D,E, (and CVD)....Staff NHLBI 301-496-4236
Vitamins/Minerals....Corwin, Emil FDA 202-205-4144
Vitamins....Nesbitt, Elizabeth USITC 202-205-3355
Vitiligo....Staff NIAMS 301-496-8188
Vitrectomy....Staff NEI 301-496-5248
Vitreous Detachment....Staff NEi 301-496-5248
Vocal Cord Paralysis....Staff NINDS 301-496-5751
Vocal Cord Paralysis....Staff NIDCD 301-496-7243
Vocal Temor....Staff NIDCD 301-496-7243
Vocational Rehabilitation (Drug Related)....Staff NIDA 301-443-6245
Vogt-Koyanagi Disease....Staff NEI 301-496-5248
Voice Disorders....Staff NIDCD 301-496-5248
Volunteerism....Kharfen, Michael ACF 202-401-9215
Volunteers (Patients)....Staff CC 301-496-4763
Von Hipple-Lindau Disease....Staff NINDS 301-496-5751
Von Recklinghausen's Disease....Staff NINDS 301-496-5751
Von Willebrand's Disease....Staff NHLBI 301-496-4236
Voting and Registration....Jennings, Jerry CENSUS 301-457-2434
Voting Districts....McCully, Cathy CENSUS 301-457-1099
Voyager Flight Project....Doyle, Jim NASA 818-354-5011
Vulnerable Populations (Drug Abuse)....Staff NIDA 301-443-6245

W

Waardenburg Syndrome...Staff NIDCD 301-496-7243
Wage Developments, Current, Comp. and Working Cond....Cimini, Michael LABOR 202-606-6275
Wages/Industrial Relations, Collect Barg Settlements, Major....Devine, Janice M. LABOR 202-606-6276
Wages/Industrial Relations, Collect Barg Agreements Analysis....Cimini, Michael LABOR 202-606-6275
Wages/Industrial Relations, Current Wage Developments....Cimini, Michael LABOR 202-606-6275
Wages/Industrial Relations, Empl Benefit Surv, Other Benefits....Houff, James LABOR 202-606-6238
Wages/Industrial Relations, Empl Benefit Surv, Pension Plans....Houff, James LABOR 202-606-6238

Wages/Industrial Relations, Employment Cost Index....Shelly, Wayne LABOR 202-606-6206
Wages/Industrial Relations, Health Studies....Webber, William LABOR 202-606-6162
Wages/Industrial Relations, Special Projects....Webber, William LABOR 202-606-6162
Wages/Industrial Relations, Unions, Membership....Cimini, Michael LABOR 202-606-6275
Wages/Industrial Relations, Work Stoppages....Cimini, Michael LABOR 202-606-6275
Waldenstroms Macroglobulinemia....Staff NCI 301-496-5583
Walking sticks....Spalding, Josephine USITC 202-205-3498
Wall coverings, of rubber or plastics....Raftery, Jim USITC 202-205-3365
Wallets, Billfolds, Flatgoods....Byron, James E. COMMERCE 202-482-4034
Wallets....Seastrum, Carl USITC 202-205-3493
Walleye....Staff NEI 301-496-5248
Wallpaper....Twarok, Chris USITC 202-205-3314
Warm Air Heating Eqmt....Vacant COMMERCE 202-482-3509
Warts....Staff NIAID 301-496-5717
Washington issues....Callahan, Christopher UMD 301-405-2432
Waste and Chemical Policy Division....Staff EPA 202-260-5422
Waste and scrap (metals)....Lundy, David USITC 202-205-3439
Waste Detoxification....Lytle, Jill-Ellman NEIC 202-586-0370
Waste Heat Recovery....Lytle, Jill-Ellman NEIC 202-586-0370
Waste Management....Greeves, John T. NRC 301-425-7437
Waste Material Management....Sisson, Kurt NEIC 202-586-6750
Waste or scrap....Spalding, Josephine USITC 202-205-3498
Waste Products Utilization....Lytle, Jill-Ellman NEIC 202-586-0370
Waste Reduction Technologies....Lytle, Jill-Ellman NEIC 202-586-0370
Waste, textile: cotton....Sweet, Mary Elizabeth USITC 202-205-3455
Waste, textile: manmade fiber....Sweet, Mary Elizabeth USITC 202-205-3455
Waste, textile: silk....Shelton, Linda USITC 202-205-3457
Waste, textile: wool....Shelton, Linda USITC 202-205-3457
Waste Treatment and Disposal....Staff EPA 703-308-8434
Wastepaper....Stanley, Gary COMMERCE 202-482-0375
Watches....Harris, John COMMERCE 202-482-1178
Watches....Luther, Dennis USITC 202-205-3497
Watches....Scwartz, Stanley CUSTOMS 212-466-5895
Water and Sewage Treatment Plants....Vacant COMMERCE 202-482-3509
Water Division....Staff EPA 202-260-5700
Water Enforcement Division....Staff EPA 202-564-8304
Water Environmental Laws....Staff NEIC 202-586-4996
Water Hardness (and CVD)....Staff NHLBI 301-496-4236
Water Pollution....Staff EPA 202-260-2756
Water Projects, Federal....Staff FWS 703-358-1719
Water Quality Information Center....Makuch, Joseph NAL 301-504-6077
Water Resource Equipment....Vacant COMMERCE 202-482-3509
Water Resource Usage and Analysis....Staff FWS 703-358-1710
Water Rights Agreements, Fish and Wildlife....Staff FWS 703-358-1719
Water Supply....Staff OD/ORS 301-496-3537
Waterway rescues....McCormack, Michael USCG 202-267-1948
Waterway searches....McCormack, Michael USCG 202-267-1948
Waterway Services....Staff Coast Guard Hotline 800-368-5647
Wave communications systems....Tarcza, Thomas C. PTO 703-308-1689
Wave Energy....Loose, Ronald NEIC 202-586-5348
Wax, articles of....Spalding, Josephine USITC 202-205-3498
Waxes....Brownchweig, Gilbert CUSTOMS 212-466-5744
Waxes....Randall, Rob USITC 202-205-3366
Weapons and Crime....Taylor, Bruce Justice Stat 202-616-3498
Weapons and Crime....Rand, Michael Justice Stat 202-616-3494
Weapons Testing....Staff NEIC 301-903-3441
Weapons....Jordan, Charles PTO 703-308-0918
Wearing Apparel: Boys (sizes 2-7 only)....Kirschner, Bruce CUSTOMS 212-466-5865
Wearing Apparel: Girls (sizes 2-7 only)....Kirschner, Bruce CUSTOMS 212-466-5865
Wearing Apparel: Infants....Kirschner, Bruce CUSTOMS 212-466-5865
Weather....Whatley, David FAA 202-267-9090
Weatherization Assistance - Elderly....Staff NEIC 202-426-1698
Weatherization Assistance - Handicapped....Staff NEIC 202-426-1698
Weatherization Assistance - Low Income Individuals....Staff NEIC 202-426-1698
Weatherization Assistance....Staff NEIC 202-426-1698
Weaving machines....Greene, William USITC 202-205-3405
Weber-Christian Disease....Staff NIAID 301-496-5717
Weber-Christian Disease....Staff NIAMS 301-496-8188
Weekly and Annual Earnings--Current Pop. Survey....Mellor, Earl LABOR 202-606-6378

Weekly issue (new US patents)....Harris, Patricia PTO 703-305-7458
Wegener's Granulomatosis....Staff NIAMS 301-496-8188
Wegener's Granulomatosis....Staff NIAID 301-496-5717
Wegener's Granulomatosis....Staff NHLBI 301-496-4236
Weighing machinery....Lusi, Susan USITC 202-205-2334
Welding apparatus....Mata, Ruben USITC 202-205-3403
Welding/Cutting Apparatus....Abrahams, Edward COMMERCE 202-482-0312
Welfare and AFDC JOBS Programs....Checkan, Jane ACF 202-401-9215
Werdnig-Hoffmann Disease....Staff NINDS 301-496-5751
Werner's Syndrome....Staff NIDDK 301-496-3583
Wernicke's Disease....Staff NINDS 301-496-5751
West Bank....Roberts, Nigel Cnty World Bank 202-473-2241
West Bank....Young, Dorothy Cnty AID 202-663-2620
Western Europe/trade matters....Richards, Timothy US Trade Rep 202-395-3320
Western European Union (WEU)....Staff Cnty State 202-736-7299
Western Hemisphere Affairs....Huenemann, Jonathan US Trade Rep 202-395-5190
Western Hemisphere (policy planning)....Surobrodie, Carmen US Trade Rep 202-395-3900
Western Hemisphere Programs, Fish and Wildlife....Staff FWS 703-358-1754
Western Hemisphere/trade matters....Ives, Ralph US Trade Rep 202-395-5190
Western Hemisphere/trade matters....Allgeier, Peter US Trade Rep 202-395-6135
Western Sahara....Dolley, Thomas Cnty Mines 202-501-9690
Western Sahara....Staff Cnty State 202-647-3407
Western Samoa (Apia)....Staff Cnty State 202-647-3546
Western Samoa....Berghage, Jeff Peace Corps 202-606-1098
Western Samoa....Davies, Irene Cnty World Bank 202-458-2481
Western Samoa....Imam, Fahmila Cnty Export-Import Bank 202-565-3738
Western Samoa....Rahman, Talaat Cnty TDA 703-875-4357
Western Samoa....Shelton, Alison Cnty Treasury 202-622-0354
Western Samoa....Slade, Tuiloma Neroni Cnty Embassy 212-599-6196
Western Samoa....Stewart, Andrea W. Cnty Embassy 212-599-6196
Wetlands Division....Staff EPA 202-260-1799
Wetlands Inventory, National....Staff FWS 703-358-2201
Wetlands Protection Hotline....Staff EPA 800-832-7828
Whalebone, articles of....Spalding, Josephine USITC 202-205-3498
Wheat with options....Sepsey, Judy CFT 312-353-9025
Wheat....Reeder, John USITC 202-205-3319
Wheel goods: motorized....Hagey, Michael USITC 202-205-3392
Wheel goods: non-motorized....Seastrum, Carl USITC 202-205-3493
Whiplash....Staff NINDS 301-496-5751
Whipple's Disease....Staff NINDS 301-496-5751
Whipple's Disease....Staff NIAID 301-496-5717
Whips....Spalding, Josephine USITC 202-205-3498
Whiskey....Harney, Amy USITC 202-205-3465
Whistleblower Hotline....Staff EPA 800-424-4000
White Collar Crime....Kaplan, Carol Justice Stat 202-307-0759
Wholesale services....Luther, Dennis USITC 202-205-3497
Wholesale Trade, Census....Trimble, John CENSUS 301-457-2694
Wholesale Trade, Current Sales and Inventories....Piesto, Nancy CENSUS 301-457-2799
Wholesale Trade....Burroughs, Helen COMMERCE 202-482-1542
Whooping Cough....Staff NIAID 301-496-5717
Wilderness Planning, Fish and Wildlife....Staff FWS 703-358-1786
Wilderness Planning....Twiss, John FS 202-205-1422
Wildlife Assistance....Staff FWS 703-358-1713
Wildlife, Exotic....Staff FWS 703-358-1718
Wildlife Health Research....Staff FWS 202-208-5634
Wildlife, Injurious....Staff FWS 703-358-1718
Wildlife, Law Enforcement....Staff FWS 703-358-1949
Wildlife Management, Refuges....Staff FWS 703-358-2043
Wildlife Permits....Staff FWS 703-358-2104
Wildlife Protection....Staff FWS 703-358-1718
Wildlife, Range and Fish Habitat Research....Lennartz, Michael R. FS 202-205-1524
Wildlife, Refugees....Staff FWS 703-358-1744
Wildlife Research....Lennartz, Michael R. FS 202-205-1524
Wildlife....Kilbourne, James C. Justice 202-272-4421
William's Syndrome....Staff NHLBI 301-496-4236
Wilms' Tumor....Staff NCI 301-496-5583
Wilson Disease....Staff NIDDK 301-496-3583
Wilson Disease....Staff NINDS 301-496-5751
Wind Energy....Loose, Ronald NEIC 202-586-5348
Wind Engineering....Lew, H.S. NIST 301-975-6061
Windmill Components....Garden, Les COMMERCE 202-482-0556
Wines....Harney, Amy USITC 202-205-3465
Wire and Wire Products....Garden, Les COMMERCE 202-482-0556
Wire Cloth, Industrial....Reise, Richard COMMERCE 202-482-3489

Wire Cloth....McCauley, Patrick COMMERCE 202-482-0132
Wire Rods....Fitzgerald, John CUSTOMS 212-466-5492
Wire rods....Yost, Charles USITC 202-205-3442
Wire....Fitzgerald, John CUSTOMS 212-466-5492
Wire....Yost, Charles USITC 202-205-3442
Wireless Cable Applications....Staff FCC 202-418-1600
Wireless Microphones (licensed)....Staff FCC 717-337-1212
Wiring sets....Cutchin, John USITC 202-205-3396
Wiskott-Aldrich Syndrome....Staff NCI 301-496-5583
Wolff-Parkinson-White Syndrome (WPW)....Staff NHLBI 301-496-4236
Wollastonite....Potter, Michael J. MINES 202-501-9387
Women and Drugs....Staff NIDA 301-443-6245
Women, Employment/Unemployment Statistics....Hayghe, Howard LABOR 202-606-6378
Women in journalism....Beasley, Maurine UMD 301-405-2413
Women Owned Businesses....Emanuel, Elaine CENSUS 301-763-5726
Women, Population....Smith, Denise CENSUS 301-457-2378
Women's Businesses....Myers, Elizabeth SBA 202-205-6673
Women's Health and Fertility....Peterson, Herbert B. CDC 404-488-5250
Women's Health Initiative....Staff OD 301-402-3168
Women's Health Issues....Staff OD 301-402-1770
Women's Ownership Policy....Staff FCC 202-416-0934
Women's Sports....Staff Women's Sport Foundation 800-227-3988
Wood (densified)....Hoffmeier, Bill USITC 202-205-3321
Wood Containers....Wise, Barbara COMMERCE 202-482-0375
Wood Preserving....Wise, Barbara COMMERCE 202-482-0375
Wood Products, Misc.....Wise, Barbara COMMERCE 202-482-0375
Wood products, rough primary....Hoffmeier, Bill USITC 202-205-3321
Wood Products....Garretto, Paul CUSTOMS 212-466-5779
Wood Products....Wise, Barbara COMMERCE 202-482-0375
Wood pulp....Rhodes, Richard USITC 202-205-3322
Wood Technology....Howard, James FS 202-205-1558
Wood veneers....Hoffmeier, Bill USITC 202-205-3321
Wood Working Machinery....Cosslet, Patrick COMMERCE 202-482-0680
Wool and Mohair....Skinner, Robert Agri 202-219-0840
Wool and Mohair....Lawler, John Agri 202-219-0840
Wool and Mohair....Simpson, Linda Agri 202-720-3578
Wool grease, sulfonated or sulfated....Land, Eric USITC 202-205-3349
Wool....Shelton, Linda USITC 202-205-3457
Wool....Steller, Rose USITC 202-205-3323
Wool....Warlick, William USITC 202-205-3459
Word processors....Baker, Scott USITC 202-205-3386
Work Experience, Employment/Unemployment Stats....Mellor, Earl LABOR 202-606-6378
Work Injuries, Reports and Surveys of, Comp. and Work....Jackson, Ethel LABOR 202-606-6167
Work Injury, Report Surveys, Comp and Working Cond.....Jackson, Ethel LABOR 202-606-6167
Work-life Estimates, Employment Statistics....Horvath, Francis LABOR 202-606-6345
Work Stoppages, Compensation and Working Conditions....Cimini, Michael LABOR 202-606-6275
Workers, Older, Empl/Unempl. Stats.....Rones, Philip LABOR 202-606-6378
Working Conditions, Employment Cost Data....Shelly, Wayne LABOR 202-606-6206
Working Conditions, Safety and Health, Asst.Comm.....Eisenberg, William M. LABOR 202-606-6304
Working Conditions....Cimini, Michael LABOR 202-606-6275
Working Poor, Employment/Unemployment Statistics....Herz, Diane LABOR 202-606-6378
Workplace Drug Abuse....Staff NIDA 301-443-6245
Works of Art....Mushinske, Larry CUSTOMS 212-466-5739
Wound Healing (LDBA)....Staff NIDR 301-496-4261
Woven Outerwear: Boys'....Raftery, William CUSTOMS 212-466-5851
Woven Outerwear: Men's....Raftery, William CUSTOMS 212-466-5851
Woven Outerwear: Women's....Raftery, William CUSTOMS 212-466-5851
Wryneck (Torticollis)....Staff NINDS 301-496-5751

X

X-ray Crystallography....Staff NCRR 301-594-7934
X-ray, Radiation Effects on Fetus....Staff FDA 301-594-3533
X-ray Technician....Staff HRSA/BHPr 301-443-5794
X-ray apparatus....Johnson, Christopher USITC 202-205-3488
Xanthinuria....Staff NIDDK 301-654-4415
Xanthomatosis....Staff NHLBI 301-496-4236

Be patient. If any phone number is incorrect, call (area code) 555-1212 and request the new listing.

1449

Xeroderma Pigmentosum....Staff NIAMS 301-496-8188
Xeroderma Pigmentosum....Staff NCI 301-496-5583
Xerophthalmia....Staff NEI 301-496-5248
Xeroradiography....Staff NCI 301-496-5583
Xerostomia (Dry Mouth)....Staff NIDR 301-496-4261
Xylene....Raftery, Jim USITC 202-205-3365
Xylenol....Matusik, Ed USITC 202-205-3356

Y

YAG Laser....Staff NEI 301-496-5248
Yarns....Konzet, Jeffrey CUSTOMS 212-466-5885
Yarns....Shelton, Linda USITC 202-205-3457
Year 2000 Research and Development....Keeley, Catherine CENSUS 301-457-4036
Yeast Infections....Staff NIAID 301-496-5717
Yeast....Janis, William V. COMMERCE 202-482-2250
Yellow Fever....Staff NIAID 301-496-5717
Yellow Page Advertising....Staff FCC 202-632-7553
Yellowcake....Greenblatt, Jack USITC 202-205-3353
Yemen (Aden)/Minerals....Michalski, Bernadette Cnty Mines 202-501-9699
Yemen A.R.....Maybury-Lewis, Anthony Cnty Export-Import Bank 202-565-3739
Yemen Arab Republic (Sanaa)....Staff Cnty State 202-647-6572
Yemen, Republic of....Mukherjee, Mohua Cnty World Bank 202-473-3022
Yemen, Republic of....Thanos, Paul Cnty Commerce 202-482-1860
Yemen (Sana)/Minerals....Michalski, Bernadette Cnty Mines 202-501-9699
Yemen....Alaini, Mohsin Cnty Embassy 202-965-4760
Yemen....DiMeo, Pam Peace Corps 202-606-3196
Yemen....Mercer, Dorothy Cnty Treasury 202-622-0184
Yemen....Nasher, Ahmed Abdo Cnty Embassy 202-965-4761
Yemen....Schildwachter, Christy Peace Corps 202-606-3196
Yemen....Squire, Margo Cnty USIA 202-619-5529
Yemen...Vacant Cnty AID 202-663-2620
YMCA....Staff YMCA of the USA 800-872-9622
Youth Conservation Corps, Fish and Wildlife....Staff FWS 703-358-2029
Youth Development Information Center....Kane, John NAL 301-504-6400
Youth, Employment Statistics....Cohany, Sharon LABOR 202-606-6378
Youth, Students, and Dropouts, Empl./Unempl. Stats....Cohany, Sharon LABOR 202-606-6378
Youth with disabilities....Staff NCYD 800-333-6293
Yttrium....Hedrick, James B. MINES 202-501-9412
Yugoslavia (Belgrade)....Staff Cnty State 202-647-4138
Yugoslavia/Minerals....Steblez, Walter Cnty Mines 202-501-9671
Yugoslavia....Jackson, Juhka Cnty Treasury 202-622-0766
Yugoslavia....Keller, Jeremy Cnty Commerce 202-482-4915
Yugoslavia....Popovic, Zoran Cnty Embassy 202-462-6566
Yugoslavia....Vujovic, Nebojsa Cnty Embassy 202-462-6566

Z

Zaire/Minerals....Heydari, Michael Cnty Mines 202-501-9688
Zaire, Republic of (Kinshasa)....Staff Cnty State 202-647-2080
Zaire....Esposito, Dina Cnty AID 202-647-7887
Zaire....Henning, Herman Cnty USIA 202-619-5926
Zaire....Kotze, Joan Cnty Treasury 202-622-0333
Zaire....Maybury-Lewis, Anthony Cnty Export-Import Bank 202-565-3739
Zaire....Michelini, Philip Cnty Commerce 202-482-4388
Zaire....Tatanene, Manata Cnty Embassy 202-234-7690
Zaire...Grau, William J. Cnty World Bank 202-473-3309
Zambia (Lusaka)....Staff Cnty State 202-647-8432
Zambia/Minerals....Antonides, Lloyd Cnty Mines 202-501-9686
Zambia....Anderson, Sydney Cnty AID 202-647-2965
Zambia....Bezek, Jill Cnty TDA 703-875-4357
Zambia....Holm-Olsen, Finn Cnty Commerce 202-482-4228
Zambia....Jones, Donald Peace Corps 202-606-3256
Zambia....Kamana, Dunstan Weston Cnty Embassy 202-265-9717
Zambia....Kotze, Joan Cnty Treasury 202-622-0333
Zambia....Maybury-Lewis, Anthony Cnty Export-Import Bank 202-565-3739
Zambia....Nzala, George R. Cnty Embassy 202-265-9719
Zambia....Pomerantz, Phyllis Cnty World Bank 202-473-7170
Zambia....Schwartz, Larry Cnty USIA 202-619-6904
Zeolites....Virta, Robert MINES 202-501-9384
Zimbabwe (Harare)....Staff Cnty State 202-647-9429
Zimbabwe/Minerals....Izon, David Cnty Mines 202-501-9692
Zimbabwe....Burns, Paul Peace corps 202-606-3634
Zimbabwe....Holm-Olsen, Finn Cnty Commerce 202-482-4228
Zimbabwe....Jewett, Wood Peace Corps 202-606-3635
Zimbabwe....Keeys, Lynn Cnty AID 202-647-4289
Zimbabwe....Marongwe, Mark G. Cnty Embassy 202-332-7100
Zimbabwe....Maybury-Lewis, Anthony Cnty Export-Import Bank 202-565-3739
Zimbabwe....Midzi, Amos Bernard Muvengwa Cnty Embassy 202-332-7100
Zimbabwe....Patel, Praful C. Cnty World Bank 202-473-4250
Zimbabwe....Rauch, Margie Cnty Treasury 202-622-0251
Zimbabwe....Schwartz, Larry Cnty USIA 202-619-6904
Zimbabwe....Younge, Nathan Cnty TDA 703-875-4357
Zinc compounds....Greenblatt, Jack USITC 202-205-3353
Zinc....Jasinski, Stephen MINES 202-501-9418
Zinc....Larrabee, David Commerce 202-482-0607
Zinc....White, Linda USITC 202-205-3427
Zip Codes, Economic Data....Russell, Anne CENSUS 301-457-2687
Zip Codes, Demographic Data....Staff CENSUS 301-457-4100
Zip Codes, Geographic Relationships....Quarato, Rose CENSUS 301-457-1128
Zippers....Shildneck, Ann USITC 202-205-3499
Zirconium compounds....Greenblatt, Jack USITC 202-205-3353
Zirconium....DeSapio, Vincent USITC 202-205-3435
Zirconium....Gambogi, Joseph MINES 202-501-9390
Zollinger-Ellison Syndrome....Staff NIDDK 301-496-3583
Zoonoses....Staff NIAID 301-496-5717
Zoris....Sundar, Shetty USITC 202-205-3486

Index

Index

The thousands of studies in the Current Events Chapter and Experts Chapter are <u>not</u> listed in this Index.

Index

Allergies, 513, 963, 1197
  publications, 535
  research grants, 285
  slide set, 535
Alloys, improved, 982
Alternative fuels
  commercial development, 1056
Alzheimer's Disease, 508, 513, 962
  clearinghouse, 552
  long-term care, 535
  research, 553
  treatments, 553
  videos, 552
American Indians
  see also Native Americans
  arts and crafts, 1263, 1268
  drug abuse, 591
  drug education, 588
  enterprise development, 827
  exhibits, 1268
  health services, 505
  housing, 126
  land areas, 1268
  tribal school drug education, 588
American Samoa
  arts agency, 305
  pesticide agencies, 1148
Americans with Disabilities Act, 121
AmeriCorps, 195
AMTRAK, 409
  Internet access, 1219
  public information office, 69
Ancient cultures
  slides, 1279
Anesthesia research, 562
Angiography, 956
Animal Welfare Licensee System, 1209
Animals
  see also Pets
  air travel, 1240
  biomedical research, 569
  dealer licensing, 1209
  diseases, 150, 1008
  drug testing, 1008, 1240
  drugs, 1239
  endangered species, 962, 1135, 1197, 1256
  ethical issues, 1008, 1240
  health, 1014
  library, 1203
  livestock, 1013
  parasitology, 1008
  poison control, 1140, 1238
  research alternatives, 507, 955
  research facilities, 1209
  research grants, 279
  sickness, 1240
  veterinary services, 1013
  welfare, 1016
Annual Governors Conferences, 722
Annuities
  tax forms, 468
Anorexia nervosa, 513, 962, 1197
Ansel Adams Prints, 25
Antarctica
  geologic maps, 1088
  research expeditions, 289, 391, 404, 972
  science stations, 907, 1094, 1130
Anthracite, 1212
Anthropology
  education, 163
Anti-toxins, 936
Antitrust
  airlines, 772
  business reviews, 607
  consumers, 605
  guidelines, 1223
  investigations, 605

joint research ventures, 606
  nuclear industry, 1065
  senate committee, 1178
Apartments
  experimental construction, 134
  loans, 132
Apheresis, 957
Apnea, sleep, 507
Apollo missions
  slides, 1280
  video, 1287
Appalachian Region
  economic development, 336
  grants for research, 359, 375
Apparel, 840
Appliances
  energy standards, 1038, 1044
  labeling, 1038
Apprenticeships
  science and engineering, 947
Aquaculture, 148, 751, 790, 962, 1008
  African, 1005
  database, 1108
  national association, 1014
Arc-welding, 996
Archaeology, 195, 934, 1120
  artifacts, 993
  database, 298
  grants, 298
  import controls, 313
  National Parks policy, 310
  slides, 1279
Architects, 630
Architecture
  Capitol, U.S., 301, 310
  drawings archives, 290, 299, 310, 1085
  grants, 294
  library, 299
  photographs, 292-293
  transportation, 289, 393, 812, 816, 1105
Archives
  American art, 309, 311
  archival training course, 245, 302
  art photographs, 292
  diplomatic, 910
  economic data, 859
  educational research, 179
  Eliot Elisofon Photographic
    Archives, 290, 309
  federal laws, 611, 1186
  federal motion pictures, 290
  Folkways Records, 300, 313
  genealogy research, 642
  German Army records, 308
  legislative, 1185
  maps, 290
  military, 942
  military data files, 302, 308
  military service records, 641
  Moses and Frances Asch
    Collection, 291, 313
  motion picture, 291
  National Air and Space Archives, 298
  National Anthropological Archives, 303
  prisoner-of-war records, 643
  records management, 300
  Security and Exchange Commission
    records, 433
  security-classified records, 299
  ship passenger arrival records, 643
  Smithsonian Institution, 305
  sound recordings, 290
  state historical records, 305
  vice-presidential papers, 307
  Vietnam War, 307
Arctic
  foreign policy issues, 907, 1094, 1130

oil and gas exploration, 956
  research expeditions, 289, 391, 404
  research missions, 972
Arizona
  adult education centers, 171
  agency on aging, 555
  agricultural offices, 1031
  arts agency, 305
  arts grants, 318
  banking department, 437
  bill status information, 1189
  Board of Pharmacy, 664
  Bureau of Land Management office, 688
  company directories, 658
  consumer protection office, 101
  corporation information, 653
  crime statistics, 871
  Department of Commerce, 138
  Department of Education, 230
  Department of Health Services, 664
  Department of Revenue, 631
  environmental library, 1103
  federal procurement assistance, 827
  freedom of information office, 1170
  general information, 724
  geoscience agency, 979
  health statistics, 881
  highway department offices, 886
  housing programs, 138
  insurance department, 678
  international trade offices, 850
  Internet access, 1235
  IRS hotline, 460
  labor office, 875
  licensed professionals, 631
  maps, 1089
  money for students, 210
  motor vehicles division, 636
  pesticide agencies, 1148
  public health office, 541
  public utilities, 670
  radon office, 1114
  securities division, 661
  small business advocate, 724
  small business development centers, 725
  state data centers, 890
  state information, 35
  state planning office, 899
  state procurement office, 832
  state tax assistance, 494
  statistical abstracts, 896
  surplus property auctions, 699
  tax form distribution center, 466
  tax forms and publications, 487
  unclaimed property office, 705
  uniform commercial code department, 626
  water resources district office, 1118
  weights and measures office, 675
  wildlife refuges, 1136
Arkansas
  adult education centers, 171
  agency on aging, 555
  agricultural offices, 1031
  arts agency, 305
  arts grants, 318
  banking department, 438
  bill status information, 1189
  Board of Pharmacy, 664
  company directories, 658
  consumer protection office, 101
  corporation information, 653
  crime statistics, 871
  Department of Education, 230
  Department of Health, 664
  environmental library, 1103
  federal procurement assistance, 827
  freedom of information office, 1170

  The thousands of studies in the Current Events Chapter and Experts Chapter are not listed in this Index.

Index

Index

Index

The thousands of studies in the Current Events Chapter and Experts Chapter are not listed in this Index.

Index

Index

The thousands of studies in the Current Events Chapter and Experts Chapter are not listed in this Index.

kidney and urologic diseases, 546
labor, 1214
labor-management issues, 254
legal briefs, 616
Library of Congress, 1193
medical devices, 563
medical hotlines, 503
medical literature, 497, 501
medical subjects, 502
MEDLINE, 501
mental health, 530
microcomputers, 942, 961
military research and development, 937
minerals, 979
mining and minerals, 442, 803, 938
National Coal Resources Data System, 802,
    1042, 1060
National Electronic Injury Surveillance
    System, 108
National Institute of Occupational Safety
    and Health, 262
National Occupational Hazard Survey, 261
non-nuclear survivability/vulnerability
    data, 941
nuclear energy, 1067
nuclear facilities, 1066
nuclear power, 1073
nuclear power plants, 1071
Nuclear Regulatory Commission, 1065
nuclear waste, 1047
Nutrient Data Bank, 520
nutrition, 517, 1020
occupational health, 506
ocean science, 962
oceanography, 795, 1081
online, 724, 737, 739, 743, 748
osteoporosis, 554
overseas security information, 406
ozone, 1113
patent and trademark, 964, 1004
PDQ, 502
pesticides, 1015, 1143
Peter A. Juley and Son Collection, 290, 310
phase diagram, 993
pipeline safety, 811, 1063, 1101, 1143
plant genetic research, 1015
poisoning incidents, 108
polymers, 946, 962
POPLINE, 502
power fields, 1052
railroads, 819
Registry of Toxic Effects of Chemical
    Substances (RTECS), 502, 566, 567
research in progress, 955
research referrals, 939, 953
residential energy consumption, 1054
Rural Electrification Administration, 780
science and technology, 176, 1047, 1197
scientific grants, 569
Securities and Exchange Commission, 433
securities transactions, 433
securities, lost or stolen, 430
semiconductors, 942, 961
SERLINE, 501
SIDILINE, 502
small business, 712
Smithsonian art index, 310
Smithsonian slides and photographs, 290,
    310
smoking and health, 550
space shuttle, 1250, 1252, 1283
speech recognition, 998
standard reference data, 998
stolen art, 606
superconductivity, 1096
sustainable agriculture, 150, 1017
swimming pool-related deaths of
    children, 108

tactical weapons, 950
technology, 1047, 1066
thermochemical tables, 999
toxicology, 262, 1102, 1117, 1145, 1149
TOXLINE, 349, 502, 566
TOXLIT, 502
TOXNET, 502
trade leads, 850
traffic accidents, 886
transportation research, 345, 810
treasury securities, 436
TRI, 502
TRIFACTS, 502
U.S. supplier lists, 1027
unemployment insurance, 253
union contracts, 239, 258
veterans medical data, 383
volcanoes, 1228
water quality, 1117
weather, 1078-1079, 1083
workplace air quality, 262
world agricultural economics, 1029
world population, 869
Daylight saving time, 1040
Deafness
    see also Disabled, Handicapped
    clearinghouse, 559
    closed-captioned videos, 559
    education materials, 153
    grants for interpreters, 188
    interpreters, 198
    rehabilitation services, 559
    research grants, 283
    TDD Directory, 561
Deaths
    alcohol and drug use, 575
    consumer products, 504
    grieving process, 529
    highway fatalities, 575
    infant, 523
    medical devices, 1215
    minorities and Blacks, 505
    national statistics, 571
    on-the-job, 1210
    overseas, 852
    pregnancy-related, 526
Debt
    collateral, 625
    collection, 95, 1211
    federal, 435
    online search access, 625
    personal or corporate, 625
    U.S. government, 1240
Deer, 1252
Defense
    arms control, 1199
    Internet information sites, 1220
    issues and policy, 939
    national security, 947
    nuclear weapons, 1066
    security assistance, 948
Defense cuts
    home loans, 133
Defense Logistics Agency, 826
Defense Nuclear Facilities Safety Board
    public information office, 62
Defense Reutilization and Marketing sales, 693
Delaware, 636
    adult education centers, 171
    agency on aging, 556
    agricultural offices, 1032
    arts agency, 305
    arts grants, 319
    banking department, 438
    bill status information, 1189
    Board of Pharmacy, 665
    company directories, 658

consumer protection office, 101
corporation information, 654
crime statistics, 871
Department of Education, 230
Department of Public Health, 665
Division of Professional Regulation, 631
Division of Securities, 661
environmental library, 1103
federal procurement assistance, 827
freedom of information office, 1171
general information, 727
geoscience agency, 979
health statistics, 881
highway department offices, 886
housing programs, 139
insurance department, 679
international trade offices, 850
Internet access, 1235
IRS hotlines, 460
labor office, 876
licensed professionals, 631
maps, 1089
money for students, 212
motor vehicles division, 637
pesticide agencies, 1146
public health office, 542
public utilities, 671
radon office, 1114
small business advocate, 727
small business development centers, 727
state data centers, 891
state information, 35
state planning office, 899
state procurement office, 832
state tax assistance, 494
statistical abstracts, 896
surplus property auctions, 699
tax form distribution center, 466
tax forms and publications, 487
unclaimed property office, 706
uniform commercial code section, 626
water resources district office, 1118
weights and measures office, 675
wildlife refuges, 1137
Dementia, 508
    brain aging, 553
    causes and treatment, 535
    experimental therapies, 540
Demographics
    Center for Population Research, 525
    crime, 870
    food consumption, 1213
    foreign, 843
    global, 845
    international, 840
    Internet information sites, 1222
    population research, 525
    research grants, 282
    state data, 721
    statistics, 33
    students, 229
Dental
    care, 27
    implants, 27
    laboratories, 1215
    records, 609
Dental school
    disadvantaged students, 201
    loan repayment, 199
    residency training, 201
Dentistry
    AIDS, 533
    audiovisual materials, 290
    child health, 524
    dental health, 516, 547
    education and practice, 242
    educational grants, 192

The thousands of studies in the Current Events Chapter and Experts Chapter are not included in this Index.

Index

The thousands of studies in the Current Events Chapter and Experts Chapter are <u>not</u> listed in this Index.

Index

The thousands of studies in the Current Events Chapter and Experts Chapter are not listed in this Index.

Index

Index

The thousands of studies in the Current Events Chapter and Experts Chapter are <u>not</u> listed in this index.

Index

The thousands of studies in the Current Events Chapter and Experts Chapter are not listed in this Index.

drug companies, 565
Environmental Protection Agency, 1096
exclusions, 1155
exemptions, 1150, 1153-1154, 1159
Farm Credit Administration, 1011
federal civilian employment, 1160
federal contracts, 1160
Federal Information Center, 1157
Federal Labor Relations Authority, 255, 267
Federal Mediation and Conciliation
    Service, 255
federal offices, 1164
fee waivers, 1152
fees, 1152, 1158
financial information, 1154
financial institutions, 1155
geological information, 1155
informant records, 1156
judicial appeals, 1156, 1161
law enforcement, 1155
lawsuits, 1154
limitations, 1151
litigation records, 1160
making requests, 1152
maps, 1150
medical records, 1160
military service, 1160
National Labor Relations Board, 256
National Mediation Board, 255
Nuclear Regulatory Commission, 1067
Occupational Safety and Health Review
    Commission, 264
Office of Federal Register, 1158
Pension Benefit Guaranty Corporation, 250
personal privacy, 1155
personnel rules, 1154
photographs, 1150
Postal Rate Commission, 113
Privacy Act, 1150, 1155, 1157-1161
protected information, 1154
radiation, 563
Railroad Retirement Board, 271
requests, 1150-1153, 1156, 1158, 1160, 1161
responses, 1153
sample request letters, 1163
scope of, 1151
security classification, 1154
state offices, 1151-1153, 1156, 1170
state open records laws, 1150
tax code, 1154
violations, 1151
Fuel efficiency, 99, 813, 1045
Fuels
    alcohol plants permits, 1038
    alcohol, 1048
    alternative fuels technology, 1064
    alternative, 808, 1059-1060
    alternatives from farm crops, 1011
    automotive efficiency, 1059
    biofuels, 1053
    biomass, 1039
    compressed natural gas, 808
    consumption, 988, 1060
    diesel pricing, 815, 1041
    distilled spirits, 765
    economy standards in motor vehicles, 93,
        808, 1039
    ethanol, 808
    files online, 1042
    fuel cycle plants, 1067
    grain based, 1038
    hardwood trees, 1011
    loans, 1038
    methanol, 808
    motor, 1061
    motor vehicle usage, 817
    synthetic, 962, 1040

tax credits, 489
taxes, motor vehicles, 817
thermodynamic properties, 1000
unleaded, 1056, 1116
winter, 1212
wood, 962, 1040, 1197
Fugitives
    drug charges, 599
Fulbright grants, 184
Fulbright scholarships, 300
Fulbright-Hays
    seminars, 185
    training grants, 185
Fundraising
    tax implications, 445
Funerals, 94
    consumer rules, 96
Fusion, 956, 1048, 1067

G

Gale Research Inc
    Encyclopedia of Associations, 8, 649
Gallstones
    surgery, 541
Gambling, 606
    tax forms, 468
Games of chance, 99
Gardening, 148, 150, 1007, 1239
    classes, 149
    disease diagnosis assistance, 150
    free assistance, 148
    growing vegetables, 151
    herb, 150, 962, 1197
    insects and bugs, 149, 1013
    landscape, 150, 962, 1197
    mulches, 151
    rose culture, 150, 513, 962, 1197
    weed control, 1015
    workshops, 149
Gas exploration, 793, 1112, 1133
Gasohol, 956
Gasoline
    octane posting, 99
    sales, 817
Gemini missions
    videos, 1287
Gemstones, 98
Genealogy, 302, 642
    military service records, 641, 642, 941, 946
    Native Americans, 301
    research guides, 642
    workshops, 27, 642
General Accounting Office, 862
    annual report, 862
    bid protests, 824
    congressional assistance, 1185
    history, 299
    reports, 1185
General contractor loans, 722
General Motors
    repairs, 96
General Obligation Bonds, 720
General Services Administration
    foreign gifts, 697
    government contracts, 824
    Internet access, 1222
    miscellaneous property, 693
    public information office, 65
    regional offices, 694
Genetics, 1046
    animal, 1020
    applied, 1017
    Cooley's Anemia, 540
    disorders, 569
    engineering, 1008, 1098

fish, 1132
fundamental process, 569
heritable mutations, 955
international development, 922
mapping, 508, 955
plants, 1015
research, 524
research grants, 285
spina bifida, 547
testing, 508, 955
therapy, 508, 955
toxicology, 566
workplace screening, 515
Geodesy, 1082
Geographic Names Information Database, 28
Geographic names, 1213, 1214
Geography, 1080, 1086, 1087, 1100
    aerial photographs, 340, 1238, 1087
    census maps, 868
    census products, 855
    education, 163
    exhibits, 1088
    foreign names, 1213
    foreign policy issues, 914, 1087
    information systems, 1086
    land cover, 1086
    naming information, 337, 1088
    publication for parents, 1266
    reference works, 1089
    U.S. maps, 1091
Geology, 1080, 1100, 1254
    Antarctic, 979, 1239
    caves, 979, 1081, 1239
    continental margins, 805, 1062
    cores, 976
    earthquakes, 977, 1091
    energy resources, 977, 1091
    environmental, 977
    Exclusive Economic Zone of the United
        States, 805, 1062
    exhibits, 1088
    field records, 977
    hazards, 96, 1141
    information centers, 978
    international, 979
    landslides, 979
    library, 1201
    maps, 977, 1091
    marine, 977-979, 1081, 1239
    mineral resources, 977, 1091
    naming and classification, 977, 1088
    offshore drilling, 805, 1062
    publications, 978
    rock collecting, 1240
    scientific publications, 978
    teaching aids, 978, 1254, 1266, 1288
    teaching materials, 177, 976
    videos, 978
    volcanoes, 977, 1091
Geophysics, 967, 977, 1080, 1100
    land/marine data, 1088
    solid earth, 978
Georgia
    adult education centers, 171
    agency on aging, 556
    agricultural offices, 1032
    arts agency, 306
    arts grants, 320
    banking department, 438
    bill status information, 1189
    Board of Pharmacy, 665
    Clerk of Superior Court, 625-626
    company directories, 658
    consumer protection office, 102
    corporation information, 654
    crime statistics, 871
    Department of Agriculture, 665

The thousands of studies in the Current Events Chapter and Experts Chapter are not listed in this Index.

Index

The thousands of studies in the Current Events Chapter and Experts Chapter are not listed in this index.

Index

Index

The thousands of studies in the Current Events Chapter and Experts Chapter are not listed in this Index.

Index

Labor relations
    foreign visitor program, 235
Labor surplus areas, 826
Labor unions
    bargaining unit, 254
    Certification of Representative (RC), 256
    drug abuse programs, 586
    elections, 256
    employer petition, 256
    representation elections, 256
    unit clarification, 256
    withdrawal of union-shop authority, 256
Labor-management
    mediation cases, 616
Laboratories
    federal consortium, 954
    federal, 1211
    Lawrence Berkeley Laboratory, 960
    medical, 1215
    voluntary accreditation, 1000
Lakes
    Kentucky, 1260
Lands
    cadastral surveys, 1123
    foreign-owned agricultural, 1214
    management issues, 1202
    public management, 1132
    public, 1127, 1179
    reclamation, 1179
Landmarks
    historic, 301
    national registry, 303
    natural, 1100
Landscaping, 150, 962, 1053
    assistance, 149
Landslides, 979, 1141
Language, 195
    disorders, 507
    grants for teachers, 187
Languages
    educational grants, 184, 185
    foreign research grants, 185
Larceny, 606
Laser surgery, 564
Lasers, 769, 945, 949
    development, 994
    high energy, 960
    interferometer, 995
    research, 942, 949, 961
Latin America, 782
    field research fellowships, 166
    health activities, 916
    marketing, 840
    research project histories, 908
    small and micro enterprises, 916
Law
    Americans arrested abroad, 404
    ancient, 613, 917, 1187, 1195
    banking and finance, 416-417
    campaign finance, 641, 1184
    canon, 613, 917, 1187, 1195
    Chinese, 613, 917, 1187, 1195
    civil, 613, 917, 1187, 1195
    Coast Guard, U.S., 607
    constitutional, 615
    education grants, 188
    education organizations, 152, 162
    enforcement overseas, 918
    environmental, 1096, 1097, 1099
    Far Eastern, 1187
    FDIC liquidation litigation, 420
    Freedom of Information, 1150-1152, 1153,
        1156, 1158, 1160, 1161
    history of, 605
    insanity defense, 607
    international arms control, 928
    Islamic, 613, 917, 1187, 1195

Jewish, 613, 917, 1187, 1195
judicial research, 616
juvenile justice, 589
Law School Clinic program, 616
legal assistance for the poor, 616
legal services, 616, 617
legal suits abroad, 408
maritime enforcement, 941
medieval, 613, 917, 1187, 1195
mining, 801, 806, 1128
Occupational Safety and Health Review
    Commission, 263
poverty law, 616
Privacy Act, 1150
respect for laws, 589
Roman, 613, 917, 1187, 1195
water resources, 1120
Law enforcement
    program grants, 356
Law school
    money programs, 197
Lawn care, 149
Lawn workshops, 30
Lawrence Berkeley Laboratory, 1048
Lawyers, 630
    see also Attorneys
Layaways, 766
Lead in drinking water, 1111
Lead based paint, 125
Lead poisoning, 504, 1142
    grants, 366
Learning disabilities, 957
Leasing
    gas, 1062, 1064, 1127
    long term, 132
    mineral, oil, gas, 1125
    offshore oil leases, 1126
    oil, 1062, 1064, 1127
    onshore leasing program, 1063
    outer continental shelf, 805, 1062, 1123
Legal Services Corporation, 616
Legalization
    grants, 376
Legislation
    aerospace, 971
    animal welfare, 1008, 1016, 1240
    aquaculture products, 148
    arms control and disarmament, 929
    asbestos, 1094
    banking and finance, 416, 420
    biotechnology, 1008
    child protection, 610
    children's rights, 610
    civil rights, 622
    coal, 1060
    consumer protection, 94
    cost estimates of, 861
    currency issues, 1179
    database, 1173
    disability community, 154
    disabled individuals, 560
    document rooms, 1183
    education issues, 1179
    energy, 1044, 1048, 1056
    environmental, 1018, 1096, 1098-1099, 1101
    federal, 1173, 1174
    federal elections, 1178, 1184
    fiscal consequences, 1181
    higher education, 167
    history of, 1183, 1186, 1195, 1200
    immigration, 916
    Internal Revenue Service, 448-449
    Internet information sites, 1223
    labor, 1179
    legal assistance to the poor, 616
    legislative process, 1185
    mail, 113

minimum wage, 1179
nuclear, 1072
pesticides, 1015, 1143
petroleum industry, 1063
public attendance at hearings, 392
public lands, 1125
publications, 1206
school lunch programs, 1179
security assistance, 947
senate committees, 1176
state-level, 339, 1188
superfund, 1148
taxes, 447, 452
telecommunications, 766, 780
transportation, 99, 809
women's issues, 240
Legislative Branch
    public information offices, 39
Libraries
    African art, 309, 1199
    Agency for International Development, 906
    agriculture, 33, 964, 1215
    air pollution, 1108
    Alzheimer's Disease, 552
    American history, 310
    Army Corps of Engineers, 934
    Army Materials and Mechanics Research
        Center, 936, 953
    Army Materiel Command, 950, 964
    Army Medical Library, 934
    Arson Resource Center, 346, 606
    art slides, 292, 316
    arts and museum management, 1199
    aviation, 931
    aviation history, 966
    banking law, 416
    Bell-Henry Library, 298
    binational centers, 404, 908, 1199
    Botanic Garden, U.S., 148
    Bureau of Land Management, 1125
    Bureau of Mines, 805
    Bureau of the Census, 766, 855
    business, 33
    career training grants, 186
    catalog cards, 1194
    catalog numbers, 1196
    Census depositories, 856
    Chesapeake Bay, 1109
    child abuse, 1210
    children's useage, 162
    Coast Guard law, 607
    commodity futures, 441
    construction grants, 364
    Consumer Product Safety Commission, 108
    Department of Commerce, 765, 766
    Department of Housing and Urban
        Development, 125
    Department of Labor, 237
    Department of Transportation, 813
    Doris and Henry Dreyfuss Study Center
        and Library, 299
    education, 160
    Edwards Air Force Base, 950
    energy, 1048
    energy online, 1041
    energy research, 1048
    Environmental Protection Agency law, 1099
    Environmental Protection Agency, 1096
    Environmental Research Laboratory, 1098
    environmental research, 1098, 1100, 1102,
        1117, 1145, 1149
    Farm Credit Administration, 1011
    Federal Depository Libraries, 1206
    Federal Election Commission, 641, 1184
    Federal Labor Relations Authority, 255
    Fire Research Information Service, 996
    funds for resources, 169

The thousands of studies in the Current Events Chapter and Experts Chapter are <u>not</u> listed in this Index.

Index

Index

The thousands of studies in the Current Events Chapter and Experts Chapter are not included in this Index.

Index

The thousands of studies in the Current Events Chapter and Experts Chapter are not listed in this Index.

Index

Index

The thousands of studies in the Current Events Chapter and Experts Chapter are not listed in this Index.

The thousands of studies in the Current Events Chapter and Experts Chapter are not included in this Index.

The thousands of studies in the Current Events Chapter and Experts Chapter are not listed in this Index.

Index

The thousands of studies in the Current Events Chapter and Experts Chapter are not listed in this Index.

The thousands of studies in the Current Events Chapter and Experts Chapter are not listed in this Index.

Index

The thousands of studies in the Current Events Chapter and Experts Chapter are not listed in this Index.

Index

The thousands of studies in the Current Events Chapter and Experts Chapter are not listed in this Index.

The thousands of studies in the Current Events Chapter and Experts Chapter are not included in this Index.

1511

Index

The thousands of studies in the Current Events Chapter and Experts Chapter are not listed in this Index.

The thousands of studies in the Current Events Chapter and Experts Chapter are <u>not</u> included in this Index.

Index

The thousands of studies in the Current Events Chapter and Experts Chapter are <u>not</u> listed in this Index.